KEY TO ABBREVIATIONS

+	continued on later pages of same issue
abp	archbishop
abr	abridged
Ag	August
Ap	April
arch	architect
assn	association
Aut	Autumn
av	avenue
bart	baronet
bibliog	bibliography
bibliog f	bibliographical foot-notes
bi-m	bimonthly
bi-w	biweekly
bldg	building
bp	bishop
co	company
comp	compiled, compiler
cond	condensed
cont	continued
corp	corporation
D	December
dept	department
ed	edited, edition, editor
F	February
Hon	Honorable
il	illustrated, illustration, illustrator
inc	incorporated
introd	introduction, introductory
Ja	January
Je	June
Jl	July
jr	junior
jt auth	joint author
ltd	limited
m	monthly
Mr	March
My	May
N	November
no	number
O	October
por	portrait
pseud	pseudonym
pt	part
pub	published, publisher, publishing
q	quarterly
rev	revised
S	September
semi-m	semimonthly
soc	society
Spr	Spring
sq	square
sr	senior
st	street
Sum	Summer
sup	supplement
supt	superintendent
tr	translated, translation, translator
v	volume
w	weekly
Wint	Winter
yr	year

Readers' Guide to
Periodical Literature

MARCH 1967—FEBRUARY 1968

READERS' GUIDE TO
PERIODICAL LITERATURE

Cumulated Volumes

READERS' GUIDE TO
PERIODICAL LITERATURE

An Author and Subject Index

MARCH 1967 — FEBRUARY 1968

Edited by
ZADA LIMERICK

Indexers
ANNE W. FURNESS
DEREK A. HANDLEY
LINDA LACK HOY
MURIEL M. PHILLIPS

THE H. W. WILSON COMPAN
NEW YORK   19

PRINTED IN THE UNITED STATES OF AMERICA

Library of Congress Catalog Card No. (6-8232)

ACKNOWLEDGMENTS

In addition to the staff members whose names appear on the title page we wish to acknowledge the contributions of Ann F. Dietz, Lovisa J. Jenkins, Berta Pisciattano, Virginia Turrell, and Barbara Stanley Welch who indexed for this volume.

Z. L.

20984

ABBREVIATIONS OF PERIODICALS INDEXED

March 1967—February 1968

FOR FULL INFORMATION, CONSULT PAGES IX-XI

ALA Bul—ALA Bulletin
Aero Tech—Aerospace Technology
    Formerly Technology Week including Missiles and Rockets
Am Artist—American Artist
Am City—American City
Am Ed—American Education
Am For—American Forests
*Am Heritage—American Heritage
Am Hist R—American Historical Review
Am Home—American Home
Am Rec G—American Record Guide
America—America
Américas—Américas
Ann Am Acad—Annals of the American Academy of Political and Social Science
Antiques—Antiques
Arch Forum—Architectural Forum
Arch Rec—Architectural Record
Art N—Art News
*Atlan—Atlantic
Audubon—Audubon
Aviation W—Aviation Week & Space Technology

Bet Hom & Gard—Better Homes and Gardens
Bsns W—Business Week
Bul Atomic Sci—Bulletin of the Atomic Scientists

Cath World—Catholic World
*Changing T—Changing Times
Christian Cent—Christian Century
Commentary—Commentary
Commonweal—Commonweal
Cong Digest—Congressional Digest
*Consumer Bul—Consumer Bulletin
*Consumer Rep—Consumer Reports
Craft Horiz—Craft Horizons
Cur Hist—Current History

Dance Mag—Dance Magazine
Dept State Bul—Department of State Bulletin
Design—Design
Duns R—Dun's Review
    Formerly Dun's Review and Modern Industry

Ebony—Ebony
Electr World—Electronics World
Esquire—Esquire

*Farm J—Farm Journal (Central edition)
Field & S—Field & Stream
Flower Grower—Flower Grower, The Home Garden
    Continued as Home Garden & Flower Grower Feb '67
Flying—Flying
Focus—Focus
*For Affairs—Foreign Affairs
Fortune—Fortune

*Good H—Good Housekeeping

*Harper—Harper's Magazine
Harvard Bsns R—Harvard Business Review
*Hi Fi—High Fidelity incorporating Musical America
Hobbies—Hobbies
*Holiday—Holiday
Home Gard—Home Garden & Flower Grower
*Horizon—Horizon
Horn Bk—Horn Book Magazine
Horticulture—Horticulture
Hot Rod—Hot Rod
House & Gard—House & Garden incorporating Living for Young Homemakers
House B—House Beautiful

Int Concil—International Conciliation

*Ladies Home J—Ladies' Home Journal
Library J—Library Journal

Life—Life
Liv Wildn—Living Wilderness
*Look—Look (Middle Atlantic edition)
McCalls—McCall's
Mlle—Mademoiselle
Mo Labor R—Monthly Labor Review
Mod Phot—Modern Photography
Motor B—Motor Boating
Motor T—Motor Trend

NEA J—NEA Journal
N Y Times Mag—New York Times Magazine
*Nat Geog Mag—National Geographic Magazine
Nat Parks Mag—National Parks Magazine
Nat R—National Review (44p issue only, pub. in alternate weeks)
Nation—Nation
Nations Bsns—Nation's Business
*Natur Hist—Natural History incorporating Nature Magazine
Negro Hist Bul—Negro History Bulletin
New Repub—New Republic
New Yorker—New Yorker
*Newsweek—Newsweek

Opera N—Opera News
Outdoor Life—Outdoor Life

PTA Mag—PTA Magazine
Parents Mag—Parents' Magazine and Better Homemaking
Parks & Rec—Parks & Recreation
Plays—Plays
Poetry—Poetry
Pop Electr—Popular Electronics
Pop Gard—Popular Gardening & Living Outdoors
*Pop Mech—Popular Mechanics
Pop Phot—Popular Photography
Pop Sci—Popular Science Monthly
Pub W—Publishers' Weekly

*Read Digest—Reader's Digest (Great Lakes edition)
Redbook—Redbook
*Reporter—The Reporter

Sat Eve Post—Saturday Evening Post
Sat R—Saturday Review
Sch & Soc—School and Society
Sch Arts—School Arts
Sci Am—Scientific American
Sci Digest—Science Digest
Sci N—Science News
Science—Science
*Seventeen—Seventeen
Sky & Tel—Sky and Telescope
*Sports Illus—Sports Illustrated
Sr Schol—Senior Scholastic (Teacher edition)
Suc Farm—Successful Farming (Eastern edition)
Sunset—Sunset (Central edition)

Tech W—Technology Week including Missiles and Rockets
    Continued as Aerospace Technology, Jl 17 '67
Time—Time
Todays Health—Today's Health
Travel—Travel

UN Mo Chron—UN Monthly Chronicle
UNESCO Courier—UNESCO Courier
U S Camera—U.S. Camera & Travel
U S News—U.S. News & World Report

Vital Speeches—Vital Speeches of the Day
Vogue—Vogue

Wilson Lib Bul—Wilson Library Bulletin
*Writer—Writer

Yachting—Yachting
Yale R—Yale Review

* Available for blind and other physically handicapped readers on talking books, in braille, or on magnetic tape. For information address Division for the Blind and Physically Handicapped, Library of Congress, Washington, D.C. 20542

LIST OF PERIODICALS INDEXED

All data as of latest issue received

ALA Bulletin—available only to members. m (bi-m Jl-Ag) American Library Association, 50 E Huron St, Chicago 60611

Aerospace Technology—$6. bi-w Aerospace Technology, 1001 Vermont Av, NW, Washington, D.C. 20005
Formerly Technology Week including Missiles and Rockets

America—$10. w (bi-w year-end issue) America Press, 106 W 56th St, New York 10019

The American Academy of Political and Social Science Annals—$10. free to members. bi-m American Academy of Political and Social Science, 3937 Chestnut St, Philadelphia 19104

American Artist—$8. m (S-Je) American Artist, 2160 Patterson St, Cincinnati, Ohio 45214

The American City—$10. m Buttenheim Pub. Corp, 757 3d Av, New York 10017

American Education—$3.75. m (bi-m D, Jl) American Education, Superintendent of Documents, U.S. Government Printing Office, Washington, D.C. 20402

American Forests—$6. m American Forestry Association, 919 17th St, NW, Washington, D.C. 20006

*American Heritage—$16.50. bi-m American Heritage, 383 W Center St, Marion, Ohio 43302

The American Historical Review—$15. free to members of the American Historical Association, 5 times a yr (O, D, F, Ap, Je) The Macmillan Co, 866 3d Av, New York 10022

The American Home—$3. m (bi-m Ja, Jl) The American Home, Independence Sq, Philadelphia 19105

The American Record Guide—$4.50. m American Record Guide, P.O. Box 319, Radio City Station, New York 10019

Américas—$5. m Pan American Union, Washington, D.C. 20006

Antiques—$12. m Straight Enterprises, Inc, 551 5th Av, New York 10017

The Architectural Forum—$12. m (bi-m Ja, Jl) The Architectural Forum, 111 W 57th St, New York 10019

Architectural Record—$6. m (semi-m My) Architectural Record, P.O. Box 430, Hightstown, N.J. 08520

Art News—$11.50. m (S-Je) Art News, 444 Madison Av, New York 10022

*The Atlantic—$8.50. m Atlantic Monthly Co, 8 Arlington St, Boston 02116

Audubon—$7. bi-m National Audubon Society, 1130 5th Av, New York 10028

Aviation Week & Space Technology—$10. w Aviation Week, P.O. Box 430, Hightstown, N.J. 08520

Better Homes and Gardens—$3. m Better Homes and Gardens, 1716 Locust St, Des Moines, Ia. 50303

Bulletin of the Atomic Scientists—$7. m (S-Je) Bulletin of the Atomic Scientists, 935 E 60th St, Chicago 60637

Business Week—$10. w Business Week, P.O. Box 430, Hightstown, N.J. 08520

The Catholic World—$6. m Catholic World, Harristown Road, Glen Rock, N.J. 07452

*Changing Times—$6. m Changing Times, The Kiplinger Magazine, Editors Park, Md. 20782

The Christian Century—$8.50. w Christian Century Foundation, 407 S Dearborn St, Chicago 60605

Commentary—$9. m American Jewish Committee, 165 E 56th St, New York 10022

Commonweal—$9. w (bi-w year-end issue, mid-Jl-mid-S) Commonweal Pub. Co, Inc, 232 Madison Av, New York 10016

Congressional Digest—$10. m (S-Je) Congressional Digest Corp, 3231 P St, NW, Washington, D.C. 20007

*Consumer Bulletin—$5. m Consumers' Research, Inc, Washington, N.J. 07882

*Consumer Reports—$6. m Consumers Union of U.S, Inc, 256 Washington St, Mount Vernon, N.Y. 10550

Craft Horizons—$8. bi-m American Craftsmen's Council, 44 W 53d St, New York 10019

Current History—$8.50. m Current History, Inc, 1822 Ludlow St, Philadelphia 19103

Dance Magazine—$8. m Dance Magazine, 268 W 47th St, New York 10036

The Department of State Bulletin—$10. w Department of State Bulletin, Superintendent of Documents, U.S. Government Printing Office, Washington, D.C. 20402

Design—$4.50. bi-m (S-Je) Design Magazine, 1100 Waterway Blvd, Indianapolis, Ind. 46202

Dun's Review—$5. m P.O. Box 3088, Grand Central Station, New York 10017
Formerly Dun's Review and Modern Industry

Ebony—$5. m Johnson Pub. Co, Inc, 1820 S Michigan Av, Chicago 60616

Electronics World—$6. m Electronics World, Portland Pl, Boulder, Colo. 80301

Esquire—$7.50. m Esquire, Portland Pl, Boulder, Colo. 80301

*Farm Journal (Central edition)—$1. m Farm Journal, Inc, 230 W Washington Sq, Philadelphia 19105

Field & Stream—$4. m Holt, Rinehart and Winston, Inc, 383 Madison Av, New York 10017

Flower Grower, The Home Garden—$3.50. m Flower Grower, 1031 Broadway, Albany, N.Y. 12201
Continued as Home Garden & Flower Grower Feb '67

Flying—$6. m Flying, Portland Pl, Boulder, Colo. 80301

Focus—$2. m (S-Je) American Geographical Society, Broadway at 156th St, New York 10032

*Foreign Affairs—$8. q Council on Foreign Relations, Inc, 58 E 68th St, New York 10021

Fortune—$14. m (semi-m Je, S) Fortune, 540 N Michigan Av, Chicago 60611

*Good Housekeeping—$5. m Good Housekeeping, Box 517, New York 10019

*Harper's Magazine—$8.50. m Harper's Magazine, 381 W Center St, Marion, Ohio 43302

Harvard Business Review—$10. bi-m Harvard Business Review, 108 10th St, Des Moines, Ia. 50305

*High Fidelity incorporating Musical America—$12. m High Fidelity, 2160 Patterson St, Cincinnati, Ohio 45214

Hobbies—$5. m Lightner Pub. Corp, 1006 S Michigan Av, Chicago 60605

*Holiday—$5.95. m Holiday, Independence Sq, Philadelphia 19105

Home Garden & Flower Grower—$3.50. m Home Garden, 1031 Broadway, Albany, N.Y. 12201

*Horizon—$16. q Horizon, 379 W Center St, Marion, Ohio 43302

The Horn Book Magazine—$6. bi-m Horn Book, Inc, 585 Boylston St, Boston 02116

Horticulture—$5. m Horticulture, 300 Massachusetts Av, Boston 02115

Hot Rod—$5. m Petersen Pub. Co, 5959 Hollywood Blvd, Los Angeles 90028

House & Garden incorporating Living for Young Homemakers—$6. m House & Garden, Boulder, Colo. 80301

House Beautiful—$6. m House Beautiful, P.O. Box 560, New York 10019

International Conciliation—$2.75. 5 times a yr (S, N, Ja, Mr, My) Carnegie Endowment for International Peace, 345 E 46th St, New York 10017

*Ladies' Home Journal—$4. m Ladies' Home Journal, Independence Sq, Philadelphia 19105

Library Journal—$10. semi-m (m Jl-Ag) R. R. Bowker Co, 1180 Avenue of the Americas, New York 10036

Life—$7.75. w (except one issue at year end) Life, 540 N Michigan Av, Chicago 60611

The Living Wilderness—$5. q The Wilderness Society, 729 15th St, NW, Washington, D.C. 20005

*Look (Middle Atlantic edition)—$5. bi-w Look, Look Bldg, Des Moines, Ia. 50304

McCall's—$3. m McCall's, McCall St, Dayton, Ohio 45401

Mademoiselle—$5. m Mademoiselle, Boulder, Colo. 80301

Modern Photography—$6. m Modern Photography, 2160 Patterson St, Cincinnati, Ohio 45214

Monthly Labor Review—$7.50. m Superintendent of Documents, U.S. Government Printing Office, Washington, D.C. 20402

Motor Boating—$6. m Motor Boating, P.O. Box 544, New York 10019

Motor Trend—$5. m Petersen Pub. Co. 5959 Hollywood Blvd, Los Angeles 90028

NEA Journal—available only to members. m (S-My) National Education Association of the United States, 1201 16th St, NW, Washington, D.C. 20036

The Nation—$10. w (bi-w Jl-Ag) Nation Associates, Inc, 333 6th Av, New York 10014

*National Geographic Magazine—$8. m The Secretary, National Geographic Society, Washington, D.C. 20036

National Parks Magazine—$5. m National Parks Association, 1701 18th St, NW, Washington, D.C. 20009

National Review—$10. bi-w (44p issue) National Review, 150 E 35th St, New York 10016

Nation's Business—$23.75. (3 yrs) m Chamber of Commerce of the U.S, 1615 H St, NW, Washington, D.C. 20006

*Natural History incorporating Nature Magazine—$7. m (bi-m Je-S) American Museum of Natural History, Central Park W at 79th St, New York 10024

The Negro History Bulletin—$3. m (O-My) Association for the Study of Negro Life and History, Inc, 1538 9th St, NW, Washington, D.C. 20001

The New Republic—$10. w (except the last week in Jl, the second and fourth weeks in Ag and the last week in D) New Republic, 381 W Center St, Marion, Ohio 43302

The New York Times Magazine—$39. w (complete Sunday ed; not sold separately) New York Times, Times Bldg, 229 W 43d St, New York 10036

The New Yorker—$8. w New Yorker Magazine, Inc, 25 W 43d St, New York 10036

*Newsweek—$10. w Newsweek, 117 E 3d St, Dayton, Ohio 45402

Opera News—$8. w (27 issues S 9-Je 15) The Metropolitan Opera Guild, Inc, 1865 Broadway, New York 10023

Outdoor Life—$4. m Outdoor Life, Boulder, Colo. 80312

The PTA Magazine—$2. m (S-Je) The PTA Magazine, 700 N Rush St, Chicago 60611

Parents' Magazine and Better Homemaking—$4. m Parents' Magazine, Bergenfield, N.J. 07621

Parks & Recreation—$5. m National Recreation and Park Association, 1700 Pennsylvania Av, NW, Washington, D.C. 20006

Plays—$7. m (O-My) Plays, Inc, 8 Arlington St, Boston 02116

Poetry—$10. m (bi-m Ap-My) Modern Poetry Association, 1018 N State St, Chicago 60610

Popular Electronics—$5. m Popular Electronics, Portland Pl, Boulder, Colo. 80302

Popular Gardening & Living Outdoors—$2. q Holt, Rinehart & Winston, Inc, 383 Madison Av, New York 10017

*Popular Mechanics—$4. m Popular Mechanics, Box 646, New York 10019

Popular Photography—$6. m Popular Photography, Portland Pl, Boulder, Colo. 80302

Popular Science Monthly—$4. m Popular Science, P.O. Box 1083, Boulder, Colo. 80302

Publishers' Weekly—$15. w (bi-w year end issue) R. R. Bowker Co, 1180 Avenue of the Americas, New York 10036

*Reader's Digest (Great Lakes edition)— $3.97. m Reader's Digest Association, Inc, Pleasantville, N.Y. 10570
     Enlarged type edition available from Xerox Corp, P.O. Box 3300, Grand Central Station, New York, N.Y. $4.50 a month or $25.65 for six months

Redbook—$3. m Redbook, McCall St, Dayton, Ohio 45401

*The Reporter—$7. bi-w (2 summer issues omitted) The Reporter, 660 Madison Av, New York 10021

The Saturday Evening Post—$3.95. 26 issues per year The Saturday Evening Post, Independence Sq, Philadelphia 19105

Saturday Review—$8. w Saturday Review, Inc, 380 Madison Av, New York 10017

School & Society—$9.50. bi-w (O-My, including summer annual) Society for the Advancement of Education, Inc, 1860 Broadway, New York 10023

School Arts—$7. m (S-Je) School Arts, Printers Bldg, Worcester, Mass. 01608

Science—$12. w American Association for the Advancement of Science, 1515 Massachusetts Av, NW, Washington, D.C. 20005

Science Digest—$5. m Science Digest, Box 654, New York 10019

Science News—$6.50. w Science Service, Inc, 1719 N St, NW, Washington, D.C. 20036

Scientific American—$8. m Scientific American, 415 Madison Av, New York 10017

Senior Scholastic—(Teacher education)—$5. w (S-My) Senior Scholastic, 902 Sylvan Av, Englewood Cliffs, N.J. 07632

*Seventeen—$6. m Seventeen, Radnor, Pa. 19088

Sky and Telescope—$6. m Sky Pub. Corp, 49-50-51 Bay State Road, Cambridge, Mass. 02138

*Sports Illustrated—$9. w (except one issue at year end) Sports Illustrated, 540 N Michigan Av, Chicago 60611

Successful Farming (Eastern edition)—$1. m Successful Farming, 1716 Locust St, Des Moines, Ia. 50303

Sunset (Central edition)—$3. in Calif, Ore, Wash, Idaho, Ariz, Nev, Utah, Hawaii. $5 in other states m Sunset Magazine, Menlo Park, Calif. 94025

Technology Week including Missiles and Rockets—$6. w (bi-w year-end issue) Technology Week, 1001 Vermont Av, NW, Washington, D.C. 20005
     Continued as Aerospace Technology Jl 17 '67

Time—$12. w Time, 540 N Michigan Av, Chicago 60611

Today's Health—$4. m Today's Health, 535 N Dearborn St, Chicago 60610

Travel—$6. m Travel, Travel Bldg, Floral Park, N.Y. 11001

UN Monthly Chronicle—$7. m (except in Ag) United Nations Publications, Room 1059, New York 10017

The UNESCO Courier—$5. m (bi-m Ag-S) UNESCO Pub. Center, 317 E 34th St, Department WS, New York 10016

U.S. Camera & Travel—$5. m U.S. Camera & Travel, Box 562, Des Moines, Ia. 50302

U.S. News & World Report—$12. w U.S. News & World Report, 435 Parker Av, Dayton, Ohio 45401

Vital Speeches of the Day—$8. semi-m City News Pub. Co, Inc, 1 Wolf's Lane, Pelham, N.Y. 10803

Vogue—$10. semi-m (m My-Jl, D) Vogue, Boulder, Colo. 80301

Wilson Library Bulletin—$5. m (S-Je) The H. W. Wilson Co, 950 University Av, Bronx, N.Y. 10452

*The Writer—$6. m The Writer, Inc, 8 Arlington St, Boston 02116

Yachting—$7. m Yachting Pub. Corp, 50 W 44th St, New York 10036

The Yale Review—$5. q Yale Review, 92-A Yale Station, New Haven, Conn. 06520

* Available for blind and other physically handicapped readers on talking books, in braille, or on magnetic tape. For information address Division for the Blind and Physically Handicapped, Library of Congress, Washington, D.C. 20542

KEY TO ABBREVIATIONS

+	continued on later pages of same issue	jr	junior
		jt auth	joint author
abp	archbishop		
abr	abridged	ltd	limited
Ag	August		
Ap	April	m	monthly
arch	architect	Mr	March
assn	association	My	May
Aut	Autumn	N	November
av	avenue	no	number
bart	baronet	O	October
bibliog	bibliography		
bibliog f	bibliographical footnotes	por	portrait
		pseud	pseudonym
bi-m	bimonthly	pt	part
bi-w	biweekly	pub	published, publisher, publishing
bldg	building		
bp	bishop	q	quarterly
co	company	rev	revised
comp	compiled, compiler		
cond	condensed	S	September
cont	continued	semi-m	semimonthly
corp	corporation	soc	society
		Spr	Spring
D	December	sq	square
dept	department	sr	senior
ed	edited, edition, editor	st	street
		Sum	Summer
F	February	sup	supplement
		supt	superintendent
Hon	Honorable		
il	illustrated, illustration, illustrator	tr	translated, translation, translator
inc	incorporated	v	volume
introd	introduction, introductory		
		w	weekly
Ja	January	Wint	Winter
Je	June		
Jl	July	yr	year

Sample entry: **CIGARETTES**
Your teen-ager and smoking. R. H. Roach. il
Todays Health 46:68-70+ Ja '68

Explanation: An illustrated article on the subject **CIGA-RETTES** entitled "Your teen-ager and smoking," by R. H. Roach, will be found in volume 46 of Todays Health, pages 68-70 (continued on later pages of the same issue) the January 1968 number

READERS' GUIDE TO
PERIODICAL LITERATURE

March 1967 — February 1968

AAAS. See American association for the advancement of science

AADC. See Association of American dance companies

AAF. See American advertising federation

AAFSS (advanced aerial fire support system) See Airplanes, Military—Armaments

AAHPER. See American association for health, physical education and recreation

AALL. See American association of law libraries

AASA. See American association of school administrators

AASL. See American association of school librarians

AAUP. See Association of American university presses; American association of university professors

A and P company. See Great Atlantic and Pacific tea company

ABA. See American bar association; American basketball association; American booksellers association

ABC. See American broadcasting company

ABM (anti-ballistic missile) See Guided missiles—Defenses

ABPC. See American book publishers council

AC electronics division. See General motors corporation—AC electronics division

A. C. Nielsen company. See Nielsen, A. C. company

ACC. See United Nations—Administrative committee on co-ordination

ACE. See American council on education

ACLU. See American civil liberties union

ACOG. See American college of obstetricians and gynecologists

ACT. See American conservatory theatre

ACTH
  Regulation of the adrenal cortex secretory pattern by adrenocorticotropin. H. R. Fevold. bibliog il Science 156:1753-5 Je 30 '67

ACWA. See Amalgamated clothing workers of America

A/D converters. See Computers—Input-output equipment

ADA. See Americans for democratic action

ADC (aid to dependent children) See Child welfare—United States

ADL. See B'nai b'rith—Anti-defamation league

A. E. pseud.
  Bring in the whiskey now. Mary. F. O'Connor. New Yorker 43:38-40+ Ag 12 '67

AEC. See United States—Atomic energy commission

AFA. See Air force association; American forestry association

AFBF. See American farm bureau federation

AFCEA. See Armed forces communications and electronics association

AFDC (aid to families with dependent children) See Child welfare—United States

AFDOUS. See Association of food and drug officials of the United States

AFL. See American football league

AFL-CIO. See American federation of labor and Congress of industrial organizations

AFT. See American federation of teachers

AFTRA. See American federation of television and radio artists

AHA. See American heart association

AIA. See American institute of architects

AIA-Sunset Western home awards. See Western home awards

AIAA. See Aerospace industries association of America

AICPA. See American institute of certified public accountants

AID. See Association for international development; United States—Agency for international development

AIDS (aircraft integrated data systems) See Aeronautic instruments

AIGA. See American institute of graphic arts

AILS (advanced integrated landing system) See Airplanes—Landing

AILSS (advanced integrated life support system) See Life support systems (space environment)

AIP. See American institute of planners

ALA. See American library association

ALARR (air-launched air-recoverable rocket) See Rockets—Use in research

ALPA. See Air line pilots association, International

ALPO. See Association of lunar and planetary observers

ALS (anti-lymphocyte serum) See Serum

ALSEP (Apollo lunar surface experiment package) See Moon—Surface

AMA. See American management association; American medical association

AMC. See American motors corporation

AOCA. See Associated opera companies of America

AOPA. See Aircraft owners and pilots association

AP. See Associated press

APA. See Association of producing artists

ARL group. See Association of research libraries

ARPA. See United States—Defense, Department of—Advanced research projects agency

ARTS (advanced radar traffic system) See Radar in aviation

A-scan. See Aeronautic instruments

ASCD. See Association for supervision and curriculum development

ASCS. See United States agricultural stabilization and conservation service

ASMS (advanced surface missile system) See Guided missiles—Launching from ships

ASPCA. See American society for the prevention of cruelty to animals

ASW (anti-submarine warfare) See Submarine warfare

AT and T. See American telephone and telegraph company

ATA. See Air transport association of America

ATM (Apollo telescope mount) See Artificial satellites—Astronomical applications

ATPI. See American textbook publishers institute

ATS (applications technology satellites) See Artificial satellites

AUPS. See American university press service, incorporated

AWACS (airborne warning and control system) See Radar defense networks

AWOL cases. See United States—Army—Desertion

AALTO, Alvar
  Man standing in the center. W. McQuade. por Arch Forum 126:112 Ja '67
  Timeless masterwork; Maire Gullichsen's Villa Mairea; reprint. F. Gutheim. il House B 110:82-7 Ja '68

AARDVARKS
  Aardvark, as in A. il Sci N 92:499 N 18 '67
  Its name has eight letters and comes first in Webster's. por Life 63:47 O 13 '67

AARKROG, A. and Lippert, J.
  Europium-155 in debris from nuclear weapons.
    bibliog Science 157:425-7 Jl 28 '67
AARON, Hank
  Homer of the Braves. H. L. Masin. por Sr
    Schol 91:28 S 21 '67
AARONS, Leroy F.
  Adoption laws. New Repub 156:10-11 Ja 28
    '67
AASE, Georgia Mae
  Pine cones and glass crafts. Design 69:16-19
    Wint '67
ABALONES
  Giant pinks. H. D. Brown. Hobbies 72:126 Ag
    '67
  Making bowls of abalone shells. il Sunset
    139:115 N '67
ABANDONED towns
  Centennial year for old Hamilton, Nevada. il
    Sunset 139:50 O '67
ABANDONMENT. See Desertion and non-sup-
    port
ABBE, Kathryn
  And all through the house. E. Galligan. il
    U S Camera 30:44-5 D '67
ABBEY, Edward
  West's land of surprises. Read Digest 90:61-5
    F '67
ABBOT, J. Lloyd, Jr
  Flight into Antarctic darkness. Nat Geog Mag
    132:732-8 N '67
ABBOTT, R. Tucker, and Jensen, Russell
  Molluscan faunal changes around Bermuda.
    bibliog Science 155:687-8 F 10 '67
ABBOTT, Thelma
  Regional report. Home Gard 54:50 Jl '67
ABBOTT, William L.
  Not all of labor agrees with Meany. New
    Repub 157:15-16 N 25 '67
ABDUCTIN. See Proteins
ABDULLAH, Mohammad
  Lion on the loose. il Newsweek 71:38 Ja 15
    '68
  Song of India. Nat R 20:16 Ja 16 '68
ABEL, Carlos A. and Grey, H. M.
  Carboxy-terminal amino acids of αA and αM
    heavy chains. bibliog Science 156:1609-10 Je
    23 '67
ABEL, I. W.
  Abel, ready and willing. por Newsweek 70:
    90+ S 25 '67
ABEL, Lionel
  Liberal anti-communism revisited. Com-
    mentary 44:32-3 S '67
  Varieties of reason. Commentary 44:106+ D
    '67
ABELES, Benjamin
  Inventor of the month. S. V. Jones. il por
    Sci Digest 61:17 F '67
ABELL, Bess
  Ghost hostess. il pors Newsweek 69:33-4 F
    20 '67
ABELL, Elizabeth (Clements)
  Able Bess's spectacular. il por Time 90:26-7
    D 8 '67
  White House's able Mrs Abell. G. Astor. il
    pors Look 31:74-7 Je 27 '67
ABERFAN, Wales
  Aberfan; happiness ended last October. T.
    Coleman. il Sat Eve Post 240:91-5 O 21 '67
  Aberfan's sad dispute over money; disaster
    fund. L. Wainwright. Life 63:28B S 15 '67
  Ghosts of Aberfan; one year later. W. Dan-
    forth. il McCalls 95:98-103+ N '67
  Village that lost its children. L. Lee. il Red-
    book 130:58-60+ Ja '68
ABERNETHY, Thomas Gerstle
  Speech that touched a tender nerve in Con-
    gress; excerpts from address, July 25, 1967.
    por U S News 63:33 Ag 7 '67
ABERT squirrels. See Squirrels
ABILENE, Kan.
  See also
  Eisenhower museum
ABILENE, Tex.
  9, 8, 7 . . stop. R. G. Taylor. il Am City
    82:129 My '67
ABILITY
  Alienation in the low-ability classroom. R. J.
    Mueller and A. H. Frerichs. bibliog f Sch
    & Soc 95:254-6 Ap 15 '67
  Biographical predictors of scientific per-
    formance. C. W. Taylor and R. L. Ellison.
    bibliog il Science 155:1075-80 Mr 3 '67
  Theory of educability. M. Schwebel. bibliog f
    Sch & Soc 95:306-9 Sum '67
    See also
  Creative ability
  Great men
ABILITY. Influence of age on
  Vintage mind; excerpts from The new years.
    A. W. Simon. il McCalls 95:75 Ja '68

ABILITY grouping in education
  Ability grouping and the average child; with
    a parent's comments. J. W. Wrightstone.
    il NEA J 57:9-11+ Ja '68
  D.C. may drop track system. Sr Schol 90:
    sup2+ Ap 14 '67
  Tracked or railroaded? civil-rights groups
    challenge system. il Newsweek 69:59 Ap
    24 '67
  What's new in grouping; with study-discus-
    sion program by D. Harris and E. Harris.
    H. A. Thelen. bibliog il PTA Mag 62:22-5,
    33 S '67
ABILITY tests
  See also
  Intelligence tests
  Maze tests
ABINGDON press
  Abingdon press institutes new award. Pub W
    191:56 F 13 '67
ABISCH, Roz
  Bookmaking exhibition on developing a pic-
    ture book. il por Pub W 191:98 F 6 '67
ABLATION shielding. See Shielding (heat)
ABLE, Bernard Renault
  Cold way to new life. L. Wainwright. Life
    62:16 Ja 27 '67
ABLON, Ralph E.
  Corporation of the future; address, October
    24, 1967. Vital Speeches 34:73-6 N 15 '67
ABNORMAL psychology. See Psychology, Path-
    ological
ABNORMALITIES (animals)
  Congenital malformations induced by mes-
    caline, lysergic acid diethylamide, and
    bromolysergic acid in the hamster. W. F.
    Geber. bibliog il Science 158:265-7 O 13 '67
  LSD: injection early in pregnancy produces
    abnormalities in offspring of rats. G. J.
    Alexander and others. bibliog il Science
    157:459-60 Jl 28 '67; Reply with rejoinder.
    J. A. DiPaolo. 158:522 O 27 '67
  Lysosomal enzyme inhibition by trypan blue:
    a theory of teratogenesis F. Beck and
    others. bibliog il Science 157:1180-2 S 8 '67
ABNORMALITIES (man) See Deformities
ABOLAFIA, Louis
  Abolafia for president. New Yorker 43:39-41
    My 13 '67
  Al Capp on the hippie economics. A. Capp.
    il Nations Bsns 55:64-7 S '67
ABOLITIONISTS
  Family divided; Grimké family. J. Steven-
    son. il Am Heritage 18:4-25+ Ap '67
ABOMINABLE snowman. See Animals, Myth-
    ical
ABORIGINES, Australian. See Australia—Na-
    tive races
ABORTION
  Abortion: a biological view; a legal view.
    T. L. Hayes; R. M. Byrn. Commonweal 85:
    676-81 Mr 17 '67
  Abortion and mental health. America 116:
    239 F 18 '67
  Abortion & pluralism. Commonweal 85:582-3
    F 24 '67; Discussion. 85:667-8+; 86:27-8 Mr
    17-24 '67
  Abortion beyond assumptions; symposium.
    Commonweal 86:408-23 Je 30 '67
  Abortion by consent? Christian Cent 84:132
    F 1 '67
  Abortion can be costly. America 116:411-12
    Mr 25 '67
  Abortion, Catholics, and the law. N. St John-
    Stevas. Cath World 206:149-52 Ja '68
  Abortion debate and tough ecumenism.
    America 116:336 Mr 11 '67
  Abortion gets its first thorough U.S. airing;
    report on International conference on abor-
    tion. Sci N 92:297-8 S 23 '67
  Abortion is not enough. M. Novak. Christian
    Cent 84:430-1 Ap 5 '67
  Abortion; laws and attitudes. P. Kerby. Na-
    tion 204:754-6 Je 12 '67
  Abortion, legal and free; British House of
    commons passes bill. Newsweek 70:32 Jl 24
    '67
  Abortion: one girl's story. V. Yudkin. Read
    Digest 91:69-72 Jl '67
  Abortion; symposium; with editorial com-
    ment. America 117:706-19 D 9 '67
  Abortion: unchangeable social custom. F.
    Marley. il Sci N 91:526-7 Je 3 '67
  Babies, for and against. il Sat Eve Post 240:
    96 Je 3 '67
  Campaign to make legal abortion easier.
    Good H 164:191-3 Mr '67
  Conference without consensus; International
    conference on abortion. R. A. McCormick.
    America 117:320-1 S 23 '67
  Coping with abortion; panel discussion. Mlle
    65:172-3+ O '67
  Crucial question about abortion. T. A. Wass-
    mer. Cath World 206:57-61 N '67

ACCELERATION (electrons, etc)—*Continued*
Heavy atoms and high energy. C. Behrens. il Sci N 91:484-5 My 20 '67
Hidden flaw; Enrico Beach, Mich. Sci Am 217:59 N '67
Japan moves forward; electron accelerator. S. Griffin. il Sci N 92:329 S 30 '67
Japanese join in. Sci N 92:127 Ag 5 '67
Linear accelerators for protons: new developments. D. E. Nagle. bibliog il Science 157:145-9 Jl 14 '67
Low-power accelerators. il Sci N 91:199 F 25 '67
Making a mockery of Title VI; question of a site for government's proposed atomic accelerator plant. Christian Cent 84:886 Jl 12 '67
New medical tool. Electr World 79:93 Ja '68
Onward to element 126; omnitron. Sci Am 217:50+ O '67
Particle physics balance shifts. il Sci N 92:295 S 23 '67
Streamer chamber; particle detector at Stanford linear accelerator. D. Yount. il Sci Am 217:38-46 bibliog(p 156) O '67
300 bev: compromise, progress, competition. Sci N 92:33-4 Jl 8 '67
200-BeV accelerator. Sci Am 216:56-7 F '67
200-bev accelerator: moving into a WASP's nest? B. Nelson. il Science 156:1713-16 Je 30 '67
200 bev: close Senate vote defeats effort to delay Weston project. B. Nelson. Science 157:294-5 Jl 21 '67; Discussion. 158:48+ O 6 '67
200 bev full steam. Sci N 91:471-2 My 20 '67
200 bev: harmony prevails as physicists close ranks. D. S. Greenberg. Science 155:983-5 F 24 '67
ACCEPTANCE. See Conduct of life
ACCESSORIES, Dress. See Dress accessories
ACCESSORIES, Household. See Household furnishings
ACCESSORIES, Photographic. See Photography—Apparatus and supplies
ACCIDENT litigations. See Actions and defenses
ACCIDENT; story. See Eclov, S.
ACCIDENT; story. See Gallant, M.
ACCIDENT law
    See also
Damages
ACCIDENTS
Accident-prone child. D. I. Manheimer and G. D. Mellinger. il Parents Mag 43:52-3+ Ja '68
Hidden habits of women; facts about home accidents. C. B. Hicks. il Todays Health 45:28-31+ D '67
How safe are your child's toys? T. J. Rakstis. il Todays Health 45:20-3 D '67
Why you need a safety program; Milwaukee; excerpts from address. H. G. Hatcher. il Am City 82:103-5 Ag '67
    See also
Collisions at sea
First aid in illness and injury
Sprains
Traffic accidents
    also subhead Accidents, or Accidents and injuries under various subjects, e.g. Aviation—Accidents

        Anecdotes, facetiae, satire, etc.
Springtime classic; home accidents during spring cleaning. W. Stanton. Look 31:14 Ap 18 '67
        Prevention
Rubber floors and rubber heels help to prevent falls. Consumer Bul 50:29-30 Ap '67
Safety in use of household chemicals. il Consumer Bul 50:19 S '67
Safety tips for tub and shower. Good H 165:184 S '67
Watch every step! C. Elliott. il Outdoor Life 140:44-5+ Ag '67
    See also
Safety devices and measures
    also subhead Safety devices and measures under various subjects, e.g. Automobiles—Safety devices and measures
ACCIDENTS, Liability for. See Liability (law)
ACCOUNTANTS
Accountant of tomorrow; address, April 25, 1966. J. W. Queenan. Vital Speeches 33:200-8 Ja 15 '67
Accounting: the other side of the ledger; embattled CPAs. il Duns R 89:36-7+ Mr '67
Maybe you need an accountant. il Changing T 21:45-7 N '67
ACCOUNTING
Accountant of tomorrow; address, April 25, 1966. J. W. Queenan. Vital Speeches 33:200-8 Ja 15 '67

Control by accountants. D. Wolfle. Science 156:895 My 19 '67
    See also
Billing
Bookkeeping
Corporations—Accounting
Cost accounting
ACCOUNTING, Household. See Budget, Household; Domestic finance
ACCOUNTING office, General. See United States—General accounting office
ACCOUNTING principles board. See American institute of certified public accountants
ACCREDITATION, College. See Colleges and universities—Accreditation
ACCREDITATION of library schools. See Library schools and education
ACCULTURATION
    See also
Americanization
ACCUTRON electric watches. See Watches, Electric
ACE, Goodman
Top of my head. See issues of Saturday review
Way back in '68. Sat Eve Post 240:22 O 21 '67
ACER saccharum. See Maple
ACETYLCHOLINE
Acetylcholine receptor: similarity in axons and junctions. P. Rosenberg and H. G. Mautner. bibliog il Science 155:1569-71 Mr 24 '67
Ionic mechanism of cholinergic inhibition in molluscan neurons. D. J. Chiarandini and H. M. Gerschenfeld. bibliog il Science 156:1595-6 Je 23 '67
Ionic mechanisms of cholinergic excitation in molluscan neurons. D. J. Chiarandini and others. bibliog il Science 156:1597-9 Je 23 '67
ACETYLCHOLINESTERASE
Acetylcholinesterase: method for demonstration in amacrine cells of rabbit retina. C. W. Nichols and G. B. Koelle. bibliog il Science 155:477-8 Ja 27 '67
Cholinergic binding capacity of proteolipids from isolated nerve-ending membranes. E. D. P. de Robertis and others. bibliog il Science 158:928-9 N 17 '67
Electrical phenomena associated with the activity of the membrane-bound acetylcholinesterase. T. Podleski and J. P. Changeux. bibliog il Science 157:1579-81 S 29 '67
ACHESON, Dean Gooderham
Acheson on negotiation; excerpts from televised interview. Reporter 37:28-9 D 28 '67
Criticize Greek leaders? excerpts from letter to The Washington post. por U S News 64:11 Ja 1 '68
Negotiate with the reds? Dean Acheson's advice; interview. por U S News 63:50-1 D 18 '67
        about
On the subject of pain. N. Cousins. Sat R 50:22 D 23 '67
ACHIEVEMENT tests
National assessment of educational progress: some technical deficiencies. C. A. Anderson. bibliog f Sch & Soc 95:48-50 Ja 21 '67
ACHIEVEMENTS, Student. See Student achievements
ACHILLEA. See Yarrows
ACHILLES, Tendon of. See Tendons
ACHLYA ambisexualis. See Molds (botany)
ACID phosphatases. See Phosphatases
ACIDOSIS
Metabolic aspects of acid-base change. W. D. Lotspeich. bibliog il Science 155:1066-75 Mr 3 '67
ACIDS, Fatty
Fatty acids in eleven species of blue-green algae: geochemical significance. P. L. Parker and others. bibliog il Science 155:707-8 F 10 '67
ACIDS, Organic
Isoprenoid acids in recent sediments. M. Blumer and W. J. Cooper. bibliog il Science 158:1463-4 D 15 '67
ACKERMAN, Edward A.
Population, natural resources, and technology. bibliog f Ann Am Acad 369:84-97 Ja '67
ACKERMAN, Michael
Opinion: on the hippie put-on. por Mlle 65:40+ S '67
ACKERMAN, William
Bradford ornamental pear. Horticulture 45:32 N '67
ACKLEY, Gardner
Now: an upturn in business; interview. pors U S News 63:34-9 S 4 '67

ACKLEY, Gardner—*Continued*

about

Good-by to LBJ's Mr Chips. il por Newsweek 71:57-8 Ja 15 '68
Ivied council. Time 91:11 Ja 12 '68
ACME visible records, incorporated
Turning deaf ear to rich suitors. il Bsns W p 148-50 Ja 14 '67
ACONCIO, Giacomo
Jacopo Aconcio as an engineer. L. White, jr. bibliog f Am Hist R 72:425-44 Ja '67
ACORN worms. See Balanoglossus
ACOSTA, Elizabeth Cleland
James Thurber, I love you. Sat Eve Post 240:88-9 My 20 '67
ACOSTA, Gus
Land and the sky. il U S Camera 30:54-5 D '67
ACOUSTICAL holography. See Holography
ACOUSTICAL waves. See Sound waves
ACOUSTICS. See Music—Acoustics and physics
ACOUSTICS, Architectural
Architects of silence. C. Stramentov. il UNESCO Courier 20:8-12 Jl '67
Lively arts; interview, ed. by R. Hemming. S. Skrowaczewski. Sr Schol 90:21 Mr 17 '67
Noise control in architecture: more engineering than art. il Arch Rec 142:193-203 O '67
Orchestra hall remodeled: the eye is pleased, but . . . ; Chicago report. R. C. Marsh. Hi Fi 17:MA20-1 Ja '67
Sound decay. S. V. Jones. il Sci Digest 63:94 Ja '68
ACQUISITIONS, Corporate. See Corporate acquisitions
ACQUISITIONS, Library. See Libraries—Acquisitions
ACRYLAMIDE
Artifact produced in disc electrophoresis by ammonium persulfate. J. M. Brewer. bibliog il Science 156:256 Ap 14 '67
ACRYLIC-latex additives. See Plastics
ACT of charity; story. See O'Connor, F.
ACT of self-defense; story. See Ford, J. H.
ACTING
Anthony Newly: inside out; ed. by E. Miller. A. Newley. il Seventeen 26:124-5+ O '67
Beaut of a British bird; ed. by E. Miller. L. Redgrave. il Seventeen 26:98-9+ D '67
Dean Martin talks about: his drinking, the Mafia, Frank Sinatra, women, Bobby Kennedy; interview, ed. by O. Fallaci. D. Martin. il Look 31:78-85+ D 26 '67
English Fox captures Hollywood! ed. by E. Miller. J. Fox. il Seventeen 26:140-1+ Mr '67
Hollywood scene; ed. by E. Miller. T. Stamp. il Seventeen 26:56-7 N '67
It doesn't come easy; ed. by E. Miller. D. Hemmings. il Seventeen 26:152-3+ My '67
It's a mad, mad world, old boy; interview, ed. by C. Brossard. R. Burton. Look 31:69-70 Je 27 '67
Jack Lemmon: most serious funnyman in the flicks; interview, ed. by C. Brossard. J. Lemmon. il Look 31:66-71 F 7 '67
Last visit with two undimmed stars; interview, ed. by J. Hamilton. K. Hepburn; S. Tracy. il Look 31:26-30+ Jl 11 '67
Theatre in Europe; English format. H. Clurman. Nation 204:797-8 Je 19 '67
You get what you go after; ed. by E. Miller. G. Lockwood. Seventeen 26:142-3+ F '67

Study and teaching

Clap hands, here comes Strasberg; method acting classes in Paris. il Time 90:78 O 6 '67
ACTINOMYCETES fossil. See Micropaleontology
ACTINOMYCIN
Actinomycin D blocks formation of memory of shock-avoidance in goldfish. B. W. Agranoff and others. bibliog il Science 158:1600-1 D 22 '67
Actinomycin D effect on amino acid absorption from rat jejunal loops. C. Yamada and others. bibliog il Science 158:129-30 O 6 '67
Temperature effect on protein synthesis in a heat-synchronized protozoan treated with actinomycin D. J. E. Byfield and O. H. Scherbaum. bibliog il Science 156:1504-5 Je 16 '67
Thyroxine interaction with actinomycin D and possible biological implications. K. H. Kim and others. bibliog il Science 156:245-6 Ap 14 '67

ACTION in art
Art in motion: Y. Agam's paintings. C. Willard. il Look 31:48-50 Ap 18 '67
ACTION painting. See Art, Abstract
ACTION photography. See Photography of moving objects
ACTIONS and defenses
Après-ski legality. il Time 89:45 Ja 27 '67
Gadflies who put the bite on business; plaintiffs' lawyers. il Bsns W p 124-6 O 14 '67
See also
Damages
ACTIVATED sludge. See Sewage disposal—Activated sludge method
ACTIVITIES, Playground. See Playground activities
ACTIVITIES, Student. See Student activities
ACTIVITY rhythms. See Periodicity
ACTOMYOSIN
Heat inactivation or the relaxing site of actomyosin: prevention and reversal with dithiothreitol. H. M. Levy and E. M. Ryan. bibliog il Science 156:73-4 Ap 7 '67
ACTORS and actresses
Show must go on, but not too long; Broadway stars balk at lengthy runs. J. Hallowell. il Life 63:41-2 Jl 21 '67
What's happening. G. Shalit. See issues of Ladies' home journal
You can see that I'm not twenty years old. B. Weinraub. il Sat Eve Post 240:38-41 F 25 '67
See also
Acting
American theatre wing
Children as actors
Children of actors and actresses
Moving picture actors and actresses
Television broadcasting—Performers
Theatrical agencies
Vaudeville
also names of actors and actresses, e.g. B. Lahr

Psychology

Manner of speaking: sadness of the performer. J. Ciardi. Sat R 50:12-13 Je 24 '67
ACTORS and actresses, Negro. See Negro actors and actresses
ACTOR'S workshop. See San Francisco—Theater
ACTRESSES. See Moving picture actors and actresses
ADAIR, Doug
Cesar Chavez's biggest battle. Nation 205:627-8 D 11 '67
ADAIR, Eugene
Preservation; interview. New Yorker 43:31-3 F 25 '67
ADAM, David P. and others
Enclosed bark as a pollen trap. bibliog Science 157:1067-8 S 1 '67
ADAM, Robert
Adam revolution in furniture. E. Stillinger. il por Antiques 91:218-22 F '67
Statuary for an Adam house. R. Davidson. il Antiques 91:186 F '67
ADAMANTANAMINE. See Amantadine hydrochloride
ADAMO, S. J.
Press. See issues of America
Story of Charles Davis. America 116:777-80 My 27 '67
ADAMS, Abigail (Smith)
Portraits of John and Abigail Adams: a quest for a likeness. A. Oliver. il pors Antiques 91:476-80 Ap '67
ADAMS, Alice
Young couple with class; story. Redbook 129:72-3 S '67
ADAMS, Alice, 1931-
Stitching. Craft Horiz 27:26-31 S '67

about

Woven structures of Alice Adams. B. Kafka. il Craft Horiz 27:14-17 Mr '67
ADAMS, Ansel
Ansel Adams. Pop Phot 61:82-3 Jl '67

about

California exposed: Eloquent light exhibition at the Boston museum of fine arts. M. R. Weiss. il por Sat R 50:50-3 S 23 '67
David in Adamsland. D. Vestal. il Pop Phot 61:90-101+ D '67
ADAMS, Armenta
Africa revisited. por Hi Fi 17:MA26-7 Ag '67
ADAMS, Eleanor
Sex education: the Swedish system. Sr Schol 90:sup 16-17 Ap 21 '67
ADAMS, Frederick B. Jr
Family friend of all the world. por Wilson Lib Bul 41:573-5 F '67

ADAMS, Hazard
  Place and movement. Poetry 110:42-4 Ap '67
  Wreath of elegies. Poetry 109:310-16 F '67
ADAMS, Henry
  Letters, and life, of Henry Adams. L. Kronenberger. por Atlan 219:80-4+ Ap '67
ADAMS, J. Donald
  In the shadow of Sagamore Hill. Sat R 50:33 My 6 '67
ADAMS, John
  Portraits of John and Abigail Adams: a quest for a likeness. A. Oliver. il pors Antiques 91:476-80 Ap '67
ADAMS, Lillian S.
  If FLES is to succeed. NEA J 56:72 D '67
ADAMS, Marguerite Gay
  Christmas-lost; poem. Good H 165:234 D '67
ADAMS, Molly
  Living with plants. il Horticulture 45:34-5+ S '67
ADAMS, Phoebe Lou
  Points North. Atlan 219:99-100+ Mr '67
  Potpourri. See issues of Atlantic
ADAMS, Robert Martin
  Cowley as critic. New Repub 156:24-6 Mr 11 '67
ADAMS, Russell E. Jr
  Substrata communications. Pop Electr 28:45-8+ Ja '68
ADAMS, Samuel
  Firebrand of the revolution. A. Winston. il por Am Heritage 18:60-4+ Ap '67
ADAMS, William P.
  Store techniques stressed at CBA convention. Pub W 192:26-7 S 4 '67
ADAMS, William Taylor
  Authors vs critics: children's books in the 1870's; excerpt from The rise of children's book reviewing in America, 1865-1881. R. L. Darling. il por Pub W 192:25-7 O 16 '67
ADAPTATION (biology)
  Ornithine-urea cycle activity in xenopus laevis: adaptation in saline. R. L. McBean and L. Goldstein. bibliog il Science 157:931-2 Ag 25 '67
  Serum osmolality in the coelacanth, latimeria chalumnae: urea retention and ion regulation. G. E. Pickford and F. B. Grant. bibliog il Science 155:568-70 F 3 '67
  Terrestrial adaptations of crustaceae: symposium in memory of Warren J. Gross. il Science 157:1592-3 S 29 '67
  Visceral tissue vascularization: an adaptive response to high temperature. R. O. Rawson and others. il Science 158:1203-4 D 1 '67
  See also
  Evolution
  Genetics
ADAPTATION (botany)
  Euglena gracilis: a novel lipid energy reserve and arachidonic acid enrichment during fasting. A. Rosenberg. bibliog il Science 157:1189-91 S 8 '67
ADAPTATION, Social. See Adjustment, Social
ADAPTIVE machines. See Perceptrons
ADARKAR, Vivek B.
  Let's just say I've been around; story. Seventeen 26:148-9 Ap '67
ADCOCK, Cynthia L.
  Third-party expectations. Nation 205:186-8 S 4 '67
ADCOCK, George
  Ambulance crisis. Todays Health 45:25-7+ Mr '67
ADDAMS, Charles
  Mother Goose; illustrations. Sat Eve Post 240:36-41 O 21 '67
ADDANKI, Somasundaram, and others
  Passive transport of 5,5-dimethyl-2,4-oxazolidinedione into beef heart mitochondria. bibliog Science 155:1678-9 Mr 31 '67
ADDICTS, Drug. See Narcotic addicts
ADDING machines
  Electric adding machines. il Consumer Rep 32:486-90 S '67
ADDISON'S disease
  More light on a JFK ailment. U S News 63:9 Jl 24 '67
  Pathologist-sleuth reopens Kennedy controversy; suggests J. F. Kennedy suffered from Addison's disease. Sci N 92:79-80 Jl 22 '67
  Postmortem on JFK. il Newsweek 70:54 Jl 24 '67
ADDITIONS, House. See Houses, Remodeled
ADDITIVES. See Gasoline—Additives; Storage batteries—Additives
ADDITIVES, Food. See Food additives
ADDONIZIO, Hugh J.
  Lethal indifference. L. M. Moroze. Nation 205:105-7 Ag 14 '67
ADDRESSEE unknown; story. See McInerny, R.

ADE, Ginny
  Strip mining in Pennsylvania. Nat Parks Mag 41:15-17 Mr '67
ADEL, Alf
  Cutting, punching and drilling of printed circuit boards. Pop Electr 28:57-9 Ja '68
ADELPHI university, Garden City, N.Y.
  College or career for dancers? Adelphi's answer. E. Stodelle. il Dance Mag 41:60-3 Mr '67
  Dorne collection. Am Artist 31:6 Mr '67
ADEM, A. A.
  Solid-state flashers for light displays. Electr World 78:83-4 Ag '67
  Solid-state ring counters and chasers for light displays. Electr World 78:84-5 S '67
ADEN
  Aden is a little Vietnam for Britain. H. Smith. il N Y Times Mag p 12-14+ Jl 23 '67
  Aden: keeping the peace, and tempers. il Life 62:36-7 Ap 14 '67
  Aden: the way it was. A. Waugh. Nat R 19:855 Ag 8 '67
  As the British pull out: another big vacuum. J. Law. il U S News 63:64-5 N 27 '67
  At full flood; anti-British rioting. il Time 89:45-6 Ap 14 '67
  Case history of terror. G. DeCarvalho. il Life 63:94A+ D 8 '67
  Competition of hate. il Time 89:39 Mr 10 '67
  Coveted pesthole. il Newsweek 69:54+ Mr 13 '67
  Desert feud that's explosive. il U S News 62:65-6 Ap 17 '67
  Nasser's drive for south Arabia. L. Mosher. il Reporter 36:24-7 F 9 '67
  New power play? il Newsweek 69:63 Ap 17 '67
  Storm in the Crater. il Newsweek 70:38+ Jl 3 '67
  Under siege. A. Higbee. Newsweek 69:62+ Mr 27 '67
  Violence greets U.N. team: opposition to Britain's plan for granting independence to Aden and states of the South Arabian protectorate. il Sr Schol 90:14-15 Ap 21 '67
  Where more conflict is brewing in Mideast. U S News 63:9 Jl 10 '67
  See also
  United Nations—Aden
ADENAUER, Konrad
  Europe's elder statesman sizes up today's world; summary of interview, ed. by K. Lachmann. por U S News 62:63 F 13 '67

  about
  Adenauer dies. il pors Sr Schol 90:17-18 My 5 '67
  Adenauer 1876-1967. J. Bell. il pors Life 62:119-20 Ap 28 '67
  Adenauer's tragedy. C. Amery. Nation 204:580 My 8 '67
  Burying Der Alte, and an era. il Newsweek 69:50-1+ My 8 '67
  Death of Der Alte. America 116:668 My 6 '67
  Gathering at the grave. il Time 89:28-9 My 5 '67
  Imperishable place. il por Time 89:32+ Ap 28 '67
  Konrad Adenauer. G. Bailey. Reporter 36:12-13 My 4 '67
  Konrad Adenauer. W. S. Schlamm. Nat R 19:457 My 2 '67
  Man who put Germany where it is today. por U S News 62:22 My 1 '67
  Summoning up to judgment. il por Newsweek 69:32-3 My 1 '67
  To honor Der Alte. il por Life 62:34-8 My 5 '67
  Why Adenauer turned against U.S. por U S News 62:89 My 15 '67
ADENOHYPOPHYSITIS. See Pituitary body—Diseases
ADENOSINE phosphates
  Adenosine 3',5'-cyclic phosphate: stimulation of steroidogenesis in sonically disrupted adrenal mitochondria. S. Roberts and others. bibliog il Science 158:372-4 O 20 '67
ADENOSINE triphosphatase
  Cochlear function and sodium and potassium activated adenosine triphosphatase. W. Kuijpers and others. bibliog il Science 157:949-50 Ag 25 '67
  Sodium- and potassium-activated adenosine triphosphatase of gills: role in adaptation of teleosts to salt water. F. H. Epstein and others. bibliog il Science 156:1245-7 Je 2 '67
  Sodium and potassium effects on skeletal muscle microsomal adenosine triphosphatase and calcium uptake. B. B. Rubin and A. M. Katz. bibliog il Science 158:1189-90 D 1 '67

ADENOSINE triphosphatase—*Continued*
Sodium-potassium adenosine triphosphatase: acyl phosphate intermediate shown to be L-glutamyl-γ-phosphate. A. Kahlenberg and others. bibliog il Science 157:434-6 Jl 28 '67
ADENOSINE triphosphate
Adenosine triphosphate usage by flagella. C. J. Brokaw. bibliog il Science 156:76-8 Ap 7 '67
Muscle-spindle histochemistry. B. Nyström. bibliog il Science 155:1424-6 Mr 17 '67
ADENOVIRUSES
Adenovirus endocarditis in mice. Z. R. Blailock and others. bibliog il Science 157: 69-70 Jl 7 '67
Adenovirus tumorigenesis: role of the viral genome in determining tumor morphology. W. A. Strohl and others. bibliog il Science 156:1631-3 Je 23 '67
Transforming activity of green monkey SA7, C8 adenovirus in tissue culture. A. D. Alstein and others. bibliog il Science 158:1455-7 D 15 '67
ADENYL cyclase. See Enzymes
ADHESIVE tape
Handyman how-to. il Bet Hom & Gard 45: 38+ Mr '67
ADHESIVES
Guide to household adhesives. il Consumer Rep 32:230-2 Ap '67
ADIRONDACK forest preserve. See Forests, State
ADIRONDACK MOUNTAINS
Adirondack spring; with photographs. E. Porter. Audubon 69:32-7 Mr '67
Adirondacks; forever wild? with editorial comment. J. T. Cunningham. il Audubon 69:4, 38-43 Mr '67
Forever wild: the Adirondacks, by E. Porter. Review
  Liv Wildn 30:32-3 Aut '66. P. Strain
ADIRONDACK park. See New York (state)—Parks and reserves
ADJUSTMENT (psychology)
What kind of mates will our teen-agers be? T. Irwin. il Todays Health 45:20-3 S '67
ADJUSTMENT, Economic
  See also
Job satisfaction
ADJUSTMENT, Social
American woman: her breaking point. F. F. Flach. Vogue 149:248+ My '67
Children in crisis. J. R. Komaiko. il Parents Mag 42:35-7+ F '67
Christine discovers love. J. K. Besterman. il Good H 164:60+ My '67
Girl who can't say yes; questions and answers. A. Wood. Seventeen 26:170+ F '67
How is youth to be served? H. Fairlie. New Repub 156:12-14 Ap 8 '67
How you can beat fatigue. A. Lake. il Seventeen 26:112-13+ Je '67
I want to be liked for myself alone; questions and answers. A. Wood. Seventeen 26:146+ O '67
I'll never live among strangers again. V. Hancock. McCalls 94:20+ S '67
I'm tired of it all; questions and answers. A. Wood. Seventeen 26:178+ My '67
In my opinion; teen-agers take themselves too seriously. K. Callanan. Seventeen 26: 262 My '67
Missionary's predicament: how far to adapt? H. Horan. America 117:197-200 Ag 26 '67
On becoming a social being; with study-discussion program, by R. Strang. L. J. Yarrow. bibliog il PTA Mag 61:18-20, 30 F '67
Program for a prom dropout; questions and answers. A. Wood. Seventeen 26:124+ D '67
Roots of student despair; reprint. S. L. Halleck. il Sci Digest 62:65-70 S '67
Strange celebration. Mrs I. M. M. Gilbert. McCalls 95:38+ D '67
Take it easy with teen-agers. H. Thomson. il Todays Health 45:33-5 F '67
Tiny tots a go-go; group adjustment program for four & five year olds; Mountain View, Calif. D. Gale. il Parks & Rec 2:26-7+ Ag '67
What teenage friendships are all about. E. G. Neisser. il Parents Mag 42:48-50+ Jl '67
  See also
Aged—Adjustment problems
College students—Adjustment
Conformity
High school students—Adjustment
Individual and society
Maturity
Security and insecurity (psychology)
ADJUSTORS, Debt. See Debtor and creditor
ADLAI Stevenson Institute of International affairs
Living memorial. Newsweek 69:46 F 20 '67
Stevenson institute of international affairs. B. Ward. Christian Cent 84:862-3 Jl 5 '67

ADLER, Bill
Laugh a day; excerpts from Treasury of medical wit and humor. Todays Health 45: 40-1 Ap; 52-3 My '67
(comp) Young hearts and valentines. Good H 164:84-5 F '67
ADLER, Emma Morel
Trustees' garden village. Antiques 91:331 Mr '67
ADLER, Hans
Rebirth of a salesman; poem. Christian Cent 85:38 Ja 10 '68
ADLER, Kurt Herbert
San Francisco sound; interview, ed. by F. Merkling. pors Opera N 32:18-19 S 23 '67
ADLER, Larry
Seeking a mark. il por Time 89:48-9 Je 30 '67
ADLER, Lee
Systems approach to marketing. bibliog f Harvard Bsns R 45:105-18 My '67
ADLER, Leopold, 2d
Historic Savannah foundation, inc. Antiques 91:334-8 Mr '67
ADLER, Renata
Letter from Israel. New Yorker 43:114+ Je 17 '67
Letter from the Palmer house. New Yorker 43:56-8+ S 23 '67
Reporter at large. New Yorker 43:116+ F 25; 55-8+ Ap 15 '67
  about
Rigors of criticism. por Time 90:38 D 1 '67
Youth movement. il por Newsweek 70:99-99A D 4 '67
ADLER, Robert Philip
Mightier than the pencil. por Time 89:92+ Mr 17 '67
ADLER, Stella
Women worth watching. por(p30) McCalls 95:104 Ja '68
ADMINISTRATION, Public
United Nations programme in public administration. UN Mo Chron 4:25-6 F '67
  See also
Bureaucracy
Government spending policy
ADMINISTRATION of justice. See Justice, Administration of
ADMINISTRATIVE ability. See Executive ability
ADMINISTRATIVE and budgetary committee. See United Nations—Administrative and budgetary committee
ADMINISTRATIVE and political divisions
  See also
Apportionment (election law)
ADMINISTRATIVE assistants to the president. See Public officers
ADMINISTRATIVE committee on co-ordination. See United Nations—Administrative committee on co-ordination
ADMINISTRATIVE communication. See Communication in management
ADMINISTRATIVE remedies
  See also
Ombudsman
ADMINISTRATORS, College. See College officials
ADMINISTRATORS, Government. See Public officers
ADMISSIONS; story. See Frank, J.
ADOLESCENCE
Adults cause most teen-age problems. Sch & Soc 95:512+ D 23 '67
Alienated youth. J. Down. il Sch & Soc 95: 252-4 Ap 15 '67
Casanova, junior grade. G. Porter. il Read Digest 90:81-3 Ap '67
Getting the kids we deserve. E. J. Anthony. il N Y Times Mag p57+ Ja 22 '67
On turning thirteen. J. A Zill. il Look 31: 50-2 Ag 22 '67
Our troubled youth; address. August 18, 1967. R. W. Menninger. Vital Speeches 34:121-5 D 1 '67
What adolescents should know about adolescence; symposium; with a study-discussion program by C. Smallenburg and H. Smallenburg. R. Armour. bibliog il PTA Mag 62:10-13, 33-4 S '67
  See also
Boys
Girls
Puberty
Youth
ADOLESCENT literature. See Childrens literature
ADOLESCENT medicine. See Youth—Health and hygiene
ADOLESCENTS. See Youth
ADOLPH, E. F.
Heart's pacemaker; with biographical sketch. Sci Am 216:19, 32-7 bibliog(p 150) Mr '67

ADOPTED children. See Children, Adopted

ADOPTION

Adoption laws; case of the Liuni family. L. F. Aarons. New Repub 156:10-11 Ja 28 '67

Child is a child, is a child. P. Garland. il Ebony 22:44-6+ Ap '67

Cradle of 10,000 babies; placement service in Evanston, Ill. L. Wolters. il Todays Health 45:47-8 Ag '67

Half a home is better than none; adoption by a single parent. il Time 90:44+ D 8 '67

Mixed adoptions; Los Angeles County department of adoptions program. Newsweek 69:58 Ap 24 '67

Moment of doubt. Redbook 130:8+ Ja '68

New ease in adoptions. il Time 89:76 Ja 27 '67

One parent is better than none. L. D. Armstrong. il Good H 164:69+ F '67

Our outdated adoption laws. M. Gross. il Parents Mag 42:64-5+ N '67

Should an adopted child match the parents' background? il Good H 165:172 Ag '67

They asked us to give up our child. M. Liuni. il Ladies Home J 84:92-3+ Ap '67

What's new in adoption? C. Carner. bibliog il Todays Health 45:44-7+ Ag '67

See also

Children, Adopted

ADOPTION of cities. See Intercommunity cooperation

ADRENAL cortex

See also

Corticosteroids

ADRENAL glands

Regulation of the adrenal cortex secretory pattern by adrenocorticotropin. H. R. Fevold. bibliog il Science 156:1753-5 Je 30 '67

Renin-like enzyme in the adrenal gland. J. W. Ryan. bibliog il Science 158:1589-90 D 22 '67

ADRENAL mitochondria. See Mitochondria

ADRENOCORTICOTROPIC hormones. See ACTH

ADRIAN, Max

GBS; one man show. Newsweek 70:115 O 23 '67

ADSORBENTS

Carbon dioxide removal unit developed by Ham Standards; molecular selves. Tech W 20:29 Ap 10 '67

ADULT education

Continuing education; address, December 16, 1966. H. A. Moreen. Vital Speeches 33:244-7 F 1 '67

From mop to typewriter; pilot clerical training unit at the University of California at Los Angeles. L. A. W. Darling. il NEA J 56:28-9 O '67

Lights are on; and the whole family goes to school at night; Operation Reach M. A. Marlar. il Am Ed 3:21-4 My '67

Make way for drop-ins. V. Hartke. il NEA J 56:22-3 N '67

New university of the air; project in Great Britain. Sch & Soc 95:519+ D 23 '67

Rickover on universal adult education. W. W. Brickman. Sch & Soc 95:169 Mr 18 '67

Sister from Carlisle; nun teaches illiterates in Carlisle, England. W. D. Boutwell. PTA Mag 62:10 D '67

Unesco's program; forty-eight countries participate to eradicate adult illiteracy. Sch & Soc 95:480+ D 9 '67

Year we went back to school. L. Santalo. il Redbook 128:10+ F '67

You're reading, Mr Mitchell! Greenleigh project to test reading systems for adult illiterates. M. W. Clark. NEA J 56:16-19 My '67

See also

Labor and laboring classes—Education

Trade schools

United States—Armed forces—Education

University extension

Library participation

Books for adults beginning to read. Wilson Lib Bul 41:83-7 S '66; Correction. 41:671 Mr '67

Limited adult reader; Cleveland public library's Reading centers program. T. E. Barensfeld. il Library J 92:3004-7 S 15 '67

Orientation of the out-of-school adult to the use of public libraries; preconference workshop sponsored by the Adult services division, Reference service division, with cooperation of Public library association. M. C. Hannigan. ALA Bul 61:829-30 Jl '67

ADULT music study See Music—Instruction and study

ADULT-youth relationship. See Youth-adult relationship

ADULTERY

Four cases in the new morality; excerpts from You and the new morality. J. A. Pike. Ladies Home J 84:104-5+ My '67

Testing of a marriage. McCalls 95:18+ Ja '68

You shall not commit adultery. H. A. Bosley. Read Digest 91:139-42 O '67

ADULTHOOD. See Maturity

ADVANCED integrated life support system. See Life support systems (space environment)

ADVANCED management courses. See Executives—Training

ADVANCED management program, Harvard university. See Harvard university—Graduate school of business administration

ADVANCED radar traffic system. See Radar in aviation

ADVANCED research and technology, Office of. See United States—National aeronautics and space administration—Advanced research and technology, Office of

ADVANCED research projects agency. See United States—Defense, Department of—Advanced research projects agency

ADVANCEMENT schools. See Schools, Experimental

ADVENT

As Advent approaches; reality of the Advent message. N. Pittenger. Christian Cent 84:1522-4 N 29 '67

ADVENTURE and adventurers

Old man and the sea. il Newsweek 69:61-5 Je 12 '67

ADVERTISEMENTS. See Advertising

ADVERTISING

Bristol-Myers' hard sell. T. A. Wise. il Fortune 75:118-21+ F '67

Can you claim equality with competitor's product? H. F. Pilpel. Pub W 191:86 Ja 30 '67

News behind the ads. See issues of Changing times

Parochial stigma; advertising in Catholic newspapers. S J. Adamo. America 117:44 Jl 8 '67

University of Chicago press drops black Chicago ad. il Pub W 192:246-7 Ag 28 '67

War of the suds; Lite vs. Lite. il Newsweek 70:80-1 O 2 '67

Welcome to the consumption community; excerpt from The Americans: the world experience. D. J. Boorstin. il Fortune 76:118-20+ S 1 '67

What nudists look at; advertisement for Sony portable television set. il Newsweek 70:66 Jl 24 '67

See also

Communication

Newspapers—Advertising policy

Photography in advertising

Public relations

Television advertising

also subhead Advertising under various subjects, e.g. Books—Advertising

Anecdotes, facetiae, satire, etc.

Coils of fate. Christian Cent 84:607 My 3 '67

Tell me, pretty billboard. N. Perrin. New Yorker 43:163-4+ Ap 22 '67

Bibliography

Books in communications. A. Balk. See issues of Saturday review

Costs

Color the ad dollar a paler green. Bsns W p93-4 Ag 26 '67

When $30-million walks the plank; strike causes cutback in Ford TV advertising. il Bsns W p38 S 16 '67

History

Lost: two anvils; growth from a 1704 newspaper ad to multi-billion-dollar industry. Sr Schol 90:5 Ap 28 '67

Laws and regulations

New watchdog for the admen? highlights of AAF annual meeting. il Bsns W p94-6 F 18 '67

Moral aspects

See Advertising ethics

Psychological aspects

Art of bamboozlement; concerning theories of John Kenneth Galbraith. R. L. Shayon. Sat R 50:37 Jl 29 '67

Psychology

Kooky creator of antic advertising. il Bsns W p76+ Je 10 '67

Mini-sell on Madison avenue. J. Weingarten. il Duns R 90:27-8+ Jl '67

ADVERTISING—*Continued*

Social aspects
Service of suggestions; economic and social effects of advertising. J. W. Hobson. Duns R 89:93-4 Ap '67

Europe, Eastern
Running it up the Danube. Time 90:62 S 1 '67

Israel
War is over, courtesy of Wissotzky tea. il Time 89:67 Je 30 '67

ADVERTISING, Classified
Classified experiment; Philadelphia evening bulletin. Newsweek 70:52 Ag 28 '67
Make your classified ad get action. il Changing T 21:23-4 D '67

ADVERTISING, Direct mail
Licking the postage hike; third-class mailers. Bsns W p52 D 9 '67
Select list for advertisers; Metromail group. Bsns W p92 My 27 '67

ADVERTISING, Fraudulent
Roadside bargain; misleading roadside advertising. J. Heath. il Consumer Bul 50:18-19 Jl '67

ADVERTISING, Municipal. See Municipal advertising

ADVERTISING, Outdoor
Of many things; upgrading outdoor advertising. P. Weber. America 117:inside cover Jl 1 '67
See also
Billboards

ADVERTISING, Political
Ad-itorial voices. Newsweek 70:84-5 N 6 '67
Good, the true and the beautiful; causes of the right. J. G. Dunne. Sat Eve Post 240:16+ Ag 12 '67

ADVERTISING, Public service
SR's fifteenth annual advertising awards. W. D. Patterson. il Sat R 50:76-83 Ap 8 '67

ADVERTISING, Radio. See Radio advertising

ADVERTISING agencies
Adman who plays with paper airplanes: H. Gossage of board of Shade tree corp, San Francisco. il Bsns W p74-6+ F 11 '67
Agency love, on the rocks? shuffling of accounts. G. Lazarus. Sat R 50:94-5 My 13 '67
It's new, different, and it's all mine. G. Lazarus. Sat R 50:93-4 N 11 '67
Preventive maintenance in client-ad agency relations. M. P. Ryan and R. H. Colley. Harvard Bsns R 45:66-74 S '67
See also names of advertising agencies, e.g. Wells, Rich, Greene, incorporated

Advertising
Now ad men plug their own wares; self-promotion to bring in new business. il Bsns W p 178+ My 6 '67

Consolidations and mergers
Foot in Detroit's door; Leo Burnett co.-D.P. Brother & co. merger. Newsweek 69:82 Mr 27 '67
Marriage, agency style. G. Lazarus. il Sat R 50:58-9 S 9 '67

Finance
Ad men shiver as profits melt. il Bsns W p36-7 D 23 '67

ADVERTISING art
Fashion illustrating. M. Meixner. il Design 68:22-4 Ja '67

ADVERTISING campaigns
Color her blood; success of Clairol campaigns. Newsweek 69:70 Je 19 '67
Dear friends; Avis and Hertz, truce or ruse? il Newsweek 69:88 F 13 '67
Take that! gas and oil firms feud. il Newsweek 69:84 My 8 '67

ADVERTISING cards
Trade cards; comp. by W. G. McLoughlin. il Am Heritage 18:48-63 F '67

ADVERTISING ethics
Advertising; let's stop tampering with the machinery; address, February 8, 1967. C. L. Gould. Vital Speeches 33:434-8 My 1 '67
See also
Advertising, Fraudulent

ADVERTISING in politics. See Advertising, Political

ADVERTISING mediums

Catholic press
Chancery office clout; problem of obtaining advertising for diocesan news-weeklies. S. J. Adamo. America 117:584-5 N 11 '67

Labels
Labels of John Elliott jr. J. C. Hughes. il Antiques 91:514-17 Ap '67

Newspapers
Can a newspaper claim copyright in ads? H. F. Pilpel. Pub W 191:87 Ja 30 '67
See also
Advertising, Classified
Newspapers—Advertising policy

Packaging
Best-dressed packages go out most often. G. Lazarus. il Sat R 50:103-5 Je 10 '67

Periodicals
New leaf in catalogue sales; Gamble-Aldens catalogue inserted in the Saturday evening post. Bsns W p44 Ag 19 '67

ADVERTISING research
Defending the big advertiser; with charts. Bsns W p98+ Ap 15 '67

ADVICE columns. See Newspapers—Advice columns

ADVISORY board on national parks, historic sites, buildings and monuments. See United States—Advisory board on national parks, historic sites, buildings and monuments

AEDES aegypti. See Mosquitoes

AEGEAN ISLANDS
Cruising and chartering the Greek islands. B. Robinson. il Yachting 121:42-5+ F '67
See also
Hydra (island)

AEGYPTOPITHECUS zeuxis. See Apes, Fossil

AEOLIAN corporation
Way grandpa played it. Time 90:76 Ag 4 '67

AEPYORNIS titan. See Birds, Extinct

AERIAL cableways. See Cableways

AERIAL cameras. See Cameras

AERIAL mapping. See Mapping, Aerial

AERIAL photography. See Photography, Aerial

AERIAL reconnaissance
Needs outpace strong Viet recon gains. C. Brownlow. il Aviation W 86:19-22 Mr 13 '67
USAF boosts North Viet ECM jamming. C. Brownlow. il Aviation W 86:22-5 F 6 '67

AERIAL reconnaissance cameras. See Cameras

AERIAL routes. See Airways

AERIAL tramways. See Cableways

AERO spacelines, incorporated
Johnston to head Aero spacelines. Aviation W 87:30 N 20 '67
Mini Guppy begins certification testing. G. S. Hunter. il Aviation W 87:72-3+ Jl 3 '67

AEROCARS. See Airplanes, Light—Automobile combinations

AERODYNAMICS
Subsonic aeronautics enters renaissance. W. S. Beller. il Tech W 20:38-9 Ap 10 '67
Wide range of speeds covered in studies. R. Pay. il Tech W 20:92+ Mr 27 '67
See also
Air flow

AEROFLOT (airline) See Airlines—Russia

AEROJET-General corporation
Aerojet moving into water purification. J. F. Judge. il Tech W 20:26-8 Mr 6 '67
Computer-controlled manikin developed by Aerojet, USC. il Tech W 20:20 Ap 3 '67
Subcontracts on SST and 747 keynote Aerojet diversification. Aviation W 87:28 D 25 '67
Where the people are; Watts manufacturing co. to employ Negroes. il Newsweek 70:84 S 18 '67

AERONAUTIC associations. See Aviation associations

AERONAUTIC charts
Washington clipboard; standardizing government-produced aeronautical charts. R. Burkhardt. Flying 80:20 My '67

AERONAUTIC conferences. See Aviation conferences

AERONAUTIC education. See Aviation education

AERONAUTIC engineering. See Aviation engineering

AERONAUTIC exhibitions. See Aviation—Exhibitions

AERONAUTIC instruments
Advanced avionics used widely in AH-56A. C. M. Plattner. il Aviation W 86:28-31 My 15 '67
Airborne collision avoidance systems. P. J. Klass. il Aviation W 87:85-8+ Jl 10; 97+ Jl 17 '67
Airline anti-collision units seen in 1974. Aviation W 86:24 Je 26 '67

AERONAUTIC instruments—*Continued*
Airlines expected to tell collision avoidance needs. H. Taylor. il Tech W 20:18-19 Je 26 '67
Altitude programer developed by Pan Am. K. J. Stein. il Aviation W 87:76-7 Jl 31 '67
Anti-collision system uses atomic clock. P. J. Klass. il Aviation W 86:70-1+ F 6 '67
Army will test multiple approach system: A-scan. K. J. Stein. il Aviation W 87:72-3+ Ag 7 '67
Attack angle system set for Gulfstream 2. R. G. O'Lone. il Aviation W 87:89+ O 9 '67
Bendix offers dual-mode flight director. K. J. Stein. il Aviation W 86:81-2+ Mr 13 '67
Concorde flight instruments developed: combination horizon-flight director and combination heading and navigation situation display. il Aviation W 86:218+ My 29 '67
EROS, an airborne collision avoidance system. J. H. Wujek, jr. il Electr World 78:35-8+ D '67
Existing hardware pushed for AWADS. Aviation W 88:23 Ja 1 '68
Expanded AIDS use planned by American; aircraft integrated data systems. Aviation W 87:41 S 18 '67
Flight tests of army LOH avionics begin. P. J. Klass. il Aviation W 86:65+ Je 12 '67
Fractionalization marks French industry. P. J. Klass. il Aviation W 86:89+ Je 5 '67
Infrared under study for pilot warning. P. J. Klass. Aviation W 87:6-7 D 25 '67
ILAAS sets new management patterns; IHAS system under development. K. J. Stein. il Aviation W 86:273+ Mr 6 '67
IR device tested as turbulence detector: infrared scanning radiometer to detect clear air turbulence. R. D. Hibben. il Aviation W 86:61+ F 20 '67
Low-airspeed device designed for VTOLS. il Aviation W 88:59-60 Ja 8 '68
Mid-air payoff: new mid-air collision-avoidance system. il Time 90:62 Jl 21 '67
NASA seeks low-cost collision warning. D. A. Brown. il Aviation W 87:114-15+ S 18 '67
Navy to test autonavigator on carrier. C. D. LaFond. il Tech W 20:28-9 Mr 13 '67
New data yield clues to reliability. P. J. Klass. il Aviation W 86:80-1+ F 13 '67
New recorder developed for large jets. K. J. Stein. il Aviation W 87:52-4 D 25 '67
New vertical-scale instruments ordered by TWA for 747 engines. il Aviation W 87:39 D 11 '67
Pan Am plans to evaluate turbulence detector on 707. Aviation W 86:35 Ap 10 '67
Pilots to demand more SST operating data; acceleration in development of supersonic instruments urged. H. J. Coleman. Aviation W 87:69+ D 11 '67
Safer skies: collision-avoidance system. Newsweek 70:53 Jl 24 '67
T-33s used to check aerospace systems. G. S. Hunter. il Aviation W 86:97-8+ F 6 '67
Time to fly; Automatic fuel-range computer. il Flying 81:82+ S '67
Traffic control of advanced SST studied. K. J. Stein. il Aviation W 86:79-82 My 22 '67
See also
Altimeters
Automatic pilot (airplanes)
Compass
Gyro compass
Inertial guidance systems
Radio telephone on aircraft
Tacan

Display systems
Bullseye GCA radar uses phased array; new precision approach radar to simplify ground control approach. P. J Klass. il Aviation W 87:56-7+ Jl 3 '67
CSF offers head-up display for operational flight tests. D. E. Fink. il Aviation W 88:68-9+ Ja 8 '68
Head-up unit tried in Category 3 system; incorporation of display in Douglas all-weather landing equipment. il Aviation W 86:60-1+ Je 26 '67
Plastic lenses cut F-111B display weight; vertical display indicator group system. R. G. O'Lone. il Aviation W 86:69-72 F 27 '67
Texas instruments readying display system for AAFSS. Tech W 20:36 Je 12 '67

Testing
IHAS prototype flight tests under way. B. Miller. il Aviation W 87:80-1+ D 4 '67
Net barrier system to be tested in France. W. C. Wetmore. il Aviation W 87:113+ D 11 '67
USAF tests digital flight instruments. K. J. Stein. il Aviation W 87:89+ D 11 '67

AERONAUTIC laboratories
See also
Cornell aeronautical laboratory, incorporated
AERONAUTIC meteorology. See Meteorology, Aeronautic
AERONAUTIC research
NACA si, NASA no. W. J. Coughlin. Tech W 20:132 Mr 27 '67
NASA engine work keyed to components. M. L. Yaffee. il Aviation W 87:64-5+ S 4 '67
NASA expanding aeronautical research. il Aviation W 86:34 Ja 30 '67
NASA moves to upgrade general aviation technology. Tech W 21:18-19 Jl 3 '67
NASA reshapes aeronautics role; termination of X-15. W. J. Normyle. Aviation W 88:26-7 Ja 15 '68
New emphasis directed toward propulsion and aerodynamics. W. S. Beller. il Tech W 20:35-6 Ja 30 '67
U.K. industry join in anti-noise research. H. J. Coleman. il Aviation W 87:61+ Ag 14 '67
See also
Rand corporation
AERONAUTICS
See also
Aviation

Accidents
See Aviation—Accidents

Charts
See Aeronautic charts

Exhibitions
See Aviation—Exhibitions

History
Offspring of Icarus. il UNESCO Courier 20:18-19 My '67

Safety devices and measures
See Aviation—Safety devices and measures

Study and teaching
See also
Air pilots—Training
Aviation education
AERONAUTICS, Commercial
IATA discussions focus on giant jet transports. Aviation W 87:29 D 25 '67
North Atlantic edges near 5-million year. J. W. Carter. il Aviation W 87:24-5 D 25 '67
747 economies seen sacrificed to frills. Aviation W 87:31 O 2 '67
SST and the government: critics shout into a vacuum. R. J. Samuelson. il Science 157:1146-51 S 8 '67; Discussion. 158:313+ O 20 '67
See also
Air freight service
Air travel
Airlines

Federal aid
SST sets precedents in fund recovery. H. D. Watkins. il Aviation W 87:44-5+ O 16 '67

International aspects
See Aviation—International aspects

Non-scheduled operations
See Local service airlines

Europe, Western
Heavy industry key to European market. D. E. Fink. il Aviation W 86:297+ Mr 6 '67
Spurt seen in European general aviation. il Aviation W 86:342-5 My 29 '67

Iran
See also
Airlines—Iran

Russia
See also
Airlines—Russia

United States
Economic gains forecast for SST. il Aviation W 86:26-7 My 22 '67
Hub airport congestion splits user ranks; difficulties confronting air taxi and commuter airline operators. D. A. Brown. Aviation W 86:121+ Je 12 '67
Martin withdraws as SST subcontractor. Aviation W 87:23 S 25 '67
Ten urgent aeronautical tasks. C. L. Johnson. Tech W 20:66-7 Ja 23 '67
Transportation, challenge to air travel: address, June 26, 1967. F. D. Hall. Vital Speeches 33:656-9 Ag 15 '67
See also
Airlines—United States

AERONAUTICS, Military
Advanced aircraft, ground equipment creating new demands. C. D. LaFond and R. Barnhart. il Tech W 20:79-81+ Mr 27 '67
Six acrobatic teams display skills in precision flying; photographs by J. H. Pickerell. Aviation W 87:62-9 Ag 21 '67
Variety of techniques marks team flying. W. H. Gregory. il Aviation W 87:50-1+ Ag 21 '67
    See also
Airplanes, Military
Helicopters—Military applications

Great Britain
Healey's procurement policy under fire; joint Anglo-French variable-geometry aircraft program. H. J. Coleman. Aviation W 86:20-1 F 20 '67

Iran
Neutral Iran will add F-4Ds to strengthen air defense. H. D Watkins. il Aviation W 87:50-1+ Ag 7 '67

Israel
Israelis relied on helicopters for movement of troops, logistics support, pilot rescue. W. C. Wetmore. il Aviation W 87:90-1+ Ag 7 '67
    See also
Israeli-Arab war, 1967—Aerial operations

Russia
Weapons on display: voluntary & involuntary; Moscow show. il Time 90:34+ Jl 21 '67
    See also
Aircraft, Military—Russia

United States
AMSA future keyed to penetration study; advanced manned strategic aircraft. M. Getler. Tech W 20:12-14 F 13 '67
Congress told new conflict would strain air resources. D. C. Winston. Aviation W 86:18 My 22 '67
Military aeronautics, technology for the 70's. il Tech W 20:37-43+ Mr 27 '67
Services face deep program cuts. C. Brownlow. Aviation W 87:22-3 Ag 7 '67
Strategic planning centers on missiles. E. H. Kolcum. il Aviation W 86:69-74 Mr 6 '67
Subsonic aeronautics enters renaissance. W. S. Beller. il Tech W 20:38-9 Ap 10 '67
    See also
Air bases
Airplanes, Military—United States

Vietnam (Republic)
    See also
Vietnamese war, 1957- Aerial operations
AEROSOL generators. See Electric generators
AEROSOLS
Detergent to spray with care; Fantastik spray cleaner. Consumer Rep 32:461-3 S '67
Purse dispenser for spray products. il Consumer Rep 32:348 Jl '67
Trips that kill; fumes from cocktail-glass chiller. il Time 90:77 O 13 '67
What can't they can? directory of aerosols for photographers. H. Zucker. Pop Phot 60:118 My '67
AEROSPACE education. See Aviation education
AEROSPACE industries
Loan restriction imperils exports. D. C. Winston. Aviation W 87:26-7 S 18 '67
    See also
Airplane industry and trade

Employees
Industry job total to reach 1.4 million. Aviation W 87:32 S 18 '67

Finance
Companies report record sales, profits. Aviation W 86:318 Mr 6 '67
Industry expansion problems to squeeze profit margins. W. H. Gregory. il Aviation W 86:82-5+ Mr 6 '67
Profit margins rise in fourth quarter. Aviation W 86:114 Ap 24 '67
6.8 per cent rise forecast for aerospace sales. Aviation W 87:18-19 D 25 '67
United offering spotlights capital need. W. H. Gregory. il Aviation W 87:24-5 S 4 '67

Oceanographic activities
Industry investing heavily in oceanology. il Aero Tech 21:44+ S 25 '67

Securities
Bond market attracting aerospace firms. W. H. Gregory. il Aviation W 86:103-5+ Ap 10 '67

Wall Street: ABC's of the ABM. C. Morgello. Newsweek 70:77 O 2 '67
Widely varying views given on aerospace stock outlook. H. M. David. il Tech W 20:24-5 Je 19 '67

Europe
Special report: Europe shifts basic patterns; symposium. il Aviation W 86:84-9+ My 29 '67

Europe, Western
Cooperation urged for European industry. Aviation W 87:81-2+ S 25 '67
Europe's techno-politics. R. Hotz. Aviation W 87:11 O 2 '67
Production consortiums emerge as new hope in aerospace. L. Doty. il Aviation W 86:84-9+ My 29 '67
Status of major U.S. European defense, aerospace programs. Aviation W 86:62-6 Mr 6 '67
Timidity slowing technological decisions; European aerospace cooperative programs. H. J. Coleman. il Aviation W 86:94-5+ My 29 '67
    See also
Eurospace

France
France's CFTH-HB emphasizing exports. il Aviation W 86:296-301 My 29 '67
French consolidate aerospace industry to gird for joint development efforts. il Aviation W 86:90-2 Mr 6 '67
French industry ties to U.S. seen strong; with editorial comment by R. Hotz. Aviation W 86:11, 22+ Je 19 '67

Germany (Federal Republic)
R&D curtailment jolts German industry. L. Doty. Aviation W 86:24-5 Mr 13 '67
West German industry being consolidated. il Aviation W 86:149+ My 29 '67

Great Britain
Aerospace firms face U.K. profits test. H. J. Coleman. Aviation W 87:34 Jl 10 '67
Aerospace industry faces U.K. inquiry. Aviation W 87:34 Ag 14 '67
Britain is seeking to stabilize industry. H. J. Coleman. il Aviation W 86:97+ Mr 6 '67
U.K. industry leaders cite trade imbalance with U.S. Aviation W 87:23 D 18 '67

Sweden
Swedegroup moves to increase exports. il Aviation W 86:183-4 My 29 '67

United States
Aerospace firms prominent at OECON. il Tech W 20:32-3 F 20 '67
Aerospace industry: its future. U S News 63:45 N 6 '67
Aerospace industry sets course to new peaks. R. Hotz. Aviation W 86:60-1 Mr 6 '67
Aerospace shoots for diversity. il Bsns W p 150-2 D 9 '67
Bond market attracting aerospace firms. W. H. Gregory. il Aviation W 86:103-5+ Ap 10 '67
Companies report record sales, profits. Aviation W 86:318 Mr 6 '67
Complex-complex; distrust of military-industrial complex. M. Getler. Aero Tech 21:58 Ja 1 '68
Economists debate military-industrial concentration. Sci N 93:33-4 Ja 13 '68
Faithless men. Nation 204:547-8 My 1 '67
Industry expansion problems to squeeze profit margins. W. H. Gregory. il Aviation W 86:82-5+ Mr 6 '67
Industry investing heavily in oceanology. il Aero Tech 21:44+ S 25 '67
Industry offers wide range of space rescue system plans. H. M. David. Tech W 20:30-1 Mr 20 '67
Industry sales hit $27.3 billion in 1967. Aero Tech 21:11 Ja 1 '68
Industry told of responsibility to continue space program. W. S. Beller and C. D. LaFond. il Tech W 20:46-7 My 15 '67
Message for industry; excerpts from address. R. H. Charles. Aviation W 86:11 Mr 13 '67
NASA lists top 100 contractors. Aviation W 87:69-70+ O 2 '67
New aerospace products. See issues of Aviation week & space technology
New market for aerospace technology; symposium; with editorial comment. il Tech W 20:20-4+, 66 Je 5 '67
1967, a year of decision. R. W. Martin, jr. Aviation W 86:11 F 20 '67
Outlook for 1968. R. Hotz. Aviation W 88:11 Ja 1 '68
Profit margins rise in fourth quarter. Aviation W 86:114 Ap 24 '67

AEROSPACE industries—United States—*Cont.*
Salute to the transistor. P. J. Klass. Aviation W 88:21 Ja 15 '68
Space: what's in it for industry; address, October 16, 1967. J. R. Moore. Vital Speeches 34:76-9 N 15 '67
Spending with aerospace industry climbs to record total of $37.3 billion. il Tech W 20: 14-15 Ja 30 '67
Status of major U.S. European defense, aerospace programs. Aviation W 86:62-6 Mr 6 '67
Ten urgent aeronautical tasks. C. L. Johnson. Tech W 20:66-7 Ja 23 '67
Turbulent summer; effect of nation's grave problems. R. Hotz. Aviation W 87:11 Jl 31 '67
U.S. aerospace exports; tables. Aviation W 87:66 Ag 28 '67
U.S. move to hard sell in Paris pays off. C. Brownlow. Aviation W 86:37 Je 12 '67
War, changes strain aerospace industry. M. L. Yaffee. il Aviation W 86:77-81 Je 5 '67
    See also names of aerospace firms, e.g. McDonnell aircraft corporation
AEROSPACE industries association of America
Modest goals, benefits seen key to future. J. Rhea. il Aero Tech 21:21-2+ S 11 '67
AEROSPACE materials. See Materials
AEROSPACE medical division. See United States—Air force—Systems command
AEROSPACE technology (periodical)
Letter to our readers; change of name from Technology week to Aerospace technology. W. W. Parrish. Tech W 21:8 Jl 3 '67
AEROSPACE telemetry. See Space telemetry
AESCHYLUS
House of Atreus: a point of view. J. Lewin. il Cath World 206:118-20 D '67
Oresteia; adaptation. See Lewin, J. House of Atreus
Prometheus bound; adaptation. See Lowell, R.
AESTHETIC values. See Worth
AESTHETICS
Art and beauty; excerpt from The book of art. il Design 68:33-5 Mr '67
Esthetics in traditional Africa. R. F. Thompson. il Art N 66:44-5+ Ja '68
Mind: an essay on human feeling, by S. K. Langer. Review
    New Yorker 43:98+ Ag 12 '67. W. Sargeant
Missing element; standards of taste and morality. B. W. Tuchman. PTA Mag 61:20-2 My '67
    See also
Architecture—Philosophy
Art—Philosophy
Harmony (aesthetics)
Music—Philosophy and aesthetics
Romanticism
AFFECTIONATE divorce; story. See Rodgers, M. A.
AFFECTIONATELY, Harold; story. See Shelnutt, E.
AFFLERBACH, Lois. See Bry, I. jt. auth.
AFGHAN dancing. See Dancing, Afghan
AFGHANISTAN
    See also
Economic assistance in Afghanistan
Theater—Afghanistan

Foreign relations
Prime Minister of Afghanistan visits the United States; exchange of greetings, exchange of toasts, and joint statement, March 28, 1967. M. H. Maiwandwal; L. B. Johnson. Dept State Bul 56:627-32 Ap 17 '67
AFRICA
Africa and the African genius: symposium. il UNESCO Courier 20:4-37 Je '67
Fact sheet on newly independent Africa. il Sr Schol 91:7-8 O 5 '67
Monthly report on Africa. P. McStallworth. Negro Hist Bul 30:19-20 Ja '67
New Africa; address, November 9, 1966. J. Palmer. Vital Speeches 33:272-8 F 15 '67
    See also
Agriculture—Africa
Americans in Africa
Arts and crafts—Africa
Asians in Africa
Colleges and universities—Africa
Copyright—Africa
Economic assistance in Africa
Education—Africa
Guerrillas—Africa
Hunting—Africa
National parks and reserves—Africa
Natural resources—Africa
Science—Africa
Slavery—Africa

Socialism—Africa
South Africa
Sports—Africa
States (Africa)
Tourist trade—Africa
United Nations—Africa
Zoology—Africa

Antiquities
Protection of Africa's artistic heritage; address, April 1966. E. Eyo. il UNESCO Courier 20:2, 16-19 Je '67

Bibliography
African bookshelf. G. M. Carter. Nation 205:90-2 Jl 31 '67

Civilization
View from outside. J. Burnham. Nat R 19: 128 F 7 '67

Description and travel
Captain Canot, American slave-trader, visits the African town of Timbo. T. Canot. il Negro Hist Bul 30:10 O '67
Marvin Newman in Africa. E. Galligan. il U S Camera 30:61+ My '67
New films: focus on Africa. V. M. Falconer. il Sr Schol 91:sup 18-19 O 5 '67

Discovery and exploration
All for the love of a lady; walking from Cape Town to Cairo. B. O'Brien. il Field & S 72:32-3+ Ja '68

Economic conditions
Africa and America; address, March 31, 1967. J. Palmer. 2d. Dept State Bul 56:646-51 Ap 24 '67
    See also
United Nations—Economic commission for Africa

Foreign opinion
Certain apprehension; possible effects of execution of M. Tshombe. il Time 90:26 Ag 4 '67

Foreign relations
Africa in the world arena. K. W. Grundy. bibliog f Cur Hist 52:129-35+ Mr '67
    See also
Africa—Neutrality

History
Bibliography
Articles and other books received; comp. by D. E. Gardinier. See issues of American historical review

Historiography
Current problems of African historiography; address, October 22, 1965. C. G. Contee. bibliog il Negro Hist Bul 30:5-10 Ap '67
Scientific study of Africa's history. K. O. Dike. il UNESCO Courier 20:8-13 Je '67

Maps
Africa 1967: independent states. UNESCO Courier 20:20-1 Je '67
Map of Africa (cont) Sr Schol 91:26 O 5 '67

Native races
Day in the life of a bushman. J. D. Ratcliff. il Read Digest 91:29-30+ S '67
Dressing up the Masai. il Time 90:40 N 24 '67
    See also
Hausas

Neutrality
Africa and the world: nonalignment reconsidered; address, April 1967, with questions and answers. F. L. Hadsel. Ann Am Acad 372:93-104 Jl '67

Photographs
African image. Mod Phot 32:64-9 Ja '68

Politics
Africa and America; address, March 31, 1967. J. Palmer. 2d. Dept State Bul 56:646-51 Ap 24 '67
African affairs; a confusion of colonels. E. Huxley. Nat R 19:466-7 My 2 '67
Entering 1968. E. Huxley. Nat R 20:33+ Ja 16 '68
Man, we've got enough problems of our own! S. Lewin. Sr Schol 91:8 O 5 '67
Report on Africa; symposium. bibliog f il Cur Hist 52:129-74+ Mr '67
Will Africa make the transition? E. M. von Kuehnelt-Leddihn. Nat R 19:1114 O 17 '67
    See also
Organization of African unity
Tricontinental conference, Havana, 1966

AFRICA—*Continued*

Race problems

See also
Asians in Africa
    also subhead Race problems under
    names of African countries, e.g. South
    Africa—Race problems

Religious institutions and affairs
World around us. Christian Cent 84:1574 D
    6 '67
See also
Church of England in Africa
Missions—Africa

Social conditions
See also
Slavery—Africa

Study and teaching
Africa and slave trade in the classroom. W.
    L. Katz. Negro Hist Bul 30:11 O '67
AFRICA, EAST
See also
Hunting—Africa, East
Mozambique
Public opinion—Africa, East
Research—Africa, East
Science—Africa, East
Zoology—Africa, East

Description and travel
Easy adventure: East Africa. S. M. Howland.
    il Travel 128:30-5 N '67

Economic integration
Seeds of hope; formation of the East African
    economic community. il Newsweek 70:53
    D 11 '67
Smart new club; East African economic com-
    munity. il Time 90:33 D 22 '67

Politics
Uncommon cry; East African community
    created. il Time 89:42 Je 16 '67

Race problems
Black resentment for the Asians. il Time 89:
    32+ F 24 '67
AFRICA, NORTH
Other Africa: the Maghreb; address, May 9,
    1967. J. Palmer. 2d. Vital Speeches 33:522-7
    Je 15 '67; Same. Dept State Bul 56:806-14
    My 29 '67
See also
Sahara Desert
Tunisia
World war, 1939-1945—Campaigns and battles
    —Africa
Politics
Arab vs. Arab: gain for Russia; Soviet arms.
    il U S News 63:67 Jl 24 '67
Trends in north Africa. W. H. Lewis. Cur
    Hist 52:136-41+ Mr '67
World's next danger area. il U S News 62:
    62-4 Ap 17 '67
AFRICA, NORTHEAST
Trouble in Northeast Africa. il U S News
    62:52-4 Je 19 '67
AFRICA, NORTHWEST
See also
Spanish Sahara
AFRICA, SOUTHEAST
See also
Swaziland
AFRICA, SOUTHERN
See also
Botswana
Lesotho
South Africa

Economic relations
Africa: new nations and new alignments: As-
    sociation of Botswana, Lesotho and Swazi-
    land with South Africa. N. Mostert. il
    Reporter 36:27-31 Je 29 '67

Foreign relations
Lost heritage: African good will. R. E. Dodge.
    Christian Cent 84:1395-6 N 1 '67

Race problems
Africa's guerrillas extend their fight. A.
    Delius. il Reporter 37:38-40 O 5 '67
International seminar on apartheid, racial dis-
    crimination and colonialism in southern
    Africa; United Nations. UN Mo Chron 4:40-7
    Ag '67
Now guerrilla war threatens white Africa. il
    U S News 63:122-3 S 25 '67

United States, the United Nations and
    southern Africa; address, January 27, 1967.
    A. J. Goldberg. Dept State Bul 56:289-94 F
    20 '67
U.S. viewpoint on four current world prob-
    lems; statement, September 21, 1967. A. J.
    Goldberg. Dept State Bul 57:488-9 O 16 '67
AFRICA, WEST
See also
Angola
Food supply—Africa, West
Ivory Coast
Niger River
Nigeria
Science—Africa, West

Social history
Africa remembered, ed. by P. D. Curtin. Re-
    view
    Sat R 50:39-41 Je 10 '67. C. Miller
AFRICA and the United States
America and Africa: the New World and the
    newer world; address, May 26, 1967. N. D.
    Katzenbach. Dept State Bul 56:954-9 Je 26
    '67; Same. Vital Speeches 33:622-5 Ag 1 '67
America's understanding of Africa, address,
    October 21, 1967. J. Palmer. 2d. Dept State
    Bul 57:656-60 N 13 '67
AFRICAN affairs, Bureau of. See United
    States—State, Department of—African af-
    fairs, Bureau of
AFRICAN architecture. See Architecture,
    African
AFRICAN art. See Art, African
AFRICAN authors. See Authors, African
AFRICAN banded mongooses. See Mongooses
AFRICAN languages
Vernacular languages in a changing society.
    P. Diagne. il UNESCO Courier 20:29-32 Je
    '67
AFRICAN literature
Dawn, the totem, the drums. W. Cartey.
    Commonweal 86:227-30 My 12 '67
Trends in present-day African literature;
    excerpts from African literature. E.
    Mphahlele. il UNESCO Courier 20:22-3+ Je
    '67
See also
Childrens literature—Africa

Bibliography
African bookshelf. UNESCO Courier 20:37 Je
    '67
AFRICAN millipedes. See Millipeds
AFRICAN scientists. See Scientists, African
AFRICAN students in the United States. See
    Foreign students in the United States
AFRICAN violets
African violets. H. Van Zele. il Horticulture
    45:24-6 D '67
New African-violets. il Home Gard 54:57
    O '67
What you should know to grow African-
    violets. J. T. Neal. Home Gard 54:41 O '67
AFRICANS
East Africa turns on with khat. L. Fellows.
    il N Y Times Mag p22-3+ Jl 9 '67
AFTER the rain; drama. See Bowen, J.
AFTERNOON newspapers. See Newspapers
AGA Khan IV
Three faces of the fourth Aga; with report
    by T. Thompson. il pors Life 63:43-6+ N
    17 '67
AGAINST a backdrop; story. See White, W.
AGAM, Yaacov
Art in motion. C. Willard. il por Look 31:
    48-50 Ap 18 '67
AGAN, Jennette
My mother, the pie maker. Parents Mag 42:
    90-3+ N '67
AGAR
Disulfur monoxide: production by desulfo-
    vibrio. W. P. Iverson. bibliog il Science 156:
    1112-14 My 26 '67
AGASSI, Joseph
Kirchhoff-Planck radiation law. bibliog Sci-
    ence 156:30-7, Ap 7 '67
AGATES
Gem color and forest fires. H. D. Brown. il
    Hobbies 72:126 O '67
Manhattan onyx. H. D. Brown. Hobbies 72:
    125 Ap '67
AGATHE'S tale; ballet. See Ballets—Criticisms
AGATTU ISLAND
Agattu military mission? Nat Parks Mag
    41:21 Ja '67

AGE
    See also
    Age groups
    Aging
    Longevity
    Middle age
    Old age
AGE (animals)
    Tell age of cattle by their teeth. J. Herrick.
    il Suc Farm 65:50H Ap '67
AGE (plants)
    Lupinus arcticus Wats. grown from seeds of
    pleistocene age. A. E. Porsild and others.
    bibliog il Science 158:113-14 O 6 '67
AGE (psychology)
    In my opinion: there's no disgrace in dating
    younger boys. J. Brentlinger. Seventeen
    26:198 O '67
AGE, School. See School age
AGE, Voting. See Suffrage—United States
AGE and ability. See Ability, Influence of age
    on
AGE and employment
    Job redesign for older workers: case studies.
    H. J. Rothberg. Mo Labor R 90:47-51 Ja
    '67
    Near-forgotten aged; Project FIND. D. San-
    ford. New Repub 158:13-14 Ja 6 '68
    Speaking out; I'm old and I'm glad of it.
    J. Daniels. Sat Eve Post 240:8+ F 25 '67
        See also
    Retirement from business, etc.

        Anecdotes, facetiae, satire, etc.
    Old story. G. Ace. Sat R 50:8 My 6 '67
AGE determination by radioactivity. See
    Radioactive dating
AGE groups
    Population shifts: business effect. il U S
    News 62:52-3 Je 26 '67
AGE of the earth. See Earth—Age
AGED
    Aged buyers to get help. Sci N 91:101 Ja 28
    '67
    Charles le vieux. il Time 90:45 Ag 4 '67
    Escalating the lease-on-life. W. Holbrook.
    Atlan 220:89-90 Ag '67
    First 124 years are the hardest; 'oldest liv-
    ing American'. C. Smith, L. Root and A.
    Ash. il Sat Eve Post 240:79-80+ Je 17 '67
    Live as long as you want to. O. A. Battista.
    Farm J 91:66R Mr '67
        See also
    Aging
    Old age
    Retirement from business, etc.

        Adjustment problems
    Does the U.S. treat its senior citizens fairly?
    pro and con discussion. Sr Schol 90:12-13
    My 12 '67
    Preparing for health needs after age sixty-
    five. Bet Hom & Gard 45:122+ S '67
    Speaking out; I'm old and I'm glad of it.
    J. Daniels. Sat Eve Post 240:8+ F 25 '67

        Anecdotes, facetiae,
        satire, etc.
    Oldies but goodies. F. P. Tullius. New Yorker
    43:56 D 9 '67

        Care and hygiene
    Preparing for health needs after age sixty-
    five. Bet Hom & Gard 45:122+ S '67
    Yes, you can go home again; a community
    program serving the elderly and chronically
    ill of Rochester and Monroe County, N.Y.
    M. A. Brice. Todays Health 45:54-6 D '67

        Economic conditions
    Does the U.S. treat its senior citizens fairly?
    pro and con discussion. Sr Schol 90:12-13
    My 12 '67
    Near-forgotten aged; Project FIND. D. San-
    ford. New Repub 158:13-14 Ja 6 '68

        Housing
    Ecumenism at work in Leisure World. M.
    Chapman. Christian Cent 85:60-1 Ja 10 '68
AGEE, Doris
    But we're alive! Read Digest 90:104-8 Je '67
AGENCE France-presse. See News agencies
AGENCIES
    See also
    Travel agencies
AGENCIES, Advertising. See Advertising
    agencies
AGENCIES, Employment. See Employment
    agencies
AGENCIES, Federal. See United States—Execu-
    tive departments

AGENCIES, Regulatory. See Independent regu-
    latory commissions
AGENCY for international development. See
    United States—Agency for international de-
    velopment
AGENTS, Literary. See Literary agents
AGENTS, Moving picture. See Theatrical
    agents
AGENTS, Photographers. See Photographers
    agents
AGENTS, Real estate. See Real estate agents
AGENTS, Talent. See Theatrical agencies
AGFACHROME films. See Photography—Films
AGGIORNAMENTO; story. See Christman, E.
AGGLUTINATION
    Agglutinating specificity for LW factor in
    guinea pig and rabbit anti-Rh serums.
    P. Levine and M. J. Celano. bibliog il
    Science 156:1744-6 Je 30 '67
AGGLUTININS
    Effect of amantadine hydrochloride on the
    response of human lymphocytes to phyto-
    hemagglutinin. W. E. Rawls and others.
    bibliog il Science 158:506-7 O 27 '67
    Hemagglutinating 7S subunits of 19S cold
    agglutinins. A. G. Cooper. bibliog il Science
    157:933-5 Ag 25 '67
    Lambda chains in cold agglutinins. T. Feizi.
    bibliog il Science 156:1111-12 My 26 '67
    Viral inhibition of lymphocyte response to
    phytohemagglutinin. J. R. Montgomery and
    others. bibliog il Science 157:1068-70 S 1
    '67
AGGRESSION (international law)
    Definition of aggression; Assembly begins
    consideration of item. UN Mo Chron 4:57-
    62 D '67
    Open letter to Konrad Lorenz. E. Rabino-
    witch; discussion. Bul Atomic Sci 23:35-6
    Ap '67
    Reconfirmations. J. Burnham. Nat R 19:788
    Jl 25 '67
        See also
    United Nations—Committee on the question of
    defining aggression
AGGRESSIVENESS (psychology)
    Human aggression: the need for a species-
    specific framework. R. L. Holloway, jr.
    Natur Hist 76:40-4 bibliog(p69) D '67
    Human idiosyncrasy, anthropologists con-
    clude. Sci N 92:583-4 D 16 '67
    Origins of human bonds. S. Fraiberg. Com-
    mentary 44:47-57 D '67
    Scaling data on inter-nation action. L. E.
    Moses and others. bibliog il Science 156:
    1054-9 My 26 '67
    War is not in our genes; animal and human
    aggressiveness; theories of Konrad Lorenz,
    Robert Ardrey and others. S. Carrighar. il
    N Y Times Mag p74-5+ S 10 '67; Discus-
    sion. p 12+ O 1; 22+ O 22 '67
        See also
    Fighting (psychology)
AGHA Khan IV. See Aga Khan IV
AGHAJANIAN, George K. and others
    Serotonin: release in the forebrain by stimu-
    lation of midbrain raphé. bibliog Science
    156:402-3 Ap 21 '67
AGING
    Genetics slows aging. B. Frisch. il Sci Di-
    gest 61:52-3 Mr '67
    Young science looks at aging; gerontologists
    step up research. il Bsns W p 118-20+ Ag
    26 '67
AGNELLI, Giovanni, 1921-
    Everybody works for Gianni; interviews, ed.
    by E. Hughes and P. Dragadze. pors Life
    63:41-2+ N 24 '67

        about
    In Italy, Agnelli is the man to see. il por
    Bsns W p 128-9+ My 13 '67
AGNELLI, Marella (Caracciolo)
    Rococo getaway for Donna Marella Agnelli,
    in Italy. V. Lawford. il pors Vogue 150:218-
    25 O 1 '67
AGNELLI empire. See Italy—Industries
AGNES, Sister
    Appearances; poem. America 116:853 Je 17
    '67
    Parable: for Robert; poem. America 116:587
    Ap 22 '67
    Pomegranate seeds for Christmas morning;
    poem. America 117:765 D 23 '67
    Time is a bone in the sun; poem. Common-
    weal 87:439 Ja 12 '68
    To stop the rose; poem. America 117:415 O
    14 '67
AGNEW, Harold
    Weapons and world stability; excerpts from
    address. Aviation W 86:11 Mr 27 '67

AGNEW, Spiro T.
Maryland library board backed by Agnew veto. Library J 92:2108 Je 1 '67

AGNON, Samuel Joseph
Books: S. Y. Agnon: Noble laureate. L. Kahn. Cath World 205:245-7 Jl '67
Man touched by God. E. Feldman. por Sat R 50:94-7 Ap 22 '67
Reflections on S. Y. Agnon. G. Scholem. Commentary 44:59-66 D '67

AGOSTINI, Giacomo
Viva! but hide your women. B. Ottum. il por Sports Illus 26:32-4+ My 15 '67

AGRANOFF, Bernard W.
Memory and protein synthesis; with biographical sketch. Sci Am 216:14, 115-22 Je '67
—and others
Actinomycin D blocks formation of memory of shock-avoidance in goldfish. bibliog Science 158:1600-1 D 22 '67

AGREEMENTS, International. See Treaties

AGRICULTURAL administration
Closing the world food gap. L. Soth. Bul Atomic Sci 23:40-2 N '67
Population and food supply; excerpts from papers submitted to the United Nations world population conference. C. Taeuber. bibliog f il Ann Am Acad 369:73-83 Ja '67
World outlook for conventional agriculture. L. R. Brown. bibliog il Science 158:604-11 N 3 '67

Brazil
Report from South America. W. E. Swegle. Suc Farm 65:18+ D '67

India
Fight for food. M. Zim. il Fortune 75:71-2+ F '67
Must India starve? aims of new program. J. E. Frazer and P. Friggens. Read Digest 91:117-21 Jl '67

Poland
Middle ground. Newsweek 71:34+ Ja 15 '68

Russia
New look at today's Russia. R. K. Brome. U S News 62:72 Je 5 '67

United States
Dairy report from Washington. Farm J 91:D16 Je '67
Farm controls can taper off. Life 62:4 Mr 31 '67
Farm follies. Reporter 37:16 S 21 '67
Freeman answers cheap food charges. O. L. Freeman. Farm J 91:35-6+ Ag '67
Last minute report straight from Washington. See issues of Farm journal
Plight of plenty; call for collective bargaining to raise farm prices. Time 90:20 D 22 '67
Rich get richer; call for $10,000 ceiling on all direct farm subsidies. Time 89:19 Je 30 '67
We are losing our uniqueness. D. Hanson. Suc Farm 65:6+ Je '67
What government will and won't do for you. F. Bailey, jr. Suc Farm 65:58-9 Mr '67
What happens when The plan moves in? G. Lorang. Farm J 91:D2 D '67
What the big corn crop means; ed. by R. D. Wennblom. Farm J 91:27+ S '67
What the experts told the President. Farm J 91:54 S '67
See also
Farm produce—Prices
United States—Agriculture, Department of

AGRICULTURAL chemicals
Handling and storing chemicals safely. Suc Farm 65:99 Mr '67
How long to keep garden chemicals? Sunset 139:218 N '67
New chemicals make the garden behave. S. Schuler. House B 109:174+ S '67
See also
Fungicides
Herbicides
Weeds—Chemical control

AGRICULTURAL chemistry
See also
Plants—Chemical analysis

AGRICULTURAL clubs
See also
4-H clubs

AGRICULTURAL contracts. See Contracts, Agricultural

AGRICULTURAL cooperation, International. See Agriculture—International aspects

AGRICULTURAL economics. See Agriculture—Economic aspects

AGRICULTURAL education
Americans not everybody knows, Samuel W. Johnson and others. C. W. Ferguson. PTA Mag 62:17-19 S '67

AGRICULTURAL engineering

Study and teaching
Those industrious young men and their farming machines. J. Farrar. il Am Ed 3:22-4+ O '67

AGRICULTURAL exhibitions
Leaky-roof circuit; county-fair shows. A. Higgins. il Sports Illus 27:50-2+ Jl 3 '67

AGRICULTURAL experiment stations
Americans not everybody knows, Samuel W. Johnson and others. C. W. Ferguson. PTA Mag 62:17-19 S '67

AGRICULTURAL experimentation. See Agricultural research

AGRICULTURAL extension work
See also
4-H clubs

AGRICULTURAL forecasts
Agricultural; the year 2000 AD: address, January 20, 1967. O. L. Freeman. Vital Speeches 33:290-4 Mr 1 '67
Agrobiology: specialization or systems analysis? N. F. Jensen. bibliog Science 157:1405-9 S 22 '67
Big turn. Farm J 91:104 Ja '67
Farmcast. See issues of Farm journal
Power farming U.S.A. G. W. Wormley. Farm J 91:32-36A Ja '67
What farmers plan to plant this spring. Farm J 91:46 My '67
What's ahead for '68? C. W. Gifford. Farm J 91:27+ D '67

AGRICULTURAL labor. See Farm labor

AGRICULTURAL laws and legislation
Laws to control farm wastes; are they coming? D. Malena. Suc Farm 65:31 Ag '67
Meet the new man behind farm laws; interview. W. R. Poage. Farm J 91:47 Je '67

AGRICULTURAL machinery
Get better field efficiency from your machinery; questions and answers. P. B. Jones. Suc Farm 65:42-3+ My '67
Machinery parade; photographs. See issues of Farm journal
Preview for 1967. G. W. Wormley. il Farm J 91:32-36A Ja '67
Speed-up-ideas for spring planting. P. B. Jones. il Suc Farm 65:56-7 Mr '67
Toward the square tomato; new machines on the farm. il Time 90:78-83 Ag 18 '67
What's new. See issues of Successful farming
See also
Feed handling
Harvesting machinery
Hay making machinery
Motor trucks
Seeding machinery

Care
See Agricultural machinery—Maintenance and repair

Cost of operation
Quick ways to figure machinery costs. Suc Farm 65:83 Ja '67

Leasing
Custom farming: will this new trend replace leasing? B. Brantley. il Suc Farm 65:33+ My '67
Custom hiring, when it pays. Suc Farm 65:58E F '67

Maintenance and repair
Hints for faster fall harvest. P. B. Jones. il Suc Farm 65:50-1 S '67
Maintenance, key to longer life, more profit. il Suc Farm 65:61+ Ja '67
Putting machinery away? P. B. Jones. il Suc Farm 65:28-9 D '67
Trade or fix up, here's how to decide. il Suc Farm 65:56-7 Ja '67

Prices
Decision-making help on what size to buy. il Suc Farm 65:52-3 Ja '67

Repairing
See Agricultural machinery—Maintenance and repair

Storage
Putting machinery away? P. B. Jones. il Suc Farm 65:28-9 D '67

AGRICULTURAL mechanics. See Agricultural engineering

AGRICULTURAL museums
See also
Farmers' museum, Cooperstown, N.Y.

AGUILAR, Luis E.
Regis Debray: where logic failed. Reporter 37:31-2 D 28 '67
AHERN, Eugene J.
To be perfectly frank. America 116:753-4 My 20 '67
AHIDJO, Ahmadou
President of Cameroon visits the United States; exchange of toasts, October 24, 1967. Dept State Bul 57:655-6 N 13 '67
AHLANDER, Leslie Judd
Up to their ears in the arts. Am Ed 3:29-31 N '67
AHLERS, Arvel W.
Classy glassy movies. Mod Phot 1:76-7+ Jl '67
Money, pictures. Pop Phot 60:83+ My; 61: 68+ Ag '67
Pro movie effects: easy does it. Mod Phot 31:86-7+ Ap '67
AHMANSON, Howard Fieldstead
Emperor in private. il por Time 90:96+ N 10 '67
Millionaire, California style; I've never added it all up. il por Newsweek 70:84-5 D 11 '67
AHMED, Deed
Wind and the trees; Why does it happen so? poems, tr. by A. Ali. Horn Bk 43:237-8 Ap '67
AID to dependent children (program) See Child welfare—United States
AID to families with dependent children (program) See Child welfare—United States
AIDA; opera. See Verdi, G.
AIDES, Teachers. See Teachers aides
AIDS (aircraft integrated data systems) See Aeronautic instruments
AIDS in teaching. See Teaching—Aids and devices
AIGNER, Lucien
Maneuvering in miniature. Pop Mech 129: 136-7 Ja '68
New home for old inventions. Pop Mech 128: 102-5 Ag '67
AIKEN, Conrad
Conrad Aiken: our best known unread poet. L. Untermeyer. por Sat R 50:28-9+ N 25 '67
Lowry/Aiken symbiosis. R. H. Costa. Nation 204:823-6 Je 26 '67
AIKEN, George David
Occupation: farmer; avocation: Senator. J. Herbers. il pors N Y Times Mag p24-5+ Ja 29 '67
AIMÉE, Anouk
Aimée, it means to be loved; with report by M. Durham. il pors Life 62:85-6 My 19 '67
Fellini talks about the face of Anouk Aimée. F. Fellini. por Vogue 150:160-1 O 1 '67
AIMS in education. See Education—Aims and objectives
AIMS of recreation. See Recreation—Aims and objectives
AINSWORTH, Ed
Remembering Uppie. Sat R 50:32-3 S 30 '67
AINTREE race course. See Race tracks
AINTREE steeplechase. See Horse racing
AINUS. See Japan—Native races
AIR
    See also
Fog
AIR, Ionized
    Physiological effect
Black box that turns you on; anti-fatigue device. il Bsns W p79-80 My 6 '67
AIR agreements. See Aviation—International aspects
AIR analysis
Radio-controlled model boat samples air and plankton. H. E. Schlichting, jr. and J. E. Hudson, jr. il Science 156:238-9 Ap 14 '67
AIR bases
Air force North Vietnam effort dependent on Thai bases. C. Brownlow. il Aviation W 86:26-9 Ap 3 '67
Backlash of Mideast war: Libya turns on the U.S; Wheelus field at stake. il U S News 63:48 Ag 21 '67
Is U.S. to lose its last air base in Africa? Wheelus air base, Libya. il U S News 62:6 Je 26 '67
Major U.S. bastion springs up in Thailand. il Bsns W p38-9 My 13 '67
TAC profiting from Nellis' expanded role. C. M. Plattner. il Aviation W 86:98-9+ My 8 '67
Thai ally; major U.S. installations in Thailand. F. Sully. il Newsweek 69:51 Mr 27 '67
Thailand grants U.S. permission to use U Tapao airbase; statement, March 22, 1967. D. Rusk. Dept State Bul 56:597-8 Ap 10 '67

USAF expands Vietnam repair capability; USAF bases in South Vietnam and Thailand. il Aviation W 86:74-8 My 22 '67
AIR California
Competing with the freeways. il Time 89:105 Je 9 '67
AIR cargo containers. See Containers for shipping
AIR compressors
In a spin over research; examining turbulent airflow in working model of gas turbine compressor. il Sci N 91:234 Mr 11 '67
AIR conditioning
Air conditioning: a new interpretation for architects. il Arch Rec 142:153-7+ Jl; 125-9+ Ag '67
Air conditioning does more than cool. il Farm J 91:40 Je '67
Don't be switch-happy with central cooling. Bet Hom & Gard 45:108 Je '67
    See also subhead Air conditioning under various subjects, e.g. Automobiles—Air conditioning
    Study and teaching
Education: undergraduate, post-graduate, professional. il Arch Rec 142:135-6 Ag '67
    Terminology
Glossary of heating and air conditioning terms. Arch Rec 142:158 Jl '67
Glossary of terms related to package equipment. Arch Rec 142:130 Ag '67
AIR conditioning equipment
Air conditioners. il Consumer Rep 32:300-7 Je '67
Air conditioning: a cool appraisal. il McCalls 94:96-7 My '67
Air conditioning: a new interpretation for architects. il Arch Rec 142:153-7+ Jl; 125-9+ Ag '67
Evaporative-type car air coolers. Consumer Bul 50:36 Jl '67
How to buy an air conditioner. Parents Mag 42:86-7 My '67
More air conditioners. il Consumer Rep 32: 378-9 Jl '67
Room air conditioners. il Consumer Bul 50: 9-14 Je '67
Room air conditioners. il Consumer Rep 32: 137-44 D '67
This gas-flame air conditioner both heats and cools. R. W. Denniston. il Pop Sci 191: 94-5 O '67
Tips on buying air conditioners. Am Home 70:80+ Jl '67
AIR coolers. See Air conditioning equipment
AIR-cushion landing system. See Airplanes—Landing gear
AIR cushion vehicles. See Ground effect machines
AIR education. See Aviation education
AIR fields. See Aviation landing stations
AIR filters
Air vacuum cleaner. il Sci Digest 61:30 Ap '67
AIR filters, Automobile
Keep it clean; washable air cleaners. E. Rickman. il Hot Rod 20:110 O '67
AIR flow
In a spin over research; examining turbulent airflow in working model of gas turbine compressor. il Sci N 91:234 Mr 11 '67
AIR force academy. See United States air force academy, Colorado Springs
AIR force association
AFA convention demands new strategy, cites technology. W. E. Wilks. Tech W 20:17 Mr 20 '67
AIR force bases. See Air bases
AIR force eastern test range. See Proving grounds
AIR force pilots. See Air pilots
AIR force satellite test center. See Proving grounds
AIR frame industry. See Airplane industry and trade
AIR France. See Airlines—France
AIR freight handling. See Freight handling
AIR freight service
Air cargo sees a higher ceiling. il Bsns W p 106-8+ My 13 '67
All-cargo profits follow shrinking trend. Aviation W 87:34 N 27 '67
Cargo, charter proposals hit by airlines. H. D. Watkins. Aviation W 87:37 D 4 '67
Cargos cases watched closely for trends. H. D. Watkins. Aviation W 87:32-3 Jl 24 '67
CAB mood spurs route filings from three all-cargo carriers. H. D. Watkins. Aviation W 86:27-8 My 1 '67

AIR freight service—*Continued*

Computer maker exports principally by air. J. W. Carter. il Aviation W 86:65+ F 13 '67

Domestic military cargo increase sought. H. D. Watkins. Aviation W 88:27 Ja 1 '68

Giant jets spur air shippers to form New York cooperative. J. W. Carter. Aviation W 88:30 Ja 1 '68

Improvements in cost analysis urged for air-freight industry. Aviation W 87:49 S 18 67

MAC-freed aircraft used in new rules. Aviation W 87:43 D 11 '67

New boom on the airlines: rising tide of freight. il U S News 62:100-1 Je 12 '67

New York seeks tighter airport security. R. F. Coburn. Aviation W 88:35 Ja 1 '68

North Atlantic air cargo and mail data, year 1966; table. Aviation W 86:54-5 Mr 20 '67

Off-route charter rule easing proposed. H. D. Watkins. Aviation W 86:38-9 My 15 '67

Transpacific route case: three all-cargo carriers aim at major market in Pacific case; proposals by Airlift international, Flying Tiger line and Seaboard world airlines. H. D. Watkins. il Aviation W 86:48-50+ Je 12 '67

U.S. air traffic to grow; so may costs; with tables. J. W. Carter. il Aviation W 86:250-1+ Mr 6 '67

U.S. cargo growth rate lagging. J. W. Carter. il Aviation W 86:36-7 My 15 '67

See also
Airlift international, incorporated
Airplanes, Freight
Flying Tiger line, incorporated
Helicopter freight service

Rates

Freight rate cuts seen aiding industry. J. W. Carter. Aviation W 86:28-9 My 22 '67

Pacific cargo rate cut expected. J. W. Carter. Aviation W 86:36-7 Ap 17 '67

AIR freight terminals. See Airport buildings

AIR glow. See Airglow

AIR guns

Forerunner rifle; V-L air rifle fires bullets without cartridges. il Time 89:33 Je 30 '67

Look what they've done to the BB gun. D. C. Fales. il Pop Mech 127:114-15 Je '67

Try a new air rifle. P. Wahl. il Pop Sci 192: 92-5 Ja '68

200-shot Daisy and the ultimate plink. J. Shepherd. il Field & S 72:66-7+ S '67

AIR-India international. See Airlines—India

AIR inter (airline) See Airlines—France

AIR-launched air-recoverable rocket. See Rockets—Use in research

AIR line pilots association, International

ALPA studies low-cost systems to warn against small aircraft. Aviation W 86:24 Je 26 '67

Conflict over 737 crew size intensifies. Aviation W 87:37-8 S 11 67

AIR mail service

CAB cuts domestic airmail rates. L. Doty. Aviation W 87:34 S 11 '67

More mail awards planned for air taxis. E. J. Bulban. Aviation W 87:85-6 D 18 '67

North Atlantic air cargo and mail data, year 1966; table. Aviation W 86:54-5 Mr 20 '67

U.S. air traffic to grow; so may costs; with tables. J. W. Carter. il Aviation W 86:250-1+ Mr 6 '67

Sweden

Via rocket mail to . . ; celebrating 50th anniversary. il Life 63:67-8 D 8 '67

AIR pilot shortage. See Air pilots—Supply and demand

AIR pilots

Carrier pilots show little stress in North Vietnam raids. C. M. Plattner. il Aviation W 86:80-1+ Ap 24 '67

Flying spacewatchers. J. Eberhart. il Sci N 92:179 Ag 19 '67

Getting a lecture from the pilot; K. Ruppenthal, Stanford business lecturer. il Bsns W p68-9+ Ja 28 '67

Pilots, captains and accidents. R. Blodget. Flying 81:110 D '67

Pilots to demand more SST operating data; acceleration in developmnt of supersonic instruments urged. H. J. Coleman. Aviation W 87:69+ D 11 '67

Pro's nest; accident prone pilots. T. Boxter. Flying 82:20 Ja '68

Safety check; controlling pilot panic. Flying 82:94-5 Ja '68

Sky is their limit. R. N. Buck. Read Digest 90:68-72 Ap '67

Viet demands cut USAF pilot manning. Aviation W 87:28 Ag 7 '67

See also
Airplane crews
Airplanes—Piloting
Aviation—Physiological aspects
Drinking and airplane accidents
Helicopter pilots
Women as air pilots

Anecdotes, facetiae, satire, etc.

Games pilots play. R. Starnes. il Field & S 72:44-5+ Je '67

Legal status, laws, etc.

Wide open airspaces? R. Burkhardt. Flying 81:30 N '67

Licenses

Basic question; improvement of present pilot certification system. R. B. Parke. Flying 80:32 Mr '67

Basic reaction. R. Burkhardt. Flying 81:32 S '67

FAA proposes sweeping use fees; new system of licensing. D. A. Brown. Aviation W 86: 26 My 1 '67

Physical examinations

Crash report urges better medical tests. Aviation W 86:39 Ap 10 '67

Supply and demand

Empty seats in the cockpit. G. Jennings. il Read Digest 90:127-31 Je '67

Military pilot shortage; low supply forces inefficient employment. D. A. Brown. il Aviation W 86:66-7+ My 8 '67

Military pilot shortage; services search for long-term solutions. D. A. Brown. Aviation W 86:83+ Je 5 '67

Military pilot shortage; Viet needs, civil lure pinch USAF, army. D. A. Brown. il Aviation W 86:94-5+ My 15 '67

Pilot pinch; dwindling supply of military aviators. Time 89:35 Ap 14 '67

Viet-caused pilot shortage draws Senate unit rebuke. Aviation W 87:30 S 18 '67

Training

American to build central facility to handle heavy training loads. il Aviation W 87:40 N 13 '67

Danny Kaye's own story: if I can learn to fly, you can learn to fly. D. Kaye. il Pop Sci 190:76-9+ Ja '67

Dornier designs military-civil jet trainer. E. H. Kolcum. il Aviation W 87:61+ N 13 '67

FAA urges training at remote airports. Aviation W 86:45+ Ap 24 '67

FAA weighs proficiency checks, added training for general pilots. Aviation W 88:20 Ja 1 '68

Follow me through. R. Blodget. See issues of Flying

Foreign accent; flight instruction, British style. J. Fricker. Flying 81:102 D '67

Forward controllers to train in OV-10A. B. K. Thomas, jr. Aviation W 88:71-3 Ja 1 '68

Learning to fly. S. Wilkinson. il Holiday 41:100-6 Je '67

MAC prepares for C-5 crew training. Aviation W 87:172 N 20 '67

National aviation training program urged. Aviation W 87:87-8 S 4 '67

New training concepts studied for 747. il Aviation W 87:159+ N 20 '67

Pro's nest; checking on continuing proficiency. T. Baxter. Flying 81:26 D '67

Snobs. R. Blodget. Flying 80:30 F '67

See also
Airplanes, Training
Aviation schools
Flight simulators

AIR plants
See also
Bromeliads

AIR pollution

Air pollution. Nat R 19:234 Mr 7 '67

Air pollution can kill, New York study suggests. Todays Health 45:85 My '67

Air pollution: where the problems are worst. Science 157:785 Ag 18 '67

Air quality act of 1967: a step forward, but don't expect immediate improvement of your air. B. Nelson. il Science 158:355-7 O 20 '67

America's healthiest cities. N. Faber. Ladies Home J 84:178+ O '67

Apathy clouds the air. Sci N 91:593-4 Je 24 '67

Automobile internal-combustion engine and the interest of the American people are on a collision course. J. T. Middleton. il Pop Sci 190:96-9+ My '67

AIR traffic control—*Continued*

Human problems in traffic control. D. A. Brown. il Aviation W 87:44-5+ O. 2; 100-1+ O 9; 102-3+ O 16 '67

Near miss; congestion problem of private planes at commercial airports. New Repub 157:8 Ag 19 '67

Proposed design could add ATC function. P. J. Klass. il Aviation W 87:97+ Jl 17 '67

Pro's nest; midair collision. T. Baxter. Flying 81:24 O '67

SSTs may force traffic control changes. Aviation W 86:49-50 Ap 3 '67

Traffic control of advanced SST studied. K. J. Stein. il Aviation W 86:79-82 My 22 '67

Trial center tests Eurocontrol concept. H. J. Coleman. il Aviation W 86:80-2 F 6 '67

Unsafe skies? Newsweek 69:57 Ap 3 '67
    See also
Airports—Traffic control

AIR traffic control, Military

New towers adding flexibility to air forces's 407L system; mobile air traffic control tower. J. A. Strasser. il Aero Tech 21:32-3 D 18 '67

AIR traffic controllers (persons)

Air traffic controller. Flying 82:40 Ja '68

FAA readies new controller screening test. Aviation W 87:45 O 2 '67

Ghana's control tower girl. il Ebony 22:115-16+ S '67

Personnel ability limits technology gain. D. A. Brown. il Aviation W 87:44-5+ O 2 '67

AIR transport agreements. See Aviation—International aspects

AIR transport association of America

ATA urges major control improvements. Aviation W 87:36 Ag 28 '67

ATA weighs proposal to back high-speed baggage system. R. F. Coburn. Aviation W 86:40 Ja 23 '67

Airlines challenge general aviation fees. H. D. Watkins. Aviation W 87:36-7 O 23 '67

Can airports cope with the jet age? special report. il Bsns W p54-6+ Jl 22 '67

Carriers, forwarders to meet on extra cargo services, costs. Aviation W 86:40 Ap 10 '67

Consideration of ILS replacement urged. Aviation W 87:41+ O 23 '67

Major carriers confront CAB with financial problem forecast. Aviation W 87:40 D 4 '67

AIR-transportable docks. See Aviation landing stations—Landing mats

AIR transportation. See Aeronautics, Commercial

AIR travel

Can airports cope with the jet age? special report. il Bsns W p54-6+ Jl 22 '67

Global jet-away. I. Wolfert. il Travel 128:65-6+ N '67; Same abr. with title What it's like to fly around the world. Read Digest 91:219-20+ N '67

Handwriting on the air terminal wall. C. Leedham. il N Y Times Mag p28-9+ My 21 '67

How your family can enjoy air travel more. Bet Hom & Gard 45:30 F '67

Is this the coming way to run an airline? you bet it is. R. Joseph. Esquire 68:139-40 O '67

Let's travel: to Europe. Mlle 64:173-6 F '67

Problems of prosperity; excerpts from address. S. G. Tipton. Aviation W 87:21 D 11 '67

SST: travelers' boon or sonic boom? pro and con discussion. il Sr Schol 90:12-14 Mr 17 '67

Supersonic travel: will the gamble pay off? il U S News 63:74-5 S 11 '67

Tomorrow's traveler. H. Sutton. il Sat R 51:41-2+ Ja 6 '68

Travel notes; predictions made in 1957. R. Joseph. Esquire 68:68+ O '67

Welcome aboard, austerity class. S. Alexander. Life 62:16A F 3 '67
    See also
Aeronautics, Commercial
Airlines
Aviation
Private flying

Physiological aspects
See Aviation—Physiological aspects

Asia

SAS expects Bangkok flights to triple. E. H. Kolcum. il Aviation W 87:29+ N 27 '67

Bahama Islands

Bahamas Baedeker; George Town, Exuma. E. D. Muhfeld. il Flying 81:74-7 S '67

Caribbean Region

Gone flying, Caribbean by Skyknight; a spendthrift's tour of the islands. J. Gilbert. il Flying 81:70-8 Ag '67

Let's travel: to the Caribbean. il Mlle 65:194 My '67

Route decision laid to lag in development. L. Doty. Aviation W 87:26-7 N 6 '67

Japan

Tokyo-Osaka traffic rising from slump. R. F. Coburn. Aviation W 87:41+ D 4 '67

Russia

Aeroflot registers traffic, profit gains. il Aviation W 87:27-9 O 2 '67

New York-Moscow flights may start soon. J. W. Carter. il Aviation W 87:26-7 S 25 '67

Thailand

Bangkok planning new airport. Aviation W 87:31-2 N 27 '67

United States

Blizzard snarls Northeast traffic. Aviation W 86:43+ F 13 '67

AIR turbulence. See Atmospheric turbulence

AIR vacuum cleaners. See Air filters

AIRBUSES. See Airplanes, Jet propelled

AIRCRAFT
    See also
Balloons
Gliders (aeronautics)

AIRCRAFT carriers

Carrier JFK: quarter-billion blunder? il U S News 63:89 Jl 17 '67

Carriers launch strikes against Vietnam; photographs. Aviation W 86:50-3 F 27 '67

Death of the Yorktown; excerpts from Incredible victory. W. Lord. il Look 31:32-6+ Ag 22 '67

U.S.S. John F. Kennedy, remarks, May 27, 1967. L. B. Johnson Dept State Bul 56:959-60 Je 26 '67

Yankee station: inviting retaliation; in the Gulf of Tonkin. T. W. Pew. jr. Nation 205:141-2 Ag 28 '67

Fires and fire protection

Fire! fire! flight deck aft! Forrestal disaster. T. Armbrister. il Sat Eve Post 240:34-7 O 7 '67

Fire on the Forrestal. Time 90:20 Ag 4 '67

Fire on the Forrestal. il Newsweek 70:37 Ag 7 '67

Fire on the hangar deck! D. Moser. il Read Digest 90:100-5 Mr '67

Hell aboard CVA-59; Forrestal fire; with report by H. Wingo. il Life 63:20-7 Ag 11 '67

World gone wrong; Forrestal fire. il Newsweek 70:30 Ag 14 '67

Launching

John F. Kennedy; new carrier. il Newsweek 69:26-7 Je 5 '67

AIRCRAFT computers. See Computers—Aeronautic applications

AIRCRAFT engines. See Airplane engines

AIRCRAFT gas turbines. See Gas turbines, Aircraft

AIRCRAFT integrated data systems. See Aeronautic instruments

AIRCRAFT owners and pilots association

AOPA seeks new standards to aid safety. Aviation W 87:16 S 4 '67

AIRCRAFT shows. See Aviation—Exhibitions

AIRCRAFT video tape recorders. See Video tape recorders and recording

AIRD, John S.

Estimating China's population. bibliog f Ann Am Acad 369:61-72 Ja '67

AIRFIELDS. See Aviation landing stations

AIRFLOW. See Air flow

AIRFREIGHT. See Air freight service

AIRGLOW

New Airglow observatory in Pennsylvania. W. A. Feibelman. il Sky & Tel 33:340-2 Je '67

AIRLIFT International, Incorporated

MAC cutback spurs airlift pilot dispute. Aviation W 87:39 O 23 '67

Transpacific route case: three all-cargo carriers aim at major market in Pacific case. H. D. Watkins. il Aviation W 86:48-50+ Je 12 '67

AIRLINE hostesses. See Airlines—Hostesses

AIRLINE maintenance. See Airplanes—Maintenance and repair

AIRLINE mergers.   See Airlines—Consolidations and mergers
AIRLINE passenger clerks.   See Airlines—Passenger service
AIRLINE strike. See Strikes—United States—Airlines

AIRLINES
Airlines eye Pacific as next plum. il Bsns W p50-2+ F 11 '67
Giant jets to force new concepts. L. Doty. il Aviation W 87:39-45 N 20 '67
Let's travel: to Europe. Mlle 64:173-6 F '67
See also
Air travel

Advertising
Fearful sell; Pacific air lines advertisements. Newsweek 69:83-4 My 8 '67
Hey there, sweaty palms! Pacific air lines campaign. Time 89:90 My 12 '67
Pacific fear of flying drive criticized; executive resigns. Aviation W 86:30-1 My 8 '67

Anecdotes, facetiae, satire, etc.
Ticket or the tiger; reduced fare for the wife. G. Ace. Sat R 50:3 D 23 '67

Consolidations and mergers
Allegheny, Henson plan route exchange. Aviation W 87:29-30 Ag 21 '67
Bonanza, West Coast, Pacific merger urged. Aviation W 87:37 D 11 '67
Braniff control may go to LTV. Aviation W 87:47 Ag 14 '67
Court challenge nears in Eastern acquisition of Remmert-Werner. D. A. Brown. Aviation W 88:22-3 Ja 1 '68
Examiner urges board approve Air West plan. Aviation W 88:52 Ja 15 '68
How to make ten from three; merger of Pacific with Phoenix's Bonanza and Seattle's West coast. Time 90:59 S 1 '67
Merger rumors spurred by new aircraft. L. Doty. Aviation W 87:32-3 D 25 '67
More blue in Braniff's yonder; Braniff-Pan American-Grace airways merger. il Bsns W p 102-6+ Ja 21 '67
Pacific and West Coast airlines trying for third time to merge. Aviation W 86:22 Je 26 '67

Costs
Improvements in cost analysis urged for airfreight industry. Aviation W 87:49 S 18 '67

Employees
BOAC workers call management remote. Aviation W 87:39 Ag 28 '67
Migrant workers to be trained for aircraft production jobs. Aviation W 87:127-8 Ag 14 '67
See also
Airlines—Hostesses

Fares
Basic IATA traffic conference structure faces severe testing. L. Doty. Aviation W 87:40 O 9 '67
Board's blackout investigation hinges on future United position. Aviation W 88:45 Ja 15 '68
Carriers see slight relief in fare order. Aviation W 87:27 D 25 '67
CAB conditionally approves IATA fares. Aviation W 86:31 Mr 31 '67
Dumping the discounts. il Time 90:95-6 N 24 '67
Falling yield may spur push for fare rise. W. H. Gregory. il Aviation W 87:37-9 O 9 '67
Family air fares. Bet Hom & Gard 46:14+ Ja '68
Fare structure study ready; preliminary CAB findings due. Aviation W 86:37-8 Ap 10 '67
Filings snarl excursion fare plans. R. F. Coburn. Aviation W 86:38 Ap 3 '67
High flying fares. G. B. Friedman. New Repub 156:19-21 Mr 4 '67
Mixed earnings cloud fare issue. H. D. Watkins. Aviation W 87:25-6 N 27 '67
New filings threaten U.S. fare structure. Aviation W 87:31 N 20 '67
Pacific fare cuts approved by IATA. Aviation W 87:36 Ag 7 '67
Separate fare structure seen for SSTs. Aviation W 87:30-1 D 18 '67
Steady fare cuts spur Atlantic growth. L. L. Doty. Aviation W 86:49-50 Ja 23 '67
U.S. air traffic to grow; so may costs; with tables. J. W. Carter. il Aviation W 86:250-1+ Mr 6 '67
Youth fare extensions approved. Aviation W 86:45 Ja 30 '67

Federal aid
CAB withdraws subsidy from Northeast. J. W. Carter. Aviation W 88:29 Ja 8 '68
Further subsidy drop seen in fiscal 1968. il Aviation W 88:30 Ja 8 '68
See also
Local service airlines—Federal aid

Feeder airlines
See Local service airlines

Finance
Airline financing activity at peak. Aviation W 88:26 Ja 1 '68
Airline income and expense; tables (title varies) See occasional issues of Aviation week & space technology
Airlines face rising SST funding. Aviation W 86:42-3 Je 12 '67
Airlines shift to more equity financing. L. Doty. Aviation W 87:26-8 Ag 21 '67
Airlines' striking figures Fortune 75:287 Je 15 '67
Airlines widen use of lease financing. Aviation W 87:55 D 11 '67
All-cargo profits follow shrinking trend. Aviation W 87:34 N 27 '67
Credit restoration will aid trunklines. Aviation W 86:42 Mr 20 '67
Demand, jets, new authority spur growth; U.S. supplemental airlines. H. D. Watkins. il Aviation W 87:40-1+ Ag 28 '67
Domestic trunks studying shrinking revenue returns. L. Doty. Aviation W 87:28 O 30 '67
Eastern stretches turn-around schedule; four airlines show increases in traffic and revenues. W. H. Gregory. Aviation W 86:29 My 1 '67
Eastern TWA to cooperate on Concorde, 747 support. Aviation W 87:38 D 4 '67
Falling yield may spur push for fare rise. W. H. Gregory. il Aviation W 87:37-9 O 9 '67
High-flying revenues lose some altitude. il Bsns W p70-1 Ag 12 '67
How airlines ranked in revenues, profits, 1966: table. Aviation W 87:69 Jl 10 '67
Increases in airline operating revenues, 1966 over 1965; table. Aviation W 86:48 My 8 '67
Insurance firms financing airlines; banks engaged in financing carriers; tables. Aviation W 87:27 Ag 21 '67
IATA carriers show concern on profits. Aviation W 87:39-40 D 4 '67
Major carriers confront CAB with financial problem forecast. Aviation W 87:40 D 4 '67
Mixed earnings cloud fare issue. H. D. Watkins. Aviation W 87:25-6 N 27 '67
Net loss of $82.6 million recorded for airline strike. Aviation W 87:24 Jl 31 '67
Rumors bring capitalization questions. Aviation W 87:33 D 25 '67
Slipping loads imperil profitability. H. D. Watkins. il Aviation W 87:34-6 D 11 '67
Straining to pay for tomorrow. Time 91:72 Ja 5 '68
Summary of airline indebtedness; table. Aviation W 87:28 Ag 21 '67
Supplemental airline surge. H. D. Watkins. il Aviation W 87:40-1+ Ag 28; 32-4+ S 4 '67
Survey finds war in Vietnam increases airline revenue 5 per cent. il Aviation W 87:40 O 23 '67
TWA completes major financing program. Aviation W 87:31 D 25 '67
Trunkline profit & loss, July, 1967; table. Aviation W 87:33 O 2 '67
Turbojet, turbofan aircraft 1966 operating expense; table. Aviation W 86:49+ My 15 '67
Turbojet, turbofan aircraft operating expense; tables. Aviation W 87:56-7 N 13 '67
Turboprop aircraft 1966 operating expense, dollars per total aircraft hour; table. Aviation W 86:32-3 My 22 '67
U.S. airline assets and liabilities; tables (cont) Aviation W 86:53 My 8; 87:34 S 25 '67
U.S. airline operating revenues and expenses, 1966; table. Aviation W 86:30-1 My 1 '67
U.S. airline rate of return; chart. Aviation W 88:49 Ja 15 '68
See also
Airlines—Securities

Food service
Booked for travel: Braniff's and Pan American's cuisine. H. Sutton. Sat R 50:48 Mr 4 '67

Freight service
See Air freight service; Airplanes, Freight

Hostesses
Coffee, tea, but not me! il Newsweek 71:55 Ja 1 '68

AIRLINES—Hostesses—*Continued*
High flying, but not flighty; original stewardesses. il Sr Schol 90:5 My 12 '67
Person to person: by air; stewardess's life. il Seventeen 26:249 F '67
Stewardesses seek change in airline role. il Aviation W 87:34-6 Ag 28 '67
Teen travel talk; fashion flies highest for the stewardess corps. il Seventeen 26:74 N '67
Up from Betty Grable; American airlines stewardesses' new uniforms. il Newsweek 70:58 S 4 '67
Up in the air. R. Hoffmann. il Mlle 64:128-9+ F '67
Vive la différence. il Time 89:52 Ap 14 '67

Anecdotes, facetiae, satire, etc.
My career as a girl-watcher. R. Armour. il Read Digest 91:21-2+ Ag '67

International aspects
See Aviation—International aspects

Maintenance and repair
See also
Airplanes, Jet propelled—Maintenance and repair

Management
Demand, jets, new authority spur growth; U.S. supplemental airlines. H. D. Watkins. il Aviation W 87:40-1+ Ag 28 '67
Supplemental airline surge. H. D. Watkins. il Aviation W 87:40-1+ Ag 28; 32-4 S 4 '67

Anecdotes, facetiae, satire, etc.
Is this any way to run an airline? (don't ask me) R. Lemon. il Sat Eve Post 240:24 Ap 22 '67

Passenger service
Aeroflot registers traffic, profit gains. il Aviation W 87:27-9 O 2 '67
ATA weighs proposal to back high-speed baggage system. R. F. Coburn. Aviation W 86:40 Ja 23 '67
Airlines preview electronic redcap; computer-controlled baggage handler. il Bsns W p 126+ Ag 19 '67
Bumpy departures on the airlines; failure to honor reservations. Consumer Rep 32:565-6 N '67
CAB service scrutiny concerns carriers. H. D. Watkins. Aviation W 86:41+ Ap 3 '67
Come fly to Europe with me in the new jumbo jet. D. Francis. il Pop Sci 190:98-101+ Mr '67
Complaint surge concerns board. H. D. Watkins. il Aviation W 86:37-8 Mr 20 '67
Dumping the discounts. il Time 90:95-6 N 24 '67
End to free drinks, movies on airlines? il U S News 62:16 My 1 '67
Flying with Dan McGrew; Golden Nugget promotion scheme of Alaska airlines. il Newsweek 70:78 D 11 '67
Ground barrier; CAB investigates VIP lounges. il Newsweek 70:72 Ag 14 '67
Onward & upward with Inflight; movies on planes. R. Levy. il Duns R 89:55-6 F '67
RIP for VIP? lounges or clubs at airports. il Newsweek 69:86+ F 13 '67
Sky writing; airlines publishing their own magazines. il Newsweek 70:86 Jl 17 '67
Stretched DC-8s posing airline problems J. W. Carter. il Aviation W 87:56-8+ D 4 '67
Two worst headaches in air travel; overbooked flights and misdirected baggage. il Changing T 21:33-6 F '67
United high-speed bag system installation at O'Hare delayed. R. F. Coburn. Aviation W 86:50 Ap 17 '67
Vive la différence. il Time 89:52 Ap 14 '67
Welcome aboard, austerity class. S. Alexander. Life 62:16A F 3 '67
Who's got the bags? plan for automated baggage delivery system. Time 90:68-9 Jl 14 '67

Rates
See Air freight service—Rates; Airlines—Fares

Regulation
See Aviation—Laws and regulations

Reservation systems
Board proposes substantial hike in airline overbooking penalties. H. D. Watkins. Aviation W 86:39 Ja 23 '67

Routes
See Airways

Safety devices and measures
See Aviation—Safety devices and measures

Securities
Calculating the point of takeoff. il Bsns W p 113-14 D 16 '67

Shuttle service
American claims 27 per cent of New York-Boston air market. J. W. Carter. il Aviation W 86:24-9 Mr 27 '67
Dogfight? Eastern air lines vs. American. Newsweek 69:77 F 20 '67
Here comes the mini-airliner; short haul airlines. W. Langewiesche. Read Digest 92:189-93+ Ja '68
Shuffle on the shuttle; guaranteed-seat shuttle on New York-Boston run. Bsns W p31 F 11 '67
Shuttle battle; American and Eastern service between Boston and New York. il Time 89:86+ F 17 '67

Statistics
Airline traffic; tables. See issues of Aviation week & space technology
Boardings by U.S. carriers in selected areas outside the continental U. S; tables Aviation W 87:62+ D 11 '67
Growth in U.S. air passengers; tables. Aviation W 87:34 O 30 '67
How airlines ranked in revenues, profits, 1966; table. Aviation W 87:69 Jl 10 '67
Increases in operating revenues; table. Aviation W 87:45 S 18 '67
International airline North Atlantic passengers, load factors, year 1966; table. Aviation W 86:52-3 Mr 20 '67
1966 air passengers between the United States, other countries by flag of carrier; table. Aviation W 87:56-7 D 11 '67
Turbojet aircraft 1966 operations; traffic statistics; table. Aviation W 86:54-5+ Ap 3 '67
Turbojet and turbofan load factors in scheduled service; tables. Aviation W 87:30-1 O 30 '67
Turboprop aircraft 1966 operations and traffic statistics; table. Aviation W 86:52-3 Ap 3 '67
Turboprop load factors in scheduled service; tables. Aviation W 87:39 O 30 '67
U.S. airline operations and traffic statistics, year 1966; table. Aviation W 86:50-1 Mr 20 '67
U.S. airline scheduled service load factors; table. Aviation W 87:45 S 11 '67
U.S. airline scheduled service traffic growth; table. Aviation W 87:47 S 11 '67
U.S. airline traffic scores August gains. Aviation W 87:35 S 18 '67

Terminals
See Airports

Tickets
Carriers adopt systems concept; including standard, computerized ticketing equipment. R. F. Coburn. Aviation W 87:40 Jl 10 '67
Hot tickets; tickets stolen from travel agencies. Time 90:76-7 Jl 28 '67
See also
Airlines—Reservation systems

Traffic
Airlines reinstating service to Tel Aviv. Aviation W 86:19 Je 19 '67
Airlines study peaking pattern changes. W. H. Gregory. il Aviation W 86:76-7+ My 29 '67
Airlines urged to act now on congestion. E. H. Kolcum. Aviation W 87:42-3 O 16 '67
Atlantic traffic may hit 5 million. J. W. Carter. il Aviation W 86:36-7 Ap 24 '67
Choking on prosperity; congestion of major airports. R. Hotz. Aviation W 87:11 Ag 21 '67
CAB hurls legal rebuff at Alitalia. L. Doty. Aviation W 87:35 O 23 '67
CAB plans more innovation in policies. H. D. Watkins. il Aviation W 86:223-31+ Mr 6 '67
Complaint surge concerns board. H. D. Watkins. il Aviation W 86:37-8 Mr 20 '67
Holiday traffic surge sets mark. Aviation W 88:25-6 Ja 8 '68
JAL urges balanced capacity in Pacific. R. F. Coburn. Aviation W 87:49-50 D 11 '67
One trillion passenger miles; growth prospects and requirements of the airline industry to the year 1990; excerpts from address. J. C. Maxwell. Aviation W 87:21 Jl 10 '67
Passenger traffic records set by airlines for Easter weekend. Aviation W 86:39 Ap 3 '67
Slipping loads imperil profitability. H. D. Watkins. il Aviation W 87:34-6 D 11 '67

AIRLINES—Traffic—*Continued*
Steady fare cuts spur Atlantic growth. L. L. Doty. Aviation W 86:49-50 Ja 23 '67
Summer traffic forecast clouded; mixed domestic June returns. H. D. Watkins. Aviation W 87:30 Jl 3 '67
Tokyo-Osaka traffic rising from slump. R. F. Coburn. Aviation W 87:41+ D 4 '67
U.S. lags behind in global route outlook. L. Doty. il Aviation W 86:243-5+ Mr 6 '67
U.S. trunks expecting another big year. W. H. Gregory. il Aviation W 88:24-6 Ja 1 '68
See also
Aviation—Transatlantic flights

Alaska
See also
Alaska airlines

China (People's Republic)
Fast boat to China; China airlines' new Boeing 727. il Time 89:98 Ap 14 '67

Czechoslovakia
New routes to Asia, Africa set by CSA. Aviation W 87:39 Ag 28 '67

France
Bumpy flight toward *la gloire;* Air France management shake-up. il Bsns W p 153-4 My 27 '67
Maiden flight; first lady pilot employed by Air inter. il Time 90:79 Jl 28 '67

Great Britain
Four U.K. carriers seek Atlantic routes. H. J. Coleman. Aviation W 87:33-4 Ag 21 '67

India
Air-India sees advanced jets forcing close small-carrier ties. Aviation W 86:30 F 27 '67

Iran
Major challenges face Iranian effort to build carrier; Iran national airlines. il Aviation W 86:42-3+ Je 26 '67

Italy
Alitalia buys maintenance data recorder. K. J. Stein. Aviation W 86:83 F 6 '67
CAB hurls legal rebuff at Alitalia. L. Doty. Aviation W 87:35 O 23 '67

Japan
JAL urges balanced capacity in Pacific. R. F. Coburn. Aviation W 87:49-50 D 11 '67

Micronesia
Continental outlines Micronesia service. il Aviation W 87:27 N 27 '67

Pakistan
PIA sets resumption of Atlantic service. Aviation W 87:30-1 O 30 '67

Poland
Business trips bring bulk of LOT traffic. Aviation W 88:52 Ja 15 '68

Russia
Aeroflot battles press on cause for flight delays, poor service. Aviation W 86:43 F 6 '67
Aeroflot registers traffic, profit gains. il Aviation W 87:27-9 O 2 '67
America to Moscow nonstop: what it's like to fly Russian; Aeroflot. R. K. Brome. il U S News 62:62-4 My 29 '67
Getting together with Aeroflot; commercial air service between Russia and the U.S. il Bsns W p 139-40 D 2 '67
Landing right problem to cause delay in Il-62 New York service. Aviation W 86:28 F 20 '67
Visitor from Russia; Ilyushin-62 in the U.S. il Time 90:108 D 1 '67

Scandinavia
See also
Scandinavian airlines system

Thailand
Thai airways plans expansion. il Aviation W 87:43 D 11 '67

United States
CAB plans more innovation in policies. H. D. Watkins. il Aviation W 86:223-31+ Mr 6 '67
Eastern stretches turn-around schedule; four airlines show increases in traffic and revenues. W. H. Gregory. Aviation W 86:29 My 1 '67

High-flying supplementals. il Time 89:62+ Je 30 '67
New Northwest/Southwest awards generate protests. Aviation W 86:39 My 15 '67
Supplemental airline surge. H. D. Watkins. il Aviation W 87:40-1+ Ag 28; 32-4+ S 4 '67
U.S. air traffic to grow; so may costs; with tables. J. W. Carter. il Aviation W 86:250-1+ Mr 6 '67
U.S. airline operating revenues and expenses, 1966; table. Aviation W 86:30-1 My 1 '67
U.S. airline operations and traffic statistics, year 1966; table. Aviation W 86:50-1 Mr 20 '67
U.S. airlines push buy American. L. Doty. il Aviation W 88:42-4 Ja 15 '68
U.S. lags behind in global route outlook. L. Doty. il Aviation W 86:243-5+ Mr 6 '67
Whoosh! success of U.S. charter companies. il Newsweek 70:66 Jl 3 '67
See also
Aeronautics, Commercial—United States
Air transport association of America
Local service airlines
also names of airlines, e.g. Eastern air lines

Anecdotes, facetiae, satire, etc
Is this any way to run an airline? (don't ask me) R. Lemon. il Sat Eve Post 240:24 Ap 22 '67

AIRLINES, Local service. See Local service airlines
AIRPLANE accidents. See Aviation—Accidents
AIRPLANE building. See Airplanes—Manufacture
AIRPLANE cabins
Architectural treatment provides room-like 747 cabin. il Aviation W 87:46-7 N 20 '67

Pressurization
See Airplanes—Pressurization
AIRPLANE carriers. See Aircraft carriers
AIRPLANE collisions. See Aviation—Accidents
AIRPLANE compass. See Compass
AIRPLANE construction. See Airplanes—Manufacture
AIRPLANE crews
Conflict over 737 crew size intensifies. Aviation W 87:37-8 S 11 '67
Evaluation plan may decide 737 crew. R. G. O'Lone. Aviation W 87:32-3 D 18 '67
AIRPLANE engines
Amazing new five-cylinder, two-stroke radial engine; design for lightplanes. J. W. Wright. il Pop Sci 191:45-7+ D '67
Higher-thrust J65 set for navy A-4s. Aviation W 87:30 Ag 7 '67
Low-weight rotary powerplant developed. M. L. Yaffee. il Aviation W 86:55-6+ Mr 13 '67
More on engine handling. J. A. Diblin. Flying 80:92-3 Je '67
NASA studying advanced engine for general aviation aircraft. Aviation W 87:113 Ag 28 '67
Three engines seen for airbus. Aviation W 87:35 Ag 7 '67
U.S. reciprocating engines; specifications (cont) Aviation W 86:195-6 Mr 6 '67
See also
Gas turbines, Aircraft

Fuel
Fuel shortage may increase costs. il Aviation W 87:32-4 Ag 7 '67
What can PFA 55MB do for you? alcohol blend eliminates fuel icing problems. A. Trammell. il Flying 80:44-5+ F '67

Fuel feeding
Prime consideration. T. R. Cole, jr. Flying 80:92 Ap '67

History
Power for flight; with editorial comment. A. Trammell. il Flying 80:6, 48-62+ My '67

Maintenance and repair
Instant overhaul; engine exchange plan. il Flying 81:24+ N '67
Jet stream to Vietnam via Miami; airport engine plants overhaul planes for speedy return to combat. il Bsns W p 112-14 Ja 14 '67
Running out of TBO? time between overhaul. J. Diblin. Flying 82:63-4 Ja '68

Repairing
See Airplane engines—Maintenance and repair

AIRPLANE engines—*Continued*

Superchargers

Last word in power turbocharging. J. Diblin. il Flying 80:77-80 F '67

Testing

New products: Alcor's engine analyzer. Flying 82:24+ Ja '68

AIRPLANE fares. See Airlines—Fares

AIRPLANE hangars. See Hangars

AIRPLANE hostesses. See Airlines—Hostesses

AIRPLANE industry and trade

Business jet firms vie for export trade; competition at the Paris air show. C. Brownlow. Aviation W 86:35 Je 5 '67

Fighting for the short haul; short-haul jets. il Time 89:92 Ap 21 '67

Foreign accent. J. Fricker. See issues of Flying

See also
Helicopter industry and trade

Consolidations and mergers

Douglas bullish over McDonnell merger plan. W. E. Wilks. il Tech W 20:36-7 F 6 '67

Federal agencies weigh terms of Douglas-McDonnell merger. I. Stone. Aviation W 86:34 Ja 23 '67

McDonnell, Douglas to merge. Tech W 20:23 Ja 23 '67

McDonnell holders to get added stock; merger agreement between McDonnell and Douglas aircraft co. Aviation W 86:31 Mr 27 '67

McDonnell moves in; McDonnell-Douglas merger. Bsns W p36 Ja 21 '67

Federal aid

Boom that's brewing a storm; Boeing's SST. il Bsns W p64-5+ O 28 '67

SST sets precedents in fund recovery. H. D. Watkins. il Aviation W 87:44-5+ O 16 '67

Finance

747 risk tops billion dollars. Aviation W 87: 59 N 20 '67

International aspects

DOD studies international fighter. Aviation W 86:16-17 Mr 13 '67

Statistics

U.S. business & utility aircraft shipments; tables. See occasional issues of Aviation week & space technology

Czechoslovakia

Czechs use western sales techniques in export push. D. E. Fink. il Aviation W 86: 167+ My 29 '67

Europe

Special report: Europe shifts basic patterns; symposium. il Aviation W 86:84-9+ My 29 '67

Europe, Western

Europe seeks new collaborative efforts; excerpts from address. A. H. C. Greenwood. il Aviation W 87:61+ O 2 '67

$15-billion aviation market seen. Aviation W 87:63 O 2 '67

Foreign accent; production of aerobatic airplanes. J. Fricker. il Flying 80:24+ My '67

Heavy industry key to European market. D. E. Fink. il Aviation W 86:297+ Mr 6 '67

Out-of-joint projects; Britain suffers rebuffs from Paris. Time 90:85 Jl 14 '67

France

French engine companies strong, growing. il Aviation W 86:265+ My 29 '67

French industry ties to U.S. seen strong; with editorial comment by R. Hotz. Aviation W 86:11, 22+ Je 19 '67

French order for 100 Mirage F-1s seen. il Aviation W 86:261+ My 29 '67

Vive le avion. J. Fricker. il Flying 81:26+ S '67

Germany (Federal Republic)

Fund cut stalls West German VTOL work. il Aviation W 86:284-5+ My 29 '67

Politics alter German air force plans. D. E. Fink. Aviation W 86:35-6 Ap 3 '67

R&D curtailment jolts German industry. L. Doty. Aviation W 86:24-5 Mr 13 '67

VFW 614 rollout set for mid-1969; development of short-range turbofan transport. Aviation W 86:293+ My 29 '67

Great Britain

Boost in Beagle Pup production planned. il Aviation W 86:101 Je 26 '67

Concorde financing bill planned in Britain. H. J. Coleman. Aviation W 87:29 D 18 '67

Hawker Siddeley pushes Trident 3 effort. il Aviation W 86:47-8 Ap 10 '67

Latest de Gaulle blow at Britain; supersonic military project canceled. U S News 63:11 Jl 17 '67

Out-of-joint projects; Britain suffers rebuffs from Paris. Time 90:85 Jl 14 '67

Israel

Fledgling industry takes wing in Israel; Aero Jet Commander plant. il Bsns W p 127 O 7 '67

Israelis acquire Jet Commander program. Aviation W 87:34 S 18 '67

Netherlands

Fokker to begin F-28 marketing campaign. il Aviation W 86:224-5+ My 29 '67

Poland

Poland sees reduced dependence on USSR aircraft assistance. Aviation W 86:109+ Ja 23 '67

Russia

Forging, press highlight Russian metalworking advances. M. L. Yaffee. il Aviation W 87:70-9 Jl 10 '67

Soviet salesmen buzz West's airplane market; Soviet SST to Paris international air show. il Bsns W p64-6+ Mr 18 '67

Soviets continue low-key export effort. il Aviation W 86:157-8+ My 29 '67

Will Russia win the SST race? interview, ed. by B. Kocivar. N. Halaby. il Look 31: 72+ F 7 '67

Sweden

Saab ready to show new 105XT for major sales drive. W. C. Wetmore. il Aviation W 87:40-1+ S 25 '67

Strong export potential seen for Viggen; Sweden's Saab aircraft company. W. C. Wetmore. il Aviation W 86:234-5+ My 29 '67

Sweden builds powerful military turbofan. il Aviation W 86:278-81 My 29 '67

United States

Anteing up for SST. Bsns W p33-4 F 11 '67

Business aircraft exports hold. il Aviation W 86:101+ Je 5 '67

Corporate jet competition stiffening. E. J. Bulban. il Aviation W 86:279-81+ Mr 6 '67

Economic curbs imperil industry; with editorial comment C. Brownlow. Aviation W 88:11, 16-19 Ja 8 '68

General aviation seeks problem accord. D. A. Brown. Aviation W 88:27 Ja 8 '68

Giant jets; the next revolution in air transport; special report; with editorial comment. il Aviation W 87:21, 35-47+ N 20 '67

Lockheed to brief subcontractors on L-1011 risk-sharing program. il Aviation W 87:37 D 11 '67

New military aircraft market potential tops $30 billion; DOD decisions awaited. M. Getler. il Tech W 20:37-43+ Mr 27 '67

North American support for Concorde set. Aviation W 88:31 Ja 1 '68

Piston aircraft sales growth rate may drop in 1967. il Aviation W 86:288-9+ Mr 6 '67

Redesign crucial in U.S. export efforts. E. J. Bulban. il Aviation W 86:143+ My 29 '67

Sound off; new light business aircraft. J. C. Fletcher. Flying 80:88-9 Ap '67

Subcontractor role grows in 747 work. R. G. O'Lone. il Aviation W 87:99-101+ N 20 '67

U.S. firms study European airbus market. C. M. Plattner. Aviation W 86:43 Je 5 '67

U.S. move to hard sell in Paris pays off. C. Brownlow. Aviation W 86:37 Je 12 '67

Where do all the airplanes go; distributor-dealer network. S. Buegeleisen. il Flying 81:84-7 Jl '67

See also names of airplane manufacturing companies, e.g. Beech aircraft corporation

AIRPLANE instruments. See Aeronautic instruments

AIRPLANE insurance. See Insurance, Aviation

AIRPLANE mechanics

Mechanic recruiting stressed. Aviation W 87: 84 Jl 31 '67

AIRPLANE models

Big boys at play; first international paper-airplane competition. il Time 89:58 Mr 3 '67

Plane and fancy; Scientific American's first international paper airplane competition. il Newsweek 69:70 Ja 30 '67

AIRPLANE parts

C-5A to revolutionize U.S. military airlift. J. D. Hendricks. il Aviation W 87:167-9 N 20 '67

AIRPLANE parts—*Continued*
Innovations aid Boeing-Wichita 747 task. il
    Aviation W 87:141+ N 20 '67
Rohr expanding for 747 nacelle program. Aviation W 87:133-4 N 20 '67
Spare parts policy overhaul urged. R. G.
    O'Lone. il Aviation W 86:73 My 29 '67
AIRPLANE racing
Confessions of a Powderpuffer; All woman
    transcontinental air race. S. Buegeleisen. il
    Flying 81:58-63 D '67
Homemade highflyers. il Time 90:92-3 O 6
    '67
Lady AWTAR comes of age; All-woman
    transcontinental air race better known as
    the Powder puff derby. E. D. Muhlfeld. il
    Flying 80:100-3 Ap '67
Racing gets hot: Cleveland report. J. Gilbert.
    il Flying 82:46-53 Ja '68
Reno '66: Reno national championship air
    races. F. Tallman. il Flying 80:40-3 F '67
Shades of Smilin' Jack; National air races.
    il Newsweek 70:66 O 9 '67
AIRPLANE seats. See Airplanes—Seats
AIRPLANE selling. See Airplane industry and
    trade
AIRPLANE sheds. See Hangars
AIRPLANE travel. See Air travel
AIRPLANE warranty. See Warranty
AIRPLANE wings
Bonding stressed at Fairchild. il Aviation W
    87:136 N 20 '67
New wing promises design breakthrough.
    B. K. Thomas, jr. il Aviation W 87:25-6
    Jl 24 '67
SST wing pivot seen easily maintainable.
    I. Stone. il Aviation W 87:109-11+ D 4 '67
Use of early data speeds tooling design. il Aviation W 87:144 N 20 '67
AIRPLANES
Leading international aircraft; specifications
    (cont) Aviation W 86:216-19 Mr 6 '67
New Cessna models include Reims rocket. il
    Aviation W 87:89+ D 18 '67
Saga of the Spruce Goose. il Newsweek 69:
    39 F 13 '67
USSR military and civil aircraft; specifications (cont) Aviation W 86:214 Mr 6 '67
U.S. commercial transports; specifications
    (cont) Aviation W 86:205 Mr 6 '67
    See also
Aviation
Flying machines
Seaplanes

Accidents
See Aviation—Accidents

Automobile combinations
See Airplanes, Light—Automobile combinations

Bird collisions
See Aviation—Bird hazards

Cabins
See Airplane cabins

Chartering
Buying better airlift; excerpt from address,
    March 31, 1967. R. H. Charles. Aviation
    W 86:21 Ap 3 '67
Cargo; charter proposals hit by airlines.
    H. D. Watkins. Aviation W 87:37 D 4 '67
CAB eases backhaul limitations for overseas
    military charters. H. D. Watkins. Aviation W 87:28 N 6 '67
Demand for cargo charter seen continuing
    downward trend. Aviation W 87:29 O 30 '67
Demand, jets, new authority spur growth;
    U.S. supplemental airlines. H. D. Watkins.
    il Aviation W 87:40-1+ Ag 28 '67
Sagging MAC cargo hits charters; Transpacific piston operations suspended. H. D.
    Watkins. Aviation W 86:27-8 Je 19 '67
Supplemental airline surge. H. D. Watkins.
    il Aviation W 87:40-1+ Ag 28; 32-4+ S 4 '67
Supplemental sees rising tour business. Aviation W 86:41 Ja 23 '67
Supplementals mount drive for routes. H. D.
    Watkins. Aviation W 87:26-7 D 25 '67
Whoosh! success of U.S. charter companies.
    il Newsweek 70:66 Jl 3 '67
You don't have to own an airplane. T. Trueblood. il Field & S 72:50-1+ Je '67
    See also
Airplanes, Freight—Chartering

Construction
See Airplanes—Manufacture

Control
See also
Automatic pilot (airplanes)

Cost of operation
Annual business aircraft operating costs;
    table. Aviation W 86:86-7 My 22 '67
Cost of flying. T. F. Widmer. il Flying 80:94-7
    F '67
Turbojet, turbofan aircraft 1966 operating
    costs; table. Aviation W 86:46 My 15 '67
Turboprop aircraft 1966 operating costs; table.
    Aviation W 86:34 My 22 '67

Crews
See Airplane crews

Design
Biography of a hired gun. R. Bach. il Flying 80:40-3 Ap '67
By design; Aircraft design-induced pilot error.
    R. B. Parke. Flying 82:34 Ja '68
NAA may help produce and sell VFW 614.
    Aviation W 87:31 Jl 24 '67
Soviets break tradition in Yak-40 design;
    three-engine, short-haul transport using
    turbofan engines. W. H. Gregory. il Aviation W 86:30-2 Je 19 '67
    See also
Airplanes, Jet propelled—Design
Helicopters—Design

Electronic equipment
ADF credibility gap. M. M. Goldsmith. Flying 80:67+ Je '67
Effort embraces spectrum from SST to
    private planes. il Aero Tech 21:56-7 N 20
    '67
New avionic products. See occasional issues
    of Aviation week & space technology
    See also
Computers—Aeronautic applications

Emergency landing
See Airplanes—Landing

Engines
See Airplane engines

Equipment
He always leaves them laughing. T. Severino.
    Flying 80:94-5 Ap '67
747 economies seen sacrificed to frills. Aviation W 87:31 O 2 '67
    See also
Aeronautic instruments
Oxygen apparatus
Radio telephone on aircraft

Escape devices
Control loss in F-111A forces crewmen to
    eject in module. E. J. Bulban. il Aviation W
    87:21-2 O 30 '67
Escape at low speed, altitude still challenges
    designers. il Aero Tech 21:41-2 Jl 17 '67
Services strive to better their crew ejection
    systems. H. M. David. il Tech W 20:89-91
    Mr 27 '67

Exhibitions
See Aviation—Exhibitions

Fires and fire protection
Cool pilot brought this one down safely; Eastern air lines DC-8. il Life 62:34-5 Ap 21 '67
System fills jet cabin with foam. il Aviation W 87:45+ N 13 '67

Flaps
See Flaps, Airplane

Fuel
See Airplanes engines—Fuel

Fuel tanks
Fuel tank safety systems required. Aviation
    W 87:75 S 4 '67

Fuselage
Innovations aid Boeing-Wichita 747 task. il
    Aviation W 87:141+ N 20 '67
LTV effort equals A-7 level. Aviation W 87:
    134-5 N 20 '67
Norair expands for 747 fuselage effort. il Aviation W 87:121-3+ N 20 '67

History
See Aeronautics—History

Hydraulic equipment
Users report on BAC 111 hydraulic gear. il
    Aviation W 86:75+ Ja 23 '67

Ice protection
Cessna using 411 to test rain-removal, de-icing units. il Aviation W 87:80-1 Jl 3 '67

AIRPLANES—*Continued*

Inspection

Beech 18 grounding disrupts schedules. Aviation W 86:41 My 15 '67
DC-6, -7 inspection easing restrictions. Aviation W 86:322 Mr 6 '67

Instrument flying

See Aviation—Instrument flying

Instruments

See Aeronautic instruments

Insurance

See Insurance, Aviation

Landing

AIL develops compact, solid-state ILS. K. J. Stein. il Aviation W 86:87+ F 13 '67
Army evaluates portable beacon system. K. J. Stein. il Aviation W 86:98-9+ Mr 20 '67
Army will test multiple approach system: A-scan. K. J. Stein. il Aviation W 87:72-3+ Ag 7 '67
Bell testing remote site landing system; simplified aircraft instrument landing system tested in conjunction with interim remote area terminal equipment. R. Barnhart. il Tech W 20:32 Mr 13 '67
Brakes and how to use them. T. Smith. Flying 81:71-2 D '67
CSF moves to exploit landing aids need. il Aviation W 86:305+ My 29 '67
Consideration of ILS replacement urged. Aviation W 87:41+ O 23 '67
Downtown VTOL service faces obstacles. D. A. Brown. il Aviation W 86:101+ Ja 23 '67
FAA testing calibrator for airport ILS. P. J. Klass. il Aviation W 86:92-3+ Mr 20 '67
New antenna aids LaGuardia approaches. K. J. Stein. il Aviation W 86:74+ Je 26 '67
Safer landings; tactical landing approach radio. S. V. Jones. il Sci Digest 61:80 Je '67
Stitch in time. R. Gottlieb. Flying 81:88+ Ag '67
There are no strange airports. R. Blodget. Flying 81:84 N '67
When there's nowhere to go but down; forced landings. A. Trammell. il Flying 81:54-7 N '67
Where would you put it? R. Blodget. Flying 81:98-9 S '67
  See also
Airplanes, Jet propelled—Landing
Airplanes, Military—Landing
Airports—Lighting

Landing gear

Air cushion landing gear flight tested. il Aviation W 87:24 Ag 21 '67
Landing gear capacity called inadequate. Aviation W 87:32-3 S 11 '67
Landing without wheels; air-cushion landing gear. il Time 90:76 Ag 25 '67
Piper Cherokee arrow. J. Gilbert. il Flying 81:34+ Ag '67

Landing on carriers

  See Airplanes, Military—Landing on carriers

Landing on ships

  See also
Helicopters—Landing on ships

Lighting

USAF, navy test new formation lights; electroluminescent tape. K. J. Stein. il Aviation W 88:72-3+ Ja 15 '68

Lightning hazards

See Aviation—Lightning hazards

Maintenance and repair

  See also
Airplane engines—Maintenance and repair
Airplanes, Business—Maintenance and repair
Airplanes, Jet propelled—Maintenance and repair
Airplanes, Military—Maintenance and repair

Manufacture

Flap tracks involve complex processing. il Aviation W 87:128 N 20 '67
Homebuilder and his craft. A. Trammell and J. Gilbert. il Flying 81:36-52 S '67
LTV designs forming machine to do work of four presses. il Aviation W 88:70 Ja 1 '68
Manufacturing effort for 747 calls for new techniques, vast investment in facilities. il Aviation W 87:108-9+ N 20 '67
Raising the pressure fourfold. il Bsns W p 126-8 F 18 '67

Use of early data speeds tooling design. il Aviation W 87:144 N 20 '67
  See also
Airplanes, Supersonic—Manufacture

Anecdotes, facetiae, satire, etc.

Feasible flying machine; if the Wright brothers had built their airplane under government contract. S. Dryer. il Sat Eve Post 240:18 N 4 '67

Materials

Advanced materials control C-5A weight. il Aviation W 87:228-9+ N 20 '67
New high-temperature materials studied. Aviation W 88:41 Ja 1 '68
  See also
Airplanes, Light—Materials
Airplanes, Supersonic—Materials

Noise

Airport area housing criticized. Aviation W 87:55-7 N 13 '67
Coast noise verdict may set precedent. Aviation W 88:35 Ja 1 '68
Computer graphics aid solution to DC-9 cabin noise problem. il Aviation W 87:69+ Jl 17 '67
Jet noise is getting awful. R. Sherrill. il N Y Times Mag p24-5+ Ja 14 '68
NASA begins major engine noise project. M. L. Yaffee. il Aviation W 87:38-9+ Ag 21 '67
NASA seeks quiet aircraft engine design. W. S. Beller. il Tech W 20:20-1 Je 19 '67
Noise study focuses on intakes, exhaust. Aviation W 86:24 Je 19 '67
Street and air traffic noise, and what we can do about it. L. L. Beranek. il UNESCO Courier 20:12-17+ Jl '67
U.K. industry join in anti-noise research. H. J. Coleman. il Aviation W 87:61+ Ag 14 '67

Operation

See Airplanes—Piloting

Parts

See Airplane parts

Passenger service

See Airlines—Passenger service

Piloting

Flight in the fabulous Phantom. G. G. O'Rourke. il Atlan 220:57-60 Jl '67
Hotshot Charlie rides again; pilots of F-4C Phantom and Spad XIII. D. Stone. il Esquire 68:111-15 O '67
I learned about flying from that. See issues of Flying
Listen to the engine. G. Hill. Flying 81:87 O '67
Pilots, captains and accidents. R. Blodget. Flying 81:110 D '67
Snobs. R. Blodget. Flying 80:30 F '67
Snowstorm! R. E. Brown. Flying 81:91 D '67
What's so special about special VFR? reprint. Flying 81:47 N '67
Winter's tale; special problems for aviators. il Flying 81:134-5 D '67
  See also
Drinking and airplane accidents
Meteorology, Aeronautic

Power supply

Rule of thumb for power settings. W. K. Kershner. il Flying 80:98 Ap '67

Pressurization

Light-aircraft pressure unit developed; cabin pressurization system. G. S. Hunter. il Aviation W 88:91+ Ja 15 '68
Pressure loss study spurs rule proposal. B. K. Thomas, jr. il Aviation W 86:68-9+ My 1 '67

Private ownership

Cost of flying. T. F. Widmer. il Flying 80:94-7 F '67
Plane in every garage. J. Roe. il House B 109:34+ S '67
Separate airports for private planes? U S News 63:73 O 9 '67
  See also
Airplanes in business
Private flying

Purchasing

Bargain-basement planes. J. Gilbert. il Flying 80:34-43 Je '67
Just do it. K. Connes. il Flying 80:76-7 Je '67

Racing

See Airplane racing

AIRPLANES—*Continued*

Radar equipment
See Radar in aviation

Registration and transfer
Numbers please; FAA aircraft registry N-numbers. A. Trammell. il Flying 80:54-5 Ap '67

Renting
Rental pilots, beware. D. H. Scott. Flying 81:63-4 S '67

Rocket propulsion
See Rocket propulsion

Safety devices and measures
Airlines expected to tell collision avoidance needs. H. Taylor. il Tech W 20:18-19 Je 26 '67
Better cabin restraint systems sought. D. A. Brown. il Aviation W 86:91+ Mr 27 '67
FAA maps a route to more air safety. Bsns W p40 S 23 '67
Fuel tank safety systems required. Aviation W 87:75 S 4 '67
How high are you? altimeter accuracy. P. Turner. Flying 81:82-3 N '67
Net barrier system to be tested in France. W. C. Wetmore. il Aviation W 87:113+ D 11 '67
New FAA standards set guidelines. Sci N 92:344 O 7 '67
New safety rules may spark fund battle. D. A. Brown. il Aviation W 87:24-5 S 25 '67
See also
Airplanes—Escape devices
Airplanes—Ice protection
Aviation—Safety devices and measures

Seats
Boeing studies growth versions of 747. R. G. O'Lone. il Aviation W 86:45+ Mr 20 '67
Seat makers emphasize reduced weight. G. S. Hunter. il Aviation W 87:39+ D 18 '67
Upholstered torture rack; the jet seat. Life 64:4 Ja 19 '68

Skidding
Will test grooves for skid resistance. il Am City 82:22 F '67

Specifications
C-5A calls for precision in requirements. Aviation W 87:237+ N 20 '67
Specifications on twenty-seven popular homebuilts. Flying 81:48-9 S '67

Speed
Biography of a hired gun. R. Bach. il Flying 80:40-3 Ap '67
Soviet E-266 shown with record pilots. il Aviation W 87:54-5 D 18 '67
Wide range of speeds covered in studies. R. Pay. il Tech W 20:92+ Mr 27 '67
See also
Airplanes, Supersonic

Spinning
Stalls and spins. R. Blodget. Flying 80:56-7 Je '67

Stalling
Stalls and spins. R. Blodget. Flying 80:56-7 Je '67

Storage
Where ghosts come back to life; Military aircraft storage & disposition center, Davis-Monthan air force base. il Bsns W p58-60 Je 17 '67

Storm hazards
See Aviation—Storm hazards

Submarine combination
See Submarine boats—Airplane combination

Take-off
See also
Airplanes, Vertical take-off and landing

Testing
See also
Airplanes, Business—Testing

Weight
Boeing to cut weight of 747 with use of paper honeycomb. Aviation W 87:43 Jl 10 '67
Wary airlines hopeful Boeing can solve 747 weight problem. R. G. O'Lone. Aviation W 87:31 Jl 3 '67

Wheels
Follow me through; third wheel. R. Blodget. Flying 81:98-9 Ag '67

Windshields
Stretched acrylic windshield adapted for 747. Aviation W 87:135 N 20 '67

Wings
See Airplane wings

AIRPLANES, Amphibious
Amphibian rebuilder finds strong demand; planning a turboprop conversion of the Mallard. R. G. O'Lone. il Aviation W 87:111+ Jl 10 '67
German navy interest raises hopes for Do.324 production; STOL amphibian aircraft design. Aviation W 86:293 My 29 '67

AIRPLANES, Atomic powered
Possible nuclear aircraft roles analyzed. il Aviation W 87:41+ O 30 '67

AIRPLANES, Business
Aviation week pilot report:
Cessna aims at comfort, economy in 421. D. A. Brown. il Aviation W 87:98-9+ Ag 7 '67
Beech acting to give aircraft sales a lift. E. J. Bulban. il Aviation W 87:105+ N 13 '67
Best of two worlds; MU-2; pride of Japan's Mitsubishi ltd. and Texas' Mooney aircraft corp. R. Blodget. il Flying 81:40-7 Jl '67
Business aircraft exports hold. il Aviation W 86:101+ Je 5 '67
Business jet firms vie for export trade; competition at the Paris air show. C. Brownlow. Aviation W 86:35 Je 5 '67
Company finds King Air valuable tool. il Aviation W 86:357 My 29 '67
Corporate experience aids Gulfstream 2. D. A. Brown. il Aviation W 87:56-7+ O 9 '67
Corporate jet competition stiffening. E. J. Bulban. il Aviation W 86:279-81+ Mr 6 '67
Corporate jet set; hopes for surge in sales. il Time 89:62 Je 30 '67
European interest rises in business show; first International general aviation salon Gosselies airport, Belgium. il Aviation W 87:97+ O 2 '67
How goes it with the jet set. J. Gilbert. il Flying 81:66-71 O '67
Israelis acquire Jet Commander program. Aviation W 87:34 S 18 '67
Leading turbine-powered business aircraft; specifications (cont) Aviation W 86:208 Mr 6 '67
Pan Am prepares for next business jet. D. A. Brown. il Aviation W 87:81+ Jl 31 '67
Piaggio nears selection of outlets in drive to sell PD-808 in U.S. C. M. Plattner. Aviation W 88:103-5 Ja 15 '68
Pilot report: King Air. A. Trammell. il Flying 81:42-6 N '67
Private lines. Aviation W 87:114-15 Ag 21: 88 S 4: 101-2 O 2: 94-5 O 9: 92-3+ O 30: 86 D 18: 57 D 25 '67; 88:105 Ja 15 '68
Rockwell pushing new Turbo Commander. il Aviation W 87:117-19 Ag 14 '67
Sound off; new light business aircraft. J. S. Fletcher. Flying 80:88-9 Ap '67
Supersonic jets studied at Georgia tech. D. A. Brown. il Aviation W 86:106-7+ Ap 24 '67
Trend to small jets emerging at NBAA. D. A. Brown. Aviation W 87:33 O 16 '67
Trying harder with number two; bizjet. J. Gilbert. il Flying 80:84-8 F '67
U.S. business, personal and utility aircraft; specifications (cont) Aviation W 86:207 Mr 6 '67
Variable-geometry business jet studied. il Aviation W 86:77+ My 1 '67
When does an airplane make business sense? Flying 81:120 O '67
World jet agreement to sell PD-808 in U.S. is canceled. Aviation W 86:21 F 20 '67
See also
Airplanes in business

Cost of operation
See Airplanes—Cost of operation

Design
B.206S U.S. sales bid keyed to service. D. A. Brown. il Aviation W 87:129+ S 11 '67
Hawker Siddeley unveils improved HS 125. il Aviation W 87:111 Ag 28 '67
Single-engine family expanded by Cessna. E. J. Bulban. il Aviation W 87:32-4 O 9 '67

Electronic equipment
Building-block control system marketed. D. A. Brown. il Aviation W 87:91+ Jl 24 '67

AIRPLANES, Business—*Continued*

Maintenance and repair

Atlantic stresses maintenance flexibility. D. A. Brown. il Aviation W 86:106-8 F 13 '67
Cooperative group improves maintenance. R. F. Coburn. Aviation W 86:75-6 F 27 '67

Testing

Aviation week pilot report:
Hansa jet enters business aircraft fleet. H. J. Coleman. il Aviation W 86:351+ My 29 '67
Corporate experience aids Gulfstream 2. D. A. Brown. il Aviation W 87:56-7+ O 9 '67
Pilot report:
Commander Turbo II. R. B. Weighman. il Flying 81:52-4 O '67
DH-125 series 3AR. J. Gilbert. il Flying 81-50-3 D '67
Merlin IIA. A. Trammell. il Flying 81:56-9 Ag '67
T-33s used to check aerospace system s. G. S. Hunter. il Aviation W 86:97-8+ F 6 '67
Well-tempered Hansa jet. J. Fricker. il Flying 81:46-51 O '67

AIRPLANES, Convertible

747 incorporates proven techniques, new technology. C. M. Plattner. il Aviation W 87:62-3+ N 20 '67

AIRPLANES, Drone

Navy plans purchase of advanced drones. M. Getler. il Tech W 20:23 Ap 17 '67
U.S. drones and target missiles; specifications (cont) Aviation W 86:190 Mr 6 '67

AIRPLANES, Experimental

NASA may increase thrust for new X-15; rocket engine power for hypersonic research aircraft. il Aviation W 86:77+ Ap 17 '67
NASA reshapes aeronautics role; termination of X-15. W. J. Normyle. Aviation W 88: 26-7 Ja 15 '68
Over the top; first man to die in an X-15. il Time 90:27 N 24 '67
Several design studies expected for AX; close-air-support aircraft. C. M. Plattner. Aviation W 86:29-30 Ap 3 '67

Testing

NASA planning to test AiResearch ramjet in X-15A-2. I. Stone. il Aviation W 86: 74-5+ Ja 30 '67

AIRPLANES, Freight

C-5A commercial cargo version planned. il Aviation W 87:213-14 N 20 '67
Facilities stressed in L-500 concept. il Aviation W 87:214+ N 20 '67
Mini Guppy begins certification testing. G. S. Hunter. il Aviation W 87:72-3+ Jl 3 '67
Soviets add two new versions to growing An-24 family; twin-turboprop transport. W. G. Gregory. il Aviation W 87:54-5+ Jl 10 '67
Stretched Hercules offered by Lockheed. W. H. Gregory. il Aviation W 87:85+ S 11 '67
Transall proposed as cargo feederliner; twin-turboprop transport. il Aviation W 86:34 Je 19 '67
See also
Airplanes, Convertible
Airplanes, Military transport

Chartering

Flying Tiger defends back-haul charters. H. D. Watkins. Aviation W 86:38-9 Ap 24 '67
MAC charter demands take dip. H. D. Watkins. Aviation W 87:22-3 S 25 '67

AIRPLANES, Hypersonic. See Airplanes, Supersonic

AIRPLANES, Jet propelled

Airline demand for more seats brings stretch in L-1011 design. C. M. Plattner. Aviation W 87:22 D 18 '67
BEA pushes for BAC 211 order approval. H. J. Coleman. Aviation W 87:38 Ag 28 '67
Come fly to Europe with me in the new jumbo jet. D. Francis. il Pop Sci 190:98-101+ Mr '67
DC-10 airbus effort confirmed. Aviation W 87:29 N 6 '67
Delivery delay looming for 737. Aviation W 87:27 O 30 '67
Fighting for the short haul; short-haul jets. il Time 89:92 Ap 21 '67
Giant jets; the next revolution in air transport; special report; with editorial comment. il Aviation W 87:21, 35-47+ N 20 '67
Global jet-away. I. Wolfert. il Travel 128: 65-6+ N '67; Same abr. with title What it's like to fly around the world. Read Digest 91:219-20+ N '67
Here comes the bus; Lockheed's air bus. il Time 90:96 S 22 '67

Large economy size; Douglas aircraft DC-8-61. il Time 89:90 Mr 3 '67
Lockheed's airbus. Newsweek 70:76 S 18 '67
New entry in the compact-jet market; F-228 short-haul jet. il Time 89:88 F 10 '67
New Yak-40 details disclosed by Soviets. Aviation W 86:47 Ap 24 '67
Prowling mind of Henri Coanda. G. H. Stine. il Flying 80:64-8 Mr '67
$690-million order will give United all-jet fleet in 1969. J. W. Carter. Aviation W 87:28 Jl 31 '67
Spars on 737 reinforced. Aviation W 87:29 N 6 '67
Stretched DC-8s posing airline problems. J. W. Carter. il Aviation W 87:56-8+ D 4 '67
Transpacific route case; Braniff keys proposal to advanced jets. E. J. Budban. il Aviation W 86:33-4+ Mr 27 '67
TWA plans to buy ten more 747s in $455-million Boeing purchase. Aviation W 87:37 O 23 '67
Trend to small jets emerging at NBAA. D. A. Brown. Aviation W 87:33 O 16 '67
Two carriers add 727-200 to New York-Florida battle il Aviation W 87:30 D 25 '67
United buys seventy-nine new jets. Bsns W p29 Jl 29 '67
U.K. pushing airbus plan; BEA bid for BAC 211 hit. H. J. Coleman. Aviation W 86:30 Mr 27 '67
See also
Airplanes, Business

Design

Airbus designers and carriers warned of LaGuardia problems. Aviation W 87:66 Jl 17 '67
Airbus wins tentative approval; Britain, France, Germany agree on design. H. J. Coleman Aviation W 87:25 Jl 31 '67
Boeing moves delivery of first 727-200 to December. C. M. Plattner. il Aviation W 87:40-1+ S 11 '67
Boeing 737 design includes innovations. il Aviation W 87:59 S 18 '67
Boeing studies growth versions of 747. R. G. O'Lone. il Aviation W 86:45+ Mr 20 '67
Boeing wrestled with double-deck layout, finally settled on single deck for 747. il Aviation W 87:60-1 N 20 '67
British studying new transport family. H. J. Coleman. il Aviation W 87:35-6 Jl 3 '67
Dornier designs military-civil jet trainer. E. H. Kolcum. il Aviation W 87:61+ N 13 '67
Douglas proposes two versions of airbus. C. M. Plattner. il Aviation W 86:26-9 Je 26 '67
Douglas pushes DC-10 airbus plan. il Aviation W 87:36-9 N 13 '67
Douglas seeks to stretch DC-8-63 range. C. M. Plattner. il Aviation W 86:30 Mr 13 '67
F-228 jet aimed at regional market; short-haul turbofan transport. J. W. Carter. il Aviation W 86:37-8 F 6 '67
Hawker Siddeley pushes Trident 3 effort. il Aviation W 86:47-8 Ap 10 '67
L-1011 designed for cross-country role. il Aviation W 87:36-40 S 18 '67
Lockheed airbus uses current technology. I. Stone. il Aviation W 86:30-3 Je 26 '67
Production goal set at 500 for Jetstream. il Aviation W 87:89 S 4 '67
747 incorporates proven techniques, new technology. C. M. Plattner. il Aviation W 87:62-3+ N 20 '67
Soviets add two new versions to growing An-24 family; twin-turboprop transport. W. H. Gregory. il Aviation W 87:54-5+ Jl 10 '67
Tomorrow's buses get wings; airbus displayed at Paris air show. il Bsns W p64+ Jl 1 '67
U.S. firms pushing trade-off studies of medium-range jet. Aviation W 86:29 Mr 13 '67
U.S. firms study European airbus market. C. M. Plattner. Aviation W 86:43 Je 5 '67

Equipment

Boeing moves delivery of first 727-200 to December. C. M. Plattner. il Aviation W 87:40-1+ S 11 '67
Major component suppliers for Boeing 737. Aviation W 87:65 S 18 '67
747 incorporates proven techniques, new technology. C. M. Plattner. il Aviation W 87:62-3+ N 20 '67

Hydraulic equipment
See Airplanes—Hydraulic equipment

Instrument flying

Head-up unit tried in Category 3 system; incorporation of display in Douglas all-weather landing equipment. il Aviation W 86:60-1+ Je 26 '67

AIRPLANES, Jet propelled—*Continued*

Landing

Head-up unit tried in Category 3 system; incorporation of display in Douglas all-weather landing equipment. il Aviation W 86:60-1+ Je 26 '67

Maintenance and repair

Airlines seek test methods to cut maintenance costs. J. F. Judge. il Tech W 20:35-6 Je 12 '67

Preparing for the superjets; Eastern air lines and Trans World airlines joint project to reduce cost of maintaining future superjet fleets. Time 90:102 D 8 '67

Noise

See Airplanes—Noise

Parts

See Airplane parts

Seats

See Airplanes—Seats

Testing

Boeing presses 737 flight test program. il Aviation W 86:40-1 Ap 17 '67

Boeing 737 at midpoint in flight testing. C. M. Plattner. il Aviation W 87:56-7+ S 18 '67

F-28 test program ahead of schedule. Aviation W 87:40 S 18 '67

Fokker to begin F-28 marketing campaign. il Aviation W 86:224-5+ My 29 '67

Testing to stress size, control response. il Aviation W 87:147+ N 20 '67

Used airplanes

See Airplanes, Used

Weight

See Airplanes—Weight

AIRPLANES, Light

Beech 99 interest signals market battle. Aviation W 86:31 My 8 '67

Better cabin restraint systems sought. D. A. Brown. il Aviation W 86:91+ Mr 27 '67

Boost in Beagle Pup production planned. il Aviation W 86:101 Je 26 '67

Bushmaster drawing corporate interest. Aviation W 87:92 O 30 '67

Cherokee knights of the roundtable. il Flying 80:14-15 Je '67

Citabria's giant strides; Mustang rumble. il Flying 81:12-14 Jl '67

Foreign accent; hypothetical baby plane market. J. Fricker. il Flying 80:24+ Je '67

Foreign accent; sales of American lightplanes in Britain. J. Fricker. Flying 81:27 Ag '67

Get up and go: new models. R. B. Parke. Flying 81:32 N '67

Gone flying, Caribbean by Skyknight; a spendthrift's tour of the islands. J. Gilbert. il Flying 81:70-8 Ag '67

Handley Page Jetstream. J. Fricker. il Flying 81:68-70 Jl '67

Meet the Yankee. J. Gilbert. il Flying 81:64-70 N '67

Mountain hopping to Aspen in a hot new Debonair. R. B. Weeghman. il Flying 80:34-9 Ap '67

Navions unite; American navion society. S. S. Weinberg. il Flying 80:70-1 Ap '67

Peruvian firm studies clean-wing twins. D. A. Brown. il Aviation W 86:94-5 Ja 30 '67

Pilot report:

Beagle B.206-S. J. Gilbert. il Flying 81:34-7 D '67

Cardinal. A. Trammell. il Flying 81:30-3 D '67

Cassutt racer. J. Gilbert. Flying 81:52 S '67

Centurion. A. Trammell. il Flying 81:47-9+ D '67

421. R. B. Parke. il Flying 81:38-9 D '67

Mooney Mustang. A. Trammell. il Flying 81:38-41 O '67

Mustang II. R. Weeghman. Flying 81:50+ S '67

Piper Navajo. R. B. Weeghman. il Flying 81:42-5 O '67

Ranger. A. Trammell. il Flying 81:44-6 D '67

Skyservant. J. Fricker. il Flying 81:40-3 D '67

Smith miniplane. J. Gilbert. Flying 81:47+ S '67

Turbo Viking. R. B. Weeghman. il Flying 81:54-5 D '67

Volpar Turboliner. R. Blodget. il Flying 81:58-60 O '67

Wittman W-8 tailwind. R. Weeghman. Flying 81:47 S '67

Pilot report: Cessna turbo-system Super Skymaster. A. Trammell. il Flying 81:74-7 Jl '67

Pilot report: the Cherokee 140-4. R. B. Weeghman. il Flying 81:54-8 Jl '67

Piper Cherokee arrow. J. Gilbert. il Flying 81:34+ Ag '67

Piper offers retractable-gear Cherokee. il Aviation W 86:97 Je 19 '67

Piston aircraft sales growth rate may drop in 1967. il Aviation W 86:288-9+ Mr 6 '67

Progress report: the Aero Stars. R. Blodget. il Flying 80:82-3 My '67

Tin goose comes back; Buckmaster. il Pop Sci 191:60-1 Jl '67

U.S. business, personal and utility aircraft; specifications (cont) Aviation W 86:207 Mr 6 '67

Vive le avion. J. Fricker. il Flying 81:26+ S '67

Who's pushing for Musketeers? il Flying 80:14-15 My '67

See also
Airplanes, Business

Accidents

See Aviation—Accidents

Automobile combinations

Car that makes its own expressway; Molt Taylor's Aerocar. D. MacDonald. il Motor T 19:84-6 Mr '67

Design

British pressing own program for variable-geometry fighter. H. J. Coleman. il Aviation W 87:31 O 9 '67

HP-137 Jetstream aimed at new markets. il Aviation W 86:345+ My 29 '67

Homebuilder and his craft. A. Trammell and J. Gilbert. il Flying 81:36-52 S '67

Russians to use Be-30 as micro-airbus. il Aviation W 87:30-1 N 6 '67

Yak-18T features several modifications. W. H. Gregory. il Aviation W 87:107-8 Jl 17 '67

Engines

See Airplane engines

Inspection

See Airplanes—Inspection

Landing

See Airplanes—Landing

Maintenance and repair

How to be a winner at the maintenance game. C. Banfe. il Flying 81:50-2 Jl '67

Manufacture

See Airplanes—Manufacture

Materials

Bellanca. R. B. Weeghman. il Flying 80:46-51 F '67

Testing

Beechcraft model 60 Duke. A. Trammell. il Flying 81:48-9 Jl '67

Cessna 411-A. R. Blodget. il Flying 80:48-52 Je '67

Cessna using 411 to test rain-removal, de-icing units. il Aviation W 87:80-1 Jl 3 '67

Pilot report:

Cessna Skyhawk. A. Trammell. il Flying 80:32-6 My '67

Lark 95. N. Leatham. il Flying 80:44-8 Mr '67

AIRPLANES, Military

Aircraft, the one indispensable arm of the entire anti-submarine warfare team. S. Thurmond. Aero Tech 21:23-4 D 4 '67

Canadians eye Northrop F-5 successor. M. Getler. il Tech W 20:16-17 Ap 10 '67

DOD studies international fighter; concept based on FX. Aviation W 86:16-17 Mr 13 '67

Dogfight: U.S. and France in aircraft sales race. il Newsweek 70:76 D 18 '67

European interest sought for Northrop 530 fighter. Aviation W 87:26 Ag 7 '67

France's Mid-East arms ban hits Sud and Dassault hardest. Aviation W 87:19 D 18 '67

Problems cloud future of V/STOL fighter; proposed U.S.-West German V/STOL tactical fighter. C. Brownlow. il Aviation W 86:106-7+ My 29 '67

See also
Airplanes, Restored
Airplanes, Vertical take-off and landing

Accidents

See Aviation—Accidents

AIRPLANES, Military—Continued

Armaments

AC-47 broadens Viet attack envelope. C. Brownlow. il Aviation W 86:54-5+ Ap 17 '67
Day H-bombs fell on Palomares. L. Azancot. il Sat R 50:21-7+ Ja 28 '67
Day they lost the H-bomb, by C. Morris. Review
  Sat R 50:40 Ja 28 '67. O. R. Reid
Go-ahead is imminent for improved A-7; integrating the avionics system. W. Andrews. il Tech W 20:16-17 Je 19 '67
Gunship success spurs advanced models. il Aviation W 87:27 Ag 14 '67
100-bullet-a-second machine gun. J. Crane. il Pop Sci 190:86-7 Ap '67
One of our H-bombs is missing, by F. Lewis. Review
  Sat R 50:39 Ja 28 '67. O. R. Reid
Plane design seen ignoring ordnance role. H. Taylor and others. il Tech W 20:105-6 Mr 27 '67
Suit underscores proprietary data issue; Comac armament control. K. J. Stein. Aviation W 86:56-7+ F 27 '67
Texas instruments readying display system for AAFSS; advanced aerial fire support system. Tech W 20:36 Je 12 '67
USAF tests automatic flare dispenser. C. M. Plattner. il Aviation W 86:99+ F 13 '67

Testing
Weapons test boosts F-111A for war role. il Aviation W 88:17-18 Ja 1 '68

Control
Air force expects big gains from AIDS; aircraft integrated data system. W. Andrews. il Tech W 20:16-18 Je 26 '67
F-111A flies land profile supersonically. P. J. Klass. il Aviation W 86:84-5+ Ja 23 '67

Design
Britain, France agree to build variable-sweep-wing fighter. Aviation W 86:35 Ja 23 '67
Longer FB-111 with AMSA engines studied; advanced manned strategic aircraft. M. Getler. Tech W 20:14 F 20 '67
Plane design seen ignoring ordnance role. H. Taylor and others. il Tech W 20:105-6 Mr 27 '67
Saab ready to show new 105XT for major sales drive. W. C. Wetmore. il Aviation W 87:40-1+ S 25 '67
USAF seeks design for A-1 replacement. C. M. Plattner. Aviation W 86:41+ Ja 30 '67
U.S.-German fighter systems reviewed; concerning V-STOL tactical fighter design. D. E. Fink. Aviation W 86:18-19 Je 26 '67
Why the flak around the F-111. R. Witkin. il N Y Times Mag p32-5+ Ap 2 '67

Electronic equipment
ARC-98 transceiver awarded to Hoffman. Aviation W 87:103+ Jl 17 '67
Advanced aircraft, ground equipment creating new demands. C. D. LaFond and R. Barnhart. il Tech W 20:79-81+ Mr 27 '67
Air force expects big gains from AIDS; aircraft integrated data system. W. Andrews. il Tech W 20:16-18 Je 26 '67
Air force tests new F-105 avionics. Aero Tech 21:18 D 4 '67
Electronic warfare gains key Viet role. il Aviation W 88:48-9+ Ja 1 '68
Microcircuit ILS/VOR unit in development for air force. K. J. Stein. il Aviation W 87:100-1+ S 18 '67
Two firms will get CF/CD work on VSX. W. Andrews. il Aero Tech 21:21-2 Ag 28 '67
VSX go-ahead spurs A-NEW competition; avionics equipment on carrier-based antisubmarine warfare aircraft. Aero Tech 21:14 D 4 '67
Viet operations spur new A-6 interest. C. Brownlow. il Aviation W 86:67+ Ap 24 '67

Testing
Navy set to brief industry on huge new VAST program. Aero Tech 21:52+ S 11 '67
Wide use of navy's new test system seen. P. J. Klass. il Aviation W 87:75-7+ O 16 '67

Equipment
A-New system readied for tests on P-3C. C. M. Plattner. il Aviation W 86:72-3+ Mr 27 '67
Compact searchlights designed by Xerox for Viet battle needs. Aviation W 86:23 Je 26 '67
ILAAS sets new management patterns; IHAS system under development. K. J. Stein. il Aviation W 86:273+ Mr 6 '67

Mustangs modified for anti-guerrilla role. B. K. Thomas, jr. il Aviation W 87:67+ O 16 '67
Saab 105XT offers combat versatility. H. J. Coleman. il Aviation W 87:60-1+ S 25 '67
Viet-generated advances reach theater; testing sensors and electronic-countermeasures hardware. C. Brownlow. il Aviation W 86:68-9+ My 22 '67
  See also
Aeronautic instruments
Airplanes, Military—Electronic equipment

Escape devices
See Airplanes—Escape devices

Landing
Monitor aids C-141 all-weather landing. K. J. Stein. il Aviation W 86:80-1+ Ap 3 '67

Landing on carriers
Aviation week pilot report: navy tests routine automatic landings; all-weather carrier landing system (AWCLS) B. K. Thomas, jr. il Aviation W 86:88-9+ My 15 '67

Maintenance and repair
A-7A maintenance test may set trend. E. J. Bulban. il Aviation W 87:79+ S 18 '67
Jet stream to Vietnam via Miami; airport engine plants overhaul planes for speedy return to combat. il Bsns W p 112-14 Ja 14 '67
USAF expands Vietnam repair capability. il Aviation W 86:74-8 My 22 '67

Manufacture
Air force seeks metalworking advances. M. L. Yaffee. Aviation W 86:53-4+ F 6 '67
Big press argument explodes again at air force meeting. il Tech W 20:25-6 Ja 23 '67
200,000-ton forging press seen needed. M. L. Yaffee. Aviation W 86:78-9+ Ja 30 '67

Materials
Air force seeks metalworking advances. M. L. Yaffee. Aviation W 86:53-4+ F 6 '67
Composite materials turning point seen. G. S. Hunter Aviation W 87:47-9 O 30 '67
Quality control, testing seen key to future aeronautical advances. J. F. Judge. il Tech W 20:63-4+ Mr 27 '67

Piloting
See Airplanes—Piloting

Radar equipment
See Radar in aviation

Repair
See Airplanes, Military—Maintenance and repair

Safety devices and measures
Smoke danger spurs changes for AC-47. Aviation W 87:17 D 18 '67
Survivability studies accelerated. C. Brownlow. Aviation W 87:16-17 D 18 '67

Speed
See Airplanes—Speed

Storage
See Airplanes—Storage

Testing
A-7A maintenance test may set trend. E. J. Bulban. il Aviation W 87:79+ S 18 '67
JTF-2 begins new tests of low level penetration capabilities. W. E. Wilks. il Aero Tech 21:28-9 Ag 14 '67
Military tests may preview SST problems. C. M. Plattner. Aviation W 87:61-2+ O 16 '67
NASA assumes XB-70 research effort. Aviation W 86:38-9 F 13 '67
Saab 105XT offers combat versatility. H. J. Coleman. il Aviation W 87:60-1+ S 25 '67
TAC profiting from Nellis' expanded role. C. M. Plattner. Aviation W 86:98-9+ My 8 '67

Australia
A-4Gs, S-2Es bought by Australian navy. il Aviation W 87:21 Jl 31 '67

Austria
Austria buying more Swedish aircraft. Aviation W 87:23 Jl 31 '67

Denmark
Danes nearing jet choice for air force. Aviation W 87:35-6 O 9 '67

AIRPLANES, Military transport—*Continued*

Design

Five new C-5A versions proposed. C. Brownlow. Aviation W 87:16-17 Jl 31 '67

Electronic equipment

Self-contained avionics broaden scope of C-5 missions. K. J. Stein. il Aviation W 87: 192-6+ N 20 '67

AIRPLANES, Model. See Airplane models

AIRPLANES, Private. See Airplanes—Private ownership

AIRPLANES, Remodeled

Mustangs modified for anti-guerrilla role. B. K. Thomas, jr. il Aviation W 87:67+ O 16 '67

Pilot report: Geronimo Apache. A. Trammell. il Flying 81:70-3 S '67

Stretched Hercules offered by Lockheed. W. H. Gregory. il Aviation W 87:85+ S 11 '67

USAF lets contract to modify O-2 for improved performance. Aviation W 88:38 Ja 15 '68

AIRPLANES, Restored

Great antiques:
Nieuport 28. F. Tallman. il Flying 81: 64-7 Jl '67

Great antiques: Fokker D.VII. J. Gilbert. il Flying 80:102-7 Mr '67

Where ghosts come back to life: Military aircraft storage & disposition center, Davis-Monthan air force base. il Bsns W p58-60 Je 17 '67

AIRPLANES, Short take-off and landing

Armed Porter studied for Vietnam role. C. Brownlow. il Aviation W 87:67+ Je 25 '67

Bonn studying new STOL fighter. Aviation W 87:26-7 D 11 '67

Civil Buffalo pushed as intercity STOL. il Aviation W 87:55 S 11 '67

Revisions urged in STOL requirements. D. A. Brown. il Aviation W 87:111+ Ag 21 '67

STOL version C-119 proposed. Aviation W 86: 72 Je 5 '67

STOLs demonstrate versatility at Paris; photographs. Aviation W 86:92-3+ Je 19 '67

Speeding up air travel; Breguet 941, STOL transport. il Time 90:57 Ag 11 '67

Stretched, twin-engine Porter designed. D. E. Fink. il Aviation W 87:77-8+ O 9 '67

U.S. and Canadian STOL aircraft; specifications (cont) Aviation W 86:209 Mr 6 '67

V/STOL technology. il Tech W 20:53-8+ Mr 27 '67

AIRPLANES, Supersonic

Accelerating the jet age; interview. W. Allen. Nations Bsns 55:58-9+ Ag '67

Anteing up for SST. Bsns W p33-4 F 11 '67

Approval of SST by Congress held likely. H. Taylor. Tech W 20:16 My 8 '67

Ban the boom? F. Mount. il Nat R 19:850-4 Ag 8 '67

British, French rely on Concorde lead. il Aviation W 86:194-5+ My 29 '67

Concorde gets on its mark. il Bsns W p 120-1 D 16 '67

Concorde rolls out: first supersonic transport. Sci N 92:609-10 D 23 '67

Economic gains forecast for SST. il Aviation W 86:26-7 My 22 '67

Expanding jet age: financial and economic implications: address, October 9, 1967. T. A. Wilson. Vital Speeches 34:88-92 N 15 '67

Faith in hypersonic aircraft seen stimulus to development. W. S. Beller. il Tech W 20: 24-5 Mr 13 '67

$15 billion SST market predicted by FAA official. il Tech W 20:17 My 22 '67

$4-billion machine that reshapes geography. J. Mecklin. il Fortune 75:113-16+ F '67

Full SST funding approval expected. Aero Tech 21:11 Jl 31 '67

Funding request for SST seen imminent. H. D. Watkins. il Aviation W 86:35-6 Ja 30 '67

GE accumulating SST engine test time. il Tech W 20:28-9 Ap 3 '67

Hands across channel groom SST for flight; British and French jointly produced Concorde. il Bsns W p 158-60+ O 28 '67

How the SST will be financed. Time 89:88-9 My 26 '67

Incredible SST. W V. Shannon. Commonweal 86:462-3 Jl 28 '67

International SST cooperation considered. K. Johnsen. Aviation W 86:28-9 F 27 '67

Major base changes unforeseen for SST. Aviation W 86:27-8 My 22 '67

One trillion passenger miles; growth prospects and requirements of the airline industry to the year 1990; excerpts from address. J. C. Maxwell. Aviation W 87:21 Jl 10 '67

Raising the pressure fourfold. il Bsns W p 126-8 F 18 '67

Russians want a piece of U.S. SST market. Sci N 91:256-7 Mr 18 '67

Senate approval seen assured for SST. D. C. Winston. Aviation W 86:38 Ap 17 '67

Showing off the Concorde. il Time 90:98 D 15 '67

Soviet salesmen buzz West's airplane market; Soviet SST to Paris international air show. il Bsns W p64-6+ Mr 18 '67

Special report: Concorde rollout; symposium; with editorial comment. il Aviation W 87:11, 24-31 D 18 '67

Supersonic aircraft studied as launchers. W. J. Normyle. Aviation W 86:54+ Je 26 '67

Supersonic transport. K. H. Hohenemser; reply with rejoinder. R. A. McDonnell. Bul Atomic Sci 23:64 My '67

SST and the government; critics shout into a vacuum. R. J. Samuelson. il Science 157: 1146-51 S 8 '67; Discussion. 158:313+ O 20 '67

Supersonic transport: blind stakes in the poker game. K. M. Ruppenthal. Nation 204:786-9 Je 19 '67

SST flies to hill. il Sci N 91:449 My 13 '67

Supersonic transport: heat, cold, radiation & the boom. K. M. Ruppenthal. il Nation 204: 685-9 My 29 '67

SST payments held no fare rise cause. Aviation W 86:49 Mr 13 '67

SST program responsibility shifts; with editorial comment. H. D. Watkins. il Aviation W 86:11, 28-9 My 8 '67

SST pushed by Johnson. Bsns W p 176 My 6 '67

SST technical group to include non-U.S. airlines ordering 2707. Aviation W 87:31 Ag 7 '67

Supersonic travel: will the gamble pay off? il U S News 63:74-5 S 11 '67

SST: travelers' boon or sonic boom? pro and con discussion. il Sr Schol 90:12-14 Mr 17 '67

SSTs may force traffic control changes. Aviation W 86:49-50 Ap 3 '67

Traffic control of advanced SST studied. K. J. Stein. il Aviation W 86:79-82 My 22 '67

U.S. SST seen more economical than Concorde, some subsonics. Aviation W 86:39+ Mr 20 '67

U.S. suppliers for Concorde prototypes. Aviation W 86:28 Mr 27 '67

Up in the clouds with the SST. E. Clark. il Sat R 51:47-8+ Ja 6 '68

What about the SST and national priorities? Am City 82:6 N '67

When the SST is too slow; planning hypersonic transport. J. Eberhart. il Sci N 91:528-9 Je 3 '67

Will Russia win the SST race? interview, ed. by B. Kocivar. N. Halaby. il Look 31: 72+ F 7 '67

See also
Airplanes, Business
Sonic boom

Control

Concorde flight instruments developed; combination horizon-flight director and combination heading and navigation situation display. il Aviation W 86:218+ My 29 '67

Cost

Airline funding aid called critical to SST. H. D. Watkins. Aviation W 86:41 F 6 '67

Airlines face rising SST funding. Aviation W 86:42-3 Je 12 '67

British emphasize Concorde cost control. il Aviation W 86:203-5 My 29 '67

Lift for the SST. Newsweek 69:89 F 13 '67

On the line. Time 89:88 F 10 '67

President readies SST message. il Aviation W 86:26-7 F 20 '67

President to seek $250 million for SST. H. Taylor. il Tech W 20:16 F 13 '67

Supersonic transport; billion-dollar dilemma. K. M. Ruppenthal. il Nation 204:652-6 My 22 '67

SST corp. considered to finance production versions of aircraft. K. Johnsen. Aviation W 87:41+ Jl 10 '67

SST prototype costs detailed; industry to pay $300 million. H. Taylor. Tech W 20:15 F 20 '67

Design

Concorde interior shown in mockup; photographs. Aviation W 87:40-3 Jl 3 '67

Final SST prototype design established. R. G. O'Lone. il Aviation W 87:34-6 D 4 '67

Passenger capacity in Concorde being cut to add baggage space. il Aviation W 87:27 N 6 '67

AIRPLANES, Supersonic—Design—*Continued*
SST design changes. Sci N 92:101-2 Jl 29 '67
SST design refined by Boeing. il Aero Tech 21:16 D 4 '67
Swing wing winner. il Sr Schol 89:17 Ja 20 '67

Electronic equipment
Electronic challenges in the SST program. J. H. Wujek, jr. Electr World 78:26-7+ Jl '67
NASA spells out SST electronics needs. Tech W 20:21 My 8 '67
New designs evolving for SST antennas. B. M. Elson. il Aviation W 87:91+ N 13 '67

Engines
See Jet airplane engines

Equipment
Avionics for advanced SST under study. Aviation W 86:49 Ap 17 '67
Tantalum elevon built for 3,000F test. M. L. Yaffee. il Aviation W 88:36-9+ Ja 1 '68

Lubrication
Lubricants sought for advanced aircraft. M. L. Yaffee. il Aviation W 86:71+ Ap 3 '67

Manufacture
Latest de Gaulle blow at Britain; supersonic military project canceled. U S News 63:11 Jl 17 '67
Martin withdraws as SST subcontractor. Aviation W 87:23 S 25 '67
SST sets precedents in fund recovery. H. D. Watkins. il Aviation W 87:44-5+ O 16 '67

Materials
Tantalum elevon built for 3,000F test. M. L. Yaffee. il Aviation W 88:36-9+ Ja 1 '68
Titanium seen boosting SST lightning risk. Aviation W 87:95 N 13 '67

Testing
Hypersonic aircraft hardware tests set. Aviation W 86:32 Je 19 '67
Insulated X-15A-2 ready for speed tests. C. M. Plattner. il Aviation W 87:74-81 Jl 24 '67
Military tests may preview SST problems. C. M. Plattner. Aviation W 87:61-2+ O 16 '67
Two of a special kind; test series of the X-15 and the XB-70. il Time 90:38-9 S 1 '67

AIRPLANES, Training
TC-4C to boost A-6A crew proficiency. K. J. Stein. il Aviation W 86:84-5+ My 1 '67

AIRPLANES, Used
Bargain-basement planes. J. Gilbert. il Flying 80:34-43 Je '67
Comanche 180; a used aircraft pilot report. R. B. Weeghman. il Flying 80:50-3 Ap '67
Just do it! K. Connes. il Flying 80:76-7 Je '67
Market warms up for secondhand jets. il Bsns W p56+ S 2 '67
Paint your aircraft sale green. C. Banfe. Flying 80:72 Ap '67

Testing
Used aircraft pilot report:
Fairchild 24. J. Gilbert. il Flying 81:44-9 Ag '67
Used aircraft pilot report; Cessna 170. J. Gilbert. il Flying 82:54-7 Ja '68
Used aircraft pilot report; the Apache. J. Gilbert. il Flying 80:44-7 My '67

AIRPLANES, Vertical take-off and landing
Bell X-22 V/STOL shows versatility in 20-kt. gusts. il Aviation W 86:32-3 My 15 '67
Burgeoning of V/STOL efforts reflected at Paris show; military and commercial aircraft. C. Brownlow. il Aviation W 86:72-3+ Je 19 '67
Composite aircraft seen emerging as next basic VTOL. M. L. Yaffee. il Aviation W 86:60-1+ My 1 '67
Downtown VTOL service faces obstacles. D. A. Brown. il Aviation W 86:101+ Ja 23 '67
Europe seeks new collaborative efforts; excerpts from address. A. H. C. Greenwood. il Aviation W 87:61+ O 2 '67
Europe stressing quick helicopter sales; VTOL research declining. il Aviation W 86:322-3+ My 29 '67
Foster backs V/STOL use for search and rescue task. M. Getler. il Tech W 20:16-17 Mr 6 '67
Fund cut stalls West German VTOL work. il Aviation W 86:284-5+ My 29 '67
Problems cloud future of V/STOL fighter. C. Brownlow. il Aviation W 86:106-7+ My 29 '67
Subsonic aeronautics enters renaissance. W. S. Beller. il Tech W 20:38-9 Ap 10 '67

Supertrain meets VTOL. il Newsweek 70:58 N 6 '67
U.K. Harrier emerges as weapons system; vertical takeoff and landing strike fighter. H. J. Coleman. il Aviation W 86:26-7 Je 5 '67
U.S. and Canadian VTOL aircraft; specifications (cont) Aviation W 86:212 Mr 6 '67
U.S.-German fighter systems reviewed; concerning V/STOL tactical fighter design. D. E. Fink. Aviation W 86:18-19 Je 26 '67
V/STOL gets big lift in expanding aviation work. W. Andrews. il Aero Tech 21:88+ N 20 '67
V/STOL technology. il Tech W 20:53-8+ Mr 27 '67
VTOLS go back to the boards. il Bsns W p60-2 Ap 8 '67
See also
Autogiros

Control
Pilot role grows in VTOL control concept. G. S. Hunter. il Aviation W 86:92-3+ Ap 10 '67

Testing
Further Do. 31 tests clouded by funding. il Aviation W 87:67 N 13 '67

AIRPLANES in agriculture
U.S. agricultural aircraft; specifications (cont) Aviation W 86:209 Mr 6 '67

AIRPLANES in astronomy
Flying spacewatchers. J. Eberhart. il Sci N 92:179 Ag 19 '67

AIRPLANES in business
Annual report to the single-engine stockholders. R. Blodget. il Flying 81:34-7 O '67
Bowaters utilizes jet on two continents. D. A. Brown. il Aviation W 86:120-1+ Ap 17 '67
Firms urged to monitor air taxi service; supplemental air transportation. Aviation W 86:99+ Je 5 '67
French study center pushes aviation use. Aviation W 86:359 My 29 '67
Hennessey's Queen Air aids distribution. il Aviation W 86:348-9 My 29 '67
New commuter airline planning MSC-Houston airport shuttle. Aviation W 87:86 Jl 3 '67
Pro's nest (cont of) For love and money. T. Baxter. See issues of Flying
See also
Airplanes, Business
National business aircraft association

AIRPLANES in camping
Exploring north of nowhere. F. Perry and L. Perry. il Field & S 72:46-9+ Je '67

AIRPLANES in fishing. See Airplanes in hunting and fishing

AIRPLANES in hunting and fishing
Flying for sportsmen; symposium il Field & S 72:37-51+ Je '67
Winged safari for Arctic char. D. Barnes. il Sports Illus 26:48-55 My 15 '67

AIRPLANES in rescue work
Aerial rescue gain seen in debris study; upper atmospheric nuclear debris studies may yield experience in midair retrieval. B. K. Thomas, jr. il Aviation W 87:83+ Ag 21 '67
Air rescue flights begin in Fairbanks. Aviation W 87:30 Ag 21 '67
First C-141 rescue mission aids Indians. Aviation W 88:20 Ja 1 '68
See also
Helicopters in rescue work

AIRPORT buildings
Airlines get ready for new VIP; air freight terminal. il Bsns W p 116-18+ My 13 '67
Architecture for the new itinerants. G. Nelson. il Sat R 50:30-1+ Ap 22 '67
Booked for travel, new terminal for National airlines. H. Sutton. Sat R 50:48-9 Mr 4 '67
BOAC aims to speed 747 passenger flow. W. C. Wetmore. il Aviation W 87:47+ D 4 '67
High-speed Heathrow cargo complex set. H. J. Coleman. il Aviation W 86:43+ Ja 23 '67
Service firm building two new hangars. Aviation W 87:123+ Ag 14 '67

AIRPORT landing fees. See Airports—Finance
AIRPORT thefts. See Stealing
AIRPORTS
Airports, the Twin Cities way. V. M. Draper. il Flying 80:82-5 Je '67
Choking on prosperity; congestion of major airports. R. Hotz. Aviation W 87:11 Ag 21 '67
Fighting trim. R. B. Parke. Flying 80:32 Ap '67
Great airport dilemma. D. W. Butwin. il Sat R 51:49-50+ Ja 6 '68
Limbo of a great airport. L. Wainwright. Life 64:12 Ja 5 '68

AIRPORTS—*Continued*
Stretched DC-8s posing airline problems. J. W. Carter. il Aviation W 87:56-8+ D 4 '67
See also
Aviation landing stations
Hangars
Heliports

Automation
Atlanta tests support automation plans. P. J. Klass. il Aviation W 87:51+ S 4 '67

Buildings
See Airport buildings

Control towers
Better view at airports. il Fortune 75:159-60 F '67

Design
Airports of the future. il U S News 63:70-3 O 9 '67
Redesigning American airports. W. Von Eckardt. Harper 234:66-8+ Mr '67
Tomorrow's airports vs. the ground barrier. G. A. W. Boehm. Read Digest 91:123-7 S '67

Equipment
Fiscal 1969 fund talks crucial for ATC. P. J. Klass. il Aviation W 87:76-7+ Ag 28 '67

Federal aid
ATA urges major control improvements. Aviation W 87:36 Ag 28 '67
FAA will aid 386 U.S. airports; Alaska, Texas top beneficiaries. Aviation W 87:17-18 S 4 '67
Fiscal 1969 fund talks crucial for ATC. P. J. Klass. il Aviation W 87:76-7+ Ag 28 '67
See also
Federal airport corporation (proposed)

Finance
Airlines challenge general aviation fees. H. D. Watkins. Aviation W 87:36-7 O 23 '67
Airlines, others criticize new regulations. D. A. Brown. Aviation W 87:26-7 N 27 '67
FAA proposes sweeping use fees; new system of licensing. D. A. Brown. Aviation W 86:26 My 1 '67
FAA said to request inadequate funding. Aviation W 87:32 Jl 31 '67
Near miss; congestion problem of private planes at commercial airports. New Repub 157:8 Ag 19 '67

Landscape gardening
Skirts flying; airport landscaping. S. Buegeleisen. Flying 80:94 My '67

Lighting
Low-cost approach light rules produce mixed airline reaction. Aviation W 87:47 N 13 '67
Washington clipboard; improving runway lighting. R. Burkhardt. Flying 82:26 Ja '68

Location
Copenhagen may move airport; relocation of airport to Saltholm island. il Aviation W 86:52 My 8 '67
Great Swamp of New Jersey; jetports and progress; statement before Fish and wildlife service hearing. T. M. Edison. Nat Parks Mag 41:18 My '67

Planning
Airlines urged to act now on congestion. E. H. Kolcum. Aviation W 87:42-3 O 16 '67
Airport five-year plan to cost $1.5 billion. Aviation W 86:50 Ap 24 '67
Airport planning: a growing field for architects. il Arch Rec 142:93-4+ S '67
Choice of Stansted sparks controversy. Aviation W 86:30 My 22 '67
Homing in on the airport crisis. il Bsns W p 115-16+ N 18 '67
Joint planning urged for large airports. E. J. Bulban. il Aviation W 86:42-3 Ap 24 '67
747 to intensify airport space problems. H. D. Watkins. il Aviation W 87:49+ N 20 '67
Systems approach to airport snarl urged. B. M. Elson. Aviation W 88:47+ Ja 15 '68
Tomorrow's airports vs. the ground barrier. G. A. W. Boehm. Read Digest 91:123-7 S '67
See also
Airports—Location

Runways
Will test grooves for skid resistance. il Am City 82:22 F '67

Safety devices and measures
See also
Radar in aviation

Surfaces
Instant airport; use of Rapid site. il Sci Digest 61:79-80 Ap '67

Traffic
Airlines challenge general aviation fees. H. D. Watkins. Aviation W 87:36-7 O 23 '67

Traffic control
Air traffic control improvements outlined. C. D. LaFond. Tech W 20:20+ Ap 24 '67
Approach reports may be mandatory. il Aviation W 86:29 Je 19 '67
Better view at airports; FAA is now well into a $20-million program to build air-traffic control towers. il Fortune 75:159-60 F '67
Breaking the ground barrier. il Time 90:56+ S 8 '67
CSF moves to exploit landing aids need. il Aviation W 86:305+ My 29 '67
FAA to seek proposals on terminal radar control. W. Andrews. Aero Tech 21:16-17 N 6 '67
General aviation seeks problem accord. D. A. Brown. Aviation W 88:27 Ja 3 '68
Hub airport congestion splits user ranks; difficulties confronting air taxi and commuter airline operators. D. A. Brown. Aviation W 86:121+ Je 12 '67
See also
Air traffic controllers (persons)

Transportation problems
Automatic trains to transport travelers at Houston terminal. il Aviation W 87:61 D 11 '67
Passport to nineteen-eighty; symposium. il Esquire 68:84-91 Ag '67
Possible solutions to improve New York airport access cited. F. Cogan. il Aviation W 86:33 My 1 '67
Taking off from downtown; advantages of VTOL and Sikorsky-Budd helicopter. il Life 62:36-7 My 12 '67
We've got to lick the airport crisis! il Changing T 21:43-6 D '67

California
See also
Los Angeles—Airports

Canada
See also
Montreal—Airports

Denmark
Copenhagen may move airport; relocation of airport to Saltholm island. il Aviation W 86:52 My 8 '67
See also
Copenhagen—Airports

Great Britain
Choice of Stansted sparks controversy. Aviation W 86:30 My 22 '67
U.K. airports group reports earnings. Aviation W 87:55 S 18 '67

Ireland
Irish firm in ban on U.S. rights to Dublin. W. J. Normyle. il Aviation W 87:39+ Jl 31 '67

New York (state)
See also
New York (city)—Airports

United States
Airport jam. R. Brady. Duns 90:5 O '67
Can airports cope with the jet age? special report. il Bsns W p54-6+ Jl 22 '67
Major base changes unforeseen for SST. Aviation W 86:27-8 My 22 '67
Skirts flying; airport landscaping. S. Buegeleisen. Flying 80:94 My '67
To control the swarm; Senate aviation subcommittee's proposals. il Time 90:12-13 D 29 '67
U.S. airport crisis. il Newsweek 69:80-2+ My 15 '67
We've got to lick the airport crisis! il Changing T 21:43-6 D '67
See also subhead Airports under names of cities, e.g. Los Angeles—Airports

AIRPORTS, Floating
Floating airports. il Sci Digest 62:65 O '67

AIRWAYS
Aeroflot flying over Scandinavia. D. C. Winston. Aviation W 86:28 Mr 13 '67
Airlines eye Pacific as next plum. il Bsns W p50-2+ F 11 '67
Allegheny route bid supported. Aviation W 87:41 O 16 '67
Atlantic traffic may hit 5 million. J. W. Carter. il Aviation W 86:36-7 Ap 24 '67

AIRWAYS—*Continued*

Board bureau urges intensified competition in transpacific case. Aviation W 87:35-6 Ag 7 '67

Cargo cases watched closely for trends. H. D. Watkins. Aviation W 87:32-3 Jl 24 '67

CAB defers major Northwest awards. Aviation W 86:39 Ap 17 '67

CAB faces problem in Pan Am route bid. R. G. O'Lone. Aviation W 86:39 My 1 '67

CAB mood spurs route filings from three all-cargo carriers. H. D. Watkins. Aviation W 86:27-8 My 1 '67

CAB will tighten route case procedures. J. W. Carter. Aviation W 87:38-9 O 23 '67

Continental spreads its wings; applies for routes to the Pacific. il Bsns W p 120-2+ N 18 '67

Gold rush over Pacific; for tourist traffic. il U S News 62:88-9 Mr 6 '67

New Northwest/Southwest awards generate protests. Aviation W 86:39 My 15 '67

New routes awarded three local airlines. Aviation W 87:41 S 18 '67

New York-Moscow flights may start soon. J. W. Carter. il Aviation W 87:26-7 S 25 '67

Northeast emphasizing route expansion. Aviation W 87:41+ N 13 '67

Northwest passage. Newsweek 69:90 Ap 24 '67

NW-SW rights proposed for seven. Aviation W 87:32 N 27 '67

Pacific plum; new routes; competitors; CAB hearings. Newsweek 69:84 Mr 27 '67

Plan for southern route case disputed. H. D. Watkins. Aviation W 86:45 Ap 17 '67

Policy shift seen in Hawaii awards. Aviation W 87:41 S 18 '67

Restructuring of U.S. airspace considered by FAA to meet rising traffic fund pinch. D. A. Brown. il Aviation W 87:102-3+ O 16 '67

Route decision laid to lag in development. L. Doty. Aviation W 87:26-7 N 6 '67

SAS expects Bangkok flights to triple. E. H. Kolcum. il Aviation W 87:29+ N 27 '67

Soviets, West Germany renew route clash. Aviation W 87:27 S 25 '67

Steady fare cuts spur Atlantic growth. L. L. Doty. Aviation W 86:49-50 Ja 23 '67

Supplementals mount drive for routes. H. D. Watkins. Aviation W 87:26-7 D 25 '67

Transpacific route case: American seeks U.S. traffic protection. H. D. Watkins. il Aviation W 86:48-9+ Ja 30 '67

Transpacific route case: Braniff keys proposal to advanced jets. E. J. Bulban. il Aviation W 86:33-4+ Mr 27 '67

Transpacific route case: Continental cites regional identification. R. G. O'Lone. il Aviation W 86:33-4+ My 8 '67

Transpacific route case: Eastern stresses less competitive areas. H. D. Watkins. il Aviation W 86:53+ Ap 10 '67

Transpacific route case: Pan Am aims to keep top role in Pacific. J. W. Carter. il Aviation W 86:40-1+ Je 19 '67

Transpacific route case: three all-cargo carriers aim at major market in Pacific case; proposals by Airlift international, Flying Tiger line and Seaboard world airlines. H. D. Watkins. il Aviation W 86:48-50+ Je 12 '67

Transpacific route case: TWA stresses forging round-the-world service link. H. D. Watkins. il Aviation W 86:32-4+ F 20 '67

Transpacific route case: Western ties route bid to fare-cut plan. R. G. O'Lone. il Aviation W 86:54-5+ F 13 '67

U.S.-Italy conflict will set pattern. L. Doty. Aviation W 87:39-40 O 16 '67

U.S. lags behind in global route outlook. L. Doty. il Aviation W 86:243-5+ Mr 6 '67

See also

Aviation—Transatlantic flights

Traffic control

See Air traffic control

AKADEMGORODOK, Siberia

Science city rises from the Siberian taiga. il UNESCO Courier 20:32-6 N '67

Siberia's oasis for scientists; Academic town. il Bsns W p74-6+ Jl 22 '67

AKAI, Hiromu, and others

Virus-like particles in normal and tumorous tissues of drosophila. bibliog Science 157:810-13 Ag 18 '67

AKER, Suzanne

Data on the dangerous pantin, paper doll that dances. Dance Mag 41:50-3 D '67

AKHMATOVA, Anna

Reading Hamlet; July 1914; Heart's memory of sun. .; poems, tr. by S. Kunitz. Nation 204:528 Ap 24 '67

AKRIDGE, Clavis E.

Cry in the night. por Outdoor Life 139:54-5+ F '67

AKRON, Ohio

Education

Mediterranean; teaching classics at Walsh Jesuit H.S. A Prosen. il Sr Schol 90:sup 18 My 5 '67

ALABAMA

See also

Education—Alabama
Fishing—Alabama
Gardens—Alabama
Justice, Administration of—Alabama
Law—Alabama
Macon County

Politics and government

Third party in '68? the George Wallace story; with interview. il U S News 62:54-8+ Mr 20 '67

Race problems

After the agitators left Greensboro. J. K. Batten. il Reporter 37:31-3 Ag 10 '67

Demons in Alabama. Time 89:50 My 5 '67

Social conditions

Outsiders; doctors report on health of rural children. New Repub 157:4 Jl 15 '67

ALABAMA. University, Tuscaloosa

His and hers. New Repub 156:8-9 My 27 '67

Loaded for Bear. H. L. Masin. il Sr Schol 91:25 O 26 '67

Rose red with anger; F. Rose's feud with legislators. Time 89:49 Ap 21 '67

There are 300 Negroes at the University of Alabama. G. Samuels. il N Y Times Mag p32-3+ My 14 '67

Visit to Tuscaloosa. N. Cousins. Sat R 50:20+ My 27 '67

ALAMEDA college, Alameda, Calif.

Alameda college, a mall campus with built-in student mix. il Arch Rec 142:158 N '67

ALAMEIN, Battle of. See World war, 1939-1945—Campaigns and battles—Africa

ALANINE. See Amino acids

ALARMS

See also

Burglar alarms
Electric alarms
Fire alarms

ALASKA

Alaska: a challenge in conservation, by R. A. Cooley. Review

Liv Wildn 30:31-2 Aut '66. M. E. Murie

Atomic energy in Alaska; Conservation society's opposition to atomic experimentation. Nat Parks Mag 41:25 Ap '67

There's a frontier waiting in Alaska. il Changing T 21:7-11 Mr '67

Way North; Alaska's centennial exposition. il Time 89:17 Je 2 '67

See also

Architecture, Domestic—Alaska
Arts and crafts—Alaska
Camping—Alaska
Dams—Alaska
Earthquakes—Alaska
Education—Alaska
Fairbanks
Fisheries—Alaska
Floods—Alaska
Glacier Bay National Monument
Housing—Alaska
Hunting—Alaska
Klondike gold fields
McKinley, Mount
Mount McKinley National Park
Natural resources—Alaska
Pribilof Islands
Saint Lawrence Island
Tourist trade—Alaska
Wilderness areas—Alaska
Zoology—Alaska

Antiquities

See Indians of North America—Antiquities—Alaska

Description and travel

Alaska journey. S. Turner. il Sr Schol 90:sup20-1 Mr 17 '67

Alaska's boating centennial. H. E. McLean. il Motor B 119:25-7+ F '67

Going places, finding things in Alaska. H. Johnson. il House & Gard 131:40-4+ My '67

Gone flying to Alaska. R. Blodget. il Flying 80:34-9+ Mr '67

Passage to the Yukon. K. Lamott. il Holiday 41:68-9+ My '67

ALASKA—*Continued*

Economic conditions

Alaska tries to break the ice. il Bsns W p 150-2+ N 4 '67

History

Warm celebration for Seward's icebox. il Sr Schol 90:6-7 Mr 31 '67

Industries

Report from Alaska; Japanese investors. J. Gooding. il Fortune 76:49+ S 1 '67
See also
Fisheries—Alaska

ALASKA airlines
Flying with Dan McGrew; Golden Nugget promotion. il Newsweek 70:78 D 11 '67

ALASKA beaches. See Beaches

ALASKA Methodist university, Anchorage
Mountain climbing not limited to experts. R. L. Linder. il Parks & Rec 2:30-1+ Mr '67

ALASKA RANGE
See also
Mount McKinley National Park

ALASKA. University
Call of the wild. il Newsweek 70:44 Ag 21 '67

ALASKAN glaciers. See Glaciers

ALASKANS
Alaska journey. S. Turner. il Sr Schol 90: sup20-1 Mr 17 '67

ALATEEN (organization)
When a parent drinks too much. J. Locke. il Parents Mag 42:44-5+ Jl '67

ALBANIA
Albania and China: the incongruous alliance. A. Logoreci. bibliog f Cur Hist 52:227-31+ Ap '67
Lock on the door. R. Flamini. il Time 89: 32+ My 26 '67
Mediterranean Maoists. D. Egli. il Newsweek 70:49 Ag 14 '67

ALBANY, N.Y.

City planning

New York rebuilds its capital. il Fortune 75: 173-4+ My '67

Education

Academy for hard cases; Philip Schuyler high school. il Time 89:38 Ap 7 '67
Teaching Russian in junior high schools; Maplewood, N.Y, a suburb. L. J. Cerri. Sr Schol 90:sup21 My 5 '67

Newspapers

Reluctant crusaders. Time 89:88+ Ap 28 '67
Uncle Dan's feud with the Albany newspapers. J. Kapstein. il Reporter 36:37-40 Mr 9 '67

ALBARET, Céleste
Three friends of Proust. P. Kolb. il pors Vogue 149:86-87 Mr 15 '67

ALBATROSSES
Nature note. il Sci N 92:94 Jl 22 '67

ALBEE, Edward
Angry playwright in a soft spell. T. B. Morgan. il pors Life 62:90-90B+ My 26 '67
Delicate balance. Criticism
Nat R 19:99 Ja 24 '67
Everything in the garden; adaptation of play by G. Cooper. Criticism
America 118:19 Ja 6 '68
Commonweal 87:444+ Ja 12 '68
Nation 205:669 D 18 '67
New Repub 157:25-7 D 16 '67
Newsweek il 70:96 D 11 '67
Reporter 37:38-9 D 28 '67
Sat R 50:24 D 16 '67
Time 90:96 D 8 '67
He can try anything. por Newsweek 69:90+ My 29 '67

ALBERDI, Juan Bautista
Alberdi, Pan Americanist. P. F. Lavin. il por Américas 19:30-4 Ap '67

ALBERT, Samuel L.
Ordinarily this would be otherwise; poem. Atlan 219:111 My '67
She does; poem. Atlan 219:113 F '67

ALBERT and Mary Lasker foundation
Lasker largesse. il Newsweek 70:103-4+ N 20 '67

ALBERT Bonniers förlag. See Publishers and publishing—Sweden

ALBERT Einstein award
Einstein award winner. Sci N 91:279 Mr 25 '67

ALBERT Lasker awards
Lasker lens. il Time 90:57 N 17 '67
Two doctors and a senator. il Sci N 92:488-9 N 18 '67

ALBERTA

Industries

Now Canada strikes it rich in oil; Athabaska tar sands and Rainbow Lake area. il U S News 62:108-10 My 22 '67

ALBERTI, Rafael
Hispanic chronicle. W. Branstone. Poetry 111:46-55 O '67

ALBERTS, William E.
Are the churches failing today's teenagers? Parents Mag 42:50-2+ F '67

ALBERTZ, Heinrich
Hero's decline. por Newsweek 70:38+ O 9 '67

ALBINO, Joseph
Four-footed radar in Vietnam. Pop Mech 128:76-80+ S '67
Two new dairy systems from scratch. il Suc Farm 65:100B Ja '67

ALBINOS and albinism
Snowflake; the world's first white gorilla. A. J. Riopelle. il Nat Geog Mag 131:442-8 Mr '67
Tyrosinase inhibition: its role in suntanning and in albinism. L. T. Y. Chian and G. F. Wilgram. bibliog il Science 155:198-200 Ja 13 '67

ALBRECHT, Margaret
Don't be an over-anxious parent. Parents Mag 42:58-9+ Ap '67

ALBRIGHT, Ivan Le Lorraine
No single fact is as it seems. K. Kuh. il pors Sat R 50:23-7 F 11 '67

ALBRIGHT-Knox art gallery, Buffalo, N.Y.
Albright-Knox-Buffalo: work in progress. B. Townsend. il Art N 65:30-45+ Ja '67; Correction. 66:6 Mr '67

ALBROOK, Robert C.
Participative management: time for a second look. Fortune 75:166-70+ My '67
Secretary Fowler's crusade for monetary reform. Fortune 76:78-80+ Ag '67

ALBUMIN Naskapi. See Blood—Proteins
ALBUQUERQUE, N.Mex.

Education

That girl in Albuquerque; Carol Chinberg: brilliant in school, housemother for her motherless family. il Look 31:M18+ Ap 4 '67

ALCATRAZ (Island)
Rock of ages. J. Didion. Sat Eve Post 240:24-5 Jl 1 '67

ALCINDOR, Lewis
Alcindor the awesome. il pors Ebony 22:91-2+ Mr '67
Alone in a crowd. W. J. McKean. il pors Look 31:95-8 F 21 '67
Big Lew measures his lonely world; with account by J. Riley. il pors Life 62:105-6+ F -17 '67
Making of a legend. il pors Newsweek 69: 59-62 F 27 '67
Proof of the promise. il por Time 89:42 F 10 '67
Terror in the air. F. Deford. Sports Illus 26: 16-21 Ap 3 '67
UCLA wraps it up. Newsweek 69:56 Ap 3 '67

ALCOCK, George
Triumph of a stargazer. L. Wainwright. Life 63:24B N 24 '67

ALCOHOL

Physiological effects

Maternal behavior in the domestic cock under the influence of alcohol. J. K. Kovach. bibliog il Science 156:835-7 My 12 '67
What every woman should know about drinking. J. Brothers. Good H 164:50+ Ap '67
See also
Alcoholism
Drinking and traffic accidents

ALCOHOL in the body
Britain survives the breathalyser. L. Wainwright. Life 63:20A O 20 '67
Drawing the line for drivers. Time 90:86 S 22 '67
Letter from London; law imposing breathalyser tests. M. Panter-Downes. New Yorker 43:228 N 11 '67
None for the road; European drivers obliged to submit to random curbside breathalyser tests. il Time 90:33 O 20 '67
Spreading: tests for drinking drivers. il U S News 63:13 O 16 '67

ALCOHOLIC drinks. See Liquors
ALCOHOLICS
Public drunkenness: crime or health problem? G. Stern. bibliog f Ann Am Acad 374:147-56 N '67

ALCOHOLICS—*Continued*

Rehabilitation
Dealing with drunks. il Time 90:72 Jl 28 '67
Gary Crosby, a man's victory over alcoholism. M. Davidson. il Good H 165:92-3+ S '67
LSD, one way trip for alcoholics? F. R. Schreiber and M. Herman. il Sci Digest 62:60-4 Jl '67

ALCOHOLISM
Alcohol in perspective. Consumer Rep 32:97-9 F '67
Churchmen consider study on alcoholism; views presented at Middle Atlantic institute on alcohol studies. W. B. Gray. Christian Cent 84:1475-6 N 15 '67
Temptation of Dr Johnson; his consumption of alcohol. Sci Am 217:44 Ag '67
What happens when you drink. C. Williamson. il Redbook 129:62-3+ Jl '67
See also
Alateen (organization)

Research
Neither wet nor dry; Cooperative commission on the study of alcoholism. Sci N 92:416-17 O 28 '67

Therapy
Alcoholism: the small beginnings of a significant federal program. B. Nelson. il Science 158:475-7 O 27 '67
Alcoholism therapy; Finland. D. A. Ehrlich. Sci N 92:260 S 9 '67
Drinking license, please. Sci Digest 62:63 D '67
LSD for sociopaths. Sci N 91:352 Ap 15 '67
LSD, one way trip for alcoholics? F. R. Schreiber and M. Herman. il Sci Digest 62:60-4 Jl '67
Public drunkenness: crime or health problem? G. Stern. bibliog f Ann Am Acad 374: 147-56 N '67
Sot: his psyche or his genes? Eizopride as a cure. R. Kirk. Nat R 19:808 Jl 25 '67

ALCOHOLS
See also
Threitol

ALCOTT, Louisa May
Authors vs critics: children's books in the 1870's; excerpt from The rise of children's book reviewing in America, 1865-1881. R. L. Darling. il por Pub W 192:25-7 O 16 '67

ALDABRA ISLAND
Aldabra: biology may lose a unique island ecosystem. J. Walsh. il Science 157:788-90 Ag 18 '67
Aldabra: reprieve for an island. J. Walsh. Science 158:1164 D 1 '67
Can Aldabra be protected? letter. D. J. Zinn. Science 157:8 Jl 7 '67
Fighting for Aldabra. il Time 90:60 O 20 '67
Indispensable atoll. Nation 205:516 N 20 '67
Of tortoises and men. J. Ludwigson. il Sci N 92:156-7 Ag 12 '67
Saved by the pound; reprieve for ecology of Aldabra. Sci N 92:584 D 16 '67
Secret war for Aldabra Island. il Sci N 92: 391-2 O 21 '67
Tortoise and the jet. D. Wolfie. Science 157: 255 Jl 21 '67

ALDAN, Daisy
Vertical is our new sight; Your letter; Cometary script; Everywhere in constancy, he is intoning, look! look! poems. Poetry 111:150-6 D '67

ALDEBURGH, England
Britten and the Aldeburgh miracle. E. Greenfield. il Hi Fi 17:MA24-6 S '67
Britten at Aldeburgh; Snape Maltings concert hall. I. Kolodin. il Sat R 50:41-3 Jl 29 '67
Britten country; photographs. Opera N 31: 12-15 F 11 '67

ALDEBURGH festival. See Music festivals—England

ALDEHYDES
Glutaraldehyde activation of nuclear acid phosphatase in cultured plant cells. D. W. De Jong and others. bibliog il Science 155: 1672-4 Mr 31 '67
Photooxidation of hydrocarbons in the presence of aliphatic aldehydes. A. P. Altshuller and others. bibliog il Science 156:937-9 My 19 '67

ALDER
Don't call red alder a weed! W. B. Morse. il Am For 73:38-40+ S '67

ALDERFER, Richard D.
Value of high school debate. NEA J 56:39 Mr '67

ALDERMEN. See Councilmen

ALDOLASE
Aldolase reaction with sugar diphosphates. A. H. Mehler and M. E. Cusic, jr. bibliog il Science 155:1101-3 Mr 3 '67

ALDOSTERONE
Control of aldosterone secretion by the pituitary gland. W. P. Palmore and P. J. Mulrow. bibliog il Science 158:1482-4 D 15 '67

ALDOUS, Lucette
Music to my ears. I. Kolodin. Sat R 50:24 Je 17 '67

ALDRICH, L. T. See Hart, S. R. jt. auth.

ALDRICH, Samuel R.
How fertilizer affects crop quality. Suc Farm 65:44H Ja '67

ALDRICH, Winthrop W.
Suez crisis; a footnote to history. For Affairs 45:541-52 Ap '67

ALDRIDGE, James
Braver time; story. Redbook 129:149 My '67

ALDRIDGE, John W.
How I made it to true literary happiness. Life 64:8 Ja 12 '68
Kennedy drama: matrix for novelists. Life 62:8 F 3 '67

ALEUTIAN ISLANDS
See also
Agattu Island
Amchitka

ALEUTIAN ISLANDS national wildlife refuge.
See Wildlife sanctuaries

ALEWIVES (fishes)
Alewife explosion. il Time 90:56 Jl 7 '67
Dead fish by the ton; ecology of Lake Michigan. il Sci N 92:9-10 Jl 1 '67
Something fishy: alewives die in Lake Michigan. il Newsweek 70:23-4 Jl 31 '67

ALEXANDER the Great, king of Macedonia
In the footsteps of Alexander the Great. H. Schreider and F. Schreider. il pors Nat Geog Mag 133:1-65 Ja '68

ALEXANDER, Benjamin H.
Research scientist lends a hand to capital's poor. il pors Ebony 22:124-6+ Mr '67

ALEXANDER, Bob
Bob Alexander on damage control. Yachting 121:125 Je '67

ALEXANDER, Bruce K. See Bowers, J. M. jt. auth

ALEXANDER, Clifford L. Jr
Broader effort on job bias. por Bsns W p56+ Jl 15 '67

ALEXANDER, D. E. See Wilson, C. M. jt. auth.

ALEXANDER, George J. and others
LSD: injection early in pregnancy produces abnormalities in offspring of rats. bibliog il Science 157:459-60 Jl 28 '67

ALEXANDER, Jules
Advertising photographer. il por U S Camera 30:58-9 Ag '67

ALEXANDER, Mary
Must children read in packs? Pub W 191: 120-1 F 20 '67

ALEXANDER, R. W.
Short-short story. Writer 80:17-18 Ag '67
When it really counts; story. Good H 164:84-5 Je '67

ALEXANDER, Raymond Pace
Tribute to Mother Katharine Drexel; address, February 10, 1966. por Negro Hist Bul 29: 181-2+ Fall '66

ALEXANDER, Richard G.
Four stripes in the graveyard. por Time 91: 14 Ja 19 '68
Question of tradition. por Newsweek 71:28 Ja 22 '68

ALEXANDER, Shana
Feminine eye. See issues of Life

ALEXANDER, Tom
McNamara's expensive economy plane. Fortune 75:88-91+ Je 1 '67
New ways for the shipyards. Fortune 76:114-21 Jl '67
Wild plan for South America's wilds. Fortune 76:148-50+ D '67

ALEXANDER, W. O.
Competition of materials; with biographical sketch. Sci Am 217:54, 254-6+ S '67

ALEXANDER'S department stores, incorporated
Way they made their boutique tick; 59th St. bridge boutique. il Life 68:89 O 20 '67

ALEXANDROV, A. P.
Heroic deed. Bul Atomic Sci 23:10-13 D '67

ALFALFA
Honeybees resent alfalfa kicks. Sci N 91: 195 F 25 '67
What's new in alfalfa varieties. W. D. Pardee. Suc Farm 65:58A F '67

ALFALFA weevils
Nature note: weevil killer. il Sci N 91:564 Je 17 '67

ALFORD, Ruth Burgar
Island is a place apart. Home Gard 54:52-3 Jl '67

ALFRED the Great, king of England
On writing about King Alfred. C. W. Hodges.
  por Horn Bk 43:178-82 Ap '67
ALFRED, L. J. and Gelboin, H. V.
Benzpyrene hydroxylase induction by poly-
  cyclic hydrocarbons in hamster embryonic
  cells grown in vitro. bibliog Science 157:75-6
  Jl 7 '67
ALFRED, Theodore M.
Checkers or choice in manpower management.
  bibliog f Harvard Bsns R 45:157-8+ Ja '67
ALFRED A. Knopf, Incorporated. See Knopf,
  Alfred A., incorporated
ALFRED I. duPont awards
DuPont awards: finis? R. L. Shayon. Sat R
  50:110 Mr 11 '67
ALFREDA Marie, Sister
Myth in the New Testament. por Cath World
  205:171-5 Je '67
ALFVÉN, Hannes
Antimatter and cosmology; with biographical
  sketch. Sci Am 216:15, 106-12+ Ap '67

about

Antimatter and creation.   A. Ewing. il por
  Sci N 91:64+ Ja 21 '67
ALGAE
Aztecs ate algacake. W. V. Farrar. Sat R
  50:55 Mr 4 '67
Bromophenols from red algae. J. S. Craigie
  and D. E. Gruenig. bibliog il Science 157:
  1058-9 S 1 '67
Chlamydomonas reinhardi: heterozygous diploid strains. W. T. Ebersold. bibliog il
  Science 157:447-9 Jl 28 '67
Cytoplasmic and chloroplast ribosomes of
  chlamydomonas; ultracentrifugal characterization. R. Sager and M. G. Hamilton. bibliog il Science 157:709-11 Ag 11 '67
Fatty acids in eleven species of blue-green
  algae: geochemical significance. P. L.
  Parker and others. bibliog il Science 155:
  707-8 F 10 '67
Glycerol excretion by symbiotic algae from
  corals and tridacna and its control by the
  host. L. Muscatine. bibliog il Science 156:
  516-19 Ap 28 '67
Membranes of valonia ventricosa: apparent
  absence of water-filled pores. J. Gutknecht.
  bibliog il Science 158:787-8 N 10 '67
New high-temperature chlorella. C. Sorokin.
  bibliog il Science 158:1204-5 D 1 '67
U.S., Russian scientists view algae as principal
  space food. H. J. Coleman. Aviation W 87:
  88-9 Ag 14 '67
  See also
Diatoms
Euglena
Lichens
ALGAE, Fossil
Algal stromatolites: use in stratigraphic cor-
  relation and paleocurrent determination. P.
  Hoffman. bibliog il Science 157:1043-5 S 1
  '67
Stromatolites; report on conference. R. N.
  Ginsburg. Science 157:339-40 Jl 21 '67
ALGAE as food
Aztecs ate algacake. W. V. Farrar. Sat R 50:
  55 Mr 4 '67
ALGEBRA, Boolean
Logic demon; duplicating the logic functions
  of giant electronic computers. D. Lan-
  caster. il Pop Electr 25:41-5+ D '66
Non-Cantorian set theory; analogy with non-
  Euclidean geometry. P. J. Cohen and R.
  Hersh. il Sci Am 217:104-6+ bibliog(p 160)
  D '67
ALGER, Fred
Young millionaires of finance. por Bsns W
  p76-9 D 30 '67
ALGER, Horatio, 1832-1899
Homilies of Horatio. M. Klein. Reporter 37:
  53-4 S 7 '67
ALGER, Leclaire G. See Leodhas, S. N. pseud.
ALGERIA
Algerian on dead center. A. De Borchgrave.
  il Newsweek 70:52+ N 13 '67
  See also
Socialism—Algeria
Women—Algeria

Economic conditions

Algeria revisited. E. M. von Kuehnelt-
  Leddihn. Nat R 19:437 Ap 4 '67
Algerian socialism's slow leak. J. Harriss.
  New Repub 156:19 My 6 '67

Foreign relations
Congo (capital Kinshasa)

Too hot to handle? Nat R 19:890 Ag 22 '67

History
Rebellion, 1954-1962

From Algeria to Vietnam. J. Kaplow. Commonweal 86:260-2 My 19 '67

Politics and government

To the barricades again. il Time 91:35 Ja 5 '68

Social conditions

  See also
Women—Algeria
ALGONQUIAN Indians
  See also
Cree Indians
ALGONQUIN hotel. See New York (city)—
  Hotels, restaurants, etc.
ALGONQUIN PROVINCIAL PARK
Mike Frome; voices of wolves. M. Frome.
  Am For 73:5+ Ja '67
ALHAMBRA
Gardens of Moorish yesterdays.   D. A. Nes-
  bett. Sat R 50:52+ Ja 28 '67
ALI, Ahmed
Children's reading in Pakistan. Horn Bk
  43:235-7 Ap '67
(tr) See Ahmed, D. Wind and the trees;
  Why does it happen so?
ALI, Muhammad. See Clay, C.
ALICE Long's dachshunds; story. See Spark,
  M.
ALIENATION, Social. See Social isolation
ALIMONY
Alimony for men? New York bill for alimony
  reform. Newsweek 71:58 Ja 8 '68
GH poll: do our alimony laws need reform-
  ing? S. H. Hofstadter. Good H 165:24+ S
  '67
ALINSKY, Saul David
Alinsky denounces reconciliation. Christian
  Cent 84:861 Jl 5 '67; Discussion. 84:1195-6
  S 20 '67
Episcopal editor denounces Saul Alinsky.
  Christian Cent 84:1452 N 15 '67
FIGHT against Kodak. B. Carter. il Reporter
  36:28-31 Ap 20 '67
FIGHT-Kodak fight. D. Livadas. Nat R 19:
  683 Je 27 '67
From worse to worse. Christian Cent 84:166
  F 8 '67; Reply. G. E. Kurtz. 84:444 Ap 5
  '67
Shepherds vs. flocks. W. C. Martin. Atlan 220:
  54-9 D '67
ALIOTO, Joseph
Flower of the West? il por Newsweek 71:24
  Ja 22 '68
ALIPHATIC aldehydes. See Aldehydes
ALISKY, Marvin
Mexican-Americans make themselves heard.
  Reporter 36:45-6+ F 9 '67
ALISON, Grover
Bookshop in Puerto Rico. il por Pub W 191:
  60-2 Je 26 '67
ALITALIA (airline). See Airlines—Italy
ALKALINE phosphatases. See Phosphatases
ALKALOIDS
Biosynthesis of the morphine alkaloids. G.
  W. Kirby. bibliog il Science 155:170-3 Ja 13
  '67
ALKEMA, Chester Jay
Crayon & chalk stencil technique. il Sch Arts
  66:38-41 Mr '67
Let's progress beyond the lollipop tree.
  Design 68:4-8 Sum '67
Tooling aluminum. Design 68:28-9 Sum '67
ALL-America cities
1966 All America cities. D. Chapman. il Look
  31:72-9 Ap 18 '67
ALL America selections. See Plants—All Amer-
  ica selections
ALL-American racing team.   See Motor boat
  racing
ALL-expense tours. See Travel
ALL-Japan audio fair. See Audio fairs
ALL-star team. See Baseball players
ALL the lovely possibilities; story. See Lyons,
  A. W.
ALL-woman transcontinental air race. See Air-
  plane racing
ALL year schools. See School year
ALLAIRE state park. See New Jersey—Parks
  and reserves
ALLAN, Donald A.
Cause for rejoicing. Reporter 36:37-8 My 4 '67
ALLAN, Maud
Salome and the king. E. R. Simmons and
  D. J. Holland. pors Dance Mag 41:52-3 N
  '67
ALLAND, Alexander, Jr
War and disease: an anthropological perspec-
  tive. Natur Hist 76:58-61 bibliog(p70) D '67
ALLARD, William Albert
Yellowstone wildlife in winter. il Nat Geog
  Mag 132:636-61 N '67
ALLEGHANY corporation
Corporate marine. Time 91:71 Ja 5 '68

ALLEGHENY commuter airlines
Allegheny, Henson plan route exchange. Aviation W 87:29-30 Ag 21 '67
Allegheny route bid supported. Aviation W 87:41 O 16 '67

ALLEGIANCE
See also
Citizenship

ALLEGIANCE, Oaths of. See Loyalty, Oaths of

ALLELES. See Allelomorphism

ALLELOMORPHISM
Twin meiosis and other ambivalences in the life cycle of schizosaccharomyces pombe. H. Gutz. bibliog il Science 158:796-8 N 10 '67

ALLEN, Anne
This way out. Am Ed 3:2-4+ Jl '67

ALLEN, Arthur T.
Literature for children: an engagement with life. Horn Bk 43:732-7 D '67

ALLEN, Charles M.
Unity in a university: the two cultures; address, April 25, 1967. Vital Speeches 33: 730-4 S 15 '67

ALLEN, Elizabeth
Art hidden in a bramble patch. il pors Life 63:76-9 Ag 18 '67
Patchwork prophecies. il por Time 89:53 Je 2 '67

ALLEN, Evelyn Young
Child with speech defects. NEA J 56:35-6 N '67

ALLEN, George and Unwin, limited
Behind the scenes at Britain's best shipper; distribution center. H. F. Scott. il Pub W 192:27-9 O 23 '67

ALLEN, Gina
To the planets for gold; reprint. Sci Digest 62: 39-44 O '67

ALLEN, Ivan, 1911-
Troubled cities, and their mayors. il por(p39) Newsweek 69:42 Mr 13 '67

ALLEN, James E.
Obituary of F. B. Henderson. Negro Hist Bul 30:20 F '67

ALLEN, John Alexander
Long farewell to Mrs Milliken; poem. Reporter 36:57 F 9 '67

ALLEN, Larry
Troubleshooting new color chassis. Electr World 79:38-40+ Ja '68

ALLEN, Linda
(ed) The look you like; questions and answers. See issues of Today's health

ALLEN, Maury
Teacher with class. Sr Schol 90:26 Mr 10 '67

ALLEN, Merton, and Solke, Kenneth
Disinfection by electrohydraulic treatment. Science 156:524-5 Ap 28 '67

ALLEN, Michael
Chaplain to the cool world. G. Astor. il pors Look 31:79-84 O 31 '67

ALLEN, Sir Peter Christopher
Sirs Paul and Peter. por Time 90:94+ N 17 '67

ALLEN, Richard D.
Million dollar copycats. il pors Ebony 23:74-6+ Ja '68

ALLEN, Richie
Batman to the rescue. H. L. Masin. por Sr Schol 90:24 My 12 '67

ALLEN, Robert V.
(comp) Articles and other books received: Soviet Union. See issues of American historical review

ALLEN, Sally Lyman
Genomic exclusion: a rapid means for inducing homozygous diploid lines in tetrahymena pyriformis, syngen 1. bibliog Science 155:575-7 F 3 '67

ALLEN, Sara Van Alstyne
Bronze hawk; poem. America 117:616 N 18 '67
Child and the book; poem. Horn Bk 43:433 Ag '67

ALLEN, William
Puberty is . . . Read Digest 92:99-101 Ja '68

ALLEN, William M.
Accelerating the jet age; interview. pors Nations Bsns 55:58-9+ Ag '67
Men who made the world move. H. Bigart. por Sat R 50:61-2 Ap 22 '67

ALLEN, Woody
Spring bulletin. New Yorker 43:38-9 Ap 29 '67

about

Woody. P. O'Neil. il pors Life 62:92-4+ Ap 28 '67
Woody Allen's bed of neuroses. J. Reddy. por Read Digest 91:113-16 Jl '67
Woody, Woody, everywhere il por Time 89: 90-1 Ap 14 '67

ALLEN university, Columbia, S.C.
Fight for quality on two Negro campuses. P. Clancy. il Reporter 37:37-9 Jl 13 '67

ALLENBAUGH, Naomi
Learning about movement. NEA J 56:48+ Mr '67

ALLENSWORTH, Calif.
Death threatens western town. L. Robinson. il Ebony 22:60-2+ Je '67

ALLERGIC encephalomyelitis. See Encephalomyelitis

ALLERGIC rhinitis. See Rhinitis

ALLERGY
Are you allergic to clothes? R. W. Crane. il Todays Health 45:30-2 F '67
Cytotoxic effect of lymphocyte-antigen interaction in delayed hypersensitivity. N. H. Ruddle and B. H. Waksman. bibliog il Science 157:1060-2 S 1 '67
Delayed hypersensitivity in man: a correlate in vitro and transfer by an RNA extract. D. E. Thor. bibliog il Science 157:1567-9 S 29 '67
If a pet causes an allergy. il Good H 165: 170 Ag '67
Sneezin' season is here. D. L. Unger. Todays Health 45:3 Jl '67

ALLEY, Walter, and Day, Richard
Servicing the new disk brakes. Pop Sci 190: 168-71+ Ja '67

ALLIANCE for progress
Alliance after six years: progress or not? pro and con discussion. Sr Schol 90:14-16 Ap 14 '67
Alliance for progress: dramatic start and hopeful future; address, August 21, 1967. S. M. Linowitz. Dept State Bul 57:321-4 S 11 '67
Alliance for progress moves on: a report on developments since the summit meeting; address, November 14, 1967. C. T. Oliver. Dept State Bul 57:754-8 D 4 '67; Same with title Latin America: the Alliance moves on. Vital Speeches 34:135-8 D 15 '67
Alliance for progress notes. See issues of Américas
Alliance that lost its way. E. F. Montalva. For Affairs 54:437-48 Ap '67
Alliance without progress. N. Miller. New Repub 157:8-9 S 9 '67
American Chiefs of state meet at Punta del Este; statements, April 11-14, 1967; with text of Declaration of the presidents of America. L. B. Johnson. Dept State Bul 56:706-21 My 8 '67
Best advisor of the Alliance. G. de Zéndegui. Américas 19:inside cover N '67
Business of development; address, September 13, 1967. C. T. Oliver. Dept State Bul 57: 470-5 O 9 '67
CIAP chairman installed. G. Meek. Américas 19:45 My '67
CIAP meeting. G. Meek. Américas 19:44-5 N '67
Contours of change in the home hemisphere; excerpts from address, December 7, 1967. C. T. Oliver. Dept State Bul 58:3-10 Ja 1 '68
Dialogue on the Alliance; meeting of American chiefs of state. A. Morales-Carrión. Américas 19:inside cover Jl '67
Foreign ministers of the American republics meet at Buenos Aires; statement, February 21, 1967, with resolution of meeting of foreign ministers, February 26, 1967. E. Bunker. Dept State Bul 56:472-6 Mr 20 '67
Guerrillas of peace and hope; presentation of diplomas to the twenty-nine young winners of essay contest. G. de Zéndegui. Américas 19:inside cover S '67
Hemisphere cooperation through the Alliance for progress; address, October 19, 1967. S. M. Linowitz. Dept State Bul 57:616-20 N 6 '67
Institution-building and the Alliance for progress; address, June 7, 1967. C. T. Oliver. Dept State Bul 57:102-7 Jl 24 '67
Latin American integration and the Alliance. J. M. Hunter. bibliog f il Cur Hist 53:257-62+ N '67
Latin American summit meeting; message to Congress, March 13, 1967. L. B. Johnson. Dept State Bul 56:540-5 Ap 3 '67
Our stake in a big awakening. R. N. Goodwin. il Life 62:66-8+ Ap 14 '67
Pan American day and Pan American week, 1967; proclamation. L. B. Johnson. Dept State Bul 56:632-3 Ap 17 '67
Sixth anniversary of the Alliance for progress; remarks, August 17, 1967. L. B. Johnson. Dept State Bul 57:287-8 S 4 '67
Trinidad and Tobago country review. G. Meek. Américas 19:45 N '67
Yankee goes home: Ecuador vs. ambassador. Sr Schol 91:20-1 O 26 '67

ALLIANCE of Reformed churches throughout the world holding the Presbyterian system
World Presbyterian area meeting. D. H. Rayner. Christian Cent 84:250+ F 22 '67

ALLIANCES
Fact sheet on U.S. alliances. Sr Schol 91:11-12 O 5 '67
See also
Central treaty organization
North Atlantic treaty organization

ALLIED chemical corporation
Firecracker for Allied. Newsweek 69:77+ F 6 '67

ALLIED stores corporation
Big-city store takes fashion into a barn; Stern brothers' East Hampton green. il Bsns W p32-3 My 27 '67

ALLIGATORS
American alligator. A. P. Hutt. il Nat Parks Mag 41:14-17 D '67
Serious situation of the American alligator. Nat Parks Mag 41:20 F '67
Troubled alligator. G. Laycock. il Field & S 71:49+ Ap '67

ALLILUEVA, Svetlana. See Stalina, S. I.

ALLIN, Roger W.
Inadequate water supply threatens Everglades National Park. Parks & Rec 2:37+ O '67

ALLIS-Chalmers manufacturing company
Allis-Chalmers pushes fuel cell efforts. R. D. Hibben. il Aviation W 86:65+ Ja 23 '67
Alphabet soup; Signal and Allis-Chalmers merge. Newsweek 70:85-6 D 11 '67
Hidden appeal of Allis-Chalmers. S. H. Brown. il Fortune 76:155-7+ N '67
Ling raises the ante; attempt to acquire Allis-Chalmers. Bsns W p36 Ag 19 '67
Signal accomplishment. il Time 90:104+ D 8 '67
Teaching Ling a thing; Ling-Temco-Vought takeover offer refused. il Time 90:68-9 Ag 25 '67
Wallflower; General dynamics discussions fall through. Newsweek 70:76+ S 18 '67

ALLISON, Anthony
Lysosomes and disease; with biographical sketch. Sci Am 217:20, 62-72 N '67

ALLISON, Harry W.
Ministers: a 200-hour view. Christian Cent 84:533-5 Ap 26 '67

ALLISON, John M.
Apathetic alert. Sat R 50:31+ Je 3 '67
Emperor and the inevitable. Sat R 50:44 S 30 '67
Foreign service with finesse. Sat R 50:47-8 F 4 '67
Problem of unlimited warfare. Sat R 50:43 N 4 '67

ALLIUMS
They're spectacular and they're onions. il Sunset 139:211 N '67

ALLOPURINOL
End, at last, to gout? A. Q. Maisel. Read Digest 90:113-17 Je '67

ALLOWANCES, Childrens. See Childrens allowances

ALLOWANCES, Duty free. See Duty free importation

ALLOWANCES, Family. See Family allowances

ALLOWAY, Lawrence
In the art world: the young crowd. House B 109:118-20 Jl '67

ALLOWAY, Thomas M. and Routtenberg, Aryeh
Reminiscence in the cold flour beetle, tenebrio molitor. bibliog Science 158:1066-7 N 24 '67

ALLOYS
See also
Aluminum alloys
Steel alloys

ALLPORT, Peter W.
What have you done for me lately? address, January 31, 1967. Vital Speeches 33:339-43 Mr 15 '67

ALLSHOUSE, Merle F.
False alarm? Christian Cent 84:142 F 1 '67

ALLSPICE
Add flavor with pimientos. Am Home 70:111 Jl '67

ALLUMS, Gail
On cue; Iowa U. coed becomes pool star. il pors Ebony 22:63-5+ Ag '67

ALLUVIAL rivers. See Rivers

ALM, A. A. and Schantz-Hansen, R.
Tubelings for tomorrow. pors Am For 73:16-18 S '67

ALMA, Mich.
Water, ground, surface, treated or raw. J. D. McNaughton. il Am City 82:104-6 Mr '67

ALMANACS
Time of the Almanac. Newsweek 70:94 N 20 '67
See also
World almanac and book of facts

ALMENDRADO. See Desserts

ALMONDS
Elegant almond. Am Home 70:114 Ja '67

ALONSO, Alicia
Alonso: near return of a Cuban star. W. Terry. il pors Sat R 50:40-1 Jl 15 '67

ALONSO, Braulio
Commitment to action. por NEA J 56:29 S '67

ALONSO, Lou
Child with impaired vision. NEA J 56:42-3 N '67

ALOR, Jerjes Pantoja-. See Pantoja-Alor, J.

ALPER, Clifford D.
Family resemblance. Opera N 31:21-3 F 18 '67

ALPERT, Hollis
Hollywood in Budapest. Sat R 50:20-1+ D 23 '67
How useful are film festivals? Sat R 50:56-8 Jl 8 '67
SR goes to the movies. See issues of Saturday review

ALPERT, Richard
Non-communication. P. Michelson. New Repub 156:35-8 Mr 4 '67

ALPHA ecdysone. See Hormones, Plant

ALPHA-glycerophosphate dehydrogenase. See Dehydrogenases

ALPHA Helix (ship) See Ships, Research

ALPHA Helix expedition. See Scientific expeditions

ALPHA-hematite. See Hematite

ALPHA macroglobulins. See Globulins

ALPHA particle dating. See Radioactive dating

ALPHABET
From Aardvark to Zymurgy. D. Thomas. bibliog il Library J 92:4582-6 D 15 '67
Gothic ABC. B. Byfield. il Atlan 219:62-8 Mr '67
They still wont teach the ABC's the modern way; I.T.A. experiment. il Ladies Home J 84:78+ My '67
Wuns upon a tiem; initial teaching alphabet. P. McBroom. Sci N 91:145 F 11 '67; Reply. C. Thomas. 91:390 Ap 22 '67

History
Tigris to Danube; single system of writing. Sci Am 217:40 Ag '67

ALPORT, Cuthbert James McCall Alport, baron
Incredible envoy. Newsweek 70:44 Jl 3 '67

ALSMILLER, R. G. Jr
Nucleon-meson cascade and shielding. bibliog Science 157:1399-405 S 22 '67

ALSOP, Joseph
Books (cont) New Yorker 42:112+ Ja 28 '67
No more nonsense about ghetto education! New Repub 157:18-23 Jl 22; 44 S 2; 18-23 N 18 '67; Same abr. with title Can Negro children make the grade? Read Digest 91:81-4 N '67
Reaction to the Coleman report; reprint. NEA J 56:27-8 S '67

ALSOP, Stewart
Affairs of state. See issues of Saturday evening post
But if twenty-five trucks fanned out... Sat Eve Post 240:18 O 21 '67; Same abr. with title Day the U.S. was destroyed. Read Digest 92:92-4 Ja '68
Our only real ally. Read Digest 91:43-5 S '67
Supreme court asks a question; is it fair? Sat Eve Post 240:42-4+ O 21 '67

ALSTEIN, A. D. and others
Transforming activity of green monkey SA7, C8 adenovirus in tissue culture. bibliog Science 158:1455-7 D 15 '67

ALTAMONT, N.Y.
Train station and the community. E. Cowley. il Sch Arts 66:35-8 My '67

ALTBACH, Philip G.
Spies for C.I.A. or deserving students? Christian Cent 84:352-4 Mr 15 '67

ALTER, Robert
In the community (cont) Commentary 43:67-71 Ja; 75-80 Mr; 66-71 Je; 44:46-52 O '67
Ousted by age from old intrigue. Sat R 50:40 O 21 '67

ALTERNATORS. See Electric generators, Alternating current

ALTHOUSE, Jack
Introducing the FET set. Pop Electr 26:27-30 My '67

ALTHOUSE, John
Electronics in oceanography. Electr World 77:44-6+ Mr '67
Temperature-depth measurements in the ocean. Electr World 78:33-6+ S '67
ALTIMETERS
How high are you? altimeter accuracy. P. Turner. Flying 81:82-3 N '67
New laser altimeter earmarked for 1968. Aero Tech 21:57 S 11 '67
Radar reassurance. il Flying 80:22+ Je '67
ALTINTEPE excavations. See Turkey—Antiquities
ALTITUDE, Influence of
Altitude and athletics. Sci Am 218:51 Ja '68
IBP: setting the stage; effects of high altitudes on human physiology. Sci N 92:512-13 N 25 '67
Plague of high altitudes; disappointments for Olympic athletes in Mexico city. B. J. Culliton. Sci N 92:587 D 16 '67
Up in the air; contest at 1968 Olympic site in Mexico city. il Newsweek 70:82 N 6 '67
ALTITUDE programers. See Aeronautic instruments
ALTMAN, China
296 stringers help us cover the world. G. P. Hunt. por Life 62:5 F 24 '67
ALTMAN, Harold
Portfolio of etchings; with biographical sketch. Am Artist 31:62-7 O '67
ALTMAN, Jack, and Ziporyn, Marvin
Mind of a murderer; excerpt from Born to raise hell. Sat Eve Post 240:27-31+ Jl 1; 38-40+ Jl 15 '67
ALTRUISM
What nature reveals about peacemaking; theories of W. Trotter. J. F. Wharton. Sat R 50:14-16 My 27 '67
ALTSCHUL, Aaron M.
Food proteins: new sources from seeds; address, December 26, 1966. bibliog Science 158:221-6 O 13 '67
ALTSCHUL, Frank
Advice and dissent. Sat R 50:33 F 11 '67
How right was U.S. might? Sat R 50:64 Je 10 '67
Once-over on the globe. Sat R 50:34-5 O 21 '67
ALTSHULLER, A. P. and others
Photooxidation of hydrocarbons in the presence of aliphatic aldehydes. bibliog Science 156:937-9 My 19 '67
ALUMINUM
Aluminum-26 and beryllium-10 in Greenland ice. R. McCorkell and others. bibliog il Science 158:1690-2 D 29 '67
Aluminum-26 in Pacific sediment: implications. J. T. Wasson and others. bibliog il Science 155:446-8 Ja 27 '67
New know-how you need for aluminum wiring. G. Daniels. il Pop Sci 191:159-61 S '67
Shape up! working with aluminum while building a dragster body. E. Dahlquist. il Hot Rod 20:66-9 Mr; 100-2+ Ap '67

Prices
Aluminum expects to resume its climb. il Bsns W p 142+ D 16 '67
ALUMINUM, Structural
Weathering of aluminum based on long-term tests in both industrial and seacoast atmospheres; excerpts from technical report. il Arch Rec 141:175-6 F '67
ALUMINUM alloys
Weathering of aluminum based on long-term tests in both industrial and seacoast atmospheres; excerpts from technical report. il Arch Rec 141:175-6 F '67
Wider use of cryogenic quenching seen. M. L. Yaffee. il Aviation W 86:81+ Ap 10 '67
ALUMINUM antimonide
Superconductivity of metallic aluminum antimonide. J. Wittig. bibliog il Science 155:685-6 F 10 '67
ALUMINUM cans
See also
Beer containers
ALUMINUM coated mirrors. See Mirrors for telescope
ALUMINUM company of America
Growing with an organization; interview. J. D. Harper. il Nations Bsns 55:64-8 D '67
ALUMINUM industry and trade
Metal of future is getting there. il Bsns W p 116-18+ Je 24 '67

France
Pechiney's progress. J. Ross-Skinner. Duns R 89:61-2+ Je '67

United States
Aluminum expects to resume its climb. il Bsns W p 142+ D 16 '67

ALUMINUM work
Firing glass enamels on aluminum. E. Winter. il Design 68:12-16 Mr '67
Tooling aluminum. C. J. Alkema. il Design 68:28-9 Sum '67
ALUMNI. See College graduates
ALVARD, Julien
Paris. See issues of Art news
What does Miro do with what he sees? Art N 66:32-3+ N '67
ALVAREZ, A.
Speaking out. por Sat Eve Post 240:10+ S 9 '67
ALVAREZ, Arturo Jacinto
I remember Beau Geste; story. Américas 19:28-31 N '67
ALVAREZ, Enrique Zuleta
Poet of the New World. Américas 19:10-18 F '67
ALVAREZ, Walter C.
Can you work yourself to death? Farm J 91:66J Mr '67
ALVEOLAR cells. See Cells
ALWIN Nikolais dance company. See Dance companies
AMABILE, George
Snowfall: four variations; poem. New Yorker 43:46 Mr 4 '67
AMALFI excursion. See Italy—Description and travel
AMALGAMATED clothing workers of America
Sewing machines & union machines. H. Hill. il Nation 205:18-19 Jl 3 '67
AMANTADINE hydrochloride
Breakthrough by Du Pont: a drug that blocks viruses. A. Rosenfeld. il Life 62:60A-61 F 10 '67
Effect of amantadine hydrochloride on the response of human lymphocytes to phytohemagglutinin. W. E. Rawls and others. bibliog il Science 158:506-7 O 27 '67
Epidemic may test drug; test of the controversial anti-viral drug. Sci N 92:228 S 2 '67
AMAPÁ, Brazil
Brazil's magic mountain. K. Seegers and S. Seegers. il Américas 19:20-7 Mr '67
AMARA, Lucine
Music to my ears; recital in Carnegie Hall. I. Kolodin. Sat R 50:107 O 14 '67
AMARAL, Olga
Olga Amaral. N. Znamierowski. il por Craft Horiz 27:28-31+ My '67
AMARO, Manuel, pseud.
Symbol of good will: the Antarctic treaty. Américas 19:1-9 F '67
AMARYLLIS
House plant spectacular. il Flower Grower 54:32-3 Ja '67
AMATEUR astronomers. See Astronomers, Amateur
AMATEUR athletic union of the United States
Sanctions and sanctimony: Sullivan award to J. Ryun. Sports Illus 26:11 Mr 6 '67
AMATEUR golf. See Golf
AMATEUR moving pictures. See Moving pictures, Amateur
AMATEUR photomicrography. See Photomicrography
AMATEUR radio operators. See Radio operators, Amateur
AMATEUR radio stations. See Radio stations, Amateur
AMATEUR tennis. See Tennis
AMATEUR theatricals
Opportunity please knock: youth gang produces lively show with guidance of O. Brown, jr. il Ebony 22:104-7 Ag '67
AMATEURISM (sports)
Pay's the thing; pro tennis has gone big time. Time 89:69 Je 23 '67
Ready for breaking; International Olympic committee's new amateur pledge. Time 90:70 Jl 28 '67
Tennis, everyone? British lawn tennis association erases distinction between amateur and professional. il Newsweek 70:49 D 25 '67
Two little words: British lawn tennis association deletes amateur and professional division. Time 90:45 D 22 '67
Vote for the 19th century: USLTA against open tennis. B. Collins. Sports Illus 26:76-7 Je 12 '67
AMAYA, Mario
Alien art. Opera N 32:26-9 Ja 20 '68
AMAZON RIVER
Adventure trips to the far outposts: to the Amazon Basin and Antarctica; with report by M. Leatherbee. il Life 63:78-87+ S 8 '67
Amazon River: environmental factors that control its dissolved and suspended load. R. J. Gibbs. bibliog il Science 156:1734-7 Je 30 '67

AMAZON RIVER—*Continued*
South from the Spanish Main, ed. by E. P. Hanson. Review
  Sat R 50:41-2 O 7 '67. R. E. Crist

AMBASSADORS
Mr & Mrs Ambassador: the Bunkers of Nepal and Vietnam. il Life 62:118-19+ Je 9 '67
Their excellencies. J. H. Plumb il Horizon 10:64-5 Wint '68
  See also
Negro ambassadors
United States—Diplomatic and consular service

AMBASSADORS wives
Diplomacy with dash. il Vogue 149:178-83 My '67
Fruitful life of Lady Carter; wife of ambassador of Guyana. il Ebony 22:40-2+ Jl '67

AMBER
X-ray diffraction study of some fossil and modern resins. J. W. Frondel. il Science 155:1411-13 Mr 17 '67

AMBERLEY, John Russell, viscount
Lord Russell and Lord Amberley. P. Toynbee; reply. P. A. Ternahan. New Repub 156:38 F 11 '67

AMBLER, Eric
Dirty story; novel. Sat Eve Post 240:23-7 Ag 26; 50-61 S 9; 70-2 S 23 '67

AMBROSIA (botany) See Ragweed

AMBROSIA beetle. See Beetles

AMBROTYPES
Ambrotypes: the positive. il Pop Phot 60:98+ My '67

AMBULANCES
Ambulance crisis. G. Adcock. il Todays Health 45:25-7+ Mr '67
Needed: first aid for ambulance services. I. Ross. il Read Digest 90:98-102 F '67
What are your chances in a medical emergency? C. Remsberg and B. Remsberg. il Good H 165:100-1+ N '67

AMCHITKA
We repeat, leave Aleutians alone! second underground nuclear explosion planned. Audubon 69:5 Mr '67

AMDURSKY, Ralph
So, rent a helicopter! D. S. Gelatt. il Pop Phot 60:94-9 F '67

AMEBA
Chaos chaos. E. V. Gravé. il Natur Hist 76:48-9 O '67
Optical differentiation of amoebic ectoplasm and endoplasmic flow. W. R. Baker, jr. and J. A. Johnson, jr. bibliog il Science 156:825-6 My 12 '67; Discussion. 158:142-3 O 6 '67

AMEBIASIS
Travel well. E. N. Dye. Travel 128:67 O '67

AMEBIC dysentery. See Amebiasis

AMENDMENTS to the Constitution. See United States—Constitution—Amendments

AMER, Abdul Hakim
Fateful friendship. Newsweek 70:50+ S 25 '67
Tough times for Nasser. por Time 90:31-2 S 22 '67
Voice from the grave; excerpts from document said to be last testament. Time 90:38 D 15 '67

AMERICA
  See also
United States

      Antiquities
  See also
Mayas
North America—Antiquities

      Discovery and exploration
Amazing discovery! American history depicted on playing cards. D. Powills. il Hobbies 72:114-15+ O '67
October 12, 1492; with editorial comment. H. Martínez-Montero. il Américas 19:inside cover, 1-4 O '67
Passion of Hernando de Soto; excerpt from Explorers of the Mississippi. T. Severin. il Am Heritage 18:26-31+ Ap '67
Was America a mistake? great debates of the enlightenment. H. S. Commager. il Horizon 9:30-3+ Aut '67
  See also
Vikings

AMERICA (periodical)
Danger ahead; NCCM-NCORT tension. Commonweal 87:372-3 D 22 '67

AMERICA (schooner) See Schooners

AMERICA hurrah; drama. See Van Itallie, J.-C.

AMERICAN (Chicago) See Chicago American

AMERICAN academy of achievement
Brainy brother act to heal the heart. il Life 62:35-6+ Ja 27 '67

AMERICAN academy of arts and sciences
Dædalus: marking a decade of journeys from the labyrinth. B. Nelson. il Science 156:770-3 My 12 '67

AMERICAN advertising federation
New watchdog for the admen? highlights of AAF annual meeting. il Bsns W p94-6 F 18 '67

AMERICAN airlines, Incorporated
American claims 27 per cent of New York-Boston air market. J. W. Carter. il Aviation W 86:24-9 Mr 27 '67
American gains in shuttle market battle; New York-Washington commuter market. J. W. Carter. Aviation W 87:35-6 S 11 '67
American to build central facility to handle heavy training loads. il Aviation W 87:40 N 13 '67
American way; new president. Time 91:84-5 Ja 19 '68
American's new pilot. Newsweek 71:75 Ja 22 '68
Shuttle scuffle; service along northeast travel corridor. il Newsweek 70:88 N 20 '67
Trade winds; standby passengers. J. Beatty, jr. Sat R 50:12 S 30 '67
Transpacific route case: American seeks U.S. traffic protection. H. D. Watkins. il Aviation W 86:48-9+ Ja 30 '67

AMERICAN anthropological association
Anthropologists overwhelmingly approve research ethics statement. B. Nelson. Science 156:365 Ap 21 '67

AMERICAN architecture. See Architecture, American

AMERICAN art. See Art, American

AMERICAN art-union, New York
Collecting American-nineteenth-century art. J. W. Middendorf, 2d. il Antiques 92:680-8 N '67

AMERICAN artist (periodical)
Reflections on our thirtieth birthday. N. Kent. Am Artist 31:3+ Ap '67
To instruct and inspire; editorial on 311th issue. N. Kent. Am Artist 32:5 Ja '68

AMERICAN artists. See Artists, American

AMERICAN association for health, physical education, and recreation
Project spotlights smoking dangers. Sr Schol 90:sup9 Ap 14 '67

AMERICAN association for the advancement of science
AAAS notes. Sci N 93:35-6 Ja 13 '68
AAAS officers, committees, and representatives for 1967. Science 155:857-60 F 17 '67
Public information service. T. C. Heatwole. Science 155:869-70 F 17 '67
Upward spiral of costs and dues; letter with reply. E. B. Hook; D. Wolfle. Science 158:854-5 N 17 '67
Whither AAAS annual meetings? W. G. Berl. Science 157:1379 S 22 '67

      Meetings, 1966
AAAS council meeting, 1966. D. Wolfle. il Science 155:855-6 F 17 '67
Report of the eighth Washington meeting. R. L. Taylor. il Science 155:860-9 F 17 '67
Reports of sections and societies. Science 155:871-90+ F 17 '67
Revolution is here. H. Pryor. il Sci Digest 61:13-17 Mr '67

      Meetings, 1967
American association for the advancement of science and affiliated societies 1967 annual meeting, New York city, 26-31 December. Science 157:586-8 Ag 4 '67
AAAS general and sectional symposia. il Science 158:1218-19 D 1 '67
AAAS 1967 annual meeting. il Science 158:1078-86 N 24 '67
AAAS section programs. Science 158:1493-5 D 15 '67
Annual meeting; tentative schedule of sessions, December 26-31, 1967. Science 157:1468-71 S 22 '67
Association affairs. Science 157:222-3 Jl 14 '67
Behavioral research, New York zoological park. R. Penney. il Science 158:144-5 O 6 '67
Election of AAAS officers. il Science 157:1594-600 S 29 '67
For 1968, the scope is global; 134th annual meeting. il Bsns W p36-8+ Ja 6 '68
Hazards of iodine-131 fallout in Utah; Norman Bauer memorial symposium. E. W. Pfeiffer. Science 158:397-8 O 20 '67
Intelligent man's guide to the 1967 AAAS meeting; with program. W. G. Berl. Science 158:1342-67 D 8 '67
Psychochemical research strategies in man; symposium, 28-29 December. AAAS annual meeting. A. J. Mandell. Science 158:1496-7 D 15 '67

AMERICAN association for the advancement of science—Meetings, 1967—*Continued*
Weather modification. J. E. Fletcher. il Science 158:276-7 O 13 '67
Web-building spiders, symposium, 29-30 December 1967, AAAS annual meeting, New York city. P. N. Witt. il Science 158:1216-17 D 1 '67

AMERICAN association of blood banks
Rare blood to the rescue. P. Brady. il Todays Health 45:34-8 My '67

AMERICAN association of law libraries
Panel quartet; 60th annual meeting. E. Bander. il Library J 92:2736-7 Ag '67

AMERICAN association of school administrators
AASA attacks assessment; Harvard groups protest. Library J 92:829-30 F 15 '67
AASA re-examines the issues; 99th convention, with editorial comment. W. D. Boutwell. Sr Schol 90:sup2, sup5 Mr 10 '67
AASA vs. National assessment plan. Sch & Soc 95:288-9 Sum '67
Focus on teacher at AASA convention. Sr Schol 90:sup4 F 10 '67
National assessment: national controversy. Sr Schol 90:sup2 F 3 '67

AMERICAN association of school librarians
San Francisco beat; ALA report. Library J 92:3115-16 S 15 '67

AMERICAN association of theological schools
Seminary and preseminary education: analyses of two A.A.T.S. reports. T. C. Oden; L. G. Tait. Christian Cent 84:536+ Ap 26 '67

AMERICAN association of university professors
AAUP report on 1966-67 salary survey. il Science 156:1072 My 26 '67
AAUP statement on St John's university. Sch & Soc 95:170+ Mr 18 '67

AMERICAN association of women ministers
Women ministers in 48th session. E. T. Culver. Christian Cent 84:1108 Ag 30 '67

AMERICAN astronautical society
Commercial development of space urged. il Aviation W 86:67+ My 15 '67
Exploitation of space technology boosted; special report: AAS annual meeting; with editorial comment. W. J. Coughlin and others. il Tech W 20:18-20, 50 My 8 '67
Industry told of responsibility to continue space program. W. S. Beller and C. D. LaFond. il Tech W 20:46-7 My 15 '67
NASA official raps Soviets at AAS meeting. Aero Tech 21:47 D 4 '67
Voyager teams to be picked within year. H. Taylor. il Tech W 20:18-19 Mr 20 '67

AMERICAN astronomical society
American astronomers report; highlights of some papers (cont) il Sky & Tel 33:162-3; 34:143-6, 213-14 Mr, S-O '67

AMERICAN athletes. See Athletes

AMERICAN authors. See Authors, American

AMERICAN ballads. See Ballads, American

AMERICAN ballet theatre
ABT returns, exhilarating! season at the New York city center. W. Terry. Sat R 50:53+ D 16 '67
America's ballet royalty. W. Terry. il Sat R 50:44-5 O 28 '67
Catch up with. L. Lerman. Mlle 65:148-9 Ag '67
Harbingers and history; spring season at New York state theater. M. Marks. il Dance Mag 41:34-40 Jl '67
Musical events; opening of season at City Center. W. Sargeant. New Yorker 43:226 D 9 '67
Musical events; performance of Les sylphides, Concerto, Balcony scene and Rodeo. W. Sargeant. New Yorker 43:135 My 27 '67
New stars. W. Terry. il Sat R 50:24+ Je 3 '67
Swans on Lake Michigan. il Newsweek 69:100 F 27 '67
Toe to toe; season in New York. H. Saal. il Newsweek 69:88-9 Je 5 '67
World of dance: Ballet theatre finale. W. Terry. il Sat R 50:45 Je 24 '67
World of dance: production of Swan lake at New York state theater. W. Terry. il Sat R 50:22+ My 27 '67
World of dance; review of New York season. W. Terry. il Sat R 50:84-5 Je 10 '67

AMERICAN bankers association
Bankers hedge bets. il Bsns W p34 S 30 '67
Plea to stem dollar flow. Bsns W p 108 Ag 5 '67

AMERICAN Baptist convention. See Baptists in the United States

AMERICAN bar association
Glacial progress. Time 90:49-50 Ag 18 '67

AMERICAN basketball association
ABA: playing the game called survival. T. Brody. Sports Illus 27:46-7 O 23 '67
Bay of bigs. Sports Illus 26:17 Je 12 '67
Labor pains of a new league. J. Jares. il Sports Illus 26:56-7 F 13 '67
Shooting for three; first ABA season. F. Deford. il Sports Illus 27:22-3 N 27 '67

AMERICAN bishops' conference. See National conference of Catholic bishops

AMERICAN bison. See Buffaloes

AMERICAN black walnut trees. See Walnut trees

AMERICAN book company
Litton, American book sign merger plan. Pub W 191:229 Ja 23 '67

AMERICAN book publishers council
ABA and ABPC criticize new postal rate bill. Pub W 192:29 N 20 '67
ABPC cites 1966 book boom; juvenile sales up 50 percent. Library J 92:4206+ N 15 '67
ABPC estimates 1966 sales, reports five-year trends; with tables. Pub W 192:28-31 O 16 '67
ABPC examines plans and structure; 1967 annual meeting. il Pub W 191:26-31 Je 12 '67
Data transfer: explosion and remedies; conference at Arden house. il Pub W 191:35-41 Ap 10 '67
Future of federal aid explored at D.C. briefing; conference. il Library J 92:3790-2 O 15 '67
International crisis in copyright; report of meeting by ABPC's technical, scientific and medical publishers group. S. Wagner. Pub W 192:16-17 D 4 '67
Management of change; case histories. il Pub W 191:22-7 My 1; 28-33 My 8 '67
1966 in review. Pub W 191:52 Ja 30 '67
U.S. education programs past, present and future: report of conference, with editorial comment. il Pub W 192:21-6, 36 O 2 '67

Religious publishers group
Book examination centers urged at RPG meeting. Pub W 192:29-30 O 30 '67
College market for religious and related books; summaries of addresses at luncheon. Pub W 191:74-5 F 27 '67
Factors in marketing viewed at RPG workshop; symposium. il Pub W 191:26-32 Ap 3 '67
RPG spring workshop planned on marketing. Pub W 191:77 F 27 '67

AMERICAN booksellers association
ABA and ABPC criticize new postal rate bill. Pub W 192:29 N 20 '67
ABA convention draws record registration of 3500, Miss Fitz-Gibbon is keynote speaker. Pub W 191:33-4 Je 12 '67
ABA holds a regional meeting in Houston. il Pub W 192:18-22 D 4 '67
Comments on the survey of bookstore operating ratios. D. Melcher; reply. J. B. Kobak. Pub W 191:159 Ja 23 '67
Debate that reflects real needs. C. B. Grannis. Pub W 192:49 S 18 '67
Disillusioned first-timer comments on the ABA convention. S. R. Vance. Pub W 192:172-3 Jl 10 '67; Discussion. 192:45-7 Jl 31; 17-18 Ag 14; 185-8 Ag 28 '67
1966 in review. Pub W 191:53-4 Ja 30 '67
67th ABA: in the future, change, growth. EDP. il Pub W 191:34-9 Je 26 '67
67th ABA: year's review, success and problems; symposium. il Pub W 191:46-55 Je 19 '67
Trade winds; annual convention. J. Beatty, jr. Sat R 50:10-11 Je 24 '67

AMERICAN book-Stratford press, incorporated
AB-SP adds a bindery to its Saddle Brook plant. il Pub W 192:78+ Ag 7 '67

AMERICAN broadcasting company
ABC-ITT merger. America 117:759 D 23 '67
Broken engagement for ITT and ABC; corporate marriage ended. Bsns W p24 Ja 6 '68
Bumpy days at ABC. Newsweek 71:94 Ja 22 '68
Networks take cue from Stage 67; ABC's success with cultural TV series. il Bsns W p60-2+ F 25 '67
Voice of ITT; probable effect of merger on independence. J. Ridgeway. New Repub 157:17-19 Jl 8 '67

AMERICAN broadcasting company-International telephone and telegraph merger. See Business consolidations and mergers

AMERICAN businessmen. See Businessmen

AMERICAN businessmen, Hall of fame for. See Michigan. University, Ann Arbor—Business hall of fame (proposed)

AMERICAN can company
Bargaining brightens in can talks; wages on productivity basis. Bsns W p 101-2 Ja 13 '68
Knock at metal box. Time 89:94 Je 23 '67
AMERICAN cancer society
Idle millions; hoarding by California division. S. Pelletiere. Nation 205:401-3 O 23 '67
AMERICAN catholicism. See Catholic church in the United States
AMERICAN Catholics. See Catholics in the United States
AMERICAN centennial exposition, Philadelphia. See Philadelphia—Centennial exhibition, 1876
AMERICAN citizenship. See Citizenship
AMERICAN city (periodical)
American city awards to be announced soon. il Am City 82:81 D '67
Eleven win merit awards. il Am City 82:63-6 Ja '67
New Jersey engineer wins the American city award. il Am City 82:111 N '67
AMERICAN civil liberties union
ACLU supports review of Michigan censorship verdict. Pub W 191:226 Ja 23 '67
Battle over the Bill of rights. F. Powledge. il Life 62:22-5+ Mr 31 '67
Civil liberties and uncivility in school. W. W. Brickman. Sch & Soc 95:102 F 18 '67
Whither loyalty oaths? Sr Schol 90:sup4 Mr 3 '67
AMERICAN college of obstetricians and gynecologists
Infertility: the other challenge. A. Kerr. il McCalls 95:54+ Mr '67
Pill; highlights of questionnaire sent to ACOG. A. Lake. il McCalls 95:96-7+ N '67; Same abr. with title How safe is the pill? Read Digest 92:48-52 Ja '68
AMERICAN college of surgeons
Fat down; transplants up. Sci N 92:370 O 14 '67
AMERICAN college students. See College students
AMERICAN committee for cultural freedom
Cultural cold war; excerpt from Towards a new past. C. Lasch. Nation 205:202-12 S 11 '67; Discussion. 205:309, 340-1 O 2-9 '67
AMERICAN Communist party. See Communist party (United States)
AMERICAN conservatism. See Conservatism
AMERICAN conservatory theatre
Floating permanent company. H. Hewes. Sat R 50:76 Ap 22 '67
On the Ball. il Newsweek 70:118+ N 20 '67
AMERICAN cookery. See Cookery, American
AMERICAN council of learned societies
Research library needs to be studied. Library J 92:1398 Ap 1 '67
AMERICAN council on education
American council of education urges defiance of HUAC. Christian Cent 84:988 Ag 2 '67
Selective service and student deferment; statement, April 25, 1967. Sch & Soc 95:428-30 N 11 '67
Statement on confidentiality of student records; July 7, 1967. Sch & Soc 95:504-6 D 9 '67
AMERICAN cyanamid company
Siverd of American cyanamid. il Fortune 76:59 N '67
AMERICAN dance festival. See Dance festivals
AMERICAN dancing. See Dancing
AMERICAN design. See Design
AMERICAN designers. See Costume designers
AMERICAN drama
Time for comedy. L. Kronenberger. Atlan 219:63-6 My '67
See also
Dramatists, American
AMERICAN eagles. See Eagles
AMERICAN economic assistance. See Economic assistance, American
AMERICAN economic association
Pathfinders for tomorrow's economics; John Bates Clark medalists. Bsns W p57 Ja 6 '68
AMERICAN education week
American education week, 1967, proclamation. L. B. Johnson. Am Ed 3:back cover O '67
AMERICAN elk. See Elk
AMERICAN Elsevier publishing company
Policing the consequences of science; New York company to publish technological forecasting journal. J. Lear. Sat R 50:67 D 2 '67
AMERICAN exiles. See Exiles
AMERICAN farm bureau federation
Farm bureau, NFO settle on next moves. Farm J 91:37 Ja '67
Harvest of scandal. R. G. Sherrill. Nation 205:496-500 N 13 '67

AMERICAN federation of labor and Congress of industrial organizations
Abel, ready and willing. Newsweek 70:90+ S 25 '67
AFL-CIO gets wooed for 1968. il Bsns W p76+ D 16 '67
Big labor's pitch at the bargaining table; wage negotiation manifesto of AFL-CIO. il Nations Bsns 55:42-3+ My '67
Big worry for unions; conservative gains in '68. il U S News 63:66-7 D 25 '67
Bone in Meany's throat. H. Rowen. New Repub 156:9-10 My 6 '67; Correction. 156:42 Je 3 '67
Can AFL-CIO win its textile siege? il Bsns W p94+ Mr 25 '67
Can outcast unions come home again? pressures to bring major independent unions back into fold of AFL-CIO. il Bsns W p 136+ Ja 14 '67
GM fight delays a family battle; Meany-Reuther confrontation. il Bsns W p57-8 D 2 '67
Inside story of the Reuther-Meany fight. il U S News 62:93-5 F 20 '67
Labor at Bal Harbour. B. J. Widick. Nation 206:6-8 Ja 1 '68
Labor girds for 1968, and a sea of troubles. il Newsweek 70:82-3 D 18 '67
Labor in the bag: the Meany-Johnson romance. S. Lens. Commonweal 87:432-3 Ja 12 '68
Labor maps a try harder strategy. Bsns W p 152+ Mr 4 '67
Labor's newest split: the price of a Reuther walkout. U S News 62:76-8 F 27 '67
Labor's top council sticks out its chin; strong opposition on Labor-Commerce merger. Bsns W p32-3 F 25 '67
Marriage on the rocks. Time 89:20-1 F 10 '67
Most of the way with L.B.J. Time 90:27 D 15 '67
Now: unions to police employers. U S News 62:80 F 13 '67
On labor horizon for '68: big demands, turmoil, strikes; biennial convention of the AFL-CIO. U S News 63:105-7 D 18 '67
Reuther takes a walk. Newsweek 69:80 F 13 '67
Reuther vs. Meany, a labor rift widens. U S News 62:10 F 13 '67
Reuther vs. Meany: background to labor's showdown. B. J. Widick. Nation 204:614-16 My 15 '67
Reuther vs. Meany; open break. S. Lens. Commonweal 85:557-9 F 17 '67
Reuther walks out, but doesn't shut the door; UAW resignations from AFL-CIO posts. il Bsns W p66-8 F 11 '67
Rift in AFL-CIO; Reuther vs. Meany. Sr Schol 90:21-2 F 24 '67
Situs picketing nears a showdown; trades unions pushing hard for bipartisan backing of Taft-Hartley amendment. Bsns W p 158 Ap 15 '67
Split in labor. W. V. Shannon. Commonweal 85:584-5 F 24 '67
Split labor faces a big year. il Newsweek 69:82-5 F 20 '67
Strong arm squad; longshoremen and anti-war demonstrators. New Repub 158:11 Ja 6 '68
Together again; A.F.L.-C.I.O. and the Democrats. Time 89:24 Mr 3 '67
Union furor over CIA money. U S News 62:86 My 22 '67
Union strength: at a new peak. U S News 63:97 D 11 '67
UAW goes out on two long limbs: Reuther's program. il Bsns W p99-100+ Ap 29 '67
Walter Reuther tries to build a fire. S. Lens. Commonweal 86:253-4 My 19 '67
War stirs union doves; opposition to AFL-CIO's backing of war. Bsns W p36 N 18 '67
Who's angry? support for Democrats. il Newsweek 69:63-4 Mr 6 '67

United farm workers organizing committee

Actos: Teatro campesino, a theatrical part of the United farmworkers organizing committee. New Yorker 43:23-5 Ag 19 '67
Cesar Chavez's biggest battle. D. Adair. Nation 205:627-8 D 11 '67
Unionizing the farm; Di Giorgio signs an AFL-CIO contract. il Bsns W p 164+ Ap 22 '67
Workers on the farms; agreement with the Western conference of teamsters. N. C. Mills. New Repub 157:9 S 23 '67
AMERICAN federation of priests
Restless clergy. G. Zimmermann. il Look 31:25-7 F 7 '67

AMERICAN federation of teachers
AFT in caucus and convention: new style for 1967. B. S. Julian. Mo Labor R 90:19-20 N '67
AFT wants new standards; annual convention. J. H. Lloyd. Sr Schol 91:sup2 S 28 '67
First cooperative conference. Negro Hist Bul 30:20 Ap '67
Professor and collective negotiations. J. F. Day and W. H. Fisher. bibliog f Sch & Soc 95:226-9 Ap 1 '67
St John's congress postponed till May; library school boycott by UFCT continues. Library J 92:517+ F 1 '67
Union response to academic mass production. P. Janssen. il Sat R 50:64-6+ O 21 '67
Unionizing the academics. J. Brann. New Repub 156:10-11 F 25 '67
Washington report. J. Lloyd. Sr Schol 91:sup20 S 28 '67
When the votes are counted... R. J. Flynn. NEA J 56:48+ My '67

AMERICAN federation of television and radio artists
AFTRA the fact. New Repub 156:7 Ap 29 '67
Due to circumstances; AFTRA strike. il Newsweek 69:86 Ap 10 '67
Hour of amateurs. il Time 89:88 Ap 14 '67
Management takes to the microphones. il Bsns W p28 Ap 8 '67
Portrait of the artists. il Time 89:46 Ap 7 '67
Show-stopper; AFTRA strike ends. Sr Schol 90:22-3 Ap 28 '67
Still out. Newsweek 69:119 Ap 17 '67
When $100,000-a-year men go on strike. il U S News 62:98-9 Ap 17 '67

AMERICAN fiction
Books in the field: American fiction. M. Klein. bibliog il Wilson Lib Bul 42:467-76 Ja '68
Five for year's end. G. Hicks. Sat R 50:19-20 D 30 '67
Novel as a function of American democracy; address, March 23, 1967. R. Ellison. Wilson Lib Bul 41:1022-7 Je '67
See also
Best sellers

History
Lachrymose ladies; address, September 15, 1966. J. Manthorne. bibliog Horn Bk 43:375-84, 501-13, 622-30 Je-Ag, O '67

AMERICAN film institute
Onward and upward with the institute. H. Alpert. Sat R 50:50 Je 24 '67
Rising sun in film's firmament; first meeting of the Board of trustees. A. Knight. Sat R 50:37 Ag 26 '67
Show of concern. Newsweek 70:74+ S 4 '67

AMERICAN flag. See Flags—United States
AMERICAN folk songs. See Folk songs, American

AMERICAN football league
Flag fury, bearing down in A.L.'s hottest race. il Life 63:16-25 S 8 '67
Merry-go-rounds; NFL and AFL common draft of college players. il Time 89:43 Mr 24 '67
Real draft beef; NFL and AFL draft college players. Newsweek 69:89 Mr 27 '67
Sporting scene; defeat of Kansas City Chiefs by Green Bay Packers in Los Angeles. H. W. Wind. New Yorker 42:102+ F 4 '67

AMERICAN forestry association
AFA's Distinguished service award for 1967, Mrs Lyndon B. Johnson. il Am For 73:76 N '67
AFA's 92nd annual meeting; report from Las Vegas. il Am For 73:16-17+ D '67
John Aston Warder, first president. L. S. V. Banks. il Am For 73:10-13+ N '67
Prime-time Smokey program: Ballad of Smokey the bear. Am For 73:4 Ja '67
Redwoods and the American forestry association: Redwood National Park. J. B. Craig. Am For 73:8-9 Ap '67
Sounding board; Operation Golden Eagle award given to AFA. il Am For 73:40 Ap '67
This I believe. W. E. Towell. Am For 73:11 F '67
Where AFA's records will be kept; Sterling memorial library, Yale. il Am For 73:3 Ja '67

AMERICAN foundation for management research, Incorporated
Mapping management to the 21st century. il Bsns W p 112-14 S 2 '67

AMERICAN foundation of religion and psychiatry
Where religion and psychiatry join hands. C. W. Hall. Read Digest 90:122-6 Mr '67

AMERICAN Friends service committee
On both sides of the lines; celebrating 50th anniversary. Christian Cent 84:524 Ap 26 '67
Operation friendship; Chicago's Preadolescent enrichment program. S. Olds. il Parents Mag 42:56-7+ Ap '67
Vietnam's war-ravaged children; refugee center at Quang Ngai. C. Brossard. il Look 31:22-5 Ap 18 '67

AMERICAN furniture. See Furniture, American
AMERICAN geographical society
Geographical dinner. New Yorker 43:37-8 D 16 '67
AMERICAN glass. See Glassware
AMERICAN heart association
Scientists hear of new hopes to cut heart toll. il Bsns W p88-90 O 28 '67
AMERICAN horse shows association
High times at the National; Madison Square garden. A. Higgins. Sports Illus 27:66 N 20 '67
AMERICAN house decoration. See House decoration, American
AMERICAN humor. See Humor, American
AMERICAN imperialism. See Imperialism
AMERICAN Indian fund
See also
Association on American Indian affairs, incorporated
AMERICAN institute for foreign study
Chaperoning for credit. E. Kolowrat. il Sr Schol 90:sup8 Mr 3 '67
AMERICAN institute of aeronautics and astronautics
Aerospace convention in Boston. R. N. Watts, jr. Sky & Tel 33:96-7 F '67
AIAA meeting hears call for steps to regulate submersibles. R. W. Niblock. Aero Tech 21:50 N 6 '67
New emphasis directed toward propulsion and aerodynamics. W. S. Beller. il Tech W 20:35-6 Ja 30 '67
AMERICAN institute of architects
A.I.A. honors twenty buildings in national awards program. il Arch Rec 141:50-1+ Je '67
A.I.A. revises basic contract documents. Arch Rec 141:81-2 Ja '67
A.I.A.-Sunset Western home awards. il Sunset 139:74-89 O '67
Architects analyze new means of influence; annual convention. il Arch Rec 141:35-6+ Je '67
For once I'll give in and indulge in criticism; proposed new headquarters building. E. Goble. il Arch Rec 142:9 Ag '67
AMERICAN institute of certified public accountants
Changing the rules. il Fortune 75:227-8 Ap '67
AMERICAN institute of graphic arts
Covers 1966 at AIGA show. il Pub W 191:74-6+ Ap 3 '67
AMERICAN institute of graphic arts children's book show. See Book exhibits
AMERICAN institute of physics
New committee on physics and society. Sch & Soc 95:377-8 O 28 '67
That noise you hear may be pollution; scientists fighting noise pollution. il Bsns W p40-1 Ap 22 '67
AMERICAN institute of planners
Environment for man, ed. by W. R. Ewald, jr. Review
Sat R 50:23-4 Jl 29 '67. J. H. Plumb
Future: still cloudy; Washington conference on the next fifty years. Sci N 92:368-9 O 14 '67
AMERICAN intellectuals. See Intellectuals
AMERICAN international pictures (firm)
Z as in zzzz, or zowie. il Time 89:61 My 5 '67
AMERICAN Italian anti-defamation league
Italians, American style. M. Puzo. il N Y Times Mag p7+ Ag 6 '67; Discussion. p 12+ Ag 20; 12 Ag 27; 62+ S 10 '67
AMERICAN-Japanese exchanges. See Educational exchanges
AMERICAN Jews in Israel. See Americans in Israel
AMERICAN legion
Parting of the ways. J. O'Gara. Commonweal 85:618 Mr 3 '67
To teach the unknowing; address, August 31, 1967. W. E. Galbraith. Vital Speeches 34:11-13 O 15 '67
AMERICAN liberalism. See Liberalism
AMERICAN library association
ALA awards (cont) il Wilson Lib Bul 42:25+ S '67
ALA committee appointments. R. H. McDonough. ALA Bul 61:909 S '67
ALA goals for action, 1967; with statement by N. Cousins. ALA Bul 61:951-4 S '67

AMERICAN library association—*Continued*
ALA organization and information 1967-68.
  ALA Bul 61:1123-6+ N '67
Awards, citations, and scholarships. il Library J 92:2729-30 Ag '67
Bugles at credibility gap. K. Nyren. Library J 92:1555 Ap 15 '67
Cooperation betweeen ALA and state library associations; address, September 1966. R. Warncke. ALA Bul 61:191-6 F '67
Libraries unlimited; address, July 1, 1967. F. E. Mohrhardt. bibliog ALA Bul 61:811-19 Jl '67
News from the divisions. See issues of ALA bulletin
1967 ALA awards winners. il ALA Bul 61:872-6 Jl '67
1967: ALA election of officers. il Library J 92:2728 Ag '67
1967: ALA officers and awards; youth divisions. il Library J 92:3118 S 15 '67
1966 in review. Pub W 191:55 Ja 30 '67
Nominations requested for 1968 ALA awards. Library J 92:3588-90, 3799-800 O 15 '67; Same. Wilson Lib Bul 42:263+ N '67

Meetings

How ALA selects a conference site. C. J. Hoy. ALA Bul 61:423-5 Ap '67

Meetings, 1967

ALA: bright future. L. E. Hunt. Sr Schol 91:sup 10 S 21 '67
ALA conference: feast or famine? K. Molz. Wilson Lib Bul 42:80-3+ S '67
ALA conference roundup (title varies) Library J 92:1568, 1790, 1884, 2108 Ap 15-Je 1 '67
ALA conference studies library manpower crisis. il Pub W 192:28-9 Ag 14 '67
ALA meets in San Francisco. Wilson Lib Bul 41:1044-5 Je '67
ALA midwinter report. E. Moon; S. Havens. il Library J 92:731-42 F 15 '67
ALA midwinter report. K. Molz. Wilson Lib Bul 41:608-12 F '67
ALA youth divisions plan convention programs. Library J 92:1284 Mr 15 '67
[Continuing education for librarians; symposium] bibliog ALA Bul 61:259-81+ Mr '67
Council in quandary. E. Moon; K. Nyren. il Library J 92:2689, 2720-3 Ag '67
Division in depth; RTSD. K. Nyren. il Library J 92:2724-7 Ag '67
Exhibitors oppose plan for ALA midwinter exhibits. Library J 92:722 F 15 '67
Lips will move again; pre-conference on Intellectual freedom and the teenager. E. Moon. Library J 92:1980 My 15 '67
Manpower is major issue at ALA annual conference. Pub W 191:60-1 Je 19 '67
Manpower: the big show. S. Havens. il Library J 92:2713-19 Ag '67
Midwinter highlights. Library J 92:833-6 F 15 '67
Midwinter in New Orleans: highlights of the midwinter meeting. il ALA Bul 61:289-319 Mr '67
Myths and realities. E. Moon. Library J 92:2319 Je 15 '67
Phronemophobic ALA; fear of thinking. J. Shera. Wilson Lib Bul 42:85+ S '67
San Francisco beat; ALA report on the youth divisions: AASL, CSD, YASD. il Library J 92:3114-18 S 15 '67
San Francisco conference: council, preconferences, program meetings, divisions, committees, roundtables. ALA Bul 61:820-33+ Jl '67; Correction 61:1008 O '67
San Francisco conference program plans. ALA Bul 61:321-4 Mr '67
San Francisco '67. S. Havens. il Library J 92:2707-12 Ag '67; Reply. P. Hiatt. 92:3349 O 1 '67
Tentative program of the 86th annual ALA conference. ALA Bul 61:469+ My '67
Youth programs set for ALA conference. Library J 92:1692 Ap 15 '67

Meetings, 1968

ALA midwinter meeting 1968: tentative program. ALA Bul 61:1340-1 D '67
1968 ALA midwinter meeting Bal Harbour, Miami Beach, Florida, January 8-13. il ALA Bul 61:982-4 S '67

Meetings, 1973

You're going on a spree in 1973: council decision to hold conference in Las Vegas, Nev; ALA midwinter report. J. Shera. Wilson Lib Bul 41:723+ Mr '67; Reply. H. G. Morehouse. 41:887 My '67

Adult services division

Books for adults beginning to read. Wilson Lib Bul 41:83-7 S '66; Correction. 41:671 Mr '67
Notable books of 1966. Pub W 191:49 Mr 6 '67; Same. ALA Bul 61:329-31 Mr '67; NEA J 56:48+ Ap '67; Wilson Lib Bul 41:763-4 Ap '67; Library J 92:1102 Mr 15 '67; Discussion. 92:1099, 1775 Mr 15, My 1 '67

Children services division

Notable children's books of 1966. il ALA Bul 61:415-18 Ap '67; Same. Library J 92:1685-6+ Ap 15 '67
San Francisco beat; ALA report. Library J 92:3116 S 15 '67
World of storytelling. D. Anderson. ALA Bul 61:828-9 Jl '67

Commission on a national plan for library education

Report for the Commission on a national plan for library education. ALA Bul 61:419-22 Ap '67

Committee on copyright issues

Copyright grab bag, II: a new kind of lend-lease. C. F. Gosnell. bibliog ALA Bul 61:707-12 Je '67
Senate copyright hearings under way. G. Krettek and E. D. Cooke. Wilson Lib Bul 41:981-2+ My '67
Workable copyright bill expected by ALA. Library J 92:1783 My 1 '67

Constitution and bylaws committee

Constitution and bylaws committee report. ALA Bul 61:561 My '67

Council

ALA council action. ALA Bul 61:150-1 F '67
Council in quandary; ALA conference. E. Moon; K. Nyren. il Library J 92:2689, 2720-3 Ag '67
Location of ALA headquarters; with case for, and two cases against moving to Washington. ALA Bul 61:929-41 S '67
Open letter to the ALA council. L. M. Morsch. ALA Bul 61:1276 D '67
San Francisco conferences. ALA Bul 61:820-4
Tale of two cities: ALA midwinter report. E. Moon. il Library J 92:731-7 F 15 '67 Jl '67
You're going on a spree in 1973: decision to hold conference in Las Vegas, Nev; ALA midwinter report. J. Shera. Wilson Lib Bul 41:723+ Mr '67; Reply. H. G. Morehouse. 41:887 My '67

Finance

ALA endowment funds. ALA Bul 61:1338-9 D '67
ALA headquarters classification and pay plan. ALA Bul 61:1328-30 D '67
Treasurer's report (cont) ALA Bul 61:1331-7 D '67

Headquarters

ALA headquarters classification and pay plan. ALA Bul 61:1328-30 D '67
ALA headquarters move faces membership vote. Library J 92:2696+ Ag '67
ALA mail vote materials distributed to members. Library J 92:3355 O 1 '67
Breakdown of membership vote on location of ALA headquarters. il Library J 92:1298-9 D '67
Location of ALA headquarters; with case for, and two cases against moving to Washington. ALA Bul 61:929-41 S '67
Midstream or Midwest? E. Moon. Library J 92:2859+ S 1 '67
San Francisco conference; council vote to move ALA headquarters from Chicago to Washington, D.C. ALA Bul 61:820-2 Jl '67

Information and automation division

Information science and automation: the newest division. S. R. Salmon. ALA Bul 61:637-42 Je '67

Intellectual freedom committee

ALA freedom committee awaits NCTE conference. Library J 92:723 F 15 '67
Library bill of rights: reasons for revision; with present text, proposed text. E. J. Gaines. Library J 92:984-5 Mr 1 '67; Same. ALA Bul 61:409-11 Ap '67; Reply. Z. Horn. Library J 92:1875-6 My 15 '67

International relations office

ALA-IRO charts program for foreign activities. Library J 92:3580 O 15 '67

AMERICAN library association—*Continued*

Library technology program

LTP's annual report lists 1968 projects. Pub W 193:47 Ja 8 '68
Library technology program announces 1968 plans. Library J 92:4094 N 15 '67

Membership

ALA membership statistics. il ALA Bul 61: 426+ Ap '67
Focus on ALA-PLA membership. A. B. Martin. il ALA Bul 61:1095-101 O '67
Playgirl of the western world. J. Shera. Wilson Lib Bul 42:529+ Ja '68

Program evaluation and budget committee

Hand out to the has beens. P. S. Dunkin. Library J 92:4481 D 15 '67

Public library association

Focus on ALA-PLA membership. A. B. Martin. il ALA Bul 61:1095-101 O '67
Public library standards; ALA meeting, letter to the editor. P. Hiatt. Library J 92:3349 O 1 '67

Resources and technical services division

Division in depth: RTSD; ALA conference. K. Nyren. il Library J 92:2724-7 Ag '67
RTSD issues call for new ideas. Library J 93:143 Ja 15 '68

Young adult services division

Best books for young adults. NEA J 56:66-7 Mr '67; Same. Pub W 191:50 Mr 6 '67; Library J 92:1282+ Mr 15 '67; Wilson Lib Bul 41:769 Ap '67
San Francisco beat; ALA report. Library J 92:3116-17 S 15 '67

AMERICAN literature

New lit; giving fictitious names to people who may be recognizable. G. Ace. Sat R 50:5 Mr 18 '67
Pop goes America; absurdity in literature. P. Michelson. New Repub 157:23-6+ S 9 '67
Re-appraisals. by M. Green. Review
    Reporter 36:55-6 F 9 '67. M. Bradbury
World elsewhere, by R. Poirier. Review
    Commentary 44:110-12+ O '67. W. Berthoff
    See also
American fiction
American poetry
Authors, American
Negro literature

Appreciation and interpretation

World elsewhere, by R. Poirier. Review
    Nation 205:58-9 Jl 17 '67. A. Trachtenberg

History

American 1890s, by L. Ziff. Review
    Reporter 36:51-2 F 23 '67. R. Sklar
Chicago renaissance, by D. Kramer. Review
    Nation 204:184-6 F 6 '67. D. Levin
Think back on us, by M. Cowley. Review
    New Repub 156:24-6 Mr 11 '67. R. M. Adams
    Sat R 50:31-2 Mr 11 '67. G. Hicks

Translations into Russian

Little girl migrates; V. Nabokov's Lolita. C. Brown. New Repub 158:19-20 Ja 20 '68

California

Penmen of the golden West. J. K. Hutchens; K. Rexroth. il Sat R 50:34-6+ S 23 '67

Southern states

John Peale Bishop & the other thirties. L. A. Fiedler. Commentary 43:74+ Ap '67
With the bark on, comp. by J. Q. Anderson. Review
    Sat R 50:54 Je 10 '67. P. Flowers

AMERICAN management association

Manager training facility relies on library; Donald W. Mitchell memorial library, Hamilton, N.Y. Library J 92:3580+ O 15 '67
Role of business in society's perfectibility; excerpt from address. N. W. Chamberlain. Mo Labor R 90:41-3 Ap '67

AMERICAN medical association

AMA: some doctors are in revolt, but revolution is not in sight. E. Langer. Science 157: 285-8 Jl 21 '67; Discussion. 157:1261-3 S 15 '67
Doctors report: what's new in medicine; annual convention. U S News 63:12 Jl 3 '67

Easing abortion rules; AMA policy changed. Newsweek 70:51 Jl 3 '67
Food for thought and vice versa; nutrition lecture series. J. L. Breeling. il Todays Health 45:14-15 S '67
Helping trim drug bills. F. J. L. Blasingame. Todays Health 45:88 My '67
Medical education and the AMA. M. O. Rouse. Todays Health 45:88 O '67
Physicians gather in Atlantic City. F. Marley. Sci N 91:579 Je 17 '67
Progress report; new president-elect. il Time 89:44 Je 30 '67

Institute for biomedical research

AMA research institute: trouble on the road to Utopia. P. M. Boffey. il Science 158: 1653-8 D 29 '67

AMERICAN merchant marine. See Merchant marine—United States
AMERICAN military assistance. See Military assistance, American
AMERICAN minorities. See Minorities
AMERICAN motorcycle association

Please don't die now, baby. K. Chapin. il Sports Illus 27:30-1 O 16 '67

AMERICAN motors corporation

AMC puts money men at wheel. Bsns W p40 Ja 14 '67
Auto firm's call for help from union. U S News 63:85 Ag 21 '67
Can Roy Chapin salvage AMC? il Bsns W p 144-6+ Ap 8 '67
Changing the tag; new Ramblers. il Time 89: 88 Mr 3 '67
Detroit's no. 4 holds on. il Bsns W p42-3 N 18 '67
Drastic measures; proposed sale of Kelvinator and Redisco. Newsweek 69:80 Ap 17 '67
Hope at American; Javelin specialty car. il Time 90:67-8 Ag 25 '67
Irreverence at American; Javelin advertising campaign. il Time 90:93-4 S 22 '67
Next: the Voltswagon? AMC's Amitron. il Time 90:69-70 D 22 '67
Rambler gets a push. Bsns W p33 My 6 '67
Rambler takes a gamble; cuts prices by $200. Bsns W p39 F 25 '67
Rambling into the gap. Time 89:87 F 10 '67
Shifting the image. il Newsweek 69:59 Je 26 '67
69-cent special; low priced Rambler. il Newsweek 69:64 Mr 6 '67
Sledge-hammer sell; with report by N. Belliveau. il Life 63:101-2+ O 27 '67
Some strikes should never be called. B. L. Masse. America 117:497 N 4 '67
Uphill & getting steeper; financial crisis. Time 89:90 My 12 '67
What hath Rambler wrought? Javelin and AMX. J. Schmidt. il Motor T 19:30-2 S '67
Will the Javelin pull AM back on the road? il Bsns W p24-5 Ag 26 '67

AMERICAN museum of natural history, New York

George E. Peterson; material for the new Hall of man of Africa. J. L. Stoutenburgh. Hobbies 71:116+ F '67
Mineral show. New Yorker 43:53-4 N 11 '67
What goes on in a large museum. J. L. Stoutenburgh. Hobbies 72:114 Jl '67

AMERICAN music. See Music, American
AMERICAN national opera company

America sings: Sarah Caldwell's National opera; grant awarded by National council on the arts. H. Kupferberg. il Atlan 220: 120-2 S '67
American national opera company. A. Darack. il Hi Fi 17:MA20-1 D '67
And we quote; interview, ed. by P. J. Smith. S. Caldwell. Hi F¦ 17:MA17 O '67
Caldwell look for Lulu, Falstaff. I. Kolodin. Sat R 50:54 O 21 '67
Indianapolis. R. D. Daniels. il Opera N 32:22-3 O 14 '67
Musical events; performances of Verdi's Falstaff, Berg's Lulu and Puccini's Tosca. W. Sargeant. New Yorker 43:154+ O 14 '67
Report: New York: production of Tosca at the Brooklyn academy. S. Jenkins, jr. Opera N 32:24 N 25 '67
What they did to Berg's Lulu. G. Perle. il Sat R 50:45 D 30 '67

AMERICAN navion society. See Aviation clubs
AMERICAN Negro visitors in Africa. See Foreign visitors in Africa
AMERICAN Negroes. See Negroes in the United States
AMERICAN Negroes in Africa. See Americans in Africa
AMERICAN newspaper publishers association

Percy; convention; with statements by C. H. Percy. New Yorker 43:38-40 My 6 '67

AMERICAN newspapers. See Newspapers—
United States
AMERICAN novels. See American fiction
AMERICAN opera. See Opera, American
AMERICAN opera society
Adventure on the high C; E. Suliotis in
Norma. Time 90:65 N 17 '67
Music to my ears:
Performance of Giulio Cesare. I. Kolodin.
Sat R 50:55 Ap 8 '67
Performance of Gluck's Orfeo ed Euridice.
I. Kolodin. Sat R 50:82+ Ap 22 '67
Performance of Maria Stuarda. I.
Kolodin. Sat R 50:35 D 23 '67
Production of Norma. I. Kolodin. Sat R
50:75+ N 25 '67
Musical events; concert performance of Bel-
lini's Norma in Carnegie Hall. W. Sar-
geant. New Yorker 43:221-2 N 18 '67
Musical events; concert performance of
Donizetti's Maria Stuarda. W. Sargeant.
New Yorker 43:152 D 16 '67
Musical events; concert performance of
Handel's Giulio Cesare. W. Sargeant. New
Yorker 43:124 Ap 1 '67
Musical events; performance of Gluck's Orfeo
ed Euridice. W. Sargeant. New Yorker 43:
169 Ap 15 '67
New York; Gluck's Orfeo ed Euridice. F.
Merkling. Opera N 31:28 My 13 '67
New York; Handel's Giulio Cesare, at
Carnegie Hall. R. D. Daniels. Opera N 31:
28 My 13 '67
Report: New York; performance of Maria
Stuarda in Carnegie Hall. R. D. Daniels.
Opera N 32:31 Ja 6 '68
Report: New York; performance of Norma at
Carnegie Hall. R. D. Daniels. Opera N 32:
30 D 16 '67
AMERICAN painting. See Painting, American
AMERICAN philosophy. See Philosophy, Ameri-
can
AMERICAN physical society
Physicists. New Yorker 42:35 F 18 '67
AMERICAN poetry
Completed pattern. M. Benedict. Poetry 109:
262-6 Ja '67
Dead horses and live issues. L. Simpson. Na-
tion 204:520-2 Ap 24 '67
Difficulties of being major; the poetry of
Robert Lowell and James Dickey. P. Davi-
son. il Atlan 220:116-21 O '67
Do you have a poem book. . ? G. Davenport.
Nat R 19:858-9 Ag 8 '67
Five anthologies. R. J. Mills, jr. Poetry 109:
345-50 F '67
New poets, by M. L. Rosenthal. Review
Sat R 50:45 Je 10 '67. R. D. Spector
Varieties of criticism. L. L. Martz. Poetry
110:254-7 Jl '67
See also
Ballads, American

Bibliography
Debuts and encores. C. Philbrick. Sat R 50:
32-4 Je 3 '67
AMERICAN poets. See Poets, American
AMERICAN political science association
Political science: CIA, ethics stir otherwise
placid convention. R. J. Samuelson. Science
157:1414-17 S 22 '67
AMERICAN portraits. See Portraits, American
AMERICAN power boat association
APBA action report. J. D. Paris. See issues
of Motor boating
More power to you. M. Crook. See issues of
Yachting
AMERICAN property in Mexico
Mexican border towns lure gringo industry.
il Bsns W p 120-2 D 2 '67
AMERICAN public opinion. See Public opinion
—United States
AMERICAN public works association
Which trees and what street surfacing;
regional APWA meeting E. F. Spitzer. il
Am City 82:97+ Jl '67
AMERICAN reporters. See Reporters and
reporting
AMERICAN research and development cor-
poration
General Doriot's dream factory. G. Bylinsky.
il Fortune 76:103-7+ Ag '67
AMERICAN revolution. See United States—His-
tory—Revolution
AMERICAN Royal (horse show) See Horse
shows
AMERICAN SAMOA
Samoa. C. Stinnett. il Holiday 42:54-5+ Jl
'67
See also
Education—American Samoa

AMERICAN school in Japan
Library of the American school in Japan.
L. D. Downs. Horn Bk 43:576-9 O '67
AMERICAN schools abroad
American schools abroad. P. Deutschman. il
Holiday 42:105-10 O '67
Road to Taipei; University-to-school project.
R. Forbes and H. R. Wire. il Am Ed 3:5-7
N '67
AMERICAN scientists. See Scientists, American
AMERICAN sculpture. See Sculpture, American
AMERICAN shipbuilding company
Takeover on the lakes; G. Steinbrenner, chief
executive officer. il Bsns W p29-30 Ag 26
'67
AMERICAN silverware. See Silverware
AMERICAN slang. See Slang
AMERICAN society for the prevention of cruel-
ty to animals
Great meddler; founder of the ASPCA. G.
Carson. il Am Heritage 19:28-33+ D '67
AMERICAN society of magazine photographers
Photographer pleads his case; new rates. C.
E. Rotkin. il Pub W 191:90-1+ F 6 '67
AMERICAN society of newspaper editors
Bargain basement? annual convention. News-
week 69:64 Mv 1 '67
AMERICAN stock exchange
Big casino. il Time 90:94 N 17 '67
Dead men tell no tales; investigating the
price rigging of eight stocks. il News-
week 69:83 My 8 '67
Speculative spree alarms Amex. il Bsns W
p36-7 Jl 15 '67
Stock scandal, '67 style; charges of rigging
price of Pentron electronics corp. stock.
Newsweek 69:71 Je 12 '67
Why big board hopes to tame a paper tiger;
using extra time to catch up with back
office work. il Bsns W p96 Ag 12 '67
AMERICAN students. See College students
AMERICAN students in foreign countries
See also
Foreign study
AMERICAN students in Great Britain; Amer-
ican students in Russia; etc. See Foreign
students in Great Britain; Foreign students
in Russia; etc.
AMERICAN symphony orchestra
Musical events (cont) W. Sargeant. New
Yorker 43:232 N 11 '67
Musical events; concert in Carnegie Hall,
conducted by J. Eger. W. Sargeant. New
Yorker 43:219 N 25 '67
AMERICAN tape duplicating company
Million dollar copycats. il Ebony 23:74-6+
Ja '68
AMERICAN teachers in foreign countries
See also
National education association—Teach corps
AMERICAN technical assistance. See Tech-
nical assistance, American
AMERICAN telephone and telegraph company
Ceiling on earnings for AT&T: the effects. il
U S News 63:42 Jl 17 '67
David and Goliath; FCC orders cuts in
profits on Bell telephone system and
charges for long-distance and overseas
calls. Newsweek 70:73 Jl 17 '67
Decoding FCC's signal; commission's decision
on AT&T's rate structure. il Bsns W p 120+
Jl 15 '67
Lessons of history; public relations depart-
ment. L. L. L. Golden. Sat R 50:62 Jl 8
'67
Mother Bell gets a message; FCC orders
reduction of charges. Time 90:79-80 Jl 14
'67
Plot to bury the Bell system. il Parks & Rec
2:17-18 D '67
Sovereign state of Bell. N. L. Parks. Nation
205:430-5 O 30 '67
Wall Street: the FCC drops a shoe; rules
that AT&T's rates should be lowered.
C. Morgello. il Newsweek 70:74 Jl 17 '67
Who will Bell the colossus? N. L. Parks
Nation 205:391-3 O 23 '67
Why Ma Bell looks good again; AT&T's stock
perking up. il Bsns W p 152+ Mr 11 '67
See also
Bell telephone laboratories
Government investigations—American tele-
phone and telegraph company
AMERICAN textbook publishers institute
ATPI-NACS: problems of order-fulfillment.
Pub W 191:31-2 Mr 13 '67
ATPI: past, present and future at 25th an-
niversary meeting; symposium; with edi-
torial comment. il Pub W 191:26-40, 48 My
29 '67

AMERICAN textbook publishers institute—
Continued
Educational publishers study the role of universities; two day conference. il Pub W 192:21-4 D 25 '67
1966 in review. il Pub W 191:52-3 Ja 30 '67
AMERICAN theatre wing
Tony comes of age. il Time 89:51 Ap 7 '67
AMERICAN tobacco company
Sold, American; merger spree of American tobacco co. Time 89:73 F 3 '67
AMERICAN tourists. See Travelers
AMERICAN university of Beirut
Grinding in English, unwinding in Arabic. G. Buckman. il Mlle 64:148-9+ F '67
AMERICAN university press service, Incorporated
Services and committee work; summary of reports. Pub W 192:25-6 Jl 3 '67
AMERICAN visitors in Canada; American visitors in Finland; etc. See Foreign visitors in Canada; Foreign visitors in Finland; etc.
AMERICAN water works association
AWWA nominates new officers. il Am City 82:162+ Mr '67
AWWA taps Eric Johnson to succeed Ray Faust. il Am City 82:96+ Ag '67
AMERICAN wines. See Wine
AMERICAN women. See Women—United States
AMERICAN writers. See Authors, American
AMERICAN youth hostels. See Youth hostels
AMERICANA (antiques) See Antiques
AMERICANISM
But what of the dream? excerpt from address, October 12 1967. J. W. Gardner. Read Digest 92:37-41 Ja '68
Challenges & opportunities; address, December 1, 1966. C. L. Gould. Vital Speeches 33:217-23 Ja 15 '67
Manhattan serenade; Support our men in Viet Nam parade. il Time 89:31 My 19 '67
Pop goes America. P. Michelson. New Repub 157:25-8 S 2 '67
Reflections on a parade; parade of 70,000 in support of the men in Vietnam. America 116:774-5 My 27 '67
Responsibilities of national greatness; a citizen's obligations and the bepuzzlements of identification. K. Burke. il Nation 205:46-50 Jl 17 '67
To teach the unknowing; address, August 31, 1967. W. E. Galbraith. Vital Speeches 34: 11-13 O 15 '67
What should an American citizen be; address, January 3, 1967. J. E. Davis. Vital Speeches 33:238-40 F 1 '67
See also
Patriotism
AMERICANIZATION
World tries the American way. il U S News 63:32-5 Ag 21 '67
AMERICANS
American rediscovers America. F. C. Painton. il U S News 63:58-62 S 4 '67
Americans not everybody knows: E. Blackwell. N. Stack. il PTA Mag 61:26-7 F '67
Americans, why aren't you liked? Y. Chabas. Christian Cent 84:1127-8 S 6 '67
Far-off places are calling again. il Bsns W p 176+ My 20 '67
Good times, but people are unhappy; findings of nationwide survey. il U S News 62:50-5 My 22 '67
How America lives. G. Cameron. See Issues of Ladies' home journal
Mood of the country as poll takers find it; findings of Gallup polls. il U S News 63:91-2 D 11 '67
Pop goes America. P. Michelson. New Repub 157:25-8 S 2 '67
Sin-drome: America, nation of the sin bores. R. Baker. McCalls 95:5 Ja '68
Some questions about the study of American character in the twentieth century. D. Riesman. bibliog f Ann Am Acad 370:36-47 Mr '67
Speaking out; we've lost the art of friendship. H. Calisher. il Sat Eve Post 240:10+ Ag 26 '67
Uneasy America; why? what a nationwide survey shows. il U S News 63:42-6+ S 18 '67
What the people want. D. Lawrence. U S News 63:100 Ag 21 '67
See also
Californians
Northerners
United States
Women—United States
AMERICANS for democratic action
ADA defers; question of L. B. Johnson's renomination. New Repub 157:5-6 O 7 '67; Discussion. 157:11-12 O 14; 34-6 O 28 '67

ADA's agony. Nat R 19:726 Jl 11 '67
ADA's options. New Repub 157:6-7 D 23 '67
Non-debate; annual convention. K. Crawford. Newsweek 69:46 Ap 17 '67
AMERICANS in Africa
When an American Negro returns to Africa. E. Dunbar. il Look 31:55-8+ Ap 4 '67
AMERICANS in Australia
What to expect if you emigrate to Australia. il U S News 63:76-7 Jl 17 '67
AMERICANS in Austria
Romance: off-key; memories of being in Vienna when in the twenties. L. Rosten. Look 31:12 My 30 '67
AMERICANS in Cairo. See Americans in Egypt
AMERICANS in Egypt
Cairo diary of U.S. humiliation. T. Thompson. il Life 62:70+ Je 23 '67
War that never was; American press corps in Cairo during Israeli-Arab war. G. Montgomery. Sat R 50:54-6 Ag 12 '67
We will kill you Americans, too! Americans in Cairo. J. Law il U S News 62:30-1 Je 26 '67
AMERICANS in England
Dig we must! teen-ager's summer job at archeological excavations. J. Shumsky. il Seventeen 26:146-7+ S '67
I-A in London. H. Greer. Nation 205:487-8 N 13 '67
See also
United States—Armed forces—Forces in Great Britain
AMERICANS in Ethiopia
See also
United States—Armed forces—Forces in Ethiopia
AMERICANS in Europe
Going to Europe, the hard way; summer job. D. Klein. il Seventeen 26:152-3 D '67
Anecdotes, facetiae, satire, etc.
American in Paris, and elsewhere; the composer abroad. G. Kubik. il Opera N 32:8-13 N 4 '67
AMERICANS in foreign countries
How to transplant your home; moving abroad. M. M Hemingway. il House & Gard 131: 148-9+ Ap '67
Return of the native; American girls who have grown up abroad. J. Steinberg. il Mlle 64:216-17+ Ap '67
See also
United States—Armed forces—Forces in foreign countries

Anecdotes, facetiae, satire, etc.
East of New York, south of Madrid, down to Kenya. F. R. Buckley. Vogue 149:82-5 Ap 1 '67
AMERICANS in France
American in Paris; B. Washburne, ambassador during Franco-Prussian war. S. Hess. il Am Heritage 18:18-27+ F '67
Conscientious AWOLs. T. Land. Nation 205: 488-91 N 13 '67
Twenties in Montparnasse; lives of young American writers. M. Cowley. il Sat R 50: 51+ Mr 11 '67
See also
United States—Air force—Forces in France
United States—Army—Forces in Europe
AMERICANS in Germany
See also
United States—Armed forces—Forces in Europe
AMERICANS in India
Report: India's holy men; American tyagis. F. Levine. Atlan 220:23-4+ O '67
AMERICANS in Israel
American Jews in Israel, by H. R. Isaacs. Review
New Repub 157:30-2 N 18 '67. E. Grossman
I fell in love with kibbutzniks; Ramat ha Shofet. S. Lo Bello. il Seventeen 26:136-7+ Mr '67
Israeli notebook. H. Brandon. Sat R 50:20 S 30 '67
AMERICANS in Japan
Gone native. il Newsweek 70:37 O 30 '67
AMERICANS in Latin America
Legacy of Che Guevara; civil and military presence. N. Gall. bibliog f Commentary 44:39-44 D '67
AMERICANS in Nepal
Tibetan tea. J. Hoffman. il Sr Schol 90:sup 17 My 5 '67
AMERICANS in Paris. See Americans in France

AMERICANS in Polynesia
Reformed publisher; interview. E. H. Dodd, jr. New Yorker 43:47-8 O 28 '67
AMERICANS in Saigon. See Americans in Vietnam
AMERICANS in Spain
Incident at Villaviciosa. R. Lynes. Harper 235:26+ O '67
AMERICANS in Thailand
Air of intrigue; increasing suspicion about disappearance of J. Thompson. Time 89:32+ My 5 '67
American abroad; J. H. W. Thompson. il Newsweek 69:54 Ap 10 '67
Another Vietnam. W. Pfaff. Commonweal 85: 550-1 F 17 '67
Walk in the jungle; J. Thompson missing in the Cameron Highlands of Malaysia. il Time 89:27 Ap 7 '67
See also
United States—Armed forces—Forces in Thailand
AMERICANS in the Congo
Christmas with the Walkers; traveling in Belgian Congo in early nineteen-thirties. E. Hahn. New Yorker 43:152+ My 20 '67
Pawpaw pie; traveling in Belgian Congo in early nineteen-thirties. E. Hahn. New Yorker 43:47-54 Ap 15 '67
AMERICANS in the Korean war. See Korean war. 1950-1953—American participation
AMERICANS in the Middle East
As Americans fled the Mideast turmoil. il U S News 62:8 Je 19 '67
Exodus, economy-class; anti-American outbursts cause evacuations. il Time 89:18-19 Je 16 '67
Notice to U.S. travelers to the Middle East. Dept State Bul 56:952-3 Je 26 '67
AMERICANS in Turkey
In Turkey, everything comes up roses; experiences in small Turkish seacoast village. A. Friendly. il Harper 234:85-9 F '67
AMERICANS in Vienna. See Americans in Austria
AMERICANS in Vietnam
Bell of decision rings out in Vietnam. T. H. White. il Life 63:54-6+ S 1 '67
Checkmate in Vietnam. W. Pfaff. Commonweal 85:585-6 F 24 '67
Do-gooders with a difference. il Time 89: 18-19 Ap 7 '67
Mark of Zorthian; with report by M. Parker. il Life 62:51-2+ My 12 '67
Mildred Harrison's Viet Nam ordeal. P. Avery. il Ebony 22:88-90+ My '67
U.S. support of pacification effort in Viet-Nam reorganized; statement, May 11, 1967. E. Bunker. Dept State Bul 56:844-5 Je 5 '67
Viet-Nam civilian service awards presented by President Johnson; remarks, August 16, 1967. L. B. Johnson. Dept State Bul 57:288-90 S 4 '67
See also
United States—Armed forces—Forces in Vietnam
United States—Army—Forces in Vietnam
AMERICA'S cup race. See Yacht racing
AMERICUS, pseud.
President dumping. New Repub 157:11-13 O 28 '67
AMERSON, Lucius
Kind of black power in Macon County, Ala. G. Roberts. il pors N Y Times Mag p32-3+ F 26 '67
New look in southern sheriffs. il pors Ebony 22:120-2+ My '67
AMERY, Carl, pseud. See Mayer, C.
AMES, Ed
Him Mingo. il por Time 90:80+ S 29 '67
AMES, Ezra
Group portraits; Ames and Hogarth. I. F. Cortelyou. il Antiques 92:632+ N '67
AMES, Louise Bates
Is your child in the wrong grade? excerpts. Ladies Home J 84:119-20+ Je '67
AMES, Morgan
Simon & Garfunkel in action. Hi Fi 17:62-6 N '67
AMES research center. See United States—National aeronautics and space administration—Ames research center
AMEX. See American stock exchange
AMFT, M. J.
Calm makes the world go round; story. Seventeen 26:126-7 O '67
Forget it ever happened; story. Seventeen 26: 116-17 Je '67
Injured party; story. Seventeen 26:146-7 N '67
Little learning; story. Seventeen 26:306-7 Ag '67

Something else; story. Seventeen 26:154-5 S '67
To keep your cool; story. Seventeen 26:152-3 F '67
AMHERST, Mass.
Housing
Planned unit development means better communities. M. C. Huntoon, jr. il Am Home 70:124+ Mr '67
AMHERST college, Amherst, Mass.
Two decades of Amherst admissions. Sch & Soc 95:344-5 O 14 '67
AMICHAI, Yehuda
Nina of Ashkelon; story. Commentary 44:40-7 Jl '67
AMINES
Biogenic amines and emotion. J. J. Schildkraut and S. S. Kety. bibliog il Science 156:21-30 Ap 7 '67
Clathrate hydrates of some amines. G. A. Jeffrey and others. bibliog il Science 155: 689-91 F 10 '67
Imine-bonding in membrane transport of monosaccharides; invalidity of kinetic evidence. P. G. LeFevre. bibliog il Science 158:274-5 O 13 '67
AMINO acids
Actinomycin D effect on amino acid absorption from rat jejunal loops. C. Yamada and others. bibliog il Science 158:129-30 O 6 '67
Amino acid coding in sarcina lutea and saccharomyces cerevisiae. W. E. Groves and E. S. Kempner. bibliog il Science 156:387-90 Ap 21 '67
Amino acid transport: evidence for genetic control of two types in human kidney. C. R. Scriver and O. H. Wilson. bibliog il Science 155:1428-30 Mr 17 '67
Amino acids and the spikes from the retinal ganglion cells. K. Kishida and K. I. Naka. bibliog il Science 156:648-50 My 5 '67
Aminoaciduria resulting from cycloleucine administration in man. R. R. Brown. bibliog il Science 157:432-4 Jl 28 '67
Carboxy-terminal amino acids of γA and γM heavy chains. C. A. Abel and H. M. Grey. bibliog il Science 156:1609-10 Je 23 '67
Chemical modification of yeast alanine-tRNA with a radioactive carbodiimide. S. W. Brostoff and J. M. Ingram. bibliog il Science 158:666-9 N 3 '67
Evolution of structure and function of proteases. H. Neurath and others. bibliog il Science 158:1638-44 D 29 '67
Hemoglobin gun hill: deletion of five amino acid residues and impaired heme-globin binding. T. B. Bradley, jr. and others. bibliog il Science 157:1581-3 S 29 '67
Immunoglobulin structure: variation in amino acid sequence and length of human lambda light chains. F. W. Putnam and others. bibliog il Science 157:1050-3 S 1 '67
Suppressor selection for amino acid replacements expected on the basis of the genetic code. H. Berger and C. Yanofsky. bibliog il Science 156:394-7 Ap 21 '67
See also
Cystine
Tryptophan
Tyrosine
AMINOFF, Cary A.
Restraint in resuming US aid to Indonesia. New Repub 156:13-14 F 11 '67
AMINOGLYCOSIDIC antibiotics. See Antibiotics
AMINOMETHANE. See Methylamines
AMINOPEPTIDASES. See Peptidases
AMIS, Kingsley
Why Lucky Jim turned right. Nat R 19:1121-2+ O 17 '67
about
Lucky Jim Bond. il por Newsweek 69:61 My 8 '67
AMISH Mennonites. See Mennonites
AMMER, Dean S.
Entering the new economy. Harvard Bsns R 45:2-4+ S '67
AMMETERS
Electronic kinks. R. O. Pedersen. il Pop Mech 129:144 Ja '68
Throw together a Quintupler; placing a shunt across the milliammeter. F. H. Tooker. il Pop Electr 28:64 Ja '68
AMMONIA as fuel. See Fuel
AMMONIUM persulfate
Artifact produced in disc electrophoresis by ammonium persulfate. J. M. Brewer. bibliog il Science 156:256 Ap 14 '67
AMMONS, A. R.
Love song; Love song (2); Mission; poems. Poetry 110:153-4 Je '67

AMMONS, A. R.—*Continued*

about

Four poets. H. Carruth. Poetry 111:43-5 O '67

Interior and exterior worlds. J. Logan. Nation 204:541-2 Ap 24 '67

AMMUNITION
See also
Bullets
Projectiles

AMNESIA
Amnesic effects of small bilateral brain puncture in the mouse. M. Bohdanecka and others. bibliog il Science 157:334-6 Jl 21 '67

Permanence of retrograde amnesia produced by electroconvulsive shock. M. W. Luttges and J. L. McGaugh. bibliog il Science 156: 408-10 Ap 21 '67

Recovery of memory after amnesia induced by electroconvulsive shock. S. Zinkin and A. J. Miller; reply with rejoinder. M. J. Herz and H. V. S. Peeke. Science 156:1396-7 Je 9 '67

Retrograde amnesia produced by intraperitoneal injection of physostigmine. M. D. Hamburg. bibliog il Science 156:973-4 My 19 '67

Strange struggle of Sy Patt. B. Remsberg and C. Remsberg. il Good H 166:88-9+ Ja '68

AMNUAI, Paul Sithi-. See Sithi-Amnuai, P.

AMOEBA. See Ameba

AMOEBIASIS. See Amebiasis

AMON, James H.
Small mammal exhibits feature moats and grottoes. Parks & Rec 2:45 O '67

AMORPHOUS materials. See Materials

AMORPHOUS solids. See Solids

AMORTIZATION deductions
How to avoid tax traps. Farm J 91:56A Ja '67

Now: first aid for business; request to reinstate tax credit and fast-depreciation rules. il U S News 62:53 Mr 20 '67

Trade or fix up, here's how to decide. il Suc Farm 65:56-7 Ja '67
See also
Investment tax credit

AMORY, Cleveland
First of the month. See issues of Saturday review

AMOS, D. Bernard. See Bach, F. H. jt. auth.

AMOSOV, Nikolai Mikhailovich
Open heart of Dr Amosoff. L. Gross. il pors Look 31:122-3+ O 3 '67

Soul of a Soviet surgeon. B. R. Boylan. Sat R 50:51 F 25 '67

AMPEX corporation
Ampex makes a play for the home market. il Bsns W p 164-6+ Je 17 '67

Replaying for profit. il Time 89:96 Ap 14 '67

AMPHENOL corporation
Bitten by a bug. Newsweek 70:85-6 N 20 '67

When a suitor knocks; courtship of Amphenol by Solitron. il Bsns W p 121-2 N 11 '67

Written in the stars. il Newsweek 70:85 O 16 '67

AMPHETAMINES
Addicted! addiction to diet pills. Good H 164:12+ My '67

D-men on the road; illegal peddling of amphetamine tablets. Time 89:69 My 5 '67

Dangerous rush. Sci Digest 62:59-60 N '67

2,5-Dimethoxy-4-methyl-amphetamine, STP: a new hallucinogenic drug. S. H. Snyder and others. bibliog il Science 158:669-70 N 3 '67

Drugs that even scare hippies. A. Rosenfeld. Life 63:81-2 O 27 '67

Effects of magnesium pemoline and dextroamphetamine on human learning. J. T. Burns and others. bibliog il Science 155: 849-51 F 17 '67

Pills and Olympians. Sci N 91:353 Ap 15 '67

Putting the brakes on speed; government to restrict the flow of illegal drugs. Bsns W p92+ O 28 '67

Speed kills; Methedrine. il Newsweek 70:87 O 30 '67

Unsafe at any speed; Methedrine. il Time 90:54+ O 27 '67

AMPHIBIA

Orientation

See Orientation

AMPHIBIAN airplanes. See Airplanes, Amphibious

AMPHIBIOUS automobiles. See Automobiles, Amphibious

AMPHIBIOUS motor vehicles. See Motor vehicles, Amphibious

AMPHIBOLES
Amphibole: first occurrence in a meteorite. E. Olsen. bibliog il Science 156:61-2 Ap 7 '67

Fractionation of potassium/rubidium by amphiboles: implications regarding mantle composition. S. R. Hart and L. T. Aldrich. bibliog il Science 155:325-7 Ja 20 '67

AMPLIFIER circuits. See Electronic circuits

AMPLIFIERS
Aah-chooo! not another pepper? outboard BCB preamp peps up auto reception. G. McClellan. il Pop Electr 27:60-1 Jl '67

Acoustech add-a-kit solid-state integrated hi-fi amplifier. il Pop Electr 27:47-8 Jl '67

Audio integrated circuits, what's available? D. E. Lancaster. il Electr World 78:34-6 O '67

Brute-70; solid-state power amplifier for mono or stereo hi-fi. E. G. Louis. il Pop Electr 26:41-6+ F '67

Build CB audio leveler. D. Meyer. il Pop Electr 26:55-8+ F '67

Build the electronic stethoscope; sound amplifier to track down mechanical vibrations. S. Stella. il Pop Electr 26:33-5 My '67

Build the mule box; converter to increase CB talk power. D. Meyer. il Pop Electr 26:45-50+ Mr '67

Build the two-by-two stereo preamplifier. D. Meyer. il Pop Electr 26:69-73+ Mr '67

Characteristics of limiter amplifiers. il Electr World 77:86-7 Mr '67

Common-sense design of transistor amplifiers. D. L. Carlson. il Electr World 77:48-50+ Je '67

Design of an electronic guitar system. J. Arndt. il Electr World 77:26-7+ F '67

Dyna's new solid state amp and pre-amp kits. H. Samuels. il Pop Sci 192:106-7 Ja '68

Electronic guitars and amplifiers. D. Queen. il Electr World 77:38-41 F '67

Hi-fi amplifier terms and definitions. L. Feldman. Electr World 77:27+ Ja '67

Hi-fi product report; Eico model 3070 Cortina amplifier. il Electr World 78:22 D '67

Integrated-circuit i.f. amplifier used in new FM receiver. D. R. Von Recklinghausen. il Electr World 77:34-6+ Ap '67

Knight-kit KG-895 superba amplifier. il Electr World 78:16+ Ag '67

Neutralizing the cascode amplifier. L. R. Bishop. il Electr World 78:66 Jl '67

Operational amplifier: circuits & applications. D. E. Lancaster. il Electr World 78:49-52+ Ag '67

Parametric light amplification. il Electr World 78:88 N '67

Problems of matching speakers to solid-state amplifiers. V. Brociner. il Electr World 77:23-6+ Ja '67

Selecting amplifiers and splitters. il Pop Electr 26:48-9+ Je '67

Solid-state hi-fi amplifier directory. Electr World 77:28-9 Ja '67

Solid-state line-operated audio amplifier. L. E. Greenlee. il Pop Electr 26:40-2 Je '67

Solid-state microphone transformer. J. B. Wood. il Electr World 77:68 Mr '67

You can build a super-simple headphone stereo amplifier. R. M. Benrey. il Pop Sci 190:130-1+ My '67
See also
Lasers

AMPLIFIERS, Fluid. See Fluid amplifiers

AMPLITUDE modulation tester. See Testing instruments

AMPUTEES
One man's impossible triumph; case of F. Ellis. B. Merson. il Good H 165:74-5+ Ag '67

Rehabilitation

See Rehabilitation

AMRAM, David
Music-making swinger; interview, ed. by D. Lurie. pors Life 63:33-4+ Ag 11 '67

AMSBERG, Claus Georg von. See Claus, prince of the Netherlands

AMSTERDAM, Netherlands

Music

Amsterdam; Netherlands opera foundation's Götterdämmerung. J. Mindszenthy. il Opera N 31:30 Mr 4 '67

AMURAO, Corazon
House of death. il por Newsweek 69:43-4 Ap 17 '67

Masakit in Peoria. il por Time 89:36 Ap 14 '67

AMUSEMENT parks
Happy parks. H. Sutton. il Sat R 50:40-2 Je 3; 80-2 Je 10 '67

AMUSEMENT parks—*Continued*
Independence Hall reconstruction sound system; Knott's berry farm, Calif. J. P. Nelson. il Electr World 78:32-3 Jl '67
Tory and old Whig fun; Berry farm and ghost town. R. Kirk. Nat R 19:911 Ag 22 '67
See also
Coney Island
Disneyland park, Anaheim, Calif.

AMUSEMENTS
See also
Childrens amusements
Games
Play
Recreation

AMY Loveman national award
Amy Loveman awards: who says books are dying. J. F. Fixx. Sat R 50:26 Jl 15 '67

ANABAPTISTS
Holy terrors of Munster. E. Stillman. il Horizon 9:90-5 Sum '67

ANABLE, Tony, Jr
America cup report: the pace increases. Motor B 119:126+ My '67
Bahamas 500. Motor B 119:42-3 My '67

ANACONDA copper mining company
River of poison; pollutants released in Clark Fork River by strike at copper mine. il Newsweek 70:70 Ag 28 '67
Toward the future. Time 89:90 Mr 3 '67

ANAEMIA. See Anemia

ANAEROBIC bacteria. See Bacteria, Anaerobic

ANAHEIM, Calif.
We send out bills in envelopes automatically. J. E. Willis. il Am City 82:149+ O '67
See also
Disneyland park

ANALGESICS
Dangers of analgesics. il Time 89:74+ F 24 '67
New painkiller better than morphine? pentazocine. U S News 63:11 Jl 31 '67
Relief without addiction? pentazocine. Time 90:67 Jl 7 '67

ANALYZERS, Engine. See Airplane engines—Testing

ANAPHYLATIC shock. See Anaphylaxis

ANAPHYLATOXIN. See Toxins and antitoxins

ANAPHYLAXIS
How it feels to die; clinical death resulting from penicillin-induced anaphylactic shock. D. Snell. Life 62:38-40+ My 26 '67; Same abr. Read Digest 19:106-10 Ag '67
Release of slow-reacting substance of anaphylaxis in the rat: polymorphonuclear leukocyte. R. P. Orange and others. bibliog il Science 157:318-19 Jl 21 '67

ANAPLASMOSIS
Anaplasmosis vaccine available. Suc Farm 65:63 Je '67

ANARCHISM and anarchists
Is the U.S. drifting toward anarchy? il U S News 63:50-2 D 4 '67
See also
Industrial workers of the world

ANARCHISTS. See Anarchism and anarchists

ANARGYROS, Spero
Sculpture of Spero Anargyros. F. Whitaker. il por Am Artist 31:32-7+ F '67

ANASTASI, Richard William
Well, ma, I'm still here. H. H. Martin. il por Sat Eve Post 240:67a N 18 '67

ANATOMICAL models
Almost man: the doctor trainer. C. Carner. il Todays Health 45:16-18 My '67
Computer-controlled manikin developed by Aerojet, USC. il Tech W 20:20 Ap 3 '67
Computerized dummy. il Sci Digest 61:inside cover Je '67
Deathproof patient for student doctors. il Life 63:87+ D 8 '67
Electronic pigeon's eye developed. Sci N 91:412 Ap 29 '67
Phantom student has photogenic skeleton. il Todays Health 45:8 Mr '67
Robot of life & death: Sim one. il Time 89:41 Mr 31 '67
Versatile computer is a patient; computerized manikin, University of Southern California's school of medicine. il Am Ed 3:18 N '67

ANATOMY
See also
Cadavers
Skeleton
also names of organs and regions of the body, e.g. Heart

Study and teaching
See also
Anatomical models

ANATOMY, Artistic
See also
Human figure in art

ANATONE, Wash.
Small school, big curriculum; use of self-study education kits at Anatone high school. J. Guernsey. il Am Ed 3:11+ O '67

ANCHOR post products, incorporated
On the fence. M. B. Keiser. il Parents Mag 42:26+ F '67

ANCHORAGE, Alaska
Newspapers
Cheechako takes over. il Time 89:43 Je 30 '67

ANCHORING. See Boats—Mooring

ANCHORS
Anchors and anchoring. R. D. Ogg. il Yachting 121:79+ Ja '67
Experiences with sea anchors. P. B. Sheldon. il Yachting 123:92-3+ Ja '68

ANCIENT civilization. See Civilization, Ancient

AND be a good boy; story. See McMorrow, F.

AND their fathers who begat them; story. See Targan, B.

ANDENAES, Tonnes
Norwegian scholarly publishing; summary of address. Pub W 192:29-30 Jl 24 '67

ANDEREGG, Gene
Most in fishing ever; interview. il Field & S 71:42-5+ F '67

ANDERS, Arthur F.
Rehearsal for World war II. D. Perry. il por Am Heritage 18:40-5+ Ap '67

ANDERSEN, Hans Christian
Emperor and the nightingale; dramatization. See Leech, M. T.
Snow queen; dramatization. See Leech, M. T.
Swineherd; dramatization. See Thane, A.

ANDERSEN, Karl
If a body . . . H. Lindsay. Sat R 50:8+ Ap 8 '67

ANDERSEN, Yvonne
Film animation at the Yellow ball workshop. Design 69:7-11 Fall '67

ANDERSON, Albert D. See Davidson, G. T. jt. auth.

ANDERSON, Arthur J. O.
(tr) See Sahagún, B. de. Feather merchants
(tr) See Sahagún, B. de. Goldworkers and lapidaries

ANDERSON, Barry. See Hyman, R. jt. auth.

ANDERSON, C. Arnold
National assessment of educational progress: some technical deficiencies. bibliog f Sch & Soc 95:48-50 Ja 21 '67

ANDERSON, Dee
American souvenir spoons. Hobbies 72:34-5 Je '67

ANDERSON, Don L.
Phase changes in the upper mantle. bibliog Science 157:1165-6+ S 8 '67

ANDERSON, Donald Jack
Cottontails are tough critters. Field & S 72:56-7+ S '67
Great ginseng trade. Field & S 72:52-3+ N '67
Hounds to trail ghosts! Field & S 72:48-9+ O '67
Old fishing hole. Field & S 72:45-7+ Jl '67
Sam the potlicker. Field & S 72:54-5+ Ag '67

ANDERSON, Donald P.
Unit on religion. NEA J 57:35 Ja '68

ANDERSON, Duwayne M. and others
Frost phenomena, on Mars. bibliog Science 155:319-22 Ja 20 '67

ANDERSON, Eugenie (Moore)
Trust Territory of the Pacific Islands; statement, June 8, 1967. Dept State Bul 57:365-6 S 18 '67

ANDERSON, Frank
Life with an encyclopedist; summary of address. Pub W 191:86-7 Je 12 '67

ANDERSON, Glenn B.
How to stop suburban soil erosion. Am City 82:102+ D '67

ANDERSON, Harold C.
Obituary
Liv Wildn por 30:33 Wint '66

ANDERSON, Jervis
Polarities. Commentary 43:100-4 Mr '67
Voices of Newark. Commentary 44:85-90 O '67

ANDERSON, John Firth
Role of the library in the study of social and urban problems. Wilson Lib Bul 41:942-3 My '67

ANDERSON, Jon
...In the time that I lived there so successfully disguised to myself as a child. . ; poem. Horn Bk 43:232 Ap '67
Monument to resignation; Looking for Jonathan; poems. Poetry 110:379-81 S '67

ANDERSON, Joseph B. Jr
Anderson platoon. il pors Ebony 22:69-72+ O '67

ANDERSON, Kenneth A.
How to fish with a sky hook. Pop Mech 128: 90-1 Ag '67

ANDERSON, Kenneth N.
Computers: they supply answers when your doctor needs to know. Pop Mech 127:134-7 Mr '67; Same with title Instant medicine by electronic brain. Sci Digest 61:9-14 Ap '67
Earthquakes made to order. Pop Mech 127: 78-81+ Je '67
How to avoid the twelve most common skiing accidents. Sci Digest 62:7-12 D '67

ANDERSON, Leonard J. and others
Space search. Sch Arts 67:21-4 S '67

ANDERSON, Maxwell
Elizabeth the queen. Criticism
    Nat R 19:99 Ja 24 '67

ANDERSON, Patricia
Role playing in the library. Library J 93:267 Ja 15 '68

ANDERSON, Patrick
Ralph Nader, crusader; or, The rise of a self-appointed lobbyist. N Y Times Mag p25+ O 29 '67

ANDERSON, Quentin
Frost's way: making the most of it. Nation 204:182-4 F 6 '67

ANDERSON, Robert Orville
As oil industry looks away from the uncertain Mideast; interview. U S News 63:54-5 Jl 31 '67

about
American westerns, 1967. il pors Vogue 149: 244-5 My '67
Kingdom for .8 of a calf. il por Time 90:94+ O 20 '67

ANDERSON, Robert T.
Recent trends in ethnology. bibliog f Ann Am Acad 369:141-8 Ja '67

ANDERSON, Robert Woodruff
You know I can't hear you when the water's running. Criticism
    America 116:793 My 27 '67
    Christian Cent 84:1048-9 Ag 16 '67
    Commonweal 86:175-6 Ap 28 '67
    Life 62:23 Ap 28 '67
    Nation 204:444 Ap 3 '67
    New Yorker 43:119 Mr 25 '67
    Newsweek il 69:110 Mr 27 '67
    Reporter 36:43.4 Ap 20 '67
    Sat R 50:42 Ap 1 '67
    Time 89:69 Mr 24 '67

ANDERSON, Sherwood
Small towns as points of departure. G. Hicks. Sat R 50:23-4 D 9 '67

ANDERSON, Sid
Practical skin-diving. Yachting 122:58-9+ N '67

ANDERSON, Stephen S.
Economic reform in Yugoslavia. bibliog f Cur Hist 52:214-19+ Ap '67
Soviet Russia and the two Europes. Cur Hist 53:203-7+ O '67

ANDERSON, Tom
(ed) See Wallace, G. Wallace on Reagan an' NR

ANDERSON, Wayne J.
Teaching styles we parents practice. PTA Mag 61:8-10 bibliog(p34) Mr '67

ANDES MOUNTAINS
See also
Saloya Valley

ANDIRONS
Hearth warming andirons. il House & Gard 132:280-1 N '67

ANDORRA
Day the prince came. il Time 90:30 N 3 '67
Two in one. il Newsweek 70:48 N 6 '67
See also
Fishing—Andorra

ANDRADE, Carlos Drummond de
Hispanic chronicle. W. Barnstone. Poetry 111:46-55 O '67

ANDRÉ, John
Benedict Arnold: how the traitor was unmasked; excerpt from George Washington in the American revolution. J. T. Flexner. il pors Am Heritage 18:8-15 O '67
Your excellencys most obedient...servant. H. H. Peckham. por Wilson Lib Bul 41:586-9 F '67

ANDREA Doria (ship) See Shipwrecks

ANDREAS, Dwayne Orville
Little bank with big connections. il por Bsns W p49-50 F 4 '67

ANDREOTTI, Dante
Our war was with the police department. E. Carruth. il por Fortune 77:195-7 Ja '68

ANDRETTI, Mario
Indy, where the big money is. por Pop Sci 190:70-1 Mr '67
Pontiac Firebird: the GTO gets a little brother. Pop Sci 190:90-3 F '67

about
Andretti: vroom at the top. il por Newsweek 69:64-6+ My 29 '67
Demolition run at Daytona. K. Chapin. Sports Illus 26:20-1 Mr 6 '67
Dueling with slingshots at 180 mph. J. Skow. il pors Sat Eve Post 240:70-5 Je 3 '67
Mario vs. the whooshmobile. B. Ottum. il por Sports Illus 26:30-3 My 22 '67
What is this danger? il Time 89:57 Ap 21 '67
Young man in a hurry. J. McFarland. il pors Hot Rod 20:56-8 Ag '67

ANDREW, Agnellus
Wizard of Hatch End. J. McLaughlin. America 117:140-inside back cover Ag 5 '67

ANDREW and his son; story. See Weesner, T.

ANDREW Low's house. See Savannah, Ga.—Historic houses, etc.

ANDREWS, Dean
Shutting up big-mouth. por Time 90:48+ Ag 25 '67

ANDREWS, Emmett
In the wake of the skipjacks. W. B. Matthews, jr. il Motor B 119:32-3+ Ap '67

ANDREWS, James E.
Blake outer ridge: development by gravity tectonics. bibliog Science 156:642-5 My 5 '67

ANDREWS, Julie
My London; interview, ed. by S. Robinson. McCalls 94:46+ Ap '67

about
Julie plays Gertie. J. A. Zill. il pors Look 31:63-8 S 19 '67
Long-winded lady; movie-making in Algonquin hotel. New Yorker 43:21-3 Je 17 '67

ANDREWS, Michael F.
18th INSEA world congress in Prague, Czechoslovakia. Sch Arts 66:32-7 Mr '67

ANDREWS, Walter
Raytheon gets nod on Sam-D development. Tech W 20:18-19 My 29 '67

ANDREWS, Wayne
Last word on architecture. Sat R 50:40-2 Mr 11 '67

ANDRIC, Ivo
Allegories of Ivo Andric. D. Devereux. Christian Cent 84:208 F 15 '67

ANDROGENS
Antiandrogen implanted in brain stimulates male preproductive system. G. J. Bloch and J. M. Davidson. bibliog il Science 155: 593-5 F 3 '67

ANDROMACHE; story. See Dubus, A.

ANDROMEDA galaxy. See Galactic systems

ANDROS ISLAND, Bahama Islands
Shoal water secrets of South Andros. N. Hayes. il Motor B 120:32-5 D '67

ANECDOTES
My magic box. L. Rosten. il Look 31:22-3 Mr 7 '67
Twice (and more!)-told tales. M. Giesy. Writer 80:29-30+ My '67
See also subhead Anecdotes, facetiae, satire, etc. under various subjects, e.g. Opera—Anecdotes, facetiae, satire, etc.

ANELLO, Douglas A.
Excerpt from statement before Communications subcommittee, October 12, 1967. Cong Digest 46:297+ D '67

ANEMIA
Heme and globin synthesis control: observations in vivo in beta thalassemia. M. Kreimer-Birnbaum and R. M. Bannerman. bibliog il Science 155:1116-18 Mr 3 '67; Reply with rejoinder. T. G. Gabuzda and others. 157:1079 S 1 '67
Lambda chains in cold agglutinins. T. Feizi. bibliog il Science 156:1111-12 My 26 '67
Microincision of sickled erythrocytes by a laser beam. W. N. Jensen and others. bibliog il Science 155:704-7 F 10 '67
Riddle of the dangerous bean; enzyme deficiency as cause of hemolysis and favism in specific ethnic groups. J. R. Marcus and G. Cohen. Harper 234:98-102 Je '67

ANEMIA phylitidis. See Ferns

ANEMONES, Sea. See Sea anemones

ANESTHESIA
Anesthetization of porpoises for major surgery. S. H. Ridgway and J. G. McCormick. bibliog il Science 158:510-12 O 27 '67
Radio pulses to kill pain. il Life 69:97-8 Je 16 '67

ANIMALS—*Continued*

Diseases and pests

Transmission and passage of experimental kuru to chimpanzees. D. Gajdusek and others. bibliog il Science 155:212-14 Ja 13 '67

See also Dogs—Diseases and pests and similar headings

Economic value

See Zoology, Economic

Food

Association of illness with prior ingestion of novel foods. S. H. Revusky and E. W. Bedarf. bibliog il Science 155:219-20 Ja 13 '67

Chemical-cue preferences of inexperienced snakes; comparative aspects. G. M. Burghardt. bibliog il Science 157:718-21 Ag 11 '67

Ecological significance of sexual dimorphism in size in the lizard anolis conspersus. T. W. Schoener. bibliog il Science 155:474-7 Ja 27 '67

Gekkonid lizards adapt fat storage to desert environments. H. R. Bustard. bibliog Science 158:1197-8 D 1 '67

Institute reports on: a well-balanced diet for your pet. il Good H 164:6 Ja '67

Pets in the pantry. P. O'Keefe. Am Home 70:38 S '67

Habits and behavior

Animal world of darkness; pavilion at New York's Bronx zoo. il Sci Digest 62:32-6 D '67

Barometric pressure fluctuations: effects on the activity of laboratory mice. R. L. Sprott. bibliog il Science 157:1206-7 S 8 '67

Behavior development in the dog: an interspecific analysis. R. B. Cairns and J. Werboff. bibliog il Science 158:1070-2 N 24 '67

Behavior of captive white-footed mice. J. L. Kavanau. bibliog il Science 155:1623-39 Mr 31 '67

Behavior of vervet monkeys and other cercopithecines. T. T. Struhsaker. bibliog il Science 156:1197-203 Je 2 '67

Christians and violence. S. Windass. Commonweal 86:11-13 Mr 24 '67

Collectors; xenophora the carrier shell. P. Villiard. il Audubon 69:85-7 My '67

Crazy, mixed-up adolescents of the wild. J. George. il Read Digest 92:159-62+ Ja '68

Do animals feel emotion? Sci N 92:533-4 D 2 '67

Experiential deprivation and later behavior. J. L. Fuller. bibliog il Science 158:1645-52 D 29 '67

Fossil behavior; some fossils represent the tracks or burrows of ancient animals. A. Seilacher. il Sci Am 217:72-6+ Ag '67

Konrad Lorenz. E. Stillman. il Horizon 9:60-5 Spr '67

Lions? elephants? hyenas? how much do you know that isn't so? il Pop Mech 128:92-3 S '67

Mystery of Mima mounds. R. C. Davids. il Farm J 91:17 Ag '67

Mystique of aggression. D. L. Wallace. Christian Cent 84:503-5 Ap 19 '67

Naturalist at large; concerning K. Lorenz's On aggression and R. Ardrey's Territorial imperative. M. Bates. Natur Hist 76:14+ Ap '67

Nonhormonal basis of maternal behavior in the rat. J. S. Rosenblatt. bibliog il Science 156:1512-14 Je 16 '67; Reply. F. A. Beach. 157:1591 S 29 '67

On aggression, by K. Lorenz. Review
Commentary 43:89-93 F '67. W. J. Dannhauser; Discussion. 44:8+ Ag '67
Sci Am 216:135-6+ F '67. S. A. Barnett; Discussion. 216:8+ My '67

On ethology. Sci N 91:472 My 20 '67

Rehumanized chimps. il Time 89:64 Ap 21 '67

Reporter at large; Japan monkey center at Inuyama. E. Kahn. New Yorker 43:126-33 S 23 '67

Study of animal behavior. J. Oppenheimer. il UNESCO Courier 20:30-1 My '67

Trials of a zebra herd stallion. R. D. Estes. il Natur Hist 76:58-65 N '67

War is not in our genes; animal and human aggressiveness; theories of Konrad Lorenz, Robert Ardrey and others. S. Carrighar. il N Y Times Mag p74-5+ S 10 '67; Discussion. p 12+ O 1; 22+ O 22 '67

See also
Biotelemetry
also Fishes—Habits and behavior and similar headings

Language

See Animal communication

Migration

See also
Orientation

Orientation

See Orientation

Photographs

Family of white wolves. S. Wayman. Life 62:50-7 Je 2 '67

Gallery of the great; portfolio of stallions. J. Cooke. Sports Illus 27:34-41 Ag 14 '67

Wild world; symposium. Life 63:20-33+ D 22 '67

Protection

Fun furs; danger of extermination, in the interests of fashion, of spotted cats. New Yorker 43:32-3 My 20 '67

How to get a cat out of a tree. il Changing T 21:24 My '67

Occurrence; rescue of dog from East River by drivers from Wells Fargo. New Yorker 42:20-3 Ja 21 '67

Time is short and the water rises; condensation. J. Walsh and R. Gannon. il Read digest 91:213-22+ Jl '67

See also
American society for the prevention of cruelty to animals
Animal experimentation
Animals—Treatment
Wildlife sanctuaries

Quarantine

See Quarantine, Veterinary

Sight

See Sight (animals)

Training

Attention shift and errorless reversal learning by the California sea lion. R. J. Schusterman. bibliog il Science 156:833-5 My 12 '67

How to teach your dog tricks. P. O'Keefe. Am Home 70:12 Je '67

Lovingest animal lover; I. Tors training ground for animal performers. il Life 63:41-2+ S 29 '67

Training without reward: traditional training of pig-tailed macaques as coconut harvesters. M. Bertrand. il Science 155:484-6 Ja 27 '67

Tuffy, the navy's deep sea lifeguard. T. Stimson. il Pop Mech 128:66-9+ Jl '67

See also
Animals in moving pictures
Bears—Training

Treatment

Kindness and cruelty in Great Britain. G. Carson. il Natur Hist 76:6+ bibliog(p 105) D '67

Sharper bite for lab animals; federal law regulating treatment. il Bsns W p 132+ F 18 '67

ANIMALS, Abnormalities of. See Abnormalities (animals)

ANIMALS, Aquatic. See Marine fauna

ANIMALS, Cruelty to. See Animals—Treatment

ANIMALS, Domestication of. See Domestication

ANIMALS, Experimentation. See Animal experimentation

ANIMALS, Experiments on. See Animal experimentation

ANIMALS, Extinct
Overkill, not overchill; theories of Paul Martin. il Time 90:94 D 8 '67

Pleistocene overkill; extinction of North America's large mammals. P. S. Martin. il Natur Hist 76:32-8 bibliog(p 105) D '67; Reply with rejoinder. L. S. B. Leakey. 77:73-5 Ja '68

See also
Eohippus
Paleontology

ANIMALS, Infancy of
Chemical-cue preferences of inexperienced snakes; comparative aspects. G. M. Burghardt. bibliog il Science 157:718-21 Ag 11 '67

Maternal and environmental influences on the adrenocortical response to stress in weanling rats. S. Levine. bibliog il Science 156:258-60 Ap 14 '67

Protein metabolism in the developing brain: influence of birth and gestational age. R. J. Schain and others. bibliog il Science 156:984-6 My 19 '67

ANIMALS, Mythical
Modern monsters, some are real some are not.
D. Cohen. il Sci Digest 61:14-20 My '67
More monsters, please! S. Alexander. Life
63:30B D 8 '67
ANIMALS, Nocturnal. See Animals—Habits and
behavior
ANIMALS, Performing. See Animals—Training
ANIMALS, Predatory
Predators and scavengers; carnivores of
Ngorongoro Crater in Africa. R. D. Estes.
il Natur Hist 76:20-9 F; 38-47 bibliog(p70)
Mr '67
See also
Coyotes
Wolves
ANIMALS, Prehistoric. See Animals, Extinct
ANIMALS, Rescue of. See Animals—Protection
ANIMALS, Training. See Animals—Training
ANIMALS, Treatment of. See Animals—Treatment
ANIMALS as carriers of infection
Diseases we catch from animals. R. W.
Crane. il Todays Health 45:56-7+ Mr '67
Regulating exotic pets; British problem. F. C.
Livingstone. Sci N 92:540 D 2 '67
See also
Rats as carriers of infection
Rodents as carriers of infection
ANIMALS' Christmas tree; drama. See Robertson, O. J.
ANIMALS in art
Dogs in his trailer. M. Hunn. il Design 69:
4-6 Fall '67
Operation Sunshine; E. Reinhardt's murals
for children's infirmaries and state hospitals. C. W. Wittman. il Am Artist 31:
27-31 F '67
Searle's cats; with drawings by R. Searle.
Look 31:58-9 S 19 '67
See also
Birds in art
ANIMALS in boating
Dog's day; pets and boats can go together.
J. W. Goris. il Motor B 120:42-3+ Jl '67
ANIMALS in captivity. See Zoological gardens
ANIMALS in literature
Hanuman, leader of the monkeys, beloved
by millions; excerpts from Epics, myths
and legends of India. P. Thomas. il
UNESCO Courier 20:16-17 D '67
ANIMALS in moving pictures
King of the beasties; I. Tors, producer of
outdoor adventure films. il Time 89:67-8 Je
16 '67
ANIMALS on television programs
King of the beasties; I. Tors, producer of
outdoor adventure films. il Time 89:67-8 Je
16 '67
ANIMATED cartoons. See Moving pictures—
—Animated cartoons; Television broadcasting—Animated cartoons
ANISFIELD-Wolf awards
Anisfield-Wolf awards. J. F. Fixx. Sat R 50:25
My 13 '67
ANKLE fractures. See Fractures
ANKRAH, Joseph Arthur
General Ankrah of Ghana visits the United
States; exchange of toasts, October 10,
1967. Dept State Bul 57:572 O 30 '67

about

New start. il por Time 91:22+ Ja 12 '68
ANN ARBOR film festival. See Moving picture
festivals
ANNAPOLIS, Md.
Annapolis; commuters, midshipmen and colonial charm. J. Hay. il Holiday 42:68-73+
O '67
ANNE ARUNDEL COUNTY, Md.
Developers help county acquire recreation
sites. W. W. Kershow. Parks & Rec 2:4
F '67
ANNEALING
Quartz; extreme preferred orientation produced by annealing. H. W. Green. 2d. bibliog il Science 157:1444-7 S 22 '67
X-ray fabric analysis of hot-worked and
annealed flint. H. R. Wenk and others. il
Science 157:1447-9 S 22 '67
ANNELIDS
Reef builders; sabellaria. D. W. Kirtley. il
Natur Hist 77:40-5 Ja '68
Sabellariid worm. Sci N 92:413 O 28 '67
ANNEXATION, Municipal. See Cities and
Towns—Growth
ANNIVERSARIES
See also
Wedding anniversaries
ANNIVERSARY gifts. See Gifts
ANNUAL meetings, Stockholders. See Stockholders meetings

ANNUAL reports, Corporate. See Corporation
reports
ANNUAL wage plans. See Wages—Annual wage
ANNUALS (plants)
Make your garden the talk of the town with
the 1967 All-America annuals. il Pop Gard
18:8 Mr '67
Unusual annuals. E. C. Volz. il Horticulture
45:22-3 Ap '67
Whole summer full of color. H. Mason. and
others. il Bet Hom & Gard 45:52-3 Ap '67
ANNUALS, High school. See High school annuals
ANNUITIES
Inflationproof annuities. Changing T 21:25-9
F '67
Life companies fight back at mutual funds;
pushing variable annuity plans. il Bsns W
p 122+ My 13 '67
ANOLIS conspersus. See Lizards
ANONYMOUS telephone calls. See Telephone
calls
ANOTHER story. See Cheever, J.
ANOUILH, Jean
Cavern. *Criticism*
Nation 205:125-6 Ag 14 '67
ANSCOCHROME films. See Photography—Films
ANSOFF, H. Igor, and Stewart, J. M.
Strategies for a technology-based business.
Harvard Bsns R 45:71-83 N '67
ANSTIS, S. M.
Visual adaptation to gradual change of intensity. Science 155:710-11 F 10 '67
ANSWERING service, Telephone. See Telephone—Answering service
ANSWERS to questions. See Questions and
answers
ANTARCTIC exploration
First conquest of Antarctica's highest peaks.
N. B. Clinch. il Nat Geog Mag 131:836-63
Je '67
Scott of the Antarctic, by R. Pound. Review
Sci Digest il 62:85-6 Jl '67
ANTARCTIC REGIONS
Antarctic notes; U.S. Antarctic research program. Sci N 92:586 D 16 '67
Antarctica; the urgency of protecting life
on and around the great southerly continent. R. C. Murphy. il Natur Hist 76:21-
31 Je '67
Massive scientific effort. B. A. Leerburger,
jr. il Sci N 92:635-6 D 30 '67
New kind of southern cruise, to wild Antarctica. il Life 63:84-7 S 8 '67
Puzzle of Antarctica's desert valleys; reprint.
W. J. Perkinson. il Sci Digest 61:32-6 Ap '67
Space man's look at Antarctica; Wright Dry
Valley studied as a possible proving ground
for space instruments. W. Von Braun.
il Pop Sci 190:114-16+ My '67
Symbol of good will; the Antarctic treaty.
M. Amara. il Américas 19:1-9 F '67
See also
Antarctic exploration
Aviation—Antarctic Regions
Ice—Polar Regions
ANTARCTIC research. See Polar research
ANTARCTIC treaty, 1959
Symbol of good will; the Antarctic treaty.
M. Amaro. il Américas 19:1-9 F '67
U.S. appoints observers for Antarctic inspections. Dept State Bul 56:71 Ja 9 '67
U.S. observers inspect Antarctic stations. il
Dept State Bul 56:633-4 Ap 17 '67
ANTEATERS
Nature note; last of the numbats; myrmecobius fasciatus. il Sci N 91:542 Je 10 '67
Two for extinction. il Sci Digest 61:22-4 F
'67
ANTELOPE hunting
Gemsbok in the Kalahari. J. O'Connor. il
Outdoor Life 140:28-9+ Jl '67
See also
Pronghorn hunting
ANTELOPES, American. See Pronghorns
ANTENNAE
Antennae and sexual receptivity in drosophila
melanogaster females. A. Manning. bibliog
il Science 158:136-7 O 6 '67
ANTENNAS (electronics)
And now the mini-antenna. il Time 89:124 My
19 '67
New designs evolving for SST antennas. B.
M. Elson. il Aviation W 87:91+ N 13 '67
See also
Radar—Antenna and scanning mechanisms
Radio antennas
Television antennas

ANTHERIDIA
Anemia phyllitidis: inducibility of physiological state antagonistic to antheridium formation. U. Näf. bibliog il Science 156:1117-19 My 26 '67

ANTHOLOGIES
Five anthologies. R. Dana. Poetry 110:47-51 Ap '67
Five anthologies. R. J. Mills, jr. Poetry 109: 345-50 F '67
How an anthology is made. T. M. H. Blair. Writer 80:16-20+ Mr '67

ANTHONY, Dart
Showing off The show-offs. V. H. Swisher. il pors Dance Mag 41:24-5+ My '67

ANTHONY, E. James
Parent and child. N Y Times Mag p57+ Ja 22 '67

ANTHONY, Mother Mary. See Mary Anthony, Mother

ANTHRAX
Bacteria around the Cape; cases in dock workers unloading bone shipments. Time 90:57 N 17 '67

ANTHROP, Donald F.
Redwood National Park. Liv Wildn 31:36-47 Spr '67

ANTHROPOGEOGRAPHY
National character in the perspective of cultural geography. J. O. M. Broek. bibliog f Ann Am Acad 370:8-15 Mr '67

ANTHROPOLOGISTS
Cross-cultural research and government policy. R. L. Beals. Bul Atomic Sci 23: 18-24 O '67
See also names of anthropologists, e.g. L. C. Eiseley

ANTHROPOLOGY
Anthropological perspectives on national character. E. A. Hoebel. bibliog f Ann Am Acad 370:1-7 Mr '67
Myth of the machine, by L. Mumford. Review New Repub 156:18+ Ap 29 '67. S. Kauffmann
Savage mind, by C. Lévi-Strauss. Review Natur Hist 76:58+ My '67. C. M. Turnbull
See also
Anthropogeography
Civilization
Man
Man, Prehistoric
Man, Primitive
Manners and customs

Bibliography
Books for Christmas; an anthropologist's choice. M. Mead. Redbook 130:22+ D '67

Research
Anthropologists' debate: concern over future of foreign research. B. Nelson; discussion. Science 156:1032-5; 157:251-2 My 26, Jl 21 '67

Study and teaching
Venture in cultural anthropology. P. F. Mayer. Negro Hist Bul 29:179-80+ Fall '66

ANTHROPOMETRY
See also
Body size

ANTI-AMERICANISM. See United States—Foreign opinion

ANTIANDROGENS. See Androgens

ANTIBALLISTIC missile system. See Guided missiles—Defenses

ANTIBIOTICS
Antibiotics in the laboratory-rearing of cecropia silkworms. L. M. Riddiford. bibliog Science 157:1451-2 S 22 '67
Failure of cycloheximide to induce tyrosine transaminase in the anesthetized rat. C. Mavrides and E. A. Lane. bibliog il Science 156:1376-8 Je 9 '67; Reply with rejoinder. S. Fiala and E. S. Fiala. 157:1591 S 29 '67
Memory in mice analyzed with antibiotics. L. B. Flexner and others. bibliog il Science 155:1377-83 Mr 17 '67
Phosphorylative inactivation of aminoglycosidic antibiotics by escherichia coli carrying R factor. H. Umezawa and others. il Science 157:1559-61 S 29 '67
R factors mediate resistance to mercury, nickel, and cobalt. D. H. Smith. bibliog il Science 156:1114-16 My 26 '67
Streptonigrin; effect on the first meiotic metaphase of the mouse egg. G. Jagiello. bibliog il Science 157:453-4 Jl 28 '67
Toxicity of antibiotics in laboratory rodents. V. A. A. Killby and P. H. Silverman. Science 156:264 Ap 14 '67; Reply with rejoinder. R. Donovick. 157:338 Jl 21 '67
See also
Penicillin
Streptomycin

ANTIBODIES. See Antigens and antibodies

ANTI-COLLISION systems. See Aeronautic instruments

ANTI-COMMUNISM in literature. See Communism in literature

ANTI-COMMUNIST measures. See Communism—Anti-Communist measures

ANTI-COMMUNIST measures in the United States. See Communism—United States—Anti-Communist measures; United States—Foreign relations—Anti-Communist measures

ANTI-COMMUNIST movements
Decline of the anti-Communist left. M. Geltman. il Nat R 19:79-83 Ja 24 '67

Greece, Modern
It's neat in Greece. R. F. McDonald. New Repub 157:15-17 Jl 22 '67

Indonesia
Indonesia's night of terror. H. Sutton. il Sat R 50:25-8+ F 4 '67

Latin America
Campus communism: Latin America's Trojan horse. E. Cárdenas. Read Digest 90:92-6 Je '67

ANTICORROSIVES. See Corrosion and anticorrosives

ANTI-DEFAMATION league. See B'nai b'rith—Anti-defamation league

ANTI-DEFAMATION league, American Italian. See American Italian anti-defamation league

ANTIDEPRESSANTS
Antidepression drugs. Consumer Rep 32:547-8 O '67

ANTI-DEPRESSION measures. See United States—Economic policy

ANTI-EARTHQUAKE building. See Earthquakes and building

ANTI-EVOLUTION controversy. See Tennessee evolution controversy

ANTI-EVOLUTION legislation. See Evolution—Laws and legislation

ANTIFLU drug. See Amantadine hydrochloride

ANTI-FREEZE solutions
Antifreeze and coolants for automobiles. il Consumer Bul 50:4-6+ N '67
Water makes good antifreeze. B. Wennerstrom. il Motor T 19:95 D '67

ANTIFRICTION bearings. See Bearings (machinery)

ANTIGENS and antibodies
Adjuvant activity of erythrocyte isoantigens. L. W. Schierman and R. A. McBride. bibliog il Science 156:658-9 My 5 '67
Altered response to pneumococcal polysaccharide in offspring of immunologically paralyzed mice. R. Kerman and others. bibliog il Science 156:1514-16 Je 16 '67
Antibodies to rabbit cytochrome c arising in rabbits. A. Nisonoff and others. bibliog il Science 155:1273-5 Mr 10 '67
Antibody formation: stimulation by polyadenylic and polycytidylic acids. W. Braun and M. Nakano. bibliog il Science 157:819-21 Ag 18 '67
Antibody-producing cells in division. A. J. Claflin and O. Smithies. bibliog il Science 157:1561-2 S 29 '67
Antibody variability; excerpts from address, June 3, 1967. O. Smithies. bibliog il Science 157:267-73 Jl 21 '67
Antigenic competition: cellular or humoral. J. Radovich and D. W. Talmage. bibliog il Science 158:512-14 O 27 '67
Antigenic study of the protein from a defective strain of tobacco mosaic virus. I. Rappaport and M. Zaitlin. bibliog il Science 157:207-8 Jl 14 '67
Autologous immune-complex pathogenesis of experimental allergic glomerulonephritis. T. S. Edgington and others. bibliog il Science 155:1432-4 Mr 17 '67
Autoradiographic plaques for the detection of antibody formation to soluble proteins by single cells. E. Pick and J. D. Feldman. bibliog il Science 156:964-6 My 19 '67
Cancer and immunology. B. J. Culliton. il Sci N 91:310 Ap 1 '67
Cell-bound immunity to autologous and syngeneic mouse tumors induced by methylcholanthrene and plastic discs. I. Hellström and K. E. Hellström. bibliog il Science 156: 981-3 My 19 '67
Circumventing immunity; lymph drainage and anti-lymphocyte treatment. il Time 89: 63-4 Mr 10 '67
Cytotoxic effect of lymphocyte-antigen interaction in delayed hypersensitivity. N. H. Ruddle and B. H. Waksman. bibliog il Science 157:1060-2 S 1 '67

ANTIGENS and antibodies—*Continued*
Delayed hypersensitivity: bone marrow as the source of cells in delayed skin reactions. D. M. Lubaroff and B. H. Waksman. bibliog il Science 157:322-3 Jl 21 '67
Delayed hypersensitivity in man: a correlate in vitro and transfer by an RNA extract. D. E. Thor. bibliog il Science 157:1567-9 S 29 '67
Drug-induced tolerance for skin allografts across the H-2 barrier in adult mice. G. L. Floersheim. bibliog il Science 156:951-4 My 19 '67
Efficiency of the first component of complement, of C'1, in the hemolytic reaction. H. R. Colten and others. bibliog il Science 158:1590-2 D 22 '67
Electrical recordings from meningioma cells during cytolytic action of antibody and complement. A. Prieto and others. bibliog il Science 157:1185-7 S 8 '67
Gastrin antibodies: induction, demonstrations, and specificity. D. R. Schneider and others. bibliog il Science 156:391-2 Ap 21 '67
Genetic background and expressivity of histocompatibility genes. W. K. Silvers and R. E. Billingham. bibliog il Science 158:118-19 O 6 '67
Hemagglutinating 7S subunits of 19S cold agglutinins. A. G. Cooper. bibliog il Science 157:933-5 Ag 25 '67
Heterophile reactive antigen in infectious mononucleosis. J. H. Peters. bibliog il Science 157:1200-2 S 8 '67
Histocompatibility antigen transfer in utero: tolerance in progeny and sensitization in mother. C. Tai and N. A. Halasz. bibliog il Science 158:125-6 O 6 '67
Hu-1: major histocompatibility locus in man. F. H. Bach and D. B. Amos. bibliog il Science 156:1506-8 Je 16 '67
Immunization with skin isografts taken from tolerant mice. D. Steinmuller. bibliog il Science 158:127-9 O 6 '67
Lambda chains in cold agglutinins. T. Feizi. bibliog il Science 156:1111-12 My 26 '67
Lead on schizophrenia. Sci N 91:141 F 11 '67
Loss of thymus-distinctive serological characteristics in mice under certain conditions. M. Schlesinger and V. K. Golakai. bibliog il Science 155:1114-16 Mr 3 '67
Lymphocytic choriomeningitis: production of antibody by tolerant infected mice. M. B. A. Oldstone and F. J. Dixon. bibliog il Science 158:1193-5 D 1 '67
Mechanism of antibody synthesis: size differences between mouse kappa chains. W. R. Gray and others. bibliog il Science 155:465-7 Ja 27 '67
Minuscule molecules sidestep antibodies. Sci N 92:59 Jl 15 '67
Mouse immunoglobulin allotypes: detection with rabbit antiserums. J. E. Coe. bibliog il Science 155:562+ F 3 '67
New organs for old; ways to break through the immunity barrier. M. Clark. il Newsweek 69:92 Mr 13 '67
Red cells coated with immunoglobulin G: binding and sphering by mononuclear cells in man. A. F. LoBuglio and others. bibliog il Science 158:1582-5 D 22 '67
Requirement for two cell types for antibody formation in vitro. D. E. Mosier. bibliog il Science 158:1573-5 D 22 '67
Solid-phase radioimmunoassay in antibody-coated tubes. K. Catt and G. W. Tregear. bibliog il Science 158:1570-2 D 22 '67
Specific binding activity of isolated light chains of antibodies. T. J. Yoo and others. bibliog il Science 157:707-9 Ag 11 '67
Structure of antibodies. R. R. Porter. il Sci Am 217:81-7+ O '67
Tryout kidney. Newsweek 69:67 Mr 20 '67
See also
Complement fixation
Rh factors
ANTIHYPERTENSIVE agents
How drugs can control blood pressure. J. H. Winchester. Read Digest 91:143-6 D '67
ANTI-IMPERIALISM. See Imperialism
ANTI-INFLATION measures. See Inflation (finance)
ANTILLES. See West Indies
ANTI-LYMPHOCYTE serum. See Serum
ANTIMALARIALS
Tiny enemy in Vietnam. il Life 63:53-4+ N 24 '67
ANTIMISSILE defense system. See Guided missiles—Defenses
ANTI-MISSILE missile programs. See Guided missiles—Defenses
ANTI-NEGRO prejudice. See Race prejudice

ANTIOCH college, Yellow Springs, Ohio
Antioch college. A. Karlen. il Holiday 41:46-9+ Je '67
Face of justice; Cincinnati protest, December 1967. A. L. Denman. New Repub 158:12 Ja 20 '68
Libraries
Latin American collection; adaptation of address, June 1967. C. Dearnaley and P. Bixler. Wilson Lib Bul 42:417-21 D '67
ANTI-PARTICLES. See Particles (nuclear physics)
ANTIPASTO. See Appetizers
ANTI-POLLUTION devices. See Air pollution control equipment
ANTI-POVERTY program, 1964-
Biting the bloodhounds; House of representatives approves poverty program. il Time 90:23-4 N 24 '67
Bosses and boll weevils; poverty bill passed. Reporter 37:9-10 N 30 '67
Critique of cost-benefit analyses of training; excerpt from Training the poor. D. O. Sewell. bibliog f Mo Labor R 90:45-51 S '67
Domestic pacification. New Repub 157:7 Jl 1 '67
Drumming up votes for the poverty program. E. K. Shanahan. New Repub 156:7-8 Je 17 '67; Reply. R. A. Levine. 157:34 Jl 1 '67
It can be done! conquering poverty in the US by 1976. J. Tobin. New Repub 156:14-18 Je 3 '67; Reply. L. H. Keyserling. 156:33-4 Je 10 '67
Jobs for the hard-core poor; in private industry and elsewhere. Bsns W p48 Mr 18 '67
Lawyers for the poor; legal services program. New Repub 157:9-10 N 11 '67
Lessons of the long hot summer; proposals to widen war on poverty. B. Rustin. Commentary 44:39-45 O '67
New criticism of the antipoverty program. U S News 63:8 N 20 '67
No escalation. il Time 89:24 Ap 21 '67
No margarine either. New Repub 157:5-7 N 25 '67
Now your taxes train pickets; unions infiltrating poverty programs. il Nations Bsns 55:37-9+ Mr '67
Other pacification, to cool U.S. cities; with report by S. McBee. il Life 63:30-34A Ag 25 '67
Other war; criticism of war on poverty program. il Time 89:28-9 My 19 '67
Poverty warfare; cuts in appropriations. Newsweek 70:35 N 27 '67
Programs and priorities. S. A. Levitan and G. L. Mangum. il Reporter 37:20-2 S 7 '67; Reply. L. H. Keyserling. 37:8 S 21 '67
Vietnam and the poor. Sat Eve Post 240:98 F 25 '67
War on poverty. I. Mothner. il Look 31:26-34+ Je 13 '67
Where poverty program is doing poorly; interview. P. M. Landrum. Nations Bsns 55:52+ O '67
See also
California—Anti-poverty program
Chicago—Anti-poverty program
Los Angeles—Anti-poverty program
Mississippi—Anti-poverty program
New York (city)—Anti-poverty program
Washington, D.C.—Anti-poverty program
ANTIPSYCHOTIC drugs. See Chlorpromazine
ANTIQUE dealers
Twelve suggestions for successful antique buying by mail order; excerpt from Successful selling of antiques by mail. Hobbies 72:80-1+ Ag '67
What records you must keep; excerpt from Successful selling of antiques by mail. Hobbies 72:120-1 S '67
ANTIQUE dolls. See Dolls
ANTIQUE jewelry. See Jewelry
ANTIQUES
Antiques book preview; The American heritage history of colonial antiques. M. B. Davidson. il Antiques 92:341-7 S '67
Antiques of tomorrow. M.-L. Mastai. Am Home 70:112 N '67
Antiques; questions & answers. L. A. Boger. See issues of House & garden incorporating Living for young homemakers
Caveat emptor Judaeus; lively manufacturing trade in Jewish antiques. C. Roth. Commentary 43:84-6 Mr '67
Don't throw it away too soon; junk in your barnyard. G. Logsdon. il Farm J 91:74B+ Mr '67
History in houses:
General Dodge house. B. S. Utley. il Antiques 92:210-13 Ag '67
Hyde hall, Otsego County, N.Y. D. R. Kent. il Antiques 92:187-93 Ag '67

ANTIQUES—*Continued*
History in houses: Locust Grove, near Louisville, Kentucky. S. W. Thomas. il Antiques 91:223-7 F '67
History in houses, the Bolduc house in Ste Genevieve, Mo. G. R. Brooks. il Antiques 92:96-9 Jl '67
How to judge antiques the way a dealer does. P. C. Flayderman and B. Flayderman. il House B 109:54-5+ S '67
Interim report from Washington, D.C; diplomatic reception rooms in the Department of state's building. E. P. Birk. il Antiques 91:724+ Je '67
Letter from London (cont) J. Stuart. il Antiques 91:440, 556+; 92:308+, 464+, 648+, 766+ Ap-My, S-D '67
Living with antiques:
Chestnut Hill home of Mrs Thomas D. Thacher. E. Stillinger. il Antiques 91:503-7 Ap '67
Detroit home of Mr and Mrs Charles H. Gershenson. D. F. Gershenson. il Antiques 91:637-41 My '67
Hofwyl plantation in Brunswick, Ga. C. M. Theus. il Antiques 92:194-7 Ag '67
Hosmer house in Montreal. E. H. Turner. il Antiques 92:91-5 Jl '67
Montgomery place the home of Major and Mrs John White Delafield. A. Delafield. il Antiques 91:234-9 F '67
New Hampshire home of Mr and Mrs John Hodgson. A. D. Hodgson. il Antiques 92:182-6 Ag '67
Pennsylvania home of Mr and Mrs Charles J. Fox, 2d. E. Stillinger. il Antiques 92:214-17 Ag '67
Pennsylvania home of Mr and Mrs Walter L. Wolf. L. Solis-Cohen. il Antiques 92:336-40 S '67
Ross house in York County, Pa. W. D. Garrett. il Antiques 92:203-7 Ag '67
Living with antiques in England; Essex home of E. Clare Hanley. J. Vickers. il Antiques 92:208-9 Ag '67
Not-quite-antiques: for $150 or less. B. Plumb. il N Y Times Mag p64-5 Mr 26 '67
Treasury of American antiques. il McCalls 94:88-93 Jl '67
See also
Shelburne museum, Shelburne, Vt.

Bibliography
Books about antiques. See issues of Antiques

Collectors and collecting
American antiques in the collection of Mr and Mrs Charles L. Bybee. J. L. Fairbanks. il Antiques 92:832-9 D '67 (to be cont)

Exhibitions
American decorative arts in Florida: exhibition at University of Miami. E. P. Birk. il Antiques 91:158+ F '67
Calendar of shows. See issues of Antiques
Current and coming. E. P. Birk. See issues of Antiques

Tariff
See Tariff on antiques
ANTIQUES, Forged
Caveat emptor Judaeus; lively manufacturing trade in Jewish antiques. C. Roth. Commentary 43:84-6 Mr '67
How not to buy an early American dry sink; suggestions of G. Grotz. Time 89:76-7 Ja 27 '67
ANTIQUES, Reproductions of
Instant antiques; Ateliers d'art A. Mailfert Amos, manufacturers of French furniture. il Newsweek 69:60 My 15 '67
ANTIQUES dealers. See Antique dealers
ANTIQUITIES. See Archeology;*also* subhead Antiquities under names of countries, states, etc. e.g. Egypt—Antiquities
ANTIQUITY of man. See Man—Origin and antiquity
ANTI-RIOT devices. See Police—Equipment and supplies
ANTI-SATELLITE weapons systems. See Weapons systems
ANTI-SEMITISM
American Catholics and anti-Semitism in the 1930's. D. J. O'Brien. Cath World 204:270-6 F '67
Anti-Semitism and the Gospel; language of the New Testament. M. D. Zeik. Commonweal 86:16-18 Mr 24 '67; Reply. C. H. Bishop. 86:138-9+ Ap 21 '67
Between hammer and sickle, by B. Ami. Review
Sat R il 50:35 S 2 '67. R. I. Rubin

Christian education and the Jewish people; address before American academy of religion. L. D. Streiker. Christian Cent 84:168-71 F 8 '67
De Gaulle and the Jews. Newsweek 70:47 D 11 '67
Facts and fallacies: Negro anti-Semitism. G. T. Marx. Nation 206:11-13 Ja 1 '68
Gentile beast. Christian Cent 84:299-300 Mr 8 '67
Germans are worrying the world again; neo-Nazism: National democratic party (NPD) J. Roddy. il Look 31:17-21 Mr 21 '67
Hate literature in Spanish. America 116:201 F 11 '67
If some, then all; draft convention on the elimination of all forms of religious intolerance. Christian Cent 84:1451 N 15 '67
Jews and Christians in suburbia. R. Stark and S. Steinberg. Harper 235:73-8 Ag '67; Discussion. 235:4+ O '67
Negroes are anti-Semitic because they want a scapegoat. R. Gordis. il N Y Times Mag p28-9+ Ap 23 '67; Discussion. p 12+ My 21 '67
Negroes are anti-Semitic because they're anti-white. J. Baldwin. il N Y Times Mag p26-7+ Ap 9 '67; Discussion. p 12+ My 21 '67
Poland's anti-Semitic Maoist underground. S. L. Shneiderman. il Reporter 36:21-3 Ja 26 '67
Prevalence of scapegoats: Negro anti-Semitism. Nation 206:5 Ja 1 '68
Trouble in Wayne; concerning defeat of Jews in school board election. il Newsweek 69:80 F 27 '67
See also
Jews—Persecutions
ANTI-SLAVERY. See Slavery
ANTI-SLAVERY movement. See Slavery—United States
ANTI-SLAVERY society for the protection of human rights
Slavery: the crime the world ignores. N. Mostert. il Reporter 38:29-31 Ja 11 '68
ANTI-SMOG devices. See Automobile engines—Exhaust
ANTI-SMOKING clinics. See Smoking
ANTI-STRIKE legislation. See Labor laws and legislation; Labor laws and legislation—United States
ANTI-SUBMARINE warfare. See Submarine warfare
ANTITRUST division. See United States—Justice, Department of—Antitrust division
ANTITRUST legislation. See Trusts, Industrial—Law
ANTI-VIETNAM demonstrations. See Vietnamese war, 1957- —Protests, demonstrations, etc. against
ANTIVIRAL proteins. See Interferon
ANTIVIVISECTION. See Vivisection
ANTLERS
Antlered dinnerware. D. Shiner. il Design 69:18-19 Fall '67
Antlers of Nara. il Natur Hist 76:30-3 F '67
New light on mystery of antlers. R. J. Goss. il Outdoor Life 139:54-5+ Mr '67
ANTONAKOS, Stephen
Light brigade. E. C. Baker. il Art N 66:52-5+ Mr '67
ANTONELLO da Messina
Still another art find: a priceless work by Antonello da Messina. il Life 62:30-30A Ja 27 '67
ANTONINI, Eraldo
Hemoglobin and its reaction with ligands. bibliog Science 158:1417-25 D 15 '67
ANTONIONI, Michelangelo
Antonioni talks about his work. por Life 62:66-7 Ja 27 '67
about
Adventurous Antonioni. L. Barzini. por Holiday 41:99-100+ Ap '67
Antonioni's hypnotic eye on a frantic world. il pors Life 62:62B-65 Ja 27 '67
Watching Antonioni. R. Garis. Commentary 43:86-9 Ap '67; Reply with rejoinder. P. Warshow. 44:14-17 Ag '67
ANTONY and Cleopatra; drama. See Shakespeare, W.—Plays
ANTONY and Cleopatra; opera. See Barber, S.
ANTROPOLOGIA. See Mexico (city)—Galleries and museums
ANTS
Ant stridulations and their synchronization with abdominal movement. H. G. Spangler. bibliog il Science 155:1687-9 Mr 31 '67
Fire ant venom: synthesis of a reported component of solenamine. P. E. Sonnet. bibliog il Science 156:1759-60 Je 30 '67

ANTS—*Continued*
Living doors; phragmosis in ants. W. S.
Creighton. il Natur Hist 76:71-3 bibliog
(p 105) D '67

ANTS, Fossil
First mesozoic ants. E. O. Wilson and others. bibliog il Science 157:1038-40 S 1 '67
Most ancient ant. il Sci N 92:276 S 16 '67
Up from the wasp. Sci Am 217:60+ O '67

ANTS, White. See Termites

ANTUNES, Augusto Tranjano de Azevedo. See
Azevedo Antunes, A. T. de

ANTWERP
Description
Stopping off in Antwerp. N. Braybrooke. Sat
R 50:45 Jl 22 '67

ANXIETY
Alleviating the college student's anxiety.
M. Katahn. NEA J 57:17-18 Ja '68
Student anxiety. P. H. Abelson. Science 158:
1139 D 1 '67
When parents have to leave. B. Spock. il Redbook 128:41+ Ap '67
Which age of anxiety? J. H. Plumb. il Horizon 9:88-9 Aut '67
See also
Fear

ANZA-BORREGO DESERT state park. See
California—Parks and reserves

ANZUS council
ANZUS council discusses political and security
problems; text of communique, April 22,
1967. Dept State Bul 56:749-50 My 15 '67

AORTA
Corridors of the heart; with photographs by
L. Nilsson. Life 64:22-31 Ja 19 '68

APACHE airlines
Board denies air taxi jet weight limit exemption. Aviation W 86:29 F 27 '67

APALACHICOLA, Fla.
Gadfly with a sting; Apalachicola times campaigns against domination of Du Pont
estate. il Time 89:40 Je 23 '67

APARTHEID. See South Africa—Race problems

APARTMENT houses
Anyone for singles; South Bay club in Torrance. Calif. il Newsweek 69:70 My 8 '67
Apartment building on upswing again. G. A.
Christie. il Arch Rec 142:83 S '67
Apartment in the Rockies. il House B 109:
112-13 Ag '67
Boys & girls together; apartments for singles-
only; South Bay clubs, Los Angeles. C.
Mangel. il Look 31:M8+ Ag 22 '67
New apartment community. il House B 109:
108-9+ Ag '67
What it's like to live in an experiment;
Habitat of Expo 67. D. Jacobs. il N Y Times
Mag p50-1+ Je 4 '67
Why Miami's visitors sign up for the year.
il Bsns W p 169-70+ O 14 '67
See also
Apartments
Row houses

Condominium plan ownership
California: planned pleasure; new condominium communities. D. Messinesi. Vogue 150:
76-8 Ag 15 '67
Condominiums take to skis; Vail and Dillon,
Colo. il Bsns W p 196-8 N 18 '67

Cooperative ownership
Two apartments by the sea; Fort Lauderdale
and Palm Beach. il House B 109:114-15 Ag
'67
See also
Apartment houses—Condominium plan ownership

Designs and plans
Two residential developments in Florida. il
Arch Rec 142:155-60 O '67

Employees
See also
Strikes—United States—Apartment house employees

Noise
Lease and quiet; ways to circumvent construction flaws and restrictions. J. H. Ingersoll. il House B 109:122-4 Ag '67
Old folks at, home? life in a Manhattan
apartment. E. G. Smith. il Atlan 220:118-
19 D '67

APARTMENT houses, Prefabricated
Habitat and after; with account by R. Boyd.
il Arch Forum 126:34-44 My '67

APARTMENT houses, Remodeled
Upper West side story; architect Earl Burns
Combs. B. Plumb. il N Y Times Mag p 122-
3 S 10 '67

APARTMENTS
Apartment life, Italian style. il House B 109:
98-9 Ag '67
Apartment with a view to the future. il
Good H 164:144-51 Mr '67
Art of fooling the eye. il Am Home 70:60-1
S '67
Art scholar's loft; the New York apartment
of William Rubin. il Vogue 149:136-43+
Mr 15 '67
Country in the city; architect Eduard H.
Bullerjahn's home on Beacon Hill. P. Doherty. il House B 109:74-9 Ag '67
Editor shows how to have a luxury apartment. il Redbook 130:69-72 Ja '68
English contemporary; duplex in London's
Pimlico section. il House B 109:96-7 Ag '67
Family apartment, château style; Mr and Mrs
Harold Toppel's New York apartment. M.
Gough. il House B 109:84-9 Ag '67
France today, savoir-vivre; home of Daniel
Kiener in Paris. H. Morrison. il House B
109:92-5 Ag '67
Full of tricks. B. Plumb. il N Y Times Mag
p 114:15 Ap 9 '67
Green scene; apartment of Arnold Scaasi. J.
Peter. il Look 31:M12 Ag 22 '67
In Stockholm, a designer's apartment. il
House B 110:104-5 Ja '68
Larry Rivers' living room; block-deep floor
in Manhattan loft building. M. Simons. il
Look 31:M20+ Mr 21 '67
Look of a garden, five floors up; apartment
of J. Bennett. il House & Gard 132:100-3
Ag '67
Making a scene. B. Plumb. il N Y Times Mag
p40-1 Jl 9 '67
Manhattan apartment, country-house charm.
F. Heard. il House B 109:126-9 Mr '67
Modern American classic; overlooking the
ocean in Atlantic City. E. Sverbeyeff. il
House B 109:90-1+ Ag '67
Modern updated. B. Plumb il N Y Times
Mag p20-1 D 31 '67
Money isn't everything; railroad flat in Greenwich Village. B. Plumb. il N Y Times Mag
p40-1 Je 25 '67
Paul's pacesetter; architect, Paul Rudolph's
New York apartment. E Plumb. il N Y
Times Mag p42-3 Jl 23 '67
Problem apartment. F. Heard. il House B
109:100-5 Ag '67
Renaissance plus. R. Reif. il N Y Times Mag
p56-7 Ag 13 '67
Sense of serenity; home of Mr and Mrs Peter
Lewis, overlooking San Francisco Bay. J. L.
Hendrix. il House B 109:80-3 Ag '67

Anecdotes, facetiae, satire, etc.
Mrdr'd in full kitch, acc. to grdn. S. Blackburn. New Yorker 43:205-7 N 25 '67

APARTMENTS, Remodeled
Upper West side story; architect Earl Burns
Combs. B. Plumb. il N Y Times Mag p 122-
3 S 10 '67

APATITE
Apatite crystallites: effects of carbonate on
morphology. R. Z. LeGeros and others. bibliog il Science 155:1409-11 Mr 17 '67
Lepidocrocite, an apatite mineral, and magnetite in teeth of chitons, polyplacophora.
H. A. Lowenstam. bibliog il Science 156:
1373-5 Je 9 '67

APERTIFS. See Liquors

APES, Fossil
Ancient ancestor; skull of Aegyptopithecus
zeuxis. il Time 90:62 N 24 '67
Earliest apes. E. L. Simons. il Sci Am 217:28-
35 D '67
Man's earliest known ancestor; Aegyptopithecus zeuxis. il Sci N 92:514 N 25 '67

APFELBAUM, Ben. See Sale, J. K. jt. auth.

APGAR, Virginia
Of miracles and medicine. il pors Todays
Health 46:30-1 Ja '68

APHASIA
Electronics and aphasia; teaching stroke victims to talk. J. Frye. Electr World 78:54-5
D '67

APHIDS. See Plant lice

APHORISMS and apothegms
Poor woman's almanac. B. Pfizer. il Ladies
Home J 84:8 Ap; 32 Ag; 74 S; 91 N; 8 D '67

APHRODISIAS
Ancient Aphrodisias and its marble treasures.
K. T. Erim. il Nat Geog Mag 132:280-94
Ag '67
Aphrodisias revisited. il Newsweek 71:72 Ja
15 '68

APOLLINAIRE, Guillaume, pseud.
French chronicle. P. Zweig. Poetry 111:124-9
N '67

APOLLO (space vehicle) See Space vehicles

APOLLO lunar exploration office. See United States—National aeronautics and space administration—Apollo lunar exploration office (proposed)

APOLLO lunar module. See Space vehicles—Landing systems—Moon

APOLLO lunar surface experiment package. See Moon—Surface

APOLLO project. See Space flight to the moon

APOLLO telescope mount. See Artificial satellites—Astronomical applications

APOMIXIS. See Parthenogenesis (plants)

APOMORPHINE
Kicking drugs: a very personal story. W. S. Burroughs. Harper 235:39-42 Jl '67

APOPEROXIDASE. See Peroxidases

APOSTASY
Defection: protest or treason? F. X. Murphy; discussion. America 116:198-9 F 11 '67
Father Davis and the servant church. J. B. Sheerin. Cath World 204:324-5 Mr '67
Loss to us all; the Charles Davis case. R. M. Brown. Commonweal 86:92-4 Ap 7 '67
McCabe affair; after Charles Davis; with editorial comment. J. M. Cameron. Commonweal 85:653-5 Mr 10 '67
No time to leave; the Charles Davis case. J. G. Lawler. Commonweal 86:87-92 Ap 7 '67; Discussion. 86:221+ My 12 '67
Psychoanalysis causes a break; monks of the Benedictine monastery at Cuernavaca renouncing their vows. America 117:5 Jl 1 '67
Story of Charles Davis. S. J. Adamo. America 116:777-80 My 27 '67

APOSTLES
Miracle of the Twelve. E. O. Hauser. il Read Digest 91:85-90 D '67
See also
Peter, Saint

APOTHEGMS. See Aphorisms and apothegms

APPALACHIAN MOUNTAINS
See also
Cumberland Plateau

APPALACHIAN REGION
Girl from V.I.S.T.A; experiences of J. Honrath as a worker in the mountains of eastern Kentucky. F. Powledge. il Redbook 129:80-1+ Jl '67
To the hills and hollows; story of the Appalachia educational laboratory. C. M. Singleton and S. M. Brown. il Am Ed 3:22-5 Jl '67
Who needs people? J. Ridgeway. New Repub 156:10-12 My 13 '67
See also
Education—Appalachian Region

Recovery program, 1965-
Grants for regional development extended. G. Krettek and E. D. Cooke. Wilson Lib Bul 42:337-8 N '67
Opportunity and action in Appalachia. Mo Labor R 90:III-IV Ja '67

APPALACHIAN regional commission. See United States—Appalachian regional commission

APPALACHIAN trail
New Hampshire's White Mountain huts. A. E. Kessler. il Travel 127:37-40 Je '67

APPALACHIAN volunteers. See Volunteers in service to America

APPARATUS for the blind. See Blind, Apparatus for the

APPARATUS for the deaf. See Deaf, Apparatus for the

APPARENT death. See Death, Apparent

APPARITIONS, Photography of. See Photography of apparitions

APPEASEMENT. See International relations

APPEL, Regis
Luther: liturgical reformer. Cath World 206: 68-70 N '67

APPEL, S. H. and others
Brain polysomes: response to environmental stimulation. bibliog Science 157:836-8 Ag 18 '67

APPENDICITIS
Appendicitis still kills. Sci Digest 62:71 D '67

APPETIZERS
Appetizer nibble munch guide. R. Holmberg. il Bet Hom & Gard 46:54-5 Ja '68
Deluxe dips. il Bet Hom & Gard 45:107-8 Jl '67
Flavorful but not calorie-full; with recipes. il Sunset 138:174 F '67
Hors d'oeuvres can make a meal. V. T. Habeeb. il Am Home 70:100-1+ Je '67
It's antipasto; with recipe. il Sunset 138: 156 F '67
Melons and; meat with melon as appetizer. il Sunset 139:60-1 S '67

Nine to make merry. il McCalls 95:112-13+ N '67
Pick-a-dilly; with recipes. il Seventeen 26: 182-3+ S '67
Start-a-party hors d'oeuvres. Good H 165:156 D '67
Steak tartare: beef rarer than rare for the cocktail hour; with recipes. E. Alston. il Look 31:82-3 S 19 '67
Tasty dips. il Ebony 22:122+ S '67
See also
Canapés

APPLAUSE
Bravo! bravo! reasons why people applaud. Newsweek 69:70 Je 26 '67

APPLE, R. W. jr
New light on wrangle over civilian casualties; concerning report in New York times. U S News 62:11 Mr 6 '67

APPLE tree; musical comedy. See Musical comedies, revues, etc.—Criticisms, plots, etc.

APPLEBAUM, Max H.
Percent modulation nomogram. Electr World 77:31 Ja '67

APPLEGATE, Irvamae (Vincent)
President Applegate comments on: the proposed dues increase. NEA J 56:35-8 My '67

APPLES
Apple fruit-set: evidence for a specific role of seeds. F. G. Dennis, jr. bibliog il Science 156:71-3 Ap 7 '67
It's apple time. il Sunset 139:50-7 S '67
See also
Cookery—Fruit

APPLETON, Frank M.
Washington's Canadian corner. Travel 127: 50-1+ My '67

APPLETON, William S.
Nervous habits are assets. A. J. Snider. il Sci Digest 62:68 D '67

APPLETON, Wis.
Substations can be good neighbors. W. C. Rasmussen. il Am City 82:142 O '67

APPLETON-Century-Crofts, incorporated
Appleton-Century publishes U.S. funds-to-school guide. Pub W 191:35 Ja 2 '67; Correction. 191:230 Ja 23 '67

APPLEY, Lawrence A.
Management expert talks about managing a family; interview. por Changing T 21: 30-5 O '67

APPLIANCE warranties. See Warranty

APPLICATION to elysium; story. See Berger, T.

APPLICATIONS for admission to colleges. See Student selection

APPLICATIONS for positions
Aim for the job you want, and land it. Changing T 21:21-3 My '67
Job hunting by chain letter; letter (cont) P. L. Petrakis. Science 157:1119+ S 8 '67

APPLICATIONS technology satellites. See Artificial satellites

APPLIED art. See Design, Industrial

APPLIED mathematics. See Mathematics

APPLIED science. See Technology

APPORTIONMENT (election law)
Constitutional convention, the facts with interview with E. Dirksen. il U S News 62:62-6 Je 5 '67
Cooling reapportionment: rules confined to state level. il Time 89:54 Je 2 '67
Dirksen caper. New Repub 156:2 Ap 29 '67
Emergence of Conyers; stand on bill H.R. 208. Nation 205:6 Jl 3 '67
How Chief Justice Warren changed his mind; excerpt from address, October 20, 1948. E. Warren. U S News 62:66 Je 5 '67
One man, one vote. E. S. Cahn and J. C. Cahn. New Repub 156:11-12 Ap 8 '67
One-man, one-vote shakes up Maryland. N. K. Herzfeld. Commonweal 86:142-3 Ap 21 '67
Some lessons of reapportionment; Tennessee. B. Kovach. Reporter 37:26+ S 21 '67
States fight back; one man, one vote. Sr Schol 90:18-19 Ap 7 '67
Strong start; E. Dirksen urges Congress to modify the reapportionment rulings. il Time 89:25-6 My 19 '67

APPRAISAL. See Assessment; Valuation

APPRAISAL of books. See Book reviews

APPRAISAL of public schools. See Evaluation (education)

APPRECIATION of art. See Art—Appreciation

APPRECIATION of music. See Music—Appreciation

APPRECIATION of nature. See Nature

APPRENTICES
Cram course for Negro apprentices; Joint apprenticeship program of the Workers defense league and the A. Philip Randolph education fund. il Bsns W p88-90+ N 25 '67
Job program that works; New York city's Joint apprenticeship program. T. R. Brooks. il Reporter 37:28-30 N 16 '67
See also
Employees—Training
APPROPRIATIONS
See also subhead Appropriations and expenditures under names of countries and departments of government. e.g. United States—Air force—Appropriations and expenditures
APRICOTS
See also
Cookery—Fruit
APRIL trombone; story. See Boles, P. D.
APRONS
Apron for a young cook. il Sunset 139:94+ D '67
What does an apron mean? M. Holmes. il Todays Health 45:62-3 F '67
APTE, Stu
New world record tarpon on a fly. Outdoor Life 140:30-3+ Ag '67
APTECKER, George
Abstractions by Aptecker. M. Orovan. il U S Camera 30:56-7 Mr '67
APTHEKER, Bettina
Modest role; letter. New Repub 156:34-5 Je 10 '67
about
Sinister hand. New Repub 156:3-4 Ap 29 '67
APTHEKER, Herbert
Note on the history. Nation 205:375-6 O 16 '67
APTITUDE. See Ability
APTITUDE tests
Problems of high school students in relation to grade achievement; prediction from differential aptitude tests. J. C. Marshall. bibliog f il Sch & Soc 95:237-8 Ap 1 '67
S.A.T.s under fire. Time 91:66 Ja 5 '68
Test your mechanical aptitude. M. Schultz. il Pop Mech 128:78-81+ Ag '67

Anecdotes, facetiae, satire, etc.
How to get into college. P. Hamburger. New Yorker 43:36-7 My 20 '67
AQUA gliders. See Gliders (aeronautics)
AQUADROMES. See Airports, Floating
AQUANAUTS
I became an aquanaut, third class. D. C. Fales. il Pop Mech 127:110-11+ My '67
Now, the ocean; Sealab III. J. Ludwigson. il Sci N 92:40-1 Jl 8 '67
Undersea hardware still untrustworthy; Sealab 2 experiment. il Sci N 91:408-9 Ap 29 '67
Clothing
Litton drawing on space role to develop underwater suit. S. Montgomery. il Tech W 20 39-41 My 29 '67
AQUAPLANES
Build this underwater aquaplane. W. Morris il Pop Mech 128:142-3 Jl '67
AQUARIUMS
Labs: Osborn laboratories of marine sciences. Coney Island. New Yorker 43:48 N 4 '67
New York aquarium and Osborn laboratories of marine sciences. G. D. Ruggieri. il Science 158:675-6 N 3 '67
Undersea in Santa Barbara; Undersea Gardens. il Sunset 139:19 N '67

Finance
Impact of homo sapiens upon an alligator wishing well; Steinhart aquarium, San Francisco, Calif. E. S. Herald and others. il Parks & Rec 2:30+ S '67
AQUARIUMS, Salt water. See Aquariums
AQUATIC animals. See Marine fauna
AQUATIC plants
Plants for ponds and stream sides. W. O. Coon. il Horticulture 45:32-3+ Ag '67
Rear-guard ecology; man-made lakes create new problems in West and Central Africa. C. Weiss. il Sci N 91:595 Je 24 '67
So long, myriophyllum exalbescans. il Sci Digest 62:58-9 D '67
See also
Algae
Water snowflake
AQUATIC snails. See Snails

AQUATIC sports
See also
Boats and boating
Motor boat racing
Sailing
Surf riding
Water polo
AQUATOMETERS. See Magnetometers
AQUINAS, Thomas, Saint. See Thomas Aquinas, Saint
ARAB-Israeli war, 1948-1949. See Israeli-Arab war, 1948-1949
ARAB-Israeli war, 1967. See Israeli-Arab war, 1967
ARAB-Israeli war in literature. See War and literature
ARAB-Jewish relations. See Jewish-Arab relations
ARAB league. See Arab states
ARAB refugees. See Refugees, Arab
ARAB states
Arab unity thwarted by old enmities. il Life 62:87 Je 16 '67
Beginning to face defeat. Time 90:21 S 8 '67
Daring voices in Khartoum. America 117:261 S 16 '67
Divided in defeat; Arabs receive more Russian arms. il Time 89:23-4 Je 30 '67
Losers. il Newsweek 69:20-1 Je 26 '67
Running from defeat. il Time 89:26-7 Je 23 '67
See also
Finance—Arab states
Jewish-Arab relations
Armed forces
Picking up the pieces. Time 90:24-5 Jl 7 '67
Commerce
Backlash of defeat roils Arab world. il Bsns W p 112-14 Je 17 '67
Defenses
Arabs' new arms. il Time 90:28 O 20 '67
Economic conditions
Backlash of defeat roils Arab world. il Bsns W p 112-14 Je 17 '67
Oil: when is a ban not a ban? il Newsweek 69:57+ Je 26 '67
Foreign relations
Arab bloc realignments. G. Lenczowski. Cur Hist 53:346-51+ D '67
Arabs in disarray: who let who down? il Newsweek 70:36 Jl 3 '67
Arabs-Israelis muzzle to muzzle. il Life 62: 30-1 Je 2 '67
Bitter seeds; conference of foreign ministers of thirteen Arab states. il Newsweek 70:34+ Ag 14 '67
Blunt business; request that U.S. supply arms for moderate Arab states. il Time 90: 13 S 1 '67
Coping in Khartoum: meeting of Arab foreign ministers. il Time 90:21 Ag 11 '67
Distant peace. Time 90:38 S 15 '67
Israel's strategy for the future. il U S News 63:40-2 D 18 '67
Silence of the moderates. A. Hottinger. New Repub 156:7-8 Je 24 '67
Summitry, Arab style. il Newsweek 70:44 S 4 '67
U.N. condemns violations of Middle East cease-fire; statements, October 24, 25, 1967. A. J. Goldberg. Dept State Bul 57:690-2 N 20 '67
Israeli occupation, 1967-
Dialogue of the deaf; growing Arab terrorism in Israeli-occupied territory. il Time 90:34 O 6 '67
Greater Israel. il Newsweek 70:32 D 25 '67
Israel's tough stand on captured territories. A. Perlmutter. New Repub 158:12-14 Ja 13 '68
Return to Etzion; Israel's occupation problems. il Newsweek 70:38 O 9 '67
Unusual occupation. il Time 90:19 D 29 '67
Politics
Arab bloc realignments. G. Lenczowski. Cur Hist 53:346-51+ D '67
Arab world girds for second round against Israel. J. Law. il U S News 63:27-8 Jl 10 '67
Losers' summit, a peaceless truce. il Newsweek 70:29+ Jl 24 '67
Middle East crisis: a trial balance. L. Binder. il Bul Atomic Sci 23:2-7+ S '67
New Arab world. W. Rogers. il Look 31:31-3 O 17 '67
See also
Middle East crisis, 1967
ARABIA
Eastern Arabia. A. Melamid. bibliog il Focus 18:1-6 N '67

ARABIA—*Continued*

History

See also
European war, 1914-1918—Arabia
ARABIA, SOUTH (Federation)   See South
Arabia (Federation)
ARABIAN horses. See Horses
ARABIAN nights: musical comedy. See Musical
comedies, revues, etc.—Crticisms, plots, etc.
ARABS
Arabs, 1967. J. S. Badeau. Atlan 220:102-4+
D '67
Jerusalem: experiment in coexistence. S.
De Gramont. il N Y Times Mag p 14-18+
Jl 30 '67; Discussion. p 12+ Ag 27; 70+
S 10 '67
See also
Arab states
Jewish-Arab relations

History

Arabia decepta: a people self-deluded;
Time essay. Time 90:24-5 Jl 14 '67
ARABS in Israel
Arabs under Israeli rule. A. de Borchgrave.
il Newsweek 70:38+ S 11 '67
Bridge on the River Jordan. H. Swados. il
N Y Times Mag p32-3+ N 26 '67
Israel's strategy for the future. il U S News
63:40-2 D 18 '67
Moshe and the mukhtars: problems of Arab
refugees and those remaining. il Newsweek
70:37-8 Jl 3 '67
Sense amid the shambles; Palestinian Arabs
to begin negotiations with Israeli authori-
ties. il Time 90:32+ S 22 '67
Shaky bridge. Newsweek 70:45-6 O 2 '67
ARANGO, Gonzalo
Where pirates roamed. Américas 19:38-42 Ag
'67
ARARAT, MOUNT
Ancient Ararat. T. Özgüç. il Sci Am 216:38-
46 bibliog(p 150) Mr '67
ARBERG, Harold W. and Carleton, C. S.
Sonata for two clarinets. Am Ed 3:30-2 F '67
ARBITRAGE
Wall Street: caution, men at work. C. Morgel-
lo. il Newsweek 70:65 Jl 3 '67
ARBITRATION, Industrial
See also
Industrial relations
Labor courts
Lockouts

United States

Better way than strikes? an idea that is
growing: voluntary arbitration; with ex-
cerpts from address by R. C. Cooper. U S
News 63:109-12 N 27 '67
Can Congress settle the rails? impasse be-
tween carriers and the shopcraft unions.
Bsns W p92+ My 13 '67
Can you force labor peace? views of experts
in labor, management, and government. il
Bsns W p 128+ Ja 21 '67
Crucial copper talks move to Washington;
to end eight-week-old copper strike. Bsns
W p33 S 9 '67
How to avoid the picket lines: voluntary
arbitration. Bsns W p83 O 21 '67
See also
United States—Federal mediation and con-
ciliation service
ARBITRATION, International
Intermediaries, by O. R. Young. Review
Sat R 50:40 Ag 12 '67. L. Roberts
See also
Disarmament
Peace
ARBOUSSIER, Gabriel Marie d'
Birth of a new Africa. por UNESCO
Courier 20:4-8+ Je '67
ARBOVIRUSES. See Viruses
ARBUCKLE, Ernest C.
Dean's new desk. il por Time 90:99 O 27 '67
ARBUS, Diane
Telling it as it is. il Newsweek 69:110 Mr
20 '67
ARBUZOV, Aleksei Nikolaevich
Promise; tr. by A. Nicolaeff. Criticism
Commonweal 87:358-9 D 15 '67
Nation 205:605-6 D 4 '67
New Yorker 43:149 N 25 '67
Newsweek 70:105 N 27 '67
Sat R 50:24 D 2 '67
Vogue 151:62 Ja 1 '68
ARC, Electric. See Electric arc
ARC de triomphe. See Paris—Monuments,
statues, etc.
ARC welders. See Welders
ARC welding. See Electric welding

ARCADES
Arches and arcades form protective sun-
shades. il House & Gard 131:146-7 F '67
Cleveland arcade; reprint. M.-P. Schofield.
il Arch Forum 127:60-5 S '67
Sunny arcades and secret gardens in a ro-
mantic house in Texas. il House & Gard
132:242-7 N '67
ARCHAEOLOGY. See Archeology
ARCHEOLOGICAL research
Archeology and dating by hydration of
obsidian. J. W. Michels. bibliog il Science
158:211-14 O 13 '67
ARCHEOLOGICAL smuggling. See Smuggling
ARCHEOLOGISTS

Anecdotes, facetiae, satire, etc.
Don't believe all they dig up. B. Boothroyd.
Atlan 219:111-12 Je '67
ARCHEOLOGY
Archaeological notes. Sci N 93:64 Ja 20 '68
Atlantis and the searchers. il Newsweek 70:
52-5 Jl 31 '67
Cave life on the Palouse; salvage archeolo-
gists win a race with builders of Lower
Monumental Dam on the Snake River. G. H.
Grosso. il Natur Hist 76:38-43 F '67
Old stones: tale of human continuity. G.
Green. Holiday 42:8+ S '67
Salvage archeology in the Missouri River
basin. W. R. Wedel. bibliog il Science 156:
589-97 My 5 '67
See also
Cave drawings and paintings
Cave dwellers
Cities and towns. Ruined, extinct, etc.
Earthworks (archeology)
Excavations (archeology)
Indians of North America—Antiquities
Man, Prehistoric
Mummies
Numismatics, Ancient
Stone age
X rays—Archeological applications
also subhead Antiquities under names of
continents, countries. states, etc. e.g. Is-
rael—Antiquities
ARCHEOLOGY, Submarine
Diving for treasure in the pirate city; Port
Royal, Jamaica. H. H. Martin. il Sat Eve
Post 240:63-7 Ag 12 '67
Rescuing sunken history. W. Hartley and E.
Hartley. il Sci Digest 63:24-30 Ja '68
ARCHEOMAGNETISM. See Magnetism, Ter-
restrial
ARCHER, Joey
Repeat for the best negative fighter around.
M. Kram. il por Sports Illus 26:44-6 F 6 '67
ARCHERD, William Dale
Insulin shocker. il por Newsweek 70:25-6 D
25 '67
One coincidence too many. il por Time 90:18-19
Ag 11 '67
ARCHERY
Under-cover archery. G. H. Gillelan. il Out-
door Life 140:94+ D '67
See also
National archery association

Equipment
Archery hunting in 1925. S. Pope. Field & S
72:45+ Ja '68
Bowfishing gear. G. H. Gillelan. il Outdoor
Life 139:12+ My '67
See also
Bow and arrow

Safety devices and measures
Safety for archers. G. H. Gillelan. il Out-
door Life 139:34+ Mr '67
ARCHERY ranges. See Shooting ranges
ARCHES
Arches and arcades form protective sun-
shades. il House & Gard 131:146-7 F '67
L'ARCHITECTE et l'Empereur d'Assyrie;
drama. See Arrabal, F.
ARCHITECTS
Architects come into their own. il Newsweek
69:90-2 Mr 20 '67
Current architecture draws a new picture.
E. Goble. Arch Rec 141:9 Je '67
Factors shaping the future for architects.
G. A. Christie. il Arch Rec 141:83 Je '67
How much should the architect know about
air conditioning? il Arch Rec 142:132+ Ag
'67
Is there comprehension of architects and
their work? E. Goble. Arch Rec 141:9 F '67
John Hall, a busy man in Baltimore. R. C.
Smith. il Antiques 92:360-6 S '67
Museum of modern art discovers Harlem; ex-
hibition. The new city: architecture and
urban renewal. C. R. Hatch. il Arch Forum
126:38-47 Mr '67

ARCHITECTS—*Continued*
Our uncommon profession; address, May 16,
1967. C. Luckman. Arch Rec 141:93-4 Je;
93-4 Jl '67
Where do architects look for new clients?
E. Goble. Arch Rec 141:9 My '67
See also
Women as architects
also names of architects, e.g. O. Nie-
meyer

Fees
Action is taken on contracts, costs and fees.
Arch Rec 141:81-2 F '67
Congress moves slowly on the federal fee
structure. Arch Rec 142:81-2 S '67
World's biggest client needs professional brief-
ing. Arch Rec 141:81-2 Ap '67
ARCHITECTS collaborative, The
Challenging collaboration for TAC. M. F.
Schmertz. il Arch Rec 142:159-64 S '67
ARCHITECTURAL acoustics. See Acoustics,
Architectural
ARCHITECTURAL competitions. See Architec-
ture—Competitions
ARCHITECTURAL conferences
On the calendar. See issues of Architectural
record
ARCHITECTURAL criticism
Civic consciences; the urban reporter-critic.
Time 89:66+ Mr 31 '67
ARCHITECTURAL decoration. See Decoration
and ornament, Architectural; Ironwork
ARCHITECTURAL design. See Architecture
ARCHITECTURAL designs. See Architecture—
Designs and plans; Architecture, Domestic
—Designs and plans
ARCHITECTURAL drawing
Architects and drawings; will there be a
change? E. Goble. Arch Rec 142:9 O '67
ARCHITECTURAL drawing instruments
Today's new tools for tomorrow's practice;
excerpts from address. C. H. Wheeler, jr. il
Arch Rec 142:93-4 D '67
ARCHITECTURAL engineering. See Structural
engineering
ARCHITECTURAL firms
Our uncommon profession; address, May 16,
1967. C. Luckman. Arch Rec 141:93-4 Je;
93-4 Jl '67
Practice. See issues of Architectural record
Practice; office management. H. A. Golemon.
il Arch Rec 141:93-4 F; 93-4 Mr '67
Seven common errors in architectural office
management. D. Hurst. Arch Rec 141:93-4
Ap '67
See also
Architects collaborative
also names of architectural firms, e.g.
Roth, Emery, and sons
ARCHITECTURAL plans. See Architecture,
Domestic—Designs and plans
ARCHITECTURAL space. See Space (archi-
tecture)
ARCHITECTURE
Architectural business. See issues of Archi-
tectural record
Buildings in the news. See issues of Architec-
tural record
Focus; monthly review of notable buildings.
See issues of Architectural forum
Forum; monthly review of events and ideas.
See issues of Architectural forum
Know your architecture. N. A. Hecht. il
Am Home 70:24 Mr '67
Modern antiques; 20th century landmarks. C.
Robinson. il Arch Forum 126:74-82 Je '67
Modern antiques; 20th century landmarks.
P. Blake. il Arch Forum 126:80-7 My '67
Selective eye of Marcel Breuer. P. Blake. il
House B 109:152-9+ Mr '67
Structure & design. See issues of Fortune
See also
Airport buildings
Church architecture
City planning
College architecture
Courthouses
Department stores
Domes
Factories
Foundations
Functionalism
Glass construction
Hotels, taverns, etc.
Industrial buildings
Loft buildings
Marine structures
Orientation (architecture)
Pavilions
Remodeling (architecture)
School buildings
Stone construction
Subway stations
Swimming pools

Theater buildings
Theological schools
    also subhead Architecture under vari-
    ous subjects. e.g. Museums—Architecture;
    also under names of cities, e.g. Chicago—
    Architecture

Anecdotes, facetiae, satire, etc.
Summer architecture. W. McQuade. il Arch
Forum 126:86 Je '67 (to be cont)

Appreciation
Two great architects hit by public taste. E.
Goble. Arch Rec 141:9 Mr '67

Bibliography
Books. See issues of Architectural forum
Last word on architecture. W. Andrews.
Sat R 50:40-2 Mr 11 '67
Required reading. See issues of Architectural
record
View the local architectural marvels. il Chang-
ing T 21:20-1 Je '67

Competitions
A.I.A. honors twenty buildings in national
awards program. il Arch Rec 141:50-1+
Je '67
A.I.A.-Sunset Western home awards. il Sunset 139:74-89 O '67
Bold bastion; Boston's new city hall. il Time
90:36 D 29 '67
Notes and comment; competition for the design of an educational and recreational
center incorporating dual purpose fallout
shelter space. New Yorker 43:47-8 O 14 '67
Philadelphia firm wins competition for Bir-
ingham-Jefferson civic center. il Arch Rec
142:40-1 Jl '67
Prize folly; house competition of the
American institute of architects. B. Plumb.
il N Y Times Mag p54-5 Ja 22 '67

Composition, proportion, etc.
Architect's specialty; scale of things to come.
E. Goble. Arch Rec 142:9 N '67

Conservation and restoration
Boscobel; Garrison-on Hudson, New York. C.
Pintchman. il Horticulture 45:36-7+ D '67
Bringing back the heritage; restoration of
town houses in Charleston and Savannah.
il Time 90:49 S 1 '67
Building the past. il Time 91:15 Ja 19 '68
Bureau of public roads, devastator. R. Kirk.
Nat R 19:202 F 21 '67
By the past inspired; town house in Milan.
B. Plumb. il N Y Times Mag p60-1 Ag 27
'67
Children must understand the past to create
a better future. G. E. Howard. Parents
Mag 42:38+ Mr '67
Deserted village; Allaire, part of Allaire
state park. H. W. Hoffman. il Sch Arts
66:20-2 Mr '67
Is Venice sinking? excerpt from Antiquities
in peril. T. L. Christie. il Sat R 50:40+
Mr 25 '67
Old Salem. A. Stagg. il House & Gard 131:20+
Je '67
Preservation; Canada 1967. B. S. Delaney. il
Antiques 92:100-5 Jl '67
Preservation; the necessary art. il Fortune
75:159-62 Mr '67
Preserve it, if it's great architecture. E.
Goble. Arch Rec 141:9 Ja '67
Train station and the community; conversion
to community center, Altamont, N.Y. E.
Cowley. il Sch Arts 66:35-8 My '67
Trustees' garden village; Savannah, Ga. E.
M. Adler. il Antiques 91:331 Mr '67

Designs and plans
Architects come into their own. il Newsweek
69:90-2 Mr 20 '67
Architecture strongly manipulated in space
and scale; Christian science organization
building, Urbana, Ill. il Arch Rec 141:137-
42 F '67
Eggs are coming; egg-shaped buildings. il
Time 89:53 Je 16 '67
For concerts, dance and drama; flexible de-
sign; ed. by M. F. Schmertz. il Arch Rec
141:115-30 F '67
Rudolph style; unpredictable. D. Jacobs. il
N Y Times Mag p46-7+ Mr 26 '67

Details
See also
Facades

Exhibitions
Architecture; The Zähringer new towns,
sponsored by Swiss federal institute of
technology. E. Galantay. Nation 204:283-5
F 27 '67

ARCHITECTURE—Exhibitions—*Continued*
INTERAMA exposition hailed as full-scale experiment in urban design; permanent exposition of the western hemisphere nations between Miami and Miami Beach. il Arch Rec 141:40-3 Mr '67
Museum of modern art discovers Harlem; exhibition, The new city: architecture and urban renewal. C. R. Hatch. il Arch Forum 126:38-47 Mr '67
See also
Montreal—Worlds fair, 1967—Architecture

Modular design

See Modular coordination (architecture)

Philosophy

[Address at centennial convention of the AIA, May 16, 1957] H. R. Luce. Arch Forum 126:38-9 Je '67
Architects analyze new means of influence. il Arch Rec 141:35-6+ Je '67
Architecture in the electronic age; interview, ed. by J. Barnett. M. McLuhan. Arch Rec 141:151-2 Mr '67
Art of human use. N. Silver. Nation 204:629-31 My 15 '67
Dreams of tomorrow. R. B. Riley. il Arch Forum 126:66-7+ Ap '67
For once I'll give in and indulge in criticism. E. Goble. il Arch Rec 142:9 Ag '67
Frank Lloyd Wright, by N. K. Smith. Review Nation 204:121-2 Ja 23 '67. S. Paul
World around us: toward an architecture of joy and human sensibility. B. Thompson. il Arch Rec 142:153-8 S '67

Terminology

Is there comprehension of architects and their work? E. Goble. Arch Rec 141:9 F '67

Africa

See also
Architecture, African

Brazil

Two from the first team; new public buildings by O. Niemeyer and A. E. Reidy. il Time 90:90-3 D 8 '67

California

Making of a city. M. Roberts. il Sat R 50: 72-4 S 23 '67

Canada

Canada's new turn in architecture. E. Kaufmann, jr. il Harper 234:62-8 My '67
Mammoth building program marks observance of Canadian centennial. il Arch Rec 141:42-3 F '67

France

See also
Architecture, Domestic—France

Germany

See also
Stuttgart, Germany—Architecture

Ireland

Magic box; Trinity college library, Dublin. J. Donat. il Arch Forum 127:78-85 O '67

Japan

Design governor; new buildings at Takamatsu. il Time 89:94-5 My 19 '67

Mexico

Useless towers of Mexico; Satellite city. il Fortune 75:166 F '67

Russia

Building the Soviet society; excerpts from The Soviet Union, the fifty years. A. L. Huxtable. il Arch Forum 127:34-41 N '67
New forms & materials. il UNESCO Courier 20:26-7 N '67

Scotland

Austere and monumental church in Scotland; East Kilbride. il Arch Rec 141:133-6 Ja '67

South Carolina

Strong marble verticals for a state office building. il Arch Rec 141:178-9 Je '67

Switzerland

Centre Le Corbusier; Zurich. U. Roth. il Arch Forum 127:82-7 S '67

United States

Buildings in the news. See issues of Architectural record
Civic architecture. il Arch Rec 142:107-30 D '67

U.S. architecture: a progress report. P. Herrera. il Fortune 76:123-6 S 1 '67
See also
American institute of architects
Architecture, American
also subhead Architecture under names of cities, e.g. New York (city)—Architecture

ARCHITECTURE, African

African architecture old and new. il UNESCO Courier 20:14-16 Je '67

ARCHITECTURE, American

Five buildings by Alden B. Dow; interview. A. B. Dow. il Arch Rec 142:165-76 S '67
Greek revival. N. A. Hecht. il Am Home 70: 24 Mr '67
Recent work of Evans Woollen; with foreword by E. Woollen. il Arch Rec 141:139-50 My '67

ARCHITECTURE, Colonial

Atlanta women design their dream home. il Parents Mag 42:83-5+ My '67
Boston women design their dream home; a Garrison colonial house. il Parents Mag 42:80-3+ Je '67
See also
Architecture, Georgian

ARCHITECTURE, Domestic

Their second Breuer. B. Plumb. il N Y Times Mag p62-3 F 12 '67
Two rebels with a lovely cause; Johnston's planless house, Moonhole on Bequia island. C. Phinizy. il Sports Illus 26:42-6 F 27 '67
Your next house; portfolio. J. De Long. House B 109:132-7 S '67
See also
Apartment houses
Apartments
Architecture, Modern
Bathrooms
Beach architecture
Buildings, Round
Cabins
Concrete houses
Courtyards
Houses
Houses, Prefabricated
Houses, Remodeled
Parsonages and rectories
Row houses
Skylights
Summer homes

Conservation and restoration

See Architecture—Conservation and restoration

Designs and plans

Architects' own houses. il Arch Rec 142:143-5 N '67
Award winning home; built by Scholz homes, inc. il Parents Mag 42:74-9 S '67
Built with minimum strain on the budget. il Sunset 138:134 F '67
Dollar-stretching blueprint house il Am Home 70:68-9 Ja '67
Family houses specially designed for Better homes and gardens. N. Seney. il Bet Hom & Gard 46:30-5 Ja '68
Home improvement 1967! il Bet Hom & Gard 45:55-63 F '67
H&G's Hallmark house for 1967; home of the Marshall Steves; with report by J. Norman. il House & Gard 131:125-39+ Ap '67
House beautiful presents five great-value houses; architect-designed homes under $30,000. J. De Long. il House B 109:111-21 F '67
House in my head; excerpts. D. Rodgers. il House B 109:124-30 S; 208-15+ O; 70+ N '67
House planned for cars as well as people. il Arch Rec 141:143-6 F '67
Ideas in houses (cont) il Life 62:84-7+ Mr 24; 100-3+ My 5; 80-3+ Je 30; 63:108-11+ S 8; 98-100+ O 6; 116-17+ N 24 '67
Low-cost land inspires two unique houses. il Am Home 70:64-7 Ja '67
New shapes to live in. il House & Gard 131: 142-7 F '67
Record houses of 1967. Arch Rec 141:41-114 mid-My '67
This is a very adaptable house plan. N. Seney. il Bet Hom & Gard 45:138+ Ap '67
Today's house breaks out of the box. il House & Gard 133:94-105 Ja '68
Today's well-spent building dollar. il House B 109:100-10+ F '67
Updating the big old house. il Am Home 70: 92-5 My '67
Well-built, well-kept house. J. H. Ingersoll. il House B 109:38+ N; 12 D '67

Exhibitions

See also
Montreal—Worlds fair, 1967—Architecture

ARCHITECTURE, Domestic—*Continued*

Alaska

Big, bold as all Alaska; Willis Harpel's house in Anchorage; with report by J. Fincher. il Life 63:98-100+ O 6 '67

Arizona

Gonzales house, Paradise Valley, Arizona. il Arch Rec 141:94-7 mid-My '67

In the desert, a hacienda for 1967; with account by J. Bonfante. il Life 62:84-7+ F 10 '67

British Columbia

Magnificent timber pavilion. J. De Long. il House B 109:236-41 O '67

California

Alcorn obtains low cost by unconventional plan. il Arch Rec 142:148-9 N '67

Box house unboxed. il House & Gard 131: 156-9 Mr '67

California house with a cross-country future. il Good H 165:114-25+ N '67

Campbell solves tight site and budget problems with a compact, three-level, expansible home; house in Sausalito. il Arch Rec 142: 143-5 N '67

Fantasy house down to earth. J. De Long. il House B 109:118-19 Je '67

In an old garage-laundry an architect finds space for his family to grow. il House B 109:126-31 Je '67

In California's Marin hills two handsome award winners. il Sunset 139:84-9 O '67

In his former studio an artist creates an art-filled second home. il House B 109:132-5 Je '67

Karas house, Monterey, California. il Arch Rec 141:104-7 mid-My '67

Killingsworth gains spaciousness with garden rooms. il Arch Rec 142:152-4 N '67

Los Angeles women design their dream home. il Parents Mag 42:88-90+ Mr '67

Open house with cloistered privacy. J. De Long. il House B 109:274-9 N '67

Privacy, California style. il Ladies Home J 84:82-5 Jl '67

Private residence, Sherman Oaks, California. il Arch Rec 141:86-7 mid-My '67

Sculptured house for a collecting family. il House B 109:152-9 Ap '67

Seaside fortress; with report by R. Wernick. il Life 62:100-3+ My 5 '67

Sierra chalet. J. De Long. il House B 109: 146-9 D '67

Small house that's tall indoors. il Sunset 138: 86-7 Ap '67

There is always room at the top. il House & Gard 131:148-55 Mr '67

This big house is crowded with ideas; pavilion house. il Sunset 139:88-92 N '67

White elegance in a firehouse. il House & Gard 131:112-17 Je '67

Woo house, Los Angeles. il Arch Rec 141:92-3 mid-My '67

Young place, full of sun. F. Heard. il House B 109:82-7 Jl '67

Colorado

Bold design reflects the Rockies; Denver; designed by Charles Haertling. J De Long. il House B 109:116-17 F '67

Garden for all seasons; open design house in Boulder. B. Plumb. il N Y Times Mag p52-3 Je 18 '67

Home is a shelter; Colorado Rockies at Carbondale. B. Plumb. il N Y Times Mag p 106-7 Mr 5 '67

Small wood-and-stone house relates well to a mountain site. il Arch Rec 141:181-4 Ap '67

Wagener house, Boulder, Colorado. il Arch Rec 141:104-7 mid-My '67

Connecticut

Art and an open kitchen. il House & Gard 131:132-3 My '67

Chateau the sounds of music built: R. Rodgers' house. J. Peter. il Look 31:44-7 O 31 '67

Colonial charm with plans you can buy. il Am Home 71:62-3 Ja '68

Freidin uses trim simplicity to make the most of a modest budget. il Arch Rec 142: 150-1 N '67

Glass house that's fine in winter too. A. C. Borg. il Am Home 70:60-3 D '67

How to delight your guests; visiting the Talbots of Washington, Conn. A. Stagg. il House & Gard 132:65-71 Jl '67

Illusion of doubled space. il House & Gard 131:134-5 My '67

More than modern, hip baroque; Charles W. Moore's remodeled house in New Haven. B. Plumb. il N Y Times Mag p79-81 F 26 '67

New slant on space. il Am Home 70:54-7 S '67

Private residence Connecticut. il Arch Rec 141:42-7 mid-My '67

River house revisited. il Am Home 70:82-3 Je '67

Serene facade conceals pools, fountains and spatial excitement. il Arch Rec 142:185-8 S '67

Stillman house, Litchfield, Connecticut. il Arch Rec 141:54-7 mid-My '67

Denmark

Artist's garden home. M. Duckett. il House B 110:98-9+ Ja '68

Cool and simple; Poul Kjaerholm's house. B. Plumb. il N Y Times Mag p 104-5 Ap 16 '67

Spare and individual; a publisher's manor outside of Copenhagen. il House B 110:92-3 Ja '68

England

Be it ever so stately...manor house, called Lypiatt Park. B. Plumb. il N Y Times Mag p36-7 Jl 16 '67

Finland

Modern great-house; lakeside estate near Helsinki. il House B 110:112-15 Ja '68

Timeless masterwork; Maire Gullichsen's Villa Mairea; reprint. F. Gutheim. il House B 110:82-7 Ja '68

Vacation house in the woods; year-round hideaway in Finland. il House B 110:102-3 Ja '68

Florida

Compact contemporary with exceptional style. J. Reedy. il Bet Hom & Gard 45:32+ Jl '67

Cube-shaped house with expanded spaces. il Arch Rec 142:135-8 D '67

New use of an ageless form: honeycomb house. il House & Gard 132:118-21+ Ag '67

Paradise found on a 50-foot plot. J. DeLong. il House B 109:78-81 Jl '67

Seclusion in the sun. J. H. Ingersoll. il House B 109:38+ N '67

France

Bringing the past to new life; remodeling of an ancient stone house in France's Dordogne valley. il House B 109:160-3 Je '67

Mill on the Marne. B. Plumb. il N Y Times Mag p56-7 F 5 '67

Overlooking the Mediterranean, a house of six pavilions. il House & Gard 132:114-17 Ag '67

Riviera house on a hilltop. il Arch Rec 141: 148-50 Je '67

Georgia

Atlanta women design their dream house. il Parents Mag 42:83-5+ My '67

Magic of levels. il Am Home 70:62-3 S '67

Greece, Modern

Island retreat from Athens; commuting by hydrofoil. il House B 109:100-1 Ja '67

Illinois

Chicago mothers design their dream home. il Parents Mag 42:53-6+ F '67

Karlin house, Chicago; multi-level town-house. il Arch Rec 141:76-7 mid-My '67

New geometry in stone and glass. il House B 109:178-82 Ap '67

Ireland

See also
Architecture, Georgian

Italy

Escape to the Mediterranean; a three-room grotto. il House B 109:102-5 Ja '67

Rococo getaway for Donna Marella Agnelli, in Italy. V. Lawford. il Vogue 150:218-25 O 1 '67

Vacation villa; house on Lake Como. B. Plumb. il N Y Times Mag p70-1 Je 11 '67

Jamaica

Jamaican pavilion. il House B 109:116-19 Ja '67

Kansas

One-third of the floor space is core; farm home. R. Martens. il Farm J 91:67-71+ O '67

Long Island, N.Y.

Antique treasure, modern workings; Mulford-Baker house, East Hampton, L.I. il House B 109:170-7 Ap '67

Escape to the Atlantic shore; six faces to the sun. J. L. Hendrix. il House B 109:94-9 Ja '67

ARCHITECTURE, Domestic—Long Island, N.Y.—*Continued*
Flowering of a modern manoir; home of Mrs F. Carpenter. J. L. Hendrix. il House B 109:130-7+ My '67
Living in a work of art; G. Bunshaft's weekend home. J. Peter. il Look 32:64-6 Ja 9 '68
Luxe without fuss. il House & Gard 131:98-101 Je '67
Making of a man or house; conversion of a silo and a cattle barn at Southampton. F. Heard. il House B 109:138-45 D '67
Not far out on Long Island; Woodmere. il Arch Forum 126:76-9 Ap '67
Palace on the beach; house of the John O'Toole's; with report by S. Mahoney. il Life 62:80-3+ Je 30 '67
Today's well-spent building dollar; vacation house designed by Harry Bates. il House B 109:100-3+ F '67

Maine

Harby house, York Harbor, Maine. il Arch Rec 141:72-5 mid-My '67

Maryland

Inventive shapes of present and future. M. Gough. il House B 109:158-61 S '67

Massachusetts

Be authentic with traditional; 18th-century Massachusetts farmhouse. il Am Home 70:84-7 O '67
Boston women design their dream home; a Garrison colonial house. il Parents Mag 42:80-3+ Je '67
Huygens creates a strong modern house with a traditional form. il Arch Rec 142:146-7 N '67
Pleasures of detail in a thoughtfully planned house. il House & Gard 131:120-7+ F '67
Stubbins house, Cambridge, Massachusetts. il Arch Rec 141:88-91 mid-My '67
Welch house, Harvard, Massachusetts. il Arch Rec 141:100-3 mid-My '67

Michigan

Detroit women design their dream home. R. Charles. il Parents Mag 42:68-70+ Jl '67
Interlocking beam system makes possible greater roof spans and clerestories. A. B. Dow. il Arch Rec 142:174-6 S '67
Prefabricated system allows variety in house design. A. B. Dow. il Arch Rec 142:170-1 S '67

Minnesota

Munsons designed their farm home for efficiency. J. LemMon. il Suc Farm 65:74-7 S '67

Missouri

Obata house, St Louis. il Arch Rec 141:48-51 mid-My '67
This split-entry house is different. N. B. Seney. il Bet Hom & Gard 45:64-7 Mr '67

Nevada

Tahoe's Incline leans on total sport; Incline Village launched on impetus of sport. P. Knight. il Sports Illus 27:42-6 S 25 '67

New Jersey

Development house, Morris Township, New Jersey. il Arch Rec 141:98-9 mid-My '67
For the new horizon: a sculptured profile. E. Sverbeyeff. il House B 109:140-5 S '67
Ten lessons from a superb house. A. C. Borg. il Am Home 70:82-7 Mr '67

New York (state)

Case house, Van Hornesville, New York. il Arch Rec 141:78-81 mid-My '67
House and site integrated by sensitive design, meticulous detailing. il Arch Rec 142:105-8 Ag '67
Island residence, Long Island Sound, New York. il Arch Rec 141:66-71 mid-My '67
Open-faced pavilion against a hillside; Bedford Village; designed by Frank Edward Dushin. J. De Long. il House B 109:120-1 F '67
Private residence, Rye, New York. il Arch Rec 141:62-5 mid-My '67
Riverside viewpoint; house in Rockland County overlooking the Hudson. B. Plumb. il N Y Times Mag p84-5 O 29 '67
Rouse house, Clayton, New York. il Arch Rec 141:108-11 mid-My '67
See also
Architecture, Domestic—Long Island, N.Y.

Ohio

Tall house accentuates the horizontal; Cuyahoga Falls; Gerald Rembowski's design. J. De Long. il House B 109:112-13 F '67

Up-to-date colonial; home of the Thomas Fryes in Columbus; with report by G. Moore. il Life 63:116-17+ N 24 '67

Oregon

Dimensional Mondrian; Portland; designed by William Hawkins. il House B 109:118-19 F '67
Little house with a big view; Portland; designed by Saul Zaik. J. De Long. il House B 109:114-15 F '67
Priestley house, Lake Oswego, Oregon. il Arch Rec 141:52-3 mid-My '67
Up and up, from lake level to lookouts above. il Sunset 138:102-3 My '67

Pennsylvania

Eighty-year house decorated for today. V. D. Hahn. il Am Home 70:88-9 My '67

Sardinia

Vacation fortress on Sardinia. il Arch Forum 126:64-5 Je '67

Spain

Executive's castle in Spain; house of Geoffrey Parsons. il Fortune 75:167-9 Ap '67

Sweden

In suburban Stockholm; cosmopolitan apartment in Stockholm. il House B 110:95-7 Ja '68
Water-lily house; a prefabricated contemporary. il House B 110:78-81 Ja '68

Texas

Brick-walled oasis, cool, green heart. il House B 109:165-9 Ap '67
Escape to the Texas prairie; open-and-shut shelter. J. DeLong. il House B 109:80-1+ Ja '67
H&G's Hallmark house for 1967; home of the Marshall Steves; with report by J. Norman. il House & Gard 131:125-39+ Ap '67
House full of light. il House & Gard 132:226-31 O '67
In Texas a house and lot become a private estate. il House B 109:146-9 Je '67
Sunny arcades and secret gardens in a romantic house in Texas. il House & Gard 132:242-7 N '67

Tunisia

Oasis in Tunisia. il House B 109:113-15 Ja '67

United States

Habitat, U.S.A; with introd. by S. T. Lee. il House B 109:151-82 Ap '67
Homes for all season. il Holiday 42:62-5 O '67
This house was built for peace and quiet. N. Seney. il Bet Hom & Gard 45:62-3 S '67
Today's house breaks out of the box. House & Gard 133:94-105 Ja '68
Togetherness to a point; prize winning house designed by architect George Nemeny. il N Y Times Mag p 112-13 My 14 '67
Very smart small house. J. A. Hufnagel. il Bet Hom & Gard 45:124 O '67
Very special two-story house. N. B. Seney. il Bet Hom & Gard 45:86-9 N '67

Vermont

Escape to the snows of Vermont; the ivory tower. E. Sverbeyeff. il House B 109:82-7 Ja '67
Ski house in the sun. B. Plumb. il N Y Times Mag p 110-12 N 12 '67
See also
Cabins

Virginia

Farmhouse for a lively family. il House & Gard 132:182-7 S '67
Future-minded hillside house. il House B 109:88-91 Jl '67
Townhouses, Reston, Virginia. il Arch Rec 141:58-61 mid-My '67

Washington, D.C.

House on the Hill. B. Plumb. il N Y Times Mag p68-9 Je 4 '67
Newmyer house, Washington, D.C. il Arch Rec 141:82-5 mid-My '67
Two houses become one. il Am Home 70:84-7 My '67

Washington (state)

Architectural sleight-of-hand, this really is a two-story house. il Sunset 139:64-5 S '67
Here is a lesson in low cost building; they got their beautiful house for $11 per foot. il Sunset 138:82-3 Mr '67
House stands free of the beach, facing into the weather. il Sunset 138:106-8 Ap '67
Major face-lift. il Am Home 70:80-1 My '67

ARCHITECTURE, Domestic—Washington
(state)—*Continued*
Timber treehouse, oriental serenity. J. De
Long. il House B 109:160-4 Ap '67
Turned back to front. A. C. Borg. il Am Home
70:78-9 My '67
You can't quite tell where the house stops
and the garden begins. il Sunset 139:126-8
Jl '67

Western states
See also
Western home awards
ARCHITECTURE, Ecclesiastical. See Church
architecture
ARCHITECTURE, English
See also
Architecture, Georgian
ARCHITECTURE, Fantastic
Cloud busters in Houston; designs by three
18th century French architects. il Time 90:
61+ N 3 '67
ARCHITECTURE, French
Some new directions in French architecture.
L. A. Weismehl. il Arch Rec 142:161-8 O '67
ARCHITECTURE, Georgian
Georgian: D. Guinness of Irish Georgian so-
ciety. New Yorker 43:41-2 O 7 '67
ARCHITECTURE, German
Frei Otto designs 1,864 million cubic feet of
air; German pavilion at Expo 67. il Arch
Forum 126:58-65 Ap '67
ARCHITECTURE, Greek
City as an act of will; excerpts from Design
of cities. E. N. Bacon. il Arch Rec 141:
114-23 Ja '67
ARCHITECTURE, Hillside. See Hillside ar-
chitecture
ARCHITECTURE, Hotel. See Hotels, taverns,
etc.
ARCHITECTURE, Japanese
Miniature megastructure; Yamanashi com-
munications center. V. C. Mahler. il Arch
Forum 127:35-43 S '67
Palace on the beach; house of the John
O'Toole's on Long Island; with report by
S. Mahoney. il Life 62:80-3+ Je 30 '67
ARCHITECTURE, Landscape. See Landscape
gardening
ARCHITECTURE, Modern
Architecture: a twentieth-century flop. P.
Johnson. Look 32:30 Ja 9 '68
Breuer: the last modern architect. C. Jones.
il Horizon 9:32-41 Sum '67
Current architecture and its communication.
E. Goble. Arch Rec 141:9 Ap '67
Current architecture draws a new picture.
E. Goble. Arch Rec 141:9 Je '67
Municipal building that breaks with tradition;
Glendale, Calif. il Am City 82:92-3 Jl '67
Not far out on Long Island; Woodmere. il
Arch Forum 126:76-9 Ap '67
ARCHITECTURE, School. See School buildings
ARCHITECTURE, Spanish American (United
States)
H&G's Hallmark house for 1967; home of the
Marshall Steves; with report by J. Nor-
man il House & Gard 131:125-39+ Ap '67
ARCHITECTURE, Tunisian
Takrouna. M. H. Goldfinger. il Arch Forum
127:98-106 Jl '67
ARCHITECTURE and climate
Wind, sun, rain and the exterior wall. il
Arch Rec 142:205-16 S '67
ARCHITECTURE and state. See Art and gov-
ernment
ARCHITECTURE in art
Portfolio of drawings of old mills. N. Kent.
il Am Artist 31:30-5+ S '67
ARCHIVES
Sound archive for piano rolls: International
piano library. P. G. Davis. Hi Fi 17:22 Ap
'67
See also
Oral history
United States
Public authorities' records not to be open
in N.Y. Pub W 192:37 O 9 '67
See also
Presidential libraries
ARCHOSAURIA. See Reptiles, Fossil
ARCTANDER, Erik H.
Go-go engines that power motorcycles. Pop
Sci 191:102-7 Ag '67
ARCTIC char fishing. See Char fishing
ARCTIC REGIONS
See also
Alaska
Antarctic Regions
Birds—Arctic Regions
Fishing—Arctic Regions
Greenland
Ice—Polar Regions
Yukon

Description and travel
Land of perpetual sunshine. H. French. Holi-
day 41:6 Je '67
Maps
World: polar projection. Sr Schol 91:28 O 5
'67
ARCTIC research. See Polar research
ARDATOVSKY, Vadim
Challenge of peace. UNESCO Courier 20:22-7
Ag '67
ARDEATINE caves massacre. See World war,
1939-1945—Atrocities
ARDEN, John
Waters of Babylon. Criticism
Nation 204:574 My 1 '67
ARDENNE, Manfred von
Cancer is bad for you. J. Medelman. Esquire
68:111+ N '67
ARDERY, Philip, Jr
Focus on Kentucky. Nat R 19:1318 N 28 '67
ARDOIN, John
Set to go. Opera N 31:6-7 Mr 18 '67
Time for decision. Hi Fi 17:MA18 F '67
AREA studies
Foreign area research guidelines adopted;
announcement, December 19, 1967. Dept
State Bul 58:55-9 Ja 8 '68
See also
Canadian studies
Southeast Asian studies
AREES, Edward A. and Mayer, Jean
Anatomical connections between medial and
lateral regions of the hypothalamus con-
cerned with food intake. bibliog Science
157:1574-5 S 29 '67
ARELLANO, Jorge Eduardo
Light Nicaraguan poets. Américas 19:33-9
O '67
ARENA stage. See Washington, D.C.—Theater
ARENAS, Sports. See Stadiums
ARENDT, Hannah
Reflections. New Yorker 43:49-52+ F 25 '67
about
Eichmann trial. L. Poliakov. Commentary
43:86-8+ Ja '67
ARENDTSVILLE, Pa.
New tank goes in an old one; reservoir. R. M.
Best. il Am City 82:125-6 O '67
ARFFA, Marvin S. See Snelbecker, G. E. jt.
auth.
ARGENTINA
See also
Censorship—Argentina
Córdoba (city)
Education and state in Argentina
Fishing—Argentina
Legislation—Argentina
Tierra del Fuego
Trade unions—Argentina
Economic conditions
Revolution in Argentina? A. Cohen. bibliog f
Cur Hist 53:283-90 N '67
Economic policy
Argentina: the politics of late industrializa-
tion. E. Kenworthy. For Affairs 45:463-76
Ap '67
Economic relations
U.S.-Argentine trade committee holds second
meeting; text of joint communique, July 5,
1967. Dept State Bul 57:146-7 Jl 31 '67
Politics and government
Argentina: the politics of late industrializa-
tion. E. Kenworthy. For Affairs 45:463-76
Ap '67
Revolution in Argentina? A. Cohen. bibliog f
Cur Hist 53:283-90 N '67
See also
Legislation—Argentina
ARGENTINE literature
See also
Borges, J. L.
ARGERICH, Martha
Scaling the mountain. il por Newsweek 70:
91-2 S 18 '67
ARGOW, Keith A.
Our forestry schools. Am For 73:28-9 Ap '67
ARGUE, Gary R. See Owens, B. B. jt. auth.
ARGUMENT
See also
Controversy

ARGUS, M. K.
Thief. Sat R 50:4 Ja 28 '67
ARGUS research corporation
Independent advice lures brokers. il Bsns W
p 101-2+ F 11 '67
ARGYRIS, Chris
We must make work worthwhile. Life 62:
56+ My 5 '67
ARIABELLA; story. See Steers, N. A.
ARIAS, Abelardo
Reaction & reform in Colombia. il por Time
89:60 Mr 3 '67
ARIAS DE SAAVEDRA, Hernando. See Hernandarias
ARID regions
Is man changing the climate of earth? adaptation of address. R. A. Bryson. il Sat R
50:52-5 Ap 1 '67
Plants for dry places.   G. W. Kelly. il
Horticulture 45:32-3 Jl '67
See also
Irrigation
ARISAEMA triphyllum. See Jack-in-the-pulpits
ARISTOCRACY
See also
Great Britain—Nobility
Upper classes
ARISTOTLE
Belief and Mr Dewart. M. Novak. Commonweal 85:485-8 F 3 '67; Discussion. 85:634+;
86:103 Mr 10, Ap 7 '67
Truth of belief. E. MacKinnon. America 116:
553-6 Ap 15 '67
ARITHMETIC
High-speed math short cuts. A. P. Armagnac.
il Pop Sci 190:119-26 Mr '67
See also
Division
ARITHMETIC, Mental
CERN's human computer: W. Klein. D. A.
Ehrlich. il Sci N 93:72-3 Ja 20 '67
ARIZONA
See also
Architecture, Domestic—Arizona
Booksellers and bookselling—Arizona
Canyon de Chelly National Monument
Gardens—Arizona
Glen Canyon
Grand Canyon
Hunting—Arizona
Petrified Forest National Park
Roads—Arizona

Antiquities
See Indians of North America—Antiquities
—Arizona

Description and travel
Arizona's Turquoise triangle. K. McClure. il
Travel 128:41-3+ O '67

Historic houses, etc.
Navajos have traded here for ninety-one
years; Hubbell trading post national historic site. il Sunset 139:26 O '67

Legislature
Gung-ho legislators. Time 89:25 Mr 10 '67
ARIZONA (battleship) See Warships—United
States
ARIZONA Desert botanical garden. See Botanical gardens
ARJOMAND, Lily Jahanara
Libraries for the children of Iran. Wilson Lib
Bul 41:1055-61 Je '67
ARKANI-HAMED, J. See Toksöz, M. N. jt.
auth.
ARKANSAS
See also
Fishing—Arkansas
Hunting—Arkansas
Law—Arkansas
Prisons—Arkansas

Parks and reserves
Arkansas' mountain-top playgrounds. P. Crittenden. il Travel 128:30-4 O '67

Politics and government
Big Rock of Little Rock. Read Digest 90:111-
15 Mr '67
On to 1968; tour of Arkansas by Governor
Winthrop Rockefeller. il Time 90:25 Jl 21
'67
Rocky of Little Rock; gubernatorial candidates. T. Dearmore. il Reporter 37:14-18
O 5 '67
ARKANSAS RIVER
Oklahoma's stairway to the sea; Arkansas
River project. il Bsns W p 186-8+ Ap 22
'67

ARKANSAS RIVER VALLEY regional library,
Dardanelle, Ark.
From Buttermilk to Gum Log; bookmobiles
tote more than books. W. M. Lewis. il Am
Ed 3:8-11 Je '67
ARKIN, Alan
Alan Arkin talks about what it's like to be
a star. B. Weinraub. il pors N Y Times
Mag p30-1+ Mr 12 '67
ARKUS-DUNTOV, Zora
Man and his legend. J. McFarland. il pors
Hot Rod 20:36-9 S '67
ARLEDGE, Roone Pinckney
Locker in the living room. il Time 90:73 O
20 '67
ARLEN, Michael J.
Air (cont) New Yorker 42:75-6+ Ja 21; 136+
F 18; 43:148+ Mr 4; 187-8 Mr 18; 135-8 Ap
1; 184+ Ap 15; 158+ Ap 29; 182-8 My 13;
139-42+ My 27; 161-4+ S 30; 173-80+ O 21;
185-8 N 4; 143-4+ N 18; 215-18 D 2; 100+
D 16; 54+ D 30 '67
ARLINGHAUS, Ralph B. and Polatnick, Jerome
Detergent-solubilized RNA polymerase from
cells infected with foot-and-mouth disease
virus bibliog Science 158:1320-2 D 8 '67
ARLINGTON, Va.
See also
Pentagon building

National cemetery
No room to spare. Newsweek 69:44+ F 20
'67
See also
Kennedy, J. F.—Tomb
ARLINGTON, Vt.
See also
Martha Canfield free memorial library
ARLINGTON HEIGHTS, Ill.
Meter collection uses sealed bags. L. A. Hanson. il Am City 82:126+ F '67
ARMAGNAC, Alden P.
Atom sleuths seek secret treasures in the
pyramids. Pop Sci 190:88-90 Mr '67
Beating the spacecraft fire peril. Pop Sci 190:
96-8+ Je '67
ARMAMENTS
See also
Airplanes, Military—Armaments
Disarmament
Warships—Armaments
ARMBRISTER, Trevor
Fire! fire! flight deck aft! Sat Eve Post 240:
34-7 O 7 '67
Great Bolivian fever mystery; ed. by D. S.
Stroetzel. Read Digest 90:165-6+ F '67
Is this plane a billion-dollar blunder? Sat Eve
Post 240:23-5+ Je 17 '67
Letter from Saigon. Sat Eve Post 240:64-5
S 9 '67
ARMCHAIRS. See Chairs
ARMED forces
See also subhead Armed forces under
names of countries, e.g. United States—
Armed forces
**ARMED forces communications and electronics
association**
Big comsat advances predicted at AFCEA. il
Tech W 20:22 Je 12 '67
ARMED forces education program. See United
States—Armed forces—Education
ARMED forces museum and park (proposed)
See Smithsonian institution
ARMED forces news bureau. See United States
—Armed forces news bureau
ARMED forces radio service. See Radio stations, Military
ARMED robbery. See Robberies and assaults
ARMED services committee. See United States
—Congress—House of representatives—
Armed services committee
ARMENIA
See also
Foreign visitors in Armenia
ARMIES
See also subhead Army under names of
countries, e.g. Israel—Army

Officers
See also
Generals
ARMOR. See Arms and armor
ARMORED automobiles. See Automobiles,
Armored
ARMORED vessels
Ironclads rise again! river battleships for
Vietnam duty. R. Zimmerman. il Pop Mech
128:96-9 D '67
ARMORIES
How a city took care of itself; reaction to
closure of armory. il Nations Bsns 55:48-51
S '67

ARMOUR, Richard
Author on TV. por Pub W 192:48-9 D 25 '67
Friendly advice to new fathers from an old
pro. Parents Mag 42:48-9+ Je '67
Houses I have known and loved. Parents
Mag 42:72-4 O '67
My career as a girl-watcher. Read Digest 91:
21-2+ Ag '67
Time for laughter. PTA Mag 62:10-11 S '67
Turning on the light. Writer 80:33-5+ Ap '67

ARMOUR, Toby
Toby Armour; Judson memorial church.
J. Maskey. Dance Mag 42:23+ Ja '68

ARMOUR and company
Adjustment to plant closure; excerpt from
report to the Automation fund committee.
J. L. Stern. Mo Labor R 90:42-6 Ja '67
Quick truce; new agreement with two unions.
Newsweek 69:33 Mr 13 '67

ARMS and armor
Ceramics puts a shield under 'copter crews;
carbide ceramic armor. il Bsns W p80
D 9 '67
Stopping bullets with nylon. Time 90:57 Ag 11
'67

ARMS and the man; drama. See Shaw, G. B.

ARMS control. See Disarmament

ARMS control legislation. See Firearms—Laws
and regulations

ARMS sales. See Purchasing, Military

ARMSTRONG, Charlotte
Your plot is contrived. Writer 80:17-19 O '67

ARMSTRONG, Edwin Howard
Inventor's vindication. il por Newsweek 70:70
O 30 '67

ARMSTRONG, Janet L.
How team teaching works in Tulsa. Sr Schol
90:sup 17 Ap 14 '67

ARMSTRONG, Lois Dickert
One parent is better than none. Good H 164:
69+ F '67

ARMSTRONG, Louis
Everybody's Louie. L. L. King. por Harper
235:61-9 N '67

ARMSTRONG, Marion
Movies (cont) Christian Cent 84:112, 144-5,
240+, 313, 440-1, 597, 628, 726, 754-5, 945,
1000, 1198-9, 1256, 1326, 1468+, 1632-3;
85:52-3 Ja 25-F 1, 22, Mr 8, Ap 5, My 3-10,
31-Je 7, Jl 19, Ag 2, S 20, O 4, 18, N 15,
D 20 '67, Ja 10 '68

ARMSTRONG, O. K.
Landmark decision in the war on pornography. Read Digest 91:93-7 S '67
Victory over the smut peddlers. Read Digest
90:147-8+ F '67

ARMSTRONG, Richard
Soviet Russia, 1917-1967. Sat Eve Post 240:
25-38+ N 4 '67
Vietnam: believe me, he can kill you. Sat
Eve Post 240:29-35+ Mr 25 '67

**ARMSTRONG-JONES, Antony Charles Robert,
1st earl of Snowdon.** See Snowdon, A. C.
R. A.-J.

ARMY (football) See Football

ARMY barracks. See United States—Army—
Barracks and quarters

ARMY dogs. See Dogs, War use of

ARMY engineers. See United States—Army—
Corps of engineers

ARMY food. See United States—Army—Commissariat

ARMY libraries. See United States—Army—
Libraries

ARMY life
See also
Soldiers

ARMY of the Cumberland. See United States—
History—Civil war—Regimental histories

ARMY rations. See United States—Army—Commissariat

ARMY research office. See United States—
Army research office

ARMY reserves. See United States—Army—
Reserves

ARMY rifles. See Rifles

ARNDT, Jack
Design of an electronic guitar system.
Electr World 77:26-7+ F '67

ARNESON, Robert
Picasso the craftsman. Craft Horiz 27:28-33
N '67

ARNESS, Virginia
From the Oasis. pors Ebony 22:112-14+ O '67

ARNETT, Carroll
My horse William; poem. Sat R 50:37 Ag 26
'67
about
Five poets. E. Blum. Poetry 109:340 F '67

ARNHEIM, N. Jr, and others
Molecular size of hagfish muscle lactate
dehydrogenase. bibliog Science 157:568-9
Ag 4 '67

ARNHEITER, Marcus Aurelius
Arnheiter incident. il por Time 90:18-19 D 1
'67
Raising Caine. por Newsweek 70:31A D 4 '67

ARNHOLM, Ronald
Ronald Arnholm: maker of word paintings.
E. M. Ettenberg. il por Am Artist 31:66-70
N '67

ARNO, Stephen F.
North Cascades. Nat Parks Mag 41:4-9 Je '67
Some animals of Olympic Park. Nat Parks
Mag 41:10-14 Mr '67

ARNOLD, Anne
How to outwit a toddler. Parents Mag 42:41-
3+ Mr '67

ARNOLD, Benedict
Benedict Arnold: how the traitor was unmasked; excerpt from George Washington
in the American revolution. J. T. Flexner.
il pors Am Heritage 18:6-15 O '67
Benedict Arnold: the aftermath of treason.
M. Lomask. bibliog il por Am Heritage
18:16-17+ O '67

ARNOLD, Elliott
One brief, shining moment; excerpts from
interview, ed. by H. Frankel. por Sat R
50:22 S 2 '67

ARNOLD, Henry A.
Manned submersibles for research. bibliog
Science 158:84-90+ O 6 '67

ARNOLD, Margaret (Shippen)
Benedict Arnold: how the traitor was unmasked; excerpt from George Washington
in the American revolution. J. T. Flexner.
il pors Am Heritage 18:6-15 O '67
Benedict Arnold: the aftermath of treason.
M. Lomask. bibliog il Am Heritage 18:16-
17+ O '67

ARNOLD, Mark
Anti-war demonstrations: address, May 22,
1967. Vital Speeches 33:565-6 Jl 1 '67

ARNOLD, Martin
City Councilman John Santucci is a man in a
wind tunnel. N Y Times Mag p56-7+ Ap
16 '67
Lindsay inner circle. N Y Times Mag p32-
3+ O 15 '67
Report: New York. Atlan 219:22+ Je '67

ARNOLD, Rus
Camera abroad. U S Camera 30:52-3+ Mr '67
F/stop. il U S Camera 30:40-1+ Ap '67

ARNOLD, Walter
Selective objection and the public interest.
Christian Cent 84:1218-21 S 27 '67

ARNOLD Palmer enterprises, incorporated. See
Palmer, Arnold, enterprises, incorporated

ARNOLD Schwinn and company. See Schwinn,
Arnold and company

ARNOTT, Robert J.
Squeeze play. por Newsweek 69:61 Ja 30 '67

ARNSTEIN, George E.
American education placement service. bib-
liog f Sch & Soc 95:298-301 Sum '67
NEA search locates teachers and jobs; in-
terview, ed. by J. Lloyd. Sr Schol 91:sup4+
O 26 '67

AROMATIC compounds
Hydroxylation-induced migration: the NIH
shift. G. Guroff and others. bibliog il Science 157:1524-30 S 29 '67

ARONOFF, S. See Lee, S. jt. auth.

ARONOW, Don
More power to you. E. H. Nabb. il Yachting
122:32+ D '67

ARONOWITZ, Alfred G.
Pop music: the most? or just a mess? Sat
Eve Post 240:70-5 Jl 15 '67

ARONSON, Boris
Boris. B. Atkinson. il por Sat R 50:23 Je 10 '67

ARONSON, Jerome M. and others
Glucans of oomycete cell walls. bibliog Science 155:332-5 Ja 20 '67

AROUND the world flights. See Aviation—
World flights

ARPINO, Gerald
Ballet menus. W. Terry. Sat R 50:53-4 S 30
'67

ARRABAL, Fernando
L'architecte et l'Empereur d'Assyrie. Crit-
icism
New Yorker 43:176+ Ap 15 '67
European literary scene. R. J. Clements.
Sat R 50:29 My 6 '67

ARRANGEMENT; story. See Boughton, A.

ARRANGEMENT of flowers. See Flowers, Arrangement of

ARRANGEMENT of furniture. See Furniture,
Arrangement of

ARRAU, Claudio
Performer looks at psychoanalysis. pors Hi Fi 17:50-4 F '67
ARRIGHI typeface. See Type and typefounding
ARROW points. See Arrowheads
ARROWHEADS
Check your broadheads. G. H. Gillelan. il Outdoor Life 140:66+ Ag '67
Indian relics. C. Miles. il Hobbies 72:109-10+ N '67
ARRUPE, Pedro
Black pope. J. Kobler. il pors Sat Eve Post 240:30-4+ Mr 11 '67
ART
It's pretty, but is it art? random art. S. Angus. il Sat R 50:14-15 S 2 '67
Sound and fury in the arts; symposium; ed. by A. Hurlburt and P. Coffin. il Look 32: 13-30+ Ja 9 '68
What is art? R. Barrio. il Design 69:32-5 Fall '67
See also
Aesthetics
Animals in art
Architecture
Artists
Childrens art
Classicism
Composition (art)
Cubism
Design
Drawings
Engravings
Federal art project
Frescoes
Glass painting and staining
Graffiti
Impressionism (art)
Light in art
Originality (in art)
Paintings
Pen drawing
Performing arts
Photography, Artistic
Portraits
Posters
Sculpture
Vietnamese war, 1957-   —Art
also subhead Art under names of cities, e.g. Paris—Art

Appreciation
Anecdotes, facetiae, satire, etc.
Avoidism in the arts. R. Price. Look 32:78 Ja 9 '67
Bibliography
Book review section. See issues of Design
Book reviews. See issues of American artist
Books. See issues of School arts
News of books. See issues of School arts
Of art and anti-art. G. H. Hamilton. il Sat R 50:38+ N 25 '67

Collections
See Art—Private collections

Competitions
Competitions and awards. See issues of American artist
1967 Scholastic art awards. il Sr Schol 90:18-19 My 19 '67
See also
Childrens art—Competitions

Conservation and restoration
Art of re-creativity. M. Strage. il Esquire 69: 92-7 Ja '68
Florence: mending damaged treasures. K. Kuh. il Sat R 50:11-21 Jl 22 '67
Florence rises from the flood. J. Judge. il Nat Geog Mag 132:1-43 Jl '67
In Florence, new troubles and new treasures. il Life 62:54-9 Je 30 '67
Painting hospital in the lemon grove. H. J. Plenderleith. il UNESCO Courier 20:24-34 Ja '67
Protection of Africa's artistic heritage; address, April 1966. E. Eyo. il UNESCO Courier 20:2, 16-19 Je '67
To the rescue of art; Italy's Central institute of restoration. R. Deardorff. il Holiday 41: 29-30+ Ap '67

Education
See Art education

Exhibitions
American Artist travelogue. il Am Artist 31: 79-85+ Ap '67
Art. M. Kozloff. See issues of Nation
Art festival brightens busy city square; Washington, D.C. C. Walker. il Parks & Rec 2:24-5+ S '67

Art of Africa for the whole world; First world festival of Negro arts. P. Cooke. il Negro Hist Bul 29:171-2+ Fall '66
Art under Mussolini; Florence exhibition. Modern art in Italy, 1915-1935. K. Kuh. il Sat R 50:42-3 Je 24 '67
Art world. H. Rosenberg. New Yorker 43:99-100+ F 25; 179-80+ Mr 25; 162+ My 6; 112+ Je 3; 76+ Jl 29; 90+ Ag 26; 145-6+ S 23; 189-92+ O 21; 225-8+ N 18; 138+ D 16 '67
Bulletin board. See issues of American artist
Coming soon, art exhibits. See issues of Design
Current and coming. E. P. Birk. See issues of Antiques
Dialogue in a museum; Museum of contemporary crafts' tenth anniversary exhibition. K. K. Hui; J. Crumrine. il Craft Horiz 27:18-22+ Jl '67
Drawn from Dublin; master drawings from the National gallery of Ireland at Wildenstein. J. Ashbery. il Art N 66:46 D '67
Embattled heritage; Italian heritage exhibition at New York's Wildenstein gallery for CRIA. il Newsweek 69:89 My 29 '67
Founders of the American tradition; exhibition of two hundred years of American painting at Hirschl & Adler, New York. H. A. LaFarge. il Art N 66:36-7+ D '67
Gallery exhibitions. Am Artist 31:16+ F; 30-1+ Ap; 24-5+ My; 14+ Je '67
Goings on about town. See issues of New Yorker
Impressions from a Caribbean tour; Horizon club conference afloat exhibit. R. Kornfeld. il Sch Arts 67:29 N '67
International in Pittsburgh; Carnegie prize-winners. il Time 90:60-1 N 3 '67
Letter from London (cont) J. Stuart. il Antiques 91:684+ Je '67
Little Ferndale will get lively this month. il Sunset 138:48-50 My '67
Museum calendar. See issues of American artist
Pittsburgh's mini-international. K. Kuh. il Sat R 50:45-7 D 2 '67
Pranksters; silly season in Manhattan galleries. il Time 89:75 My 26 '67
Reviews and previews. See issues of Art news
Russell W. Porter exhibit. D. Milon. il Sky & Tel 34:226-8 O '67
Shape for the future; São Paulo bienal. il Time 90:96-7+ S 29 '67
That old feeling; Phillips academy, Andover, Mass, art show called Feelies. il Newsweek 69:98-9 Ap 3 '67
Where and when to exhibit. See issues of Art news
Williamstown-sur-Seine; loans from Sterling and Francine Clark art institute in Williamstown, Mass. J. Ashbery. il Art N 65: 44-7+ F '67
Year-end notes from a critic's diary. K. Kuh. il Sat R 50:34-5 D 30 '67
See also
Montreal—Worlds fair, 1967—Art
also names of museums, e.g. Museum of modern art, New York: *also* subhead Exhibitions under various subjects e.g. Childrens art—Exhibitions

Expertising
Dating and authenticating works of art by measurement of natural alpha emitters. B. Keisch and others. bibliog il Science 155: 1238-42 Mr 10 '67
How science uncovers art fakes. B. Frisch. il Sci Digest 62:6-11 Ag '67
See also
Forgery of works of art

Galleries and museums
Art; conflicts and tensions in the museum world today. M. Kozloff. Nation 205:570-2 N 27 '67
Boom in U.S. university museums; with editorial comment. E. Bryant. il Art N 66:25, 30-47+ S '67
Electronic museum. A. Schoener. il Pop Phot 60:84-7 Ap '67
In the museums. R. Davidson. See issues of Antiques
Museums display the art of selling; craft shops. il Bsns W p82-4+ Ap 8 '67
Notes on Canadian activities in the arts. E. P. Birk. il Antiques 92:32+ Jl '67
Taste on the campus. il Time 90:50-1 Jl 21 '67
Tourist tips. C. J. McNaspy. America 117: 23-4 Jl 1 '67

ART—Galleries and museums—*Continued*
Trial marriage with art; new role for museums: renting and selling. H. Katz and M. Katz. House B 109:30+ F '67
  See also names of museums, e.g. Brooklyn museum

Architecture
See Museums—Architecture

History
Study and teaching
Instructional resources in the teaching of art history. R. M. Diamond. il Sch Arts 66:24-8 Je '67

Philosophy
Antihierarchical American. A. Goldin. il Art N 66:48-50+ S '67
Art and style; reprint. il Design 68:32-5 Ja '67
Art; attitudes of C. Oldenburg and A. Kaprow. M. Kozloff. Nation 205:27-9 Jl 3 '67
Art in a hairshirt. A. Goldin. Art N 65:26+ F '67
Astonish me Sunday: a sermon. P. Halsman. il Pop Phot 60:69-71+ Mr '67
Ceramics photography. J. Schlanger. il Craft Horiz 27:24-9 Ja '67
Coming to terms with the new art. E. Genauer. House B 109:183+ Ap '67
History by contact. F. C. Castle. Art N 66:48-51+ O '67
Manner of speaking; sadness of the performer. J. Ciardi. Sat R 50:12-13 Je 24 '67
Mind, by S. K. Langer. Review
  Sat R 50:32-3 Jl 15 '67 H. Read
Serial rights; concepts and feelings behind the new serial art first showing at Finch college. D. Lee. il Art N 66:42-5+ D '67
What is design? R. M. Pearson. il Design 68:23-4 Mr '67
Why scale? Los Angeles County museum's survey of U.S. sculpture. J. Wechsler. il Art N 66:32-5+ Sum '67
  See also
Aesthetics

Private collections
Americans in faraway places; Roderic H. D. Henderson collection. W. H. Gerdts. il Antiques 91:647-9 My '67
Bonanza for Boston; the Nasli and Alice Heeramaneck collection. R. Lynes. Harper 234:22+ F '67
Collecting American nineteenth-century art. J. W. Middendorf, 2d. il Antiques 92:630-3 N '67
Diary of an art dealer, by R. Gimpel. Review
  New Yorker 43:182+ Ap 22 '67. H. Rosenberg
French touch; collection of Dr and Mrs Harry Bakwin. il Art N 66:32-3+ O '67
Fresh-air fun; outdoor sculpture of American collectors. il Time 90:72-7 S 8 '67
Governor lectures on art; excerpt from address at the New school for social research, New York. N. A. Rockefeller. il N Y Times Mag p28-31+ Ap 9 '67
House of a thousand treasures; the Berg collection. W. Wilson. il House B 109:124-7+ F '67
In quest of beauty; collecting 19th- and 20th-century French painting; with reproductions of paintings. P. Mellon. il Nat Geog Mag 131:372-85 Mr '67
Letter from Paris; exhibition of French painting from Swiss collectors at the Orangerie. Genêt. New Yorker 43:141-2+ Je 10 '67
Mellon collection. il Fortune 76:135-42 D '67
Newest ancient art; exhibition of objects from J. C. Leff collection of Ancient art of Latin America at the Brooklyn museum. J. H. Kay. il Américas 19:9-16 Ap '67
124 rooms, twenty baths, elevators, central heating, fit for a prince; Liechtenstein collection. J. Wechsberg. il Esquire 68:217-21+ D '67
Personal touch; T. Edward Hanley collection. il Newsweek 69:99 Ja 30 '67
Wrightsman collection, by F. J. B. Watson. Review
  Antiques il 91:620-7 My '67. R. Davidson
  See also
Art in the home
Pierpont Morgan library

Psychology
See also
Art therapy

Scholarships and fellowships
Competitions and awards. See issues of American artist
Competitions, scholarships. See issues of Art news

Social aspects
See Art and society

Study and teaching
Art and a high school humanities program. J. Warwick. il Sch Arts 66:5-8 Je '67
Cubism as a class project. L. J. Miller. il Design 69:36-7 Wint '67
Cutting edge of curriculum; art program in Newton, Mass. A. Hurwitz. il Sch Arts 67:9-12 O '67
Engaging art in dialogue. E. B. Feldman. il Sat R 50:60-1+ Jl 15 '67
Head start to what? role of art activities. P. J. Smith. il Sch Arts 66:9-10 Je '67
Let's progress beyond the lollipop tree. C. J. Alkema. il Design 68:4-8 Sum '67
On art in the schools. G. F. Horn. il Sch Arts 67:6-18 S '67
Saturday high school art classes at the Massachusetts college of art. J. Grepp. il Sch Arts 66:5-8 Ja '67
Special assignment: creative arts in the disadvantaged elementary school. H. Topper. il Sch Arts 66:5-8 F '67
Student teacher named Gail. D. Barclay. il Sch Arts 66:3-4 Ja '67
Teaching art through film making. G. S. Wright, jr. il Sch Arts 66:36-9 Je '67
Teen-age artists; summer art honors program. H. Weiler. il Sch Arts 67:38-9 O '67
Up to their ears in the arts; Ambler experimental project for high school students. L. J. Ahlander. il Am Ed 3:29-31 N '67
Very small happening at Forty Mile Bend; Fla. A. Hurwitz. il NEA J 56:71-2 S '67
Young start in art. E. Sharpe. il Todays Health 45:58-61 S '67
  See also
Art education
Colleges and universities—Art departments
Sculpture—Study and teaching, and similar headings

Materials
Color inventions. W. H. Tomajan. il Sch Arts 66:29-30 Ja '67
Crayon & chalk stencil technique. C. J. Alkema. il Sch Arts 66:38-41 Mr '67
Hot crayon fantasies. E. E. Welch. il Design 68:30-2 Mr '67
Metal-scrap animals. T. Pokorny, jr. il Sch Arts 66:29-30 Mr '67
Things with string. M. Snow. il Sch Arts 66:13-14 Ja '67
Two heads are better than one. H. Ringgenberg. il Design 68:14-16 Ja '67
Unique new teaching tool: Moby Lynx kit. H. E. Jackson. il Design 69:29-31 Fall '67

Projects
Classroom cathedral; slides of stained glass windows. A. Heidt. il Sch Arts 66:11 Je '67
Diorama depicting scene of Battle of Monmouth. L. E. Eben. il Sch Arts 66:31-2 F '67
Film; the place in the school art program. G. S. Wright, jr. il Sch Arts 66:31-5 Ja '67
Illustration: an art form. J. E. Miller. il Design 69:12-13 Fall '67
Motivation to the abstract. S. Zirlin and J Todak. il Sch Arts 66:29-31 Je '67
3-D art. P. S. Zakroff. il Design 68:17-19 Mr '67
What's on my mind? a three-dimensional collage structure. E. G. Rice and B. Rice. il Sch Arts 66:5-11 Mr '67
  See also
Christmas decorations
Enamel and enameling
Masks (for the face)
Mural painting and decoration
Puppets and puppet plays
Wire sculpture

Technique
Art and style; reprint. il Design 68:32-5 Ja '67
Blues for Yves Klein. L. Rivers. il Art N 65:32-3+ F '67
Let's arrange a counterchange. J. S. Lorr. il Design 68:4-6 Ja '67
Tips for artists. F. C. Matranga. il Design 68:38 Ja '67

Themes
Anatomy of an assassination; display in Manhattan's Dintenfass gallery. il Time 90:96 S 29 '67
Drawings of Richard Welling. N. Kent. il Am Artist 31:52-9 F '67
  See also
Negroes in art
Plants in art
Venice in art
West in art

ART—*Continued*

Therapeutic use
See Art therapy

Valuation
Taxman loseth; value of a triptych donated to the Houston museum of fine arts by Mrs S. C. Blaffer. il Time 89:49 Mr 3 '67

Africa
See also
Arts and crafts—Africa

California
Art bloom. J. Coplans. il Vogue 150:184-7+ N 1 '67
English sculpture in California. il Antiques 92: 736+ N '67
Explosion that never went boom. W. Wilson. il Sat R 50:54-6 S 23 '67

Canada
Notes on Canadian activities in the arts. E. P. Birk. il Antiques 92:32+ Jl '67

Europe, Western
American Artist travelogue; Europe. il Am Artist 31:84-5+ Ap '67

Germany (Federal Republic)
Germany. J. Claus. Art N 66:60 Mr '67

Great Britain
Letter from London (cont) J. Stuart. il Antiques 91:176+; 92:308+, 464+, 648+, 766+ F, S-D '67

Italy
See also
Florence—Art
Painting, Italian

Japan
See also
Arts and crafts—Japan

Russia
Art world; retour de l'U'R.R.S: a metaphysical excursion. H. Rosenberg. New Yorker 43:69-73 Jl 1 '67
See also
Painting, Russian

Switzerland
Letter from Paris; exhibition of French painting from Swiss collectors at the Orangerie. Genêt. New Yorker 43:141-2+ Je 10 '67

United States
American Artist travelogue; events. il Am Artist 31:80-4 Ap '67
Artist in American society: the formative years, 1790-1860. by N. Harris. Review
Nation 204:565-6 My 1 '67. A. Trachtenberg
Op, pop and the real thing. R. Berenson. il Nat R 19:648+ Je 13 '67
See also
Art, American
Painting, American
    also subhead Art under names of cities, e.g. Chicago—Art

ART, Abstract
Art world; action painting wing of abstract expressionism. H. Rosenberg. New Yorker 43:145-6+ S 23 '67
Bluhm's light; abstract painter draws the figure. N. Edgar. il Art N66:48-9+ Sum '67
Cool and concrete from the 'thirties. S. Burton. il Art N 66:34-5+ Ap '67

ART, African
Esthetics in traditional Africa. R. F. Thompson. il Art N 66:44-5+ Ja '68
See also
Arts and crafts—Africa

ART, Amateur

Anecdotes, facetiae, satire etc.
Apes of God invade U.S; excerpts from The apes of God, ed. by T. B. Hess. W. Lewis. Art N 66:25 Mr '67

ART, American
Boom in American art. il U S News 62:68-71 Ap 10 '67
Explosion that never went boom. W. Wilson. il Sat R 50:54-6 S 23 '67
Homage to Hans Hofmann; contemporary art scene. H. Rosenberg. il Art N 65:49+ Ja '67
See also
Art, Negro (American)
Artists, American
Painting, American
Sculpture, American

Collectors and collecting
Collecting American art for the Metropolitan: 1961-1966. J. Biddle. il Antiques 91:481-6 Ap '67

ART, Ancient
See also
Art, Greek

ART, Applied. See Design, Industrial

ART, Asian
Epics in the art of south Asia. B. N. Goswamy. il UNESCO Courier 20:18-29+ D '67

ART, Bhutanese
Secrets of Shangri-La. il Time 90:60-1 Ag 18 '67

ART, British
See also
Painting, British

ART, Buddhist
See also
Art, Tibetan
Sculpture, Buddhist

ART, Byzantine
Kariye Djami. by P. A. Underwood. Review
Art N il 66:40-1+ D '67. J. Beckwith

ART, Canadian
Musée imaginaire of Canadian art; Three hundred years of Canadian art. E. P. Birk. il Antiques 92:268+ S '67

ART, Chinese
See also
Painting, Chinese

ART, Commercial
See also
Art and industry

ART, Cuban
See also
Painting, Cuban

ART, Decorative. See Design, Decorative

ART, Egyptian
See also
Portraits, Egyptian

ART, Eskimo. See Eskimos—Art

ART, French
See also
Painting, French

ART, Gothic
Cathedrals as living drama; theories of H. Kraus. il Time 90:88+ N 17 '67

ART, Greek
Recapturing the ardor of Greece. K. Kuh. il Sat R 50:42-4 O 28 '67

ART, Illusionary. See Modernism (art)

ART, Indian (East Indian)
Bonanza for Boston; the Nasli and Alice Heeramaneck collection. R. Lynes. Harper 234:22+ F '67

ART, Influence of. See Art therapy

ART, Irish
Rose go bragh: exhibition of modern painting and ancient Celtic art, Dublin. J. Russell. il Art N 66:22+ Ja '68

ART, Italian
Art under Mussolini; Florence exhibition. Modern art in Italy, 1915-1935. K. Kuh. il Sat R 50:42-3 Je 24 '67
See also
Painting, Italian

ART, Jewish
See also
Jewish art and symbolism

ART, Latin American
Art. See issues of Américas

ART, Medieval
Cleveland's medieval treasure. il Time 89: 72-3 Ja 27 '67

ART, Minoan
See also
Crete—Antiquities

ART, Modern. See Modernism (art)

ART, Negro
Art of Africa for the whole world; First world festival of Negro arts. P. Cooke. il Negro Hist Bul 29:171-2+ Fall '66
See also
Negro artists

ART, Negro (American)
American Negro art in progress. L. J. Pierre-Noel. il Negro Hist Bul 30:6-9 O '67
See also
Tanner, H. O.

ART, Oriental
From the farthest East. M. B. Davidson. il Antiques 92:344-8 S '67

ART, Persian
World of fabulous fables; London's Victoria and Albert museum exhibition of Persian miniatures. il Time 90:54 Ag 25 '67

ART, Pre-Columbian
See also
Sculpture, Pre-Columbian

ART, Primitive
Art of primitive arts; with portfolio of works in Museum of primitive art, N.Y. R. Sieber. Art N 66:28-43+ Ja '68
Generalić, a Croatian peasant painter. A. Werner. il Am Artist 31:40-5+ F '67
Primitive, primitive art. il Sci Digest 62:20-1 S '67
See also
Cave drawings and paintings
Eskimos—Art
ART, Religious. See Christian art and symbolism
ART, Rococo
Boucher's lovers in a park. E. Mongan. il Art N 66:50-1+ Sum '67
ART, Russian
In the beginning there was art. J. Berger. Nation 206:88-9+ Ja 15 '68
Russians are coming; H. L. Carlsruh contract to import and sell Russian art in the United States. il Newsweek 69:108 Ap 10 '67
See also
Painting, Russian
ART, Tibetan
Lamaist art; the Panchen Lama. G. Kaler. il Hobbies 72:50 Je '67
Talisman and testament; Tibetan ritual objects of every-day use. G. Kaler. il Hobbies 72:50 S '67
Tibetan Lamaism. G. Kaler. il Hobbies 72:50-1 My '67
ART and children. See Children and art
ART and government
Civic architecture. D. P. Moynihan. Arch Rec 142:107 D '67
ART and industry
Boom in American art. il U S News 62:68-71 Ap 10 '67
Business in the arts awards, and a new progress report. A. Gingrich. Esquire 68:6+ Jl '67
Corporation and the arts, by R. Eells. Review Nation 205:468-9 N 6 '67. P. Clecak Sat R 50:35+ N 4 '67. A. A. Berle
Esquire's 1966 Business in the arts award. Esquire 68:28-9 Jl '67
Onward and upward with business in the arts. A. Gingrich. Esquire 69:6+ Ja '68
Thing of beauty is a profit forever. il Newsweek 69:76-8 Je 5 '67
Where is new Bohemia going? J. Gruen. Vogue 150:101+ Ag 1 '67
See also
Design, Industrial
ART and libraries. See Libraries and art
ART and morals
See also
Theater—Moral and religious aspects
ART and photography
Astonish me Sunday; a sermon. P. Halsman. il Pop Phot 60:69-71+ Mr '67
Camera and the brush. K. Young. il U S Camera 30:34 D '67
Ceramics photography. J. Schlanger. il Craft Horiz 28:24-9 Ja '67
Frustrated artist? try line drawings. P. Farber. U S Camera 30:20 Je '67
Nonphotographer looks at the medium; interview, ed. by J. Deschin. E. Mandelbaum. Pop Phot 60:22+ Je '67
Picasso & photography; excerpts from Picasso & co. Brassaï. il Pop Phot 60:78-80+ My '67
Should the camera interpret art? N. Rothschild. Pop Phot 61:78 Jl '67
ART and politics
Art world; politics in the art of our time. H. Rosenberg. New Yorker 43:138+ D '67
Week of the angry artist. C. Harnack. Nation 204:245-8 F 20 '67; Discussion. 204:322+ Mr 13 '67
ART and religion
Art of the future; uniting secular and sacred art. R. Dunavon. America 117:740-2 D 16 '67
Liturgy and the arts: a unique relationship. J. W. Moody. Cath World 205:303-9 Ag '67
Miracles of faith. il Vogue 150:180-91 D '67
Theology and the arts, by D. Harned. Review Christian Cent 83:1575 D 21 '66. P. Meinke; Reply. B. T. Dahlberg. 84:145-6 F 1 '67
ART and science
Science for art's sake; scientists collaborate with artists in using new materials, techniques. il Bsns W p56 O 21 '67
ART and society
Art and alienation, by H. Read. Review Sat R 50:29-30 D 2 '67. J. K. Simon
Art in a hairshirt. A. Goldin. Art N 65:26+ F '67
Art of measuring the arts. A. Toffler. Ann Am Acad 373:141-55 S '67

Artist in American society: the formative years, 1790-1860, by N. Harris. Review Nation 204:565-6 My 1 '67. A. Trachtenberg
Cultivating the arts of poverty. F. A. J. Ianni. il Sat R 50:60-2+ Je 17 '67
Theater of commitment; excerpt from address. E. Bentley; discussion. Commentary 43:6+ Mr '67
Where is the avant-garde? C. Greenberg. Vogue 149:112-13+ Je '67
ART and state
Aid for artists: but is it really art? il U S News 63:11 Ag 28 '67
First steps in legislation for the arts. L. J. Lefkowitz; discussion. Art N 65:6 O; 6 D '66; 6 Ja '67
See also
United States—National foundation on the arts and the humanities
ART appreciation. See Art—Appreciation
ART auctions. See Art sales
ART books. See Art literature
ART center college of design, Los Angeles
School where cars are born. N. Willatt. il Duns R 89:45-6+ Ap '67
ART centers
Irving Center for the arts. B. Waldo. il Parks & Rec 2:17+ Je '67
Old barn with a new bias; Simon's Rock arts center, Great Barrington, Mass. il Arch Forum 126:100-3 Ja '67
ART collecting. See Art—Private collections
ART competitions. See Art—Competitions
ART criticism
See also
Art—Appreciation
ART critics
Renderings in three-dimensional form; excerpts from Painting lessons from the great masters. H. L. Cooke. il Am Artist 31:32-5 D '67
ART dealers
By appointment only; private dealers. il Newsweek 70:80 S 4 '67
Diary of an art dealer, by R. Gimpel. Review New Yorker 43:182+ Ap 22 '67. H. Rosenberg
See also
Sotheby and company
ART dealers association of America
Editor's letters; reply. R. F. Colin. Art N 65:6 Ja '67
ART education
Arthur Lismer, artist and art-educator: a reflection on his life, work and philosophy. H. G. Hinterreiter. il Sch Arts 66:21-8 Ja '67
Building aesthetic qualities in the school art program. C. L. Hallberg. il Sch Arts 67:19-20 S '67
Hand them a *frobish*; learning through the five senses. R. M. Bilenker. il NEA J 56:30-1+ O '67
How much rubbed off? art teacher at Phillips academy, Andover, Mass. il Time 89:76+ Je 16 '67
John Dewey and education through art. J. S. Keel. bibliog il Sch Arts 66:33-7 F '67
On behalf of art. R. T. McGee. il NEA J 57:36-7 Ja '68
What makes a good junior high art program? C. Mulford. il NEA J 56:14-17 Mr '67
See also
Art—Study and teaching
Children and art
National art education association
ART exhibitions. See Art—Exhibitions
ART exhibitions, Traveling. See Exhibitions, Traveling
ART festivals. See Art—Exhibitions
ART forgeries. See Forgery of works of art
ART galleries and museums. See Art—Galleries and museums
ART glass. See Glass, Ornamental
ART in motion
Drawing in the dark; kinetic art produced by a laser beam. il Time 90:64 O 27 '67
Infinity in eight minutes; J. de Rivera's sculpture piece in front of Smithsonian institution's new Museum of history and technology. il Time 89:66 Ap 7 '67
Labyrinthine fun house; J. Le Parc's work. il Time 89:66 Mr 24 '67
Motionless motion; R. Breer's kinetic sculpture. H. Rosenstein. il Art N 66:37+ N '67
Movement in art. H. Rosenberg. Vogue 149:170-1+ F 1 '67
Twittering galaxy of electronic sculptures. il Life 62:112-14+ Ap 7 '67

ART in public buildings
Art in striped pants; art for embassies. il Newsweek 70:107-8 O 9 '67

ART in the home
Collector's collector. il House B 109:130-3 Mr '67
Great art in Los Angeles. il Vogue 150:156-9 Ag 15 '67
In his former studio an artist creates an art-filled second home. il House B 109:132-5 Je '67
Light science, and space. A. Michelson. il Vogue 149:142-3+ Mr 15 '67
Living with antiques; the Pennsylvania home of Mr and Mrs Walter L. Wolf. L. Solis-Cohen. il Antiques 92:336-40 S '67
Serene house: unexpected detail. il House & Gard 131:110-15 F '67
Talent for Christmas; home of the Vincent Prices. il House & Gard 132:136-43 D '67

ART institute, Chicago. See Chicago art institute

ART literature
Notes for young designers about art books. S. Salter. Pub W 192:90+ S 4 '67
See also
Publishers and publishing—Art literature

ART loans
Art; selection from Tunisian national museum to be in the United States for two years. M. Grosser. Nation 204:634-6 My 15 '67
Morals and mime; essential Hogarth. J. Summerson. il Art N 65:22-5+ F '67
Noble Metropolitan visitors; old masters loaned to the Met from private collections in America and abroad. H. A. La Farge. il Art N 65:27-31+ F '67
Williamstown-sur-Seine; loans from Sterling and Francine Clark art institute in Williamstown, Mass. J. Ashberry. il Art N 65:44-7+ F '67

ART materials. See Artists materials

ART metal work
Philolaos. E. Benson. il Craft Horiz 27:32-3+ S '67
Woven structures of Alice Adams. B. Kafka il Craft Horiz 27:14-17 Mr '67
See also
Aluminum work
Enamel and enameling
Filigree
Jewelry
Wire sculpture

ART museums. See Art—Galleries and museums

ART objects
Where is it? L. Lerman. il Mlle 65:103-5 Je '67
See also
Antiques
Art in the home
Relics and reliquaries

Conservation and restoration
See Art—Conservation and restoration

ART objects, British
Letter from London. J Stuart. il Antiques 91:440, 556+ Ap-My '67

ART objects, Chinese
Chinese art from a royal collection; masterpieces belonging to King Gustaf VI Adolf of Sweden on tour to American museums. H. Trubner. il Antiques 91:644-6 My '67

ART objects, Reproductions of. See Reproductions of works of art

ART objects, Russian
Russian treasures in London; exhibition at the Victoria and Albert museum. J. Stuart. il Antiques 91:556+ My '67

ART of the book foundation, Frankfort on the Main. See Book industries and trade—Germany (Federal Republic)

ART project, Federal. See Federal art project

ART sales
Art game, by R. Wraight. Review
New Repub 156:29-30 F 18 '67. F. Getlein
Back to market; A. H. Meadows buys paintings for Southern Methodist university. il Time 89:84 Je 9 '67
Coming auctions. See issues of Art news
Double & triple; sale of Monet's The terrace at Ste Adresse. il Time 90:93 D 8 '67
$532,000 Picasso. il Newsweek 69:92 My 8 '67
Price of a Picasso; Mother and child by the sea. il Time 89:60 My 5 '67
Russians are coming; H. L. Carlsruh contract to import and sell Russian art in the United States. il Newsweek 69:108 Ap 10 '67
Sotheby's touch in St Louis; auction for benefit of City museum. il Bsns W p 140-1 D 9 '67

ART schools
Art school directory. 1967. Am Artist 31:SDI-16 [75–90] Mr '67

Art schools; Sunday painters versus men of passion. D. Holden. il Am Artist 31:52-3+ Mr '67
Art schools; the charges against the universities. D. Holden. il Am Artist 31:72-3+ Ap '67
See also
Art center college of design, Los Angeles

ART smuggling. See Smuggling

ART students
Letter from London; exhibition at the Tate: annual Young contemporaries show. M. Panter-Downes. New Yorker 42:152 F 11 '67

ART studios. See Artists studios

ART teachers
Artist-teacher in America John Sloan. D. G. Byrd. bibliog il Sch Arts 66:25-30 F '67
Too good to teach? D. Manzella. il Sch Arts 66:12-13 Mr '67

Education
Art education laboratory. E. Cohen. il Sch Arts 66:32-5 Je '67

ART teachers, Student. See Student teachers

ART thefts

Anecdotes, facetiae, satire, etc.
Anyway, they're available on slides. G. Gotler. New Yorker 42:36-7 F 18 '67

ART therapy
Letter from Paris; exhibition of art by schizophrenic or psychopathic patients from special institutions in the Musée des arts décoratifs of the Louvre. Genêt. New Yorker 43:169-70 Ap 29 '67

ART trade
Buyers, sellers, and forgers. M. Esterow. Harper 234:83-6 Je '67
See also
Art dealers
Art sales

ARTEMIA. See Shrimps

ARTERIES
Humoral agent from calf lung producing pulmonary arterial vasoconstriction. E. D. Robin and others. bibliog il Science 156:827-30 My 12 '67
See also
Aorta

ARTERIOSCLEROSIS
Binding the cholesterol; use of cholestyramine, Time 90:77 O 13 '67
Prevention of induced atherosclerosis by peroxidase. J. Caravaca and others. bibliog il Science 155:1284-7 Mr 10 '67

ARTHAUD editions. See Publishers and publishing—France

ARTHRITIS
Human collagenase: identification and characterization of a enzyme from rheumatoid synovium in culture. J. M. Evanson and others. bibliog il Science 158:499-502 O 27 '67
Inroads against a crippler; rheumatoid arthritis. F. Marley. il Sci N 92:68-9 Jl 15 '67
Why arthritis hurts. Newsweek 69:92 Je 19 '67

Therapy
Closing in on rheumatoid arthritis, the number one crippler. J. L. Decker. il Todays Health 45:44-7+ Je '67

ARTHROPODS
Water balance in desert arthropods. E. B. Edney. bibliog il Science 156:1059-66 My 26 '67

ARTICHOKES
See also
Cookery—Vegetables

ARTICLES for periodicals. See Periodical literature

ARTIFICIAL fog. See Fog, Artificial

ARTIFICIAL fur. See Fur, Artificial

ARTIFICIAL gill. See Respiratory apparatus

ARTIFICIAL grass courts. See Tennis courts

ARTIFICIAL heart valves. See Heart—Surgery

ARTIFICIAL hearts. See Hearts, Artificial

ARTIFICIAL insemination
A.I. made this top herd better. O. Bay. Farm J 91:72M F '67
Demand growing for hog A.I. D. Hagen. Farm J 91:74 Ap '67

ARTIFICIAL insemination, Human
Sperm banks debated. B. J. Culliton. il Sci N 92:208-9 Ag 26 '67
Test tube children; a new kind of orphan; reprint. H. P. Gouldner. il Sci Digest 62:16-22 Jl '67

ARTIFICIAL insemination, Human—*Continued*

Laws and regulations

Child of artificial insemination; status and rights. il Time 89:79-80 Ap 14 '67

ARTIFICIAL islands
Aerospace firms prominent at OECON. il Tech W 20:32-3 20 '67

ARTIFICIAL kidneys. See Kidneys, Artificial

ARTIFICIAL lakes. See Lakes, Artificial

ARTIFICIAL larynx. See Larynx, Artificial

ARTIFICIAL lawns. See Turf, Artificial

ARTIFICIAL limbs
Back on their feet. F. Marley. il Sci N 91: 120-1 F 4 '67
Electric limbs; implanted electronic pickup. F. C. Livingstone. Sci N 92:495 N 18 '67

ARTIFICIAL respiration. See Respiration, Artificial

ARTIFICIAL respirator. See Respiratory apparatus

ARTIFICIAL rubber. See Rubber, Artificial

ARTIFICIAL satellites
Annual world aerospace encyclopedia 1967. Aero Tech 21:21-32+ Jl 31 '67
ATS-C satellite to carry device to measure mirror deterioration. G. S. Hunter. il Aviation W 86:73 Mr 13 '67
Astrolog; current status of U.S. missile and space programs. il Aero Tech 21:35-8 Ja 1 '68
Big savings seen in TTS check of Apollo network; Test and training satellite. il Aero Tech 21:30 D 18 '67
Boeing interplanetary Orbiter suggested for 1971 launch. K. Voss. il Tech W 20:25 Mr 6 '67
Crack in able; plan for a gigantic mirror to be in orbit and beam sun's rays down to earth. Sci N 91:304 Ap 1 '67
Daddy longlegs; Applications technology satellites. Newsweek 70:62 D 11 '67
First applications technology satellite. R. N. Watts, jr. il Sky & Tel 33:288-9 My '67
Go-ahead set for $100-million ATS in '68. Aero Tech 21:23 D 18 '67
Historic color portrait of earth from space; DODGE satellite. K. F. Weaver. il Nat Geog Mag 132:726-31 N '67
NASA studies ATS-3 switch to new position over Pacific. B. K. Thomas, jr. Aviation W 87:20 N 27 '67
Reflecting satellite; NASA study causes concern among astronomers. B. Nelson. il Science 155:304+ Ja 20 '67
Roster of space activity. R. N. Watts, jr. il Sky & Tel 35:13-15 Ja '68
Satellite beacon silenced; ATS-1 is carrying on a multitude of experiments. R. N. Watts, jr. Sky & Tel 33:215 Ap '67
Satellite club; international satellite launches, except U.S.S.R; chart. Sci N 93:48 Ja 13 '68
Satellite elongation into a true Sky-Hook. J. D. Isaacs and others; discussion. Science 152:800; 158:946-7 My 6 '66, N 17 '67
10-100 GHz band windows seen increasing data rates; experiment for applications technology satellite. W. S. Beller. il Tech W 20:38-9 F 27 '67
Trend to smaller satellites seen emerging. J. Rhea. il Aero Tech 21:36-7 Ag 14 '67
See also
Space vehicles

Agricultural applications

Eye in the sky helps you; photographs taken from satellites giving information about crops and soils. L. Lane. Farm J 91:12 Ag '67

Astronomical applications

Dragonflies in space; Orbiting geophysical observatory series. il Time 90:56 Ag 11 '67
Long-boom antennas to map cosmic noise; radio astronomy explorer satellite. W. S. Beller. il Tech W 20:34-5 F 20 '67
Long-legged eye in the sky; radio astronomy explorer. il Sci N 91:378 Ap 22 '67
Manned observatory in space; Apollo telescope mount. W. Von Braun. il Pop Sci 192:98-100+ Ja '68
NASA postpones OAO launch to make changes in spacecraft. K. Johnsen. Aviation W 86:17 Mr 13 '67
NASA still trying to solve problem of re-entry blackout; OSO launch set. il Aero Tech 21: 50 O 23 '67
New observatory, earth resource satellite planned. J. A. Strasser. il Aero Tech 21: 46-7+ N 20 '67
New window to heavens; ultraviolet experiments to be carried on OAO. A. Ewing. il Sci N 91:504-5 My 27 '67

Nine OSO 4 experiments tested. Aviation W 87:26 O 30 '67
OAO gets a new look. il Sci N 91:499 My 27 '67
OGO-4 reaches near-Polar orbit to study solar activity effects. Aviation W 87:30 Ag 7 '67
OSO 4 ultraviolet solar observations. il Sky & Tel 34:362-5 D '67
OSO reveals the sun in ultraviolet. il Sci N 92:559 D 9 '67
Radio measurements in space; radio astronomy explorer satellite. J. H. Wujek, jr. il Electr World 77:46-7+ My '67
Sun and space solar measurements. J. H. Wujek, jr. il Electr World 78:32-3 O '67
Two more OSO's. R. N. Watts, jr. Sky & Tel 33:215 Ap '67

Attitude control systems
See Artificial satellites—Control systems

Communication applications
See Communications satellites

Control systems
Three-axis attitude system developed for ATS F and G. R. Pay. il Tech W 20:38-9 My 1 '67

Detection
Radar signature analysis; White Sands missile range in New Mexico. E. A. Lacy. il Electr World 77:23-5+ F '67

Electronic equipment
Big savings seen in TTS check of Apollo network; Test and training satellite. il Aero Tech 21:30 D 18 '67
Fairchild Hiller readying SERT hardware; module to perform all support functions. J. Rhea. il Aero Tech 21:34-6 D 18 '67
Test of aircraft satellite navaid planned. P. J. Klass. il Aviation W 88:75-6+ Ja 8 '68

Equipment
Suicide timer used on ERS. Aero Tech 21:42 D 4 '67

Launching
French allot funds for six Diamant Bs. Aviation W 87:41 Jl 17 '67
Italy's African space triumph; launch from sea-borne pad; with report by M. Durham. il Life 62:101-2+ My 26 '67

Mapping applications
Honeywell working on orbital scanner; satellite system to measure horizon in infrared band. J. Rhea. il Aero Tech 21:25-6 N 6 '67
International satellite geodesy. R. N. Watts, jr. il Sky & Tel 33:214 Ap '67
New Nimbus, Geos satellites planned. Aero Tech 21:16 Ja 1 '68
Shape of the earth. D. King-Hele. il Sci Am 217:67-72+ O '67

Meteorological applications
Filling a weather gap; launching of ESSA-4. Sci N 91:135 F 11 '67
Future of weather satellites. R. N. Watts, jr. Sky & Tel 34:157 S '67
New Nimbus, Geos satellites planned. Aero Tech 21:16 Ja 1 '68
New Nimbus metsat competition planned. H. M. David. Tech W 20:19 Ap 10 '67
Pioneer 7 doubling as sun weatherman. R. Pay. il Tech W 20:20+ F 27 '67
Satellites could triangulate on weather. W. S. Beller. il Tech W 20:26-7 F 6 '67
Sea Robin tests resumed; mooring problems stressed. il Aero Tech 21:25-6 Jl 17 '67
Tiros M design broadens capabilities. K. J. Stein. il Aviation W 86:103-7 My 8 '67
Tracking by satellite; using Nimbus for non-weather applications. Sci N 92:19 Jl 1 '67
Weather surveillance by satellite; Tiros, Nimbus, and successor ESSA satellites are providing global weather information. J. H. Wujek, jr. il Electr World 77:23-5 Mr '67

Military applications
Bombs in orbit. T. M. Conrad. Commonweal 87:332-4 D 8 '67
MOL increases opportunities in military space activities. il Aviation W 86:117-19 Mr 6 '67
Moving right along; U.S. and U.S.S.R. nuclear programs. New Repub 158:7-8 Ja 13 '68
Nike gets new anti-satellite role. il Aviation W 87:62+ O 23 '67
Russian spy satellite launch rate levels. Aviation W 87:26 Jl 24 '67
Russia's orbital bomb. Newsweek 70:34 N 13 '67

ARTIFICIAL satellites—Military applications—
Continued
Satellites at war. Sci N 92:176-7 Ag 19 '67
Shadow of the FOBS; bombs in orbit; Russian
system. Sci N 92:487-8 N 18 '67
Soviet payloads overfly Nike-X test site;
FOBS launches. P. J. Klass. il Aviation W
87:81+ D 11 '67
Space bomb; fractional orbital bombardment
system. il Time 90:24-5 N 10 '67
Tactical comsat terminals readied for soldier
in field. Aero Tech 21:37+ Ag 14 '67
USAF reconnaissance satellites. il Aviation
W 86:116 Mr 6 '67
USAF to orbit two advanced Velas in April.
G. S. Hunter. il Aviation W 86:71+ F 13 '67

Navigational applications
Navigation satellite study set. Aviation W
86:117+ Ap 17 '67
New satellite Navaid tested successfully. P.
J. Klass. il Aviation W 87:63-4 N 27 '67
Sailing by satellite; Transit satellite naviga-
tional system. il Time 90:56-7 Ag 11 '67
Wide civilian use seen for navy Navsat.
R. W. Niblock. Aero Tech 21:20 Ag 14 '67

Testing
Deadline nears for role in ESRO Comsat.
D. E. Fink. il Aviation W 87:28-31 S 11
'67

Tracking
America's big eye on the sky. D. Robinson.
il Read Digest 90:155-6+ F '67
ATS tracking system accurate to 0.5 meter.
C. D. LaFond. il Tech W 20:37-9 Ja 30 '67
Radar signature analysis; White Sands missile
range in New Mexico. E. A. Lacy. il Electr
World 77:23-5+ F '67

Use in research
Ariel 3 measures atmosphere, ionosphere;
third in a series of U.S.-U.K. cooperative
projects. W. J. Normyle. il Aviation W
86:364-7+ My 29 '67
Ark in orbit. il Time 90:54+ S 22 '67
EROS project initial funding seen in fiscal
'69 by Udall; earth resources observation
satellite. A. Hill. Tech W 20:29-30+ Ap 17
'67
Earth resources satellite far from reality.
J. Rhea. il Tech W 20:34+ F 13 '67
Earth resources vehicle efforts pushed. Avia-
tion W 87:75+ N 13 '67
Experimenters begin evaluation of specimens
from Biosatellite. Aviation W 87:29 S 18
'67
Explorer 35 orbiting with seven experiments.
Aviation W 87:29 Jl 24 '67
Eyes in the sky will help feed world; Earth
resources satellites. W. Von Braun. il Pop
Sci 191:80-2 Jl '67
French design payload for Soviet booster;
agreement on plan to launch Roseau radio
observatory satellite. D E. Fink. Aviation
W 87:33 Jl 10 '67
Happy landings; Surveyor 5 and Biosatellite 2.
Newsweek 70:98 S 25 '67
Interest grows in low-cost OV program. R.
Pay. il Tech W 20:24-5+ F 13 '67
IMP launch set for May 24 will warn of solar
flares. Tech W 20:19 My 22 '67
NASA wins battle over resource satellite
work. Aero Tech 21:21 O 9 '67
New observatory, earth resource satellite
planned. J. A. Strasser. il Aero Tech 21:
46-7+ N 20 '67
Of gnats and moonbeams; Surveyor 5 and
Biosatellite 2. il Newsweek 70:67 S 18 '67
RCA bidding for ERS job with vidicon. Aero
Tech 21:42 O 23 '67
Satellite eye on the sea. il Sci Digest 62:41-3
D '67
Soviets intensify near-earth investigations.
Aviation W 87:27-8 O 23 '67
SESP plans at least three '68 shots; air
force's space experiment support program.
F. Burnham. il Aero Tech 21:17-18 Ja 1 '68
ARTIFICIAL satellites, Australian
Satellite club; Australia's first satellite,
WRESAT. il Sci N 93:48 Ja 13 '68
ARTIFICIAL satellites, British
Ariel 3 measures atmosphere, ionosphere;
third in a series of U.S.-U.K. cooperative
projects. W. J. Normyle. il Aviation W
86:364-7+ My 29 '67
ARTIFICIAL satellites, European
Deadline nears for role in ESRO Comsat.
D. E. Fink. il Aviation W 87:28-31 S 11 '67
ESRO II satellite scheduled for WTR launch
in April. J. A. Redeker. Tech W 20:24-5
Ap 3 '67
ESRO's first satellite. Sci N 91:544 Je 10 '67

ARTIFICIAL satellites, French
French space program begins new phase;
scientific mission of Diademe series. W. C.
Wetmore. il Aviation W 86:50-1+ Mr 27
'67
ARTIFICIAL satellites, Italian
Italy's African space triumph; launch from
sea-borne pad; with report by M. Durham.
il Life 62:101-2+ My 26 '67
ARTIFICIAL satellites, Russian
Maser in orbit; a Russian first. il Sci N 92:
153 Ag 12 '67
Soviets intensify near-earth investigations.
Aviation W 87:27-8 O 23 '67
USSR initiates national satellite TV net. D. C.
Winston. il Aviation W 87:39+ N 27 '67
See also
Space probes, Russian
ARTIFICIAL sweeteners. See Sugar substitutes
ARTIFICIAL teeth. See Teeth, Artificial
ARTIFICIAL turf. See Turf, Artificial
ARTILLERY
See also
Projectiles
ARTISTIC photography. See Photography, Ar-
tistic
ARTISTS
Diary of an art dealer, by R. Gimpel. Review
New Yorker 43:182+ Ap 22 '67. H. Rosen-
berg
[Fine art reproductions] A. Saarinen. il Mc-
Calls 94:52-4 Je; 132-5 Jl; 114-15 Ag; 30-1 S;
95:38-9 O; 42-3 N; 78-9 D '67; 41-2 Ja '68
In the art world; the young crowd. L. Allo-
way. House B 109:118-20 Jl '67
Masters in the art news. See issues of Art
news
Renderings in three-dimensional form; ex-
cerpts from Painting lessons from the great
masters. H. L. Cooke. il Am Artist 31:32-5
D '67
Where is the avant-garde? C. Greenberg.
Vogue 149:112-13+ Je '67
Who, what, where and when? Inquiries about
artists. N. Kent. Am Artist 31:5 S '67
See also
Bohemianism
Engravers
ARTISTS, American
Art bloom. J. Coplans. il Vogue 150:184-6+
N 1 '67
New New York art scene; who makes it?
excerpts from New York; the new art scene.
A. Solomon. il Vogue 150:102-7+ Ag 1 '67
Way-out West; interviews with four San
Francisco artists. J. Raffaele and E. Baker.
il Art N 66:38-41+ Sum '67
See also
Artschwager, R.
Bearden, R.
Beckett, S.
Gablik, S.
Painting, American
Sculpture, American
Tawney, L.
White, C.
Zahourek, J.
ARTISTS, British
See also
Beardsley, A. V.
ARTISTS, German
Paris on the Rhine; artists' community in
Düsseldorf. il Time 89:50-3 Je 2 '67
ARTISTS, Japanese
See also
Hiroshige, A.
ARTISTS, Latin American
From the River Plate to the Seine. D. C.
Bayón. il Américas 19:22-7 Ag '67
ARTISTS materials
Art mart. See issues of American artist
Constructions in chrome; J. Seley's automobile
bumper sculptures. il Time 89:66 Mr 10 '67
1967 buyer's guide. Sch Arts 66:41-6 F '67
Ralph Mayer's technical question & answer
page. R. Mayer. See issues of American
artist
Supplies for painting and sketching. Good H
165:158 Jl '67
Tips for artists. F. C. Matranga. il Design
68:38 Ja '67
What's new, where to buy it. See issues of
Design
Works of art from skulls and eggshells. F.
Martin. il Design 68:10-11 Mr '67
See also
Paper
ARTISTS studios
Art city; help for space-seeking artists in
New York. il Newsweek 70:63 Ag 21 '67
Indoor-outdoor painting studio. il Sunset 138:
132 F '67

ARTISTS studios—*Continued*
Lofty solutions; projects to provide accommodation for New York artists. il Time 90: 60 Ag 18 '67

ARTS, Fine. See Art

ARTS and crafts
Bread & wine. il McCalls 94:102-7 Mr '67
Holiday world bazaar. See issues of Holiday World's fair of crafts. il Craft Horiz 27:24-7 My '67
See also
Batik
Block printing
Decoration and ornament
Enamel and enameling
Handicraft
Jewelry
Needlework
Weaving

Bibliography
Book review section. See issues of Design
Books (cont) Craft Horiz 27:58 Mr; 8 My '67

Exhibitions
Calendar; Where to show. See issues of Craft horizons
California arts commission: first crafts exhibition. B. Kester. il Craft Horiz 27:24-7+ Mr '67
Exhibitions. See issues of Craft horizons

Study and teaching
Travel & study; lists of schools and colleges in the U.S.A. and abroad. il Craft Horiz 27:11-21 My '67

Africa
Protection of Africa's artistic heritage; address, April 1966. E. Eyo. il UNESCO Courier 20:2, 16-19 Je '67

Alaska
Going places, finding things in Alaska. H. Johnson. il House & Gard 131:40-4+ My '67

Europe, Western
Shopping in Europe. E. Benson. Craft Horiz 27:23+ My '67

Finland
Anonymity. K. Franck. il Craft 27:34-5 Mr '67

Ireland
First harvest from Ireland's brilliant new design workshop, Kilkenny. M. Gough and J. Hendrix. il House B 109:242-5 O '67

Japan
Living treasures of Japan. R. Beardwood. il Fortune 76:130-5 N '67

Latin America
Showcase in Spain; Institute of Hispanic culture, Madrid. N. López Pellón. il Américas 19:32-5 N '67

Nepal
Folk art of Nepal. S. Peterson. il Craft Horiz 27:36-9 Mr '67

New England
Craft sampling in New England. R. Deardorff. il Redbook 129:42 Jl '67

Peru
Folk arts of Peru. F. L. Phelps. il Américas 19:18-25 Jl '67

Philippines
Showcase in Spain; Institute of Hispanic culture, Madrid. N. López Pellón. il Américas 19:32-5 N '67

United States
Artists at work; craftsmen of the Southwest. R. Deardorff. Redbook 130:43 N '67
Today's originals. D. L. Brightbill. il Am Home 70:16+ O '67
See also
Museum of contemporary crafts, New York

History
American habitat; excerpts from Taste in America. I. Ross. il House B 109:200-2 Ap '67

ARTSAY, Alda Favia-. See Favia-Artsay, A.

ARTSCHWAGER, Richard
Artschwager's mental furniture. E. C. Baker. il por Art N 66:48-9+ Ja '68

ARUNDEL, Jocelyn
Washington national zoological park has star performers; reprint. Parks & Rec 2:17+ F '67

AS you like it; drama. See Shakespeare, W.—Plays

ASBELL, Bernard
Case of the wandering IQs. Redbook 129:31+ Ag '67
Dick Lee discovers how much is not enough. N Y Times Mag p6-7+ S 3 '67
Medical training costs too much; excerpt from Case studies in change. Am Ed 3: 5-6 Mr '67

ASBURY, Francis
Francis Asbury, by L. C. Rudolph. Review
Christian Cent 84:474 Ap 12 '67. C. Bangs

ASCARIASIS
WHO aims at worms. D. A. Ehrlich. Sci N 92:115 Jl 29 '67

ASCENSION day
Ascension day charade. Christian Cent 84: 675-6 My 24 '67; Discussion. 84:942-3 Jl 19 '67

ASCENSION of Jesus Christ. See Jesus Christ —Resurrection and ascension

ASCOLI, Max
Editorial. See issues of The Reporter

ASCOMYCETES
Growth and sporulation of a pyrimidine spore color mutant of sordaria fimicola. A. S. El-Ani. bibliog il Science 156:88-90 Ap 7 '67

ASH, Agnes. See Root, L. jt. auth.

ASH, David
On a clear day you will see the electric car. N Y Times Mag p22+ Ja 29 '67

ASH, Roy Lawrence
Let's make foreign aid count. Duns R 90:43+ O '67
Nation building; address, November 8, 1967. Vital Speeches 34:181-4 Ja 1 '68

ASHANTI blood. See Mussaenda erythrophylla

ASHBERY, John
Cornell: the cube root of dreams. Art N 66: 56-9+ Sum '67

ASHBROOK, John Milan
Excerpt from address, March 8, 1966. Cong Digest 46:87+ Mr '67

ASHBROOK, Joseph
Astronomical scrapbook. See issues of Sky and telescope

ASHBY, Lyle W.
Deputy executive secretary Lyle W. Ashby. P. N. Mathless. por NEA J 56:51 O '67

ASHBY, Warren
Secrets of their hearts. Christian Cent 84: 310-12 Mr 8 '67
Theological existence among the ruins. Christian Cent 84:368-71 Mr 22 '67

ASHBY, William C. and others
Ecological dosimetry: radiation levels influenced by plant growth. bibliog Science 155:1430-2 Mr 17 '67

ASHCROFT, Samuel C.
Handicapped in the regular classroom. NEA J 56:33-4 N '67

ASHE, James
R.F. sniffer. Pop Electr 26:55-6 Je '67

ASHEIM, Lester E.
Manpower: a call for action; excerpts from address, February 1967. por Library J 92: 1795-7 My 1 '67

ASHLAND, Ore, Shakespeare festival. See Shakespeare festivals

ASHLAND oil and refining company
Outworking the competition. il Time 90:99-100 N 10 '67

ASHLEY, Audrey M. D.
Big paint job. Sch Arts 66:39 My '67

ASHLEY, Patricia
Music and musicians of Canada. Sat R 50:66-7 Ap 29 '67

ASHLEY, Stephen
Black palace; poem. Horn Bk 43:632 O '67

ASHLEY, Thomas L.
Excerpt from remarks, January 17, 1967. Cong Digest 46:180+ Je '67

ASHMOLEAN museum. See Oxford, England—Galleries and museums

ASHMORE, Harry Scott
Department gives facts regarding Ashmore-Baggs contracts with Hanoi. Dept State Bul 57:462-3 O 9 '67
Perils of probing. por Time 90:22 S 29 '67
Rover boys retaliate. Nat R 19:1054+ O 3 '67
Voice from the think tank. por Newsweek 70:21-2 O 2 '67
When an ex-editor made a bid for peace. por U S News 63:12 O 2 '67

ASHTON, Sir Frederick
Royal pair. H. Saal. il Newsweek 69:83-4 My 1 '67

ASHWORTH, Raymond B. and Cormier, M. J.
Isolation of 2,6-dibromophenol from the marine hemichordate, balanoglossus biminiensis. bibliog Science 155:1558-9 Mr 24 '67

ASIA

New opportunities in Asia; address, October 4, 1967. W. S. Gaud. Dept State Bul 57:579-84 O 30 '67
See also
Air travel—Asia
Bhutan
Children—Asia
Development banks—Asia
East and West
Economic assistance in Asia
Education—Asia
United Nations—Economic commission for Asia and the Far East
United States—Armed forces—Forces in Asia

Economic conditions

East Asia today; address, January 20, 1967. W. P. Bundy. Dept State Bul 56:323-7 F 27 '67

Economic integration

First steps toward an Asian Common market. D. Warner. Reporter 36:24+ My 18 '67

Economic policy

Japan's Prime Minister talks of Vietnam and the future of Asia; excerpts from address, November 15, 1967. E. Sato. U S News 63: 55-6 N 27 '67

Foreign opinion
American

Time is on our side in Asia. E. O. Reischauer. Read Digest 90:55-60 F '67

Foreign relations

Asian perspective; address, July 11, 1967. H. Kaplan. Dept State Bul 57:230-5 Ag 21 '67
Japan's Prime Minister talks of Vietnam and the future of Asia; excerpts from address, November 15, 1967. E. Sato. U S News 63: 55-6 N 27 '67
What is our pictture of Asia? A. Axelbank. New Repub 158:17-19 Ja 6 '68

History
Bibliography

Articles and other books received; east Asia; comp. by C. Hobbs. See issues of American historical review
Articles and other books received; south Asia; comp. by H. Conroy. See issues of American historical review

Maps

Map of Asia (cont) Sr Schol 91:27 O 5 '67

Politics

Asia after Vietnam. R. M. Nixon. For Affairs 46:111-25 O '67; Same. il U S News 63:86-91 O 23 '67
See also
Tricontinental conference, Havana, 1966

Religious institutions and affairs

World around us. Christian Cent 84:1605 D 13 '67

Riots

Overflowing revolution; neighboring countries suffer Maoist riots. il Time 90:20-1 Jl 28 '67

Social life and customs

Corruption in Asia; Time essay. Time 90:24-5 Ag 18 '67; Same abr. with title Is corruption inevitable in Asia? Read Digest 91:163-6 N '67

ASIA, CENTRAL

Communism's great divide. A. Parry. il Reporter 36:29-32 Je 1 '67
See also
Uzbekistan

ASIA, SOUTHEASTERN

ANZUS council discusses political and security problems; text of communique, April 22, 1967. Dept State Bul 56:749-50 My 15 '67
Asian diary. J. Mander. Commentary 44:90-5 O '67
U.S. commitment in southeast Asia; symposium. bibliog f Cur Hist 54:1-47+ Ja '68
Vietnam as a matter of conscience; progress toward economic, political and social stability. America 118:5-6 Ja 6 '68
War for southeast Asia. R. Hotz. Aviation W 86:21 Ap 24 '67
See also
Chinese in southeastern Asia
Communism—Asia, Southeastern
Guerrillas—Asia, Southeastern
Medical service—Asia, Southeastern
Mekong River
Opium trade—Asia, Southeastern

Antiquities

Southeast Asia and the West; prehistoric and early historic relations. W. G. Solheim, 2d. bibliog il Science 157:896-902 Ag 25 '67

Defenses

Australia's defense role after Harold Holt. D. Warner. il Reporter 38:24-6 Ja 11 '68

Economic conditions

Success for the U.S. il U S News 62:38-40 My 8 '67

Economic relations

First steps toward an Asian Common market. D. Warner. Reporter 36:24+ My 18 '67
Sports-shirt diplomacy; new, five-nation economic alliance. il Time 90:27 Ag 18 '67

Foreign relations

Neutralization in southeast Asia: problems and prospects, by C. E. Black and others. Review
   Bul Atomic Sci 23:29-32 Ap '67. A. S. Lall
Southeast Asia. G. Zimmermann. il Look 31: 54-6+ Jl 11 '67
Vice President Humphrey visits Viet-Nam, Malaysia, and Indonesia; remarks, toast, and joint communique, October 30-November 6, 1967. H. H. Humphrey. Dept State Bul 57:789-92 D 11 '67

History

Making of South East Asia, by G. Coedes. Review
   New Yorker 42:112+ Ja 28 '67. J. Alsop
Southeast Asia and the West; prehistoric and early historic relations. W. G. Solheim, 2d. bibliog il Science 157:896-902 Ag 25 '67

Maps

Strife-torn Viet Nam and its neighbors. il Nat Geog Mag 131:190-3, sup(folded map) F '67

Politics

New face of Buddha, by J. Schecter. Review
   Sat R 50:38 Ag 5 '67. L. Landry
Regional solution for Viet Nam. Vu-van-Thai. For Affairs 46:347-61 Ja '68
Southeast Asia. G. Zimmermann. il Look 31: 54-6+ Jl 11 '67
Struggle for power; US-USSR influences. H. Brandon. Sat R 50:11 Ag 12 '67

Religious institutions and affairs
See also
Buddha and Buddhism

ASIA and the United States

Fourteen experts look at U.S. future in Asia; report by Freedom house public affairs institute. U S News 64:29-31 Ja 1 '68
Partnership in east Asia and the Pacific; address, July 28, 1967. W. P. Bundy. Dept State Bul 57:195-200 Ag 14 '67

ASIA MINOR

Antiquities
See also
Aphrodisias

History

In the footsteps of Alexander the Great. H. Schreider and F. Schreider. il Nat Geog Mag 133:1-65 Ja '68

ASIAN art. See Art, Asian

ASIAN dancing. See Dancing, Asian

ASIAN development bank. See Development banks—Asia

ASIAN flu. See Influenza

ASIAN flu virus. See Influenza virus

ASIAN music. See Music, Asian

ASIANS

Asia. G. Zimmermann. il Look 31:37-53 Jl 11 '67
See also
Chinese

ASIANS in Africa

Asians go home. il Newsweek 70:55 S 25 '67
Black resentment for the Asians. il Time 89:32+ F 24 '67
Duka-wallas are outcasts in Africa. L. Fellows. il N Y Times Mag p20-2+ Je 25 '67

ASIATICS. See Asians

ASILIDAE. See Flies

ASIMOV, Isaac

After Apollo, a colony on the moon. N Y Times Mag p30-2+ My 28 '67; Same. Sci Digest 62:44-8+ S '67
Can you please give an explanation of the unified field theory? Sci Digest 61:86 F '67
Humanness of man. NEA J 56:6-8+ D '67

ASIMOV, Isaac—*Continued*
Isaac Asimov explains (cont of) Please explain; questions and answers. See issues of Science digest
Moon exploration: advent of the new engineering. por Tech W 20:46-8 Ja 23 '67
Over the edge of the universe. Harper 234: 97-8+ Mr '67
Views on science books. See issues of Horn book magazine to October 1967
about
Translator. por Time 90:55-6 Jl 7 '67
ASINOF, Eliot
From rabbit to real pro. N Y Times Mag p54-5+ S 10 '67
ASOFSKY, Richard, and Small, P. A. Jr
Colostral immunoglobulin-A: synthesis in vitro of T-chain by rabbit mammary gland. bibliog Science 158:932-3 N 17 '67
ASOLO theater comedy festival. See Drama festivals
ASPARAGINASE. See Enzymes
ASPARAGUS
Asparagus & rhubarb. D. Brooks. il Home Gard 54:35-6 Je '67
See also
Cookery—Vegetables
ASPEN, Colo.
Mountain hopping to Aspen in a hot new Debonair. R. B. Weeghman. il Flying 80: 34-9 Ap '67
ASPEN (periodical)
Box pop. il Newsweek 69:91 F 20 '67
ASPER, Ken, and Hayes, Jim
Big trout are my meat. pors Outdoor Life 139:66-9+ Ap '67
ASPHALT shingles. See Shingles
ASPIRIN
Aspirin: wonder drug nobody understands. G. A. W. Boehm. Read Digest 90:116-18 Mr '67
Fighting aspirin ads three ways; proposed FTC rules. il Bsns W p38 Jl 15 '67
ASSASSINATION
See also
Kennedy, J. F.—Assassination
ASSASSINATION in art. See Art—Themes
ASSEMBLAGE. See Sculpture
ASSEMBLY, Right of
See also
Free speech
ASSEMBLY plants, Automobile. See Automobile assembly plants
ASSESSMENT
Property tax scandals: bad laws & crafty assessors. M. Harris. Nation 204:210-12 F 13 '67
What does the assessed value of property mean? il Good H 165:160 Jl '67
What if you're near a city? B. Brantley. Suc Farm 65:54 My '67
ASSESSORS
Property tax scandals: bad laws & crafty assessors. M. Harris. Nation 204:210-12 F 13 '67
ASSIS CHATEAUBRIAND BANDEIRA DE MELO, Francisco de
Empire from the ground up. por Bsns W p88 Je 17 '67
ASSISI, Italy
Assisi that nobody knows. N. Braybrooke. il Sat R 50:35-6 Jl 29 '67
ASSOCIATED opera companies of America
City of firsts; production of Boris Godunov in Baltimore. A. M. Lingg. il Opera N 32:16-19 N 4 '67
ASSOCIATED press
Live wires. il Newsweek 71:46-7 Ja 15 '68
ASSOCIATION and associations. See Associations
ASSOCIATION for international development
Summer in Bogotá. W. M. Barbieri. America 117:274-7 S 16 '67
ASSOCIATION for school, college and university staffing
American education placement service. G. E. Arnstein. bibliog f Sch & Soc 95:298-301 Sum '67
ASSOCIATION for supervision and curriculum development
Meeting, 1967. D. Burleson. Sr Schol 90:sup2 Ap 14 '67
ASSOCIATION for the study of Negro life and history
First cooperative conference. Negro Hist Bul 30:20 Ap '67
1966 annual meeting; the 51st anniversary session of the association. Negro Hist Bul 30:21 Ja '67
ASSOCIATION of American dance companies
Building an organization; National endowment's initial grants. M. B. Siegel. Dance Mag 41:51+ Ag '67

ASSOCIATION of American law schools
New trends in law schools. Sch & Soc 95: 290 Sum '67
ASSOCIATION of American library schools
ALA midwinter report. K. Molz. Wilson Lib Bul 41:611-12 F '67
ASSOCIATION of American medical colleges
University medicine; letter. R. C. Berson. Sat R 50:71 My 6 '67
ASSOCIATION of American university presses
AAUP program features professional sessions. Pub W 191:67-8 Ap 24 '67
AAUP views publishing scene in Canada and abroad; symposium. il Pub W 192:27-31 Jl 24 '67
Editorial management: four problem areas; reports of editorial seminars il Pub W 192: 39-46 Jl 17 '67
1966 in review Pub W 191:53 Ja 30 '67
Period of youthful aging. C. Kerr. Sat R 50: 34 Je 10 '67
Presidents of the American association of university presses; 1943-1967. il Sat R 50: 32-3 Je 10 '67
Preview of Toronto. J. K. Hutchens. Sat R 50:28-9+ Je 10 '67
Professional seminars mark annual meeting of AAUP; symposium; with editorial comment. il Pub W 192:22-33, 38 Jl 3 '67
Third annual exhibition of university press books. il Pub W 191:64-5+ Je 12 '67
See also
American university press service, incorporated
ASSOCIATION of Catholic teachers
Meanwhile, back in Philadelphia. A. Swidler. Commonweal 86:191-2 My 5 '67
ASSOCIATION of Chicago priests
New witness. Commonweal 86:277 My 26 '67
Priestly pace-setters. America 116:866 Je 24 '67
Priests opt for relevancy. America 116:769 My 27 '67
ASSOCIATION of college and research libraries
Total of seventy-five grants; gifts to college and university libraries by Grants committee. Wilson Lib Bul 41:554 F '67
ASSOCIATION of food and drug officials of the United States
Frank industry talk on frozen food sins. Consumer Rep 32:124-5 Mr '67
ASSOCIATION of lunar and planetary observers
ALPO anniversary. Sky & Tel 33:229 Ap '67
ASSOCIATION of Pittsburgh priests
Another association. America 116:203 F 11 '67
ASSOCIATION of producing artists
APA-Phoenix nest. H. Hewes. Sat R 51:26 Ja 6 '68
APA-Phoenix season. A. Pryce-Jones. Vogue 149:112 F 1 '67
APA's big season. M. Gussow. il Newsweek 71:57 Ja 1 '68
Broadway's APA and Hollywood's mom. R. Kotlowitz. il Harper 234:115-17 Ap '67
ASSOCIATION of research libraries
National commission hears ARL group. Library J 92:2493-4 Jl '67
ASSOCIATION on American Indian affairs, incorporated
Equal rights for this American too; American Indian. Christian Cent 84:429 Ap 5 '67
ASSOCIATIONS
Aslib for America: solution to problem of proliferation of specialized organizations and their overlapping membership. J. Shera. Wilson Lib Bul 41:1063-4 Je '67
See also
Communist organizations

Federal aid
Evasion by definition. Nation 204:452 Ap 10 '67
How to care for the CIA orphans; Time essay. Time 89:42-3 My 19 '67
Public-private organizations. D. Wolfle. Science 156:587 My 5 '67
ASSUMPTION of the Virgin Mary. See Mary, Virgin—Assumption
ASSYRO-Babylonian music. See Music, Assyro-Babylonian
ASTAIRE, Fred
Special for the special. V. H. Swisher. il pors Dance Mag 42:24-6 Ja '68
ASTARTE; ballet. See Ballets—Criticisms
ASTEROIDS
Duck, here comes Icarus! Sci Digest 62:33 O '67
Icarus, strange swinger. Sci N 92:490 N 18 '67
Minor planet Icarus in 1968. il Sky & Tel 35: 21 Ja '68
Rotation of Vesta. Sky & Tel 35:3+ Ja '68

ASTHMA
Asthmatic child. G. D. Barkin and J. P. McGovern il NEA J 56:40-1 N '67
Cutting coughs; environmental-control unit. Newsweek 70:54 Ag 28 '67
Facts about childhood asthma. E. F. Ellis. il Parents Mag 42:76-7+ N '67
Kids who conquer asthma. S. M. Spencer. il Sat Eve Post 240:88-90 F 25 '67
Winning the battle against asthma. D. Ducas. il Todays Health 45:28-32 Ag '67; Same. Sci Digest 62:76-80 O '67
 See also
Miners asthma

ASTIER DE LA VIGERIE, Emmanuel d'
Svetlana, as I know her. Ladies Home J 84:61+ Ag '67

ASTIZ, Carlos Alberto
Changing face of Latin American higher education. Bul Atomic Sci 23:4-8 F '67

ASTON, Roy, and Hibbeln, Phyllis
Induced hypersensitivity to barbital in the female rat. bibliog Science 157:1463-4 S 22 '67

ASTOR, Gerald
Reverend Fay Hill and his lace pants mob. Look 31:71-6 O 31 '67

ASTOR, William Waldorf, family
Decline and fall; closing of Cliveden. il Newsweek 69:38 My 29 '67

ASTRAKHAN coat; drama. See Macaulay, P.

ASTRIN, Kenneth H. See Doolittle, R. F. jt. auth.

ASTROGRAPHIC lenses. See Lenses, Astrographic

ASTROJET classic. See Golf—Tournaments

ASTROLOGY
Family food horoscope; with recipes. B. M. Stover. il Parents Mag 43:60-5 Ja '68
Horoscopes. S. Leek. See issues of Ladies' home journal
Horoscopes for mothers. S. Leek. Ladies Home J 84:12+ My '67
Is astrology nonsense? H. Van Horne. Redbook 130:20+ Ja '68
Is astrology scientific? D. Cohen. il Sci Digest 61:30-2 F '67
Opinion: on your year. C. V. Cotta. Mlle 66:42-3+ Ja '68
Party in your future; with recipes. il Ladies Home J 84:120-1+ O '67

Anecdotes, facetiae, satire, etc.
Hard-core astrology. J. Mathewson. il Look 31:M14 N 14 '67

ASTRONAUTICS. See Space flight

ASTRONAUTS
Apollo 204. J. G. Dunne. Sat Eve Post 240:20+ Je 17 '67
Apollo's final seconds. il Newsweek 69:96+ F 13 '67
Fire kills three astronauts. il Sr Schol 90:16 F 10 '67
Inquest on Apollo. il Time 89:18-19 F 10 '67
Is moon program in real trouble? il U S News 62:29-32 F 13 '67
On tragedy; deaths of the Apollo astronauts. W. J. Coughlin. Tech W 20:50 F 6 '67
Put them high on the list of men who count: V. Grissom, E. White, R. Chaffee. il Life 62:18-27 F 3 '67
Three astronomers picked to become astronauts. Sky & Tel 34:135 S '67
To strive, to seek, to find, and not to yield. il Time 89:13-16 F 3 '67
Tragedy at the Cape. R. Hotz. Aviation W 86:17 F 6 '67
We knew that someday. . . Sci N 91: 112 F 4 '67
 See also
Cunningham, W.
Eisele, D.
Komarov, V.
Schirra, W. M.

Clothing
Air force studying hybrid, two-gas suit. H. M. David. il Tech W 20:18 F 27 '67
Four firms deliver spacesuits for MOL. H. M. David. Tech W 20:38-9 F 13 '67
Jet shoes studied as astronaut EVA aid. il Aviation W 87:81+ S 11 '67
Nonflammable suit material under evaluation for Apollo. il Tech W 20:20-1 My 29 '67
Robot flexes thirty-five joints to test space suits. T. Anderson. il Pop Sci 190:128-9 My '67
Space suit and life support projects escape trimming. il Aero Tech 21:100-5 N 20 '67
Two-way stretch in space. H. Manchester. il Pop Mech 127:136-9 Ap '67

Salaries
Now, a big pay cut for the astronauts. il U S News 62:19 My 15 '67

Training
Schirra's team carries on for Apollo. il Life 62:32-5 My 19 '67

ASTRONOMERS
Three astronomers picked to become astronauts. Sky & Tel 34:135 S '67
 See also
Horn-D'Arturo, G.
Women as astronomers

ASTRONOMERS, Amateur
Amateur astronomers. See issues of Sky and telescope
Canadian amateurs visit Mexico. J. A. Dumas. il Sky & Tel 34:91 Ag '67
Gleanings for ATM's; ed. by R. E. Cox. See issues of Sky and telescope
Here and there with amateurs (cont) Sky & Tel 34:233-8+ O '67
 See also
Association of lunar and planetary observers

ASTRONOMICAL charts. See Astronomy—Charts, diagrams, etc.

ASTRONOMICAL conferences
Convention at Long Beach; joint meeting of Western amateur astronomers and Association of lunar and planetary observers.. J. W. Goodman. il Sky & Tel 34:223-4 O '67
Fourth Texas symposium. L. C. Green. il Sky & Tel 34:84-8, 153-6 Ag-S '67

ASTRONOMICAL distances
Quasar distance measured. il Sci N 92:607 D 23 '67
Sun's distance. Sky & Tel 34:355 D '67
Twinkling galaxy: quasar distance observation. Sci Am 217:49-50 D '67

ASTRONOMICAL instruments
Radio astronomy: NSF scrutinizing proposals for six major instruments. V. K. McElheny. Science 157:782-4 Ag 18 '67
What is the true shape of the sun? J. Ashbrook. bibliog il Sky & Tel 34:229-30 O '67; Discussion. 34:371 D '67
 See also
Interferometers
Telescope

ASTRONOMICAL league
Convention in Washington. P. V. Rizzo. il Sky & Tel 34:139-42 S '67

ASTRONOMICAL lenses. See Lenses, Astrographic

ASTRONOMICAL measurements
Measuring the position angle of a double star. G. Gleason. il Sky & Tel 33:117-18 F '67

ASTRONOMICAL models
Intensity fluctuations of a relativistically expanding source. A. G. Petschek. bibliog Science 156:239 Ap 14 '67
Rapid rotation of the solar interior. A. J. Deutsch. bibliog Science 156:236-7 Ap 14 '67
Rotation of the sun. P. Goldreich and G. Schubert. bibliog il Science 156:1101-2 My 26 '67; Reply. R. H. Dicke. 157:960 Ag 25 '67
Stellar evolution: comparison of theory with observation. I. Iben, jr. bibliog il Science 155:785-96 F 17 '67
3-D star display. W. E. Broderick il Sky & Tel 34:288 N '67

ASTRONOMICAL observatories
High-energy cosmic rays. A. N. Bunner. il Sky & Tel 34:204-8 O '67
Lindheimer astronomical research center. il (p269) Sky & Tel 33:271 My '67
New Airglow observatory in Pennsylvania. W. A. Feibelman. il Sky & Tel 33:340-2 Je '67
Night at the observatory; studying quasars at Mount Palomar. H. S. F. Cooper, jr. il Horizon 9:108-16 Sum '67
Steward observatory's new 90-inch reflector; at Kitt Peak. R. L. Hilliard. il Sky & Tel 34:79-81 Ag '67
World's biggest camera; Kitt Peak national observatory solar telescope. C. M. Cardon. il Arch Forum 127:44-9 O '67
 See also
National radio astronomy observatory, Green Bank, W.Va.
Smithsonian institution—Astrophysical observatory

Australia
Two 150-inch telescopes for southern hemisphere. Sky & Tel 34:71 Ag '67
Two well-equipped observatories in Australia. R. E. Cox. il Sky & Tel 35:48-53 Ja '68

ASTRONOMICAL observatories—*Continued*

Chile
Corning fabricating mirror for European observatory; European southern observatory, La Silla Mountain, Chile. il Tech W 20:36-7 Mr 6 '67
Two 150-inch telescopes for southern hemisphere. Sky & Tel 34:71 Ag '67

France
Great French astronomer; the late A. Danjon, former director of Paris observatory. J. Kovalevsky. il Sky & Tel 33:347-9 Je '67
Lunar photography at Pic du Midi observatory. Z. Kopal. il Sky & Tel 33:216-19 Ap '67

Germany (Federal Republic)
Roger Barry and the Mannheim observatory. J. Ashbrook. il Sky & Tel 33:228-9 Ap '67

Mexico
Mexican observatory to move. Sky & Tel 34:361 D '67
Observatory moves; National astrophysical observatory. E. Zubryn. Sci N 92:178 Ag 19 '67

Russia
New Soviet observatory at Shemakha, Azerbaijan. C. S. Gillmor. il Sky & Tel 34:215 O '67

ASTRONOMICAL photography
All-reflection Schmidt telescope for space research. L. C. Epstein. il Sky & Tel 33:204-7 Ap '67
Astrophotography with a short-focus lens. G. E. Shaw. il Sky & Tel 33:394-5 Je '67
Giant prominence photographed in March. il Sky & Tel 33:276-7 My '67
Kitt Peak's new photoelectric guider. W. F. Ball and A. A. Hoag. il Sky & Tel 35:22-4 Ja '68
Meteor photography in the Netherlands. F. H. Naber. il Sky & Tel 35:54-7 Ja '68
More about color moon movies. J. F. Bridges. il Sky & Tel 33:254-5 Ap '67
Photograph exploding stars. il Sci Digest 62:32 O '67
Photographing star spectra. R. Waber and R. McPherson. il Sky & Tel 33:322-5 My '67
Resolution of NGC 205. G. S. Mumford. il Sky & Tel 33:160 Mr '67
Shooting stars. K. Poli. il Pop Phot 61:96-7+ S '67
Some hints on amateur meteor photography. D. Milon. il Sky & Tel 34:115-16 Ag '67
Swiss amateur's cooled-emulsion camera. H. Eggeling. il Sky & Tel 34:382-3 D '67
Techniques tomorrow; telephoto lenses as used by astronomers. B. Sherman. Mod Phot 31:32+ Ap '67
1200mm. L. Mulvehill. il U S Camera 30:64-5+ F '67

ASTRONOMICAL research
Opening up the southern heavens; three large telescopes to be built in southern hemisphere Time 90:62 Jl 21 '67
Optical astronomy in perspective. H. W. Babcock. bibliog il Science 156:1317-22 Je 9 '67
Science in search of itself; gamma-ray astronomy. A. Ewing. il Sci N 92:117 Jl 29 '67
Science versus spectaculars; concerning statements of B. Lovell and Fred Hoyle. Nation 204:612 My 15 '67
See also
Astrophysics

ASTRONOMICAL societies
See also
American astronomical society
Astronomical league
International astronomical union

ASTRONOMICAL society of Mexico
Canadian amateurs visit Mexico. J. A. Dumas. il Sky & Tel 34:91 Ag '67

ASTRONOMY
Astronomy. J. Stokley. See issues of Science news
Astronomy notes. Sci N 92:611 D 23 '67
Join the in-group and look to the stars. G. Heberton. il Pop Gard 18:50-3+ Ag '67
See also
Airplanes in astronomy
Asteroids
Astronomical research
Comets
Cosmogony
Earth
Life on other planets
Nebulae
Occulations
Radar in astronomy
Radio astronomy

Satellites
Sun
Universe

Atlases
See Stars—Atlases

Bibliography
Books and the sky. See issues of Sky and telescope

Charts, diagrams, etc.
Position in the H-R diagram. M. Hack. Sky & Tel 33:354 Je '67
Sky and telescope's new star charts. G. Lovi. Sky & Tel 35:34-6 Ja '68
Sky reporter. T. D. Nicholson. See issues of Natural history incorporating Nature magazine
Southern stars. See issues of Sky and telescope
Stars for [the month] See issues of Sky and telescope
See also
Stars—Atlases

Exhibitions
Space astronomy at Expo 67. P. A. Leavens. il Sky & Tel 34:72-8 Ag '67

History
Cosmic vision of Robert Burton. J. Ashbrook. Sky & Tel 33:92 F '67
Ejnar Hertzsprung, measurer of stars. A. V. Nielsen. il Sky & Tel 35:4-6 Ja '68

Observations
Backyard astronomer; finding celestial objects. J. S. Pickering. il Natur Hist 76:54+ Mr '67
Observing Mars in 1967. C. F. Capen. il Sky & Tel 33:208-10 Ap '67
See also
Interferometers
Moon—Observations
Space flight—Astronomical observations
Sun—Observations

Study and teaching
Astronomy for juniors in Brooklyn. J. S. Levine. il Sky & Tel 34:291-2 N '67
Theoretical astronomy; new institute in Cambridge. J. Walsh. Science 157:1286-8 S 15 '67
See also
Planetariums

Tables, etc.
Events of 1968 in the Graphic time table. Sky & Tel 35:31-3 Ja '68

ASTRONOMY, Nautical. See Nautical astronomy

ASTRONOMY, Spherical and practical
See also
Azimuth

ASTROPHOTOGRAPHY. See Astronomical photography

ASTROPHYSICAL observatories. See Astronomical observatories

ASTROPHYSICS
Cosmologists; 1967 Texas symposium on relativistic astrophysics. New Yorker 42:31 F 11 '67
Fourth Texas symposium; relativistic astrophysics. L. C. Green. il Sky & Tel 34:84-8, 153-6 Ag-S '67
Gravitational collapse. K. S. Thorne. il Sci Am 217:88-92+ bibliog(p 154+) N '67
Joint institute for laboratory astrophysics; National bureau of standards and University of Colorado. R. H. Garstang. il Sky & Tel 33:150-2 Mr '67
Macro meets micro. Sci N 91:160 F 18 '67
Relativistic astrophysics; report on 1967 symposium. S. P. Maran and A. G. W. Cameron. bibliog il Science 157:1517-24 S 29 '67
See also
Magnetic fields (cosmic physics)

ASTROS (baseball) See Baseball clubs

ASTURIAS, Miguel Ángel
Guatemalan author wins Nobel prize for literature. Pub W 192:30 O 30 '67
Myth for mankind. R. G. Mead, jr. por Sat R 50:32 N 4 '67
Tendency of commitment. por Time 90:42 O 27 '67

ASTURIAS
Unspoiled Asturias. V. E. Condon. il Travel 127:58-60 Ja '67

ASYLUM, Right of
Declaration on territorial asylum; Sixth committee approves draft. UN Mo Chron 4:110 D '67
Is there sanctuary in the church? Christian Cent 84:1389 N 1 '67
Right of asylum; resolution adopted by General assembly. UN Mo Chron 4:139 Ja '67

AT midnight; ballet. See Ballets—Criticisms

AT the drop of another hat; revue. See Musical comedies, revues, etc.—Criticisms, plots, etc.

AT-the-table cookery. See Cookery

ATABRINE
Quinacrine, atebrin: mode of action. J. Ciak and F. E. Hahn. bibliog il Science 156:655-6 My 5 '67

ATCHESON, Richard
Bennington college. Holiday 42:46-9+ S '67
Cartagena on the Spanish Main. Holiday 43:20+ Ja '68
Fascination of Fiji. Holiday 42:26+ Jl '67
Florida's back-yard jungle. Holiday 42:16+ N '67
North Carolina: Outer Banks and inner peaks. Holiday 42:16+ S '67
Rothenburg: time remembered. Holiday 42:20+ D '67
Spirit of Old Town. Holiday 41:66-9+ Mr '67

ATCHISON, Topeka and Santa Fe railway
Purveyor to the West; Harvey houses. L. Beebe. il Am Heritage 18:28-31+ F '67

ATEBRIN. See Atabrine

ATHABASCA oil sands. See Bituminous sand

ATHEISM
Atheism and criticism. R. O. Johann. America 116:506 Ap 1 '67
Difficult dialogue with non-believers. R. Butler. Cath World 205:95-100 My '67
God and contemporary philosophy. J. Collins. Commonweal 85:528-34 F 10 '67

ATHENAGORAS I, patriarch
His embrace is universal. il pors Life 62:30-2+ Mr 31 '67
I hear secret voices that speak of love; interview, ed. by P. Dragadze. il por Life 62:38 Mr 31 '67
Reunion in Rome. Time 90:84 N 3 '67

ATHENS, Greece
City as an act of will; excerpt from Design of cities. E. N. Bacon. il Arch Rec 141:114-19 Ja '67
Antiquities
Hellenic highlights. M. M. Davis. il Travel 128:24-30+ Ag '67
Piecing together an ancient puzzle; the tower of the winds. D. J. de S. Price. il Nat Geog Mag 131:586-96 Ap '67
Description
Hellenic highlights. M. M. Davis. il Travel 128:24-30+ Ag '67

ATHENS festival. See Music festivals—Greece, Modern

ATHEROSCLEROSIS. See Arteriosclerosis

ATHERTON, Calif.
Pin money for paperbacks; Menlo-Atherton high school. M. Hegland. il Library J 92:2000-1 My 15 '67
Why we can't wait; Atherton high school; letter to the editor. M. Hegland. Library J 92:1267-8 Mr 15 '67

ATHLETES
And the melody lingered on. B. Ottum. il Sports Illus 27:18-21 Ag 14 '67
Best-kept secrets; decathlon men. J. Underwood. il Sports Illus 26:82-6+ Je 12 '67
Bright faces of the future; high school athletes. il Sports Illus 26:44-51 Je 26 '67
Bully buildup in old Mexico; preparations for 19th Olympic games. B. Ottum. il Sports Illus 27:20-3 O 30 '67
Play is the thing! athletes as musicians. H. L. Masin. il Sr Schol 90:32 Ap 28 '67
Smashing start to the season; best dash men met in San Francisco. P. Axthelm. il Sports Illus 28:46-7 Ja 15 '68
That glamorous devil and his chorus line; J. C. Killy and French girls. D. Jenkins. il Sports Illus 26:22-5 Mr 20 '67
See also
Amateurism (sports)
Baseball players
Basketball players
Football players
Jewish athletes
Negro athletes
Recruiting
Fumbled ball; address, December 1, 1966. A. Brundage. Vital Speeches 33:411-16 Ap 15 '67
Jays turned into eagles; Hopkins Blue jays vs United States naval academy. G. Ronberg. il Sports Illus 26:28-9 My 22 '67
See also
Football players—Recruiting
Salaries
See also
Baseball players—Salaries

ATHLETES, Jewish. See Jewish athletes

ATHLETES, Negro. See Negro athletes

ATHLETES, Women. See Women as athletes

ATHLETIC buildings. See Gymnasiums

ATHLETIC fields
New dome for field track area; University of Pennsylvania. il Parks & Rec 2:34+ My '67

ATHLETICS
See also
Gymnastics
Pentathlon
Rowing
Running
School athletics
Track athletics

ATHLETICS for girls and women. See Physical education and training of Women

ATKINS, Robert J. See Hamburg, M. jt. auth.

ATKINSON, Brooks
Boris. Sat R 50:23 Je 10 '67
Grand Canyon. Natur Hist 76:38-9 N '67
Great swamp is good for nothing, but life, knowledge, peace and hope. N Y Times Mag p32-6+ F 12 '67
On speaking the speech. Sat R 50:30-1 Mr 4 '67
Realm of the irregular. Sat R 50:42 F 11 '67

ATKINSON, Robert E.
Regional report. Home Gard 54:55 S '67

ATKINSON, W. R. See Sartor, J. D. jt. auth.

ATLANTA
Architecture
Arts crunch: Memorial cultural center. G. Bradshaw. il Vogue 150:126-9+ S 15 '67
Big ideas that give downtown a new look; Peachtree Center project. il Bsns W p100-2+ F 25 '67
Building with air; new Regency Hyatt house. il Time 89:50 Je 2 '67
Communicable disease center
See United States—Communicable disease center
Hotels, restaurants, etc.
Building with air; new Regency Hyatt house. il Time 89:50 Je 2 '67
Georgia peach; Regency Hyatt house. il Newsweek 70:62 Jl 3 '67
Hotel that's all razzle-dazzle; Regency Hyatt house. il Life 63:78-80 Jl 21 '67
Music
Atlanta (cont) C. White. Opera N 32:23 O 14 '67
Atlanta's Aida. il Newsweek 70:98+ S 11 '67
See also
Atlanta symphony orchestra
Negroes
Atlanta's Negroes rock the boat. J. H. Baird. il Reporter 37:32-4 D 14 '67
Religious institutions and affairs
Parish without bounds; Community of Christ our Brother. C. Foust. Commonweal 86:514-15 Ag 25 '67
Riots
Accusing finger. il Newsweek 70:30-2 Jl 3 '67
Recipe for riot. il Time 89:20-1 Je 30 '67
Stores
Rich rewards; Rich's. il Newsweek 69:80-2 F 6 '67
Store with its heart in its work; Rich's. Time 89:89-90 Je 23 '67
Theater
Theatre; Theatre Atlanta. J. Novick. Nation 204:509 Ap 17 '67

ATLANTA Braves (baseball) See Baseball clubs

ATLANTA civic ballet (organization)
Atlanta's burgeoning ballets. W. Terry. il Sat R 50:56-8+ O 21 '67
Atlanta's Municipal theatre presents Giselle. D. Hering. il Dance Mag 41:26+ O '67

ATLANTA 500. See Automobile racing

ATLANTA symphony orchestra
Downbeat for a new era. il Time 90:53 O 27 '67

ATLANTIC and Pacific tea company. See Great Atlantic and Pacific tea company

ATLANTIC aviation corporation
Atlantic stresses maintenance flexibility. D. A. Brown. il Aviation W 86:106-8 F 13 '67

ATLANTIC cables. See Cables, Submarine

ATLANTIC Coast line-Seaboard merger. See Railroads—Consolidations and mergers

ATLANTIC community
Concert and conciliation: the next stage of the Altantic alliance; address, September 11, 1967. E. V. Rostow. Dept State Bul 57:422-30 O 2 '67; Same. Vital Speeches 34:13-18 O 15 '67
De Gaulle, non! Britain's application to join the Common market. A. Lejeune. Nat R 19:637+ Je 13 '67
Europe plays a stronger hand. il Bsns W p37-8 Mr 11 '67
Framework of East-West reconciliation. Z. Brzezinski. bibliog f For Affairs 46:256-75 Ja '68
On allies and enemies. M. Ascoli. Reporter 36:12 Je 1 '67
Pity of it. S. Alsop. Sat Eve Post 240:16 D 16 '67

ATLANTIC continental shelf. See Continental shelf

ATLANTIC fault. See Faults (geology)

ATLANTIC flights. See Aviation—Transatlantic flights

ATLANTIC monthly press
What is the Atlantic monthly press? P. Davison. il Pub W 192:32-4 O 16 '67

ATLANTIC OCEAN
Magnetic boundaries in the North Atlantic Ocean, J. R. Heirtzler and D. E. Hayes. bibliog il Science 157:185-7 Jl 14 '67
See also
Gulf Stream

ATLANTIC recording corporation
Turkish tycoons of "Soul". il Time 90:43 Jl 28 '67

ATLANTIC refining company
And they lived happily ever after: merger of Atlantic refining and Richfield oil. il Bsns W p 156-8+ Ap 29 '67

ATLANTIC salmon. See Salmon

ATLANTIC states
See also
Fishing—Atlantic states
Northeastern states

Description and travel
Washington and the two Virginias. il Bet Hom & Gard 45:80-1 Mr '67

ATLANTIC union (proposed)
Latest idea for Britain: a Common market with U.S. il U S News 64:46-7 Ja 1 '68

ATLANTIS
Atlantis and the searchers. il Newsweek 70:52-5 Jl 31 '67
Atlantis beneath the vineyard. il Sci N 92:125-6 Ag 5 '67
Economy-size Atlantis; Minoan city unearthed on island of Thera. il Time 90:68-9 Jl 28 '67
Explosion that changed the world; Santorini explosion. R. Schiller. il Read Digest 91:122-7 N '67
Is this Atlantis? D. Cohen. il Sci Digest 62:66-9 O '67
Volcano that shaped the western world; Santorini eruption; theories of A. Galanopoulos. J. Lear; discussion. Sat R 49:93-4 D 3 '66; 50:74 F 4; 55-6 Ap 1 '67

ATLANTIS II deep. See Ocean bottom

ATLAS (periodical)
Atlas's world. il Newsweek 69:58 Ap 3 '67

ATLASES
Inexpensive atlas; Scholastic world atlas. il Consumer Bul 50:34 Ag '67

ATLASES, Astronomical. See Stars—Atlases

ATMOSPHERE
Evolution of the earth's atmosphere; report on Lloyd V. Berkner memorial symposium. S. I. Rasool. il Science 157:1466-7 S 22 '67
See also
Fog
Sun—Atmosphere

ATMOSPHERE, Upper
Composition measurements of the topside ionosphere. J. H. Hoffman. il Science 155:322-4 Ja 20 '67
Ionospheric sounding rocket use gains. W. J. Normyle. il Aviation W 86:87+ Mr 20 '67
Ionospherically propagated sea scatter. L. H. Tveten. bibliog il Science 157:1302-4 S 22 '67
Radio reflection by free radicals in earth's atmosphere. J. D. Barry and others. bibliog il Science 156:1730-2 Je 30 '67; Reply with rejoinder. P. L. Bender. 158:1487-8 D 15 '67
See also
Airglow
Rockets—Use in research

ATMOSPHERIC electricity
Electric currents accompanying tornado activity. M. Brook. bibliog il Science 157:1434-6 S 22 '67

Temperature-dependence of the polarity of electrical charges on ice crystals. F. K. Odencrantz and R. W. Buecher. bibliog il Science 158:256-7 O 13 '67
Tornadoes: mechanism and control. S. A. Colgate. bibliog il Science 157:1431-4 S 22 '67
See also
Auroras
St Elmo's fire
Thunderstorms

ATMOSPHERIC ions. See Ions

ATMOSPHERIC pollution. See Air pollution

ATMOSPHERIC pressure
Barometric pressure fluctuations: effects on the activity of laboratory mice. R. L. Sprott. bibliog il Science 157:1206-7 S 8 '67

ATMOSPHERIC research
Aerial rescue gain seen in debris study; upper atmospheric nuclear debris studies may yield experience in midair retrieval. B. K. Thomas, jr. il Aviation W 87:83+ Ag 21 '67
Ionosphere after IQSY: London meetings review findings. N. Calder. Science 157:666-8 Ag 11 '67
NASA studying bids for sounding system. Aviation W 87:113 O 16 '67
Position of planets linked to solar flare prediction. R. Pay. il Tech W 20:35-8 My 15 '67
Preparation of submicroscopic spider threads for particle studies. M. J. Saunders and P. E. Prettyman. bibliog il Science 155:1124-5 Mr 3 '67
Supersonic Martlet/Scramjet set for first flight in Canada; Project HARP research program to gather atmospheric data. R. Barnhart. il Tech W 20:22-3 My 8 '67
See also
National center for atmospheric research
Rockets—Use in research

ATMOSPHERIC temperature
Climate modification by atmospheric aerosols. R. A. McCormick and J. H. Ludwig. bibliog Science 156:1358-9 Je 9 '67
Temperature-dependence of the polarity of electrical charges on ice crystals. F. K. Odencrantz and R. W. Buecher. bibliog il Science 158:256-7 O 13 '67

ATMOSPHERIC turbulence
Clear-air turbulence: simultaneous observations by radar and aircraft. J. J. Hicks and others. bibliog il Science 157:808-9 Ag 18 '67
IR device tested as turbulence detector; infrared scanning radiometer to detect clear air turbulence. R. D. Hibben. il Aviation W 86:61+ F 20 '67
NASA to coordinate pilot-aircraft studies; attack on clear air turbulence. B. K. Thomas, jr. il Aviation W 86:103-4 Mr 20 '67
Nature note; CAT, monster in the sky. Sci N 92:6 Jl 1 '67
Pan Am plans to evaluate turbulence detector on 707. Aviation W 86:35 Ap 10 '67
Scanning the CAT. il Time 90:55 Jl 7 '67

ATOLLS. See Coral reefs and islands

ATOMIC age
Ambiguous anniversary. il Newsweek 70:94-6 D 4 '67
Coming of age. il Time 90:28-9 D 8 '67
Education and the challenge of the future; creative living in the nuclear age. A. W. Munk. Sch & Soc 95:180-2 Mr 18 '67
Life with the atom: after twenty-five years. il U S News 63:64-6 D 11 '67
Nuclear age celebrates silver anniversary. I. Asimov. il Sci Digest 62:44-8 D '67

ATOMIC blasting
A-blast for copper. il Time 90:45 N 3 '67
A-blast for gas; Project Gasbuggy. il Newsweek 70:51 D 25 '67
A-bomb in the gas field; Gasbuggy. Sci N 92:610 D 23 '67
AEC sets Project Gasbuggy, first Plowshare experiment; underground nuclear detonation to produce natural gas. Aero Tech 21:43 N 6 '67
Atomic explosions for peace rescheduled. Sci N 92:558 D 9 '67
Good start for Gasbuggy. il Time 90:66-7 D 22 '67
H-bomb goes commercial; Gasbuggy blast. Bsns W p70-2 D 16 '67
Mining by atomic explosion: a 4.5-million experiment; Gasbuggy project. il U S News 63:107 N 20 '67
Project Gasbuggy. N. Carlisle and J. Carlisle. il Pop Mech 128:102-5+ S '67
Special report on Plowshare. D. R. Inglis and C. L. Sandler. Bul Atomic Sci 23:46-53 D '67

ATOMIC bomb shelters
  Chicken coop; Defense department's civil defense shelter program. Nation 205:69 Jl 31 '67
  Fallout shelter survey; Civil defense says there is no place like home. K. Sperry. Science 158:894-5 N 17 '67
  Notes and comment; competition for the design of an educational and recreational center incorporating dual purpose fallout shelter space. New Yorker 43:47-8 O 14 '67
  Sheltered life; study of human behavior in fallout shelters. il Newsweek 70:47 Jl 3 '67

ATOMIC bombs
  Incredible story of How China got the bomb; excerpts. W. L. Ryan and S. Summerlin. il Look 31:19-25 Jl 25 '67
  Nuclear age celebrates silver anniversary. I. Asimov. il Sci Digest 62:44-8 D '67
  Twenty-five years with the bomb; interview, ed. by A. Wolff. E. P. Wigner. Look 31:58+ D 26 '67
  See also
  Hydrogen bombs

Manufacture
  Building the bomb: an Indian view. S. J. Narayan. Bul Atomic Sci 23:25-6 F '67
  From Hahn to Hiroshima. il Newsweek 69:57 Ap 3 '67
  Igor Kurchatov, 1903-1960. E. Rabinowitch; A. P. Alexandrov; I. Golovin. Bul Atomic Sci 23:8-18 D '67
  Manhattan project, by S. Groveff. Review
  Atlan 219:149 Ap '67. O. Handlin
  Sat R 50:29+ Je 3 '67. B. G. Lall

Testing
  Bang no. 7; one more Chinese atomic test. Time 91:34+ Ja 5 '68
  Bugs in red China's bomb? il U S News 64:53 Ja 8 '68
  China explodes a hydrogen bomb; communiqué, June 17, 1967. Cur Hist 53:169+ S '67
  Chinese bomb blasts pact hopes. D. C. Winston. Aviation W 86:16-18 Je 26 '67
  Muted thunder; China's seventh nuclear shot. Newsweek 71:48 Ja 15 '68
  Peking adds potent punch to its arsenal. il Bsns W p36-7 Je 24 '67
  What China can hit with H-bomb; with interview with C. Y. Cheng. il U S News 63:35-8 Jl 3 '67

Testing, Detection of
  Excitation of surface waves by events in southern Algeria. R. C. Liebermann and P. W. Pomeroy. bibliog il Science 156:1098-100 My 26 '67
  Test detection: decoupling theory verified, but does it matter? L. J. Carter. Science 155:438-40 Ja 27 '67
  USAF to orbit two advanced Velas in April. G. S. Hunter. il Aviation W 86:71+ F 13 '67

Testing, Suspension of
  See also
  Nuclear test ban treaty, 1963

Testing, Underground
  How to hide underground tests; decoupling theory, Project Sterling. Bsns W p54+ Ja 14 '67
  Underground A-tests may be making us radioactive. N. Wadsworth. il Sci Digest 62:13-17 S '67

ATOMIC clocks
  Anti-collision system uses atomic clock. P. J. Klass. il Aviation W 86:70-1+ F 6 '67

ATOMIC energy. See Atomic power

ATOMIC energy agency. See International atomic energy agency

ATOMIC nuclei
  Nuclear theory. il Sci N 91:424 My 6 '67
  Polarized protons as nuclear probes. L. Rosen. bibliog il Science 157:1127-34 S 8 '67

ATOMIC power
  December 2, 1967; twenty-fifth anniversary. R. Stern. Nation 205:645+ D 18 '67
  Life with the atom; after twenty-five years. il U S News 63:64-6 D 11 '67
  Nuclear power: key to a golden age of mankind; address, December 2, 1967. L. B. Johnson. Dept State Bul 57:862-4 D 25 '67
  See also
  Atomic bombs
  Nuclear fission
  Nuclear fusion
  Nuclear reactors

Economic aspects
  Atom is gaining on oil and coal in energy race. il U S News 63:86-8 Ag 7 '67
  Atom's challenge to the coal industry. B. Kovach and N. Caldwell. Reporter 36:39-41 F 23 '67
  Dormant nuclear revolution. E. Teller. il Tech W 20:39-42 Ja 23 '67
  Dwight Eisenhower's proposal for our time; atomic desalting plants for the Near East. L. L. Strauss. il Nat R 19:1008-10 S 19 '67
  International control of civil nuclear power. M. Willrich. il Bul Atomic Sci 23:31-8 Mr '67
  Is the nuclear nonproliferation treaty enough? G. H. Quester. Bul Atomic Sci 23:35-7 N '67
  Nuclear age celebrates silver anniversary. I. Asimov. il Sci Digest 62:44-8 D '67
  Nuclear power goes critical. il Fortune 75:116-19 Mr '67
  Power push at PG&E. N. Willatt. il Duns R 90:39-40+ Ag '67
  Proposal for the Middle East: atomic desalting plants. Nation 205:322 O 9 '67
  See also
  Atomic blasting
  Atomic power plants
  Nuclear reactors
  Ships, Atomic powered

Industrial aspects
  See Atomic power—Economic aspects

International aspects
  Nuclear fuel-for-all. L. Beaton For Affairs 45:662-9 Jl '67
  To be nuclear or not. B. T. Feld. Bul Atomic Sci 23:60-2 My '67
  See also
  European atomic energy community
  International atomic energy agency

International control
  Counting the plutonium; IAEA inspection of nuclear facilities. Sci N 92:584 D 16 '67
  Gap, the drain and non-proliferation. il Sci N 91:445-6 My 13 '67
  International control of civil nuclear power. M. Willrich. il Bul Atomic Sci 23:31-8 Mr '67
  Latest A-bomb worry; spread of nuclear arms. il U S News 62:92 Ap 17 '67
  Nuclear proliferation: the real danger. Fortune 76:66 Ag '67
  Nuclear spread. J. R. Schlesinger. Yale R 57:66-84 O '67
  See also
  United States—Atomic energy commission

China (People's Republic)
  Bugs in red China's bomb? il U S News 64:53 Ja 8 '68

Germany (Federal Republic)
  Into the atomic lead? il Newsweek 71:58 Ja 15 '68
  Nuclear blackball. Newsweek 69:48-9 F 20 '67

Great Britain
  Nuclear energy: new study assails British program. J. Walsh. Science 156:1350-2 Je 9 '67

Mexico
  Nuclear progress: snail's pace. E. Zubryn. Sci N 92:379 O 14 '67

New Zealand
  Nuclear age begins; long pull ahead; nuclear energy generation. W. A. Scholes. Sci N 92:471+ N 11 '67

United States
  See Atomic power

ATOMIC power plants
  Atomic power-plants for your town? nuclear electricity is practical, but there are problems. il Changing T 21:39-41 Ap '67
  Electric power: new uses, new sources, more demand; interview. W. J. Clapp. il U S News 62:74-8 Mr 27 '67
  Europe's nuclear battle. J. Ross Skinner. il Duns R 89:65-6+ Mr '67
  More fuel for new-reactor race; fast breeder reactor for commercial power. il Bsns W p46+ Ja 13 '68
  Nuclear plants turn up the juice. il Bsns W p64-6+ Mr 11 '67
  Nuclear power go-ahead; West Germany. Sci N 92:276 S 16 '67
  Taming the H-bomb for power; generating electricity from nuclear fusion. il Bsns W p 102-4+ Mr 18 '67
  Thermal pollution: Senator Muskie tells AEC to cool it. B. Nelson. Science 158:755-6 N 10 '67

ATOMIC power plants—*Continued*
Third generation of breeder reactors. T. R. Bump. il Sci Am 216:25-33 My '67
Worldwide nuclear power; progress and problems. G. T. Seaborg. il Dept State Bul 56:90-7 Ja 16 '67

Location

Nuclear power on salmon rivers. A. Netboy. il Nation 205:337-9 O 9 '67
ATOMIC power plants, Portable. See Space vehicles—Atomic power plants
ATOMIC powered airplanes. See Airplanes, Atomic powered
ATOMIC powered ships. See Ships, Atomic powered
ATOMIC powered submarines. See Submarine boats, Atomic powered
ATOMIC powered warships. See Warships, Atomic powered
ATOMIC research
AEC centrifuge ban puts industry in spin. il Bsns W p99-100 Je 10 '67
AEC revamps warheads to penetrate ABM defenses. Tech W 20:20 F 6 '67
Atomic energy in Alaska; Conservation society's opposition to atomic experimentation. Nat Parks Mag 41:25 Ap '67
Books; life of Niels Bohr. O. R. Frisch. Sci Am 216:145-8+ Je '67
Bottling up the atom; AEC determination to control production of enriched uranium-235 in gas centrifuges. il Newsweek 69:86 Je 19 '67
Fusion research; an international affair. Bsns W p 106 Mr 18 '67

China (People's Republic)

Chinese H-bomb. Nation 205:4 Jl 3 '67
Reds' big priority; a nuclear missile. il U S News 63:37 O 2 '67

Europe, Western

See also
European atomic energy community
European organization for nuclear research

Germany

From Hahn to Hiroshima. il Newsweek 69:57 Ap 3 '67

Great Britain

Alone or together; development of a national program in Britain. D. Fishlock. Sci N 92:328 S 30 '67

India

Building the bomb; an Indian view. S. J. Narayan. Bul Atomic Sci 23:25-6 F '67

Japan

Japan moves forward; electron accelerator. S. Griffin. il Sci N 92:329 S 30 '67

Russia

Igor Kurchatov, 1903-1960. E. Rabinowitch; A. P. Alexandrov; I. Golovin. Bul Atomic Sci 23:8-18 D '67
Man with an atomic reactor. C. S. Wren. il Look 31:M19-22 O 3 '67

Scandinavia

Hope for small nations; regional cooperation. H. J. Barnes. Sci N 92:326-8 S 30 '67

United States

See Atomic research
ATOMIC research laboratories
British fusion research; cuts may reveal a pattern; cutback at Culham laboratory. J. Walsh. Science 157:665-6 Ag 11 '67
Fusion lab fund cut; cutback at Culham, Britain. D. Fishlock. Sci N 92:204 Ag 26 '67
See also
Oak Ridge national laboratory
United States—Atomic energy commission
ATOMIC test ban treaty. See Nuclear test ban treaty, 1963
ATOMIC warfare
But if twenty-five trucks fanned out... S. Alsop. Sat Eve Post 240:18 O 21 '67; Same abr. with title Day the U.S. was destroyed. Read Digest 92:92-4 Ja '68
Can U.S. survive red H-bombs? effects of imaginary attack on U.S. C. Hosmer. il U S News 63:60 Jl 31 '67
Nuclear time bomb; excerpts from report on the effects of possible use of nuclear weapons, and security and economic implications of wider acquisition and further development. il Sat R 50:16-19+ D 9 '67
Ultimate escalation. Nation 204:451-2 Ap 10 '67
See also
Atomic weapons

Casualties

Fatalities in U.S.-Soviet nuclear war; Defense dept. estimates of probable U.S. and Soviet fatalities. il Aviation W 87:57 O 23 '67

Defenses

Atomic arms race, a mad momentum may be under way. R. L. Gilpatric. il N Y Times Mag p54-5+ D 3 '67
Chinese H-bomb. Nation 205:4 Jl 3 '67
Dollars vs. lives; a U.S. choice; interview. E. Teller. il U S News 62:44-8 My 29 '67
Fireballs, matzohballs & Nike-X. M. Getler. Tech W 20:50 Je 26 '67
How to prevent a nuclear war; warning to Americans by Joint chiefs of staff; with statement by E. G. Wheeler. il U S News 62:31-3 My 15 '67
New thoughts on missile defense. D. G. Brennan. Bul Atomic Sci 23:10-15 Je '67
Nuclear defense; while U S. lags, Soviets rush ahead; excerpts from article in Izvestia. V. I. Chuikov. U S News 63:61 Jl 31 '67
Twenty-five years with the bomb; interview, ed. by A. Wolff. E. P. Wigner. Look 31:58+ D 26 '67

Ethical aspects

Visit with the great Kahn. S. Paradise. Christian Cent 84:1556-8 D 6 '67

Social aspects

International suicide? D. Lawrence. U S News 63:116 O 2 '67

Terminology

Fighting a nuclear war of the words; Strangelovisms. il Newsweek 69:47 Mr 27 '67

ATOMIC waste. See Radioactive waste disposal
ATOMIC weapons
Atomic arms race, a mad momentum may be under way. R. L. Gilpatric. il N Y Times Mag p54-5+ D 3 '67
China and the hydrogen bomb. N. Cousins. Sat R 50:16 Jl 8 '67
Chinese statement on nuclear proliferation; reprint. Bul Atomic Sci 23:53-4 My '67
Cold war is dead, but the arms race rumbles on. J. B. Wiesner. Bul Atomic Sci 23:6-9 Je '67
FOBS, ABM, etc; hearings on weapons developments before the Military applications subcommittee on the Joint committee on atomic energy. New Repub 157:8-9 N 18 '67
How much danger for the U.S.? M. S Johnson. U S News 63:34 Jl 24 '67
Last chance on nuclear nonproliferation? A. Larson. Sat R 50:21-4 O 7 '67
Moving right along; U.S. and U.S.S.R. nuclear programs. New Repub 158:7-8 Ja 13 '68
Neither will I again smite every thing living. S. Alsop. il Sat Eve Post 240:16 Je 17 '67
Nuclear spread. J. R. Schlesinger. Yale R 57:66-84 O '67
Nuclear time bomb; excerpts from report on the effects of possible use of nuclear weapons, and security and economic implications of wider acquisition and further development. il Sat R 50:16-19+ D 9 '67
One-upmanship; new Russian and U.S. nuclear weapons. il Sci Am 218:44 Ja '68
Paradoxes de la paix, by P. M. Gallois. Review
Nat R 19:1125-6 O 17 '67. S. T. Possony
Pastore's ABM plea; excerpts from remarks. J. O. Pastore. Aviation W 87:21 S 18 '67
Peace and the strategy conflict, by W. R. Kintner. Review
Nat R 19:1387-8 D 12 '67. F. J. Johnson
Sino-Soviet threat; testimony. R. S. McNamara. Aviation W 86:11 F 27 '67
Soviets prepare space weapon for 1968; with editorial comment. C. Brownlow. il Aviation W 87:21, 30-1 N 13 '67
U.S.-Soviet megaton gap rises again; summary of report prepared for the House armed services committee by the American security council. Aero Tech 21:10 Jl 17 '67
Warning signals fly for U.S. in the nuclear race; excerpts from report, with charts. U S News 63:32-3 Jl 24 '67
See also
Guided missiles

International control

ABM, some arms control issues. L. S. Rodberg. Bul Atomic Sci 23:16-20 Je '67
Bomb spreads. il Sci N 92:7-8 Jl 1 '67
Conference of non-nuclear weapon states; committee adopts report. UN Mo Chron 4:13-14 O '67

ATOMIC   weapons—International   control—
Continued
Convention on prohibition of nuclear weapons; consideration by First committee. UN Mo Chron 4:69-72 D '67
Denuclearization of Latin America; consideration in First committee. UN Mo Chron 4:18-22 N '67
Denuclearization of Latin America; First committee's recommendation to Assembly. UN Mo Chron 4:72-3 D '67
Denuclearization of Latin America; text of message to Preparatory commission for the denuclearization of Latin America. Thant. UN Mo Chron 4:13-14 F '67
Denuclearization in Latin America; Treaty for the prohibition of nuclear weapons in Latin America. H. Bowser. Sat R 50:32 My 20 '67
End of the treaty? Newsweek 69:38+ My 29 '67
Ending the cold war; Vietnam need not slow the thaw. W. C. McWilliams; reply. R. D. Masters. Commonweal 85:547+ F 17 '67
Gap, the drain and non-proliferation. il Sci N 91:445-6 My 13 '67
General assembly adopts resolutions; with texts. UN Mo Chron 4:27-35 Ja '67
Haves v. have-nots; non-proliferation treaty. Time 89:29-30 Mr 3 '67
H-bomb warnings. Commonweal 86:435-6 Jl 14 '67
Hope on nuclear treaty. Bsns W p38 Ag 19 '67
Last chance on nuclear nonproliferation? A. Larson. Sat R 50:21-4 O 7 '67
Latin America bans the bomb; Treaty of Tlatelolco. L. Eder. Nation 204:371-2 Mr 20 '67
Letter from Geneva; Eighteen-nation disarmament conference; enactment of nonproliferation treaty. D. Lang. New Yorker 43:70+ Ag 5 '67
Nineteen seventy-five; what is holding up agreement on a non-proliferation treaty. G. Lichtheim. Commentary 44:64-7 Jl '67
1966 international negotiations for arms control and disarmament; letter of transmittal, February 17, 1967 with excerpt from report. L. B. Johnson. Dept State Bul 56:568-77 Ap 3 '67
Non-proliferation: hopes and fears. il Newsweek 69:40+ Mr 6 '67
NATO nuclear planning group holds first ministers meeting; statement, April 3, 1967; with text of communique, April 7, 1967. R. S. McNamara. Dept State Bul 56:686-8 My 1 '67
Nuclear bans and the technology gap. il Sci N 91:183-4 F 25 '67
Nuclear blackball; non-proliferation treaty. Newsweek 69:48-9 F 20 '67
Nuclear fuel-for-all. L. Beaton. For Affairs 45:662-9 Jl '67
Nuclear spread: quest for a treaty is receiving new attention. J. Walsh. Science 157:288-90 Jl 21 '67
Pledge: no first use. B. T. Feld. Bul Atomic Sci 23:46-8 My '67. Reply with rejoinder. E. Young. 23:37-8 N '67
President Johnson renews call for nonproliferation treaty; message, February 21, 1967. L. B. Johnson. Dept State Bul 56:447-8 Mr 20 '67
Tangled treaty; U.S.-NATO allies disagree on nonproliferation treaty. Newsweek 69:37-8 My 1 '67
What have we learned? N. Cousins. Sat R 50:20+ Je 24 '67
Withdraw missile submarines? E. W. Crawford. Bul Atomic Sci 23:39 N '67

Testing
AEC digs deep for big blast; new test series. il Bsns W p 140+ S 16 '67
Enlarged nuclear test capability being developed by AEC, DOD. K. Johnsen. Aviation W 87:31 D 11 '67
How scientists play games with names; naming nuclear weapons tests. il Bsns W p66 D 30 '67
Rockets developed in case nuclear tests are resumed. R. Pay. il Tech W 20:26-9 Ap 17 '67

ATOMIC weapons and disarmament
ABM decision. R. Gomer. Bul Atomic Sci 23:29 N '67
ABM, some arms control issues. L. S. Rodberg. Bul Atomic Sci 23:16-20 Je '67
Antiproliferation. Sci Am 217:48 O '67
Arms control and European unity: the next ten years; excerpts from Arms control and the Atlantic alliance. K. W. Deutsch. Bul Atomic Sci 23:21-4 My '67
Chinese bomb blasts pact hopes. D. C. Winston. Aviation W 86:16-18 Je 26 '67

Congressional interest in ABM heightens. D. C. Winston. Aviation W 87:68-9 O 23 '67
Convention on prohibition of nuclear weapons; consideration by First committee. UN Mo Chron 4:69-72 D '67
Denuclearization of Latin America, by A. G. Robles. Review
Bul Atomic Sci 23:32-3 N '67. P. Barnes
General assembly adopts resolutions; with texts. UN Mo Chron 4:27-35 Ja '67
Hopes run high for limiting nuclear club. Bsns W p35-6 My 6 '67
International suicide? D. Lawrence. U S News 63:116 O 2 '67
Is the nuclear nonproliferation treaty enough? G. H. Quester. Bul Atomic Sci 23:35-7 N '67
Missile-defense debate intensifies. C. Brownlow. il Aviation W 87:55-6+ O 23 '67
Missile defense: LBJ's bid to curb arms race gains support. L. J. Carter. Science 155:1651-4 Mr 31 '67
Nuclear bans and the technology gap. il Sci N 91:183-4 F 25 '67
Outer space, strategy, and arms control. W. C. Clemens, jr. Bul Atomic Sci 23:24-8 N '67
Tangled treaty; U.S.-NATO allies disagree on nonproliferation treaty. Newsweek 69:37-8 My 1 '67
U.S. discusses effect of ABM deployment on arms control efforts; statement, September 19, 1967. A. S. Fisher. Dept State Bul 57:543-5 O 23 '67
U.S. gives views on Soviet proposal for convention on nonuse of nuclear weapons; statement, November 20, 1967. A. S. Fisher. Dept State Bul 58:26-30 Ja 1 '68
U.S. viewpoint on four current world problems; statement, September 21, 1967. A. J. Goldberg. Dept State Bul 57:487-8 O 16 '67
See also
Conference of the Eighteen-nation committee on disarmament, Geneva, 1962-
ATOMIC workers
Radiation protection; report on symposium. R. L. Kathren. Science 156:544-6+ Ap 28 '67
ATOMS
Atom reactions in flow tubes. B. A. Thrush. bibliog il Science 156:470-3 Ap 28 '67
Comparative X-ray and neutron diffraction study of bonding effects in s-triazine. P. Coppens. bibliog il Science 158:1577-9 D 22 '67
Nature of ceramics. J. J. Gilman. il Sci Am 217:112-18+ S '67
Solid state. N. Mott. il Sci Am 217:80-9 S '67
See also
Atomic nuclei
Matter
Molecules
Protons
ATOMS for peace awards
Atoms for peace: Russian declines award. il Science 158:360 O 20 '67
ATONEMENT in action. See Volunteer service, International
ATRAZINE. See Weeds—Chemical control
ATROCITIES of war. See War; World war, 1939-1945—Atrocities
ATROPINE
Circadian pattern of plasma 17-hydroxycorticosteroid: alteration by anticholinergic agents. D. T. Krieger and H. P. Krieger. bibliog il Science 155:1421-2 Mr 17 '67
ATSUSHI, Iwamatsu. See Yashima. T. pseud.
ATTACHED houses. See Row houses
ATTACHMENT and garnishment
How garnisheed workers fare under arbitration. R. W. Fisher. bibliog f Mo Labor R 90:1-6 My '67
ATTARDI, Domenica G. and others
Submaxillary gland of mouse: properties of a purified protein affecting muscle tissue in vitro. bibliog Science 156:1253-5 Je 2 '67
ATTEBERY, James E.
We're switching to diesel-driven refuse trucks. Am City 82:79-80 Ag '67
ATTENTION
How to teach listening skills; discriminating listening to records and tapes. J. Muri. il Sr Schol 90:sup 14 Mr 10 '67
Learn the useful art of listening. il Changing T 21:40-2 D '67
Perceptual deficit during a mental task. D. Kahneman and others. bibliog il Science 157:218-19 Jl 14 '67
Successiveness discrimination as a two-state, quantal process. A. B. Kristofferson. bibliog il Science 158:1337-9 D 8 '67
Who is listening? address, April, 1967. S. L. Wallace. Wilson Lib Bul 42:295-300 N '67
ATTENUATORS, Radio. See Radio attenuators

ATTICS
Renovation of a garret. il House B 110:120-1 Ja '68
Ventilation for a sun-baked attic. il Sunset 138:134+ My '67

Anecdotes, facetiae, satire, etc.
Manner of speaking. J. Ciardi. Sat R 50:16+ S 16 '67

ATTITUDES
Alienated vs. society; symposium. bibliog f il Sch & Soc 95:252-68 Ap 15 '67
Are we having a nervous breakdown? H. Cox. McCalls 95:6+ Ja '68
Case for young rebels. J. Brothers. Good H 164:61-2 Je '67
Challenge of fear. A. Paton. Sat R 50:19-21+ S 9 '67
Children's views of foreign peoples, by W. E. Lambert and O. Klineberg. Review
  Wilson Lib Bul il 42:187-93 O '67. L. Minturm
I just don't understand these kids; attitude toward money. E. Weston. McCalls 95:8 D '67
Mood at Berkeley. C. J. McNaspy. America 116:817-18 Je 3 '67
Odd-couple: image-obsessed world. D. Newman and R. Benton. il Mlle 65:18 Je '67
Shortchanged children of suburbia, by A. Miel. Review
  Sat R 50:89 My 20 '67. J. H. Martin
To a giver from a taker. U S News 64:100 Ja 15 '68
See also
Frustration
Moral attitudes
Political attitudes
Public opinion
Value (psychology)

ATTLEE, Clement Richard Attlee, 1st earl
Egalitarian example. por Time 90:34+ O 20 '67
Obituary
Newsweek por 70:51 O 16 '67
President Johnson expresses sorrow at death of Lord Attlee; statement, October 8, 1967. L. B. Johnson. Dept State Bul 57:568 O 30 '67

ATTOE, O. J.
New long-term plant feeding. Horticulture 45:45 O '67

ATTORNEY General (United States) See United States—Justice, Department of

ATTORNEYS. See Lawyers

ATTRACTANTS, Insect. See Insect sex attractants

ATTUCKS, Crispus
Boston massacre and the martyrdom of Crispus Attucks. por Negro Hist Bul 30:4 Mr '67

ATTWOOD, William
Labyrinth in foggy bottom; excerpts from The reds and the blacks. por Atlan 219:45-50 F '67; Same abr. Read Digest 90:121-4 Je '67
about
Dialogue with the third world. T. P. Melady. Sat R 50:64 Ap 8 '67

ATWATER, James D. See Wilkinson, C. B. jt. auth.

AUBREY, John
Theatre; Roy Dotrice's impersonation. E. Oliver. New Yorker 43:46 D 30 '67
Theatre; R. Dotrice's impersonation. H. Clurman. Nation 206:92-3 Ja 15 '68

AUCHINCLOSS, Hugh D. family
How the remarkable Auchincloss family shaped the Jacqueline Kennedy style. S. Birmingham. il Ladies Home J 84:91-3+ Mr '67

AUCHINCLOSS, Louis
Collector of innocents; story. McCalls 94:102-3+ Ap '67

AUCTIONEERS. See Auctions

AUCTIONS
Classic action at a vintage auction; first auction of automobiles conducted in this country. J. Wilson. il Motor T 19:74-7 Ap '67
Ill-starred treasure comes into its own; auction of items of K. Wagner's Spanish treasure trove at New York's Parke-Bernet galleries. il Life 62:100-2 Mr 10 '67
Joint purchasing leads to joint selling; Lower Bucks County, Pa. R. Zweig. il Am City 82:96 F '67
Look what's happening to purebred auctions! il Farm J 91:40-1+ O '67
Record prices mark Charles Hamilton's 1966-67 auctions. K. V. Hostick. il Hobbies 72:108-9 D '67
1740 Canary & all that; vintage wine auctions in London. Time 89:62 Je 9 '67

Trove come true; salvage of an armada wrecked in 18th century off Florida at Manhattan's Parke-Bernet galleries. il Time 89:74-5+ F 10 '67
When old wine pours like gold; London auction at Christie's. il Bsns W p 152-5 Je 10 '67
See also
Book sales

AUCTIONS, Art. See Art sales

AUDEN, Wystan Hugh
Afterword. Horn Bk 43:176-7 Ap '67
Citizen of the republic of letters; address, November 30, 1967. por Library J 92:4508-9 D 15 '67
Real world; excerpt from address. New Repub 157:25-7 D 9 '67
about
Artemis and harlequin. H. Kenner. Nat R 19:1432-3 D 26 '67
Auden at sixty. J. Hollander. por Atlan 220:84-7 Jl '67
W. H. Auden awarded National medal for literature. Pub W 191:35 My 1 '67
W. H. Auden receives National literature medal. por Pub W 192:24 D 4 '67

AUDIENCES
People and their feelings; Lincoln Center student program. R. A. Tuggle. il Opera N 31:8-13 Mr 4 '67
Why opera? J. Barzun. il Opera N 31:6-10 Ja 28 '67
See also
Applause
Television audiences

AUDIO amplifiers. See Amplifiers

AUDIO dealers
What makes an audio dealer? N. Eisenberg. Hi Fi 17:111 O '67

AUDIO fairs
Hi-fi in the halls of Hilton; New York hi-fi show. I. Berger. il Sat R 50:66-8 S 16 '67
New York high fidelity music show. Consumer Bul 50:28-9 F '67
N.Y. hi-fi show. W. A. Stocklin. Electr World 78:6 S '67
Old show in new package; high fidelity exhibition at New York's Statler Hilton hotel. il Hi Fi 17:36+ D '67
Other side; 1967 fair in London. T. Heintz. Sat R 50:71+ Ap 29 '67
Progress and renaissance, audio 1967; New York hi-fi show. I. Berger. Sat R 50:61+ O 28 '67
Show stoppers; New York high fidelity show at Statler-Hilton. H. Fantel. Opera N 32:27 N 4 '67
Tokyo's hi-fi show. il Hi Fi 18:30+ Ja '68

AUDIO fidelity records. See Video tape recordings

AUDIO oscillators. See Oscillators

AUDIO-visual aids
Audio-visual communications: trends and possibilities. il Arch Rec 141:167-70 F '67
Audiovisual guide. Library J 92:4283-94 N 15 '67
New educational materials (cont) Sr Schol 90:sup 18-20 F 3; sup30+ F 17; sup 16+ Mr 10; sup23-4+ Ap 14; sup 19 Ap 21; sup 17-19 My 12; sup21 My 19; 91:sup33-5 S 28; sup20 O 5; sup 15 O 19; sup 10-12 O 26; sup 17 N 16 '67
New media: help students come to their senses: aids for teaching composition. D. A. Sohn. il Sr Schol 90:sup 16-17 My 19 '67
Sex education: new teaching materials. D. Burleson. il Sr Schol 90:sup 14 Ap 21 '67
See also
Educational media index
Instructional materials centers
Libraries and audio-visual materials

AUDIO-visual equipment
Expo 67, preview of the future for audio-video? N. Eisenberg. Hi Fi 17:16 D '67

AUDIO-visual instruction
Agents for change: producer or consumer? W. Howell. Library J 92:3812-14 O 15 '67
English, education and the electronic revolution; excerpts. E. J. Farrell. Sr Schol 91:sup 12-13 S 28 '67
Media fellowships offered under Higher ed. act. Library J 92:1287 Mr 15 '67
New university of the air; project in Great Britain. Sch & Soc 95:519+ D 23 '67
Video tape: mass medium for individualized instruction. G. Pensinger. il Sr Schol 91:sup22-3 O 26 '67
See also
Computers—Educational applications
Libraries and audio-visual materials
Moving pictures in education
National education association—Department of audio-visual instruction
Television in education

AUDIO-visual materials, Cataloging of. See Cataloging
AUDITING
 See also
 Tax auditing
 United States—General accounting office
AUDITIONS. See Theatrical production
AUDITIONS, Metropolitan. See Singing—Competitions
AUDITORIUM theater, Chicago. See Chicago—Theater
AUDITORIUMS
 For concerts, dance and drama: flexible design; by M. F. Schmertz. il Arch Rec 141: 115-30 F '67
 When conventioneers hit town. il Bsns W p 158-60+ Ja 14 '67
 See also
 Concert halls
AUDUBON medal
 A. Starker Leopold Audubon medalist, 1966. C. W. Buchheister. il Audubon 69.20-1 Ja '67
AUDUBON nature centers
 City kids take to the farm: Aullwood children's farm. J. Lauzon. il Parents Mag 42: 50-1+ D '67
AUDUBON societies
 See also
 National Audubon society
AUERBACH, C.
 Chemical production of mutations. bibliog Science 158:1141-7 D 1 '67
AUERBACH, Robert, and Rugowski, J. A.
 Lysergic acid diethylamide: effect on embryos. bibliog Science 157:1325-6 S 15 '67
AUERBACH, Sylvia
 Knee by any other name. Atlan 220:123-4 O '67
AUERSWALD, Wilhelm, and Doleschel, Walter
 Lactones as inhibitors of the fibrinolytic system. bibliog Science 156:1244-5 Je 2 '67
AUFORTH, Frederick C.
 Idle millions. S. Pelletiere. Nation 205:401-3 O 23 '67
AUGENSTEIN, Leroy
 Shall we play God? Christian Cent 84:1314-18 O 18 '67
AUGERS
 Make your own auger bits. W. E. Burton. il Pop Mech 127:188 F '67
AUGHANBAUCH, John
 All about hickory. Am For 73:28-30+ Jl '67
AUGSPURGER, George L.
 Damping factor debate. Electr World 77:46-7 Ja 67
AUGSTEIN, Rudolf
 Mirror of Germany. il por Newsweek 70:99-99A+ O 23 '67
AUGUSTA, Ga.
  Music
 See also
 Augusta opera company
AUGUSTA national golf club course. See Golf courses
AUGUSTA opera company
 Report: Augusta, Ga. R. J. Croan. Opera N 32:21 N 4 '67
AUGUSTINE, Saint
 St Augustine & the new religion. P. W. Schmidtchen. il por Hobbies 72:104-5+ Ja '68
AULESTIA, Patricia
 From the grass roots. J. Anderson. il por Dance Mag 41:14-16+ Ag '67
AULLWOOD children's farm, Ohio. See Audubon nature centers
AUMENTE, Jerome
 Following the Moselle. Travel 127:34-6 Je '67
 Ghetto is people. Nation 205:555-7 N 27 '67
 Majestic Norse course. Travel 128:42-4 Ag '67
AURORA, Colo.
 Lighting gets more people in the swim. T. R. Knapp. il Am City 82:130+ Je '67
AURORAS
 Lights in the sky: still enigmatic. il Sci N 92:58 Jl 15 '67
 Rockets bombard the aurora; Aerobee and Javelin. il Sci Digest 61:38-9 My '67
 Two fine auroral displays in January. il Sky & Tel 33:184-6 Mr '67
 Variation in atmospheric carbon-14 activity relative to a sunspot-auroral solar index. J. R. Bray. bibliog il Science 156:640-2 My 5 '67
 White-light solar flare and the May 25th aurora. il Sky & Tel 34:57-9 Jl '67
 See also
 Airglow
AUSCHWITZ atrocities. See World war, 1939-1945—Atrocities
AUSCHWITZ concentration camp. See Concentration camps—Poland

AUSTEN, Alice
 Cottage. New Yorker 43:35-6 S 30 '67
AUSTEN, Jane
 Pride and prejudice; dramatization. See Newman, D.
AUSTIN, Alex
 Something about heaven; story. Mlle 64: 176-7 Mr '67
AUSTIN, Cassius
 Cassius Austin: warden. L. Dietz. por Field & S 72:44-5+ N '67
AUSTIN, Eleanor S. and Sanders, F. G.
 Florage, a collage of pressed flowers. il Horticulture 45:28-9+ D '67
AUSTIN, Tex.
  Banks
 Banking empire in Lyndon Johnson's future? il U S News 63:59-60 Jl 24 '67
AUSTIN Peay state college, Clarksville, Tenn.
 Austin Peay: aesthetics and flexibility. J. Givens. il Library J 92:4360-2 D 1 '67
AUSTRALIA
 Australia; country of champs; with report by G. Johnston. il Vogue 150:158-66+ S 15 '67
 Books in review; Australia and the islands. H. M. Van Deusen. Natur Hist 76:64-9 Mr '67
 Changing face of Australia. C. B. Hagan. il Cur Hist 52:295-301 My '67
 See also
 Airplanes, Military—Australia
 Astronomical observatories—Australia
 Birds—Australia
 Book industries and trade—Australia
 Colleges and universities—Australia
 Cotton growing—Australia
 Education—Australia
 Fishing—Australia
 Frontier and pioneer life—Australia
 Great Barrier Reef
 Hunting—Australia
 Immigrants in Australia
 Iron mines and mining—Australia
 Libraries—Australia
 Melbourne
 Military service, Compulsory—Australia
 Mines and mineral resources—Australia
 National parks and reserves—Australia
 New South Wales
 Sports—Australia
 Sydney
 Water supply—Australia
 Yachts and yachting—Australia
 Zoology—Australia

  Defenses
 Australia's defense role after Harold Holt. D. Warner. il Reporter 38:24-6 Ja 11 '68

  Description and travel
 Personal business; Australia in the springtime. Bsns W p 165-6 S 23 '67
 Their shining Eldorado, by E. Huxley. Review
  Sat R il 50:30-1 S 9 '67. O. Prescott

  Economic conditions
 Australia strikes it rich. il U S News 62:74-7 My 1 '67

  Industries
 See also
 Broken Hill proprietary company
 Mines and mineral resources—Australia

  Military policy
 See also
 Australia—Defenses

  Native races
 Aboriginal activity; constitutional amendments improve status. il Time 89:42 Je 16 '67

  Politics and government
 Australia looks ahead, as much support for U.S? il U S News 64:22-3 Ja 1 '68
 See also
 Australia—Prime ministers
 Political parties—Australia

  Prime ministers
 New pilot. il Newsweek 71:43+ Ja 22 '68
 Succession; contenders. Newsweek 71:32 Ja 1 '68

  Religious institutions and affairs
 World around us (cont) Christian Cent 84: 820-2, 1612-13 Je 21, D 13 '67

  Social conditions
 Australasian character. J. Forster. bibliog f Ann Am Acad 370:156-63 Mr '67
 What to expect if you emigrate to Australia. il U S News 63:76-7 Jl 17 '67

AUSTRALIA and the United States
Australia looks ahead, as much support for
U.S? il U S News 64:22-3 Ja 1 '68
How a Yank reacts to the Aussies. U S News
64:5 Ja 1 '68
AUSTRALIA library association. See Library
association of Australia
AUSTRALIA, National library. See National li-
brary of Australia
**AUSTRALIA, New Zealand, and United States
treaty council.** See ANZUS council
AUSTRALIAN desert mice. See Mice, Desert
AUSTRALIAN literature
See also
Childrens literature—Australia
AUSTRALIAN lungfishes. See Lungfishes
AUSTRALIAN poetry
More poems from Down Under. P. Smith. il
Am For 73:38-9 My '67
AUSTRALIAN slang. See Slang
AUSTRALIANS
Australasian character. J. Forster. bibliog f
Ann Am Acad 370:156-63 Mr '67
Personal business; Australia in the spring-
time. Bsns W p 165-6 S 23 '67
AUSTRALOPITHECUS africanus. See Man,
Prehistoric
AUSTRIA
See also
Airplanes, Military—Austria
Americans in Austria
Music—Austria
Opera—Austria
Public opinion—Austria
Tyrol
Vienna
Vorarlberg

Description and travel
Austria Austrians know. N. S. Hazelton.
Nat R 19:1123 O 17 '67
Travel's picture portfolio. Travel 127:52-7 My
'67

History
Bibliography
Articles and other books received; comp. by
A. H. Price. See issues of American his-
torical review

Politics and government
Otto and the Austrian psyche. E. v. Kuehnelt
Leddihn. Nat R 19:1326 N 28 '67
See also
Fascism—Austria
AUSTRIAN cookery. See Cookery, Austrian
AUSTRIAN literature
Transformation of the garden: ideal and so-
ciety in Austrian literature; address, Sep-
tember 1965. C. E. Schorske. bibliog f Am
Hist R 72:1283-320 Jl '67
AUSTRIAN TYROL. See Tyrol
AUTHORITARIANISM
Be like me! be free! J. G. Milhaven. Amer-
ica 116:584-6 Ap 22 '67; Discussion. 116:784-
90 My 27 '67
AUTHORITY
Try the spirits. R. Kirk. Nat R 19:1211 O 31
'67
See also
Authoritarianism
AUTHORS
Authors & editors. See issues of Publishers'
weekly
Lance for hire; freelance writers. il Time 90:
78+ S 15 '67
Medium as she is massaged; excerpts from
Authors take sides on Vietnam. Nat R 20:
18-19 Ja 16 '68
Most important questions unpublished writers
ask. M. Pollack. Writer 80:14-16+ F '67
Rights and permissions; views on not-writers;
ed. by P. Nathan. M. Cowley. Pub W 193:
33 Ja 1 '68
See also
Authorship
Editors and editing
Historians
Literary agents
Literature
Novelists
PEN club
Poets
Royalties
Women as authors

Homes and haunts
See Literary landmarks
AUTHORS, African
Africa's black writers. T. Sterling. Holiday
41:131-40 F '67

Present-day writers of tropical Africa. il
UNESCO Courier 20:24-5 Je '67
See also
African literature
AUTHORS, American
American 1890s, by L. Ziff. Review
Reporter 36:51-2 F 23 '67. R. Sklar
Après la guerre finie; American writers in
World war I. M. Cowley. il Horizon 10:
112-19 Wint '68
Endowing the arts; National council on the
arts program of assistance to writers. D.
Dempsey. Sat R 50:25 Ag 12 '67
John Peale Bishop & the other thirties. L. A.
Fiedler. Commentary 43:74+ Ap '67
Lachrymose ladies; address, September 15,
1966. J. Manthorne. bibliog Horn Bk 43:375-
84, 501-13, 622-30 Je-Ag. O '67
Penmen of the golden West. J. K. Hutchens;
K. Rexroth. il Sat R 50:34-6+ S 23 '67
Think back on us, by M. Cowley. Review
New Repub 156:24-6 Mr 11 '67. R. M.
Adams
Sat R 50:31-2 Mr 11 '67. G. Hicks
Trade winds; American writers who came
to a violent end; ed. by H. R. Mayes. W.
Brockway. Sat R 50:16 N 4 '67
When poets looped the loop; the Chicago
renaissance. J. K. Hutchens. Sat R 50:35-6
Ja 28 '67
Young American writers, by R. Kostelanetz.
Review
Sat R 50:25-6 D 2 '67. G. Hicks
See also
American literature
Burgess, T. W.
Dahlberg, E.
Dos Passos. J.
Federal writers project
Hoffer, E.
Hughes, L.
James, H.
Mailer, N.
Melville, H.
Negro authors
Sendak. M.
Sinclair, U.
Still, J.
Warren, R. P.
Wolfe, T.
AUTHORS, Argentine
See also
Mallea, E.
AUTHORS, Austrian
See also
Austrian literature
AUTHORS, British. See Authors, English
AUTHORS, English
See also
Christie, A.
Dickens, C.
Ewing, J. H. G.
Lucas. F. L.
Russell, B. R.
Walton, I.
Wells, H. G.
Wilde, O.
AUTHORS, European
Author! author! eastern Europe's nervous
stable of writers. il Time 89:33-4 Mr 17 '67
AUTHORS, French
Literary life in Paris. H. R. Lottman. il
Pub W 192:21-3 N 27 '67
AUTHORS, German
See also
German literature
AUTHORS, Greek
See also
Kazantzakis, N.
AUTHORS, Guatemalan
See also
Asturias, M. A.
AUTHORS, Irish
See also
Joyce. J.
O'Faolain. S.
AUTHORS, Italian
See also
Goldoni, C.
AUTHORS, Mexican
Literary life south of the Rio Grande. J.
K. Hutchens. il Sat R 50:42-4 F 25 '67; Dis-
cussion. 50:26 Mr 25 '67
AUTHORS, Negro. See Negro authors
AUTHORS, Russian
Chain reaction. il Newsweek 71:29-31 Ja 8 '68
Moscow trial; the perils of literature. il News-
week 71:35 Ja 22 '68
Off with the mask; trial of intellectuals
accused of anti-Soviet agitation. il Time
91:21-2 Ja 19 '68
Other country inside Russia; Soviet writers.
S. Kunitz. il N Y Times Mag p24-5+ Ag
20 '67

AUTHORS, Russian—*Continued*
Shaming their elders; imprisoned Soviet writers. il Time 91:36 Ja 5 '68
Svetlana era; Soviet intellectuals swear never again. J. Laber. Commonweal 86:390-2 Je 23 '67
See also
Bulgakov, M.
Grinevskiĭ, A. S.
Makarenko, A. S.
Olesha, ĬŪ. K.
Pasternak, B. L.

AUTHORS, South African
See also
Abrahams, P.

AUTHORS, Southern. See Authors, American
AUTHORS agents. See Literary agents
AUTHORS and politics
Books; fashion for authors to come out with pontifical declarations on public affairs. M. Muggeridge. Esquire 68:54+ D '67
Reactionaries, by J. Harrison. Review
Commentary 44:82+ Ag '67. D. Donoghue; Nation 204:792-3 Je 19 '67. S. Paul
Nat R II 19:809+ Jl 25 '67. J. Hart
New Repub 157:19-20+ S 16 '67; I. Howe; Reply with rejoinder. C. M. Silverman. 44:8+ N '67

AUTHORS and publishers
Author's right of access to publication. H. F. Pilpel. Pub W 193:23 Ja 1 '68
I mean, my God, if you can't produce a great American novel for two hundred thou, presold to the flicks, what the hell hope is there for American literature? S. Braun. il Esquire 67:76-7+ F '67
Inconclusive skirmish of the war on poverty. A. Gingrich. Esquire 67:6 F '67
Publisher and the pep talk. E. O'Connor. Writer 80:31-2 Ap '67
When you query, write it right! L. Olfson. Writer 80:14-15+ Mr '67
See also
Literary agents
Royalties

AUTHORS conferences
European literary scene; international congress on romanticism, Budapest. R. J. Clements. Sat R 50:31 N 4 '67
Evolution and ideation; twenty-fifth annual World science fiction convention. New Yorker 43:38 S 16 '67
Guide to writers' conferences. D. J. Willcox. Writer 80:46-8 Ap '67
Latin American writer's congress: a dialog tries to fill a void. R. Morrison. Pub W 191:18-19 My 15 '67
Workshops for writers; preview of summer conferences. G. Munson. il Sat R 50:37-9+ Ap 29 '67
Writers' conferences 1967. Writer 80:49-54 Ap '67

AUTHORS tours. See Books—Advertising
AUTHORSHIP
Aim for the heart. P. Gallico. Writer 80:11-12+ S '67
Amber notebooks. D. Myers. Esquire 67:146-7 F '67
Block, failure, and depression. P. Highsmith. Writer 80:23-6 O '67
Books: the reader and the writer. W. Ready. Writer 80:21-3+ Jl '67
Changes and constants in a writer's life. M. C. Banning. Writer 80:11-13 N '67
From facts to fiction; physician turned writer; reprint. W. Percy. Writer 80:27-8+ O '67
In praise of a café-au-lait bat; books every writer should own. L. Conger. Writer 80:9-10 Jl '67
Iron snake selection. J. G. Dunne. Sat Eve Post 240:22-3 N 4 '67
Letter to a fiction writer. B. J. Chute. Writer 80:9-12 O '67
Re-learning the basics. N. Benchley. Writer 80:28-30 Ap '67
Restoration of a writer. P. S. Curry. Writer 80:13-15 S '67
Second million words. W. E. Barrett. Writer 80:9-12 My '67
This Oscar (sob) really belongs to all those who . . . L. Conger. Writer 80:9-10 Ag '67
Where to sell manuscripts. See issues of Writer
Why free-lance writers get nervous. J. N. Bell. Sat R 50:91-2 N 11 '67; Discussion. 51:108-9 Ja 13 '68
Writer's requisites. A. Seton. Writer 80:19+ Ag '67
Writing a first novel; symposium. Writer 81: 20-6 Ja '68 (to be cont)

Writing for the greeting card market. L. Hardt. Writer 80:28-9 Mr '67
See also
Authors
Authors conferences
Childrens literature—Technique
Drama—Technique
Fiction—Technique
Letter writing
Literary research
Plagiarism
Plots (drama, novel, etc)
Short stories
Style, Literary
Television authorship

Anecdotes, facetiae, satire, etc.
Six burrs in the blanket. F. Flora. Writer 80:24-6 Ag '67

Bibliography
Writer's library. See issues of Writer

Collaboration
Ghost writers give boss the word. il Bsns W p72-4 Ja 21 '67

AUTISM
Empty fortress, by B. Bettelheim. Review
Commonweal 86:283-6 My 26 '67. W. Ryan
New Repub 156:23-4 Mr 4 '67. R. Coles
World without I; University of Chicago's Orthogenic school for autistic children. il Newsweek 69:70-1 Mr 27 '67

AUTO radios. See Automobiles—Radio equipment

AUTOBIOGRAPHY
At the piano; excerpts. I. Newton. il Opera N 31:6-7 Je 10 '67
Peripatetic reviewer. E. Weeks. Atlan 220: 135 O '67
See also
Diaries

AUTO-engine analyzer. See Automobile engines—Testing

AUTOGIRO company of America
Autogiro flies once again, in the courts: battling helicopter industry over patent rights. il Bsns W p78-80+ My 27 '67

AUTOGIROS
James Bond's amazing one-man autogyro. D. Scott. il Pop Sci 190:66-9+ Je '67
Mostly for fun, rarely for business. il Bsns W p80 My 27 '67
Wild new flying machines: gyrodynes. J. L. Kent. il Sci Digest 61:64-8 F '67

AUTOGRAPHS
Record prices mark Charles Hamilton's 1966-67 auctions. K. V. Hostick. il Hobbies 72: 108-9 D '67
See also
Signatures (writing)

AUTOLITE technical service institute
Auto tech; Autolite's new self-study delivery of automotive fundamentals. J. McFarland. il Hot Rod 20:82 Je '67

AUTOMATIC alarms. See Electric alarms
AUTOMATIC automobile control. See Automobiles—Control
AUTOMATIC cargo handling. See Freight handling
AUTOMATIC checkout equipment

Display systems
See Information display systems

AUTOMATIC control
See also
Automation
Cybernetics
Hydraulic control
Inertial guidance systems
also subhead Automatic control under various subjects, e.g. Waterworks—Automatic control

AUTOMATIC elevators. See Elevators
AUTOMATIC exposure meters. See Exposure meters
AUTOMATIC light fader. See Electric lighting —Control
AUTOMATIC machinery. See Machinery, Automatic
AUTOMATIC pilot (airplanes)
Case for PC; positive control as standard equipment on all Mooney aircraft. Flying 80:15-16 My '67
Monitor aids C-141 all-weather landing. K. J. Stein. il Aviation W 86:80-1+ Ap 3 '67
AUTOMATIC speech recognition
Computers that hear. C. Behrens. il Sci N 91:214 Mr 4 '67
Voice-controlled computer is teachable; Litton's Mellonics div. system. R. Lindsey. Aero Tech 21:52-3 O 9 '67

AUTOMATIC sprinkler corporation of America
Fireball on the acquisition front: H. E. Figgie. il Bsns W p78-81 Ag 12 '67
AUTOMATIC teaching. See Teaching machines
AUTOMATIC train control. See Railroads—Automatic train control
AUTOMATIC transmission. See Automobiles—Transmission
AUTOMATIC washing machines. See Washing machines
AUTOMATION
Automation: a tool dedicated to the service of man; address, September 12, 1967. V. W. Bearinger. Vital Speeches 34:50-3 N 1 '67
Automation syndrome. il Sci Digest 61:82 My '67
Capital and economic growth; address, February 16, 1967. G. Champion. Vital Speeches 33:330-3 Mr 15 '67
Most notorious victory, by B. B. Seligman. Review
Commentary 44:86-8 Ag '67. R. Lekachman
What comes next in the computer age; interview. J. Diebold. il U S News 62:54-7 Je 26 '67
See also
Computers—Industrial applications
Hospitals—Automation
Libraries—Automation
Machinery, Automatic
Retail trade—Automation
School libraries—Automation
Unemployment, Technological
AUTOMATONS
Anyone for yo-ho-ho? computerized robots at Disneyland. il Life 63:138-9+ S 15 '67
Difference of man and the difference it makes, by M. J. Adler. Review
Sat R 50:30-1 N 18 '67. H. Read
Extending man's grasp. il Time 89:46 F 24 '67
Maxwell's demon. W. Ehrenberg. il Sci Am 217:103-10 bibliog(p 156) N '67
Mechanical calf. S. V. Jones. il Sci Digest 61:74 My '67
Robot with muscles. Sci Digest 61:26-7 Mr '67
Robots: Unimation, inc, makers of Unimate industrial robot; interview. T. H. Lindbom. New Yorker 43:20-2 Je 24 '67
Unimation head sees 5,000 full-time robots in five years. R. Barnhart. il Tech W 20:38-9 F 20 '67
What robots do now for industry. il Bsns W p 114-16 My 20 '67
See also
Perceptrons
AUTOMOBILE accessories. See Automobiles—Equipment
AUTOMOBILE accidents. See Traffic accidents
AUTOMOBILE air filters. See Air filters, Automobile
AUTOMOBILE assembly plants
Auto assembly plant set in tree-bounded park; Volkswagen assembly plant, Palma Solo-Moron, Venezuela. il Arch Rec 144:164-6 Ja '67
AUTOMOBILE boat trailers
Long distance trailing. D. Jay. il Yachting 122:62-3+ D '67
1968 trailers. il Motor B 121:172-3 Ja '68
Rigging up for the road; hitches to link car and trailer. F. M. Paulson. il Field & S 72:90-3 Ag '67
Trailer information. Yachting 121:433 Ja '67
AUTOMOBILE bodies. See Automobiles—Bodies
AUTOMOBILE brakes. See Brakes, Automobile
AUTOMOBILE buying. See Automobiles—Purchasing
AUTOMOBILE clubs
Big week for the beat-up best; SCCA championships at Daytona. B. LaFontaine. il Sports Illus 27:92+ D 4 '67
AUTOMOBILE dealers
Dealer woes. il Newsweek 69:86+ Mr 20 '67
Ford dealers battle the storm; lack of new cars to sell. il Bsns W p44-5 O 21 '67
How to buck the trend in autos; Galpin square Ford in the San Fernando Valley. il Bsns W p 132-3 Mr 18 '67
'68 buyer's guide; the dealer & the deal. il Motor T 19:20+ N '67
See also
National automobile dealers association
AUTOMOBILE drivers
Drive-aways; benefits and risks of bargain car-transport opportunities. F. A. Tinker. il Travel 128:61-2+ O '67
Hot rod's 1967 top ten. il Hot Rod 21:78-9 Ja '68
How young is too young? T. Stimson. il Pop Mech 128:132-5+ O '67

Keep a grip on yourself. il Pop Mech 128:114-15 N '67
Overheard in suburbia; sports-car mechanic. D. Chapman. Look 31:109 My 16 '67
Pills drivers shouldn't take. E. M. Wylie. Read Digest 90:83-5 F '67
Woman who hit and ran. J. Robbins and J. Robbins. il McCalls 94:112-13+ F '67
Young killers; high accident rate and death toll of young male drivers. il Time 90:46 Ag 25 '67
See also
Drinking and traffic accidents

Anecdotes, facetiae, satire, etc.
Carrie's war against the clutch. N. Hartshorne. il Good H 164:42+ Mr '67

Licenses
Highway murder; reform proposals. J. Kelner. New Repub 157:13 S 2 '67
Soon: national standards for drivers. il U S News 62:90-2 Je 19 '67
AUTOMOBILE driving
Drivin' with Dan; questions and answers. D. Gurney. See issues of Popular mechanics
Driving tips. Hot Rod 20:142 O '67
How safe is your driving? quiz. P. A. Gagnon and J. H Pollack. Ladies Home J 84:180 N '67
How you can be an expert night driver. P. W. Kearney. il Pop Sci 190:82-5 Mr '67
Is your night driving in focus? W. J. Toth. Am Home 70:31+ S '67
Notes and comment; driving with a police escort. New Yorker 43:21 Jl 15 '67
Safer ways to drive at night. il Changing T 21:15-16 Mr '67
Take our automotive quiz. W. J. Toth. Am Home 71:30-1 Ja '68
Taking a drive in an electric. il U S News 62:75 Mr 20 '67
U.S. and the automobile; driving research laboratory in Providence, R.I. Sci Am 216:58+ My '67
What should you do if suddenly..? G. E. Hollister. Motor T 19:78-9 O '67
What you should know about driving the interstate highways. D. L. Gregg. Bet Hom & Gard 45:30+ Je '67
See also
Automobile drivers
Automobiles—Speed

Competitions
Car-rally craze. E. Stevenson. il Mlle 65:148-50+ Je '67

Laws and regulations
See Automobile laws and regulations

Research
See United States—Public health service—Driving research laboratory

Safety devices and measures
Danger on the highways; interview. W. Haddon, jr. il U S News 63:66-9 O 16 '67
Drive, and stay safe. H. Pyle. Parents Mag 42:30 Jl '67
Improved auto safety is wasted on unimproved drivers. E. N. Dye. Travel 127:63+ Je '67
Look ma, no driver; electronic control of driving. J. O'Connell. America 117:638-40 N 25 '67

Study and teaching
Can driving be taught? Time 90:49 N 3 '67
Driver education in the schools: how good? il Changing T 21:43-7 O '67
Fastest school in the world; National school of safe high performance driving. B. Kilpatrick. il Pop Mech 129:94-7+ Ja '68
Personal business; teen-age driving. Bsns W p 111-12 Jl 1 '67
What driver education teaches you. W. J. Toth. Am Home 70:74-5 D '67
AUTOMOBILE engines
Big Ford into little Ford. E. Rickman. il Hot Rod 20:50+ Ap '67
Big hauler. J. Thawley. il Hot Rod 20:66-7 My '67
Biggest engine of them all: Cadillac. J. G. Schmidt. il Motor T 19:80-1 D '67
Biggy for early 'Vettes. J. Thawley. il Hot Rod 20:94-5 D '67
Chevy gets ahead. J. McFarland. il Hot Rod 20:92-3 Ap '67
Chevy II plus; to install a 283 or 327 Chevy V8. J. Thawley. il Hot Rod 20:56 Mr '67
Chevy's moustache curlers. J. McFarland. il Hot Rod 20:28-32 D '67
Clearance checking; rebuilding an engine. B. Lang. il Hot Rod 20:88-9 D '67

AUTOMOBILE engines—*Continued*
Corveight; Corvair with Olds V8 engine. E. Dahlquist. il Hot Rod 21:64-6 Ja '68
Dart sharpener; 273 wedge engine snap. J. Thawley. il Hot Rod 20:68-70 O '67
Engines in your future. J. Ethridge. il Motor T 19:38-43 Ap '67
Fin city; chrome trim for engine compartments. B. Lang. il Hot Rod 20:76 Ag '67
First test: NSU's twin-rotor Wankel-powered sedan. D. Scott. il Pop Sci 191:90-1+ S '67
Ford F-1 engine. G. Borgeson. il Motor T 19:40-3 S '67
Ford's new clean machine. D. Shattuck. il Motor T 19:74-6 D '67
Four-cam V-6 powers new Fiat sports car. J. P. Norbye. il Pop Sci 192:68-9 Ja '68
Hold it! press-fit studs. B. Lang. il Hot Rod 20:86 Jl '67
Inside the '68s: new brakes, suspensions, engines, and body details. J. P. Norbye and J. Dunne. il Pop Sci 191:111-18 O '67
Liveable lifters; hydraulic lifters. E. Rickman. il Hot Rod 20:87 O '67
Motor racing: more slowdowns; engine rulings. K. W. Purdy. il Atlan 220:119-21 D '67
New car for a new engine; RO-80 sedan by Germany's NSU. il Bsns W p72-4 S 2 '67
1968 engine & gearing data; table. Motor T 19:94-5 N '67
Performance fundamentals. J. McFarland. See issues of Hot rod
Putten der growl in der beetle. J. Thawley. il Hot Rod 20:92-5 F; 60-1 Ap; 98-9 My '67
Rivals to the Wankel; a roundup of rotary engines. J. P. Norbye. il Pop Sci 190:80-5 Ja '67
Simplified swapping; bigger engines in the family pickup. E. Rickman. il Hot Rod 20:96-7 S '67
Sizzlin's sixes; six-cylinder Chevys. J. Thawley. il Hot Rod 20:40-2 Mr '67
Swapping the semi-hemi. E. Rickman. il Hot Rod 20:50-1 F '67
383 wedge work; bolt-on equipment. E. Rickman. il Hot Rod 20:60-2 O '67
Wankel wager; NSU non-piston gas engine. il Time 90:94 S 8 '67
Warning: danger ahead! head milling. J. Thawley. il Hot Rod 20:92-4 Jl '67
See also
Carburetors
Cranks and crankshafts
Gas turbines, Automotive
Manifolds
Motor truck engines
Piston rings
Tachometers

Air supply
Better breathing. B. Lang. il Hot Rod 20:48-50 Mr '67
Keeping track of the air. il Hot Rod 20:111+ S '67
Memo to Mustangers; manifold and blower replacement. J. Thawley. il Hot Rod 20:102 O '67

Care
Auto shop cartunes. J. McFarland. il Hot Rod 20:100-3 Je '67
Engine tune-ups, what they should include and when your car needs one D. L. Gregg. il Bet Hom & Gard 45:28+ N '67
How to cure power loss during acceleration. M. Schultz. il Pop Mech 128:122-5 S '67
How you can find those hidden causes of engine overheating. M. Schultz. il Pop Mech 127:140-3+ Je '67
Make a four-point winter checkout for quick cold starts. M. Schultz. il Pop Mech 129:146-9+ Ja '68
New wrinkles for an old smoothie; small-block Chevy V8. J. McFarland. il Hot Rod 20:52-3 N; 76-7 D '67
Tune that two-stroke. Hot Rod 20:138+ My '67
VW tuning tips. J. Thawley. il Hot Rod 20:92-3 O '67
When stock cars don't finish, they tell about your car's weaknesses. S. Yunick. il Pop Sci 191:65-9+ N '67

Cooling
How to keep your engine cool. H. Carrier. il Pop Sci 191:95-8 Ag '67
How you can find those hidden causes of engine overheating. M. Schultz. il Pop Mech 127:140-3+ Je '67

Exhaust
ABCs of smog-control devices. R. W. Temple. il Pop Mech 128:154-9+ N '67
Automobile internal-combustion engine and the interest of the American people are on a collision course. J. T. Middleton. il Pop Sci 190:96-9+ My '67

Billion-dollar smog hoax! J. M. Callahan. il Motor T 19:68-70 Mr '67
California's still choking. P. Hager. New Repub 156:10-11 F 11 '67
Cars are poison. Sci N 91:162 F 18 '67
Detroit bets it can clean up its engines. il Bsns W p88-90+ S 23 '67
Fighting auto fumes; the latest prescription. il U S News 63:64-5 O 30 '67
Ford's new clean machine. D. Shattuck. il Motor T 19:74-6 D '67
New relief from auto fumes due soon; setback for the electric car? il U S News 63:76-7 Jl 24 '67
Publisher's memo. R. Brock. Hot Rod 20:6 Mr '67
Pursuing the possible; autos and air pollution. Sci N 92:441-2 N 4 '67
Respiratory exposure to lead: epidemiological and experimental dose-response relationships. J. R. Goldsmith and A. C. Hexter. bibliog il Science 158:132-4 O '67
Revolt against the internal-combustion engine. L. Lessing. il Fortune 76:78-83+ Jl '67
Standards at the edge of the art. il Sci N 93:61-2 Ja 20 '68
Tightening exhaust control; exhaust-manifold reactor. Time 91:37 Ja 12 '68
What smog control will cost you. J. M. Callahan. il Motor T 19:60-1+ S '67

Filters
See Air filters, Automobile

Fuel
Fuel ratios vs. temperature. B. Lang. il Hot Rod 20:70 F '67

Fuel consumption
NASCAR at night. J. McFarland. il Hot Rod 20:62-3 My '67
Why does your gas mileage drop in the winter? H. T. Gurley. il Pop Sci 190:168-9 F '67

Fuel feeding
Electronic brains promise comeback for fuel injection. J. P. Norbye and D. Scott. il Pop Sci 192:74-9 Ja '68
Fifteen ways to cure rough idle. M. Schultz. il Pop Mech 127:140-3+ F '67
Injecting fuel into the VW; computer-directed fuel injection system. il Bsns W p44 S 23 '67
See also
Fuel pumps

History
Origin of the automobile engine. L. Bryant. il Sci Am 216:102-10+ bibliog(p 152) Mr '67

Ignition
Electronic ignition systems. R. L. Carroll. il Electr World 77:47-9+ F '67
Engine power, mileage and life depend on your timing techniques. M. Schultz. il Pop Mech 127:166-9+ Ap '67
Fifteen ways to cure rough idle. M. Schultz. il Pop Mech 127:140-3+ F '67
How to replace and adjust distributor points. H. Carrier. il Pop Sci 190:91-5 Je '67
Igniter rebuild; rebuild your own distributor. J. Thawley. il Hot Rod 20:84-5 N '67
Ignition control; method of taking illegally parked cars to the pound without using tow trucks. New Yorker 43:28-9 My 27 '67
Keepers of the flame. J. McFarland. il Hot Rod 20:82-5 D '67
Low-cost capacitive-discharge ignition system. B. F. Cawifield. il Electr World 78:30-2 N '67
Solving electrical and ignition problems. M. Schultz. il Pop Mech 127:144-7 My '67
Timing is basic; ignition timing. Hot Rod 20:139 O '67
Universal wiring for automotive ignition systems. C. C. Morris. il Electr World 78:48 Ag '67
See also
Spark plugs

Lubrication
See Automobiles—Lubrication

Mounting
Four-bolt caps; bolt-on accessory. B. Lang. il Hot Rod 20:70 Je '67
Mount up! B. Lang. il Hot Rod 20:46-7 O '67

Repairing
Cold crack repairing; cracked head or block. J. Thawley. il Hot Rod 21:98-9 Ja '68

AUTOMOBILE engines—Repairing—*Continued*
New wrinkles for an old smoothie; small-block Chevy V8. J. McFarland. il Hot Rod 20:52-3 N; 76-7 D '67
Shop talk. J. McFarland. See issues of Hot rod

Superchargers

Get belted; multiple-belt blower drive of poly-urethane. E. Rickman. il Hot Rod 20:76 Ap '67
Supercharging by jet. R. Huntington. il Hot Rod 20:42-4 Jl '67

Testing

Build the electronic stethoscope; sound amplifier to track down mechanical vibrations. S. Stella. il Pop Electr 26:33-5 My '67
How the 429 really performs. S. Kelly. il Motor T 19:77 D '67
It's spring tune-up time; EICO auto analyzer kit. il Pop Electr 26:66 My '67

Valves

Better breathing. B. Lang. il Hot Rod 20: 48-50 Mr '67
M/T's three valve threat. B. Lang. il Hot Rod 20:34-6 Je '67
Toughening torqueflites. E. Dahlquist. il Hot Rod 20:64-6 S '67
AUTOMOBILE exhibitions. See Automobiles—Exhibitions
AUTOMOBILE factories
Good design and amenity for a vast auto plant; Ford stamping plant. il Arch Rec 141: 156-7 Ja '67
See also
Ford motor company

Employees

Automakers focus on Detroit's jobless. R. W. Irvin. Reporter 37:29-30 D 28 '67
Is early retirement popular? what auto industry is finding. il U S News 62:62+ Ap 3 '67
Two halves; problems of newly hired slum dwellers. Time 90:28 D 8 '67
What worries Detroit. B. J. Widick. Nation 205:68 Jl 31 '67
See also
Automobile industry and trade—Wages and hours
AUTOMOBILE gages. See Gages
AUTOMOBILE industry and trade
Road test for auto trade accord; U.S.-Canada pact. il Bsns W p55-6 Je 17 '67

Advertising

Irreverence at American; Javelin advertising campaign. il Time 90:93-4 S 22 '67
Sledge-hammer sell; Wells, Rich, Greene-A.M.C. campaign; with report by N. Belliveau. il Life 63:101-2+ O 27 '67
You go your way; I'll go mine; Chevy's new television-commercial car. il Pop Mech 128: 88-9+ S '67

Employees
See Automobile factories—Employees

Finance

Pact that might have been; proposed G.M.-Ford-Chrysler mutual aid pact. Time 91:86 Ja 19 '68
Public interest and the Ford strike. S. Lens. Commonweal 86:598-9 S 29 '67

History

How Leland lost Lincoln to Ford. G. Borgeson. il Motor T 19:58-62+ F '67

Public relations

Germans spread red carpet at auto plants; Daimler-Benz, VW coddle customers. il Bsns W p56-8+ My 6 '67
Way we see it. D. MacDonald. Motor T 19:4 F '67

Quality control

Detroit tools up drive to cut costly callbacks. il Bsns W p 102-4+ F 4 '67; Same abr. with title How do you build a better car? Read Digest 90:39-40+ Je '67

Used cars

Used car buyer's guide; symposium. il Motor T 19:38-54 Je '67

Wages and hours

Accord at Ford, a slippery road. il Newsweek 70:69 O 30 '67
And now for G.M. il Time 90:96 N 17 '67
Any way in sight to head off an auto strike? il U S News 62:93-5 My 1 '67

Auto workers shrug at the big issues; will strike if they have to. il Bsns W p 152-3+ Ag 19 '67
Best contract we've ever had. il Newsweek 70:85 N 20 '67
Biggest pay demand in history? Reuther states his terms. il U S News 63:72-4 Jl 24 '67
Detroit's labor talks race down to the wire; threshing out compromises. il Bsns W p21-2 S 2 '67
Down to the wire in Detroit; Ford-UAW. il Newsweek 70:67-8 S 11 '67
Ford sets costly pattern; GM and Chrysler next on UAW's bargaining calendar; with editorial comment. il Bsns W p37-9, 164 O 28 '67
How UAW has propped up income; protections for pay, health, and old age. il Bsns W p83-4+ N 11 '67
Labor peace in '68? il Bsns W p 17-18 D 23 '67
Long, large & difficult; U.A.W. labor demands. il Time 90:67 Jl 21 '67
Men with the skills get restive over pay; craftsmen in the auto industry. il Bsns W p83-4 Mr 11 '67
One down, two to go. Newsweek 70:71-2 N 6 '67
Peace; General motors and UAW reach agreement without strike. Time 90:69 D 22 '67
Public interest and the Ford strike. S. Lens. Commonweal 86:598-9 S 29 '67
Reuther delivers the goods; contracts by UAW with Ford motor co. and Caterpillar tractor co. il Bsns W p51-2+ N 4 '67
Salaried workers; one union's plan. U S News 63:69 Jl 31 '67
Settlement at GM. Newsweek 70:53 D 25 '67
Squeeze, squeeze, squeeze. il Time 90:91 N 3 '67
Target; UAW rejects industry's offer. Time 90:86 S 8 '67
Toward a strike. il Time 90:58 S 1 '67
Trading blue collars for white; guaranteed annual wage and salaries. UAW goals in 1967 bargaining. il Bsns W p43-4+ Ap 1 '67
UAW's special prebargaining convention. W. L. Tillery. Mo Labor R 90:33-5 Jl '67
Where the auto talks are going smoothly; negotiators at Livonia. il Bsns W p 146+ S 23 '67
See also
Collective bargaining—Automobile industry

Brazil

Driving down to Rio; Ford buys majority interest in Willys-Overland do Brasil. Time 90:79 Ag 4 '67
Lot of car buying by lot. il Time 90:71 Jl 21 '67

Czechoslovakia

Competing with the West; Skoda's output. il Time 89:88 Mr 10 '67

Europe, Eastern

Cars for the Kremlin; European automakers rich market behind the iron curtain. J. Ross-Skinner. il Duns R 89:67-8+ My '67
Report from east Europe; automania. W. Rademaekers. il Fortune 76:77+ O '67

Europe, Western

Cars for the Kremlin; European automakers rich market behind the iron curtain. J. Ross-Skinner. il Duns R 89:67-8+ My '67
European hot line. See issues of Motor trend
Gloom amid the chrome. il Time 89:86 Mr 24 '67
Safety rules brake foreign auto makers. Bsns W p 119-20 Ag 12 '67
Threat from the East; Japanese cars on European market. il Time 90:91-2 N 3 '67

France

Citroen drives hard to keep its place. il Bsns W p 120-2 O 7 '67

Germany (Federal Republic)

Germans spread red carpet at auto plants; Daimler-Benz, VW coddle customers. il Bsns W p56-8+ My 6 '67
Mercedes in overdrive. il Time 90:70 D 22 '67
New boss for the bug; Volkswagen. Time 89: 100 Ap 14 '67
New car for a new engine; RO-80 sedan by Germany's NSU. il Bsns W p72-4 S 2 '67
New class on the autobahn; Bayerische motoren werke. il Time 90:79-80 Ag 4 '67
Volkswagen drives east; negotiating with Bulgaria. Bsns W p76 F 18 '67

AUTOMOBILE industry and trade—*Continued*

Great Britain
See also
Ford motor company, limited, Dagenham, England
Rootes motors, incorporated

Italy
Car to fugit in: the Lamborghini GT. il Newsweek 69:102+ Ap 17 '67
Fiat in fourth. il Time 90:98 N 17 '67
Great auto race. il Newsweek 70:70+ O 30 '67
Souped-up Fiat models seek European sales. il Bsns W p 137 My 13 '67
Swift cars built in slow motion; Maserati, top name in Italy's Gran Turismo. il Bsns W p62-3 Ja 21 '67
Victory by Fiat; biggest car maker outside Detroit. Bsns W p20 D 30 '67

Japan
Here come the Japanese. S. M. Robards. il Fortune 75:114-15 Je 1 '67
Into third place. il Time 89:94 Mr 3 '67
Threat from the East; Japanese cars on European market. il Time 90:91-2 N 3 '67

Russia
Report from the CIA. Newsweek 69:78 Mr 13 '67
What the auto means to Ivan. il Bsns W p 110+ F 11 '67

South Africa
South Africa raises ante on autos. il Bsns W p96+ N 18 '67

Sweden
Driving lessons: Volvo and SAAB. Fortune 76:215 S 15 '67

United States
April brings smiles to Detroit. il Bsns W p32-3 My 6 '67
Auto dealers fret over '67 performance; confusion over callbacks, credit and Vietnam. il Bsns W p32-3 F 4 '67
Auto sales stay in low; fell 25 per cent in early March. Bsns W p48 Mr 18 '67
Autos bank on a brighter spring; sales off badly so far this year. il Bsns W p32-3 Mr 4 '67
Dealer woes. il Newsweek 69:86+ Mr 20 '67
Detroit hopes for winner in '68. il Bsns W p33-4 Je 3 '67
Detroit listening post. B. Irvin. See issues of Popular mechanics
Detroit sees hopeful signs; auto sales up. Bsns W p46 Ap 29 '67
Detroit's turn to cheer; forecasts for 1968. il Bsns W p41-2 D 9 '67
Dividends, profits and wages: UAW proposal. B. L. Masse. America 116:849 Je 17 '67
Does a General motors agreement mean full speed ahead for autos? U S News 63:68 D 25 '67
Eyes on Detroit. il Fortune 76:39-40 O '67
How auto industry sees '68. il U S News 64:43 Ja 1 '68
Living with recalls. il Time 89:62 Je 2 '67
Looking toward spring. Time 89:92 Mr 17 '67
Modest, mixed, but unmistakable; spring-time upturn in sales. Time 89:87 Je 23 '67
New auto rules: safe or sorry? il Newsweek 69:79 F 13 '67
New autos race for a head start. il Bsns W p32-3 Ag 12 '67
1968: the year of the big if. B. Kilpatrick. il Pop Mech 128:94-7+ O '67
Outlook as auto dealers see it. il U S News 62:108 F 13 '67
Outlook for auto sales, prices. il U S News 63:42 N 6 '67
Plight of some auto makers; makers of specialty autos. il U S News 62:52-3 Ap 17 '67
Pushing the captives; Detroit subsidiaries abroad market in the U.S. il Bsns W p 19 Jl 1 '67
'68 cars: how new will they be? B. Irvin. il Pop Mech 127:59-62+ Je '67
Slow getaway for the auto market. J. Main. il Fortune 75:110-15+ Je 1 '67
Those sporty, swinging specialty cars! il Motor T 19:26-7 My '67
Truce and progress; concerning safety requirements. il Time 89:87 F 10 '67
UAW goes out on two long limbs: Reuther's program. il Bsns W p99-100+ Ap 29 '67
Where car sales are heading. il U S News 62:43 Mr 27 '67
See also
Automobile dealers
Automobiles—Manufacture
Automobiles—Prices

Collective bargining—Automobile industry
Strikes—United States—Automobile industry and trade
United automobile, aerospace and agricultural implement workers of America
also names of automobile manufacturing companies, e.g. Ford motor company

AUTOMOBILE industry strikes. See Strikes—United States—Automobile industry and trade

AUTOMOBILE insurance. See Insurance, Automobile

AUTOMOBILE laws and regulations
Billion-dollar smog hoax! J. M. Callahan. il Motor T 19:68-70 Mr '67
Cars and the law. R. J. Gottlieb. See issues of Motor trend to October 1967
Drive-aways; benefits and risks of bargain car-transport opportunities. F. A. Tinker. il Travel 128:61-2+ O '67
What the law means to consumers. Consumer Rep 32:192-4 Ap '67
See also
Traffic regulations

Europe
None for the road; European drivers obliged to submit to random curbside breathalyser tests. il Time 90:33 O 20 '67

Great Britain
Britain survives the breathalyser. L. Wainwright. Life 63:20A O 20 '67
Letter from London; law imposing breathalyser tests. M. Panter-Downes. New Yorker 43:228 N 11 '67
Virtues of sobriety. Time 90:41 N 17 '67

AUTOMOBILE mechanics (persons)
How important is the color of a man's collar? il Good H 165:20+ N '67
Mechanic's check. M. Lamm. Motor T 19:52 Je '67
Piecework mechanic caper. J. Joseph. il Motor T 19:52-3+ Ag '67
Squires to the knights of the roaring road; riding mechanics. G. Borgeson. il Motor T 19:92+ O '67
Where there's fire, there's Smokey; S. Yunick. J. McFarland. il Hot Rod 21:48-50 Ja '68

Training
Auto tech; Autolite's new self-study delivery of automotive fundamentals. J. McFarland. il Hot Rod 20:82 Je '67

AUTOMOBILE motors. See Automobile engines

AUTOMOBILE owners
Stars' cars. il Time 90:86 S 29 '67

AUTOMOBILE ownership
Should you buy, rent, or lease a car? W. J. Toth. Am Home 70:50-1 My '67
Some factors affecting housing density and auto ownership; excerpt from Postwar metropolitan development: housing preferences and auto ownership. J. F. Kain. Mo Labor R 90:45-6 Mr '67

AUTOMOBILE painting. See Automobiles—Painting

AUTOMOBILE parking
Air rights help to solve a parking problem; San Mateo, Calif. P. N. Bay. il Am City 82:84-5 N '67
At last, a parking place! H. Mason and others. il Bet Hom & Gard 45:64-5 Ap '67
Clean the snow off the parking lots first; St Cloud, Minn. S. Knapp. il Am City 82:86-7 Ag '67
Cure for parking lots? W. Von Eckardt. Am Home 70:45-7 N '67
Double-decked village; Kingsbury green, London. il Arch Forum 126:46-51 Ap '67
Ignition control; method of taking illegally parked cars to the pound without using tow trucks. New Yorker 43:28-9 My 27 '67
International incident; New York city parking restrictions. Newsweek 69:41 F 6 '67
Parking mall that..; Columbia, S.C. C. C. Burnett. il Am City 82:74-6 Ja '67
See also
Parking meters

AUTOMOBILE parts
Headers-in pieces yet. J. Thawley. il Hot Rod 20:78 S '67
Motor trend's special awards; features and accessories. il Motor T 19:42-3 F '67
Press-on styling. E. Rickman. il Hot Rod 20:82 My '67

AUTOMOBILE phonograph. See Automobiles—Phonograph equipment

AUTOMOBILE picnics. See Picnics

AUTOMOBILE racing
AHRA grand nationals. E. Rickman. il Hot Rod 20:40-1 Ag '67

AUTOMOBILE racing—*Continued*
AHRA '67 nationals notes. E. Dahlquist. il Hot Rod 20:64-5 O '67
A.J. again. il Newsweek 70:68 D 11 '67
A.J. in the afternoon; United States auto club championship. E. Dahlquist. il Hot Rod 20:52-4 D '67
All-American success; Dan Gurney wins Belgian Grand prix. il Time 89:55 Je 30 '67
Andretti: vroom at the top. il Newsweek 69:64-6+ My 29 '67
Apple pie, mom and Mr Gurney; victory in Belgian Grand prix. B. Ottum. il Sports Illus 26:28-9 Je 26 '67
Auto racing around the world; symposium, ed. by J. P. Norbye. il Pop Sci 190:69-74 Mr '67
Bad day at Bonneville. J. Thawley. il Hot Rod 20:96 F '67
Bakersfield. J. Thawley. il Hot Rod 20:46-7 My '67
Big bad Baja; first annual Mexican 1000 rally. J. Thawley. il Hot Rod 21:46-7 Ja '68
Big week for the beat-up best; SCCA championships at Daytona. B. LaFontaine. il Sports Illus 27:92+ D 4 '67
Boss racing, a couple of little known southern races. E. Dahlquist. il Hot Rod 20:52-4+ Jl '67
Boy with a silver spanner; Darlington Southern 500. il Time 90:58 S 15 '67
Bruce and Denny show makes a fast buck; New Zealanders in the Can-Am series. B. Ottum. il Sports Illus 27:70-3 O 2 '67
Bud Moore, the man who makes the Mercurys tick. B. Lang. il Hot Rod 20:44-6 Ap '67
Can the independents win at Daytona? il Pop Mech 127:89-92+ F '67
Can we beat the British at the brickyard? 1967 Indy 500. R. Ward. il Pop Mech 127:116-18+ My '67
Caper at Carlsbad. J. Thawley. il Hot Rod 20:68-70 Jl '67
Champ with a feel for the rattlesnake; R. Petty, winner at Daytona. Sports Illus 26:36-8 F 27 '67
Charlotte National 500. B. Myers. il Motor T 20:52-4 Ja '68
Charlotte world 600. R. Brock. il Hot Rod 20:50-2 Ag '67
Chip off the old block; R. Petty's stock-car racing record. il Newsweek 70:46 Ag 21 '67
Climb to the clouds. R. Brock. il Hot Rod 20:62-3 S '67
Crowned king of the road; New Zealander, D. Hulme at Mexican Grand prix. K. Chapin. il Sports Illus 27:53-4 O 30 '67
Danger, spectators; East African safari. Time 89:60 Ap 7 '67
Darlington Southern 500. B. Myers. il Motor T 19:66-9 Jl '67
David. E. Dahlquist. il Hot Rod 20:72-4 Je '67
Day of truth in racing. L. Collins and D. Lapierre. il N Y Times Mag p8-9+ Jl 9 '67; Same abr. with title Greatest auto race of all. Read Digest 91:121-6 O '67
Daytona '67. E. Dahlquist. il Hot Rod 20:38-40+ My '67
Deadly antiques; Monaco Grand prix course. il Time 89:83 My 19 '67
Demolition run at Daytona; 500-mile stock-car race. K. Chapin. il Sports Illus 26:20-1 Mr 6 '67
Dragsters only, please! Bakersfield. E. Dahlquist. il Hot Rod 20:48-50 O '67
Duel at Le Mans. G. Borgeson. il Motor T 19:54-7 S '67
Dueling with slingshots at 180 mph. J. Skow. il Sat Eve Post 240:70-5 Je 3 '67
Easy five-0-0; Darlington Southern 500. R. Brock. il Hot Rod 20:64-5 N '67
500-mile journey into an artist's eye; reproductions of paintings by B. Stanley; with account by R. Crozier. Sports Illus 26:74-81+ My 29 '67
For want of a shaft; Daytona Continental. il Time 89:55 F 17 '67
Ford races to a big showdown; ready to tackle Ferraris at Le Mans. B. Ottum. il Sports Illus 26:34-5 Ap 10 '67
Gentlemen, junk your engines; Jones, in turbine car, loses 500 to Foyt. B. Ottum. il Sports Illus 26:30-3 Je 12 '67
Georgia on our minds: Ford-Chrysler; NASCAR races. E. Dahlquist. il Hot Rod 20:62-4 Je '67
Glorious double; Ford winners at Le Mans. B. Ottum. il Sports Illus 26:14-17 Je 19 '67
Gold country classic. B. Lang. il Hot Rod 20:96-8 Ag '67
Hail the new MT 500 king! Jones dethrones Gurney, but it took two Sundays to do it. J. Ethridge. il Motor T 19:68-70 Ap '67

Hamming it up at a stock car race; taking pigs along as passengers. M. Lamm. il Pop Mech 128:88-9 Jl '67
Holy spectacle; 4-wheel-drive Grand prix. E. Rickman. il Hot Rod 20:68-9 Je '67
Hot rod magazine drags. S. Kelly. il Motor T 19:72-3 Jl '67
I shall be back for another bash; ed. by K. Chapin. J. Clark. il Sports Illus 27:26-7 N 6 '67
In the Lions' den; 200 MPH club meet. E. Dahlquist. il Hot Rod 20:42-3 F '67
Indy '67. J. McFarland. il Hot Rod 20:30-5 N '67
Indy: the waiting game. J. McFarland. il Hot Rod 20:32-5 Ag '67
Jet threat; turbine car at Indianapolis 500. il Newsweek 69:57 Je 12 '67
Joy ride: Le Mans race. Newsweek 69:64 Je 26 '67
Kalittascope; interview, ed. by J. McFarland. C. Kalitta. il Hot Rod 20:56-8 My '67
King. W. Youst. il Hot Rod 20:80-2 Mr '67
Mario vs. the whooshmobile; Indianapolis 500. B. Ottum. il Sports Illus 26:30-3 My 22 '67
Matchless Minis; Monte Carlo rally. il Newsweek 69:69 Ja 30 '67
Motor trend, Riverside 500. E. Dahlquist. il Hot Rod 20:64-5 Ap '67
Motorsports. See issues of Motor trend
Motorsports; the Atlanta 500; symposium. il Motor T 19:108-10 Je '67
NASCAR at night. J. McFarland. il Hot Rod 20:62-3 My '67
NASCAR's wet Nat's. E. Dahlquist. il Hot Rod 20:90-1 N '67
News on wheels; stock car races. M. Spiegel. il Sr Schol 91:19 D 14 '67
Oahu wahoo. J. McFarland. il Hot Rod 20:46-7 Mr '67
Polar drags; Anchorage, Alaska. B. Lang. il Hot Rod 20:38-40 D '67
Race to the title; Jack Brabham wins Canada's Mosport park Grand prix. il Newsweek 70:56 S 11 '67
Racer in a far-out country; J. Hall of Texas. C. Phinizy. il Sports Illus 26:30-2+ My 1 '67
Racewatchers guide to competition cars. il Pop Mech 127:95-101 Mr '67
Racing bug; Volkswagen powered racing cars. il Newsweek 70:105 O 30 '67
Racing's fabulous invalid; Mario Andretti and A. J. Foyt at dirt-track raing. W. Johnson. il Sports Illus 27:32-3 S 18 '67
Roddin' at random. See issues of Hot rod
Roundy-round corner. E. Dahlquist. See issues of Hot rod
Rufus and the turbine. J. McFarland. il Hot Rod 20:40-2 N '67
Salt '67; Bonneville speed week. J. Thawley. il Hot Rod 20:54-6 N '67
Second for Ford; win at Le Mans. il Time 89:69 Je 23 '67
Shootout at the Riverside corral; fourth annual Hot rod magazine championship drags. J. Thawley. il Hot Rod 20:44-7 Je '67
Show & go. See issues of Hot rod
Silence is not always golden; Indy 500. J. Ethridge. il Motor T 19:42-9 Ag '67
Six cars in search of an image; sports-personal cars in competition. J. Wright. il Motor T 20:40-2 Ja '68
'67 Super stock nationals; weenies and Cecil. J. McFarland. il Hot Rod 20:52-4 S '67
So, what's so tough about stock-car racing? J. W. Wright. il Pop Sci 191:108-11+ Ag '67
Someone up there said, let's race, and lo . . . Ford came flying. B. Ottum. il Sports Illus 27:26-32 D 25 '67
Springnationals, y'all. J. Thawley. il Hot Rod 20:32-5 S '67
Stirling Moss on racing. S. Moss. See issues of Motor trend to June 1967
Stockers; winners and hopefuls. il Motor T 19:108-11 N '67
Tailgating at three miles a minute; Daytona 500, photographs. Sports Illus 26:32-6 F 27 '67
There's a turbine in their future; A. J. Foyt wins Indianapolis 500. il Time 89:56+ Je 9 '67
Those great pictures in Grand prix, how they were made. R. Dempewolff. il Pop Mech 127:77-81+ Mr '67
Three of a kind; Daytona Continental. il Newsweek 69:87 F 20 '67
To catch a ghost; drivers compete for positions in Memorial day 500. il Time 89:56+ My 26 '67
Tulsa, the end of the trail. J. McFarland. il Hot Rod 21:58-61 Ja '68
Virginia 500. B. Myers. il Motor T 19:66-8+ Jl '67

AUTOMOBILE racing—*Continued*
Wee Jimmy's big, beautiful win at the Glen; U.S. Grand prix. B. Ottum. il Sports Illus 27:60+ O 9 '67
What is this danger? hottest racing driver in the world. il Time 89:57 Ap 21 '67
What makes Nicholson run. J. Thawley. il Hot Rod 20:58-61 F '67
When a dream race became a nightmare; Charlotte, N.C. K. Chapin. il Sports Illus 27:22-3 O 23 '67
When stock cars don't finish, they tell about your car's weaknesses. S. Yunick. il Pop Sci 191:65-9+ N '67
Which way will it go? 1968 Motor trend-Riverside 500. B. Sanders. il Motor T 20:76 Ja '68
Win for Cougar, a wild ride for Camaro; Trans-American racing championship. K. Chapin. il Sports Illus 27:58-60 Ag 14 '67
Winternationals; '67 veni, vidi, Ford! J. McFarland. il Hot Rod 20:40-3 Ap '67
World 600; the rub was in the rubber. B. Myers. il Motor T 19:56-7 Ag '67
See also
Automobile speed records
Automobiles, Racing
Speedways
Women in automobile racing

Economic aspects
Daytona 500. D. MacDonald. il Motor T 19:68-72 My '67
Racing's elusive pot of gold. B. Thomas. il Motor T 19:46-8+ F '67

History
Hot rod twentieth anniversary; scrapbook, 1948-1968. J. McFarland. il Hot Rod 21:28-39 Ja '68
Squires to the knights of the roaring road; riding mechanics. G. Borgeson. il Motor T 19:92+ O '67

Terminology
Drag racing lingo. Hot Rod 21:111 Ja '68 (to be cont)
Oval track lingo. Hot Rod 20:134 N '67
Voice of the racers. Hot Rod 20:158-9 O '67
AUTOMOBILE radios. See Automobiles—Radio equipment
AUTOMOBILE rallies. See Automobile driving —Competitions
AUTOMOBILE renting. See Automobiles—Renting
AUTOMOBILE service stations
Answer to your car-repair problem: car clinics. il U S News 62:90-1 Je 26 '67
Automobile diagnostic center. L. Solomon. il Electr World 77:48-52+ My '67
Canadian service station is pleasingly concealed by built-up earth berms. il Arch Rec 141:182-3 My '67
Prototype for service stations: Mobil tests effect of design on sales at fifty-eight locations; with comment by Rawleigh Warner, jr. il Arch Rec 141:172-5 My '67
Step by step through a diagnostic center. il Bet Hom & Gard 45:76-7+ Ap '67
Those clinics for sick cars; ills electronically traced. il Changing T 21:31-4 Ap '67
Those fancy diagnostic centers: are they really better than Joe's garage? E. D. Fales, jr. il Pop Mech 128:92-6+ Ag '67
Toward a better community, must gas stations be garish? W. Von Eckardt. il Am Home 70:40+ Je '67
AUTOMOBILE shows. See Automobiles—Exhibitions
AUTOMOBILE signals
See also
Automobiles—Signal lights
AUTOMOBILE speed records
How we broke 266 speed records with Camaros. S. Yunick. il Pop Sci 192:102-5+ Ja '68
AUTOMOBILE speeding. See Automobiles—Speed
AUTOMOBILE speedways. See Speedways
AUTOMOBILE stealing. See Automobiles, Theft of
AUTOMOBILE styling. See Automobiles—Design
AUTOMOBILE thefts. See Automobiles, Theft of
AUTOMOBILE tires. See Tires, Automobile
AUTOMOBILE touring
Notes for nomads. See issues of Travel

Anecdotes, facetiae, satire, etc.
Driving to rack and ruin. R. Atcheson. il Holiday 42:20+ O '67

Canada
Four family planned auto tours. il Bet Hom & Gard 45:76-7 Mr '67

Middle western states
Milwaukee and the lakes country. il Bet Hom & Gard 45:78-9 Je '67

Portugal
Touring Portugal by car, a 1,500 mile loop. il Sunset 138:38+ Mr '67

Russia
Along a Russian road. C. S. Wren. il Look 31:117-21 O 3 '67
By car through Russia; journey into past. W. MacDougall. il U S News 63:86-7 N 20 '67

United States
Four family planned auto tours. il Bet Hom & Gard 45:76-83 Mr '67
On the go, by car. M. Bernstein. il U S Camera 30:46-7+ My '67
Two more family-planned auto tours. il Bet Hom & Gard 45:152-5 Ap; 74-7 My; 76-9 Je '67

Western states
Salt Lake and the mountains. il Bet Hom & Gard 45:76-7 Je '67
AUTOMOBILE towing. See Towing
AUTOMOBILE traffic. See Road traffic; Street traffic
AUTOMOBILE trailer hitches. See Automobiles —Equipment
AUTOMOBILE trailers
Choosing a recreation vehicle for family use. C. M. Edwards. il Consumer Bul 50:36-40 Mr '67
Immobile and mundane. Newsweek 69:84 F 27 '67
Living in a mobile home in Florida. E. T. Kienz. il Consumer Bul 50:35-6 Ag '67
My piggyback boat hauler tows a travel trailer, too. F. A. Barnes. il Pop Sci 191:102-3 Jl '67
Put the car in shape to pull that trailer. il Changing T 21:37-9 Jl '67
Race trailers. B. Lang. il Hot Rod 20:88-90 Ap '67
Travel trailer hauling and necessary auxiliary equipment. J. B. Miller. il Consumer Bul 50:21-4 F '67
What to know about using a trailer. Good H 165:151 Jl '67
See also
Automobile boat trailers

Equipment
Add this boat rack to your tent trailer. J. Mudrock. il Pop Mech 127:132-3 My '67
AUTOMOBILE trips. See Automobile touring
AUTOMOMILE warranty. See Warranty
AUTOMOBILE wheels. See Automobiles—Wheels
AUTOMOBILE wiring. See Automobiles—Electric wiring
AUTOMOBILE workers. See Automobile factories—Employees
AUTOMOBILES
As the curtain goes up on '68 autos: the outlook. il U S News 63:32-3 S 4 '67
Autos: high hopes, and worries. il U S News 63:105 S 25 '67
Autos 1967. il Consumer Rep 32:188-90 Ap '67
Buick GS400. B. Kilpatrick. il Pop Mech 127:88-91+ Mr '67
Camaro pace car. il Hot Rod 20:133 Ag '67
Camaro: stage last. J. McFarland. il Hot Rod 20:46-8 Ag '67
Car talk. il Changing T 21:24-5 S '67
Cars à la carte. See issues of Motor trend
Cars in your family. D. L. Gregg. See issues of Better homes and gardens
Cars of the stars. J. Joseph. il Motor T 19:89-92 Jl '67
Chevota. J. Thawley. il Hot Rod 20:60-1 Jl '67
Chevrolet Impala. B. Hartford. il Pop Mech 127:94-6+ My '67
Cougar & Firebird. J. Ethridge. il Motor T 19:34-7 My '67
Detroit serves up the '68 models. Changing T 21:6 S '67
Detroit's best-kept secrets for '68. J. Dunne. il Pop Sci 191:48-9+ Ag '67
Dodge Polara: thirsty diamond in the rough. B. Hartford. il Pop Mech 128:116-18+ Ag '67
Facts and figures on the '68 cars. Pop Sci 191:92-5 N '67

AUTOMOBILES—*Continued*

Firebird. E. Dahlquist. il Hot Rod 20:44-5 F '67

Ford Falcon: more faithful than flashy. B. Hartford. il Pop Mech 127:84-6+ Je '67

Ford's ultimate super cars. E. Dahlquist. il Hot Rod 20:58-60 N '67

Four 1967 automobiles; Chevrolet Impala V-8; Ford Galaxie 500 V-8; Plymouth Fury II V-8; Mercury Cougar V-8. il Consumer Bul 50:10-16 F '67

Four of a kind; Oldsmobiles. E. Dahlquist. il Hot Rod 20:32-6 Ap '67

Fun cars you can build from a kit. J. W. Wright. il Pop Sci 190:61-5+ F '67

GTO, crossbreed bomb. E. Dahlquist. il Hot Rod 20:60-1 My '67

Gyron 1; two-wheel action with passenger car comfort. D. MacDonald. il Motor T 19:23-4 Je '67

Holy Toledo, a jazzy jeep! A. Markovich. il Pop Mech 128:92-4+ Ag '67

If I had a million dollars, I'd buy a Cadillac. D. Francis. il Pop Sci 190:72-3 F '67

Ignition '68. M. Spiegel. il Sr Schol 91:35-8+ O 12 '67

Intermediate year; 1968 models. il Time 90:91-2 S 15 '67

Latest on '68 cars, and a look at five of them. il U S News 63:118 S 18 '67

McCall's 1968 report on automobiles; woman's guide to easier maintenance and more driving pleasure. il McCalls 95:34+ N '67

Marlin & Charger. B. Schilling. il Motor T 19:38-40 My '67

Mercury's new Cougar. B. Kilpatrick. il Pop Mech 127:110-12+ Je '67

More people are choosing intermediates for family use. J. Dunne. il Pop Sci 190:103-5 F '67

Most from your automobile. W. J. Toth. See issues of American home

Mustang, Camaro & Barracuda. J. Ethridge. il Motor T 19:28-33 My '67

News on wheels. D. Chu. il Sr Schol 90:32 F 10 '67

1968 autos: safer models with appeal to youth. il Ebony 23:90-4+ Ja '68

1968 cars. il Changing T 21:25-32 D '67

1968 cars are here. W. J. Toth. Am Home 70:48-9 O '67

1967 cars. il Consumer Bul 50:16-26 Ap '67

1967 full-size cars. il Consumer Bul 50:16-25 My '67

Olds Cutlass: performance yes, economy no! B. Hartford. il Pop Mech 127:102-4+ My '67

Ordeal of the short distance; oversized and overpowered cars. N. Cousins. Sat R 50:28-9 F 11 '67

Personal business; 1968 models. Bsns W p 103 S 2 '67

PM owners report:
Chevrolet Camaro. B. Kilpatrick. il Pop Mech 128:122-4+ Jl '67
Chrysler Newport. B. Kilpatrick. il Pop Mech 127:92-5+ Ap '67
Dodge Charger. B. Kilpatrick. il Pop Mech 127:101-3+ F '67
Plymouth Fury. B. Kilpatrick. il Pop Mech 128:70-2+ Jl '67
Rambler American. B. Hartford. il Pop Mech 129:117-19+ Ja '68

Practical size, good visibility, but problems with noise and discomfort. J. Dunne. il Pop Sci 190:107-9 Ap '67

Rambler Rebel. B. Kilpatrick. il Pop Mech 127:120-3+ Ap '67

Really new ones. B. Kilpatrick. il Pop Mech 128:101-3+ O '67

Return of the Jeepster. V. L. Oertle. il Motor T 19:64-5 Mr '67

Rum running, basic training for stockers. B. E. Myers. il Motor T 19:48-9+ Mr '67

Show goes on; 1968 models. il Time 90:93 S 22 '67

Six 1967 automobiles: Dodge Coronet deluxe V-8, Falcon Futura six, Ford Fairlane 500 V-8, Oldsmobile F-85 V-8, Plymouth Belvedere II 6, Rambler American 440 six. il Consumer Bul 50:24-32 Mr '67

'68 cars: some chopped, others stretched, all sportier. J. Dunne. il Pop Sci 191:50-3 Jl '67

'68 Cobra GTs. S. Kelly. il Motor T 19:58-9 N '67

'68 General motors, Ford, American motors, Chrysler. E. Dahlquist. il Hot Rod 20:32-8+ O '67

'68 new car buyer's guide. il Motor T 19:35-50+ N '67

'68s are here; symposium. il Motor T 19:36-54+ O '67

68s; more facts on next year's cars. D. Mac-Donald. il Motor T 19:30-9 Ag '67

'68s pass their first test. il Bsns W p34-5 O 7 '67

68s vs 67s. D. MacDonald. il Motor T 19:20-9 S '67

'67-X prize custom. S. Kelly. il Motor T 19:64-5 Ag '67

Sports-personal cars: what lies ahead? R. W. Irvin. il Motor T 20:21-3 Ja '68

Sporty cars: special packages. il Motor T 19:41-2 My '67

Twelfth annual Look automotive preview: the '68's. A. Rothenberg. il Look 31:82-95 O 17 '67

What's new. See issues of Successful farming

What's new from Detroit? a preview of 1968 cars. R. Huntington. il Consumer Bul 50:20-6 O '67

Which cars will be the stars in '68? J. P. Norbye and J. Dunne. il Pop Sci 191:98-110 O '67

Your first peek at the '68 cars. J. Dunne. il Pop Sci 190:70-3 Je '67

Your friend the Camaro. J. McFarland. il Hot Rod 20:62-4 F '67

See also
Motor trucks
Sports cars
Taxicabs

Accessories
See Automobiles—Equipment

Accidents
See Traffic accidents

Advertising
See Automobile industry and trade—Advertising

Air conditioning
On keeping your cool at a bargain price. D. MacDonald. il Motor T 19:100-1 Jl '67

Airplane combinations
See Airplanes, Light—Automobile combinations

Anecdotes, facetiae, satire, etc.
Decline and fall of Becky. B. Bernstein. Esquire 67:22+ F '67

Those were the pleasant years. E. H. Bowers. Sat R 50:43-4 Je 17 '67

Axles
Tube axles for Chevys. B. Lang. il Hot Rod 20:66-7 Ap '67

Bodies
Basic body dimensions (cont) il Consumer Rep 32:208-10 Ap '67

How to fix those dents in your car. J. Burroughs. il Pop Sci 190:138-41 Mr '67

1968 body dimensions; table. Motor T 19:98 N '67

Shape up! working with aluminum while building a dragster body. E. Dahlquist. il Hot Rod 20:66-9 Mr; 100-2+ Ap '67

Brakes
See Brakes, Automobile

Bumpers
Splash instead of crash? water-filled bumper is claimed to soften the blow. J. Ethridge. il Motor T 19:64 Jl '67

Tiger with a pussycat nose; rubber bumper of '68 GTO. J. Ethridge. il Motor T 19:58-9 S '67

Water bumpers, new automotive safety device. il Am City 82:184+ S '67

Burglar alarms
See Burglar alarms

Camping equipment
Camping gear: it's come a long, long way. D. L. Gregg. il Bet Hom & Gard 45:12+ My '67

Now, a camper for sedans. il Pop Sci 191:123 Ag '67

Carburetors
See Carburetors

Care
ABCs of keeping your car in tune. H. Carrier. See issues of Popular science monthly

Care fare: excerpts from Britain's Automobile association-published magazine Drive. il Time 89:95 My 5 '67

How to get more for your old car. J. B. Colborne. il Pop Mech 127:130-3+ Ap '67

Prepare your car for sale or trade. M. Lamm. Motor T 19:50-1 Je '67

Saturday mechanic. M. Schultz. See issues of Popular mechanics

Something wrong with your car? trouble signs. G. Hollister. Motor T 19:34-5 O '67

AUTOMOBILES—Care—Continued
Tips for your home and family. E. Maxwell. Todays Health 45:77-8 My '67
Twelve sure ways to cut truck and car expenses. P. B. Jones. il Suc Farm 65: 40-1 Je '67

Chassis
Woody carves a chassis. J. Thawley. il Hot Rod 20:70-2 Mr '67

Clutches
Freewheeling alternator. E. Rickman. il Hot Rod 20:80 Ap '67
Slippin' and slidin'; sliding clutch. E. Dahlquist. il Hot Rod 20:48-50 D '67
True science friction. J. McFarland. il Hot Rod 20:90-3 My '67

Collectors and collecting
Classic action at a vintage auction. J. Wilson. il Motor T 19:74-7 Ap '67
Truly Nolen: exterminator of classics? R. A. Latimer. il Motor T 19:84-6+ My '67

Anecdotes, facetiae, satire, etc.
To park a classic. S. Hilt. Motor T 19:78 Mr '67

Control
Look ma, no driver; electronic control of driving. J. O'Connell. America 117:638-40 N 25 '67

Cost of operation
Isky's wailin' street Chevy. E. Rickman. il Hot Rod 20:48-51 S '67

Design
Design/engineering trend setters. il Motor T 19:44-5 F '67
Detroit spotlight. See issues of Motor trend
Detroit: the shape of '68. il Newsweek 69:80-81A Ap 10 '67
Family cars: they just keep rollin' along. B. Kilpatrick. il Pop Mech 128:114-17+ O '67
First look at the '68s. D. MacDonald. il Motor T 19:43-53 Jl '67
Hatching a firebird. D. MacDonald. il Motor T 19:35-7 Mr '67
Hope at American; Javelin specialty car. il Time 90:67-8 Ag 25 '67
How car makers hope to foil auto thieves. U S News 62:15 My 1 '67
In the works for '68: more personal cars. U S News 62:16-17 Ap 10 '67
Intermediates; right, ready and rarin' to go. B. Kilpatrick. il Pop Mech 128:110-13+ O '67
Luxury by the ton: bigger engines, more gadgets. B. Kilpatrick. il Pop Mech 128:118-19+ O '67
Metaphysics of automotive design. N. Thimmesch. il Esquire 68:188-9+ D '67
Nine lives of Cougar. il Motor T 19:34-8 F '67
Personal-ity plus sportiness, scoot spell success. B. Kilpatrick. il Pop Mech 128:106-9 O '67
Plight of some auto makers; makers of specialty autos. il U S News 62:52-3 Ap 17 '67
Report on '68 cars; the changes. il U S News 62:42-4 My 22 '67
School where cars are born. N. Willatt. il Duns R 89:45-6+ Ap '67
Tear for the convertible. il Time 90:77 Jl 28 '67
Ten old-time losers. M. Lamm. il Motor T 19:98-101+ Je '67
Toronado limo. S. Kelly. il Motor T 19:32-3 Jl '67
You go your way: I'll go mine; Chevy's new television-commercial car. il Pop Mech 128: 88-9+ S '67
See also
Automobiles—Safety devices and measures

Differential
See Automobiles—Transmission

Driveshafts
See Automobiles—Propeller shafts

Driving
See Automobile driving

Electric equipment
Current discussion on car electricity. J. McFarland. il Hot Rod 20:82-5 F '67
Lights out! automatic unit to turn off car lights. E. Rickman. il Hot Rod 20:108 D '67
Master fuse for safety. il Hot Rod 20:122 Ap '67
Solving electrical and ignition problems. M. Schultz. il Pop Mech 127:144-7 My '67

Electric wiring
How to keep the accessories working. H. Carrier. il Pop Sci 192:123-7 Ja '68
How to take care of the electrical system. H. Carrier. il Pop Sci 191:101-5+ N '67
Universal wiring for automotive ignition systems. C. C. Morris. il Electr World 78:48 Ag '67
Wired in. J. Thawley. il Hot Rod 20:74 Mr '67

Electronic equipment
Automotive electronics. R. M. Brown. il Electr World 77:23-9 My '67
Make your own six to twelve volt up-verter. B. Richards. il Pop Electr 27:67-70 O '67

Equipment
Achtung! examenhaben das VW shiftenleber; shift-stick. J. McFarland. il Hot Rod 20:66 N '67
Deluxe engine stand. il Hot Rod 20:82 N '67
If your car's rear end scrapes. il Sunset 138: 98 Je '67
Instant spoiler; a race-bred kit to give the fastback Mustang a racing look. B. Lang. il Hot Rod 20:54 Ap '67
Load-equalizing trailer hitch you can make. A. F. Gimbel. il Pop Sci 191:127-30 Jl '67
Loads & loads of extras for your car. il Changing T 21:35-8 N '67
Motor trend's special awards; features and accessories. il Motor T 19:42-3 F '67
New things for your car. (title varies) See issues of Motor trend
1968 car prices, options & accessories; table. Motor T 19:96-7 N '67
Options: which ones are worth the extra cost? il Consumer Rep 32:198-201 Ap '67
Put the car in shape to pull that trailer. il Changing T 21:37-9 Jl '67
Rigging up for the road; hitches to link car and trailer. F. M. Paulson. il Field & S 72:90-3 Ag '67
Tow bars. B. Lang. il Hot Rod 20:70 Ag '67
Trailer hitch that's easy on a car. V. L. Oertle. il Pop Sci 190:158-9 Je '67
Travel trailer hauling and necessary auxiliary equipment. J. B. Miller. il Consumer Bul 50:21-4 F '67
Triple-duty armrest for your car. W. B. Sill. il Pop Sci 191:121 N '67
Vital car accessories for your vacation. D. L. Gregg. Bet Hom & Gard 45:28 Jl '67
What's new. See issues of Hot rod
Wide-angle rear-view mirror for autos. Consumer Bul 51:19 Ja '68
Wink mirror; wide angle rear-view mirror. E. Rickman. il Hot Rod 20:91 D '67
See also
Automobiles—Electric equipment
Automobiles—Tape equipment
Odometers

Exhaust
See Automobile engines—Exhaust

Exhibitions
Cars, cars, cars; international auto show. C. H. Simonds. Nat R 19:757-8 Jl 11 '67
Chrome-plated year for the imports. new lines at New York's auto show. il Bsns W p30-1 Ap 8 '67
Custom cars; sixth annual National custom car show at the Coliseum. New Yorker 43: 53-4 D 2 '67
Farrago of motors; International automobile show in Coliseum. New Yorker 43:42-3 Ap 15 '67
Show & go. See issues of Hot rod
Tire kicker on the prowl; International automobile show, New York. L. Wainwright. Life 62:24B Ap 14 '67

Four wheel drive
New Jeepster: a tough and glamorous powerhouse. J. Dunne. il Pop Sci 190:88-9 My '67

Front wheel drive
Is front-wheel drive for you? round two; Toronado. H. P. Luckett. il Pop Sci 190:110-11 Ja '67

Fuel systems
See Automobile engines—Fuel feeding

Gearing
Gearbox rebuilding. B. Lang. il Hot Rod 20: 48-50 Je '67
1968 engine & gearing data; table. Motor T 19:94-5 N '67
Short shifts; VW shifter. J. Thawley. il Hot Rod 20:78 Je '67
Tooth or consequences; standard-shift transmission. J. McFarland. il Hot Rod 20:86-9 Ag '67
See also
Automobiles—Transmission

AUTOMOBILES—*Continued*

Headers
See Automobile parts

Heating and ventilation
Ventilating system for your car. H. T. Gurley. il Pop Mech 128:160 Ag '67

History
Classics of the '50s. D. MacDonald. il Motor T 20:55-9 Ja '68
Dodge's war wagon. F. X. Tolbert. il Motor T 19:78-9 D '67
Goggles & side curtains. G. Carson. il Am Heritage 18:32-9+ Ap '67
Ralph Stein on vintage cars. R. Stein. See issues of Motor trend
Supercharged Duesenberg 35 SJ. R. Stein. Motor T 19:72-3 D '67
Ten old-time losers. M. Lamm. il Motor T 19:98-101+ Je '67

Ignition
See Automobile engines—Ignition

Inspection
Sad state of state inspection. J. Joseph. Motor T 19:86+ Je '67

Insurance
See Insurance, Automobile

Leasing
Car renting vs ownership: which is best? Good H 164:187 My '67
Should you buy, rent, or lease a car? W. J. Toth. Am Home 70:50-1 My '67
When leasing autos for municipal use; Chicago. F. J. Casey. Am City 82:153-4 F '67

Lighting
See also
Automobiles—Signal lights

Lubrication
Additives; miracle workers in a can? D. MacDonald. il Motor T 19:82-4+ O '67
Dry-sumpthin' else; oil pumps. B. Lang. il Hot Rod 20:102-3 Jl '67
Oil for your car. C. P. Gilmore. Pop Sci 191: 67-71+ S '67
Oily issue. B. Lang. il Hot Rod 20:96-7 My '67
Swinging Chevy plan. D. Nowell. il Hot Rod 20:90-1 Mr '67

Manufacture
Suddenly, autos grow scarcer. il U S News 63:50 Jl 17 '67
See also
Automobile factories
Automobile industry and trade

Materials
Get belted; multiple-belt blower drive of polyurethane. E. Rickman. il Hot Rod 20:76 Ap '67
It's...it's plastic car. il Motor T 19:36 S '67
Tiger with a pussycat nose; rubber bumper of '68 GTO. J. Ethridge. il Motor T 19: 58:9 S '67

Painting
Pearl for pennies; pearl paint job. E. Rickman. il Hot Rod 20:62-3 N '67

Parking
See Automobile parking

Phonograph equipment
Facts about car stereo. B. Hartford. il Pop Mech 127:106-9+ My '67

Prices
Adventure in the auto marketplace; fiction of list prices. Consumer Rep 33:4 Ja '68
Detroit guarantees less. il Bsns W p40 S 30 '67
Higher prices coming for '68 cars. il U S News 63:12 S 11 '67
1968 car prices, options & accessories; table. Motor T 19:96-7 N '67
Now a bargain season for U.S. autos. il U S News 62:112-13 Ap 24 '67
Rambler takes a gamble; cuts prices by $200. Bsns W p39 F 25 '67
Saving money with your car. W. J. Toth. Am Home 70:46-7 Ja '67
Shuffle & cut. Time 90:101 O 6 '67
Suddenly, autos grow scarcer. il U S News 63:50 Jl 17 '67
Why car prices will rise; Henry Ford gives reasons; statements. H. Ford, 2d. U S News 62:22 My 29 '67

Propeller shafts
Driveshaft building. B. Lang. il Hot Rod 20: 115-16 O '67
How to get the clunk! out of your driveline. M. Schultz. il Pop Mech 128:158-61+ D '67

Purchasing
About auto financing; buying a used car. Sr Schol 90:39 Ap 21 '67
Autos; what to know in buying a new car. il Good H 164:202-3 Ap '67
Cars in your family; new car shopping guide. D. L. Gregg. il Bet Hom & Gard 45:20+ F '67
How to buy a new car. Consumer Rep 32: 409-12 D '67
How to save money buying a car. R. O'Brien. Read Digest 91:69-72 S '67
Is now the best time to trade in your car? il Pop Sci 190:122 Je '67
'68 buyer's guide; the dealer & the deal. il Motor T 19:20+ N '67
'68 new car buyer's guide. il Motor T 19:35-50+ N '67
'67 leftovers, are they a good buy? R. Schilling. il Motor T 19:34+ S '67
Used car buyer's guide; symposium. il Motor T 19:38-54 Je '67
Why not buy a used car? il Changing T 21: 7-11 Ag '67
See also
Automobile ownership

Radio equipment
Aah-chooo! not another pepper? outboard BCB preamp peps up auto reception. G. McClellan. il Pop Electr 27:60-1 Jl '67
FM in the car works better now. Consumer Rep 32:65-6 F '67
Put FM in your car. D. J. Sweeney. il Pop Electr 27:83-4 N '67

Rating
Ratings of compact-sized specialty V8s. Consumer Rep 32:358 Jl '67
Ratings of the 1967 US cars. il Consumer Rep 32:213-23 Ap '67

Renting
Avis vs. Hertz: Madison avenue's favorite feud. M. Mayer. Harper 236:40-4 Ja '68
Car renting vs ownership: which is best? Good H 164:187 My '67
Middle management gets a chauffeur; chauffeur-driven cars. il Bsns W p 142 S 9 '67
Should you buy, rent, or lease a car? W. J. Toth. Am Home 70:50-1 My '67
We'll never be no. 1! C. B. Hicks. il Pop Mech 128:86-8+ Ag '67
See also
Avis rent a car
Hertz corporation
National car rental systems, incorporated

Repairing
Automotive activity in recreation. E. G. West. il Parks & Rec 2:32-3 Ja '67
Differential rebuild. B. Lang. il Hot Rod 21: 74-6 Ja '68
Frequency-of-repair records: 1961 to 1966 models. il Consumer Rep 32:224-6 Ap '67
Gus Wilson's model garage (title varies) M. Bunn. See issues of Popular science monthly
How to fix those dents in your car. J. Burroughs. il Pop Sci 190:138-41 Mr '67
Linkage lingo. J. McFarland. il Hot Rod 20:96-9 Jl '67
Most common car trouble signs. il Good H 164:157 F '67
Piecework mechanic caper. J. Joseph. il Motor T 19:52-3+ Ag '67
Saturday mechanic. M. Schultz. See issues of Popular mechanics
Say, Smokey; questions and answers. S. Yunick. See issues of Popular science monthly
Shop talk. J. McFarland. See issues of Hot rod
See also
Automobile mechanics (persons)
Automobile service stations

Safety devices and measures
Aerospace skills utilized in safety car. R. D. Hibben. il Aviation W 87:60-3 D 25 '67
Auto safety devices cut head-on injuries. Todays Health 45:12 D '67
Auto-safety rule: can it be met? U S News 62: 14 Mr 20 '67
Auto-safety standards. M. Friedman. Newsweek 69:80 Je 5 '67
Auto safety; the truth and the hokum. il Chamberlain. il Nat R 19:343-6 Ap 4 '67

AUTOMOBILES—Safety devices and measures
  —*Continued*
Auto safety: will next year's cars be safer?
  Consumer Rep 32:190-2 Ap '67
Automatic light blinker. M. Chan. il Pop
  Electr 27:56 Ag '67
Automotive safety: community action; ad-
  dress, June 5, 1967. B. J. Nichols. Vital
  Speeches 33:628-31 Ag 1 '67
Can anyone build really safe cars? J. Ethridge.
  il Motor T 19:52-6+ Ap '67
Car safety measures lose their sharp bite.
  Bsns W p30-1 F 4 '67
Coming: federal controls over used automo-
  biles. il U S News 63:61 D 18 '67
Comparison of safety features in the specialty
  cars. Consumer Rep 32:357 Jl '67
Danger on the highways; interview. W. Had-
  don, jr. il U S News 63:66-9 O 16 '67
Driver's friends, passengers help save lives.
  Todays Health 45:86-7 My '67
Headrest combats whiplash. il Sci N 91:343
  Ap 8 '67
Horsetrading? car safety deadline. il Sr Schol
  89:16-17 Ja 20 '67
How good are auto safety gimmicks? A. R.
  Roalman. il Todays Health 45:38-41 S '67
Inside the '68s: new brakes, suspensions, en-
  gines, and body details. J. P. Norbye and
  J. Dunne. il Pop Sci 191:111-18 O '67
LBJ's safety boss: babe in bureaucracy's
  jungle. A. Rothenberg. il Look 31:101-3 My
  30 '67
Nader takes potshots at the '67s. R. W. Ir-
  vin. il Motor T 19:79-81 Mr '67; Discussion.
  19:82 Mr; 30 Je '67
New auto rules: safe or sorry? il Newsweek
  69:79 F 13 '67
Notes and comment. New Yorker 42:23 F 4
  '67
100 million straps, 30 million extra lights.
  A. Rothenberg. il Look 31:96 O 17 '67
Proposals & prototypes. il Time 90:100 D 8
  '67
Proven again: safety is still up to people.
  A. H. Sypher. il Nations Bsns 55:27-8 Jl '67
Quick, inexpensive way to skidproof any
  car! D. L. Gregg. il Bet Hom & Gard 45:
  42+ S '67
Republic's safety car unveiled. il Aero Tech
  21:15+ D 4 '67
Safer at any speed; progress report on safety
  program. il Newsweek 71:40-1 Ja 1 '68
Safer autos in '68; the changes coming. il
  U S News 62:12 F 13 '67
Safer cars in 1968. S. H. Brams. il Parents
  Mag 42:78-81+ N '67
Safety, and antisafety features. Consumer
  Rep 32:277 My '67
Safety: is it for real? il Pop Mech 128:98-100
  '67
Safety: some changes made, and to come. il
  Consumer Rep 33:34-5 Ja '68
Speed, safety, and sense! M. Spiegel. il Sr
  Schol 91:26 N 2 '67
Truce and progress; concerning safety re-
  quirements. il Time 89:87 F 10 '67
Water bumpers, new automotive safety
  device. il Am City 82:184+ S '67
Way we see it. D. MacDonald. Motor T 19:6
  Mr '67
What smog control will cost you. J. M. Calla-
  han. il Motor T 19:60-1+ S '67
What the new auto safety laws will mean
  to you. J. P. Norbye and others. il Pop
  Sci 190:80-4+ Je '67
Where war has been declared on hoodlums.
  U S News 64:9 Ja 8 '68
Why auto safety legislation was necessary.
  il Consumer Bul 50:33-5 Je '67
Wraparound safety; scatterblankets. J. Mc-
  Farland. il Hot Rod 21:87 Ja '68
  See also
Automobile driving—Safety devices and
  measures
Automobiles—Testing
Automobiles, Foreign—Safety devices and
  measures
Safety belts

Quotations, maxims, etc.
Of autos and auto safety; comp. by E. F.
  Murphy. N Y Times Mag p81 Ja 22 '67

Service stations
See Automobile service stations

Shock absorbers
Suspended sentence; coil/shock suspension
  system. B. Lang. il Hot Rod 20:100-1 Ag '67

Shows
See Automobiles—Exhibitions

Signal lights
Add 1-2-3 turn signals to your car. R. F.
  Graf. il Pop Sci 190:128-30 Ja '67

Take your turn; sequential turn indicators.
  E. Rickman. il Hot Rod 20:91 O '67
Telltale for your car's tail lights. H. Zave.
  il Pop Sci 191:98-100 Jl '67
Turn indicator flasher unit. W. P. Mitchell.
  il Pop Electr 27:66 O '67

Skidding
Farewell to wet-weather skids; longitudinal
  grooves in California. J. Root. il Pop Mech
  127:124-7+ Mr '67
Stop skidding! new research is whipping your
  greatest driving hazard. D. Francis. il Pop
  Sci 190:80-4 F '67

Social aspects
Sex and the single car. J. Joseph. il Motor T
  19:44-7 Ap '67

Specifications
Guide to the specifications table (cont) il
  Consumer Rep 32:202-5 Ap '67
1967 cars. il Consumer Bul 50:16-26 Ap '67
1967 full-size cars. il Consumer Bul 50:16-25
  My '67

Speed
How fast is too fast? T. Stimson. il Pop
  Mech 128:71-4+ S '67
Speed, safety, and sense! M. Spiegel. il Sr
  Schol 91:26 N 2 '67
  See also
Automobile speed records
Speed indicators

Springs and suspension
Suspended sentence; coil/shock suspension
  system. B. Lang. il Hot Rod 20:100-1 Ag
  '67

Starting
How to solve hard starting. M. Schultz. il
  Pop Mech 128:118-21 Jl '67

Steering gear
Guide line; steering unit. B. Lang. il Hot Rod
  20:88-9 N '67
Your next car may have variable-ratio
  steering. J. Dunne. il Pop Sci 191:88-91
  Jl '67
Your steering linkage. M. J. Schultz. il Pop
  Mech 127:164-7+ Mr '67

Stopping
Stalling: how to find and fix the trouble.
  M. Schultz. il Pop Mech 128:144-7+ N '67

Tape equipment
Facts about car stereo. B. Hartford. il Pop
  Mech 127:106-9+ My '67
Stereo-8 on the go! stereo tape-cartridge
  systems in cars. R. Hemming. Sr Schol
  90:32 My 12 '67
Tapes hit the road. H. Kupferberg. il Atlan
  220:130+ O '67

Testing
American dream; Javelin. E. Dahlquist. il
  Hot Rod 20:34-7 D '67
As auto makers step up their tests for safety.
  il U S News 62:34-5 F 6 '67
Barracuda 383. J. Schmidt. il Motor T 19:52-
  3 S '67
Beep! beep! Road Runner. E. Dahlquist. il
  Hot Rod 20:36-9 N '67
Buick LeSabre, Chrysler Newport, Mercury
  Monterey, Olds Delmont. il Consumer Rep
  32:273-9 My '67
Chevelle Malibu V-8, America's most popu-
  lar intermediate. J. P. Norbye and J.
  Dunne. il Pop Sci 191:54-6 D '67
Chevrolet's Chevelle, Ford's Fairlane, and
  Plymouth's Belvedere. J. P. Norbye. il Pop
  Sci 190:100-3 F '67
Dodge R/T. E. Dahlquist. il Hot Rod 20:34-
  6+ F '67
Fastback filly; Mustang. E. Dahlquist. il Hot
  Rod 20:34-6+ Mr '67
Five full-sized V8 sedans; Dodge, Ambas-
  sador, Chevrolet, Ford, Pontiac. il Consumer
  Rep 33:24-33 Ja '68
Five luxury specialty cars. J. Ethridge. il
  Motor T 19:68-73 Ag '67
Four-wheel safari test in the rugged Rock-
  ies. S. James. il Pop Mech 127:119-22+ My
  '67
Gordon Johncock tests the new Corvette. G.
  Johncock. il Pop Mech 129:108-10+ Ja '68
Horsing around with the Mustang six. A.
  Miller. il Hot Rod 20:91-3 Je; 48-50 Jl '67
How and why of CU's auto tests. il Consumer
  Rep 32:206-7 Ap '67
Instant sporty cars are practical, and fun.
  J. Dunne. il Pop Sci 190:110-13 Mr '67
Jackie Stewart tests:
  Pontiac's flashy Firebird. J. Stewart. il
  Pop Mech 127:98-100+ F '67

AUTOMOBILES—Testing—*Continued*
Javelin SST: an exciting new sportster for '68. P. Jones. il Pop Sci 191:76-9 S '67
MT road test:
American look-alikes. S. Kelly. il Motor T 19:75-8 F '67
Dana 427 Camaro. J. Ethridge. il Motor T 19:60-1 Jl '67
Dodge Dart GT revisited. R. Schilling. il Motor T 19:50-1 Ag '67
Dodge's dreadnoughts. J. Ethridge. il Motor T 19:56-8 Je '67
Firebreathing bird from Pontiac. J. Ethridge. il Motor T 19:30-4 Mr '67
How do you say PFST? Pontiac Firebird Sprint Turismo. S. Kelly. il Motor T 19:54-5 Jl '67
Olds swings a pair of keen Cutlasses. J. Ethridge. il Motor T 19:53-6 F '67
Ramming air to a Firebird to make it fly. S. Kelly. il Motor T 19:40-1 Ag '67
Rogue runner. S. Kelly. il Motor T 19:76-7 Je '67
Skylark & GS 400. S. Kelly. il Motor T 19:59-62 Ap '67
Three faces of Fairlane. R. Schilling. il Motor T 19:78-80+ Je '67
Three of a kind; Chevy, Ford and Plymouth. S. Kelly. il Motor T 19:38-46 Mr '67
Tres Chevelles. R. Schilling. il Motor T 19:56-9 Jl '67
Two rockin' puritans from Plymouth. D. MacDonald. il Motor T 19:63-6 F '67
Yankee doodle dandies. S. Kelly. il Motor T 19:64-6 S '67
News on wheels; General motors proving ground. M. Spiegel. il Sr Schol 91:38-9 S 28 '67
$1839 Rambler. S. Kelly. il Motor T 19:54 Ag '67
Pontiac Catalina, Mercury Monterey, and Dodge Polara. J. P. Norbye; J. Dunne. il Pop Sci 190:96-101 Ja '67
Pontiac Firebird: the GTO gets a little brother. M. Andretti. il Pop Sci 190:90-3 F '67
PUREformance trials: were they? D. MacDonald. il Motor T 19:48-51 Ap '67
Rambler Rebel 770, practical, sturdy, and quiet. J. P. Norbye and J. Dunne. il Pop Sci 191:57-9 D '67
Road testing five intermediate-sized V8s; Buick Special, Chevelle Malibu, Ford Fairlane, Plymouth Belvedere, Rambler Rebel. il Consumer Rep 32:82-7 F '67
Rodger Ward tests the Charger R/T. R. Ward. il Pop Mech 128:73-5 D '67
Super cars; testing the Pontiac GTO, Charger R/T, Buick GS 400, Torino GT, Chevelle SS 396, Road Runner, Olds 4-4-2, Dodge R/T. il Motor T 19:23-41 D '67
Testing six sporty cars; Mustang, Camaro, Barracuda, Javelin, Cougar, Firebird. il Motor T 20:24-39 Ja '68
These family sedans pack some surprises; Impala, Fury III, Galaxie 500, and Ambassador SST. J. P. Norbye and J. Dunne. il Pop Sci 192:86-91 Ja '68
Tough Rogue to go; Rambler Rebel. E. Dahlquist. il Hot Rod 20:38-40+ Je '67
Two champagne cars: $15,000 vs. $4000; Mercury's new Cougar XR7 and Aston Martin DB-6. R. Ward. il Pop Mech 127:114-17 Mr '67
What the pure oil tests prove about performance. B. Kilpatrick. il Pop Mech 127:96-9 Ap '67
When better cars are built: Buick GS 400. E. Dahlquist. il Hot Rod 21:40-2 Ja '68
World's most revealing car tests: Union Pure oil performance trials. J. P. Norbye. il Pop Sci 190:88-91 Ap '67

Tires
See Tires, Automobile

Towing
See Towing

Traction
$9 traction bars. B. Warrick. il Hot Rod 20:78 O '67

Transmission
Building a two-speed trans. B. Lang. il Hot Rod 20:98-9 D '67
Carve a shaft; transmission pilot shaft to align clutch disc. B. Lang. il Hot Rod 21:62 Ja '68
Differential rebuild. B. Lang. il Hot Rod 21:74-6 Ja '68
Overdriving. J. Thawley. il Hot Rod 20:100-1 O '67
Throttle-body science; automatic transmissions. J. McFarland. il Hot Rod 20:72 D '67

Tooth or consequences; standard-shift transmission. J. McFarland. il Hot Rod 20:86-9 Ag '67
Toughening torqueflites. E. Dahlquist. il Hot Rod 20:64-6 S '67

Transportation
Drive-aways; benefits and risks of bargain car-transport opportunities. F. A. Tinker. il Travel 128:61-2+ O '67

Upholstery
Time to switch? Color hit, bus upholstery experiment. E. Rickman. il Hot Rod 20:76 Mr '67

Ventilation
See Automobiles—Heating and ventilation

Wheels
Alignment and wheel balance. D. L. Gregg. Bet Hom & Gard 45:44+ S '67
Make 'em fit; wheel adapters. il Hot Rod 20:85 Ag '67
Wide-base wheels. B. Lang. il Hot Rod 20:92-3 S '67

Wrecking
Super street litter needs a special hauler; junked cars, Miami, Fla. il Am City 82:56 O '67

AUTOMOBILES, Amphibious
I drove through a flood in a car that swims. R. Gannon. il Pop Sci 191:76-9+ Ag '67

AUTOMOBILES, Armored
Peacekeeper is here! Nation 205:517-18 N 20 '67

AUTOMOBILES, Care of. See Automobiles—Care

AUTOMOBILES, Compact
Chevy II, Falcon, Valiant, Rambler American. il Consumer Rep 32:325-31 Je '67
Compacts: good things, little packages. B. Kilpatrick. il Pop Mech 128:104-5+ O '67
New Ford Cortina: lotsa car for little money. J. P. Norbye. il Pop Sci 190:112-13 My '67
Pacer from Ford's British stable; compact Cortina. il Bsns W p98+ N 25 '67
Ratings of the 1967 US cars. il Consumer Rep 32:214-15 Ap '67
'68 compacts. il Motor T 19:76-9 N '67
Truth about the compact cars: Plymouth Valiant, Chevy II, and Rambler American. J. P. Norbye. il Pop Sci 190:104-7 Ap '67
Youthful not-so-compacts: Dodge Dart GT, Ford Falcon Futura, Rambler Rebel SST. J. P. Norbye. il Pop Sci 190:108-11 Mr '67

Testing
Five specialty cars; Ford Mustang, Chevrolet Camaro, Mercury Cougar, Plymouth Barracuda and Pontiac Firebird. il Consumer Rep 32:352-6+ Jl '67
Imported economy cars: Ford Cortina, Fiat 124, Renault 10, Datsun RL-411 and Sunbeam Arrow and for comparison the Rambler American. il Consumer Rep 32:437-47 Ag '67

AUTOMOBILES, Electric
A.C. motor drive for electric cars. R. M. Brown. il Electr World 77:28-9 My '67
Case for the electric automobile. D. E. Carr. il Atlan 219:92-5 Je '67; Reply. P. N. Gammelgard. 220:50-1 O '67
D.C. motor drive for electric cars. J. Mungenast. il Electr World 77:25 My '67
Electric autos, not yet. J. Ludwigson. il Sci N 91:338-9 Ap 8 '67
Electric cars; are they kidding? R. Dunlop. il Pop Mech 127:118-21+ Je '67
Electric cars; coming back? T. F. Walsh. il Todays Health 45:56-9+ My '67
Electric cars: they're cleaner, but. . . il Sci N 91:232 Mr 11 '67
Gar Wood: an old sea dog is up to new tricks. J. Fix. il Pop Mech 128:82-5+ Jl '67
GM makes an electric Corvair. il Pop Sci 190:132-3 Ja '67
Here's Ford's first electric. D. Scott. il Pop Sci 191:106-7+ S '67
Here's one for the road; Westinghouse Markette. il Bsns W p33 Ap 8 '67
How you'll drive the amazing Urbmobile. C. P. Gilmore. il Pop Sci 191:75-8+ O '67
New relief from auto fumes due soon; setback for the electric car. il U S News 63:76-7 Jl 24 '67
Next: the Voltswagon? AMC's Amitron. il Time 90:69-70 D 22 '67
On a clear day you will see the electric car. D. Ash. il N Y Times Mag p22+ Ja 29 '67
Plug-in, pollution-less car in your future? il Sr Schol 90:8-9 Mr 17 '67
Revolt against the internal-combustion engine. L. Lessing. il Fortune 76:78-83+ Jl '67

AUTOMOBILES, Racing—*Continued*
Kalittascope; interview, ed. by J. McFarland.
 C. Kalitta. il Hot Rod 20:56-8 My '67
Motor racing; more slowdowns; engine rul-
 ings. K. W. Purdy. il Atlan 220:119-21 D
 '67
Motorsports; the Atlanta 500; symposium. il
 Motor T 19:108-10 Je '67
Pair of dandy's; '68 Dodges. E. Dahlquist. il
 Hot Rod 21:54-6 Ja '68
Project altered; car owned by Explorer post
 14, San Fernando, Calif. il Hot Rod 20:46-7
 Jl '67
Racer in a far-out country; J. Hall of Texas.
 C. Phinizy. il Sports Illus 26:30-2+ My 1
 '67
Racewatchers guide to competition cars. il
 Pop Mech 127:95-101 Mr '67
Racing's fabulous invalid; Mario Andretti
 and A. J. Foyt at dirt-track racing. W.
 Johnson. il Sports Illus 27:32-3 S 18 '67
Reining in the turbine; regulation sets new
 limits on the power of turbine engines.
 Time 90:65 Jl 7 '67
Roddin' at random. See issues of Hot rod
Second-hand super cars. W. Thoms. Motor T
 19:44-5 Je '67
Shootout at the Riverside corral; fourth an-
 nual Hot rod magazine championship
 drags. J. Thawley. il Hot Rod 20:44-7 Je '67
Silence is not always golden; Indy 500. J.
 Ethridge. il Motor T 19:42-9 Ag '67
Sizzlin' sixes; six-cylinder Chevys. J. Thawley.
 il Hot Rod 20:40-2 Mr '67
Sudden revenge for Ferrari; victory at Day-
 tona international speedway. K. Chapin.
 il Sports Illus 26:22-5 F 13 '67
Target: 200 mph Mustang. J. Thawley. il Hot
 Rod 20:30-2 F '67
Wee Jimmy's wee bomb; record average
 speed in Lotus. il Time 91:36 Ja 12 '68
What makes Indy run. J. Ethridge. il Motor
 T 19:68-70+ Je '67
When a dream race became a nightmare;
 Charlotte, N.C. L. Chapin. il Sports Illus
 27:22-3 O 23 '67
Win for Cougar, a wild ride for Camaro;
 Trans-American racing championship. K.
 Chapin. il Sports Illus 27:58-60 Ag 14 '67
Winter champs, AHRA style. J. Thawley. il
 Hot Rod 20:56-7 Ap '67
Woody carves a chassis. J. Thawley. il Hot
 Rod 20:70-2 Mr '67
 See also
Karts (midget cars)

Care

Free tenths; tips for running a stocker. E.
 Dahlquist. il Hot Rod 20:36-8 Ag '67

Exhibitions

Hot rods in Mexico. R. Brock. il Hot Rod
 21:71 Ja '68

History

Stutz's great hours at Le Mans. G. Borgeson. il Motor T 19:72-4+ Mr '67

Repairing
 See also
Automobile mechanics (persons)

Safety devices and measures

SEMA and you; Specialty equipment manu-
 facturer's association. D. Francicso. Hot
 Rod 20:120-1 D '67
AUTOMOBILES, Remodeled
Bite and life for drag 'Vettes J. Thawley. il
 Hot Rod 20:60-1 Ag '67
Bolting some stinger onto the 'Stang. J.
 Thawley. il Hot Rod 20:58-60 S '67
Building MoPar's muscle. E. Dahlquist. il
 Hot Rod 20:62-4 Ag '67
Camaro, stage III. J. McFarland. il Hot Rod
 20:58-60 De '67
Camaro, stage two. J. McFarland. il Hot Rod
 20:68-70 Ap '67
Chevy snap for a jumpin' jeep. J. Thawley.
 il Hot Rod 20:94-5 Je '67
Corveight; Corvair with Olds V8 engine. E.
 Dahlquist. il Hot Rod 21:64-6 Ja '68
Double-duty dandy; Pontiac Invader. il Hot
 Rod 20:40-1 Jl '67
Gull-wing Toronado. S. Kelly. il Motor T
 19:22-3 F '67
Horsing around with the Mustang six. A.
 Miller. il Hot Rod 20:91-3 Je; 48-50 Jl '67
Shape up! working with aluminum while
 building a dragster body. E. Dahlquist. il
 Hot Rod 20:66-9 Mr; 100-2+ Ap '67
Sizzlin' sixes; six-cylinder Chevys. J. Thawley.
 il Hot Rod 20:40-2 Mr '67
Sleeper swap. J. Thawley. il Hot Rod 20:
 94-5 Ag '67
Thunderbug; customized VW. il Hot Rod 20:
 108-9 N '67

AUTOMOBILES, Second-hand. See Automo-
 biles, Used
AUTOMOBILES, Steam
Will steamers make it back on auto market?
 il Bsns W p85-6 D 9 '67
AUTOMOBILES, Theft of
Computer combats auto thefts. B. M. Crit-
 tenden. il Am City 82:116-17 Je '67
Insure against auto theft for $1; simple
 do-it-yourself alarm systems. G. E. Hollister.
 il Motor T 19:72 F '67
Secrets of a car thief. M. Lamm. Motor T
 19:68+ F '67
Stamp out auto theft. R. L. Winklepleck. il
 Pop Electr 26:59-61 Mr '67
Stop thief! E. Rickman. il Hot Rod 20:62-3
 Jl '67
Ways to avoid car theft. Good H 165:198 O '67
AUTOMOBILES, Toy
Eight tips to tuning a winning slot car. il Pop
 Mech 129:178-80 Ja '68
AUTOMOBILES, Used
Buying a used super car. M. Lamm. il
 Motor T 19:59-62 D '67
Coming: federal controls over used automo-
 biles. U S News 63:61 D 18 '67
How to buy a used car. il Consumer Rep 32:
 412-38 D '67
I'll cheat you if you don't watch out. il Pop
 Sci 191:76-9+ D '67
Nine-point check for used cars. Suc Farm 65:
 110 Mr '67
Used cars and the wise buyer. il Sr Schol
 90:25-7+ Ap 21 '67
Why not buy a used car? Changing T 21:
 7-11 Ag '67

Depreciation
 See Depreciation

Prices

Seasonal demand and used car prices. il Mo
 Labor R 90:12-16 O '67
Some used-car prices. Changing T 21:10 Ag
 '67
Twenty-four best used car buys. M. Lamm.
 il Motor T 19:40 Je '67
AUTOMOTIVE diesel engines. See Diesel en-
 gines, Automotive
AUTOMOTIVE gas turbines. See Gas turbines,
 Automotive
AUTOMOTIVE immortality; story. See Mid-
 wood, B.
AUTOMOTIVE industry. See Automobile in-
 dustry and trade
AUTOMOTIVE mathematics. See Mathematics
AUTONAVIGATORS. See Aeronautic instru-
 ments
AUTOPEN signatures. See Signatures (writing)
AUTOPILOTS. See Automatic pilot (airplanes)
AUTOPSY
Learning from the dead. il Newsweek 70:62-3
 S 11 '67
Lessons from the dead. Time 90:70 S 8 '67
AUTOSOMES. See Chromosomes
AUTOSPORES. See Spores (botany)
AUTUMN
Autumn in the Rockies. J. E Dwyer. il Pop
 Gard 18:52-5+ D '67
Summer's lease. A. Waugh. Nat R 19:1212 O
 31 '67
AUTUMN sortie; story. See Frater, A.
AUXINS
Acropetal movement of auxin: dependence
 on temperature. G. W. Keitt, jr. and R. A.
 Baker. bibliog il Science 156:1380-1 Je 9
 '67
Induction of coiling in tendrils by auxin and
 carbon dioxide. L. Reinhold. bibliog il Sci-
 ence 158:791-3 N 10 '67
 See also
Indoleacetic acid
AVALANCHE photodiodes. See Diodes
AVALANCHES
Nature note; white death. Sci N 91:84 Ja 28
 '67
 See also
Landslides
AVANT garde (periodical)
No hits, no runs, no Eros. B. Brower. Life
 63:18 D 1 '67
AVANT-garde literature. See Literature
AVANT-garde moving pictures. See Moving
 pictures
AVANT-garde music. See Music
AVANT-garde sculpture. See Sculpture
AVANT-garde theater. See Theater
AVCO corporation
Avco strike heats up pressure for a law. il
 Bsns W p 114 Jl 1 '67

AVEDON, Richard
Beatles; a color folio. Look 32:32-41 Ja 9 '68
AVERAGES, Stock. See Stocks—Price indexes and averages
AVERILL, Lloyd J.
Confidence man revisited. Christian Cent 84: 277-8 Mr 1 '67
AVERY, Lydia
Role of secular institutes. America 116:187-8 F 4 '67
AVERY, Paul
Mildred Harrison's Viet Nam ordeal. Ebony 22:88-90+ My '67
AVERY, T. Eugene
Silhouettes of distinctive trees. Am For 73: 24-6 S '67
AVIATION
Aviation jetstream. K. V. Brown. See issues of Popular mechanics
Aviation off the record; fantasy and reality of aviation. R. Bach. Flying 82:72-4 Ja '68
General aviation seeks to fight criticism. D. A. Brown. Aviation W 88:101-2 Ja 15 '68
Scott's corner. D. H. Scott. See issues of Flying
Senator and the reporter; interview, ed. by R. Peterson. B. M. Goldwater. il Flying 81:56-61 S '67
Traffic pattern; news and views. See issues of Flying
See also
Air travel
Airways
Gliding and soaring
Private flying
    also headings beginning Aeronautic, Aeronautics, Airplane, Airplanes

Accidents
Accident report; pilot's errors. R. B. Parke. Flying 80:32 Je '67
Bombs of Palomares, by T. Szulc. Review New Repub 156:36-7 My 20 '67. W. K. Wyant, jr
British accident report: cause of Viscount crash undetermined. Aviation W 87:123+ S 18 '67
British ministry of aviation report; overshoot focal point of Vanguard inquiry. Aviation W 86:81+ F 20 '67
British ministry of aviation report; pilot, training cited in Vanguard crash. il Aviation W 86:80-7+ F 27 '67
British safety report: medical factor studied in Bellanca crash. Aviation W 87:105+ D 11 '67
Cincinnati crashes not believed involved with design of airport. D. A. Brown. Aviation W 87:36 D 11 '67
CAB accident investigation report:
    Beechraft crash in box canyon kills NASA official, two others. Aviation W 86:93 Mr 27 '67
    Fuselage failure cited in Mantz crash; Winterhaven, Calif. July 8, 1965. Aviation W 86:97+ Ja 30 '67
    Pilot's coronary problem cited in crash. Aviation W 88:75-83+ Ja 1 '68
Can flying be safer? il Bsns W p98+ Jl 29 '67
Crash report urges better medical tests. Aviation W 86:39 Ap 10 '67
Crashes probed in Ohio, Liberia. Aviation W 86:31 Mr 13 '67
Crowded sky; mid-air collision near Hendersonville, N.C. Time 90:16 Jl 28 '67
Day H-bombs fell on Palomares. L. Azancot. il Sat R 50:21-7+ Ja 28 '67
Day they lost the H-bomb, by C. Morris. Review
    Sat R 50:40 Ja 28 '67. O. R. Reid
Dear diary; Oiens' plane crash in California. il Newsweek 70:35 O 16 '67
Death in Trinity Mountains; crash of Alvin Oien's plane. il Time 90:30 O 13 '67
Delta crash involved airline training trip. Aviation W 86:38 Ap 10 '67
Engine failure, load cited in C-46 crash. Aviation W 87:29 O 30 '67
Excessive speed of TWA DC-9 cited in airport midair crash; Dayton's Cox municipal airport. Aviation W 86:43 Je 12 '67
FBI probing blast on American flight. Aviation W 87:30 N 20 '67
Hills of Hebron; Convair 880 crashes in Kentucky. Time 90:17-18 D 1 '67
Homecoming; Delta airlines DC-8 crash in New Orleans. il Newsweek 69:35-6 Ap 10 '67
Japanese investigation commission report: severe gust blamed for 707 Tokyo crash. il Aviation W 87:115+ Ag 28 '67
Mid-air! mid-air! mid-air! K. Wheeler. il Read Digest 90:127-31 F '67

NASA accident report: pilot work load cited in M2-F2 crash. il Aviation W 87:129-32+ O 9 '67
NASA says X-15A exceeded structure limits before crash. Aviation W 87:24 N 27 '67
National safety board report: descent in West coast crash unexplained. Aviation W 88: 106-9+ Ja 15 '68
NTSB fails to find cause in 727 crash. Aviation W 88:52 Ja 15 '68
Navy, Vertol analyze accidents of CH-46. Aviation W 87:45 Jl 24 '67
One man's impossible triumph; case of F. Ellis. B. Merson. il Good H 165:74-5+ Ag '67
One of our H-bombs is missing, by F. Lewis. Review
    Sat R 50:39 Ja 28 '67. O. R. Reid
Over the top; first man to die in an X-15. il Time 90:27 N 24 '67
Pilot distraction seen in M2-F2 accident. C. M. Plattner. Aviation W 87:29 Ag 7 '67
Please hurry, someone; ordeal of A. Oien family after crash in mountains of northern California. H. H. Martin. il Sat Eve Post 241:30-2+ Ja 13 '68
Poison ivy can be deadly. Flying 81:86 N '67
Possible problem with bleed air cited in BAC 111 crash hearing. Aviation W 87:33 D 18 '67
Pro's nest; midair collision. T. Baxter. Flying 81:24 O '67
Scott's corner; collision between a Boeing 727 and a Cessna 310 in North Carolina. D. H. Scott. Flying 81:88-9 O '67
Ten minutes to live; mid-air collision of Eastern airlines Constellation, December 4, 1965. W. R. Young. il Read Digest 90:198-200+ My '67
Transportation dept. investigation report: maintenance cited in JAL engine blast. il Aviation W 88:88-9+ Ja 8 '68
See also
Drinking and airplane accidents
Parachuting—Accidents and injuries
Survival after airplane accidents, shipwrecks, etc.

Altitude flying
See also
Airplanes—Pressurization

Bibliography
Book reviews. See issues of Flying

Bird hazards
Birdwatching seriously. il Sci N 91:245 Mr 11 '67
Forecasting birds. il Time 89:73 Mr 17 '67
Fowl weather for flying. Newsweek 70:98+ S 25 '67
Runway rabbit hunt. J. S. Flannery. il Outdoor Life 139:74-6 Mr '67

Blind flying
See Aviation—Instrument flying

Clubs
See Aviation clubs

Communications systems
See Radio in aviation

Competitions
Bahamas flying treasure hunt; another winner. E. D. Muhlfeld. il Flying 80:70 F '67
See also
National intercollegiate flying association

Cost
See Airplanes—Cost of operation

Exhibitions
Air race into the future; 27th Paris air show. W. D. Patterson. Sat R 50:15 Jl 8 '67
Air show '67. R. Blodget. il Flying 80:66-7 Ap '67
Aircraft compete in international showcase; Paris air show. il Aviation W 87:50-5 Jl 24 '67
Americans are coming! 27th Salon de l'aeronautique et de l'espace. J. Fricker. il Flying 80:44-7 Je '67
Best of shows; Paris air show. R. B. Parke. il Flying 80:118-19+ Mr '67
Blue sky salesmen; 27th biennial Paris air show. il Newsweek 69:78 Je 5 '67
Challenge to U.S. arrayed at air show; with editorial comment by R. Hotz. il Aviation W 86:53, 58-68 My 29 '67
Echoes from Domodedovo; Soviet national aviation day air show. R. Hotz. Aviation W 87:21 Jl 17 '67

AVIATION—Exhibitions—*Continued*
European interest rises in business show; first International general aviation salon Gosselies airport, Belgium. il Aviation W 87:97+ O 2 '67
Foreign accent; bizjets to biplanes. European air shows. J. Fricker. il Flying 82:30-1 Ja '68
Image building at the big show; 27th Paris air show. il Time 89:64 Je 2 '67
Limits on flying cloud 1969 Paris show; with editorial comment by R. Hotz. W. H. Gregory. il Aviation W 86:21, 26-34 Je 12 '67
Litton to run $830 million Greek development program; plans revealed at Paris air show. H. Taylor. il Tech W 20:17-19 Je 12 '67
Moscow air show. il Aero Tech 21:11 Jl 17 '67
Paris air show draws praise of U.S. aerospace companies. D. E. Fink. Aviation W 87: 22-3 Ag 21 '67
Paris air show; Soviet displays again dominate exposition. H. Taylor. il Tech W 20: 12-15 Je 5 '67
Paris air show; special report; with editorial comment by R. Hotz. Aviation W 86:17, 22-39 Je 5 '67
Paris air show; Vostok booster, V/STOL fighter debut. H. Taylor. il Tech W 20:16-17 My 29 '67
Paris '67. J. Fricker. il Flying 81:84-7+ Ag '67
Russian air show. Aviation W 87:58-63+ Jl 31 '67
Russian air show; symposium. il Aviation W 87:16-24+ Jl 24 '67
Russian air show; with account by C. Brownlow. il Aviation W 87:26-39 Jl 17 '67
Six acrobatic teams display skills in precision flying; photographs by J. H. Pickerell. Aviation W 87:62-9 Ag 21 '67
Soviet salesmen buzz West's airplane market; Soviet SST to Paris international air show. il Bsns W p64-6+ Mr 18 '67
Soviets demonstrate vertical envelopment capability with An-22 heavy transport. il Aviation W 87:52-5 Ag 14 '67
Soviets preen feathers, with VTOLS, swingwing craft, at Moscow show. il Bsns W p37 Jl 15 '67
Stealing the show in Paris; Russians display space vehicles. il Time 89:87 Je 9 '67
U.S. turns it on at Paris air show. il Bsns W p 195-6 My 13 '67
Variety of Russian spacecraft displayed; Paris air show; photographs. Aviation W 86:84-5+ Je 12 '67
Variety of techniques marks team flying. W. H. Gregory. il Aviation W 87:50-1+ Ag 21 '67
Winds aloft; Reading national maintenance & operations meeting. il Flying 81:13-14+ Ag '67
Yakovlev faults U.S. display at Paris air show. Aviation W 87:44 Jl 24 '67

Fog problem
Warm fog suppression in large-scale laboratory experiments. R. J. Pilié and others. il Science 157:1319-20 S 15 '67

History
See Aeronautics—History

Ice problem
See Airplanes—Ice protection

Instrument flying
Aviation week pilot report: blind-flight orienter uses magnetic field. B. K. Thomas, jr. il Aviation W 86:91-4+ Ap 17 '67
Follow me through; concerning instrument rating. R. Blodget. Flying 80:88 My '67
IFR and the single man. M. W. Horowitz. Flying 80:78-9 Ap '67
Pilot report:
Link's new GAT I; general aviation trainer I. R. B. Weeghman. il Flying 80:72-4 My '67

International aspects
Aeroflot flying over Scandinavia. D. C. Winston. Aviation W 86:28 Mr 13 '67
Aeroflot permit recommended. Aviation W 86:37 Ap 17 '67
Airbus wins tentative approval; Britain, France, Germany agree on design. H. J. Coleman. Aviation W 87:25 Jl 31 '67
Cargo cases watched closely for trends. H. D. Watkins. Aviation W 87:32-3 Jl 24 '67
CAB denies Seaboard protest on lease; aviation policies of the Italian government. L. Doty. Aviation W 87:38 D 11 '67
CAB hurls legal rebuff at Alitalia. L. Doty. Aviation W 87:35 O 23 '67

Cooperation urged for European industry. Aviation W 87:81-2+ S 25 '67
European interest sought for Northrop 530 fighter. Aviation W 87:26 Ag 7 '67
Europeans agree to start airbus project. il Aviation W 87:30 O 2 '67
Getting together with Aeroflot; commercial air service between Russia and the U.S. il Bsns W p 139:40 D 2 '67
Irish firm in ban on U.S. rights to Dublin. W. J. Normyle. il Aviation W 87:39+ Jl 31 '67
JAL urges balanced capacity in Pacific. R. F. Coburn. Aviation W 87:49-50 D 11 '67
Landing right problem to cause delay in Il-62 New York service. Aviation W 86:28 F 20 '67
Saigon's squeeze play; refused landing clearance to Pan Am commercial flight. Time 89:90 Mr 3 '67
SAS gains Moscow-Tokyo route; with editorial comment. Aviation W 86:21, 36-7 Ja 23 '67
Soviet pact may snarl SAS talks. L. Doty. Aviation W 86:27-8 F 27 '67
State dept. to press for new talks on U.S. rights to Dublin. J. W. Carter. Aviation W 86:38-9 Ja 23 '67
Technical talks on New York-Moscow air service successfully completed. Dept State Bul 57:820 D 18 '67
Travel cuts could blunt airline growth. L. Doty. Aviation W 88:19-21 Ja 8 '68
Tu-114 avionic lack may delay U.S.-Moscow route. Aviation W 86:40 Ap 3 '67
U.S. airlines push buy American. L. Doty. il Aviation W 88:42-4 Ja 15 '68
U.S. and Italy terminate air transport agreement; text of joint communique, May 31, 1967. Dept State Bul 56:965 Je 26 '67
United States and Panama amend air transport agreement; joint statement, June 7, 1967. Dept State Bul 56:965-6 Je 26 '67
U.S.-Italy conflict will set pattern. L. Doty. Aviation W 87:39-40 O 16 '67
U.S. stand on liability draws more fire; fatal accident. Aviation W 87:30 S 4 '67
Visitor from Russia; Ilyushin-62 in the U.S. il Time 90:108 D 1 '67
See also
International air transport association
International civil aviation organization

Laws and regulations
Air taxis, commuters face new rules. Aviation W 86:43 Ap 17 '67
Cargo, charter proposals hit by airlines. H. D. Watkins. Aviation W 87:37 D 4 '67
Long-term inclusive tour plans clouded. H. D. Watkins. Aviation W 87:29 Jl 31 '67
Murphy urges continued airlines, CAB independence. H. D. Watkins. Aviation W 88:28 Ja 8 '68
Washington clipboard. R. Burkhardt. See issues of Flying
See also
Air pilots—Legal status, laws, etc.
Air traffic control
Airports—Traffic control
United States—Civil aeronautics board
United States—Federal aviation administration

Lightning hazards
Titanium seen boosting SST lightning risk. Aviation W 87:95 N 13 '67

Medical aspects
Carrier pilots show little stress in North Vietnam raids. C. M. Plattner. il Aviation W 86:80-1+ Ap 24 '67

Meteorological aspects
See Meteorology, Aeronautic

Night flying
Stitch in time. R. Gottlieb. Flying 81:88+ Ag '67

Periodicals
See also
Aviation week and space technology (periodical)

Physiological aspects
Heart strain greater in landing on carrier than bombing. C. M. Plattner. il Aviation W 86:60-1+ Mr 13 '67
It's just a simple cold. R. J. Slencak. Flying 81:74 N '67
When not to take a plane trip. Good H 165: 170 Ag '67
See also
Aviation—Medical aspects

Safety devices and measures
Air accidents; House commerce committee hearing. J. Ridgeway. New Repub 157:12-14 Ag 5 '67

AVIATION—Safety devices and measures
—*Continued*
Air safety goes down two roads: on land and in planes. Bsns W p56 Jl 22 '67
Air safety problems; excerpts from address. A. S. M. Monroney. Aviation W 87:11 Jl 3 '67
Can air travel be kept safe? problem posed by new planes. il U S News 64:54-6 Ja 1 '68
New moves to make air travel safer. U S News 63:15 O 2 '67
Proven again: safety is still up to people. A. H. Sypher. il Nations Bsns 55:27-8 Jl '67
Requests, advice complicate ATC effort. Aviation W 87:101 O 9 '67
Safer air; new FAA rules. il Newsweek 70:80 O 2 '67
Safer skies. Time 90:59 S 22 '67
Safety check. See issues of Flying
Safety first; FAA announces stringent new regulations. il Time 90:88 S 29 '67
Skirts flying; safety seminar. S. Buegeleisen. il Flying 82:22 Ja '68
Washington clipboard; opposition to General aviation pilot education program. R. Burkhardt. Flying 81:24 Ag '67
What's a swinger like you doing on the ground? light aircraft accidents. A. R. Roalman. il Todays Health 45:28-31+ O '67
See also
Airplanes—Ice protection
Airplanes—Safety devices and measures
Oxygen apparatus

Snowstorm hazards
See Aviation—Storm hazards

Speed
See Airplanes—Speed

Storm hazards
Blizzard snarls Northeast traffic. Aviation W 86:43+ F 13 '67
Japanese investigation commission report; severe gust blamed for 707 Tokyo crash. il Aviation W 87:115+ Ag 28 '67
Rescue in the clouds. J. P. Blank. Read Digest 91:73-7 S '67
Snowstorm! R. E. Brown. Flying 81:91 D '67
Stones from clouds; hailstones. il Sci Digest 62:23 S '67
Storm warning; problem of a thunderstorm. F. C. Bates. il Flying 80:94-7 Je '67
Winter's tale; special problems for aviators. il Flying 81:134-5 D '67
See also
Aviation—Lightning hazards

Stunt flying
Six acrobatic teams display skills in precision flying; photographs by J. H. Pickerell. Aviation W 87:62-9 Ag 21 '67
Variety of techniques marks team flying. W. H. Gregory. il Aviation W 87:50-1+ Ag 21 '67

Transatlantic flights
Flight that tied the world together; Lindbergh flight. K. V. Brown. il Pop Mech 127:84-7 My '67
Four U.K. carriers seek Atlantic routes. H. J. Coleman. Aviation W 87:33-4 Ag 21 '67
Lucky Lindy's luckiest day. il Sr Schol 90:16 My 19 '67
Tomorrow's traveler. H. Sutton. il Sat R 51:41-2+ Ja 6 '68
USAF HH-3s make record helicopter Atlantic flight; photographs. Aviation W 86:38-9 Je 12 '67

Transcontinental flights
Transcontinental battle breeds shuttle. J. W. Carter. il Aviation W 87:36-8 Ag 14 '67

Transoceanic flights
See also
Aviation—Transatlantic flights

World flights
Around the world. L. Rockefeller il Flying 81:58-62+ N '67

Antarctic Regions
Flight into Antarctic darkness. J. L. Abbot, jr. il Nat Geog Mag 132:732-8 N '67

Great Britain
Labor government repels AFVG censure. H. J. Coleman. il Aviation W 87:82-5 Jl 24 '67

Mexico
Mexico. M. H. Bearns, 3d. il Flying 80:44-7 Ap '67

Russia
Foreign accent. J. Fricker. il Flying 80:22+ Ap '67

United States
See also
Airlines—United States
Airports—United States

AVIATION, Commercial. See Aeronautics, Commercial

AVIATION, Military. See Aeronautics, Military

AVIATION and health. See Aviation—Physiological aspects

AVIATION associations
Aerospace calendar. See issues of Aviation week & space technology
Calendar. See issues of Flying
Flight plan '67-'68 (cont) Flying 80:107 F '67; 82:88-9 Ja '68
See also
International astronautical federation

AVIATION clubs
How to start a flying club. L. Davis. il Flying 80:48-9 Ap '67
Learning to fly. S. Wilkinson. il Holiday 41:101-6 Je '67
Navions unite; American navion society. S. S. Weinberg. il Flying 80:70-1 Ap '67

AVIATION conferences
Ninety-nines international convention. S. Buegeleisen. Flying 81:20 S '67

AVIATION education
Baby talk; learning to fly. T. Baxter. Flying 81:28 N '67
Skirts flying; aerospace education workshop. S. Buegeleisen. Flying 81:24 D '67
Too young to fly? R. B. Parke. il Flying 80:68-71 My '67
Who me fly? C. Lofting. il Flying 81:34-41 N '67
See also
Air pilots—Training
Aviation schools

AVIATION engineering
Soviet educator urges engineer rewards; excerpts from Izvestia. I. F. Obraztsov. Aviation W 87:115+ S 11 '67

AVIATION engines. See Airplane engines

AVIATION exhibitions. See Aviation—Exhibitions

AVIATION fuel. See Airplane engines—Fuel

AVIATION industry. See Airplane industry and trade

AVIATION instructors. See Air pilots—Training

AVIATION instruments. See Aeronautic instruments

AVIATION insurance. See Insurance, Aviation

AVIATION landing stations
Jungle flattop. K. V. Brown. il Pop Mech 127:64-7 Je '67

Landing mats
C-5A forward-area dock set. il Aviation W 87:58 N 27 '67

AVIATION research. See Aeronautic research

AVIATION schools
From the tower; Aero commander ground school. E. D. Muhfeld. il Flying 82:6 Ja '68
Helicopter school, first class. R. Blodget. il Flying 80:58-61 Mr '67
Home work; choosing a qualified pilot training school. R. B. Parke. Flying 81:28 D '67
Learning to fly. S. Wilkinson. il Holiday 41:101-6 Je '67
See also
Warhawk aviation service, incorporated

AVIATION week and space technology (periodical)
Big sky beat. il Time 90:34 Ag 11 '67
Laurels for 1967. R. Hotz. Aviation W 87:11 D 25 '67
1967, a year of decision. R. W. Martin, jr. Aviation W 86:11 F 20 '67

AVIATORS, Military. See Air pilots

AVINERI, Shlomo
One man's Israel. Commentary 44:92-4+ D '67

AVIONICS. See Airplanes—Electronic equipment

AVIS rent a car
Avis vs. Hertz; Madison avenue's favorite feud. M. Mayer. Harper 236:40-4 Ja '68
Is no. 2 really trying harder? basketball series in Pittsburgh between Hertz and Avis. il Bsns W p38-9 F 18 '67

AVISON, Margaret
Seven poets. R. Tillinghast. Poetry 110:265-6 Jl '67

AVITAL, Samuel
Dialogue between mime and skeptic. J. Anderson. pors Dance Mag 41:20-1 Ag '67

AVIZANDUM; story. See Henderson, R.
AVOCADOS
Unexploited avocado; with recipes. E. Alston. il Look 31:77 My 30 '67
AVON, Anthony Eden, 1st earl of
When the sun set... G. A. Craig. Reporter 37:37-8 N 30 '67
AVONDALE shipyards, incorporated
Speeding the schedule of seagoing cargo; the Lash and the Seabee. il Bsns W p 124+ Ag 26 '67
AWARE, incorporated
Blacklisted! story of J. H. Faulk; condensation of The jury returns. L. Nizer. il Read Digest 90:201-4+ Mr '67
AXELBANK, Albert
Marchers of Tokyo. Nation 206:41-3 Ja 8 '68
On the eve of balloting in South Korea. New Repub 156:9-11 Ap 29 '67
What is our picture of Asia? New Repub 158:17-19 Ja 6 '68
AXILROD, Gertrude D. See Rothberg, S. jt. auth.
AXLES
See also
Automobiles—Axles
AXTHELM, Pete
Cross country. Sports Illus 27:72-3 D 11 '67
Harness racing. Sports Illus 27:68+ Jl 17: 48-9 Jl 31; 60+ Ag 28; 64+ O 2; 72-3 O 16 '67
Hockey. Sports Illus 26:61-4 My 15 '67; 28: 40-1 Ja 8 '68
Horse racing. Sports Illus 26:45-8 Ja 23 '67
Track & field (title varies) Sports Illus 26: 66+ Je 5; 56+ Je 26 '67; 28:46-7 Ja 15 '68
When the real McGuire stood up. Sports Illus 26:74-8+ Mr 20 '67
AYER, Ethan
Treasure dream; story. New Yorker 43:167-8 Mr 11 '67
AYERS, Jake
Struggle that changed Glen Allan. D. Nevin. il por Life 63:108+ S 29 '67
AYNESWORTH, Hugh
JFK conspiracy. Newsweek 69:36+ My 15 '67
AYURVEDIC medicine. See Medicine, Hindu
AZALEAS
Blazing Oregon trail; native color, azaleas and rhododendrons. R. Friedman. il Home Gard 54:45 Je '67
Grow azaleas and rhododendrons. il Pop Gard 18:55 My '67
Taming the wild azaleas. il House & Gard 131:140-1+ Ap '67
AZANCOT, Leopoldo
Day H-bomb fell on Palomares. Sat R 50:21-7+ Ja 28 '67
AZERBAIJANI language
Native language instruction in Azerbaijan is inadequate. Sch & Soc 95:450-1 N 25 '67
AZEVEDO ANTUNES, Augusto Tranjano de
Brazil's magic mountain. K. Seegers and S. Seegers. il por Américas 19:20-7 Mr '67
AZIMUTH
Gyrocompass azimuth finders challenge astronomy methods. il Tech W 20:40 Mr 20 '67
AZTEC literature
Way of Quetzalcóatl. T. de Gerez. il Horn Bk 43:171-5 bibliog(p 132) Ap '67
AZTECS
Feather merchants; excerpt from the 16th century Aztec manuscript; tr. by C. E. Dibble and A. J. O. Anderson. B. de Sahagún. il Craft Horiz 27:18-23+ Mr '67
Goldworkers and lapidaries; excerpt from the 16th century Aztec manuscript; tr. by C. E. Dibble and A. J. O. Anderson. B. de Sahagún. il Craft Horiz 27:16-21 S '67
AZURE mutants. See Mutation (bacteria)

B

BART (Bay area rapid transit) See San Francisco—Rapid transit
BB guns. See Air guns
BBB. See Better business bureaus
BBC. See British broadcasting corporation
BCIE. See Central American bank for economic integration
B. F. Goodrich company. See Goodrich, B. F, company
BIE. See Bureau of international expositions
BIS. See Bank for international settlements
BLM. See United States—Land management, Bureau of

BMI. See Book manufacturers' institute
BMW. See Automobile industry and trade— Germany (Federal Republic)
BRI. See Building research institute
BSC. See British steel corporation
BVD company
Up from underwear. Fortune 75:324 Je 15 '67
BABB, Sanora
Challenge of words. Writer 81:12-13 Ja '68
BABBITT, Hank
Fishing. Sports Illus 27:67-8+ O 9 '67
BABBITT (literary character) See Characters in literature
BABCOCK, Barbara Allen
More leeway for the police? New Repub 156: 24-6 Ap 1 '67
BABCOCK, Horace W.
Optical astronomy in perspective. bibliog Science 156:1317-22 Je 9 '67
BABCOCK, John
We don't read water meters any more. Am City 82:86-7 Jl '67
BABE in the wilderness; story. See Flynn, R.
BABE the blue ox; story. See Fowles, J.
BABIES. See Infants
BABIES hospital, New York. See New York (city)—Columbia-Presbyterian medical center
BABY bottle warmers
Dangerous warmers for baby bottles. il Consumer Rep 32:67 F '67
BABY care. See Infants—Care and hygiene
BABY pants. See Infants—Clothing
BABY sitters
Baby-sitter's bonanza: two months in Europe, including five-week cruise of Adriatic and Aegean aboard chartered yacht. L. Gross. il Look 31:85-6+ Mr 21 '67
Ways to save costs on baby-sitters. il Good H 165:187 S '67

Anecdotes, facetiae, etc.
Innocent curse of Peggy Dobell. L. Rosen. Look 31:6-7 S 19 '67
BABYHIP; story. See Wells, P.
BABYLONIAN inscriptions. See Cuneiform inscriptions
BACCALAUREATE addresses
Enough food, enough wealth, enough time; address, June 11, 1967. J. A. Hannah. Vital Speeches 33:684-6 S 1 '67
Most likely to commence; Washington's most popular commencement speakers. Newsweek 69:51 My 1 '67
Playing it safe. il Newsweek 69:78-9 Je 26 '67
BACCARAT paperweights. See Paperweights
BACCHARIS pilularis. See Coyote brush
BACH, Fritz H. and Amos, D. B.
Hu-1: major histocompatibility locus in man. bibliog Science 156:1506-8 Je 16 '67
BACH, George R.
Caifornia woman. Ladies Home J 84:63+ Jl '67
We can close the generation gap. Ladies Home J 85:36+ Ja '68
BACH, Johann Sebastian
Bach bargains, nine cantatas on five discs. P. L. Miller. Am Rec G 33:570+ Mr '67
J. S. Bach up to date. R. Sabin. Am Rec G 34:157 O '67
Musical events; performance of Brandenburg concertos and other items by Berlin philharmonic. W. Sargeant. New Yorker 43: 225-6 D 9 '67
Records:
Easter oratorio. Opera N 31:34 Mr 25 '67
St John passion; St Mark passion. Opera N 31:34 Mr 25 '67
BACH, Richard
Aviation off the record. Flying 82:72-4 Ja '68
BACH festivals
Thirtieth Bach festival: ready, willing, and Abel; Carmel report. K. D. Wallace. Hi Fi 17:MA22-3+ O '67
BACHAR, Shlomo
On the boards. W. Como. por Dance Mag 41: 24 O '67
BACHELORS. See Single men
BACILLUS subtilis
Sporulation mutations induced by heat in bacillus subtilis. J. Northrop and R. A. Slepecky. bibliog il Science 155:838-9 F 17 '67
Transforming activity in both complementary strands of bacillus subtilis DNA. M.-D. Chilton. bibliog il Science 157:817-19 Ag 18 '67
BACK
First aid. C. J. Potthoff. Todays Health 45: 74 F '67
See also
Backache
Spine

BACK yards
  Country club in your own backyard. il House
    & Gard 132:126-8 Jl '67
  Landscape ideas U.S.A. from Oregon. J. Fan-
    ning. il Pop Gard 18:34-9 Mr '67
  Magic change for a small back yard. il Pop
    Gard 18:12-13 Ag '67
    See also
  City gardens
BACKACHE
  Backache. Am Home 71:32 Ja '68
  Biped's burden. il Newsweek 70:59 O 16 '67
  Personal business. Bsns W p 165-6 O 21 '67
BACKBONE. See Spine
BACKGROUND for Nancy; drama. See Mann-
  ing, S.
BACKGROUND in fiction. See Fiction—Tech-
  nique
BACKHOES. See Excavating machinery
BACKLIN-LANDMAN, Hedy
  Art museum, Princeton university. Antiques
    92:670-9 N '67
BACKMAN, Jules
  Defending the big advertiser. il Bsns W p98+
    Ap 15 '67
BACKMEYER, D. P.
  Time-tested maintenance tips. Am City 82:
    96-100 Ap '67
BACKWARD children. See Mentally handi-
  capped children; Slow learning children
BACKWARD heart; story. See Holland, B.
BACON, Edmund Norwood
  City as an act of will; excerpts from Design
    of cities. Arch Rec 141:113-27 Ja '67
BACON, Vinton W.
  How Chicago saved $2.5 million. Am City 82:
    16 O '67
  Separate storm and sanitary sewers not the
    answer in Chicago. Am City 82:67 Ja '67
BACON, W. Stevenson
  Science newsfront. See issues of Popular
    science monthly
BACON
  Out of the frying pan; shock hazard in the
    Reddi-bacon package. il Consumer Rep 32:64
    F '67
    See also
  Cookery—Meat
BACTERIA
  Growth of a thermophilic bacterium on hy-
    drocarbons: a new source of single-cell
    protein. R. I. Mateles and others. bibliog il
    Science 157:1322-3 S 15 '67
  Mechanisms of enzymatic bacteriolysis. J. L.
    Strominger and J. M. Ghuysen. bibliog il
    Science 156:213-21 Ap 14 '67
  Polyribosomes of growing bacteria. C. P.
    Flessel and others. bibliog il Science 158:
    658-60 N 3 '67
  Selective release of enzymes from bacteria.
    L. A. Heppel. bibliog Science 156:1451-5 Je
    16 '67
  Tools of conjugation; pili of gram-negative
    bacteria. Sci Am 217:55 D '67
    See also
  Bacillus subtilis
  Escherichia coli
  Microorganisms
  Mutation (bacteria)
  Viruses
        Metabolism
  Evolutionary significance of metabolic con-
    trol systems. J. L. Cánovas and others. bib-
    liog il Science 156:1695-9 Je 30 '67
        Mutation
    See Mutation (bacteria)
        Nomenclature
  Recommendations on nomenclature of the
    order mycoplasmatales; subcommittee on
    the taxonomy of mycoplasmatales. bibliog
    Science 155:1694-6 Mr 31 '67
        Resistance
  Infectious drug resistance. T. Watanabe. il
    Sci Am 217:19-27 D '67
BACTERIA, Anaerobic
  Anaerobic chamber for bug studies; research
    at National heart institute. Sci N 91:197
    F 25 '67
  Conversion of DDT to DDD pathogenic and
    saprophytic bacteria associated with plants.
    B. T. Johnson and others. bibliog il Sci-
    ence 157:560-1 Ag 4 '67
BACTERIA, Fossil. See Micropaleontology
BACTERIA, Pathogenic
  Crystallization of a sulfate-binding protein
    (permease) from salmonella typhimurium.
    A. B. Pardee. bibliog il Science 156:1627-8
    Je 23 '67

Lack of end-product inhibition and repres-
  sion of leucine synthesis in a strain of sal-
  monella typhimurium. R. A. Calvo and J.
  M. Calvo. bibliog il Science 156:1107-9 My
  26 '67
On your vacation, eat with care! Consumer
  Bul 50:27-8 J '67
Salmonella chase your calves. L. A. Baker.
  Farm J 91:D10 Ag '67
What's behind that salmonella scare. R.
  Wilmore. Farm J 91:27+ Ja '67
  See also
Pneumococci
BACTERIA, Photosynthetic
  Carotenoid biosynthesis in rhodospirillum
    rubrum: effect of pteridine inhibitor. N. A.
    Nugent and R. C. Fuller. bibliog il Science
    158:922-4 N 17 '67
BACTERIAL viruses. See Bacteriophage
BACTERIOLOGICAL warfare. See Biological
  warfare
BACTERIOLOGY
    See also
  Sea water—Bacteriology
BACTERIOLYSIS
  Cell lysis: another function of the coat
    protein of the bacteriophage f2. N. D.
    Zinder and L. B. Lyons. bibliog il Science
    159:84-6 Ja 5 '68
BACTERIOPHAGE
  Azure mutants: a type of host-dependent
    mutant of the bacteriophage f2. K. Horiuchi
    and N. D. Zinder. bibliog il Science 156:1618-
    23 Je 23 '67
  Bacteriophage S13: a seventh gene. I. Tess-
    man and others. bibliog il Science 156:824-5
    My 12 '67
  Building a bacterial virus. W. B. Wood and
    R. S. Edgar. il Sci Am 217:60-6+ Jl '67
  Cell lysis: another function of the coat
    protein of the bacteriophage f2. N. D.
    Zinder and L. B. Lyons. bibliog il Science
    159:84-6 Ja 5 '68
  Chemistry and structure of nucleic acids of
    bacteriophages. J. A. Cohen. bibliog il Sci-
    ence 158:343-51 O 20 '67
  Direction of translation in bacteriophage
    S13. I. Tessman and others. bibliog il Sci-
    ence 158:267-8 O 13 '67
  Replication of viral RNA: RNA synthetase
    from escherichia coli infected with phage
    MS2 or Qβ. G. Feix and others. bibliog il
    Science 157:701-3 Ag 11 '67
BAD cold; story. See Spencer, E.
BADEAU, John S.
  Arabs, 1967. Atlan 220:102-4+ D '67
BADMINTON (game)
  Judy takes a final curtain call; retires from
    the game. K. Chapin. il Sports Illus 26:65-
    7 Ap 24 '67
el-BADRY, M. A.
  Population projections for the world, devel-
    oped and developing regions: 1965-2000.
    bibliog f Ann Am Acad 369:9-15 Ja '67
BAEHNER, Robert L. and Nathan, D. G.
  Leukocyte oxidase: defective activity in
    chronic granulomatous disease. bibliog
    Science 155:835-6 F 17 '67
BAER, Richard A. Jr
  Church and conservation. J. B. Craig. Am
    For 73:13 O '67
BAEZ, Joan
  Non-violent soldier; interview. New Yorker
    43:44-6 O 7 '67
BAGDIKIAN, Ben H.
  American newspaper is neither record, mir-
    ror. . . nor herald of the day's events.
    Esquire 67:124-8+ Mr '67
  Black immigrants. Sat Eve Post 240:25-9+ Jl
    15 '67
  Justice on the bench in Mississippi. New
    Repub 156:12-13 F 18 '67
BAGGAGE. See Luggage
BAGGAGE bicycles. See Motor scooters
BAGGS, William C.
  (ed) See Ho-chi-Minh. Talk with Ho Chi
    Minh
BAGHDAD
        Galleries and museums
  Custodian for the Fertile Crescent; Iraq mu-
    seum. il Time 89:86-9 Mr 31 '67
BAGPIPES
  Skirling the blues; R. Harley. il Newsweek
    69:97-8 Ja 30 '67
BAGS
    See also
  Plastic bags
BAHAMA ISLANDS
  Exploring a coral atoll; Hogsty Reef in the
    southern Bahamas. W. M. Stephens. il
    Yachting 121:62-4+ F '67

BAHAMA ISLANDS—*Continued*
Mafia: shadow of evil on an island in the
sun. B. Davidson. il Sat Eve Post 240:
27-37 F 25 '67
Scandal in the Bahamas. R. Oulahan and
W. Lambert. il Life 62:58-66+ F 3 '67
See also
Air travel—Bahama Islands
Andros Island
Elections—Bahama Islands
Exuma (islands)
Nassau
San Salvador Island
Tourist trade—Bahama Islands

Description and travel
Bahamas: winter vacation wonderland. il
Ebony 23:36-8+ Ja '68
Bahamian fortnight. G. Merrill. il Motor B
120:41-3+ O '67
Discovering the Bahamas. H. Bradshaw and
V. Bradshaw. il Todays Health 45:42-5+
D '67
Gunkholing; lazy drifting in the Bahama
Banks. B. Glowacki. il Travel 128:40-4 N '67
More of sea than of land: the Bahamas. C.
Mitchell. il Nat Geog Mag 131:218-67 F '67
Out Out islands. P. Davis. Yachting 122:44-
5+ N '67
Those in Out Islands. B. De Holguin. il
Travel 127:40-4 F '67
Twenty feet can go a long way; Bahamian
Out Islands. J. Hennesey. il Yachting 122:
48-9+ N '67

Politics and government
Consultant's paradise lost; former minister
accused of accepting bribes. il Time 90:
25-6 S 8 '67

Race problems
Black vote revolt in the Bahamas. L. Bennett, jr. il Ebony 22:68-70+ Je '67

BAHAMAS 500 race. See Motor boat racing

BAHAMAS flying treasure hunt. See Aviation—
Competitions

BAHER, Constance Whitman
Cinder-rabbit; drama. Plays 26:61-9 Mr '67

BAIBAKOV, Nikolai Konstantinovich
Making the Soviet future work. il pors Bsns
W p 128-30+ Je 10 '67

BAIER, Martin
Zip code, new tool for marketers. Harvard
Bsns R 45:136-40 Ja '67

BAIL
Bugs in bail reform; new federal bail reform
act. Time 89:47 F 3 '67

BAILEY, Anthony
Profiles; F. E. Hood. New Yorker 43:34-6+
Ag 26 '67
Profiles: through the great city. New Yorker
43:35-42+ Jl 22; 35-8+ Jl 29; 32-6+ Ag 5 '67
Swinging. Ladies Home J 84:8 Jl '67

BAILEY, C. B.
Siliceous urinary calculi in calves: prevention
by addition of sodium chloride to the diet.
bibliog Science 155:696-7 F 10 '67

BAILEY, Clay
Mexican classic. Opera N 31:6 F 18 '67

BAILEY, F. Lee
F. Lee Bailey: a new breed of hero; interview, ed. by M. McLaughlin. pors Mlle 65:
64-5+ Jl '67

about
Bailey & the Boston strangler. il Time 89:40
Ja 27 '67
Bailey for the defense. il pors Newsweek
69:35-6+ Ap 17 '67
Brash newcomer to the ranks of great de-
fenders. D. Jackson. il pors Life 62:45-6+
F 17 '67
Case in point. G. Ace. Sat R 50:7 Ap 1 '67
Handbook of success, chapter III. il por
Time 89:91 My 19 '67
Mary Coppolino's own story; ed. by E. Linn.
M. Coppolino. Good H 165:128+ Ag '67
Unaccustomed defeat. Newsweek 69:30 Ja 30
'67

BAILEY, George
Devaluing the pound, and labour. Reporter
37:20-2 D 14 '67
East Germany: the plan collapses. Reporter
36:19-24 Ap 20; 8 Je 1 '67
Konrad Adenauer. Reporter 36:12-13 My 4 '67
Puritan revolt in Greece. Reporter 36:19-23
My 18 '67
Report from three battlefronts. Reporter 36:
13-15 Je 29 '67
Strange interlude in Athens. Reporter 37:34-7
Ag 10 '67
Strange world of UNRWA. Reporter 37:20-3
N 16 '67
Titoism's failure. Reporter 36:16-20 Ja 26 '67

BAILEY, Howald
Dreamer. Opera N 32:24-5 D 23 '67

BAILEY, J. W.
Dairy health first aid kit. Suc Farm 65:135-
6 Mr '67
Veterinary helps. See occasional issues of
Successful farming
Why animals are sold subject or condemned.
Suc Farm 65:46 I Mr '67
Why bulls or cows fail to breed. Suc Farm
65:70 Mr '67

BAILEY, James
Stacked switches and their ganged arrays.
por Electr World 78:50-2 O '67

BAILEY, John Moran
Bailed out. Newsweek 69:33 F 6 '67

BAILEY, Joseph C.
Clues for success in the president's job. Harvard Bsns R 45:97-104 My '67

BAILEY, Pearl
Big new deal for Dolly, hello, Pearl; with
report by T. Prideaux. il pors Life 63:128-
30+ D 8 '67
Dolly rediviva. il por Time 90:56 N 24 '67
Hello, Dolly! R. Lantz. il pors Ebony 23:83-9
Ja '68
Pearl in the raw. por Newsweek 70:110 D 4
'67

BAILEY, R. W.
Period-frequency graph. Electr World 78:27
S '67

BAILEY, Ralph
Gardener goes to South America. House &
Gard 132:168-9+ D '67

BAILEY, Robeson
I taught my grouse dog to quit hunting. Field
& S 71:174-5 Ap '67

BAILKEY, Nels
Early Mesopotamian constitutional development. bibliog f Am Hist R 72:1211-36 Jl '67

BAIN, Barbara
TV's Barbara Bain: computer-age Mata
Hari. S. Gordon. il pors Look 31:73-4+ N
28 '67

BAIN, George S.
Common paradox: white-collar organization in
Britain; excerpt from Trade union growth
and recognition. bibliog f Mo Labor R 90:
42-7 O '67

BAIRD, Bil
People is the thing the world is fullest of.
T. Lewis. America 116:354 Mr 11 '67

BAIRD, Cora
People is the thing the world is fullest of.
T. Lewis. America 116:354 Mr 11 '67

BAIRD, Donald, and Carroll, R. L.
Romeriscus, the oldest known reptile. bibliog
Science 157:56-9 Jl 7 '67

BAIRD, Irene
Canada's Far North: a land on the move.
UNESCO Courier 20:14-17+ Ap '67

BAIRD, Joseph H.
Atlanta's Negroes rock the boat. Reporter
37:32-4 D 14 '67
Lester Maddox: Puritan in the Statehouse.
Reporter 37:19-22 O 5 '67

BAIT
Art of worm fishing. W. Davis. il Outdoor
Life 139:78+ Mr '67
Bass are everywhere; but can you catch
them? W. Davis. il Outdoor Life 139:60-3+
Ap '67
Deadly bait for bass; lamprey eel. L. Green.
il Outdoor Life 139:52-3+ Je '67
Natural baits for trout. T. Trueblood. il Field
& S 71:26+ Ap '67
Suckers for muskies. F. M. Stephey. il Out-
door Life 139:148 Mr '67

BAJUSZ, Eörs, and Homburger, Freddy
Cardiomyopathies. Science 156:1649-50+ Je 23
'67

BAKAL, Carl
Bang! bang! you're dead. Esquire 68:44-5 Jl
'67
How to understand your home insurance.
House B 109:123+ F '67
Philadelphia story: do gun control laws really
work? Sat R 50:20-1+ Ap 22; 27 My 13; 33
My 20 '67

BAKER, Augusta
To Mississippi in the interest of children and
books. G. Woods. il Wilson Lib Bul 41:
1028-33 Je '67

BAKER, Donald W.
Five poets. Poetry 109:401-6; 111:195-202 Mr,
D '67
Waiting; Seventeen; Soldier; poems. Poetry
110:244-8 Jl '67

BAKER, Elizabeth C.
Light brigade. Art N 66:52-5+ Mr '67
—See Raffaele, J. jt. auth.

BAKER, Elzie Wylie, Jr
Charlotte National 500. B. Myers. il pors
Motor T 20:52-4 Ja '68

BAKER, Frederick D. and Hotchin, John
Slow virus kidney disease of mice. bibliog
Science 158:502-4 O 27 '67

BAKER, Hollis M.
We bought a very small castle, then the
fun began. House & Gard 131:142-5 Ap '67

BAKER, J. A.
Peregrine; excerpts. Audubon 69:26-41 S '67

BAKER, Jack
House of fresh-cut color. M. White. il Ladies
Home J 84:84-7 F '67

BAKER, Joan
Joan Baker and John Herbert McDowell.
Judson memorial church. J. Anderson.
Dance Mag 41:78-9 Mr '67

**BAKER, Jocelyn King. See Norris, D. M. jt.
auth.**

BAKER, Lyle A.
Looks like milk fever, but it isn't. Farm J
91:D16 Ap '67
You can stop IBR. por Farm J 91:D9+ F '67

BAKER, Mary Ann, and Hayward, J. N.
Autonomic basis for the rise in brain tem-
perature during paradoxical sleep. bibliog
Science 157:1586-8 S 29 '67

**BAKER, Philip John Noel-. See Noel-Baker,
P. J.**

**BAKER, Robert A. See Keitt, G. W. jr, jt.
auth.**

BAKER, Robert Gene
And the moral of the Baker case is. . . R.
Harwood. New Repub 156:17-19 F 4 '67
Baker case: a glimpse of inside politics. il
por U S News 62:42-3 F 6 '67
Baker found guilty. Sr Schol 90:22 F 24 '67
Bobby Baker has it made. M. Viorst. por
Esquire 68:90-2+ Jl '67
Bobby Baker trial: a rare look at politics
behind the scenes. il por U S News 62:8+
Ja 30 '67
Friend in need. Newsweek 69:29 Ja 30 '67
Guilty. il por Newsweek 69:33-4 F 6 '67
Inside the Baker case: the jurors' story. il por
U S News 62:39 F 13 '67
Just a bad dream. Newsweek 69:37 F 13 '67
Secret of box G-302. Time 89:20-1 F 3 '67
T.R.B. from Washington. New Repub 156:6
Ja 28 '67
Token comeuppance; sentence. Time 89:37 Ap
14 '67

BAKER, Russell
March madness. Read Digest 90:15-16 Mr '67
Sin-drome. McCalls 95:5 Ja '68
Wayward Washington; excerpt from Wash-
ington: the New York times guide to the
Nation's capital. Holiday 41:64-9+ F '67
You, too, can be anti-American. N Y Times
Mag p36-7+ Ap 23 '67

about

Quiet subversive. por Time 91:60 Ja 19 '68

BAKER, Samm Sinclair
African safari view of the U.N. Sat R 50:41-
2 S 9 '67

BAKER, W. R. jr, and Johnston, J. A. jr
Optical differentiation of amoebic ectoplasm
and endoplasmic flow. bibliog Science 156:
825-6; 158:143 My 12, O 6 '67

BAKER and Taylor company
Baker & Taylor to sponsor preview in August.
Pub W 191:60 Je 19 '67
Baker & Taylor will open second new plant.
il Pub W 191:229 Ja 23 '67

BAKERS and bakeries
Sweet Vienna: Demel's cake shop; with reci-
pes. E. Alston. il Look 31:70-2 D 26 '67
See also
National biscuit company

BAKERSFIELD race. See Automobile racing

BAKING
See also
Bread
Cake
Gingerbread
Pie

BAKING industry. See Bakers and bakeries

BAKING utensils. See Kitchen utensils

BAKKEN, James
King of the kickers. il por Newsweek 70:90 O
16 '67

BAKLAVA. See Cookery, Middle Eastern

BAKOS, Augustus
Doctor and his garden. W. Radcliffe. il por
Pop Gard 18:69-71 D '67

**BAKWIN, Harry, collection. See Art—Private
collections**

BALAGUER, Joaquín
President Balaguer talks candidly about his
country's future; interview. por Nations
Bsns 55:51 D '67

about

Balaguer: the first nine months. S. Rodman.
New Repub 156:19-23 Mr 25 '67
Rule of personalismo. Time 90:32+ S 29 '67
Santo Domingo revisited. S. Huck. por Nat
R 19:471-2 My 2 '67

BALAKIAN, Anna
Sponge for the world's tears. Sat R 50:38
Jl 22 '67
Those who evaluate. Sat R 50:71-2 Je 10 '67

**BALANCE (physiology) See Equilibrium
(physiology)**

BALANCE of nature
Close look at wildlife in America; with edi-
torial note. B. Gilbert. il Sat Eve Post 240:
32-6, 74 S 9 '67
International biological program. R. Revelle.
Science 155:957 F 24 '67
Nutrient cycling. F. H. Bormann and G. E.
Likens. bibliog il Science 155:424-9 Ja 27 '67

BALANCE of payments
Balance of payments, 1967. Duns R 89:17-18+
My '67
Barriers up & down. il Time 89:95 F 10 '67
Beggar thy neighbor; from the allies, cau-
tious reassurance. il Newsweek 71:73+ Ja
22 '68
Better than gold; Lyndon Johnson's proposals
to cut deficit. New Repub 158:5-6 Ja 13 '68
Buck stops here. il Newsweek 71:64-6 Ja 15
'68
Cooperation for balance-of-payments equili-
brium; statement, November 30, with text
of communique, December 1, 1967. E. V.
Rostow. Dept State Bul 57:876-83 D 25 '67
Defending the pound; Britain's balance-of-
trade deficit. Newsweek 70:58 Ag 7 '67
Deficit context. Commonweal 87:460-1 Ja 19
'68
Dissecting the balance. il Fortune 75:36+ Mr
'67
Driving down the deficit; U.S. trade and
financial policies, with editorial comment.
il Bsns W p 13-15, 102 Ja 6 '68
Financial prohibition; proposal for tax on im-
ports as well as on tourism. H. C. Wallich.
Newsweek 71:76 Ja 22 '68
Gold and the dollar. W. F. Butler and J. V.
Deaver. For Affairs 46:181-92 O '67
Helping the U.S. hold up the dollar; with
editorial comment. il Bsns W p 17-20, 132
Ja 13 '68
How Fowler pushes for balance. Bsns W p
18 Ja 13 '68
Is a world slump in the cards? Bsns W
p 105-6 D 9 '67
L.B.J. and his soft dollar; measures to re-
duce deficit. Life 64:4 Ja 19 '68
More imbalance in payments. Bsns W p36
My 20 '67
Octopus in a blanket; change in U.S. gold
policy. il Time 89:95-6 Ap 14 '67
Our evolving international strategy; address,
April 6, 1967. R. A. Peterson. Vital Speeches
33:429-34 My 1 '67
Payments gap grows but the worries ebb.
il Bsns W p36-4 Ja 14 '67
Payments plan wins backers abroad. Bsns W
p21-2 Ja 13 '68
Pentagon escalates war on payments gap;
overseas sales of military equipment. il
Bsns W p22-3 Ja 13 '68
Plan to stop the gold drain. N. R. Danielian.
Read Digest 91:154-8 D '67
Price of protectionism; letter, October 18,
1967. H. H. Fowler. Dept State Bul 57:650-
2 N 13 '67
Report of Council of economic advisers. il
Dept State Bul 56:339-48 F 27 '67
Smaller gap on payments; second-quarter im-
provement. Bsns W p44 Ag 19 '67
Stanching the flood. il Time 91:10-11 Ja 12 '68
Stormy weather for the dollar; with panel
discussion by H. Wallich; P. A. Samuelson;
M. Freidman. il Newsweek 69:86-8+ Ap 17
'67
Test of intelligence and will; painful policy
decisions on U.S. fiscal affairs. Bsns W
p 160 D 2 '67
U.S. balance of payments; can we plug the
gold drain? il Sr Schol 91:8-11 D 7 '67
What the restrictions mean. il Time 91:54-5
Ja 12 '68
World monetary system; address, March 17,
1967. H. F. Fowler. Vital Speeches 33:455-
62 My 15 '67
World trade and finance and U.S. prosperity;
address, December 6, 1967. L. B. Johnson.
Dept State Bul 58:6-7 Ja 1 '68
Wrong way to solve the gold problem. Bsns
W p 174 Ap 29 '67

BALANCE of power
Arms: is U.S. lead shrinking? il U S News
63:61 S 25 '67

BALANCE of power—*Continued*
How much danger for the U.S? M. S. Johnson.
U S News 63:34 Jl 24 '67
Israeli victory. New Repub 156:1-2 Je 17 '67
National security; address, October 11, 1967.
H. M. Jackson. Vital Speeches 34:34-7 N 1
'67
Struggle for power; US-USSR influences in
Asia and the Middle East. H. Brandon. Sat
R 50:11 Ag 12 '67
Weapons and world stability; excerpts from
address. H. Agnew. Aviation W 86:11 Mr
27 '67
    See also
Great powers
BALANCE of trade. See Balance of payments
BALANCE sheets. See Financial statements
BALANCED diet. See Diet
BALANCHINE, George
Balanchine's latest. I. Kolodin. Sat R 50:24
Ap 29 '67
Jewels by Balanchine. H. Saal. il News-
week 69:105 Ap 24 '67
World of dance. W. Terry. Sat R 50:40 Jl
29 '67
BALANOGLOSSUS
Isolation of 2,6-dibromophenol from the mar-
ine hemichordate, balanoglossus biminiens-
is. R. B. Ashworth and M. J. Cormier.
bibliog il Science 155:1558-9 Mr 24 '67; Re-
ply J. S. Webb. 158:522 O 27 '67
BALD cypress
Bald cypress swamp in Indiana. C. S. Wat-
son, jr. il Nat Parks Mag 41:13 Ag '67
Sentinel of the swamp. C. H. Giles. il Nat
Parks Mag 41:9 My '67
BALD eagles. See Eagles
BALDING, Ivor Godfrey
Booking Bugged bets brings a Balding
bonanza. W. Tower. Sports Illus 27:68+
N 27 '67
BALDNESS

    Quotations, maxims, etc.
Time himself is bald. . ; comp. by H. Block.
il N Y Times Mag p 126-7 Ap 9 '67
BALDRIGE, Malcolm, 1922-
How to beat Parkinson's law. Duns R 89:46-
7+ Je '67
BALDWIN, Charles L. and Runkle, R. S.
Biohazards symbol: development of a biologi-
cal hazards warning signal. Science 158:
264-5 O 13 '67
BALDWIN, Dave
Side-door entrance to the major leagues. L.
Shecter. il por Sports Illus 27:61-2+ Jl 17
'67
BALDWIN, Hanson Weightman
Great missile debate. Reporter 36:23-6 Je 29 '67
Poseidon, new chapter in missilery. Read
Digest 92:120-4 Ja '68
Vietnam balance sheet. Reporter 37:14-18 O
19 '67
    about
Outward bound. Nat R 19:1310+ N 28 '67
BALDWIN, James
Negroes are anti-Semitic because they're
anti-white. N Y Times Mag p26-7+ Ap 9
'67
Tell me how long the train's been gone;
story; excerpt from novel. McCalls 94:118-19
F '67
    about
Dialectic of The fire next time. A. Gayle,
jr. Negro Hist Bul 30:15-16 Ap '67
BALDWIN, Ralph B.
Ranger VIII and gravity scaling of lunar
craters. bibliog Science 157:546-7 Ag 4 '67
BALDWIN, Roger N.
Norman Thomas; a combative life. New Re-
pub 158:11-12 Ja 13 '68
BALFOUR, John Patrick Douglas, 3d baron
Kinross. See Kinross, J. P. D. B.
BALI
Bali. R. McKie. il Holiday 42:48-53+ Jl '67
Indonesia's night of terror. H. Sutton. il
Sat R 50:25-8+ F 4 '67
BALIN, Robert P.
Baffling quiz. Pop Electr 28:60+ Ja '68
Color code quiz. Pop Electr 27:70+ N '67
Electronic angle quiz. Pop Electr 27:55+ S '67
Electronic measurements quiz. Pop Electr
27:96+ Ag '67
Electronic switching quiz. Pop Electr 27:52+
O '67
International electronics quiz. Pop Electr 27:
46+ Jl '67
BALINT, Nicholas G.
(comp) As others see us. See issues of Satur-
day review

(comp) Letters to the world's editors. Sat R
50:45 Jl 8; 40 S 9; 54 O 7; 64-5 N 11; 51 D
9 '67; 51:99 Ja 13 '68
BALIO, Tino T.
Public confrontation of Hermann J. Muller.
Bul Atomic Sci 23:8-12 N '67
BALIS, M. Earl, and others
Urinary metabolites in congenital hyper-
uricosuria. bibliog Science 156:1122-3 My 26
'67
BALISH, Jacquelyn
Bruce Downes; a critical appraisal. Pop Phot
61:124-7+ N '67
Photographica. bibliog Pop Phot 60:94-5+
My '67
BALK, Alfred
American tragedy, 1967. Sat R 50:34 S 16 '67
Books in communications. See issues of
Saturday review
God is rich. Harper 235:69-73 O '67
BALKAN STATES
Back to normal. F. Y. Blumenfeld. il News-
week 69:58+ Ap 17 '67
    See also
Turkey
BALL, George Wildman
Opinion: on fighting the problem. por Mlle
65:200+ Ag '67
Promise of the multinational corporation; ex-
cerpts from address. por Fortune 75:80 Je 1
'67
Trade with U.S.S.R; address, April 20, 1967.
Vital Speeches 33:546-50 Jl 1 '67
BALL, Judith A. See Murray, R. F. jr, jt.
auth.
BALL, Robert
Declining art of concealing the figures. For-
tune 76:136-9+ S 15 '67
BALL, W. Macmahon
Japan in Asia's future. Nation 206:82-4 Ja 15
'68
BALL, Warren F. and Hoag, A. A.
Kitt Peak's new photoelectric guider. Sky &
Tel 35:22-4 Ja '68
BALL, William
On the Ball. il por Newsweek 70:118+ N 20
'67
BALL, William B.
Examination of the church-state issues in
federal aid to education. Wilson Lib Bul
41:694-9 Mr '67
BALL lightning. See Lightning
BALL of fire; story. See Liben, M.
BALL state university, Muncie, Ind.
Ball state story, by G. White. Review
Sat R 50:87 N 18 '67. P. Woodring
BALLADS, American
Casey at the bat; excerpts from The anno-
tated Casey at the bat. M. Gardner. il Am
Heritage 18:64-8 O '67
Second version of Lucy Terry's early ballad.
B. Katz. Negro Hist Bul 29:183-4 Fall '66
BALLADS, English
Traditional tunes of the child ballads, by B.
H. Bronson. Review
Am Rec G 33:845-7 My '67. H. Yurchenco
BALLADS, Scottish
Traditional tunes of the child ballads, by
B. H. Bronson. Review
Am Rec G 33:845-7 My '67. H. Yurchenco
BALLANTINE, William
Finger Lakes country. Holiday 41:62-7+ My
'67
BALLANTYNE, Michael
Prescription for success: hard work, imag-
ination; reprint. Pub W 191:49-50 Ap 17
'67
BALLARD, Charles
What management should know about labor;
address, February 10, 1967. Vital Speeches
33:316-20 Mr 1 '67
BALLARD, Ernesta Drinker
Gardening under lights and in the green-
house. Harper 234:132-6 Mr '67
My sunporch plants. il Horticulture 45:22-5
N '67
BALLARD, L. A. T. and Lipp, A. E. G.
Seed dormancy: breaking by uncouplers and
inhibitors of oxidative phosphorylation.
bibliog Science 156:398-9 Ap 21 '67
BALLARD, Lowell Clyne
Who's next; poem. Negro Hist Bul 30:15 O
'67
BALLERINAS. See Dancers
BALLET
Delightful dilemmas; American ballet theater
and Royal ballet at Lincoln Center. il Time
89:103 My 19 '67
Don't you even speak to me; ballet in pro-
ductions at the Metropolitan opera and the
New York city opera. D. Hering. il Dance
Mag 41:24+ D '67
Presstime news. See issues of Dance maga-
zine

BALLET—*Continued*
Regional ballet, U.S.A. D. Hering. See issues of Dance magazine
Reviews. See issues of Dance magazine
Sisters under the skin; opera and ballet. C. Barnes. il Opera N 31:8-13 Ap 15 '67
Three pamphlets collected, by L. Kirstein. Review
  Dance Mag 41:13+ N '67. J. Anderson
Toe to toe; outstanding dance season in New York. H. Saal. il Newsweek 69:88-9 Je 5 '67
Views of a dancing Dane; ed. by E. Miller. E. Bruhn. il Seventeen 26:148-9+ N '67
We who travel. R. Page. Dance Mag 41:62+ Je '67
  See also
Choreography
Dancing

History

Alien art. M. Amaya. il Opera N 32:26-9 Ja 20 '68
Augusta Bournonville: a life in Paris, 1846. F. Hjorth. il Dance Mag 41:59-61 Je '67
Lillian Moore: a joyous searching; American theatrical dance. S. J. Cohen. il Dance Mag 41:34-7 S '67

Study and teaching

Face to face with a girl on her toes. L. Rudnick. Seventeen 26:157 N '67
Question and answer; dance as part of elementary and secondary school curriculum. Y. Yourlo and E. Yourlo. Dance Mag 41:18 F '67
Summer on pointe; Fokine ballet camp. W. Como. il Dance Mag 41:68-9 F '67
Teacher personalities: Cossack on Long Island. Dance Mag 41:86-7 Ap '67
Who is a ballet master? N. Beriozoff. J. Anderson. il Dance Mag 42:54-7+ Ja '68

Canada

That unavoidable decade, Les grands ballet canadiens; Salle Wilfrid Pelletier, Montreal. D. Hering. il Dance Mag 41:34-8 Ag '67
  See also
National ballet of Canada

China (People's Republic)

Ballet in Communist China. M. G. Swift. il Dance Mag 41:60-5 N '67

Ecuador

From the grass roots; director of Ecuador's ballet folklorico encourages village dance groups. J. Anderson. il Dance Mag 41:14-16+ Ag '67

Europe, Western

Open letter: jobs in Europe, anyone? A. Hutchinson. Dance Mag 41:18-20 Jl '67

France

Paris ballet star: Norman de Joie of Les ballets modernes de Paris. il Ebony 23:67-8+ D '67

Great Britain

Swinging London has its critics; reviewing the dance. F. Hall. il Dance Mag 41:50-3+ O '67
  See also
Royal ballet, Great Britain

Mexico

  See also
Ballet folklóre of Mexico

Russia

Report from Russia. E. Souritz. il Dance Mag 41:28-9+ S '67
BALLET and state. See Theater and state
BALLET companies
Alas, poor Shakespeare; State ballet of Rhode Island. W. Terry. il Sat R 50:46 D 9 '67
I go to the studio and try out my dreams; Los Angeles junior ballet. V. H. Swisher. il Dance Mag 42:64-7 Ja '68
In their infinite variety; personalities in America's regional ballet companies. D. Hering. il Dance Mag 41:68-71 S '67
Prelude to a dancing dynasty; performance by the Ballet romantique. W. Terry. il Sat R 50:37-8 Jl 8 '67
Regional ballet, U.S.A. D. Hering. See issues of Dance magazine
Repertory for six; 92nd street Y. M. Marks. Dance Mag 41:38+ Ap '67
There's more than sand and sagebrush here! Utah civic ballet. J. Anderson. il Dance Mag 41:42-5+ Ag '67

Village theater ballet; Village theatre.   J. Maskey. Dance Mag 41:34 F '67
  See also
American ballet theatre
Atlanta civic ballet (organization)
Boston ballet company
City Center Joffrey ballet
Harkness ballet (organization)
Manhattan festival ballet
National ballet
National ballet of Canada
New York city ballet
Pennsylvania ballet company
Royal ballet, Great Britain
Washington ballet (organization)
BALLET dancers. See Dancers
BALLET festivals. See Dance festivals
BALLET folklorico of Ecuador. See Ballet—Ecuador
BALLET folklórico of Mexico
Ballet folklorico of Mexico; Metropolitan opera house. D. Hering. Dance Mag 41:28 Ag '67
World of dance; U.S. tour, program. W. Terry. il Sat R 50:45-6 Je 17 '67
BALLET notation. See Dance notation
BALLET production. See Dance production
BALLET romantique. See Ballet companies
BALLET schools. See Dance schools
BALLET theatre. See American ballet theatre
BALLETS
Balanchine's latest. I. Kolodin. Sat R 50:24 Ap 29 '67
Gem dandy; première of Balanchine's untitled work il Time 89:89 Ap 21 '67

Choreographies
  See Choreography

Criticisms

Agathe's tale
  Sat R il 51:96 Ja 13 '68
Astarte
  Dance Mag il 41:34-6 N '67
  New Yorker 43:91 S 30 '67
  Sat R 50:50-1 O 7 '67
At midnight
  Dance Mag il 42:52-3 Ja '68
  Newsweek 70:115 D 11 '67
  Sat R il 50:37 D 23 '67
Brandenburg nos. 2 and 4
  Sat R 50:45 Je 3 '67
Cello concerto
  Sat R 50:53-4 S 30 '67
Cinderella
  New Yorker 43:134 Ap 29 '67
  Sat R 50:26 My 6 '67
Concerto
  Sat R 50:53+ D 16 '67
Coppelia
  Dance Mag il 41:59-62 Ap '67
Dance for three people
  Sat R il 50:48 N 4 '67
Danses concertantes
  Sat R 50:53 D 16 '67
Devanagari
  Sat R il 50:48-9 N 4 '67
Diversion of angels
  Sat R il 50:43+ S 9 '67
Don Quixote
  Dance Mag 41:57+ Mr '67
  Dance Mag il 41:70 F '67
Dream
  New Yorker 43:157 My 6 '67
Elergy
  Sat R 50:53-4 S 30 '67
Flower festival
  Sat R 50:52 D 2 '67
Four moons
  Dance Mag 41:54-5+ D '67
  Sat R il 50:60-1+ N 18 '67
Glinkiana
  Sat R 50:79 D 16 '67
Gnossiennes
  Sat R 50:62 My 20 '67
Golden age
  New Yorker 43:220 N 25 '67
Gymnopédies
  Sat R 50:62 My 20 '67
Hamlet
  Sat R il 50:46 D 9 '67
Harbinger
  Sat R il 50:24 Je 3 '67
Las Hermanas
  Sat R 50:53 D 16 '67
Jeux
  Dance Mag 41:84 Mr '67
Jewels
  New Yorker 43:177 Ap 22 '67
  New Yorker 43:219 N 25 '67
  Newsweek il 69:105 Ap 24 '67
  Sat R 50:40 Jl 29 '67

BALLETS—Criticisms—*Continued*
Lento
  Sat R 51:96 Ja 13 '68
Das lied von der erde. See Song of the earth, below
Mass for the present time
  Time 90:87 D 15 '67
Moves
  Sat R 50:104 O 14 '67
Nutcracker
  Dance Mag 41:84 Mr '67
  Sat R il 50:51 D 2 '67
  Time il 90:63 D 22 '67
Paradise lost
  New Yorker 43:163 Ap 15 '67
  Sat R il 50:22+ My 27 '67
  Time il 89:43 Mr 3 '67
Pas de deesses
  Sat R 50:50-1 O 7 '67
Prologue
  Dance Mag 41:57 Mr '67
  Dance Mag il 41:35-8 F '67
  Sat R 50:73 Ja 28 '67
Ragtime
  Dance Mag 41:57 Mr '67
Romeo and Juliet
  New Yorker 43:134 My 27 '67
Shadowplay
  Sat R 50:62 My 20 '67
Sleeping beauty
  New Yorker 43:134 Ap 29 '67
  Sat R 50:26 My 6 '67
Song of the earth
  New Yorker 43:157 My 6 '67
  Sat R 50:28 My 13 '67
  Time il 89:90 My 5 '67
Swan lake
  Dance Mag 41:30-1 My '67
  Newsweek il 69:100 F 27 '67
  Sat R 50:22+ My 27 '67
  Sat R 50:45 Je 3 '67
Translucens
  Sat R 51:96 Ja 13 '68
La ventana
  Dance Mag 42:30 Ja '68

History
[Story of La Péri: 1843, 1912, 1967] il Dance Mag 41:39-44 Ap '67

Production and direction
See Dance production

BALLETS modernes de Paris. See Ballet—France
BALLHAUS, William Francis
Tall man in the saddle. N. Willatt. por Duns R 90:35-6 Jl '67
BALLIETT, Whitney
Jazz. New Yorker 43:130-2 Mr 18; 96 Ag 12; 86 Ag 19; 74 Ag 26 '67
Jazz concerts (cont) New Yorker 42:109-11 Ja 28; 43:125-6 Mr 25; 163-5 Ap 8; 80 Ag 5 '67
Jazz records (cont) New Yorker 43:221-2+ N 25 '67
Musical events. New Yorker 43:74+ Jl 22 '67
Profiles; B. Rich. New Yorker 42:35-6+ Ja 21 '67
BALLINGER, Harry Russell
Planning and painting a seascape; excerpts from Painting sea and shore. Design 68:4-9 Mr '67
BALLISTIC-glide reentry vehicle. See Guided missiles—Defenses
BALLISTIC systems division. See United States —Air force—Ballistic systems division
BALLISTICS
Breezes bend bullets. H. G. Tapply. il Field & S 72:60 N '67
Un BALLO in maschera; opera. See Verdi, G.
BALLOON racing
Balloonacy! G. Stokes. il Travel 127:60-2 Ap '67
BALLOONS
Airlift for logs. il Fortune 75:150-1 F '67
Balloonacy! G. Stokes. il Travel 127:60-2 Ap '67
Pop goes the balloon; fire-propelled balloons. Newsweek 69:87 Mr 6 '67
Space balloon scientist. il Ebony 22:44-6+ Mr '67
Trial balloons in the southern hemisphere. V. E. Lally. il Science 155:456-9 Ja 27 '67

Use in research
And all from fission-track dating. A. Ewing. il Sci N 91:266-7 Mr 18 '67
Far-infrared surveys of the sky. W. F. Hoffmann and others. bibliog il Science 157:187-9 Jl 14 '67
BALLOONS in lumbering
Highways in the sky. R. H. Forbes. il Am For 73:16-18+ Je '67

BALLOT
See also
Voting machines
BALLPARKS. See Stadiums
BALLROOM dancing. See Dancing
BALLS
See also
Golf balls
BALLS (parties)
Evening of splendor for the love of Venice; fund raising ball for artisan flood victims. il Life 63:40-5 S 22 '67
For sweet charity's sake; Ballo in maschera to aid Venetian artisans. il Newsweek 70:104+ S 25 '67
Party: Truman Capote receives. G. Steinem. il Vogue 149:50-7+ Ja 15 '67
Politics of the Capote ball. W. F. Buckley, jr. il Esquire 68:159-64+ D '67
BALNAVES, John
Leader in cooperation. bibliog por Library J 92:4117-19 N 15 '67
BALTHUS
Balthus: the solitary scandal. C. Estienne. il Art N 66:39-41+ My '67
BALTIC STATES
See also
Estonia

Russian occupation
Voice from a Baltic grave; exposing the hypocrisy of Kosygin's address on June 19, 1967. America 117:30 Jl 8 '67
BALTIMORE

Galleries and museums
See also
Walters art gallery

Historic houses, etc.
Oval room from Willow Brook; excerpts from catalogue. W. V. Elder, 3d. il Antiques 91:496-9 Ap '67

Music
City of firsts: production of Boris Godunov. A. M. Lingg. il Opera N 32:16-19 N 4 '67
See also
Peabody institute

Poor
Baltimore clamps down; fraud charges against overpaid recipients. New Repub 156:6-7 Ap 29 '67

Sanitary affairs
Eliminated: one expensive rehandling operation; four-wheel sweepers clean the streets and haul the debris. E. Moore. il Am City 82:76-7 Jl '67

Theater
New theater: a center for Baltimore; Charles center theater. J. M. Dixon. il Arch Forum 126:72-9 My '67
BALTIMORE Bullets (basketball team) See Basketball teams
BALTIMORE civic opera company
Report: Baltimore; new production of Mussorgsky's Boris Godunov. F. C. Smith. Opera N 32:28 D 16 '67
BALTIMORE Colts (football club) See Football clubs
BALTIMORE COUNTY, Md.
Cooperation builds a target range. W. E. Fornoff. il Am City 82:64 Ap '67
BALTIMORE Orioles (baseball) See Baseball clubs
BALTUSROL golf course, Springfield, N.J. See Golf courses
BAMBERGER, Gay
Symphony for New York's elder population. Parks & Rec 2:32+ My '67
BAMBOO
Dwarf bamboos and how to restrain them. il Sunset 138:205 Je '67
Spirit of bamboo; interview. C. Sie. New Yorker 43:36-7 My 6 '67
BAMBOO fences. See Fences
BANANAS, Joe. See Bonanno, J.
BANANAS
Mellow yellow; banana skins; newest ticket to a psychedelic trip. il Newsweek 69:93 Ap 10 '67
Top banana; commendation seal to Chiquita brand. M. B. Keiser. il Parents Mag 42:46-7 S '67
Tripping on banana peels; mellow yellow craze. il Time 89:52 Ap 7 '67
Yes, they sell more bananas. il Bsns W p90-2+ Jl 8 '67
BAND instruments
See also
Drum

BAND music
See also
Phonograph records—Band music
BANDA, Hastings Kamuzu
President of Malawi visits the United States;
exchange of toasts, June 8, 1967. Dept State
Bul 57:42-4 Jl 10 '67

about
Heroes or Neros? il por Time 89:46 Ap 14
'67
BANDEIRA DE MELO, Francisco de Assis Cha-
teaubriand. See Assis Chateaubriand Ban-
deira de Melo, F. de
BANDER, Edward J.
Panel quartet. Library J 92:2736-7 Ag '67
BANDERA, Tex.
Where whooping cranes winter. H. Sutton. il
Sat R 50:39-40 Ap 1 '67
BANDS (music)
Best of the dance bands; New Mayfair orches-
tra. N. McCaffrey. Nat R 19:1082-5 O 3 '67
Big bands and Miles. M. Williams. Sat R 50:
71 S 30 '67
Jazz; Ellington's stand at the Rainbow grill.
W. Balliett. New Yorker 43:86 Ag 19 '67
Jazz orchestra; Thad Jones-Mel Lewis alli-
ance. B. Korall. il Sat R 50:116-17+ Mr 11
'67
Jazz; quintet led by J. Steig at L'intrigue.
W. Balliett. New Yorker 43:130-2 Mr 18 '67
Jefferson airplane loves you; new San
Francisco sound: love rock. J. Luce. il
Look 31:58-62 My 30 '67
Luvs story; girls' band. M. English. il
Look 31:M14-16+ My 2 '67
New sounds of brass, woodwind, and per-
cussion. J. Krance. House B 109:46+ Ap '67
New surge for a tired old idiom; Charles
Lloyd and jazz. R. Saltonstall, jr. Life 62:15
Je 9 '67
New voice from the barrios; Afro-Latin music
of the Eddie Palmieri ensemble. R. F.
Thompson. il Sat R 50:53-5+ O 28 '67
Play it again, Sam; age of the big bands.
il Time 90:106+ N 24 '67
Profiles; B. Rich. W. Balliett. New Yorker
42:35-6+ Ja 21 '67
Return of the big bands. G. Lees. Hi Fi 17:
32 S '67
Trills, toots & oompah-pahs; outdoor summer
band concerts. il Time 90:61 S 8 '67
When big bands were big. J. O'Hara. il Holi-
day 41:20+ Ap '67
Where the big bands are. G. Lees. il Hi Fi
17:100 S '67
Competitions
Battle of the bands; teen-age groups rock
for the U.S. title. il Life 63:131-2 S 29 '67
BANDS, School
Sonata for two clarinets; student composers
take over. H. W. Arberg and C. S. Carle-
ton. il Am Ed 3:30-2 F '67
BANDSAWS. See Saws
BANDURA, Albert
Behavioral psychotherapy; with biographical
sketch. Sci Am 216:19, 78-82+ bibliog (p 150)
Mr '67
BANFE, Chuck
How to be a winner at the maintenance game.
Flying 81:50-2 Jl '67
Paint your aircraft sale green. Flying 80:72
Ap '67
BANFF-Jasper highway. See Roads—Canada
BANGKOK
Airports
Bangkok planning new airport. Aviation W
87:31-2 N 27 '67
BANGOR, Me.
Curriculum breakthrough in the humanities.
L. C. Comeau and others. il Sr'Schol 90:sup
13-14 Ap 7 '67
BANGS, Carl
Casualties of Catholic reform. Christian Cent
84:1554-6 D 6 '67
Methodist Nehemiah. Christian Cent 84:474
Ap 12 '67
BANISTER, Manly
Build this sleekly styled split-level typing
desk. Pop Mech 129:156-9+ Ja '68
Don't sell your bandsaw short. Pop Mech
128:160-2 Jl '67
Don't sell your drill press short. Pop Mech
127:188-92 My '67
Get double duty from your portable saw. Pop
Mech 128:184-6 O '67
BANK Americards. See Credit cards
BANK buildings
Four buildings for banking. il Arch Rec 142:
127-32 Jl '67
Monumental small bank; Hernando, Miss. il
Arch Rec 141:167-70 My '67

BANK checks. See Checks
BANK consolidations and merger
Blow to bank mergers; Supreme court backs
Justice's antitrusters, takes a dim view
of Bank merger act of 1966. Bsns W p23
Ap 1 '67
Time of decision on bank mergers; Justice
dept. claims that 1966 law did not relax
rules on mergers. il Bsns W p 100+ Ja 28
'67
BANK credit. See Credit
BANK credit cards. See Credit cards
BANK failures
Beirut: the unfamiliar taste of humble pie;
failure of the Intra bank. il Bsns W p83
Ja 21 '67
Fall of the genius from Jerusalem. G. De
Carvalho. il Life 62:87-9 Ja 27 '67
BANK for international settlements
Basel club. il Time 89:93 Je 23 '67
BANK loans. See Loans, Bank
BANK of England
Defensive boost; raises discount rate. News-
week 70:69-70 O 30 '67
Squeeze play in London. Bsns W p 150 S 30
'67
BANK rates. See Interest
BANK reserves
Economy: a boost and a blow; $1.1 billion in
federal construction funds released. News-
week 69:79 Ap 17 '67
Fed takes a fresh step toward ease; reducing
reserve requirements of banks. il Bsns W
p34-5 Mr 4 '67
BANK robberies. See Robberies and assaults
BANKER, Robert E.
Techniques in sales of rights; address, March
22, 1967. por Pub W 191:30-2 Ap 3 '67
BANKERS
See also
American bankers association
Negro bankers
Semenenko, S.
BANKIER, William
Replacement; story. Ladies Home J 85:98-
100 Ja '68
BANKING and currency committee. See United
States—Congress—Senate—Banking and cur-
rency committee
BANKING law
Brouhaha at the bank; Mercantile bank of
Canada. Newsweek 69:80 F 6 '67
Citibank row boils over in Ottawa; Mercan-
tile bank in Canada owned by New York's
First national city bank. Bsns W p 120
Ja 28 '67
Leeching Lytton back to health. Bsns W
p 130+ N 11 '67
BANKRUPTCY
New idea: mass bankruptcy, and the damage
it could do; personal bankruptcies, particu-
larly Negroes. il U S News 63:124-5 S 25 '67
Why so many people are going bankrupt. il
U S News 62:83-5 Ap 3 '67
Wizard of Paterson; Inter-City transporta-
tion co. bankruptcy. Newsweek 70:72 N 6
'67
See also
Business failures
BANKRUPTCY, Fraudulent. See Fraudulent
conveyances
BANKS, Barbara
Trays can simplify your life. House B 109:41-3
S '67
—and Warkentin, Adena
Mentally retarded children aren't all alike.
Parents Mag 42:56-8+ Mr '67
BANKS, Ernie
New life for an old man. D. Llorens. il pors
Ebony 22:100-2+ O '67
BANKS, Laura Stockton (Voorhees)
John Aston Warder, first president of the
American forestry association. por Am For
73:10-13+ N '67
BANKS, Lynne Reid
Only son; story. Ladies Home J 84:100-1 My
'67
BANKS, The (islands) See Outer Banks (is-
lands)
BANKS, Coin
Old mechanical banks. F. H. Griffith. See
issues of Hobbies
BANKS and banking
Banking and the antitrust laws. W. T.
Lifland. bibliog f Harvard Bsns R 45:138-44
My '67
See also
Credit
Interest

BANKS and banking—See also—*Continued*
Investment banking
Loans, Bank
Money
Postal savings banks
 also headings beginning Bank

Branch banking

Chase tries instant branching; big gains abroad. il Bsns W p 112-17 Ap 29 '67
Other war for U.S. bankers; in Vietnam, Chase Manhattan and Bank of America fight inflation. il Bsns W p92+ O 14 '67

Checking accounts
See also
Checks

Foreign subsidiaries

Bache gets its foot in the door; Bankhaus Bache & co, Frankfurt. il Bsns W p 104-5+ My 20 '67
Chase tries instant branching; big gains abroad. il Bsns W p 112-17 Ap 29 '67
First real international bankers; American banks. J. Main. il Fortune 76:143-6+ D '67

Public relations

No more starched collars; professional public relations department of Chase Manhattan bank. L. L. L. Golden. Sat R 50:76 F 11 '67

Regulation

Squeeze play in London. Bsns W p 150 S 30 '67

Reserve requirements
See Bank reserves

Savings departments
See also
Savings deposits

Service

Bank checking services. Bet Hom & Gard 45:105 D '67

Canada

Brouhaha at the bank; Mercantile bank of Canada. Newsweek 69:80 F 6 '67
Canada gives bankers more room to swing; revision of Canada's bank act. Bsns W p62+ My 27 '67
Citibank row boils over in Ottawa; Mercantile bank in Canada owned by New York's First national city bank. Bsns W p 120 Ja 28 '67
Why the First national city bank took the rap in Canada. M. Clark. il Fortune 75:75+ Ap '67

France

Paris bank with a flair for empire; Banque de Paris et des Pays-Bas (Bank of Paris and the Netherlands) il Bsns W p78+ F 18 '67
Tiger in the bank; Banque de Paris et des Pays-Bas. il Time 89:68-9 Ja 27 '67
See also
Rothschild family

Germany (Federal Republic)

Bache gets its foot in the door; Bankhaus Bache & co, Frankfurt. il Bsns W p 104-5+ My 20 '67
Two *sprecher* for one; Deutsche bank names two associate speakers. il Time 89:88+ Je 16 '67

Great Britain
See also
Bank of England

Italy

More than a touch of honesty; Banca d'America e d'Italia small-loan program. il Time 89:96+ My 5 '67

Lebanon

Beirut: the unfamiliar taste of humble pie; failure of the Intra bank. il Bsns W p83 Ja 21 '67
Fall of the genius from Jerusalem. G. De Carvalho. il Life 62:87-9 Ja 27 '67
Inscribed in gold; Intra bank to be managed by investment company. Newsweek 70:83 O 23 '67
Reopening at Intra. Time 91:71 Ja 5 '68
Rescue in Beirut; Intra bank revisited as international investment company. il Time 90:91-2 O 20 '67

Michigan

Parsons group. il Time 90:98+ N 17 '67

Sweden

Wallenberg boys, and how they grew; Sweden's premier industrial dynasty. il Bsns W p 114-18+ F 25 '67

Switzerland

Now even Swiss banks are under fire, but—. il U S News 63:82-3 Jl 31 '67
Why Zurich's gnomes attract all that money. il Bsns W p52-3+ Jl 8 '67

United States

Beleaguered bankers. il Fortune 75:81-2+ Je 15 '67
Preaching what you practice; interview. G. Champion. Nations Bsns 55:48-9+ Mr '67
Tough new challenger threatens the banks; House hearings on proposed federal savings associations. il Bsns W p42+ O 14 '67
See also
American bankers association
Banking law
Export-import bank of Washington
Federal deposit insurance corporation
Federal reserve banks
Monetary policy
Money—United States
Savings banks
Transamerica corporation
United States—Federal reserve board
 also subhead Banks under names of cities, e.g. New Orleans—Banks

BANKS and banking, International
See also
Bank for international settlements
International commercial bank

BANNERMAN, Robin M. See Kreimer-Birnbaum, M. jt. auth.

BANNING, Margaret Culkin
Changes and constants in a writer's life. Writer 80:11-13 N '67

BANNISTER, Dwight
Mark, I love you! excerpts. H. Painter. il Good H 164:93-5+ Ap '67

BANNISTER, Rosella
Man-sized meals in a girl-sized galley. por Motor B 120:44-5+ Jl '67

BANQUE de Paris et des Pays-Bas (Bank of Paris and the Netherlands) See Banks and banking—France

BANTA, Martha
House of the seven ushers and how they grew: a look at Jamesian Gothicism. Yale R 57:56-65 O '67

BANVEL D. See Dicamba

BANVILLE, Robert R.
For whose interests? Christian Cent 84:118+ Ja 25 '67

BAPTISM
Baptist Saturn. Christian Cent 84:1011 Ag 9 '67; Reply. G. T. Sparkman. 84:1194 S 20 '67

BAPTIST general conference. See Baptists in the United States

BAPTIST Sunday school board
Baptist board's plans for NLW completed. Pub W 191:96 F 27 '67

BAPTISTS
See also
Anabaptists

BAPTISTS in Russia
Muted centennial for Russian Protestants. M. Bourdeaux. Christian Cent 84:1500+ N 22 '67

BAPTISTS in the United States
A.B.C. president supports negotiation in Vietnam. Christian Cent 84:772 Je 14 '67
Baptist division in Minnesota. Christian Cent 84:709 My 31 '67
Baptist indomitability. Christian Cent 84:927 Jl 12 '67
Baptist Saturn. Christian Cent 84:1011 Ag 9 '67; Reply. G. T. Sparkman. 84:1194 S 20 '67
Baptists reject federal funds. Christian Cent 84:957 Jl 26 '67
Fence walking North Carolina Baptists; North Carolina Baptist state convention. Christian Cent 84:1620 D 20 '67
Keeping the pulpit free; Home mission board withdraws from South Africa crusade. Newsweek 69:88 Ap 24 '67
Money, principle and Southern Baptists; dilemma over federal aid. J. Brann. New Repub 157:10 Jl 15 '67
Social concern in the S.B.C; annual convention. Christian Cent 84:805 Je 21 '67
Southern Baptist seminaries challenged. G. H. Shriver, jr. Christian Cent 84:601-2 My 3 '67
Southern Baptists withdraw from South Africa crusade. Christian Cent 84:581-2 My 3 '67
Split in the ranks; ABC. Newsweek 69:64 F 20 '67

BAR-ILLAN, David
Impassioned Israelis. Hi Fi 17:47-50 Jl '67

BARAK, James. See Beck, C. E. jt. auth.

BARBADOS
Barbados: a small great American nation. G. de Zéndegui. Américas 19:inside cover D '67
See also
United Nations—Barbados

Description and travel
Barbados: twenty-third member state of the OAS. W. A. Simmonds. il Américas 19:3-12 D '67

Foreign relations
Barbados a new member; OAS council approval. G. Meek. il Américas 19:44 N '67

BARBECUE carts. See Serving carts

BARBECUE cookery
Barbecue. il Ebony 22:108+ Jl '67
Barbecue ideas from Pakistan. Sunset 138:164 Je '67
Chicken over the coals. P. Dittberner. il Bet Hom & Gard 45:86 Jl '67
Great from the grill. R. Holmberg. il Bet Hom & Gard 45:68-9+ Ag '67
If your barbecue resembles any of these, here's how to use it to do your turkey. il Sunset 139:138-40 N '67
Meat loaves on the barbecue; with recipes. il Sunset 130:120 S '67
Scallop shish kebab; with menu and recipes by E. Graves. il Life 63:126-7+ S 22 '67
Smoke cooking; excerpts from Smoke cooking. M. Kramer and R. Sheppard. il Ladies Home J 84:90-1+ Jl '67
Splendid results every time from under the hood; with recipes. il Sunset 139:112-14 S '67
Swish, kaboing! il Bet Hom & Gard 45:92 Je '67
Two from the barbecue. il Bet Hom & Gard 45:107 Je '67
What's on the grill? chicken, fish, ribs, turkey halves, lamb; with recipes. il Sunset 138:84 Je '67
Why not some birds on the barbecue? with recipes. il Sunset 139:96-7 Jl '67

BARBECUE grills
It's big, simple, portable, inexpensive, and it works. il Sunset 138:82-4 Je '67
New designs for outdoor chefs. il Pop Gard 18:44-7 My '67
Splendid results every time from under the hood; with recipes. il Sunset 139:112-14 S '67

BARBER, Carter
Long morning after. Sports Illus 26:45-8+ My 1 '67

BARBER, Samuel
Antony and Cleopatra. Criticism
Am Rec G por 33:871-2+ My '67

BARBER, Steve
No hits, no luck. il por Time 89:66 My 12 '67

BARBER, Willard F.
Books. Bul Atomic Sci 23:56-7 Je '67

BARBER shop phobia. See Phobias

BARBERS and barber shops
Profiles; P. Molé. W. Whitworth. New Yorker 43:63-4+ O 21 '67

BARBET, Raymond
France's Communists make a formidable comeback. H. Tanner. il N Y Times Mag p54-5+ N 19 '67

BARBIERI, William M.
Summer in Bogotá. America 117:274-7 S 16 '67

BARBIROLLI, Sir John
Butterfly by Barbirolli. R. Jacobson. Sat R 50:56-7+ O 28 '67

BARBITURATES
Induced hypersensitivity to barbital in the female rat. R. Aston and P. Hibbeln. bibliog il Science 157:1463-4 S 22 '67

BARBOUR, Ian G.
Significance of Teilhard. Christian Cent 84:1098-102 Ag 30 '67

BARBOUR, Thomas L.
Nevada's neglected bonanzaland. Travel 127:45-9 Ja '67

BARCELONA

Galleries and museums
Barcelona's Catalonian treasure house; Museum of fine arts. K. Kuh. Sat R 50:40-2 Ag 26 '67

Music
Catalan spice and a new young orchestra. E. Haines. il Hi Fi 17:MA24-5+ Ja '67
Orchestra revamped, a season in full swing. E. Haines. il Hi Fi 17:MA24-5 Ag '67

Stores
Spain's shoppers say *bienvenido* to Sears. il Bsns W p92-4+ Ap 15 '67

BARCLAY, Doris
Student teacher named Gail. Sch Arts 66:3-4 Ja '67

BARCLAY, M. and others
Plasma membranes of rat liver; isolation of lipoprotein macromolecules. bibliog Science 156:665-7 My 5 '67

BARD, Bernard
Brooklyn's bus to equality. Sat R 50:78-9 F 18 '67
New York's superblock: 114th street, Harlem. Good H 166:134 Ja '68

BARD, G. Terry
What a minister really does. L. David. il pors Good H 164:60-1+ Ja '67

BARDACH, J. E. and others
Orientation by taste in fish of the genus ictalurus. bibliog Science 155:1276-8 Mr 10 '67

BARDEN, John
Second chance for Cleveland. Commonweal 87:103-4 O 27 '67

BARDEN, William
Digital U.H.F. frequency measurements. Electr World 78:48-50 N '67
High-speed punched-card readers. Electr World 77:42-5 Ja '67

BARDSLEY, Dorothy
Frozen image: filmstrips in the school library. Library J 92:856-7+ F 15 '67

BARE, C. and others
Interferometer experiment with independent local oscillators. bibliog Science 157:189-91 Jl 14 '67

BARENBOIM, Daniel
Beyond dexterity. por Time 90:36 Ag 11 '67
Music to my ears; playing of Beethoven's Emperor concerto with the Philadelphia orchestra in Philharmonic Hall. I. Kolodin. Sat R 51:37 Ja 6 '68

BARENSFELD, Thomas E.
Limited adult reader; Cleveland public library's Reading centers program. por Library J 92:3004-7 S 15 '67

BARG, Herbert
B for boxed-in executives. Duns R 90:55-6+ O '67

BARGAINING power. See Collective bargaining

BARGE amphibious resupply cargo. See Motor vehicles, Amphibious

BARGELLINI, Piero
Mayor of Florence; interview. New Yorker 43:39-41 Ap 22 '67

BARGER, Vernon D. and Cline, D. B.
High-energy scattering; with biographical sketch. Sci Am 217:14, 76-9+ D '67

BARGHOORN, Elso S. See Schopf, J. W. jt. auth.

BARGHOORN, Frederick C.
Cultural exchanges between Communist countries and the United States. bibliog f Ann Am Acad 372:113-23 Jl '67

BARING, George Rowland Stanley, 3d earl of Cromer. See Cromer. G. R. S. B.

BARITZ, Loren
Our Puritan roots. Nation 204:699-700 My 29 '67

BARIUM
See also
Fresnoite

BARK
Uncharted worlds on the face of a tree; with photographs and comments by N. Cousins. C. C. Calkins. Home Gard 54:35-7 N '67
See also
Birch bark

BARK, Photography of. See Nature photography

BARK beetles. See Beetles

BARK paper in religion, folklore, etc. See Paper in religion, folklore, etc.

BARKA, Mehdi Ben. See Ben Barka, M.

BARKAN, Manuel
Art educator award, NAEA 1967. por Sch Arts 66:4 Je '67

BARKÉ, Harvey E.
Beneficial insects? Horticulture 45:34-5+ F '67

BARKER, B. Devereux, 3d
(ed) America's cup news. See issues of Yachting
Deep water racing. See issues of Yachting

BARKER, Elliott S.
Poems; Wilderness calls; Horseback riding. Am For 73:44 Ap '67

BARKER, Eric
The laugh; poem. Sat R 50:29 F 11 '67

BARKER, George
Flight 462; poem. Poetry 110:38 Ap '67

BARKER, John W.
Case for Greek musicality. Am Rec G 33:843-4 My '67

BARR, Browne
Bury the parish? Christian Cent 84:199-202 F 15 '67
BARR, Donald
Tale of the headmaster. Sat R 50:70-1 Ap 15 '67
Traffic jam in the private schools. R. Schickel. il por N Y Times Mag p26-7+ Mr 12 '67; Discussion. p 14+ Ap 2 '67
What did we do wrong? N Y Times Mag p36-7+ N 26 '67
BARR, Isabel Harriss
Gravely, but with hope; poem. Cath World 206:76 N '67
BARR, Joseph Walker
Financing a college education; address, February 4, 1967. Vital Speeches 33:348-52 Mr 15 '67
BARR, Richard H. and Du Von, Jay
Education and the bond market. See issues of American education to March 1967
—and Edelman, Edward
Bond market (cont of) Education and the bond market. See issues of American education
BARRACKS
    See also
United States—Army—Barracks and quarters
BARRACUDA fishing
How to catch a cuda. S. Clements. il Field & S 72:56-7+ O '67
BARRAND'S landing; story. See Morgan, B.
BARRAX, Gerald William
Two poems: Gunsmoke: 1957; Butterflies: 1965; From Five-part invention. Poetry 110:164-8 Je '67
BARRED; story. See O'Hara, J.
BARRETT, Alan H.
Radio observations of interstellar hydroxyl radicals. bibliog Science 157:881-9 Ag 25 '67
BARRETT, Clifton Waller
Book collecting anyone? J. T. Winterich. por Sat R 50:129-30 Mr 11 '67
BARRETT, David B.
African reformation. il Newsweek 71:66-7 Ja 8 '68
BARRETT, J. Edward
Credibility of the Communist conspiracy. Christian Cent 84:500-1 Ap 19 '67
BARRETT, Peter
They sail to win. Yachting 121:60+ Ja '67
BARRETT, William Edmund
Second million words. Writer 80:9-12 My '67
BARRETT, William Joseph
William J. Barrett 1895-1967. T. D. Brophy. por Craft Horiz 27:9 Mr '67
BARRIER REEF, GREAT. See Great Barrier Reef
BARRINGTON, R. I.
Ninety-four per cent vote aye; disposable refuse-sack system. il Am City 82:78-9 Jl '67
BARRINGTON college, Rhode Island
Quiet design for a small, rural school: master plan and physical education building for Barrington college. il Arch Rec 141:196-7 Ap '67
BARRIO, Raymond
Constructing a wood relief. Design 68:25-9 Ja '67
What is art? il por Design 69:32-5 Fall '67
BARRIS, Chuck
Games pretty people play. il por Newsweek 70:56 Jl 31 '67
BARRON, John
Tyranny in the Internal revenue service. Read Digest 91:42-9 Ag '67
BARROW, Clyde
Onward and upward with the arts. P. Kael. New Yorker 43:147-8+ O 21 '67
BARROW, William J.
Obituary
Pub W 192:40 O 16 '67
BARROWS, Alben
He makes decisions after twenty years behind bars. D. Llorens. il pors Ebony 23:44-6+ Ja '68
BARROWS, David
Gardener's synopsis of useful succulents. Home Gard 54:26-34 Jl '67
It pays to give a tree a proper start. Home Gard 54:40 N '67
Thirty seven good ideas for your garden. Home Gard 54:27-34 S '67
BARRUS, G. A.
Cutthroats of southeast arm. por Field & S 72:34-5+ Jl '67
BARRY, J. Dale, and others
Radio reflection by free radicals in earth's atmosphere. bibliog Science 156:1730-2; 158: 1488 Je 30, D 15 '67
BARRY, Joseph Amber
Twilight princess and the Sun King. Horizon 9:106-11 Spr '67
(tr) See Chanel, G. Collections by Chanel

BARRY, Les
Travel. See issues of Popular photography
BARRY, Richard Francis, 3rd. See Barry, Rick
BARRY, Rick
Education of Mr Barry. il por Sports Illus 27:22-4+ Ag 14 '67
Fastest gun in the West. R. Wurlitzer. il pors Sat Eve Post 240:80-2 Mr 11 '67
High jump. Newsweek 70:70 Jl 3 '67
Razor-cut idol of San Francisco. F. Deford. il por Sports Illus 26:32-5 F 13 '67
Super soph! H. L. Masin. il por Sr Schol 90:32 F 24 '67
BARRY, Roger
Roger Barry and the Mannheim observatory. J. Ashbrook. il Sky & Tel 33:228-9 Ap '67
BARRY, Thomas
Memo from the Mary's last stowaway. Look 31:122 N 14 '67
BARS, Snack. See Snack bars
BARS and barrooms
Dating bars. il Time 89:47 F 17 '67
If you behave yourself they might serve you a drink; new breed of New York bartender. G. Frazier, 4th. il Esquire 68:150-3 N '67
In London, lunch at a pub. il Sunset 139:50+ N '67
It's great to be in Galena at Christmas. R. Bissell. il Holiday 42:26+ D '67
Overheard in suburbia: bartender. L. Botto. Look 31:M27 My 16 '67
Prefab pubs; market overseas. il Time 90:72 Ag 25 '67
Pub fare: London. il Look 31:60-1 My 2 '67
Recalling the Borstal boy; Dublin pubs. H. Sutton. Sat R 50:48-9 D 2 '67
BARS for the home
Bar bit; equipment. il House B 109:96+ N '67
Bar; now you see it, now you don't. il House B 109:195-6 My '67
Build a bar just for the fun of it. W. C. Leckey. il Pop Mech 128:136-42 Ag '67
Ideas for home bars. il Am Home 70:16+ N '67
BARSI, Carol
Permanent resident. Atlan 220:100-1 Jl '67
BARTA, W. J.
Water-rail coordination; address, September 6, 1967. Vital Speeches 34:4-7 O 15 '67
BARTEL, Virginia
Sixth graders make terrific tutors. Parents Mag 42:56-7+ S '67
BARTELT engineering company
Sharing the risk in packaging war; Riegel paper. il Bsns W p 132-4 Jl 8 '67
BARTER, Robert H.
Is it safe to have surgery during pregnancy? Redbook 129:52+ Jl '67
BARTER
Confessions of a horse trader. N. Dean. il Pop Phot 61:89+ D '67
BARTH, John
Literature of exhaustion. Atlan 220:29-34 Ag '67
Lost in the funhouse; story. Atlan 220:73-82 N '67
Title; story. Yale R 57:213-21 D '67

            about
Existentialist comedian. il por Time 89:109 Mr 17 '67
What happened to John Barth? R. Garis; discussion. Commenatry 43:16+ Ja '67
BARTH, Karl
At the feet of greatness. J. C. Evans. Christian Cent 84:335 Mr 15 '67
BARTH, Peter S.
Effect of economic change on the Michigan labor force. Mo Labor R 90:29 Mr '67
BARTHA, Richard, and Pramer, David
Pesticide transformation to aniline and azo compounds in soil. bibliog Science 156:1617-18 Je 23 '67
BARTHEL, Joan
After nineteen TV years, only Ed Sullivan survives. N Y Times Mag p24-5+ Ap 30 '67
John Wayne, superhawk. N Y Times Mag p4-5+ D 24 '67; 4+ Ja 14 '68
Show business puts its holiday foot forward. Good H 165:54+ D '67
What makes a gardener dig. N Y Times Mag p28-30+ Mr 5 '67
BARTHELME, Donald
Dolt; story. New Yorker 43:56-8 N 11 '67
Few moments of sleeping and waking; story. New Yorker 43:24-6 Ag 5 '67
Report; story. New Yorker 43:34-5 Je 10 '67
Snow White; story. New Yorker 42:38-50 F 18 '67
BARTHOLOMEW, Carol
Most of us are mainly mothers; excerpts. Ladies Home J 84:80 S; 36 O; 156 N '67

BARTHOLOMEW, Cecilia
Can writing be taught? Writer 80:18-20+ S
'67

BARTHOLOMEW, Warren M.
Recreation education in selected junior or
community colleges. Parks & Rec 2:25-6+
Ja '67

BARTIMOLE, Roldo S. and Gruber, Murray
Cleveland: recipe for violence. Nation 204:814-
17 Je 26 '67

BARTLETT, Des. See Bartlett, J. jt. auth.

BARTLETT, Grant A.
Scanning electron microscope: potentials in
the morphology of microorganisms. bibliog
Science 158:1318-19 D 8 '67

BARTLETT, Jen, and Bartlett, Des
Other Africa; excerpts from Nature's paradise. il Audubon 69:68-75 S '67

BARTLETT, William Henry
William H. Bartlett and his imitators; ex-
cerpts. M.-E. Earl. il Antiques 92:722-5
N '67

BARTON, Bruce
Classic optimist. il por Time 90:18 Jl 14 '67
Word man. il por Newsweek 70:78-9 Jl 17 '67

BARTON, G.
Hybridizing dahlias. Horticulture 45:28-30 S
'67

BARTON, John
Reconsideration of the criteria for deterrence.
Bul Atomic Sci 23:41-4 D '67

BARTSCH, Jürgen
How secret the confessional? il por Time 90:
51 D 22 '67

BARWELL meteorite. See Meteorites

BARZEL, Ann
Looking at television. See issues of Dance
magazine
Paul Taylor sends Decatur. Dance Mag 42:
42-3 Ja '68

BARZINI, Luigi
Adventurous Antonioni. Holiday 41:99-100+
Ap '67

BARZUN, Jacques
Why opera? Opera N 31:6-10 Ja 28 '67

BASALLA, George
Spread of western science. bibliog Science
156:611-22 My 5 '67

BASALT
Crystalline basalts. H. D. Brown. il Hobbies
72:126-7 S '67
Oceanic basalt leads: a new interpretation
and an independent age for the earth. T.
J. Ulrych. bibliog il Science 158:252-6 O 13
'67

BASALTIC lavas. See Lava

BASEBALL
Big-leaguer big in the boondocks; Birdie
Tebbetts manages Marion, Va. Mets of
Appalachian rookie league. D. Wolf. il Life
63:28-31 S 1 '67
Oddities for openers; new baseball season.
Time 89:65 Ap 14 '67
See also
Baseball clubs
Little leagues
National baseball hall of fame and museum
Pitching (baseball)
World series (baseball)

Accidents and injuries
Birds fall down on broken wings. J. Jares. il
Sports Illus 27:26-8+ Jl 17 '67

Anecdotes, facetiae, satire, etc.
Marital pastime. G. Ace. Sat R 50:14 Ap 2
'67

Photographs
Splash of strange hues in baseball's most
frantic week. J. G. Zimmerman. Sports
Illus 27:26-31 O 9 '67

Rules
All antiseptic. Time 90:42 D 8 '67
It happens every spring; changes in scoring
rules. R. L. Tobin. Sat R 50:67-8 F 11 '67

Tickets
Winning the World series business. il Bsns
W p33 O 7 '67

BASEBALL clubs
All odds & ends; Cincinnati Reds lead the
National league. il Time 89:56 My 26 '67
American league frenzy; best pennant race in
years. il Sports Illus 27:20-5 S 11 '67
Baseball is the waiting game.   R. Lardner.
il N Y Times Mag p30-2+ Jl 30 '67; Dis-
cussion. p9 Ag 13; 10 Ag 20 '67
Baseball 1967: form chart, American league.
il Sports Illus 26:69-72 Ap 17 '67
Baseball 1967: form chart, National league.
il Sports Illus 26:65-8 Ap 17 '67

Baseball roundup 1967: tools of ignorance. il
Ebony 22:128-30+ Je '67
Baseball's week. H. Weiskopf. See issues of
Sports illustrated published during baseball
season
Behind the bold Red uprising in Cincinnati.
W. Leggett. il Sports Illus 26:65-8 My 22 '67
Better from the neck up. E. Stanky and
W. Leggett. il Sports Illus 27:18-23 Ag 28
'67
Big pitch by a baseball baby; B. Von Hoff's
training for New York Mets. W. J. McKean.
il Look 31:53-8 Je 27 '67
Birds are flying; St Louis Cardinals. il News-
week 70:76 Ag 14 '67
Birds fall down on broken wings. J. Jares.
il Sports Illus 27:26-8+ Jl 17 '67
Brat's new world; manager of Chicago White
Sox. il Time 90:64 Jl 7 '67
Can good management rally the Yankees?
M. Burke. il Duns R 89:38-9+ My '67
Captain Bligh's boys: the Red Sox. il News-
week 70:81 Ag 7 '67
Cardinals against, who? American league
four-team pennant race. W. Leggett. il
Sports Illus 27:18-21 O 2 '67
Cardinals in spring plumage; il Time 89:75
Ap 28 '67
Cha Cha goes boom, boom, boom! O. Cepeda,
pride of St Louis. M. Mulvoy. il Sports Illus
27:18-21 Jl 24 '67
Chaos in the American league. W. Leggett.
il Sports Illus 26:28-30+ My 8 '67
Charlie O. Finley follies; the A's fired, hired
and fired a manager. B. Musburger. il
Sports Illus 27:50-2 S 4 '67
Daddy for the Twins; Minnesota Twins share
lead in American league. il Time 90:57 Ag 25
'67
Dark's outlook is young and bright; manager
of the Athletics. W. Leggett. il Sports
Illus 26:50-2+ Mr 13 '67
Decline and fall of the New York Yankees, by
J. Mann. Review
New Repub 156:25-6 Je 24 '67. M. Renek
Detroit's refrain is Mayo and Sain; new
manager and a shrewd coaching staff for
Tigers. W. Leggett. il Sports Illus 26:26-7
Ap 3 '67
Dizzy days at the top; American league pen-
nant race. il Newsweek 70:62 S 18 '67
Dodger story. B. Bavasi and J. Olsen. il
Sports Illus 26:78-82+ My 15; 44-6+ My 22;
30-4+ My 29; 46-50+ Je 5 '67
Finley's follies. il Newsweek 70:68-9 S 4 '67
Five for the flag; American league pennant
race. W. Leggett and others. il Sports Illus
27:14-19 Ag 7 '67
Four for one; American league standings. il
Time 90:57 S 15 '67
Gashouse revisited; St Louis Cardinals. il
Time 90:50 Ag 11 '67
Good hitters can't hit good pitchers; annual
all-star game. Time 90:53-4 Jl 21 '67
Hero of baseball's hottest pennant race; C.
Yastrzemski of Boston Red Sox. il News-
week 70:62-6 O 2 '67
How the Cards stack up; St Louis Cardinals,
National league pennant winners. il News-
week 70:65 O 2 '67
Keeping CBS in the big leagues; trying to
rebuild New York Yankees into a winner.
il Bsns W p80-2+ Ap 15 '67
League of the absurd. il Time 90:40 Ag 4 '67
Mets find a young phenom. J. Jares. Sports
Illus 26:64-6 Je 26 '67
Most happy brat; E. Stanky, manager of the
White Sox. il Newsweek 70:53 Jl 17 '67
Nay for quality; American league to expand.
Time 90:69 O 27 '67
Now it was Detroit's turn to be king of the
hill; Tigers rallied from black Sunday in
Chicago to first place. P. Waldmeir. Sports
Illus 27:64 S 25 '67
Oddball season. il Newsweek 69:91-2 My 22
'67
Olé, Adolfo! Chicago Cubs improve. il News-
week 69:64 Je 26 '67
Orioles in the American! Pirates in the Na-
tional! H. L. Masin. Sr Schol 90:30 Ap 7 '67
Out in front in fun and games; St Louis
Cardinals in National league pennant race.
W. Leggett. il Sports Illus 27:22-4+ S 4 '67
Percentage player makes his pitch for K.C;
E. Kauffman. T. O'Leary. Sports Illus 28:
42-3 Ja 8 '68
Pirates: Pittsburgh's confidence guys. I. R.
McVay. il Look 31:64-9 My 30 '67
Play by play; Boston newspapers' coverage of
Red Sox games. il Newsweek 70:88 S 18 '67
Poor Sam, what a weird week; Minnesota
Twins. J. Jares. il Sports Illus 26:24-6+
My 1 '67
Red and his roomie, and the pennant; St
Louis Cardinals. J. Brosnan. il N Y Times
Mag p36-7+ S 17 '67

BASEBALL clubs—*Continued*
Roar for Roger in St Louis. W. Leggett. il
    Sports Illus 26:22-7 Ap 24 '67
St Louis card-sharps. H. L. Masin. il Sr
    Schol 91:42 O 5 '67
Slight revival of hope in Boston; Red Sox
    disciplined by tough-guy manager D. Wil-
    liams. J. Jares. il Sports Illus 26:66-8+ My
    15 '67
Sore arms and no cigarettes; Hank Bauer's
    pitchers are hurting, but things really don't
    look bad for the Orioles. J. Jares. il Sports
    Illus 26:36-7 Ap 10 '67
Sporting scene; World series: St Louis
    Cardinals vs. Boston Red Sox. R. Angell.
    New Yorker 43:176+ O 28 '67
Stanley, the general manager; St Louis Car-
    dinals. W. Leggett. il Sports Illus 26:66+
    Mr 20 '67
Ten-percenters; St Louis Cardinals. il Time
    89:54-5 Je 30 '67
Things are different in Atlanta; P. Richards
    in charge of Braves. M. Mulvoy. Sports
    Illus 26:53-4 Mr 27 '67
Those big Tiger muscles; A. Kaline and his
    Detroit teammates. W. Leggett. il Sports
    Illus 26:24-7 Je 5 '67
Trade in winter, hope in spring. W. Leggett.
    il Sports Illus 26:44-8 Ap 17 '67
Up again down again; American league pen-
    nant race. W. Leggett. il Sports Illus 27:
    26-9 S 18 '67
Virtue is rewarded; Boston Red Sox in the
    pennant race. M. Mulvoy. il Sports Illus 27:
    12-17 Ag 21 '67
What team is that? the Cubs? third place?
    L. Durocher's Cubs. T. C. Brody. il Sports
    Illus 26:64+ My 29 '67
Wild finale, and it's Boston! American league
    pennant race. W. Leggett. il Sports Illus
    27:32-4+ O 9 '67
Winners all around; American league season
    predictions. Time 89:80 Je 16 '67
Wynn of the losers; Houston Astros. il Time
    90:64 Jl 7 '67
Yoweee Chicago! Cubs in first place. J. Jares.
    il Sports Illus 27:14-17 Jl 10 '67
    See also
World series (baseball)
BASEBALL fans
New breed of baseball fan. C. Einstein. il
    Harper 235:69-70+ Jl 1 '67
BASEBALL farm clubs. See Baseball
BASEBALL hall of fame. See National baseball
    hall of fame and museum
BASEBALL managers
Harry the hat; H. Walker. J. R. McDermott.
    il Life 62:105-8+ Ap 7 '67
    See also
Dark, A. R.
Durocher, L.
Mele, S.
Stanky, E.
Stengel, C.
Tebbetts, B.
Walker, H.
Williams, D.
BASEBALL players
Always they want more, more, more; J.
    Marichal of San Francisco Giants. A. Stump.
    il Sat Eve Post 240:68-71 Jl 29 '67
Baseball is the waiting game. R. Lardner.
    il N Y Times Mag p30-2+ Jl 30 '67; Dis-
    cussion. p9 Ag 13; 10 Ag 20 '67
Baseball 1967: form chart, American league.
    il Sports Illus 26:69-72 Ap 17 '67
Baseball 1967: form chart, National league. il
    Sports Illus 26:65-8 Ap 17 '67
Baseball roundup 1967: tools of ignorance. il
    Ebony 22:128-30+ Je '67
Behind the bold Red uprising in Cincinnati.
    W. Leggett. il Sports Illus 26:65-8 My 22 '67
Better from the neck up. E. Stanky and
    W. Leggett. il Sports Illus 27:18-23 Ag 28
    '67
El Birdos fly high; St Louis Cardinals vs
    Boston Red Sox. W. Leggett. il Sports
    Illus 27:22-9 O 16 '67
Cardinals against, who? American league
    four-team pennant race. W. Leggett. il
    Sports Illus 27:18-21 O 2 '67
Chaos in the American league. W. Leggett.
    il Sports Illus 26:28-30+ My 8 '67
Coach me a little bit. il Newsweek 69:88-92
    Ap 10 '67
Dodger story. B. Bavasi and J. Olsen. il
    Sports Illus 26:78-82+ My 15; 44-6+ My 22;
    30-4+ My 29; 46-50+ Je 5 '67
Four aces in the wildest windup. il Life
    63:28D-29 S 29 '67
From spikes to a blue suit. J. Conlan and R.
    Creamer. il Sports Illus 27:36-9 Jl 3 '67

Hero of baseball's hottest pennant race; C.
    Yastrzemski of Boston Red Sox. il News-
    week 70:62-6 O 2 '67
Highlight; Jim McGlothlin of the California
    Angels. il Sports Illus 26:77 Je 19 '67
Highlight; reliever Ted Abernathy of the
    Cincinnati Reds. por Sports Illus 26:99
    My 15 '67
Highlight; Steve Barber of the Orioles. il
    Sports Illus 26:85 My 8 '67
Infamous spitter; illegal but popular spitball.
    H. Weiskopf. il Sports Illus 27:12-17 Jl 31
    '67
Koufax the incomparable; Jews and high
    holiday games. M. Richler; discussion. Com-
    mentary 43:6+ F '67
Long, wet summer; spitball pitchers. il Time
    90:52-3 S 1 '67
New kind of numbers game. W. Leggett. il
    Sports Illus 26:58+ Je 19 '67
1967 rookie cookies. H. L. Masin. Sr Schol
    90:24 Mr 31 '67
On the tee: an error and a fumble; football
    and baseball players at Astrojet classic.
    D. Jenkins. il Sports Illus 26:16-19 F 27 '67
Out in front in fun and games; St Louis
    Cardinals in National league pennant race.
    W. Leggett. il Sports Illus 27:22-4+ S 4 '67
Pirates: Pittsburgh's confidence guys. I. R.
    McVay. pors Look 31:64-9 My 30 '67
St Louis card-sharps. H. L. Masin. il Sr
    Schol 91:42 O 5 '67
Signs of spring; provocative questions. il
    Time 89:50-1 Mr 31 '67
Sore arms and no cigarettes; Hank Bauer's
    pitchers are hurting, but things really don't
    look bad for the Orioles. J. Jares. il Sports
    Illus 26:36-7 Ap 10 '67
Sporting scene; World series: St Louis
    Cardinals vs. Boston Red Sox. R. Angell.
    New Yorker 43:176+ O 28 '67
Thunderation of sluggers; voting for National
    league all-star team. W. Leggett. il Sports
    Illus 27:14-17 Jl 3 '67
Trade in winter, hope in spring. W. Leggett.
    il Sports Illus 26:44-8 Ap 17 '67
When baseball went to war; World war II.
    F. Graham, jr. il Sports Illus 26:78-82+
    Ap 17 '67
    See also
National baseball hall of fame and museum
    also names of baseball players, e.g. W.
    Monbouquette
    Photographs
Old faces in new uniforms. il Sports Illus 26:
    48-64 Ap 17 '67
    Recruiting
Fresh breezes from the free-agent draft;
    poorer teams have equal chance to sign top
    talent. W. Leggett. Sports Illus 26:26 My 1
    '67
Real secret of trading. B. Bavasi and J. Ol-
    sen. il Sports Illus 26:46-50+ Je 5 '67
    Salaries
Maximum ado over minimums. L. Shecter. il
    Sports Illus 27:58+ D 18 '67
Money makes the player go. B. Bavasi and
    J. Olsen. il Sports Illus 26:44-6+ My 22 '67
BASEBALL rules. See Baseball—Rules
BASEBALL stadiums. See Stadiums
BASEBALL teams. See Baseball clubs
BASEBALL umpires. See Umpires (sports)
BASEL, Switzerland
    Art
Putting Pablo to the vote: city to buy
    Picassos. il Time 90:46 D 29 '67
BASEMENTS and cellars
Build a basement that's easy to remodel. M.
    C. Huntoon, jr. Am Home 70:141 O '67
Greenhouse enclosed, and a basement finished.
    il House B 109:152-3 Je '67
This basement is part of the upstairs.
    J. Reedy. il Bet Hom & Gard 45:70-1 O '67
This basement really lives! il Bet Hom &
    Gard 45:14 S '67
Warm way to finish your basement. H. Shuld-
    iner. il Pop Sci 191:128-32+ S '67
BASES, Air. See Air bases
BASES, Military. See Military bases
BASHAM, Arthur L.
    Mahabharata and the Ramayana. UNESCO
    Courier 20:4-10+ D '67
BASHLINE, Jim
    Best ways to hunt rabbits East to West.
    Field & S 72:46-7+ Ja '68
BASHLINE, L. James
    Bear by the square mile. Field & S 72:42-3+
    Ag '67

BASIC protection plan. See Insurance, Automobile

BASKERVILLE, John
Writing master turned master printer. P. W. Schmidtchen. il pors Hobbies 72:104-5 My '67

BASKET making
Budget basket; how to make a simple flower basket. M. M. Ridenour. il Home Gard 54: 14 My '67
See also
Indians of North America—Basket making

BASKETBALL
All together now, a big whompf for Norfolk state. C. Kirkpatrick. il Sports Illus 28:20 Ja 8 '68
Basketball's week. M. Hyman. il Sports Illus 27:98-9 D 11 '67
Chapel Hill's tobacco rogues: L&M kids. B. Lewis and L. Miller. F. Deford. il Sports Illus 26:24-6+ F 20 '67
College basketball 1968. il Sports Illus 27: 34-46+ D 4 '67
Getting the Vandy treatment; Duke vs Vanderbilt. C. Kirkpatrick. il Sports Illus 27: 18-21 D 25 '67
Guy named Pete; Maravich of Louisiana state university. il Time 91:33 Ja 19 '68
High-climbing Ivy; Princeton. il Newsweek 69:90 F 13 '67
Hoopla in Texas; UCLA to play University of Houston. il Newsweek 71:77 Ja 22 '68
Icemen; freeze or stall tactics. Time 89:55 F 17 '67
In from the Three I league; Salukis of Southern Illinois university. J. Jares. il Sports Illus 26:18-19 Ja 30 '67
In search of Naismith's game. F. Deford. il Sports Illus 26:24-6+ Mr 6 '67
Is no. 2 really trying harder? basketball series in Pittsburgh between Hertz and Avis. il Bsns W p38-9 F 18 '67
Old Harvard earns a Bluenose; college basketball's last tournament in chilly Nova Scotia. C. Kirkpatrick. il Sports Illus 28: 16-17 Ja 15 '68
Pallacanestro is the rage. J. Olsen. il Sports Illus 26:62-6+ F 13 '67
Razor-cut idol of San Francisco; R. Barry. F. Deford. il Sports Illus 26:32-5 F 13 '67
Small world; Southern Illinois university. il Time 89:60+ F 3 '67
Stallball, a game to sleep by; UCLA vs USC. J. Jares. il Sports Illus 26:28-30 Mr 13 '67
Terror in the air; UCLA's L. Alcindor. F. Deford. il Sports Illus 26:16-21 Ap 3 '67
That Providence cannonball; J. Walker. F. Deford. il Sports Illus 26:18-19 Ja 23 '67
They're still at it in Indiana; Hoosiers lose to Kentucky in annual high school Allstar game. K. Chapin. il Sports Illus 26:30-1 Je 26 '67
Tiger in the house of Ivy; Princeton team. J. Jares. il Sports Illus 26:20-3 F 27 '67
Two to go for Lew. F. DeFord. il Sports Illus 26:14-17 Mr 27 '67
See also
American basketball association

Equipment
Case for the twelve-foot basket. M. Hyman. il Sports Illus 27:78-80+ D 4 '67

Rules
Knocking the stuffing out; rules for college game. Sports Illus 26:24 Ap 10 '67
Lew's still loose; college basketball rules. il Time 89:68 Ap 14 '67

BASKETBALL coaches. See Coaches (athletics)

BASKETBALL fans
Fans get the booby prize; partisan spectators at NBA pro playoffs. F. Deford. il Sports Illus 26:28-31 Ap 24 '67

BASKETBALL players
All America basketball. I. R. McVay. pors Look 31:71-5 Mr 21 '67
Bay of bigs. Sports Illus 26:17 Je 12 '67
Black supremacy; all-Negro schools in Deep South play in white tournaments. Sports Illus 26:8 Mr 27 '67
Case for the twelve-foot basket. M. Hyman. il Sports Illus 27:78-80+ D 4 '67
College basketball 1968. il Sports Illus 27:34-46+ D 4 '67
In search of Naismith's game. F. Deford. il Sports Illus 26:24-6+ Mr 6 '67
Just too much giant; W. Chamberlain and B. Russell; with report by J. Larner. il Life 62:82-4+ Ap 21 '67
Look who's down there; shorter men. il Time 89:69 Mr 3 '67
Making of a legend: towering Lew Alcindor. il Newsweek 69:59-62 F 27 '67

New spirit of the 76ers; defeat of Celtics in the Eastern division pro playoffs. F. Deford. il Sports Illus 26:28-31 Ap 17 '67
Next year's stars are here; college basketball's freshman teams. C. Kirkpatrick. il Sports Illus 26:18-21 F 6 '67
1967 All-American H.S. basketball squad. H. L. Masin. il Sr Schol 90:36 My 19 '67
Pallacanestro is the rage. J. Olsen. il Sports Illus 26:62-6+ F 13 '67
Pro basketball; NBA vs. ABA=prosperity. il Ebony 23:64-6+ Ja '68
Pro basketball preview. il Sports Illus 27: 28-40+ O 23 '67
Shooting for the top; UCLA opponents. H. L. Masin. il Sr Schol 91:24 D 7 '67
Tiger in the house of Ivy; Princeton team. J. Jares. il Sports Illus 26:20-3 F 27 '67
Two to go for Lew. F. DeFord. il Sports Illus 26:14-17 Mr 27 '67
See also names of basketball players, e.g. C. Murphy

BASKETBALL scouting
Scouting reports (cont) Sports Illus 27:37-40+ O 23; 44-6+ D 4 '67

BASKETBALL teams
And the big good Bruins. il Time 91:43 Ja 5 '68
Big Bill's debut; Knickerbockers against St Louis Hawks. il Newsweek 70:49 D 25 '67
Big Z and his misfiring Pistons. M. Cope. il Sports Illus 27:26-8+ D 18 '67
Curtains for the Celtics. il Time 89:57 Ap 21 '67
Education of Mr Barry; legal fight between San Francisco warriors and Oakland Oaks. F. Deford. il Sports Illus 27:22-4+ Ag 14 '67
Fans get the booby prize; partisan spectators at NBA pro playoffs. F. Deford. il Sports Illus 26:28-31 Ap 24 '67
Fast start for Ben's Hawks. F. Deford. il Sports Illus 27:24-5 N 13 '67
Fastest gun in the West; San Francisco Warriors R. Barry. R. Wurlitzer. il Sat Eve Post 240:80-2 Mr 11 '67
High jump; Oakland Oaks lures Bruce Hale and R. Barry. Newsweek 70:70 Jl 3 '67
It's Earl, Earl, Earl the pearl; rookie shooter of Baltimore Bullets. F. Deford. il Sports Illus 27:18-19 O 30 '67
New spirit of the 76ers; defeat of Celtics in the Eastern division pro playoffs. F. Deford. il Sports Illus 26:28-31 Ap 17 '67
New York gets a top team at last; the Knickerbockers. F. Deford. il Sports Illus 27:28-31 O 23 '67
No. twenty-four, a new man for New York; B. Bradley of New York Knickerbockers. F. Deford. il Sports Illus 27:18-19 D 18 '67
Pro basketball; NBA vs. ABA=prosperity. il Ebony 23:64-6+ Ja '68
Pro basketball preview. il Sports Illus 27: 28-40+ O 23 '67
Sonic boom in Seattle; SuperSonics. F. Deford. il Sports Illus 27:38-40+ O 9 '67
Sweet revenge; W. Chamberlain with Philadelphia 76ers. Time 89:40 My 5 '67
Tough grind to the big time; New Jersey Americans. W. J. McKean. il Look 32:78-81 Ja 23 '68
Waiting made it sweeter; 76ers dethroned the Celtics. F. Deford. il Sports Illus 26: 54-6 My 8 '67
See also
American basketball association

BASKETBALL tournaments
BVD boys shoot down a hex; North Carolina's Tar Heels capture Far West classic in Portland. J. Jares. il Sports Illus 28:18-19+ Ja 8 '68
Black supremacy; all-Negro schools in Deep South play in white tournaments. Sports Illus 26:8 Mr 27 '67
NCAA; twenty-two teams after Alcindor. F. Deford. il Sports Illus 26:28-30+ Mr 20 '67
UCLA wraps it up. Newsweek 69:56 Ap 3 '67

BASKETS
See also
Basket making

BASKING sharks. See Sharks

BASQUE provinces
Basques. M. H. Levine. il Natur Hist 76:44-51 Ap '67

BASQUES
Basques. M. H. Levine. il Natur Hist 76:44-51 Ap '67
New Basques. il Time 89:31 Ap 7 '67

BASS, William M See Kerley, E. R. jt. auth.

BASS
Striped bass in canvas chronicle; paintings by S. Meltzoff; with account by D. Barnes. Sports Illus 27:34-9 S 4 '67

BATS
Radio tracking of homing bats. T. C. Williams and J. M. Williams. bibliog il Science 155:1435-6 Mr 17 '67
BATS, Fossil
50,000,000-year-old bat. il Sci Digest 62:61-2 O '67
BATTEN, James K.
After the agitators left Greensboro. Reporter 37:31-3 Ag 10 '67
BATTEN, Joe, and Hudson, L. C.
How to live a fuller life. Nations Bsns 55:78-80 F '67
BATTEN, W. E.
Economics of information retrieval; adaptation of address, November 22, 1965. por Library J 92:974-5 Mr 1 '67
BATTEN, William M.
Responsible retailing. Duns R 89:83-6 Mr '67

about
How they minted the new Penney. J. McDonald. il por Fortune 76:110-13+ Jl '67
BATTERIES, Electric. See Electric batteries
BATTERY chargers. See Storage battery chargers
BATTERY charging. See Electric batteries—Charging
BATTERY-powered tape recorders. See Magnetic recorders and recording
BATTING records. See Sports records
BATTIST, Sondra
Curandera artist. Américas 19:36-40 My '67
BATTISTA, O. A.
Live as long as you want to. Farm J 91:66R Mr '67
BATTLE fatigue. See Neuroses
BATTLE of the sexes. See Women and men
BATTLEFIELDS
Second battle of Antietam; controversy over location of the transmission lines. Nat Parks Mag 41:20-1 O '67
Souvenir detectors; Civil war memento collectors in the South. il Time 89:53 Mr 24 '67
BATTLESHIPS. See Warships
BAUER, Erwin A.
Adventuring westward. por Outdoor Life 139:49-51+ Ap; 50-3+ My; 33-5+ Je '67
Christmas on a houseboat. pors Outdoor Life 140:42-5+ D '67
Great coon hunt. Outdoor Life 140:48-9+ N '67
Jump the gun for bass. Outdoor Life 139:44-7+ Mr '67
Safari, anyone? il Audubon 69:22-7 Jl '67
Sunset of the snail kite. Field & S 72:58-60 Ag '67
They've whipped those beginner's blues. Field & S 71:54-7+ F '67
Two hours on an African island. il Audubon 69:64-7 S '67
Who says hunting's finished around here? Outdoor Life 140:38-41+ Ag '67
—and East, Ben
Blight on the land. Outdoor Life 140:35-7+ D '67 (to be cont)
BAUER, Joseph A. Jr. See Held, R. jt. auth.
BAUER, Raymond A.
Societal feedback. bibliog f Ann Am Acad 373:180-92 S '67
—and Greyser, S. A.
Dialogue that never happens. bibliog f Harvard Bsns R 45:2-4+ N '67
BAUGH, James O. and others
Single fallout particles and zirconium-95 from the Chinese nuclear explosion of 9 May 1966. bibliog Science 155:1405-7 Mr 17 '67
BAUM, Gregory
Book of the month. Cath World 205:310-11 Ag '67
Laying foundations for a theology of renewal. Commonweal 86:564-5 S 22 '67
BAUM, Lyman Frank
Trade winds. H. R. Mayes. Sat R 50:10-11 Jl 29 '67
BAUMAN, John Nevin
Hard drive of White motor. J. Berry. il por Duns R 88:37-8+ D '66
BAUMEISTER, Mary
Survival of a family. por McCalls 94:28 F '67
BAUR, Esther
Fader plan: Detroit style. bibliog Library J 92:3119-21 S 15 '67
BAUR, John Ireland Howe
New impresario for the showcase. il Time 90:64 N 24 '67
BAUXITE
Fossiliferous bauxite in glacial drift, Martha's Vineyard, Massachusetts. C. A. Kaye. bibliog il Science 57:1035-7 S 1 '67

BAVASI, Buzzie. See Bavasi, E. J.
BAVASI, Emil Joseph, and Olsen, Jack
Dodger story. Sports Illus 26:78-82+ My 15; 44-6+ My 22; 30-4+ My 29; 46-50+ Je 5 '67
BAVIER, Robert Newton, 1918-
IYRU adopts three new classes. Yachting 123:117+ Ja '68
Special art of match racing; excerpts from A view from the cockpit. Yachting 122:62-4+ S '67
BAXANDALL, Lee
(tr) See Weiss, P. Song of the Lusitanian bogey
BAXTER, Percival Proctor
Tribute to Gov. Baxter; letter to the editor. H. M. Albright. Am For 73:3 Ja '67
BAXTER, Tom
Pro's nest. See issues of Flying
BAXTER laboratories, incorporated
Company with a heart. R. Levy. il Duns R 90:49 Ag '67
BAY, Paul N.
Air rights help to solve a parking problem. Am City 82:84-5 N '67
BAY area rapid transit. See San Francisco—Rapid transit
BAY windows. See Windows
BAYBERRY
Bayberries and bayberry candles. H. W. Dengler. il Am For 73:4-7+ D '67
BAYBERRY candles. See Candles
BAYER, Ann
Quints on a picnic. Sat Eve Post 240:24-31 S 9 '67
The rich have beards, and the poor walk droopy. Sat Eve Post 240:12+ D 30 '67
Woman who gave of herself; story. Sat Eve Post 240:62-4 My 20 '67
BAYERISCHE motoren werke. See Automobile industry and trade—Germany (Federal Republic)
BAYH, Birch
Excerpt from address, May 15, 1967. Cong Digest 46:274+ N '67
Quizzing of suspects: here's a new way; excerpts from statement, February 7, 1967. U S News 62:14 F 20 '67
BAYLEY, Nancy
Rare study tracks half a lifetime. il Sci N 92:275-6 S 16 '67
BAYNE, Jacky C.
Back from the dead. por Newsweek 70:99 N 13 '67
BAYÓN, Damián Carlos
From the River Plate to the Seine. Américas 19:22-7 Ag '67
BAYONNE, N.J.
Asbestos fibers toughen thin overlays. il Am City 82:66 Je '67
BAYREUTH festival
After Wieland, business as usual? W. B. Rios. il Hi Fi 17:MA22-3 N '67
Bayreuth; productions of the Ring, Tristan and Parsifal. E. Davidson. il Opera N 32:25 S 23 '67
Clouds over Valhalla. il Time 90:40 Ag 25 '67
Two about Bayreuth. G. L. Mayer. Am Rec G 33:1120-1 Ag '67
BAZELON, David Lionel
Justice for juveniles; adaptation of address. New Repub 156:13-16 Ap 22 '67
BAZELON, David T.
Clients against lawyers. Harper 235:104+ S '67
Legal survey. Commentary 44:102+ D '67
Liberal anti-communism revisited. Commentary 44:33-6 S '67
BE, Nguyen-van-. See Nguyen-van-Be
BE honest with me; story. See Lee, M.
BEA, Augustin, cardinal
Paths to ecumenism. por Sat R 50:8-11 Jl 8 '67
BEACH, Garnet, and Kimble, D. P.
Activity and responsivity in rats after magnesium pemoline injections. bibliog Science 155:698-701 F 10 '67
BEACH architecture
Escape to the Atlantic shore; six faces to the sun. J. L. Hendrix. il House B 109:94-9 Ja '67
Harby house, York Harbor, Maine. il Arch Rec 141:72-5 mid-My '67
House stands free of the beach, facing into the weather. il Sunset 138:106-8 Ap '67
Island residence, Long Island Sound, New York. il Arch Rec 141:66-71 mid-My '67
Narrow beach lot; special design problems. il Sunset 139:58-63 Jl '67
Palace on the beach; house of the John O'Toole's on Long Island; with report by S. Mahoney. il Life 62:80-3+ Je 30 '67
Summer cottage grows up. il Am Home 70:82-3 My '67

BEATLES—*Continued*
Beatles, op. 15; Sgt. Pepper's lonely hearts club band. G. Lees. pors Hi Fi 17:94 Ag '67
Beatles vs. Stones; Roling Stones as rivals. J. Kroll. il Newsweek 71:62-3 Ja 1 '68
Fab? chaos; the TV film. Magical mystery tour. il Time 91:60-1 Ja 5 '68
Facing the music. P. Schrag. Sat R 50:61 Ag 19 '67
It's getting better. J. Kroll. il Newsweek 69:70 Je 26 '67
Messengers. il pors Time 90:60-2+ S 22 '67; Same abr. with title Four little Beatles and how they grew. Read Digest 91:229-30+ D '67
Mix-master to the Beatles. il Time 89:67 Je 16 '67
New far-out Beatles. T. Thompson. il Life 62:100-2+ Je 16 '67
Other noises, other notes. il Time 89:63 Mr 3 '67
Secular music. R. Christgau. Esquire 68:283-6 D '67
Sgt. Pepper; latest album. New Yorker 43:22-3 Je 24 '67
Those Beatles again. H. Yurchenco. pors Am Rec G 34:248 N '67
BEATNIKS
Nothing more to declare, by J. C. Holmes. Review
    Newsweek il 69:112+ Mr 13 '67. S. K. Oberbeck
Up-down-and-off-Beatniks. Sci Digest 62:75 Jl '67
When Beatniks land in the army. il U S News 62:52-4 Je 5 '67
    See also
Hippies
BEATON, Cecil
Interview, ed. by A. Fatt. por Dance Mag 41:48-9 F '67
My first trip. McCalls 94:36+ My '67
BEATON, Leonard
Nuclear fuel-for-all. For Affairs 45:662-9 Jl '67
BEATRICE foods company
Beatrice foods savors a zestier cupboard. il Bsns W p 122+ D 16 '67
Beatrice the acquisitive. Fortune 75:252 Je 15 '67
BEATTY, Jerome, Jr
Hanging up on Hemingway. Esquire 67:116 F '67
Trade winds. See issues of Saturday review
BEATTY, John
Two-headed monster. P. Beatty. Horn Bk 43:96-101 F '67
BEATTY, Patricia
Two-headed monster. Horn Bk 43:96-101 F '67
BEATTY, Warren
Warren Beatty. pors Vogue 150:94-7 N 15 '67
Will the real Warren Beatty please shut up. R. Reed. il pors Esquire 68:92-6+ Ag '67
BEAUGÉ, L. A. See Sjodin, R. A. jt. auth.
BEAUTIFICATION of cities. See Municipal improvement
BEAUTIFICATION of landscape. See Landscape improvement
BEAUTY. See Aesthetics
BEAUTY, Personal
Are you ready to be seen? S. Harney. Ladies Home J 84:34 Ag '67
Basic beauty course for girls. il Sr Schol 91:30 S 21; 24 N 2 '67
Beauty at home. See issues of American home
Beauty bulletin. See issues of Vogue
Beauty checkout. See issues of Vogue
Beauty gossip: Paris, Rome, London, New York. il Vogue 149:128-32 Mr 15 '67
Beauty pack-in. il Mlle 65:252 Ag '67
Beauty stopover; Linda Roy, winner in the Westinghouse science talent search. il Seventeen 26:228 My '67
Big beauty debate: husbands vs bachelors; ideas of what constitutes a really good-looking woman. il McCalls 94:54+ My '67
Crash beauty; crash course in beauty at the U. of Pennsylvania. il Mlle 66:106+ Ja '68
Dear beauty editor. See issues of Seventeen
Dressing table talk. See issues of Seventeen
For your most romantic party look: ribbons, ringlets and radiance. il Good H 165:106-7 N '67
Four facets of spring beauty. il Good H 164:118-19 Ap '67
Girl who discovered her own beauty. il Redbook 128:88-91 F '67
Having a beautiful time. il Seventeen 26:76-81 Je '67
How cool can you get? thirty beauty ideas. il Good H 165:78-9 Jl '67
How to mend your midsummer beauty mishaps. il Seventeen 26:94-5 Jl '67
How to stay young. D. Day. il Ladies Home J 84:72+ My '67

The look you like; questions and answers; ed. by L. Allen. See issues of Today's health
100 ways of summer. il Mlle 65:134-47 My '67
Private lives of several beauties. il Vogue 150:132-5 O 15 '67
Quest for beauty in Dahomey. J. Maquet. il Vogue 150:218-27+ D '67
$750 worth of beauty advice from fifteen experts. S. Harney. il Ladies Home J 84:52+ Ag '67
Stay young & beautiful. A. F. Cronin. il Parents Mag 43:24+ Ja '68
Stay young & beautiful. V. S. Stitt. il Parents Mag 42:40 O; 54 N; 18 D '67
Stephanie Farrow. il Seventeen 26:164-5 Ap '67
Take a day for beauty. il Redbook 129:74-5+ My '67
Time for beauty; schedules of essential beauty care. il Redbook 130:92-3+ N '67
To be a beauty; all me and nobody else; symposium. il Seventeen 26:90-5 O '67
What's good for the gander; hints for good looks of men. il Vogue 149:144-7 Je '67
You remind me of someone. il McCalls 94:88-9 S '67
Your special look. il Seventeen 26:176-7 S '67
    See also
Baths
Beauty shops
Cosmetics
Exercise
Hairdressing
Make-up
Skin
BEAUTY contests
New trend toward black beauties. il Ebony 23:164-6+ D '67

    Anecdotes, facetiae, satire, etc.
Nothing like a dame: NLW plan for Miss Library universe of 1968; with editorial comment. P. S. Dunkin. Library J 92:1591 Ap 15 '67
BEAUTY culture
Crash beauty; crash course in beauty at the U. of Pennsylvania. il Mlle 66:106+ Ja '68
Svengali of the skin; E. Laszlo's Institute for cosmetology; with report by D. Lurie. il Life 62:35-6+ Je 23 '67
BEAUTY in nature. See Nature
BEAUTY preparations. See Cosmetics
BEAUTY shops
I spa; or, how to profit from a visit to one of America's super bodyshops: The greenhouse, the Neiman-Marcus-supervised pavilion. Vogue 149:178+ Ap 1 '67
Svengali of the skin; E. Laszlo's Institute for cosmetology; with report by D. Lurie. il Life 62:35-6+ Je 23 '67
BEAVER ISLAND
Diving for wolves in ice water. B. Gilbert. il Sports Illus 26:62-6+ F 20 '67
BEAVER Mark IV (research vehicle) See Submarine boats, Research
BEBAN, Gary
All the way with O.J. D. Jenkins. il Sports Illus 27:16-21 N 27 '67
Great one confronts O.J. D. Jenkins. il por Sports Illus 27:32-4+ N 20 '67
Great one. por Time 90:44 O 20 '67
One more great play. D. Jenkins. il Sports Illus 27:14-19 S 25 '67
Technocrat. J. Bonfante. il pors Life 63:90A-90B+ N 17 '67
Three for the trophy. il Newsweek 70:94 N 27 '67
UCLA's mad bomber. H. L. Masin. por Sr Schol 91:19-O 19 '67
BEBERMAN, Max
Measuring academic productivity. Sat R 50:68-9 Jl 15 '67
BÉCAUD, Gilbert
Great Becaud. G. Lees. por Hi Fi 17:118 F '67
BÉCHET, Sidney
Bechet the prophet. M. Williams. por Sat R 50:64-5 F 11 '67
BECHTEL, Steve
Discovery; poem. Horn Bk 43:385 Je '67
BECK, A. and others
Phosphorylation with inorganic phosphates at moderate temperatures. bibliog Science 157:952 Ag 25 '67
BECK, Carlton E. and Barak, James
Place of values in the study of society. bibliog f Sch & Soc 95:122-3 F 18 '67
BECK, Charles B. See Pettitt, J. M. jt. auth.
BECK, F. and others
Lysosomal enzyme inhibition by trypan blue: a theory of teratogenesis. bibliog Science 157:1180-2 S 8 '67

BECK, Joan
Babies love to learn; excerpt from How to raise a brighter child. Parents Mag 42:58-9+ S '67
Guarding the unborn. Todays Health 46:38-41+ Ja '68
BECK, Lois Weekes
That other Las Vegas. Travel 128:36-8 D '67
BECK, Ray
Brainy black duck. Outdoor Life 140:42-3+ N '67
BECK, Theodric Romeyn
Early vision of public education; letter. W. A. Brumfield. Science 157:874 Ag 25 '67
BECKENBACH, Edwin Ford
Upgrading mathematics education. por Sch & Soc 95:410-11 N 11 '67
BECKER, Ben
Academy for hard cases. il por Time 89:38 Ap 7 '67
BECKER, Ernest
Class hires a scholar. il Time 89:58 Mr 10 '67
BECKER, F. F. and Broome, J. D.
L-Asparaginase: inhibition of early mitosis in regenerating rat liver. bibliog Science 156:1602-3 Je 23 '67
BECKER, Gary S.
Pathfinders for tomorrow's economics. Bsns W p57 Ja 6 '68
BECKER, Howard S.
Existentialist therapy. Sat R 50:27-8 Ag 12 '67
BECKERT, Wilhelm M.
U.S. hosts Boy scouts world jamboree. Parks & Rec 2:21 Je '67
BECKET, James
Chile's mini-revolution. Commonweal 87:406-8 D 29 '67
BECKET, Welton
Portrait of the artist as a businessman. R. Sheehan. il por Fortune 75:144-8+ Mr '67
BECKETT, Sheilah
Sheilah Beckett: classicist. N. Kent. il por Am Artist 31:38-44+ Ap '67
BECKHARD, Richard
Confrontation meeting. Harvard Bsns R 45:149-55 Mr '67
BECKMAN instruments, incorporated
Tall man in the saddle. N. Willatt. Duns R 90:35-6 Jl '67
BECKWITH, John
Djami jewel. Art N 66:40-1+ D '67
BECKWITH, Jonathan R.
Regulation of the lac operon. bibliog Science 156:597-604 My 5 '67
BECLCH; drama. See Owens, R.
BED linens. See Linen, Household
BED-sitting rooms. See Bedrooms
BEDARF, E. W. See Revusky, S. H. jt. auth.
BEDAS, Yusef K.
Beirut: the unfamiliar taste of humble pie. il Bsns W p83 Ja 21 '67
Fall of the genius from Jerusalem. G. De Carvalho. il por Life 62:87-9 Ja 27 '67
BEDAU, Hugo Adam
Issue of capital punishment. bibliog f Cur Hist 53:82-7+ Ag '67
BEDDING
Modern bedding: designed for your ease. il Good H 164:209-10 F '67
See also
Mattresses
Sheets
BEDELL, Eugenia
Going places, finding things in Corsica. House & Gard 133:10+ Ja '68
BEDFORD, James H.
Cold way to new life. L. Wainwright. Life 62:16 Ja 27 '67
Never say die. il Time 89:57 F 3 '67
BEDFORD, N.Y.

Education
Strongly stated structural framework encloses flexible environment for a middle school; Fox Lane middle school. il Arch Rec 141:178-9 Mr '67
BEDIENT, Calvin
Gaze behind the lens. Nation 205:59-60 Jl 17 '67
Representative Lowell. Nation 204:442-3 Ap 3 '67
Sunny side of Marxism. Nation 205:534-5 N 20 '67
BEDROOM furnishings. See Household furnishings
BEDROOMS
Chez Mlle: nesting habits of the college bird. D. Hampton. il Mlle 65:100-1 Ag '67
Color it happy. il Am Home 70:122 Jl '67
Dear home editor. il Seventeen 26:200 My; 391+ Ag '67
Four ways to do one room. il Seventeen 26:146-9+ Mr '67

How to change your scene to super. il Seventeen 26:100-1+ Je '67
Join the hunt. il Seventeen 26:110-13 O '67
New in your room: switched-ons. il Seventeen 26:168-71 My '67
Paper's the thing; how to decorate quickly, colorfully, inexpensively. il Seventeen 26:188 My '67
Take a bed, make a bedroom. D. Hampton. il Mlle 66:16-17 Ja '68
Tune in to the newest. il Seventeen 26:234 My '67
See also
Guest rooms
BEDS
Instant guestroom. E. Kinard. il House B 109:106-7+ Ag '67
Sleep for swingers; bed show at the Museum of contemporary crafts in New York city. il Sci Digest 63:72-3 Ja '68

Anecdotes, facetiae, satire, etc.
Bedtime tales. F. L. Remington. il Todays Health 46:64-7 Ja '68
BEDSPREADS. See Coverlets
BEDTIME reading. See Books and reading
BEDWETTING. See Urine—Incontinence
BEE-balm. See Horsemint
BEEBE, Forest
I was the dog; ed. by B. East. Outdoor Life 140:68-9+ D '67
BEEBE, Lucius
Purveyor to the West. Am Heritage 18:28-31+ F '67
about
Purple Pepys of El Morocco. J. K. Hutchens. por Sat R 50:27-8 D 16 '67
BEEBE, Robert
Flopperstoppers for seagoing motorboats. il Motor B 119:42-4+ F '67
Passagemaker's summer cruise. Motor B 119:86+ F '67
BEECH, Keyes
Flying young man on the Saigon trapeze Read Digest 91:75-9 Jl '67
BEECH aircraft corporation
Beech 99 interest signals market battle Aviation W 86:31 My 8 '67
BEECHAM, Sir Thomas
Beecham discography. W. Botsford. Am Rec G 33:745-7, 930-2, 1009-12, 1078-81; 34:150-1, 244-5 My-Ag, O-N '67
Sir Thomas Beecham: a half-century of recordings. W. Botsford. por Am Rec G 33 742-5 My '67
BEECHER, William
McNamara's innovations. Reporter 36:51-2 Mr 23 '67
BEECHER ISLAND, Battle of, 1868
Don't let them ride over us. G. M. Heinzman. il Am Heritage 18:44-7+ F '67
BEECK, Frans Jozef van
Continuity in the Dutch church. America 117:266-9+ S 16 '67
BEEF
Before you broil, you must choose. il Sunset 139:84-5 Ag '67
See also
Cookery—Meat

Prices
See Meat—Prices
BEEF heart mitochondria. See Mitochondria
BEEF industry. See Meat industry and trade
BEEF stew. See Stew
BEELINE fashions, incorporated
Apparel salesmen take samples to the party il Bsns W p 148-50+ Jl 15 '67
BEEM, Wendell Bruce
Aunt Irene. Horn Bk 43:429-33 Ag '67
BEEMAN, W. W. See Lake, J. A. jt. auth.
BEER
Aquavit and beer. R. J. Misch. il House B 110:124+ Ja '68
Beer: a draught of mild midsummer magic. W. Clifford. House B 109:120-1+ Ag '67
Saving the bread for the sandwich; Rheingold's no-carbohydrate beer. il Time 90:74-5 Jl 7 '67
Things you never knew about beer. C. P. Gilmore. il Pop Sci 191:58-61+ Ag '67
See also
Brewing industries
Skol international corporation

BEER containers
Metals fight to hold their beer; steel-aluminum competition for the multi-billion-can beer and soft-drink market. il Bsns W p92+ Mr 18 '67

BEERY, Clinton D.
Floodlighting a courthouse. Am City 82:118 Ag '67

BEES
Deadly bee. il Sci Digest 61:83-4 My '67
Evolution of bee language. H. Esch. il Sci Am 216:96-102+ bibliog(p 148) Ap '67
Honey bees: do they use the direction information contained in their dance maneuver? D. L. Johnson. bibliog il Science 155:844-7 F 17 '67
Honeybees: do they use direction and distance information provided by their dancers? K. v. Frisch; A. M. Wenner; D. L. Johnson. bibliog il Science 158:1072-7 N 24 '67
Honey bees: do they use the distance information contained in their dance maneuver? A. M. Wenner. bibliog il Science 155:847-9 F 17 '67
Honeybees resent alfalfa kicks. Sci N 91:195 F 25 '67
Natural history; the honey bee. Hobbies 72:119 Ag '67
Tailor-made honeybees: bred to pollinate a particular crop. Sci N 92:202 Ag 26 '67

BEESON, Jack
Lizzie Borden. Criticism
Hi Fi il 18:MA7 Ja '68
New Yorker 43:189-90 N 4 '67
Records:
Lizzie Borden; Hello out there. Opera N 31:34 Ap 1 '67

BEETHOVEN, Ludwig van
Again. Schmidt-Isserstedt's great Beethoven. M. N. Kanny. Am Rec G 33:576-7 Mr '67
Beethoven as I knew him, by A. F. Schindler. Review
Am Rec G 33:830+ My '67. M. N. Kanny
Beethoven out of Mahler by Steinberg. J. Diether. Am Rec G 33:386-7 Ja '67
Beethoven quartets, by J. Kerman. Review
New Repub 156:38-9 F 25 '67. R. Evett
Faithful to Fidelio. Time 90:42 Ag 18 '67
Jacqueline Du Pré and Stephen Bishop; individually and together. M. N. Kanny. il Am Rec G 33:548-9 Mr '67
Leonore/Fidelio of 1805. B. Jacobson. Hi Fi 17:MA12 O '67
Music to my ears; Cleveland orchestra's performance of Missa solemnis. I. Kolodin. Sat R 50:62 F 25 '67
Ormandy and Steinberg complete their Beethoven nine. H. Goldsmith. Hi Fi 17:84-5 Ja '67
Outstanding; Bishop alone. M. N. Kanny. Am Rec G 33:549-50 Mr '67
Prime Casals from Marlboro. M. N. Kanny. Am Rec G 33:489 F '67
Records:
Fidelio. Opera N 31:34 Ap 8 '67
Missa solemnis. Opera N 31:34 My 13 '67
Tanglewood. S. Jenkins. Opera N 32:20 S 23 '67
Two views of the nine Beethoven symphonies. M. N. Kanny. Am Rec G 33:646-8 Ap '67

BEETLES
Diets for rearing the ambrosia beetle xyleborus ferrugineus (fabricius) in vitro. J. L. Saunders and J. K. Knoke. bibliog il Science 157:460+ Jl 28 '67
Sex attractants in frass from bark beetles; with reply by D. L. Wood and others. J. P. Vité. bibliog Science 156:105 Ap 7 '67
Symbiosis; effects of a mutualistic fungus upon the growth and reproduction of xyleborus ferrugineus. D. M. Norris and J. K. Baker. bibliog Science 156:1120-2 My 26 '67
See also
Carpet beetles
Flour beetles

BEFORE you go; drama. See Holofcener, L.

BEGGS, Franklin Delano
Divorce, American style. il por Newsweek 70:30 O 16 '67

BEGINNING of tomorrow; story. See Turner, C.

BEGONIAS
Bright begonias for shady places. L. A. Deming. il Home Gard 54:66-7 F '67
Color your windows begonia. E. Kondonellis. il Am Home 70:68-9 N '67
Winter-flowering begonias. J. L. Martin. il Home Gard 54:20-1 O '67

BEHAN, Brendan
Recalling the Borstal boy. H. Sutton. Sat R 50:48-9 D 2 '67

BEHAVIOR (psychology)
Behavioral psychotherapy. A. Bandura. il Sci Am 216:78-82+ bibliog(p 150) Mr '67

Causality, consciousness, and cerebral organization. W. R. Hess. bibliog Science 158:1279-83 D 8 '67
Emotional first aid? L. L. Prina. il N Y Times Mag p 112+ Ap 2 '67
How to handle a crisis. D. A. Sugarman and R. Hochstein. Seventeen 26:150-1+ S '67
Mystique of aggression. D. L. Wallace. Christian Cent 84:503-5 Ap 19 '67
Naturalist at large; concerning K. Lorenz's On aggression and R. Ardrey's Territorial imperative. M. Bates. Natur Hist 76:14+ Ap '67
On ethology. Sci N 91:472 My 20 '67
Origins of human bonds. S. Fraiberg. Commentary 44:47-57 D '67
Secrets; why you need them. A. West. Vogue 150:127+ Ag 15 '67
Split-level American family. U. Bronfenbrenner. Sat R 50:60-6 O 7 '67
Wayward Puritans, by K. T. Erikson. Review
Nation 205:316-17 O 2 '67. A. Guttmann
What nature reveals about peacemaking; theories of W. Trotter. J. F. Wharton. Sat R 50:14-16 My 27 '67
See also
Human nature
Motivation (psychology)
Psychobiology
Social norm

BEHAVIOR, Animal. See Animals—Habits and behavior

BEHAVIOR, Criminal. See Criminal psychology

BEHAVIOR of animals. See Animals—Habits and behavior

BEHAVIOR therapy. See Psychotherapy

BEHAVIORAL sciences
Behavioral sciences and family planning. M. Snyder. Science 158:677-80+ N 3 '67
Behavioral sciences notes. Sci N 93:14 Ja 6 '68
Privacy and behavioral research; preliminary summary of the report of the panel on privacy and behavioral research. Science 155:535-8 F 3 '67

BEHIND-the-lens meters. See Exposure meters

BEHME, Bob
First bear in the Yolla Bollys. Field & S 72:56-9 N '67
Go to beat the bandtails. Field & S 72:62-5 Je '67
Jarbidge deer hunt. Field & S 72:50-1+ O '67
Should we save the Salton? Field & S 72:8-10+ Ag '67
That surprising Eagle Lake. Field & S 72:38-9+ Je '67

BEHN, Harry
Definition implied. Horn Bk 43:561-4 O '67

BEHRENDT, John C.
Gravity increase at the South Pole. bibliog Science 155:1015-17 F 24 '67

BEHRENS, Carl
Plethora of particles. Sci N 92:342-6 S 30 '67
Violence studies frustrating. Sci N 92:381 O 14 '67

BEIDAS, Yusef K. See Bedas, Y. K.

BEIDLEMAN, Richard G.
Thomas Nuttall. Horticulture 45:36-7+ Je '67

BEIDLER, Barbara
Poetic Venture. por Newsweek 69:64 F 27 '67

BEINECKE rare book and manuscript library. See Yale university—Libraries

BEIRUT
Banks
See Banks and banking—Lebanon

Hotels, restaurants, etc.
Flackery in the Levant; opening of the Phoenicia hotel; excerpt from Throw away the key. M. Hampton. Sat R 50:47-9+ Ap 15 '67

BEIRUT agreement. See Duty free importation

BEISNER, Robert L.
Gloom, gloom, gloom, and scarce one ray of light; excerpts from The anti-imperialists; twelve against empire, 1898-1900. Am Heritage 18:65-71 Ag '67

BEISWENGER, John L.
Sensitive low-cost indicators. Pop Electr 27:49-50+ Jl '67

BEITZ, Berthold
New man of iron at Krupp. il por Bsns W p 106-8 Ag 12 '67

BÉJART, Maurice
Joke in the midst of prayer. il Time 90:87 D 15 '67

BELANGER, Albert J.
Home and school. Cath World 206:17-18 O '67

BELAÚNDE, Victor Andrés
Tributes in the United Nations. por UN Mo Chron 4:140-1 Ja '67
BELAÚNDE TERRY, Fernando
Peru's misfired guerrilla campaign. N. Gall. Reporter 36:36-8 Ja 26 '67
Peru's path to progress. D. G. Stroetzel. il por Read Digest 91:167-70+ S '67
Swirl of trouble. il por Time 90:32 N 3 '67
BELCH, David E.
Public library phoenix. por Library J 92:2365-8 Je 15 '67
BELCHER, Donald J.
Rivers of fresh water. Sat R 50:46 Jl 1 '67
BELDEN, Louise C.
Verplanck cup. Antiques 92:840-2 D '67
BELENKY, Robert
Heroes of a bad time. Nation 205:188-9 S 4 '67
BELFAST
Hospitals
Immediate counterattack; Belfast's mobile heart unit. il Time 90:32 S 1 '67
BELFER, Nancy
Thoughts on designing for textiles. Sch Arts 66:34-7 Ap '67
BELFORD, Barbara
Centennial for Nebraska. Travel 127:32-7 Ap '67
BELGIAN cookery. See Cookery, Belgian
BELGIAN Grand prix. See Automobile racing
BELGIUM
See also
Brussels
Casteau
Chemical industries—Belgium
Investments, Foreign (in Belgium)
Television broadcasting—Belgium
Defenses
Politics clouding Belgian order. Aviation W 87:23 D 25 '67
Description and travel
Travel's picture portfolio. Travel 127:52-7 Mr '67
History
Bibliography
Articles and other books received; comp. by P. Rosenfeld. See issues of American historical review
Industries
See also
Chemical industries—Belgium
BELGIUM and the United States
See also
United States—Foreign opinion—Belgian
BELIEF and doubt
Faith and doubt. A. Dulles. America 116:350 Mr 11 '67
BELIEF in God. See Faith
BELIEVERS church. See Church unity
BELIK, John
New dimensions in sculpture. Sch Arts 66:9-12 Ja '67
BELITT, Ben
Dog in the manger; Flower market: Cuernavaca; Termites: taxco; Gayossa ambulance service: emergency; poems. Poetry 110:71-7 My '67
Papermill graveyard; poem. New Yorker 43:46 My 20 '67
(tr) See Neruda, P. Sonnet XXIX
BELIZE, British Honduras
Belize. J. Russell. il Travel 128:56-60 O '67
BELL, Arthur
Young man remembers May Massee. Pub W 191:84-5 F 20 '67
BELL, Daniel
Liberal anti-communism revisited. Commentary 44:36-9 S '67
Toward a communal society. Life 62:112-14+ My 12 '67
about
Intellectuals' intellectual. G. P. Hunt. por Life 62:3-My 12 '67
BELL, James
Adenauer 1876-1967. Life 62:119-20 Ap 28 '67
Fall of the House of Krupp. Fortune 76:72-7+ Ag '67
BELL, Joseph N.
Lifeline for would-be suicides. Todays Health 45:30-3+ Je '67
War on narcotics. pors Todays Health 45:48-62 Jl '67
Why free-lance writers get nervous. Sat R 50:91-2 N 11 '67
BELL, Léonie
Dreambooks for gardeners. House B 109:126-7+ Ja '67

Growing up in a garden. House B 109:49-51 S '67
Snows of spring, fresh with fragrance. Home Gard 54:38-9 Ap '67
BELL, Louise Price
Jogging down into the Grand Canyon. Redbook 130:42 N '67
BELL, Marvin
Picture of soldiers; War piece; Memories of Bragg and Klein; Water, winter, fire; Difference; Travel; On returning to teach; Give back, give back; poems. Poetry 110:6-13 Ap '67
BELL aerosystems company
Bell expanding air cushion vehicle effort. M. L. Yaffee. il Aviation W 86:61+ Mr 20 '67
BELL and Howell company
Merrill to be acquired by Bell & Howell company. Pub W 191:122 F 20 '67
BELL telephone hour (television program) See Television broadcasting—Music
BELL telephone laboratories
Bell, Western electric play key Nike role. il Aviation 87:118-23 O 23 '67
Biggest mirror ever, Holmdel, N.J. il Arch Forum 126:33-41 Ap '67
BELL telephone system
Employment and wage trends in Bell system companies. L. E. Lewis and J. C. Bush. il Mo Labor R 90:38-41 Mr '67
Sovereign state of Bell. N. L. Parks. Nation 205:430-5 O 30 '67
Who will Bell the colossus? N. L. Parks. il Nation 205:391-3 O 23 '67
BELLINGRATH gardens, Theodore, Ala. See Gardens—Alabama
BELLINI, Vincenzo
Beatrice di Tenda. G. L. Mayer. il Am Rec G 34:180-2 N '67
High emotions, radiant melos, in a first Beatrice di Tenda. P. J. Smith. por Hi Fi 17:76+ D '67
Report: New York; performance of Norma at Carnegie Hall. R. D. Daniels. Opera N 32:30 D 16 '67
Sutherland's Beatrice. H. Weinstock. il Sat R 50:57 O 28 '67
BELLIVEAU, Nancy
Sledge-hammer sell. Life 63:101-2+ O 27 '67
BELLO, Ann H.
Rose success in easy stages. Flower Grower 54:52-3+ Ja '67
BELLOCCHIO, Marco
Current cinema. P. Kael. New Yorker 43:90+ Ja 13 '68
Welcome, Bellocchio. J. Morgenstern. Newsweek 71:84 Ja 22 '68
BELLONI, Manuel
Inner silence of Eduardo Mallea. Américas 19:20-7 O '67
BELLOTTO, Bernardo
Vagabond vedutista. il Time 90:96-7+ S 29 '67
BELLOW, Gary
U.S. letter: McFarland. C. Trillin. New Yorker 43:173-4+ N 4 '67
BELLS
Collectors and collecting
One bell collector's luck. L. E. Springer. il(p 1) Hobbies 72:123 S '67
BELLUSCHI, Pietro
Tradition-free architcture for a free church: a Unitarian center by Pietro Belluschi. il Arch Rec 141:135-40 Mr '67
BELMONT, August, 1908-
Revival of a grand old name. V. Kraft. il por Sports Illus 27:49-50+ Ag 7 '67
BELMONT stakes. See Horse racing
BELOIT college, Beloit, Wis.
Beloit's successful trimester. il Time 90:58 Ag 11 '67
BELT, Forest H.
Radio & television news. Electr World 79:23-4 Ja '68
BELTRAMI, Giacomo Constantino
Preposterous pathfinder; excerpt from Explorers of the Mississippi. T. Severin. il Am Heritage 19:56-63 D '67
BELTS, Safety. See Safety belts
BELTSVILLE research center. See United States—Agricultural research center, Beltsville, Md.
BELVIN, William, and Klein, Art
Houseboating is a family affair. il Motor B 121:102-4 Ja '68
BEN, Philip
Franco will have no choice. New Repub 156:13-14 F 18 '67
General assembly debate. New Repub 157:15-16 S 30 '67
High cost of historic rights. New Repub 156:13-14 Ja 28 '67

BEN, Philip—*Continued*
Israel and Nasser. New Repub 157:20-2 S 9
'67
Israel's will to survive. New Repub 156:12-13
Ap 15 '67
They're all afraid of America. New Repub
156:7-8 My 13 '67
Two Italys. New Repub 156:11-12 F 25 '67
Unsettlement is the Middle East prospect.
New Repub 157:10-11 N 25 '67
Waiting for a compromise. New Repub 157:
9-10 Jl 1 '67
What can and can't be done. New Repub 156:
6-7 Je 24 '67
BEN-AZIZ, A.
Nobiletin is main fungistat in tangerines
resistant to mal secco. bibliog Science 155:
1026-7 F 24 '67
BEN BARKA, Mehdi
L'affaire est finie. Time 89:39 Je 16 '67
BEN GURION, David
Travel notes. R. Joseph. Esquire 68:31-2+
S '67
Traveler, consider my Israel; ed. by R.
Joseph. pors Esquire 68:94-5+ Jl '67
BEN YAHMED, Bechir
Problems of independence; a look at the
third world; interview. por U S News 63:
80-1 S 4 '67
BENARDE, Melvin A. and Goldberg, H. S.
Chemical disinfection in industry, food, and
agriculture. Science 155:490 Ja 27 '67
BENCE, A. E. See Hollister, L. S. jt. auth.
BENCE Jones proteins. See Proteins
BENCH saws. See Saws
BENCHES
Build a storage bench for lounging. il Pop
Gard 18:76-7 My '67
How to make the sailmaker's bench. H.
Wicks. il Pop Sci 191:122-3 Jl '67
BENCHLEY, Nathaniel
Ombudsman; story. New Yorker 43:33-5 Jl
1 '67
Re-learning the basics. Writer 80:28-30 Ap '67
BENCHLEY, Peter
Shark! Holiday 42:68-9+ N '67
BENCI, Ginevra
Leonardo's Ginevra. W. Karp. il Horizon 9:24-
9 Aut '67
Notes and comment. New Yorker 43:39 Mr
25 '67
BENDER, Horace, pseud. See Greenough, H.
BENDER, Marylin
How Jacqueline Kennedy influences the way
you look. Redbook 129:52+ Ag '67
BENDINER, Elmer
America absurd. Nation 204:441-2 Ap 3 '67
Cult of the majority. Nation 205:57-8 Jl
17 '67
Machismo. Nation 205:283-4 S 25 '67
BENDINER, Robert
Thirties; when culture came to Main Street;
excerpt from Just around the corner. Sat
R 50:19-21 Ap 1 '67
about
Happy days. S. Maloff. il Newsweek 69:106+
My 8 '67
Ironical chronicle. Time 89:112 Ap 28 '67
BENEDICT, Mary
Freedom of the high school press? NEA J
56:64-6 D '67
BENEDICT, Nelson
With the sport fishermen. See issues of
Yachting
BENEDIKT, Michael
Completed pattern. Poetry 109:262-6 Ja '67
Some litanies; Fraudulent days; From a win-
dow; Visual face; poems. Poetry 110:78-82
My '67
BENEFIT performances of opera. See Opera—
Benefit performances
BENEFIT societies
Unfraternal takeover; fight for management
control at Lutheran brotherhood. Bsns W
p 177 S 30 '67
BENESH notation. See Dance notation
BENET, James
Googol! Am Ed 3:9-10 O '67
BENGALIS
Atlantic report. F. Levine. Atlan 219:24+ Mr
'67
BENITEZ, Helena H. See Murray, M. R. jt.
auth.
BENITÉZ, Manuel. See Cordobés
BENITO Cereno; drama. See Lowell, R.
BENJAMIN, Annette Francis
Health in the home. See issues of American
home

BENJAMIN, Mary A.
Autopen; excerpts from The collector. Hob-
bies 72:108-9+ O '67
BENJAMIN, Selma
How many blocks to New York? Library J
93:265-6 Ja 15 '68
BENJELLOUN, Othman
Morocco's first modern industrialist. il por
Fortune 75:79 F '67
BENKO, Gregor
Keyboard in perspective. Am Rec G 33:870-1
My '67
—and Santaella, William
Piano roll legacy. Hi Fi 17:51-3 Jl '67
BENNETT, Arnold
Writer by trade, by D. Barker. Review
New Yorker 43:189-90+ Ap 15 '67. V. S.
Pritchett
BENNETT, Bruce
Variations on a theme; poem. Nation 204:604
My 8 '67
BENNETT, C. Faye
Bird Island; poem. Cath World 204:295 F '67
BENNETT, Charles Edward
Keeping Congress honest. D. Bonafede. il
Newsweek 69:29-30 Ap 3 '67
BENNETT, Doug
But how do I cool the water? U S Camera
30:28+ D '67
BENNETT, Edna
Woman on the run. U S Camera 30:44-5+
S '67
BENNETT, Gordon C.
Exploring history's heartland. Travel 128:56-
60 Jl '67
BENNETT, Hank
Short-wave listening. See issues of Popular
electronics
BENNETT, Joan
Look of a garden, five floors up. il por House
& Gard 132:100-3 Ag '67
BENNETT, John
On D. H. Lawrence and his snake; poem.
New Yorker 43:46 Ap 22 '67
BENNETT, John C.
Christians look at revolution. Christian Cent
84:137-8 F 1 '67
about
Earl lectures are heard by 1,000. E. T.
Culver. Christian Cent 84:293-4 Mr 1 '67
BENNETT, Leon
Red cell slip at a wall in vitro. bibliog Sci-
ence 155:1554-6 Mr 24 '67
BENNETT, Lerone, Jr
Black vote revolt in the Bahamas. Ebony
22:68-70+ Je '67
How to stop riots. Ebony 22:29-32+ O '67
Negro in textbooks; reading, 'riting and
racism. Ebony 22:130-2+ Mr '67
What's in a name? Negro vs. Afro-American
vs. black. Ebony 23:46-8+ N '67
BENNETT, Paul A.
Grabhorns; their methods and best books.
Pub W 191:96+ Mr 6 '67
BENNETT, Richard Rodney
Britain's avant-garde. P. L. Miller. Am Rec
G 33:623 Ap '67
Penny for a song. Criticism
Hi Fi il 18:MA24+ Ja '68
BENNETT, Robert LaFollette
New era for the American Indian. por Natur
Hist 76:6-8+ F '67
BENNETT, Rowena
Waking the daffodil; drama. Plays 26:73-4 Ap
'67
BENNETT, W. Tapley, Jr
United States and Portugal amend cotton
textile agreement. Dept State Bul 57:548-9
O 23 '67
BENNETT, Wallace Foster
Vietnam; world war III, Communist style;
address, October 23, 1967. por U S News
63:108-13 N 6 '67
BENNINGTON college, Bennington, Vt.
Bennington college. R. Atcheson. il Holiday
42:46-9+ S '67
Bennington college dance group, 92nd street Y.
D. Hering. Dance Mag 41:29-30 Ag '67
BENOIT, Emile
East-West business cooperation. New Repub
156:21-3 F 18 '67
BENOLKEN, R. M. and Russell, C. J.
Tetrodotoxin blocks a graded sensory response
in the eye of limulus. bibliog Science 155:
1576-7 Mr 24 '67
—See Malawista, S. E. jt. auth.
BENSCH, Klaus G. and others
Absorption of intact protein molecules across
the pulmonary air-tissue barrier. bibliog
Science 157:1204-6 S 8 '67
BENSON, Arnold
Upper hand; story. Redbook 129:84-5 Jl '67

BENSON, Charles S.
Why the schools flunk out. Nation 204:463-6
Ap 10 '67
BENSON, Dennis C.
Waynesburg: a study in religion on the
campus. J. P. Park. Christian Cent 84:1084-6
Ag 23 '67
BENSON, Elaine
Philolaos. Craft Horiz 27:32-3+ S '67
Shopping in Europe. **Craft Horiz 27:23+ My**
'67
BENSON, Emanuel
Julio Le Parc; the craft of light. Craft Horiz
27:26-9 Jl '67
BENSON, Hal Johns
Hal Johns Benson exploits his marine back-
ground; with biographical sketch. il por Am
Artist 31:42-3+ D '67
BENSON, Philip F. and Young, P. M.
Suppression by actidione of development of
rat liver L-tyrosine: 2-oxoglutarate amino-
transferase activity. biblog Science 159:97
Ja 5 '68
BENTLEY, Eric
Theater of commitment; excerpt from ad-
dress. Commentary 42:63-72 D '66; 43:10+
Mr '67
(tr) See Biermann, W. Four ballads of Wolf
Biermann: Ballad on the poet Francois
Villon; Brigitte; Early morning; Ballad of
the man
about
Bentley award. Nation 204:229 F 20 '67
BENTLEY, Lloyd K.
Pictures & poetry; photographs. Pop Phot
61:77-80 D '67
BENTLEY, Nelson
Five poets. D. W. Baker. Poetry 109:401-2
Mr '67
BENTON, Robert
Dynamic duo. il por Newsweek 70:84 N 6
'67
—See Newman, D. jt. auth.
BENTWOOD furniture. See Furniture, Bent-
wood
BENVENUTI, Nino
Arrivederci. Nino Benvenuti. T. **Maule.** il
por Sports Illus 26:20-3 My 1 '67
Mamma mia! il por Newsweek 69:94 My 1 '67
Never a champ like Nino. T. Thompson. il
pors Life 62:78+ Je 2 '67
BENZEDRINE. See Amphetamines
BENZENE triethiodide. See Gallamine triethio-
dide
BENZINGER, M. G.
Old roses to treasure. Home Gard 54:47+ F
'67
BENZPYRENE hydroxylase. See Enzymes
BEQUESTS. See Wills
BEQUIA (island)
St Vincent and Bequia. J. Egan. il Atlan
220:122-3+ D '67
Two rebels with a lovely cause; Johnston's
planless house, Moonhole. C. Phinizy. il
Sports Illus 26:42-6 F 27 '67
BERANEK, Leo L.
Street and air traffic noise, and what we
can do about it. UNESCO Courier 20:12-17+
Jl '67
BERBERIAN, Cathy
Bel canto & the Beatles. il por Time 89:58
Je 2 '67
BERCHTESGADEN
Berchtesgaden revisited; how the Nazi play-
ground passed into private hands. il News-
week 69:85 F 20 '67
BERDOY, Pierre
Berdoy portfolio. il Craft Horiz 27:17-23 Ja '67
BEREAVEMENT
Broken heart syndrome. Newsweek 70:92 O
23 '67
Portion of thyself. A. Silberman. Read Digest
90:157-60 Mr '67
BERENDT, John
If they've found another assassin, let them
name names and produce their evidence.
Esquire 68:80-2+ Ag '67
BERENSON, Ruth
Art. Nat R 19:648+, 1028+, 1434-7 Je 13,
S 19, D 26 '67
Op, pop, and the real thing. Nat R 19:648+
Je 13 '67
BERENSTAIN, Janice. See Berenstain, S. jt.
auth.
BERENSTAIN, Stanley, and Berenstain, Janice
It's all in the family. See issues of McCall's
BERG, Alan D.
Malnutrition and national development. For
Affairs 46:126-36 O '67
BERG, Alban
From Butterfly to Wozzeck. H. Kupferberg.
il Atlan 220:124+ N '67

Lulu. Criticism
New Repub 157:31-2 Jl 15 '67
New Yorker 43:64 Jl 1 '67
New Yorker 43:154+ O 14 '67
Sat R 50:32 Jl 8 '67
Sat R 50:54 O 21 '67
Sat R il 50:43-5 D 30 '67
Pierre Boulez conducts Wozzeck. A. Sperber.
il Am Rec G 33:1064-6 Ag '67
Records:
Wozzeck. Opera N 32:38 D 9 '67
Three views of Wozzeck. G. **Perle.** il Sat R
50:54-5 D 2 '67
BERG, Barbara Anne
Legacy; poem. Mlle 65:306 Ag '67
BERG, Phil
House of a thousand treasures. W. Wilson.
il House B 109:124-7+ F '67
BERG, Roland H.
For us, the big change is now! Look 31:41-2
Mr 21 '67
Where did all the nurses go? Nurse in train-
ing. Look 32:26+ Ja 23 '68
Why Americans hide behind a chemical cur-
tain. Look 31:12-13 Ag 8 '67
BERG, Stephen
Between us; poem. New Yorker 42:132 F 11 '67
BERG, P, collection. See Art—Private collec-
tions
BERGAMO, Italy
Music
Revivals: Donizetti and Paisiello. W. **Wea-**
ver. Hi Fi 17:MA27 Ja '67
BERGAMOT oil
Bergamot country; Reggio. L. Gardiner. At-
lan 220:104-5 Jl '67
BERGANZA, Teresa
Breath of spring; interview, ed. by G. Fitz-
gerald. por Opera N 31:16 F 25 '67
BERGDORF Goodman company. See New York
(city)—Stores
BERGEN, Candice
Africa: Safari. por Vogue 149:146-7+ Ap 1 '67
Is Bel Air burning? il por Esquire 68:138-41+
D '67
about
Candy Bergen, golden girl. R. Hochstein. il
pors Good H 164:34+ My '67
BERGEN international festival. See Music
festivals—Norway
BERGENDOFF, Conrad
Luther and Lutheranism today. Cath World
206:63-7 N '67
BERGENIA
Winter blooming garden standby. il Sunset
138:232 F '67
BERGER, Arthur
Entertainment culture. Nation 205:228-9 S 18
'67
Politics of entertainment. Nation 205:422-4
O 30 '67
BERGER, Hillard, and Yanofsky, Charles
Suppressor selection for amino acid replace-
ments expected on the basis of the genetic
code. biblog Science 156:394-7 Ap 21 '67
BERGER, Ivan
Affording high fidelity. Sat R 50:62 Je 24 '67
Automatic transports. Sat R 50:51 Jl 29 '67
Doctor Dolby's dilly. Sat R 50:74-5 Mr 25 '67
Hi-fi. Esquire 67:36+ Mr '67
Hi-fi; FM. Esquire 68:18+ N '67
Hi-fi in the halls of Hilton. Sat R 50:66-8
S 16 '67
How high the hi-fi sights. Sat R 50:73+ Ap
29 '67
Progress and renaissance, audio 1967. Sat R
50:61+ O 28 '67
Recording off the air. Sat R 50:72-3 Ja 28 '67
Sound of sound-on-sound. Sat R 50:57 D 2
'67
Years of stereo and solid state. Sat R 50:70-1
Ag 26 '67
Zero VU. Sat R 50:87 F 25 '67
BERGER, John
In the beginning there was art. Nation 206:
88-9+ Ja 15 '68
Notes for an essay on Rodin. Nation 205:
661-3 D 18 '67
BERGER, Rainer. See Taylor, R. E; Wells,
P. V. jt. auths.
BERGER, Robert J.
Winterizing your power mower. Am Home
70:142+ O '67
BERGER, Thomas
Application to elysium; story. Esquire 68:
214-16 D '67
BERGER, Wolfgang H.
Foraminiferal ooze: solution at depths. biblog
Science 156:383-5 Ap 21 '67
—and Soutar, Andrew
Planktonic foraminifera: field experiment on
production rate. biblog Science 156:1495-7
Je 16 '67

BERGES, Ruth
    Poet as music critic. Am Rec G 33:692-6+
      My '67
BERGESON, C. A.
    Guide to silicone masonry water repellents.
      Arch Rec 141:181-2 Ja '67
BERGGRAV, Karl
    Grow philodendrons in many varieties. Horti-
      culture 45:20-1+ Mr '67
BERGH, Henry
    Great meddler. G. Carson. il por Am Heritage
      19:28-33+ D '67
BERGMAN, Ingrid
    New heartbreak in Ingrid Bergman's life. M.
      S. Davis. il pors Good H 164:54-7+ Ja '67
    One thing at a time. pors Time 90:53 S 8 '67
    Shining return for Ingrid. T. Prideaux. il pors
      Life 63:63-4+ O 13 '67
BERGMAN, Ray
    Ray Bergman says goodbye. pors Outdoor Life
      139:4+ My '67
                    about
    Obituary
        Outdoor Life por 139:4 My '67
BERGQUIST, G. William
    Obituary
        Pub W 191:37 Je 12 '67
BERGQUIST, Laura
    Cuba. Look 31:32-40+ D 12 '67
BERGS, Victor V. and Scotti, T. M.
    Virus-induced peliosis hepatis in rats. bibliog
      Science 158:377-8 O 20 '67
BERGSTRÖM, Sune
    Prostaglandins: members of a new hormonal
      system. bibliog il Science 157:382-91 Jl 28 '67
BERIĬA, Lavrentii Pavlovich
    Real man from Smersh. R. Conquest. il
      pors N Y Times Mag p36-7+ N 5 '67
    Twenty letters to a friend, by S. Allilueva.
      Review
        Sat R 50:33-4+ O 7 '67. H. E. Salisbury
BERING glacier, Alaska. See Glaciers
BERING ISLAND
    See also
    Zoology—Bering Island
BERING SEA REGION
    Bering land bridge: evidence of spruce in
      late-Wisconsin times. P. A. Colinvaux. bib-
      liog il Science 156:380-3 Ap 21 '67
BERIO, Luciano
    Music. E. Boretz. Nation 204:123-4 Ja 23 '67
    Music to my ears; Passaggio presented at
      Juilliard school. I. Kolodin. Sat R 50:56+
      Ja 28 '67
    Musical events. W. Sargeant. New Yorker
      42:105 Ja 21 '67
BERIOZOFF, Nicholas
    Who is a ballet master? J. Anderson. il por
      Dance Mag 42:54-7+ Ja '68
BERKE, Jacqueline
    Tourist in the wake of war. Sat R 50:40-1+
      O 14 '67
BERKELEY, Mary Emlen (Lowell) Lloyd
      Berkeley, countess of
    From Boston to Berkeley square. E. Weeks.
      Atlan 220:136 O '67
BERKELEY, Molly. See Berkeley, M. E. L. L.
    B. countess of
BERKELEY Baptist divinity school. See
    Theological schools
BERKES, Ross N.
    Indian-Pakistani relations. bibliog f Cur Hist
      52:289-94+ My '67
BERKNER, Lloyd Viel
    Lloyd Berkner dies at 62. J. Anderson. il por
      Science 156:1349 Je 9 '67
BERKSHIRE community college, Pittsfield,
    Mass.
    Berkshire college, a rural campus with urban
      vitality. il Arch Rec 142:166-7 N '67
BERKSHIRE symphonic festival
    Faithful to Fidelio; original score conducted
      by E. Leinsdorf at Tanglewood. Time 90:42
      Ag 18 '67
    Tanglewood; first version of Beethoven's Fi-
      delio. S. Jenkins. Opera N 32:20 S 23 '67
BERL, Walter G.
    Intelligent man's guide to the 1967 AAAS
      meeting. Science 158:1342 D 8 '67
BERLAND, Theodore
    Fog that saves lives. Read Digest 90:33-4+
      Mr '67
    Lifesaving jobs where you earn as you
      learn. Todays Health 45:36-41+ F '67
    Professionals who help humanity. Todays
      Health 45:52-5+ Ap '67
    Roentgen's magic rays. Todays Health 45:58-
      9+ Mr '67
    Rural patient gets a break. Todays Health
      45:62-7 O '67
    Schooled to save lives. Todays Health 45:50-
      5+ Mr '67
    When your skin turns dry. Todays Health 46:
      12-15 Ja '68

BERLE, Adolf Augustus
    Analyzing the corporate-complex. Sat R 50:
      29-30 Je 24 '67
    Uncharted esthetics. Sat R 50:35+ N 4 '67
BERLIN, Irving
    He wanted to murder the bugler. B. Catton.
      il por Am Heritage 18:50-5+ Ag '67
    Sheet music. A. Debus. il por Hobbies 72:125
      Ag '67
BERLIN

                    Description
    Thomas Wolfe's Berlin. C. H. Holman. il
      Sat R 60:66+ Mr 11 '67
    Two faces of Berlin. J. Faber. il U S Camera
      30:56-7+ Ag '67

                Economic conditions
    Is West Berlin's economic life gradually ebb-
      ing away? il Bsns W p 124-7 Ap 1 '67

                    History
                Allied occupation, 1945-
    See also
    Berlin wall, 1961-
BERLIN (East Berlin)
    Letter from Berlin (cont) J. Wechsberg. New
      Yorker 43:197-200+ N 18 '67
    Preposterous scar of a going city; the Berlin
      wall. G. P. Hunt. Life 62:3 Mr 3 '67
    Tale of two half cities. J. C. Evans. Chris-
      tian Cent 84:135-6 F 1 '67
    Two million people in a pen! C. P. Streeter.
      il Farm J 91:62A-62B Ap '67

                    Music
    Berlin. J. H. Sutcliffe. Opera N 31:31 Mr 4
      '67
    Berlin; East Berlin's Staatsoper. J. H. Sut-
      cliffe. Opera N 31:32 Ap 8 '67
    Komische oper; near-perfect. P. Moor.
      Hi Fi 17:MA24-MA25 F '67
    Theatre in Europe; Verdi's La Traviata at
      the Komische oper. H. Clurman. Nation
      205:92-4 Jl 31 '67

                    Theater
    Theater in Europe; productions at the Ber-
      liner ensemble. H. Clurman. Nation 205:
      92-4 Jl 31 '67
BERLIN (West Berlin)
    Memo from Berlin; the new threat from
      within. W. Long. Look 31:110 D 12 '67
    Tale of two half cities. J. C. Evans. Chris-
      tian Cent 84:135-6 F 1 '67

                    Churches
    Germany 1967; Kaiser Wilhelm Gedächtnis-
      kirche. D. P. Moynihan. Atlan 219:43-4 My
      '67

                Economic conditions
    Mission to Moscow; West Germany improv-
      ing trade through International fashion
      festival. il Time 90:38-9 S 15 '67
    West Berlin; the story of a city in decline.
      il U S News 63:81-2 D 4 '67

                    Music
    Berlin. J. H. Sutcliffe. il Opera N 31:31 Mr
      4; 28 Ap 15 '67
    Notes from our correspondents. P. Moor. il
      Hi Fi 17:16+ Mr '67
    Report: Berlin; scheduled world premieres
      and revivals. J. H. Sutcliffe. Opera N 32:
      32 D 16 '67

                Politics and government
    Hero's decline; mayor resigns. Newsweek 70:
      38+ O 9 '67
    Problems for a protégé. il Time 90:34-5 O
      27 '67

                Public buildings
    Letter from Berlin; new cultural center. J.
      Wechsberg. New Yorker 43:192-7 N 18 '67
BERLIN festival. See Music festivals—Ger-
    many (Federal Republic)
BERLIN film festival. See Moving picture fes-
    tivals
BERLIN free university. See Colleges and uni-
    versities—Germany (Federal Republic)
BERLIN philharmonic orchestra
    Music to my ears; Bach programs in Car-
      negie Hall. I. Kolodin. Sat R 50:38-9 D 16
      '67
    Musical events; performance of Brandenburg
      concertos and other Bach items. W. Sar-
      geant. New Yorker 43:225-6 D 9 '67
BERLIN question, 1945-
    Is West Berlin's economic life gradually ebb-
      ing away? il Bsns W p 124-7 Ap 1 '67
    See also
    Berlin wall, 1961-

BERLIN wall, 1961-
Berlin, by E. L. Dulles. Review
  Sat R 50:44 Je 10 '67. L. L. Snyder
Design for a nightmare; new wall. il Time
  90:35 D 8 '67
Preposterous scar of a going city.   G. P.
  Hunt. Life 62:3 Mr 3 '67
Two million people in a pen! C. P. Streeter.
  il Farm J 91:62A-62B Ap '67
West Berlin; the story of a city in decline.
  il U S News 63:81-2 D 4 '67
BERLINERS
Is West Berlin's economic life gradually ebb-
  ing away? il Bsns W p 124-7 Ap 1 '67
BERLIOZ, Hector
Boom in Berlioz. E. Greenfield. Hi Fi 17:
  MA26+ Ap '67
Musical events; performance of The damna-
  tion of Faust by N.Y. philharmonic. W.
  Sargeant. New Yorker 43:193-4 D 2 '67
Les Troyens (Trojan men) Criticism
  Hi Fi 17:MA22-3 Ja '67
BERLITZ schools of languages
Berlitz taught me Russian in a hurry. J.
  Roddy. Look 31:M6+ O 3 '67
Brainwashing to teach; Total immersion
  course. il Time 89:63-4 F 17 '67
BERLOWITZ, Laurence, and Birnstiel, M. L.
Histones in the wild-type and the anucleolate
  mutant of xenopus laevis. bibliog Science
  156:78-80 Ap 7 '67
BERMAN, Emile Zola
Where are they now? il por Newsweek 69:12
  F 6 '67
BERMAN, Eugene
Interview; ed. by A. Fatt. il por Dance Mag
  41:52 Mr '67
BERMAN, Harold J. and Garson, J. R.
Road to trade. Nation 204:626-8 My 15 '67
BERMAN, Helen M. and others
Anomeric bond-character in the pyranose
  sugars. bibliog Science 157:1576-7 S 29 '67
BERMAN, Michael B.
Moorestown builds modern neighborhood cen-
  ter. por Parks & Rec 2:36-7 My '67
BERMUDA
Beautiful, busybody Bermuda. A. Bester.
  il Holiday 42:46-55+ N '67
Bermuda's off-shore isles. A. R. Pastore, jr.
  il Travel 128:35-6 O '67
News from Bermuda. J. Silver. Mlle 66:37-8
  Ja '68
Old flame: Bermuda. G. Bradshaw. Vogue 149:
  231+ Mr 1 '67
BERMUDA to Denmark race. See Yacht racing
BERMÚDEZ, José Ygnacio
Bermúdez-Dignac exhibits in Caracas. il por
  Américas 19:41 N '67
BERN, Howard A.
Hormones and endocrine glands of fishes.
  bibliog Science 158:455-62 O 27 '67
BERNAC, Pierre
Poulenc and Bernac, French song, with pure
  pleasure the aim. N. Rorem. il pors Hi Fi
  17:85-6 N '67
Stuff of legend. R. Gelatt. Reporter 37:45 S
  7 '67
BERNAD, Miguel A.
Blunder in Laos. America 117:766-9 D 23 '67
BERNADOTTE AF WISBORG, Lennart, greve
Mike Frome. M. Frome. Am For 73:3+ Ag
  '67
BERNANOS, Georges
Bernanos: the writer as child. R. Coles. New
  Repub 156:23-7 Ap 15 '67
BERNARD, Ian
Chocolates. Criticism
  Commonweal 86:126 Ap 14 '67
  New Yorker 43:148 Ap 22 '67
BERNARD, Jessie, and Lobsenz, N. M.
Why husbands and wives remain strangers.
  Redbook 129:60-1+ O '67
BERNARD, Sidney
Poet at the podium. Nation 204:534-6 Ap 24 '67
Poetry, drama in Harlem. Nation 204:826-7
  Je 26 '67
Sholom Aleichem in the park. Nation 205:
  124-5 Ag 14 '67
**BERNARD Geis associates. See Geis, Bernard,
  associates**
BERNARDI, Herschel
Commercial for Herschel. New Yorker 43:42-3
  Mr 25 '67
BERNE, Eric
Games analysis adds flavor to psychiatry.
  P. McBroom. il por Sci N 91:308-9 Ap 1 '67
BERNE copyright convention. See Copyright
BERNHARD, Arnold
Value Line vs. all comers. por Fortune 76:
  240+ N '67

BERNHARDT, Sarah
Madame Sarah, by C. O. Skinner. Review
  Nation 204:472-3 Ap 10 '67. H. Clurman
  Reporter 36:58+ F 9 '67. G. Culligan
  Vogue 149:44 Ja 15 '67. M. Mannes
Madame Sarah; condensation. C. O. Skinner.
  il por Read Digest 90:227-30+ Ap '67
BERNINGHAUSEN, David K.
Teaching a commitment to intellectual free-
  dom; adaptation of address, January 14,
  1967. por Library J 92:3601-5 O 15 '67
BERNS, William A.
Where film buyers meet sellers. Sat R 50:45
  D 23 '67
BERNSTEIN, Burton
Decline and fall of Becky. Esquire 67:22+
  F '67
BERNSTEIN, Irving
Comparison of industrial and race conflict.
  Mo Labor R 90:39-40 Jl '67
BERNSTEIN, Leonard
Mahler: his time has come. Hi Fi 17:51-4
  S '67
          about
Bernstein to relinquish post in 1969 (or be-
  fore?) por Hi Fi 17:MA2 Ja '67
Bernstein's Mahler: a prophecy fulfilled.
  M. N. Kanny. il por Am Rec G 34:278-81
  D '67
Bernstein's majestic Mahler 8th. I. Kolodin.
  il Sat R 50:65 Ja 28 '67
Blinding facility of Leonard Bernstein. M.
  Mayer. por Esquire 67:66-8+ F '67
How to think about Leonard Bernstein. J.
  Roddy. por Look 32:74-7 Ja 9 '68
Lively arts. R. Hemming. il por Sr Schol 89:
  22 Ja 20; 91:21-2 D 7 '67
Musical events; shared conducting of concert
  by New York philharmonic. W. Sargeant.
  New Yorker 43:203-4 O 21 '67
Once and future Bernstein. R. Gelatt. Re-
  porter 36:49-51 F 23 '67
Recordings. M. Mayer. Esquire 67:38 F '67
Triumph by Lenny and Mahler. S. Kanfer.
  Life 63:12 N 3 '67
BERNSTEIN, Marion
On the go, by car. il U S Camera 30:46-7+
  My '67
BERNSTEIN, Merton C.
Pensions: unsafe at any age? Duns R 89:
  32-3+ Ja '67
BERNSTEIN, Victor H.
Reunion in Warsaw; remembering Nurem-
  berg. Nation 204:112-16 Ja 23 '67
TV editorials: How brave & free? Nation 205:
  170-3, 318 S 4, O 2 '67
Where have all the flowers gone? Redbook
  128:78-9+ Mr '67
BERREMAN, Gerald D.
On the role of women. Bul Atomic Sci 22:26-
  8 N '66; 23:28-9 Mr '67
BERRIAULT, Gina
Watched: the new student president. Esquire
  68:93+ S '67
BERRIES
What you should know about buying and
  caring for fresh berries. H. McCully.
  House B 109:173 My '67
          See also
Cookery—Fruit
  also names of berries, e.g. Blueberries
BERRIGAN, Daniel
I am never complete; Unfinished man; Of
  fair love the mother; Somehow; This
  crucifix; Wedding; poems. Poetry 111:31-5
  O '67
          about
Authors & editors. por Pub W 191:43 F 27 '67
BERRIGAN, Philip
Musings from Baltimore city jail. Common-
  weal 87:195-6 N 17 '67
          about
News and views; fund raising to defray ex-
  penses for coming trial. J. Deedy. Com-
  monweal 87:426 Ja 12 '68
BERRISFORD, Anthony
Poland. Travel 127:56-61 Je '67
BERRY, Graham
Explosion in astronomy. Sci Digest 61:43-54
  My '67
BERRY, James R.
How to walk on the moon. Pop Mech 128:
  228+ O '67; Same. Sci Digest 62:6-8 N '67
Infrared: lighting up the invisible. Sci Di-
  gest 62:40-7+ N '67
Lightning is as deadly as ever. Pop Mech 128:
  64-7+ Ag '67
New electronic war on burglars. Pop Mech
  128:86-9 D '67

BERRY, James R.—*Continued*
They dive for wrecks. Pop Mech 127:92-4+ Mr '67
What sun glare can do to your driving. Pop Mech 128:78-80+ Jl '67
BERRY, Joe
Parents who love other people's children. J. Devaney. il por Redbook 130:48-9+ D '67
BERRY, Michael
Just for laughs. Look 31:72 Je 27 '67
BERRY, Walter
Happy scrappers. il por Time 89:72 F 10 '67
BERRY, Warren
Soccer business kicks off. Duns R 90:49-50+ N '67
BERRY, Wendell
Marriage; Grace; Burial of the old; To think of the life of a man; Dead calf; Do not be ashamed; poems. Poetry 110:148-52 Je '67
Response to a war. Nation 204:527-8 Ap 24 '67
Stones; poem. Nation 205:312 O 2 '67
BERRYMAN, John
Three sonnets; They may suppose because I would not cloy your ear; Our Sunday morning when dawn-priests were applying; A broken heart, but can a heart break now? Mlle 64:154 Ap '67
about
Whisky and ink, whisky and ink. J. Howard. il pors Life 63:67-8+ Jl 21 '67
BERSON, Minnie Perrin
Save them young. Am Ed 3:5-8 Jl '67
BERSON, Robert C.
University medicine; letter. Sat R 50:71 My 6 '67
BERTHOFF, Warner
Ambitious scheme. Commentary 44:110-12+ O '67
BERTMAN, Bernard, and Guyer, R. A.
Solid helium. Sci Am 217:84-95 Ag '67
BERTOLUCCI, Bernardo
Current cinema. P. Kael. New Yorker 43:94-5 Ja 13 '68
BERTRAND, Mireille
Training without reward: traditional training of pig-tailed macaques as coconut harvesters. bibliog Science 155:484-6 Ja 27 '67
BERTRANDE Meyers, Sister. See Meyers, B.
BERUBE, Maurice R.
Bundy's plan for New York schools. Commonweal 87:349-50 D 15 '67
De facto anticlimax. Commonweal 86:438-9 Jl 14 '67
Education and the poor. Commonweal 86:46-8 Mr 31 '67
Quiet revolution. New Repub 156:26-8 Mr 25 '67
BERWYN, Ill.
Melter makes the snow disappear. il Am City 82:45 D '67
BERYLLIUM
Aluminum-26 and beryllium-10 in Greenland ice. R. McCorkell and others. bibliog il Science 158:1690-2 D 29 '67
Beryllium-10 in a manganese nodule. B. L. K. Somayajulu. bibliog il Science 156:1219-20 Je 2 '67
BESHIRI, Patricia
Eight ways to have an extra vacation without leaving town. Parents Mag 42:36-7+ Jl '67
BESPALOFF, Alexis
Wines to drink young. House & Gard 132:260+ N '67
BESS, Donovan
Rage for awareness. Nation 204:243-4+ F 20 '67
BESSON, Frank Schaeffer, 1910–
From factory to foxhole: a 10,000-mile pipeline to war; excerpts from address, May 12, 1967. por U S News 62:98-9 Je 19 '67
BEST, Raymond M.
New tank goes in an old one. Am City 82:125-6 O '67
BEST books. See Books and reading—Best books
BEST of sports; drama. See Cable, H.
BEST play awards. See New York drama critics circle
BEST regards to Mr Cary Grant; story. See Madocs, R.
BEST sellers
Best sellers of the week. See issues of Publisher's weekly
Court denies injunction against Chicago tribune; alleged improper listing of The arrangement. Pub W 192:157-8 Jl 10 '67
Hardcover best sellers of 1966 in the U.S. book trade. A. P. Hackett. il Pub W 191:40-2 Ja 30 '67

Little red book; world sales of Quotations from chairman Mao Tse-tung. S. K. Oberbeck. Newsweek 69:102 Je 5 '67
1966 paperback best sellers in the bookstores. Pub W 191:43-6 Ja 30 '67
Sneak preview of the fall's best sellers. McCalls 94:6+ Ag '67
Stein and Day sues Chicago tribune; alleged improper listing of The arrangement. Pub W 191:44 My 29 '67
Trade winds. H. R. Mayes. Sat R 50:10 My 13 '67
Trade winds; 1927 season. H. R. Mayes. Sat R 50:14 S 9 '67
World of books. L. Friedman. Writer 81:4+ Ja '68

Anecdotes, facetiae, satire, etc.
How to write a best seller. L. Rosten. Look 31:12 Ag 22 '67
BESTER, Alfred
Beautiful, busybody Bermuda. Holiday 42:46-55+ N '67
Chicago sights and delights. Holiday 41:133-7 Mr '67
BESTERMAN, Jean K.
Christine discovers love. Good H 164:60+ My '67
BETA sitosterol. See Sitosterols
BETHE, Hans Albrecht
Oppenheimer: where he was there was always life and excitement. Science 155:1080-4 Mr 3 '67
about
Nobel prizes; physics. V. F. Weisskopf. por Science 158:745-6 N 10 '67
Quick and the cosmic. por Newsweek 70:106+ N 13 '67
Stoking mechanism of stellar furnaces. por Sci N 92:463-4 N 11 '67
BETHEL, Paul D.
Can Castro start a new Vietnam? Nat R 19:130-4 F 7 '67
BETHESDA, Md.

Architecture
Unforced simplicity for a Unitarian church. il Arch Rec 144:129-32 Ja '67
BETHLEHEM, Jordan
Take the no. 22 bus to Bethlehem! il Look 31:32 D 26 '67
BETJEMAN, John
Subaltern's love-song. N Y Times Mag p25 Ag 13 '67
about
Betjeman phenomenon. W. Petschek. il por N Y Times Mag p24-5+ Ag 13 '67; Reply. E. V. Halbmeier. p62 S 10 '67
BETTAUER, Arthur
Strategy for divestments; address, October 5, 1966. Harvard Bsns R 45:116-24 Mr '67
BETTELHEIM, Bruno
Dialogue with mothers. See issues of Ladies' home journal
Parent and child. N Y Times Mag p65+ F 12 '67
Speaking out. por Sat Eve Post 240:10+ Mr 11 '67
Survival of the Jews. New Repub 157:23-30 Jl 1 '67
about
World without I. il por Newsweek 69:70-1 Mr 27 '67
BETTER boys foundation
Small awakening. il Ebony 22:154-5 Je '67
BETTER business bureaus
Don't fall for home-repair gyps. il Changing T 21:13-16 My '67
BETTING. See Gambling
BETTIS, Joseph Dabney
New ethical vision. Christian Cent 84:208-10 F 15 '67
BEUM, Robert
May song. Commonweal 86:284 My 26 '67
BEV accelerators. See Accelerators (electrons, etc)
BEVER, Thomas G. See Mehler, J. jt. auth.
BEVERAGE industry. See Soft drink industry
BEVERAGES
Cooling drinks of summer and how to keep them icy. J. A. Beard. il House & Gard 132:112 Jl '67
Fresca blizzard. Newsweek 70:63 D 25 '67
Fresh fruit shakes; with recipes. il Seventeen 26:120-1+ Je '67
Frosty coolers men like. K. Schaller. il Farm J 91:56 Je '67
Hot beverages. il Bet Hom & Gard 45:120 N '67

BEVERAGES—*Continued*
How to make the beverages on our cover. il
Bet Hom & Gard 45:21 Je '67
Refreshing coolers for torrid days. G. Maddox. il Todays Health 45:14-17 Jl '67
Summer drinks, on the citrus circuit. W.
Clifford. House B 109:156-7+ Je '67
See also
Beer
Coffee
Punch (beverage)
Tea
Wine
BEVERLY HILLS, Calif.
Social life and customs
Is Bel Air burning? C. Bergen. il Esquire
68:138-41+ D '67
BEVERLY HILLS Friars club. See Los Angeles—Clubs
BEVINS, E. Marshall
Priest who practiced what he preached. W.
Peters. por Good H 165:82-3+ Ag '67
BEWLEY, Lois M.
Public library and the planning agency. bibliog por ALA Bul 61:968-74 S '67
BEYM, Richard
Teaching of English abroad. Américas 19:17-
19 Mr '67
BEZ, Frank
Camera takes a trip. M. Laurance. il U S
Camera 30:48-9 D '67
BEZZANT, Robert G.
Flood control brings beauty. Am City 82:73
Jl '67
BHAGAVADGITA. See Mahabharata—Bhagavadgita
BHASKAR
Bhaskar & co: dances of India; Village
theatre. J. Anderson. Dance Mag 41:30 Jl
'67
BHATIA, Krishan
India adrift. For Affairs 45:652-61 Jl '67
BHATNAGAR, Rajendra S. and others
Intracellular pool of unhydroxylated polypeptide precursors of collagen. bibliog Science 158:492-4 O 27 '67
BHUMIBOL Adulyadej, king of Thailand
United States and Thailand pledge to continue close cooperation to promote peace;
exchange of greetings and exchange of
toasts, June 27, with joint statement, June
29, 1967. Dept State Bul 57:62-4 Jl 17 '67
about
Visit with the king & queen of Thailand. G.
Zimmermann. il pors Look 31:86-91 Je 27 '67
BHUTAN
See also
Costume—Bhutan
Royal family
H.M. the queen of Bhutan, and her children.
il Vogue 150:84-7 Jl '67
BHUTANESE art. See Art, Bhutanese
BIALEK, Robert
View from a record dealer's window. Am Rec
G 34:92-4 O '67
BIANCHI, Eugene C.
Democracy in the church: why it must
work. America 117:79-82 Jl 22 '67
BIANCHI Y PÉREZ DE CASTRO, Manuel.
See Amaro, M. pseud.
BIASINY, Charles
Camera in the city; photographs. U S Camera
30:76-7 D '67
BIBBY, Geoffrey
Body in the bog. Horizon 10:44-51 Wint '68
BIBESCO, Marthe Lucie (Lahovary) princesse
Three friends of Proust. P. Kolb. il por Vogue
149:90-1 Mr 15 '67
BIBLE
Post-biblical Christianity. D. Callahan; discussion. Commonweal 85:359+, 606-7 Ja 6,
F 24 '67
Antiquities
See also
Israel—Antiquities
Jerusalem—Antiquities
Jordan—Antiquities
Bibliography
Bibles and related books for the fall. il
Pub W 192:70-3 S 25 '67
Bibles and related books for the spring. il
Pub W 191:67-70 F 27 '67
Biography
Isaac and Ishmael: 1967. N. B. McLeod.
Christian Cent 84:959-61 Jl 26 '67

Criticism, interpretation, etc.
Adam's fall: the task of reinterpretation. M.
Flick. Cath World 205:42-6 Ap '67
Bibles and related books for the fall. il
Pub W 192:73-5 S 25 '67
Bibles and related books for the spring. il
Pub W 119:67-72 F 27 '67
Exodus as autobiography. A. R. Gold. Commentary 43:46-51 My '67
Jerusalem and Athens; beginning of the Bible
and its Greek counterparts. L. Strauss.
Commentary 43:45-57 Je '67
Middle of the road. D. Meade. Christian
Cent 84:1436+ N 8 '67
Myth in the New Testament. Sister Alfreda
Marie. Cath World 205:171-5 Je '67
You shall be as Gods, by E. From. Review
Commentary 43:99-101 My '67. E. Isaac
Geography
Journey into the living world of the Bible.
M. B. Grosvenor. il Nat Geog Mag 132:494-
507 O '67
Lands of the Bible today. il Nat Geog Mag
132:796-7, sup(folded map) D '67
Hermeneutics
Fox and hedgehog. S. Keen. Christian Cent
84:344-5 Mr 15 '67
Language, hermeneutic, and word of God,
by R. W. Funk. Review
Christian Cent 84:142 F 1 '67. M. F. Allshouse
History
At last: one Bible for all Christians. J. Daniel.
il Read Digest 90:112-16 My '67
Inspiration
We're up to Deuteronomy. J. Shallit. Read
Digest 91:19-20+ Jl '67
Interpretation
See Bible—Criticism, interpretation, etc.
Philology
See Hebrew language
Reading
We're up to Deuteronomy. J. Shallit. Read
Digest 91:19-20+ Jl '67
Versions
At last: one Bible for all Christians; RSV.
J. Daniel. il Read Digest 90:112-16 My '67
Oxford's New Scofield: reference Bible. K.
Haselden. Christian Cent 84:582 My 3 '67
Scofield Bible; revised after fifty years. il
Pub W 191:67-72 F 27 '67
Old Testament
Justifying man's ways to man. B. Mandelbaum. Sat R 50:57-8 F 25 '67
Manuscripts
See also
Dead Sea scrolls
Exodus
Exodus as autobiography. A. R. Gold. Commentary 43:46-51 My '67
Ezekiel
Letter to Zeke: a commentary on Ezekiel.
R. M. Davidson. Cath World 206:153-4 Ja
'68
New Testament
See also
Apostles
Jesus Christ
Versions
Anti-Semitism and the Gospel; language of
the New Testament. M. D. Zeik. Commonweal 86:16-18 Mr 24 '67; Reply. C. H. Bishop
86:138-9+ Ap 21 '67
Gospels
See also
Jesus Christ—Miracles
Miracles
John
St John and faith. V. P. McCorry. America
117:360-inside back cover S 30 '67
Singular witness. V. P. McCorry. America
116:513-14 Ap 1 '67
Spiritual Gospel. V. P. McCorry. America
116:inside back cover Ap 8 '67
BIBLE characters. See Bible—Biography
BIBLICAL maps. See Bible—Geography
BIBLIOGRAPHY
Tabby cat and the elephant; basic meaning.
P. S. Dunkin. Library J 92:751 F 15 '67
See also subhead Bibliography under various subjects, e.g. Dogs—Bibliography

BIBLIOTHERAPY
See also
Libraries, Hospital
BICKEL, Alexander M.
Antitrust slowdown? New Repub 156:15-18 My 20; 33 Je 10 '67
CBS on the Warren report. New Repub 157: 29-30 Jl 15; 32+ Ag 19 '67
Death penalty litigation. New Repub 157:13-14 Ag 19 '67
Failure of the Warren report. Commentary 42:31-9 O '66; 43:23-6+ Ap '67
Law and prudence in the Powell case. New Repub 156:9-10 F 25 '67
Lawyers and more lawyers. New Repub 157: 24-5 S 23 '67
Obscenity cases. New Repub 156:15-17 My 27 '67
Premature verdict on Warren. New Repub 157:36-7 O 7 '67
Return to Dallas. New Repub 157:34 D 23 '67
Skelly Wright's sweeping decision. New Repub 157:11-12 Jl 8; 43 Ag 5 '67
Supreme court: internal security cases. New Repub 158:21-2 Ja 6 '68
BICKERS, Jack
Latest way to kill soybean weeds. Farm J 91:33+ Ap '67
BICKMORE, Lee S.
Turning men into decision-makers; interview. por Nations Bsns 55:88-90+ O '67
BICYCLE racing
Brutal business; cyclists and dope. Sports Illus 27:7 Ag 14 '67
Champion on wheels; O. Martin, jr. il Ebony 22:108+ S '67
Little something; Tom Simpson dies on Tour de France. Time 90:54 Jl 21 '67
Racing through dairyland; National bicycle championships. H. Peterson. il Sports Illus 27:20-1 Ag 21 '67
BICYCLE trails. See Trails
BICYCLE trips. See Cycling trips
BICYCLES
How to create a high-rise bike. il Pop Sci 191:125 N '67
BICYCLING. See Cycling
BIDAULT, Georges
Angry man. J. Blocker. por Newsweek 70: 42+ S 11 '67
Cry from quixotic exile. Time 90:110 S 29 '67
Pitiful caricature. R. G. Hazo. Nation 205: 537-8 N 20 '67
Second resistance of Georges Bidault. S. DeGramont. il pors N Y Times Mag p46-7+ O 8 '67; Reply with rejoinder. J. Soustelle. p 16+ D 17 '67
BIDDING, Competitive. See Contracts, Government
BIDDLE, Francis
Frenchman from Savannah. New Repub 157: 26-30 N 11 '67
BIDDLE, James
Collecting American art for the Metropolitan: 1961-1966: Antiques 91:481-6 Ap '67

about

Building the past. il Time 91:15 Ja 19 '68
BIDERMAN, Albert D.
Surveys of population samples for estimating crime incidence. bibliog f Ann Am Acad 374:16-33 N '67
—and Reiss, A. J. Jr
On exploring the dark figure of crime. bibliog f Ann Am Acad 374:1-15 N '67
BIDERMAN, Sol
Mestre Noza. Américas 19:5-7 N '67
BIEBERMAN, Lisa
Psychedelic experience. New Repub 157:17-19 Ag 5 '67
BIEGA, B. C.
Selecting the right constant-voltage transformer. Electr World 78:42-3+ D '67
BIEHL, Art
At sea without a rudder; interview, ed. by D. Selby. Yachting 121:94+ Ap '67
BIENNALE, Venice. See Music festivals—Italy
BIERCE, Ambrose
Ambrose Bierce's devilish definitions; excerpts from Enlarged devil's dictionary; ed. by E. J. Hopkins. Am Heritage 18:112 Ap '67

about

Misanthrope; with excerpts from The devil's dictionary. por Time 89:102 My 5 '67
BIERMAN, Jacquin D.
How to buy property insurance. por Parents Mag 42:18+ My '67
Money matters. por Parents Mag 42:28+ Ap; 20+ Jl; 32+ S; 12+ N '67
Value of fringe benefits. por Parents Mag 42:16+ Je '67

BIERMANN, Wolf
Four ballads of Wolf Biermann: Ballad on the poet Francois Villon; Brigitte; Early morning; Ballad of the man; tr. by E. Bentley. Nation 205:532-3 N 20 '67
BIEVER, Vern
Packer snapper. D. Schreiner. il U S Camera 30:60-1+ N '67
BIG BEAVER ISLAND. See Beaver Island
BIG BEND NATIONAL PARK
Big Bend jewel in the Texas desert. N. T. Kenney. il Nat Geog Mag 133:104-33 Ja '68
Colima warbler census in Big Bend's Chisos Mountains. R. H. Wauer. il Nat Parks Mag 41:8-10 N '67
Wax makers. N. C. Newman. il Nat Parks Mag 41:14-15 Ja '67
BIG bloody cockbird; story. See Weeks, J.
BIG business. See Capitalism; Corporations; Trusts, Industrial
BIG Cypress swamp, Florida
Last great strand; Corkscrew swamp sanctuary. P. Matthiessen. il Audubon 69:64-71 Mr '67
BIG girl; story. See Chidester, A.
BIG HOLE RIVER DAM (proposed) See Dams
BIG SUR, Calif.
They saved the Big Sur. F. J. Taylor. il Read Digest 91:170-5 N '67
BIG white naked bird; story. See Robinson, B.
BIGART, Homer
Men who made the world move. Sat R 50:54+ Ap 22 '67
BIGELOW, Robert P.
Legal & security issues posed by computer utilities. bibliog f Harvard Bsns R 45:150-2+ S '67
BIGHORNS. See Mountain sheep
BIGOS, Michele
Makeup today is subtle, natural. por Farm J 91:58-9 Ag '67
BIHAR, India
On the edge of starvation. il U S News 62: 66-7 Je 26 '67
BIHLER, Penny
Calendar; poem. Good H 164:181 Je '67
BIKINIS. See Bathing suits
BILENKER, Ruth M.
Hand them a *frobish*. NEA J 56:30-1+ O '67
BILHARZIASIS. See Schistosomiasis
BILINGUAL instruction
Bilingual education; legislative proposals. New Repub 157:9 O 21 '67; Discussion. 157:44-5 N 18 '67
Knocking down the language walls; proposed amendment to ESEA to establish bi-lingual education programs. F. M. Cordasco. Commonweal 87:6-8 O 6 '67
BILINGUALISM
Bilingualism and language learning; FLICS project at Michigan university. Sch & Soc 95:294 Sum '67
BILIRUBIN
Oxidative phosphorylation in experimental bilirubin encephalopathy. I. Diamond and R. Schmid. bibliog il Science 155:1288-9 Mr 10 '67
BILL, Arthur
Pestalozzi children's village. Sch & Soc 95: 502-3 D 9 '67
BILL of rights (United States) See United States—Constitution—Bill of rights
BILLARD, Jules B.
Buenos Aires, Argentina's melting-pot metropolis. Nat Geog Mag 132:662-95 N '67
Montreal greets the world. Nat Geog Mag 131: 600-21 My '67
BILLBOARD (periodical)
Top ten, and how they get there; selections from Billboard. Hi Fi 17:49 F '67
BILLBOARD lobbying. See Lobbying
BILLBOARDS
Highway billboards, blight or boon? Consumer Bul 50:33-4 Ag '67
How about a billboards national park? Life 62:4 My 19 '67
How Britain controls billboards. il Am City 82:109 Je '67
Signs of the times; wrangle over which billboards to outlaw. New Repub 156:8 Ap 15 '67
Visual pollution; sometimes it hides the scars. il Pop Gard 18:24-5 D '67
Why the scenic route can't be seen; lobby works to weaken billboard control legislation. il Bsns W p 106-8 Je 17 '67

Anecdotes, facetiae, satire, etc.

Tell me, pretty billboards. N. Perrin. New Yorker 43:163-4+ Ap 22 '67

BILLERA, I. John
Conscience of a conglomerate. R. Levy. por
Duns R 90:42-3+ Ag '67
Taking USI out of the limelight. por
Bsns W p51-2+ Ja 21 '67
BILLETER, Erika
Third international tapestry biennial. Craft
Horiz 27:8-15 Jl '67
BILLFOLDS. See Purses
BILLIARDS
Grandma shot out the lights; U.S. Open
pocket billiards championship. T. O'Leary.
il Sports Illus 27:52-4 Jl 10 '67
On cue: Iowa U. coed becomes pool star. il
Ebony 22:63-5+ Ag '67
Shooting out the lights with Wimpy; ed. by
B. Ottum. L. Lassiter. il Sports Illus 27:50-9
O 16 '67
BILLING
Order processing systems; summary of dis-
cussions on automation at AAUP annual
meeting. Pub W 192:31-2 Jl 3 '67
We send out bills in envelopes automatic-
ally; Anaheim, Calif. J. E. Willis. il Am
City 82:149+ O '67
BILLINGHAM, R. E. See Silvers, W. K. jt.
auth.
BILLINGS, John Shaw
Luce raised the level of photographic art. P.
Stackpole. U S Camera 30:14+ Je '67
BILLINGS, W. D. and Godfrey, P. J.
Photosynthetic utilization of internal carbon
dioxide by hollow-stemmed plants. bibliog
Science 158:121-3 O 6 '67
BILLINGTON, James H.
Beneath the panoply of power, the intel-
ligentsia hits out at the old order. Life
63:70-2+ N 10 '67
Historian's assessment of a Soviet family
chronicle. Life 63:106A+ S 22 '67
BILLIPP, Betty
End of August; poem. McCalls 94:128 Ag '67
Unfair competition; poem. McCalls 94:128
S '67
BILLMAN, B. D.
Free collective bargaining; address, March 10,
1967. Vital Speeches 33:631-5 Ag 1 '67
BILORA'S motorama. See Photography of mov-
ing objects
BIMONTE, Richard
Damaged in transit from stage to screen.
Reporter 37:39-40+ O 19 '67
Stage. Commonweal 86:321-3 Je 2 '67
BIMS, Hamilton J.
Indian uprising for civil rights. Ebony 22:
64-5+ F '67
BINARY counters. See Counting machines and
devices
BINARY number system. See Numeration
BINARY stars. See Stars, Double
BINDER, Alan B. and Cruikshank, D. P.
Mercury: new observations of the infrared
bands of carbon dioxide. bibliog Science
155:1135 Mr 3 '67
BINDER, Carmen
Theodor Binder: Peru's Albert Schweitzer. A.
J. Carley. il por Américas 19:1-7 Mr '67
BINDER, David
Best collective in Hungary: the Lenin farm.
N Y Times Mag p32-3+ Mr 12 '67
BINDER, Leonard
Middle East crisis: a trial balance. Bul
Atomic Sci 23:2-7+ S '67
BINDER, Theodor
Theodor Binder: Peru's Albert Schweitzer.
A. J. Carley. il pors Américas 19:1-7 Mr '67
BINDING (books) See Bookbinding
BING, Dave
Pistons' Bing. il por Newsweek 71:68 Ja 8 '68
BING, Geoffrey Henry Cecil
Ignoring the storm warnings. Nation 205:594-
6 D 4 '67
BING, Rudolf
Mr Bing's birthday. il por Opera N 31:28-9
F 18 '67
BING Crosby national pro-amateur champion-
ship. See Golf—Tournaments
BINGHAM, George Caleb
George Caleb Bingham: a new find. J. Wil-
merding. il Antiques 92:556-7 O '67
BINGHAM, June
Intelligent square's guide to hippieland. N Y
Times Mag p25+ S 24 '67
Opinion on home truths. por Mlle 65:52+ Je
'67
Other Vietnam. Mlle 65:179+ O '67
BINI, Dante
Bini shell; interview. New Yorker 43:28-9 Je
3 '67
BINKLEY, Virgil W.
(ed) See McDonald, M. Old Bruie's last visit

BINNS, R. A.
Farmington meteorite: cristobalite xenoliths
and blackening. bibliog Science 156:1222-6
Je 2 '67
BINOCULARS. See Field glasses
BINSFELD, Edmund L.
Question for John; poem. Christian Cent 84:
1431 N 8 '67
BINSTOCK, L. and Goldman, L.
Giant axon of myxicola: some membrane
properties as observed under voltage clamp.
bibliog Science 158:1467-9 D 15 '67
BIOASTRONAUTICS. See Space flight—Phys-
iological aspects
BIOCHEMICAL fuel cells. See Fuel cells
BIOCHEMISTRY
Chemical production of mutations. C. Auer-
bach. bibliog Science 158:1141-7 D 1 '67
Life sciences notes. See issues of Science
news, June 3, 1967-
Pi complexes in biological systems; report of
discussion group sponsored by New York
academy of sciences. J. Harris and others.
Science 158:1707-8 D 29 '67
See also
Biosynthesis
Blood—Analysis and chemistry
Molecular biology
Proteins
Urine—Analysis
BIOELECTRONICS. See Medical electronics
BIOFLAVONOIDS
Bitter pills for vitamins. Bsns W p28+ Ja 13
'68
BIOGRAPHICAL dictionaries
See also
Who's who in library service
Who's who in the USSR
BIOGRAPHY
Books. M. Muggeridge. Esquire 67:24+ Mr '67

Anecdotes, facetiae, satire, etc.
Day in the life of Roger Angell. R. Angell.
New Yorker 43:28-31 Ag 19 '67

Bibliography
Biography (cont) F. J. Gallagher. America
116:693+ My 6 '67

History
Davy's biographers: notes on scientific
biography. J. Z. Fullmer. bibliog il Science
155:285-91 Ja 20 '67
BIOHAZARDS symbol. See Labels
BIOLOGICAL apparatus and supplies
Apparatus for solid-phase peptide synthesis.
M. C. Khosla. bibliog il Science 156:253-4
Ap 14 '67
Calcium-selective electrode with liquid ion ex-
changer. J. W. Ross. bibliog il Science 156:
1378-9 Je 9 '67
Capillary-tube scanner for mechanized micro-
biology. R. L. Bowman and others. bibliog
il Science 158:78-83 O 6 '67
Protein structure in days. il Sci N 92:151-2
Ag 12 '67
Sequential slice of life; cell sectioning
process. il Sci Digest 62:60 D '67
Solid-phase radioimmunoassay in antibody-
coated tubes. K. Catt and G. W. Tregear.
bibliog il Science 158:1570-2 D 22 '67
BIOLOGICAL balance. See Balance of nature
BIOLOGICAL chemistry. See Biochemistry
BIOLOGICAL clocks. See Periodicity
BIOLOGICAL constitution of man. See Man—
Constitution
BIOLOGICAL control of insects. See Insects,
Injurious and beneficial—Control
BIOLOGICAL control systems
Biocommunications: one-way street. B. J.
Culliton. Sci N 91:426 My 6 '67
BIOLOGICAL cycles. See Periodicity
BIOLOGICAL laboratories
Jackson: a lab that links mice and men. il
Bsns W p 192-4 S 9 '67
Marine lab in East Africa; Kanduchi, Tan-
zania. C. Weiss. il Sci N 91:552-3 Je 10 '67
See also
Woods Hole, Mass. marine biological labora-
tory
BIOLOGICAL physics
See also
Biological control systems
Molecular biology
BIOLOGICAL research
Adaptation of an insect cell line. Grace's an-
theraea cells, to medium free of insect
hemolymph. C. E. Yunker and others. il
Science 155:1565-6 Mr 24 '67

BIOLOGICAL research—*Continued*
Antireductionism and molecular biology. K. F. Schaffner. bibliog Science 157:644-7 Ag 11 '67; Discussion. 158:857+ N 17 '67
Biology's grandiose plan; international biological program. B. J. Culliton. il Sci N 91:556-7 Je 10 '67
Double helix; the discovery of the structure of DNA; excerpts, with editorial comment. J. D. Watson. il Atlan 221:76-94+ Ja '68 (to be cont)
Fracture planes in an ice-bilayer model membrane system. D. W. Deamer and D. Branton. bibliog il Science 158:655-7 N 3 '67
Psychochemical research strategies in man, symposium. 28-29 December. AAAS annual meeting. A. J. Mandell. Science 158:1496-7 D 15 '67
Report: science: insects, animals, and man. D. E. Carr. Atlan 219:31-3 My '67
Skin. R. F. Rushmer and others; reply. C. A. Larson. Science 155:488 Ja 27 '67
  See also
Biotelemetry
Salk institute for biological studies, San Diego, Calif.
BIOLOGICAL specimens
Fracture planes in an ice-bilayer model membrane system. D. W. Deamer and D. Branton. bibliog il Science 158:655-7 N 3 '67
BIOLOGICAL telemetry. See Biotelemetry
BIOLOGICAL warfare
Chemical and biological warfare: the research program. E. Langer. il Science 155:174-6+, 299-303 Ja 13-20 '67
Chemical and biological weapons; once over lightly on Capitol hill. E. Langer. Science 156:1073+ My 26 '67; Reply. D. R. McKeen. 157:875 Ag 25 '67
CBW, Vietnam evoke scientist's concern. E. Langer. Science 155:302 Ja 20 '67; Discussion. 156:167. 1029-30 Ap 14, My 26 '67
Ecological warfare: defoliation and crop destruction by U.S. forces in Vietnam. Sci Am 218:44-6 Ja '68
5,000 scientists vs. CBW. Sci N 91:185 F 25 '67
Gas and germ warfare: controversy over research contracts. S. Hersh. New Repub 157:12-14 Jl 1 '67
Just a drop can kill: secret work on gas and germ warfare; research at military installations, colleges, universities and private firms. S. M. Hersh. New Repub 156:11-15 My 6 '67
BIOLOGISTS
What man can make of man; genetic programing; competence of biologists to determine the optimal genotype. K. H. Hertz. Christian Cent 84:807-10 Je 21 '67
BIOLOGY
Information and control processes in living systems; report on conferences. D. M. Ramsey. Science 158:1706-7 D 29 '67
Life sciences notes. See issues of Science news. June 3, 1967-
  See also
Biological research
Biomathematics
Cell division (biology)
Embryology
Environment
Genetics
Mutation (biology)
Natural history
Polymorphism (biology)
Psychobiology
Regeneration (biology)
Space biology
    Philosophy
Biology of ultimate concern, by T. Dobzhansky. Review
  Natur Hist 76:62+ O '67. J. Oppenheimer
    Study and teaching
Skin-out, skin-out. M. Bates. Natur Hist 76:20-3 O '67
BIOLOGY, Molecular. See Molecular biology
BIOMACROMOLECULES. See Molecules
BIOMATHEMATICS
Biomathematics and computer science; report on fifth annual symposium. L. D. Cady, jr. Science 156:1265-6 Je 2 '67
BIOMEDICAL engineering
Beyond the life island. il Sci N 91:168 F 18 '67
Heart strain greater in landing on carrier than bombing. C. M. Plattner. il Aviation W 86:60-1+ Mr 13 '67
Medicine moves toward systems techniques. J. A. Shannon. il Tech W 20:72-3+ Ja 23 '67
New medicine and its weapons. il Newsweek 69:60-8 Ap 24 '67

BIOMEDICAL research. See Medical research
BIOMETRY
  See also
Biomathematics
BIOMOLECULES. See Molecules
BIOSATELLITE. See Artificial satellites—Use in research
BIOSYNTHESIS
Biosynthesis of polyketides and related compounds; excerpts from address, June 28, 1966. A. J. Birch. bibliog il Science 156:202-6 Ap 14 '67
Biosynthesis of the morphine alkaloids. G. W. Kirby. bibliog il Science 155:170-3 Ja 13 '67
Carotenoid biosynthesis in rhodospirillum rubrum: effect of pteridine inhibitor. N. A. Nugent and R. C. Fuller. bibliog il Science 158:922-4 N 17 '67
Direction of chain growth in polysaccharide synthesis. P. W. Robbins and others. bibliog il Science 158:1536-42 D 22 '67
Gamma globulins: structure and control of biosynthesis. F. W. Putnam. Science 158:813-14 N 10 '67
Insulin biosynthesis: evidence for a precursor. D. F. Steiner and others. bibliog il Science 157:697-700 Ag 11 '67
Isoprenoid biosynthesis in a cell-free system from pea shoots. J. E Graebe. bibliog il Science 157:73-5 Jl 7 '67
Lack of end-product inhibition and repression of leucine synthesis in a strain of salmonella typhimurium. R. A. Calvo and and J. M. Calvo. bibliog il Science 156:1107-9 My 26 '67
Progesterone: its possible role in the biosynthesis of cardenolides in digitalis lanata. E. Caspi and D. O. Lewis. bibliog il Science 156:519-20 Ap 28 '67
Rabbit hemoglobin biosynthesis: use of human hemoglobin chains to study molecule completion. J. R. Shaeffer and others. bibliog il Science 158:488-90 O 27 '67
Skin-pigment regulation of vitamin-D biosynthesis in man. W. F. Loomis. bibliog il Science 157:501-6 Ag 4 '67
Structural basis for the inhibition of protein biosynthesis: mode of action of tubulosine. A. P. Grollman. bibliog il Science 157:84-5 Jl 7 '67
BIOTELEMETRY
Implant biotelemetry and microelectronics. W. H. Ko and M. R. Neuman. bibliog il Science 156:351-60 Ap 21 '67
Radio pill: symbol of a new science; R. S. Mackay's radio telemetry. Todays Health 45:1105 Mr 15 '67
BIOTELEMETRY
Tuning-in on wildlife secrets. H. Bradshaw and V. Bradshaw. il Pop Mech 129:114-16+ Ja '68
BIOTITE
Biotite flakes: alteration by chemical and biological treatment. J. R. Boyle and others. bibliog il Science 155:193-5 Ja 13 '67
BIRCH, A. J
Biosynthesis of polyketides and related compounds; excerpts from address, June 28, 1966. bibliog Science 156:202-6 Ap 14 '67
BIRCH bark
Birch-bark bonus. R. Cochran. il Outdoor Life 139:24 Je '67
BIRD, Henry L.
Lucky Bird. D. Graham. New Repub 157:9-10 D 23 '67
BIRD, Isabella Lucy. See Bishop, I. L. B.
BIRD, John
Birth of a super-food. Sat Eve Post 240:62+ Jl 1 '67
Don't flood our Grand Canyon. Sat Eve Post 240:24-9+ Ag 12 '67
Unyielding Amish: we want to be left alone. Sat Eve Post 240:28-36 Je 17 '67
When children can't learn. Sat Eve Post 240:27-31+ Jl 29 '67
BIRD, John, 1937?-
Bird of prey. pors Time 90:68 N 17 '67
BIRD, Junius B.
Littorina littorea: occurrence in a northern Newfoundland beach terrace, predating Norse settlements. Science 159:114 Ja 5 '68
BIRD, Laurel Ellen
Definition; poem. Christian Cent 84:1423 N 8 '67
BIRD, Michael J.
Biggest blast before the A-bomb; excerpts from The town that died. Pop Mech 128:81-3 D '67
BIRD, Robert S.
Robert F. Kennedy: at home with the heir apparent. Sat Eve Post 240:28-35 Ag 26 '67

BIRD, Thomas E.
Big brother vs. the Melkites. Commonweal 86:509-10 Ag 25 '67

BIRD, Tracy
Auto insurance. Motor T 19:50+ My '67

BIRD accidents. See Birds—Accidents and hazards

BIRD calling
Pied Piper from down East: G. Soule. D. Barnes. il Sports Illus 28:34-7 Ja 8 '68

BIRD dogs
Dogs. D. M. Duffey. See issues of Outdoor life
Dogs for the prairies. D. M. Duffey. il Outdoor Life 139:178-83 Ap '67
Son of October. C. Ford. il Field & S 72:70-1 O '67

Training
See Dogs—Training

BIRD feeders. See Feeders (birds)

BIRD houses
Four houses and a feeder. C. Conley. il Field & S 72:109 N '67
House to build; bluebird house. il Home Gard 54:65 My '67
What are the best bird houses? E. A. Mason. Horticulture 45:22-3+ Mr '67
Would you believe a bird bottle? il Home Gard 54:46 D '67

BIRD in the hand; story. See Clay, G. R.

BIRD photography. See Photography of birds

BIRD populations
Control
Foolproof control of pigeons and starlings; Columbia, Mo. M. R. Sanford. il Am City 82:116-17 Mr '67
Notes and comment; purple martins mistaken for starlings in Missouri. New Yorker 43:35 S 9 '67

BIRD protection. See Birds—Protection

BIRD sanctuaries
Hawaii's bird paradise; Kipuka Puaulu, in Hawaii Volcanoes National Park. W. B. Fletcher. il Nat Parks Mag 41:10-14 O '67
Potomac eagle refuges; proposed Potomac bald eagle refuge at Mason Neck. Va. Liv Wildn 30:45 Aut '66
Some place to hide; a home in the Danube delta. F. V. Grunfeld. il Reporter 37:32-4 N 30 '67
Trumpeter returns from oblivion; at Red Rock Lakes national wildlife refuge. R. C. Murphy. il Read Digest 90:190-2+ Je '67
See also
Wildlife sanctuaries

BIRD shooting. See Shooting

BIRD shot. See Shot

BIRD study
Bird finding. O. S. Pettingill, jr. See issues of Audubon
Birders: a more civilized breed. R. T. Peterson. il N Y Times Mag p65+ D 17 '67
Getting the bird; 24-hour period count of species. il Time 89:47 Je 2 '67
My logging boss husband is a bird watcher. A. Colwell. il Am For 73:30-1+ Ap '67
Trip afield with a young Thoreau. T. Browne. Nat Parks Mag 41:14 N '67
See also
Photography of birds

BIRD watching. See Bird study

BIRDHOUSES. See Bird houses

BIRDS
Bird finding. O. S. Pettingill, jr. See issues of Audubon
Birds are happy to join you. il Sunset 139: 166-7 S '67
See also
Game birds
Shore birds
also names of birds, e.g. Quails

Accidents and hazards
Ecological disaster; Torrey Canyon disaster. il Sci Digest 61:26 Je '67
Shed few tears; statistical view of bird mortality. H. Mayfield. il Audubon 69:61-5 My '67
Tragedy of errors; effect of Torrey Canyon disaster on sea life. J. Fisher and S. Charlton. il Audubon 69:72-85 N '67

Anecdotes, facetiae, satire, etc.
Willie, the uncommon thrush; picture story. N. Rockwell. McCalls 94:76-83 Ap '67

Care
Good care advice for pet birds. il Good H 164:155 F '67

Collision with airplanes
See Aviation—Bird hazards

Extermination
Now you can get new bait starlings. Farm J 91:50F O '67

Food and feeding
Birds are happy to join you. il Sunset 139: 166-7 S '67
Science proves it, the robin sees the worm. F. Heppner. il Audubon 69:86-8+ S '67
Thanksgiving for birds. M. D. Hodgins. il Home Gard 54:43 N '67

Growth and development
Avian pineal gland: progonadotropic response in the Japanese quail. A. Sayler and A. Wolfson. bibliog il Science 158:1478-9 D 15 '67

Habits and behavior
Brain lesions in birds: effects on discrimination acquisition and reversal. L. J. Stettner and W. J. Schultz. bibliog il Science 155: 1689-92 Mr 31 '67
Heronry in the house. G. B. Schaller. il Audubon 69:66-7 Jl '67
Visual isolation in gulls. N. G. Smith. il Sci Am 217:94-102 O '67
See also
Birds—Food and feeding
Courtship of birds
Periodicity

Hazards
See Birds—Accidents and hazards

Language
See Birds—Habits and behavior

Migration
Birdwatching seriously. il Sci N 91:245 Mr 11 '67
See also
Orientation

Orientation
See Orientation

Protection
Huge slick, spreading with tide and current; efforts to save British birds affected by Torrey Canyon's oil invasion. J. Hicks. il Life 62:33-5 Ap 14 '67
Public support is needed to save the ivorybill. Audubon 69:4 N '67
See also
Bird sanctuaries

Sight
See Sight (birds)

Stories
Single destiny; Brave Thomas, the tikki bird. R. Nathan. Sat R 50:4 Mr 18 '67
That quail, Robert; excerpt. M. A. Stanger. il Read Digest 90:122-7 Ap '67

Study
See Bird study

Training
Training and maintenance of keypecking in the pigeon by negative reinforcement. H. Rachlin and P. N. Hineline. bibliog il Science 157:954-5 Ag 25 '67

Arctic Regions
Footprint thieves. G. M. Sutton. il Audubon 69:53-7 N '67

Australia
Fantasyland finds. H. E. Mercer. il Travel 128:59-60+ D '67

Connecticut
Regional report:
New Britain, Conn. A. T. Daley. Home Gard 54:58 D '67

Guam
Guam, boondocks unspoiled. O. S. Pettingill, jr. il Audubon 69:8-12+ S '67

Guyana
Guyana, plain, rain forest and savanna. O. S. Pettingill, jr. il Audubon 69:6-10+ My '67

Hawaii
Hawaii's bird paradise; Kipuka Puaulu, in Hawaii Volcanoes National Park. W. B. Fletcher. il Nat Parks Mag 41:10-14 O '67

Japan
Where ocean birds climb island trees. M. J. Kilgour. il Audubon 69:70-7 Jl '67

BIRDS –*Continued*

Nepal

Tail-wagging warbler; re-emergence of the harish bird. R. G. G. Price. il Atlan 221: 100-1 Ja '68

New Zealand

New Zealand spring. O. S. Pettingill, jr. il Audubon 69:6-10+ Ja '67

Newfoundland

Way down East. O. S. Pettingill, jr. il Audubon 69:6-10+ Mr '67

Oregon

Cascades, sagebrush, lava, sea. O. S. Pettingill, jr. il Audubon 69:6-8+ N '67

Trinidad (island)

Steel bands and tropical birds; my Eden. D. R. Eckelberry. il Audubon 69:44-7 Mr '67

Trinidad galaxy; paintings. D. R. Eckelberry. il Audubon 69:48-53 Mr '67

Utah

Virgin River country. O. S. Pettingill, jr. il Audubon 69:6-10+ Jl '67

BIRDS, Extinct

Re-creating Madagascar's giant extinct bird. A. Wetmore. il Nat Geog Mag 132:488-93 O '67

Tail-wagging warbler; re-emergence of the harish bird. R. G. G. Price. il Atlan 221: 100-1 Ja '68

BIRDS, Injurious and beneficial

War with the birds. P. Wagner. il Harper 234:80-4 Ap '67

BIRDS, Symbolism of. See Symbolism

BIRDS in art

Owl and the artists; excerpt from Centuries of owls. F. Medlin. il Natur Hist 76:32-9 O '67

Parrot show; exhibition: Polly imagists, at Cordier & Ekstrom gallery; interview. A. H. Ekstrom. New Yorker 43:18 Ja 6 '68

Talent of Robert Verity Clem. R. M. Mengel. il Audubon 69:56-61 S '67

BIRDS of prey

See also

Eagles
Hawks
Kites (birds)

BIRENBAUM, William M.

Behind the scenes at Long Island U. J. Ridgeway. New Repub 156:10-11 Ap 15 '67

Duel at LIU. Newsweek 69:68+ Ap 10 '67

BIRK, Eileen P.

Current and coming. See issues of Antiques

BIRKS, Roy

Canal holiday in Britain. Motor B 119:114 F '67

BIRMINGHAM, Mary Louise

Selected list of children's books. Commonweal 87:176-85 N 10 '67

BIRMINGHAM, Stephen

How the remarkable Auchincloss family shaped the Jacqueline Kennedy style. Ladies Home J 84:91-3+ Mr '67

Our crowd; excerpt. Ladies Home J 84:165-70 N '67

Sudden fame of Michael Caine. Holiday 41: 81-2+ Je '67

Sun Valley set. Holiday 42:62-7+ N '67

Where did babies come from? McCalls 94: 65+ S '67

BIRMINGHAM, Ala.

Negroes

More grounds for hope in Birmingham. R. F. Fulton. Christian Cent 84:1412-14 N 1 '67

BIRMINGHAM, England, public library

Birmingham public library starts construction in '68. Library J 93:22 Ja 1 '68

BIRNBAUM, Hubert C.

Seeing red in black & white. U S Camera 30: 42-3+ O '67

BIRNBAUM, Martha Kreimer-. See Kreimer-Birnbaum, M.

BIRNBAUM, Norman

Eastern Europe & the death of God. Commentary 44:69-73 Jl '67

BIRNN, Roland

U.S. Coast guard auxiliary. See issues of Yachting

BIRNSTIEL, Max L. See Berlowitz, L. jt. auth.

BIRRELL, Lowell McAfee

Birrell verdict. Newsweek 71:55 Ja 8 '68

Birrell's day in court. Newsweek 70:83 D 18 '67

BIRSTEIN, Ann

Conversations with Katey. McCalls 94:22+ Mr '67

Movies (cont) Vogue 149:44 Ja 15; 62 F 15; 55 Mr 15; 49 Ap 15; 77 Je; 150:42 Ag 1; 68 O 15; 73 N 15 '67

BIRTH. See Childbirth

BIRTH, Multiple

Trillion-to-one change; Sepúlveda octuplets. Time 89:67 Mr 17 '67

See also

Parabiosis

BIRTH control

Behavioral sciences and family planning. M. Snyder. Science 158:677-80+ N 3 '67

Best time to be told. Time 90:69-70 S 8 '67

Birth control: losing support of Negroes? U S News 63:13 Ag 7 '67

Birth control: U.S. programs off to slow start. E. Langer. Science 156:765-7 My 12 '67

Champion of birth control; S. M. Keeny; with excerpts from interview; ed. by F. Andrews. il Life 63:39+ O 6 '67

Character of modern fertility. N. B. Ryder. bibliog f il Ann Am Acad 369:26-36 Ja '67

Ecologist's view of the population problem. D. L. Lyon. Liv Wildn 31:31-5 Spr '67

Equalizing opportunity for family planning. A. J. Lesser. il PTA Mag 61:20-2 Ap '67

For zero growth. il Time 90:70 N 24 '67

Is pregnancy the time to think about spacing children? S. G. Kohl. Redbook 130:29+ N '67

Population crisis: reasons for hope. F. W. Notestein. For Affairs 46:167-80 O '67

Population policy: will current programs succeed? excerpts from address, March 14, 1967. K. Davis. bibliog il Science 158:730-9 N 10 '67

Prospects for population control. J. M. Stycos. Christian Cent 84:1458-62 N 15 '67

Statement on population growth. Thant. UN Mo Chron 4:105-6 Ja '67

Women in a contraceptive culture. P. Koval. Commonweal 87:381-2 D 22 '67

See also

Abortion

Contraceptives

International planned parenthood federation

Religious aspects

Abortion is not enough. M. Novak. Christian Cent 84:430-1 Ap 5 '67; Reply. J. R. Bodo. 84:727 My 31 '67

Birth control and the Catholic church. C. B. Luce. McCalls 94:48+ F '67

Birth control crisis; reprint. D. O'Callaghan. Cath World 204:326-34 Mr '67; Discussion. 205:66-7, 131, 194-5 My-Jl '67

Birth control; what a secret report says. U S News 62:17 My 1 '67

Calling for contraception; Roman Catholic laymen. Time 90:73 O 27 '67

Contraception and the synod of bishops. America 117:339 S 30 '67; Discussion. 117: 454+, 627 O 28, N 25 '67

How U.S. Catholics view birth control. il Newsweek 69:71-2 Mr 20 '67

New freedom for Catholic women. Christian Cent 84:1549 D 6 '67

News and views; Populorum progressio and statement of U.S. bishops. Commonweal 86:162 Ap 28 '67

No pipeline from heaven. R. Y. O'Brien. America 116:313 Mr 4 '67; Discussion. 116: 487-8 Ap 1 '67

No. 2 moral issue of today. G. H. Williams. America 116:452-3 Mr 25 '67

Personalist view of marriage. J. Gilbert. Cath World 205:365-70 S '67

Pope and the pill. Bsns W p48 Ap 22 '67

Pope's conscience. J. T. Noonan, jr. Commonweal 85:559-60 F 17 '67; Discussion. 86:68 Mr 31 '67

Report revealed; theological summary of Pope Paul's 1966 birth-control commission report. Newsweek 69:61-2 My 1 '67

Symbol of birth control. Commonweal 86:163-4 Ap 28 '67

Time for a change; pontifical commission's report. Time 89:62 Ap 28 '67

Vatican II, contraception and Christian marriage. T. Mackin. America 117:54-7 Jl 15 '67; Discussion. 117:314-17, 362-3 S 23, O 7 '67

Voice and torment of a rebel priest; interview, ed. by B. Rutherford. il Life 63:33-4+ S 8 '67

What price aggiornamento? R. M. Brown. Commonweal 86:549-50 S 8 '67

With all deliberate speed? Nat R 19:454+ My 2 '67

BIRTH control—*Continued*

India

Anybody want a radio? proposed mandatory sterilization for fathers. Newsweek 70:44 Jl 31 '67

Enterprise in birth control; companies distribute government-subsidized rubber condoms. il Time 89:32+ Je 23 '67

India's haphazard birth-control program. G. W. S. Trow. Reporter 37:35-6 D 14 '67

It's God's will; why interfere? J. Lelyveld. il N Y Times Mag p28-9+ Ja 14 '68

Must India starve? aims of new program. J. E. Frazer and P. Friggens. Read Digest 91:117-21 Jl '67

Too many people, is India facing disaster? interview. S. Chandrasekhar. il U S News 62:90-3 Ap 3 '67

Japan

How Japan solves population problem. il U S News 62:64-5 Je 12 '67

Underdeveloped areas

Prospects for reducing natality in the underdeveloped world. D. Kirk. bibliog f il Ann Am Acad 369:48-60 Ja '67

Science toys urged for poorer nations. Sci N 91:111 F 4 '67

United States

See Birth control

BIRTH defects. See Deformities

BIRTH order
See also
Children, First-born

BIRTH rate
Character of modern fertility. N. B. Ryder. bibliog f il Ann Am Acad 369:26-36 Ja '67
Population growth and educational development. B. A. Liu. il Ann Am Acad 369:109-20 Ja '67
See also
Population, Increase of

India
See also
Birth control—India

Korea (Republic)

Birthrate cut; other diseases remain problem. Sci N 92:130 Ag 5 '67

Rumania

Back to puritanism; low birth rate. Newsweek 69:60 F 6 '67

Unplanned production. Newsweek 70:48+ S 18 '67

Underdeveloped areas

Combustibility of humans; how to avoid world famine and population crisis. H. Brown. Sat R 50:14-17+ Je 24 '67

Reproductive performance and reproductive capacity in less industrialized societies. G. W. Roberts. bibliog f il Ann Am Acad 369:37-47 Ja '67

United States

As U.S. baby boom comes to an end. U S News 62:20 Mr 13 '67

Can U.S. cope with unfettered stork? Bsns W p 103 N 4 '67

End of baby boom. il Sci Digest 62:81-2 S '67

There'll be fewer little noses. P. Woodring. il Sat R 50:54-5 Mr 18 '67

Why the U.S. population isn't exploding. L. A. Mayer. il Fortune 75:162-6+ Ap '67

BIRTHDAY parties. See Childrens parties; Entertaining

BIRTHDAY party; drama. See Pinter, H.

BIRTHPLACES
Going home again. A. Brien. Holiday 42:12+ N '67
Try to be more like Pittsburgh; birthplaces of celebrated persons. W. Stanton. New Yorker 43:57-9 D 23 '67

BISCAYNE NATIONAL MONUMENT (proposed) See National monuments

BISCHOFF. Ilse
Vigée-Lebrun and the women of the French court. Antiques 92:706-12 N '67

BISCUIT and cracker industry
See also
National biscuit company

BISHKO, C. J.
(comp) Articles and other books received; Spain and Portugal. See issues of American historical review

BISHOP, Claire Huchet
Homage to May Massee. Commonweal 87:173-4 N 10 '67

BISHOP, H. D.
Blessed Trinities. Am For 73:36-7+ O '67
Roadside trout fishing, what's wrong with it? Am For 73:6-7+ Je '67
Snake River submarines. Am For 73:24-5+ Je '67
Super Skunk. Am For 73:18-20 My '67

BISHOP, Henry
Lonely youth in the rural South. G. Goodman. il pors Ebony 22:71-2+ Ag '67

BISHOP, Isabella Lucy (Bird)
Love in the park; excerpt from A gallery of dudes. M. Sprague. il Am Heritage 18:8-13+ F '67

BISHOP, Jim
Day in the life of President Johnson. McCalls 94:88-91+ Ap '67

BISHOP, Joey
Here's Johnny. Newsweek 69:114 My 8 '67

BISHOP, John Peale
John Peale Bishop & the other thirties. L. A. Fiedler. Commentary 43:74+ Ap '67

BISHOP, Jordan
Régis Debray. Commonweal 87:164-6 N 10 '67
Sprouting slums. Commonweal 86:172-3 Ap 28 '67

BISHOP, Lee R.
Neutralizing the cascode amplifier. Electr World 78:66 Jl '67

BISHOP, Morris
Essay: what is important in history? Am Heritage 19:2-3 D '67

BISHOP, Stephen
Jacqueline Du Pré and Stephen Bishop; individually and together. M. N. Kanny; J. Diether. il por Am Rec G 33:548-51 Mr '67
Young excitement in music. A. Rich. por House B 109:102-3+ Jl '67

BISHOP, Thomas
Critic's choice. Sat R 50:28 Je 24 '67
Famous ancestor of the new novel. Sat R 50:56-7 N 25 '67

BISHOP, William Warner
Office of the librarian; address, June 28, 1967. F. E. Mohrhardt. bibliog por Wilson Lib Bul 42:391-6 D '67

BISHOP college, Dallas, Tex.
Tiny Bishop prospers in new soil. il Ebony 22:82-4+ Mr '67

BISHOPS
America's Catholic bishops. D. Callahan. Atlan 219:63-6+ Ap '67
Canadian bishops show the way. America 116:573 Ap 22 '67
Challenge to Rome; European council of bishops. Newsweek 70:71 Jl 24 '67
Choosing a successor. il Time 90:88+ D 15 '67
More Episcopal power? pastoral responsibility for presiding bishop. il Newsweek 69:62 My 1 '67
Naming bishops for an open church. America 116:827 Je 10 '67
Nominating bishops. America 116:365 Mr 18 '67
Of many things; Episcopal seminar held at Fordham university. C. J. McNaspy. America 117:inside cover Jl 22 '67
Of many things; preparing for Episcopal synod. America 116:197+ F 11 '67
On selecting American bishops. J. T. Ellis. Commonweal 85:643-9 Mr 10 '67; Reply. N. W. Logal. 86:75+ Ap 7 '67
Open letter to the U.S. bishops. R. M. Brown. Commonweal 85:547-9 F 17 '67; Discussion. 85:671-3; 86:28 Mr 17-24 '67; America 116:334 Mr 11 '67
Privilege of the faith cases; proposal to authorize local bishops to grant a divorce. America 117:702 D 9 '67
St Louis Catholics speak up. Christian Cent 84:886-7 Jl 12 '67
Up bishops' sleeves; National conference of Catholic bishops. Newsweek 69:88 Ap 24 '67
See also
Chanceries, Diocesan
National conference of Catholic bishops

BISMARCK, Mona Strader (Bush) Williams, countess
Garden of the heart. V. Lawford. il pors Vogue 149:182-7+ Ap 1 '67

BISMARCK, Otto, fürst von
Blood and iron chancellor, by L. L. Snyder. Review
Sat R 50:28 Ag 19 '67. H. Kohn

BISON, American. See Buffaloes

BISPLINGHOFF, Raymond L.
Budapest brain in aerodynamics. Sat R 50:29-30 O 14 '67

BISQUE-headed dolls. See Dolls

BISSELL, Richard
It's great to be in Galena at Christmas. Holiday 42:26+ D '67

BITES, Dog. See Dog bites

BITES, Venomous. See Venom

BITS, Auger. See Augers

BITS, Boring. See Drilling and boring machinery

BITTERMAN, M. E. See Lowes, G; Potts, A. jt. auths.

BITTLE, Camilla R.
Divorce for Rob Phillips; story. Good H 164: 76-7 F '67

BITUMINOUS sand
Alberta oil: the cup runneth over; huge finds in Rainbow-Zama region. il Bsns W p68-73 Jl 1 '67
From an icy quagmire, half the world's oil; Fort McMurray plant. il Newsweek 70:78-80 O 2 '67
New frontier: the tar sands; Athabaska oil sands. J. Lear. il Sat R 50:57 S 2 '67
Unlocking oil from Canada's tar sands; Athabasca sands; reprint. J. H. Carmical. il Sci Digest 61:56-9 Je '67

BIVINS, Doris, and Ergun, Sabri
Magnetic susceptibilities of coals. bibliog Science 159:83 Ja 5 '68

BIXLER, Paul. See Dearnaley, C. jt. auth.

BIZET, Georges
Carmen. Criticism
New Yorker 43:54 D 23 '67
Newsweek il 70:68 D 25 '67
Sat R 50:38-9 D 30 '67
Time il 90:50 D 22 '67

BIZJETS. See Airplanes, Business

BIZZI, Emilio
Discharge of frontal eye field neurons during eye movements in unanesthetized monkeys. bibliog Science 157:1588-90 S 29 '67

BJOERKMAN, Aake
Soviet streets are the cleanest. Am City 82: 102-3 Je '67

BJORKLUND, Lorence F.
Recollections of an Old West illustrator. por Pub W 192:76-8+ N 6 '67

BLACK, A. H.
Transfer following operant conditioning in the curarized dog. bibliog Science 155:201-3 Ja 13 '67

BLACK, Barbara
Seeds. Horticulture 45:28-9+ F '67

BLACK, Craig C.
Middle and late eocene mammal communities: a major discrepancy. bibliog Science 156:62-4 Ap 7 '67

BLACK, Donald J. See Reiss, A. J. jr. jt. auth.

BLACK, Helena, pseud.
Short story of a short war: the aftermath. Nat R 19:1255-6 N 14 '67

BLACK, Hillel
What our children read; excerpt from The American schoolbook. Sat Eve Post 240:27-9+ O 7 '67

BLACK, Hugo La Fayette
Justice under law. P. W. Romero. por Negro Hist Bul 30:12-14 F '67
Shift in the Supreme court; what one new justice can mean. il por U S News 62:67-8 Ap 24 '67

BLACK, Keith
That old Black's magic. J. McFarland. il pors Hot Rod 20:72-4 Jl '67

BLACK, Richard G. See Halpern, L. M. jt. auth.

BLACK, Roe C.
Are you being squashed by over-feeding? Farm J 91:B4-5+ My '67

BLACK, Shirley (Temple) See Temple, S.

BLACK, Stuart C. See Bretthauer, E. W. jt. auth.

BLACK
Radiant solar energy and the function of black homeotherm pigmentation: an hypothesis. W. J. Hamilton. 3d and F. Heppner. bibliog il Science 155:196-7 Ja 13 '67

BLACK bear hunting. See Bear hunting

BLACK bears. See Bears

BLACK CANYON OF THE GUNNISON NATIONAL MONUMENT
Lower Black Canyon of the Gunnison. W. R. Hansen. il Nat Parks Mag 41:14-19 Jl '67
Lower Black Canyon of the Gunnison River. Nat Parks Mag 41:21 S '67

BLACK comedy; drama. See Shaffer, P.

BLACK duck shooting. See Duck shooting

BLACK eagles. See Eagles

BLACK eye. See Eye—Injuries

BLACK flies See Flies

BLACK Hawks (hockey team) See Hockey teams

BLACK magic. See Witchcraft

BLACK marlin fishing. See Fishing

BLACK Muslim movement
I am not worried about Ali; ed. by T. Maule. B. Russell. il Sports Illus 26:18-21 Je 19 '67

BLACK nationalism. See Nationalism—Negro race

BLACK Panther party for self defense
Call of the Black Panthers. S. Stern. il N Y Times Mag p 16-11+ Ag 6 '67

BLACK power. See Nationalism—Negro race; Negroes in the United States; Race relations

BLACK SEA REGION
See also
Tourist trade—Black Sea Region

BLACK walnut trees. See Walnut trees

BLACKBALLING. See Blacklisting

BLACKBURN, Paul
Collioure; poem. Nation 204:822 Je 26 '67
Crossing; poem. New Yorker 43:50 My 13 '67
(tr) See Cortázar, J. Night face up

BLACKBURN, Sara
Mrdr'd in full kitch. acc. to grdn. New Yorker 43:205-7 N 25 '67

BLACKETT, Patrick Maynard Stuart
Ever widening gap; address. December 27, 1966. bibliog Science 155:959-64 F 24 '67

BLACKLISTING
Blackballing the Fiedlers. B. Jackson. New Repub 157:13-14 S 9 '67
Blacklisted! story of J. H. Faulk; condensation of The jury returns. L. Nizer. il Read Digest 90:201-4+ Mr '67
See also
Boycott

BLACKMAIL. See Extortion

BLACKOUTS (electric power.) See Electric power

BLACKSTOCK, Paul W.
Super-sleuths. Sat R 50:32-3 N 18 '67

BLACKSTONE Rangers. See Gangs

BLACKWELL, Charles R.
Air force alumnus. il U S Camera 31:78-9 Ja '68

BLACKWELL, Elizabeth
Americans not everybody knows. N. Stack. por PTA Mag 61:26-7 F '67

BLACKWELL, R. Quentin, and others
Hemoglobin variants in Koreans: hemoglobin G Taegu. bibliog Science 158:1056-7 N 24 '67

BLADDER
Surgery
Peeling technique; useful in bladder cancers. Sci N 91:430 My 6 '67

BLADES, Helicopter. See Helicopters—Blades

BLAIBERG, Philip
Cape Town's second. il por Time 91:38 Ja 12 '68
Philip Blaiberg. Time 91:51 Ja 19 '68
Surgery and show biz. il por Newsweek 71: 49 Ja 15 '68

BLAILOCK, Z. R. and others
Adenovirus endocarditis in mice. bibliog Science 157:69-70 Jl 7 '67

BLAINE amendment. See New York (state)—Constitution

BLAIR, Edith
(ed) See Quant, M. Chez Mlle: Mary Quant at home

BLAIR, Eric. See Orwell, G. pseud.

BLAIR, Gary
In defense of the windward plane. por Yachting 122:23+ N '67

BLAIR, Newell
Questions and answers on the NEA mutual fund; interview. NEA J 56:41-2 O '67

BLAIR, T. M. H.
How an anthology is made. Writer 80:16-20+ Mr '67

BLAIR, William McCormick, Jr
Depth and durability of U.S.-Philippine relations; address, June 29, 1967. Dept State Bul 57:203-7 Ag 14 '67

BLAIR House. See Washington, D.C.—Historic houses, etc.

BLAKE, Donald P.
Anybody with a camera can be a newsman! Pop Phot 60:81-3+ F '67
Twisted terminology. U S Camera 30:65 Ap '67

BLAKE, Eugene Carson
Pan-Christian papacy? R. M. Brown. Commonweal 86:446+ Jl 14 '67
Tragically self-defeating policy. Christian Cent 84:643-4 My 17 '67

BLAKE, Hector
Keep your eye on an exciting game; ed. by M. Mulvoy. por Sports Illus 27:38-45 N 6 '67

BLAKE, Patricia
Fifth ace. New Repub 157:31 Jl 1 '67

BLAKE, Peter
Selective eye of Marcel Breuer. House B
109:152-9+ Mr '67
BLAKE, Robert
Two unknowns seek movie fame as killers;
In cold blood. S. Gordon. il pors Look 31:
114+ Je 13 '67
BLAKE, William
Dialogue with a flea; notebook of Blake
sketches. il Time 89:72 Ap 21 '67
New Apocalypse: the radical Christian vision
of William Blake, by T. J. J. Altizer. Re-
view
Christian Cent 84:1070 Ag 23 '67. M. S.
Hall
New Blake letter. F. W. Hilles. Yale R 57:
85-9 O '67
BLAKE plateau. See Ocean bottom
BLAKELY, R. J.
Wit to win; address, 1966. bibliog f por ALA
Bul 61:152-4+ F '67
BLAKESLEE, Alton L.
Today's health news. See issues of Today's
health
BLAKEY, G. Robert
Organized crime in the United States. bib-
liog f Cur Hist 52:327-33+ Je '67

about

Official cover-up: a flagrant case in point.
Life 63:103 S 8 '67
BLANCH, Lesley
Patchouli. Vogue 150:184-5+ O 1 '67
BLAND, Edith (Nesbit) See Nesbit, E.
BLANDY, Richard. See Noah, H. J. jt. auth.
BLANK, Joseph P.
Ill wind in Indiana. Read Digest 90:66-71 Mr
'67
Rescue in the clouds. Read Digest 91:73-7
S '67
Speaking of weather: some like it cold. Look
31:44+ Mr 7 '67
Unborn baby's fight to live. Redbook 128:74-
5+ Mr '67
BLANKETS
Space stadium blanket. il Consumer Bul 50:
16-17 N '67
See also
Electric blankets, coverlets, etc.
BLANQUET, Paul, and others
Iodine determined in purified thyrocalcitonin.
bibliog Science 158:381-3 O 20 '67
BLASINGAME, Francis James Levi
Helping trim drug bills. Todays Health 45:88
My '67
You ought to take some time off and go
fishing! Field & S 71:52-3 F '67
BLASSINGAME, John W.
Selection of officers and non-commissioned
officers of Negro troops in the Union army,
1863-1865. bibliog f Negro Hist Bul 30:8-11
Ja '67
BLASTING
Blasting can save money. W. J. Fletcher. il
Suc Farm 65:93 F '67
See also
Atomic blasting
BLASTOCYSTS. See Ovum
BLASTOKININ. See Proteins
BLASTOMYCES dermatitidis.   See   Fungi,
Pathogenic
BLATNIK, John A.
Man-made highway hazards that kill. por
Pop Sci 191:84-8+ N '67
BLATT, Burton, and Mangel, Charles
Tragedy and hope of retarded children. Look
31:96-9+ O 31 '67
BLAU, Herbert
Saturn eats his children. R. Brustein. New
Repub 156:34-5 Ja 28 '67
BLAUKOPF, Kurt
Notes from our correspondents. See issues of
High fidelity incorporating Musical America
BLAW, Michael E. and others
Experimental allergic encephalomyelitis in
agammaglobulinemic chickens. bibliog Sci-
ence 158:1198-200 D 1 '67
BLAZER, Rexford Sydney
Outworking the competition. il por Time 90:
99-100 N 10 '67
BLAZER buttons. See Buttons
BLEACHING materials
Chlorine bleach: a fresh view of what it can
do. il Good H 165:6 O '67
BLEEDERS disease. See Hemophilia
BLENDERS, Electric. See Electric apparatus
and appliances, Domestic
BLENKINSOPP, Joseph
Sex and the Christian. Commonweal 87:435-9
Ja 12 '68
BLESS this house; story. See Rodgers, M. A.

BLESSING, Leo B. and others
But, judge, what is proper discipline? Read
Digest 91:157-8+ S '67
BLEVINS, Winfred
High camp, straight Bach & Stravinsky. Hi
Fi 17:MA24-5+ N '67
BLIGHT, Fire. See Fire blight
BLIND
Handicapped American of the year. il Ebony
22:101-2+ Ap '67
Pittsburgh's seeing eye dog pioneer. il Ebony
22:80-2+ F '67
See also
Dogs as guides
Libraries—Work with blind

Education

School where blind children see; Blind chil-
drens center, Los Angeles. E. M. Dean. il
Todays Health 45:50-3 F '67
Sounds and shadows; blind student on geog-
raphy camping trip; Montgomery Blair H.S.
Silver Springs, Md. P. L. Jones. il Sr Schol
90:sup 19 My 5 '67
BLIND, Apparatus for the
Electronic eyes for the blind. J. Hazelwood. il
Sci N 91:456-7 My 13 '67; Reply. L. M.
Clark. 92:5-6 Jl 1 '67
Light probe for the blind. il Electr World 78:
77 N '67
Liquid level indicator for the blind; electronic
device. T. V. Cranmer. il Pop Electr 26:
59-60 My '67
Phone device aids deaf-blind persons; tactile
speech indicator. Todays Health 45:87 Mr
'67
Reading machine, laser beam help blind see.
Todays Health 46:73 Ja '68
BLIND, Books for the
See also
Talking books
United States—Library of Congress—Division
for the blind and physically handicapped
BLIND, Periodicals for the
Fashion show for blind teens: Seventeen's
first. il Seventeen 26:261 My '67
See also
Talking books
BLIND childrens center, Los Angeles. See Blind
—Education
BLIND flying. See Aviation—Instrument flying
BLIND riveting. See Rivets and riveting
BLINDERMAN, Abraham
From touchdown to take-off. U S Camera
30:70-1+ F '67
BLINKING lights. See Electric lamps, Flashing
BLISS, Edith
Galley-west. Yachting 121:83+ My '67
BLISS and Laughlin Industries, Incorporated
How to get out of a steel-lined rut; diver-
sification by acquisition. Bsns W p86+ Jl
15 '67
BLIVEN, Naomi
Books (cont) New Yorker 43:189-90+ Mr 18;
170+ S 9 '67; 85-6+ Ja 6 '68
BLIZZARDS. See Snowstorms
BLOATING
Bloat control without feeding. Farm J 91:47
My '67
Bloat stopper now OK for mixed feeds. Farm
J 92:54 Ja '68
How to treat bloat in cattle. J. W. Bailey.
Suc Farm 65:62-3 O '67
BLOCH, Ernst
Ernst Bloch: philosopher of the not-yet. S. P.
Schilling. Christian Cent 84:1455-8 N 15 '67;
Discussion. 84:1663 D 27 '67
Semblance of a resemblance. O. Daniel. Sat R
50:113 O 14 '67
BLOCH, George J. and Davidson, J. M.
Antiandrogen implanted in brain stimulates
male reproductive system. bibliog Science
155:593-5 F 3 '67
BLOCK, H. & R, incorporated
Storefront tax service earns a good return.
il Bsns W p 196-8+ Mr 25 '67
BLOCK, Joseph L.
Block bows out. por Newsweek 70:80-1 N 6
'67
Maverick steps out. il por Time 90:94+ N 3
'67
BLOCK, Louis
Louis Block. il por Time 91:50 Ja 19 '68
BLOCK, Ruth
(comp) Fine art of memory. N Y Times Mag
p32 Ja 7 '68
(comp) Of crime and the criminal. N Y Times
Mag p 104-5 Mr 12 '67
(comp) Time himself is bald. . . N Y Times
Mag p 126-7 Ap 9 '67
BLOCK, Victor
How doctors keep up. Todays Health 45:56-
60 Ag '67

BLOCK ISLAND
Holiday discovery of the month. il Holiday 42:74-5 Ag '67
BLOCK parties
Accent the fun in giving a fund-raising block party. il Seventeen 26:74-7+ Jl '67
BLOCK printing
Fine printmaking with wood. C. Kehne, jr. il Sch Arts 67:34-6 O '67
Printing with a soap eraser. P. A. Lee. il Sch Arts 67:28-9 O '67
Put the grain to work; woodblock printing. J. L. Fonville. il Sch Arts 67:16-17 O '67
Reach to the bottom of the barrel; neoprene prints. G. F. Gates. il Sch Arts 67:24-6 O '67
Scrap block printing. J. F. Warwick. il Sch Arts 67:14-15 O '67
See also
Linoleum block printing
BLOCKS (engine) See Automobile engines
BLOCKS, Toy. See Toys
BLODGET, Robert
Follow me through. See issues of Flying
about
Publisher's memo. E. D. Muhlfeld. por Flying 80:6 Ap '67
BLOEDEL, J. R. See Llinás, R. jt. auth.
BLOMDAHL, Karl Birger
Aniara. Criticism
New Yorker 43:81-3 Je 24 '67
Opera N il 31:14-15 My 13 '67
BLOOD
Food intake controlled by a blood factor. J. D. Davis and others. bibliog il Science 156:1247-8 Je 2 '67
Red cells coated with immunoglobulin G: binding and sphering by mononuclear cells in man. A. F. LoBuglio and others. bibliog il Science 158:1582-5 D 22 '67
See also
Eosinophils
Erythropoiesis

Analysis and chemistry
Annals of medicine; the orange man; first recorded victim of carotenemia-lycopenemia, through excessive eating of carrots and tomatoes. B. Roueché. New Yorker 43:100+ My 27 '67

Circulation
Blood viscosity: influence of erythrocyte aggregation. S. Chien and others. bibliog il Science 157:829-31 Ag 18 '67
Blood viscosity: influence of erythrocyte deformation. S. Chien and others. bibliog il Science 157:827-9 Ag 18 '67
Distribution of circulation rates within a single tissue type. B. A. Hills. bibliog il Science 157:942-3 Ag 25 '67
Flow characteristics of human erythrocytes through polycarbonate sieves. M. I. Gregersen and others. bibliog il Science 157:825-7 Ag 18 '67
Hemorrheology; report on first meeting of the International society of hemorrheology. H. Goldsmith. Science 155:1443-4 Mr 17 '67
Microcirculation and shock; report on international, interdisciplinary conference. D. Shepro and G. P. Fulton. Science 157:1211-12 S 8 '67
Red cell slip at a wall in vitro. L. Bennett. bibliog il Science 155:1554-6 Mr 24 '67
60,000 miles of blood vessels; research on microcirculation. J. Hixson. il Sci N 92:546-7 D 2 '67
Venous system. J. E. Wood. il Sci Am 218:86-8+ Ja '68
See also
Thrombosis

Coagulation
Thick blood disease; risk of clot-caused strokes high among people with elevated-hemoglobin levels. Newsweek 70:65 N 6 '67

Collection and preservation
Frozen for transfusion; blood components. il Time 90:86 S 22 '67
In cold blood; freeze-thaw process devised by C. E. Huggins. il Newsweek 69:82 My 1 '67

Corpuscles and platelets
Glutathione reductase in red blood cells: variant associated with gout. W. K. Long. bibliog il Science 155:712-13 F 10 '67
Ultrastructure of thrombosthenin, the contractile protein of human blood platelets. D. Zucker-Franklin and others. bibliog il Science 157:945-6 Ag 25 '67
See also
Erythrocytes
Lymphocytes

Diseases
See also
Anemia
Hemophilia
Leukemia

Pigments
See also
Hemoglobin

Plasma
Cholinesterase in plasma; first reported absence in the Bantu; half-life determination. T. Jenkins and others. bibliog il Science 156:1748-50 Je 30 '67
Fibrinogen from human plasma: preparation by precipitation with heavy-metal coordination complex. M. E. Brown and F. Rothstein. bibliog il Science 155:1017-19 F 24 '67

Pressure
See Blood pressure

Proteins
Autosomal linkage between the albumin and Gc loci in humans. K. Kaarsalo and others. bibliog il Science 158:123-5 O 6 '67
Protein uptake in multivesicular bodies in the molt-intermolt cycle of an insect. M. Locke and J. V. Collins. bibliog il Science 155:467-9 Ja 27 '67
Selective phagocytosis: a new concept in protein catabolism. H. Gans and others. bibliog il Science 159:107-10 Ja 5 '68
See also
Taraxein

Serum
See Serum

Storage
See also
Blood, Frozen

Transfusion
Breakthrough in transfusion: plasmapheresis. Todays Health 45:42 S '67
Man with 586 blood brothers. il Ebony 22:56-8+ F '67
Unborn baby's fight to live. J. Blank. il Redbook 128:74-5+ Mr '67
BLOOD, Frozen
In cold blood; freeze-thaw process devised by C. E. Huggins. il Newsweek 69:82 My 1 '67
BLOOD alcohol level. See Alcohol in the body
BLOOD banks
See also
American association of blood banks
BLOOD cells. See Blood—Corpuscles and platelets
BLOOD clotting. See Blood—Coagulation
BLOOD groups
See also
Rh factors
BLOOD in urine. See Hematuria
BLOOD pressure
How drugs can control blood pressure. J. H. Winchester. Read Digest 91:143-6 D '67
BLOOD substitutes
Blood substitute. Sci Digest 61:38-9 F '67
BLOOD tumors. See Leukemia
BLOOD vessel transplants. See Transplantation of organs, tissues, etc.
BLOOD vessels
See also
Vascular system
Veins
BLOODWORTH, Dennis
China is like the Chinese language. N Y Times Mag p 10-11+ Je 18 '67
Chinese Unicorn. Horizon 9:117-19 Sum '67
BLOOM, Arthur D. and others
Lactic dehydrogenase and metabolism of human leukocytes in vitro. bibliog Science 156:979-81 My 19 '67
BLOOM, Eleanor Olson
Keyboard composition. NEA J 56:73-4 D '67
BLOOM, Gerald E. and others
Ring D chromosome: a second case associated with anomalous haptoglobin inheritance. bibliog Science 156:1746-8 Je 30 '67
BLOOM, Murray Teigh
Good pupils, poor teachers. Redbook 128:72-3+ F '67
How other women diet. Redbook 129:70-1+ O '67
How seven families beat the high cost of living; with case histories and interviews. McCalls 94:66-7+ Je '67
Joint tenancy: can it work for you? Read Digest 91:163+ O '67
Our sick jails can be cured. Read Digest 90:181-2+ F '67
BLOOMINGDALES (store) See New York (city)—Stores

BOATBUILDING—*Continued*
From dream to reality (cont) E. L. Parks.
il Motor B 119:50-2+ F '67
Jobs in pleasure boating. C. Peet. Pop Mech
127:28+ F '67
Profiles; F. E. Hood. A. Bailey. New Yorker
43:34-6+ Ag 26 '67
Story of Ona. G. F. McClish. il Motor B 121:
93-6+ Ja '68
Yachting interviews: Jon Van Hoboken. B.
Robinson. il Yachting 122:41+ Ag '67
See also
Chrysler corporation
Shipbuilding
Yacht building
BOATING clubs. See Boat clubs
BOATING industry
Facts and the figures. J. E. Choate. Yacht-
ing 123:55+ Ja '68
BOATS

Care
Annual maintenance; symposium. il Yachting
121:65-77+ Ap '67
Best in fitting-out. il Motor B 119:27-40 Mr;
34-42 Ap '67
Care now, save $ $ later. E. S. Maloney.
il Motor B 120:46-7+ S '67
Problem and the cure for galvanic corrosion.
C. F. Kelley. il Yachting 122:50-1+ O '67

Bibliography
Sources of maintenance information. E. Horan.
il Yachting 121:73+ Ap '67

Chartering
Tips on chartering boats. G. Heinold. il Outdoor Life 140:22+ S '67

Collectors and collecting
Floating Smithsonian; antique powerboats
make colorful one-day show in the Thousand Islands. C. E. Carpenter. il Yachting
122:57+ Jl '67

Design
Design showcase. See issues of Motor boat-
ing
Designs. W. H. deFontaine. See issues of
Yachting
Handy Andy. J. Emmett. il Motor B 120:36-7
D '67
1967 boats: fast bottoms, more push. A. Mike-
sell. il Pop Mech 127:146-52 F '67

Documentation
See Boats—Registration

Electric equipment
Electric power aplenty for the small boat;
ship's-generator system. W. L. Hensley. il
Pop Sci 191:86-8 D '67
Electrified cruising. J. West. il Yachting 121:
75-7+ Ap '67
Give your boat that electric look. F. M.
Paulson. il Field & S 72:112-16 O '67
When I pushed the starter nothing happened.
E. B. Forsyth. il Motor B 119:34-5+ My
'67
See also
Electric currents—Grounding

Electronic equipment
Auto pilot, able assistant for the skipper.
E. S. Maloney. il Motor B 120:42-5 D '67
Electrified cruising. J. West. il Yachting 121:
75-7+ Ap '67
Electronics boon for boatmen. D. Kendall.
il Motor B 119:29-32 F '67
1968 electronics. il Motor B 121:174-81+ Ja '68
What's new in electronics. J. Gribbins. il
Motor B 120:34-6+ S '67

Equipment
Best in fitting-out. il Motor B 119:34-5 Ap
'67
Cabin talk. M. Wiley. See issues of Yacht-
ing
Fine points of buying a boat. F. M. Paulson.
il Field & S 71:138-40+ Mr '67
Four good ideas for boatsmen. il Pop Sci 191:
142-3 N '67
Gadgets and gilhickies. H. deFontaine. See
issues of Yachting
Great impact; how developments in offshore
powerboat racing have been passed down
to pleasure boating. E. H. Nabb. il Yacht-
ing 123:80-2+ Ja '68
Man-sized meals in a girl-sized galley. R.
Bannister. il Motor B 120:44-5+ Jl '67
New checklist for a long wet summer. P.
Czura. il Esquire 67:94-7 F '67
New gadgets and gear for your boat. il Pop
Mech 127:164-5 F '67

New gear for the new year. F. M. Paulson.
il Field & S 71:114-19 F '67
1968 equipment & accessories. il Motor B 121:
182-95+ Ja '68
Priceless record; checklist of model number,
size, serial number, etc. of boat parts. R.
O. Cox. il Motor B 119:30-1+ My '67
Rig for night running. T. Gibbs. il Motor B
120:26-9+ Jl '67
Rig to dunk the dinghy. B. Fleischhauer. il
Motor B 119:52 Mr '67
Rig your boat for hunting. J. A. Emmett. il
Outdoor Life 140:18+ N '67
Rust: the uninvited guest. A. P. Smith. Yacht-
ing 121:68+ Ap '67
Small-boat hoist you can build. H. Clark. il
Pop Sci 190:132-3 Mr '67
Tips on towing. C. W. Smith. il Outdoor
Life 140:118 O '67
Use of lines in maneuvering. C. F. Chapman.
il Motor B 120:50-2 Ag '67
Waterfront news. M. Wiley. See issues of
Yachting
What's new. J. Gribbins. See issues of Motor
boating
What's new in boating. il Pop Sci 190:118-21
Ja '67
See also
Anchors
Burglar alarms
Depth indicators

Exhibitions
Boat show calendar. Yachting 123:119+ Ja '68
Boat show 1968. il Motor B 121:125-96+ Ja '68
Boats, people, & portents; National boat
show. il Motor B 119:124-8 Mr '67
Chicago show loops the loop. il Motor B
119:124 My '67
Floating Smithsonian; antique powerboats
make colorful one-day show in the Thou-
sand Islands. C. E. Carpenter. il Yachting
122:57+ Jl '67
London's international boat show. E. F. Hay-
lock. il Motor B 119:130+ Mr '67
Seattle boat show. E. Crimmin. il Motor B
119:134-5 Mr '67
Yachting's boat show. il Yachting 121:123-6+
Ja '67
See also
Motor boats—Exhibitions

Heating and ventilation
Meeting the new ventilation standards.
Motor B 119:40 Mr '67
Ventilation. W. M. Crook. il Yachting 121:
94-5+ Ja '67

Hulls
See Hulls (naval architecture)

Inspection
Surveying: truth or consequences. R. W. Carrick. il Yachting 121:70-2+ Ap '67

Launching
See also
Yachts—Launching

Materials
Early fiberglass boats. B. Cobb. jr. il
Yachting 121:104-6+ Ja '67
Fiberglass; surface imperfections. B. Cobb, jr.
il Yachting 121:66-7+ Ap '67
Judging fiberglass. B. Cobb, jr. il Yachting
123:86-7+ Ja '68
Miniboats. F. M. Paulson. il Field & S 72:
136-9 My '67
This dinghy's a featherweight. G. Daniels. il
Pop Sci 191:142-5+ Ag '67
Tolly serves up a sandwich hull. J. Roe. il
Pop Sci 191:108-10+ S '67
Upkeep of teak. J. Emmett. Yachting 121:
69+ Ap '67
See also
Protective coatings

Mooring
Anchoring out. J. Emmett. il Yachting 122:
37+ O '67
How to secure your boat at a dock or float
or slip. C. F. Chapman. il Motor B 120:86-9
Jl '67
Making fast. G. S. Smith. il Motor B 119:122
My '67
Marina docking; maneuvering single screw
craft. J. Emmett. il Yachting 121:77-9+
My '67
Picking up a mooring or making a dock. H.
deFontaine. il Yachting 121:103 Ja '67
Safe way to anchor a canoe. J. A. Emmett.
il Outdoor Life 139:160 Ap '67
Slip-away-six feet of nylon gets you out of
tricky moorings single-handed. F. W.
Fleischhauer. il Pop Sci 190:136-7 Ap '67

Noise
See Motor boats—Noise

BOATS—*Continued*

Painting

1968 finishing touches. il Motor B 121:196+ Ja '68

Propellers

See Propellers

Purchasing

Fine points of buying a boat. F. M. Paulson. il Field & S 71:138-40+ Mr '67

How to buy your first boat; symposium. il Pop Mech 127:153-7+ F '67

Secondhand buying tips. J. A. Emmett. il Outdoor Life 140:120-1+ O '67

What to know in selecting a family's first boat. il Good H 164:194 Je '67

See also

Yachts—Purchasing

Registration

New simplified procedures for the measurement and documentation of pleasure craft. Motor B 120:96-7 Jl '67

Repairing

Best in fitting-out. il Motor B 119:27-40 Mr '67

Reconstructing a Flying Dutchman. F. W. Schroeder, jr. il Yachting 121:74-5+ Ja '67

See also

Calking

Sanitation

Pollution predicament; marine sanitary systems. R. W. Carrick. Yachting 121:112+ Ja '67

Small boat pollution control. il Motor B 119: 37 Mr '67

Speed

Constructing a speed curve. il Motor B 119: 102-5 Je '67

Transportation

Long distance trailing. D. Jay. il Yachting 122:62-3+ D '67

My piggyback boat hauler tows a travel trailer, too. F. A. Barnes. il Pop Sci 191: 102-3 Jl '67

100,000 miles for pay and pleasure; Small craft deliveries, ltd. D. B. Mellonie. il Motor B 120:31+ D '67

Tow your boat to a northern wilderness. G. Laycock. il Field & S 72:158-61+ My '67

See also

Automobile boat trailers

Ventilation

See Boats—Heating and ventilation

BOATS, Ice. See Ice boats and ice boating

BOATS, Remodeled

See also

Yachts, Remodeled

BOATS, Submarine. See Submarine boats

BOATS, Used

Secondhand buying tips. J. A. Emmett. il Outdoor Life 140:120-1+ O '67

See also

Yachts, Used

BOATS and boating

Alaska's boating centennial. H. E. McLean. il Motor B 119:25-7+ F '67

Among the snags and shoals. J. A. Emmett. il Outdoor Life 140:94-6 Ag '67

Another sex triangle; man, woman, and boat. H. Resnik. Vogue 150:345+ S 1 '67

Bahamas bearings. G. F. McClish. See issues of Motor boating

Boat handling with the seasoned skipper; excerpts from Piloting, seamanship and small boat handling. C. F. Chapman. il Motor B 120:86-9 Jl '67 (to be cont)

Boating. J. A. Emmett. See issues of Outdoor life

Boating; ed. by F. M. Paulson. See issues of Field & stream

Calendar of coming events; comp. by R. Smith. See issues of Motor boating

Chesapeake log. W. B. Matthews, jr. See issues of Motor boating

Days of fun ahead; some major boating events of 1967. il Motor B 119:22-6 Mr '67

Dory boat surfing offers newest water sports fun. A. Wechter. il Motor B 120:107+ S '67

Downhill to Enchilada; reproductions of paintings; with account by C. Barber. M. Simont. Sports Illus 26:40-8+ My 1 '67

First aid afloat. P. B. Sheldon. Yachting 121: 61-5 Je '67

First family boat. B. D. Barker, 3d. il Yachting 121:114-15+ Ja '67

Getting started in boating: A's to your Q's. J. Roe. il Pop Sci 190:114-17+ Ja '67

Great impact; how developments in offshore powerboat racing have been passed down to pleasure boating. E. H. Nabb. il Yachting 123:80-2+ Ja '68

How big a boat should I buy? il Pop Sci 190:117 Ja '67

How to get your keel wet. C. S. Wren. il Look 31:98-100 Je 13 '67

Man and his boat. H. C. Langer, jr. il Yachting 121:71-3+ Ja '67

Midwest watch. Motor B 119:157-9 Ap '67

News from yachting centers. See issues of Yachting

1967 logbook. il Motor B 121:61-76 Ja '68

Northern Cal roundup. J. Schmale. See issues of Motor boating

Northwest gales. E. Crimmin. See issues of Motor boating

Notes for nomads. See issues of Travel

Off my chest. See issues of Yachting

Out of a clear blue sky; gales at Sand Pit, Lloyds Neck, Long Island. F. Nostrand. il Yachting 122:42-3+ O '67

Outboard the Bahamas. F. M. Paulson. il Field & S 72:68-71 My '67

Rig for night running. T. Gibbs. il Motor B 120:26-9+ Jl '67

Seasoned skipper. See issues of Motor boating

Shakedown cruise family style; buying and getting to know a new cabin cruiser. F. Sweeney. il Yachting 121:91-3+ Ja '67

'67 fleet's in! J. Roe. il Pop Sci 190:70-5 Ja '67

Southward ho. J. Wilson. See issues of Motor boating

TLC. P. Smyth. Motor B 120:46 D '67; 121:322 Ja '68

Under the lee of the longboat. See issues of Yachting

Westward ho. B. Ruskauff. See issues of Motor boating

What's new. J. Gribbins. See issues of Motor boating

What's new in boating. il Pop Sci 190:118-21 Ja '67

Yachting eyes a boat. See issues of Yachting

You can be a boatman for less than you think. F. M. Paulson. il Field & S 72:38-9+ Ja '68

See also

Canoes and canoeing

Children in boating

Cookery, Marine

Cruising

Fishing boats

House boats

Indians of North America—Boats

Inland navigation

Marinas

Motor boats

River trips

Rowing

Sailboats

Sailing

Sails

United States—Coast guard—Boats

Women in boating

Yachts and yachting

Accidents

At sea without a rudder; interview, ed. by D. Selby. A. Biehl. il Yachting 121:94+ Ap '67

Beware the big ones! E. R. Greeff. il Yachting 121:170-1+ Mr '67

Cape Mendocino crisis. B. Inch and D. Selby. il Yachting 122:60+ N '67

Getting unstuck. I. M. Johnson. il Yachting 123:84-5+ Ja '68

How to avoid getting in trouble with your boat: condensation from Rescue at sea. J. M. Waters, jr. il Pop Mech 127:161-3+ F '67

How to handle a boating emergency. G. Emory. il Pop Mech 128:61-5 Jl '67

Man overboard! J. M. Williams. Yachting 121:82+ My '67

Man who didn't come to dinner; interview, ed. by C. West. P. L'Esperance. il Yachting 121:65+ Mr '67

Saved by a whisker. H. Waters. il Motor B 119:74+ Mr '67

So Kit sank. F. B. Thurber. il Yachting 123: 90+ Ja '68

Water skiing and the law. M. M. Dolan. il Motor B 120:34-5 Jl '67

Anecdotes, facetiae, satire, etc.

Fallen oak. G. Crandall. il Motor B 119:44-5+ Ap '67

Anecdotes, facetiae, satire, etc.

Commodore buys a boat; interview, ed. by W. H. deFontaine. H. Ford. il Yachting 122:60-1+ D '67

BOATS and boating—Anecdotes, facetiae, satire, etc.—*Continued*
Report on the boating habits of the adult American male. G. K. Gould. il Motor B 121:113-15+ Ja '68

Bibliography
Book notes and reviews. See issues of Yachting

Laws and regulations
Pollution pickle revisited. R. Stone and J. Napier. il Motor B 121:318-19 Ja '68
Portents for boat owners; National association of state boating law administrators seventh annual conference. il Motor B 121:320-1 Ja '68
Washington report. W. T. Stone. See issues of Yachting

Safety devices and measures
Big blow coming! J. A. Emmett. il Outdoor Life 140:114-16 S '67
Drownproof your crew. W. C. Chasey, jr. il Yachting 122:27+ Jl '67
Hazards and emergencies. J. A. Emmett. il Outdoor Life 139:80+ Je '67
How to handle a boating emergency. G. Emory. il Pop Mech 128:61-5 Jl '67
On avoiding collisions. J. S. Letcher, jr. il Yachting 121:72-3+ Mr '67
Start with safety. G. Manning. il Motor B 119:34-5 Ap '67
Suppose your boat swamps. J. A. Emmett. il Outdoor Life 139:38+ Ap '67
Young skippers set a safety record. J. O'Brien. il Motor B 119:32-3+ My '67
See also
Canoes and canoeing—Safety devices and measures

Statistics
Facts and figures. J. E. Choate. Yachting 121:428-30 Ja '67

Study and teaching
Free boating education; United States power squadrons and the U.S. Coast guard auxiliary. il Motor B 120:106 Ag '67
Young skippers set a safety record. J. O'Brien. il Motor B 119:32-3+ My '67
Youngster's first boat. J. A. Emmett. il Outdoor Life 139:112+ Mr '67

BOAZ, Martha
Librarian in Vietnam. Wilson Lib Bul 41:962-7 My '67
BOBBY; story. See Whitehill, J.
BOBCAT hunting
Tallyho, the bobcat. L. Miracle. il Outdoor Life 140:70-3+ O '67
BOBCATS
Chat mysterieux, uncanny cat. R. Rood. Audubon 69:86-8+ N '67; Same abr. with title Wildcat: wraith with claws. Read Digest 91:25-6+ N '67
Nice pussy, twenty pounds of dynamite. S. P. Young. il Am For 73:10+ O '67
BOBWHITE shooting. See Quail shooting
BOCCA, Geoffrey
Those were the years that were: vets, jets, mods, and minis. Sat R 50:47+ Ap 22 '67
BOCCE. See Bowling
BÖCK, A. and Neidhardt, F. C.
Genetic mapping of phenylalanyl-sRNA synthetase in escherichia coli. bibliog Science 157:78-9 Jl 7 '67
BODE, Carl
Passage; poem. New Repub 158:32 Ja 6 '68
BODE, Elroy
How will I know my true love? story. Redbook 129:36-7 Ag '67
BODIES, Dead. See Cadavers
BODMAN, Henry T.
U.S. dollar: address, September 22, 1967. Vital Speeches 34:42-4 N 1 '67
BODY chemistry. See Biochemistry
BODY fat. See Fat
BODY fluids
Nature's sleeping potion? humoral factor. Sci Am 217:56+ O '67
See also
Perspiration
BODY size
Another size for man? R. J. Hansen and M. J. Holley, jr. il Sat R 50:74-5 D 2 '67
Earlier maturation in man. J. M. Tanner. il Sci Am 218:21-7 Ja '68
BODY snatching
Body snatchers; excerpts from The doctors' story. T. Gallagher. il Am Heritage 18:64-73 Je '67
BODY temperature. See Temperature, Animal and human
BODY weight. See Weight (physiology)
BOEHLKE, Kenneth W. See Eleftheriou, B. E. jt. auth.

BOEHM, Ann E. See White, M. A. jt. auth.
BOEHM, George A. W.
Aspirin: wonder drug nobody understands. Read Digest 90:116-18 Mr '67
Tomorrow's airports vs. the ground barrier. Read Digest 91:123-7 S '67
BOEHM, Paul
Experimental programs. Parks & Rec 2:37-8+ D '67
BOEHM-OLLER, Emma
Francisco Oller: Puerto Rican impressionist. Américas 19:22-7 S '67
BOEING company
AC Carousel chosen as 747 nav system. P. J. Klass. il Aviation W 86:68-71+ F 20 '67
Accelerating the jet age; interview. W. Allen. Nations Bsns 55:58-9+ Ag '67
Boeing award means $100 million for AC. il Tech W 20:38-9 F 6 '67
Boeing focuses top talent on 747. Aviation W 87:100-1 N 20 '67
Boeing's electronics capability growing. J. Rhea. Aero Tech 21:40 O 9 '67
Boom that's brewing a storm; SST. il Bsns W p64-5+ O 28 '67
Expanding jet age: financial and economic implications; address, October 9, 1967. T. A. Wilson. Vital Speeches 34:88-92 N 15 '67
Giant jets: the next revolution in air transport; special report; with editorial comment. il Aviation W 87:21, 35-47+ N 20 '67
Lot of people for a lot of plane; 747 successfully marketed. il Time 89:86 Je 16 '67
Megalopolis comes to the Northwest. P. Herrera. il Fortune 76:118-23+ D '67
Subcontractor role grows in 747 work. R. G. O'Lone. il Aviation W 87:99-101+ N 20 '67
SST program responsibility shifts; with editorial comment. H. D. Watkins. il Aviation W 86:11 28-9 My 8 '67
BOELLSTORFF, Ruth
Shall we go inside? Farm J 91:37 Jl '67
BOES, Robert J. See Pak, W. L. jt. auth.
BOESCHENSTEIN, Harold
Owens-Corning molds an industry. il pors Bsns W p 120-2+ Mr 4 '67
BOETH, Richard
Inquisition of an aphorist; poem. Atlan 219:114 F '67
BOETTINGER, Henry M.
Big gap in economic theory. bibliog f Harvard Bsns R 45:51-8 Jl '67
BOG vegetation
Sea, sand and bog; Long Island bog flowers. D. G. Schleisner. il Audubon 69:34-5 Jl '67
BOGACHIEL VALLEY. See Olympic National Park
BOGAN, Louise
Three songs: Little Lobelia's song; Psychiatrist's song; Masked woman's song. New Yorker 43:45 Ap 1 '67
Verse (cont) New Yorker 43:160-2 Mr 4 '67
BOGART, Humphrey
In my opinion. E. Roseman. Seventeen 26:268 F '67
BOGER, Louise Ade
Antiques; questions & answers. See issues of House & Garden incorporating Living for young homemakers
BOGGESS, William P.
Screen-test your credit risks. Harvard Bsns R 45:113-22 N '67
BOGGIANO, Gian
Civilized teacher's lament; poem. Christian Cent 84:716 My 31 '67
Low-priced admission; poem. Christian Cent 84:136 F 1 '67
BOGGS, Jean Sutherland
Europe's Canada. Art N 66:47-9 N '67
BOGIE, Thomas M.
Discussion in Dallas. por Library J 92:2127-30 Je 1 '67
BOGOTÁ, Colombia

Social conditions
Summer in Bogotá; Association for international development (AID) W. M. Barbieri. America 117:274-7 S 16 '67
BOGS
Bog; Rockland Bog, Me. L. Dietz. il Field & S 72:56-7+ My '67
See also
Bog vegetation
Peat bogs
BOGUNOVIC, Branko
Fall of a China-watcher. il por Time 90:48-9 Jl 21 '67
BOHDANECKA, Milada, and others
Amnesic effects of small bilateral brain puncture in the mouse. bibliog Science 157:334-6 Jl 21 '67

La BOHÈME; opera. See Puccini, G.

BOHEMIA
Romance with reality. G. McSlroy. il Opera
N 31:8-12 F 4 '67
BOHEMIAN buns. See Buns
BOHEMIANISM
Romance with reality. G. McElroy. il Opera
N 31:8-12 F 4 '67
Romantic rebels: an informal history of
Bohemianism in America, by E. Hahn. Review
Sat R il 50:42 F 11 '67. B. Atkinson
Where is new Bohemia going? J. Gruen.
Vogue 150:101+ Ag 1 '67
See also
Beatniks
BOHLEN UND HALBACH, Alfred Krupp von.
See Krupp von Bohlen und Halbach, A.
BÖHM, Karl
Böhm's Bayreuth Tristan. R. Lawrence.
Sat R 50:63 Ja 28 '67
Musical events; shared conducting of concert
by New York philharmonic. W. Sargeant.
New Yorker 43:203-4 O 21 '67
BOHR, Niels Henrik David
Books. O. R. Frisch. Sci Am 216:145-8+ Je '67
BOIARDO, Ruggiero
Macabre home of a capo, monument to mob
murder. il por Life 63:16-17 S 1 '67
BOIGNY, Félix Houphouet-. See Houphouet-
Boigny, F.
BOIKO, Claire
Book that saved the earth: drama. Plays
27:37-42 Ja '68
Cupivac; drama. Plays 26:59-64 My '67
How to choose a boy; drama. Plays 27:67-70
Ja '68
Lady Moon and the thief; drama. Plays 27:
77-82 O '67
Roamin' Jo and Juli; or, How the West was
lost; drama. Plays 24:1-14 Ap '67
Snowman who overstayed; drama. Plays 26:
70-4 Mr '67
Young Abe's destiny; drama. Plays 26:43-8
F '67
BOILEAU, Helen Houston
Thirty ways to make food more enticing.
Parents Mag 42:80-1 O '67
BOILS
Boils. E. Maxwell. Todays Health 45:77-8 N
'67
BOIS, Paul J.
Building a wood-disk patio? treat it right!
Am For 73:32-3+ Ap '67
BOISE Cascade corporation
Profit lovely as a tree. Time 90:68-9 Jl 21 '67
BOLACK, Thomas Felix
Two millionaires, East and West. il pors Sat
Eve Post 240:26-7 D 30 '67
BOLES, Paul Darcy
April trombone; story. Seventeen 26:160-1 Ap
'67
Million guitars; story. Seventeen 26:134-5
O '67
Somewhere music; story. Seventeen 26:82-3
Jl '67
BOLEX 16 pro cameras. See Moving picture
cameras
BOLGER, Ray
Hey, Ray, how 'bout Once in love with Amy!
G. Frazier. pors Esquire 68:110-11 S '67
BOLIDES. See Meteors
BOLIN, Rolf L.
From the log of the Te Vega; with biographical sketch. Natur Hist 76:6, 24-31 Ag '67
BOLIVIA
Bolivia under Barrientos. D. B. Heath. bibliog f Cur Hist 53:275-82+ N '67
See also
Communism—Bolivia
Guerrillas—Bolivia
Trials—Bolivia

Economic conditions
Problems in La Paz. il Newsweek 70:40+
O 30 '67

Politics and government
Benefits of subversion. Time 91:25 Ja 19 '68
BÖLL, Heinrich
Rain is hard. Esquire 67:100 Mr '67
BOLL weevils
Hampea Schlecht: possible primary host of
the cotton boll weevil. P. A. Fryxell and
M. J. Lukefahr. bibliog Science 155:1568-9
Mr 24 '67
BOLLING, Richard
Bolling is right. New Repub 157:8-9 N 11 '67
BOLLWORMS, Pink
Isolation of N,N-diethyl-m-toluamide, deet,
from female pink bollworm moths. W. A.
Jones and M. Jacobson. bibliog il Science
159:99-100 Ja 5 '68

BOLOGNA, Italy
Music
Rome, Bologna. F. Nuzzo. Opera N 31:33 Mr
11 '67
BOLOGNA book fair for children and youth.
See Book fairs
BOLSHEVISM. See Communism—Russia
BOLSHOI opera company. See Opera—Russia
BOLTON, Charles M.
Tight sheathing tops tunneling. Am City 82:
159-60 Je '67
BOLTON, Isabel, pseud. See Miller, M. B.
BOMAR, Cora Paul
Senate ESEA hearings near conclusion; excerpts from testimony, August 15, 1967,
ed. by G. Krettek and E. D. Cooke. Wilson Lib Bul 42:229 O '67
BOMARZO; opera. See Ginastera, A.
BOMB shelters. See Atomic bomb shelters
BOMBARDMENT satellites. See Artificial satellites—Military applications
BOMBAY
Music
Reporter at large; jazz. V. Mehta. New
Yorker 43:209-10+ D 9 '67
BOMBERGER, Phil
Riflery included in indoor recreation program.
Parks & Rec 2:40+ Ap '67
BOMBING planes. See Airplanes, Military
BOMBS
Deadly mementos; unexploded bombs in Germany. il Newsweek 69:60 Mr 27 '67
BON voyage parties. See Entertaining
BONANNO, Joseph
How Joe Bonanno schemed to kill, and lost.
il por Life 63:18-19 S 1 '67
BONAVENA, Oscar
Bean-can bout in Frankfurt. M. Kram. il
pors Sports Illus 27:20-3 S 25 '67
BONAVENTURA, Joseph, and Riggs, Austen
Polymerization of hemoglobins of mouse and
man: structural basis. bibliog Science 158:
800-2 N 10 '67
BOND, Harold
Glove; poem. New Yorker 43:60 N 4 '67
BOND, Horace Julian. See Bond, J.
BOND, James (literary character) See Spies in
literature
BOND, Julian
Representative; interview. New Yorker 43:
34-5 Ap 1 '67
about
Infamous Mr Bond. M. Frady. il pors Sat
Eve Post 240:94-6+ My 6 '67
BOND analysts. See Investments—Advisers
BOND campaigns. See Municipal bonds
BONDARCHUK, Sergei
Movers. A. Sarris. por Sat R 50:14 D 23 '67
BONDS
Bargain days again in bonds. il U S News
63:82-4 Jl 3 '67
Bargains in bonds, for how long? what investors can earn on bonds now. il U S News
63:34-5 Jl 17 '67
Bond men sweep out the shop. il Bsns W
p93-4 Jl 1 '67
Bonds vs. stocks: growing dilemma. il U S
News 63:87-9 D 18 '67
Bull market in bonds. il Fortune 75:212-13
Mr '67
Buyers' market in bonds. C. Morgello. il
Newsweek 71:47 Ja 1 '68
Crucial bond rates. il Fortune 75:40+ My '67
Markets run scared as tax bill falters. il
Bsns W p30-1 N 4 '67
Nervous scramble. Time 90:90+ O 27 '67
Wall Street: the bonds test. C. Morgello.
Newsweek 69:89 Mr 20 '67
See also
Municipal bonds
State bonds

Marketing
When half a loaf is the answer; Textron
bond issue. il Bsns W p 118+ Jl 8 '67

Rating
Bargains in bonds, a look at today's record
yields. il U S News 63:116+ N 6 '67
Money tightens, bond yields up. U S News 62:
96 Je 26 '67
BONDS, Convertible
Cloud over convertible debentures. il Bsns W
p 143-4+ O 7 '67
Ins & outs of convertible securities. il
Changing T 21:43-5 Mr '67
Wall Street: closing the convertible loophole. C. Morgello. il Newsweek 70:75 N 6
'67

BONDS, Government
All about Treasury's new savings bonds. il
    U S News 62:35-6 Mr 6 '67
Bond yields: rising again. U S News 62:87
    Mr 6 '67
Breaking the impasse: Bonn to buy medium-
    term U.S. Treasury bonds to offset bal-
    ance of payments. Newsweek 69:60 Mr 27
    '67
Savings bonds are different now. il Changing
    T 21:45-6 Ag '67
Staid U.S. treasurys get speculative dash. il
    Bsns W p 115-16 D 2 '67
    See also
State bonds

Russia
Betting on the czar; bonds issued by Russia's
    Czarist government. Newsweek 69:76 F 27
    '67

BONDS, Industrial development
Bond doggle. P. Stern. New Repub 156:8-9
    My 6 '67
Industrial bonds win fans; to lure new in-
    dustry. Bsns W p 108 Ag 26 '67
Tax incentive that's coming under fire. il U S
    News 62:94-6 Je 12 '67
BONDS, Municipal. See Municipal bonds
BONDS, Revenue
Borrowing at the ballot box. Time 90:101 N 17
    '67
Calling the shots on the cities; Moody's in-
    vestors service, inc. and Standard & Poor's
    corp. evaluate cities' financial strength. il
    Bsns W p88-90 S 2 '67
    See also
Bonds, Industrial development
BONDS, School. See School finance
BONDS, State. See State bonds
BONE, Hugh A.
American party politics, elections, and vot-
    ing behavior. bibliog f Ann Am Acad 372:
    124-37 Jl '67
BONE
Infrared analysis of rat bone; age depend-
    ency of amorphous and crystalline mineral
    fractions. J. D. Termine and A. S. Posner;
    reply with rejoinder. D. McConnell. Sci-
    ence 155:607-8 F 3 '67
BONE cancer. See Cancer
BONE marrow. See Marrow
BONERS. See Blunders
BONES

Diseases
Battling the bone-thinner; osteoporosis. G. D.
    Whedon. il Todays Health 45:66-8 S '67
    See also
Paget's disease
BONFANTE, Jordan
Hail to the new king of Tonga. Life 63:58-65
    Jl 21 '67
Most unlikely lark. Life 63:117-18+ S 22 '67
O.J. Life 63:74A-74B+ O 27 '67
Technocrat. Life 63:90A-90B+ N 17 '67
Walls within walls, but everywhere a view.
    Life 62:89-90 F 10 '67
BONHAM, Margaret
Wish for an afternoon; story. Good H 165:
    62-5 Ag '67
BONHOEFFER, Dietrich
Bonhoeffer's love letters. Time 90:100 D 1 '67
Catholic looks at Bonhoeffer. W. Kuhns. Chris-
    tian Cent 84:330-2 Je 28 '67
Changing mind. W. E. Hull. Christian Cent
    84:920-1 Jl 12 '67
He inspired the death of God. J. Pelikan.
    Sat R 50:30+ Mr 18 '67
Martyr's love. por Newsweek 70:84 D 4 '67
BONIN ISLANDS
Changing flags. il Sr Schol 91:18 D 7 '67
Complete meeting of the minds. il Newsweek
    70:49-50 N 27 '67
Something for the hat. il Time 90:24 N 24 '67
U.S. and Japan reaffirm common objectives
    and pledge continued cooperation. L. B.
    Johnson; E. Sato. Dept State Bul 57:742-7
    D 4 '67
What U.S. is giving back to Japan. il U S
    News 63:54 N 27 '67
BONIS, L. J. and Duga, J. J.
Fundamental phenomena in the materials
    sciences. Science 155:357-9+ Ja 20 '67
BONN, Myrtle
Have traveled, will teach. Am Ed 3:1-3 F
    '67
Teachers then and now. Am Ed 3:13-19 O '67
BONN

Music
Bonn; production of Strauss' Elektra. H.
    Koegler. Opera N 31:29 Mr 18 '67

BONNER, James, and others
Biology of isolated chromatin. bibliog Science
    159:47-56 Ja 5 '68
BONNER, Paul H. Jr
Apocryphal diary: entries Harold Nicholson
    never wrote. Vogue 150:229 N 1 '67
BONNET, Honoré
Encore Napoleon. il por Time 89:43-4 Mr 24
    '67
BONNEVILLE national races. See Automobile
    racing
BONNIERS, Albert, förlag. See Publishers and
    publishing—Sweden
BONSAI. See Trees, Dwarf
BONUS system
Bonus plan where performance counts; pie
    that GM's managers share. il Bsns W p58+
    My 13 '67
Rare blending of carrot and stick; annual
    meeting of the nation's largest independ-
    ent distributor of plumbing and heating
    equipment. il Bsns W p 132+ Mr 4 '67
BOOBY traps, Military. See Mines, Military
BOODLEY, James W.
Surfactants help make water wetter. Horti-
    culture 45:28-9 Jl '67
BOOHER, Edward E.
Decades ahead from a publisher's view; ex-
    cerpts from address, June 22, 1967. Science
    158:882-4 N 17 '67
BOOK advertising. See Books—Advertising
BOOK art foundation, Frankfort on the Main.
    See Book industries and trade—Germany
    (Federal Republic)
BOOK auctions. See Book sales
BOOK awards. See Literary prizes
BOOK awards, National. See National book
    awards
BOOK binding. See Bookbinding
BOOK buying for libraries. See Libraries—
    Acquisitions
BOOK censorship. See Censorship
BOOK clubs
    See also
Book-of-the-month club
BOOK collecting
Amy Loveman awards: who says books are
    dying? J. F. Fixx. Sat R 50:26 Jl 15 '67
Book collecting anyone? three noted col-
    lectors. J. T. Winterich. il Sat R 50:129-
    30+ Mr 11 '67
    See also
Book sales
BOOK covers
Covers 1966 at AIGA show. il Pub W 191:74-
    6+ Ap 3 '67
Nonfiction jackets dominate Turck & Rein-
    field contest winners. il Pub W 191:81-2
    My 1 '67
Six outstanding book jackets designed in
    1967. M. R. Kraner. il Pub W 193:68 Ja 1 '68
Torn jackets hinder sales of books. Pub W
    191:49 Mr 27 '67
Variable look: covers of Bantam books.
    R. G. G. Price. il Atlan 219:112 F '67

Anecdotes, facetiae, satire, etc.
Book jacket of the month club. K. Haugaard.
    Sat R 50:3 Jl 8 '67
BOOK design
Approach to Americana at Kentucky press.
    il Pub W 191:102 My 1 '67
Architectural design in Walker gift book. il
    Pub W 191:94-5 Je 12 '67
Designers assess scholarly books: AAUP book
    show. C. B. Grannis. Pub W 192:65 Jl 3
    '67
Designer's corner. S. Salter. See first issue of
    each month of Publishers' weekly
Doctor Maurice Spitzer: pioneer of the Ju-
    daic book art. I. Soifer. il Pub W 192:83-
    4+ S 4 '67
Jan Tschichold: proponent of asymmetry and
    tradition. P. Standard. il Pub W 191:88-92+
    My 1 '67
Magazine approach for rocketry book. il Pub
    W 191:95+ Je 12 '67
Making of In memory of my feelings. G.
    Williams, jr. il Pub W 193:60+ Ja 1 '68
Quality in book production; address, Septem-
    ber 20, 1967. H. Williamson. Pub W 192:80+
    O 2 '67
    See also
William Addison Dwiggins award
BOOK exhibits
AIGA children's book show. il Pub W 192:72-
    4+ O 2 '67
Baker & Taylor to sponsor preview in August.
    Pub W 191:60 Je 19 '67

BOOK exhibits—*Continued*
Children as authors; exhibition of books written and made by sixth graders in the Laboratory school at the University of Chicago. Z. Sutherland. Sat R 50:35 Mr 18 '67
Children's books selected for AIGA tour. il Library J 92:4564-6 D 15 '67
Conventions and exhibits; symposium. Pub W 191:28 Ap 3 '67
Designers assess scholarly books; AAUP book show. C. B. Grannis. Pub W 192:65 Jl 3 '67
Fifty books: great quality, less innovation. il Pub W 191:72+ Je 12 '67
First international art book exhibit; Paris. Pub W 192:33 S 4 '67
New England book show, books tour the region; award to Burton Jones. Pub W 191:90+ Mr 6 '67
1967 ABA convention trade exhibit; photographs. Pub W 191:36-7 Je 26 '67
Taste and a sense of history; western books; Western books exhibition. il Pub W 191:88+ Je 12 '67
Third annual exhibition of university press books. il Pub W 191:64-5+ Je 12 '67
    See also
Library exhibits
BOOK fairs
Bookman abroad; report on British bookshops, booksellers, and the Frankfurt book fair. R. Smith. il Pub W 192:44-8 N 20 '67
Frankfort book fair; latest edition. C. Northcott. Christian Cent 84:1472 N 15 '67
Frankfurt fair, 1967; books, politics & demonstrations. J. Daves. il Pub W 192:19-22 N 20 '67
Midwest book festival stimulates sales. il Pub W 192:31-2 O 9 '67
Plans for fifth Bologna fair for children's books. Pub W 193:47 Ja 8 '68
Religious publishers group views Frankfurt fair. Pub W 193:27 Ja 1 '68
BOOK illustration. See Illustration of books and periodicals
BOOK indexes. See Indexes
BOOK industries and trade
BMI report part II; symposium. il Pub W 192:50-2+ D 4 '67
Bookmaking. See first issue of each month of Publishers' weekly
SRA designer cites use of industrial techniques; summary of address. W. Zbdeblick. Pub W 191:95-6 Ap 3 '67
Supplies for bookmaking, a look into the future. P. De Florez. Pub W 191:86-7 Mr 6 '67
    See also
Bookbinding
Books—Prices
Books—Reprints
Booksellers and bookselling
Printing
Printing industry
Publishers and publishing

Advertising
See Books—Advertising

Law
But can you do that? H. F. Pilpel. See occasional issues of Publishers' weekly

Statistics
ABPC cites 1966 book boom; juvenile sales up 50 percent. Library J 92:4206+ N 15 '67
Needed: more statistical information; summary of address. R. M. Peck. Pub W 192:27 N 20 '67

Africa
See also
Copyright—Africa

Australia
Books in Australia. B. Reid. il Library J 92:4123-6 N 15 '67

France
See also
Publishers and publishing—France

Germany (Federal Republic)
Book art foundation; Frankfurt. S. Salter. Pub W 192:82-3 D 4 '67

Spain
See also
Publishers and publishing—Spain

United States
Book industry in 1968; six leaders view the future; symposium. il Pub W 193:15-19 Ja 1 '68

Stressing a cost-effectiveness analysis; summary of address. H. F. Drury. il Pub W 192:26-7 N 20 '67
    See also
Book manufacturers' institute
BOOK jackets. See Book covers
BOOK jobbers
Complex world of book wholesaling. R. H. Smith. Pub W 192:43 O 9 '67
    See also
Baker and Taylor company
BOOK lending, Library. See Libraries—Circulation, loans, etc.
BOOK lists. See Books and reading—Best books; Childrens literature—Bibliography; Reading lists
BOOK making (betting)
Frankie Carlin, the bookie. J. Flaherty. il N Y Times Mag p28-9+ Ap 2 '67
$7 billion from illegal bets and a blight on sports; Cosa nostra involvement. il Life 63:92-3 S 8 '67
    See also
Ladbroke and company
BOOK manufacturers' institute
BMI report, part 1: troubles of '67, forecasts for '68. il Pub W 192:23-8 N 20 '67
BMI report, part 11: sweeping internal changes are voted. il Pub W 192:50-2 D 4 '67
1966 in review. Pub W 191:54-5 Ja 30 '67
BOOK numbers
Copyright, book numbering; remarks. P. Du Sautoy. Pub W 192:27-8 Jl 24 '67
Literary information systems; summary of addresses and panel discussion at ABPC conference. Pub W 191:35-7 Ap 10 '67
Standard book numbering approved for U.S.A. Pub W 192:76 S 25 '67
Standards group to study book numbering. Pub W 192:35 O 16 '67
Uniform encoding planned for paperback backstraps. il Pub W 191:63 Je 19 '67
BOOK-of-the-month club
B-O-M club's fulfillment moving to Pennsylvania. Pub W 192:34 S 4 '67
BOMC pays record price for Alliluyeva memoirs. Pub W 191:40-1 My 22 '67
BOOK postage. See Postal rates—United States
BOOK prices. See Books—Prices
BOOK prizes. See Literary prizes
BOOK processes in libraries. See Libraries—Technical processes
BOOK rarities
Books. P. W. Schmidtchen. See issues of Hobbies
Sampling of rare books; symposium. il Wilson Lib Bul 41:566-607+ F '67

Facsimiles
Facsimile from Orion is first machine-made Blake. il Pub W 192:94+ N 6 '67
Franklin's Bagatelles in facsimile. il Pub W 193:66-7 Ja 1 '68
Limited editions, unlimited prices. D. Dempsey. Sat R 50:31 My 13 '67
BOOK repairing. See Books—Conservation and restoration
BOOK restoration. See Books—Conservation and restoration
BOOK reviewers. See Critics
BOOK reviews
Book world supplement for Washington, Chicago. Pub W 192:34 Jl 3 '67
Books; choosing books for review. M. Muggeridge. Esquire 67:44+ F '67
New showcase for WJT's book coverage. Pub W 191:36 Ap 17 '67
What I did to books and vice versa; experiences of former editor of Book week. R. Kluger; discussion. Harper 234:8+ F '67
WLB review of books; symposium. bibliog Wilson Lib Bul 42:466-524 Ja '68
    See also
New York review of books (periodical)
Newspapers—Sections, columns, etc.
BOOK sales
Going, going, gone! bidding at book auction. P. W. Schmidtchen. il Hobbies 72:104+ S '67
BOOK selection
Book examination centers urged at RPG meeting. Pub W 192:29-30 O 30 '67
Choosing for our youngest. A. Rusk. il Library J 92:1294-5 Mr 15 '67
Examination of methods used in a study of decision-making; science library materials. M. B. Snyder. il ALA Bul 61:1319-23 D '67
Must children read in packs? M. Alexander. Pub W 191:120-1 F 20 '67

BOOK selection—*Continued*
Nervous Nellies on race relations? school libraries. A. G. Mims. bibliog Library J 92:1291-3+ Mr 15 '67
100 miles an hour in the fog. K. Nyren. Library J 92:513 F 1 '67
Standard lists, an unstandardized view. J. Shera. Wilson Lib Bul 41:615+ F '67
Trade winds; guidelines offered by R. H. Viguers on choosing a book for a child. J. Beatty, jr. Sat R 50:12+ N 11 '67
    See also
Booksellers and bookselling—Stock
Libraries—Acquisitions

BOOK series. See Series, Book

BOOK tariff
    See also
Duty free importation

BOOK that saved the earth; drama. See Boiko, C.

BOOK thefts
Security survey indicates turnstiles widely used; academic libraries. Library J 92:3362+ O 1 '67

BOOK trade. See Book industries and trade

BOOK week
Book week on a budget; suggestions from Pennsylvania state library. R. Fink. il Library J 92:3124-5 S 15 '67
Children's book week promotion and fairs. il Pub W 192:122 Jl 10 '67
Story of two weeks. E. S. Hendryson. PTA Mag 62:13 N '67

BOOK wholesalers. See Book jobbers

BOOKBINDING
Adhesive binding: some advantages and aspirations; panel discussion. il Pub W 191:86-8 F 6 '67
AB-SP adds a bindery to its Saddle Brook plant. il Pub W 192:78+ Ag 7 '67
Binding standards seen ineffective. Library J 93:26 Ja 1 '68
Binding trends cited at Philadelphia clinic. Pub W 191:94-5 Ap 3 '67
Bookbinding by Kurt Londenberg. H. Halbey. il Craft Horiz 27:30-3 Ja '67
Consent agreement ends U.S. library bindings suit. Pub W 192:28 O 30 '67
Eighteen publishers of children's books charged with price fixing by Justice department; the library market. il Library J 92:1982-5 My 15 '67
Flex binding: its uses in hand bookbinding. P. Lada-Mocarski. Pub W 192:82 Ag 7 '67
Libraries make a noise; suits over setting net prices for specially bound library editions. Bsns W p39 My 6 '67
Library binding suit drags on in Chicago. Library J 92:1103 Mr 15 '67
Net pricing and the salesman. D. Melcher. Library J 92:1979-80 My 15 '67
New bindery triples Spaulding-Moss capacity. il Pub W 191:116 F 6 '67
New plaintiffs debate entering library binding suit; state of Michigan joins; Detroit library withdraws. Pub W 191:76 F 27 '67
New standards for library binding. il Pub W 191:77-8 Je 12 '67
Proposed standards for library bindings: what is strong enough? D. Melcher. il Pub W 192:18-20 D 11 '67
Publishers advise binders to specialize; manufacturer-publisher relations; summary of panel discussion. il Pub W 191:106-7 F 6 '67
Publishers consent decrees override legal suits; high prices for children's books in library editions. Library J 92:4563-4 D 15 '67
Real issues in the library bindings cases. D. Melcher. Pub W 191:37 My 1 '67
St Crispin bindery branches out. Pub W 192:35 O 23 '67
U.S. sues eighteen publishers on library bindings, net prices. Pub W 191:32-3 My 1 '67
    See also
St Crispin bindery, incorporated

BOOKBINDING machinery
Some new advances in bindery technology; report of seminar. F. B. Myrick. il Pub W 193:50-1+ Ja 1 '68
Tools of the trade; Charlton casemaker. il Pub W 191:101-2 Je 12 '67

BOOKER, Simeon
Adam Clayton Powell, the man behind the controversy. Ebony 22:27-30+ Mr '67
I'm a soul brother. Ebony 22:150-4 Ap '67
What Republican victory means to the Negro. Ebony 22:88-90+ F '67

BOOKKEEPERS. See Accountants

BOOKKEEPING
Dance teacher in the community. D. R. Sellars. Dance Mag 42:84-5 Ja '68

Financial record-keeping simplified; method for dancers. R. Gorewitz. il Dance Mag 41:78-9 S; 90-3 O; 90-2 N '67; 42:88-90 Ja '68

BOOKLETS. See Pamphlets

BOOKMAKING. See Book making (betting)

BOOKMOBILES
Bookmobile service to schools. G. K. Schenk. Wilson Lib Bul 41:853+ Ap '67
Bookmobiles and bookmobile service, by E. F. Brown. Review
    Wilson Lib Bul 41:1073-4 Je '67. G. K. Schenk
From Buttermilk to Gum Log; bookmobiles tote more than books to Arkansas River Valley families. W. M. Lewis. il Am Ed 3:8-11 Je '67
IMC on wheels; El Rancho school district, Pico Rivera, Calif. J. H. Moody. il Library J 92:304-5 Ja 15 '67
Joy on wheels. L. Conger. Writer 80:7+ D '67
Pioneering with the Job corps; camp near Curlew, Wash; North central regional library, Wenatchee, Wash. J. H. Pardee. il Library J 92:748-9 F 15 '67

BOOKS
    See also
Best sellers
Royalties
Textbooks

Advertising

Aspects of direct mail; summary of talks on direct mail methods. W. R. Hooper; D. M. Hannawalt; A. Arau. Pub W 191:29-30 Ap 3 '67
But does it sell books? buttons as a vehicle for publicity and other means of promotion. D. Dempsey. Sat R 50:26-7 Mr 18 '67
FTC hits false advertising of health books. S. Wagner. Pub W 192:35-6 Jl 24 '67
Leading promotions June—August. il Pub W 191:46-66 Ap 24 '67
Lovitt's advice to publishers at NABE meeting; summary of address. G. Lovitt. Pub W 192:31-2 N 20 '67
Major promotions for January books. il Pub W 192:17-27 O 30 '67
PPA workshop panel gives tips on author tours. Pub W 192:33-4 N 6 '67
Rights and wrongs of advertising and translation; concerning The master and Margarita by M. Bulgakov; letter. M. Ginsburg. Pub W 193:45-6 Ja 15 '68
Rodale seeks court review of free speech issue in book advertsing. S. Wagner. Pub W 192:36-7 O 9 '67
September books; some early fall campaigns. il Pub W 191:106-41 Je 5 '67
Spring highspots: calendar of 275 leading campaigns from February to May. il Pub W 191:178-208 Ja 23 '67
Stein & Day happening cannot happen in park. Pub W 192:36 S 4 '67
275 fall highspots: October—December books. il Pub W 192:200-31 Ag 28 '67

Care

ABC's of caring for books. Am Home 70:122 Mr '67

Classification
See Classification

Collectors and collecting
See Book collecting

Conservation and restoration

Book restoration in Florence. B. A. Bannon. il Pub W 192:27-8 N 6 '67
Cleaning and preserving bindings and related materials: on the care of valuable books. il Consumer Bul 51:32 Ja '68
Florence rises from the flood. J. Judge. il Nat Geog Mag 132:1-43 Jl '67
Grant to LC launches Brittle book study. Pub W 191:117 Mr 6 '67
Libraries of Florence, November 1966; with recommendations and resolution passed by ALA council. A. T. Hamlin. il ALA Bul 61:141-51 F '67
Library crisis in Italy; inaction in Rome, serious threat to the National library of Florence. A. T. Hamlin. il Library J 92:2516-22 Jl '67
Operation Booklift; fire aftermath projects of the Jewish theological seminary of America. D. Dempsey. il Sat R 50:39-41 Ap 15 '67
Painting hospital in the lemon grove. H. J. Plenderleith. il UNESCO Courier 20:24-34 Ja '67

BOOKS—Conservation and restoration—*Cont.*
Reproduction vs. preservation; excerpt from Care and preservation of books. J. Alden; reply. J. B. Blake. Library J 92:507-8 F 1 '67
Saving the libraries of Florence; Committee to rescue Italian art (CRIA) C. Horton. bibliog il Wilson Lib Bul 41:1034-43 Je '67
Tale of two cities: council meetings; ALA midwinter report. E. Moon. il Library J 92:731-2 F 15 '67

Exhibitions
See Book exhibits

Large print books
See Printing—Legibility

Prices
Eighteen publishers of children's books charged with price fixing by Justice department; the library market. il Library J 92:1982-5 My 15 '67
Libraries make a noise; suits over setting net prices for specially bound library editions. Bsns W p39 My 6 '67
Library binding suit drags on in Chicago. Library J 92:1103 Mr 15 '67
Net pricing and the salesman. D. Melcher. Library J 92:1979-80 My 15 '67
New plaintiffs debate entering library binding suit; State of Michigan joins; Detroit library withdraws. Pub W 191:76 F 27 '67
Price averages, 1966, cited in major categories. il Pub W 191:54-5 F 13 '67
Publishers consent decrees override legal suits; high prices for children's books in library editions. Library J 92:4563-4 D 15 '67
Real issues in the library bindings cases. D. Melcher. Pub W 191:37 My 1 '67
U.S. sues eighteen publishers on library bindings, net prices. Pub W 191:32-3 My 1 '67

Repairing
See Books—Conservation and restoration

Reprints
Reprint pitfalls. E. Moon. Library J 92:4311 D 1 '67
Techniques in sales of rights; address, March 22, 1967. R. E. Banker. il Pub W 191:30-2 Ap 3 '67
That solid backlist title: how many to print? L. Shatzkin. Pub W 191:31-2 Je 12 '67

Statistics
See Book industries and trade—Statistics

Storage
See also
Warehouses

Transportation
Using the trucking industry more effectively; summary of address. J. D. Brothers. Pub W 192-56 D 4 '67

BOOKS, Art. See Art literature
BOOKS, Filmed. See Film adaptations
BOOKS, Illustrated. See Illustrated books
BOOKS, Illustration of. See Illustration of books and periodicals
BOOKS, Privately printed. See Privately printed books
BOOKS, Rare. See Book rarities
BOOKS and reading
Big books of '67: sumptuous and serious; coffee-table books. R. A. Sokolov. il Newsweek 70:105+ D 11 '67
Books. See issues of Vogue
Books. M. Muggeridge. See issues of Esquire
Books and the learning process; address, June 27, 1961. I. Hunt. Horn Bk 43:424-9 Ag '67
Coming attractions. il Time 91:60 Ja 12 '68
In praise of a café-au-lait bat; books every writer should own. L. Conger. Writer 80:9-10 Jl '67
Life book review. See issues of Life
Miseries of being bookbound S. Alexander. Life 62:29 Mr 17 '67
Notes and comment; good books to read in bed. New Yorker 43:31 Ap 8 '67
Outlook tower; books of interest to high school students; comp. by M. C. Scoggin. See issues of Horn book magazine
Reading: a commitment to consciousness; address, April 28, 1967. B. De Mott. il Wilson Lib Bul 42:74-9 S '67
Reading time: three minutes between classes. L. Conger. Writer 80:9-10 Je '67
Throw out the textbooks. A. Gordon. il Am Ed 3:5-7 S '67

What did a young critic read? W. H. Chamberlin. il Sat R 50:78-9 F 11 '67
What? study on my vacation? summer courses or summer reading. D. Klein. il Seventeen 26:252-3 Ap '67
WLB review of books; symposium. bibliog Wilson Lib Bul 42:466-524 Ja '68
See also
Best sellers
Bibliography
Biography
Book selection
Childrens literature
Childrens reading
College students—Reading
Fiction
Immoral literature and pictures
Libraries
Libraries and readers
Moving pictures and reading
National book committee
Reading lists
Reference books
Travel literature
Youth—Reading

Anecdotes, facetiae, satire, etc.
Books please. P. S. Dunkin. Library J 92:2373 Je 15 '67

Best books
ALA picks 1966's notable children's books. Pub W 191:34-5 Ap 3 '67
America's survey of new spring books. America 116:686+ My 6 '67
America's survey of notable fall books (cont) America 117:652-66 N 25 '67
Award-winning books for children. PTA Mag 62:31 S '67
Best books for young adults. NEA J 56:66-7 Mr '67; Same. Pub W 191:50 Mr 6 '67; Library J 92:1282+ Mr 15 '67; Wilson Lib Bul 41:769 Ap '67
Book review; ed. by M. Cooley. See issues of Library journal
Books; critics' choices for Christmas (cont) Commonweal 87:307-17 D 1 '67
Books 1966. il Nat R 19:136-9 F 7 '67
Five for year's end. G. Hicks. Sat R 50:19-20 D 30 '67
Notable books of 1966. Pub W 191:49 Mr 6 '67; Same. ALA Bul 61:329-31 Mr '67; NEA J 56:48+ Ap '67; Wilson Lib Bul 41:763-4 Ap '67; Library J 92:1102 Mr 15 '67; Discussion. 92:1099, 1775 Mr 15, My 1 '67
See also
Best sellers

Bibliography
Adult books for young adults; ed. by M. Trahan and R. Minudri. Library J 92:2209-15, 3870-2+, 4272-8, 4636-40; 93:313-16 S 15, O 15, N 15, D 15 '67, Ja 15 '68
Books for adults beginning to read (cont) Wilson Lib Bul 41:83-7 S '66; Correction. 41:671 Mr '67
Books for Christmas. G. Davenport. Nat R 19:1340-2 N 28 '67
Books for spring reading. R. Girson. il Sat R 50:46-7+ F 25 '67
Books for summer reading. Sr Schol 90:sup 16 My 12 '67
Books for summer reading; symposium. Sr Schol 90:sup 17-18+ Ap 28 '67
Books for young adults. Library J 92:4580-1 D 15 '67
Books to come; ed. by J. Putnam. Library J 92:611-90, 2194-256, 3465-555 F 1, Je 1, O 1 '67
Bookworm's boutique. House & Gard 132:42+ D '67
Curl up and read. See issues of Seventeen
Gift giving at $5 top. H. Frankel. Sat R 50:36-7 N 25 '67
Good buys in books for Christmas. Am Home 70:36 D '67
Involving students with books; ed. by J. Foster. il Sr Schol 90:sup9-16 Mr 31 '67
Merry schizmas to booksellers! current adult and children's titles. Pub W 192:39-40 Ag 21 '67
New books for fall reading. il Sr Schol 91:sup37+ S 28 '67
New books for high school students. Sr Schol 90:sup 12 Ap 14; 91:sup 11 D 7 '67
New Yorker lists at this season some books by its contributors published during the year (cont) New Yorker 43:221 D 2 '67
1968 spring preview: January through June. il Pub W 192:232-45 Ag 28 '67
Of power, freedom, ideology, and the American way of life. R. M. Perdew. il Sr Schol 90:sup25-36 Mr 31 '67
Paperbacks for slow readers. H. M. McDonnell. il Sr Schol 89:sup27 Ja 20 '67

BOOKS and reading—Bibliography—*Continued*
Potpourri. P. Adams. See issues of Atlantic
Roundup of new fall books. il Sr Schol 91:
   sup 17-21+ N 30 '67
SR's check list of holiday gift books; comp.
   by N. Sofian. Sat R 50:22+ N 25 '67
SR's check list of the week's new books;
   comp. by N. Sofian. See issues of Saturday
   review
Seasonal shelf; coffee-table volumes. il Time
   90:112+ D 15 '67
Second look. il Time 90:64+ D 29 '67
Slick-paper pages of the past. N. Samstag.
   il Sat R 50:50+ N 25 '67
Summer bookshelf. Sr Schol 90:40 My 19 '67
This week. See issues of Christian century
Time listings. See issues of Time
Trade winds. J. Beatty, jr. Sat R 50:6 D 23
   '67

International aspects

International book institute committee is
   named. Library J 92:2328+ Je 15 '67
International book programs; symposium. Pub
   W 191:34-5 My 29 '67
U.S. sets policy on int'l. book programs. Pub
   W 191:90 Ja 30 '67

Reading aloud

Oral interpretation. E. Worrell. il NEA J
   56:37-9 Mr '67
Special language. I. Neuman. Horn Bk 43:
   498-500 Ag '67

United States

See Books and reading

BOOKS and reading, Influence of. See Literature, Influence of

BOOKS as gifts
Books for Christmas: an anthropologist's
   choice. M. Mead. Redbook 130:22+ D '67
In the beginning was the word. P. Heins.
   Horn Bk 43:707 D '67

BOOKS for children. See Childrens literature

BOOKS for the people fund, incorporated
Literacy programs in Colombia; adaptation of
   report. M. D. Shepard. il Wilson Lib Bul
   41:829-33 Ap '67

BOOKS for the sick
   See also
   Libraries, Hospital

BOOKSELLERS and bookselling
ATPI-NACS: problems of order-fulfillment.
   Pub W 191:31-2 Mr 13 '67
Bookstore as learning center. R. H. Smith.
   Pub W 192:28 D 4 '67
Clerk's eye view; or, The fine art of book-
   selling. S. Auerbach. il Pub W 192:48-50
   O 16 '67; Reply. L. Russ. 192:40-1 O 30 '67
Factors in successful selling. Pub W 191:26-
   8 Ap 3 '67
New device perfected for detecting thieves.
   Pub W 191:67 F 13 '67
Take a bow: Anne Udin. G. Goulder. il Pub W
   191:54-5 My 8 '67
World of books; making your book sell. L.
   Friedman. Writer 80:5-6 N '67
You too can buy by mail; the publisher and
   the mail-order market. D. Dempsey. Sat R
   50:30+ Jl 15 '67
   See also
   College bookstores
   Libraries and booksellers

Accounting

Teletypewriters for bookstores: improving
   communications. il Pub W 192:41-2 Ag 21
   '67

Catholic literature

See also
Booksellers and bookselling—Religious literature

Childrens literature

Children's books: who is the audience? sum-
   mary of discussion at ABA. Pub W 191:38
   Je 26 '67
Why Rex Harrison is Dr Dolittle. L. Russ.
   Pub W 192:22 D 11 '67

Cookbooks

Personal approach for selling cookbooks.
   T. M. Crager. il Pub W 192:60-1 S 11 '67

Finance

Getting along with bankers: advice from two
   experts; William W. Lyon and Philip Mc-
   Callum. Pub W 192:65-6 Ag 21 '67

Paperback books

Paperback sales & circulation; letter to the
   editor. R. C. Woodward. Library J 92:1776
   My 1 '67

Small paperback shop that survives on low
   overhead; Savran's paperback shop, Minneapolis. E. Cottle. il Pub W 191:65-6 F 6
   '67
Titles, trouble and timber! or, Life among
   the paperbacks S. Auerbach. Pub W 192:
   43-4 O 23 '67

Publicity

Program of the week; panel on publicity. il
   Pub W 191:33-5 Mr 20 '67

Religious literature

Detroit Cokesbury marks its first year at new
   address. il Pub W 191:95-6 F 27 '67
Linz urges joint action to aid Catholic bookselling; summary of talk at National church
   goods association convention. W. Linz.
   Pub W 191:78 F 27 '67
New Presbyterian bookstore serves the whole
   person; Atlanta. B. R. Hooper. il Pub W
   192:90-1 S 25 '67
Religious books: new opportunities; summary
   of addresses. J. J. Delaney: L. Cassels; E.
   M. Merritt. il Pub W 191:53-5 Je 19 '67
Today's religious books: worth the bookseller's effort and experiment. C. B. Grannis. Pub W 192:79 S 25 '67

Returns policy

Golden press initiates non-returnable policy
   on books at longer discount; seller has
   option. Pub W 191:31 My 1 '67

Statistics

Comments on the survey of bookstore operating ratios. D. Melcher; reply. J. B. Kobak.
   Pub W 191:159 Ja 23 '67
Retail business goes up in third quarter of
   1967 but falls below increases in 1966 third
   quarter. Pub W 192:36-7 N 27 '67
Stores gain in second quarter but fall below
   1966 figures. Pub W 192:267 Ag 28 '67

Stock

Data processing for the bookstore; summary
   of panel discussion. il Pub W 191:34-5 Je 26
   '67
Five-point plan overcomes excess inventory
   problem. il Pub W 192:52-4 O 9 '67
Non-book items in the college store; symposium. Pub W 191:30 My 22 '67
Our stock control system is invaluable; John
   Mistletoe bookshop in Albany. H. D. Greene,
   3d. il Pub W 191:35-7 My 15 '67
Short cut to inventory control for retail booksellers. Coqui. il Pub W 192:29-31 D 25 '67

Study and teaching

Recruitment and training: a sound, practical
   plan. C. B. Grannis. Pub W 191:38 Je 12 '67

Wages and hours

Minimum wage laws and NACS stores; symposium. Pub W 191:34-5 My 22 '67

Africa

Institutional distributor to serve Middle East.
   Pub W 191:59 Ap 10 '67

Arizona

B. Dalton Phoenix store is new, spacious and
   fun. il Pub W 192:45 Ag 7 '67

California

Bookshop for nautical buffs; Barkentine book
   shop in Marina del Rey. il Pub W 191:75-6
   Je 19 '67
Cheesecake builds unique bookshop; Thunder-
   bird book shop, Carmel Valley. A. Brilliant.
   il Pub W 193:58-9 Ja 8 '68
Hunter's doing well in handsome new home;
   Beverly Hills. il Pub W 192:66-7 Ag 21 '67
La Jolla shop moves into charming old
   house; Johu Cole's book & craft shop.
   Pub W 191:49+ Mr 27 '67
Martindale's Century City branch: casual,
   quiet, and profitable. il Pub W 192:61-2
   Jl 17 '67
New Sather Gate shop thriving despite side-
   street locale; Berkeley. F. H. Potter. il
   Pub W 192:33-4 D 4 '67
Robert Campbell and Louis Epstein are
   honored at West coast dinner. il Pub W
   191:68+ Ap 24 '67
Take a bow Bob Campbell, Lou Epstein. il
   Pub W 191:103-5 Je 5 '67
Triburon books is a family-run store. Pub W
   191:250 Ja 23 '67

Canada

Canadian booksellers: a coming of age. J. Wilentz. Pub W 191:55-7 Je 19 '67
Classic shops set pace in Montreal. il Pub W
   193:76-9 Ja 15 '68

BOOKSELLERS and bookselling—Canada—
Continued
Prescription for success: hard work, imagination; reprint. M. Ballantyne. Pub W 191:49-50 Ap 17 '67
Selling books at Expo 67; British book shop. L. Melzack. il Pub W 192:44-5 O 23 '67
Selling scholarly books in Canada. Pub W 192:28-9 Jl 3 '67

Colorado
No structural changes needed for new store front; Chinook bookshop in Colorado Springs. il Pub W 191:66-7 F 6 '67

Florida
Elson's book store opened in Jacksonville. il Pub W 191:165 Je 5 '67
Posh bookstore in an elegant shopping center; Elson's book store, Palm Beach. il Pub W 191:66-7 F 13 '67

France
Books a la mode in Paris. R. Smith. il Pub W 192:35-6 N 27 '67
Direct mail bookselling threatened in France. H. R. Lottman. Pub W 191:30-2 Mr 27 '67
Fine bookstores in Paris? *mais oui! et beaucoup*. H. R. Lottman. il Pub W 193:34-7 Ja 1 '68

Georgia
Atlanta bookseller is star in USIA film for overseas. il Pub W 192:42 N 6 '67
New Presbyterian bookstore serves the whole person; Atlanta. B. R. Hooper. il Pub W 192:90-1 S 25 '67

Great Britain
Bookman abroad; report on British bookshops, booksellers, and the Frankfurt book fair. R. Smith. il Pub W 192:44-8 N 20 '67
See also
Booksellers and bookselling—Scotland

Illinois
Chestnut court, Winnetka thriving in its 30th year. il Pub W 192:67-8 N 13 '67
Lively promotion helps old-fashioned store; Landfield's book stall in Quincy. Pub W 192:41 Ag 14 '67

Maryland
Baltimore bookman fights against KKK terrorism; New era bookshop. Pub W 191:35-6 Mr 27 '67
Baltimore to protect beleaguered bookstore. Pub W 191:34 Ap 3 '67

Michigan
Detroit: a riot-torn city survives and bounces back. il Pub W 192:264-7 Ag 28 '67
Detroit Cokesbury marks it first year at new address. il Pub W 191:95-6 F 27 '67

Middle East
Institutional distributor to serve Middle East. Pub W 191:59 Ap 10 '67

Minnesota
Small paperback shop that survives on low overhead; Savran's paperback shop, Minneapolis. E. Cottle. il Pub W 191:65-6 F 6 '67

Missouri
B. Dalton, bookseller opens in St Louis area; St Ann. il Pub W 191:137-8 F 20 '67
B. Dalton chain grows: third store opened; St Louis suburb of Crestwood. il Pub W 191:49 My 1 '67

Montana
Montana store moves; expands paperback section; Val's book & magazine center, Great Falls. il Pub W 191:49 Mr 27 '67

New Jersey
Book house: inventory control boosts profits. il Pub W 191:85-6 Ap 24 '67
McGraw-Hill opens second bookstore, in New Jersey. il Pub W 191:50 Je 12 '67

New York (state)
Large crowds drawn to opening of Marboro bookshop; New York city. il Pub W 191:97 F 27 '67
Laurel book center: metamorphosis of a bookshop. il Pub W 191:64-6 Mr 6 '67
New Anderson's: making of a bookshop; store in Larchmont, N.Y. il Pub W 192:25-7 Ag 14 '67
Our stock control system is invaluable; John Mistletoe bookshop in Albany. H. D. Greene, 3d. il Pub W 191:35-7 My 15 '67
Rizzoli on Fifth avenue acquires more space. Pub W 191:250-1 Ja 23 '67

Service is key to Sci-Tech success. il Pub W 191:72-3 Ap 10 '67
Unusual window display stirs controversy, pickets; Taylor's paperback books, New York city. il Pub W 191:50 F 6 '67

Ohio
Chagrin Falls supports thriving book store. il Pub W 192:46 Ag 7 '67

Pennsylvania
Book boutique in old Philadelphia; Book and print shop. il Pub W 192:36-7 D 11 '67

Puerto Rico
Bookshop in Puerto Rico. il Pub W 191:60-2 Je 26 '67

Scotland
Near the Royal Mile; Thin's Edinburgh. P. Johnson. jr. il Pub W 192:33-5 O 9 '67

United States
ABA holds a regional meeting in Houston. il Pub W 192:18-22 D 4 '67
Annual crisis season; Christmas. R. H. Smith. Pub W 192:27 D 11 '67
Booksellers assay sales of Manchester book. Pub W 191:51 Mr 13 '67
Bookstores report: Manchester book sales mixed. Pub W 191:166 Je 5 '67
Can it hit 1-million? W. Manchester's The death of a President. Bsns W p28 Ap 1 '67
Comments on the survey of bookstore operating ratios. D. Melcher; reply. J. B. Kobak. Pub W 191:159 Ja 23 '67
How Mideast-crisis books sell. Pub W 192:47 Jl 24 '67
List of commission salesmen. Pub W 191:82-5 Ja 30 '67
New shops opened in 1966; West was most popular area. Pub W 191:106 Ja 30 '67
1966 Christmas business; the best in many years. il Pub W 191:104-6 Ja 30 '67
Publishers, booksellers exchange views. il Pub W 191:35+ Je 26 '67
Recruitment and training for bookselling. C. B. Grannis. Pub W 191:54 Je 26 '67
Retailing (cont of) Bookselling. See issues of Publishers' weekly
Twenty unread letters; disappointing sales of Svetlana's story. il Newsweek 70:80A D 4 '67
Who's who among the travelers; publishers' salesmen. Pub W 191:66-82 Ja 30; 56 F 13; 124 F 20; 80 F 27 '67
World of books. L. Friedman. Writer 80:5-6 N; 10 D '67; 81:4+ Ja '68
See also
American booksellers association
Christian booksellers association
College bookstores
Women's national book association

Vermont
Vermont bookshops promote book about Vt. bookshop. Pub W 191:52 Mr 27 '67

Washington. D.C.
Woodward & Lothrop and Dayton co. talking of merging. Pub W 191:250 Ja 23 '67

Washington (state)
Competition: stimulus to successful Seattle shop; Lea's bookshop. il Pub W 191:53 My 8 '67

BOOKSELLING in libraries
Library as marketplace; proposal that commercial bookstores be established in public libraries. N. Kirin. il Wilson Lib Bul 41:617-21+ F '67

BOOKSTORES. See Booksellers and bookselling; College bookstores

BOOLEAN algebra. See Algebra, Boolean

BOONE, R. E.
Rapid-bloc system accelerates treatment. Am City 82:80-3 Ja '67

BOONTLING. See Slang

BOONVILLE, Calif.
Quiet Boonville country, and boontling. il Sunset 138:30+ Mr '67

BOORE, J. P.
Old glass paperweights (cont) Hobbies 72:84-5+ Ag '67

BOORMAN, Howard L. and Boorman, S. A.
Strategy and national psychology in China. bibliog f Ann Am Acad 370:143-55 Mr '67

BOORMAN, Scott A. See Boorman, H. L. jt. auth.

BOORSTIN, Daniel J.
Welcome to the consumption community; excerpt from The Americans: the world experience. Fortune 76:118-20+ S 1 '67

BOORSTIN, Daniel J.—*Continued*
about
Non-communications. P. Michelson. New Repub 156:35-8 Mr 4 '67
BOOSTERS for space vehicles. *See* Space vehicles—Propulsion systems
BOOTH, Albie
My most unforgettable character. M. A. Stevens. il Read Digest 91:198-200+ N '67
BOOTH, Arch N.
(ed) *See* Jennings, J. Q. Pay vs. profit: where the Nation's money really goes
BOOTH, David A.
Localization of the adrenergic feeding system in the rat diencephalon. bibliog Science 158:515-17 O 27 '67
BOOTH, Gene
What's with those new tires? Pop Mech 128: 96-9+ S '67
BOOTH, Newell S. Jr
Middle ground in the Middle East? Christian Cent 84:1188-92 S 20 '67
BOOTH, Paul
New politics goes local. Nation 204:682-5 My 29 '67
BOOTH, Philip
Misery of mechanics; poem. Poetry 111:19-20 O '67
about
Opposite methods. H. Carruth. Poetry 109: 400-1 Mr '67
BOOTLEGGING
Five flashes east; goings-on along the Florida coast in the rum-running era. H. Waters. il Yachting 123:76-7+ Ja '68
Rum running, basic training for stockers. B. E. Myers. il Motor T 19:48-9+ Mr '67
See also
Smuggling
BOOTS and shoes. *See* Shoes
BORA-BORA (island)
Bora-Bora a paradise on a precipice. C. Phinizy. il Sports Illus 28:24-31 Ja 15 '68
BORCH, F. J.
80ist man; address, November 15, 1967. Vital Speeches 34:187-90 Ja 1 '68
BORDEN company
Borden company vs. chicken little; USDA vs Wyler's chicken noodle soup mix. Consumer Rep 32:349 Jl '67
Borden's land of milk & honey. R. Levy. il Duns R 89:42-4+ My '67
Chemical reaction at Borden; company's chemical and plastics operations built up. Bsns W p200+ F 18 '67
BORDER patrol
Bridge at Lo Wu; Hong Kong. C. Lucas. il Sat R 50:82+ O 14 '67
BORDER war, Indian-Chinese. *See* Sino-Indian border dispute, 1957–
BORDINAT, Eugene, 1920–
Metaphysics of automotive design. N. Thimmesch. il por Esquire 68:188-9+ D '67
BORDUA, David J.
Recent trends: deviant behavior and social control. bibliog f Ann Am Acad 369:149-63 Ja '67
BOREDOM
Is there a life after marriage? B. Head. Mlle 66:91+ Ja '68
BORETOS, John W. and Pierce, W. S.
Segmented polyurethane: a new elastomer for biomedical applications. bibliog Science 158:1481-2 D 15 '67
BORETZ, Benjamin
Music. Nation 204:445-6; 205:157-8 Ap 3, Ag 28 '67
Records (cont) Nation 204:221-2, 349-50; 205: 603-5 F 13, Mr 13, D 4 '67
Records 1967. Nation 205:698-700 D 25 '67
BORG-Warner corporation
Soothing the pains of growing too fast. il Bsns W p 190-2+ F 18 '67
BORGE, Victor
Copenhagen: a native returns. Holiday 43:32+ Ja '68
about
Boat for St Croix. B. Robinson. il por Yachting 122:46+ N '67
BORGES, Jorge Luis
Journey without an end. por Time 89:90 Mr 24 '67
Literature of exhaustion. J. Barth. Atlan 220:30-4 Ag '67
Maze of the unreal and real. R. G. Mead, jr. Sat R 50:44-5 My 13 '67
Moments of truth. S. Maloff. por Newsweek 69:92-3 Ap 3 '67
BORGESE, Elisabeth Mann
Elephants seldom forget. Holiday 41:30+ F '67
Pacem in terris II. Nation 205:74-9 Jl 31 '67

BORGESON, Griffith
European hot line. Motor T 19:75 Ag '67
—*See* Cahler, B. jt. auth.
BORGZINNER, Jon
From Mao to 3-D oᴅ or Twiggy. Life 63:42-3 S 1 '67
His sitar sound rocks the U.S. Life 63:35-6+ Ag 18 '67
Leaf, a lemon drop, a cartoon is born. Life 62:78B+ Mr 17 '67
Life movie review. Life 62:15 Je 16 '67
Limerick lad in Arthur's court. Life 63:76+ S 22 '67
Overheard sound became her greatest friend. Life 62:112 Ap 14 '67
BORIC acid
High-pressure dissociation of carbonic and boric acids in seawater. C. Culberson and others. bibliog il Science 157:59-61 Jl 7 '67
BORING bits. *See* Drilling and boring machinery
BORIS Godunov; opera. *See* Musorgskiĭ, M. P.
BORK, Robert H.
Supreme court versus corporate efficiency. Fortune 76:92-3+ Ag '67
BORLAND, Hal
Artistry of ice. Audubon 69:50-3 Ja '67
Book essay: the naturalist's library. Natur Hist 77:68-70 Ja '68
Hill country homilies. Audubon 69:66-77 My '67
Now in December; excerpt from Sundial of the seasons. Read Digest 91:43-4+ D '67
Plenty of the land. Audubon 69:30-5 N '67
Waiting for the woodcock. Audubon 69:56-7 Mr '67
BORMANN, Adolf Martin
In the forest of fear. E. R. F. Sheehan. il pors Sat Eve Post 240:30-2+ Ag 12 '67
BORMANN, F. H. and Likens, G. E.
Nutrient cycling. bibliog Science 155:424-9 Ja 27 '67
BORMANN, Martin
In the forest of fear. E. R. F. Sheehan. il por Sat Eve Post 240:30-2+ Ag 12 '67
BORN, Max
On Max Born's reflections. L. Williams. Bul Atomic Sci 23:27-8 F '67
BORNEO
Native races
Home for the boomerang; Dayak tribesmen massacre Chinese. Time 90:34+ D 15 '67
Trojan horse; Chinese slaughtered by Dyaks. M. Parker. il Newsweek 70:36-7 D 25 '67
BORODIN, Aleksandr Porfir'evich
Prince Igor. Criticism
New Yorker 43:144-6 S 9 '67
Sat R 50:73 S 16 '67
BOROME, Joseph A.
Robert Purvis & his early challenge to American racism. Negro Hist Bul 30:8-10 My '67
BORON
Facility to put UAC in boron filament field. il Aero Tech 21:48 Ja 1 '68
See also
Plants, Effect of boron on
BORON carbide. *See* Ceramic materials
BOROWSKI, Tadeusz
People who walked; story. Commentary 43: 65-9 F '67
BORREGO state park. *See* California—Parks and reserves
BORROWING of money. *See* Credit; Loans
BORST, L. B. *See* Sauer, G. E. jt. auth.
BORTON, Terry
What turns kids on? Sat R 50:72-4+ Ap 15 '67
BORU, Thomas
We are proud my wife and I; poem. Nat R 19:464 My 2 '67
BOSCH, Hieronymus
Bosch ors Hertogenbosch. il Newsweek 70: 107 O 9 '67
Web of meanings. T. M. Folds. il Redbook 130:62-3+ D '67
BOSCH, Juan
Liberals in wonderland. R. Shereff. Commonweal 86:198-9+ My 5 '67
Overtaken by events, by J. B. Martin. Review
Nat R 19:152 F 7 '67. J. B. Burnham
BOSCO, Giovanni, Saint
Don Bosco, by L. von Matt and H. Bosco. Review
Cath World 205:313-14 Ag '67 C. Murray
BOSCOBEL (historic house) *See* New York (state)—Historic houses, etc.
BOSLEY, Harold A.
You shall not commit adultery. Read Digest 91:139-42 O '67
BOSMAJIAN, Haig A.
Nonmorality of cruelty and killing. Christian Cent 84:1065-7 Ag 23 '67

BOSOM. See Breast

BOSTON, Larry
Goal for '67: no more measles. Todays Health 45:48-51 My '67

BOSTON

Banks
$1,000,000 misunderstanding; loans by S. Semenenko of First national. Time 90:75 Ag 18 '67

City hall
Bold bastion. il Time 90:36 D 29 '67

Crime
Brinksmanship; looting of armored car. il Newsweek 69:33 Je 5 '67
Overkill in Boston; fratricide among racketeers. Time 89:21 F 10 '67
Victims of a gang feud, deadly items in a startling report: crime U.S; findings of National crime commission; with report by R. B. Stolley. il Life 62:22-9 F 24 '67

Description
Walk with Paul Revere, in Boston. il Sunset 138:57-8+ My '67

Education
Balancing act in Boston. E. Sigel. il Reporter 36:22-4 My 4 '67; Reply with rejoinder. J. Lee. 36:10-11 Je 15 '67
Busing kids to the suburbs; Boston's METCO program. H. Spergel. il Am Ed 3:2-5 Ap '67
Death at an early age; excerpts. J. Kozol. Atlan 220:49-55, 107-10 S, O '67
Education: notes on community schools. J. Featherstone. New Repub 157:16-17 D 9 '67
Instant expert; views of J. Kozol. il Time 90: 56 N 10 '67
Progressive unprogressive school; Boston Latin school. il Sr Schol 90:3 F 10 '67
Requiem for the urban school; experiences of J. Kozol. E. Z. Friedenberg. il Sat R 50:77-9+ N 18 '67
Scholae Latinae Bostoniensis vita aeterna sit! Boston Latin school. il Time 91:67 Ja 5 '68
Summer school integration in a suburb. G. E. Snelbecker and M. S. Arffa. il Sch & Soc 95:303-5 Sum '67
Village school downtown, by P. Schrag. Review
New Repub 156:33-5 My 20 '67. J. Kozol
Sat R 50:90 My 20 '67. R. Coles
Whipping boys; book attacks practice of rattaning. il Newsweek 70:94 O 16 '67

Elections
Grace note from Louise. il Newsweek 70:67 N 20 '67
Narrow margin. Nation 205:515 N 20 '67

Finance
Parking enforcement pays. T. J. Murphy. il Am City 82:116 Ag '67

Galleries and museums
See also
Museum of science

Gardens
On Beacon hill, the Women's city club of Boston has a garden. G. Hollett. il Horticulture 45:18 N '67

Historic houses, etc.
Second Harrison Gray Ottis house, Boston. S. Parsons and W. D. Garrett. il Antiques 92:536-41 O '67

History
When Christmas was banned in Boston. D. P. Marriott. il Am Heritage 19:107-11 D '67

Hospitals
Early-warning system; studies of patients at Levine cardiac center, Peter Bent Brigham hospital. il Newsweek 69:62 Ja 30 '67

Intellectual life
Problem of Boston, by M. Green. Review Reporter 36:56-7 F 9 '67. M. Bradbury

Libraries
See also
Boston public library

Music
U.S. premiere: Moses and Aaron. C. L. Osborne. il Hi Fi 17:MA8+ F '67
See also
Opera company of Boston

Negroes
Balancing act in Boston. E. Sigel. il Reporter 36:22-4 My 4 '67; Reply with rejoinder. J. Lee. 36:10-11 Je 15 '67

It was a long, hot summer; playground aide; with Commonwealth service corps. B. Kantrowitz. il Seventeen 26:114-15+ Je '67

Newspapers
Boston strangle; Traveler merges with morning Herald. Newsweek 70:52 Jl 3 '67
Farewell, Traveler; combines to form new morning paper, called the Herald traveler. Time 90:71 Jl 7 '67

Politics and government
Athenian democracy; Mrs Hicks wins primary. il Newsweek 70:28+ O 9 '67
Backlash in Boston, and across the U.S. il Newsweek 70:29-30+ N 6 '67
Crowded field; mayoralty campaign. Time 90:17-18 Jl 14 '67
Every little breeze; candidates for mayor. il Newsweek 70:37+ S 18 '67
Harangues and hurrahs in Boston; candidates for mayor. J. McLellan. Commonweal 86:405-6 Je 30 '67
Hicks in Boston; mayoral campaign. New Repub 157:10-11 O 28 '67
In Cleveland and Boston, the issue is race. B. Rice. il N Y Times Mag p31+ N 5 '67
Louise Day Hicks gets out the vote. M. Nolan. il Reporter 37:22-4 O 19 '67
Round one was a breeze for Louise. J. Howard. il Life 63:89-90+ O 13 '67
Southies' comfort; Mrs Hicks wins primary. il Time 90:28 O 6 '67

Public buildings
Boston gives engineers an eyeful. J. F. Flaherty. il Am City 82:95-8 S '67
Gropius' split tower is hub of Boston center; John F. Kennedy federal office building. il Arch Rec 141:184-6 Je '67
Walk with Paul Revere, in Boston. il Sunset 138:57-8+ My '67

Riots
Battle of Grove Hall. il Newsweek 69:30 Je 12 '67
Blue Hill blues; Roxbury Negro district riots. il Time 89:20 Je 16 '67
Nights of Negro riots, and more ahead? il U S News 62:16 Je 19 '67
Violence in Roxbury. H. MacMullen, jr. Christian Cent 84:876-8 Jl 5 '67

Sanitary affairs
Boston gives engineers an eyeful. J. F. Flaherty. il Am City 82:95-8 S '67

Schools
See Boston—Education

Stores
Boston shoe store remodeling accomplished for total budget of $20,000. il Arch Rec 141: 176-7 My '67
See also
Pierce, S. S, company

Theater
Theater; Theatre company of Boston's production of Tango, by S. Mrozek. H. Hewes. Sat R 50:34 Jl 29 '67

BOSTON ballet company
Boston ballet company, Back Bay theatre. D. Hering. Dance Mag 41:32-3 Mr '67
Boston ballet; Hunter college playhouse. D. Hering. Dance Mag 41:30-1 D '67
World of dance; New York debut at the Hunter college playhouse. W. Terry. il Sat R 50:80 N 11 '67

BOSTON Bruins (hockey team) See Hockey teams

BOSTON city hall competition. See Architecture—Competitions

BOSTON Latin school. See Boston—Education

BOSTON marathon. See Running

BOSTON massacre, 1770
Boston massacre and the martyrdom of Crispus Attucks. Negro Hist Bul 30:4 Mr '67
Boston, 1770. F. M. Henley. America 117:150 Ag 12 '67

BOSTON museum of fine arts
Birthdays are important. N. Kent. Am Artist 31:3+ Mr '67

BOSTON museum of science. See Museum of science, Boston

BOSTON Patriots (football club) See Football clubs

BOSTON public library
Adding to the heritage; new addition. il Time 89:78 F 24 '67
Addition to the Boston public library. il Arch Rec 142:110-11 D '67

BOSTON Red Sox (baseball) See Baseball clubs

BOSTON theological institute
Major ecumenical move in theological educa-
tion. Christian Cent 84:1646 D 27 '67
Uniting for economy & ecumenism. Time 90:
26 D 29 '67
BOSTON venereal diseases campaign. See
Venereal diseases, Campaign against
BOSWELL, Charles
There was more than one race; excerpts from
America, the story of the world's most
famous yacht. Yachting 122:70-1+ S '67
BOSWELL, Victor R.
U.S.D.A. agricultural research center, Belts-
ville, Md. Horticulture 45:36-7 F '67
BOSWORTH, Allan R.
Authors & editors. Pub W 191:39 F 6 '67
BOTANICAL apparatus
Plant moisture stress; evaluation by pressure
bomb. R. H. Waring and B. D. Cleary.
bibliog il Science 155:1248+ Mr 10 '67
BOTANICAL chemistry
See also
Alkaloids
BOTANICAL gardens
Desert botanical garden, Phoenix, Arizona. E.
E. Brockway. il Horticulture 45:18-19+ Ag
'67
How to use a botanical garden. P. Clark.
Horticulture 45:46-7 Je '67
Huntington botanical; where many gardens
grow as one. il Home Gard 54:24-5 O '67
See also
Holden arboretum, Mentor, Ohio
Missouri botanical garden
New York botanical garden
BOTANICAL research
See also
Agricultural research
Boyce Thompson institute for plant research
BOTANICAL societies
See also
Horticultural societies
BOTANICAL stamps. See Postage stamps
BOTANISTS
See also
Nuttall, T.
BOTANY
See also
Adaptation (botany)
Chromosomes (botany)
Mutation (botany)
also headings beginning Plant, Plants

Bibliography
Onward and upward in the garden (cont)
K. S. White. New Yorker 43:113-14+ D 16
'67

Ecology
Habitat selection by chemically differentiated
races of lichens. W. L. Culberson and C. F.
Culberson. bibliog il Science 158:1195-7 D 1
'67

Morphology
See also
Antheridia

Nomenclature
Carl Linnaeus, May 1707-Jan 1778; symposium.
il Home Gard 54:34-6 My '67
Hedera helix hibernica? Pop Gard 18:14-15
Mr '67

Physiology
Leaf epicuticular waxes. G. Eglinton and R.
J. Hamilton. bibliog il Science 156:1322-35
Je 9 '67
Wax microchannels in the epidermis of white
clover. D. M. Hall. bibliog il Science 158:
505 O 27 '67
See also
Chloroplasts
Differentiation (botany)
Plants—Translocation

Terminology
If you don't know a petal from a sepal, or a
bract from a catkin, here's an introduction
to flower talk. il Sunset 138:226+ Mr '67

Korea
People and plants of Korea. R. W. Lighty. il
Horticulture 45:14-17+ Ag '67

Southwestern states
Native plants of the Southwest. F. B. Widmoyer and D. T. Sullivan. il Horticulture
45:46-9 Ap '67

Western states
See also
Sagebrush
BOTANY, Medical
Making medicines from plants. il Good H
166:167 Ja '68
See also
Ginseng

BOTHWELL, Hazel
Child with impaired hearing. NEA J 56:44-6
N '67
BOTSFORD, Stephen B.
Obituary
New Yorker 43:92 Ja 6 '68
BOTSFORD, Ward
Beecham discography. Am Rec G 33:745-7,
930-2, 1009-12, 1078-81; 34:150-1, 244-5 My-
Ag, O-N '67
Sir Thomas Beecham. Am Rec G 33:742-5
My '67
BOTSWANA
Africa: new nations and new alignments. N.
Mostert. il Reporter 36:27-31 Je 29 '67
BOTTICELLI, Sandro
Mystical Nativity. A. Saarinen. il McCalls
95:78-9 D '67
BOTTLE messages
Mystique of messages in bottles. F. A. Mont-
gomery, jr. il Motor B 120:48-9 D '67
BOTTLE-nosed dolphins. See Dolphins (mam-
mals)
BOTTLE warmers. See Baby bottle warmers
BOTTLES
Instead of a full-rigged ship, why not a pear
in the bottle? il Sunset 138:92-3 My '67
Plastic bottles with a built-in surprise. Con-
sumer Rep 32:296-7 Je '67
BOTTOM fishing. See Fishing
BOTTOME, Edgar M.
Mythology of the A.B.M. Commonweal 87:74-
6 O 20 '67
BOTTS, Percival R.
Thank you, Wadi Botts! C. McCormick. Re-
porter 37:41-4+ O 5 '67
BOUCHARD, Emily
Miss Bouchard protests. T. W. Moore. Chris-
tian Cent 84:1288-90 O 11 '67
BOUCHER, François
Boucher's lovers in a park. E. Mongan. il Art
N 66:50-1+ Sum '67
BOUGHTON, Alfred C.
Memo from the publisher (title varies) (cont)
Tech W 20:11 Mr 6 '67
BOUGHTON, Audrey A.
Arrangement; story. McCalls 94:94-5 F '67
BOULAY, Peter
Good enough for Galileo. Am Ed 4:15-18 D '67
BOULDER, Colo.

Architecture
Pueblo for highbrows; NCAR complex. il
Time 90:78-9 S 22 '67
BOULDING, Kenneth E.
Ask not what . . . excerpts from address. New
Repub 157:7 O 7 '67
BOULEVARD solitude; opera. See Henze, H.
W.
BOULEZ, Pierre
Boulez as composer, conductor, hero. S. Lowe.
il por Hi Fi 17:MA18-19 Ag '67
Boulez, live and recording. T. Heintz. Sat R
50:71 Ap 29 '67
Prophet in exile.   E. Salzman. por Opera N
32:8-11 Ja 20 '68
So soon, a classic: Le marteau sans maître
(The masterless hammer) P. L. Miller. por
Am Rec G 33:639 Ap '67
BOULWARE, Marcus H.
Minister Malcolm; orator profundo. Negro
Hist Bul 30:12-14 N '67
BOUMEDIENNE, Houari
Algerian on dead center. A. De Borchgrave. il
por Newsweek 70:52+ N 13 '67
Algerian socialism's slow leak. J. Harriss.
New Repub 156:19 My 6 '67
Messiah in motion. por Newsweek 70:37-8
Jl 31 '67
To the barricades again. il por Time 91:35
Ja 5 '68
BOUNDARIES
See also subhead Boundaries under
names of countries, states, etc. e.g. India
—Boundaries
BOUNDARY waters canoe area. See Recrea-
tion areas
BOUQUETS, Dried. See Flowers, Dried
BOURBON whiskey. See Whiskey
BOURDEAUX, Michael
Eastern Catholics in the Ukraine. America
116:344-5 Mr 11 '67
Russia gives China anti-Moslem label. Chris-
tian Cent 89:1108-9 Ag 30 '67
BOURDENS, Henri
Long voyage home. por Newsweek 69:64-5 Ap
17 '67
BOURDENS, José
Long voyage home. por Newsweek 69:64-5 Ap
17 '67
BOURDON, David
Cantilevered rainbow. Art N 66:28-31+ Sum
'67

BOURDON, David—*Continued*
Dandy who drew a decadent age. Life 62:52+
F 24 '67
Enigmatic bachelor of Utopia parkway. Life
63:63+ D 15 '67
Mute paintings, scathing diatribes and un-
yielding dogma. Life 62:52 F 3 '67
Simple quality, like Mantle hitting a homer.
Life 64:50A Ja 19 '68
BOURDON, Robert
Robert Bourdon blacksmith in wrought iron.
D. J. Willcox. il Am Artist 32:32-7 Ja '68
BOURGUIBA, Habib ben Ali
Art of plain talk. il por Time 90:40 S 29 '67
Tunisia and Egypt. il Atlan 219:28+ Ap '67
BOURJAILY, Vance
Governor from Ida Grove. N Y Times Mag
p34-5+ F 26 '67
In the summer of the valve trombone; story;
excerpt from The man who knew Kennedy.
Ladies Home J 84:93-8 F '67
Lover's mask; story. Sat Eve Post 240:84-6
My 6 '67

about

Authors & editors. por Pub W 191:38-9 F 6
'67
BOURKE, George
From tip to top in Florida. See issues of
Travel
BOURNE, Peter G.
Stress in fight & flight. il por Time 89:57 Ap
14 '67
BOURNONVILLE, August
Bournonville revisited; excerpts from letters.
F. Hjorth and E. Aschengreen. il Dance
Mag 41:22-3 Jl '67
Souvenir de ton pére. por Dance Mag 41:50-4
My '67
BOURNONVILLE, Augusta
Augusta Bournonville: a life in Paris, 1846. F.
Hjorth. il Dance Mag 41:59-61 Je '67
Souvenir de ton pére. A. Bournonville. il por
Dance Mag 41:50-4 My '67
BOUSH, G. M. See Matsumura, F. jt. auth.
BOUTIQUE house. See Houses, Prefabricated
BOUTWELL, William D.
What's happening in education? See issues
of PTA magazine
BOVINE mastitis. See Mastitis
BOVINE rhinotracheitis. See Cattle—Diseases
and pests
BOW, Frank Townsend
Excerpt from address, January 24, 1967. Cong
Digest 46:107+ Ap '67
BOW; story. See Walker, T.
BOW and arrow
Selecting a bow for the target archer. K. C.
Schuyler. il Consumer Bul 50:15-18 Je '67
BOW hunting. See Hunting with bow and
arrow
BOW sights
Hunt with a bowsight? G. H. Gillelan. il
Outdoor Life 140:26+ O '67
BOWEN, Elizabeth
Mirrors are magic. House & Gard 132:112-13
Ag '67
BOWEN, Ezra
Hello, Jimmy, said the machine, I've been
waiting for you. Life 62:70+ Ja 27 '67
Western powder. Mlle 66:189-90+ N '67
BOWEN, Jean
Holcman collection. Sat R 50:53-5 My 27 '67
BOWEN, John
Baltic states. Travel 127:37-40 My '67
Valley of the Swedes. Travel 128:37-40 O '67
BOWEN, John, 1924-
After the rain. Criticism
America 117:723-4 D 9 '67
Christian Cent 84:1527-8 N 29 '67
New Yorker 43:81 O 21 '67
Newsweek 70:113 O 23 '67
Sat R 50:46 O 28 '67
BOWEN, Mary
Coloma: a sawmill restored. Nat Parks Mag
41:15-17 N '67
BOWEN, William
U.S. economy enters a new era. Fortune 75:
110-15+ Mr '67
BOWER, Eli M.
Magic of symbols. NEA J 57:28-31+ Ja '68
BOWERING, George
White station wagon strophes; poem. Poetry
110:88-9 My '67
BOWERS, E. H.
Those were the pleasant years. Sat R 50:43-4
Je 17 '67
BOWERS, Faubion
Looking and listening. See issues of House
& garden incorporating Living for young
homemakers

Makeup: the reality of illusion. Opera N 31:
8-12 Mr 11 '67
Scriabin's opera. Opera N 31:6-7 Mr 4 '67
BOWERS, J. Michael, and Alexander, B. K.
Mice: individual recognition by olfactory cues.
bibliog Science 158:1208-10 D 1 '67
BOWERS, John
Big city thieves. Harper 234:50-4 F '67
Notre Dame: we're number one! Sat Eve
Post 240:85-9 O 7 '67
Sexy little me. Sat Eve Post 240:26-31 My 6
'67
BOWFISHING. See Fishing with bow and
arrow
BOWKER, R. M.
Briton tells what's wrong with his country.
por U S News 62:70-2 F 27 '67
BOWKER, R. R. and company
Bowker stockholders approve sale to Xerox
corporation. Pub W 193:24 Ja 1 '68
Salute to Congress launches politics direc-
tory. il Pub W 192:38 O 16 '67
See also
Carey-Thomas award
BOWL football games. See Football
BOWLER, Joe
Joe Bowler: illustrator. D. Holden. il por
Am Artist 31:54-60+ N '67
BOWLES, Chester
Who owns the land? Read Digest 91:143-4 O
'67
BOWLES, Paul Frederic
Brilliant hobbyist of modern infernos. M.
Maddocks. Life 63:8 Jl 21 '67
Desert within. T. Solotaroff. New Repub 157:
29-31 S 2 '67
BOWLING, Becky
In my opinion. por Seventeen 26:450 Ag '67
BOWLING
Alley fighter; National championship at Madi-
son Square Garden. Newsweek 70:92 D 18 '67
Bocce, Italy's favorite pastime. A. Hine. il
Holiday 43:56-7+ Ja '68
Bowling: International masters championship.
G. S. Brown. il Sports Illus 27:74+ D 11 '67
Lawn bowls. T. N. Davis, 3d. il Parks & Rec
2:29-30 N '67
Lead up to a lifetime sport; junior bowling.
J. White. il Parks & Rec 2:30-1+ Ag '67
Over thirty is over the hill; Akron's $100,000
Tournament of champions. G. Ronberg. il
Sports Illus 26:86-8 Ap 10 '67
Senior citizens bowling; Newington, Conn.
senior citizens club. C. M. Lemire. il Parks
& Rec 2:33+ My '67
BOWLING GREEN state university, Ohio
Wedding cake in Bowling Green. A. R.
Rogers. il Library J 92:4353-4 D 1 '67
BOWLS
Making a copper enamel bowl. E. Winter. il
Design 69:23-8 Fall '67
BOWMAN, Eldon
Pleasure horses in the parks. Nat Parks
Mag 41:4-6 N '67
BOWMAN, Robert L. and others
Capillary-tube scanner for mechanized mi-
crobiology. bibliog Science 158:78-83 O 6 '67
BOWMAN, Tibby
Where to get... Motor B 119:112-14+ Ap '67
BOWRA, Sir Cecil Maurice
Greats man. J. Wain. New Repub 157:25-8
N 18 '67
BOWRA, Sir Maurice. See Bowra, C. M.
BOWSER, Hallowell
Denuclearization in Latin America. Sat R
50:32 My 20 '67
Lambaréné since Schweitzer. Sat R 50:30 N
25 '67
BOWSKY, William M.
Medieval commune and internal violence; po-
lice power and public safety in Siena, 1287-
1355. bibliog f Am Hist R 73:1-17 O '67
BOX (plant) See Boxwood
BOX cameras. See Cameras
BOX gardening. See Flower boxes, planters,
etc.
BOX shelves. See Shelves
BOXERS
Babyweights; world title holders in lightest
weights. il Newsweek 70:68 Jl 24 '67
Lady is a champ; A. Eaton. M. Kram. il
Sports Illus 27:76-8+ N 6 '67
Once and future king? scramble for Ali's title.
T. Maule. il Sports Illus 27:18-21 Jl 10 '67
Then there were six; tournament to pick suc-
cessor to Muhammad Ali. M. Kram. il
Sports Illus 27:12-15 Ag 14 '67
See also names of boxers, e.g. J. Frazier
BOXES, cases, etc.
Silver box is not square. il Vogue 149:158-9+
Je '67
You decorate gift canisters. il Sunset 138:129
F '67

BOXING

After Muhammad, a graveyard; Clay-Folley fight. M. Kram. il Sports Illus 26:28-9 Ap 3 '67

After the bell; riot at Dick Tiger-José Torres fight. Sports Illus 26:11 My 29 '67

Ali takes a crown and a cause. A. Dundee and T. Maule. il Sports Illus 27:36-40 Ag 21 '67

Arrivederci, Nino Benvenuti; Benvenuti-Griffith fight. T. Maule. il Sports Illus 26:20-3 My 1 '67

Bean-can bout in Frankfurt; Mildenberger vs Bonavena. M. Kram. il Sports Illus 27:20-3 S 25 '67

Book fighter who may change Ali's style: challenger Z. Folley. M. Kram. il Sports Illus 26:71-2 Mr 20 '67

Cruel Ali with all the skills; Clay-Terrell fight. T. Maule. il Sports Illus 26:18-21 F 13 '67

Devil had a left jab; Benvenuti-Griffith fight. G. Rogin. il Sports Illus 27:50+ O 9 '67

Gypsy Joe: fire and music and miniculture; J. Harris-C. Cokes fight. M. Kram. il Sports Illus 26:77-9 Ap 10 '67

Hate & love; Clay-Terrell fight. Time 89:55 F 17 '67

Have a piece of Georgie boy; Chuvalo-Frazier fight. M. Kram. il Sports Illus 27:26-8 Jl 31 '67

He could go to jail and still be champ; Muhammad Ali. A. Dundee and T. Maule. il Sports Illus 27:32-4+ Ag 28 '67

Impossible dream; C. Clay-Z. Folley fight. Time 89:49 Mr 31 '67

Jimmy Ellis gets his own show: beats Oscar Bonavena in heavyweight elimination tournament. M. Kram. il Sports Illus 27:34-6+ D 11 '67

Last campaign of boxing's last angry man; fight manager. J. Hurley. W. C. Heinz. il Sat Eve Post 240:38-42+ F 11 '67

Left that was; Terrell-Clay fight. T. Maule. il Sports Illus 26:14-17 F 6 '67

Life in a hot corner; C. Clay. A. Dundee and T. Maule. il Sports Illus 27:64-72 Ag 14 '67

Mamma mia! world middleweight fight. il Newsweek 69:94 My 1 '67

No weighty problems for Carlos. M. Kram. Sports Illus 27:48-50 Jl 10 '67

Once and future king? scramble for Ali's title. T. Maule. il Sports Illus 27:18-21 Jl 10 '67

Promises, promises; Griffith vs. Benvenuti. Time 90:93 O 6 '67

Repeat for the best negative fighter around; J. Archer loses to E. Griffith. M. Kram. il Sports Illus 26:44-6 F 6 '67

Right man in the right place, at last; R. Rouse to meet champion Dick Tiger. G. Rogin. il Sports Illus 27:32-4+ N 13 '67

Sad farewell, a glad hello; Jones-Frazier fight. M. Kram. il Sports Illus 26:44+ Mr 6 '67

Saviors; Ali-Patterson rematch killed by governors of Nev. and Penn. Sports Illus 26:11 Ap 24 '67

Spiritually set for a new go; middleweight champion Nino Benvenuti to fight challenger Emile Griffith. G. Rogin. il Sports Illus 27:34-6+ S 25 '67

Theater of cruelty; Clay-Terrell fight. il Newsweek 69:87 F 20 '67

Then there were six; tournament to pick successor to Muhammad Ali. M. Kram. il Sports Illus 27:12-15 Ag 14 '67

They're still waiting for Jerry; Quarry-Patterson fight. M. Kram. il Sports Illus 27:20-3 N 6 '67

Tiger hammers home a sermon; Tiger-Rouse fight. G. Rogin. il Sports Illus 27:24-6+ N 27 '67

Title for Trieste; Giovanni Benvenuti wins middleweight championship. il Time 89:75 Ap 28 '67

Tokyo's new honorable rage; fighting Harada and boxing. il Sports Illus 26:22-4 Ja 23 '67

Vicente bored in but Ernie merely bored; Saldivar vs Winstone, Terrell vs Ramos. B. Ottum. Sports Illus 27:66-8 O 23 '67

What next? Clay-Folley fight. il Newsweek 69:56 Ap 3 '67

Will Joe Frazier be the next champ? B. J. Friedman. il Sat Eve Post 240:97-101 S 23 '67

You sweeter than wine, Joe. M. Kram. il Sports Illus 26:32-4+ Je 19 '67

Zora Folley ranks Muhammad Ali as no. 1; ed. by M. Sharnik. Z. Folley. Sports Illus 26:32 Ap 10 '67
See also
World boxing association

Refereeing
See Sports officiating

BOXING fans. See Sports fans

BOXWOOD

For hedges and edges for neatly tailored lumps and bumps. il Sunset 139:120-1 Ag '67

BOY scouts

Be prepared; World jamboree in Farragut state park. il Newsweek 70:23-4 Ag 14 '67

Boy scouts enrole in cycle driving course; program in Los Angeles. il Todays Health 45:13 N '67

Do boy scouts rate a badge for retailing? il Bsns W p72-4 Ag 12 '67

Jamboree '67. J. L. Collier. il Read Digest 91:121-4 Ag '67

Old scoutmaster in action; H. Humphrey acts to prevent Roosevelt camp closure. il Life 62:77-8 Je 16 '67

U.S. hosts Boy scouts world jamboree. W. M. Beckert. il Parks & Rec 2:21 Je '67
See also
Boys life (periodical)

Explorer scouts
Project altered; car owned by Explorer post 14, San Fernando, Calif. il Hot Rod 20:46-7 Jl '67

BOYCE, Irene
Unborn baby's fight to live. J. Blank. il por Redbook 128:74-5+ Mr '67

BOYCE, Richard
Taping the scene abroad. Hi Fi 17:41-6 Ag '67

BOYCE, Stephen G. See Plass, W. T. jt. auth.

BOYCE Thompson institute for plant research, Incorporated
Boyce Thompson institute for plant research, inc. G. L. McNew. il Science 158:1489-92 D 15 '67

BOYCOTT

Galled by de Gaulle; consumer backlash against things French. il Bsns W p22 D 30 '67

How to hurt a Frenchman. H. Moffett. il Life 64:34-34B Ja 19 '68

Peaceful plan to clobber business; bill before Congress. il Nations Bsns 55:38-9+ Je '67

Will boycott rule put brake on technology? labor's right to resist automation. il Bsns W p 104+ Ap 29 '67
See also
Blacklisting

BOYD, Alan Stephenson
Back scratching. New Repub 157:7-8 O 7 '67

Hot seat. R. B. Parke. il por Flying 80:30 My '67

Welcome to chaos. W. J. Coughlin. Tech W 20:50 Je 19 '67

BOYD, Catharine
Selling touch. Writer 81:16-17+ Ja '68

BOYD, David
Painting with smoke. J. Jones. il pors Design 69:36-7 Fall '67

BOYD, James
Tragedy of Thomas Dodd; excerpt from Above the law. por Sat Eve Post 241:19-25 Ja 13; 58-62+ Ja 27 '68 (to be cont)

UN and the have-nots: alternatives to explosion. Nation 204:562-4 My 1 '67

BOYD, Malcolm
Movies (cont) Christian Cent 84:178-9, 346-7, 1164, 1560-1 F 8, Mr 15, S 13, D 6 '67

What we have to do is try not to lie; dialogue with J. Coburn. por Redbook 129:64-5+ O '67

about
Authors & editors. por Pub W 191:42 F 27 '67

BOYD, Natasha
Family in the wilderness. il Liv Wildn 30:36-41 Wint '66

BOYD, Robin
Habitat's cluster. Arch Forum 126:36-41 My '67

BOYDEN, Frank Learoyd
Headmaster, by J. McPhee. Review
Sat R il por 50:70-1 Ap 15 '67. D. Barr

BOYDEN associates, incorporated. See Employment agencies

BOYER, David S.
Micronesia: the Americanization of Eden. Nat Geog Mag 131:702-44 My '67

BOYKIN John E.
Karts with rocket power. Pop Mech 127:120-1 Mr '67

BOYKO, Hugo
Salt-water agriculture; with biographical sketch. Sci Am 216:19, 89-94+ Mr '67

BOYLAN, Barbara
On the boards. W. Como. il por Dance Mag 41:22 My '67

BOYLAN, Brian Richard
Next door to Watts. Sat R 50:30 Jl 8 '67
Soul of a Soviet surgeon. Sat R 50:51 F 25 '67

BOYLE, A. J. F. See Johnstone, B. M. jt. auth.

BOYLE, J. R. and others
Biotite flakes: alteration by chemical and biological treatment. bibliog Science 155: 193-5 Ja 13 '67

BOYLE, Kay
Man in the wilderness. Nation 204:693-4 My 29 '67

BOYLE, Robert
Robert Boyle. M. B. Hall. il por Sci Am 217: 96-102 Ag '67

BOYLE, Robert H.
Fishing (cont) Sports Illus 26:42 Ja 23; 59-60 My 8 '67
Kind and canny canines. Sports Illus 28:50-6 Ja 15 '68

BOYS
Can you ever really trust a boy? questions and answers. A. Wood. Seventeen 26:122+ Je '67
Happy times. T. Trueblood. il Field & S 71: 24+ F '67
How different are they? excerpt from Development of sex differences, ed. by E. E. Maccoby. S. F. Yolles. il N Y Times Mag p64-5+ F 5 '67
How to move a boy to action; questions and answers. A. Wood. Seventeen 26:168+ N '67
What makes boys masculine. B. Bettelheim. Ladies Home J 84:41-2 S '67
What makes boys so different. A. Lake. il Seventeen 26:108-9+ O '67
What to do till the next boy comes along; questions and answers. A. Wood. Seventeen 26:174+ Ap '67
See also
Adolescence
Runaway boys and girls
Youth

Health and hygiene
Why some boys should stay off the team. F. V. Hein. Todays Health 45:72+ Ag '67

BOYS as actors. See Children as actors

BOYS camps. See Camps

BOYS haircuts. See Haircutting

BOYS life (periodical)
How Boys' life grows without trying. Bsns W p74 Ag 12 '67

BOYS parties. See Entertaining

BRA. See Brassieres

BRABHAM, Jack
Best racing: Grand prix. por Pop Sci 190:69 Mr '67

BRACELAND, Francis J.
Fixed resolve not to quit. Sat R 50:37 My 13 '67

BRACEROS. See Migrant labor

BRACES. See Orthopedic apparatus

BRACEWELL, R. N. See Swenson, G. W. jr. jt. auth.

BRACKEN, Peg
Peg Bracken's appendix to the I hate to cook book. See issues of Ladies' home journal

BRACKEN. See Ferns

BRACKMAN, Arnold C.
Vietnam: an end in itself? Sat R 50:32-4+ O 28 '67

BRACKMAN, Jacob
Graffiti to print. N Y Times Mag p97-9 F 12 '67
Onward and upward with the arts. New Yorker 43:34-6+ Je 24 '67

BRADBURY, Malcolm
Opinion: on looking foreign. por Mlle 64:98+ F '67
Perceptions and provocations. Reporter 36:55-7 F 9 '67

BRADBURY, Marilee Jean
Problems approach to geography. NEA J 56:39-40 Ap '67

BRADBURY, Ray
At what temperature do books burn? reprint. Writer 80:18-20 Jl '67
Impatient Gulliver above our roofs. Life 63: 31-7 N 24 '67
about
Count Dracula and Mr Ray Bradbury. R. Kirk. Nat R 19:365 Ap 4 '67

BRADBURY, Wilbur
Overdue idea put on a scratch pad. Life 62: 115-16 My 19 '67

BRADEN, Thomas W.
Speaking out. por Sat Eve Post 240:10+ My 20 '67
about
Come the revelations. New Repub 156:7-8 My 27 '67

BRADERMAN, Eugene M.
U.S. and Philippines begin talks on future economic relations; statement, November 20, 1967. Dept State Bul 58:11-12 Ja 1 '68

U.S.-Philippine relations: where we stand today; address, March 9, 1967. Dept State Bul 56:660-4 Ap 24 '67

BRADFIELD, Robert B. and others
Morphological changes in human scalp hair roots during deprivation of protein. bibliog Science 157:428-9 Jl 28 '67

BRADFORD ornamental pears. See Pears

BRADLEY, Bill
And you too, Bill. il Time 90:45 D 22 '67
Big Bill's debut. il por Newsweek 70:49 D 25 '67
He's a stubborn idealist with a romantic streak. J. Larner. il pors Life 64:57-8 Ja 19 '68
No. twenty-four, a new man for New York. F. Deford. il pors Sports Illus 27:18-19 D 18 '67
Scholar athlete. Newsweek 69:73 My 8 '67

BRADLEY, Kitty. See Bradley, O. N. jt. auth.

BRADLEY, Omar Nelson
Ike's tactics: hot pursuit in Vietnam; television interview. por U S News 63:22 D 11 '67
—and Bradley, Kitty
My visit to Vietnam; ed. by W. Rogers. pors Look 31:29-35 N 14 '67

BRADLEY, Sam
Invitation to meeting; poem. Christian Cent 84:1042 Ag 16 '67
Sailor not Christian on a cruel sea; poem. Sat R 50:53 N 11 '67
This man of fear, a man of faith; poem. Christian Cent 84:1622 D 20 '67
about
Five poets. E. Blum. Poetry 109:341 F '67

BRADLEY, Thomas B. jr, and others
Hemoglobin gun hill: deletion of five amino acid residues and impaired heme-globin binding. bibliog Science 157:1581-3 S 29 '67

BRADSHAW, George
Arts crunch. Vogue 150:126-9+ S 15 '67
Old flame: Bermuda. Vogue 149:231+ Mr 1 '67
Paintings in a paper bag; story. Vogue 150: 248-51 O 1 '67

BRADSHAW, Hank
Blizzard perch. Field & S 72:52-3+ D '67
Dangerous bass of Lake Cumberland. Field & S 71:40-1+ Ap '67
Deer drive. Outdoor Life 139:52-3+ F '67
Ice fishing a la cart. Pop Mech 129:132-4+ Ja '68
Moose a mile. Field & S 72:36-7+ Ag '67
One small gun for all small game. por Field & S 72:54-5+ N '67
—and Bradshaw, Vera
Discovering the Bahamas. il Todays Health 45:42-5+ D '67
Tuning-in on wildlife secrets. Pop Mech 129: 114-16+ Ja '68

BRADSHAW, Vera. See Bradshaw, H. jt. auth.

BRADSTREET, Anne (Dudley)
Benevolent phantom. por Time 90:84 Jl 7 '67

BRADY, Charles
Crossmess parzle; poem. America 117:764 D 23 '67

BRADY, Diamond Jim. See Brady, J. B.

BRADY, Edward L. and Wallenstein, M. B.
National standard reference data system. bibliog Science 156:754-62 My 12 '67

BRADY, James Buchanan
Feast of the season. A. Gingrich. Esquire 68: 6+ D '67

BRADY, Philip
Rare blood to the rescue. Todays Health 45: 34-8 My '67

BRADY, Raymond
Look what's happening to glass! Read Digest 91:175-6+ D '67

BRADY, Rodney H.
Computers in top-level decision making. Harvard Bsns R 45:67-76 Jl '67

BRADY, William T.
They don't have to starve. Nations Bsns 55: 88-90+ Mr '67

BRAESTRUP, Peter
How the guerrillas came to Koh Noi. N Y Times Mag p30-1+ D 10 '67
Report: Laos. Atlan 220:10+ Ag '67

BRAHM, Walter
Habits and attitudes. por Library J 92:1804-5 My 1 '67

BRAHMS, Johannes
Decca's Brahms Fourth, the cream of the crop. M. N. Kanny. Am Rec G 33:475 F '67
Farewell to all that. A. Sperber. Am Rec G 33:756-7+ My '67
First complete recording of the Brahms trios and other chamber works. M. N. Kanny. il Am Rec G 34:208-10+ N '67
Records:
Eighteen songs. Opera N 32:30 S 9 '67
Szell's complete Brahms symphonies. M. N. Kanny. il Am Rec G 33:912-14 Je '67

BRAILLE periodicals.   See Blind, Periodicals for the
BRAIN, Dennis
Inimitable Dennis Brain.   I. Kolodin. il por Sat R 50:59+ My 27 '67
BRAIN
Autonomic basis for the rise in brain temperature during paradoxical sleep. M. A. Baker and J. N. Hayward. bibliog il Science 157:1586-8 S 29 '67
Brain builders; building a miniature brain in salamanders. il Sci Digest 62:71-2 S '67
Brain lesions in birds: effects on discrimination acquisition and reversal. L. J. Stettner and W. J. Schultz. bibliog il Science 155: 1689-92 Mr 31 '67
Brain polysomes: response to environmental stimulation. S. H. Appel and others. bibliog il Science 157:836-8 Ag 18 '67
Brain research; report on fourth visiting seminar of the International brain research organization. P. B. Dews and others. Science 158:951-2+ N 17 '67
Endoplasmic reticulum: United States-Japan cooperative science program; report on symposium. G. Palade and K. Porter. Science 156:106-10 Ap 7 '67
Humanness of man. I. Asimov. il NEA J 56: 6-8+ D '67
Magnesium pemoline: failure to affect in vivo synthesis of brain RNA. N. R. Morris and others. bibliog il Science 155:1125-6 Mr 3 '67
Mind, brain, and humanist values. R. W. Sperry; discussion. Bul Atomic Sci 23:33-4 Ja; 26 F; 34 Ap; 43-4 O '67
Mind-mapping the dolphin; first complete atlas of its brain. L. Gebhart. il Sci N 92: 206-7 Ag 26 '67
New view of the brain cell; new light mircoscope. Sci N 92:128 Ag 5 '67
Oxygen tension changes evoked in the brain by visual stimuation. K. J Gijsbers and R. Melzack. bibliog il Science 156:1392-3 Je 9 '67
Pemoline levels in brain: enhancement by dimethyl sulfoxide. J. J. Brink and D. G. Stein. bibliog il Science 158:1479-80 D 15 '67
Protein metabolism in the developing brain: influence of birth and gestational age. R. J. Schain and others. bibliog il Science 156: 984-6 My 19 '67
Radio control of the brain. J. Reinert. il Sci Digest 61:32-6 Je '67
Serotonin: release in the forebrain by stimulation of midbrain raphé. G. K. Aghajanian and others. bibliog il Science 156:402-3 Ap 21 '67
Steroid-sensitive single neurons in rat hypothalamus and midbrain: identification by microelectrophoresis. K. Ruf and F. A. Steiner. bibliog il Science 156:667-9 My 5 '67
Successiveness discrimination as a two-state, quantal process. A. B. Kristofferson. bibliog il Science 158:1337-9 D 8 '67
Tetrodotoxin: effects on brain metabolism in vitro. S. L. Chan and J. H. Quastel. bibliog il Science 156:1752-3 Je 30 '67
Thinking about how we think. P. McBroom. il Sci N 92:544-5 D 2 '67
Thinking machine. I. Asimov. Sci Digest 62: 73-4 D '67
Tiliqua scincoides: temperature-sensitive units in lizard brain. M. Cabanac and others. bibliog il Science 158:1050-1 N 24 '67
Two brains per person. Sci Digest 62:23 N '67
See also
Cerebral cortex
Hypothalamus

Diseases

Oxidative phosphorylation in experimental bilirubin encephalopathy. I. Diamond and R. Schmid. bibliog il Science 155:1288-9 Mr 10 '67
What to do about brain diseases. J. G. Clark. Farm J 91:B8-9 My '67
See also
Cerebral hemorrhage
Hydrocephalus

Localization of functions

Brain stem structures responsible for the electroencephalographic patterns of desynchronized sleep. O. Candia and others. bibliog il Science 155:720-2 F 10 '67
Localization of the adrenergic feeding system in the rat diencephalon. D. A. Booth. bibliog il Science 158:515-17 O 27 '67
Neural correlates of food and water intake in the rat. J. N. Coury. bibliog il Science 156:1763-5 Je 30 '67
Short-term memory, parsing, and the primate frontal cortex. K. H. Pribram and W. E. Tubbs. bibliog il Science 156:1765-7 Je 30 '67

Split brain in man. M. S. Gazzaniga. il Sci Am 217:24-9 Ag '67
Visual form discrimination after removal of the visual cortex in cats. S. S. Winans. bibliog il Science 158:944-6 N 17 '67

Surgery

Dead body & the living brain; with questions and answers. O. Fallaci. il Look 31:99-101+ N 28 '67

Weight

Relative brain size: a new measure. L. Radinsky. bibliog il Science 155:836-8 F 17 '67

Wounds and injuries

Amnesic effects of small bilateral brain puncture in the mouse. M. Bohdanecka and others. bibliog il Science 157:334-6 Jl 21 '67
Starvation and the brain: permanent brain damage from improper diets. il Sci N 91: 307 Ap 1 '67
BRAIN, Transplantation of. See Transplantation of organs, tissues, etc.
BRAIN damaged children
In most newborn babies: brain damage can be prevented; Neonatal intensive care unit. Babies hospital. T. Irwin. il Look 31:61-7+ S 5 '67
New hope for brain-damaged children? O. James. il Parents Mag 42:72-5+ N '67
New lease on life. il Good H 164:20+ F '67
Patterning treatment for brain-damaged stirs controversy. Todays Health 45:80-1 D '67

Education

Potential for what? Doman-Delacato theory attacked in AMA journal. il Newsweek 70: 98-9 N 13 '67
When children can't learn; crawl-and creep therapy helping retarded and brain-damaged youngsters. J. Bird. il Sat Eve Post 240:27-31+ Jl 29 '67
BRAIN hemorrhage. See Cerebral hemorrhage
BRAIN hormones. See Hormones
BRAIN stimulation. See Stimulus and response
BRAIN surgery. See Brain—Surgery
BRAIN transplantation. See Transplantation of organs, tissues, etc.
BRAIN tumors. See Tumors
BRAINARD, Joe
Joe Brainard: quotes and notes. J. Schuyler. il Art N 66:56-7+ Ap '67
BRAINWASHING
Hanoi's Pavlovians; apparent attempts to brainwash U.S. prisoners held in the North. il Time 89:33-4 Ap 14 '67
BRAITHWAITE, Edward R.
Teacher in slum school; interview, ed. by M. Ronan. il por Sr Schol 90:sup6 Ap 7 '67
BRAKES, Airplane
Brakes and how to use them. T. Smith. Flying 81:71-2 D '67
BRAKES, Automobile
ABCs of brakes. R. W. Temple. il Pop Mech 127:138-42+ My '67
Inside the '68s: new brakes, suspensions, engines, and body details. J. P. Norbye and J. Dunne. il Pop Sci 191:111-18 O '67
Split braking system failure. J. Ethridge. il Motor T 19:66-7 Mr '67
What's the scoop? fiberglass kit to aerate Mustang rear binders. B. Lang. il Hot Rod 20:88-9 F '67
Why can't American cars have brakes like these? R. P. Crossley. il Pop Mech 127:130-1+ Mr '67

Care

Servicing the new disk brakes. W. Alley and R. Day. il Pop Sci 190:168-71+ Ja '67
BRALY, Malcolm
Economics of burglary; interview, ed. by W. H. Manville. Sat Eve Post 240:50 D 30 '67
about
Authors & editors. por Pub W 192:16-17 O 2 '67
BRAMLETTE, M. N.
Primitive microfossils or not? Science 158: 673-4 N 3 '67
BRAMS, Stanley H.
Safer cars in 1968. Parents Mag 42:78-81+ N '67
BRANAN, Karen
Day nurseries: what to look for. Todays Health 45:48-9+ O '67
BRANCH banking. See Banks and banking—Branch banking

BRANCH libraries. See Libraries—Branches and stations

BRANCH stores. See Department stores—Branch stores

BRANCO, Humberto Castello. See Castello Branco, H.

BRAND names. See Trade names

BRANDEIS university, Waltham, Mass.
Brandeis at nineteen. Newsweek 70:94-5 O 16 '67
Builder in a hurry; president to retire. il Time 90:64 S 29 '67
Theater; presentation of John Arden's The workhouse donkey. H. Hewes. Sat R 50:49 My 27 '67

BRANDENBURG nos. 2 and 4; ballet. See Ballets—Criticisms

BRANDON, Henry
From Trotsky to Vietnam, Averell Harriman is still very much the ambassador at large. N Y Times Mag p22-3+ Mr 5 '67
State of affairs. See issues of Saturday review
(ed) See Johnson, C. A. T. Talk with the First lady
(ed) See Longworth, A. R. Talk with an eighty-three-year-old enfant terrible

BRANDON, S. G. F.
Paul and his opponents. Horizon 10:106-11 Wint '68

BRANDT, Bill
Shadow of light by Bill Brandt. N. Hall; R. Hattersley. il Pop Phot 61:102-3+ S '67

BRANDT, Philip W. and Freeman, A. R.
Plasma membrane: substructural changes correlated with electrical resistance and pinocytosis. bibliog Science 155:582-5 F 3 '67

BRANDT, Steven C.
Are they really learning the ropes? Nations Bsns 55:75-7 Ag '67

BRANDT, Thomas O.
Competition for graduate fellowships. Sch & Soc 95:394 O 28 '67

BRANDT, Willy
After two world wars; address, October 6, 1967. Vital Speeches 34:106-11 D 1 '67

about
Fox and the bear are cautious partners. P. Shabecoff. il pors N Y Times Mag p20-1+ F 5 '67

BRANDY
Brandies. il Consumer Rep 32:603-6 N '67
Brandy cook book. J. A. Beard. il House & Gard 132:261+ N '67
Instead of a full-rigged ship, why not a pear in the bottle? il Sunset 138:92-3 My '67

BRANIFF international airways
Booked for travel; new ideas in flying eating. H. Sutton. Sat R 50:48 Mr 4 '67
Braniff automates for full-scale move into cargo market. E. J. Bulban. il Aviation W 87:30-2 Jl 31 '67
Braniff control may go to LTV. Aviation W 87:47 Ag 14 '67
Transpacific route case: Braniff keys proposal to advanced jets. E. J. Bulban. il Aviation W 86:33-4+ Mr 27 '67

BRANIFF-Panagra merger. See Airlines—Consolidations and mergers

BRANN, James
Money, principle and Southern Baptist. New Repub 157:10 Jl 15 '67
National rally for student power. Nation 205: 658-60 D 18 '67
San Jose: the bullhorn message. Nation 205: 465-7 N 6 '67
Unionizing the academics. New Repub 156: 10-11 F 25 '67

BRANNEN, G. K.
Build PM's Jumper sailboard. Pop Mech 127: 160-3+ Ap '67

BRANSFORD, George
Some new battles are boiling in the Coral Sea. V. Kraft. il por Sports Illus 27:54+ D 18 '67

BRANT, Freddie Michael
Beloved impostor M.D. gives up his practice. il pors Life 64:32-3 Ja 12 '68
Médecin malgré lui. il por Newsweek 70:24-5 D 25 '67

BRANTLEY, William R. and Butler, J. R.
Coast guard's Christmas carol. Pop Mech 128: 76-80+ D '67

BRANTON, Daniel. See Deamer, D. W. jt. auth.

BRASILIA, Brazil
Brasilia: a capital investment. il Sr Schol 90:3 Ap 21 '67
Brasilia comes of age. G. Delmas. il Reporter 36:25-6+ F 23 '67
Human touch. D. Bonafede. il Newsweek 70: 62 D 18 '67

BRASS work
See also
Candlesticks

BRASSAÏ
Picasso & photography; excerpts from Picasso & co. por Pop Phot 60:78-80+ My '67

BRASSIERES
Sticky situation with a strapless bra; Bleumette bra. Consumer Rep 32:411 Ag '67

BRATSK, Russia
Three weeks in a Russian town. L. Gross. il Look 31:76-82+ O 3 '67

BRATTAIN, William E.
Madrigal singers celebrate the yuletide on college campuses. Parks & Rec 2:8-9+ D '67

BRAUD, Jorge Lara-. See Lara-Braud, J.

BRAUER, Donald G.
Completely automated watering systems. Am City 82:96-7 Mr '67

BRAUN, Peter
Regional refuse-disposal solution. Am City 82: 96-7 D '67

BRAUN, Saul
I mean, my God, if you can't produce a great American novel for two hundred thou, presold to the flicks, what the hell hope is there for American literature? Esquire 67: 76-7+ F '67
Transmogrification of Soupy Sales. Esquire 68:104-7+ O '67

BRAUN, Werner, and Nakano, Masayasu
Antibody formation: stimulation by polyadenylic and polycytidylic acids. bibliog Science 157:819-21 Ag 18 '67

BRAUN engineering company
High-pressure process wins Detroit's heart; cold extrusion technique for steel. il Bsns W p 112-13 My 6 '67

BRAVE little tailor; drama. See Thane, A.

BRAVER time; story. See Aldridge, J.

BRAVERMAN, Maxwell H.
Books. Sci Am 216:135-6+ Ap '67

BRAVO, Francisco
Laymen. . . is what it takes! America 116: 524-8 Ap 8 '67

BRAWERMAN, George. See Drews, J. jt. auth.

BRAY, J. Roger
Variation in atmospheric carbon-14 activity relative to a sunspot-auroral solar index. bibliog Science 156:640-2 My 5 '67

BRAY, Olin E.
Studying the black bear in Yellowstone National Park. Nat Parks Mag 41:10-12 Ag '67

BRAYBROOKE, Neville
Assisi that nobody knows. Sat R 50:35-6 Jl 29 '67
Stopping off in Antwerp. Sat R 50:45 Jl 22 '67
Tennyson's Isle of Wight. Sat R 50:60-1+ Mr 11 '67

BRAZIL
Inside Brazil; excerpt from Inside South America. J. Gunther. il Read Digest 90: 119-24 My '67
Testing place. il Time 89:29-33 Ap 21 '67
See also
Agricultural administration—Brazil
Amapá
Amazon River
Architecture—Brazil
Automobile industry and trade—Brazil
Brasilia
Cooperative associations—Brazil
Finance—Brazil
Government investigations—Brazil
Hunting—Brazil
Land tenure—Brazil
Peasantry—Brazil
Poor—Brazil
Research—Brazil
Taxation—Brazil
Television broadcasting—Brazil
Television industry—Brazil
Trials—Brazil

Constitution
Dictatorial powers? il Newsweek 69:48+ Ja 30 '67

Description and travel
Unexpected Brazil. J. Dos Passos. il Holiday 42:52-9+ S '67

Economic conditions
Brazil's miserable northeast. H. W. Flannery. Cath World 205:276-81 Ag '67
Facade in Brazil; effects of industrialization in the northeast. J. Page. New Repub 157: 8 S 9 '67
Report; Northeast Brazil. J. A. Page. Atlan 221:20-3 Ja '68
See also
Finance—Brazil

BRAZIL—*Continued*

Economic policy

Brazil: not yet through the wringer; new government expected to continue tough austerity program. il Bsns W p 102-4+ Ja 14 '67

Culture and development: the Brazilian example. G. de Zéndegui. il Américas 19:1-2 Jl '67

Quiet revolution. J. W. F. Dulles. Nat R 19: 299-300 Mr 21 '67

See also
Finance—Brazil

Foreign relations

President-elect of Brazil visits the United States; exchange of toasts, January 26, 1967. A da Costa e Silva; L. B. Johnson. Dept State Bul 56:242-4 F 13 '67

Industries

Instant coffee brews a quarrel; dispute between the U.S. and Brazil. il Bsns W p 180 S 30 '67

See also
Sugar industry and trade

Intellectual life

Culture and development: the Brazilian example. G. de Zéndegui. il Américas 19:1-2 Jl '67

Native races

See Indians of South America—Brazil

Politics and government

Brazil: not yet through the wringer; new government expected to continue tough austerity program. il Bsns W p 102-4+ Ja 14 '67

Brazil's Catholic left. T. G. Sanders. America 117:598-601 N 18 '67

Brazil's dilemma; political system. R. Graham. bibliog f Cur Hist 53:291-7+ N '67

Fun or folly? Newsweek 69:56+ My 8 '67

Post of moral command. il Time 89:29-30 Mr 24 '67

Price of unpopularity. Time 90:30 Jl 28 '67

Tragic end of Travancas the Terrible. Time 90:24 D 29 '67

See also
Brazil—Constitution

Religious institutions and affairs

World around us (cont) Christian Cent 84: 482-3, 731-4, 919, 1236, 1541-2 Ap 12, My 31, Jl 12, S 27, N 29 '67

See also
Catholic church in Brazil
Methodist church in Brazil

Social conditions

Brazilian national character in the twentieth century. G. Freyre. bibliog f Ann Am Acad 370:57-62 Mr '67

See also
Peasantry—Brazil
Poor—Brazil

BRAZILIAN students

Happening in São Paulo; priests arrested for association with Communist students. G. H. Dunne. America 117:306-9+ S 23 '67

BRAZILIANS

Brazilian national character in the twentieth century. G. Freyre. bibliog f Ann Am Acad 370:57-62 Mr '67

Unexpected Brazil. J. Dos Passos. il Holiday 42:52-9+ S '67

See also
Lebanese in Brazil

BREACH of promise

Old class; case of William H. Brown. il Newsweek 69:38-9 Mr 6 '67

Once again into the breach; case of William Henry Brown. Time 89:50 Mr 3 '67

BREAD

Almond rolls. S. M. Rule. il Good H 164:146 F '67

Americans not everybody knows: Sylvester Graham; first notable health lecturer. C. W. Ferguson. PTA Mag 61:14-16 Mr '67

La belle brioche. il McCalls 94:106-7+ Ap '67

Braided holiday bread. il Good H 165:194 N '67

Bread & wine. il McCalls 94:102-7 Mr '67

Breads with a foreign flavor. B. S. Brown. Good H 164:155 My '67

Corny but good; cornbread or johnnycake. C. B. Colby. Outdoor Life 139:27 Je '67

Crêpe rolls to make ahead; with recipe. Sunset 138:136 Je '67

Dough handles easily because it's chilled. il Sunset 139:106 D '67

Fancy dinner rolls, easy! il Bet Hom & Gard 45:92 Mr '67

Festive breads cook book. D. Franz. il House & Gard 131:163+ My '67

Hearthside cookbook; Christmas breads. Good H 165:140+ D '67

Hot breads; with recipes. il Sunset 138:154+ Je '67

How to make a two-color twist loaf. il Sunset 138:210 Ap '67

Nut breads. il Bet Hom & Gard 45:92+ D '67

Quick brioches. il Bet Hom & Gard 45:100 My '67

Shortcut breads. il Bet Hom & Gard 45:95-6 Ap '67

Special-occasion yeast breads. B. L. Henry. il Farm J 91:66-7+ D '67

Successful recipes. il Suc Farm 65:109-10 Ja '67

Successful recipes, holiday breads. il Suc Farm 65:51-2 D '67

Super-fast yeast breads; with recipes. il Ladies Home J 84:112-13+ S '67

They are upside down pinwheels; bolas; with recipe. il Sunset 138:193 F '67

Two quick breads made with honey. Sunset 138:162 Ap '67

Yeast breads with glamor. B. L. Henry. il Farm J 91:110-11 F '67

See also
Buns
Gingerbread
Toast

BREAKAWAY lighting standard. See Street lighting fixtures

BREAKFAST foods. See Cereal foods

BREAKFASTS

Breakfast come-ons. il Parents Mag 42:84-5 S '67

Goodbye to breakfast. Sci Digest 62:80-1 S '67

Graduation galas; morning after breakfast; with menu and recipes. il McCalls 94:92-3+ Je '67

Have a million-dollar New Year's eve and a matching breakfast; with recipes and menu. il McCalls 95:98-9+ D '67

Hearty breakfasts on the run. il Am Home 71:88+ Ja '68

See also
Brunches

BREAKING free; story. See McInerny, R.

BREAM, Julian

Master of the solo guitar in music of modern masters. S. Fleming. por Hi Fi 17:89 N '67

Phantom troubadour. il por Time 90:116+ D 1 '67

BREAST

Hope for flat-chested; silicone implants. Sci Digest 62:69 D '67

BREAST feeding. See Infants—Nutrition

BREATHING. See Respiration

BREATHING apparatus. See Respiratory apparatus

BRECHER, Edward M.

LSD: danger to unborn babies. McCalls 94: 70-1+ S '67

With a life at stake. McCalls 95:96-7+ O '67

BRECHT, Bertolt

Alas, poor Bertolt Brecht! F. Ewen. Nation 204:213-14 F 13 '67

Drums in the night. Criticism
New Yorker 43:106 Je 3 '67

Galileo. Crticism
America 116:793-4 My 27 '67
Christian Cent 84:657-8 My 17 '67
Nation 204:603-4 My 8 '67
New Repub 156:28-30 My 6 '67
New Yorker 43:146 Ap 22 '67
Newsweek 69:107 Ap 24 '67
Reporter 36:50-2 My 18 '67
Sat R 50:46 Ap 29 '67
Time il 89:83 Ap 21 '67
Vogue 149:76 Je '67

Puntila and his hired man. Criticism
Time il 89:83 Ap 21 '67

Schweyk in the second World war. Criticism
Sat R 50:71 N 25 '67

BRECK, John H, Incorporated

Consumer service bureau report; something special in shampoos. M. B. Keiser. il Parents Mag 42:8+ Ag '67

BRECKENRIDGE, W. R. See Davey, K. G. jt. auth.

BREED, William J.

Canyon and the river. Natur Hist 76:50-1 N '67

BREED of giants; story. See Stranger, J.

BREEDER reactors. See Nuclear reactors

BREEDING

Conventional wisdom: how wise? animal breeding in captivity. il Sci N 91:217 Mr 4 '67

BREEDING—*Continued*
Farm becomes the factory; confinement breeding of pigs, poultry, and cattle. il Bsns W p68-70 Ag 19 '67
See also
Cattle breeding
Dog breeding
Eugenics
Genetics
Horse breeding
Swine breeding

BREEDLOVE, Nancey Grannis
New roses to treasure. Home Gard 54:46+ F '67

BREELING, James L.
Food for thought and vice versa. Todays Health 45:14-15 S '67

BREER, Robert
Motionless motion. H. Rosenstein. il Art N 66:37+ N '67

BREESE, Sydney S. Jr
Biomacromolecules: views and models. Science 157:727 Ag 11 '67

BREINER, Sheldon, and Kovach, R. L.
Local geomagnetic events associated with displacements on the San Andreas fault. bibliog Science 158:116-18 O 6 '67

BREISKY, Bill
Please don't strike the teacher. Sat Eve Post 240:21 D 2 '67

BREK, C. L.
How to get full value from a home tractor. Pop Sci 191:166+ Jl '67

BREMENTOWN litterbug; drama. See Creegan, G. R.

BRENNAN, D. G.
New thoughts on missile defense. Bul Atomic Sci 23:10-15 Je '67

BRENNAN, Francis
Slaughter on Park avenue. Sat R 50:18 Je 24 '67

BRENNAN, Garnet E.
Case of the pot-smoking school principal. S. Alexander. Life 63:25 N 17 '67

BRENNAN, John
Death of a President; a dissent. Nat R 19: 415 Ap 18 '67
Non-news explosion. Nat R 19:849 Ag 8 '67

BRENNAN, Maeve
Children are there, trying not to laugh; story. New Yorker 43:24-5 Ja 13 '68
Door on West Tenth street; story. New Yorker 43:54-7 O 7 '67
Snowy night on west Forty-ninth street; story. New Yorker 42:28-34 Ja 21 '67

BRENNAN, Niall
Australia's deep divisions. Commonweal 86: 79-80 Ap 7 '67

BRENTLINGER, Judy
In my opinion. por Seventeen 26:198 O '67

BRESLIN, Jimmy
Breslin at bat. S. W. Little. Sat R 50:66 Ag 12 '67

BRESSLER, Doris
When a child's teeth need straightening. Parents Mag 42:82-3+ N '67

BRESSON, Henri Cartier-. See Cartier-Bresson, H.

BRESSOUD, Ed
Teacher with class. M. Allen. por Sr Schol 90:26 Mr 10 '67

BRETHREN. Church of the. See Church of the Brethren

BRETT, Robin, and Higgins, G. T.
Cliftonite in meteorites: a proposed origin. bibliog Science 156:819-20 My 12 '67

BRETTHAUER, Erich W. and Black, S. C.
Polonium-210: removal from smoke by resin filters. bibliog Science 156:1375-6 Je 9 '67

BREUER, Herb
Assignment Bahamas. il U S Camera 30:56-7 Je '67
When the living is easy. il U S Camera 30: 40-1 Jl '67

BREUER, Marcel
Back to the drawing board; efforts rejected. Time 89:44 F 3 '67
Breuer: the last modern architect. C. Jones. il por Horizon 9:32-41 Sum '67
Selective eye of Marcel Breuer. P. Blake. il House B 109:152-9+ Mr '67
Small office building by Marcel Breuer sophisticated use of precast concrete. il Arch Rec 141:131-6 F '67
Two great architects hit by public taste. E. Goble. Arch Rec 141:9 Mr '67

BREUER, Robert
Richard Strauss: grandeur and grossness. Sat R 50:56+ My 27 '67

BREUGHEL, Peeter. See Brueghel, P.

BREWER, Carson
Smokies, hike to discovery. por Liv Wildn 30:3-8 Aut '66

BREWER, Gay, Jr
How to hit golf's best shot; ed. by M. Mulvoy. pors Sports Illus 27:30-7 Ag 7 '67
about
Gay's green jacket. Newsweek 69:70 Ap 24 '67
Glory day for Gay. D. Jenkins. il por Sports Illus 26:22-7 Ap 17 '67
Positively. por Time 89:57-8 Ap 21 '67
Sporting scene. H. W. Wind. New Yorker 43:145-8+ Ap 29 '67

BREWER, John M.
Artifact produced in disc electrophoresis by ammonium persulfate. bibliog Science 156: 256 Ap 14 '67

BREWERIES
You can take it with you; Britain's Allied breweries. Time 91:73 Ja 5 '68

BREWING industries
Cosmopolitan brew: Skol lager beer. Fortune 76:190 S 15 '67
Tapping profits; Britain's no. 2 brewery introduces radical changes. Time 89:108 Je 9 '67
See also
Beer
Breweries

BREWSTER, Daniel Baugh
Should paid witnesses say so. il por Bsns W p 168+ S 9 '67

BREWSTER, Kingman, 1919-
Pressures on university trustees; excerpts from address, May 1967. Sch & Soc 95:404 N 11 '67
about
Anxiety behind the façade. il por Time 89: 78-80+ Je 23 '67; Same abr. with title Can our colleges close the dollar gap? Read Digest 91:87 S '67
Present and future of Kingman Brewster. M. Levitas. il pors N Y Times Mag p30-1+ F 12 '67

BREYTENBACH, Breyten
Fettered spirit. por UNESCO Courier 20:27-9 Mr '67

BREZHNEV, Leonid Il'ich
Soviet view of NATO; address, April 24, 1967. Vital Speeches 33:514-22 Je 15 '67
Thus spake Leonid Brezhnev; excerpts from address, November 3, 1967. Reporter 37:19 D 14 '67

BRIANT, Sister Mary, and others
Some college planetariums. pors Sky & Tel 34:158-61 S '67

BRIANT, Peter C.
Reflections on professional organization; excerpt from address. Mo Labor R 90:22-5 S '67

BRIANT, Roger
On the gypsy circuit. W. Como. por Dance Mag 41:20 Ap '67

BRIBERY
Are some of our best friends gamblers? Life 63:8 S 22 '67
Fumbled ball; address, December 1, 1966. A. Brundage. Vital Speeches 33:411-16 Ap 15 '67
Long palm of the law. N. Pileggi. il Esquire 67:132-5+ Ap '67
See also
Politics, Corruption in

BRICE, Edward Warner
Girl scouts pitch in. Am Ed 3:32 Jl '67

BRICE, Mary Anne
Calling it quits. Mlle 64:192-3+ Ap '67
Lifetime guarantees, gift or gimmick? Duns R 90:65-6 N '67
Midnight market. Duns R 90:39-40 Jl '67
Yes, you can go home again. Todays Health 45:54-6 D '67

BRICK. See Bricks

BRICK construction
Brick-walled oasis, cool, green heart. il House B 109:165-9 Ap '67

BRICK pavements. See Pavements, Brick

BRICKMAKING
Brick kiln builds up its speed; first automated plant. il Bsns W p72-4 Jl 15 '67

BRICKMAN, William W.
Foreign books for educators. Sch & Soc 95: 192-5+, 395-8 Mr 18, O 28 '67
Khrushchev's vision of the future Soviet school. bibliog f Sch & Soc 95:461-74 N 25 '67
U.S. books for educators (cont) Sch & Soc 94:502+; 95:324-6+ D 24 '66, Sum '67

BRICKS
New face of brick. il House B 109:166-7+ S '67

BRIDE of Christ; story. See Gordimer, N.
BRIDGE (game)
Caution: bid this with care. C. Goren. il Sports Illus 27:74 N 6 '67
Chinese finesse: unsound but oh so useful; addiction to bridge. C. Goren. il Sports Illus 27:43 Jl 3 '67
Flashy leghorn diamond; artificial Italian system. C. Goren. il Sports Illus 26:51 F 6 '67
Italian sings the blues; concern about the break up of Italy's famed Blue team. B. Garozzo. il Sports Illus 26:50+ Ja 23 '67
Jeremy the kingmaker. C. Goren. il Sports Illus 27:57 S 4 '67
Masterful move by two master-point aces. C. Goren. il Sports Illus 26:74 My 15 '67
Mr Goren is doubling you. C. Goren. il Sports Illus 27:50-2+ D 25 '67
One that might have been and one that hurt. C. Goren. il Sports Illus 26:36-7 Je 12 '67
Schenken just rolls along. C. Goren. il Sports Illus 26:52-3 F 27 '67
Sit where you choose, and lose. C. Goren. il Sports Illus 26:48 Mr 6 '67
Trapped when the king turned tyrant; World championship in Miami Beach. C. Goren. il Sports Illus 26:64-5 My 8 '67
Winning debut for K and K; Edgar Kaplan and Norman Kay. C. Goren. il Sports Illus 26:62 Ap 24 '67
See also
Bridge clubs
BRIDGE clubs
Cataclysm at the Cavendish club. C. Goren. il Sports Illus 26:74 Ap 10 '67
BRIDGE design. See Bridges—Design
BRIDGE players
Detectives give a hand in a chase; McKenney trophy for B. Crane. C. Goren. il Sports Illus 27:98+ D 4 '67
Good team must have a good bench; World championship team. C. Goren. il Sports Illus 27:46-7 Jl 24 '67
Italian sings the blues; concern about the break up of Italy's famed Blue team. B. Garozzo. il Sports Illus 26:50+ Ja 23 '67
Masterful move by two master-point aces; Tobias and Jan Stone first and second in the McKenney trophy race. C. Goran. il Sports Illus 26:74 My 15 '67
One way of filching a hand in the Flitch; London husband-and-wife championship winners: Richard Anthony and Jane Priday. C. Goren. il Sports Illus 26:54-5 Je 19 '67
Pulling a fast one. S. Goren. il Sports Illus 27:96-7 S 11 '67
Sir Pete is unhorsed. C. Goren. il Sports Illus 27:104+ S 18 '67
Team trials became a Philadelphia story. C. Goren. il Sports Illus 27:74+ O 16 '67
Winning debut for K and K; Edgar Kaplan and Norman Kay. C. Goren. il Sports Illus 26:62 Ap 24 '67
BRIDGE tournaments
Congress cup runneth over the border; Montreal, winner of intercity championship. C. Goren. il Sports Illus 27:62 Ag 14 '67
Detectives give a hand in a chase; McKenney trophy for B. Crane. C. Goren. il Sports Illus 27:98+ D 4 '67
French came set for a fight; first round of 1967 World bridge championship. C. Goren. il Sports Illus 26:72+ Je 5 '67
Knocked out by a big swing. C. Goren. il Sports Illus 26:68 Je 26 '67
Last hand that is a handful; Blue ribbon pair championship. C. Goren. il Sports Illus 27:67 D 18 '67
Masterful show of the wizardry of Ozzie. C. Goren. il Sports Illus 27:61 O 30 '67
Nowhere to go but down; Masters knockout team championship, Montreal. C. Goren. il Sports Illus 27:54-5 Ag 21 '67
One way of filching a hand in the Flitch; London husband-and-wife championship winners: Richard Anthony and Jane Priday. C. Goren. il Sports Illus 26:54-5 Je 19 '67
Singing blues in the night; World bridge championship. H. Peterson. il Sports Illus 26:36-8 Je 12 '67
Slam that spoiled an expert's lunch. C. Goren. il Sports Illus 26:94 Ap 17 '67
Story of an accusation, by T. Reese. Review
Nation 205:251-2 S 18 '67. D. Cort
Team trials became a Philadelphia story. C. Goren. il Sports Illus 27:74+ O 16 '67
There was nothing they could do about Lew; L. Mathe winner of the Vanderbilt cup. C. Goren. il Sports Illus 26:56-7 Ap 3 '67

Trapped when the king turned tyrant; World championship in Miami Beach. C. Goren. il Sports Illus 26:64-5 My 8 '67
World championship: just color it blue; Italy's Blue team. C. Goren. il Sports Illus 26:72 My 29 '67
BRIDGER wilderness area. See Wilderness areas—Wyoming
BRIDGES
Exclusively for horses; equestrian crossing on highway bridge. il Am City 82:30 D '67
See also
Drawbridges
also subhead Bridges under names of cities, e.g. St Louis—Bridges

Accidents

At Point Pleasant; Ohio River's Silver bridge investigation. il Newsweek 71:41 Ja 1 '68
Collapse of the Silver bridge; Ohio River. il Time 90:20 D 22 '67
Thunder on the Ohio; Ohio River bridge. il Newsweek 70:25 D 25 '67

Design

Anecdotes, facetiae, satire, etc.

Bad bridgework; British bridges. R. Gordon. Sat R 50:4+ S 16 '67

Floors

Epoxy sandwich protects bridge decks; New Jersey turnpike. il Am City 82:27 My '67

Maintenance and repair

Stronger than the original; bridge buffeted by waves and weather gets gunite rehabilitation; Long Key bridge, Fla. il Am City 82:121 Je '67

Photographs

Bridges. U S Camera 30:68-9 Je '67
BRIDGES, Lift. See Drawbridges
BRIDWELL, Margaret M.
Oliver Frazer, early Kentucky portrait painter. Antiques 92:718-21 N '67
BRIE cheese. See Cheese
BRIEF lives (dramatic reading) See Dramatic readings
BRIEN, Alan
Going home again. Holiday 42:12+ N '67
Pleasures and miseries of hotels. Holiday 43:10+ Ja '68
Sex and money: the modern equation. Holiday 42:12+ O '67
What's in a face? Holiday 42:10+ D '67
about
Nobody quite like him. il por Newsweek 69: 76-8 Mr 20 '67
BRIENZA, Paul
Waterproofing a parking garage. Am City 82: 142-3 S '67
BRIER, Herbert S.
Amateur radio. See issues of Popular electronics
BRIGGS, L. I. and Pollack, H. N.
Digital model of evaporite sedimentation. Science 155:453-6 Ja 27 '67
BRIGHAM, Besmilr
Floating big sail-high sea birds; poem. Atlan 219:87 Je '67
BRIGHT, John
Disney's fantasy empire. Nation 204:299-303 Mr 6 '67
BRIGHT, Richard Louis
Time is now. Am Ed 3:12-14 N '67
BRIGHT children. See Children, Gifted
BRILL, Earl H.
Cold feet in the promised land; excerpt from Sex is dead and other postmortems. Christian Cent 84:432-5 Ap 5 '67
Is marriage dying, too? excerpt from Sex is dead and other postmortems. Christian Cent 84:268-70 Mr 1 '67
BRILL, Harry
San Francisco redevelopment blues. Commonweal 86:383-4 Je 23 '67
BRILLIANT, Alan
Cheesecake builds unique bookshop. Pub W 193:58-9 Ja 8 '68
BRIMMER, Andrew F.
Money men. il pors Ebony 22:65-6+ S '67
BRINE. See Salt
BRINE shrimps. See Shrimps
BRINER, William
Building of a town. S. A. Parvin. il Hobbies 71:110 F '67
BRINHART, Betty
Grow your own from seed. Home Gard 54: 64+ Ap '67
Regional report. Home Gard 54:52-3 N '67

BRINK, Carol Ryrie
Keep the bough green. Horn Bk 43:447-53 Ag '67
BRINK, John J. and Stein, D. G.
Pemoline levels in brain: enhancement by dimethyl sulfoxide. bibliog Science 158: 1479-80 D 15 '67
BRINKLEY, David
Dilemma of being very, very rich. por Ladies Home J 84:204 N '67
BRINKMAN, Albert R.
Worried look at workbooks. PTA Mag 61: 8-10 bibliog(p36) Ap '67
BRINK'S robberies. See Robberies and assaults
BRINNIN, John Malcolm
My father, my son; poem. New Yorker 43: 51-3 O 7 '67
BRIOCHE. See Bread
BRISKIN, Jacqueline
Captive; story. Seventeen 26:148-9 F '67
Knight in unshining armor; story. Seventeen 26:148-9 S '67
BRISTLECONE pine. See Pine
BRISTOL, Conn.
You have to want industry. H. J. Wojtusik. il Am City 82:86-7 D '67
BRISTOL-Myers company
Bristol-Myers' hard sell. T. A. Wise. il Fortune 75:118-21+ F '67
She does; radiantly red hair colors campaign launched. il Time 90:69 Ag 11 '67
BRISTOL Siddeley engines, limited
Excess-profit action stirs U.K. parliament. H. J. Coleman. Aviation W 86:33-4 Ap 3 '67
Ministry, engine firm criticized in excess-profit investigation; Parliamentry committee. Aviation W 87:19 Jl 31 '67
BRISTOW, William H.
Happy hundred! Sr Schol 90:sup 13 F 10 '67
BRITISH
    See also
English
BRITISH aircraft corporation
Airports, money stall BEA re-equipment. il Aviation W 86:46 F 6 '67
BRITISH airports authority. See Great Britain —British airports authority
BRITISH amateur golf tournament. See Golf—Tournaments
BRITISH art objects. See Art objects, British
BRITISH artificial satellites. See Artificial satellites, British
BRITISH broadcasting corporation
Britains blubby blup; Radio one. Newsweek 70:116 O 23 '67
This is the network that is. il Time 89:50 Mr 10 '67
    See also
Listener (periodical)
BRITISH COLUMBIA
    See also
Architecture, Domestic—British Columbia
Inside Passage
    Description and travel
North to adventure. T. H. Inkster. il Travel 127:41-5 Je '67
    Industries
New empire rises in Canada's west. il U S News 63:64-8 Jl 17 '67
    Parks and reserves
Up and up to the Garibaldi flowers; Garibaldi provincial park. il Sunset 138:30+ Je '67
BRITISH Commonwealth. See Commonwealth of nations
BRITISH cookery. See Cookery, English
BRITISH European airways corporation
Airports, money stall BEA re-equipment. il Aviation W 86:46 F 6 '67
BEA pushes for BAC 211 order approval. H. J. Coleman. Aviation W 87:38 Ag 28 '67
BRITISH HONDURAS
    See also
Belize
Fishing—British Honduras
BRITISH in China. See English in China
BRITISH in India. See English in India
BRITISH Labor party. See Labor party (Great Britain)
BRITISH military bases. See Military bases, British
BRITISH money. See Money—Great Britain
BRITISH museum
London's surfeit of riches. il Time 90:85 D 1 '67
BRITISH national theatre. See Theater—Great Britain

BRITISH Open. See Golf—Tournaments
BRITISH overseas airways corporation
Brickbats at BOAC. il Time 89:88 Mr 24 '67
BOAC posts record earnings in year; U.K. dividend doubles. Aviation W 87:47 Ag 14 '67
BOAC workers call management remote. Aviation W 87:39 Ag 28 '67
BRITISH poetry
British chronicle. R. Howard. Poetry 110:195-203 Je '67
New poets, by M. L. Rosenthal. Review Sat R 50:45 Je 10 '67. R. D. Spector
    See also
English poetry
BRITISH press. See Newspapers—Great Britain
BRITISH press council. See Newspapers—Great Britain
BRITISH royal ballet. See Royal ballet, Great Britain
BRITISH sculpture. See Sculpture, British
BRITISH singers. See Singers
BRITISH steel corporation
Britain creates its own big steel; nationalization of fourteen companies. Bsns W p30-1 Ag 5 '67
British socialism's last grasp. Fortune 76:205 S 15 '67
Lord of steel. il Time 90:70 Ag 11 '67
BRITISH steeplechase. See Horse racing
BRITISH VIRGIN ISLANDS
British Virgin Islands. H. Wilson. il Travel 127:42-5 My '67
Marina Cay. P. M. Young. il Travel 127:65-6 Ja '67
BRITTANY
Goose and gander; call for Breton independence. Newsweek 70:41 Ag 14 '67
Letter from Paris; two departments: Côtes du Nord and Finistère devastated areas, because of wreck of Torrey Canyon. Genêt. New Yorker 43:166+ Ap 29 '67
Le petit bélon; shortage of oysters. P. Brown. il Holiday 41:56-7+ Je '67
BRITTEN, Benjamin
Communicator; interview, ed. by E. Forbes. Opera N 31:16 F 11 '67
        about
Britten and the Aldeburgh miracle. E. Greenfield. il Hi Fi 17:MA24-6 S '67
Britten and the bard, a new Midsummer night. D. Hamilton. il Hi Fi 17:128-9 O '67
Britten at Aldeburgh. I. Kolodin. il Sat R 50:41-3 Jl 29 '67
Britten country; photographs. Opera N 31: 12-15 F 11 '67
Burning fiery furnace. Criticism
    Hi Fi 17:MA13 S '67
Many facets of Benjamin Britten. H. Kupferberg. il Atlan 220:126+ D '67
Music to my ears; performance of Schubert's Die winterreise in the Hunter college playhouse. I. Kolodin. Sat R 50:107 O 14 '67
Music to my ears; performance of War requiem by the Philharmonic orchestra. I. Kolodin. Sat R 50:26 My 6 '67
Musical events; performance of War requiem by N.Y. philharmonic. W. Sargeant. New Yorker 43:134+ Ap 29 '67
Peter Grimes. Criticism
    Hi Fi il 17:MA8-9 Ap '67
    New Yorker 42:104 Ja 28 '67
    Opera N 31:12 Ja 7 '67
    Opera N 31:17-20 F 11 '67
    Opera N 31:24-5 F 11 '67
    Sat R 50:57 F 4 '67
Rape of Lucretia. Criticism
    Opera N il 31:12-13 Ja 7 '67
Records:
    Britten: A midsummer night's dream. Opera N 32:34 Ja 13 '68
BRITTER, Marguerite S.
(ed) Book notes and reviews. Yachting 121: 80 F; 118 Ap '67
BROAD-leaved evergreens. See Evergreens
BROADBENT, Robert V.
News for sheep hunters. Outdoor Life 140:107 D '67
Scarface. pors Outdoor Life 140:66+ D '67
BROADHEADS. See Arrowheads
BROADWAY. See New York (city)—Streets
BROADWAY actors and actresses. See Actors and actresses
BROADWAY-Hale stores, Incorporated
California's tailor-made store chain. il Bsns W p88-90+ My 27 '67
BROCINER, Victor
Problems of matching speakers to solid-state amplifiers. Electr World 77:23-6+ Ja '67

BROCK, Alan
Strange legacy of Conrad Cantzen. Read Digest 90:41-2+ F '67
BROCK, Carol
Party planner. See issues of Good housekeeping
BROCK, Lou
Winning Card. il por Newsweek 69:66-7 Je 5 '67
BROCK, Thomas D.
Life at high temperatures. bibliog Science 158:1012-19 N 24 '67
BROCKMAN, James
Favorite pioneer recording artists. J. Walsh. il por Hobbies 72:38-9+ O '67
BROCKTON, Mass.
Instrumentation for today and tomorrow; sewage-treatment plant. il Am City 82:113-15 F '67
BROCKWAY, Edith E.
Desert botanical garden. il Horticulture 45:18-19+ Ag '67
BROCKWAY, Wallace
Le jongleur returns. Opera N 31:6-7 Ap 15 '67
Trade winds; ed. by H. R. Mayes. Sat R 50:16 N 4 '67
BRODE, Wallace Reed
Brode to head chemical society. por Sci N 92:584 D 16 '67
BRODEN, Diana
Sophocles and the sixth graders. NEA J 56:15 N '67
BRODER, David S. See Hess, S. jt. auth.
BRODER, Nathan
For Handel's organ works, Archive thinks of everything. Hi Fi 17:78C-78D F '67
BRODERICK, Albert
From a friend who never met him. America 117:246-8 S 9 '67
BRODERICK, Dorothy M.
Books for the early years. PTA Mag 62:22-4 bibliog(p34) N '67
Librarian in today's society; excerpts from address, November 7, 1966. por Library J 92:1413-16 Ap 1 '67
Plus ça change: classic patterns in public/school library relations. bibliog por Library J 92:1995-7 My 15 '67
BRODERICK, William E.
3-D star display. il Sky & Tel 34:288 N '67
BRODEUR, Paul
Snow in Petrograd; story. New Yorker 42:136 F 11 '67
BRODIE, Bernard
How not to lead an alliance. Reporter 36:18-24 Mr 9 '67
BRODIE, Bernard Beryl
Bridging two disciplines. B. J. Culliton. il pors Sci N 92:476-7 N 11 '67
Lasker awards. por Sci N 92:488-9 N 18 '67
Lasker largesse. por Newsweek 70:104+ N 20 '67
Lasker lens. il por Time 90:57 N 17 '67
BRODIE, Fawn M.
Ronald Reagan plays surgeon. Reporter 36:11-16 Ap 6 '67
BRODIE, John
Long live the king. H. Wilner. il pors Sat Eve Post 240:85-9 N 18 '67
BRODSKY, Bernard. See Ryan, O. jt. auth.
BRODY, Sidney F. family
Great art in Los Angeles. il pors Vogue 150:156-9 Ag 15 '67
BRODY, Thomas C.
Baseball. Sports Illus 26:64+ My 29 '67
C. B. DeMille of the pros. Sports Illus 27:74-6+ N 20 '67
College football. Sports Illus 27:48-9 Jl 3; 52+ N 27 '67
Handball. Sports Illus 26:90+ Ap 17 '67
Marathon. Sports Illus 26:62-3+ My 1 '67
Swimming. Sports Illus 26:56+ Mr 27 '67
Track & field (title varies) Sports Illus 26:58-9 F 13; 51-4 Mr 6; 64-6 Mr 13 '67
Two guys named Jim had the same idea. Sports Illus 26:34-5 Je 12 '67
BROECKER, W. L.
Into each movie some rain should fall. Pop Phot 60:125+ Je '67
Moving camera. il Pop Phot 61:122-5+ O '67
BROECKER, Wallace S. and others
Radium-226 and radon-222: concentration in Atlantic and Pacific oceans. bibliog Science 158:1307-10 D 8 '67
BROEK, Jan O. M.
National character in the perspective of cultural geography. bibliog f Ann Am Acad 370:8-15+ Mr '67
BROEKMEIJER, M. W. J. M.
GI's in Vietnam: praise from a Dutch general; excerpts from report. U S News 63:14 O 16 '67

BROGAN, Colm
Common market and a horse named Arkle. Nat R 19:252-4 Mr 7 '67
Letter from London. Nat R 19:1065-6, 1423-4 O 3, D 26 '67
BROGAN, Sir Denis William
English sickness. Harper 234:57-62 Je '67
Naiveté versus reality in Vietnam; excerpts from Worlds in conflict. Atlan 220:48-55 Jl '67
BROILERS, Electric. See Electric apparatus and appliances, Domestic
BROILING
How to broil without a broiler. il Ladies Home J 84:34 Je '67
BROKAW, C. J.
Adenosine triphosphate usage by flagella. bibliog Science 156:76-8 Ap 7 '67
BROKEN bones. See Fractures
BROKEN HILL proprietary company
Striking it rich Down Under; world's fifth largest steelmaker. il Bsns W p56+ Mr 4 '67
BROKEN homes
Seven mistakes divorced parents make. J. H. Pollack. il Parents Mag 42:48-9+ Mr '67
When parents separate; common sins committed by divorced parents. J. H. Pollack. il Todays Health 45:16-19+ Je '67
BROKERS
Bob Cratchit hours; Stock exchange shorten daily trading sessions to help paperwork delays. il Time 90:75 Ag 18 '67
Don't cuss your broker for everything. Bsns W p 129-30 D 9 '67
Hot market's blizzard of paper. il Newsweek 70:51 Ag 21 '67
Stockbroker test: Shearson Hammill stockbroker aptitude. New Yorker 43:40-1 D 16 '67
This is a kids' market. They're all under 30. A. Smith. il Life 63:47-8 Jl 28 '67
Wall Street's own watchdogs; compliance men to prevent stock frauds. il Bsns W p90-2+ Jl 29 '67
Young millionaires of finance; new men in Wall Street. il Bsns W p76-9 D 30 '67
See also
Campbell, D. A. company
Clark, Dodge and company
Harris, Upham and company
Hutton, E. F. and company
Salomon brothers and Hutzler (firm)
Stock exchange
Women as brokers

Commissions

Are give-ups on the way out? SEC rules against commission splitting with regional exchanges. il Bsns W p 125-6+ Ja 14 '67
Reforming the funds. P. A. Samuelson. Newsweek 69:74 Mr 6 '67
So prosperous it hurts. il Time 90:91 O 20 '67
BROKERS, Real estate. See Real estate agents
BROMELIADS
Bromeliads. V. Padilla. il Horticulture 45:22-5+ Ag '67
Growing your own Christmas ornaments. il Sunset 139:180 D '67
Introducing five more of the showy bromeliads. il Sunset 138:230 F '67
BROMIGE, David
Weight less than the shadow; poem. Poetry 110:30-2 Ap '67
BROMINE molecules. See Molecules
BROMMER, Gerald F.
Wrap it up. Sch Arts 67:12-15 N '67
BROMOPHENOLS. See Phenols
BRONCHIAL asthma. See Asthma
BRONCHIOLAR cells. See Cells
BRONFENBRENNER, Urie
New morality. Sat R 50:47 Jl 1 '67
Split-level American family. Sat R 50:60-6 O 7 '67
BRONOW, J. A.
Separate those sewers. Am City 82:94-6 F '67
BRONOWSKI, Jacob
Second scientific revolution. UNESCO courier 20:20-4 My '67
Wondrous reach of imagination; excerpt from address, May 25, 1966. Read Digest 91:128-31 S '67
BRONTË, Charlotte
Jane Eyre; dramatization. See Olfson, L.
BRONTË, Emily
Wuthering Heights; dramatization. See Olfson, L.
BRONX, N.Y.
Hospitals
See New York (city)—Hospitals

BRONX State hospital. See Hospitals, Psychiatric

BRONX zoo. See New York zoological park

BRONZES
Gold age bronze; Greek and Roman bronzes at the Fogg museum. S. Nodelman. il Art N 66:26-9 D '67
Lamaist art; the Panchen Lama. G. Kaler. il Hobbies 72:50 Je '67
Portrait in bronze; Kuan Ti, Chinese god of war. G. Kaler. il Hobbies 72:50+ Mr '67
Portraits in bronze; Tibetan figures. G. Kaler. il Hobbies 72:50 Ap '67

BROOCHES
It's after four and that's a daisy; pop art brooches. il Sunset 138:140 Ap '67
Late nineteenth century brooch. L. F. Reals. il Hobbies 72:98W N '67

BROOK, Marvin G.
Getting on talking terms. PTA Mag 62:14-16 bibliog(p32) S '67

BROOK, Marx
Electric currents accompanying tornado activity. bibliog Science 157:1434-6 S 22 '67

BROOK, Peter
Lively arts; interview, ed. by M. Ronan. il Por Sr Schol 90:21 Mr 31 '67

BROOKE, Edward William
After the long, hot summer, where do we go? pors Look 31:24-7 S 5 '67
Low income programs; address, August 7, 1967. Vital Speeches 33:719-22 S 15 '67

about
Change of heart; concerning maiden address. por Newsweek 69:28 Ap 3 '67
Halt Vietnam bombing? por U S News 62:15 Ap 3 '67
I'm a soul brother. S. Booker. il pors Ebony 22:150-4 Ap '67
Individual who happens to be a Negro. il pors Time 89:20-3 F 17 '67
with title Senator who happens to be a Negro. Read Digest 90:99-102 My '67
Senator Brooke and Dr King. Nation 204:452-3 Ap 10 '67
Three Negro senators of the United States; with biographical sketch. por Negro Hist Bul 30:4-5+ Ja '67

BROOKER, Clarence
Death of a dropout. J. Sideman. New Repub 156:11-14 Je 3 '67

BROOKHOUSE, Christopher
Man in the ocelot suit; poem. Harper 235:38 S '67

BROOKINGS institution
Schoolmaster to the government. P. McBroom. il Sci N 92:232-3 S 2 '67

BROOKLYN
See also
Coney Island

Courts
Case of the debatable Brooklyn D.A. T. J. Fleming. il N Y Times Mag p32-3+ Mr 19 '67

Education
Brooklyn's bus to equality; white children taken to P.S. 20 in Negro neighborhood. B. Bard. il Sat R 50:78-9 F 18 '67

Galleries and museums
See also
Brooklyn museum

Housing
Comprehensive district planning privately sponsored guides rehabilitation of six blocks in Brooklyn. il Arch Rec 142:142-9 Jl '67
To save a slum; Bedford-Stuyvesant restoration corp. il Newsweek 70:48 N 20 '67

Parks and playgrounds
Prospect park; interview. C. Lancaster. New Yorker 43:48-50 O 28 '67
Will a park die in Brooklyn? Brooklyn's Prospect park. J. J. Shomon. il Audubon 69:80-1 Mr '67

BROOKLYN botanic garden

Children's garden
Children garden at the Brooklyn botanic garden. F. M. Miner. il Horticulture 45:34-8 Ap '67

BROOKLYN museum
Bequest to Brooklyn; collection of Mrs Albert C. Barnes. il Newsweek 69:106-7 Ap 24 '67
Newest ancient art; exhibition of objects from J. C. Leff collection of Ancient art of Latin America at the Brooklyn museum. J. H. Kay. il Américas 19:9-16 Ap '67

Rare rugs; reception at opening of exhibition. New Yorker 43:38-9 My 13 '67
Wrecker, spare that frieze! rescued relics by Anonymous arts recovery society in Frieda Schiff Warburg Memorial sculpture garden. R. S. Gallagher. il Am Heritage 18:60-4+ Ag '67

BROOKLYN public library
Brooklyn gambit; decision by professional librarians to join AFL-CIO American federation of state, county and municipal employees. K. Nyren; discussion. Library J 92:508+ F 1 '67
Brooklyn library staff pickets in protest il Library J 92:2493 Jl '67
Brooklyn trustees and union approve contract. Library J 92:2981-3 S 15 '67; Reply. L. Brandwein. 92:3935 N 1 '67
Reaching the nonuser. H. Franklin. Wilson Lib Bul 41:943-6 My '67
Year of library change reported by Brooklyn; summary of annual report. J. C. Frantz. Library J 92:3584+ O 15 '67

BROOKS, Alan
Girl watching. E. Galligan. il U S Camera 30:48-9 O '67

BROOKS, David William
Super-farmer attacks global poverty. A. Rankin. por Read Digest 92:25-6+ Ja '68

BROOKS, Dori
Asparagus & rhubarb. Home Gard 54:35-6 Je '67
Easy recipes for summer. Home Gard 54:44-5 Jl '67
Fresh corn on the cob. Home Gard 54:47 Ag '67
From the fall food garden. Home Gard 54:44 O '67
On revitalizing vegetables. Home Gard 54:26 S '67
Sage and honeyed thoughts. Home Gard 54:42 N '67

BROOKS, George R.
History in houses. Antiques 92:96-9 Jl '67

BROOKS, Gladys
Best of many lives. G. Hicks. Sat R 50:39-40 F 25 '67

BROOKS, Gwendolyn
Langston Hughes. Nation 205:7 Jl 3 '67

BROOKS, Harvey
Applied science and technological progress; excerpt from report. bibliog Science 156:1706-12 Je 30 '67

BROOKS, Iris
Soup and salad supper cook book. House & Gard 131:179+ Mr '67

BROOKS, Joe
Man with drag. Outdoor Life 139:66-7+ Mr '67

BROOKS, John
Profiles; Xerox corporation, formerly Haloid company. New Yorker 43:46-50+ Ap 1 '67

BROOKS, John Gaunt
Building muscle with outside help. il pors Bsns W p93-4+ S 16 '67

BROOKS, Patricia
Our Miss Brooks; interview, ed. by R. D. Daniels. pors Opera N 32:14-15 N 4 '67

about
Save a pair for Verdi. D. Hering. il por Dance Mag 41:29-30+ Mr '67

BROOKS, Patricia K.
Grand tour; as it may be. Sat R 51:61 Ja 6 '68
Julian the tranquil slept here. Sat R 50:66+ N 25 '67

BROOKS, Paul
Copper company vs. the North Cascades. Harper 235:48-50 S '67
Fight for America's Alps. Atlan 219:87-90+ My '67
Seed of a conscience; excerpt from Manual of outdoor interpretation. Audubon 69:36-7 N '67

BROOKS, Phyllis
To relinquish; poem. Poetry 110:243 Jl '67

BROOKS, Richard
In hot water. J. Jacobs. Reporter 38:38 Ja 11 '68

BROOKS, Thomas R.
Can parents run New York's schools? Reporter 38:20-2 Ja 11 '68
Caseworker and the client. N Y Times Mag p26-7+ Ja 29 '67
Job program that works. Reporter 37:28-30 N 16 '67
Numbers, the game that only the mobsters win. Read Digest 91:79-82 S '67

BROOKS, Van Wyck
Best of many lives. G. Hicks. Sat R 50:39-40 F 25 '67
If strangers meet, by G. Brooks. Review Vogue 149:144 My '67. A. Kazin

BROOME, Harvey
Harvey Broome addresses the save our Smokies hikers; text of address. Liv Wildn 30:8 Aut '66

BROOME, J. D. See Becker, F. F. jt. auth.

BROOMFIELD, William S.
U.N. objectives for unification of Korea reaffirmed; statement, November 16, 1967. Dept State Bul 57:844-5 D 18 '67

BROPHY, Marjorie
Every day is mother's day. See issues of Good housekeeping

BROPHY, Thomas D'Arcy
William J. Barrett 1895-1967. Craft Horiz 27: 9 Mr '67

BROSNAN, Jim
Red and his roomie, and the pennant. N Y Times Mag p36-7+ S 17 '67

BROSSIN DE MÉRÉ, Andrée
Thinking in colour... il por Vogue 150:98-9 Ag 15 '67

BROSTOFF, Steven W. and Ingram, V. M.
Chemical modification of yeast alanine-tRNA with a radioactive carbodiimide. bibliog Science 158:666-9 N 3 '67

BROTEN, N. W. and others
Long base line interferometry: a new technique. Science 156:1592-3 Je 23 '67

BROTHERHOOD of man

Bibliography
Books for brotherhood (cont) il Commonweal 85:592-3 F 24 '67

BROTHERHOOD of painters, decorators and paperhangers of America
Painters' union. B. Hall. il Nation 205:81-4 Jl 31 '67

BROTHERHOODS
See also
Vocation (in religion)

BROTHERS, J. David
Using the trucking industry more effectively; summary of address. por Pub W 192:56 D 4 '67

BROTHERS, Joyce
On being a woman. See issues of Good housekeeping

BROTHERS and sisters. See Siblings

BROUGHTON, James
Our land & our sea & hallelujah. R. RoselIep. Poetry 111:190-2 D '67

BROUGHTON, T. Alan
Waking to day; poem. Commonweal 87:439 Ja 12 '68

BROUGHTON, T. Robert S.
(comp) Articles and other books received; ancient. See issues of American historical review

BROWDER, Joan
Don't pull the plug on the Everglades. Am For 73:12-15+ S '67

BROWER, Brock
Bullheaded leader of aerospace labor. Life 64:60-2+ Ja 19 '68
Needed home for new writing. Life 63:22 S 22 '67
No hits, no runs, no Eros. Life 63:18 D 1 '67
Northerner's North. Holiday 41:10+ My '67
Puzzling front runner. Life 62:84-8+ My 5 '67

about
Governor Romney ran him ragged. G. P. Hunt. por Life 62:3 My 5 '67

BROWER, Millicent
Noise pollution: a growing menace. Sat R 50:17-19 My 27 '67

BROWER, Nancy
Getting there is more than half the fun. Motor B 120:29-31+ O '67
Key West. Travel 128:24-9 D '67

BROWN, Allan H.
Post-Apollo era, decisions facing NASA. Bul Atomic Sci 23:11-16 Ap '67

BROWN, B. E.
Neuromuscular transmitter substance in insect visceral muscle. bibliog il Science 155: 595-7 F 3 '67

BROWN, Barry
Barry Brown tests the Scoopic 16, designed to be held. Pop Phot 61:138-41 N '67

BROWN, Bianca S.
[Foods] with a foreign flavor. See issues of Good housekeeping

BROWN, Bruce
Happy tycoon takes off; with report by G. Moore. il pors Life 63:37-8+ Ag 25 '67

BROWN, Clarence
Chekhov among the convicts. New Repub 157:26-8+ O 21 '67

Little girl migrates. New Repub 158:19-20 Ja 20 '68
Observations. Commentary 44:80 Ag '67

BROWN, Claude
Nobody worries about integration anymore! Look 31:28 Je 27 '67
Power of blackness. Look 31:22-7 Je 27 '67

BROWN, David S.
Is your business too organized? Nations Bsns 55:76-8 Mr '67

BROWN, Deming
Poets, red and white. N Y Times Mag p6+ My 28 '67

BROWN, Dolores
Campfire inside. pors Outdoor Life 140:50-3+ D '67

BROWN, Dorothy Foster
Button collecting. See issues of Hobbies

BROWN, Edwin J.
College of whose choice? Parents Mag 42:40-1+ D '67

BROWN, G. W. Jr, and Brown, S. G.
Urea and its formation in coelacanth liver. bibliog Science 155:570-3 F 3 '67

BROWN, George Alfred
Middle East crisis; address, June 21, 1967. Vital Speeches 33:586-9 Jl 15 '67

about
Bitter aftertaste. il Time 90:18 D 29 '67
Destiny catches up with George Brown. C. Brogan. Nat R 19:1423-4 D 26 '67
I am what I am. il pors Newsweek 70:46+ O 16 '67
One of those weeks. il por Newsweek 70:50-1 N 13 '67
Troubled times of George Brown. B. Wenham. New Repub 157:11-13 N 18 '67
Unchangeable George. il por Time 90:37 O 13 '67

BROWN, George Edward, 1920-
I am tired of your gimmicks. por Nation 205: 614-17 D 11 '67

BROWN, Gwilym S.
Bowling. Sports Illus 27:74+ D 11 '67
Golf (cont) Sports Illus 26:52-3 F 20; 27:64-5 O 23 '67
Marathon. Sports Illus 27:70-1 O 16 '67
Track & field (title varies) (cont) Sports Illus 26:48-50 F 27 '67

BROWN, H. Douglas
Gems and minerals. See issues of Hobbies

BROWN, H. Rap
If you have any doubts about Rap Brown inciting riots; excerpts from news conference, July 27, 1967. por U S News 63:8 Ag 7 '67

about
Black militants talk of guns and guerrillas. il U S News 63:32 Ag 7 '67
Firebrand. il por Newsweek 70:28 Ag 7 '67
Man from SNCC. Newsweek 69:45 My 22 '67
Man with a match. il por Time 90:23 S 22 '67
Two for a monologue; Governor Kirk interrupts speech by H. R. Brown. il por Time 90:21 Ag 18 '67

BROWN, Harold O. J.
'Tis the season to be surly. Nat R 19:1424-7 D 26 '67

BROWN, Harrison
Combustibility of humans. Sat R 50:14-17+ Je 24 '67
International cooperation: the new ICSU program on critical data; excerpts from address, December 29, 1966. Science 156: 751-4 My 12 '67
Political-economic web: crisis in development; text of address. Bul Atomic Sci 23: 2-7 D '67

BROWN, Harry Darrow, and others
Erythrocyte abnormality in human myopathy. bibliog Science 157:1577-8 S 29 '67

BROWN, J. E. and others
Photoelectric potential from photoreceptor cells in ventral eye of limulus. bibliog Science 158:665 N 3 '67

BROWN, James Oliver
Literary agents. Writer 80:15-17 Jl '67

BROWN, Jeff
Do forget to write. Holiday 41:80-1 Ap '67

BROWN, Jimmy
Brown power. il por Newsweek 71:75+ Ja 15 '68
Footage instead of yardage for Jim Brown; with report by W. Warga. il pors Life 62:103-4+ My 19 '67

BROWN, Joanna
Girl's guide to men-on-the-make. Mlle 66:120-1+ D '67

BRUEMMER, Fred
Sable Island; with biographical sketch. il
Natur Hist 76:6, 54-9 Ag '67
Strange cod of Ogac Lake. Outdoor Life 140:
56-9 N '67
BRUHN, Erik
Views of a dancing Dane; ed. by E. Miller.
pors Seventeen 26:148-9+ N '67

about

World of dance. W. Terry. il Sat R 50:84-5
Je 10 '67
BRUMBERG, Abraham
Despite the thaw. Reporter 36:60-2 Mr 9 '67
BRUMMELL, O. B.
Folk music (cont)   Hi Fi 17:136 Ja; 112+
Mr; 112+ Ap; 106+ My; 106+ Je; 92 Jl; 110
Ag; 118 S; 138-9 N; 134 D '67; 18:108-9 Ja
'68
Marvelous music of Hungary. Hi Fi 17:85
Ja '67
BRUN, Helen L.
Discover Ontario's Land O'Lakes. Motor B
119:22-3+ Je '67
BRUNCHES
Brunch is a breakfast that doesn't look it. il
Sunset 138:216+ My '67
Come to brunch! N. C. Gray. il Am Home
70:58-9 N '67
Company's coming to brunch. Am Home 70:
102 Ja '67
Easter Sunday brunch; with recipes. il Seven-
teen 26:162-3+ Mr '67
For winter health and energy plan bigger
better brunches; with recipes. K. Smith.
il Pop Gard 18:72-5+ Mr '67
Relax and entertain with Sunday brunch;
with recipes and menus. G. Maddox. il To-
days Health 45:60-5 Mr '67
Sunday brunch: easy-going party for people
on-the-go; with recipes. il Ladies Home J
84:80-1+ O '67
BRUNDAGE, Avery
Fumbled ball; address, December 1, 1966.
Vital Speeches 33:411-16 Ap 15 '67

about

Last living amateur is still a king among
kings. L. Griggs. il por Sports Illus 26:70+
My 22 '67
BRUNEI (sultanate)
Shellfare state. M. Parker. il Newsweek 71:
38-9 Ja 8 '68
BRUNK, C. F. and Hanawalt, P. C.
Repair of damaged DNA in a eucaryotic cell:
tetrahymena pyriformis. bibliog Science 158:
663-4 N 3 '67
BRUNK, Max E.
New look in meat; excerpt from address. por
Farm J 91:54N Ap '67
Who best speaks for the consumer? address,
September 20, 1966. Vital Speeches 33:247-52
F 1 '67
BRUNS, Bill
God likes a winner, said dad to the rabbi.
Life 63:50 S 15 '67
U.S. men are losers. Life 63:109+ S 22 '67
World's greatest designer who wants no
geraniums. Life 63:65 Jl 28 '67
BRUNSWICK, Ga.

Historic houses, etc.

Living with antiques; Hofwyl plantation in
Brunswick, Ga. Mrs C. M. Theus. il An-
tiques 92:194-7 Ag '67
BRUSH fires
Siege season; southern California. Time 90:28
N 10 '67
BRUSHES
Three hair brushes with power assist. il Con-
sumer Rep 32:409-10 Ag '67
BRUSHING of teeth. See Teeth—Care and
hygiene
BRUSILOW, Anshel
And we quote; ed. by B. Jacobson. por Hi Fi
17:MA14 F '67
BRUSSELS
Brussels: a U.S. business beachhead. Bsns W
p78 S 16 '67
NATO learns to live in exile from France. il
Bsns W p46-8 O 21 '67

Description

Going places, finding things in Brussels. R.
Pomeroy. il House & Gard 132:76+ O '67

Music

Brussels. L. Mueller. Opera N 31:28 Ap 15 '67
Brussels; production of Die fledermaus. L.
Mueller. Opera N 31:32 F 11 '67
Report: Brussels; production of Rossini's
Comte Ory. L. Mueller. il Opera N 32:32
D 30 '67

BRUSSELS department store fire. See Fires
BRUSTEIN, Robert
Theatre. See issues of New republic
about
Theatre. J. Novick. Nation 204:381-2 Mr 20
'67
Up at Yale, way off off off Broadway. A. Levy.
il por N Y Times Mag p30-1+ My 21 '67
BRUTUS, Dennis
Seeds of wrath. por UNESCO Courier 20:23-4
Mr '67
BRUYA, Ethel L.
Gift for Clewiston. Library J 92:4369 D 1 '67
BRY, Ilse, and Afflerbach, Lois
Links between the humanities and the litera-
ture of the human sciences. Wilson Lib
Bul 42:510-25 Ja '68
BRYAN, C. D. B.
1-A or 2-S, the draft and the student. N Y
Times Mag p26-7+ Mr 19 '67
Why the generation gap begins at thirty.
N Y Times Mag p 10-11+ Jl 2 '67
BRYAN, Diana
Notes for the hostess. See issues of House &
garden incorporating Living for young home-
makers to August 1967
BRYAN, Harrison
American automation in action; reprint. bib-
liog Library J 92:189-96 Ja 15 '67
Gloomy conclusion? bibliog por Library J 92:
4113-16 N 15 '67
BRYAN, J. 3d
Arch of triumph. Holiday 43:62-3+ Ja '68
What price tulips? Holiday 41:62-3 Ap '67
BRYAN, James E.
New ALA officer. ALA Bul 61:868+ Jl '67
BRYANT, Deborah
Miss America one year later. J. Canaday.
pors McCalls 94:80+ F '67
BRYANT, Edward
Boom in U.S. university museums. Art N 66:
30-47+ S '67
BRYANT, Farris
States-man. Newsweek 69:35-6 Mr 20 '67
Wooing the governors: LBJ style. il por U S
News 62:19 Mr 20 '67
BRYANT, H. Stafford, Jr
What college bookmen are up to in 1967. Pub
W 191:42-5 F 13 '67
BRYANT, J. A. Jr
Class of '67: the gentle desparadoes. Nation
204:779 Je 19 '67
BRYANT, Lynwood
Origin of the automobile engine; with
biographical sketch. Sci Am 216:19, 102-10+
bibliog(p 152) Mr '67
BRYANT, Robert H.
History and theology. Christian Cent 84:944-
5 Jl 19 '67
BRYNES, Asher
Pacification primer. New Repub 156:39-41 Ap
8 '67
BRYNNER, Irena
Jewelry by Sepp Schmölzer. Craft Horiz 27:
14-15 S '67
BRYSON, Reid A.
Is man changing the climate of earth? adapta-
tion of address. por Sat R 50:52-5 Ap 1
'67
BRZEINSKI, Joseph E. and others
Should Johnny read in kindergarten? NEA J
56:23-5 Mr '67
BRZEZINSKI, Zbigniew
American transition. New Repub 157:18-21
D 23 '67
Framework of East-West reconciliation. bib-
liog f For Affairs 46:256-75 Ja '68
Implications of change for United States for-
eign policy; remarks, May 22, 1967. Dept
State Bul 57:19-23 Jl 3 '67
Toward a community of the developed na-
tions. Dept State Bul 56:414-20 Mr 13 '67
BUBBLE bath. See Bath preparations
BUBBLES, John
Bubbles: survivor of Buck & Bubbles, the
great song-and-dance team; interview. New
Yorker 43:21-3 Ag 26 '67
BUBBLES, Soap. See Soap bubbles and films
BUCHAN, Alastair
Future of NATO. bibliog f por(back cover)
Int Concil 565:5-61 N '67
BUCHANAN, Doris
We learned at school. Yachting 123:83+ Ja
'68
BUCHANAN, Ian
Family quiz game. See issues of Parents'
magazine and better homemaking
BUCHANAN, William J.
One last time, amigo. Read Digest 90:61-5
My '67

BUCHANAN, Mich.
Bright lights. brighter future. D. D. Tammen.
il Am City 82:158 O '67
BUCHAREST declaration. See Warsaw pact,
1955
BUCHER, Carlton G.
Coffee table that solves a problem. Pop Sci
191:124-7 D '67
BUCHER, Nancy L. R. See Moolten, F. L. jt.
auth.
BUCHHEISTER, Carl W.
Presidents reports. See issues of Audubon to
January, 1967
about
Buchheister to retire. Nat Parks Mag 41:
20 Ja '67
Carl W. Buchheister, a tribute. R. T. Peter-
son. por Audubon 69:54-5 Mr '67
BUCHMAN, Frank Nathan Daniel
They're out to remake the world; condensa-
tion. C. W. Hall. por Read Digest 92:145-
56+ Ja '68
BUCHSBAUM, Walter H. and Henn, W. D.
Troubleshooting integrated circuits. Electr
World 78:34-6+ Jl; 37-40 Ag '67
BUCHWALD, Art
Boy who had his haircut. Lades Home J 84:52
Je '67
Feminine mistaque. Read Digest 91:55-6 O '67
Incredible Caribbean adventures of one Art
Buchwald and family. pors Ladies Home J
84:106-7+ N '67
BUCK (singer)
Bubbles: survivor of Buck & Bubbles, the
great song-and-dance team; interview.
J. Bubbles. New Yorker 43:21-3 Ag 26 '67
BUCK, Pearl (Sydenstricker)
Children America forgot. Read Digest 91:108-
10 S '67
Stranger, come home; story. Good H 165:84-5
D '67
BUCK, Robert N.
Sky is their limit. Read Digest 90:68-72 Ap
'67
BUCK, Robina H.
Club on Corfu. Sr Schol 91:sup 11 N 2 '67
Fugue in varied tempos. Sr Schol 90:sup
14-15 My 5 '67
BUCK, Tom
But daddy; excerpts. por Ladies Home J 85:
47-50+ Ja '68
**BUCK ISLAND REEF NATIONAL MONU-
MENT**
Dive at Buck Island. M. W. Williams. il
Nat Parks Mag 41:4-7 Ag '67
BUCKETS (pails)
Ice buckets. il House & Gard 132:35-6 S '67
BUCKHOLDT, Johann. See John of Leiden
BUCKHOUT, Robert
Thailand: where we came in. Nation 205:305-8
O 2 '67
BUCKINGHAM, Gregory F.
Stanford's big new splash. K. Chapin. por
Sports Illus 26:24-5 Ap 3 '67
BUCKLEY, Charles Anthony
Last of a breed. il por Newsweek 69:41-2 F
6 '67
BUCKLEY, Fergus Reid
East of New York, south of Madrid, down
to Kenya. Vogue 149:82-5 Ap 1 '67
BUCKLEY, Marylou
Mortal love; poem. America 117:415 O 14 '67
On a friend gone early to seed; poem. Amer-
ica 117:616 N 18 '67
Song for a separation; poem. Cath World
206:164 Ja '68
BUCKLEY, Michael
French opinion on an American war. America
116:810-11 Je 3 '67
U.S. troops leave France. America 116:563-4
Ap 15 '67
BUCKLEY, Patricia (Taylor)
How would you like your daughter to marry
William F. Buckley, jr? E. Harris. il pors
Look 31:112+ Mr 7 '67
Pat Buckley: oasis for a caustic conserva-
tive. C. Mangel. il pors Look 31:108-11 Mr
7 '67
BUCKLEY, Priscilla L.
Theater. Nat R 19:976-8 S 5 '67
BUCKLEY, Thomas
Men of third squad, second platoon, C com-
pany, third battalion. il N Y Times Mag
p34-5+ N 5 '67
Robin Olds and his battle aces. Esquire 68:
117-19 O '67
Transsexual operation. Esquire 67:111-15+ Ap
'67
BUCKLEY, William Frank, 1925-
Non-Latin mass. Commonweal 87:167-9 N 10
'67

Notes & asides. Nat R 19:1314. 1369, 1418 N
28-D 26 '67
On civil disobedience, 1967. N Y Times Mag
p27 N 26 '67
On the right. See issues of National review
Politics of the Capote ball. Esquire 68:159-
64+ D '67
Reagan: a relaxing view. Nat R 19:1319-25+
N 28 '67
Speaking out. por Sat Eve Post 240:4+ D 30
'67
about
Buckley, Buckley, bow wow wow. G. Wills.
por Esquire 69:72-6+ Ja '68
God. man. and William F. Buckley. L. L.
King. Harper 234:53-61 Mr '67
How would you like your daughter to marry
William F. Buckley, jr? E. Harris. il por
Look 31:112+ Mr 7 '67
Pat Buckley: oasis for a caustic conserva-
tive. C. Mangel. il pors Look 31:108-11 Mr
7 '67
Sniper. il pors Time 90:70-2+ N 3 '67
BUCKMAN, Gertrude
Grinding in English. Unwinding in Arabic.
Mlle 64:148-9+ F '67
BUCKS COUNTY, Pa.
Joint purchasing leads to joint selling. R.
Zweig. il Am City 82:96 F '67
BUCKVAR, Felice
Best of friends: worst of enemies. Parents
Mag 42:42-3+ D '67
How to talk to your child's teacher. Parents
Mag 42:64-5+ S '67
BUCKWALTER, Len
Selecting a CB transceiver. Electr World 77:
40-3 Mr '67
What to look for in a miniscreen TV. Pop
Mech 128:90-3+ D '67
BUDAPEST
Description
Interlude in Budapest. L. Hellman. Holiday
42:60-1 N '67
Music
Report: Budapest; operatic productions. J.
Boraros. il Opera N 32:32 Ja 6 '68
BUDD company
High-speed bid for business. il Bsns W p
126-8 F 4 '67
BUDD railcars. See Railroads—Trains
BUDDHA and Buddhism
New face of Buddha, by J. Schecter. Review
Sat R 50:38 Ag 5 '67. L. Landry
See also
Zen Buddhism
BUDDHIST sculpture. See Sculpture, Buddhist
BUDDHISTS
Ky v Buddhists. round two. Tran-van-Dinh.
New Repub 156:15-19 My 13 '67
BUDÉ, Guillaume
Guillaume Budé and the first historical school
of law. D. R. Kelley. bibliog f Am Hist R
72:807-34 Ap '67
BUDGET
Germany (Federal Republic)
Mifrifi to the rescue; eliminating budget def-
icit. Time 90:96 S 15 '67
Siege of the Pentabonn; projected cuts in de-
fense budget. il Time 90:27-8 Jl 28 '67
Great Britain
Aiming the ax. Newsweek 71:34 Ja 15 '68
Britain holds the line; no easing in austerity
program. Bsns W p42 Ap 15 '67
British budget cuts to focus on defense. H.
J. Coleman. Aviation W 88:34 Ja 15 '68
Letter from London (cont) M. Panter-
Downes. New Yorker 43:49-50 D 23 '67
More freeze & squeeze. il Time 89:98 Ap 21
'67
Steady as she goes. Newsweek 69:86 Ap 24 '67
United States
Balancing act. Newsweek 70:21-2 O 30 '67
Balancing act. H. C. Wallich. Newsweek 69:
82 F 6 '67
Big-guns budget. Nation 204:164 F 6 '67
Budget for a tough year. Life 62:4 F 3 '67
Budget message of the President, January
24, 1967; excerpts; with excerpts from The
budget of the United States government
for the fiscal year ending June 30, 1968.
L. B. Johnson. il Dept State Bul 56:230-6
F 13 '67; Cong Digest 46:106+ Ap '67
Budget mystery for fiscal 1967. America 117:
124-5 Ag 5 '67
Budgetary note. R. Saulnier. Nat R 19:508
My 16 '67
Charlie Schultze's $135 billion book. H. Sidey.
il Life 62:32B F 10 '67

BUDGET—United States—*Continued*
Congress and the budget. Sr Schol 90:15-16 F 24 '67
Declining deficit. il Fortune 76:40+ D '67
Deficit comes home to roost; new economics; with editorial comment. G. Burck. il Fortune 76:67, 90-3+ S 1 '67
First peek at peak budget; defense spending at $73-billion. Bsns W p33 Ja 21 '67
$40-billion the budget leaves out. il Bsns W p55-6+ F 25 '67
GOP zeroes in on the budget; to reduce government spending. il Bsns W p24-5 Ap 1 '67
Great society's wondrous war budget. C. Stevenson. Read Digest 90:49-54 Ap '67
Hard choice; guns instead of the Great society. New Repub 156:7-8 F 4 '67
How the budget deficit could escalate. il U S News 62:44 Je 5 '67
How to cut the U.S. budget; Time essay. Time 90:38 D 8 '67
Johnson faces critical choices on new budget. Bsns W p53 D 16 '67
Johnson gives nation a new kind of budget. il Bsns W p30-2 Ja 28 '67
Johnson swings the ax on spending; cut federal budget to win tax increase. il Bsns W p30-1 Jl 15 '67
Lots of red ink. il Fortune 75:20+ Je 1 '67
LBJ's answer. Newsweek 70:79+ N 27 '67
LBJ's war budget and its new math. il Newsweek 69:30-1 F 6 '67
New economics takes over the budget; with charts. U S News 62:90-2 F 6 '67
New frame for the budget; proposal for unified system, with editorial comment. il Bsns W p 152-4, 200 O 21 '67
Now, a merged budget for U.S.? U S News 63:98 O 30 '67
Old budget plans quickly fade away. il Bsns W p44+ My 20 '67
Paring the deficit; 1968 budget revision. il Bsns W p23-4 Ag 26 '67
Putting the budget in sharper forcus. Bsns W p48 D 16 '67
Shaping a simpler budget. il Bsns W p95-6+ Ag 5 '67
State of the budget and the economy; excerpts from message to the Congress, August 3, 1967. L. B. Johnson. Dept State Bul 57:266-8 Ag 28 '67
Tax increase: the federal budget; address. September 19, 1967. R. J. Saulnier. Vital Speeches 34:39-41 N 1 '67
This month's feature: Congress and the fiscal 1968 budget. il Cong Digest 46:99-128 Ap '67
Three federal budget concepts; address, March 3, 1967. R. J. Saulnier. Vital Speeches 33:400-4 Ap 15 '67
Tough year. il Time 89:17-18 Ja 27 '67
U.S. budget: a runaway deficit? Newsweek 69:73-4 My 29 '67
U.S. taxpayer: fit to be tithed. il Newsweek 70:65-6+ Ag 14 '67
What's $172 billion? il U S News 62:25-7 F 6 '67
Why budget problems may raise your taxes. U S News 64:85-6 Ja 8 '68
See also
Taxation—United States
United States—Appropriations and expenditures
United States—Budget, Bureau of the

BUDGET, Household
Family money management. See issues of Better homes and gardens
How seven families beat the high cost of living; with case histories and interviews. M. T. Bloom. il McCalls 94:66-7+ Je '67
How to save money on food. J. Roper. il Redbook 128:66-7+ Mr '67
How to stop fighting over money. J. L. Schimel and S. Blum. il Redbook 130:72-3+ N '67
New city worker's family budget; tables. P. Groom. bibliog il Mo Labor R 90:1-8 N '67
Take a new look at your income for 1967. M. Feeley. il Am Home 70:58+ Ja '67
What a young family should do with its money; advice by financial experts. il Changing T 21:17-21 D '67

BUDGET, Military

United States
See United States—Armed forces—Appropriations and expenditures

BUDGET, Personal
Budgets; how to best plan ahead. Good H 164:198 Ap '67
How to manage your money; excerpts from The hardship of accounting. J. B. Harjes. Seventeen 26:236+ My '67

Those money miseries; questions and answers. A. Wood. Seventeen 26:106+ Jl '67
See also
Finance, Personal
Saving and savings

BUDGET, School. See School finance

BUDGET, State
Where the money comes from. il Time 89:17-18 F 10 '67

BUDGET bureau (United States) See United States—Budget, Bureau of the

BUDLONG, Torrey
Excommunicated; poem. Mlle 64:97 F '67

BUDWORMS, Spruce. See Spruce budworms

BUECHER, Roger W. See Odencrantz, F. K. jt. auth.

BUECHLER, James
Sound of the story. Writer 80:19-21 Je '67

BUEGELEISEN, Sally
Skirts flying. See issues of Flying
Where do all the airplanes go. Flying 81:84-7 Jl '67

BUELL, Don Carlos
MacBird: an historical review. New Repub 156:27-8 F 18 '67

BUENA PARK, Calif.
Optics operate signals in emergencies. J. W. Verbeck. il Am City 82:125+ Mr '67

BUENOS AIRES

Description
Buenos Aires, Argentina's melting-pot metropolis. J. B. Billard. il Nat Geog Mag 132:662-95 N '67

Music
Buenos Aires. G. Knepler. Opera N 32:26 S 23 '67
Report: Buenos Aires; performance of Wagner's Ring des Nibelungen. G. Knepler. il Opera N 32:31 D 23 '67

BUENOS AIRES. University. See Colleges and universities—Argentina

BUFFALO, N.Y.

Banks
M.&T.'s puzzling acceptances. Fortune 75:237-8 Je 15 '67

Galleries and museums
See also
Albright-Knox art gallery

Riots
Just a rampage. Time 90:17 Jl 7 '67

BUFFALO Bills (football club) See Football clubs

BUFFALO hunting
Buffalo hunt; excerpt from Blessed McGill. E. Shrake. il Sports Illus 27:60-70 D 25 '67
Indestructible buffalo. J. O'Connor. il Outdoor Life 139:52-5+ Ap '67

BUFFALO philharmonic orchestra
Musical events; concert in Carnegie Hall. W. Sargeant. New Yorker 43:166+ My 13 '67

BUFFALO university. See New York (state) State university—University at Buffalo

BUFFALOES
Buffalo is back! B. Surface. il Read Digest 90:189-92+ My '67
See also
Water buffaloes

BUFFET meals
Beefing up the ham, etc. J. Hewitt. il N Y Times Mag p49 Ag 13 '67
Cocktail buffet in a garage. il House & Gard 132:220-1 N '67
Feast for dieters; with recipes. il Ladies Home J 84:82-3+ O '67
Make-ahead buffets leave you free on the party day; with menus and recipes. il Sunset 138:184-6+ My '67
Plan your party buffet with kitchen props. il Good H 165:166+ D '67
See also
Suppers

BUFFETS (furniture)
Buffet? dining table? here are both in one. R. E. Schultz. il Pop Sci 191:165-9 N '67
How to style up an old buffet. il Farm J 92:65 Ja '68
How you can add a Spanish-style buffet to your dining area. il Pop Sci 191:168-77 S '67

BUFFUM, William Burnside
U.N. condemns use of Angola as base for Congo mercenaries; statement, November 8, 1967. Dept State Bul 57:807-8 D 11 '67
U.N. security council condemns recruitment of mercenaries; statements, July 6, 10, 1967. Dept State Bul 57:151 Jl 31 '67

BUFO marinus. See Toads

BUGANDA, Kabaka of. See Mutesa II, king of Buganda

BUGANDA
King's story; President Obote decrees total abolition of Buganda. Newsweek 70:45 Jl 3 '67

BUGELSKI, B. R.
Traffic signals and depth perception. bibliog Science 157:1464-5 S 22 '67

BUGG, Ralph T.
Danger rides the school bus. Todays Health 45:20-3+ N '67
Mending hearts at home. Todays Health 45:52-5 N '67
They're mending hearts with exercise. Todays Health 45:50-5 O '67

BUHAGIAR, Marion
Xerox annual report: a guided tour. Fortune 75:184-7+ Je 15 '67

BUICK, Barbara
Indigenous children's literature. bibliog Library J 92:4219-21 N 15 '67

BUILDING
Architectural business. See issues of Architectural record
Countrywide look at the stir in home building. U S News 62:92-4 Ja 30 '67
Forum; monthly review of events and ideas. See issues of Architectural forum
Going looks rough for home builders. U S News 64:10 Ja 8 '68
Rebound in housing. il Fortune 75:40+ Ap '67
Structure & design. See issues of Fortune
You can afford your dream house, just build it yourself. D. Huff. il Pop Sci 192:63-7+ Ja '68
See also
Glass construction
Home ownership
Strains and stresses
Walls
Wood construction

Contracts and specifications
A.I.A. revises basic contract documents. Arch Rec 141:81-2 Ja '67
Building components; selecting interior finishes for college buildings; New York's State university construction fund. Arch Rec 141:197-8 My '67
Comment and contract tabulation. G. A. Christie. il Arch Rec 141:83 Ja '67
Legal background of document revisions. Arch Rec 141:93-4 Ja '67

Cost
Builders fear money drought. il Bsns W p99-100 O 14 '67
Building costs. L. C. Jaquith; W. H. Edgerton. See issues of Architectural record
Financing home improvements. T. Irwin. Am Home 70:87+ My '67
Here is a lesson in low cost building; they got their beautiful house for $11 per foot. il Sunset 138:82-3 Mr '67
How to stretch your building dollar. Am Home 70:63 Ja '67
If you think of building a house, what costs are doing. il U S News 63:74-5 D 4 '67
Other ways to save building money. D. X. Manners. House B 109:104 F '67
Planned cost control: an instrument for good design. Arch Rec 141:81 Mr '67
Proposed guide for square-foot cost calculations. L. C. Jaquith. Arch Rec 142:87-8 D '67
Today's well-spent building dollar. il House B 109:100-10+ F '67

Estimates
Computerized cost estimating. J. Barnett. il Arch Rec 141:163-6 Mr '67

Finance
Action is taken on contracts, costs and fees. Arch Rec 141:81-2 F '67
Easier loans for commercial/industrial properties? Arch Rec 142:R1-2 Jl '67
Homebuilding's happy future; special report. il Bsns W p84-5+ My 6 '67
See also
Mortgages

Regulations
See Building laws and regulations

Statistics
Building activity (title varies) G. A. Christie. See issues of Architectural record
Current trends in construction. G. A. Christie. See issues of Architectural record
F. W. Dodge construction outlook: 1968. il Arch Rec 142:81-4 N '67

BUILDING and earthquakes. See Earthquakes and building

BUILDING-block houses. See Modular coordination (architecture)

BUILDING codes. See Building laws and regulations

BUILDING costs. See Building—Cost

BUILDING finance. See Building—Finance

BUILDING fittings
Clever remodeling and building ideas. W. C. Leckey. il Pop Mech 128:142-5 S '67
Product reports. See issues of Architectural record
Today in industry, tomorrow at home. J. H. Ingersoll. il House B 109:168-9+ S '67
See also
Hardware

Bibliography
New literature for house planning. Arch Rec 141:26+ mid-My '67

BUILDING industry
Aftermath of the credit squeeze. G. A. Christie. il Arch Rec 142:83 O '67
All of a sudden, houses are getting scarce. il U S News 63:48-9 O 9 '67
Builders fear money drought. il Bsns W p99-100 O 14 '67
Building the Soviet society; excerpts from The Soviet Union, the fifty years. A. L. Huxtable. il Arch Forum 127:34-41 N '67
Down the up staircase; home-building industry. il Fortune 76:44+ O '67
European methods for controlling the construction cycle. Arch Rec 141:88 Je '67
Homebuilding's happy future; special report. il Bsns W p84-5+ My 6 '67
Italy exports its building knowhow; Italian construction companies working around the globe. il Bsns W p91-2+ N 18 '67
It's a slow start for housing upturn. Bsns W p38-9 Ap 15 '67
Modules gain ground in housing landscape; modular construction turning into assembly-line industry. il Bsns W p78-81 Ja 6 '68
One-man show in empire building. il Bsns W p 122-3+ S 16 '67
Profit lovely as a tree; Boise Cascade acquires Indianapolis' U.S. land inc. Time 90:68-9 Jl 21 '67
Recovering, slowly. il Time 89:96 Ap 28 '67
Revolutionizing an industry; interview. W. J. Levitt. il Nations Bsns 55:54-6+ F '67
Seasonality and construction. R. J. Myers and S. Swerdloff. il Mo Labor R 90:1-8 S '67
Tight money again; trouble for building industry. il U S News 62:70-1 Je 12 '67
What's ahead for the construction industry. G. A. Christie. Arch Rec 141:93-6 My '67
Where building wages are heading. U S News 63:78 Ag 28 '67
Worst is over in housing; Fed and White House push recovery. il Bsns W p27 Ja 21 '67
See also
Dillingham corporation
Houses, Prefabricated

Employees
Job program that works; New York city's Joint apprenticeship program. T. R. Brooks. il Reporter 37:28-30 N 16 '67

Labor conditions
Will boycott rule put brake on technology? labor's right to resist automation. il Bsns W p 104+ Ap 29 '67

Wages and hours
Deferred wage increases: a step toward greater stability? L. C. Jaquith. Arch Rec 141:87-8 F '67
$500 a week for highway work? U S News 62:83 Je 5 '67
Study shows weight of wages in building costs. L. C. Jaquith. il Arch Rec 142:93-4 N '67
Study weighs the effect of wage rates on building costs. Arch Rec 142:71-2 Ag '67
Where pay is going up faster. U S News 63:105 O 9 '67

BUILDING laws and regulations
Building permits for tree houses! Life 63:4 Jl 14 '67
Safety in the trees; building inspector requires parents to obtain tree-house building permits. il Time 90:68+ Jl 7 '67
These codes cost you money. C. P. Gilmore. Read Digest 91:91-5 D '67
See also
Zoning

BUILDING logs, Toy. See Toys
BUILDING lots. See Building sites
BUILDING machinery industry and trade
   See also
   Clark equipment company
BUILDING materials
   Building components; selecting interior finishes for college buildings; New York's State university construction fund. Arch Rec 141:197-8 My '67
   Drop city: new life for junked cars. C. Trego. il Arch Forum 127:74-5 S '67
   Imported materials: new flavor or national threat? Arch Rec 142:87-8 Jl '67
   Product reports. See issues of Architectural record
   Today in industry, tomorrow at home. J. H. Ingersoll. il House B 109:168-9+ S '67
   Two new materials for the home builders. il Pop Mech 128:38 Ag '67
   Warm way to finish your basement. H. Shuldiner. il Pop Sci 191:128-32+ S '67
      See also
   Bricks
   Concrete
   Shingles
   Siding (building)
   Stone construction
   Tiles
   Wood
      Bibliography
   New literature for house planning. Arch Rec 141:26+ mid-My '67
      Prices
   Building slowdown has small effect on materials prices. L. C. Jaquith. Arch Rec 141:87-8 Ja '67
BUILDING permits. See Building laws and regulations
BUILDING research
   Engineering approach to designing glass for wind. il Arch Rec 141:163-6 F '67
   Research shows how to construct successful tile-metal lath partitions. il Arch Rec 142:181-2 N '67
      See also
   Housing research
BUILDING research institute
   Building research institute gets a reprieve. Arch Rec 141:213-14 Ap '67
BUILDING sites
   Air rights structure for the Department of labor; over the freeway tunnel. il Arch Rec 142:116-19 D '67
   Builders fish profits from man-made lakes; booming market for second homes on artificial lakes. il Bsns W p 186-9 Mr 4 '67
   Building for the National park service: designed to respect an historic site; Interpretive facilities building. Harpers Ferry, W.Va. il Arch Rec 142:136-9 O '67
   Covered-bridge house over a ravine. il Am Home 70:64-5 Ja '67
   Cube-shaped house with expanded spaces. il Arch Rec 142:135-8 D '67
   Escape to the snows of Vermont; the ivory tower. E. Sverbeyeff. il House B 109:82-7 Ja '67
   Federal office building designed to span a freeway. il Arch Rec 142:120-3 D '67
   Freidin uses trim simplicity to make the most of a modest budget. il Arch Rec 142:150-1 N '67
   House and site integrated by sensitive design, meticulous detailing. il Arch Rec 142:105-8 Ag '67
   Is that lot safe to build on? soil survey can tell you before it's too late. il Changing T 21:22-4 Ag '67
   Magnificent timber pavilion. J. De Long. il House B 109:236-41 O '67
   Mini-garden acts big. E. Kondonellis. il Am Home 70:64-5 S '67
   Narrow beach lot; special design problems. il Sunset 139:58-63 Jl '67
   Obata house, St Louis. il Arch Rec 141:48-51 mid-My '67
   Paradise found on a 50-foot plot. J. De Long. il House B 109:78-81 Jl '67
   Priestley house, Lake Oswego, Oregon. il Arch Rec 141:52-3 mid-My '67
   Private residence Connecticut. il Arch Rec 141:42-7 mid-My '67
   Right side of the tracks: urban space over open railroad tracks and highways. il Time 89:69 Mr 10 '67
   River house revisited. il Am Home 70:82-3 Je '67
   There is always room at the top. il House & Gard 131:148-55 Mr '67

Turned back to front. A. C. Borg. il Am Home 70:78-9 My '67
Up and up and up, from lake level to lookouts above. il Sunset 138:102-3 My '67
Why settle for less? M. A. Guitar. il Am Home 70:52-3+ S '67
   See also
Hillside architecture
Libraries—Location
Marine structures
BUILDING trades. See Building industry
BUILDING trades unions
   How to rescue America from plumbers, carpenters and people like that. J. Fischer; discussion. Harper 234:6+ Mr '67
   Job program that works; New York city's Joint apprenticeship program. T. R. Brooks. il Reporter 37:28-30 N 16 '67
   Peaceful plan to clobber business; bill before Congress. il Nations Bsns 55:38-9+ Je '67
BUILDING workers
   See also
   Building industry
BUILDINGS
   Focus: monthly review of notable buildings. See issues of Architectural forum
   Modern antiques: 20th century landmarks. C. Robinson. il Arch Forum 126:74-82 Je '67
   Modern antiques: 20th century landmarks. P. Blake. il Arch Forum 126:80-7 My '67
      See also
   Architecture
   Industrial buildings
   Mechanical equipment of buildings
   Office buildings
   School buildings
   Theater buildings
      Cleaning
   U.S.-made steam unit cleans flood-begrimed Florence. il Am City 82:94 D '67
      Equipment
   See Building fixtures
      Height
   Letter from Paris. Genêt. New Yorker 43:172+ My 13 '67
BUILDINGS, Fireproof. See Fireproof construction
BUILDINGS, Moving of. See Moving of structures, etc.
BUILDINGS, Prefabricated
   Building with boxes. J. Bailey. il Arch Forum 126:46-51 My '67
   Instant hotel; San Antonio's Hilton palacio del rio. il Time 90:96+ N 24 '67
   New town; Grand Isle, prefabricated mining town in the Gulf of Mexico. J. Johansen. il Arch Forum 127:44-53 S '67
      See also
   Apartment houses, Prefabricated
   Houses, Prefabricated
BUILDINGS, Remodeled
   How business is helping to rebuild cities. il U S News 62:90-2 Mr 20 '67
   Luncheon in a one-time church. il House & Gard 132:226-7 N '67
      See also
   Houses, Remodeled
BUILDINGS, Restoration of. See Architecture —Conservation and restoration
BUILDINGS, Round
   Tower of stone in Sun Valley. H. Morrison. il House B 109:154-7 D '67
BUILDINGS, Wrecking of. See Wrecking
BUILDINGS in art. See Architecture in art
BUILT in furniture. See Furniture, Built in
BUILT-in vacuum system. See Vacuum cleaners
BUJOLD, Genevieve
   Canada's Joan of Arc. L. Williams. il pors Look 31:M16-19 D 12 '67
BUKOVSKII, Vladimir
   Chain reaction. il Newsweek 71:31 Ja 8 '68
BUKSTEIN, Ed
   Digital computer logic; what the symbols mean. Electr World 78:46-7 Ag '67
BUL (periodical) See Periodicals—Israel
BULBS
   Holland's great spring bulb show. il Sunset 138:31-2 My '67
   How a bare ledge became a spring bulb garden. il House & Gard 132:232-4 S '67
   If you act this October, here is spring '68. il Sunset 139:222-3 O '67
   Little bulbs: you grow them just for the fun of it. il Sunset 139:90-1 O '67
   New bulb culture research. W. Meachem. Horticulture 45:22-3 O '67

BULBS—*Continued*
Plant two months of spring color now. H. Mason and R. O'Harra. il Bet Hom & Gard 45:64-7 S '67
Set the stage for spring. il House B 109:69 O '67
Some are true miniatures, and some are just little. il Sunset 139:230 O '67
Spring bulbs was a rocky ledge with a sea of color. il House & Gard 132:180-1 S '67
This is the scene that's set in September and will bloom in the spring for years. il Home Gard 54:41-3 S '67
Uncommon bulbs next fall. G. S. Wister. il Horticulture 45:18-21+ Ap '67
See also
Amaryllis
Crocuses
Hyacinths
Tulips

Storage
It's time to dig dahlias. il Sunset 139:206 N '67

BULGAKOV, Mikhail
Books. A. Goldman. Vogue 151:58 Ja 1 '68
Out of the drawer, into the light. E. J. Simmons. por Sat R 50:35-6+ N 11 '67
Painful voices. Time 89:44 Ap 14 '67

BULGARIA
See also
Opera—Bulgaria

Economic conditions
Report from east Europe: western ways are catching on. A. Kucherov. il U S News 63:48-50 Jl 10 '67

Politics and government
Balkan kaleidoscope. A. Z. Rubinstein. Cur Hist 52:224-6+ Ap '67

Religious institutions and affairs
World around us. Christian Cent 84:318+ Mr 8 '67

Social conditions
Report from east Europe: western ways are catching on. A. Kucherov. il U S News 63:48-50 Jl 10 '67

BULL, Hedley
Arms and influence. Bul Atomic Sci 23:25-6 Mr '67

BULL fights. See Bullfights

BULL trout fishing. See Trout fishing

BULLARD, Eugene
Incredible life of Monsieur Bullard. M. H. Smith. il pors Ebony 23:120-2+ D '67

BULLDOGGING. See Rodeos

BULLET park; story. See Cheever, J.

BULLETIN, Philadelphia
Classified experiment. Newsweek 70:52 Ag 28 '67

BULLETIN boards
Her pin-ups are magnets; fabric-covered magnetic board. il Sunset 138:126 F '67

BULLETPROOF clothes. See Arms and armor

BULLETS
Magic bullet; uranium flechettes. il Time 90:90 O 6 '67
See also
Cartridges
Shot

BULLFIGHTERS
Matador. B. Conrad. il Holiday 43:68-71+ Ja '68
Ten toreros in need of a bull; with glossary of Spanish terms. J. McCormick. il Sports Illus 27:34-9 Jl 24 '67
See also
Ostos, J.

BULLFIGHTS
Bullfight; N. Mailer's Book/record album. W. D. Patterson. Sat R 51:105 Ja 13 '68
Ten toreros in need of a bull; with glossary of Spanish terms. J. McCormick. il Sports Illus 27:34-9 Jl 24 '67

BULLFIGHTS, Photography of. See Photography of sports

BULLHEADS
Chemical communication in social behavior of a fish, the yellow bullhead (ictalurus natalis) J. H. Todd and others. bibliog il Science 158:672-3 N 3 '67
Orientation by taste in fish of the genus ictalurus. J. E. Bardach and others. bibliog il Science 155:1276-8 Mr 10 '67

BULLITT, Stimson
Brave man in Seattle. Nation 204:99-100 Ja 23 '67

BULLITT, William C.
Books. G. Steiner. New Yorker 42:111-14+ Ja 21 '67
Bullitt to Wilson. R. Coles. New Repub 156:27-30 Ja 28 '67
Can history use Freud? the case of Woodrow Wilson. B. W. Tuchman. Atlan 219:39-44 F '67

BULLOCK, Paul
Poverty in the ghetto, the view from Watts. Mo Labor R 90:26 F '67

BULLOUGH, Vern L.
Egypt: bruises and suspicions. Nation 205:394-5 O 23 '67
Trouble in Egypt. Nation 204:647-9 My 22 '67

BULLRIDING. See Rodeos

BULLS
Onward & upward; Charolais breeding bull, Sam 951. il Time 89:92 Ap 7 '67

BULOVA watch company
Good time; increased sales and earnings. il Time 89:85-6 Je 16 '67

BUMBRY, Grace
Bizet or bizarre, Carmen's the star. I. Kolodin. Sat R 50:38-9 D 30 '67
In the cards. E. Salzman. por Opera N 32:26-7 D 16 '67

BUMP, T. R.
Third generation of breeder reactors; with biographical sketch. Sci Am 216:21, 25-33 My '67

BUMPERS, Automobile. See Automobiles—Bumpers

BUMPUS, F. Merlin. See McCubbin, J. W. jt. auth.

BUNCHE, Ralph
Crisis; interview. New Yorker 43:22-3 Jl 29 '67

BUNDY, McGeorge
Problems of success; excerpts from address. Time 90:25 D 8 '67

about
Bundy report. B. Stretch. por Sat R 50:70-1 D 16 '67
Bundy's plan for New York schools. M. R. Berube. Commonweal 87:349-50 D 15 '67
Mini-school districts. Reporter 37:8-9 N 30 '67
More brainpower for every buck. il pors Bsns W p46-8+ Ja 6 '68
Trouble shooter Bundy; the job: peace in Mideast. por U S News 62:21 Je 19 '67
Where East may meet West. por Bsns W p39 My 13 '67

BUNDY, Mary Lee
Factors influencing public library use. por Wilson Lib Bul 42:371-82 D '67
Metropolitan public library use. bibliog Wilson Lib Bul 41:950-61 My '67
—See Wasserman, P. jt. auth.

BUNDY, William Putnam
Bundy comments on Galbraith's plan. N Y Times Mag p31+ N 12 '67
East Asia today; address, January 20, 1967. Dept State Bul 56:323-7 F 27 '67
Mr Bundy discusses Viet-Nam on Meet the press; transcript of interview, August 27, 1967. Dept State Bul 57:352-7 S 18 '67
Partnership in east Asia and the Pacific; address, July 28, 1967. Dept State Bul 57:195-200 Ag 14 '67
Path to Viet-Nam: a lesson in involvement; address, August 15, 1967. Dept State Bul 57:275-87 S 4 '67; Same. Vital Speeches 33:706-13 S 15 '67
Seventeen years in east Asia; address, May 3, 1967. Dept State Bul 56:790-5 My 22 '67
Vietnamese election campaign; statement, August 11, 1967. Dept State Bul 57:260-1 Ag 28 '67
Why U.S. is in Vietnam: an official explanation. por U S News 63:48-9 D 18 '67

BUNGE, Charles A.
Library education and reference performance. por Library J 92:1578-81 Ap 15 '67

BUNKER, Caroline Clendening (Laise) See Laise, C. C.

BUNKER, Ellsworth
Ambassador Bunker assesses current situation in Viet-Nam; news conference, November 13, 1967. Dept State Bul 57:748-51 D 4 '67
Ambassador Bunker dedicates new U.S. embassy at Saigon; remarks, September 29, 1967. Dept State Bul 57:584-5 O 30 '67
Foreign ministers of the American republics meet at Buenos Aires; statement, Feburary 21, 1967. Dept State Bul 56:472-3 Mr 20 '67
Report on Viet-Nam: address, November 17, 1967. Dept State Bul 57:781-4 D 11 '67

BUNKER, Ellsworth—*Continued*
Secretary Rusk and Ambassador Bunker discuss Viet-Nam in TV-radio interviews; transcript of interview, September 10, 1967. Dept State Bul 57:416-21 O 2 '67
U.S. support of pacification effort in Viet-Nam reorganized; statement, May 11, 1967. Dept State Bul 56:844-5 Je 5 '67

about

Burgeoning boss picks an old hand. H. Sidey. il por Life 62:32B Mr 24 '67
Ellsworth Bunker in Saigon. W. Lippmann. Newsweek 69:25 Mr 27 '67
Mr & Mrs Ambassador. il pors Life 62:118-19+ Je 9 '67
New faces, new mood? por Sr Schol 90:19 Mr 31 '67
New team for the U.S. in Vietnam. por U S News 62:20 Mr 27 '67
Our new team in Saigon. D. Warner. il Reporter 37:25-6+ S 7 '67
Quiet American goes to Vietnam. R. Eder. il pors N Y Times Mag p28-9+ Mr 26 '67

BUNN, Martin
Gus Wilson's model garage (title varies) See issues of Popular science monthly

BUNNER, Alan N.
High-energy cosmic rays. Sky & Tel 34:204-8 O '67

BUNS
Classic kolache; Bohemian specialty. il Bet Hom & Gard 45:116 Jl '67

BUNSHAFT, Gordon
Living in a work of art. J. Peter. il pors Look 32:64-6 Ja 9 '68

BUNTING, Basil
Never a boast or a see-here. H. Kenner. Nat R 19:1217-18 O 31 '67

BUONOMO, Jeannette Ramos. See Ramos Buonomo, J.

BUOYANCY
Buoyancy and pressure; questions and answers. J. Daugherty and M. Daugherty. il Sci Digest 62:91-2 Jl '67

BUOYS

Mooring

Sea Robin tests resumed; mooring problems stressed. il Aero Tech 21:25-6 Jl 17 '67

BURACK, W. Richard
Has drug industry met its Nader? il Bsns W p 104+ Je 10 '67
What's in a name is the question. por Bsns W p 109 Je 10 '67

BURAWA, Alexander W. See Jensen, N. P. jt. auth.

BURCHELL, S. C.
Last waltz in Vienna. Horizon 10:82-101 Wint '68

BURCHETT, Wilfred
Mouthpiece for reds: the strange role of Wilfred Burchett. il por U S News 62:19-20 F 27 '67
Who is Wilfred Burchett? D. Warner. il por Reporter 36:18-21 Je 1 '67

BURCHFIELD, Charles Ephraim
Cover; An April mood. il Am Artist 31:4 Je '67

BURCHINAL, Lee G.
ERIC and the need to know. NEA J 56:65-72 F '67

BURCK, Gilbert H.
Challenging east European market. Fortune 76:122-4+ Jl '67
East Europe's struggle for economic freedom. Fortune 75:124-7+ My '67
Good living begins in the wine cellar. Fortune 75:122-9 Je 1 '67
Perils of the multi-market corporation. Fortune 75:130-5+ F '67

BURCKLE, Lloyd H. and others
Tertiary sediment from the East Pacific rise. bibliog Science 157:537-40 Ag 4 '67

BURDETTE, Walter J. and Yoon, J. S.
Mutations, chromosomal aberrations, and tumors in insects treated with oncogenic virus. bibliog Science 155:340-1 Ja 20 '67

BURDICK, William
This is the dance that was. M. Marks. il pors Dance Mag 41:44-9 Jl '67

BUREAU of African affairs. See United States —State, Department of—African affairs, Bureau of

BUREAU of customs. See Customs service— United States

BUREAU of international expositions
President asks Senate approval of U.S. membership in BIE; letter, November 28, 1967. L. B. Johnson. Dept State Bul 58:52-3 Ja 8 '68

BUREAU of research. See United States— Education, Office of—Research, Bureau of

BUREAUCRACY
Administration of federal aid: a monstrosity has been created. D. S. Greenberg. Science 157:43-5+ Jl 7 '67
Air pollution. Nat R 19:234 Mr 7 '67
Federal paper-work explosion: new form bothers universities. B. Nelson. Science 156:1468-9 Je 16 '67
Hospitals, doctors reveal: medicare's maladies. il Nations Bsns 55:44-6+ Mr '67
How the Pentagon works. A. Yarmolinsky. Atlan 219:56-61 Mr '67
Private responsibility for public management. F. B. Morse. bibliog f Harvard Bsns R 45:6-8+ Mr '67

BUREAUS of the United States government. See name of bureau, inverted under United States, e.g. United States—Land management, Bureau of

BURFORD, William
Five poets. D. W. Baker. Poetry 111:196-8 D '67

BURGELIN, Henri
International structures for a nuclear age. Christian Cent 84:748-50 Je 7 '67

BURGER, Chester
How much their eyes tell us! Pop Phot 60:106-7+ F '67
Photographer's guide to Expo 67. Pop Phot 60:74-7+ Ap '67

BURGER, Warren E.
What to do about crime in U.S; excerpts from address, 1967. por U S News 63:70-3 Ag 7 '67

BÜRGER Schippel; drama. See Sternheim, C.

BURGESS, Anthony
Brothers Grimm and their famous law for linguists. Horizon 10:66-72 Wint '68
Gibraltar. Holiday 41:70-1+ F '67
Murder most fair by Agatha the good. Life 63:8 D 1 '67
Travel 18th century style. Holiday 42:72-7+ N '67

about

Fertile world of Anthony Burgess. G. Hicks. Sat R 50:27-9+ Jl 15 '67

BURGESS, Bobby
On the boards. W. Como. il por Dance Mag 41:22 My '67

BURGESS, H. F.
Counterclockwise; poem. Christian Cent 84:782 Je 14 '67

BURGESS, Lorraine Marshall
Bold green look indoors. il Home Gard 54:38-9 F '67
Butterflies in your garden. il Horticulture 45:26-7 Jl '67
You can paint a flower. Home Gard 54:60-1 Mr '67

BURGESS, Thornton Waldo
Unforgettable Thornton W. Burgess. L. Levine. il por Read Digest 91:100-5 O '67

BURGHARDT, Gordon M.
Chemical-cue preferences of inexperienced snakes: comparative aspects. bibliog Science 157:718-21 Ag 11 '67

BURGHARDT, Walter J.
He lived with wisdom. America 117:248-9 S 9 '67

BURGHAUSER, Hugo
Honored guest; interview, ed. by A. M. Lingg. por Opera N 31:29 Ap 1 '67

BURGLAR alarms
How to protect your valuables from burglary. D. B. Burns. il Pop Sci 191:80-3+ S '67
Insure against auto theft for $1; simple do-it-yourself alarm systems. G. E. Hollister. il Motor T 19:72 F '67
Machine senses robber's footfall. F. C. Livingstone. Sci N 92:229 S 2 '67
Personal business; auto theft. Bsns W p 129-30 Jl 22 '67
Stamp out auto theft; auto sentinel alarm. R. L. Winklepleck. il Pop Electr 26:59-61 Mr '67
Stop thief! E. Rickman. il Hot Rod 20:62-3 Jl '67
Thief alarm systems for boats. H. deFontaine. il Yachting 121:99+ Je '67 (to be cont)

BURGLARY and burglars
Big city thieves. J. Bowers. Harper 234:50-4 F '67
Murf the Surf and his jewel-studded jinx. K. Wheeler and S. Smith. il Life 62:92-4+ Ap 21 '67
To catch a thief. P. B. Rummel. il Mlle 65:106-7+ Je '67

BURGNER, Jack
Printing for the child. Design 68:10-13 Ja '67

BURIAL
See also
Funeral rites and ceremonies
Tombs

BURTON, Sister Dolores Marie
Medium is absurd. Commonweal 86:340-2 Je
9 '67
BURTON, John F. X.
Philadelphia, farewell. R. A. Schroth. America
116:176 F 4 '67; Discussion. 116:173-4, 330
F 4, Mr 11 '67
BURTON, Philip
He tamed an Irish audience. Sat R 50:29
Je 17 '67
BURTON, Richard
His Liz: a scheming charmer. por Life 62:78-9
F 24 '67
It's a mad, mad world, old boy; interview,
ed. by C. Brossard. por Look 31:69-70 Je
27 '67

about

Burtons in Dahomey. L. Rasponi. il por
Vogue 149:92-3+ Ap 15 '67
Happy anniversary, Elizabeth and Richard;
tributes from their friends. por McCalls 94:
68-9+ Je '67
On location with Richard and Liz: why
they're never dull. C. Brossard. il pors
Look 31:64-7 Je 27 '67
Peter Glenville talks about the Burtons.
P. Glenville. il por Vogue 150:282-5+ S 1 '67
Voyage with the Burtons. C. G. Pepper. il
pors McCalls 95:56-60+ Ja '68
BURTON, Sir Richard Francis
Devil drives, by F. M. Brodie. Review
Sat R 50:27 Jl 8 '67. O. Prescott
Fantastic life. P. D. Zimmerman. pors News-
week 69:94+ Je 12 '67
Saga of Ruffian Dick. il por Time 90:82 Ag 4
'67
BURTON, Robert
Cosmic vision of Robert Burton. J. Ash-
brook. Sky & Tel 33:92 F '67
BURTON, Scott
Cool and concrete from the 'thirties. Art N
66:34-5+ Ap '67
George McNeil and the figure. Art N 66:38-9+
O '67
Herman Rose: telling and showing. Art N
66:36-7+ Sum '67
See-through sculpture. Art N 66:36-7+ Mr
'67
Two for May: Dunn, Hendler. Art N 66:55+
My '67
BURTON, Walter E.
Eighteen ways to get more from your portable
drill. Pop Mech 128:152-5 Ag '67
Flat turnings from round stock. Pop Mech
127:186-7 My '67
How to grind work with micrometer preci-
sion. Pop Mech 128:194-7 N '67
How to squeeze more from your plier wrench.
Pop Mech 127:186-9 Ap '67
Make an inclinometer, and get those angles
straight! Pop Mech 128:176-9 D '67
Make this handy indicator for your shop. Pop
Mech 129:196-9 Ja '68
Make your own auger bits. Pop Mech 127:188
F '67
New windows and doors slide on air. Pop
Sci 190:158-9 Ap '67
Shorty tripod for shooting low. Pop Mech 128:
104-5 Jl '67
Special-shaped punches you can make. Pop
Mech 128:172-4 D '67
BURTON parish church. See Williamsburg,
Va.—Churches
BURY, John
Moses, Mozart, Pinter; interview, ed. by E.
Rizzo. por Opera N 32:16 Ja 13 '68
BUS lines. See Motor bus lines
BUSBY, Roswell F.
Undersea penetration by ambient light, and
visibility. Science 158:1178-80 D 1 '67
BUSCH, Noel F.
Hirohito, emperor of Japan. Read Digest 91:
102-6 D '67
Hong Kong: fragrant harbor of the Orient.
Read Digest 90:182-4+ Je '67
Lilliputian world of the bonsai. Read Digest
91:182-6+ S '67
BUSCH, Richard
He lost his own bigotry in the army. Life
63:44+ D 15 '67
BUSCH memorial stadium. See Stadiums
BUSH, Monroe
Burdened acres, the people question. Liv
Wildn 31:28-31 Spr '67
Reading about resources. See issues of
American forests
BUSH-Holley house. See Greenwich, Conn.—
Historic houses, etc.
BUSHMAN trance dancers. See Medicine men
BUSHMEN. See Africa—Native races

BUSINESS
Better year coming for business: a preview
of the gains and losses. il U S News 64:29-
31 Ja 8 '68
Creativity in business. J. D. Gray. Duns R
89:26+ Mr '67
Does business need more brains, muscle or
ideals? F. Morley. il Nations Bsns 55:35-6
O '67
For the birds? concerning college students
attitudes. L. L. Golden. Sat R 50:93 Ap
8 '67
Sparks from the campus; R. Galvin's cor-
poration-campus dialogue. il Newsweek 69:
79+ Ap 3 '67
See also
Capitalism
Christmas business
Corporations
Free enterprise
Industrial mobilization
Marketing
Money
Profit
Retail trade

Bibliography

Books to come; ed. by J. Putnam. Library J
92:1067-73, 2637-41. 4064-8 Mr 1, Jl, N 1 '67
Business books of 1966; comp. by A. Malkin.
Library J 92:976-8 Mr 1 '67
Business highspots: November to March books.
il Pub W 192:47-9 N 13 '67
Businessman's bookshelf. E. C. Bursk. Sat R
51:81 Ja 13 '68
Executive bookshelf. See issues of Dun's
review

Exhibitions

See Exhibitions

Foreign expansion

American challenge; American industry in
Europe. il Time 90:32 N 24 '67
Europe's obsession with U.S. economic power.
E. Taylor. il Reporter 37:25-7 D 28 '67
Foreign scout for the small man; E. M. Lang
of Resources & facilities corp. il Bsns W
p 131-2+ O 21 '67
French business smiles at Canada; French-
owned companies in Canada. il Bsns W p24-
6 Jl 22 '67
How they won the West, and more; engaged
in at least eighty-five ventures in thirty-
three countries. il Bsns W p 178-80+ Ja 28
'67
Spending overseas holds to rapid pace; Mc-
Graw-Hill survey; with editorial comment.
il Bsns W p 104-5, 132 Ag 5 '67
See also
Corporations—Foreign subsidiaries

Forms, blanks, etc.

Foreigner is no. 1 in a U.S. market; Toronto's Moore corp, largest maker of business forms. il Bsns W p 171-2+ S 23 '67

Handbooks, manuals, etc.

Most efficient data bank. C. B. Grannis. Pub
W 192:56 N 13 '67

International aspects

Cooperation or stagnation? address, November 15, 1967. R. A. Peterson. Vital Speeches
34:165-8 Ja 1 '68
East-West business cooperation; a new approach to Communist Europe. E. Benoit.
New Repub 156:21-3 F 18 '67
Great American purchase; massive and continuing penetration of Europe. A. de Borchgrave. il Newsweek 69:36-8 F 27 '67
How business schools welcome the world;
education for international business. il
Bsns W p 118-19+ D 9 '67
International business. il Duns R 89:53-5 Ja;
47-8+ F; 65-6+ Mr '67
International business. J. Ross-Skinner. See
issues of Dun's review
Multinational enterprises & national sovereignty. R. Vernon. Harvard Bsns R 45:156-
8+ Mr '67
Not much pain for big business; borrowing
money overseas to finance continued investments. il Bsns W p 16-17 Ja 6 '68
One slice of the pie; businesses' potential to
handle internationalism. il Time 90:95 N 24
'67
Shorter strides for the giants? problems of
U.S.'s multinational companies. il Bsns W
p40-2 D 30 '67
This changing world; the role of business,
address, October 5, 1967. T. J. Watson, jr.
Vital Speeches 34:48-50 N 1 '67; Excerpts.
U S News 63:60-1 N 13 '67

BUSINESS—*Continued*

Periodicals
See also
Fortune (periodical)

Political aspects
Can the Republicans win back business? interviews with businessmen and politicians; ed. by G. R. Rosen. il Duns R 89:32-5+ My '67
Johnson treatment. T. Levitt. il Harvard Bsns R 45:114-18+ Ja '67
$30 billion for whom? politics, profits and the anti-missile missile. F. W. Collins. New Repub 156:13-15 Mr 11 '67
What LBJ thinks about businessmen now. Nations Bsns 55:46-9 D '67
See also
Lobbying

Public relations
American forecast; symposium. il Sat R 51:31-4+ Ja 13 '68
Corporate disclosure; insider trading. A. Fleischer, jr. bibliog f Harvard Bsns R 45:129-35 Ja '67
Dow chemical company: sales and worries are up. R. J. Samuelson. Science 158:1031-2 N 24 '67
From inside out. L. L. L. Golden. Sat R 50:95-6 N 11 '67
How Mr Housewares woos his customers; W. H. Sahloff of GE. il Bsns W p98-100+ Jl 1 '67
Only by public consent, by L. L. L. Golden. Review
   Sat R 51:80 Ja 13 '68. J. A. Livingston
Perspective on public relations. K. Henry. bibliog f Harvard Bsns R 45:14-16+ Jl '67
Public relations; a help for management; address, April 5, 1967. B. C. Goss. Vital Speeches 33:426-9 My 1 '67

Small business
See Small business

Social aspects
American forecast; symposium. il Sat R 51:31-4+ Ja 13 '68
Business and youth. R. L. Cutler. Duns R 89:24+ Ap '67
Business at work in the Twin Cities. P. Herrera. il Fortune 76:123-4+ Ag '67
Business rebuilds the slums. il Nations Bsns 55:40-1+ Je '67
Business sets up its own Great society. il U S News 62:73-5 Ap 3 '67; Same abr. Read Digest 90:89-91 Je '67
Business zeroes in on poverty. Life 63:4 D 15 '67
Businesslike approach to poverty; Nelson A. Rockefeller's conference on social welfare. R. Stein. Sat R 50:20 D 9 '67
Cities outlook; businessmen ponder the city's ills. Bsns W p83 D 2 '67
Congress and the crisis in our cities. J. Bailey. Arch Forum 127:54-7 S '67
Corporation: sociological and technological developments; address, April 20, 1967. T. J. Gordon. Vital Speeches 33:500-5 Je 1 '67
Creative competition. G. Champion. bibliog f Harvard Bsns R 45:61-7 My '67
Crisis in the cities: does business hold the key? with comments by business leaders. il Duns R 90:31-5 N '67
Deeper shame of the cities. M. Ways. Fortune 77:132-5+ Ja '68
DEW line for business. L. L. L. Golden. Sat R 50:60 S 9 '67
Getting to the ghettos; private industry to create jobs for hard-core unemployed. Bsns W p38 O 7 '67
Hallelujah, amen! Nat R 19:1109 O 17 '67
How business helps customers. Nations Bsns 55:35-7 Jl '67
How to clean up the Nation's slums? il Newsweek 70:64-5+ Ag 28 '67
Industry and environment. D. Wolfle. Science 156:1441 Je 16 '67; Reply. A. R. Gregory. 157:628+ Ag 11 '67
Instant city; corporate builders of new towns. P. Herrera. il Fortune 75:135-8 Je 1 '67
Keeping cities cool. il Bsns W p46+ Je 10 '67
Luring business into the ghettos. il Newsweek 70:77 O 16 '67
New business for busniess: reclaiming human resources. G. Burck. il Fortune 77:158-61+ Ja '68
New industrial state, by J. K. Galbraith. Review
   Newsweek 69:75C+ Je 26 '67. S. Maloff

Role of business in society's perfectibility; excerpt from address. N. W. Chamberlain. Mo Labor R 90:41-3 Ap '67
Second shock wave; address, January 26, 1967. W. O. Robertson. Vital Speeches 33:408-11 Ap 15 '67
Social-industrial complex. M. Harrington. Harper 235:55-60 N '67; Discussion. 236:4 Ja '68
Social role for business. America 117:432-3 O 21 '67
Stick-in-the-HUDs; tax inducements to private enterprise to provide jobs in the ghettoes. Nat R 19:1056 O 3 '67
They don't have to starve; private enterprise, blueprint for feeding the world's hungry. W. T. Brady. il Nations Bsns 55:88-90+ Mr '67
Urban unrest: whose problem is it? address, August 25, 1967. L. W. Moore. Vital Speeches 33:749-52 O 1 '67
Violence in the city: a better place to live; address, July 31, 1967. J. V. Lindsay. Vital Speeches 33:674-7 S 1 '67
See also
Business and race problems

Taxation
See Business tax

Terminology
New babel of business. R. Levy. il Duns R 90:38-9 O '67
BUSINESS, Retirement from. See Retirement from business, etc.
BUSINESS administration. See Business management and organization
BUSINESS airplanes. See Airplanes, Business
BUSINESS and art. See Art and industry
BUSINESS and education
Close-up: executives, educators and youth; interview. J. F. Oates, jr. il Duns R 89:10-11+ Ja '67
Education for a new era. T. A. Vanderslice; J. B. Conant. il Sat R 51:48+ Ja 13 '68
Educator and the industrialist. R. E. Slaughter. il NEA J 56:27-9 F '67
Industry and education. F. Keppel; W. Howell. il Library J 92:3807-14 O 15 '67
Kids, computers, and corporations. P. Schrag. il Sat R 50:78-80+ My 20 '67
Lot more than a sheepskin; graduation industry. il Bsns W p 124-6 Je 24 '67
Private industry's factory classrooms. R. Gustaitis. il Reporter 37:23-4 S 7 '67
Realities of the learning market; address, August 9, 1966. H. Howe, 2d. il Library J 92:297-301 Ja 15 '67
Social-industrial complex. M. Harrington. Harper 235:55-60 N '67; Discussion. 236:4 Ja '68
Where businessmen gave their community a future; Scottsbluff, Neb. il Nations Bsns 55:92-4+ F '67
Who feeds the golden goose? address, February 1, 1967. A. F. Jacobson. Vital Speeches 33:306-9 Mr 1 '67
See also
College students and business
Corporations—Charitable contributions

International aspects
This changing world: the role of business; address, October 5, 1967. T. J. Watson, jr. Vital Speeches 34:48-50 N 1 '67; Excerpts. U S News 63:60-1 N 13 '67
U.S. business taking over Europe? excerpts from American challenge. J. J. Servan-Schreiber. il U S News 63:103-4 N 20 '67
BUSINESS and golf. See Golf and business
BUSINESS and professional women
Executive sweets; South Vietnamese businesswomen. il Time 90:70 Jl 21 '67
Lotus blossoms; Harvard business school course for Vietnamese women. il Newsweek 70:65-6 Jl 24 '67
Woman intellectual and the church; symposium. Commonweal 85:446-56+ Ja 27 '67; Discussion. 85:611+ Mr 3 '67
Working girl, 1967. L. B. Johnson. il McCalls 94:78-9+ My '67
See also
Married women—Employment
Secretaries
Women as executives

Anecdotes, facetiae, satire, etc.
Confessions of a business thing. S. Alexander. Life 63:18 Ag 11 '67

BUSINESS consultants
Building muscle with outside help. il Bsns W p93-4+ S 16 '67
Consultants with a flair for math; Planning research corp. il Bsns W p 196-8+ S 16 '67
Does this Mother know best? F. Zappa, leader of the Mothers of Invention rock group. W. H. Manville. il Sat Eve Post 241:56-7 Ja 13 '68
Learning from Experience, inc; management consulting company run by retirees. il Bsns W p106+ My 27 '67
People and jobs. J. Tebbel. il Sat R 50:11-12+ D 30 '67
Rosser Reeves returns; heads Tiderock corp. il Newsweek 70:56-7 Ag 21 '67
See also
McKinsey and company

BUSINESS cooperation
Brinkmanship in business. B. D. Henderson. Harvard Bsns R 45:49-55 Mr '67

BUSINESS costs. See Cost

BUSINESS crime. See Commercial crimes

BUSINESS cycles
New economics: can it beat the business cycle? il Sr Schol 91:20+ O 12 '67
Productivity in manufacturing. M. Ziegler. il Mo Labor R 90:1-5 O '67
Variability by skill in cyclical unemployment. M. S. Cohen and W. H. Gruber. bibliog f il Mo Labor R 90:8-11 Ag '67
What the business outlook means for you. il Nations Bsns 55:90-1+ S '67

BUSINESS depression
Just what is a recession, anyway? Bsns W p42 Mr 25 '67
Recession? what latest facts show. il U S News 62:33-5 Ap 10 '67
Semantic stew: a crabwise mini-slump? Newsweek 69:63 Mr 6 '67
Time for a new economic miracle; Germany's recession. il Bsns W p78-80+ Jl 8 '67

BUSINESS districts
Mall-transitway constructed by force account; Nicollet mall, Minneapolis. H. Erickson. il Am City 82:134-6 S '67
New enclosed-mall shopping center is designed as a small commercial city; West Oak plaza shopping center. Neiman-Marcus store, Houston, Tex. il Arch Rec 141:142-3 Mr '67
Parking mall that . . . ; Columbia, S.C. C. C. Burnett. il Am City 82:74-6 Ja '67
Semi-pedestrian mall; El Monte, Calif. il Am City 82:102 Ag '67
See also
Shopping centers

BUSINESS economics, Office of. See United States—Business economics, Office of

BUSINESS economy. See Business management and organization

BUSINESS education
How business schools welcome the world; education for international business il Bsns W p 118-19+ D 9 '67
How to rise fast: by degrees; master's degree in business administration. il Newsweek 70:60-2 D 25 '67
Xerox U; listening courses prepared by the Xerox corp. il Time 91:73 Ja 5 '68
See also
Corporate seminars, incorporated
Distributive education
Executives—Training
Harvard university—Graduate school of business administration
Stanford university, Stanford, Calif.—Graduate school of business

BUSINESS enterprises, New
Hippie business. D. Sanford. New Repub 156:7-8 Je 10 '67

BUSINESS entertaining
Office cheer spreads a bit wider. il Bsns W p22 D 23 '67

BUSINESS ethics
Case of the disloyal executive. T. J. Murray. Duns R 90:35-7+ D '67
Community responsibilities of business; address, October 24, 1967. J. R. Cortelyou. Vital Speeches 34:148-50 D 15 '67
Corporate disclosure; insider trading. A. Fleischer, jr. bibliog f Harvard Bsns R 45:129-35 Ja '67
Luck of Clarence Jackson; businessman in dispute with Sears, Roebuck. il Time 90:64 S 1 '67
Marketing ethics & the consumer. E. A. Clasen. Harvard Bsns R 45:79-86 Ja '67
See also
Advertising ethics
Better business bureaus

BUSINESS expenses. See Expense accounts (business)

BUSINESS failures
Business failures. R. Wyant. See issues of Dun's review
Why businesses fail. Sr Schol 90:16 My 12 '67
Zeckendorf revisited; Mortimer Caplin to sue Zeckendorf and others. Newsweek 69:80 My 1 '67

BUSINESS flying. See Airplanes in business

BUSINESS forecasting
As business leaders look ahead. U S News 62-49 My 22 '67
Best bets for 1967. il Duns R 89:95-6+ Ja '67
Business: a look ahead. See issues of Nation's business
Business at bottom; upturn next? il U S News 63:40-1 Ag 7 '67
Business prospects around U.S; effects of money upset. il U S News 63:44-5 D 4 '67
Business prospects in 1967, as LBJ looks ahead. U S News 62:32-3 F 6 '67
Business upturn: will it be checked? il U S News 63:28-9 Ag 21 '67
Businessmen's expectations (cont) L. Humphries. il Duns R 88:13 D '66; 89:13 Mr; 13 Je; 90:15 S; 13 D '67
Commerce secretary forecasts new era for business; interview. A. B. Trowbridge. Nations Bsns 55:30-3 Ag '67
Continued uneasy prosperity. Time 91:56-7 Ja 12 '68
Experts say of '67: a good year; excerpts from testimony. H. Fowler; W. M. Martin. jr. U S News 62:116 F 20 '67
Forecasting and strategy of change; company forecasting. il Pub W 191:23-4 My 1 '67
Foresight vs. footwork. H. C. Wallich. Newsweek 69:86 My 8 '67
How to keep the bloom on the boom; forecast from top executives. il Nations Bsns 55:42-4+ Ap '67
How's business? a close look at the trends. il U S News 62:41-2 Mr 27 '67
In spite of everything, business will pick up. il Nations Bsns 55:76-81 Jl '67
Latest look at business prospects. il U S News 63:33-4 N 27 '67
Life in the old boom yet; drops in NBER's leading indicators. il Bsns W p39-42 Mr 25 '67
Longest boom: can it last? with charts. U S News 63:40-2 O 30 '67
New signals: spur boom, instead of curbing it. U S News 62:74 Mr 13 '67
Next upturn, when? il U S News 62:48-51 Ap 24 '67
Now: an upturn in business; interview. G. Ackley. U S News 63:34-9 S 4 '67
Picking up speed. il Time 89:87 My 12 '67
Retailers smile uneasily. il Bsns W p29-30 Ag 19 '67
Rising hopes and crossed fingers. il Newsweek 69:75 My 15 '67
Setback in business ahead? U S News 62:25-7 Mr 6 '67
Six stocks for growth. il Duns R 89:81-2 F '67
Through a glass, brightly. R. Brady. Duns R 89:5 Ja '67
Tight money ahead? what it will do to the boom. il U S News 63:109-10 O 23 '67
Trend of American business. See issues of U.S. news & World report
Veteran fund manager views the market; interview. T. R. Price. il Duns R 90:47-9 D '67
We'll have to run fast to keep up. il Nations Bsns 55:44-7 O '67
What the business outlook means for you. il Nations Bsns 55:90-1+ S '67
What twelve top forecasters expect for '68; symposium. il U S News 64:32-8 Ja 8 '68
Where are tomorrow's markets? F. R. Sullivan. Duns R 90:40-1+ N '67
Where business is headed. U S News 63:44-6 O 9 '67
Where fastest growth will come; industries. il U S News 62:46 F 20 '67
Which way for stocks in '68? C. Mathews. Duns R 90:36-7+ N '67
See also
Forecasts (economics)

BUSINESS forms. See Business—Forms, blanks, etc.

BUSINESS games. See Management games

BUSINESS gifts. See Gifts in business

BUSINESS hall of fame. See Michigan. University, Ann Arbor—Business hall of fame (proposed)

BUSINESS hours
Midnight market. M. A. Brice. il Duns R 90:39-40 Jl '67

BUSINESS in the arts award
Esquire's 1966 Business in the arts award. Esquire 68:28-9 Jl '67
Esquire's second annual Business in the arts awards. il Esquire 69:30-1 Ja '68

BUSINESS intelligence
Organizational intelligence. by H. L. Wilensky. Review
Reporter 37:54-6 N 2 '67. G. A. Craig

BUSINESS libraries. See Libraries, Business

BUSINESS location. See Location in business and industry

BUSINESS management and organization
Computers: no impact on divisional control; excerpts from The impact of computers on management. J. Dearden. bibliog Harvard Bsns R 45:99-104 Ja '67
Corporate planning at a crossroads. D. W. Ewing. bibliog f Harvard Bsns R 45:77-86 Jl '67
Corporation of the future; address, October 24, 1967. R. E. Ablon. Vital Speeches 34:73-6 N 15 '67
Crises in a developing organization. G. L. Lippitt and W. H. Schmidt. il Harvard Bsns R 45:102-12 N '67
EOS eyes new markets as Xerox unit. J. F. Judge. Tech W 20:36 My 8 '67
Entering the new economy. D. S. Ammer. Harvard Bsns R 45:2-4+ S '67
Executive trends. See issues of Nation's business
Experience, difficult art of management; address, July 27, 1967. H. C. Krannert. Vital Speeches 33:651-4 Ag 15 '67
Federated, and the consumer comeback. J. Poindexter. il Duns R 90:38-42+ D '67
Go-go world of the risk manager. R. Levy. il Duns R 90:38-9+ N '67
Good managers don't make policy decisions; excerpts from address, April 27, 1967. H. E. Wrapp. Harvard Bsns R 45:91-9 S '67
How to beat Parkinson's law. M. Baldrige. il Duns R 89:46-7+ Je '67
How to set up a project organization. C. J. Middleton. il Harvard Bsns R 45:73-82 Mr '67
Is the gap technological? gap between Europe and the United States. J. Diebold. For Affairs 46:276-91 Ja '68
Is your business too organized? D. S. Brown. il Nations Bsns 55:76-8 Mr '67
Management of change; case histories. il Pub W 191:22-7 My 1; 28-33 My 8 '67
Management problems of tomorrow; presidents' panel. T. J. Murray. il Duns R 89:24-6+ F '67
Management's next generation. R. J. Weston; R. H. Mulford. il Sat R 51:32-4 Ja 13 '68
Market planning and the role of government; excerpt from The new industrial state. J. K. Galbraith. Atlan 219:69-72+ My '67
New industrial state, by K. Galbraith. Review
Life 63:4 Jl 7 '67
Nation 205:246-8 S 18 '67. H. Magdoff
Sat R 50:29-30 Je 24 '67. A. A. Berle
New industrial state; excerpt. J. K. Galbraith. Atlan 219:51-7 Ap '67
New management job: the integrator. P. R. Lawrence and J. W. Lorsch. il Harvard Bsns R 45:142-51 N '67
New venture management in a large company. R. W. Peterson. il Harvard Bsns R 45:68-76 My '67
Participative management: time for a second look. R. C. Albrook. il Fortune 75:166-70+ My '67
Patterns of organization change; excerpts from study. L. E. Greiner. bibliog il Harvard Bsns R 45:119-22+ My '67
Putting action into planning. R. H. Schaffer. Harvard Bsns R 45:158-60+ N '67
R for boxed-in executives; concept of functional management, Aldon rug mills. H. Barg. il Duns R 90:55-6+ O '67
Regional management overseas. C. R. Williams. il Harvard Bsns R 45:87-91 Ja '67
Short, happy life of the long-range planner. J. Berry. Duns R 89:36-8 Ja '67
So, you think you're indispensable. il Nations Bsns 55:56-8+ D '67
So you're going to have a planning department! R. F. Vancil. il Harvard Bsns R 45:88-96 My '67
Strategies for a technology-based business. H. I. Ansoff and J. M. Stewart. il Harvard Bsns R 45:71-83 N '67
Strategy for divestments; address, October 5, 1966. A. Bettauer. il Harvard Bsns R 45:116-24 Mr '67
Three years beyond George Orwell: corporate world of 1987. L. H. Schoenhofen, jr. il Duns R 89:43-4+ Mr '67

We must make work worthwhile. C. Argyris. Life 62:56+ My 5 '67
Why do mergers miscarry? J. Kitching. il Harvard Bsns R 45:84-101 N '67
See also
American management association
Bonus system
Business consultants
Business cooperation
Conflict of interests (business)
Corporate acquisitions
Corporations
Cost accounting
Department stores—Management
Diversification in industry
Executive ability
Executives
Factory management
Industrial management and organization
Industrial relations
Inventories
Marketing
Office management
Systems management

Charts, graphs, etc.
Who works with whom? D. I. Cleland and W. Munsey. Harvard Bsns R 45:84-90 S '67

BUSINESS organization. See Business management and organization

BUSINESS recession. See Business depression

BUSINESS research
R: social research. H. G. Hohorst; D. C. Burnham. il Sat R 51:56+ Ja 13 '68
See also
Market research
Operations research
System simulation

BUSINESS risks. See Risk

BUSINESS schools. See Business education

BUSINESS secrets. See Trade secrets

BUSINESS seminars. See Seminars

BUSINESS service industries. See Service industries

BUSINESS statistics
Figures of the week. See issues of Business week
See also
Business forecasting

BUSINESS success. See Success

BUSINESS tax
Common market gets common tax: switch to French-style tax on value added. il Bsns W p65-6+ D 9 '67

BUSINESSMEN
Businessmen in the news. See issues of Fortune
Capitalist chameleons; Communist China. il Time 89:74-5 F 3 '67
Company spirits perk up again; proposal to restore the 7 per cent investment credit. il Bsns W p34-6 Mr 18 '67
How to succeed in business? work in Washington. il Fortune 75:127-33 Mr '67
Long summer commute; businessmen's weekend visits to families in summer homes. il Time 90:58 Jl 21 '67
SR's businessman of the year. W. D. Patterson. Sat R 51:67-8+ Ja 13 '68
Top businessmen, as voted by 500 leaders. il U S News 63:16 Jl 17 '67
Wry look at Americans. F. Kearton. il Duns R 89:27 F '67
See also
Capitalists and financiers
Executives
Michigan. University, Ann Arbor—Business hall of fame (proposed)
Negro businessmen

Recruiting
See Employment systems

BUSONI, Ferruccio
Report: New York. F. Merkling. il Opera N 32:23-4 N 25 '67
Turandot. Criticism
Sat R 50:50 O 28 '67

BUSTARD, H. Robert
Gekkonid lizards adapt fat storage to desert environments. bibliog Science 158:1197-8 D 1 '67

BUSTIN, Edouard
Confrontation in the Congo. Cur Hist 52:168-74 Mr '67

BUSWELL, James Oliver, 1947?-
Double life. H. Saal. por Newsweek 69:83 My 1 '67
Musical events; recital in Philharmonic Hall. W. Sargeant. New Yorker 43:137 Ap 29 '67
Truth seeker. il por Time 89:54 Ap 28 '67

C

CF. See Cystic fibrosis

CF&I steel corporation
New spur for steel's also-ran. il Bsns W p 188-90+ My 13 '67

CIA. See United States—Central intelligence agency

CIAP (Inter-American committee on the Alliance for progress) See Alliance for progress

CIT financial corporation
C.I.T. financial corp. to buy Grosset & Dunlap. Pub W 192:32 O 2 '67

CLA. See California library association

CLR. See Council on library resources, incorporated

CMH. See Medal of honor (United States)

CNI (communications, navigation and identification system) See Radio apparatus on aircraft

CNLA. See Council of national library associations

COCU. See Consultation on church union

COG (councils of government) See Municipal government

COR. See Committee of responsibility to save war-burned and war-injured Vietnamese children

CORE. See Congress of racial equality

COSATI (committee on scientific and technical information) See United States—Federal council for science and technology

COSPAR. See International council of scientific unions—Committee on space research

CPM (critical path method) See Critical path analysis

CRAM (comprehensive random achievement monitor) See Student achievements

C-rations. See United States—Army—Commissariat

CRIA. See Committee to rescue Italian art

CSD. See American library association—Children's services division

CU. See Consumers union of United States

CUNY. See New York (city) City university of New York

CAB drivers. See Taxicab drivers

CABALLÉ, Montserrat
Day with Caballé; interview, ed. by G. Fitzgerald. pors Opera N 31:14-16 Mr 11 '67

about
Caballé in Trovatore. I. Kolodin. Sat R 50:62 F 25 '67

CABANAC, M. and others
Tiliqua scincoides: temperature-sensitive units in lizard brain. bibliog Science 158:1050-1 N 24 '67

CABARET; musical comedy. See Musical comedies, revues, etc.—Criticsms, plots, etc.

CABEZA PRIETA game range. See Game preserves

CABINET (Great Britain) See Great Britain—Cabinet

CABINET (United States) See United States—Cabinet

CABINET officers
President's cabinet. il Sr Schol 91:36-7 O 5 '67
See also
United States—Cabinet

CABINET work
See also
Cabinetmakers

CABINETMAKERS
Check list of Savannah cabinetmakers prior to 1830. Antiques 91:369 Mr '67
John Hall, a busy man in Baltimore. R. C. Smith. il Antiques 92:360-6 S '67
Wood: the friendly mystery. J. Krenov. il Craft Horiz 27:28-9+ Mr '67
See also
Adam, R.

CABINETS (furniture)
Cabinet for all outdoors. K. C. Schuyler. il Outdoor Life 139:12 F '67
Lockup gun cabinet. il Pop Sci 191:166-7 O '67
Three smart cabinets for stereo components. il Bet Hom & Gard 46:80-1 Ja '68
See also
Kitchen cabinets
Television cabinets

CABINS
Cabins and vacation houses. il Consumer Bul 50:17 Jl '67
Hideout: newest piece of ski equipment, for use all year. M. Simons. il Look 31:58-9 F 7 '67
Room where skiers arrive and depart. il Sunset 138:118 F '67

Ski house in the sun. B. Plumb. il N Y Times Mag p 110-12 N 12 '67
Tree-house ski house; designed by David Sellers; with report by F. Kappler. il Life 62:84-7+ Mr 24 '67

CABINS, Airplane. See Airplane cabins

CABLE, Harold
Best of sports; drama. Plays 26:1-14 My '67
Deputy for Broken Bow; drama. Plays 27:13-22 N '67

CABLES, Submarine
Cables and satellites prepare for the mat; new transatlantic line, U.S. global satellite system. Bsns W p 139-40 D 16 '67
Pressure rises for new cable approval. K. Johnsen. Aviation W 88:19 Ja 1 '68

CABLEWAYS
America's longest and highest thrill ride; Jackson Hole's new aerial tramway. S. James. il Pop Mech 127:118-19 F '67

CABOT, Godfrey Lowell
Only to God, by L. Harris. Review
Atlan 220:132-4 D '67. E. Weeks

CABRILLO music festival. See Music festivals—California

CABRILLO NATIONAL MONUMENT
Go to Cabrillo on a clear day following a winter storm. il Sunset 138:26+ F '67

CACCINI, Giulio
Opera's first step was a stumble. G. Jennings. il Opera N 31:6-7 F 11 '67

CACHE VALLEY
America's most beautiful valley. S. Storm. il Am For 73:38-40+ Ja '67

CACTUS
Cactus. H. G. Yocum. il Horticulture 45:34-5 Je '67
Grafting cacti. A. B. Greenberg. il Horticulture 45:40-2 D '67
Mexican cacti in trouble. E. Zubryn. il Sci N 92:280-1 S 16 '67

CADAVERS
Body snatchers; excerpts from The doctors' story. T. Gallagher. il Am Heritage 18:64-73 Je '67
Concerning an ultimate question. America 116:274-5 F 25 '67
Logistics of dying. D. Sudnow. il Esquire 68:102-3+ Ag '67

CADDEN, Vivian
Most unexpected threat to a good marriage. McCalls 94:94-5+ Jl '67

CADLE, Dean
Man on troublesome. Yale R 57:236-55 D '67

CADMAN, John D. and Goodman, R. E.
Landslide noise. bibliog Science 158:1182-4 D 1 '67

CADY, Lee D. Jr
Biomathematics and computer science. Science 156:1265-6 Je 2 '67

CAESAR, Gene
Scandal in the Job corps. Read Digest 90:118-22 F '67

CAESAREAN section. See Cesarean section

CAFE curtains. See Curtains and draperies

CAFES. See Restaurants

CAFFREY, John
Computers in higher education; excerpt from The computer in American education. Sch & Soc 95:319-23 Sum '67
Higher education and the computer. NEA J 56:30-2 F '67

CAGE, John
John Cage: stories and sayings; excerpts from A year from Monday. Dance Mag 41:34-6 D '67
about
Sound, silence, time. por Newsweek 70:68+ D 25 '67

CAGE; drama. See Cluchey, R.

CAGLE, William R.
James Whitcomb Riley, notes on the early years; reprint. Hobbies 72:108-9+ Jl '67

CAGNEY, James
Yankee Doodle Cagney. R. C. Roman. il pors Dance Mag 41:58-61+ Jl '67

CAHIER, Bernard
Fiat's sassy 125 sedan. Motor T 19:38 S '67
—and Borgeson, Griffith
European showcase. Motor T 20:62-7 Ja '68

CAHILL, Tom
Tom Cahill: Army's accidental coach. T. Cohane. il por Look 31:116-19+ N 28 '67

CAHN, Edgar S. and Cahn, J. C.
One man, one vote. New Repub 156:11-12 Ap 8 '67

CAHN, Jean Camper. See Cahn, E. S. jt.

CAHN, Robert D.
Detergents in membrane filters. bibliog Science 155:195-6 Ja 13 '67

CAIN, Stanley A.
Fiftieth anniversary of the National park service 1916-1966. por Liv Wildn 30:16-18 Aut '66

CAINE, Marcella
Inner inquiry; poem Negro Hist Bul 30:5 F '67
Question '66; poem. Negro Hist Bul 30:20 F '67

CAINE, Michael
Michael Caine talks about... interview, ed. by O. Fallaci. pors Look 31:84-7+ My 30 '67

about
Caine mutiny. M. W. Lear. por McCalls 94: 86-7+ Mr '67
Hot actor for a cool time. C. McCarry. il pors Sat Eve Post 240:94-7 My 20 '67
New roughneck breed of ladies' men. P. Hamill. por Good H 165:94-5+ O '67
Sudden fame of Michael Caine. S. Birmingham. pors Holiday 41:81-2+ Je '67
Young man shows his medals. il por Time 89:66 F 17 '67

CAIRNS, Elton J.
Anodic oxidation and molecular structure: influence on performance of normal saturated hydrocarbons in fuel cells. bibliog Science 155:1245-6 Mr 10 '67

CAIRNS, Robert B. and Werboff, Jack
Behavior development in the dog: an interspecific analysis. bibliog Science 158:1070-2 N 24 '67

CAIRO
Description
Israeli pilot's panoramic souvenir; with aerial photographs. Life 63:52B-52C Jl 14 '67

CAKE
Bourbon in the sweet. J. Hewitt. il N Y Times Mag p60 Ja 22 '67
Bride makes pineapple upside-down cake. il McCalls 94:44 Ap '67
Carrousel ginger cake. il Bet Hom & Gard 45:100 My '67
Double-take cake; with recipes. il Seventeen 26:166-7+ N '67
First step to famous pastries is this buttery cake; genoise; with recipes. il Sunset 138: 214+ Ap '67
From central Europe: three bakers' classics. il Sunset 138:190-1 Mr '67
Frozen cake starts you off; festive torte. il Sunset 139:139-40 D '67
Fruitcake snowflakes; with recipes. il Seventeen 26:122-3+ D '67
Fruitcakes for the holidays. il Sunset 139:189 N '67
Hearthside cookbook Christmas 1967. il Good H 165:138-40 D '67
Holiday cakes from old Europe; effortless Christmas baking. il Ladies Home J 84: 90-1+ D '67
How the Greeks bake with yogurt; with recipes. Sunset 138:195 F '67
It's a buttery raisin cake; with recipe. il Sunset 138:158 F '67
Just reach in the freezer for one. il Sunset 139:88-9 Ag '67
Kicky conversation cakes. K. Schaller. il Farm J 91:78-9+ My '67
Now's the time to make fruitcake. P. Cannon. il Ladies Home J 84:122-3+ N '67
Occasion cake. il Ladies Home J 84:90-1+ Je '67
October's the time for onion cake. il Sunset 139:170 O '67
Old-world dessert; torte. J. Hewitt. il N Y Times Mag p 130+ O 8 '67
Regal almond cake. il Bet Hom & Gard 46:62 Ja '68
So you're learning to cook. il Am Home 70: 80 Ja; 124 My '67
Spiced chocolate pound cake. V. V. Voboril. il Good H 164:130 F '67
Successful recipes, feather-light cakes. il Suc Farm 65:61-2 Je '67
Sweden's frying-pan cake; laggtarta. C. Claiborne. il N Y Times Mag p 100+ N 12 '67
Sweet Vienna: Demel's cake shop; with recipes. E. Alston. il Look 31:70-2 D 26 '67
Viennese treasure; sacher torte. C. Claiborne. il N Y Times Mag p70 D 17 '67
You make it with cooky dough and raspberry jam: Viennese Linzertorte. il Sunset 138:172 Ap '67

See also
Coffee cake
Gingerbread
Pastry
Shortcake

CAKE mixes. See Food mixes

CALABRIA, Italy
Calabrian days with Norman Douglas. H. R. Lottman. il Sat R 50:61+ Mr 11 '67

CALAM, John
New books. Sat R 50:66 Ag 19; 94-5 S 16; 82 O 21; 88 N 18; 74 D 16 '67

CALAMITIES. See Disasters

CALCAREOUS deposits. See Sedimentation and deposition

CALCIFICATION
Calcified tissues; report on Gordon research conference. G. Nichols, jr. Science 157: 961-2 Ag 25 '67
Secondary calcification in the foraminiferal genus globorotalia. W. N. Orr. bibliog il Science 157:1554-5 S 29 '67

CALCITONIN
Calcitonin from ultimobranchial glands of dogfish and chickens. D. H. Copp and others. bibliog il Science 158:924-5 N 17 '67

CALCIUM carbonate
Calcareous septa formed in snail shells by larvae of snail-killing flies. L. V. Knutson and others. bibliog il Science 156:522-3 Ap 28 '67

CALCIUM cyanamide
Build a weed free lawn. Pop Gard 18:65 My '67

CALCIUM electrodes. See Electrodes

CALCIUM in the body
Calcium-induced activation of phosphorylase in rat hearts. A. J. D. Friesen and others. bibliog il Science 155:1108-9 Mr 3 '67
Crayfish muscle: permeability to sodium induced by calcium depletion. J. P. Reuben and others. bibliog il Science 155:1263-6 Mr 10 '67
Heat inactivation of the relaxing site of actomyosin: prevention and reversal with dithiothreitol. H. M. Levy and E. M. Ryan. bibliog il Science 156:73-4 Ap 7 '67
Plasma membrane: substructural changes correlated with electrical resistance and pinocytosis. P. W. Brandt and A. B. Freeman. bibliog il Science 155:582-5 F 3 '67
Sarcoplasmic reticulum of striated muscle: localization of potential calcium binding sites. C. W. Philpott and M. A. Goldstein. bibliog il Science 155:1019-21 F 24 '67
Sodium and potassium effects on skeletal muscle microsomal adenosine triphosphatase and calcium uptake. B. B. Rubin and A. M. Katz. bibliog il Science 158:1189-90 D 1 '67
Vitamins D₂ and D₃ in New World primates: influence on calcium absorption. R. D. Hunt. and others. bibliog il Science 157:943-5 Ag 25 '67

CALCIUM metabolism
Interpopulation variations in calcium metabolism in the stream limpet, ferrissia rivularis (Say) W. R. Hunter and others. bibliog il Science 155:338-40 Ja 20 '67

CALCULATING devices
See also
Slide rule

CALCULATING machines. See Computers

CALCULI, Urinary
Siliceous urinary calculi in calves: prevention by addition of sodium chloride to the diet. C. B. Bailey. bibliog Science 155:696-7 F 10 '67

CALCULUS
Calculus in high school. Sci N 91:246 Mr 11 '67

CALCUTTA
Intellectual life
Atlantic report. F. Levine. Atlan 219:24+ Mr '67

CALDECOTT medal.
Evaline Ness. A. Durell. il Library J 92: 1298-9 Mr 15 '67
Evaline Ness, the Caldecott medalist for 1967. J. H. Michel. il Am Artist 31:32-7+ Je '67
Newbery and Caldecott award winners. ALA Bul 61:358 Ap '67
Newbery and Caldecott winners: Irene Hunt, Evaline Ness. il Pub W 191:34-5 Mr 13 '67
Newbery-Caldecott party. il Pub W 191:38 Mr 27 '67
Newbery-Caldecott winners. il Wilson Lib Bul 41:783 Ap '67

CALDER, Alexander
Calder. J. Peter; E. Alston. il pors Look 32: 60-3 Ja 9 '68
Calder. J. Russell. il pors Vogue 150:110-15+ Jl '67

CALDERAS. See Craters

CALDERISI, David. See Halliwell, D. jt. auth.

CALDWELL, Daniel W. family
Negro; three families. J. A. Williams. il Holiday 41:58-61+ Mr '67

CALDWELL, Helen
All-important first year. Parents Mag 42:
38-9+ F '67
CALDWELL, Nat. See Kovach, B. jt. auth.
CALDWELL, Sarah
And we quote; interview, ed. by P. J. Smith.
por Hi Fi 17:MA17 O '67
about
America sings: Sarah Caldwell's National
opera. H. Kupferberg. il Atlan 220:120-2
S '67
American national opera company. A.
Darack. il Hi Fi 17:MA20-1 D '67
Caldwell look for Lulu, Falstaff. I. Kolodin.
Sat R 50:54 O 21 '67
Musical events; performances by American
national opera company at Brooklyn acad-
emy of music. W. Sargeant. New Yorker
43:154+ O 14 '67
CALENDARS
Block printing calendars. L. J. Miller. il De-
sign 69:9 Wint '67
Getting the new year on paper; companies
use of calendars and diaries. il Bsns W
p96-8 D 30 '67
CALEY, Earle R. and Easby, D. T. Jr
Indium as an impurity in ancient western
Mexican tin and bronze artifacts and in
local tin ore. bibliog Science 155:686-7 F 10
'67
CALGARY, Alberta
Calgary's planetarium and museum. S. Wieser.
il Sky & Tel 34:14-15 Jl '67
CALHOUN, John Caldwell
Faces from the past. R. M. Ketchum. por
Am Heritage 18:18-19 O '67
CALIAN, Carnegie Samuel
Dialogue on an age of convergence. Christian
Cent 84:681-3 My 24 '67
CALIFANO, Joseph Anthony, 1931-
How new laws are conceived. P. Lisagor. por
Nations Bsns 55:19-20 Ag '67
CALIFORNIA
California revolution; post-1945 scene. il Na-
tion 204:133-8, 178-81, 206-10, 243-4+, 272-5,
299-303, 336-40+ Ja 30-Mr 13 '67
California: the nation within a nation; sym-
posium. il Sat R 50:16-28+ S 23 '67
State of go: California. il Vogue 150:128-31
Ag 15 '67
See also
Agriculture—California
American literature—California
Architecture—California
Architecture, Domestic—California
Art—California
Booksellers and bookselling—California
Colleges and universities—California
Death Valley National Monument
Education—California
Fishing—California
Gardens—California
Geology—California
Housing—California
Hunting—California
Justice, Administration of—California
Klamath Mountains
Land—California
Law—California
Libraries—California
Marin County
Monterey Peninsula
Music festivals—California
Paleontology—California
Pinnacles National Monument
Roads—California
Salton Sea
San Francisco Bay Region
Sequoia National Park
Skis and skiing—California
Taxation—California
Water supply—California
Whiskeytown Lake
Wilderness areas—California
Yosemite National Park

Anti-poverty program
Champion of the rural poor; California rural
legal assistance agency. Time 90:75 D 15 '67
Poverty politics in California. A. Kopkind.
New Repub 156:19-20 F 18 '67
U.S. letter: McFarland; California rural
legal assistance program. C. Trillin. New
Yorker 43:173-4+ N 4 '67
Why Reagan's mad; California rural legal
assistance program. New Repub 157:13-14
O 21 '67

Antiquities
See Indians of North America—Antiquities
—California

Arts commission
California arts commission; first crafts exhi-
bition. B. Kester. il Craft Horiz 27:24-7+
Mr '67
Climate
Climate and clothes. ALA Bul 61:731 Je '67

Descripton and travel
California: the nation within a nation; sym-
posium. il Sat R 50:16-28+ S 23 '67
Cooling off at Resting Springs. il Sunset 139:24
N '67
From Tulelake to Death Valley; the unknown
California. R. Kirk. Redbook 130:37-9 N '67
If you head for L.A. in March, here are
detours. il Sunset 138:48-9 Mr '67
Late winter auto exploring in the coast
ranges. il Sunset 138:64 F '67

Economic conditions
California slows down; a new look at the
pace-setting state. il U S News 62:66-8 Je
12 '67
Economic policy
In the black, with crust. il Time 89:24-5 Mr
17 '67
Ronald Reagan faces life. A. J. Reichley. il
Fortune 76:98-103+ Jl '67

Education, Department of
Swim'st thou in wealth; California's school
library puzzle. F. D. Largent and J. W.
May. il Am Ed 3:12-13 Je '67

Historic houses, etc.
Coloma: a sawmill restored. M. Bowen. il
Nat Parks Mag 41:15-17 N '67

Industries
Home with the winos; wineries. H. Sutton.
il Sat R 50:44-5 Ag 12 '67
See also
Aerospace industries—United States
Agriculture—California

Parks and reserves
California's Anza-Borrego Desert state park.
O. F. Oldendorph. il Nat Parks Mag 41:4-9
D '67
Easy spelunking in the Mojave; Mitchell Cav-
erns state reserve. il Sunset 139:20+ N '67
So big and so empty; Anza-Borrego desert
state park. il Sunset 138:84-91 Mr '67
See also
Disneyland park, Anaheim

Politics and government
Black out; primary election results. New
Repub 157:7 N 25 '67
California countdown; efforts to start two
new parties. il Newsweek 71:13-14 Ja 1 '68
CDC convention. Nation 205:356 O 16 '67
Coming up with a slate in California; Cali-
fornia Democratic council convention. J.
Ridgeway. New Repub 157:9-10 O 14 '67; Re-
ply. F. W. Neal. 157:29 D 16 '67
Credibility in Sacramento; two staff members
suspected of homosexuality forced to resign.
il Time 90:27 N 10 '67
Democratic disaster area. J. Phelan. il Re-
porter 37:18-21 N 2 '67
Dismay for L.B.J; split in Democratic party.
Time 89:14-15 Je 2 '67
Fast start: end of Governor R. Reagan's suc-
cessful 1967 session. il Time 90:17 Ag 11 '67
Getting out of the shade; action of Lt. Gov.
Finch. il Newsweek 70:23 Ag 14 '67
Governor no; R. Reagan to defend cutbacks
of medical aid. Reporter 37:12-13 O 19 '67
Governor Reagan's slightest vestige. A. Rosin
and R. H. Simmons. New Repub 156:10 Je
24 '67
Guide to Reagan country; the political culture
of southern California. J. Q. Wilson. Com-
mentary 43:37-45 My '67; Discussion. 44:
18+ S '67
Lolliplop; San Mateo County election. il
Newsweek 70:35 N 27 '67
Miscasting of Shirley; election in San Mateo
County. Nation 205:580-1 D 4 '67
Not great, not brilliant, but a good show. J.
Duscha. il N Y Times Mag p28-9+ D 10 '67
Now that Reagan is governor, how's he
doing? R. Evans and R. Novak. il Sat Eve
Post 240:40-2+ Jl 1 '67
Peace & war in San Mateo. il Time 90:26
N 24 '67
Politics in the Palmlands; biographical
sketches. H. Sutton. il Sat R 50:22-7+ S 23
'67
Reagan, ex-radical. A. Kopkind. New Repub
157:17-21 Jl 15 '67

CALIFORNIA—Politics and government—*Cont.*
Reagan in the State house. W. F. Buckley, jr. Nat R 19:787 Jl 25 '67
Reagan: squeeze on spending. il U S News 63: 60-2 O 30 '67
Reagan takes a look ahead: and explains some '67 decisions. U S News 64:11 Ja 8 '68
Revolt against the poor. P. Kerby. Nation 205:262-7 S 25 '67
Ronald Reagan faces life. A. J. Reichley. il Fortune 76:98-103+ Jl '67
Ronald Reagan, governor; over-acting? A. V. Krebs, jr. Commonweal 85:639-41 Mr 10 '67
Spots on Mr Clean; Reagan denies homosexual ring in executive office. il Newsweek 70:34-5 N 13 '67
Star is born. Newsweek 69:36+ F 6 '67
Welcome to the fraternity; *détente* between Kuchel and Reagan. il Time 89:30 My 19 '67
Who is Ronald Reagan? por Read Digest 90: 102-6 Ap '67

Population
Californians: where they come from. U S News 62:21 Ap 24 '67
Dynamics of repulsion. D. B. Luten. il Nation 204:134-8 Ja 30 '67

Social history
Guide to Reagan country: the political culture of southern California. J. Q. Wilson. Commentary 43:37-45 My '67; Discussion. 44: 18+ S '67

Social life and customs
California woman; symposium. il Ladies Home J 84:61-81+ Jl '67
Freckled superwoman; concerning Ladies' home journal report on California women. Time 90:67 Jl 28 '67
Rage for awareness; movements in California. D. Bess. il Nation 204:243-4+ F 20 '67

CALIFORNIA, LOWER
See also
Fishing—California, Lower
Libraries—California, Lower
Paleontology—California, Lower

CALIFORNIA center for community development
Poverty politics in California. A. Kopkind. New Repub 156:19-20 F 18 '67

CALIFORNIA earthquakes. See Earthquakes—United States

CALIFORNIA encephalitis virus. See Encephalitis virus

CALIFORNIA holly. See Toyon

CALIFORNIA institute of technology, Pasadena
JPL scientists challenge sterilization goals. H. M. David. Tech W 20:32-3 My 1 '67

CALIFORNIA library association
California. L.A. study asks major changes. Library J 93:140 Ja 15 '68

CALIFORNIA literature. See American literature—California

CALIFORNIA. State college, San Jose
San Jose: the bullhorn message; Negro campaign against discrimination. J. Brann. Nation 205:465-7 N 6 '67

CALIFORNIA. University
Angry aftermath at Cal; firing of C. Kerr. Time 89:42 F 3 '67
Berkeley story; facts on a big university. il U S News 62:54-5 F 6 '67
California draws a blank. H. Draper. Nation 205:682-5 D 25 '67
California oath controversy, by D. P. Gardner. Review
   Nation 204:795-6 Je 19 '67. G. R. Stewart
   Sat R 50:80 O 21 '67. F. Fertig
Cal's Kerr ousted. il Sr Schol 90:13-14 F 17 '67
Clark Kerr tells his story; interview, ed. by W. Flynn and J. M. Russin. C. Kerr. Newsweek 69:64-5 F 6 '67
Coordinator for Cal; new president. il Time 90:64 S 29 '67
Cut-rate California; Ronald Reagan and the budget. New Repub 157:9-10 Ag 5 '67
Failure of a peacemaker; California's board of regents dismiss Kerr. il Time 89:60 Ja 27 '67
Free education. M. Friedman. Newsweek 69:86 F 20 '67
Free for whom? R. Moley. Newsweek 69:112 Mr 20 '67
Hitch in time? C. J. Hitch and Alex C. Sherriffs appointments. Newsweek 71:37-8 Ja 1 '68
Kerr affair. H. Brandon. Sat R 50:13 F 11 '67
Manager for Cal. Newsweek 70:53 O 2 '67
Reagan retreats. Newsweek 69:80-1 O 27 '67
Reagan uses his broom. Bsns W p38 Ja 28 '67

Reagan vs. the Regents; compromise on plan to impose tuition fees. Newsweek 70:80 S 11 '67
Reagan's lesson; result of sacking Kerr and advocating tuition. Nation 204:166 F 6 '67
Report from California: the Governor and the university. E. Langer, il Science 155: 1220-4 Mr 10 '67; Discussion. 156:581-2 My 5 '67
Ronald Reagan plays surgeon. F. M. Brodie. il Reporter 36:11-16 Ap 6 '67
Squabble over semantics; rejects Gov. Reagans' plan to levy tuition charge. Time 90: 64 S 8 '67
Three Rs in California; Reagan, the Regents, and the right. W. Trombley. il Sat R 50:47-8+ Mr 18 '67
Tragedy at Cal: a fiscal & presidential crisis. il Time 89:44-5 F 24 '67
Turmoil in higher education; interview, ed. by G. B. Leonard and T. G. Harris. C. Kerr. il Look 31:17-21 Ap 18 '67
What Reagan hath wrought. J. Duscha. New Repub 156:10-12 F 4 '67
Wounded are many; Kerr fired. il Newsweek 69:87-8 Ja 30 '67

Berkeley campus
As Berkeley awaits Ronald Reagan. R. Stith. Commonweal 85:443-4 Ja 27 '67
B-school throws away the book; Berkeley's advanced management training program. il Bsns W p 104-6+ Ap 22 '67
Berkeley, how do students really live? S. Van Der Ryn and M. Silverstein. il Arch Forum 127:90-7 Jl '67
Class hires a scholar; students' efforts to retain. E. Becker. il Time 89:58 Mr 10 '67
Decline of freedom at Berkeley (cont) L. S. Feuer; discussion. Atlan 218:105-11 O; 38+ N '66; 219:44 Mr '67
Good for Berkeley; students conservation activities. Reporter 37:14 D 28 '67
How to prevent riots; student-faculty committee report. il Time 91:34 Ja 19 '68
Failing university; faculty-student commission's report. Newsweek 71:59 Ja 22 '68
Molecular biology: U.S. and Italy to establish new graduate school. J. Walsh. il Science 156:1582-3 Je 23 '67
Mood at Berkeley. C. J. McNaspy. America 116:817-18 Je 3 '67
Oakland: how to lose in winning; Berkeley student sit-in at induction center. J. S. Hadsell. Christian Cent 84:1476-8 N 15 '67
Ph.D. language requirements: California survey results; letter. D. G. Nichols and T. Everson. Science 156:1549 Je 23 '67
Rebellion and responsibility. B. Rubenstein and M. Levitt. Yale R 57:16-30 O '67
Walk-yourself tour of Berkeley's changing campus. il Sunset 139:52 O '67

School of librarianship
Berkeley L.S. students unite against censors. Library J 92:4318 D 1 '67

Strawberry Canyon recreation area
Impact of a distinctive university recreation area. T. S. Yukic. il Parks & Rec 2:35-6 N '67

Libraries
Instant college libraries; new campuses at Santa Cruz and Irvine; interview, ed. by J. Cushman. D. T. Clark; J. E. Smith. il Library J 92:240-3 F 1 '67
See also
California. University—Los Angeles campus—Libraries
California. University—Santa Cruz campus—Libraries

Los Angeles campus
Beauty & bongos; UCLA campus outdoor sculpture court. il Time 89:70 Je 16 '67
From mop to typewriter; pilot clerical training unit. L. A. W. Darling. il NEA J 56:28-9 O '67
Shooting for the top; UCLA opponents. H. L. Masin. il Sr Schol 91:24 D 7 '67
UCLA's committee on fine arts productions brings performances to school and community. V. H. Swisher. il Dance Mag 41:33-5 Je '67
UCLA's outstanding displays of modern sculpture. il Sunset 138:96-7 F '67
U.C.L.A.'s 20-year plan for health science. il Arch Rec 142:198-201 S '67

Libraries
Climbing the ladder; excerpt from Fortune and friendship. L. C. Powell. il Library J 93:49-53 Ja 1 '68

CALIFORNIA. University—*Continued*

Santa Cruz campus

New and spacious campus inspires a fresh approach. il Arch Rec 141:198-205 Ap '67

Libraries

Santa Cruz: redwoods and a bay view. il Library J 92:4356-7 D 1 '67

CALIFORNIA university bookstores. See College bookstores

CALIFORNIA Western railroad
Super Skunk. H. D. Bishop. il Am For 73:18-20 My '67

CALIFORNIA wines. See Wine

CALIFORNIANS
Guide to Reagan country: the political culture of southern California. J. Q. Wilson. Commentary 43:37-45 My '67; Discussion. 44:18+ S '67
How to be a California girl; Robynne Hoover's regimen. R. J. Kaiser. il Look 31:M20-2+ D 26 '67
Memoirs of a recent migrant. H. Brucker. il Sat R 50:20-1+ S 23 '67
Powers that make California go. H. Sutton. il Vogue 150:148-53 Ag 15 '67

CALISHER, Hortense
Speaking out. por Sat Eve Post 240:10+ Ag 26 '67

CALKING
Caulking Rx for leaky seams. H. Harris. il Yachting 121:50-2+ F '67
How to choose the right boat caulk. G. Emory. il Pop Mech 127:164-7+ My '67
See also
Sealing compositions

CALKINS, Carroll C.
Bouquets in the air. House B 109:184-7 Ap '67
How to give your piano the attention it deserves. House B 109:64+ Mr '67
Shades of a lath house, and carpets of color. House B 109:88-9 Ja '67
Thomas D. Church; the influence of 2,000 gardens. House B 109:140-5 Mr '67
Twenty best trees to plant. House B 109:128-31+ F '67
Uncharted worlds on the face of a tree. Home Gard 54:35 N '67

CALKINS, Frank
Wassail for woolly worms. il Field & S 72:58-9+ Je '67

CALKINS, Myron D.
Let's pave more streets. Am City 82:88-9 Ag '67

CALL to a stranger; story. See Park, M.

CALLA lilies
Now's the time to plant callas. il Sunset 139:232 O '67

CALLAGHAN, James
Britain holds the line. por Bsns W p42 Ap 15 '67

CALLAHAN, Daniel
America's Catholic bishops. Atlan 219:63-6+ Ap '67
Crisis in Catholic education. N Y Times Mag p34-5+ Ap 23 '67
New directions. Commonweal 85:621-2+; 86:287-90 Mr 3, My 26 '67
Parochial education. Commentary 43:81-3 Ja '67
Priests question the rule of celibacy. N Y Times Mag p36-7+ O 22 '67
Revolution in the cloth. Sat R 50:24-5 Jl 29 '67

CALLAHAN, Joseph M.
Billion-dollar smog hoax! Motor T 19:68-70 Mr '67
What smog control will cost you. Motor T 19:60-1+ S '67

CALLAN, John H.
Faculty participation in college administration. Sch & Soc 95:121-2 F 18 '67

CALLAN, Pat
How to buy a ski boat. Pop Mech 127:155-6+ F '67

CALLANAN, Kathleen
In my opinion. por Seventeen 26:262 My '67

CALLAWAY, John D.
New reformation and the myth of media objectivity. Christian Cent 84:1349-52 O 25 '67

CALLING, Animal. See Animal calling

CALLISON, Charles H.
National outlook. See issues of Audubon

about

Callison named society's top administrator. Audubon 69:19 Ja '67

CALM makes the world go round; story. See Amft, M. J.

CALOREN, Fred
Nationalism in Quebec, 1967. Christian Cent 84:913-19, 1102 Jl 12, Ag 30 '67

CALORIES, Food. See Diet; Food values

CALVERT family
Maryland, their Maryland: with paintings. W. E. Wilson. Am Heritage 18:8-19+ Ag '67

CALVES

Care

Buildings save calves and time. J. Russell. il Farm J 91:D4-6 Ag '67
Calf mortality takes a licking. A. H. McDaniel. il Farm J 91:D12-13 Ag '67
Cut death losses with these tips. N. Reeder. Farm J 91:D8 Ag '67
Ten ways you can save more calves. il Farm J 91:96+ Mr '67

Diseases and pests

Salmonella chase your calves. L. A. Baker. Farm J 91:D10 Ag '67

Feeding

Calf mortality takes a licking. A. H. McDaniel. il Farm J 91:D12-13 Ag '67
Calves don't need hay. J. Bickers. il Farm J 91:D15 Ag '67
Cool milk before you feed it? A. Phelps. il Farm J 91:D2 O '67
Revolution in calf feeding. A. Phelps. il Farm J 91:D13-14 Ag '67

CALVES, Mechanical. See Automatons

CALVIN, John
Books. P. W. Schmidtchen. il por Hobbies 72:104+ Jl '67
Keep the church out of, what? L. DeKoster. por Christian Cent 84:404-7 Mr 29 '67

CALVIN, William H. and Stevens, C. F.
Synaptic noise as a source of variability in the interval between action potentials. bibliog Science 155:842-4 F 17 '67

CALVINISM
Keep the church out of, what? L. DeKoster. Christian Cent 84:404-7 Mr 29 '67
Our Puritan roots. L. Baritz. Nation 204:699-700 My 29 '67
See also
Mercersburg theology

CALVO, Joseph M. See Calvo, R. A. jt. auth.

CALVO, R. A. and Calvo, J. M.
Lack of end-product inhibition and repression of leucine synthesis in a strain of salmonella typhimurium. bibliog Science 156:1107-9 My 26 '67

CAMBODIA
Awkward facts; Communists use Cambodia as base area and sanctuary. il Newsweek 70:46 D 4 '67
Buildup on the border; North Vietnamese infiltrators. il Time 90:27-8 D 1 '67
Frangipani & bafflegab; J. Kennedy's visit. il Time 90:29 N 10 '67
Letter from Cambodia. R. Shaplen. New Yorker 43:66+ Ja 13 '68
Living theater; visit of J. Kennedy. il Newsweek 70:57-8 N 13 '67
Now that Jackie Kennedy has visited Cambodia. il U S News 63:20 N 13 '67
Princely sum-ups. il Time 89:39 Ap 14 '67
Travels of Jackie. il Newsweek 70:76-7 N 20 '67
See also
Communism—Cambodia
Theater—Cambodia

Foreign relations

About, face! N. Sihanouk changes his tune. Newsweek 71:41 Ja 8 '68
Ant's progress; anti-Chinese moves. Newsweek 70:48+ S 25 '67
Borderline success; violations to be investigated by ICC. il Newsweek 71:32 Ja 22 '68
Cambodia: growing base for Vietnam reds. il U S News 63:62-3 D 11 '67
Fair weather friend. Nat R 20:17 Ja 16 '68
How Peking doublecrosses a friend. il U S News 62:26 Ap 24 '67
In hot pursuit; reactions to U.S. pursuit of North Vietnamese inside borders. A. Campbell. New Repub 158:19-21 Ja 13 '68
Just a baby step; plan to authorize U.S. troops to enter Cambodia. il Newsweek 70:38 D 25 '67
New balance. il Newsweek 71:14-15 Ja 15 '68
Prince and US; new wolf at Cambodia's door? D. G. Porter. Commonweal 87:442-3 Ja 12 '68
Wider war in southeast Asia? Communists use neighboring countries as sanctuaries. il Bsns W p20-1 Ja 6 '68

CAMBODIA—*Continued*

Politics and government
He is the state: Sihanouk's relations with government. Newsweek 69:57 My 15 '67

CAMBODIAN sculpture. See Sculpture, Cambodian

CAMBRIDGE, Godfrey MacArthur
Godfrey Cambridge wins battle of bulges, loses 117 pounds. L. Robinson. il pors Ebony 22:160-2+ O '67

CAMBRIDGE, Md.
Black militants talk of guns and guerrillas. il U S News 63:32 Ag 7 '67
Firebrand. il Newsweek 70:28 Ag 7 '67

CAMBRIDGE, Mass.
Harvard square, where all Boston makes the scene; shopping center. il Bsns W p 144-6 O 28 '67

CAMBRIDGE research laboratories. See United States—Air force—Cambridge research laboratories

CAMBRIDGE. University
Theoretical astronomy: new institute in Cambridge. J. Walsh. Science 157:1286-8 S 15 '67
Xerox director named first American Magdalene fellow. Pub W 192:25 D 11 '67

CAMDEN, N.J.
It helps to be in trouble. il Am City 82:67-8 N '67

CAMELLIA exhibits. See Flower exhibits

CAMELLIAS
Gift camellia, in a container. il Sunset 139:158 D '67
Here is a grand door to open, to find the new hybrid camellias. Sunset 139:194+ N '67
Here's help in choosing camellias. il Sunset 138:200+ F '67
New ways to use camellias. M. Marko and J. Past. il Horticulture 45:22-3+ F '67
Stunning japonicas. il Sunset 138:82-5 F '67
You can tinker with camellias. il Sunset 139:160-1 S '67

CAMELOT project. See Project Camelot

CAMERA cases
Getting ready for the underwater camera trip. P. Stackpole. U S Camera 30:16+ Jl '67

CAMERA clubs
Taking a memo to Neptune; Grand Bahama underwater explorers club. L. Barry. il Pop Phot 60:46+ F '67

CAMERA lenses. See Lenses, Photographic

CAMERA shutters
Automation vs. reciprocity failure. C. W. Kennedy il Pop Phot 60:50+ F '67
Camera shutters: will electronics take over? A. Goldsmith. il Pop Sci 191:120-2+ S '67
Secrets of long shutter life. N. Goldberg. il Pop Phot 61:104-5 Ag '67
Smart way to check a camera shutter: use your TV. J. W. Hamblen. il Pop Sci 191:106-7+ D '67

Testing
Simple test for shutter speed. C. Welch. il Pop Mech 128:168-9 S '67

CAMERA stores. See Photographic apparatus industry and trade

CAMERA tripods
Improvised camera supports. C. W. Kennedy. il Pop Phot 60:157 Mr '67
Shorty tripod for shooting low. W. E. Burton. il Pop Mech 128:104-5 Jl '67

CAMERAS
Annual guide to forty-five top cameras. il Mod Phot 31:63-108 D '67
Anything you can do I can do better; no you can't! T. Karp. il Mod Phot 31:78-81+ F '67
Baby view does a man's work; miniature Cambo view camera. J. S. Forney. il Pop Phot 62:84 Ja '68
Beat and offbeat (title varies) N. Rothschild. Pop Phot 61:34+ Ag; 58+ D '67
Behind the scenes. il Mod Phot 31:14+ Mr '67
Big show? Chicago dealer exhibit. il Mod Phot 31:76-82 Je '67
Bruce Davidson: my Leica, the movie camera. H. V. Fondiller. il Pop Phot 60:130-3+ My '67
Camera buyers want technical advice & discussion. Consumer Bul 50:28-30 S '67
Camera that photographers helped design; Koni-Omega M. H. Zucker. il Pop Phot 61:104-7 N '67
Camera with a take-charge flash; Minolta Autopak. H. Zucker. il Pop Phot 62:87 Ja '68

Chrislin insta camera. C. W. Kennedy. il Pop Phot 61:44+ Ag '67
Chrislin: rival to Polaroid? D. L. Miller. il Mod Phot 31:46+ Jl '67
Christmas shopping guide. il Mod Phot 31:137-8 D '67
Collect data before buying cameras abroad. W. Lane. Travel 128:65 O '67
Customs list aids camera shopping. W. Lane. Travel 128:69 N '67
Ed Scully on basics. E. Scully. Mod Phot 31:44+ Ap '67
Exakta vs Exakta: which is the phony? West German Exakta vs. the Dresden. H. Keppler. il Mod Phot 31:40+ Je '67
First Kodak box. E. Bennett. il U S Camera 30:56 My '67
How to buy the right camera. W. Lane. Travel 127:70 My '67
If I were the camera industry ... N. Rothschild. il Pop Phot 62:112-13+ Ja '68
Inside Photokina: way-out cameras make news. A. Goldsmith. il Pop Sci 190:134-7 Ja '67
Instant pictures, well, almost; Chrislin insta-camera. il Consumer Rep 32:408 Ag '67
Is your camera a Paris original? N. Goldberg. il Pop Phot 61:116+ Jl '67
Kodak's new shirt-pocket Instamatics. E. H. Ortner. il Pop Sci 190:142-3 My '67
Large camera. A. Feininger. See issues of Modern photography
Large camera; how to build a format close-up camera. A. Feininger. il Mod Phot 31:40+ My '67
Large camera; right equipment for photographing paintings and sculpture. A. Feininger. Mod Phot 31:28+ F '67
Leica M4 makes debut. il U S Camera 30:38 Jl '67
Leica M4: new and fast. B. Pierce. il Pop Phot 61:76-7+ Ag '67
Low-cost still cameras. il Consumer Rep 32:597-601 N '67
Meyers on technique. E. Meyers. Mod Phot 31:22+ Mr '67
Modern tests. See issues of Modern photography
New products. See issues of U.S. camera & travel
Now there's a Leica M4. K. Poli. il Pop Phot 61:56 Jl '67
On the go, by bus. I. Desfor. il U S Camera 30:42-3+ My '67
120-size cameras fight back. E. H. Ortner. il Pop Sci 191:132-5+ O '67
Personal-use report: Instamatic 804. P. Wahl. il Pop Sci 190:126-7 F '67
Photo beat. W. Hanson; N. Rothschild; B. Pierce. See issues of Popular photography
Pre-shrunk! Instamatic compacts. il Pop Phot 60:120-1 My '67
Price is right; Singlex TLS. H. Zucker. il Pop Phot 62:78-9 Ja '68
Progress in copy cameras; CLR issues contract. Library J 92:3368-9 O 1 '67
Reconnaissance camera focused on traffic. il Tech W 20:35-6 Ap 3 '67
Rollei 35: bigger inside than outside? B. Pierce. il Pop Phot 61:100-1+ Ag '67
Seen in Chicago. il U S Camera 30:41+ Je '67
Simon says; Hasselblad superwide, a favorite. N. Simon. Mod Phot 31:30+ D '67
Small & handy, it's a dandy. H. Zucker. il Pop Phot 62:79 Ja '68
Spot meter inside the Contarex. H. Zucker. il Pop Phot 62:76-7 Ja '68
Still cameras. il Consumer Rep 32:322-38 D '67
Swiss amateur's cooled-emulsion camera. H. Eggeling. il Sky & Tel 34:382-3 D '67
Test reports. See issues of Popular photography
35mm. E. Bennett. il U S Camera 30:60+ My '67
Underwater testing for six weeks at Bermuda. P. Stackpole. U S Camera 30:26+ N '67
U.S. camera & travel test reports. See issues of U.S. camera & travel
What cameras do Russians prefer? survey results. H. Keppler. Mod Phot 31:41 Ag '67
See also
Electronic cameras
Eye camera
Mirrors for cameras
Moving picture cameras
Polaroid Land cameras
Single-lens reflex cameras
Twin-lens cameras
View finders

CAMERAS—*Continued*

Care

Face-lifting for cameras. M. D. Grennan. il Pop Phot 60:76-7+ Mr '67
Lubrication: experts only. N. Goldberg. il Pop Phot 62:66 Ja '68
Undercover camera; how to keep it, and yourself, dry in wet weather. il Pop Phot 60:124 Je '67

Collectors and collecting

Camera collectors and why they grow. C. Schwalberg. il U S Camera 30:48-9+ S '67

Loading

Super 8 boom. G. Gilbert. il U S Camera 30:63-7+ S '67

Renting

Meyers on technique. E. Meyers. Mod Phot 32:26 Ja '68

Repairing

Camera overboard! and what to do next. N. Goldberg. il Pop Phot 61:104-5 S '67
First aid for cameras. N. Goldberg. il Pop Phot 61:66-7 Jl '67

Testing

Buying a camera? check it! D. L. Miller. il Mod Phot 31:122-3+ D '67
Keppler on the SLR. H. Keppler. Mod Phot 31:22+ My '67
Keppler on the SLR; tests by CU. H. Keppler. il Mod Phot 31:12+ Je '67
Smart way to check a camera shutter: use your TV. J. W. Hamblen. il Pop Sci 191:106-7+ D '67
Techniques tomorrow; home tests of equipment? B. Sherman. Mod Phot 31:50+ Je '67
Test your camera and film before you travel. W. Lane. il Travel 127:70 Mr '67

CAMERAS, Used

Good buys in used SLR's. il Mod Phot 31:72-3+ S '67
Shopping the used camera market. E. Hannigan. U S Camera 30:16+ Jl '67

CAMERAS on space vehicles. See Space vehicles—Equipment

CAMERON, A. G. W. See Maran, S. P. jt. auth.

CAMERON, Barry

Fossilization of an ancient, Devonian, soft-bodied worm. bibliog Science 155:1246-8 Mr 10 '67

CAMERON, Gail

How America lives. See issues of Ladies' home journal
What it takes to be a Kennedy. Ladies Home J 84:76-7+ F '67
Why good sons become draft dodgers; excerpts from interviews. Ladies Home J 84:72-3+ Ag '67

CAMERON, J. M.

Jesus and the church. Commonweal 87:269-74 N 24 '67
McCabe affair. Commonweal 85:653-5 Mr 10 '67

CAMERON, James

Isle of deadlock. Sat Eve Post 241:58-9+ Ja 13 '68
—and others
Infant vocalizations and their relationship to mature intelligence. bibliog Science 157:331-3 Jl 21 '67

CAMERON, Jamie

(ed) See Reed, A. Fish is caught

CAMEROON REPUBLIC

President of Cameroon visits the United States; exchange of toasts, October 24, 1967. L. B. Johnson; A. Ahidjo. Dept State Bul 57:654-6 N 13 '67

CAMEROTA, Elaine

Play's the thing to catch kids' minds and make them swing. Sr Schol 90:sup 16-17 Mr 17 '67

CAMOUGIS, George, and others

Potency difference between the zwitterion form and the cation forms of tetrodotoxin. bibliog Science 156:1625-7 Je 23 '67

CAMP cookery

Bean-hole beans. C. B. Colby. Outdoor Life 139:34 My '67
Campfire bakery. B. Riviere. il Field & S 71:64 F '67
Campfires for cooking. C. B. Colby. il Outdoor Life 139:28+ Ap '67
How to be a great cook in a camper! Bet Hom & Gard 45:94-5 My '67
Now you're cooking on wood. E. W. Smith. il Field & S 71:56-7+ Mr '67

CAMP equipment. See Camping outfits

CAMP fire girls

Impressions from a Caribbean tour; art exhibit. R. Kornfeld. il Sch Arts 67:29 N '67

CAMP stoves

Let's buy a grill and cook out! il Changing T 21:29-30 Je '67

CAMPAIGN funds

Back scratching; philosophy of A. S. Boyd New Repub 157:7-8 O 7 '67
By Long possessed; fight against repeal of campaign-fund law. Newsweek 69:26 My 15 '67
Clean money for Congress. J. Wright. il Harper 234:98-102+ Ap '67
Congressional ethics: who can afford to be honest? Time essay. Time 89:24-5 Mr 31 '67
Demeaning indulgence; R. Long's crusade. Time 89:19-20 My 12 '67
Dinner dunner; testimonial dinner for Gov. Peabody. il Newsweek 69:38 Je 26 '67
Dulski dinner. Newsweek 70:28 Ag 21 '67
Elections for sale; taxpayers contributions bill. K. Crawford. Newsweek 69:40 Ap 10 '67
End of plan to give tax funds to politicians? U S News 62:16 Ap 24 '67
Filling the bill; irrelevant amendment. Newsweek 69:24+ My 1 '67
Financing campaigns; L. B. Johnson's new plan. New Repub 156:2 Je 10 '67
Footing the bill. New Repub 157:9-10 S 30 '67
How to finance political campaigns. J. N. Eller. America 116:869 Je 24 '67
Lesson in practical politics; reprint. R. Long. il U S News 63:61 Jl 3 '67
Long enough; 1966 campaign-fund bill remains inoperative. Newsweek 69:26 My 22 '67
LBJ: million-a-week fund raiser. il U S News 63:34 Jl 10 '67
Now is the time for all good men . . ; Time essay. Time 91:44-5 Ja 5 '68
One man, one vote, one dollar. M. Nolan. Reporter 36:28-9 My 4 '67
Paying for campaigns; Presidential election campaign fund act. Newsweek 69:34 Ap 17 '67
Paying for politics, Ashmore-Goodell bill. New Repub 157:4 Jl 22 '67
Pipers and payers. New Repub 156:5-6 Mr 25 '67; Reply. O. R. Reid. New Repub 156:42-3 Ap 8 '67
Repenting in leisure; fight to repeal Presidential election campaign fund act. Time 89:24 Ap 21 '67
Senate election reform bill America 117:369 O 7 '67
Senate's rising star loses bid for power; Senator R. Long loses presidential campaign financing law. Bsns W p35-6 My 13 '67
Tax dollars for politics, slush fund or reform? il U S News 62:36 My 8 '67
Ticklish problem of political fund-raising, and spending. D. D. Eisenhower. Read Digest 92:64-9 Ja '68
Where the tax bill bogged down; Senate fight over repeal of campaign financing law. Bsns W p35 Ap 22 '67
Will taxpayers have to foot the bill for political campaigns? U S News 63:14 S 25 '67

CAMPAIGNE, Jameson G.

Our fighting men understand. Read Digest 91:143-4 Jl '67

CAMPAIGNS, Advertising. See Advertising campaigns

CAMPAIGNS, Money raising. See Fund raising

CAMPAIGNS, Political. See Political campaigns

CAMPAIGNS, Presidential. See Presidential campaigns

CAMPAU, DuBarry

Is Canada cultured? Sat R 50:58-60 Ap 29 '67

CAMPBELL, Alex

British take stock. New Repub 156:3-5 Je 17 '67
Fulbright versus Taylor. New Repub 156:26-7 F 25 '67
G. K. Shesterton protests. New Repub 156:36+ Ap 8 '67
In hot pursuit. New Repub 158:19-21 Ja 13 '68
Life with father. New Repub 157:25-6 O 14 '67
Poverty of nations. New Repub 156:32+ Je 3 '67
Report from Israel. New Repub 156:8-10 Je 10 '67
Republicanism's new frontier. New Repub 157:15-17 N 18 '67

CAMPBELL, Alex—*Continued*
Stone's throw. New Repub 158:37+ Ja 6 '68
Toynbee the biographer. New Repub 156:26-7
Je 24 '67
Tragedy of errors. New Repub 157:32 S 9 '67
Walt Whitman Rostow. New Repub 157:15-17
N 4 '67
War games. New Repub 157:30+ Jl 22 '67
CAMPBELL, Charles
To train a firefighter. Am City 82:102-3 Mr
'67
CAMPBELL, Sir Clifford
New tenants in government house. E. B.
Thompson. il por Ebony 22:80 O '67
CAMPBELL, D. A, company
Setting odds on mutual funds for fun and
profit. il Bsns W p49-50 Ja 14 '67
CAMPBELL, Edwina
Curl up and read. Seventeen 26:234 S '67
CAMPBELL, Howard W. See Suga, N. jt. auth.
CAMPBELL, John C.
Soviet-American relations: conflict and co-
operation. bibliog f Cur Hist 53:193-202+
O '67
CAMPBELL, John F.
Spy who returned to the fold; story. Atlan
219:84-6 Je '67
CAMPBELL, Lawrence
Alexander Liberman in orbit. Art N 66:40-1+
Ap '67
CAMPBELL, Lucille
3D woven forms. Sch Arts 66:17-18 My '67
CAMPBELL, Rex
Sign on my barn. Farm J 91:38 F '67
CAMPBELL, Robert
How the computer gets the answer. Life
63:60-72 O 27 '67
CAMPBELL, Robert B.
Robert Campbell and Louis Epstein are
honored at West coast dinner. il por Pub
W 191:68+ Ap 24 '67
Take a bow Bob Campbell, Lou Epstein. por
Pub W 191:103-5 Je 5 '67
CAMPBELL, Shirley Aley
Way of all flesh. il por Newsweek 70:115 S
25 '67
CAMPBELL, T. L.
Basic science in mission-oriented endeavor.
Science 156:670-2 My 5 '67
CAMPBELL-Ewald company
Ad agency emerging from Chevy's shadow. il
Bsns W p94-6+ Je 3 '67
Shaking up Campbell-Ewald. Bsns W p37
D 23 '67
CAMPERS and coaches, Truck
Big news in camp coaches. B. W. Dalrymple.
il Outdoor Life 140:32-5+ Jl '67
Build an expandable camper. A. S. Ryan. il
Pop Sci 190:162-6+ My '67
Campers: roughing it in style. A. Rothenberg.
il Look 31:79-80 Ag 22 '67
Choosing a recreation vehicle for family
use. C. M. Edwards. il Consumer Bul 50:
36-40 Mr '67
Elegant pickups: your next family car? il Pop
Sci 191:54-7 Ag '67
How to add a kitchen to a camper. A. S.
Ryan. il Pop Sci 190:160-2 Je '67
Meet PM's high-tailer. il Pop Mech 127:110-15
Ap '67
Notes for nomads. See issues of Travel
Pampered campers; camper buses. il Time
89:62 Je 9 '67
Pickup and co. M. Gresham and G. Gresham.
il Field & S 71:54-5+ Mr '67
Take to the open road in a '67 camper. il
Pop Sci 190:181-3 My '67
They made a camper out of a Greyhound. J.
Ingersoll. il Pop Mech 127:128-31 My '67
Turn turtle: carry your house on your back.
E. Logan. il Sr Schol 90:sup20 My 12 '67

Equipment
Campers: twelve ways to add comfort and
convenience. T. Stimson. il Pop Mech 127:
124-7+ My '67

Renting
Why it pays to rent a vacation camper. V. L.
Oertle. il Pop Sci 190:176-80+ My '67

CAMPING
Best things in life are free, or almost. M.
Gough. il House B 109:64+ Jl '67
Boat camping. P. Perrett. il Yachting 121:
84-5+ My '67
Camping. C. B. Colby. See issues of Outdoor
life
Collier's laws for happy camping. J. L.
Collier. Read Digest 90:171-5 Je '67
Discover Ontario's Land O'Lakes. H. L. Brun.
il Motor B 119:22-3+ Je '67

Great camping debate; John Steinbeck vs.
Erle Stanley Gardner. J. Steinbeck; E. S.
Gardner. Pop Sci 190:160-1+ My '67
Rehearsal for camping. C. B. Colby. Outdoor
Life 139:36+ F '67
Snowmobiles start a new camping craze. H.
Shuldiner. il Pop Sci 191:148-50+ D '67
Tips for camping out. il Ebony 22:168 Je '67
Tulip poplars and protozoa on the Chopa-
wamsic; educational camping at Prince
William Forest park. P. Thomson. il NEA
J 56:32-3 O '67
See also
Airplanes in camping
Camping outfits
Guides

Activities
Virginia City, how to run a day camp program based on a popular theme. J. Hasz.
il Parks & Rec 2:24-5+ Ap '67

Anecdotes, facetiae, satire, etc.
Those were the pleasant years. E. H.
Bowers. Sat R 50:43-4 Je 17 '67

Educational aspects
Sounds and shadows; blind student on geog-
raphy camping trip; Montgomery Blair
H.S. Silver Springs, Md. P. L. Jones. il
Sr Schol 90:sup 19 My 5 '67

Safety devices and measures
Travel well. E. N. Dye. Travel 128:63-4 Ag
'67

Alaska
Survival in the North. R. Blodget. il Flying
80:40-1 Mr '67

Canada
Camping the calendar highway. G. Laycock.
il Field & S 71:40-3 Mr '67
Easy camping in the Canadian bush. N.
Karas. il Field & S 71:62-3+ Mr '67
You can't beat canoe camping. J. R. Gregg.
il Field & S 71:46-7+ Mr '67

Europe
We camped our way through Europe. J.
Linkletter. il Pop Mech 129:128-31+ Ja '68

Europe, Western
We camped Europe. P. Lippman. il Field &
S 72:52-5+ Je '67

Idaho
Family in the wilderness; camping in the
Selway-Bitterroot wilderness area. N. Boyd.
il Liv Wildn 30:36-41 Wint '66

Middle western states
Camping guide to the U.S; the Midwest.
M. Frome. il Holiday 41:145-52 My '67

United States
Are you up on today's camping? quiz. D.
Du Bois. Outdoor Life 139:66-8+ Je '67
Look what's happened to camping. C. Mangel.
il Look 31:74-6 Ag 22 '67
Vacation wonderlands for family camping. il
Parents Mag 42:72-5+ Ap '67
CAMPING outfits
Are you up on today's camping? quiz. D.
Du Bois. Outdoor Life 139:66-8+ Je '67
Art of the picnic; with recipes. il Sunset
139:38-45 Ag '67
Be ready for rain. C. B. Colby. il Outdoor
Life 140:108-11+ S '67
Get a good sleep. C. B. Colby. il Outdoor Life
140:104-8 N '67
Get geared up for camping. P. Czura. il To-
days Health 45:34-9+ Jl '67
Let's look ahead. C. B. Colby. il Outdoor
Life 140:16+ O '67
More new gear for '67. C. B. Colby. il Out-
door Life 139:20+ Je '67
New camping gear for '67. C. B. Colby. il
Outdoor Life 139:80+ My '67
New hardware for campers. il Pop Mech
127:134-5 My '67
Seven-in-one camp tool. C. Conley. il Field &
S 72:123 S '67
Shoestring camping. C. B. Colby. il Outdoor
Life 139:28+ Mr '67
Small things that help. C. B. Colby. il Out-
door Life 140:80-3 Jl '67
Smooth way to rough it. H. Shuldiner. il
Pop Sci 191:148-51 Jl '67
See also
Automobiles—Camping equipment
Colorado outdoor sports corporation
Packs
Sleeping bags

CAMPION, Donald R.
Jesuit grass-roots renewal. America 116:286 F 25 '67
CAMPOS, Leo F.
Water utility will offer air conditioning and steam heating. Am City 82:75-7 D '67
CAMPOS, Roberto de Oliveira
Man to remember. Newsweek 69:59 Mr 20 '67
CAMPS
Lifetime sports camps. il Parks & Rec 2:24+ F '67
Miseries of an overweight child; John Occhipinti's summer at Camp Tahoe. B. Kocivar. il Look 31:36-8+ N 14 '67
Now's the time to choose next summer's camp. S. S. Rosenberg. il Parents Mag 42: 42-3+ Jl '67
Personal business; time to think about summer camp. Bsns W p 177-8 F 18 '67
Summer camps. L. W. Sauer. PTA Mag 61: 33 Je '67
Virginia City, how to run a day camp program based on a popular theme. J. Hasz. il Parks & Rec 2:24-5+ Ap '67
See also
Labor camps
CAMPS, Refugee
Return visit to despair; Palestinian refugees at Ein el Hilweh camp, Lebanon. J. Bell. il Time 90:20 D 29 '67
Whom the gods love; North Vietnamese refugee camp at Duc Co. J. F. Mason. il Reporter 37:21-5 S 21 '67
CAMPS for the handicapped
New dimensions in camping for the physically handicapped; Easter seal society. F. M. Robinson. il Parks & Rec 2:21+ F '67
CAMPUS courier
Digest that! tactics used to get the Courier off the ground. New Repub 156:6 Ap 29 '67
Fallen Courier. New Repub 157:10 Ag 5 '67
Reader's digest goes to college. J. Teppel. il Sat R 50:92-3 My 13 '67; Discussion. 50:94-5 Je 10 '67
CAMPUS life. See Student life
CAMPUS planning
Architecture on the campus; symposium. il Arch Forum 127:46-75+ Jl '67
Campus architecture shaped by master plans. Arch Rec 141:185 Ap '67
Instant campus; a remedy for junior college growing pains. J. H. Sofokidis. il Am Ed 3:15-19 S '67
Nine community colleges. il Arch Rec 142: 155-71 N '67
Something new in college campuses; State university of New York at Albany. il U S News 63:54-6 S 4 '67
CAMPUS slang. See Slang
CAMUS, Albert
Can we survive nihilism? T. Merton. Sat R 50:17-19 Ap 15 '67
CAN company, American. See American can company
CANADA
Canada at a century. C. D. W. Goodwin. bibliog f il Cur Hist 52:282-8+ My '67
Canada discovers itself; Time essay. Time 89:26-7 My 5 '67
Canada's next one-hundred years. il U S News 62:86-90 Ap 10 '67
Happy hundred! symposium. il Sr Schol 90: sup6-7, 13-16+ F 10 '67
Making up for apathy; centennial celebrations. Time 90:32 Jl 7 '67
See also
Architecture—Canada
Ballet—Canada
Banks and banking—Canada
Booksellers and bookselling—Canada
Camping—Canada
Church unity—Canada
Colleges and universities—Canada
Electric power—Canada
Festivals—Canada
Foreign visitors in Canada
France—Foreign relations—Canada
Gardens—Canada
Gaulle, C. de—Visit to Canada, 1967
Hunting—Canada
Immigration and emigration—Canada
Labor laws and legislation—Canada
Library schools and education—Canada
New Brunswick
Petroleum—Canada
Police—Canada
Publishers and publishing—Canada
Quebec (province)
Research—Canada
Saskatchewan
Taxation—Canada
Trade unions—Canada
Transportation—Canada
Yachts and yachting—Canada

Armed forces
Lesson for U.S? a blueprint for better, cheaper defense. il U S News 62:12 Je 12 '67
Bibliography
Canada: an exciting teaching opportunity. F. S. Gross. il Sr Schol 90:sup 16 F 10 '67
Canadian publications. R. Davidson. Antiques 92:106+ Jl '67
Civilization
Growing independence in Canadian-American relations. J. W. Holmes. For Affairs 46: 151-66 O '67
Report; identity crisis and cultural emergence. B. Stock. il Atlan 220:10+ Jl '67; Reply with rejoinder. J. W. Bacque. 220: 48+ O '67
See also
Canada—Intellectual life
Commerce
Canada and the United States; address, October 31, 1966. R. Winters. Vital Speeches 33:214-17 Ja 15 '67
Canadian's case for an Atlantic free-trade area; interview, ed. by R. K. Brome. J. V. Clyne. U S News 64:48-50 Ja 1 '68
Common market for U.S. and Canada? interview. D. Rockefeller. U S News 63:88-9 Ag 21 '67
World's big wheat crops: a worry for Canada. il U S News 63:64 O 23 '67
Commercial treaties and agreements
Road test for auto trade accord. il Bsns W p55-6 Je 17 '67
Defenses
Canada; collective security; address, November 13, 1967. P. Martin. Vital Speeches 34:133-5 D 15 '67
Lesson for U.S? a blueprint for better, cheaper defense. il U S News 62:12 Je 12 '67
Description and travel
Canada exposed: the look of the young nation; excerpts from Portrait of a period: a collection of Notman photographs, ed. by R. Harper. Am Heritage 18:13-25 Je '67
Canada's centennial fever. S. Robinson. il McCalls 94:70+ Mr '67
Montreal and Canada's Expo 67; travel information. il Bet Hom & Gard 45:76-7 Mr '67
One hundredth year: Canada celebrates birthday. L. Jonckheere. il Sr Schol 90:sup 18-19 F 10 '67
St Lawrence River: key to Canada. H. LaFay. il Nat Geog Mag 131:622-67 My '67
Tall trip in short takes. J. Scott and L. Scott. il Motor B 119:28-31+ Ap '67
This proud land, this Canada. I. Mothner. il Look 31:20-31 Ag 22 '67
Economic conditions
Canadians face big tax boost. U S News 63: 114 D 11 '67
Drab reality that Expo masked. il Bsns W p33-4 D 30 '67
Icing on Canada's cake. il Bsns W p53-4 Jl 15 '67
See also
Wages—Canada
Economic policy
Canada tries to cool it; efforts to dampen inflation. Bsns W p46 N 18 '67
Canadian economy and incomes policy; excerpt from Prices, productivity and employment. Mo Labor R 90:55-7 Ap '67
Economic relations
United States
Canada and the United States; address, October 31, 1966. R. Winters. Vital Speeches 33:214-17 Ja 15 '67
Resentful partner: Canada fights its orbit. C. W. Gonick. Nation 204:489-94 Ap 17 '67
See also
Joint United States-Canadian committee on trade and economic affairs
Foreign relations
France
Le grand faux pas of le grand Charles. M. Clark. il Life 63:44B-44C Ag 4 '67
United States
Canada and the United States, a centennial retrospective. B. Hutchison. il Am Heritage 18:6-12+ Je '67

CANADIANS—*Continued*
Canadian character in the twentieth century. J. Porter. bibliog f Ann Am Acad 370:48-56 Mr '67
Canadian culture. W. French. il Christian Cent 84:906-10 Jl 12 '67
It helps if you know both of the languages; English-speaking Canadians flocking to French classes. il Bsns W p96-7 N 25 '67
Report; identity crisis and cultural emergence. B. Stock. il Atlan 220:10+ Jl '67; Reply with rejoinder. J. W. Bacque. 220:48+ O '67
This proud land, this Canada. I. Mothner. il Look 31:20-31 Ag 22 '67

CANAL cruising. See Cruising
CANAL ZONE. See Panama Canal Zone
CANALETTO, 1720-1780. See Bellotto, B.
CANALS
    See also
Panama Canal
Suez Canal
            Canada
    See also
Rideau Canal
        Central America
    See also
United States—Interoceanic canal commission
        Europe, Western
Floating across the Continent: seeing western Europe by waterway; with account by M. Leatherbee. il Life 62:50-61+ Je 23 '67
            Florida
    See also
Florida Ship Canal project
        Great Britain
Canal holiday in Britain. R. Birks. il Motor B 119:114 F '67
        New York (state)
    See also
Erie Canal
            Ohio
Mike Kirwan's big ditch; Lake Erie-Ohio River Canal. W. Schulz. Read Digest 90:59-64 Je '67
        United States
    See also
Erie Canal

CANALS; story. See Sillitoe, A.
CAN-Am series. See Automobile racing
CANAPÉS
Redbook's complete guide to fabulous sandwiches; with recipes. il Redbook 129:93-5+ Je '67
CANARY ISLANDS
Well worth the trip. M. Gough. House B 109:96+ F '67
CANAVAN, Francis
To make a university great. America 117:57-60, 230 Jl 15, S 9 '67
CANAVERAL, CAPE. See Kennedy, Cape
CANBERRA, Australia. Commonwealth national library. See National library of Australia
CANBY, Vincent
Czar of the movie business. N Y Times Mag p38-9+ Ap 23 '67
CANCELL, Benton Russell
She's hauling! N. Willatt. por Dung R 90:54-5+ N '67
CANCER
Cancer and immunology. B. J. Culliton. il Sci N 91:310 Ap 1 '67
Endocrine-induced regression of cancers; address, December 13, 1966. C. Huggins. bibliog il Science 156:1050-4 My 26 '67
International cancer atlas. Sci N 91:318 Ap 1 '67
Milk-like fluid in a mammary adenocarcinoma: biochemical characterization. R. Hilf. bibliog il Science 155:826-7 F 17 '67
    See also
Cancer research
            Causes
Clearing the air; lung cancer not caused by air pollution. Newsweek 70:41 D 25 '67
Evidence of cancer-immunology link. Sci N 92:163 Ag 12 '67
Is uranium mining a hazard to health? il Bsns W p 107-8+ Je 3 '67
Popular insecticides potential causes of cancer. Consumer Bul 51:38-40 Ja '68
What the cigarette commercials don't show. H. J. Mooney. Read Digest 92:71-4 Ja '68
            Diagnosis
Cancer signals? malignancy-associated changes. Newsweek 69:56 F 27 '67

Detection of oral cancer: a way to save lives. Good H 164:192 My '67
Direct inspection; cervical cancer detected by colposcopy. Time 89:66 Ap 21 '67
Let's close our tragic cancer gap. A. C. Williams. Todays Health 45:88+ Ap '67
Operation unneeded; suspicious lung masses. Sci Digest 61:28-9 Mr '67
Simple smear test detects oral cancer. Todays Health 45:87 D '67
Who gets cancer checkups? Sci Digest 62:74 O '67
        Prevention and control
Let's close our tragic cancer gap. A. C. Williams. Todays Health 45:88+ Ap '67
            Therapy
And then there was one. A. Lake. il Good H 164:90-1+ Mr '67
Apply-it-yourself salve for skin cancer; methotrexate. il Life 62:87-8 Mr 3 '67
Cancer is bad for you; hypothermia treatment. J. Medelman. Esquire 68:111+ N '67
Case of the unlicensed vaccine. il Time 89:57 Mr 3 '67
Four that lived. Sci Digest 61:59 Ap '67
Heat on cancer; heating up blood to 110 degrees. Newsweek 70:110 S 18 '67
Inflammatory cure; skin cancer. il Time 89:74 F 24 '67
Selective cancer killer; l-asparagine. Newsweek 69:55 Ap 3 '67
Starving out cancer; low-phenylalanine diet. Newsweek 69:68 Je 26 '67
Thin blood a blow to cancer. Sci Digest 63:83 Ja '68
What parents should know about childhood cancer; new drugs and radiological techniques. W. S. Ross. Read Digest 90:83-7 Mr '67
            Vaccines
FDA seizes anticancer drug; Rand coupled fortified antigen. Sci N 91:142-3 F 11 '67
Vaccine for cancer. Sci N 91:317-18 Ap 1 '67
Vaccine loses; Rand cancer vaccine. Sci N 91:258 Mr 18 '67

CANCER cells
First film of cancer cells in action; taken by Russell Sherwin. il Life 63:57-8+ N 17 '67
Transmission. Sci N 91:430 My 6 '67
CANCER producing substances
5-Oxo-5H-benzo[e]isochromeno-[4,3-b] indole, a new type of highly sarcomagenic lactone. A. Lacassagne and others. bibliog il Science 158:387-8 O 20 '67
Malignant transformation in vitro by carcinogenic hydrocarbons. C. Heidelberger and P. T. Iype. bibliog il Science 155:214-17 Ja 13 '67
Molecular pathology and carcinogenesis; report on first New Zealand international symposium. J. H. Weisburger and C. M. Goodall. Science 159:115-16 Ja 5 '68
Phenotypic expression of transformation: induction in cell culture by a phorbol ester. A. Sivak and B. L. Van Duuren. bibliog il Science 157:1443-4 S 22 '67
CANCER research
Animals smoke, and die. F. Marley. il Sci N 92:158-9 Ag 12 '67
Assault on viral leukemia. il Sci N 91:174-5 F 18 '67
Cancer cells starved in enzyme treatment. Sci N 91:351-2 Ap 15 '67
Cancer dissemination; report on meeting. H. G. Mandel. Science 158:958-60 N 17 '67
Cancer immunity. Sci Digest 61:36-7 F '67
Cancer, the longest fight. D. Zimmerman. Newsweek 69:118-19 Ap 17 '67
Challenge to man of the neoplastic cell; address, December 13, 1966. P. Rous. bibliog Science 157:24-8 Jl 7 '67
Comparative oncology. Sci N 91:461 My 13 '67
Enzyme starves cancer cells; L-asparaginase. Sci N 92:582-3 D 16 '67
Hormones and heart attacks. Sci N 92:175 Ag 19 '67
Improved in vitro survival of normal, functional spleen cells. B. Mohit and G. H. Sato. bibliog il Science 157:449-51 Jl 28 '67
Induction of cancer by viruses. R. Dulbecco. il Sci Am 216:28-37 bibliog(p 146) Ap '67
Keto-aldehydes and cell division. A. Szent-Györgyi and others. bibliog Science 155:539-41 F 3 '67
Lab creates life in a test tube. il Bsns W p58 D 23 '67
Oral cancer; chewing tobacco in India. K. S. Nayar. Sci N 92:495 N 18 '67
Secret from the guinea pigs; L-asparaginase. il Time 89:57-8+ Ap 14 '67

CANCER research—*Continued*
Viruses and cancer. il Sci N 91:448 My 13 '67
World cancer fight; new International cancer research agency affiliated with World health organization. D. A. Ehrlich. Sci N 91:574+ Je 17 '67
See also
Roswell Park memorial institute
Sloan-Kettering institute for cancer research
CANCER tests. See Cancer—Diagnosis
CANCER viruses
Genetics fights cancer. B. Frisch. il Sci Digest 61:48 Mr '67
Virus-like particles in established murine cell lines: electron-microscopic observations. D. A. Kindig and W. H. Kirsten. bibliog il Science 155:1543-5 Mr 24 '67
CANDELILLAS
Wax makers. N. C. Newman. il Nat Parks Mag 41:14-15 Ja '67
CANDIA, O. and others
Brain stem structures responsible for the electroencephalographic patterns of desynchronized sleep. bibliog Science 155:720-2 F 10 '67
CANDID photography. See Photography—Portraits
CANDIDATES, Political
Do we need peace candidates? T. C. Sorensen; A. I. Waskow. Sat R 50:32-3 F 4 '67
Doves in trouble? their problem in '68. il U S News 62:78-9 Je 5 '67
Entertainment culture. A. Berger. Nation 205:228-9 S 18 '67
Family affair; G. W. McGee's 1958 campaign in Wyoming. D. McGee. il Reporter 36:43-8 Mr 9 '67
Fulbright's prospects. J. Witcover. New Repub 156:4-5 Je 10 '67
Harangues and hurrahs in Boston; candidates for mayor. J. McLellan. Commonweal 86:405-6 Je 30 '67
Hoffa taint; Missouri senatorial contenders. D. L. Spritzer. New Repub 156:5 Je 10 '67
Hometown advice; L. P. Williams replaces J. Meredith as Harlem candidate. Newsweek 69:39-40 Mr 27 '67
How do you fight Shirley Temple? campaigning in San Mateo County. J. Duscha. il Reporter 37:21-3 N 2 '67
Man nobody knows; congressional candidates in San Mateo County. New Repub 157:11-12 O 21 '67
Mrs Black & the neighbors. il Time 90:27-8 N 10 '67
NR poll: conservatives preferences for the 1968 Republican nomination. Nat R 19:236-7, 340-1, 456, 559, 678, 786 Mr 7, Ap 4, My 2, 30, Je 27, Jl 25 '67
New politics goes local. P. Booth. Nation 204:682-5 My 29 '67
Politics of entertainment. A. Berger. Nation 205:422-4 O 30 '67
Rocky of Little Rock; gubernatorial candidates in Arkansas. T. Dearmore. il Reporter 37:14-18 O 5 '67
Score one for Stokes, and Negroes up for mayor. il Life 63:36-41 O 13 '67
Seven sitting doves; Democrats who speak out. P. F. Healy. New Repub 156:8-10 Je 3 '67
State races: key to the White House in 1968? with chart. il U S News 63:41-2 S 4 '67
Strange bedfellows; Ronald Reagan and Shirley Temple. G. Ace. Sat R 50:8 O 21 '67
See also
Political campaigns
Presidential candidates
Vice-presidential candidates
also names of political candidates, e.g. L. D. Hicks
CANDLES
Bayberries and bayberry candles. H. W. Dengler. il Am For 73:4-7+ D '67
How to make marbled candles, ice-mold candles, waffle candles. il Sunset 139:80+ D '67
CANDLESTANDS. See Candlesticks
CANDLESTICKS
Brass household candlesticks of the gothic period. J. K. Richardson. il Antiques 92:818-21 D '67
How to build a Shaker candlestand, and candlestick, too. D. Warren. il Pop Sci 191:144-5 N '67
Sconce of fat round candles. il Sunset 139:86 D '67
CANDY
Easy-to-make gift toffee. il Sunset 139:145 D '67
Hearthside cookbook. Good H 165:183-4+ D '67
This year give chocolates with a professional look. il Farm J 91:68-9 D '67

CANDY Industry and trade
Sweet justice; Britain's major candymakers ordered to end resale price maintenance. il Time 90:80 Ag 4 '67
See also
Paul. Peter, incorporated
Russell Stover candies, incorporated
CANFIELD, Cass
Reflections on reaching the age of 150. Harper 234:14+ Je '67

about
Catching the 4:52. il por Newsweek 70:69-70 Jl 24 '67
CANFIELD Martha free memorial library. See Martha Canfield free memorial library, Arlington, Vt.
CANHAM, Erwin D.
Public looks at labor. Duns R 89:81+ Ja '67
CANISTERS. See Boxes, cases, etc.
CANNED food
Check salmon cans for a health hazard. Consumer Rep 32:185 Ap '67
Family dinners off the pantry shelf. il Good H 166:102-18 Ja '68
Work wonders with canned and frozen poultry products. il Ladies Home J 84:101+ F '67
See also
Heinz, H. J, company
CANNES international film festival
Ars longa...censoring of Ulysses. il Time 89:49 My 12 '67
Cannes '67. H. Alpert. Sat R 50:50+ My 27 '67
Letter from Paris; showing of Jeu de Massacre, Mouchette, and J'ai Tué Raspoutine. Genêt. New Yorker 43:127-9 My 27 '67
CANNING, Curtis
To Becky with love from all the Harvards. M. Riley. il Sports Illus 27:44 Jl 10 '67
CANNING and preserving
Tips on canning. il Suc Farm 65:55 Ag '67
CANNON, Poppy
Line a day. See issues of Ladies' home journal
Meal a day. See issues of Ladies' home journal
CANOE trips
Down the Raccoon River by canoe. R. P. Cushman. il Parents Mag 42:64-5+ O '67
CANOES, Sailing. See Sailboats
CANOES and canoeing
Canoe built from siding. G. Daniels. il Pop Sci 191:149-53+ N '67
Canoe craft primer. F. M. Paulson. il Field & S 72:110-15 Je '67
Escape to discovery. B. Geagan. il Field & S 72:42-3+ D '67
Redwood canoe...a beauty you can build. F. McGuckin and J. Payne. il Pop Sci 190:171-5+ Mr '67
You can't beat canoe camping. J. R. Gregg. il Field & S 71:46-7+ Mr '67
See also
Indians of North America—Boats

Safety devices and measures
Saddle mount; a deep-water canoe entry. J. T. Santoro. il Parks & Rec 2:25+ Je '67
CANON law
Changing law in a changing church; updating the Code of canon law. P. M. Shannon. America 116:248-50 F 18 '67
Constitutionalism and the church; call by the Canon law society of America and Fordham university. America 117:432 O 21 '67
Let's be honest about the canon. R. L. Morgan. Christian Cent 84:717-19 My 31 '67; Discussion. 84:1068-9 Ag 23 '67
Reform of canon law; reprint. P. M. Shannon. Cath World 206:53-6 N '67
See also
Divorce (canon law)
CANONS for the mass. See Mass
CANOT, Theodore
Captain Canot, American slave-trader, visits the African town of Timbo. Negro Hist Bul 30:10 O '67
CANOVA, Antonio
Defrosting Canova; acquisition of Perseus by Metropolitan museum. il Newsweek 70:90 S 18 '67
Footnotes. il(cover) Am Artist 31:6+ N '67
Marble for the Met. il Time 90:77 S 15 '67
Under wraps, the Met's newest star. il Life 63:125-6 S 15 '67
CANOVAS, J. L. and others
Evolutionary significance of metabolic control systems. bibliog Science 156:1695-9 Je 30 '67

CANTATAS
Cantata with lyrics, by Hitler: The rise and fall of the Third Reich, by L. Schifrin. H. Siders. Life 63:14 S 29 '67
Heads or tails. L. C. Schifrin's Rise and fall of the Third Reich. il Newsweek 70:92 Ag 14 '67

CANTELON, Philip L.
Greetin's, cousin George. Am Heritage 19:6-11+ D '67

CANTON, China
Cantonment in Canton. Time 89:24-5 Mr 24 '67
End of a truce. Newsweek 71:34 Ja 1 '68
Lurid tales from Canton. il Time 90:39-40 S 29 '67
Visit to Canton. J. Cantwell. Time 90:35 O 6 '67
Who's on first? trouble in Canton. Newsweek 69:48+ Je 5 '67

CANTOR, Georg
Non-Cantorian set theory; analogy with non-Euclidean geometry. P. J. Cohen and R. Hersh. il Sci Am 217:104-6+ bibliog (p 160) D '67

CANTORS, Jewish
Art of the cantor; cantorial recordings. P. Kwartin. Sat R 50:91 F 25 '67

CANTRELL, Lana
Two for the show. por Time 89:63-4 Mr 3 '67

CANTUA
It's a plant to walk under. il Sunset 138:269 Ap '67

CANTWELL, John
Visit to Canton. Time 90:35 O 6 '67

CANTWELL, Mary
Eat. Mlle 66:78 N; 56+ D '67; 18+ Ja '68

CANTWELL, Robert
Nature. Sports Illus 26:47-8+ Mr 27 '67

CANTZEN, Conrad
Strange legacy of Conrad Cantzen. A. Brock. il Read Digest 90:41-2+ F '67

CANVASSING
Aiming at mom to sell books. il Bsns W p56-7+ Jl 29 '67
Apparel salesmen take samples to the party; Beeline fashions, a door-to-door purveyor of ready-to-wear. il Bsns W p 148-50+ Jl 15 '67
As American as apple strudel; door-to-door peddlers. Consumer Rep 32:348-9 Jl '67

Anecdotes, facetiae, satire, etc.
Give me an old-fashioned peddler. M. Holmes. il Todays Health 45:68-70 My '67

CANYON DE CHELLY NATIONAL MONUMENT
Boom... C. Foley. il Am For 73:4+ Mr '67

CANYONLANDS NATIONAL PARK
Canyonlands. R. L. Reynolds. il Am Heritage 18:52-63 O '67
Unlocking the canyon country. il Sunset 138:82-91 My '67

CANYONS
See also
Grand Canyon

CAPA, Robert
Capa: his traditions remain. il Pop Phot 60:87+ Je '67
Death comes to Robert Capa; excerpt from Twelve at war. R. Hood. il por Pop Phot 60:84-6+ Je '67

CAPE, Dempsey
Footrace with a caribou. por Outdoor Life 140:48-9+ S '67

CAPE, William H.
Future role of the city clerk. Am City 82:174+ S '67

CAPE COD
Charles Dickens would have loved this house. A. McArdle. il Am Home 70:48-9 D '67

CAPE COD NATIONAL SEASHORE
Cape Cod. B. B. Chamberlain. il Natur Hist 76:24-33 bibliog(p67) My '67

CAPE KENNEDY. See Kennedy, Cape

CAPE MAY, N.J.
Victorian New Jersey. H. P. Koenig. il Travel 128:42-5+ S '67

CAPEN, Charles C. and Young, D. M.
Thyrocalcitonin; evidence for release in a spontaneous hypocalcemic disorder. bibliog Science 157:205-6 Jl 14 '67

CAPEN, Charles F.
Observing Mars in 1967. Sky & Tel 33:208-10 Ap '67

CAPILLARY circulation. See Blood—Circulation

CAPILLARY-tube scanners. See Biological apparatus and supplies

CAPITAL cable company
Johnson TV firm that's losing money. U S News 63:8 Jl 17 '67

CAPITAL development fund. See United Nations—Capital development fund

CAPITAL gains tax. See Income tax—Capital gains tax

CAPITAL investments
Business outlays get back on the high road; 1968 capital spending up 5 per cent. il Bsns W p44-5 N 11 '67
Business' plans for new plants and equipment, 1967-1970. Arch Rec 141:81-2 My '67
Capital investment stays on the track; proposed 6 per cent surcharge is having little effect on capital spending plans. Bsns W p40+ Ja 28 '67
Cooling things by spending less, or taxing more? il Newsweek 70:57-8 S 4 '67
Cutbacks ahead. Newsweek 70:96 S 25 '67
How much should a corporation earn? J. J. Scanlon. il Harvard Bsns R 45:4-6+ Ja '67
Outlays throw a curve; highlights of Commerce-SEC capital spending survey. il Bsns W p40 Mr 11 '67
R&D looms big in fiscal budgets; McGraw-Hill survey. il Bsns W p68-9+ My 13 '67
Spending looks peppier; 1967 capital spending plans; McGraw-Hill survey. il Bsns W p25-6 F 11 '67
Spring stirs bright hopes; McGraw-Hill capital spending survey. il Bsns W p33-4 Ap 22 '67
Still on a high plateau; how capital spending shapes up for 1967. il Bsns W p40 S 9 '67
Too much capacity. il Fortune 76:36+ D '67
Waiting for the next half. il Bsns W p43 Je 10 '67
Which way for capital spending? J. Weingarten. il Duns R 90:33-5+ O '67
See also
Investment tax credit

CAPITAL punishment
Answers for J. W. Christian Cent 84:131-2 F 1 '67
Death penalty litigation. A. M. Bickel. New Repub 157:13-14 Ag 19 '67
Dying death penalty. Time 89:50 F 17 '67
Forbidding fruits of capital punishment. J. E. Starrs. Cath World 205:286-92 Ag '67
Issue of capital punishment. H. A. Bedau. bibliog f il Cur Hist 53:82-7+ Ag '67
Killing the death penalty. il Time 90:47-8 Jl 7 '67
See also
Executions and executioners

CAPITAL spending. See Capital investments

CAPITALISM
Capitalism, socialism, and the future of the industrial state; excerpts from The new industrial state. J. K. Galbraith. Atlan 219:61-7 Je '67
Creeping capitalism in the Soviet Union? excerpts from address, 1967. H. Landreth. bibliog f Harvard Bsns R 45:133-40 S '67
Limits of American capitalism, by R. L. Heilbroner. Review
Commentary 43:92-5 Ja '67. E. S. Mason
Three big ism's and how they grew. il Sr Schol 91:16-21+ S 28 '67
See also
Free enterprise

CAPITALISM and communism. See Communism and democracy

CAPITALISTS and financiers
Our crowd, by S. Birmingham. Review
Life 63:6 Jl 14 '67. P. Lyon
Proprietors in the world of big business. R. Sheehan. il Fortune 75:178-83+ Je 15 '67
See also
Businessmen
Millionaires
Rich, The

CAPITOL (United States) See United States—Capitol

CAPITOL records, incorporated
Capitol gains. Newsweek 69:76+ F 27 '67
Happy twenty-fifth. G. Lees. il Hi Fi 17:116 D '67

CAPITOLS
See also
United States—Capitol

CAPON, Robert Farrar
Of many things. America 116:130 Ja 28 '67
Secular and the sacred. America 116:307-12 Mr 4 '67

CAPOTE, Truman
Extreme magic; cruising up the Yugoslavian coast. por Vogue 149:84-9+ Ap 15 '67
Go right ahead and ask me anything; interview, ed. by G. Steinem. por McCalls 95:76-7+ N '67
Miriam; story; reprint. Mlle 65:142-3 O '67
Thanksgiving visitor; story. McCalls 95:75 N '67
Truman Capote reports on the filming of In cold blood. por Sat Eve Post 241:62-5 Ja 13 '68
Voice from a cloud. Harper 235:99-100+ N '67

CAPOTE, Truman—*Continued*

about

Capote and the Perrys. L. Lerman. il por Mlle 65:141 O '67
Party. G. Steinem. il pors Vogue 149:50-7+ Ja 15 '67
Politics of the Capote ball. W. F. Buckley, jr. il Esquire 68:159-64+ D '67

CAPOTOSTO, John
Six weekend projects to improve your home. Pop Mech 127:134-7 F '67

CAPOTOSTO, Rosario
How to put down an instant lawn. Pop Sci 191:178-81 O '67

CAPP, Al
Al Capp on the hippie economics. il Nations Bsns 55:64-7 S '67

CAPP, Arthur O. jr
Electrical contact considerations. Electr World 77:49-53 Ap '67

CAPP, Grayson L. and others
Hemoglobin Portland 1: a new human hemoglobin unique in structure. bibliog Science 157:65-6 Jl 7 '67

CAPPADOCIA
Troglodytes; putting architecture underground. B. Rudofsky. il Horizon 9:28-39 Spr '67

CAPRI
Capri today. A. Waugh. Nat R 19:1076+ O 3 '67

CAPTAN
Fungicide danger. il Sci N 91:568 Je 17 '67

CAPTIVE; story. See Briskin, J.

CAPURRO, Daryl E.
Voice of a soldier in Vietnam; letter. U S News 62:112 Je 5 '67

CAR operating costs. See Automobiles—Cost of operation

CAR rallies. See Automobile driving—Competitions

CARACAS, Venezuela

Music

Caracas: production: Andrea Chénier, Tosca and Forza del destino. N. S. Koslovs. Opera N 31:32 Ja 28 '67

CARAMOOR festivals. See Music festivals—New York (state)

CARAS, Jimmy
Grandma shot out the lights. T. O'Leary. il Sports Illus 27:52-4 Jl 10 '67

CARAVACA, Josefina, and others
Prevention of induced atherosclerosis by peroxidase. bibliog Science 155:1284-7 Mr 10 '67

CARAVAN routes. See Trade routes

CARAWAY
Using caraway in sweet baking; with recipes. Sunset 139:206 O '67

CARBACHOL
Food and water intake after intrahypothalamic injections of carbachol in the rabbit. S. R. Sommer and others. bibliog il Science 156:983-4 My 19 '67

CARBODIIMIDE. See Imides

CARBOHYDRASES
Mechanisms of enzymatic bacteriolysis. J. L. Strominger and J. M. Ghuysen. bibliog il Science 156:213-21 Ap 14 '67

CARBOHYDRATES
Carbohydrate supply as a regulator of rat liver phosphoenolpyruvate carboxykinase activity. E. Shrago and others. bibliog il Science 158:1572-3 D 22 '67

CARBON

Isotopes

Atmospheric transfer of carbon-14: a problem in fungus translocation studies. C. P. P. Reid and F. W. Woods. bibliog il Science 157:712-13 Ag 11 '67
Carbon isotope composition of carbonaceous matter from the Precambrian of the Witwatersrand system. J. Hoefs and M. Schidlowski. bibliog il Science 155:1096-7 Mr 3 '67
Carbon-13, rich diagenetic carbonates in miocene formations of California and Oregon. K. J. Murata and others. bibliog il Science 156:1484-6 Je 16 '67
Deuterium isotope effect on carbon isotope fractionation in photosynthesis. R. A. Uphaus and J. J. Katz. bibliog il Science 155:324-5 Ja 20 '67
Variation in atmospheric carbon-14 activity relative to a sunspot-auroral solar index. J. R. Bray. bibliog il Science 156:640-2 My 5 '67
Variations in the isotopic composition of carbon in urban atmospheric carbon dioxide. L. Friedman and A. P. Irsa. bibliog il Science 158:263-4 O 13 '67

CARBON dioxide
Carbon dioxide, oxygen separation: facilitated transport of carbon dioxide across a liquid film. W. J. Ward, 3d. and W. L. Robb. bibliog il Science 156:1481-4 Je 16 '67
Carbon dioxide removal unit developed by Ham Standard. Tech W 20:29 Ap 10 '67
Control of spiracles in silk moths by oxygen and carbon dioxide. B. N. Burkett and H. A. Schneiderman. bibliog il Science 156:1604-6 Je 23 '67
Ethylene and carbon dioxide: mediation of hypocotyl hook-opening response. B. G. Kang and others. bibliog il Science 156:958-9 My 19 '67
Industrial emission of carbon dioxide in the United States: a projection; use of fossil fuels. F. A. Rohrman and others. bibliog il Science 156:931-2 My 19 '67
Variations in the isotopic composition of carbon in urban atmospheric carbon dioxide. L. Friedman and A. P. Irsa. bibliog il Science 158:263-4 O 13 '67

See also
Photosynthesis
Plants, Effect of carbon dioxide on

CARBON dioxide lasers. See Lasers

CARBON monoxide
Carbon monoxide: report on conference. J. R. Goldsmith. Science 157:842-4 Ag 18 '67

CARBONATES
Apatite crystallites: effects of carbonate on morphology. R. Z. LeGeros and others. bibliog il Science 155:1409-11 Mr 17 '67
See also
Lithium carbonate

CARBONIC acid
High-pressure dissociation of carbonic and boric acids. in seawater. C. Culberson and others. bibliog il Science 157:59-61 Jl 7 '67

CARBORUNDUM company
Carborundum philosophy of fit. W. H. Wendel. il Duns R 89:38 Ap '67

CARBOXYLIC acids
Isoprenoid and dicarboxylic acids isolated from Colorado Green River shale (Eocene) P. Haug and others. bibliog il Science 158:772-3 N 10 '67

CARBURETORS
Holley hints; four-barrel carburetors. J. Thawley. il Hot Rod 20:100-1 S '67
How to clean and adjust your carburetor. H. Carrier. il Pop Sci 191:123-6 S '67
Secondary chance; new Holley 3-barrel. J. McFarland. il Hot Rod 20:74 F '67

CARCASSONNE, France
At Carcassonne; overnight in the fourteenth century. il Sunset 138:66+ F '67

CARCINOGENIC substances. See Cancer producing substances

CARD sharping. See Cardsharping

CARDBOARD star; drama. See Phillips, O.

CARDENAS, Eduardo
Campus communism: Latin America's Trojan horse. Read Digest 90:92-6 Je '67

CARDENOLIDES. See Sterols

CARDIAC diseases. See Heart—Diseases

CARDIAC pacers. See Pacemaker, Artificial (heart)

CARDIAC rate meter. See Medical instruments and apparatus

CARDIAC resuscitation
Who shall die? il Newsweek 70:92 O 9 '67

CARDILLAC; opera. See Hindemith, P.

CARDINAL, Paul J. jr
Incinerator's role in sludge disposal; excerpt from paper presented before American society of sanitary engineering. Am City 82:108-10 D '67

CARDINALS
Bigger role for American Catholics? il U S News 62:16 Je 12 '67
Fine papal art of creating new cardinals. il Time 89:94 Je 9 '67
New American cardinals. America 116:824 Je 10 '67
New red hats. il Newsweek 69:85 Je 12 '67
See also
Popes—Election

CARDINALS (baseball) See Baseball clubs

CARDINALS (football club) See Football clubs

CARDINALS, College of. See Cardinals

CARDIOVASCULAR diseases. See Heart—Diseases

CARDON, Charlotte M.
World's biggest camera. Arch Forum 127:44-9 O '67

CARDS
Cardsharp, or vice versa; excerpt from The diary of the American revolution, 1775–1781, ed. by J. A. Scott. F. Moore. il Am Heritage 19:112 D '67
Gift from Hiroshige. D. Powills. il Hobbies 72:114-15+ D '67
Hobbies guide 1939-1966; alphabetical index of topics. D. Powills. il Hobbies 72:122-3 Je '67
Hobbies guide, 1939-1966; themes of Playing cards. D. Powills. il Hobbies 72:122-3 My '67
Playing cards. D. Powills. See issues of Hobbies

See also
Bridge (game)
Cardsharping
Chicago playing card collectors, incorporated
Gambling

Collectors and collecting
Collecting playing cards, by S. E. Mann. Review
  Hobbies il 71:126-7+ F '67. D. Powills
Pack of rebels. il Am Heritage 18:28-9 Je '67

History
Button collecting; the queen of hearts. D. F. Brown. il Hobbies 72:52+ S '67
Packs of fun, by B. Severn. Review
  Hobbies il 72:116-17+ S '67. D. Powills
Visit to Bielefeld; Playing card museum. F. G. Taylor. il Hobbies 72:122-3 Ag '67

CARDS, Advertising. See Advertising cards
CARDS, Catalog. See Catalog cards
CARDS, Greeting. See Greeting cards
CARDSHARPING
Story of an accusation, by T. Reese. Review
  Nation 205:251-2 S 18 '67. D. Cort
CARDULLO, Mario W.
Clergy manpower for the future. America 117:546-7+ N 11 '67
CAREER children. See Children, Professional
CAREER counseling. See Vocational guidance
CAREER girls. See Business and professional women
CAREERS. See Occupations
CAREERS, incorporated
Mr Brain drain. il Life 62:101-2 Mr 17 '67
CAREERS for women. See Woman—Occupations
CAREERS in agriculture. See Agriculture as a profession
CAREY, Donald E. See Myers, R. M. jt. auth.
CAREY, Ron
Laughing matter? por Newsweek 69:55 My 29 '67
CAREY, William D.
Roles of the Bureau of the budget; excerpts from address, September 30, 1966. Science 156:206-8+ Ap 14 '67
Toward a responsible future. por Parents Mag 43:32+ Ja '68
CAREY-Thomas award
Carey-Thomas award presentation. il Pub W 191:145 Je 5 '67
Creative publishing award goes to Braziller. Library J 92:2110 Je 1 '67
CARGO airlines. See Air freight service
CARGO handling. See Container system (freight handling); Freight handling
CARGO parachuting. See Parachuting, Cargo
CARGO planes, Military. See Airplanes, Military transport
CARGO terminals. See Airport buildings
CARGO vessels. See Freight vessels
CARIBBEAN cruises. See Cruising
CARIBBEAN fruit fly. See Fruit flies
CARIBBEAN green turtles. See Turtles, Green
CARIBBEAN REGION
Happy calypso of new semi-states. il Life 62:36-9 Mr 17 '67
Let's travel: Caribbean cruise. B. T. Blackwell. Mlle 65:195-9 My '67
New mini-states of the Caribbean. W. P. Carty and N. Raymond. Reporter 36:40-2 Mr 9 '67
Where the melting pot has melted. F. Morley. il Nations Bsns 55:23-4 Jl '67

See also
Air travel—Caribbean Region
Gardens—Caribbean Region
Investments, Foreign (in the Caribbean Region)
Puerto Rico
Real property—Caribbean Region
Tourist trade—Caribbean Region
West Indies

Description and travel
Caribbean vacation on a budget. R. J. Gunder. Redbook 128:48+ Mr '67
Chartering, Caribbean style. P. Smyth. il Motor B 120:26-8+ O '67
Favorite harbors of the Caribbean. J. C. Kozlick. il Motor B 121:97-101+ Ja '68
Islands down wind. E. Hiscock. il Yachting 121:58-60+ F '67
Tropical island vacations close to home. M. Vennum. il Bet Hom & Gard 45:143-6 O '67
Undiscovered Caribbean: eight islands in the sun. G. Astor and J. Shepherd. il Look 31:60-6+ F 21 '67
Well worth the trip. M. Gough. House B 109:161 F '67
CARIBOU hunting
Footrace with a caribou. D. Cape. il Outdoor Life 140:48-9+ S '67
Instant record; majestic Newfoundland bull. B. Knutson. il Outdoor Life 140:20-3+ Jl '67
CARICATURES and cartoons
Bestiary. W. Steig. New Yorker 43:52-3 Mr 11 '67
Feiffer. J. Feiffer. See issues of New republic
Inept heroes, winners at last; C. M. Schulz's Peanuts characters; with report by J. Borgzinner. il Life 62:74-8+ Mr 17 '67
Letter from the publisher; political jockeys on Time's cover. J. R. Shepley. Time 89:25 Ap 14 '67
Some cartoons of 1967. Nation 206:14-15 Ja 1 '68
Wordless workshop. R. Doty. See issues of Popular science monthly
See also
Johnson, L. B.—Caricatures and cartoons
Vietnamese war, 1957- —Caricatures and cartoons
CARINGELLA, Charles
Build the beginner's FET Regen receiver. Pop Electr 27:40-6+ S '67
CARL, Herbert A. See Fry, R. M.; Price, P. P. jt. auths.
CARLETON, Charles S. See Arberg, H. W. jt. auth.
CARLETON, R. Milton
Annual vines. Horticulture 45:26-7+ F '67
Equipment, the extra hand that helps you; excerpt from Vegetables for today's gardens. Home Gard 54:58-9+ Mr '67
Truth about organic gardening. Pop Gard 18:12-13+ My '67
CARLETON, William G.
Cultural roots of American law enforcement. bibliog f Cur Hist 53:1-7+ Jl '67
CARLEY, Austin J.
Theodor Binder: Peru's Albert Schweitzer. Américas 19:1-7 Mr '67
CARLINSKY, Dan, and Lefkowitz, Bernard
Painting the ocean red, etc. at Columbia university. Esquire 68:99+ S '67
CARLISI, Catherine
Prayer of a retarded child; poem. Cath World 205:236 Jl '67
CARLISLE, Jon. See Carlisle, N. jt. auth.
CARLISLE, Kitty
To tell the truth; interview, ed. by R. D. Daniels. por Opera N 31:26 Ja 7 '67
CARLISLE, Norman, and Carlisle, Jon
Project Gasbuggy. Pop Mech 128:102-5+ S '67
CARLISLE, Thomas John
Holy night; poem. America 117:764 D 23 '67
Promised land; poem. Sat R 50:17 Ag 19 '67
Reprimand; poem. Christian Cent 84:719 My 31 '67
With Dickens; poem. Sat R 50:54 My 6 '67
CARLSBAD World series race. See Automobile racing
CARLSON, Carol
From Three afternoons; poem. Mlle 66:124 N '67
CARLSON, Donald L.
Common-sense design of transistor amplifiers. Electr World 77:48-50+ Je '67
CARLSON, Elliot
Games in the classroom. Sat R 50:62-4+ Ap 15 '67
CARLSON, James E.
Current trends in construction. Arch Rec 142:88 N '67
CARLSON, Leland H.
(comp) Articles and other books received; British Commonwealth and Ireland. See issues of American historical review
CARLSON, Stanley D. and others
Vitamin A deficiency: effect on retinal structure of the moth manduca sexta. bibliog Science 158:268-70 O 13 '67

CARLSON, Warren, family
They have joy to spare, and share. J. Gillies.
il Farm J 91:54-5 D '67
CARLSSON, Gösta
Swedish character in the twentieth century.
bibliog f Ann Am Acad 370:92-8 Mr '67
CARMEL Bach festival. See Bach festivals
CARMEN; opera. See Bizet, G.
CARMER, Carl
This hollowed-out ground. Am Heritage 18:
58-9+ Je '67
CARMICAL, J. H.
Unlocking oil from Canada's tar sands; re-
print. Sci Digest 61:56-9 Je '67
CARMICHAEL, Stokely
Black mischief. il por Newsweek 70:58 N 27
'67
Go for the honkies. Newsweek 69:28 Ap 24
'67
Rising demand: crack down on Carmichael.
il pors U S News 63:6-7 D 25 '67
Road to hell. il por Time 90:28 D 15 '67
We're going to shoot the cops. por U S News
62:10 My 29 '67
Which way for the Negro? il por Newsweek
69:27-8+ My 15 '67
Whip of black power; with report by G.
Parks. il pors Life 62:76A-78+ My 19 '67
—and Hamilton, Charles
Dynamite; excerpt from Black power; the
politics of liberation in America. Atlan 220:
98-102 O '67
CARMICHEL, Jim
Watauga walleyes. Field & S 72:128-31+ Je
'67
CARNE seca. See Cookery, Mexican
CARNEGIE corporation of New York
Antidote to boredom; report on educational
television. New Repub 156:7-8 F 11 '67
Blueprint for public TV. il Newsweek 69:89
F 6 '67
Boost for poor brother; ETV. Time 89:55 F 3
'67
Candid camera on TV; report on educational
television. Nation 204:324 Mr 13 '67
Carnegie report urges national ETV setup.
Sr Schol 90:sup4 F 10 '67
Clark Kerr heads study of U.S. higher edu-
cation. Pub W 191:47 F 6 '67
Closing the TV quality gap. R. L. Tobin.
Sat R 50:73-4+ Ap 8 '67
Postman is the proctor for millions of corre-
spondence students; recent study. B. H.
Pearse. il Am Ed 3:10-12 F '67
Public television. J. McLaughlin. America
116:567 Ap 15 '67
Public TV: a wasteland oasis. Life 62:4 F 17
'67
Public TV around the corner? concerning re-
port of Carnegie commission on educational
TV. il U S News 62:91 Mr 13 '67
CARNEGIE foundation for the advancement
of teaching
Six decades of the Carnegie foundation. Sch
& Soc 95:141+ Mr 4 '67
CARNEGIE institute of technology, Pittsburgh
Funds for the younger faculty. Sch & Soc
95:170 Mr 18 '67
CARNEGIE international exhibition of art.
See Art—Exhibitions
CARNEGIE university, Pittsburgh
Carnegie university: new institution emerging
in Pittsburgh. B. Nelson. il Science 155:673-
6 F 10 '67
CARNELL, Edward John
Edward John Carnell: an evaluation. A. B.
Haines. Christian Cent 84:751 Je 7 '67
Obituary
Christian Cent 84:612 My 10 '67
CARNER, Charles
Almost-man: the doctor trainer. Todays
Health 45:16-18 My '67
Choosing your psychiatrist. Todays Health
45:30-3 Jl '67
Don't be surprised by after-baby blues. To-
days Health 45:32-5 D '67
Surprise inside: strange effects of drugs.
Todays Health 45:56-9+ Ap '67
Tomorrow's hospitals of today. Todays
Health 45:30-7 Mr '67
What's new in adoption? bibliog Todays
Health 45:44-7+ Ag '67
CARNER, Donald C.
Making hospitals more efficient, and pro-
ficient. Todays Health 45:88+ Mr '67
CARNETT, George S.
Is our math inferior? Am Ed 3:1-3 Mr '67
CARNEY, Christin
Perfect wife. por Redbook 129:12+ S '67
CARNIVALS
Lot of quarters; James E. Strates carnival.
W. K. Zinsser. il Look 31:18 S 5 '67

School carnivals in Honolulu. il Sunset 138:23
F '67
Time to think winter; Quebec winter carnival.
L. Barry. il Pop Phot 61:26+ O '67
CARNIVORA
Predators and scavengers; carnivores of
Ngorongoro Crater in Africa. R. D. Estes. il
Natur Hist 76:20-9 F; 38-47 Mr '67
CAROB
Behind them is a carob screen. il Sunset
139:114 Ag '67
CARONI RIVER
Rivers in the making. H. F. Garner. il Sci
Am 216:84-8+ Ap '67
CAROTENE
Annals of medicine; the orange man; first re-
corded victim or carotenemia-lycopenemia,
through excessive eating of carrots and
tomatoes. B. Roueché. New Yorker 43:110+
My 27 '67
CAROTENOIDS
Carotenoid biosynthesis in rhodospirillum
rubrum; effect of pteridine inhibitor. N. A.
Nugent and R. C. Fuller. bibliog il Science
158:922-4 N 17 '67
CAROTID bodies
5-Hydroxytryptamine in the carotid body of
the cat. S. R. Chiocchio and others. bibliog
il Science 158:790-1 N 10 '67
CAROUSEL; musical comedy. See Musical com-
edies, revues, etc.—Criticisms, plots, etc.
CAROUSEL inertial navigation system. See In-
ertial guidance systems
CARP, Frances M.
Retirement crisis. Science 157:102-3 Jl 7 '67
CARP fishing
Hottest fly fishing anywhere; Lake Michigan.
M. Ellis il Field & S 72:50-1+ Jl '67
CARPENTER, Clifford E.
Floating Smithsonian. Yachting 122:57+ Jl
'67
CARPENTER, Curt
Best ways to hunt rabbits East to West.
Field & S 72:46-7+ Ja '68
CARPENTER, Mrs Francis
Flowering of a modern manoir. J. L. Hendrix.
il House B 109:130-7+ My '67
CARPENTER, Lois
Commitment; poem. Farm J 91:44 N '67
CARPENTRY
Strange tools and exotic secrets of Japanese
carpentry. il Pop Sci 190:138-40 Ja '67
See also
Joints (carpentry)
CARPET beetles
Sex attractant of the black carpet beetle.
R. M. Silverstein and others. bibliog il
Science 157:85-7 Jl 7 '67
CARPET underlays. See Rug pads
CARPETS, Outdoor. See Rugs and carpets,
Outdoor
CARPETS. See Rugs and carpets
CARPETS for libraries. See Library furniture
and equipment
CARPORTS. See Garages
CARR, Archie
Caribbean green turtle, imperiled gift of the
sea. pors Nat Geog Mag 131:876-90 Je '67
100 turtle eggs; excerpts from So excellent
a fishe; with biographical sketch. Natur
Hist 76:6, 46-51 Ag; 40-3+ O '67
CARR, Donald Eaton
Case for the electric automobile. Atlan 219:
92-5 Je '67
Report: science: insects, animals, and man.
Atlan 219:31-3 My '67
CARR, John Dickson
Murder fancier recommends. Harper 235:90-2
Jl '67
CARR, William George
Century of cooperation. NEA J 56:61-2 S '67
about
Tributes to William G. Carr; symposium. por
NEA J 56:8-11 My '67
CARRELS, Study. See School libraries
CARREÑO, Virginia, pseud.
Hernandarias. Américas 19:27-35 My '67
CARRICK, Robert W.
Pollution predicament. Yachting 121:112+ Ja
'67
Reception committee for the Dame. Motor B
120:34-5+ Ag '67
Surveying: truth or consequences. Yachting
121:70-2+ Ap '67
Whaler-sailer? Yachting 123:106-8+ Ja '68
CARRICKNABAUNA (dramatic reading) See
Dramatic readings
CARRIER, Herb
ABCs of keeping your car in tune. See issues
of Popular science monthly

CARRIER, Robert
Connoisseur's cookbook; excerpts. por Ladies
Home J 84:88-9+ D '67
about
Cook of the walk. R. A. Sokolov. il por
Newsweek 70:102+ D 4 '67
CARRIER pigeons. See Pigeons
CARRIER shell. See Mollusks
CARRIERS
See also
Transportation
CARRIERS, Aircraft. See Aircraft carriers
CARRIERS of Infection
See also
Animals as carriers of infection
CARRIGHAR, Sally
War is not in our genes. N Y Times Mag
p74-5+ S 10; 40 O 22 '67
CARRIKER, Melbourne R. and others
Gastropod urosalpinx: pH of accessory boring
organ while boring. bibliog Science 158:
920-2 N 17 '67
CARRIÓN, Arturo Morales-. See Morales-Car-
rión, A.
CARRITT, D. E. See Green, E. J. jt. auth.
CARROL, Regina
Showing off The show-offs; V. H. Swisher. il
pors Dance Mag 41:24-5+ My '67
CARROLL, Corky
Surfmanship and salesmanship. R. Sherrill.
il por N Y Times Mag p 12-14+ Jl 16 '67
CARROLL, Diahann
Gallic-American spectacular. il pors Ebony
22:36+ Ap '67
CARROLL, Harold W. and Kimeldorf, D. J.
Protection through parabiosis against the
lethal effects of exposure to large doses of
X-rays. bibliog Science 156:954-5; 157:582
My 19, Ag 4 '67
CARROLL, J. Speed
Bright boy from Yazoo. New Repub 157:32-4
N 18 '67
CARROLL, James
Matthew ten, twenty-three; poem. Cath World
205:106 My '67
CARROLL, James D.
Process values of university research. bibliog
Science 158:1019-24 N 24 '67
CARROLL, James J.
Second look at black nationalism. America
117:84-5 Jl 22 '67
CARROLL, John
Enchanted bicycle; drama. Plays 27:83-8 O
'67
CARROLL, Joseph
Gentle Irish. Sports Illus 27:40-6+ Ag 28 '67
CARROLL, Mark
Notes on Turkish publishing; summary of
address. Pub W 192:31 Jl 24 '67
CARROLL, Robert L. See Baird, D. jt. auth.
CARROLL, Ronald L.
Electronic ignition systems. Electr World 77:
47-9+ F '67
New approach to engine tachometers. Electr
World 78:71 S '67
CARROLL, Thomas Sylvester
Carroll of lever brothers. por Fortune 75:51
Ap '67
CARRUTH, Eleanore
Great fashion explosion. Fortune 76:162-5+
O '67
CARRUTH, Hayden
Four poets. Poetry 111:43-6 O '67
Louis Zukofsky. Poetry 110:420-2 S '67
Mystical candor. Nation 205:473-4 N 6 '67
On a picture of Ezra Pound. Poetry 110:103-5
My '67
Opposite methods. Poetry 109:400-1 Mr '67
Poetry of abstraction. Poetry 110:184-6 Je '67
Spring 1967; poem. Nation 205:214 S 11 '67
To solve experience. Poetry 109:267 Ja '67
CARS (automobiles) See Automobiles
CARSE, James P.
Interracial marriage; a Christian view. Chris-
tian Cent 84:779-82 Je 14 '67
CARSON, David
Comparative marketing, a new-old aid. bib-
liog Harvard Bsns R 45:22-4+ My '67
CARSON, Gerald
Goggles & side curtains. Am Heritage 18:32-
9+ Ap '67
Great meddler. Am Heritage 19:28-33+ D '67
Kindness and cruelty in Great Britain; with
biographical sketch. por Natur Hist 76:4-
6+ bibliog(p 105) D '67
CARSON, Mrs Gerald
N.Y. trustee disqualified after eight years
service. Library J 93:22 Ja 1 '68
CARSON, John B.
When giving flowers. Horticulture 45:46 N '67

CARSON, Johnny
Misery is a blind date; excerpts. McCalls
94:56 S '67
Redbook dialogue. por Redbook 130:74-5+
N '67
Trouble with $1,500,000 a year; interview, ed.
by B. Walters. il por Ladies Home J 84:
168+ O '67
about
Here's Johnny. Newsweek 69:114 My 8 '67
Here's Johnny. il Time 89:104 Ap 28 '67
Johnny Carson: the battle for TV's midnight
millions. H Van Horne. il pors Look 31:78-
9+ Jl 11 '67
Midnight idol. il pors Time 89:104-6+ My
19 '67; Same abr. with title Johnny Car-
son: TV's midnight idol. Read Digest 91:
153-7 Ag '67
Prince of wails. il por Time 89:88 Ap 14 '67
Vice-President; appearance on Tonight show
and meeting with participants of Double
discovery. New Yorker 43:23-5 Ag 12 '67
Wherrrr's Johnny? il por Newsweek 69:119
Ap 17 '67
CARTAGENA, Colombia
Cartagena on the Spanish Main. R. Atcheson.
il Holiday 43:20+ Ja '68
For centuries it was Spain's new world
stronghold. il Sunset 138:65 Ap '67
Where pirates roamed. G. Arango. il Améri-
cas 19:38-42 Ag '67
CARTELS, International. See Trusts, Indus-
trial—International trusts
CARTER, Barbara
FIGHT against Kodak. Reporter 36:28-31
Ap 20 '67
Junior colleges are blooming in the sunshine
state. NEA J 56:22-4 My '67
CARTER, Carolyn
Bellingrath gardens. Home Gard 54:23-5 N
'67
CARTER, Chester C.
Washington's red carpet diplomat. il pors
Ebony 22:104-6+ Je '67
CARTER, Edward William
California's tailor-made store chain. il por
Bsns W p88-90+ My 27 '67
CARTER, Elliott, 1908-
Music; new piano concerto. B. Boretz.
Nation 204:445-6 Ap 3 '67
CARTER, Everitt A.
Adventures of Nick Carter. T. J. Murray. por
Duns R 89:50-2+ Ap '67
CARTER, Gwendolen M.
African bookshelf. Nation 205:90-2 Jl 31 '67
CARTER, Kenneth LeMesurier
Tax plan for Canada switches the burden.
il por Bsns W p40 Mr 4 '67
Tax reform; Canada shows the way. D. G. M.
Coxe. il Nat R 19:688-90 Je 27 '67
CARTER, Manfred A.
Dice of Villon; poem. Christian Cent 84:1157
S 13 '67
Parade of gods; poem. Christian Cent 84:
1348 O 25 '67
CARTER, Mary
Polar zone; story. McCalls 94:84-5 Jl '67
Sound and light; story. McCalls 95:88-9 O '67
CARTER, Purvis M.
Robert Lloyd Smith and the Farmers' im-
provement society, a self-help movement in
Texas. bibliog Negro Hist Bul 29:175-6 Fall
'66
CARTER, Robert L.
School integration is still on the agenda. Sat
R 50:70-2+ O 21 '67
CARTER, Sara Lou Harris, lady
Fruitful life of Lady Carter. il pors Ebony
22:40-2+ Jl '67
CARTER, Thomas Henry
Cultural shock. Newsweek 70:30 O 2 '67
CARTER, William A. and Lery, H. B.
Ribosomes: effect of interferon on their in-
teraction with rapidly labeled cellular and
viral RNA's. bibliog Science 155:1254-7 Mr
10 '67
CARTERETTE, Edward C. and Jones, M. H.
Visual and auditory information processing in
children and adults. bibliog Science 156:986-8
My 19 '67
CARTEY, Wilfred
Dawn, the totem, the drums. Commonweal
86:227-30 My 12 '67
CARTHEW, Anthony
Double-think, Egyptian style. N Y Times
Mag p 19-21+ Ag 20 '67
Plight of tourist guide no. 25. Sat R 50:42-3
O 14 '67
There is no false courage left in Egypt. N Y
Times Mag p45-7+ D 3 '67
Through darkest America with camera and
checkbook. N Y Times Mag p30-1+ Ag 27
'67

CARTIER, John O.
Don't bet on a muskie. Outdoor Life 139:50-1+ Je '67
Fall steelheads are back. Outdoor Life 140:58-9+ O '67
Spring specktacular. Outdoor Life 139:76-8+ My '67
(comp) That's where I want to fish. Outdoor Life 139:84-7 Ap '67
We wanted a western hunt. pors Outdoor Life 140:29-31+ S '67
White bass fever in the Bluegrass. por Outdoor Life 139:74-5+ Ap '67

CARTIER, Warren A.
Cochise choice. Outdoor Life 140:48-51+ O '67

CARTIER-BRESSON, Henri
People of a proud land; photographs. Holiday 42:66-73 D '67

about

Cartier-Bresson today. B. Schwalberg; D. Vestal; M. Korda. il Pop Phot 60:108-9+ My '67
Henri Cartier-Bresson's Japan. il Look 31:28-33 F 7 '67

CARTILAGE
Synovial cell synthesis of a substance immunologically like cartilage proteinpolysaccharide. R. Janis and others. bibliog il Science 158:1464-7 D 15 '67

CARTOGRAPHY
Regional cartographic conference; fifth United Nations regional cartographic conference for Asia and the Far East. UN Mo Chron 4:65-6 Ap '67

CARTON, Aaron S.
Poverty programs, civil rights, and the American school. Sch & Soc 95:108-9 F 18 '67

CARTONNAGE. See Paper work

CARTOON drawing. See Drawing

CARTOONISTS
See also
Caricatures and cartoons

CARTOONS. See Caricatures and cartoons

CARTRIDGE, Phonograph. See Phonograph—Pickup

CARTRIDGE loaded tape. See Magnetic tape

CARTRIDGES
Long pants for the 6 mm.'s. W. Page. il Field & S 71:120-4 F '67
Mild cartridges. J. O'Connor. il Outdoor Life 139:122+ Ap '67
No flowers, please W. Page il Field & S 72:88-91 Jl 67
Reload your ammunition and save. il Am City 82:57 D '67
The .270 in Africa. J. O'Connor. il Outdoor Life 139:118-22 Mr '67

CARTRIDGES, Stereo. See Phonograph—Stereophonic pickup

CARTS
Wheels in the garden. il Sunset 138:78-9 Je '67

CARTS, Serving. See Serving carts

CARTWRIGHT, Gary
Great chili championship fix. Sports Illus 27:80-2+ D 11 '67

CARTY, Winthrop P. and Raymond, Nicholas
New mini-states of the Caribbean. Reporter 36:40-2 Mr 9 '67
—See Raymond, N. jt. auth.

CARUBELLI, R. and Griffin, M. J.
Sialic acid in HeLa cells: effect of hydrocortisone. bibliog Science 157:693-4 Ag 11 '67

CARUSO, Mike
Mighty mouse leads the way. G. Ronberg. il por Sports Illus 26:59-60 F 20 '67

CARUSO, Nino
Workshop: expanded polystyrene for ceramic production. Craft Horiz 27:34-5 S '67

CARVER, George Washington
George Washington Carver; a boy who wished to know why. R. L. Love. por Negro Hist Bul 30:13-15 Ja; 15-18 F; 15-19 Mr '67

CARVEYOR. See Railroads—Passenger traffic

CARVING (meat, etc)
Cooking lesson: how to carve roasts. il Am Home 70:78+ D '67
How to carve a ham. il Bet Hom & Gard 45:80 D '67
Meet our master chef. V. T. Habeeb. il Am Home 70:104-5 Jl '67
Turkey. il Redbook 130:102-4 N '67

CASALS, Pablo
Tribute to Pablo Casals. H. H. Humphrey. il por Hi Fi 17:MA4 Ap '67

CASAMASSIMA, Emanuele
Library crisis in Italy. A. T. Hamlin. il Library J 92:2516-22 Jl '67

CASANOVA DE SEINGALT, Giacomo Girolamo
Venetian Don Juan. B. Grebanier. Sat R 50:38-9 O 21 '67

CASCADE particles. See Particles (nuclear physics)

CASCADE RANGE
Classic Cascades wilderness walk. il Sunset 139:31-2 Ag '67
Fight for America's Alps; preserving the North Cascades in Washington. P. Brooks. il Atlan 219:87-90+ F '67; Same abr. Read Digest 90:104-8 My '67
North Cascades. S. F. Arno. il Nat Parks Mag 41:4-9 Je '67
Park for the North Cascades? meeting the test of national park eligibility. C. F. Brockman; reply. S. F. Arno. Am For 73:3-4 Ja '67

CASCODE amplifiers. See Amplifiers

CASE, Clifford Philip
Why unthinkable? Nation 204:482-3 Ap 17 '67

CASE, Jay
Pain in Spain. Commonweal 85:561-3 F 17 '67

CASE method
Group case study method in political education. R. Y. Fluno. il Sch & Soc 95:188-91 Mr 18 '67

CASES, Tool. See Tool boxes, racks, etc.

CASEWIT, Curtis W.
New exhilaration: skiing at sixty! Travel 127:37-9 F '67
We take to the hills. Parents Mag 42:48-9+ Ag '67

CASEY, Francis J.
Stationary melter licks snow-disposal problem. Am City 82:118+ F '67

CASEY, Frank J.
When leasing autos for municipal use. Am City 82:153-4 F '67

CASEY, Genevieve M.
Michigan: opening up resources. por Library J 92:2523-5 Jl '67

CASEY, Robert Randolph
Excerpt from remarks, March 20, 1967. Cong Digest 46:219+ Ag '67

CASEY at the bat (ballad) See Ballads, American

CASH, Wilbur Joseph
W. J. Cash, by J. L. Morrison. Review New Repub 157:28-30 D 9 '67. C. V. Woodward

CASPER, Billy
Beating seventeen greens and a brown. A Wright. il Sports Illus 27:46-7 Jl 10 '67

CASPI, E. and Lewis, D. O.
Progesterone: its possible role in the biosynthesis of cardenolides in digitalis lanata. bibliog Science 156:519-20 Ap 28 '67

CASS, James
Fordham university: renaissance in the Bronx. Sat R 50:52-4+ Je 17 '67
—See Woodring, P. jt. ed.

CASSEBEER, F. W.
Siberian iris. il Horticulture 45:22-5+ Jl '67

CASSELL, Frank H.
Development of jobs; address, September 2, 1967. bibliog f Vital Speeches 34:59-64 N 1 '67
Manpower planning; address, May 9, 1967. Vital Speeches 33:559-65 Jl 1 '67

CASSEM, N. H.
Black, green and red rebellions. America 118:33-5 Ja 13 '68

CASSEROLE cookery
Collector's casseroles; with recipes. il McCalls 95:116-17+ O '67
Cooking for two. il Bet Hom & Gard 45:103-4 Mr '67
Creative casseroles make quick, tasty meals; with recipes. G. Maddox. il Todays Health 45:32-7 O '67
From Persia, two splendid casseroles. Sunset 138:181+ Ap '67
Our very favorite casseroles. R. Holmberg. il Bet Hom & Gard 45:78-83+ F '67
Successful recipes, main dish casseroles. il Suc Farm 65:85-6 Ap '67

CASSIDY, Charles E.
In a class by themselves. Sr Schol 90:sup 10-11 Ap 14 '67

CASSIDY, Claudia
Lyric opera wins by a Chicago margin. Sat R 51:100-1 Ja 13 '68

CASSIDY, William A.
Meteorite field studies at Campo del Cielo. il Sky & Tel 34:4-10 Jl '67

CASSIRER, Henry R.
Television's role in education. Sch & Soc 95:354-8 O 14 '67

CASSITY, Turner
Art in transition. L. Lieberman. Poetry 109: 396-7 Mr '67
CASTAWAYS
See also
Survival (after airplane accidents, shipwrecks, etc)
CASTEAU, Belgium
SHAPE takes shape; new headquarters. M. Mok. il Life 62:105-6+ Je 9 '67
CASTELLO BRANCO, Humberto
Dictatorial powers? por Newsweek 69:48+ Ja 30 '67
Price of unpopularity. Time 90:30 Jl 28 '67
Quiet revolution. J. W. F. Dulles. Nat R 19:299-300 Mr 21 '67
CASTILLO, Vicente Levi. See Levi Castillo, V.
CASTING (fishing)
Pause that catches. G. Heinold. il Outdoor Life 140:98-100 D '67
Placing the cast. A. J. McClane. il Field & S 72:104-6 S '67
See also
Fly casting
CASTING (sculpture)
Sandcasting. B. E. Johnson. il Sch Arts 66: 18-20 Je '67
CASTING, Continuous. See Continuous casting
CASTING, Precision. See Lost wax process
CASTING molds. See Molds (for casting)
CASTLE, Frederick C.
History by contact. Art N 66:48-51+ O '67
What's that, the '68 Stella? wow! Art N 66: 46-7+ Ja '68
CASTLE, Wendell
Wood: George Sugarman. Craft Horiz 27: 30-3 Mr '67
CASTLE HARBOUR Islands. See Bermuda
CASTLEFORD pottery. See Pottery, English
CASTLES
Ancient castles; post cards. B. Finnegan il Hobbies 72:119-21 D '67
At Schloss Fasanerie; centuries of royal family treasure in Germany. V. Lawford. il Vogue 150:142-9+ O 15 '67
Castle hunting in little England beyond Wales. il House & Gard 131:196-8 Ap '67
Ruspolis; castle. Vignanello. il Vogue 150: 322-5 S 1 '67
We bought a very small castle, then the fun began. H. M. Baker. il House & Gard 131: 142-5 Ap '67
CASTRATION
See also
Skoptsi
CASTRO, Fidel
My curious row with Fidel; interview, ed. by L. Bergquist. Look 31:50-1 D 12 '67

about
Anniversary song. por Newsweek 70:47 Ag 7 '67
Anniversary thoughts. por Newsweek 71:38+ Ja 15 '68
Authors & editors; concerning L. Lockwood's book. il por Pub W 191:21 My 1 '67
Castro revolution, export model. Life 63:4 Ag 11 '67
Castro's Cuba, Cuba's Fidel, by L. Lockwood. Review
Sat R 50:27-8 Jl 29 '67. S. Halper
Fidel Castro's comeback; where it's headed. il por U S News 63:86-7 Ag 21 '67
History and Herbert Matthews. Nat R 19: 1004-5 S 19 '67
Is Castro behind guerrilla war in U.S. cities? il U S News 63:23-5 Ag 14 '67
Playing to the crowd. Newsweek 70:33-4 Ag 21 '67
Reporting on Cuba J. Yglesias. New Repub 157:23-6 Jl 8 '67
What Castro is plotting: the fight for a hemisphere. il por U S News 63:42-3 O 9 '67
CASTRO, José R.
BCIE: five years of progress. Américas 19:28-31 Ag '67
CASUALTIES. See Vietnamese war, 1957- — Casualties
CAT tails. See Cattails
CATA, Alfonso
Amelia and YASNY. A. Fatt. il por Dance Mag 41:54-5 O '67
ÇATAL Hüyük excavations. See Turkey—Antiquities
CATALINA ISLAND. See Santa Catalina Island
CATALOG cards
LC calls for proposals for new card system. Library J 92:4325-6 D 1 '67

Library of Congress cards to segment Dewey numbers. Library J 92:176 Ja 15 '67
Three A/V companies begin to issue catalog cards: McGraw-Hill films, Encyclopaedia Britannica films, and Tweedy transparencies. Library J 92:1985-6 My 15 '67
CATALOG codes. See Cataloging
CATALOG houses. See Mail order business
CATALOGING
LC duplicating two machine-readable cataloging files. E. Hamer and A. McCormick. ALA Bul 61:1295 D '67
Marc II cataloging format recommended as standard. Library J 93:136 Ja 15 '68
Three A/V companies begin to issue catalog cards: McGraw-Hill films, Encyclopaedia Britannica films, and Tweedy transparencies. Library J 92:1985-6 My 15 '67
See also
Subject headings

Study and teaching
Automation and authority vs. autonomy. J. E. Daily. il Library J 92:3606-9 O 15 '67; Reply. O. K. Ruxin. 93:127 Ja 15 '68
Map librarianship. W. W. Ristow. bibliog il Library J 92:3610-14 O 15 '67
CATALOGS, College. See College catalogs
CATALOGS, Mail order
See also
Mail order business

Anecdotes, facetiae, satire, etc.
Lower forty sports catalogue. C. Ford. il Field & S 71:8+ F '67
CATALOGS, Publishers
Sex in the syllabus; concerning the Grove press school and college catalog. J. H. Plumb. Sat R 50:27-8 Mr 25 '67; Reply. B. Rosset. 50:26 Ap 29 '67
CATALOGS, Seed and plant
Catalogs. R. G. Hands. Horticulture 45:50+ D '67
Dreambooks for gardeners. L. Bell. il House B 109:126-7+ Ja '67
Shop here for best plants of 1968. Home Gard 54:50-7 D '67
CATALOGS, Star. See Stars—Catalogs
CATALONIAN museum of fine arts. See Barcelona—Galleries and museums
CATALYSIS
Molecular uniformity in biological catalyses. W. D. McElroy and others. bibliog il Science 157:150-60 Jl 14 '67
CATAMARANS
Are two hulls better than one? B. Kocivar. il Look 31:95-7 Je 13 '67
Car propels homemade catamaran. il Pop Sci 191:100-1 D '67
Chris Wilson on spinnakers for small catamarans; excerpt from The international book of catamarans and trimarans. C. Wilson. il Yachting 121:48-9+ Mr '67
CATASTROPHES. See Disasters
CATCH a falling star; story. See Fritz, J.
CATCH me a star; story. See Deal, B. H.
CATECHISMS
See also
Catholic church—Catechisms
CATECHOLAMINES
Brain catecholamines: relation to defense reaction evoked by acute brainstem transection in cat. D. J. Reis and others. bibliog il Science 156:1768-70 Je 30 '67
Inhibition of lipolytic action of growth hormone and glucocorticoid by ultraviolet and X-radiation. J. N. Fain. bibliog il Science 157:1062-4 S 1 '67
See also
Dopamine
CATERERS and catering
America's huge catered affair. il Newsweek 70:60-2 S 4 '67
Dishing up 5-million meals every week; Saga administration corp. il Bsns W p 188-90 My 6 '67
Money in the kitchen: dial-a-dinner; with recipes. il Seventeen 26:72-3+ Jl '67
Overheard in surburbia; caterer. B. Rollin. Look 31:M27 My 16 '67
Party giving? relax and hire a manager. Bsns W p 135-6 D 2 '67
CATERING. See Caterers and catering
CATERPILLAR tractor company
Agile Cat. il Time 90:75 Jl 7 '67
Guaranteed wage catches on: the way it will work. U S News 63:84+ N 6 '67

CATERPILLARS
Butterflies and plants. P. R. Ehrlich and P.
H. Raven. il Sci Am 216:104-11+ Je '67
See also
Moths

CATFISH fishing
Cats that swim. J. B Kemmerer. Field & S
72:30-1+ Jl '67

CATHA edulis. See Kat

CATHEDRAL of Christ the King. See Liverpool
—Cathedral of Christ the King

CATHEDRAL of St John the Divine. See New
York (city)—St John the Divine, Cathedral
of

CATHEDRALS
England
See also
Liverpool—Cathedral of Christ the King

United States
Pros & cons of cathedrals. il Time 91:49 Ja 12
'68

CATHER, Willa
Excerpts from The kingdom of art: Willa
Cather's first principles and critical statements, 1893-1896. por Horizon 9:116-19 Spr
'67

CATHODE ray tubes
Cathode ray display speeds SRAM data;
USAF short-range attack missile. R. G.
O'Lone. il Aviation W 86:74-5+ Mr 13 '67
New developments in CRT phosphors. J. R.
Collins. il Electr World 77:48-52+ Ja '67
See also
Television camera tubes

CATHOLIC action
See also
Laity—Catholic church

CATHOLIC association for International peace
CAIP what is its future? P. W. McCloskey.
Commonweal 87:194-5 N 17 '67
News and views. J. Deedy. Commonweal 86:
596 S 29 '67; Reply. W. V. O'Brien. 87:67+
O 20 '67

CATHOLIC authors
See also
Catholic historians

CATHOLIC church
Aggiornamento. See issues of Catholic world
Anger of a rebel. Time 90:50 Jl 7 '67
Are you a Catholic? questioning by a Protes-
tant philosopher. F. Sontag. America 117:
502-5 N 4 '67; Discussion. 118:13-16 Ja 6 '68
Arrogant, smug, angry. K. L. Woodward. il
Newsweek 69:69 Je 26 '67
Ascent to God after the council. H. F. Smith.
America 116:283-5 F 25 '67
Catholic crisis; whole nature of leadership.
E. J. Hughes. Newsweek 69:21 Mr 6 '67
Catholic dilemma. il Newsweek 69:75 Mr 20 '67
Changing law in a changing church. P. M.
Shannon. America 116:248-50 F 18 '67
Church and sect. D. Callahan. Commonweal
87:140-3 N 3 '67; Discussion. 87:317-18 D
1 '67
Concerning an ultimate question. America
116:274-5 F 25 '67
Corrupt church; concerning editorial in New
blackfriars. Commonweal 85:612 Mr 3 '67;
Discussion. 86:3+, 66-8 Mr 24-31 '67
Defection: protest or treason? F. X. Murphy;
discussion. America 116:198-9 F 11 '67
Faith and new opinions. A. Dulles. America
117:479 O 28 '67
Have we loved the past too long? L. Dewart;
discussion. America 116:70-2, 424-8+ Ja 21,
Mr 25 '67
In defense of institutions. E. Fontinell. il
America 116:314-16 Mr 4 '67
Instant renewal? J. O'Gara. Commonweal 86:
112 Ap 14 '67
Jacques Maritain on aggiornamento. R. A.
Graham. America 116:348-9 Mr 11 '67
Jesus and the church. J. M. Cameron. Com-
monweal 87:269-74 N 24 '67
Laughing matter? church as subject for
comedians. il Newsweek 69:55 My 29 '67
Let's be honest about the canon. R. L. Mor-
gan. Christian Cent 84:717-19 My 31 '67;
Discussion. 84:1068-9 Ag 23 '67
Loss to us all; the Charles Davis case. R. M.
Brown. Commonweal 86:92-4 Ap 7 '67
McCabe affair; after Charles Davis; with
editorial comment. J. M. Cameron. Common-
weal 85:653-5 Mr 10 '67
Miniature Luthers. Christian Cent 84:1243-4
O 4 '67
Modern priest looks at his outdated church,
by J. Kavanaugh. Review
Cath World 205:310-11 Ag '67. G. Baum
Christian Cent 84:999 Ag 2 '67. C. M.
Smith
Commonweal 86:473-4 Jl 28 '67. R. Horch-
ler

Modern priest looks at his outdated church;
excerpts. J. Kavanaugh. il Look 31:54-8+
Je 13 '67
New church essays in Catholic reform, by
D. Callahan. Review
Cath World 204:307-8 F '67. T. Molnar
Christian Cent 84:177-8 F 8 '67. W. R.
Miller
No time to leave; the Charles Davis case.
J. G. Lawler. Commonweal 86:87-92 Ap 7
'67; Discussion. 86:221+ My 12 '67
Of many things; church's attitude toward
truth and truthfulness. T. N. Davis; dis-
cussion. America 116:267, 496-501 F 25, Ap
1 '67
Of many things, concerning The church and
civilization. V. S. Kearney. America 116:in-
side cover Ap 8 '67
Of many things; preparing for Episcopal syn-
od. America 116:197+ F 11 '67
Of many things; revolution within the church.
T. N. Davis. America 117:229+ S 9 '67
Quiet Catholic question; unpublicized Pentecost. E. C. Kennedy. America 116:147-8 Ja
28 '67
Renewal mess. D. Callahan. Commonweal 85:
621-2+ Mr 3 '67; Discussion. 86:63-5 Mr 31
'67
Revolution in the cloth; books which press
for reforms. D. Callahan. il Sat R 50:24-
5 Jl 29 '67
Story of Charles Davis. S. J. Adamo. America
116:777-80 My 27 '67
Testimony of a 20th century Catholic. M. L.
West. America 117:678-81+ D 2 '67
Theological road show; Catholic congress on
the theology of church renewal at the
University of Toronto. il Newsweek 70:79
S 4 '67
Trojan horse in the City of God, by D. von
Hildebrand. Review
Nat R 19:863-4 Ag 8 '67. T. Molnar
Turmoil for Catholics all over the world. il
U S News 62:62-3 Mr 27 '67
Wheat or weeds? V. P. McCorry. America
117:587-8 N 11 '67
Word to the old breed. J. O'Gara. Common-
weal 86:386 Je 23 '67
Wounded priest, wounded church; discussion.
America 116:132-3, 296 Ja 28, Mr 4 '67
Year of faith; papal proclamation. America
117:51-2 Jl 15 '67
See also
Confession
Councils and synods
Ecumenical movement
Encyclicals
Excommunication
Jesuits
Laity—Catholic church
Mass
Modernism
Opus Dei
Orthodox Eastern church
Papacy
Pilgrims and pilgrimages
Priests
Sacred Heart, Devotion to
Saints
Sisterhoods
Synod of bishops, 1967
Vatican council, 2d
Vocation (in religion)
Women and the church

Authority
See Church—Authority

Byzantine rite
Big brother vs. the Melkites. T. E. Bird.
Commonweal 86:509-10 Ag 25 '67; Reply.
W. Birmingham. 87:43+ O 13 '67

Byzantine rite (Ruthenian)
Bishop in exile. il Time 90:60 Jl 21 '67
Elko fiasco. Commonweal 86:330-1 Je 23 '67
Same old Rome; Byzantine Catholicism.
Commonweal 87:429 Ja 12 '68

Catechisms
Catechism in Dutch. Newsweek 69:61 Ja 30
'67
Catechism in Dutch; one of the year's
religious best-sellers. Time 90:100 D 1 '67
Come to the Father; a new catechetical program. Sister Jeanette Marie. il Cath World
205:47-51 Ap '67
Confusion over a catechism; new Dutch
catechism. America 117:674 D 2 '67
From rote to reality; Come to the Father
series. il Time 89:56+ F 17 '67
History lesson; controversy over new third-
grade catechism. Word and worship. Newsweek 70:58 Ag 21 '67

CATHOLIC church—Catechisms—*Continued*
New catechetical program tested in fifty dioceses; Come to the Father. Pub W 191:77 F 27 '67
Sophisticating the catechism; Dutch catechism. J. L. McKenzie. Commonweal 87:201-2 N 17 '67

Ceremonies and practices
How U.S. Catholics view their rites. Newsweek 69:70 Mr 20 '67

Clergy
Letter from Vatican City. X. Rynne. New Yorker 43:119-20+ S 9 '67
Now for Catholics, deacons again. U S News 63:6 Jl 10 '67
Of many things; filling parish vacancies. T. N. Davis. America 116:inside cover My 27 '67
Priests question the rule of celibacy. D. Callahan. il N Y Times Mag p36-7+ O 22 '67
Up-dating the clergy; how far is up? J. F. Byrnes. America 118:8-10 Ja 6 '68
See also
Association of Chicago priests
Association of Pittsburgh priests
Bishops
Cardinals
Priests
Vocation (in religion)

Converts
See also
Converts, Catholic

Dioceses
After Spellman? contenders, and plans for the future of the Archdiocese of New York. il Newsweek 71:38-9 Ja 1 '68
Lansing renewal program. C. E. Rhodes. America 117:202-3 Ag 26 '67
Opening the books; Baton Rouge diocesan finances. Time 90:85 S 22 '67
Priests' associations go regional. J. J. Hill. Commonweal 87:69-70 O 20 '67
Report on a workshop; Vatican II's Constitution on the church. America 116:549 Ap 15 '67
See also
Chanceries, Diocesan

Discipline
End of the imprimatur. il Time 90:26 D 29 '67
Of many things; psychological freedom. J. McLaughlin. America 117:453 O 28 '67
Philadelphia, farewell. R. A. Schroth. America 116:176 F 4 '67; Discussion. 116:173-4, 330 F 4, Mr 11 '67
Priests question the rule of celibacy. D. Callahan. il N Y Times Mag p36-7+ O 22 '67
See also
Indulgences
Obedience (canon law)

Education
Aggiornamento on campus; developments in American Catholic universities. Sat R 50: 95 F 18 '67
America's 1967 directory of Catholic colleges. America 117:556-8 N 11 '67
America's 1967 directory of Catholic junior colleges. America 116:644 Ap 29 '67
Campus corner. M. P. Sheridan. America 116:722; 117:318 My 13, S 23 '67
Catholic college education; system, style & Christianity; address, June 11, 1967. J. P. Leary. Vital Speeches 33:635-8 Ag 1 '67
Catholic education in crisis; conference sponsored by National Catholic education association. J. H. Lloyd. Sr Schol 91:sup2 D 7 '67
Catholic junior college. W. H. Conley. America 116:645-6 Ap 29 '67
Catholic schools and brotherhood. C. J. Hayes. Cath World 206:165-6 Ja '68
Catholic university of today; text of IFCU statement with introd. by N. G. McCluskey. America 117:154-6 Ag 12 '67
Cool generation and the church; symposium, with editorial comment. Commonweal 87:5, 19-22 O 6 '67
Dead issue? state grants to church-related colleges. J. O'Gara. Commonweal 85:445 Ja 27 '67; Reply. W. J. Van Cleve. 85:575 F 17 '67
Ferment on the campus; disputes at St John's university; University of Dayton; Catholic university of America. P. A. Grant, jr. Cath World 205:293-7 Ag '67
Financial crisis in Catholic colleges. N. G. McCluskey. America 117:298-304 S 23 '67; Discussion. 117:426 O 21 '67

Future of an illusion; Catholic universities face the fate of the papal states; adaptation of address. J. Cogley. Commonweal 86: 310-16 Je 2 '67; Discussion. 86:435+ Jl 14 '67; America 117:inside cover Ag 5 '67
In praise of some Catholic colleges. R. Kirk. Nat R 19:1338 N 28 '67
Is secularization the answer for Catholic colleges? Christian Cent 84:165 F 8 '67
Jesuit university; time for some changes. M. F. Larréy. Commonweal 86:43-5 Mr 31 '67
Laicization of Catholic colleges. A. M. Greeley. Christian Cent 84:372-5 Mr 22 '67
Lay control of Catholic colleges. G. J. Dalcourt. America 117:412-14 O 14 '67
Layman in Catholic higher education. J. P. Leary. America 116:251-3 F 18 '67
Louder voice for laymen; mixed lay-clerical board. il Time 89:50 F 3 '67
Marist brothers: an omen? America 117:629 N 25 '67
Meanwhile, back in Philadelphia; strike of lay teachers in the diocesan high school system. A. Swidler. Commonweal 86:191-2 My 5 '67
Myths and fads in Catholic higher education. A. M. Greeley. America 117:542-5 N 11 '67; Reply. G. Bugge. 117:726-7 D 16 '67
Neoterism in Catholic colleges. R. Kirk. Nat R 19:963 S 5 '67
New approach to teaching religion. W. M. Roche. America 116:376-7 Mr 18 '67; Discussion. 116:571 Ap 22 '67
New Catholic college. N. G. McCluskey. America 116:414-17 Mr 25 '67; Discussion. 116:571-2 Ap 22 '67
Parochial education. D. Callahan. Commentary 43:81-3 Ja '67
Philosophy in the Catholic university. J. Donceel; discussion. America 115:470-1; 116:99+, 580-2, 767-8 O 22 '66, Ja 21, Ap 22, My 27 '67
Problem of Catholic U. N. K. Herzfeld. Commonweal 86:39-41 Mr 31 '67
Religious instruction; faith vs. training. F. McQuilkin; G. Moran. Commonweal 86:48-50+ Mr 31 '67
Revolt in some Catholic colleges; what's back of it all. il U S News 62:58-60 My 8 '67
Shape of Catholic higher education, ed. by R. Hassenger. Review
   Sat R 50:68 Je 17 '67. J. Cogley
Sharing responsibilities at Catholic universities. America 116:173 F 4 '67
Sharing the power; laymen on college boards. il Newsweek 69:90 F 6 '67
Student freedom. M. P. Sheridan. America 116:856 Je 17 '67
Theology and academic freedom. M. P. Sheridan. America 116:681-2 My 6 '67
Today's Catholic schools. R. C. Spitzer. Cath World 206:167-70 Ja '68
See also
Catholic university of America
Dayton, Ohio. University
Fordham university
Manhattan college, New York
National Catholic educational association
Notre Dame, Ind. University
Parochial schools, Catholic
St John's university, Jamaica, N.Y.
St Mary's Dominican college, New Orleans
Webster college, Webster Groves, Mo.

Eucharist
On the worship of the eucharist. America 116:847-8 Je 17 '67

Finance
Church investments. Commonweal 87:44 O 13 '67
Churches and public financial reports. America 117:6 Jl 1 '67
Opening the books; Baton Rouge diocesan finances. Time 90:85 S 22 '67
Problem of parish support. America 116:271 F 25 '67
Taxing our credulity and taxing the churches. America 116:408-9 Mr 25 '67
Vatican puts its books in order; bringing centralized management to the business affairs. Bsns W p32 Ag 26 '67

Government
Challenge to Rome; European council of bishops. Newsweek 70:71 Jl 24 '67
Church management systems. P. M. O'Meara. America 116:835-7 Je 10 '67
Constitutionalism and the church; call by the Canon law society of America and Fordham university. America 117:432 O 21 '67

CATHOLIC church—Government—*Continued*
Democracy in the church. W. L. Doty; E. C.
Bianchi. America 117:76-82 Jl 22 '67
St Louis Catholics speak up. Christian Cent
84:886-7 Jl 12 '67

History

Economic growth, capital investment, and the
Roman Catholic church in nineteenth-cen-
tury Ireland. E. Larkin. bibliog f il Am
Hist R 72:852-84 Ap '67

Infallibility

Speaking out; Catholicism is right, so why
change it? F. D. Wilhelmsen. Sat Eve Post
240:10+ Jl 15 '67

Liturgy and ritual

Barbarous English; excerpts from letter to
William F. Buckley, jr. H. Kenner. Com-
monweal 87:371+ D 22 '67
Cool generation and the church; symposium,
with editorial comment. Commonweal 87:5,
11-18 O 6 '67
Kind of mecca; Emmaus house in Manhat-
tan's East Harlem. il Newsweek 70:92 N
27 '67
Liturgical experimentation. America 116:275,
304-5 F 25-Mr 4 '67
Liturgy: a long way to go. America 116:237
F 18 '67
Liturgy and the arts: a unique relationship.
J. W. Moody. Cath World 205:303-9 Ag '67
Open experiments, openly arrived at; with
editorial comment. R. Haughton. Common-
weal 86:507, 511-13 Ag 25 '67; Discussion.
86:597+ S 29 '67
Positive and open approach; liturgical renewal.
America 116:302 Mr 4 '67
Quest for community; new forms of liturgy.
C. J. McNaspy. America 117:174-5 Ag 19 '67
Reformation Roman-style; excerpt from
Methodist observer at Vatican II. Cath
World 204:341-5 Mr '67
Time to create. P. J. Hallinan. Commonweal
87:47-9 O 13 '67
Underground church. il Time 90:53 S 29 '67
   See also
Liturgical language
Liturgical movement—Catholic church
Liturgical week
Mass
Bibliography
Book reviews. C. J. McNaspy. America 117:
183-4 Ag 19 '67

Membership
See Church membership

Missions

Aid to the Latin American church. J. J.
Considine. America 117:352-4 S 30 '67
In the forest of fear; son of M. Bormann
as a Catholic missionary in the Congo.
E. R. F. Sheehan. il Sat Eve Post 240:30-
2+ Ag 12 '67
Missionary's predicament: how far to adapt?
H. Horan. America 117:197-200 Ag 26 '67
Seamy side of charity. I. Illich; discussion.
America 116:296-8, 317-19, 444-6+ Mr 4,
25 '67
Why missions? P. Hebblethwaite. Cath World
205:335-9 S '67
   See also
Association for international development
Jesuits—Missions
Music
See Church music

Negroes
Church and the Negro. America 117:28 Jl 8
'67
   See also
National Catholic conference for interracial
justice
Relations
Jews
Again, silence in the churches. A. R. Eckardt
and A. L. Eckardt. Christian Cent 84:970-3,
992-5 Jl 26-Ag 2 '67
Arab-Israeli war and Catholic-Jewish dia-
logue. J. B. Sheerin. Cath World 205:260-2
Ag '67
Dissent and discovery; concerning publication
Guidelines for Catholic-Jewish relations. il
Newsweek 69:60 Ap 3 '67
Let the guidelines truly guide; eight prin-
ciples to govern Catholic-Jewish relations.
America 116:493 Ap 1 '67
Three popes and the Jews, by P. E. Lapide.
Review
   Sat R 50:27-8 S 9 '67. B. E. Olson

Lutheran church
Luther and the church today; symposium.
Cath World 206:63-71+ N '67
Orthodox Eastern church
Pope and Patriarch. America 117:105-6 Jl 29
'67
Protestant churches
Another hole in the head; Protestant fomenter
of anti-Catholic bigotry. Christian Cent 84:
525 Ap 26 '67
Can we learn from Mariology? P. K. Jewett.
Christian Cent 84:1019-21 Ag 9 '67
Christian unity: ups and downs; Anglican-
Roman Catholic reunion. America 116:172
F 4 '67
Fátima and Populorum progressio; ecumeni-
cal setback. R. J. Mollar. Christian Cent 84:
1025-6 Ag 9 '67
How to belittle the Pope; forbidding partici-
pation of Catholics in ecumenical prayer
services in Rome. America 116:204 F 11 '67
Pope as leader of all Christians? U S News
62:15 Je 19 '67

Relations (diplomatic)
Vatican and the third world; ally in their
struggle against underdevelopment. T. P.
Melady. America 117:641-3 N 25 '67

China (People's Republic)
Reopening the door to China. W. J. Richardson. America 116:850-2 Je 17 '67

Germany
Three popes and the Jews, by P. E. Lapide.
Review
   Sat R 50:27-8 S 9 '67. B. E. Olson

Israel
Jews and Rome. il Newsweek 70:72 Jl 31
'67
Russia
Soviet president at the Vatican. America 116:
202 F 11 '67
United States
Delegate leaves. Commonweal 86:358 Je 16 '67
Pope's fraternal eyes; new apostolic delegate
to the U S. Time 90:62 Jl 14 '67

Yugoslavia
New era in Yugoslavia; signing of agreement
between Tito's government and the Vati-
can. G. J. Prpic. America 116:528-30 Ap 8
'67
Roman curia
Addenda on the curia. Christian Cent 84:1117
S 6 '67
Changing the old guard. Time 91:58 Ja 19 '68
Curbing the curia. Newsweek 70:57 Ag 28 '67
Letter from Vatican City (cont) X. Rynne.
New Yorker 43:126+ S 9 '67
Reform, but not yet, Lord. G. MacEoin.
Commonweal 86:515-18 Ag 25 '67
Shake-up in the curia. il Newsweek 71:78-9
Ja 22 '68
Shattering tradition. il Time 90:38 Ag 25 '67
Vatican puts its books in order; bringing
centralized management to the business af-
fairs. Bsns W p32 Ag 26 '67
Woman's angle; four nuns named to curia.
il Newsweek 70:72 O 16 '67

Ruthenian rite
See Catholic church—Byzantine rite (Ru-
thenian)
Societies
See also
Catholic association for international peace
National council of Catholic men
Secular institutes

Anecdotes, facetiae, satire, etc.
Awful confessions of an anti-organization
Catholic. P. J. Laux. il America 117:108-10
Jl 29 '67
Statistics
Church in statistics, 1967. America 116:747
My 20 '67
No shortage of vocations? America 116:800 Je
3 '67
Theology
See Theology

Ukrainian rite
See Catholic church—Byzantine rite (Ruthenian)
CATHOLIC church and art. See Art and religion

CATHOLIC church and communism
Oh, what a lovely dialogue; the Catholic Marxism of Slant. P. Steinfels; reply. B. Wicker. Commonweal 85:475+ F 3 '67

CATHOLIC church and economics. See Christianity and economics

CATHOLIC church and labor. See Church and labor

CATHOLIC church and politics. See Church and politics

CATHOLIC church and race problems. See Church and race problems

CATHOLIC church and social problems. See Church and social problems

CATHOLIC church and the press. See Church and the press

CATHOLIC church and war. See War and religion

CATHOLIC church in Brazil
Bishops speak out. Time 90:40 D 15 '67
Brazil's Catholic left. T. G. Sanders. America 117:598-601 N 18 '67
Happening in São Paulo; priests arrested for association with Communist students. G. H. Dunne. America 117:306-9+ S 23 '67
Priests with pricked consciences. E. K. Long. Christian Cent 85:82-3 Ja 17 '68

CATHOLIC church in Canada
Happening in Toronto; institute on renewal in the church. America 117:234 S 9 '67
Quebec: secular and free; excerpt from Four o'clock lectures. P. Doucet. Christian Cent 84:910-13 Jl 12 '67

CATHOLIC church in Colombia
Reaction & reform in Columbia. il Time 89:60 Mr 3 '67

CATHOLIC church in Czechoslovakia
Catholic persistence in Czechoslovakia. Christian Cent 84:699-700 My 24 '67
Church in Czechoslovakia today; priest collaborators. T. Zubek. America 117:115-17 Jl 29 '67

CATHOLIC church in England
Of many things; Catholic press in England. D. L. Flaherty. America 116:295 Mr 4 '67

CATHOLIC church in France
Talking back; criticizing Vatican heresyhunters. Newsweek 69:63 F 13 '67

CATHOLIC church in Germany (Federal Republic)
Uneasy alliance. C. Amery. Commonweal 87:45-6 O 13 '67

CATHOLIC church in Great Britain
English Catholic tours the U.S. A. Lunn. Nat R 19:87-90 Ja 24 '67
Letter from London: Catholic crisis. R. Williams. Nation 205:51-2 Jl 17 '67
Of many things; Fr. Giarchi's sermons for London's teen-agers. T. N. Davis. America 117:425 O 21 '67

CATHOLIC church in Ireland
Economic growth, capital investment, and the Roman Catholic church in nineteenth-century Ireland. E. Larkin. bibliog f il Am Hist R 72:852-84 Ap '67

CATHOLIC church in Latin America
Aid to the Latin American church. J. J. Considine. America 17:352-4 S 30 '67
Changing role of the church in Latin America. il U S News 63:94-5 O 16 '67
Latin America: rise of a new non-Communist left. G. A. Geyer. Sat R 50:22-3+ Jl 22 '67
Latin-American church and renewal. C. Hoinacki. Cath World 206:27-31 O '67
Latin American diary; changes in six cities along Latin America's Pacific coast. E. K. Culhane. America 116:243-6 F 18 '67
Seamy side of charity. I. Illich; discussion. America 116:296-8, 317-19, 444-6+ Mr 4, 25 '67

CATHOLIC church in Peru
Reaching the 90 per cent. P. C. Kelly. America 116:873 Je 24 '67

CATHOLIC church in Poland
Polish Catholic left. J. J. Kulczycki. America 116:556-9 Ap 15 '67
Polish church and Communist state: cardinal vs. Communist boss. H. H. Ward. Christian Cent 84:288+ Mr 1 '67
Report. D. R. Shanor. Atlan 220:36+ D '67

CATHOLIC church in South America. See Catholic church in Latin America

CATHOLIC church in Spain
Change in Spain. C. J. McNaspy. America 117:111 Jl 29 '67

CATHOLIC church in the Netherlands
Catechism in Dutch. Newsweek 69:61 Ja 30 '67
Continuity in the Dutch church. F. J. van Beeck. America 117:266-9+ S 16 '67
Dutch pastoral council. I. Van Rijn. America 116:373-5 Mr 18 '67

Monks are coming to town; experiment among Trappists. America 117:193 Ag 26 '67
More sparks from Holland. il Time 90:58 Ag 18 '67
Radical, revolutionary church of the Netherlands. il Time 89:36 Mr 31 '67
Those Dutch Catholics. G. Zimmermann. il Look 32:22-4 Ja 23 '68
Will the Dutch change Catholicism in America? excerpts from Exploding church. F. Franck. il Look 32:17-21 Ja 23 '68

CATHOLIC church in the United States
America's Catholic bishops. D. Callahan. Atlan 219:63-6+ Ap '67
At last; one Bible for all Christians; RSV for the gospel and epistle readings at mass. J. Daniel. il Read Digest 90:112-16 My '67
Big brother vs. the Melkites. T. E. Bird. Commonweal 86:509-10 Ag 25 '67; Reply. W. Birmingham. 87:43+ O 13 '67
Catholic super-patriots. J. O'Gara. Commonweal 86:226 My 12 '67
English Catholic tours the U.S. A. Lunn. Nat R 19:87-90 Ja 24 '67
Friction in Philadelphia; another head rolls. A. Swidler. Commonweal 87:463-4 Ja 19 '68
Growing unrest in the Catholic church. il U S News 62:59-63 Mr 27 '67
How U.S. Catholics view their church; major findings of survey. il Newsweek 69:68-75 Mr 20 '67
Jesuit grass-roots renewal; meeting at St Mary's college, St Marys, Kan. D. E. Campion. America 116:286 F 25 '67
Let these voices be heard. America 116:551 Ap 15 '67
Message from the bishops; pastoral letter. Time 91:59 Ja 19 '68
Plaintive letter; bishops' last letter. Newsweek 71:79 Ja 22 '68
Punt on the five-yard line; four Paulist priests fired from diocese by Bishop Gorman. il Time 89:56 Je 16 '67
Reporter looks at American Catholicism. by B. McGurn. Review Sat R 50:28-9 S 9 '67. P. K. Cuneo
Theology: made in U.S.A. T. F O'Meara. Cath World 205:231-6 Jl '67
Underground church. il Time 90:53 S 29 '67
U.S. bishops' pastoral; How will it be received? America 118:23 Ja 13 '68
Will the Dutch change Catholicism in America? excerpts from Exploding church. F. Franck. il Look 32:17-21 Ja 23 '68
See also
Catholics in the United States
Church unity—United States
National Catholic office for motion pictures

History
John F. Kennedy and American Catholicism. by L. H. Fuchs. Review America 116:507-8 Ap 1 '67. J. T. Ellis Sat R il 50:32 My 6 '67. E. Wakin

CATHOLIC church in Yugoslavia
Agreement between the Holy See and Yugoslavia; tr. by Z. Damjanov. F. Franic. Cath World 205:353-7 S '67

CATHOLIC college professors and instructors. See College professors and instructors

CATHOLIC colleges. See Catholic church—Education

CATHOLIC education. See Catholic church—Education

CATHOLIC encyclopedia
See also
New Catholic encyclopedia

CATHOLIC high schools. See Catholic church—Education

CATHOLIC historians
Luther and Catholic historians. W. W. MacDonald. America 117:434-6 O 21 '67

CATHOLIC hospitals. See Hospitals

CATHOLIC humor. See Humor, Catholic

CATHOLIC intellectuals. See Intellectuals

CATHOLIC inter-American cooperation program. See Religious conferences

CATHOLIC interracial councils
Cody all alone; withdrawing support from the Catholic interracial council of Chicago. Christian Cent 84:302 Mr 8 '67
Indicative concession. Christian Cent 84:709 My 31 '67

CATHOLIC junior colleges. See Catholic church—Education

CATHOLIC laymen. See Laity—Catholic church

CATHOLIC learning and scholarship
See also
Catholics—Intellectual life

CATHOLIC library association
See also
Regina award

CATHOLIC literature
Longing for spring again; interview. G. Fielding. Cath World 204:296-300 F '67
No laughing matter. V. P. McCorry. America 116:218-19 F 11 '67
See also
Publishers and publishing—Catholic literature

Bibliography
Catholic world of books for Lent. V. Kendall. Cath World 204:288-9 F '67
Preview of Catholic books. P. K. Cuneo. America 117:384+ O 7 '67
Religion (cont) E. S. Stanton. America 116:697-700 My 6 '67
Suggestions for Lenten reading. America 116:220+ F 11 '67

CATHOLIC newspapers. See Catholic press
CATHOLIC periodicals. See Catholic press
CATHOLIC philosophy. See Philosophy
CATHOLIC press
Catholic press troubles. Newsweek 70:59 Jl 17 '67
Dialog, but blandly; controversy over editorial policy. J. Deedy. Commonweal 86:484-6 Ag 11 '67
Merry-go-round; Twin circle. S. J. Adamo. America 117:451-2 O 21 '67
Nationals. S. J. Adamo. America 117:693-4 D 2 '67
New crusade on the Catholic right; new national weekly newspaper, Twin circle. Christian Cent 84:1341 O 25 '67
New voice on the right; Twin circle, a new national weekly. Newsweek 70:116 S 25 '67
News and views; resignation of J. O'Connor as editor of Delmarva dialog. J. Deedy. Commonweal 86:378 Je 23 '67
Of many things; end of Sacred Heart messenger. D. F. X. Meenan. America 117:670 D 2 '67
Parochial stigma; advertising in Catholic newspapers. S. J. Adamo. America 117:44 Jl 8 '67
Press. S. J. Adamo. See issues of America
Storm over Delaware; Delmarva dialog controversy. S. J. Adamo. America 117:120 Jl 29 '67
Too much too soon; resignation of editor of the Delmarva dialog. S. J. Adamo. America 116:860-1 Je 17 '67
Whither or wither; concerning Catholic diocesan newspapers. S. J. Adamo. America 116:226-8 F 11 '67
See also
Commonweal (periodical)
Ramparts (periodical)
Wanderer (periodical)

CATHOLIC relief services. See National Catholic welfare conference
CATHOLIC schools. See Parochial schools, Catholic
CATHOLIC students
Evolution of the high school student. D. Travers. Cath World 205:139-44 Je '67
Gap between the generations; ed. by L. F. McKernan. Cath World 205:134-8 Je '67
Open-minded Catholic students. Sch & Soc 95:518 D 23 '67
Student involvement in the liturgy; survey findings of attitudes of Catholic college freshmen toward the mass. W. J. Farrell. il Cath World 205:199-204 Jl '67
Students in social action. M. P. Sheridan. America 117:565 N 11 '67

CATHOLIC students' opinion. See Student opinion
CATHOLIC universities. See Catholic church—Education
CATHOLIC university of America
Blow-up at Catholic U; with editorial comment. N. K. Herzfeld. Commonweal 86:187-91 My 5 '67
Cause for revolt. il Newsweek 69:61 My 1 '67
Change strikes Catholic university. J. B. Sheerin. Cath World 205:132-3 Je '67
High noon at Catholic U. M. I. Urofsky. Nation 205:303-5 O 2 '67
Reaching the cherubim; Father Charles E. Curran reinstated. Newsweek 69:113 My 8 '67
Time for Boy scouts? il Time 89:62 Ap 28 '67
Victory at C.U. Time 89:84 My 5 '67
What happened at Catholic U. D. M. Knight. America 116:723-5 My 13 '67
Zeroing in on freedom; can the Charles Currans be freed? symposium. Commonweal 86:316-21 Je 2 '67

CATHOLICISM. See Catholic church

CATHOLICS
Testimony of a 20th century Catholic. M. L. West. America 117:678-81+ D 2 '67
Today's layman: an uncertain Catholic. D. J. Thorman; discussion. America 116:231-2 F 18 '67

Intellectual life
Woman intellectual and the church; symposium. Commonweal 85:446-56+ Ja 27 '67; Discussion. 85:611+ Mr 3 '67

CATHOLICS in England
Disciples of Christ & Marx; England's New left Catholics. il Time 89:93 Mr 10 '67
R.C.'s: a report on the Roman Catholics in Britain today, by G. Scott. Review America 116:812-13 Je 3 '67. D. J. Dooley

CATHOLICS in Hungary
More arrests in Hungary. America 116:170 F 4 '67

CATHOLICS in India
India's elections. America 116:331-2 Mr 11 '67

CATHOLICS in Latin America
Primitives: Catholicism's submerged third. J. Tuck. Cath World 204:284-8 F '67

CATHOLICS in South Africa
Another vile Vatican plot; Catholic immigrants to South Africa. America 116:713 My 13 '67

CATHOLICS in the United States
American Catholics and anti-Semitism in the 1930's. D. J. O'Brien. Cath World 204:270-6 F '67
Catholic statistical profile. Christian Cent 84:676-7 My 24 '67
How U.S. Catholics view their church; major findings of survey. il Newsweek 69:68-75 Mr 20 '67
O blessed deviation. N. Rambusch. Commonweal 86:363-6 Je 16 '67

Statistics
Clergy manpower for the future. M. W. Cardullo. America 117:546-7+ N 11 '67; Reply. W. J. Mehok 117:726 D 16 '67

CATHOLICS in Vietnam
Viet Catholics speak out. America 116:574 Ap 22 '67
Vietnam's Catholics. America 117:290 S 23 '67

CATLIN, George
O-kee-pa; excerpts, with editorial comment. Am Heritage 18:30-7+ O '67
Tragic prescience of George Catlin; ed. by R. S. Gallagher. Am Heritage 18:72 O '67

CATO, pseud.
Focus on Washington. See issues of National review

CATOIR, John T.
Church and second marriage. Commonweal 86:113-17 Ap 14 '67

CATS
Gray princess; excerpts from Particularly cats. D. Lessing. il McCalls 94:110-11+ Mr '67
How to get a cat out of a tree. il Changing T 21:24 My '67
Pet news; theories of Milan Greer. J. Kuh. Ladies Home J 84:58 Mr '67
Simon at seventeen. S. Burnford. Ladies Home J 84:40+ O '67
See also
Save a cat league, incorporated

Photographs
Candid cats on camera. il Good H 165:206 D '67

CATS in art. See Animals in art
CATSKILL MOUNTAINS
Catskills of New York: past, present, potential. S. S. Chase. il Am For 73:22-5+ Ag '67

CATT, Kevin J. and Tregear, G. W.
Solid-phase radioimmunoassay in antibody-coated tubes. bibliog Science 158:1570-2 D 22 '67
—and others
Human growth hormone and placental lactogen: structural similarity. bibliog Science 157:321 Jl 21 '67

CATTAILS
Photosynthetic system II: racial differentiation in typha latifolia. S. J. McNaughton. bibliog il Science 156:1363 Je 9 '67

CATTANO, Billy
Murf the Surf and his jewel-studded jinx. K. Wheeler and S. Smith. il por Life 62:92-4+ Ap 21 '67

CATTELL, David T.
Fiftieth anniversary; a Soviet watershed? Cur Hist 53:224-9+ O '67

CATTERSON, James M. Jr
  Reporter at large. R. Harris. New Yorker
  43:48-50+ Ap 8 '67
CATTLE

Age
See Age (animals)

Breeding
See Cattle breeding

Breeds
This month's cover story; Charolais cattle.
  D. Malena. il Suc Farm 65:68 Mr '67

Diseases and pests
Breakthrough on shipping fever; new vac-
  cines. R. C. Black. il Farm J 91:22+ Jl '67
How these four beefmen prevent disease. D.
  Malena. il Suc Farm 65:50-1 O '67
How these four dairymen handle herd health
  problems. J. R. Borcherding. il Suc Farm
  65:56-8 O '67
How to cope with two big summer problems;
  dust and heat stress. J. G. Clark. Farm J
  91:B10 Jl '67
PC feeder boom, good news for you. R. C.
  Black. il Farm J 91:B8+ S '67
Preconditioning is only part of the battle. J.
  Clark. il Farm J 91:B14-15 N '67
Pre-treated feeders, dividends and dangers.
  J. G. Clark. Farm J 91:B20-1 S '67
Stop those cowlot hippies; stomach worms.
  L. A. Baker. Farm J 91:D8 D '67
What to do about brain diseases. J. G. Clark.
  Farm J 91:B8-9 My '67
You can stop IBR; infectious bovine rhino-
  tracheitis. L. A. Baker. Farm J 91:D9+
  F '67
    See also
Anaplasmosis
Bloating
Foot-and-mouth disease

Feeding
All concentrate; benefits and risks. Farm J
  92:B12 Ja '68
Are you being squashed by over-feeding? R.
  C. Black. il Farm J 91:B4-5+ My '67
Best start-up ration, roughage or concen-
  trate? J. G. Clark. Farm J 92:B10 Ja '68
Build your ration by the bell; electronic load
  cells. D. K. O'Brien. il Farm J 91:B13
  S '67
Cattle finish fast on all-corn ration. il Farm J
  91:B19 S '67
Easiest way to figure out what to feed cat-
  tle. Suc Farm 65:38-9 Ja '67
How good are the cooked grains? il Farm J
  91:B12 Ja '67
Net energy; new yardstick for feed values.
  R. C. Black. il Farm J 91:B4-5 Jl '67
Partners, not competitors; farmer-feeders and
  commercial feedlots. R. C. Black. il Farm J
  91:B3+ N '67
Slower gains on high-moisture corn. Farm J
  91:B10 N '67
They cut this feeder's cost of gain. D. Malena.
  il Suc Farm 65:24-5 D '67
They'll put you in feeding for $10 a head. il
  Farm J 91:B 10+ Mr '67
Tour shows more beef; less labor. Suc Farm
  65:86+ O '67
Your beef business. J. A. Rohlf. il Farm J
  91:B16 My '67
    See also
Calves—Feeding
Cows—Feeding

Marketing
Three easy ways you can hedge cattle. O. Bay.
  il Farm J 91:50V+ O '67

Performance records and registration
Look what's happening to purebred auctions!
  il Farm J 91:40-1+ O '67
    See also
Cattle, Beef—Performance records and registration

Prices
More money for your cows. D. Hagen. Farm
  J 91:D16 O '67
Pricecast. See issues of Farm journal
Some sunshine through the clouds. il Farm J
  91:B19 N '67
What do the numbers really mean? il Farm J
  91:B23 S '67

Transportation
    See also
Cattle, Beef—Shrinkage
CATTLE, Beef
Dairy blood in your beef future? il Farm J
  91:34-5+ S '67

Eight farmers tell how to start a beef herd.
  D. Malena. il Suc Farm 65:42-3 Ap '67
Feeder shortage? R. C. Black. il Farm J
  92:B13 Ja '68
How to cope with cold weather. J. Clark. il
  Farm J 91:B11 Ja '67
Partners, not competitors; farmer-feeders and
  commercial feedlots. R. C. Black. il Farm
  J 91:B3+ N '67
What's new. See issues of Successful farming

Feeding
See Cattle—Feeding

Grading and standardization
Cutability gets a price tag. R. C. Black. il
  Farm J 91:37+ O '67
More muscle, less bone. R. C. Black. Farm J
  91:46X My '67

Marketing
Now, better cattle market reports. il Suc
  Farm 65:50+ N '67
Selling cattle grade and yield. D. Malena
  and R. J. Fee. il Suc Farm 65:50-1 F '67
Ten ways to hit a better market. Farm J 91:
  46 Je '67

Performance records and registration
Performance records; easier way to bigger
  profits. D. Malena. il Suc Farm 65:30-1 Jl
  '67
Records have kept me in business. C. E. Ball.
  il Farm J 91:28-9+ Je '67

Prices
See Cattle—Prices

Shrinkage
Least-shrink way to handle replacements.
  Farm J 91:B6 S '67

Weight
See Cattle, Weight and measurements of
CATTLE, Cooling of. See Livestock, Cooling
  of
CATTLE, Weight and measurements of
Look what's under the hide! D. Seim. il
  Farm J 91:B4-5 S '67
    See also
Cattle, Beef—Shrinkage
CATTLE auctions. See Auctions
CATTLE barns. See Barns and stables
CATTLE breeding
Beef crossbreeding; they make it work. D.
  Malena. il Suc Farm 65:36-7+ Je '67
Dairy blood in your beef future? il Farm J
  91:34-5+ S '67
For beef, new details on using. .; artificial
  insemination, estrus control hormones,
  fertility testing, pregnancy testing. D.
  Malena. il Suc Farm 65:40-1 My '67
Should you use a heat-control drug this year?
  il Farm J 91:32+ Ap '67
We don't care what a cow looks like. . . C. E.
  Ball. il Farm J 91:22-3+ Ag '67
Why bulls or cows fail to breed. J. W. Bailey.
  Suc Farm 65:70 Mr '67
Will fall calving pay? they found out! D.
  Malena. il Suc Farm 65:32-3 O '67
    See also
Bulls
CATTLE driving
Australia's lonely sheep country. B. L. Bur-
  man. il Read Digest 90:204-6+ Ap '67
CATTLE handling
Corral that saves labor. G. Lorang. il Farm J
  92:R2 Ja '68
Least-shrink way to handle replacements.
  Farm J 91:B6 S '67
PC feeder boom, good news for you. R. C.
  Black. il Farm J 91:B8+ S '67
CATTLE industry and trade
Beef extra. See issues of Farm journal
Cattle feeders, ten feet tall. R. C. Black. il
  Farm J 91:B6 My '67
Could a beef herd up your profits? D. Malena.
  il Suc Farm 65:48-9+ Mr '67
Factory that turns out beef steers. N. Reeder.
  il Farm J 91:B6-7+ N '67
For beef, new details on using. .; artificial
  insemination, estrus control hormones,
  fertility testing, pregnancy testing. D.
  Malena. il Suc Farm 65:40-1 My '67
He raises 6½ pounds more beef per acre. R.
  Alleman and D. Malena. il Suc Farm 65:45
  Ja '67
How soon the sun? Farm J 91:B15 My '67
How to make more money growing out cattle.
  D. D. Hubbard. Farm J 91:B14 Mr '67

CATTLE industry and trade—*Continued*
Kingdom for .8 of a calf; Atlantic Richfield co. Time 90:94+ O 20 '67
New guidelines for fair wintering deals. Farm J 91:B17 N '67
Plain talk about using beef futures. F. Bailey, jr. il Suc Farm 65:42-3 N '67
Where are they all coming from? il Farm J 91:B19 Mr '67
Your beef business. J. A. Rohlf. See issues of Farm journal
See also
Western testing, incorporated

History
King of ranchers: H. Miller. B. Taper. il Am Heritage 18:20-3+ Ag '67

Great Britain
In Britain a plague's grim pileup; foot-and-mouth epidemic. il Life 64:26-9 Ja 5 '68
Letter from London; foot-and-mouth epidemic. M. Panter-Downes. New Yorker 43:52-3 D 23 '67
New crisis in Britain: deadly cattle disease. U S News 63:14 D 18 '67

CATTLE manures. See Fertilizers and manures
CATTLE ranches. See Ranches
CATTLEMEN
See also
Cowboys
CATTON, Bruce
Army of the Cumberland: a panorama show by W. D. T. Travis. Am Heritage 19:40-9 D '67
He wanted to murder the bugler. Am Heritage 18:50-5+ Ag '67
Reading, writing, and history. Am Heritage 18:82-3 Ap; 56-7+ Je; 80-2 O '67
CAU, Jean
Françoise Hardy; tr. by A. Foulke. Vogue 149:166-7+ Mr 1 '67
Marvellous trickery; tr. by A. Foulke. Vogue 149:140-1+ Ap 15 '67
CAUCASUS
Friendship is climbing a Soviet mountain. C. S. Wren. il Look 31:64 O 3 '67
CAUDILL, Harry M.
Lilly's wood. Audubon 69:24-7 My '67
CAUDILL, Rebecca
Report from Pikeville, Kentucky; testimony. ed. by K. Molz. Wilson Lib Bul 42:399-402 D '67
CAULFIELD, Patricia
Caulfield on color. See issues of Modern photography
Grand Canyon; photographs. Natur Hist 76: 41-8 N '67
Nature and the camera. Natur Hist 76:60-1 O; 77:64+ Ja '68
Uncommon eye of Richard Selby. Mod Phot 31:76-81 Ap '67
(ed) See Porter, E.   Art and technique of Eliot Porter
CAULKING. See Calking
CAUSES of death. See Death—Causes
CAUTE, David
Final solution. Harper 235:92+ Jl '67
CAVAGLIERI, Giorgio
Pair of talented preservers. por Fortune 75:162 Mr '67
CAVALLERIA rusticana; opera. See Mascagni, P.
CAVANAGH, Jerome Patrick
Detroit's mayor: he went all out to help the poor, but... il por U S News 63:16 Ag 7 '67
Mary quite contrary. por Newsweek 69:44-5 Je 19 '67
Troubled cities, and their mayors. il por Newsweek 69:42-3 Mr 13 '67
Young mayor seeks an answer in the ashes. N. Thimmesch. il por Life 63:56+ Ag 11 '67
CAVANAUGH, Arthur
Element of you. Writer 80:22-3 Ag '67
Twenty-five cent job; story. McCalls 94:58-9 Ag '67
CAVE, Hugh
Island of Eve; story. Good H 165:87-9 O '67
Summer serenade; story. Good H 165:72-3 Jl '67
CAVE, W. L.
Rage of a bear. Outdoor Life 140:26-9+ Ag '67
CAVE drawings and paintings
Oldest paintings in the Americas; Juxtlahuaca cave discoveries by C. E. T. Gay and G. Griffin. il Life 62:107-8+ My 12 '67
Oldest paintings of the New World; Juxtlahuaca cave, Mexico. C. T. E. Gay. il Natur Hist 76 28-35 Ap '67

Pictograph cave in Kings Canyon National Park. C. W. Stouffer. il Nat Parks Mag 41:16-17 My '67
CAVE dwellers
Troglodytes; putting architecture underground. B. Rudofsky. il Horizon 9:28-39 Spr '67
CAVENDISH club. See Bridge clubs
CAVERN; drama. See Anouilh, J.
CAVES
Flash flood underground; exploring the Sauvajou in the French Pyrenees. I. Treat. Holiday 42:48-9+ O '67
Oldest paintings of the New World; Juxtlahuaca cave, Mexico. C. T. E. Gay. il Natur Hist 76:28-35 Ap '67
Russell cave dedicated; new visitor center named for Gilbert H. Grosvenor. il Nat Geog Mag 132:440-2 S '67
See also
Mammoth Cave National Park
CAVIAR
Russian caviar: fish eggs at ermine prices. E. Alston. il Look 31:100-1 O 3 '67
CAWLFIELD, Billy F.
Low-cost capacitive-discharge ignition system. il Electr World 78:30-2 N '67
CAYMAN ISLANDS
Reporter at large; voyage to Miskito Bank, Nicaragua for green turtle fishing. P. Matthiessen. New Yorker 43:120+ O 28 '67
See also
Grand Cayman (island)
CEAUSESCU, Nicolae
Two in one. Newsweek 70:61 D 18 '67
Winner take all. Time 90:39 D 15 '67
CECCHETTI council of America
Summer teacher sessions. W. Como. il Dance Mag 41:70 O '67
CECIL, Robert, 1st earl of Salisbury. See Salisbury. R. C.
CECIL family
England's second family. L. B. Smith. il pors Horizon 9:68-79 Aut '67
CECROPIA. See Silkworms
CEDAR
Dancing deodars. il Sunset 139:152-4 D '67
CEDAR CITY, Utah, Shakespeare festival. See Shakespeare festivals
CEDAR RAPIDS, Ia.

Sanitary affairs
Better than the pilot model. J. W. Gerlich. il Am City 82:94-6 O '67
CEFIS, Eugenio
Cefis of E.N.I. por Fortune 76:31 Ag '67
CEILINGS
Ceilings: a new role to play. J. H. Ingersoll. il House B 109:188-91+ Ap '67
How you can install an illuminated ceiling. il Pop Mech 128:163-6 O '67
Suspended ceiling. il Sunset 138:146+ Ap '67
CELANO, M. J. See Levine, P. jt. auth.
CELEBRATIONS
See also
Festivals
CELEBRITIES
Admired women I don't admire. M. Mannes. McCalls 94:40+ Ap '67
Censorship by boredom. A. Gingrich. Esquire 67:6 Je '67
Do celebrities make good parents? J. Brothers. Good H 165:34+ S '67
If you could give a child only one precious gift, what would it be? celebrities' answers; comp. by M. Davidson. il Good H 165:80-2 Jl '67
Men, now. il Vogue 150:88-103 N 15 '67
NR's annual guide to unsatisfactory people; comp. by C. H. Simonds. il Nat R 19:1428-9 D 26 '67
Pets and peeves: the bigger they are, the more enticing targets they make; J. Fairchild's targets. il Life 62:46 Mr 17 '67
Profiles; P. Molé, barber with famous customers. W. Whitworth. New Yorker 43:63-4+ O 21 '67
Seventh annual dubious achievement awards for 1967. il Esquire 69:49-55 Ja '68
Sun Valley set. S. Birmingham. il Holiday 42:62-7+ N '67
Try to be more like Pittsburgh; birthplaces of celebrated persons. W. Stanton. New Yorker 43:57-9 D 23 '67
Very small, very famous. il Good H 165:40-1 D '67
What's happening. G. Shalit. See issues of Ladies' home journal
See also
Great men
Women, Famous

CELEBRITIES—*Continued*

Anecdotes, facetiae, satire, etc.

Namesmanship. N. Hartshorne. Look 31:M8 My 30 '67

CELESTIAL photography. *See* Astronomical photography

CELIBACY

Bachelor psychosis; concerning Pope Paul's new encyclical, Sacerdotalis celibatus. Commonweal 86:436-7 Jl 14 '67

Celibacy explosion. J. O'Gara; reply. J. A. Miles. Commonweal 85:689-91 Mr 17 '67

Encyclical on Priestly celibacy. America 117: 29 Jl 8 '67

How U.S. Catholics view celibacy. il Newsweek 69:73 Mr 20 '67

In defense of celibacy; Pope Paul's Sacerdotalis celibatus. il Newsweek 70:72-3 Jl 3 '67

Modern church, outdated priest? T. E. Clarke. America 116:758 My 20 '67

On being single in South Bend; Notre Dame symposium on clerical celibacy. J. Groutt. Commonweal 86:600-1 S 29 '67

Priests question the rule of celibacy. D. Callahan. il N Y Times Mag p36-7+ O 22 '67

Psychoanalyst's case for celibacy. J. B. Rosenbaum. Cath World 205:107-10 My '67

Reverend James Kavanaugh, broadcaster. J. McLaughlin. America 117:42-4 Jl 8 '67

Something missing? Roman church and the cult of the sexless. R. T. Gill. America 116: 837 Je 10 '67

Speaking out; priests shouldn't marry. E. C. Kennedy. Sat Eve Post 241:8+ Ja 27 '68

Symposium on celibacy. T. E. Clarke. America 117:305 S 23 '67; Discussion. 117:490-1 N 4 '67

Talk within the club; North American academy of ecumenists. Time 89:56-7 Je 30 '67

Talking back to Rome. Time 90:66 S 15 '67

Thoughts on priestly celibacy. J. J. Evoy. America 117:114 Jl 29 '67

Toward a chosen celibacy. America 116:519 Ap 8 '67

CÉLINE, Louis Ferdinand, pseud. *See* Destouches, L. F.

CELIS, Pérez

Pérez Celis: an image of the Americas. F. Demaria. il Américas 19:38-9 D '67

CELL division (biology)

Antibody-producing cells in division. A. J. Claflin and O. Smithies. bibliog il Science 157:1561-2 S 29 '67

L-Asparaginase: inhibition of early mitosis in regenerating rat liver. F. F. Becker and J. D. Broome. bibliog il Science 156:1602-3 Je 23 '67

Cell division: direct measurement of maximum tension exerted by furrow of echinoderm eggs. R. Rappaport. bibliog il Science 156:1241-3 Je 2 '67

Cell synchrony; report on Second international conference. G. L. Whitson and others. Science 157:1219-20+ S 8 '67

Chlamydomonas reinhardi: heterozygous diploid strains. W. T. Ebersold. bibliog il Science 157:447-9 Jl 28 '67

Contact inhibition in colony formation. H. W. Fisher and J. Yeh. bibliog il Science 155:581-2 F 3 '67

Control of cell division. Sci Am 217:44 Jl '67

Distribution of chromatids at mitosis. J. A. Heddle and others. bibliog il Science 158: 929-31 N 17 '67

Keto-aldehydes and cell division. A. Szent-Györgyi and others. bibliog Science 155: 539-41 F 3 '67

Mototic reactivation of the terminal bud and cambium of white ash. H. B. Tepper and C. A. Hollis. bibliog il Science 156:1635-6 Je 23 '67

Streptonigrin: effect of the first meiotic metaphase of the mouse egg. G. Jagiello. bibliog il Science 157:453-4 Jl 28 '67

CELL sorter. *See* Physiological apparatus

CELLARS. *See* Basements and cellars

CELLARS, Wine. *See* Wine cellars

CELLISTS

Prodigy comes of age. il Time 89:75 Mr 10 '67

See also
Rostropovich, M.

CELLO concerto; ballet. *See* Ballets—Criticisms

CELLO music
See also
Phonograph records—Cello music

CELLS

Autoradiographic plaques for the detection of antibody formation to soluble proteins by single cells. E. Pick and J. D. Feldman. bibliog il Science 156:964-6 My 19 '67

Bronchiolar and large alveolar cell in pulmonary phospholipid metabolism. A. H. Niden. bibliog il Science 158:1323-4 D 8 '67

Cell aggregation: its enhancement by a supernatant from cultures of homologous cells. J. E. Lilien and A. A. Moscona. bibliog il Science 157:70-2 Jl 7 '67

Cells of mice and men; hybridization. Sci Am 218:51 Ja '68

Cellular dynamics: hormones; report on conference. L. D. Peachey. Science 155:226+ Ja 13 '67

Cellular dynamics; report on fifth conference. P. R. Gross. Science 157:7-8 Ag 11 '67

Collagen-coated cellulose sponge: three-dimensional matrix for tissue culture of Walker tumor 256. J. Leighton and others. bibliog il Science 155:1259-61 Mr 10 '67

Collagen synthesis by cells synchronously replicating DNA. L. M. Davies and others. bibliog il Science 159:91-3 Ja 5 '68

Electrical recordings from meningioma cells during cytolytic action of antibody and complement. A. Prieto and others. bibliog il Science 157:1185-7 S 8 '67

Frog cerebellum: absence of long-term inhibition upon Purkinje cells. R. Llinás and J. R. Bloedel. bibliog il Science 155: 601-3 F 3 '67

Genomic exclusion: a rapid means for inducing homozygous diploid lines in tetrahymena pyriformis, syngen 1. S. L. Allen. bibliog il Science 155:575-7 F 3 '67

Giant-cell centrioles. J. L. Matthews and others. bibliog il Science 155:1423-4 Mr 17 '67

Hexagonal pattern in cell walls of escherichia coli B. D. A. Fischman and G. Weinbaum. bibliog il Science 155:472-4 Ja 27 '67

Improved in vitro survival of normal, functional spleen cells. B. Mohit and G. H. Sato. bibliog il Science 157:449-51 Jl 28 '67

Langerhans cells: uptake of tritiated thymidine. L. Giacometti and W. Montagna. bibliog il Science 157:439-40 Jl 28 '67

Mechanisms of enzymatic bacteriolysis. J. L. Strominger and J. M. Ghuysen. bibliog il Science 156:213-21 Ap 14 '67

Molecular aspects of lens cell differentiation. J. Papaconstantinou. bibliog il Science 156: 338-46 Ap 21 '67

Nuclear-cytoplasmic interaction in DNA synthesis. D. M. Prescott and L. Goldstein. bibliog il Science 155:469-70 Ja 27 '67

Radiation chimeras and genetics of somatic cells. A. Lengerová. bibliog il Science 155: 529-35 F 3 '67

Sialic acid in HeLa cells: effect of hydrocortisone. R. Carubelli and M. J. Griffin. bibliog il Science 157:693-4 Ag 11 '67

Sickle-cell trait in human biological and cultural evolution; excerpt from address, January 1967. S. L. Wiesenfeld. bibliog il Science 157:1134-40 S 8 '67

Spectrophotometric cell sorter. L. A. Kamentsky and M. R. Melamed. bibliog il Science 156:1364-5 Je 9 '67

Stearic acid as plasma replacement for intracellular in vitro culture of plasmodium knowlesi. W. A. Siddiqui and others. bibliog il Science 156:1623-5 Je 23 '67

Strophanthidin-sensitive transport of cesium and sodium in muscle cells. R. A. Sjodin and L. A. Beaugé. bibliog il Science 156: 1248-50 Je 2 '67

Synovial cell synthesis of a substance immunologically like cartilage proteinpolysaccharide. R. Janis and others. bibliog il Science 158:1464-7 D 15 '67

Transverse tubule apertures in mammalian myocardial cells: surface array. D. G. Rayns and others. bibliog il Science 155: 656-7 My 5 '67

Virus-like particles in established murine cell lines: electron-microscopic observations. D. A. Kindig and W. H. Kirsten. bibliog il Science 155:1543-5 Mr 24 '67

See also
Cancer cells
Cell division (biology)
Chromatin
Lymphoid cells
Membranes (biology)
Mitochondria
Nerve cells

Culture
See Tissues—Culture

CELLULOSE sponges. *See* Sponges, Artificial

CELTIC-Rangers fans. *See* Soccer

CELTIC twilight; story. *See* Ostrow, J.

CEMENT
See also
Concrete

CEMENT Industry and trade
Dundee solves a weighty problem; world's largest cement-making kiln. il Bsns W p 150+ N 25 '67
CEMENT kilns
Dundee solves a weighty problem; world's largest cement-making kiln. il Bsns W p 150+ N 25 '67
CENNI di Pepo. See Cimabue
CENSORSHIP
ACLU supports review of Michigan censorship verdict. Pub W 191:226 Ja 23 '67
Controlling crime news; excerpts from The crime war. R. M. Cipes. Atlan 220:47-53 Ag '67
1966 in review; censorship and the freedom to read. Pub W 191:50-2 Ja 30 '67
School censorship in Fascist Italy and the U.S. G. L. Williams. bibliog f il Sch & Soc 95:185-8 Mr 18 '67
Some words of warning anent privacy. H. F. Pilpel. Pub W 191:45-6 Mr 6 '67
See also
Freedom of the press
Government and the press
Immoral literature and pictures
Information, Freedom of
Libraries—Censorship
Library bill of rights
Moving picture censorship
School libraries—Censorship

Argentina
Sex & the strait-laced strongman. il Time 90:33 Ag 18 '67

Czechoslovakia
Czech writers. Nation 205:453 N 6 '67
Purifying Prague. Newsweek 70:51 O 16 '67

England
On iniquity, by P. H. Johnson. Review New Repub 156:25-6 Mr 25 '67. H. Tracy

Greece, Modern
Safe & censored; military government censors theater. il Time 90:32 Jl 7 '67

Ireland
Irish censorship: the case of John McGahern. B. Cook. Cath World 206:176-9 Ja '68

Italy
School censorship in Fascist Italy and the U.S. G. L. Williams. bibliog f il Sch & Soc 95:185-8 Mr 18 '67

Russia
Chain reaction. il Newsweek 71:29-31 Ja 8 '68
Man of courage: Solzhenitsyn's denunciation of Soviet censorship. Newsweek 69:44 Je 12 '67
Shaming their elders; imprisoned Soviet writers. il Time 91:36 Ja 5 '68
Soviet censors on the defensive; fight against literary censorship. Life 63:4 Jl 28 '67

Spain
Ambivalence in Spain. Time 89:40+ Ap 7 '67
Rights and permissions; Spanish publishing. P. Nathan. Pub W 192:56 O 9 '67

United States
See Censorship

Yugoslavia
Resilient critics; Tito waging campaign against liberals. il Time 89:35 Ap 28 '67
CENSORSHIP (canon law)
End of the imprimatur. il Time 90:26 D 29 '67
CENSORSHIP, Library. See Libraries—Censorship
CENSORSHIP of mail. See Postal censorship
CENSUS
See also
United States—Census
CENSUS bureau (United States) See United States—Census, Bureau of the
CENTENNIAL exhibition, Philadelphia. See Philadelphia—Centennial exhibition, 1876
CENTENNIALS
Canada: almost inside the whale. D. Fisher. il Christian Cent 84:889-93 Jl 12 '67
Centennial for Nebraska. B. Belford. il Travel 127:32-7 Ap '67
CENTER for cultural and technical interchange between East and West. See Hawaii, University—East-West center
CENTER for editions of American authors. See Modern language association of America

CENTER for inter-American relations, New York
Inter-American activities. E. P. Birk. il Antiques 92:616 N '67
Our common commitment; excerpts from address, September 18, 1967. H. H. Humphrey. il Américas 19:1-4 N '67
CENTER for the study of democratic institutions, Santa Barbara, Calif.
California dreaming. J. Didion. Sat Eve Post 240:26+ O 21 '67
Ill-starred peace meeting; Pacem in terris convocation in Geneva. M. McGrory. America 116:829 Je 10 '67
Of many things; convocation in Geneva. H. J. Sievers. America 116:inside cover Je 3 '67
Peace on earth at Geneva. America 116:845 Je 17 '67
CENTERPIECES. See Table decoration
CENTERS for the performing arts
For concerts, dance and drama: flexible design; ed. by M. F. Schmertz. il Arch Rec 141:115-30 F '67
See also
Saratoga performing arts center
CENTRAL AMERICA
See also
Fishing—Central America

Economic integration
See Latin America—Economic integration

Economic policy
See also
Central American program of economic integration
CENTRAL AMERICAN bank for economic integration
BCIE: five years of progress. J. R. Castro. il Américas 19:28-31 Ag '67
CENTRAL AMERICAN program of economic integration
Central American regional integration. J. S. Nye, jr. bibliog f il Int Concil 562:5-66 Mr '67
Historical roots of Latin American integration; Central American common market. H. Martínez-Montero. il Américas 19:17-23 Ap '67
CENTRAL and southern Florida flood control district
Winds of change; south Florida's drought. Newsweek 69:56 My 29 '67
CENTRAL ARIZONA project (proposed)
Arizona water project blocked. il Sci N 92:55-6 Jl 15 '67
Canyon controversy: second round. il Sci N 91:302-3 Ap 1 '67
Hayden moves. New Repub 157:8 O 14 '67
Hayden's rough rider; Central Arizona project attached to public-works bill. Time 90:16 O 20 '67
CENTRAL ASIA. See Asia, Central
CENTRAL CITY, Colo.
Traveler's choice. V. F. Rees. Travel 127:68 Mr '67
CENTRAL CITY festival. See Music festivals—Colorado
CENTRAL-Eastern Europe. See Europe, Eastern
CENTRAL EUROPE
See also
Balkan states
CENTRAL Intelligence agency. See United States—Central intelligence agency
CENTRAL national bank, Chicago. See Chicago—Banks
CENTRAL OREGON community college, Bend, Ore.
Central Oregon college, a community college for commuter and resident students. il Arch Rec 142:160-1 N '67
CENTRAL park. See New York (city)—Parks and playgrounds
CENTRAL railroad company of New Jersey
Little railroad that couldn't: bankruptcy of Jersey central. il Bsns W p70-2 Ap 1 '67
CENTRAL treaty organization
CENTO economic committee meets at Washington; statement, March 14, 1967, and communique. W. S. Gaud. Dept State Bul 56:668-71 Ap 24 '67
Present viability of NATO, SEATO, and CENTO; address, April 1967, with questions and answers. A. E. P. Duffy. Ann Am Acad 372:33-9 Jl '67
CENTRAL WASHINGTON state college, Ellensburg
Nine stories hang from steel straps for two high-rise dormitories. il Arch Rec 142:151-2 D '67

CENTRALIZED purchasing. See Purchasing,
Municipal
CENTRALIZED schools. See Consolidated
schools
CENTRIFUGE process. See Foundry practice
CENTRIFUGES
Air force readies precision centrifuge. Tech W
21:38-9 Jl 3 '67
Sandia designs centrifuge for 100-lb. units.
W. E. Wilks. il Aero Tech 21:45 Ag 28 '67
Tight lid on U-235 production method; using
gas centrifuge for uranium separation. il Sci
N 91:327-8 Ap 8 '67
CENTRIOLES. See Cells
CEPEDA, Orlando
Cha Cha goes boom, boom, boom! M. Mulvoy.
il pors Sports Illus 27:18-21 Jl 24 '67
Proof of the pluses. il por Time 90:73-4 N 17
'67
CEPHALONIA (island)
Editor's report: Grecian find. M. M. Davis.
il Travel 128:58-62 S '67
CEPHEIDS
Cepheids in the small Magellanic cloud. il
Sky & Tel 33:149 Mr '67
RU camelopardalis, a unique cepheid vari-
able. M. Hack. il Sky & Tel 33:350-4 Je '67
See also
Stars, Variable
CERAMI, Charles A.
Preparing your children for tomorrow's world.
Parents Mag 43:35-8+ Ja '68
CERAMIC coating. See Enamel and enameling
CERAMIC costume jewelry. See Jewelry
CERAMIC materials
Ceramics puts a shield under 'copter crews;
carbide ceramic armor. il Bsns W p80 D
9 '67
CERAMICS. See Pottery
CERASO, John
Interference theory of forgetting; with bio-
graphical sketch. Sci Am 217:19, 117-21+
bibliog (p 156) O '67
CERATONIA siliqua. See Carob
CERCOPITHECINES. See Monkeys
CERDAN, Marcel, jr
Le petit Cerdan. il por Newsweek 70:65 N 13
'67
CEREAL foods
Fight for a place at the breakfast table. S.
Zalaznick. il Fortune 76:128-31+ D '67
Money wasted on unneeded vitamins. B. J.
Culliton. il Sci N 91:146 F 11 '67
Rich, crunchy goodness: $10 million a bowl.
il Newsweek 70:76-7 N 6 '67
CEREBELLUM
Frog cerebellum: absence of long-term in-
hibition upon Purkinje cells. R. Llinás
and J. R. Bloedel. bibliog il Science 155:
601-3 F 3 '67
Synaptic vesicles of inhibitory and excitatory
terminals in the cerebellum. L. M. H.
Larramendi and others. bibliog il Science
156:967-9 My 19 '67
CEREBRAL cortex
Discharge of frontal eye field neurons during eye movements in unanesthetized monkeys. E. Bizzi. bibliog il Science 157:1588-90
S 29 '67
Intracellular olfactory response of hippocampal neurons in awake, sitting squirrel
monkeys. T. Yokota and others. bibliog il
Science 157:1072-4 S 1 '67
Perceived number and evoked cortical potentials. M. R. Harter and C. T. White. bibliog il Science 156:406-8 Ap 21 '67
Prostaglandins: localization in subcellular
particles of rat cerebral cortex. K. Kataoka
and others. bibliog il Science 157:1187-9
S 8 '67
Responses of human somatosensory cortex to
stimuli below threshold for conscious sensa-
tion. B. Libet and others. bibliog il Science
158:1597-600 D 22 '67
Short reactions stay unconscious; neurological
basis in sensory cortex for unconscious processes. Sci N 92:631-2 D 30 '67
Visual form discrimination after removal of
the visual cortex in cats. S. S. Winans.
bibliog il Science 158:944-6 N 17 '67
CEREBRAL hemorrhage
Patricia Neal: suddenly I wanted to live! S.
Frank. Good H 165:70-1+ Jl '67
CEREMONY of innocence; drama. See Ribman,
R.
CERF, Bennett Alfred
Bennett Cerf's views on trends in publish-
ing. Pub W 192:36 O 16 '67
CERN (Conseil européen pour la recherche nu-
cléaire) See European organization for nu-
clear research

CERRI, Lawrence J.
Teaching Russian in junior high schools. Sr
Schol 90:sup21 My 5 '67
CERRUTI, James
Jamaica goes it alone. Nat Geog Mag 132:
842-73 D '67
CERTIFICATES, Aviators. See Air pilots—
Licenses
CERTIFICATES of deposit
False alarm in CDs? A. H. Hauser. il Duns R
88:43-4+ D '66
CERTIFICATION of teachers. See Teachers—
Certification
CERTIFIED public accountants. See Account-
ants
CERUMEN. See Earwax
CERUTI, Giacomo
Barons and beggars of Giacomo Ceruti. L.
Mallé. il Art N 66:26-9+ Mr '67
CERVANTES, Alfonso J.
To prevent a chain of super-Watts. bibliog f
Harvard Bsns R 45:55-65 S '67; Excerpts.
por U S News 63:108-11 O 9 '67
CERVICITIS. See Cervix—Diseases
CERVI'S Rocky Mountain Journal
Why in hell; criticism of Denver newspapers.
il Newsweek 70:64 S 4 '67
CERVIX
Diseases
Cervicitis: a common condition in women.
Good H 165:203 O '67
CESAREAN section
What are the hazards of childbirth by sur-
gery? Todays Health 45:86 Ap '67
CESIUM in the body
Strophanthidin-sensitive transport of cesium
and sodium in muscle cells. R. A. Sjodin
and L. A. Beaugé. bibliog il Science 156:
1248-50 Je 2 '67
CESSNA, Perry A.
County water system proved best. Am City
82:105-7+ F '67
CESTODA
Neurosecretory cells in a cestode, hymenolepis
diminuta. K. G. Davey and W. R. Breck-
enridge. bibliog il Science 158:931-2 N 17 '67
CETACEA
Immobilizing drugs lethal to swimming mam-
mals; letter. W. E. Schevill and others.
bibliog Science 157:630-1 Ag 11 '67
CEYLON
Letter from Ceylon. M. Connelly. Holiday
42:51-4 D '67
See also
Colombo

Description and travel
Ceylon sidetrip. E. S. Smith. il Travel 128:
30-5+ S '67
CHABAS, Yves
Americans, why aren't you liked? Christian
Cent 84:1127-8 S 6 '67
CHABE, Alexander M.
Evaluating Soviet education. bibliog f Sch &
Soc 95:458-61 N 25 '67
CHABRIER, Alexis Emmanuel
Records:
Education manquée. Opera N 31:34 Ja 7
'67
CHADWICK, Ruth
Anticlimax; poem. McCalls 94:124+ Ag '67
Who keeps in trim? poem. McCalls 94:177
Mr '67
CHAE, Myung Shin
Korean general tells how to beat the Viet
Cong; interview, ed. by G. C. Troelstrup.
por U S News 62:56-7 My 15 '67
CHAFFEE, Roger Bruce
Chaffee. il pors Life 62:20-1 F 3 '67
Fire in the spacecraft! il pors Newsweek
69:25-9 F 6 '67
For the heroes, salute and farewell. il Life
62:20-1+ F 10 '67
To strive, to seek, to find, and not to yield.
il por Time 89:13-16 F 3 '67
We knew that someday... Sci N 91:112 F 4 '67
CHAFING dish cookery
Chafing dish cook book. R. C. Bateman. il
House & Gard 132:245+ O '67
CHAGALL, Marc
Chagall's Magic flute. I. Kolodin. Sat R 50:
46-7 Mr 4 '67
Flowery Flute; sets and costumes for The
magic flute. il Time 89:43+ Mr 3 '67
Mozart and Chagall. il Newsweek 69:75 Mr
6 '67
CHAGLA, Mahomedali Currim
Tower of Babel. por Newsweek 70:53 S 18
'67
CHAGNON, Napoleon A.
Yanomamö social organization and warfare.
Natur Hist 76:44-8 bibliog(p69) D '67

CHAI, F. Y.
 Crisis; interview. New Yorker 43:22 Jl 29 '67
CHAIN letters
 Luck be a prayer tonight. G. Ace. Sat R 50:
 10 S 30 '67
CHAIN saws. See Saws
CHAIN stores
 High cost of eating. B. B. Seligman. Commentary 44:48-52 Jl '67; Discussion. 44:6+
 O '67
 Partners in sales; John Lewis chain of stores throughout Britain. il Time 90:100+ D 8 '67
 See also
 Broadway-Hale stores, incorporated
 Penney, J. C. company
CHAINS
 Chain bag is a kneeling pad. il Sunset 138:
 105 F '67
CHAIR cars. See Railroads—Cars
CHAIRS
 Don't just sit there . . . il Redbook 129:78-81+
 S '67
 Eclectic chair; exhibition at New York's Museum of modern art. il Newsweek 70:96 O 9
 '67
 How to buy recliner chairs. Am Home 70:34
 D '67
 Scandinavian design: still making waves. il
 House B 110:106-7 Ja '68
CHALFONT, Alun Arthur Gwynne Jones, baron. See Chalfont, A. G. J.
CHALFONT, Arthur Gwynne Jones, baron
 Troubled times of George Brown. B. Wenham.
 New Repub 157:12-13 N 18 '67
CHALK, O. Roy
 Rey Tiza. por Newsweek 70:84+ Jl 17 '67
CHALL, Jeanne S.
 Helping Johnny read. Newsweek 70:66 N 6 '67
CHAMBER music
 See also
 Phonograph records—Chamber music
CHAMBER orchestras
 Music to my ears; performance of The good soldier Schweik by the Chamber symphony of Philadelphia. I. Kolodin. Sat R 50:38
 D 16 '67
 Report: New York; revival of The good soldier Schweik. J. W. Freeman. Opera N
 32:31 D 30 '67
CHAMBERLAIN, Barbara Blau
 Cape Cod; with biographical sketch. Natur Hist 76:4, 24-33 bibliog(p67) My '67
CHAMBERLAIN, Francis P.
 Catholic education in Latin America. America
 116:750-3 My 20 '67
CHAMBERLAIN, Gary L.
 Crime, confessions and the Supreme court.
 America 117:32-4 Jl 8 '67
CHAMBERLAIN, Gary M.
 Not-so-fireproof buildings. Am City 82:119-
 21+ S '67
 Riot control. Am City 82:87-9+ F; 107-9 Mr '67
CHAMBERLAIN, John
 Auto safety; the truth and the hokum. Nat R
 19:343-6 Ap 4 '67
 Is there a statute of limitations on justice?
 Nat R 19:1257-8 N 14 '67
CHAMBERLAIN, Neil W.
 Role of business in society's perfectibility; excerpt from address. Mo Labor R 90:41-3 Ap
 '67
CHAMBERLAIN, Wilt
 Just too much giant; with report by J. Larner.
 il pors Life 62:82-4+ Ap 21 '67
 Shoot, Wilt. Time 90:45 D 22 '67
 Sweet revenge. Time 89:40 My 5 '67
 Waiting made it sweeter. F. Deford. il por
 Sports Illus 26:54-6 My 8 '67
CHAMBERLIN, Anne
 And now, for the consumer, Miss Betty Furness! Sat Eve Post 240:26-7 Je 17 '67
 Big dude drive in the Crazies. por Sat Eve
 Post 240:32-7 Jl 29 '67
 Dance wildly, Queen Mary's about to die.
 Sat Eve Post 240:72-3 D 16 '67
 Enough is enough, Tom Edison. Sat Eve Post
 240:91-2 My 20 '67
 Expo 67: the big blast up north. Sat Eve Post
 240:30-7 Ap 22 '67
 Swinging Americans. Mlle 64:222-3+ Ap '67
CHAMBERLIN, J. Gordon
 Ecumenical tangle. Christian Cent 85:75-7 Ja
 17 '68
CHAMBERLIN, Thomas
 Owner's comments. Yachting 122:52-3 O '67
CHAMBERLIN, William Henry
 Edmund Burke: friend of freedom. Sat R 50:
 22-3 Ap 15 '67
 John Stuart Mill: independent radical. Sat R
 50:30-1 My 20 '67

Medicare; foretaste of 1984? Nat R 19:413 Ap
 18 '67
What did a young critic read? Sat R 50:78-9
 F 11 '67
CHAMBERS, Sir Paul
 International trade and investment; address,
 March 7, 1967. Vital Speeches 33:371-5 Ap
 1 '67
 about
 Sirs Paul and Peter. por Time 90:94+ N 17
 '67
CHAMBERS, Whittaker
 Friendship and fratricide, by M. A. Zeligs.
 Review
 Atlan por 220:54-7 Ag '67. G. Rees; Reply with rejoinder. M. A. Zeligs. 220:47-8
 D '67
 Nat R 19:295-8+ Mr 21 '67. E. Van Den
 Haag
 Nation 204:373-4 Mr 20 '67. D. Cort
 Newsweek il por 69:92-3 Ja 30 '67. S.
 Maloff
 Sat R por 50:34-5 F 11 '67. M. Harris
 Time por 89:102+ F 10 '67
CHAMBERS of commerce
 Executive trends. Nations Bsns 55:16+ F '67
CHAMBERS'S encyclopaedia
 Chambers's fourth edition promoted in U.S.
 market. Pub W 191:38+ Mr 13 '67
CHAMELEONS
 Chameleon. C. Gans. il Natur Hist 76:52-9 Ap
 '67
CHAMETZKY, Jules
 Old Jew in new times. Nation 205:436-8 O 30
 '67
CHAMPA, Kermit S.
 Olitski: nothing but color. Art N 66:36-8+
 My '67
CHAMPAIGN, Ill.
 Ripper chews through frozen clay. J. T.
 Kearns. il Am City 82:60 F '67
CHAMPION, George
 Capital and economic growth; address, February 16, 1967. Vital Speeches 33:330-3 Mr
 15 '67
 Creative competition. bibliog f Harvard Bsns
 R 45:61-7 My '67
 Our obsolete welfare state; address, October
 29, 1967. Vital Speeches 34:111-14 D 1 '67
 Preaching what you practice; interview. por
 Nations Bsns 55:48-9+ Mr '67
 U.S. in the world market place; address, April
 24, 1967. Vital Speeches 33:505-8 Je 1 '67
CHAMPION papers incorporated-United States plywood corporation merger. See Business consolidations and mergers
CHAMPLAIN, LAKE
 From sword to scythe in Champlain country.
 E. A. Starbird. il Nat Geog Mag 132:153-201
 Ag '67
CHAMPLAIN waterway. See Waterways—United States
CHAMPTOCÉ, France
 Soul of France. E. Butler. Holiday 42:92+ S
 '67
CHAMULA Indians. See Indians of Mexico
CHAN, Melvin
 Automatic light blinker. Pop Electr 27:56 Ag
 '67
 Multi-waveform generator. Pop Electr 27:52-
 4+ S '67
 Transistor curve tracer. Electr World 79:
 55-8+ Ja '68
CHAN, S. L. and Quastel, J. H.
 Tetrodotoxin: effects on brain metabolism in vitro. bibliog Science 156:1752-3 Je 30 '67
CHANCE, Britton, 1913-, and others
 Sailing yacht research. Science 156:411-12 Ap
 21 '67
CHANCE, Britton, family
 Sailing by Chance. E. S. Gillingham, jr. il
 Motor B 119:88-90+ Ap '67
CHANCE, Dean
 New Dean on the list of great nonhitters. C.
 Kirkpatrick. il por Sports Illus 27:42-3 Jl 24
 '67
CHANCE, Norman A.
 Changing world of the Cree; with biographical sketch. Natur Hist 76:4, 16-23 My '67
CHANCE
 See also
 Probabilities
CHANCELLOR, John William
 Honest persuader views an imprecise instrument; interview, ed. by A. Henehan. Sr
 Schol 90:20 Ap 28 '67
 How the U.S. tells its story to the world;
 interview. por U S News 62:76-9 F 20 '67
 International broadcasting and the changing world audience; address, April 1967, with questions and answers. Ann Am Acad 372:
 72-9 Jl '67

CHANCELLOR, John William—*Continued*

about

Change of voice. por Time 89:41 Je 2 '67
Leaving the Voice. por Newsweek 69:63 My 29 '67

CHANCERIES, Diocesan
Those faceless chanceries. J. O'Donoghue. Commonweal 86:167-71 Ap 28 '67

CHANDLER, Otis
New winds in the South, new splash in the North. W. L. Rivers. il Sat R 50:75-6+ S 23 '67

CHANDRASEKHAR, S.
Too many people, is India facing disaster? interview. por U S News 62:90-3 Ap 3 '67

CHANEL, Gabrielle
Collections by Chanel; tr. by J. Barry. por McCalls 94:12 Je; 44 Jl; 40 Ag; 54 S; 95:24 O; 72 D '67

CHANGE
Montessori suey. R. G. G. Price. Atlan 220: 124-5 O '67
We had better be better! address, October 16, 1967. H. R. Hall. Vital Speeches 34:125-8 D 1 '67

CHANGE, Economic. See Economic change
CHANGE, Social. See Social change
CHANGE, Technological. See Technological change
CHANGE of life in women. See Menopause
CHANGE of sex
Transsexual operation. T. Buckley. Esquire 67:111-14+ Ap '67
Twilight people. il Newsweek 70:55-6 O 2 '67

CHANGEUX, J. P. See Podleski, T. jt. auth.
CHANNEL ISLANDS (English Channel)
Norman Island. C. N. Parkinson. Atlan 220: 92-4 Ag '67

CHANNEL ISLANDS, Calif. See Santa Barbara Islands

CHANNING, Carol
Full evening of brotherliness; President's annual party for the Chief Justice, the Speaker of the House and the Vice President at the White House. H. Sidey. il por Life 62:30D Ja 27 '67
Operation Big daddy. il por Time 89:19-20 Ja 27 '67

CHAO, Chung-yao
Incredible story of How China got the bomb; excerpts. W. L. Ryan and S. Summerlin. il Look 31:19-25 Jl 25 '67

CHAO, E. C. T.
Shock effects in certain rock-forming minerals. bibliog Science 156:192-202 Ap 14 '67

CHAPEL, I. C.
Clatter stopper. Pop Electr 26:57-8 Je '67

CHAPIN, Emerson
Korea: tenacity pays off. Reporter 37:25-6+ D 14 '67

CHAPIN, Katherine Garrison
Parting in summer; poem. New Repub 156:22 Ap 29 '67
Perse in flight. New Repub 157:26-8 S 23 '67

CHAPIN, Kim
Badminton. Sports Illus 26:65-7 Ap 24 '67
Boating. Sports Illus 27:96-7 D 4 '67
Motor sports (cont) Sports Illus 27:58-60 Ag 14; 62-3 S 25; 53-4 O 30 '67
Please don't die now, baby. Sports Illus 27: 30-1 O 16 '67
Swimming. Sports Illus 26:97-9 Ap 17; 27:48+ Ag 21 '67
Tennis (cont) Sports Illus 26:56 Je 19; 27: 44-5 Jl 24; 97-8+ S 18 '67
They're still at it in Indiana. Sports Illus 26: 30-1 Je 26 '67

CHAPIN, Roy Dikeman, 1915-
Can Roy Chapin salvage AMC? il pors Bsns W p 144-6+ Ap 8 '67

CHAPIN, Suzy
Adjustable diet cookbook; excerpts. Ladies Home J 85:72-3+ Ja '68

CHAPLAINS, College. See Colleges and universities—Religious life
CHAPLAINS, Industrial
Industrial chaplain. Newsweek 69:81A Ap 10 '67

CHAPLAINS, Military
Chaplaincy agencies defend high standards. Christian Cent 84:101 Ja 25 '67

CHAPLAINS, Prison
Breakthrough for prison chaplains; Cyril Engler's suggestions. America 117:235 S 9 '67

CHAPLIN, Charles
Ageless master's anatomy of comedy; interview; ed. by R. Meryman. pors Life 62:80-4+ Mr 10 '67

about

Anatomy of tepidity. H. Kenner. por Nat R 19:599-600 My 30 '67

CHAPMAN, A. R.
Oak in paradise. Am For 73:27+ S '67

CHAPMAN, Bruce K.
Why not abolish the draft? Nat R 19:303-5 Mr 21 '67

CHAPMAN, Charles Frederic
Piloting, seamanship and small boat handling; excerpts. Motor B 120:86-9 Jl; 50-2 Ag; 48-51 O; 76-9 D '67

CHAPMAN, Clark R. See Cruikshank, D. P. jt. auth.

CHAPMAN, Colin
Briton views American schools. Am Ed 3:23-6 Je '67

CHAPMAN, Leonard F. Jr
Cerebral commandant. il por Time 90:25 D 15 '67
Management marine. por Newsweek 70:33 D 18 '67
Marines get a new leader. il por U S News 63:18 D 18 '67

CHAPPELL, Eleanor
Taking care of your teeth. Am Home 71:103 Ja '68

CHAPPELLE, Emmett W. and others
Prevention of protein denaturation during exposure to sterilization temperatures. bibliog Science 155:1287-8 Mr 10 '67

CHAR fishing
Big three of cold-water sport fishing: trout, char, salmon. A. J. McClane. il Field & S 72:45+ My '67
Winged safari for Arctic char. D. Barnes. il Sports Illus 26:48-55 My 15 '67

CHARACTER
Where I stand, and why. B. Spock. Redbook 129:20+ Jl '67
See also
Christian life
Ethics
Personality

CHARACTER analysis
Venus and you. A. Star. il Seventeen 26:144-5 S '67

CHARACTER education. See Moral education
CHARACTER reading. See Character analysis; Graphology
CHARACTER tests
See also
Personality tests

CHARACTERIZATION
Elusive secret; creating memorable characters. H. D. Jordan. Writer 80:24-6 D '67
New lit; giving fictitious names to people who may be recognizable. G. Ace. Sat R 50:5 Mr 18 '67
Verbs and people. F. Rickett. Writer 80:11-13 Ja '67

CHARACTERS in literature
Collision: child's and the adult world; concerning Ellen Grae by Vera and Bill Cleaver. J. A. Rowell. Library J 92:3126 S 15 '67
Dear characters. J. Cunningham. Horn Bk 43:233-4 Ap '67
If the name fits. J. O'Hara. il Holiday 41:28+ My '67
Is Babbitt dead? survey reveals what real estate people think of their reflected images. L. S. Burns. bbiliog f Harvard Bsns R 45: 14-16+ S '67
Micawber sahib; Mehta's Delinquent Chacha. A. Fremantle. il Reporter 36:46 My 4 '67
Multiple hero. J. L. Collier. il Holiday 41:10+ Ap '67
Tarzan phenomenon: success in the overseas market but not in United States; letter to the editor. R. M. Hodes. Library J 92:1876 My 15 '67
Tarzan, son of Kala. S. Maloff. il Newsweek 69:100+ Ap 10 '67
Tom Jones. K. Rexroth. Sat R 50:13 Jl 1 '67
Who is Doris Grumbach? real faces behind the names in fiction. M. Janeway. Atlan 220: 90-1 Ag '67
See also
Characterization
Fiction
Shakespeare, W.—Characters
Spies in literature

CHARACTERS in moving pictures
Dream that never died; Gone with the wind; Melanie and others. O. De Havilland. il Look 31:113-14 D 12 '67

CHARACTERS in opera
Flashes of lightning; Verdi goes to the heart of his characters. S. Jenkins, jr. il Opera N 32:24-5 Ja 20 '68

CHEATING
See also
Fraud
CHEATING at cards. See Cardsharping
CHEATING in schoolwork
Crack in the façade; latest cheating scandal.
il Newsweek 69:117 Mr 13 '67
Scandal in Colorado Springs. Time 89:66 Mr
3 '67
Why the cadets cheat. J. A. Heise. il Nation
204:622-6 My 15 '67; Discussion. 205:2+ Jl
3 '67

CHECKERBOARDS
Make this tile-top chess and checkerboard.
E. Waltner and W. Waltner. il Pop Mech
128:146-7+ D '67

CHECKLEY, Bob
Auto news makers. D. MacDonald. por Motor T 19:98 Jl '67

CHECKS
Bank checking services. Bet Hom & Gard
45:105 D '67
Cashing in on the checkless society. R. L.
Kramer and W. P. Livingston. bibliog f
Harvard Bsns R 45:141-9 S '67
Money goes electronic in the 1970s; check-
less, cashless society. il Bsns W p54-6+
Ja 13 '68
Who's afraid of the big blank check? attempt
to stamp out uncoded checks. Time 90:95
S 15 '67

CHECKUP, Medical. See Physical examinations

CHEESE
Cheese: best of both worlds; Parmesan and
Brie. C. W. Morton. il Atlan 219:116+ Mr
'67
This cheese and butter won't make you fat.
Farm J 91:74P Mr '67
See also
Cookery—Cheese

CHEETAH (periodical)
Grownups in hippieland. il Time 91:56 Ja 5
'68

CHEEVER, John
Another story. New Yorker 43:42-8 F 25 '67
Bullet park; story. New Yorker 43:56-9 N 25
'67
Sophia, Sophia, Sophia. Sat Eve Post 240:32-5
O 21 '67

CHEFS. See Cooks

CHEKHOV, Anton Pavlovich
Chekhov's plays. K. Rexroth. Sat R 50:18 Jl
8 '67

CHELMINSKI, Rudolph
Not so bad to be different. Life 63:54-5 Ag 18
'67

CHELONIA mydas. See Turtles, Green
CHELSEA, London. See London
CHELSEA theatre center. See New York (city)
—Theater

CHEMICAL abstracts (periodical)
Services of professional societies; summary of
addresses at ABPC conference. N. E. Cottrell; F. J. Weyl. Pub W 191:39-40 Ap 10 '67

CHEMICAL apparatus and supplies
Atom reactions in flow tubes. B. A. Thrush.
bibliog il Science 156:470-3 Ap 28 '67

CHEMICAL bonds
Chemical bonding information from photoelectron spectroscopy. C. S. Fadley and others. bibliog il Science 157:1571-3 S 29 '67
Fission-fragment synthesis of a new nitrogen-fluorine compound. A. R. Miller and
others. bibliog Science 155:688 F 10 '67
Spectroscopy, molecular orbitals, and chemical bonding; address, December 12, 1966. R.
S. Mulliken. bibliog il Science 157:13-24 Jl
7 '67

CHEMICAL elements
Onward to element 126; omnitron. Sci Am
217:50+ O '67
See also names of chemical elements,
e.g. Mendelevium

Atomic element 101
See Mendelevium

Atomic no. 102
See Nobelium

Nomenclature
Discovery, undiscovery, rediscovery. il Sci N
92:274-5 S 16 '67

CHEMICAL geology. See Geochemistry

CHEMICAL industries
Chemical makers come to a boil; tariff deals
in Kennedy round. Bsns W p36+ My 27 '67

Chemical makers try a new price formula.
Bsns W p42 S 16 '67
See also
Diamond alkali company
Dow chemical company
Du Pont de Nemours, E. I, and company
Grace, W. R. and company
Imperial chemical industries, limited
Monsanto company
Union carbide corporation

Finance
Hopeful formula for chemicals. il Bsns W p34-
5 Jl 15 '67

Belgium
Organic change at Solvay. Fortune 76:198 S
15 '67

Germany (Federal Republic)
Another no. 2 tries harder; Germany's Bayer
and Hoechst, competing to control Chem-
ische werke Huels. Bsns W p 35-6 N 4 '67
Chemical trio thrives on booming foreign
sales. il Bsns W p80 Jl 8 '67

CHEMICAL instruments. See Chemical apparatus and supplies

CHEMICAL lighting. See Lighting

CHEMICAL reactions
Defining sections of the chemical blur. Sci N
92:464-5 N 11 '67
Transition-state models and hydrogen-isotope
effects. R. E. Weston, jr. bibliog il Science
158:332-42 O 20 '67
See also
Oxidation reduction reaction

CHEMICAL reagents
Complement: substitution of the terminal
component in immune hemolysis by 1,10-
phenanthroline. U. Hadding and H. J.
Müller-Eberhard. bibliog il Science 157:442-3
Jl 28 '67

CHEMICAL research
See also
Gordon research conferences

CHEMICAL warfare
Chemical and biological warfare: the research
program. E. Langer. il Science 155:174-6+;
299-303 Ja 13-20 '67; Discussion. 155:1196+;
156:582 Mr 10, My 5 '67
Chemical and biological weapons; once over
lightly on Capitol hill. E. Langer. Science
156:1073+ My 26 '67; Reply. D. R. McKeen.
157:875 Ag 25 '67
CBW, Vietnam evoke scientist's concern. E.
Langer. Science 155:302 Ja 20 '67; Discussion. 156:167, 1029-30 Ap 14, My 26 '67
5,000 scientists vs. CBW. Sci N 91:185 F 25
'67
Gas and germ warfare; controversy over research contracts. S. Hersh. New Repub 157:
12-14 Jl 1 '67
Herbicides in Vietnam. A. W. Galston. New
Repub 157:19-21 N 25 '67
Just a drop can kill; secret work on gas and
germ warfare; research at military instal-
lations, colleges, universities and private
firms. S. M. Hersh. New Repub 156:11-15
My 6 '67
More against chemical warfare; petition
signed by more than 5,000 U.S. scientists.
Sci Am 216:48 Ap '67
Prospect beyond the poisons. N. Cousins.
Sat R 50:20 Ag 19 '67
This way to hell; use of napalm bombs.
Christian Cent 84:1036-7 Ag 16 '67

CHEMICALS
Manufacture
See also
Chemical industries

Physiological effects
First aid: chemical injuries to eyes or skin.
C. J. Potthoff. Todays Health 45:84 Ap '67
See also
Pharmacology

Prices
Chemical makers try a new price formula.
Bsns W p42 S 16 '67

CHEMICALS, Agricultural. See Agricultural
chemicals

CHEMISTRY
See also
Biochemistry
Geochemistry
Photographic chemistry
Radicals (chemistry)

Study and teaching
Chemical education in Negro colleges. E. O.
Woolfolk and L. S. Smith. il Negro Hist Bul
30:7-11 F '67

CHEMISTRY, Analytic
See also
Radioactivation analysis
Spectrophotometry
CHEMISTRY, Medical and pharmaceutical
See also
Pharmacology
CHEMISTRY, Organic
See also
Aromatic compounds
Electroorganic chemistry
CHEMISTRY, Physical and theoretical
Chemical properties of materials. H. Reiss.
il Sci Am 217:210-14+ S '67
See also
Solution (chemistry)
Thermodynamics
CHEMISTRY, Surface. See Surface chemistry
CHEMWAY corporation
Chemway's way. R. Levy. il Duns R 88:45+
D '66
CHEN, Francis F.
Leakage problem in fusion reactors; with
biographical sketch. Sci Am 217:10, 76-88
bibliog(p 134+) Jl '67
CHEN, Jane L. and Wildman, S. G.
Functional chloroplast polyribosomes from
tobacco leaves. bibliog Science 155:1271-3
Mr 10 '67
CHEN, Raymond F. and others
Fluorescence decay times: proteins, co-
enzymes, and other compounds in water.
bibliog Science 156:949-51 My 19 '67
CHEN, Yi
Survival course. por Newsweek 69:48 Je 12 '67
CHENEY, Frances Neel
Current reference books. See issues of Wilson
library bulletin
CHENEY, Louis T.
Telfair and its paintings. Antiques 91:353-9
Mr '67
CHENG, Chu-yuan
Cultural revolution and China's economy.
bibliog f Cur Hist 53:148-54+ S '67
Expert size-up of red China as a nuclear
power; interview. por U S News 63:38 Jl 3
'67
CHERKASKY, Martin
City should get out of the hospital business.
N Y Times Mag p52-3+ O 8 '67
CHERRY trees
Cherry trees hoard water. Sci N 91:195 F 25
'67
CHERT
Hydrous sodium silicates from Lake Magadi,
Kenya: precursors of bedded chert. H. P.
Eugster. bibliog il Science 157:1177-80 S 8
'67
CHERUBINI, Luigi
Medea. Criticism
Opera N il 32:29 D 16 '67
CHESAPEAKE BAY
Chesapeake: colonial haven. L. Jonckheere.
il Sr Schol 91:sup 14-16+ S 28 '67
In the wake of the skipjacks. M. B.
Matthews, jr. il Motor B 119:32-3+ Ap
'67
CHESHIRE, Maxine
Living it up in Washington. Nations Bsns
55:58-9 Jl '67
CHESKIN, Louis
Conducting a marketing survey for a market-
ing book. por Pub W 193:59-60 Ja 15 '68
CHESLER, Mark, and Fox, Robert
Teacher peer relations and educational
change. NEA J 56:25-6 My '67
CHESS
Chess corner. A. Horowitz. See issues of
Saturday review
Further adventures of terrible-tempered
Bobby; international tournament in Tunisia.
T. Matthews. Sports Illus 27:69-70+ N 20 '67
Problems that are built on the knight's move
in chess. M. Gardner. il Sci Am 217:128-32
O '67
CHESS and checkerboards. See Checkerboards
CHEST
Diseases
Your chest pain may not be heart trouble.
J. D. Wassersug. il Sci Digest 62:74-8 S
'67
CHESTERFIELD, Ind.
Another all-mercury city. il Am City 82:128
N '67
CHESTERTON, Gilbert Keith
Index to G. K. Chesterton; ed. by J. W.
Sprug. Review
New Repub 156:36+ Ap 8 '67. A. Campbell
CHESTS
Build this two-in-one chest-crib. D. Schack-
muth. il Pop Mech 127:172-5 My '67

CHEVALIER, Lois R. and Cohen, Leonard
Terrible trouble with the birth-control pills.
Ladies Home J 84:43-5+ Jl '67
CHEYENNE Indians
Photographs
Assignment #1. H. Keppler. il Mod Phot 31:
58-65 F '67
CHIAN, Lucia T. Y. and Wiigram, G. F.
Tyrosinase inhibition: its role in suntanning
and in albinism. bibliog Science 155:198-200
Ja 13 '67
CHIANG, Ching-kuo
His father's son. por Newsweek 70:50+ D
11 '67
CHIANG, Kai-shek
Ready & waiting. por Time 89:28+ Ja 27 '67
CHIANG, Kai-shek, Mme. See Chiang, M. L. S.
CHIANG, Mei-ling (Sung)
Valor of truth; reprint. U S News 63:108+
S 11 '67
CHIANG Ching. See Mao, T. T. Mme
CHIAPPETTA, Jerry
Coho craze in Michigan. Field & S 72:42-3+
Ja '68
Stud tires for sportsmen. Field & S 72:58-9+
S '67
CHIARA, Alan R.
Alan R. Chiara favors a design concept; with
biographical sketch. il por Am Artist 31:52-
3+ N '67
CHIARANDINI, D. J. and Gerschenfeld, H. M.
Ionic mechanism of cholinergic inhibition in
molluscan neurons. bibliog Science 156:1595-6
Je 23 '67
—and others
Ionic mechanisms of cholinergic excitation in
molluscan neurons. bibliog Science 156:1597-
9 Je 23 '67
CHICAGO
Chicago digs itself out. il Bsns W p36 F 4 '67
New Chicago; symposium. il Holiday 41:13-
17+ Mr '67
When leasing autos for municipal use. F. J.
Casey. Am City 82:153-4 F '67
Worst snow in Chicago's history. il Life 62:
62-70 F 10 '67

Airports

Can airports cope with the jet age? Chicago
story. il Bsns W p63-4 Jl 22 '67
Midway readied for early airline return. Aviation W 87:39 S 11 '67

Anti-poverty program

Needed: a poverty plumber. il Life 63:35 Ag 25
'67

Architecture

Chicago's multi-use giant; John Hancock center. il Arch Rec 144:137-44 Ja '67
They'll commute by elevator in 100-story
tower; John Hancock center. A. P. Armagnac. il Pop Sci 190:100-1 My '67

Art

Chicago. J. Kind. Art N 65:27+ Ja; 66:59+
Mr; 61 Sum '67
Chicago's Picasso. il Life 63:85-6 Ag 25 '67
Troubled arts. W. Murray. il Holiday 41:
62-5+ Mr '67
See also
Chicago—Monuments, statues, etc.

Banks

Chicago's credit card crisis; mass replacement
of cards. Bsns W p35 Jl 15 '67
Nicest thing since money; banks credit-cards
encourage fraud. Newsweek 70:73 Jl 17 '67

City planning

Old neighborhood swings back to life; Chicago's old town section. il Bsns W p80-2
Ag 26 '67

Crime

Arrested by detectives Valesares and Sullivan,
charge: murder. B. J. Friedman. il Sat Eve
Post 240:38-42+ Ap 22 '67
Nicest thing since money; banks credit-cards
encourage fraud. Newsweek 70:73 Jl 17 '67
Normal week for crime. R. Rice. il N Y Times
Mag p8-9+ Je 18 '67

Description

Chicago sights and delights. A. Bester. il
Holiday 41:133-7 Mr '67
Illinois: the city and the plain. R. P. Jordan.
il Nat Geog Mag 131:745-97 Je '67
New Chicago. A. Karlen. il Holiday 41:46-53
Mr '67
Spirit of Old Town. R. Atcheson. il Holiday
41:66-9+ Mr '67

CHICAGO—*Continued*

Education

Chicago: legacy of an ice age; excerpt from Our children's burden. C. Remsberg and B. Remsberg. il Sat R 50:73-5+ My 20 '67; Discussion. 50:50+ Je 17 '67
Chicago plans desegregation. Sat R 50:73-4 O 21 '67
Mixed classes; broadest plan so far. U S News 63:10 S 4 '67
New Trier, East and West; schools in Chicago's exclusive North Shore suburbs. il Newsweek 69:90 My 22 '67
What about ghetto? school integration. Newsweek 70:49 S 4 '67

Education, Board of

Chicago: legacy of an ice age; excerpt from Our children's burden. C. Remsberg and B. Remsberg. il Sat R 50:73-5+ My 20 '67; Discussion. 50:50+ Je 17 '67

Elections

Data processing speeds the election process. J. E. Murphy. il Am City 82:100 My '67
King Richard the fourth. il Time 89:36 Ap 14 '67
Making book on Mr Daley. E. S. Gilbreth. Nation 204:395-8 Mr 27 '67
Once and future king; R. J. Daley re-elected. Newsweek 69:46 Ap 17 '67

Fires

See Fires

Galleries and museums

See also
Chicago art institute
Museum of contemporary art, Chicago

Hotels, restaurants, etc.

Dining in Chicago. S. Spitzer. il Holiday 41:84-6+ Mr '67
Personal business; business trip to Chicago. Bsns W p 169-70 Ja 28 '67

Housing

Tenant unions seek to put an end to slums. S. Olds. Christian Cent 84:1579-82 D 6 '67

Intellectual life

When poets looped the loop; the Chicago renaissance. J. K. Hutchens. Sat R 50:35-6 Ja 28 '67

Libraries

Chicago area librarians score use by outsiders. Library J 92:1558+ Ap 15 '67
See also
Chicago public library

McCormick Place

Conventioneers lose their biggest home. il Bsns W p28-30 Ja 21 '67
McCormick Place sparks new fire; controversy over rebuilding. il Bsns W p90-1 D 16 '67

Mayors

Making book on Mr Daley. E. S. Gilbreth. Nation 204:395-8 Mr 27 '67

Monuments, statues, etc.

Chicago prepares for biggest Picasso of all; 136-ton sculpture to Chicago's new Civic center. il Bsns W p 122-3 My 6 '67
Old maestro's magic; Picasso's sculpture in civic center. il Time 90:54-5 Ag 25 '67
Picasso in the steelworks; sculpture piece for Chicago's civic center. il Fortune 76:111-13 Ag '67

Music

Chicago. J. W. Stedman and G. McElroy. Opera N 31:27 Ap 15 '67
Grandiose musical muddle. R. C. Marsh. Hi Fi 17:MA20+ Ag '67
See also
Chicago symphony orchestra
Lyric opera of Chicago

Negroes

Apostle of economics; J. Jackson's Operation Breadbasket. D. Llorens. il Ebony 22:78-80+ Ag '67
Homesick in freedomland; voter-registration drive. il Newsweek 69:37-8 F 13 '67
Organization men; Blackstone Rangers of Chicago gang, renounces violence. il Newsweek 69:34 Je 5 '67
Shocking rise of murder. J. Star. il Look 31:28-34 S 19 '67
Wall of respect; artists of Organization of black American culture paint mural in Chicago ghetto. il Ebony 23:48-50 D '67

Newspapers

Fighting to lose least. il Time 90:54 Ag 18 '67
See also
Chicago American (newspaper)
Chicago tribune

Parks and playgrounds

Lincoln park; photographs. D. Kirkland. Holiday 41:74-83 Mr '67

Police

Arrested by detectives Valesares and Sullivan, charge: murder. B. J. Friedman. il Sat Eve Post 240:38-42+ Ap 22 '67
Criminology lesson; superintendent retires. Newsweek 69:32-3 My 29 '67
Shocking rise of murder. J. Star. il Look 31:28-34 S 19 '67

Politics and government

See also
Chicago—Elections

Prisons and reformatories

Cook County horrors. il Time 90:75-6 D 15 '67

Religious institutions and affairs

Getting your visa for Chicago. B. Cook. Commonweal 86:5-7 Mr 24 '67; Discussion. 86:158-9 Ap 21 '67
See also
Ecumenical institute, Chicago

Sanitary affairs

How Chicago saved $2.5 million; chlorination facilities. V. W. Bacon. il Am City 82:16 O '67
Separate storm and sanitary sewers not the answer in Chicago. V. W. Bacon. il Am City 82:67 Ja '67

Social conditions

Division street: America, by S. Terkel. Review
America 116:381 Mr 18 '67 R. A. Schroth
Nation 204:376-8 Mr 20 '67. R. Stern
Reporter 36:53-4 Ap 20 '67. A. M. Greeley
My Chicago. J. B. Martin. il Holiday 41:54-7+ Mr '67
New Chicago. A. Karlen. il Holiday 41:46-53 Mr '67

Social life and customs

Chicago after dark. G. P. Gates. il Holiday 41:70-3+ Mr '67

Social work

Detroit, 1967; students community organization activities in Lawndale. R. A. Schroth. America 117:152-3 Ag 12 '67

Theater

Auditorium reborn. R. C. Marsh. Hi Fi 18:MA22+ Ja '68
Chicago's Auditorium theater reborn. W. Terry. il Sat R 50:81-3 N 25 '67
Raising the curtain in Chicago; Auditorium theater restored. il Time 90:68 N 10 '67

Transportation

Mileage meters cut bus costs. il Am City 82:134 My '67

Worlds Columbian exposition, 1893

Columbian exposition. B. Finnegan. il Hobbies 72:120+ Ag '67

CHICAGO American (newspaper)
New front page. il Newsweek 69:67 Ap 10 '67
CHICAGO and North Western-Chicago Great Western merger. See Railroads—Consolidations and mergers
CHICAGO and North Western railway
Broadening the rails; acquisition of Essex wire corp. il Time 89:88 Je 23 '67
Looking younger. Time 90:82 Jl 14 '67
CHICAGO art institute
Continental decorative arts at the Art institute of Chicago. A. Wardwell. il Antiques 92:508-23 O '67
Illuminating the impressionists. il Time 90:96-8 D 1 '67
CHICAGO authors. See Authors, American
CHICAGO Bears (football club) See Football clubs
CHICAGO Black Hawks (hockey team) See Hockey teams
CHICAGO board of trade
Booming bedlam in commodity trading. il Bsns W p72-3+ Mr 4 '67
New job, old territory. il Time 89:91-2 Mr 17 '67

CHICAGO conference of laymen. See Laity—
Catholic church
CHICAGO Cubs (baseball) See Baseball clubs
CHICAGO McCormick Place fire. See Fires
CHICAGO Orchestra hall. See Concert halls
CHICAGO playing card collectors, incorporated
CPCC's deck of decks. D. Powills. Hobbies 72:
114-15 N '67
CHICAGO public library
Bookworm turns; amnesty on fines for over-
due books. Newsweek 71:32 Ja 15 '68
Chicago public library bans art again. Li-
brary J 92:1783 My 1 '67
Democratic interregnum promised Chicago
P.L. Library J 92:2874 S 1 '67
Shakeup in Chicago: Gscheidle resigns. Li-
brary J 92:2698 Ag '67
Strike threat cancelled at Chicago public li-
brary. Library J 92:1398-9 Ap 1 '67
CHICAGO symphony orchestra
Lively arts; new direction in Chicago? inter-
view, ed. by R. Hemming. J. Martinon. Sr
Schol 90:22 F 10 '67
Recordings. M. Mayer. Esquire 68:26 Ag '67
Reunion at Orchestra Hall. R. C. Marsh.
Hi Fi 17:MA25 Mr '67
CHICAGO tribune
Book world supplement for Washington, Chi-
cago. Pub W 192:34 Jl 3 '67
Court denies injunction against Chicago
tribune; alleged improper listing of The ar-
rangement. Pub W 192:157-8 Jl 10 '67
How to pack the pews; concerning an edi-
torial. Christian Cent 84:1011 Ag 9 '67
Stein and Day sues Chicago tribune; alleged
improper listing of The arrangement. Pub
W 191:44 My 29 '67
CHICAGO truck drivers' and chauffeurs' union
Tough man ties up the teamsters; E. Fenner,
head of independent drivers' union. Bsns W
p 158+ My 6 '67
CHICAGO. University
Chicago names new president. R. J. Samuel-
son. Science 157:1415 S 22 '67
Happy marriage in Chicago; E. H. Levi new
president. Time 90:44+ S 22 '67
Local boy makes good; E. H. Levi is new
president. Newsweek 70:75-6 S 25 '67
CHICAGO university bookstore. See College
bookstores
CHICAGO university press
University of Chicago press drops black Chi-
cago ad. il Pub W 192:246-7 Ag 28 '67
CHICAGO White Sox (baseball) See Baseball
clubs
CHICAGOANS
Division street: America, by S. Terkel. Re-
view
Reporter 36:53-4 Ap 20 '67. A. M. Greeley
Sat R 50:36-7 Ja 28 '67. H. Mitgang
CHICHESTER, Sir Francis Charles
Tale of two heroes, Gipsy Moth IV and her
one-man crew. il pors Life 62:28-37+ Je 9
'67; Same abr. with title Around the world
with Gipsy Moth IV. Read Digest 91:46-52
S '67
about
Derring-do off Cape Horn. il Time 89:71 Mr
31 '67
14,000 miles singlehanded; reprint. G. Chi-
chester. il pors Yachting 121:62-5+ My '67
Home is the sailor. L. Wainwright. Life 62:
26A Je 9 '67
Loneliness of the long-distance sailor. H.
Gordon. il por N Y Times Mag p30-2+ Ja
22 '67
Old man and the sea. il pors Newsweek 69:61-
5 Je 12 '67
Treasure from the sea. il por Time 89:48
Je 9 '67
Voyage completed. G. Chichester. il por Yacht-
ing 122:38-40+ Ag '67
CHICHESTER, Giles
14,000 miles singlehanded; reprint. Yachting
121:62-5+ My '67
Voyage completed. por Yachting 122:38-40+
Ag '67
CHICK embryos. See Embryology—Birds
CHICKEN as food. See Cookery—Poultry
CHICKEN livers. See Cookery—Poultry
CHICKEN salads. See Salads
CHICKENMAN (radio program) See Radio
broadcasting—Humor
CHICKERING, Sherman B.
New American male. Mlle 66:66-7+ Ja '68

CHIDESTER, Ann
Big girl; story. por Good H 166:66-9 Ja '68
Scent of ginger; story. McCalls 94:112-13 Mr
'67
CHIEFS (football club) See Football clubs
CHIEFS of staff. See United States—Joint
chiefs of staff
CHIEN, Shu, and others
Blood viscosity: influence of erythrocyte ag-
gregation. bibliog Science 157:829-31 Ag 18
'67
Blood viscosity: influence of erythrocyte de-
formation. bibliog Science 157:827-9 Ag 18
'67
CHIKUNGUNYA virus. See Viruses
CHILD, Julia
Everyone's in the kitchen with Julia. il Read
Digest 90:66-70 F '67
Julia Child way to plan your own ready-
ahead dinner. il pors Ladies Home J 84:88+
O '67
CHILD accidents. See Accidents
CHILD-adult relationship
Needed: heroic examples for the young; ex-
cerpts from address. J. F. Kauffman. NEA
J 56:16-17 O '67
Split-level American family. U. Bronfenbren-
ner. Sat R 50:60-6 O 7 '67
We're scared of our kids: a Journal readers'
poll. Ladies Home J 85:5 Ja '68
See also
Youth-adult relationship

Bibliography
Books for adults. PTA Mag 62:34 S; 37 O
'67
Choice for readers. PTA Mag 62:37 N '67
Introducing the older generation to children.
NEA J 56:82-3 D '67
CHILD beating. See Cruelty to children
CHILD care centers. See Foster day care
CHILD delinquency. See Juvenile delinquency
CHILD development group of Mississippi. See
Project Head Start
CHILD guidance. See Child study
CHILD labor
United States
Illegal to hire neighbors' kids? Farm J 91:
84 S '67
CHILD obesity. See Corpulence
CHILD photography. See Photography of chil-
dren
CHILD placing. See Adoption; Foster home
care
CHILD portraiture. See Portrait painting
CHILD psychiatry
Boys nobody wanted. S. S. Rosenberg. il
Parents Mag 42:35-7+ Ja '67
When child psychiatry is wasted money. D.
J. Holmes. il Ladies Home J 84:62+ O '67
See also
Mentally handicapped children
CHILD psychology. See Child study
CHILD psychotherapy. See Psychotherapy
CHILD study
Babies love to learn; excerpt from How to
raise a brighter child. J. Beck. il Parents
Mag 42:58-9+ S '67
Baby's mind: the crucial first months; ex-
cerpt from The crucial years. M. Pines.
il McCalls 94:74-5+ Ap '67
Building the child's self-concept. S. G. Ells-
worth. il NEA J 56:54-6 F '67
Children's views of foreign peoples, by O.
Klineberg and W. E. Lambert. Review
N Y Times Mag il p72+ My 21 '67. M.
Pines
Wilson Lib Bul il 42:187-93 O '67. L. Min-
turn
Child's inhumanity to child; with study-dis-
cussion program, by E. Harris and D. Har-
ris. C. Gregory. bibliog il PTA Mag 62:22-
5, 35 D '67
Does your room talk? Sci Digest 62:62 D '67
How to help the child who wets his bed. J.
Mendels. il Parents Mag 42:38-9+ Jl '67
In praise of preschoolers. C. Blunt. il Parents
Mag 42:60-1+ O '67
Our happy underachiever. J. Lewis. il Parents
Mag 42:48-9+ Ap '67
Shortchanged children; excerpt from Short-
changed children of suburbia. A. Miel and
E. Kiester, jr. il N Y Times Mag p99-
100+ Ap 16 '67; Discussion. p21 Ap 30; 12+
My 7 '67
Split-level American family. U. Bronfenbren-
ner. Sat R 50:60-6 O 7 '67

CHILD study—*Continued*
Unlocking early learning's secrets. il Life 62: 40-7 Mr 31 '67
When parents have to leave. B. Spock. il Redbook 128:41+ Ap '67
See also
Children, First-born
Childrens questions
Parent-child relationship
Psychology, Educational
CHILD suicide. See Suicide
CHILD-to-child tutoring program. See Tutors and tutoring
CHILD welfare
True sprit of Christmas; United Nations Declaration of the rights of the child; ed. by A. B. Heath. P. Heath and others. Nat R 19:1420-1 D 26 '67
See also
Adoption
Cruelty to children
Foster day care
Foster home care
Juvenile courts
Pestalozzi children's village
United Nations children's fund

United States

Birth of a movement. R. A. Cloward and F. F. Piven. il Nation 204:582-8 My 8 '67
Children of divorce, what rights have they? with Milwaukee's bill of rights for children in divorce actions. R. W. Hansen. Read Digest 90:181-3+ Mr '67
Dealing out the poor; proposed reforms to the aid to dependent children program. Nation 205:164 S 4 '67
Do we want children's allowances? with table. J. Tobin. New Repub 157:16-18 N 25 '67; Reply with rejoinder. J. C. Vadakin. 157:15-18 D 23 '67
Here's the rub; social-security bill restricts aid to families with dependent children. il Newsweek 71:16 Ja 15 '68
New welfare: women and children last; amendments to new social security bill. R. A. Cloward and F. F. Piven. Commonweal 86:541-2 S 8 '67
Now there's a White House plan for the Nation's children. il U S News 62:80-1 F 20 '67
President Johnson's special message to Congress; children and youth. L. B. Johnson. il PTA Mag 61:20-2 Mr; 12-14+ Ap '67
Taking it out on the kids; Maryland's decision on Aid to dependent children. New Repub 157:9 O 7 '67
See also
Fresh air charity

Vietnam (Republic)

No ordinary man; Arthur N. McMellon memorial orphanage in Vietnam. H. A. Mulligan. il Read Digest 91:127-31 Jl '67
CHILDBIRTH
As frail as a sparrow. C. S. Shade. il McCalls 94:74+ Mr '67
Childbirth: what is done in routine and complicated births. il Good H 164:142-3 Ja '67
Emergency childbirth. E. Maxwell. Todays Health 45:79-80 F '67
First hours. B. Spock. il Redbook 130:65-71+ N '67
How I almost became a midwife in Africa. V. L. Franklin. il Redbook 129:74-5+ O '67
Protecting the infant; symposium. il Todays Health 46:29-57+ Ja '68
Relieving pressure & pain; use of decompression unit. il Time 90:36 D 22 '67
Stork realities. F. L. Remington. Todays Health 45:16-17 Mr '67
What happens during labor? A. B. Gerbie. Redbook 129:33-4 My '67
See also
Cesarean section
Midwives
Obstetrics
Pregnancy
CHILDERS, Joanne
Moving mother out; poem. Commonweal 85: 652 Mr 10 '67
CHILDHOOD memories. See Reminiscence
CHILDLESSNESS. See Sterility
CHILDREN
Children must be protected from the harm of race. B. Spock. Negro Hist Bul 30:14 Ap '67
Divorce from three to six. J. F. McDermott, jr. il N Y Times Mag p99+ O 22 '67

Little shopper; fifteen month old Thomas Raymond Koeniges, jr. in department store. il Look 31:M16+ Ap 18 '67
See also
Adoption
Boys
Cookery by children
Family, Size of
Family life
Fathers
Infants
Mothers
Moving pictures for children
Music and children
Negro children
Nursery schools
Parents
Play
Preschool children
Presidents—United States—Children
Problem children
School children
Siblings
Stepparents
Television broadcasting and children
Travel with children

Accidents
See Accidents

Adjustment
See Adjustment, Social

Amusements
See Childrens amusements

Anxiety
See Anxiety

Care and hygiene
Better health for all babies; Collaborative perinatal project, U.S. Public health service. T. C. Wilson and K. Niehans. Parents Mag ≤2:68-9+ N '67
Getting children medically ready for school. il Good H 165:185 S '67
Growing pains. See issues of Today's health
LBJ's message on youth: pointing a new path for medical practice. B. Nelson. Science 155:811-12 F 17 '67
Pediatrician's almanac. L. H. Smith. McCalls 95:34 Ja '68
Summer checkup for school beginners. M. McKinlock. il Parents Mag 42:40-1+ Ag '67
Ways to use medicine safely with children. il Good H 166:170 Ja '68
Why don't we save these mothers and babies? W. Goodman. il Redbook 128:68-9+ Ap '67
Your child's health. L. W. Sauer. See issues of PTA magazine
See also
Children—Management and training
Children—Preparation for medical and dental care
Infants—Care and hygiene
Public schools—Health service

Caricatures and cartoons
Small wonders. R. Marcus. See issues of Good housekeeping

Day care
See Day nurseries; Nursery schools

Development
See Children—Growth and development

Diseases
Your child's health. L. W. Sauer. See issues of PTA magazine
See also
Communicable diseases
Infants—Care and hygiene
also names of children's diseases, e.g. Convulsions

Education
See Education, Elementary; Education of children

Etiquette
See Etiquette for children and youth

Food
See Children—Nutrition

Growth and development
Children in crisis. J. R. Komaiko. il Parents Mag 42:35-7+ F '67
Cognitive capacity of very young children. J. Mehler and T. G. Bever. bibliog il Science 158:141-2 O 6 '67
Earlier maturation in man. J. M. Tanner. il Sci Am 218:21-7 Ja '68

CHILDREN—Growth and development—*Cont.*
Emotional first aid? L. L. Prina. il N Y Times Mag p 112+ Ap 2 '67
Farewell to babyhood; with study-discussion program by R. Strang. A. Graham. bibliog PTA Mag 61:25-7. 35 My '67
Growing and learning. H. E. Rie and E. D. Rie. Cath World 206:13-16 O '67
Growth: the short and tall of it; report prepared in cooperation with the American academy of pediatrics. A. Kerr. il McCalls 94:50+ Ap '67
New research that is changing old ideas about child behavior. Good H 164:196 Mr '67
On becoming a social being; with study-discussion program by R. Strang. L. J. Yarrow. bibliog il PTA Mag 61:18-20, 30 F '67
Slow growth; psychic impact on growth. Sci N 92:63 Jl 15 '67
What children learn when they play; excerpt from Conspiracy against childhood. E. LeShan. il Redbook 129:66-7+ Jl '67
  See also
Child study
Infants—Growth and development

Hairdressing
See Hairdressing

Health
See Children—Care and hygiene

Hospitals
Operation Sunshine; E. Reinhardt's murals for children's infirmaries and state hospitals. C. W. Wittman. il Am Artist 31:27-31 F '67
Plastic surgery brings brighter lives to thousands of youngsters; services provided by the Children's hospital medical center, Boston. Todays Health 45:41 Mr '67

Law
  See also
Adoption
Juvenile courts
Juvenile delinquency
Parent and child (law)

Management and training
Are we spoiling our kids? with group discussion program, by E. J. Le Shan. il Parents Mag 42:46-7+, 84-5 Ja '67
Back to baby farming? F. R. Schreiner and M. Herman. Sci Digest 61:25-6 Ap '67
Bringing up baby for a million mothers; interview, ed. by S. O'Quin. L. Smith. il Life 64:38-9+ Ja 19 '68
California woman: how she raises her superchildren. B. Walters. Ladies Home J 84:77+ Jl '67
Child on drugs. B. W. Wyden. il N Y Times Mag p63+ Ag 20 '67
Child's inhumanity to child; with study-discussion program, by E. Harris and D. Harris. C. Gregory. bibliog il PTA Mag 62:22-5, 35 D '67
Dialogue with mothers, what eating problems are really all about. B. Bettelheim. Ladies Home J 84:78+ N '67
Don't be an over-anxious parent; with discussion group program by E. J. Leshan. M. Albrecht. il Parents Mag 42:33-4+, 58-9+ Ap '67
Family clinic. See issues of Parents' magazine and better homemaking
Friendly advice to new fathers from an old pro. R. Armour. il Parents Mag 42:48-9+ Je '67
Goals of discipline; with study discussion program. E. G. Neisser. il Parents Mag 42:66-7+, 90 O '67
Growing pains. See issues of Today's health
How are children disciplined in other cultures. M. Mead. Redbook 129:10 Ag '67
How children learn the joy of giving. B. Spock. il Redbook 129:41-3+ S '67
How I beat my kids. N. Howe. il Redbook 129:10+ Je '67
How to outwit a toddler. A. Arnold. il Parents Mag 42:41-3+ Mr '67
How to talk childrenese. K. D Fishman. il N Y Times Mag p 105+ My 14 '67
If it were my child. See issues of Ladies' home journal
Letter killeth. R. Coles. New Repub 157:18-23 N 4 '67
Mistaken kindness; when a mother tries to do too much for her children. il Good H 165:24+ O '67

Most of us are mainly mothers; excerpts. C. Bartholomew. Ladies Home J 84:80 S; 36 O; 156 N '67
Neglect of children as a cause of crime; report of National crime commission. D. Lawrence. U S News 62:96 Mr 6 '67
Perfect child. E. J. LeShan. il N Y Times Mag p63-4+ Ag 27 '67
Persistent child; excerpt adapted from Temperament and behavior disorders in children. A. Thomas and others. il Parents Mag 42:35-7+ D '67
Redbook dialogue. J. Lemmon; C. Schulz. il Redbook 130:50-1+ D '67
Setting rules that work. C. Himber. il N Y Times Mag p 114+ N 19 '67
Speaking out; children should learn about violence. B. Bettelheim. Sat Eve Post 240:10+ Mr 11 '67
Teacher's case against discipline; excerpts from Freedom, not license! A. S. Neill. il Redbook 128:61+ Ap '67
Teaching styles we parents practice; with study-discussion program, by R. Strang. W. J. Anderson. bibliog il PTA Mag 61:8-10, 34 Mr '67
What did we do wrong? D. Barr. il N Y Times Mag p36-7+ N 26 '67; Discussion. p22+ D 10; 12+ D 17 '67
What the Soviet Spock taught; A. S. Makarenko's teachings. T. Frankel. il N Y Times Mag p93-6 My 7 '67
What to do with the children until company comes. B. B. Smith. il Redbook 129:6+ Ag '67
When bedtime brings problems... J. J. Cox. il Todays Health 45:39-41 My '67
You have to be taught to hate. J. M. Eagan. il Parents Mag 42:32+ F '67
  See also
Child study
Childrens allowances
Corporal punishment
Discipline
Parent-child relationship
Problem children

Bibliography
Books for parents. P. Pinson. See issues of Parents' magazine and better homemaking

Memories
See Reminiscence

Mortality
  See also
Infant morality

Nutrition
Feeding young children can be easy and fun; with recipes. M. C. Newsom. il Parents Mag 42:62-5+ My '67
Malnutrition and national development. A. D. Berg. For Affairs 46:126-36 O '67
More power to you. il Sr Schol 91:40-1 S 28 '67
Starvation and the brain; permanent brain damage from improper diets. il Sci N 91:307 Ap 1 '67
V.I.P. dinner; with recipes. il Ladies Home J 84:130-2+ O '67
  See also
Eating, Psychology of

Only child problem
Myth of the only child; with discussion group program by M. R. Sherwin. A. Loomer. il Parents Mag 42:28+, 54-5+ Mr '67

Photographs
Caution: baby at play. Good H 164:57-8 Je '67
  See also
Photography of children

Preparation for medical and dental care
What parents can do to take the scare out of surgery. J. L. Whatley. il Todays Health 45:40-4 Jl '67
Who's afraid of doctors? many children fear doctors. B. Bettelheim. Ladies Home J 84:20+ Jl '67

Psychiatry
See Child psychiatry

Psychology
See Child study

Religion
Mixed marriages. L. M. Örsy. America 117:242-5 S 9 '67; Discussion. 117:398, 589 O 14, N 18 '67
What children think of God. Time 91:62 Ja 5 '68

CHILDREN—*Continued*

Sayings

Christmas grows on many trees. H. Dunn. il NEA J 56:20-1 D '67

Class of 1984 (now 5) looks ahead. O. Ryan and B. Brodsky. il N Y Times Mag p6-7+ D 31 '67

No one slept with mom while you were gone, dad! excerpts from Oops! or life's awful moments. A. Linkletter. Ladies Home J 84: 36+ Ag '67

The rich have beards, and the poor walk droopy. A. Bayer. il Sat Eve P⸱st 240:12+ D 30 '67

Volcanos give us hot java. H. Dunn. il Sci Digest 61:62-5 Mr '67

Sleep

See Sleep

Suicide

See Suicide

Surgery

See also
Children—Preparation for medical and dental care
Infants, Newborn—Surgery

Training

See Children—Management and training

Asia

Children America forgot; illegitimate children fathered and abandoned by U.S. servicemen. P. S. Buck. Read Digest 91:108-10 S '67

France

Allons, enfants; rating Charles de Gaulle. il Newsweek 71:31-2 Ja 8 '68

Hong Kong

Encounter in Hong Kong. L. Lennon. il Good H 165:32+ N '67

Japan

Every child a prodigy. D. Chapman. il Look 31:M24+ N 28 '67

Korea (Republic)

Korea's 2½-year-old genius; Kim Ung Yong. F. Dandridge. il Look 31:M8-10 F 7 '67

United States

See also
Child labor—United States
Child welfare—United States

Vietnam (Republic)

See also
Child welfare—Vietnam (Republic)

CHILDREN, Adopted
Adopted children are different. H. H. Work. il Parents Mag 42:42-3+ F '67
Test tube children: a new kind of orphan; reprint. H. P. Gouldner. il Sci Digest 62:16-22 Jl '67

CHILDREN, Adoption of. See Adoption

CHILDREN, Backward. See Slow learning children

CHILDREN, Cruelty to. See Cruelty to children

CHILDREN, Deaf. See Deaf

CHILDREN, Delinquent. See Juvenile delinquency

CHILDREN, Education of. See Education of children

CHILDREN, Exceptional
Karl's handicap, the impediment of creativity. R. E. Samples. il Sat R 50:56-7+ Jl 15 '67; Discussion. 50:51+ Ag 19 '67
See also
Children, Gifted

CHILDREN, Firstborn
Were you the oldest child? E. Kaplan. il Sci Digest 61:72-6 F '67

CHILDREN, Gifted
Korea's 2½-year-old genius; Kim Ung Yong. F. Dandridge. il Look 31:M8-10 F 7 '67
See also
Children as musicians

Education

Bright kids. G. C. Keller. il Am Ed 3:28-32 Mr '67

CHILDREN, Handicapped
See also
Brain damaged children

Education

Education of the handicapped. il Am Ed 3:30-1 Jl '67

In a class by themselves: Tele-class program, Los Angeles; reprint. C. E. Cassidy. il Sr Schol 90:sup 10-11 Ap 14 '67
Physically handicapped child; symposium. il NEA J 56:33-48 N '67
See also
Brain damaged children—Education

CHILDREN, Illegitimate. See Illegitimacy

CHILDREN, Mentally superior. See Children, Gifted

CHILDREN, Missing. See Missing persons

CHILDREN, Painting of. See Portrait painting

CHILDREN, Photography of. See Photography of children

CHILDREN, Preschool. See Preschool children

CHILDREN, Problem. See Problem children

CHILDREN, Professional
Career child. R. Kramer. il N Y Times Mag p 107+ Ap 9 '67

CHILDREN, Refugee. See Refugee children

CHILDREN, Retarded. See Mentally handicapped children

CHILDREN, Runaway. See Runaway boys and girls

CHILDREN, Sick. See Sick, The

CHILDREN and art
Exciting world of art. V. D'Amico. il Parents Mag 42:48-9+ D '67

CHILDREN and death
How children feel about death. G. Krupp. il Parents Mag 42:54-5+ Ap '67
What four brave women told their children. B. Remsberg and C. Remsberg. il Good H 164:94-6+ My '67

CHILDREN and music. See Music and children

CHILDREN and parents. See Parent-child relationship

CHILDREN and race relations. See Interracial cooperation

CHILDREN and religion. See Children—Religion

CHILDREN and television. See Television broadcasting and children

CHILDREN and war. See Vietnamese war, 1957-—Children

CHILDREN are there, trying not to laugh; story. See Brennan, M.

CHILDREN as actors
Hair-raising class of 1830; shooting Oliver; with report by J. Hicks. il Life 64:72-6 Ja 19 '68
To a dear child...; E. Leslie, America's first child star. J. Douglass. Horn Bk 43:571-5 O '67
Where are they now? child stars. N. Zierold. il Good H 165:154 S '67
See also
Dramatization in education

CHILDREN as artists. See Childrens art

CHILDREN as authors
Children as authors. Z. Sutherland. Sat R 50:35 Mr 18 '67
Small voices; comp. by J. Berger and D. Berger. Review
Horn Bk 43:303+ Je '67. R. H. Viguers
True sprit of Christmas; United Nations Declaration of the rights of the child; ed. by A. B. Heath. P. Heath and others. Nat R 19:1420-1 D 26 '67
See also
Childrens poems (by children)

CHILDREN as musicians
Conqueror of the classics; pianist. K. Hutchinson. il Ebony 23:38-40+ N '67
Every child a prodigy. D. Chapman. il Look 31:M24+ N 28 '67
Hi, hi, Hornets, eight-year-old Steve Calvert on drums for his three-brother rock combo. W. Hedgepeth. il Look 31:M21-22 O 17 '67

CHILDREN as photographers
Flying photographer. J. Collison. il Flying 81:115 D '67
Learning through the lens; disadvantaged New York children's summer workshop conducted by Susan Wood. M. R. Weiss. il Sat R 50:55+ Je 17 '67
Shooting from a floating resort; cruise. L. Barry. il Pop Phot 61:20+ Ag '67
Through the eyes of children. J. Hays. il U S Camera 30:58-9+ O '67

CHILDREN in art
Four children, three artists. J. Dolmetsch. il Antiques 91:500-2 Ap '67
Two-year-old summer; paintings. D. Schwartz. McCalls 94:72-7 My '67

CHILDREN in boating
Cruising with the very young. T. Gibbs. il Motor B 119:24-7+ Je '67
Junior yachting. See issues of Yachting
Setting up a junior program. il Yachting 121:196 Mr; 250+ Ap; 204-5 My; 186+ Je; 122:134 Ag; 163-4 D '67; 123:378-9 Ja '68
She sails while he drives; interview, ed. by S. Lowell. M. D. G. Muncey. il Motor B 120:44-5+ S '67
Young skippers set a safety record. J. O'Brien. il Motor B 119:32-3+ My '67

CHILDREN of actors and actresses
My kids are the real stars; F. Henderson's children. G. M. Landau. il Parents Mag 42:42-5+ Ag '67

CHILDREN of diplomats
Race problem for the diplomatic corps. U S News 63:18 N 6 '67

CHILDREN of migrant laborers

Education
Children of neglect; a plea. P. M. Stern. Parents Mag 42:30+ Ja '67
Educating migratory children. Sch & Soc 95:484 D 9 '67
Mees, you goin' to be real teacher now, don'cha? A. Parker. il Am Ed 3:14-16 My '67; Same abr. with title Worst bunch in school. Read Digest 91:182-4+ Jl '67
Remembering forgotten Americans; Leoti, Kan. C. Loyd. NEA J 56:58-9 D '67
School grants for migrants. Sat R 50:64 Jl 15 '67
We open doors for migrant children. W. E. Newsome. NEA J 56:27-8 Ap '67

CHILDRENS allowances
Helping your children to learn about money. B. Spock. Redbook 130:29+ D '67

CHILDRENS amusements
Cruising with the very young. T. Gibbs. il Motor B 119:24-7+ Je '67
Forget TV, children, let's play: creative fun for kids; concerning play books by Barbara Kruger Bate. D. Oliver. Life 63:11 S 1 '67
Ways to entertain children indoors. il Good H 165:168-9 Ag '67
See also
Christmas projects
Nature study
Play
Playgrounds
Story telling
Television broadcasting—Childrens programs
Toys

CHILDRENS art
Artists. il Sch Arts 67:30-1 D '67
Burlap bags and boys. Sister Marie Clarence. il Sch Arts 67:36-7 D '67
Civil rights is also a state of mind. R. Coles. il N Y Times Mag p32-4+ My 7 '67
Drawings by Charlotte Daley. C. Daley. il Sch Arts 66:9-12 F '67
Illustration: an art form. J. E. Miller. il Design 69:12-13 Fall '67
Pint-size Picassos. T. Gezari. il Parents Mag 42:52-3+ Mr '67
Pre-school children paint. il Sch Arts 66:19-20 Ja '67
Primitive, primitive art. il Sci Digest 62:20-1 S '67
Sculpture for a school atrium. M. F. Tressler. il Sch Arts 66:15-18 Ja '67
Stitchery for the young child. E. Madsen. il Sch Arts 67:12-13 D '67
Student art on display; sculpture exhibit of San Mateo city school district, Calif. D. Sperisen. il Sch Arts 67:29 D '67
See also
Sand sculpture

Competitions
Art education accessible to all: creative activity on the seashore; project among vacationing youngsters in Egypt. L. Zaky. bibliog il Sch Arts 66:19-23 My '67
Young artists in orbit; painting the universe competition. M. J. Steinbaum. il Sch Arts 67:32-3 O '67

Exhibitions
School artist; Young in art at the Philadelphia Civic Center museum. il Sch Arts 67:4 N '67

CHILDREN'S asthma research Institute and hospital, Denver
Kids who conquer asthma. S. M. Spencer. il Sat Eve Post 240:88-90 F 25 '67

CHILDRENS attitudes. See Attitudes

CHILDREN'S book council
Children's book council issues '67 vacation kit. Pub W 191:124 F 20 '67

CHILDRENS book departments. See Booksellers and bookselling—Childrens literature
CHILDRENS book exhibits. See Book exhibits
CHILDRENS book fairs. See Book fairs
CHILDRENS book week. See Book week
CHILDRENS books. See Childrens literature
CHILDRENS camps. See Camps
CHILDRENS courts. See Juvenile courts
CHILDRENS fears. See Fear
CHILDRENS furniture. See Furniture, Childrens
CHILDRENS games. See Games
CHILDRENS gardens
Graduation: New York botanical garden's ceremony for Children's gardencraft classes. New Yorker 43:36 S 30 '67
See also
Brooklyn botanic garden—Children's garden
CHILDRENS haircuts. See Haircutting
CHILDRENS hats. See Hats
CHILDRENS hospital, Boston. See Children—Hospitals
CHILDRENS letters (by children) See Letters by children
CHILDRENS libraries. See Libraries, Childrens
CHILDRENS literature
ABPC cites 1966 book boom; juvenile sales up 50 percent. Library J 92:4206+ N 15 '67
Another Charlotte's web, please: a grandmother's letter to Santa Claus. L. Russ. Pub W 192:23 D 4 '67
Attention, attention ... A. Dobrin. il Horn Bk 43:27-30 F '67
Aunt Irene. W. B. Beem. il Horn Bk 43:429-33 Ag '67
Books, children, and women. R. H. Viguers. Horn Bk 43:152-3 Ap '67
Books for the early years; with study-discussion program, by R. Strang. D. M. Broderick. bibliog il PTA Mag 62:22-4, 34 N '67
Child-concerning world; symposium. bibliog il Wilson Lib Bul 42:164-205+ O '67
Children's editor looks at excellence in children's literature. J. Karl. Horn Bk 43:31-41 F '67
Choosing the best in children's books. J. P. Elwart. il Parents Mag 42:60+ Ap '67
Confessions of a book fiend; films and filmstrips based on children's books. M. Schindel. Library J 92:858-9 F 15 '67
Didacticism in modern dress. J. R. Townsend. Horn Bk 43:159-64 Ap '67
Homage to May Massee. C. H. Bishop. il Commonweal 87:173-4 N 10 '67
How to raise a bookworm. M. Nash. il Redbook 128:63+ Mr '67
Literature for children; an engagement with life. A. T. Allen. Horn Bk 43:732-7 D '67
One world for youth. Z. Sutherland. il Sat R 50:48-9 S 16 '67
Realism in children's literature. E. Enright. Horn Bk 43:165-70 Ap '67
Teen-age and young adult market: editorial needs and requirements; symposium. Writer 80:43-5 Ap '67
Through a glass, darkly; representation of the Negro in books for children. D. H. Millender. bibliog il Library J 92:4571-6 D 15 '67
To America, with daughter: in search of Robert McCloskey. R. Stokes. il Horn Bk 43:419-23 Ag '67
To Mississippi in the interest of children and books; three trips to speak at University of Mississippi on the Negro child in children's books. G. Woods. il Wilson Lib Bul 41:1028-33 Je '67
Trade books surpass texts in treatment of minorities. Library J 92:1284-5 Mr 15 '67
Two-headed monster. P. Beatty. Horn Bk 43:96-101 F '67
Writer comments. E. C. Haugaard. Horn Bk 43:444-6 Ag '67
See also
Book selection
Book week
Booksellers and bookselling—Childrens literature
Childrens poetry
Childrens reading
Fairy tales
Horn book magazine
Libraries, Childrens
Newbery medal
Picture books for children
Publishers and publishing—Childrens literature
Scientific literature for children

CHILDRENS literature—*Continued*

Bibliography

Award-winning books for children. PTA Mag 62:31 S '67
Best books of the year; selected by the editors of SLJ book review. il Library J 92:4577-81 D 15 '67
Book review. See second issue of each month of Library journal
Book week awards announced. Library J 92:1986 My 15 '67
Booked for Christmas. il Library J 92:3818-20 O 15 '67
Booklist (title varies) comp. by R. H. Viguers and others. See issues of Horn book magazine
Books (cont) J. Malcolm. New Yorker 43:157-60+ D 16 '67
Books for boys and girls. D. E. Leland. See issues of Parents' magazine and better homemaking
Books for children. R. Gagliardo. il PTA Mag 62:29-30 Ja '68
Books for young people. Z. Sutherland. See issues of Saturday review
Books to brighten winter weather. PTA Mag 61:35-6 F '67
Books to come; ed. by J. C. Thomson. Library J 92:1341-79 Mr 15 '67
Books to come; ed. by S. A. Roth. Library J 92:3879-912+ O 15 '67
Bountiful harvest of children's books. E. Sheehan. America 117:514+ N 4 '67
Children's books. C. H. Simonds. Nat R 19:1342-3 N 28 '67
Children's books for fall. il Pub W 192:123-56 Jl 10 '67
Children's books of 1966-67. NEA J 56:74-7 N '67
Children's books selected for AIGA tour. il Library J 92:4564-6 D 15 '67
Childrens' Christmas book selection. Christian Cent 84:1601-2 D 13 '67
Children's paperbacks; comp. by J. C. Thomson (cont) Library J 92:367-9 Ja 15 '67
Children's paperbacks; comp. by M. Philips. Library J 93:320-4 Ja 15 '68
Children's paperbacks; comp. by S. Roth. Library J 29:2053-4+, 3137-9 My 15, S 15 '67
Editors' choice: the SLJ book review editors select best children's books of the spring season. il Library J 92:1998-9 My 15 '67
Fall books for young people. Z. Sutherland. il Sat R 50:40-51 N 11 '67
Juvenile book awards: 1966. Library J 92:1303 Mr 15 '67
1967 non-definitive list. H. Yglesias. Nation 205:663-5 D 18 '67
Notable children's books of 1966. il ALA Bul 61:415-18 Ap '67; Same. Library J 92:1685-6+ Ap 15 '67
Paperbacks and other inexpensive books for children. PTA Mag 62:36-7 O '67
Peculiar list of children's books. L. Russ. Pub W 193:19-21 Ja 1 '68
Selected list of children's books (cont) E. M. Graves. il Commonweal 86:293-303 My 26 '67
Selected list of children's books. M. L. Birmingham. il Commonweal 87:176-85 N 10 '67
Some leading spring children's books. il Pub W 191:86-119 F 20 '67
Spring books for young people; comp. by Z. Sutherland. il Sat R 50:47-8+ My 13 '67
Stocking full of wealth. Z. Sutherland. il Sat R 50:34-6 D 16 '67
Teaching of children's literature. E. H. Gross. il Wilson Lib Bul 42:199-205 O '67
See also
Reading lists

Exhibitions

See Book exhibits

History

Inheritance of our children. E. Nesbitt. Horn Bk 43:328-35 Je '67

History and criticism

Authors vs critics: children's books in the 1870's excerpt from The rise of children's book reviewing in America, 1865-1881. R. L. Darling. il Pub W 192:25-7 O 16 '67

Illustrations

See Illustrations of books and periodicals

Study and teaching

Teaching of children's literature. E. H. Gross. bibliog il Wilson Lib Bul 42:199-205 O '67

Technique

Fiction for teen-agers. N. Hentoff. il Atlan 220:136+ D '67

Progress report from underground. L. Conger. Writer 80:7-8 My '67
Why did you end your story that way? E. Yates. Horn Bk 43:709-14 D '67
Writing a book; excerpt from address. P. Pearce. Horn Bk 43:317-22 Je '67
Writing for children. C. Zolotow. Writer 80:36-8 Ap '67

Themes

See Literature—Themes

Translating

Marriage of Draupadi; excerpt from Tales from Indian classics, book 1. Savitri. il UNESCO Courier 20:8-9 D '67
Russians publish their version of the children's classic, A. A. Milne's Vinni-Pukh. P. Young. il Life 63:107 S 8 '67

Africa

Beyond the colonial bias. A. Pellowski. il Library J 92:4228-31+ N 15 '67

Australia

Indigenous children's literature. B. Buick. bibliog il Library J 92:4219-21 N 15 '67

India

Marriage of Draupadi; excerpt from Tales from Indian classics, book 1. Savitri. il UNESCO Courier 20:8-9 D '67

Latin America

Books for Miguel. T. de Gerez. bibliog Library J 92:4587-9+ D 15 '67
Center on children's cultures; agency within framework of United States committee for UNICEF. A. Pellowski. bibliog il Wilson Lib Bul 42:209-13 O '67

Pakistan

Children's reading in Pakistan. A. Ali. Horn Bk 43:235-7 Ap '67

Russia

Russians publish their version of the children's classic, A. A. Milne's Vinni-Pukh. P. Young. il Life 63:107 S 8 '67

Spain

Center on children's culture; agency within framework of United States committee for UNICEF. A. Pellowski. bibliog il Wilson Lib Bul 42:209-13 O '67

CHILDRENS literature, influence of
Books and the learning process; address June 27, 1967. I. Hunt. Horn Bk 43:424-9 Ag '67
Keep the bough green. C. R. Brink. Horn Bk 43:447-53 Ag 67

CHILDRENS manners. See Etiquette for children and youth

CHILDRENS meals. See Meals

CHILDRENS museums
Meet the raccoon; new kind of nature museum. M. Gross. il Parents Mag 42:46-7+ F '67

CHILDRENS national book week. See Book week

CHILDRENS parties
Birthday parties around the world; with recipes. il Ladies Home J 84:108-12 O '67
Happy birthday! with study-discussion program, by R. Strang. G. D. Ewing. bibliog il PTA Mag 61:17-19, 35 Ap '67
Kids' parties, winter style. Bet Hom & Gard 45:112 F '67
Trick of treating; with recipes. il Ladies Home J 84:114+ O '67

CHILDRENS phonograph records. See Phonograph records—Childrens records

CHILDRENS pillows. See Pillows

CHILDRENS plays
Texts
Middle grades; lower grades. See issues of Plays

CHILDRENS poems (by children)
Bringing poetry out of hiding; excerpts from Miracles, ed. by R. Lewis. il NEA J 56:12-14 F '67
Horn book league. See issues of Horn book magazine
Wind and the trees; Why does it happen so? tr. by A. Ali. D. Ahmed. Horn Bk 43:237-8 Ap '67

CHILDRENS poems (for children)
See also
Mother Goose
Nursery rhymes

CHILDRENS poetry
Place for poetry. R. Lewis. Pub W 192:119-20 Jl 10 '67
  See also
Childrens poems (by children)
CHILDRENS questions
What youngsters' questions tell us. F. R. Schreiber. il Todays Health 45:34-7 N '67
CHILDRENS reading
Baby dolls are gone; effect of TV. N. Larrick. bibliog il Library J 92:3815-17 O 15 '67
Honest audience. J. P. Wood. Horn Bk 43: 612-16 O '67
Library of the American school in Japan. L. D. Downs. Horn Bk 43:576-9 O '67
Must children read in packs? M. Alexander. Pub W 191:120-1 F 20 '67
Who are the early readers? A. P. Eliasberg. il N Y Times Mag p74+ F 19 '67
  See also
Childrens literature
Comics (books, strips, etc)
Libraries, Childrens
CHILDRENS religion. See Children—Religion
CHILDRENS responsibility. See Responsibility
CHILDRENS rooms
Home learning center. il House & Gard 132: 198-201 S '67
CHILDRENS sayings. See Children—Sayings
CHILDRENS scooters. See Scooters, Childrens
CHILDREN'S services division, American library association. See American library association—Children's services division
CHILDRENS shoes. See Shoes
CHILDRENS spring book festival awards. See Rewards, prizes, etc.
CHILDRENS stories

Technique
  See Childrens literature—Technique
CHILDRENS success. See Success
CHILDRENS thefts. See Shoplifting
CHILDRENS thinking. See Thought and thinking
CHILDRENS villages
  See also
Pestalozzi children's village
CHILDRENS zoos. See Zoological gardens
CHILDRESS, William
Captive; poem. Reporter 36:39 Ap 6 '67
Quarry; poem. Reporter 36:56 Je 15 '67
CHILDS, Marquis W.
Mr Reston on the press. New Repub 156: 23-4 Ap 29 '67
CHILDS, Richard D.
(ed) See Philpott, G. Vietnamese school gongs sound
CHILDS bill of rights. See Child welfare
CHILE
  See also
Astronomical observatories—Chile
Colleges and universities—Chile
Elections—Chile
Geology—Chile
Juan Fernández Islands
Land tenure—Chile
Political parties—Chile
Public health—Chile
Skis and skiing—Chile
Tierra del Fuego

Economic conditions
Can Chile show the way to rest of Latin America? il U S News 63:74-6 Jl 10 '67

Foreign relations
  See also
Project Camelot

Politics and government
Chilean Christian democracy. W. R. Duncan. bibliog f Cur Hist 53:263-9+ N '67
Chile's mini-revolution; Christian democratic reign. J. Becket. Commonweal 87:406-8 D 29 '67
Eduardo Frei is trying a revolution without the execution wall. B. Collier. il N Y Times Mag p30-1+ F 19 '67
Frei's visit vetoed. il Sr Schol 90:16-17 F 10 '67
Last, best hope, by L. Gross. Review
  New Repub 157:30-1 D 23 '67. J. A. Page
President regrets; concerning rejection of President's trip. il Newsweek 69:53 Ja 30 '67
Setback for Frei. Time 89:49 Ap 14 '67
Stalemate in Chile. G. W. Grayson, jr. New Repub 156:14 F 4 '67

Travel ban. Time 89:36 Ja 27 '67
What next in Chile? New Repub 156:6 Ap 22 '67
  See also
Elections—Chile
Political parties—Chile

Population
Pills, coils and abortion; planned parenthood world conference. W. V. D'Antonio. Commonweal 86:193-4 My 5 '67

Religious institutions and affairs
World around us. Christian Cent 84:1328-30 O 18 '67
  See also
Church and state in Chile

Social conditions
  See also
Chile—Population
CHILEAN poetry

Translations into English
Sonnet XXIX; you come from the destitute South, from the house, tr. by B. Belitt. P. Neruda. Nation 205:697 D 25 '67
CHILI con carne. See Cookery—Meat; Cookery, Mexican
CHILTON, Mary-Dell
Transforming activity in both complementary strands of bacillus subtilis DNA. bibliog Science 157:817-19 Ag 18 '67
CHIMNEYS
Height makes might for new chimneys. il Fortune 75:158-9 My '67
It's a chimney wrap-around. il Sunset 138: 154+ Mr '67
CHIMPANZEES
Hemoglobin polymorphism in chimpanzees and gibbons. H. A. Hoffman and others. bibliog il Science 156:944 My 19 '67
Rehumanized chimps. il Time 89:64 Ap 21 '67
Transferrin polymorphism and population differences in the genetic variability of chimpanzees. M. Goodman and others. bibliog il Science 156:98-100 Ap 7 '67
CHINA
  See also
Peasantry—China
Taiwan

Antiquities
Treasure from a Chinese tomb; Ch'u silk manuscript. il Time 90:39 S 1 '67

Civilization
China's next phase. R. S. Elegant. For Affairs 46:137-50 O '67
Science and civilization in China, by J. Needham. Review; with excerpts
  Horizon il 10:52-63 Wint '68. D. J. de S. Price

Foreign population
  See also
English in China

Foreign relations
Strategy and national psychology in China. H. L. Boorman and S. A. Boorman. bibliog f Ann Am Acad 370:143-55 Mr '67

Russia
Russia & China; ancient rivalry for the Asian land mass. H. Schwartz. il Horizon 10:4-21 Wint '68

History
Chinese looking glass, by D. Bloodworth. Review
  Newsweek il 70:73 Jl 24 '67. S. K. Oberbeck
Through China's looking glass. C. P. Fitzgerald. Nation 206:24-6 Ja 1 '68

Bibliography
Chinese and Japanese historiography: some trends, 1961-1966. A. F. Wright and J. W. Hall. bibliog f Ann Am Acad 371:178-93 My '67
New books on Chinese history. W. K. Richards. Sr Schol 91:sup 12 N 30 '67

Historiography
Chinese and Japanese historiography: some trends, 1961-1966. A. F. Wright and J. W. Hall. bibliog f Ann Am Acad 371:178-93 My '67

Politics and government
Strategy and national psychology in China. H. L. Boorman and S. A. Boorman. bibliog f Ann Am Acad 370:143-55 Mr '67

CHINA—*Continued*

Social conditions

See also
Peasantry—China

Social history

Mind of China; Time essay. Time 89:28-9 Mr 17 '67

CHINA (People's Republic)

Cruelty and insanity made me a fugitive. S. T. Ma. il Life 62:24-9+ Je 2 '67
Fact sheet on red China. D. Chu. Sr Schol 91:5-6 O 5 '67
Incredible story of How China got the bomb; excerpts. W. L. Ryan and S. Summerlin. il Look 31:19-25 Jl 25 '67
Report on mainland China; symposium. bibliog f il Cur Hist 53:129-66+ S '67

See also
Airlines—China (People's Republic)
Atomic research—China (People's Republic)
Ballet—China (People's Republic)
Canton
Catholic church—Relations (diplomatic)—China (People's Republic)
Colleges and universities—China (People's Republic)
Communism—China (People's Republic)
Communist party (China [People's Republic])
Education—China (People's Republic)
Foreign visitors in China
Korean war, 1950-1953—Chinese participation
Macao
Mass media—China (People's Republic)
Music—China (People's Republic)
Research—China (People's Republic)
Science—China (People's Republic)
Sports—China (People's Republic)
United Nations—China (People's Republic)
Youth movement—China (People's Republic)

Armed forces

China's army: confusion in the ranks. il Newsweek 69:50+ Je 19 '67
China's military posture; People's liberation army (PLA) S. M. Chiu. bibliog f Cur Hist 53:155-60 S '67
Collision course. Newsweek 70:44 Ag 14 '67
Divided army. il Time 90:26 Ag 11 '67
Long march of Lin Piao. L. Fessler. il N Y Times Mag p64-5+ S 10 '67
More power for the army. il Time 89:34+ Je 16 '67
Testing the gun. il Newsweek 69:48-9 F 13 '67

Army

Army: huge but unwieldy; principal strength behind Communist party Chairman Mao Tse-tung. Bsns W p78 Jl 15 '67
Army in command. il Time 90:37-8 N 24 '67
Red China's divided army. R. S. Elegant and S. C. Liu. il Reporter 37:13-16 Ag 10 '67
Restraining the red generals. H. Schwartz. Sat R 50:40 Jl 22 '67

Boundaries

Tension on the Sino-Soviet border. C. P. Fitzgerald. il For Affairs 45:683-93 Jl '67
War of nerves; Sino-Soviet border. il Newsweek 69:44+ Mr 6 '67

Commerce

Chestnuts and jellyfish: Canton trade fair wins trade for Japan. Newsweek 69:72 Je 5 '67
Doing business with Mao. Newsweek 70:75-7 S 11 '67

Defenses

Peking adds potent punch to its arsenal. il Bsns W p36-7 Je 24 '67
Peking's big blast; first hydrogen bomb. Time 89:27-8 Je 23 '67

See also
Atomic warfare—Defenses

Description and travel

China. E. Moreira Salles. il Vogue 149:142-4+ Ap 1 '67

Diplomatic and consular service

Hazardous duty. il Time 90:31 Jl 7 '67

Economic conditions

As red China plunges deeper into chaos; impact of disorders. il U S News 63:36-8 O 2 '67
China return. R. H. Solomon. Yale R 57:148-60 O '67
Downfall of red China? interview. L. La Dany. il U S News 62:35-7 F 27 '67

Havoc and hunger. Newsweek 70:43 Jl 3 '67
Havoc that Mao has wrought. il Bsns W p76-8+ Jl 15 '67
Pure but poor. il Newsweek 69:56-7 F 20 '67
Red China: no yellow peril; views from Asia. il U S News 63:66-7 D 4 '67

Economic policy

Capitalists & managers in Communist China. B. M. Richman. Harvard Bsns R 45:57-78 Ja '67
China's economic situation. D. Wilson. Bul Atomic Sci 23:3-8 N '67
Cultural revolution and China's economy. C. Y. Cheng. bibliog f il Cur Hist 53:148-54+ S '67
Technology in China. G. Uchida; reply with rejoinder. P. F. Drucker. Sci Am 216:8-9 F '67

Foreign opinion

China must update its own fable. Life 63:4 S 29 '67
Politics. D. MacDonald. Esquire 67:64+ Ap '67

Foreign relations

China must update its own fable. Life 63:4 S 29 '67
China, Russia & the U.S. O. Gass. bibliog f Commentary 43:65-73 Mr '67
China's next phase. R. S. Elegant. For Affairs 46:137-50 O '67
Dragon's breath. Newsweek 70:42 S 4 '67
Great week for insults. il Time 90:30 S 22 '67
H-bomb, now: red China. Sr Schol 91:32+ S 28 '67
Life in a fishbowl; isolation of foreign diplomats in Peking. il Newsweek 70:43+ S 11 '67
Overflowing revolution; neighboring countries suffer Maoist riots. il Time 90:20-1 Jl 28 '67
Politics; China's global strategy. D. MacDonald. Esquire 67:18+ F '67
Red China: no yellow peril; views from Asia. il U S News 63:66-7 D 4 '67
Red China vs. Britain; what's ahead now? il U S News 63:10 S 11 '67
Red guards and Vietnam. Commonweal 85:441-2 Ja 27 '67
Reopening the door to China. W. J. Richardson. America 116:850-2 Je 17 '67
Ultimatum & anarchy: Peking's behavior to British and other diplomats. Time 90:20 S 1 '67
Will red China now risk war? il U S News 62:38-40 My 29 '67
Yellow peril revisited; excerpts from Pax Americana. R. Steel. Commentary 43:58-65 Je '67

See also
China (People's Republic)—Boundaries

Asia

China in Asia. C. P. FitzGerald. Cur Hist 53:129-34+ S '67
Myth of Chinese aggression. O. M. Lee. Nation 205:459-63 N 6 '67

Asia, Southeastern

Chinese threat to world order; address, April 8, 1967. S. Nimmanheminda. il Ann Am Acad 372:59-63 Jl '67

Burma

Trouble in Burma. il Newsweek 70:53+ N 27 '67

Great Britain

Mao's bullies get a bit of their own medicine. il Life 63:28-28A S 8 '67
Squeeze: in Peking and Hong Kong. il Newsweek 70:41-2 S 4 '67
Standing firm; anti-British demonstrations. il Newsweek 69:42+ My 29 '67
Will Hong Kong become Peking duck? R. Terrill. New Repub 157:14-15 S 2 '67

See also
Hong Kong—Boundaries

India

Delegation of donkeys; diplomats expelled from Peking and New Delhi. R. Ramanujam. il Newsweek 70:44 Jl 3 '67

Russia

As the turmoil in China keeps growing. il U S News 62:6 F 6 '67
Closer to a final split. il Time 89:26 F 17 '67
High invective. il Time 89:25 F 3 '67
Mao baits the Russian Bear. il Newsweek 69:47-8 F 13 '67
Moscow and the current Chinese crisis. F. Michael. bibliog f Cur Hist 53:141-7+ S '67

CHINA—Foreign relations—Russia—*Continued*
Ridicule and bullets widen the great rift.
il Life 62:30-1 F 24 '67
Russia vs. red China: what's actually going
on; with analysis by F. B. Stevens. il U S
News 62:36-40 F 20 '67
Russian charge: Peking is hijacking Soviet
jets. il U S News 62:12 Mr 6 '67
Sabbath of witches, a canceling of Christmas.
il Time 89:31 F 10 '67
Significance of the rift between the Chinese
Communist regime and the Soviet Union;
address, April 1967, with questions and an-
swers. S. K. Chow. Ann Am Acad 372:64-71
Jl '67
Tension on the China-Soviet border. A. D.
Barnett. il Look 31:40-2+ O 3 '67

United States

China and Vietnam. R. Terrill. New Repub
155:16-20 O 29 '66; Correction. 156:37 Ja 28
'67
China: the people's middle kingdom and the
U.S.A., by J. K. Fairbank. Review
Sat R 50:45 S 30 '67. C. T. Hu
China's cautious American policy. I. C. Ojha.
bibliog f Cur Hist 53:135-40+ S '67
Dragon under glass: time for a new China
policy. J. C. Thomson, jr. Atlan 220:55-61
O '67
War with China. H. E. Salisbury. New Re-
pub 156:25-8 My 20 '67

Vietnam (Democratic Republic)

China and North Vietnam: the limits of the
alliance. I. C. Ojha. bibliog f Cur Hist
54:42-7 Ja '68

Vietnam (Republic)

Will China intervene? the stakes in Vietnam.
W. C. McWilliams. Commonweal 85:553-5
F 17 '67

Intellectual life

We are slaves who have been betrayed;
destruction of intellectuals under Mao. S.
T. Ma. il Life 63:64-6+ Jl 14 '67

Politics and government

Approaching a showdown; Mao's naked power
struggle. il Time 89:24 F 3 '67
As the turmoil in China keeps growing. il
U S News 62:6 F 6 '67
Cadres, bureaucracy, and political power in
Communist China, by A. D. Barnett and
E. Vogel. Review
New Repub 157:23-5 D 16 '67. J. W. Lewis
Can Mao win? M. Omori. New Repub 156:
14-16 F 25 '67
Chaos in Canton. Time 90:26 Ag 25 '67
Chaos in Canton. il Newsweek 70:54 S 18 '67
Chaos spreads: Mao calls on the army. il
Newsweek 69:48+ F 6 '67
China in turmoil. il Sat Eve Post 240:90
Mr 11 '67
China puzzle: old man in a hurry. C. P.
Fitzgerald. il Nation 204:326-9 Mr 13 '67
China, Russia & the U.S. O. Gass. bibliog f
Commentary 43:65-73 Mr '67
China: signs of moderation. il Newsweek 70:
34-6 O 9 '67
China's economic situation. D. Wilson. Bul
Atomic Sci 23:3-8 N '67
China's military posture. S. M. Chiu. bibliog
f Cur Hist 53:155-60 S '67
China's next phase. R. S. Elegant. For Affairs
46:137-50 O '67
Chou takes the reins; Mao's cultural revolu-
tion backfired. il Bsns W p39 Mr 11 '67
Death of Li; principle of social order. il
Time 89:27-8 Ja 27 '67
Diagnosing the dragon; U.S.-China watchers.
il Time 89:21-2 Ja 27 '67
Downfall of red China? interview. L. La
Dany. il U S News 62:35-7 F 27 '67
Edge of chaos; further political and social
chaos. il Time 90:23 Ag 4 '67
End of a truce; fresh disorders in Canton.
Newsweek 71:34 Ja 1 '68
Evening at the ballet; public appearance of
Mao and violence. il Time 89:32 My 5 '67
Growing mystery of Communist China. il U S
News 63:36-8 Ag 21 '67
In rough waters. Newsweek 69:45-6 F 27
'67
Intermission. Newsweek 70:50 D 11 '67
Into the dustbin! onto the garbage heap! re-
newed attacks on Liu by Red guards. Time
89:40+ Ap 14 '67
Liberate the Southwest! fighting in Szech-
wan. Time 89:35-6 My 19 '67
Life in Peking: report from a long nose. J.
L. Vincent. il N Y Times Mag p25-7+ F
26 '67

Long way to go. Time 89:25-6 F 24 '67
Look through the bamboo curtain. H.
Schwartz. Sat R 50:51-2 My 6 '67
Mao and the struggle for China. il News-
week 69:32-9+ Ja 30 '67
Mao baits the Russian Bear. il Newsweek 69:
47-8 F 13 '67
Mao Tse-tung's last revolution. V. S. Kear-
ney. America 116:215-17 F 11 '67
Mao vs. Liu: who holds the guns? il U S News
63:13 Ag 28 '67
Maoists make a tactical retreat. R. S.
Elegant. il Reporter 36:32-5 Mr 23 '67
Mao's cultural revolution. C. P. Fitzgerald.
Nation 205:325-8 O 9 '67
Mao's revolution: keeping China safe for com-
munism. J. R. Townsend. il Nation 204:781-6
Je 19 '67
Mao's worst crisis. M. Omori. New Repub
156:17-19 Ja 28 '67
More power for the army. il Time 89:34+ Je
16 '67
Rectifying the revolution. Time 91:22 Ja 19 '68
Sabbath of witches, a canceling of Christmas.
il Time 89:31 F 10 '67
Spreading chaos in Communist China; China's
trouble spots. il U S News 62:8 F 13 '67
Summon to the army. Time 89:27 F 17 '67
There's no future in Maoism. Life 62:4 Ja
27 '67
Time of summing up. il Time 90:36 O 13 '67
Trouble in all directions. il Time 90:26 D 22 '67
Understanding Mao; or, look back to Stalin.
H. R. Trevor-Roper. il N Y Times Mag
p28-9+ D 12 '67
Upheaval in China. B. I. Schwartz. Com-
mentary 43:55-62 F '67
We're not sure what will happen next. il
Newsweek 69:43 Ap 3 '67
What's really going on now in red China;
symposium. il U S News 62:46-50+ Ja 30 '67
Who's on first? trouble in Canton. Newsweek
69:48+ Je 5 '67
Wounded tigers. il Newsweek 70:46-7 Ag 7 '67
Writhing dragon. Nat R 19:70+ Ja 24 '67
See also
Communism—China (People's Republic)
Communist party (China [People's Republic])

Population

Estimating China's population. J. S. Aird.
bibliog f Ann Am Acad 369:61-72 Ja '67

Social conditions

As red China plunges deeper into chaos; im-
pact of disorders. il U S News 63:36-8
O 2 '67
China: stories from the inside. M. London.
Nat R 19:744-6 Jl 11 '67
Edge of chaos; further political and social
chaos. il Time 90:23 Ag 4 '67
Fields of battle; effect of cultural revolution
on farmers. il Newsweek 69:58 My 15 '67
Havoc and hunger. Newsweek 70:43 Jl 3 '67
See also
Communism—China (People's Republic)

Territorial expansion

Communism's great divide. A. Parry. il Re-
porter 36:29-32 Je 1 '67
CHINA (People's Republic) and Russia. See
Russia and China (People's Republic)
CHINA (People's Republic) and the United
States
Who knows the truth about red China? in-
terview. F. Pardinas. Cath World 205:36-41
Ap '67
CHINA (porcelain) See Pottery
CHINA cow. See Soybeans
CHINA trade porcelain. See Pottery, Chinese
CHINA trade; story. See Hogan, D.
CHINATOWN, San Francisco. See San Fran-
cisco—Chinatown
CHINESE
Asian diary. J. Mander. Commentary 44:90-5
O '67
China is like the Chinese language. D. Blood-
worth. il N Y Times Mag p 10-11+ Je 18 '67
Chinese finesse: unsound but oh so useful;
addiction to bridge. C. Goren. il Sports
Illus 27:43 Jl 3 '67
Strategy and national psychology in China.
H. L. Boorman and S. A. Boorman. bibliog
f Ann Am Acad 370:143-55 Mr '67
See also
Peasantry—China
CHINESE art objects. See Art objects, Chinese
CHINESE atomic bomb test. See Atomic bombs
—Testing

CHINESE bronzes. See Bronzes
CHINESE businessmen. See Businessmen
CHINESE cookery. See Cookery, Chinese
CHINESE dancing. See Dancing, Chinese
CHINESE drama
    What the villain did; plot of Hai Jui dis-
    missed from office, by H. Wu. il News-
    week 69:43 My 1 '67
CHINESE enamels See Enamels and enameling
CHINESE furniture. See Furniture, Chinese
CHINESE hibiscus. See Hibiscus
CHINESE hydrogen bomb. See Hydrogen bombs
CHINESE in Indonesia
    Firmer hand. il Time 90:36 O 20 '67
    Home for the boomerang; Dayak tribesmen
    massacre Chinese. Time 90:34+ D 15 '67
    Indonesia after Sukarno. D. Warner. il Re-
    porter 36:36-7 Je 15 '67
    Trojan horse; Chinese slaughtered by Dyaks.
    M. Parker. il Newsweek 70:36-7 D 25 '67
CHINESE in southeastern Asia
    Chinese threat to world order; address, April
    8, 1967. S. Nimmanheminda. il Ann Am
    Acad 372:59-63 Jl '67
CHINESE in the United States
    See also
San Francisco—Chinatown
CHINESE-JAPANESE war, 1937-1945
                Aerial operations
    See also
Panay (gunboat) incident
CHINESE language
    Chinese say it how-how.   L. A. Harlow.
    Travel 127:60-2+ Mr '67
                Dictionaries
    Chinese Unicorn. D. Bloodworth. il Horizon
    9:117-19 Sum '67
              Terms and phrases
    Chinese Unicorn. D. Bloodworth. il Horizon
    9:117-19 Sum '67
                  Writing
    China is like the Chinese language. D. Blood-
    worth. il N Y Times Mag p 10-11+ Je 18 '67
CHINESE literature
    From the East. R. E. Teele. Poetry 109:272
    Ja '67
    Lessons through the barrel of a gun; sacred
    writings of Mao Tse-tung. G. Woodcock. il
    Commonweal 86:81-4 Ap 7 '67
CHINESE military assistance. See Military as-
    sistance, Chinese
CHINESE paintings. See Painting, Chinese
CHINESE philosophers. See Philosophers
CHINESE philosophy. See Philosophy, Chinese
CHINESE pottery. See Pottery, Chinese
CHINESE refugees. See Refugees, Chinese
CHINESE studies (Sinology)
    Forms of modern Sinology. J. Mirsky. Nation
    204:468-70+ Ap 10 '67
CHINESE symbolism. See Symbolism
CHINESE writing. See Chinese language—
    Writing
CH'ING Hsüan-t'ung, emperor of China
    20th day of the 10th moon; excerpt from
    The last Manchu. Sat R 50:50 F 25 '67
                  about
    Emperor's conversion. M. H. Fried. Sat R
    50:50-1 F 25 '67
CHINNOCK, Frank
    Pat Smith's special war in Vietnam. Read
    Digest 90:195-6+ Je '67
CHINOOK salmon fishing. See Salmon fishing
CHIOCCHIO, Sara R. and others
    5-Hydroxytryptamine in the carotid body of
    the cat. bibliog Science 158:790-1 N 10 '67
CHIONODOXA. See Glory of the snow
CHIRICO, Giorgio de
    Surrealist Quixote. S. Koch. Nation 204:120-
    1 Ja 23 '67
CHIROPRACTORS
    Medical dispute about treatment by chiro-
    practors. Good H 164:185-7 My '67
CHISELS
    How to convert old chisels to serve new uses.
    W. E. Burton. il Pop Mech 129:200 Ja '68
CHISHOLM, Jean B.
    Three poems: Tortoise; Hippopotamus; Dor-
    mouse. Good H 164:267 Ap '67
CHITONS teeth. See Teeth (animals)

CHIU, S. M.
    China's military posture. bibliog f Cur Hist
    53:155-60 S '67
CHLAMYDOMONAS. See Algae
CHLORELLA. See Algae
CHLORIDES
    Seizure discharges evoked in vitro in thin
    section from guinea pig hippocampus. C.
    Yamamoto and N. Kawai. bibliog il Science
    155:341-2 Ja 20 '67
CHLORINATED insecticides. See Insecticides
CHLORINE
    Chlorination of unsaturated compounds in
    nonpolar media. M. L. Poutsma. bibliog
    il Science 157:997-1005 S 1 '67
    See also
Sewage disposal—Chlorination
CHLORINE bleach. See Bleaching materials
CHLORITES (mineral)
    Transformation of gibbsite to chlorite in
    ocean bottom sediments. L. D. Swindale
    and P.-F. Fan. bibliog il Science 157:799-
    800 Ag 18 '67
CHLOROPHENYLALANINE.   See Phenyl-
    alanine
CHLOROPHYL
    See also
Chloroplasts
CHLOROPLASTS
    Functional chloroplast polyribosomes from
    tobacco leaves. J. L. Chen and S. G.
    Wildman. bibliog il Science 155:1271-3 Mr 10
    '67
    Galactosyl diglycerides: their possible func-
    tion in euglena chloroplasts. A. Rosenberg.
    bibliog il Science 157:1191-6 S 8 '67
    Phenotypic variations among chloroplasts of
    a single cell. A. Gibor. bibliog il Science 155:
    327-9 Ja 20 '67
CHLORPROMAZINE
    Antipsychotic drugs. Consumer Rep 32:548-50
    O '67
CHOAS (ameba) See Ameba
CHOATE, Joseph E.
    Facts and figures. Yachting 121:428-30 Ja '67;
    123:55+ Ja '68
CHOCOLATE
    See also
Cookery—Chocolate
CHOCOLATES. See Candy
CHOCOLATES; drama. See Bernard, I.
CHODOROV, Frank
    Death of a teacher; eulogy. W. F. Buckley,
    jr. por Nat R 19:84-5+ Ja 24 '67
CHOICE (psychology)
    Are the experts destroying our judgment?
    M. Lerner. McCalls 95:26+ N '67
CHOICE of college. See College, Choice of
CHOICE of occupations. See Occupations; Vo-
    cational guidance
CHOICE of wars; drama. See Shaw, I.
CHOIRS
    See also
Church music
CHOLERA
    Cholera threatens. D. A. Ehrlich. il Sci N
    92:43 Jl 8 '67
CHOLESTEROL
    Binding the cholesterol; use of cholestyra-
    mine. Time 90:77 O 13 '67
    Cholesterol. A. Talmey. Vogue 150:148-9 S
    15 '67
    Cholesterol study sparks FDA policy review;
    report to the AMA meeting. Sci N 92:11
    Jl 1 '67
    Cocktail for cholesterol; use of cholestyra-
    mine. Newsweek 70:59 O 16 '67
    Conversion of beta sitosterol to cholesterol
    blocked in an insect by hypocholesterolemic
    agents. J. A. Svoboda and W. E. Robbins.
    bibliog il Science 156:1637-8 Je 23 '67
    Drug hits heart menace. Sci Digest 63:32 Ja
    '68
    Fat in the foods we eat. il Consumer Bul
    50:37-40 Jl '67
    Saturation in milk and meat fats. S. Patton
    and E. M. Kesler. bibliog il Science 156:
    1365-6 Je 9 '67
    Shedding new light on heart disease. il Bsns
    W p 110+ Je 24 '67
CHOLINE
    Anticholinergic blockade of centrally induced
    thirst. R. A. Levitt and A. E. Fisher; re-
    ply with rejoinder. A. Routtenberg. bibliog
    il Science 157:838-41 Ag 18 '67
    Choline in the cell wall of a bacterium: novel
    type of polymer-linked choline in pneumoc-
    occus. A. Tomasz. bibliog il Science 157:
    694-7 Ag 11 '67

CHOLINESTERASE
Cholinesterase in plasma: first reported absence in the Bantu; half-life determination. T. Jenkins and others. bibliog il Science 156:1748-50 Je 30 '67
Heritability of plasma cholinesterase activity in inbred mouse strains. C. R. Angel and others. bibliog il Science 156:529-30 Ap 28 '67

CHOLLA cactus. See Cactus

CHOMSKY, Noam
On civil disobedience, 1967. N Y Times Mag p27-8 N 26 '67

CHONDRITES. See Meteorites

CHONGOS. See Cookery, Mexican

CHOOKASIAN, Lili
Armenian diary. G. Gavejian. il pors Opera N 32:14-16 D 23 '67

CHOPIN, Frédéric François
Chopin's mazurkas: a new miraculous reading from Rubinstein. H. Goldsmith. il Hi Fi 17:73-4 Ap '67
Josef Hofmann, memorable Chopin. R. Kammerer. il Am Rec G 33:556-7 Mr '67

CHOPS. See Cookery—Meat

CHORAL music
  See also
Church music
Phonograph records—Choral music

CHORAL singing
  See also
Operas—Choral singing

CHOREOGRAPHY
Association of black choreographers. Clark center for the performing arts. J. Maskey. Dance Mag 41:29 Ag '67
Concert of dance; Judson memorial church. J. Anderson. Dance Mag 41:32+ S '67
Concert of new choreographers, Henry street settlement playhouse. J. Anderson. Dance Mag 41:31-2 Jl '67
Dance '67: 92nd street Y. J. Maskey. Dance Mag 42:30 Ja '68
Dance uptown; Minor Latham playhouse. J. Maskey. Dance Mag 41:31 D '67
New choreographers concert. Clark center for the performing arts. J. Maskey. Dance Mag 41:36 My '67; 42:78 Ja '68
On the move; polemic on dancing. K. King. il Dance Mag 41:56-8 Je '67
Report from Boston; Vestris prize for choreography. P. Marmein. Dance Mag 41:20+ S '67
Testament to Tamiris; 92nd street Y. M. Marks. Dance Mag 41:88 Je '67
Tudor and the Royal ballet. S. J. Cohen. il Sat R 50:74-5 My 13 '67
Works by Eve Gentry, Elizabeth Keen, Christine Loizeaux, Rudy Perez & Barbara Roan; Clark center for the performing arts. J. Anderson. Dance Mag 41:30-1 Ag '67
World of dance; J. Clouser's venture at the Y. W. Terry. il Sat R 50:44-5 Je 24 '67
You are always somewhere, hopefully; work of J. Hunter. R. Hartley. il Dance Mag 41:62-5 S '67
  See also
Dance notation

CHOSEN; story. See Potok, C.

CHOU, En-lai
Chou En-lai. K. Y. Hsu. New Repub 156:21-5 Ap 8 '67
Chou takes the reins. il por Bsns W p39 Mr 11 '67
Middle way. il pors Newsweek 69:54 Mr 13 '67
People of the week. U S News 62:21 Mr 20 '67
Third man. il por Time 89:34 Mr 3 '67
We're not sure what will happen next. il por Newsweek 69:43 Ap 3 '67

CHOU, Shi-ming
Myxovirus-like structures in a case of human chronic polymyositis. bibliog Science 158: 1453-5 D 15 '67

CHOW, Shu-kai
Significance of the rift between the Chinese Communist regime and the Soviet Union; address, April 1967, with questions and answers. Ann Am Acad 372:64-71 Jl '67

CHRIS-CRAFT corporation
Yachting interviews: Jon Van Hoboken. B. Robinson. il Yachting 122:41+ Ag '67

CHRISLIN insta cameras. See Cameras

CHRISS, Nicholas C. See Cohen, J. jt. auth.

CHRIST. See Jesus Christ

CHRIST, Carl F.
Econometrics and model-building. bibliog Ann Am Acad 370:164-75 Mr '67

CHRIST-JANER, Victor Frederick
Lake Erie, constituent imagery determines campus design. Arch Forum 127:62-7 Jl '67

CHRISTENING. See Baptism

CHRISTENSEN, Arthur R.
Rustic hourglass. Pop Sci 192:172-3+ Ja '68

CHRISTENSEN, J. A.
East high school's drama workshop. Sr Schol 90:sup 13 Mr 17 '67

CHRISTGAU, Robert
Anatomy of a love festival. Esquire 69:60-7+ Ja '68
Life styles: the boxing fan. Esquire 67:120-3 My '67
Secular music. Esquire 67:16+ Je; 68:54+ O; 283-6 D '67
Tune up, turn disestablishmentarian, drop out. Esquire 68:104-5+ S '67

CHRISTIAN, George
Christian way. il por Newsweek 69:93 Ap 24 '67
Compleat Johnson man. il por Time 89:74-5 Je 16 '67

CHRISTIAN advertising. See Religious advertising

CHRISTIAN art and symbolism
Liturgy and the politics of the kingdom. R. J. Neuhaus. Christian Cent 84:1623-7 D 20 '67
Miss Bouchard protests; exhibition of International congress on religion, architecture and the visual arts. T. W. Moore. Christian Cent 84:1288-90 O 11 '67
  See also
Art and religion
Glass painting and staining
Stations of the cross

CHRISTIAN booksellers association
Store techniques stressed at CBA convention. W. P. Adams. il Pub W 192:26-7 S 4 '67

CHRISTIAN Brothers wine. See Wine

CHRISTIAN century (periodical)
Changing mind. W. E. Hull. Christian Cent 84:920-1 Jl 12 '67

CHRISTIAN character. See Christian life

CHRISTIAN colleges. See Denominational colleges

CHRISTIAN council of India. See National Christian council of India

CHRISTIAN democrats (Chile) See Political parties—Chile

CHRISTIAN democrats (Latin America) See Political parties—Latin America

CHRISTIAN doctrine. See Theology

CHRISTIAN education. See Religious education

CHRISTIAN ethics
Christian maturity. B. Häring. America 117: 240-1 S 9 '67
Christians and violence. S. Windass. Commonweal 86:11-13 Mr 24 '67
Ethical teaching of Jesus. C. E. Curran. Commonweal 87:248-50+ N 24 '67
God is evolving, not dead; with excerpt from If this be heresy, by J. A. Pike. K. S. Latourette. Sat R 50:45-6 S 16 '67
Is marriage still sacred? what does love mean? A. Whitman. Redbook 128:68-9 F '67
Life control and the Christian. C. P. Kindregan. America 117:406-8 O 14 '67
Marriage in the modern world; address. July 1966. D. Burke. Cath World 205:101-6 My '67
Virtue does stand in the middle. America 117:370 O 7 '67
Word. V. P. McCorry. See issues of America
  See also
Church and social problems
Conscience
Humility
Love (theology)
War and religion

CHRISTIAN giving
  See also
Stewardship, Christian

CHRISTIAN life
As Advent approaches; reality of the Advent message. N. Pittenger. Christian Cent 84:1522-4 N 29 '67
Ascent to God after the council. H. F. Smith. America 116:283-5 F 25 '67
Christian maturity. B. Häring. America 117: 240-1 S 9 '67
Faith or works? question of what makes a Christian. R. Haughton. Cath World 205: 263-7 Ag '67
Rejoice and be glad; excerpt from The quantity of a hazelnut. F. E. Malania. Redbook 130:35-42 Ja '68
Spiritual death? V. P. McCorry. America 117: inside back cover Ag 26 '67
Temporary rain and fog. V. P. McCorry. America 117:188 Ag 19 '67
Valor of truth; reprint. M. L. Chiang. U S News 63:108+ S 11 '67

CHRISTIAN life—*Continued*
What is an anonymous Christian? P. Hebblethwaite. Cath World 205:90-4 My '67
See also
Conversion
Faith
Hypocrisy
Stewardship, Christian
CHRISTIAN love. See Love (theology)
CHRISTIAN missions. See Missions
CHRISTIAN movements, Student. See Student Christian movements
CHRISTIAN names. See Names, Personal
CHRISTIAN pacifism. See Pacifism
CHRISTIAN Science
Impact of Christian Science on the American churches, 1880-1910. R. J. Cunningham. bibliog f Am Hist R 72:885-905 Ap '67
CHRISTIAN socialism. See Socialism, Christian
CHRISTIAN stewardship. See Stewardship, Christian
CHRISTIAN theological seminary, Indianapolis
Seminary drama and the God is dead theme. R. A. Fangmeier. Christian Cent 84:846-7 Je 28 '67
CHRISTIAN unity. See Church unity
CHRISTIAN year
See also
Advent
CHRISTIANITY
Black power and the American Christ. V. Harding; discussion. Christian Cent 84: 214 F 15 '67
Letter to Zeke: a commentary on Ezekiel. R. M. Davidson. Cath World 206:153-4 Ja '68
Militant anti-Christianity. N. Pittenger. Christian Cent 84:712-14 My 31 '67
Theological existence among the ruins. W. Ashby. Christian Cent 84:368-71 Mr 22 '67; Reply. B. F. Lewis. 84:624 My 10 '67
Where all else ends; excerpt from The crucified answer. O. Hartman. Christian Cent 84:259 Mr 1 '67
See also
Apostles
Catholic church
Christian ethics
Christian life
Fundamentalism
Jesus Christ
Missions
Paul, Saint—Teaching
Protestantism
Religion and science
Theology
CHRISTIANITY, Primitive. See Church history—Primitive and early church
CHRISTIANITY and communism. See Communism and religion
CHRISTIANITY and culture
Christian critique of American culture, by J. N. Hartt. Review.
    Cath World 205:371-3 S '67. R. C. Neville
Importance of being earnest about Christian myth. G. Dudley, 3d. Christian Cent 84:1215-18 S 27 '67
Poets, theologians and the nature of myth; seminar on Myth in religion and literature. T. Stoneburner. Christian Cent 85:54+ Ja 10 '68
CHRISTIANITY and economics
Changing role of the church in Latin America. il US News 63:94-5 O 16 '67
Laissez-faire is not enough; widening gap between rich nations and poor nations. S. L. Parmar. Christian Cent 84:587-9 My 3 '67
CHRISTIANITY and international affairs. See Church and international relations
CHRISTIANITY and other religions
Again, silence in the churches. A. R. Eckardt and A. L. Eckardt. Christian Cent 84:970-3, 992-5 Jl 26–Ag 2 '67
Arabs, Israelis, Christians: letters to editors on the Middle East crisis. Christian Cent 84:1128-30 S 6 '67
Christians and the Mideast crisis. W. G. Oxtoby. Christian Cent 84:961-5 Jl 26 '67; Reply. D. Lieber. 84:1193-4 S 20 '67
Communication between faiths; Jewish-Christian relations. L. D. Streiker. Sat R 50:37 N 11 '67
Dialogue with Mecca; France's Fraternity of Abraham. il Time 89:56-7 Je 2 '67
Did Christians fail Israel? R. L. Rubenstein. Commonweal 87:297-8 D 1 '67; Discussion. 87:420-1+ D 29 '67
For better communication; American Judaism to step up communications with Christianity and the Negro ghettos. Time 90:72 N 24 '67

God is not enough? I. J. Gerber. Christian Cent 84:684-7 My 24 '67; Discussion. 84:676, 997-8, 1524-5 My 24, Ag 2, N 29 '67
Judaism and the Christian predicament, by B. Z. Bokser. Review
    New Repub 156:25-6+ My 6 '67. R. Hazelton
Judaism, Christianity, and the western tradition. H. Jonas. Commentary 44:61-8 N '67
Morning after; effect of Israeli-Arab war on Christian-Jewish relations. il Newsweek 70: 73 Jl 3 '67
What is the meaning of the people of Israel? J. Haughey. America 117:218-20 S 2 '67
Words fitly spoken; Jewish-Christian dialogues. Christian Cent 84:1277 O 11 '67
CHRISTIANITY and politics. See Church and politics
CHRISTIANITY and science. See Religion and science
CHRISTIANITY and social problems. See Church and social problems
CHRISTIANITY today (periodical)
Mr Inside. Newsweek 71:71-2 Ja 15 '68
CHRISTIANS
Christian and the hippie. J. Hitchcock. Christian Cent 84:1040-2 Ag 16 '67

Anecdotes, facetiae, satire, etc.

Ploys for the pious; concerning the book Games Christians play. Time 89:58 F 17 '67
CHRISTIANS and Jews. See Christianity and other religions
CHRISTIANS in Africa
See also
Protestants in Africa
CHRISTIANS in Ghana
How Ghana's churches failed their testing. K. E. Ankrah; reply. A. Y. Wurapa. Christian Cent 84:242+ F 22 '67
CHRISTIANS in Japan
See also
United church of Christ in Japan
CHRISTIANS in Nigeria
Technicolored Christian; as Nigerian sees the American. E. G. Dalbey, jr. Christian Cent 84:1158-60 S 13 '67
CHRISTIANS in Russia
Religion in Russia: the status of Christians. J. D. Windhausen. il Nat R 19:1174-5 O 31 '67
Struggle for religious faith in the Soviet Union today. H. A. Bosley. Christian Cent 84:1082-4 Ag 23 '67
CHRISTIANS in Tanganyika. See Christians in Tanzania
CHRISTIANS in Tanzania
Communicating the word in Tanzania. W. B. Gray. Christian Cent 84:414 Mr 29 '67
CHRISTIANSEN, Godtfred Kirk
Toys for Jutland. il por Time 90:72 D 22 '67
CHRISTIE, Agatha
Third girl; story. Redbook 128:139 Ap '67
    about
Murder most fair by Agatha the good. A. Burgess. Life 63:8 D 1 '67
CHRISTIE, George A.
Building activity (title varies) See issues of Architectural record
Comment and contract tabulation. Arch Rec 141:83 Ja '67
Current trends in construction. See issues of Architectural record
CHRISTIE, Julie
Strange, empty success of Julie Christie; interview, ed. by O. Fallaci. por Look 31: 66-9 Mr 21 '67
    about
Lusty new role for Julie Christie. S. Flink. il pors Look 31:59-65 Mr 21 '67
CHRISTIE, Trevor L.
Generals and the news spy. Sat R 50:60-1+ Jl 8 '67
Is Venice sinking? excerpt from Antiquities in peril. Sat R 50:40+ Mr 25 '67
Once and future ships. Sat R 51:51-2+ Ja 6 '68
Tauchnitz rises again. Sat R 50:35-6 D 23 '67
Troika and the tourists. Sat R 50:44-6 O 14 '67
What's left after the tornado? Sat R 50:41 O 14 '67
World travel calendar, 1968. Sat R 51:74+ Ja 6 '68
CHRISTINA, queen of Sweden
Queen Christina. J. H. Elliott. il pors Horizon 9:66-79 Sum '67
CHRISTMAN, Elizabeth
Aggiornamento; story. Reporter 37:34-6 D 28 '67

CHRISTMAS decorations—*Continued*
Mama's little workshop. J. L. O'Neill. Am Home 70:25 D '67
Nine ways to deck a door. il Bet Hom & Gard 45:40-3 D '67
Non-stop festivities. il House & Gard 132:156-7 D '67
Paper ornaments you can make. il House & Gard 132:36 D '67
Pine cones and glass crafts; suggestions for the holiday hobbyist. G. M. Aase. il Design 69:16-19 Wint '67
Sconce of fat round candles. il Sunset 139:86 D '67
Swinging tree trims! il Bet Hom & Gard 45:52-4 D '67
Talent for Christmas; home of the Vincent Prices. il House & Gard 132:136-43 D '67
Woven ojos de dios; Mexican ornaments. G. J. Moody. il Sch Arts 67:8-9 D '67
  See also
Christmas greens
Christmas trees

CHRISTMAS decorations, Outdoor
Artful doorways. il McCalls 95:122-3 D '67
Decorate your tree outdoors. V. Reynolds. il & Home Gard 54:47 D '67
Glow that only garden lights can give. B. C. Kilvert, jr. il Home Gard 54:20-1 D '67
How to light up your home for Christmas. W. C. Leckey. il Pop Mech 128:134-7 D '67

CHRISTMAS desserts. See Desserts

CHRISTMAS dinners
American turkey; at home in Europe. H. McCully. il House B 109:172-7+ D '67
As the British feast at Christmas; with recipes. il McCalls 95:132-4+ D '67
December meal plan idea. il Bet Hom & Gard 45:77-8+ D '67

CHRISTMAS entertainments
Strange celebration. Mrs I. M. M. Gilbert. McCalls 95:38+ D '67

CHRISTMAS eve
Hospital Christmas eve. C. McCullers. McCalls 95:96-7 D '67

CHRISTMAS gifts
Best buy gifts (cont) il Consumer Rep 32:572-3 N '67
Best Christmas ever. il Parents Mag 42:58-61+ D '67
Child's garden of things-to-make for Christmas. il Good H 165:116-21 D '67
Enchantments. il House B 109:128-37 D '67
Famous bright-idea gift list. il Good H 165:10+ D '67
For campers at Christmas. C. B. Colby. il Outdoor Life 140:16+ D '67
For Christmas; gift ideas & shopping tips. il Changing T 21:7-12 D '67
Forty-two gifts they'll be glad you made. il Good H 165:108-13+ N '67
Gift from the heart. N. V. Peale. il Read Digest 92:95-8 Ja '68
Gift ideas, to please a weeder, and even to start a non-weeder off on weeding. il Sunset 139:162+ D '67
Gifts crafted by hand. E. Kinard. il House B 109:168-9 D '67
Gifts from museums (cont) il Consumer Rep 32:594-6 N '67
Gifts from the transistor age. N. Craig. il House B 109:170-1 D '67
Gifts! gifts! for everyone! L. Lerman. il Mlle 66:146-9 N '67
Gifts that last a lifetime. T. Trueblood. il Field & S 72:12+ D '67
Gifts you never thought of. il McCalls 95:68+ D '67
Great gift: a good bag; sleeping bags. il Sunset 139:33+ D '67
Guide for last-minute shoppers. Bsns W p 133 D 16 '67
Here's hoping. L. B. Johnson. il McCalls 95:84+ D '67
How to cope with the high cost of Christmas. L. Lane. Farm J 91:57 D '67
In San Francisco's North Beach, unusual gifts each $10 or less. il Sunset 139:28-30 D '67
Last minute! great romantic gifts. L. Lerman. Mlle 66:124-5 D '67
Merry Christmas, with many happy returns. M. Feeley. Am Home 70:26-7 N '67
Ninety-nine gift ideas, peanuts-to-emeralds price-tags. Vogue 150:122-4+ N 15 '67
Off on a shopping spree. il Seventeen 26:130+ D '67
Presents for pilots. P. L. Demarest. il Flying 81:67-70 D '67
Small gifts to sew. il Good H 165:198+ D '67

What's new in gift ideas for Christmas. Outdoor Life 140:90+ N '67
Who'll spool? you'll! il Seventeen 26:162-3+ N '67
  See also
Books as gifts
Christmas projects
Food as gifts
Gifts in business
Plants as gifts
Wine as gifts
Wrapping of packages

  Anecdotes, facetiae, satire, etc.
Christmas present. J. A. Michener. il Read Digest 91:60-3 D '67

CHRISTMAS gifts for children
Choices for a child's Christmas. il House B 109:164-7 D '67
Off the track and into the slot; slot-car racing sets and dolls most popular presents. il Time 90:49 D 15 '67
On and off the avenue (cont) New Yorker 43:105-6+ D 9 '67
Special stocking gifts for under $2. il Good H 165:189-90 D '67
'Tis the season to be cranky. R. Kramer. il N Y Times Mag p 109-10+ N 26 '67
Workshop wonders; colorful storage racks, toy cabinet, mice-people and doll's house. il Bet Hom & Gard 45:56-8 D '67
  See also
Books as gifts
Toys

CHRISTMAS gifts for men
Christmas gifts for yourself. il Pop Mech 128:175 D '67
Extravagances for a gentleman's stocking. il House & Gard 132:282-3 N '67
For the best brother in the world (yours or somebody else's) with love at Christmas. il Seventeen 26:116-17 D '67
Gifts for craftsmen. J. H. Ingersoll. il House B 109:180-1 D '67
Go gifts for the car. McCalls 95:146 D '67
Men's fragrances: the numbers game. il Mlle 66:109-11 D '67
PS previews the Christmas gifts you'd like to get. il Pop Sci 191:111-23 D '67
Twenty-two ways to please a trout fisherman. il Sunset 139:25 D '67

CHRISTMAS gifts for pets
Merry Christmas dear Fido! P. O'Keefe. Am Home 70:44 D '67
Pet gifts: don't forget Fido. Good H 165:194 D '67

CHRISTMAS gifts for the home
Christmas gifts from your workshop. il Pop Mech 128:176-80 N '67
For making coffee the hard way. il Sunset 139:70-1 D '67
Forty-nine under-the-tree terrifics for under $16. il House & Gard 132:232-3 N '67
Forty-two reasons for mistletoe bussing, all under $36. il House & Gard 132:234-5 N '67
Good gifts for the family. il Bet Hom & Gard 45:15+ D '67
Good gifts for the family; furniture. C. Garner. il Bet Hom & Gard 45:56+ N '67
Joy of giving; eighty beguilements under $6. il House & Gard 132:228-31 N '67
Last minute gifts: very, very special. il House & Gard 132:30 D '67
On and off the avenue (cont) New Yorker 43:157-8+ D 2 '67
Small wonders; miniature appliances. M. Davidson. il Ladies Home J 84:76-7 D '67
Stereo Christmas goodies under $30. M. Sherwin. il Hi Fi 17:64-6 D '67
Twenty-eight splendiferous cadeaux with price tags to match. il House & Gard 132:236-7 N '67
Two unusual gifts: carving board, beverage server. il Pop Sci 191:118-19 N '67

CHRISTMAS gifts for women
For every girl on your Christmas list. il Seventeen 26:118-19 D '67
Gleamies for the giving. il Seventeen 26:144 D '67
Little frivolities for a lady's stocking. il House & Gard 132:284-5 N '67
On and off the avenue (cont) New Yorker 43:159-60+ N 25 '67
One for the toe. il Ladies Home J 84:54+ D '67
Step into la giftique fantastique. il Seventeen 26:96-7+ D '67

CHRISTMAS greens
Decorate with material from your garden. P. Frese. il Horticulture 45:16-23 D '67

CHRISTMAS in art
Christmas radiance at the White House. S. F. Smith. il House & Gard 132:134-5+ D '67

CHRISTMAS lighting. See Christmas decorations

CHRISTMAS meals
Best Christmas ever. il Parents Mag 42:56+ D '67
Candlelight cookbook of glamorous recipes and glowing tables for your holiday entertaining. il Good H 16f:88-107 D '67
Christmas gift cook book; with recipes. J. A. Beard. il House & Gard 132:173+ D '67
Christmas in Santa Claus land. N. S. Hazelton. Nat R 19:1398 D 12 '67
Festive food, changeabout centerpieces; with menus and recipes. il Farm J 91:64-5+ D '67
Gifts for gastronomes. il House & Gard 132: 148-9 D '67
Good food will abound; with recipes. V. T. Habeeb. il Am Home 70:89-90+ N '67
Great roasts! with menus. V. T. Habeeb. il Am Home 70:76-7+ D '67
Redbook's holiday hostess cookbook. il Redbook 130:111-26 D '67
Traditional holiday dinner for all, even those on special diets. il Good H 165:223-5 D '67
Yule feasts for weight watchers; with recipes. G. Maddox. il Todays Health 45:46-51 D '67
See also
Christmas dinners
Christmas suppers

CHRISTMAS music
See also
Phonograph records—Christmas music

CHRISTMAS pageant; story. See Robinson, B.

CHRISTMAS plays
Texts
Animals' Christmas tree. O. J. Robertson. Plays 27:67-9 D '67
Cardboard star. O. Phillips. Plays 27:1-11 D '67
Christmas carol; dramatization of story by C. Dickens. W. Hackett. Plays 27:81-90 D '67
Christmas shopping early. M. Hark and N. McQueen. Plays 27:49-58, 65 D '67
Santa and the efficiency expert. F. B. Watts. Plays 27:59-65 D '67
Silent night. L. Hollingsworth. Plays 27: 91-6 D '67
Sleepy little elf. O. J. Robertson. Plays 27:70-2 D '67

CHRISTMAS poetry
Aftermath: Christmas morning. B. Colquitt. Christian Cent 84:1622 D 20 '67
Christmas eve. D. Moffatt. Ladies Home J 84:119 D '67
Christmas-lost. M. G. Adams. Good H 165: 234 D '67
Christmas, 1967. S. Moon. Christian Cent 84: 1622 D 20 '67
Christmas poems. America 117:764-5 D 23 '67
Christmas tree. N. Foster. Horn Bk 43:778 D '67
Computer people's Christmas. K. Louchheim. McCalls 95:155 D '67
Meditation on the manger. E. Day. il Horn Bk 43:730-1 D '67
Night after Christmas. P. McGinley. il McCalls 95:42 D '67
On the Nativity. Sister Mary Frances. Christian Cent 84:1622 D 20 '67
Sonnet on Christmas morning. P. Meinke. Ladies Home J 84:117 D '67
Visit from St Nicholas. C. C. Moore. il McCalls 95:107 D '67
Worried ones. M. Haney. Christian Cent 84: 1629 D 20 '67

CHRISTMAS presents. See Christmas gifts

CHRISTMAS projects
Christmas crafts for children. M. Garrity. il Bet Hom & Gard 45:84-5 N '67
Christmas is something you make yourself. E. D. Craster and M. Garrity. il Bet Hom & Gard 45:36-63+ D '67
These are ice lights; tin can Christmas lanterns. il Sunset 139:62-3 D '67

CHRISTMAS savings plan. See Christmas clubs

CHRISTMAS shopping
I saw mommy kicking Santa Claus. J. Kerr. il McCalls 95:89+ D '67

CHRISTMAS shopping early; drama. See Hark, M. and McQueen, N.

CHRISTMAS stories
Booked for Christmas. il Library J 92:3818-20 O 15 '67
Christmas pageant. B. Robinson. il McCalls 95:112-13 D '67
My son, the shepherd. I. Woodley. il Redbook 130:52-3 D '67
Season of renewal. J. Fritz. il McCalls 95: 126-7 D '67

Stranger, come home. P. S. Buck. il Good H 165:84-5+ D '67
Tom Tinker Ellis. A. Moray. il Mlle 66:100-1+ D '67
Transient nativity. F. A. Raborg, jr. Horn Bk 43:772-8 D '67
What mistletoe? W. Stanton. il Ladies Home J 84:64-5 D '67

CHRISTMAS suppers
Double supper party, when the clan gathers. il Sunset 139:110-11 D '67

CHRISTMAS television programs. See Television broadcasting—Christmas programs

CHRISTMAS toys. See Toys

CHRISTMAS tree lights. See Christmas decorations

CHRISTMAS tree ornaments. See Christmas decorations

CHRISTMAS trees
California first; National community Christmas tree. il Am For 73:30-1 F '67
Classic Swedish cooky tree makes a grand all-family project. il Sunset 139:66-9 D '67
Commercial Christmas trees. B. M. Huey. il Am For 73:12-15+ D '67
Decorate your tree outdoors. V. Reynolds. il Home Gard 54:47 D '67
Extra green crop for Christmas; Santa's forests, Wisconsin concern. il Bsns W p48-9 D 23 '67
Forestry research in West Virginia; is there a Christmas tree gap? R. C. Byrd. il Am For 73:8-9+ D '67
Personal-signature Christmas tree. M. Gough. il House B 109:124-7 D '67
Pick the perfect Christmas tree. Am Home 70:93 D '67
To keep the green of the Christmas tree. Home Gard 54:26 D '67
Trim a juniper to make a miniature Christmas tree. il Sunset 139:156 D '67
Yarn tree isn't difficult. il Sunset 139:72 D '67

Safety devices and measures
Is your Christmas tree safe? Todays Health 45:18 D '67

CHRISTMAS wrappings. See Wrapping of packages

CHRISTMAS wreaths
Pine cones and glass crafts; suggestions for the holiday hobbyist. G. M. Aase. il Design 69:16-19 Wint '67

CHRISTOLOGY. See Jesus Christ

CHRISTOPHE, Henri, king of Haiti
Christophe, king of Haiti, by H. Cole. Review Newsweek por 70:95+ N 6 '67 R. A. Sokolov

CHRISTOPHER, Jordan
Four most likely to succeed. L. Lerman. il por Mlle 65:158-9 S '67

CHRISTUS, Petrus
Saint Eligius. McCalls 94:114-15 Ag '67

CHROMATIDS. See Chromosomes

CHROMATIN
Biology of isolated chromatin. J. Bonner and others. bibliog il Science 159:47-56 Ja 5 '68

CHROMATOGRAPHIC analysis
Chromatographic silica gel; surface area determined by adsorption. R. L. Hoffmann and others. bibliog il Science 157:550-1 Ag 4 '67
Continuous gas chromatography. M. V. Sussman and C. C. Huang. bibliog il Science 156: 974-6 My 19 '67
How to construct a gas chromatograph that can measure one part in a million. C. L. Stong. il Sci Am 217:283-6+ S '67

CHROMOSOMES
Autosomal deletion mapping in man. W. E. Nance and E. Engel. bibliog il Science 155:692-4 F 10 '67
Chromosomal abnormalities in leukocytes from LSD-25 users. S. Irwin and J. Egozcue. bibliog il Science 157:313-14 Jl 21 '67
Chromosomal breakage induced by extracts of human allogeneic lymphocytes. P. J. Fialkow. bibliog il Science 155:1676-7 Mr 31 '67
Chromosomal damage in human leukocytes induced by lysergic acid diethylamide. M. M. Cohen and others. bibliog il Science 155: 1417-19 Mr 17 '67
Chromosome abnormality in rat leukemia induced by 7,12-dimethylbenz[a]anthracene. T. Sugiyama and others. bibliog il Science 158:1058-9 N 24 '67
Chromosome studies on Marshall islanders exposed to fallout radiation. H. Lisco and R. A. Conard. bibliog il Science 157:445-7 Jl 28 '67

CHROMOSOMES—*Continued*
Chromosomes and crime. J. A. M. Graham. il Sci Digest 62:38-40 D '67
Chromosomes and leukocytes; report on conference. M. A. Kelsall. Science 155:1039-40 F 24 '67
Close look at heredity; photographs of human chromosomes. Time 90:61 N 24 '67
Crime chromosome; genetic abnormality ex plains criminal behavior. Sci N 91:258 Mr 18 '67
Distribution of chromatids at mitosis. J. A. Heddle and others. bibliog il Science 158:929-31 N 17 '67
Drugs & chromosomes. Time 90:84-5 S 15 '67
Leukocytes of humans exposed to lysergic acid diethylamide: lack of chromosomal damage. W. D. Loughman and others. bibliog il Science 158:508-11 O 27 '67
LSD and the unborn. il Newsweek 70:110 S 18 '67
LSD: danger to unborn babies. E. M. Brecher. McCalls 94:70-1+ S '67
LSD: growing menace to teenagers; with study discussion program. W. W. Zeller. Parents Mag 42:49-50, 70-1+ N '67
Mammalian X-chromosomes: change in patterns of DNA replication during embryogenesis. R. N. Hill and J. J. Yunis. bibliog il Science 155:1120-1 Mr 3 '67
Mosaic in X & Y; Polish athlete barred on medical grounds. il Time 90:70 S 29 '67
Ring D chromosome: a second case associated with anomalous haptoglobin inheritance. G. E. Bloom and others. bibliog il Science 156:1746-8 Je 30 '67
Segregation of sister chromatids in mammalian cells. K. G. Lark and others; discussion. Science 156:1133-4 My 26 '67
Sex chromosomes in lizards. C. J. Cole and others. bibliog il Science 155:1028-9 F 24 '67
Streptonigrin: effect on the first meiotic metaphase of the mouse egg. G. Jagiello. bibliog il Science 157:453-4 Jl 28 '67
Survival despite autosome lack; retardation due to missing autosome. il Sci N 92:393 O 21 '67
Twilight people. il Newsweek 70:55-6 O 2 '67
See also
Chromatin
Crossing over (genetics)
Genes
CHROMOSOMES (botany)
Making elms compatible. il Time 90:91 O 6 '67
Platyzoma: a new look at an old link in ferns. A. F. Tryon and G. Vida. bibliog il Science 156:1109-10 My 26 '67
CHROMOSPHERE. See Sun—Atmosphere
CHRONICALLY ill

Care and treatment
Yes you can go home again; a community program serving the elderly and chronically ill of Rochester and Monroe County, N.Y. M. A. Brice. Todays Health 45:54-6 D '67
CHRONICLE, San Francisco. See San Francisco chronicle
CHRYSANTHEMUMS
History of chrysanthemums. D. S. Manks. il Horticulture 45:16-17+ S '67
Home garden notebook. B. C. Kilvert, jr. il Home Gard 54:61-2 My '67
Increasing chrysanthemums; you have a choice. il Sunset 138:242 Mr '67
Instant chrysanthemums, ready now. Sunset 139:116 Ag '67
Plant in spring to flower in fall. il Home Gard 54:79 Mr '67
CHRYSLER corporation
And now for G.M. il Time 90:96 N 17 '67
Best contract we've ever had. il Newsweek 70:85 N 20 '67
Chrysler corp. assembles a new identity; Pentastar as symbol. il Bsns W p59+ Ap 29 '67
Chrysler in '68: a new concept. il Bsns W p54 S 2 '67
More than half American; Rootes motors ltd. Time 89:69-70 Ja 27 '67
On land, on sea; Chrysler success in pleasure-boat field. il Newsweek 69:76 Je 19 '67
Reuther escalates his war on auto companies. il U S News 63:85-6 N 13 '67
CHRYSSA, 1933-
Chryssa, D. Cyr. il pors Sch Arts 66:23-8 Mr '67
Light brigade. E. C. Baker. il Art N 66:52-5+ Mr '67
CHU, Dan
News on wheels (cont) Sr Schol 90:32 F 10; 32 Mr 31; 32 My 12 '67

CHUCK hunting. See Woodchuck hunting
CHUIKOV, Vasilii Ivanovich
Nuclear defense: while U.S. lags, Soviets rush ahead; excerpts from article in Izvestia. por U S News 63:61 Jl 31 '67
CHUKOVSKII, Kornei Ivanovich
Department of amplification. New Yorker 42:81-2+ Ja 21 '67
about
Department of amplification and correction, M. Morton. New Yorker 43:166+ Ap 8 '67
CHUNG, Il Kwon
U.S and Korea pledge continued friendship and cooperation; exchange of greetings, exchange of toasts, with joint statement, March 14, 1967. Dept State Bul 56:549-53 Ap 3 '67
about
From a U.S. ally, a warning to appeasers. por U S News 62:20 Mr 27 '67
CHUNG, Kyung Wha
Cookie & Pinky come through. por Time 89:78 My 26 '67
CHURCH, Frank
From the U.S.A. to all the world, with love. Esquire 68:83-4+ Jl '67
about
Dove versus a dogcatcher. W. B. Furlong. il pors N Y Times Mag p6-7+ Je 25 '67
Fighting dove. il por Newsweek 69:28-9 Je 5 '67
Recall Senator Church? W. F. Buckley, jr. Nat R 19:628 Je 13 '67
CHURCH, R. J. Harrison
Guinea. bibliog Focus 17:1-6 Mr '67
CHURCH, Thomas D.
Put personality into your garden. il Horticulture 45:16-21 O '67
about
Thomas D. Church; the influence of 2,000 gardens. C. Calkins. il por House B 109:140-5 Mr '67
CHURCH
See also
Catholic church
Women and the church

Authority
Catholic dilemma. il Newsweek 69:75 Mr 20 '67
Democracy in the church. W. L. Doty; E. C. Bianchi. America 117:76-82 Jl 22 '67
How U.S. Catholics view the Pope. il Newsweek 69:74 Mr 20 '67
Orthodoxy and Catholicity, by J. Meyendorff. Review
Cath World 205:57-60 Ap '67. R. Marshall
Plea for intramural dialogue; removal of Paulist fathers challenged by laymen in Richardson, Tex. B. Hasbrouck. America 117:38-9 Jl 8 '67
Restless clergy. G. Zimmermann. il Look 31:25-7 F 7 '67
Word to the unwise; challenge to authority of Catholic hierarchy. Commonweal 87:289-90 D 1 '67
CHURCH, Negro. See Negroes in the United States—Religion
CHURCH administration. See Church government
CHURCH and art. See Art and religion
CHURCH and education
Church or college: either, but not both. P. H. Sherry. Christian Cent 84:1247-50 O 4 '67; Discussion. 84:1597-9 D 13 '67
See also
Catholic church—Education
Parochial schools, Catholic
Public schools and religion
CHURCH and international relations
Reinhold Niebuhr plays Hamlet; possibility of world government. J. P. Speer. Christian Cent 84:336-9 Mr 15 '67; Discussion. 84:591-2 My 3 '67
CHURCH and labor
Economic leverage of the churches; Project Equality. America 116:714 My 13 '67
News and views; Project Equality. J. Deedy. Commonweal 86:458 Jl 28 '67
See also
Chaplains, Industrial
CHURCH and libraries. See Libraries—Work with churches
CHURCH and politics
Activism is no virtue. il Time 90:75 N 10 '67
Biblical basis of the Geneva conference; Conference on church and society. H. Cox. Christian Cent 84:435-7 Ap 5 '67

CHURCH and state—*Continued*
Constitutional crisis in New York. **Christian Cent** 84:1387-8 N 1 '67
Cuius regio eius religio; resolution of interstate conflict. H. S. Reuss. Christian Cent 84:1346-8 O 25 '67
Lord of Lords; excerpt from The carpenter's son. C. Marney. Christian Cent 84:195 F 15 '67
North Carolina High court denies pastoral immunity. Christian Cent 84:166 F 8 '67
State's top court upholds N.Y. text law. Pub W 191:33 Je 12 '67
'Tis the season to be surly. H. O. J. Brown. Nat R 19:1424-7 D 26 '67
Two walls, not one; separation between church and state. America 117:674 D 2 '67
See also
Church of England
Church property
Public schools and religion
Secularization

CHURCH and state in Brazil
See also
Catholic church in Brazil

CHURCH and state in Chile
Church and state in Peru and Chile since 1840; a study in contrasts. F. B. Pike. bibliog f Am Hist R 73:30-50 O '67

CHURCH and state in Czechoslovakia
See also
Catholic church in Czechoslovakia

CHURCH and state in Germany (Federal Republic)
Shadow of the concordat; Catholic schools and German bishops. C. Wilpert. Commonweal 86:333-4 Je 9 '67
Uneasy alliance. C. Amery. Commonweal 87:45-6 O 13 '67

CHURCH and state in Greece
New primate of Greece. America 116:769-70 My 27 '67

CHURCH and state in Israel
Battle of the bodies; autopsy one of the bitterest religious controversies. il Time 89:62+ Ap 28 '67

CHURCH and state in Peru
Church and state in Peru and Chile since 1840: a study in contrasts. F. B. Pike. bibliog f Am Hist R 73:30-50 O '67

CHURCH and state in Poland
See also
Catholic church in Poland

CHURCH and state in Russia
Orthodox face a crisis at Kirov. M. Bourdeaux. Christian Cent 84:478 Ap 12 '67

CHURCH and state in Spain
Pain in Spain; Franco and the church. J. Case. Commonweal 85:561-3 F 17 '67
Religious freedom in Spain. America 117:47 Jl 15 '67

CHURCH and state in Turkey
Turks harass the Orthodox. America 116:773-4 My 27 '67

CHURCH and state in Vietnam (Republic)
Ky v Buddhists, round two. Tran-van Dinh. New Repub 156:15-19 My 13 '67

CHURCH and state in Yugoslavia
New era in Yugoslavia; signing of agreement between Tito's government and the Vatican. G. J. Prpic. America 116:528-30 Ap 8 '67
See also
Catholic church in Yugoslavia

CHURCH and synagogue library association
Church and synagogue LA founded in Philadelphia. Library J 92:3957 N 1 '67

CHURCH and the press
Bishops and the press. J. O'Connor. America 116:180-2 F 4 '67; Discussion. 116:330 Mr 11 '67
Of many things; Catholic press in England. D. L. Flaherty. America 116:295 Mr 4 '67

CHURCH architecture
Aftermath of the church building boom. J. R. Scotford. Christian Cent 84:1650-3 D 27 '67
Austere and monumental church in Scotland; East Kilbride. il Arch Rec 141:133-6 Ja '67
Church ceiling form shaped by acoustics; Presbyterian church, Dearborn. A. B. Dow. il Arch Rec 142:168-9 S '67
Church that turned a corner; Church of the Epiphany, New York. il Arch Forum 127:82-7 N '67
Elk Grove United Presbyterian church: a skillful assembly of adapted forms. il Arch Rec 142:134-5 O '67
Miracles of faith. il Vogue 150:180-91 D '67
New architecture for the changing church? M. F. Schmertz. Arch Rec 142:129 N '67

Tradition-free architecture for a free church; a Unitarian center by Pietro Belluschi. il Arch Rec 141:135-40 Mr '67
Turning point; International congress on religion, architecture and the visual arts. T. F. Mathews. America 117:393-6 O 7 '67
Unforced simplicity for a Unitarian church; Bethesda, Md. il Arch Rec 141:129-32 Ja '67
See also
International congress on religion, architecture and the visual arts
Synagogues

CHURCH art. See Christian art and symbolism

CHURCH attendance
Church attendance on the upturn? Gallup poll findings. Christian Cent 85:68 Ja 17 '68

Anecdotes, facetiae, satire, etc.
Excuses that keep people from church. N. G. Long. Farm J 91:72E F '67

CHURCH colleges. See Denominational colleges

CHURCH committees
Democracy in the church: will it work? W. L. Doty. America 117:76-8 Jl 22 '67

CHURCH conferences. See Religious conferences

CHURCH cooperation. See Religious cooperation

CHURCH councils. See Councils and synods

CHURCH decoration and ornament
See also
Glass painting and staining

CHURCH drama. See Religious drama

CHURCH finance
Churches flex monetary muscles Christian Cent 84:1245 O 4 '67
Inflation hits your church. il Changing T 21:21-3 Jl '67
See also
Catholic church—Finance

CHURCH going. See Church attendance

CHURCH government
Hierarchy and laity; verticality as a theological category. J. W. Dixon, jr. il Christian Cent 84:1353-6+ O 25 '67
Roman Catholic and Protestant church structures compared. R. C. Dodds. Cath World 205:327-34 S '67
See also
Catholic church—Government

CHURCH history
See also
Catholic church—History
Missions
United States—Church history

Primitive and early church
Paul and his opponents. S. G. F. Brandon. il Horizon 10:106-11 Wint '68

CHURCH membership
Church and sect. D. Callahan. Commonweal 87:140-3 N 3 '67; Discussion. 87:317-18 D 1 '67
See also
Confirmation

CHURCH music
Church music revisited. R. Thibodeau. Commonweal 86:204-6 My 5 '67; Reply. T. J. Gilheany. 86:357+ Je 16 '67
Has jazz a place in the church? H. Dance. il Sat R 50:46-7 Jl 15 '67
Something heavy; religious rock. il Time 90:50 D 29 '67
Universa Laus: Spain, August, 1967; conference on liturgical music. D. A. Kister. America 117:522-3 N 4 '67
See also
Phonograph records—Church music

CHURCH of England
Britain's Methodists go Episcopal. C. Northcott. Christian Cent 84:613-14 Mv 10 '67
Church of England rebuffs critics. Christian Cent 84:1013-14 Ag 9 '67
Disestablishment for the Church of England? C. Northcott. Christian Cent 84:303 Mr 8 '67
Preacher for the empire's parish: dean of St Paul's cathedral. Time 89:63-4 Je 23 '67

CHURCH of England in Africa
Intercommunion in Central Africa. G. White. Christian Cent 84:1301-2 O 11 '67

CHURCH of England in Canada
Anglican church in Canada general synod. J. R. Mutchmor. Christian Cent 84:1411-12 N 1 '67
Church-without-God minister without church; E. Harrison refused permission to officiate in the diocese of Toronto. Christian Cent 84:334 Mr 15 '67

CHURCH of Jesus Christ of Latter-day saints.
See Mormons and Mormonism

CHURCH of the Brethren
Church of the Brethren annual conference.
B. W. Crist. il Christian Cent 84:1050-1 Ag
16 '67

CHURCH of the Holy Sepulcher. See Jerusalem—Church of the Holy Sepulcher

CHURCH of the Nativity, Bethlehem. See
Bethlehem, Jordan

CHURCH property

Taxation

Are churches fudging on tax exemption?
Christian Cent 84:427 Ap 5 '67
God is rich. A. Balk. Harper 235:69-73 O '67
Rendering unto Caesar. Christian Cent 84:
1244 O 4 '67; Discussion. 84:1570 D 6 '67
Should church property be taxed? il U S
News 63:46-7 Jl 10 '67
Tax the churches too? Christian Cent 84:396-7
Mr 29 '67; Discussion. 84:625, 840 My 10,
Je 28 '67
Taxing the churches: the law and the facts.
America 116:801 Je 3 '67

CHURCH-related colleges. See Denominational
colleges

CHURCH-related housing projects. See Housing
projects

CHURCH renewal
Renewal and the dynamic of the provisional.
G. H. Shriver. Christian Cent 84:1551-3 D 6
'67
Renewal in Europe. D. Fisher. Cath World
206:101-4 D '67

CHURCH schools
See also
Catholic church—Education
Education and state
Parochial schools

CHURCH services
Drive-in devotion. il Time 90:83-4 N 3 '67
Secular sermons. il Time 89:93-4 Mr 10 '67

CHURCH symbolism. See Christian art and
symbolism

CHURCH unity
Christian unity. Commonweal 86:381-2 Je 23
'67
Deliberation on the believers church. M. Shelly. Christian Cent 84:1077-8+ Ag 23 '67
Two commandments and a question. V. P.
McCorry. America 117:inside back cover S
9 '67
Unity at Uppsala; assembly to consider universal implications of unity. Christian Cent
84:739-40 Je 7 '67
See also
Church renewal
Community churches
Consultation on church union
Ecumenical movement
Religious cooperation

Canada

Ecumenical movement in Canada. A. B. B.
Moore. Christian Cent 84:902-5 Jl 12 '67

Great Britain

Dallying on union, Anglican-Methodist conversations. C. Northcott. Christian Cent 84:
1309-10 O 18 '67
Why not Presbyterian? union between Congregational and Presbyterian churches of
England and Wales. C. Northcott. Christian
Cent 84:1550 D 6 '67

United States

American church? J. E. McCaw. America
117:498-501 N 4 '67

CHURCH women united (organization)
Church women united; no longer United
church women? M. Frakes. Christian Cent
84:990-1 Ag 2 '67

CHURCH work
Bury the parish? B. Barr. Christian Cent 84:
199-202 F 15 '67; Discussion. 84:411-12 Mr
29 '67
What a minister really does. L. David. il
Good H 164:60-1+ Ja '67
See also
Church and social problems

CHURCH work with migrants
Migrants: directions '67. J. F. Conway. Cath
World 205:31-5 Ap '67

CHURCH work with youth
Are the churches failing today's teenagers?
W. E. Alberts. il Parents Mag 42:50-2+ F
'67
Of many things; Fr. Giarchi's sermons for
London's teen-agers. T. N. Davis. America
117:425 O 21 '67

CHURCH world service
Seeks church aid for war victims. Christian
Cent 84:861 Jl 5 '67

CHURCHES
See also
Church architecture

Fires and fire protection

Eye for an eye; trouble in Lowndes County,
Ala. Newsweek 69:34+ Ap 3 '67

Greenland

Leif Ericsson and his relatives; Thjodhild's
church; with report by M. Steinmann. il
Life 63:53-4+ S 15 '67

Latin America

Stone, iron, wood, poverty, truth; how windows of A. Winternitz unite with other
mediums of sacred art. C. Rodriguez Saavedra. il Américas 19:20-6 My '67

United States

Aftermath of the church building boom. J. R.
Scotford. Christian Cent 84:1650-3 D 27 '67
Soviet view of U.S. churches. Christian Cent
84:1014 Ag 9 '67

CHURCHES, Suburban. See Suburban churches
CHURCHGOING. See Church attendance

CHURCHILL, Creighton
Five prima donnas of the wine world. House
B 109:150-1+ Mr '67
Wine primer; excerpts from The world of
wines. House B 109:58+ Jl '67

CHURCHILL, Lord Randolph Henry Spencer
Reminiscence. S. Leslie. Nat R 19:1392-3 D 12
'67

CHURCHILL, Sarah
Thread in the tapestry; excerpt. por Ladies
Home J 84:108-9+ S '67

CHURCHILL, Vernon
Quick and the dead. il por Newsweek 70:35
N 13 '67

CHURCHILL, Sir Winston Leonard Spencer
Churchill library in 5″ time capsule. Library J 92:182 Ja 15 '67
They made our world. L. Rosten. pors Look
31:84-5+ F 7 '67
Thread in the tapestry; excerpt. S. Churchill.
il por Ladies Home J 84:108-9+ S '67
Winston S. Churchill: companion vol. I, by
R. S. Churchill. Review
Sat R 50:34+ N 18 '67. A. Nevins
Winston S. Churchill: young statesman 1901-
1914, by R. S. Churchill. Review
Atlan 220:144-6 D '67. O. Handlin
Sat R 50:34 N 18 '67. Lord Rowley
Winston S. Churchill: youth, 1874-1900, by
R. S. Churchill. Review
Commentary 44:84-9 Jl '67. L. Malkin
Reporter por 36:54+ Mr 9 '67. G. A. Craig

CHURCHILL, Winston Spencer, 1940-
Winston is back. il por Newsweek 70:32 O
30 '67

CHUSID, Frederick and company
Tough questions for recruiters; is an employment counselor an employment agency? Bsns W p42 D 23 '67

CHUTE, B. J.
Letter to a fiction writer. Writer 80:9-12
O '67

CHUVALO, George
Have a piece of Georgie boy. M. Kram. il por
Sports Illus 27:26-8 Jl 31 '67

CHUYEN, Le-xuan-. See Le-xuan-Chuyen

CIAK, Jennie, and Hahn, F. E.
Quinacrine, atebrin; mode of action. bibliog
Science 156:655-6 My 5 '67

CIARDI, John
About the blabberhead; On developing a positive personality; Meeting; Aliquod; Shark;
poems. Sat R 50:16 O 21 '67
Lines from the beating end of the stethoscope;
poem. Sat R 50:12 N 18 '67
Manner of speaking. See issues of Saturday
review

CIBA foundation
World health service proposed by Ciba head
Sci N 91:431 My 6 '67

CICADA killers. See Wasps

CICADAS
Nature note. il Sci N 92:318 S 30 '67

CICERO, Ill.
Siege of Cicero; racism. B. J. Oudes. il Nation 204:398-401 Mr 27 '67

CIEMBRONIEWICZ, J. and Kolar, O.
Eosinophilic response in glioblastoma tissue
culture after addition of autologous lymphocytes. bibliog Science 157:1054-5 S 1 '67

CIGAR factories. See Factories
CIGARETTE filters
Columbia and its new filter: smoke over Morningside Heights. R. J. Samuelson. il Science 157:520-4 Ag 4 '67
Columbia filter raises a cloud of questions. Bsns W p20-1 Jl 22 '67
Columbia filter: university takes a second look. R. J. Samuelson. Science 157:1541-2 S 29 '67
Filtering out the facts; Strickman's damages suit against NBC. il Newsweek 71:52 Ja 1 '68
New cigarette filter, a university's dilemma. A. Rosenfeld. il Life 63:50-1 Jl 28 '67
New dark horse entry; low-tar filter. il Sci N 92:104-5 Jl 29 '67
New safe cigarette filter: what you should know about it and what parents should tell their children. L. David. Good H 165:92-3+ N '67
Notes and comment; doubts about Columbia filter program. New Yorker 43:47 O 21 '67
Polonium-210: removal from smoke by resin filters. E. W. Bretthauer and S. C. Black. bibliog il Science 156:1375-6 Je 9 '67
Safer smoking? claims for a new filter. il U S News 63:8-9 Jl 24 '67
Second thoughts: Columbia university's financial interest in new cigarette filter. Newsweek 70:50 S 4 '67
Second thoughts; Strickman filter. Newsweek 71:49-50 Ja 15 '68
Strickman filter. il Time 90:43 Jl 21 '67
Toward a safe smoke? il Newsweek 70:54 Jl 24 '67
CIGARETTE machines. See Cigarette-making machines
CIGARETTE-making machines
Cigarette-making machines. il Consumer Bul 50:18-20 Mr '67
CIGARETTE smoke
Damaging source of air pollution. P. H. Abelson. Science 158:1527 D 22 '67
Promising new attack on the cigarette hazard; chemistry of smoking. H. Fantel. il Sci Digest 61:50-5 Je '67
CIGARETTE smoking. See Smoking
CIGARETTE smuggling. See Smuggling
CIGARETTES
Animals smoke, and die. F. Marley. il Sci N 92:158-9 Ag 12 '67
Another tar derby? new report ranks brands according to tar and nicotine levels. il Bsns W p37 Mr 18 '67
Antismoke signals. L. W. Sauer. PTA Mag 61:27-8 Ap '67
Beauty checkout; you minus cigarettes. Vogue 151:30 Ja 1 '68
Burning questions; government analysis of cigarettes. il Newsweek 70:56 D 11 '67
Burning up over those extra puffs; new 100mm. cigarettes. il Bsns W p 172+ F 25 '67
Cigarette prohibition? mounting pressure against tobacco industry. Newsweek 70:64-5 N 6 '67
Classroom-tested techniques for teaching about smoking. il NEA J 56:37-50 D '67
Government pressing toward a safer smoke. il Sci N 92:227 S 2 '67
Hazards of smoking; mass of additional evidence. Sci Am 217:48-50 O '67
Hidden battles, subtle foes; A. Palmer's experience in giving up cigarettes. M. H. McCormack. il Sports Illus 26:54-6+ Mr 20 '67
If you don't want your children to smoke ... H. S. Diehl. il Parents Mag 42:40 Ap '67
It is safe to smoke, by L. Mallan. Review New Repub 156:28-30 Mr 25 '67. M. Mintz
King-size problem; concerning TV interview by D. T. Fredrickson. G. Ace. Sat R 50:7 D 2 '67
New smoking tactic. il Sci N 91:447-8 My 13 '67
New tar derby is off and running. il Bsns W p94-6+ D 16 '67
New warning for cigarette smokers. il U S News 63:40 S 4 '67
No smoking! smoking among children and youth. il Am Ed 3:7 My '67
Please hold this magazine a little further away; 100-mm. size cigarettes. il Time 89:97 Ap 28 '67
Polonium-210 in bronchial epithelium of cigarette smokers; with reply by R. B. Holtzman. J. B. Little and E. P. Radford, jr. bibliog Science 155:606-7 F 3 '67
Preventive puff; Howard Steinbach's Cancer brand. Newsweek 69:62 Ap 3 '67

Promising new attack on the cigarette hazard. H. Fantel. il Sci Digest 61:50-5 Je '67
Search for a safer cigarette. G. Bylinsky. il Fortune 76:146-9+ N '67
Smoke signs: the signal remains red; excerpts from address. D. Horn. PTA Mag 62:25 S '67
Tar, nicotine & butts; government-established levels of cigarette tar and nicotine content. il Time 90:102+ D 8 '67
Tar, nicotine & filters; with table. Time 89:51 Mr 24 '67
You can stop smoking & stay thin. P. Deutsch and R. Deutsch. il Ladies Home J 84:80+ Mr '67; Same abr. with title Do you really want to stop smoking? Read Digest 91:97-101 N '67
Your teen-ager and smoking. R. H. Roach. il Todays Health 46:68-70+ Ja '68

Advertising

Anti-cigarette advertising. America 117:433 O 21 '67
Can FTC stunt growth of smokers? Bsns W p34 Jl 8 '67
Cigarette advertising: should it be curbed? pro and con discussion. Sr Schol 91:12-13+ N 16 '67
Cigarette issue; health agencies failure to support FCC rule. R. L. Shayon. Sat R 50:58 O 21 '67
FCC ruling on cigarette ads: health groups react warily. L. J. Carter. Science 158:888-92 N 17 '67
FCC smoke ruling; radio and television stations must represent antismoking groups. Newsweek 69:84 Je 12 '67
Like your cigarette should; the Winston slogan; reprint. R. L. Tobin. Writer 80:34 Ja '67
Notes and comment; proposed bills to limit cigarette advertising on television. New Yorker 43:41 S 23 '67
Silly milly; campaign for 100-mm. cigarettes. il Time 90:96-7 O 20 '67
Smoking and health: FCC demands an antidote to cigarette ads. L. J. Carter. il Science 157:406-8 Jl 28 '67
Time for the truth. New Repub 156:7 Je 17 '67
What the cigarette commercials don't show. H. J. Mooney. Read Digest 92:71-4 Ja '68

Prices

How smokers get hooked. Time 90:102 O 6 '67
CIGNA, Gina
Historical records. A. Favia-Artsay. por Hobbies 72:36 Mr '67
CILIA and ciliary motion
Guanine nucleotide associated with the protein of the outer fibers of flagella and cilia. R. E. Stevens and others. bibliog il Science 156:1606-8 Je 23 '67
Modified cilia in sensory organs of juvenile stages of a parasitic nematode. M. M. R. Ross. bibliog il Science 156:1494-5 Je 16 '67
CIMABUE, 1240-1302?
Seven centuries-old masterpiece ruined. il UNESCO Courier 20:17 Ja '67
CINCHONA
Quinine cartel on the record. il Sci N 91:302 Ap 1 '67
CINCINNATI

Libraries

See also
Cincinnati and Hamilton County, Ohio, public library

Music

See also
Cincinnati symphony orchestra

Police

Morale rearmament; law firm and public relations company gain improvements for force. il Time 89:69 My 26 '67

Street traffic

Computer traffic control a hit with baseball fans. J. Scheinson. il Am City 82:152+ O '67

Theater

Theatre; Playhouse in the park presents J. Anouilh's The cavern. J. Novick. Nation 205:125-6 Ag 14 '67

Water supply

Tight sheating tops tunneling. C. M. Bolton. il Am City 82:159-60 Je '67
CINCINNATI AND HAMILTON COUNTY, Ohio, public library
Borrowing department store techniques to promote library service. R. W. Rodger. il Wilson Lib Bul 42:304-8 N '67

CITIES and towns, Medieval
Architecture; Zähringer towns, Switzerland.
E. Galantay. Nation 204:283-5 F 27 '67
CITIES and towns, Ruined, extinct, etc.
Wanted: paying guests to trace the lost
cities of Peru. R. Joseph. il Esquire 68:138-9
S '67
See also
Pajatén, Peru
Petra, Jordan
Teotihuacán, Mexico
Troy
CITIZENS associations
Ghetto is people; involving the community in
planning. J. Aumente. Nation 205:555-7 N
27 '67
CITIZENS band radio. See Citizens radio
service
CITIZENS committee for peace with freedom
Peace with freedom. Nation 205:483-4 N 13
'67
Peace with freedom: a middle way. America
117:632 N 25 '67
Unleashing the silent center. Nat R 19:1246-7
N 14 '67
Voice from the silent center. il Time 90:15-16
N 3 '67
Voices of silence. J. N. Eller. America 117:
541 N 11 '67
CITIZENS housing and planning council of
New York, incorporated
Failure in the slums. W. F. Buckley, jr. Nat
R 19:341 Ap 4 '67
CITIZENS obligations. See Citizenship
CITIZENS radio service
Amateur radio for CB'ers. W. F. Lange. il
Pop Electr 26:51-8 My; 59-63 Je '67
CB'ers are wondering about; questions and
answers. Pop Electr 27:69-70 Ag '67
FCC bears down on CB. W. A. Stocklin.
Electr World 77:6 My '67
FCC proposes CB type acceptance; manu-
facturers blamed for CB malpractices; with
editorial comment. il Pop Electr 26:78-9
My '67
Jam that the FCC can't spread; citizen's
band and small-business airwaves jammed.
il Bsns W p176-8 F 25 '67
On the citizens band. M. P. Spinello. See
issues of Popular electronics

Equipment
Annual report on CB equipment. il Pop Electr
27:71-8 Ag '67
Build CSB audio leveler. D. Meyer. il Pop
Electr 26:55-8+ F '67
Build the mule box; converter to increase
CB talk power. D. Meyer. il Pop Electr 26:
45-50+ Mr '67
Getting the most from your CB rig; tuning
your transmitter. D. Meyer. il Pop Electr
26:72-3+ Ap '67
Selecting a CB transceiver. L. Buckwalter.
il Electr World 77:40-3 Mr '67
Two-way radios you can tuck anywhere. B.
Hartford. il Pop Mech 128:170-2+ Jl '67
CITIZENS scholarship foundation of America,
incorporated
Dollars for scholars. J. Cass. Sat R 50:60
Ap 15 '67
CITIZENSHIP
Approving dual citizenship. Time 89:76 Je
9 '67
At the grass roots; citizen participation in
community affairs Sr Schol 89:7 Ja 20 '67
But what of the dream? excerpt from address,
October 12, 1967. J. W. Gardner. Read
Digest 92:37-41 Ja '68
How do you score as a citizen? quiz. Chang-
ing T 21:26 S '67
Independence day: good citizen; address,
July 4, 1967. H. V. Prochnow. Vital Speeches
33:664-6 Ag 15 '67
Responsibilities of national greatness; a citi-
zen's obligations and the bepuzzlements of
identification. K. Burke. il Nation 205:46-50
Jl 17 '67
See also
Patriotism
Self determination, National
CITIZENSHIP, Education for
Education and public service. J. W. Eaton.
bibliog f Sch & Soc 95:358-60 O 14 '67
New curriculum for citizenship education;
Culver military academy. L. K. Moore. il
Sr Schol 90:sup 14-15 My 19 '67
Watts, the schools, and citizenship educa-
tion. J. F. Ohles. Sch & Soc 95:256 Ap 15
'67
See also
League of women voters, of the United States
Political science—Study and teaching

CITRUS drinks. See Beverages
CITRUS flavonoids. See Bioflavonoids
CITRUS fruit industry
Orange crush; growers face catastrophe.
Time 89:67 Ja 27 '67
CITRUS fruit trees, Dwarf. See Fruit trees,
Dwarf
CITRUS fruits
See also
Cookery—Fruit

Diseases and pests
See also
Mal secco disease of citrus
CITY advertising. See Municipal advertising
CITY and country
Climate of cities. W. P. Lowry. il Sci Am
217:15-23 Ag '67
Sisters under the skin. P. Swiggum. Farm J
91:55 Ag '67
See also
Country life
Suburban life
CITY and town life
City; photographs. J. Romeo. Fortune 77:
136-9 Ja '68
Pros and cons of apartment living. il Good H
164:152 Mr '67
See also
Church and social problems
CITY bonds. See Municipal bonds
CITY Center Joffrey ballet
Ballet menus. W. Terry. Sat R 50:53-4 S 30 '67
Company rhythm; a review of the City Cen-
ter Joffrey ballet; New York city center.
D. Hering. il Dance Mag 41:59-62+ My '67
Maiden in the cake of ice; fall season. D.
Hering. il Dance Mag 41:34-7+ N '67
Musical events; performance of Astarte. W.
Sargeant. New Yorker 43:91 S 30 '67
Musical events; performances of Green ta-
ble; Pas des déesses; Sea shadow and Arcs
and angels. W. Sargeant. New Yorker 43:
125 Mr 25 '67
Ritual in rock. il Time 90:48 O 6 '67
CITY churches
Wall Street priest. il Newsweek 70:58 O 30
'67
See also
Suburban churches
CITY cleaning. See Cleaning of cities
CITY clerks. See Municipal officers
CITY council, New York. See New York (city)
—Council
CITY gardens
Little by little we created a privacy. S.
Wilks. il Home Gard 54:68-70 Mr '67
To beautify America: proud park in Steel-
ville, Mo. J. Pursley. Home Gard 54:48
Je '67
Urban gardens. A. W. Smith. Nat Parks
Mag 41:2 O '67
See also
Roof gardens
CITY growth. See Cities and towns—Growth
CITY halls
New city hall that borrows from the past;
Eugene, Ore. R. L. Norton. il Am City 82:
108-9 Ag '67
CITY improvement. See Municipal improvement
CITY life. See City and town life
CITY magazines. See Periodicals—United
States
CITY managers
Recent city manager appointments. See is-
sues of American city
CITY markets. See Markets, Municipal
CITY models. See Models of cities, towns, etc.
CITY noise. See Noise
CITY OF REFUGE NATIONAL HISTORICAL
PARK
God Lono has many faces. il Sunset 139:29+
O '67
CITY parks. See Parks
CITY planners
See also
Doxiadis, C. A.
Rouse, J. W.
CITY planning
Big cities do have a future; symposium. il
U S News 62:46-50 Je 26 '67
Business and the big cleanup; need for busi-
ness initiative in reshaping country's en-
vironment. Fortune 75:101-2 Mr '67
Can today's big cities survive? conference
sponsored by the Lions international. il U S
News 63:54-8 N 6 '67

CITY planning—*Continued*
Cities under glass; A. Spilhaus's scheme for solving problems of urban sprawl. il Newsweek 71:44-5 Ja 8 '68
Cities: what will they be like? J. Hay. il Parents Mag 43:44-5+ Ja '68
City as an act of will; excerpts from Design of cities. E. N. Bacon. il Arch Rec 141:113-27 Ja '67
City meets the space age; summer study on science and urban development. Woods, Hole, Mass. J. Bailey. Arch Forum 126: 60-3+ Ja '67
Coming era of ecumenopolis. C. A. Doxiadis. Sat R 50:11-14 Mr 18 '67
Design of cities, by E. N. Bacon. Review New Repub 157:32-4 S 2 '67. F. Gutheim
Do your city planners know about air pollution? A. N. Heller. il Am City 82:91-4 Ap '67
Environment for man, ed. by W. R. Ewald, jr. Review Sat R 50:23-4 Jl 29 '67. J. H. Plumb
Hanging cities ahead? space cities. il UNESCO Courier 20:14-15 F '67
How to make a city come alive. T. P. F. Hoving. il Parents Mag 42:50-1+ Ap '67
Life in the instant cities. T. Roszak. il Nation 204:336-40+ Mr 13 '67
Model cities. $11 million appropriated for planning. Parks & Rec 2:31+ D '67
New Greek oracle of urban planning; C. Doxiadis. il Bsns W p66-8+ Jl 15 '67
New towns: an urban frontier. P. McBroom. il Sci N 92:64-5 Jl 15 '67
Planned pathways bring leisure and safety; Litchfield Park, Ariz. A. E. Patterson. il Parks & Rec 2:22-3 Je '67
Profiles; C. Abrams. B. Taper. New Yorker 42:38-42+ F 4 '67
Public library and the planning agency. L. M. Bewley. bibliog ALA Bul 61:968-74 S '67
Should U.S. cities be torn down? U S News 64:10 Ja 8 '68
Streets and spaces; conditions in Latin America. J. M. F. Pastor. il Américas 19:5-11 O '67
Toward a better community; space in the city. W. Von Eckardt. il Am Home 70:12+ S '67
Toward a national design policy; Senate committee testimony. A. C. Rogers. Arch Rec 141:187-90 Je '67
Urban housing design for new towns and old neighborhoods. il Arch Rec 142:133-52 Jl '67
Urgent future, by A. Mayer. Review Arch Rec 142:131-4 D '67. L. Mumford
What kind of city? R. Moley. Newsweek 70:72 Ag 21 '67
What the big cities must do to stay alive; interview. R. Moses. il U S News 64:66-8 Ja 8 '68
Where have all the flowers gone? V. H. Bernstein. il Redbook 128:78-9+ Mr '67
See also
Cities and towns
Regional planning
Suburbs
Urban renewal
also subhead City planning under names of cities, e.g. Oakland, Calif.—City planning

CITY products corporation
Teaching the ladies helps pull in traffic; furniture retailers give courses in homemaking. il Bsns W p 124-7 Ja 13 '68

CITY school systems. See Public schools

CITY traffic. See Street traffic

CITY transit. See Rapid transit

CITY trees. See Trees in cities

CITY university of New York. See New York (city) City university of New York

CIVEN, Morton, and others
Circadian rhythms of liver enzymes and their relationship to enzyme induction. bibliog Science 157:1563-4 S 29 '67

CIVIC advertising. See Municipal advertising

CIVIC centers. See Municipal centers

CIVIC education. See Citizenship, Education for

CIVIL aeronautics board. See United States— Civil aeronautics board

CIVIL air patrol. See United States—Civil air patrol

CIVIL and political rights, International covenant on. See International covenant on civil and political rights

CIVIL aviation. See Aeronautics, Commercial

CIVIL defense
Workable civil defense and disaster relief program; Denver. T. Currigan. il Am City 82:108-9 N '67
See also
Atomic bomb shelters
also subhead Defenses under names of cities, e.g. Oklahoma City—Defenses

Russia
Nuclear defense: while U.S. lags, Soviets rush ahead; excerpts from article in Izvestia. V. I. Chuikov. U S News 63:61 Jl 31 '67

CIVIL disobedience. See Lawlessness; Passive resistance to government

CIVIL liberties. See Civil rights

CIVIL liberties union, American. See American civil liberties union

CIVIL procedure
See also
Jury

CIVIL rights
Civil liberties. M. R. Konvitz. bibliog f Ann Am Acad 371:38-58 My '67
Freedom at home and freedom abroad. America 118:24-5 Ja 13 '68
Human rights conventions; statement, February 23, 1967. A. J. Goldberg. Dept State Bul 56:524-9 Mr 27 '67
Real nature of the world revolution; the drive for human rights; what this portends for U.S. policy. A. Larson. Sat R 50:15-18 Je 3 '67
Regional seminar in Warsaw on economic and social rights. UN Mo Chron 4:69 Ag '67
United Nations High Commissioner for human rights; concerning proposal to create institution. UN Mo Chron 4:31 F '67
See also
Due process of law
Free speech
Human rights day and week
Inter-American commission on human rights
International covenant on civil and political rights
International covenant on economic, social and cultural rights
Privacy
Students—Civil rights
Universal declaration of human rights

Study and teaching
Subject: human rights. J. H. Sofokidis. il Am Ed 4:12-14 D '67
Teacher fired over civil rights. Sr Schol 91: sup 14 O 12 '67

Great Britain
Letter from London; tougher new laws against racial discrimination. M. Panter-Downes. New Yorker 43:80 Ag 19 '67

Haiti
Human rights in Haiti. Américas 19:45 S '67

United States
Civil rights & consumer messages. Time 89:18 F 24 '67
Civil rights bill of 1967. America 116:303 Mr 4 '67
Fair housing again in rights bill. il U S News 62:69 F 27 '67
Peace and the racial revolution. Sch & Soc 95:138 Mr 4 '67
Racists' rights; Maryland Court of appeals rules ten-month ban violates rights of States' rights party. Time 90:38+ Jl 14 '67
Something borrowed: Presidential message on civil rights. Newsweek 69:27-8 F 27 '67
Un-American activities: court rule aids Stamler in contempt case. K. Sperry. Science 158:1294-5 D 8 '67
Weston, Jackson, the F.C.C. and Pastore. N. Sharp. Christian Cent 84:1268 O 4 '67
See also
American civil liberties union
Negroes in the United States—Civil rights
United States—Commission on civil rights
United States—Constitution—Bill of rights

CIVIL rights act of 1964
Mediation in civil rights disputes. J. T. Barrett. Mo Labor R 90:44-6 Jl '67

CIVIL rights candidates. See Candidates, Political

CIVIL rights commission. See United States— Commission on civil rights

CIVIL rights demonstrations
Cities in '68; M. L. King's 1968 plan to march on Washington by poor Negroes. New Repub 157:5-7 D 16 '67
Poverty, paternalism and protest. M. A. Seng. Cath World 204:352-5 Mr '67

CIVIL rights division. See United States— Justice, Department of—Civil rights division

CIVIL rights organizations
...And Kodak will ask, how high? troubles
with FIGHT. Fortune 75:78 Je 1 '67
Black power and the American Christ. V.
Harding; discussion. Christian Cent 84:214
F 15 '67
Economic leverage of the churches; Project
Equality. P. J. Flynn. America 116:823 Je
10 '67
Evolving Negro solidarity; what lies behind
the support of Adam Clayton Powell.
Christian Cent 84:395-6 Mr 29 '67
FIGHT against Kodak. B. Carter. il Report-
er 36:28-31 Ap 20 '67
Fight that swirls around Eastman Kodak;
battle over more jobs for Negroes. il
Bsns W p38-41 Ap 29 '67
Mediation in civil rights disputes. J. T. Bar-
rett. Mo Labor R 90:44-6 Jl '67
New threat for employers? what a Negro
group seeks from Kodak; FIGHT dispute
over hiring agreement. il U S News 62:74-5
My 8 '67
Of many things; Kodak and FIGHT agree-
ment. R. A. Schroth. America 117:inside
cover Jl 8 '67
Self-doubt and black pride; Eastman Kodak
and the FIGHT organization. R. A. Schroth.
America 116:502-5 Ap 1 '67; Reply with re-
joinder. P. A. Mallon. 116:664-5 My 6 '67
Shepherds vs. flocks; church involvement in
FIGHT assault on Kodak. W. C. Martin.
Atlan 220:53-9 D '67
What the Kodak fracas means; job prob-
lems of Negroes. Bsns W p 192 My 6 '67
Which way for the Negro? il Newsweek 69:
27-8+ My 15 '67
See also
Lowndes County freedom organization
Student non-violent coordinating committee
CIVIL rights workers
...Because he was black and I was white;
symposium, ed. by E. Sutherland. Mlle 64:
224-5+ Ap '67
How the white problem spawned black power.
A. F. Poussaint. il Ebony 22:88-90+ Ag '67
Philadelphia murders; lynching of three civil
rights workers. il Newsweek 70:32-3 O 23
'67
Prison note, by B. Deming. Review
Esquire 68:42+ O '67. D. Macdonald
Stranger at the gates, by T. Sugarman. Re-
view
New Repub 156:28+ F 4 '67. E. Suther-
land
Time of trial; charges of conspiracy to de-
prive slain civil rights workers of con-
stitutional rights. il Time 90:22 O 20 '67
See also
Student non-violent coordinating committee
CIVIL service
See also
Bureaucracy
United States
Contractor support service called illegal.
Aviation W 87:19-20 30 '67
U.S. civil service: rebels on the Potomac. R.
G. Sherrill. Nation 204:265-8 F 27 '67
U.S. civil service: Washington's bland bond-
age. R. G. Sherrill. Nation 204:239-42 F 20
'67; Reply with rejoinder. J. W. Macy, jr.
204:418+ Ap 3 '67
See also
Government employees
Public officers
CIVIL service commission. See United States—
Civil service commission
CIVIL war currency. See Paper money—United
States—History
CIVIL war souvenirs. See Souvenirs
CIVILIAN morale. See Morale, National
CIVILIAN review board. See New York (city)
—Police department
CIVILIZATION
Birth of Europe, by R. S. Lopez. Review
New Yorker 43:100-2+ Je 24 '67. P. Gay
Man's new dialogue with man; Time essay.
Time 89:34-5 Je 30 '67
University and development. A. Morales-
Carrión. il Américas 19:8-13 S '67
Where is biology taking us? excerpts from
address, October 1966. R. S. Morison.
Science 155:429-33 Ja 27 '67; Discussion.
156-11 Ap 7 '67
See also
Anthropology
Atomic age
History
Humanism
Intellectual life
Manners and customs
Popular culture
Religions
Technology and civilization
also subhead Civilization under names of
countries, e.g. China—Civilization

History
Great men, great events (cont) il UNESCO
Courier 20:27-9 O '67
CIVILIZATION, Ancient
Old stones; tale of human continuity. G.
Green. Holiday 42:8+ S '67
CIVILIZATION, Chinese. See China—Civiliza-
tion
CIVILIZATION, Christian
See also
Christianity and culture
CIVILIZATION, Minoan
Atlantis and the searchers. il Newsweek 70:
52-5 Jl 31 '67
Atlantis beneath the vineyard. il Sci N 92:
125-6 Ag 5 '67
Economy-size Atlantis; Minoan city un-
earthed on island of Thera. il Time 90:68-9
Jl 28 '67
Explosion that changed the world; Santorini
explosion. R. Schiller. il Read Digest 91:
122-7 N '67
Is this Atlantis? D. Cohen. il Sci Digest 62:
66-9 O '67
See also
Crete—Antiquities
CIVILIZATION and science. See Science and
civilization
CIVILIZATION and technology. See Technol-
ogy and civilization
CLAFLIN, Alice J. and Smithies, Oliver
Antibody-producing cells in division. bibliog
Science 157:1561-2 S 29 '67
CLAIBORNE, Craig
Food. See issues of New York times magazine
CLAIMS
See also
Restitution claims
CLAIRVOYANCE
My psychic friends; excerpts from A search
for the truth. R. Montgomery. Read Digest
90:151-2+ Ap '67
See also
Extrasensory perception
CLAMPS
See also
Holding devices (machine work)
CLAMS
How the state of Washington conserves its
razor clam population. J. Copland. il Parks
& Rec 2:41+ Mr '67
See also
Cookery—Shellfish
CLANCY, Joseph P.
Graves; poem. Commonweal 86:171 Ap 28 '67
Poem for Patricia. Commonweal 86:285 My
26 '67
CLANCY, Paul
Can the southern Negro exodus be stemmed?
Reporter 37:27-8+ N 2 '67
Fight for quality on two Negro campuses.
Reporter 37:37-9 Jl 13 '67
CLAPP, William J.
Electric power: new uses, new sources, more
demand; interview.por U S News 62:74-8
Mr 27 '67
CLARA, Miss.
It's coniped, in a photo finish; water tank of
modern design. il Am City 82:34 O '67
CLARA'S reverse psychology; story. See Hu-
lett, G.
CLARENCE, Sister Marie. See Marie Clarence,
Sister
CLARION music society
Musical events; concert performance of
Croesus, by R. Keiser. W. Sargeant. New
Yorker 43:152-4 D 16 '67
Report: New York: performance of Reinhard
Keiser's Croesus in Town Hall. F. Merk-
ling. Opera N 32:31 D 30 '67
CLARK, Bob
Nightmare journey. pors Ebony 22:121-4+ O
'67
CLARK, Brian F. C. and Marcker, K. A.
How proteins start; with biographical
sketches. Sci Am 218:19, 36-42 bibliog(150)
Ja '68
CLARK, Collin
New beat for the teen: library rock. Li-
brary J 92:1706-7 Ap 15 '67
CLARK, Cortelia
Street singer. il por Newsweek 69:117 Ap 17
'67
CLARK, Darthela
John Evelyn esq; fellow of the Royal society.
Horticulture 45:34-5+ D '67
CLARK, David, company
Two-way stretch in space. H. Manchester.
il Pop Mech 127:136-9 Ap '67
CLARK, Dodge and company
Wall Street gets a capital idea. il Bsns W
p 150-2 Ja 28 '67

CLARK, Donald E.
Books behind the bars. J. W. Kling. il Library J 92:1424-5 Ap 1 '67
CLARK, Donald T.
Instant college libraries; interview, ed. by J. Cushman. por Library J 92:540-3 F 1 '67
CLARK, Earl
How Seattle is beating water pollution. Harper 234:91-5 Je '67
Last frontier: the Olympic Peninsula. Todays Health 45:34-9+ Ag '67
CLARK, Edward
When a Texas-style diplomat hits Australia. H. Gordon. il pors N Y Times Mag p48-9+ O 8 '67
CLARK, Evert
Up in the clouds with the SST. Sat R 51:47-8+ Ja 6 '68
CLARK, Fred C. Jr
Customizing the open runabout. Yachting 121:92-3+ Ap '67
Flexible fuel system for your outboard. Pop Sci 190:135-7 Ap '67
Gunkholing the Glens. Yachting 122:48-50+ Ag '67
CLARK, Gordon
We filled page four. Reporter 36:37-40 Ap 6 '67
CLARK, Grenville
Legacy of a great American; interview; ed. by R. D. Heffner. por McCalls 94:64+ Ap '67
CLARK, Hank
Build this double-deck boat port. Pop Mech 129:152-3 Ja '68
Small-boat hoist you can build. Pop Sci 190:132-3 Mr '67
CLARK, J. J.
Marianas turkey shoot; excerpt from Carrier admiral. por Am Heritage 16:26-9+ O '67
CLARK, Jim, 1936-1968
I shall be back for another bash; ed. by K. Chapin. por Sports Illus 27:26-7 N 6 '67

about
Wee Jimmy's wee bomb. il por Time 91:36 Ja 12 '68
CLARK, Jim, 1941?-
Exploring the Peace River. pors Field & S 72:40-1+ Ja '68
CLARK, Joseph G.
Best start-up ration, roughage or concentrate? por Farm J 92:B10 Ja '68
How to cope with cold weather. por Farm J 91:B11 Ja '67
Preconditioning is only part of the battle. por Farm J 91:B14-15 N '67
What to do about brain diseases. por Farm J 91:B8-9 My '67
CLARK, Joseph S.
America's foreign aid program; address, January 14, 1967. Vital Speeches 33:299-303 Mr 1 '67
CLARK, Kenneth Bancroft
Search for identity. Ebony 22:39-40+ Ag '67
What business can do for the Negro; interview. por Nations Bsns 55:66-70 O '67

about
Hallelujah, amen! Nat R 19:1109 O 17 '67
Our last hope? L. L. L. Golden. Sat R 51:116 Ja 13 '68
CLARK, M. Edward
Home from Vietnam: June 14, 1967. Christian Cent 84:1067-8 Ag 23 '67
CLARK, Marguerite
Crisis in the hospitals. Sat R 50:40-1 My 20 '67
General practice for profit. Sat R 50:38 Mr 11 '67
CLARK, Marie Wynne
You're reading, Mr Mitchell! NEA J 56:16-19 My '67
CLARK, Mark Wayne
Do truce talks mean peace? interview. por U S News 62:42-4 Mr 20 '67
What it takes to be a leader; excerpt from address. Read Digest 91:160-2 Jl '67
CLARK, Marsh
Le grand faux pas of le grand Charles. Life 63:44B-44C Ag 4 '67
Why the First national city bank took the rap in Canada. Fortune 75:75+ Ap '67
CLARK, Mary
Our cruising houseboat. Yachting 121:80-1+ Ap '67
CLARK, Petula
Petula; with report by R. B. Stolley. il pors Life 62:79-80+ Je 9 '67
Search for Petula Clark. G. Gould. il por Hi Fi 17:67-71 N '67
CLARK, Phil
How to use a botanical garden. Horticulture 45:46-7 Je '67

CLARK, Ramsey
Civil rights: we haven't really improved, we may have slipped; excerpts from address, April 13, 1967. por U S News 62:50-1 My 1 '67

about
All in the family. por Time 89:22 Mr 10 '67
How will Clark tip the scales? por Bsns W p 160+ Mr 11 '67
Juridical chairs. por Newsweek 69:36-7 Mr 13 '67
Low-key and liberal. F. P. Graham. il pors N Y Times Mag p30-1+ Ap 2 '67
Mr Clark: what kind of attorney general? por U S News 62:22 Mr 13 '67
Watch on the Attorney General. C. Fritchey. Harper 235:38+ N '67
Wrong guy for the wrong post at the wrong time? V. S. Navasky. il pors Sat Eve Post 240:74-5+ D 16 '67
CLARK, Robert
Last citadel. il por Newsweek 71:23 Ja 15 '68
CLARK, Sidney
Kyushu. Travel 127:46-9+ Je '67
CLARK, Thomas Campbell
All in the family. por Time 89:22 Mr 10 '67
Juridical chairs. por Newsweek 69:36-7 Mr 13 '67
CLARK, Thomas D.
Colonial gadfly. Sat R 50:48-9 Je 10 '67
CLARK, Tom
Fig 1; Song; Sonnet; Death in the family; City; Lake: coda; poems. Poetry 111:143-9 D '67
Poetry chronicle. Poetry 110:105-11 My '67
Purgatory; Inferno; Poem: Like musical instruments; poems. Poetry 109:363-6 Mr '67
CLARK, Willard
Lens lines. See issues of U.S camera & travel
CLARK, Sterling and Francine, art Institute. See Sterling and Francine Clark art institute. Williamstown, Mass.
CLARK equipment company
He oils the wheels at Clark equipment; financial vice-president, J. Wood. Bsns W p70-1+ Ap 15 '67
CLARK HILL, LAKE. See Lakes, Artificial
CLARK Institute. See Sterling and Francine Clark art institute. Williamstown, Mass.
CLARKE, Arthur Charles
Colossus; interview. New Yorker 43:25 My 27 '67
CLARKE, Elizabeth
Cylburn wildflower preserve and garden center. Horticulture 45:40-1+ Ap '67
CLARKE, Gary H.
Operation Noah's ark. Parks & Rec 2:27+ Je '67
CLARKE, Margaret. See McMullin, M. D. jt. auth.
CLARKE, Thomas A. and others
Ecological studies during Project Sealab II. bibliog Science 157:1381-9 S 22 '67
CLARKE, Thomas E.
Humanity of Jesus. Commonweal 87:237-41 N 24 '67
Modern church, outdated priest? America 116:758 My 20 '67
CLARKSON family
Clarkson coat-of-arms. H. K. Eilers. il Hobbies 72:116-17+ O '67
CLASEN, Earl A.
Marketing ethics & the consumer. Harvard Bsns R 45:79-86 Ja '67
CLASON, Elsie D.
Traveler's choice. (cont) Travel 128:11 Jl '67
CLASS distinction. See Social classes
CLASS reunions. See College graduates
CLASS trips. See School excursions
CLASSES, Special. See Special classes and special schools
CLASSICAL education
See also
Greek language—Study and teaching
Latin language—Study and teaching
CLASSICAL literature
Classics revisited (cont) K. Rexroth. Sat R 50:21 Mr 4; 24 Ap 22; 14-15 My 13; 13 Jl 1; 18 Jl 8; 20 Jl 29; 42+ Ag 19; 44 S 2; 28 S 16; 24+ S 30; 10+ N 11; 23 D 2; 56 D 9 '67; 51:92 Ja 6 '68
Mediterranean; teaching classics at Walsh Jesuit H.S. Akron, Ohio. A. Prosen. il Sr Schol 99:sup 18 My 5 '67
CLASSICAL Rome. See Rome
CLASSICISM
Recapturing the ardor of Greece. K. Kuh. il Sat R 50:42-4 O 28 '67
CLASSICS, The. See Classical literature

CLEGHORN, Reese, and Watters, Pat
Impact of Negro votes on southern politics.
Reporter 36:24-5+ Ja 26 '67
CLELAND, David I. and Munsey, Wallace
Who works with whom? Harvard Bsns R
45:84-90 S '67
CLEM, Robert Verity
Talent of Robert Verity Clem. R. M. Mengel.
il Audubon 69:56-61 S '67
CLEMATIS
Clematis. M. M. Taylor. il Horticulture 45:
54+ D '67
Shrubby clematis for perennial gardens. E. M.
Schroeder. Home Gard 54:57 Mr '67
CLEMENS, Cyril
My visit with John F. Kennedy. Hobbies 72:
109+ Ap '67
CLEMENS, Lynwood G. and others
Mating behavior: facilitation in the female
rat after cortical application of potassium
chloride. bibliog Science 157:1208-9 S 8 '67
CLEMENS, Samuel Langhorne
The adventures of Tom Sawyer: dramatiza-
tion. See Hackett. W Glorious whitewasher
            about
Huckleberry Finn. K. Rexroth. Sat R 50:14-
15 My 13 '67
Major author in a minor key. C. Neider. il
por Sat R 50:34-5 Mr 25 '67
Mr Clemens and Mr Twain, by J. Kaplan.
Review
Nation 205:24-6 Jl 3 '67. J. Martin
CLEMENS, Walter C. Jr
Outer space, strategy, and arms control. Bul
Atomic Sci 23:24-8 N '67
CLEMENT, Saint, bp of Okhrid
Clement of Ohrid, Slavic educator. por Sch &
Soc 95:175-6 Mr 18 '67
CLEMENT, Anthony C. and Tyler, Albert
Protein-synthesizing activity of the anucleate
polar lobe of the mud snail ilyanassa obso-
leta. bibliog Science 158:1457-8 D 15 '67
CLEMENT, Ora A.
Nebraska's man-made forest. Nat Parks Mag
41:18-19 N '67
CLEMENTE, Roberto Walker
Old aches & pains. il por Time 89:56 My 26
'67
Viva, Roberto! il pors Ebony 22:38-41 S '67
CLEMENTS, Julia
Flower arranging in England. por Horticulture
45:28-31+ Mr '67
CLEMENTS, Robert J.
European literary scene. See issues of Satur-
day review
—See Rousseas, S. W. jt. auth.
CLEMENTS, Sid
How to catch a cuda. Field & S 72:56-7+ O
'67
CLEMENTS library of American history. See
Michigan. University. Ann Arbor—Clements
library of American history
CLEMMITT, Marcia
Curl up and read. Seventeen 26:14 Ap '67
CLEPPER, Henry
Conservation's grand lodge. por Am For 73:
22-7+ O '67
Homage to Basswood Lake. Am For 73:24-7+
Mr '67
Profile of a forester: Charles A. Gillett. Am
For 73:31+ Jl '67
CLERGY
Apostle to the affluent; suburban minister.
W. Hedgepeth. Look 31:41 My 16 '67
Concerned clergy seek peace in Washington;
Clergyman's education-action mobilization
on Vietnam. Christian Cent 84:100 Ja 25 '67
Draft the clergy too; World alliance of re-
formed churches proposal. Christian Cent
84:133-4 F 1 '67
End of the apartment house ministry. G. A.
Goodman. Christian Cent 84:615-17 My 10
'67; Reply. G. J. Micheaels. 84:871-2 Jl 5 '67
Lutheran clergyman looks at marriage; re-
ply. R. Moynihan. Cath World 205:2-3 Ap
'67
Ministers under the microscope. Christian
Cent 84:1061 Ag 23 '67
Of many things; interfaith symposium on
Who speaks for the church. H. J. Sievers.
America 117:inside cover D 16 '67
Should ministers be draft-exempt? il Time
89:70+ Ap 7 '67
Supports automatic social security for minis-
ters; House bill introduced by George M.
Rhodes. Christian Cent 84:398 Mr 29 '67
What a minister really does. L. David. il
Good H 164:60-1+ Ja '67
    See also
Catholic church—Clergy
Celibacy
Parishes
Preaching
Priests
Protestant Episcopal church—Clergy
Theologians

Anecdotes, facetiae, satire, etc.
Things that make a preacher laugh. N. G.
Long. Farm J 91:381 Je '67

Costume
Of many things; garb of European priests.
J. McLaughlin. America 117:inside cover O
7 '67; Discussion. 117:528 N 11 '67
On wearing the Roman collar. P. J. Weber.
America 116:560-2 Ap 15 '67

Education
Ministers: a 200-hour view. H. W. Allison.
Christian Cent 84:533-5 Ap 26 '67
Refresher course in theology; survey spon-
sored by the Midwest association of
theological schools. C. Wessels. il America
116:648-9 Ap 29 '67
Seminary community: a critique. L. B.
Mead. Christian Cent 84:563+ Ap 26 '67

Salaries
    See also
Priests—Salaries
CLERICAL dress. See Clergy—Costume
CLERODENDRUM. See Glory bowers
CLERON, Victor
Rest are simply left to die. J. Robbins and
J. Robbins. Redbook 130:80-1+ N '67
CLEVELAND, Harlan
Golden rule of consultation; address, June 20,
1967. Dept State Bul 57:141-6 Jl 31 '67
Official view of U.S: still vital to western de-
fense; excerpt from address, August 23,
1967, with questions and answers. por U S
News 63:61-4 S 11 '67
CLEVELAND

Architecture
Cleveland arcade; reprint. M.-P. Schofield. il
Arch Forum 127:60-5 S '67
Erieview plaza; il Arch Rec 141:153-6 Mr '67

Art
    See also
Cleveland museum of art

Crime
Bombs and suburbs; incident in Cleveland
Heights. N. C. Mills. Nation 204:817 Je
26 '67

Elections
Black power at the polls; Stokes, Hatcher
victories. C. L. Sanders; A. Poinsett. il
Ebony 23:23-6+ Ja '68
Cleveland and Gary. Newsweek 70:66-7 N
20 '67
Historic Election day for America. D. Jack-
son. il Life 63:36-7 N 17 '67
Real black power. il Time 90:23-7 N 17 '67

Galleries and museums
    See also
Cleveland museum of art

Housing
How to become a target city; Hough area
problems. R. H. Giles. il Reporter 36:38-41
Je 15 '67
New kind of team: three trade associations,
a non-profit citizens' group and HUD, com-
bine to rehab slum. il Arch Rec 142:150-2
Jl '67
Promise denied; urban renewal program.
Time 89:34 Je 9 '67

Libraries
    See also
Cleveland public library

Music
Blossom center: old dream come true; Cleve-
land summer orchestra's new pavilion. B.
Murray. Hi Fi 17:MA22-3 Ap '67
    See also
Cleveland orchestra

Negroes
Cleveland: recipe for violence. R. S. Bartimole
and M. Gruber. Nation 204:814-17 Je 26 '67
Memo from Cleveland: you can't stop the
riot that's coming. J. Star. Look 31:96+
My 30 '67
Question in the ghetto: can Cleveland escape
burning? J. Skow. il Sat Eve Post 240:38-
42+ Jl 29 '67
Sitting on the lid in Cleveland. R. Stock.
Commonweal 86:358-9 Je 16 '67

Newspapers
    See also
Cleveland plain dealer

CLEVELAND—*Continued*

Police

Cleveland: recipe for violence. R. S. Bartimole and M. Gruber. Nation 204:814-17 Je 26 '67

Politics and government

Black breakthrough. Newsweek 70:30+ O 16 '67

Focus on Cleveland. S. Friedman. Nat R 19:1335-6 N 28 '67

In Cleveland and Boston, the issue is race. J. M. Naughton. il N Y Times Mag p30+ N 5 '67

Into the mud; mayoralty race. Time 90:19 N 3 '67

Negro marches toward city hall; C. Stokes wins primary. il Bsns W p36-7 O 7 '67

Question in the ghetto: can Cleveland escape burning? J. Skow. il Sat Eve Post 240:38-42+ Jl 29 '67

Rematch in Cleveland; Negro contender for mayor. Time 90:24 S 15 '67

Second chance for Cleveland. J. Barden. Commonweal 87:103-4 O 27 '67

Stokes in Cleveland; mayoral campaign. New Repub 157:11 O 28 '67

Stokes on trial in Cleveland; first Negro mayor. il Bsns W p41 N 18 '67

U.S. letter: Cleveland; C. Stokes winner of Democratic mayoralty nomination. C. Trillin. New Yorker 43:210-14+ O 14 '67

Vindicative victory; C. Stokes wins Democratic nomination. il Time 90:29 O 13 '67

See also
Cleveland—Elections

Poor

Friendly town; vacation and medical examination programs for disadvantaged children. M. Slivka. il PTA Mag 61:8-10 Je '67

Public health

Friendly town; medical care for the poor. M. Slivka. PTA Mag 61:10 Je '67

Recreation

Tobogganing in your shirtsleeves; chutes in Cleveland's Rocky River reservation. O. D. Graham. il Parks & Rec 2:23+ My '67

Riots

Memo from Cleveland: you can't stop the riot that's coming. J. Star. Look 31:96+ My 30 '67

Riots, violence & civil rights. S. S. Friedman. Nat R 19:898-904+ Ag 22 '67

Social conditions

Helping hand of Jim Redding; activities in the Hough area. V. Pizer. il Read Digest 90:99-103 Je '67

How to become a target city; Hough area problems. R. H. Giles. il Reporter 36:38-41 Je 15 '67

Riots, violence & civil rights. S. S. Friedman. Nat R 19:898-904+ Ag 22 '67

Sitting on the lid in Cleveland. R. Stock. Commonweal 86:358-9 Je 16 '67

See also
Cleveland—Negroes

Social work

Friendly town; vacation and medical examination programs for disadvantaged children. M. Slivka. il PTA Mag 61:8-10 Je '67

CLEVELAND HEIGHTS

Things are happening in Cleveland Heights; Roxboro junior high school. il Sr Schol 91:sup8-9 S 21 '67

Education

Thriving youth theater; Cleveland Heights-University Heights city school district. L. Freyman. il NEA J 57:26-7 Ja '68

CLEVELAND museum of art

Anatomy lessons & elephant tusks; new acquisitions. il Time 90:46-7 D 29 '67

Cleveland's medieval treasure. il Time 89:72-3 Ja 27 '67

Keeping behind the times in Cleveland. A. Z. Silver. Reporter 36:40+ Je 29 '67

CLEVELAND orchestra

Music to my ears; performance of Missa solemnis. I. Kolodin. Sat R 50:62 F 25 '67

Musical events; concert in Carnegie Hall, conducted by G. Szell. W. Sargeant. New Yorker 43:146 Mr 4 '67

Musical events; two concerts in Carnegie Hall under M. Rudolph. W. Sargeant. New Yorker 42:105-6+ Ja 28 '67

CLEVELAND plain dealer

Cordial welcome for Newhouse; purchase of the 125-year-old paper. il Time 89:47 Mr 10 '67

Plain and fancy dealing. Newsweek 69:78 Mr 13 '67

CLEVELAND public library

Limited adult reader; public library's Reading centers program. T. E. Barensfeld. il Library J 92:3004-7 S 15 '67

CLEVELAND symphony orchestra. See Cleveland orchestra

CLEWISTON, Fla, public library

Gift for Clewiston; Harry T. Vaughn building. E. L. Bruya. il Library J 92:4369 D 1 '67

CLIBURN, Van

Triumphant Cliburn recital. C. J. Luten. il por Am Rec G 33:397 Ja '67

CLICHE verres. See Glass prints

CLICHES. See English language—Terms and phrases

CLIFF dwellers and cliff dwellings

Cliff dwelling model. P. S. Zakroff and E. Gell. il Design 69:6-8 Wint '67

CLIFFORD, Clark McAdams

Mr Clifford and General Taylor report on talks on Viet-Nam with allied leaders; transcript of press conference, August 5, 1967. Dept State Bul 57:256-60 Ag 28 '67

CLIFFORD, Francis, pseud.

World of action. Writer 80:17-18 N '67

CLIFFORD, N. K.

Crisis in Canadian theological education. Christian Cent 84:897-9 Jl 12 '67

CLIFFORD, William

Beer. House B 109:120-1+ Ag '67

Four-day outing from New York. Atlan 219:114-16+ Je '67

Gift of cheer. House B 109:163+ D '67

Summer drinks, on the citrus circuit. House B 109:156-7+ Je '67

CLIFT, Montgomery

Montgomery Clift: a small place in the sun. R. Thom. por Esquire 67:104-5+ Mr '67

CLIFTONITE

Cliftonite in meteorites; a proposed origin. R. Brett and G. T. Higgins. bibliog il Science 166:819-20 My 12 '67

CLIGNET, Remi

Hazards of educational planning. Sat R 50:59-60+ Ag 19 '67

CLIMATE

Antarctic radiolaria, magnetic reversals, and climatic change. J. D. Hays and N. D. Opdyke. bibliog il Science 158:1001-11 N 24 '67

Climate modification by atmospheric aerosols. R. A. McCormick and J. H. Ludwig. bibliog Science 156:1358-9 Je 9 '67

Climate of cities. W. P. Lowry. il Sci Am 217:15-23 Ag '67

Is man changing the climate of earth? adaptation of address. R. A. Bryson. il Sat R 50:52-5 Ap 1 '67

Tree ring indices: a circumpolar comparison. R. K. Haugen. bibliog il Science 158:773-5 N 10 '67

Ups and downs of climate; climatic oddities. J. Daugherty and M. Daugherty. il Sci Digest 62:88-90 Ag '67

See also
Temperature
Weather

CLIMATOLOGY. See Climate

CLIMBING plants

Annual vines. R. M. Carleton. il Horticulture 45:26-7+ F '67

Induction of coiling in tendrils by auxin and carbon dioxide. L. Reinhold. bibliog il Science 158:791-3 N 10 '67

Luxurious flowering vines. il Am Home 70:60+ My '67

To grace a wall or window. H. V. Wilson. il Home Gard 54:48-9 Ag '67

Two vines get mixed up together. il Sunset 139:124 Jl '67

Vines for privacy and vines for shade. il Sunset 139:150-2 S '67

Ways to tie your vines and some handsome vines to tie. il Sunset 138:194-5 Je '67

You can use vines everywhere. H. O. Perkins. il Horticulture 45:18-21 Je '67

See also
Clematis
Glory bowers
Grapes
Wax plants

CLINCH, Nicholas B.

First conquest of Antarctica's highest peaks. Nat Geog Mag 131:836-63 Je '67

CLINE, David B. See Barger, V. D. jt. auth.

CLINE, Ralph
What is a principal? J. Poppy. il pors Look 31:34-40 O 17 '67

CLINICAL laboratories. See Medical laboratories

CLINICAL medicine. See Medicine, Clinical

CLINICAL research. See Medical research

CLINICS. See Health clinics

CLINTON, George
This hollowed-out ground. C. Carmer. il por Am Heritage 18:58-9+ Je '67

CLINTON, Sir Henry
This hollowed-out ground. C. Carmer. il por Am Heritage 18:58-9+ Je '67
Your excellencys most obedient. . .servant. H. H. Peckham. Wilson Lib Bul 41:586-9 F '67

CLITOCYBE rivulosa. See Fungi

CLIVEDEN (estate) See Country estates—England

CLOCK and watch makers
Curtis and Dunning, clockmakers. R. N. Hill. il Antiques 91:214-17 F '67
See also
Bulova watch company

CLOCK radios. See Radio receivers

CLOCKS
English clocks. L. W. Slaughter. il Hobbies 71:46-7 F; 72:46-7 Mr; 46-7+ Ap '67

Collectors and collecting
Collecting old time-pieces (cont) L. W. Slaughter. il Hobbies 72:46-7 Mr '67

History
Collecting old time-pieces; German clocks. L. W. Slaughter. il Hobbies 72:46-7+ Ag; 46-7+ S; 46-7 O '67; 46-7+ Ja '68
Collecting old time-pieces; German clocks (Netherlands) L. W. Slaughter. il Hobbies 72:46-7+ N; 46-7+ D '67

CLOCKS, Atomic. See Atomic clocks

CLOROX company
Clorox case; Supreme court dissolves P&G-Clorox merger. il Consumer Rep 32:360-3 Jl '67
High court dissolves a sudsy conglomerate; P&G-Clorox merger decision. il Bsns W p40-1 Ap 15 '67
No guidelines in sight; ten-year-old Procter & Gamble-Clorox chemical merger. Time 89:92+ Ap 21 '67
Now, a tougher barrier to big mergers? U S News 62:12+ Ap 24 '67

CLOSE-up photography. See Photography, Close-up

CLOSED circuit television. See Television, Closed circuit

CLOSED-end investment companies. See Investment trusts

CLOSED shop. See Open and closed shop

CLOSETS
Closet ideas: worth looking into; linen closets. il Ladies Home J 84:67 Mr '67
Here is where the linen goes. il Sunset 138: 138 Ap '67

CLOTHES dryers
What to look for in washers and dryers. V. T. Habeeb. il Am Home 70:138 O '67

CLOTHES hampers
Wall hamper stows clothes and soap. R. Fish. il Pop Mech 128:163 D '67

CLOTHES hangers
Tender loving hangers. il House & Gard 131: 67-8+ Mr '67

CLOTHES washing machines. See Washing machines

CLOTHING, Cold weather
Ways to dress warmly in cold weather. il Good H 165:200 N '67
What you should know about winter health care. il Pop Gard 18:50-1 Mr '67
See also
Clothing and dress—Sports clothes
Underwear

CLOTHING, Industrial. See Clothing and dress—Work clothes

CLOTHING and dress
Aglow: electronic clothes; interview. D. Dew. New Yorker 42:26-8 Ja 28 '67
Are you allergic to clothes? R. W. Crane. il Todays Health 45:30-2 F '67
As Wall Street watches hemlines; corresponding highs and lows in Dow-Jones average. il U S News 62:94 My 29 '67
Civil liberties and uncivility in school. W. W. Brickman. Sch & Soc 95:102 F 18 '67

Clothes that glisten; dresses of foil. il Consumer Bul 50:35 N '67
Exotic departures; English girls and boys in their teens and twenties. M. Spark. New Yorker 42:31-2 Ja 28 '67
Institute report on paper clothing. il Good H 165:6 Ag '67
It really is paper! N. L. Pouch. il Good H 165:144 Ag '67
Mini-looking in London. L. Wainwright. Life 62:24 My 26 '67
News: paper fashions; wrap your world in paper. il Seventeen 26:142-5 My '67
Now it's the little paper dress; disposable garments. il Bsns W p 132-4+ Jl 22 '67
Paper at the Lotos; paper saris. New Yorker 43:29-30 My 27 '67
Paper caper. A. Chamberlin. il Sat Eve Post 240:32-7 D 2 '67
Paper chase, the boom in disposable clothing. il Consumer Bul 50:4-6 Jl '67
Paper posh: disposable elegance. J. A. Zill. il Look 31:80-2+ Mr 7 '67
Questions about fashion and clothes bring surprising answers. il Redbook 130:61+ Ja '68
Real live paper dolls; paper clothing. il Time 89:52 Mr 17 '67
Redbook dialogue. P. Diller and R. Gernreich. il Redbook 129:58-9+ My '67
Short-cut pantsuit. il Life 62:43-4+ Je 23 '67
Take a fashion lesson; how to choose double-time travel clothes. Seventeen 26:232 My '67
Tips for trying on clothes. il Good H 165: 168-9 Ag '67
Toss-aways for the poolside and seaside life. il House & Gard 131:106-7 Je '67
Turn on your dress, Diana! electronic clothes. T. Hyman. il Sat Eve Post 241:26-9 Ja 13 '68
Wardrobes for the wastebasket. R. Levy. il Duns R 89:59 Je '67
See also
Bathing suits
Clothing industry
Costume design
Fashion
Fashion as a profession
Hats
Kilts
Scarves
Sewing

Anecdotes, facetiae, satire, etc.
All the nudes that fit the print; paper dresses. G. Ace. Sat R 50:6 Jl 22 '67

Children
See also
Infants—Clothing

Color
How now? brown. Time 90:84 N 24 '67
Your best fashion colors. il Seventeen 26: 122-3 O '67

Men
Civil liberties and uncivility in schools. W. W. Brickman. Sch & Soc 95:102 F 18 '67
Is mod dead? il Newsweek 69:73-4 Mr 6 '67
Living it up in Washington. M. Cheshire. il Nations Bsns 55:58-9 Jl '67
Memo on menswear: news, views and advice. B. Ullmann. il Good H 166:156-7 Ja '68
Men, now. il Vogue 150:88-103 N 15 '67
Men's fashions for spring and summer; a Mexican fiesta of color. il Ebony 22:115-18+ Ap '67
Opinion: on looking foreign. M. Bradbury. Mlle 64:98+ F '67
Personal business; dinner wear's flights of fancy. Bsns W p 171-2 N 18 '67
Sense of style; list of best dressed men in Men's bazaar. G. Frazier. Esquire 68:62+ S '67
Turtlenecks for men. il Time 89:59 Mr 3 '67
What revolution in men's clothes? R. Lynes. Harper 234:26+ My '67
Woman's guide to men's sport shirts and sweaters. Good H 165:176-9 D '67
See also
Shirts
Underwear

History
New look at the old mod. J. Dolmetsch. il Antiques 92:854-7 D '67

Prices
Clothing; staying in fashion on a modest budget. il Good H 164:201 Ap '67

Purchasing
How to stretch your clothing dollar. M. Feeley. Am Home 70:20-1 S '67

CLOTHING and dress—*Continued*

Sports clothes

Best ski news. D. Messinesi. Vogue 151:46 Ja 1 '68
Clothes for bowmen. G. H. Gillelan. il Outdoor Life 140:82+ S '67
Clothing for boatmen. J. A. Emmett. il Outdoor Life 140:102-3+ D '67
Life with the Jax pack. D. Jenkins. il Sports Illus 27:56-62 Jl 10 '67
Sixty miles per hour while standing still; ski clothes. il Sports Illus 27:34-6+ D 18 '67
Sporting look. See issues of Sports Illustrated
Take a fashion lesson; ski clothing. il Seventeen 26:186 N '67

Work clothes

Liquid-cooled suit. Sci Digest 61:28-9 Ap '67

CLOTHING industry
Beautiful people, by M. Bender. Review
    Reporter 37:39-40+ N 30 '67. G. Culligan
Reporter at large; Twiggy in New York. T. Whiteside. New Yorker 43:64-6+ N 4 '67

Wages and hours

Pay raises, higher clothing prices. U S News 62:84 Je 5 '67

France

Le crocodile; sporting goods company. il Time 90:62 S 1 '67
New body: more woman than you'd think; Courrèges dancing mannequins. il Vogue 150:137-9 N 15 '67

Great Britain

Biba: London's mini mecca. H. Ehrlich. il Look 31:92-5+ N 14 '67
Cohen the kiltmaker; Glasgow factory of D. & H. Cohen ltd. il Time 90:98 S 15 '67

Russia

Miniskirts in Moscow; Soviet Union's first international fashion festival. il Newsweek 70:43-4 S 4 '67
Russia's five-year fashion leap. J. A. Zill. il Look 31:40-5+ Je 27 '67

United States

Apparel salesmen take samples to the party; Beeline fashions, Bensenville, Ill. il Bsns W p 148-50+ Jl 15 '67
Great fashion explosion. E. Carruth. il Fortune 76:162-5+ O '67
    See also
Amalgamated clothing workers of America
BVD company
Genesco, incorporated
International ladies' garment workers' union
Logan, Jonathan, incorporated
Magnin, Joseph, company
New York (city)—Industries

CLOTHING prices. See Clothing and dress—Prices
CLOTTING of blood. See Blood—Coagulation
CLOTURE rule. See United States—Congress—Senate—Rules and practice
CLOUD, Preston E. Jr, and Nelson, C. A.
Phanerozoic-cryptozoic and related transitions: new evidence. bibliog Science 154:766-70; 157:958 N 11 '66, Ag 25 '67
CLOUD, Wallace
Artificial gills: they'll let you breathe like a fish. Pop Mech 128:69-72+ D '67
Tiger sharks strike in the Vietnam swamps. Pop Mech 128:131-4+ N '67
CLOUD seeding. See Rain making
CLOUDS
Photography of the earth's cloud satellites from an aircraft. C. Wolff and others. bibliog il Science 157:427-9 Jl 28 '67
Temperature measurements in noctilucent clouds. J. S. Theon and others. il Science 157:419-21 Jl 28 '67
CLOUGH, Barbara M.
Accepted or rejected? interview, ed. by D. Klein. por Seventeen 26:134-5+ Mr '67
CLOUGH, Roy L. Jr
Toy steam engine has a secret. Pop Sci 191:124 N '67
CLOUSER, James
Evening of new works by James Clouser and Louis Falco. 92nd street Y. D. Hering. Dance Mag 41:30 Ag '67
World of dance. W. Terry. il por Sat R 50:44-5 Je 24 '67
CLOWARD, Richard A. and Piven, F. F.
Birth of a movement. Nation 204:582-8 My 8 '67
Corporate imperialism for the poor. Nation 205:365-7 O 16 '67

Mississippi: starving by the rule book. Nation 204:429-31 Ap 3 '67
New welfare: women and children last. Commonweal 86:541-2 S 8 '67
We've got rights! New Repub 157:23-7 Ag 5 '67
—See Piven, F. F. jt. auth.
CLOWES, Allen
Culture comes to Indianapolis. R. Gover. il por N Y Times Mag p6-7+ D 24 '67
CLOWES memorial hall for the performing arts. See Indianapolis—Clowes memorial hall for the performing arts
CLOWNS
Eggshell library for clowns; International circus clowns club. T. Conway. il Design 68:36-7 Sum '67
CLUB apartments. See Apartment houses
CLUB Méditerranée. See Vacation villages
CLUB-plan vacation homes. See Vacation villages
CLUBS
Fifth dimension; Hullabaloo teen-age dance clubs. il Newsweek 69:100 Ap 17 '67
    See also
Agricultural societies
Boat clubs
Bridge clubs
Country clubs
Yacht clubs
    also subhead Clubs under names of cities, e.g. London—Clubs
CLUCHEY, Rick
Cage. Criticism
    New Repub 158:34+ Ja 13 '68
CLUE of daffodils; story. See Hinchman, J.
CLURMAN, Harold Edgar
Star of Paris. Nation 204:472-3 Ap 10 '67
CLUSTER housing. See Housing projects—Site planning
CLUSTERS of stars. See Stars—Clusters
CLUTCHES, Automobile. See Automobiles —Clutches
CLUTTER, Herbert William, family
Truman Capote reports on the filming of In cold blood. T. Capote. il Sat Eve Post 241:62-5 Ja 13 '68
CLUYTENS, André
Obituary
    Opera N 32:28 S 9 '67
CLYMER, Adam
Primer on prying. Reporter 36:50-1 Ap 20 '67
CLYNE, John V.
Canadian's case for an Atlantic freetrade area; interview, ed. by R. K. Brome. por U S News 64:48-50 Ja 1 '68
CO, Nguyen-huu-. See Nguyen-huu-Co
COACH with the six insides; drama. See Erdman, J.
COACHES (athletics)
Expo of a different kind; U.S. coaches in Canada. T. C. Brody. il Sports Illus 27:48-9 Jl 3 '67
Fighting Illini; slush fund for football and basketball players. D. Jenkins. il Sports Illus 26:16-19 Mr 6 '67
Lock the doors! here comes Tommy! UCLA's controversial T. Prothro. M. Durslag. il Sports Illus 27:40-4 S 4 '67
Out. Time 89:49 Mr 31 '67
Slipping in slush; use of alumni-financed slush fund to support needy Illinois athletes. il Time 89:78 Mr 10 '67
Stallball, a game to sleep by; UCLA vs USC. J. Jares. il Sports Illus 26:28-30 Mr 13 '67
Taste of that not-so-old college spirit. J. Underwood. Sports Illus 27:20-1 N 27 '67
This year the fight will be in the open; importance of national rankings. D. Jenkins. il Sports Illus 27:28-52+ S 11 '67
    See also
Cohen, H.
Daugherty, D.
Lombardi, V.
Mackenzie, J.
Moses, W.
Parker, H.
Parseghian, A.
Sain, J.
COACHES and coaching
When the coachman was a millionaire; with watercolors by M. Klepper. Am Heritage 18:20-5+ O '67
COAL
Magnetic susceptibilities of coals. D. Bivins and S. Ergun. bibliog il Science 159:83 Ja 5 '68
COAL industry
Great Britain
Lord Coal's role. il Time 90:84 Ag 18 '67

COAL industry—*Continued*
United States
Atom's challenge to the coal industry. B. Kovach and N. Caldwell. Reporter 36:39-41 F 23 '67

COAL mines and mining
Stripping operations
Blight on the land. E. A. Bauer and B. East. il Outdoor Life 140:35-7+ D '67 (to be cont)
Legacy of torment. il Time 89:90 Mr 31 '67
Sparring with spoilers; Kentucky's new ruling. Time 90:13 D 29 '67
Strip mining in Pennsylvania. G. Ade. il Nat Parks Mag 41:15-17 Mr '67
These murdered old mountains; effects of strip mining operations in Kentucky. D. Nevin. il Life 64:54-60+ Ja 12 '68
Who needs people? not the strippers of Appalachia. J. Ridgeway. New Repub 156:10-12 My 13 '67

United States
Coal's boom creates a new kind of town. il Bsns W p 164+ S 16 '67

Wales
Ghosts of Aberfan; one year later. W. Danforth. il McCalls 95:98-103+ N '67
Terrifying ineptitude; National coal board blamed for disaster at Aberfan, Wales. Sci N 92:204 Ag 26 '67

COANDA, Henri
Prowling mind of Henri Coanda. G. H. Stine. il por Flying 80:64-8 Mr '67

COAST and geodetic survey. See United States—Coast and geodetic survey

COAST changes
Pleistocene shoreline sediments in coastal Georgia: deposition and modification. J. H. Hoyt and J. R. Hails. bibliog il Science 155:1541-3 Mr 24 '67

COAST defense
See also
United States—Coast guard

COAST guard. See United States—Coast guard

COAST guard academy, United States. See United States coast guard academy, New London, Conn.

COAST guard auxiliary. See United States—Coast guard auxiliary

COASTAL marshes. See Salt marshes

COASTING
Ghostly go for the bobs; world bobsled championships on new Olympic run at Alpe d'Huez, France. B. Ottum. il Sports Illus 26:16-21 F 20 '67
Ti-leaf sliding in Hawaii. il Sunset 139:26 D '67
See also
Toboggans and tobogganing

COASTS
How long is the coast of Britain? statistical self-similarity and fractional dimension. B. Mandelbrot. bibliog il Science 156:636-8 My 5 '67
See also
Estuaries
United States
Call of the coast. C. Davis. il Holiday 42:56-9+ O '67

COATES, Bill, and Roth, Bernie
How does the land lie? Outdoor Life 140:30-1+ Jl '67

COATES, James M. Jr
Little Rock ten years later. J. Egerton. il por Sat R 50:60-1 D 16 '67

COATES, Joseph. See Sagalyn, A. jt. auth.

COATES, Robert M.
Our far-flung correspondents. New Yorker 43:102+ Je 17 '67
Setting-in of winter; story. New Yorker 43:60-8 D 9 '67

COATING materials. See Protective coatings

COATINGS, Protective. See Protective coatings

COATS
See also
Fur coats, wraps, etc.

COBB, Boughton, Jr
Early fiberglass boats. Yachting 121:104-6+ Ja '67
Fiberglass; surface imperfections. Yachting 121:66-7+ Ap '67
Judging fiberglass. Yachting 123:86-7+ Ja '68
New fiberglass spars. Yachting 122:41+ O '67

COBB, Lillord
Big gamble of Lillord Cobb. il pors Ebony 22:63-4+ O '67

COBBAN, Alfred
Many lives of Georges Lefebvre. G. Shapiro. bibliog f Am Hist R 72:502-14 Ja '67

COBLE, Tom
Time for the gentle people. Criticism Commonweal 86:394 Je 23 '67

COBLENTZ, Stanton A.
Green conquest; poem. Liv Wildn 31:35 Spr '67

COBURN, James
What we have to do is try not to lie; dialogue with Father Boyd. por Redbook 129:64-5+ O '67
about
Beyond the ego. il por Time 89:76 My 26 '67

COCA-COLA company
Fresca blizzard. Newsweek 70:63 D 25 '67

COCCOLITHS, Fossil. See Flagellates, Fossil

COCHELL, Shirley
Getting students into the act. Sr Schol 90:sup8 Mr 17 '67
How to develop students' storytelling skills. Sr Schol 90:sup24 Mr 31 '67
New books for teaching English. Sr Schol 90:sup22 Ap 7 '67
Student-built halls of fame. Sr Schol 90:sup28 F 17 '67

COCHLEA. See Ear

COCHRAN, William G.
Footnote; address, December 29, 1966. bibliog Science 156:1460-2 Je 16 '67

COCKBURN, Aidan
Latent diseases rise up. Sci N 92:608 D 23 '67

COCKCROFT, Sir John
Sir John Cockcroft dies at seventy. G. Parrillo. por Science 157:1416 S 22 '67
On the pioneering generation. E. Rabinowitch. Bul Atomic Sci 23:2 N '67

COCKRILL, W. Ross
Water buffalo; with biographical sketch. Sci Am 217:15, 118-25 D '67

COCKROACHES
Cockroaches, ugh! Changing T 21:34 N '67
Durable hazard. F. Marley. il Sci N 92:304-5 S 23 '67
Fighting and death from stress in a cockroach. L. S. Ewing. bibliog il Science 155:1035-6 F 24 '67
Horde uncountable. N. B. Bates. Natur Hist 76:20+ N '67

COCKTAIL parties. See Entertaining

COCKTAIL pianists. See Pianists

COCKTAILS
State of the American cocktail. H. J. Grossman. House B 109:196-7 Ap '67
Wine, women & so on. P. Cannon. Ladies Home J 84:60 O '67

COCONUT crabs. See Crabs

COCOONS
Cocoon surrounding desert-dwelling frogs. A. K. Lee and E. H. Mercer. bibliog il Science 157:87-8 Jl 7 '67

COCTEAU, Jean
Camera eye. S. Maloff. por Newsweek 70:73-73A+ Jl 24 '67
Notes on a spiritual odyssey. W. Fowlie. il por Sat R 50:28-9 Je 17 '67

COD fishing
Strange cod of Ogac Lake. F. Bruemmer. il Outdoor Life 140:56-9 N '67

CODATA. See International council of scientific unions—Committee on data for science and technology

CODE instruments. See Radio telegraph

CODES (ciphers) See Ciphers

CODY, George D.
Inventor of the month. S. V. Jones. il por Sci Digest 61:17 F '67

CODY, John Patrick, abp
Cody all alone. Christian Cent 84:302 Mr 8 '67
Getting your visa for Chicago. B. Cook. Commonweal 86:5-7 Mr 24 '67; Discussion. 86:158-9 Ap 21 '67
Indicative concession. Christian Cent 84:709 My 31 '67

COE, John E.
Mouse immunoglobulin allotypes. detection with rabbit antiserums. bibliog Science 155:562+ F 3 '67

COE, Michael D. and others
Olmec civilizations, Veracruz, Mexico: dating of the San Lorenzo phase. bibliog Science 155:1399-401 Mr 17 '67

COEDUCATION
Better coed than dead; college rush toward coeducation. il Time 89:57 My 5 '67
Celibacy, sacred and profane. J. O'Hara. Holiday 42:28-9 Ag '67

COELACANTHS
Living fossil. I. Asimov. Sci Digest 63:86-7 Ja '68
Serum osmolality in the coelacanth, latimeria chalumnae: urea retention and ion regulation. G. E. Pickford and F. B. Grant. bibliog il Science 155:568-70 F 3 '67
Urea and its formation in coelacanth liver. G. W. Brown, jr. and S. G. Brown. bibliog il Science 155:570-3 F 3 '67

COERR, Wymberley DeRenne
Yankee goes home. Sr Schol 91:20-1 O 26 '67

COEVOLUTION. See Evolution

COEXISTENCE. See World politics, 1945-

CO-EXISTENCE policy. See United States—Foreign relations—Russia

COFFEE
Beauty bean. R. Starnes. Field & S 72:20+ N '67
How coffee affects your health. Todays Health 45:70 Ap '67
How to brew a great cup of coffee. V. T. Habeeb. il Am Home 71:72+ Ja '68
Instant coffee brews a quarrel; dispute between the U.S. and Brazil. il Bsns W p 180 S 30 '67

Prices
Coffee crisis. Américas 19:43 Mr '67
Cure for coffee. il Time 89:75 F 3 '67

COFFEE cake
One-bowl coffee cake. il Sunset 138:187+ Mr '67
So-good coffee cakes. R. Hanna. il Suc Farm 65:116-17+ Mr '67
Stop by for coffee. il Parents Mag 42:68-9 Ja '67
Sweet and sour. C. Claiborne. il N Y Times Mag p68 Je 11 '67

COFFEE pots, percolators, etc.
Buyer's guide to coffee makers. il Am Home 71:76 Ja '68
For making coffee the hard way. il Sunset 139:70-1 D '67
Porcelain pots for brewing and warming coffee. H. Newman. il Antiques 92:329-31 S '67
Take the guesswork out of coffeemaking. il House B 109:182-4 My '67

COFFEE table books. See Books and reading

COFFEE tables. See Tables

COFFEE trade
Second annual report on the International coffee agreement transmitted to Congress; with letter of transmittal, January 19, 1967, by L. B. Johnson. il Dept State Bul 56:250-60 F 13 '67
See also
International coffee council

COFFEE vending machines. See Vending machines

COFFER, Helene Lewis
True and lasting kind; story. Good H 165:94-5 N '67

COFFEY, J. I.
Anti-ballistic missile debate. For Affairs 45:403-13 Ap '67

COFFEY, J. Russell, and Renaux, Robert
Small industry provides summer recreation. Parks & Rec 2:33-4 Je '67

COFFEY, Raymond
Vietnam's not-so-free press. Sat R 50:122-3+ O 14 '67

COFFEY, Warren
Aeschylus I'm maybe not. Commonweal 86:231-2 My 12 '67
Incompleat novelist. Commentary 44:98+ S '67
Oxford boys. Commonweal 87:112-13 O 27 '67

COFFIN, Robert P. Tristram
Prize pumpkin; story. PTA Mag 62:31-2 N '67

COFFIN, Tristram
Congress: its lost sacred powers. Bul Atomic Sci 23:35-7 D '67

COFFIN, William Sloane, 1924-
Buckley, Buckley, bow wow wow. G. Wills. por Esquire 69:72-6+ Ja '68
Coffin and man at Yale. il por Newsweek 70:67 N 13 '67

COGEN, Charles, and Selden, David
American federation of teachers' position paper; statement; July 18-20, 1966. pors Sch & Soc 95:87-91 F 4 '67

COGGAN, Frederick Donald, abp
Commencement address; Archbishop of York speaks at General theological seminary in New York city. America 116:846 Je 17 '67

COGGESHALL, Roger G.
Enjoy the satisfaction of successful plant grafting. Horticulture 45:24-5+ Mr '67

COGLEY, John
Dissent is not enough. N Y Times Mag p28 N 26 '67
Future of an illusion; adaptation of address. Commonweal 86:310-16 Je 2 '67
Identity crisis in the Catholic college. Sat R 50:68 Je 17 '67
John Courtney Murray. America 117:220-1 S 2 '67

COGNITION. See Knowledge, Theory of

COHELEACH, Guy
Hawks of southern North America; paintings; with biographical sketch. il por Audubon 69:41-6 Ja '67

COHEN, Abraham
Challenge of the rival educators. Library J 92:853-5 F 15 '67
Screenings; 8mm. Library J 92:3833-5, 4595-6 O 15, D 15 '67

COHEN, Alexander Henry
Run-through. New Yorker 43:21-2 Jl 8 '67

COHEN, Alvin
Revolution in Argentina? bibliog f Cur Hist 53:283-90 N '67

COHEN, Daniel
Is this Atlantis? Sci Digest 62:66-9 O '67

COHEN, David
Magnetic fields around the torso: production by electrical activity of the human heart. bibliog Science 156:652-4 My 5 '67

COHEN, Elaine
Art education laboratory. Sch Arts 66:32-5 Je '67

COHEN, Gerald. See Marcus, J. R. jt. auth.

COHEN, Harlan
Playing it the Japanese way. G. Ronberg. il Sports Illus 26:30-1 Je 5 '67

COHEN, Harry B. and others
Sleep: the effect of electroconvulsive shock in cats deprived of REM sleep. bibliog Science 156:1646-8 Je 23 '67

COHEN, Harry D. and Barondes, S. H.
Puromycin effect on memory may be due to occult seizures. bibliog Science 157:333-4 Jl 21 '67

COHEN, Hennig
Visions of depravity. Reporter 36:39-40+ My 4 '67

COHEN, J. A.
Chemistry and structure of nucleic acids of bacteriophages. bibliog Science 158:343-51 O 20 '67

COHEN, Jacob Gershon-. See Gershon-Cohen, J.

COHEN, Jerry, and Chriss, N. C.
New Orleans: act I. Reporter 36:17-20 Ap 6 '67

COHEN, Joel H.
One child, one vote. Parents Mag 42:40-1+ Ja '67

COHEN, Leonard. See Chevalier, L. R. jt. auth.

COHEN, Lita H. Solis-. See Solis-Cohen, L. H.

COHEN, Maimon M. and others
Chromosomal damage in human leukocytes induced by lysergic acid diethylamide. bibliog Science 155:1417-19 Mr 17 '67

COHEN, Martin
Here comes Hoving! Read Digest 91:98-102 S '67
Redbook's guide to Canada's fair. Redbook 128:19-26 Ap '67

COHEN, Melvin J. See Jacklet, J. W. jt. auth.

COHEN, Morris
That coming boom in housing. Fortune 75:134-7+ My '67

COHEN, Paul J. and Hersh, Reuben
Non-Cantorian set theory; with biographical sketch. Sci Am 217:15, 104-6+ bibliog(p 160) D '67

COHEN, Robert David
Alchemical child; poem. New Yorker 43:218 D 2 '67
Path; poem. New Yorker 43:136 S 16 '67
Poem for father's going. New Yorker 43:111 S 30 '67

COHEN, Selma Jeanne
Both art and education. Dance Mag 41:48-9 Ag '67
Lillian Moore: a joyous searching. Dance Mag 41:34-7 S '67
Project Rocket. Dance Mag 41:39-41+ F '67
Tudor and the Royal ballet. Sat R 50:74-5 My 13 '67

COHEN, Sheldon S.
Easier tax paying coming; interview. por Nations Bsns 55:42-3+ Mr '67
129 billion dollars in taxes; the miracle of April 15; excerpts from address, March 17, 1967. por U S News 62:100-1 Ap 17 '67
To tax and to please; address, December 15, 1966. Vital Speeches 33:268-72 F 15 '67

COHEN, Wilbur J.
Education and learning. bibliog f Ann Am
Acad 373:79-101 S '67
COHERER
Coherer; early history of radio communica-
tions. H. B. Davis. il Pop Electr 26:47-9
My '67
COHN, Arthur
Four works from Poland, one of them a
masterpiece. Am Rec G 34:26-7 S '67
Gilt-edged aural securities. Am Rec G 33:
731-2 My '67
On four records from two labels, seven works
by Janáček. Am Rec G 33:379+ Ja '67
Via Nonesuch, a trip to another brave new
world. Am Rec G 34:190-1 N '67
COHN, Emma
Outlook tower. Horn Bk 43:226-8, 367-9 Ap,
N '67
COHN, Harry
King Cohn, by B. Thomas. Review
Life 62:11+ Mr 3 '67. B. Schulberg
Sat R 50:30 Mr 18 '67. A. Knight
Time por 89:118+ Ap 14 '67
COHN, Lawrence
Mississippi John Hurt: 1892-1966. Sat R
50:90 F 25 '67
(comp) Recommended recordings, Christmas
1967. Sat R 50:49 D 16 '67
Recordings reports: folk and blues LPs (cont)
Sat R 50:86 F 25; 54 D 30 '67
COHN, Morris M.
In an emergency, call a contractor. Am City
82:84-5 Ag '67
COHN, Victor
(ed) See Wright, P. M. Medicine today
COHO fishing. See Salmon fishing
COIFFURE. See Hairdressing
COILS, Electric. See Electric coils
COILS, Radio. See Radio coils
COIN collecting. See Numismatics
COINAGE. See Coins
COINS
Canada's switch to nickel coins. U S News
62:101 Je 19 '67
Coin quiz. C. French. See issues of Hobbies
Heraldic terms help identify foreign coins.
C. French. Hobbies 72:102 D '67
Numismatics. C. French. See issues of Hobbies
Sweden's coinage. C. French. Hobbies 72:
102 My '67

Collectors and collecting
See Numismatics
COIT, Margaret L.
Holding fortress America. Sat R 50:25-6 D 9
'67
November 22, 1963. Sat R 50:30-1 Ap 15 '67
Winds of change are bitter. Sat R 50:64+
Je 10 '67
COKES, Curtis
Gypsy Joe: fire and music and miniculture.
M. Kram. il Sports Illus 26:77-9 Ap 10 '67
COLACINO, Dick
On the boards. W. Como. por Dance Mag
41:24 O '67
COLBORNE, James B.
How to get more for your old car. Pop
Mech 127:130-3+ Ap '67
COLBURN, D. S. and others
Diamagnetic solar-wind cavity discovered
behind moon. bibliog Science 158:1040-2 N 24
'67
COLBURN, Edwin B.
Wilson company changes. Wilson Lib Bul
41:661-2 Mr '67
COLBY, Carroll B.
Camping. See issues of Outdoor life
COLCHICINE
Human polymorphonuclear leukocytes: de-
monstration of microtubules and effect of
colchicine. S. E. Malawista and K. G.
Bensch. bibliog il Science 156:521-2 Ap 28
'67
Making elms compatible. il Time 90:91 O 6
'67
COLD
See also
Low temperature research
Physiological effects
Time measurement in insect photoperiodism:
reversal of a photoperiodic effect by chill-
ing. D. S. Saunders. bibliog il Science 156:
1126-7 My 26 '67
What you should know about winter health
care. il Pop Gard 18:50-1 Mr '67
Therapeutic applications
Icy cure; cryotherapy used for herpetic
keratitis. Time 90:44 Jl 21 '67
See also
Cryogenic surgery

COLD (disease)
How to cope with children's colds. A. Kerr.
McCalls 95:56+ O '67
I prescribe for coughs and colds. J. D.
Wassersug. il Sci Digest 61:67-71 Mr '67
Protect your family against colds. G. Nicholas.
il Suc Farm 65:103+ F '67
When sniffles can be beautiful; Contac, cold
remedy by Menley & James division of
Smith, Kline & French. il Bsns W p69-70+
Ja 14 '67
COLD drinks. See Beverages
COLD flour beetles. See Flour beetles
COLD frames
Winter color in your coldframe. M. Hellein-
er. il Horticulture 45:25-6 N '67
COLD soups. See Soups
COLD treatment of steel. See Steel—Cold
working
COLD viruses
More cold viruses. Sci N 91:472 My 20 '67
COLD war. See World politics, 1945-
COLD war (United States and Russia) See
United States—Foreign relations—Russia
COLD wax batik. See Batik
COLD weather
Brrr! coldest weather in forty years. il
Newsweek 71:23 Ja 22 '68
Speaking of weather; some like it cold;
International Falls, Minn. J. P. Blank. il
Look 31:44+ Mr 7 '67
COLD weather clothing. See Clothing, Cold
weather
COLDFRAMES. See Cold frames
COLDS. See Cold (disease)
COLE, Mrs Amedee J.
Plant your color. House B 109:174-5 My '67
COLE, Charles J. and others
Sex chromosomes in lizards. bibliog Science
155:1028-9 F 24 '67
COLE, Edward Nicholas
GM: test for a new team. por Newsweek
70:83 N 13 '67
G.M.'s new line-up. il por Time 90:93 N 10 '67
New leaders for a mammoth corporation. por
U S News 63:19 N 13 '67
COLE, Fred C.
New CLR president. ALA Bul 61:788 Jl '67
COLE, Jack
Reflections on a Broadway flop. R. Estrada.
il pors Dance Mag 42:58-61 Ja '68
COLE, LaMont C.
Oxygen crisis. Newsweek 71:45 Ja 8 '68
COLE, Mary
Summer in the city. Cath World 205:223-30
Jl '67
COLE, Sally M.
Cooking with corn syrup. Am Home 70:116d
Ja '67
COLE, Truman R. Jr
Prime consideration. Flying 80:92 Ap '67
COLEAN, Miles
Should you buy, build, or rent now? House
B 109:122+ F '67
COLEMAN, Denny
Ornette Coleman: father and son. M. Wil-
liams. Sat R 50:45 Jl 29 '67
COLEMAN, Douglas Leonard
Hope from diabetic mice. il Sci N 92:154
Ag 12 '67
COLEMAN, Earl
Model of a sage man; story. Esquire 69:77
Ja '68
COLEMAN, Elliott
From Rose Demonics; poem. Poetry 109:237-40
Ja '67
Line of light. Poetry 110:416-19 S '67
Montale; the longest glow, the longest shad-
ows. Poetry 109:268-70 Ja '67
COLEMAN, James S.
Controversial report on education; what it
really means. por U S News 63:44-5 D 25
'67
Games: new tools for learning. por Sr Schol
91:sup9 N 9 '67
(ed) Games in the classroom. Sr Schol 91:
sup3+ N 9 '67
COLEMAN, Kenneth
Savannah, Georgia's port city. Antiques 91:
322-3 Mr '67
COLEMAN, Ornette
Four lives in the bebop business, by A. B.
Spellman. Review
Nation 204:378-9 Mr 20 '67. B. Kremen
Jazz concerts; quartet and the Philadelphia
woodwind quintet at the Village theatre.
W. Balliett. New Yorker 43:125-6 Mr 25 '67
Ornette Coleman: father and son. M. Wil-
liams. Sat R 50:45 Jl 29 '67

COLEMAN, Sheldon
  Businessman looks at the business of pleasure; address, October 31, 1966. por Am For 73:18-21+ Ja '67
COLEMAN, Terry
  Aberfan; happiness ended last October. Sat Eve Post 240:91-5 O 21 '67
  Stay tuned for the princess. Sat Eve Post 240:28-9 D 16 '67
COLEMAN company
  Smooth way to rough it. H. Shuldiner. il Pop Sci 191:148-51 Jl '67
COLEMAN'S scouts. See United States—History—Civil war—Secret service—Confederate States
COLEOPTILES
  Separation of transit of auxin from uptake: average velocity and reversible inhibition by anaerobic conditions. M. H. M. Goldsmith. bibliog il Science 156:661-3 My 5 '67
COLES, Christie Lund
  Gentle years; poem. Ladies Home J 84:165 Mr '67
COLES, Robert
  Bernanos: the writer as child. New Repub 156:23-7 Ap 15 '67
  Children of the American ghetto. Harper 235:16+ S '67
  Civil rights is also a state of mind. N Y Times Mag p32-4+ My 7 '67
  Danilo Dolci: the politics of grace. New Repub 157:23-6 Ag 19 '67
  Drugs: flying high or low. Yale R 57:38-46 O '67
  Hero of our time. New Repub 156:23-4 Mr 4 '67
  In the name of education. Sat R 50:90 My 20 '67
  Knut Hamsun: the beginning and the end. New Repub 157:21-4 S 23 '67
  Letter killeth. New Repub 157:19-23 N 4 '67
  Life's madness. New Repub 156:24-8+ My 13 '67
  Maddox of Georgia. New Repub 157:19-22 Ag 5 '67
  Maybe God will come and clean up this mess. Atlan 220:103-6 O '67
  Mississippi frontier. New Repub 157:41-2+ N 11 '67
  More on southern politics. New Repub 157:20-3 D 16 '67
  Stripped bare at the follies. New Repub 158:18+ Ja 20 '68
  When the southern Negro moves North. N Y Times Mag p25-7+ S 17 '67
  White pieties and black reality. Sat R 50:57-9+ D 16 '67
  Who's to be born? New Repub 156:10-12 Je 10 '67
COLGATE, Stirling A.
  Tornadoes: mechanism and control. bibliog Science 157:1431-4 S 22 '67
COLGATE-Rochester divinity school
  Suggestions for seminaries. America 116:617 Ap 29 '67
COLGATE university, Hamilton, N.Y.
  Colgate's high school high ability seminars. J. E. Rexine. il Sch & Soc 95:316-18 Sum '67
COLGRASS, Michael
  Music to my ears; E. Leinsdorf's performance of As quiet as. I. Kolodin. Sat R 50:41 Mr 18 '67
COLIAS eurytheme. See Butterflies
COLIC
  Q's and A's about colic. D. Kligler. il Parents Mag 42:44-5+ My '67
COLIMORE, Benjamin
  World soul on film: the fifth New York film festival. Cath World 206:171-5 Ja '68
COLIN, Ralph F.
  Editor's letters (cont) Art N 65:6 Ja '67
COLINVAUX, Paul A.
  Bering land bridge: evidence of spruce in late-Wisconsin times. bibliog Science 156:380-3 Ap 21 '67
COLISTRO, James
  On the boards. W. Como. por Dance Mag 41:16 Jl '67
COLITIS
  Secret of caring for the patient; ulcerative colitis; ed. by W. S. Ross. M. J. Lepore. il Todays Health 45:38-42+ N '67
COLLABORATION with the enemy. See Treason
COLLADO, Emilio G.
  Toward a more productive dialogue. Sat R 51:62 Ja 13 '68
COLLAGE
  Action from the gluepot; work of Marca-Relli. il Time 90:76-7 O 20 '67

Art: boxes of J. Cornell. M. Kozloff. Nation 204:701-2 My 29 '67
Black persephone; R. Bearden's painted collages. R. Pomeroy. il Art N 66:44-5+ O '67
Contemporary craftsman and fabric collage. M. R. Papas. il Sch Arts 66:11-14 Ap '67
Content as combination; S. Gablik's collage-paintings. J. Russell. il Art N 66:52-3+ O '67
Cornell: the cube root of dreams; show of boxes and collages at the Guggenheim. J. Ashbery. il Art N 66:56-9+ Sum '67
Figure in the center; work of Marca-Relli. E. Mandelbaum. il Art N 66:58-9+ S '67
Imagined universe stored in boxes; J. Cornell's boxes; with report by D. Bourdon. il Life 63:52-61 D 15 '67
Paradise regained; exhibition of boxes at New York's Guggenheim museum. J. Kroll. il Newsweek 69:86 Je 5 '67
What's on my mind? a three-dimensional collage structure. E. G. Rice and B. Rice. il Sch Arts 66:5-11 Mr '67
COLLAGEN
Collagen-derived membrane: corneal implantation. M. W. Dunn and others. bibliog Science 157:1329-30 S 15 '67
Collagen-like fragments: excretion in urine of patients with Paget's disease of bone. S. M. Krane and others. bibliog il Science 157:713-16 Ag 11 '67
Collagen proline hydroxylase in wound healing, granuloma formation, scurvy, and growth. E. Mussini and others. bibliog il Science 157:927-9 Ag 25 '67
Collagen synthesis by cells synchronously replicating DNA. L. M. Davies and others. bibliog il Science 159:91-3 Ja 5 '68
Corneas from calf skin. Time 89:68+ Ap 28 '67
Fever chart for fossils; analysis of collagen to calculate temperatures of extinct species. Time 90:32+ S 8 '67
Human collagenase: identification and characterization of an enzyme from rheumatoid synovium in culture. J. M. Evanson and others. bibliog il Science 158:499-502 O 27 '67
Intracellular pool of unhydroxylated polypeptide precursors of collagen. R. S. Bhatnagar and others. bibliog il Science 158:492-4 O 27 '67
COLLAGEN-coated cellulose sponges. See Sponges, Artificial
COLLE, Royal D.
Color on TV. Reporter 37:23-5 N 30 '67
COLLECTING. See Collectors and collecting
COLLECTION of blood. See Blood—Collection and preservation
COLLECTIVE bargaining
Bargaining hurdles that are still ahead; trucking settlement boosts demands in other industries. il Bsns W p 160+ Ap 22 '67
Big labor's pitch at the bargaining table; wage negotiation manifesto of AFL-CIO. il Nations Bsns 55:42-3+ My '67
Collective bargaining on the farm. Mo Labor R 90:III-IV Je '67
Creative unionism; address. September 20, 1967. I. Stern. Vital Speeches 34:157-60 D 15 '67
Divide and conquer isn't so easy. Bsns W p59-60 Je 10 '67
How to avoid the picket lines; voluntary arbitration. Bsns W p83 O 21 '67
Libraries and labor unions. K. Nyren. il Library J 92:2115-21 Je 1 '67
Mr Kheel's defense of strikes. B. L. Masse. America 117:431 O 21 '67
More strikes, more inflation: collision course on the labor front. A. H. Raskin. Sat R 50:32-5+ F 25 '67
More tough talk in bargaining; 1968 negotiations, with charts. Bsns W p56-9 D 30 '67
Other employees in the school: nonteacher bargaining; excerpt from Teachers, administrators, and collective bargaining. E. B. Shils and C. T. Whittier. Mo Labor R 90:42-4 S '67
Public looks at labor. E. D. Canham. Duns R 89:81+ Ja '67
Rank and file flexes its muscle; reject negotiated settlements for heftier contracts. Bsns W p61-2 S 9 '67
Trade-off becomes the word. B. L. Masse. America 116:520 Ap 8 '67
Trend to autonomy in collective bargaining. M. A. Kelly. Mo Labor R 90:24-5 F '67

COLLECTIVE bargaining—*Continued*
Who wins a strike? I. Ross. Read Digest 91:
101-5 Ag '67
Why we're having strikes. **J. W. Keener.** il
Duns R 90:50-1 D '67
See also
National railway labor conference
Trade agreements
Trade unions

Automobile Industry
Bargaining without a bludgeon; UAW and
GM. il Bsns W p42-3 D 9 '67
Big one begins; auto industry and UAW
negotiations. il Bsns W p29-30 Jl 15 '67
Shape of the salary plan; UAW guaranteed
annual salary scheme. il Bsns W p 102-3 Jl
29 '67
UAW opens act II; negotiations with Chrys-
ler and GM. Bsns W p31 N 4 '67

Paper Industry
Crossfire catches paper companies; contract
negotiations held up. il Bsns W p 118+ F
4 '67

Steel Industry
Better way than strikes? an idea that is
growing: with excerpts from address by
R. C. Cooper. U S News 63:109-12 N 27 '67
Free collective bargaining; address, March 10,
1967. B. D. Billman. Vital Speeches 33:631-5
Ag 1 '67
Steel prospects harden; future bargaining.
Bsns W p 136 D 9 '67

Teachers
Professor and collective negotiations. J. F.
Day and W. H. Fisher. bibliog f Sch & Soc
95:226-9 Ap 1 '67
Teacher-Board of ed. contract talks; National institute on collective negotiations in
public education conferences. Sr Schol 91:
sup4 O 12 '67

COLLECTIVE bargaining, Industry wide
Bigger guns for bargaining wars; coordinated
multi-group teams vs offensive lockout. Bsns
W p49-50 Ag 12 '67
R. Conrad Cooper speaks his mind; blames
union misuse of power. il Bsns W p 152+
O 7 '67

COLLECTIVE farms

Hungary
Best collective in Hungary: the Lenin farm.
D. Binder. il N Y Times Mag p32-3+ Mr
12 '67

COLLECTIVE settlements
See also
Shakers

Israel
I fell in love with kibbutzniks; Ramat ha
Shofet. S. Lo Bello. il Seventeen 26:136-7+
Mr '67

COLLECTIVISM
See also
Individualism

COLLECTOR of innocents; story. See Auchincloss, L.

COLLECTORS and collecting
Antiques' travel guide. See issues of Antiques
Collections make vacation memories. E. C.
Robinson. Am Home 70:118 Jl '67
Collector's collector. il House B 109:130-3
Mr '67
Collectors' notes; ed. by E. Gaines. See is-
sues of Antiques
Confessions of a trivialist. S. Rosenberg. il
Life 62:66-8+ F 24 '67
Don't throw that away! somebody collects
it. Changing T 21:45-6 Jl '67
Is your collection showing? il Bet Hom &
Gard 45:44 F '67
They live as they like; C. and R. Di Rosa.
il House & Gard 131:140-7 Mr '67
Today's trivia, tomorrow's..? B. La Fontaine.
il N Y Times Mag p82+ D 3 '67
Treasure hunt. J. Mebane. See issues of Bet-
ter homes and gardens
See also
Art—Private collections
Book collecting
also subheads Collection and preserva-
tion, or Collectors and collecting under
various subjects, e.g. Insects—Collection
and preservation; *also* names of articles collected e.g. Miniature objects

COLLEEN Moore doll house. See Doll houses

COLLEGE, Choice of
College & careers. D. Klein. See issues of
Seventeen
College of whose choice? E. J. Brown. il Par-
ents Mag 42:40-1+ D '67

College of whose choice? J. Cass. Sat R 50:
69 N 18 '67
In my opinion; maybe you shouldn't go away
to college. C. L. Craven. Seventeen 26:140
Jl '67
Still time to get into a good college. B. Fine.
Harper 234:50-4 Ap '67
What the college catalogues won't tell you:
a student's-eye view of American cam-
puses. il McCalls 94:100-1 Mr '67
Where is the ivy greenest? D. Klein. il
Seventeen 26:152-3+ N '67
Where to get bad advice about college; high
school guidance counselor. J. F. Scott. il
Ladies Home J 84:76+ N '67
Which personality succeeds in college? D.
Klein. il Seventeen 26:148-9+ My '67
See also
College admissions center, Evanston, Ill.

COLLEGE administration. See Colleges and
universities—Administration

COLLEGE administrators. See College officials

COLLEGE admission. See Colleges and universities—Entrance requirements

COLLEGE admissions center, Evanston, Ill.
Data on college vacancies; program con-
ducted by educational service bureau in
Illinois. Sch & Soc 95:7 Ja 7 '67

COLLEGE alumni. See College graduates

COLLEGE and school drama
New approaches to teaching drama; sympo-
sium. il Sr Schol 90:sup7-8+ Mr 17 '67
Teaching aid: live drama. Sr Schol 90:sup2
Mr 17 '67
Thriving youth theater; Cleveland Heights-
University Heights city school district. L.
Freyman. il NEA J 57:26-7 Ja '68
See also
College theater

Texts
Junior and senior high. See issues of Plays

COLLEGE and school journalism
Freedom of the high school press? M. Bene-
dict. NEA J 56:64-6 D '67
Freedom underground; unauthorized papers
of high school students. il Time 89:65 Mr
31 '67
Middle of the journey. R. Kirk. Nat R 19:857
Ag 8 '67
New candor, j.g. il Newsweek 70:66-7 D 25 '67
To make a university great; prescription of-
fered by Fordham's student newspaper, the
Ram. F. Canavan. America 117:57-60 Jl 15
'67; Discussion. 117:141-2, 230+ Ag 12, S
9 '67
Word gets out. M. Lydon. Esquire 68:106-7+
S '67
See also
Campus courier

COLLEGE and the community. See Colleges
and universities—Public relations

COLLEGE aptitude tests. See Aptitude tests

COLLEGE architecture
Albany: New York state university center
on the way up. B. Nelson. il Science 155:
1521-5 Mr 24 '67; Reply. R. F. Creegan.
156:893 My 19 '67
Architecture on the campus; symposium. il
Arch Forum 127:46-75+ Jl '67
Building to walk through. il Arch Forum
127:60-3 O '67
Building types study (cont) il Arch Rec 141:
185-212 Ap '67
Campus boom: a new college a week. il Newsweek 69:65-73 F 20 '67; Same abr. with
title New college a week. Read Digest 90:
161-4 Je '67
Harvard completes a course in urban design.
D. Canty. il Arch Forum 126:64-77 Ja '67
Nine community colleges. il Arch Rec 142:
155-71 N '67
Something new in college campuses; State
university of New York at Albany. il U S
News 63:54-6 S 4 '67
Structure and form express the three-way
function of this office building; Fisher ad-
ministrative center, University of Detroit.
il Arch Rec 142:109-14 Jl '67
$28-billion program for the class of '77. T.
O'Hanlon. il Fortune 76:155-61 O '67
See also
Dormitories
Gymnasiums

COLLEGE art galleries. See Art—Galleries and
museums

COLLEGE athlete recruiting. See Athletes—
Recruiting

COLLEGE athletics
Fighting Illini; slush fund for football and
basketball players at University of Illinois. D. Jenkins. il Sports Illus 26:16-19 Mr
6 '67

COLLEGE athletics—*Continued*
Fumbled ball; address, December 1, 1966. A. Brundage. Vital Speeches 33:411-16 Ap 15 '67
This year the fight will be in the open; importance of national rankings. D. Jenkins. il Sports Illus 27:28-52+ S 11 '67
See also
Basketball
Football
Wrestling

COLLEGE attendance. See Colleges and universities—Attendance

COLLEGE bookstores
Berkeley backlash comes to Midwest U; new policy on quantity of textbooks to be ordered. R. H. Smith. Pub W 191:55 Mr 6 '67
Bomb blast rocks bookstore at University of Chicago. Pub W 191:50 My 1 '67
Bookselling in a two-year college; Corning community college, N.Y. P. Johnson, jr. il Pub W 192:46-8 D 25 '67
Cafeteria now bookstore at University of Florida. J. Solomon. il Pub W 192:68-9 N 13 '67
CIA subsidized college bookstore co-op. Pub W 191:48 Mr 6 '67
College store and the trade book. P. Johnson. il Pub W 191:46-8 F 13 '67
College stores cannot afford to give rebates on books. Pub W 191:66 Mr 6 '67
Data processing can save money. G. Lee il Pub W 191:52-4 Mr 20 '67
For a growing campus; Santa Barbara bookstore. J. Goldstein. il Pub W 192:56-8 S 18 '67
Harvard coop's expansion means progress and growth. il Pub W 192:46-8 O 2 '67
Illinois bill restricts merchandise in college stores. Pub W 191:36-7 My 8 '67
Johns Hopkins' book center. P. Johnson, jr. il Pub W 191:56-8 My 22 '67
NACS, Chicago publishers, oppose college store bill. Pub W 191:34 Je 12 '67
NACS plans for expansion in growing market; annual convention. il Pub W 191:24-39 My 22 '67
One-third of the sales, 85 per cent of the paperwork; survey at Yale co-op. R. H. Smith. Pub W 192:36 Ag 7 '67
Presses and the college stores; summary of discussions at AAUP annual meeting. Pub W 192:30-1 Jl 3 '67
Separate stores at Univ. of Toronto. il Pub W 192:50-2 Jl 3 '67
Vote postponed on college store bill. Pub W 191:60 Je 19 '67
See also
National association of college stores

COLLEGE buildings. See College architecture

COLLEGE business managers. See College officials

COLLEGE catalogs

Anecdotes, facetiae, satire, etc.
Spring bulletin. W. Allen. New Yorker 43:38-9 Ap 29 '67

COLLEGE catering. See Caterers and catering

COLLEGE counselors. See Personnel service in education

COLLEGE courses. See Colleges and universities—Curriculum

COLLEGE discipline
College crime, and punishment. J. Steinberg. Mlle 65:316+ Ag '67
Crackdown starts on student riots; with interview with J. H. Reinoehl. il U S News 64:34-7 Ja 1 '68
Tough line on protests. il Sat R 50:69 D 16 '67

COLLEGE dormitories. See Dormitories

COLLEGE dropouts. See Dropouts

COLLEGE education
Campus corner. M. P. Sheridan. America 116:877 Je 24 '67
End the grading system? education chief urges change; excerpts from address, August 22, 1967. H. Howe, 2d. U S News 63:14 S 4 '67
Higher education and the computer. J. Caffrey. il NEA J 56:30-2 F '67
Technology in higher education: the winds of change blow stronger; report of conference sponsored by the American educational publishers institute. il Pub W 193:35-8 Ja 8 '68
What's going on in schools & colleges. See issues of Changing times
See also
Coeducation
Colleges and universities—Curriculum
Colleges and universities—Teaching
Junior colleges
Liberal education
Technical education

Aims and objectives
Modern university: concerns for the future. S. B. Gould. Science 155:1511-14 Mr 24 '67
Responsibility of colleges and universities; address, October 29, 1966. R. H. Wick. Vital Speeches 33:240-4 F 1 '67
Time to serve; adaptation of address, September 18, 1966. R. F. Goheen. Sch & Soc 95:296-8 Sum '67
Unity in a university: the two cultures; address, April 25, 1967. C. M. Allen Vital Speeches 33:730-4 S 15 '67
University: an intellectual community; address, March 17, 1967. R. M. Hutchins. vital Speeches 33:475-8 My 15 '67
University and the multiversity; adaptation of address. R. M. Hutchins. New Repub 156:15-17 Ap 1 '67

COLLEGE education, Cost of
Building a college fund. Changing T 21:48-inside back cover S '67
College: what it costs, how to pay for it. il Changing T 21:7-13 S '67
Educational loans. R. C. Jancauskas. America 116:440-1+ Mr 25 67
Financing a college education; address, February 4, 1967. J. W. Barr. Vital Speeches 33:348-52 Mr 15 '67
Getting into college in '67: the cost, the problems. il U S News 62:60-2 F 13 '67
How much should you save to send your child to college? P. Lindberg. Bet Hom & Gard 45:6 Ag '67
Paying for college, price goes up and up. il U S News 62:80 Ap 10 '67
Tuition and educational hierarchy in California. R. Kirk. Nat R 19:421 Ap 18 '67
Who should pay for higher education? P. Woodring. Sat R 50:71 My 20 '67

COLLEGE education, Value of
Should every youngster go to college? J. M. Lynch, jr. il Parents Mag 42:46-7+ Mr '67
University: power and innocence. P. Schrag. Sat R 50:68-9+ O 21 '67

COLLEGE enrollment. See Colleges and universities—Attendance

COLLEGE entrance requirements. See Colleges and universities—Entrance requirements

COLLEGE faculties. See College professors and instructors

COLLEGE fees. See Colleges and universities—Finance

COLLEGE football. See Football

COLLEGE fraternities
Intellectual work in fraternities. Sch & Soc 95:282+ Sum '67
See also
Sigma delta chi

COLLEGE freshmen. See College students

COLLEGE graduates
After graduation, a job in New York? A. Grant. il Mlle 65:144-5+ Je '67
Bidding for brains; competitive college-recruiting by business. il Time 90:82 Jl 14 '67
Class of '67; the gentle desperadoes; symposium. il Nation 204:775-81 Je 19 '67
Eggheads with the beer; alumni reunions. il Time 89:76 Je 16 '67
Job market for class of '67: more openings, better pay. il U S News 62:77-8 Mr 6 '67
Jobs for college grads; with list of occupations, salaries and information sources. il Ebony 22:81-2+ Je '67
Most frenzied year in history; rush by business to sign up graduates. il Bsns W p54-6+ Ap 8 '67
Old Boys' dinner; the English institution contrasted with American class reunions. A. Waugh. Nat R 19:750 Jl 11 '67

COLLEGE graduates, Women
Career expectations of Negro women graduates; excerpt from report. J. H. Fichter. bibliog f il Mo Labor R 90:36-42 N '67
Women college graduates seven years later. J. A. Wells. il Mo Labor R 90:28-32 Jl '67

COLLEGE librarians. See Librarians

COLLEGE libraries
Fancy gothic fiction; adaptation of remarks, December 2, 1966. J. W. Gardner. Library J 92:1896-7 My 15 '67
Gloomy conclusion? surveying Australian university libraries. H. Bryan. bibliog il Library J 92:4113-16 N 15 '67
Junior college libraries: development, needs, and perspectives; preconference. R. Christensen. ALA Bul 61:830-1 Jl '67
Libraries of the future for the liberal arts college; faculty vs. librarians. R. T. Jordan. il Library J 92:537-9 F 1 '67; Correction. 92:1096 Mr 15 '67; Reply. L. Hubbard. 92:1392 Ap 1 '67

COLLEGE libraries—*Continued*
Lighting and ventilation; adaptation of address, May 16, 1966. E. Mason. il Library J 92:201-6 Ja 15 '67
Overloaded bandwagon. R. Z. Sellers. il Wilson Lib Bul 41:915-19 My '67
Stress and strain in academic librarianship; adaptation of address, October 1967. G. R. Lyle. bibliog Library J 93:158-61 Ja 15 '68
University social role: report omits libraries. Library J 92:4458 D 15 '67
Well-wrought interior design; adaptation of address, May 16, 1966. E. Mason. il Library J 92:743-7 F 15 '67

Administration
See Library administration

Architecture
See Library architecture

Automation
American automation in action; reprint H. Bryan. bibliog il Library J 92:189-96 Ja 15 '67

Anecdotes, facetiae, satire, etc.
Trial by computer; excerpts from address, April 1967. B. Stuart-Stubbs. il Library J 92:4471-4 D 15 '67

Book selection
See Book selection

Cooperation
New England state university libraries' regional processing center. D. E. Vincent. ALA Bul 61:672-3 Je '67

Finance
$24.5 million for college library materials, HEA Title II-grant A allocations. Pub W 192:48-9 Jl 17 '67

Foreign language collections
Latin American collection; adaptation of address, June 1967. C. Dearnaley and P. Bixler. Wilson Lib Bul 42:417-21 D '67

Moving picture collections
Films for the community college library. H. Wheeler. Wilson Lib Bul 42:411-14 D '67

Reference work
College reference librarian and the faculty. D. J. Smith. il Library J 92:1588-92 Ap 15 '67

Science collections
Examination of methods used in a study of decision-making; science library materials. M. B. Snyder. il ALA Bul 61:1319-23 D '67

Statistics
Academic library building in 1967. J. Orne. il Library J 92:4345-50 D 1 '67

COLLEGE libraries and research. See Libraries and research

COLLEGE libraries and state
Library materials grants to colleges tripled. Library J 92:2863+ S 1 '67

COLLEGE library architecture. See Library architecture

COLLEGE life. See Student life

COLLEGE loyalty oaths. See Loyalty, Oaths of

COLLEGE museums
Boom in U.S. university museums; with editorial comment. E. Bryant. il Art N 66:25, 30-47+ S '67

COLLEGE of cardinals. See Cardinals

COLLEGE of physicians and surgeons, Columbia university. See Columbia university—College of physicians and surgeons

COLLEGE officials
College business managers. Sch & Soc 95:212-13 Ap 1 '67
Unknown rulers; state-university regents. il Time 89:52 My 12 '67
See also
College presidents

COLLEGE operas, revues, etc.
Bloomington; Indiana university opera theater productions. W. Mootz. Opera N 31:32 F 25; 32:22 S 23 '67
Chicago; production of Peri's Euridice by the University of Chicago's Collegium musicum. G. McElroy. Opera N 31:33 Mr 25 '67
Does L.A. want opera? H. Stevens. il Hi Fi 17:MA22+ F '67
Report: Cincinnati; production of Borodin's Prince Igor. W. Mootz. il Opera N 32:30 Ja 6 '68

Report: Los Angeles; U.S.C. opera theater production of Berg's Wozzeck. A. Goldberg. Opera N 32:31 Ja 20 '68
Report: New York; Brooklyn college opera theater performances of Der freischütz. A. M. Lingg. Opera N 32:30 Ja 20 '68
Report: New York; Brooklyn college opera theater presentation of Antonio Salieri's Prima la musica poi le parole and world premiere of Thomas Pasatieri's Padrevia. A. M. Lingg. il Opera N 32:30 D 23 '67
Singing in the plains; University of Illinois Opera group. J. W. Stedman. il Opera N 31:29-31 F 25 '67

COLLEGE presidents
Picking presidents; internship program sponsored by the American council on education. il Time 90:88 N 24 '67
Pursuit of presidents. il Time 89:74 Ap 14 '67
Salesman, philosopher, riot preventer. A. Hacker. il N Y Times Mag p26-7+ My 7 '67
University presidency, 1966. Sch & Soc 95:27 Ja 7 '67
Visit to Tuscaloosa. N. Cousins. Sat R 50:20+ My 27 '67

COLLEGE professors and instructors
College reference librarian and the faculty. D. J. Smith. il Library J 92:1588-9 Ap 15 '67
Inducting graduate students into college training. J. R. Egner and D. R. Pierce. bibliog f Sch & Soc 95:55-6 Ja 21 '67
Is there a statute of limitations on justice? J. Chamberlain. Nat R 19:1257-8 N 14 '67
Laicization of Catholic colleges. A. M. Greeley. Christian Cent 84:372-5 Mr 22 '67
Layman in Catholic higher education. J. P. Leary. America 116:251-3 F 18 '67
Life of Professor Riley. M. Mayer. Harper 235:88-9 O '67
Malcontent professors. I. Kristol. Fortune 76:229-30 D '67; Reply with rejoinder. C. Leinenweber. 77:121 Ja '68
Nineteen-year-old professor teaches philosophy at Stanford university. il Life 63:111-12 O 27 '67
Scholars and soldiers, a crisis of values. M. Windmiller. Nation 205:651-4 D 18 '67
TA; teaching assistants. il Newsweek 70:50 O 30 '67
Theological ferment in Canada? J. A. Davidson. Christian Cent 84:900-2 Jl 12 '67
Time to leave the house; physicist Rabi leaves Columbia university. il Time 89:46+ My 26 '67
Unionizing the academics. J. Brann. New Repub 156:10-11 F 25 '67
See also
Academic freedom
Colleges and universities—Teaching
Teachers and students
Women as college professors and instructors

Anecdotes, facetiae, satire, etc.
Up the Ivy, by A. Mentor. Review
Nat R 19:1343-4 N 28 '67. T. Day

Education
Intern program for college teachers. A. N. Gilbert. il Sch & Soc 95:417-20 N 11 '67

Leaves of absence
Constructive use of faculty mobility; new guidelines concerning sabbatical and special leaves. R. H. Farber. Sch & Soc 95:183 Mr 18 '67

Pensions
See also
Carnegie foundation for the advancement of teaching

Political activities
Guerrilla war on the campus; reprisals against activators. New Repub 156:6-7 My 20 '67
Point of view; address, December 13, 1967. J. W. Fulbright. Science 158:1555 D 22 '67

Rating
Best minds in higher education. A. J. Dibden. Sch & Soc 95:83-4 F 4 '67

Salaries
AAUP report on 1966-67 salary survey. il Science 156:1072 My 26 '67
End of living endowment? re-examination of policy in U.S. Catholic universities. America 116:269 F 25 '67
Soaring salaries. il Time 89:58 Mr 10 '67

COLLEGE professors and instructors—*Cont.*

Selection and appointment

Dissent threshold; Chicago state college denies teaching job to historian. il Newsweek 70:46-7 Jl 31 '67

Supply and demand

Faculty recruitment; science and engineering. D. Wolfle. Science 157:1125 S 8 '67

Harvard: beginning to worry about maintaining its faculty. B. Nelson. Science 156:922-5 My 19 '67

COLLEGE readiness. See Readiness for learning

COLLEGE recruiting. See Employment systems

COLLEGE reports and records

Students' records: ACE calls for confidentiality. E. Langer. Science 157:525 Ag 4 '67

Students' rights; they should have more, establishment agrees. E. Langer. Science 157:524-6 Ag 4 '67

COLLEGE reunions. See College graduates

COLLEGE slang. See Slang

COLLEGE sports. See College athletics

COLLEGE statistics. See Colleges and universities—Statistics

COLLEGE stores association. See National association of college stores

COLLEGE student activities. See Student activities

COLLEGE student forums. See Forums (discussion and debate)

COLLEGE students

Activism among college students. W. W. Brickman. Sch & Soc 95:4 Ja 7 '67

Annual attempt to bridge the generation gap. A. Gingrich. Esquire 68:6+ S '67

Be like me! be free! J. G. Milhaven. America 116:584-6 Ap 22 '67; Discussion. 116:784-90 My 27 '67

Campus turmoil: a religious dimension. T. A. Langford. Christian Cent 84:172-4 F 8 '67

Chorus of whimpers; campus revolts on the wane. Time 89:39 Ap 7 '67

Clark Kerr calls it the exaggerated generation. C. Kerr. il N Y Times Mag p28-9+ Je 4 '67

Class of '67: the gentle desperadoes; symposium. il Nation 204:775-81 Je 19 '67

College freshmen 1966; findings from questionnaire survey. America 116:137 Ja 28 '67

Convenient myths: today's students; address, May 19, 1967. A. C. Sherriffs. Vital Speeches 33:669-72 Ag 15 '67

Drugs on campus: a Gallup poll. F. Dickenson. Read Digest 91:114-15 N '67

Drugs on the campus. J. Shepherd. il Look 31:14 Ag 8 '67

Drugs on campus; underground agents at Cornell and Fairleigh Dickinson universities. il Time 89:36+ Mr 24 '67

Editor's bookshelf; concerning books by Nevitt Sanford and Mervin B. Freedman. P. Woodring. il Sat R 50:65-6 Ag 19 '67

Education of wombats. P. West. Commonweal 87:143-6 N 3 '67

Five college students speak out; questions and answers, ed. by L. F. McKernan; discussion. Cath World 205:134-8 Je '67

Freshman profile. il Sch & Soc 95:149-50 Mr 4 '67

Friendly grasp of hand to junior college transferees. R. L. Loughlin. bibliog f Sch & Soc 95:352 O 14 '67

From where I sit; college students and the generational gap. E. Raushenbush. Mlle 66:61+ Ja '68

Grinding in English, unwinding in Arabic. G. Buckman. il Mlle 64:148-9+ F '67

Life in the pressure cooker. il Newsweek 69:82-4 Ap 3 '67

Of many things; exaggerated picture of sexual indulgence. J. McLaughlin. America 117:527 N 11 '67

On the campus: fear and anger; effect of war. il Newsweek 70:87-8+ Jl 10 '67

Open letter to flunk-outs and patriots. Esquire 68:89 S '67

Potted ivy; alienated students smoking marihuana. il Time 89:98+ My 19 '67

Profile of the college freshman. W. W. Brickman. Sch & Soc 95:287 Sum '67

Rights and responsibilities. Sch & Soc 95:247-8 Ap 15 '67

Secretary Rusk redefines United States policy on Viet-Nam for student leaders; text of letter to 100 student leaders, January 4, 1967; with text of students' letter to President Johnson, December 29, 1966. D. Rusk. Dept State Bul 56:133-7 Ja 23, '67; Correction. 56:192 F 6 '67

Sex on campus; a new ethic but not sex for kicks. J. L. Walsh. Commonweal 85:590-1+ F 24 '67

Something to talk about on campus. J. Romer and P. Roth. il Mlle 65:320-3 Ag '67

Sparks from the campus; R. Galvin's corporation-campus dialogue. il Newsweek 69:79+ Ap 3 '67

Speaking out; our students have no utopia. B. G. Gallagher. il Sat Eve Post 240:8+ My 6 '67

Standards of conduct. Sch & Soc 95:244+ Ap 15 '67

To Mr Jovanovich; activist protest in the 'sixties. M. R. Killingsworth. Harper 235:60+ O '67

Turmoil in higher education; interview, ed. by G. B. Leonard and T. G. Harris. C. Kerr. il Look 31:17-21 Ap 18 '67

War on campus; symposium. il Nation 205:645-60 D 18 '67

Who are the activists? E. Van Loon. il Am Ed 4:2-4+ D '67

Who says college kids have changed? G. Moore. il Life 62:90-90B+ My 19 '67

Why a revolt on college campuses; with excerpts from address by S. L. Halleck. il U S News 62:71-5 My 29 '67

Worried about today's young people? il U S News 63:44-6 O 30 '67

See also
Coeducation
College athletics
College fraternities
Foreign students in the United States
Foreign study
German students
Graduate students
Self government in education
Student achievements
Student activities
Student Christian movements
Student demonstrations
Student life
Student unions
Study
Teachers and students
United States national student association
Young Americans for freedom (organization)

Adjustment

Alleviating the college student's anxiety. M. Katahn. NEA J 57:17-18 Ja '68

Beginning in doubt. R. Kirk. Nat R 19:306 Mr 21 '67

College dropout phenomenon. W. Dalrymple. il NEA J 56:11-13 Ap '67

Rebellion and responsibility. B. Rubenstein and M. Levitt. Yale R 57:16-30 O '67

Roots of student despair; reprint. S. L. Halleck. il Sci Digest 62:65-70 S '67

Student anxiety. P. H. Abelson. Science 158:1139 D 1 '67

This way out; slum youngsters choose college; three students at the University of California. A. Allen. il Am Ed 3:2-4+ Jl '67

Touching base with our youth. E. F. McKibbin. Sch & Soc 95:424-5 N 11 '67

Unrest in college. Sch & Soc 95:246-7 Ap 15 '67

What makes freshman year so dangerous? D. Klein. il Seventeen 26:158-9+ S '67

Aid

See Student aid; Student loans; Theological students—Aid

Civil rights

See Students—Civil rights

Communist activities

Campus communism: Latin America's Trojan horse. E. Cárdenas. Read Digest 90:92-6 Je '67

Happening in São Paulo; priests arrested for association with Communist students. G. H. Dunne. America 117:306-9+ S 23 '67

How a campus terrorized a city; Central university in Caracas. Read Digest 90:94-5 Je '67

Dating

See Dating

COLLEGES and universities—_Continued_
University and the multiversity; adaptation of address. R. M. Hutchins. New Repub 156:15-17 Ap 1 '67

See also
Academic freedom
College education
College students
College year
Colleges for women
Free universities
Summer schools
Theological schools
University presses
also names of colleges and universities, e.g. Columbia university; _also_ types of colleges, e.g. Medical colleges

Accreditation
Penalizing Parsons. Newsweek 69:69 Ap 17 '67

Administration
Federal paper-work explosion: new form bothers universities. B. Nelson. Science 156:1468-9 Je 16 '67
Government of colleges and universities. Sch & Soc 95:168-70 Mr 18 '67
Laicization of Catholic colleges. A. M. Greeley. Christian Cent 84:372-5 Mr 22 '67
Megaversity's struggle with itself; running Michigan state. D. Norton-Taylor. il Fortune 75:160-5+ My '67
Modern university: concerns for the future. S. B. Gould. Science 155:1511-14 Mr 24 '67
Pitt picks chancellor: agrees that modesty is the best policy. B. Nelson. il Science 155: 541-4 F 3 '67
Presidential leadership in academe. A. R. Dykes. bibliog f il Sch & Soc 95:223-6 Ap 1 '67
Problem of Catholic U. N. K. Herzfeld. Commonweal 86:39-41 Mr 31 '67
Rebellion and responsibility. B. Rubenstein and M. Levitt. Yale R 57:16-30 O '67
Sharing responsibilities at Catholic universities. America 116:173 F 4 '67
Who should control? Commonweal 85:475-6 F 3 '67
Why a revolt on college campuses: with excerpts from address by S. L. Halleck. il U S News 62:71-5 My 29 '67

See also
College presidents
College trustees
Self government in education

Faculty participation
College faculty participation in academic governance. C. A. Hickman. NEA J 56:46-8 O '67
Faculty participation in college administration. J H. Callan. Sch & Soc 95:121-2 F 18 '67; Reply. J. R. Seeley. 95:414-15 N 11 '67

Student participation
See Self government in education

Admission standards
See Colleges and universities—Entrance requirements

Appraisal
See Evaluation (education)

Art departments
Art schools: Sunday painters versus men of passion. D. Holden. il Am Artist 31:52-3+ Mr '67
Art schools: the charges against the universities. D. Holden. il Am Artist 31:72-3+ Ap '67
Tomorrow's baroque; staff of practicing artists at Manhattan's Hunter college. il Time 89:66 Ap 7 '67

Attendance
College students wanted. Newsweek 70:66 S 18 '67
Statistics of attendance in American universities and colleges, 1966-67. G. G. Parker. il Sch & Soc 95:9-24. 124-5 Ja 7. F 18 '67
U.S. pushes its lead in higher education; student numbers in U.S. and European universities. il U S News 63:84-5 Jl 31 '67

See also
Student selection

Business schools
See Business education

Choice
See College, Choice of

Cooperation
Oceanography: Woods Hole and MIT pool their resources. L. J. Carter. il Science 157:1154-7 S 8 '67
State coordination of higher education Sch & Soc 95:134+ Mr 4 '67
Vassar-Yale match? Sch & Soc 95:280+ Sum '67

Curriculum
Academe's cult of innovation. W. N. Potter. Sch & Soc 95:80-2 F 4 '67
And still the roaring gut; college courses offering easy credits. Time 90:46 D 15 '67
Colleges that are doing new things. Changing T 21:28-9 Ap '67
Curriculum power; student demands for new course offerings. Time 90:50+ S 15 '67
Flexible college curriculum. Sch & Soc 95: 6-7 Ja 7 '67
Life in the pressure cooker. il Newsweek 69: 82-4 Ap 3 '67
Preparatory colleges? Carnegie corporation grant for study of the question. America 116:800 Je 3 '67
Shaking the world with an 8-mm. camera. E. Lester. il N Y Times Mag p44-5+ N 26 '67

See also
Area studies
Free universities
Oriental studies

Desegregation
Civil rights: higher education comes under scrutiny. K. Sperry. Science 157:1293 S 15 '67
Courting the Negro. il Time 89:59 Ap 28 '67
Man in the fish fry parlor; T. Marshall's registration of dozen Negro students at Louisiana state university. W. Rogers. Look 31: 115 O 17 '67
May queens and effigies; Negroes on southern campuses. il Newsweek 69:98+ Je 5 '67
Michigan: ruckus over race has relevance to other universities. B. Nelson. Science 156: 1209-12 Je 2 '67
Tiny Bishop prospers in new soil. il Ebony 22:82-4+ Mr '67

Discipline
See College discipline

Drama departments
See Drama—Study and teaching

Enrollment
See Colleges and universities—Attendance

Entrance requirements
Accepted or rejected? interviews, ed. by D. Klein. C. Vroman; B. M. Clough; R. L. Jackson. il Seventeen 26:134-5+ Mr '67
Admissions and the private college. G. D. Nicoll. Sch & Soc 95:148-9 Mr 4 '67
College entrance mania. S. Kelman. il Life 63:61+ N 24 '67
Getting into college in '67; the cost, the problems. il U S News 62:60-2 F 13 '67
Getting your letter. il Newsweek 69:51 My 1 '67
Internationally recognized university entrance test? Sch & Soc 95:486 D 9 '67
It's easier to get into college: reports from the campus. il U S News 64:56-8 Ja 8 '68
Needed: a university for the C+ student. H. A. Fitzgerald. il Look 32:52 Ja 23 '68
Pretense and honesty in college admissions; excerpts from address, May 11, 1967. E. D. Eddy. Sch & Soc 95:415-17 N 11 '67
Problems of college admission. il Sch & Soc 95:106-7 F 18 '67
Racy correspondence. W. F. Buckley, jr. Nat R 19:1253 N 14 '67
Two decades of Amherst admissions. Sch & Soc 95:344-5 O 14 '67

See also
Student selection

Extension
See University extension

Faculties
See College professors and instructors

Federal aid
See Federal aid to education

Finance
Anxiety behind the façade. il Time 89:78-80+ Je 23 '67; Same abr. with title Can our colleges close the dollar gap? Read Digest 91:85-8 S '67

COLLEGES and universities—*Continued*

Statistics

Higher education, excelsior! Sch & Soc 94:478 D 24 '66
See also
Colleges and universities—Attendance

Teaching

From logs to logistics; excerpts from address, December 9, 1965. J. Seidlin. Sch & Soc 95:420-3 N 11 '67
He liked students; excerpt from the teacher. J. Fischer. NEA J 56:68 D '67
Human learning in a natural setting. Sch & Soc 95:41-2 Ja 21 '67
Innovation in undergraduate teaching. E. M. Williams. bibliog il Science 155:974-9 F 24 '67
Leadership; address, March 7, 1967. M. Tarcher. Vital Speeches 33:404-8 Ap 15 '67
Of students, professors, and computers. C. Fincher. il Sch & Soc 95:144-8 Mr 4 '67
Teaching, research, and academic freedom. J. D. Garwood. Sch & Soc 95:413-14 N 11 '67
What about college teaching? questions and answers. D. Klein. il Seventeen 26:258-9 F '67
See also
College professors and instructors

Trustees

See College trustees

Africa

Today's schools prepare tomorrow's African scientists. N. C. Otieno. il UNESCO Courier 20:33-6 Je '67

Alabama

See also
Alabama. University, Tuscaloosa

Alaska

See also
Alaska Methodist university, Anchorage
Alaska. University

Argentina

Report to the American academic community; excerpt from A report to the American academic community on the present Argentine university situation. Bul Atomic Sci 23:40-4 Ap '67

Australia

Gloomy conclusion? surveying Australian university libraries. H. Bryan. bibliog il Library J 92:4113-16 N 15 '67

California

Knowledge bonanza. M. Wax. il Nation 204:178-81 F 6 '67
Public education. M. Friedman. Newsweek 69:86 Mr 13 '67
Tuition and educational hierarchy in California. R. Kirk. Nat R 19:421 Ap 18 '67
See also
Alameda college, Alameda
Art center college of design, Los Angeles
California. State college, San Jose
Laney college, Oakland
Merritt college, Oakland
Mills college, Oakland
Southern California university, Los Angeles
Stanford university

Canada

Crisis in Canadian theological education. N. K. Clifford. Christian Cent 84:897-9 Jl 12 '67
Hark to the elder institutions! letters. L. Kerwin; E. O. Dodson. Science 155:265 Ja 20 '67
See also
Toronto. University

Chile

Chile's regional universities. K. A. Herath. il Américas 19:18-20 N '67
Oral Roberts U. in Chile! P. Zottele. Christian Cent 84:734 My 31 '67

China (People's Republic)

Chinese university: target of the cultural revolution. C. T. Hu. il Sat R 50:52-4+ Ag 19 '67

Colorado

See also
Colorado. University, Boulder

Connecticut

See also
Wesleyan university, Middletown
Yale university

Delaware

See also
Delaware. University, Newark

England

Magic of Mod U; University of Sussex. il Newsweek 69:61 Mr 20 '67
See also
Cambridge. University
Oxford. University

Europe

Rebellion in Europe. il Time 90:39 D 22 '67

Florida

Junior colleges are blooming in the sunshine state. B. Carter. il NEA J 56:22-4 My '67
See also
Miami-Dade junior college, Miami
Nova university, Fort Lauderdale

Georgia

See also
Emory university, Atlanta
Georgia state college, Atlanta
Morehouse college, Atlanta

Germany (Federal Republic)

Letter from Berlin; West Berlin's free university. J. Wechsberg. New Yorker 43:165-6+ N 18 '67
Speak of the devil; students at Free university of Berlin riot at trial of F. Teufel. Newsweek 70:49 D 11 '67
Student movement, German style; Socialist student union of the Free university of Berlin. H. Brandon. Sat R 50:10+ S 9 '67

Great Britain

British universities confront a dilemma. H. C. Noble. Christian Cent 84:701 My 24 '67

Illinois

See also
North Park college, Chicago
Southern Illinois university
Wheaton college, Wheaton

Indiana

See also
Ball state university, Muncie
Notre Dame, Ind. University

Iowa

See also
Iowa state university of science and technology, Ames
Parsons college, Fairfield

Ireland

Dublin: winds of change; concerning Catholic ban on Trinity college. America 116:669 My 6 '67
Magic box; Trinity college library, Dublin. J. Donat. il Arch Forum 127:78-85 O '67

Italy

Molecular biology: U.S and Italy to establish new graduate school. J. Walsh. il Science 156:1582-3 Je 23 '67

Japan

I.C.U. crisis. H. Post. Christian Cent 84:1505+ N 22 '67
Mass production in Tokyo. il Time 90:81+ N 17 '67

Kansas

See also
Washburn university, Topeka

Kentucky

See also
Kentucky Southern college, Louisville

Latin America

Campus communism: Latin America's Trojan horse. E. Cárdenas. Read Digest 90:92-6 Je '67
Changing face of Latin America higher education. C. A. Astiz. Bul Atomic Sci 23:4-8 F '67
Higher education in Latin America. Sch & Soc 95:426-7 N 11 '67
Yanqui universities. R. Hilton. il Nation 205:145-8 Ag 28 '67

Lebanon

See also
American university of Beirut

COLLEGES and universities—*Continued*

Louisiana
See also
Grambling college, Grambling
Louisiana state university, Baton Rouge

Maryland
See also
Maryland. University, College Park
Washington college, Chestertown

Massachusetts
See also
Amherst college, Amherst
Berkshire community college, Pittsfield
Brandeis university, Waltham
Harvard university
Massachusetts college of art, Boston
Massachusetts institute of technology, Cambridge
Massachusetts. University, Amherst
Radcliffe college, Cambridge
Tufts university, Medford

Michigan
See also
Detroit. University
Kalamazoo college
Michigan state university, East Lansing
Michigan. University, Ann Arbor
Oakland community college, Union Lake

Minnesota
See also
Minnesota. University, Minneapolis

Missouri
See also
Missouri. University, Columbia
Washington university, St Louis
Webster college, Webster Groves

Montana
See also
Montana. University, Missoula

Nebraska
See also
Hiram Scott college, Scottsbluff

New England
New England state university libraries' regional processing center. D. E. Vincent. ALA Bul 61:672-3 Je '67
Six little universities, and how they grew. il U S News 62:56-8 F 6 '67
To visit New England's colleges. il Sunset 139:57-8 O '67

New Hampshire
See also
New Hampshire. University, Durham

New Jersey
New hope in New Jersey; first chancellor of higher education. il Time 90:58 Ag 25 '67
See also
Douglass college, New Brunswick
Princeton university

New York (state)
See also
Adelphi university, Garden City
Barnard college
Colgate university, Hamilton
Columbia university
Cornell university, Ithaca
Corning community college
Fordham university
New York (state). State university
Rochester, N.Y. University
Vassar college, Poughkeepsie

Ohio
See also
Antioch college, Yellow Springs
Dayton, Ohio. University
Lake Erie college, Painesville
Marietta college, Marietta
Ohio state university, Columbus
Ohio university, Athens
Western Reserve university, Cleveland

Oklahoma
See also
Oklahoma. University, Norman

Oregon
See also
Central Oregon community college, Bend
Oregon graduate center, Portland
Reed college, Portland

Pennsylvania
See also
Carnegie university, Pittsburgh
Duquesne university, Pittsburgh
Haverford college
Pittsburgh. University
Waynesburg college

Poland
Intellectual revolt in Poland. T. Szamuely. il Reporter 36:32-4 Je 1 '67

Rhode Island
See also
Barrington college
Rhode Island. University, Kingston

Russia
Problems of higher education in the Soviet Union; excerpt from The school and state in the U.S.S.R. H. C. Rudman. bibliog f il Sch & Soc 95:153-4+ Mr 4 '67
Science students at Moscow U. E. M. Ifft. Bul Atomic Sci 23:37-40 Ap '67
Soviet higher education: ideal and reality; excerpts from book. L. Froese. Sch & Soc 95:455-8 N 25 '67

Southern states
Expanding southern universities. Sch & Soc 95:408-10 N 11 '67
May queens and effigies; Negroes on southern campuses. il Newsweek 69:98+ Je 5 '67

Spain
Feeding the fire; riots at University of Madrid. Newsweek 69:36+ My 29 '67

Tennessee
See also
Austin Peay state college, Clarksville

Texas
See also
Angelo state college, San Angelo
Bishop college, Dallas
Houston. University
Mountain View college, Dallas

United States
Campus boom: a new college a week. il Newsweek 69:65-73 F 20 '67; Same abr. with title New college a week. Read Digest 90:161-4 Je '67
Campus corner. M. P. Sheridan. America 116:279 F 25 '67
Clark Kerr heads study of U.S. higher education. Pub W 191:47 F 6 '67
College scene (cont) il Sci Digest 61:25 F '67
Colleges in action (cont of) College scene. See issues of Science digest
Colleges that still have room. il Changing T 21:44-7 My '67
Crackdown starts on student riots; with interview with J. H. Reinoehl. il U S News 64:34-7 Ja 1 '68
Educational publishers study the role of universities; two day conference, sponsored by American textbook publishers institute. il Pub W 192:21-4 D 25 '67
Growing pains of the multiversity. W. Willcox. Atlan 220:45-7 Jl '67
In defense of the multiversity. R. Rapoport. Atlan 219:73-4 Je '67
Latest growth industry, colleges in U.S. il U S News 63:86-8 Jl 17 '67
Mapping the varieties of innocence from Antioch to Bob Jones. il Esquire 68:102-3 S '67
Mascatine's challenge to universities. Sch & Soc 95:168 Mr 18 '67
Measuring colleges qualitatively; the Gourman report. R. Kirk. Nat R 19:695 Je 27 '67
New Catholic college. N. G. McCluskey. America 116:414-17 Mr 25 '67; Discussion. 116:571-2 Ap 22 '67
New kind of college; small college on a university's campus. Seventeen 26:202+ My '67
Off-campus speaker policy. America 117:403-4 O 14 '67
Reforming the universities; views of P. Goodman. P. Clecak. Nation 204:407-11 Mr 27 '67
Responsibility of colleges and universities; address, October 29, 1966. R. H. Wick. Vital Speeches 33:240-4 F 1 '67
What is right in higher education? I. D. Weeks. Sch & Soc 95:353-4 O 14 '67
What the college catalogues won't tell you: a student's-eye view of American campuses. il McCalls 94:100-1 Mr '67
What's ahead for higher education? L. B. Mayhew. il NEA J 56:16-18 D '67
What's going on in schools & colleges. See issues of Changing times
Yanqui universities. R. Hilton. il Nation 205:145-8 Ag 28 '67
See also
Coeducation
Colleges and universities, State
Colleges for women
Denominational colleges
Medical colleges
Summer schools

COLLEGES and universities—*Continued*

Utah
See also
Utah. University, Salt Lake City

Venezuela
How a campus terrorized a city; Central university in Caracas. Read Digest 90:94-5 Je '67

Vermont
See also
Bennington college, Bennington

Virginia
See also
Virginia. University, Charlottesville

Washington, D.C.
See also
Howard university

Washington (state)
See also
Central Washington state college, Ellensburg

Wisconsin
See also
Beloit college, Beloit
Wisconsin. University, Madison

COLLEGES and universities, Municipal
See also
New York (city) City university of New York

COLLEGES and universities, State
Ideas and the state university. E. M. Oboler. Sch & Soc 95:78-80 F 4 '67
New England state university libraries' regional processing center. D. E. Vincent. ALA Bul 61:672-3 Je '67
Six little universities, and how they grew; New England. il U S News 62:56-8 F 6 '67
See also names of state colleges and universities, e.g. Bowling Green state university, Ohio

COLLEGES for Negroes. See Negroes in the United States—Education

COLLEGES for women
Seven sisters: is the ivy overgrown? M. A. Guitar. il Mlle 65:268-9+ Ag '67
Women's college. D. Klein. il Seventeen 26: 176+ Ag '67; Correction. 26:4 O '67
See also names of women's colleges, e.g. Mills college, Oakland, Calif.

COLLEY, Russell H. See Ryan, M. P. jt. auth.

COLLIER, Barnard Law
Eduardo Frei is trying a revolution without the execution wall. N Y Times Mag p30-1+ F 19 '67

COLLIER, James Lincoln
Collier's laws for happy camping. Read Digest 90:171-5 Je '67
Jamboree '67. Read Digest 91:121-4 Ag '67
Multiple hero. Holiday 41:10+ Ap '67

COLLIER, P. F, and son, corporation. See Crowell Collier and Macmillan, incorporated

COLLIES
Kind and canny canines. R. H. Boyle. il Sports Illus 28:50-6 Ja 15 '68
Pet news; white collie called Blanco, pet of Lyndon Johnson. R. Schoenstein. il Ladies Home J 84:47 F '67

COLLINS, A. Gene, and Egleson, G. C.
Iodide abundance in oilfield brines in Oklahoma. bibliog Science 156:934-5 My 19 '67

COLLINS, Bud
Tennis. Sports Illus 26:76-7 Je 12; 27:44-6 Jl 3 '67

COLLINS, Carter Compton
Electronic eyes for the blind. J. Hazelwood. il por Sci N 91:456-7 My 13 '67

COLLINS, Frederic W.
$30 billion for whom? New Repub 156:13-15 Mr 11 '67

COLLINS, J. V. See Locke, M. jt. auth.

COLLINS, James Daniel
God and contemporary philosophy. Commonweal 85:528-34 F 10 '67
Maritain asks some questions. America 118: 29-32 Ja 13 '68

COLLINS, John Frederick
Harangues and hurrahs in Boston. J. McLellan. Commonweal 86:405-6 Je 30 '67

COLLINS, John R.
Advances in magnetic materials. Electr World 78:49-52+ D '67
Infrared radiometry. Electr World 78:23-7+ O '67
New developments in CRT phosphors. Electr World 77:48-52+ Ja '67

COLLINS, Lawrence, and Lapierre, Dominique
Day of truth in racing. N Y Times Mag p8-9+ Jl 9 '67; Same abr. with title Greatest auto race of all. Read Digest 91:121-6 O '67
France's small farmers never had it so bad. N Y Times Mag p8-9+ D 24 '67

COLLINS, Ruby L. See Forman, S. jt. auth.

COLLINS, William, sons and company, limited
Rights and permission; Book-of-the-month choices. P. Nathan. Pub W 192:43 N 20 '67

COLLISION indicators. See Aeronautic instruments

COLLISION insurance. See Insurance, Automobile

COLLISIONS, Airplane. See Aviation—Accidents

COLLISIONS at sea
Biggest blast before the A-bomb; excerpts from The town that died. M. J. Bird. il Pop Mech 128:81-3 D '67
On avoiding collisions. J. S. Letcher, jr. il Yachting 121:72-3+ Mr '67

COLLISON, Jim
Flying photographer (cont) Flying 81:115 D '67

COLMENARES, Jose
(ed) See Schulberg, B. It could happen in the schools

COLOBAEA. See Flies

COLOGNE, Germany

Antiquities
Under the haberdashery by the city gate; funeral monument of Lucius Poblicius. il Time 90:54+ D 1 '67

Hospitals
Cologne's drive-in hospital: traffic in three dimensions. il Arch Rec 142:190-3 S '67

COLOGNE. See Perfumery

COLOMA mill. See California—Historic houses, etc.

COLOMBIA
See also
Cartagena
Economic assistance in Colombia
Education—Colombia
Indians of South America—Colombia
Protestant churches—Colombia
San Jorge River
Tota, Lake

Economic conditions
Taking a stand. il Time 89:39 F 17 '67

Religious institutions and affairs
See also
Catholic church in Colombia

COLOMBIAN Indians. See Indians of South America—Colombia

COLOMBO, Ceylon
Reporter at large; Dehiwala zoological gardens. E. Hahn. New Yorker 43:96+ S 23 '67

COLONIAL architecture. See Architecture, Colonial

COLONIAL architecture, Spanish. See Architecture, Spanish American (United States)

COLONIAL dependencies. See Colonies

COLONIAL houses. See Architecture, Colonial

COLONIAL life and customs
See also
Williamsburg, Va.

COLONIALISM. See Colonies

COLONIES
Mission histories. F. D. Lueking. Christian Cent 84:176 F 8 '67
United Nations and the decolonization of non-self-governing territories. J. W. S. Malecela. UN Mo Chron 4:84-96 Ag '67
See also
Imperialism
United Nations—Committee on information from non-self-governing territories
United Nations—Special committee on the situation with regard to implementation of declaration on granting of independence to colonial countries and peoples
United Nations—Trusteeship council
also subhead Colonies under names of countries, e.g. Portugal—Colonies

COLOR
Olitski: nothing but color. K. S. Champa. il Art N 66:36-8+ My '67
Total and complex: three young colorists. H. Rosenstein. il Art N 66:52-4+ My '67
What is color? E. P. Herman. il Design 68: 7-9 Ja '67
See also
Black
Clothing and dress—Color

COLOR—*Continued*

Psychology

Stimulus preferences and imprinting. P. H. Klopfer. bibliog il Science 156:1394-6 Je 9 '67

COLOR and music. See Music and color

COLOR film processing. See Photography—Developing and developers

COLOR film processors. See Photography—Apparatus and supplies

COLOR films. See Photography—Films

COLOR filters. See Light filters

COLOR in gardens. See Gardens—Color

COLOR in house decoration
Brimming with gaiety. il House & Gard 131: 92-5 Je '67
Color adventures that take more nerve than money. il House & Gard 132:170-5 S '67
Color! how to break the rules and still be right. P. Rumely and N. Cordts. il Bet Hom & Gard 46:36-47 Ja '68
Color it happy. il Am Home 70:122 Jl '67
Color it...vivid. B. Plumb. il N Y Times Mag p80-1 My 21 '67
Constant color, true blue. il McCalls 94:120-7 F '67
Cover it colorful. il Good H 164:144-50 Ap '67
Flowering of a modern manoir; home of Mrs F. Carpenter. J. L. Hendrix. il House B 109:130-7+ My '67
Foreshadowing a future of white-on-white, its optical surprises. il House B 109:148-9 S '67
Fresh bright look. il House & Gard 132:194-201 O '67
Furniture for the instant eclectic. F. Heard. il House B 109:292-5 N '67
Glistening news: silver walls. il House & Gard 131:136-9 F '67
House of fresh-cut color. M. White. il Ladies Home J 84:84-7 F '67
How to wake up an old-fashioned house without spending a fortune: color and pattern. il House & Gard 131:116-19 F '67
In a remodeled barn: lots of comfort and a bit of humor. il House & Gard 132:212-19 N '67
Innocents and the wickeds. il House B 109: 141-57 My '67
Living with red. M. White. il Ladies Home J 84:90-3 S '67
Magical power of the accent. il House & Gard 132:156-63 S '67
One big house, one basic color scheme. il Am Home 70:74-9 Mr '67
Punch of black & white. M. White. il Ladies Home J 84:98-9 Ap '67
Seven great ways to brighten your windows with H&G's sunshine colors. il House & Gard 131:136-9+ Mr '67
Spirited decorating. P. Rumely and N. Cordts. il Bet Hom & Gard 45:50-61 S '67
Sure-fire formula for smart decorating: black and white plus a color. P. Rumely and N. Cordts. il Bet Hom & Gard 45:46-53 Ag '67
Two approaches to color. V. D. Hahn. il Am Home 70:66-73 Mr '67
White elegance in a firehouse. il House & Gard 131:112-117 Je '67
Young place, full of sun. F. Heard. il House B 109:82-7 Jl '67

COLOR in house painting. See House painting

COLOR in landscape
It's a colorful, colorful world. M. Gough. il House B 109:126+ My '67

COLOR in textile fabrics. See Textile fabrics—Color

COLOR me loving; story. See Edwards, S.

COLOR music. See Music and color

COLOR of animals
Origin of iridescent colors on the indigo snake. E. A. Monroe and S. E. Monroe. bibliog il Science 159:97-8 Ja 5 '68

COLOR of man
Skin-deep; effect of vitamin D production on skin pigmentation. Newsweek 70:80 Ag 14 '67
Skin-pigment regulation of vitamin-D biosynthesis in man. W. F. Loomis. bibliog il Science 157:501-6 Ag 4 '67; Reply with rejoinder. F. R. Freemon. 158:579-80 N 3 '67
Vitamin D & the races of man. il Time 90: 52-3 Ag 18 '67
Vitamin D, key to color? Sci N 92:177 Ag 19 '67
    See also
Negro race

COLOR of snakes. See Color of animals

COLOR photography
Caulfield on color. P. Caulfield. See issues of Modern photography
Color clinic. D. B. Eisendrath, jr. See issues of Popular photography
Creative color. A. Rothstein. See issues of U.S. camera & travel
Freedom to find pictures; portfolio by freelancers. Pop Phot 62:90-9 Ja '68
Harvey Lloyd: what he believes about his craft. H. Lloyd. il Pop Phot 61:90-9 Ag '67
How to get the most out of Anscochrome 500. N. Rothschild. il Pop Phot 61:110-13+ D '67
How to see a picture in color. L. Friedel. il Mod Phot 31:84-9+ F '67
How to shoot flashy color without a flash. P. Wahl. il Pop Mech 129:160-1+ Ja '68
Lawrence Fried's live color. il Pop Phot 60: 100-5+ F '67
New color; symposium. il Pop Phot 61:77-113 Jl '67
Rothschild a la carte. N. Rothschild. il Pop Phot 60:84-93+ My '67
Ten color films: and how they're different! H. Keppler. il Mod Phot 31:72-5+ My '67
There's more to autumn than the leaves on the trees. B. Randall. il U S Camera 30: 38-41+ O '67
Turner; excerpts from address. P. Turner. il Pop Phot 60:90-9+ Mr '67

History

Nostalgic look at the medium; thirtieth anniversary of Popular photography. D. B. Eisendrath, jr. Pop Phot 60:54+ My '67

COLOR photography printing. See Photography—Printing processes

COLOR photomicrography. See Photomicrography

COLOR prejudice. See Race prejudice

COLOR prints (reproductions) See Reproduction of works of art

COLOR sense
Goldfish retina: organization for simultaneous color contrast. N. W. Daw. bibliog il Science 158:942-4 N 17 '67
Monocular and binocular aftereffects of chromatic adaptation. R. L. De Valois and J. Walraven. il Science 155:463-5 Ja 27 '67

COLOR television. See Television, Color

COLOR television receivers

Manufacture

See Television apparatus—Manufacture

COLOR television receivers. See Television receivers—Color receivers

COLORADO
    See also
Architecture, Domestic—Colorado
Black Canyon of the Gunnison National Monument
Booksellers and bookselling—Colorado
Estes Park
Fishing—Colorado
Hunting—Colorado
Law—Colorado
Music festivals—Colorado

COLORADO outdoor sports corporation
From outer space to open space; from equipment for planes, missiles, and space vehicles to outdoor camping equipment. il Bsns W p98-100 N 11 '67

COLORADO RIVER
Adventure as you like it. C. Conley. il Field & S 72:26-31 Ja '68
Colorado River fight nears climax; compromise solution. il Bsns W p 162+ Ap 29 '67
Dams and the Colorado. J. Ludwigson. il Sci N 91:167 F 18 '67
Down the Colorado. F. Leydet. il Holiday 41: 50-5+ Je '67
    See also
Central Arizona project (proposed)
Grand Canyon
Salton Sea

COLORADO. University, Boulder
Joint institute for laboratory astrophysics; National bureau of standards and University of Colorado. R. H. Garstang. il Sky & Tel 33:150-2 Mr '67
Where the air is clear. il Newsweek 69:95 F 13 '67

COLORATURA. See Embellishment (vocal music)

COLORED glass. See Glass, Colored

COLORED paper. See Paper

COLORED people (U.S.). See Negroes in the United States

COLPOSCOPY. See Cancer—Diagnosis

COLQUITT, Betsy
Aftermath: Christmas morning; poem. Christian Cent 84:1622 D 20 '67

COLT, Priscilla Crum
Giving the past a future. H. Meeker. il Arch Forum 126:56-61 My '67

COLT industries, incorporated
How the army zeroed in on the M-16. Bsns W p68 Je 24 '67

COLT revolvers. See Revolvers

COLTEN, Harvey R. and others
Efficiency of the first component of complement, C'1, in the hemolytic reaction. bibliog Science 158:1590-2 D 22 '67

COLTRANE, Jim
33,000-volt shock wins two award of $½ million. A. Peters. il pors Ebony 23:112-14+ N '67

COLTRANE, John William
Death of a jazzman. P. D. Zimmerman. por Newsweek 70:78-9 Jl 31 '67
John Coltrane: 1926-1967. A. B. Spellman. Nation 205:119-20 Ag 14 '67
Legacy of John Coltrane. M. Williams. por Sat R 50:69+ S 16 '67
Requiem for 'Trane. P. Garland. il pors Ebony 23:66-8+ N '67

COLTS (football) See Football clubs

COLUM, Padraic
Poet captain: Thomas MacDonagh; poem. Poetry 110:251-3 Jl '67
Tradition that existed in my grandmother's house. New Yorker 43:28-31 D 23 '67

about
Off Broadway. E. Oliver. New Yorker 43: 138+ Ap 8 '67

COLUMBIA, Md.
Cities: what will they be like? J. Hay. il Parents Mag 43:44-5+ Ja '68
Hail Columbia. il Newsweek 69:65 Je 26 '67
Messianic master builder: J. Rouse and his instant city. J. Rouse. il Life 62:35-6+ F 24 '67
New city, new church; ecumenical church planning. T. Mathews. Commonweal 86: 518-20+ Ag 25 '67
New towns: an urban frontier. P. McBroom. il Sci N 92:64-5 Jl 15 '67
Only in Columbia, the next America. J. Bailey. il Arch Forum 127:42-7 N '67
Profiles: through the great city. A. Bailey. New Yorker 43:50-2+ Ag 5 '67

COLUMBIA, Mo.
Foolproof control of pigeons and starlings. M. R. Sanford. il Am City 82:116-17 Mr '67

COLUMBIA, S.C.

City planning
Parking mall that... C. C. Burnett. il Am City 82:74-6 Ja '67

COLUMBIA broadcasting system
Air; CBS documentary, Vietnam perspective: air war in the North. M. J. Arlen. New Yorker 43:148+ Mr 4 '67
Air; drama: The final war of Olly Winter. M. J. Arlen. New Yorker 42:136+ F 18 '67
CBS buys books; acquisition of Holt, Rinehart & Winston. il Time 89:85 Mr 10 '67
CBS proposes merger with Holt. Pub W 191: 37 Mr 13 '67
CBS widens its lead; A. C. Nielsen co. ratings. il Bsns W p48+ O 28 '67
CBS wins some bullish reviews. il Bsns W p 121-3 Ja 21 '67
Due to circumstances beyond our control, by F. W. Friendly. Review
America 116:564 Ap 15 '67. J. McLaughlin
Nation 204:476-7 Ap 10 '67. J. Horn
Sat R 50:30-1 Ap 1 '67. R. J. Landry
Fred Friendly and Friendlyvision. H. Swados. il N Y Times Mag p30-1+ Ap 23 '67
Friendly persuasion; concerning book Due to circumstances beyond our control. R. L. Shayon. Sat R 50:71 Ap 8 '67
Great sellout to soap opera; excerpt from Due to circumstances beyond our control. F. W. Friendly. il Life 62:84+ Mr 17 '67
Keeping CBS in the big leagues; trying to rebuild New York Yankees into a winner. il Bsns W p80-2+ Ap 15 '67
Retrieving a lost rocket; excerpt from Due to circumstances beyond our control... F. W. Friendly. il Life 62:70-2+ Mr 24 '67
TV editorials: How brave & free? V. H. Bernstein. Nation 205:170-3 S 4 '67; Reply with rejoinder. D. J. Trageser. 205:290+ O 2 '67

COLUMBIA-Presbyterian medical center. See New York (city)—Columbia-Presbyterian medical center

COLUMBIA records, incorporated
He makes music pay at CBS; G. Lieberson. il Bsns W p 106-7+ O 7 '67
Twelve tones of Christmas; Columbia's releases of far-out music. il Time 90:52 D 8 '67

COLUMBIA RIVER
Crisis on the Columbia; huge annual fish loss. T. Trueblood. il Field & S 72:10-12+ Jl '67

COLUMBIA university
Columbia and its new filter: smoke over Morningside Heights. R. J. Samuelson. il Science 157:520-4 Ag 4 '67
Columbia choice; controversial sponsorship of new cigarette filter. il Time 90:43 Jl 21 '67
Columbia filter raises a cloud of questions. Bsns W p20-1 Jl 22 '67
Columbia filter: university takes a second look. R. J. Samuelson. Science 157:1541-2 S 29 '67
Columbia, pleonexia on the acropolis. C. R. Hatch. il Arch Forum 127:68-75 Jl '67
Columbia's neighbors: the slums of academe. R. Gustaitis. il Reporter 37:34-8 O 5 '67; Discussion. 37:10 N 2 '67
Gronk! session of non-verbal communication sponsored by the Social atmosphere committee. New Yorker 43:32-4 Ap 1 '67
New cigarette filter, a university's dilemma. A. Rosenfeld. il Life 63:50-1 Jl 28 '67
New dark horse entry; low-tar filter. il Sci N 92:104-5 Jl 29 '67
New safe cigarette filter: what you should know about it and what parents should tell their children. L. David. Good H 165: 92-3+ N '67
Notes and comment; doubts about filter program. New Yorker 43:47 O 21 '67
Painting the ocean red, etc. at Columbia university; Warmth movement. D. Carlinsky and B. Lefkowitz. Esquire 68:99+ S '67
Recasting at Columbia; new provost. il Newsweek 69:111-12 Je 19 '67
Revolt in the ranks; opposition to class ranking. il Newsweek 69:69 Ap 17 '67
Second thoughts; financial interest in new cigarette filter. Newsweek 70:50 S 4 '67
Weep, lion, weep; Columbia football. il Newsweek 70:90+ D 18 '67
Who's on top? Columbia ends ranking. Sr Schol 90:16 Ap 21 '67
See also
Teachers college, Columbia university

College of physicians and surgeons
Body snatchers; excerpts from The doctors' story. T. Gallagher. il Am Heritage 18: 64-73 Je '67

Lamont geological observatory
Lamont geological observatory. J. L. Worzel. il Science 150:948-9 N 17 '67

COLUMBIA-Viking desk encyclopedia
Encyclopedia revision within modest cost limit. il Pub W 193:67-8 Ja 1 '68

COLUMBIAN exposition of 1893. See Chicago—Worlds Columbian exposition, 1893

COLUMBUS, Christopher
October 12, 1492; with editorial comment. H. Martinez-Montero. il Américas 19:inside cover, 1-4 O '67
Pearls of Margarita; reprint. C. P. Idyll. il Américas 19:8-14 Ag '67
Voyage. W. J. Coughlin. Tech W 20:50 My 29 '67

COLUMBUS, Ind.

Architecture
Inspired renaissance in Indiana; with report by M. Wellemeyer. il Life 63:74-84+ N 17 '67
Skyline rises in a Corn Belt town. il Bsns W p 138-40+ N 18 '67

Education
School that will vanish; Lincoln elementary school. J. M. Dixon. il Arch Forum 127:48-53 N '67

Parks and playgrounds
School that will vanish; Lincoln elementary school. J. M. Dixon. il Arch Forum 127:48-53 N '67

COLUMNISTS. See Newspapers—Sections, columns, etc.

COLUMNS (architecture)
Classic columns in minutes. il Pop Mech 127:215 F '67

COLUMNS (newspapers) See Newspapers—Sections, columns, etc.

COLVIN, Elizabeth W.
  In limbo of learning. Sat R 50:72 D 16 '67
COLVIN, Francis
  Bicycle boy; poem. Commonweal 86:288 My
  26 '67
COLVIN, Thomas E.
  Designer's comments. Yachting 121:92-3+ Je
  '67
COLVIN, William
  New school try. Time 90:104 N 24 '67
COLWELL, Alice
  My logging boss husband is a bird watcher.
  por Am For 73:30-1+ Ap '67
COLWELL, Don
  My logging boss husband is a bird watcher.
  A. Colwell. il pors Am For 73:30-1+ Ap '67
COLWELL, Robert N.
  Remote sensing of natural resources; with
  biographical sketch. Sci Am 218:19, 54-69 Ja
  '68
COMA
  Unconsciousness. C. J. Potthoff. Todays
  Health 45:68 O '67
COMAC armament control. See Airplanes, Mili-
  tary—Armaments
COMANCHE Indians
  Buffalo hunt; excerpt from Blessed McGill.
  E. Shrake. il Sports Illus 27:60-70 D 25 '67
COMAY, Joan
  Israel for the tourist. Holiday 42:137-40+ D '67
COMBAT fatigue. See Neuroses
COMBAT neuroses. See Neuroses
COMBES, Harry
  Fighting Illini. D. Jenkins. il por Sports Illus
  26:16-19 Mr 6 '67
COMBINATION rooms. See Rooms
COMBINES. See Harvesting machinery
COMBS, Cecil
  These murdered old mountains. D. Nevin. il
  por Life 64:54-60+ Ja 12 '68
COMBUSTIBLE materials. See Inflammable
  materials
COMBUSTION
  Getting inside a flame; sulfur oxidation. Sci
  Digest 62:25 N '67
COME back if it doesn't get better; story. See
  Gilliatt, P.
COME back to San Francisco; story. See Ewen,
  L. S.
COME live with me; drama. See Minoff, L.
  and Price, S.
COMEAU, Lesa C. and others
  Curriculum breakthrough in the humanities.
  Sr Schol 90:sup 13-14 Ap 7 '67
COMEDIANS
  When they really knew how to laugh; 1920s
  revisited. C. Ford. il McCalls 95:82-3+ N
  '67
    See also
  Allen, W.
  Bird, J.
  Freberg, S.
  Lahr, B.
  Negro comedians
  Paulsen, P.
  Rickles, D.
  Rivers, J.
  Smothers brothers
  Vernon, J.
COMEDY
  Ageless master's anatomy of comedy; inter-
  view; ed. by R. Meryman. C. Chaplin. il
  Life 62:80-4+ Mr 10 '67
  Hat: tenth anniversary of collaboration; in-
  terview. M. Flanders; D. Swann. New
  Yorker 43:46-8 Mr 11 '67
  Time for comedy. L. Kronenberger. Atlan 219:
  63-6 My '67
  Tragedy and comedy, by W. Kerr. Review
  Life 62:18 My 19 '67. T. Prideaux
    See also
  Comedians
  Humor
  Moving pictures—Comedy
  Television broadcasting—Humor
COMER, James P.
  Social power of the Negro; with biograph-
  ical sketch. Sci Am 216:14, 21-7 bibliog
  (p 146) Ap '67
COMETS
  Another for the amateurs; Ikeya-Seki 1967n.
  il Time 91:37 Ja 12 '68
  Comets and the IQSY. F. C. Livingstone.
  Sci N 92:160 Ag 12 '67
  Comets simulated. il Sci N 91:402 Ap 29 '67
  Hertzsprung's enigmatic object. J. Ashbrook.
  il Sky & Tel 34:382-3 D '67
  Naked-eye comet 1967f. il Sky & Tel 34:83
  Ag '67
  Observations of comet 1967f. il Sky & Tel
  34:190-2 S '67

One hundred periodic comets. B. G. Marsden.
  bibliog il Science 155:1207-13 Mr 10 '67
Re-finding comets. Sci N 92:393 O 21 '67
Two more comets. Sky & Tel 33:227 Ap '67
Were comets the midwives at the birth of
  man? theories of R. J. Uffen. J. Lear. il Sat
  R 50:57-62 My 6 '67; Discussion. 50:52-6
  Ag 5 '67
    See also
Halley's comet
COMIC book heroes. See Comics (books, strips,
  etc)
COMIC literature. See Humor
COMIC strips. See Comics (books, strips, etc)
COMICS (books, strips, etc)
  Funnies on Capitol hill. D. S. Greenberg.
  Science 155:1222 Mr 10 '67
  Inept heroes, winners at last; C. M. Schulz's
  Peanuts characters; with report by J.
  Borgzinner. il Life 62:74-8+ Mr 17 '67
  New Peanuts happiness book; excerpt. C. M.
  Schulz. il McCalls 95:90-1 O '67
  You're a good man, Charlie Schulz. B. Con-
  rad. il N Y Times Mag p32-5+ Ap 16 '67;
  Same abr. Read Digest 91:168-72 Jl '67
    Educational applications
  Comics scene; magazines in the library. ed.
  by B. Katz. A. E. Prentice. Library J 93:
  59 Ja 1 '68
COMING-out party; story. See Sullivan, P. W.
COMINSKY, J. R.
  Doris Nash Wortman, 1890-1967. Sat R 50:
  19 Je 24 '67
COMMAGER, Henry Steele
  How not to be a world power. N Y Times Mag
  p28-9+ Mr 12 '67
  Issue is integrity; statement, February 20,
  1967; ed. by C. B. Grannis. Pub W 191:42
  Mr 13 '67
  On the evils of a foreign education. Sat R
  50:83-4+ F 18 '67
  On the way to 1984. Sat R 50:68-9+ Ap 15
  '67
  Was America a mistake? Horizon 9:30-3+
  Aut '67
COMMEMORATIVE medals. See Medals
COMMEMORATIVE stamps. See Postage
  stamps
COMMENCEMENT addresses. See Baccalaure-
  ate addresses
COMMENCEMENTS
  Commencement '67; absence of luminaries.
  Nation 204:741 Je 12 '67
COMMENTARY (periodical)
  Letter. N. Podhoretz. Harper 234:11 My '67;
  Reply with rejoinder. R. Ellison. 235:4+ Jl
  '67
COMMERCE
  Business around the globe. See issues of
  Fortune
  Cotton in the world trade arena; address,
  March 10, 1967. A. M. Solomon. Dept State
  Bul 56:555-60 Ap 3 '67
  International trade and investment; address,
  March 7, 1967. P. Chambers. Vital Speeches
  33:371-5 Ap 1 '67
  New perspectives on trade and development.
  I. Frank. For Affairs 45:520-40 Ap '67
  Progress in a generation of peril; address,
  October 23, 1967. L. B. Johnson. Dept State
  Bul 57:631-3 N 13 '67
  U.S. in the world market place; address,
  April 24, 1967. G. Champion. Vital Speeches
  33:505-8 Je 1 '67
  U.S. in world trade; address, March 22, 1967.
  B. K. Wickstrum. Vital Speeches 33:535-8
  Je 15 '67
  Where the surpluses are. il Time 91:70 Ja 5
  '68
  World economy; marking time. L. A. Mayer.
  il Fortune 76:31-2+ S 15 '67
  World trade and finance and U.S. prosperi-
  ty; address, December 6, 1967. L. B. John-
  son. Dept State Bul 58:6-7 Ja 1 '68
    See also
  Balance of payments
  Competition, International
  Corporations
  Free trade and protection
  Investments, Foreign
  Merchant marine
  Money
  Reciprocity
  Stock exchange
  Tariff
  Trade missions
  World trade week
    also subhead Commerce under names of
    countries, e.g. Japan—Commerce

COMMERCE committee. See United States—Congress—House of representatives—Commerce committee
COMMERCE department (United States) See United States—Commerce, Department of
COMMERCIAL credit company
Journey for Muecke. R. Levy. Duns R 90:56-8 D '67
COMMERCIAL crimes
Business crime. R. Nader. New Repub 157: 7-8 Jl 1 '67; Reply with rejoinder. L. N. Cutler. 157:34-5 S 9 '67
COMMERCIAL ethics. See Business ethics
COMMERCIAL investment trust corporation. See CIT financial corporation
COMMERCIAL law
See also
Trusts, Industrial—Law
Warranty
COMMERCIAL missions. See Trade missions
COMMERCIAL photography. See Photography, Commercial
COMMERCIAL products
How to price industrial products. A. W. Walker. il Harvard Bsns R 45:125-32 S '67
Is U.S. technology a threat to Europe? Read Digest 90:137-40 Je '67
Months ahead; guide for your work and personal living. See issues of Changing times
See also
Marine resources
Products, New
Quality of products

Testing
See also
Consumers union of United States
COMMERCIAL travelers
Breadwinner on tour; guidebooks for the business man. H. Sutton. Sat R 50:42-3 Jl 15 '67
COMMERCIAL treaties and agreements
East-West trade pulls a switch; barter-type trade agreements. il Bsns W p 123-4+ Mr 11 '67
See also
General agreement on tariffs and trade
Tariff
also subhead Commercial treaties and agreements under names of countries, e.g. United States—Commercial treaties and agreements
COMMERCIALS. See Television advertising
COMMISSION on faith and order. See World council of churches
COMMISSION of the European communities
Pragmatic prophet of a federalist Europe; J. Rey; with editorial comment. il Bsns W p74-6+, 202 S 16 '67
COMMISSIONS, independent regulatory. See Independent regulatory commissions
COMMISSIONS of inquiry, International
Methods of fact-finding; Sixth committee consideration. UN Mo Chron 4:111 D '67
COMMISSIONS of the United Nations. See name of the commission as subhead under United Nations, e.g. United Nations—Commission on human rights
COMMISSIONS of the United States government. See name of the commission as subhead under United States, e.g. United States—Commission of fine arts
COMMITTEE for a sane nuclear policy. See National committee for a sane nuclear policy
COMMITTEE for economic development
American forecast; symposium. il Sat R 51: 31-4+ Ja 13 '68
Business and public policy, by K. Schriftgiesser. Review
Sat R 51:79-80 Ja 13 '68. A. Prager
COMMITTEE for environmental information
Scientist and citizen: St Louis group broadens educational role. B. Nelson. Science 157:903-5+ Ag 25 '67
COMMITTEE for nuclear information. See Committee for environmental information
COMMITTEE of responsibility to save war-burned and war-injured Vietnamese children
Children of Viet Nam; mission to find war-injured children suitable for medical treatment in the U.S. il Time 89:62 My 26 '67
C.O.R.'s score. il Time 90:57 D 8 '67
News and views. J. Deedy. Commonweal 86: 330 Je 9 '67
News and views; difficulties bringing children to U.S. medical centers. J. Deedy. Commonweal 86:562 S 22 '67
Truth about wounded Vietnamese children. Christian Cent 84:740 Je 7 '67

COMMITTEE of twenty-four. See United Nations—Special committee on the situation with regard to implementation of declaration on granting of independence to colonial countries and peoples
COMMITTEE on copyright issues. See American library association—Committee on copyright issues
COMMITTEE on information from non-self-governing territories. See United Nations—Committee on information from non-self-governing territories
COMMITTEE on invisibles and financing relating to trade. See United Nations conference on trade and development
COMMITTEE on non-governmental organizations. See United Nations—Economic and social council
COMMITTEE on potential contamination and interference from satellites. See National academy of sciences—Committee on potential contamination and interference from satellites
COMMITTEE on space research. See International council of scientific unions—Committee on space research
COMMITTEE on the peaceful uses of outer space. See United Nations—Committee on the peaceful uses of outer space
COMMITTEE to rescue Italian art
Editorial: for CRIA. H. M. Franc. Art N 65:29+ Ja '67
Embattled heritage; Italian heritage exhibition at New York's Wildenstein gallery for CRIA. il Newsweek 69:89 My 29 '67
Saving the libraries of Florence. C. Horton. bibliog il Wilson Lib Bul 41:1034-43 Je '67
COMMITTEES, Congressional. See United States—Congress—Committees
COMMODITIES. See Commercial products
COMMODITIES price index. See Index numbers
COMMODITY exchanges. See Exchanges
COMMODITY speculation. See Speculation
COMMON law marriage. See Marriage, Common law
COMMON market in Central America. See Central American program of economic integration
COMMON market in Latin America. See Latin American free trade association
COMMON market in western Europe. See European economic community
COMMON stocks. See Stocks
COMMONWEAL (periodical)
Change of editors. J. O'Gara. Commonweal 86:255-6 My 19 '67
Commonweal papers. Commonweal 85:498-519+ F 10 '67; Discussion. bibliog 85:636; 87:224-50+ Mr 10, N 24 '67
COMMONWEALTH Edison company
Pathfinder for nuclear power; Chairman J. H. Ward. il Bsns W p76-8 Mr 11 '67
COMMONWEALTH of nations
Britain and the Commonwealth; symposium. bibliog f il Cur Hist 52:257-301+ My '67
COMMUNAL prayer. See Prayer
COMMUNICABLE disease center, Atlanta. See United States—Communicable disease center
COMMUNICABLE diseases
Latent diseases rise up; evolutionary approach to infectious diseases. Sci N 92:608 D 23 '67
Protecting your child from contagious diseases. B. Spock. il Redbook 129:20+ My '67
U.S. wages world war on epidemics; Atlanta's Communicable disease center. il Bsns W p 104-6+ Mr 11 '67
See also
Animals as carriers of infection
also names of communicable diseases, e.g. Cholera
COMMUNICABLE diseases in animals
Diseases we catch from animals. R. W. Crane. il Todays Health 45:56-7+ Mr '67
COMMUNICATION
Air. M. J. Arlen. New Yorker 43:135-8 Ap 1 '67
Communications; ed. by R. L. Tobin. See issues of Saturday review
Language and communication. J. J. Gumperz. bibliog f Ann Am Acad 373:219-31 S '67
Language and silence, by G. Steiner. Review
Time 89:112+ Ap 28 '67
McLuhan montage. il Library J 92:1701-3 Ap 15 '67
Marshall McLuhan: communications explorer. N. P. Hurley. America 116:241-3 F 18 '67
Medium is the massage, by M. McLuhan and Q. Fiore. Review
Cath World 205:177-8 Je '67. D. J. Leary

COMMUNICATION—*Continued*
Medium is the message; excerpts from Understanding media. M. McLuhan. NEA J 56: 24-7 O '67
Message of Marshall McLuhan. il Newsweek 69:53-7 Mr 6 '67
Needed: more human communication. il Ebony 22:108-9 Mr '67
Notes and comment; fashionableness of the world dialogue. il New Yorker 43:23 S 2 '67
Reading: a commitment to consciousness; address, April 28, 1967. B. De Mott. il Wilson Lib Bul 42:74-9 S '67
Understanding McLuhan (in part) R. Kostelanetz. il N Y Times Mag p 18-19+ Ja 29 '67; Discussion. p 12+ F 12 '67
Understanding Marshall McLuhan; or, Will TV put a zombie in your future? Sr Schol 90:13-16 Ap 28 '67
Vision 67: communications' role in man's survival and growth; report of conference. Pub W 192:58-9 D 4 '67
What's happening with mixed media? A. Rothstein. U S Camera 30:14-15 N '67
Who is listening? address, April, 1967. S. L. Wallace. Wilson Lib Bul 42:295-300 N '6

See also
Communications research
Communications satellites
Cybernetics
Mass media
Public relations
Radio communication
Teletype
United States—Federal communications commission
United States—President's task force on communication policy

International aspects
Lines, hot, cold, tepid. Sci N 92:82 Jl 22 '67
Mallard may help close technology gap. W. Andrews. Aero Tech 21:22-3 O 23 '67
See also
Hot line (Washington and Moscow)

Pakistan
Pakistani communications to be upgraded. Electr World 78:99 N '67
COMMUNICATION, Animal. See Animal communication
COMMUNICATION and traffic
See also
Telecommunication
COMMUNICATION in education
Communications technology: a social force; address, October 10, 1967. R. W. Sarnoff. Vital Speeches 34:94-6 N 15 '67
Communications: the undiscovered country; adaptation of address, 1966. D. M. Grieco. bibliog il Library J 92:845-8 F 15 '67
Schoolman's guide to Marshall McLuhan. J. M. Culkin. il Sat R 50:51-3+ Mr 18 '67
COMMUNICATION in government
How Johnson brings the world to his desk; information-gathering system. il Bsns W p 178-80+ Mr 4 '67
Washington; L. B. Johnson's policies. R. Evans and R. Novak. Atlan 220:6+ O '67
COMMUNICATION in management
Authors & editors; projected series of business communication books. Pub W 192: 19-20 N 13 '67
Confrontation meeting. R. Beckhard. Harvard Bsns R 45:149-55 Mr '67
Frustrating warfare of business; with report by C. Argyris. il Life 62:40-53+ My 5 '67
Laws of probability and bureaucratic style. H. Nugent. Atlan 219:118+ Mr '67
What management should know about labor; responsibilities in communication; address, February 10, 1967. C. Ballard. Vital Speeches 33:316-20 Mr 1 '67
COMMUNICATION in medicine
How doctors keep up. V. Block. il Todays Health 45:56-60 Ag '67
COMMUNICATION in science
Advancement of the Nation's health. P. H. Abelson. Science 158:53 O 6 '67
Civilian technology: NASA study finds little spin-off. D. S. Greenberg. Science 157: 1016-18 S 1 '67; Discussion. 158:438 O 27 '67
Information exchange groups to be discontinued; letter. E. A. Confrey; reply. W. V. Thorpe. Science 155:1195-6 Mr 10 '67
Information functions of an international meeting. B. E. Compton and W. D. Garvey. Science 155:1648-50 Mr 31 '67
Matthew effect in science; address, August 1967. R. K. Merton. bibliog Science 159:56-63 Ja 5 '68

National standard reference data system. E. L. Brady and M. B. Wallenstein. bibliog il Science 156:754-62 My 12 '67
Quick-access pool for world data; Washington study urges system for scientific and engineering information. Bsns W p78+ Je 17 '67
Science critics; excerpts from address, October 19, 1966. R. Dubos; reply. H. E. Evans. Science 155:1058 Mr 3 '67
Scientific communication as a social system; excerpt from address, November 22, 1966. W. D. Garvey and B. C. Griffith. bibliog Science 157:1011-16 S 1 '67
COMMUNICATIONS, Military
Mallard contracts let; Gander studied; multination integrated communications systems. J. Rhea. Aero Tech 21:21-2 O 23 '67
Mallard may help close technology gap. W. Andrews. Aero Tech 21:22-3 O 23 '67
See also
Radio communication, Military
United States—Air force—Communication systems
COMMUNICATIONS, navigation and identification system. See Radio apparatus on aircraft
COMMUNICATIONS research
Ears and eyes in your skin; concept of a cutaneous language revived. A. J. Snider. il Sci Digest 61:75-6 Je '67
COMMUNICATIONS satellite corporation
Communications policy; message to Congress. L. B. Johnson. Dept State Bul 57:296-301 S 4 '67
Comsat cash spurs diversification drive. Aviation W 86:98 Je 26 '67
Comsat domestic satellite plan scheduled for early FCC ruling. K. Johnsen. Aviation W 87:20 S 25 '67
Comsat faces U.S. overseas challenge. K. Johnsen. il Aviation W 86:165+ Mr 6 '67
Comsat keeps sending them up. il Bsns W p 186+ O 14 '67
Comsat reveals advanced satellite plans. K. Johnsen. Aviation W 87:21 N 6 '67
Comsat seeks to broaden types of satellite services. Aviation W 87:29 O 16 '67
Comsat shows its hand. Bsns W p98+ Ag 5 '67
Eurospace urges regional Comsat system. D. E. Fink. Aviation W 87:29-30 Ag 28 '67
More talk, more TV via Comsat's birds. U S News 62:13 Ja 30 '67
New Comsat unit to manage global net. Aviation W 88:39 Ja 15 '68
Soviets adding civil satellites. Aero Tech 21: 24 Ag 28 '67
U.S. dominance seen hindering Intelsat. R. G. O'Lone. Aviation W 87:31 Ag 28 '67
COMMUNICATIONS satellites
Canadian report urges domestic comsat. K. Johnsen. Aviation W 86:59+ Mr 27 '67
Cinderella in the sky; satellite-to-home broadcasting. L. Lessing. il Fortune 76:130-3+ O '67
Communications satellites; introduction. E. Rabinowitch. Bul Atomic Sci 23:2-3 Ap '67
Comsat domestic satellite plan scheduled for early FCC ruling. K. Johnsen. Aviation W 87:20 S 25 '67
Costs of broadcast satellites linked to locale, TV quality. R. Pay. il Tech W 20:36-7 F 20 '67
Data are coming. W. J. Coughlin. Tech W 20:50 F 13 '67
Help wanted: domestic; potential benefit of domestic satellites for all forms of communications. M. Getler. Aero Tech 21:66 Ag 28 '67
Lani Bird 2 successful. R. N. Watts, jr. il Sky & Tel 33:140 Mr '67
Little bird that casts a big shadow. C. E. Silberman. il Fortune 75:108-11+ F '67
NAR, Hughes offer new comsat designs. il Aero Tech 21:18+ N 6 '67
Prodigious satellites: Comsat, ma Bell and ETV. E. B. Lambeth. il Nation 204:109-12 Ja 23 '67
Soviet union starting comsat network. Aviation W 87:17 Jl 31 '67
Soviets adding civil satellites. Aero Tech 21: 24 Ag 28 '67
Space talkers. il Newsweek 70:90-1 O 23 '67
TV broadcast satellite study proposals evaluated at Marshall. I. Stone. Aviation W 86:118-19 Je 12 '67
TV direct from satellite to your home; it could be soon. il U S News 62:68-9 Je 26 '67
10,000-circuit comsat studied by Lockheed for Intelsat use. il Aviation W 86:32 Ap 10 '67

COMMUNICATIONS satellites—*Continued*
Three domestic communication satellite plans will be proposed; Communications satellite corp, Ford foundation and National broadcasting co. K. Johnsen Aviation W 86:33 Ap 10 '67
USSR initiates national satellite TV net. D. C. Winston. il Aviation W 87:39+ N 27 '67
Versatile satellite; communications system for commercial aircraft. Sci Digest 61:25 Mr '67
Vista; a new look at satellite TV; visual-talking system. Electr world 77:84 Ap '67

See also
Communications satellite corporation
International telecommunications satellite consortium

Electronic equipment
Mechanically despun antenna readied for Intelsat III launch. Aero Tech 21:38+ D 4 '67
Sat-com tests to help decide on voice, data transmissions. P. J. Klass. il Aviation W 87:84-6+ N 13 '67

International aspects
Cables and satellites prepare for the mat; new transatlantic line, U.S. global satellite system. Bsns W p 139-40 D 16 '67
Communications satellite dogfight. J. McLaughlin. America 117:227-inside back cover S 2 '67
Communications satellites: a new institutional setting. H. I. Schiller. Bul Atomic Sci 23:4-8 Ap '67
Europe unifying policy for Intelsat talks. D. E. Fink. Aviation W 87:69-70 N 27 '67
Eurospace urges regional Comsat system. D. E. Fink. Aviation W 87:29-30 Ag 28 '67
Franco-German comsat project bolstered. D. E. Fink. Aviation W 87:27-8 Jl 24 '67
French ask U.S. help for comsat. D. E. Fink. Aviation W 86:22-3 Je 5 '67
Italy sets up 1st independent Comsat link. R. Lindsey. il Aero Tech 21:28+ N 6 '67
New Comsat unit to manage global net. Aviation W 88:39 Ja 15 '68
New monitor on communications; study of nation's communications policy. Bsns W p40 Ag 19 '67
Prodigious satellites: Comsat, ma Bell and ETV. E. B. Lambeth. il Nation 204:109-12 Ja 23 '67
Systems development dispute delays NATO Comsat effort. Aviation W 87:28 Ag 7 '67
TV programme girdling the world; Our world. P. de Latil. UNESCO Courier 20:38 N '67
Three international programs. R. N. Watts, jr. Sky & Tel 33:363-4 Je '67

Military applications
Big comsat advances predicted at AFCEA. il Tech W 20:22 Je 12 '67
Choice of contractor for U.K. military comsat due shortly. Tech W 20:34 Ja 30 '67
DOD decision on interim comsat slips again. Tech W 20:18 Je 5 '67
DOD strives for phase II Comsat award by year's end. Aero Tech 21:23-4 Ag 28 '67
Eighteen IDCSP satellites in orbit; initial defense communications satellite system. Aviation W 87:39 Jl 10 '67
IDCSP network completed; DOD eyes advanced comsats. J. Rhea. Aero Tech 21:20 Jl 17 '67
NATO plans to buy two U.S. comsats. il Aero Tech 21:14+ N 20 '67
Tactical comsat terminals readied for soldier in field. Aero Tech 21:37+ Ag 14 '67
Tactical utilization of comsat faces test. P. J. Klass. il Aviation W 88:66-7+ Ja 15 '68

Tracking
Bid requests due in February for NATO comsat stations. Aviation W 87:22-3 D 25 '67

COMMUNICATIONS satellites, Canadian
Canadian industry urges comsat decision. K. Johnsen. Aviation W 86:97-8 Je 26 '67

COMMUNICATIONS satellites, European
NATO ready to act on satellite project. D. E. Fink. Aviation W 86:24 My 1 '67

COMMUNICATIONS satellites, Russian
Control loss suspected on Molniya. P. J. Klass. Aviation W 86:23 My 1 '67

COMMUNION. See Catholic church—Eucharist

COMMUNISM
Benign face of communism. America 116:672 My 6 '67
Cruising the carbuncles; 100th anniversary of publication of Das Kapital. il Time 90:35 S 22 '67

Is communism dead? G. Lichtheim. bibliog f Commentary 44:62-7 O '67
Karl Marx was all wet. il Nations Bsns 55: 100-2+ N '67
Revolution in the third world; ed. by P. P. Ardrey, jr. il Nat R 19:1188-200 O 31 '67
Three big ism's and how they grew. il Sr Schol 91:16-21+ S 28 '67
Thus spake Leonid Brezhnev; excerpts from address, November 3, 1967. L. Brezhnev. Reporter 37:19 D 14 '67
What is left of communism? G. Lichtheim. For Affairs 46:78-94 O '67

See also
Communist parties
Socialism

Anecdotes, facetiae, satire, etc.
Beginner's guide to Mao Tse-tung. il Esquire 68:209-13 D '67
Next fifty years: a preview? C. FitzGibbon. il Nat R 19:1201-4 O 31 '67

Anti-Communist measures
Come the revelations; concerning T. Braden's Saturday evening post article and statements. New Repub 156:7-8 My 27 '67
OAS council: report recommends anti-Communist measures: study of the first Tricontinental conference, Havana. January 1966. G. Meek. il Américas 19:42-3 Ja '67
OAS foreign ministers take steps against Cuban subversion; statements, September 23, 24 with text of final act, September 24, 1967. D. Rusk. Dept State Bul 57:490-8 O 16 '67
Speaking out, I'm glad the CIA is immoral. T. W. Braden. Sat Eve Post 240:10+ My 20 '67

See also
United States—Foreign relations—Anti-Communist measures

History
Books. M. Muggeridge. Esquire 67:52+ Ap '67

Africa, Southern
Now guerrilla war threatens white Africa. il U S News 63:122-3 S 25 '67

Asia
We cannot accept a Communist seizure of Vietnam. R. A. Scalapino; discussion. New Repub 155:5-7 D 24 '66; N Y Times Mag p 12+ Ja 22 '67

Asia, Southeastern
Guerrilla warfare and Peking. J. M. Van Der Kroef. Nat R 20:34-5 Ja 16 '68
If war now spreads in Asia; bigger burden for U.S. il U S News 64:29-31 Ja 15 '68
President Johnson holds talks with Australian Prime Minister; remarks, June 1, 1967. L. B. Johnson; H. E. Holt. Dept State Bul 56:960-3 Je 26 '67

Bolivia
Debray convicted. il Sr Schol 91:20 D 7 '67
Guevara: new martyr, or a symbol of Communist failure? il U S News 63:20 O 23 '67
Is Ché Guevara in Bolivia? il Sr Schol 91:6 O 12 '67
Latin America: how many Vietnams? D. James. Nat R 19:949-51 S 5 '67
What 100 Castro-type guerrillas can do. il U S News 62:84-5 Je 26 '67

Anti-Communist measures
Convincing the cynics; campaign to flush out Communist guerrillas. il Newsweek 69: 43-4 Ap 24 '67

Cambodia
Cambodia: more and more a haven for attacks on South Vietnam. il U S News 63:10 D 4 '67
Cambodia: next theater of war? il U S News 63:25 Ag 28 '67
Next, hot pursuit of the Communists? U S News 64:6 Ja 8 '68
Rumblings on the periphery. il Time 91:26+ Ja 5 '68

China (People's Republic)
China: is history repeating itself? J. K. Fairbank. New Repub 156:13-14 F 25 '67
China, the surprising country, by M. Roper. Review
Nat R 19:149-52 F 7 '67. K. A. Wittfogel
Continuing Chinese revolution. H. M. Vinacke. Cur Hist 53:161-6+ S '67

COMMUNISM—China   (People's   Republic)—
Continued
Fanshen, by W. Hinton. Review
   Nation 205:184-5 S 4 '67. C. P. FitzGerald
For Mao's sake; interview. M. Kriz. Nat R
   19:944-5 S 5 '67
Forms of modern Sinology. J. Mirsky. Nation
   204:468-70+ Ap 10 '67
Havoc that Mao has wrought. il Bsns W
   p76-8+ Jl 15 '67
I fought in red China's sports war; ed. by
   L. Velie. P. S. Shih. Read Digest 90:73-8
   Je '67
Interrupted   cruise;   encounter   with   Red
   guards of the Chinese coast. C. Hancke and
   B. Hancke. il Yachting 122:44-5+ Ag '67
Lessons through the barrel of a gun; sacred
   writings of Mao Tse-tung. G. Woodcock.
   il Commonweal 86:81-4 Ap 7 '67
Maoism: the religious analogy. D. E. Mac-
   Innis. Christian Cent 85:39-42 Ja 10 '68
Out of chaos: end of an era for red China.
   il U S News 62:36 F 13 '67
We are slaves who have been betrayed; de-
   struction of intellectuals under Mao. S. T.
   Ma. il Life 63:64-6+ Jl 14 '67
   See also
Communist party (China [People's Repub-
   lic])

Cuba

Castro revolution, export model. Life 63:4 Ag
   11 '67
Cost of eight years of Castro. M. de Medici.
   Read Digest 91:89-93 Jl '67
Cuba. L. Bergquist. il Look 31:32-40+ D 12 '67
Cuban diary: bringing up Castro's new man.
   J. Reston. il N Y Times Mag p 11-13+
   Ag 13 '67
Faces of Fidelismo. L. Eder. il Nation 205:
   173-7 S 4 '67
Rentaguerrilla, inc. Nat R 19:890+ Ag 22 '67
Who won the missile confrontation? Nat R
   19:838 Ag 8 '67

Czechoslovakia

Nervous reaction. Time 90:37-8 S 29 '67
Unchecked exchange in Czechoslovakia. J. C.
   Evans. Christian Cent 84:774-5 Je 14 '67
   See also
Communist party (Czechoslovakia)

Europe, Western

Mao power; Europe's newest significant
   political philosophy. il Newsweek 70:48-50
   N 6 '67

France

   See also
Communist party (France)

Greece, Modern

   See also
Anti-Communist movements—Greece, Modern

Hong Kong

Mao-think v. the stiff upper lip. il Time 89:
   30+ My 26 '67
Red China turns on Britain; with interview
   with D. Trench. il U S News 62:36-7 My
   29 '67
Seeing it through. il Newsweek 69:48 Je 5
   '67
Will Hong Kong become Peking duck? R.
   Terrill. New Repub 157:14-15 S 2 '67
   See also
Communist party (Hong Kong)

Hungary

Hungary: the mechanism and the marionettes. C. Sterling. Reporter 36:25-7 My 4
   '67

India

   See also
Communist party (India)

Indonesia

   See also
Anti-communist movements—Indonesia
Communist party (Indonesia)

Italy

Searchers: conflict and communism in an
   Italian town, by B. Paulson and A. Ricci.
   Review
   Sat R 50:41-2 F 4 '67. C. F. Delzell
   See also
Communist party (Italy)

Japan

   See also
Communist party (Japan)

Laos

End of a myth; war in Laos. il Newsweek
   70:36+ O 23 '67
Rumblings on the periphery. il Time 91:26+
   Ja 5 '68

Latin America

Anniversary song; Cuba's plans to extend
   Communist revolution throughout Latin
   America. il Newsweek 70:47 Ag 7 '67
Can Castro start a new Vietnam? P. D.
   Bethel. Nat R 19:130-4 F 7 '67
Cracking down on Castro; OAS resolutions.
   Nation 205:324-5 O 9 '67
Fact sheet on Latin America. Sr Schol 91:9
   O 5 '67
Havana: fanning the guerrilla flames; meet-
   ing of the Organization for Latin American
   solidarity. il Newsweek 70:33-4 Ag 14 '67
OAS foreign ministers take steps against
   Cuban subversion; statements, September
   23, 24 with text of final act, September 24,
   1967. D. Rusk. Dept State Bul 57:490-8 O 16
   '67
Playing to the crowd; conflict among OLAS
   delegates. Newsweek 70:33-4 Ag 21 '67
President Johnson welcomes OAS foreign
   ministers; toast, September 22, 1967. L.
   B. Johnson. Dept State Bul 57:498-9 O 16
   '67
Régis Debray; Latin American Marxist. J.
   Bishop. Commonweal 87:164-6 N 10 '67
Regis Debray; where logic failed. L. E.
   Aguilar. Reporter 37:31-2 D 28 '67
Split-level subversion; Conference on Latin
   American solidarity. Time 90:26+ Ag 4 '67
United States and the Latin American left
   wings. J. J. Johnson. Yale R 56:321-35
   Mr '67
What Castro is plotting: the fight for a
   hemisphere. il U S News 63:42-3 O 9 '67
Who won the missile confrontation? Nat R
   19:838 Ag 8 '67
Wild cry from Havana: more revolutions;
   Latin American solidarity organization con-
   ference. il Life 63:30-1 Ag 18 '67
   See also
Anti-Communist movements—Latin America

Middle East

Enemy is the same. M. Geltman. Nat R 19:
   748 Jl 11 '67

Philippines

   See also
Hukbalahaps

Poland

   See also
Communist party (Poland)

Russia

Dissenting view of the day that shook the
   world; November 7, 1917. J. Lukacs. il N Y
   Times Mag p32-3+ O 22 '67; Discussion.
   p 12+ N 12 '67
Fifty years after: communism has failed,
   it is being destroyed by life itself; interview. A. Kerensky. il U S News 62:66-9
   Mr 13 '67
Horror of communism, as Stalin's daughter
   tells it. S. Stalina. U S News 62:22 My 8
   '67
In the Soviet union; forces of the future;
   with reports by P. Young and J. H.
   Billington. il Life 63:41-54+ N 10 '67
Ironies of history, by I. Deutscher. Review
   Commentary 43:84-6 Je '67. M. Rush
Russia: the next fifty years. il Bsns W p81-
   2+ Ap 29 '67
Soviet Russia, 1917-1967; fifty years of
   thunder. R. Armstrong. il Sat Eve Post
   240:25-38+ N 4 '67
Twenty letters to a friend, by S. Alliluyeva.
   Review
   Nation 205:469-70 N 6 '67. A. Werth
Unfinished revolution, by I. Deutscher. Re-
   view
   Nation 206:85-6 Ja 15 '68. D. Joravsky
What is left of communism? G. Lichtheim.
   For Affairs 46:78-94 O '67
Where Russia is headed; with interview with
   G. W. Nutter. il U S News 63:68-77 N 6 '67
Workers' paradise lost, by E. Lyons. Review
   Nat R 19:1283-5 N 14 '67. S. T. Possony
Workers' paradise lost; condensation. E.
   Lyons. il Read Digest 91:233-7+ N '67
   See also
Communist party (Russia)

Bibliography

USSR: the first half-century. R. Barnes. il
   Sat R 50:22-3 D 30 '67

Thailand

Another Vietnam. W. Pfaff. Commonweal 85:
   550-1 F 17 '67
Hopes and fears in booming Thailand. P. T.
   White. il Nat Geog Mag 132:76-125 Jl '67

COMMUNISM—Thailand—_Continued_
Letter from Bangkok. R. Shaplen. New Yorker 43:142+ Mr 18 '67
More soft spots. il Time 90:25-6 N 3 '67
Rumblings on the periphery. il Time 91:26+ Ja 5 '68
South also rises; Communist insurgency. il Newsweek 70:55 N 6 '67
Thailand: privileged sanctuary. O. Schell. New Repub 157:18-19 S 30 '67
Tightrope in Thailand. E. Klein. il Newsweek 69:52-3 Je 19 '67

Underdeveloped areas

Revolution in the third world; ed. by P. P. Ardrey, jr. il Nat R 19:1188-200 O 31 '67
T.R.B. from Washington; theory of Value line. New Repub 157:2 Jl 8 '67

United States

And further ... Nat R 19:452 My 2 '67
Black power; tool for the Communists? il U S News 64:14 Ja 15 '68
Did Communists spark the Pentagon march? U S News 63:16 D 4 '67
Friendship and fratricide, by M. A. Zeligs. Review
  Nat R 19:295-8+ Mr 21 '67. E. Van Den Haag
Who are the new pro-Communists? W. F. Buckley, jr. Nat R 19:127 F 7 '67
See also
Communist party (United States)

Anti-Communist measures

. . . And in Congress; Willis bill passed. New Repub 157:9 D 9 '67
Angelic vision of the Warren court; New York laws designed to keep subversives off the staffs and faculties of public schools and state colleges declared unconstitutional. Nat R 19:122 F 7 '67
Communists beat the rap; U.S. Court of appeals reverse conviction for violating McCarran act. America 116:367 Mr 18 '67
Liberty v. security; effectiveness of McCarran act reduced. Time 90:19 D 22 '67
McCarran act, RIP. Nat R 19:396 Ap 18 '67
Notes on the CIA shambles. J. Burnham. Nat R 19:294 Mr 21 '67
See also
United States—Foreign relations—Anti-Communist measures

Venezuela

How a campus terrorized a city; Central university in Caracas. Read Digest 90:94-5 Je '67

Vietnam (Republic)

End to enemy expansion in Vietnam? U S News 62:9 F 6 '67
Unrepentant, unyielding; interview with Viet Cong prisoners, after destruction of Ben-Suc in Iron triangle. B. B. Fall. New Repub 156:19-24 F 4 '67

Anti-Communist measures
See also
Vietnamese war, 1957-

Yugoslavia

Now Tito cracks down on old-line Communists. il U S News 64:93-4 Ja 15 '68
Titoism's failure. G. Bailey. il Reporter 36: 16-20 Ja 26 '67
See also
Communist party (Yugoslavia)

COMMUNISM and democracy
Credibility of the Communist conspiracy. J. E. Barrett. Christian Cent 84:500-1 Ap 19 '67
Framework of East-West reconciliation. Z. Brzezinski. bibliog f For Affairs 46:256-75 Ja '68
Happiness? reprint. D. Lawrence. U S News 63:128 S 25 '67
May day; address, May 1, 1967. A. A. Grechko. Vital Speeches 33:508-9 Je 1 '67
Origins of the cold war. A. Schlesinger, jr. For Affairs 46:22-52 O '67; Reply. W. A. Williams. Nation 205:492-5 N 13 '67
Other Vietnams. J. Burnham. Nat R 19:465 My 2 '67
Peace and the strategy conflict, by W. R. Kintner. Review
  Nat R 19:1387-8 D 12 '67. F. J. Johnson
Soviet view of NATO; address, April 24, 1967. L. I. Brezhnev. Vital Speeches 33: 514-22 Je 15 '67
Understanding people's wars. G. W. Shepherd, jr. Christian Cent 84:1185-8 S 20 '67

Vietnam: study in ironies. R. Niebuhr. New Repub 156:11-12 Je 24 '67
What is sauce for the goose is sauce for the gander. E. Rabinowitch. Bul Atomic Sci 23:41-3 S '67

COMMUNISM and nationalism
Soviet achievement; excerpt from The Soviet achievement, 1917-1967. J. P. Nettl. Harper 235:90-4+ O '67

COMMUNISM and religion
Breaking the Christian-Communist silence; Christian-Marxist dialogue. Christian Cent 84:1451 N 15 '67; Discussion. 85:45-6 Ja 10 '68
Can Christians talk to Communists? C. S. Wren. il Look 31:36+ My 2 '67
Dialogue in an age of convergence. C. S. Calian. Christian Cent 84:681-3 My 24 '67
Eastern Europe & the death of God; conference of Marxist sociologists of religion in Prague. N. Birnbaum. Commentary 44: 69-73 Jl '67
Marxists at Santa Clara; Christian-Marxist dialogue. America 117:534 N 11 '67
Religious reform in eastern Europe? M. Bourdeaux. Christian Cent 84:186-7 F 8 '67
Struggle for religious faith in the Soviet Union today. H. A. Bosley. Christian Cent 84:1082-4 Ag 23 '67
See also
Catholic church in Poland

COMMUNISM in literature
Fifty years: a literary tribute; selections from the literature of anti-communism. il Nat R 19:1176-87 O 31 '67

COMMUNIST aggression. See Aggression (international law)

COMMUNIST countries
When revisionists go hunting; Tito & Ceauşecu oppose Moscow's plans for world conference. il Time 91:21 Ja 12 '68
See also
Europe, Eastern
Investments, Foreign (in Communist countries)

Commerce

Capitalizing on communism. A. De Borchgrave. il Newsweek 70:30-2 D 25 '67
East-West relations; address, December 11, 1966. F. D. Kohler. Vital Speeches 33:196-200 Ja 15 '67
East-West trade: an avenue toward world peace; address, May 4, 1967. A. B. Trowbridge. Dept State Bul 56:881-5 Je 12 '67
Teaming up for trade; Rockefeller, Eaton groups join to push East-West deals. Bsns W p40 Ja 21 '67
This month's feature: moves to expand U.S.-Soviet-bloc trade. Cong Digest 46:162-92 Je '67

Religious institutions and affairs
See also
Europe, Eastern—Religious institutions and affairs

Travel regulations
See Travel regulations

COMMUNIST countries and the West. See World politics, 1945-

COMMUNIST organizations
. . . And in Congress; Willis bill passed. New Repub 157:9 D 9 '67
Antiwar protests: a weapon for Communists. U S News 63:12 N 13 '67

COMMUNIST parties
By the waters' edge; meeting at Karlovy Vary. Newsweek 69:55 My 8 '67
New comintern? L. M. Taubinger. Nat R 19: 909 Ag 22 '67
Red nations agree on one thing: hate U.S; meeting of Europe's Communists in Karlovy Vary, Czechoslovakia. il U S News 62:59-60 My 15 '67

COMMUNIST party (China [People's Republic])
China: Maoists vs. Maoists. il Newsweek 69:45 Je 26 '67
Chou En-lai. K. Y. Hsu. New Repub 156:21-5 Ap 8 '67
Conspiracy in Peking; May 16 group. il Newsweek 70:61-2 D 18 '67
Convulsion in Communist China, and what it means to the U.S. D. Chu. Sr Schol 90: 6-11+ Mr 3 '67
Eleventh plenary session communiqué, 1966; Eight Central committee; excerpts. Cur Hist 53:167-9 S '67
Making it official, President Liu out. Time 90:26+ Jl 7 '67
Mao turns China to turmoil. il Bsns W p32-3 Ja 14 '67

COMO, William
On the gypsy circuit. See issues of Dance magazine

COMPACT cars. See Automobiles, Compact

COMPAGNIE des machines Bull. See Electronic apparatus industry and trade—France

COMPANIES. See Corporations

COMPANION crops
Space-saving idea: onions among my tulips. E. M. Schroeder. Home Gard 54:69 My '67

COMPANY magazines. See House organs

COMPANY names. See Corporations—Names

COMPANY planes. See Airplanes, Business

COMPANY towns
Gulf buys itself a new town; Reston, Va. Bsns W p50 S 9 '67

COMPARATIVE education. See Education, Comparative

COMPARATIVE marketing. See Marketing

COMPASS
Marine compasses. il Consumer Rep 32:427-31 Ag '67
Mariner's compass; excerpts from Piloting, seamanship and small boat handling. C. F. Chapman. il Motor B 120:48-51 O '67
Navigating by sun stone; Viking aid to navigation. Sci Am 217:44 Jl '67
New direction; aviation compass with 400 lockers. R. A. Noblett. il Flying 80:78-80 Je '67

COMPASS, Gyroscopic. See Gyro compass

COMPASSION. See Sympathy

COMPATIBILITY (marriage) See Marriage

COMPENSATION (law)
See also
Damages

COMPENSATION for victims of crime. See Reparation

COMPETITION
See also
Free enterprise
Price cutting

COMPETITION, International
Toward one world of business. Fortune 76:105-6 S 15 '67

COMPETITIONS
Anybody seen Wayne Walker? oil companies' giveaway contests. Time 91:41+ Ja 19 '68
Mademoiselle's college competitions. Mlle 66:47 N '67
Triviaddiction; second annual Ivy league-Seven sisters Trivia contest. il Time 89:69-70 Mr 10 '67
Value Line vs. all comers; stock performance contest. Fortune 76:240+ N '67
See also subhead Competitions under various subjects, e.g. Aviation—Competitions

COMPETITIVE bidding. See Contracts, Government

COMPLEMENT fixation
Anaphylatoxin in its relation to the complement system. J. Jensen. bibliog il Science 155:1122-3 Mr 3 '67
Deficient complement fixation by aggregated gamma globulin from hypogammaglobulinemic patients. R. J. Pickering and others. bibliog il Science 157:454-5 Jl 28 '67
Virus particles and murine leukemia virus complement-fixing antigen in neoplastic and nonneoplastic cell lines. W. T. Hall and others. bibliog il Science 156:85-8 Ap 7 '67

COMPLEMENTS (immunity)
Complement: substitution of the terminal component in immune hemolysis by 1,10-phenanthroline. U. Hadding and H. J. Müller-Eberhard. bibliog il Science 157:442-3 Jl 28 '67
Efficiency of the first component of complement, C'1, in the hemolytic reaction. H. R. Colten and others. bibliog il Science 158:1590-2 D 22 '67

COMPLEXION. See Skin

COMPONENTS construction. See Houses, Prefabricated

COMPOSERS
Disreputable romantics. F. Cooper. il Hi Fi 18:48-50 Ja '68
I am society's child; J. Ian. il Life 63:53-4+ O 27 '67
Over twenty-one: little known prolific opera composers. F. Kabalin. il Opera N 31:8-12 F 18 '67

Anecdotes, facetiae, satire, etc.
American in Paris, and elsewhere. G. Kubik. il Opera N 32:8-13 N 4 '67

COMPOSERS, American
See also
Hawkins, M.
Schuller, G.
Walker, W. S.

COMPOSERS, Argentine
See also
Schifrin, L. C.

COMPOSERS, Australian
See also
Williamson, M.

COMPOSERS, Austrian
See also
Berg, A.
Bruckner, A.
Mahler, G.
Mozart, J. C. W. A.
Schubert, F. P.
Webern, A. von

COMPOSERS, British
See also
Composers, English

COMPOSERS, Czech
From the banks of the Vlatava. O. Daniel. Sat R 50:76-7 F 25 '67
See also
Dvořák, A.
Janáček, L.

COMPOSERS, Danish
See also
Nielsen, C.

COMPOSERS, English
Britain's musical revival. H. Kupferberg. Atlan 219:135-8 Ap '67
English musical renaissance, by F. Howes. Review
Reporter 37:47-8 O 5 '67. R. Gelatt
See also
Britten, B.
Delius, F.
Holst, G.
Josephs, W.

COMPOSERS, Finnish
See also
Sibelius, J. J. C.

COMPOSERS, French
See also
Berlioz, H.
Boulez, P.
Lalande, M. de
Messiaen, O.
Poulenc, F.

COMPOSERS, German
See also
Händel, G. F.
Henze, H. W.
Humperdinck, E.
Lortzing, A.
Stockhausen, K.
Strauss, R.

COMPOSERS, Italian
See also
Bellini, V.
Caccini, G.
Dallapiccola, L.
Donizetti, G.
Geminiani, F.
Monteverdi, C.
Verdi, G.

COMPOSERS, Japanese
See also
Takemitsu, T.

COMPOSERS, Korean
See also
Yun, I.

COMPOSERS, Mexican
See also
Chávez, C.

COMPOSERS, Polish
See also
Penderecki, K.
Szymanowski, K.

COMPOSERS, Russian
See also
Prokof'ev, S. S.
Rimskii-Korsakov, N. A.
Skriabin, A. N
Stravinsky, I. F.
Tchaikovsky, P. I.

COMPOSERS, Spanish
See also
Granados, E.

COMPOSING machines. See Typesetting machines

COMPOSITE materials. See Materials

COMPOSITION (art)
Notes on composition for the young landscape painter. P. L. Martin. il Am Artist 31:50-5 S '67
On composition in landscape; excerpts from Starting with watercolor. R. Hilder. il Am Artist 31:42-7 My '67
What makes an object interesting? D. Kingman. il Design 68:20-1 Ja '67

COMPOSITION (music)
Composer uses printing presses for inspiration. il Pub W 191:116-17 Mr 6 '67
Diary of a young man of fashion; pages from an advanced composer's notebooks, 1987. P. J. Korn. Hi Fi 17:60-3 S '67
Family resemblance; similarities of Verdi's operas. C. D. Alper. il Opera N 31:21-3 F 18 '67
Hit from Hamburg; a U.S. opera; G. Schuller's The visitation. P. Moor. Life 62:11 Je 30 '67
Opera is born; Ginastera's Bomarzo. P. Hume. il Américas 19:34-7 Jl '67
Peripatetic reviewer; composition demands of the new musical theater on Broadway. E. Weeks. Atlan 220:108 Jl '67
Sonata for two clarinets; student composers take over. H. W. Arberg and C. S. Carleton. il Am Ed 3:30-2 F '67

COMPOSITION (photography)
Ambiguous image. H. M. Kinzer. il Pop Phot 60:78-85 Mr '67
Avoid the shape trap. R. Arnold. il U S Camera 30:58-61+ Jl '67
Caulfield on picture taking; contrived vs candid. P. Caulfield. Mod Phot 31:18 D '67
Compositions are arrangements that work. E. Scully. il Mod Phot 31:50-7 S '67
Graphics are crucial! so is emotional impact! J. Scully. il Mod Phot 31:52-61+ My '67
In search of knowledge. il U S Camera 30:86-7 O '67
Large camera; check list to prevent errors. A. Feininger. Mod Phot 31:46+ N '67
Look at it another way. R. E. Mayer. il U S Camera 30:46-7+ Ap '67
Master of timing, master of light. P. Caulfield. il Mod Phot 31:52-9 Mr '67
Op goes the easel. R. W. Parsons. il Pop Phot 60:88-9+ F '67
Pictures that make you wonder. il Pop Phot 61:108-15 N '67
Seven ways to see a chair. M. Orovan. il U S Camera 30:62-3 F '67
Shoot through the hole. J. R. Oswald. il U S Camera 30:68-9 O '67
Wait? for what? J. Scully. il Mod Phot 31:60-5 Ap '67
World's greatest pictures; Stravinsky by Newman. J. Scully. il Mod Phot 31:70-1+ My '67
See also
Photography—Still life

COMPOSITION, English. See English language —Composition

COMPOST
See also
Fertilizers and manures
Refuse as fertilizer

COMPREHENSION
See also
Learning, Psychology of

COMPREHENSIVE random achievement monitor. See Student achievements

COMPRESSED air
See also
Air compressors

COMPRESSORS, Air. See Air compressors

COMPTON, Bertita E. and Garvey, W. D.
Information functions of an international meeting. Science 155:1648-50 Mr 31 '67

COMPTON, Dick
Super-veep. Atlan 219:118+ Ap '67

COMPTON, Sir Edmund
Tough cheese. por Newsweek 71:32 Ja 8 '68

COMPTON, Gardner
Film dance and things to come. Dance Mag 42:34-7 Ja '68

COMPTON, Neil
Expo 67. Commentary 44:32-9 Jl '67
Observations (cont) Commentary 43:77-9 Ja '67

COMPTON, Wilson Martindale
Hymn to an Ohioan. por Am For 73:6-7+ Ap '67

COMPTON, Calif.
Negroes
Ill-at-ease in Compton, by R. M. Elman. Review
Sat R 50:30 Jl 8 '67. B. R. Boylan

COMPULSORY arbitration. See Arbitration, Industrial

COMPULSORY education
Washington report; require learning by federal law? J. Lloyd. Sr Schol 90:sup6 My 5 '67
See also
School age

COMPULSORY military service. See Military service, Compulsory

COMPULSORY retirement from business, etc. See Retirement from business, etc.

COMPUTER-assisted instruction. See Computers—Educational applications

COMPUTER golf. See Golf, Indoor

COMPUTER industry
Computer-leasing stocks. A. M. Louis. il Fortune 76:167-8+ Jl '67
Mini-computer runs some big totals. il Bsns W p78 N 25 '67

Employees
See Computer workers

Securities
Grow-grow computer makers. il Duns R 90:71-2 Ag '67

France
France: first the bomb, then the Plan Calcul. J. Walsh. Science 156:767-70 My 12 '67
French computer industry faces dilemma. il Aviation W 86:317-19 My 29 '67
GE learns a lesson in France; spiraling costs force slow down of computer making. Bsns W p76+ Ja 21 '67

COMPUTER lease and rental services. See Computers—Renting

COMPUTER logic. See Algebra, Boolean

COMPUTER match-making. See Computers—Social applications

COMPUTER process control. See Computers—Industrial applications

COMPUTER processing. See Electronic data processing

COMPUTER programming. See Programming (computers)

COMPUTER schools. See Programming (computers)—Study and teaching

COMPUTER workers
Computer revolution wants you. H. Shuldiner. il Pop Sci 191:86-8+ S '67
Eerie interface of man and machine. R. Campbell. il Life 63:60-72 O 27 '67
Help wanted: 50,000 programmers. G. Bylinsky. il Fortune 75:140-3+ Mr '67
How good are computer schools? il Bsns W p97-8+ O 7 '67
Skill requirements for computer manufacturing. H. Greenspan. il Mo Labor R 90:52-4 S '67
Software gets a hardsell approach. il Bsns W p 171-2+ O 21 '67
Software snarl; shortage of programmers. il Time 90:75-6 Ag 18 '67

COMPUTERIZED manikin. See Anatomical models

COMPUTERS
Big IBM job won't compute. Bsns W p54 Mr 25 '67
Computer ogre or tool? M. A. Jensen. Park & Rec 2:22+ S '67
Computer science; letter. A. Newell and others. Science 157:1373-4 S 22 '67
Computermania; eastern Europe is beginning to click. Newsweek 69:84-5 Mr 27 '67
Computers go to court; legal hassle between Honeywell and Sperry Rand over patent licensing. Bsns W p 150 Je 10 '67
Computers today. S. L. Englebardt. il Sci Digest 61:41-8+ F '67
Computers viewed as ripe for more creative usage. Aero Tech 21:26 Ag 14 '67
Copyright and computers. D. Wolfie. Science 156:319 Ap 21 '67
Domain walls in computers of the future. A. Ewing. il Sci N 91:436-7 My 6 '67
How the computer gets the answer. R. Campbell. il Life 63:60-72 O 27 '67
Logic demon; duplicating the logic functions of giant electronic computers. D. Lancaster. il Pop Electr 25:41-5+ D '66
New computer borrows present programs; using Miniflow language. il Tech W 20:40-1 Ja 30 '67
New frontiers. H. Fantel. Opera N 32:29 S 23 '67
No nonsense; interview. C. P. Lecht. New Yorker 43:25-7 Ag 19 '67
Russians researching laser computers. Sci N 92:303 S 23 '67
Think tank gets a new brain wave; SDC. il Bsns W p58-60 Ag 26 '67
Thinking machine. I. Asimov. Sci Digest 62:73-4 D '67
What comes next in the computer age; interview. J. Diebold. il U S News 62:54-7 Je 26 '67
See also
Automatic speech recognition
Control data corporation
Cybernetics
Electronic data processing
Magnetic memory (computers)
Perceptrons
Programming (computers)
Punched card systems

COMPUTERS—*Continued*

Aeronautic applications

Atlanta tests support automation plans. P. J. Klass. il Aviation W 87:51+ S 4 '67

Attack angle system set for Gulfstream 2. R. G. O'Lone. il Aviation W 87:89+ O 9 '67

BOAC is using computers to plan world SST routes. Aviation W 87:28 D 18 '67

Carriers adopt systems concept; including standard, computerized ticketing equipment. R. F. Coburn. Aviation W 87:40 Jl 10 '67

Color TV generated by computer to evaluate spaceborne systems. B. M. Elson. il Aviation W 87:78+ O 30 '67

Computer graphics aid solution to DC-9 cabin noise problem. il Aviation W 87:69+ Jl 17 '67

CDC readies Phoenix computer production; fire-control computer for air-to-air missile system. C. D. LaFond. il Tech W 20:24-5 My 8 '67

Four versions of autonetics D26J shown; airborne digital computers. il Aero Tech 21:34 D 4 '67

Radar simulator uses digital computer. B. M. Elson. il Aviation W 87:97+ O 16 '67

Univac modifying computer for use in A-7A avionics. C. D. LaFond. il Tech W 20:17 F 13 '67

Agricultural applications

Computer cuts my paperwork. O. Bay. il Farm J 91:A4 N '67

Computer farming in your future? R. J. Fee. Suc Farm 65:39+ S '67

Computer watches 42,000 layers. Farm J 91:48J Ja '67

Instant answers for your farm; portable teletype attached to home phone. il Farm J 91:23+ Jl '67

Will you listen to a computer? D. Hanson. Suc Farm 65:8 F '67

Anecdotes, facetiae, satire, etc.

Priests' union threatens strike; computerized confessional. P. J. Laux. il America 117:550-1 N 11 '67

Architectural applications

Computer-aided building design: where do we go from here? J. Barnett. Arch Rec 141:219-20 Ap '67

Computerized cost estimating. J. Barnett. il Arch Rec 141:163-6 Mr '67

Art applications

Electronic museum. A. Schoener. il Pop Phot 60:84-7 Ap '67

Electronic museum: Museum computer network project. il Newsweek 70:42 D 25 '67

Banking applications

Cashing in on the checkless society. R. L. Kramer and W. P. Livingston. bibliog f Harvard Bsns R 45:141-9 S '67

Money goes electronic in the 1970s; checkless, cashless society. il Bsns W p54-6+ Ja 13 '68

Soon you'll never see money at all; cashless, checkless society. il Changing T 21:7-11 O '67

Bibliographic applications

Computer and copyright: the next five years. C. H. Lieb. Pub W 192:40-2 S 18 '67

Fair use: McClellan bill proposals. S. Kauffmann. New Repub 157:24+ O 7 '67

Grant given for computer library language study. Pub W 191:117 F 6 '67

Literary information systems: summary of addresses and panel discussion at ABPC conference. Pub W 191:35-7 Ap 10 '67

Biological applications

Talking without a voice. il Sci Digest 61:41 Mr '67

Botanical applications

Electronic herbarium; National university of Mexico. E. Zubryn. il Sci N 92:161 Ag 12 '67

Business applications

Automation improves customer service: Philadelphia suburban water co, Bryn Mawr, Pa. G. H. Dann. il Am City 82:122-3+ Je '67

Business trends: knowledge-computer revolution; address. July 21, 1967. E. H. Wasson. Vital Speeches 33:694-7 S 1 '67

Computers in top-level decision making. R. H. Brady. il Harvard Bsns R 45:67-76 Jl '67

Computers: no impact on divisional control; excerpts from The impact of computers on management. J. Dearden. bibliog Harvard Bsns R 45:99-104 Ja '67

Model for branch store planning. M. Sawits. il Harvard Bsns R 45:140-3 Jl '67

New intellectual climate; address, April 20, 1967. O. Helmer. Vital Speeches 33:497-9 Je 1 '67

Communication applications

Philco-Ford installing twelve AUTODIN centers; automatic digital network. il Tech W 20:33 F 6 '67

Control applications

GE details MTF's Apollo logistics program; computerized provisioning system. J. F. Judge. il Aero Tech 21:48+ O 9 '67

On the production line; direct digital control of industrial processes. C. Behrens. Sci N 92:539 D 2 '67

Raytheon's new RAC-230 uses Poseidon computer technology. J. A. Strasser. il Aero Tech 21:46-7 Ja i '68

Cooperative use

Charts for time-sharers; GE computer centers to offer use of digital plotters to customers. Bsns W p 174 Je 24 '67

Computer time-sharing catches on; multiplecustomer computer-sharing. il Bsns W p 177-8+ Ap 15 '67

Computer time-sharing, everyman at the console. J. Main. il Fortune 76:88-91+ Ag '67

Computers and security. C. Behrens. il Sci N 91:532-3 Je 3 '67

I used a real computer at home, and so will you. C. P. Gilmore. il Pop Sci 190: 90-4+ My '67

Criminal investigation applications

See also
United States—Federal bureau of investigation—National crime information center

Design

Raytheon's new RAC-230 uses Poseidon computer technology. J. A. Strasser. il Aero Tech 21:46-7 Ja i '68

Digital computers

Digital computer logic; what the symbols mean. E. Bukstein. il Electr World 78:46-7 Ag '67

How the computer gets the answer. R. Campbell. il Life 63:60-72 O 27 '67

I used a real computer at home, and so will you. C. P. Gilmore. il Pop Sci 190:90-4+ My '67

Nike-X will use hyper-speed computers. il Aviation W 87:124-7 O 23 '67

Penultimate automatic keyer. P. A. Stark and others. il Electr World 77:36-8+ Je '67

Philco-Ford installing twelve AUTODIN centers; automatic digital network. il Tech W 20:33 F 6 '67

Radar simulator uses digital computer. B. M. Elson. il Aviation W 87:97+ O 16 '67

3-D tic-tac-toe; playing games with UNIVAC 1107. il Sci Digest 62:25-6 Jl '67

Educational applications

Aerospace techniques may meet needs. J. Rhea. il Tech W 20:28-9 F 27 '67

Campus computers. il Sat R 50:76 Ap 15 '67

Challenge of technology; excerpts. Todays Health 45:57 S '67

Communications technology: a social force; address, October 10, 1967. R. W. Sarnoff. Vital Speeches 34:94-6 N 15 '67

Computer and the chancellor. J. Shera. Wilson Lib Bul 41:837+ Ap '67

Computer as a tutor; with an account of the Brentwood, Calif. program by E. Bowen. il Life 62:68-70+ Ja 27 '67

Computer tutors for ghetto pupils. A. Poinsett. il Ebony 23:91-4+ D '67

Computerized classrooms are almost here. il Changing T 21:24-8 Mr '67

Computers and the schools; symposium. bibliog il NEA J 56:15-32 F '67

Computers find school is tough. il Bsns W p 106-8 Jl 1 '67

Computers in high education; excerpt from The computer in American education. J. Caffrey. Sch & Soc 95:319-23 Sum '67

Computers to track education research. Aero Tech 21:32 Jl 17 '67

Fifteen little Indians: Westinghouse computer project on Menominee reservation. Wisconsin. New Repub 156:6 Je 17 '67; Reply. A. C. Turner. 157:34-5 Jl 1 '67

Flexibility for class time; Stanford school scheduling system. il Time 90:110 D 8 '67

COMPUTERS—Educational applications—*Cont*
Formulas for learning. il Sci N 91:406-7 Ap 29 '67
Harper, RCA to develop computer-based programs. Pub W 191:50 Je 26 '67
Human learning in a natural setting. Sch & Soc 95:41-2 Ja 21 '67
Kids, computers, and corporations. P. Schrag. il Sat R 50:78-80+ My 20 '67
More computers for the campus. il Sci N 91:326-7 Ap 8 '67
New B.M.O.C.s: big machines on campus. il Time 89:98 My 19 '67
1968 seen critical for computer education. J. Rhea. il Aero Tech 21:20-2 Ja 1 '68
Of students, professors, and computers. C. Fincher. il Sch & Soc 95:144-8 Mr 4 '67
Technology in higher education: the winds of change blow stronger; report of conference sponsored by the American educational publishers institute. il Pub W 193:35-8 Ja 8 '68
There's a computer in your future; symposium. il Am Ed 3:11-25 N '67
See also
Electronic data processing
Teaching machines

Government applications

Big brother reads the tax returns. G. Astor. il Look 31:82+ Ap 18 '67
City where computers will know about everybody; New Haven project: UMIS for Urban management information system. il U S News 62:78-9 My 15 '67
Computerized man: cause of privacy; address, May 20, 1967. W. Douglas. Vital Speeches 33:700-4 S 1 '67
Don't tell it to the computer; V. Packard; discussion. N Y Times Mag p 12+ Ja 29 '67
Feasibility study on clearinghouse for copyrights and computers; with editorial comment. Pub W 192:33, 38 S 4 '67
Prototype project for copyrights and computers: feasibility study of mechanism to handle requests for copyright clearances. Pub W 192:35 Jl 31 '67
Unhappy returns from the IRS' computers; income tax returns checked by central data processing machines. il Bsns W p73-4+ F 25 '67

Industrial applications

Computer model for new product demand. M. Hamburg and R. J. Atkins. Harvard Bsns R 45:107-10+ Mr '67
From design to finished product; automated metalworking factory. il Bsns W p88-90 D 30 '67
See also
Computers—Control applications

Input-output equipment

Communicating with computers. J. Kyle. il Electr World 77:50-2+ F '67
Computer's little helpers multiply. il Bsns W p 116-20 Ag 5 '67
CDC airborne A/D converter under evaluation by air force. J. Rhea. il Aero Tech 21:33-4 D 4 '67
Digital plotting techniques. L. E. Frenzel, jr. il Electr World 77:47-50+ Mr '67
NEL testing display methods. Aero Tech 21:36 O 9 '67

International aspects

Quick-access pool for world data; Washington study urges system for scientific and engineering information. Bsns W p78+ Je 17 '67

Investment applications

Buttons are a broker's best friend; electronic inquiry terminals. il Bsns W p 123-4+ N 4 '67
Investment future of America; address, May 1, 1967. G. K. Funston. Vital Speeches 33:554-9 Jl 1 '67
Setting odds on mutual funds for fun and profit; D. A. Campbell co.'s brokerage firm. il Bsns W p49-50 Ja 14 '67

Mathematical applications

Computer-generated motion pictures. B. R. Groves. il Science 155:1662-3 Mr 31 '67

Medical applications

Automating medicine; excerpt from Ferment in medicine. R. M. Magraw and D. B. Magraw. Sat R 50:66-9 O 7 '67
Computer diagnosis; detecting brain tumors. F. C. Livingstone. Sci N 91:558 Je 10 '67

Computerized physicals. Sci Digest 63:81-2 Ja '68
Computers: they supply answers when your doctor needs to know. K. N. Anderson. il Pop Mech 127:134-7 Mr '67; Same with title Instant medicine by electronic brain. Sci Digest 61:9-14 Ap '67

Anecdotes, facetiae, satire, etc.
Computer, spare that physician. R. Goulart. Sat R 50:4 Jl 29 '67

Meteorological applications

Surprise answer in the lab; cause of sudden warmings. il Sci N 92:631 D 30 '67

Military applications

AC delivers first SRAM computer. il Aero Tech 21:15 O 23 '67
Air force to centralize software services under new command. D. C. Winston. Aviation W 87:30 D 11 '67
Baptism of fire for computers. il Bsns W p 128-30+ Ap 22 '67
Nike-X will use hyper-speed computers. il Aviation W 87:124-7 O 23 '67
Second $100 million computer buy looms. M. Getler. Tech W 20:14 Ap 24 '67
Senator charges DOD analysis may be damaging U.S. security. Aviation W 87:27 S 18 '67
TACFIRE computer role may expand. Aero Tech 21:12 N 20 '67

Miniaturization

Mini-computer runs some big totals. il Bsns W p78 N 25 '67

Municipal applications

Computerized voter registration; Flint, Mich. W. R. Penberthy. il Am City 82:78-9 N '67
Data processing speeds the election process; Chicago. J. E. Murphy. il Am City 82:100 My '67
Get the tax bills out on time; use of electronic tax rolls in Oakland, Calif. E. V. Waring. il Am City 82:110-11 Je '67
How to purchase data-processing equipment. J. E. Enright. Am City 82:127-8 Ap '67
Plan before you put a computer to work; Memphis, Tenn. C. R. Henze. il Am City 82:100-1 Mr '67
Water utility will offer air conditioning and steam heating; San Antonio, Tex. L. F. Campos. il Am City 82:75-7 D '67

Museum applications
See Computers—Art applications

Musical applications
See also
Phonograph records—Electronic music

Photographic applications
Computer-generated motion pictures. B. R. Groves. il Science 155:1662-3 Mr 31 '67

Police applications
Computer combats auto thefts. B. M. Crittenden. il Am City 82:116-17 Je '67

Printing applications
Alphanumeric introduces new composing program. Pub W 191:114 F 6 '67
AAUP: computer-aided composition; summary of address, June 12, 1967. A. H. Gray. il Pub W 192:78+ Jl 3 '67
Break-even point in computer composition; summary of report. J. W. Seybold. Pub W 191:73 Ap 3 '67
Forces of change; shaping the publishers' world. il Pub W 191:22-3 My 1 '67
Future of scientific journals. W. S. Brown and others. bibliog Science 158:1153-9 D 1 '67
Harris-Intertype introduces electronic-controlled press. il Pub W 192:84 N 6 '67
New processes and old stupidity. R. L. Tobin. Sat R 50:93-4 Je 10 '67
New York times index to go on computer. Pub W 193:46 Ja 8 '68
PIA computer section studies Seybold report. Pub W 191:118 F 6 '67
Printing is turning the page; Videocomp. il Bsns W p 122-4+ S 9 '67
Publishing goes electronic. C. Behrens. il Sci N 92:44-5 Jl 8 '67
Rocappi completes new typesetting program. Pub W 191:117 F 6 '67
Using the computer for the appropriate job; report of second International conference on computerized typesetting. il Pub W 192:64+ D 4 '67
Visible word; excerpts from address. H. Spencer. Pub W 192:62 D 4 '67

COMPUTERS—*Continued*

Renting

Leasing game. il Time 90:95 S 15 '67
New name is computer leasing; J. Diebold. Bsns W p41 S 9 '67

Scientific applications

Automation in the laboratory. R. J. Spinrad. il Science 158:55-60 O 6 '67
Biomathematics and computer science; report on fifth annual symposium. L. D. Cady, jr. Science 156:1265-6 Je 2 '67
Computerizing lobsters. il Sci Digest 62:25 D '67
Distortion of a splashing liquid drop. F. H. Harlow and J. P. Shannon. bibliog il Science 157:547-50 Ag 4 '67
Nautical computer; IBM-1800 data and control system. il Sci Digest 62:39 N '67
Redstone reports success in library computer use. Library J 93:142 Ja 15 '68

Social applications

Computer; individual privacy; address, March 6, 1967. S. J. Ervin, jr. Vital Speeches 33: 421-6 My 1 '67
Human values in the computer age: the negative income tax; address, November 30, 1967. A. Miller. Vital Speeches 34:190-2 Ja 1 '68
Made-to-order matches; computer dating. M. Durant. il Mlle 64:114-15+ F '67
Post office box; electronic dating services. N White. New Repub 157:21 Ag 19 '67

Space flight applications

All-digital displays studied for NASA mission center. il Tech W 20:22 F 20 '67
America's big eye on the sky. D. Robinson. il Read Digest 90:155-6+ F '67
Cathode ray display speeds SRAM data; USAF short-range attack missile. R. G. O'Lone. il Aviation W 86:74-5+ Mr 13 '67
Computer tells launch vehicle readiness. il Tech W 20:36-7 Ap 17 '67
MOL computer weds two technologies. R. Pay. il Tech W 20:26-7 Ap 3 '67
100-ft.-lb.-sec. momentum produced by 65-lb. CMG. il Aero Tech 21:40-1 Ag 28 '67

Sports applications

Computers & quarterbacks. R. Levy. il Duns R 90:63 S '67
Numbers game for the tour; IBM sports information service. A. Wright. il Sports Illus 27:76-8 N 13 '67

Time sharing systems

Legal & security issues posed by computer utilities. R. P. Bigelow. bibliog f Harvard Bsns R 45:150-2+ S '67

Traffic control applications

Computer puts more go on city streets; Wichita Falls, Tex. R. L. Wilshire. il Am City 82:116+ N '67
Computer to control tunnel traffic; Liverpool. il Am City 82:130-1 Mr '67
Computer traffic control a hit with baseball fans; Cincinnati, Ohio. J. Scheinson. il Am City 82:152+ O '67
Computer will control airport traffic; New York city's John F. Kennedy airport. il Am City 82:140+ Je '67
Digital computer designed to control traffic only; Fort Lauderdale, Fla. il Am City 82: 100+ Ja '67
Turin tries computer traffic control; Italy. il Am City 82:136 Ap '67

Transportation applications

Computed highway. Sci Digest 62:29-30 Ag '67
Computers for commuters. il Am City 82:104 Jl '67

COMPUTERS, Used
Boom in used computers? A. Hershman. il Duns R 90:63-4 D '67

COMPUTERS on aircraft. See Computers—Aeronautic applications

COMSAT. See Communications satellite corporation

COMSTOCK, Henry B.
Field day for engineers. il Pop Mech 127:88-92 My '67
Huge new sports center: how the Garden grew. il Pop Mech 128:140-3+ N '67
Slow train to Great Slave. Pop Mech 128:110-13 Jl '67

CON men. See Fraud

CONANT, Barbara M.
Trials and tribulations of textbook price indexing. ALA Bul 61:197-9 F '67

CONANT, James Bryant
Are schools getting better? interview. por U S News 63:102-4+ O 23 '67
Comprehensive high school; interview. por Sr Schol 90:sup 18-19 My 19 '67
Conant cites unique role of U.S. high school library; excerpts from Comprehensive high school. Library J 92:3098+ S 15 '67
Conant revisited. T. Ferrer. por Sat R 50: 56-7+ Mr 18 '67
about
End of orthodoxy. Sat R 51:50 Ja 13 '68

CONANT, Ralph W.
Sociological and institutional changes in American life: their implications for the library. por ALA Bul 61:528-36 My '67

CONCANAVALIN
Concanavalin A reaction with human normal immunoglobulin G and myeloma immunoglobulin G. M. A. Leon. bibliog il Science 158:1325-6 D 8 '67

CONCENTRATION. See Attention

CONCENTRATION camp atrocities. See World war, 1939-1945—Atrocities

CONCENTRATION camps

Germany

Germany 1967; visit to Dachau. M. Decter. Atlan 219:50-3 My '67
Last trip to Ravensbruck. W. Hangen. il Holiday 41:70-1+ Ap '67

Poland

Auschwitz, by B. Neumann. Review Sat R 50:43-4 F 4 '67. L. L. Snyder
Nazi war victims on trial; concerning Treblinka, by J. F. Steiner. A. Donat. Sat R 50: 32-4 My 13 '67
Reader's choice; concerning Treblinka by Jean-François Steiner. O. Handlin. Atlan 219:128 Je '67
Revolt at Treblinka; excerpts from Treblinka. tr. by H. Weaver. J. F. Steiner. il Sat Eve Post 240:34-6+ My 20; 38-40+ Je 3 '67
Survival of the Jews; concerning J. Steiner's Treblinka. B. Bettelheim. New Repub 157: 23-30 Jl 1 '67; Discussion. 157:32+ Jl 15; 34+ S 30 '67
Treblinka, by J. F. Steiner. Review Harper 235:92+ Jl '67. D. Caute
Treblinka: heroism or fantastic apology? J. Greenfeld. Life 62:8+ My 19 '67

Russia

Journey into the whirlwind, by E. S. Ginzburg. Review Time 90:118+ D 1 '67

CONCENTUS musicus (ensemble) See Instrumental ensembles

CONCEPTION
Baby she'd always wanted. A. Levy. il Good H 164:48+ F '67

CONCERT artists. See Pianists

CONCERT halls
Arts crunch: Memorial cultural center, Atlanta. G. Bradshaw. il Vogue 150:126-9+ S 15 '67
Blossom center: old dream come true; Cleveland summer orchestra's new pavilion. B. Murray. Hi Fi 17:MA22-3 Ap '67
Britten and the Aldeburgh miracle; Maltings at Snape. E. Greenfield. il Hi Fi 17:MA24-6 S '67
Britten at Aldeburgh; Snape Maltings concert hall. I. Kolodin. il Sat R 50:41-3 Jl 29 '67
For concerts, dance and drama: flexible design; ed. by M. F. Schmertz. il Arch Rec 141:115-30 F '67
Jesse H. Jones hall: the most sophisticated building of its kind anywhere in the world. il Arch Rec 141:116-21 F '67
Maltings at Snape: old malthouses converted into a concert hall for Aldeburgh music festival. il Arch Forum 127:66-71 N '67
New hall at Snape; notable events in the hall. T. Heinitz. il Sat R 50:49+ Jl 29 '67
New halls under way; Queen Elizabeth hall and Purcell room. E. Greenfield. il Hi Fi 17: MA22-3 Je '67
Orchestra hall remodeled: the eye is pleased, but. . ; Chicago report. R. C. Marsh. Hi Fi 17:MA20-1 Ja '67
Other side; London's Queen Elizabeth Hall. T. Heinitz. il Sat R 50:76 Mr 25 '67

Acoustics

See Acoustics, Architectural

CONCERT managers
Concert managers convene. S. Fleming. Hi Fi 17:MA9 Mr '67

CONCERT singers. See Singers

CONCERTO; ballet. See Ballets—Criticisms

CONCERTOS
Music; new piano concerto by E. Carter. B. Boretz. Nation 204:445-6 Ap 3 '67
See also
Phonograph records—Concertos

CONCHOLOGY. See Shells (conchology)

CONCILIATION, International. See Arbitration, International

CONCORD, Mass.
Thoreau lyceum founded. Liv Wildn 30:43 Aut '66

CONCORDE airliner. See Airplanes, Supersonic

CONCRETE
How to get better concrete. A. Muehling. il Suc Farm 65:48-9 Je '67
Stupid questions about bag mixes. S. J. Howard. il Pop Mech 127:178-80 Ap '67

Coloring
Concrete can be colorful. P. McCafferty. il Pop Sci 190:184-8 Ap '67

Repairing
See Concrete construction—Repairing

CONCRETE, Precast
Concrete in the garden, using precast panels. il Sunset 138:92 Je '67
Finally: a low-cost component system for housing that really works; Techcrete. il Arch Rec 141:187-94 Mr '67
Small office building by Marcel Breuer: sophisticated use of precast concrete; Torrington manufacturing co. il Arch Rec 141: 131-6 F '67

CONCRETE, Reinforced
Acrylic-latex additives create extra-strength new concretes. il Arch Rec 141:199-200 Mr '67

CONCRETE construction

Repairing
Patching concrete and masonry. B. Gladstone. Am Home 70:150 O '67

CONCRETE floors. See Floors, Concrete

CONCRETE houses
Instant concrete house. G. X. Sand. il Pop Mech 127:116-17 Je '67

CONCRETE music. See Music, Concrete

CONCRETE ornaments, Garden. See Garden ornaments

CONCRETIONS
Concretions. il Sci N 92:196 Ag 26 '67

CONDENSATION
Condensation of atmospheric moisture from tropical maritime air masses as a freshwater resource. R. D. Gerard and J. L. Worzel. bibliog il Science 157:1300-2 S 15 '67; Reply. R G. W. Willcocks. 158:1525 D 22 '67

CONDIE, Kent C.
Composition of the ancient North American crust. bibliog Science 155:1013-15 F 24 '67

CONDITIONED reflexes. See Conditioned response

CONDITIONED response
Actinomycin D blocks formation of memory of shock-avoidance in goldfish. B. W. Agranoff and others. bibliog il Science 158: 1600-1 D 22 '67
Audiogenic seizure susceptibility induced in C57B1/6J mice by prior auditory exposure. K. R. Henry. bibliog il Science 158:938-40 N 17 '67
Babies are novelty-digesting machines from the first day. il Life 62:42-3 Mr 31 '67
Brain lesions in birds: effects on discrimination acquisition and reversal. L. J. Stettner and W. J. Schultz. bibliog il Science 155: 1689-92 Mr 31 '67
Building on Pavlov. P. McBroom. il Sci N 91:498-9 My 27 '67
Conditioning with delayed vitamin injections. J. Garcia and others. bibliog il Science 155: 716-18 F 10 '67
Discrimination learning and inhibition. H. S. Terrace; reply with rejoinder. J. A. Deutsch. Science 156:988-9 My 19 '67
Effects of visual form on the evoked response. E. R. John and others. bibliog il Science 155:1439-42 Mr 17 '67
Electrocortical correlates of stimulus response and reinforcement. K. H. Pribram and others. bibliog il Science 157:94-6 Jl 7 '67; Discussion. 158:394-5 O 20 '67
Lateral hypothalamic stimulation in satiated rats: the rewarding effects of self-induced drinking. J. Mendelson. il Science 157:1077-9 S 1 '67

Learning-set formation by mink, ferrets, skunks, and cats. B. A. Doty and others. bibliog il Science 155:1579-80 Mr 24 '67
Magnesium pemoline: effect on avoidance conditioning in rats. P. W. Frey and V. J. Polidora. bibliog il Science 155:1281-2 Mr 10 '67
Magnesium pemoline; enhancement of learning and memory of a conditioned avoidance response. N. Plotnikoff; discussion. bibliog il Science 153:902; 155:603-5; 157:958-9 Ag 19 '66, F 3, Ag 25 '67
Modulation of elicited behavior by a fixed-interval schedule of electric shock presentation. W. H. Morse and others. bibliog il Science 157:215-17 Jl 14 '67
Motivated forgetting mediated by implicit verbal chaining; a laboratory analog of repression. S. Glucksberg and L. J. King. il Science 158:517-19 O 27 '67
Perceptual deficit during a mental task. D. Kahneman and others. bibliog il Science 157:218-19 Jl 14 '67
Puromycin and retention in the goldfish. A. Potts and M. E. Bitterman. bibliog il Science 158:1594-6 D 22 '67
Reversal learning and forgetting in bird and fish. R. C. Gonzalez and others. bibliog il Science 158:519-21 O 27 '67
Reward and learning in the goldfish. G Lowes and M. E. Bitterman. bibliog il Science 157:455-7 Jl 28 '67
Stimulus preferences and imprinting. P. H. Klopfer. bibliog il Science 156:1394-6 Je 9 '67
Training and maintenance of keypecking in the pigeon by negative reinforcement. H. Rachlin and P. N. Hineline. bibliog il Science 157:954-5 Ag 25 '67

CONDITIONING therapy. See Psychotherapy

CONDODINA, Alice
Ayako Uchiyama co; Alice Condodina and co. Clark center for the performing arts. J. Maskey. Dance Mag 41:31-2 Ag '67

CONDOMINIUM plan ownership. See Apartment houses—Condominium plan ownership

CONDON, Eddie
Eddie. R. Gehman. por Sat R 50:55-6 Ap 15 '67

CONDON, Edward U.
Books. Bul Atomic Sci 23:34-5 O '67

about
Flying saucers. W. Rogers. il Look 31:76-80 Mr 21 '67
Great UFO probe. H. Shuldiner. il por Pop Sci 191:120-3 O '67
UFO-watcher watcher. J. Piel. il Newsweek 69:111 Mr 20 '67

CONDON, Richard
Geneva stares down the future. Holiday 42: 28+ O '67

CONDON, Vesta E.
Unspoiled Asturias. Travel 127:58-60 Ja '67

CONDON-Wadlin act. See Labor laws and legislations—New York (state)

CONDORS
Nature note; California condor. Sci N 91: 300 Ap 1 '67
San Rafael and the condor; concerning the proposed San Rafael primitive area. Audubon 69:57 My '67

CONDRY, William
Kites of Europe; with biographical sketch. Natur Hist 76:5, 46-51 bibliog (p67) My '67

CONDUCT of life
Catholic college education: system, style & Christianity; address, June 11, 1967. J. P. Leary. Vital Speeches 33:635-8 Ag 1 '67
Cricket in academe; address, June 11, 1967. G. Pelletier. Vital Speeches 34:24-6 O 15 '67
Dream; excerpts. H. A. Hartwick. il Ladies Home J 84:81+ Ap '67
Four choices for young people. J. Fischer. Harper 235:12-15 Ag '67; Same abr. Read Digest 91:177-8+ N '67
Hang-loose ethic; excerpts from It's happening. J. L. Simmons and B. Winograd. NEA J 56:18-20+ O '67
How to live a fuller life. J. Batten and L. C. Hudson. Nations Bsns 55:78-80 F '67
Interview with Barbara Ward; ed. by R. D. Heffner. B. Ward. McCalls 94:48+ Je '67
Respect for life. il Ebony 22:112-13 Ap '67
Secret of self-renewal. A. Gordon. Read Digest 90:103-6 F '67
Standards of conduct. Sch & Soc 95:244+ Ap 15 '67
Two words to avoid, two to remember. A. Gordon. Read Digest 92:53-6 Ja '68
Way of acceptance. A. Gordon. Read Digest 90:136-9 My '67

CONDUCT of life—*Continued*
What four brave women told their children. B. Remsberg and C. Remsberg. il Good H 164:94-6+ My '67
What options do youth have? symposium; with study-discussion program, by C. Smallenburg and H. Smallenburg. bibliog il PTA Mag 62:2-5+, 34 Ja '68
See also
Altruism
Anger
Charity
Christian life
Conscience
Courage
Ethics
Forgiveness
Friendship
Generosity
Good will (ethics)
Habit
Human relations
Humility
Hypocrisy
Love
Loyalty
Patriotism
Responsibility
Selfishness
Sportsmanship
Sympathy
Truthfulness

CONDUCTING (music)
Lively arts; who says the best conductors can't be American? interview, ed. by R. Hemming. D. Johanos. Sr Schol 90:24 My 5 '67
Maestro von Karajan is always turned on. M. Mayer. il N Y Times Mag p50-1+ D 3 '67
Mystiques and techniques of conducting. W. S. Kimmel. Am Rec G 33:853-5 My '67
Profiles; Z. Mehta. W. Sargeant. New Yorker 43:53-4+ D 16 '67
Toscanini legacy. Hi Fi 17:41 Mr '67
See also
Conductors (music)

Competitions
See Music—Competitions
CONDUCTIVITY, Electric. See Electric conductivity
CONDUCTIVITY, Heat. See Heat conductivity
CONDUCTORS (music)
But which conductor? foremost maestros, leading challengers, gone but not forgotten. il Sr Schol 90:22-3 My 5 '67
Conductors: fifth annual Dimitri Mitropoulos international competition for conductors; with interview with J. F. M. Vonk. New Yorker 42:28-30 Ja 28 '67
Great conductors, by H. C. Schonberg. Review
Life 63:24 S 15 '67. H. Kupferberg
Gypsy boy. il Time 91:76-80 Ja 19 '68
Lively arts; Philharmonic guessing game: who will succeed Bernstein. R. Hemming. il Sr Schol 89:22 Ja 20 '67
Maestro on the rise. il Ebony 22:112-14+ My '67
Musical events: concert conducted by assistant conductors of New York philharmonic: S. Caduff, J. P. Izquierdo, and A. Lombard. W. Sargeant. New Yorker 43:126 Ap 1 '67
Musical events; three guests over three symphony orchestras: P. Kletzki, I. Kertesz, and R. Kubelik. W. Sargeant. New Yorker 42:119-21 F 4 '67
Philharmonic sweepstakes; search for Bernstein's successor. il Newsweek 70:114+ D 18 '67
See also
Bernstein, L.
Böhm, K.
Davis, C.
Goberman, M.
Golschmann, V.
Haitink, B.
Karajan, H. von
Kertesz, I.
Klemperer, O.
Maazel, L.
Martinon, J.
Mehta, Z.
Previn, A.
Skrowaczewski, S.
Szell, G.
Toscanini, A.
CONE, Richard A.
Early receptor potential: photoreversible charge displacement in rhodopsin. bibliog Science 155:1128-31 Mr 3 '67

CONE dwellers. See Cave dwellers
CONES, Volcanic. See Volcanoes
CONEY, Mattie Rice
One Negro woman's advice to her people. il pors U S News 62:68-9 Mr 27 '67
CONEY ISLAND
Where the fun was. J. Bruce. il Sports Illus 27:68-76 Ag 28 '67
CONEY ISLAND aquarium. See Aquariums
CONFECTIONERY industry and trade   See Candy industry and trade
CONFEDERATE States of America
Beyond the aid of history; concerning introduction by Allan Nevins to new edition of Richardson's 1905 Messages and papers of the Confederacy. F. E. Vandiver. il Sat R 50:34 My 6 '67
Jefferson Davis: private letters, 1823-1889, selected and ed. by H. Strode. Review
Am Heritage 18:56-7+ Je '67. B. Catton

Secret service
See United States—History—Civil war—Secret service—Confederate States
CONFERENCE for human welfare. See Southern conference for human welfare
CONFERENCE of governors.   See Governors conference, 1967
CONFERENCE of non-nuclear-weapon states (proposed)
First meeting of Preparatory committee. UN Mo Chron 4:16 Mr '67
CONFERENCE of the Eighteen-nation committee on disarmament, Geneva, 1962-
Ambassador Foster discusses nonproliferation treaty; transcript of a press conference, August 11, 1967. W. C. Foster. Dept State Bul 57:291-4 S 4 '67
Bomb spreads. il Sci N 92:7-8 Jl 1 '67
Disarmament; resumption of work in Geneva. UN Mo Chron 4:14-16 Mr '67
Draft adrift. Newsweek 70:44-5 S 4 '67
Draft treaty on nonproliferation of nuclear weapons submitted to Geneva disarmament conference; statements, August 24, 1967; with text of draft treaty. L. B. Johnson; W. C. Foster. Dept Stae Bul 57:315-20 S 11 '67
ENDC at the General assembly. H. A. Jack. il Bul Atomic Sci 23:30-3 F '67
Geneva conference, five years later; excerpt from report. H. A. Jack. Bul Atomic Sci 23:38-42 Ja '67
Hope on nuclear treaty. Bsns W p38 Ag 19 '67
Letter from Geneva; Eighteen-nation disarmament conference (cont) D. Lang. New Yorker 43:70+ Ag 5 '67
Neutrals and the test-ban negotiations, by M. S. Ahmed. Review
Bul Atomic Sci 23:33-4 D '67. A. S. Lall
1966 international negotiations for arms control and disarmament; letter of transmittal, February 17, 1967 with excerpt from report. L. B. Johnson. Dept State Bul 56:568-77 Ap 3 '67
Pledge: no first use. B. T. Feld. Bul Atomic Sci 23:46-8 My '67
President Johnson renews call for nonproliferation treaty; message, February 21, 1967. L. B. Johnson. Dept State Bul 56:447-8 Mr 20 '67
Promise of a gift; U.S. and Russian negotiators agree on draft treaty to prevent the spread of nuclear weapons. Time 90:19-20 S 1 '67
Treaty nears final stage; Soviet-U.S. joint draft. Sci N 92:228 S 2 '67
Who'll buy the nuclear pact? U.S.-Soviet draft treaty on nuclear nonproliferation. Bsns W p25 S 2 '67
CONFERENCE of the solidarity of peoples of Asia, Africa and Latin America, 1966. See Tricontinental conference, Havana, 1966
CONFERENCE on Latin American solidarity, 1967. See International conferences
CONFERENCE on the concept of the believers church. See Religious conferences
CONFERENCES
Coming events. See issues of Parks & Recreation
See also Library conferences; Scientific conferences; and similar headings
CONFERENCES on science and world affairs. See Pugwash conferences on science and world affairs
CONFESSION
Confession to counseling. il Time 90:50 O 13 '67
How secret the confessional? case of murders by J. Bartsch in Germany. il Time 90:51 D 22 '67

CONFESSION—*Continued*
Of many things. J. Moffitt. America 116:
359 Mr 18 '67
Secrecy of the confessional. America 118:25
Ja 13 '68
CONFESSION (law)
Citizen on trial: the new confession rules. Y.
Kamisar. bibliog f Cur Hist 53:76-81+ Ag
'67
Cops, courts, and Congress; effects of Su-
preme court decisions. J. O. Newman. New
Repub 156:16-20 Mr 18 '67; Discussion. 156:
24-6 Ap 1; 44-5 Ap 8 '67
Crime, confessions and the Supreme court:
Miranda decision. G. L. Chamberlain.
America 117:32-4 Jl 8 '67
Does silence mean guilt? tacit-admission
rule voided in Pennsylvania. Time 89:52
My 5 '67
Father is not a counsel: boy's confession of
murder barred in Oklahoma. Time 90:51
D 1 '67
Negotiated guilty plea. A. Rosett. Ann Am
Acad 374:70-81 N '67
CONFESSION; story. See McMorrow, F.
CONFESSIONS of faith. See Creeds
CONFESSIONS of Nat Turner; novel. See Sty-
ron, W
CONFIDENCE men. See Fraud
CONFINEMENT breeding. See Breeding
CONFIRMATION
Age for confirmation. America 116:338 Mr 11
'67; Reply. A. Landay. 116:545 Ap 15 '67
Awaiting confirmation. Newsweek 69:64 F 27
'67
What age for Christian soldiers? il Time 89:
72-3 F 24 '67
CONFLICT (psychology)
Theology of conflict. J. J. Lally. Common-
weal 87:355-8 D 15 '67
CONFLICT, Social. See Social conflict
CONFLICT of interests (business)
Protesting too much? ABC-ITT pressure
newsmen covering merger. Newsweek 69:
69-70 My 1 '67
CONFLICT of interests (public office)
Governor Reagan's slightest vestige. A. Rosin
and R. H. Simmons. New Repub 156:10 Je
24 '67
CONFORMITY
Education of wombats. P. West. Commonweal
87:143-6 N 3 '67
Lively arts; interview, ed. by M. Ronan. V.
Redgrave. Sr Schol 91:17-18 O 19 '67
One and only you? excerpt from The Seven-
teen guide to knowing yourself. D. A. Sug-
arman and R. Hochstein. il Seventeen 26:
300-1+ Ag '67
Open letter to the father of a boy who won't
get his hair cut. M. Groves. Good H 165:
62+ N '67
See also
Dissenters

Anecdotes, facetiae, satire, etc.
How to be a nonconformist; excerpts. E. J.
Karg. il Seventeen 26:383+ Ag '67
CONFORMITY (religion) See Dissenters, Re-
ligious
CONGAR, Georges Yves. See Congar, M. J.
CONGAR, Marie Joseph
Interview with Yves Congar; ed. by P. Gran-
field. America 116:676-80 My 6 '67
CONGAR, Yves Marie Joseph. See Congar, M. J.
CONGDON, Kirby
Books. Américas 19:38-9 Ja '67
CONGENITAL malformations. See Deformities
CONGER, Dean
Siberia: Russia's frozen frontier. il Nat Geog
Mag 131:297-345 Mr '67
CONGER, Lesley
Heart of the family; story. Good H 164:
106-7 Ap '67
Off the cuff. See issues of Writer
CONGO (capital Kinshasa)
Congo is still an active volcano. H. Tanner. il
N Y Times Mag p52-3+ S 10 '67; Same abr.
Read Digest 91:135-8 D '67
One down, one to go. Time 90:28 Jl 21 '67
Report from the Congo: war-drum days
ahead. R. W. Howe. Look 31:106 O 31 '67
U.N. condemns use of Angola as base for
Congo mercenaries; statement, November 8,
1967; with text of resolution. W. B. Buf-
fum. Dept State Bul 57:807-8 D 11 '67
See also
Copper industry and trade—Congo (capital
Kinshasa)

Economic assistance in the Congo (capital
Kinshasa)
United Nations—Congo (capital Kinshasa)

Economic policy
Confrontation in the Congo. E. Bustin. Cur
Hist 52:168-74 Mr '67

Expropriation policy
Politics of copper; proxy fight in the Congo.
P. Semonin. Nation 204:303-6 Mr 6 '67

Foreign relations
Question of price; conditions for delivery of
M. Tshombe. il Newsweek 70:44 Ag 14 '67

Industries
About-face; continued operation of Union
minière by S.G.M. il Time 89:94 Mr 3 '67
Politics of copper; proxy fight in the Congo.
P. Semonin. Nation 204:303-6 Mr 6 '67

Politics and government
Abduction in the air; Tshombe's kidnaping.
il Time 90:19-20 Jl 14 '67
Africa in black and white; concerning K.
Nkrumah's book Challenge of the Congo.
C. Miller. il Sat R 50:28-30 Mr 25 '67
Cause for optimism. Time 90:30 D 1 '67
Confrontation in the Congo. E. Bustin. Cur
Hist 52:168-74 Mr '67
Death to all whites. il Time 90:32+ Ag 25 '67
Jungle victory; mercenaries beaten at Bu-
kavu. Newsweek 70:78 N 20 '67
Last stand; Red cross plans to evacuate rebels
from Bukavu. il Newsweek 70:50+ N 6 '67
Mercenaries change sides. S. Meisler. il Na-
tion 205:689-91 D 25 '67
Misfortunes of Mobutu. il Newsweek 70:44
Ag 28 '67
No sad farewells; mercenary brigade leaves.
Time 90:38 O 13 '67
Plot and counter-plot. K. Kyle. New Repub
157:13-16 S 16 '67
Revolt in the Congo. Newsweek 70:33-4 Jl 17
'67
Second front; white mercenaries and black
rebels in Katanga. il Newsweek 70:51 N 13
'67
Shrinking giants; white mercenaries willing
to call off revolt in exchange for amnesty
and safe conduct. Time 90:24 S 1 '67
Tshombe scowls in Algerian detention as
Congo writhes. il Life 63:32B Jl 21 '67
Ultimatum from Bukavu; white mercenaries
revolt. il Time 90:30 Ag 18 '67
Victory for Mobutu. il Newsweek 70:34-5 Jl 24
'67
What the Congo flare-up is all about. il U S
News 63:7 Jl 17 '67
Who are the mercenaries? J. Burnham. Nat
R 19:959 S 5 '67
CONGO mercenaries. See Mercenary troops
CONGREGATIONAL Christian churches
National association of Congregational Chris-
tian churches. H. Conn. Christian Cent
84:1075 Ag 23 '67
CONGRESS (United States) See United States
—Congress
CONGRESS for cultural freedom
Cultural cold war; excerpt from Towards a
new past. C. Lasch. Nation 205:198-212 S 11
'67; Discussion. 205:309, 340-1 O 2-9 '67
Insufficiency of frankness; CIA subsidies. Na-
tion 204:678 My 29 '67; Reply. S. Spender.
204:802+ Je 26 '67
Literary Bay of Pigs; CIA subsidies. A.
Werth. Nation 204:711 Je 5 '67; Reply. S.
Spender. 204:802+ Je 26 '67
CONGRESS for recreation and parks
Congress capsule calendar, December 3-7.
1967. il Parks & Rec 2:30-1 O '67
Dates and site selected plans start for 1967
Congress. il Parks & Rec 2:23+ F '67
CONGRESS of racial equality
CORE leaps without looking; annual conven-
tion. Christian Cent 84:931-2 Jl 19 '67
Successor to Floyd McKissick may not be so
reasonable. F. C. Shapiro. il N Y Times
Mag p32-3+ O 1 '67
CONGRESS of theology, Toronto. See Religious
conferences
CONGRESS of writers. World. See PEN club
CONGRESS on religion, architecture and the
visual arts. See International congress on
religion, architecture and the visual arts
CONGRESS on the theology of the renewal of
the church. See Religious conferences
CONGRESS party. See Political parties—India
CONGRESSIONAL candidates. See Candidates,
Political

CONGRESSIONAL committees. See United States—Congress—Committees
CONGRESSIONAL ethics. See Political ethics
CONGRESSIONAL immunity. See United States —Congress—Privileges and immunities
CONGRESSIONAL interns. See Interns (civil service)
CONGRESSIONAL investigations. See Government investigations
CONGRESSIONAL joint committees. See United States—Congress—Committees
CONGRESSIONAL library. See United States— Library of Congress
CONGRESSIONAL medal of honor. See Medal of honor (United States)
CONGRESSIONAL procedure. See United States—Congress—Rules and practice
CONGRESSIONAL record
    Reading the Record. K. Crawford. Newsweek 70:37 N 6 '67
CONGRESSMEN
    Advice to congressmen. Nation 205:5-6 Jl 3 '67
    Best congressmen of the year. Nation 206:34-5 Ja 8 '68
    Congress: a soft, easy job; address, February 7, 1967. B. H. Oehlert, jr. Vital Speeches 33: 472-5 My 15 '67
    Congressional ethics: who watches the watchdog? Sr Schol 90:12-13 F 24 '67
    Dear congressman: is Doddism dead? L. L. King. il N Y Times Mag p26-7+ Ap 16 '67
    Elephant gets glamor; freshmen lawmakers giving the Grand old party new image. W. Martin. il Nations Bsns 55:38-9+ My '67
    Grades for the frosh; new GOP freshmen. Newsweek 70:21 S 25 '67
    GOP freshmen congressmen. R. Bauman and D. Franke. il Nat R 19:356-9 Ap 4 '67
    GOP shows its hand; Republican leaders in Congress. Bsns W p32-3 Ja 21 '67
    How ethical should Congress be? A. H. Sypher. il Nations Bsns 55:31-2 Je '67
    Key men in the 90th Congress. il Sr Schol 90:8-9 F 24 '67
    Members of the 90th Congress; tables. Sr Schol 91:34-5 O 5 '67
    Midsummer soundings; congressmen find out what is on their constituents' minds. il Time 90:13-14 Jl 14 '67
    Soul brothers; black power antagonists on Capitol hill. Reporter 37:10 Ag 10 '67
    Speak up to your congressmen. F. N. Ikard. Nations Bsns 55:38-9 D '67
    Speaking out; Congress is hypocritical. L. L. King. Sat Eve Post 240:10+ Ap 8 '67
    Wobble on the war on Capitol hill; congressional mind-changing on Vietnam. D. Oberdorfer. il N Y Times Mag p30-1+ D 17 '67
    See also
    United States—Congress

    Ethics
    See Political ethics

    Salaries, allowances, etc.
    Congressional ethics gap; need for financial relief. Life 62:4 Je 30 '67
CONGRESSMEN, Letters to. See Lobbying
CONIFERS
    Cascades' green mantle. W. F. Heald. il Am For 73:12-15+ Ap '67
CONJURING

    Apparatus and supplies
    Conjurers put magic touch on sales. il Bsns W p 100-2 D 16 '67
CONKLIN, Bill
    Caught in the act. Sat Eve Post 240:18 Ag 26 '67
CONKLIN, Paul
    Good day at Rough Rock. Am Ed 3:4-9 F '67
CONLAN, Jocko, and Creamer, Robert
    Jocko; excerpts. Sports Illus 26:70-2+ Je 26; 27:36-9 Jl 3 '67
CONLEY, Clare
    Is flying for you? Field & S 72:56-7+ Je '67
    Memory for muleys. Field & S 72:38-9+ Ag '67
CONLEY, James. See Wagner, B. A. jt. auth.
CONLEY, William H.
    Catholic junior college. America 116:645-6 Ap 29 '67
CONN, Frances G. See Lauren, C. jt. auth.
CONNABLE, Roma
    Newest campus: the world. Mlle 65:180-1+ O '67
CONNALLY, John Bowden, 1917-
    Why Kennedy went to Texas. por Life 63:86A-86B+ N 24 '67

    about
    Back to Dallas. Time 90:54-5 N 24 '67
CONNAUGHTON, Jack
    Bowling. G. S. Brown. il por Sports Illus 27: 74+ D 11 '67
CONNEAUT, Ohio
    Pumping polyelectrolytes is tricky. C. P. Baugher. Am City 82:28 Jl '67
CONNECTICUT
    See also
    Architecture, Domestic—Connecticut
    Education—Connecticut
    Fishing—Connecticut
    Gardens—Connecticut
    Natural history—Connecticut
    Prisons—Connecticut

    Historic houses, etc.
    See also
    Greenwich, Conn.—Historic houses, etc.
CONNECTICUT furniture. See Furniture, American
CONNECTICUT opera association
    Hartford; production of Bohème. W. D. Miranda. Opera N 31:30 Ja 28 '67
    Hartford; production of La figlia del reggimento. W. Miranda. il Opera N 31:23 Je 10 '67
    Hartford; production of La Traviata. W. D. Miranda. il Opera N 31:31 Mr 11 '67
    Report: Hartford; production of Tosca. W. D. Miranda. Opera N 32:30 D 16 '67
CONNECTICUT RIVER
    Main stream of New England. E. S. Grant. il Am Heritage 18:46-59+ Ap '67
    Pollution in the East: once upon a river. E. S. Grant. il Am For 73:4-7+ Jl '67
CONNECTIVE tissues. See Tissues
CONNECTORS
    Lanyard system dominates $50 million umbilical market. Aero Tech 21:36-7 O 23 '67
CONNELL, Cynthia Colleen
    Poem; Sing and sing without a sound. Horn Bk 43:779 D '67
CONNELL, E. J.
    Accident-prevention program that works. Am City 82:147+ O '67
CONNELL, W. E. and Patrick, W. H. Jr
    Sulfate reduction in soil: effects of redox potential and pH. bibliog Science 159:86-7 Ja 5 '68
CONNELLY, Dolly
    Nature. Sports Illus 27:64+ N 27 '67
CONNELLY, Marc
    Caravan circuses of Europe. Holiday 43:64-7+ Ja '68
    Letter from Ceylon. Holiday 42:51-4 D '67
CONNER, Bruce
    Savonarola in nylon skeins. il Time 91:50 Ja 5 '68
CONNER, Caryl
    Teacher corps. Am Ed 3:13-19 Ap '67
CONNER, John G.
    Convert your All-American 5 for 120-meter marine band. Pop Electr 26:71-2+ F '67
CONNES, Keith
    Just do it! por Flying 80:76-7 Je '67
CONNIFF, Frank
    Jackie exclusive; interview in New York world journal tribune. il Time 89:63-4 Mr 24 '67
CONNIFF, James C. G.
    Most hazardous days of your life; reprint. Sci Digest 61:31-7 My '67
    (ed) See Goddard, J. L. Are you wasting money on worthless health aids
CONNOLLY, Frank A.
    Obituary
    Am For por 73:63 Ja '67
CONNOR, Frances P.
    Crippled and health-impaired children. NEA J 56:37-9 N '67
CONNOR, John Thomas
    Connor of Allied. Time 89:70+ F 3 '67
    Firecracker for Allied. Newsweek 69:77+ F 6 '67
    Honorable discharge. por Newsweek 69:77-8 Ja 30 '67
CONNOR, Patricia. See Pearson, K. jt. auth.
CONOVER, Grandin
    Party on Greenwich avenue. Criticism New Yorker 43:140 My 20 '67
CONOVER, H. S.
    Good ground maintenance; address, October 1966. Parks & Rec 2:38+ Ap '67
CONOVER, Willis
    Music at Monterey. Sat R 50:109+ O 14 '67

    about
    Sound of music. il por Newsweek 69:50+ Je 5 '67

CONQUEST, Robert
Real man from Smersh. N Y Times Mag p36-7+ N 5 '67

CONRAD, Barnaby
Matador. Holiday 43:68-71+ Ja '68
You're a good man, Charlie Schulz. N Y Times Mag p32-5+ Ap 16 '67; Same abr. Read Digest 91:168-72 Jl '67

about
Barnaby Conrad: painter. F. Whitaker. il por Am Artist 31:40-5+ N '67

CONRAD, John P.
Prisons and prison reform. bibliog f Cur Hist 53:88-93+ Ag '67

CONRAD, Joseph
Molded by painful reality. S. Weintraub. por Sat R 50:37-8+ Je 10 '67

CONRAD, Paul
Letter from the publisher. J. R. Shepley. il(cover) pors Time 89:25 Ap 14 '67

CONRAD, Robert A. See Lisco, H. jt. auth.

CONRAD, Thomas M.
Bombs in orbit. Commonweal 87:332-4 D 8 '67

CONROY, Frank
Short, bumpy ride with Steve McQueen. Esquire 67:108-10+ Je '67

about
Early self-portrait. S. Kauffmann. New Repub 157:16+ N 11 '67

CONROY, Hilary
(comp) Articles and other books received; east Asia. See issues of American historical review

CONSCIENCE
Question of conscience. D. A. Sugarman and R. Hochstein. il Seventeen 26:140-1+ F '67
Role of conscience in the modern world; conference in Boston under Catholic, Jewish and Protestant sponsorship. America 116:746 My 20 '67
Thomas More: conscientious objector; conscience and the civil law, topic at Ecumenical conference on the role of conscience. J. B. Sheerin. Cath World 205:196-8 Jl '67

CONSCIENTIOUS objectors
Beating General Marsbars; draft-counseling and resistance centers. il Time 90:15 S 8 '67
Brush with the R.O.T.C. W. C. Findley. Christian Cent 84:1222-3 S 27 '67
Conscience and the draft. J. M. Swomley, jr. Christian Cent 84:833-5 Je 28 '67
Conscience and the war. New Repub 156:7-8 Ap 15 '67
Countdown on Noyd. D. Sanford. New Repub 157:14-15 O 21 '67
Doctors' dilemma; Levy case and medical students who refuse to serve in Vietnam. Nation 204:676-7 My 29 '67
Draft-age dilemma. O. S. Johnson. McCalls 94:34+ Ag '67
Draft board theology. M. Novak. Commonweal 86:467-8 Jl 28 '67; Discussion. 86:563+ S 22 '67
Goals of dissent; evaluation of the Vietnam protest movement. L. Grauman, jr. Nation 205:617-21 D 11 '67
Isolation without splendor; international organizations assisting draft resisters and deserters from U.S. forces. Nation 205:484 N 13 '67
Must conscientious objectors be pacifists? J. B. Sheerin. Cath World 206:146-7 Ja '68
Resistance movement: draft resistance unions on campuses around the country. New Repub 156:5-6 My 27 '67
Resister/deserter underground; Americans in Europe. H. Greer; T. Land. Nation 205:487-91 N 13 '67
Selective C.O. J. Greenfield. New Repub 157:15-16 Jl 1 '67
Selective conscientious objector; injustices perpetuated by Military selective service act of 1967. America 117:73 Jl 22 '67
Selective objection and the public interest; present law is unconstitutional. W. Arnold. Christian Cent 84:1218-21 S 27 '67
Via the underground to Canada; American draft resisters. Christian Cent 84:1388-9 N 1 '67
Vietnam: pacifist on the killing ground; Gary Malbach. C. S. Wren. il Look 31:36-8 D 26 '67
Why good sons become draft dodgers; excerpts from interviews. G. Cameron. il Ladies Home J 84:72-3+ Ag '67
See also
Military service, Compulsory

CONSCIOUSNESS
See also
Subconsciousness

CONSCRIPTION, Military. See Military service, Compulsory

CONSEIL européen pour la recherche nucléaire. See European organization for nuclear research

CONSERVATION as a profession. See Natural resources—Vocational guidance

CONSERVATION associations
Beating back the bulldozers; movements in California. H. Gilliam. il Sat R 50:67-9 S 23 '67
Conservation comes of age; California movement. S. Thurber. il Nation 204:272-5 F 27 '67
See also
Environmental defense fund
Sierra club

CONSERVATION foundation
Future environments of North America; ed. by F. F. Darling and J. P. Milton. Review Am For 73:41+ Ja 67. M. Bush

CONSERVATION law. See Conservation of resources—Legal aspects

CONSERVATION of resources
Audubon cause. E. Mitchell. il Audubon 69:92-3 S '67
Audubon view. Audubon 69:4 Mr '67
Church and conservation. J. B. Craig. Am For 73:13 O '67
Communication with our outdoor heritage; address, November 1, 1966. H. Hatcher. il Am For 73:14-17+ Ja '67
Conservation, a new perspective; address, June 13, 1967. M. E. Stone. Vital Speeches 33:625-8 Ag 1 '67
Conservation: a rationed tomorrow? il Sr Schol 91:4-7 D 14 '67
Conservation; ed. by H. Titus. See issues of Field & stream to December 1967
Crisis in beauty; excerpt from Moment in the sun. R. Rienow and L. T. Rienow. Liv Wildn 31:50-4 Spr '67
Economic development and its long-run environmental implications. J. H. Cumberland. il Nat Parks Mag 41:11-13 N '67
Estuaries protection a must in Congress. Audubon 69:5 Jl '67
Estuaries: will Congress save them from encroachments? L. J. Carter. il Science 156:1717+ Je 30 '67
Help save our heritage. il Mod Phot 31:80-1+ O '67
How to stop the pillage of America. R. H. Boyle. il Sports Illus 27:40-2+ D 11 '67
Its name is mud. R. Starnes. Field & S 71:18+ Ap '67
Last ditch fight for vanishing estuaries. il Sci N 92:103-4 Jl 29 '67
Let's not gamble with our natural resources; proper management of public lands. J. B. Craig. Am For 73:9 N '67
Mike Frome. M. Frome. Am For 73:3+ F; 3+ Jl '67
Mike Frome: trip in Alaska. M. Frome; reply. R. E. Bell. Am For 73:62-3 Ja '67
Mr Freeman looks ahead. O. Freeman. Am For 73:10-11+ Ap '67
National outlook. C. H. Callison. See issues of Audubon
News and commentary. See issues of National parks magazine
Politics of conservation. M. Frome. il Holiday 41:78-9+ F '67
Politics of conservation, by F. E. Smith. Review Am For 73:45 Ja '67. R. E. Wolf
Report of president and general counsel to the general membership of National parks association, May 25, 1967. A. W. Smith. Nat Parks Mag 41:I-IV Ap '67
Sustained yield and balanced use. W. E. Towell. Am For 73:11 S '67
Tax laws: conservationists must step gingerly on Capitol hill. L. J. Carter. Science 155:179-81 Ja 13 '67
Where do we go from here? A. J. McClane. il Field & S 71:10-12+ F '66
See also
Forest conservation
Landscape protection
Natural resources—United States
Preservation of landmarks, scenery, etc.—United States
White House youth conference on natural beauty and conservation
Wilderness areas
Wildlife conservation

Anecdotes, facetiae, satire, etc.
Mike Frome: activities of the exclusive riverways guild. M. Frome. Am For 73:6 N '67

CONSERVATION of resources—*Continued*

Legal aspects

Environmental pollution: scientists go to court. L. J. Carter. il Science 158:1552-6 D 22 '67

Study and teaching

In defense of nature; OAS and Inter American press association technical center, sponsors of first Round table on conservation information. G. de Zéndegui. Américas 19: inside cover Ag '67

Wake up foresters, you're needed! J. J. Shomon. il Am For 73:12-15+ My '67

Africa

Destruction of Eden. L. Brown. il Audubon 69:36-53 Jl '67

To save an Eden, wildlife must pay. L. Brown. il Audubon 69:42-9 S '67

California

Beating back the bulldozers. H. Gilliam. il Sat R 50:67-9 S 23 '67

Good for Berkeley; students conservation activities. Reporter 37:14 D 28 '67

Florida

Don't pull the plug on the Everglades. J. Browder. il Am For 73:12-15+ S '67

Indiana

Conservation laws enacted by Indiana. J. A. Blatt. Parks & Rec 2:16 S '67

Iowa

Abundance of the prairie; Hayden Kalsow Cayler, and Sheeder prairies. K. B. Gale. il Horticulture 45:34-5 Ag '67

Russia

Nyet raskhititelyam prirody (no to the plunderers of nature) S. Ostrander and L. Schroeder. il Audubon 69:63-5 Jl '67

Texas

Dredging up a Texas squabble; oyster shells from Galveston Bay. E. Shrake. il Sports Illus 27:43-8 Ag 14 '67

Washington (state)

Copper company vs. the North Cascades. P. Brooks. il Harper 235:48-50 S '67

North Cascades National Park; copper mining vs. conservation. K. Sperry. il Science 157: 1021-4 S 1 '67; Discussion. 158:205; 159:31-2+ O 13 '67, Ja 5 '68

CONSERVATION of works of art. See Art—Conservation and restoration

CONSERVATISM

Accent the negative. F. S. Meyer. Nat R 19:135 F 7 '67

Coalition for victory in '68: will LBJ get Republican votes? H. Paolucci. Nat R 19:630-1 Je 13 '67

Conservatism and Republican candidates. F. S. Meyer. Nat R 19:1385 D 12 '67

Conservative tradition in America, by A. Guttmann. Review
Nat R 19:1214-16 O 31 '67. P. P. Witonski
Nation 205:535-7 N 20 '67. L. Kampf

Conservatives crash the gates. Nat R 19:1312 N 28 '67

Danger on the home front. Christian Cent 84: 99-100 Ja 25 '67; Reply. B. Graham. 84: 410-11 Mr 29 '67

Genesis of German conservatism, by K. Epstein. Review
Nat R 19:700-1 Je 27 '67. S. J. Tonsor

Liberal-Conservatives; address, August 11, 1967. R. M. Roelfs. Vital Speeches 33:746-9 O 1 '67

Operation 1968. W. A. Rusher. il Nat R 19: 1115-17+ O 17 '67
See also
Right and left (political science)
Young Americans for freedom (organization)

Periodicals

Some hope for the rising generation. R. Kirk. Nat R 19:255 Mr 7 '67

CONSERVATIVE party (Canada)

Pragmatist for the Tories. Time 90:36 S 22 '67

Tory turnaround. Newsweek 70:53 S 18 '67

CONSERVATIVE party (Great Britain)

Big victory in Britain for the Conservatives. U S News 62:16+ Ap 24 '67

Conservative comeback. Time 89:40+ Ap 21 '67

Honeymoon ends; local elections; Tory victory. Newsweek 69:44+ Ap 24 '67

Tories prove a thesis; annual conference. Time 90:35-6 O 27 '67

CONSIDINE, Bob

Jackie exclusive; interview in New York world journal tribune. il Time 89:63-4 Mr 24 '67

CONSIDINE, John J.

Aid to the Latin American church. America 117:352-4 S 30 '67

CONSIDINE, Millie

Thoroughly peripatetic Millie. H. Sutton. Sat R 50:41-2 Jl 8 '67

CONSOLIDATED aquanauts vital equipment.
See Life support systems (submarine environment)

CONSOLIDATED Edison company of New York

Can Con Edison give up smoking? pollution problems the New York utility faces. il Bsns W p 106-8+ F 25 '67

Case of Con Edison; public relations department. L. L. L. Golden. Sat R 50:96 My 13 '67

Con Edison: the arrogance of power; findings of the Arnold H. Hirsch report. A. Prisendorf. il Nation 204:401-4 Mr 27 '67

CONSOLIDATED schools

Educational park concept. M. Wolff. Wilson Lib Bul 42:173-5+ O '67

CONSOLIDATIONS, Business. See Business consolidations and mergers

CONSORTIUM (finance) See Syndicates (finance)

CONSPIRACY

Fearsome five; conspiracy charge against Benjamin Spock and others. New Repub 158:7-8 Ja 20 '68

Meaning of conspiracy. il Time 91:65 Ja 19 '68

CONSTANCE Lindsay Skinner award

Constance Lindsay Skinner award presented to Mildred L. Batchelder. il Pub W 191:142 Je 5 '67

Mildred L. Batchelder will receive Skinner award. Pub W 191:124 F 20 '67

CONSTANT-current diode. See Diodes

CONSTANT voltage transformers. See Electric transformers

CONSTANTINE II, king of the Hellenes

King tells how his coup failed. pors Life 64: 52-4 Ja 5 '68

about

Besieged king. il pors Time 89:28-31 Ap 28 '67

Checking the king. il por Newsweek 69:58 Je 5 '67

Constantine and the colonels; on the eve of civil war. R. C. Macridis. Nation 206:8-11 Ja 1 '68

Coup that collapsed. il por Time 90:24-5 D 22 '67

Greece: a tragic hour. il por Newsweek 69: 34+ My 1 '67

Greece: under the knife. il por Newsweek 69:48+ My 8 '67

Greek vs. Greek; the U.S. stake. il por U S News 63:28 D 25 '67

King & the coup. i. Shenker. Time 89:31 My 12 '67

King Constantine: is he Prince Hal? Hamlet? Macbeth? R. Eder. il pors N Y Times Mag p23+ Je 11 '67

King on the spot? il por Sr Schol 90:18 My 12 '67

King's move; end game? il por Newsweek 70:27-9 D 25 '67

King's visit: pleasant but unproductive. il por Newsweek 70:42 S 25 '67

New Greek goals. il por Sr Schol 91:34 S 28 '67

Question of terms. il por Newsweek 71:30 Ja 1 '68

CONSTELLATIONS

On the reported gamma-ray source in Cygnus. G. S. Mumford. Sky & Tel 33:159 Mr '67

Sky is for looking. R. Starnes. Field & S 72: 12+ Ja '68
See also
Orion (constellation)

CONSTITUTION (United States) See United States—Constitution

CONSTITUTIONAL amendments. See United States—Constitution—Amendments

CONSTITUTIONAL conventions
See also
United States—Constitutional convention (proposed)

CONSTITUTIONAL law
See also
Judicial review

CONSTITUTIONS, State
See also
New York (state)—Constitution

CONSTRUCTION Industry. See Building industry

CONSTRUCTION materials. See Building materials

CONSTRUCTION toys. See Toys

CONSULAR service. See United States—Diplomatic and consular service

CONSULATES (buildings) See Embassies (buildings)

CONSULTANTS, Business. See Business consultants

CONSULTANTS, Library. See Library consultants

CONSULTATION on church union
Boost for COCU. Christian Cent 84:227-8 F 22 '67; Discussion. 84:470 Ap 12 '67
Church of the Brethren annual conference. B. W. Crist. il Christian Cent 84:1050-1 Ag 16 '67
COCU assaulted in its cradle. Christian Cent 84:803-4 Je 21 '67; Discussion. 84:1073 Ag 23 '67
COCU's navel; concerning an article by James Montgomery Boice. Christian Cent 84:611-12 My 10 '67
Expanding COCU; Christian Methodist Episcopal church admitted. Christian Cent 84:398 Mr 29 '67
Hoop rolling at Cambridge. K. Haselden. Christian Cent 84:645-7 My 17 '67

CONSULTATION on technology and human values. See National council of the churches of Christ in the United States of America

CONSUMER advisory council. See United States—Consumer advisory council

CONSUMER buying surveys. See Consumer surveys

CONSUMER credit. See Credit

CONSUMER education
Buying guide issue (cont) il Consumer Rep 32:1-441 D '67
Saving face; series called Your dollar's worth for NET. il Time 90:86 N 3 '67
What it takes to be a smart shopper. il Changing T 21:39-44 S '67
    See also
Consumer protection

CONSUMER electronics show. See Electronic apparatus industry and trade—Exhibitions

CONSUMER federation of America
Consumers try to organize. il Bsns W p56 N 11 '67

CONSUMER frauds. See Fraud

CONSUMER goods. See Commercial products

CONSUMER preferences. See Consumers preferences

CONSUMER price index. See Price indexes

CONSUMER protection
Advertising; let's stop tampering with the machinery; address, February 8, 1967. C. L. Gould. Vital Speeches 33:434-8 My 1 '67
Betty Furness. New Repub 156:8-9 Mr 18 '67
Betty opens a new door. il Newsweek 69:92+ Mr 20 '67
Betty's blockbuster. Newsweek 71:57 Ja 8 '68
Can Betty Furness help the consumer? il Consumer Rep 32:256-8 My '67
Dialogue that never happens; marketing and its critics. R. A. Bauer and S. A. Greyser. bibliog f Harvard Bsns R 45:2-4+ N '67
Docket; notes on government actions taken to enforce consumer protection laws. See issues of Consumer reports
How business helps customers. Nations Bsns 55:35-7 Jl '67
How much federal protection do consumers want? Consumer Bul 50:26-8 My '67
Johnson's shield for consumers. il Bsns W p34-5 F 25 '67
Kidding the consumer. Nation 204:421 Ap 3 '67
Lady with a sympathetic ear; B. Furness. Bsns W p68+ S 23 '67
LBJ's package for consumers. il Newsweek 69:69 F 27 '67
Meet Ralph Nader. il Newsweek 71:65-7+ Ja 22 '68
Open letter to Betty Furness. Nations Bsns 55:44-5 My '67
Post office protects consumers against fraud. Consumer Bul 50:19-20 N '67
Responsible retailing. W. M. Batten. Duns R 89:83-6 Mr '67
Standards and the public interest; address, February 13, 1967. J. H. Hollomon. Vital Speeches 33:364-8 Ap 1 '67
Super protection; address, November 15, 1967. R. W. Darrow. Vital Speeches 34:171-4 Ja 1 '68
What have you done for me lately? address, January 31, 1967. P. W. Allport. Vital Speeches 33:339-43 Mr 15 '67
What lawmakers plan for you. Changing T 21:6 Mr '67

What LBJ proposes to protect consumers. U S News 62:8 F 27 '67
Who best speaks for the consumer? address, September 20, 1966. M. E Brunk. Vital Speeches 33:247-52 F 1 '67
Who speaks for the consumer now? il Changing T 21:41-4 Jl '67
Words from the White House. Nat R 19:233-4 Mr 7 '67
    See also
Better business bureaus
Consumer federation of America
Consumers union of United States

CONSUMER surveys
Bit more bounce; University of Michigan survey. il Bsns W p30 Ap 1 '67
Gauging how people will spend; Census bureau's quarterly survey of consumer intentions. il Bsns W p 156+ O 21 '67
New guide to the consumer's mind; Census bureau's survey of consumer buying intentions. il Bsns W p 128+ O 7 '67
Sliding in under higher tags; study by the Survey research center of the University of Michigan. il Bsns W p31 Jl 8 '67
Stronger air of caution; University of Michigan survey. il Bsns W p21-2 Ja 6 '68
Your voice and your vote; annual questionnaire. Consumer Rep 32:367 Jl '67
    See also
Consumers preferences

CONSUMERS
Changing mood of the American buying public; interview. G. Katona. U S News 63:39-40 Jl 17 '67
Consumer: king or vassal of the economy? il Sr Schol 90:13-15+ F 10 '67
Long, cold spring for retailers; consumer spending. il Bsns W p34-5 Je 3 '67
Marketing ethics & the consumer. E. A. Clasen. Harvard Bsns R 45:79-86 Ja '67
Nice people to do business with. il Consumer Rep 32:332-3 Je '67
Now may be the time for thrifty consumers to buy! Consumer Bul 50:15-16 O '67
Saving comes back into style. il Bsns W p28-9 F 11 '67
Speaker for the house. C. Montgomery. See issues of Good housekeeping
Waste not, have not? Read Digest 90:33-4+ F '67
    See also
Consumer education
Consumer protection

CONSUMERS, Negro. See Negro market

CONSUMERS credit. See Credit

CONSUMERS preferences
Admen try eye-spy to read buyer's mind; using mind-reading Eye camera. il Bsns W p 142-4 Ag 19 '67
Defending the big advertiser; with charts. Bsns W p98+ Ap 15 '67
Russia loosens its belt. il Bsns W p64-8+ S 30 '67

CONSUMERS union of United States
Consumers union puts on muscle. il Bsns W p84-6 D 23 '67
CU's annual meeting and election of directors. Consumer Rep 32:615 N '67
CU's annual meeting, plus. Consumer Rep 32:462 S '67
Keppler on the SLR; tests of cameras and lenses. H. Keppler. il Mod Phot 31:12+ Je '67

CONSUMPTION (economics)
Chary consumers. il Fortune 75:32+ Mr '67
Consumers hold back. il Bsns W p27 F 11 '67
Home goods; but what will they think of next? L. A. Mayer. il Fortune 76:114-18+ Ag '67
Low earners and their incomes. V. C. Perrella. il Mo Labor R 90:35-40 My '67
Opening the closed fist; retail sales. Time 90:71-2 D 22 '67
Retailers' three percent. il Fortune 76:40+ O '67
Tracking the habit of consumers. il Bsns W p60-1 D 30 '67
Welcome to the consumption community; excerpt from The Americans; the world experience. D. J. Boorstin. il Fortune 76:118-20+ S 1 '67
    See also
Consumer surveys
Consumers
Supply and demand

CONTACT lenses
Are contact lenses for you? il Changing T 21:34-7 Mr '67
Contact lenses. Consumer Rep 32:168-73 Mr '67
I like my contact lenses. B. Christensen. Farm J 91:74 My '67

CONTACT printing. See Photography—Printing processes

CONTACTORS, Electric. See Electric contactors

CONTAGION and contagious diseases. See Communicable diseases

CONTAGIOUS diseases. See Communicable diseases

CONTAINER corporation of America
Container seeks a bigger package. il Bsns W p 186-8+ O 21 '67

CONTAINER system (freight handling)
Let's take our ships out of the bottle. L. Velie. Read Digest 90:132-6 F '67
Maritime industry's expensive new box; trailer-size cargo containers. H. B. Meyers. il Fortune 76:150-4+ N '67
Revolution in shipping: can it save U.S. merchant marine? il U S News 62:116-17 My 15 '67

CONTAINERIZATION. See Container system (freight handling)

CONTAINERIZED cargoes. See Container system (freight handling)

CONTAINERS
Packaging's puckering plastic ploy; Cubitainers. H. Zucker. Pop Phot 60:119 My '67
See also
Beer containers

CONTAINERS, Pressurized. See Aerosols

CONTAINERS for shipping
Glass-fiber cargo container use set. Aviation W 87:38 S 11 '67

CONTAMINATION of Mars. See Mars (planet)—Contamination

CONTAMINATION of Venus. See Venus (planet)—Contamination

CONTAREX cameras. See Single-lens reflex cameras

CONTARINO, A. F.
Miniature switches. por Electr World 78:37-9 O '67

CONTEE, Clarence G.
Current problems of African historiography; address, October 22, 1965. bibliog Negro Hist Bul 30:5-10 Ap '67

CONTEMPORARY Christian art, incorporated
Miss Bouchard protests; exhibition of International congress on religion, architecture and the visual arts. T. W. Moore. Christian Cent 84:1288-90 O 11 '67

CONTEMPORARY drama. See Drama

CONTEMPORARY music. See Music

CONTERIS, Hiber
Ideology and faith: a confrontation. Christian Cent 84:995-7 Ag 2 '67

CONTI, C. C.
Cornucopia; poem. Christian Cent 84:1486 N 22 '67

CONTINENT, Lost. See Atlantis

CONTINENTAL airlines
Continental spreads its wings; applies for routes to the Pacific. il Bsns W p 120-2+ N 18 '67
Transpacific route case: Continental cites regional identification. R. G. O'Lone. il Aviation W 86:33-4+ My 8 '67

CONTINENTAL can company
Bargaining brightens in can talks; wages on productivity basis. Bsns W p 101-2 Ja 13 '68

CONTINENTAL drift
Advice for the Establishment; excerpt from address. J. T. Wilson. Sat R 50:50-1 S 2 '67
Africa and South America linked by rock-age studies. G. S. Mumford. Sky & Tel 34:221 O '67
Canada's unappreciated role as scientific innovator; magnetic surveys and the theory of convection in the earth's mantle; theories of J. T. Wilson and L. W. Morley. J. Lear. il Sat R 50:45-50 S 2 '67
Drifting theories shake up geology. il Sci N 91:399 Ap 29 '67
East is going west. il Sci Digest 61:28-9 Je '67
Fractured fossils give up a secret; evidence of horizontal movement in the earth's crust across Central America. il Sci Digest 62:77-8 Jl '67
Geology along the North Atlantic: Gander conference; report on international conference. H. P. Woodward. Science 158:1368+ D 8 '67
Gondwanaland fitted. Sci Am 216:58 F '67
Piecing continents together. il Time 90:36 Ag 18 '67
Stop-and-go continents. Sci Am 217:50+ D '67
Strong new evidence. Sci N 92:175 Ag 19 '67
Test of continental drift by comparison of radiometric ages. P. M. Hurley and others. bibliog il Science 157:495-500 Ag 4 '67

CONTINENTAL Illinois national bank and trust company of Chicago. See Chicago—Banks

CONTINENTAL oil company
Spurring growth with imagination; interview. L. F. McCollum. Nations Bsns 55: 46-7+ Ap '67

CONTINENTAL shelf
Elephant teeth from the Atlantic continental shelf. F. C. Whitmore, jr. and others. bibliog il Science 156:1477-81 Je 16 '67
Elephants under the sea. il Sci Digest 61:15-16 Ap '67
Freshwater peat on the continental shelf. K. O. Emery and others. bibliog il Science 158:1301-7 D 8 '67
Off-the-shelf proposal. M. Getler. Aero Tech 21:90 S 25 '67
Secrets of sunken lands; studies off the Atlantic coast reveal history and wealth of the shelf. B. Tufty. il Sci N 91:77-9 Ja 21 '67
Seismic refraction profile in Coral Sea basin. G. G. Shor, jr. bibliog il Science 158:911-13 N 17 '67

CONTINENTAL slope. See Continental shelf

CONTINENTS
Antipodal location of continents and oceans. C. G. A. Harrison; reply with rejoinder. R. Thompson. Science 156:263-4 Ap 14 '67
See also
Continental drift

CONTINUOUS casting
Ingot mold maker casts new horoscope; Valley mould & iron corp. il Bsns W p74-6+ Ag 5 '67

CONTINUOUS video recorders. See Video tape recorders and recording

CONTOR, Roger J.
Proposed Tutimaba wilderness. Liv Wildn 30: 3-10 Wint '66

CONTOSKI, Victor
Eastern European poetry. Poetry 110:52-5 Ap '67

CONTRACEPTION. See Birth control

CONTRACEPTIVES
Beyond the pill. W. R. Young. il McCalls 90:90-1+ Mr '67
Birth control: an up-to-date summary of contraceptive methods. il Good H 164:144-5 Ja '67
Birth control and your emotions. J. Brothers. il Good H 165:50+ Jl '67
Birth control crisis; reprint. D. O'Callaghan. Cath World 204:326-34 Mr '67; Discussion. 205:66-7, 131, 194-5 My-Jl '67
Dual pill mechanism; tests with Enovid. Sci N 91:280 Mr 25 '67
Estrogens' double life; morning-after birth control. Sci N 92:343 O 7 '67
Evaluate loops and coils. Sci N 91:116 F 4 '67
First complete guide to modern birth control. W. L. Fielding. Ladies Home J 84: 46-7 Jl '67
Freedom from fear; the pill. il Time 89: 78-80+ Ap 7 '67
How safe is the pill? G. J. Langmyhr. Parents Mag 42:58-9+ O '67
Intrauterine devices: effects on ultrastructure of human endometrium. R. M. Wynn. bibliog il Science 156:1508-10 Je 16 '67; Reply with rejoinder. W. A. Krotoski. 157: 1465 S 22 '67
Intrauterine devices; report on meeting. P. A. Corfman and S. Segal. Science 156:1136 My 26 '67
News of the pill. Time 89:66 Ap 21 '67
Next in birth control. il Sci N 91:349-50 Ap 15 '67
No moral revolution discovered, yet. Sci N 93:60-1 Ja 20 '68
Pill & strokes. Time 90:33 D 29 '67
Pill and the girl next door. D. Hubert. il Mlle 64:162-3+ Mr '67
Pill: early breakthroughs; letters. S. R. M. Reynolds; S. H. Sturgis. Science 155:1361 Mr 17 '67; Reply with rejoinder. C. G. Hartman. 156:1435 Je 16 '67
Pill for men; temporary sterility induced by drug compound. J. Reinert. Sci Digest 61:69-71 F '67
Pill for teens. Sci N 91:473 My 20 '67
Pill; highlights of questionnaire sent to ACOG. A. Lake. il McCalls 95:96-7+ N '67; Same abr. with title How safe is the pill? Read Digest 92:48-52 Ja '68
Pill is safe but... Sci Digest 61:79 Je '67
Pill; latest experiments in birth control. A. Talmey. Vogue 149:114-15 Ap 15 '67
Prospects for population control. J. M. Stycos. Christian Cent 84:1458-62 N 15 '67

CONTRACEPTIVES—*Continued*
Putting a brake on runaway birth rates; U.S. to supply developing nations with contraceptives. il Bsns W p76-8 S 23 '67
Scientists' cliche blocks family planning; problem of impoverished women. Sci N 92:344-5 O 7 '67
Search for a birth control method to replace the pill. Good H 165:179-81 S '67
Search for the superpill; Ford foundation grants. il Newsweek 70:98+ N 20 '67
Should birth control be available to unmarried women? with discussion. F. C. Wood, jr. Good H 164:12+ F '67
Should doctors prescribe contraceptives for unmarried girls? F. R. Talbot. il Ladies Home J 85:37+ Ja '68
Terrible trouble with the birth-control pills. L. R. Chevalier and L. Cohen. Ladies Home J 84:43-5+ Jl '67; Discussion. 84:92+ N '67
Turning off sperm. B. J. Culliton. il Sci N 92:452-3 N 4 '67
Use of oral contraception in the United States, 1965. N. B. Ryder and C. F. Westoff; reply with rejoinder. H. Rather. Science 155:951 F 24 '67
Warning signs; relationship between oral contraceptives and thromboembolism. Newsweek 69:82 Je 5 '67

Anecdotes, facetiae, satire, etc.
Birth control solution hailed; Swedish pill called ZIP. P. J. Laux. il America 117:551 N 11 '67

CONTRACT bridge. See Bridge (game)
CONTRACT packaging. See Packaging
CONTRACTS
Before you sign that contract. R. Gottlieb il Motor T 19:52-4 Je '67
See also
Put and call transactions
Subcontracting
Teachers—Contracts
CONTRACTS, Agricultural
Contract cropping: what's behind it? il Farm J 91:26-7+ Jl '67
CONTRACTS, Government
Bell, Western electric play key Nike role. il Aviation W 87:118-23 O 23 '67
Business gears up for the Nike-X; $5-billion anti-missile system for 15,000 companies. il Bsns W p38-9 S 30 '67
Contracts and procurements (title varies) See issues of Technology week including Missiles and rockets
Cost disclosure showdown nears; government's attempt to widen inspection of data on fixed-price contracts. D. C. Winston. Aviation W 87:16-17 O 2 '67
Defense contracts under fire. Bsns W p32 Jl 29 '67
Defense orders start to peak out. il Bsns W p44-6 O 28 '67
Excess of excess profits; British government contracts. Time 89:100+ Ap 14 '67
F-111 contractor penalties may be pressed by Congress. Aero Tech 21:13+ S 25 '67
GAO cries for help. Nation 204:389 Mr 27 '67
Grand Coulee project stirs up a tempest; Russia's request to be allowed to bid. il Bsns W p59 Ap 15 '67
Hows and whys of bidding; Milwaukee procedure. A. L. Lehrbaummer. il Am City 82:168+ O '67
Kick from defense; $3-billion in extra military ordering. Bsns W p39 Ap 15 '67
McDonnell Douglas led DOD '67 awards. il Aero Tech 21:14-16 D 18 '67
Major Nike-X contractors. Aviation W 87:64 O 23 '67
Martin wins Apollo applications integration contract. Aero Tech 21:10 Jl 31 '67
NASA lists 100 top contractors. il Aviation W 87:69+ D 18 '67
Phrase rediscovered; the military-industrial complex; profiting from defense contracts. Nation 205:402-1 O 30 '67
Power play; Russian interest in Grand Coulee turbines contract. Newsweek 69:76 Ap 10 '67
Probing Pentagon's buying practices; buying in, deliberate bidding at a known loss. il Bsns W p 121-2 Mr 18 '67
Procurement policy questions stem from Hughes LOH bid. H. M. David. Tech W 20:19 Mr 6 '67
Public interest. New Repub 157:5-6 D 2 '67
R&D and the contract state; throwing away the yardstick; excerpt from Science, stagnation, and the contract state. H. L. Nieburg; reply with rejoinder. W. T. Bonney. Bul Atomic Sci 23:28-9 F '67

Rickover tells GE to weigh anchor; manufacturers of propulsion equipment decline to bid. Bsns W p 105+ Je 24 '67
Senate to probe federal role in technology transfer. Tech W 20:23 Je 12 '67
SST flies to hill. il Sci N 91:449 My 13 '67
$30 billion for whom? politics, profits and the anti-missile missile. F. W. Collins. New Repub 156:13-15 Mr 11 '67
Top 100 U.S. Defense department contractors. il Aviation W 88:72-3 Ja 1 '68
Truth-in-negotiation enforcement sought. Aviation W 87:26 Ag 7 '67
Voyager teams to be picked within year. H. Taylor. il Tech W 20:18-19 Mr 20 '67
What Vietnam is teaching Philco; transport and warehousing for the military. il Bsns W p 100+ S 9 '67
When a giant stumbles; North American aviation and the Apollo contract. Newsweek 69:63 My 1 '67
See also
Government investigations—Government contracts
United States—National aeronautics and space administration—Procurement

Accounting
Closer eye on contractors; non-competitive fixed-price contracts. Bsns W p 158 O 21 '67
Picking the winners with a new system; life cycle costing vs traditional low-bid practice. il Bsns W p62+ My 13 '67

Anecdotes, facetiae, satire, etc.
Feasible flying machine; if the Wright brothers had built their airplane under government contract. S. Dryer. il Sat Eve Post 240:18 N 4 '67

Subcontracting
Pentagon shot that misfired; Defense dept. study of geographic distribution of defense work. il Bsns W p38 Ap 8 '67

Great Britain
Excess-profit action stirs U.K. parliament. H. J. Coleman. Aviation W 86:33-4 Ap 3 '67

CONTRACTS, Teachers. See Teachers—Contracts
CONTRERAS, Gloria
Gloria Contreras dance group; 92nd street Y. M. Marks. Dance Mag 42:81 Ja '68
CONTROL data corporation
Computer maker exports principally by air. J. W. Carter. il Aviation W 86:65+ F 13 '67
CDC takes peripheral road to growth. il Bsns W p 118 Ag 5 '67
CONTROL moment gyroscopes. See Gyroscopes
CONTROL of credit. See Credit
CONTROL of insects. See Insects, Injurious and beneficial—Control
CONTROL of production. See Factory management
CONTROL systems, Biological. See Biological control systems
CONTROL towers, Airport. See Airports—Control towers
CONTROLLERS, Air traffic. See Air traffic controllers (persons)
CONTROVERSY
Christian controversy. V. P. McCorry. America 116:861-2 Je 17 '67
CONVENIENCE foods. See Food—Ready-to-cook food
CONVENTION halls. See Auditoriums
CONVENTIONS
McCormick Place sparks new fire; controversy over rebuilding. il Bsns W p90-1 D 16 '67
When conventioneers hit town. il Bsns W p 158-60+ Ja 14 '67
CONVENTIONS (treaties) See Treaties
CONVENTIONS, Constitutional. See Constitutional conventions
CONVENTIONS, Political. See National conventions (political); Political conventions
CONVENTS and nunneries
In 1968: let the sisters be. America 118:26 Ja 13 '68
New voices from the convent; for democratic reforms in the structure of the church. Nation 205:677 D 25 '67
CONVERSATION
Getting on talking terms; with study-discussion program by R. Strang. M. G. Brook. bibliog il PTA Mag 62:14-16, 32 S '67
Onward and upward with the arts; the put-on. J. Brackman. New Yorker 43:34-6+ Je 24 '67
See also
Gossip

COOKERY—*Continued*
Family tested recipe. Parents Mag 42:70-1+ Ja; 61-3+ F '67
Fifty ways to stretch food dollars. Redbook 130:67+ Ja '68
Fondue for fall. J. Hewitt. il N Y Times Mag p90 O 29 '67
Food to cry into. N. S. Hazelton. Nat R 19:364+ Ap 4 '67
For a small dinner, why not cook right at the table? with recipes. il Sunset 139:162-3 O '67
For winter health and energy plan bigger better brunches; with recipes. K. Smith. il Pop Gard 18:72-5+ Mr '67
Four favorites: roast veal menagere; grilled pork chops; sour cream coffeecake; salade nicoise. C. Claiborne. il N Y Times Mag p86-7 Ja 7 '68
From the fall food garden. D. Brooks. Home Gard 54:44 O '67
Hearty one-dish meal; Seville rice and chicken. B. L. Henry. il Farm J 91:80 Ja '67
How do you read a recipe? Bet Hom & Gard 45:126 Ap '67
How to follow a recipe. il Seventeen 26:170 N '67
How to put extra appeal into every meal. R. Holmberg. il Bet Hom & Gard 45:78-83+ My '67
How to save time in your kitchen; common-sense tips. Bet Hom & Gard 45:100-1 Ag '67
How to teach your children to enjoy the wonderful world of food; with recipes. B. L. Henry. il Farm J 91:120-1+ Mr '67
If food looks good, family will cheer; with recipes. il Redbook 130:76-7+ Ja '68
Impressive but quick; with recipes. il Am Home 71:86-7+ Ja '68
Introducing a new measure of heat for Redbook recipes. il Redbook 128:92-3+ F '67
Just the right touch for appetite appeal. K. Schaller. il Farm J 91:122-3 Mr '67
Keep-cool cookbook of do-ahead dishes. il Good H 165:92-108 Ag '67
Last-minute meals that busy women can prepare and serve in less than an hour; with recipes. il Redbook 129:90-4+ S '67
Line a day. P. Cannon. il Ladies Home J 84:106-7+ F '67
Low or high calorie meals; with recipes. B. L. Henry and D. Groves. il Farm J 92:70-2 Ja '68
Masterpiece recipes. il Redbook 129:78-83+ My '67
Menus for entertaining. N. S. Hazelton. il Nat R 19:587+ My 30 '67
Menus in the making; with recipes. H. McCully. il House B 109:194-5+ Ap '67
Money in the kitchen: dial-a-dinner; with recipes. il Seventeen 26:72-3+ Jl '67
[Month] menus; with recipes. See issues of Sunset
No time to cook. il McCalls 94:54 Ap; 42 My; 36 Je '67
Nobody ever tells you these things; questions and answers. H. McCully. See issues of House beautiful
Paula Peck's art of good cooking; excerpts. P. Peck. il Ladies Home J 84:118-19+ My '67
Peg Bracken's appendix to the I hate to cook book. P. Bracken. See issues of Ladies' home journal
Recipes for success; Menus by mail. A. Geracimos. il Sat Eve Post 241:28-9 Ja 27 '68
Redbook's timesaver cookbook; with recipes. il Redbook 128:99-112 Mr '67
Sage and honeyed thoughts, and a dash of Worcestershire. D. Brooks. Home Gard 54: 42 N '67
Season's fare. H. S. Witty. See issues of Flower grower, the home garden (cont as) Home garden & flower grower
So you're learning to cook. il Am Home 70: 112 Mr '67
Something old is something new; clay-pot cooking. J. Hewitt. il N Y Times Mag p 110+ D 10 '67
Summer meals to remember. il McCalls 94: 96-106+ Jl '67
Summer party cook book; with recipes. J. A. Beard. il House & Gard 132:113+ Jl '67
Sunday dinner, step-by-step; with menu and recipes. R. Holmberg. il Bet Hom & Gard 45:76-83 S '67
Sunset's kitchen cabinet. See issues of Sunset
They'll tell the world you're a wonderful cook! il Good H 164:118-32 My '67

Think mint! il Bet Hom & Gard 45:89 S '67
Thirty ways to make food more enticing. H. H. Boileau. Parents Mag 42:80-1 O '67
Three for the stuffing; with recipes. il Parents Mag 42:86-7+ S '67
Tips for the cook. il Suc Farm 65:83 S '67
We trim a snack tree; with recipes. il Farm J 91:78-9 Ja '67
When the chefs cook for themselves; with menus. H. McCully. il House B 109:174-6+ Mr '67
Who's cooking? excerpts from The ballet cook book, with introductory statement by L. Joel. T. LeClercq. il Dance Mag 41:57-9+ N '67
Wise shopping, good eating; with recipes. V. T. Habeeb. il Am Home 70:94-6+ Ja '67
Wise ways to stretch your food dollar; with recipes. G. Maddox. il Todays Health 46: 58-63 Ja '68
Work wonders with milk products; with recipes. il Ladies Home J 84:120-1+ Mr '67
World of fine cooking. M. Field. See occasional issues of McCall's
You can cook and all without a measuring spoon; with recipes. il Seventeen 26:170-3+ Ap '67

See also
Barbecue cookery
Bread
Breakfasts
Broiling
Cake
Canapés
Casserole cookery
Christmas cookery
Christmas dinners
Christmas meals
Cookbooks
Cookies
Diet
Dinners and dining
Dumplings
Electronic cooking
Entertaining
Gingerbread
Ice cream, ices, etc.
Meals
Mincemeat
Olives
Pie
Pressure cooking
Salads
Sandwiches
Sauces
Shortcake
Soups
Suppers
Thanksgiving dinners
Tomato sauce
Waffles

Anecdotes, facetiae, satire, etc.
Christmas goose. C. Ford. il Field & S 72:6+ D '67
Moral virtue in the kitchen. N. S. Hazelton. Nat R 19:251 Mr 7 '67

Bibliography
See Cookbooks—Bibliography

Competitions
Great chili championship fix. G. Cartwright. il Sports Illus 27:80-2+ D 11 '67

Measurements
Common measuring mistakes. il Ladies Home J 84:68 Ap '67
For good measure; kitchen measurers. B. Wadsworth. il Ladies Home J 84:134 N '67

Study and teaching
So you're learning to cook. See issues of American home

Cheese
Cheese choices. il Bet Hom & Gard 45:95-6 Ap '67
Cheese with a foreign flavor. B. S. Brown. il Good H 165:180 N '67
Cooking with cheese. M. Field. il Holiday 41:105-10 F '67
Cooking with ricotta cheese; with recipes. il Sunset 138:144+ F '67
Successful recipes, cheese treats. il Suc Farm 65:79-80 O '67

Chocolate
Chocolate takes the cake. C. Claiborne. il N Y Times Mag p41 Jl 16 '67
Cooking with chocolate. M. Field. il McCalls 95:66+ D '67

COOKERY—Chocolate—*Continued*
New hip dip: chocolate fondue. E. Alston.
il Look 31:82-3 F 7 '67
Ten luscious desserts, two tempting breads,
and a quick hot drink, all chocolate. R.
Holmberg and D. Eby. il Bet Hom & Gard
45:94-100+ N '67

Eggs

American classic: eggs Benedict; with recipe.
C. Claiborne. il N Y Times Mag p94 S 24
'67
Chef d'oeuf: best omelet maker in the land.
il Time 91:68-9 Ja 5 '68
Eggs are our dish; with recipes. M. W.
Goodman. il Parents Mag 42:62-3 Mr '67
Elegant ways with eggs. il Ebony 22:156+ My
'67
Five great egg dishes. B. L. Henry. il
Farm J 91:92-3+ Ap '67
Five-minute omelet breakfast. il Good H
164:175 Mr '67
French omelet. il Am Home 70:74 S '67
In each dish the surprise is a delicious pre-
poached egg. il Sunset 138:206+ My '67
Other half of the egg; excerpt. H. McCully
and others. il Ladies Home J 84:114-15+ S
'67
Peppers and eggs: for a western omelet or
Basque pipérade; with recipes. E. Alston. il
Look 31:96-7 N 28 '67
See also
Soufflés

Fish

Big culinary catch; with recipes. H. McCully.
il House B 109:120-1+ Ja '67
Bluegill banquet. C. B. Colby. il Outdoor
Life 139:36 Ap '67
Delicate fish filets. V. T. Habeeb. il Am
Home 70:91-3+ S '67
Fish tricks; with recipes. il Redbook 128:
96-8+ F '67
Fish with a flair. il Ebony 22:110+ Mr '67
Net raves with these fish dishes; with rec-
ipes. G. Maddox. il Todays Health 45:52-5
Je '67
New ways with fish. P. Cannon. il Ladies
Home J 84:122-3+ Mr '67
Pleasure from a poached fish; with recipes
and menu by E. Graves. il Life 63:76-7+
Ag 11 '67
Salmon party ball. il Bet Hom & Gard 45:99
My '67
Seafood is great food, fresh, frozen or
canned. il Parents Mag 42:60-3+ F '67
Seafood with a foreign flavor. B. S. Brown.
il Good H 164:214 Ap '67
Table fare from the ocean floor; with recipes.
L. Heinold. il Outdoor Life 139:46-7 Ap '67
Taste of luxury. C. Claiborne. il N Y Times
Mag p 110-11 Ap 9 '67
Tuna and salmon spectaculars; prize tested
recipes. il Bet Hom & Gard 46:64+ Ja '68
Twenty fishes of the Pacific. il Sunset 138:
176-8+ Mr '67
Two delicious ways to cook a whole salmon;
with recipes. il Sunset 139:52-5 Jl '67
Warm-water fish story; with recipes. il Look
31:92-3 F 21 '67
Why not fish for compliments? with recipes.
il McCalls 94:134-5+ F '67
Work wonders with tuna. il Ladies Home J
84:92+ Je '67
You can't cook a fish too soon. T. Trueblood.
il Field & S 72:24+ My '67
See also
Caviar
Cookery—Shellfish

Fruit

Apple charlotte. H. McCully. il House B 109:
69 Ap '67
Apple charlotte with apricot sauce. V. V.
Voboril. il Good H 166:120 Ja '68
Down East delicacy: blueberry pie; with
menu and recipes by E. Graves. il Life
63:62-5 Jl 7 '67
Flavorful raisin recipes. Am Home 70:111
Mr '67
Fruit: so cool, so lovely. il Am Home 70:
106-7+ Jl '67
Good berrying ahead; with recipes. H. Mc-
Cully. il House B 109:172-3+ My '67
Good companion for lamb or beef: apricots.
il Sunset 138:162 F '67
Great apple ideas. J. McCloskey. il Suc Farm
65:60-1 N '67
Harvest fruits and vegetables; with recipes.
il McCalls 95:112-13+ O '67
If you have loquats; with recipes. Sunset
138:142 Je '67
Making your own apricot purée. Sunset 138:
174+ Je '67

Nectarines three ways. R. Holmberg. il Bet
Hom & Gard 45:78-9+ Ag '67
New ways with citrus fruits. R. Hanna. il
Suc Farm 65:108-9+ F '67
Seedless grape pie surprises. il Sunset 139:
98+ Ag '67
Spectacular strawberry dishes. il Farm J 91:
54-5+ Je '67
Successful recipes, peach specials. il Suc
Farm 65:63-4 Ag '67
Tasty berry tarts. il Sunset 138:110-11 My
'67
Two Danish fruit desserts. Sunset 138:233
Ap '67
Versatile lemon. H. McCully. il House B 109:
154-5+ Je '67
Watermelon; with recipes. E. Alston. il Look
31:60-1 Je 27 '67

Game

Fare: game. C. Claiborne. il N Y Times Mag
p23 D 24 '67
Game for dinner: pheasant and venison; with
recipes. E. Alston. il Look 31:46-7 N 14 '67
Little dove is big eating. C. B. Colby. il Out-
door Life 140:107 N '67
Pointers on partridge. C. B. Colby. Outdoor
Life 139:32 Mr '67
Presto, rabbit. C. Claiborne. il N Y Times
Mag p73 Je 4 '67
Quail with mushrooms. C. B. Colby. il Out-
door Life 140:18 Ag '67
To cook a porcupine. C. B. Colby. il Out-
door Life 140:20 D '67
Woodchucks are for eating. C. B. Colby. il
Outdoor Life 140:24 O '67

Leftovers

Michael Field's culinary classics and improvisations; excerpt. M. Field. il McCalls 95:
110-11+ O '67
Stir-fry dinner using leftovers; with recipes.
Sunset 139:177 O '67
Work wonders with leftover turkey. il Ladies Home J 84:96+ D '67

Meat

Bacon baking and other tricks. il Ladies
Home J 84:77 My '67
Banquet in white. C. Claiborne. il N Y Times
Mag p58 My 28 '67
Beau repast. C. Claiborne. il N Y Times Mag
p 124 N 19 '67
Beef from cattle range to kitchen range.
il Suc Farm 65:56-7 Jl '67
Beef patties Parmesan. il Bet Hom & Gard
45:105 My '67
Beef rib supreme. R. Holmberg. il Bet Hom
& Gard 45:84-5+ Mr '67
Bravura dish: tournedos Rossini. C. Claiborne.
il N Y Times Mag p99 N 5 '67
British? mais oui; steak and kidney pie. C.
Claiborne. il N Y Times Mag p35 S 3 '67
Broiled flank steak mignonettes. il Good H
164:194 Ap '67
Budget beef; with recipes. P. Cannon. il
Ladies Home J 84:110-11 S '67
Carver's delight. J. Hewitt. il N Y Times
Mag p 107+ Ap 2 '67
Caveman style: charcoal or charred wood
cookery. C. Claiborne. il N Y Times Mag
p42 Jl 9 '67
Company beef roast in a crust. K. Schaller.
il Farm J 91:89 Ap '67
Crown roast of pork. R. Holmberg. il Bet
Hom & Gard 45:86-7+ Mr '67
Dinner on the double. D. Eby. il Bet Hom &
Gard 45:96 My '67
Dinner party pot roasts. il Good H 164:100-15
F '67
Discovered: new values in veal. il Ladies
Home J 84:116-17+ Ap '67
Experts reveal good news of the new pig.
P. Cannon. il Ladies Home J 84:104-5+ F
'67
Fabulous franks. il Bet Hom & Gard 45:93-4
Ag '67
First-rate franks. P. Dittberner. il Bet Hom
& Gard 45:108 My '67
For a juicy, tender pork loin roast. Sunset
139:151 N '67
Fresh, smoked, spicy or mild; sausages. il
Redbook 129:90-1+ Jl '67
Gala ham. H. McCully. il House B 109:306-8+
N '67
Great chili championship fix. G. Cartwright.
il Sports Illus 27:80-2+ D 11 '67
Great roasts! with menus. V. T. Habeeb. il
Am Home 70:76-7+ D '67
Hamburger do's & donts. Good H 164:134-
40 Ap '67

COOKERY—Meat—*Continued*
Hamburger, thrifty, versatile, sure to please. K. G. Winton. il Parents Mag 42:70-1+ Ja '67
High-flying veal. J. Hewitt. il N Y Times Mag p99 Mr 5 '67
Holiday roasts. il Bet Hom & Gard 45:90 D '67
Hot dog; frankfurter dishes; with recipes. il McCalls 94:86-7+ Je '67
Hottest steak. C. Claiborne. il N Y Times Mag p68 Ag 20 '67
It's a dill-flavored meat pie. il Sunset 138: 222 Ap '67
Lamb and veal specials. il Bet Hom & Gard 45:91-2 My '67
Lamb's pork. C. Claiborne. il N Y Times Mag p39 Jl 23 '67
Leg of Lamb. R. Holmberg. il Bet Hom & Gard 45:88-9+ Mr '67
Leg, rack, or shoulder: here are three delicious ways with spring lamb. il Sunset 138:212-13 Ap '67
Make your own liverwurst. il Sunset 139:210 O '67
Menu shortcuts, with cold cuts. L. Anderson. il Bet Hom & Gard 45:100 Je '67
Nifty dishes: from thrifty ground meats; with recipes. il Good H 164:126-41 Ap '67
Nobody knows more about chili than I do. H. A. Smith. Holiday 42:68-9+ Ag '67
Restaurateur; beef in America better than in his native Italy; interview. A. Prantera. New Yorker 43:43-4 Mr 18 '67
Roast them just as if you were roasting ribs. il Sunset 138:92-3 Mr '67
Roasting time and temperature chart. Bet Hom & Gard 45:128 Mr '67
Roasts to carve before company comes. S. Sarvis. il Farm J 91:60-2 N '67
Rolled veal and pork roast. R. Holmberg. il Bet Hom & Gard 45:90+ Mr '67
Sausage, homemade and easy; with recipes. il Sunset 139:168-9 O '67
Sausage standouts. il Bet Hom & Gard 45:122 N '67
Splendid neglected roast; loin of pork; with menu and recipes by E. Graves. il Life 63: 124-5+ N 17 '67
Steak crusty with pepper; with recipe and menu by E. Graves. il Life 62:104-5+ Mr 17 '67
Steak rarity. C. Claiborne. il N Y Times Mag p 100 Ap 23 '67
Successful recipes, meat roll-ups. il Suc Farm 65:111-12 F '67
Successful recipes, unusual meat loaves. il Suc Farm 65:119-20 Mr '67
Three meals from a lamb leg; with recipes. il Sunset 139:200+ O '67
Twenty-five great things to do with ground beef. il McCalls 94:108-11+ Ap '67
Veal Italian style. V. T. Habeeb. il Am Home 70:117-19+ O '67
Veal with a foreign flavor. il Good H 165:172 D '67
When dinner's for eight. C. Claiborne. il N Y Times Mag p 100-1 O 22 '67
Why not serve steaming chile? Sunset 139:166 N '67
Why not try lamb? with recipes. J. McCloskey. il Suc Farm 65:78-9 S '67
Work wonders with sausages; with recipes. il Ladies Home J 85:76+ Ja '68
See also
Barbecue cookery
Broiling
Cookery—Game
Stew

Mushrooms
In search of cantharellus cibarius & company. P. Knight. il Sports Illus 27:80-3 O 16 '67
Work wonders with mushrooms. il Ladies Home J 84:122+ My '67

Nuts
Cooking with nuts. M. Field. il McCalls 94: 72+ F '67
Nuts are so elegant for cooking. H. McCully. il House B 109:246-7+ O '67

Poultry
Bride serves golden-fried chicken. il McCalls 94:42 Jl '67
Bride serves golden roast turkey. il McCalls 95:58 N '67
Chicken classics the lazy way. il Ladies Home J 84:120-1+ My '67
Chicken cookbook. il Good H 164:116-37 Je '67
Chicken dishes with a foreign flavor. B. S. Brown. il Good H 164:178 F '67

Choice chick. C. Claiborne. il N Y Times Mag p64 Ja 14 '68
For menu variety try versatile chicken; with recipes. G. Maddox. il Todays Health 45: 32-7 S '67
Frozen turkeys. il Consumer Rep 32:568-71 N '67
How to roast that holiday turkey. il Bet Hom & Gard 45:124 N '67
If you like chicken livers. il Sunset 138:184+ Ap '67
It can be supreme. C. Claiborne. il N Y Times Mag p 126+ Mr 19 '67
Man talks turkey; with recipes. E. Alston. il Look 31:98-9 Mr 7 '67
Pacesetter, golden orange chicken. R. Holmberg. il Bet Hom & Gard 45:78-9 S '67
Seasoned with summer; chicken paysanne. C. Claiborne. il N Y Times Mag p36 Je 25 '67
Smoked turkey dinner. il Bet Hom & Gard 45:86 Je '67
Soy-seasoned and delicious; chicken teriyaki; with recipes. il Sunset 139:182 O '67
Superb cooking starts here. V. T. Habeeb. il Am Home 70:103-5+ Jl '67
Tempting new chicken dish. B. L. Henry. il Farm J 91:75 S '67
Try a new holiday stuffing. Farm J 91:63 N '67
Turkey. il Redbook 130:105-6 N '67
Want to try a new stuffing? Sunset 139:180 N '67
Well garnished squab; with menu and recipes. E. Graves. il Life 63:90-1+ D 15 '67
Why not some birds on the barbecue? with recipes. il Sunset 139:96-7 Jl '67
With game hens from your freezer. il Sunset 139:142 D '67
Work wonders with canned and frozen poultry products. il Ladies Home J 84:101+ F '67
You cook your chicken in a pomegranate sauce. il Sunset 139:159-60 N '67
See also
Barbecue cookery

Rhubarb
Get ready for rhubarb! il Bet Hom & Gard 45:114 My '67

Rice
Easy-to-prepare rice dishes. D. Hutcheson. Am Home 70:108 S '67
Risottos and pilafs. P. Peck. il House & Gard 133:127-9+ Ja '68
So you can't cook rice? il Ladies Home J 84:108+ F '67

Shellfish
Bride makes lobster thermidor. il McCalls 94:38 S '67
Favorite ways with oysters. il Bet Hom & Gard 45:74-5 D '67
For the two of you, an oyster roast; with recipe. Sunset 139:187 O '67
How a visiting Frenchman and a visiting Italian might make magic with our fresh Pacific clams; with recipes. il Sunset 139: 92-3 O '67
Little shrimps and big. C. Claiborne. il N Y Times Mag p72 F 19 '67
Lobster red; with recipes. C. Claiborne. il N Y Times Mag p84 S 17 '67
Lobster tails with hollandaise. il Sunset 139: 109 D '67
Pasta by the sea. C. Claiborne. il N Y Times Mag p 110 O 15 '67
S is for summer, and shrimp. C. Claiborne. il N Y Times Mag p50 Jl 30 '67
Scallop shish kebab; with menu and recipes by E. Graves. il Life 63:126-7+ S 22 '67
Sea fare at the dock. V. T. Habeeb. il Am Home 70:102+ Je '67
Shrimp specialties. il Bet Hom & Gard 45:95 F '67
Take twenty-four cherrystones. C. Claiborne. il N Y Times Mag p55 Ja 29 '67
They still clamor for clams. C. Claiborne. il N Y Times Mag p 130+ D 3 '67
What is this delicious surprise? fried squid. il Sunset 139:86 Ag '67

Vegetables
Art of asparagus cooking. P. Cannon. il Ladies Home J 84:112-13+ Ap '67
Asparagus, fresh as spring! with recipes. D. Eby. il Bet Hom & Gard 45:34 Ap '67
At the root of it all. M. Field. McCalls 94: 60+ Mr '67
Bean-hole beans. C. B. Colby. Outdoor Life 139:84 My '67
Bonus in beans. il Ebony 22:96+ F '67
Brilliant red bell peppers for color and flavor; with recipes. il Sunset 139:198-9 O '67

COOKERY—Vegetables—*Continued*
Chinese cabbage is something else! with recipes. il Bet Hom & Gard 45:96 S '67
Chinese cut up with vegetables; with recipes. E. Alston. il Look 31:64-5 Jl 11 '67
Do-ahead dinner vegetables. il Sunset 138:192+ Ap '67
Endive; with recipes. E. Alston. il Look 31:82-3 Ap 4 '67
Fresh corn on the cob. D. Brooks. Home Gard 54:47 Ag '67
Fresh tomato specials; with recipes. il Bet Hom & Gard 45:99-100 S '67
Fresh vegetables in fritters. il Sunset 138:221 Ap '67
Green and wax beans. il Bet Hom & Gard 45:107-8 Jl '67
Harvest fruits and vegetables; with recipes. il McCalls 95:112-13+ O '67
Idea vegetables. R. Holmberg. il Bet Hom & Gard 45:74-5+ Ag '67
Imagine crunchy artichokes; with recipes. il Sunset 139:205 O '67
Is there a vegetable hater in the house? il McCalls 94:112-13+ Ap '67
Kraut a la française. C. Claiborne. il N Y Times Mag p70 My 21 '67
Looking for a gourmet treat? consider the lowly potato. G. Maddox. il Todays Health 45:54-9 F '67
New ideas with onions. B. Zache. il Bet Hom & Gard 45:122 F '67
Offbeat artichoke; with menu and recipes by E. Graves. il Life 62:114-15+ Ap 14 '67
Okra for color and crispness; with recipes. Sunset 139:172+ O '67
On revitalizing vegetables. D. Brooks. il Home Gard 54:26 S '67
Peppers and eggs: for a western omelet or Basque pipérade; with recipes. E. Alston. il Look 31:96-7 N 28 '67
Please handle with care. il Am Home 70:94+ S '67
Season's fare. H. S. Witty. Home Gard 54:6+ My '67
Spinach pie? certainly. and also leek, carrot, and mushroom pies. il Sunset 138:203-4 Mr '67
Successful recipes, fall squash. il Suc Farm 65:63-4 N '67
T is for tomatoes. J. Paulson. il Ladies Home J 84:98 Je '67
Vegetables at their garden best. il Farm J 91:52-3 Ag '67
Winter vegetable cook book. N. S. Hazelton. il House & Gard 131:149+ F '67
Work wonders with packaged potato products. il Ladies Home J 84:118+ Ap '67
   See also
Stew
      Water chestnuts
Water chestnuts! with recipes. il Bet Hom & Gard 45:100+ Ap '67
      Wine
Brandy cook book. J. A. Beard. il House & Gard 132:261+ N '67
COOKERY, American
Cooking Dutch with a blender; Pennsylvania Dutch dishes. il Good H 165:120+ Ag '67
Milky way or alimentary canal? pretensions of foreign cooking. J. Wechsberg. Sat R 50:64+ F 25 '67
National treasury of cookery; excerpt. il Ladies Home J 84:118-19+ N '67
No time to cook; New England dinner; menu with recipes. il McCalls 94:42 My '67
Restaurateur: beef in America better than in his native Italy; interview. A. Prantera. New Yorker 43:43-4 Mr 18 '67
When meals were meals; excerpts. M. Dickinson. il Ladies Home J 84:78-9+ Ag '67
COOKERY, Austrian
Eggs whipped, baked, delicious; Salzburg dumplings. il Sunset 139:176 N '67
Secret recipes from Vienna. Vogue 150:94 N 1 '67
Sweet Vienna: Demel's cake shop; with recipes. E. Alston. il Look 31:70-2 D 26 '67
Viennese treasure; sacher torte. C. Claiborne. il N Y Times Mag p70 D 17 '67
When Vienna eats, it's cake. M. C. Morton. il Holiday 42:74-6+ S '67
COOKERY, Belgian
Dutch & Belgian cook book. K. S. Nelson. il House & Gard 132:203+ S '67
COOKERY, Canadian
Zesty Canadian luncheon, halibut royale. R. Holmberg and E. Craster. il Bet Hom & Gard 45:82-3+ O '67
COOKERY, Chinese
Chinese cooking, family style; with recipes. il Good H 165:106-19 S '67

Chinese cut up with vegetables; with recipes. E. Alston. il Look 31:64-5 Jl 11 '67
Everybody cooks his own in the hot pot; with recipe and menu. il Sunset 138:72-5 Je '67
Joy of Chinese cooking; with recipes. C. Claiborne. il N Y Times Mag p 116-17 S 10 '67
Thousand recipe Chinese cookbook; excerpt. G. B. Miller. il Ladies Home J 84:124-5+ Mr '67
COOKERY, Danish
On loan from Copenhagen, the smørrebrød; with recipes. R. Holmberg and E. Craster. il Bet Hom & Gard 45:76-7+ O '67
COOKERY, Dutch
Dutch & Belgian cook book. K. S. Nelson. il House & Gard 132:203+ S '67
Little rascals and other Dutch delights. il Sunset 139:118+ D '67
COOKERY, English
Aftermath. L. Saalburg. Esquire 67:62+ My '67
As the British feast at Christmas; with recipes. il McCalls 95:132-4+ D '67
Old-fashioned treats for new-fashioned carolers. P. Cannon. il Ladies Home J 84:66-7+ D '67
Pub fare: London. il Look 31:60-1 My 2 '67
COOKERY, European
Blue Danube cookbook; excerpt. M. K. Donovan. il Ladies Home J 84:102-3+ F '67
Education of the American palate: of mousse and menu. J. Wechsberg. il Sat R 50:37-8+ Ap 22 '67
Food of love; favorite foods of operatic composers, tr. by F. Merkling. H. Schraemli. Opera N 32:6-7 D 30 '67
Holiday cakes from old Europe; effortless Christmas baking. il Ladies Home J 84:90-1+ D '67
COOKERY, Finnish
Traditional holiday foods; Finnish Christmas cookery. J. McCloskey. il Suc Farm 65:48-9 D '67
COOKERY, Foreign. See Cookery, International
COOKERY, French
Aftermath. L. Saalburg. Esquire 67:62+ My '67
Bravura dish: tournedos Rossini. C. Claiborne. il N Y Times Mag p99 N 5 '67
Everyone's in the kitchen with Julia. il Read Digest 90:66-70 F '67
Fine art of French cooking; with recipes. il McCalls 94:98-106+ S '67
Finest food of France. S. Spitzer. il Holiday 42:70-1+ N '67
French way with french fries; summary. with recipes; ed. by E. Alston. R. Randall. il Look 31:111-12 O 17 '67
Grow a little gourmet at home; with recipes from Three stars for babies and juniors by C. Ripault. il Life 62:80-4+ Mr 10 '67
In Calder's kitchen: homemade tools, homegrown food; with recipes. E. Alston. il Look 32:62-3 Ja 9 '68
Man talks turkey; with recipes. E. Alston. il Look 31:98-9 Mr 7 '67
Menus and recipes of Mme Van de Kemp. Vogue 150:133+ Ag 1 '67
COOKERY, German
German dinner featuring Königsberger klops. R. Holmberg and E. Craster. il Bet Hom & Gard 45:74-5+ O '67
COOKERY, Greek
Great finish for a Grecian feast, karidopita. R. Holmberg and E. Craster. il Bet Hom & Gard 45:88-9+ O '67
Greek stews with low calorie sauces. Sunset 139:186 N '67
How the Greeks bake with yogurt; with recipes. Sunset 138:195 F '67
COOKERY, Hungarian
Hungarian accent. C. Claiborne. il N Y Times Mag p 102 Ap 16 '67
COOKERY, Indian (East Indian)
Classic from India, curried lamb dinner. R. Holmberg and E. Craster. il Bet Hom & Gard 45:86-7+ O '67
Curry: hot or not; with recipes. E. Alston. il Look 31:78-80 S 5 '67
Serve curry on a cart. V. T. Habeeb. il Am Home 70:99+ Je '67
COOKERY, International
[Foods] with a foreign flavor. B. S. Brown. See issues of Good housekeeping
How to please a crowd; with recipes. il Redbook 129:84-6+ My '67
Milky way or alimentary canal? pretensions of foreign cooking in the United States. J. Wechsberg. Sat R 50:64+ F 25 '67

COOKERY, International—*Continued*
Pick the country, and have a party! with recipes. R. Holmberg and E. Craster. il Bet Hom & Gard 45:74-89+ O '67
World's fare: international favorites from Expo 67; with recipes. il McCalls 94:94-100+ Ag '67

COOKERY, Iranian
From Persia, two splendid casseroles. Sunset 138:181+ Ap '67

COOKERY, Italian
Countess Bismarck's recipes. Vogue 149: 205+ Ap 1 '67
Milanese mix. C. Claiborne. il N Y Times Mag p 114 N 26 '67
No time to cook; dinner Italian style. il McCalls 94:80 Mr '67
Off the beaten path. C. Claiborne. il N Y Times Mag p91 My 7 '67
Pasta for the virtuoso; with recipes and menu by E. Graves. il Life 62:106-7+ My 26 '67
Pizza making, and the pizza eating; with recipe. il Sunset 138:138-9 Je '67
Treasury of Italian cooking; with recipes. il McCalls 94:120-30+ Mr '67
Veal Italian style. V. T. Habeeb. il Am Home 70:117-19+ O '67
Viva pasta. C. Claiborne. il N Y Times Mag p62-3 F 5 '67
Wonderfully Italian, a Ravello dinner; with recipes. R. Holmberg and E. Craster. il Bet Hom & Gard 45:78-9+ O '67
See also
Macaroni

COOKERY, Japanese
Japanese feast. il House & Gard 131:82-3 Je '67
One-dish tempura for the family. il Sunset 139:108+ S '67
Soy-seasoned and delicious; chicken teriyaki; with recipes. il Sunset 139:182 O '67

COOKERY, Marine
Galley-west. E. Bliss. il Yachting 121:83+ My '67
Jerry Pendleton on the commissary. J. Pendleton. il Yachting 121:125-7 Je '67
Man-sized meals in a girl-sized galley. R. Bannister. il Motor B 120:44-5+ Jl '67

COOKERY, Mexican
Company's coming to a Mexican dinner. Am Home 70:128 O '67
Dinner at the Quintanillas; with recipes. S. A. Fertitta. il Look 31:31-3 Mr 21 '67
Fiesta Mexican dessert, almendrado. R. Holmberg and E. Craster. il Bet Hom & Gard 45:80-1+ O '67
It's tostadas for supper. il Sunset 138:240 My '67
Making and using Mexico's *carne seca*; with recipe. il Sunset 138:189 F '67
Making your own fresh tortillas with a tortilla press; with recipe. il Sunset 138:153 F '67
Party picnics go Mexican. B. M. Stover. il Parents Mag 42:54-5+ Jl '67
This simple Mexican dessert consists of delicious lumps; chongos. il Sunset 138:178 My '67
Why not serve steaming chile? Sunset 139:166 N '67

COOKERY, Middle Eastern
Making Persian baklava; with recipe. il Sunset 138:165-6 F '67

COOKERY, Moroccan
Tea therapy, accompanied by sweet pastries; with recipes. E. Alston. il Look 31:80-1 Ap 18 '67

COOKERY, Oriental
See also
Cookery, Chinese
Cookery, Japanese

COOKERY, Ornamental
Christmas gift cook book; with recipes. J. A. Beard. il House & Gard 132:173+ D '67
Christmas treat; edible trees. il Ebony 23: 158+ D '67
Fairy-tale castle cake. il McCalls 95:128-9+ D '67
Festive breads cook book. D. Franz. il House & Gard 131:163+ My '67
Friendly beasts; fairy-tale scene from cookies. il Ladies Home J 84:74-5+ D '67
Goodies, pretty to look at, luscious to eat. il Am Home 70:58-9+ D '67
Kicky conversation cakes. K. Schaller. il Farm J 91:78-9+ My '67
Merry Christmas cookies! merry gingerbread! merry children. il Redbook 130:78-81+ D '67
Party tricks from our chef. il Am Home 70:96 N '67

Spooky but tasty gingerbread house for Halloween; with recipes. il Sunset 139:164+ O '67
You build your Christmas bread tree or wreath the way you shingle a roof. il Sunset 139:60-1 D '67
See also
Cake

COOKERY, Outdoor
Cook-and-dine table. il House & Gard 131:84-5 Je '67
Cookouts for the young set. K. Smith. il Pop Gard 18:56-9 Ag '67
Exciting summer furniture, food, projects, equipment. D. Popplestone. il Bet Hom & Gard 45:46-65+ Je '67
Garden parties for weight watchers. K. Smith. il Pop Gard 18:48-51+ My '67
Sesame trout and sourdough; Bridger wilderness; photographs by Bruce Davidson; with account by P. Knight. il Sports Illus 27:30-3+ Jl 31 '67
See also
Barbecue cookery
Camp cookery
Outdoor meals

Equipment and supplies
In look for outdoor cooking. il Am Home 70: 88 Je '67
See also
Camp stoves

Safety devices and measures
Safety tips for cooking outdoors. il Good H 165:152-3 Jl '67

COOKERY, Pakistani
Barbecue ideas from Pakistan. Sunset 138: 164 Je '67

COOKERY, Polynesian
Party picnics go Polynesian. B. M. Stover. il Parents Mag 42:58-9 Jl '67
Polynesian buffet, a hoolaulea; with recipes. R. Holmberg and E. Craster. il Bet Hom & Gard 45:84-5+ O '67

COOKERY, Quantity

Bibliography
Books. M. F. K. Fisher. New Yorker 43:207-8+ O 21 '67

COOKERY, Russian
Eastern Easter; dessert called paschka. C. Claiborne. il N Y Times Mag p98-9 Ap 30 '67
Russians do it differently. il Sunset 138:198 Mr '67

COOKERY, Scandinavian
Elegant and earthy. H. McCully. il House B 110:122-3+ Ja '68
Great Scandinavian cook book; excerpts. ed. by J. A. Ellison. K. Fredrikson. il Ladies Home J 84:88-9+ Je '67
Party picnics go Scandinavian. B. M. Stover. il Parents Mag 42:56-7 Jl '67

COOKERY, Scottish
Happy New Year buffet; with recipes. il Ladies Home J 85:74-5+ Ja '68

COOKERY, Spanish
Costa Brava cooking; with recipes. E. Alston. il Look 31:54-6 Ag 22 '67
Feast for the infanta. R. A. De Groot. il Esquire 68:184-7+ D '67

COOKERY, Turkish
Delights of the Ottoman table; excerpt from Rice, spice, and bitter oranges. Mediterranean foods and festivals. L. Perl. il Sat R 50:61-2 O 14 '67

COOKERY, Viennese. See Cookery, Austrian

COOKERY, West Indian
Menu from Martinique. C. Claiborne. il N Y Times Mag p77 F 26 '67

COOKERY books. See Cookbooks

COOKERY by children
Cooking kids; Home economics nursery school. Douglass college. New Brunswick, N.J. M. English. il Look 31:M24+ N 14 '67
Extra pair of hands in the kitchen. il Sunset 138:94-5 F '67
Merry Christmas cookies! merry gingerbread! merry children. il Redbook 130:78-81+ D '67
Mini-meals for the now generation. il Parents Mag 42:64-5 Ag '67
Our teenage cook. See issues of Good housekeeping

COOKERY by men
Chefs of the West. See issues of Sunset
Father's day in the kitchen; with recipes. il Parents Mag 42:66-9+ Je '67
Food of love; favorite foods of operatic composers. tr. by F. Merkling. H. Schraemli. Opera N 32:6-7 D 30 '67
Summer bachelor; Tuck Colby's favorites; with recipes. E. Alston. il Look 31:76 Ag 8 '67

COOKERY by men—*Continued*

Anecdotes, facetiae, satire, etc.
Father-by-himself cookbook. R. Lemon. il
  Sat Eve Post 240:14 Ag 12 '67
COOKERY contests. See Cookery—Competitions
COOKERY on yachts. See Cookery, Marine
COOKFAIR, Arthur S.
  Tesla's thermomagnetic motor. Pop Electr
  25:70-1+ D '66
COOKIE cutters
  Holiday cookie cutters. W. E. Homan. il
  Hobbies 72:98J-98K+ N '67
COOKIE rebellion; story. See Stanton, W.
COOKIE trees. See Christmas trees
COOKIES
  Big recipe, big cookies. il Farm J 91:90 Ap
  '67
  Bride makes cookies for tea; petit-fours;
  with recipe. il McCalls 94:130 Je '67
  Christmas cheer with a cooky cutter. D.
  Brooks. Home Gard 54:37 D '67
  Classic Swedish cooky tree makes a grand
  all-family project. il Sunset 139:66-9 D '67
  Friendly beasts; fairy-tale scene from cook-
  ies. il Ladies Home J 84:74-5+ D '67
  Hearthside cookbook Christmas 1967. il Good
  H 165:133-7 D '67
  Jiffy cookies and bars. il Farm J 92:68-9
  Ja '68
  Little rascals and other Dutch delights. il
  Sunset 139:118+ D '67
  Make-ahead refrigerator cookies; with rec-
  ipes. il Sunset 138:130 Je '67
  Playful cookies and pop (corn) art. R. Holm-
  berg and P. Dittberner. il Bet Hom & Gard
  45:64-6 D '67
  To help you bake cookies. il House & Gard
  132:286-7 N '67
COOKING. See Cookery
COOKING, Pressure. See Pressure cooking
COOKING utensils. See Kitchen utensils
COOKING utensils, Electric. See Electric ap-
  paratus and appliances, Domestic
COOKS
  Crisis in the kitchen; chef shortage. il News-
  week 70:66+ S 4 '67
  When the chefs cook for themselves; with
  menus. H. McCully. il House B 109:174-6+
  Mr '67
    See also
  Carrier, R.
  Haller, H.
COOLEY, Katherine
  Negro's plea; poem. Negro Hist Bul 30:21 Ap
  '67
COOLEY, Margaret
  (ed) Book review. See issues of Library jour-
  nal
COOLEY, R. C. and others
  Observations of the andromeda galaxy at
  11-centimeter wavelength. bibliog Science
  156:1087-8 My 26 '67
COOLIDGE, Clark
  Landscape and language. R. Sward. Poetry
  109:410-11 Mr '67
COOLIDGE, Coit, and Coolidge, Nancy
  New library buildings in the San Francisco
  Bay area. ALA Bul 61:738-9 Je '67
COOLIDGE, Nancy. See Coolidge, C. jt. auth.
COOLING of livestock. See Livestock, Cooling
  of
COOMBS, Philip H.
  Global revolution. Sat R 50:49-50 Ag 19 '67
COON, William O.
  Plants for ponds and stream sides. Horti-
  culture 45:32-3+ Ag '67
COON hunting. See Raccoon hunting
COONEY, A. M. See Wilson, R. B. jt. auth.
COONS, Betty Cannon, and Guy, F. C.
  Memorial exhibit in Richmond. Antiques 92:
  542-5 O '67
COONS. See Raccoons
COOPER, Amiel G.
  Hemagglutinating 7S subunits of 19S cold
  agglutinins. bibliog Science 157:933-5 Ag 25
  '67
COOPER, David
  Nobody wanted school desegregation. Am Ed
  3:2-4 Je '67
  North Carolina kills its dream. Nation 206:
  77-9 Ja 15 '68
COOPER, Frank
  Disreputable romantics. Hi Fi 18:48-50 Ja
  '68
COOPER, Giles
  Everything in the garden; adaptation. See
  Albee, E.

COOPER, Gordon
  Astronauts' vacation house. il por Pop Mech
  127:142-5 Ap '67
COOPER, Henry S. F. Jr
  Night at the observatory. Horizon 9:108-16
  Sum '67
COOPER, James C.
  Economy: a minority view. Duns R 89:40-1+
  My '67
COOPER, James Fenimore
  Leather-stocking trails. D. Ford. il Travel
  127:45-9 Mr '67
COOPER, Jane
  No more elegies; poem. New Yorker 43:30
  Ja 13 '68
  Weather of six mornings; poem. New Yorker
  43:43 S 9 '67
COOPER, Jed Arthur
  Mugwump or full participant? NEA J 56:18
  Mr '67
COOPER, Joseph D.
  More problems of instant medicine. por Sat R
  50:56-61 Je 3 '67
COOPER, R. Conrad
  Steel strike? industry offers a substitute; ex-
  cerpts from address, November 13, 1967.
  por US News 63:109-10 N 27 '67
    about
  R. Conrad Cooper speaks his mind. pors Bsns
  W p 152+ O 7 '67
COOPER, R. M. and Taylor, L. H.
  Thalamic reticular system and central grey:
  self-stimulation. bibliog Science 156:102-3
  Ap 7 '67
COOPER, W. J. See Blumer, M. jt. auth.
COOPER, William R.
  Duquesne, dramatic change in campus scale.
  Arch Forum 127:78-85 Jl '67
COOPER union for the advancement of science
  and art

  Museum for the arts of decoration
  Cooper union museum's treasures. E. P.
  Birk. il Antiques 92:144 Ag '67
  Smithsonian outpost. New Yorker 43:49-50 O
  21 '67
COOPERATION
  See also
  Business cooperation
  Industrial cooperation
  Inter-American cooperation
  International cooperation year
  Interracial cooperation
  Library cooperation

  United States
  Limits of individualism. A. Nevins. Sat R
  50:25-7+ N 25 '67
COOPERATION in education. See Colleges and
  universities—Cooperation
COOPERATIVE apartment houses. See Apart-
  ment houses—Cooperative ownership
COOPERATIVE associations
  See also
  Cotton producers association
  Marketing, Cooperative
  Poor peoples corporation
  Southwest Alabama farmers cooperative asso-
  ciation

  Brazil
  Brazil's miserable northeast. H. W. Flan-
  nery. Cath World 205:276-81 Ag '67
COOPERATIVE commonwealth federation. See
  Political parties—Canada
COOPERATIVE marketing. See Marketing, Co-
  operative
COOPERATIVE municipal purchasing. See Pur-
  chasing, Municipal
COOPERATIVE research. See Research, Co-
  operative
COOPERSTOWN, N.Y.
  Leather-stocking trails. D. Ford. il Travel
  127:45-9 Mr '67
    See also
  National baseball hall of fame and museum
COOS BAY
  Coos Bay. il Sunset 139:26-8 Ag '67
COPE, Jack
  Black butterflies. Mlle 64:167+ Mr '67
  Khotso's millions. Reporter 37:41-4 D 14 '67
COPE, Myron
  Agent 26250, where are you? pors Sports
  Illus 27:74-6+ O 2 '67
  Big Z and his misfiring Pistons. Sports Illus
  27:26-8+ D 18 '67
  Would you let this man interview you?
  Sports Illus 26:70-2+ Mr 13 '67
COPE, Oliver
  Future of medical education. Harper 235:98-
  9+ O '67

COPE Allman International, limited
Conglomerate, London-style. il Time 90:96 O 13 '67
Socialist tycoon. Newsweek 70:85 O 16 '67

COPELAND, Harold
Heaths & heathers for all-season bloom. Home Gard 54:76-8 Mr '67

COPENHAGEN
Copenhagen: a native returns. V. Borge. il Holiday 43:32+ Ja '68

Airports
SAS plans new Copenhagen cargo center. J. W. Carter. il Aviation W 86:50-1 My 8 '67

Music
Notes from our correspondents. R. Naur. il Hi Fi 17:14+ Ap '67

Parks and playgrounds
Happy parks: Tivoli. H. Sutton. il Sat R 50:40-2 Je 3 '67

COPENHAGEN 800th anniversary festival. See Festivals—Denmark

COPLAND, Aaron
Bernstein's Copland Third. C. J. Luten. por Am Rec G 33:933 Je '67
Copland at the Bowl. Samuel at Cabrillo. I. Kolodin. Sat R 50:45 S 9 '67
Music to my ears; performance of Inscape. I. Kolodin. Sat R 50:50 N 4 '67

COPLAND, Jeri
How the state of Washington conserves its razor clam populations. Parks & Rec 2:41+ Mr '67

COPLANS, John
Art bloom. Vogue 150:184-7+ N 1 '67

COPLEY, John Singleton
Mr and Mrs Thomas Mifflin. A. Saarinen. il McCalls 95:38-9 O '67

COPLON, Judith
Coplon case dismissed. D. Kraslow. New Repub 156:10-11 F 18 '67

COPP, D. H. and others
Calcitonin from ultimobranchial glands of dogfish and chickens. bibliog Science 158:924-5 N 17 '67

COPPELIA; ballet. See Ballets—Criticisms

COPPENS, P.
Comparative X-ray and neutron diffraction study of bonding effects in s-triazine. bibliog Science 158:1577-9 D 22 '67

COPPER
Elusive shortage. il Time 90:94+ O 27 '67
See also
Scrap metal

COPPER industry and trade
Toward stability for copper. Time 89:91-2 Je 16 '67

Congo (capital Kinshasa)
Congo takes heat off copper; compromise with Belgian company. Bsns W p42 F 25 '67

United States
Accounting for copper. Fortune 75:333 Je 15 '67
Little union-busting? copper workers strike. Nation 206:70 Ja 15 '68
Strain of a five-month strike. il Bsns W p 160-2+ N 18 '67
Strange story of a two-month strike. U S News 63:95-6 S 18 '67
Strike that adds to the dollar's troubles. il U S News 64:78-9 Ja 15 '68
Toll of a five-month strike: who is hurt and how much. il U S News 63:94-6 D 11 '67
Tough stands stymie a copper settlement; workers set to strike eight companies. il Bsns W p 111-12 Jl 8 '67
Unions mass for copper showdown; rubber walkout is stalemated. Bsns W p 156+ My 20 '67
See also
Anaconda copper mining company

COPPER miners strike. See Strikes—United States—Miners

COPPER mines and mining
A-blast for copper. il Time 90:45 N 3 '67
How White Pine got to pay dirt. il Bsns W p 120-2 Jl 29 '67
See also
Anaconda copper mining company
Kennecott copper corporation

Congo (capital Kinshasa)
About-face; continued operation of Union minière by S.G.M. il Time 89:94 Mr 3 '67
Politics of copper: proxy fight in the Congo. P. Semonin. Nation 204:303-6 Mr 6 '67
What goes on in the Congo? nationalization of Union minière. Nation 204:196 F 13 '67

COPPER range company
How White Pine got to pay dirt. il Bsns W p 120-2 Jl 29 '67

COPPERWELD steel company
501st company. Fortune 75:254 Je 15 '67

COPPOLINO, Carl Anthony
Bailey for the defense. il por Newsweek 69:35-6 Ap 17 '67
Mary Coppolino's own story; ed. by E. Linn. M. Coppolino. Good H 165:72-3+ Ag '67

COPPOLINO, Mary
Mary Coppolino's own story; ed. by E. Linn. por Good H 165:72-3+ Ag '67

COPPOLINO trial. See Trials (murder)

COPULATORY behavior. See Sex behavior

COPYING processes
Centralized duplicating; Garden Grove, Calif. G. Wiesner. il Am City 82:98-9 F '67
Copying computers' words; Xerox 2400-IV, will duplicate and collate copies of computer print-out sheets at rate of forty a minute. Bsns W p68 Mr 4 '67
Copying methods manual, by W. R. Hawken. Review
Consumer Bul 50:35 Ap '67
Reprography: regulation is needed; report of second International congress on reprography, Cologne. F. B. Myrick. il Pub W 192:70-2+ D 4 '67
See also
Photography—Copying
Transparencies—Copying

COPYRIGHT
Confusion from Stockholm. R. H. Smith. Pub W 192:33 Ag 14 '67
International crisis in copyright; report of meeting by ABPC's technical, scientific and medical publishers group. S. Wagner. Pub W 192:16-17 D 4 '67
Stockholm is host for Berne copyright revision. H. R. Lottman. Pub W 192:31-2 Jl 31 '67
Turning point for international copyright. R. H. Smith. Pub W 193:28 Ja 1 '68

Addresses
See Copyright—Lectures, sermons, etc.

Advertisments
Who owns the ads: advertiser or newspaper? H. F. Pilpel. Pub W 192:28-9 S 4 '67

Artistic performance
Copyright dilemma; record companies and performers protection drive. R. L. Shayon. Sat R 50:66 N 11 '67
Personality can be appropriated. H. F. Pilpel. Pub W 191:49 Je 26 '67

Broadcasting rights
Radio: a paradoxical parasite. G. Lees. il Hi Fi 17:162 O '67

Duration
Case that might have been decided either way. H. F. Pilpel. Pub W 192:31 O 2 '67

Government employees
See Copyright, Government employees

Government information
See also
Copyright, Government employees

Lectures, sermons, etc.
Who owns the substance of lecture notes? H. F. Pilpel. Pub W 192:30 O 2 '67

Music
See also
Copyright—Broadcasting rights

Phonograph records
Copyright dilemma; record companies and performers protection drive. R. L. Shayon. Sat R 50:66 N 11 '67
See also
Copyright—Broadcasting rights

Radio rights
See Copyright—Broadcasting rights

Renewal
See Copyright—Duration

Unauthorized reprints
Bootleg Secret life draws Grove suit. Pub W 191:80 F 27 '67

Africa
Copyright, book numbering; remarks. P. Du Sautoy. Pub W 192:27-8 Jl 24 '67

COPYRIGHT—*Continued*

United States

Appeals court upholds CATV's copyright liability. Pub W 191:143 Je 5 '67
But can you do that? H. F. Pilpel. Pub W 191:41-2 My 29 '67
Can a newspaper claim copyright in ads? H. F. Pilpel. Pub W 191:87 Ja 30 '67
Computer and copyright: the next five years. C. H. Lieb. Pub W 192:40-2 S 18 '67
Copyright and computers. D. Wolfle. Science 156:319 Ap 21 '67
Copyright bill in 90th Congress. Sr Schol 90:sup2 F 17 '67
Copyright grab bag. II: a new kind of lend-lease. C. F. Gosnell. bibliog ALA Bul 61:707-12 Je '67
Copyright revision: one and a half cheers for the House. R. H. Smith. Pub W 191:72 Ap 24 '67
Copyright revision: the great giveaway? R. H. Smith. Pub W 191:40 My 8 '67
Copyright revisited. J. J. Marke. il Wilson Lib Bul 42:34-45 S '67
Fair use; McClellan bill proposals. S. Kauffmann. New Repub 157:24+ O 7 '67
Feasibility study on clearinghouse for copyrights and computers; with editorial comment. Pub W 192:33, 38 S 4 '67
Information as a property; address, 1967. W. Jovanovich. il Wilson Lib Bul 42:46-55 S '67
Nearer to the dust, by G. A. Gipe. Review Sat R 50:63 Jl 8 '67. S. W. Little
New copyright law creeps nearer. il Bsns W p 126+ Ag 5 '67
New copyright law for the new Congress. H. E. Wigren. Sch & Soc 95:50-1 Ja 21 '67
Prototype project for copyrights and computers; feasibility study of mechanism to handle requests for copyright clearances. Pub W 192:35 Jl 31 '67
Rights and permissions. P. Nathan. See issues of Publishers' weekly
Senate copyright hearings study fair use and education, computers, ETV. Pub W 191:34-5 My 8 '67
Senate gets bill for new copyright commission. Pub W 192:43 Ag 21 '67
Senate hearings, July 25, on copyright commission. Pub W 192:34 Jl 3 '67
Senate hearings scheduled on copyright revision. Pub W 191:49 Mr 6 '67
Senate subcommittee opens hearings on general copyright revision bill. Pub W 191:33 Ap 3 '67
Status of copyright revision; excerpts from a discussion. L. Deighton; B. Linden. il Pub W 191:29-30 My 29 '67
Time limit on copyright filings extended for German citizens. Dept State Bul 57:171 Ag 7 '67
    See also
American library association—Committee on copyright issues

COPYRIGHT, Government employees
Implications of the latest Rickover ruling; question of right to copyright speeches made on own time while in public office. H. F. Pilpel. Pub W 192:33-4 Jl 31 '67
COPYRIGHT issues committee. See American library association—Committee on copyright issues
Le COQ d'or; opera. See Rimskiĭ-Korsakov, N. A.
COQUI, pseud.
Sales supervision: suggestions for managers. Pub W 192:42-4 S 18 '67
Short cut to inventory control for retail booksellers. Pub W 192:29-31 D 25 '67
CORAL GABLES, Fla.
New buses rid city of red ink. T. C. Hall. il Am City 82:37 Ap '67

Industries
Companies hark to Coral Gables' Spanish accent; base for directing Latin American operations. il Bsns W p 123-4+ Ap 22 '67
CORAL reefs and islands
Bermuda's southern aeolianite reef tract. D. J. Stanley and D. J. P. Swift. bibliog il Science 157:677-81 Ag 11 '67
Coral corral? proposal to raise plankton-eating whales. Sci Am 216:52+ Mr '67
Exploring a coral atoll; Hogsty Reef, in the southern Bahamas. W. M. Stephens. il Yachting 121:62-4+ F '67
Glycerol excretion by symbiotic algae from corals and tridacna and its control by the host. L. Muscatine. bibliog il Science 156:516-19 Ap 28 '67

Holocene changes in sea level; evidence in Micronesia. F. P. Shepard and others. bibliog il Science 157:542-4 Ag 4 '67
Zonation of uplifted pleistocene coral reefs on Barbados, West Indies. K. J. Mesolella. bibliog il Science 156:638-40 My 5 '67
    See also
Great Barrier Reef
Line Islands
Midway (islands)
CORAL SEA
Seismic refraction profile in Coral Sea basin. G. G. Shor, jr. bibliog il Science 158:911-13 N 17 '67
CORALLO, Antonio
Mafia scandal; new trouble for Lindsay. US News 64:10 Ja 1 '68
Mob finds a patsy in a mayor's inner circle. S. Smith and W. Lambert. il Life 64:46-51 Ja 5 '68
CORBETT, Edward P. J.
Book reviews. America 117:720 D 9 '67
CORBIT, John D. jr, and others
What's wrong with American hospitals? asking a computer. Sat R 50:67-9 F 4 '67
CORBMAN, Myrtle
Mutiny, decorous and decorative, on the Bountiful. por Motor B 120:44-7 O '67
CORBUSIER, Le. See Le Corbusier
CORCORAN, Barbara
You can't put a black jack on a black queen; story. Redbook 129:40-1 Ag '67
CORCORAN, Judy
Fitness time in Topeka. Am Ed 3:21-3+ S '67
CORD (consortium research development) See Educational research
CORDASCO, Frank M.
Knocking down the language walls. Commonweal 87:6-8 O 6 '67
Puerto Rican pupils and American education; adaptation of address, August 30, 1966. bibliog f Sch & Soc 95:116-19 F 18 '67
CORDIALS. See Liqueurs
CORDIERITE
Magical stones of the sun; cordierite identified as Viking navigation aid. il Time 90:58 Jl 14 '67
CORDINER, Ralph Jarron
Man who recast Reagan. il pors Newsweek 69:16 My 22 '67
CORDLESS shavers. See Razors
CÓRDOBA (city), Argentina
Cordoba (Argentina) takes noise abatement by the horns. G. L. Fuchs. il UNESCO Courier 20:21-2 Jl '67
el CORDOBÉS
Back to battle the bulls. il pors Life 62:107-8+ Ap 28 '67
Matador. B. Conrad. il pors Holiday 43:68-71+ Ja '68
CORDS, Electric. See Electric cords
CORDTZ, Dan
Antidisestablishmentarianism at Wheeling steel. Fortune 7:104-9+ Jl '67
But what do we do about the Arabs. Fortune 76:74-9+ S 1 '67
It's now or never for the post office. Fortune 75:134-9+ Mr '67
Social security drifting off course. Fortune 76:104-7+ D '67
CORDY, D. R. See Richards, W. P. C. jt. auth.
CORE construction. See Unit construction
CORELLI, Franco
Franco Corelli in and out of costume. C. L. Osborne. il pors Hi Fi 17:63-7 F '67
COREOPSIS
Bright yellow and free-blooming. Sunset 138:236 F '67
CORES, Magnetic. See Magnetic memory (computers)
CORFAM. See Leather substitutes
CORFMAN, Eunice Luccock
To be an athlete; story. Harper 235:86-94 N '67
CORFMAN, Philip A. and Segal, Sheldon
Intrauterine devices. Science 156:1136 My 26 '67
CORFU (island)
Club on Corfu; a Club Méditerranée village. R. H. Buck. il Sr Schol 91:sup 11 N 2 '67
CORITA, Sister. See Kent, M. C.
CORKETT, Tom
Tom Corkett on crew selection. Yachting 121:124 Je '67
CORKSCREW swamp sanctuary. See Wildlife sanctuaries
CORLEY, Bob
Instant sketches from photo prints. Pop Mech 128:156-7 D '67

CORLISS, Richard
 Etc. Commonweal 86:234-6 My 12 '67
 Movies in brief. Nat R 19:153-5, 917-19 F
  7, Ag 22 '67
 Pop music: what's been happening. Nat R
  19:371-4 Ap 4 '67
 Raggedy Andy Warhol. Commonweal 86:469-70
  Jl 28 '67
—and Jensen, Paul
 Medley of unsung films. Nat R 19:814+ Jl
  25 '67
CORMAN, Roger
 Psychedelia. H. Alpert. Sat R 50:39 S 2 '67
CORMIER, Milton J. See Ashworth, R. B. jt.
  auth.
CORN, Hilda
 First lady; story. Redbook 130:90-1 N '67
CORN
 Light-enhanced potassium absorption by corn
  leaf tissue. D. W. Rains. bibliog il Science
  156:1382-3 Je 9 '67
 Oats compete with corn? D. F. Wilken and
  H. Guither. Suc Farm 65:98 F '67
 Ribonuclease activity in normal and opaque-
  2 mutant endosperm of maize. C. M. Wilson
  and D. E. Alexander. bibliog il Science 155:
  1575-6 Mr 24 '67
 Ribonuclease activity in the developing seeds
  of normal and opaque-2 maize. A. Dalby
  and I. ab I. Davies. bibliog il Science 155:
  1573-5 Mr 24 '67
 Subcellular structure of endosperm protein
  in high-lysine and normal corn. M. J.
  Wolf and others. bibliog il Science 157:556-7
  Ag 4 '67

Cultivation
 Beans vs. corn; which will net you most in
  1967? A. G. Mueller and H. Guither. il Suc
  Farm 65:104 Mr '67
 Corn. D. Seim. il Farm J 91:46H+ My '67
 Corn yields: are you aiming high enough?
  G. Johnson and J. Russell. il Farm J 91:
  40-1+ Mr '67
 Don't go wild on irrigation! P. B. Jones.
  Suc Farm 65:52-3 F '67
 Doyle Smith grows 20-inch row corn. C. E.
  Sommers. il Suc Farm 65:54-5+ Mr '67
 How the big operators grow corn. D. Seim.
  il Farm J 91:66H+ Mr '67
 Mick, the dreamer; a story of the soil. J.
  Stuart. il Am For 73:34-7+ F '67
 107-bu. corn after 65-bu. wheat the same
  year. J. Russell. il Farm J 91:64P-64Q+
  F '67
 Pop-up; will it become the starter? fertilizer
  directly with the seed. J. Russell. il Farm J
  91:54+ Ap '67
 Thirty tons of silage from broadcast corn.
  D. Hagen. Farm J 91:74K Mr '67
 What made the big corn crop? ed. by R. D.
  Wennblom. il Farm J 91:32-3+ D '67
 What the experts recommend for corn this
  year. il Suc Farm 65:37 Ap '67

Diseases and pests
 How to control corn insects. Suc Farm 65:
  90+ Mr '67
 Sow later, reap more; Israel's hybrid corn
  disease caused by virus. Time 90:56+ Jl 14
  '67

Drying
 Fast new way to dry corn. N. Reeder. Farm J
  92:48 Ja '68

History
 Birth of wheat and maize farming. J. Hawkes.
  il UNESCO Courier 20:6-7 My '67

Hybrids
 Heterosis: complementation by mitochondria.
  R. G. McDaniel and I. V. Sarkissian; dis-
  cussion. Science 155:722; 156:263 F 10, Ap 14
  '67
 How to select the right corn hybrid. W.
  Messerly. il Suc Farm 65:78 F '67

Seeding
 They went to equal-distance corn spacing.
  C. E. Sommers. il Suc Farm 65:32-3 Ja '67
 What farmers think of 20-inch row corn.
  C. E. Sommers. il Suc Farm 65:40-1+ Ja
  '67

Storage
 Cold corn, how its working; refrigerated
  storage. W. J. Fletcher. il Suc Farm 65:33
  Je '67
 How to handle overflow corn. P. B. Jones. il
  Suc Farm 65:40-1 O '67
CORN, Sweet
 How to get the most out of corn. G. Morri-
  son. il Horticulture 45:34-5+ My '67
 Why corn ears go wrong. Sunset 139:252 O
  '67
 See also
 Cookery—Vegetables

CORN bread. See Bread
CORN coleoptiles. See Coleoptiles
CORN dance. See Indians of North America—
  Dances
CORN rootworms
 Split-season control kills more corn root-
  worms. D. Seim. il Farm J 91:72D+ F '67
CORN silage. See Silage
CORN syrup. See Syrups
CORNEAL lenses. See Contact lenses
CORNEAL transplants. See Transplantation of
  organs, tissues, etc.
CORNELL, Jack
 Controlled solarization. U S Camera 30:46-7+
  S '67
CORNELL, Joseph
 Art; exposition in the Guggenheim. M. Koz-
  loff. Nation 204:701-2 My 29 '67
 Art world; exhibition at the Guggenheim
  museum. H. Rosenberg. New Yorker 43:112+
  Je 3 '67
 Cornell: the cube root of dreams. J. Ashbery.
  il Art N 66:56-9+ Sum '67
 Imagined universe stored in boxes; with re-
  port by D. Bourdon. il por Life 63:52-61
  D 15 '67
 Paradise regained; exhibition of boxes at
  New York's Guggenheim museum. J. Kroll.
  il Newsweek 69:86 Je 5 '67
CORNELL aeronautical laboratory, incorporated
 CAL readying radar system to study micro-
  wave, plasma. R. Barnhart. Tech W 20:30+
  My 29 '67
CORNELL university, Ithaca, N.Y.
 Cornell ends parent role. Sat R 50:86 N 18 '67
 Cornell's new student housing forms unified
  residential complex. il Arch Rec 141:148-50
  Mr '67
 Pot bust at Cornell. D. Sanford. New Repub
  156:17-20 Ap 15 '67; Discussion. 156:26-7
  Ap 29; 34 My 6 '67
CORNETT, Lilly
 Lilly's wood. H. M. Caudill. il Audubon 69:
  24-7 My '67
CORNETT, R. Orin
 Cued speech. A. C. Miles. Am Ed 3:26-8 N '67
CORNFELD, Bernard
 Empire at Bernie-Voltaire. il por Time 90:
  110-11 O 6 '67
 Strategic retreat. por Newsweek 69:72 Je 5 '67
CORNING community college, N.Y.
 Bookselling in a two-year college. P. John-
  son, jr. il Pub W 192:46-8 D 25 '67
CORNING glass center, Corning, N.Y.
 New acquisitions at the Corning museum of
  glass. il Hobbies 72:98X-98Z N '67
 Special collection somewhat off the beaten
  track; Corning museum of glass. P. N.
  Perrot. il Wilson Lib Bul 41:593-7 F '67
CORNING museum of glass. See Corning glass
  center, Corning, N.Y.
CORNISH, Geoffrey S. and Robinson, W. G.
 Country club look for public golf courses.
  Parks & Rec 2:28-9+ My '67
CORNUS kousa. See Dogwood
CORNWALL, Barbara
 Cyprus: no change. New Repub 158:10 Ja 13
  '68
CORONA, Solar. See Sun—Corona
CORONADO trail. See Roads—Arizona
CORONARY artery disease. See Arteriosclerosis
CORONARY heart disease. See Heart—Diseases
CORONATION of Poppea; opera. See Mon-
  teverdi, C.
CORONATIONS
 Hail to the new king of Tonga. J. Bonfante.
  il Life 63:58-65 Jl 21 '67
 On a tropical isle, big week for a big king.
  il U S News 63:16 Jl 17 '67
 What a king should be; coronation of
  Tupou IV in Tonga. il Time 90:32 Jl 14 '67
 See also
 Mohammed Reza Pahlevi, shah of Iran—
  Coronation
CORPORAL punishment
 Cane & the strap; corporal punishment in
  British schools. il Time 90:62+ S 8 '67
 Whipping boys; book attacks practice of rat-
  taning in Boston schools. il Newsweek 70:
  94 O 16 '67
CORPORATE acquisitions
 Antidisestablishmentarianism at Wheeling
  steel. D. Cordtz. il Fortune 76:104-9+ Jl '67
 Beatrice foods savors a zestier cupboard. il
  Bsns W p 122+ D 16 '67
 CBS buys books; acquisition of Holt, Rinehart
  & Winston. il Time 89:85 Mr 10 '67
 Empire builders: conglomerate mergers. H. C.
  Wallich. Newsweek 70:56 Ag 21 '67

CORPORATE acquisitions—*Continued*

Fire that stirred Holly sugar to action; unsuccessful corporate take-over by International systems & controls corp. il Bsns W p 151-2+ N 18 '67

Geneen's machine; ITT's appetite for acquisitions. il Newsweek 70:66-8 Ag 7 '67

How to get out of a steel-lined rut; Bliss & Laughlin's diversification by acquisition. Bsns W p86+ Jl 15 '67

In a single stroke; Ling-Temco-Vought acquires Wilson & co. il Time 89:94 Mr 17 '67

Killing; National car rental sold to Greatamerica corp. Newsweek 70:78 O 23 '67

Laird of the epicurean manner; S. S. Pierce bought by Laird industries inc. il Time 89:88-9 Je 23 '67

LTV blitzes its way into ranks of giants; take-over of Chicago-based Wilson & co. il Bsns W p 178-80+ Mr 18 '67

Making big waves with small fish; H. E. Singleton of Teledyne. il Bsns W p36-9 D 30 '67

Medicine man at Indian Head; R. W. Lear. il Bsns W p84+ Ag 19 '67

Meshulam Riklis: how to build an empire without cash; acquisition of Manhattan's Lerner stores by McCrory corporation. il Duns R 90:21 Jl '67

Profits from a pigmy; Williams brothers buys Great Lakes pipe line. Fortune 75:326 Je 15 '67

Tactics of cash takeover bids. S. L. Hayes, 3d. and R. A. Taussig. il Harvard Bsns R 45:135-48 Mr '67

Takeover tycoon: I win because I intend to win. Duns R 90:35 S '67

Tenneco lands Kern County. Bsns W p96-8+ Jl 22 '67

CORPORATE giving. See Corporations—Charitable contributions

CORPORATE liability. See Liability (law)

CORPORATE ombudsman. See Ombudsman

CORPORATE planning. See Business management and organization

CORPORATE seminars, incorporated

New school try. Time 90:104 N 24 '67

CORPORATION lawyers. See Lawyers

CORPORATION management. See Business management and organization

CORPORATION presidents. See Corporations—Presidents

CORPORATION reports

Changing the rules. il Fortune 75:227-8 Ap '67

Declining art of concealing the figures; annual reports of foreign companies. R. Ball. il Fortune 76:136-9+ S 15 '67

Gesture of friendship; foreign-language editions of annual reports. L. L. L. Golden. Sat R 50:102 Je 10 '67

Xerox annual report; a guided tour. M. Buhabiar. il Fortune 75:184-7+ Je 15 '67

CORPORATIONS

Big corporations can have their own CIA. New Repub 156:18 F 18 '67

Corporation of the future; address, October 24, 1967. R. E. Ablon. Vital Speeches 34:73-6 N 15 '67

Corporation: sociological and technological developments; address, April 20, 1967. T. J. Gordon. Vital Speeches 33:500-5 Je 1 '67

Corporations: where the game is growth. il Bsns W p98-100+ S 30 '67

Down near the up sign; sales and earnings. Time 90:74 Ag 4 '67

Gadflies who put the bite on business; plaintiffs' lawyers. il Bsns W p 124-6 O 14 '67

Galbraith speaks; summary of address. il Pub W 191:25-6 My 22 '67

Keeping their success in the family; privately held companies. Bsns W p96-8 D 9 '67

New industrial state, by J. K. Galbraith. Review
  Fortune 76:90-1+ Jl '67. I. Kristol
  Time 89:74 Je 30 '67

Professor Galbraith stirs memories of Pius XI; re-examination of encyclical On reconstructing the social order. B. L. Masse. America 117:196 Ag 26 '67

Top of the top. il Fortune 75:194-5 Je 15 '67

See also
Bonds
Business consolidations and mergers
Executives
Monopolies
Proxies
Trusts, Industrial

Accounting

Accounting: the other side of the ledger; embattled CPAs. il Duns R 89:36-7+ Mr '67

Cost controls that cost money. E. C. Schleh. il Duns R 89:49+ Ap '67

Profit reporting by divisions? T. J. Murray. il Duns R 89:29-31+ My '67

Put people on your balance sheet. J. S. Hekimian and C. H. Jones. bibliog f il Harvard Bsns R 45:105-13 Ja '67

Advertising

Agency love, on the rocks? shuffling of accounts. G. Lazarus. Sat R 50:94-5 My 13 '67

Graphic art of corporate image. il Fortune 76:127-8+ Jl '67

Charitable contributions

Corporate giving: a growing problem. J. Weingarten. il Duns R 90:31-2+ Ag '67

Number one to the Met; Eastern air lines gives the Met $500,000. il Time 89:87 My 26 '67

When big business makes gifts, tax-deductible. A. Hacker. il N Y Times Mag p34-5+ N 12 '67

See also
Foundations, Charitable and educational

Directories

Fortune directory. Fortune 75:196-225 Je 15 '67

Fortune directory of the 200 largest industrials outside the U.S. Fortune 76:140-6 S 15 '67

Directors

Legal liabilities of executives. M. Feuer. il Duns R 89:48-9+ My '67

Finance

Adding to the records. Time 89:88+ F 17 '67

America's most profitable companies. J. B. Weiner. il Duns R 89:32-3+ Ap '67

Battle reports; third-quarter earnings. il Time 90:92+ N 3 '67

Boom on bootstrap finance. il Duns R 90:19-20+ Jl '67

Corporate squeeze; first-quarter sales. il Bsns W p 150 My 6 '67

Corporations keep their cool on profits; with editorial comment. il Bsns W p34-5, 204 F 18 '67

Corporations scramble for cash. il Bsns W p 151-2+ Mr 25 '67

Costs go under the microscope: second-quarter earnings. il Bsns W p26-8 Jl 8 '67

Credit risks & opportunities. R. M. Kaplan. il Harvard Bsns R 45:83-8 Mr '67

Earnings move up again, at a crawl; third-quarter profit reports. il Bsns W p39-40 O 28 '67

Earnings take a dip. il Bsns W p29 Ap 8 '67

First quarter; profits. Time 89:96 Ap 28 '67

Gloom was overdone; second quarter profits. il Bsns W p 19 Jl 22 '67

How McDonnell won Douglas. T. A. Wise. Fortune 75:155-6+ Mr '67

How much should a corporation earn? J. J. Scanlon. il Harvard Bsns R 45:4-6+ Ja '67

How to beat Parkinson's law. M. Baldrige. il Duns R 89:46-7+ Je '67

Investing in a dividend boost. G. E. MacDougal. il Harvard Bsns R 45:87-92 Jl '67

Latest on profits; signs of an end to the decline. il U S News 63:60 N 6 '67

Latest on profits: the squeeze is still on; with chart. U S News 63:67 Ag 7 '67

Market shrugs off profit dip. il Bsns W p28-9 Jl 29 '67

Mixture with a minus flavor. il Time 90:75-6 Jl 28 '67

Profit picture: many companies squeezed, but... il U S News 62:81 F 13 '67

Profits add up to less. Bsns W p39 My 20 '67

Profits: cutting out the cookies; cost-cutting programs. il Newsweek 70:60-1 Jl 3 '67

Reminders & records; 1966 prosperous year. Time 89:69-70 F 3 '67

Special circumstances; third-quarter earnings. Time 90:92-3 O 27 '67

Squeeze on profits continues. il Bsns W p 137 Je 17 '67

Tactics that win that extra nickel. il Bsns W p76-8+ Ag 19 '67

Tax speedups & corporate liquidity. J. E. Miles. il Harvard Bsns R 45:2-4+ Jl '67

Tumbling profits. il Fortune 75:36+ Ap '67

Two-tone; profits. Time 89:87-8 My 5 '67

Using credit for profit making. M. T. Weishans. il Harvard Bsns R 45:141-7+ Ja '67

What happens to profits? D. Lawrence. U S News 62:96 Ap 3 '67

When stock issues miss the boat. il Bsns W p 162+ Ap 15 '67

CORPORATIONS—Finance—*Continued*
  Where profits are being squeezed the hardest;
    with table. il U S News 62:102-3 My 1 '67
  Why stocks feel better; first-quarter earn-
    ings. il Bsns W p42 Ap 22 '67
  Will '67 earnings dip? 1966 fourth quarter
    report. il Bsns W p28 F 4 '67

  See also
  Bankruptcy
  Capital investments
  Corporations—Accounting
  Dividends
  Executives—Salaries
  Profit

  Foreign expansion
  See Business—Foreign expansion

  Foreign subsidiaries
  ¿Cómo está, RCA? J. Ross-Skinner. il Duns R
    89:63 Ap '67
  Dollar invades Europe. J. D. Phillips. Nation
    205:242-5 S 18 '67
  Europe and America: partners in technology;
    address, November 10, 1966. G. C. McGhee.
    Dept State Bul 56:148-53 Ja 23 '67
  Gesture of friendship; foreign-language edi-
    tions of annual reports. L. L. L. Golden.
    Sat R 50:102 Je 10 '67
  Global company in a changing world. T. J.
    Murray. il Duns R 90:27-8+ Ag; 46-7+ S
    '67
  Going multinational; Ford sets up European-
    based subsidiary. Time 89:69 Je 30 '67
  How ITT tightens its spreading net; ITT
    Europe's business plan. il Bsns W p58-60+
    Je 24 '67
  International VP: man on the run; Honey-
    well's E. Spencer. il Bsns W p48+ Ag 26
    '67
  Long-term view from the 29th floor; U.S.
    corporations in overseas markets. il Time
    90:56-9+ D 29 '67
  Multinational enterprises & national sover-
    eignty. R. Vernon. Harvard Bsns R 45:
    156-8+ Mr '67
  Politics of private foreign investment. L.
    Model. il For Affairs 45:639-51 Jl '67
  Pushing the captives; Detroit subsidiaries
    abroad market in the U.S. il Bsns W p 19
    Jl 1 '67
  Regional management overseas. C. R. Wil-
    liams il Harvard Bsns R 45:87-91 Ja '67
  South Africa raises ante on autos. il Bsns
    W p96+ N 18 '67
  What U.S. companies are doing abroad. See
    issues of U.S. news & World report
  Why the climate is changing for U.S. invest-
    ment. W. Guzzardi, jr. il Fortune 76:112-
    17+ S 15 '67

  Names
  Cringe: odd corporation names for fleet-owned
    taxicabs. New Yorker 43:39 S 16 '67
  Problem: updating names of organizations for
    twenty-first century. New Yorker 43:23-4
    S 2 '67

  Presidents
  Clues for success in the president's job. J. C.
    Bailey. Harvard Bsns R 45:97-104 My '67
  Dilemma of the young presidents. il Duns R
    90:41+ Ag '67
  Making of a corporation president. A.
    Hacker. il N Y Times Mag p26-7+ Ap 2
    '67
  Men who run the top twenty manufacturing
    companies. il Bsns W p 115 S 30 '67
  Why don't executives get off dead center?
    T. J. Murray. il Duns R 89:29-31+ Ap '67

  Public relations
  See Business—Public relations

  Real estate operations
  How business is helping to rebuild cities. il
    U S News 62:90-2 Mr 20 '67
  Real estate: growing sideline for big corpora-
    tions. il U S News 63:90-2 Ag 21 '67

  Size
  New industrial state; excerpt. J. K. Gal-
    braith. Atlan 219:51-7 Ap '67

  Social aspects
  See Business—Social aspects

  Taxation
  Scaling the Alps for tax havens; principality
    of Liechtenstein. il Bsns W p66-7+ O 21 '67
  Struggling with the surcharge; with editorial
    comment. il Bsns W p124+, 192 S 23 '67

CORPORATIONS, Foreign
  Decade of dazzling growth. E. K. Falter-
    mayer. il Fortune 76:128-35+ S 15 '67
  Stocks of the 200. J. Main. il Fortune 76:
    151-2+ S 15 '67
  See also
  Corporations, International

CORPORATIONS, International
  Promise of the multinational corporation; ex-
    cerpts from address. G. W. Ball. Fortune
    75:80 Je 1 '67
  See also
  Corporations, Foreign

CORPORATIONS, Nonprofit
  Politics of consortium; community corpor-
    ations. M. Miles. New Repub 157:12-13 S
    9 '67

CORPORATIONS, Private. See Corporations

CORPORATIONS, Stealing from. See Stealing

CORPORATIONS and education. See Business
  and education

CORPS of engineers. See United States—Army—
  Corps of engineers

CORPSES. See Cadavers

CORPULENCE
  Butterballs, stay fat. A. J. Snider. Sci Digest
    61:28 Mr '67
  Chemistry of fatness; controlling weight with
    hormones. Newsweek 69:82 My 1 '67
  Curing the obese; diuretics questioned. D. A.
    Ehrlich. Sci N 92:377+ O 14 '67
  Future in the scale; obese adolescents. E.
    W. Buzbee. il N Y Times Mag p97+ Mr
    12 '67
  Godfrey Cambridge wins battle of bulges,
    loses 117 pounds. L. Robinson. il Ebony 22:
    160-2+ O '67
  If you're overweight, you don't know how to
    eat. G. M. Knox. il Bet Hom & Gard 46:
    24+ Ja '68
  Miseries of an overweight child; John Oc-
    chipinti's summer at Camp Tahoe. B. Ko-
    civar. il Look 31:36-8+ N 14 '67
  Program for overweight teens. Sci Digest 62:
    74 Jl '67
  Regulation of food intake and obesity. J.
    Mayer and D. W. Thomas. bibliog il Science
    156:328-37 Ap 21 '67
  Speaking out; more people should be fat.
    L. Louderback. il Sat Eve Post 240:10+
    N 4 '67
  Think fat, be fat. il Sci Digest 62:81 Ag '67
  Why some mothers fatten their children. G.
    R. Krupp. il Todays Health 45:56-7+ N '67
  Why some people get fat; eating experi-
    ment. il Sci Digest 62:31-2 N '67
  See also
  Weight watchers, incorporated

CORPUS CHRISTI, Tex.
  Treasure of pleasure. P. Crittenden. il Travel
    127:41-4 Mr '67

  Libraries
  Square-on-square in Corpus Christi; Green-
    wood branch of public library. P. S. Burson.
    il Library J 92:4377-8 D 1 '67

CORREAS, Edmundo
  Rugendas; historian with pencil and paint.
    bibliog Américas 19:12-19 O '67

CORRECTIONAL institutions. See Reformatories

CORRESPONDENCE. See Letters

CORRESPONDENCE schools and courses
  Postman is the proctor for millions of cor-
    respondence students; recent study by the
    Carnegie corporation. B. H. Pearse. il Am
    Ed 3:10-12 F '67
  See also
  Autolite technical service institute

CORRESPONDENTS, Foreign. See Foreign
  correspondents

CORRESPONDENTS, War. See War correspondents

CORROSION and anticorrosives
  Merc's robot corrosion fighter. A. Mikesell. il
    Pop Mech 129:150-1+ Ja '68
  Problem and the cure for galvanic corro-
    sion. C. F. Kelley. il Yachting 122:50-1+
    O '67
  Rust: the uninvited guest. A. P. Smith.
    Yachting 121:68+ Ap '67
  Wanted: a cure for corrosion. il Bsns W p88+
    S 30 '67
  Your personal battle with rust. J. Hand. il
    Pop Sci 190:186+ Mr '67

CORRUPTION in politics. See Politics, Corruption in

CORRY, John
  Cardinal Spellman and New York politics.
    Harper 235:74-80+ D '67
  Manchester papers. Esquire 67:83-91+ Je '67

CORRY, John—*Continued*

about

Corry papers. G. Talese. il Esquire 67:92-4+ Je '67

CORSARO, Frank
Avoiding the patterns; interview, ed. by E. R. Rizzo. por Opera N 31:16 Mr 25 '67

CORSICA
Catch-22 revisited. J. Heller. il Holiday 41: 45-55 Ap '67
Election fever; Gaullist victories on Corsica. il Newsweek 69:59 Mr 27 '67
Going places, finding things in Corsica. E. Bedell. il House & Gard 133:10+ Ja '68
Offbeat Corsica. P. Korn. il U S Camera 30: 58-9+ S '67

CORSON, Hazel Wyman
Dame Fortune and Don Money; dramatization of a Spanish folk tale. Plays 26:55-61 Ap '67
Fish in the forest; dramatization of a Russian folk tale. Plays 27:43-9 O '67
Green glass ball; dramatization of an Irish folk tale. Plays 27:43-9 Ja '68
Triumph for two; dramatization of a Bohemian folk tale. Plays 26:37-44 Mr '67

CORSON, James W.
Look to youth. Parks & Rec 2:20-2+ D '67

CORT, David
Of guilt and resurrection. Nation 204:373-4 Mr 20 '67
Signal danger. Nation 205:251-2 S 18 '67
Ultimate joke. Nation 205:633-4 D 11 '67

CORTADA, James N. and Hope, A. G.
Foreign service institute: patterns of professional development. Dept State Bul 56:218-23 F 6 '67

CORTAZAR, Julio
I am an axolotl; story; excerpt from End of the game. Vogue 149:124-5 F 15 '67
Night face up; story, tr. by P. Blackburn. New Yorker 43:49-52 Ap 22 '67

about

Author. P. Méras. por Sat R 50:36 Jl 22 '67

CORTELYOU, Irwin F.
Group portraits: Ames and Hogarth. Antiques 92:632+ N '67

CORTELYOU, John R.
Community responsibilities of business; address, October 24, 1967. Vital Speeches 34: 148-50 D 15 '67

CORTEX, Cerebral. See Cerebral cortex

CORTICOSTEROIDS
Adenosine 3', 5'-cyclic phosphate: stimulation of steroidogenesis in sonically disrupted adrenal mitochondria. S. Roberts and others. bibliog il Science 158:372-4 O 20 '67
Circadian pattern of plasma 17-hydroxycorticosteroid: alteration by anticholinergic agents. D. T. Krieger and H. P. Krieger. bibliog il Science 155:1421-2 Mr 17 '67
Enzyme induction by corticosteroids in embryonic cells: steroid structure and inductive effect. A. A. Moscona and R. Piddington. bibliog il Science 158:496-7 O 27 '67
Inhibition of lipolytic action of growth hormone and glucocorticoid by ultraviolet and X-radiation. J. N. Fain. bibliog il Science 157:1062-4 S 1 '67
Polycystic renal disease: a new experimental model. D. Y. E. Perey and others. bibliog il Science 158:494-6 O 27 '67

CORTNER, Jean A. See Davidson, R. G. jt. auth.

CORVALLIS, Ore.
Warm-hearted city; mapping the heat island. Sci Am 216:52 Ap '67

CORWIN, R. D. and Duchoviner, M. E.
Bike exerciser you can build. Pop Sci 191: 176-7 O '67

CORWIN, R. David
Dilemma of the Iroquois; with biographical sketch. Natur Hist 76:4, 6-7+ Je '67

COSA nostra. See Mafia

COSBY, Bill
Private world of Bill Cosby. J. Stang. il pors Good H 164:26+ Je '67
Silver throat's crusade. il por Newsweek 70:78 S 4 '67
Spy off duty. J. M. Flagler. il pors Look 31:M16-17+ My 30 '67

COS COB. See Greenwich, Conn.

COSELL, Howard
Would you let this man interview you? M. Cope. il por Sports Illus 26:70-2+ Mr 13 '67

COSER, Lewis A.
Labor pains. Commentary 43:91-3 Je '67
Liberal anti-communism revisited. Commentary 44:39-41 S '67

COSMETIC factories. See Factories

COSMETIC industry and trade
Key man in cosmetics. J. Ross-Skinner. il Duns R 90:65 D '67
Poisons & cosmetics: adventures in the skin trade. T. Stabile. Nation 206:16-19 Ja 1 '68
See also
Chemway corporation
Holiday magic organic cosmetics

COSMETIC surgery. See Surgery, Plastic

COSMETICS
Beauty checkout. See issues of Vogue
Beauty memo. Mlle 64:90 F '67
Hand creams and lotions. Consumer Rep 32: 526-7 O '67
How to buy cosmetics you'll really use. il Good H 165:104-5 S '67
Newly minted makeup shade; copper. il McCalls 94:78-9 Ag '67
Poisons & cosmetics: adventures in the skin trade. T. Stabile. Nation 206:16-19 Ja 1 '68
Stay young & beautiful. V. S. Stitt. il Parents Mag 42:40 O; 54 N; 18 D '67
Suntan preparations. il Consumer Rep 32: 364-7 Jl '67
Suntan preparations. Consumer Rep 32:223-6 D '67

See also
Make-up
Toilet preparations

Anecdotes, facetiae, satire, etc.

Star is born: new line of cosmetics. il Mlle 64:186-7+ Ap '67

COSMETICS for men
Blade shave without lather; Amazing liquid shaving lotion. Consumer Rep 32:186 Ap '67
Checking out the men. Vogue 149:64+ Je; 150: 58 N 15 '67
Fads and faces. R. Lynes. il Harper 235:26+ S '67

See also
Perfumery for men

COSMETOLOGISTS. See Beauty shops

COSMETOLOGY. See Beauty culture

COSMIC dust. See Matter, Interstellar

COSMIC harmony. See Harmony of the spheres

COSMIC physics
See also
Astrophysics
Magnetic field (cosmic physics)

COSMIC radio noise. See Radio astronomy

COSMIC rays
High-energy cosmic rays. A. N. Bunner. il Sky & Tel 34:204-8 O '67
Is cosmic ray bombardment dangerous? I. Asimov. Sci Digest 61:87-8 Je '67
Isotropy of cosmic background radiation at 4080 megahertz. R. W. Wilson and A. A. Penzias. bibliog il Science 156:1100-1 My 26 '67
Paleomagnetic field reversals and cosmic radiation. C. J. Waddington. bibliog Science 158:913-15 N 17 '67
Smooth sea of cosmic radiation. Sci Am 216: 54-5 My '67
Tracks of cosmic rays in plastics. R. L. Fleischer and others. bibliog il Science 155: 187-9 Ja 13 '67

Measurement

Search for 21-centimeter radiation near cosmic X-ray sources. R. W. Hobbs and J. P. Hollinger. bibliog il Science 155:448-9 Ja 27 '67

COSMOGONY
Cosmic evolution. R. Jastrow. il Natur Hist 77:32-9 bibliog(p76) Ja '68
Evolution of the earth's atmosphere; report on Lloyd V. Berkner memorial symposium. S. I. Rasool. il Science 157:1466-7 S 22 '67
Infrared stars; interaction between stars and interstellar clouds. H. L. Johnson. bibliog il Science 157:635-8 Ag 11 '67
Over the edge of the universe. I. Asimov. Harper 234:97-8+ Mr '67
Scientists study data linking earth, moon. il Aviation W 87:29-30 O 9 '67

COSMOLOGY
Antimatter and cosmology. H. Alfvén. il Sci Am 216:106-12+ Ap '67
Background radiation and the birth of the universe. Sci N 92:582 D 16 '67
History of the universe; with letters. G. Gamow. bibliog il Science 158:766-9 N 10 '67
See also
Universe

COSMOS (satellites) See Artificial satellites, Russian

COSPAR. See International council of scientific unions—Committee on space research

COST

Costs go under the microscope; second-quarter earnings. il Bsns W p26-8 Jl 8 '67

See also
Labor cost

COST (law)

Bitter Candy; collateral demands of P. Foreman. il Time 89:64 Ap 7 '67

COST accounting

Cost controls that cost money. E. C. Schleh. il Duns R 89:49+ Ap '67

GAO cries for help. Nation 204:389 Mr 27 '67

Physical distribution, forgotten frontier. R. P. Neuschel. il Harvard Bsns R 45:125-34 Mr '67

Profits: cutting out the cookies; cost-cutting programs. il Newsweek 70:60-1 Jl 3 '67

See also
Value analysis

COST control. See Cost accounting

COST of advertising. See Advertising—Costs

COST of airplane operation. See Airplanes—Cost of operation

COST of automobile operation. See Automobiles—Cost of operation

COST of college education. See College education, Cost of

COST of food. See Food—Prices

COST of living

See also
Budget, Household
Clothing and dress—Prices
Domestic finance
Food—Prices
Income
Prices
Standard of living

United States

Consumer and wholesale prices; tables. See issues of Monthly labor review

Cost push. il Fortune 76:40+ N '67

How living standards have risen. il Nations Bsns 55:95 N '67

How much cost of living will go up; interview. A. M. Ross. il U S News 63:70-2+ N 13 '67

Living cost rise at a dangerous level? U S News 63:14 D 11 '67

Living costs get critical again. il Bsns W p62+ F 11 '67

Living costs, wages, and wage policy. H. M. Douty. bibliog f il Mo Labor R 90:1-7 Je '67

Moderate life: $9,191 a year. il Newsweek 70:71 N 6 '67

New city worker's family budget; tables. P. Groom. bibliog il Mo Labor R 90:1-8 N '67

Now may be the time for thrifty consumers to buy! Consumer Bul 50:15-16 O '67

Quite a lot more; Bureau of labor statistics report. il Time 90:92 N 3 '67

What it costs to live: a survey of thirty-nine places. il U S News 63:52-3 N 6 '67

Where the cost of living is heading. il U S News 63:31-3 S 11 '67

Where the living is easiest; comparing costs in 140 cities. il Bsns W p 103-4 My 13 '67

See also
Food—Prices
Price indexes
Prices—United States

COST of medical service. See Medical service, Cost of

COST of sickness. See Medical service, Cost of

COSTA, Richard Hauer

Lowry/Aiken symbiosis. Nation 204:823-6 Je 26 '67

COSTA E SILVA, Artur da

President-elect of Brazil visits the United States; text of toast, January 26, 1967. Dept State Bul 56:243-4 F 13 '67

about

Fun or folly? por Newsweek 69:56+ My 8 '67

Post of moral command. il por Time 89:29-30 Mr 24 '67

Testing place. il pors Time 89:29-33 Ap 21 '67

COSTA MESA, Calif.

Night inspections weed out traffic hazards. il Am City 82:122 N '67

COSTA RICA

Antiquities

See Indians of Central America—Antiquities—Costa Rica

COSTUME

See also
Fashion

History

Lady and the marten; fur ornaments of 16th-century. H. A. LaFarge. il Art N 66:40-1 N '67

250 years of costume. R. Davidson. il Antiques 92:872+ D '67

Bhutan

H.M. the queen of Bhutan, and her children. il Vogue 150:84-7 Jl '67

Great Britain

Mini-looking in London. L. Wainwright. Life 62:24 My 26 '67

Hungary

All strictly from Hungary. il Life 63:72-81 D 8 '67

India

Paper at the Lotos; paper saris. New Yorker 43:29-30 My 27 '67

Spain

Daring romantics in Spain: Luis and Alvaro Figueroa. il Vogue 150:64-5 Ag 1 '67

Surinam

Surinam's language of the hat. il Ebony 22:36-8 My '67

Tanzania

Dressing up the Masai. il Time 90:40 N 24 '67

Zambia

Minicultural revolution; Zambian campaign against miniskirts. il Time 89:29 Je 30 '67

COSTUME, Theatrical

Costumes by Karinska; reprint. J. A. Rubin. il Dance Mag 41:49-51+ Je '67

Erté. R. D. Daniels. il Opera N 32:11-13 S 23 '67

Julie plays Gertie; filming of Star! J. A. Zill. il Look 31:63-8 19 '67

Masked & bared; drawings from Duke of Devonshire's collection on display at Washington's National gallery. il Time 89:82 Ap 14 '67

New house; wardrobe department. F. Stevenson. il Opera N 31:30-1 Ja 7 '67

COSTUME accessories. See Dress accessories

COSTUME caper; drama. See Martens, A. C.

COSTUME design

Aglow: electronic clothes; interview. D. Dew. New Yorker 42:26-8 Ja 28 '67

All strictly from Hungary. il Life 63:72-81 D 8 '67

Anyone she wants to be; U.S.-designed collections of fall and winter clothes. il Time 89:75 Je 23 '67

Beardsley back in bloom again; with report by D. Bourdon. il Life 62:46-52+ F 24 '67

Bosom rediscovered. il Time 89:48 F 17 '67

Exciting innovations in Italian style spark fashion rebellion '67. il Ebony 22:141+ O '67

Face to face with a busy boutique-owner. M. Millet. il Seventeen 26:145 Mr '67

Fiona's Paris favorites. il Life 62:91-7 Mr 3 '67

Flick chick; influence of movies. il Newsweek 70:113 D 18 '67

Galanos runs a good gamut. il Life 62:105-6 Mr 10 '67

Is Paris burning? new collections for spring and summer. il Time 89:55+ F 10 '67

It's Andre & Yves; Paris fashion world. il Time 90:42-3 Ag 11 '67

Mary Quant, limited, kinky success story. M. Cleave. il N Y Times Mag p28-9+ Mr 19 '67; Same abr. with title Mary Quant, London's kooky success story. Read Digest 90:109-12 Je '67

New Valentino. il Time 89:70 Mr 10 '67

No-bra look. il Newsweek 70:98+ O 16 '67

Paris boost for legs. il Life 63:61-3+ S 1 '67

Ruffles. il Life 63:87-8 D 15 '67

Russia's five-year fashion leap. J. A. Zill. il Look 31:40-5+ Je 27 '67

Skirting the issue; spring showings in Paris. il Newsweek 69:70 F 13 '67

Sly fox in fashion's chicken house; interview; ed. by D. Lurie. J. Fairchild. il Life 62:43-4+ Mr 17 '67

Steel for style; Paco Rabanne's styles. il Life 62:49-50+ My 26 '67

Up, up & away. il Time 90:70-8+ D 1 '67

V for Valentino. il Life 63:91-4+ D 1 '67

See also
Costume, Theatrical

Study and teaching

Fashion-design schools: getting the fantasy out of your system. P. Rifield. il Mlle 65:120-1+ S '67

COSTUME designers
America's best: fashion at the top. T. Owett.
il Ladies Home J 84:94-7 Ap '67
Designers for the dance; with interviews. ed.
by A. Fatt. il Dance Mag 41:42-50 F; 50-5
Mr; 55-8 Ap '67
You can make it only if it sells. A. Grant.
il Mlle 65:122-4+ S '67

See also
De La Renta, O.
Erté
Garavani, V.
Gernreich, R.
Quant, M.
Rabanne, P.
Rikki
Stewart, E.
Valentino

COTABISH, Matthew I.
Excerpt from testimony, July 25, 1966. Cong
Digest 46:23+ Ja '67

CÔTE D'AZUR. See Riviera

COTLER, Gordon
Anyway, they're available on slides. New
Yorker 42:36-7 F 18 '67
Don't call us, we'll recall you. New Yorker
43:65 D 2 '67
Little Kwanda does it again. New Yorker
43:26-7 Jl 8 '67
Love comes to the United Nations. Sat Eve
Post 240:18 Je 17 '67
Man and his matrix. New Yorker 43:164-7
S 9 '67
More big news from out there. New Yorker
42:28-9 F 4 '67
Victory no. 743 at sea. New Yorker 43:128+
Ap 1 '67; Same. Yachting 122:58+ Jl '67

COTONOU, Dahomey
On location with Richard and Elizabeth (&
145 friends) filming of Comedians. L. Garrison. il N Y Times Mag p30-1+ My 7 '67

COTTA, Clara V.
Opinion: on your year. por Mlle 66:42-3+
Ja '68

COTTAGE cheese
Work wonders with cottage cheese; with
recipes. il Ladies Home J 84:116+ S '67

COTTLE, Evelyn
Small paperback shop that survives on low
overhead. Pub W 191:65-6 F 6 '67

COTTON
Crop allotments: power behind the cotton.
P. Marcuse. il Nation 206:43-6 Ja 8 '68

COTTON boll weevils. See Boll weevils

COTTON growing
Australia
Cotton finds another throne Down Under. il
Bsns W p46-8+ Ag 5 '67

COTTON industry and trade
Cotton in the world trade arena; address,
March 10, 1967. A. M. Solomon. Dept State
Bul 56:555-60 Ap 3 '67
Department opposes elimination of import
quotas on extra long staple cotton; state-
ment, July 12, 1967. E. V. Rostow. Dept
State Bul 57:236-9 Ag 21 '67
U.S. and China exchange notes on cotton
textile agreements. il Dept State Bul 57:
694-7 N 20 '67
United States and India sign new cotton textile agreement; announcement, with text of
U.S. note, August 31, 1967. il Dept State Bul
57:398-400 S 25 '67
United States and Israel sign new cotton
textile agreement; Department announcement, with text of U.S. note. Dept State
Bul 57:243-5 Ag 21 '67
United States and Jamaica sign new cotton
textile agreement. il Dept State Bul 57:
622-4 N 6 '67
U.S. and Pakistan conclude new cotton textile agreement; Department announcement
and text of U.S. note. il Dept State Bul
57:114-16 Jl 24 '67
United States and Portugal amend cotton
textile agreement. W. T. Bennett, jr. il Dept
State Bul 57:548-9 O 23 '67
United States and Spain sign cotton textile
agreement. il Dept State Bul 57:726-8 N 27
'67
U.S. and Yugoslavia exchange notes on cotton textile arrangements. il Dept State Bul
57:586-9 O 30 '67
U.S. Philippines exchange notes on cotton
textile arrangements. il Dept State Bul 57:
511-14 O 16 '67

COTTON producers association
Super-farmer attacks global poverty. A.
Rankin. Read Digest 92:25-6+ Ja '68

COTTON workers
Off the land; plight of the Negroes in the
Mississippi Delta. Nation 204:261 F 27 '67

COTTONTAIL hunting. See Rabbit hunting

COTTRELL, A. H.
Nature of metals; with biographical sketch.
Sci Am 217:48, 90-100 S '67

COUCHING See Embroidery

COUGAR hunting. See Puma hunting

COUGARS. See Pumas

COUGHLAN, Robert
Equivocal hero of science: Robert Oppenheimer. Life 62:34-34A Mr 3 '67

COUGHLIN, Charles Edward
American Catholics and anti-Semitism in the
1930's. D. J. O'Brien. Cath World 204:270-
6 F '67

COUGHLIN, George G.
What every trial juror should know. Read
Digest 91:145-9 Ag '67

COUGHLIN, William J.
Editorial. See issues of Technology week including Missiles and rockets
Memo from the publisher. il Tech W 20:9 Mr
27 '67
Memo from the publisher. A. C. Boughton.
por Tech W 20:11 Mr 6 '67

COULDOCK, Charles W.
Silence is not always golden. H. Lindsay.
Sat R 50:6 S 30 '67

COUNCIL BLUFFS, Iowa

Historic houses, etc.
History in houses; General Dodge house.
B. S. Utley. il Antiques 92:210-13 Ag '67

COUNCIL for economic mutual assistance
Coordinated planning for science in Communist Europe. L. F. Jordan. bibliog il Science 155:796-802 F 17 '67; Reply. K.
Deutsch. 156:454+ Ap 28 '67

COUNCIL of community churches. See International council of community churches

COUNCIL of economic advisers. See United
States—Council of economic advisers

COUNCIL of foreign ministers, Geneva, 1954
Two Vietnams or one? letter. M. Gordon. New
Repub 157:36-7 Jl 22 '67

COUNCIL of governments, Washington. See
Washington, D.C.—Politics and government

COUNCIL of national library associations
National library council proposed by committee. Library J 92:2104+ Je 1 '67

COUNCIL on library resources, incorporated
Bibliographical projects backed by CLR. Pub
W 192:38-9 O 9 '67
CLR ends first decade; thirty-three projects
launched. Library J 92:2870 S 1 '67
CLR grants. Wilson Lib Bul 41:776+ Ap '67
New CLR president. F. C. Cole. ALA Bul
61:788 Jl '67
Progress in copy cameras; CLR issues con-
tract. Library J 92:3368-9 O 1 '67
Recent grants by Council on library resources.
Pub W 192:36-7 O 16 '67

COUNCIL on youth opportunity. See United
States—President's council on youth opportunity

COUNCILMEN
City Councilman John Santucci is a man in
a wind tunnel. M. Arnold. il N Y Times
Mag p56-7+ Ap 16 '67

COUNCILS and synods
Dutch pastoral council. I. Van Rijn. America
116:373-5 Mr 18 '67
Hopes for the bishops' synod. America 116:
410 Mr 25 '67
Next step: an American council. R. W.
Gilsdorf. America 116:277-9 F 25 '67

See also
Diocesan synods
Synod of bishops
Vatican council, 2d

COUNCILS of government. See Municipal government

COUNSELING
Young living; questions and answers. A.
Wood. See issues of Seventeen
See also
Personnel service in education
Vocational guidance

COUNSELING service, School. See Personnel
service in education

COUNSELORS
See also
Personnel service in education

COUNTERFEIT drugs. See Drugs

COUNTERFEIT money. See Counterfeits and
counterfeiting

COUNTERFEITS and counterfeiting
Funny money; counterfeit greenbacks in
eastern Europe. Newsweek 70:36+ Ag 28 '67

COUNTERFEITS and counterfeiting—*Cont.*
Funny money is no joke. il Nations Bsns 55:95 Je '67
How to make money; forgeries of U.S. dollar circulating in eastern Europe. Time 90:35 Jl 21 '67
See also
Forgery of works of art
Fraud

COUNTERREVOLUTIONS. See Revolutions

COUNTERS (electrons, ions, etc)
Frequency measurements with the electronic counter. A. W. Edwards. il Electr World 77:84 Ja '67
Stream chamber; particle detector at Stanford linear accelerator. D. Yount. il Sci Am 217:38-46 bibliog(p 156) O '67

COUNTING. See Numeration

COUNTING machines and devices
Want to build an integrated circuit binary counter? D. Lancaster. il Pop Electr 25: 57-61+ D '66

COUNTRIES. See Nations

COUNTRY clubs
Personal business; breaking 90 in club management. Bsns W p 145-6 Ap 29 '67

COUNTRY doctors. See Physicians

COUNTRY estates

England
Decline and fall; closing of Cliveden. il Newsweek 69:38 My 29 '67
Noble zoo of the mad marquess; Longleat. il Life 62:63-4+ Je 30 '67

Finland
Lived-in landmark; Ammine manor house. il House B 110:108-9 Ja '68

Norway
Graceful heirloom; manor-house of Nils Frederik Aalls. il House B 110:74-7 Ja '68

COUNTRY girl; drama. See Odets, C.

COUNTRY hospitals. See Hospitals, Rural

COUNTRY life
Blueprint of paradise; mountain farm. R. Starnes. Field & S 72:16+ Jl '67
Hill country harvest, by H. Borland. Review Sat R 50:33 S 2 '67. R. L. Perkin
Plenty of the land. H. Borland. il Audubon 69:30-5 N '67
They live as they like; C. and R. Di Rosa. il House & Gard 131:140-7 Mr '67
See also
Farm life
Recreation, Rural

Anecdotes, facetiae, satire, etc.
Simple life. S. J. Harris. Read Digest 91:24B Ag '67

COUNTRY music. See Folk music, American

COUNTRY of the heart; story. See Knowlton, R. A.

COUNTRY schools. See Rural schools

COUNTRY towns. See Cities and towns

COUNTS, George S.
Creation of the new Soviet man. Sch & Soc 95:438-44 N 25 '67

COUNTY agents
Agents of the other war; U.S. in Viet Nam. Time 89:23 Ja 27 '67

COUNTY fairs. See Agricultural exhibitions

COUNTY jail libraries. See Prison libraries

COUNTY libraries. See Libraries, County

COUNTY officers
See also
Sheriffs

COUNTY park systems. See Parks

COUPLINGS, Electric
Selecting amplifiers and splitters. il Pop Electr 26:95 Je '67

COUPONS
Where there's smoke; British government to abolish cigarette coupons. il Time 90:94 N 3 '67

COURAGE
Apollo, the destroyer; moral horror that afflicts our society. D. J. Stewart. New Repub 156:15 F 18 '67
Courage of Karla Little. J. G. Hubbell. il Read Digest 91:149-54 Jl '67

COURNOYER, Yvan
Deadeye dude of the North. P. Axthelm. il pors Sports Illus 26:43-5 Ap 3 '67

COURSEN, Herbert R. Jr
How they die in Vietnam. New Repub 158: 23-6 Ja 13 '68

COURSES of study
Editor's bookshelf; proposals of Arthur R. King, jr. and John I. Goodlad. P. Woodring. Sat R 50:67 Jl 15 '67
Little relief in sight. M. H. Jennison. Todays Health 45:65 S '67
Teaching in America; need for curriculum reform. M. Tumin. il Sat R 50:77-9+ O 21 '67
What Sputnik did to our schools. F. M. Hechinger. il McCalls 95:106-7+ O '67
What turns kids on? Philadelphia cooperative schools curriculum of concerns program. T. Borton. il Sat R 50:72-4+ Ap 15 '67
What's happening in education? content. W. Abraham. il Todays Health 45:44-6+ S '67
See also
Association for supervision and curriculum development
Colleges and universities—Curriculum
High schools—Curriculum
Vocational education

COURT buildings. See Courthouses

COURT houses. See Courthouses

COURT reporting (by newspapers) See Newspaper court reporting

COURT tennis. See Tennis

COURTESY
Quotations, maxims, etc.
Be nice! comp. by E. F. Murphy. N Y Times Mag p42 Mr 5 '67

COURTHOUSES
Courthouse sets the tone of community beautification; Sacramento County, Calif. M. T. Scimens. il Am City 82:129 O '67
Justice on a pedestal; U.S. tax court building. il Arch Forum 127:76-9 S '67

COURTS
See also
Criminal procedure
Judges
Jury
Justice, Administration of—United States
Juvenile courts
Traffic courts

Southern states
Civil-rights setback in southern courts; efforts to deny northern lawyers right to practice. G. B. Driesen. il Reporter 36:18-22 F 23 '67

United States
Change down South; C. F. Clayton, new member of Fifth circuit court of appeals. Time 90:80+ N 24 '67
Courts: pyramid of U.S. justice. il Sr Schol 91:18-20 N 30 '67
Rights for prisoners. Time 91:46+ Ja 5 '68
Thirty minutes to nowhere; Washington's federal courts employ alert system. Time 90:47 Jl 21 '67
See also
Courts, State
Small claims courts
United States—Court of military appeals
United States—Supreme court

COURTS, Industrial. See Labor courts

COURTS, Military. See Courts martial

COURTS, State
Rising crime and the courts; state justices take a stand; text of resolution. U S News 63:53 Ag 28 '67

COURTS martial
Back to business; Nuremberg issue fails. il Newsweek 69:30+ Je 5 '67
Conviction of Captain Levy. N. Von Hoffman. New Repub 156:9-11 Je 17 '67
Court-martial of Captain Levy: medical ethics v. military law. E. Langer. il Science 156: 1346-50 Je 9 '67; Discussion. 157:140 Jl 14 '67
Guilty as charged; case of Howard Brett Levy. il Time 89:33 Je 9 '67
Guilty minority; first U.S. war crimes trial to come out of Vietnam. il Time 91:31-2 Ja 5 '68
Men at war; war crimes defense fails in case of Captain Howard Brett Levy. Time 89:15-16 Je 2 '67
Nuremberg revisited; case of Capt. H. Levy. il Newsweek 69:23-4 My 29 '67
Nürnberg & Viet Nam; case of Captain Howard Levy. il Time 89:20 My 26 '67
To the stockade. Newsweek 69:33 Je 12 '67
Two sides of atrocity; Americans committing atrocities receive sentences. il Time 90:38 Jl 14 '67

COURTS of small claims. See Small claims courts

COURTSHIP
See also
Dating
Love
Love letters

COURTSHIP of birds
Dawn rendezvous on the lek. P. A. Johnsgard. il Natur Hist 76:16-21 Mr '67
Waiting for the woodcock. H. Borland. il Audubon 69:56-7 Mr '67

COURTSHIP of insects
Antennae and sexual receptivity in drosophila melanogaster females. A. Manning. bibliog il Science 158:136-7 O 6 '67
Preferential mating versus mimicry: disruptive selection and sex-limited dimorphism in papilio glaucus. J. M. Burns; reply with rejoinder. T. Prout. Science 156:534 Ap 28 '67
Volatile principle from oak leaves: role in sex life of the polyphemus moth. L. M. Riddiford and C. M. Williams. bibliog il Science 155:589-90 F 3 '67

COURTYARDS
It's an entry, a patio, and a garden room. il Sunset 138:121 Je '67

COURY, John N.
Neural correlates of food and water intake in the rat. bibliog Science 156:1763-5 Je 30 '67

COUSINS, Margaret
Christmas is (not) for children. Ladies Home J 84:59 D '67

COUSINS, Norman
Uncharted worlds on the face of a tree; photographs. Home Gard 54:35-7 N '67
View of the American library; statement. ALA Bul 61:953 S '67
about
American editor's odyssey. B. Moyers. Sat R 50:30-1+ N 11 '67

COUSY, Bob
Are some of our best friends gamblers? Life 63:8 S 22 '67

COUVE DE MURVILLE, Maurice
Middle East crisis; address, June 22, 1967. Vital Speeches 33:589-91 Jl 15 '67

COVE PALISADES STATE PARK. See Oregon
—Parks and reserves

COVE vitamin and pharmaceutical, incorporated
Calories author guilty; faces jail and fine. Pub W 191:40 My 22 '67

COVENANT on civil and political rights. See International covenant on civil and political rights

COVENANT on economic, social and cultural rights. See International covenant on economic, social, and cultural rights

COVENT Garden opera company
Music to my ears; production of King Priam at Covent Garden. I. Kolodin. Sat R 50:24 Je 17 '67

COVER, John H.
Commentary on the recent International conference on water for peace. Nat Parks Mag 41:22 Ag '67

COVER design. See Book covers

COVER plants
Evergreen groundcovers. D. Wyman. il Horticulture 45:14-17 N '67
Six best all-around groundcovers. il Home Gard 54:48 O '67

COVERLETS
He's Smokey the bear-spread. il Sunset 139:93 D '67
Sunflower coverlet to crochet and embroider. il Good H 165:148+ O '67

COVERS, Book. See Book covers

COVINA, Calif.
Public buildings
This city yard is neighborly. M. Hubiak. il Am City 82:114-15 Je '67

COW stanchions. See Barns and stables—Equipment

COWAN, Paul
Public & private. Commentary 44:89+ Jl '67

COWARD, Noel
Epitaph for an elderly actress; poem. Mlle 66:46 Ja '68

COWARDICE. See Fear

COWBOYS
Outback. D. Moser. il Life 63:56-69+ D 22 '67
See also
Dightman, M.
Rodeos

COWBOYS (football club) See Football clubs

COWLEY, Malcolm
Après la guerre finie. por Horizon 10:112-19 Wint '68
Rights and permissions; views on not-writers; ed. by P. Nathan. Pub W 193:33 Ja 1 '68

COWLEY, Robert
Our dancing daughters. Horizon 9:98-9 Aut '67

COWLES, Virginia
Malta, the unique. Vogue 149:99+ F 1 '67

COWLES communications, incorporated
Cowles to publish new education magazine. Library J 92:1985 My 15 '67

COWLEY, Edward
Train station and the community. il Sch Arts 66:35-8 My '67

COWLEY, Malcolm
Papa and the parricides. Esquire 67:100-1+ Je '67
Twenties in Montparnasse. Sat R 50:51+ Mr 11 '67
about
Art and the book reviewer. L. Kriegel. Nation 204:732-3 Je 5 '67
Thirties, thirty years later. G. Hicks. Sat R 50:31-2 Mr 11 '67

COWS
How we pick high-producing long-wearing dairy cattle. M. Green and others. il Suc Farm 65:32-3 D '67
See also
Dairying
Diseases and pests
Looks like milk fever, but it isn't; grass diseases. L. A. Baker. Farm J 91:D16 Ap '67
See also
Mastitis
Feeding
Can you pass this feeding quiz? D. Braun. il Farm J 91:D6+ F '67
Corn silage, the only roughage cows need. N. Reeder. il Farm J 91:32-3+ N '67
How to squeeze more milk from your feed. M. E. McCullough. il Farm J 91:D10-11 Ap '67
Lead feed, but keep costs in line. H. H. Van Horne. Suc Farm 65:66 S '67
More milk from the same feed. J. Bickers. il Farm J 91:20-1 Je '67
No more parlor feeding for us. B. Fowler. il Farm J 91:28-9+ Ja '67
Put some fat on those cows. Farm J 91:D11 O '67
Self feeds according to production. N. Reeder. il Farm J 91:D4-5 F '67
Spring dairy feeding tips. F. Foreman. Suc Farm 65:49 My '67

Milk production
See Milk—Production

COWS in religion, folklore, etc.
Myth of the sacred cow. M. Harris. il Natur Hist 76:6-8+ Mr '67
Sacred cow. B. Griffiths. Commonweal 85:483-4 F 3 '67

COWSILLS (singers) See Singers

COX, Allan, and Kawai, Naoto
Paleomagnetism: United States-Japan committee on scientific cooperation. Science 155:724 F 10 '67
—and others
Reversals of the earth's magnetic field; with biographical sketches. Sci Am 216:22, 44-54 bibliog(p 146) F '67

COX, Arthur N. and Cox, J. P.
Cepheid pulsations. Sky & Tel 33:278-82 My '67
—and others
Racing the moon's shadow. Sky & Tel 33:85-9 F '67

COX, Donald F. and Good, R. E.
How to build a marketing information system. Harvard Bsns R 45:145-54 My '67

COX, Edwin
Murder and jasmine. Sat R 50:63-4+ N 18 '67

COX, Eleanor W.
Tobaccos that satisfy. Horticulture 45:42-3 O '67

COX, Harvey
Are we having a nervous breakdown? McCalls 95:6+ Ja '68
Biblical basis of the Geneva conference. Christian Cent 84:435-7 Ap 5 '67
Guernica to Vietnam: the capacity for horror. Commonweal 86:164-5 Ap 28 '67
Kinesthetic happening: art or atrocity? Commonweal 87:44-5 O 13 '67

COX, Harvey—*Continued*
McLuhanite Christianity at Expo 67. Commonweal 86:277-9 My 26 '67
Open letter to Allen Ginsberg. Commonweal 86:147-9 Ap 21 '67

about

Secular city debate; ed. by D. Callahan. Review
Cath World 205:54+ Ap '67. D. J. Leary
COX, James J.
When bedtime brings problems. . . Todays Health 45:39-41 My '67
COX, John P. See Cox, A. N. jt. auth.
COX, John W.
Problem: how hard does a baseball fall? Sci Digest 62:12-13+ Ag '67
COX, Prentiss G. See Simpson, S. B. jr, jt. auth.
COX, Robert E.
(ed) Gleanings for ATM's. See issues of Sky and telescope
COX, Robert O.
Priceless record. Motor B 119:30-1+ My '67
COX, William
Magi hangup; story. New Yorker 43:44-6 D 23 '67
COX, William S.
Intrepid a likely winner. Sports Illus 26:38-9 Je 26 '67

about

Boat is born. il Sports Illus 26:32-7 Je 26 '67
COXE, Donald G. M.
Tax reform: Canada shows the way. Nat R 19:688-90 Je 27 '67
COXE, Louis
Et in Acadia: Champlain to the sagamore Membertou; poem. Yale R 56:551 Je '67
Lady of the freesias; poem. New Repub 156: 28 Ap 8 '67
On a photograph of a soldier whose best friend has just been killed in combat. Vietnam; poem New Repub 157:24 Jl 1 '67

about

Four poets. H. Carruth. Poetry 111:43-5 O '67
COYLE, J. J.
Ninety day mistress. Criticism Newsweek 70:121 N 20 '67
COYNE, Walter A.
Build now pay later. Am Ed 3:6-8+ Ap '67
Presidential scholars. Am Ed 3:27-8 Je '67
COYOTE brush
Better coyote brush. il Sunset 139:264 O '67
COYOTE hunting
Little wolves. A. L. Livingston. il Outdoor Life 140:38-41+ D '67
COYOTES
Wanderlust from the plains. S. P. Young. il Am For 73:10+ Ja '67
COYOTES, Photography of. See Photography of animals
CRAB nebula. See Nebulae
CRABB, A. L.
Last last day. PTA Mag 62:19-21 D '67
CRABS
Coconut crab. Sci N 92:388 O 21 '67
CRABS, King. See King crabs
CRABTREE, Bruce
Small boat paradise. Yachting 121:73+ My '67
(ed) See Driscoll, G. Yachting interviews: Columbia's Gerry Driscoll
CRADLES
Cradles. J. Mebane. il Bet Hom & Gard 45:32 Ap '67
CRAFT, Robert
Stravinsky. por Look 31:50-4+ D 26 '67
CRAFTS. See Arts and crafts; Handicraft
CRAGER, Tess M.
Personal approach for selling cookbooks. por Pub W 192:60-1 S 11 '67
CRAIG, Alan K.
Lithophagic snail from southern British Honduras. bibliog Science 158:795-6 N 10 '67
CRAIG, George B. jr
Mosquitoes: female monogamy induced by male accessory gland substance. bibliog Science 156:1499-501 Je 16 '67
CRAIG, Gordon A.
Churchill on Churchill. Reporter 36:54+ Mr 9 '67
Communication gap. Reporter 37:54-6 N 2 '67
Definitive Disraeli. Reporter 36:48-50 Ap 6 '67
Kennan looks back. Reporter 37:45-6+ D 14 '67
When the sun set. . . Reporter 37:37-8 N 30 '67

CRAIG, H.
Isotope separation by carrier diffusion. bibliog Science 159:93-6 Ja 5 '68
—See Longinelli, A. jt. auth.
CRAIG, James B.
Place in the sun. Am For 73:10-13+ Ag '67
CRAIG, William
Don't dig in on gentleman Jim. Sat Eve Post 240:70-3 S 9 '67
Fall of Japan; excerpt. Sat Eve Post 240: 36-8+ Ag 26 '67
CRAIGHEAD, John
Sharing the lives of wild golden eagles. Nat Geog Mag 132:420-39 S '67
CRAIGIE, J. S. and Gruenig, D. E.
Bromophenols from red algae. bibliog Science 157:1058-9 S 1 '67
CRAIN, Robert L. and Inger, Morton
Urban school integration: strategy for peace Sat R 50:76-7+ F 18; 97 My 20 '67
CRAMP, Writers. See Writers cramp
CRAMPS. See Menstruation—Disorders
CRANBERG, Gilbert
What did the Supreme court say?. Sat R 50: 90-2 Ap 8 '67
CRANBERG, Lawrence
P-M bomb. Bul Atomic Sci 23:37-40 D '67
CRANDALL, Gil
Fallen oak. Motor B 119:44-5+ Ap '67
CRANDON park zoo, Miami, Fla. See Zoological gardens
CRANE, Barry
Detectives give a hand in a chase. C. Goren. il Sports Illus 27:98+ D 4 '67
CRANE, George Washington, 1901-
What, me worry? Christian Cent 84:823 Je 21 '67
CRANE, H. R.
g Factor of the electron; with biographical sketch. Sci Am 218:19, 72-4+ bibliog(p 150) Ja '68
CRANE, Julian C. See Maxie, E. C. jt. auth.
CRANE, Paul
Clobbering of Harold Wilson. America 116: 683 My 6 '67
Labor's dilemma in Britain. America 117:409 O 14 '67
CRANE, R. W.
Are you allergic to clothes? Todays Health 45:30-2 F '67
Diseases we catch from animals. Todays Health 45:56-7+ Mr '67
CRANE, Ralph
Cry for help from the proud Navajo; photographs. Life 64:14-23 Ja 5 68
East side of the wall; photographs. Life 62: 58-69 My 26 '67

about

Back home again after thirty-two years. G. P. Hunt. por Life 62:3 My 26 '67
Into the blizzard, fresh from the jungle. G. P. Hunt. por Life 64:2 Ja 5 '68
CRANE, Stephen
Short story was his medium. G. Hicks. Sat R 50:31-2 Jl 22 '67
CRANE, William B. Jr
World's most compact workshop. il pors Pop Mech 128:138-41 D '67
CRANES (birds)
Back from the brink; breeding whooping cranes in captivity. il Sci N 91:592 Je 24 '67
Crane hunting in Mexico. W. Page. il Field & S 72:36-7+ N '67
Wildlife exploitation and the sandhill crane. Audubon 69:5 S '67
CRANHAM, Gerry
Where the action is. il U S Camera 30:56-7 S '67
CRANK calls. See Telephone calls
CRANKS and crankshafts
352 skiddoo, hello 428; stock crank and pistons. J. Thawley. il Hot Rod 20:42 Ag '67
CRANKSHAW, Edward
Coup that changed the world. N Y Times Mag p26-7+ F 19 '67
CRANMER, T. V.
Liquid level indicator for the blind. Pop Electr 26:59-60 My '67
CRANSTON family
Cranston coat-of-arms. H. K. Eilers. il Hobbies 72:118-19+ My '67
CRAPE myrtle
Crape myrtle isn't one to droop. il Sunset 139:124-5 Ag '67
CRAPPIE fishing
Spring specktacular. J. O. Cartier. il Outdoor Life 139:76-8+ My '67
They've whipped those beginner's blues. E. A. Bauer. il Field & S 71:54-7+ F '67

CRATERS
Nevada's ancient Lunar Crater. il Sunset 139:39 N '67
CRATERS, Moon. See Moon—Surface
CRATERS OF THE MOON NATIONAL MONUMENT
Proposed Tutimaba wilderness. R. J. Contor. il Liv Wildn 30:3-10 Wint '66
CRAVEN, Carol Lynne
In my opinion. por Seventeen 26:140 Jl '67
CRAVENS, Gwyneth. See Cravens, R. jt. auth.
CRAVENS, Jay
Sawmill in Vietnam; excerpt from letter. Am For 73:8+ S '67
CRAVENS, Richard, and Cravens, Gwyneth
Underground, incorporated. Mlle 64:164-5+ Ap '67
CRAVIOTO, Humberto, and others
Metachromatic leukodystrophy sulfatide lipidoses, cultured in vitro. bibliog Science 156:243-5 Ap 14 '67
CRAWDADDY (periodical)
Crawdaddy! Newsweek 70:114 D 11 '67
CRAWFISH. See Crayfish
CRAWFORD, H. D.
George Mason country. il Am For 73:18-21+ N '67
CRAWFORD, Jack, jr
Surf rider; poem. Poetry 111:157-8 D '67
CRAWFORD, John S.
Duel in the Rockies. il Outdoor Life 140:54-7+ O '67
CRAWFORD, Kenneth
Washington. See issues of Newsweek
CRAWFORD, Leslie
Gentle art of handkissing. Ebony 22:91-2 O '67
CRAWFORD, Michael
I'd fall thirty floors for a good laugh. T. Prideaux. il por Life 62:70D Mr 10 '67
Pleasure bumps. il por Time 89:41 Je 2 '67
CRAWL and creep therapy. See Brain damaged children—Education
CRAYFISH
Crayfish muscle: permeability to sodium induced by calcium depletion. J. P. Reuben and others. bibliog il Science 155:1263-6 Mr 10 '67
Regeneration in crustacean motoneurons; evidence for axonal fusion. R. R. Hoy and others. bibliog il Science 156:251-2 Ap 14 '67
CRAYON painting. See Encaustic painting
CREAL, Margaret
Summer days; story. Reporter 36:35-9 Je 29 '67
CREAM puffs. See Pastry
CREAMER, Robert. See Conlan, J. jt. auth.
CREASING of textiles
See also
Textile fabrics, Wrinkle resistant
Woolen and worsted fabrics—Creasing
CREATINE
Creatine phosphokinase in thyroid: isoenzyme composition compared with other tissues. F. A. Craig and J. C. Smith. bibliog il Science 156:254-5 Ap 14 '67
CREATION
See also
Cosmogony
Earth
CREATION (literary, artistic, etc)
Art and style; reprint. il Design 68:32-5 Ja '67
Biographical predictors of scientific performance. C. W. Taylor and R. L. Ellison. bibliog il Science 155:1075-80 Mr 3 '67
Ceramics photography. J. Schlanger. il Craft Horiz 27:24-9 Ja '67
Creative writer today. C. Quigley. Cath World 206:111-17 D '67
Experiment with brainstorming: creative playground activities. B. A. Wagner and J. Conley. il Parks & Rec 2:21+ S '67
Moose-hunting. Dean Rusk, and the Arabian delegate. L. Conger. Writer 80:14-16 Ap '67
My art is my feelings made visible. E. Taylor. il Farm J 91:106-7+ Mr '67
Opinion: a defense of fad. D. M. Davis. Mlle 65:50+ O '67
Perfection of performance. N. Kent. Am Artist 31:5 D '67
Second million words. W. E. Barrett. Writer 80:9-12 My '67
Squeezing the orange. D. W. Parr. Writer 80:25-6 S '67
Voice from a cloud. T. Capote. Harper 235:99-100+ N '67
What if and if only. L. Conger. Writer 80:6-8 Mr '67
See also
Creative ability
English language—Composition—Creative activities
Inspiration

CREATIVE ability
Kari's handicap, the impediment of creativity. R. E. Samples. il Sat R 50:56-7+ Jl 15 '67; Discussion. 50:51+ Ag 19 '67
Questions of passion; turning an audience on. R. Kotlowitz. Harper 235:120-3 O '67
CREATIVE carvings, incorporated
Masterpieces in metal; three-dimensional wildlife ornaments. M. C. Gethman. il Field & S 72:48-9+ D '67
CREATIVE dramatics. See Dramatization in education
CREATIVE education
National report: gains and goals in education; PACE projects. N. Estes. il Parents Mag 42:53-5+ S '67
Washington report; overview of ESEA Title III projects to advance creativity in education (PACE) J. Lloyd. Sr Schol 90sup6 Ap 28 '67
CREATIVE playthings, incorporated
Ph.D.'s in toyland; educational toys. il Newsweek 69:101 My 29 '67
CREATIVE teaching. See Creative education
CREATIVE thinking. See Thought and thinking
CREATIVE writing. See English language—Composition—Creative activities
CRÈCHES. See Christmas cribs
CREDIBILITY gap (game) See Games
CREDIT
Are you making the best use of your credit? P. Lindberg. il Bet Hom & Gard 46:6+ Ja '68
Big hole in truth-in-leading; costs of revolving credit. il Consumer Rep 32:470-4 S '67
Borrowing costs: up, and up. U S News 63:112+ D 11 '67
Consumer credit. Consumer Rep 32:396-8 D '67
Consumer credit: let the buyer beware! Sr Schol 90:12-14 Mr 3 '67
Cost of money adds to case for a tax boost. il Bsns W p40-1 Je 24 '67
Credit; the different kinds and their cost. il Good H 164:204 Ap '67
Demand for loans softens. il Bsns W p 117-18 Ag 19 '67
Fed gets set to pull harder on reins. Bsns W p45-6 D 9 '67
Fed may lighten its touch. Bsns W p29-30 F 4 '67
Fed will play it tight, but not overdo it. il Bsns W p86-7 D 30 '67
How business weathered the money crisis. il U S News 62:50-2 F 13 '67
Is a money crunch on its way? il Bsns W p35-6 S 30 '67
Is another big squeeze on money in offing? il Bsns W p 130-2 Je 3 '67
Old crusader; opening of House hearings on truth-in-lending legislation. Newsweek 70:51-2 Ag 21 '67
$123 television set with $297 interest; truth-in-lending bill. Life 63:4 Jl 28 '67
Personal business; so you want to borrow some money. Bsns W p 111 F 4 '67
Selective stimulus; Federal reserve board eases cost of money. Time 89:86-7 Mr 10 '67
Shylock was a piker; truth-in-lending bill passed by Senate. Time 90:23 Jl 21 '67
Signs of strain. Time 89:87 My 26 '67
Survey shows truth about lending. E. R. McAlister. il Nations Bsns 55:116-20 My '67
Tight money: a breathing spell, but next... il U S News 62:100+ Je 5 '67
Tighter money coming; the effects. il U S News 63:108+ N 13 '67
Using credit for profit making. M. T. Welshans. il Harvard Bsns R 45:141-7+ Ja '67
Wall Street: a temporary roadblock? C. Morgello. il Newsweek 69:80 F 20 '67
When you borrow on your assets. Changing T 22:22 Ja '68
See also
Checks
Debtor and creditor
Instalment plan
Loans, Bank
Loans, Foreign
Monetary policy

Rating
How good is your credit? Am Home 71:10+ Ja '68
Screen-test your credit risks. W. P. Boggess. il Harvard Bsns R 45:113-22 N '67
What the credit bureaus know about you. J. A. Morris. Read Digest 91:85-9 N '67
When credit is flatly refused. Consumer Rep 32:244-5 My '67

CREDIT bureaus
What the credit bureaus know about you.
J. A. Morris. Read Digest 91:85-9 N '67
CREDIT cards
All about credit cards. il Good H 164:200 Je
'67
Chicago's credit card crisis; mass replacement of cards. Bsns W p35 Jl 15 '67
Do you really benefit from bank credit-card plans? P. Lindberg. Bet Hom & Gard 45:6 N '67
Easy go; use of bank credit cards. il Time 89:91-2 Ap 21 '67
Flood of bank credit cards. U S News 63:101 D 4 '67
Guard those credit cards! il Changing T 21:24 Ag '67
Here's a new way to say charge it; bank credit cards. il U S News 62:103-5 My 22 '67
Money goes electronic in the 1970s; checkless, cashless society. il Bsns W p54-6+ Ja 13 '68
Nicest thing since money; Chicago's banks credit-cards encourage fraud. Newsweek 70: 73 Jl 17 '67
Now, livestock credit cards. R. C. Black. Farm J 91:B12+ S '67
Souping up gas credit cards; tie-in with motels. il Bsns W p66+ F 25 '67
See also
Diners' club, incoroporated
CREDIT counseling. See Debtor and creditor
CREDIT life insurance. See Insurance, Life—Credit aspects
CREDIT unions
Washington hides truth in lending. il Nations Bsns 55:38-9+ F '67
CREDITOR. See Debtor and creditor
CREE Indians
Changing world of the Cree; Algonquian-speaking Cree Indians of the Mistassini and Waswanipi bands. N. A. Chance. il Natur Hist 76:16-23 My '67
CREEDS
New creeds for new times. B. L. Masse. America 117:596 N 18 '67
CREEGAN, George R.
Brementown litterbug; drama. Plays 26:82-4 Mr '67
CREELEY, Robert
Enough; Eye; Water; Here; Of years; Intervals; Song; poems. Poetry 109:287-98 F '67
CREEPING plants
Colorful creeper and climber. il Sunset 139:148 S '67
CREIGHTON, William S.
Living doors; with biographical sketch. por Natur Hist 76:4, 71-3 bibliog(p 105) D '67
CREPES. See Griddle cakes
CRESPO, Paulo
Brazil's miserable northeast. H. W. Flannery. Cath World 205:277-81 Ag '67
CRESSEY, Donald Ray
Methodological problems in the study of organized crime as a social problem. bibliog f Ann Am Acad 374:101-12 N '67
CRETACEOUS period. See Paleontology—Cretaceous
CRETANS
Gnarled face of Crete; with account by M. Leatherbee. il Life 62:62-72+ F 17 '67
CRETE
Gnarled face of Crete; with account by M. Leatherbee. il Life 62:62-72+ F 17 '67
See also
Sphakia
Antiquities
Found: a gold ring; unearthed in the burial chamber of a Minoan princess. J. Sakellarakis. il Horizon 10:102-5 Wint '68
Promise of Thera. E. Vermeule. Atlan 220: 83-4+ D '67
CREWS, Airplane. See Airplane crews
CRIB deaths. See Infant mortality
CRIBS (beds)
Build this two-in-one chest-crib. D. Schackmuth. il Pop Mech 127:172-5 My '67
CRICHTON, Robert
You got to be a hero. Sat Eve Post 240:30-2+ D 30 '67
CRICK, Francis Harry Compton
Double helix; the discovery of the structure of DNA; excerpts, with editorial comment. J. D. Watson. il por Atlan 221:76-94+ Ja '68 (to be cont)
CRICKET (game)
England's colonial legacy, cricket. A. Waugh. il Nat R 19:198+ F 21 '67

CRILL, Wayne E. and Kennedy, T. T.
Inferior olive of the cat: intracellular recording. bibliog Science 157:716-18 Ag 11 '67
CRIME and criminals
Chromosomes and crime. J. A. M. Graham. il Sci Digest 62:38-40 D '67
See also
Body snatching
Burglary and burglars
Capital punishment
Conspiracy
Counterfeits and counterfeiting
Crime prevention
Criminal law
Criminal psychology
Fraud
Impostors and imposture
Justice, Administration of—United States
Juvenile delinquency
Mafia
Murder
Perjury
Police
Prisoners
Prisoners, Discharged
Punishment
Robberies and assaults
Self defense
Shoplifting
Stealing
Trials

Bibliography
Readings on crime. Cur Hist 53:46-8+, 111+ Jl-Ag '67

Economic aspects
Mob; money gathering sources of the Cosa nostra; with report by S. Smith. il Life 63:91-102+ S 8 '67

Identification
See Identification

International aspects
See also
International criminal police organization

Law
See Criminal law
Quotations, maxims, etc.
Of crime and the criminal; comp. by R. Block. il N Y Times Mag p 104-5 Mr 12 '67

Statistics
See Criminal statistics

Florida
How to win the war? intra-gang violence. il Newsweek 70:32 Jl 3 '67
Messiah in open town. il Time 89:24 Ap 28 '67
She didn't scream; motorcycle gang crucify girl. il Newsweek 70:33 D 11 '67
When a state opens its own war on crime. il U S News 62:61-2 My 22 '67
Where war has been declared on hoodlums. U S News 64:9 Ja 8 '68

Georgia
Death of a dogged man; investigator of crime in Jackson County. il Newsweek 70: 26-7 Ag 21 '67
Paroles for sale; corruption on Georgia parole board. il Newsweek 71:15-16 Ja 1 '68

Germany (Federal Republic)
Katzenjammer kops; nationwide drive to round up most wanted criminals. Newsweek 70:54 D 18 '67

Great Britain
Life without the hangman; murder rate drops. Time 90:48 Jl 7 '67
What the British are doing to crack down on crime; interview. R. Jenkins. U S News 62:86 F 6 '67

Italy
Medieval commune and internal violence; police power and public safety in Siena; 1287-1355. W. M. Bowsky. bibliog f Am Hist R 73:1-17 O '67

Japan
See also
Tokyo—Crime

Louisiana
Carlos Marcello: king thug of Louisiana. il Life 63:94-7 S 8 '67
From a governor and a D.A. an offer of resignation; reactions to articles concerning Cosa nostra's empire. S. Smith. il Life 63: 34-6 S 29 '67

CRIME and criminals—*Continued*

Mexico
Acapulco's other side, army drive to round up all the arms in the state of Guerrero. il Time 90:35-6 S 22 '67

New England
See also
Mafia

Russia
See also
Prisons—Russia

Sweden
See also
Prisons—Sweden

United States
Angry Congress seeks tougher crime laws; rising sentiment against Supreme court rulings. il Bsns W p 138+ Ap 22 '67
Blamed in crime rise: civil-rights excesses; excerpts from address. C. E. Whittaker. U S News 62:15 F 27 '67
Challenge of crime in a free society. Report by the President's commission on law enforcement and administration of justice. Review
    New Repub 156:38-40 My 20 '67. F. Remington
Combating crime; symposium, ed. by L. E. Ohlin and H. S. Ruth, jr. bibliog f il Ann Am Acad 374:1-184 N '67
Community-based correctional treatment: rationale and problems. E. K. Nelson, jr. bibliog f Ann Am Acad 374:82-91 N '67
Crime; a contemporary responsibility; address, October 16, 1967. H. C. Donnelly. Vital Speeches 34:114-16 D 1 '67
Crime & affluence: case of the culpable victim. M. Fooner. il Nation 204:307-8 Mr 6 '67
Crime & counterforce. Time 91:23-4 Ja 5 '68
Crime and politics; findings of the President's commission on law enforcement and the administration of justice. G. Geis. Nation 205:115-16 Ag 14 '67
Crime and punishment; action against the spreading epidemic of street violence. il Newsweek 71:24-5 Ja 8 '68
Crime & the Great society; findings of President's commission on law enforcement and administration of justice; Time essay. Time 89:20-1 Mr 24 '67
Crime and the lawbreaking mentality. il Sr Schol 90:7-10+ F 17 '67
Crime in our communities. J. Moorhead. PTA Mag 61:2-3 Ap '67
Crime in the city: can it be controlled? address, June 5, 1967. H. R. Leary. Vital Speeches 34:22-4 O 15 '67
Crime; interview, by W. Rogers. N. D. Katzenbach. Look 31:101-4+ Mr 7 '67
Crime up, punishment down. il U S News 62:72 Ap 10 '67
Criminal and the community. G. Tyler. Cur Hist 53:102-6+ Ag '67
Era of growing strife in U.S. il U S News 63:41-3 S 25 '67
FBI warns about: the Christmas trade no business wants; planned bankruptcy. J. E. Hoover. il Nations Bsns 55:44-6+ N '67
He knows in his heart; concerning Johnson's message on crime. Newsweek 69:32-3 F 20 '67
High crime, poor justice. P. McBroom. il Sci N 91:186-7 F 25 '67
Johnson sets strategy for a war on crime. Bsns W p82-3 F 11 '67
Johnson's crime message. New Repub 156:10 F 18 '67
Johnson's war on crime. il U S News 62:48 F 20 '67
Mob; empire of organized crime, its power, structure, tactics; with report by S. Smith. il Life 63:15-23+ S 1; 91-102+ S 8 '67
Murf the Surf and his jewel-studded jinx. K. Wheeler and S. Smith. il Life 62:92-4+ Ap 21 '67
National goals and indicators for the reduction of crime and delinquency. D. Glaser. bibliog f il Ann Am Acad 371:104-26 My '67
New evidence of the terrific spurt of crime in America. il U S News 63:12 Ag 21 '67
Only half-civilized. Christian Cent 84:523-4 Ap 26 '67
Organized crime: on the defensive? Sr Schol 90:10 F 17 '67
Police. S. Blum. il Redbook 128:76-7+ F '67
President on crime; Crime commission's proposals. Reporter 36:14+ F 23 '67

Response to crime. Sci N 91:172 F 18 '67
Shocking balance sheet on crime; recommendations of National crime commission report. Life 62:6 F 24 '67
To redeem the worst, to better the best; concerning Presidential message to Congress. Time 89:19 F 17 '67
U.S. crime: a renaissance? il Newsweek 69:31-3 F 27 '67
U.S. crime: its scope and causes; symposium. bibliog f il Cur Hist 52:321-58+ Je '67
Victims of a gang feud, deadly items in a startling report: crime U.S., findings of National crime commission; with report by R. B. Stolley. il Life 62:22-9 F 24 '67
Violence in America; Time essay. Time 90:18-19 Jl 28 '67
What to do about crime in U.S; excerpts from address, 1967. W. E. Burger. il U S News 63:70-3 Ag 7 '67
    See also
Automobiles, Theft of
Criminal statistics
Gambling
Gangs
Mafia
Negroes in the United States—Crime
Racketeering
United States—Federal bureau of investigation
United States—President's commission on law enforcement and administration of justice
    also subhead Crime under names of cities, e.g. Chicago—Crime

Wisconsin
Death of a warden; Bob Markle. D. Duffey. il Outdoor Life 139:41-3+ F '67

CRIME and the press
Bad news at the breakfast table. Esquire 68:40-1 Jl '67
Controlling crime news; excerpts from The crime war. R. M. Cipes. Atlan 220:47-53 Ag '67
Crime and publicity, by A. Friendly and R. Goldfarb. Review
    New Repub 157:34-7+ S 2 '67. H. L. Will
Crime and publicity; defendant's right to fair trial often violated. il Newsweek 69:65 Je 5 '67
Trial by headline. L. Nizer. il McCalls 94:93+ F '67
    See also
Newspaper court reporting

CRIME commission. See United States—President's commission on law enforcement and administration of justice

CRIME detection. See Criminal investigation; Identification

CRIME films. See Moving pictures— Crime films

CRIME in literature
Pause, now, and consider some tentative conclusions about porno-violence. T. Wolfe. Esquire 68:59+ Jl '67
    See also
Detective and mystery stories

CRIME novels. See Detective and mystery stories

CRIME prevention
Aerospace methods eyed for crime fighting. J. Rhea. il Tech W 20:37-8 Ap 24 '67
Crime control in our community; suggested program for a PTA meeting or public meeting sponsored by a PTA or council of PTA's. PTA Mag 61:30-1 Ap '67
Crime control: task force urges use of science and technology. J. Anderson. Science 156:1579-82 Je 23 '67
Crusading in Indianapolis; News editor leads Anti-crime crusade. il Time 89:38+ Je 23 '67
Delicate balance: President says local police have responsibility for keeping the peace. il Newsweek 70:30 S 25 '67
Genesis of crime. R. K. Woetzel. Cur Hist 52:321-6 Je '67
National goals and indicators for the reduction of crime and delinquency. D. Glaser. bibliog f il Ann Am Acad 371:104-26 My '67
Plan of action. E. M. Kennedy. Sat Eve Post 240:28-9 F 11 '67
President on crime: Crime commission's proposals. Reporter 36:14+ F 23 '67
Prevention of crime and treatment of offenders: Advisory committee's second session. UN Mo Chron 4:125-6 Ja '67
Science vs. crime: new twists in an old war. il Changing T 21:54-5 Jl '67
Space-age vigilantes; shotgun squads protect shops from holdup men in Houston. il Time 89:34-5 Je 9 '67

CRIME prevention—*Continued*
Support for the professionals; Johnson's federal crime and gun laws. Time 90:23 S 22 '67
This month's feature: Congress & the national crime problem. Cong Digest 46:193-224 Ag '67
U.S. crime: punishment and prevention; symposium. bibliog f il Cur Hist 53:65-110+ Ag '67
War on crime. Sr Schol 90:23 F 24 '67
  See also
Juvenile delinquency—Prevention
Police

CRIME syndicates. See Crime and criminals—United States

CRIME wave. See Crime and criminals—United States

CRIMEA
  See also
Yalta

CRIMES, Business. See Commercial crimes

CRIMES, Commercial. See Commercial crimes

CRIMES, Political. See Political crimes and offenses

CRIMINAL behavior. See Criminal psychology

CRIMINAL identification. See Identification

CRIMINAL investigation
Crime control: task force urges use of science and technology. J. Anderson. Science 156: 1579-82 Je 23 '67
Federal role in criminal investigation procedures. A. S. Nanes. Cur Hist 53:107-10+ Ag '67
Governor Kirk's not-so-secret police; controversy over special investigators to fight crime in Florida. F. Murray. il Reporter 36:27-30 Mr 23 '67
Is the U.S. coddling criminals? pro and con discussion. Sr Schol 90:11-12 F 17 '67
Quizzing of suspects: here's a new way; excerpts from statement, February 7, 1967. B. Bayh. U S News 62:14 F 20 '67
Squad-car lawyers. il Time 89:79 Ap 14 '67
Technology and control of crime. D. Wolfle. Science 156:1687 Je 30 '67
Video tape recorders used in tests by Miami police. il Tech W 20:29 Je 19 '67
Wood wizard; tracking down Lindbergh kidnapper by wood analysis. J. B. Craig. il Am For 73:28-30+ O '67
  See also
Electronics in criminal investigation, espionage, etc.
Identification
Police questioning
Television in criminal investigation
United States—Federal bureau of investigation

      Anecdotes, facetiae, satire, etc.
Caught in the act. B. Conklin. il Sat Eve Post 240:18 Ag 26 '67

CRIMINAL law
Angry Congress seeks tougher crime laws; rising sentiment against Supreme court rulings. il Bsns W p 138+ Ap 22 '67
Armed and dangerous; amended bill. New Repub 157:8+ N 25 '67
Criminal and the law; excerpts from Lawyers and laws. M. Mayer. il Sat Eve Post 240: 25-7+ F 11 '67
GOP steals a march with crime; crime control proposals. Bsns W p 130+ Ag 19 '67
  See also
Capital punishment
Conspiracy
Juvenile courts
Obscenity (law)
Perjury

CRIMINAL lawyers. See Lawyers

CRIMINAL procedure
Catching up with Miranda; Court frees confessed murderer. Time 89:49 Mr 3 '67
Crime, confessions and the Supreme court; Miranda decision. G. L. Chamberlain. America 117:32-4 Jl 8 '67
Floriot loses one. il Time 90:72-3 Jl 28 '67
Immunity of prosecutors; case of L. E. Miller, jr. il Time 89:72 Mr 31 '67
In the matter of Gault; excerpts from United States Supreme court decision and from the dissent, May 15, 1967. Cur Hist 53:112-13+ Ag '67
Interrogation and the criminal process. A. J. Reiss, jr. and D. J. Black. bibliog f Ann Am Acad 374:47-57 N '67
Negotiated guilty plea. A. Rosett. Ann Am Acad 374:70-81 N '67

Perjury routine; police perjury. I. Younger. il Nation 204:596-7 My 8 '67
Police, judges tell Congress: criminals get the breaks; excerpts from hearings by Senate judiciary committee's subcommittee on criminal laws and procedures. il U S News 62:44-5 Mr 27 '67
Pot bust at Cornell; R. Thaler's entrapment methods for possessing marijuana. D. Sanford. New Repub 156:17-20 Ap 15 '67; Discussion. 156:26-7 Ap 29; 34 My 6 '67
Speaking out; after the riots: force won't settle anything. R. Girardin. Sat Eve Post 240:10+ S 23 '67
Systems analysis and the criminal justice system. A. Blumstein. bibliog f Ann Am Acad 374:92-100 N '67
U.S. courts and criminal justice. W. M. Beaney. bibliog f Cur Hist 53:65-9+ Ag '67
We can break the grip of the mob. Life 63: 4 S 8 '67
What happens when rioters get into court. il U S News 63:52 Ag 28 '67
What the British are doing to crack down on crime; interview. R. Jenkins. U S News 62:86 F 6 '67
When defendants testify. Time 90:51 N 3 '67
  See also
Grand jury
Jury
Speedy trial

CRIMINAL psychology
Crime chromosome; genetic abnormality explains criminal behavior. Sci N 91:258 Mr 18 '67
Independent offender. R. W. England, jr. bibliog f il Cur Hist 52:334-40+ Je '67
On iniquity, by P. H. Johnson. Review Commentary 43:107-11 My '67. M. Ellmann
  Reporter 36:39-40 My 18 '67. W. L. Gundersheimer
  Sat R 50:34 Ap 15 '67. D. Lyons
  See also
Forensic psychiatry

CRIMINAL statistics
Crime and politics; findings of the President's commission on law enforcement and the administration of justice. G. Geis. Nation 205:115-16 Ag 14 '67
Crime statistics; a numbers game? Sr Schol 90:8-9 F 17 '67
Crisis worse than anyone imagined; report of the National crime commission. R. B. Stolley. il Life 62:24-5 F 24 '67
Great juggling act. J. Leo. Commonweal 87: 9-10 O 6 '67
On exploring the dark figure of crime. A. D. Biderman and A. J. Reiss, jr. bibliog f Ann Am Acad 374:1-15 N '67
Survey of population samples for estimating crime incidence. A. D. Biderman. bibliog f il Ann Am Acad 374:16-33 N '67
Who commits the crime? repeaters, says the FBI; findings of study. il U S News 62:52 My 8 '67

CRIMINALS. See Crime and criminals

CRIMMIN, Eileen
Northwest gales. See issues of Motor boating
Puget Sound heritage cruise. Motor B 119: 22-7+ My '67
Seattle boat show. Motor B 119:134-5 Mr '67
What you can do about the virus. Sci Digest 61:77-80 F '67

CRIMMINS, Alice
Modern Medea? il pors Newsweek 70:34 S 25 '67

CRIPPLES
  See also
Orthopedic apparatus

      Rehabilitation
  See Rehabilitation

CRIST, Judith (Klein)
Critic-at-large. See issues of Ladies' home journal
Movies. Vogue 150:226 S 1; 68 S 15; 142 O 1; 135 N 1; 163 N 15; 174 D '67
Movies: where anything goes. Look 32:22-5 Ja 9 '68
      about
Critic around the clock. por Newsweek 69:95 Mr 27 '67

CRIST, Raymond E.
Men, motives and missions. Sat R 50:41-2 O 7 '67
Paraguay. bibliog Focus 18:1-6 D '67
—and Taylor, Alice
Ecuador. bibliog Focus 18:1-6 O '67
Peru. bibliog Focus 17:1-6 Ap '67

CRISTOBALITE
Farmington meteorite: cristobalite xenoliths and blackening. R. A. Binns. bibliog il Science 156:1222-6 Je 2 '67
CRISTOFV, Cristjo
Black box that turns you on. il Bsns W p79-80 My 6 '67
CRITES, Stephen
Going-out of a recluse; poem. Christian Cent 84:656 My 17 '67
Religious noise; poem. Christian Cent 84:529 Ap 26 '67
CRITICAL path analysis
CPM for new product introductions. W. Dusenbury. il Harvard Bsns R 45:124-39 Jl '67
CPM; the earlier, the better; practice in modern construction economics. L. C. Jaquith. Arch Rec 142:87-8 O '67
Third generation. PERT/LOB. P. P. Schoderbek and L. A. Digman. il Harvard Bsns R 45:100-10 S '67
CRITICISM
  See also
Educational criticism
Literary criticism
Television criticism
CRITICISM, Personal. See Self evaluation
CRITICISM, Political. See Opposition (political science)
CRITICS
Amiable springboard; theater critics. M. Gussow. Newsweek 70:96+ D 18 '67
End of one-man's opinion; two theater critics of New York times. il Time 89:51 Mr 17 '67
Enter Clive Barnes. Newsweek 69:109 Mr 20 '67
French new criticism, by L. LeSage. Review Sat R 50:71-2 Je 10 '67. A. Balakian
Of criticism and dance. E. M. Ferdun. Dance Mag 41:51 F '67
Prince Uncharming: music critic, B. H. Haggin. Time 90:59 Jl 21 '67
Role of the critic. R. Eyer. il Opera N 31:8-12 F 25 '67
Swinging London has its critics; reviewing the dance. F. Hall. il Dance Mag 41:50-3+ O '67
Youth movement; critical departments of New York times. il Newsweek 70:99-99A D 4 '67
  See also
Bentley, E.
Literary criticism
CRITTENDEN, B. M.
Computer combats auto thefts. Am City 82:116-17 Je '67
CRITTENDEN, Pauline
Arkansas' mountain-top playgrounds. Travel 128:30-4 O '67
Treasure of pleasure. Travel 127:41-4 Mr '67
CROAN, Robert
Small slice of the moderns. Hi Fi 17:MA20 Je '67
CROATIAN language. See Serbo-Croation language
CROCE, Arlene
Movies (cont) Nat R 19:482-5 My 2 '67
Off off-Broadway, New York. Nat R 19:261-5 Mr 7 '67
Theater. Nat R 19:99-100; 20:43-4 Ja 24 '67, Ja 16 '68
—and Simonds, C. H.
(comps) Lest you forget ... Nat R 19:1205-6 O 31 '67
CROCUSES
Crocus for fall and spring. il(cover) Home Gard 54:19 S '67
Nature note. il Sci N 91:252 Mr 18 '67
Plant a crocus spring! il Am Home 70:38 O '67
CROLEY, Victor A.
Blueberries for the South. Home Gard 54:16 Ap '67
Pole sallet: spring greens, wild & cultivated. Home Gard 54:78+ Ap '67
CROMER, George Rowland Stanley Baring, 3d earl of
For the Yankee dollar. Time 90:92 S 29 '67
CROMPTON, A. W. and Jenkins, F. A. Jr
American Jurassic symmetrodonts and Rhaetic pantotheres. bibliog Science 155:1006-9 F 24 '67
CRONIN, Ann Ferrell
Stay young & beautiful. Parents Mag 43:24+ Ja '68
CRONIN, John F.
Father Cronin leaves Washington. America 116:492 Ap 1 '67
CRONIN, Michael C.
Surf safety school. Parks & Rec 2:16-17+ Jl '67

CRONIN, Sean
Baggot street bard. Commonweal 87:447-8 Ja 12 '68
Cool, courageous and an excellent shot. Nation 206:20-1 Ja 1 '68
MacDiarmid: Highland red. Nation 204:728-30 Je 5 '67
O'Casey's benevolent blasts. Nation 205:315-16 O 2 '67
CRONIN, Vincent
Fire and flood on the Arno. Sat R 50:24 D 30 '67
CRONKITE, Nancy
Untitled poem. Mlle 65:208 Ag '67
CRONKITE, Walter, 1916-
Twenty-first century: the world you'll live in. pors Pop Sci 190:98-101 Ap '67

            about
Cronkite's alarm. Nation 204:260-1 F 27 '67
CRONOSCOPE. See Electric lamps, Photoflash
CROOK, Mel
More power to you. See issues of Yachting
CROP forecasts. See Agricultural forecasts
CROP reports. See Agriculture—Statistics
CROP yields
How fertilizer affects crop quality. S. R. Aldrich. Suc Farm 65:44H Ja '67
CROPS
News. See issues of Farm journal
What's new. See issues of Successful farming
  See also names of crops, e.g. Soybeans

          Statistics
  See Agriculture—Statistics
CROPS, Surplus. See Food supply
CROPSEY, Jasper Francis
Jasper F. Cropsey, child of the Hudson River school. W. S. Talbot. Antiques 92:713-17 N '67
CROQUET
Mallets across the blinkin' sea; Britain's Hurlingham club vs Westhampton mallet club of Long Island. S. Pileggi. il Sports Illus 27:22-5 Jl 31 '67
Sport of stings. P. Maas. il Holiday 42:50-3+ O '67
CROSBY, Gary
Gary Crosby, a man's victory over alcoholism. M. Davidson. il por Good H 165:92-3+ S '67
CROSBY, John
Aftermath. L. Saalburg. Esquire 67:62+ My '67
CROSS, Farrell
How to get more out of weekends. Read Digest 92:125-8 Ja '68
CROSS, Frank L. Jr, and Ross, Roger
Fight air pollution before it starts. por Am City 82:101-3 S '67
CROSS, Wilbur. See Graham, J. A. M. jt. auth.
CROSS, Way of the. See Stations of the cross
CROSS country running. See Running
CROSS pollination. See Fertilization of plants
CROSSING over (genetics)
Autosomal linkage between the albumin and Gc loci in humans. K. Kaarsalo and others. bibliog il Science 158:123-5 O 6 '67
Orientation of nonsense codons on the genetic map of the lac operon. D. Zipser. bibliog il Science 157:1176-7 S 8 '67
Tetrahymena: effect of freezing and subsequent thawing on breeding performance. E. M. Simon. bibliog il Science 155:694-6 F 10 '67
  See also
Chromosomes
CROSSINGS; story. See Minot, S.
CROSSLEY S-D surveys
Peace of mind. New Repub 157:11 N 18 '67
CROSSMAN, Carl L.
Rose medallion and mandarin patterns in China trade porcelain. Antiques 92:530-5 O '67
CROSSMAN, Patricia R.
Gold-headed cane; story. McCalls 94:118-19 Mr '67
CROSWELL, Harry
Verdicts of history. T. J. Fleming. il por Am Heritage 19:22-7+ D '67
CROTON bugs. See Cockroaches
CROUSE, John O.
Griffith race, serene but surprising. Motor B 119:96-8 Ap '67
CROW, C. P.
Justice of sorts. Reporter 37:37-41 D 14 '67

CROW Indians
Two Leggings: the making of a Crow warrior, by P. Nabokov. Review
Am Heritage 18:80-2 O 67. B. Catton
CROW shooting
Bad day for crows. B. W. Dalrymple. il Outdoor Life 139:64-5+ Mr '67
CROWDS
Perils of crowd counting; H. A. Jacobs method of estimating the size of a crowd. il Time 89:44 Ap 7 '67
CROWE, Frederick E.
Christology and contemporary philosophy. Commonweal 87:242-7 N 24 '67
CROWELL Collier and Macmillan, Incorporated
Calif. enjoins Collier's encyclopedia sales pitch. Pub W 191:39 Mr 20 '67
Crowell Collier to buy science materials firm. Pub W 191:37 Ap 17 '67
CROWN Zellerbach corporation
Paper profits. il Time 89:88+ My 5 '67
CROWS
Garrick! says the crow, and also bah! humbug! R. Cantwell. il Sports Illus 26:47-8+ Mr 27 '67
CROWTHER, Bosley
Case of Crowther. H. Alpert. Sat R 50:111 S 23 '67
Rigors of criticism. por Time 90:38 D 1 '67
CROWTHER, Clarence Edward, bp
Bishop Crowther deported. J. Squire. Christian Cent 84:1001-2 Ag 2 '67
CROYDEN, Margaret
Fashion of peeping Toms. Nation 205:568-9 N 27 '67
CROZIER, Bob
Shears of fate, the loom of life. Sports Illus 26:79-81+ My 29 '67
CRUDE oil. See Petroleum
CRUELTY to animals. See Animals—Treatment
CRUELTY to children
Abused child. J. W. Gardner. il McCalls 94:96-7+ S '67
Battered child syndrome. America 116:236 F 18 '67
CRUICKSHANK, Marjorie
Influence of tradition: comparisons of English and Scottish education; excerpts from address, July 19, 1966. bibliog f Sch & Soc 95:498-502 D 9 '67
CRUIKSHANK, Dale P. and Chapman, C. R.
Mercury's rotation and visual observations. Sky & Tel 34:24-6 Jl '67
—See Binder, A. B. jt. auth.
CRUISERS. See Motor boats; Yachts and yachting
CRUISERS, Fishing. See Fishing boats
CRUISES. See Cruising
CRUISING
Adventure trips to the far outposts; to the Amazon Basin and Antarctica; with report by M. Leatherbee. il Life 62:78-87+ S 8 '67
Baby-sitter's bonanza: two months in Europe, including five-week cruise of Adriatic and Aegean aboard chartered yacht. L. Gross. il Look 31:85-6+ Mr 21 '67
Bahamian fortnight. G. Merrill. il Motor B 120:41-3+ O '67
Barefoot cruising in the Virgins. il Newsweek 69:64-9 Ja 30 '67
By sea, to see the elephants; cruise among the islands off the California coast. S. Murray. il Yachting 122:52-5+ Jl; 46-7+ Ag '67
Cruising and chartering the Greek Islands. B. Robinson. il Yachting 121:42-5+ F '67
Cruising in northern Florida. E. White. il Motor B 119:42-5+ Mr '67
Cruising to Expo 67. W. Richards. il Motor B 119:154 F '67
Cruising to the Garden of the Hesperides. R. Kelton. il Motor B 119:28-9+ My '67
Cruising unlimited; from Olympia, Wash. northwestward to Alaska. W. Dawson. il Yachting 121:68-70+ Ja '67
Everglades expedition. R. T. Fisher. il Yachting 121:61-4+ Mr; 82-5+ Ap '67
Facts to know about winter cruises. il Good H 165:196-7 O '67
Floating across the Continent; seeing western Europe by waterway; with account by M. Leatherbee. il Life 62:50-61+ Je 23 '67
Fun³, a big time in the Bahamas. E. Horan. il Yachting 122:50-1+ N '67
Gales for Christmas. D. J. Tinius. il Motor B 120:39+ D '67
Getting there is more than half the fun. N. Brower. il Motor B 120:29-31+ O '67

Gunkholing the lesser Antilles. D. M. Street, jr. il Yachting 122:52-3+ N '67
In the wake of the skipjacks. W. B. Matthews, jr. il Motor B 119:32-3+ Ap '67
Islands down wind. E. Hiscock. il Yachting 121:58-60+ F '67
Leisurely cruise around St John. J. C. Kozlick. il Motor B 120:38-9+ O '67
Midwesterner cruises east. J. R. Witmer. il Yachting 122:52-4+ D '67
Motor boating cruise sampler. Motor B 119:22-3 Ap '67
Passagemaker's summer cruise. R. Beebe. Motor B 119:86+ F '67
Puget Sound heritage cruise. E. Crimmin. il Motor B 119:22-7+ My '67
Southward from Maine. E. Hiscock. il Yachting 122:58-9+ D '67 (to be cont)
To Texas, by ICW. P. A. Hathorn. il Motor B 120:52-5 O '67 (to be cont)
To the cruise centennial (with oceans of love) A. Gingrich. Esquire 68:134-5+ N '67
Trailer boating the Bruce Peninsula. F. M. Paulson. il Field & S 72:36-9 Jl '67
Twenty feet can go a long way; Bahamian Out Islands. J. Hennesey. il Yachting 122:48-9+ N '67
Whaler-sailer? R. W. Carrick. il Yachting 123:106-8+ Ja '68
Woolpacks and wonders in New Brunswick. D. W. Gardner. il Motor B 119:24-7+ Ap '67
See also
River trips

Anecdotes, facetiae, satire, etc.
Winter cruise. J. G. Dunne. Sat Eve Post 241:16 Ja 27 '68
CRUISING houseboats. See House boats
CRUM, Gertrude
Recipes for success. A. Geracimos. il por Sat Eve Post 241:28-9 Ja 27 '68
CRUMMIE, John H.
Space balloon scientist. il pors Ebony 22:44-6+ Mr '67
CRUMPET, Peter
Stub on the toe of the lion. Nat R 19:361-3 Ap 4 '67
CRUMRINE, James
Dialogue in a museum. Craft Horiz 27:18-22+ Jl '67
CRUSE, Heloise
Heloise, the most-heeded housewife. J. Howard. il pors Life 62:39+ Ap 21 '67
CRUST of the earth. See Earth—Surface
CRUSTACEA
Amateur scientist; how to photograph tiny live crustaceans. P. Rowe. il Sci Am 216:143-4+ My '67
Terrestrial adaptations of crustacea; symposium in memory of Warren J. Gross. il Science 157:1592-3 S 29 '67
See also
Crayfish
Eye (crustacea)
Ostracods
CRUTCHFIELD, James A.
Economic considerations. Bul Atomic Sci 23:17-21 S '67
CRUZ, Mario
Brazil's magic mountain. K. Seegers and S. Seegers. il por Américas 19:20-7 Mr '67
CRUZIC, Kathleen
Caring for a sick baby. Parents Mag 42:44-5+ Mr '67
CRY of silence; story. See Greenberg, J.
CRYOGENIC detectors. See Detectors
CRYOGENIC research. See Low temperature research
CRYOGENIC surgery
Super-cold: hottest thing in surgery. S. L. Englebardt. Read Digest 90:131-5 My '67
CRYOGENICS. See Low temperatures
CRYONICS society of California
Cold way to new life; body of J. H. Bedford frozen shortly after death. L. Wainwright. Life 62:16 Ja 27 '67
Never say die; body of J. H. Bedford frozen. il Time 89:57 F 3 '67
CRYOSURGERY. See Cryogenic surgery
CRYOTHERAPY. See Cold—Therapeutic applications
CRYPTANALYSIS. See Cryptography
CRYPTOGRAPHY
Codebreakers, by D. Kahn. Review
Sat R 50:32-3 N 18 '67. P. W. Blackstock
When BOMB is 6214. il Newsweek 70:48 O 2 '67

CRYPTO-JEWS. See Maranos

CRYPTOLOGY. See Cryptography

CRYSTAL palace exhibition, 1851. See London
—Great exhibition of the works of industry of all nations, 1851

CRYSTALLIZATION
Crystallization of a sulfate-binding protein (permease) from salmonella typhimurium. A. B. Pardee. bibliog il Science 156:1627-8 Je 23 '67
Crystallization of human lysozyme. E. F. Osserman. bibliog il Science 155:1536-7 Mr 24 '67

CRYSTALLOGRAPHY
Amateur scientist; on growing crystals of salt. J. Bailey. il Sci Am 218:131-2 Ja '68
Clathrate hydrates of some amines. G. A. Jeffrey and others. bibliog il Science 155: 689-91 F 10 '67
Electronic properties of amorphous materials. J. Tauc. bibliog il Science 158:1543-8 D 22 '67
Fresnoite: unusual titanium coordination. P. B. Moore and J. Louisnathan. bibliog il Science 156:1361-2 Je 9 '67
Nature of ceramics. J. J. Gilman. il Sci Am 217:112-18+ S '67
Nature of glasses. R. J. Charles. il Sci Am 217:126-30+ S '67
Nature of metals. A. H. Cottell. il Sci Am 217:90-100 S '67
Pi electron systems at high pressure. H. G. Drickamer. bibliog il Science 156:1183-9 Je 2 '67
Staurolite: sectoral compositional variations. L. S. Hollister and A. E. Bence. bibliog il Science 158:1053-6 N 24 '67
See also
Liquid crystals
Polymorphism
X ray studies
Apatite crystallites: effects of carbonate on morphology. R. Z. LeGeros and others. bibliog il Science 155:1409-11 Mr 17 '67
Crystal structure of the 1 : 1 complex of 5-fluorouracil and 9-ethylhypoxanthine. S. H. Kim and A. Rich. bibliog il Science 158:1046-8 N 24 '67
Crystal structure of the solid electrolyte, RbAg₄I₅. S. Geller. bibliog il Science 157: 310-12 Jl 21 '67
Solid state. N. Mott. il Sci Am 217:80-9 S '67
Synthetic zeolites: growth of larger single crystals. J. Ciric. il Science 155:689 F 10 '67
X-ray diffraction study of some fossil and modern resins. J. W. Frondel. il Science 155: 1411-13 Mr 17 '67
X-ray fabric analysis of hot-worked and annealed flint. H. R. Wenk and others. il Science 157:1447-9 S 22 '67

CRYSTALS. See Crystallography

CRYSTALS, Liquid. See Liquid crystals

CRYSTALS, Snow. See Snow

CUADRA, Pablo Antonio
Dante discovers America. Américas 19:32-9 F '67

CUATRECASAS, Pedro, and Segal, Stanton
Electrophoretic heterogeneity of mammalian galactose dehydrogenase. bibliog Science 154:533-5; 156:1518 O 28 '66, Je 16 '67

CUBA
Anniversary thoughts. Newsweek 71:38+ Ja 15 '68
Reporting on Cuba. J. Yglesias. New Repub 157:23-6 Jl 8 '67
See also
Communism—Cuba
Foreign visitors in Cuba
Immigration and emigration—Cuba
Science—Cuba
Tourist trade—Cuba

Economic conditions
As Russia tightens up on Castro. il U S News 64:55 Ja 15 '68
Cost of eight years of Castro. M. de Medici. Read Digest 91:89-93 Jl '67
Fidel Castro's comeback: where it's headed. il U S News 63:86-7 Ag 21 '67
How life has changed in a Cuban sugar mill town. J. Yglesias. il N Y Times Mag p8-9+ Jl 23 '67
Time for diversion. il Time 91:26 Ja 19 '68
See also
Communism—Cuba

Economic relations
Fidel Castro's comeback: where it's headed. il U S News 63:86-7 Ag 21 '67

Foreign relations
Can Castro start a new Vietnam? P. D. Bethel. Nat R 19:130-4 F 7 '67
Cool days at the Havana summit. il U S News 63:12 Jl 10 '67
Cuban intervention cited in report. Américas 19:45 S '67
Does a deal bar U.S. from action against Cuba? il U S News 63:54-5 Ag 28 '67
Foreign ministers condemn Cuba; twelfth meeting of consultation of ministers of foreign affairs. G. Meek. il Américas 19:43-4 N '67
Stopover in Havana; Kosygin visits Castro. il Time 90:26 Jl 7 '67

History
Presidential leadership in foreign affairs: William McKinley and the Turple-Foraker amendment. P. S. Holbo. bibliog f Am Hist R 72:1321-35 Jl '67
Rebel without hatred. J. A. Del Regato. il Américas 19:29-35 Ja '67

Industries
See also
Sugar industry and trade

Intellectual life
Situation of Cuba's intellectuals; tr. by J. Lara-Braud. M. Maldonado-Denis. Christian Cent 85:78-80 Ja 17 '68

Politics and government
As Russia tightens up on Castro. il U S News 64:55 Ja 15 '68
Free territory of America. America 116:171 F 4 '67
One millionaire and twenty beggars; excerpts from Pax Americana. R. Steel. Harper 234:81-7 My '67
Presidential leadership in foreign affairs: William McKinley and the Turpie-Foraker amendment. P. S. Holbo. bibliog f Am Hist R 72:1321-35 Jl '67

Social conditions
Cost of eight years of Castro. M. de Medici. Read Digest 91:89-93 Jl '67
Time for diversion. il Time 91:26 Ja 19 '68
See also
Communism—Cuba

CUBAN crisis, 1962
Does a deal bar U.S. from action against Cuba? il U S News 63:54-5 Ag 28 '67

CUBAN painting. See Painting, Cuban

CUBAN refugees. See Refugees, Cuban

CUBANS in the United States
See also
Refugees, Cuban
Tampa, Fla.—Ybor City

CUBISM
Art; The sculpture of Picasso. M. Kozloff. Nation 205:441-4 O 30 '67
Cubism as a class project. L. J. Miller. il Design 69:36-7 Wint '67
London; cubist art from Czechoslovakia at the Tate. J. Russell. Art N 66:51 N '67
They came from inner space; exhibition at Knoedler. J. Ashbery. il Art N 66:48-50+ D '67

CUBS (baseball) See Baseball clubs

CUCKOOS
See also
Road runners (birds)

CUCUMBERS
Cucumbers on a trellis. il Home Gard 54:12 Ap '67

CUED speech. See Deaf—Means of communication

CUENCA, Spain
Julian the tranquil slept here. P. Brooks. Sat R 50:66+ N 25 '67

CUERNAVACA, Mexico
Cuernavaca, eternal springtime. M. Oberon. Vogue 149:43 Ja 15 '67

CUEVAS, José Luis
Two young rebels in Mexican painting. A. de Neuvillate. il por Américas 19:8-16 Mr '67

CUFF, Sergeant, pseud. See Winterich, J. T.

CULBERSON, C. and others
High-pressure dissociation of carbonic and boric acids in seawater. bibliog Science 157: 59-61 Jl 7 '67

CULBERSON, Chicita F. See Culberson, W. L. jt. auth.

CULBERSON, William Louis, and Culberson, C. F.
Habitat selection by chemically differentiated races of lichens. bibliog Science 158:1195-7 D 1 '67

CULHANE, Eugene K.
Latin American diary. America 116:243-6 F 18 '67
CULKIN, John M.
Schoolman's guide to Marshall McLuhan. Sat R 50:51-3+ Mr 18 '67

about

Kidbirds, cinemates and seeing-eye children. D. S. Gelatt. il Pop Phot 62:100-3+ Ja '68
CULLEN, Thomas L.
How harmful is natural radioactivity? America 116:280-2 F 25 '67
CULLIGAN, Glendy
Spinach is the message. Reporter 37:39-40+ N 30 '67
Undivinable Sarah. Reporter 36:58+ F 9 '67
CULLINAN, Elizabeth
Sunday like the others; story. New Yorker 43:26-33 Ag 26 '67
CULLITON, Barbara J.
Consent: it's the law. Sci N 92:88-9 Jl 22 '67
Man and his science. Sci N 91:91 Ja 28 '67
Sperm banks debated. Sci N 92:208-9 Ag 26 '67
CULLMAN, Joseph Frederick, 1912-
Machine that will sell anything. il por(cover) Bsns W p92-4+ Mr 4 '67
CULP, Gordon, and Hansen Sigurd
How to clean wastewater for reuse. bibliog Am City 82:96-9 Je '67
CULSHAW, John
Project of the decade, singer of the century; excerpt from Ring resounding. Sat R 50: 72-5 Ag 26 '67
CULTS
Ping is the thing; A. LaVey's new Satanic religion. S. Alexander. Life 62:31 F 17 '67
Rage for awareness: movements in California. D. Bess. il Nation 204:243-4+ F 20 '67
CULTS, Negro
See also
Black Muslim movement
CULTURAL anthropology. See Ethnology
CULTURAL education. See Liberal education
CULTURAL evolution. See Social change
CULTURAL exchanges. See Exchange of persons programs
CULTURAL relations
Elegant lady: scholars and artists; address, October 19, 1967. S. D. Ripley. Vital Speeches 34:184-7 Ja 1 '68
Man does not live by politics alone; excerpts from address, April 9, 1950. J. Nehru. il UNESCO Courier 20:46-8+ Ag '67
See also subhead Cultural relations under names of countries, e.g. Russia—Cultural relations
CULTURALLY deprived children. See Socially handicapped children
CULTURE
Art of measuring the arts. A. Toffler. Ann Am Acad 373:141-55 S '67
Venture in cultural anthropology. P. F. Mayer. Negro Hist Bul 29:179-80+ Fall '66
See also
Civilization
History
Popular culture
Society, Primitive
also subheads Civilization; Intellectual life, under names of countries, e.g. Canada —Intellectual life
CULTURE, Primitive. See Indians of North America—Culture
CULTURE and Christianity. See Christianity and culture
CULTURE and war. See War and civilization
CULTURE of cells. See Tissues—Culture
CULTURE pearls. See Pearls
CULVER, Elsie Thomas
Fourth National workshop for Christian unity. Christian Cent 84:698-9 My 24 '67
Women ministers in 48th session. Christian Cent 84:1108 Ag 30 '67
CULVER, John
Best congressmen of the year. Nation 206:34-5 Ja 8 '68
CULVER, Katherine B.
Making and using transparencies. Sr Schol 91:sup 10-11 S 28 '67
CULVER military academy. See Military schools
CUMBERLAND, John H.
Economic development and its long-run environmental implications. Nat Parks Mag 41:11-13 N '67
CUMBERLAND ISLAND NATIONAL SEA-SHORE (proposed) See National parks and reserves—United States

CUMBERLAND MOUNTAINS. See Cumberland Plateau
CUMBERLAND PLATEAU
Lilly's wood. H. M. Caudill. il Audubon 69: 24-7 My '67
These murdered old mountains; effects of strip mining operations in Kentucky. D. Nevin. il Life 64:54-60+ Ja 12 '68
CUMMINGS, Samuel
Arms merchant to the world. S. De Gramont. il N Y Times Mag p38-9+ S 24 '67
CUMMINS, Paul
Advice; poem. New Repub 157:26 N 18 '67
CUMMINS engine company
Skyline rises in a Corn Belt town. il Bsns W p 138-40+ N 18 '67
CUNARD steamship company
Dance wildly, Queen Mary's about to die. A. Chamberlin. il Sat Eve Post 240:72-3 D 16 '67
Death of the Queens. il Time 89:122 My 19 '67
Great Cunard gamble. R. Nuttall. il Duns R 90:51+ N '67
Long live the Q; Q-4 to be launched. il Time 90:104 S 22 '67
Long live the Queen. il Newsweek 70:72 O 2 '67
Luxury era fades at sea; plan to scrap Cunard's Queens. il Bsns W p 122-4 My 20 '67
Successor to the Queens; Cunard's new luxury liner, Q4. il Pop Mech 128:106-8+ S '67
Sun sets on two ocean monarchs; Queen Mary and Queen Elizabeth. il Bsns W p44 My 13 '67
CUNEIFORM inscriptions
Music ages a thousand years. il Sci N 91: 400 Ap 29 '67
CUNEO, Paul K.
Death of a President: review of the reviews. America 116:684-5 My 6 '67
New style in Catholicism. Sat R 51:34 Ja 6 '68
Of many things. America 116:328 Mr 11; inside cover Ap 1 '67
Orthodoxy and the grass roots. Sat R 50:28-9 S 9 '67
CUNETTA, Joseph
Big but compact. Am City 82:137-9 O '67
CUNNINGHAM, George E.
Constitutional disenfranchisement of the Negro in Louisiana (cont) Negro Hist Bul 29: 174+ Fall '66
CUNNINGHAM, Glenn
Mail sex behavior. Reporter 37:12+ N 16 '67
CUNNINGHAM, James F.
New books. J. Kane. Cath World 205:251 Jl '67
CUNNINGHAM, John T.
Adirondacks: forever wild. Audubon 69:38-43 Mr '67
CUNNINGHAM, Julia
Dear characters. Horn Bk 43:233-4 Ap '67
CUNNINGHAM, Merce
José and others. D. Hering. il Dance Mag 41:34 O '67
CUNNINGHAM, Raymond J.
Impact of Christian Science on the American churches, 1880-1910. bibliog f Am Hist R 72:885-905 Ap '67
CUNNINGHAM, Walt
Freshmen in the crew: two self-made men who finally have the jobs they want. il pors Life 62:36 My 19 '67
CUPBOARDS
Secret cupboards I have known. E. M. Jarrett. il Pop Sci 190:160-2 F '67
See also
Kitchen cabinets
CUPIT, William G.
Operation Home Start. NEA J 56:53-4 S '67
CUPIVAC; drama. See Boiko, C.
CUPS
Verplanck cup. L. C. Belden. il Antiques 92: 840-2 D '67
CURARE
Transfer following operant conditioning in the curarized dog. A. H. Black. bibliog il Science 155:201-3 Ja 13 '67
CURIA romana. See Catholic church—Roman curia
CURIE, Eve
Marie Curie; excerpts from Madame Curie, tr. by V. Sheean. UNESCO Courier 20:14-16+ O '67
CURIE, Marie (Skłodowska)
Rarest, most precious vital force; preamble of memorandum, June 16, 1926. UNESCO Courier 20:16-17 O '67

about

First great woman scientist and much more. S. Raven. il pors N Y Times Mag p52-3+ D 3 '67

CURIE, Marie (Skłodowska)—about—*Cont.*
Maria Skłodowska: the dreamer in Warsaw. L. Infeld. il UNESCO Courier 20:20-2 O '67
Marie Curie; excerpts from Madame Curie, tr. by V. Sheean. E. Curie. il pors UNESCO Courier 20:14-16+ O '67
Woman we called *la patronne.* M. Perey. il por UNESCO Courier 20:22-4 O '67

CURIE, Pierre
Marie Curie; excerpts from Madame Curie, tr. by V. Sheean. E. Curie. il pors UNESCO Courier 20:14-16+ O '67

CURLERS, Hair. See Hair curlers

CURLEY, Daniel
Now that the children are nearly grown; poem. America 116:587 Ap 22 '67

CURLEY, Walter W.
Total blueprint. por Library J 92:1807 My 1 '67

CURNOW, Hugh
(ed) See Uggams, L. Why I married an Australian

CURRAN, Charles E.
Ethical teaching of Jesus. Commonweal 87: 248-50+ N 24 '67
about
Blow-up at Catholic U; with editorial comment. N. K. Herzfeld. Commonweal 86: 187-91 My 5 '67
Cause for revolt. il por Newsweek 69:61 My 1 '67
Of many things. T. N. Davis America 116: 663+ My 6 '67
Time for Boy scouts? il por Time 89:62 Ap 28 '67
What happened at Catholic U. D. M. Knight. America 116:723-5 My 13 '67
Zeroing in on freedom; symposium. Commonweal 86:316-21 Je 2 '67

CURRAN, Joseph Edwin
Curran's NMU; headquarters vs. the men at sea. D. J. Fliegel. il por Nation 204:143-7 Ja 30 '67

CURRENCY. See Money

CURRENCY convertibility
An authority tells: what to do to strengthen the dollar. il U S News 64:53 Ja 1 '68

CURRENCY question
Agony of the pound. il Time 90:29-32 N 24 '67
Britain devalues the pound. il Sr Schol 91: 17-18 D 7 '67
Devaluation: crisis of the mini-pound; with report by C. Welles. il Life 63:34-7 D 1 '67
Dollar and pound. il Nat R 19:1365-6 D 12 '67
How markets acted when pound fell. il U S News 63:37 D 4 '67
If the dollar were devalued. il U S News 64:47-8 Ja 8 '68
Letter from London; pound devalued. M. Panter-Downes. New Yorker 43:150-3 D 2 '67
Letter from Paris; fall of the pound sterling. Genêt. New Yorker 43:95-6+ D 9 '67
Sterling's lesson for the dollar. Life 63:4 D 1 '67
Weathering the fallout. il Time 90:105-6 D 1 '67
Will the dollar slip, too? il U S News 63:33-6 D 4 '67
Wilson devalues the pound, what price the damage? il Newsweek 70:73-4+ N 27 '67
World and the mini-pound. il Newsweek 70: 73-4+ D 4 '67

CURRENT events
Affairs of state. S. Alsop. See issues of Saturday evening post
March of the news; front page of the week. See issues of U.S. news & World report
Month in review. See issues of Current history
1967 contemporary affairs test. Sr Schol 91: 39-40 S 21 '67
People and events. See issues of Senior scholastic
Press section; excerpts from newspapers and periodicals. See issues of Reader's digest

CURRICULAR guidance. See Educational guidance

CURRICULUM. See Colleges and universities—Curriculum; Courses of study; High schools—Curriculum

CURRICULUM development, Association for. See Association for supervision and curriculum development

CURRIER, Audrey
Resonance of charity. L. Wainwright. Life 62:21 F 24 '67

CURRIER, Ruth
Ruth Currier & dance co, Village theatre. J. Anderson. Dance Mag 41:30 Ag '67

CURRIER, Stephen R.
Eulogy. il por Arch Forum 126:47 Ja '67
Resonance of charity. L. Wainwright. Life 62:21 F 24 '67

CURRIGAN, Thomas Guida
Workable civil defense and disaster relief program. Am City 82:108-9 N '67

CURRY, Peggy Simson
Restoration of a writer. Writer 80:13-15 S '67

CURRY, Russell D.
Progress report. Dance Mag 41:64-5 O '67

CURRY, Tom
Viewing with alarm. Writer 80:29-30 Jl '67

CURRY
Curry: hot or not; with recipes. E. Alston. il Look 31:78-80 S 5 '67
Serve curry on a cart. V. T. Habeeb. il Am Home 70:99+ Je '67

CURSILLOS de christiandad (movement)
Attack on the cursillo. America 116:616 Ap 29 '67

CURTAIN and drapery fixtures
How to buy drapery hardware. Am Home 70: 46 S '67

CURTAIN walls. See Walls

CURTAINS and draperies
All about drapery linings. Am Home 70:113 My '67
Cool and compatible cafes. il Bet Hom & Gard 45:121 Jl '67
Fiber glass fabrics: a drapery favorite. Good H 165:6 S '67
Tambour curtains. il House & Gard 131:204-5 Mr '67
Window treatments. Am Home 70:78-9 N '67
Window wizardry. il House & Gard 131:128-39+ Mr '67

CURTIS, C. Michael
Alternatives to apathy. Sat R 50:27-8 S 2 '67
Nation blemished. Sat R 50:63+ Ap 8 '67
Writing non-fiction. Writer 80:22-9 Ja '67

CURTIS, Joseph E.
Cowardly lion. Parks & Rec 2:18+ Ag '67

CURTIS, K. D.
Parakiting! Travel 128:40-1 S '67

CURTIS, Lemuel
Curtis and Dunning, clockmakers. R. N. Hill. il Antiques 91:214-17 F '67

CURTIS, Paul
Kansas quail renaissance. Field & S 72:58-9+ O '67

CURTIS, Robert
Candid kids. il U S Camera 30:50-1 My '67

CURTIS, Thomas B.
Excerpt from address, December 9, 1966. Cong Digest 46:233+ O '67
about
Voices of doubt. Nation 205:548 N 27 '67

CURTIS, Victor
Revelry in Washington. Travel 127:50-1 F '67

CURTIS, William
Kokanee keep things jumping. Outdoor Life 139:25-6+ Mr '67

CURVATURE of the spine. See Spine—Abnormities and deformities

CURVED space. See Relativity (physics)

CURVES
See also
Frequency curves

CUSACK, Isabel Langis
Shell game; story. Sat Eve Post 240:58-61 D 2 '67
What a way to go! story. McCalls 95:104-5 O '67

CUSHING, Richard James, cardinal
Cardinal Cushing TV portrait. America 117: 630 N 25 '67

CUSHIONS
See also
Pillows

CUSHMAN, Jerome
Ex New Orleans librarian blasts board, friends; excerpts from letter. Library J 92: 1403 Ap 1 '67

CUSHMAN, Robert P.
Down the Raccoon River by canoe. Parents Mag 42:64-5+ O '67

CUSIC, Marshall E. Jr. See Mehler, A. H. jt. auth.

CUSTARDS
Custard & its regal cousins. P. Cannon. il Ladies Home J 84:116-17+ My '67
Happy ending: Danish, Spanish, or Greek custard. il Sunset 138:196-7+ Ap '67
So you're learning to cook. il Am Home 70:86 Je '67

CUSTODIAN account. See Trusts and trustees

CUSTOM farming. See Agricultural machinery—Leasing

CUSTOMER relations
Preventive maintenance in client-ad agency relations. M. P. Ryan and R. H. Colley. Harvard Bsns R 45:66-74 S '67
CUSTOMS. See Manners and customs
CUSTOMS (tariff) See Tariff
CUSTOMS bureau. See Customs service—United States
CUSTOMS service

United States
One Washington bureau that turns a profit. Nations Bsns 55:94 O '67
CUSTOMS service and tourists
Camera abroad. R. Arnold. il U S Camera 30: 52-3+ Mr '67
Caveat tourist; new rules for tourist discount in France. Time 90:107-8 D 8 '67
Customs list aids camera shopping. W. Lane. Travel 128:69 N '67
Traveler's $100 misunderstanding. House & Gard 131:27-8 My '67
Well traveled camera; getting past customs. Mod Phot 31:112+ F '67
CUT flowers. See Flowers—Cut flowers
CUT off saw. See Saws
CUTANEOUS communication. See Communications research
CUTLERY
See also
Knives
CUTTING boards
Proper cutting-board care. Good H 165:206 N '67
CUTTING tools
Here's an easy way to make an abrasive cut-off machine. R. Shoberg. il Pop Mech 128: 184-5 N '67
See also
Knives
CUTTINGS, Plant. See Plant propagation
CWALINA, Gustav E. and others
Pharmacy, serving man and medicine. Todays Health 45:54-5+ My '67
CYBERNETICS
Biocommunications: one-way street. B. J. Culliton. Sci N 91:426 My 6 '67
Cybernetic age: an optimist's view. G. T. Seaborg. Sat R 50:21-3 Jl 15 '67
Riddle for tomorrow's world: how to lead a good life; excerpts from address. E. F. Zeigler. Parks & Rec 2:28+ S '67
CYCLADES (islands)
See also
Delos
Thera (island)
CYCLAMATE. See Sugar substitutes
CYCLES, Biological. See Periodicity
CYCLES. Business. See Business cycles
CYCLING
See also
Bicycle racing

Anecdotes, facetiae, satire, etc.
Passion on a bicycle. H. S. Resnik. Atlan 221:104-5 Ja '68

Safety devices and measures
Safety first for the bike brigade. F. E. Hawthorne. il Parents Mag 42:50-1+ Ag '67
CYCLING trips
Cycling; for community service and for fun. S. Lustig. il Parks & Rec 2:23+ Ap '67
Cycling out to sea: from Philadelphia to Outer Banks of North Carolina. B. A. Roth. il Travel 128:45-9 Ag '67
CYCLOHEXIMIDE. See Antibiotics
CYGNUS (constellation) See Constellations
CYLBURN wildflower preserve and garden center, Baltimore, Md.
Cylburn wildflower preserve and garden center. E. Clarke. il Horticulture 45:40-1+ Ap '67
CYMBALS
Status cymbals: Avedis Zildjian co. il Newsweek 71:76-7 Ja 22 '68
CYPERUS papyrus. See Papyrus
CYPHERS. See Ciphers
CYPRESS
See also
Bald cypress
CYPRUS
Clerical delay; settlement between the Turks and Greeks. il Time 90:32+ D 8 '67
Cyprus: no change. B. Cornwall. New Repub 158:10 Ja 13 '68

Greek-Turkish crisis: boon for Russia, threat to U.S? il U S News 63:8 D 4 '67
Greek word for Cyprus: shame. il Newsweek 70:50+ D 18 '67
Grivas trouble. Nat R 19:1364-5 D 12 '67
Isle of deadlock. J. Cameron. il Sat Eve Post 241:58-9+ Ja 13 '68
Out of the past: Cyprus on the brink. il Newsweek 70:37-8 D 4 '67
Peace on an isle of hate? il Sr Schol 91:14-15 D 14 '67
Radically changed situation. il Time 90:37-8 D 15 '67
Shadows of war. il Time 90:22-3 D 1 '67
Still ticking; Paradise lost. il Newsweek 70: 48-9 D 11 '67
That tragic land. Reporter 37:8+ D 28 '67
U.S. joins in efforts to avert war in eastern Mediterranean; statements. December 5, 1967. L. B. Johnson; C. R. Vance. Dept State Bul 57:859-60 D 25 '67
Where war threatens next: the Mediterranean and beyond. il U S News 63:44-6 D 11 '67
Who'll end up ruling Cyprus? T. Sage. Nat R 19:569-71 My 30 '67
See also
United Nations—Armed forces—Forces in Cyprus
United Nations—Cyprus
Water supply—Cyprus
CYR, Don
Chryssa. Sch Arts 66:23-8 Mr '67
(ed) See Krushenick, N. Conversation
(ed) See Segal, G. Conversation with George Segal
CYSTIC fibrosis
Nail test for a child killer. il Life 63:95-6 N 10 '67
Sodium transport: inhibitory factor in sweat of patients with cystic fibrosis. J. A. Mangos and N. R. McSherry. bibliog il Science 158:135-6 O 6 '67
CYSTINE
Increased cystine in leukocytes from individuals homozygous and heterozygous for cystinosis. J. A. Schneider and others. bibliog il Science 157:1321-2 S 15 '67
CYSTINURIA. See Intestines—Diseases
CYTOCHROMES
Antibodies to rabbit cytochrome c arising in rabbits. A. Nisonoff and others. bibliog il Science 155:1273-5 Mr 10 '67
CYTOKININS. See Peptides
CYTOSINE
Transport and phosphorylation as factors in the antitumor action of cytosine arabinoside. D. Kessel and others. bibliog il Science 156:1240-1 Je 2 '67
CZARIST bonds. See Bonds, Government—Russia
CZECH fiction
Letter from Prague. J. Skvorecky. Nation 205:470-3 N 6 '67
CZECH film festival. See Moving picture festivals
CZECH literature
Laughter and endurance; excerpts from Short stories from Czechoslovakia (Nouvelles Tchèques et Slovaques) A. Hoffmeister. il UNESCO Courier 20:24-6 Ap '67
CZECH painting. See Painting, Czech
CZECHOSLOVAKIA
Czechoslovakia: paths in dialogue opening. R. H. Bryant. Christian Cent 84:604-6 My 3 '67
See also
Airlines—Czechoslovakia
Airplane industry and trade—Czechoslovakia
Automobile industry and trade—Czechoslovakia
Censorship—Czechoslovakia
Communism—Czechoslovakia
Communist party (Czechoslovakia)
Industrial management and organization—Czechoslovakia
Jews in Czechoslovakia
Moving picture industry—Czechoslovakia
Moving pictures—Czechoslovakia
Youth—Czechoslovakia

Economic conditions
Rickety Czech new model. C. Sterling. il Reporter 36:22-4 Je 1 '67

Economic policy
Czechoslovakia's half century. V. E. Mares. bibliog f il Cur Hist 52:200-7 Ap '67

History
Czechoslovakia's half century. V. E. Mares. bibliog f il Cur Hist 52:200-7 Ap '67

CZECHOSLOVAKIA—*Continued*

Industries

See also
Industrial management and organization—
Czechoslovakia

Intellectual life

Czech writers. Nation 205:453 N 6 '67
Nettles of Prague. J. Dornberg. Nation 206:50-
2 Ja 8 '68
Purifying Prague. Newsweek 70:51 O 16 '67

Politics and government

Some interesting happenings in Prague. R.
Eder. il N Y Times Mag p32-3+ N 12 '67

Religious institutions and affairs

See also
Catholic church in Czechoslovakia

Social conditions

Unchecked exchange in Czechoslovakia. J. C.
Evans. Christian Cent 84:774-5 Je 14 '67
CZECHOSLOVAKIAN airlines. See Airlines—
Czechoslovakia
CZECHS
See also
Bohemia
CZURA, Pete
Best duck bargain. Outdoor Life 140:62-5 O '67
Big horn of birds. por Field & S 72:104-6+
D '67
Get geared up for camping. Todays Health
45:34-9+ Jl '67
Ice fishing quick and easy. Field & S 72:66-8
Je '67
New checklist for a long wet summer. Esquire
67:94-7 F '67
—and Kowalski, J. M.
Field & stream six-week conditioning pro-
gram for sportsmen. Field & S 72:47-53
Ag '67

D

D. A. Campbell company. See Campbell, D. A,
company
DAVI. See National education association—De-
partment of audio-visual instruction
DCEV (direct-current electronic voltmeters)
See Voltmeters
DDC (direct digital control) See Computers—
Control applications
DDT (insecticide)
Conversion of DDT to DDD by pathogenic and
saprophytic bacteria associated with plants.
B. T. Johnson and others. bibliog il Science
157:560-1 Ag 4 '67
Dechlorination of DDT in frozen blood. D. J.
Ecobichon and P. W. Saschenbrecker. bib-
liog il Science 156:663-5 My 5 '67

Injurious effects

Death from DDT. C. W. Buchheister. Audubon
69:5 Ja '67
Environmental pollution: scientists go to
court. L. J. Carter. il Science 158:1552-6
D 22 '67
Gathering storm over DDT. F. Graham, jr.
New Repub 156:15-17 Je 24 '67
Poisoning with DDT: effect on reproductive
performance of artemia. D. S. Grosch. il
Science 155:592-3 F 3 '67
Toxic substances and ecological cycles. G. M.
Woodwell. Sci Am 216:6+ Je '67
Uncertain defenders. F. Graham, jr. il Audu-
bon 69:28-37 My '67

Physiological effects

DDT: interaction with nerve membrane conductance changes. T. Narahashi and H. G.
Haas. bibliog il Science 157:1438-40 S 22 '67

Residues

Anaerobic biodegradation of DDT to DDD in
soil. W. D. Guenzi and W. E. Beard. bibliog
il Science 156:1116-17 My 26 '67
DDT residues in an East coast estuary: a
case of biological concentration of a persistent insecticide. G. M. Woodwell and
others. bibliog il Science 156:821-4 My 12 '67
DDTV (dry diver transport vehicle) See Submarine boats
DESP. See National education association—
Department of elementary school principals

DMSO. See Methyl sulfoxide
DNA. See Deoxyribonucleic acid
DODGE (Department of defense gravity experi-
ment) See Artificial satellites
DSRV (deep submergence rescue vehicle) See
Submarine boats
DACEY, Norman F.
Don't let probate take your money away.
Ladies Home J 84:70+ Ap '67
about
Appeals court upholds ban on How to avoid
probate! Pub W 192:29 N 6 '67
Defrocking Dacey. Time 90:46 Jl 21 '67
How to avoid probate! decision to be ap-
pealed. Pub W 192:47 Jl 17 '67
Issues in the probate verdict. R. H. Smith.
Pub W 193:51 Ja 8 '68
Law group seeks to enjoin How to avoid pro-
bate. Pub W 191:36 Ap 17 '67
Taking Dacey off the hook. Time 91:29 Ja 12
'68
DACHAU concentration camps. See Concen-
tration camps—Germany
DADDARIO, Emilio Quincy
Congress faces space policies. Bul Atomic Sci
23:11-16 My '67
DADE COUNTY, Fla.
Employee suggestions win cash. il Am City
82:80 Ag '67

Parks and reserves

Progressive park and recreation system embraces 1967 congress host city. il Parks &
Rec 2:27-8 O '67

Recreation

Dade County's lifetime sports program holds
communty and individual interests. il Parks
& Rec 2:46+ O '67
DAEDALUS (periodical)
Daedalus: marking a decade of journeys from
the labyrinth. B. Nelson. il Science 156:770-3
My 12 '67
DAFFODILS. See Narcissus
DAGHESTAN
Mountain men. J. Korengold. il Newsweek 69:
44+ Je 12 '67
DAGUERREOTYPES
Daguerreotypes: silvered mirrors. il Pop Phot
60:98+ My '67
DAHLBERG, Edward
Return to Kansas City. Holiday 41:16+ Je '67
about
Five poets. D. W. Baker. Poetry 109:403-5
Mr '67
Man in the wilderness. K. Boyle. Nation 204:
693-4 My 29 '67
Windmills in the head. A. Kerrigan. Nat R
19:1027 S 19 '67
DAHLIAS
Dahlias. il Home Gard 54:71-2 Ap '67
Hybridizing dahlias. G. Barton. il Horticul-
ture 45:28-30 S '67
It's D-day for dahlias. B. Black. il Pop Gard
18:10-11 Ag '67
It's time to dig dahlias. il Sunset 139:206 N
'67
May's the last call to plant dahlias for Aug-
ust and fall color. il Sunset 138:274 My '67
DAHLQUIST, Eric
Roundy-round corner. See issues of Hot rod
DAHOMEY
Political ocean; cooperative enterprise in Afri-
can fishing village. America 116:825 Je 10 '67
Quest for beauty in Dahomey. J. Maquet. il
Vogue 150:218-27+ D '67
Seasonal coup. Time 90:24 D 29 '67
See also
Cotonou
DAILY, Jay E.
Automation and authority vs. autonomy. por
Library J 92:3606-9 O 15 '67
Many changes, no alteration. bibliog por Li-
brary J 92:3961-3 N 1 '67
DAILY news, New York
Signs of life in New York; afternoon news-
paper. Time 91:60 Ja 19 '68
DAIMLER-Benz, ag. See Automobile industry
and trade—Germany (Federal Republic)
DAIRY barns. See Barns and stables
DAIRY farm management
Dairy comment. D. Braun. Farm J 91:D16 Ag
'67
Low-cost setup for 200 cows. J. R. Borcherd-
ing. il Suc Farm 65:32-3+ Jl '67
Now we're ready for 100 cows. J. R. Bor-
cherding. il Suc Farm 65:48-9 S '67
Outlook. il Farm J 91:D1 Je '67
Who makes the most money dairying? N.
Reeder. il Farm J 91:D6+ Ap '67

DAIRY farm records
  See also
  Dairying—Economic aspects
DAIRY farming. See Dairying
DAIRY farms
  Cream in dairies. il Duns R 89:97-9 Mr '67
  Ideas ready to use. il Farm J 91:D19 O '67
  Two new dairy systems from scratch. J. Albino. il Suc Farm 65:100B Ja '67
  See also
  Dairy farm management
DAIRY industry and trade
  Dairy extra; symposium. See issues of Farm journal
DAIRY machinery
  See also
  Milking machines
DAIRY parlors. See Milking parlors
DAIRY products
  Business report. C. W. Gifford. Farm J 91: D2 Ag '67
               Prices
  See also
  Milk—Prices
DAIRYING
  Dairy extra; symposium. See issues of Farm journal
  Discontent in dairyland. il Newsweek 69:44+ My 8 '67
  News. See issues of Farm journal
  Raising and selling veal. R. Vilstrup and J. Crowley. il Suc Farm 65:46L Mr '67
  What's new. See issues of Successful farming
  See also
  Cows—Feeding
  Dairy farm management
  Dairy farms
            Economic aspects
  Business report. C. W. Gifford. Farm J 91:D2 Ap '67
DAISIES, Shasta. See Shasta daisies
DAKOTA Indians
  Dispatch from Wounded Knee; Pine Ridge reservation, S.D. C. Kentfield. il N Y Times Mag p28-31+ O 15 '67
DALBEY, E. Gordon, jr
  Technicolored Christian. Christian Cent 84: 1158-60 S 13 '67
DALBY, Arthur, and Davies, I, ab I.
  Ribonuclease activity in the developing seeds of normal and opaque-2 maize. bibliog Science 155:1573-5 Mr 24 '67
DALCOURT, Gerard J.
  Lay control of Catholic colleges. America 117:412-14 O 14 '67
DALE, Edwin L. jr
  LBJ's tax dilemma. New Repub 156:8-10 Ap 1 '67
  Three reasons for prosperity. N Y Times Mag p38-9+ N 5 '67
  U.S. economic giant keeps growing. N Y Times Mag p30-1+ Mr 19 '67
  Who gets what from the Kennedy round? New Repub 156:15-16 F 11 '67
DALE'S penthouse restaurant fire. See Fires
DALEY, Amelia T.
  Regional report. Home Gard 54:58 D '67
DALEY, Charlotte
  Drawings by Charlotte Daley. Sch Arts 66:9-12 F '67
DALEY, Richard J.
  King Richard the fourth. il por Time 89:36 Ap 14 '67
  Making book on Mr Daley. E. S. Gilbreth. por Nation 204:395-8 Mr 27 '67
  Once and future king. Newsweek 69:46 Ap 17 '67
  Troubled cities, and their mayors. il por(p39) Newsweek 69:41 Mr 13 '67
DALEY, Robert
  Brave and the beautiful. Vogue 149:114-19+ Je '67
  Race it like it was, baby. Vogue 149:110-11+ Ja 15 '67
  World's greatest tenor. Life 63:74-6+ D 15 '67
DALI, Salvador
  Interview; ed. by A. Fatt. il por Dance Mag 41:54-5 Mr '67
DALL sheep hunting. See Mountain sheep hunting
DALLAPICCOLA, Luigi
  Solo flight; interview,ed. by W. Weaver. pors Opera N 31:13 Mr 11 '67
                about
  New York. Q. Eaton. il Opera N 31:26 Ap 15 '67
  Night flight (Volo di notte) Criticism
    New Yorker 43:124+ Mr 18 '67

DALLAS
  Scene of the crime. il Newsweek 70:31B-32+ D 4 '67
               Gardens
  In Dallas, a burst of bloom. il House B 109: 170-3 Mr '67
               Hospitals
  Death of a President, by W. Manchester. Review
    Reporter 36:37-9 My 18 '67. R. West
  Parkland hospital; case no. 24740; excerpts from The death of a President. W. Manchester. il Look 31:40-6+ F 7 '67
               Music
  Time for decision. J. Ardoin. il Hi Fi 17: MA18 F '67
  See also
  Dallas civic opera company
        Politics and government
  Dallas scores; Goals for Dallas program. il Am City 82:130-1+ N '67
               Recreation
  Dallas benefits from Lifetime sports program. W. Keeling. il Parks & Rec 2:20+ Jl '67
     Religious institutions and affairs
  Paulists and the Dallas affair. J. B. Sheerin. Cath World 205:319-20 Ag '67
  Paulists depart, but tensions linger in Dallas. A. V. Krebs, jr. Commonweal 87:68-9 O 20 '67
               Stores
  Merchant prince of Dallas; S. Marcus. il Bsns W p 114-16+ O 21 '67
DALLAS civic opera company
  Report: Dallas. J. Ardoin. il Opera N 32:30 D 30 '67
  Report: Dallas; revival of Cherubini's Medea. J. Ardoin. il Opera N 32:29 D 16 '67
DALLAS Cowboys (football club) See Football clubs
DALLAS public library
  Discussion in Dallas. T. M. Bogie. il Library J 92:2127-30 Je 1 '67
  Displays; the book as art. il Wilson Lib Bul 42:334-5 N '67
DALLAS symphony orchestra
  Lively arts; who says the best conductors can't be American? interview ed. by R. Hemming. D. Johanos. Sr Schol 90:24 My 5 '67
DALPHIN, Marcia
  Children's library. Horn Bk 43:55 F '67
  Undebatable joy. Horn Bk 43:120+ F '67
DALRYMPLE, Byron W.
  Bad day for crows. Outdoor Life 139:64-5+ Mr '67
  Big news in camp coaches. pors Outdoor Life 140:32-5+ Jl '67
  Birds and bows. por Field & S 72:42-5+ Jl '67
  Ute Lake; New Mexico's newest hotspot. Field & S 72:64-5+ My '67
DALRYMPLE, Willard
  College dropout phenomenon. NEA J 56:11-13 Ap '67
D'ALTILIO, Michael D.
  New Jersey engineer wins the American city award. por Am City 82:111 N '67
DALTON, Kathie
  On the boards. W. Como. por Dance Mag 41: 23 S '67
DALTON schools, New York. See Private schools
DALY, John
  Voice of America; memorandum to John Daly. R. J. Walton. il Nation 205:135-8 Ag 28 '67; Reply with rejoinder. J. Chancellor. 205:258+ S 25 '67
DALY, John W. and Myers, C. W.
  Toxicity of Panamanian poison frogs (dendrobates); some biological and chemical aspects. bibliog Science 156:970-3 My 19 '67
DAMAGES
  How courts decide the value of a husband's life. M. Mayer. il Redbook 129:72-3+ Je '67
  Reaming-out Drano; Mrs Frances Moore awarded $930,000 damages because of misconduct by Drackett company. Time 89:92 My 19 '67
  See also
  Liability (law)
  Negligence
D'AMBOISE, Jacques
  Prologue; the day before the day before the premiere. J. Anderson. il pors Dance Mag 41:35-8 F '67
DAME Fortune and Don Money; drama. See Corson, H. W.

D'AMICO, Victor
Exciting world of art. Parents Mag 42:48-9+
D '67

DAMJANOV, Zvonimir
(tr) See Franic, F. Agreement between the
Holy See and Yugoslavia

DAMMEYER, John
Frustrating warfare of business. il pors Life
62:40-53 My 5 '67

D'AMOUR, O'Neil C.
Image of the teaching religious. America 116:
418 Mr 25 '67

DAMPIER, Louie
Life of Riley, and Dampier. H. L. Masin. il
por Sr Schol 90:20 F 10 '67

DAMPING (mechanics)
See also
Sound waves—Damping

DAMS
Canyon dams: dissents from Arizona sci-
entists. L. J. Carter. Science 157:46 Jl 7 '67
Cave life on the Palouse; salvage archeol-
ogists win a race with builders of Lower
Monumental Dam on the Snake River. G.
H. Grosso. il Natur Hist 76:38-43 F '67
Dam that talks back: Oroville Dam. W. S.
Griswold. il Pop Sci 190:86-8 F '67
Dam the Big Hole, full speed ahead. G. Lay-
cock. il Field & S 72:12-16+ My '67
Dams and the Colorado. J. Ludwigson. il
Sci N 91:167 F 18 '67
Dams and wild rivers: looking beyond the
pork barrel. L. J. Carter. il Science 158:
233-6+ O 13 '67
Day they pulled the plug. R. Starnes. il
Field & S 72:28+ O '67
Don't flood our Grand Canyon; dam builders
vs conservationists. J. Bird. il Sat Eve
Post 240:24-9+ Ag 12 '67
Farewell to Hells Canyon; taming Snake River
by a new dam. J. Skow. il Sat Eve Post
240:76-83 Jl 1 '67
Grand Canyon: dam it or not? proposed
Hualapai (formerly Bridge Canyon) and
Marble Canyon Dams; pro and con discus-
sion. il Sr Schol 90:6-7 F 3 '67
Grand Canyon dams go. Sci N 91:135 F 11
'67
Grand Canyon still threatened; letter. W. C.
Bradley. Science 156:451 Ap 28 '67
High court questions need of dam on Snake
River. Am For 73:38 Jl '67
High Mountain Sheep; dam on Snake River
in Idaho. Nat Parks Mag 41:20 N '67
Hooker Dam. Liv Wildn 31:61 Spr '67
In search of a subsidy machine: or, Why
the Grand Canyon must be dammed; ex-
cerpt from address, March 17, 1967. L. I.
Moss. Bul Atomic Sci 23:25-30 Je '67
Mike Frome; Tellico Dam across the Little
Tennessee River. M. Frome. Am For 73:7+
Mr '67
No dams! Grand Canyon. il Am For 73:8 Mr
'67
Old rock dams on the Potomac River. H. P.
Hobbs, jr. il Nat Parks Mag 41:14-19 Ag '67

Alaska
Rampart dam; administration against con-
struction of the proposed Rampart Dam on
Yukon River. Nat Parks Mag 41:20 Ag '67

Pakistan
Dam at Mangla. il Time 90:113-14 D 1 '67

DANA, Bill
Pop goes the network. il por Newsweek 69:
90+ My 15 '67

DANA, Robert
Five anthologies. Poetry 110:47-51 Ap '67

DANCE, Helen
Mid-month recordings. Sat R 50:46-7 Jl 15 '67

DANCE, Stanley
Granz rides again. Sat R 50:57 Ap 15 '67
Recordings reports: jazz LPs. See issues of
Saturday review

DANCE and state. See Theater and state

DANCE bands. See Bands (music)

DANCE camps
Summer on pointe; Fokine ballet camp. W.
Como. il Dance Mag 41:68-9 F '67

DANCE caravan U.S.A. See Dance institutes
and workshops

DANCE clubs. See Clubs

DANCE companies
Dance theater workshop. Theater 80 St
Marks. J. Maskey. Dance Mag 41:83 Mr
'67

Dance uptown, Minor Latham playhouse. J.
Maskey. Dance Mag 41:81 Mr '67

Dances of and by youth; Alwin Nikolais
dance company. W. Terry. il Sat R 50:36
D 30 '67
Eleo Pomare dance company; 92nd street Y.
M. Marks. Dance Mag 41:74-5 Je '67
Financial record-keeping simplified; business
organization. R. Gorewitz. Dance Mag 41:
90-2 N '67
First chamber dance quartet, Hunter col-
lege playhouse. D. Hering. Dance Mag 41:
36-7 Mr '67
James E. Murphy jr. dance company, Clark
center for the performing arts. J. Maskey.
Dance Mag 41:29 Ag '67
Judson dance theatre; Judson memorial
church. J. Maskey. Dance Mag 41:87 Je '67
Mariano Parra ballet espanol; Village the-
atre. J. Anderson. Dance Mag 41:72+ Je '67
Mariko Sanjo & co, 92nd st Y. J. Anderson.
Dance Mag 41:89 Je '67
Uni trio with Barbara Greer; Marian Sarach
& co. Judson memorial church. J. Ander-
son. Dance Mag 41:80 Mr '67
See also
Ballet companies

DANCE conferences
Connecticut commission on the arts ventures
a seminar. E. Stodelle. il Dance Mag 41:
30-1+ O '67
Three giant steps; Dance magazine reports
on three government funded conferences;
symposium. Dance Mag 41:46-51+ Ag '67

DANCE costume designers. See Costume
designers

DANCE costumes. See Costume, Theatrical

DANCE critics. See Critics

DANCE educators of America, incorporated
Summer teacher sessions. W. Como. il Dance
Mag 41:66-7 O '67

DANCE festivals
Calendar of summer international dance
events. il Dance Mag 41:40-4+ My '67
Cherokee, Choctaw, Shawnee, Osage; Indian
ballerina festival. D. Hering. il Dance Mag
41:54-5+ D '67
Erotic dances in the starlight; presentations
at Caramoor, N.Y. W. Terry. il Sat R 50:
49-50 Jl 22 '67
Four moons; Oklahoma Indian ballerina fes-
tival. W. Terry. il Sat R 50:60-1+ N 18 '67
In the light of a kindred humanity; LA's
international folk dance festival. V. H.
Swisher. il Dance Mag 41:46-9 Mr '67
International ballet evening; Long Island
festival. J. Anderson. Dance Mag 41:76-7+
S '67
Jacob's Pillow dance festival. J. Maskey.
Dance Mag 41:36-7 O '67
José and others; American dance festival.
D. Hering. il Dance Mag 41:33-5+ O '67
Kathryn won the booby prize; Southeastern
regional ballet festival. D. Hering. il Dance
Mag 41:62-9 Jl '67
Learn walk; learn run; 5th annual South-
western regional ballet festival. D. Hering.
il Dance Mag 41:63-5 Je '67
O, brother sun and sister moon; Jacob's Pil-
low dance festival. W. Terry. il Sat R 50:
39-40 Jl 29 '67
Perfection by the Thames; American dance
festival. W. Terry. il Sat R 50:43+ S 9 '67
Rebekah Harkness foundation dance festival
Delacorte theater. M. Marks. Dance Mag
41:37+ O '67
There will be only one of you; 8th annual
Northeast regional ballet festival. D.
Hering. il Dance Mag 41:66-71 Je '67
Turkey on the tennis court; Pacific-Western
regional ballet festival. D. Hering. il Dance
Mag 41:56-63 Ag '67
World of dance; Jacob's Pillow dance
festival's current season. W. Terry. il Sat R
50:41-2 Ag 5 '67
World of dance; seventh program in the
Jacob's Pillow series. W. Terry. Sat R 50:
39 Ag 26 '67

DANCE for three people; ballet. See Ballets—
Criticisms

DANCE halls
Roseland; the eternal prom. R. Kotlowitz.
Harper 235:133-6 N '67

DANCE institutes and workshops
Connecticut commission on the arts ventures
a seminar. E. Stodelle. il Dance Mag 41:
30-1+ O '67
Dances of and by youth; Dance theater
workshop. W. Terry. il Sat R 50:36-7 D
30 '67
Entertainment: a dividend; Harkness, Jacob's
Pillow and Connecticut college summer
workshops. W. Terry. il Sat R 50:62-3 S
16 '67

DANCE institutes and workshops—*Continued*
Louisiana experiment; Invitational repertory workshop. E. H. Haslam. Dance Mag 41: 32+ O '67
1967 summer teacher sessions; Dance caravan U.S.A. il Dance Mag 41:72-3 N '67
Saturdays at nine; Dance theater workshop. J. Maskey. Dance Mag 42:75+ Ja '68
See also
Dancers' workshop of San Francisco

DANCE magazine
Dance magazine's annual awards 1966. il Dance Mag 41:38-43+ Mr '67
Distinguished, dedicated gathering; Dance magazine's annual awards party. il Dance Mag 41:45-9+ My '67

DANCE masters of America
Summer teacher sessions. W. Como. il Dance Mag 41:68-9 O '67

DANCE notation
Choreologist at the Met; Benesh system. R. Holden. il Dance Mag 41:39-41 Ag; 24-6+ S '67
Enquiry into movement notation, by G. F. Curl. Review
    Dance Mag 41:76-9 O '67. R. Holden
    Reply. A. Hutchinson. 41:20+ D '67

DANCE of death; drama. See Strindberg, A.

DANCE production
Showing off The show-offs; how three bright young dancers put together a new nightclub act. V. H. Swisher. il Dance Mag 41:24-5+ My '67
Who is a ballet master? N. Beriozoff. J. Anderson. il Dance Mag 42:54-7+ Ja '68

DANCE records. See Phonograph records— Dance music

DANCE schools.
Dance teacher in the community. D. R. Sellars. Dance Mag 41:74-6 D '67; 42:84-5 Ja '68
Face to face with a girl on her toes. L. Rudnick. Seventeen 26:157 N '67
Meet Robin Howard; British modern dance movement. J. Percival. Dance Mag 41:22-3+ Mr '67
See also
North Carolina school of the arts, Winston -Salem

Finance
Financial record-keeping simplified. R. Gorewitz. il Dance Mag 41:90-3 O '67

DANCE studios
Financial record-keeping simplified; business organization. R. Gorewitz. Dance Mag 41: 90-2 N '67

DANCE teachers
Dance teacher in the community. D. R. Sellars. Dance Mag 41:68-9 N; 74-6 D '67
1967 summer teacher sessions. il Dance Mag 41:72-7 N '67
See also
Cecchetti council of America
Dance educators of America, incorporated
Dance masters of America
National council of dance teacher organizations

Education
Ways to learn; Dance teachers' club of Boston inc. il Dance Mag 41:52-3 Ag '67

DANCE theater workshop. See Dance institutes and workshops

DANCE workshops. See Dance institutes and workshops

DANCERS
Alien art. M. Amaya. il Opera N 32:26-9 Ja 20 '68
Blue belles. il Newsweek 69:101 Je 12 '67
Brief biographies. S. Goodman. See issues of Dance magazine
Financial record-keeping simplified. R. Gorewitz. il Dance Mag 41:78-9 S; 90-3 O; 90-2 N '67; 42:88-90 Ja '68
For 2¢ a kick; Rockettes' strike. il Time 90: 80 S 29 '67
Go-go girls; going thing in nightspots. il Newsweek 69:99-100 Mr 13 '67
Hoof and mouth disease: food, diet and dancers. A. Fatt. il Dance Mag 41:39 Je; 24-5 Jl; 23 Ag; 30+ S '67
Illustrious dance alumni of P.A. W. Terry. il Sat R 50:32-3 Jl 1 '67
In the news; photographs. See issues of Dance magazine
In their infinite variety; personalities in America's regional ballet companies. D. Hering. il Dance Mag 41:68-71 S '67
Line at Radio City music hall; Rockettes. G. Jonas. il N Y Times Mag p 114+ N 12 '67; Reply. A. E. Kurland. p39 D 10 '67

Moon maidens; five part Indian ballerinas. il Newsweek 70:101-2 N 6 '67
New stars. W. Terry. il Sat R 50:24+ Je 3 '67
On the gypsy circuit. W. Como. See issues of Dance magazine
Open letter: jobs in Europe, anyone? A. Hutchinson. Dance Mag 41:18-20 Jl '67
Presstime news. See issues of Dance magazine
Tax man cometh; dancers' income tax. R. Gorewitz. il Dance Mag 41:26-7 Ag '67
World of dance; Harkness ballet dancers. W. Terry. il Sat R 50:46-7 D 9 '67
See also
Negro dancers
also names of dancers, e.g. A. Alonso

Salaries
Tax man cometh; dancers' income tax. R. Gorewitz. il Dance Mag 41:26-7 Ag '67

DANCERS' workshop of San Francisco
Dancers' workshop of San Francisco in Parades and changes, Hunter college. D. Hering. il Dance Mag 41:36-7+ Je '67

DANCHIN, R. V.
Chromium and nickel in the fig tree shale from South Africa. bibliog Science 158:261-2 O 13 '67

DANCING
Dance; with a gravure portfolio of photographs by H. Migdoll. W. Sorell. Horizon 9:96-105 Sum '67
Erick Hawkins addresses a new-to-dance audience. E. Hawkins. il Dance Mag 41:40- 4 Je '67
Katherine Litz; interview. ed. by O. Maynard. K. Litz. il Dance Mag 41:56-60+ F '67
On the move; polemic on dancing. K. King. il Dance Mag 41:56-8 Je '67
Orange grove gavotte; California scene. W. Terry. il Sat R 50:47-8+ S 23 '67
Out of the rain; intersection between modern dance and ballet by Paul Taylor's dance company. il Time 91:55 Ja 5 '68
Presstime news. See issues of Dance magazine
Reviews. See issues of Dance magazine
UCLA's committee on fine arts productions brings performances to school and community; dance attractions. V. H. Swisher. il Dance Mag 41:33-5 Je '67
World of dance. W. Terry. See issues of Saturday review
World of dance; J. Clouser's venture at the Y. W. Terry. il Sat R 50:44-5 Je 24 '67
See also
Ballet
Choreography
Dance notation
Folk dancing
Moving pictures—Dancing
Television broadcasting—Dancing

Aesthetics
See Dancing—Philosophy

Bibliography
Dancer's bookshelf (cont) Dance Mag 41:45+ Ap '67
Dancer's bookshelf. J. Anderson. il Dance Mag 41:48-53 S; 18+ N; 37+ D '67

History
Lillian Moore: a joyous searching; American theatrical dance. S. J. Cohen. il Dance Mag 41:34-7 S '67
This is the dance that was; technique of W. Burdick. M. Marks. il Dance Mag 41: 44-9 Jl '67

Philosophy
Dance has many faces; excerpts. Dance Mag 41:74-5 S '67
John Martin at school. E. Rothschild. il Dance Mag 42:38-40 Ja '68
Who am I? why do I dance? F. Jackson. il Dance Mag 41:54-7+ S '67

Production and direction
See Dance production

Study and teaching
Awareness of dignity; new uses and meanings of dance education. il Dance Mag 41:38-41 N '67
Both art and education; second Developmental conference on dance. S. J. Cohen. Dance Mag 41:48-9 Ag '67
Boys like to dance. K. V. Powell. il Dance Mag 41:73 Mr '67

DANCING—Study and teaching—*Continued*
College or career for dancers? Adelphi's answer. E. Stodelle. il Dance Mag 41:60-3 Mr '67
Dance in our schools: how long before the issue is faced? B. King. il Dance Mag 41:62-6+ D '67
Dance vacation: experiences in Hawaii, the Philippines and Japan. L. Mattlage. il Dance Mag 41:27-8+ Jl '67
How to win friends and influence dancers; teacher brings American modern dance to three near eastern nations. P. Nirenska. il Dance Mag 41:28-9+ Je '67
Is it just for jobs? Dance project of M.F.Y. R. A. Rodgers. il Dance Mag 41:26-8 Ap '67
Making cultural exchange a real exchange; teaching modern dance in Asia. il Dance Mag 41:21-3 O '67
Mrs Potts and her dancing tots: social-dancing classes in Wyoming, Ohio. B. Rollin. il Look 31:105-7 My 16 '67
Paul Taylor sends Decatur; Harper theatre dance festival, Illinois. A. Barzel. il Dance Mag 42:42-3 Ja '68
Project Rocket; report of Developmental conference on dance S. J. Cohen. il Dance Mag 41:39-41+ F '67
Question and answer; a son's interest in dancing. Y. Yourlo and E. Yourlo. Dance Mag 41:30-1 Ap '67
Souvenir de ton pére; A. Bournonville's parental advice to his daughter. A. Bournonville. il Dance Mag 41:50-4 My '67
This is the dance that was; technique of W. Burdick. M. Marks. il Dance Mag 41:44-9 Jl '67
Trial by testing; second Conference on dance education and summer Institute for advanced study in dance education. F. W. Hatch. Dance Mag 41:49-50 Ag '67
Who am I? why do I dance? F. Jackson. il Dance Mag 41:54-7+ S '67
See also
Dance schools
Dance studios

Taiwan

A! and I spend a year in Taiwan. il Dance Mag 41:47+ N '67

DANCING, Afghan
Theatrical nights with the Afghans. G. Wright. Sat R 51:91-2 Ja 13 '68

DANCING, Asian
Epics in the art of south Asia. B. N. Goswamy. il UNECO Courier 20:18-29+ D '67

DANCING, Chinese
On a roof in Hong Kong. E. Worth. il Dance Mag 41:30-2 Je '67

DANCING, Indian (East Indian)
Bhaskar & co: dances of India; Village theatre. J. Anderson. Dance Mag 41:30 Jl '67
Indian rasa for U.S. students. J. Anderson. il Dance Mag 41:28-30 F '67
Kathakali and the dance-drama of India; Ramayana and the Mahabharata. C. K. Nair. il UNESCO Courier 20:36-42 D '67
Visit to India. R. Renouf. il Dance Mag 42:48-51 Ja '68

DANCING, Japanese
Patterns in pastel; Odori festival at the Almanson theater, Los Angeles. W. Terry. Sat R 50:38 Ag 26 '67

DANCING, Mexican
See also
Ballet folklorico of Mexico

DANCING, Religious. See Dancing in religion, folklore, etc.

DANCING, Spanish
Holiday bounty. W. Terry. il Sat R 51:36+ Ja 6 '68
Lucero Tena and ensemble; Henry Miller's theatre. D. Hering. Dance Mag 41:30 D '67
Mariano Parra ballet espanol; Village theatre. J. Anderson. Dance Mag 41:72+ Je '67
On the boards. W. Como. il Dance Mag 41:17 Ag '67
Teresita La Tana & Spanish dance co; 92nd street Y. M. Marks. Dance Mag 41:70 Jl '67
See also
Molina, J.

DANCING, Yugoslav
Lado: Yugoslav national dance and folk ensemble; New York city center. D. Hering. Dance Mag 41:30+ N '67

DANCING clubs. See Clubs

DANCING in moving pictures. See Moving pictures—Dancing

DANCING in religion, folklore, etc.
Song of songs; Judson memorial church. M. Marks. Dance Mag 41:88-9 Je '67
See also
Indians of North America—Dances

DANCING in television See Television broadcasting—Dancing

DANE, L. Achilles
Appliance insurance: the best policy. House B 109:193 O '67

DANFORTH, Herman L.
Refuse trains. better, faster, safer. Am City 82:102-4 N '67

DANFORTH, Wendy
Ghosts of Aberfan. McCalls 95:98-103+ N '67

D'ANGELO, Lou
Visit from La Befana. Sat R 50:8+ D 16 '67

DANGER for Santa Claus; story. See Lenz, S.

DANGERFIELD, George
Gents of the disestablishment. Nation 204:437-8 Ap 3 '67

DANGEROUS Archipelago. See Tuamotu Islands

DANIEL, A. Mercer
Quotes from John Brown; address, October 16, 1966. Negro Hist Bul 30:6-7 My '67

DANIEL, Annette
We won the rock fight. Home Gard 54:62-3 Mr '67

DANIEL, James
Appliance no home should be without. Read Digest 90:141-4 Je '67
At last: one Bible for all Christians. Read Digest 90:112-16 My '67
How to save money on milk. Read Digest 90:79-82 Mr '67
Martin Luther: a magnet for all Christians. Read Digest 92:181-2+ Ja '68

DANIEL, Joseph C. Jr. See Krishnan, R. S. jt. auth.

DANIEL, Margaret (Truman)
Margaret Truman's new life. G. Shalit. il pors Look 31:26-8 Ap 18 '67

DANIEL, Oliver
Contents of Kontarsky. Sat R 50:47+ D 30 '67
Denmark, post Nielsen. Sat R 50:52 D 16 '67
From the banks of the Vlatava Sat R 50:76-7 F 25 '67
New sound of music. Sat R 50:64-5 O 28 '67
On discovering Szymanowski. Sat R 50:54-5 Je 24 '67
Semblance of a resemblance. Sat R 50:113 O 14 '67
Six by Chávez. Sat R 50:89-90 Ag 26 '67

DANIELEVITCH, Vladimir
(tr) See Kudriavtzeff, I. Ivan and the three bears

DANIELIAN, N. R.
Plan to stop the gold drain. Read Digest 91:154-8 D '67

DANIELS, George
Canoe built from siding. Pop Sci 191:149-53+ N '67
Facts about all kinds of faucets. Pop Sci 191:141-6 D '67
New know-how you need for aluminum wiring. Pop Sci 191:159-61 S '67
This dinghy's a featherweight. Pop Sci 191:142-5+ Ag '67
—and Weaver, Loyd
Home-plumbing know-how. Pop Sci 190:169-74 Ap; 169-73 My; 131-6 Je; 191:133-8 Jl; 113-17 Ag '67
—See Weaver, L. jt. auth.

DANIELS, George H.
Pure-science ideal and democratic culture. bibliog Science 156:1699-705 Je 30 '67
Scientific profession in early nineteenth-century America; excerpt from American science in the age of Jackson. bibliog Sch & Soc 95:523-36 D 23 '67

DANIELS, Jonathan
Speaking out. por Sat Eve Post 240:8+ F 25 '67

DANINOS, Pierre
Guide to the U.S.A. for Frenchmen only. Read Digest 91:25-6+ O '67

DANISH cookery. See Cookery, Danish

DANISH music. See Music, Danish

DANISH pastry. See Pastry

DANJON, André
Great French astronomer. J. Kovalevsky. il por Sky & Tel 33:347-9 Je '67

DANKWORTH, Margaret A.
Primer congreso mundial de zoological. por Parks & Rec 2:26+ Jl '67

DANN, George H.
Automation improves customer service. Am City 82:122-3+ Je '67

DANNHAUSER, Werner J.
Of geese and men. Commentary 43:89-93 F
'67
Studying society. Commentary 43:101-4 Ap
'67
DANNON milk products, incorporated
Dannon fattens up on nothing but yogurt.
il Bsns W p82+ S 9 '67
DANSES concertantes; ballet. See Ballets—
Criticisms
DANSTEDT, Rudolph T.
Excerpt from statement, July 1966. Cong Di-
gest 46:30 Ja '67
DANTE Alighieri
Dante discovers America. P. A. Cuadra. il
Américas 19:32-9 F '67
DANTON, Georges Jacques
Danton, by R. Christophe. Review
Newsweek por 70:92 S 11 '67. S. Maloff
DANTON, J. Periam
Test of research. Wilson Lib Bul 41:914-15
My '67
D'ANTONIO, William V.
Pills, coils and abortion. Commonweal 86:
193-4 My 5 '67
DANZER, Emmerich
Crystal and steel on the ice. B. Ottum. il
Sports Illus 26:24-7 Mr 13 '67
DANZIGER, Harris
Body and song. Opera N 32:8-11 Ja 13 '68
DAPHNE in cottage D; drama. See Levi, S.
DARACK, Arthur
American national opera company. Hi Fi 17:
MA20-1 D '67
Life and death of a meteor. Sat R 50:32-3
S 9 '67
May festival: ovations and paid bills. Hi Fi
17:MA21+ Ag '67
On the road with the Met national company.
Hi Fi 17:MA18+ Ja '67
Passion for all things Czech. Sat R 50:57 N
25 '67
DARBY, James M.
Reflections on the Dayton situation. America
116:650-2 Ap 29 '67
DARD Hunter paper museum, Appleton, Wis.
Dard Hunter paper museum. Am Artist 31:
68-9 O '67
DARGAN, Michael J.
747 economies seen sacrificed to frills. Avia-
tion W 87:31 O 2 '67
DARIEN, Conn.

Education

Skilled use of pop-up roofs gives good scale
and visual-aids projection space for a K-6
school; Ox Ridge elementary school. il Arch
Rec 141:182-3 Mr '67
DARIO, Rubén
Bust of Nicaraguan poet dedicated. G. Meek.
il Américas 19:47 Mr '67
1967: Rubén Darío year. G. de Zéndegui. por
Américas 19:inside cover Ja '67
Poet of the New World. E. Z. Alverez. il pors
Américas 19:10-18 F '67
Ruben Dario and the resurrection of Hispa-
no-American poetry. E. Rodriguez-Mone-
gal. por UNESCO Courier 20:24-6 O '67
DARK, Alvin Ralph
Charlie O. Finley follies. B. Musburger. il
Sports Illus 27:50-2 S 4 '67
Dark's outlook is young and bright. W. Leg-
gett. il por Sports Illus 26:50-2+ Mr 13 '67
Finley's follies. il por Newsweek 70:68-9 S 4
'67
DARK, Harris Edward
Your youngster and the motorcycle. Todays
Health 45:20-4 My '67
DARK glasses. See Sun glasses
DARKROOM equipment. See Photography—Ap-
paratus and supplies
DARKROOMS. See Photography—Studios and
darkrooms
DARLING, Lu Ann W.
From mop to typewriter. NEA J 56:28-9 O
'67
DARLING, Richard L.
Authors vs critics: children's books in the
1870's; excerpt from The rise of children's
book reviewing in America, 1865-1881. Pub
W 192:25-7 O 16 '67
DARLINGTON Southern 500. See Automobile
racing
DARLINGTONIA. See Pitcher plants
DARRÉ, Jeanne Marie
Music to my ears; Carnegie Hall recital. I.
Kolodin. Sat R 50:58 N 18 '67
DARRELL, Robert Donaldson
Sonic showcase. See issues of High fidelity
incorporating Musical America
Tape deck. See issues of High fidelity in-
corpating Musical America

DARRICARRÈRE, Roger
Decorative glass of Roger Darricarrere; with
biographical sketch. J. Lovoos. il por Am
Artist 31:48-53+ My '67
DARROW, Charles B.
It's orchids for Monopoly's inventor. il por
Bsns W p 182 Mr 25 '67
DARROW, George M.
Strawberries. Horticulture 45:16-17+ Jl '67
DARROW, Judson S.
How to spot a good used gun. Pop Mech 128:
106-9 Ag '67
DARROW, Richard W.
Super protection; address, November 15,
1967. Vital Speeches 34:171-4 Ja 1 '68
DART, Francis E. and Pradhan, P. L.
Cross-cultural teaching of science. bibliog
Science 155:649-56 F 10 '67
DART, Justin Whitlock
Life in a banana peel factory. por Duns R
89:50-1+ Ap '67
DART, Laren
I, surveyor; poem. Sky & Tel 33:161 Mr '67
DART, Richard Pousette-. See Pousette-Dart,
R.
DARTMOUTH college, Hanover, N.H.

Hopkins center

Diddlidong at Dartmouth. il Time 90:38 Jl
28 '67
Henze at Hanover: the creative experience.
B. Jacobson. il Hi Fi 17:MA18-19 O '67
DARVALL, Denise Ann
Gift of a heart. il por Life 63:24-7 D 15 '67
DARWIN, Charles Robert
Darwin sidelight: the shape of the young
man's nose. S. E. Hyman. Atlan 220:96-
100+ N '67
Question: Darwinism revisited; letter with
reply. N. Macbeth; E. S. Deevey, jr. Yale
R 56:616-40 Je '67
DARWINISM. See Evolution
DAS, Deb K.
India: out of the straitjacket. Nat R 19:290-1
Mr 21 '67
DASH, Samuel
Excerpt from address, April 22, 1966. Cong
Digest 46:212+ Ag '67
DASHBOARD gages. See Gages
DASSEN ISLAND
Two hours on an African island. E. A. Bauer.
il Audubon 69:64-7 S '67
DATA display systems. See Information display
systems
DATA processing. See Punched card systems
DATA processing, Electronic. See Electronic
data processing
DATA-processing equipment. See Computers
DATA processing workers. See Computer work-
ers
DATA storage and retrieval systems. See In-
formation storage and retrieval systems
DATA transmission systems
    See also
Telephone—Data transmission systems
DATE with Washington; drama. See Hark,
M. and McQueen, N. jt. auths.
DATES (fruit)
Date festival soon in Indio. il Sunset 138:42
F '67
DATING
Can you ever really trust a boy? questions
and answers. A. Wood. Seventeen 26:122+
Je '67
Dating bars. il Time 89:47 F 17 '67
How to move a boy to action; questions and
answers. A. Wood. Seventeen 26:168+ N
'67
In my opinion. J. Brentlinger. Seventeen 26:
198 O '67
In my opinion; going steady rates another
look. B. Bowling. Seventeen 26:450 Ag '67
Made-to-order matches; computer dating. M.
Durant. il Mlle 64:114-15+ F '67
Man talk: come to dinner. D. Newman and R.
Benton. Mlle 66:70 N '67
Man talk; imitation of life: college love life
and work life simultaneously. D. Newman
and R. Benton. Mlle 65:134 Ag '67
Man talk; the put-down. D. Newman and R.
Benton. Mlle 65:96+ O '67
New rules for the single game; helping singles
meet each other. il Life 63:60-6 Ag 18 '67
Post office box; electronic dating services.
N. White. New Repub 157:21 Ag 19 '67
Program for a prom dropout; questions and
answers. A. Wood. Seventeen 26:124+ D
'67
Talking it over with Gay Head; questions and
answers. Gay Head. See issues of Senior
scholastic

DATING—*Continued*
Too much sex too soon? dating in adolescence. B. Spock. Redbook 130:26+ Ja '68
What to do till the next boy comes along; questions and answers. A. Wood. Seventeen 26:174+ Ap '67
See also
Automobiles—Social aspects

Anecdotes, facetiae, satire, etc.
Affair of the heart; eleven-year-old Marcie. J. Grayson. il Good H 164:33-4+ Ap '67
DATSUN (automobile) See Automobiles, Foreign
DAUGHERTY, Duffy
Win one for aunt Mary Margaret! G. Holland. il pors Sat Eve Post 240:84-7 N 4 '67
DAUGHERTY, Hugh Duffy. See Daugherty, D.
DAUGHERTY, John, and Daugherty, Molly
Fooling with light; quiz. Sci Digest 61:93-6 F '67
Quiz. See issues of Science digest
DAUGHERTY, Molly. See Daugherty, J. jt. auth.
DAUGHTER of the regiment; opera. See Donizetti. G.
DAUGHTERS
Harem in the house; condensation. G. Porter. il Read Digest 91:245-51+ D '67
Not a case history, not a statistic: our daughter. J. March. il McCalls 94:76-7+ Ag '67
See also
Fathers
DAUGHTERS and mothers. See Parent-child relationship
DAUGHTERS and parents. See Parent-child relationship
DAVENEL, George
Can you predict your child's future? Parents Mag 42:33-5+ Ag '67
DAVENPORT, Arthur
New fish for the Northeast. Field & S 71: 38-9+ Ap '67
DAVENPORT, Edgar Loomis
Favorite pioneer recording artists. J. Walsh. por Hobbies 72:35-6+ Ag; 37-9 S; '67; Correction. 72:36+ D '67
DAVENPORT, Guy
Do you have a poem book. .? Nat R 19:858-9 Ag 8 '67
Resurrection in Cookham churchyard; poem. Poetry 110:321-7 Ag '67
Romantic in an unromantic age. Nat R 19: 1389+ D 12 '67
DAVENPORT, John, 1904-
Radical economics of Milton Friedman. Fortune 75:130-2+ Je 1 '67
Report from Grenoble. Fortune 75:69-70+ Mr '67
DAVENPORT, Marcia
Divine autocrat. Opera N 31:6-13 Mr 25 '67
Soaring of a great spirit. Opera N 32:24-5 Ja 6 '68
about
Passion for all things Czech. A. Darack. Sat R 50:57 N 25 '67
DAVENPORT, Iowa
Mini-megalopolis rises along the Mississippi; thriving Quad-cities of Iowa and Illinois. il Bsns W p 168-70 F 25 '67
DAVENPORT house. See Savannah, Ga.—Historic houses, etc.
DAVES, Joan
Frankfurt fair, 1967: books, politics & demonstrations. Pub W 192:19-22 N 20 '67
DAVEY, K. G. and Breckenridge, W. R.
Neurosecretory cells in a cestode, hymenolepis diminuta. bibliog Science 158:931-2 N 17 '67
DAVID, D. W.
Night train to Chittagong. Read Digest 91: 95-9 O '67
DAVID, E. E. Jr, and Truxal, J. G.
Man-made world, a new course for high schools. Science 156:914-20 My 19 '67
DAVID, Jacques Louis
David: the Napoleon of French painting; excerpts from Lives of the painters. J. Canaday. il por Horizon 9:48-59 Sum '67
J. L. David's portrait of the Marquise de Pastoret. J. Maxon. il Art N 66:44-6 N '67
DAVID, Lester
New safe cigarette filter. Good H 165:92-3+ N '67
What a minister really does. Good H 164: 60-1+ Ja '67
DAVID, Sherrie May
Weaving with a straw loom. Sch Arts 67:4-5 D '67
DAVID Clark company. See Clark, David, company

DAVIDS, Richard C.
Coming: community colleges for everyone? Farm J 91:32-3+ My '67
In praise of pigs. Read Digest 91:223-4+ D '67
DAVIDSON, Ben
Mustache to the attack! il pors Life 64:48A-49+ Ja 12 '68
DAVIDSON, Bill
Coming soon on TV. Sat Eve Post 240:30-3 O 7 '67
Hell, no, we won't go! Sat Eve Post 241:21-6 Ja 27 '68
Hidden evils of LSD. Sat Eve Post 240: 19-23 Ag 12 '67
I'm nuts and I know it. Sat Eve Post 240: 66-72+ Je 17 '67
It was that damned book. Sat Eve Post 240: 81-9 Ap 8 '67
Jackie Gleason: anything I can't lick appeals to me. Sat Eve Post 240:30-7 F 11 '67
Mafia: how it bleeds New England. Sat Eve Post 240:27-31 N 18 '67
Mafia: shadow of evil on an island in the sun. Sat Eve Post 240:27-37 F 25 '67
Professorial policeman. Holiday 41:13-17+ Mr '67
DAVIDSON, Bruce
Bruce Davidson: my Leica, the movie camera. H. V. Fondiller. il pors Pop Phot 60: 130-3+ My '67
DAVIDSON, Gerald T. and Anderson A. D.
Venus: volcanic eruptions may cause atmospheric obscuration. bibliog Science 156:1729-30; 158:396 Je 30, O 20 '67
DAVIDSON, Gustav
Celebration of angels; adapted from A dictionary of angels. Ladies Home J 84:60-1+ D '67
DAVIDSON, Homer L.
Pocket CB meter. Pop Mech 127:182-3+ Mr '67
DAVIDSON, J. A.
Theological ferment in Canada? Christian Cent 84:900-2 Jl 12 '67
DAVIDSON, Jesse
Go to the races. W. Johnson. il pors Sports Illus 27:102-4+ D 4 '67
DAVIDSON, Julian M. See Bloch, G. J. jt. auth.
DAVIDSON, Marshall B.
Antiques book preview. Antiques 92:341-7 S '67
DAVIDSON, Muriel
Gary Crosby, a man's victory over alcoholism. Good H 165:92-3+ S '67
What eighteen smart women think of Ronald Reagan. Good H 166:78-9+ Ja '68
DAVIDSON, Robert M.
Letter to Zeke; a commentary on Ezekiel. Cath World 206:153-4 Ja '68
DAVIDSON, Ronald G. and Cortner, J. A.
Mitochondrial malate dehydrogenase: a new genetic polymorphism in man. bibliog Science 157:1569-71 S 29 '67
DAVIDSON, Ruth
In the museums. See issues of Antiques
DAVIDSON, William R. See Doody, A. F. jt. auth.
DAVIES, Gerald R.
Postmark: Pall Mall. Pub W 191:23-4 My 15 '67
DAVIES, Iolo ab I. See Dalby, A. jt. auth.
DAVIES, Lois M. and others
Collagen synthesis by cells synchronously replicating DNA. bibliog Science 159:91-3 Ja 5 '68
DAVIES, Nigel
Justin looks at Twiggy. Mlle 65:76 Jl '67
about
Reporter at large: Twiggy in New York. T. Whiteside. New Yorker 43:64-6+ N 4 '67
DAVIES, Peter Maxwell
Britain's avant-garde. P. L. Miller. Am Rec G 33:623 Ap '67
DAVIS, Bertram H.
Bertram H. Davis, general secretary, AAUP. por Sch & Soc 95:343 O 14 '67
DAVIS, Charles
Father Davis and the servant church. J. B. Sheerin. Cath World 204:324-5 Mr '67
about
Are you a Catholic? F. Sontag. America 117: 502-5 N 4 '67
Book reviews. A. Dulles. America 117:568+ N 11 '67
Ex-priests on the attack. il por Time 90:70+ O 27 '67

DAVIS, Charles—about—*Continued*
Letter from London. R. Williams. Nation 205:51 Jl 17 '67
Loss to us all. R. M. Brown. Commonweal 86:92-4 Ap 7 '67
McCabe affair; with editorial comment. J. M. Cameron. Commonweal 85:653-5 Mr 10 '67
No time to leave. J. G. Lawler. Commonweal 86:87-92 Ap 7 '67; Discussion. 86:221+ My 12 '67
Quiet Catholic question. E. C. Kennedy. America 116:147-8 Ja 28 '67
Story of Charles Davis. S. J. Adamo. America 116:777-80 My 27 '67
Wounded priest, wounded church; discussion. America 116:132-3, 296 Ja 28, Mr 4 '67

DAVIS, Chester
How to build a provincial-style desk. Pop Sci 191:182-5+ O '67

DAVIS, Christopher
Call of the coast. Holiday 42:56-9+ O '67
Memorial day. Holiday 41:60-1+ My '67

DAVIS, Clarence A.
Excerpt from statement before Subcommittee on constitutional amendments, July 25, 1967. Cong Digest 46:283+ N '67

DAVIS, Colin
Labor of love; interview. ed. by J. W. Freeman. por Opera N 31:26 F 11 '67

about
Fire in the belly. por Time 89:78 Ja 27 '67
Inflamed by music. por Newsweek 69:98 F 6 '67
Recordings. M. Mayer. Esquire 67:74+ My '67
Return of Peter Grimes. I. Kolodin. Sat R 50:57 F 4 '67

DAVIS, Dave
Alley fighter. Newsweek 70:92 D 18 '67

DAVIS, David
Other culture. B. Farrell. il Life 62:88+ F 17 '67

DAVIS, Dorothy Crane
Predicting tomorrow's children. Todays Health 46:32-7 Ja '68

DAVIS, Douglas M.
Opinion: a defense of fad. por Mlle 65:50+ O '67

DAVIS, E. Dexter
Safety is the watchword. Pop Gard 18:82-3 My '67

DAVIS, Ed
How Ed Davis retired. S. A. Parvin. il Hobbies 72:110 Mr '67

DAVIS, Foster
Darkness on the Delta. Reporter 37:35-7 S 21 '67

DAVIS, Hazel
Profile of the American public school teacher, 1966. NEA J 56:12-15 My '67

DAVIS, Henry B.
Coherer. Pop Electr 26:47-9 My '67

DAVIS, Jack
Redwoods: old clichés and new confusions. Am For 73:32-3+ Ag '67

DAVIS, Jefferson
Jeff Davis: the man behind the image. B. Catton. il por Am Heritage 18:56-7+ Je '67

DAVIS, Jerome
Young man on the go. il pors Ebony 22:56-8+ S '67

DAVIS, John D. and others
Food intake controlled by a blood factor. bibliog Science 156:1247-8 Je 2 '67

DAVIS, John E.
What should an American citizen be; address, January 3, 1967. Vital Speeches 33:238-40 F 1 '67

DAVIS, John Warren
Samuel Frances, revolutionary, patriot and citizen-extraordinary; excerpt from address, August 16, 1966. Negro Hist Bul 30:11 N '67

DAVIS, Joseph A. See Eisner, T. jt. auth.

DAVIS, Kay
Meet the Thompsons of rural route surprise. Farm J 91:42-3 Jl '67
(ed) See Golden, L. Golden is our valley

DAVIS, Kingsley
Population policy: will current programs succeed? excerpts from address, March 14, 1967. bibliog Science 158:730-9 N 10 '67

DAVIS, Lou
How to start a flying club. Flying 80:48-9 Ap '67

DAVIS, Malcolm McTear
Hellenic highlights. Travel 128:24-30+ Ag '67

DAVIS, Melton S.
New heartbreak in Ingrid Bergman's life. Good H 164:54-7+ Ja '67

DAVIS, Millard C.
Autumn; poem. Liv Wildn 30:33 Aut '66
Influence of Emerson, Thoreau, and Whitman on the early American naturalists John Muir and John Burroughs. bibliog Liv Wildn 30:18-23 Wint '66

DAVIS, Ossie
English language is my enemy! Negro Hist Bul 30:18 Ap '67

DAVIS, Paul
Kentucky Derby; paintings. Sports Illus 26:36-40 My 8 '67

DAVIS, Paul W.
Treasure house; poem. Sky & Tel 33:82 F '67

DAVIS, Peggy
Out Out islands. Yachting 122:44-5+ N '67

DAVIS, Peter G.
At the Met: new Elektra and old friends. Hi Fi 17:MA9+ Ja '67
Bolshoi: thinking big. Hi Fi 17:MA18-19+ N '67
Burning fiery furnace. Hi Fi 17:MA13 S '67
Notes from our correspondents. See issues of High fidelity incorporating Musical America
Record producers. Hi Fi 18:38-43 Ja '68
Repeat performance. See issues of High fidelity incorporating Musical America
Wunderlich's Lieder, an artistry almost fully in flower. Hi Fi 17:83-4 Ja '67

DAVIS, Richard Harding
Around the world with swash and buckle. R. Waldron. il pors Am Heritage 18:56-9+ Ag '67

DAVIS, Robert Gorham
Leslie Fiedler's fictions. Commentary 43:73-7 Ja '67

DAVIS, Robert L.
Books in the field: mathematics. bibliog Wilson Lib Bul 42:497-509 Ja '68

DAVIS, Roy L.
Smoking and health education: a national overview; excerpt from address, September 22, 1967. PTA Mag 62:27-8 D '67

DAVIS, Samuel
Mother, I do not hate to die. J. C. Phifer. il por Am Heritage 18:32-3+ F '67

DAVIS, Sandra
On the road with Yevtushenko. G. P. Hunt. il por Life 62:3 F 17 '67

DAVIS, Stanley N. See Marsden, S. S. jr. jt. auth.

DAVIS, Thomas N. 3d
Lawn bowls. Parks & Rec 2:29-30 N '67

DAVIS, Watson
Obituary
Sci N pors 92:28-9 Jl 8 '67
Watson Davis 1896-1967. pors Sci N 92:28-9 Jl 8 '67

DAVIS, Wynn
Angling. See issues of Outdoor life
Bass are everywhere. Outdoor Life 139:43-5+ My '67

DAVIS cup. See Tennis

DAVISON, Endicott Peabody
Endicott Davison elected new NRPA president. il Parks & Rec 2:18+ Jl '67
Presidential profile. por Parks & Rec 2:3 Jl '67

DAVISON, Peter
Difficulties of being major. Atlan 220:116-21 O '67
Time and the poet. Writer 80:20-1 Ag '67
What is the Atlantic monthly press? por Pub W 192:32-4 O 16 '67

DAVISON, William Edward
Wild Bill. R. Gehman. por Sat R 50:69+ Ag 26 '67

DAVITT, J. Alan
Lay leader's view: Catholic schools today; interview, ed. by H. Ravis. Sr Schol 90:sup4 Mr 31 '67

DAVY, Sir Humphry, bart
Davy's biographers: notes on scientific biography. J. Z. Fullmer. bibliog il por Science 155:285-91 Ja 20 '67

DAW, Nigel W.
Goldfish retina: organization for simultaneous color contrast. bibliog Science 158:942-4 N 17 '67

DAWES, Robert Taylor
Knotty problem of shoelaces. il Changing T 21:37-8 O '67

DAWES mansion. See Evanston, Ill.—Historic houses, etc.

DAWIDOWICZ, Lucy S.
Musical Hebraism. Commentary 44:73-7 Jl '67

DAWKINS, Cecil
Displaced person; dramatization of short stories by F. O'Connor. Criticism America 116:160-1 Ja 28 '67

DAWSON, Robert
Five poets. D. W. Baker. Poetry 111:195-6
D '67
DAWSON, Samuel
High life at Saratoga, 1837; excerpt from
letter. Am Heritage 18:107 Je '67
DAWSON, Will
Cruising unlimited. il Yachting 121:68-70+ Ja
'67
DAWSON, Yukon
Frozen El Dorado. J. Lotz. il Américas 19:
21-7 N '67
Lure of the Klondike. A. M. Lingg. il Opera N
31:6-7 My 13 '67
DAY, A. Grove
Literary adventures in paradise: the beach-
comber books. Holiday 42:6+ Jl '67
DAY, Beth
Dare to make mistakes. Read Digest 91:83-4
S '67
—See Liley, M. jt. auth.
DAY, Doris
How to stay young. pors Ladies Home J 84:
72+ My '67
DAY, Dorothy
Death of a peacemaker. Commonweal 86:14-16
Mr 24 '67
DAY, Eileen
Meditation on the manger; poem. Horn Bk
43:730-1 D '67
DAY, James F. and Fisher, W. H.
Professor and collective negotiations. bib-
liog f Sch & Soc 95:226-9 Ap 1 '67
DAY, R. H. and others
Behavioral compensation with monocular vi-
sion. bibliog Science 156:1129-30 My 26 '67
DAY, Richard. See Alley, W. jt. auth.
DAY, Thomas
Playing the academic game. Nat R 19:1343-4
N 28 '67
DAY, Virgil B.
Labor-management relations; address, Feb-
ruary 8, 1967. Vital Speeches 33:309-13 Mr
1 '67
What's ahead for labor-management rela-
tions. Mo Labor R 90:45-6 Ap '67
DAY-LEWIS, Cecil
Laurels for Cecil. il por Newsweek 71:74
Ja 15 '68
Mr Day Lewis' pale fire. J. Wain. New
Repub 156:21-4 Je 24 '67
Poetic breadwinner. por Time 91:20-1 Ja 12
'68
DAY camps. See Camps
DAY care for children. See Foster day care;
Day nurseries
DAY dreams. See Daydreams
DAY in the death of Joe Egg; drama. See
Nichols, P.
DAY lilies
Day-lilies are her delight. H. V. Wilson. il
Home Gard 54:37 Jl '67
Daylilies flamboyant and shy. il Am Home
70:44+ Je '67
Few are the flowers that ask so little. il
Home Gard 54:35-6 Jl '67
How to hybridize hemerocallis. D. L. Fer-
rick. il Horticulture 45:30-1+ Je '67
DAY nurseries
Day nurseries: what to look for. K. Branan.
il Todays Health 45:48-9+ O '67
See also
Foster day care
Nursery schools
DAY of magic; story. See Oppenheimer, M.
DAY schools, Jewish. See Jews—Education
DAYAKS. See Borneo—Native races
DAYAN, Moshe
What Dayan says about Vietnam; statements.
por U S News 62:58 Je 26 '67

about

Dayan: turning mice into lions. C. Pepper.
il por Newsweek 69:32-3 Je 19 '67
Father and hero. Y. Dayan. il pors Look
31:15-19 Ag 22 '67
Hawk of Israel. C. G. Pepper. il pors N Y
Times Mag p5+ Jl 9 '67
Hopeful truths of the new reality. por Life
63:120-120B S 29 '67
Israel's Dayan: mastermind of victory. por
U S News 62:21 Je 19 '67
DAYAN, Ruth (Schwarz)
When my mother, Rachel, went down to
Jericho. por McCalls 94:24+ S '67
DAYAN, Yaël
Father and hero. pors Look 31:15-19 Ag 22
'67

about

People are talking about. por Vogue 150:280-1
S 1 '67

DAYDREAMS
Your dreams both day and night. D. A.
Sugarman and R. Hochstein. il Seventeen
26:84-5+ Jl '67
DAYHOFF, Margaret O. and others
Venus: atmospheric evolution. bibliog Sci-
ence 155:556-8 F 3 '67
DAYLIGHT saving
Daylight saving April 30 for whole U.S,
almost. il U S News 62:54 Mr 27 '67
Referendum row; Michigan petition suspends
anti-daylight saving law. Time 90:47 Jl
7 '67
Running to daylight; Uniform time act. il
Time 89:58+ My 12 '67

Anecdotes, facetiae, satire, etc.

Top of my head. G. Ace. Sat R 50:8 Ap 29
'67
DAYLIGHTING. See Lighting
DAYLILIES. See Day lilies
DAYS of hope and glamour; story. See Weiss,
M.
DAYTON, Ohio

City planning

Giving the past a future; Burns-Jackson.
H. Meeker. il Arch Forum 126:56-61 My '67
DAYTON, Ohio. University
Dayton imbroglio. America 116:548 Ap 15 '67
Reflections on the Dayton situation. J. M.
Darby. America 116:650-2 Ap 29 '67
DAYTON trial. See Tennessee evolution con-
troversy
DAYTONA BEACH Journal
Case in point. B. H. Bagdikian. Esquire 67:
125-8+ Mr '67
DAYTONA 500. See Automobile racing
DEAD bodies. See Cadavers
DEAD SEA scrolls
Battle of the scrolls; the Dead Sea discov-
eries reconsidered. C. Raphael. il Atlan 219:
88-92+ My '67
Temple scroll; discovery of new scroll. il
Time 90:83 N 3 '67
DEADWOOD, S.D.
Deadwood, South Dakota. il Bet Hom &
Gard 45:24+ Ag '67
DEAF
Lifting the curtain of silence. J. D. Ratcliff.
il Todays Health 45:66-8+ N '67; Same abr.
with title Doctor I can hear! Read Digest
91:189-90+ N '67

Education

Child with impaired hearing. H. Bothwell. il
NEA J 56:44-6 N '67

Means of communication

Cued speech; new communication method.
A. C. Miles. il Am Ed 3:26-8 N '67

Sign language

See Deaf—Means of communication
DEAF, Apparatus for the
Electronics for speech and hearing therapy.
L. G. Lawrence. il Electr World 78:44-5+
S '67
Phone device aids deaf-blind persons; tactile
speech indicator. Todays Health 45:87 Mr
'67
See also
Hearing aids
DEAF, Theater for the
See also
National theater of the deaf
DEAFNESS
Hearing help; child deafness caused by
rubella. il Time 89:68 Ap 28 '67
New hope for the deafened. H. G. Earl. il
Sci Digest 63:7-13 Ja '68
See also
Deaf
Hearing aids
DE AGUIRRE, Emiliano, and Butzer, K. W.
Problematical pleistocene artifact assemblage
from northwestern Spain. bibliog Science
157:430 Jl 28 '67
DEAKIN, James
Big brass lambs. Esquire 68:144-8+ D '67
Dark side of L.B.J. Esquire 68:45-8+ Ag '67
DEAL, Babs H.
Catch me a star; story. Good H 165:84-5 S
'67
DEALERS, Art. See Art dealers
DEALERS, Automobile. See Automobile dealers
DEALERS in antiques. See Antique dealers

DEAMER, David W. and Branton, Daniel
Fracture planes in an ice-bilayer model membrane system. bibliog Science 158:655-7 N 3 '67

DEAN, Charles O.
Regional report. Home Gard 54:54 S '67

DEAN, Edith M.
School where blind children see. Todays Health 45:50-3 F '67

DEAN, Nicholas
Confessions of a horse trader. Pop Phot 61:89+ D '67

DEAN, Sir Patrick
British economy; address, November 6, 1967. Vital Speeches 34:150-3 D 15 '67
Outer space treaty signed by sixty nations at White House ceremony; text of statement, January 27, 1967. Dept State Bul 56:268-9 F 20 '67

DEAR Paulina, tenting tonight; story. See Mechem, J.

DEARBORN, Mich.
Hubbard's hotel. Newsweek 70:80A-80B D 4 '67

DEARDEN, John
Computers: no impact on divisional control; excerpts from The impact of computers on management. bibliog Harvard Bsns R 45:99-104 Ja '67

DEARDORFF, Robert
Artists at work. Redbook 130:43 N '67
Craft sampling in New England. Redbook 129:42 Jl '67
Fabulous cottages of Newport. Redbook 129:39 Jl '67
Rome's Riviera. Travel 128:61-3 Jl '67
Step by step through Philadelphia. Travel 128:36-41+ Jl '67
Step by step through Washington. Travel 128:30+ Jl '67
To the rescue of art. Holiday 41:29-30+ Ap '67

DEARMORE, Tom
Rocky of Little Rock. Reporter 37:14-18 O 5 '67

DEARNALEY, Carolyn, and Bixler, Paul
Latin American collection; adaptation of address, June 1967. Wilson Lib Bul 42:417-21 D '67

DEATH
Logistics of dying. D. Sudnow. il Esquire 68:102-3+ Ag '67
See also
Bereavement
Children and death
Funeral rites and ceremonies
Suicide

Causes
Broken heart syndrome. Newsweek 70:92 O 23 '67
See also
Violent deaths

DEATH (biology)
Answer to immortality? il Sci Digest 62:82-3 Ag '67
When are you really dead? il Newsweek 70:87 D 18 '67
When is a person dead? A. J. Snider. il Sci Digest 62:70-1 O '67

DEATH, Apparent
Back from the dead. il Newsweek 70:99 N 13 '67

DEATH and children. See Children and death

DEATH of God theology
Funny thing happened on the way to the library. W. Hamilton. Christian Cent 84:469-70 Ap 12 '67
God is dead debate in Japan. G. K. Chapman. Christian Cent 84:123-4 Ja 25 '67
Modernity demythologized. R. Goetz. Christian Cent 84:691-2+ My 24 '67
Radical theology and the death of discourse. L. T. Howe. Christian Cent 84:583-6 My 3 '67
Radical understanding. J. A. Phillips. Christian Cent 84:869-70 Jl 5 '67
Secular and the sacred. R. F. Capon. il America 116:307-12 Mr 4 '67; Discussion. 116:515 Ap 8 '67
Seminary drama and the God is dead theme; musical commissioned by Christian theological seminary. R. A. Fangmeier. Christian Cent 84:846-7 Je 28 '67

DEATH penalty. See Capital punishment

DEATH rate. See Mortality; Infant mortality

DEATH taxes. See Inheritance tax

DEATH VALLEY NATIONAL MONUMENT
Ground afire. O. F. Oldendorph. il Nat Parks Mag 41:4-9 Jl '67

DEAVER, John V. See Butler, W. F. jt. auth.

DEBATES and debating
Buckley, Buckley, bow wow wow; Buckley-Coffin debate at Yale. G. Wills. il Esquire 69:72-6+ Ja '68
Value of high school debate. R. D. Alderfer. NEA J 56:39 Mr '67
See also
Controversy
Forums (discussion and debate)

DEBAYLE, Anastasio Somoza. See Somoza Debayle, A.

DEBENTURES, Convertible. See Bonds, Convertible

DEBIASI, Victor
Is there a marine turbine in your future? Motor B 120:27-30 D '67

DEBLER, Walter R.
Gauge to measure tiny changes in gas pressure. Sci Am 217:110-11 Ag '67

DE BOLT, James
Brief biography. S. Goodman. pors Dance Mag 41:64-5 Ap '67

DE BOLT, William Walter
War with a puzzle; poem. Christian Cent 84:829 Je 28 '67

DEBRAY, Jules Regis
Case of Régis Debray. por Newsweek 70:47-8 Ag 7 '67
Case of Régis Debray. il por Time 90:24 S 1 '67
Cracking down on Castro. Nation 205:324-5 O 9 '67
Debray convicted. il por Sr Schol 91:20 D 7 '67
Hot potato; Debray captured by government forces in Bolivia. Newsweek 69:61 My 8 '67
In Bolivia, captured Marxist becomes a cause célèbre. L. Hall. il por Life 63:32-4 Ag 18 '67
Judgment on Régis Debray. Newsweek 70:60 N 27 '67
One hundred for one? il por Newsweek 70:46 S 4 '67
Régis Debray. J. Bishop. Commonweal 87:164-6 N 10 '67
Regis Debray: where logic failed. L. E. Aguilar. Reporter 37:31-2 D 28 '67
Terms of trade. il Newsweek 71:43 Ja 15 '68
Unusual prisoner. por Time 91:25 Ja 12 '68
Unwitting betrayal. il por Time 90:33-4 N 24 '67
Who, me? Newsweek 70:42 O 9 '67

DEBT
See also
Bankruptcy
Credit
Debtor and creditor

DEBT; story. See Panos, D.

DEBT counseling. See Debtor and creditor

DEBT of honor; story. See Pritchett, V. S.

DEBTOR and creditor
Debt clinics; Rx for the poor. J. H. Pollack. il Nations Bsns 55:75-7 D '67
See also
Attachment and garnishment

DEBTS, Public

United States
Annual debt ceiling hocus-pocus. Bsns W p 180 Je 17 '67
Battle at budget gap. il Bsns W p38 Je 17 '67
Debt limit: how it got where it is. il U S News 62:106 F 27 '67
Defeat for LBJ in the House: new pressure for spending cuts; vote to reject raising limit on the national debt. U S News 62:102 Je 19 '67
National debt: getting lighter as it grows? il Sr Schol 90:15-16+ Mr 17 '67
Once too often; House votes against proposal to raise ceiling. Newsweek 69:70 Je 19 '67
Paying the store; Mills wins passage of bill to raise maximum debt. Time 89:17 Je 30 '67
Public debt: what does it mean? M. Mayer. Bet Home & Gard 45:28 Mr '67
Scraping the ceiling. Newsweek 69:78 Ja 30 '67
Spending crisis for LBJ? a rebellion in Congress; use of federal debt ceiling to force cut. U S News 69:95-6 Je 26 '67
Why myths about public debt hurt us. H. L. Lutz. il Nations Bsns 55:50-3 Ag '67

DEBUS, Allen
Sheet music. Hobbies 72:125 Ag '67

DEBUSSY, Claude
Piano works of Claude Debussy, by E. R. Schmitz. Review
Am Rec G 33:855 My '67. D. A. Klein

DEBYE, Peter
Peter Debye, an appreciation. F. A. Long. por Science 155:979-80 F 24 '67

DE CAMP, L. Sprague
Isle of eyeless watchers. Sci Digest 62:6-12 O '67
Lost city of the Incas. Sci Digest 62:68-72 Ag '67
DE CARVALHO, George
Case history of terror. Life 63:94A+ D 8 '67
Fall of the genius from Jerusalem. Life 62: 87-9 Ja 27 '67
DECATHLON. See Track athletics
DECAUX, Lucile, pseud. See Bibesco, M. L. L.
DECAY, Radioactive
See also
Fluorescence—Decay
DECCA navigation
Seaboard to equip DC-8s with Omnitrac. K. J. Stein. il Aviation W 86:45 Ap 10 '67
DECEIT. See Fraud
DECEMBER
Now in December; excerpt from Sundial of the seasons. H. Borland. il Read Digest 91: 43-4+ D '67
DECENTRALIZATION in school administration. See School management and organization
DECENTRALIZING authority in business. See Business management and organization
DE CICCO, Marie-Pierre
Mexico. por Vogue 149:145+ Ap 1 '67
DECISION (periodical)
How about that? Christian Cent 84:828 Je 28 '67
DECISION making
Better decisions with preference theory. J. S. Hammond, 3d. bibliog f il Harvard Bsns R 45:123-41 N '67
Computers in top-level decision making. R. H. Brady. il Harvard Bsns R 45:67-76 Jl '67
Educational decision making; symposium. NEA J 56:22-31 D '67
Effective decision. P. F. Drucker. Harvard Bsns R 45:92-8 Ja '67
Guide to decision-making. A. Guerry, jr. il Duns R 90:53+ N '67
Marketing ethics & the consumer, E. A. Clasen. Harvard Bsns R 45:79-86 Ja '67
Operations research in marketing. P. Kotler. bibliog f Harvard Bsns R 45:30-4+ Ja '67
Their decision-making process bothers some of the British. J. Walsh. Science 155:1654-6 Mr 31 '67
See also
Choice (psychology)
DECISION making (political science)
Democratic participation. S. Verba. bibliog f il Ann Am Acad 373:53-78 S '67
DECK, John
Greased samba; story. Atlan 220:76-80 S '67
DECKER, John L.
Closing in on rheumatoid arthritis. por Todays Health 45:44-7+ Je '67
Motility of the turtle embryo, chelydra serpentina linne. bibliog Science 157:952-4 Ag 25 '67
DECKER, William B.
Authors & editors. por Pub W 192:33 S 18 '67
DECKERS, Jeanine. See Luc Dominique
DECKS (outdoor rooms) See Outdoor rooms
DECLAN, Peter, pseud.
Trial by laicization. Commonweal 87:328-31 D 8 '67
DECLARATION of Geneva. See Child welfare
DECLARATION of human rights. See Universal declaration of human rights
DECLARATION of war. See War, Declaration of
DECOMPRESSION chambers
Useful work at 600-ft. depths demonstrated by Westinghouse. il Tech W 20:38 Je 19 '67
DECOMPRESSION domes. See Medical instruments and apparatus
DECONTAMINATION (from gases, chemicals, etc)
See also
Space vehicles—Sterilization
DECORATION and ornament
Jewels for the house. il House & Gard 133: 108-9 Ja '68
Mart art's; avant-garde décor. il McCalls 95: 76-81 Ja '68
Shell decorations. A. G. Melvin. il Hobbies 72:125+ Ja '68
See also
Arts and crafts
Christmas decorations
Design
Filigree
Flowers, Arrangement of
House decoration
Jewelry
Wood carving

DECORATION and ornament, Architectural
Architectural art in Germany; exhibition at the Museum of contemporary crafts. F. Mitchell. il Craft Horiz 27:10-13 Ja '67
Architectural iron works; excerpts from a century old building front catalog. il Arch Forum 126:63-70 My '67
Cantilevered rainbow; R. Grosvenor's constructions. D. Bourdon. il Art N 66:28-31+ Sum '67
Wrecker, spare that frieze! rescued relics by Anonymous arts recovery society in Fried Schiff Warburg Memorial sculpture garden. R. S. Gallagher. il Am Heritage 18:60-4+ Ag '67
DECORATION and ornament, Personal
Skin game; Tatu transfers. il Newsweek 70: 78-9 Jl 24 '67
DECORATION day. See Memorial day
DECORATIONS, Christmas. See Christmas decorations
DECORATIONS of honor
Fruit salad. C. W. Morton. il Atlan 220:110 S '67
DECORATIVE design. See Design, Decorative
DECORATIVE hardware. See Hardware
DECOSTA, Victor
Television. J. Horn. Nation 206:59 Ja 8 '68
DECOYS (hunting)
Pied Piper from down East: G. Soule. D. Barnes. il Sports Illus 28:34-7 Ja 8 '68
DE CRISTOFORO, R. J.
Case for buying a good miter box. Pop Sci 190:154-7 Ja '67
How Teflon-S improves power-saw blades. Pop Sci 191:138-40 D '67
How to cut rabbet-miter joints. Pop Sci 190: 151-5 My '67
How to set up a one-motor shop. Pop Sci 192: 156-9 Ja '68
Nineteen smart tricks with a router. Pop Sci 191:140-5 Jl '67
Rip-fence stop jig. Pop Sci 190:140-1 F '67
Three good accessories for a drill press. Pop Sci 191:138-40 N '67
What spade bits can do for you. Pop Sci 190: 126-9 Je '67
DECTER, Midge
Germany 1967. Atlan 219:50-3 My '67
Sex, my daughters, and me. Harper 235:27-32 Ag '67
DEEDY, John
News and views. Commonweal 86:330, 402 Je 9, 30 '67
DEEP Diver (submersible) See Submarine boats
DEEP fat frying. See Frying
DEEP in the heart of Texas; story. See Saint, N.
DEEP-lift paving. See Pavements
DEEP sea deposits
Confirmation from afar; hot brines and heavy metal deposits in deeps of the Red Sea. E. T. Degens and D. A. Ross. il Sat R 50:52 S 2 '67
Geological exploration in an East coast submarine canyon from a research submersible. J. V. A. Trumbull and M. J. McCamis. bibliog il Science 158:370-2 O 20 '67
Knoll and sediment drift near Hudson canyon. A. Lowrie, jr .and B. C. Heezen. bibliog il Science 157:1552-3 S 29 '67
Manganese and related elements in the interstitial water of marine sediments. B. J. Presley and others. bibliog il Science 158: 906-10 N 17 '67
Opal phytoliths in a North Atlantic dust fall. D. W. Folger and others. bibliog il Science 155:1243-4 Mr 10 '67
Sediment distribution on the mid-ocean ridges with respect to spreading of the sea floor. J. Ewing and M. Ewing. bibliog il Science 156:1590-2 Je 23 '67
Signs test applied to Caribbean deep-sea core A 172-6. R. Yalkovsky. bibliog il Science 155:1408-9 Mr 17 '67
Zodiacal dust and deep-sea sediments. S. F. Singer. bibliog il Science 156:1080-3 My 26 '67
DEEP sea diving. See Diving, Submarine
DEEP sea fishing. See Salt water fishing
DEEP-sea tides. See Tides
DEEP submergence rescue vehicle. See Submarine boats
DEEPSTAR. See Oceanographic research—Equipment
DEER
See also
Antlers
Game, Dressing of

DEER hunting
Big-game hunting for everyone. G. Dovel. il Field & S 72:52-3+ S '67
Buck picked me. T. Janes. il Outdoor Life 140:40-1+ N '67
Buck wore black. J. Mears. Outdoor Life 139:10 My '67
Cochise choice; mule deer and white-tail, too. W. A. Cartier. il Outdoor Life 140: 48-51+ O '67
Cuyler hill monster. S. Mawson. il Outdoor Life 139:56-7+ My '67
Deer drive; Black Hills and whitetails. H. Bradshaw. il Outdoor Life 139:52-3+ F '67
Deer hunt I'll never forget. F. McKinley. il Field & S 72:60-1+ Je '67
Getting ahead. W. Page. il Field & S 72:70-3 Ag '67
Hunt in the North Kaibab. V. Kraft. il Sports Illus 27:54-7 N 20 '67
Hunting the ridge runners. C. F. Waterman. il Field & S 72:44-5+ O '67
Jackpot hunt for $48. B. Holden. il Outdoor Life 140:56-9+ S '67
Jarbidge deer hunt. B. Behme. il Field & S 72:50-1+ O '67
Luck of the Willeys. H. Willey, jr. il Outdoor Life 140:56-7+ D '67
Memory for muleys. C. Conley. il Field & S 72:38-9+ Ag '67
Muzzle-loader deer hunt. C. Elliott. il Outdoor Life 139:48-51+ Mr '67
Nine natives and the hard buck. L. Dietz. il Field & S 71:54-5+ Ap '67
Prepare now for deer. G. H. Gillelan. il Outdoor Life 140:60+ Jl '67
Ten rules for mule deer. T. Trueblood. il Field & S 72:32+ O '67
Three bucks for the book. E. Morgan. il Outdoor Life 140:54-5+ N '67
We wanted a western hunt. J. O. Cartier. il Outdoor Life 140:29-31+ S '67
Whitetails along the border. W. Page. il Field & S 72:46-7+ O '67

Anecdotes, facetiae, satire, etc.
Dear me, it's deer hunting season again! H. Stieve. il Farm J 91:45+ N '67
DEER park; drama. See Mailer, N.
DEERING, William
Convention exhibit notes; NCSS. Sr Schol 91: sup 14 D 14 '67
DEETZ, James, and Dethlefsen, E. S.
Death's head, cherub, urn and willow; with biographical sketches. Natur Hist 76:5, 28-37 Mr '67
DEEVEY, Edward S. jr
Question: Darwinism revisited; reply: letter from Birnam Wood. Yale R 56:631-40 Je '67
DEEVEY, Robert J.
Thief in the store. Pub W 191:38 My 22 '67
DEFAMATION. See Libel and slander
DEFECTORS, Political
Blow to the reds; Stalin's daughter defects. il U S News 62:19 Mr 20 '67
Chase: Stalin's daughter, Svetlana, in Switzerland. Time 89:30 Mr 24 '67
Coming on over; Viet Cong defecting to allied side. Time 89:39 Ap 14 '67
Crossing the Potomac; János Radványi obtains asylum. il Time 89:20 My 26 '67
Cruelty and insanity made me a fugitive. S. T. Ma. il Life 62:24-9+ Je 2 '67
Defectors: East and West. Sr Schol 90:15 Mr 31 '67
Her journey of no return: S. Stalin. M. H. Zim. il Life 62:66-7 Mr 24 '67
How Viet Cong fare when they defect. il U S News 63:38 O 23 '67
I was a Red guard; ed. by L. Velie. C. T. Wang. Read Digest 90:55-60 My '67
Model defector; J. Radvanyi. Newsweek 69: 22-3 My 29 '67
Nobody dared stop us; defector from Red guards; interview, ed. by K. M. Chrysler. C. T. Wang. U S News 62:57 Ja 30 '67
Peking's defectors abroad. L. M. Taubinger. Nat R 19:414 Ap 18 '67
Search for Svetlana. il Newsweek 69:62 Mr 27 '67
Stalin's daughter. il Newsweek 69:51-2 Mr 20 '67
Surprise from the past; Svetlana Iosifovna Stalin. il Time 89:32 Mr 17 '67
Svetlana's trip to freedom; with report by R. Korengold. il Newsweek 69:21-4 My 1 '67
Terror at the hands of the Red guard; case of Ma Sitson. il Life 62:22-3 Je 2 '67

We are slaves who have been betrayed. S. T. Ma. il Life 63:64-6+ Jl 14 '67
Why I defected from the Vietcong; interview, ed. by N. Turner. Le-xuan-Chuyen. Read Digest 91:91-6 N '67
Why I fled from Communist North Korea; interview, ed. by K. M. Chrysler. S. K. Lee. il U S News 62:60-1 My 29 '67
With open arms; Chieu Hoi program to encourage guerrillas to defect. il Newsweek 69:52 Mr 27 '67
DEFENDI, V. and Jensen F.
Oncogenicity by DNA tumor viruses: enhancement after ultraviolet and cobalt-60 radiations. bibliog Science 157:703-5 Ag 11 '67
DEFENSE, Department of. See United States—Defense, Department of
DEFENSE appropriations. See United States—Armed forces—Appropriations and expenditures
DEFENSE buying. See United States—Armed forces—Procurement
DEFENSE contracts. See Contracts, Government
DEFENSE electronics, incorporated
Portable VHF receiver from DEI weighs less than 10 lbs. C. D. LaFond. il Tech W 20:32-3 Ap 3 '67
DEFENSE industries. See Munitions industries
DEFENSE intelligence agency. See United States—Defense, Department of—Defense intelligence agency
DEFENSE laboratories. See Military research
DEFENSE mechanisms (biology)
Alarm reaction of the top smelt, atherinops affinis: reexamination. R. H. Rosenblatt and G. S. Losey, jr. bibliog il Science 155:671-2 N 3 '67
Defensive use of a fecal shield by a beetle larva. T. Eisner and others. bibliog il Science 158:1471-3 D 15 '67
Erratic display as a device against predators. D. A. Humphries and P. M. Driver. bibliog Science 156:1767-8 Je 30 '67
Role differentiation in copulating cicada killer wasps. N. Lin. bibliog il Science 157:1334-5 S 15 '67
DEFERRED payment plan. See Instalment plan
DEFICIENT diet. See Diet, Deficient
DEFICIT spending. See Government spending policy
DEFINITIONS

Anecdotes, facetiae, satire, etc.
Understanding our cultural revolution. R. R. Lingeman. il N Y Times Mag p6+ My 14 '67
DE FLOREZ, Peter
Supplies for bookmaking, a look into the future. por Pub W 191:86-7 Mr 6 '67
DEFONTAINE, Ham
Gadgets and gilhickies. See issues of Yachting
DEFONTAINE, W. H.
Designs. See issues of Yachting
DEFORD, Frank
Pro basketball. Sports Illus 26:54-6 My 8 '67
Tennis (cont) Sports Illus 27:68+ D 11 '67
DEFORMITIES
Autosomal deletion mapping in man. W. E. Nance and E. Engel. bibliog il Science 155: 692-4 F 10 '67
Baby who was born twice; case of Lori Lee Grant. T. Morris. Redbook 129:64-5+ Je '67
Chances of a defective child. il Time 89:57 Mr 3 '67
Medical help that prevents birth of defective children. Good H 165:193-5 O '67
Mutant enzymatic and cytological phenotypes in cultured human fibroblasts. J. G. Leroy and R. I. DeMars. bibliog il Science 157:804-6 Ag 18 '67
Sulfite oxidase deficiency in man: demonstration of the enzymatic defect. S. H. Mudd and others. bibliog il Science 156:1599-602 Je 23 '67
Virus etiology of congenital malformations; report on conference. S. C. Mitchell and G. L. Woodside. Science 157:1337-8 S 15 '67
DEGAS, Edgar
Artificial heart. il Time 89:72-3+ Mr 3 '67
Ballerinas and bathers; works in the show Drawings by Degas. A. Werner. Reporter 36:44+ Ap 20 '67
Degas; illustrious and unknown; with excerpt from La Cigale by H. Meilhac and L. Halévy. L. Tannenbaum. il Art N 65:50-5+ Ja '67
Draughtsmanship of Edgar Degas. A. Werner. il Am Artist 31:47-53+ O '67

DE GAULLE, Charles. See Gaulle, C. de

DEGENHARDT, Bob
Bear of the decade. pors Outdoor Life 140: 36-9+ Jl '67

DEGENS, Egon T. and Ross, D. A.
Confirmation from afar. Sat R 50:52 S 2 '67

DEGLER, Carl N.
Princeton's president. New Repub 157:32-3 D 23 '67

DE GOGORZA, Emilio Edoardo
Collectors' releases.   A. Favia-Artsay. por Hobbies 72:36+ Ap '67

DE GRAAFF, Jan
Lilies for every clime. Home Gard 54:39 Ag '67

DE GRAMONT, Sanche
Arms merchant to the world. N Y Times Mag p38-9+ S 24 '67
Battle for Jerusalem. Sat Eve Post 240:70-5 Ag 12 '67
Britain and France build a common market of youth. N Y Times Mag p7+ Jl 16 '67
Deserters go underground. Sat Eve Post 241:27 Ja 27 '68
Does R.F. mean *république française* or Rothschild frères? N Y Times Mag p8-9+ Je 25 '67
How to play a lottery. N Y Times Mag p24-5+ My 7 '67
Jerusalem: experiment in coexistence. N Y Times Mag p 14-18+ Jl 30; 72 S 10 '67
Re-enter: Mendès-France, hoping. N Y Times Mag p25+ Ap 16 '67
Second resistance of Georges Bidault. N Y Times Mag p46-7+ O 8 '67
Three candidates in a test of Gaullism. N Y Times Mag p26-7+ Mr 5 '67

DEGREES, Academic
Exporting Ph.D's: is it profitable? letter. A. W. Shurcliff. Science 157:138+ Jl 14 '67
Language requirements for the Ph.D; letter. S. Ross and C. W. Shillings; discussion. Science 154:1603; 155:1492 D 30 '66, Mr 24 '67
Ph.D. language requirements: California survey results; letter. D. G. Nichols and T. Everson. Science 156:1549 Je 23 '67; Reply. T. Page. 157:1373 S 22 '67
Ph.D. reform in social sciences. Sci N 91: 375-6 Ap 22 '67
Suggested intermediate graduate degree. H. Putnam. bibliog f Sch & Soc 95:182 Mr 18 '67

DEGREES, Honorary
Kudos. Time 89:90+ Je 9; 79 Je 16; 85 Je 23 '67

DE GROOT, Roy Andries
Cordials and liqueurs, most luxurious of drinks. House B 109:262+ N '67
Feast for the infanta. Esquire 68:184-7+ D '67
Four marvelous ways to eat outdoors. Sat Eve Post 240:30-7 Jl 15 '67
How to make the perfect pousse-café. House B 109:80 N '67

about
Feast of the season. A. Gingrich. Esquire 68:6+ D '67

DE HAVILLAND, Olivia
Dream that never died. pors Look 31:113-14 D 12 '67

DE HOLGUIN, Beatrice
Picturesque Panama. Travel 127:40-4 Ja '67
Those in Out Islands. Travel 127:40-4 F '67

DEHYDRATION (physiology)
Heat exacts a toll; death by dehydration in Mexico's spring heat waves. E. Zubryn. Sci N 91:558 Je 10 '67

DEHYDROGENASES
Alpha-glycerophosphate dehydrogenase and glucose-6-phosphate dehydrogenase in tissues of the Weddell seal. G. H. Fried and others. bibliog il Science 155:1560-1 Mr 24 '67
Athens variant of glucose-6-phosphate dehydrogenase. G. Stamatoyannopoulos and others. bibliog il Science 157:831-3 Ag 18 '67
Autosomal phosphogluconic dehydrogenase polymorphism in the cat, felis catus L. H. C. Thuline and others. bibliog il Science 157:431-2 Jl 28 '67
Electrophoretic heterogeneity of mammalian galactose dehydrogenase. P. Cuatrecasas and S. Segal; discussion. bibliog il Science 156:1516-18 Je 16 '67
Electrophoretic variants of α-glycerophosphate dehydrogenase in drosophila melanogaster. E. H. Grell. bibliog il Science 158: 1319-20 D 8 '67
Embryonic enzyme patterns: characterization of the single lactate dehydrogenase isozyme in preimplanted mouse ova. J. Rapola and O. Koskimies. bibliog il Science 157:1311-12 S 15 '67

Enzymatic identification of fish products. A. C. Wilson and others. bibliog il Science 157:82-3 Jl 7 '67
Genetic control of lactate dehydrogenase formation in the hagfish eptatretus stoutii. S. Ohno and others. bibliog il Science 156:96-8 Ap 7 '67
Glyceraldehyde-3-phosphate dehydrogenase variants in phyletically diverse organisms. H. G. Lebherz and W. J. Rutter. bibliog il Science 157:1198-200 S 8 '67
Lactic dehydrogenase and metabolism of human leukocytes in vitro. A. D. Bloom and others. bibliog il Science 156:979-81 My 19 '67
Malic dehydrogenase isozymes: distribution in developing nucleate and anucleate halves of sea urchin eggs. G. W. Patton, jr. and others. bibliog il Science 156:400-1 Ap 21 '67
Mitochondrial malate dehydrogenase: a new genetic polymorphism in man. R. G. Davidson and J. A. Cortner. bibliog il Science 157:1569-71 S 29 '67
Molecular size of hagfish muscle lactate dehydrogenase. N. Arnheim, jr. and others. bibliog il Science 157:568-9 Ag 4 '67
Rabbit lactate dehydrogenase isozymes: effect of pH on activity. P. J. Fritz. bibliog il Science 156:82-3 Ap 7 '67
See also
Enzymes

DE-ICERS. See Airplanes—Ice protection

DEIGHTON, Lee C.
ATPI president stresses special school market; summary of address. Pub W 191:61 Je 19 '67

DE JOIE, Norman
Paris ballet star. il pors Ebony 23:67-8+ D '67

DE JONG, D. W. and others
Glutaraldehyde activation of nuclear acid phosphatase in cultured plant cells. bibliog Science 155:1672-4 Mr 31 '67

DEJONG, David Cornel
Erelong remembered; Direction north; Every Saturday; All American; poems. Poetry 111: 21-7 O '67
Windows; poems. Nation 204:574 My 1 '67

DE KOONING, Willem
Art world; exhibition at Knoedler's. H. Rosenberg. New Yorker 43:140+ Jl 16 '67
De Kooning's derring-do. il por Time 90:88-9 N 17 '67
Don Quixote in springs. D. L. Shirey. il por Newsweek 70:80-1 N 20 '67
Light of de Kooning. L. Finkelstein. por Art N 66:28-31+ N '67

DEKOSTER, Lester
Keep the church out of, what? Christian Cent 84:404-7 Mr 29 '67

DELACATO, Carl H.
When children can't learn. J. Bird. il pors Sat Eve Post 240:27-31+ Jl 29 '67

DELAFIELD, Anita
Living with antiques. Antiques 91:234-9 F '67

DELANEY, Barbara Snow
Municipal art society of New York, 1892-1967. Antiques 91:642-3 My '67
Preservation: Canada 1967. Antiques 92:100-5 Jl '67

DELANY, Ron
Running of the green. pors Sports Illus 28: 18-23 Ja 15 '68

about
Where are they now? il por Newsweek 69:14 F 20 '67

DE LA RENTA, Oscar
Everybody's Oscar. il por Time 90:69 N 10 '67

DE LAVALLADE, Carmen
Carmen de Lavallade with guests; Village theatre. J. Anderson. Dance Mag 41:30-1 Jl '67
Dance magazine's annual awards 1966. por Dance Mag 41:40-1+ Mr '67

DELAWARE
See also
Fishing—Delaware
Gardens—Delaware

DELAWARE, Ohio
Putting the flimflam on the slickers from the city; Little brown jug harness race. P. Axthelm. il sports Illus 27:64+ O 2 '67

DELAWARE RIVER VALLEY
Valley of the Swedes. J. Bowen. il Travel 128:37-40 O '67

DELAWARE, University, Newark
Student participation. Sch & Soc 95:214 Ap 1 '67

DELEGATES to the United Nations. See United Nations—Delegates

DELFT, Netherlands
Traveler's choice. D. M. Young. Travel 127:9 Je '67
DELFT ware
Pottery shopping in Holland. il Sunset 139:38 S '67
DELICATE balance; drama. See Albee, E.
DELINQUENT children. See Juvenile delinquency
DE LIPSKI, Vladimir
Unesco in the service of peace. UNESCO Courier 20:28-30 F '67
DELIUS, Anthony
Africa's guerrillas extend their fight. Reporter 37:38-40 O 5 '67
Drawn-out fight for South-West Africa. Reporter 36:20-1 My 4 '67
Paving Tanzania's way with good intentions. Reporter 37:41-3 Jl 13 '67
DELIUS, Frederick
Musical events; performance of Mass of life. W. Sargeant. New Yorker 42:154+ F 11 '67
DELMAN, David
Jilting; story. Redbook 129:62-3 Je '67
DELMARVA dialog (newspaper) See Catholic press
DELMAS, Gladys
Brasilia comes of age. Reporter 36:25-6+ F 23 '67
DELMONICO'S. See New York (city)—Hotels, restaurants, etc.
DEL OLMO, Filomena Peloro, and Del Olmo, Guillermo
FLES programs. NEA J 56:42-3 My '67
DEL OLMO, Guillermo. See Del Olmo, F. P. jt. auth.
DE LONG, James
House beautiful presents five great-value houses. House B 109:111-21 F '67
DELONG, Richard
Live virus vaccines, benefactors with a catch. bibliog Sci Digest 63:33-8 Ja '68
DELORENZO, Anthony George
Auto news makers. D. MacDonald. por Motor T 19:8 Je '67
DELOS
City as an act of will; excerpt from Design of cities. E. N. Bacon. il Arch Rec 141:122-3 Ja '67
DE LOYO, Conté
On the boards. W. Como. il por Dance Mag 41:17 Ag '67
DELPHI, Greece
Delphi; the oracle revealed. W. Golding. il Holiday 42:60-1+ Ag '67
DELPHI technique. See Operations research
DEL PIERRE, Francine
Francine Del Pierre; interview, ed. by F. Frank. Craft Horiz 27:10-13+ Mr '67
DEL REGATO, Juan Angel
Rebel without hatred. Américas 19:29-35 Ja '67
DEL RIO, Dolores
Dolores Del Rio; excerpts. J. Gómez-Sicre. il pors Américas 19:8-17 N '67
DELTA Aquarids. See Meteors
DELZELL, Charles F.
Cause for Castelfuoco. Sat R 50:41-2 F 4 '67
DE MAEYER, Edward. See De Maeyer-Guignard, J. jt. auth.
DE MAEYER-GUIGNARD, Jaqueline, and De Maeyer, Edward
Depression of circulating interferon response in Balb/c mice after urethan treatment. bibliog Science 155:482-4 Ja 27 '67
DEMANTIUS, Christoph
Real sleeper from Nonesuch. J. W. Barker. Am Rec G 33:492-3 F '67
DEMARIA, A. J. and others
Ultrashort light pulses. bibliog Science 156:1557-68 Je 23 '67
DEMARIA, Fernando
Pérez Celis; an image of the Americas. Américas 19:38-9 D '67
DEMARIS, Ovid. See Wills, G. jt. auth.
DEMARS, Robert I. See Leroy, J. G. jt. auth.
DEMBER, William N. and Purcell, D. G.
Recovery of masked visual targets by inhibition of the masking stimulus. bibliog Science 157:1335-6 S 15 '67
DE MEDICI, Marino. See Medici, M. de
DEMERS, Louis A.
Street records that work. Am City 82:130-2 O '67
DEMIKHOV, Vladimir Petrovich
Tissue rejection challenged. il Sci N 91:282 Mr 25 '67

DEMOCRACY
Anti-politics in America, by J. H. Bunzel. Review
  Nation 204:827-8 Je 26 '67. H. S. Kariel
Can democracy work? J. Burnham. Nat R 19:510 My 16 '67
Democratic participation. S. Verba. bibliog f il Ann Am Acad 373:53-78 S '67
Eugene McCarthy's mission. W. Lippman. Newsweek 70:25 D 18 '67
Freedom and order; a commentary on the American political scene, by H. S. Commager. Review
  Sat R 50:37-8 Ja 28 '67. D. Young
Novel as a function of American democracy; address, March 23, 1967. R. Ellison. Wilson Lib Bul 41:1022-7 Je '67
Policy and the people. N. A. Rockefeller. For Affairs 46:231-41 Ja '68
  See also
Communism and democracy
DEMOCRACY and communism. See Communism and democracy
DEMOCRATIC party
Democrat appraises his party's chances. U S News 63:44 N 27 '67
Democratic disaster area; California. J. Phelan. il Reporter 37:18-21 N 2 '67
Democrats in 1968. W. Lippmann. Newsweek 71:9 Ja 1 '68
Dismay for L.B.J; split in Democratic party in California. Time 89:14-15 Je 2 '67
Dump-Johnson movement. S. V. Roberts. Commonweal 87:106-7 O 27 '67
Dump LBJ? il Newsweek 70:24-5 O 9 '67
Gene McCarthy. New Repub 157:7-8 N 18 '67
Governor from Ida Grove; H. Hughes of Iowa. V. Bourjaily. il N Y Times Mag p34-5+ F 26 '67
Hitched to LBJ? case for not renominating L. B. Johnson. New Repub 157:1+ S 30 '67
Johnny Appleseeds; anti-Johnson organizations New Repub 157:9-10 O 28 '67
McCarthy bomb. K. Crawford. Newsweek 70:32 D 4 '67
McCarthy in Chicago; Conference of Concerned Democrats. P. R. Wieck. New Repub 157:9-11 D 16 '67
Marxists from Multnomah. Time 90:30 O 13 '67
Minus for the Democrats; District of Columbia Democratic central committee and White House pressure. New Repub 158:9 Ja 20 '68
Move to dump Johnson. il Newsweek 70:25-8 N 27 '67
Muskie of Maine. M. Nolan. Reporter 37:44-6 Jl 13 '67
Now is the time. New Repub 157:7-8 D 9 '67
Our larger than life President. New Repub 156:15-17 Ap 29 '67
Party that thinks it owns the place. H. Sidey. Life 63:28B S 8 '67
Ready, willing and able; anti-Johnson Democrats at Conference of Concerned Democrats. D. Ireland. Commonweal 87:375-6 D 22 '67
Temper of the times. il Time 89:27-33 Ap 14 '67
They never go back; Kennedy Democrats-in-exile. K. Crawford. Newsweek 70:27 Ag 14 '67
Voice for dissent. Time 90:21-2 D 8 '67
War, riots, crime, taxes; why Democrats worry about '68. il U S News 63:46-7 Ag 21 '67
What's happening to the Democrats? il U S News 63:31-3 D 18 '67
Where Johnson is facing political danger in 1968. U S News 63:42-3 N 13 '67
Whose stalking horse? E. McCarthy to enter primary in Massachusetts. Newsweek 70:32 D 18 '67
Why it will be a Johnson-Humphrey ticket again in '68. il U S News 62:40-3 F 13 '67
Will Bobby's friends trip up LBJ in '68? il U S News 62:53-4 Ap 10 '67
  See also
National conventions, Democratic
Tammany Hall
DEMOCRATIC study group. See Political clubs and associations
DEMOGRAPHY
Demographic aspects of urbanization; recommendations for United Nations work programme. UN Mo Chron 4:31 O '67
Demographic aspects of urbanization; UN ad hoc committee. UN Mo Chron 4:67 Ag '67
John Graunt's offspring; three centuries of demography. B. Urlanis. il UNESCO Courier 20:4-9 F '67

DENVER—*Continued*

Libraries

See also
Denver public library

Music

See also
Denver symphony orchestra

Newspapers

Why in hell; criticism of Denver newspapers. il Newsweek 70:64 S 4 '67

Public health

New kind of care; neighborhood health center. R. H. Berg. il Look 31:36-40 Mr 21 '67

Streets

No more paving secrets or underground mysteries. F. A. Wikgren. il Am City 82:28 Mr '67

DENVER and Rio Grande Western railroad
High-mountain railroad with profits to match. il Bsns W p 174-6+ Je 10 '67

DENVER post
High noon in Denver; fight for control. Newsweek 70:70-1 Ag 7 '67

DENVER public library
Get rich quick scheme in the American West; concerning French manuscript, Memoire sur La Louisiane. Mrs A. Freeze. il Wilson Lib Bul 41:603-5 F '67

DENVER symphony orchestra
Pros & cons of the Golschmann era; Denver report. A. Young. Hi Fi 17:MA18 Jl '67

DENVER zoological gardens.   See Zoological gardens

DENZER, Peter W.
Notes from a flood journal. Yale R 56:475-80 Mr '67

DEODAR. See Cedar

DEODORANTS
Perspiration, everybody's problem. M. Lederer. il Todays Health 45:12-14 Ag '67

DEOXYRIBONUCLEIC acid
Closer to synthetic life; active DNA synthesized. il Time 90:66 D 22 '67
Collagen synthesis by cells synchronously replicating DNA. L. M. Davies and others. bibliog il Science 159:91-3 Ja 5 '68
Disease theory skips DNA; study of kuru and scrapie. F. Marley. il Sci N 91:169-70 F 18 '67
Dormin (abscisin II) inhibitor of plant DNA synthesis? J. van Overbeek and others. bibliog il Science 156:1497-9 Je 16 '67
Double helix; the discovery of the structure of DNA; excerpts, with editorial comment. J. D. Watson. il Atlan 221:76-94+ Ja '68 (to be cont)
Electron spin resonance of gamma-irradiated oriented DNA prepared by wet spinning. A. Ehrenberg and others. bibliog il Science 157:1317-19 S 15 '67
Fungicide danger; captan's genetic effect. il Sci N 91:568 Je 17 '67
Genetic passenger. Sci Am 216:57-8 F '67
Genetic recombination in escherichia coli; clone heterogeneity and the kinetics of segregation. T. H. Wood. bibliog il Science 157:319-21 Jl 21 '67
How proteins start. B. F. C. Clark and K. A. Marcker. il Sci Am 218:36-42 bibliog (p 150) Ja '68
In vitro synthesis of DNA: a perspective on research. M. F. Singer. il Science 158:1550-1 D 22 '67
Induction of cancer by viruses. R. Dulbecco. il Sci Am 216:28-37 bibliog(p 146) Ap '67
Induction of mutants with altered DNA composition: effect of ultraviolet on bacterium paracoli 5099. G. F. Gause and others bibliog il Science 157:1196-7 S 8 '67
Interlocked DNA; molecules of DNA from mitochondria. Sci Am 218:46+ Ja '68
Lab creates life in a test tube. il Bsns W p58 D 23 '67
Life in a tube; synthetic DNA. il Newsweek 70:50 D 25 '67
Mammalian X-chromosomes: change in patterns of DNA replication during embryogenesis. R. N. Hill and J. J. Yunis. bibliog il Science 155:1120-1 Mr 3 '67
Mitochondrial-satellite and circular DNA filaments in yeast. J. H. Sinclair and others. bibliog il Science 156:1234-7 Je 2 '67
Nuclear-cytoplasmic interaction in DNA synthesis. D. M. Prescott and L. Goldstein. bibliog il Science 155:469-70 Ja 27 '67

Photoreactivation in vivo of pyrimidine dimers in paramecium DNA. B. M. Sutherland and others. bibliog il Science 158:1699-700 D 29 '67
RNA and DNA synthesis in developing eggs of the milkweed bug, oncopeltus fasciatus (Dallas) S. E. Harris and H. S. Forrest. bibliog il Science 156:1613-15 Je 23 '67
Repair of DNA. P. C. Hanawalt and R. H. Haynes. il Sci Am 216:36-43 bibliog(p 146) F '67
Repair of damaged DNA in a eucaryotic cell; tetrahymena pyriformis. C. F. Brunk and P. C. Hanawalt. bibliog il Science 158:663-4 N 3 '67
Synthesis of DNA: how they spread the good news. D. S. Greenberg. il Science 158:1548-50 D 22 '67
Transforming activity in both complementary strands of bacillus subtilis DNA. M.-D. Chilton. bibliog il Science 157:817-19 Ag 18 '67
Tritiated thymidine: effect of decomposition by self-raiolysis on specificity as a tracer for DNA synthesis. M. Wand and others. bibliog il Science 157:436-8 Jl 28 '67
Ultraviolet irradiation of DNA in vitro and in vivo produces a third thymine-derived product. A. J. Varghese and S. Y. Wang. bibliog il Science 156:955-7 My 19 '67
Viable synthetic DNA; with editorial comment. il Sci N 92:629-30 D 30 '67

DEOXYRIBONUCLEIC virus
Oncogenicity by DNA tumor viruses: enhancement after ultraviolet and cobalt-60 radiations. V. Defendi and F. Jensen. bibliog il Science 157:703-5 Ag 11 '67

DE PAOLO, Ron
Into the blizzard, fresh from the jungle. G. P. Hunt. por Life 64:2 Ja 5 '68

DEPARTMENT of economic and social affairs. See United Nations—Department of economic and social affairs

DEPARTMENT of housing and urban development. See United States—Housing and urban development, Department of

DEPARTMENT stores
See also
Alexander's department stores, incorporated
Federated department stores, incorporated
Mail order business
Retail trade
also subhead Stores under names of cities. e.g. Atlanta—Stores

Art departments

Buyers, sellers, and forgers. M. Esterow. Harper 234:83-6 Je '67

Branch stores

Big-city store takes fashion into a barn; Stern brothers' East Hampton green. il Bsns W p32-3 My 27 '67
Model for branch store planning. M. Sawits. il Harvard Bsns R 45:140-3 Jl '67
Store designers help ring the cash registers; suburban branches in the U.S. il Bsns W p42-6+ Jl 1 '67

Employees

Fifty ways employes steal from their store. il Life 63:70-1 D 15 '67

Management

Behind the scenes at the big store. il Changing T 21:39-40 Mr '67

DE PAULA, Paulo
My happy blues; story. Américas 19:29-31 F '67

DEPENDENCIES. See Colonies

DEPENDENTS schools overseas. See American schools abroad

DEPORTATION
Bitter tea of Dr Tsien. M. Viorst. Esquire 68:125-9+ S '67

DEPOSIT stations, Library. See Libraries—Branches and stations

DEPOSITION (geology) See Sedimentation and deposition

DEPOSITORY libraries. See Libraries, Depository

DEPPE, Frederick
Inspector Deppe and the smoky boiler. New Yorker 42:32-3 F 11 '67

DEPRECIATION
Make depreciation work for you; a used car's potential depreciation. M. Lamm. il Motor T 19:48-50 Je '67
See also
Amortization deduction

DEPRECIATION (currency) See Money

DEPRESSANTS. See Antidepressants

DEPRESSION, Business. See Business depression

DEPRESSION, Mental
Don't be surprised by after-baby blues. C. Carner. il Todays Health 45:32-5 D '67
How to cure depression. F. R. Schreiber and M. Herman. Sci Digest 61:12-15 F '67
Lithium vs. manic-depression. P. McBroom. il(p561) Sci N 91:575 Je 17 '67
Postpartum depression. S. H. Gardiner. Redbook 129:31+ O '67
To beat the blues. J. Graham. Read Digest 90:39-40+ Ap '67
See also
Antidepressants

DEPRIVATION, Maternal. See Maternal deprivation

DEPTH indicators
Finding your way with sounders. J. West. il Yachting 122:47-9+ O '67

DEPTH of field. See Photography—Focusing

DEPTH perception. See Space perception

DEPTH sounders. See Depth indicators

DEPUTY for Broken Bow; drama. See Cable, H.

DERAIN, André
London. J. Russell. Art N 66:60 O '67

DERECKTOR, Bob
Man and his boat. Wild Goose. A. R. Mansfield, jr. il Yachting 121:78-9+ Ap '67

DERIVATION of words. See English language—Etymology

DE RIVERA, José
Infinity in eight minutes. il por Time 89:66 Ap 7 '67

DERRICK, M.
Superconducting magnets in high-energy physics. bibliog Science 158:325-31 O 20 '67

DERRY, D. M. and Wolfe, L. S.
Gangliosides in isolated neurons and glial cells. bibliog Science 158:1450-2 D 15 '67

DERSHOWITZ, Rita
To Mr Lippmann. Harper 235:46-7 O '67

DERTHICK, Lawrence Gridley
Assistant executive secretary for educational services. A. C. Harding. por NEA J 57:45 Ja '68

DE RUTH, Jan
Painting a nude in an alla prima technique: excerpt from Painting the nude. Am Artist 31:44-9+ Je '67

DESAI, Morarji
Crown of thorns. il Newsweek 69:65-6 Mr 27 '67
Karma of Maraji Desai. J. Lelyveld. il pors N Y Times Mag p30-1+ S 24 '67

DESAIX, Pierre
Tank testing America. por Yachting 122:69+ S '67

DESALTING of sea water. See Sea water—Desalting

DESALVO, Albert
Bailey & the Boston strangler. il por Time 89:40 Ja 27 '67
Call for F. Lee. por Newsweek 69:37-8 Mr 6 '67
Return of the strangler. il por Time 89:26-7 Mr 3 '67
Unaccustomed defeat. Newsweek 69:30 Ja 30 '67

DESCENT from the hill; story. See Rosselli, A.

DESCH, Robert P.
Sonnet for a Sabbath, 30 A.D. Christian Cent 84:367 Mr 22 '67

DE SCHAUNSEE, Max
Lion of Pisa. Opera N 31:26-7 Ap 8 '67

DESCHIN, Jacob
Viewpoint. See issues of Popular photography

DESEGREGATION. See Colleges and universities—Desegregation; Public schools—Desegregation

DESEGREGATION decision, 1954. See United States—Supreme court—Decisions

DESEGREGATION of libraries. See Libraries and Negroes

DESERET news, Salt Lake City
Stern Mormon view. il Time 90:72 Ag 4 '67

DESERET; opera. See Kastle, L.

DESERET arthropods. See Arthropods

DESERT botanical garden, Arizona. See Botanical gardens

DESERT fauna
Brush-up on desert critters. il Sunset 138:42+ Ap '67
See also
Lizards
Mice, Desert

DESERT frogs. See Frogs

DESERT iguanas. See Iguanas

DESERT mice. See Mice, Desert

DESERT sheep. See Mountain sheep

DESERT vegetation
See also
Cactus
Succulent plants

DESERTION, Naval. See United States—Navy—Desertions

DESERTION and non-support
Million fathers desert; family desertion in Mexico. E. Zubryn. Sci N 93:10 Ja 6 '68

DESERTS
West's land of surprises. E. Abbey. Read Digest 90:61-5 F '67
See also
Arid regions
Desert fauna
Great Karoo
Namib Desert
Sahara Desert

DESFOR, Irving
On the go, by bus. il U S Camera 30:42-3+ My '67

DESIGN
Design as a public relations tool. S. N. Fujita. Wilson Lib Bul 42:293-4 N '67
North of the border; Canadian design. B. Plumb. il N Y Times Mag p 106-7 Ap 30 '67
What is design? R. M. Pearson. il Design 68:23-4 Mr '67
See also
Costume design

DESIGN, Book. See Book design

DESIGN, Decorative
Bertil Vallien: gentle fantasies done with daring and delight. D. Smith. il Craft Horiz 27:8-13+ S '67
Continental decorative arts at the Art institute of Chicago. A. Wardwell. il Antiques 92:508-23 O '67
Lines & developments. E. J. Dorsey. il Design 68:24-6 Sum '67
Manhole cover artist. F. R. Kemp. il Design 68:36-7 Ja '67
See also
Arts and crafts
Textile design
Textile fabrics
Animal forms
Horses & riders. D. F. Brown. il Hobbies 71:52-3+ Jl '66; Correction. 71:52 F '67
How to make owl stones. J. W. Klages. il Design 68:18-19 Ja '67

DESIGN, Industrial
Pursuit of tastelessness. C. M. Cloban. Design 68:17 Sum '67
Putting design on the track; Sundberg-Ferar designs. il Bsns W p94-6+ F 25 '67

DESIGN in photography. See Composition (photography)

DESIGN of airplanes. See Airplanes—Design

DESIGN of automobiles. See Automobiles—Design

DESIGNED facilities corporation
Building with boxes. J. Bailey. il Arch Forum 126:46-51 My '67

DESIGNERS
Boris; B. Aronson. B. Atkinson. il Sat R 50:23 Je 10 '67
Designers for the dance; with interviews, ed. by A. Fatt. il Dance Mag 41:42-50 F; 50-5 Mr; 55-8 Ap '67
Renaissance skipper; industrial designer, W. T. Snaith. il Time 90:101-2 S 22 '67
See also
Costume designers

DESIGNS, Architectural. See Architecture—Designs and plans

DESILU productions, incorporated
G&W loves Lucy. il Newsweek 69:70 F 27 '67
Into new territory; Gulf & Western's take-over. il Time 89:86 F 24 '67

DE SILVA, Anil
Collective dream of a continent. il UNESCO Courier 20:13-15+ D '67

DESIRE caught by the tail; drama. See Picasso, P.

DESK diaries. See Diaries

DESK furnishings
Chez Mlle; home desk area. B. Plumb. il Mlle 64:70-1 Mr '67

DESKS
Build this sleekly styled split-level typing desk. M. Banister. il Pop Mech 129:156-9+ Ja '68

DESKS—*Continued*
Chez Mlle; home desk area. B. Plumb. il Mlle 64:70-1 Mr '67
Desk on poles; desk on the wall. il Sunset 138:120 F '67
How to build a provincial-style desk. C. Davis. il Pop Sci 191:182-5+ O '67
DE SOTO, Hernando. See Soto, H. de
DESPAIR in literature. See Literature—Themes
DESPRES, Emile
How sound is the dollar? the U.S. view; interview. por U S News 63:59-60 D 11 '67
DESSERTS
Apple charlotte. H. McCully. il House B 109: 69 Ap '67
Assorted desserts. il Bet Hom & Gard 45: 102 My '67
Butterscotch desserts. il Bet Hom & Gard 45:95 F '67
Chocolate fondue for dessert; with recipe. il Sunset 138:140 Je '67
Classic desserts with a new idea! with recipes. R. Holmberg and B. Zache. il Bet Hom & Gard 45:78-83+ Ap '67
Come for dessert & coffee; with recipes. il McCalls 94:138-9+ F '67
Come for dessert; with recipes. il Farm J 91:102-3+ F '67
Cooking with candy. il Bet Hom & Gard 45: 115-16 O '67
Cool summer desserts; freezer desserts; with recipes. il Redbook 129:92-4+ Ag '67
Dessert of the month. V. V. Voboril. See issues of Good housekeeping
Desserts and snacks for the keep-slim crowd; with recipes. il Good H 164:120-33 Mr '67
Desserts to make in camp; with recipes. Sunset 138:135 Je '67
Eggs whipped, baked, delicious; Salzburg dumplings. il Sunset 139:176 N '67
From Mexico, a puff pudding; almendrado; with recipe. il Sunset 138:219 Ap '67
How to make fresh fruit mousse; with recipe. il Sunset 138:126+ Je '67
Making desserts with citrus; with recipes. il Sunset 138:184+ F '67
No-cook desserts from your freezer. il Ladies Home J 84:80-1+ Ag '67
No time to lose; desserts for Christmas gifts. il McCalls 95:116-20+ N '67
Peach desserts. il Bet Hom & Gard 45:93-4 Ag '67
Peaches and cream in a cooky crust; with recipes. Sunset 139:125 S '67
Plum-lovely desserts. R. Holmberg. il Bet Hom & Gard 45:76-7+ Ag '67
Present from a pear tree. C. Claiborne. il N Y Times Mag p22 D 31 '67
Prune whip, as you like it. il Bet Hom & Gard 45:94 Mr '67
Successful recipes, pineapple desserts. il Suc Farm 65:59-60 Jl '67
Sure-fire desserts; flaming foods. il Ladies Home J 84:10 D '67
Sweets with a switch. il Am Home 70:118+ My '67
This simple Mexican dessert consists of delicious lumps; chongos. il Sunset 138:178 My '67
Using caraway in sweet baking; with recipes. Sunset 139:206 O '67
With the early strawberries. il Sunset 138: 170 Ap '67
See also
Cake
Cookery—Fruit
Ice cream, ices, etc.
Pie
Puddings
Shortcake
Tarts
DESTOUCHES, Louis Ferdinand
Black comic years before his time. W. Goodman. Life 62:10 Ja 27 '67
DESTRIAU effect. See Electroluminescence
DESTROYERS. See Warships
DETECTIVE and mystery plays
Looking glass murder. J. Murray. Plays 27: 11-25 Ja '68
Purloined portrait. E. J. Dias. Plays 27:23-34 N '67
DETECTIVE and mystery stories
Large print program initiated by Walker. Library J 92:2345 Je 15 '67

Bibliography
Criminal record. J. T. Winterich. See last issue of each month of Saturday review
Murder fancier recommends. J. D. Carr. il Harper 235:90-2 Jl '67
Mystery, detective and suspense. M. K. Grant. See first issue of each month of Library journal

Technique
Ideas for mystery fiction. S. Ellin. Writer 80:11-13 D '67
Who is your hero? D. MacKenzie. Writer 81:18-19 Ja '68
Writing the police-routine novel. D. Shannon. Writer 80:11-13+ Mr '67
DETECTIVES
Governor Kirk's not-so-secret police; controversy over special investigators to fight crime in Florida. F. Murray. il Reporter 36:27-30 Mr 23 '67
Governor Kirk's private eyes; the Wackenhut corporation. F. J. Cook. il Nation 204: 616-22 My 15 '67
See also
Pinkerton's incorporated
DETECTORS
Army begins tests of new mortar locator. R. Barnhart. il Aero Tech 21:43-4 Jl 17 '67
Cryogenic detector. Sci N 91:325-9 Ap 8 '67
Radar and vegetation; radar in large-scale surveys of vegetation. Sci Am 217:40 Ag '67
Treasure finders: do they really work? E. Jensen. il Pop Mech 128:112-14+ Ag '67
See also
Counters (electrons, ions, etc)
Metal detectors
DETERGENTS
Battle of Lake Erie: eutrophication and political fragmentation. K. Sperry. il Science 158:351-5 O 20 '67
Detergent to spray with care; Fantastik spray cleaner. Consumer Rep 32:461-3 S '67
Fight grime with the lighter, righter touch! il Redbook 129:88-9+ S '67
LAS detergents relieve stream-foam problems; biodegradability and removal from sewage treatment plants. il Am City 82: 107+ N '67
Liquid dishwashing detergents. il Consumer Rep 32:424-6 Ag '67
DETERMINISM. See Free will and determinism
DETERRENCE (strategy) See Strategy
DETHLEFSEN, Edwin S. See Deetz, J. jt. auth.
DETROIT
Crime
Kids in trouble; suburban youth. G. Astor. il Look 31:34-6 My 16 '67
Maintaining the public welfare; exposés by L. Gordon. Time 90:51 S 22 '67

Economic conditions
Detroit's economic disaster. il Newsweek 70: 57 Ag 7 '67

Education
Community action sets criteria for zoned high school; Eastern senior high school. il Arch Rec 142:184-5 O '67
Fader plan: Detroit style; Highland Park high school. E. Baur. bibliog il Library J 92:3119-21 S 15 '67
Innovative school design breaks the box by use of satellite classroom units and concrete curves; Amelia Earhart junior high school. il Arch Rec 141:180-1 Mr '67
ST reports: Detroit's extended school program. E. Logan. Sr Schol 90:sup7 Ap 28 '67
Where no bells ring; Troy high. Newsweek 69:96+ My 8 '67

Education, Board of
Quasi-boycott of Kingsport press in Detroit Pub W 191:89 Ja 30 '67

Housing
Condemned house and Hobart street; clergy under arrest. H. E. Berg. Christian Cent 84:157-8 F 1 '67
Detroit ends a twenty-year demonstration; Gratiot project. R. Montgomery. il Arch Forum 126:82-7 Ja '67
Pre-fab housing and the church in Detroit. H. H. Ward. Commonweal 86:602-3 S 29 '67

Libraries
See also
Detroit public library

Negroes
Automakers focus on Detroit's jobless. R. W. Irvin. Reporter 37:29-30 D 28 '67
Behind the riots; a sociological study; excerpt of address. R. V. Smith. il Am Ed 3:2-4+ N '67
Detroit: up from the ashes; New Detroit committee program. il Newsweek 71:48-50 Ja 1 '68

DETROIT—Negroes—*Continued*
Detroit's marry-in; program for legalizing common-law marriages. Newsweek 70:61 S 18 '67
How Detroit gropes toward racial peace. il Bsns W p83-4 N 25 '67

Newspapers
Detroit's press profiteers. W. Serrin and G. Goltz. il Reporter 38:32-3 Ja 11 '68
Too impatient to talk; two strike-prone newspapers closed down. il Time 90:84+ D 8 '67
See also
Strikes—United States—Newspapers

Police
Nightmare journey; violence against Negroes during riots. B. Clark. il Ebony 22:121-4+ O '67
Personal touch in police communications. E. Soldan. il Am City 82:36 Je '67
When policemen strike in a big city. il U S News 63:73-4 Jl 3 '67

Politics and government
Mary quite contrary; Detroit's mayor fights recall petition. Newsweek 69:44-5 Je 19 '67

Riots
After due reflection, Detroit and the riots. G. M. Lenox. Christian Cent 84:1300-1 O 11 '67; Reply. G. E. Ireland. 84:1572 D 6 '67
American tragedy, 1967: Detroit: with eyewitness report by J. Dotson. il Newsweek 70:18-27 Ag 7 '67
Autopsy report; investigation of riot fatalities. il Newsweek 70:40+ S 18 '67
Detroit. il Life 63:16-25 Ag 4 '67
Detroit: a riot-torn city survives and bounces back. il Pub W 192:264-7 Ag 28 '67
Detroit aftermath; with report by M. Thimmesch. il Life 63:54-8+ Ag 11 '67
Detroit gropes its way. il Bsns W p25 Ag 5 '67
Detroit, 1967. R. A. Schroth. America 117: 151-2 Ag 12 '67
Fire this time. il Time 90:13-18 Ag 4 '67
Guard under fire; House armed services subcommittee investigation of handling of riots. il Newsweek 70:22 S 4 '67
Last night in Detroit city. F. Mount. il Nat R 19:905-8 Ag 22 '67
Looting, burning, now guerrilla war. il U S News 63:23-7 Ag 7 '67
Motown blues. B. J. Widick. il Nation 205: 102-4 Ag 14 '67
Nightmare journey; violence against Negroes during riots. B. Clark. il Ebony 22:121-4+ O '67
Romney-LBJ feud; who played politics in the rioting? il U S News 63:14 Ag 14 '67
Two Vietnams, one there, the other here; reprint. S. Friedman. U S News 63:25 Ag 14 '67
Ugly aftermath. Time 90:20 Ag 18 '67
Whitey hasn't got the message. J. A. Lukas. il N Y Times Mag p24-5+ Ag 27 '67; Discussion. p39 S 17 '67
Who are the rioters? a study of two cities. il U S News 63:40-1 S 11 '67
Who is really to blame in the rioting? il U S News 63:10 Ag 7 '67
Why the Detroit riots got out of hand. il U S News 64:16 Ja 15 '68

Social conditions
Behind the riots; a sociological study; excerpt of address. R. V. Smith il Am Ed 3: 2-4+ N '67

Stores
Merchants count up the losses; riot damages. Bsns W p28 Ag 5 '67

Transportation
Bus-shelter program woos new riders. il Am City 82:138 Je '67
DETROIT diesel engine division. See General motors corporation—Detroit diesel engine division
DETROIT newspaper strike. See Strikes—United States—Newspapers
DETROIT Pistons (basketball team) See Basketball teams
DETROIT public library
Detroit Metro project periled by squabble. Library J 92:4326 D 1 '67
DETROIT Tigers (baseball) See Baseball clubs
DETROIT. University
Structure and form express the three-way function of this office building; Fisher administrative center. il Arch Rec 142:109-14 Jl '67

DETZER, Karl
False alarm, the prank that kills. Read Digest 91:113-17 S '67
DEUTERIUM
Deuterium and oxygen-18 in natural waters: analyses compared. E. Halevy and B. R. Payne. il Science 156:669 My 5 '67

Isotopes
Deuterium isotope effect on carbon isotope fractionation in photosynthesis. R. A. Uphaus and J. J. Katz. bibliog il Science 155: 324-5 Ja 20 '67
DEUTERIUM oxide
Deuterium oxide: direct action on sympathetic ganglia isolated in culture. M. R. Murray and H. H. H. Benitez. bibliog il Science 155:1021-4 F 24 '67
Hopeful plunge into heavy water; Canada's chemical plant, Glace Bay. il Bsns W p 164+ My 13 '67
DEUTEROPHOMA tracheiphila. See Mal secco disease of citrus
DEUTSCH, Armin J.
Rapid rotation of the solar interior. bibliog Science 156:236-7 Ap 14 '67
DEUTSCH, Karl W.
Arms control and European unity: the next ten years; excerpts from Arms control and the Atlantic alliance. Bul Atomic Sci 23:21-4 My '67
DEUTSCH, Patricia, and Deutsch, R. M.
Does emotional tension make you ill? Read Digest 91:122-5 D '67
Does your child have hidden heart trouble? Read Digest 90:92-6 My '67
One man's fight against hemophilia. Todays Health 45:40-3 Ag '67; Same abr. with title Doctor Thelin's fight against hemophilia. Read Digest 91:90-4 Ag '67
San Diego. Redbook 129:64-5+ My '67
Shocking facts about VD. Parents Mag 42: 44-5+ Ja '67
You can stop smoking & stay thin. Ladies Home J 84:80+ Mr '67; Same abr. with title Do you really want to stop smoking? Read Digest 91:97-101 N '67
DEUTSCH, Ronald M.
Who's to blame for nutrition nonsense? Todays Health 45:66-7 My '67
—See Deutsch, P. jt. auth.
DEUTSCH bank. See Banks and banking—Germany (Federal Republic)
DEUTSCHER, Isaac
Deutscher and Zilliacus. Nation 205:166+ S 4 '67
DEUTSCHER forstverein. See Fernow award
DEUTSCHMAN, Paul
American schools abroad. Holiday 42:105-10 O '67
DE VALOIS, Russell L. and Walraven, Jan
Monocular and binocular aftereffects of chromatic adaptation. Science 155:463-5 Ja 27 '67
DEVALUATION. See Money
DEVALUATION of currency. See Currency question
DEVANAGARI; ballet. See Ballets—Criticisms
DEVANEY, John
Parents who love other people's children. Redbook 130:48-9+ D '67
DEVAS, Nicolette
Bohemian girl. Time 89:98+ Ap 7 '67
She adopted Augustus John. H. T. Moore. Sat R 50:66 Ap 8 '67
DEVELOPING (photography) See Photography—Developing and developers
DEVELOPING nations. See Underdeveloped areas
DEVELOPING tanks. See Photography—Apparatus and supplies
DEVELOPMENT, Economic. See Economic development
DEVELOPMENT and resources corporation
Economic situation in Viet-Nam. L. B. Johnson; D. E. Lilienthal; R. W. Komer. Dept State Bul 56:467-71 Mr 20 '67
Mr Lilienthal discusses Viet-Nam's economic development program; news briefing, December 6, 1967. D. E. Lilienthal. Dept State Bul 57:864-7 D 25 '67
Selling self-help at a profit. il Bsns W p54-6+ Ag 12 '67
DEVELOPMENT banks

Asia
Asian development bank. T. Watanabe. UN Mo Chron 4:33-7 F '67

DEVELOPMENT banks—Asia—*Continued*
Asian development bank immunities defined. L. B. Johnson. Dept State Bul 56:563 Ap 3 '67
Asian development bank: message to Congress, September 26, 1967. L. B. Johnson. Dept State Bul 57:508-11 O 16 '67
DEVELOPMENT of children. See Children—Growth and development
DEVELOPMENT program of the United Nations. See United Nations—Development program
DEVEREUX, Don
Allegories of Ivo Andric. Christian Cent 84: 208 F 15 '67
DEVEREUX, Ian
Temperature measurements from oxygen isotope ratios of fish otoliths. Science 155: 1864-5 Mr 31 '67
DE VEUVE, Laura
The best is yet to be. Christian Cent 84: 866-7 Jl 5 '67
DEVIANT behavior. See Behavior (psychology)
DEVIL In literature
Can we survive nihilism? J. Milton's Satan and A. Camus's Sisyphus. T. Merton. Sat R 50:16-19 Ap 15 '67
DE VILLENEUVE, Justin. See Davies, N.
DEVILLERS, Philippe
Generals sing an old song. Nation 205:233-8 S 18 '67
about
What's your plan? Nation 205:644 D 18 '67
DE VILLIERS, Marq
House of apartheid. Nation 204:741-4 Je 12 '67
DEVILS; drama. See Whiting, J.
DEVIL'S disciple; drama. See Shaw, G. B.
DEVLIN, Joseph. See Griffin, G. A. jt. auth.
DEVLIN, Polly
Midsummer dream. Vogue 149:152-7+ Je '67
Penelope Tree. Vogue 150:162-5 O 1 '67
Twiggy haute couture. Vogue 149:64-5+ Mr 15 '67
DEVLIN, Sandra
On the boards. W. Como. por Dance Mag 41:22 Je '67
DEVLIN, Wende
Beat poems of a beat mother (cont) Good H 164:40 Mr '67
DEVONIAN period. See Paleobotany—Devonian; Paleontology—Devonian
DEVOTION to the Sacred Heart. See Sacred Heart, Devotion to
DEVRIES, Arthur L. See Somero, G. N. jt. auth.
DE VRIES, Peter
Nothing to write home about; story. Harper 235:68-72 Ag '67
Reuben, Reuben; dramatization. See Shumlin, H. Spofford
DEW, Diana
Aglow; interview. New Yorker 42:26-8 Ja 28 '67
about
Turn on your dress, Diana! T. Hyman. il por Sat Eve Post 241:26-9 Ja 13 '68
DEW, Dick
He bought a bus. Sat R 50:58-9+ Je 17 '67
DEWART, Leslie
God and the supernatural. Commonweal 85: 523-8 F 10 '67
about
Belief and Mr Dewart. M. Novak. Commonwal 85:485-8 F 3 '67; Discussion. 85:634+; 86:103 Mr 10, Ap 7 '67
Truth of belief. E. MacKinnon. America 116: 553-6 Ap 15 '67
DEWEY, Horace W.
Lenin's journey in the sealed train. N Y Times Mag p26-7+ Mr 26 '67
DEWEY, John
John Dewey and education through art. J. S. Keel. bibliog il Sch Arts 66:33-7 F '67
DEWS, P. B. and others
Brain research. Science 158:951-2+ N 17 '67
DEWSON, James H. 3d, and others
Rapid eye movement sleep deprivation: a central-neural change during wakefulness. bibliog Science 156:403-6 Ap 21 '67
DEXTROAMPHETAMINE. See Amphetamines
DIABETES research
Hope from diabetic mice. il Sci N 92:154 Ag 12 '67
DIADEME (satellite) See Artificial satellites, French
DIAGNE, Pathé
Vernacular languages in a changing society. por UNESCO Courier 20:29-32 Je '67

DIAGNOSIS
In the lab; too many defective tests. il Time 89:75 F 17 '67
Patients who want to be sick; excerpt from Patients, doctors and families. F. C. Lewis. il Todays Health 46:20-3 Ja '68
Tests that fail. Newsweek 69:62 F 20 '67
See also
Computers—Medical applications
Photography, Medical
Ultrasonic waves—Medical applications
DIAGNOSIS, Urinary. See Urine—Analysis
DIAGNOSTIC instruments. See Medical instruments and apparatus
DIAL telephone. See Telephone, Dial
DIALOGUE
Fine art of eavesdropping. G. Gordon and M. Gordon. Writer 80:16-17+ S '67
Sound of the story. J. Buechler. Writer 80: 19-21 Je '67
DIALYSIS
See also
Kidneys, Artificial
DIAMOND, Edwin
Interpretation of dreams. N Y Times Mag p26-7+ F 12 '67
Long day's journey into the insomniac's night. N Y Times Mag p30-1+ O 1 '67; Same abr. with title Inside insomnia. Read Digest 92: 131-4 Ja '68; Same with title Insomniac's nightmare. sleep. Sci Digest 63:62-7 Ja '68
Singing those Christmas holiday blues. N Y Times Mag p32-3+ D 17 '67
DIAMOND, Ivan, and Schmid, Rudi
Oxidative phosphorylation in experimental bibirubin encephalopathy. bibliog Science 155:1288-9 Mr 10 '67
DIAMOND, Martin
Challenge to the Court. Nat R 19:642-4 Je 13 '67
DIAMOND, Robert M.
Instructional resources in the teaching of art history. Sch Arts 66:24-8 Je '67
DIAMOND alkali company
Bird's-eye view helps win sales and savings; new practitioners of physical distribution. il Bsns W p66-9 Ap 8 '67
CPM for new product introductions. W. Dusenbury. il Harvard Bsns R 45:124-39 Jl '67
DIAMOND Head lighthouse. See Lighthouses
DIAMOND tools. See Diamonds, Industrial
DIAMOND watch; story. See Mather, B.
DIAMONDBACKS. See Rattlesnakes
DIAMONDS
Abundance of type II diamonds. S. Tolansky and H. Komatsu. il Science 157:1173-5 S 8 '67
Hexagonal diamonds in meteorites. Sci N 91: 226 Mr 11 '67
Hexagonal diamonds in meteorites: implications. R. E. Hanneman and others. bibliog il Science 155:995-7 F 24 '67
Huge diamond becomes family's best friend; New York trip for Africans. il Ebony 23: 110-15 Ja '68
Petrus and Ernestine find a diamond as big as an egg. il Life 63:36-7 N 10 '67
Whose best friend? finding and selling of the Lesotho diamond. il Newsweek 70:42 O 30 '67
DIAMONDS, Industrial
Diamond tool machines ablative shields. J. F. Judge. il Tech W 20:34 Mr 13 '67
DIAMONSTEIN, Barbaralee D.
Champion of the impossible dream. Sat R 50:50+ Je 10 '67
DIAPER rash. See Skin—Diseases
DIAPERS, Infants
Disposable diapers. il Consumers Rep 33:36-8 Ja '68
DIARIES
Getting the new year on paper; companies use of calendars and diaries. il Bsns W p96-8 D 30 '67
Gold rush diary. by E. D. Perkins. Review Sat R 50:27-8 My 27 '67. J. K. Hutchens
My magic box. L. Rosten. il Look 31:22-3 Mr 7 '67
Anecdotes, facetiae, satire, etc.
Apocryphal diary; entries Harold Nicolson never wrote. P. H. Bonner, jr. Vogue 150: 229 N 1 '67
Oxford boys. W. Coffey. Commonweal 87:112-13 O 27 '67
El DIARIO-la Prensa
Rey Tiza. Newsweek 70:84+ Jl 17 '67
DIARRHEA
Diarrhea deadly; worst killer of child life. D. A. Ehrlich. Sci N 92:403 O 21 '67

DIAS, Earl J.
Martha Washington's spy; drama. Plays 26: 59-67 F '67
My fair monster; drama. Plays 26:1-12 F '67
Purloined portrait; drama. Plays 27:23-34 N '67
Sand dune hillbillies; drama. Plays 26:15-26, 36 My '67

DIATOMS
Diatom. il Sci N 92:293 S 23 '67

DIAZ ORDAZ, Gustavo
Challenge to the opulent nations; summary of address. America 117:538 N 11 '67
Mexican president honored; excerpts from address, October 26, 1967, ed. by G. Meek. Américas 19:40 D '67
President Diaz Ordaz' visit to Washington; remarks, toast, and address, October 26, 27, 1967. Dept State Bul 57:674-80 N 20 '67

about
Amigos. Newsweek 70:27 N 6 '67
Amigos reunited, Diaz Ordaz and LBJ. il U S News 63:28 N 6 '67

DIBBLE, Charles E.
(tr) See Sahagún, B. de. Feather merchants
(tr) See Sahagún, B. de. Goldworkers and lapidaries

DIBBLE, Vernon K.
In the wasps' nest. Nation 204:439-41 Ap 3 '67

DIBDEN, Arthur J.
Best minds in higher education. Sch & Soc 95:83-4 F 4 '67

DIBELIUS, Otto Friedrich Karl, bp
Defender of the church. il por Time 89:48+ F 10 '67

DIBLIN, Joe A.
Last word in power turbocharging. Flying 80:77-80 F '67
More on engine handling. Flying 80:92-3 Je '67
Running out of TBO? Flying 82:63-4 Ja '68

DICAMBA
New ally in the war against weeds; Banvel D. W. H. Zick. il Parks & Rec 2:32-3 Ap '67

DICE
Spots before your eyes. D. Lancaster. il Pop Electr 27:29-34 S '67

DICE games. See Gambling

DICHLORODIPHENYLTRICHLOROETHANE. See DDT (insecticide)

DICHTER, Misha
Lively arts; interview, ed. by R. Hemming. il por Sr Schol 90:21-2 Ap 14 '67
about
Young Americans with Russian medals. P. G. Davis. por Hi Fi 17:20+ Ja '67

DICK, Lois Hoadley
Advice to pulpit-pretenders; poem. Christian Cent 84:535 Ap 26 '67

DICKE, Robert Henry
Challenging Einstein. por Newsweek 69:98+ F 13 '67
Einstein under siege. C. Behrens. il Sci N 91:144 F 11 '67
Was Einstein wrong? reprint. W. Sullivan. il por Sci Digest 61:75-8 Ap '67
—See McDonald, B. E. jt. auth.

DICKENS, Charles
Christmas carol; dramatization. See Hackett, W.
about
Christmas carol; excerpt from introduction to A Christmas carol in two Christmas classics. E. Johnson. por Sat R 50:13+ D 30 '67
Early, miserable life of Charles Dickens; excerpt from The making of Charles Dickens. C. Hibbert. il Horizon 9:90-7 Aut '67

DICKENSON, Fred
Drugs on campus; a Gallup poll. Read Digest 91:114-15 N '67
Tantalizing treasure of the Andrea Doria. Read Digest 91:150-3 N '67

DICKERMAN, Ernest M.
Beneficial alternate proposal for a Great Smokies road. Liv Wildn 30:42-4 Wint '66

DICKERMAN, Sherwood
How the marines fight the other war. Reporter 36:31-3 Ap 6 '67
Taste of what's to come in the ugly Delta war. Reporter 36:37-9 F 23 '67

DICKERSON, Earl, family
Negro; three families. J. A. Williams. il Holiday 41:58-61+ Mr '67

DICKERSON, George
City emotion; poem. Mlle 64:128 Mr '67

DICKERSON, Nancy
Nancy Dickerson; Washington's most serious butterfly. B. Rollin. il pors Look 31:28-30 S 5 '67

DICKEY, David Dale
(ed) See Moses, F. How to stump the ducks

DICKEY, James
Dark ones; poem. Sat Eve Post 240:72 Ap 8 '67
Falling; poem. New Yorker 42:38-40 F 11 '67
May day sermon to the women of Gilmer County by a lady preacher leaving the Baptist church; poem. Atlan 219:90-7 Ap '67
Power and light; poem. New Yorker 43:60-1 Mr 11 '67
Snakebite; poem. New Yorker 43:44 F 25 '67
Sun; poem. New Yorker 42:32 Ja 28 '67
about
Difficulties of being major. P. Davison. por Atlan 220:116-21 O '67
Inventing the American heart. M. Goldman. Nation 204:529-30 Ap 24 '67
Pilot into poet. R. Tillinghast. New Repub 157:28-9 S 9 '67
Way of seeing and saying. L. Untermeyer. Sat R 50:31+ My 6 '67

DICKINSON, David B. and others
Dimethyl sulfoxide protects tightly coupled mitochondria from freezing damage. bibliog Science 156:1738-9 Je 30 '67

DICKINSON, Emily
Magic prison. A. MacLeish. por Sat R 50: 21-3 O 28 '67

DICKINSON, Joan Younger
Letter from Hong Kong. Holiday 42:24+ S '67

DICKINSON, Maude
When meals were meals; excerpts. Ladies Home J 84:78-9+ Ag '67

DICKINSON, William R. and Hatherton, Trevor
Andesitic volcanism and seismicity around the Pacific. bibliog Science 157:801-3 Ag 18 '67

DICKSON, James
Commission report on the character assassination of President Lyndon B. Johnson. Esquire 67:69-73 Mr '67

DICKSON, Larry L. See McGinnis, S. M. jt. auth.

DICKSON, Robert B.
Out of trouble to win a double. A. Wright. Sports Illus 27:94-5 S 11 '67

DICTAPHONE corporation
Great dictator. R. Levy. il Duns R 90:48-50 S '67

DICTATING machines
Miniature dictation recorders. J. Frye. Electr World 78:64-6 Ag '67
See also
Dictaphone corporation

DICTATORSHIP
Toward Caesarism; effects of war. Christian Cent 84:579-80 My 3 '67

DICTIONARIES
See also subhead Dictionaries under various subjects, e.g. Musicians—Dictionaries

DICTIONARY of scientific biography
Scientific biography; work will contain articles on 5000 scientists. K. Sperry. Science 157:1417-18 S 22 '67

DICYANOMETHYLENE indanedione. See Indanedione

DID anybody miss me? story. See Stanton, W.

DIDACTIC literature
Didacticism in modern dress. J. R. Townsend. Horn Bk 43:159-64 Ap '67

DIDION, Joan
Hippie generation. Sat Eve Post 240:25-31+ S 23 '67
—and Dunne, J. G.
Points West. pors Sat Eve Post 240:8-9+ Je 3; 20+ Je 17; 24-5 Jl 1; 20+ Jl 29; 20+ Ag 26; 22-3 S 23; 26+ O 21; 24+ N 18; 24+ D 2; 18 D 16; 14 D 30 '67; 241:14 Ja 13 '68
—See Dunne, J. G. jt. auth.

DIEBOLD, John
Is the gap technological? For Affairs 46:276-91 Ja '68
What comes next in the computer age; interview. por U S News 62:54-7 Je 26 '67
about
New name in computer leasing. por Bsns W p41 S 9 '67

DIEBOLD, William, Jr
Britain on a budget. Sat R 50:37 Mr 4 '67

DIEDRICH, Edward C.
Rose-colored world of Intourist. Nat R 19: 638-9+ Je 13 '67

DIEFENBACH, Viron L.
Fluoridation story: putting the smile on young faces. Todays Health 45:60-1 F '67

DIEHL, Harold S.
If you don't want your children to smoke. . . por Parents Mag 42:40 Ap '67

DIEHL, Marie A.
Guardian of a doll family. Hobbies 72:39-40+ Jl '67

DIEHNELT, Walter
More room for your money. Farm J 91:34-5 N '67

DIELDRIN
Dieldrin: degradation by soil microorganisms. F. Matsumura and G. M. Boush. bibliog il Science 156:959-61 My 19 '67

DIENBIENPHU, Battle of. See Indochina. French—History—Civil war, 1946-1954

DIENER, T. O. and Raymer, W. B.
Potato spindle tuber virus: a plant virus with properties of a free nucleic acid. bibliog Science 158:378-81 O 20 '67

DIERKS, Donald
U.S. premiere: Henze's Young lord. Hi Fi 17:MA26-7+ My '67

DIESEL engines, Automotive
Diesel engines step up power. il Bsns W p64-6 Je 3 '67

DIESEL engines, Marine
Diesel dollars and sense. R. Mensch. il Yachting 123:98-9+ Ja '68

DIESKAU, Dietrich Fischer-. See Fischer-Dieskau, D.

DIET
Adjustable diet cookbook; excerpts. S. Chapin. il Ladies Home J 85:72-3+ Ja '68
All-time best reducing diets for you, for him, for the whole family. il Good H 164:97-108 My '67
Basic beauty course for girls. il Sr Schol 91:30 S 21; 24 N 2 '67
Beauty checkout; add up ounces, subtract pounds. Vogue 151:34 Ja 1 '68
Clipped cream diet; eight holiday recipes. Vogue 150:152+ D '67
Curing the obese; diuretics questioned. D. A. Ehrlich. Sci N 92:377+ O 14 '67
Daily rhythm in tyrosine concentration in human plasma; persistence on low-protein diets. R. J. Wurtman and others. bibliog il Science 158:660-2 N 3 '67
Diet you can live with; and exercises you might even enjoy; excerpts from Guide to modern physical fitness. C. B. Wilkinson and J. D. Atwater. il Look 31:99-100+ O 17 '67
Dieters' clipboard. See issues of Seventeen
Do it by exercise. Time 90:62 Ag 11 '67
Do you really know how to diet the smart way? Bet Hom & Gard 45:14+ F '67
Doctors' own diet. P. Wyden and B. Wyden. Ladies Home J 84:61+ F '67
Editor's diet. il Mlle 64:184-5 Ap '67
Facts on quacks: how to lose weight without diet, and other myths. il Todays Health 45:16-18 N '67
Feast for dieters; with recipes. il Ladies Home J 84:82-3+ O '67
Good eating & basic-four reducing plan. R. H. Smithies. il Good H 166:193-5 Ja '68
Gourmet diet cook book. E. Ross. il House & Gard 131:127+ Je '67
Hambletonian wonder-week diet; with recipes and menus. il Ladies Home J 84:126+ Mr '67
Hoof and mouth disease: food, diet and dancers. A. Fatt. il Dance Mag 41:39 Je; 24-5 Jl; 23 Ag; 30+ S '67
How other women diet. M. T. Bloom. il Redbook 129:70-1+ O '67
If you're overweight, you don't know how to eat. G. M. Knox. il Bet Hom & Gard 46:24+ Ja '68
Low or high calorie meals; with recipes. B. L. Henry and D. Groves. il Farm J 92:70-2 Ja '68
Slim down, shape up; with sixty-eight diet tips and eight lazy exercises. il Good H 164:154-8 Ja '68
Weight watchers cook book; excerpts. J. Nidetch. il Ladies Home J 84:114-15+ Ap; 128 My '67
Weight watching for wanderers. J. H. Winchester. il Travel 128:49-51 N '67
What to do about fat: plus the commonsense diet. A. Talmey. Vogue 149:126-7 Mr 15 '67
What to do when some are fat and some are thin. M.-L. Reiner. il Parents Mag 42:94-5 N '67
Wise woman's diet for summer slimming. il Redbook 129:48-9 Jl '67
Wise woman's diet: sure, simple, safe; with recipes. il Redbook 130:78+ Ja '68

You and your diet. See issues of Good housekeeping
Zinc retention in rabbits; effect on previous diet. E. R. Graham and P. Telle. bibliog il Science 155:691-2 F 10 '67
See also
Children—Nutrition
Corpulence
Food fads
Food habits
Nutrition
Nutrition research
Oils and fats, Edible
Proteins
Weight reducing preparations
Weight watchers, incorporated

Anecdotes, facetiae, satire, etc.
Let George do it, diet that is. J. L. O'Neill. Am Home 70:50-1 Mr '67

DIET, Deficient
Morphological changes in human scalp hair roots during deprivation of protein. R. B. Bradfield and others. bibliog Science 157:438-9 Jl 28 '67
Starving on the installment plan: malnutrition and Food for peace. il Sr Schol 91:6-7 N 9 '67

DIET in disease
Diet & the heart. Time 89:47 Je 30 '67
Medical diets for common problems. A. F. Benjamin. Am Home 70:57 Mr '67

DIET pills. See Drugs

DIETHER, Jack
Babi Yar. Am Rec G 34:4-6+ S '67
Beethoven out of Mahler by Steinberg. Am Rec G 33:386-7 Ja '67
Gustav Holst. Am Rec G 33:1002-4 Jl '67
Leinsdorf's Mahler Third. Am Rec G 34:100-2 O '67
Messiah. Am Rec G 33:630-3 Ap '67
Neville Cardus on Mahler. Am Rec G 33:834+ My '67
Notes from our correspondents. Hi Fi 17:24+ S '67
Three at once: Das lied. Am Rec G 33:722-7 My '67
Two views of MacBird! Am Rec G 33:974+ Je '67
Vaughan Williams: four works, one, a first on records. Am Rec G 33:552-4 Mr '67

DIETHYL toluamide
Isolation of N,N-diethyl-m-toluamide, deet, from female pink bollworm moths. W. A. Jones and M. Jacobson. bibliog il Science 159:99-100 Ja 5 '68

DIETRICH, Marlene
Kraut. J. Kroll. por Newsweek 70:113 O 23 '67
Old gal in town. por Time 90:84 O 20 '67

DIETS. See Diet

DIETZ, Howard
Something to remember them by. I. Kolodin. il por Sat R 50:60 F 11 '67

DIETZ, Lew
Bog. Field & S 72:56-7+ My '67
Cassius Austin: warden. Field & S 72:44-5+ N '67
Nine natives and the hard buck. Field & S 71:54-5+ Ap '67
Okefenokee. Field & S 71:60-1+ Ap '67

DIEUZAIDE, Jean
Picture stations; photographs. Pop Phot 61:120-1 D '67

DIFFERENCES, National. See National characteristics

DIFFERENCES, Racial. See Racial differences

DIFFERENT one; story. See Engle, K.

DIFFERENTIAL aptitude tests. See Aptitude tests

DIFFERENTIATION (biology)
Epithelial-mesenchymal interactions: report on eighteenth Hahnemann symposium. R. Fleischmajer. Science 157:1472+ S 22 '67
Hormone-dependent differentiation of immature mouse mammary gland in vitro. A. E. Voytovich and Y. J. Topper. bibliog il Science 158:1326-7 D 8 '67
Hormone-dependent differentiation of mammary gland: sequence of action of hormones in relation to cell cycle. D. H. Lockwood and others. bibliog il Science 156:945-6 My 19 '67

DIFFERENTIATION (botany)
Habitat selection by chemically differentiated races of lichens. W. L. Culberson and C. F. Culberson. bibliog il Science 158:1195-7 D 1 '67

DIFFUSION
Anodic oxidation and molecular structure: influence on performance of normal saturated hydrocarbons in fuel cells. E. J. Cairns. bibliog il Science 155:1245-6 Mr 10 '67

DIFFUSION—*Continued*
Diffusion of water in zeolites. C. Parravano and others. bibliog il Science 155:1535-6 Mr 24 '67
Isotope separation by carrier diffusion. H. Craig. bibliog il Science 159:93-6 Ja 5 '68
Silicone rubber: oxygen, carbon dioxide, and nitrous oxide measurement in gas mixtures. H. S. Winsey and J. Folkman. bibliog il Science 157:203-4 Jl 14 '67

DIFFUSION bonding. See Metal bonding

DIGESTIVE system
Painful bubbles; gas in the digestive tract. il Time 90:58+ D 8 '67

Diseases
I prescribe. . .for ulcers and indigestion. J. D. Wassersug. il Sci Digest 61:69-73 My '67

DIGHTMAN, Myrtis
Eight seconds on a barrel of dynamite. il pors Ebony 23:35-6+ D '67
Lonely bull rider. il por Newsweek 69:89-90 Je 19 '67

DI GIOVANNI, Norman Thomas
Sacco-Vanzetti. Nation 205:108 Ag 14 '67

DIGITAL computers. See Computers—Digital computers

DIGITAL converters. See Computers—Input-output equipment

DIGITAL flight instruments. See Aeronautic instruments

DIGITAL voltmeters. See Voltmeters

DIGITALIS lanata. See Foxgloves

DIGITALIS purpurea. See Foxgloves

DIGLYCERIDES. See Glycerides

DIGMAN, Lester A. See Schoderbek, P. P. jt. auth.

DIGNAC, Geny
Bermúdez-Dignac exhibits in Caracas. il Américas 19:41 N '67

DIKE, K. Onwuka
Scientific study of Africa's history. por UNESCO Courier 20:8-13 Je '67

DILANTIN
10,000-to-1 payoff; therapy for emotional disturbance. A. Rosenfeld. il Life 63:121-2+ S 29 '67

DILCO. See Dillingham corporation

DILLENER, John A.
Saigon water-works psychology. Am City 82:92-4 My '67

DILLER, Phyllis
Redbook dialogue. pors Redbook 129:58-9+ My '67

DILLINGHAM corporation
Hawaiian operation with a global punch. il Bsns W p 182-4+ Ap 15 '67

DILLON, Bruce
Helping hand for the Torrey pine. Nat Parks Mag 41:16-17 S '67

DILLON, Jack
Wasn't he nice, Pete? wasn't he nice? story. McCalls 94:82-3 S '67

DILLON, Richard H.
Fine art of abdicating responsibility; adaptation of address, June 23, 1967. por Library J 92:2885-8 S 1 '67
San Francisco a la carte. por Library J 92:2353-60 Je 15 '67

DILTS, Peggy. See Hudson, P.

DILWORTH, Joseph Richardson
Greener look for Yale blue. il Bsns W p 143-4 S 30 '67

DILWORTH, Richardson
Where are they now? por Newsweek 69:22 Mr 13 '67

DIMANCESCU, Dan
Kayak odyssey from the Inland Sea to Tokyo. pors Nat Geog Mag 132:295-337 S '67

DIMATTEO, L. P. and Stewart, M. W.
Prepare to go 100 per cent underground. Am City 82:62+ O '67

DIMENT, Adam
Authors & editors. il por Pub W 192:15 D 4 '67

DIMETHYL benzanthracene
Chromosome abnormality in rat leukemia induced by 7,12-dimethylbenz[a]anthracene. T. Sugiyama and others. bibliog il Science 158:1058-9 N 24 '67

DIMETHYL sulfoxide. See Methyl sulfoxide

DIMETHYLAMINO group
Weird light you can pour from a bottle; tetrakisdimethylaminoethylene. W. S. Bacon. il Pop Sci 191:84-5 S '67

DIMETHYLOXAZOLIDINEDIONE. See Oxazolidinedione

DIMITRI Mitropoulos International music competition. See Music—Competitions

DINERS' club, incorporated
Charge! gang defrauds Diners club. Time 90:80 N 24 '67

DINGHIES, Sailing. See Sailboats

DINGHY racing. See Boat racing

DINGLE, Hugh, and Haskell, J. B.
Phase polymorphism in the grasshopper melanoplus differentialis. bibliog Science 155:590-2 F 3 '67

DINGOES
Red dog dingo. D. Stivens. Holiday 42:105-6+ S '67

DINH, Tran-van-. See Tran-van-Dinh

DINING. See Dinners and dining

DINING tables. See Tables

DINNER at eight; drama. See Kaufman, G. S. and Ferber, E.

DINNERS and dining
Best things come from the oven! il Good H 164:124-6 F '67
Black-tie dinner at Baby Jane's; with recipes. il Ladies Home J 84:126-9 O '67
Black-tie dinner plus fun and games. il House & Gard 132:224-5 N '67
Budget-minded meals he's sure to like. il Good H 164:74-91 Ja '67
Company's coming to dinner; with recipes. Am Home 70:112 Jl; 106 S '67
Cooking for two; with recipes. il McCalls 94:136-7+ F '67
Couples who cook; with menus and recipes. H. McCully. il House B 109:104-7+ Jl '67
Dinner-for-two cookbook; with menus and recipes. E. Ross. il House & Gard 131:173+ Ap '67
Dinner triumph; with recipes. il N Y Times Mag p80 O 1 '67
Dinner's ready in only an hour, or less. il Good H 165:130-45 O '67
Dress-up dinners; with recipes. il Mlle 65:190-2 O '67
Elegant steak dinner for two. il Sunset 138:237 My '67
Feast of Easter. C. Claiborne. il N Y Times Mag p 100 Mr 12 '67
For the last-minute shopper; with menu. V. T. Habeeb. il Am Home 70:104+ Mr '67
From shopping bag to the table in under 30 minutes; with recipes. il Sunset 138:150-1 F '67
Great dinners. E. Graves. See issues of Life
Home at 6, dinner at 8; with recipes. E. Alston. il Look 31:80-2 D 12 '67
January meal plan idea. il Bet Hom & Gard 46:75-6 Ja '68
Julia Child way to plan your own ready-ahead dinner; with recipes. il Ladies Home J 84:88+ O '67
Let's have hotspyot; simmer dinners; with recipes. il Sunset 138:98-100 F '67
Light-hearted entertaining on a gold-plated shoestring; menus with recipes. N. S. Toop. il Parents Mag 42:78-9+ O '67
Meal a day; menus. P. Cannon. il Ladies Home J 84:131 Mr; 125 Ap '67
Menus men like, when company comes. il Redbook 128:92-6+ Ap '67
Movable feast in a winery. il House & Gard 132:222-3 N '67
No time to cook; menu with recipes. See issues of McCall's
Perfect summer dinner; with recipes. il Bet Hom & Gard 45:78-9+ Jl '67
Progressive dinner; with recipes. il McCalls 94:140-2+ F '67
Sunday dinner, step-by-step; with menu and recipes. R. Holmberg. il Bet Hom & Gard 45:76-83 S '67
Two spring dinners, roast pork or roast chicken. il Sunset 138:210+ My '67
V.I.P. dinner; with recipes. il Ladies Home J 84:130-2+ O '67
When dinner's for eight. C. Claiborne. il N Y Times Mag p 100-1 O 22 '67
With all the fixin's holiday dinner. il McCalls 95:114-15+ N '67
See also
Food, Frozen
Outdoor meals
Thanksgiving dinners

DINOSAURS
Baja California; late cretaceous dinosaurs. W. J. Morris. bibliog il Science 155:1539-41 Mr 24 '67
Old bones store sells out; dinosaur store at Utah university. il Sci Digest 62:65-6 Ag '67
What is the iguanodon? Sci Digest 62:74-5 D '67

DIOCESAN chanceries. See Chanceries, Diocesan

DIOCESAN synods
Synod in Atlanta. America 116:576 Ap 22 '67
DIOCESES
See also
Catholic church—Dioceses
Chanceries, Diocesan
DIODES
Gunn oscillators. D. L. Heiserman. il Electr World 78:42-3 S '67
Higher gain avalanche photodiodes. Electr World 78:86 N '67
Light-emitting diodes. D. L. Heiserman. il Electr World 79:36-7+ Ja '68
LSA diodes: new source of microwave power; limited space charge accumulation. il Electr World 77:29 Je '67
Silicon-carbide light diode. Electr World 77:61 Mr '67
Using the new constant-current diodes. D. E. Lancaster. il Electr World 78:30-1+ O '67

Testing
Breakdown reverse voltage transistor and diode tester. C. D. Rakes. il Pop Electr 26:67-71 My '67
DIORAMAS
Diorama depicting scene of Battle of Monmouth. L. E. Eben il Sch Arts 66:31-2 F '67
Miniatures are big in our family. Mrs D. J. Moe. il Hobbies 72:109-110 Ag '67
Paul Revere's shop in miniature. R. Davidson. il Antiques 92:176 Ag '67
DIOSPYROS. See Persimmons
DIPHENAMID. See Herbicides
DIPHOSPHOPYRIDINE nucleotide
Sot: his psyche or his genes? Enzopride as a cure for alcoholism. R. Kirk. Nat R 19:808 Jl 25 '67
DIPLOMACY
Public diplomacy at the United Nations; address, July 27, 1967. A. J. Goldberg. Dept State Bul 57:262-5 Ag 28 '67
See also
Diplomatic and consular service
European war, 1914-1918—Diplomatic history
International relations
DIPLOMATIC and consular service
Life in a fishbowl; isolation of foreign diplomats in Peking. il Newsweek 70:48+ S 11 '67
Red China vs. Britain; what's ahead now? il U S News 63:10 S 11 '67
Ultimatum & anarchy; Peking's behavior to British and other diplomats. Time 90:20 S 1 '67
See also
Ambassadors
also subhead Diplomatic and consular service under names of countries, e.g. Great Britain—Diplomatic and consular service
DIPLOMATIC recognition. See Recognition (international law)
DIPLOMATS
See also
Ambassadors
Russia—Diplomatic and consular service
United States—Foreign service
DIPLOMATS children. See Children of diplomats
DIPOLE antennas. See Radio antennas
DIRECT digital control. See Computers—Control applications
DIRECT election of presidents. See Presidents —United States—Election
DIRECT energy conversion
Science pacemaker. P. Pierce. il Ebony 22: 52-4+ Ap '67
See also
Fuel cells
DIRECT mail advertising. See Advertising, Direct mail
DIRECT selling. See Canvassing
DIRECTION, Sense of. See Orientation
DIRECTION finding apparatus
See also
Radio in navigation
DIRECTORIES
See also subhead Directories under various subjects, e.g. Theological schools— Directories
DIRECTORS. See Moving picture directors
DIRECTORS, Corporation. See Corporations— Directors
DIRKSEN, Everett McKinley
Case for school prayer. Good H 164:30 Mr '67
Excerpt from radio-television report, March 6, 12, 1967. Cong Digest 46:268+ N '67

Rewrite the U.S. Constitution? interview. por U S News 62:63-6 Je 5 '67
State of the Union; a Republican appraisal; address, January 19, 1967. Vital Speeches 33:258-60 F 15 '67; Excerpts. por U S News 62:72 Ja 30 '67
about
Dirksen and LBJ, strange allies; with interview with M. Mansfield. il pors U S News 63:72-5 D 11 '67
Dirksen caper. New Repub 156:2 Ap 29 '67
Dirksen's first bill. Christian Cent 84:101 Ja 25 '67
Ev-and-Lyndon show. il por Newsweek 70:27 O 30 '67
Ev and the everlasting. Christian Cent 84: 1589 D 13 '67
Everett Dirksen is a happening! records. W. Hedgepeth. il pors Look 31:M24+ D 12 '67
Mister Republican; relationship with L. B. Johnson. New Repub 157:4 D 2 '67
90th GOP style: Republican State of the Union message. il por Newsweek 69:19-20 Ja 30 '67
No consensus: G.O.P. State of the Union message. il por Time 89:18 Ja 27 '67
Old man Dirksen. K. Crawford. Newsweek 71:27 Ja 8 '68
Package of mischief. New Repub 157:4 S 23 '67
Sing Loo, sweet Senator. il por Time 89: 21 F 10 '67
Smell of battle. Nat R 20:16 Ja 16 '68
Soul brothers. Reporter 37:10 Ag 10 '67
Strong start. il Time 89:25-6 My 19 '67
Unconventional convention. Reporter 36:6-8 Ap 6 '67
DI ROSA, Carolyn
They live as they like. il pors House & Gard 131:140-7 Mr '67
DI ROSA, René
They live as they like. il pors House & Gard 131:140-7 Mr '67
DIRTY story; novel. See Ambler, E.
DISABLED. See Handicapped
DISACCHARIDASES. See Intestines—Diseases
DISADVANTAGED children. See Socially handicapped children
DISARMAMENT
Inquiry into a disarmed world. il UNESCO Courier 20:5-9 Ag '67
Science and disarmament. P. Noel-Baker. bibliog f il UNESCO Courier 20:10-21+ Ag '67
Strategy for arms control; recommendations of White House panel on arms control and disarmament, 1965. J. B. Wiesner. Sat R 50:17-20 Mr 4 '67
See also
Atomic weapons and disarmament
Conference of the Eighteen-nation committee on disarmament, Geneva, 1962-

Latin America
Denuclearization in Latin America; Treaty for the prohibition of nuclear weapons in Latin America. H. Bowser. Sat R 50:32 My 20 '67
Latin America bans the bomb; Treaty of Tlatelolco. L. Eder. Nation 204:371-2 Mr 20 '67
Latin American nations conclude nuclear free zone treaty; statement, February 13, 1967. F. Freeman. Dept State Bul 56:436 Mr 15 '67
Latins ban bomb. Sr Schol 90:15+ Mr 3 '67
DISASTERS
Aberfan; happiness ended last October. T. Coleman. il Sat Eve Post 240:91-5 O 21 '67
Alert system that blankets a borough; Red Bank, N.J. F. E. Brower, jr. il Am City 82:30 My '67
Ghosts of Aberfan; one year later. W. Danforth. il McCalls 95:98-103+ N '67
Major air pollution disasters. Sr Schol 90:7 Mr 17 '67
Operation anti-disaster. E. D. Mills. il UNESCO Courier 20:16-17+ F '67
Village that lost its children; Aberfan, Wales. L. Lee. il Redbook 130:58-60+ Ja '68
See also
Bridges—Accidents
Hurricanes
Shipwrecks
DISC brakes. See Brakes, Automobile
DISC electrophoresis. See Electrophoresis
DISC jockeys
Decibelters. il Time 90:81 O 27 '67
Le deejay; M. Pasternak's Paris-based program. il Newsweek 69:52 My 1 '67

DISC Jockeys—*Continued*
Deejays and teen radio; WQAM, teen music station in south Florida. L. M. Savary. America 117:444-5 O 21 '67
Larry Josephson; interview. L. Josephson. New Yorker 43:25-6 Je 17 '67
See also
Kaufman, M.

DISCHARGED prisoners. See Prisoners, Discharged

DISCIPLES. See Apostles

DISCIPLES of Christ
Disciples launch basic change; 118th assembly of the International convention of Christian churches. H. E. Fey. Christian Cent 84:1421-3 N 8 '67

DISCIPLINE
But, judge, what is proper discipline? L. B. Blessing and others. Read Digest 91:157-8+ S '67
His and hers of discipline; setting standards and enforcing them. J. Brothers. Good H 166:36+ Ja '68
New approach to discipline; with discussion group program by C. W. Mattuck. R. Thomas. bibliog il Parents Mag 42:28+, 58-9+ My '67
See also
Children—Management and training
College discipline

DISCIPLINE, Industrial. See Labor discipline

DISCIPLINE, Library. See Library administration

DISCOTHEQUES. See Night clubs

DISCOUNT
Fed sticks to its course. il Bsns W p36-7 Ap 15 '67

DISCOUNT houses (retail trade)
See also
Korvette, E. J, incorporated

DISCOVERIES in geography
See also
Explorations

DISCOVERIES in science. See Inventions

DISCRIMINATION
If some, then all; draft convention on the elimination of all forms of religious intolerance. Christian Cent 84:1451 N 15 '67
See also
Jews and Negroes
United Nations—Sub-commission on prevention of discrimination and protection of minorities

DISCRIMINATION, Racial. See Race discrimination

DISCRIMINATION in education
Fair educational practice act is dead. E. S. Wilson. il Sat R 50:85-6 S 16 '67
San Jose: the bullhorn message; Negro campaign against discrimination. J. Brann. Nation 205:465-7 N 6 '67

DISCRIMINATION in employment
Bigger stick to fight job bias. il Bsns W p84+ Mr 18 '67
Broader effort on job bias; new chairman of Equal employment opportunity commission. C. L. Alexander, jr. Bsns W p56+ Jl 15 '67
Comparing racial employment. il Sch & Soc 95:340 O 14 '67
Debate is over. P. M. Klutznick. il Sat R 51: 54+ Ja 13 '68
Discriminatory promotion systems. P. B. Doeringer. Mo Labor R 90:27-8 Mr '67
Economic leverage of the churches; Project Equality. America 116:714 My 13 '67; Reply. P. J. Flynn. 116:823 Je 10 '67
Hiring and promotion policies under FEP legislation; excerpt from Patterns of discrimination in employment. Mo Labor R 90:53-6 F '67
Negro and apprenticeship, by F. R. Marshall and V. M. Briggs, jr. Review
Reporter 37:56+ N 2 '67. K Goodall
Of many things; Kodak and FIGHT agreement. R. A. Schroth. America 117:inside cover Jl 8 '67
Processing employment discrimination cases. A. W. Blumrosen. Mo Labor R 90:25-6 Mr '67
Racial policies of American industry. H. R. Northrup. Mo Labor R 90:41-3 Jl '67
Sex and equal employment rights. Mo Labor R 90:111-1V Ag '67
Slough of equality. Nation 204:196-7 F 13 '67
Tomorrow becomes yesterday; complaints about refusal to promote or train because of color. Time 90:99-100 D 8 '67
Tougher stand on discrimination? U S News 63:82 Ag 7 '67
See also
Negroes in the United States—Employment

DISCRIMINATION in housing
California's fair-housing follies. G. V. Kennard. America 117:204-6 Ag 26 '67
Fair housing again in rights bill. il U S News 62:69 F 27 '67
Fair housing showdown in the West. G. V. Kennard. America 116:142-6 Ja 28 '67
Ghettos in the U.S, or propaganda? il U S News 63:63 Ag 21 '67
House in Paddock Woods; case of J. Jones before Supreme court. Newsweek 70:42 D 18 '67
Louisville happening; Derby runs scared; open housing issue. L. Grauman, jr. il Nation 204:639-92 My 29 '67
McNamara's Negroes; Pentagon's dilatory efforts to end off-base housing segregation. New Repub 156:6 My 6 '67
Mac's other war; Negro servicemen in off-base housing. Time 90:24 S 29 '67
Mr Jones goes to Washington; Supreme court will hear arguments in major open-housing case. J. Galloway. Commonweal 87:374-5 D 22 '67
Off-base housing; policy of the Defense department. New Repub 157:9 Ag 5 '67
Open issue; Supreme court reverses California's 1964 initiative vote on open housing. Newsweek 69:30+ Je 12 '67
Opening roads for open housing; state courts. Time 89:47 F 3 '67
Property rights and human rights. R. K. Taylor. Christian Cent 84:1120-2 S 6 '67; Reply. R. G. Lapp. 84:1320 O 18 '67
Reflections on open housing. America 117: 295-6 S 23 '67; Discussion. 117:426 O 21 '67
200-bev accelerator; moving into a WASP's nest? B. Nelson. il Science 156:1713-16 Je 30 '67
200 bev; close Senate vote defeats effort to delay Weston project. B. Nelson. Science 157:294-5 Jl 21 '67; Discussion. 158:48+ O 6 '67
Unfair housing authority. J. Eisen. Commonweal 87:8-9 O 6 '67
Whose Kentucky home? il Newsweek 69:27-8 My 1 '67
See also
Housing—Desegration
Negroes in the United States—Housing

DISCRIMINATION learning. See Learning, Psychology of

DISCUS, pseud.
Music in the round. See issues of Harper's magazine

DISCUSSION
John Stuart Mill on intemperate discussion. J. S. Mill. Commonweal 87:379 D 22 '67
See also
Conversation

DISCUSSION groups. See Forums (discussion and debate)

DISCUSSION method (education)
University of Texas philosophical colloquia. il Sch & Soc 94:476+ D 24 '66

DISEASES
What's new in medicine. A. Kerr. See issues of McCall's
See also
Animals as carriers of infection
Mortality
War and disease
also names of diseases, e.g. Anemia

Causes and theories of causation

Lysosomes and disease. A. Allison. il Sci Am 217:62-72 N '67
Riddle of the dangerous bean; enzyme deficiency as cause of hemolysis and favism in specific ethnic groups. J. R. Marcus and G. Cohen. il Harper 234:98-102 Je '67
Sickle-cell trait in human biological and cultural evolution; excerpt from address, January 1967. S. L. Wiesenfeld. bibliog il Science 157:1134-40 S 8 '67

History

Latent diseases rise up; evolutionary approach to infectious diseases. Sci N 92:608 D 23 '67

DISEASES, Hereditary. See Heredity of disease

DISEASES, Industrial
Improving occupational health in Chile; Institute of occupational health and air pollution research. Santiago. il UN Mo Chron 4:79-84 Mr '67
Industry doctors try new approach; environmental health. il Bsns W p80-2+ My 13 '67
Is uranium mining a hazard to health? il Bsns W p 107-8+ Je 3 '67

DIVERSIFICATION in industry
Appetite for more; ITT buys Levitt & sons. il Time 90:74-5 Ag 4 '67
Borden's land of milk & honey. R. Levy. il Duns R 89:42-4+ My '67
Broadening the rails; Chicago & North Western railway acquiring Essex wire corp. il Time 89:88 Je 23 '67
Case for conglomerates. Fortune 75:163-4 Je 15 '67
Changing face of W. R. Grace. R. Levy. il Duns R 90:22-4+ Jl '67
Conglomerate, London-style; Cope Allman. il Time 90:96 O 13 '67
Container seeks a bigger package. il Bsns W p 186-8+ O 21 '67
Double the profits, double the pride. il Time 90:86-8+ S 8 '67
Empire builders; conglomerate mergers. H. C. Wallich. Newsweek 70:56 Ag 21 '67
Freeport says it with sulfur. il Bsns W p72-6 N 4 '67
Greyhound's new route; other businesses. il Time 89:89 My 26 '67
Incubating industry in Mexico; B. Quintana's Industria del Hierro. il Bsns W p86-8 Je 24 '67
Ling's latest; Ling-Temco-Vought, inc. proposal to buy Greatamerica corp. Newsweek 70:72+ Ag 14 '67
Odd news about conglomerates. T. O'Hanlon. il Fortune 75:174-7 Je 15 '67
Olin's grand designer; G. Grand. W. Berry. Duns R 89:50-2 My '67
Perils of the multi-market corporation. G. Burck. il Fortune 75:130-5+ F '67
Sharp edge of Gillette. R. Levy. il Duns R 89:43-4+ Ap '67
Steel goes afield. il Bsns W p42+ S 30 '67
Stepping out of a silvery past; Handy & Harman processor. il Bsns W p 144-6 N 25 '67
Westinghouse plugs in. il Bsns W p94-6+ Je 17 '67

DIVERSION of angels; ballet. See Ballets—Criticisms

DIVESTITURE. See Trusts, Industrial—Law

DIVIDENDS
Dividends feel the pressure. il Bsns W p59-60+ Mr 18 '67
How much can your savings earn? il Changing T 21:12-13 Mr '67
Investing in a dividend boost. G. E. MacDougal. il Harvard Bsns R 45:87-92 Jl '67
Wall Street; unyielding rise in yields. C. Morgello. il Newsweek 69:71 Ap 3 '67

DIVINE comedy. See Dante Alighieri

DIVINE love. See Love (theology)

DIVING, Submarine
Dive at Buck Island. M. W. Williams. il Nat Parks Mag 41:4-7 Ag '67
Diver's dream come true; Underwater explorers club on Grand Bahama. C. Phinizy. il Sports Illus 26:38-41 F 6 '67
Diving women of Korea and Japan. S. K. Hong and H. Rahn. il Sci Am 216:34-43 My '67
Modern argonauts. V. D. Smith. il Ebony 22:99-102+ Mr '67
Sunken time bombs full of oil! D. C. Fales. il Pop Mech 128:97-101+ N '67
They dive for wrecks. J. R. Berry. il Pop Mech 127:92-4+ Mr '67
Useful work at 600-ft. depths demonstrated by Westinghouse. il Tech W 20:38 Je 19 '67
See also
Aquanauts
Archeology, Submarine
Skin diving

Physiological aspects
Endurance limits underwater. B. Frisch. il Sci Digest 61:48-53 Ap '67

DIVING apparatus
Aquanauts get liquid air; cryogenic breathing units. J. Eberhart. il Sci N 92:138-9 Ag 5 '67
Cryogenic scuba; liquid air rig. il Time 89:53 Je 16 '67
Practical skin-diving. S. Anderson. il Yachting 122:58-9+ N '67
See also
Respiratory apparatus
Submarine vehicles

DIVING platforms, boards, etc.
Build this low-cost diving board. il Pop Mech 127:170-1 My '67

DIVING suits
Navy gets radioisotope heater for divers. R. W. Niblock. il Aero Tech 21:42-3 O 23 '67

DIVINING rod
Psychologists examine the secrets of water witching. R. Hyman and E. Z. Vogt. il Sci Digest 63:39-45 Ja '68

DIVINITY of Christ. See Jesus Christ—Divinity

DIVINITY schools. See Theological schools

DIVINITY students. See Theological students

DIVISION
To avoid long division, use this short-cut table. A. P. Armagnac. Pop Sci 190:124-5 Mr '67

DIVISION for the blind. See United States—Library of Congress—Division for the blind and physically handicapped

DIVISION for the physically handicapped. See United States—Library of Congress—Division for the blind and physically handicapped

DIVISION of library services and educational facilities. See United States—Education, Office of—Library services and educational facilities, Division of

DIVORCE
Church and second marriage. J. T. Catoir. Commonweal 86:113-17 Ap 14 '67
Divorce for Catholics. Newsweek 69:80+ Mr 6 '67
Divorce from three to six. J. F. McDermott, jr. il N Y Times Mag p99+ O 22 '67
Divorce: no longer unthinkable. R. Ruether. Commonweal 86:117-19+ Ap 14 '67
Rational ethics says no. G. G. Grisez. Commonweal 86:122-5 Ap 14 '67
See also
Alimony
Broken homes

Italy
No divorce, Italian style. G. D. Kumlien. Commonweal 86:279-80 My 26 '67

New York (state)
Help wanted; divorce counselor. M. M. Hunt; discussion. N Y Times Mag p21 Ja 22 '67
Rush to Juárez. Time 90:64 S 1 '67
Sadness in Juárez. Newsweek 70:31-2 S 4 '67

United States
California woman. G. Greene. Ladies Home J 84:62+ Jl '67
Children of divorce, what rights have they? with Milwaukee's bill of rights for children in divorce actions. R. W. Hansen. Read Digest 90:181-3+ Mr '67
Divorce and the Negro woman. P. Pierce. il Ebony 22:84-6+ Jl '67
Divorce suburban style; Kay Biocini. G. B. Leonard. il Look 31:30-3 My 16 '67
Divorced woman, American style. il Newsweek 69:64-6+ F 13 '67
How U.S. Catholics view divorce. Newsweek 69:73-4 Mr 20 '67

DIVORCE (canon law)
Privilege of the faith cases; proposal to authorize local bishops to grant a divorce. America 117:702 D 9 '67

DIVORCE for Rob Phillips; story. See Bittle, C. R.

DIVORCEES
Divorced woman, American style. il Newsweek 69:64-6+ F 13 '67
New public health problem. Sci N 92:560 D 9 '67

DIXON, Dave
Tonic for a game with tired blood. F. Deford. por Sports Illus 27:68+ D 11 '67

DIXON, Eddie, and Hamilton, Bus
Grizzly scalped me. por Outdoor Life 139:76-7+ Ap '67

DIXON, Frank J. See Oldstone, M. B. A. jt. auth.

DIXON, Jeane
Gullibility in Washington. C. Fritchey. Harper 234:34-8 Je '67

DIXON, John W. jr
Hierarchy and laity. Christian Cent 84:1353-6+ O 25 '67

DIXON, Paul Rand
Little old lady with a tough new look. il por Newsweek 70:82-3 O 23 '67

DIXON, Calif.
City-school cooperation builds a park two years sooner. J. M. Lesher. il Am City 82:80-1 N '67

DJILAS, Milovan
Conversation with Djilas; interview, ed. by S. Cohen. por Newsweek 69:44 Ap 3 '67
about
Allegories of Ivo Andric. D. Devereux. Christian Cent 84:208 F 15 '67
Tito foe freed. il por Sr Schol 89:18 Ja 20 '67

DLAMINI, Khotso Sethuntsa. See Khotso

DO-it-yourself building. See Building

DO-it-yourself work
Four weekend projects with pipe. J. Burroughs. il Pop Mech 127:178-83 My '67
Homebuilder and his craft. A. Trammell and J. Gilbert. il Flying 81:36-52 S '67
Six weekend projects to improve your home. J. Capotosto. il Pop Mech 127:134-7 F '67
You, too, can build a fireplace. W. C. Leckey. il Pop Mech 128:148-53+ D '67 (to be cont)
See also
Kit building

DOAR, John Michael
Exit John Doar. il por Newsweek 70:32 D 11 '67
Following the action. Time 90:27 D 8 '67

DOBRIN, Arnold
Attention, attention... Horn Bk 43:27-30 F '67
My approach to children's books. il Am Artist 31:30-5 Mr '67

DOBRYNIN, Anatolii Fedorovich
Outer space treaty signed by sixty nations at White House ceremony; text of statement, January 27, 1967. Dept State Bul 56:269 F 20 '67

DOBZHANSKY, Theodosius
Changing man; excerpts from address, December 26, 1966. bibliog Science 155:409-15; 157:6 Ja 27, Jl 7 '67
Evolution: implications for religion. Christian Cent 84:936-41 Jl 19 '67

about
Watching a new species develop? il por Time 89:37 Ap 7 '67

DOCKING in space. See Orbital rendezvous (space flight)

DOCKS
Build this double-deck boat port. H. Clark. il Pop Mech 129:152-3 Ja '68
Picking up a mooring or making a dock. H. deFontaine. il Yachting 121:103 Ja '67

DR Cook's garden; drama. See Levin, I.

DR McGrath; drama. See Wilson, E.

DR Seuss, pseud. See Geisel, T. S.

DOCTORS. See Physicians

DOCTRINAL theology. See Theology

DOCTRINE, Religious. See Theology

DOCUMENTARY films. See Moving pictures—Documentary films

DOCUMENTARY phonograph records. See Phonograph records—Documentary records

DOCUMENTARY photography. See Photography, Documentary

DOCUMENTARY television programs. See Television broadcasting—Documentary programs

DODD, Edward H, Jr
Reformed publisher; interview. New Yorker 43:47-8 O 28 '67

DODD, Frank C.
Obituary
Pub W por 193:64-5 Ja 15 '68

DODD, Mead and company
Reformed publisher; interview. E. H. Dodd, jr. New Yorker 43:47-8 O 28 '67

DODD, Thomas Joseph
Case of Senator Dodd: the charges and a reply; excerpts. U S News 62:44-5 Je 26 '67
Excerpt from address, February 9, 1967. Cong Digest 46:216+ Ag '67

about
Anti-Dodd report. W. F. Buckley, jr. Nat R 19:560 My 30 '67
At Dodd hearings: the accusations, the senator's defense. il por U S News 62:8 Mr 27 '67
At the bar of the Congress. Nat R 19:336-7 Ap 4 '67
Beginning of the end. por Newsweek 69:36 My 8 '67
But for the grace of Dodd. por Newsweek 69:37 Je 26 '67
Censure. il Newsweek 70:23 Jl 3 '67
Censure for Dodd? Sr Schol 90:19 My 12 '67
Committee for justice for Dodd. Nat R 19:555-6 My 30 '67
Congressional ethics gap. Life 62:4 Je 30 '67
Crime and punishment in the club. R. Yoakum. New Repub 156:8-9 My 13 '67
Different kind of censure debate. M. McGrory. America 117:31 Jl 8 '67
Dodd and mammon. F. Mount. il pors Nat R 19:731-7 Jl 11 '67
Dodd and Powell. Nation 204:387-8 Mr 27 '67
Dodd dilemma. Commonweal 86:404 Je 30 '67

Dodd is not being persecuted. Nation 204:805-6 Je 26 '67
Dodd report revisited. Nat R 19:624-5 Je 13 '67
Dodd that failed. R. Yoakum. New Repub 156:10-13 Ap 1 '67
Dodd's defense. il por Time 89:16-17 Je 23 '67
Dogging Dodd. Newsweek 69:26-7 Ap 24 '67
Findings in the Dodd case; with text of resolution of censure. il por U S News 62:70-1 My 8 '67
Issue beyond Senator Dodd. America 117:29-30 Jl 8 '67
Oft-blurred line. il por Time 89:16-17 Mr 24 '67
Pearson the conqueror. Nat R 19:507 My 16 '67
Powell and Dodd cases, how they differ. il por U S News 62:35-7 My 1 '67
Senate judgment: Dodd is censured. por U S News 63:22 Jl 3 '67
Senator Dodd and the informers. por Sat Eve Post 241:70 Ja 27 '68
Senator Dodd's censure. W. F. Buckley, jr. Nat R 19:509 My 16 '67
Taps for Tom. il por Time 89:18 Je 30 '67
Testifying for Dodd. R. Yoakum. New Repub 156:12-13 Mr 18 '67
To tell or not to tell. W. V. Shannon. Commonweal 86:308-9 Je 2 '67
Tragedy of Thomas Dodd; excerpt from Above the law. J. Boyd. il por Sat Eve Post 241:19-25 Ja 13; 58-62+ Ja 27 '68 (to be cont)
Undoing of Dodd. il por Time 89:21-2 My 5 '67
What Dodd did. il por Newsweek 69:30-1 Mr 27 '67
What hath Dodd wrought? R. Yoakum. por New Repub 157:13-16 Jl 8 '67

DODD hearings. See United States—Congress—Senate—Standards and conduct, Committee on

DODDS, Robert C.
Roman Catholic and Protestant church structures compared. Cath World 205:327-34 S '67

DODECANESE (islands)
See also
Kasos (islands)

DODGE, F. W. corporation
F. W. Dodge construction outlook: 1968. il Arch Rec 142:81-4 N '67

DODGE, Mary (Mapes)
Hans Brinker, or The silver skates; dramatization. See Thane, A. Gift for Hans Brinker

DODGE, Natt N.
New Guadalupe Mountains National Park. Nat Parks Mag 41:4-7 F '67

DODGE, Ralph E. bp
Lost heritage: African good will. Christian Cent 84:1395-6 N 1 '67

DODGERS (baseball) See Baseball clubs

DOERINGER, Peter B.
Discriminatory promotion systems. Mo Labor R 90:27-8 Mr '67

DOES a tiger wear a necktie? drama. See Peterson, D.

DOG Argentine. See Hunting dogs

DOG bites
Beware the dogs; Goodman children killed. il Newsweek 71:15 Ja 1 '68
Tragedy at Lynchburg; Goodman brothers killed by dogs. il Time 90:13 D 29 '67

DOG breeding
Breeding your hunting dog. J. Griffen. il Field & S 72:178-9+ My '67
Mongrels for progress; Ventura County dog fanciers association. Sports Illus 26:7 Ja 23 '67

DOG breeds. See Dogs

DOG days. See Hot weather

DOG fleas. See Fleas

DOG houses. See Kennels

DOG racing
Belle of the mushers; 1966 World championship sled dog race in Anchorage, Alaska. V. Kraft. il Sports Illus 26:54-63 Ja 23 '67

DOG shows
Big bark in the Garden; Westminster kennel club show. R. H. Boyle. Sports Illus 26:48-50 F 13 '67

Quotations, maxims, etc.
Dogs in review; comp. by E. F. Murphy. il N Y Times Mag p 128 My 14 '67

DOG sleds and sledding
Dogsled derby: hills, chills, spills, thrills. R. Gannon and E. D. Fales, jr. il Pop Sci 190:106-9 F '67

DOLLS—*Continued*
Dolls for the Christmas trade in 1892. C. H. Fawcett. il Hobbies 72:39+ D '67
Inventive approach; dolls from nylon hose and cotton stuffing. K. R. Morrison. il Design 68:23 Sum '67
Little brother. il Time 90:68 N 10 '67
Little brother comes to America; boy doll with sex organs. B. W. Wyden. il N Y Times Mag p77+ O 29 '67; Discussion. p40 N 12; 12 N 19 '67
More about some 19th century mechanical dolls. C. H. Fawcett. il Hobbies 72:38-9 Ag '67
School for doll makers; San Francisco's Japantown. il Sunset 139:8 O '67
Some German bisque-headed dolls and doll marks. C. H. Fawcett. il Hobbies 72:40-1 My '67
Some of Mrs Kears' mechanical dolls. C. H. Fawcett. il Hobbies 72:40 Je '67
Some unforgettable dolls of long ago; portrait dolls. C. H. Fawcett. il Hobbies 72:40+ Ap '67
Watch out for this platinum blonde; Slick Chick. il Consumer Rep 32:566 N '67
    See also
Paper dolls
DOLLS, Paper. See Paper dolls
DOLLY Varden trout fishing. See Trout fishing
DOLMATCH, Theodore Bieley
Smaller firm and its corporate plan. por Pub W 191:30-3 My 8 '67
DOLMETSCH, Joan
Four children, three artists. Antiques 91:500-2 Ap '67
New look at the old mod. Antiques 92:854-7 D '67
DOLOMITE (mineral)
Marine dolomite of unusual isotopic composition. K. L. Russell and others. bibliog il Science 155:189-91 Ja 13 '67
DOLORES Marie Burton, Sister. See Burton, D. M.
DOLPHINS (mammals)
Anesthetization of porpoises for major surgery. S. H. Ridgway and J. G. McCormick. bibliog il Science 158:510-12 O 27 '67
Dolphin talk. Newsweek 70:61 Ag 21 '67
Mind-mapping the dolphin; first complete atlas of its brain. L. Gebhart. il Sci N 92:206-7 Ag 26 '67
Tuffy, the navy's deep sea lifeguard. T. Stimson. il Pop Mech 128:66-9+ Jl '67
DOLT; story. See Barthelme, D.
DOM Juan, or The feast of the statue; drama. See Molière, J. B. P.
DOMAIN, Eminent. See Eminent domain
DOMAIN theory. See Magnetism
DOMAN-Delacato system. See Brain damaged children—Education
DOMES
Expo named Buckminster Fuller. D. Jacobs. il N Y Times Mag p32-3+ Ap 23 '67
Frei Otto designs 1,864 million cubic feet of air; German pavilion at Expo 67. il Arch Forum 126:58-65 Ap '67
New dome for field track area; University of Pennsylvania. il Parks & Rec 2:34+ My '67
DOMESTIC animals
    See also
Dogs
Domestication
DOMESTIC appliances. See Electric apparatus and appliances, Domestic; Household appliances
DOMESTIC economic assistance. See Economic assistance, Domestic
DOMESTIC employees. See Household employees
DOMESTIC finance
Check up on your family spending. Changing T 21:48 Ap '67
Does it pay for a wife to work? F. Henle. Am Home 70:44-5+ S '67
Facts every wife should learn about widowhood. Good H 165:154 Jl '67
Family money management. See issues of Better homes and gardens
Financing home improvements. T. Irwin. Am Home 70:87+ My '67
Her money power. P. H. Douglas. Vogue 149:249+ My '67
Making the most of your family's money. Good H 164:197 Ap '67
Money management. M. Feeley. See issues of American home
Money management. T. Irwin. Am Home 71: 10+ Ja '68
Money matters. J. D. Bierman. Parents Mag 42:28+ Ap; 20+ Jl; 42+ S '67

Money matters; managing your family's finances. K. McKenna. Parents Mag 42:22+ Mr '67
Money trap. il Good H 165:22 Jl '67
1967, the year to stretch your dollar; symposium. il Am Home 70:57-79+ Ja '67
Population shifts: business effect; how age groups are changing. il U S News 62:52-3 Je 26 '67
Renee married a tight-fisted man. D. C. Disney. il Ladies Home J 84:40+ My '67
Spending your money; questions and answers. S. Porter. See issues of Ladies' home journal
Twenty-six ways to economize over the holidays. il Good H 165:193 D '67
What went wrong in dreamland? Larkdale, Ill. B. Remsberg and C. Remsberg. il Good H 164:74-5+ F '67
Where does money trouble start? inability to predict the future. M. Mayer. Bet Hom & Gard 45:84 My '67
Young marriages; what happens when parents pay the bills? S. Grafton. il McCalls 94:67+ Ap '67
    See also
Budget, Household
Budget, Personal
Cost of living
Saving and savings
DOMESTIC peace corps. See Volunteers in service to America
DOMESTIC relations
    See also
Divorce
Family
Family life
Husbands
Marriage
Wives
DOMESTICATION
Early domestication of animals. J. Hawkes. il UNESCO Courier 20:7-8 My '67
DOMICILE
Residence requirements drop for city jobs. R. V. Sherman. il Am City 82:108+ Je '67
DOMINIC, C. J.
Reserpine: inhibition of olfactory blockage of pregnancy in mice. bibliog Science 152: 1764-5; 155:852 Ja 24 '66, F 17 '67
DOMINICA (island)
Let's travel: to Dominica. J. Silver. Mlle 65: 84+ Je '67
DOMINICAN REPUBLIC
    See also
Economic assistance in the Dominican Republic
Government ownership—Dominican Republic
Technical assistance in the Dominican Republic

Economic conditions

Balaguer's burden: the Trujillo holdings. N. Raymond and W. P. Carty. Reporter 37: 26-8 N 30 '67
Dominican turnabout: now it's Yanqui, sí; commie, no. il Nations Bsns 55:50+ D '67

Economic relations

    See also
Joint Dominican Republic-Puerto Rican economic commission

Foreign relations

Balaguer's burden: the Trujillo holdings; resentment of U.S. N. Raymond and W. P. Carty. Reporter 37:27-8 N 30 '67

Politics and government

Balaguer: the first nine months. S. Rodman. New Repub 156:19-23 Mr 25 '67
Balaguer's Dominican Republic. J. N. Goodsell. bibliog f Cur Hist 53:298-302+ N '67
Liberals in wonderland; crisis over the Dominican Republic. R. Shereff. Commonweal 86:198-9+ My 5 '67
Overtaken by events, by J. B. Martin. Review Nat R 19:152 F 7 '67. J. B. Burnham
President Balaguer talks candidly about his country's future; interview. J. Balaguer. Nations Bsns 55:51 D '67
Rule of personalismo. Time 90:32+ S 29 '67
Santo Domingo revisited. S. Huck. Nat R 19:471-2 My 2 '67
DOMINIONS, British. See Commonwealth of nations
DOMINIS, John
Cheat River; photographs. Life 63:110-19+ D 22 '67
DOMINY, Floyd E.
Tapping the rivers of the sky. Am City 82: 98-101 Jl '67
Unusual pipe-bedding technique. Am City 82:90-3 F '67 (to be cont)

DOMMEN, Arthur J.
Japan's Communists: rich and cautious. Reporter 36:33-4+ Ap 6 '67
DOMS, Keith
Needed: a fuller knowledge of the user and the nonuser. Wilson Lib Bul 41:931-2 My '67
DON Giovanni; opera. See Mozart, J. C. W. A.
DON Juan
Rake's progress; photographs. Opera N 31:21-3 Ja 28 '67
DON Quixote; ballet. See Ballets—Criticisms
DON Rodrigo; opera. See Ginastera, A.
DONALD, David
Historical synthesis. Commentary 44:94+ S '67
DONAT, Alexander
Hunters become the hunted. Sat R 50:32-3 Ap 15 '67
Nazi war victims on trial. Sat R 50:32-4 My 13 '67
DONAT, John
Magic box. Arch Forum 127:78-85 O '67
DONCEEL, Joseph
Philosophy in the Catholic university. America 115:330-1; 116:580-2 S 24 '66, Ap 22 '67
DONELLI, Aldo
Weep, lion, weep. il Newsweek 70:90+ D 18 '67
DONEN, Adelle
Beautiful pacesetter of the London whirl; with account by D. Lurie. il pors Life 62:48-51+ F 10 '67
DONEN, Stanley, family
Other Adelle who retreats to the English countryside. il pors Life 62:52-3 F 10 '67
DONG, Pham-van-. See Pham-van-Dong
DONIS, Miles
Madness of us alone; story. Mlle 65:146-7 S '67
DONIZETTI, Gaetano
Daughter of the regiment. Criticism
Opera N il 31:14-15 Mr 4 '67
Donizetti's Pia de' Tolomei. W. Weaver. il Hi Fi 17:MA31 N '67
Freni-Gedda Elisir. R. Lawrence. Sat R 50:56 O 28 '67
Lucia di Lammermoor. Criticism
Opera N il 32:30 Ja 13 '68
Music to my ears; performance of Maria Stuarda. I. Kolodin. Sat R 50:35 D 23 '67
Records:
Campanello. Opera N 31:34 Ja 7 '67
L'elisir d'amore. Opera N 32:34 D 16 '67
DONLEAVY, J. P.
Traveler, consider my Dublin. .; ed. by R. Joseph. pors Esquire 67:122-3+ Ap '67
DONN, William L.
Causes of the ice ages. Sky & Tel 33:221-5 Ap '67
DONNEL, Roscoe J.
Cooke triplet astrographic lens for the amateur. Sky & Tel 33:312-19 My '67
DONNELLY, H. C.
Crime; address, October 16, 1967. Vital Speeches 34:114-16 D 1 '67
DONNER, Frank J.
Case of the private I. Nation 205:629-33 D 11 '67
DONNER, Frederic G.
Competitive innovation, key to progress; excerpts from address, July 13, 1967. por Nations Bsns 55:68-9 S '67
DONOGHUE, Denis
Literary fascism. Commentary 44:82+ Ag; 11 N '67
DONOVAN, Hedley
Vietnam: slow, tough but coming along. Life 62:68+ Je 2 '67
DONOVAN, Maria Kozslik
Blue Danube cookbook; excerpt. Ladies Home J 84:102-3+ F '67
DOODLES (sketches) See Psychoanalysis
DOODY, Alton F. and Davidson, W. R.
Next revolution in retailing. Harvard Bsns R 45:4-6+ My '67
DOOLEY, D. J.
Catholics have a right to a point of view. America 116:812-13 Je 3 '67
DOOLITTLE, James Harold
25th reunion toast for Doolittle's raiders. il por Life 62:42 Ap 28 '67
DOOLITTLE, Jerome H.
Lament for good old-fashioned smut. Esquire 67:32+ F '67
DOOLITTLE, Russell F. and Astrin, K. H.
Light chains of rabbit immunoglobulin: assignment to the kappa class. bibliog Science 156:1755-7 Je 30 '67
DOOR on West Tenth street; story. See Brennan, M.

DOOR to door selling. See Canvassing
DOORS
Making an entrance; exterior door designs. il House B 109:43+ N '67
New faces for your front door. il Pop Mech 127:160-1 My '67
New windows and doors slide on air. W. E. Burton. il Pop Sci 190:158-9 Ap '67
DOORWAYS
Artful doorways. il McCalls 95:122-3 D '67
Key to kitchen traffic problems: move the back entrance. J. Gillies. il Farm J 92:66 Ja '68
DOORYARD gardens. See Gardens
DOPAMINE
Dopamine protects mice against whole-body irradiation. K. N. Prasad and M. H. Van Woert. bibliog il Science 155:470-2 Ja 27 '67
DOPPLER effect
Ionospherically propagated sea scatter. L. H. Tveten. bibliog il Science 157:1302-4 S 15 '67
DORAL Open tournament. See Golf—Tournaments
DORAN, Jeffrey
Under another's sky; story. Atlan 221:68-75 Ja '68
DOREN, David MacNeil
Inside the mountains, outside the law. Sat R 50:52-4+ O 14 '67
Why learn the language? Atlan 221:102-3 Ja '68
DORFE, pseud.
Angel winging on the moon. Design 69:25 Wint '67
DORIES. See Boats and boating
DORIOT, Georges F.
General Doriot's dream factory. G. Bylinsky. il por Fortune 76:103-7+ Ag '67
DORMAN, Sonya
Burglar; poem. Sat R 50:62 Je 10 '67
DORMIN. See Growth inhibiting substances (plants)
DORMITORIES
Berkeley, how do students really live? S. Van Der Ryn and M. Silverstein. il Arch Forum 127:90-7 Jl '67
Cornell's new student housing forms unified residential complex. il Arch Rec 141:148-50 Mr '67
Nine stories hang from steel straps for two high-rise dormitories. il Arch Rec 142:151-2 D '67
Pedestrian mall links housing clusters to form a community at University of Michigan. il Arch Rec 141:147 Mr '67
Stanford university: housing cluster. il Arch Rec 141:210-12 Ap '67
State university residence hall: spatial complexity on a low budget. il Arch Rec 142:142-4 O '67
Two dormitories at Ohio state. il Arch Rec 142:153-4 D '67
DORN, Edward
Sundering U.P. tracks: First note; poems. Poetry 109:359-62 Mr '67
DORNBERG, John
Nettles of Prague. Nation 206:50-2 Ja 8 '68
DORNQUAST, Robert
Very superior pike! por Field & S 72:54-5+ D '67
DORROS, Sidney
How good is your child's school? il NEA J 56:37-52 S '67
Legacy of honor. por Negro Hist Bul 30:6-7 Ja '67
DORSEY, Edna J.
Lines & developments. Design 68:24-6 Sum '67
DORY boat surfing. See Surf riding
DOSAGE. See Drugs—Dosage
DOSIMETERS. See Radiometers
DOSIMETRY. See Radiology, Medical
DOS PASSOS, John
Unexpected Brazil. Holiday 42:52-9+ S '67
What makes a novelist; address upon receiving the Feltrinelli award. Nat R 20:29-32 Ja 16 '68
about
John Dos Passos. J. Hart. por Nat R 19:93+ Ja 24 '67
Return to paradise. D. Wakefield. por Atlan 219:102-4+ F '67
DOSS, Margot Patterson
Where it's at. por Library J 92:2361-4 Je 15 '67
DOSTAL, H. C. and Leopold, A. C.
Gibberellin delays ripening of tomatoes. bibliog Science 158:1579-80 D 22 '67
DOSTOEVSKII, Fedor Mikhailovich
Id of Dostoevsky. A. Nin. por Sat R 50:35+ Je 10 '67

DOWLING, John E.
Nobel prize: three named for medicine, physiology award. Science 158:468-9 O 27 '67
Site of visual adaptation. bibliog Science 155:273-9; 157:584-5 Ja 20, Ag 4 '67

DOWN, Jack
Alienated youth. Sch & Soc 95:252-4 Ap 15 '67

DOWN in the dumps; story. See Harington, D.

DOWNES, Bruce
Bruce Downes; a critical appraisal. J. Balish. pors Pop Phot 61:124-7+ N '67

DOWNES, Edward
Music that laughs and capers. Opera N 32:24-5 D 16 '67
Sign of the storm. Opera N 31:24-5 Mr 11 '67

DOWNES, Mollie Panter-. See Panter-Downes, M.

DOWNES, Rackstraw
Welliver's travels. Art N 66:34-6+ N '67

DOWNEY, Leo R.
Financial problems of the parochial school network. Sch & Soc 95:305-6 Sum '67

DOWNIE, Freda
Bereavement; poem. New Repub 156:27 F 25 '67

DOWNIE, Mary Alice
Mrs Ewing in Canada. Horn Bk 43:721-5 D '67

DOWNING, Thomas N.
Merchant marine; address, February 13, 1967. Vital Speeches 33:478-80 My 15 '67

DOWNS, Hugh
At home abroad: Portugal. Travel 128:42-4 D '67

DOWNS, Jim
Rabbit hunt, Indian style. Outdoor Life 139:54-5+ Je '67

DOWNS, Lavinia Davis
Library of the American school in Japan. Horn Bk 43:576-9 O '67

DOWNS, Marion P.
Hunt to catch a handicap. Todays Health 46:46-51 Ja '68

DOWN'S syndrome. See Syndromes

DOWNTOWN areas. See Business districts

DOWTY, Leonhard
Audrey Hepburn makes the scene. Good H 165:84-6 Ag '67
Love song. Good H 164:232 My '67

DOXIADIS, Constantinos Apostolos
Coming era of ecumenopolis. Sat R 50:11-14 Mr 18 '67
House is to live in, a home is to love; ed. by J. Robbins and J. Robbins. Redbook 129:51+ My '67
Life in the year 2000. NEA J 56:12-14 N '67

about
New Greek oracle of urban planning. il pors Bsns W p66-8 Jl 15 '67

DOYLE, Sir Arthur Conan
Conan Doyle, by P. Nordon. Review
Nat R 19:915-16 Ag 22 '67. S. Leslie
Short but wild history of spirit photography. M. Gardner. por Pop Phot 61:65 O '67

DOYLE, Patricia Jansen
Real world of Jacqueline Grennan. Sat R 50:58-9 Jl 15 '67

DRABBLE, Margaret
Voyage to Cythera; story. Mlle 66:98-9 D '67

DRACKETT family
Cincinnati Dracketts. il Fortune 75:121 F '67

DRACKETT company
Reaming-out Drāno. Time 89:92 My 19 '67

DRAFT, Military. See Military service, Compulsory

DRAFT law. See Military service, Compulsory —United States

DRAFT resisters. See Military service, Compulsory—United States

DRAFTEES. See Soldiers

DRAFTING boards, tables, etc. See Drawing boards, tables, etc.

DRAG racing. See Automobile racing

DRAGGING (fishing) See Trawls and trawling

DRAGIN, John Peter
Hard drive of White motor. J. Berry. il por Duns R 88:37-8+ D '66

DRAGON ships. See Viking ships

DRAINAGE
See also
Runoff

DRAINAGE, House
How to open clogged house drains. G. Daniels and L. Weaver. il Pop Sci 191:133-8 Jl '67
New types of drainage systems. L. Weaver and G. Daniels. il Pop Sci 192:151-4 Ja '68

DRAKE, Francis Vivian
Let's fight to win in Vietnam. Read Digest 90:67-72 My '67
—and Drake, Katherine
Wonderland of Australia's Great Barrier Reef. Read Digest 90:162-4+ Mr '67

DRAKE, James
Journey into speed; photographs. Sports Illus 27:32-43 D 25 '67
Time to go to Cooperstown; photographs. Sports Illus 27:28-32 Jl 24 '67

DRAKE, Katharine
Our flying Nightingales in Vietnam. Read Digest 91:73-9 D '67
—See Drake, F. V. jt. auth.

DRAKE PASSAGE
Geostrophic transport through the Drake Passage. A. L. Gordon. bibliog il Science 156:1732-4 Je 30 '67

DRAMA
Take a letter: cardinal rule of the theater. G. Ace. Sat R 50:12 Ja 28 '67
Theater of dislike; contemporary drama. D. J. Leary. Cath World 205:217-22 Jl '67
See also
College and school drama
Comedy
Literature
Television broadcasting—Drama
Tragedy
    also Chinese drama; Russian drama; etc.

Study and teaching
Talent hunt in the East Village. R. Kotlowitz. Harper 234:141-4 Mr '67
Tomorrow's stars: on campus today. M. A. Guitar. il Mlle 66:158-9+ N '67
See also
College and school drama

Technique
Theater of commitment; excerpt from address. E. Bentley; discussion. Commentary 43:6+ Mr '67
Two people in a room: playwriting; interview. H. Pinter. New Yorker 43:34-6 F 25 '67
Writing and playwriting. G. P. Elliott. Writer 80:17-18 F '67

Themes
Broadway malady; generation gap themes. G. Ace. Sat R 50:6 N 11 '67
Playwright who drops political blockbusters; R. Hochhuth. M. Esslin. il N Y Times Mag p48-9+ N 19 '67
Probing Pinter's play: The homecoming; with interview with H. Pinter; ed. by H. Hewes. il Sat R 50:56+ Ap 8 '67
Psychiatrist looks at The homecoming. A. N. Franzblau. Sat R 50:58 Ap 8 '67
Theater is the victim of a plot; staleness of new plays. W. Kerr. il N Y Times Mag p 10-11+ Je 25 '67

DRAMA, Religious. See Religious drama

DRAMA departments in colleges and universities. See Drama—Study and teaching

DRAMA festivals
All this and Expo, too: summer repertory schedule, 1967. H. Hewes. Sat R 50:44 Je 3 '67
Theater; Florida state university and the Asolo theater festival association's summer festival. H. Hewes. Sat R 50:22 Ag 5 '67

DRAMA in education. See Dramatization in education

DRAMA reading. See Books and reading—Reading aloud

DRAMAS
Dr McGrath. E. Wilson. Commentary 43:60-7 My '67
Kingdom of earth. T. Williams. Esquire 67:98-100+ F '67
Latent heterosexual. P. Chayefsky. Esquire 68:49-56+ Ag '67
Not enough rope. E. May. Mlle 66:152-3+ N '67
See also
Happenings (theater)
Spring—Drama

Criticisms, plots, etc.
Goings on about town. See issues of New Yorker
Life theater review. T. Prideaux. See issues of Life
Off Broadway. E. Oliver. See issues of New Yorker
Stage. See issues of Commonweal

DRAMAS—Criticisms, plots, etc.—*Continued*
Theater (cont) Nat R 19:99-100, 261-6, 316-17, 702-3, 1393-5 Ja 24, Mr 7-21, Je 27, D 12 '67
Theatre. See issues of Vogue
Theatre. B. Gill. New Yorker 43:57 Ja 13 '68
Theater. H. Hewes. See issues of Saturday review
Theatre. J. McCarten. See issues of New Yorker to December 23, 1967
Theatre. R. Brustein. See issues of New republic
Theatre. T. Lewis. See issues of America
Time listings. See issues of Time
See also
London—Theater
New York (city)—Theater
Shakespeare, W.—Plays

Single works
See name of author for full entry
After the rain. J. Bowen
America hurrah. J.-C. Van Itallie
L'architecte et l'Empereur d'Assyrie. F. Arrabal
Arms and the man. G. B. Shaw
Astrakhan coat. P. Macaulay
Beard. M. McClure
Bećlch. R. Owens
Before you go. L. Holofcener
Benito Cereno. See Old Glory, below
Birthday party. H. Pinter
Black comedy. P. Shaffer
Bürger Schippel. C. Sternheim
Cage. R. Cluchey
Cavern. J. Anouilh
Ceremony of innocence. R. Ribman
Chocolates. I. Bernard
Choice of wars. I. Shaw
Coach with the six insides. J. Erdman
Come live with me. L. Minoff and S. Price
Country girl. C. Odets
Dance of death. A. Strindberg
Daphne in cottage D. S. Levi
Day in the death of Joe Egg. P. Nichols
Deer park. N. Mailer
Delicate balance. E Albee
Desire caught by the tail. P. Picasso
Devils. J. Whiting
Devil's disciple. G. B. Shaw
Dinner at eight. G. S. Kaufman and E. Ferber
Displaced person. C. Dawkins
Dr Cook's garden. I. Levin
Does a tiger wear a necktie? D. Peterson
Drums in the night. B. Brecht
Duchess of Malfi. J. Webster
East wind. L. Lehman
Eleonora Duse. M. Fratti
Elizabeth the queen. M. Anderson
Everything in the garden. E. Albee
Exit the king. E. Ionesco
Experiment. D. Halliwell and D. Calderisi
Les femmes savantes. J. B. P. Molière
Fortune and men's eyes. J. Herbert
Fragments. M. Schisgal
Galileo. B. Brecht
Girl in the Freudian slip. W. F. Brown
Glass menagerie. T. Williams
Government inspector. N. Gogol
Great white hope. H. Sackler
Guimpes and saddles. E. A. Molloy
Halfway up the tree. P. Ustinov
Hamp. J. Wilson
Happiness. M. Simon
Happy faculty. J. Nourse and P. Nourse
Herakles. A. MacLeish
Homecoming. H. Pinter
House of Atreus. J. Lewin
How to be a Jewish mother. S. Vall
Iphigenia in Aulis. Euripides
Junebug graduates tonight! A. Shepp
Keep it in the family. B. Naughton
Killing of Sister George. F. Marcus
Lie. See Le mensonge, below
Little foxes. L. Hellman
Little murders J. Feiffer
MacBird! B. Garson
Man in the glass booth. R. Shaw
Man who washed his hands. W. C. Thompson
Le mensonge. N. Sarraute
Mrs Wilson's diary. R. Ingrams and J. Wells
More stately mansions. E. G. O'Neill
My kinsman, Major Molineux. See Old Glory, below
My sweet Charlie. D. Westheimer
Natural look. L. Thuna
Niggerlovers. G. Tabori
Ninety day mistress. J. J. Coyle
Not a way of life. J. Rush
Of love remembered. A. Sundgaard
Old Glory. R. Lowell
Oresteia. See House of Atreus, above
Ox cart. R. Marques

Pantagleize. M. de Ghelderode
Party on Greenwich avenue. G. Conover
Plebeians rehearse the uprising. G. Grass
Poker session. H. Leonard
Prometheus bound. R. Lowell
Promise. A. N. Arbuzov
Puntila and his hired man. B. Brecht
Le roi se meurt. See Exit the king, above
Rimers of Eldritch. L. Wilson
Rose tattoo. T. Williams
Rosencrantz and Guildenstern are dead. T. Stoppard
Saint Joan. G. B. Shaw
Schweyk in the second World war. B. Brecht
Scuba duba. B. J. Friedman
Servant of two masters. C. Goldoni
Show-off. G. E. Kelly
Le silence. N. Sarraute
Soldiers. R. Hochhuth
Something different. C. Reiner
Song of the Lusitanian bogey. P. Weiss
Spofford. H. Shumlin
Staircase. C. Dyer
Star-spangled girl. N. Simon
Stephen D. H. Leonard
Strong breed. W. Soyinka
Tango. S. Mrozek
Tartuffe. J. B. P. Molière
Tenth man. P. Chayefsky
That summer, that fall. F. D. Gilroy
There's a girl in my soup. T. Frisby
Thomas Cranmer of Canterbury. C. Williams
Tiger or disciple. J. Giraudoux
Time for the gentle people. T. Coble
'Tis pity she's a whore. J. Ford
To clothe the naked. L. Pirandello
Trials of Brother Jero. W. Soyinka
Two character play. T. Williams
Unknown soldier and his wife. P. Ustinov
US. America 116:760-1 My 20 '67
Viet rock. M. Terry
Walking to Waldheim. M. Simon
War and peace. A. Neumann and others
Waters of Babylon. J. Arden
We bombed in New Haven. J. Heller
What did we do wrong? H. Denker
White House happening. L. Kirstein
White lies. P. Shaffer
Who's happy now? O. Hailey
Wicked cooks. G. Grass
Wild duck. H. Ibsen
You know I can't hear you when the water's running. R. W. Anderson

One-act plays
Getting students into the act. S. Cochell. il Sr Schol 90:sup8 Mr 17 '67
DRAMATIC art. See Acting
DRAMATIC criticism
See also
George Jean Nathan award
DRAMATIC education. See Drama—Study and teaching
DRAMATIC festivals. See Drama festivals
DRAMATIC play. See Dramatization in education
DRAMATIC production. See Theatrical production
DRAMATIC production (in education) See Dramatization in education
DRAMATIC readings
Off Broadway: Carricknabauna. E. Oliver. New Yorker 43:138+ Ap 8 '67
Off Broadway; I must be talking to my friends. E. Oliver. New Yorker 43:147-9 D 2 '67
Theatre; R. Dotrice's impersonation of J. Aubrey. H. Clurman. Nation 206:92-3 Ja 15 '68
Theatre; Roy Dotrice's impersonation of J. Aubrey. E. Oliver. New Yorker 43:46 D 30 '67
See also
Poetry readings
DRAMATIC sopranos. See Opera singers
DRAMATICS in schools. See College and school drama; Dramatization in education
DRAMATISTS, American
Off-off-Broadway: it's in. M. Gussow. il Newsweek 69:88+ My 1 '67
See also
Albee, E.
Friedman, B. J.
Melfi. L.
O'Neill, E. G.
DRAMATISTS, English
See also
Pinter, H.
DRAMATISTS, German
See also
Hauptmann, G. J. R

DRAMATISTS, Italian
See also
Goldoni, C.
DRAMATIZATION in education
Florida findings: Asolo company's audience-development projects. H. Hewes. Sat R 50: 22 Mr 18 '67
Playmaking with a purpose; creative dramatics. D. DuVal. il Parents Mag 43: 54-6+ Ja '68
Role-playing as a learning method for disadvantaged children; excerpt from Role-playing for social values; decision making in the social studies. F. R. Shaftel and G. Shaftel. bibliog f Sch & Soc 94:494-8 D 24 '66
Role playing in the library; Reo and Michigan avenue schools, Lansing, Mich. P. Anderson. Library J 93:267 Ja 15 '68
DRAMATIZATION of history
Saturday, June 14, 1800; historical background of Puccini's Tosca. O. Rachleff. Opera N 32:24-5 Ja 13 '68
DRANE, James F.
Voice and torment of a rebel priest; interview, ed. by B. Rutherford. pors Life 63:33-4+ S 8 '67
about
What price aggiornamento? R. M. Brown. Commonweal 86:549-50 S 8 '67
DRANOV, Paula
Taste of college. Am Ed 3:25-7 Ap '67
DRAPEAU, Jean
Flags for Canada. R. Mercer. il por Opera N 31:8-13 My 13 '67
Mayor. New Yorker 43:33-4 Ap 29 '67
Twenty-first century comes to Montreal. R. Gustaitis. il Reporter 36:36-40 F 9 '67
DRAPER, Charles Stark
Remedial technology must be supported by information. por Tech W 20:56-8+ Ja 23 '67
DRAPER, Hal
California draws a blank. Nation 205:682-5 D 25 '67
DRAPER, Theodore
American crisis: Vietnam, Cuba & the Dominican Republic. bibliog f Commentary 43:27-48 Ja; 12+ My '67
Israel and world politics. bibliog Commentary 44:19-48 Ag; 18+ D '67
DRAPER, V. M.
Airports, the Twin Cities way. Flying 80:82-5 Je '67
DRAPER, William H. Jr
Overpopulation: threat to survival. por Parents Mag 42:30 Ag '67
DRAPERIES. See Curtains and draperies
DRAWBRIDGES
Vertical-lift bridge without towers; St Paul avenue bridge, Milwaukee. il Am City 82:50 Jl '67
DRAWING
From pencil note to painting: how to use pencils and crayons in developing sketches. H. Gasser. il Design 69:20-4 Wint '67
Scribble cartoons. H. Riggenberg. il Design 69:14-15 Wint '67
See also
Architectural drawing
Pen drawing
Tracing
DRAWING, Childrens. See Childrens art
DRAWING boards, tables, etc.
Drafting table folds against the wall. il Sunset 138:106+ Mr '67
DRAWING Instruments
Gears within gears draw fantastic ornaments; new drawing set, Spirograph. A. P. Armagnac. il Pop Sci 191:72-4 S '67
See also
Architectural drawing instruments
DRAWINGS
Drawings of Richard Welling. N. Kent. il Am Artist 31:52-9 F '67
Leonardo's lost notebooks. il Life 62:24-31 Mr 3 '67
Nameless evil; M. Lasansky's Nazi drawings on exhibit at Manhattan's Whitney museum. il Time 89:86 Mr 31 '67
Portfolio of drawings of old mills. N. Kent. il Am Artist 31:30-5+ S '67
Portfolio of drawings of Vietnam. J. Nielsen. il Am Artist 31:58-63 Ap '67
Sheilah Beckett; classicist. N. Kent. il Am Artist 31:38-44+ Ap '67

Exhibitions
Ballerinas and bathers; works in the show Drawings by Degas. A. Werner. Reporter 36:44+ Ap 20 '67

God made manifest; J. Pollock at the Museum of modern art. F. Getlein. New Repub 156: 26-7 Ap 22 '67
Visions of depravity; Lasansky, Goya and Beardsley shows. H. Cohen. Reporter 36: 39-40+ My 4 '67
Why Aubrey Beardsley is back; exhibition coming to Gallery of modern art. J. Russell. il N Y Times Mag p 14-17+ F 5 '67
DREAM; ballet. See Ballets—Criticism
DREAM of kings; story. See Petrakis, H. M.
DREAM of Liu-Tung; opera. See Yun, I.
DREAMING sleep. See Sleep
DREAMS
Dreams & nightmares; child, with study-discussion program, by R. Strang. A. Graham. bibliog il PTA Mag 62:24-6, 33 O '67
Dreams, art and mental telepathy. P. McBroom. il Sci N 92:424-5 O 28 '67
In dreams: does seven mean conception? F. O'Connor. Vogue 150:164-5+ N 1 '67
Interpretation of dreams. E. Diamond. il N Y Times Mag p26-7+ F 12 '67
What your dreams do for you. L. Galton. il Pop Sci 191:98-100+ S '67
Your dreams both day and night. D. A. Sugarman and R. Hochstein. il Seventeen 26:84-5 Jl '67
See also
Sleep
DREELE, W. H. von
Understanding the Holy Land; poem. Nat R 19:785 Jl 25 '67
DREHER, Carl
Chastening of NASA. Nation 205:269-73 S 25 '67
It's getting noisier. Nation 205:238-42 S 18 '67
Lady vanished. Nation 204:374-6 Mr 20 '67
Pulitzer power. Nation 205:502-5 N 13 '67
DRENNAN, Henry Thomas
(ed) Federal library legislation, programs, and services (cont) ALA Bul 61:1049-57+ O '67
--and Reed, S. R.
Library manpower; address, June 1967. bibliog ALA Bul 61:957-65 S '67
DRENTLUSS, Lester
Lester Drentluss, a Jewish boy from Baltimore, attempts to make it through the summer of 1967. C. Trillin. Atlan 221:43-5 Ja '68
DRESS accessories
Newest tack; hardware look. il Time 90:57 Ag 18 '67
Shoes and belts that jingle, jangle, jingle; newest accouterments for sporting wardrobes. il Sports Illus 26:56-7 My 15 '67
DRESS and waist industry. See Clothing industry
DRESS design. See Costume design
DRESS designers. See Costume designers
DRESS patterns. See Patterns (dress)
DRESSING of game. See Game, Dressing of
DRESSING rooms
Dressing room and bath in compartments. il Sunset 138:126 Ap '67
DRESSMAKING
Quick tricks with neckline facings. C. Houck. il Parents Mag 42:57 N '67
See also
Costume design
Patterns (dress)
Sewing
DREW, Elizabeth Brenner
Atlantic report: Washington. Atlan 219:6+ Mr '67
Civil rights commission. Atlan 220:16-19 Ag '67
Health syndicate. Atlan 220:75-82 D '67
Is the FCC dead? Atlan 220:29-36 Jl '67
Report: Washington. Atlan 219:6+ Mr; 220: 4+ N '67
DREW theological seminary. See Drew university, Madison, N.J.
DREW university, Madison, N.J.
Drew controversy gets wider airing; dismissal of dean C. W. Ranson. T. Cooper. Christian Cent 84:451-4 Ap 5 '67
Drew professors resign in protest. T. S. Cooper. Christian Cent 85:92-4 Ja 17 '68
Drew's dean summarily dismissed. Christian Cent 84:102 Ja 25 '67; Reply. R. P. Scharlemann. 84:317 Mr 8 '67
Student boycott hits Drew university; concerning president Robert F. Oxnam's dismissal of dean C. W. Ranson. Christian Cent 84:526 Ap 26 '67
DREWS, Elizabeth Monroe
Reaching and teaching the gifted. NEA J 56: 8-11+ N '67

DREWS, Jürgen, and Brawerman, George
Messenger RNA patterns in rat liver nuclei before and after treatment with growth hormone. bibliog Science 156:1385-6 Je 9 '67
DREXEL, Mother Mary Katharine
Tribute to Mother Katharine Drexel: address, February 10, 1966. por Negro Hist Bul 29: 181-2+ Fall '66
DREYFUS, Jack Jonas. 1913-
10,000-to-1 payoff. A. Rosenfeld. il pors Life 63:121-2+ S 29 '67
DRICKAMER, H. G.
Pi electron systems at high pressure. bibliog Science 156:1183-9 Je 2 '67
DRIED flowers; Dried meat; etc. See Flowers, Dried; Meat, Dried; etc.
DRIESEN, George B.
Civil-rights setback in southern courts. Reporter 36:18-22 F 23 '67
DRIFTING of continents. See Continental drift
DRILL press. See Drilling and boring machinery
DRILLING. Underwater. See Underwater drilling
DRILLING and boring (earth and rock)
See also
Mohole project
DRILLING and boring machinery
Don't sell your drill press short. M. Banister. il Pop Mech 127:188-92 My '67
Eighteen ways to get more from your portable drill. W. E. Burton. il Pop Mech 128: 152-5 Ag '67
How to machine your own D bits. H. Walton. il Pop Sci 191:172-4 O '67
More work from your drill. il Sunset 138: 117-18+ Mr '67
Portable electric drills. il Consumer Rep 32: 162-8 D '67
Self-contained drill speeds sign-post installation; New Haven, Conn. H. Skinner. il Am City 82:133 Ap '67
Three good accessories for a drill press. R. J. De Cristoforo. il Pop Sci 191:138-40 N '67
Your best buy: a ⅜" drill? H. Wicks. il Pop Sci 191:128-32+ D '67
DRINAN, Robert F.
Contemporary Protestant thinking. America 117:713-15 D 9 '67
Strategy on abortion. America 116:177-9 F 4 '67
DRINK question. See Alcoholism; Liquor problem
DRINKING, Social. See Liquor problem
DRINKING and airplane accidents
One for the air lanes. Christian Cent 84:581 My 3 '67
DRINKING and traffic accidents
After a crackdown on drinking drivers. U S News 64:9 Ja 8 '68
Britain survives the breathalyser. L. Wainwright. Life 63:20A O 20 '67
Drawing the line for drivers. Time 90:86 S 22 '67
Spreading: tests for drinking drivers. il U S News 63:13 O 16 '67
DRINKING customs
How America drinks; Time essay. Time 90: 15 D 29 '67
DRINKS. See Beverages; Liquors
DRISCOLL, Gerry
Yachting interviews: Columbia's Gerry Driscoll: interview. ed. by B. Crabtree. Yachting 121:48-9+ F '67
DRIVE-in church services. See Church services
DRIVER, P. M. See Humphries, D. A. jt. auth.
DRIVER, Tom F.
Exaltation of evil. Sat R 50:36-7+ Mr 11 '67
DRIVER training courses. See Automobile driving—Study and teaching
DRIVES (money raising) See Fund raising
DRIVESHAFTS. See Automobiles—Propeller shafts
DRIVEWAYS
Driveway design. J. B. Brimer. il Home Gard 54:71-2 F '67
These driveways are prize-winners. W. Radcliffe. il Pop Gard 18:66-8 D '67
DRIVING, Automobile. See Automobile driving
DRIVING classes. See Automobile driving—Study and teaching
DRIVING research laboratory. See United States—Public health service—Driving research laboratory
DROMM, Andrea
Is this any way to make a living? you bet it is! S. Gordon. il pors Look 31:88-90+ F 7 '67
DROPOUTS
College dropout phenomenon. W. Dalrymple. il NEA J 56:11-13 Ap '67

Death of a dropout. J. Sideman. New Repub 156:11-14 Je 3 '67
Employment of high school graduates and dropouts in 1966. E. Waldman. il Mo Labor R 90:15-21 Jl '67
Make way for drop-ins. V. Hartke. il NEA J 56:22-3 N '67
One million dropouts, the Sputnik of 1967. H. H. Humphrey. il Am Ed 3:32 S '67
Right to fail. W. K. Zinsser. Look 31:10 O 17 '67
Street academies: new way to reach the ghetto dropout; Harlem's Street academy program. P. Pierce. il Ebony 22:158-60+ Ag '67
Teacher's dedication to those whose search has failed; A. Rode's Walden school in Washington. il Life 62:76-9 Ap 28 '67
DROSERA. See Sundew
DROSOPHILA
Antennae and sexual receptivity in drosophila melanogaster females. A. Manning. bibliog il Science 158:136-7 O 6 '67
Electrophoretic variants of α-glycerophosphate dehydrogenase in drosophila melanogaster. E. H. Grell. bibliog il Science 158:1319-20 D 8 '67
Gene activation without histone acetylation in drosophila melanogaster. E. G. Ellgaard. bibliog il Science 157:1070-2 S 1 '67
Testis-specific and sex-associated hexokinases in drosophila melanogaster. R. F. Murray, jr. and J. A. Ball. bibliog il Science 156: 81-2 Ap 7 '67
Virus-like particles in normal and tumorous tissues of drosophila. H. Akai and others. bibliog il Science 157:810-13 Ag 18 '67
Watching a new species develop? experimenting with drosophila paulistorum. il Time 89: 37 Ap 7 '67
DROUGHTS
Dry Down Under; Australian drought. il Newsweek 70:84+ N 13 '67
Midwest extremes. Sr Schol 90:17 Ap 21 '67
Stillness in the Glades; Everglades National Park suffering from drought. il Time 89:30-1 My 19 '67
Wheat belt prays for rain. il Bsns W p44 Ap 15 '67
Where drought threatens a disaster. il U S News 62:10 My 22 '67
Winds of change; south Florida's drought. Newsweek 69:56 My 29 '67
DROWNING
But we're alive! D. Agee. il Read Digest 90: 104-8 Je '67
DRUCKER, Mort
Mad look at Trovatore. il Opera N 31:14-16 F 18 '67
DRUCKER, Peter F.
Effective decision. Harvard Bsns R 45:92-8 Ja '67
How the effective executive does it; excerpts from Effective executive. Fortune 75:140-3 F '67
How to double your sales. Nations Bsns 55: 80-2+ Mr '67
DRUG addicts. See Narcotic addicts
DRUG habit. See Narcotic habit
DRUG laws and legislation
Amendment fails; the idea lives on; use of generic names in federally purchased prescriptions. Sci N 92:608 D 23 '67
Computer vs. drug abuse; prescription control suggested for Sweden. Sci N 92:130 Ag 5 '67
Congress closes in on drug costs; legislation now pending. Bsns W p40 O 7 '67
Counterfeit prescriptions; traffic in substandard drugs. il Time 89:30 Je 2 '67
Curbing the drug traffic in Britain; plans to change prescription system. B. Wenham. New Repub 156:9-10 Mr 18 '67
Drug abuse reinterpreted. Sci N 91:58 Ja 21 '67
FDA gets Miltown ruling. Sci N 91:184 F 25 '67
Generic drugs favored. B. J. Culliton. Sci N 91:206-7 Mr 4 '67
Handwriting on the drugstore wall; generic vs. brand name drugs. Sci N 92:559-60 D 9 '67
Letter from London; drugs and the young. M. Panter-Downes. New Yorker 43:83-4 Ag 19 '67
New drugs: the tortuous road to approval; letter. M. B. Visscher. Science 156:313 Ap 21 '67
Putting the brakes on speed; government to restrict the flow of illegal drugs. Bsns W p92+ O 28 '67

DRURY, Michael
  Miracle; story. Good H 164:100-1 Ap '67
DRUSKA, John
  To no one whom I knew, but he is dead;
    poem. America 117:83 Jl 22 '67
DRY cell batteries. See Electric batteries
DRY cells. See Electric batteries
DRY cleaning. See Cleaning
DRY cleaning industry. See Cleaning and dye-
    ing industry
DRY diver transport vehicle. See Submarine
    boats
DRY goods
    See also
  Notions (merchandise)
DRY shavers. See Razors
DRY TORTUGAS
  Getting there is more than half the fun. N.
    Brower. il Motor B 120:29-31+ O '67
DRYER, Stan
  Feasible flying machine. Sat Eve Post 240:18
    N 4 '67
DRYERS. See Clothes dryers
DRYING (crops)
    See also
  Corn—Drying
DRYING apparatus
  Man-sized dryer blows hot or cold. H. P.
    Strand. il Pop Mech 127:192-3 Ap '67
    See also
  Clothes dryers
  Hair dryers
DRYSDALE, Don
  Great holdout. B. Bavasi and J. Olsen. il
    por Sports Illus 26:78-82+ My 15 '67
DRYWALLS. See Walls
D'SOUZA, Jerome
  Of many things. V. S. Kearney. America 116:
    inside cover Ap 8 '67
DUAL nationality. See Citizenship
DU BAY, William H.
  Death of dialogue. Christian Cent 84:1192 S
    20 '67
                  about
  Restless clergy. G. Zimmermann. il por Look
    31:25-7 F 7 '67
DUBCEK, Alexander
  Change of command. Newsweek 71:36-8 Ja 15
    '68
DUBERMAN, Martin
  Grapes of wrath. New Repub 157:23-6 D 2 '67
DUBIVSKY, Barbara
  Vacation guide to Washington, D.C; excerpts
    from Washington, the New York times'
    guide to the Nation's capital. Seventeen 26:
    130-1+ Ap '67
DUBLIN
  Traveler, consider my Dublin. .; ed. by R.
    Joseph. J. P. Donleavy. il Esquire 67:122-3+
    Ap '67
                  Description
  Dublin where James Joyce lived; excerpts
    from Ulysses. J. Joyce. il Look 31:34-40
    Ap 18 '67
  Joyce's Ireland. C. O'Brien. il Sat R 50:
    56-7+ Mr 11 '67
            Hotels, restaurants, etc.
  Recalling the Borstal boy. H. Sutton. Sat R
    50:48-9 D 2 '67
DUBLIN revolt. See Ireland—History—Sinn Fein
    rebellion, 1916
DUBLINERS. See Singers
DU BOIS, Donald
  Are you up on today's camping? Outdoor Life
    139:66-8+ Je '67
DUBOIS, William Edward Burghardt
  Credo. Negro Hist Bul 30:19 F '67
DUBOS, Rene Jules
  Can man survive life in big cities? inter-
    view. por U S News 62:64-7 My 1 '67
  Scientists alone can't do the job; excerpts
    from addresses, September 1967. Sat R 50:
    68-71 D 2 '67
DU BOUCHER, Jean
  Dry-land fleet sails the Sahara. por Nat
    Geog Mag 132:696-725 N '67
DUBRIDGE, Lee A.
  University basic research. Science 157:648-
    50 Ag 11 '67
DUBUFFET, Jean
  Jean Dubuffet's puzzles. il por Horizon 9:60-1
    Sum '67
DUBUS, Andre
  Andromache; story. New Yorker 43:22-31 Ja
    6 '68
DUCAS, Dorothy
  Winning the battle against asthma. Todays
    Health 45:28-32 Ag '67; Same. Sci Digest
    62:76-80 O '67

DUCHAC, Kenneth F.
  Manpower: a proposal; conference report. por
    Library J 92:1797-8 My 1 '67
  Public library development in Maryland. por
    Library 92:1113-16 Mr 15 '67
DUCHAMP, Gaston. See Villon, J. pseud.
DUCHAMP-VILLON, Raymond
  Duchamp-Villon: the cubist core. il por Art
    N 66:34-7+ O '66
  Gayest of us all. D. L. Shirey. il Newsweek
    70:98 O 30 '67
DUCHESS of Malfi; drama. See Webster, J.
DUCHOVINER, M. E. See Corwin, R. D. jt.
    auth.
DUCK calling. See Bird calling
DUCK decoys. See Decoys (hunting)
DUCK shooting
  Best duck bargain. P. Czura. il Outdoor Life
    140:62-5 O '67
  Brainy black duck. R. Beck. il Outdoor Life
    140:42-3+ N '67
  Great hunting; on your farm ponds. J.
    Madson. Farm J 91:23 N '67
  How to find the waterfowl hotspots. J.
    Phillips. il Field & S 72:40-1+ N '67
  How to stump the ducks; ed. by D. D.
    Dickey. F. Moses. il Outdoor Life 140:62-5
    D '67
    See also
  Bird calling
DUCKETT, Margaret
  Artist's garden home. House B 110:98-9+ Ja
    '68
DUCKS, Wild
  Welcome to the royal duck. C. Elliott. il Out-
    door Life 140:44-7 S '67
    See also
  Cookery—Game
  Duck shooting
DUDAR, Helen
  Jackie Kennedy: what people close to her
    think about her now. Good H 165:90-1+
    O '67
DUDE ranches. See Ranches
DUDLEY, Guilford, 3d
  Importance of being earnest about Christian
    myth. Christian Cent 84:1215-18 S 27 '67
DUDMAN, Richard
  Military commitment in southeast Asia. bib-
    liog f Cur Hist 54:15-21 Ja '68
  Military seminars: the mongers return. Na-
    tion 204:101-5 Ja 23 '67
DUE process of law
  Even in high school; case of student who
    cheated on regents exam. il Time 90:41 Jl
    14 '67
    See also
  Jury
DUELING
  Who killed dueling? mayor of Marseilles vs.
    a deputy. il Newsweek 69:37 My 1 '67
DUERDEN, Richard
  Song coyote stole from the Navajo; Gre-
    gorian chant 2; poems. Poetry 110:231-5
    Jl '67
DUFAULT, Peter Kane
  Amazon ants; poem. New Yorker 43:153 D 2
    '67
  Ruth; poem. New Yorker 43:36 Jl 29 '67
DUFFEY, David Michael
  Death of a warden. Outdoor Life 139:41-
    3+ F '67
  Dogs. See issues of Outdoor life
DUFFIELD, James C. See Jöbsis, F. F. jt.
    auth.
DUFFY, A. E. P.
  Present viability of NATO, SEATO, and
    CENTO; address, April 1967, with questions
    and answers. Ann Am Acad 372:33-9 Jl '67
DUFFY, Tom, and Oleksy, Jerry
  Possible impractical impossible circuit. Pop
    Electr 27:35 S '67
DUGA, Jules J. See Bonis, L. J. jt. auth.
DUGALD, James
  Constitutional crisis; annals of the West
    Bay yacht club. Motor B 119:50-1 Mr '67
  No new business. Motor B 119:47-8 F '67
  Stacked deck. Motor B 120:40-1 D '67
  Woman's touch. Motor B 119:33+ Je '67
DUGAN, Alan
  Flower grower in Aquarius; Conspiracy of
    two against the world; Working world's
    bloody flux; His hands have five knives
    each; On being out-classed by class; Bare-
    foot for a scorpion; Poem: Oh that was not
    a scrap of flying Daily news; Poem: Flower-
    ing balls! Variation of themes by Roethke
    & Eliot; On rape unattempted; On zero;
    poems. Poetry 109:217-28 Ja '67

DUGAN, Daniel O.
Sell-out in college theology. America 117:605+
N 18 '67
DUGDALE, Chester B.
Living rocks. Horticulture 45:38-9+ F '67
DUGGAN, John K. Ross-. See Ross-Duggan,
J. K.
DUGGAN, R. E. and Weatherwax, J. R.
Dietary intake of pesticide chemicals. bibliog
Science 157:1006-10 S 1 '67
DUGGER, Ronnie
Last madness of Jack Ruby. New Repub 156:
19-23 F 11 '67
New beginnings, new hopes. Harper 235:63-4
O '67
DUISBURG, Germany
Showcase for sculpture; Lehmbruck muse-
um. il Arch Forum 126:31-7 Mr '67
DUITZ, Murray
All-8 projectors. Pop Phot 60:121-5 Ap '67
Bolex 150. Pop Phot 60:117-19 Mr '67
One-man band recorder/projector integrates
slides, sound, movies. il Pop Phot 61:122-3+
D '67
DUKE, Benjamin C.
Postwar teenage student. bibliog f Sch &
Soc 95:264-8 Ap 15 '67
DUKE, Patty
Dames in the Valley of the dolls. B. Rollin.
il pors Look 31:53-6+ S 5 '67
DUKE, Paul
Powell case: bungling all around. Reporter
36:32-5 Ap 20 '67
Southern Republican strategy for 1968. Re-
porter 37:21-3 Ag 10 '67
DUKE, Robin Chandler
Diplomacy with dash. il pors Vogue 149:178-83
My '67
DUKE, Vernon
New Russian hit parade. S. Green. por Sat R
50:66 Ag 26 '67
DUKE, William Meng
Ready when you are, B.D. N. Willatt. por
Duns R 90:56-8 D '67
Thread that ties diversity together. il por
Bsns W p74-6+ D 2 '67
DUKE university, Durham, N.C.
Patriots on the campus; FBI's activities. J.
Ridgeway. New Repub 156:12-13 Mr 25 '67
DUKELSKY, Vladimir. See Duke, V.
DULBECCO, Renato
Induction of cancer by viruses; with bio-
graphical sketch. Sci Am 216:14, 28-37 bib-
liog(p 146) Ap '67
DULLES, Avery
Book reviews. America 117:568+ N 11 '67
Faith and new opinions America 117:479 O
28 '67
Jesus of history and Christ of faith. Com-
monweal 87:225-32 N 24 '67
Theology for today. America 116:350, 728; 117:
137; 118:41 Mr 11, My 13, Ag 5 '67, Ja 13 '68
DULLES, John Foster
Conversation with Dulles. L. Jefferson. por
Nat R 19:681-2 Je 27 '67
Unforgettable John Foster Dulles. R. M.
Nixon. por Read Digest 91:99-104 Jl '67
DULLES, John W. F.
Quiet revolution. Nat R 19:299-300 Mr 21 '67
DULSKI, Thaddeus J.
Dulski dinner. Newsweek 70:28 Ag 21 '67
DULUTH, Minn.
Music
Duluth: production of Il Trovatore. P.
Gainsley. Opera N 32:21 N 4 '67
DUMAS, Jacques A.
Canadian amateurs visit Mexico. Sky & Tel
34:91 Ag '67
DUMBARTON OAKS research library and col-
lection
Antiques book preview; people who lived at
Dumbarton Oaks. E. Gaines. il Antiques 92:
198-202 Ag '67
DUMMIES. See Anatomical models
DU MOND, Frank V. and Hutchinson, T. C.
Squirrel monkey reproduction: the fatted
male phenomenon and seasonal spermato-
genesis. bibliog Science 158:1067-70 N 24 '67
DUMONT, René
Ugly Frenchman. il por Newsweek 70:45 O
2 '67
DUMPLINGS
Dumplings are delightful; with recipes. J.
Hunt. il Parents Mag 42:66-7 Ap '67
DUMPS, Municipal. See Municipal dumps
DUNAVON, Robert
Art of the future. America 117:740-2 D 16 '67
DUNAWAY, Faye
Day or night Faye's a girl with go. il pors
Life 64:74 Ja 12 '68

DUNAWAY, Vic
Everglades canals for winter bass. Field & S
72:48-9+ Ja '68
DUNCAN, David Douglas
Inside the cone of fire, Con Thien. il Life
63:28D-42C O 27 '67
about
Exciting and rewarding adventure. A. Roth-
stein. U S Camera 30:12+ Mr '67
DUNCAN, Donald
I quit! from solo to chorus. A. Samuels. Na-
tion 205:284-5 S 25 '67
DUNCAN, Isadora
Vanessa Redgrave takes on Isadora. A. West.
Vogue 150:108-11 N 15 '67
DUNCAN, John Charles
Obituary
Sky & Tel por 34:283 N '67
DUNCAN, Lois
Morning of magic. Good H 165:48+ D '67
DUNCAN, Otis Dudley
Discrimination against Negroes. bibliog f Ann
Am Acad 371:85-103 My '67
DUNCAN, Robert
Interlude; poem. Atlan 221:52-3 Ja '68
Passages 28; Light; Eye of God; Passages 29;
poems. Poetry 110:141-7 Je '67
DUNCAN, Robert Blackford
Reign of Wayne. Time 91:24 Ja 5 '68
DUNCAN, W. Raymond
Chilean Christian democracy. bibliog f Cur
Hist 53:263-9+ N '67
DUNDEE, Angelo, and Maule, Tex
Ali takes a crown and a cause. Sports Illus
27:36-40 Ag 21 '67
He could go to jail and still be champ. Sports
Illus 27:32-4+ Ag 28 '67
Life in a hot corner. Sports Illus 27:64-72 Ag
14 '67
DUNDEE cement company. See Cement indus-
try and trade
DUNE buggies. See Motor vehicles
DUNES, Sand. See Sand dunes
DUNGAN, Ralph Anthony
New hope in New Jersey. por Time 90:58 Ag
25 '67
DUNHAM, David W.
Occultation highlights (cont) Sky & Tel 33:
262; 34:62; 35:63 Ap, Jl '67, Ja '68
DUNHAM, Vera
(tr) See Voznesenskii, A. Call of the lake
(tr) See Voznesenskii, A. Sketch for a poem
(tr) See Voznesenskii, A. To Bela Akhma-
dulina; Lament for two unborn poems;
Self-portrait; Note to E. Yanitskaya, for-
merly typist to Mayakovsky; Lieutenant
Zagorin
DUNHILL, Priscilla
Expressway named destruction. Arch For-
um 126:54-9 Mr '67
DUNKIN, Paul S.
Viewpoint. See second issue of each month
of Library journal to December 15, 1967
DUNLAP, Bryan
To Mr Kazin. Harper 235:55 O '67
DUNLOP, Lane
Two poems; Jacob at Beth-El; I looked over
Jordan. Yale R 57:103-4 O '67
DUNLOP, Richard
Electric cars: are they kidding? Pop Mech
127:118-21+Je '67
Fifty-one vacation stop-offs that will add real
excitement to your trip. Pop Mech 127:101-
3+ Ap '67
Follow the old road to San Antonio. Todays
Health 45:42-9+ Mr '67
Super '67 vacation: French Canada and a
world's fair too. Todays Health 45:24-9+
F '67
Wayfaring along the Ozark trail. Todays
Health 45:44-9 Ap '67
DUNLOP, Robert Galbraith
Safeguarding tomorrow's growth; address, No-
vember 16, 1966. Vital Speeches 33:252-6
F 1 '67
DUNN, A. L. and others
Electronic stethoscope and cardiac rate
meter. Electr World 78:30+ Jl '67
DUNN, Anne
Two for May; Dunn, Hendler. S. Burton. il
Art N 66:55+ My '67
DUNN, Edward B.
Erythroniums. Horticulture 45:18-19+ Mr '67
DUNN, Harold
Christmas grows on many trees. NEA J 56:
20-1 D '67
Volcanos give us hot java. Sci Digest 61:62-5
Mr '67
DUNN, Harvey
Americans not everybody knows. C. W. Fergu-
son. il PTA Mag 62:10-12 Ja '68

DUNN, Judith
Judith Dunn and the endless quest. J. Anderson. il pors Dance Mag 41:48-51+ N '67

DUNN, Michael W. and others
Collagen-derived membrane: corneal implantation. bibliog Science 157:1329-30 S 15 '67

DUNN, Stephen
Recrimination on the edge; poem. Atlan 221: 103 Ja '68

DUNNE, George H.
Happening in São Paulo. America 117:306-9+ S 23 '67

DUNNE, John Gregory
Apollo 204. por Sat Eve Post 240:20+ Je 17 '67
Strike! Sat Eve Post 240:32-6+ My 6 '67
—and Didion, Joan
Points West. pors Sat Eve Post 240:20-1 Jl 15; 16+ Ag 12; 18-19 S 9; 24+ O 7; 22-3 N 4 '67; 241:16 Ja 27 '68
—See Didion, J. jt. auth.

DUNNE, John S.
Human God: Jesus. Commonweal 85:508-11, 662-3 F 10, Mr 10 '67

DUNNING, Joseph Nye
Curtis and Dunning, clockmakers. R. N. Hill. il Antiques 91:214-17 F '67

DUNTOV, Zora Arkus-. See Arkus-Duntov, Z.

DU PLESSIX, Francine
Lucien, Octave, Victoire, Emile. New Yorker 43:26-34 Jl 29 '67

DUPLICATING processes. See Copying processes

DU PONT, Henry Francis, Winterthur museum. See Henry Francis Du Pont Winterthur museum

DU PONT, John E.
Du Pont aims for the Olympics; with report by J. R. McDermott. il pors Life 63: 62-3+ Ag 4 '67
Trials of a busy pentathlete. A. Higgins. il por Sports Illus 27:58 Ag 28 '67

DU PONT, Willis Harrington
Whole works. il por Newsweek 70:36+ O 16 '67

DU PONT DE NEMOURS, E. I. and company
Breakthrough by Du Pont: a drug that blocks viruses. A. Rosenfeld. il Life 62:60A-61 F 10 '67
DuPont goes on record with a magnetic tape; Crolyn. il Bsns W p 172 Je 24 '67
Du Pont McCoy. il Time 90:63 D 29 '67
Du Pont names a new president. Bsns W p24 D 23 '67
Du Pont stubs its toe. J. Ross-Skinner. il Duns R 89:61 Je '67
Du Pont under pressure. G. Burck. il Fortune 76:136-41+ N '67
New venture management in a large company. R. W. Peterson. il Harvard Bsns R 45:68-76 My '67
Outsider; C. B. McCoy appointment. il Newsweek 71:45-6 Ja 1 '68
Painful adjustment at Du Pont. il Time 89: 61 Je 30 '67
Sagging Du Pont casts shadow over the Dow. il Bsns W p 118+ Ap 8 '67

DU PRÉ, Jacqueline
Charismatic cellist; with report by J. Borgzinner. il pors Life 62:109-12 Ap 14 '67
Jacqueline Du Pré and Stephen Bishop; individually and together. M. N. Kanny; J. Diether. il por Am Rec G 33:548-51 Mr '67
Mistress cellist. H. Saal. il por Newsweek 69: 104+ Mr 13 '67
Music to my ears; appearance with the New York philharmonic. I. Kolodin. Sat R 50:41 Mr 18 '67
Prodigy comes of age. il por Time 89:75 Mr 10 '67

DUPRÉ, Louis
God of history. Commonweal 85:516-19+ F 10 '67

DUQUESNE university, Pittsburgh, Pa.
Duquesne, dramatic change in campus scale. W. R. Cooper. il Arch Forum 127:78-85 Jl '67

DU QUOIN, Ill.
K.D. figures out the formula; the Hambletonian trotting race at Du Quoin state fair. P. Axthelm. il Sports Illus 27:26-7 S 11 '67

DURABLE press fabrics. See Textile fabrics, Wrinkle resistant

DURABLE press household linens. See Linen, Household

DURAND, John D.
Long-range view of world population growth. bibliog f Ann Am Acad 369:1-8 Ja '67
(ed) World population. bibliog f Ann Am Acad 369:1-140 Ja '67

DURANG, John
Memoir of John Durang, American actor, 1785-1816, ed. by A. S. Downer. Review
Dance Mag il por 41:45 Ap '67. L. Moore

DURANT, Ariel
Triumph of the Will (and Ariel) B. H. Smith. Nat R 20:40-1 Ja 16 '68

DURANT, Mary
Made-to-order matches il Mlle 64:114-15+ F '67

DURANT, Will
Triumph of the Will (and Ariel) B. H. Smith. Nat R 20:40-1 Ja 16 '68

DURANTE, James
If this should be my last trip to Europe... ed. by R. Joseph. por Esquire 67:86-9+ F '67

DURATION of copyright. See Copyright—Duration

DURATION of life. See Longevity

DURDIN, Peggy, and Shaplen, J. H.
Report from Hong Kong: on the edge of the volcano. Look 31:64 D 26 '67

DURELL, Ann
Evaline Ness. Horn Bk 43:438-43 Ag '67
Evaline Ness. por Library J 92:1298-9 Mr 15 '67

DÜRER, Albrecht
Albrecht Dürer, he painted all creation. E. O. Hauser. il por Read Digest 90:146-50 Mr '67
Young hare. A. B. Saarinen. il McCalls 94: 30-1 S '67

DURHAM, Michael
Death at a house called no. 116. Life 63: 44A Ag 4 '67
Skiing is my life. I can't be afraid, you see. Life 62:62 F 24 '67
Spring in Paris, the Left Bank blooms in her image. Life 62:86 My 19 '67
They made a satellite launch look almost easy. por Life 62:102+ My 26 '67
—and Cook, Jess
Covey of spies is flushed in Germany. Life 63:65-6+ N 3 '67

DURNIAK, John
Down Under. il Pop Phot 61:116-19+ N '67

DUROCHER, Leo
Leo the lamb. il por Time 90:70-1 Jl 28 '67
They may have been a headache but they never were a bore. B. Bavasi and J. Olsen. il pors Sports Illus 26:30-4+ My 29 '67

DURSLAG, Melvin
Lock the doors! here comes Tommy! Sports Illus 27:40-4 S 4 '67

DURYEA, George F.
Lighting by which portraits are made. U S Camera 30:58-61 F '67

DU SAUTOY, Peter
Copyright, book numbering; remarks. Pub W 192:27-8 Jl 24 '67

DUSCHA, Julius
Brain banks. Sat R 50:65-6+ S 23 '67
How do you fight Shirley Temple? Reporter 37:21-3 N 2 '67
Not great, not brilliant, but a good show. N Y Times Mag p28-9+ D 10 '67
What Reagan hath wrought. New Repub 156:10-12 F 4 '67

DUSE, Eleonora
Duse returns to Asolo. H. Hewes. Sat R 50:22 Ag 5 '67

DUSENBURY, Warren
CPM for new product introductions. Harvard Bsns R 45:124-39 Jl '67

DUSHECK, George
(ed) See Freidenberg, E. Z. Irreverent dissection of libraries

DUSK. See Twilight

DUSKY grouse. See Grouse

DÜSSELDORF, Germany

Music

Dusseldorf. H. Koegler. Opera N 31:32 Ap 1 '67

DUST
Opal phytoliths in a North Atlantic dust fall. D. W. Folger and others. bibliog il Science 155:1243-4 Mr 10 '67

DUST, Interstellar. See Matter, Interstellar

DUST cloud hypothesis. See Cosmogony

DUST jackets. See Book covers

DUST spraying. See Spraying and dusting

DUTCH catechism. See Catholic church—Catechisms

DUTCH cookery. See Cookery, Dutch

DUTCH elm disease. See Elm—Diseases and pests

DUTCH Reformed church in South Africa. See Reformed church in South Africa

DUTCH sculpture. See Sculpture, Dutch
DUTCH silver. See Silverware
DUTIES (tariff) See Tariff
DUTTON, E. P. and company
Take a bow: J. F. Heidelberger. il Pub W
191:43 Mr 27 '67
DUTY
See also
Conscience
DUTY free importation
Capitol hill reception for U.S. entry into
Florence pact. il Pub W 191:122-3 F 20 '67
Improving export earnings of developing
countries; statement, January 18, 1967. W.
M. Blumenthal. Dept State Bul 56:430-6 Mr
13 '67
Treasures without tariffs; concerning Beirut
and Florence agreements. D. H. Fenn, jr.
il Am Ed 3:23-4+ Ap '67
DUVAL, Diane
Playmaking with a purpose. Parents Mag 43:
54-6+ Ja '68
DUVALIER, François
Birthday blowout. il por Time 89:43 Ap 28
'67
Coming to a boil. il por Time 90:34 Ag 25 '67
Dictator on a tightrope. il por U S News
63:44 Ag 28 '67
Haiti, next mess in the Caribbean? R. D.
Heinl, jr. Atlan 220:83-4+ N '67
Memo from Haiti: ten years of Papa Doc. E.
Dunbar. il Look 31:124 N 28 '67
Plot against Papa Doc. R. K. Brown. Nat R
19:91-2 Ja 24 '67
That old black magic. Reporter 37:11 D 14 '67
DU VON, Jay. See Barr, R. H. jt. auth.
DUVRIES, Henri L.
Five myths about your feet. Todays Health
45:49-51 Ag '67
DVORAK, Antonin
Don't fence Dvorak in. W. Weaver. il pors
Hi Fi 17:51-4 My '67
Dvorak's symphonies: the canonical five plus
the early four. D. Hamilton. Hi Fi 17:64-5
Jl '67
One of the happy composers. Discus. Harper
235:100-1 Ag '67
Two new worlds, the LSO, Kertesz, Ormandy.
E. Greenfield. Hi Fi 17:21+ F '67
DWARF fruit trees. See Fruit trees, Dwarf
DWARF irises. See Irises
DWARF plants. See Plants, Dwarf
DWARF trees. See Trees, Dwarf
DWARFS
General Tom Thumb and other midgets. V. A.
McKusick and D. L. Rimoin. il Sci Am
217:102-6+ bibliog(p 136) Jl '67
DWELL meters
Build a battery-less dwell meter. S. Wald.
il Pop Electr 27:40 N '67
DWIGGINS, William Addison award. See Wil-
liam Addison Dwiggins award
DWYER, David J.
Persistence of the sacred. Cath World 205:
298-302 Ag '67
DWYER, James E.
Autumn in the Rockies. Pop Gard 18:52-5+
D '67
DYAKS. See Borneo—Native races
DYE, Eugene N.
Travel well. See issues of Travel
DYE, James L.
Solvated electron; with biographical sketch.
Sci Am 216:22, 76-83 F '67
DYER, Charles
Staircase. Criticism
Newsweek il 71:96 Ja 22 '68
Time il 91:66 Ja 19 '68
DYER, W. Gurnee
Elephant work in South India; with biographi-
cal sketch. il Natur Hist 76:5, 38-43 My '67
DYES and dyeing
Rapid wool-dyeing. F. C. Livingstone. Sci N
92:423 O 28 '67
See also
Black
DYKES, Archie R.
Presidential leadership in academe. bibliog f
Sch & Soc 95:223-6 Ap 1 '67
DYLAN, Bob
Basic Dylan. il por Time 91:50 Ja 12 '68
Bob Dylan through a lens darkly. J. L.
Wasserman. Life 63:10 Ag 11 '67
Cinéma Vérité and film truth. A. Knight. Sat
R 50:44 S 9 '67
Sound of Bob Dylan. E. Willis. Commentary
44:71-8 N '67
DYNACHROME films. See Photography—Films

DYNAMITE
See also
Blasting
DYNAMITE tonite; musical comedy. See Musi-
cal comedies, revues, etc.—Criticisms, plots,
etc.
DYSENTERY, Amebic. See Ameblasis
DYSLEXIA. See Word blindness
DZU, Truong-dinh-. See Truong-dinh-Dzu

E

EAT. See Experiments in art and technology,
incorporated
EBF. See Encyclopaedia Britannica films,
incorporated
ECAFE. See United Nations—Economic com-
mission for Asia and the Far East
ECE. See United Nations—Economic commis-
sion for Europe
ECLA. See United Nations—Economic commis-
sion for Latin America
ECM (electrochemical machining) See Elec-
trochemical cutting
ECOSOC. See United Nations—Economic and
social council
ECS. See Education commission of the states
ECS. See Electric shock
EDC. See Education development center, in-
corporated
EDF. See Environmental defense fund
EDP. See Electronic data processing
EEC. See European economic community
EEG. See Electroencephalography
EEOC. See United States—President's equal
employment opportunity commission
E. F. Hutton and company. See Hutton, E. F,
and company
E. I. Du Pont de Nemours and company. See
Du Pont De Nemours, E. I, and company
EIB. See Export-import bank of Washington
E. J. Korvette, incorporated. See Korvette, E.
J, incorporated
ELDO. See European launcher development or-
ganization
EMG. See Electromyography
ENI (Ente nazionale indrocarburi) See Petro-
leum industry and trade—Italy
EOS. See Electro-optical systems, incorporated
E. P. Dutton and company. See Dutton, E. P.
and company
ERIC (educational resource information center)
See United States—Education, Office of—
Educational research and development, Bu-
reau of
EROS (earth resources observation satellites)
See Artificial satellites—Use in research
EROS (eliminate range zero system) See Aero-
nautic instruments
E S master. See Master E S
ESCRU. See Episcopal society for cultural and
racial unity
ESP. See Extrasensory perception
ESRO. See European space research organiza-
tion
ESSA. See United States—Environmental sci-
ence services administration
ESSA (environmental survey satellite) See Arti-
ficial satellites—Meterological applications
ETV stations. See Television stations, Educa-
tional
EVA (extravehicular activity) See Space flight—
Manned flights—Extravehicular activity
EVA (extravehicular activity) suit. See As-
tronauts—Clothing
EVR (electronic video recording) See Tele-
vision apparatus
EAGAN, James M.
You have to be taught to hate. por Parents
Mag 42:32+ F '67
EAGLE LAKE, Calif.
That surprising Eagle Lake. B. Behme. il
Field & S 72:38-9+ Je '67
EAGLES
Eagles in disguise; save-the-eagle TV com-
mercials. A. Van Dine. Sat R 51:8+ Ja 13
'68
Eagles over Hawk Mountain; excerpt from
Flashing wings. J. K. Terres. il Audubon
69:28-33 Jl '67

EAGLES—*Continued*
Hawk and eagle numbers in decline. Nat Parks Mag 41:20 Ja '67
Potomac eagle refuges; proposed Potomac bald eagle refuge at Mason Neck, Va. Liv Wildn 30:45 Aut '66
Rare black eagles on the wing. il Life 62:66B-67 Mr 3 '67
Sharing the lives of wild golden eagles. J. Craighead. il Nat Geog Mag 132:420-39 S '67
Vanishing American; bald eagle. M. J. Walker and J. Lowen. il Am For 73:6-9+ O '67

EAGLES (football club) See Football clubs

EAGLETON, Terry
Politics and the sacred. Commonweal 87:402-6 D 29 '67

EAR
Basilar membrane vibration examined with the Mössbauer technique. B. M. Johnstone and A. J. F. Boyle. bibliog il Science 158:389-90 O 20 '67
Cochlear function and sodium and potassium activated adenosine triphosphatase. W. Kuijpers and others. bibliog il Science 157:949-50 Ag 25 '67
New hope for the deafened. H. G. Earl. il Sci Digest 63:7-13 Ja '68
See also
Hearing

Diseases
See also
Deaf

Surgery
Lifting the curtain of silence. J. D. Ratcliff. il Todays Health 45:66-8+ N '67; Same abr. with title Doctor I can hear! Read Digest 91:189-90+ N '67

EAR (animals)
Pressure regulation in the middle ear cavity of sea lions; a possible mechanism. S. Odend'hal and T. C. Poulter; discussion. bibliog il Science 155:489; 157:99 Ja 27, Jl 7 '67

EARHART, Amelia
I completed Amelia Earhart's flight. A. H. Pellegreno. il por McCalls 95:48+ N '67
New disclosures on the Amelia Earhart mystery. por U S News 63:10 Jl 24 '67
Search for Amelia Earhart, by F. Goerner. Review
Nation 204:374-6 Mr 20 '67. C. Dreher

EARL, Beulah Rodgers
Quick course in exterior decorating. Pop Gard 18:18-23 Ag '67

EARL, Howard
Great rabbit war. Sci Digest 62:18-20 N '67
Watch out for this spider. Sci Digest 62:78-80 N '67

EARL, Howard G.
Taking the fear out of retirement. Todays Health 45:64-7 F '67

EARL, Mary-Ellen
William H. Bartlett and his imitators; excerpts. Antiques 92:722-5 N '67

EARLY, Tracy
Klan kludd: to be or not to be. Christian Cent 84:236 F 22 '67

EARNINGS, Corporate. See Corporations—Finance

EARPHONES
Pennant race special; four-way earphone adapter. A. F. Burr. il Pop Electr 26:31 My '67
Stereo headphones. il Consumer Rep 32:528-32 O '67

EARRINGS
Pierced ears thrill girls and jewelers. il Bens W p 100-1 Je 3 '67

EARTH
Earth and environment notes. See issues of Science news
Were comets the midwives at the birth of man? theories of R. J. Uffen. J. Lear. il Sat R 50:57-62 My 6 '67; Discussion. 50:52-6 Ag 5 '67
See also
Cosmogony
Geodesy
Magnetism, Terrestrial

Age
Oceanic basalt leads: a new interpretation and an independent age for the earth. T. J. Ulrych. bibliog il Science 158:252-6 O 13 '67
See also
Geological time

Chemical composition
See Geochemistry

Crust
See Earth—Surface

Figure
Shape of the earth. D. King-Hele. il Sci Am 217:67-72+ O '67

Internal structure
Canada's unappreciated role as scientific innovator; magnetic surveys and the theory of convection in the earth's mantle; theories of J. T. Wilson and L. W. Morley. J. Lear. il Sat R 50:45-50 S 2 '67
Phase changes in the upper mantle. D. L. Anderson. bibliog il Science 157:1165-6+ S 8 '67
See also
Mohole project

Maps
See World maps

Photographs
Crazy mixed-up planets; pictures taken by U.S. navy's DODGE satellite. Newsweek 70:58-9+ N 6 '67
First color portrait of an angry earth. Life 63:107 N 10 '67

Rotation
Geostrophic transport through the Drake Passage. A. L. Gordon. bibliog il Science 156:1732-4 Je 30 '67
Implications for geophysics of the precise measurement of the earth's rotation G. J. F. MacDonald. bibliog Science 157:304-5 Jl 21 '67
Radio method for the precise measurement of the rotation period of the earth. T. Gold. bibliog Science 157:302-4 Jl 21 '67

Shape
See Earth—Figure

Surface
Composition of the ancient North American crust. K. C. Condie. bibliog il Science 155:1013-15 F 24 '67
Fractionation of potassium/rubidium by amphiboles: implications regarding mantle composition. S. R. Hart and L. T. Aldrich. bibliog il Science 155:325-7 Ja 20 '67
Our moving continents. B. H. Frisch. il Sci Digest 63:46-8+ Ja '68
St Peter and St Paul Rocks: a high-temperature, mantle-derived intrusion. W. G. Melson and others. bibliog il Science 155:1532-5 Mr 24 '67
Seismic delay times: correlation with other data. M. N. Toksöz and J. Arkani-Hamed. bibliog il Science 158:783-5 N 10 '67
See also
Faults (geology)
Ocean bottom

EARTH, Effect of man on. See Man—Influence on nature

EARTH, Photography of. See Space photography

EARTH magnetism. See Magnetism, Terrestrial

EARTH movements
Motions of the earth's core and mantle, and variations of the main geomagnetic field. R. Hide. bibliog Science 157:55-6 Jl 7 '67
Our moving continents. B. H. Frisch. il Sci Digest 63:46-8+ Ja '68
Radiolarian evidence consistent with spreading of the Pacific floor. W. R. Riedel. bibliog il Science 157:540-2 Ag 4 '67
Sea floor spreading, topography, and the second layer. H. W. Menard. bibliog il Science 157:923-4 Ag 25 '67
Tertiary sediment from the East Pacific rise. L. H. Burckle and others. bibliog il Science 157:537-40 Ag 4 '67
Under the spreading sea floor. Sci Am 217:40+ Ag '67
See also
Seismology
Subsidences (earth movements)

EARTH moving machinery. See Excavating machinery

EARTH resources satellites. See Artificial satellites—Use in research

EARTH shine. See Earthshine

EARTH temperature
Isotopic paleotemperatures. C. Emiliani; discussion. Science 156:410; bibliog 157:722-5 Ap 21, Ag 11 '67

EARTHQUAKE research. See Earthquakes—Research

EARTHQUAKES
Man-made earthquake? possible cause of Denver tremor. Sci N 91:377 Ap 22 '67
See also
Seismic sea waves
Seismology

Research
Death without warning. il Time 90:63 Ag 4 '67
Earthquakes made to order. K. N. Anderson. il Pop Mech 127-78-81+ Je '67
Japanese program on earthquake prediction. T. Hagiwara and T. Rikitake. bibliog il Science 157:761-8 Ag 18 '67
Learning to live with earthquakes. il Bsns W p56-7 D 23 '67
Local geomagnetic events associated with displacements on the San Andreas fault. S. Breiner and R. L. Kovach. bibliog il Science 158:116-18 O 6 '67

Alaska
Shaken earth; study of 1964 earthquake. Time 90:85 N 17 '67

Japan
Japanese program on earthquake prediction. T. Hagiwara and T. Rikitake. bibliog il Science 157:761-8 Ag 18 '67

Turkey
Death at a house called no. 116. M. Durham. il Life 63:44A Ag 4 '67
Death without warning. il Time 90:63 Ag 4 '67

United States
And bust; earthquake in Gallatin national forest. M. Ericson. il Am For 73:5+ Mr '67
Sheepherder versus the geologist; the Sierra Nevada earthquake of 1872. W. R. Jones. il Audubon 69:47-9 Ja '67

EARTHQUAKES and building
Earthquakes made to order. K. N. Anderson. il Pop Mech 127:78-81+ Je '67
Skyline changes; Japan's first skyscraper able to resist earthquakes. S. Griffin. il Sci N 92:85 Jl 22 '67

EARTHSHINE
Few notes about earthshine. J. Ashbrook. il Sky & Tel 34:92-3 Ag '67

EARTHWORK
See also
Excavation

EARTHWORKS (archeology)
Pre-Columbian ridged fields; agricultural earthworks of South America. J. J. Parsons and W. M. Denevan. il Sci Am 217:92-100 Jl '67

EARWAX
Cerumen in American Indians: genetic implications of sticky and dry types. N. L. Petrakis and others. bibliog il Science 158:1192-3 D 1 '67

EASBY, Dudley T. Jr. See Caley, E. R. jt. auth.

EASELS
Easel lets you wet-mount paper for water colors. M. Banister. il Pop Mech 128:192 N '67

EASLEY, J. Allen
Southern Baptist seminaries challenged. G. H. Shriver, jr. Christian Cent 84:601-2 My 3 '67

EASON, Robert G. and others
Evoked cortical potentials: relation to visual field and handedness. bibliog Science 156:1643-6 Je 23 '67

EAST, Ben
Snakebite: the forgotten menace. Read Digest 90:132-6 Je '67
What happens to pheasants? Outdoor Life 140:34-5+ Ag '67
(ed) See Beebe, F. I was the dog
(ed) See Haataja, B. Bear to be thankful for
(ed) See Tucker, W. L. Rattlesnake jamboree
—See Bauer, E. A. jt. auth.

EAST
See also
Asia
Middle East

EAST AFRICA. See Africa, East

EAST AFRICAN academy. See Research—Africa, East

EAST AFRICAN economic community. See Africa, East—Economic integration

EAST and West
Mystical West puzzles the practical East. F. M. Esfandiary. il N Y Times Mag p22-3+ F 5 '67

EAST BERLIN. See Berlin (East Berlin)

EAST HAMPTON, N.Y.
Historic houses, etc.
Antique treasure, modern workings; Mulford-Baker house. il House B 109:170-7 Ap '67

EAST INDIANS
Indian national character in the twentieth century. D. Narain. bibliog f il Ann Am Acad 370:124-32 Mr '67

EAST MOLINE, Ill.
Mini-megalopolis rises along the Mississippi; thriving Quad-cities of Iowa and Illinois. il Bsns W p 168-70 F 25 '67

EAST PACIFIC rise. See Ocean bottom

EAST RIVER, New York (city)
New life for the river that isn't a river. M. J. Kempner. il N Y Times Mag p32-4+ Ag 6 '67

EAST ST LOUIS, Ill.
Where everything, almost, went wrong; interstate highway bridge linking St Louis and East St Louis. il Bsns W p62+ Je 10 '67

Riots
Man with a match; Rap Brown. il Time 90:23 S 22 '67

EAST-West center. See Hawaii. University—East-West center

EAST-West relations. See International relations

EAST-West trade. See Communist countries—Commerce

EAST wind; drama. See Lehman, L.

EASTER
This feast of Easter, 1967. America 116:411 Mr 25 '67
See also
Holy week
Jesus Christ—Resurrection and ascension

Drama
Cinder-rabbit. C. W. Baher. Plays 26:61-9 Mr '67
Vanishing Easter egg. H. L. Miller. Plays 26:27-36 Mr '67

Poetry
And after three days. W. L. Molton. Christian Cent 84:367 Mr 22 '67
Friday pathos. I. K. Rarden. Christian Cent 84:367 Mr 22 '67
Good Friday morning. E. Morin. Christian Cent 84:367 Mr 22 '67
J. C. A. Oerke. Christian Cent 84:367 Mr 22 '67
Sonnet for a Sabbath, 30 A.D. R. P. Desch. Christian Cent 84:367 Mr 22 '67

EASTER business. See Retail trade

EASTER dinners. See Dinners and dining

EASTER eggs
Before and after of Easter eggs. Am Home 70:123 Mr '67

EASTER ISLAND
Easter Island. W. Mulloy. il Natur Hist 76:74-81 bibliog(p 105) D '67
Isle of eyeless watchers. L. S. De Camp. il Sci Digest 62:6-12 O '67
Saving the moai & ahus. Time 90:86 O 6 '67

EASTER parties. See Entertaining

EASTERLIN, Richard A.
Effects of population growth on the economic development of developing countries. bibliog f Ann Am Acad 369:98-108 Ja '67

EASTERN air lines
Eastern acquires two resort hotels. Aviation W 87:32 O 2 '67
Eastern sees 50 per cent cargo boost with 727QCs, new facilities. Aviation W 86:37 F 27 '67
Eastern stretches turn-around schedule; four airlines show increases in traffic and revenues. W. H. Gregory. Aviation W 86:29 My 1 '67
Eastern TWA to cooperate on Concorde, 747 support. Aviation W 87:38 D 4 '67
Money from the sky; interview. ed. by F. Merkling. F. D. Hall. Opera N 32:14 N 25 '67
Number one to the Met; Eastern air lines gives the Met $500,000. il Time 89:87 My 26 '67
Preparing for the superjets; Eastern air lines and Trans World airlines joint project to reduce cost of maintaining future superjet fleets. Time 90:102 D 8 '67
Remmert acquisition by Eastern backed. Aviation W 87:29 S 4 '67

EASTERN air lines—*Continued*
Shuffle on the shuttle; guaranteed-seat shuttle on New York-Boston run. Bsns W p31 F 11 '67
Transpacific route case: Eastern stresses less competitive areas. H. D. Watkins. il Aviation W 86:53+ Ap 10 '67
EASTERN-Central Europe. See Europe, Eastern
EASTERN EUROPE. See Europe, Eastern
EASTERN music camp, Greensboro, N.C. See Music camps
EASTERN test range. See Proving grounds
EASTLAKE, William
Cleaning up Juarez. Nation 205:300-3 O 2 '67
Death of seven zipperheads. Nation 205:530-1 N 20 '67
Like a small dead man. Nation 206:13 Ja 1 '68
Lost in Vietnam. Nation 205:593-4 D 4 '67
Our Lord in Vietnam. Nation 205:491-2 N 13 '67
EASTLAND, James O.
Excerpt from address, January 19, 1967. Cong Digest 46:77+ Mr '67
EASTMAN Kodak company
. . .And Kodak will ask how high? troubles with FIGHT. Fortune 75:78 Je 1 '67
Economic leverage of the churches; Project Equality. P. J. Flynn. America 116:823 Je 10 '67
FIGHT against Kodak. B. Carter. il Reporter 36:28-31 Ap 20 '67
Fight at Kodak; company racial policies. il Newsweek 69:81+ My 8 '67
FIGHT in color; Negro employment by Kodak. il Time 89:88 My 5 '67
FIGHT-Kodak fight. D. Livadas. Nat R 19:683 Je 27 '67
Fight that swirls around Eastman Kodak; battle over more jobs for Negroes. il Bsns W p38-41 Ap 29 '67
Kodak and Fight agree to agree; plan for hiring a fixed number of Negroes. Bsns W p22 Jl 1 '67
Kodak goes Ektagraphic. il U S Camera 30:54-5 S '67
Kodak's clouded picture; London-based Kodak ltd. J. Ross-Skinner. il Duns R 89:53 Ja '67
New threat for employers? what a Negro group seeks from Kodak; FIGHT dispute over hiring agreement. il U S News 62:74-5 My 8 '67
Of many things; Kodak and FIGHT agreement. R. A. Schroth. America 117:inside cover Jl 8 '67
Peace with FIGHT. Fortune 76:66 Ag '67
Self-doubt and black pride; Eastman Kodak and the FIGHT organization. R. A. Schroth. America 116:502-5 Ap 1 '67; Reply with rejoinder. P. A. Mallon. 116:664-5 My 6 '67
Shepherds vs. flocks; church involvement in FIGHT assault on Kodak. W. C. Martin. Atlan 220:53-9 D '67
What the Kodak fracas means; job problems of Negroes. Bsns W p 192 My 6 '67
EASTMAN school of music, Rochester, N.Y.
Today's Eastman school. I. Kolodin. Sat R 50:24 Ap 29 '67
EASTON, Florence
First ladies of the Puccini premieres. M. J. Matz. por Opera N 32:6-7 Ja 13 '68
EASTWOOD, Clint
New formula for violence. il pors Life 62:95-6 Ap 14 '67
EATING
Anatomical connections between medial and lateral regions of the hypothalamus concerned with food intake. E. A. Arees and J. Mayer. bibliog il Science 157:1574-5 S 29 '67
Enterogastrone inhibits eating by fasted mice. A. V. Schally and others. bibliog il Science 157:210-11 Jl 14 '67
Localization of the adrenergic feeding system in the rat diencephalon. D. A. Booth. bibliog il Science 158:515-17 O 27 '67
Night eaters, always on the prowl. A. J. Snider. Sci Digest 63:80-1 Ja '68
Regulation of food intake and obesity. J. Mayer and D. W. Thomas. bibliog il Science 156:328-37 Ap 21 '67
Stretch receptors in the foregut of the blowfly. A. Gelperin. bibliog il Science 157:208-10 Jl 14 '67
See also
Die
Dinners and dining
Food
Meals
Outdoor meals

Anecdotes, facetiae, satire, etc.
Grape peelers and other famous food kooks. L. Lyons. Vogue 150:22+ O 15 '67
EATING, Psychology of
Conditioning with delayed vitamin injections. J. Garcia and others. bibliog il Science 155:716-18 F 10 '67
Helping children develop good eating habits. il Good H 164:192-3 Je '67
EATON, Aileen
Lady is a champ. M. Kram. il pors Sports Illus 27:76-8+ N 6 '67
EATON, Jerome A.
Greenhouse of your own. Home Gard 54:26-34 N '67
Home greenhouse. See issues of Flower grower, the home garden (cont as) Home garden & flower grower
EATON, Jerry P. See Bateman, P. C. jt. auth.
EATON, Joseph W.
Education and public service. bibliog f Sch & Soc 95:358-60 O 14 '67
EATON, Quaintance
Music in the mansions. Opera N 32:6 O 14 '67
Yankee trick. Opera N 31:6-7 Ap 1 '67
(ed) See Ulfung, R. Viking guest
(ed) See Yannopoulos, D. Greek drama
EATON, William W.
Patent problem: who owns the rights? Harvard Bsns R 45:101-10 Jl '67
EAVESDROPPING devices. See Electronics in criminal investigation, espionage, etc.
EBAN, Abba
Argument indeed: Soviet attack, Israeli retort; excerpts from address. por Life 62:25 Je 30 '67
Eban; with excerpts from address at the General assembly. New Yorker 43:25-7 Jl 1 '67
Israel's surprise weapon: envoy Eban. il por U S News 63:20 Jl 3 '67
Middle East crisis: address, June 19, 1967. Vital Speeches 33:612-19 Ag 1 '67
EBEL, Fred E.
That old regenerative set of mine. Pop Electr 28:50-1 Ja '68
EBEN, Lois E.
Diorama depicting scene of Battle of Monmouth. Sch Arts 66:31-2 F '67
EBERHARD, Hans J. Müller-. See Müller-Eberhard, H. J.
EBERHARD, Jonathan
Earth's secretive sister. Sci N 92:86-7 Jl 22 '67
EBERHART, Richard
Enigma; poem. New Yorker 43:64 N 18 '67
Haystack; poem. Nation 204:346 Mr 13 '67
Lions copulating; poem. Nation 204:520 Ap 24 '67
Mexico phantasmagoria; poem. Poetry 110:400-5 S '67
Music over words; poem. Nation 204:791 Je 19 '67
Winds: poem. Nation 204:218 F 13 '67
EBERSOLD, W. T.
Chlamydomonas reinhardi: heterozygous diploid strains. bibliog Science 157:447-9 Jl 28 '67
EBERT, Thomas A.
Negative growth and longevity in the purple sea urchin strongylocentrotus purpuratus (Stimpson) bibliog Science 157:557-8 Ag 4 '67
EBINGER, Virginia
A time to every purpose. por Redbook 128:8+ Ap '67
EBON, Martin
Svetlana's future; excerpt from Svetlana: the story of Stalin's daughter. Good H 165:79-80+ O '67
EBREY, Thomas G.
Fast light-evoked potential from leaves. bibliog Science 155:1556-7 Mr 24 '67
ECCLES, Marriner S.
Vietnam: address, August 11, 1967. Vital Speeches 33:717-19 S 15 '67
ECCLESIASTICAL architecture. See Church architecture
ECCLESIASTICAL art. See Christian art and symbolism
ECCLESIASTICAL law
See also
Canon law
ECDYSONE
Plant insecticides. Sci Am 217:54 N '67
ECHINOCEREUS. See Cactus

ECHINODERMS
Echinoderm calcite: single crystal or polycrystalline aggregate. K. M. Towe. bibliog il Science 157:1048-50 S 1 '67
See also
Embryology—Echinoderms

ECHOLOCATION (physiology)
Human echo perception. C. E. Rice. bibliog il Science 155:656-64 F 10 '67

ECK, Robert
Real masters of television. Harper 234:45-52 Mr '67; Same abr. with title Why TV is the way it is. Read Digest 90:78-82 My '67

ECKARDT, A. Roy, and Eckardt, A. L.
Again, silence in the churches. Christian Cent 84:970-3, 992-5 Jl 26-Ag 2 '67

ECKARDT, Alice L. See Eckardt, A. R. jt. auth.

ECKELBERRY, Don Richard
Steel bands and tropical birds. por Audubon 69:44-7 Mr '67
Trinidad galaxy; paintings. Audubon 69:48-53 Mr '67

ECKERT, Ralph G.
Listen world. PTA Mag 62:11-12 S '67

ECKMAN, Charley
Whistle stop. il por Newsweek 69:89-90 Mr 27 '67

ECKMAN, Fern Marja
Redgraves talk about their children. McCalls 94:86-7+ S '67

ECLIPSES, Lunar
April's total lunar eclipse. D. W. Dunham. il Sky & Tel 33:252-3 Ap '67
Lunar eclipse; April 24, 1967. il Sky & Tel 34:52-4 Jl '67
October lunar eclipse reports. il Sky & Tel 34:408-10 D '67
October's total lunar eclipse. il Sky & Tel 34: 268-9 O '67
Total moon eclipse. J. Stokley. il Sci N 92: 308-9 S 23 '67

ECLIPSES, Solar
Coronal studies at the eclipse in Bolivia. J. M. Malville. il Sky & Tel 33:136-9 Mr '67
Ground observers report on November's eclipse; symposium. il Sky & Tel 33:144-8 Mr '67
Partial solar eclipse; May 9, 1967. il Sky & Tel 34:54-6 Jl '67
Racing the moon's shadow. A. N. Cox and others. il Sky & Tel 33:85-9 F '67
Rocket observations of the eclipse in Brazil. C. A. Accardo. il Sky & Tel 33:77-82 F '67

ECLOV, Shirley
Accident: story. Redbook 129:60-1 My '67

ECOBICHON, D. J. and Saschenbrecker, P. W.
Dechlorination of DDT in frozen blood. bibliog Science 156:663-5 My 5 '67

ÉCOLE polytechnique. See Paris—Education

ECOLOGY
Ecology notes. Sci N 91:215, 235 Mr 4-11 '67
Historical roots of our ecological crisis; address, December 26, 1966. L. White, jr. Science 155:1203-7 Mr 10 '67; Discussion. 156: 737-8 My 12 '67
See also
Balance of nature
Environment
Fishes—Ecology
Insects—Ecology
Marine ecology

ECONOMETRICS. See Economics, Mathematical

ECONOMIC, social and cultural rights, International covenant on. See International covenant on economic, social and cultural rights

ECONOMIC and social council of the United Nations. See United Nations—Economic and social council

ECONOMIC assistance
Address to OECD council, Paris, April 7, 1967. H. H. Humphrey. Dept State Bul 56:683-5 My 1 '67
On foreign aid. E. Rabinowitch. Bul Atomic Sci 23:2-4 Je '67
Peaceful revolution of the 20th century; message, June 5, 1967. L. B. Johnson. Dept State Bul 57:16 Jl 3 '67
Politics of progress; address, February 20, 1967. E. V. Rostow. Dept State Bul 56:398-405 Mr 13 '67
Seminar on foreign aid. A. W. Munk. Sch & Soc 95:504 D 9 '67

ECONOMIC assistance, American
American empire; excerpts from Pax Americana. R. Steel. Commonweal 86:335-9 Je 9 '67

America's foreign aid program; reappraising its relevancy; address, January 14, 1967. J. S. Clark. Vital Speeches 33:299-303 Mr 1 '67
As Congress takes a new look at foreign aid. il U S News 63:47-8 N 13 '67
Billions for aid, clamor for more. il U S News 63:60 S 18 '67
Budget message of the President; excerpts; with excerpts from The budget of the United States government for the fiscal year ending June 30, 1968. L. B. Johnson. il Dept State Bul 56:230-6 F 13 '67
Central purpose of United States foreign policy; address, August 5, 1967. D. Rusk. Dept State Bul 57:251-5 Ag 28 '67
Challenge of foreign aid, by J. J. Kaplan. Review
Reporter 36:54-6 Je 15 '67. H. Landsberg
DOD plan would separate civil, military aid requests. D. C. Winston. Aviation W 87: 17-18 D 25 '67
Doctors in the House; cuts in foreign aid funds. Time 90:13 S 1 '67
Foreign aid; an essential element of U.S. foreign policy; address, September 30, 1967. N. D. Katzenbach. Dept State Bul 57:530-4 O 23 '67
Foreign aid and Christian responsibility. L. S. Rouner. Christian Cent 84:103-5 Ja 25 '67
Foreign aid; message to Congress, February 9, 1967. L. B. Johnson. Dept State Bul 56: 378-85 Mr 6 '67
Foreign aid seesaw. New Repub 157:9-10 N 18 '67
Foreign assistance act of 1967 signed into law; statement, November 15, 1967. L. B. Johnson. Dept State Bul 57:753 D 4 '67
Foreign assistance program for 1968; statement, May 4, 1967. D. Rusk. Dept State Bul 56:826-33 My 29 '67
Foreign assistance program; statement, July 14, 1967. D. Rusk. Dept State Bul 57:208-15 Ag 14 '67
Justice and international development, a manifesto for American action in the struggle against world poverty. Christian Cent 84:660+ My 17 '67
Let them eat their tin cups. New Repub 156:7 Mr 11 '67
Let's make foreign aid count. R. L. Ash. il Duns R 90:43+ O '67
Love your enemies; open letter to President Lyndon B. Johnson. J. W. Still. Bul Atomic Sci 23:30 Mr '67
Nation building: new economic horizon for industry; address, November 8, 1967. R. L. Ash. Vital Speeches 34:181-4 Ja 1 '68
Pacific Islands Trust Territory to receive additional funds; statement, May 10, 1967. L. B. Johnson. Dept State Bul 56:865 Je 5 '67
Peanuts for Africa. Reporter 36:16 F 23 '67
Political decay of foreign aid. J. D. Montgomery. Yale R 57:1-15 O '67
Smaller & simpler. Time 89:18 F 17 '67
Tighter wallet for foreign aid. il Bsns W p32-3 Ag 19 '67
To the marrow; lowest aid appropriation. Time 90:24 N 24 '67
U.S. in the world market place; address, April 24, 1967. G. Champion. Vital Speeches 33:505-8 Je 1 '67
What development decade? foreign-aid cuts. Nation 205:194-5 S 11 '67
Why America carries the world's burden. il U S News 62:34-7 Mr 6 '67
Why not a declaration of interdependence? America 116:577 Ap 22 '67
See also
Food relief
United States—Agency for international development
United States—President's advisory committee on foreign assistance programs

ECONOMIC assistance, Domestic
Atlantic report: Washington; too many programs. E. B. Drew. Atlan 219:6+ Mr '67
Challenge of creative federalism. L. E. Schaller. Christian Cent 84:618-22 My 10 '67
Change of heart? Senate committees vote funds for slum aid. Newsweek 70:21 S 11 '67
Great opportunity of 1965. W. F. Buckley, jr. Nat R 19:342 Ag 8 '67
Stretching the limbs; findings of task force visiting states. Time 89:19-20 Mr 31 '67
See also
Anti-poverty program, 1964-
United States—Job corps
Volunteers in service to America

ECONOMIC assistance, Japanese
Japan on the move. America 117:214 S 2 '67
Japan's new idea for co-prosperity sphere. il U S News 63:90-1 Jl 24 '67
Japan's powerful push overseas. il Bsns W p92-4+ Ag 19 '67

ECONOMIC assistance, Mexican
Mexico helps West Pakistan. Américas 19:41
My '67
ECONOMIC assistance, Russian
Where Russia is getting a toe hold in the
Mideast. il U S News 62:107-8 Mr 27 '67
ECONOMIC assistance in Afghanistan
Prime Minister of Afghanistan visits the
United States; exchange of greetings, ex-
change of toasts, and joint statement,
March 28, 1967. M. H. Maiwandwal; L. B.
Johnson. Dept State Bul 56:627-32 Ap 17
'67
Tangible tokens. il Time 89:18 Ap 7 '67
ECONOMIC assistance in Africa
Katzenbach. Dept State Bul 56:954-9 Je 26
'67; Same. Vital Speeches 33:622-5 Ag 1 '67
ECONOMIC assistance in Asia
Asian perspectives; address, July 11, 1967. H.
Kaplan. Dept State Bul 57:230-5 Ag 21 '67
Japan's quiet war against Mao. L. Velie.
Read Digest 91:116-20 Ag '67
Success for the U.S. il U S News 62:38-40
My 8 '67
U.S. economic commitment in southeast Asia.
A. Roseman. bibliog f Cur Hist 54:7-14+ Ja
'68
ECONOMIC assistance in Colombia
Summer in Bogotá; Association for inter-
national development (AID) W. M. Barbieri.
America 117:274-7 S 16 '67
ECONOMIC assistance in Europe
Birthday party; Marshall plan anniversary.
Newsweek 69:78 Je 19 '67
Historic anniversary; Marshall plan. America
116:845 Je 17 '67
Marshall plan: from the reconstruction to the
construction of Europe; address, June 6,
1967. W. A. Harriman. Dept State Bul
57:17-18 Jl 3 '67
Twenty years later; Marshall plan anniver-
sary. il Time 89:19 Je 16 '67
ECONOMIC assistance in Indonesia
Restraint in resuming US aid to Indonesia.
C. A. Aminoff. New Repub 156:13-14 F 11 '67
ECONOMIC assistance in Iran
Spreading the wealth; White revolution. S.
G. Slappey. il Nations Bsns 55:86-9 S '67
ECONOMIC assistance in Korea (Republic)
Korea's comeback, what Humphrey found.
U S News 63:13 Jl 10 '67
ECONOMIC assistance in Laos
Report; U.S. AID activities. P. Braestrup. At-
lan 220:10+ Ag '67
ECONOMIC assistance in Latin America
American Chiefs of state meet at Punta del
Este; statements, April 11-14, 1967; with
text of Declaration of the presidents of
America. L. B. Johnson. Dept State Bul
56:706-21 My 8 '67
Comedy of errors; Johnson-Fulbright clash.
il Newsweek 69:32-4 Ap 17 '67
President requests $400 million for Latin
American loans. Dept State Bul 56:887 Je
12 '67
Punta del Este revisited. L. Gordon, bib-
liog f For Affairs 45:624-38 Jl '67
Road from Punta del Este; address, May 1,
1967. S. M. Linowitz. Dept State Bul 56:
822-5 My 29 '67
Tangible tokens. il Time 89:18 Ap 7 '67
See also
Alliance for progress
Inter-American development bank
ECONOMIC assistance in Malawi
President of Malawi visits the United States;
exchange of toasts, June 8, 1967. H. K.
Banda; L. B. Johnson. Dept State Bul 57:
42-4 Jl 10 '67
ECONOMIC assistance in Nepal
Neutral cockpit. il Time 90:26+ N 3 '67
ECONOMIC assistance in North Africa
World's next danger area. il U S News 62:62-
4 Ap 17 '67
ECONOMIC assistance in Pakistan
Mexico helps West Pakistan. Américas 19:41
My '67
ECONOMIC assistance in Russia
American aid to Russia. il U S News 62:60-1
Mr 13 '67
ECONOMIC assistance in southeast Asia. See
Economic assistance in Asia
ECONOMIC assistance in Thailand
Hopes and fears in booming Thailand. P.
T. White. il Nat Geog Mag 132:76-125 Jl
'67
How the guerrillas came to Koh Noi. P.
Braestrup. il N Y Times Mag p30-1+ D 10
'67
ECONOMIC assistance in the Congo (capital
Kinshasa)
Congo looking to America, but—. il U S News
63:34 Ag 28 '67

ECONOMIC assistance in the Dominican Re-
public
Dominican turnabout; now it's Yanqui, si;
commie, no. il Nations Bsns 55:50+ D '67
ECONOMIC assistance in the Philippines
U.S. and Philippines agree on school building
project. Dept State Bul 56:850 Je 5 '67
U.S.-Philippine relations; where we stand to-
day; address, March 9, 1967. E. M. Brader-
man. Dept State Bul 56:660-4 Ap 24 '67
ECONOMIC assistance in underdeveloped areas
Challenge to the opulent nations; summary
of address. G. Díaz Ordaz. America 117:538
N 11 '67
Combustibility of humans; how to avoid
world famine and population crisis. H.
Brown. Sat R 50:14-17+ Je 24 '67
Let them eat their tin cups. New Repub
156:7 Mr 11 '67
On foreign aid. E. Rabinowitch. Bul Atomic
Sci 23:2-4 Je '67
On helping the hungry. R. M. Fagley. Chris-
tian Cent 84:811-13 Je 21 '67
Poverty of nations. A. Campbell. New Repub
156:32+ Je 3 '67
Rich and the poor. Nation 204:388 Mr 27 '67
U.S. assistance to less developed countries,
1956-65. K. M. Kauffman and H. Stalson.
il For Affairs 45:715-25 Jl '67
ECONOMIC assistance in Vietnam
AID report on Viet-Nam commodity programs
submitted to President Johnson; letter of
transmittal, January 9, 1967; with text of
report. W. S. Gaud. Dept State Bul 56:200-
16 F 6 '67
Fantasy in Vietnam. J. Osborne. New Repub
156:13-15 My 27 '67
Max the maximizer; nations assisting under
the Free world assistance program. New
Repub 157:7-8 N 25 '67
Sawmill in Vietnam; excerpt from letter.
J. Cravens. il Am For 73:8+ S '67
Selling self-help at a profit; plan for redevel-
opment of South Vietnam. il Bsns W p54-
6+ Ag 12 '67
U.S. support of pacification effort in Viet-
Nam reorganized; statement, May 11, 1967.
E. Bunker. Dept State Bul 56:844-5 Je 5 '67
U.S. to contribute to UNDP/FAO fisheries
project in Viet-Nam. Dept State Bul 56:964
Je 26 '67
Vietnam's other war; battered economy. il
Bsns W p99-102+ S 23 '67
ECONOMIC change
Effect of economic change on the Michigan
labor force. P. S. Barth. Mo Labor R 90:29
Mr '67
ECONOMIC commissions of the United Nations.
See name of commission under United Na-
tions, e.g. United Nations—Economic com-
mission for Africa
ECONOMIC conditions
Back toward normal; OECD report. Time
90:70 Jl 21 '67
Business around the world. See issues of U.S.
news & World report
Great transition; task of the first and sec-
ond postwar generations; address, Febru-
ary 23, 1967. W. W. Rostow. Dept State Bul
56:491-504 Mr 27 '67
Keeping up the pace; industrial nations in
different parts of the globe. il Bsns W
p46+ D 30 '67
Myths that keep people hungry. M. Fried-
man. Harper 234:16+ Ap '67
News, mostly good, beyond Viet Nam; Time
essay. Time 89:16-17 Ap 7 '67
Papal gaucherie; Populorum progressio. Nat
R 19:391-3 Ap 18 '67
Report of Council of economic advisers. il
Dept State Bul 56:336-50 F 27 '67
Slide toward violence in the hungering world.
H. I. Schiller. Bul Atomic Sci 23:4-6 Ja '67.
Reply with rejoinder. H. W. Salzberg. 23:
63-4 Je '67
When the world looks at U.S, a study in
power. il U S News 63:24-6 Jl 24 '67
World economic problems; Second committee
adopts five recommendations. UN Mo Chron
4:33-7 N '67
World economy; marking time. L. A. Mayer.
il Fortune 76:31-2+ S 15 '67
See also
Business conditions
Business cycles
Business depression
Cost of living
Standard of living
also subhead Economic conditions under
names of countries, states, cities, e.g. Italy
—Economic conditions

ECONOMIC cooperation. See Industrial cooperation; International cooperation

ECONOMIC cycles. See Business cycles

ECONOMIC development
Capital and economic growth; address, February 16, 1967. G. Champion. Vital Speeches 33:330-3 Mr 15 '67
Counterrevolutionary America: adaptation of address. R. L. Heilbroner. Commentary 43:31-8 Ap '67; Discussion. 44:6+ Jl '67
Development, new name for peace; excerpt from On the development of peoples, with reply by R. Maheu. Paul VI. UNESCO Courier 20:28-39 Ag '67
Economic setting. H. L. Lewis. Mo Labor R 90:1-4 F '67
Education and the wealth of nations. H. L. Enarson. Mo Labor R 90:21-4 Mr '67
Effects of population growth on the economic development of developing countries. R. A. Easterlin. bibliog f il Ann Am Acad 369:98-108 Ja '67
801st man: a man for the 21st century: address, November 15, 1967. F. J. Borch. Vital Speeches 34:187-90 Ja 1 '68
Ever widening gap; address, December 27, 1966. P. M. S. Blackett. bibliog Science 155:959-64 F 24 '67; Discussion. 156:314+, 1312-13 Ap 21, Je 9 '67
Health, population, and economic development. C. E. Taylor and M.-F. Hall. bibliog Science 157:651-7 Ag 11 '67
How much should a corporation earn? J. J. Scanlon. il Harvard Bsns R 45:4-6+ Ja '67
Huntsville: Alabama cotton town takes off into the space age. L. J. Carter. il Science 155:1224-9 Mr 10 '67
Laissez-faire is not enough; widening gap between rich nations and poor nations. S. L. Parmar. Christian Cent 84:587-9 My 3 '67
Malnutrition and national development. A. D. Berg. For Affairs 46:126-36 O '67
Modern economic growth: rate, structure, spread, by S. Kuznets. Review
Bul Atomic Sci 23:52-3 Je '67. W. P. Strassmann
Myths that keep people hungry. M. Friedman. Harper 234:16+ Ap '67
Planning without facts, by W. F. Stolper. Review
Bul Atomic Sci 23:53-4 Je '67. C. W. Kontos
Scandal of the century: rich and poor A. de Borchgrave. il Newsweek 70:38-40 O 30 '67
Slowing down: western Europe. il Time 89:87-8 F 24 '67
Society, technology, and development. M. Ras. bibliog il Américas 18:14-23 D '66; Correction. 19:48 Mr '67
Spill-over: the costs of growth. E. J. Mishan. Nation 205:558-61 N 27 '67
Three gaps: economic, technological & educational; address, February 24, 1967. R. S. McNamara. Vital Speeches 33:357-61 Ap 1 '67
Why Europe's growth tops the U.S; highlights of E. F. Denison's study. il Bsns W p 152+ Ja 14 '67
Wild plan for South America's wilds. T. Alexander. il Fortune 76:148-50+ D '67
See also
Underdeveloped areas
United States—Economic conditions

ECONOMIC equality. See Equality

ECONOMIC forecasting. See Forecasts (economics)

ECONOMIC gazette. See Periodicals—Russia

ECONOMIC growth. See Economic development

ECONOMIC imperialism. See Imperialism

ECONOMIC integration, International. See International economic integration

ECONOMIC models
New potentates rule by the numbers; econometricians. il Bsns W p56-8+ Ja 6 '68

ECONOMIC opportunity, Office of. See United States—Economic opportunity, Office of

ECONOMIC planning
Building a base for forecasters. il Bsns W p 117-19 Je 10 '67
Papal economics; concerning Pope Paul's advice on central planning. M. Friedman. Newsweek 69:87 Ap 24 '67
See also
Committee for economic development
United States—Council of economic advisers

ECONOMIC planning, International
See also
European economic community
United Nations—Economic and social council

ECONOMIC policy
Trade union approaches to income and price policy; excerpt from Non-wage incomes and prices policy. Mo Labor R 90:52-7 Ja '67
See also
Economic assistance
Industrialization
also subhead Economic policy under names of countries, e.g. United States—Economic policy

ECONOMIC relations
See also
Balance of payments
also Economic relations under names of countries, e.g. Japan—Economic relations

ECONOMIC research
See also
Brookings institution
National bureau of economic research

ECONOMIC sanctions. See Sanctions (international law)

ECONOMIC statistics
See also
Unemployment—Statistics

ECONOMIC surveys
See also
Consumer surveys

ECONOMIC theory. See Economics

ECONOMIC union. See International economic integration

ECONOMICS
Big gap in economic theory. H. M. Boettinger. bibliog f Harvard Bsns R 45:51-8 Jl '67
Economics in action. See issues of Senior scholastic
Evolution of an economist. G. Routh. Mo Labor R 90:18-22 F '67
Keeping the score. P. A. Samuelson. Newsweek 69:80 My 1 '67
Understanding and using economics (cont) M. Mayer. Bet Hom & Gard 45:42 F; 28 Mr; 36 Ap; 84 My; 128 Je '67
World is the problem. H. Wheeler. Nation 205:358-60 O 16 '67
See also
Business conditions
Consumption (economics)
Finance
Free enterprise
Marketing
Profit
Standard of living
Supply and demand
Tariff
Wages—Economic aspects
Wealth, Distribution of

Graphic methods
Throwing inflation a tricky curve; Phillips curve to gauge what must be given up in price stability for a cut in unemployment. il Bsns W p62+ Ag 19 '67

Mathematical models
Economy set to warm up; Wharton model. il Bsns W p26-7 My 27 '67

Social and ethical aspects
Puritanism: the spirit that refuses to play dead; American attitudes. il Bsns W p 194+ Ap 15 '67

Study and teaching
Teaching private enterprise. S. G. Slappey. Nations Bsns 55:87 D '67

Terminology
Knowing your economics: without it you're not with it. il Sr Schol 91:14-16+ S 21 '67

ECONOMICS, Agricultural. See Agriculture—Economic aspects

ECONOMICS, Mathematical
Econometrics and model-building. C. F. Christ. bibliog il Ann Am Acad 370:164-75 Mr '67
New potentates rule by the numbers; econometricians. il Bsns W p56-8+ Ja 6 '68
See also
Economics—Mathematical models
Interindustry economics

ECONOMICS and Christianity. See Christianity and economics

ECONOMICS and politics
Economics and politics: do they mix? Sr Schol 91:12-14 O 26 '67

ECONOMIST (London)
Thanks, but no thanks; concerning editorial praising Lyndon Johnson's Vietnam policy. New Repub 158:6 Ja 20 '68

Virgorous moderation. il Time 90:48 Jl 21 '67

ECONOMITCHESKAYA gazetta. See Periodicals—Russia

ECONOMY in government. See Government spending policy

ECTOPIC pregnancy. See Pregnancy, Complications of

ECUADOR
See also
Ballet—Ecuador
Education—Ecuador
Quito
Saloya Valley

Antiquities
See Indians of South America—Antiquities

Constitution
Sovereignty and Latin American integration. F. Galo Leoro. il Americas 19:28-33 S '67

Economic conditions
Ecuador. R. E. Crist and A. Taylor. bibliog il Focus 18:1-6 O '67

Foreign relations
Ecuador asks recall of U.S. ambassador; texts of notes. Dept State Bul 57:621-2 N 6 '67
Yankee goes home. Sr Schol 91:20-1 O 26 '67

History
Ecuador. R. E. Crist and A. Taylor. bibliog il Focus 18:1-6 O '67

Politics and government
Dynamite man; Levi Castillo. Time 89:39+ Je 16 '67
See also
Ecuador—Constitution

ECUMENICAL council, 2d. See Vatican council, 2d

ECUMENICAL institute, Chicago
Laboratory for the future. il Time 89:79 Mr 17 '67

ECUMENICAL movement
Abortion controversy: a jolt to ecumenism. J. B. Sheerin. Cath World 205:68-70 My '67
Anglican-Roman dialogue. America 117:71 Jl 22 '67
COCU assaulted in its cradle; C. K. Myers proposal. Christian Cent 84:803-4 Je 21 '67; Discussion. 84:1073 Ag 23 '67
Ecumenical crisis we face; interview. A. C. Outler. Cath World 205:20-5 Ap '67
Ecumenical revolution, by R. M. Brown. Review
    Christian Cent 84:1024 Ag 9 '67. C. Northcott
    Sat R 50:37+ N 11 '67. J. A. Hardon
Ecumenical tangle; situation in Latin America. J. G. Chamberlin. Christian Cent 85:75-7 Ja 17 '68
Episcopalian for the Pope; Bishop of California suggests all of Christianity accept the Pope as its spiritual leader. Time 89:56 Je 16 '67
Fourth National workshop for Christian unity; in California. E. T. Culver. Christian Cent 84:698-9 My 24 '67
Less than helpful. J. R. Nelson. Christian Cent 84:974+ Jl 26 '67
Midwest ecumenical symposium at Dubuque. C. M. Austin. Christian Cent 84:1614 D 13 '67
Milestone in ecumenism. America 116:335 Mr 11 '67
Pan-Christian papacy? proposal of Bishop Myers. R. M. Brown. Commonweal 86:446+ Jl 14 '67
Paths to ecumenism. A. Bea. Sat R 50:8-11 Jl 8 '67
Paul VI's secular ecumenism. R. M. Brown. Commonweal 86:262-4 My 19 '67
Pope's worst enemy. J. O'Gara. Commonweal 86:282 My 26 '67
Proposals for Uppsala; coming fourth assembly. S. C. Rose. Christian Cent 84:1123-6 S 6 '67; Discussion. 84:1402, 1558-9 N 1, D 6 '67
Reformation Roman-style; excerpt from Methodist observer at Vatican II. A. C. Outler. Cath World 204:341-5 Mr '67
Secular ecumenism and the teaching of the faith; excerpt from address, November 22, 1966. A. H. van den Heuvel. Cath World 205:14-19 Ap '67
Secular ecumenism in action; excerpt from address, November 20, 1966. G. A. Lindbeck. Cath World 205:7-13 Ap '67
Talk within the club; North American academy of ecumenists. Time 89:56-7 Je 30 '67
Unique center for ecumenism; Institute for ecumenical research at St John's abbey and university, Collegeville, Minn. America 116:270 F 25 '67

What do we mean by ecumenism? C. Northcott. Christian Cent 84:462 Ap 12 '67
Why Catholics want to dialogue with Lutherans. H. J. McSorley. Cath World 206:71+ N '67
See also
Church unity
Religious cooperation
World council of churches

Anecdotes, facetiae, satire, etc.
Duplicity decried. P. J. Laux. il America 117:552-3 N 11 '67

ECZEMA
Eczema & vaccination. Time 89:65 My 12 '67

EDDY, Edward D.
Pretense and honesty in college admissions; excerpts from address, May 11, 1967. Sch & Soc 95:415-17 N 11 '67

EDDY, Nelson
Obituary
    Opera N 31:30 Ap 15 '67

EDEL, Leon
She was an Edwardian camera. Sat R 50:29-30 Ag 12 '67
Thorn for triflers and dictators. Sat R 50:55-6 N 25 '67

EDELMAN, Edward. See Barr, R. H. jt. auth.

EDELSON, Edward
Ten smartest animals. Sci Digest 62:20-5 O '67

EDELSON, Michael
Agfachrome. U S Camera 30:64-5+ D '67
Amazing Anscochromes. U S Camera 30:48-9+ F '67
E-4 replaces E-2. U S Camera 30:62+ O '67
Kodachromes and Ektachromes. U S Camera 30:40+ Ag '67

EDELSTEIN, J. M.
Twilight in Bloomsbury. New Repub 157:26+ N 25 '67

EDEN, Anthony, 1st earl of Avon. See Avon, A. E.

EDEN, Dorothy
Shadow bride; story. Redbook 129:171-93 O '67

EDER, Linda
Faces of Fidelismo. Nation 205:173-7 S 4 '67
Latin America bans the bomb. Nation 204:371-2 Mr 20 '67

EDER, Richard
King Constantine: is he Prince Hal? Hamlet? Macbeth? N Y Times Mag p23+ Je 11 '67
Quiet American goes to Vietnam. N Y Times Mag p28-9+ Mr 26 '67

EDGAR M. Leventritt award. See Leventritt award

EDGAR, Natalie
Bluhm's light. Art N 66:48-9+ Sum '67

EDGAR, R. S. See Wood, W. B. jt. auth.

EDGERTON, Art
Handicapped American of the year. il pors Ebony 22:101-2+ Ap '67

EDGERTON, William H.
Building costs: indexes and indicators. See issues of Architectural record

EDGINGTON, Thomas S. and others
Autologous immune-complex pathogenesis of experimental allergic glomerulonephritis. bibliog Science 155:1432-4 Mr 17 '67

EDIBLE plants. See Plants, Food

EDIE, Lionel D, and company
Edie's new mind & manners. Time 89:84 Mr 24 '67

EDINA, Minn.
Completely automated watering systems. D. G. Brauer. il Am City 82:96-7 Mr '67

EDINBURGH
Music
Edinburgh. T. Urquhart. Opera N 32:26 N 4 '67
See also
International festival of music and drama

EDISON, Theodore M.
Great Swamp of New Jersey: jetports and progress; statement before Fish and wildlife service hearing. Nat Parks Mag 41:18 My '67

EDITING. See Editors and editing

EDITING amateur moving pictures. See Moving pictures, Amateur—Editing

EDITING moving pictures. See Moving pictures—Editing

EDITIONS Arthaud. See Publishers and publishing—France

EDITIONS Bernard Grasset. See Publishers and publishing—France

EDITIONS Flammarion. See Publishers and publishing—France

EDITIONS Gallimard. See Publishers and publishing—France

EDITIONS Robert Laffont. See Publishers and publishing—France

EDITORIALS
Brave man in Seattle; reaction to S. Bullitt's television editorials on Vietnam war. Nation 204:99-100 Ja 23 '67
TV editorials: How brave & free? V. H. Bernstein. Nation 205:170-3 S 4 '67

EDITORS and editing
Art of amiable persistence; E. W. Thomas, editor at Harper. il Time 89:77 My 5 '67
Author's and editor's responsibility; excerpts from A practical style guide for authors and editors. M. Nicholson. il Pub W 191:28-30 Ap 17 '67
Can editors resist the pressures to overpublish? C. B. Grannis. Pub W 192:51 Jl 17 '67
Chicago clinic panel examines different kinds of edition. D. B. Sutherland. Pub W 191:51-2 F 6 '67
Editorial management: four problem areas; reports of editorial seminars at annual meeting of Association of American university presses. il Pub W 192:39-46 Jl 17 '67
How an anthology is made. T. M. H. Blair. Writer 80:16-20+ Mr '67
Selling editor. Editor X. Pub W 192:27-8 Ag 7 '67
Too much & not enough; annual convention of the American society of newspaper editors. Time 89:88 Ap 28 '67
Why editors use form rejection slips; discussion. Writer 80:1 Ja '67
See also
Decker, W. B.
Thomas, E. W.

EDMAN, Par
Protein structure in days. il Sci N 92:151-2 Ag 12 '67

EDMUND, Norman
How to succeed in business when your hobby is photography. E. Hannigan. il por U S Camera 30:18+ Je '67

EDNEY, E. B.
Water balance in desert arthropods. bibliog Science 156:1059-66 My 26 '67

EDSON, Lee
Lone inventor with a genie complex. N Y Times Mag p28-9+ D 17 '67
Two men in search of the quark. N Y Times Mag p54-6+ O 8 '67

EDUCATION
Futuristic view. Sr Schol 91:sup5 S 28 '67
Population growth and educational development. B. A. Liu. il Ann Am Acad 369:109-20 Ja '67
See also
Books and reading
Catholic church—Education
Communication in education
Courses of study
Engineering education
Foreign study
Illiteracy
Knowledge
Knowledge, Theory of
Learning, Psychology of
Liberal education
Motivation (education)
Psychology, Educational
Special classes and special schools
Teaching
Theological education
Trade schools
also headings beginning Educational, School; *also* subhead Education under various subjects, e.g. Catholic church—Education; *also* Engineering education; Theological education; and similar headings

Aims and objectives
Another three Rs: the development of the individual; address, September 13, 1967. J. A. Howard. Vital Speeches 34:18-22 O 15 '67
Challenges to American education. F. W. Lewis. Cath World 206:11-13 O '67
Children under pressure: four doctors' views; symposium. il Todays Health 45:62-5 S '67
Current priorities in education. V. E. Strickland. Sch & Soc 95:51-3 Ja 21 '67
Devastating report on U.S. education; concerning Coleman report. il Fortune 76:181-2 Ag '67
Dialogue between public and nonpublic educators; report on convocation. J. Kaminetsky. Sch & Soc 95:425-6 N 11 '67
Education and the wealth of nations. H. L. Enarson. Mo Labor R 90:21-4 Mr '67

Education as the counterforce to alienation. W. W. Brickman. Sch & Soc 95:251 Ap 15 '67
Education for tomorrow's world. M. Mead. Redbook 129:36+ My '67
Educational decision making; symposium. NEA J 56:22-31 D '67
Education's integrative movement. J. P. Lipkin. bibliog f Sch & Soc 95:490-1 D 9 '67
Future of education: the class of 1989. M. McLuhan and G. B. Leonard. il Look 31:23-5 F 21 '67
Goals for space age education. B. J. Paschal. Sch & Soc 95:390-1 O 28 '67
Magic of symbols. E. M. Bower. il NEA J 57:28-31+ Ja '68
New directions in education. I. Supek. Bul Atomic Sci 23:31-3 My '67
Personal responsibility or education; excerpt from The world of education. R. Foy. il Sch & Soc 95:521-3 D 23 '67
Reducing the behavior gap. M. D. Fantini and G. Weinstein. NEA J 57:22-5 Ja '68
September song. P. Schrag. Sat R 50:87 S 16 '67
Special journal feature on innovation. il NEA J 56:25-33 My '67
Third of the world's children; UNESCO chief describes crisis; excerpts from address, October 1967. R. Maheu. Library J 92:4205-6 N 15 '67
Washington report: NEA all-day meeting on Education for the real world. J. Lloyd. Sr Schol 91:sup5 N 16 '67
What our children read; excerpt from The American schoolbooks. H. Black. il Sat Eve Post 240:27-9+ O 7 '67
Why the schools flunk out; concerning the Coleman report. C. S. Benson. il Nation 204:463-6 Ap 10 '67
See also
College education—Aims and objectives

Bibliography
Editor's bookshelf. P. Woodring. See issues of Saturday review
Foreign books for educators. W. W. Brickman. Sch & Soc 95:192-5+, 395-8 Mr 18, O 28 '67
New books. J. Calam. Sat R 50:66 Ag 19; 94-5 S 16; 82 O 21; 88 N 18; 74 D 16 '67
Outstanding education books of 1966; list prepared by Pi lambda theta. NEA J 56:46-7+ My '67
Professional bookshelf. Sr Schol 91:sup 12 D 7 '67
U.S. books for educators (cont) W. W. Brickman. Sch & Soc 94:502+; 95:324-6+ D 24 '66, Sum '67

Caricatures and cartoons
Innovation game, or Changing American education for fun and profit. B. Bourdeaux and T. Bourdeaux. NEA J 56:32-3 My '67

Curricula
See Courses of study

Economic aspects
This way out; slum youngsters choose college; three students at the University of California. A. Allen. il Am Ed 3:2-4+ Jl '67
See also
Colleges and universities—Finance

Exhibitions
Convention exhibit notes: NCSS, NCTE. W. Deering; H. Finch. Sr Schol 91:sup 14 D 14 '67

Experimental methods
See Education, Experimental

Federal aid
See Federal aid to education

Finance
See School finance

History
Collection of educational mementos. Sch & Soc 95:292-3 Sum '67
Historical context of educational administration; excerpt from Foundations of educational administration: a behavioral analysis. W. R. Lane and others. bibliog f Sch & Soc 94:482-92+ D 24 '66
1967 as a centennial year in the history of education. F. Parker. Sch & Soc 95:56-7 Ja 21 '67
See also
Education—United States—History

EDUCATION—*Continued*

International aspects
Come in, world. See issues of PTA magazine to November 1967
Cooperative education in developing countries: two programs; excerpts from address. A. Rich. Bul Atomic Sci 23:43-5 N '67
Editor interviews Paul A. Miller on International education act; ed. by M. S. Fenner. P. A. Miller. NEA J 56:63-4 Ap '67
Pestalozzi children's village, Trogen, Switzerland. A. Bill. il Sch & Soc 95:502-3 D 9 '67
    See also
Business and education—International aspects
International education
United Nations educational, scientific and cultural organization

International cooperation
Education: the revolution which never stops; address, October 8, 1967. L. B. Johnson. Dept State Bul 57:569-71 O 30 '67
International blueprint for education; future of education in India. Sch & Soc 95:295+ Sum '67
Unesco's program; forty-eight countries participate to eradicate adult illiteracy. Sch & Soc 95:480+ D 9 '67
    See also
Colleges and universities—International cooperation
Students, Interchange of
Teachers, Interchange of

Objectives
See Education—Aims and objectives

Periodicals
How to use professional periodicals. N. W. Hanna. NEA J 56:63-4 F '67
    See also
PTA magazine

Philosophy
Changing the pecking order: a credential society; address, October 24, 1967. H. Howe, 2d. Vital Speeches 34:70-3 N 15 '67
Jean Piaget: notes on learning; with excerpts from addresses. F. G. Jennings. il Sat R 50:81-3 My 20 '67
Power, freedom and educational revolution. M. Grandstaff. Sch & Soc 95:387-90 O 28 '67
Secrecy, sanity, and the schools. M. Grandstaff. Sch & Soc 95:142-4 Mr 4 '67

Standards
Does democracy demand degradation? F. Morley. Nations Bsns 55:29-30 S '67
Increased pressure good for children. S. C. Southard. Todays Health 45:63-4 S '67
School as a center of inquiry, by R. J. Schaefer. Review
    Sat R 50:66-7 Mr 18 '67. F. G. Jennings
Today's Catholic schools. R. C. Spitzer. Cath World 206:167-70 Ja '68
What's wrong with educational excellence? concerning United States office of education statistical study: The equality of educational opportunity. J. Shera. Wilson Lib Bul 41:969+ My '67

State control
See Education and state

Statistics
Back to school. W. V. Grant. il Am Ed 3:8-9 S '67
Current data on U.S. education. Sch & Soc 95:282 Sum '67
Magnitude of the American educational establishment, 1967-68. il Sat R 50:67 O 21 '67
Nonwhite public school population in forty-eight major cities, 1965-66 school year; table. New Repub 157:19 N 18 '67
Statistic of the month. See issues of American education
What's happening in education? progress in high schools. W. D. Boutwell. PTA Mag 61:23 My '67
    See also
Colleges and universities—Statistics
School attendance

Study and teaching
Call for a society of educologists. D. E. Denton. Sch & Soc 95:82-3 F 4 '67

Africa
Cooperative education in developing countries: two programs; excerpts from address. A. Rich. Bul Atomic Sci 23:43-5 N '67

Hazards of educational planning. R. Clignet. il Sat R 50:59-60+ Ag 19 '67
    See also
Colleges and universities—Africa

Alabama
Alabama must integrate. Time 89:64 Mr 31 '67
George vs. the court. Newsweek 69:34 Ap 3 '67
Mrs Governor faces the feds. H. Wolman. Commonweal 86:192-3 My 5 '67
NAACP sues to integrate Alabama schools. Library J 92:278 Ja 15 '67
Perils of Lurleen. Newsweek 69:36+ Ap 10 '67

Alaska
Doris D. Ray and Robert Van Houte; interview, ed. by M. S. Fenner. il NEA J 56:71-2 Mr '67

American Samoa
ETV goes way out and brings the world to Samoa. M. L. Fiedler. il Am Ed 3:14-17 Mr '67

Appalachian Region
Introduction to success; teenage trainees working with preschool youngsters. H. C. Lyon, jr. il Am Ed 3:5-6+ My '67

Argentina
    See also
Colleges and universities—Argentina

Arizona
    See also
Tucson, Ariz.—Education

Arkansas
    See also
Little Rock, Ark.—Education

Asia
Asian education explosion; report by Ruth Harris, secretary for the University world of the Methodist board of missions. Christian Cent 84:430 Ap 5 '67

Australia
School libraries: waiting in the wings. L. H. McGrath. bibliog Library J 92:4225-7 N 15 '67

California
Death Valley daze; tuition fees for elementary and secondary education. Christian Cent 84:428 Ap 5 '67
Golden age, the gathering gloom. P. Schrag. il Sat R 50:58-62+ S 23 '67
IMC on wheels; El Rancho school district, Pico Rivera. J. H. Moody. il Library J 92:304-5 Ja 15 '67
Knowledge bonanza. M. Wax. il Nation 204:178-81 F 6 '67
Pin money for paperbacks; Menlo-Atherton high school. Atherton. M, Hegland. il Library J 92:2000-1 My 15 '67
Why we can't wait; Atherton high school; letter to the editor. M. Hegland. Library J 92:1267-8 Mr 15 '67
    See also
California—Education. Department of
Los Angeles—Education

Canada
At our corner; Canadian subsidiary, Scholastic-TAB publications, ltd; tenth birthday. il Sr Schol 90:sup22 My 5 '67
What's new and different about Canadian education? F. K. Stewart. Sr Schol 90:sup2 F 10 '67
    See also
Colleges and universities—Canada

Chile
    See also
Colleges and universities—Chile

China (People's Republic)
Back to the books in China; educational-reform plan. il Time 90:58 Ag 4 '67
    See also
Colleges and universities—China (People's Republic)

Colombia
Literacy programs in Colombia; Books for the people fund, inc. and Laubach literacy, inc: adaptation of report. M. D. Shepard. il Wilson Lib Bul 41:829-33 Ap '67

Connecticut
Past and present: the twain shall meet; Enfield high school, Thompsonville, Conn. F. S. Gross. Sr Schol 91:sup 13 O 5 '67

EDUCATION—Connecticut—*Continued*
Some very special teachers' pets; three experimental federally financed education projects. E. Pinto. il Sr Schol 90:sup 16 Ap 7 '67
See also
Greenwich, Conn.—Education
West Hartford, Conn.—Education

District of Columbia
See Washington, D.C.—Education

Ecuador
Literacy and Ecuador's national development plan. R. Mathias. Sch & Soc 95:84-6 F 4 '67

England
See Education—Great Britain

Europe, Western
Field notes on the Europeans. J. Fischer. Harper 234:16+ My '67
Three gaps: economic, technological & educational; address, February 24, 1967. R. S. McNamara. Vital Speeches 33:357-61 Ap 1 '67

France
See also
Paris—Education

Gambia
See also
Education of women—Gambia

Germany (Federal Republic)
Shadow of the concordat; Catholic schools and German bishops. C. Wilpert. Commonweal 86:333-4 Je 9 '67

Great Britain
Briton views American schools. C. Chapman. il Am Ed 3:23-6 Je '67
Different integration crisis; desegregation of traditional social classes, not of races. il U S News 62:97 F 20 '67
Education reform: British reorganize secondary schools. J. Walsh. Science 159:68-70 Ja 5 '68
Happenings in education. W. D. Boutwell. il PTA Mag 62:18-19 N '67
How children learn; primary school reforms. J. Featherstone. New Repub 157:17-21 S 2 '67
Influence of tradition: comparisons of English and Scottish education; excerpts from address, July 19, 1966. M. Cruickshank. bibliog f Sch & Soc 95:498-502 D 9 '67
Schools for children: what's happening in British classrooms. J. Featherstone. New Repub 157:17-21 Ag 19 '67
Surrey with fringe benefits: two American children try British schooling. W. Froscher. il PTA Mag 61:14-16 Je '67
Teaching children to think; primary school reforms. J. Featherstone. New Repub 157:15-19 S 9 '67
See also
Adult education
Education—Scotland
Oxford. University
Public schools (endowed)—England

Illinois
See also
Chicago—Education
Evanston, Ill.—Education
Oak Park, Ill.—Education

India
Cooperative education in developing countries: two programs; excerpts from address. A. Rich. Bul Atomic Sci 23:43-5 N '67
International blueprint for education; future of education in India. Sch & Soc 95:295+ Sum '67

Ireland
See also
Colleges and universities—Ireland

Japan
Postwar teenage student. B. Duke. bibliog f il Sch & Soc 95:264-8 Ap 15 '67
U.S. ranks low in math survey. Sr Schol 90:sup4 Ap 14 '67
See also
Colleges and universities—Japan

Latin America
Catholic education in Latin America. F. P. Chamberlain. America 116:750-3 My 20 '67; Discussion. 116:745; 117:1-2 My 20, Jl 1 '67
Education hurdle. Américas 19:44 F '67
See also
Colleges and universities—Latin America

Louisiana
See also
Grambling college, Grambling

Maine
Curriculum breakthrough in the humanities; Bangor H. S. L. C. Comeau and others. il Sr Schol 90:sup 13-14 Ap 7 '67

Maryland
Luaus in the library; or, The curriculum that wasn't; Rock Creek Palisades elementary school, Kensington. M. Murray. il Library J 92:1708-10 Ap 15 '67
See also
Washington college, Chestertown

Massachusetts
See also
Boston—Education
Harvard university

Michigan
Pied Piper of paperbacks; projects of D. Fader. E. Logan. il Sr Schol 89:sup 17 Ja 20 '67
See also
Detroit—Education

Mississippi
To Mississippi in the interest of children and books; three trips to speak at University of Mississippi on the Negro child in children's books. G. Woods. il Wilson Lib Bul 41:1028-33 Je '67

Missouri
See also
St Louis—Education

Nepal
Tibetan tea. J. Hoffman. il Sr Schol 90:sup 17 My 5 '67

New Jersey
School librarian shortage in New Jersey. H. T. Gumaer. ALA Bul 61:555-7 My '67

New Mexico
See also
Albuquerque, N.Mex.—Education

New York (state)
Shared time: New York and Vermont; dual enrollment of children. America 117:127 Ag 5 '67
Tiptoe in technology; transforming library into educational materials center, through ESEA Titles II and III, at Burnt Hills-Ballston Lake junior high school. M. J. Egan. il Library J 92:1711-13 Ap 15 '67
See also
Albany, N.Y.—Education
New York (city)—Education
New York (state)—Education, Department of
New York (state). State university

North Carolina
Advancement school: North Carolina kills its dream. D. Cooper. il Nation 206:77-9 Ja 15 '68
Games work with underachievers; North Carolina advancement school. D. C. Farran. il Sr Schol 91:sup 10-11 N 9 '67

Northern Ireland
New division in North Ireland. America 117:629 N 25 '67

Ohio
See also
Akron, Ohio—Education

History
Samuel Lewis and the people's colleges. V. P. Lannie. bibliog f Sch & Soc 95:493-8 D 9 '67

Oklahoma
See also
Oklahoma. University, Norman
Tulsa, Okla.—Education

Oregon
New Oregon rhetoric curriculum. A. R. Kitzhaber. Sr Schol 90:sup 13-14 My 12 '67

Pennsylvania
Highly adaptable package; homemade media kit to provide unit on Japan. M. S. Plank and J. B. Scholl. bibliog il Library J 92:1714-17+ Ap 15 '67

Philippines
From a young American, with love; Dian Hamilton working in school for retarded children south of Manila. J. R. Moskin. il Look 31:50-2+ My 30 '67

EDUCATION—*Continued*

Poland
See also
Warsaw—Education

Russia
Education. il Look 31:48-9 O 3 '67
Facing the complexities of modern education. M. A. Prokof'ev. il UNESCO Courier 20:14-20 N '67
From illiteracy to astronautics. V. Elyutin. il UNESCO Courier 20:11-14 N '67
Half-century of Soviet education; symposium. bibliog f il Sch & Soc 95:436-74 N 25 '67
In the schools, a clamor for more freedom; with report by P. Young. il Life 63:50-3+ N 10 '67
Is it education, or indoctrination? il Newsweek 70:42 O 23 '67
Soviet educator urges engineer rewards; excerpts from Izvestia. I. F. Obraztsov. Aviation W 87:115+ S 11 '67
Transition to universal ten-year education. Sch & Soc 95:44 Ja 21 '67
See also
Colleges and universities—Russia

Scotland
Influence of tradition: comparisons of English and Scottish education; excerpts from address, July 19, 1966. M. Cruickshank. bibliog f Sch & Soc 95:498-502 D 9 '67
ST reports: how history is taught in Scotland. R. A. Page. Sr Schol 91:sup 14 O 5 '67

Sierra Leone
NEA teach corps. D. Watson. il Sr Schol 90:sup6-7 Mr 3 '67

South America
See Education—Latin America

South Carolina
See also
Allen university, Columbia
South Carolina state college, Orangeburg

Southern states
Budding confrontation; no-nonsense order of Fifth circuit court of appeals. il Time 89:20-1 Ap 7 '67
Conference report; meeting in Atlanta to discuss library education in the South, sponsored by Atlanta university's School of library service. H. Richmond and N. Kirin. Wilson Lib Bul 41:1009+ Je '67
Revolution since Little Rock. il Life 53:92-107 S 29 '67
Slow pace in Dixie; all-Negro schools. il Newsweek 70:43 Ag 21 '67
South is told now: integrate all the way. U S News 62:11 Ap 10 '67
Thirteen years after 1954; Negro pupils in South. A. Poinsett. il Ebony 22:76-7+ Ap '67
See also
Negroes in the United States—Education
Southern regional education board

Southwestern states
Help for Spanish-speaking youngsters. J. Stocker. il Am Ed 3:17-18+ My '67

Sweden
Sex education: the Swedish system. E. Adams. il Sr Schol 90:sup 16-17 Ap 21 '67

Switzerland
Problems of school organization and administration. R. Dottrens. Sch & Soc 95:177-80 Mr 18 '67
Training for engineering and technology in Switzerland; excerpt from Science in Switzerland. J. M. Luck. bibliog f il Sch & Soc 94:499-502 D 24 '66

Tennessee
See also
Nashville, Tenn.—Education
Negro schools—Tennessee

Underdeveloped areas
Eye or the finger? conference on world crisis in education. Time 90:50+ O 20 '67
Global revolution. P. H. Coombs. Sat R 50:49-50 Ag 19 '67

United States
American middle school, by S. H. Popper. Review
Sat R 50:81 O 21 '67. P. Woodring

Are schools getting better? interview. J. B. Conant. il U S News 63:102-4+ O 23 '67
Briton views American schools. C. Chapman. il Am Ed 3:23-6 Je '67
Challenges to American education. F. W. Lewis. Cath World 206:11-13 O '67
Controversial report on education; what it really means. J. S. Coleman. U S News 63:44-5 D 25 '67
Current priorities in education. V. E. Strickland. Sch & Soc 95:51-3 Ja 21 '67
Education and learning. W. J. Cohen. bibliog f il Ann Am Acad 373:79-101 S '67
Education and the challenge of the future; creative living in the nuclear age. A. W. Munk. Sch & Soc 95:180-2 Mr 18 '67
Education in America; ed. by P. Woodring and J. Cass. See issues of Saturday review
Education in America; for what, for whom, how much? il Sr Schol 91:6-11 N 16 '67
Education in 1967. W. W. Brickman. Sch & Soc 95:516-17 D 23 '67
Education in 1966. W. W. Brickman. Sch & Soc 94:468-9 D 24 '66
Education in the 1980's. Sch & Soc 95:206+ Ap 1 '67
Educational change. Sch & Soc 95:284 Sum '67
Educational changes: their implications for the library. R. J. Havighurst. ALA Bul 61:537-43 My '67
Educational equality. D. Wolfle. Science 156:19 Ap 7 '67; Reply. J. P. Gilbert and F. Mosteller. 156:1435 Je 16 '67
Educational innovation and the individual. W. W. Brickman. Sch & Soc 95:38 Ja 21 '67
Federal influences on the future of American education. F. Parker. Sch & Soc 95:383-7 O 28 '67
Imperatives remain; President's message. Sat R 50:73 F 18 '67
Look ahead in education. F. Morley. il Nations Bsns 55:27-8 Ap '67
Magnitude of the American educational establishment, 1967-68. il Sat R 50:67 O 21 '67
National assessment. A. M. Mood. Am Ed 3:11-12+ Ap '67
National assessment of educational progress: some technical deficiencies. C. A. Anderson. bibliog f Sch & Soc 95:48-50 Ja 21 '67
NEA and the real world of education; excerpts from address, October 20, 1967. S. M. Lambert. NEA J 56:34-6 D '67
News and trends. See issues of NEA journal
On libraries and learning; interview, ed. with introd. by E. Geller. H. Howe, 2d. il Library J 92:841-4 F 15 '67
People want to know. J. Moorhead. PTA Mag 61:2-3 Mr '67
Poverty programs, civil rights, and the American school. A. S. Carton. Sch & Soc 95:108-9 F 18 '67
Revolution in education: it didn't start with Sputnik. F. G. Jennings. il Sat R 50:77-9+ S 16 '67
Schools make news. See issues of Saturday review
Secrecy, sanity, and the schools. M. Grandstaff. Sch & Soc 95:142-4 Mr 4 '67
Three gaps: economic, technological & educational; address, February 24, 1967. R. S. McNamara. Vital Speeches 33:357-61 Ap 1 '67
Toward national assessment. Time 89:61 Ja 27 '67
U.S. ranks low in math survey. Sr Schol 90:sup4 Ap 14 '67
What is school for? B. Bettelheim. Ladies Home J 84:54+ O '67
What Sputnik did to our schools. F. M. Hechinger. il McCalls 95:106-7+ O '67
What's happening in education? See issues of PTA magazine
Who controls education. P. Schrag. Sat R 50:60 Mr 18 '67
See also
Colleges and universities—United States
Education—Statistics
Education—Southern states
Education and state
High schools
Indians of North America—Education
Jews—Education
Labor and laboring classes—Education
National education association
Negroes in the United States—Education
Public schools—United States
United States—Armed forces—Education
United States—Education, Office of
Vocational education
also subhead Education under names of cities, e.g. Chicago—Education

EDUCATION—United States—*Continued*

History

Collection of educational mementos. Sch & Soc 95:292-3 Sum '67

Teachers then and now. M. Bonn. il Am Ed 3:13-19 O '67

300 years at a glance; with editorial comment. il Am Ed 3:inside cover, 7-13 Mr '67

Vermont

Public-parochial combine. Sat R 50:77 Ap 15 '67

Vietnam (Republic)

Education in Vietnam: America's Dien Bien Phu? J. Naisbitt. il Sat R 50:53-5+ Jl 15 '67

Schools in Vietnam. il Newsweek 70:55 Ag 28 '67

Teaching amid terror; Hamlet school project. il Time 89:49+ Ap 21 '67

Vietnamese school gongs sound; interview, ed. by R. D. Childs. il NEA J 56:22-3 S '67

EDUCATION, Adult. See Adult education

EDUCATION, Agricultural. See Agricultural education

EDUCATION, Art. See Art education

EDUCATION, Aviation. See Aviation education

EDUCATION, Boards of. See School boards

EDUCATION, Business. See Business education

EDUCATION, College. See College education

EDUCATION, Comparative

Achievement differences in high school: U.S. and Britain. il Sch & Soc 95:71-2 F 4 '67

Briton views American schools. C. Chapman. il Am Ed 3:23-6 Je '67

International cooperative educational research. Sch & Soc 95:214-15 Ap 1 '67

Is our math inferior? global project tests the schools. G. S. Carnett. il Am Ed 3:1-3 Mr '67

Teaching children to think; informal British and progressive U.S. methods. J. Featherstone. New Repub 157:15-19 S 9 '67

EDUCATION, Compulsory. See Compulsory education

EDUCATION, Consumer. See Consumer education

EDUCATION, Distributive. See Distributive education

EDUCATION, Elementary

How children learn; primary school reforms in Great Britain. J. Featherstone. New Repub 157:17-21 S 2 '67

Is college subverting grade school? with study-discussion program by E. Harris and D. Harris. D. L. Burleson. bibliog il PTA Mag 61:8-10, 36 My '67

Schools for children: what's happening in British classrooms. J. Featherstone. New Repub 157:17-21 Ag 19 '67

Teaching children to think; primary school reforms in Great Britain. J. Featherstone. New Repub 157:15-19 S 9 '67

Teaching in America. M. Tumin. il Sat R 50: 77-9+ O 21 '67

Will we recognize tomorrow's elementary school? W. D. Hedges. il NEA J 56:9-12 D '67

See also
Courses of study
National education association—Department of elementary school principals
Nursery schools
Private schools
School children

Activity programs

Dance in our schools: how long before the issue is faced? B. King. il Dance Mag 41: 62-6+ D '67

See also
Projects (teaching)

EDUCATION, Engineering. See Engineering education

EDUCATION, Evaluation of. See Evaluation (education)

EDUCATION, Experimental

Clayton County seeks some answers. L. D. Powell and C. E. Johnson. il NEA J 56:36-7 Ap '67

Fifteen little Indians: Westinghouse computer project on Menominee reservation, Wisconsin. New Repub 156:6 Je 17 '67; Reply. A. C. Turner. 157:34-5 Jl 1 '67

Hashbury method: San Francisco's Shire school offers young hippies a libertarian education. il Newsweek 70:56 Ag 14 '67

Local associations ask about their role in innovation. D. L. Brooksby and J. H. Starie. NEA J 56:31-2 D '67

Process of innovation; case studies. G. N. Mackenzie. NEA J 56:27-31 My '67

Teacher evaluates innovations. G. A. Griffin and J. Devlin. NEA J 56:26-8 D '67

Throw out the textbooks. A. Gordon. il Am Ed 3:5-7 S '67

To the hills and hollows; story of the Appalachia educational laboratory. C. M. Singleton and S. M. Brown. il Am Ed 3:22-5 Jl '67

Up to their ears in the arts; Ambler experimental project for high school students. L. J. Ahlander. il Am Ed 3:29-31 N '67

What turns kids on? Philadelphia cooperative schools curriculum of concerns program. T. Borton. il Sat R 50:72-4+ Ap 15 '67

See also
Schools, Experimental

EDUCATION, Higher. See Colleges and universities

EDUCATION, Individual. See Individual instruction

EDUCATION, Liberal. See Liberal education

EDUCATION, Medical. See Medical education

EDUCATION, Moral. See Moral education

EDUCATION, Nutrition. See Nutrition education

EDUCATION, Office of. See United States—Education, Office of

EDUCATION, Parent. See Parent education

EDUCATION, Primary. See Education, Elementary

EDUCATION, Religious. See Religious education

EDUCATION, Safety. See Safety education

EDUCATION, Secondary

Which way to a curriculum for adolescents? F. T. Wilhelms. il NEA J 56:12-15 D '67

See also
High schools
Private schools

EDUCATION, Social. See Social education

EDUCATION, Theological. See Theological education

EDUCATION, Value of

See also
College education, Value of

EDUCATION, Vocational. See Vocational education

EDUCATION and business. See Business and education

EDUCATION and church. See Church and education

EDUCATION and economic problems. See School and social and economic problems

EDUCATION and industry. See Business and education

EDUCATION and manpower

Tomorrow is now; educating for 21st century manpower needs. H. A. Matthews. il Am Ed 3:21-2 Je '67

EDUCATION and social problems. See School and social and economic problems

EDUCATION and state

Amish, Black Muslims and Catholics. America 116:550 Ap 15 '67

Danger facing nation's schools? interview. C. F. Hansen. il U S News 63:40-6+ Jl 24 '67

Dead issue? state grants to church-related colleges. J. O'Gara. Commonweal 85:445 Ja 27 '67; Reply. W. J. Van Cleve. 85:575 F 17 '67

Delicate balance. F. D. Murphy. Sat R 51: 74+ Ja 13 '68

Financial aid to private institutions. Sch & Soc 95:42 Ja 21 '67

Higher education: more money from the state house. L. J. Carter. il Science 158:620-1 N 3 '67

Increase in support of higher education. Sch & Soc 95:132+ Mr 4 '67

More aid for the common good; taxpayer support for parochial schools. Time 89:60 Mr 3 '67

Old power play; suppression of documentary film on Catholic schools to aid repeal of Blaine amendment. Commonweal 87:67-8 O 20 '67

Plan for financing higher education. J. P. McMurray. Sch & Soc 95:489-90 D 9 '67

President's proposed education programs; excerpts from message, February 28, 1967. ed. by G. Krettek and E. D. Cooke. ALA Bul 61:383 Ap '67

Report from California: the Governor and the university. E. Langer. il Science 155: 1220-4 Mr 10 '67; Discussion. 156:581-2 My 5 '67

EDUCATION and state—*Continued*
State's top court upholds N.Y. text law. Pub W 191:33 Je 12 '67
Textbooks and libraries; loan program for children in private and public schools. America 116:846 Je 17 '67
See also
Education commission of the states
Federal aid to education
United States—Education, Office of
EDUCATION and state in Argentina
Report to the American academic community; excerpt from A report to the American academic community on the present Argentine university situation. Bul Atomic Sci 23:40-4 Ap '67
EDUCATION and state in Great Britain
Education reform: Britain tries it top to bottom. J. Walsh. Science 158:1162-5 D 1 '67
EDUCATION and travel. See Student travel
EDUCATION commission of the states
Education commission of the states. W. H. Pierce. NEA J 56:30-1 Mr '67
ECS says no to implementing national assessment. S. Holzman. Sr Schol 91:sup2 O 26 '67
EDUCATION development center, incorporated
EDC: general motors of curriculum reform. J. D. Koerner. il Sat R 50:56-8+ Ag 19 '67
EDUCATION for citizenship. See Citizenship, Education for
EDUCATION index
Educational research and the hidden author. J. W. Keating. Sch & Soc 95:350-1 O 14 '67
EDUCATION of adults. See Adult education
EDUCATION of children
Abolishing childhood; excerpts. E. J. LeShan. Todays Health 45:57 S '67
Child-concerned world; symposium. bibliog il Wilson Lib Bul 42:164-205+ O '67
See also
Camping—Educational aspects
Children—Management and training
Childrens literature
Childrens reading
Cookery by children
Education, Elementary
Education, Experimental
Montessori method of education
Museums—Work with children
Music and children
Nursery schools
Play
Preschool children—Education
Readiness for school
Safety education
Sex instruction
Social education
EDUCATION of Indian children. See Indians of North America—Education
EDUCATION of librarians. See Library schools and education
EDUCATION of Negroes. See Negroes in the United States—Education
EDUCATION of prisoners
Guru of San Quentin. E. Cleaver. Esquire 67: 88+ Ap '67
Rah! rah! rah! prisoner's request to remain for exams. il Time 89:70 My 26 '67
EDUCATION of women
See also
Colleges for women

Gambia
Gratefully yours. W. D. Boutwell. PTA Mag 62:10 D '67
EDUCATION professions development act. See School laws and legislation—United States
EDUCATIONAL acceleration
See also
High school students, Mentally superior
EDUCATIONAL achievements. See Student achievements
EDUCATIONAL administration. See School management and organization
EDUCATIONAL association publications. See Education—Periodicals
EDUCATIONAL associations
Approach to professional practices legislation. J. T. Butler. NEA J 56:43-4 F '67
King-size job for local associations. A. M. West. NEA J 56:19-20 Mr '67
Teacher-administrator relationships in the local association; symposium. NEA J 56: 49-52 F '67
Who will police the academy. P. Schrag. Sat R 50:45 Mr 18 '67
See also names of educational associations, e.g. American association of university professors
EDUCATIONAL conferences
Education conference in Buenos Aires. Sch & Soc 95:60+ Ja 21 '67

It's a date (cont) NEA J 56:6 My; 86-7 S '67; 57:63-5 Ja '68
Machines vs. people; conference on technology and the curriculum at Teachers college, Columbia university. D. L. Burleson. Sr Schol 91:sup3 D 7 '67
EDUCATIONAL cooperation
Shared time: New York and Vermont; dual enrollment of children. America 117:127 Ag 5 '67
Walls come tumbling down; team teaching center established by the Weber County school district in Ogden, Utah, under Title III grant. W. T. Greenleaf. Am Ed 3:22 Mr '67
See also
Colleges and universities—Cooperation
Education commission of the states
EDUCATIONAL criticism
All for one, one for all; support of educational critics by fellow critics. Time 90:31 D 29 '67
Constructive criticism and education. G. M. Reagan. Sch & Soc 95:423-4 N 11 '67
Education's romantic critics. P. Schrag. Sat R 50:80-2+ F 18 '67
EDUCATIONAL discrimination. See Discrimination in education
EDUCATIONAL endowments. See Endowments
EDUCATIONAL exchanges
Annual educational exchange statistics. S. K. Gorney. il Sch & Soc 95:234-7 Ap 1 '67
Educational exchange for French African administrators. T. N. Stern. Sch & Soc 95:150-2 Mr 4 '67
Foreign study, perils and possibilities; academic exchanges between the United States and Japan. N. Ukai. il Sat R 50:88+ F 18 '67
Fulbright story; Educational exchange program. R. Eyer. il Opera N 31:8-11 Ja 7 '67
Report on educational and cultural exchange sent to Congress; letter of transmittal, August 14, 1967. L. B. Johnson. Dept State Bul 57:303 S 4 '67
See also
Teachers, Interchange of
EDUCATIONAL experiments. See Education, Experimental
EDUCATIONAL extension. See Extension education
EDUCATIONAL films. See Moving pictures—Documentary films; Moving pictures in education
EDUCATIONAL games. See Games
EDUCATIONAL guidance
Can you predict your child's future? G. Davenel. il Parents Mag 42:33-5+ Ag '67
See also
Personnel service in education
EDUCATIONAL information. See Communication in education
EDUCATIONAL leadership. See Leadership
EDUCATIONAL literature
See also
Publishers and publishing—Educational literature
EDUCATIONAL lobbyists. See Lobbyists
EDUCATIONAL materials. See Teaching—Aids and devices
EDUCATIONAL media index
A/V index revamped in major media project: by USC: National information center for educational media (NICEM) Library J 92: 1280+ Mr 15 '67
EDUCATIONAL opportunity bank. See Student loans
EDUCATIONAL organization. See School management and organization
EDUCATIONAL parks. See Consolidated schools
EDUCATIONAL periodicals. See Education—Periodicals
EDUCATIONAL planning
Education: toward better schooling for all. G. M. Landau. il Parents Mag 43:39-41+ Ja '68
Hazards of educational planning. R. Clignet. il Sat R 50:59-60+ Ag 19 '67
EDUCATIONAL products information exchange. See Institute for educational development
EDUCATIONAL psychology. See Psychology, Educational
EDUCATIONAL research
Action, not research. Sch & Soc 95:213 Ap 1 '67
Advanced study of educational research. il Sch & Soc 95:40-1 Ja 21 '67
Consortia in educational research; new program called CORD. Sch. & Soc 95:172+ Mr 18 '67

EDUCATIONAL research—*Continued*
ERIC and the need to know. L. G. Burchinal. NEA J 56:65-72 F '67
Five education technology studies begin. Aero Tech 21:15 Jl 31 '67
Individual differences and education. Sch & Soc 95:248-50 Ap 15 '67
National research goals and university policies. S. B. Gould. Sch & Soc 95:347-9 O 14 '67
New federally supported Ciceronianism; criticism. W. M. French. Sch & Soc 95:349-50 O 14 '67
Regional education laboratories: bane or benefit? M. N. Freed. Sch & Soc 95:492 D 9 '67
Research clues; questions and answers. See issues of NEA journal
Washington developments in education; summaries of addresses. L. Hausman; M. Johnson; W. M. Robinson. il Pub W 191:30-4 My 29 '67
See also
Modern language association of America
EDUCATIONAL resources information center. See United States—Education, Office of—Educational research and development, Bureau of
EDUCATIONAL secretaries. See School secretaries
EDUCATIONAL segregation. See Segregation in education
EDUCATIONAL services, Incorporated. See Education development center, incorporated
EDUCATIONAL sociology
See also
Socially handicapped children—Education
EDUCATIONAL standards. See Education—Standards
EDUCATIONAL statistics. See Education—Statistics
EDUCATIONAL study tours. See Travel study courses
EDUCATIONAL surveys
Price of mathophobia; survey showing American 13-year-olds lag behind in math. il Time 89:60 Mr 17 '67
What's wrong with educational excellence? concerning United States office of education statistical study: The equality of educational opportunity. J. Shera. Wilson Lib Bul 41:969+ My '67
EDUCATIONAL television stations. See Television stations, Educational
EDUCATIONAL tests and measurements
Educational testing: national program enters critical phase. L. J. Carter. Science 156: 622-4+ My 5 '67; Reply. A. W. Vander-Meer. 157:370 Jl 28 '67
Is our math inferior? global project tests the schools. G. S. Carnett. il Am Ed 3:1-3 Mr '67
Predicting job corpsmen's performance on the tests of general education development. R. C. Pugh. Sch & Soc 95:268-9 Ap 15 '67
Rorschach tested. P. McBroom. il Sci N 92: 182-3 Ag 19 '67; Reply. L. Blank. 92:364-5 O 14 '67
Teacher-opinion poll; national testing. NEA J 56:6 S '67
Toward national assessment. Time 89:61 Ja 27 '67
Written test scores and prediction of success in college. H. R. Douglass. il Sch & Soc 95:392-4 O 28 '67
See also
Achievement tests
Aptitude tests
Grading and marking (students)
Intelligence tests
EDUCATIONAL theory. See Education—Philosophy
EDUCATIONAL toys. See Toys
EDUCATIONAL travel, Division of. See National education association—Division of educational travel
EDUCATIONAL workshops
Dateline Watts: from the ashes, a solution; Watts writers workshop. A. Nevins. il Sat R 50:79 S 23 '67
Learning through the lens; disadvantaged New York children's summer workshop conducted by Susan Wood. M. R. Weiss. il Sat R 50:55+ Je 17 '67
EDUCATORS
Elevating the education of educators. Sch & Soc 95:8 Ja 7 '67
Tale of the headmaster. D. Barr. il Sat R 50:70-1 Ap 15 '67
See also
College professors and instructors
Negro educators
Teachers
Zacharias, J. R.

EDWARD VII, king of Great Britain
Edward and the Edwardians, by P. Julian. Review
Life 63:10 Ag 4 '67. Lord Kinross
EDWARD VIII, king of Great Britain (abdicated 1936)
King who was. il por Time 89:37 My 26 '67
Return of Britain's prodigal prince. il por U S News 62:23 Je 19 '67
Weekend with H.R.H. the Duke and the Duchess of Windsor. il pors Vogue 150:98-103 N 15 '67
EDWARDS, A. W.
Frequency measurements with the electronic counter. Electr World 77:84 Ja '67
EDWARDS, Calton M.
Choosing a recreation vehicle for family use. Consumer Bul 50:36-40 Mr '67
EDWARDS, Don
Excerpt from address, April 28, 1966. Cong Digest 46:88+ Mr '67
EDWARDS, Harry
San Jose: the bullhorn message. J. Brann. Nation 205:465-7 N 6 '67
EDWARDS, Owen
Stallion's odyssey. Holiday 42:110+ S '67
EDWARDS, Paul
Authors & editors. Pub W 191:41 Mr 6 '67
EDWARDS, Phil
You should have been here an hour ago; excerpt. pors Sat Eve Post 240:32-9 Jl 1 '67
EDWARDS, Sally
Color me loving; story. Redbook 128:66-7 Ap '67
EDWARDS, Walter Meayers
Lake Powell: waterway to desert wonders. il Nat Geog Mag 132:44-75 Jl '67
EDWING, Grace D.
Happy birthday! PTA Mag 61:17-19 bibliog (p35) Ap '67
EFF, Johannes
Us loonybin jokers would rather twitch than fight it; poem. Nat R 19:249 Mr 7 '67
EFFICIENCY, Administrative
See also
Suggestion systems
EFFICIENCY, Agricultural. See Farm management
EFFICENCY, Household. See Home economics
EFFICIENCY, Industrial
Job redesign for older workers: case studies. H. J. Rothberg. Mo Labor R 90:47-51 Ja '67
See also
Personnel management
EFFIGIES, Sepulchral. See Sepulchral monuments
EGAN, James
Fortnight in Guatemala. Atlan 219:128-32 Ap '67
Making the snow scene, on or off skis. Mlle 66:171-2+ N '67
St Vincent and Bequia. Atlan 220:122-3+ D '67
EGAN, Mary J.
Tiptoe in technology. por Library J 92:1711-13 Ap 15 '67
EGBERT, Marion S.
Make yours a musical family. Suc Farm 65:101+ Ja '67
EGER, Joseph
Musical events; concert performed by the American symphony orchestra in Carnegie Hall. W. Sargeant. New Yorker 43:219 N 25 '67
EGERTON, John
Little Rock ten years later. Sat R 50:60-1 D 16 '67
TVA: the halo slips. Nation 205:11-15 Jl 3 '67
EGG shell mosaics. See Mosaics
EGGAR, Samantha
Samantha Eggar: red hair, freckles, talent to burn. il pors Vogue 149:134-5 Mr 15 '67
EGGELING, H.
Swiss amateur's cooled-emulsion camera. il Sky & Tel 34:400-3 D '67
EGGER, M. David, and Petràn, Mojmir
New reflected-light microscope for viewing unstained brain and ganglion cells. bibliog Science 157:305-7 Jl 21 '67
EGGS
See also
Cookery—Eggs
EGLESON, G. C. See Collins, A. G. jt. auth.
EGLINTON, Geoffrey, and Hamilton, R. J.
Leaf epicuticular waxes. bibliog Science 156: 1322-35 Je 9 '67
EGNER, Joan Roos, and Pierce, D. R.
Inducting graduate students into college training. bibliog f Sch & Soc 95:55-6 Ja 21 '67
EGO. See Self
EGOZCUE, Jose. See Irwin, S. jt. auth.

EGYPT
Egypt: bruises and suspicions. V. L. Bullough. Nation 205:394-5 O 23 '67
New Egypt after 1952. C. P. Harris. bibliog f Cur Hist 52:90-7+ F '67
See also
Americans in Egypt
Fishing—Egypt
Irrigation—Egypt
Morale, National—Egypt
Suez Canal
Tourist trade—Egypt

Antiquities
Return of Tut; treasures on exhibition in Paris. il Newsweek 69:118 Mr 13 '67
Tutankhamania; objects from King Tut's tomb on display at the Petit palais. il Time 89:76 Mr 17 '67
See also
Abu Simbel, Temples of
Pyramids

Defenses
Captured bases stripped of Russian gear. Aviation W 87:69-70 Jl 24 '67
Russian gifts gone to waste. il Life 62:26-7 Je 30 '67

Economic conditions
Ass in lion's skin. R. Moley. Newsweek 69:80 Je 26 '67
Cruel & difficult struggle. il Time 90:30 Ag 4 '67
Desperate act; might refuse to pay foreign-aid debts. il Time 89:37 Mr 3 '67
In the wake of war: can Nasser survive? il U S News 62:32 Je 26 '67
Report from Cairo. L. Griggs. il Fortune 75:69-70+ My '67
Trouble in Egypt. V. L. Bullough. Nation 204:647-9 My 22 '67

Economic policy
Report from Cairo. L. Griggs. il Fortune 75:69-70+ My '67

Foreign relations
Egypt and Israel; Security council resolution condemns cease-fire violation. New Repub 157:6-7 N 4 '67
Eyewitness story; journey into a forgotten war. J. Law. il U S News 62:58-60 Ap 3 '67
Flare-up jars Mideast truce; sinking of Israeli destroyer Elath and destruction of Egyptian oil installations. il Sr Schol 91:12-13 N 9 '67
Middle East: Cassandra was right; return to violence. il Newsweek 70:42+ N 6 '67
Middle East: missiles and big guns in a tinderbox. il U S News 63:10 N 6 '67
Razor's edge. il Newsweek 69:40+ My 29 '67
Tunisia and Egypt. il Atlan 219:28+ Ap '67
Why Nasser is no longer a free agent. L. Muray. New Repub 157:10-11 D 23 '67

Great Britain
See also
Sudan

Israel
Intransigence renewed. Time 90:28+ D 1 '67
Night to remember; Nasser seeks adequate policy towards Israel. Newsweek 70:40+ Ag 7 '67

United States
Cairo diary of U.S. humiliation. T. Thompson. il Life 62:70+ Je 23 '67
Desperate act; Nasser's anti-American speech. il Time 89:37 Mr 3 '67

Yemen
Focus changes. il Newsweek 69:50+ F 13 '67
Gas warfare; proof of Egyptian poison-gas attacks in Yemen. Newsweek 70:45 Ag 7 '67

History
British occupation, 1882-1936
Deal and a rebellion brought Britain in. E. Kern. il Life 63:62-9 O 6 '67
Good life as the storm gathers. E. Kern. il Life 63:84-5 O 13 '67

Invasion, 1956
Middle East ulcer; concerning three studies of the Suez crisis. A. Werth. Nation 205:311-14 O 2 '67
No end of a lesson: the inside story of Suez, by A. Nutting. Review
Sat R 50:44-5 N 4 '67. L. Roberts; Reply. A. Nutting. 50:24 D 9 '67
Suez, by H. Thomas. Review
Newsweek 70-75-6 Jl 8 '67. S. Maloff
Sat R 50:22-3+ Jl 8 '67. J. St John

Suez crisis; a footnote to history. W. W. Aldrich. For Affairs 45:541-52 Ap '67
When the sun set . . . G. A. Craig. Reporter 37:37-8 N 30 '67

Politics and government
Boss holds out. il Newsweek 70:67 O 23 '67
Double-think, Egyptian style. A. Carthew. il N Y Times Mag p 19-21+ Ag 20 '67
Fateful friendship. Newsweek 70:50+ S 25 '67
In the wake of war; can Nasser survive? il U S News 62:32 Je 26 '67
Nasser of Egypt: he has landed on his feet again. il U S News 64:32-3 Ja 1 '68
Split in Egypt. L. Muray. New Repub 157:22 S 9 '67
Tough times for Nasser. Time 90:31-2 S 22 '67
Voice from the grave; excerpts from document said to be last testament. Time 90:38 D 15 '67

EGYPT and the United States
Letter from Cairo. T. Armbrister. il Sat Eve Post 240:62-3 Jl 29 '67

EGYPTIAN portraits. See Portraits, Egyptian

EGYPTIANS
Egypt: bruises and suspicions. V. L. Bullough. Nation 205:394-5 O 23 '67

EHRENBERG, A. and others
Electron spin resonance of gamma-irradiated oriented DNA prepared by wet spinning. bibliog Science 157:1317-19 S 15 '67

EHRENBERG, W.
Maxwell's demon; with biographical sketch. Sci Am 217:20, 103-10 bibliog(p 156) N '67

EHRENBURG, Il'ia Grigor'evich
Ilya Ehrenburg: what I have learned. por Sat R 50:28-31 S 30 '67

about
Armored heart. il Newsweek 70:48 S 18 '67
Death of a survivor. por Time 90:25 S 8 '67
Do svidanyia, Ilya. A. Werth. Nation 205:344-6 O 9 '67
Obituary
    Nat R 19:1007 S 19 '67
    Pub W 192:48 S 18 '67
    Sat R 50:32 O 7 '67. R. J. Clements
Russian who dared. M. Kalb. Sat R 50:53-4 N 18 '67
Wanderer. F. Y. Blumenfeld. por Newsweek 70:106-106B O 23 '67

EHRENFELD, David W. and Koch, A. L.
Visual accommodation in the green turtle. bibliog Science 155:827-8 F 17 '67

EHRENREICH, Henry
Electrical properties of materials; with biographical sketch. Sci Am 217:52, 194-204 S '67

EHRLICH, David Alan
African food survey. Sci N 92:141 Ag 5 '67
Cholera threatens. Sci N 92:43 Jl 8 '67
New deal for women. Sci N 91:599 Je 24 '67
River blindness afflicts 200,000,000. Sci N 92:16-17 Jl 1 '67
Toward a biology CERN. Sci N 91:451 My 13 '67
World cancer fight. Sci N 91:574+ Je 17 '67
World drug law sought. Sci N 91:566 Je 17 '67
World health: bad. Sci N 91:481+ My 20 '67
WHO aims at worms. Sci N 92:115 Jl 29 '67
WHO begins research. Sci N 92:130 Ag 5 '67

EHRLICH, Paul R. and Raven, P. H.
Butterflies and plants; with biographical sketches. Sci Am 216:14, 104-11+ Je '67

EIB, George
Higher standard of maintenance. Am City 82:100-1 F '67

EIBEL, Deborah
Precious Fräulein Genoveva; poem. Horn Bk 43:101 F '67

EICHELBERGER, Clark M.
Report from the U.N. General assembly. Sat R 50:16-17 Ag 12 '67
U.N. and the sea. Sat R 50:22+ O 14 '67
U.N. summit. Sat R 50:14 Jl 1 '67

EICHMANN, Adolf
Eichmann trial. L. Poliakov. Commentary 43:86-8+ Ja '67

EIGEN, Manfred
Defining sections of the chemical blur. por (p463) Sci N 92:464-5 N 11 '67
Nobel prizes; chemistry. H. Eyring and E. M. Eyring. por Science 158:746-8 N 10 '67
Quick and the cosmic. Newsweek 70:106+ N 13 '67

800th anniversary festival, Copenhagen. See Festivals—Denmark

8mm films. See Photography—Films

EIGHTEEN-nation disarmament conference. See Conference of the Eighteen-nation committee on disarmament. Geneva. 1962-

EIGNER, Larry
Three poems: The pipes how many; The feet of Icarus; The birds. Poetry 110:18-20 Ap '67

EILERS, Hazel Kraft
At the sign of the crest. See issues of Hobbies

EIMERL, Sarel
Bond and I. Reporter 37:55-8 Jl 13 '67
Bundles from Britain. Reporter 36:40-4 Ap 6 '67
Finite variety. Reporter 36:42-5 F 23 '67
Logic and the agony. Reporter 36:47-8+ Je 1 '67

EIMON, Pan Dodd
(ed) City tells its story. See issues of American city

EIN, Daniel, and Fahey, J. L.
Two types of lambda polypeptide chains in human immunoglobulins. bibliog Science 156: 947-8 My 19 '67

EINSTEIN, Albert
On Albert Einstein; excerpt from Variety of men. C. P. Snow. Commentary 43:45-55 Mr '67
Thermodynamics in Einstein's thought. M. J. Klein. bibliog Science 157:509-16 Ag 4 '67
Unforgettable Albert Einstein. B. Hoffmann. por Read Digest 92:107-12 Ja '68
Was Einstein wrong? reprint. V' Sullivan. il Sci Digest 61:75-8 Ap '67

EINSTEIN, Charles
New breed of baseball fan. Harper 235:69-70+ Jl '67

EINSTEIN, Kurt
Grueling interview for executives after bigger jobs. C. Welles. il por Life 63:69-70+ Ag 18 '67

EINSTEIN award. See Albert Einstein award
EINSTEIN theory. See Relativity (physics)

EISELE, Donn
Freshmen in the crew: two self-made men who finally have the jobs they want. il pors Life 62:?7 My 19 '67

EISELEY, Loren C.
Immense journey of Loren Eiseley. J. Medelman. por Esquire 67:92-4+ Mr '67

EISEMAN, Alberta
(ed) See Katzenberg, J. Face to face with a boy who loves politics

EISEN, Elaine Susan
Spring; poem. Horn Bk 43:240 Ap '67

EISENBERG, Norman
Stereo mods. Hi Fi 17:62-5 Ja '67
Stereo servicing. Hi Fi 17:62-4 Ap '67
VTR topics. See issues of High fidelity incorporating Musical America

EISENBERG, Robert S. and Gage, P. W.
Frog skeletal muscle fibers: changes in electrical properties after disruption of transverse tubular system. bibliog Science 158: 1700-1 D 29 '67
—See Gage, P. W. jt. auth.

EISENBUD, Jule
Amazing weekend with the amazing Ted Serios. C. Reynolds; D. B. Eisendrath, jr. il por Pop Phot 61:81-7+ O '67

EISENDRATH, David B. Jr
Amazing weekend with the amazing Ted Serios. Pop Phot 61:85-7+ O '67
Color clinic. See issues of Popular photography

EISENHOWER, David
That's the ticket. il pors Newsweek 70:31 D 11 '67

EISENHOWER, Dwight David
Boyhood of a President; excerpt from At ease: stories I tell to friends. pors Sat Eve Post 240:32-6+ Ap 8 '67
Ike to war critics: be moderate in dissent; excerpts from news conference, October 13, 1967. por U S News 63:22 O 23 '67
Ike's tactics: hot pursuit in Vietnam; television interview. por U S News 63:22 D 11 '67
Ticklish problem of political fund-raising, and spending. Read Digest 92:64-9 Ja '68
We should be ashamed. Read Digest 91:67-71 Ag '67

about
Authors & editors; meeting members of the book trade press. Pub W 192:17 Jl 3 '67
Behind the lines. Read Digest 91:7-8 Ag '67
Ike's Gettysburg farm: a gift to the Nation. il U S News 63:17 D 11 '67
Political Ike. K. Crawford. Newsweek 71: 32 Ja 15 '68
Treasure house on the prairie. B Hibbs. il por Read Digest 90:146-52+ My '67
Underestimation of Dwight D. Eisenhower. M. Kempton. il Esquire 68:108-9+ S '67

EISENHOWER museum, Abilene, Kan.
Treasure house on the prairie; D. D. Eisenhower's boyhood home. B. Hibbs. il Read Digest 90:146-52 Mv '67

EISENMAN, Alvin
New points on paper, type; interview. por Pub W 192:62-4+ S 4 '67

EISENMAN, G. and others
Membrane structure and ion permeation. bibliog Science 155:965-74 F 24 '67

EISENPREIS, Bettijane
When do youngsters begin a second language? Parents Mag 42:66-7+ S '67

EISENSTADT, S. N.
Israeli identity: problems in the development of the collective identity of an ideological society. Ann Am Acad 370:116-23 Mr '67

EISENSTEIN, Elizabeth L.
On Who intervened in 1788? J. Kaplow. bibliog f Am Hist R 72:497-502 Ja '67

EISNER, Robert
Books. Bul Atomic Sci 23:30-2 N '67

EISNER, Thomas
Life on the sticky sundew; with biographical sketch. Natur Hist 76:4, 32-5 Je '67
—and Davis, J. A.
Mongoose throwing and smashing millipedes. bibliog Science 155:577-9 F 3 '67
—and others
Defensive use of a fecal shield by a beetle larva. bibliog Science 158:1471-3 D 15 '67

EJECTION devices (airplanes) See Airplanes
—Escape devices

EKLUND, Sigvard
Can peaceful nuclear power be kept out of bombs? interview. por U S News 62:93-4 Ap 17 '67

EKSTROM, Arne H.
Parrot show; interview. New Yorker 43:18 Ja 6 '68

EKTACHROME films. See Photography—Films

EKTACOLOR print films. See Photography—Films

EL-ANI, Arif S. See Ani, A. S.

ELAPSED-time indicators. See Timing devices

ELASMOBRANCHS
Potamtrygon spp: elasmobranchs with low urea content. T. B. Thorson and others. bibliog il Science 158:375-7 O 20 '67

ELASTASE. See Enzymes

ELBA (island)
Going places, finding things on Elba. L. J. Gartner. il House & Gard 132:30-1+ N '67

EL-BADRY, M. A. See Badry, M. A.

EL CORDOBÉS. See Cordobés

ELDADAH, Adnan H. and others
Viral hemorrhagic encephalopathy of rats. bibliog Science 156:392-4 Ap 21 '67

ELDER, William Voss, 3d
Oval room from Willow Brook; excerpts from catalogue. Antiques 91:496-9 Ap '67

ELDORADO national forest, Calif. See National forests

ELDRIDGE, Mary N.
Earl Warren: defender of human rights. Negro Hist Bul 30:11-13 My '67

ELECTION day
Press and twenty-four-hour voting; Frank Stanton's proposal for national elections. R. L. Tobin. Sat R 50:49-50 Ag 12 '67

ELECTION districts
See also
Apportionment (election law)

ELECTION expenses. See Campaign funds

ELECTION fiesta in Ultra; story. See Griffith, T.

ELECTION forecasts. See Political forecasts

ELECTION laws
See also
Voters, Registration of

United States
Let's make our elections make sense. F. Stanton. McCalls 95:8-9 D '67
Why 1968 is a dangerous year. R. L. Tobin. Sat R 50:26 O 7 '67

ELECTIONS
See also
Political campaigns
Voting

Bahama Islands
Black vote revolt in the Bahamas. L. Bennett, jr. il Ebony 22:68-70+ Je '67
Negro leader takes over; white rule in Bahamas ends. il U S News 62:16 Ja 30 '67

Chile
Classic blunder; local elections. Newsweek 69:64 Ap 17 '67

ELECTIONS—*Continued*

France

After the vote: where de Gaulle is headed. il U S News 62:35-6 Mr 20 '67

De Gaulle surveys the damage. E. Taylor. Reporter 36:29-30 Ap 6 '67

Election fever; Gaullist victories on Corsica. il Newsweek 69:59 Mr 27 '67

French elections. E. Taylor. Reporter 36:16 Mr 23 '67

French people's message to Charles de Gaulle. il U S News 62:52-3 Mr 27 '67

French vote: why be surprised? A. Werth. Nation 204:422-4 Ap 3 '67

Le grand upset: Gaullist majority down to a whisper. il Life 62:31 Mr 24 '67

Le grim Charles? Sr Schol 90:18-19 Mr 31 '67

How far will de Gaulle unbend? Bsns W p44 Mr 18 '67

Letter from Paris; candidates for parliamentary election in March. Genêt. New Yorker 42:80+ Ja 28 '67

Letter from Paris; election campaign. Genêt. New Yorker 43:110+ F 25 '67

Letter from Paris; parliamentary election campaign. Genêt. New Yorker 43:151-4 Mr 11 '67

Letter from Paris; results of parliamentary election. Genêt. New Yorker 43:172-4 Mr 25 '67

Not unspeakable pain. Time 89:29 Mr 24 '67

One for de Gaulle. Time 89:34 Mr 17 '67

Second round; first round results. Newsweek 69:45-6 Mr 20 '67

Still de Gaulle. New Repub 156:8 Mr 25 '67

Thinnest margin; National assembly results. il Newsweek 69:54+ Mr 27 '67

Germany (Federal Republic)

Ghosts in Bremen; NPD gains. Newsweek 70:43-4 O 16 '67

Grinder ground; SPD suffers losses in Lower Saxony election. Newsweek 69:54 Je 19 '67

Mixed blessings; Schleswig-Holstein and Rhineland-Palatinate state elections. Newsweek 69:53 My 8 '67

Great Britain

Honeymoon ends; local elections; Tory victory. Newsweek 69:44+ Ap 24 '67

Letter from London; elections for the Greater London council and county councils. M. Panter-Downes. New Yorker 43:177-9 My 6 '67

India

After the fall, who will lead? with report by E. Behr. il Newsweek 69:52-4 Mr 13 '67

Before chaos, one last chance; India goes to the polls. G. Woodcock. Commonweal 86:109-11 Ap 14 '67

Communism, Kerala style. J. Lelyveld. il N Y Times Mag p30-1+ Ap 30 '67

Elections cast a pall over India's future; Congress party's most humiliating defeat. il Bsns W p 164 Mr 4 '67

In the people's hands. il Newsweek 69:48 Mr 6 '67

India: out of the straitjacket. D. K. Das. Nat R 19:290-1 Mr 21 '67

Leadership jolted. il Sr Schol 90:16-17 Mr 10 '67

Marathon at the polls. il Newsweek 69:42+ F 27 '67

Massive protest. il Time 89:32+ Mr 3 '67

Me-tooism, here, too. P. C. Jain. Nat R 19:129+ F 7 '67

Strength in weakness; election setback in Congress party. il Time 89:35-6 Mr 10 '67

Upset in India; Mrs Gandhi's party hard-hit. il U S News 62:16 Mr 6 '67

Violence at the polls. Time 89:37 F 24 '67

See also

Political campaigns—India

Jamaica

One sort of moderation. Newsweek 69:50 Mr 6 '67

Wide open. Time 89:34 F 3 '67

Japan

Bouncing back. il Newsweek 69:49-50 F 13 '67

Election no. 10. il Time 89:33-4 F 3 '67

Election victory for Sato. il Sr Schol 90:13 F 17 '67

Korea (Republic)

Bid for a bigger mandate. Time 89:31-2 My 5 '67

Safe gamble. Newsweek 69:52+ My 15 '67

Shattered peace; investigation of election irregularities. Time 89:31-2 Je 23 '67

What brand do you vote? Newsweek 69:52 Je 19 '67

Netherlands

Nation of splinters. il Newsweek 69:40 F 27 '67

Philippines

Philippine elections. New Repub 157:10-11 D 9 '67

Victory for the non-candidate. Time 90:38+ N 24 '67

Spain

Experiment with democracy; 104 members to be popularly elected. Time 90:39+ O 6 '67

Politically numb. Newsweek 70:67-8 O 23 '67

Sudan

Tolerant young man. Time 89:40 Mr 17 '67

United States

After Detroit; riots' effects on elections of 1968. il Time 90:18-19 Ag 4 '67

American party politics, elections, and voting behavior. H. A. Bone. bibliog f il Ann Am Acad 372:124-37 Jl '67

Cities; States. il Time 90:28-9 N 17 '67

Congress: shades of '52, and '48; optimism of the Republican party. il Newsweek 71:23-4 Ja 8 '68

Doubleheader for George; A. Licata's victory. il Time 89:15 Je 2 '67

Elections: poor guys finish last. S. V. Roberts. Commonweal 87:291-2 D 1 '67

Elections '67: what clues for '68? with press comments. il Sr Schol 91:21-3 N 30 '67

Keeping faith with Adam; Harlem returns A. C. Powell. Newsweek 69:26 Ap 24 '67

Local scene: where the pork barrel still rules; 1968 Senate and House races. P. Carter. il Newsweek 70:39 Jl 10 '67

New revolution? shift to the Republican party. D. Lawrence. U S News 63:120 N 20 '67

Off-year vote gives few clues to 1968; election of two Negro mayors. il Bsns W p48-9 N 11 '67

On the electoral wind. Nat R 19:1308-9 N 28 '67

Press and twenty-four hour voting; Frank Stanton's proposal for national elections. R. L. Tobin. Sat R 50:49-50 Ag 12 '67

Race issue: what city voters say now. il U S News 63:35 O 16 '67

Three elections under microscope; Negro victories. Christian Cent 84:1483 N 22 '67

To the rescue; A. Licata wins special election to Michigan legislature. Newsweek 69:33 Je 5 '67

Tuesday's news; election results. Nation 205:514 N 20 '67

Two cheers; election results. New Repub 157:6 N 18 '67

Up the political ladder. il Newsweek 70:66 N 20 '67

What the '67 elections showed; Signs of change for '68. il U S News 63:31-5 N 20 '67

With the mayors. Nat R 19:1248-50 N 14 '67

See also

Candidates, Political

National conventions (political)

Nominations for office

Presidential campaigns

Presidential candidates

Presidents—United States—Election

Primaries

Public opinion polls

Suffrage—United States

Voting

also subhead Elections under names of cities, e.g. Chicago—Elections

Anecdotes, facetiae, satire, etc.

...But do as we say; observations on elective process. M. Greenfield. Reporter 37:14-16 S 7 '67

Vietnam (Republic)

American group to observe elections in Viet-Nam; background, with press interview, August 28, 1967. H. C. Lodge. Dept State Bul 57:349-51 S 18 '67

Back on the track. il Newsweek 70:46+ Ag 28 '67

Battle of ballots. il Time 89:28+ Je 23 '67

Beer in the gallery. Nation 205:357+ O 16 '67

Blood on the ballot; Communist terrorism. il Time 89:20 Ap 28 '67

Blood on the stars; Ky steps down. Newsweek 70:45-6 Jl 17 '67

Campaign kickoff. Time 90:25 Ag 11 '67

Candidates emerge; first stage of South Viet Nam's nationwide elections. il Time 89:36 Ap 28 '67

Choices get a bit clearer; Thieu-Ky victory no landslide. il Bsns W p39-40 S 9 '67

ELECTIONS—Vietnam (Republic)—*Continued*
Concerning the elections. Nat R 19:1002 S 19 '67
Death of an image; Thieu and Ky accused of hindering candidates. il Newsweek 70:41 Ag 21 '67
Democracy and the Vietnam vote. America 117:294 S 23 '67
Difference in South Vietnam; coverage by New York times. America 117:263-4 S 16 '67
Dustup at Dong Ha. il Time 90:26 Ag 18 '67
Electing a president. il Time 90:19 S 8 '67
Election, a barrier and talk of peace. il Newsweek 70:27-8+ S 18 '67
Elections in Vietnam; presidential candidates. R. S. Browne. New Repub 157:11-12 Jl 22 '67
Exercise in deception. Tran-van-Dinh. il Commonweal 86:582-4 S 22 '67
Experts; concerning U.S. election experts. Nation 205:226-7 S 18 '67
For whose interests? R. R. Banville. Christian Cent 84:118+ Ja 25 '67
From Saigon to Detroit. W. Pfaff. Commonweal 86:567-8 S 22 '67
General understanding; presidential campaign opens with television program. il Newsweek 70:28 Ag 14 '67
Jumping the gun. Newsweek 69:50 Je 26 '67
Ky decision; premier announces he will run for president. Time 89:33-4 My 19 '67
Letter from Saigon (cont) R. Shaplen. New Yorker 42:155+ F 18; 43:149-54+ O 7 '67
Letter from Saigon. T. Armbrister. il Sat Eve Post 240:64-5 S 9 '67
Letter from South Vietnam. R. Shaplen. New Yorker 43:74+ Je 17 '67
Letter to doubters; Ky's letter to Senate. Time 90:18-19 S 1 '67
Marching out the horses. K. H. Purnell. Nation 205:267-9 S 25 '67
Measuring Vietnam's elections. Life 63:4 Ag 25 '67
Mr Bundy discusses Viet-Nam on Meet the press; transcript of interview, August 27, 1967. W. P. Bundy. Dept State Bul 57:352-7 S 18 '67
Name of the game; civilian candidates return to active campaigning. il Time 90:26 Ag 25 '67
Outvoting terror; Viet Cong's terror campaign during village elections. il Newsweek 69:50 Ap 17 '67
Paucity of choice. il Time 90:19-20 S 15 '67
Peace moves next in Vietnam? W. S. Merick. il U S News 63:38-40 S 18 '67
President sends congratulations to Vietnamese chief of state; text of message, September 10, 1967. Dept State Bul 57:421 O 2 '67
Rivals; Ky and Thieu planning to run for president. Newsweek 69:46+ My 22 '67
Saigon showdown; U.S. gain or loss? il U S News 63:6 Jl 10 '67
South Vietnam exists. D. Warner. il Reporter 37:18-20 S 21 '67
South Vietnam's captive vote; candidates. Tran-van-Dinh. New Repub 157:15-16 S 2 '67
Step-down for Ky. il Newsweek 70:97 Jl 10 '67
Still no. one; presidential election campaign formally opens. il Time 90:24 Ag 4 '67
Sunday, Sept. 3. *di bau* day in Vietnam; with report by D. Moser and others. il Life 63:30-7 S 15 '67
Taking off the lid; Thieu challenges Ky. il Newsweek 69:38-9 Je 5 '67
Test of time; guerrilla attempts to frighten public away from polls. il Newsweek 70:31 S 11 '67
Then there were ten. il Newsweek 70:26 Jl 31 '67
Thieu on top. il Time 90:23-4 Jl 7 '67
Thieu vs. Ky. il Newsweek 70:39 S 4 '67
Thieu victory; divided reaction. il Sr Schol 91:30+ S 28 '67
Toward riceroots democracy. il Time 89:26-7 Ap 7 '67
Vietnam election message; peace now. A. Hassler. Christian Cent 84:1292-5 O 11 '67
Vietnam: no exit. Sat Eve Post 240:90 O 7 '67
Vietnam's Catholics. America 117:290 S 23 '67
Vote for peace. New Repub 157:5-6 S 16 '67
Vote for the future. il Time 90:28-32 S 15 '67
What the Vietnam election means. il U S News 63:21-3 S 4 '67
Why Viet Cong tried to smash election. il U S News 63:8 S 11 '67
See also
Political campaigns—Vietnam (Republic)

ELECTIONS and business conditions. See Business—Political aspects

ELECTORAL college
Case for the electoral college. A. M. Bickel. New Repub 156:15-16 Ja 28 '67; Reply. N. R. Peirce. 156:12-13 F 11 '67
Direct vote and the electoral college. R. L. Tobin. Sat R 50:24 F 18 '67
If Congress names next president. il U S News 63:34-5 D 18 '67
Next year, a funny thing could happen on the way to the White House. R. L. Strout. il N Y Times Mag p24-5 Jl 23 '67
T.R.B. from Washington. New Repub 156:2 My 20 '67
What George is doing; interest in a constitutional amendment to abolish the Electoral college. K. Crawford. Newsweek 69:45 My 22 '67
Why 1968 is a dangerous year. R. L. Tobin. Sat R 50:26 O 7 '67
Why the next man elected president may never reach the White House. C. Fritchey. Harper 235:21-4 Ag '67
Will we elect the president we vote for in 1968? E. Gossett. Read Digest 91:211-14+ N '67

ELECTRIC adding machines. See Adding machines

ELECTRIC alarms
Alarms to warn when fans fail. P. B. Jones. il Suc Farm 65:30J N '67
Horn foretells sewer overflows; McPherson, Kan. C. E. Stacy. il Am City 82:58 My '67

ELECTRIC apparatus and appliances
See also
Coherer
Electric apparatus industry
Electric equipment
Electric motors

ELECTRIC apparatus and appliances, Domestic
All-around appliance; electric skillets. V. T. Habeeb. il Am Home 70:70 D '67
All-in-one kitchen appliance center. il House & Gard 131:144 Je '67
Any advantage to a vertical rotisserie? il Consumer Rep 32:566-7 N '67
Beauty aids for the Sybarite in you. il House & Gard 132:57-8 N '67
[Blenders, broilers, coffee makers, etc] Consumer Rep 32:37-61 D '67
Clip and save; ABC's of blenders. il Seventeen 26:126 Je '67
Cooking Dutch with a blender; Pennsylvania Dutch dishes. il Good H 165:120+ Ag '67
Cooking with company. il Seventeen 26:212 S '67
Electric broilers. il Consumer Rep 32:574-8 N '67
Father's favorite, the food blender; Osterizer liquefier-blender. M. B. Keiser. il Parents Mag 42:32+ Je '67
Five idea centers. N. Craig. il House B 109:108-9 Jl '67
Great ways to use your gift appliances. il Bet Hom & Gard 45:52+ N '67
New in your room; switched-ons. il Seventeen 26:168-71 My '67
Portable electric mixers. il Consumer Bul 50:6-9 Mr '67
Tune in to the newest. il Seventeen 26:234 My '67
When dad is late. M. Davidson. il Ladies Home J 84:62+ F '67

Insurance aspects
Appliance insurance: the best policy. L. A. Dane. House B 109:193 O '67

Repairing
Appliances you can repair yourself; Proctor-Silex. Lifelong appliances. il Consumer Rep 33:51-3 Ja '68
Now; take-apart appliances you can fix yourself. S. M. Gallager. il Pop Mech 127:126-7 Je '67

ELECTRIC apparatus industry
Go-go appliances; Italy's thriving home-appliance manufacturers. il Time 90:78 Jl 7 '67
New spark at the GE of Japan; Toshiba electric. il Bsns W p 123-6+ F 11 '67
Off color. il Newsweek 69:67-8 Ap 3 '67
Weinstock wins; Britain's Associated electrical industries ltd. bought by General electric. Time 90:103 N 24 '67

ELECTRIC arc
Arc, surge, and noise suppression. R. M. Rovnyak. il Electr World 77:46-8 Ap '67

ELECTRIC automobiles. See Automobiles, Electric

ELECTRIC batteries
Test of flashlight batteries of the D size. il
Consumer Bul 50:37-40 S '67
Where tiny cells power big sales; Mallory
battery co. il Bsns W p60-2+ Ja 14 '67
See also
Fuel cells

Charging
Can dry cells be recharged? F. Shunaman. il
Pop Electr 27:41-5 Jl '67

Storage
And now, ladies & gentlemen, introducing the
electronic popsicle; keeping batteries refrigerated. P. Farber. il U S Camera 30:20+
O '67
Cool it in the refrigerator. C. W. Kennedy.
il Pop Phot 61:41-2+ N '67

ELECTRIC blankets, coverlets, etc.
Electric blankets. il Consumer Rep 32:589-93
N '67

ELECTRIC blenders. See Electric apparatus and
appliances, Domestic

ELECTRIC broilers. See Electric apparatus and
appliances, Domestic

ELECTRIC cables
See also
Electric lines

ELECTRIC capacitors

Testing
Capsnapper arrests shock hazard and protects
electrolytics. H. R. Rosenblatt. il Pop
Electr 26:23 Ap '67

ELECTRIC charges
Black box that turns you on; anti-fatigue
device. il Bsns W p79-80 My 6 '67

ELECTRIC circuit breakers
Solid-state circuit breaker operates within
microseconds. S. W. Thomas. il Electr
World 78:31 Jl '67
See also
Electric relays

ELECTRIC circuits
See also
Electric contactors
Electronic circuits
Printed circuits

ELECTRIC circus (nightclub) See Night clubs

ELECTRIC cleaners. See Vacuum cleaners

ELECTRIC coils
Relay coil considerations. M. S. Steinback.
il Electr World 77:44-5 Ap '67
See also
Radio coils

ELECTRIC conductivity
Electrical properties of materials. H. Ehren-
reich. il Sci Am 217:194-204 S '67
High-conductivity solid electrolytes: MAg4I5.
B. B. Owens and G. R. Argue. bibliog il
Science 157:308-10 Jl 21 '67
See also
Superconductivity

ELECTRIC conductors
See also
Semiconductors

ELECTRIC contactors
Electrical contact considerations. A. O. Capp,
jr. il Electr World 77:49-53 Ap '67

ELECTRIC control
See also
Remote control

ELECTRIC converters. See Electric current
converters

ELECTRIC cords
Extension cords in the household. il Consumer Bul 50:37-8 Ap '67

ELECTRIC couplings. See Couplings, Electric

ELECTRIC current converters
Build the three phaser. B. Hartford. il Pop
Mech 127:196-7 Ap '67
Make your own six to twelve volt up-verter;
equipment for automobiles. B. Richards. il
Pop Electr 27:67-70 O '67

ELECTRIC current rectifiers
Semiconductor switching of low-power circuits A. Harris. il Electr World 77:33-5 Je
'67
SCR protective circuit for hi-fi amplifier;
silicon controlled rectifier. il Electr World
77:71 Mr '67
Who's afraid of the SCR? A. A. Mangieri. il
Pop Electr 28:53-5+ Ja '68

ELECTRIC currents
See also
Electric current rectifiers

Grounding
Electrical ground requirements. C. F. Kelley.
il Yachting 121:53-5+ F '67

Improper grounding, the subtle troublespot.
M. H. Burke. il Electr World 78:82-4 N '67
What ground? R. L. Ruyle. il Pop Electr 27:
59-62 Ag '67

ELECTRIC discharges through gases
See also
Plasma (ionized gases)

ELECTRIC dish washers. See Dishwashing and
drying machines

ELECTRIC distribution
See also
Electric plants—Interconnection

ELECTRIC drills. See Drilling and boring machinery

ELECTRIC elevators. See Elevators

ELECTRIC equipment
Budget shifts reflect need for new design
approach. L. C. Jaquith. il Arch Rec 141:
87 Ap '67
Information central; questions and answers.
C. J. Schauers. il Pop Electr 26:68-70+ F:
66-8+ Mr; 76-8+ Ap; 81-3 My; 68-70 Je;
27:64-6 Jl '67
See also
Audio-visual aids
Automobiles—Electric equipment
Electric apparatus industry

ELECTRIC equipment industry
Less diversity means more prosperity for
Sola Basic. il Bsns W p82-4+ Ap 22 '67

ELECTRIC filters
See also
Radio filters

ELECTRIC generators
Commercial electric power from MHD seen
by Soviets. R. Pay. il Tech W 20:24+ Ap
10 '67
Electric power aplenty for the small boat.
W. L. Hensley. il Pop Sci 191:86-8 D '67
Electricity from a stream of air and water.
W. S. Bacon. il Pop Sci 191:80-1 Ag '67
Exotic fuels will power tomorrow. M. J.
Schultz. il Sci Digest 62:45-52 O '67
Inventor of the month; electricity for years;
generator uses thermoelectric alloy. S. V.
Jones. il Sci Digest 61:17 F '67
Jet turbine for Jacksonville, Ill. il Am City
82:18 S '67
MHD: a cloudy future. il Sci N 93:5-6 Ja 6
'68
Power from a bottled thunderstorm. S. V.
Jones. il Sci Digest 61:27 Ap '67
Power play; Russian interest in Grand Cou-
lee turbines contract. Newsweek 69:76 Ap
10 '67
Stand-by electric power. Consumer Bul 50:31-
5 Jl '67
See also
Pulse generators
Thermionic converters

ELECTRIC generators, Alternating current
Alternator, a generator turned inside out. L.
Heiner. il Yachting 122:55-7+ D '67
How to check out your alternator. M. Schultz.
il Pop Mech 128:122-5+ Ag '67

ELECTRIC hair dryers. See Hair dryers

ELECTRIC heaters
New generation of heaters. il House & Gard
132:20+ D '67
Quick ways to use electric heat. P. B. Jones.
il Suc Farm 65:44 N '67

ELECTRIC heating
All-electric high-rise demonstrates econom-
ics. il Arch Rec 141:215-18 Ap '67
Home-heating battle gets still warmer. il
Bsns W p76-7 Ag 12 '67

ELECTRIC industries
See also
Brown Boveri corporation
Electric apparatus industry
Electric power
Electric utilities
Westinghouse electric corporation

ELECTRIC interference
Arc, surge, and noise suppression. R. M.
Rovnyak. il Electr World 77:46-8 Ap '67

ELECTRIC irons
Steam irons with Teflon-coated soleplates. il
Consumer Bul 50:4-6+ S '67
Steam/spray irons. il Consumer Rep 32:68-72
F '67

ELECTRIC knives. See Knives

ELECTRIC lamps
How to get the right lamp for function and
fashion. Bet Hom & Gard 45:36-7+ F '67
More use for sodium discharge lamps. il Am
City 82:138 Ap '67
Twenty-one good questions about light bulbs.
C. P. Gilmore. il Pop Sci 190:188+ F '67

Shades
Plastic protective globes prove their worth.
il Am City 82:104+ Ja '67

ELECTRIC lamps, Flashing
Safety in a flash; Flash-O-matic. C. Conley. il Field & S 71:145 Ap '67
ELECTRIC lamps, Flashlight. See Electric lamps, Photoflash
ELECTRIC lamps, Fluorescent
Booby trap in the bathroom; improper installation instructions for fluorescent light fixtures. Consumer Rep 32:184-5 Ap '67
How to troubleshoot fluorescent lamps. P. McCafferty. il Pop Sci 190:148-9 Mr '67
Microdot making portable lamp for astronauts in space work. il Aviation W 87:117+ Ag 21 '67
ELECTRIC lamps, Mercury vapor
Mercuries shed new light on a park; South park, Buffalo, N.Y. il Am City 82:126 My '67
ELECTRIC lamps, Photoflash
Bantam that performs like a heavyweight. J. S. Forney. il Pop Phot 62:82-3 Ja '68
Camera with a take-charge flash; Minolta Autopak. H. Zucker. il Pop Phot 62:87 Ja '68
Easy to mount, and modular too. J. S. Forney. il Pop Phot 62:88-9 Ja '68
Fill-in flash indoors. C. W. Kennedy. il Pop Phot 60:33+ Je '67
Flash; most flash equipment is improperly used. P. R. Farber. il U S Camera 30:48-9+ My '67
Flashbulbs and synchronizers. R. Arnold. il U S Camera 30:59+ My '67
For better pictures in your family album. M. B. Keiser. il Parents Mag 42:17-18 Ja '67
Incredible cronoscope. P. R. Farber. il U S Camera 30:42-3+ Mr '67
Portable electronic flash bank for under $100. L. Barry. il Pop Phot 60:92-3+ F '67
Shoeless flash. B. Pierce. il Pop Phot 61:114-15 Jl '67
Speedy cronoscope again! P. Farber. il U S Camera 30:30+ Ag '67
Stingy on batteries; Trioblitz X-116. J. S. Forney. Pop Phot 62:88 Ja '68
Stop that action with a stutter strobe. P. Wahl. il Pop Mech 128:174-5+ N '67
Which low cost lighting? il Mod Phot 31:72-5 Mr '67
ELECTRIC lamps, Sodium vapor
London will try high-pressure sodium lighting. Am City 82:120+ Ag '67
ELECTRIC lamps in art
Light brigade. E. C. Baker. il Art N 66:52-5+ Mr '67
Luminal music; art has gone electric. il Time 89:78-85 Ap 28 '67
ELECTRIC light fixtures. See Lighting fixtures
ELECTRIC lighting

Control
Build a MALF; manual and automatic light fader. I. Gorgenyi. il Pop Electr 27:67-9+ S '67

Rates
See Electric utilities—Rates
ELECTRIC lines
Second battle of Antietam; controversy over location of the transmission lines. Nat Parks Mag 41:20-1 O '67
Second battle of Antietam; opposition to line towers of Potomac Edison company. Life 62:4 Je 23 '67
Second battle of Antietam: or, The fight to save our parks. B. F. Hillenbrand. Parks & Rec 2:18-19+ N '67
Second battle of Antietam; proposed Potomac Edison transmission lines. M. Frome. Am For 73:36 Jl '67
Staving off blackouts; FPC's proposed pattern of extra-high-voltage lines. Bsns W p 100 Jl 29 '67

Poles
Highway officials look at pole design. il Am City 82:102+ Jl '67

Underground
No more overhead wires! A. Hamilton. il Read Digest 91:33-4+ N '67
Prepare to go 100 per cent underground. L. P. DiMatteo and M. W. Stewart. Am City 82:62+ O '67
Transmission lines; relationship to our park and recreation facilities. G. Romney. Parks & Rec 2:17 N '67
Transmission lines; the placement of power lines and the preservation of aesthetic value. L. C. White. Parks & Rec 2:19+ D '67

ELECTRIC meters
R.F. sniffer; field strength meter. J. Ashe. il Pop Electr 26:55-6 Je '67
See also
Ammeters
Frequency meters
Voltmeters
Voltohmmeters
ELECTRIC mixers. See Electric apparatus and appliances, Domestic
ELECTRIC motors
Dremel's powerful new Moto-tool; constant-torque permanent-magnet motor. H. Walton. il Pop Sci 191:168-70 O '67
Electric motors for special jobs. W. J. Fletcher. il Suc Farm 65:54-5 F '67
How to set up a one-motor shop. R. J. De Cristoforo. il Pop Sci 192:156-9 Ja '68
Now: big electric power without phase converters. D. Hagen. il Farm J 92:44H Ja '68
Simple-minded Maggie: an electric motor with a warped, coil-less armature. D. Gierke. il Pop Electr 26:31-4+ Je '67
Two for your outboard; silent trolling motor. E. Studinka. il Pop Sci 192:120 Ja '68
See also
Automobiles, Electric
ELECTRIC motors, Alternating current

Control
A.C. motor drive for electric cars. R. M. Brown. il Electr World 77:28-9 My '67
ELECTRIC motors, Direct current

Control
D.C. motor drive for electric cars. J. Mungenast. il Electr World 77:25 My '67
ELECTRIC mowers. See Lawn mowers
ELECTRIC noise
See also
Electric interference
ELECTRIC ovens
Double-oven thirty-inch electric ranges. il Consumer Bul 50:9-15 N '67
ELECTRIC plants
See also
Electric power
Electric substations
Electric utilities

Interconnection
Guarding against more blackouts. Bsns W p54 D 30 '67
New electric age; pooling of power from several systems. R. Moley. Newsweek 69:108 My 15 '67
ELECTRIC power
Another jolt for the utilities; Middle Atlantic power failure. il Bsns W p 148-9 Je 10 '67
Darkness at noon; power failure in four eastern states. il Time 89:21 Je 16 '67
Electric power: new uses, new sources, more demand; interview. W. J. Clapp. il U S News 62:74-8 Mr 27 '67
Guarding against more blackouts. Bsns W p54 D 30 '67
Have you blackout-proofed your city? emergency standby power generation. Am City 82:10 Ag '67
It's open season on utilities; public pressure for more federal controls. il Bsns W p41-2+ Jl 22 '67
Lights out; power failure hits New Jersey, Pennsylvania, Delaware and Maryland. Newsweek 69:43 Je 19 '67
New electric age; pooling of power from several systems. R. Moley. Newsweek 69:108 My 15 '67
Power blackouts and the FPC. Nation 204:773 Je 19 '67
Power push at PG&E. N. Willatt. il Duns R 90:39-40+ Ag '67
Stand-by electric power. Consumer Bul 50:31-5 Jl '67
Staving off blackouts; FPC's proposed pattern of extra-high-voltage lines. Bsns W p 100 Jl 29 '67
When your freezer stops freezing; keep the freezer door shut. il Consumer Bul 50:40 Ag '67
Why the power failures and why more may come. il U S News 62:76-7 Je 19 '67
See also
Electric utilities

Rates
See Electric utilities—Rates

Brazil
Harnessing the Paraná; hydroelectric potential utilized. il Time 90:86 Jl 14 '67

ELECTRIC power—*Continued*
Canada
More power to Canada; vast hydroelectric power development. Sci N 91:150 F 11 '67

United States
See Electric power
ELECTRIC power lines. See Electric lines
ELECTRIC power production
Electric power from rocket blasts. il Pop Mech 128:110 Ag '67
ELECTRIC ranges. See Electric stoves
ELECTRIC rates. See Electric utilities—Rates
ELECTRIC rectifiers. See Electric current rectifiers
ELECTRIC refrigerators. See Refrigerators, Electric
ELECTRIC relays
Relays; symposium. il Electr World 77:37-60 Ap '67
See also
Electronic relays

Terminology
Relay terminology. il Electr World 77:53 Ap '67
ELECTRIC resistance
Resistor-selection nomogram. S. Salva. il Electr World 77:29 Ap '67
ELECTRIC resistors
See also
Electric contactors
ELECTRIC saws. See Saws
ELECTRIC sharpeners. See Sharpeners
ELECTRIC shavers. See Razors
ELECTRIC shock
First aid; electrocution. C. J. Potthoff. Todays Health 45:70 S '67
Modulation of elicited behavior by a fixed-interval schedule of electric shock presentation. W. H. Morse and others. bibliog il Science 157:215-17 Jl 14 '67
Permanence of retrograde amnesia produced by electroconvulsive shock. M. W. Luttges and J. L. McGaugh. bibliog il Science 156:408-10 Ap 21 '67
Recovery of memory after amnesia induced by electroconvulsive shock. S. Zinkin and A. J. Miller; reply with rejoinder. M. J. Herz and H. V. S. Peeke. Science 156:1396-7 Je 9 '67
Sleep: the effect of electroconvulsive shock in cats deprived of REM sleep. H. B. Cohen and others. bibliog il Science 156:1646-8 Je 23 '67
33,000-volt shock wins two award of $¼ million. A. Peters. il Ebony 23:112-14+ N '67
ELECTRIC signs
Solid-state ring counters and chasers for light displays. A. A. Adem. il Electr World 78:84-5 S '67
ELECTRIC skillets. See Electric apparatus and appliances, Domestic
ELECTRIC soldering iron. See Soldering apparatus
ELECTRIC stoves
Double-oven thirty-inch electric ranges. il Consumer Bul 50:9-15 N '67
Kitchen ranges. il Consumer Rep 32:8-24 D '67
See also
Electronic stoves

Testing
Electric ranges with self-cleaning ovens. il Consumer Rep 32:413-19 Ag '67
ELECTRIC substations
Substations can be good neighbors; Appleton, Wis. W. C. Rasmussen. il Am City 82:142 O '67
ELECTRIC switches
Electronic switching quiz. R. P. Balin. il Pop Electr 27:52+ O '67
Light switch that works late; Edco Escort delayed-action light switch. Consumer Rep 32:521 O '67
Speaker switch for solid-state stereo amplifiers. R. M. Benrey. il Pop Sci 191:91 Ag '67
Switches: a guide to selection & application. A. F. Hackman. il Electr World 78:47-50+ S '67
Switches; symposium. il Electr World 78:37-60 O '67
See also
Electric relays
ELECTRIC thermometers. See Thermometers and thermometry

ELECTRIC toasters
Electric toasters. il Consumer Bul 50:4-8 My '67
Toast to toasters. il Ladies Home J 84:74+ Mr '67
ELECTRIC tools, Portable
Dremel's powerful new Moto-tool; constant-torque permanent-magnet motor. H. Walton. il Pop Sci 191:168-70 O '67
Good three purpose power tool kit. il Consumer Rep 32:533 O '67
Heat gun for home use. P. McCafferty. il Pop Sci 190:158-9 Ja '67
New ideas in tools. C. Conley. il Field & S 72:87 Ja '68
Control
Pedal-operated speed control for power tools. R. M. Benrey. il Pop Sci 190:122-4 F '67
ELECTRIC toys
Build the electric tic tac toe. K. Greenberg. il Pop Electr 26:74-5 Ag '67
Anecdotes, facetiae, satire, etc.
Current happenings. D. Williamson. Sat R 50:8+ D 9 '67
ELECTRIC transformers
Selecting the right constant-voltage transformer. B. C. Biega. il Electr World 78:42-3+ D '67
ELECTRIC transmission
See also
Electric lines
Electric power
ELECTRIC utilities
New England power. W. I. Roberts. il Nation 204:818-21 Je 26 '67
Nuclear plants turn up the juice. il Bsns W p64-6+ Mr 11 '67
Pathfinder for nuclear power; Chairman J. H. Ward of Chicago's Commonwealth Edison co. il Bsns W p76-8 Mr 11 '67
See also
Consolidated Edison company of New York
Pacific gas and electric company
Advertising
Paying for power; propaganda advertising charged to consumers. New Repub 157:6 O 21 '67
Management
Overcharge, by L. Metcalf and V. Reinemer. Review
Sat R 50:32-3+ Ap 1 '67. F. J. Cook
Rates
Con Edison: the arrogance of power; findings of the Arnold H. Hirsch report. A. Prisendorf. il Nation 204:401-4 Mr 27 '67
Overcharge, by L. Metcalf and V. Reinemer. Review
New Repub 156:32+ F 4 '67. P. Millones
Sat R 50:32-3+ Ap 1 '67. F. J. Cook
Science 155:676-8 F 10 '67. L. J. Carter
Paying for power; propaganda advertising charged to consumers. New Repub 157:6 O 21 '67
Regulation
See also
United States—Federal power commission
ELECTRIC vaporizers. See Vaporizers
ELECTRIC vote counters. See Voting machines
ELECTRIC washing machines. See Washing machines
ELECTRIC watches. See Watches, Electric
ELECTRIC waves
See also
Coherer
ELECTRIC welders. See Welders
ELECTRIC welding
Equipment
Build this handy arc-welding gun. P. M. Wilson. il Pop Sci 190:149-51 F '67
ELECTRIC wire and wiring
How the third wire protects you. B. Gladstone. Am Home 70:82+ N '67
New know-how you need for aluminum wiring. G. Daniels. il Pop Sci 191:159-61 S '67
Wire your home for perfect TV and stereo. R. M. Benrey. il Pop Sci 191:162-5+ S '67
See also
Electricity in the home
ELECTRIC workers
See also
Electronic technicians
ELECTRICITY
See also
Atmospheric electricity

ELECTRICITY—*Continued*

Physiological effects
Charging the brain. Sci N 92:466 N 11 '67

Prices
See Electric utilities—Rates
ELECTRICITY, Injuries from
See also
Electric shock
ELECTRICITY, Static
Static electricity: the space age's billion-year-old gremlin. E. A. Lacy. il Electr World 78:21-3+ Jl '67
ELECTRICITY in the home
It's easy to check your wiring. il Changing T 22:19-21 Ja '68
See also
Electric wire and wiring
ELECTRICITY on boats. See Boats—Electric equipment
ELECTRICITY on the farm
Brighten your work. W. J. Fletcher. il Suc Farm 65:100-1 F '67
Select the right standby power system. W. J. Fletcher. il Suc Farm 65:72D Ja '67
ELECTRIFICATION. See Electric charges
ELECTROCHEMICAL cutting
Who will profit from new machining ideas? electrochemical machining patent suit between Anocut engineering co. and Cincinnati milling. il Bsns W p 179-80+ Ap 22 '67
ELECTROCHEMICAL devices. See Fuel cells
ELECTRO-CHEMICAL etchers. See Metal etching—Equipment
ELECTROCHEMICAL timers. See Timing devices
ELECTROCHEMISTRY
Wizard of New Rochelle: S. Ruben, specialist in electrochemistry. il Bsns W p68-70 N 4 '67
See also
Electroorganic chemistry
ELECTROCONVULSIVE shock. See Electric shock
ELECTROCUTION. See Electric shock
ELECTRODEPOSITION of metals. See Electroforming
ELECTRODES
Calcium-selective electrode with liquid ion exchanger. J. W. Ross. bibliog il Science 156:1378-9 Je 9 '67
Gastropod urosalpinx: pH of accessory boring organ while boring. M. R. Carriker and others. bibliog il Science 158:920-2 N 17 '67
ELECTRODES, Glass
Activity coefficients of aqueous potassium chloride measured with a potassium-sensitive glass electrode. P. B. Hostetler and others. bibliog il Science 155:1537-9 Mr 24 '67
ELECTROENCEPHALOGRAPHY
Averaged neural electrical activity and arousal. E. M. Podvoll and S. J. Goodman. bibliog il Science 155:223-5 Ja 13 '67
Brain stem structures responsible for the electroencephalographic patterns of desynchronized sleep. O. Candia and others. bibliog il Science 155:720-2 F 10 '67
ELECTROFORMING
Electroformed nickel motor cases cut cost. il Tech W 20:41 My 8 '67
ELECTROHYDRAULIC effect
Disinfection by electrohydraulic treatment. M. Allen and K. Soike. il Science 156:524-5 Ap 28 '67
ELECTROLUMINESCENCE
Light-emitting semiconductors. F. F. Morehead, jr. il Sci Am 216:108-13+ bibliog (p 168) My '67
USAF, navy test new formation lights. K. J. Stein. il Aviation W 88:72-3+ Ja 15 '68
ELECTROLYTES
Crystal structure of the solid electrolyte, RbAg₄I₅. S. Geller. bibliog il Science 157:310-12 Jl 21 '67
High-conductivity solid electrolytes: MAg₄I₅. B. B. Owens and G. R. Argue. bibliog il Science 157:308-10 Jl 21 '67
Pumping polyelectrolytes is tricky. C. P. Baugher. Am City 82:28 Jl '67
ELECTROMAGNETIC compatibility analysis center. See United States—Air force—Systems command
ELECTROMAGNETIC shielding. See Shielding (electricity)
ELECTROMAGNETIC theory
See also
Maxwell's equations
Unified field theories

ELECTROMYOGRAPHY
Averaged neural electrical activity and arousal. E. M. Podvoll and S. J. Goodman. bibliog il Science 155:223-5 Ja 13 '67
ELECTRON accelerators. See Accelerators (electrons, etc)
ELECTRON beams. See Electrons—Beams
ELECTRON light. See Electrons—Beams
ELECTRON microscope and microscopy
Chenopod and amaranth pollen: electron-microscopic identification. M. Tsukada. bibliog il Science 157:80-2 Jl 7 '67
Close look at heredity; photographs of human chromosomes. Time 90:61 N 24 '67
Electron microscopy: enhancement of specimen contrast by injection of atoms. J. H. Manley. il Science 158:1585-7 D 22 '67
Electron microscopy; report on sixth International congress on electron microscopy. R. M. Fisher. Science 156:673 My 5 '67
Electron's eye view. C. Behrens. il Sci N 92:131-4 Ag 5 '67
Fuzziness of fuzz: letter. J. F. A. McManus. Science 157:490-1 Ag 4 '67
Scanning electron microscope: potentials in the morphology of microorganisms. G. A. Bartlett. bibliog il Science 158:1318-19 D 8 '67
Stereoscan electron microscopy of soil microorganisms. T. R. G. Gray. bibliog il Science 155:1668-70 Mr 31 '67
Tribolium castaneum: morphology of aureate revealed by the scanning electron microscope. A. Sokoloff and others. bibliog il Science 157:443-5 Jl 28 '67
Ultrastructure of gamma M immunoglobulin and alpha macroglobulin: electron-microscopic study. S. E. Svehag and others. bibliog il Science 158:933-6 N 17 '67
ELECTRON optics
See also
Television camera tubes
ELECTRON paramagnetic resonance spectra. See Spectrum analysis
ELECTRON spin resonance. See Magnetic resonance
ELECTRONIC aids. See Electronics in navigation
ELECTRONIC apparatus and appliances
Build an electronic reverb-b-b adapter; electronically generated reverberation. D. Meyer. il Pop Electr 28:41-4 Ja '68
Build the mini-verb. D. Meyer. il Pop Electr 26:41-6 My '67
Build the R-matcher. F. H. Tooker. il Pop Electr 27:84 N '67
Build your own memo minder. R. Persing. il Pop Electr 27:49-51+ O '67
Electronic wonders for better living. M. J. Schultz. il Sci Digest 61:37-47 Je '67
EW lab tested. See issues of Electronics world
Home, sweet electronic home. Read Digest 91:113-15 Ag '67
New avionic products. See occasional issues of Aviation week & space technology
Spots before your eyes; electronic dice. D. Lancaster. il Pop Electr 27:29-34 S '67
Two one-hour projects: flashlight-battery tester; signal-injector probe. M. Lincoln; R. F. Graf. il Pop Mech 128:196-7 O '67
See also
Antennas (electronics)
Automatons
Blind, Apparatus for the
Computers
Deaf, Apparatus for the
Oceanographic instruments
    also Electronic equipment under various subjects, e.g. Automobiles—Electronic equipment

Modular design
It's easy to build electronic projects with pre-wired modules; high-gain amplifier modules. H. M. Benrey. il Pop Sci 191:140-3 O '67

Power supply
Experimenter's professional power supply. D. Lancaster. il Pop Electr 27:71-3+ N '67
Stable, low-cost reference power supplies. C. D. Todd. il Electr World 78:39-41+ D '67
Variable low-voltage power supply. M. S. Rifkin. il Electr World 78:79 O '67

Radiation hazard
Radiation and the technician. J. Frye. Electr World 78:52+ N '67
ELECTRONIC apparatus industry and trade
Value engineering for the electronics industry. F. H. Posser. il Electr World 78:41-4+ Ag '67
See also
Computer industry
    also names of electronic manufacturing companies, e.g. Teledyne, incorporated

ELECTRONIC apparatus industry and trade
—*Continued*

Exhibitions

Consumer electronics show scores with new items. il Hi Fi 17:37 S '67
See also
Western electronics show and convention

France

Fractionalization marks French industry. P. J. Klass. il Aviation W 86:89+ Je 5 '67
France aims for self-sufficient avionics industry. P. J. Klass. il Aviation W 86:130-1+ My 29 '67
G.E.'s $200-million ticket to France. G. H. Wierzynski. il Fortune 75:92-5+ Je 1 '67
More cash for Bull; money from General electric. Time 89:106 Je 9 '67
See also
Computer industry—France

Hong Kong

Hong Kong holds on. il Bsns W p34 My 27 '67

Italy

See also
Olivetti

Japan

Fruit from a bonsai; Nippon electric co. Fortune 76:195 S 15 '67
Still Akihabara, still going strong; Tokyo's electronics row. J. M. Garrott. il Pop Electr 28:40 Ja '68

Russia

NASA says Soviets have closed electronics gap. H. M. David. Tech W 20:16 Je 12 '67

United States

See also
Beckman instruments, incorporated
Litton industries, incorporated

ELECTRONIC circuits

Long-run economy seen in burn-in tests. il Aviation W 86:84-7 Ja 30 '67
Operational amplifier circuit for hi-fi. B. N. Locanthi. il Electr World 77:39-41 Ja '67
Possible impractical impossible circuit; single-diode full-wave rectifier. T. Duffy and J. Oleksy. il Pop Electr 27:35 S '67
SCR protective circuit for hi-fi amplifier; silicon controlled rectifier. il Electr World 77:71 Mr '67
See also
Printed circuits
Radio circuits
Switching systems
Television circuits
Transistor circuits

Integrated circuits

Audio integrated circuits, what's available? D. E. Lancaster. il Electr World 78:34-6 O '67
British push utilization of microcircuits. P. J. Klass. il Aviation W 86:64-7 F 27 '67
Hookup to the future; large-scale integration. il Bsns W p90-4 N 4 '67
Integrated-circuit i.f. amplifier used in new FM receiver. D. R. Von Recklinghausen. il Electr World 77:34-6+ Ap '67
Integrated circuits and the automobile. R. A. Hirschfeld. il Electr World 77:31-3+ F '67
Integrated circuits are here. R. Angus. il Hi Fi 17:47-50 My '67
IC engine tachometer and red line indicator; application of integrated circuits to automotive electronics. R. A. Hirschfeld. il Electr World 77:37-9 My '67
IC's head for industrial market. il Electr World 77:42 My '67
Integrated circuits spotlighted at WESCON. J. Rhea. Aero Tech 21:18 Ag 28 '67
Integrated circuits used in new hi-fi AM/FM receiver. W. Hannah. il Electr World 77:34-5+ Ja '67
Problems cloud timetable of large-array microcircuits. P. J. Klass. il Aviation W 87:72-3+ O 30 '67
RCA, Scott, Sony, Fisher 'n' chips. il Hi Fi 17:36 F '67
Troubleshooting integrated circuits. W. H. Buchsbaum and W. D. Henn. il Electr World 78:34-6+ Jl; 37-40 Ag '67

Testing

Troubleshooting integrated circuits: new test-equipment techniques. W. H. Buchsbaum and W. D. Henn. il Electr World 78:37-40 Ag '67

ELECTRONIC clothes. See Clothing and dress
ELECTRONIC conductors. See Semiconductors

ELECTRONIC control

Build the supertrol; sequence generator. D. Lancaster. il Pop Electr 26:41-4+ Mr '67
ELECTRONIC counters. See Counting machines and devices

ELECTRONIC cooking

How to cook electronically. il Am Home 71:68 Ja '68

ELECTRONIC data processing

Administrator and EDP. S. J. Knezevich. il NEA J 56:18-19 F '67
Army's ADSAF seen worth $100 million-plus to industry; automatic data system within the army in the field. C. D. LaFond. Tech W 20:36-7 Ap 10 '67
Booked for travel, by computer. il Bsns W p 181-2 S 9 '67
Computer's little helpers multiply. il Bsns W p 116-20 Ag 5 '67
Data processing for the bookstore; summary of panel discussion. il Pub W 191:34-5 Je 26 '67
High-volume deed recording made easy; Montgomery County, Pa. J. S. Magill. il Am City 82:90-1 Jl '67
Utilizing the computer; uses for college stores; symposium. Pub W 191:36 My 22 '67
See also
Programming languages (computers)

Libraries

See Libraries—Automation
ELECTRONIC data processing workers. See Computer workers
ELECTRONIC dice. See Dice
ELECTRONIC digital computers. See Computers—Digital computers
ELECTRONIC engine analyzers. See Automobile engines—Testing
ELECTRONIC equipment, Miniature. See Miniature electronic equipment
ELECTRONIC flash bulbs. See Electric lamps, Photoflash
ELECTRONIC flash meters. See Exposure meters
ELECTRONIC herbariums. See Herbariums
ELECTRONIC listening devices. See Electronics in criminal investigation, espionage, etc.

ELECTRONIC measurements

See also
Biotelemetry
ELECTRONIC medical apparatus. See Medical instruments and apparatus
ELECTRONIC monitoring. See Electronics in criminal investigation, espionage, etc.
ELECTRONIC music. See Music, Electronic
ELECTRONIC musical instruments. See Musical instruments, Electronic
ELECTRONIC organ. See Organ

ELECTRONIC ovens

Questions and answers about the electronic oven. il Am Home 71:70 Ja '68
Your next oven electronic? J. Gillies. il Farm J 91:38-9 Jl '67
ELECTRONIC printing machinery. See Printing machinery

ELECTRONIC relays

Magnetic reed switch; low-cost relay. N. P. Jensen and A. W. Burawa. il Pop Electr 27:47-9 S '67
Make your own reed switch-relay. N. P. Jensen and A. W. Burawa. il Pop Electr 27:49-51 S '67

ELECTRONIC research

Effort embraces spectrum from SST to private planes; aviation electronics. il Aero Tech 21:56-7 N 20 '67
ELECTRONIC scales. See Scales (weighing instruments)

ELECTRONIC service shops

Radio & TV news. See issues of Electronics world
See also
Television service shops
ELECTRONIC shutters. See Camera shutters
ELECTRONIC soldering. See Solder and soldering

ELECTRONIC stoves

Ranges that cook in record time; Institute report. il Good H 165:6 Jl '67
ELECTRONIC switches. See Electric switches
ELECTRONIC systems division. See United States—Air force—Systems command

ELECTRONIC technicians
Electronics technician shortage. R. L. Ives. il Pop Electr 27:56-61+ S '67
Occupational outlook for electronics technicians; excerpt from Occupational outlook handbook. Electr World 77:64-6 Je '67

ELECTRONIC test instruments. See Testing instruments

ELECTRONIC thermometers. See Thermometers and thermometry

ELECTRONIC timers. See Timing devices

ELECTRONIC traffic signal control. See Traffic signals—Control

ELECTRONIC typewriters. See Typewriters, Electronic

ELECTRONIC video recording. See Television apparatus

ELECTRONIC voltmeters. See Voltmeters

ELECTRONIC watches. See Watches, Electric

ELECTRONICS
Electronic angle quiz. R. P. Balin. il Pop Electr 27:55+ S '67
Electronic kinks. J. C. Keefe. il Pop Mech 128:181 S '67
Electronic properties of amorphous materials. J. Tauc. bibliog il Science 158:1543-8 D 22 '67
Home, sweet electronic home. Read Digest 91: 113-15 Ag '67
Recent developments in electronics. See issues of Electronics world
   See also
Cathode ray tubes
Cybernetics
Medical electronics
Transistors

Bibliography
Book reviews. See issues of Electronics world
Electronics library. See issues of Popular electronics

Military applications
Army's ADSAF seen worth $100 million-plus to industry; automatic data system within the army in the field. C. D. LaFond. Tech W 20:36-7 Ap 10 '67

Study and teaching
Electronics training for all. W. A. Stocklin. Electr World 78:6 D '67

Terminology
Language of electronics. E. S. Maloney. il Motor B 120:30-3 S '67

Tools
See Tools

ELECTRONICS, Medical. See Medical electronics

ELECTRONICS as a profession
   See also
Electronic technicians

ELECTRONICS in criminal investigation, espionage, etc.
Are you safe from electronic snoopers? excerpt from The intruders. E. V. Long. il Pop Sci 190:144-8+ My '67
Benchmarks. Commonweal 87:429 Ja 12 '68
Bug bomb; curtailment of the use of bugging and wiretapping in investigations by federal agencies. il Time 90:15-16 Jl 14 '67
Bug bomb; restrictions on use of bugging by federal investigators. Newsweek 70:24 Jl 17 '67
Combing out the bugs; new standards for snooping. Newsweek 71:14 Ja 1 '68
Cops, crooks and bugs. Nat R 19:676 Je 27 '67
Eavesdropping legislation: down, but not out? Time 89:45 Je 23 '67
Electronic eavesdropping. R. M. Brown. il Electr World 77:23-8+ Ap '67
Electronic eavesdropping: is ours a bugged society? il Sr Schol 90:10-13 Ap 14 '67
Electronic eavesdropping: plug in or bug out? pro and con discussion. il Sr Schol 91:8-9 bibliog(p24) D 14 '67
Intruders, by E. V. Long. Review
   Sat R il 50:31-2 Ap 1 '67. J. J. Kilpatrick
Laser ears, flying eyes. Newsweek 70:67 S 18 '67
Laying down the law to number-one lawman; trespassory eavesdrops. I. Younger. New Repub 156:11-13 Mr 4 '67
New electronic war on burglars. J. R. Berry. il Pop Mech 128:86-9 D '67
New idea in crime control: electronic techniques studied by Syracuse police-GE team. Am City 82:18+ D '67
Newsbook on privacy; findings of A. Westin. Time 90:102 S 29 '67

Right to be left alone; reasonable and balanced view on eavesdropping. America 118: 3 Ja 6 '68
Right to privacy; act suspended by opposition of prosecutors and policemen. New Repub 157:4 Ag 5 '67
Supreme court ruling that may help police. U S News 64:7 Ja 1 '68
'Tis the season to be shoplifting. il Bsns W p20+ D 23 '67
Unconstitutional bugging; Fourth amendment is applicable. New Repub 158:11 Ja 6 '68
Unplugging bugging; Supreme court's new guidelines for permissible bugging. Time 90: 43 D 29 '67
Ways to control snooping; Alan Westin's proposal. Life 62:4 Ap 21 '67
What you can do about those obscene telephone calls. W. B. Furlong. il Good H 165: 82-3+ S '67
Wiretapping and eavesdropping: pros and cons. H. Schwartz. bibliog f Cur Hist 53:31-7 Jl '67
   See also
Wire tapping

ELECTRONICS in meteorology
Sea Robin tests resumed; mooring problems stressed. il Aero Tech 21:25-6 Jl 17 '67

ELECTRONICS in navigation
Decade of marine electronics. A. N. Garden. il Yachting 121:80-2+ Ja '67
Electronic navigation. J. West. See issues of Yachting
First electronic navigation contest for the new Motor boating trophy. il Motor B 119: 40-3+ Je '67
   See also
Decca navigation

ELECTRONICS in photography. See Photography, Electronic

ELECTRONICS in surveying
Computers cut topographic survey costs. C. D. LaFond. il Tech W 20:20-1 F 20 '67

ELECTRONICS research center. See United States—National aeronautics and space administration—Electronics research center

ELECTRONS
g Factor of the electron. H. R. Crane. il Sci Am 218:72-4+ bibliog(p 150) Ja '68
Nature of metals. A. H. Cottrell. il Sci Am 217:90-100 S '67
Pi electron systems at high pressure. H. G. Drickamer. bibliog il Science 156:1183-9 Je 2 '67
Solvated electron. J. L. Dye. il Sci Am 216: 76-83 F '67
2-Dicyanomethylene-1,3-indanedione: a new electron acceptor. S. Chatterjee. bibliog il Science 157:314-16 Jl 21 '67
Stabilization of hydrated electrons in irradiated frozen sugar solutions. W. R. Elliott. bibliog il Science 157:558-9 Ag 4 '67
   See also
Atoms
Plasma (ionized gases)

Beams
Electron beams: National bureau of standards and the new technology. H. W. Koch. bibliog il Science 156:321-8 Ap 21 '67

ELECTRO-OPTICAL systems, incorporated
EOS eyes new markets as Xerox unit. J. F. Judge. Tech W 20:36 My 8 '67
New EOS vacuum chamber tests complete ion engines. il Tech W 20:33 My 29 '67

ELECTROORGANIC chemistry
Electric chemical plants. Sci Am 216:50+ Ap '67

ELECTROPHORESIS
Artifact produced in disc electrophoresis by ammonium persulfate. J. M. Brewer. bibliog il Science 156:256 Ap 14 '67
Electrophoretic heterogeneity of mammalian galactose dehydrogenase. P. Cuatrecasas and S. Segal; discussion. bibliog il Science 156:1516-18 Je 16 '67
Electrophoretic variants of α-glycerophosphate dehydrogenase in drosophila melanogaster. E. H. Grell. bibliog il Science 158: 1319-20 D 8 '67
Glyceraldehyde-3-phosphate dehydrogenase variants in phyletically diverse organisms. H. G. Lebherz and W. J. Rutter. bibliog il Science 157:1198-200 S 8 '67
Steroid-sensitive single neurons in rat hypothalamus and midbrain: identification by microelectrophoresis. K. Ruf and F. A. Steiner. bibliog il Science 156:667-9 My 5 '67

ELECTROPHYSIOLOGY

Acetylcholine receptor: similarity in axons and junctions. P. Rosenberg and H. G. Mautner. bibliog il Science 155:1569-71 Mr 24 '67

Action potentials without contraction in frog skeletal muscle fibers with disrupted transverse tubules. P. W. Gage and R. S. Eisenberg. bibliog il Science 158:1702-3 D 29 '67

Basilar membrane vibration examined with the Mössbauer technique. B. M. Johnstone and A. J. F. Boyle. bibliog il Science 158:389-90 O 20 '67

Behavioral acts elicited by stimulation of single, identifiable brain cells. A. O. D. Willows. bibliog il Science 157:570-4 Ag 4 '67

Bioelectric phenomena related to protein-fixed charge in a crab nerve fiber. E. M. Lieberman and others. bibliog il Science 156:240-2 Ap 14 '67

Crayfish muscle fiber: ionic requirements for depolarizing synaptic electrogenesis. M. Ozeki and H. Grundfest. bibliog il Science 155:478-81 Ja 27 '67

Direct synaptic connection mediating both excitation and inhibition. H. Wachtel and E. R. Kandel. bibliog il Science 158:1206-8 D 1 '67

Electrical phenomena associated with the activity of the membrane-bound acetylcholinesterase. T. Podleski and J. P. Changeux. bibliog il Science 157:1579-81 S 29 '67

Electrical recordings from meningioma cells during cytolytic action of antibody and complement. A. Prieto and others. bibliog il Science 157:1185-7 S 8 '67

Fast potential spike of frog skin generated at the outer surface of the epithelium. B. Lindemann and U. Thorns. bibliog il Science 158:1473-7 D 15 '67

Frog cerebellum: absence of long-term inhibition upon Purkinje cells. R. Llinás and J. R. Bloedel. bibliog il Science 155:601-3 F 3 '67

Frog skeletal muscle fibers: changes in electrical properties after disruption of transverse tubular system. R. S. Eisenberg and P. W. Gage. bibliog il Science 158:1700-1 D 29 '67

Inferior olive of the cat: intracellular recording. W. E. Crill and T. T. Kennedy. bibliog il Science 157:716-18 Ag 11 '67

Intracellular olfactory response of hippocampal neurons in awake, sitting squirrel monkeys. T. Yokota and others. bibliog il Science 157:1072-4 S 1 '67

Magnetic fields around the torso: production by electrical activity of the human heart. D. Cohen. bibliog il Science 156:652-4 My 5 '67

Molecular and thermal origins of fast photoelectric effects in the squid retina. W. A. Hagins and R. E. McGaughy. bibliog il Science 157:813-16 Ag 18 '67

Multiple temperature-sensitive spots innervated by single nerve fibers. D. R. Kenshalo and E. S. Gallegos. bibliog il Science 158:1064-5 N 24 '67

Neural basis of the sense of flutter-vibration V. B. Mountcastle and others. bibliog Science 155:597-600 F 3 '67

Olfactory input to the hypothalamus: electrophysiological evidence. J. W. Scott and C. Pfaffmann. bibliog il Science 158:1592-4 D 22 '67

Origin of synaptic noise. J. I Hubbard and others. bibliog il Science 157:330-1 Jl 21 '67

Photoelectric potential from photoreceptor cells in ventral eye of limulus. J. E. Brown and others. bibliog il Science 158:665 N 3 '67

Plasma membrane: substructural changes correlated with electrical resistance and pinocytosis. P. W. Brandt and A. R. Freeman bibliog il Science 155:582-5 F 3 '67

Resistance shifts accompanying the evoked cortical response in the cat. K. A. Klivington and R. Galambos. bibliog il Science 157:211-13 Jl 14 '67

Seizure discharges evoked in vitro in thin section from guinea pig hippocampus. C. Yamamoto and N. Kawai. bibliog il Science 155:341-2 Ja 20 '67

Somatosensory thalamic neurons: effects of cortical depression. H. J. Waller and S. M. Feldman. bibliog il Science 157:1074-7 S 1 '67

Synaptic noise as a source of variability in the interval between action potentials W. H. Calvin and C. F. Stevens. bibliog il Science 155:842-4 F 17 '67

Tetrodotoxin derivatives: chemical structure and blockage of nerve membrane conductance. T. Narahashi and others. bibliog il Science 156:976-9 My 19 '67

Transepithelial potentials in hydra. R. K. Josephson and M. Macklin. bibliog il Science 156:1629-31 Je 23 '67

ELECTROPLATING
See also
Electroforming

ELECTROSTIMULATION of the brain. See Electrophysiology

ELEFTHERIOU, Basil E. and Boehlke, K. W. Brain monoamine oxidase in mice after exposure to aggression and defeat. bibliog Science 155:1693-4 Mr 31 '67

ELEGANT, Robert S.
China's next phase. For Affairs 46:137-50 O '67
Maoists make a tactical retreat. Reporter 36:32-5 Mr 23 '67
—and Liu, S. C.
Red China's divided army. Reporter 37:13-16 Ag 10 '67

ELEGY; ballet. See Ballets—Criticisms

ELEMENTARY and secondary education act of 1965. See Federal aid to education

ELEMENTARY education. See Education, Elementary

ELEMENTARY school children. See School children

ELEMENTARY school libraries. See School libraries

ELEMENTARY school teachers. See Teachers

ELEMENTS, Chemical. See Chemical elements

ELEO Pomare dance company. See Dance companies

ELEONORA Duse; drama. See Fratti, M.

ELEPHANT birds. See Birds, Extinct

ELEPHANT hunting
Old Shuguli. A. Landreth. il Outdoor Life 139:48-51+ F '67

ELEPHANT seals
By sea, to see the elephants; cruise among the islands off the California coast. S. Murray. il Yachting 122:52-5+ Jl; 46-7+ Ag '67

ELEPHANTS
Elephant work in South India; employment of elephas maximus. W. G. Dyer. il Natur Hist 76:38-43 My '67
Elephants on a binge. il Time 90:29 Jl 28 '67
Elephants seldom forget. E. M. Borgese. il Holiday 41:30+ F '67
Elephants to the rescue; Special forces use elephants hired from Montagnards. R. West. il N Y Times Mag p85-7 Je 11 '67
I go back to an elephant nursery. S. Alexander. Life 62:31 Ap 7 '67

Anecdotes, facetiae, satire, etc.

Dear elephant, sir. R. Gary. il Life 63:126-39 D 22 '67
How to dismount from an elephant. R. L. Thomas. il Harper 234:102-3 My '67

ELEPHANTS, Fossil
Elephants under the sea. il Sci Digest 61:15-16 Ap '67

ELEVATORS
Faster, faster. New Yorker 43:50-1 N 4 '67

ELFANT, R. F.
INTERMAG. Science 157:1080 S 1 '67

ELFENBEIN, Josef A.
Ten-penny tragedy; drama. Plays 26:27-36 My '67

ELGAR, Sir Edward William, 1st bart
Elgar's Cello concerto. J. Diether. Am Rec G 33:550-51 Mr '67
Records:
Dream of Gerontius. Opera N 31:34 Ja 7 '67

EL GRECO. See Greco

ELIAS, Hans
Stereology. Science 156:1137+ My 26 '67

ELIASBERG, Ann Pringle
Parent and child (cont) N Y Times Mag p74+ F 19; 109+ D 10 '67

ELIOT, George Fielding
Men in battle. Nat R 19:752-3 Jl 11 '67
Pitfalls of command. Nat R 19:1024-5+ S 19 '67
Robert McNamara and the process of military decision. Nat R 19:189+ F 21 '67
Testing time. Nat R 19:256-7 Mr 7 '67

ELIOT, Thomas Stearns
T. S. Eliot, ed. by A. Tate. Review
Nat R por 19:147+ F 7 '67. H. Kenner
New Repub 156:19-25 My 20 '67. R. Poirier
T. S. Eliot's London. S. Spender. il por Sat R 50:58-9+ Mr 11 '67

ELIUTIN, Viacheslav Petrovich
From illiteracy to astronautics. UNESCO Courier 20:11-14 N '67

ELM

Diseases and pests

Dutch elm disease and you. G. E. Hafstad. il Am For 73:26-7+ Je '67
Dutch elm disease roundup. H. S. McNabb, jr. il Bet Hom & Gard 45:38+ My '67
Elms for the future. J. Ludwigson. il Sci N 92:256-7 S 9 '67
Making elms compatible. il Time 90:91 O 6 '67

Hybrids

Elms for the future. J. Ludwigson. il Sci N 92:256-7 S 9 '67

ELMAN, Richard M.
Hell's Angels. New Repub 156:30-2+ F 25 '67

EL MONTE, Calif.
Semi-pedestrian mall. il Am City 82:102 Ag '67

EL MOROCCO. See Night clubs

ELON, Amos
Letter from the Sinai front. Commentary 44:60-8 Ag '67

ELPERS, Jerry E.
Time-delay relays. por Electr World 77:37 40 Ap '67

ELROD, Carol
In living color. Christan Cent 84:375-6 Mr 22 '67

ELROY-Sparta trail. See Trails

ELSHEIMER, Adam
Man with influence. il Time 89:72 Ja 27 '67

ELSON, Edward
Atlanta bookseller is star in USIA film for overseas. il por Pub W 192:42 N 6 '67

ELSTON, Gerhard A.
Vietnam: some basic considerations. Cath World 205:78-82 My '67

ELVSTRÖM, Paul
Master touch; ed. by K. Krüger. il por Yachting 121:66-8+ Mr '67
Paul Elvström on dinghy techniques. Yachting 122:24-5+ O; 24-5+ N '67

ELWART, Joan Potter
Choosing the best in children's books. Parents Mag 42:60+ Ap '67

ELY, Nev.
Ghost town? not Ely! ed. by P. D. Elmon. il Am City 82:144+ F '67

ELYSÉE palace. See Paris—Elysée palace

ELYUTIN, Viacheslav. See Elfútin, V. P.

EMANCIPATION of women. See Woman—Equal rights

EMANS, Elaine V.
Everyday Thanksgiving; poem. Farm J 91:44 N '67
Girl graduate; poem. Good H 164:181 Je '67
Heritage; poem. Farm J 91:113 Mr '67

EMBARGO
France's Mid-East arms ban hits Sud and Dassault hardest. Aviation W 87:19 D 18 '67

EMBASSIES (buildings)
Art in striped pants; art for embassies. il Newsweek 70:107-8 O 9 '67
Balkan way; bombing of Yugoslav embassies and consulates. il Newsweek 69:39 F 13 '67
Barnes' Tabriz consulate: a sophisticated statement of ribbon arches and domes. il Arch Rec 142:93-100 Ag '67
Enclave theory? acute housing shortage in Washington. il Newsweek 69:44 Je 26 '67

EMBASSY pictures corporation
Profiles; J. Levine. C. Tomkins. New Yorker 43:55-6+ S 16 '67

EMBELLISHMENT (vocal music)
Singing voice: light and soaring. R. Rushmore. il Opera N 31:28-30 F 4 '67
Singing voice: lower and darker. R. Rushmore. il Opera N 31:24-6 F 18 '67

EMBLEN, D. L.
Fear of God and fear of man; poem. Christian Cent 84:207 F 15 '67

EMBROIDERY
Big bold stitches. il House & Gard 131:148-9 My '67
Burlap bags and boys. Sister Marie Clarence. il Sch Arts 67:36-7 D '67
Contemporary machine embroidery. E. Sturgeon. il Sch Arts 66:23-7 Ap '67
Ever hear of couching? M. Garrity. il Bet Hom & Gard 45:84+ Jl '67
Stitch in time for Christmas! M. Garrity. il Bet Hom & Gard 45:90 O '67
Stitchery for the young child. E. Madsen. il Sch Arts 67:12-13 D '67
Table embroidered is a table remembered. il House B 109:280-1 N '67
See also
Samplers

Exhibitions

Stitching; embroidery past to present at the Museum of contemporary crafts, N.Y. A. Adams. il Craft Horiz 27:26-31 S '67

EMBRYOLOGY
Marcello Malpighi and the evolution of embryology, by H. B. Adelmann. Review Sci Am 216:135-6+ Ap '67. M. H. Braverman; Reply. W. Montagna. 217:6-7 Jl '67
See also
Placenta

Birds

Cell aggregation: its enhancement by a supernatant from cultures of homologous cells. J. E. Lilien and A. A. Moscona. bibliog il Science 157:70-2 Jl 7 '67
Competent chick ectoderm: nonspecific response to RNA. H. Hillman and R. Hillman. bibliog il Science 155:1563-5 Mr 24 '67
Embryonic morphogenesis: role of fibrous lattice in the development of feathers and feather patterns. E. S. Stuart and A. A. Moscona. bibliog il Science 157:947-8 Ag 25 '67
Enzyme induction by corticosteroids in embryonic cells: steroid structure and inductive effect. A. A. Moscona and R. Piddington. bibliog il Science 158:496-7 O 27 '67
Primordial germ cells in blood smears from chick embryos. R. P. Singh and D. B. Meyer. bibliog il Science 156:1503-4 Je 16 '67

Echinoderms

Cell division: direct measurement of maximum tension exerted by furrow of echinoderm eggs. R. Rappaport. bibliog il Science 156:1241-3 Je 2 '67
Malic dehydrogenase isozymes: distribution in developing nucleate and anucleate halves of sea urchin eggs. G. W. Patton, jr. and others. bibliog il Science 156:400-1 Ap 21 '67

Insects

RNA and DNA synthesis in developing eggs of the milkweed bug, oncopeltus fasciatus (Dallas) S. E. Harris and H. S. Forrest. bibliog il Science 156:1613-15 Je 23 '67

Mammals

Benzpyrene hydroxylase induction by polycyclic hydrocarbons in hamster embryonic cells grown in vitro. L. J. Alfred and H. V. Gelboin. bibliog il Science 157:75-6 Jl 7 '67
Development of mouse ova in explanted oviducts: fertilization, cultivation, and transplantation. A. Pavlok. bibliog il Science 157:1457-8 S 22 '67
Embryonic enzyme patterns: characterization of the single lactate dehydrogenase isozyme in preimplanted mouse ova. J. Rapola and O. Koskimies. bibliog il Science 157:1311-12 S 15 '67
Intrinsic immunological tolerance in allophenic mice. B. Mintz and W. K. Silvers. bibliog il Science 158:1484-7 D 15 '67
Lysosomal enzyme inhibition by trypan blue: a theory of teratogenesis. F. Beck and others. bibliog il Science 157:1180-2 S 8 '67
Mammalian X-chromosomes: change in patterns of DNA replication during embryogenesis. R. N. Hill and J. J. Yunis. bibliog il Science 155:1120-1 Mr 3 '67

Mollusks

Protein-synthesizing activity of the anucleate polar lobe of the mud snail ilyanassa obsoleta. A. C. Clement and A. Tyler. bibliog il Science 158:1457-8 D 15 '67

Reptiles

Motility of the turtle embryo, chelydra serpentina linne. J. D. Decker. bibliog il Science 157:952-4 Ag 25 '67

EMBRYONIC tissues
Epithelial-mesenchymal interactions; report on eighteenth Hahnemann symposium. R. Fleischmajer. Science 157:1472+ S 22 '67

EMEL'ÍANOV, Vasilii Semenovich
Atoms for peace: Russian declines award. il por Science 158:360 O 20 '67

EMERGENCIES. See First aid in illness and injury

EMERGENCY communication systems
See also
Radio communication—Emergency applications

EMERGENCY landing, Airplanes. See Airplanes—Landing

EMERGENCY planning, Office of. See United States—Emergency planning. Office of

EMERGENCY powers. See Presidents—United States—Powers and duties

EMERGENCY services, Hospital. See Hospitals—Emergency services

EMERGENCY sessions of the United Nations. See United Nations—General assembly—Emergency sessions

EMERGENCY trucks. See Motor trucks, Municipal

EMERSON, William L.
Jewel for Palos Verdes. Library J 92:4379-80 D 1 '67

EMERSON Foote, incorporated. See Foote, Emerson, Incorporated

EMERY, K. O. and Garrison, L. E.
Sea levels 7,000 to 20,000 years ago. bibliog Science 157:684-7 Ag 11 '67

—and Iselin, C. O'D.
Human food from ocean and land. bibliog Science 157:1279-81 S 15 '67

—and others
Freshwater peat on the continental shelf. bibliog Science 158:1301-7 D 8 '67

EMETT, Rowland
Tower of London; cartoons. Horizon 10:73-81 Wint '68

about

Man from Far Tottering. O. Jensen. il Horizon 10:2-3 Wint '68

EMILIANI, Cesare
Isotopic paleotemperatures. bibliog Science 154:851-7; 156:410; 157:723-5 N 18 '66, Ap 21, Ag 11 '67

EMINENT domain
Second battle of Antietam; opposition to line towers of Potomac Edison company. Life 62:4 Je 23 '67
TVA: the halo slips; Land between the lakes dispute. J. Egerton. il Nation 205:11-15 Jl 3 '67

EMINENT men. See Great men

EMITTER dipper oscillators. See Oscillators

EMLEN, Alan L.
Excerpt from testimony, March 10, 1966. Cong Digest 46:61+ F '67

EMMET, Christopher
Did Moscow lose the Mideast war? Nat R 19:677 Je 27 '67
Russia's role in Vietnam. America 117:112-13 Jl 29 '67

EMMETT, J. A.
Boating. See issues of Outdoor life

EMMETT, Jim
Boats we meet: Bonita II. Yachting 121:56-7+ F '67
Handy Andy. Motor B 120:36-7 D '67
Upkeep of teak. Yachting 121:69+ Ap '67

EMMY awards. See Academy of television arts and sciences

EMORY, George
How to choose the right boat caulk. Pop Mech 127:164-7+ My '67
How to glass a boat. Pop Mech 128:129-33+ D '67
How to handle a boating emergency. Pop Mech 128:61-5 Jl '67

EMORY business school. See Emory university, Atlanta, Ga.—School of business administration

EMORY university, Atlanta, Ga.
Wonderful Wednesday; midweek free day. il Time 89:76 Ap 14 '67

School of business administration

Profits set score at B-School tournament; Emory university's annual Intercollegiate business game. il Bsns W p 156-8 Mr 18 '67

EMOTIONAL maturity. See Maturity

EMOTIONALLY disturbed children. See Mentally ill children

EMOTIONS
Biogenic amines and emotion. J. J. Schildkraut and S. S. Kety. bibliog il Science 156:21-30 Ap 7 '67
Do animals feel emotion? Sci N 92:533-4 D 2 '67
Don't be afraid of your feelings. J. K. Lagemann. Read Digest 91:137-40 Jl '67
How to handle a crisis. D. A. Sugarman and R. Hochstein. Seventeen 26:150-1+ S '67
See also
Anger
Fear
Frustration
Love
Mind and body
Photography of emotions
Security and insecurity (psychology)
Sorrow
Tempe

EMPEROR and the nightingale; drama. See Leech, M. T.

EMPHYSEMA
Battle for breath. J. L. Whatley. il Todays Health 45:42-3+ F '67

EMPIRE. See Imperialism

EMPIRE of things; story. See Mountzoures, H. L.

EMPLOYEE absenteeism. See Absenteeism

EMPLOYEE incentives. See Incentives in industry

EMPLOYEE morale
See also
Industrial relations

EMPLOYEE recreation. See Industrial recreation

EMPLOYEE rules. See Labor discipline

EMPLOYEE seniority. See Seniority, Employee

EMPLOYEE thefts. See Stealing

EMPLOYEES
See also
Job satisfaction
Personnel management
Suggestion systems
also subhead Employees under various subjects, e.g. Insurance companies—Employees

Dismissal

NLRB orders Stevens to rehire eighteen workers. Bsns W p 170 S 9 '67
See also
Labor discipline

Promotion

Blueprint to build executives. G. E. Keck. Duns R 90:45-6+ N '67
Discriminatory promotion systems. P. B. Doeringer. Mo Labor R 90:27-8 Mr '67
Hiring and promotion policies under FEP legislation; excerpt from Patterns of discrimination in employment. Mo Labor R 90:53-6 F '67

Qualifications

Changing the pecking order: a credential society; address, October 24, 1967. H. Howe. 2d. Vital Speeches 34:70-3 N 15 '67

Rating

Who really are your best employees? C. R. Grindle. il Nations Bsns 55:106-8+ My '67

Selection
See Employment systems

Training

Are they really learning the ropes? S. C. Brandt. il Nations Bsns 55:75-7 Ag '67
Bars to apprenticeship; Marshall-Briggs study on Negro participation in apprenticeship programs. America 117:538-9 N 11 '67
Dose of boot camp; three days military training feature of personnel-training in Japan. il Time 89:106 Je 9 '67
He helps the poor help themselves; interview. L. H. Sullivan. il Nations Bsns 55:42-4+ Jl '67
Labor standards and job training in foreign countries. H. Hilaski. Mo Labor R 90:36-41 S '67
Learn, baby, learn; job training programs for Watts Negroes. il Newsweek 69:79 Ap 10 '67
Manpower planning; address, May 9, 1967. F. H. Cassell. Vital Speeches 33:559-65 Jl 1 '67
Means of adjustment to technological displacement. J. A. Pichler. Mo Labor R 90:32-3 Mr '67
Migrant workers to be trained for aircraft production jobs. Aviation W 87:127-8 Ag 14 '67
Sewing machines & union machines; ILGWU and ACWA opposition to federal training in clothing trades. H. Hill. il Nation 205:18-19 Jl 3 '67
See also
Apprentices

EMPLOYEES, Transfer of
Adjustment to plant closure; excerpt from report to the Automation fund committee. J. L. Stern. Mo Labor R 90:42-6 Ja '67

EMPLOYEES as stockholders
See also
Profit sharing

EMPLOYEES magazines, handbooks, etc.
See also
House organs

EMPLOYER-employee relations. See Industrial relations; Personnel management

EMPLOYMENT

Employment and the new economics. L. H. Keyserling. il Ann Am Acad 373:102-19 S '67

Outlook for jobs. Fortune 75:40+ F '67

Why jobs stay plentiful in a business slowdown. il U S News 62:32-3 Ap 3 '67

See also

Self employed

Unemployables

Unemployment

also subhead Employment under various subjects, e.g. Youth—Employment

Government guaranty

Work and human worth. T. L. Smith. Christian Cent 84:1094-7 Ag 30 '67

Statistics

Adult men not in the labor force; special labor force report. S. S. Holland. il Mo Labor R 90:5-15 Mr '67

Buyers' market; U.S. employment in April. il Time 89:116 My 19 '67

Changes in occupational employment over the past decade. P. M. Ryscavage. il Mo Labor R 90:27-30 Ag '67

Factors affecting changes in industry employment. R. E. Kutscher and E. E. Jacobs. bibliog f Mo Labor R 90:6-12 Ap '67

Labor force and employment; tables. See issues of Monthly labor review

Reasons for nonparticipation in the labor force. R. L. Stein. il Mo Labor R 90:22-7 Jl '67

See also

Unemployment—Statistics

EMPLOYMENT, Agricultural. See Farm labor

EMPLOYMENT, Supplementary. See Supplementary employment

EMPLOYMENT agencies

Fidelity from the frat; ex-cons only. il Time 90:82-3 S 22 '67

He finds major minority talent; U. Haynes, jr, founds Management resources corp. il Bsns W p68+ O 7 '67

Making of the presidents; Boyden associates, inc. il Time 90:94+ O 13 '67

Temporaries win permanent role; companies providing temporary help. il Bsns W p64-6 D 23 '67

Tough questions for recruiters; is an employment counselor an employment agency? Bsns W p42 D 23 '67

See also

United States—Employment service

EMPLOYMENT discrimination. See Discrimination in employment

EMPLOYMENT systems

Bidding for brains; competitive college-recruiting by business. il Time 90:82 Jl 14 '67

Business isn't really selling them. J. St John. Nations Bsns 55:83 Ag '67

Computers aid employe hunt. il Ebony 22:92 Je '67

Courting the class of '67. il Newsweek 69:79-80 Ap 17 '67

Fast footwork in an industry talent hunt; National semiconductor corp.'s acquisition of top executive talent from rival Fairchild semiconductor. il Bsns W p 132+ Mr 11 '67

How retailers woo bright young talent. il Bsns W p 116-18 O 7 '67

Job show; Chicago television program offers help to unemployed. Newsweek 70:57 Jl 31 '67

Making of a corporation president. A. Hacker. il N Y Times Mag p26-7+ Ap 2 '67

Most frenzied year in history; rush by business to sign up graduates. il Bsns W p54-6+ Ap 8 '67

NEA's computer system; matching job applicants and teacher vacancies. Sch & Soc 95:284+ Sum '67

Preparation for Dow day; views presented at San Francisco state college. J. L. Shover. Nation 205:648-51 D 18 '67

Temporaries win permanent role; companies providing temporary help. il Bsns W p64-6 D 23 '67

Trends in employer manpower policies. E. R. Livernash. Mo Labor R 90:28-9 F '67

Youth gets the truth; informing students about private enterprise. il Nations Bsns 55:40-1+ Mr '67

See also

Bonus system

Discrimination in employment

Employment agencies

Guaranty of employment

See also

Employment—Government guaranty

ENAMEL and enameling

Enamel on clay. O. Johnson. il Sch Arts 67:32-5 N '67

Enamels on porcelain; Chinese ceramics. G. Kaler. il Hobbies 72:52-3+ Ja '68

Firing glass enamels on aluminum. E. Winter. il Design 68:12-16 Mr '67

Making a copper enamel bowl. E. Winter. il Design 69:23-8 Fall '67

Plique a jour enamel. G. Kaler. il Hobbies 72:52-3+ D '67

Sparkle in the storerooms; collection of renaissance enamels owned by the Walters art gallery in Baltimore. il Time 90:84-5 D 15 '67

ENAMEL and enameling (paints, etc) See Paint

ENAMELS. See Enamel and enameling

ENARSON, Harold L.

Education and the wealth of nations. Mo Labor R 90:21-4 Mr '67

ENCAUSTIC painting

Hot crayon fantasies. E. E. Welch. il Design 68:30-2 Mr '67

ENCEPHALITIS

Angiostrongylus cantonensis; proof of direct transmisssion with its epidemiological implications. D. Heyneman and B. L. Lim. bibliog il Science 158:1057-8 N 24 '67

Tragedy that wouldn't end. A. Levy. il Good H 165:42+ Jl '67

ENCEPHALITIS virus

Virus of the California encephalitis complex; isolation from culiseta inornata. O. Morgante and J. A. Shemanchuk. bibliog il Science 157:692-3 Ag 11 '67

ENCEPHALOMYELITIS

Experimental allergic encephalomyelitis in agammaglobulinemic chickens. M. E. Blaw and others. bibliog il Science 158:1198-200 D 1 '67

ENCEPHALOPATHY. See Brain—Diseases

ENCHANTED bicycle; drama. See Carroll, J.

ENCLOSURES, Loudspeaker. See Loud speaking apparatus—Cabinets

ENCOUNTER (periodical)

Books; C.I.A. cultural penetration. M. Muggeridge. Esquire 68:12+ S '67

Cultural cold war; excerpt from Towards a new past. C. Lasch. Nation 205:200-12 S 11 '67; Discussion. 205:309, 340-1 O 2-9 '67

Insufficiency of frankness; CIA subsidies. Nation 204:678 My 29 '67; Reply. S. Spender. 204:802+ Je 26 '67

Literary Bay of Pigs; CIA subsidies. A. Werth. Nation 204:710-11 Je 5 '67; Reply. S. Spender. 204:802+ Je 26 '67

ENCOURAGEMENT

This Oscar (sob) really belongs to all those who... L. Conger. Writer 80:9-10 Ag '67

ENCYCLICALS

Appeals to reason; Pope's agenda for a new humanism. New Repub 156:7-8 Ap 8 '67

Are we our brothers' keepers? Sat Eve Post 240:106 My 6 '67

Bachelor psychosis; concerning Pope Paul's Sacerdotalis celibatus. Commonweal 86:436-7 Jl 14 '67

Birth control; the Pope's latest views; excerpts from encyclical. Paul VI. U S News 62:12 Ap 10 '67

Confusion over Latin; translation of On the development of peoples. America 116:747-8 My 20 '67

Development, new name for peace; excerpt from On the development of peoples, with reply by R. Maheu. Paul VI. UNESCO Courier 20:28-39 Ag '67

Disappointing Marian development; Christi Matri Rosarii (Rosaries to the Mother of Christ) Paul VI's fourth encyclical. S. Benko; reply. L. J. White. Christian Cent 84:289 Mr 1 '67

Encyclical on priestly celibacy. America 117:29 Jl 8 '67

In defense of celibacy. il Newsweek 70:72-3 Jl 3 '67

Language of encyclicals. America 116:577-8 Ap 22 '67

On church and state. M. Ascoli. Reporter 36:18 Ap 20 '67

Papal economics. M. Friedman. Newsweek 69:87 Ap 24 '67

Papal gaucherie; Populorum progressio. Nat R 19:391-3 Ap 18 '67

Paul VI's secular ecumenism. R. M. Brown. Commonweal 86:262-4 My 19 '67

Pope and the missing businessman; concerning Pope Paul's Populorum progressio. Fortune 75:115-16 My '67

ENCYCLICALS—*Continued*
Pope Paul speaks for the have-nots; On the development of peoples. M. McGrory. America 116:552 Ap 15 '67
Pope Paul's strictures on capitalism; concerning On the development of peoples. B. L. Masse. America 116:579 Ap 22 '67
Pope's plea for poor nations; response to Populorum progressio. B. L. Masse. America 117:129-32 Ag 5 '67
Populorum progressio; fifth encyclical of Pope Paul. il Time 89:70 Ap 7 '67
Populorum progressio; Pope Paul VI's fifth encyclical On the development of peoples. Christian Cent 84:460 Ap 12 '67
Populorum progressio; Pope Paul's fifth encyclical. America 116:516 Ap 8 '67
Toward building a better world; concerning On the development of peoples. America 116:773 My 27 '67
We must make haste; Pontiff's Populorum progressio message. il Newsweek 69:84 Ap 10 '67
World is sick; concerning Pope Paul's Populorum progressio. Commonweal 86:107-8 Ap 14 '67

ENCYCLOPAEDIA Britannica
Replica edition launches Britannica's 200th year. Pub W 192-32+ N 20 '67

ENCYCLOPAEDIA Britannica educational corporation
World in Geographic filmstrips. M. M. Payne. il Nat Geog Mag 133:134-7 Ja '68

ENCYCLOPAEDIA Britannica films, incorporated
Discovery: a study in audiovisual saturation; school libraries. L. Salinger. il Library J 92:849-52 F 15 '67

ENCYCLOPAEDIA Britannica, incorporated
Britannica acquires share in Calif. technical firm. il Pub W 191:34 Ap 3 '67

ENCYCLOPAEDIA Britannica school library awards
Ten school finalists in Britannica competition. Pub W 191:123 F 20 '67

ENCYCLOPEDIAS
Bowker lecture: subscription books; address, May 18, 1967. E. J. McCabe. Pub W 191: 36-40 My 29 '67
Every home should have one. E. Pearson. Farm J 91:A9 My '67
In pursuit of truth; Great Soviet encyclopedia. Newsweek 69:54+ Ap 10 '67
Jewish knowledge. E. Isaac. Commentary 43: 99-101 Ap '67
Life with an encyclopedist; summary of addresses. W. H. Nault; F. Anderson. il Pub W 191:86-7 Je 12 '67
    See also
Chamber's encyclopaedia
New book of knowledge
New Catholic encyclopedia

END of innocence; story. See Head, A.
END of the world story. See Gallant, M.
END tables. See Tables
ENDEMIC goiter. See Goiter
ENDIVE
Do you know the Belgian endive? il Bet Hom & Gard 45:88 F '67
    See also
Cookery—Vegetables
ENDOCARDITIS
Adenovirus endocarditis in mice. Z. R. Blailock and others. bibliog il Science 157: 69-70 Jl 7 '67
ENDOCRINE glands. See Glands, Ductless
ENDOCRINOLOGY
Endocrine-induced regression of cancers; address, December 13, 1966. C. Huggins. bibliog il Science 156:1050-4 My 26 '67
Ribonucleic acid: control of steroid synthesis in endocrine tissue. D. B. Villee. bibliog il Science 158:652-3 N 3 '67
    See also
Neuroendocrinology
ENDOD
Soap and a snail killer; berries of the endod plant used in Ethiopia as soap. Sci N 91:317 Ap 1 '67
ENDOGENOUS rhythmicity. See Periodicity
ENDOMETRIUM. See Uterus
ENDOPLASMIC reticulum. See Brain
ENDOWMENTS
Greener look for Yale blue. il Bsns W p 143-4 S 30 '67
    See also
Colleges and universities—Gifts, legacies, etc.
ENDRIN
Endrin resistance in the pine mouse. R. E. Webb and F. Horsfall, jr. bibliog il Science 156:1762 Je 30 '67

ENERGY conversion, Direct. See Direct energy conversion
ENERGY resources. See Power resources
ENESCO, Georges, festival. See Music festivals —Rumania
ENFIELD, Conn.
Past and present: the twain shall meet; Enfield high school, Thompsonville. F. S. Gross. Sr Schol 91:sup 13 O 5 '67
ENFORCEMENT of law. See Law enforcement
ENGAGEMENT calendars. See Calendars
ENGEL, Eric. See Nance, W. E. jt. auth.
ENGEL, Ralph
When the lawn becomes a playground. il Home Gard 54:47 Je '67
ENGELBERT, Arthur F.
University in a windstorm. Sch & Soc 95: 119-21 F 18 '67
ENGELHARDT, John J. and others
Superconductivity and the d-shell. bibliog Science 155:191-3 Ja 13 '67
ENGELS, John
Christmas play; poem. Reporter 37:40 D 28 '67
ENGEMAN, J. P.
Laser interferometer. Electr World 77:43-5+ Je '67
ENGINE analyzers. See Airplane engines— Testing
ENGINE stand. See Automobiles—Equipment
ENGINEERING
Engineering, civilization, and society; excerpts from address, November 8, 1966. A. B. Kinzel. Science 156:1343-5 Je 9 '67
    See also
Technology
    also Aviation engineering; Systems engineering; and similar headings
        History
Jacopo Aconcio as an engineer. L. White, jr. bibliog f Am Hist R 72:425-44 Ja '67
        Study and teaching
College scene (cont) il Sci Digest 61:25 F '67
Colleges in action. See issues of Science digest
Soviet educator urges engineer rewards; excerpts from Izvestia. I. F. Obraztsov. Aviation W 87:115+ S 11 '67
    See also
Engineering education
ENGINEERING colleges
    See also names of engineering colleges, e.g. Massachusetts institute of technology, Cambridge
ENGINEERING education
Engineering degrees. N. A. Carlson. il Am Ed 3:inside back cover S '67
Literate engineering. J. H. Hollomon. il Sat R 50:40-1 Jl 1 '67
Training for engineering and technology in Switzerland; excerpt from Science in Switzerland. J. M. Luck. bibliog f il Sch & Soc 94:499-502 D 24 '66
ENGINEERING literature. See Technical literature
ENGINEERING materials. See Materials
ENGINEERING mathematics. See Mathematics
ENGINEERING models
    See also
Mechanical models
ENGINEERING research
    See also
Aeronautic research
Industrial research
ENGINEERING societies
Literature program of engineering societies; report on conference. S. Klein. Science 155: 1698-9 Mr 31 '67
ENGINEERS
Unionization of engineers and technicians. A. Kleingartner. bibliog f il Mo Labor R 90:29-35 O '67
        Fees
Congress moves slowly on the federal fee structure. Arch Rec 142:81-2 S '67
        Political activities
Scientists and engineers for L.B.J: a war and three years later. E. Langer. Science 157: 1533-6 S 29 '67
        Supply and demand
Brain drain: foreign aid for U.S. il U S News 62:78-81 My 22 '67
Brains across the sea. R. Schiller. Read Digest 90:72-6 Mr '67
British brain drain doubled in six years, survey finds. H. J. Coleman. Aviation W 87: 62-3+ O 30 '67

ENGINEERS—Supply and demand—*Continued*
Fewer brains hear U.S.A.'s siren song. il
Bsns W p 100+ My 27 '67
Help wanted: engineers and scientists. R.
Schiller. Read Digest 90:193-4+ F '67
Long-term engineering shortage seen. W. S.
Beller. il Tech W 20:28-9 Mr 20 '67
Mr Brain drain; New York firm's London re-
cruiting drives. il Life 62:101-2 Mr 17 '67
Rise in degrees. Sch & Soc 95:482+ D 9 '67

ENGINEERS, Japanese
Brain drain touches lightly; conditions in
Japan. S. Griffin. Sci N 91:480-1 My 20 '67

ENGINEERS, Professional ethics for
This business of engineering ethics. Am
City 82:6 Je '67

ENGINEERS unions. See Trade unions—United
States

ENGINES
Muscle machine; invented by Israeli sci-
entists. S. V. Jones. il Sci Digest 62:84
S '67
See also
Airplane engines
Automobile engines
Marine engines
Pistons
Rocket engines

ENGINES, Toy
Toy steam engine has a secret: hidden tur-
bine. R. L. Clough, jr. il Pop Sci 191:124
N '67

ENGLAND, Ralph W. Jr
Independent offender. bibliog f Cur Hist 52:
334-40+ Je '67

ENGLAND
See also
Aldeburgh
Architecture, Domestic—England
Censorship—England
Country estates—England
English
Great Britain
Lake District
London
Music—England
Music festivals—England
Scilly Islands
Stratford-on-Avon
Thames River
Wight, Isle of

Antiquities
See Great Britain—Antiquities

Description and travel
Preservation of natural beauty in England.
A. Netboy. il Am For 73:16-19+ Mr '67

Education
See Education—Great Britain

Galleries and museums
See also
Oxford, England—Galleries and museums

Historic houses, etc.
Follies at Stowe: the grotto. E. Gaines. il
Antiques 91:240+ F '67
Living with antiques in England; Essex home
of E. Clare Hanley. J. Vickers. il Antiques
92:208-9 Ag '67

Moral conditions
On iniquity, by P. H. Johnson. Review
New Repub 156:25-6 Mr 25 '67. H. Tracy

Religious institutions and affairs
World around us (cont) Christian Cent 84:
150+, 355-6, 483-4, 599-600, 762-4, 922, 1052,
1166+ 1332, 1578 F 1, Mr 15, Ap 12, Mv 3,
Je 7, Jl 12, Ag 16, S 13, O 18, D 6 '67
See also
Catholic church in England
Catholics in England

Social conditions
English character in the twentieth century.
G. Gorer. bibliog f Ann Am Acad 370:74-81
Mr '67

ENGLAND and Europe
Common market lure. D. Fishlock. Sci N 91:
555+ Je 10 '67

ENGLAND and the United States
See also
Americans in England
United States—Foreign opinion—British
United States—Foreign relations—Great Bri-
tain

ENGLE, Katherine
Different one; story. Redbook 129:74-5 Je '67

ENGLE, Paul
Innkeeper speaks; poem. McCalls 95:153 D '67

ENGLE, Shirley H.
Social studies look to the future; excerpts
from New frontiers in the social studies. Sr
Schol 91:sup29+ S 28 '67

ENGLEBARDT, Stanley L.
Computers today. Sci Digest 61:41-8+ F '67
Mononucleosis: separating fact from fancy.
Read Digest 91:154-7 N '67
Now, keep your teeth forever. Sci Digest 61:
55-61 Mr '67
Super-cold: hottest thing in surgery. Read
Digest 90:131-5 My '67

ENGLISH
England, the melting pot. D. Lowe. il Hori-
zon 9:56-9 Spr '67
English character in the twentieth century.
G. Gorer. bibliog f Ann Am Acad 370:74-81
Mr '67

ENGLISH ballads. See Ballads, English

ENGLISH CANADIANS. See Canadians

ENGLISH CHANNEL
Britain's big moat: the Channel. L. Ross. il
Read Digest 90:21-2+ Je '67

ENGLISH composition. See English language—
Composition

ENGLISH cookery. See Cookery, English

ENGLISH drama
Importance of writing good plays. J. Ros-
selli. il Reporter 36:44+ My 18 '67
See also
Theater—Great Britain

ENGLISH furniture. See Furniture, English

ENGLISH glass. See Glassware

ENGLISH grammar. See English language—
Grammar

ENGLISH in China
Canton more far. S. Hazzard. New Yorker
43:42-9 D 16 '67

ENGLISH in Egypt
See also
Egypt—History—British occupation, 1882-1936

ENGLISH in India
Night train to Chittagong. D. W. David. il
Read Digest 91:95-9 O '67
Ooty preserved, by M. Panter-Downes. Re-
view
New Repub 157:28-30 D 23 '67. H. Tracy
Profiles; Ootacamund, India. M. Panter-
Downes. il New Yorker 43:48-50+ Mr 4; 57-
62+ Mr 11 '67

ENGLISH language
Few ill-chosen words; address, 1964. K. M.
Ralston. Horn Bk 43:42-7 F '67
Many hues of English, by M. Pei. Review
Sat R 50:27-8 O 28 '67. G. Hicks
Modern American usage, by W. Follett and
others. Review
Am Heritage 18:82-3 Ap '67. B. Catton
Commentary 43:76-9 F '67. L. Kronen-
berger
See also
Slang
Vocabulary
Words

Composition
Bad writing. D. Wolfle. Science 155:407 Ja
27 '67
Meaningful fare for terminal students; pro-
gram built around paperback books and
films; Greenwich, Conn. H. R. Finch. Sr
Schol 91:sup 10-11 N 30 '67
New media: help students come to their
senses. D. A. Sohn. il Sr Schol 90:sup 16-17
My 19 '67
New Oregon rhetoric curriculum. A. R. Kitz-
haber. Sr Schol 90:sup 13-14 My 12 '67

Creative activities
It could happen in the schools; interview, ed.
by J. Colmenares. B. Schulberg. NEA J
56:19 D '67
Keyboard composition; composition in proper
typing techniques. E. O. Bloom. NEA J
56:73-4 D '67
Stimulating the student writer. V. E. Steahly. NEA J 56:64-6 N '67

Dialects
See also
Slang

Dictionaries
Who says it's proper English? examining the
new Random house dictionary. J. W.
Krutch. Sat R 50:19-21+ O 14 '67; Reply
J. Stein. 50:31 N 25 '67

Etymology
Tiptoe through lingo. L. Rosten. Look 31:
10-11 D 26 '67

ENGLISH language—*Continued*

Grammar

Interview with Paul Roberts. P. Roberts. Sr Schol 91:sup9+ O 19 '67
Like your cigarette should; the Winston slogan; reprint. R. L. Tobin. Writer 80:34 Ja '67
More on words. G. Hicks. Sat R 50:25-6 D 23 '67

Pronunciation

Learn a lito Englich; teaching English to Spanish speaking children. R. H. Levine. il Am Ed 4:24-5 D '67
Speaking the same language. R. I. Golden. il NEA J 56:40+ Mr '67

Study and teaching

Are English teachers teachable? National defense education act funds summer institutes for advanced study in English. R. O. Ulin. Sch & Soc 95:363-6 O 14 '67
English, hip and ofay; English exercise book. Play it cool for the ghetto child. il Newsweek 69:70 Ap 10 '67
For English teachers. J. L. Mersand. il Sr Schol 91:sup26 S 28 '67
Freshman program at Stanford. Sch & Soc 95:176+ Mr 18 '67
Good English from good books; Project English. Time 90:37 S 1 '67
How teachers make children hate reading. J. Holt. Redbook 130:50+ N '67
New English; with study-discussion program, by E. Harris and D. Harris. F. B. Freedman. bibliog il PTA Mag 62:6-8, 33-4 Ja '68
Program for overcoming the handicap of dialect. T. R. Temple. New Repub 156:11-12 Mr 25 '67
Teaching of English abroad. R. Beym. Américas 19:17-19 Mr '67
Uses of English, by H. J. Muller. Review Sat R 50:73 D 16 '67. F. G. Jennings
We ain't unteachable, just unteached; unit on prejudice and propaganda. L. Trout. il NEA J 56:24-6 Ap '67
See also
English language—Composition
English language—Grammar
English literature—Study and teaching
National council of teachers of English

Synonyms

English language is my enemy! synonyms for blackness. O. Davis. Negro Hist Bul 30:18 Ap '67

Terms and phrases

Glossary; use of affluent, ethnic, and power structure. M. Greenfield. Reporter 36:35 Je 1 '67
Is it Greek to you? L. Rosten. il Look 31:8 F 7 '67
Who says it's proper English? concerning modern expressions and Jess Stein's philosophy. J. W. Krutch. Sat R 50:19-21+ O 14 '67; Reply. J. Stein. 50:31 N 25 '67
World of the mini. G. Lazarus. Sat R 50:128 Mr 11 '67
See also
Slogans
Vocabulary
Words
Words, New

Anecdotes, facetiae, satire, etc.

Ambrose Bierce's devilish definitions; excerpts from Enlarged devil's dictionary; ed. by E. J. Hopkins. A. Bierce. Am Heritage 18:112 Ap '67

Words
History

Big mystery in small words. M. Pei. il Sat R 50:98-9+ Je 10 '67

ENGLISH language in foreign countries
Teaching of English abroad. R. Beym. Américas 19:17-19 Mr '67

ENGLISH literature
See also
English poetry

Bibliography

New books for teaching English. S. Cochell. Sr Schol 90:sup22 Ap 7 '67
New paperbacks for teaching English. il Sr Schol 89:sup 18+ Ja 20 '67

Study and teaching

Aiding unwilling readers; paperbacks do the trick; Ocean township H.S., Oakhurst, N.J. H. M. McDonnell. Sr Schol 90:sup21-2 Mr 31 '67

English, education and the electronic revolution; excerpts. E. J. Farrell. Sr Schol 91:sup 12-13 S 28 '67
Media crisis in the classroom. G. Hicks. Sat R 50:27-8 Ap 15; 19-20 Jl 8 '67
New books for teaching English. S. Cochell. Sr Schol 90:sup22 Ap 7 '67
New paperbacks for teaching English. il Sr Schol 89:sup 18+ Ja 20 '67
ENGLISH money. See Money—Great Britain
ENGLISH music. See Music, English
ENGLISH national theater. See Theater—Great Britain
ENGLISH poetry
Poetry in pamphlets. R. Hecht. Poetry 110:112-19 My '67
See also
Ballads, English
ENGLISH pottery. See Pottery, English
ENGLISH press. See Newspapers—Great Britain
ENGLISH setters. See Setters
ENGLISH silver. See Silverware
ENGLISH springer spaniel national championship. See Field trials (dogs)
ENGLISHMEN. See English
ENGLISHWOMEN. See English
ENGRAVING
William H. Bartlett and his imitators; excerpts. M.-E. Earl. il Antiques 92:722-5 N '67
See also
Engravings
ENGRAVINGS
Mestre Noza. S. Biderman. il Américas 19:5-7 N '67

Exhibitions

Mysterious engraver; 15th century anonymous German artist. il Time 90:72 S 8 '67
Mystery of the master E S; exhibition at the Philadelphia museum of art. il Life 63:87-8+ O 6 '67
ENGSTRÖM, Lars
Those new Swedish abortion pills. R. Link. por Ladies Home J 84:42+ Je '67
ENLARGING (photography) See Photography—Enlarging
ENLARGING exposure meters. See Exposure meters
ENLARGING lenses. See Lenses, Photographic
ENLARGING meters. See Photography—Enlarging
ENLIGHTENMENT
Was America a mistake? great debate of the enlightenment. H. S. Commager. il Horizon 9:30-3+ Aut '67
ENNIS, Charles
Expedition holy book. E. Gowen. il por Américas 19:1-7 S '67
ENNIS, Philip H.
Commitment to research. Wilson Lib Bul 41:898-901 My '67
ENOVID. See Contraceptives
ENRICO, Harold
Adoration; poem. Christian Cent 84:1118 S 6 '67
But Lucifer, he fell; poem. Christian Cent 84:141 F 1 '67
ENRIGHT, Elizabeth
Realism in children's literature. Horn Bk 43:165-70 Ap '67
ENRIGHT, J. T.
Temperature compensation in short-duration time-measurement by an intertidal amphipod. bibliog Science 156:1510-12 Je 16 '67
—and Hammer, W. M.
Vertical diurnal migration and endogenous rhythmicity. bibliog Science 157:937-41 Ag 25 '67
ENRIGHT, James E.
How to purchase data-processing equipment. Am City 82:127-8 Ap '67
ENROLLMENT, College. See Colleges and universities—Attendance
ENROLLMENT, School. See School attendance
ENSEMBLES (music) See Instrumental ensembles
ENSENADA, Mexico
Downhill to Enchilada; reproductions of paintings; with account by C. Barber. M. Simont. Sports Illus 26:40-8+ My 1 '67
ENSIGNS. See Flags
ENSLIN, Theodore
Degrees; Photograph of wives; This is a catbird watching a king; poems. Poetry 110:397-9 S '67
ENSTROM, Doris C. See Enstrom, E. A. jt. auth.

ENSTROM, E. A. and Enstrom, D. C.
Improving handwriting skills. Sr Schol 91:sup
10-11 O 12 '67
ENTEROGASTRONE. See Hormones
ENTERPRISE, Free. See Free enterprise
ENTERTAINERS
Stars' cars. il Time 90:85 S 29 '67
See also
Actors and actresses
Ames, E.
Beatles
Comedians
Dancers
ENTERTAINING
Complete dictionary of home entertaining. M.
S. Welch. il Redbook 129:111-18 O '67
Couples who cook; with menus and recipes.
H. McCully. il House B 109:104-7+ Jl '67
Dashing parties with little or no help. il
House & Gard 132:220-7 N '67
Drop-of-a-hat invitations. il House & Gard
132:106-11 Jl '67
Easiest parties ever, everyone cooks! il
Good H 165:146-7 O '67
Easter Sunday brunch; with recipes. il Seven-
teen 26:162-3+ Mr '67
Eat. M. Cantwell. Mlle 66:156+ D '67
Entertaining people; party ideas from every-
where (cont) il McCalls 94:19+ F; 28+
Mr; 14+ My; 10 Je; 16 Jl; 95:20 O; 34 D '67
Exciting summer furniture, food, projects,
equipment. D. Popplestone. il Bet Hom &
Gard 45:46-65+ Je '67
February is give-a-boy-a-party month; with
recipes. il Seventeen 26:164-9+ F '67
Festive breads. il House & Gard 131:158-62
My '67
Have a million-dollar New Year's eve and, a
matching breakfast; with recipes and menu.
il McCalls 95:98-9+ D '67
Having houseguests in summer. Am Home
70:116-17 Jl '67
Holiday parties. il House & Gard 132:150-7 D
'67
House in my head; excerpts. D. Rodgers.
House B 109:282-7+ N '67
How to beat the high cost of party giving.
House & Gard 132:18+ Jl '67
How to delight your guests; visiting the
Talbots of Washington, Conn. A. Stagg. il
House & Gard 132:65-71 Jl '67
How to give one big party. il Am Home
70:56-7 N '67
Lawn party; entertaining the Metropolitan
opera company. il Opera N 32:26-7 S 9 '67
Let's have a party just like that. V. D. Hahn.
il Am Home 70:62-9+ Je '67
Mini-parties with maxi-style. il Am Home 70:
52-5 N '67
Mood food; with recipes. il Seventeen 26:
142-5+ O '67
Movable feast; Pennsylvania Dutch party. il
Esquire 69:80-7 Ja '68
New party scene: the kitchen. il House &
Gard 132:234-7 O '67
Notes for the hostess. D. Bryan. See issues
of House & garden incorporating Living for
young homemakers to August 1967
Notes for the hostess. M. M. Hemingway. See
issues of House & garden incorporating
Living for young homemakers
Parties a go-go! il Bet Hom & Gard 45:96
Jl '67
The party, 1956-1966; symposium. il Es-
quire 68:152-72 D '67
Party perfect; ideas for the entertaining sea-
son. D. Hampton. il Mlle 66:76-7 N '67
Party planner. C. Brock. See issues of Good
Housekeeping
Party points, and counterpoints. S. Niren-
berg. House B 109:62+ N '67
Pick the country, and have a party! with
recipes. R. Holmberg and E. Craster. il
Bet Hom & Gard 45:74-89+ O '67
Six party ideas. il Seventeen 26:228+ F '67
Special; October party section. il Ladies
Home J 84:75-86+ O '67
Super party. il Seventeen 26:134-7+ S '67
Sure tips for successful parties. Am Home
70:111 N '67
Why not golf right at home? il Sunset 138:
112-14+ My '67
See also
Business entertaining
Caterers and catering
Christmas entertainments
Christmas meals
Dinners and dining
Games
Government entertaining
Luncheons
Suppers

Anecdotes, facetiae, satire, etc.
Cocktail party: Charles Saxon. J. Peter. il
Life 31:82-4+ My 16 '67
ENTOMOLOGY

Study and teaching
Beetle named Tarzan. J. D. Foraker. il Par-
ents Mag 42:46-7+ Jl '67
ENTRANCE drives. See Driveways
ENTRANCE halls. See Halls
ENTRANCE requirements, College. See Colleges
and universities—Entrance requirements
ENURESIS. See Urine—Incontinence
ENVERGA, Manuel S.
Philippine national policy; address, Septem-
ber 12, 1967. Vital Speeches 34:10-11 O 15
'67
ENVIRONMENT
But then came man; address, May 4, 1967.
S. L. Udall. Vital Speeches 33:569-73 Jl 1
'67
Change the weather, change the world. D.
Peters. Harper 234:98-101 My '67
Earth and environment notes. See issues of
Science news
Historical roots of our ecologic crisis;
address, December 26, 1966. L. White, jr.
Science 155:1203-7 Mr 10 '67; Discussion.
156:737-8 My 12 '67
Induction of drug-metabolizing enzymes in
liver microsomes of mice and rats by soft-
wood bedding. E. S. Vessell. bibliog il Sci-
ence 157:1057-8 S 1 '67
No place to live; HEW report. il Newsweek
69:68 Je 26 '67
Selection of social partners as a function of
peer contract during rearing. C. L. Pratt
and G. P. Sackett. bibliog il Science 155:
1133-5 Mr 3 '67
Toxic substances and ecological cycles. G. M.
Woodwell. il Sci Am 216:24-31 Mr '67; Dis-
cussion. 216:6+ Je '67
See also
Adjustment, Social
Ecology
Man—Influence of environment
Man—Influence on nature
ENVIRONMENTAL art. See Modernism (art)
ENVIRONMENTAL defense fund
Taking polluters to court. F. Graham, jr.
New Repub 158:8-9 Ja 13 '68
ENVIRONMENTAL engineering
Building designed for scenic effect; National
center for atmospheric research. J. Barnett.
il Arch Rec 142:145-54 O '67
Complexity and contradiction in the work
of Ulrich Franzen. il Arch Rec 142:133-44
O '67
Environmental pollution; West Germany, U.S.
cooperate. J. Walsh. Science 157:529-31 Ag 4
'67
Environmental quality in a growing economy,
ed. by H. Jarrett. Review
Am For 73:43 Je '67. B. F. Grossling
Five small-scale communities; projects in de-
sign by Hok; with introd. by C. Obata. il
Arch Rec 141:141-50 Mr '67
Let's see, now, your share of the bill is . . .
il Pop Gard 18:36-9 D '67
Planetary engineering. S. F. Singer. Sat R 50:
41-2 Jl 1 '67
Private responsibility for public management.
F. B. Morse. bibliog f Harvard Bsns R 45:
6-8+ Mr '67
Quality environment. A. C. Borg. il Am Home
70:92-7 O '67
Recent work of Evans Woollen; with fore-
word by E. Woollen. il Arch Rec 141:139-
50 My '67
Technology and the environment: a new con-
cern on Capitol hill. L. J. Carter. Science
157:784-6 Ag 18 '67
Toward a national design policy; Senate
committee testimony. A. C. Rogers. Arch
Rec 141:187-90 Je '67
See also
Committee for environmental information
Life support systems (space environment)
Life support systems (submarine environ-
ment)
ENVIRONMENTAL science services adminis-
tration. See United States—Environmental
science services administration
ENZENSBERGER, Hans Magnus
Two poems; The other; The end of the owls;
tr. by M. Hamburger. Mlle 65:122 My '67
ENZOPRIDE. See Diphosphopyridine nucleotide

ENZYMES

Adenyl cyclase activity in rat pineal gland: effects of chronic denervation and norepinephrine. B. Weiss and E. Costa. bibliog il Science 156:1750-2 Je 30 '67

Answers about L-asparaginase. Time 90:57 D 8 '67

L-asparaginase: inhibition of early mitosis in regenerating rat liver. F. F. Becker and J. D. Broome. bibliog il Science 156:1602-3 Je 23 '67

L-asparaginase: toxicity to normal and leukemic human lymphocytes. R. Schrek and others. bibliog il Science 155:329-30 Ja 20 '67

Benzpyrene hydroxylase induction by polycyclic hydrocarbons in hamster embryonic cells grown in vitro. L. J. Alfred and H. V. Gelboin. bibliog il Science 157:75-6 Jl 7 '67

Carbohydrate supply as a regulator of rat liver phosphoenolpyruvate carboxykinase activity. E. Shrago and others. bibliog il Science 158:1572-3 D 22 '67

Circadian rhythms of liver enzymes and their relationship to enzyme induction. M. Civen and others. bibliog il Science 157:1563-4 S 29 '67

Collagen proline hydroxylase in wound healing, granuloma formation, scurvy, and growth. E. Mussini and others. bibliog il Science 157:927-9 Ag 25 '67

Creatine phosphokinase in thyroid: isoenzyme composition compared with other tissues. F. A. Craig and J. C. Smith. bibliog il Science 156:254-5 Ap 14 '67

Elastase: production by ringworm fungi. J. W. Rippon. bibliog Science 157:947 Ag 25 '67

Enzymatic solubilization of insoluble proteins at neutral pH. S. Rothberg and G. D. Axilrod. bibliog il Science 156:90-3 Ap 7 '67

Enzyme concentrations in tissues. P. A. Srere. bibliog il Science 158:936-7 N 17 '67

Enzyme defect associated with a sex-linked human neurological disorder and excessive purine synthesis. J. E. Seegmiller and others. bibliog il Science 155:1682-4 Mr 31 '67

Enzyme regulation; report on fifth international symposium. G. Weber. Science 155:1137-8+ Mr 3 '67

Enzyme starves cancer cells; L-asparaginase. Sci N 92:582-3 D 16 '67

Enzyme v. leukemia; L-asparaginase. Time 90:67 Jl 7 '67

Enzymic oscillators. Sci Am 217:50 O '67

Evolutionary significance of metabolic control systems. J. L. Cánovas and others. bibliog il Science 156:1695-9 Je 30 '67

Glutathione reductase in red blood cells: variant associated with gout. W. K. Long. bibliog il Science 155:712-13 F 10 '67

Hexokinase isoenzymes in human erythrocytes: association of type II with fetal hemoglobin. E. W. Holmes, jr. and others. bibliog il Science 156:646-8 My 5 '67

Hexokinase isoenzymes in liver and adipose tissue of man and dog. J. Brown and others. bibliog il Science 155:205-7 Ja 13 '67

Hydroxylation-induced migration: the NIH shift. G. Guroff and others. bibliog il Science 157:1524-30 S 29 '67

Indoleacetic acid oxidase activity of apoperoxidase. B. Z. Siegel and A. W. Galston. bibliog il Science 157:1557-9 S 29 '67

Induction of drug-metabolizing enzymes in liver microsomes of mice and rats by softwood bedding. E. S. Vessell. bibliog il Science 157:1057-8 S 1 '67

Inherited diseases: on the way out. B. J. Culliton. il Sci N 92:184-5 Ag 19 '67

Lungfish neoceratodus forsteri: activities of ornithine-urea cycle and enzymes. L. Goldstein and others. bibliog il Science 157:316-17 Jl 21 '67

Malic dehydrogenase isozymes: distribution in developing nucleate and anucleate halves of sea urchin eggs. G. W. Patton, jr. and others. bibliog il Science 156:400-1 Ap 21 '67

Molecular biology: British groups push enzyme-structure studies. N. Calder. Science 156:367-9 Ap 21 '67

Oxygenases; report on colloquium. P. Feigelson. Science 155:609+ F 3 '67

Phosphoribosylamidotransferase: regulation of activity in virus-induced murine leukemia by purine nucleotides. G. H. Reem and C. Friend. bibliog il Science 157:1203-4 S 8 '67

Rabbit lactate dehydrogenase isozymes: effect of pH on activity. P. J. Fritz. bibliog il Science 156:82-3 Ap 7 '67

Reagentless substrate analysis with immobilized enzymes. S. J. Updike and G. P. Hicks. bibliog il Science 158:270-2 O 13 '67

Refsum's disease: nature of the enzyme defect. D. Steinberg and others. bibliog il Science 156:1740-2 Je 30 '67

Renin-like enzyme in the adrenal gland. J. W. Ryan. bibliog il Science 158:1589-90 D 22 '67

Riddle of the dangerous bean; enzyme deficiency as cause of hemolysis and favism in specific ethnic groups. J. R. Marcus and G. Cohen. il Harper 234:98-102 Je '67

Second hands for biological clocks; rhythms regulated by enzyme system. T. W. Hill. il Sci N 92:380-1 O 14 '67

Secret from the guinea pigs; L-asparaginase. il Time 89:57-8+ Ap 14 '67

Selective cancer killer; l-asparagine. Newsweek 69:55 Ap 3 '67

Selective release of enzymes from bacteria. L. A. Heppel. bibliog Science 156:1451-5 Je 16 '67

Valyl-transfer RNA: role in repression of the isoleucine-valine enzymes in escherichia coli. M. Freundlich. bibliog il Science 157:823-5 Ag 18 '67

What causes inflammation, and why it occurs; International inflammation club first symposium. il Time 89:60+ Je 16 '67

Why arthritis hurts. Newsweek 69:92 Je 19 '67

See also
Adenosine triphosphatase
Aldolase
Carbohydrases
Cholinesterase
Dehydrogenases
Hyaluronidase
Lysozyme
Melatonin
Mutarotase
Oxidases
Peroxidases
Phosphorylases
Proteases
Ribonuclease
Tyrosinase
Urease

EOCENE period. See Paleontology—Eocene

EOHIPPUS

Nature note: dawn horse. Sci N 91:372 Ap 22 '67

EOSINOPHILS

Eosinophilic response in glioblastoma tissue culture after addition of autologous lymphocytes. J. Ciembroniewicz and O. Kolar. bibliog il Science 157:1054-5 S 1 '67

EPERGNES

More by, and about Pitts of the epergnes. E. Gaines. il Antiques 91:748-53 Je '67

EPERYTHROZOON. See Parasites—Livestock

EPIC literature

Nathaniel Hawthorne: the absurdity of heroism. T. L. Gross. Yale R 57:182-95 D '67

EPIC poetry
See also
Mahabharata
Ramayana

EPIDEMICS

U.S. wages world war on epidemics; Atlanta's Communicable disease center. il Bsns W p 104-6+ Mr 11 '67

See also
Cholera
Influenza

EPILEPSY

Animals suited to epileptic research; gerbils' susceptibility to seizure. D. G. Robinson, jr. il Sci N 93:16-18 Ja 6 '68

Epilepsy's fading stigma. il Newsweek 69:66 My 15 '67

Victory over epilepsy. A. Hamilton. il Sci Digest 62:26-30 N '67

EPIPHANY

Twelfth night in Williamsburg, circa 1780. P. Hyde and J. L. Hendrix. il House B 109:270-3 N '67

EPISCOPAL bishops. See Bishops

EPISCOPAL church. See Protestant Episcopal church

EPISCOPAL society for cultural and racial unity

ESCRU at the crossroads. Christian Cent 84:1181 S 20 '67

EPITHELIUM

Epithelial-mesenchymal interactions; report on eighteenth Hahnemann symposium. R. Fleischmajer. Science 157:1472+ S 22 '67

EPITHELIUM—*Continued*
Fast potential spike of frog skin generated at the outer surface of the epithelium. B. Lindemann and U. Thorns. bibliog il Science 158:1473-7 D 15 '67
Purified staphylococcal alpha toxin: effect on epithelial ion transport. J. J. Rahal, jr. and others. bibliog il Science 155:1118-20 Mr 3 '67
Transepithelial potentials in hydra. R. K. Josephson and M. Macklin. bibliog il Science 156:1629-31 Je 23 '67

EPPEL, Lou
Don't leave it alone! interview, ed. by M. Crook. Yachting 121:90-1 Je '67

EPSOM derby. See Horse racing

EPSTEIN, Brian
Fifth Beatle. il por Newsweek 70:98 S 11 '67
Outsider. por Time 90:54 S 8 '67

EPSTEIN, Edward Jay
Manchester unexpurgated. bibliog f Commentary 44:25-31 Jl '67

about

Death of Lancer; concering first draft manuscript of Death of a President. por Newsweek 70:25 Jl 17 '67

EPSTEIN, Eugene E. and others
Mercury: observations of the 3,4-millimeter radio emission. bibliog Science 157:1550-2 S 29 '67

EPSTEIN, Franklin H. and others
Sodium- and potassium-activated adenosine triphosphatase of gills: role in adaptation of teleosts to salt water. bibliog Science 156:1245-7 Je 2 '67

EPSTEIN, Sir Jacob
Jacob Epstein. K. Kuh. il Sat R 50:48-9 Mr 25 '67

EPSTEIN, Joseph
After Andy Hardy. Commentary 43:94-7 Mr '67
Henry Luce and his time. bibliog f Commentary 44:35-47 N '67
Hero for our time. Commentary 43:102+ My '67

EPSTEIN, Leslie
Playground; story. Yale R 57:222-35 D '67

EPSTEIN, Lewis C.
All-reflection Schmidt telescope for space research. Sky & Tel 33:204-7 Ap '67

EPSTEIN, Louis
Robert Campbell and Louis Epstein are honored at West coast dinner. il por Pub W 191:68+ Ap 24 '67
Take a bow Bob Campbell, Lou Epstein. por Pub W 191:103-5 Je 5 '67

EPSTEIN, Mike
Mike's little rebellion. Newsweek 69:58 Je 12 '67

EPSTEIN, Seymour
Personal motif in fiction. Writer 80:11-14 Jl '67

EPTATRETUS stoutii. See Hagfish

EQUAL employment opportunity commission. See United States—President's equal employment opportunity commission

EQUAL rights for women. See Women—Equal rights

EQUAL time rule (television) See Television laws and regulations

EQUALITY
Poverty, inequality, and conflict. S. M. Miller and others. bibliog f il Ann Am Acad 373:16-52 S '67
See also
Individualism
Race relations

EQUATIONS
See also
Maxwell's equations

EQUILIBRIUM (physiology)
Gait study measures problems of balance. il Sci N 91:293 Mr 25 '67
See also
Man—Attitude and movement

EQUIPMENT, Music. See Music rooms and equipment

EQUIPMENT industries
Another boom ends. il Fortune 75:16+ Je 1 '67

EQUITY research associates
Independent advice lures brokers. il Bsns W p 101-2+ F 11 '67

ERASER block printing. See Block printing

ERASMUS, Desiderius
Preacher of the golden mean. P. W. Schmiltchen. il por Hobbies 72:104-5 Mr '67

ERB, Donald
Op. 1 from Opus one. J. Diether. Am Rec G 33:497-8 F '67

ERBES, Raymond
Microfilm: a must in the high school library. Sr Schol 90:sup 18 Ap 14 '67

ERDMAN, Jean
Coach with the six insides; dramatization of Finnegans wake, by J. Joyce. Criticism Commonweal 86:394 Je 23 '67

ERGUN, Sabri. See Bivins, D. jt. auth.

ERHARD, Ludwig
Three pragmatists. W. Lippmann. Newsweek 69:29 My 8 '67

ERHARDT, Otto
How the scene has changed; tr. by R. R. Schlein. Opera N 31:27 F 18 '67

ERIC (educational resources information center) See United States—Education, Office of—Educational research and development, Bureau of

ERICAS. See Heaths (plants)

ERICKSEN, Stanford C.
Human learning in a natural setting. por Sch & Soc 95:41-2 Ja 21 '67

ERICKSON, Hugo
Mall-transitway constructed by force account. Am City 82:134-6 S '67

ERICKSON, Richard B.
Check home zoning before you buy. Am Home 70:128 N '67

ERICSON, Mildred
And bust. Am For 73:5+ Mr '67

ERICSSON, Leif. See Leif Ericsson

ERIE, LAKE
Battle of Lake Erie: eutrophication and political fragmentation. K. Sperry. il Science 158:351-5 O 20 '67

ERIE CANAL
Lens on the locks: Erie Canal sesquicentennial exhibition. M. R. Weiss. il Sat R 50:57-9 Ag 12 '67

ERIM, Kenan T.
Ancient Aphrodisias and its marble treasures. Nat Geog Mag 132:280-94 Ag '67

about

Aphrodisias revisited. il Newsweek 71:72 Ja 15 '68

ERLICK, Everett H.
Excerpt from statement before Communications subcommittee, October 12, 1967. Cong Digest 46:299+ D '67

ERNANI; opera. See Verdi, G.

ERNEST Orlando Lawrence memorial awards
AEC award winners; five U.S. scientists to receive Lawrence memorial award for 1967. Sci N 91:331 Ap 8 '67

EROSION
Amazon River: environmental factors that control its dissolved and suspended load. R. J. Gibbs. bibliog il Science 156:1734-7 Je 30 '67
Now, check fields for these problems. G. L. Earle. il Suc Farm 65:34 D '67
Rates of surficial rock creep on hillslopes in western Colorado. S. A. Schumm. bibliog il Science 155:560-2 F 3 '67
See also
Runoff
Sinkholes

EROSION of metals
Separators tested to cut engine erosion. R. F. Coburn. il Aviation W 86:55+ My 22 '67

EROSION prevention and control
How to stop suburban soil erosion; Fairfax County, Va. G. B. Anderson. il Am City 82:102+ D '67

EROTIC literature
Dirty books list: valuable material for the first time available; letter to the editor. R. S. Bravard. Library J 92:3936 N 1 '67

ERRORS
See also
Blunders

ERRORS, Logical. See Fallacies (logic)

ERRORS, Popular
Are you wasting money on worthless health aids? interview, ed. by J. C. G. Conniff. J. L. Goddard. Pop Sci 190:92-3+ Ap '67
Doctor explodes some health-food myths; interview, ed. by C. Phillips. F. Stare. Vogue 149:120-1+ Je '67

ERTÉ
Erté. R. D. Daniels. il por Opera N 32:11-13 S 23 '67
Harbinger of tomorrow. il Time 90:58 Jl 7 '67

ERVIN, Frank
Classicist from Pekin. W. Leggett. il pors Sports Illus 26:24-6+ F 27 '67

ERVIN, Samuel James, 1896-
Computer; address, March 6, 1967. Vital Speeches 33:421-6 My 1 '67

ERVIN, Samuel James—*Continued*
Excerpt from address, May 15, 1967. Cong Digest 46:273+ N '67
Excerpt from debate, August 5, 1966. Cong Digest 46:11+ Ja '67

ERYTHROCYTES
Adjuvant activity of erythrocyte isoantigens. L. W. Schierman and R. A. McBride. bibliog il Science 156:658-9 My 5 '67
Blood viscosity: influence of erythrocyte aggregation. S. Chien and others. bibliog il Science 157:829-31 Ag 18 '67
Blood viscosity: influence of erythrocyte deformation. S. Chien and others. bibliog il Science 157:827-9 Ag 18 '67
Erythrocyte abnormality in human myopathy. H. D. Brown and others. bibliog il Science 157:1577-8 S 29 '67
Erythrocyte transfer RNA: change during chick development. J. C. Lee and V. M. Ingram. bibliog il Science 158:1330-2 D 8 '67
Flow characteristics of human erythrocytes through polycarbonate sieves. M. I. Gregersen and others. bibliog il Science 157:825-7 Ag 18 '67
Glutathione deficiency in sheep erythrocytes. J. E. Smith and B. I. Osburn. bibliog il Science 158:374-5 O 20 '67
Hexokinase isoenzymes in human erythrocytes: association of type II with fetal hemoglobin. E. W. Holmes, jr. and others. bibliog il Science 156:646-8 My 5 '67
Hydroxyethyl starch: extracellular croyophylactic agent for erythrocytes. C. T. Knorpp and others. bibliog il Science 157:1312-13 S 15 '67
Induction and survival of hemoglobin-less and erythrocyte-less tadpoles and young bullfrogs. G. Flores and E. Frieden. bibliog il Science 159:101-3 Ja 5 '68
Membranes in polyribosome formation by rabbit reticulocytes. M. L. Freedman and others. bibliog il Science 157:323-5 Jl 21 '67
Mutarotase in erythrocytes: isolation and properties. W. Sacks. bibliog il Science 158:498-9 O 27 '67

ERYTHRONIUMS. See Troutlilies

ERYTHROPOIESIS
Globin composition and synthesis of hemoglobins in developing fetal mice erythroid cells. A. Fantoni and others. bibliog il Science 157:1327-9 S 15 '67
Renal erythropoietic factor: role of ions and vasoactive agents in erythropoietin formation. E. D. Zanjani and others. bibliog il Science 156:1367-8 Je 9 '67
Virus-induced erythropoiesis in hypertransfused-polycythemic mice. E. A. Mirand. bibliog il Science 156:832-3 My 12 '67

ESALEN institute, Calif.
Joy is the prize: a trip to Esalen institute. L. E. Litwak. il N Y Times Mag p8-9+ D 31 '67
School for the senses. il Time 90:69 S 29 '67

ESCAPE devices (airplanes) See Airplanes—Escape devices

ESCAPE devices (space vehicles) See Space vehicles—Escape devices

ESCAPES
Call for F. Lee; escapee A. DeSalvo. Newsweek 69:37-8 Mr 6 '67
Lester's open house: prisoners escape from Wilkinson County prison work camp to tell Gov. Maddox about mistreatment. il Newsweek 69:24 My 1 '67

ESCAPES from death. See Survival (after airplane accidents, shipwrecks, etc)

ESCH, Harald
Evolution of bee language: with biographical sketch. Sci Am 216:15, 96-102+ bibliog(p 148) Ap '67

ESCHATOLOGY
Ernst Bloch: philosopher of the not-yet. S. P. Schilling. Christian Cent 84:1455-8 N 15 '67; Discussion. 84:1663 D 27 '67
Fox and hedgehog. S. Keen. Christian Cent 84:344-5 Mr 15 '67
New views of heaven & hell. Time 89:44+ My 19 '67
Promised end. V. P. McCorry. America 117: inside back cover N 25 '67
Protestant radicalism: eschatological witness in the world. V. Eller. Christian Cent 84: 1391-5 N 1 '67; Reply. H. Arnold. 84:1633-4 D 20 '67

ESCHEAT
Watch your money! the state might grab it. il Changing T 21:15-17 S '67

ESCHERICHIA coli
Genetic mapping of phenylalanyl-sRNA synthetase in escherichia coli. A. Böck and F. C. Neidhardt. bibliog il Science 157:78-9 Jl 7 '67

Genetic recombination in escherichia coli: clone heterogeneity and the kinetics of segregation. T. H. Wood. bibliog il Science 157:319-21 Jl 21 '67
Hexagonal pattern in cell walls of escherichia coli B. D. A. Fischman and G. Weinbaum. bibliog il Science 155:472-4 Ja 27 '67
Mutagenesis by near-visible light. H. E. Kubitschek. bibliog il Science 155:1545-6 Mr 24 '67
Mutagenesis in escherichia coli by visible light. R. B. Webb and M. M. Malina. bibliog il Science 156:1104-5 My 26 '67
Phage lambda mutants deficient in rII exclusion. B. D. Howard. bibliog il Science 158:1588-9 D 22 '67
Phosphorylative inactivation of aminoglycosidic antibiotics by escherichia coli carrying R factor. H. Umezawa and others. il Science 157:1559-61 S 29 '67
Photoinduced DNA-protein cross-links and bacterial killing: a correlation at low temperatures. K. C. Smith and M. E. O'Leary. bibliog il Science 155:1024-6 F 24 '67
Protein components in the 40S ribonucleoprotein particles in escherichia coli. E. Otaka and others. bibliog il Science 157: 1452-4 S 22 '67
Regulation of the lac operon. J. R. Beckwith. bibliog il Science 156:597-604 My 5 '67
Replication of viral RNA: RNA synthetase from escherichia coli infected with phage MS2 or Qβ. G. Feix and others. bibliog il Science 157:701-3 Ag 11 '67
Substrate binding properties of mutant and wild-type A proteins of escherichia coli tryptophan synthetase. J. K. Hardman and C. Yanofsky. bibliog il Science 156:1369-71 Je 9 '67
Suppressor selection for amino acid replacements expected on the basis of the genetic code. H. Berger and C. Yanofsky. bibliog il Science 156:394-7 Ap 21 '67
Ubiquitous bacterium: worldwide use in scientific experiments. F. Marley. il Sci N 92:231 S 2 '67
Valyl-transfer RNA: role in repression of the isoleucine-valine enzymes in escherichia coli. M. Freundlich. bibliog il Science 157: 823-5 Ag 18 '67

ESCOBAR, Marisol. See Marisol

ESCORTED tours. See Travel

ESFANDIARY, Fereidoun M.
Mystical West puzzles the practical East. N Y Times Mag p22-3+ F 5 '67

ESHKOL, Levi
Troubles for Israel in hostile Mideast; interview. por U S News 62:75-7 Ap 17 '67
What's next for Israel; interview, ed. by W. MacDougall. por U S News 63:29-31 Jl 10 '67

about
Eshkol sticks to his guns. J. Feron. il pors N Y Times Mag p34-5+ Ja 7 '68
Limited options. Newsweek 71:32+ Ja 8 '68
Nation under siege. il por Time 89:38-42 Je 9 '67

ESHLEMAN, Clayton
Nonomiya; Sensing Duncan; To Crane; Little moon worm; Poem: Woman whose open eyes at contact shy; poems. Poetry 111:76-81 N '67
Translating César Vallejo. Nation 204:540 Ap 24 '67

ESHLEMAN, Von Russel
Radar astronomy. bibliog Science 158:585-97 N 3 '67

ESKIMOS
Homogenizing the Eskimo. S. Alexander. Life 62:24A My 5 '67
Natives: even hope is scarce. il Bsns W p152 N 4 '67
Next door to Siberia. M. Miller. il Travel 128:31-7 Ag '67

Art
Artists of the tundra. il UNESCO Courier 20: 34-5 Ap '67
Homogenizing the Eskimo; visit to native carvers of Baffin land. S. Alexander. Life 62:24A My 5 '67

Education
Northern education program; pre-university education system for residents of the Northwest territories and Eskimos in northern Quebec. il Sch & Soc 95:104-5 F 18 '67

ESKIN, Arnold. See Menaker, M. jt. auth.

ESPALIERS. See Fruit trees, Training of; Trees, Training of

ESPINOLA, Elsa Wiezell de. See Wiezell de Espinola, E.

ESPIONAGE
Big haul in Bonn; Russian spy ring. il Newsweek 70:31-2 O 30 '67
Contact on Gorki street; condensation. G. Wynne. il Read Digest 91:185-90+ Ag '67
Espionage establishment; excerpt. D. Wise and T. B. Ross. il Sat Eve Post 240:29-31+ O 21; 50-3+ N 4; 76-80+ N 18 '67
From Scandinavia to Somalia, a Soviet spy network crumbles. il U S News 62:44-6 Ap 24 '67
Spies that were left behind; spy rings disclosed in West Germany. il Time 90:35 O 27 '67
See also
Electronics in criminal investigation, espionage, etc.
Secret service
Spies
Trials (espionage)

ESPIONAGE, Industrial. See Spies, Industrial

ESPY, Hilda Cole
Those wonderful shots of Killarney; story. Redbook 129:56-7 My '67

ESPY, R. H. Edwin
National council position on Middle East. Christian Cent 84:804 Je 21 '67

ESQUIRE (periodical)
Everything must go! il Esquire 67:95-9 Je '67
Look how outrageous! il Time 90:42+ Jl 14 '67
Seventh annual dubious achievement awards for 1967. il Esquire 69:49-55 Ja '68
See also
Business in the arts award

ESSAYS

Competitions
1967 Scholastic writing awards. il Sr Schol 90:21-4+ My 19 '67

ESSAYS by children. See Children as authors

ESSENCES and essential oils
See also
Bergamot oil

ESSLIN, Martin
Playwright who drops political blockbusters. N Y Times Mag p48-9+ N 19 '67

ESTAING, Valéry Giscard d'. See Giscard d'Estaing. V.

ESTATE planning
Estate planning: why you need it. il Changing T 22:25-9 Ja '68
How to avoid probate! by N. F. Dacey. Review
Consumer Rep 32:390-2 Jl '67
Personal business. Bsns W p 119 Ja 13 '68
Personal business; planning finances for a decade. Bsns W p 143 N 4 '67
Use a trust to avoid probate? Suc Farm 65: 30B N '67

ESTATE tax. See Inheritance tax

ESTATES, Unclaimed
See also
Escheat

ESTERASE polymorphism. See Polymorphism (biology)

ESTERASES
See also
Cholinesterase

ESTEROW, Milton
Buyers, sellers, and forgers. Harper 234:83-6 Je '67

ESTERQUEST, Ralph T.
Barefoot in Bal Harbour. Library J 92:2734-6 Ag '67

ESTES, Nolan
Follow through. Am Ed 3:12-14 S '67
National report: gains and goals in education. Parents Mag 42:53-5+ S '67

ESTES, Richard D.
Predators and scavengers; with biographical sketch. Natur Hist 76:5, 20-9 F; 5, 38-47 bibliog(p70) Mr '67
Trials of a zebra herd stallion. il Natur Hist 76:58-65 N '67

ESTES PARK, Colo.
Love in the park; excerpt from A gallery of dudes. M. Sprague. il Am Heritage 18:8-13+ F '67

ESTHETICS. See Aesthetics

ESTIENNE, Charles
Balthus: the solitary scandal. Art N 66:39-41+ My '67

ESTONIA
Baltic states. J. Bowen. il Travel 127:37-40 My '67
See also
Music festivals—Estonia

ESTRADA, Ric
Reflections on a Broadway flop. Dance Mag 42:58-61 Ja '68
—See Estrada, S. jt. auth.

ESTRADA, Sigrid, and Estrada, Ric
Under our eyes. Dance Mag 41:38-43+ S '67

ESTRADIOL
Sulfhydryl groups and estradiol-receptor interaction. E. V. Jensen and others. bibliog il Science 158:385-7 O 20 '67

ESTROGENS
Estrogens' double life; morning-after birth control. Sci N 92:343 O 7 '67
Feminine forever; R. A. Wilson and others' theories on estrogen therapy. il Newsweek 69:55 Ap 3 '67
Hormones and heart attacks. Sci N 92:175 Ag 19 '67
Menopause: is there a cure? B Davison. il Sat Eve Post 240:70-2 Ag 26 '67
Milk-like fluid in a mammary adenocarcinoma: biochemical characterization. R. Hilf. bibliog il Science 155:826-7 F 17 '67
Sex and the older woman; hormones to prolong femininity. F. Marley. il Sci N 91:413 Ap 29 '67
See also
Estradiol

ESTRUATION
Increased litter size in the rat X-irradiated during the estrous cycle before mating. E. W. Hahn and W. F. Ward. bibliog il Science 157:956-7 Ag 25 '67

ESTUARIES
Estuaries bill is beached by Army-Interior pact. C. H. Callison. Audubon 69:62-3 S '67
Estuaries protection a must in Congress. Audubon 69:5 Jl '67
Estuaries: will Congress save them from encroachments? L. J. Carter. il Science 156: 1717+ Je 30 '67
Interior's role strengthened in protecting estuaries. L. J. Carter. Science 157:528 Ag 4 '67
Last ditch fight for vanishing estuaries. il Sci N 92:103-4 Jl 29 '67
Vanishing tidelands. P. Redford. Atlan 219: 75-8+ Je '67; Same abr. il Read Digest 91: 134-7 S '67

ETCHING
See also
Glass prints

ETCHING, American
See also
Altman. H.

ETCHING, Dutch
See also
Seghers. H. P.

ETCHING, Glass. See Glass etching

ETHANOL
Hematuria following administration of ethanol. J. M. Orten and others. bibliog Science 157:72-3 Jl 7 '67

ETHANOLAMINE phosphoglycerides. See Glycerides

ETHICS
Code of codes reprinted from the Christmas issue of thirty-three years ago. D. Lawrence. U S News 63:80+ D 25 '67
Mad morality: an exposé. V. Eller. Christian Cent 84:1647-9 D 27 '67
Missing element: moral courage; excerpts from address. B. W. Tuchman. McCalls 94:28+ Je '67; Excerpts. PTA Mag 61:20-2 My '67
Teaching of morality has not been tabooed. D. Lawrence. U S News 62:112 F 13 '67
Where I stand, and why. B. Spock. Redbook 129:20+ Jl '67
See also
Business ethics
Christian ethics
Christian life
Conduct of life
Conscience
Forgiveness
Hypocrisy
Journalistic ethics
Labor ethics
Marriage
Medical ethics
Moral attitudes
Moral education
Patriotism
Political ethics
Responsibility
Scientists, Professional ethics for
Sexual ethics
Spirituality
Truthfulness
War, Ethics of
Woman—Social and moral questions

ETHICS committee, Senate. See United States
—Congress—Senate—Standards and con-
duct. Committee on
ETHIONINE. See Butyric acid
ETHIOPIA
Aging Lion of Judah. C. Sterling. il Reporter
36:28-30 F 9 '67
See also
United States—Armed forces—Forces in
Ethiopia
Antiquities
Journey to Ethiopia's past. R. H. Howland.
il UNESCO Courier 20:39-41 N '67

Description and travel
Ethiopia: the lion-hearted land. J. Morris. il
Holiday 41:58-67+ Je '67

Foreign relations
Emperor of Ethiopia visits the United States;
exchange of greetings, February 13, 1967;
exchange of toasts, February 14, 1967. Haile
Selassie I; L. B. Johnson. Dept State Bul
56:425-8 Mr 13 '67

Politics and government
Our man in Ethiopia. B. Hillenbrand. Com-
monweal 85:670-1 Mr 17 '67
ETHIOPIA and the United States
See also
United States—Foreign opinion—Ethiopian
ETHNIC attitudes. See Attitudes
ETHNIC types
Creative elite in America, by N. Weyl. Re-
view
Nat R 19:531-2 My 16 '67. G. Tullock
ETHNOLOGY
Componential analysis; kinship studies in cul-
tural anthropology. W. H. Goodenough. bib-
liog il Science 156:1203-9 Je 2 '67
Recent trends in ethnology. R. T. Anderson.
bibliog f Ann Am Acad 369:141-8 Ja '67
See also
Civilization
Race problems
Racial differences
Society, Primitive
ETHNOPSYCHOLOGY
See also
National characteristics
Racial differences
ETHOLOGY. See Animals—Habits and behavior
ETHYL corporation
Winner by a knockout. R. Levy. Duns R
89:42-4 Ja '67
ETHYLENE
Ethylene and carbon dioxide: mediation of
hypocotyl hook-opening response. B. G.
Kang and others. bibliog il Science 156:
958-9 My 19 '67
Ethylene formation from ethyl moiety of ethi-
onine. K. Shimokawa and Z. Kasai. bib-
liog Science 156:1362-3 Je 9 '67
Propanal may be a precursor of ethylene in
metabolism. M. Lieberman and A. T. Kun-
ishi. bibliog il Science 158:938 N 17 '67
2,4,5-Trichlorophenoxyacetic acid: effect on
ethylene production by fruits and leaves of
fig tree. E. C. Maxie and J. C. Crane. bib-
liog il Science 155:1548-50 Mr 24 '67
ETHYLHYPOXANTHINE. See Guanine
ETIQUETTE
Common sense and table manners. E. C.
Robinson. Am Home 70:126b N '67
Etiquette for polar bears; socialist book of
manners. Time 89:34+ Mr 3 '67
Mind your travel manners. L. Barry. il Pop
Phot 61:46+ Jl '67
[Monthly column] A. Vanderbilt. See issues
of Ladies' home journal
Your manners are showing. E. C. Robinson.
Am Home 70:60 Mr '67
ETIQUETTE for children and youth
Handling children who have bad manners.
B. Bettelheim. Ladies Home J 84:26+ My
'67
Mrs Potts and her dancing tots; social-
dancing classes in Wyoming, Ohio. B.
Rollin. il Look 31:105-7 My 16 '67
ETRUSCAN tombs. See Tombs
ETTER, Dave
Five poets. E. Blum. Poetry 109:342 F '67
ETTINGER, R. C. W.
Cryonics and the purpose of life. Christian
Cent 84:1250-3 O 4 '67
ETYMOLOGY. See subhead Etymology under
names of languages, e.g. English language
—Etymology
ETZIONI, Amitai, and Lehman, E. W.
Some dangers in valid social measurement.
bibliog f Ann Am Acad 373:1-15 S '67

EUCALYPTUS
Better way to plant eucalyptus. il Sunset
138:259 Ap '67
Eucalyptus in Peru. K. A. Herath. il Am For
73:20-2 Ap '67
Eucalyptus: tree of the future. L. D. Pryor.
il Am For 73:12-15+ F '67
It's Australia come to California, an almost
all-eucalyptus garden. il Sunset 138:190+
Je '67
EUCALYPTUS trees; story. See McPhee, J.
EUCHARIST. See Catholic church—Eucharist;
Lords Supper
EUCLID road machinery company
Putting the brake on GM. Bsns W p33 Ag 12
'67
EUGENE, Ore.
Architecture
New city hall that borrows from the past. R.
L. Norton. il Am City 82:108-9 Ag '67
EUGENICS
Changing man; excerpts from address,
December 26, 1966. T. Dobzhansky. bib-
liog Science 155:409-15 Ja 27 '67; Discussion.
156:581; 157:6+ My 5, Jl 7 '67
Genetics: what it will do for the next genera-
tion. B. Frisch. il Sci Digest 61:43 Mr '67
Lab creates life in a test tube. il Bsns W
p58 D 23 '67
Life control and the Christian. C. P. Kind-
region. America 117:406-8 O 14 '67
Man is not going downhill. A. J. Snider.
il Sci Digest 61:56-7 Ap '67
What man can be; excerpts from address.
B. Glass. il NEA J 56:11-14 S '67
Will society be prepared? excerpts from address. M. W. Nirenberg. Science 157:633 Ag
11 '67; Reply. J. Lederberg. 158:313 O 20 '67
EUGLENA
Euglena and the tides. J. D. Palmer. il Natur
Hist 76:60-4 F '67
Euglena gracilis: a novel lipid energy re-
serve and arachidonic acid enrichment dur-
ing fasting. R. Rosenberg. bibliog il Sci-
ence 157:1189-91 S 8 '67
Galactosyl diglycerides: their possible func-
tion in euglena chloroplasts. A. Rosenberg.
bibliog il Science 157:1191-6 S 8 '67
Mutagenic effect of visible light mediated by
endogenous pigments in euglena gracilis. J.
Leff and N. I. Krinsky. bibliog il Science
158:1332-5 D 8 '67
EUGSTER, Hans P.
Hydrous sodium silicates from Lake Magadi,
Kenya: precursors of bedded chert. bibliog
Science 157:1177-80 S 8 '67
EUPHORBIA antisyphilitica. See Candelillas
EURATOM. See European atomic energy com-
munity
EUREKA, Calif.
Virginia City. J. Hasz. il Parks & Rec 2:24-5+
Ap '67
EURIPIDES
Iphigenia in Aulis; tr. by M. Volanakis.
Criticism
Commonweal 87:409-10 D 29 '67
Nation 205:636-7 D 11 '67
New Yorker 43:147 D 2 '67
Newsweek il 70:110 D 4 '67
Sat R 50:22 D 9 '67
Time il 90:93-4 D 1 '67
EUROPE
Europe and America, 1967; address, Novem-
ber 10, 1967. J. R. Schaetzel. Dept State
Bul 57:710-15 N 27 '67
Too good to be true? pacification of Europe.
W. Lippmann. Newsweek 69:13 Ja 30 '67
See also
Airplane industry and trade—Europe
Americans in Europe
Automobile laws and legislation—Europe
Camping—Europe
Canals—Europe
Colleges and universities—Europe
Jews in Europe
Labor supply—Europe
Libraries—Europe
Music festivals—Europe
Radio broadcasting—Europe
Railroads—Europe
Tourist trade—Europe

Civilization
From Sarajevo to Potsdam, by A. J. P.
Taylor. Review
New Repub 156:19-21 Ap 29 '67. M.
Shefftz

Description and travel
Grand tour: as it was; as it is. J. Wechsberg; P. Brooks. il Sat R 51:59-61+ Ja 6
'68

EUROPE—Description and travel—*Continued*
Grand tour, by G. Trease. Review
    Newsweek il 70:78 Ag 7 '67. S. Maloff
How grand it was! excerpts from Europe:
    the grand tour. L. Martin and S. Martin.
    Sat R 50:41-3 My 27 '67
Travel 18th century style. A. Burgess. il
    Holiday 42:72-7+ N '67

Economic conditions

See also
United Nations—Economic commission for
    Europe

Economic integration

Address to Berlin House of representatives,
    April 6, 1967. H. H. Humphrey. Dept State
    Bul 56:680-1 My 1 '67
Europe going isolationist? why Humphrey
    mends fences. il U S News 62:36-7 Ap 10 '67
From the iron curtain to the open door;
    address, March 5, 1967. H. H. Humphrey.
    Dept State Bul 56:486-90 Mr 27 '67; Same
    with title New engagement. Vital Speeches
    33:386-9 Ap 15 '67
Toward a community of the developed nations.
    Z. Brzezinski. Dept State Bul 56:414-20 Mr
    13 '67
United States relations with the Soviet Union;
    address, April 21, 1967. N. D. Katzenbach.
    Dept State Bul 56:753-6 My 15 '67

Economic policy

Whatever happened to Europe? S. Freidin.
    Sat R 50:22-4 My 13 '67

History

Birth of Europe, by R. S. Lopez. Review
    Nat R 19:864-6 Ag 8 '67. J. Zola
    See also
European war, 1914-1918

Bibliography

Articles and other books received; comp. by
    O. J. Falnes. See issues of American his-
    torical review

20th century

From Sarajevo to Potsdam, by A. J. P.
    Taylor. Review
    Nat R 19:644-5 Je 13 '67. B. H. Smith
    New Repub 156:19-21 Ap 29 '67.   M.
    Shefftz

Industries

U.S. economic giant keeps growing. E. L.
    Dale, jr. il N Y Times Mag p30-1+ Mr 19
    '67

Kings and rulers

Where are they now? European kings-in-
    exile. il Newsweek 71:9 Ja 8 '68

Maps

Map of Europe (cont) Sr Schol 91:22 O 5 '67

Neutrality

Europe minus America; de Gaulle plan for
    a neutral, nuclear-free area. New Repub
    157:7-8 O 21 '67

Politics

Europe versus détente? M. D. Shulman. For
    Affairs 45:389-402 Ap '67
Persuading red China to join the U.N.
    J. B. Sheerin. Cath World 204:261-3 F '67
Seeking alternatives to de Gaulle. Life 62:4 F
    10 '67
Whatever happened to Europe? S. Freidin.
    Sat R 50:22-4 My 13 '67
    See also
European federation

Social life and customs

European odds and ends. J. C. Evans. Chris-
    tian Cent 84:958 Jl 26 '67

Union (proposed)

See European federation

EUROPE, EASTERN
Back to normal. F. Y. Blumenfeld. il News-
    week 69:58+ Ap 17 '67
East Europe, 1967; symposium. bibliog f il
    Cur Hist 52:193-240+ Ap '67
Eastern Europe: the changing climate;
    address, March 15, 1967. C. Pell. Vital
    Speeches 33:394-400 Ap 15 '67
Fissures in the eastern Europe bloc; address,
    April 1967, with questions and answers.
    N. J. G. Pounds. bibliog f il Ann Am Acad
    372:40-58 Jl '67

United States and eastern Europe in per-
    spective; address, April 29, 1967. W. A. Har-
    riman. Dept State Bul 56:815-21 My 29 '67
    See also
Advertising—Europe, Eastern
Automobile industry and trade—Europe, East-
    ern
Gambling—Europe, Eastern
Jews in Europe
Labor and laboring classes—Europe, Eastern
Morale, National—Europe, Eastern
Music, Popular (songs, etc)—Europe, Eastern
Public opinion—Europe, Eastern
Television broadcasting—Europe, Eastern

Commerce

Challenging east European market. G. Burck.
    il Fortune 76:122-4+ Jl '67
East-West trade, what it means to business.
    il U S News 62:50 Mr 27 '67
Germany and the East. C. McWilliams. Na-
    tion 205:138-41 Ag 28 '67
Revival of trade between the Communist bloc
    and the West. A. M. Solomon. bibliog f Ann
    Am Acad 372:105-12 Jl '67

Cultural relations

Cultural exchanges between Communist coun-
    tries and the United States. F. C. Barg-
    hoorn. bibliog f Ann Am Acad 372:113-23 Jl
    '67

Defenses

Ballistic missile defense and Europe. L. W.
    Martin. Bul Atomic Sci 23:42-6 My '67

Economic policy

East Europe's struggle for economic free-
    dom. G. Burck. il Fortune 75:124-7+ My '67
Why the United States should expand peace-
    ful trade with eastern Europe; address,
    March 2, 1967 A. M. Solomon. Dept State
    Bul 56:518-23 Mr 27 '67

Economic relations

Germany and the East. C. McWilliams. Na-
    tion 205:138-41 Ag 28 '67

Foreign opinion

Reality gap in eastern Europe. F. Y. Blumen-
    feld. Newsweek 70:40-1 O 9 '67

Foreign relations

Pattern of disintegration; relations with Bonn.
    Time 89:33-4 F 17 '67
Red nations agree on one thing: hate U.S.
    il U S News 62:59-60 My 15 '67
With friends like these; relations with West
    Germany. Newsweek 69:49-50 F 20 '67

History
Bibliography

Articles and other books received; comp. by
    C. Morley. See issues of American his-
    torical review

Intellectual life

Upper class in eastern Europe. L. Tyrmand.
    il Reporter 38:14-19 Ja 11 '68

Politics

Toward a community of the developed nations.
    Z. Brezezinski. Dept State Bul 56:414-20 Mr
    13 '67

Religious Institutions and affairs

Eastern Europe & the death of God; confer-
    ence of Marxist sociologists of religion in
    Prague. N. Birnbaum. Commentary 44:69-73
    Jl '67

Social life and customs

Letter from eastern Europe. R. Goldstein.
    Holiday 42:20+ N '67
Riding high; chauffeur-driven cars. Time 91:
    22 Ja 12 '68
Upper class in eastern Europe. L. Tyrmand.
    il Reporter 38:14-19 Ja 11 '68

EUROPE, WESTERN
Field notes on the Europeans. J. Fischer.
    Harper 234:14+ Mr '67
    See also
Aeronautics, Commercial—Europe, Western
Aerospace industries—Europe, Western
Art—Europe, Western
Arts and crafts—Europe, Western
Ballet—Europe, Western
Camping—Europe, Western
Communism—Europe, Western
Economic assistance in Europe
Finance—Europe, Western
Gardens—Europe, Western
Helicopter industry and trade—Europe, West-
    ern
Hotels, taverns, etc.—Europe, Western

EUROPE, Western—See also—*Continued*
Industrial management and organization—
  Europe. Western
Investments, Foreign (in Europe)
Libraries—Europe. Western
Music festivals—Europe. Western
Opera—Europe. Western
Public opinion—Europe. Western
Publishers and publishing—Europe, Western
Railroads—Europe. Western
Research—Europe. Western
Restaurants—Europe. Western
Shopping and shoppers—Europe. Western
Social and economic security—Europe, Western
Space research—Europe, Western
Television broadcasting—**Europe. Western**
Tourist trade—Europe. Western
United States—Foreign relations—Europe, Western
Youth—Europe, Western

Armed forces

See also
United States—Armed forces—Forces in Europe

Bibliography

Catch up with. L. Lerman. Mlle 64:56+ F '67

Commerce

Revival of trade between the Communist bloc and the West. A. M. Solomon. bibliog f Ann Am Acad 372:105-12 Jl '67

Defenses

Ballistic missile defense and Europe. L. W. Martin. Bul Atomic Sci 23:42-6 My '67
Disarmament; letter. R. D. Masters. Commonweal 85:547+ F 17 '67
Dynamic new policy toward the new Europe. W. Goldstein. Bul Atomic Sci 23:17-22 Ap '67
Europe looks again to U.S. leadership. A. de Borchgrave. il Newsweek 70:44-5 O 16 '67
KGK, meet LBJ; discussion of U.S. commitment to the security of Europe. il Newsweek 70:19 Ag 28 '67
Oh. what a lovely war; shore battery ruins of World war II. il Arch Forum 127:58-63 N '67
Status of major U.S. European defense, aerospace programs. Aviation W 86:62-6 Mr 6 '67
See also
North Atlantic treaty organization

Description and travel

Educated eater's Baedeker. H. Sutton. Sat R 50:30-1 Jl 1 '67
Floating across the Continent; seeing western Europe by waterway; with account by M. Leatherbee. il Life 62:50-61+ Je 23 '67
If this should be my last trip to Europe. . . ed. by R. Joseph. E. Steichen; J. Durante; J. Farley. il Esquire 67:80-93+ F '67
What's your best way to see Europe? G. Bush. il Bet Hom & Gard 45:165-8 N '67

Economic conditions

Europe: a slowdown. il Newsweek 69:82-4 Ja 30 '67
Europe bets on revival; McGraw-Hill economics dept.'s annual world survey. il Bsns W p44+ D 30 '67
In Europe's business. too. signs of an upturn. il U S News 63:96-7 S 25 '67
Slowing down. il Time 89:87-8 F 24 '67
Why Europe's growth tops the U.S; highlights of E. F. Denison's study. il Bsns W p 152+ Ja 14 '67
Will Europe see boom times again? il Bsns W p 124-6+ Ap 8 '67
See also
Unemployment—Europe Western
United Nations—Economic commission for Europe

Economic integration

Field notes on the Europeans. J. Fischer. Harper 234:16+ My '67
See also
Commission of the European communities

Economic policy

New Europe: meaning to U.S. il U S News 63:45-6 O 2 '67
See also
European economic community
Taxation—Europe. Western

Economic relations

Economic necessities and Atlantic communities. A. C. Neal. il For Affairs 45:694-705 Jl '67

Economic union

See European economic community

Foreign relations

Changing nature of Soviet and American relations with western Europe; address, April 1967, with questions and answers. D. S. McLellan. bibliog f Ann Am Acad 372:16-32 Jl '67

United States

Europe and America, 1967; address. November 10. 1967. J. R. Schaetzel. Dept State Bul 57:710-15 N 27 '67
Europe going isolationist? why Humphrey mends fences. il U S News 62:36-7 Ap 10 '67
Europe looks again to U.S. leadership. A. de Borchgrave. il Newsweek 70:44-5 O 16 '67
On three fronts; search for a stable new relationship. il Newsweek 69:49-50 My 15 '67

Historic houses, etc.

Literary past; a view from the tour bus. A. Netboy. il Sat R 50:46-7+ Mr 11 '67

Industries

Europe: a slowdown. il Newsweek 69:82-4 Ja 30 '67
House abroad. J. Ross-Skinner. Duns R 89:63-4 Ap '67
How ITT tightens its spreading net. il Bsns W p58-60+ Je 24 '67
Is U.S. technology a threat to Europe? Read Digest 90:137-40 Je '67
See also
Industrial management and organization—Europe. Western
Machine tool industry and trade
Shipbuilding

Nationalism

Europe's new nationalism. M. Ways. Read Digest 91:60-4 Jl '67

Politics

See also
Atlantic community
European federation

Popular culture

Dogheads of the West. T. Molnar. Nat R 19:1285+ N 14 '67

Religious Institutions and affairs

Renewal in Europe. D. Fisher. Cath World 206:101-4 D '67

Social life and customs

Traveling with Mlle: Europe on the cheap. L. Gottlieb. il Mlle 64:165-72+ F '67

Union (proposed)

See European federation
EUROPE, WESTERN and the United States. See Europe and the United States
EUROPE and England. See England and Europe
EUROPE and the United States
American interest in Europe; address, December 2, 1967. D. Rusk. Dept State Bul 57:855-9 D 25 '67
Cooperation or stagnation? address, November 15, 1967. R. A. Peterson. Vital Speeches 34:165-8 Ja 1 '68
Field notes on the Europeans. J. Fischer. Harper 234:18+ Mr '67
New Europe: meaning to U.S. il U S News 63:45-6 O 2 '67
Soviet view of NATO; address, April 24, 1967. L. I. Brezhnev. Vital Speeches 33:514-22 Je 15 '67
See also
Americans in Europe
United States—Foreign opinion—European
EUROPEAN aerospace industry association. See Eurospace
EUROPEAN artificial satellites. See Artificial satellites, European
EUROPEAN atomic energy community
Euratom: a cut for cooperation. J. Walsh. Science 158:1657 D 29 '67
Euratom: after ten years, still seeking the way. J. Walsh. Science 158:95-8 O 6 '67
Euratom drops out; no more fast breeder reactor research, and studies of fusion power. Sci N 93:8-9 Ja 6 '68
Euratom: nuclear integration in Europe. L. Scheinman. bibliog f il(cover) Int Concil 563:5-66 My '67

EUROPEAN atomic energy community—*Cont.*
Euratom threatened. Sci N 91:184 F 25 '67
Inspection and control in Euratom. S.
Gorove. Bul Atomic Sci 23:41-6 Mr '67
Lessons to be learned from Euratom. J.
Guéron. il Bul Atomic Sci 23:38-41 Mr '67
See also
Commission of the European communities
EUROPEAN cars. See Automobiles, Foreign
EUROPEAN center for nuclear research. See
European organization for nuclear research
EUROPEAN coal and steel community
See also
Commission of the European communities
EUROPEAN common market. See European
economic community
EUROPEAN communities, Commission of the.
See Commission of the European communities
EUROPEAN cookery. See Cookery, European
EUROPEAN economic community
Big leap; Great Britain's bid to join common market. Sr Schol 90:28 My 19 '67
Britain entering Europe. W. Lippmann.
Newsweek 69:23 My 22 '67
Britain goes to market. America 116:748 My 20 '67
Britain wants in; no choice but the Common market. S. A. Scheingold. Commonweal 86:84-6 Ap 7 '67
Britain's sad plight. Time 90:26-7 D 22 '67
British economy: world trade; address. November 6, 1967. P. Dean. Vital Speeches 34:150-3 D 15 '67
British question hangs fire; tenth anniversary meeting in Rome. il Bsns W p38 Je 3 '67
Le brushoff; de Gaulle opposes British entry. il Time 89:25-6 My 26 '67
Charlie against the tide. Fortune 75:77 Je 1 '67
Common market; Great Britain applies for membership. Nat R 19:506 My 16 '67
Common market; its effect on Britain; address, May 8, 1967. H. Wilson. Vital Speeches 33:482-94 Je 1 '67
Common market; sputters but no blow-up. Bsns W p 107-8 D 16 '67
Common thieves; swindlers collect illegal subsidies. Newsweek 69:78 F 20 '67
Cordial dislike; before Britain's talks with European common market. Nat R 19:945 S 5 '67
De Gaulle and Britain: same old stand. il Newsweek 69:34+ My 29 '67
De Gaulle dampens British bid; second move to join Common market. il Bsns W p37 My 20 '67
De Gaulle has spoken; veto of England's application for entry into the Common market. Nat R 19:554-5 My 30 '67
De Gaulle, non! Britain's application to join the Common market. A. LeJeune. Nat R 19:637+ Je 13 '67
De Gaulle's second veto; British application. il Newsweek 71:30+ Ja 1 '68
Dismal diplomacy; Britain's try for German help to gain entry to EEC. il Time 89:30 F 24 '67
European common market: the entry of Britain; address, May 16, 1967. C. de Gaulle. Vital Speeches 33:495-7 Je 1 '67
EEC steps to close the gap; technological gap between western Europe and the United States. J. R. Lambert. Sci N 92:558 D 16 '67
Exercise in persuasion; Wilson, de Gaulle & Brown. il Time 89:26+ F 3 '67
Glancing blow; first official talks on Britain's application for membership. Time 90:30 N 3 '67
Growing pains, and progress. il Newsweek 69:46-7 Ap 10 '67
Her Majesty's government decides; Britain's application to join Common market. Newsweek 69:49 My 15 '67
In lieu of an army; meeting of foreign ministers in Brussels. Newsweek 69:44 Ap 24 '67
Ironical anniversary; de Gaulle attends Rome conference. il Time 89:46 Je 9 '67
Is U.S. losing Britain as its no. 1 ally? Britain's entry into the Common market. il U S News 62:52-3 My 15 '67
Kind of Europe de Gaulle will allow. il U S News 62:22 My 29 '67
Letter from London; Common market negotiations with Britain. M. Panter-Downes. New Yorker 43:50+ D 23 '67
Letter from London; question of membership in the Common market. M. Panter-Downes. New Yorker 42:145 F 11 '67

Letter from Paris; Britain's request to be admitted to the Common market. Genêt. New Yorker 43:124+ My 27 '67
Luxembourg versus de Gaulle. J. Ross-Skinner. il Duns R 90:41-2 Jl '67
No sale; French conditions for Britain's entry. Newsweek 70:47-8 N 6 '67
Off the touchline; Britain's Common market bid. Time 89:28 My 5 '67
Possibility of an instant jump; decision that Britain apply for membership in the Common market for a second time. Time 89:29 My 12 '67
Power play in IMF; Common market nations want a louder voice. il Bsns W p31-3 S 30 '67
Report; implications of (Britain's) bid to join the Common market. D. Cook. Atlan 219:24+ My '67
Roman holiday; Common market summit. il Newsweek 69:44 Je 12 '67
Scurrying in the wings. il Time 89:26 Ja 27 '67
Shooting at Europe; de Gaulle opposes British entry to Common market. il Bsns W p37-8 Ja 28 '67
Six-movement symphony; attempts to fire West German enthusiasm for British entry. Newsweek 69:38+ F 27 '67
Standoff in Paris; British entry. il Newsweek 69:50+ F 6 '67
Ten years old. il Time 89:84 Mr 31 '67
To market; Austria's moves to join Common market. Time 89:45 Ap 21 '67
Trade with U.S.S.R. and European growth; address, April 20, 1967. G. W. Ball. Vital Speeches 33:546-50 Jl 1 '67
Troubled times of George Brown; Lord Chalfont's reputed threat if Britain refused entry. B. Wenham. New Repub 157:12-13 N 18 '67
Waiting for word from France. il Newsweek 69:51 My 22 '67
When in Rome . . . Common market summit. Newsweek 69:55 Je 5 '67
Will Europe see boom times again? il Bsns W p 124-6+ Ap 8 '67
Worst year in ten. il Time 90:106 D 1 '67
Yes or no for Europe: Harold Wilson's return from exploratory mission to the Common market countries. Time 89:31 Mr 17 '67
See also
Commission of the European communities

Anecdotes, facetiae, satire, etc.
Common market and a horse named Arkle. C. Brogan. Nat R 19:252-4 Mr 7 '67
EUROPEAN federation
Eurocrats, by A. Spinelli. Review
Sat R 50:43 Je 10 '67. H. Kohn
Europe and America, 1967; address, November 10, 1967. J. R. Schaetzel. Dept State Bul 57:710-15 N 27 '67
Framework of East-West reconciliation. Z. Brzezinski. bibliog f For Affairs 46:256-75 Ja '68
Western integration and the people's democracies. J. Lukaszewski. For Affairs 46:377-87 Ja '86
EUROPEAN launcher development organization
Europe irons out issues in initial space programs. W. C. Wetmore. il Aviation W 86:146-7+ Mr 6 '67
French trying to learn cause of Coralie misfire. Aviation W 87:35 Ag 14 '67
EUROPEAN literature
European literary scene. R. J. Clements. See issues of Saturday review
EUROPEAN machine tool exhibition, Hanover, Germany. See Machine tools—Exhibitions
EUROPEAN mail order business. See Mail order business
EUROPEAN molecular biology organization (proposed)
Toward a biology CERN. D. A. Ehrlich. Sci N 91:451 My 13 '67
EUROPEAN organization for nuclear research
CERN: regional cooperation amid tightening budgets. J. Walsh. Science 155:436-8 Ja 27 '67
CERN: the strong focus is on the 300-bev machine. J. Walsh. il Science 155:544-6 F 3 '67
CERN's human computer: W. Klein. D. A. Ehrlich. il Sci N 93:72-3 Ja 20 '68
Neutrinos: current experiments at CERN. N. Calder. Science 157:411-12 Jl 28 '67
EUROPEAN painting. See Painting, European
EUROPEAN poets. See Poets, European
EUROPEAN southern observatory. See Astronomical observatories—Chile

EUROPEAN space research organization
Deadline nears for role in ESRO Comsat. D. E.
Fink. il Aviation W 87:28-31 S 11 '67
Europe irons out issues in initial space pro-
grams. W. C. Wetmore. il Aviation W
86:146-7+ My 6 '67
ESRANGE being expanded for Skylark. K.
Lovstuhagen. il Tech W 20:40-1 F 6 '67
ESRO gets new look with management,
structure revision. J. A. Redeker. Aero
Tech 21:48+ Ag 28 '67
ESRO: space sciences research in Europe suf-
fers growing pains. J. Walsh. il Science 158:
242-4 O 13 '67
ESRO spending crisis hampers programs. J.
A. Redeker. Tech W 20:30 Je 19 '67
ESRO II satellite scheduled for WTR launch
in April. J. A. Redeker. Tech W 20:24-5 Ap
3 '67
ESRO's first satellite. Sci N 91:544 Je 10 '67
Future of ESRO hinges on July meeting. R.
Lindsey. Tech W 20:22+ Ap 3 '67
EUROPEAN student Christian movements. See
Student Christian movements
EUROPEAN union. See European federation
EUROPEAN visitors in the United States. See
Foreign visitors in the United States
EUROPEAN war, 1914-1918

American participation
See European war, 1914-1918—United
States

Causes
See also
European war, 1914-1918—Diplomatic history

Diplomatic history
Serbian campaign of 1915: its diplomatic
background. G. E. Silberstein. bibliog f Am
Hist R 73:51-69 O '67

Fiction
Après la guerre finie; American writers in
World war I. M. Cowley. il Horizon 10:112-
19 Wint '68

Medical and sanitary affairs
See also
Neuroses

Negroes
Incredible life of Monsieur Bullard; World
war I flying ace. M. H. Smith. il Ebony
23:120-2+ D '67

Peace and mediation
Thomas Woodrow Wilson, by S. Freud and
W. C. Bullitt. Review
New Repub 156:27-30 Ja 28 '67. R. Coles
New Yorker 42:111-14+ Ja 21 '67. G.
Steiner

Personal narratives
Profiles; memoirs. E. Wilson. New Yorker
43:54-6+ My 13 '67

Songs and music
He wanted to murder the bugler; I. Berlin's
show Yip Yip Yaphank, and songs by
other composers. B. Catton. il Am
Heritage 18:50-5+ Ag '67

Arabia
Desert revolt urged on by a legendary Eng-
lishman; Hejaz revolt. E. Kern. il Life 63:
54-7 O 20 '67
France
When the French army mutinied. D. John-
son. il N Y Times Mag p26-7+ My 28 '67
Russia
See also
Russia—History—Revolution, 1917-1921
Serbia
Serbian campaign of 1915: its diplomatic
background. G. E. Silberstein. bibliog f Am
Hist R 73:51-69 O '67
Turkey
On distant fronts, triumph and disaster of
a dogged defense. E. Kern. il Life 63:52-7
O 20 '67
United States
Après la guerre finie; American writers in
World war I. M. Cowley. il Horizon 10:112-
19 Wint '68
How we entered World war I. B. W. Tuch-
man. il N Y Times Mag p40-1+ Mr 5 '67
Yanks are coming. il Sr Schol 90:3+ Ap 7 '67
EUROPEAN war, 1939-1945. See World war,
1939-1945

EUROPEAN war and music. See European
war, 1914-1918—Songs and music
EUROPIUM
Europium-155 in debris from nuclear weap-
ons. A. Aarkrog and L. Lippert. bibliog il
Science 157:425-7 Jl 28 '67
EUROPORT. See Rotterdam—Harbor
EUROSPACE
Europeans firm on aerospace transporter. W.
E. Wilks. Tech W 20:36-7 Mr 13 '67
Eurospace urges regional Comsat system. D.
E. Fink. Aviation W 87:29-30 Ag 28 '67
EUTECTICS
Controlled eutectics. R. W. Kraft. il Sci Am
216:86-92 bibliog(p 146+) F '67
EUTHANASIA
Coup de grâce. M. M. Shideler; discussion.
Christian Cent 84:20, 82-3, 272-3, 471 Ja 4,
18, Mr 1, Ap 12 '67
Should mercy killing be permitted? Dr H.
Leslie Wenger says yes; with Good house-
keeping readers poll. H. L. Wenger. Good
H 164:82+ Ap '67
EUTROPHICATION. See Water pollution
EVALUATION (education)
College ratings. Sch & Soc 95:377 O 28 '67
National assessment. A. M. Mood. Am Ed
3:11-12+ Ap '67
National assessment of educational progress:
some technical deficiencies. C. A. Ander-
son. bibliog f Sch & Soc 95:48-50 Ja 21 '67
EVALUATION (psychology) See Value (psy-
chology)
EVANGELICAL church in Germany
Act of defiance; East German Evangelical
church. il Time 89:104+ Ap 14 '67
EVANGELICAL United Brethren church
Dim view of a bright prospect; the pro-
posed United Methodist church; E.U.B.-
Methodist merger. R. B. Garrison. Chris-
tian Cent 84:314-16 Mr 8 '67; Discussion.
84:501 Ap 19 '67
EVANGELICALISM
Grand alliance? evangelical leaders call for
alliance against liberal Christianity. News-
week 69:85 Je 12 '67
See also
Fundamentalism
EVANGELISTIC work
Billy's Communist rally. il Newsweek 70:71
Jl 24 '67
Graham meets communism; gathering in
Zagreb. il Time 90:60-1 Jl 21 '67
EVANOFF, Vlad
Fish 'n ships. See issues of Motor boating
EVANS, Arthur D.
Field-effect transistors. por Electr World 78:
49-52 Jl '67
EVANS, George Bird
Test your hunting know-how; questions and
answers. Field & S 72:66-7 My '67
EVANS, George E. and Kordesch, K. V.
Hydrazine-air fuel cells. bibliog Science 158:
1148-52 D 1 '67
EVANS, Griffith
Love in the park; excerpt from A gallery of
dudes. M. Sprague. il Am Heritage 18:8-13+
F '67
EVANS, Hayes, Jr
New idea in landfill operation. Am City 82:
114-15 Mr '67
EVANS, J. Claude
At the feet of greatness. Christian Cent 84:
335 Mr 15 '67
Conundrums for the ausländer. Christian
Cent 84:167 F 8 '67
Italian enigma. Christian Cent 84:710-11 My
31 '67
Messianic times? Christian Cent 84:1149-51
S 13 '67
Multiproblems in the Middle East. Christian
Cent 84:1183-4 S 20 '67
Paradigm for Russia. Christian Cent 84:679-
80 My 24 '67
Tale of two half cities. Christian Cent 84.
135-6 F 1 '67
Unchecked exchange in Czechoslovakia.
Christian Cent 84:774-5 Je 14 '67
EVANS, M. Stanton
First time out. Nat R 19:596-7 My 30 '67
Gospel according to Ayn Rand. Nat R 19:1059-
63 O 3 '67
Great divide. Nat R 19:424+ Ap 18 '67
Lean and hungry look of RFK. Nat R 19:
477+ My 2 '67
Old-fashioned oracle. Nat R 19:97-8 Ja 24
'67
EVANS, Maurice
Guestward ho. Time 90:82 D 8 '67
Million dollars worth of make-up obliterates
some famous faces; making up for Planet
of the apes. il pors Life 63:82-3 Ag 18 '67

EVANS, Robert, jr
Shuntō: Japanese labor's spring wage offensive. bibliog f Mo Labor R 90:23-8 O '67
EVANS, Rowland, and Novak, R. D.
Now that Reagan is governor, how's he doing? Sat Eve Post 240:40-2+ Jl 1 '67
Road to Miami Beach. Harper 236:21-6 Ja '68
Washington; L. B. Johnson's policies. Atlan 220:6+ O '67
EVANS products company
Why Evans products co. had a bad year. J. McDonald. il Fortune 75:138-41+ My '67
EVANSON, John M. and others
Human collagenase: identification and characterization of an enzyme from rheumatoid synovium in culture. bibliog Science 158: 499-502 O 27 '67
EVANSTON, Ill.
Education
It's a long way from the birds and bees; sex education program. W. B. Furlong. il N Y Times Mag p24-5+ Je 11 '67
Historic houses, etc.
Dawes home historical activities. il Hobbies 72:98B Mr '67
Hospitals
Evanston hospital: updating in a new wing; John J. Louis building. il Arch Rec 142:196-7 S '67
Parks and playgrounds
Mount Trashmore rises from an old clay pit. T. R. Carlson. il Am City 82:45 Jl '67
EVAPORATION
Evaporation of ice in space: Saturn's rings. H. Harrison and R. I. Schoen. bibliog Science 157:1175-6 S 8 '67
EVELYN, John
John Evelyn esq; fellow of the Royal society. D. Clark. il Horticulture 45:34-5+ D '67
EVENING and continuation schools
See also
Extension education
EVENING bulletin, Philadelphia. See Bulletin, Philadelphia
EVENING clothes. See Clothing and dress
EVERETT, Charlie J.
Crossroads toreador. il pors Ebony 22:64+ Ap '67
EVERGLADE kites. See Kites (birds)
EVERGLADES
Toughness of species; research in the Everglades. L. Gebhart. Sci N 92:355 O 7 '67
See also
Ten Thousand Islands
EVERGLADES NATIONAL PARK
Defense of the Everglades. A. W. Smith. Nat Parks Mag 41:2 Ag '67
Don't pull the plug on the Everglades. J. Browder. il Am For 73:12-15+ S '67
Everglades expedition. R. T. Fisher. il Yachting 121:61-4+ Mr; 82-5+ Ap '67
Inadequate water supply threatens Everglades National Park. R. W. Allin. il Parks & Rec 2:37+ O '67
Last chance for the Everglades. W. Stegner. il Sat R 50:22-3+ My 6 '67
Legal ruling needed on Everglades water rights. Audubon 69:5 Jl '67
National Audubon society sues to protect the Everglades. C. H. Callison. Audubon 69:56-7 My '67
Not a park to go barefoot in; Ten Thousand Islands. J. Olsen. il Sports Illus 26:58-60+ Ap 3 '67
Plug protects a park. Am City 82:60 O '67
Predicting Everglades water needs. Nat Parks Mag 41:22 S '67
Stillness in the Glades. il Time 89:30-1 My 19 '67
Threatened glories of Everglades National Park. F. K. Truslow and F. G. Vosburgh. il Nat Geog Mag 132:508-53 O '67
Water for Everglades National Park. Nat Parks Mag 41:2 D '67
Where drought threatens a disaster. il U S News 62:10 My 22 '67
Anecdotes, facetiae, satire, etc.
Florida's back-yard jungle. R. Atcheson. il Holiday 42:16+ N '67
EVERGREEN hedges. See Hedges
EVERGREENS
Evergreen groundcovers. D. Wyman. il Horticulture 45:14-17 N '67
Landscaping with evergreens. H. Mason and R. O'Harra. il Bet Home & Gard 45:58-63 O '67

Uncommon broadleaved evergreens. F. Heutte. il Horticulture 45:20-1+ Jl '67
See also
Christmas greens
Christmas trees
Conifers
Juniper
EVERLASTING delight; story. See Hazzard, S.
EVERLASTING flowers
See also
Flowers, Dried
EVERS, Myrlie B.
For us, the living; excerpts, ed. by W. Peters. por McCalls 94:86-7+ Jl; 88-9+ Ag '67
EVERSON, A. C.
How to reclaim blowout areas. Suc Farm 65:48 N '67
EVERSON, William
Seven poets. R. Tillinghast. Poetry 110:263-4 Jl '67
EVERYTHING in the garden; drama. See Albee, E.
EVETT, Robert
Music (cont) New Repub 156:38-9 F 25; 33-5 Ap 15; 28-9 Je 10; 157:30-2 Jl 15 '67
EVIDENCE (law)
Classic case of false evidence; L. E. Miller must be freed or retried for murder. Time 89:52-3 F 24 '67
Courtroom crack-up; case of H. Weinberg. il Time 90:108 N 17 '67
Gag for psychiatrists; testimony of state-employed psychiatrists. Time 90:48 Ag 25 '67
Getting it on tape; video-taped evidence. il Time 90:49 D 22 '67
Helping prosecutors; Supreme court decision on mere-evidence rule. Time 89:75 Je 9 '67
Immunity of prosecutors; case of L. E. Miller, jr. il Time 89:72 Mr 31 '67
Reliving a murder; Thomas Kidwell verdict. il Time 90:38 D 29 '67
See also
Confession (law)
Self incrimination
Wire tapping
Witnesses
EVIDENCE, Expert
See also
Witnesses
EVIL. See Good and evil
EVINRUDE, Ralph
Nine seas and an ocean. il Yachting 122:38-40+ O '67
EVINS, Joseph Landon
Representative Joe Evins: NSF and NASA get a new master of finance. L. J. Carter. il pors Science 155:806-10 F 17 '67
EVOLUTION
Biologists' statement on teaching evolution; text with comment. H. J. Muller. Bul Atomic Sci 23:39-40 F '67
Books in review; this evolving world. H. L. Shapiro. Natur Hist 76:68+ Je '67
Butterflies and plants. P. R. Ehrlich and P. H. Raven. il Sci Am 216:104-11+ Je '67
Changing man; excerpts from address, December 26, 1966. T. Dobzhansky. bibliog Science 155:409-15 Ja 27 '67; Discussion. 156:581; 157:6+ My 5, Jl 7 '67
Churches and evolution. P. Hefner. Christian Cent 84:651-6 My 17 '67
Evolution and being faithful. P. L. Holmer. Christian Cent 84:1491-4 N 22 '67; Reply. M. M. Kaplan. 85:46 Ja 10 '68
Evolution: basic to biology. W. T. Keeton; discussion. Christian Cent 84:279-80, 694+ Mr 1, My 24 '67
Evolution: implications for religion. T. Dobzhansky. Christian Cent 84:936-41 Jl 19 '67
Evolutionary science and the dilemma of freedom and determinism. L. Gilkey. Christian Cent 84:339-43 Mr 15 '67; Reply. E. C. Kemble. 84:755-7 Je 7 '67
Evolutionary significance of metabolic control systems. J. L. Cánovas and others. bibliog il Science 156:1695-9 Je 30 '67
Evolutionary view emerges; human personality. Sci N 93:6-7 Ja 6 '68
Experimental genetics and human evolution. J. Lederberg; reply with rejoinder. L. Ornstein. Bul Atomic Sci 23:57-61 Je '67
Human aggression: the need for a species-specific framework. R. L. Holloway, jr. Natur Hist 76:40-4 bibliog(p69) D '67
Immunological time scale for hominid evolution. V. M. Sarich and A. C. Wilson. bibliog il Science 158:1200-3 D 1 '67

EVOLUTION—*Continued*

John T. Scopes redivivus. Christian Cent 84:429 Ap 5 '67

Major steps in vertebrate evolution; address, December 28, 1967. A. S. Romer. bibliog il Science 158:1629-37 D 29 '67

Man, culture, evolution and environment. J. R. Jablonski. Christian Cent 84:495-8 Ap 19 '67

Question: Darwinism revisited; letter with reply. N. Macbeth; E. S. Deevey, jr. Yale R 56:616-40 Je '67

Shall we play God? L. Augenstein. Christian Cent 84:1314-18 O 18 '67; Reply. C. W. Kirkpatrick. 84:1571 D 6 '67

Significance of Teilhard. I. G. Barbour. Christian Cent 84:1098-102 Ag 30 '67

See also
Genetics
Man—Origin and antiquity
Plants—Evolution
Tennessee evolution controversy

Laws and legislation

Anti-evolution upheld; Arkansas. Sci N 91:569 Je 17 '67

End of the monkey law. Sci Am 217:42 Jl '67

Monkey business; House of Tennessee legislature repeals monkey law. il Newsweek 69:33 Ap 24 '67

See also
Tennessee evolution controversy

EVOLUTION, Social. See Social change

EVOY, John J.

Thoughts on priestly celibacy. America 117:114 Jl 29 '67

EVTUSHENKO, Evgenii Aleksandrovich

Babi Yar; poem; tr. by H. Marshall. Am Rec G 34:11 S '67

New poems; Fears; Tenderness; tr. by G. Reavey. Harper 234:65 Mr '67

Restaurant for two; Ballad about nuggets; poems, tr. by J. Updike. Life 62:33, 38 F 17 '67

Rome: Rhythms of Rome; Heat in Rome; poems, tr. by G. Reavey. Sat R 50:24-7 Jl 22 '67

What pain, my beloved; poem, tr. by G. Reavey. Good H 166:122 Ja '68

about

Poet at the podium. S. Bernard. Nation 204:534-6 Ap 24 '67

Yevtushenko and Voznesensky. G. Ruark. Poetry 111:121-4 N '67

Yevtushenko tells in two poems about his visit to America; with photographs by E. Sarsini. Life 62:32-9 F 17 '67

EWEN, Frederic

Alas, poor Bertolt Brecht! Nation 204:213-14 F 13 '67

EWEN, Lois Stuart

Come back to San Francisco; story. Good H 164:78-9 Je '67

EWING, Cortes A. M.

He liked students; excerpt from The teacher. J Fischer. NEA J 56:68 D '67

EWING, David W.

Corporate planning at a crossroads. bibliog f Harvard Bsns R 45:77-86 Jl '67

EWING, John, and Ewing, Maurice

Sediment distribution on the mid-ocean ridges with respect to spreading of the sea floor. bibliog Science 156:1590-2 Je 23 '67

EWING, Juliana Horatia (Gatty)

Mrs Ewing in Canada. M. A. Downie. il Horn Bk 43:721-5 D '67

EWING, L. S.

Fighting and death from stress in a cockroach. bibliog Science 155:1035-6 F 24 '67

EWING, Maurice. See Ewing, J. jt. auth.

EXAKTA cameras. See Cameras

EXAMINATIONS

See also
Psychological examinations

EXCAVATING machinery

How to rent a backhoe. C. E. Rhine. il Pop Sci 190:149-53+ Je '67

See also
Euclid road machinery company

EXCAVATION

Rapid excavation. T. E. Howard. il Sci Am 217:74-6+ bibliog(p 154) N '67

EXCAVATIONS (archeology)

Indian mound is excavated by high school archaeologists; coastal Miwoks of California; ed. by C. L. Stong. T. J. ONeil. il Sci Am 217:134-8 D '67

See also
Cities and towns, Ruined, extinct, etc.
Pompeii
Troy

also subhead Antiquities under names of continents, countries, states, cities, etc. e.g. Ethiopia—Antiquities

EXCELL, Raymond

Color in the kitchen sink. U S Camera 30:64-5+ Jl '67

EXCEPTIONAL children. See Children, Exceptional

EXCHANGE, Foreign. See Foreign exchange

EXCHANGE of houses. See Houses, Exchange of

EXCHANGE of persons programs

Exchange program with eastern Europe. Sch & Soc 95:345-6 O 14 '67

Making cultural exchange a real exchange; teaching modern dance in Asia. il Dance Mag 41:21-3 O '67

U.S. Romania complete 1967-68 cultural exchange arrangement; Department annoucement, with text of U.S. note. Dept State Bul 56:479-80 Mr 20 '67

U.S.-Soviet exchanges: agreement nears expiration. K. Sperry. Science 158:751 N 10 '67

See also
Educational exchanges
Students, Interchange of

EXCHANGE of students. See Students, Interchange of

EXCHANGE peace corps. See Volunteer service, International

EXCHANGES

Bonanza is over; San Francisco mining exchange. il Bsns W p28-9 Ag 26 '67

Plain talk about using beef futures. F. Bailey, jr. il Suc Farm 65:42-3 N '67

See also
Chicago board of trade
Put and call transactions
Speculation
Stock exchange

EXCHANGES, Educational. See Educational exchanges

EXCHANGES, Literary and scientific

U.S. Romania complete 1967-68 cultural exchange arrangement; Department announcement, with text of U.S. note. Dept State Bul 56:479-80 Mr 20 '67

See also
United States book exchange

EXCHEQUER (Great Britain) See Great Britain—Exchequer

EXCITEMENT at the circus; drama. See Leitner, I. A.

EXCLUSIVE agencies

Do boy scouts rate a badge for retailing? il Bsns W p72-4 Ag 12 '67

Extra green crop for Christmas; Santa's forests, Wisconsin concern. il Bsns W p48-9 D 23 '67

Franchise way. Sr Schol 90:30 My 12 '67

High court hints a softer tone; Supreme court decisions on franchising. Bsns W p40 Je 17 '67

New look in franchising. il Changing T 21:17-20 O '67

When bicycle maker peddles alone; Supreme court decision concerning Schwinn's marketing system. Bsns W p39-40 Jl 1 '67

World quaffers call for Skol. il Bsns W p74+ S 30 '67

EXCOMMUNICATION

Manner of speaking; on excommunicating demonstrators. J. Ciardi. Sat R 50:30+ Jl 22 '67

EX-CONVICTS. See Prisoners, Discharged

EXCURSION rates. See Travel—Economic aspects

EXCURSIONS

Eight ways to have an extra vacation without leaving town. P. Beshiri. il Parents Mag 42:36-7+ Jl '67

EXCURSIONS, School. See School excursions

EXECUTIONS and executioners

At San Quentin, gas chamber is back in use. il U S News 62:19 Ap 24 '67

Killing me solves nothing; interview, ed. by J. Le Blanc. A. Mitchell. il Ebony 22:121-2+ Je '67

Man of conviction; Aaron C. Mitchell's execution. Newsweek 69:29 Ap 24 '67

No. 77; execution of Luis José Monge in Colorado. Time 89:33 Je 9 '67

Stirrings on death row; execution of Aaron Mitchell at San Quentin prison. Time 89:25 Ap 21 '67

EXECUTIVE ability

Make the most of your weaknesses. A. Uris. il Nations Bsns 55:74-6 Ap '67

Moving men and nations; address, May 29, 1967. E. A. Butler. Vital Speeches 33:654-6 Ag 15 '67

EXECUTIVE departments (United States) See United States—Executive departments

EXECUTIVE jets. See Airplanes, Business
EXECUTIVE liability. See Liability (law)
EXECUTIVE office of the president. See United States—Executive office of the president
EXECUTIVE planes. See Airplanes, Business
EXECUTIVE power
Accidental President, by R. Sherrill. Review Sat R 50:59-69 Ap 8 '67. W. Johnson
See also
Presidents—United States—Powers and duties
EXECUTIVE service corps. See International executive service corps
EXECUTIVES
Case of the disloyal executive. T. J. Murray. Duns R 90:35-7+ D '67
Case of the isolated executive. B. Smith, jr. Duns R 89:34-5+ Ja '67
Corporate nomads; migrating executives. il Time 90:56 S 29 '67
Germany's managerial revolution. U S News 62:108 Je 19 '67
Ghost writers give boss the word. il Bsns W p72-4 Ja 21 '67
High cost of success; reprint. J. Barnett. il Sci Digest 62:26-9 O '67
Lessons of leadership. See issues of Nation's business
Litton: B-school for conglomerates; source of executives for other companies. il Bsns W p88-90 D 2 '67
Men on the move. See issues of Dun's review
Middle management gets a chauffeur; chauffeur-driven cars. il Bsns W p 142 S 9 '67
More room at the top? need for more executive and senior vice presidents. J. Berry. il Duns R 89:29-31 Mr '67
Muddle in management motivation. J. B. Weiner. il Duns R 88:28-31+ D '66
New service commitment. R. J. Weston. il Sat R 51:32-3 Ja 13 '68
Personal business: tax hints for executives on the move. Bsns W p 137-8 Jl 15 '67
Short, happy life of the long-range planner. J. Berry. Duns R 89:36-8 Ja '67
Three years beyond George Orwell: corporate world of 1987. L. H. Schoenhofen, jr. il Duns R 89:43-4+ Mr '67
Wanted: executive time power. F. J. Nunlist. il Duns R 90:51-2+ O '67
What business are you really in? basic challenge of T. Levitt, Harvard B-school professor. il Bsns W p 178-80+ Mr 11 '67
See also
Business management and organization
Corporations—Directors
Leadership
Negro executives
Women as executives

Anecdotes, facetiae, satire, etc.
Strange fellows, those American executives. P. Sithi-Amnuai. il Nations Bsns 55:60-2+ Jl '67

Dismissal
Do him a favor, fire him! L. L. Steinmetz. il Nations Bsns 55:96-8 N '67

Health and hygiene
See Men—Health and hygiene

Qualifications
Clues for success in the president's job. J. C. Bailey. Harvard Bsns R 45:97-104 My '67
Effective decision. P. F. Drucker. Harvard Bsns R 45:92-8 Ja '67
Eight hats of the chief executive. W. F. Rockwell, jr. il Duns R 89:40-1+ Je '67
Good managers don't make policy decisions; excerpts from address, April 27, 1967. H. E. Wrapp. Harvard Bsns R 45:91-9 S '67
How the effective executive does it; excerpts from Effective executive. P. F. Drucker. il Fortune 75:140-3 F '67
How to succeed in business by really trying; address May 3, 1967. D. H. Miller. Vital Speeches 33:531-5 Je 15 '67
Six types of bad executives; excerpts from Management and Machiavelli. A. Jay. Duns R 90:53-4 D '67
What makes a good manager? S. F. Keating. il Duns R 89:28-9+ F '67
Where is the grass the greenest? what qualifications are needed for top corporate marketing and advertising positions. G. Lazarus. Sat R 50:64 D 9 '67
Why don't executives get off dead center? T. J. Murray. il Duns R 89:29-31+ Ap '67
You can hold a good man down. C. A. Cerami. il Nations Bsns 55:69-71 D '67

Recruiting
Tough questions for recruiters; is an employment counselor an employment agency? Bsns W p42 D 23 '67

Retirement
See Retirement from business, etc.

Salaries
At the top, salaries still climb. il Bsns W p77-8+ My 20 '67
Bonus plan where performance counts; pie that GM's managers share. il Bsns W p58+ My 13 '67
Finding the right silver for the executive palm; stock-option plan still the favorite. il Bsns W p90+ Jl 22 '67
For the chief, sales set the pay; McKinsey study on executive compensation. il Bsns W p 174 S 30 '67
How top paychecks did in '66. il Bsns W p44 Ap 22 '67
Perquisites of management; executive extras. J. B. Weiner. il Duns R 89:36-7+ My '67
Personal business; deferred pay plans. Bsns W p 165-6 O 14 '67
What Britain pays its brass. Bsns W p35 N 4 '67

Selection and appointment
How to succeed. il Newsweek 69:27 Mr 20 '67
You can hold a good man down. C. A. Cerami. il Nations Bsns 55:69-71 D '67

Supply and demand
Coming scramble for executive talent. A. Patton. bibliog f il Harvard Bsns R 45:155-6+ My '67
He finds major minority talent; U. Haynes, jr. founds Management resources corp. il Bsns W p68+ O 7 '67
Personal business; switching jobs. Bsns W p 107-8 Jl 29 '67

Training
Antidote for blunders; International executive training center, France. il Time 89:100 Ap 28 '67
B-school throws away the book; Berkeley's advanced management training program. il Bsns W p 104-6+ Ap 22 '67
Big men on campus; university executive programs. il Newsweek 69:74-6 F 27 '67
Blueprint to build executives. G. E. Keck. Duns R 90:45-6+ N '67
Executive trends. Nations Bsns 55:16+ F '67
How to rise fast: by degrees; master's degree in business administration. il Newsweek 70:60-2 D 25 '67
Officers try running the office; students of Armed forces industrial college at Sperry Rand. il Bsns W p32-3 Ja 6 '68
Turning men into decision-makers; interview. L. S. Bickmore. Nations Bsns 55:88-90+ O '67
See also
Harvard university—Graduate school of business administration
EXECUTIVES as stockholders
As company officials step up sales of their own stocks; with charts. U S News 63:100-1 S 11 '67
EXECUTIVES recruiting consultants. See Employment agencies
EXECUTIVES secretaries. See Secretaries
EXECUTIVES wives. See Wives
EXEMPTION from taxation. See Taxation, Exemption from
EXERCISE
Bikini weenying. il Mlle 64:154-5 Mr '67
Diet you can live with; and exercises you might even enjoy; excerpts from Guide to modern physical fitness. C. B. Wilkinson and J. D. Atwater. il Look 31:99-100+ O 17 '67
Facts about exercise. Bet Hom & Gard 45:20+ Mr '67
Field & stream six-week conditioning program for sportsmen. P. Czura and J. M. Kowalsk. il Field & S 72:47-53 Ag '67
Get a jump on summer. il McCalls 94:76-9+ Je '67
I spa; or, how to profit from a visit to one of America's super bodyshops; The greenhouse, the Neiman-Marcus-supervised pavilion. Vogue 149:178+ Ap 1 '67
Join the thin-in. il Seventeen 26:280-1 Ag '67
Mending hearts at home. R. T. Bugg. il Todays Health 45:52-5 N '67
One exercise that does everything. E. L. Gross. il Vogue 151:118-21 Ja 1 '68

EXERCISE—*Continued*
Personal business; daily exercise to build stronger heart. Bsns W p95-6 Ja 6 '68
Run for your life. A. J. Snider. il Sci Digest 61:80-2 My '67
Slim down, shape up; with sixty-eight diet tips and eight lazy exercises. il Good H 164:154-8 Ja '67
Slim your figure for the new fall fashions. il Good H 165:90-1 Ag '67
Stay in shape and love it. il Ebony 23:107-8+ D '67
Summer exercises to keep your figure trim. il Redbook 129:84-7 Ag '67
Ten minutes a day to slimmer hips and thighs. il Seventeen 26:154-5 F '67
They're mending hearts with exercise. R. Bugg. il Todays Health 45:50-5 O '67
Travel well. E. N. Dye. Travel 127:65-6 F; 72-3 Ap '67
What to do when your looks go wrong; twenty-five good-looking women's recipes. il Vogue 149:128-31+ Ap 15 '67
    See also
Walking
            Handbooks, manuals, etc.
Guides for the flabby; exercise manuals. il Newsweek 70:90+ O 2 '67
EXERCISE, Yoga. See Yoga
EXERCISING equipment
Bike exerciser you can build. R. D. Corwin and M. E. Duchoviner. il Pop Sci 191: 176-7 O '67
EXHAUST gases. See Automobile engines—Exhaust
EXHAUST systems
    See also
Automobile engines—Exhaust
EXHIBITION buildings
    See also
Chicago—McCormick Place
Pavilions
EXHIBITION cases
Display units. J. F. Warwick. il Sch Arts 67:30-1 S '67
Paperbacks displayed diagonally. il Pub W 191:88 Ap 24 '67
EXHIBITIONS
Behind the fun at the fairs: the regulations. A. Mayor. Holiday 42:30+ N '67
DRUPA 67, the gargantuan printing fair. F. Myrick. il Pub W 192:60-1+ Ag 7 '67
Fair enough; Leipzig trade fair. il Time 89: 97 Mr 17 '67
Not another fair? Sr Schol 90:15-16 Ap 7 '67
President asks Senate approval of U.S. membership in BIE; letter, November 28, 1967. L. B. Johnson. Dept State Bul 58:52-3 Ja 8 '68
President issues executive order on international fairs program. Dept State Bul 57:827 D 18 '67
Way North; Alaska's centennial exposition. il Time 89:17 Ja 2 '67
World travel calendar, 1968. T. L. Christie. Sat R 51:74+ Ja 6 '68
    See also
Audio fairs
Book exhibits
Dioramas
London—Great exhibitions of the works of industry of all nations, 1851
Moving picture festivals
Museum exhibits
San Antonio, Tex.—HemisFair, 1968
    also subhead Exhibitions under various subjects, e.g. Machine tools—Exhibitions
EXHIBITIONS, Traveling
California arts commission; first crafts exhibition. B. Kester. il Craft Horiz 27:24-7+ Mr '67
Chinese art from a royal collection; masterpieces belonging to King Gustaf VI Adolf of Sweden on tour to American museums. H. Trubner. il Antiques 91:644-6 My '67
Jewelry by contemporary painters and sculptors; exhibit organized by New York's Museum of modern art. il Craft Horiz 27:32-9 My '67
Traveling collection of historic woodcuts. N Kent. il Am Artist 31:26-31 D '67
EXHIBITS
    See also special types of exhibits, e.g. Book exhibits
EXILES
Angry man; French political exile. G. Bidault. J. Blocker. il Newsweek 70:42+ S 11 '67
Draft-age dilemma; views of U.S. exiles in Canada. O. S. Johnson. McCalls 94:34+ Ag '67
Why good sons become draft dodgers; excerpts from interviews. G. Cameron. il Ladies Home J 84:72-3+ Ag '67

EX-IM bank. See Export-import bank of Washington
EXISTENTIALISM
Existentialism is a positivism. Christian Cent 84:237 F 22 '67
EXIT, pursued by pancakes; story. See Glenday, A.
EXIT the king; drama. See Ionesco, E.
EX-NUNS. See Ex-priests, nuns, etc.
EXOBIOLOGY. See Life on other planets; Space biology
EXODUS. See Bible—Old Testament—Exodus
EXOTICISM in literature
    See also
Robinsonades
EXPANDING universe. See Universe
EXPANSION, House. See Houses, Remodeled
EXPANSION of industry. See Industrial expansion
EXPECTING (periodical)
New magazine; guide for expectant mothers. Writer 80:27 Ag '67
EXPEDITIONS, Scientific. See Scientific expeditions
EXPENDITURES, Family. See Domestic finance
EXPENDITURES, Personal. See Budget, Personal
EXPENDITURES, State. See State finance
EXPENSE accounts (business)
Papa-san doesn't pay; standard feature of business landscape in Japan. Newsweek 70: 76+ D 18 '67
EXPERIENCE
I won't pay for the trip: no chemical routes to paradise. J. Miller. Vogue 150:286-7+ S 1 '67; Same abr. Read Digest 91:132-4 D '67
EXPERIENCE (religion)
Private sea: LSD & the search for God, by W. Braden. Review
Sat R 50:90-1 Ap 22 '67. N. W. Ross
    See also
Conversion
EXPERIENCE, Incorporated
Learning from Experience, Inc; management consulting company run by retirees. il Bsns W p106+ My 27 '67
EXPERIMENT; drama. See Halliwell, D. and Calderisi, D.
EXPERIMENT in international living (organization)
Behavior for crusaders. il Time 90:56 Jl 21 '67
EXPERIMENT stations. See Agricultural experiment stations
EXPERIMENTAL animals. See Laboratory animals
EXPERIMENTAL art. See Modernism (art)
EXPERIMENTAL automobiles. See Automobiles, Experimental
EXPERIMENTAL education. See Education, Experimental
EXPERIMENTAL medicine. See Medical research
EXPERIMENTAL psychology. See Psychology, Experimental
EXPERIMENTAL schools. See Schools, Experimental
EXPERIMENTAL surgery. See Surgery, Experimental
EXPERIMENTAL teacher education. See Teachers—Education
EXPERIMENTAL theater club. See New York (city)—Theater
EXPERIMENTATION on man. See Medical research—Experimentation on man
EXPERIMENTS in art and technology, Incorporated
Science for art's sake; scientists collaborate with artists in using new materials, techniques. il Bsns W p56 O 21 '67
EXPERTISING in art. See Art—Expertising
EXPERTS. See Specialists
EXPLODING stars. See Stars, New
EXPLORATION
    See also
Explorations
EXPLORATION, Submarine. See Diving, Submarine
EXPLORATIONS
Dawn of the geographic spirit. P. Wolff. il UNESCO Courier 20:14-15 My '67
    See also
America—Discovery and exploration
Latin America—Discovery and exploration
Polar exploration
EXPLORER scouts. See Boy scouts—Explorer scouts
EXPLORERS, American
    See also
Peary, R. E.

EXPLORERS, English
See also
Scott, R. F.
EXPLORERS club
Explorers club. New Yorker 43:51-2 N 18 '67
EXPLOSIONS
Biggest blast before the A-bomb; excerpts from The town that died. M. J. Bird. il Pop Mech 128:81-3 D '67
Measuring missile explosions. E. A. Lacy and C. N. Golub. il Electr World 78:23-6 S '67
On the edge of extinction; Port Chicago, Calif. J. G. Dunne. Sat Eve Post 240:24-5 O 7 '67
EXPLOSIONS, Underwater. See Underwater explosions
EXPLOSIVE detectors. See Detectors
EXPLOSIVES
Kilotons of TNT, 3,500 feet down. il Sci N 92:296 S 23 '67
Magnetometers locate loaded liberty ship. il Sci N 92:319 S 30 '67
See also
Blasting
Mines, Military
EXPO 67. See Montreal—Worlds fair, 1967
EXPORT and import controls. See Foreign trade regulation
EXPORT controls
Massive congressional review could cause arms export cuts. Aviation W 87:22 Jl 31 '67
EXPORT-import bank of Washington
Arms & the bank; Senate limits arms trade by the U.S. bank with underdeveloped countries. Time 90:21 Ag 18 '67
Loan restriction imperils exports. D. C. Winston. Aviation W 87:26-7 S 18 '67
Tying strings to Ex-Im deals. il Bsns W p33 Ag 19 '67
EXPORT trade. See Commerce; United States —Commerce
EXPOSITIONS. See Exhibitions
EXPOSURE (photography) See Photography—Exposure
EXPOSURE meters
Automatic exposure meters open candid world. W. Lane. Travel 127:68 Je '67
Bowens flashmeter. P. Farber. il U S Camera 31:60+ Ja '68
Case of the strange calculator dial. P. R. Farber. il U S Camera 31:44-5+ Ja '68
Center has the edge in Nikon's Photomic TN finder. H. Zucker. il Pop Phot 61:78-9+ Ag '67
Ed Scully on basics. E. Scully. Mod Phot 31:30 Jl '67
Exposure. D. Ulffers. U S Camera 30:61+ D '67
Expotrol: meter in-the-round. B. Pierce. il Pop Phot 61:94-5+ O '67
How to get the most out of a light meter. J. S. Forney. il Pop Phot 61:78-81+ S '67
How to use the S & M darkroom meter to determine proper paper contrasts for different negatives. A. Wolfman. il Mod Phot 31:14+ O '67
Ikophot T: exposure meter with back-up lights. H. Zucker. il Pop Phot 61:92-3 O '67
Keppler on the SLR: behind-the-lens meters. H. Keppler. Mod Phot 31:50+ F '67
Keppler on the SLR: spot vs integrating through-lens. H. Keppler. il Mod Phot 31:58+ D '67
Keppler on the SLR; through-the-lens meter dilemma. H. Keppler. il Mod Phot 31:34+ Jl '67
King-size-pack spot meter. J. S. Forney. il Pop Phot 62:86 Ja '68
Match-needle ease with Weston flexibility. E. Scully. il Mod Phot 31:74-5+ Jl '67
Matzkin on movies: behind-the-lens spot meter for movie cameras. M. A. Matzkin. Mod Phot 31:48 Je '67
Meyers on technique. E. Meyers. Mod Phot 31:18 Jl '67
Meyers on technique; narrow angle, spot-reading meters. E. Meyers. Mod Phot 31:18 F '67
Nikon Photomic Tn. M. Laurance. il U S Camera 30:66-7 Jl '67
1967 exposure meter guide. D. L. Miller. il Mod Phot 31:70-1 Jl '67
Reply to the SLR know-it-alls. N. Rothschild. il Pop Phot 60:71-3+ Ap '67
Spot meter inside the Contarex. H. Zucker. il Pop Phot 62:76-7 Ja '68
Tony Karp on electronic flash meters. T. Karp. il Mod Phot 31:40+ Ag '67
Use an exposure meter for flash? P. Farber. il U S Camera 30:42-3+ S '67

Wolfman on printing; enlarging exposure meters. A. Wolfman. il Mod Phot 31:26+ N '67
Would you use half a meter? P. R. Farber. il U S Camera 30:54-5+ F '67
EXPOSURE of person. See Indecent exposure
EXPRESS companies
See also
Wells Fargo express company
EXPRESS highways
Air rights structure for the Department of labor; over the freeway tunnel. il Arch Rec 142:116-19 D '67
Another victim of Vietnam; interstate highways. il U S News 62:106-7 F 13 '67
Building roads without disrupting the city; Baltimore design concept team. il Bsns W p 108+ N 18 '67
Expressway named destruction; New Orleans. F. Dunhill. il Arch Forum 126:54-9 Mr '67
Federal office building designed to span a freeway. il Arch Rec 142:120-3 D '67
Hardnosed highwaymen ride again; Interstate highway program and route planning. Life 62:4 Ap 14 '67
Housing over highways; proposed plans for San Francisco. il Arch Forum 126:96-9 Ja '67
Interstate 87; routes argument. N. Ritter. il Atlan 220:104-9 S '67
Lower Manhattan expressway. R. H. Silver. il Arch Forum 127:66-9 S '67
Perils of planned prettiness: highway beautification program. L. S. Hall. Life 62:20 My 12 '67
Problem: the Long Island expressway; solution: close down Long Island. J. McCarthy. il N Y Times Mag p34-6+ Mr 19 '67
Rising furor over superhighways. il U S News 63:14 N 27 '67
War over urban expressways; with editorial comment. il Bsns W p94-6+. 200 Mr 11 '67
What you should know about driving the interstate highways. D. L. Gregg. Bet Hom & Gard 45:30+ Je '67
EX-PRIESTS, nuns, etc.
Casualties of Catholic reform; Protestant obligations to ex-priests and nuns. C. Bangs. Christian Cent 84:1554-6 D 6 '67
World of the F.P.s. il Time 90:72 N 24 '67
EXPROPRIATION
See also
Congo (capital Kinshasa)—Expropriation policy
EXPULSION from school and college
Haverford policy on drug use. Sch & Soc 95:250+ Ap 15 '67
EXTENSION cords. See Electric cords
EXTENSION education
ST reports: Detroit's extended school program. E. Logan. Sr Schol 90:sup7 Ap 28 '67
EXTENSION ladders. See Ladders
EXTERIOR walls. See Walls
EXTERMINATION of rats. See Rats—Extermination
EXTINCT animals. See Animals, Extinct
EXTINCT birds. See Birds, Extinct
EXTINCTION of animals. See Animals, Extinct
EXTORTION
How did he do it? H. J. Karafin's activities. Newsweek 69:64-5 My 1 '67
Mr Z; bomb threats to TWA. Newsweek 69:33 Je 12 '67
Wicked and the weak. America 116:802-3 Je 3 '67
EXTRACURRICULAR activities. See Student activities
EXTRAS (opera) See Operatic production
EXTRASENSORY perception
Biological radio, ESP. D. Halacy. il Pop Electr 26:53-8+ Ap '67
Dreams, art and mental telepathy. P. McBroom. il Sci N 92:424-5 O 28 '67
Has extrasensory perception been discredited? M. Mead. Redbook 129:40 O '67
My psychic friends; excerpts from A search for the truth. R. Montgomery. Read Digest 90:151-2+ Ap '67
One photographer's ESP. E. Hannigan. il U S Camera 30:16+ My '67
EXTRAVEHICULAR activity. See Space flight —Manned flights—Extravehicular activity
EXTREMISM. See Right and left (political science)
EXTRUSION process
High-pressure process wins Detroit's heart: cold extrusion technique for steel. il Bsns W p 112-13 My 6 '67

EXUMA (islands)
Bahamas Baedeker, George Town. E. D. Muhlfeld. il Flying 81:74-7 S '67
EXURBIA. See Suburbs
EYE
Molecular aspects of lens cell differentiation. J. Papaconstantinou. bibliog il Science 156:338-46 Ap 21 '67
See also
Pupil (eye)
Retina
Visual purple

Care and hygiene
Eye care. A. F. Benjamin. Am Home 70:24 D '67
Facts about eyestrain. il Good H 164:159 F '67

Diseases and defects
Child with impaired vision. L. Alonso. il NEA J 56:42-3 N '67
See also
Onchocerciasis

Injuries
How dangerous is a black eye? Good H 165:186 S '67

Movements
Discharge of frontal eye field neurons during eye movements in unanesthetized monkeys. E. Bizzi. bibliog il Science 157:1588-90 S 29 '67
Rapid eye movement sleep deprivation: a central-neural change during wakefulness. J. H. Dewson, 3d. and others. bibliog il Science 156:403-6 Ap 21 '67
Voluntary control of microsaccades during maintained monocular fixation. R. M. Steinman and others. bibliog il Science 155:1577-9 Mr 24 '67

Surgery
Eye surgeons join sound. cold. F. Marley. il Sci N 91:72 Ja 21 '67
Icy cure; cryotherapy used for herpetic keratitis. Time 90:44 Jl 21 '67
EYE (amphibia)
Retinal ganglion cells: specification of central connections in larval xenopus laevis. M. Jacobson. bibliog il Science 155:1106-8 Mr 3 '67
Visual accommodation in the green turtle. D. W. Ehrenfeld and A. L. Koch. bibliog il Science 155:827-8 F 17 '67
EYE (animals)
Dimethyl sulfoxide: lens changes in dogs during oral administration. L. F. Rubin and P. A. Mattis; discussion. Science 154:543; 155:404 O 28 '66, Ja 27 '67
See also
Sight (animals)
EYE (crustacea)
Enhancement of flicker by lateral inhibition. F. Ratliff and others. bibliog il Science 158:392-3 O 20 '67
Photoelectric potential from photoreceptor cells in ventral eye of limulus. J. E. Brown and others. bibliog il Science 158:665 N 3 '67
Tetrodotoxin blocks a graded sensory response in the eye of limulus. R. M. Benolken and C. J. Russell. bibliog il Science 155:1576-7 Mr 24 '67; Reply with rejoinder. H. Grndfest. 156:1771 Je 30 '67
EYE (fishes)
Goldfish retina: organization for simultaneous color contrast. N. W. Daw. bibliog il Science 158:942-4 N 17 '67
EYE (insects)
Vitamin A deficiency: effect on retinal structure of the moth manduca sexta. S. D. Carlson and others. bibliog il Science 158:268-70 O 13 '67
EYE camera
Admen try eye-spy to read buyer's mind. il Bsns W p 142-4 Ag 19 '67
EYE make-up. See Make-up
EYE of love; story. See Franco, M.
EYEGLASSES
Fun glasses. il Seventeen 26:146-7 My '67
Reading glasses for the "blind." il Time 89:44 Mr 31 '67
We tried 3-D glasses; you needn't. Consumer Rep 32:244 My '67
See also
Contact lenses
Sun glasses
EYELASHES, Artificial
Fringe faking. il Mlle 64:190-1 Ap '67

EYER, Ronald
Chances to be heard. Opera N 32:14-15 Ja 6 '68
Fulbright story. Opera N 31:8-11 Ja 7 '67
Role of the critic. Opera N 31:8-12 F 25 '67
EYESIGHT. See Sight
EYNON, David. See Lasson, R. jt. auth.
EYRING, Edward M. See Eyring, H. jt. auth.
EYRING, Henry, and Eyring, E. M.
Nobel prizes; chemistry. Science 158:746-8 N 10 '67
EZEKIEL. See Bible—Old Testament—Ezekiel

F

F-111. See Airplanes, Military—United States
FAA. See United States—Federal aviation administration
FBI. See United States—Federal bureau of investigation
FCC. See United States—Federal communications commission
FDA. See United States—Food and drug administration
FDIC. See Federal deposit insurance corporation
FDL (fast deployment logistics ships) See Warships—United States
FET (field-effect transistors) See Transistors
FHA. See Future homemakers of America; United States—Federal housing administration
FIAB (Fédération international des associations des bibliothécaires) See International federation of library associations
FID. See International federation for documentation
FIGHT (Freedom, integration, God, honor, today) See Civil rights organizations
FM. See Radio frequency modulation
FM car radios. See Automobiles—Radio equipment
FM radio stations. See Radio stations, Frequency modulation
FM receivers. See Radio receivers—Frequency modulation receivrs
FM-stereo antennas. See Radio antennas
FMCS. See United States—Federal mediation and conciliation service
FNMA. See Federal national mortgage association
FPC. See United States—Federal power commission
FSLIC. See Federal savings and loan insurance corporation
FWPCA. See United States—Federal water pollution control administration
FABER, John
Two faces of Berlin. U S Camera 30:56-7+ Ag '67
FABER, Nancy
America's healthiest cities. Ladies Home J 84:178+ O '67
FABLES
Fables of a Jewish Aesop, tr. by M. Hadas. Review
Sat R 50:40 F 11 '67
FABRI, Ralph
Making paper sculpture. Am Artist 31:42-6 O '67
FABRIC collage. See Collage
FABRIC wall coverings. See Wall coverings
FABRICS. See Textile fabrics
FAÇADES
Architectural iron works; excerpts from a century old building front catalog. il Arch Forum 126:63-70 My '67
FACE
Face of the hour: the strong face. il Vogue 150:154-9 O 1 '67
What's in a face? the mind of the man behind it. A. Brien. il Holiday 42:10+ D '67
FACE lifting. See Surgery, Facial
FACIALS. See Skin—Care and hygiene
FACSIMILE transmission
Facsimile transmission project set for NY state. Library J 92:952 Mr 1 '67
Publisher, printer linked to facsimile; material for National restaurant news. Pub W 191:117 F 6 '67
Speedup: interlibrary loans by Datafax at New York public library; interview. L. P. Murphy. New Yorker 43:51-2 N 25 '67

FACSIMILES of rare books. See Book rarities
—Facsimiles

FACTORIES
Appealing environment for female employees;
Avon products center near Cincinnati. il
Arch Rec 144:152-5 Ja '67
Get inside a real mine, mill or factory. il
Changing T 21:21-2 Je '67
Windowless plant enhanced by color and
planting; cigar factory, Lima, Ohio. il Arch
Rec 144:162 Ja '67
See also
Automobile factories

Design

Streamlined factory: white streak along the
open road; Estée Lauder cosmetics plant.
J. M. Dixon. il Arch Forum 126:76-83 Mr '67

Location

See Location in business and industry

Safety devices and measures

See also
Industrial hygiene

FACTORIES, Automatic. See Machinery, Automatic

FACTORIES, Small. See Small business

FACTORIES, Underground. See Underground
factories

FACTORY management
Simulation for production. J. R. Russell and
others. bibliog Harvard Bsns R 45:162-4+
S '67
Two-way contracting. W. M. Lowry. il
Harvard Bsns R 45:131-7 My '67
See also
Inventories

FACTORY produced houses. See Houses, Prefabricated

FACTORY systems. See Factory management

FACULTIES, College. See College professors
and instructors

FADER, Daniel N.
Fader plan: Detroit style. E. Baur. bibliog il
Library J 92:3119-21 S 15 '67
Pied Piper of paperbacks. E. Logan. il Sr
Schol 89:sup 17 Ja 20 '67
Throw out the textbooks. A. Gordon. il Am
Ed 3:5-7 S '67

FADIMAN, Clifton
Doctor Moore's little masterpiece. McCalls
95:104-6 D '67

FADIMAN, William
Should American films be subsidized? Sat R
50:14-17+ Ag 5 '67

FADLEY, C. S. and others
Chemical bounding information from photoelectron spectroscopy. bibliog Science 157:
1571-3 S 29 '67

FADS
Beauty's newest fad: feather fantasies. il
McCalls 95:92-5 N '67
Button pushers. il Newsweek 69:88 Mr 27 '67
Coolest things; personality posters and psy-
chedelic posters. il Newsweek 69:87 Mr 6 '67
Follies that come with spring. il Time 89:
52-3 Mr 24 '67
Frantic romantics. A. Cooke. Mlle 66:82-3+
D '67
How to tattoo like a lady. il Redbook 130:64-5
Ja '68
Journal miss. M. Kadison. See issues of
Ladies' home journal
Pierced ears thrill girls and jewelers. il Bsns
W p 100-1 Je 3 '67
Second time around; shoop-shoop Hula-
Hoops. Newsweek 70:72 O 2 '67
Teen scene. See issues of Seventeen
Yes, darling, but who was on third? sport,
as camp as anything. G. O'Connor. il Sports
Illus 26:42-4+ Ap 24 '67
See also
College students fads
Food fads

FAESSLER, Shirley
Maybe later it will come back to my mind;
story. Atlan 219:101-4 Ap '67

FAGER, Charles E.
Movies. Christian Cent 84:1226 S 27 '67
Powell and the House: a black power vic-
tory? Christian Cent 84:175 F 8 '67

FAGLEY, Richard M.
On helping the hungry. Christian Cent 84:
811-13 Je 21 '67

FAHEY, John L. See Eln, D. jt. auth.

FAHLSTRÖM, Öyvind
Games of art. il por Time 89:68 F 24 '67

FAILE, S. P. and others
Irradiation effects in glasses: suppression by
synthesis under high-pressure hydrogen.
bibliog Science 156:1593-5 Je 23 '67

FAILURE (psychology)
Right to fail. W. K. Zinsser. Look 31:10 O 17
'67

FAILURES in business. See Business failures

FAIN, John N.
Inhibition of lipolytic action of growth hormone and glucocorticoid by ultraviolet and
X-radiation. bibliog Science 157:1062-4 S 1
'67

FAINTING
First aid: fainting. C. J. Potthoff. Todays
Health 45:66 Ag '67

FAIR educational practices. See Discrimination
in education

FAIR employment practices. See Discrimination in employment

FAIR labor standards. See Labor standards

FAIR labor standards act. See Labor laws and
legislation—United States

FAIR LAWN, N.J.
Profiles: through the great city; Radburn. A.
Bailey. New Yorker 43:50+ Jl 29 '67

FAIRBAIRN, Ann
Rights and permissions. P. Nathan. Pub W
191:64 F 6 '67

FAIRBANK, John King
China: is history repeating itself? New Repub
156:13-14 F 25 '67
Perspective on Vietnam. New Repub 158:15-
17 Ja 20 '68

FAIRBANKS, Jonathan L.
American antiques in the collection of Mr and
Mrs Charles L. Bybee. Antiques 92:832-9
D '67 (to be cont)

FAIRBANKS, Alaska
Disaster that hit Alaska's second city. il U S
News 63:10 Ag 28 '67
Soggy centennial; Fairbanks flooded. il Time
90:19 Ag 25 '67
Still waters lie on the stricken Alaskan city.
il Life 63:24-5 S 1 '67

FAIRCHILD, John Burr
Sly fox in fashion's chicken house; inter-
view; ed. by D. Lurie. pors Life 62:43-4+
Mr 17 '67
about
Man who knows all about women, and tells.
B. Walters. Ladies Home J 84:56 F '67
Shaking up Women's wear. il por Time 90:
46+ S 8 '67

FAIRCHILD camera and instrument corporation
High flier runs into turbulent air; Wall Street
is divided on its value. il Bsns W p76 D 23
'67
Reconnaissance camera focused on traffic;
applying aerial photography in Project Sky
Count. il Tech W 20:35-6 Ap 3 '67

FAIRCHILD Hiller corporation
Republic aviation sales climb as firm hits
comeback trail. R. Barnhart. il Aero Tech
21:32-3+ S 11 '67

FAIRFIELD fund, incorporated
How to succeed, but lose money. il Bsns
W p 149-50 Mr 18 '67

FAIRHURST, Janet Perry
To beautify America: a bridge becomes a
bower. Home Gard 54:10+ Ag '67

FAIRLIE, Henry
Can you believe your eyes? Horizon 9:24-7 Spr
'67; Same abr. with title Unreal world of
television news. Read Digest 91:127-30 Ag
'67
Harvard: power base for the Kennedy's? reprint from Sunday telegraph, January 15,
1967. U S News 62:37-9 Ja 30 '67
How is youth to be served? New Repub
156:12-14 Ap 8 '67
Politics in the forest. New Repub 157:13-15
O 7 '67
about
Kennedy stud farm. Nat R 19:124+ F 7 '67

FAIRMOUNT HEIGHTS, Md.
High John. E. Moon. il Library J 93:147-55
Ja 15 '68

FAIRS
See also
Audio fairs
Exhibitions

FAIRY plays
Brave little tailor; dramatization of Grimms'
fairy tale. A. Thane. Plays 26:49-58 F '67
Brementown litterbug. G. R. Creegan. Plays
26:82-4 Mr '67
Cinderella. A. Thane. Plays 27:57-68 O '67
Musicians of Bremen town. W. Roberts. Plays
27:71-4 Ja '68
Rapunzel; dramatization of Grimms' fairy
tale. A. Thane. Plays 26:79-88, 96 F '67
Sleeping Chinese beauty. K. Locke. Plays
26:81-4 My '67

FAMILY, Size of
Babes in the wood; ed. by D. C. Disney.
Ladies Home J 84:18+ F '67
But daddy; excerpts. T. Buck. il Ladies
Home J 85:47-50+ Ja '68
How to raise quints without going crazy.
G. Cameron. il Ladies Home J 84:102-3+
My '67
Swing to small families. M. Seton. il Parents
Mag 42:56-7+ O '67

FAMILY allowances
Do we want children's allowances? with table. J. Tobin. New Repub 157:16-18 N 25
'67; Reply with rejoinder. J. C. Vadakin.
157:15-18 D 23 '67
Laggard America. New Repub 157:4 S 16 '67;
Reply. M. Bassett. 157:36-7 S 30 '67
Once more, the family allowance. America
116:238 F 18 '67

FAMILY budget. See Budget, Household

FAMILY camping. See Camping

FAMILY centered maternity care. See Hospitals
—Family centered maternity care

FAMILY corporations
Federated, and the consumer comeback. J.
Poindexter. il Duns R 90:38-42+ D '67
Keeping their success in the family; privately
held companies. Bsns W p96-8 D 9 '67
Sweet, secret world of Forrest Mars. H. B.
Meyers. il Fortune 75:154-7+ My '67

FAMILY desertion. See Desertion and non-
support

FAMILY finance. See Domestic finance

FAMILY group therapy. See Family psychotherapy

FAMILY history. See Genealogy

FAMILY income. See Income

FAMILY life
And then there was one. A. Lake. il Good H
164:90-1+ Mr '67
But daddy; excerpts. T. Buck. il Ladies Home
J 85:47-50+ Ja '68
Curiosity, wonder, awareness; symposium, ed.
by M. Longwell. il Farm J 91:102-3 Mr '67.
High cost of success; reprint. J. Barnett. il
Sci Digest 62:26-9 O '67
How America lives. G. Cameron. See issues
of Ladies' home journal
How to drive your family crazy. F. R.
Schreiber and M. Herman. il Sci Digest
62:65-9 N '67
Invitation to serenity; recollection of child-
hood. S. Rama Rau. Redbook 128:65+ F
'67
My charming, freeloading brother. il Good H
164:32+ Ja '67
New heartbreak in Ingrid Bergman's life;
daughter's illness. M. S. Davis. il Good H
164:54-7+ Ja '67
No simple matter. V. P. McCorry. America
118:20-inside back cover Ja 6 '68
One child, one vote; weekly family meetings.
J. H. Cohen. il Parents Mag 42:40-1+ Ja
'67
Split-level American family. U. Bronfenbren-
ner. Sat R 50:60-6 O 7 '67
Survival of a family; experience after father
suffers cerebral hemorrhage. M. Bau-
meister. McCalls 94:28+ F '67
When a parent drinks too much. J. Locke. il
Parents Mag 42:44-5+ Jl '67
When father's a traveling man. C. Levine.
il Parents Mag 42:54-5+ Je '67
Yes, we do marry our in-laws. M. Holmes.
il Todays Health 45:38-41 Mr '67
See also
Home
Marriage counseling
Parent-child relationship
Stepparents

Anecdotes, facetiae, satire, etc.
Hello, Dali! W. Stanton. il Read Digest 90:
65-7 Je '67
Love in a small room. M. Finn. il Good H
165:56+ Jl '67
Man next door. B. Hillis. See issues of
Better homes and gardens
What does an apron mean? M. Holmes. il
Todays Health 45:62-3 F '67

Caricatures and cartoons
It's all in the family. S. Berenstain and J.
Berenstain. See issues of McCall's

FAMILY life, Education for
See also
Parent education

FAMILY planning. See Birth control

FAMILY portrait; story. See Lardner, S.

FAMILY psychotherapy
Family is the patient. F. R. Schreiber and
M. Herman. Sci Digest 61:65-9 Je '67
Treating mental illness; programs of the
Albert Einstein college. J. Ridgeway. New
Repub 156:13-5 Je 10 '67

FAMILY records
If only we had spoken. M. Parton. il McCalls
95:66+ O '67

FAMILY reunions
Lucien, Octave, Victoire, Emile; Americans
at family reunion in south of France. F. Du
Plessix. New Yorker 43:26-34 Jl 29 '67

FAMILY rooms. See Living rooms; Rooms

FAMILY therapy. See Family psychotherapy

FAMINES
Famine, 1975! by W. Paddock, and P. Pad-
dock. Review
Am For 73:27+ Jl '67. M. Bush
We are losing the race against hunger. G.
McGovern. il Look 31:86+ Mr 7 '67
World food supply; PSAC panel warns of
impending famine. L. J. Carter. Science
156:1578-9 Je 23 '67
See also
Food supply

India
Famine hits Bihar, India. Christian Cent 84:
612-13 My 10 '67
No rain, no crops, famine. V. Koilpillai.
Christian Cent 84:155-7 F 1 '67
On the edge of starvation. il U S News 62:66-
7 Je 26 '67
When famine really strikes; eyewitness story
from India. S. W. Sanders. il U S News 62:
54-6 My 1 '67

FAMOUS men. See Great men

FAMOUS women. See Women, Famous

FAN, Pow-Foong. See Swindale, L. D. jt. auth.

FANDEL, John
Clouds; poem. Cath World 205:82 My '67
Image; poem. Christian Cent 84:1039 Ag 16 '67
January-June; reparations; poem. America
118:36-7 Ja 13 '68
Stops; poem. Cath World 204:300 F '67
Veronica; poem. Cath World 205:302 Ag '67

FANGMEIER, Robert A.
Seminary drama and the God is dead theme.
Christian Cent 84:846-7 Je 28 '67

FANNIE Mae. See Federal national mortgage
association

FANNIN, Paul Jones
Excerpt from address, January 12, 1967. Cong
Digest 46:81+ Mr '67
Rhodesia; address, January 12, 1967. Vital
Speeches 33:264-7 F 15 '67

FANNING, James
Friend or foe? Horticulture 45:34-5+ O '67

FANNING, Lawrence Stanley
Cheechako takes over. il por Time 89:43 Je 30
'67

FANS
Fans in San Juan. il Hobbies 72:92 Ag '67

FANSTEEL metallurgical corporation
Changing horses, and streams; outsider W.
Hayes named president. il Bsns W p 137-
8+ Ap 1 '67

FANTASIES, Literary
Lord of the rings. R. A. Schroth. America
116:254 F 18 '67
Why Frodo lives. J. Crist. Ladies Home J
84:58 F '67

FANTASTIC architecture. See Architecture,
Fantastic

FANTASY
Risks and pleasures of fantasy. H. Gold. Holi-
day 42:6+ Ag '67
See also
Fairy tales

FANTEL, Hans H.
Audio. See issues of Opera news
Blue Danube waltzes on. Read Digest 90:174-
7+ My '67
Eye-opening discoveries about sleep. Pop
Mech 128:104-7+ N '67
Promising new attack on the cigarette
hazard. Sci Digest 61:50-5 Je '67

FANTINI, Mario D. and Weinstein, Gerald
Reducing the behavior gap. NEA J 57:22-5 Ja
'68

FANTONI, Antonio, and others
Globin composition and synthesis of hemoglobins in developing fetal mice erythroid
cells. bibliog Science 157:1327-9 S 15 '67

FAR EAST
See also
Asia
Asia, Southeastern
Tourist trade—Far East
United Nations—Economic commission for
Asia and the Far East

FAR EAST and the United States
  See also
  Pacific countries
FAR-EASTERN studies. See Oriental studies
FAR right (politics) See Right and left (political science)
FAR WEST classic. See Basketball tournaments
FARADAY, Michael
  Michael Faraday and the physics of 100 years ago; excerpts from Michael Faraday, a biography. L. P. Williams. bibliog il Science 156:1335-42 Je 9 '67
FARAGO, Ladislas
  Secrets of the secret services. Sat R 50:31-2 N 18 '67
FARAH, consort of Mohammed Reza Pahlevi, shah of Iran
  People are talking about... por Vogue 150: 110-11 O 15 '67
FARANGE, Maisie, pseud.
  Opinion: on the sex hang-up. Mlle 65:38+ Jl '67
FARB, Peter
  Nature beneath the tree. Sat R 50:44+ N 25 '67
FARBER, Emmanuel. See Stewart, G. A. jt. auth.
FARBER, Norma
  Magnified man; poem. Sat R 50:28 Jl 22 '67
FARBER, Paul R.
  Colorval. U S Camera 30:44-5+ Ap '67
  Foto facts. See issues of U.S. camera & travel
FARBER, Robert H.
  Constructive use of faculty mobility. Sch & Soc 95:183 Mr 18 '67
FARER, Tom J.
  Anti-Communist empire. Nation 205:213-15 S 11 '67
          about
  Better job for McNamara. Nation 204:674-5 My 29 '67
FARES, Airline. See Airlines—Fares
FAREWELL to the dacha; story. See Litvinov, I.
FARINA, Albert M.
  Legal aspects of recreation. por Parks & Rec 2:42-3+ Mr '67
FARKAS, Francine
  Poolside broker. il pors Newsweek 70:70-1 Ag 14 '67
FARKAS, Harold M. See McMorrow, T. jt. auth.
FARLEY, James A.
  America's destiny; address, May 14, 1967. Vital Speeches 33:686-8 S 1 '67
  If this should be my last trip to Europe... ed. by R. Joseph. por Esquire 67:90-3+ F '67
FARLEY, Jean
  Baucis & Philemon; poem. New Yorker 42:49 F 18 '67
  Cardinal; poem. Reporter 37:54 D 14 '67
FARLOW, Tal
  Reluctant return. por Time 90:50 D 22 '67
FARM buildings
  Look what happened to red barns! color coordinate your buildings. R. Wilmore. il Farm J 91:36-7 Ap '67
  See also
  Silos
  Swine farrowing crates and pens
  Swine houses
FARM bureau federation. See American farm bureau federation
FARM corporations. See Farms, Incorporated
FARM costs. See Agriculture—Economic aspects
FARM credit administration. See United States —Farm credit administration
FARM equipment
  Home-made and handy; photographs. See issues of Farm journal
  See also
  Agricultural machinery
FARM finance
  Before you sign your 1967 tax return; common oversights of farm reporting. Farm J 92:56 Ja '68
  Farm credit: enough to go around? Farm J 91:74F Mr '67
  We always operate on borrowed money. R. G. Fowler. il Farm J 91:42-3+ F '67
  Which crop will make you the most money? il Farm J 91:46N My '67
  Worried about big debt? L. Lane. Farm J 91:101+ F '67
FARM houses. See Farmhouses
FARM income. See Agriculture—Economic aspects; Income

FARM journal
  How not to write the editor. C. P. Streeter. Farm J 91:12 F '67
FARM kitchens. See Kitchens
FARM labor
  Actos: Teatro campesino, a theatrical part of the United farmworkers organizing committee. New Yorker 43:23-5 Ag 19 '67
  Agricultural minimum wage: a preliminary look. K. S. Koziara. bibliog f Mo Labor R 90:26-9 S '67
  Collective bargaining on the farm. Mo Labor R 90:III-IV Je '67
  Dairy labor plans that work. J. Russell. Farm J 92:R6 Ja '68
  Halting the flight from the land. Christian Cent 84:773-4 Je 14 '67
  How to keep hired help. R. J. Fee. il Suc Farm 65:54D S '67
  How will you hire farm labor? D. Hanson. Suc Farm 65:22 Jl '67
  Of many things: the rights of agricultural labor to organize and bargain collectively. A. P. Morris. America 118:inside cover Ja 13 '68
  Today's farm jobs and farmworkers. P. Groom. Mo Labor R 90:1-5 Ap '67
  Unionizing the farm; Di Giorgio signs an AFL-CIO contract. il Bsns W p 164+ Ap 22 '67
  Unjolly green giant; unemployment in Imperial Valley. L. T. King. Commonweal 86:461 Jl 28 '67
  See also
  American federation of labor and Congress of industrial organizations—United farm workers organizing committee
  Cotton workers
  Migrant labor
  National farm workers' association
  Strikes—United States—Farm labor
FARM leases. See Leases
FARM life
  Beautiful in the commonplace. M. Longwell. Farm J 91:108 Mr '67
  Dry stalks of autumn. A. H. Sokoloff. Sat R 50:48-9+ O 28 '67
  How to keep your marriage from slowing down. il Farm J 91:51+ Je '67
  How to listen to a husband. Farm J 91:83 Ap '67
  Is farm life worth it? K. Wilcher; discussion. Farm J 91:73-4 Ja '67
  Letters from farm women. See issues of Farm journal
  Meet the Thompsons of rural route surprise. K. Davis. il Farm J 91:42-3 Jl '67
  New perspective on spring cleaning. P. P. Leimbach. Farm J 91:63 My '67
  Not by bread alone... P. P. Leimbach. Farm J 91:101+ Mr '67
  They have joy to spare, and share; the Warren Carlsons of Winnebago County, Ill. J. Gillies. il Farm J 91:54-5 D '67
  To see America: spring's old sweet challenge; North Carolina tobacco farm; with report by C. Uzzle. il Life 62:62-72+ My 19 '67
  See also
  Country life

      Anecdotes, facetiae, satire, etc.
  Sign on my barn. R. Campbell. Farm J 91: 38 F '67
FARM machinery. See Agricultural machinery
FARM machinery insurance. See Insurance, Machinery
FARM management
  Fall fertilizer keeps your crops on schedule. R. D. Wennblom. Farm J 91:38-9+ O '67
  Farm pattern for the future. J. Harvey. Suc Farm 65:58D F '67
  Hints for faster fall harvest. P. B. Jones. il Suc Farm 65:50-1 S '67
  How we meet your changing needs. D. Hanson. Suc Farm 65:6+ Ap '67
  New sources of information, are you using them? Suc Farm 65:55 F '67
  Two-family farming: key to staying in business. il Suc Farm 65:29+ Jl '67
  See also
  Dairy farm management
  Father-son farm operating agreements
FARM management clubs. See Agricultural societies
FARM mechanics. See Agricultural engineering
FARM ownership
  Blueprint of paradise; mountain farm. R. Starnes. Field & S 72:16+ Jl '67
  Personal business; yen for the good earth? Bsns W p 111-12 Ag 26 '67

FARM ponds. See Ponds
FARM prices. See Farm produce—Prices
FARM produce
They're after your market; threat from new food products, substitutes and imitations. Farm J 91:58 Jl '67

Marketing
Food belt studies. New Repub 157:8-9 S 30 '67
What's new. R. Fee. See issues of Successful farming
What's new. R. J. Fee. Suc Farm 65:98 Ja; 58 F; 10 Mr '67
When middlemen are in the middle. il Bsns W p26-7 Ag 26 '67
See also
Marketing, Cooperative
Milk—Marketing

Prices
Falling farm income. America 117:194-5 Ag 26 '67
Family farmer fights back. M. Landy. Commonweal 87:431-2 Ja 12 '68
Food belt studies. New Repub 157:8-9 S 30 '67
Let's go with bargaining. J. D. Boyd and C. W. Gifford. Farm J 92:25+ Ja '68
Problems come with bumper crops. il U S News 63:88 S 25 '67
U.S. farmers and a hungry world. il Sr Schol 91:4-8 N 9 '67
Where low prices are causing trouble for Johnson. il U S News 62:49-50 Mr 20 '67
See also
Agricultural administration—United States
also subhead Prices under names of farm produce, e.g. Wheat—Prices

Storage
Problems come with bumper crops. il U S News 63:88 S 25 '67

FARM records
Dozen new ways to keep track of your money. il Farm J 91:44N S '67
Record keeping doesn't have to be hard work! il Suc Farm 65:60+ Ja '67

FARM subsidies. See Agricultural administration—United States

FARM tenancy
Guidelines to cash farm leasing. R. J. Fee. il Suc Farm 65:31+ O '67
See also
Leases

FARM tractors. See Tractors
FARM vacations. See Vacations
FARM wastes. See Waste products
FARM women
Give yourself a lift every month. il Farm J 91:76-7 Ja '67
Letters from farm women. See issues of Farm Journal
Rosy, going to help me this summer? R. Logsdon. il Farm J 91:64-5 My '67
She can't be real? our cover girl. N. Kleinschmidt. il Farm J 91:90 O '67

FARMER, Nan
Quincy builds a new vocational-technical curriculum. Am Ed 3:12-13+ Jl '67

FARMER-hunter relations
Proper approach. P. Alport. il Field & S 71:58-9 Ap '67

FARMERS, James
CORE leaps without looking. Christian Cent 84:931-2 Jl 19 '67

FARMERS
Why the flag flies over our farm; letters. il Farm J 91:21+ Jl '67
Young tigers in farming. G. Logsdon. il Farm J 91:29-31+ Ap '67
See also
Farm management
Strikes—United States—Farmers

Political activities
U.S. farmers and a hungry world. il Sr Schol 91:4-8 N 9 '67

FARMER'S almanac. See Almanacs
FARMERS associations. See Agricultural societies
FARMERS lunches. See Lunches
FARMERS' museum, Cooperstown, N.Y.
Farmer's museum at Cooperstown, N.Y. mirrors the country living of another century. il House & Gard 131:46-7+ Mr '67

FARMHOUSES
Farmhouse core. il Farm J 91:57-63+ S; 67-71+ O: 52-3+ N '67
How an expert remodeled his own farm home. R. Martens. il Farm J 91:70-1 My '67

Ideal farm home for a Minnesota Christmas. J. LemMon. il Suc Farm 65:44-5 D '67
Munsons designed their farm home for efficiency. J. LemMon. il Suc Farm 65:74-7 S '67

Designs and plans
More room for your money. W. Diehnelt. il Farm J 91:34-5 N '67
New ranch home with a spacious core. J. Gillies. il Farm J 91:52-3+ N '67

FARMHOUSES, Remodeled. See Houses, Remodeled
FARMINGDALE, N.Y. public library
Bircher library trustee charged with assault. Library J 92:2986 S 15 '67
Dime-store Paul Revere. E. Moon; K. Nyren. il Library J 92:3353, 3380-4 O 1 '67
FARMINGTON meteorite. See Meteorites
FARMS
See also
Dairy farms
Farm management
Farm ownership
Swine farms

Photographs
To see America: spring's old sweet challenge; North Carolina tobacco farm. B. Uzzle. Life 62:62-71 My 19 '67

Valuation
See Assessment
FARMS, Incorporated
Will we see more corporate farming? B. Brantley. Suc Farm 65:52-3+ F '67
FARNON, Robert
Farnon of England. G. Lees. il por Hi Fi 17:101 Mr '67
FARNSWORTH, Dana L.
Tensions due to what is lacking. por Todays Health 45:64 S '67
FARRAN, Dale C.
Games work with underachievers. Sr Schol 91:sup 10-11 N 9 '67
FARRAR, Donald R.
Gametophytes of four tropical fern genera reproducing independently of their sporophytes in the southern Appalachians. bibliog Science 155:1266-7 Mr 10 '67
FARRAR, Geraldine
Farewell to Farrar. A. Favia-Artsay. il pors Hobbies 72:35-6 O '67
Geraldine Farrar; February 28, 1882-March 11, 1967. F. Robinson. por Opera N 31:14-15 Ap 15 '67
FARRAR, John
Those industrious young men and their farming machines. Am Ed 3:22-4+ O '67
FARRAR, Straus and Giroux, Incorporated
Endowing the arts; government to finance forthcoming anthology. D. Dempsey. Sat R 50:25 Ag 12 '67
FARRAR, W. V.
Aztecs ate algacake. Sat R 50:55 Mr 4 '67
FARRELL, Barry
Other culture. Life 62:86-8+ F 17 '67
Pat Neal makes a radiant return. Life 62:119-20 Ap 7 '67
Secrets of the kite. Life 63:25 D 1 '67
FARRELL, Edmund J.
English, education and the electronic revolution; excerpts. Sr Schol 91:sup 12-13 S 28 '67
FARRELL, Eileen
Doing what comes naturally. W. Sargeant. por Opera N 32:28-9 D 9 '67
FARRELL, James T.
Today's disobedience is uncivil. N Y Times Mag p29 N 26 '67
FARRELL, Patricia
It's the duty of the young to be happy; story. Redbook 129:68-9 O '67
FARRELL, Ranger
Designing building exteriors with sealants in mind. Arch Rec 144:169-74 Ja '67
FARRELL, William J.
Student involvement in the liturgy. por Cath World 205:199-204 Jl '67
FARRIS, John
When Michael calls; story. Good H 165:85-7 N '67
FARROW, Mia
Mia; interview, ed. by S. Knickerbocker. pors McCalls 94:70-1+ My '67
about
Mia. T. Thompson. il pors Life 62:75-81 My 5 '67
Mia Farrow's swinging life with Frank Sinatra. V. Scott. por Ladies Home J 84:84+ My '67
Working Sinatras. J. Hamilton. il pors Look 31:86-90+ O 31 '67

FARROW, Stephanie
  Stephanie Farrow. il pors Seventeen 26:164-5
    Ap '67
FARROWING crates and pens. See Swine farrowing crates and pens
FASANA, Paul J.
  Determining the cost of library automation.
    ALA Bul 61:656-61 Je '67
FASCELL, Dante B.
  Preserving an island paradise. por Am For
    73:32-3+ Mr '67
FASCISM
  Star-spangled fascism. W. Pfaff. Commonweal
    86:487-8 Ag 11 '67

Austria
  New Austria & the old Nazis. P. Lendvai.
    Commentary 44:81-8 S '67; Reply with rejoinder. A. Werner. 44:18+ N '67

Germany
  Conversion of myths into political power: the
    case of the Nazi party, 1925-1926. D. Orlow.
    bibliog f Am Hist R 72:906-24 Ap '67
  Nuremberg party rallies, 1923-39, by H. T.
    Burden. Review
      Sat R il 50:30 D 16 '67. H. Kohn

Germany (Federal Republic)
  Germans are worrying the world again; neo-
    Nazism: National democratic party (NPD)
    J. Roddy. il Look 31:17-21 Mr 21 '67
FASHION
  Chain hangup. il Newsweek 69:89 Je 12 '67
  Great fashion explosion. E. Carruth. il Fortune 76:162-5+ O '67
  How Jacqueline Kennedy influences the way
    you look. M. Bender. Redbook 129:52+ Ag
    '67
  Mad three weeks; fall and winter styles from
    Paris. il Time 90:48 S 1 '67
  Man who knows all about women, and tells.
    B. Walters. Ladies Home J 84:56 F '67
  Next, the maxiskirt? il Time 89:57 My 12 '67
    See also
  Clothing and dress
  Costume design
  Dress accessories
  Fads
  Hairdressing
FASHION as a profession
  Jobscope; by the college and career department, fashion farrago. bibliog Mlle 65:182-3
    S '67
  You can make it only if it sells. A. Grant. il
    Mlle 65:122-4+ S '67
FASHION designers. See Costume designers
FASHION industry. See Clothing industry
FASHION magazines. See Periodicals for women
FASHION photography. See Photography,
    Fashion
FASHION shows
  Africa wows capital with fashion safari. il
    Ebony 23:167-8+ N '67
  Fashion show for blind teens; Seventeen's
    first. il Seventeen 26:261 My '67
  It's Andre & Yves; Paris fashion world. il
    Time 90:42-3 Ag 11 '67
  Miniskirts in Moscow; Soviet Union's first
    International fashion festival. il Newsweek
    70:43-4 S 4 '67
  Mission to Moscow; West Germany improving trade through International fashion
    festival. il Time 90:38-9 S 15 '67
  Paris collections, '67. Mlle 64:16+ Ap '67
  Something for the boys; K. Scott show for
    fall boutique collections in Florence. il
    Newsweek 69:58 Ap 24 '67
  Total look; New York city's fall showings. il
    Newsweek 70:74 Jl 3 '67
FASHIONABLE society. See Upper classes
FAST, Howard
  Beauty and mystery of Stonehenge. Sat R
    50:52-4 F 4 '67
FAST, Paul G.
  Ethanolamine phosphoglycerides: effect on
    the properties of myelinoid lecithin water
    systems. bibliog il Science 155:1680-1 Mr 31
    '67
FAST deployment logistics ships. See Warships—United States
FASTING
  Euglena gracilis: a novel lipid energy reserve
    and arachidonic acid enrichment during fasting. A. Rosenberg. bibliog il Science 157:
    1189-91 S 8 '67
  Fasting record. Sci Digest 61:57 Ap '67
FASTS and feasts
    See also
  Passover

FAT
  Brown and white fats: development in the
    hamster. R. L. Smalley and K. N. Smalley.
    bibliog il Science 157:1449-51 S 22 '67
  Gekkonid lizards adapt fat storage to desert
    environments. H. R. Bustard. bibliog Science 158:1197-8 D 1 '67
  Saturation in milk and meat fats. S. Patton
    and E. M. Kesler. bibliog il Science 156:1365-
    6 Je 9 '67
    See also
  Corpulence
FATE (periodical)
  Coils of Fate. Christian Cent 84:607 My 3 '67
FATHER-child relationship. See Parent-child
    relationship
FATHER-daughter relationship. See Parent-
    child relationship
FATHER hits the jackpot; drama. See
    Garver, J.
FATHER-son farm operating agreements
  Pitfalls of family partnerships. G. Logsdon.
    il Farm J 91:30-1+ D '67
FATHER-son relationship. See Parent-child
    relationship
FATHERS
  Challenge of fatherhood. R. Thomas. il
    Parents Mag 42:41-3+ Je '67
  Dialogue with mothers. B. Bettelheim. il La-
    dies Home J 84:48+ Je '67
  Familiar ritual of letting a son go. L. Wain-
    wright. Life 63:24-5 O 6 '67
  Father's role in today's society. H. H.
    Humphrey. Parents Mag 42:38 Je '67
  Friendly advice to new fathers from an old
    pro. R. Armour. il Parents Mag 42:48-9+
    Je '67
    See also
  Daughters
  Stepparents
FATHERS; story. See Mountzoures, H. L.
FATHERS day gifts. See Gifts
FATIGUE
  Are you getting enough sleep? Philip M.
    Tiller, jr. survey. J. D. Ratcliff. Read Digest
    90:109-11 My '67
  Black box that turns you on; anti-fatigue
    device. il Bsns W p79-80 My 6 '67
  Fatigue: what to do about it. A. Talmey.
    Vogue 149:98-9 F 15 '67
  Get rid of that run-down feeling. A. Uris. il
    Nations Bsns 55:82-4 Jl '67
  How you can beat fatigue. A. Lake. il Seventeen 26:112-13+ Je '67
FATIGUE, Combat. See Neuroses
FATIMA, Our Lady of. See Mary, Virgin—
    Apparitions and miracles (modern)
FATS. See Oils and fats, Edible
FATT, Amelia
  (ed) Designers for the dance; with inter-
    views. Dance Mag 41:42-50 F; 50-5 Mr; 55-8
    Ap '67
  Hoof and mouth disease. Dance Mag 41:39 Je;
    23 Ag; 30+ S '67
FATTY acids. See Acids, Fatty
FAUBUS, Orval Eugene
  Orval's pad; opens home to tourists. il por
    Time 90:21 Ag 4 '67
FAUCETS. See Plumbing
FAULK, John Henry
  Blacklisted! condensation of The jury returns.
    L. Nizer. il por Read Digest 90:201-4+
    Mr '67
FAULK, Pearl H.
  Speech education in the elementary school.
    NEA J 56:34 Mr '67
FAULKNER, William
  Wishing tree; story. Sat Eve Post 240:48-53
    Ap 8 '67
    about
  Faulkner, ed. by R. P. Warren. Review
    Sat R 50:27-8 My 6 '67. G. Hicks
  How Faulkner went his way and I went
    mine. H. Nauman. por Esquire 68:173-5 D
    '67
FAULKNER award
  Prizes authors seek. G. Hicks. Sat R 50:35-6
    My 20 '67
FAULTS (geology)
  Building to a quake? ominous silence along
    San Andreas fault. B. Tufty. il Sci N 91:
    550-1 Je 10 '67
  Local geomagnetic events associated with
    displacements on the San Andreas fault.
    S. Breiner and R. L. Kovach. bibliog il
    Science 158:116-18 O 6 '67
  Mid-Atlantic fault. Sci N 91:351 Ap 15 '67
  Pediplain in northern Chile and the Andean
    uplift. C. Galli-Olivier. bibliog il Science
    158:653-5 N 3 '67

FAURE, Maurice
French elections. E. Taylor. Reporter 36:16 Mr 23 '67

FAUST, Raymond Johns
AWWA taps Eric Johnson to succeed Ray Faust. por Am City 82:96+ Ag '67

FAUST, Robert G. and others
D-Glucose: preferential binding to brush borders disrupted with tris hydroxymethyl aminomethane. bibliog Science 155:1261-3 Mr 10 '67

FAVIA-ARTSAY, Alda
Historical records. See issues of Hobbies

FAVISM
Riddle of the dangerous bean; enzyme deficiency as cause of hemolysis and favism in specific ethnic groups. J. R. Marcus and G. Cohen. il Harper 234:98-102 Je '67

FAWCETT, Clara H.
Dollology. See issues of Hobbies

FAWCETT, Joel S.
If I had to pick one lure. pors Outdoor Life 139:54-5+ My '67

FAWZI, Mahmoud
Middle East crisis; address. June 21, 1967. Vital Speeches 33:619-21 Ag 1 '67

FAY, Paul Burgess, 1918-
Chinoiserie. Reporter 36:14 F 9 '67

FEAR
Challenge of fear. A. Paton. Sat R 50:19-21+ S 9 '67
On cowardice. P. Theroux. Commentary 43:41-4 Je '67
One last time. amigo. W. J. Buchanan. il Read Digest 90:61-5 My '67
See also
Anxiety

FEAST of lights. See Hanukkah (Feast of lights)

FEATHER behind the rock; story. See Tyler, A.

FEATHERBEDDING (industrial relations)
Unions' new goal; king-size featherbeds. il Nations Bsns 55:38-40 Jl '67

FEATHERS
Embryonic morphogenesis: role of fibrous lattice in the development of feathers and feather patterns. E. S. Stuart and A. A. Moscona. bibliog il Science 157:947-8 Ag 25 '67

FEATHERSTONE, Joseph
Bernard Malamud. Atlan 219:95-8 Mr '67
Community control of our schools. New Repub 158:16-19 Ja 13 '68
Education: notes on community schools. New Repub 157:16-17 D 9 '67
Ghetto classroom. New Repub 157:23-6+ D 23 '67
Hoffer as historian. New Repub 156:30-2 Je 3 '67
How children learn. New Repub 157:17-21 S 2 '67
Primary mathematics. New Repub 157:34-5+ N 11 '67
Schools for children; what's happening in British classrooms. New Repub 157:17-21 Ag 19 '67
Teaching children to think. New Repub 157:15-19 S 9 '67
William James as sage. New Repub 157:18-21 O 14 '67

FEATHERWORK
Feather merchants; excerpt from the 16th century Aztec manuscript; tr. by C. E. Dibble and A. J. O. Anderson. B. de Sahagún. il Craft Horiz 27:18-23+ Mr '67

FEDERAL agencies. See United States—Executive departments

FEDERAL aid. See Art and state; Federal and municipal relations; Grants-in-aid; Libraries and state; Student aid; also subhead Federal aid under various subjects, e.g. State finance—Federal aid

FEDERAL aid to education
Aid to education: planning is the key; excerpts from testimony before the House committee on education and labor, March 17, 1967; ed. by R. H. Smith. K. W. Lund. Pub W 191:40 Mr 27 '67
AASA re-examines the issues; 99th convention, with editorial comment. W. D. Boutwell. Sr Schol 90:sup2, sup5 Mr 10 '67
American federation of teachers' position paper; statement; July 18-20, 1966. C. Cogen and D. Selden. Sch & Soc 95:87-91 F 4 '67
Appleton-Century publishes U.S. funds-to-school guide. Pub W 191:35 Ja 2 '67; Correction. 191:230 Ja 23 '67
Bilingual education: legislative proposals. New Repub 157:9 O 21 '67; Discussion. 157:44-5 N 18 '67

Bills in the hopper. G. Krettek and E. D. Cooke. Wilson Lib Bul 41:849-50 Ap '67
Blaine and secular man. D. Hale. Commonweal 87:105-6 O 27 '67
Budget battle. il Sat R 50:84-5 My 20 '67
Church and school; proposed new constitution for New York state. L. Pfeffer. Nation 205:389-90 O 23 '67
Church and state; Blaine amendment. il Newsweek 70:61 N 6 '67
Church-state issue in federal aid to education; symposium. bibliog il Wilson Lib Bul 41:682-718 Mr '67; Discussion. 41:884-5, 1014-16; 42:20+, 273+ My-S, N '67
Congress shall make no law. . . W. B. Ball; L. Pfeffer; discussion. Sat R 50:74 F 18; 46+ Mr 18 '67
Decisions from the field, what OE's decentralization means to schools and colleges J. A. Turman. il Am Ed 3:20-1 Jl '67
Directory of legislative programs, fiscal year 1967. il ALA Bul 61:1075-86 O '67
Education groups propose changes in federal aid. Library J 92:827 F 15 '67
Education: the revolution which never stops; address, October 8, 1967. L. B. Johnson. Dept State Bul 57:569-71 O 30 '67
ESEA, NDEA budget; original and cut versions; this year and last; minimal cuts in 1967 ESEA budget. il Library J 92:828-9 F 15 '67
ESEA's days in Court; question of public funds for students in nonpublic schools. Sr Schol 89:sup2 Ja 20 '67
Enactments by the 89th Congress relevant to education and training below college grade, 1965-1966. C. A. Quattlebaum. Sch & Soc 95:360-3 O 14 '67
Federal aid vs. poverty. Sch & Soc 95:250 Ap 15 '67
Federal funds (cont of) Federal money for education. il Am Ed 3:22 Ap; 26-7 My; 30-1 Je '67
Federal funds; teacher training. Am Ed 3:30-1 S '67
Federal influences on the future of American education. F. Parker. Sch & Soc 95:383-7 O 28 '67
Federal responsibility in education. America 116:674 My 6 '67
Federal support for the social studies; excerpts from New frontiers in the social studies: action and analysis. J. S. Gibson. Sr Schol 90:sup9+ F 24 '67
Friends and enemies; Education act amendments introduced by E. Green. Newsweek 69:30 Je 5 '67
Funds for new graduate students. P. H. Abelson. Science 158:583 N 3 '67
Getting into the acts, continued. J. Lloyd. Sr Schol 90:sup4-5 Mr 10 '67
Getting into the acts. Sr Schol 90:sup4 Mr 17; sup6 Mr 31; sup3+ Ap 7; sup6 Ap 14; sup6 Ap 28; sup5 My 5 '67
Government and the schools. J. Justman. Sch & Soc 95:75-8 F 4 '67
Government grants and loans to colleges. Sch & Soc 94:480 D 24 '66
Graduate student stipends; excerpts from seminar, May 1965. W. R. Gruner. il Science 157:1530-3 S 29 '67
Guidelines on trial. Am Ed 3:18-20 Mr '67
He bought a bus; how L. Roberts applied federal funds to the Walden, Vt. system. D. Dew. il Sat R 50:58-9+ Je 17 '67
House votes $3.5 billion for ESEA through 1969. Pub W 191:143 Je 5 '67
How much do the Catholics want? aid to parochial schools. America 116:521 Ap 8 '67
How to get money for vocational education; National vocational student loan program. J. Moore. il Am Ed 4:10-11 D '67
Impact on foreign language teaching. Sch & Soc 95:482 D 9 '67
Johnson juggernaut; school-aid bill passed with amendments. Time 89:12-13 Je 2 '67
Kicking civil rights upstairs; proposed amendments to ESEA. P. Schrag. Sat R 50:49-50 Je 17 '67
Knocking down the language walls; proposed amendment to ESEA to establish bi-lingual education programs. F. M. Cordasco. Commonweal 87:6-8 O 6 '67
Lights are on: and the whole family goes to school at night; Operation Reach. M. A. Marlar. il Am Ed 3:21-4 My '67
LBJ: $4 billion for education. J. Lloyd. Sr Schol 90:sup5 F 17 '67
Money, principle and Southern Baptist. J. Brann. New Repub 157:10 Jl 15 '67
National research goals and university policies. S. B. Gould. Sch & Soc 95:347-9 O 14 '67

FEDERAL aid to education—*Continued*
NSF issues new education survey. D. S. Greenberg. Science 158:96 O 6 '67
Necessary separation of education; address, January 24, 1967. J. A. Howard. Vital Speeches 33:313-16 Mr 1 '67
1967 report on federal money and recent legislation for education. il Am Ed 3:13-25 F '67
No strings attached; ESEA. E. Geller. Library J 92:825 F 15 '67
Obeying the law? racial balance guidelines. D. Lawrence. U S News 62:96 F 6 '67
Our special hell: student failures; need for funds to help them. J. Nugent. Sr Schol 90:sup 13 My 19 '67
Paying for American education. H. Howe, 2d. il PTA Mag 62:5-8 S '67
Plan for financing higher education. J. P. McMurray. Sch & Soc 95:489-90 D 9 '67
Pound of cure for educational problems. B. J. Paschal. Sch & Soc 95:53-5 Ja 21 '67
Poverty-war program with too much money. U S News 62:15 Ap 17 '67
President's new ideas, and a look at the expense. il U S News 62:104-5 Mr 13 '67
Price of hope offered and then denied; curtailing or eliminating educational and social programs. R. H. Smith. Pub W 192:38 Jl 31 '67
Republican mischief; A. Quie's plan to jeopardize funds. New Repub 156:3-4 My 20 '67
Senate committee backs advance funding for ESEA. Pub W 192:26 N 27 '67
State's top court upholds N.Y. text law. Pub W 191:33 Je 12 '67
Swim'st thou in wealth; California's school library puzzle. F. D. Largent and J. W. May. il Am Ed 3:12-13 Je '67
Teaching aid: live drama. Sr Schol 90:sup2 Mr 17 '67
Themis: DOD plan to spread the wealth raises questions in academe. E. Langer. Science 156:48-50, 366 Ap 7, 21 '67; Reply. T. E. Phipps, jr. 156:1307 Je 9 '67
To the rescue; Republican plan to scuttle Elementary and secondary education act. Newsweek 69:36+ My 8 '67
$24.5 million for college library materials, HEA Title II-grant A allocations. Pub W 192:48-9 Jl 17 '67
U.S. aid to library training. Sch & Soc 95:346 O 14 '67
U.S. education aid: the debate sharpens. R. H. Smith. Pub W 192:38 Jl 24 '67
U.S. education programs past, present and future; report of American book publishers council conference, with editorial comment. il Pub W 192:21-6, 36 O 2 '67
Up the staircase; educational lobbyists. il Newsweek 69:70 My 15 '67
Walls come tumbling down; team teaching center established by the Weber County school district in Ogden, Utah, under Title III grant. W. T. Greenleaf. Am Ed 3:22 Mr '67
Washington developments in education; summaries of addresses. L. Hausman; M. Johnson; W. M. Robinson. il Pub W 191:30-4 My 29 '67
Washington report:
Title I, ESEA, Teacher corps. ERIC. J. Lloyd. Sr Schol 91:sup 11 S 21 '67
Title III ESEA (PACE) J. Lloyd. Sr Schol 91:sup 15 N 9 '67
Washington report: church-state. pride in ESEA, congressional action. J. Lloyd. Sr Schol 90:sup6 My 19 '67
Washington report: ESEA amendment proposals; minority report on ESEA. J. Lloyd. Sr Schol 90:sup8 My 12 '67
Washington report: evaluation is the word: progress with Title I funds. J. Lloyd. Sr Schol 90:sup4 Ap 21 '67
Washington report: happy 100th to USOE, ESEA accomplishments; summary of address, March 2, 1967, ed. by J. Lloyd. H. Howe, 2d. Sr Schol 90:sup6 Ap 14 '67
Washington report: Johnson's education message; summary. L. B. Johnson. Sr Schol 90:sup4 Mr 17 '67; Same. Wilson Lib Bul 41:773 Ap '67
Washington report: more money for states? J. Lloyd. Sr Schol 90:sup4 Ap 7 '67
Washington report: Title I of ESEA, report card from Education of disadvantaged children. J. Lloyd. Sr Schol 90:sup8 F 3 '67
What's happening in education? Quie controversy. W. D. Boutwell. PTA Mag 61:11-13 Je '67
See also
College libraries and state
Project Head Start
School libraries and state
Student loans

FEDERAL aid to libraries. See Libraries and state
FEDERAL aid to science. See Research—Federal aid
FEDERAL airport corporation (proposed)
Federal airport corporation urged. L. Doty. Aviation W 87:16-17 S '67
FEDERAL and municipal relations
Great disgrace. E. J. Hughes. Newsweek 70:17 Ag 7 '67
Model aid starts flowing to cities; sixty-three cities chosen. il Bsns W p86 N 25 '67
Streets lights and signs; federal grants. Am City 82:53 D '67
This month's feature: the demonstration cities controversy. Cong Digest 46:36-64 F '67
Why mayors complain they can't do business with Washington. il U S News 62:64-6 Mr 27 '67
Why the states are up in arms. il U S News 62:30 Ja 30 '67
FEDERAL and state relations
Air pollution. Nat R 19:234 Mr 7 '67
Challenge of creative federalism. L. E. Schaller. Christian Cent 84:618-22 My 10 '67
Creative federalism. R. Moley. Newsweek 69:100 Mr 6 '67
Do residents control resident game? W. E. Towell. il Am For 73:20-1+ Jl '67
New deal and the states. J. T. Patterson. bibliog f Am Hist R 73:70-84 O '67
Should Uncle share the wealth? il Nations Bsns 55:35-7+ Ap '67
States look to federal dividends; idea of unrestricted grants gaining favor among governors and economists. il Bsns W p 156-8 Ja 21 '67
Stretching the limbs; findings of task force visiting states. Time 89:19-20 Mr 31 '67
Warren making a try at fence-mending? il U S News 62:24 Ap 24 '67
Washington: a look ahead. Nations Bsns 55:7-8 D '67
What worries governors; interview. W. E. Hearnes. U S News 62:31-3 Ja 30 '67
Why the states are up in arms. il U S News 62:30 Ja 30 '67
See also
State finance—Federal aid
FEDERAL art project
Thirties: when culture came to Main Street; excerpt from Just around the corner. R. Bendiner. Sat R 50:19-21 Ap 1 '67
FEDERAL boards, bureaus, commissions, etc. of United States government. See names of boards, bureaus, etc. under United States, e.g. United States—Federal power commission
FEDERAL contract compliance. Office of. See United States—Labor. Department of—Federal contract compliance, Office of
FEDERAL courts. See Courts—United States
FEDERAL debt (United States) See Debts, Public—United States
FEDERAL deposit insurance corporation
New rules on your insured savings. il Changing T 21:49-51 D '67
FEDERAL elections. See Elections — United States
FEDERAL employees. See Government employees
FEDERAL expenditures. See United States—Appropriations and expenditures
FEDERAL farm bureau federation. See American farm bureau federation
FEDERAL government
Do we expect too much of government or too little? questions and answers. il Sr Schol 91:16-17 N 30 '67
What kind of federalism? D. Lawrence. U S News 62:104 Ja 30 '67
See also
United States—Politics and government
FEDERAL grants. See Grants-in-aid
FEDERAL highway trust fund. See Roads—Finance
FEDERAL information services. See Information services
FEDERAL judges. See Judges
FEDERAL national mortgage association
Waiting for Fanny. Fortune 76:176+ Ag '67
FEDERAL questionnaires. See Questionnaires
FEDERAL reserve bank of St Louis
Maverick in the Fed system; St Louis bank. il Bsns W p 128-9+ N 18 '67
FEDERAL reserve banks
Federal reserve: a separate government; address, October 16, 1967. W. Patman. Vital Speeches 34:138-41 D 15 '67
See also
United States—Federal reserve board

FEDERAL reserve board. See United States—Federal reserve board
FEDERAL reserve system. See Federal reserve banks
FEDERAL savings and loan insurance corporation
New rules on your insured savings. il Changing T 21:49-51 D '67
FEDERAL savings associations (proposed) See Banks and banking—United States
FEDERAL service. See Public service
FEDERAL theater project
Federal theatre, 1935-1939, by J. D. Mathews. Review
Nation 206:56-7 Ja 8 '68. H. Clurman
FEDERAL writers project
Thirties: when culture came to Main Street; excerpt from Just around the corner. R. Bendiner. Sat R 50:19-21 Ap 1 '67
FEDERALISM. See Federal government
FEDERATED department stores, incorporated
Federated, and the consumer comeback. J. Poindexter. il Duns R 90:38-42+ D '67
Shuffling the Lazari. il Time 90:90 S 29 '67
Who's watching the store. Newsweek 70:81+ O 2 '67
FÉDÉRATION internationale de documentation. See International federation for documentation
FEDERATION of American scientists
Classified research in the university; statement and recommended guidelines, July 29, 1967. Bul Atomic Sci 23:45-6 O '67
FEDERATION of Europe. See European federation
FEDERATION of Malaysia See Malaysia
FEDERATION of South Arabia. See South Arabia (Federation)
FEDERICO, Ronald
Anyone here remember trains? Sat R 50:40-1 D 30 '67
FEDORENKO, Nikolai Trofimovich
Professor Fedorenko lectures at the U.N. D. Grant. il pors N Y Times Mag p 10-11+ Jl 16 '67
FEDOROV, Evgenii Konstantinovich
Federov at WMC. il Sci N 91:423 My 6 '67
FEE, Rodney J.
What's new. See issues of Successful farming
FEED conversion. See Feed utilization efficiency
FEED handling
New conveyor keeps feed mixed. il Farm J 91:50H O '67
FEED utilization efficiency
Efficiency of feed conversion. T. C. Byerly. bibliog il Science 157:890-5 Ag 25 '67
FEEDER airlines. See Local service airlines
FEEDERS (bird)
Bird cafeteria. W. Waltner and E. Waltner. il Pop Mech 127:86 F '67
Different feeders for birds. il Good H 164:197 Je '67
Four houses and a feeder. C. Conley. il Field & S 72:109 N '67
Squirrel stopper. D. M. Nickerson. il Horticulture 45:47 F '67
FEEDING and feeding stuffs
Are drugs safe on the farm? FDA orders study of medicated feed additives. Bsns W p54 Ja 14 '67
Liquid supplements, how soon for you? R. C. Black. il Farm J 91:28-9+ D '67
See also
Calves—Feeding
Cattle—Feeding
Forage plants
Silage
Sorghum
Swine—Feeding
Urea

Contamination by drugs and pesticides
Do streptomycin and sirloin mix? Bsns W p 104-5 Jl 1 '67

Grain
Best to steam-flake grains separately Farm J 91:B16 Mr '67
FEEDING stations for birds. See Feeders (birds)
FEELEY, Mary
Money management. See issues of American home
Take a new look at your income for 1967. Am Home 70:58+ Ja '67
FEELINGS. See Emotions
FEES, Airport. See Airports—Finance
FEES, Architects. See Architects—Fees

FEES, Legal. See Cost (law)
FEIBELMAN, Walter A.
New Airglow observatory in Pennsylvania. Sky & Tel 33:340-2 Je '67
FEIFER, George
Wicked cities of the world. Holiday 43:72-83 Ja '68
Yalta, the Soviet playground. Holiday 42:66-7+ O '67
FEIFFER, Jules
Feiffer. See issues of New republic
Little murders. Criticism
Newsweek 69:116 My 8 '67
Sat R 50:66 My 13 '67
FEIGELSON, Philip
Oxygenases. Science 155:609+ F 3 '67
FEIGHT, J. J. and Sommers, C. E.
How to control soybean diseases. Suc Farm 65:40-1+ Ap '67
FEILDING, Charles R.
Better training for a better clergy. por Time 89:50 F 3 '67
FEIN, Samuel B.
Train ID, a key to better mass transit. Am City 82:106-7 Ag '67
FEINBERG, Gerald
Ordinary matter; with biographical sketch. Sci Am 216:21, 126-30+ My '67
FEININGER, Andreas
Large camera. See issues of Modern photography
FEISAL, king of Saudi Arabia
Keeping devils at bay. il Time 91:25 Ja 12 '68
Tradition and reform in Saudi Arabia. G. Lenczowski. Cur Hist 52:98-104+ F '67
FEIST, Robert
Before and after the deluge. America 116: 151-3 Ja 28 '67
FEIX, Gunter, and others
Replication of viral RNA: RNA synthetase from escherichia coli infected with phage MS2 or Qβ. bibliog Science 157:701-3 Ag 11 '67
FEIZI, Ten
Lambda chains in cold agglutinins. bibliog Science 156:1111-12 My 26 '67
FELD, Bernard T.
Pledge: no first use. Bul Atomic Sci 23:46-8 My: 38 N '67
To be nuclear or not. Bul Atomic Sci 23:60-2 My '67
FELD, Eliot
Four most likely to succeed. L. Lerman. por Mlle 65:157 S '67
Meet Eliot Feld. J. Anderson. il pors Dance Mag 41:41-3 Jl '67
Movement makers. H. Saal. il Newsweek 70: 114-15 D 11 '67
New stars. W. Terry. il por Sat R 50:24 Je 3 '67
Pulse of anguish, loving hand. D. Hering. il por Dance Mag 42:52-3 Ja '68
To transcend your own life. W. Terry. il por Sat R 50-37-8 D 23 '67
FELD, Stuart Paul
Stuart P. Feld joins Hirschl & Adler galleries. Hobbies 72:98Z-98AA N '67
FELDKAMP, Phyllis
An evening at the de Gaulles'. Atlan 219:114-18 My '67
FELDMAN, Boris Aleksandrovich
House of Pravda. W. B. Kerr. il Sat R 50: 61 D 9 '67
FELDMAN, Edmund B.
Engaging art in dialogue. Sat R 50:60-1+ Jl 15 '67
FELDMAN, Emanuel
Man touched by God. Sat R 50:94-7 Ap 22 '67
FELDMAN, Fred
Somebody up there likes you drivers. P. O'Neil. il pors Life 63:54-54B+ Ag 4 '67
FELDMAN, Joseph D. See Pick, E. jt. auth.
FELDMAN, Leonard
Buying a hi-fi tuner? Electr World 77:34+ Mr '67
Hi-fi amplifier terms and definitions. Electr World 77:27+ Ja '67
FELDMAN, Lew David
Caxton manuscript to remain in Britain: Ovid's Metamorphoses. il Wilson Lib Bul 41:548 F '67
FELDMAN, Max L.
Transportation forecast for the year 2000. Sat R 51:42 Ja 13 '68
FELDMAN, Morton
Some elementary questions. Art N 66:54-5+ Ap '67
FELDMAN, Samuel M. See Waller, H. J. jt. auth.

FELDMAN-MUHSAM, B.
Spermatophore formation and sperm transfer in ornithodoros ticks. bibliog Science 156: 1252-3 Je 2 '67

FELICANI, Aldino
Sacco-Vanzetti. N. T. Di Giovanni. Nation 205:108 Ag 14 '67
Sacco-Vanzetti: a memoir. Nation 205:108-12 Ag 14 '67

FELIX, Christopher
Unknowable CIA. Reporter 36:20-4 Ap 6 '67

FELIX, David
History lesson; Britain drops a domino. New Repub 157:10-11 N 11 '67

FELLIG, Arthur
Weegee unveils his plastic lens. H. V. Fondiller. il Pop Phot 61:115 Ag '67

FELLINI, Federico
Fellini talks about the face of Anouk Aimée. Vogue 150:160-1 O 1 '67

FELLNER, Rudolph
Act Puccini never wrote. Opera N 31:24-7 F 4 '67

FELLOWS, Lawrence
Duka-wallas are outcasts in Africa. N Y Times Mag p20-2+ Je 25 '67
East Africa turns on with khat. N Y Times Mag p22-3+ Jl 9 '67
Kenya report: market in brides. N Y Times Mag p 12+ F 19 '67

FELLOWSHIP of reconciliation
Toward Caesarism. Christian Cent 84:579-80 My 3 '67
U.S. says no; move to block Americans from sending medical supplies to civilian war victims in North Vietnam. Commonweal 86:37-8 Mr 31 '67

Les FEMMES savantes; drama. See Molière, J. B. P.

FENCES
ABC's of fence gardening. il Pop Gard 18: 38-41 My '67
Build a fence or start an ivy espalier. il Am Home 70:119 Ja '67
Fences. il House & Gard 131:120-3+ Je '67
On the fence. M. B. Keiser. il Parents Mag 42:26+ F '67
Use your fence as a landscape divider. il House & Gard 131:168-9 F '67
With bamboo poles and screening. il Sunset 138:123 Ap '67
See also
Gates

FENN, Dan H. Jr
Case of the latent lobby. Harvard Bsns R 45:22-4+ Ja '67
Treasures without tariffs. Am Ed 3:23-4+ Ap '67

FENNER, Edward
Tough man ties up the teamsters. por Bsns W p 158+ My 6 '67

FENNER, Mildred S.
(ed) Editor interviews. See issues of NEA journal

FENNESSY, E. F. Jr, and others
Humane policing. Sat R 50:48 Jl 1 '67

FENSOM, D. S.
Plant physiology: translocation in plants. Science 157:728 Ag 11 '67

FENWAY park, Boston. See Stadiums

FERAR, Montgomery
Putting design on the track. il pors Bsns W p94-6+ F 25 '67

FERARD, Nancy
Perfect punishment; story. Redbook 129:66-7 Ag '67

FERBER, Caryl, and Saler, Steve
Slum kids' hope. New Repub 156:8-10 Ap 15 '67

FERBER, Edna. See Kaufman, G. S. jt. auth.

FERBER, Ellen. See Goodman, E. jt. auth.

FERDUN, Edrie M.
Of criticism and dance. Dance Mag 41:51 F '67

FERENCY, Zolton A.
Ferency's venture. New Repub 157:8 N 4 '67; Reply. Z. A. Ferency. 157:43 N 18 '67

FERGUSON, Charles W.
Americans not everybody knows. See issues of PTA magazine

FERGUSON, David
Most special dragon; drama. Plays 27:50-4, 60 Ja '68

FERGUSON, Denzel E. See Landreth, H. F. jt. auth.

FERGUSON, Henry N.
Shock treatment for teen-agers. Todays Health 45:28-33+ Ap '67

FERGUSON, James C.
How to maintain terrazzo floors. Am City 82:92-3 Ja '67

FERGUSON, Ken
River that isn't a river. Motor B 120:34+ O '67

FERGUSON, Patrick
Patrick Ferguson; soldier and gun designer. C. G. Worman. il Hobbies 72:122-3 Ja '68

FERGUSON, R. C. and Phillips, W. D.
High-resolution nuclear magnetic resonance spectroscopy. bibliog Science 157:257-67 Jl 21 '67

FERGUSON rifles. See Rifles

FERGUSSON, Francis
Major critic. Commentary 44:79-80 Jl '67

FERKISS, Victor C.
Revolution, anyone? Commonweal 85:480-3 F 3 '67

FERLINGHETTI, Lawrence
Giacometti summer; poem. Mlle 65:118 O '67

FERMANTLE, Anne
Out of time, out of place. Reporter 37:50+ S 21 '67

FERNÁNDEZ, José Mendoza. See Mendoza Fernández, J.

FERNDALE, Calif.
Little Ferndale will get lively this month. il Sunset 138:48-50 My '67

FERNOW award
1966 Fernow award; Siegfried Graf von der Recke. il Am For 73:63 Ja '67

FERNS
Anemia phyllitidis: inducibility of physiological state antagonistic to antheridium formation. U. Näf. bibliog il Science 156: 1117-19 My 26 '67
For a show in the shade. il Sunset 139:146 S '67
Gametophytes of four tropical fern genera reproducing independently of their sporophytes in the southern Appalachians. D. R. Farrar. bibliog Science 155:1266-7 Mr 10 '67
Insect hormones: alpha ecdysone and 20-hydroxyecdysone in bracken fern J. N. Kaplanis and others. bibliog il Science 157: 1436-8 S 22 '67
Nature note. il Sci N 92:124 Ag 5 '67
Platyzoma: a new look at an old link in ferns. A. F. Tryon and G. Vida. bibliog il Science 156:1109-10 My 26 '67

FERON, James
Eshkol sticks to his guns. N Y Times Mag p34-5+ Ja 7 '68
Under new management. Sat R 50:38-9+ O 14 '67

FERRÉ, Nels F. S.
Does man really want peace? Sat R 50:10-12 Jl 1 '67

FERREIRA, Silvestre Pinheiro. See Pinheiro Ferreira, S.

FERRER, José M. 3d
Life TV review (cont) Life 62:12 F 10; 12 Mr 10; 63:16 S 15 '67
N.E.T.'s A time for burning. Life 62:12 F 10 '67

FERRER, Terry
Conant revisited. Sat R 50:56-7+ Mr 18 '67

FERRICK, Daisy L.
How to hybridize hemerocallis. Horticulture 45:30-1+ Je '67

FERRIE, David William
Carnival in New Orleans. il por Newsweek 69:32+ Mr 6 '67
Theory of an Oswald conspiracy. por Life 62:33 Mr 3 '67

FERRIES
Days of the Onitsha ferry. R. E. Morsberger. il Natur Hist 76:62-3+ Ap '67
Island-hopping off the coast of New England. M. Goodman. il Redbook 129:35-8 Jl '67

FERRIS, Barbara
People are talking about . . . por Vogue 151: 108-9 Ja 1 '68

FERRIS, C. Leo
Etching with an eraser. Design 68:17 Ja '67

FERRIS, John
Venti scudi. Opera N 31:27 Ja 28 '67
Winds of Barclay street. Sat R 50:4+ S 23 '67

FERRITE
Ferrites in GI series. Sci N 92:299 S 23 '67

FERROMAGNETISM. See Magnetism

FERROMANGANESE
Minor element composition of ferromanganese nodules. S. S. Barnes. bibliog il Science 157:63-5 Jl 7 '67

FERROTYPES. See Tintypes

FERTIG, Fred
Loyalty in the sunshine. Sat R 50:80 O 21 '67

FERTILITY, Human
Infertility: the other challenge; a report prepared in cooperation with the American college of obstetricians and gynecologists. A. Kerr. il McCalls 94:54+ Mr '67
See also
Conception

FERTILITY control. See Birth control
FERTILITY of soils. See Soil fertility
FERTILITY rite; story. See Weingarten, V.
FERTILIZATION (biology)
Development of mouse ova in explanted
oviducts: fertilization, cultivation, and trans-
plantation. A. Pavlok. bibliog il Science 157:
1457-8 S 22 '67
  See also
Spawning
FERTILIZATION of plants
New long-term plant feeding. O. J. Attoe.
Horticulture 45:45 O '67
Oxygen tension as a control mechanism in
pollen tube rupture. R. G Stanley and H.
F. Linskens. bibliog il Science 157:833-4 Ag
18 '67
Tailor-made honeybees; bred to pollinate a
particular crop. Sci N 92:202 Ag 26 '67
They conquered earth; excerpts from Living
plants of the world. L. Milne and M. Milne.
il Audubon 69:58-69 N '67
Why corn ears go wrong. Sunset 139:252 O '67
FERTILIZER industry and trade
  See also
International minerals and chemical corpora-
tion
Wages and hours
Wages in fertilizer plants, March-April 1966.
C. E. Scott, jr. il Mo Labor R 90:42-4 Mr
'67
FERTILIZER spreaders
Fertilize more and stop less with big tanks
and bulk hoppers. il Farm J 91:40-1+ F
'67
FERTILIZERS and manures
Compost. B. C. Kilvert, jr. il Home Gard 54:
45-6 O '67
Do farms cause water pollution. L. Palmer
and R. Wilmore. Farm J 91:64G+ F '67
Fall fertilizer keeps your crops on schedule.
R. D. Wennblom. Farm J 91:38-9+ O '67
Fertilizers, which type for you? C. E. Som-
mers and S. R. Aldrich. il Suc Farm 65:40-
1+ N '67
How and when to fertilize. C. E. Sommers. il
Suc Farm 65:34-5+ O '67
How fertilizer affects crop quality. S. R.
Aldrich. Suc Farm 65:44H Ja '67
Latest report on fertilizer-pesticide mixtures.
Suc Farm 65:88 Mr '67
Magic in the garden; compost heap. il Pop
Gard 18:101+ Mr '67
Mick, the dreamer; a story of the soil.
J. Stuart. il Am For 73:34-7+ F '67
Micronutrients, what's the score? C. E. Som-
mers and L. Chesnin. il Suc Farm 65:26-7+
D '67
Pop-up: will it become the starter? fertilizer
directly with the seed. J. Russell. il Farm J
91:54+ Ap '67
Ten tips on liquid manure. J. Russell.
Farm J 91:38K Je '67
  See also
Organic gardening
Soil fertility
Handling
How to handle feedlot runoff. O. Bay. Farm
J 91:44R-44S S '67
Spread fertilizer with less work. P. B. Jones.
Suc Farm 65:22D My '67
Still hauling too much manure? four ways
of breaking down more of the manure in
place. il Farm J 92:26-7+ Ja '68
Preservation and storage
Liquid pit for stanchion barns. il Farm J 91:
D14 O '67
FESSIER, Michael, Jr
Snob's guide to Hollywood. McCalls 94:70-3
Ap '67
FESSLER, Loren
Long march of Lin Piao. N Y Times Mag p64-
5+ S 10 '67
FESTIVAL Canada. See Festivals—Canada
FESTIVAL of Aquarius. See Festivals—India
FESTIVAL of the arts. See Music festivals—
Germany (Democratic Republic)
FESTIVAL of the arts, Shiraz-Persepolis. See
Music festivals—Iran
FESTIVAL of two worlds, Spoleto. See Festi-
vals—Italy
FESTIVALS
100 days of summer. L. Lerman. il Mlle 65:
125-7 My '67
World travel calendar, 1968. T. L. Christie.
Sat R 51:74+ Ja 6 '68
  See also
Dance festivals
Drama festivals
Moving picture festivals
Music festivals
Photography festivals

California
In the light of a kindred humanity; LA's in-
ternational folk dance festival. V. H.
Swisher. il Dance Mag 41:46-9 Mr '67
Canada
Flags for Canada. R. Mercer. il Opera N 31:
8-13 My 13 '67
Denmark
800th anniversary festival; Copenhagen re-
port. F. Stevenson. Hi Fi 17:MA30 Ag '67
Viking tours; Viking festival at Frederiks-
sund. il Travel 127:50-1 Mr '67
India
Festival of Dusserah. il UNESCO Courier 20:
15 D '67
India's holy men; festival of Aquarius. F.
Levine. Atlan 220:18+ O '67
Ireland
Photographing King Puck's fair. il U S Cam-
era 30:56-7 D '67
Italy
Ominous vistas; first stage settings by Henry
Moore for Don Giovanni at Spoleto. il Time
90:49 Jl 14 '67
Spoleto. F. Serpa. il Opera N 32:23 S 23 '67
Tenth Festival of two worlds; Spoleto report.
W. Weaver. Hi Fi 17:MA27+ O '67
New England
Festivals and special events. Redbook 129:41
Jl '67
Senegal
Africa revisited. A. Adams. il Hi Fi 17:
MA26-7 Ag '67
FETAL hemoglobin. See Hemoglobin
FETUS
Forecasts from the womb; specialty called
fetology being created. J. R. Hixson.
McCalls 94:60+ F '67
Most hazardous days of your life; reprint.
J. C. G. Conniff. il Sci Digest 61:31-7 My '67
Protecting the unborn baby. A. Kerr. il
McCalls 94:48+ Jl '67
Unborn baby's fight to live. J. Blank. il Red-
book 128:74-5+ Mr '67
World of the unborn. J. C. G. Conniff; dis-
cussion. N Y Times Mag p4+ Ja 29 '67
FETUS, Effects of drugs on the
Congenital malformations induced by mes-
caline, lysergic acid diethylamide, and
bromolysergic acid in the hamster. W. F.
Geber. bibliog il Science 158:265-7 O 13 '67
Drugs in pregnancy; are they safe? Con-
sumer Rep 32:432-6 Ag '67
Hidden evils of LSD; genetic damage. B.
Davidson. il Sat Eve Post 240:19-23 Ag 12
'67
Histocompatibility antigen transfer in utero:
tolerance in progeny and sensitization in
mother. C. Tai and N. A. Halasz. bibliog il
Science 158:125-6 O 6 '67
LSD & the unborn. il Time 90:60 Ag 11 '67
LSD: danger to unborn babies. E. M. Brecher.
McCalls 94:70-1+ S '67
Lysergic acid diethylamide: effect on embryos.
R. Auerbach and J. A. Rugowski. bibliog
il Science 157:1325-6 S 15 '67
New report on LSD: threat to unborn chil-
dren. il U S News 63:66 O 9 '67
FETUS, Effects of viruses on the
Virus etiology of congenital malformations:
report on conference. S. C. Mitchell and
G. L. Woodside. Science 157:1337-8 S 15 '67
FEUD; story. See Shyer, M. F.
FEUER, Lewis Samuel
Elite of the alienated. N Y Times Mag p22-
3+ Mr 26 '67
On civil disobedience, 1967. N Y Times Mag
p29+ N 26 '67
FEUER, Mortimer
Legal liabilities of executives. Duns R 89:48-
9+ My; 48-9+ Je '67
FEVOLD, H. Richard
Regulation of the adrenal cortex secretory
pattern by adrenocorticotropin. bibliog Sci-
ence 156:1753-5 Je 30 '67
FEW moments of sleeping and waking; story.
See Barthelme, D.
FEY, Harold E.
Letter from Geneva. Christian Cent 84:1014-
15 Ag 9 '67
World council and world. Christian Cent 84:
1151-2 S 13 '67
FEYNMAN, Richard Phillips
Two men in search of the quark. L. Edson. il
por N Y Times Mag p54-6+ O 8 '67

FIALKOW, Philip J.
Chromosomal breakage induced by extracts of human allogeneic lymphocytes. bibliog Science 155:1676-7 Mr 31 '67

FIAT company. See Automobile industry and trade—Italy

FIBER glass. See Glass fibers

FIBERGLASS. See Glass fibers

FIBERGLASS boatbuilding. See Boatbuilding

FIBERGLASS boats. See Boats—Materials

FIBERGLASS coatings. See Protective coatings

FIBERGLASS reinforced plastics. See Plastics, Glass reinforced

FIBRINOGEN
Fibrinogen from human plasma: preparation by precipitation with heavy-metal coordination complex. M. E. Brown and F. Rothstein. bibliog il Science 155:1017-19 F 24 '67

FIBRINOLYSIN
Lactones as inhibitors of the fibrinolytic system. W. Auerswald and W. Doleschel. bibliog il Science 156:1244-5 Je 2 '67

FIBROSIS, Cystic. See Cystic fibrosis

FICTION
The novel now, by A. Burgess. Review Sat R 50:33-4 N 25 '67. G. Hicks
Sense of an ending, by F. Kermode. Review Nation 204:730-1 Je 5 '67. D. J. Gordon
Substance of fiction; excerpts from The story: a critical anthology. M. Schorer. Writer 80:14-18+ Je '67
Your plot is contrived C. Armstrong. Writer 80:17-19 O '67

See also
Characters in literature
Christmas stories
Detective and mystery stories
Historical fiction
Negroes in literature
Novelists
Plots (drama, novel, etc)
Romanticism
Science fiction
Sex in literature
Short stories
    also American fiction; Russian fiction; etc.

Authorship
See also
Short stories

Bibliography
Fiction (cont) W. B. Hill. America 116:700-2 My 6 '67

Competitions
I mean, my God, if you can't produce a great American novel for two hundred thou, pre-sold to the flicks, what the hell hope is there for American literature? S. Braun. il Esquire 67:76-7+ F '67

Technique
Aim for the heart. P. Gallico. Writer 80: 11-12+ S '67
Background and foreground in fiction. J. C. Oates. Writer 80:11-13 Ag '67
Bond and I; techniques of Ian Fleming; Len Deighton; John Le Carré. S. Eimerl. Reporter 37:55-8 Jl 13 '67
Can writing be taught? C. Bartholomew. Writer 80:18-20+ S '67
Conversing with the people of history. L. Wibberley. Writer 80:13-14+ My '67
Doing what comes naturally. L. Ware. Writer 80:21-2 My '67
Element of you. A. Cavanaugh. Writer 80: 22-3 Ag '67
Face to face with a teen-age novelist. S. Hinton. Seventeen 26:133 O '67; Correction. 26:20 N '67
How to fight page fright. L. D. Peabody. Writer 80:25-6 F '67
How to write a novel. D. Westheimer. Writer 80:14-15+ D '67
Novelist and his trade. J. Moore. Writer 80: 13-16 O '67
One, two, three... L. Conger. Writer 80:7-8 O '67
Personal motif in fiction. S. Epstein. Writer 80:11-14 Jl '67
Rhythm of a story. M. A. Rodgers. Writer 80:19-21 N '67
Rules to write by. D. Gaines. Writer 80:14-15 Ja '67
Sense of balance. R. A. Knowlton. Writer 80:17-19+ Ap '67
Theatrical opener. T. J. McCauley. Writer 80:26-8 F '67
Ticket to Timbuktu; writing about unfamiliar places. N. Lofts. Writer 80:11-13 Je '67

World of action; suspense novel. F. Clifford. Writer 80:17-18 N '67
Writing a first novel; symposium. Writer 80: 16-18 Ja '67; 81:20-6 Ja '68 (to be cont)
Writing the Gothic novel. P. A. Whitney. Writer 80:9-13+ F '67
You-are-thereness in fiction. J. Williams. Writer 80:20-1+ Ap '67
See also
Characterization
Detective and mystery stories—Technique
Dialogue
Short stories

Themes
See Literature—Themes

FICTION, Fantasy. See Fantasies. Literary

FICTION for children. See Childrens literature

FICTION in periodicals and newspapers
Don't clean the refrigerator. G. L. Tassone. Writer 80:29-30 O '67
Writing for The Kenyon review. G. Lanning. Writer 80:31-2 O '67

FIDDLER spider. See Spiders

FIEDLER, Leslie A.
John Peale Bishop & the other thirties. Commentary 43:74+ Ap '67

about
Blackballing the Fiedlers. B. Jackson. New Repub 157:13-14 S 9 '67
Fiedler affair. por Newsweek 69:29 Je 12 '67
Leslie Fiedler's fictions. R. G. Davis. Commentary 43:73-7 Ja '67

FIEDLER, Martha L.
ETV goes way out and brings the world to Samoa. Am Ed 3:14-17 Mr '67

FIELD, Michael
Cooking with cheese. Holiday 41:105-10 F '67
Michael Field's culinary classics and improvisations; excerpt. McCalls 95:110-11+ O '67
World of fine cooking. See occasional issues of McCall's

FIELD, Sally
TV's Sally Field: The flying nun. B. Rollin. il pors Look 31:M18-20+ N 14 '67

FIELD, Stephen Johnson
Althea and the judges. B. W. Maccracken. il por Am Heritage 18:60-3+ Je '67

FIELD and stream fishing contest. See Fishing—Competitions

FIELD days, Agricultural
How to get the most out of a field day. Suc Farm 65:71 S '67

FIELD-effect current-regulator diode. See Diodes

FIELD enterprises educational corporation
Field granted injunction on salesmen's rights. Pub W 191:43-4 My 29 '67

FIELD glasses
Can a small telescope be too powerful? Consumer Bul 50:29 O '67
Little but powerful; Orvis binoculars. C. Conley. il Field & S 72:95 Ag '67

FIELD ion microscope
Field ion microscopical imaging of biomolecules. E. W. Müller and K. D. Rendulic. bibliog il Science 156:961-3 My 19 '67

FIELD strength meters. See Electric meters

FIELD trials (dogs)
Eyes have it. D. M. Duffey. il Outdoor Life 140:112-16 Ag '67
Plain folks trial. D. M. Duffey. il Outdoor Life 140:90-4 Jl '67
Revival of a grand old name; A. Belmont's dog, winner of National amateur retriever championship. V. Kraft. il Sports Illus 27: 49-50+ Ag 7 '67
Shooting-dog championship. D. M. Duffey. il Outdoor Life 139:132-6+ Je '67
Spring for the feathers; photographs by H. Carroll; with account by D. Barnes. Sports Illus 26:22-7 F 6 '67
Springer spaniel national trial. D. M. Duffey. il Outdoor Life 139:136-8+ Mr '67

FIELD trips, Educational. See School excursions

FIELDING, Gabriel, pseud. See Barnsley, A. G.

FIELDING, Henry
Tom Jones. K. Rexroth. Sat R 50:13 Jl 1 '67

FIELDING, Temple Hornaday
Profiles. J. McPhee. por New Yorker 43:32-4+ Ja 6 '68

FIELDING, Waldo L.
First complete guide to modern birth control. Ladies Home J 84:46-7 Jl '67

FIELDING travel guides. See Guidebooks

FIELDS, W. C.
Fear and laughter. O. Handlin. Atlan 221: 116+ Ja '68

FIELDS, W. C.—*Continued*
Great debunker. il pors Newsweek 69:88+ Ap 3 '67
One and only W. C. Fields; excerpt from The time of laughter, a sentimental chronicle of the twenties. C. Ford. il por Harper 245:65-8 O '67
W. C. Fields, the one and only; excerpt from The time of laughter. C. Ford. por Read Digest 91:158-62 N '67

FIERRO, Steve
Switching transistors. por Electr World 78:57-60 Jl '67

FIESER, Louis Frederick
Man who invented napalm. il por Time 91:66-7 Ja 5 '68

FIFIELD, James William, 1899-
Fifield concept of spirituality. A. B. Haines. Christian Cent 84:1332-4 O 18 '67

FIFTH avenue. See New York (city)—Streets

FIFTH committee of the General assembly. See United Nations—Administrative and budgetary committee

FIFTH constitutional amendment. See United States—Constitution—Bill of rights

FIFTY books of the year exhibit. See Book exhibits

FIGGIE, Harry E. Jr
Fireball on the acquisition front. il por Bsns W p78-81 Ag 12 '67

FIGHTER planes. See Airplanes, Military

FIGHTING (psychology)
Christians and violence. S. Windass. Commonweal 86:11-13 Mr 24 '67
Konrad Lorenz. E. Stillman. il Horizon 9:60-5 Spr '67
Mystique of aggression. D. L. Wallace. Christian Cent 84:503-5 Ap 19 '67
On aggression, by K. Lorenz. Review
 Commentary 43:89-93 F '67. W. J. Dannhauser
 Sci Am 216:135-6+ F '67. S. A. Barnett
War: the anthropology of armed conflict and aggression; symposium. bibliog il Natur Hist 76:39-70 D '67
Why men fight; concerning symposium exploring causes and consequences of armed conflict. il Newsweek 70:62 D 11 '67
 See also
Agressiveness (psychology)

FIGS
2,4,5-Trichlorophenoxyacetic acid: effect on ethylene production by fruits and leaves of fig tree. E. C. Maxie and J. C. Crane. bibliog il Science 155:1548-50 Mr 24 '67

FIGUEROA, Alvaro
Daring romantics in Spain. por Vogue 150:64-5 Ag 1 '67

FIGUEROA, Luis
Daring romantics in Spain. por Vogue 150:64-5 Ag 1 '67

FIGURAL aftereffects
Monocular and binocular aftereffects of chromatic adaptation. R. L De Valois and J. Walraven. il Science 155:463-5 Ja 27 '67
Visual adaptation to gradual change of intensity. S. M. Anstis. il Science 155:710-11 F 10 '67

FIGURE drawing
Fashion illustrating. M. Meixner. il Design 68:22-4 Ja '67

FIGURE painting. See Human figure in art

FIGURE skating. See Skating

FIJI
Fascination of Fiji. R. Atcheson. il Holiday 42:26+ Jl '67
Fun in Fiji. H. E. Mercer. il Travel 127:60-4 F '67
What happened to Friday. M. Petersen. il Motor B 119:33+ F '67
 See also
Hotels, taverns, etc.—Fiji
Tourist trade—Fiji

FIJIANS
Fun in Fiji. H. E. Mercer. il Travel 127:60-4 F '67

FILAMENTS
Filament methods called best for missiles. J. F. Judge. il Tech W 20:34-6 Ap 10 '67

FILES and filing (documents, etc)
Organize home filing this easy way. R. H. Johnson. il Parents Mag 42:76 Ag '67
Set up a farm home fact finding file. J. Fowler. il Suc Farm 65:61+ My '67

FILIBUSTERING in legislation. See United States—Congress—Senate—Rules and practice

FILICE, Alan L.
Lunar surface strength estimate from Orbiter II photograph. Science 156:1486-7 Je 16 '67

FILIGREE
Filigree, enchased and enameled. G. Kaler. il Hobbies 72:50-1 N '67

FILIPINOS
Blunder in Laos; how USAID disrupted one of the most successful programs for co-operation between Asian nations. M. A. Bernad. America 117:766-9 D 23 '67

FILM adaptations
Confessions of a book fiend; films and filmstrips based on children's books. M. Schindel. Library J 92:858-9 F 15 '67
High school principal looks Up the down staircase. H. L. Hurwitz. il Sr Schol 91:sup 16-17 O 5 '67
Rights and permissions. P. Nathan. See issues of Publishers' weekly
Ulysses in the reel world. B. McCabe. il Cath World 204:346-51 Mr '67

FILM festival, Cannes. See Cannes international film festival

FILM festivals. See Moving picture festivals

FILM library information council
Film librarians form independent organization. Library J 92:2498+ Jl '67

FILM propaganda. See Moving pictures—Propaganda films

FILM strips
Films and filmstrips for sex education. V. M. Falconer. Sr Schol 90:sup25 Ap 28 '67
Introducing the library through film; list of films and filmstrips. H. Wheeler. Wilson Lib Bul 41:197-9 O '66; Correction. 41:559 F '67
New films and filmstrips. V. M. Falconer. See occasional issues of Senior scholastic to April 14, 1967
Roundup of films and filmstrips on Canada. V. M. Falconer. il Sr Schol 90:sup20-1 F 10 '67
Screenings; filmstrips. D. Lembo. il Library J 92:3133-4, 4236-8; 93:276-7 S 15, N 15 '67, Ja 15 '68
Stepchild comes of age. D. Lembo. Library J 92:3122-3 S 15 '67
World in Geographic filmstrips. M. M. Payne. il Nat Geog Mag 133:134-7 Ja '68
 See also
Libraries and film strips

FILM washing. See Photography—Fixing

FILMS
 See also
Photography—Films

FILMS, Micro. See Microfilms

FILMS, Photographic. See Photography—Films

FILMS from books. See Film adaptations

FILMSTRIPS. See Film strips

FILSTRUP, J. Maxwell
Literary recipe; poem. Nat R 19:241 Mr 7 '67

FILTER plants
Let's update filter-design standards; excerpts from address, January 1967. J. H. Robinson. bibliog il Am City 82:105-8 Ap '67
Time-tested maintenance tips; Miami, Fla. D. P. Backmeyer. il Am City 82:96-100 Ap '67

FILTERS, Automobile. See Air filters, Automobile

FILTERS, Cigarette. See Cigarette filters

FILTERS, Light. See Light filters

FILTERS and filtration
 See also
Sewage disposal filtration

FILTERS and filtration (biological products)
Detergents in membrane filters. R. D. Cahn. bibliog il Science 155:195-6 Ja 13 '67

FINAL distance; story. See Norris, H.

FINANCE
 See also
Bonds
Church finance
Commerce
Domestic finance
Holding companies
Inflation (finance)
Interest
Investment trusts
Investments
Money
Silver as money
Stock exchange
 also subhead Finance under various subjects, e.g. Corporations—Finance

 Arab states
Shadow war on the economic front: effect of Arab-Israeli conflict. il Newsweek 69:68-70 Je 19 '67

FINANCE—*Continued*

Brazil

Report from South America: no. 1. W. E. Swegle. Suc Farm 65:22+ N '67

Canada

See also
Banks and banking—Canada

Europe, Western

Learning the secrets of companies abroad. il Bsns W p94-6+ S 9 '67

France

See also
France—Economic conditions

Great Britain

Wilson tries to wrest victory from retreat; steps after devaluation. il Bsns W p34-7 N 25 '67

See also
Bank of England
Budget—Great Britain
Money—Great Britain

United States

Fed's unenviable task. Bsns W p 174 N 11 '67
How we manage our money. il Nations Bsns 55:86-9 Jl '67
How we measure our wealth. il Nations Bsns 55:78-82 Ag '67
Plan to stop the gold drain. N. R. Danielian. Read Digest 91:154-8 D '67
Quiet economic news. Fortune 76:97 D '67
U.S. dollar: its problems and its challenges; address, September 22, 1967. H. T. Bodman. Vital Speeches 34:42-4 N 1 '67

See also
Banks and banking—United States
Budget—United States
Debts, Public—United States
Inflation (finance)
Money—United States
Silver as money
Stock exchange—New York (city)
Taxation—United States
United States—Appropriations and expenditures
United States—Budget, Bureau of the
United States—Economic conditions
United States—Federal reserve board
United States—General accounting office
also subhead Finance under names of cities, e.g. Philadelphia—Finance

Wisconsin

State-local cooperative purchasing. G. W. McGrath. il Am City 82:120+ Mr '67
FINANCE, Highway. See Roads—Finance
FINANCE, International
Can de Gaulle break the dollar? with interviews with J. Rueff and E. Despres. il U S News 63:54-6+ D 11 '67
Common market: sputters but no blow-up. Bsns W p 107-8 D 16 '67
Economic necessities and Atlantic communities. A. C. Neal. il For Affairs 45:694-705 Jl '67
Eurobonds get a young brother; European bank for medium term credit. Bsns W p 156+ S 23 '67
Europe tries to spur its capital markets; hampered by conservative stand of governments and investors. il Bsns W p 160-2 Ja 28 '67
Financial powers agree to try for easier money; U.S. British, French, German, and Italian ministers meeting at Chequers. il Bsns W p36-7 Ja 28 '67
Foreign operations weather storm; U.S. companies with overseas operations. Bsns W p 122 N 25 '67
Gold and the dollar. W. F. Butler and J. V. Deaver. For Affairs 46:181-92 O '67
Group of ten agrees on plan for creation of new international monetary reserve asset; excerpts from statements, August 28, 29; with text of communique, August 26, 1967. L. B. Johnson; H. H. Fowler. Dept State Bul 57:392-6 S 25 '67
International economic policies; excerpts from Economic report of the President and annual report of the Council of economic advisers. il Dept State Bul 56:333-50 F 27 '67
International flow of capital. UN Mo Chron 4:118-19 Jl '67
New money game; devaluation of the British pound. il Bsns W p31-2 N 25 '67
Problem of orchestration; expanding world monetary reserves. Time 89:95-6 My 5 '67

Report from Milan; Italy a bulwark of the international capital market. W. Wynn. il Fortune 76:39+ Jl '67
Reserve currencies; address, April 14, 1967. J. P. Koszul. Vital Speeches 33:682-4 S 1 '67
Shadow war on the economic front; effect of Arab-Israeli conflict. il Newsweek 69:68-70 Je 19 '67
Shock waves from the Middle East. il Time 89:88 Je 16 '67
Shrewdest man in the money market; excerpt from The money managers. G. Krefetz and R. Marossi. Harper 235:43-7 Jl '67
Thaw. il Time 89:69 F 3 '67
U.S. in the world market place; address, April 24, 1967. G. Champion. Vital Speeches 33:505-8 Je 1 '67
U.S. reaffirms international monetary co-operation; statements, November 18, 19, 1967. L. B. Johnson; H. H. Fowler. Dept State Bul 57:793 D 11 '67
Why Zurich's gnomes attract all that money. il Bsns W p52-3+ Jl 8 '67
World monetary system; address, March 17, 1967. H. F. Fowler. Vital Speeches 33:455-62 My 15 '67

See also
Balance of payments
Bank for international settlements
Foreign exchange
Inter-American development bank
International finance corporation
International monetary fund
Investments, Foreign
Liquidity, International
Money—International aspects
FINANCE, Municipal. See Municipal finance
FINANCE, Personal
Blind faith? findings of survey. Newsweek 69:82-3 My 29 '67
Do-it-yourself financial checkup; special section with facts and forms. il Changing T 21:7-20 Jl '67
How to stop fighting over money. J. L. Schimel and S. Blum. il Redbook 130:72-3+ N '67
Spending your money; questions and answers. S. Porter. See issues of Ladies' home journal
Teen-agers and money. L. Rand. NEA J 56 34 My '67

See also
Budget, Personal
FINANCE, School. See School finance
FINANCE, State. See State finance
FINANCE companies
How traders beat the 70 per cent margin; unregulated loan companies reappearing. il Bsns W p51-2 Ap 8 '67

See also
CIT financial corporation
General acceptance corporation
FINANCIAL analysts. See Investments—Advisers
FINANCIAL statements
How many have ever read a balance sheet? D. Lawrence. U S News 62:124 Ap 10 '67

See also
Corporation reports
FINANCIERS. See Capitalists and financiers
FINCH, Annie
Difference of dress; poem. Horn Bk 43:239 Ap '67
FINCH, Elfreda
When every line counts. Flower Grower 54:34-5 Ja '67
FINCH, Hardy R.
Convention exhibit notes; NCTE (cont) Sr Schol 91:sup 14 D 14 '67
Meaningful fare for terminal students. Sr Schol 91:sup 10-11 N 30 '67
FINCH, Robert H.
Getting out of the shade. il por Newsweek 70:23 Ag 14 '67
FINCHER, Cameron
Of students, professors and computers. Sch & Soc 95:144-8 Mr 4 '67
FINCHER, Jack
From hippies to Margot's mum, an uproar across the globe. Life 63:84 Jl 21 '67
I did not want to live in a box. Life 63:103-4 O 6 '67
FINDERS, View. See View finders
FINDLEY, W. Cecil
Brush with the R.O.T.C. Christian Cent 84:1222-3 S 27 '67
FINE, Benjamin
Still time to get into a good college. Harper 234:50-4 Ap '67

FINE, Irving Gifford
Musical aristocrat. R. Sabin. por **Am Reo G** 34:103 O '67
FINE, M. M.
Beneficiation of iron ores; with biographical sketch. Sci Am 218:19, 28-35 Ja '68
FINE arts. See Art
FINE piece of machinery; story. See Greenbaum, E.
FINES (penalties)
Parking enforcement pays; Boston. **T. J.** Murphy. il Am City 82:116 Ag '67
FINES, Library. See Libraries—Fines
FINES, Trade union. See Trade unions—Dues, fees, etc.
FINGER LAKES REGION, New York
Finger Lakes country. W. Ballantine. il Holiday 41:62-7+ My '67
FINGER sucking. See Thumb sucking
FINGERNAIL biting. See Nail-biting
FINGERPRINTS
Your telltale fingerprints; quiz. J. Daugherty and M. Daugherty. il Sci Digest 61:89-91 Ap '67
FINIAN'S rainbow; musical comedy. See Musical comedies, revues, etc.—Criticisms, plots, etc.
FINISHING, Wood. See Wood finishing
FINK, Janis. See Ian, J.
FINK, Ronn
Book week on a budget. Library J 92:3124-5 S 15 '67
FINKE, Walter William
Great dictator. R. Levy. il por Duns R 90: 48-50 S '67
FINKELSTEIN, Louis
Light of de Kooning. Art N 66:28-31+ N '67
FINLAND
In the giant's shadow; 50th anniversary of independence. il Time 89:46+ Je 9 '67
See also
Architecture, Domestic—Finland
Arts and crafts—Finland
Country estates—Finland
Foreign visitors in Finland
Money—Finland

Foreign relations
Other anniversary; relations with the Russians. Newsweek 70:56 D 18 '67
FINLEY, Charles O.
Charlie O. Finley follies. B. Musburger. il Sports Illus 27:50-2 S 4 '67
Finley's follies. il por Newsweek 70:68-9 S 4 '67
Nay for quality. Time 90:69 O 27 '67
FINLEY, John Huston, 1904-
Master of Eliot. il por Newsweek 69:102 My 29 '67
FINLEY, M. I.
Lost: the Trojan war. Horizon 9:50-5 Spr '67
FINLEY, Sara C. See Finley, W. H. jt. auth.
FINLEY, Wayne H. and Finley, S. C.
Inheritance. Science 156:1519 Je 16 '67
FINN, James
Human cost. Commonweal 86:573-4 S 22 '67
FINN, Michael
Swinging Europe: in and way-out. Travel 127: 30-6 F '67
FINN, Millicent
Love in a small room. Good H 165:56+ Jl '67
FINN McCool; drama. See Lynch, M.
FINNEGAN, Bob
Picture post card. See issues of Hobbies
FINNEY, Paul B. and Tompkins, J. S.
Portfolio for good, bad or rotten times; with tables. Esquire 67:128-31+ Ap '67
FINNISH baths. See Sauna
FINNISH cookery. See Cookery, Finnish
FINNISH poetry
Kalevala. K. Rexroth. Sat R 50:42+ Ag 19 '67
FINNS
Northern exposure. D. Chu. il Sr Schol 90:14-15 My 19 '67
FINO, Paul A.
Excerpt from remarks. April 10, 1967. Cong Digest 46:183+ Je '67
FIORE, Quentin
Graphics convey message in Medium is the massage; interview, with excerpts from the book. Pub W 191:62-4 Ap 3 '67
FIPPLE flute; story. See Henderson, R.
FIRE alarms
At last, a guide to home **fire alarms.** il Changing T 21:13-14 O '67
False alarm, the prank that kills. K. Detzer. il Read Digest 91:113-17 S '67

Radio waves operate fire alarms. il Am City 82:47 Jl '67
Telephones outdate sirens. Electr World 79:94 Ja '68
Watch out for fire alarm gyps! Consumer Bul 50:18 S '67
FIRE ants. See Ants
FIRE apparatus, Motor
World's mightiest fire engine; New York's Super pumper. P. Ditzel. il Pop Sci 191: 96-7+ O '67
FIRE arms. See Firearms
FIRE blight
What to do about fireblight. il Sunset 138: 245 Mr '67
FIRE departments
See also
Firemen
FIRE extinguishers
Appliance no home should be without. J. Daniel. il Read Digest 90:141-4 Je '67
Fire! extinguishers for a car fire. J. Thawley. il Hot Rod 20:75 D '67
Fire extinguishers for your home. il Consumer Bul 50:4-6 Ag '67
FIRE houses
All-wood firehouse; Tacoma, Wash. J. W. Reiser. il Am City 82:47 Jl '67
White elegance in a firehouse. il House & Gard 131:112-17 Je '67
FIRE making
Instant firepower; metal match. C. Conley. il Field & S 72:93+ Jl '67
FIRE opals. See Opals
FIRE pits. See Fireplaces, Outdoor
FIRE prevention. See Fire protection
FIRE protection
Clean up for a fireproof home. E. Maxwell. Todays Health 45:77-8 O '67
Hazardous materials; Fire protection guide on hazardous materials. Review
Consumer Bul 50:35-6 Ap '67
How to protect your house against fire. il House & Gard 131:194-5 My '67
In case of fire. Am Home 70:95 D '67
See also
Buildings, Fireproof
Fire alarms
Fire extinguishers
Fireproofing of textiles
Forest fire protection
also subhead Fires and fire protection under various subjects, e.g. Museums—Fires and fire protection
FIRE resisting textile fabrics. See Textile fabrics, Fire resisting
FIRE sprinklers
See also
Automatic sprinkler corporation of America
FIRE stations. See Fire houses
FIRE trucks. See Fire apparatus, Motor
FIREARM magazines. See Periodicals—United States
FIREARMS
Bang! bang! you're dead; mail order guns. C. Bakal. il Esquire 68:44-5 Jl '67
Firearms. See issues of Hobbies
Getting the range. J. O'Connor. See issues of Outdoor life
Shooting. J. O'Connor. See issues of Outdoor life
Shooting; ed. by W. Page. See issues of Field & stream
Test set for new flechette gun. il Aviation W 87:33 S 18 '67
Triggers and trigger control. J. O'Connor. il Outdoor Life 139:108-12 F '67
VC firepower, can we match it? M. Schultz. il Pop Mech 127:97-101+ Je '67
See also
Air guns
Colt industries, incorporated
Gunstocks
Machine guns
Pistols
Revolvers
Rifles
Shotguns

History

1883 gunsmith's guide. C. G. Worman. Hobbies 72:122 D '67
Lethal masterpieces; ornamental weaponry. il Time 90:86-9 O 6 '67
Wear gloves before firing; ornamented weapons. M. Lindsay. il Esquire 68:100-3 O '67

Laws and regulations

Arms and the disturbed man. G. Ace. Sat R 50:12 S 16 '67

FIREARMS—Laws and regulations—*Continued*
Availability of guns: a right or a fright? pro and con discussion. Sr Schol 90:14-15 Mr 10 '67
Federal control of firearms: is it necessary? A. S. Nanes. bibliog f Cur Hist 53:38-42+ Jl '67
Firearms theater of the absurd. A. Balk. Sat R 50:28+ Jl 22 '67
Glory of guns; gun magazines campaign against legal control of gun sales. il Time 90:62-3 Ag 25 '67
Gun controls: indispensable or irresponsible? pro and con discussion. bibliog il Sr Schol 91:5-7 D 7 '67
Gun (or two) in every home. Nation 206:69 Ja 15 '68
Gun owners should switch to the offense; reprint from November 1963 issue. A. Grahame. Outdoor Life 140:33-4 O '67
Guns and riots. New Repub 157:4 Ag 5 '67
Let's muffle the sound of guns; interview, ed. by W. B. Furlong. A. E. Stevenson, 3d. Good H 164:64-5+ Ja '67
Lobby on target. R. Sherrill. il N Y Times Mag p27+ O 15 '67; Discussion. p85 N 5; 42 N 19 '67
LBJ raps rioters; summary of address, September 1967. L. B. Johnson. Sr Schol 91:40-1 O 5 '67
More on gun control legislation. America 117:236 S 9 '67
Outdoor life and The death of a President; W. Manchester charges Outdoor life with hard-boiled callousness toward a national tragedy. Outdoor Life 140:32-3 O '67
Philadelphia story: do gun control laws really work? C. Bakal. Sat R 50:20-1+ Ap 22 '67; Discussion. 50:27 My 13; 33 My 20 '67
Shooter's Santa. W. Page. il Field & S 72. 70-2 D '67
Small expectations; Senate gun-control hearings. il Newsweek 70:27 Jl 24 '67
This month's feature: Congress & the national crime problem Cong Digest 46:193-224 Ag '67
Win for the gun lobby. Newsweek 70:29-30 S 4 '67
Your firearms and the plan to take them. R. Starnes. Field & S 72:12-13+ Je '67

Patents

How the army zeroed in on the M-16; negotiations with Colt to purchase the production rights. Bsns W p68 Je 24 '67

Sights

How to sight in. J. O'Connor. il Outdoor Life 140:76+ O '67
Keep things simple. J. O'Connor. il Outdoor Life 140:66+ N '67
Real scoop on scopes. P. Wahl. il Pop Mech 128:112-15+ D '67
Varmint scope. J. O'Connor. il Outdoor Life 139:88+ Je '67

FIREARMS, Used
How to spot a good used gun. J. S. Darrow. il Pop Mech 128:106-9 Ag '67

FIREBALLS. See Meteors

FIREBLIGHT. See Fire blight

FIREFLIES
Mystery of the firefly. R. Gannon. il Read Digest 91:94-7 Jl '67

FIREMAN, Philip, and others
Passive transfer of tuberculin reactivity in vitro. bibliog Science 155:337-8 Ja 20 '67

FIREMEN
Good American; address, May 20, 1967. J. H. Moehle. Vital Speeches 33:567-9 Jl 1 '67
More danger than never in being a fireman now. U S News 63:15 S 11 '67

Training

To train a firefighter; Kansas City, Mo. C. Campbell. il Am City 82:102-3 Mr '67

FIREPITS. See Fireplaces, Outdoor

FIREPLACE accessories
See also
Andirons

FIREPLACES
Built in, added on, and easy. il House B 109:50+ Je '67
How to build a fireplace fire, safely. Good H 165:190 D '67
How to pour a fireplace. D. Huff. il Pop Sci 191:132-5+ N '67
If you plan a corner fireplace. il Sunset 138: 144 Ap '67
New look in stone fireplaces. il Am Home 71: 38 Ja '68

That fireplace you've always wanted. J. A. Hufnagel and R. H. Kruse. il Bet Hom & Gard 45:75 S '67
You, too, can build a fireplace. W. C. Leckey. il Pop Mech 128:148-53+ D '67; 129:172-7 Ja '68
See also
Stoves, Franklin

Anecdotes, facetiae, satire, etc.
Where there's smoke, there's me. J. L. O'Neill. Am Home 70:37 N '67

FIREPLACES, Outdoor
New designs for outdoor chefs. il Pop Gard 18:44-7 My '67
Outdoor fireplace adds warmth to cool patio parties. il Pop Gard 18:22 Mr '67
Summer school. il Arch Forum 127:110 Jl '67
See also
Barbecue grills

FIREPROOF construction
Not-so-fireproof buildings; need for improving especially windowless structures. G. Chamberlain. il Am City 82:119-21+ S '67
Pittsburgh skyscraper achieves breakthrough in steel fireproofing; United States steel corporation. il Arch Rec 141:165-72 Ap '67

FIREPROOFING of textiles
What you should know about flammable fabrics; APOTHPC process. H. Manchester. Read Digest 90:40+ My '67

FIRES
Anti-U.S. motive in a fire disaster? Brussels department store. il U S News 62:10 Je 5 '67
Ash Wednesday; disastrous fire in Tasmania. il Time 89:29-30 F 17 '67
Big fires: a growing danger; Chicago's McCormick Place, New York city's borough of Queens. il U S News 62:12 Ja 30 '67
Chicago's fire fighters; McCormick Place. il Newsweek 69:84 Ja 30 '67
Conventioneers lose their biggest home; disastrous fire at Chicago's McCormick Place. il Bsns W p28-30 Ja 21 '67
Cost of the new Chicago fire; McCormick place. il Time 89:66 Ja 27 '67
Death in the Rue Neuve; fire in Brussels. il Time 89:27-8 Je 2 '67
Eleven-story chimney; Dale's penthouse restaurant, Montgomery, Ala. il Newsweek 69: 41+ F 20 '67
Fatal ruckus; fire at Road prison no. 32 in Florida. Time 90:16-17 Jl 28 '67
Fire hits troubled textile town; Rossville, Ga. il Bsns W p37 Je 17 '67
Fire tragedy in Brussels; L'Innovation department store. il Life 62:32-3 Je 2 '67
Genie gets out of hand; gas explosion and fire in Queens. il Bsns W p 146 Ja 21 '67
Inferno at L'Innovation. il Newsweek 69:55 Je 5 '67
Nature's blitz; Tasmania. Newsweek 69:57 F 20 '67
See also
Brush fires
Forest fires
Textile fabrics, Flammable
also subhead Fires and fire protection under various subjects, e.g. Airplanes—Fires and fire protection

FIREWORKS, Photography of. See Photography of fireworks

FIRING of employees. See Employees—Dismissal

FIRING-range timers. See Timing devices

FIRSHEIN, William, and others
Deoxycytidylate and deoxyguanylate kinase activity in pneumococci after exposure to known polyribonucleotides. bibliog Science 157:821-2 Ag 18 '67

FIRST aid in illness and injury
First aid. C. J. Potthoff. See issues of Today's health
First aid afloat. P. B. Sheldon. Yachting 121:61-5 Je '67
First aid for common home accidents. A. F. Benjamin. Am Home 70:34 S '67
First-aid for poisoning emergencies. Todays Health 45:86 O '67
How to handle emergencies in moving cars. Good H 164:195 Mr '67
Vacation time. 1967. L. W. Sauer. PTA Mag 61:33 Je '67
See also
Fainting

FIRST amendment to the Constitution. See United States—Constitution—Bill of rights

FIRST-born children. See Children, First-born

FIRST chill; story. See Randall, F. E.

FIRST committee of the General assembly. See United Nations—Political and security committee

FIRST Congregational church. See Madison, Wis.—Churches

FIRST lady; story. See Corn, H.

FIRST national bank of Boston. See Boston —Banks

FIRST national bank of Chicago. See Chicago —Banks

FIRST national city bank of New York. See New York (city)—Banks

FIRST Thanksgiving; drama. See Newman, D.

FISCHEL, Anne
Learning in a lonely place. Sat R 50:55 Ag 19 '67

FISCHER, Bobby
Further adventures of terrible-tempered Bobby. T. Matthews. Sports Illus 27:69-70 N 20 '67

FISCHER, Carl
Three ways to find gold. Field & S 72:56-7 Jl '67

FISCHER, John
Easy chair. See issues of Harper's magazine
Four choices for young people. Harper 235:12-15 Ag '67; Same abr. Read Digest 91:177-8+ N '67
He liked students; excerpt from The teacher. NEA J 56:68 D '67

FISCHER, Louis
Colorful comrade. Sat R 50:36 S 2 '67

FISCHER, Mary Ann
How to raise quints without going crazy. G. Cameron. il pors Ladies Home J 84:102-3+ My '67

FISCHER, Virlis
How to sell multiple use without half trying. Am For 73:34-5+ Ag '67
Water and the Southwest. Am For 73:14-17+ N '67

FISCHER-DIESKAU, Dietrich
Fischer-Dieskau & Moore: boffo at the box office. C. L. Osborne. il por Hi Fi 17: MA10+ Je '67
Music to my ears; recitals in Carnegie Hall and Philharmonic Hall. I. Kolodin. Sat R 50:59 Ap 1; 50 Ap 8; 82+ Ap 22 '67
Musical events; Beethoven recital in Carnegie Hall. W. Sargeant. New Yorker 43:158-9 Ap 8 '67
Records:
Eighteen songs. Opera N 32:30 S 9 '67

FISCHER quintuplets. See Quintuplets

FISCHMAN, Donald A. and Weinbaum, George
Hexagonal pattern in cell walls of escherichia coli B. bibliog Science 155:472-4 Ja 27 '67

FISCHMAN, Walter Ian
Short-ee skis, your short cut to winter fun. por Pop Sci 191:108-10+ D '67

FISH, Robert L.
Advise, and learn. Writer 80:22-4 Je '67

FISH, Experiments on. See Animal experimentation

FISH, Frozen
Frank industry talk on frozen food sins. Consumer Rep 32:124-5 Mr '67

FISH and wildlife service. See United States— Fish and wildlife service

FISH as food
See also
Cookery—Fish
Fish flour

FISH-eye lenses. See Lenses, Photographic

FISH flies. See Fishing lures, flies, etc.

FISH flour
Common wealth in ocean fisheries, by F. T. Christy, jr. and A. Scott. Review
Bul Atomic Sci 23:55-6 Je '67. G. Pontecorvo
FPC gets OK at last: FDA's regulations on fish protein concentrate. Sci N 91:138 F 11 '67
Food from the sea; fish protein concentrate. N. L. Brown. Sci N 91:154+ F 18 '67
Protein for everybody Time 89:67-8 Mr 17 '67
Turnabouts. Newsweek 69:40 F 13 '67

FISH hawks. See Ospreys

FISH hooks. See Fishhooks

FISH in the forest; drama. See Corson, H. W.

FISH industry and trade
Fishing fleet tries to cast off the past; U.S. industry in sixth place. il Bsns W p94-6+ O 21 '67
Fishmeal revolution; Mexican developed boat mounted plants. E. Zubryn. Sci N 92:475 N 11 '67
Our catch-as-catch-can fisheries. T. H. Lineaweaver, 3d. il Reporter 37:38-40 S 7 '67

Something fishy; FDA surveys of fish processing plants. R. Nader. New Repub 158: 19-21 Ja 6 '68
Where did the menhaden go? il Time 89: 87 Je 16 '67
See also
Fisheries

FISH law. See Fishery laws and legislation

FISH lines. See Fishing tackle

FISH meal
Fishmeal revolution; Mexican developed boat mounted plants. E. Zubryn. Sci N 92:475 N 11 '67

FISH mounting. See Fishes—Collection and preservation

FISH populations
Internal behavior in fish schools. W. N. McFarland and S. A. Moss. bibliog il Science 156:260-2 Ap 14 '67

FISH products. See Marine resources

FISH protein concentrate. See Fish flour

FISH schools. See Fish populations

FISH sonar. See Sonar

FISH toxins. See Toxins and antitoxins

FISHBEIN, Morris
Solving the mystery of sleep. por Sci Digest 62:43-4 Ag '67

FISHER, Adrian S.
U.S. discusses effect of ABM deployment on arms control efforts; statement, September 19, 1967. Dept State Bul 57:543-5 O 23 '67
U.S. gives views on Soviet proposal for convention on nonuse of nuclear weapons; statement, November 20, 1967. Dept State Bul 58:26-30 Ja 1 '68

FISHER, Aileen
Safety parade; drama. Plays 26:62-4 Ap '67

FISHER, Alan E. See Levitt, R. A. jt. auth.

FISHER, Desmond
Renewal in Europe. Cath World 206:101-4 D '67

FISHER, Douglas
Canada: almost inside the whale. Christian Cent 84:889-93 Jl 12 '67

FISHER, F. H.
Ion pairing of magnesium sulfate in seawater: determined by ultrasonic absorption. bibliog Science 157:823 Ag 18 '67

FISHER, Harold W. and Yeh, Jen
Contact inhibition in colony formation. bibliog Science 155:581-2 F 3 '67

FISHER, James, and Charlton, Selina
Tragedy of errors. Audubon 69:72-85 N '67

FISHER, Joseph L.
Natural environment. Ann Am Acad 371: 127-40 My '67

FISHER, Lenore Eversole
Nibblers' nemesis; poem. McCalls 94:181 Mr '67

FISHER, Lyle H.
Excerpt from statement, July 20, 1966. Cong Digest 46:17+ Ja '67

FISHER, M. F. K.
Books (cont) New Yorker 43:207-8+ O 21 '67

FISHER, Mark
Mark Fisher: an American impressionist. I. M. G. Quimby. il Antiques 91:780-3 Je '67

FISHER, R. M.
Electron microscopy. Science 156:673 My 5 '67

FISHER, Richard T.
Everglades expedition. il Yachting 121:61-4+ Mr; 82-5+ Ap '67

FISHER, Roger
John McNaughton, 1921-1967; letter. New Repub 157:43-4 Ag 5 '67

FISHER, Sir Ronald Aylmer
Footnote; address, December 29, 1966. W. G. Cochran. bibliog Science 156:1460-2 Je 16 '67
R. A. Fisher, 1890-1962: an appreciation; address, December 29,1966. J. Neyman. bibliog Science 156:1456-60 Je 16 '67

FISHER, Sally Waters
That boy who won the balloon debate. NEA J 56:32-3 Mr '67

FISHER, William H. See Day, J. F. jt. auth.

FISHERIES
Common wealth in ocean fisheries, by F. T. Christy, jr. and A. Scott. Review
Bul Atomic Sci 23:55-6 Je '67. G. Pontecorvo
Threat of the longlines. G. Heinold. il Outdoor Life 139:104+ F '67
See also
Fish industry and trade

International aspects
Convention adopted on conduct of North Atlantic fisheries. Dept State Bul 56:635-6 Ap 17 '67

FISHERIES—International aspects—*Continued*
U.S. and Japan adjourn talks on fishing in new U.S. zone. Dept State Bul 56:424 Mr 13 '67
U.S. and Mexico conclude fisheries agreement. Dept State Bul 57:685 N 20 '67
U.S. and Mexico discuss fisheries in twelve mile zone. Dept State Bul 57:475 O 9 '67
U.S. and U.S.S.R. conclude talks on fishery problems. Dept State Bul 56:331-2 F 27 '67
U.S. and U.S.S.R. extend fisheries agreements. Dept State Bul 58:67 Ja 8 '68
U.S. and U.S.S.R. hold talks on fishery problems. Dept State Bul 56:216 F 6 '67
U.S. and U.S.S.R. reviewing fisheries agreements. Dept State Bul 57:873 D 25 '67
U.S. Japan discuss operations in new U.S. fisheries zone. Dept State Bul 56:178 Ja 30 '67
U.S.-Mexican fishery talks held at Washington; joint statement, May 25, 1967. Dept State Bul 56:919 Je 19 '67

Alaska
Resource comes out of its shell in Alaska; king crab industry. il Bsns W p 132-4 O 7 '67
See also
Salmon

FISHERMEN
Sailing oystermen of Chesapeake Bay. L. Marden. il Nat Geog Mag 132:798-819 D '67
Song of the angler. A. J. McClane. **il Field** & S 72:118-22+ O '67
28,348,000 fishermen can't be wrong! interviews. il Field & S 71:60-2 F '67
Why anglers really angle. R. Ley. il Field & S 71:63+ F '67

FISHERY laws and legislation
Do residents control resident game? W. E. Towell. il Am For 73:20-1+ Jl '67
Fishing laws; United States and Canada (cont) Field & S 71:94+ Ap; 72:34+ My '67
Fishing seasons (cont) Outdoor Life 139:88-9 Ap '67

FISHES
See also headings beginning Fish; *also* names of fishes, e.g. Hagfish

Collection and preservation
Ninety minutes to mount your prize. D. C. Fales. il Pop Mech 128:100-2 Jl '67

Ecology
Alewife explosion. il Time 90:56 Jl 7 '67
Dead fish by the ton; ecology of Lake Michigan. il Sci N 92:9-10 Jl 1 '67
Fish and fishing; possible effects of Nawapa. W. F. Royce. Bul Atomic Sci 23:26-7 S '67
Internal behavior in fish schools. W. N. McFarland and S. A. Moss. bibliog il Science 156:260-2 Ap 14 '67
Something fishy; alewives die in Lake Michigan. il Newsweek 70:23-4 Jl 31 '67
Temperature measurements from oxygen isotope ratios of fish otoliths. I. Devereux. il Science 155:1684-5 Mr 31 '67
Temperature tolerance of some Antarctic fishes. G. N. Somero and A. L. DeVries. bibliog il Science 156:257-8 Ap 14 '67

Extermination
Pollution in the West: industry struggles with pollution problems. A. Netboy. il Am For 73:8-11+ Jl '67

Geographical distribution
Fish and fishing; possible effects of Nawapa. W. F. Royce. Bul Atomic Sci 23:26-7 S '67

Habits and behavior
Alarm reaction of the top smelt, atherinops affinis: reexamination. R. H. Rosenblatt and G. S. Losey, jr. bibliog il Science 158:671-2 N 3 '67
Chemical communication in social behavior of a fish, the yellow bullhead (ictalurus natalis) J. H. Todd and others. bibliog il Science 158:672-3 N 3 '67
Walking fish. il Sci Digest 62:57 S '67

Intelligence
See Animal intelligence

Metabolism
Oxygen consumption of red and white muscles from tuna fishes. M. S. Gordon. bibliog il Science 159:87-90 Ja 5 '68

Nomenclature
Twenty fishes of the Pacific. il Sunset 138:176-7 Mr '67

Physiology
Hormones and endocrine glands of fishes. H. A. Bern. bibliog il Science 158:455-62 O 27 '67
Hydrocarbons in digestive tract and liver of a basking shark. M. Blumer. il Science 156:390-1 Ap 21 '67
Lungfish neoceratodus forsteri: activities of ornithine-urea cycle and enzymes. L. Goldstein and others. bibliog il Science 157:316-17 Jl 21 '67
Piezoelectric property of otoliths. R. W. Morris and L. R. Kittleman. bibliog il Science 158:368-70 O 20 '67
Sodium- and potassium-activated adenosine triphosphatase of gills: role in adaptation of teleosts to salt water. F. H. Epstein and others. bibliog il Science 156:1245-7 Je 2 '67

Protection
Nuclear power on salmon rivers. A. Netboy. il Nation 205:337-9 O 9 '67

Stories
Exit, laughing. E. Zern. See issues of Field & stream

FISHES, Extinct
See also
Coelacanths

FISHHOOKS
Fisherman, look to your hook. H. G. Tapply. il Field & S 71:62 Ap '67

FISHING
Angling. W. Davis. See issues of Outdoor life
Don't you believe it; angling lore. T. Trueblood. il Field & S 72:22-3+ Jl '67
Fish are more interesting than politicians. S. Alsop. il Sat Eve Post 240:16 My 20 '67
Fish 'n ships. V. Evanoff. See issues of Motor boating
Fishing; ed. by A. J. McClane. See issues of Field & stream
Fishing is a contagious disease. R. Starnes. Field & S 71:20+ F '67
Flight of the snowbirds. A. J. McClane. il Field & S 71:86-92 F '67
For their first try at fishing. il Sunset 138:57-8 Ap '67
Gist of it; digest of the outdoor news: ed. by H. Moore. See issues of Outdoor life
Happy times. T. Trueblood. il Field & S 71:24+ F '67
Scourge of the seven seas. V. Kraft. il Sports Illus 27:39-43 Jl 10 '67
Sensible view of fishing. A. J. McClane. il Field & S 72:68-71 Jl '67
Sportsman's notebook. H. G. Tapply. See issues of Field & stream
What bottom fishing is, is trying your luck. il Sunset 139:47-8 N '67
Where to go fishing, vacationing, hunting; ed. by V. T. Sparano. See issues of Outdoor life
You ought to take some time off and go fishing! F. J. L. Blasingame. il Field & S 71:52-3 F '67
See also
Bait
Casting (fishing)
Fishermen
Salt water fishing
Trawls and trawling
also Bass fishing; Trout fishing; and similar headings

Anecdotes, facetiae, satire, etc.
Fisherman never lies. C. Ford. il Field & S 71:6+ Ap '67
In defense of bait fishing. B. H. Lampman. il Field & S 71:52-3 Ap '67
See also
Fishing stories

Competitions
Catch your vacation costs! E. M. Marshall. il Travel 128:46-7 S '67
1966 winners; Field & stream fishing contest. Field & S 71:34+ Mr; 68+ Ap '67

Implements and appliances
How to fish with a sky hook. K. A. Anderson. il Pop Mech 128:90-1 Ag '67
New fishing extras. D. C. Fales. il Pop Mech 127:116-19 Ap '67
Outfit for every occasion; symposium. il Field & S 71:48-51+ F '67
Tackle box with the new look. C. Conley. il Field & S 71:131 F '67

Law
See Fishery laws and legislation

FISHING—*Continued*

Alabama

Where Mr Inbetween grew up. G. Gresham. il Field & S 71:164-7+ Mr '67

Andorra

Anecdotes, facetiae, satire, etc.

Off season for izards. J. Olsen. il Sports Illus 27:70-2+ O 23 '67

Arctic Regions

Winged safari for Arctic char. D. Barnes. il Sports Illus 26:48-55 My 15 '67

Argentina

Fishing in the land of fire. E. Schwiebert. il Field & S 72:48-9+ N '67

Arkansas

Fishing was like tomorrow; Beaver Lake. C. Elliott. il Outdoor Life 139:44-7+ F '67
Float trip for rainbows. W. Davis. il Outdoor Life 139:28+ My '67

Atlantic states

Summer tide-marsh stripers. P. McLain. il Field & S 72:60-1+ My '67
That's where I want to fish; comp. by T. Janes. Outdoor Life 139:81-4 Ap '67
Tidal rivers never sleep. G. Heinold. il Outdoor Life 139:74-5+ My '67

Australia

Some new battles are boiling in the Coral Sea. V. Kraft. il Sports Illus 27:53-4+ D 18 '67

British Honduras

Troublesome tarpon. T. McNally. il Outdoor Life 139:72-3+ Mr '67

California

Deadly bait for bass; lamprey eel. L. Green. il Outdoor Life 139:52-3+ Je '67
Fishing a floating island. J. Martin. il Outdoor Life 140:42-3+ Jl '67
Fishing the Klamath Loop. M. Hayden. il Outdoor Life 140:36-9+ S '67
For the fish and for the fishing. il Sunset 138:29-30 Ap '67
It's a private fishing water; Owens River. il Sunset 138:54 Je '67
Kokanee keep things jumping. W. Curtis. il Outdoor Life 139:25-6+ Mr '67
Oh shad, poor shad. L. Green. il Field & S 72:52-5+ My '67
River of forgotten trout. J. R. Higley. il Outdoor Life 139:60-1+ F '67
Roadside trout fishing, what's wrong with it? California department of fish & game. H. D. Bishop. il Am For 73:6-7+ Je '67
Skipper called me honey. H. J. Samuels. il Outdoor Life 139:68-9+ My '67
Stripers saw pink. L. Green. il Outdoor Life 139:78-80+ Ap '67
Sundown stripers; San Pablo Bay. J. Martin. il Field & S 72:52-3+ Jl '67
That surprising Eagle Lake. B. Behme. il Field & S 72:38-9+ Je '67
What's in Fish Lake? October fish. il Sunset 139:66+ O '67

California, Lower

Strange ways for a striped marlin. J. Hardie. il Field & S 71:66-9+ Mr '67

Canada

Adventuring westward. E. A. Bauer. il Outdoor Life 139:33-5+ Je '67
Cruising Lake Nipissing. F. M. Paulson. il Field & S 71:34-5+ Ap '67
Easy campaing in the Canadian bush. N. Karas. il Field & S 71:62-3+ Mr '67
Exploring north of nowhere. F. Perry and L. Perry. il Field & S 72:46-9+ Je '67
Fish is caught: Kalum River, N.S; ed. by J. Cameron. A. Reed. il Outdoor Life 139:30-1 Je '67
Fishing light is never out. E. Park. il Outdoor Life 140:46-9+ Ag '67
Fishing the province of plenty; Nova Scotia. A. W. Prince. il Outdoor Life 139:56-9+ Je '67
High water and flies only. B. Warner. il Field & S 71:44-5+ Ap '67
I'll take seconds: Atlantic-salmon fishing in George River. B. Warner. il Outdoor Life 140:60-1+ S '67
Lakers on top: Great Bear Lake in Northwest Territories. W. Davis. il Outdoor Life 139:94+ F '67
Most in fishing ever; interview. G. Anderegg. il Field & S 71:42-5+ F '67

Strange cod of Ogac Lake. F. Bruemmer. il Outdoor Life 140:56-9 N '67
Summer exodus. A. J. McClane. il Field & S 72:82-5 Ag '67
Tow your boat to a northern wilderness. G. Laycock. il Field & S 72:158-61+ My '67
Voyage to wilderness fishing; from Ohio to Ontario. G. Lau. il Outdoor Life 140:17-19+ Jl '67
Walleyes on tap all year. W. Davis. il Outdoor Life 139:72+ Je '67
We float the Yukon and strike it rich. J. S. Flannery. il Outdoor Life 140:48-52+ Jl '67

Central America

Fishing in the Banana Republics. A. J. McClane. il Field & S 72:86-8+ D '67

Colorado

Wilderness lake cutthroat. D. Knight. il Field & S 71:36-7+ Ap '67

Connecticut

New fish for the Northeast. A. Davenport. il Field & S 71:38-9+ Ap '67
Nighttime is the time. G. Heinold. il Outdoor Life 140:128-9+ O '67
Our far-flung correspondents; waters around Salisbury. C. Rand. il New Yorker 43:152+ S 16 '67

Delaware

Ponds upon ponds of bass. T. Janes. il Outdoor Life 139:66-7+ My '67

Egypt

Shark of Araby. C. Gammon. il Sports Illus 27:88-91+ O 16 '67

Florida

Christmas on a houseboat. E. A. Bauer. il Outdoor Life 140:42-5+ D '67
Everglades canals for winter bass. V. Dunaway. il Field & S 72:48-9+ Ja '68
Make the most of mullet. W. Davis. il Outdoor Life 140:118-21 S '67
New world record tarpon on a fly. S. Apte. il Outdoor Life 140:30-3+ Ag '67

Georgia

Fish the headwaters for trout. C. Elliott. il Outdoor Life 139:58-61+ My '67
Okefenokee. L. Dietz. il Field & S 71:60-1+ Ap '67

Great Lakes Region

Boom and a blunder on Lake Michigan; coho salmon. H. Babbitt. il Sports Illus 27:67-8+ O 9 '67

Idaho

Bull trout testimonial. L. C. Newlun. il Field & S 71:56-7+ Ap '67

Indiana

Ice-out bluegills. C. Patterson. il Outdoor Life 139:52-3+ Mr '67
Saga of Willow Slough. W. C. Ligler. il Outdoor Life 140:36-7+ Ag '67

Iowa

Blizzard perch. H. Bradshaw. il Field & S 72:52-3+ D '67

Kentucky

Dangerous bass of Lake Cumberland. H. Bradshaw. il Field & S 71:40-1+ Ap '67
Midsummer night rainbows. J. Hayes. il Field & S 72:94-7+ Ja '68
White bass fever in the Bluegrass. J. O. Cartier. il Outdoor Life 139:74-5+ Ap '67

Louisiana

Utopia isle. C. Elliott. il Outdoor Life 140:44-7+ O '67

Maine

Flag is up! T. Janes. il Outdoor Life 139:74-5+ F '67

Massachusetts

Plug for jumbo blues. M. Rosko. il Outdoor Life 140:56-8+ Ag '67
Toil and treble. H. S. Moore. il Outdoor Life 140:10 S '67
World striper record tied. G. Radcliffe. il Field & S 72:68-9 S '67

Mexico

Green bottles down the Rio Grande. H. A. Smith. il Field & S 71:46-7+ F '67
Latest bass bonanza. R. B. Whitaker. il Outdoor Life 140:23-5+ Ag '67
Lure of Libertad. R. B. Whitaker. il Field & S 72:40-1+ Je '67

FISHING—*Continued*

Mexico, Gulf of

How to hunt fish by plane. G. Gresham. il Field & S 72:42-3+ Je '67

Michigan

Coho craze in Michigan. J. Chiappetta. il Field & S 72:42-3+ Ja '68
Fall steelheads are back. J. O. Cartier. il Outdoor Life 140:58-9+ O '67
Spring specktacular. J. O. Cartier. il Outdoor Life 139:76-8+ My '67
Very superior pike! R. Dornquast. il Field & S 72:54-5+ D '67

Middle western states

That's where I want to fish; comp. by J. O. Cartier. Outdoor Life 139:84-7 Ap '67

Minnesota

Bonefish of the North. J. Parry. il Field & S 72:60-1+ D '67
Ice fishing quick and easy. P. Czura. il Field & S 72:66-8 Je '67

Montana

Adventuring westward. E. A. Bauer. il Outdoor Life 139:49-51+ Ap; 50-3+ My '67 (to be cont)
Dam the Big Hole, full speed ahead. G. Laycock. il Field & S 72:12-16+ My '67
Fishing north of Yellowstone il Sunset 139:22-3 Jl '67

New Mexico

Ute Lake: New Mexico's newest hotspot. B. Dalrymple. il Field & S 72:64-5+ My '67
We fish the box at last. O. A. Washburn. il Outdoor Life 140:54-5+ D '67

New York (state)

Boss of the weed beds. W. Davis. il Outdoor Life 140:114-17+ O '67
Choosing the right rod action. W. Davis. il Outdoor Life 140:78-9+ N '67
Dig 'em out of the bushes; New York's Ausable River. W. Davis. il Outdoor Life 140:54+ Jl '67
Frostbite fishing. G. Heinold. il Outdoor Life 140:14+ N '67
Oneida, fishiest lake of them all. N. Karas. il Field & S 72:98-105 Jl '67

Northwestern states

Boom in steelheads. R. Gerlach. il Outdoor Life 139:40-3+ Je '67

Norway

Where fishing is a blood sport. E. Schwiebert. il Esquire 68:126-7+ O '67

Ohio

Jump the gun for bass. E. A. Bauer. il Outdoor Life 139:44-7+ Mr '67

Oklahoma

They've whipped those beginner's blues. E. A. Bauer. il Field & S 71:54-7+ F '67

Oregon

Beaver state bonus; Lake of the Woods. J. Martin. il Field & S 72:50-1+ D '67
Deschutes steelhead. J. Gartner. il Field & S 72:40-1+ D '67
Mackinaw on a fly. E. Park. il Field & S 71:42-3+ Ap '67

Pennsylvania

Big fly: big trout. V. C. Marinaro. il Outdoor Life 139:56-9+ Mr '67
Big trout are my meat. K. Asper and J. Hayes. il Outdoor Life 139:66-9+ Ap '67
First report: newest fishing in Pennsylvania. J. Hayes. il Field & S 71:50-1+ Ap '67
Old fishing hole. D. J. Anderson. il Field & S 72:46-7+ Jl '67
Some like it cold. J. Hayes. il Field & S 72:46-7+ D '67

South Carolina

Mission to Cape Romain. K. Osborne. il Field & S 72:48-9+ Jl '67
Renaissance at Santee-Cooper. K. Osborne. il Field & S 72:72-4+ My '67

Southern states

That's where I want to fish; comp. by C. Elliott. Outdoor Life 139:90-3 Ap '67

Tennessee

Cats that swim. J. B. Kemmerer. Field & S 72:30-1+ Jl '67

Little T for big trout. C. Elliott. il Outdoor Life 140:44-7+ N '67
Watauga walleyes. J. Carmichel. il Field & S 72:128-31+ Je '67
Yankee walleyes see red. C. Vinson. il Outdoor Life 139:44-5+ Je '67

Texas

Texas brag lake. R. Tinsley. il Outdoor Life 140:42-3+ S '67

United States

Big three of cold-water sport fishing: trout, char, salmon. A. J. McClane. il Field & S 72:43-9+ My '67
In's and out's of fishing; with drawings by D. Siegel. il Field & S 71:38-41 F '67
Man-made fishing holes answer pollution threats. il Parks & Rec 2:34-5 Mr '67
Summer exodus. A. J. McClane. il Field & S 72:82-5 Ag '67
28,348,000 fishermen can't be wrong! interviews. il Field & S 71:60-2 F '67
Voyage to wilderness fishing; from Ohio to Ontario. G. Lau. il Outdoor Life 140:17-19+ Jl '67
You should be there now. il Field & S 71:142-4+ F '67

Utah

Hottest lake in Utah; Fish Lake. L. Oertle. il Field & S 71:152-3+ Ap '67
How to fish high lakes. H. Wixom. il Outdoor Life 140:42-3+ Ag '67

Virginia

Big tumbling creek. K. Mink. il Outdoor Life 139:62-5 Je '67
Drums on the Barriers. G. Heinold. il Outdoor Life 140:20-1+ Ag '67
Good day on Mechunk creek. B. Gooch. il Outdoor Life 140:68-9+ O '67

Washington (state)

Indian uprising for civil rights. H. Bims. il Ebony 22:64-5+ F '67
Salmon for everyone. W. W. Hunter. il Field & S 71:58-9+ Mr '67

Western states

Before you go salmon fishing. Sunset 139:27 Jl '67
Glorious fish; Pacific salmon. il Sunset 139:44-51 Jl '67
Great hatch. E. W. McCray. il Outdoor Life 140:24-7+ Jl '67
Pacific striper fishing. G. Heinold. il Outdoor Life 139:12+ Je '67
That's where I want to fish; comp. by J. Mears and L. Miracle. Outdoor Life 139:93-6 Ap '67

Wisconsin

Don't bet on a muskie. J. O. Cartier. il Outdoor Life 139:50-1+ Je '67
Lesson in pints and pounds. M. Ellis. il Field & S 71:46-8+ Ap '67
Summer bass discovery. A. W. Prince. il Outdoor Life 140:40-1+ Jl '67

Wyoming

Cutthroats of southeast arm. G. A. Barrus. il Field & S 72:34-5+ Jl '67
Pain-in-the-neck pack trip. B. Milek. il Field & S 72:50-1+ My '67

FISHING, Deep sea. See Salt water fishing

FISHING, Winter

Beaver state bonus; Lake of the Woods. J. Martin. il Field & S 72:50-1+ D '67
Blizzard perch. H. Bradshaw. il Field & S 72:52-3+ D '67
Down by the old smelt stream. T. Janes. il Outdoor Life 140:48-9+ D '67
Flag is up! T. Janes. il Outdoor Life 139:74-5+ F '67
Frostbite fishing. G. Heinold. il Outdoor Life 140:14+ N '67
Hook, line and ear muffs. il Newsweek 71:77-8 Ja 22 '68
Ice fishing a la cart. H. Bradshaw. il Pop Mech 129:132-4+ Ja '68
Ice fishing quick and easy. P. Czura. il Field & S 72:66-8 Je '67
Winter walleyes. W. Davis. il Outdoor Life 140:28-30+ D '67

FISHING boats

Bass boat, a special type that borrows basic elements from Jersey sea skiffs and Maine lobster boats. il Yachting 121:53+ Je '67
Chesapeake, Skipjack regatta. B. Schill and B. Schill. il Yachting 121:200-2 F '67
Fish 'n ships. V. Evanoff. See issues of Motor boating

FISHING boats—*Continued*
How to buy a fishing boat. P. Richards. il Pop Mech 127:154+ F '67
Tartan Miss. il Motor B 119:46-7+ Je '67

Equipment
Fish 'n ships. V. Evanoff. See issues of Motor boating

FISHING industry. See Fish industry and trade

FISHING kites. See Fishing—Implements and appliances

FISHING lines. See Fishing tackle

FISHING lures, flies, etc.
Bass are everywhere. W. Davis. il Outdoor Life 139:43-5+ My '67
Big fly: big trout. V. C. Marinaro. il Outdoor Life 139:56-9+ Mr '67
Deadly plastic worm. W. Davis. il Outdoor Life 140:60+ Ag '67
Favorite flies: East to West. il Field & S 71:58-9 F '67
Flies with flash. A. Fusco. il Outdoor Life 140:52-5+ S '67
Great hatch. E. W. McCray. il Outdoor Life 140:24-7+ Jl '67
If I had to pick one lure. J. S. Fawcett. il Outdoor Life 139:54-5+ My '67
Lures with glows on. L. Green. il Field & S 71:70-1+ F '67
Make your own fishing spoons: bass and steelhead lures. C. L. Howard. il Pop Mech 127:112-14 My '67
Mayfly that will float without its hackles. R. H. Boyle. il Sports Illus 26:42 Ja 23 '67
Midsummer's meal for a largemouth bass. R. H. Boyle. il Sports Illus 26:59-60 My 8 '67
Modern fly lines. A. J. McClane. il Field & S 72:78-80+ Je '67
Revolution in salt water fishing. G. X. Sand. il Outdoor Life 139:68-71+ F '67
Ultralight fills the gap. D. C. Proper. il Outdoor Life 139:56-7+ Ap '67
Wassail for woolly worms. F. Calkins. il Field & S 72:58-9+ Je '67
Wet fly magic. W. Davis. il Outdoor Life 139:20+ Ap '67
Winter steels and the fly. R. Haig-Brown. il Outdoor Life 140:36-9+ N '67
See also
Fly casting

FISHING reels. See Fishing tackle
FISHING rods. See Fishing tackle
FISHING spoons. See Fishing lures, flies, etc.
FISHING stories
Don't fish while I'm talking. R. Manning. il Atlan 220:123 O '67

FISHING tackle
Beginner's tackle: four types of reels. A. J. McClane. il Field & S 72:102-5 N '67
Choosing the right rod action. W. Davis. il Outdoor Life 140:78-9+ N '67
Dredging with wire. H. G. Tapply. il Field & S 72:61 Ag '67
Fly-fishing reels. il Consumer Rep 32:259-63; 376-83 My, D '67
It pays to dye: marked fishing lines. T. Trueblood. il Field & S 72:18+ Je '67
Man with drag. J. Brooks. il Outdoor Life 139: 66-7+ Mr '67
New fishing extras. D. C. Fales. il Pop Mech 127:116-19 Ap '67
Rod-winding with a mousetrap. H. G. Tapply. il Field & S 72:62 D '67
Up-and-down fly lines. H. G. Tapply. il Field & S 72:70 S '67
What happened to UL? H. G. Tapply. il Field & S 72:76 My '67
Where the action is. A. J. McClane. il Field & S 71:86-8+ Mr '67

Care
Care of tackle. G. Heinold. il Outdoor Life 139: 14+ Mr '67
Store your rods safely. V. T. Sparano. Outdoor Life 139:84 Mr '67

FISHING with bow and arrow
Bowfishing gear. G. H. Gillelan. il Outdoor Life 139:12+ My '67

FISHLOCK, David
British favor 300-bev. Sci N 92:137 Ag 5 '67
Common market lure. Sci N 91:555+ Je 10 '67
Instruments: lab to shop. Sci N 92:137+ Ag 5 '67

FISHMAN, Katharine Davis
Parent and child (cont) N Y Times Mag p72+ F 26; 105+ My 14; 86+ S 24 '67
Traveling with Mlle: how to read a travel folder. Mlle 66:141-2+ D '67

FISHMEAL. See Fish meal
FISHWICK, Marshall W.
Folklore, fakelore, and poplore. Sat R 50:20-1+ Ag 26 '67
Is American history a happening? Sat R 50: 19-21 My 13 '67

FISK, Harrison S.
How to make single-concept films. Sr Schol 91:sup 12-13 O 12 '67

FISSION reactors. See Nuclear reactors
FISSION-track dating. See Radioactive dating
FISSIONABLE materials. See Radioactive substances

FIT to be tied; drama. See Martens, A. C.

FITCH, Charles Marden
Small tree for small gardens. Home Gard 54:61-2 F '67

FITCH, Lyle C.
Urban frontier. Sat R 50:26-7 Ag 5 '67

FITCH, Robert E.
Formula for the new politics. Christian Cent 84:139-41 F 1 '67
Prescription for pandemonium. Christian Cent 84:1591-2 D 13 '67

FITCH, Walter M. and Margoliash, Emanuel
Construction of phylogenetic trees. bibliog Science 155:279-84 Ja 20 '67

FITTING out boats. See Boats—Care
FITZGERALD, C. P.
China in Asia. Cur Hist 53:129-34+ S '67
China puzzle: old man in a hurry. Nation 204: 326-9 Mr 13 '67
Mao's cultural revolution. Nation 205:325-8 O 9 '67
Tension on the Sino-Soviet border. For Affairs 45:683-93 Jl '67
Through China's looking glass. Nation 206: 24-6 Ja 1 '68
Upheaval in a Chinese village. Nation 205:184-5 S 4 '67

FITZGERALD, Frances
Power set. Vogue 149:154-5+ F 1 '67
Struggle and the war. Atlan 220:72-82+ Ag '67
Viet Nam, the people. por Vogue 149:174-5+ My '67

FITZGERALD, Francis Scott Key
College of one, by S. Graham. Review Harper 234:106 F '67. A. Turnbull
Fitzgerald's Paris; excerpt from That summer in Paris, by M. Callaghan. il Sat R 50:50+ Mr 11 '67

FITZGERALD, Gerald
Verdi and the pirates. Opera N 31:14-15 F 25 '67

FITZGIBBON, Constantine
Next fifty years: a preview? Nat R 19:1201-4 O 31 '67

FITZPATRICK, Linda Rae
Linda's last trip. il por Newsweek 70:33-4 O 23 '67
Maybe somebody else can learn from it. J. A. Lukas. Read Digest 91:96-101 D '67
Speed kills. il Time 90:23 O 20 '67

FITZROY, Robert
Darwin sidelight: the shape of the young man's nose. S. E. Hyman. Atlan 220:96-100+ N '67

FITZSIMMONS, Frank
One-man rule ends for the teamsters. por Bsns W p152+ My 20 '67
Playing out Hoffa's hand. por Bsns W p81 Mr 18 '67

FIX, John
Gar Wood: an old sea dog is up to new tricks. Pop Mech 128:82-5+ Jl '67
Underwater hot rod. Pop Mech 128:100-2 D '67

FIXES, Basketball. See Bribery
FIXTURES, Bathroom. See Bathroom fixtures
FIXX, James F.
Amy Loveman awards. Sat R 50:26 Jl 15 '67
Anisfield-Wolf awards. Sat R 50:25 My 13 '67

FLACH, Frederic F.
American woman: her breaking point. Vogue 149:248+ My '67

FLAD, Harvey K. and Flad, M. F.
Preserving democracy, C.I.A. style. Commonweal 85:614-15 Mr 3 '67

FLAD, Mary Fogarty. See Flad, H. K. jt. auth.

FLAGELLA
Adenosine triphosphate usage by flagella. C. J. Brokaw. bibliog il Science 156:76-8 Ap 7 '67
Guanine nucleotide associated with the protein of the outer fibers of flagella and cilia. R. E. Stevens and others. bibliog il Science 156:1606-8 Je 23 '67

FLAGELLATES
See also
Euglena

FLAGELLATES, Fossil
Coccoliths as paleoclimatic indicators of pleistocene glaciation. A. McIntyre. bibliog il Science 158:1314-17 D 8 '67

FLAGLER, J. M.
Drugs and mysticism; visions of Saint Tim. Look 31:18+ Ag 8 '67

FLAGS
Flags and you; designing personal and club pennants. T. Gibbs. il Motor B 121:83-5+ Ja '68
New look at the yacht ensign. C. F. Chapman. il Motor B 119:43+ Ap '67

United States
After protesters burned a U.S. flag. il U S News 62:12+ My 1 '67
Burned up; bill to make flag burning a federal crime. Newsweek 70:29 Jl 3 '67
Burning issue; bill makes desecration of the flag a federal offense. Time 89:17 Je 30 '67
Flag-burning irritant; legislation hearings. Nation 204:772 Je 19 '67
Hot summers and short tempers; bill under way. Nation 205:36-7 Jl 17 '67
Oratorical overkill on the flag bill. Life 63:4 Jl 7 '67
Stars and stripes forever, and all over. il Life 62:20-1 Mr 31 '67
Test case for Old Glory; stuffed sculpture dramatizes the uses and abuses of the flag; with report by F. Powledge. il Life 62:18-19+ Mr 31 '67
Who's desecrating the flag? Christian Cent 84:771-2 Je 14 '67
Why the flag flies over our farm; letters. il Farm J 91:21+ Jl '67

Anecdotes, facetiae, satire, etc.
Fireworks. G. Ace. Sat R 50:9 Jl 1 '67

FLAGSTAD, Kirsten
Project of the decade, singer of the century; excerpt from Ring resounding. J. Culshaw. por Sat R 50:72-5 Ag 26 '67

FLAHERTY, Daniel L.
Of many things; Catholic press in England. America 116:295 Mr 4 '67
Soviet space spectacular? America 116:370-2 Mr 18 '67

FLAHERTY, Joe
Frankie Carlin, the bookie. N Y Times Mag p28-9+ Ap 2 '67
Slow bus to Bushville. N Y Times Mag p 100+ N 19 '67

FLAHERTY, John F.
Boston gives engineers an eyeful. por Am City 82:95-8 S '67

FLAMES
Musical flames may test engines, rockets. C. Behrens. il Sci N 93:43-4 Ja 13 '68
See also
Combustion

FLAMING desserts. See Desserts

FLAMINGOS
Flamingos drill in the Bahamas. il Sunset 138:74+ My '67

FLAMMABLE materials. See Inflammable materials

FLAMMABLE textile fabrics. See Textile fabrics, Flammable

FLANAGAN, Nan Riley
Cold reality. Atlan 220:117-18 N '67

FLANDERS, Michael
Hat; tenth anniversary of collaboration; interview. New Yorker 43:46-8 Mr 11 '67

about
Flann and Swanders. il por Newsweek 69:100 Ja 30 '67
Mixed bag from Britain. D. Morgan. Reporter 36:52 Mr 9 '67

FLANDES, Juan de. See Juan de Flandes

FLANNER, Janet
Departed glory of Les Halles. Life 62:82+ My 12 '67
Letter from Paris. See issues of New Yorker

FLANNERY, Harry W.
Brazil's miserable northeast. por Cath World 205:276-81 Ag '67

FLANNERY, John S.
Meet me on the Green. Outdoor Life 140:50-3+ Ag '67
Runway rabbit hunt. Outdoor Life 139:74-6 Mr '67
We float the Yukon and strike it rich. pors Outdoor Life 140:48-52+ Jl '67

FLANNERY, Kent V. and others
Farming systems and political growth in ancient Oaxaca. bibliog Science 158:445-54 O 27 '67

FLANS. See Tarts

FLAPPERS. See Girls

FLAPS, Airplane
New flap promises near-STOL capability. D. A. Brown. il Aviation W 87:119+ Jl 10 '67

FLARES
Radar-reflecting flare; may treble the chances of success of sea-air rescue. Sci Digest 61:25-6 Mr '67

FLARES, Solar. See Solar flares

FLASHBULBS. See Electric lamps, Photoflash

FLASHCUBES. See Electric lamps, Photoflash

FLASHING electric lamps. See Electric lamps, Flashing

FLASHLIGHT batteries. See Electric batteries

FLASHLIGHT photography. See Photography, Flashlight

FLATLEY, Guy
(comp) And for best director... N Y Times Mag p 174 Mr 19 '67

FLATWARE. See Silverware

FLAUBERT, Gustave
C'est moi. por Time 89:96+ F 24 '67
Famous ancestor of the new novel. T. Bishop. por Sat R 50:56-7 N 25 '67

FLAVIN, Dan
Light brigade. E. C. Baker. il Art N 66:52-5+ Mr '67

FLAVOR. See Taste

FLAVOR potentiators. See Taste

FLAW in the crust of the earth; story. See Tyler, A.

FLAXEDIL. See Gallamine triethiodide

FLAYDERMAN, Benjamin. See Flayderman, P. C. jt. auth.

FLAYDERMAN, Philip C. and Flayderman, Benjamin
How to judge antiques the way a dealer does. House B 109:54-5+ S '67

FLEAS as carriers of infection
So your neighbor has fleas? A. Hamilton. il Todays Health 45:59-61 O '67

FLECHETTE gun. See Firearms

Die FLEDERMAUS; opera. See Strauss, J. jr

FLEETWOOD, James
(ed) See Lemnitz, T. Perennial Pamina

FLEISCHER, Arthur, jr
Corporate disclosure; insider trading. bibliog f Harvard Bsns R 45:129-35 Ja '67

FLEISCHER, R. E.
Designed for six major functions. Am City 82:104-7 S '67

FLEISCHER, R. L. and others
Tracks of cosmic rays in plastics. bibliog Science 155:187-9 Ja 13 '67

FLEISCHHAUER, Bill
Rig to dunk the dinghy. Motor B 119:52 Mr '67

FLEMING, Denna Frank
When did the cold war begin? Nation 206:53-5 Ja 8 '68

FLEMING, Peggy
Crystal and steel on the ice. B. Ottum. il pors Sports Illus 26:24-7 Mr 13 '67
Elegance on ice. il por Newsweek 69:88 Mr 13 '67
Growing up & staying there. il por Time 89:76+ Mr 10 '67

FLEMING, Robben Wright
Mediator for Michigan. por Newsweek 69:68 Ap 10 '67
Mediator for Michigan. por Time 89:39 Ap 7 '67

FLEMING, Shirley
Columbia's Odyssey label starts a propitious voyage. Hi Fi 17:75-6 Ap '67
Concert managers convene. Hi Fi 17:MA9 Mr '67
Conductor Szell at the keyboard. Hi Fi 17:30+ D '67
Master of the solo guitar in music of modern masters. Hi Fi 17:89 N '67
Music at Expo, from Bach to bleeps. Hi Fi 17:MA22-3 Jl '67
Rostropovich whirlwind. Hi Fi 17:MA9+ My '67
(ed) See Simon, A. And we quote

FLEMING, Thomas J.
Case of the debatable Brooklyn D.A. N Y Times Mag p32-3+ Mr 19 '67
First in their hearts; condensation. Read Digest 90:209-12+ F '67
Fordham is trying to be Catholic with a small c. N Y Times Mag p32-3+ D 10 '67
Let me help you learn. Redbook 129:46+ O '67
Verdicts of history (cont) bibliog Am Heritage 18:65-75 Ap; 28-33+ Ag; 19:22-7+ D '67

FLEMINGER, Irwin
New art selection process. Art N 65:56-7+ Ja '67
FLESSEL, C. Peter, and others
Polyribosomes of growing bacteria. bibliog Science 158:658-60 N 3 '67
FLETCHER, J. C.
Sound off. Flying 80:88-9 Ap '67
FLETCHER, James
English and the Vietnam war. Nat R 19: 684-7+ Je 27 '67
FLETCHER, Joel E.
Weather modification. Science 158:276-7 O 13 '67
FLETCHER, Joseph Francis, 1905-
Rules and decisions. R. O. Johann. America 117:61 Jl 15 '67
FLETCHER, Winifred Bell
Hawaii's bird paradise. Nat Parks Mag 41:10-14 O '67
FLEXMAN, Ralph, and Horowitz, M. W.
Both feet on the ground. Flying 80:54-6 Mr '67
FLEXNER, James Thomas
Benedict Arnold: how the traitor was unmasked; excerpt from George Washington in the American revolution. Am Heritage 18:6-15 O '67
Providence rides a storm; excerpts from George Washington in the American revolution. Am Heritage 19:12-17+ D '67
FLEXNER, Louis B. and others
Memory in mice analyzed with antibiotics. bibliog Science 155:1377-83 Mr 17 '67
FLICK, Maurice
Adam's fall: the task of reinterpretation. Cath World 205:42-6 Ap '67
FLICKER phenomena
Enhancement of flicker by lateral inhibition. F. Ratliff and others. bibliog il Science 158: 392-3 O 20 '67
FLIEGEL, Dorian J.
Amherst community referendum. Nation 204: 757 Je 12 '67
Curran's NMU; headquarters vs. the men at sea. Nation 204:143-7 Ja 30 '67
Forgotten history of the draft. Nation 204: 454-6 Ap 10 '67
FLIES
Calcareous septa formed in snail shells by larvae of snail-killing flies. L. V. Knutson and others. bibliog il Science 156:522-3 Ap 28 '67
Hormone-mediated nutritional control of sexual behavior in male dung flies. W. Foster. bibliog Science 158:1596-7 D 22 '67
River blindness afflicts 200,000,000; biological-medical-social attack on black flies. D. A. Ehrlich. il Sci N 92:16-17 Jl 1 '67
Robber flies; asilidae. Hobbies 72:125 Jl '67
See also
Fruit flies
FLIES, Artificial. See Fishing lures, flies, etc.
FLIES, White. See White flies
FLIGHT

Physiological aspects
See Aviation—Physiological aspects
FLIGHT director. See Aeronautic instruments
FLIGHT instructors. See Air pilots—Training
FLIGHT nurses. See Nurses and nursing
FLIGHT recorders. See Aeronautic instruments
FLIGHT research center. See United States—National aeronautics and space administration—Flight research center
FLIGHT simulators
American to build central facility to handle heavy training loads. il Aviation W 87:40 N 13 '67
Both feet on the ground. R. Flexman and M. W. Horowitz. il Flying 80:54-6 Mr '67
General aviation flight trainer developed; Link General aviation trainer. K. J. Stein. il Aviation W 86:94-5+ Ap 24 '67
New simulators offer wider data range. K. J. Stein. il Aviation W 87:79+ O 2 '67
Now we can teach flying in high school. K. V. Brown. il Pop Mech 128:120-1 Ag '67
Pilot report:
Link's new GAT I; general aviation trainer I. R. B. Weeghman. il Flying 80:72-4 My '67
FLIGHT test research, incorporated
T-33s used to check aerospace systems. G. S. Hunter. il Aviation W 86:97-8+ F 6 '67
FLINDT, Flemming
Fearless Flindt and his dancing Danes. G. Rogoff. il Holiday 41:158+ Ap '67
Royal flash. il por Time 89:65+ F 24 '67

FLINK, Stanley
Lusty new role for Julie Christie. Look 31: 59-64 Mr 21 '67
FLINT, Jeremy
Jeremy the kingmaker. C. Goren. il Sports Illus 27:57 S 4 '67
FLINT, Mich.
Computerized voter registration. W. R. Penberthy. il Am City 82:78-9 N '67

Parks and playgrounds
Mr Flint; C. S. Mott lake project started. il Newsweek 69:29-30 My 1 '67
FLINT
X-ray fabric analysis of hot-worked and annealed flint. H. R. Wenk and others. il Science 157:1447-9 S 22 '67
See also
Chert
FLOATING airports. See Airports, Floating
FLOATING hospitals. See Hospital ships
FLOATS. See Rafts
FLOATS, Seaplane. See Seaplanes—Floats
FLOERSHEIM, Georg L.
Drug-induced tolerance for skin allografts across the H-2 barrier in adult mice. bibliog Science 156:951-4 My 19 '67
FLOIRAT, Sylvain
I wasn't created to lose money. il por Time 89:84 Mr 31 '67
FLOOD lighting. See Light projection
FLOOD prevention and control
Put flood-plain management first. L. Wright. il Am City 82:98-9 N '67
U.S. Mexico conclude agreement on flood control project; statement, July 6, 1967. L. B. Johnson. Dept State Bul 57:147 Jl 31 '67

United States
Flood control brings beauty; San Mateo, Calif. R. G. Bezzant. il Am City 82:73 Jl '67
See also
Muskingum watershed conservancy district
FLOODLIGHTING. See Light projection
FLOODS
See also
Rivers

Alaska
Disaster that hit Alaska's second city; Fairbanks. il U S News 63:10 Ag 28 '67
Soggy centennial; Fairbanks flooded. il Time 90:19 Ag 25 '67
Still waters lie on the stricken Alaskan city. il Life 63:24-5 S 1 '67

Brazil
No time for gaiety; Rio. Newsweek 69:66 Mr 27 '67

Italy
After the flood, the operas open. W. Weaver. Hi Fi 17:MA30 Mr '67
Again the rains. il Newsweek 70:77 N 20 '67
Artist life; Florence catastrophe. D. J. Soria. il Hi Fi 17:MA5-MA6+ F '67
Before and after the deluge. R. Feist. America 116:151-3 Ja 28 '67
Florence rises from the flood. J. Judge. il Nat Geog Mag 132:1-43 Jl '67
International campaign for Florence and Venice; symposium. il UNESCO Courier 20: 4-39 Ja '67
Letter from Florence. F. Steegmuller. New Yorker 42:50+ Ja 28 '67
Libraries of Florence, November 1966; with recommendations and resolution passed by ALA council. A. T. Hamlin. il ALA Bul 61: 141-51 F '67
Library crisis in Italy; inaction in Rome, serious threat to the National library of Florence. A. T. Hamlin. il Library J 92: 2516-22 Jl '67
Mayor of Florence; interview. P. Bargellini. New Yorker 43:39-41 Ap 22 '67
Notes from a flood journal. P. W. Denzer. Yale R 56:475-80 Mr '67
Saving the libraries of Florence; Committee to rescue Italian art (CRIA) C. Horton. bibliog il Wilson Lib Bul 41:1034-43 Je '67
Tale of two cities; council meetings; ALA midwinter report. E. Moon. il Library J 92: 731-2 F 15 '67
Unheralded disaster. R. J. Mollar. Christian Cent 84:153-5 F 1 '67
Up from the mud, a second renaissance for Florence. J. Reddy. il Read Digest 91:205-16+ O '67
Venice under water. R. Lynes. Harper 234: 33+ Mr '67

FLOODS—*Continued*

United States

Baleful toll of hurricane Beulah. il Life 63: 34-5 O 6 '67

Beulah's backlash. Newsweek 70:24 O 9 '67

Midwest extremes. Sr Schol 90:17 Ap 21 '67

Sweeping disaster along the Rio Grande; hurricane Beulah. il U S News 63:8 O 9 '67

Wild one; Beulah brings worst floods in Texas' history. il Time 90:29 O 6 '67

See also
Floods—Alaska

FLOOR coverings

Facts about modern floor coverings; Armstrong's vinyl floorings. M. B. Keiser. il Parents Mag 42:10+ D '67

Floor coverings. Consumer Rep 32:108-14 D '67

GE's new Traffic topping waterproofs a sun deck. B. W. Powell. il Pop Sci 190:138-41+ Je '67

New coverings for your floors. il Pop Sci 191:166-7 S '67

New patterns in floor coverings. il Pop Sci 190:156-7 Ap '67

Something new underfoot: Congoleum-Nairn vinyl Cushionflor. M. B. Keiser. il Parents Mag 42:34+ Mr '67

See also
Linoleum
Rubber tiles
Rugs and carpets

FLOOR waxes. See Waxes

FLOORING

Choose the right flooring for your patio. il Pop Gard 18:24-31 My '67

Wood floor finishes. il Consumer Bul 50:31-3 N '67

FLOORS

Brave new floors. il House & Gard 131:174-5 Mr '67

Elevated flooring permits impossible time schedule and great flexibility. il Arch Rec 141:227-8 Ap '67

See also
Floor coverings
Swine houses—Floors

Care

How to care for wood floors. Am Home 70:85 S '67

How to maintain terrazzo floors. J. C. Ferguson. il Am City 82:92-3 Ja '67

Institute reports on... protective coatings for kitchen floors. il Good H 164:6 Mr '67

Rubber floors and rubber heels help to prevent falls. Consumer Bul 50:29-30 Ap '67

FLOORS, Concrete

For oil stains on concrete. Sunset 139:151 O '67

FLOORS, Plywood

Plywood sandwich raises arena profits; Seattle, Wash. il Am City 82:88-9 Ja '67

FLOORS, Terrazzo. See Terrazzo

FLOORS, Tile

Now you can lay a Spanish tile floor. A. Lees. il Pop Mech 127:106-9+ Je '67

FLOORS, Wood

How to care for wood floors. Am Home 70: 85 S '67

How to refinish hardwood floors. J. P. Schenley. il Pop Mech 129:188-90 Ja '68

FLORA, Fletcher

Six burrs in the blanket. Writer 80:24-6 Ag '67

FLORA of the flower shop; drama. See Huff, B. T.

FLORAL decoration. See Flowers, Arrangement of

FLORENCE, Franklin D. R.

Self-doubt and black pride. R. A. Schroth. America 116:502-5 Ap 1 '67

FLORENCE

Fire and flood on the Arno. V. Cronin. il Sat R 50:24 D 30 '67

Flood of U.S. buyers hits Florence as usual. il Bsns W p 126-8+ Mr 18 '67

Florence rises from the flood. J. Judge. il Nat Geog Mag 132:1-43 Jl '67

Mayor of Florence; interview. P. Bargellini. New Yorker 43:39-41 Ap 22 '67

Notes from a flood journal. P. W. Denzer. Yale R 56:475-80 Mr '67

Up from the mud, a second renaissance for Florence. J. Reddy. il Read Digest 91:205-16+ O '67

Art

Artist life; Florence catastrophe. D. J. Soria. il Hi Fi 17:MA5-MA6+ F '67

Florence: mending damaged treasures. K. Kuh. il Sat R 50:11-21 Jl 22 '67

For Florence, from Florence; show at Wildenstein, for the Committee to rescue Italian art. F. Licht. il Art N 66:44-7+ My '67

Important discoveries of renaissance art in Florence. M. Meiss. il Art N 66:26-7+ Sum '67

In Florence, new troubles and new treasure. il Life 62:54-9 Je 30 '67

Letter from Florence. F. Steegmuller. New Yorker 42:60+ Ja 28 '67

To the rescue of art; Italy's Central institute of restoration. R. Deardorff. il Holiday 41:29-30+ Ap '67

Years to repair the damage. B. Molajoli. il UNESCO Courier 20:6-11 Ja '67

Churches

Dimensions of a disaster; artistic and cultural casualties suffered by Florence. il UNESCO Courier 20:14-16+ Ja '67

Education

Educational aid to flood-ravaged Florence. W. W. Brickman. Sch & Soc 95:289 Sum '67

Galleries and museums

Dimensions of a disaster; artistic and cultural casualties suffered by Florence. il UNESCO Courier 20:14-16+ Ja '67

Libraries

Book restoration in Florence. B. A. Bannon. il Pub W 192:27-8 N 6 '67

Dimensions of a disaster; artistic and cultural casualties suffered by Florence. il UNESCO Courier 20:14-16+ Ja '67

Letter from Florence. F. Steegmuller. New Yorker 42:60+ Ja 28 '67

Libraries of Florence, November 1966; with recommendations and resolution passed by ALA council. A. T. Hamlin. il ALA Bul 61: 141-51 F '67

Library crisis in Italy; inaction in Rome, serious threat to the National library of Florence. A. T. Hamlin. il Library J 92: 2516-22 Jl '67

Ricci's luxury edition aids Florence library. il Pub W 191:114 F 6 '67

Saving the libraries of Florence; Committee to rescue Italian art (CRIA) C. Horton. bibliog il Wilson Lib Bul 41:1034-43 Je '67

Tale of two cities; council meetings; ALA midwinter report. E. Moon. il Library J 92: 731-2 F 15 '67

FLORENCE agreement. See Duty free importation

FLORENTINES

Plight of the Florentine artisans. R. Keating. il UNESCO Courier 20:12-13 Ja '67

FLORES, Gustavo, and Frieden, Earl

Induction and survival of hemoglobin-less and erythrocyte-less tadpoles and young bullfrogs. bibliog Science 159:101-3 Ja 5 '68

FLORICULTURE

H&G'S gardener's month. See issues of House & garden incorporating Living for young homemakers

[Month] gardening where you live! H. Perkins. See issues of Better homes and gardens

No-work flower beds. C. G. Kenny. il Suc Farm 65:111+ Mr '67

Raised beds for cutting flowers. il Sunset 138:253 Ap '67

Regional report:
Cedar Rapids, Iowa. Home Gard 54:76 My '67
Eugene, Ore. Home Gard 54:78 My '67
Eugene, Ore. l. Prescott. Home Gard 54: 56 O '67
Fulton, Ill. T. Abbott. Home Gard 54:50 Jl '67
Jacksonville, Fla. Home Gard 54:74 My '67
La Crosse, Wis. P. Shedesky. il Home Gard 54:58-9 Ag '67
Los Angeles, Calif. R. E. Atkinson. Home Gard 54:55 S '67
Pownal, Vt. Home Gard 54:51-2 Je '67
Roanoke, Ind. Home Gard 54:53 Je '67
Spring Valley, N.Y. V. M. Quist. Home Gard 54:51 Jl '67
Springfield, Mass. C. O. Dean. Home Gard 54:54 S '67
West Hatfield, Mass. B. Brinhart. il Home Gard 54:52-3 N '67
Westport, Conn. Home Gard 54:82 My '67

See also
Bulbs
Gardening
Perennials

FLORIDA, Eugene
Barbecue cart you can build. Pop Sci 190:158-9 My '67
Getting started in model rocketry. Pop Mech 128:148-51+ Jl '67

FLORIDA
See also
Architecture, Domestic—Florida
Big Cypress swamp
Booksellers and bookselling—Florida
Colleges and universities—Florida
Crime and criminals—Florida
Everglades National Park
Gardens—Florida
Geology—Florida
Indian River
Kissimmee River
Labor and laboring classes—Florida
Land—Florida
Libraries—Florida
Miami River
Paleontology—Florida
Police—Florida
Prisons—Florida
Ten Thousand Islands
Water supply—Florida
Waterways—United States
Wilderness areas—Florida

Description and travel
Changing West coast. R. Marston. il Yachting 122:40-1+ N '67
Cruising in northern Florida. E. White. il Motor B 119:42-5+ Mr '67
From tip to top in Florida. G. Bourke. See issues of Travel
Gulf coast of Florida. G. Jahoda. il Holiday 41:70-8+ My '67

Economic conditions
Gadfly with a sting; Apalachicola times campaigns against domination of Du Pont estate. Time 89:40 Je 23 '67

History
Civilization's late arrival in south Florida. il Parks & Rec 2:39-40 Mr '67
Passion of Hernando de Soto; excerpt from Explorers of the Mississippi. T. Severin. il Am Heritage 18:26-31+ Ap '67

Land tenure
See Land tenure—United States

Legislature
I, Claudius; special election; Republican party victory. il Newsweek 69:36 Ap 10 '67

Parks and reserves
Paradise parks; state parks in the Miami area. il Parks & Rec 2:34-5+ O '67

Politics and government
Affairs of state; Governor C. Kirk. il Newsweek 69:24+ Ja 30 '67
It is a joyous thing to be a Kirk Republican! M. Frady. il Sat Eve Post 240:75-9 Jl 29 '67
New way of operating. il Time 89:19-20 Ap 7 '67
Political happening named Claude Kirk. R. Sherrill. il N Y Times Mag p34-5+ N 26 '67
See also
Florida—Legislature

FLORIDA EVERGLADES. See Everglades
FLORIDA flood control district. See Central and southern Florida flood control district
FLORIDA Indians. See Seminole Indians
FLORIDA KEYS
Ardea's world; excerpts from World of the great white heron; a saga of the Florida Keys. M. B. Sanger. il Audubon 69:54-65 Ja '67
See also
Dry Tortugas
FLORIDA power and light company
No wilderness wasted; Turkey paint development. M. Smith. Parks & Rec 2:20+ Je '67
FLORIDA SHIP CANAL project
Manatees, living lawn mowers. il Sci Digest 62:33-5 Ag '67
FLORIDA trail. See Trails
FLORIDA. University
Cafeteria now bookstore at University of Florida. J. Solomon. il Pub W 192:68-9 N 13 '67
FLORIDA West Coast inland waterway. See Waterways—United States

FLORIOT, René Edmond
Floriot loses one. il por Time 90:72-3 Jl 28 '67
FLORISTS
Customers don't say it enough; flower industry oriented to special occasions. il Bsns W p98-100+ Ap 1 '67
FLOTATION equipment. See Boats and boating—Safety devices and measures
FLOTOW, Friedrich von
Martha. Criticism
New Yorker 43:60 Ja 13 '68
FLOUR
Planning a switch to instant flour? Consumer Bul 50:30 S '67
FLOUR, Fish. See Fish flour
FLOUR beetles
Reminiscence in the cold flour beetle, tenebrio molitor. T. M. Alloway and A. Routtenberg. bibliog il Science 158:1066-7 N 24 '67
Tribolium castaneum: morphology of aureate revealed by the scanning electron microscope. A. Sokoloff and others. bibliog il Science 157:443-5 Jl 28 '67
FLOUR industry and trade
See also
Pillsbury company
FLOWER arrangements. See Flowers, Arrangement of
FLOWER baskets. See Baskets
FLOWER boxes, planters, etc.
Case for contained plantings; gardening in pots, boxes, tubs and planting beds. il Home Gard 54:27-34 Je '67
Copper sheathing cost us $1.25. il Sunset 138:167-8 Mr '67
Nursery flats into temporary planters. il Sunset 138:140+ My '67
Show your color close up. H. Mason and others. il Bet Hom & Gard 45:58-9 Ap '67
They live on a deck, but still they manage to garden in a grand way. il Sunset 139:58-9 S '67
FLOWER exhibits
Camellia shows in California. Sunset 138:204 F '67
Debut for spring; the flower shows. Home Gard 54:74 F '67
Garden events. See issues of Flower grower, the home garden (cont as) Home garden & flower grower
Garden events [in month] (title varies) See issues of Sunset
H&G'S almanac of flower shows (cont) il House & Gard 131:24+ Mr '67
Onward and upward in the garden. K. S. White. bibliog New Yorker 43:200+ N 11 '67
FLOWER festival; ballet. See Ballets—Criticisms
FLOWER gardening. See Floriculture
FLOWER painting. See Flowers in art
FLOWER photography. See Photography of flowers, plants, trees, etc.
FLOWER pot holders
Easy to build bench for pots. J. B. Brimer. il Home Gard 54:66 Mr '67
Tray for a plant container. il Sunset 138:130-1 F '67
FLOWER pots
These plant containers are from the Orient, Mexico, Europe. il Sunset 139:166+ D '67
FLOWER shops. See Florists
FLOWER shows. See Flower exhibits
FLOWER trade. See Florists
FLOWERING dogwood. See Dogwood
FLOWERING onions. See Alliums
FLOWERING shrubs. See Shrubs
FLOWERING stones
Living rocks; South African succulent plants. C. B. Dugdale. il Horticulture 45:38-9+ F '67
FLOWERING tobacco. See Nicotiana
FLOWERING trees
Bouquets in the air. C. Calkins. il House B 109:184-7 Ap '67
Good small trees for your garden. H. Rohrbach. il Horticulture 45:30-1+ O '67
FLOWERING vines. See Climbing plants
FLOWERPOTS. See Flower pots
FLOWERS, Paul
Homespun hyperboles. Sat R 50:54 Je 10 '67
FLOWERS
Flowers you never planted before. E. McDonald. il House B 109:162-3+ S '67
New flowers for 1967; cheerful eyefuls. G. Logsdon. il Farm J 91:68B-9 Ja '67

FLOWERS—*Continued*
New plants for 1967. il Flower Grower 54:38-42+ Ja '67
Newest flowers for spring. G. Logsdon. Farm J 92:58 Ja '68
See also
Annuals (plants)
Fertilization of plants
Perennials
Plant introduction
Proteas
also names of flowers, e.g. Peonies

All America selections
See Plants—All America selections

Cut flowers
How to pick flowers. Good H 164:198 Je '67
Make your cut flowers last. W. D. Holley. il Horticulture 45:22-3 Je '67
See also
Flowers, Arrangement of

FLOWERS, Arrangement of
Arrangement in fifteen minutes. il Pop Gard 18:66-7 Mr '67
Arranging flowers. il Am Home 70:125 Jl '67
Art of flower arrangement, by B. Nichols. Review
Pop Gard 18:5+ D '67. M. E. O'Brien
Fill a bowl with spring. W. Radcliffe. il Pop Gard 18:20-1 My '67
Floating flowers. il Bet Hom & Gard 45:112 Je '67
Flower arranging in England. J. Clements. il Horticulture 45:28-31+ Mr '67
Flowers for romantics. il Am Home 70:60-1 Jl '67
Make the most of a few flowers. il Farm J 91:76-7 S '67
Onward and upward in the garden. K. S. White. bibliog New Yorker 43:193-6+ N 4; 200+ N 11 '67
Quick and easy flower arrangements. il Home & Gard 54:47 Jl '67
When every line counts. E. Finch. il Flower Grower 54:34-5 Ja '67
Zinnias, formal and informal. il Bet Hom & Gard 45:103 S '67
See also
Flowers, Dried
Roses, Arrangement of

FLOWERS, Artificial
My paper flower garden. E. Finch. il Home Gard 54:82 Mr '67

FLOWERS, Dried
Arrangements that go on and on. E. D. Craster. il Bet Hom & Gard 45:72-3 O '67
Florage, a collage of pressed flowers. E. S. Austin and F. G. Sanders. il Horticulture 45:28-9+ D '67
Flowers that heed no season. il Home Gard 54:28-36 Ag '67
How to dry flowers. D. A. Froehlich. il House & Gard 131:30+ My '67
Step-by-step instructions for keeping cut flowers garden-fresh all year. il House B 109:166 Je '67
Timeless bloom. M. Gough. il House B 109:116-17 Je '67
See also
Potpourri

FLOWERS, Forcing of. See Forcing (plants)
FLOWERS, Pressed. See Flowers, Dried
FLOWERS as gifts
When giving flowers. J. B. Carson. Horticulture 45:46 N '67

FLOWERS in art
Lust for tulips. A. West. il Vogue 150:192-7+ D '67
Mary Maxwell reclines to paint her watercolors. M. Maxwell. il Am Artist 31:28-31+ Je '67
Portfolio of flower masterpieces brought to life. il House B 109:218-22 O '67
You can paint a flower. L. Burgess. il Home Gard 54:60-1 Mr '67

FLOWERS in house decoration. See Plants in house decoration
FLU. See Influenza
FLU virus. See Influenza virus
FLUID amplifiers
Control power with fluid. M. Schultz. il Pop Mech 128:114-17+ Jl '67; Same with title Next household word, fluidics. Sci Digest 62:26-30 S '67
Fluidics' drive gains momentum: control devices that work on gases and liquids. il Bsns W p 152-4 Ap 29 '67
Sperry's Utah div. expands its commercial fluidics effort. R. Barnhart. il Aero Tech 21:34 Ag 14 '67

Whole family of fluid amplifiers and a crucial link with electronics; with report by W. Bradbury. il Life 62:112-3+ My 19 '67
FLUID control. See Hydraulic control
FLUID dynamics
Undersea hot rods. J. Ludwigson. il Sci N 92:112-13 Jl 29 '67
See also
Fluid amplifiers
FLUID mechanics. See Hydromechanics
FLUIDIC amplifiers. See Fluid amplifiers
FLUIDICS. See Hydraulic control
FLUIDS
Amateur scientist; how to construct fluid models that simulate fields of force. A. D. Moore. il Sci Am 217:118-23 Jl '67
FLUIDS, Animal. See Body fluids
FLUNO, Robert Y.
Group case study method in political education. por Sch & Soc 95:188-91 Mr 18 '67
FLUORESCENCE
Specific binding activity of isolated light chains of antibodies. T. J. Yoo and others. bibliog il Science 157:707-9 Ag 11 '67

Decay
Fluorescence decay times; proteins, coenzymes, and other compounds in water. R. F. Chen and others. bibliog il Science 156:949-51 My 19 '67

FLUORESCENT lamps in art. See Electric lamps in art
FLUORIDATED salt. See Salt
FLUORIDATION. See Water supply—Fluoridation
FLUOROSCOPY
Your heart in 3-D; viewing the inside with Stereo fluoricon. il Sci Digest 61:92 F '67
FLUOROURACIL
Crystal structure of the 1 : 1 complex of 5-fluorouracil and 9-ethylhypoxanthine. S. H. Kim and A. Rich. bibliog il Science 158:1046-8 N 24 '67
FLUSHING, N.Y.
One-room school returns as dome for team teaching; Paul Klapper school. il Arch Rec 142:178-9 O '67
FLUSHING Meadows-Corona park. See Queens, N.Y.—Parks and playgrounds
FLUTE music
See also
Phonograph records—Flute music
FLUTE players
Pied Piper; J. Rampal. H. Saal. Newsweek 71:62 Ja 1 '68
See also
Steig, J.
FLY casting
Hottest fly fishing anywhere; Lake Michigan. M. Ellis. il Field & S 72:50-1+ Jl '67
FLY fishing. See Fly casting
FLY tying. See Fishing lures, flies, etc.
FLYING. See Aviation
FLYING ants. See Termites
FLYING boats. See Seaplanes
FLYING clubs. See Aviation clubs
FLYING machines
Bell developes two-man pogo for travel on moon, earth. il Tech W 21:26 Jl 3 '67
See also
Autogiros
FLYING platforms. See Flying machines
FLYING saucers
A communication concerning the UFOs; with reply by J. Lear. J. G. Fuller. Sat R 50:70-3 F 4 '67
Flying saucer from earth. il Sci N 91:453 My 13 '67
Flying saucers, are they real? J. A. Hynek. Read Digest 90:61-5 Mr '67
Flying saucers: sightings and study of UFO's. W. Rogers. il Look 31:76-80 Mr 21 '67
Flying spacewatchers. J. Eberhart. il Sci N 92:179 Ag 19 '67
Fresh look at flying saucers; Time essay. Time 90:32-3 Ag 4 '67
Great UFO probe. H. Shuldiner. il Pop Sci 191:120-3 O '67
Happening at Hoogdal; an unidentified beeping object; UFO, or, midget saw-whet owl near Sedro-Woolley, Wash. T. Beauchamp. Look 31:42-3 N 14 '67
New light on flying saucers. il U S News 62:16 Mr 20 '67
New look at the UFO enigma; ball lightning, excerpt from Light and electricity in the atmosphere. H. Hellman. il Sci Digest 62:9-15 N '67

FLYING saucers—*Continued*
Physics and metaphysics of unidentified flying objects. W. Markowitz. bibliog il Science 157:1274-9 S 15 '67; Discussion. 158:1265-6 D 8 '67
Prowling mind of Henri Coanda. G. H. Stine. il Flying 80:64-8 Mr '67
Sickies in the sky; Communist UFO observations. Time 90:28 D 22 '67
Trained eye on UFO's; letter. F. P. Hughes. Science 156:1311-12 Je 9 '67
U and the UFO. D. H. Scott. Flying 81:81-2 Ag '67
UFO phenomenon. H. Margolis. il Bul Atomic Sci 23:40-2 Je '67; Reply. J. C. Munday, jr. 23:40-1 D '67
UFO photographs, anyone? Sci Digest 62:73 S '67
UFO-watcher watcher. J. Piel. il Newsweek 69:111 Mr 20 '67
UFOs and the laws of physics; concerning views of J. Allen Hynek and William Markowitz. J. Lear. Sat R 50:59 O 7 '67
UFO's merit scientific study; letter. J. A. Hynek; discussion. Science 154:1118, 1502+; 155:404; 156:11 D 2, 23 '66, Ja 27, Ap 7 '67
UFOs: the sense and the nonsense. P. Wylie. il Pop Sci 190:76-9 Mr '67
Unidentified flying objects; reprint from Encyclopedia Americana, 1967. C. Sagan. Bul Atomic Sci 23:43-4 Je '67; Reply. J. C. Munday, jr. 23:40-1 D '67

Anecdotes, facetiae, satire, etc.

Bearfaced lie. R. Lasson and D. Eynon. Look 31:M8 Jl 25 '67
More big news from out there. G. Cotler. New Yorker 42:28-9 F 4 '67
Twinkle twinkle little UFO. N. Tripoli. Flying 81:85 S '67

FLYING schools. See Aviation schools
FLYING submarine. See Submarine boats—Airplane combination
FLYING Tiger line, incorporated
Flying Tiger defends back-haul charters. H. D. Watkins. Aviation W 86:38-9 Ap 24 '67
New tiger at the top; board chairman. il Time 90:80+ Jl 14 '67
Off-route charter rule easing proposed. H. D. Watkins. Aviation W 86:38-9 My 15 '67
Transpacific route case: three all-cargo carriers aim at major market in Pacific case. H. D. Watkins. il Aviation W 86:48-50+ Je 12 '67

FLYNN, Ralph J.
When the votes are counted... NEA J 56: 48+ My '67
FLYNN, Robert
Babe in the wilderness; story. Sat Eve Post 240:48-50 Ap 22 '67
Stampede! story. Sat Eve Post 240:52-6 Mr 25 '67

FLYTYING. See Fishing lures, flies, etc.
FOCUSING. See Photography—Focusing
FOEHN. See Winds
FOETUS. See Fetus
FOG
Nature note. Sci N 91:590 Je 24 '67
See also
Aviation—Fog problem
FO3, Artificial
Breathe easy in ultrasonic fog. il Life 62:53+ Mr 10 '67
Fog that saves lives. T. Berland. Read Digest 90:33-4+ Mr '67
FOG, Medical. See Fog, Artificial
FOG dispersal
Fogbrooms to the rescue; New Jersey turnpike experiments with moving nylon filaments. il Time 90:56 Jl 14 '67
FOGARTY, John Edward
Revolution in our schools. por Library J 92: 302-3 Ja 15 '67
about
John Edward Forgarty. P. H. Abelson. Science 155:523 F 3 '67
Obituary
Library J por 92:517 F 1 '67
Wilson Lib Bul 41:671 Mr '67. J. H. Shera
Representative Fogarty dies at 53. D. S. Greenberg. por Science 155:180 Ja 13 '67
FOGGERS, insect. See Spraying apparatus
FOIL fabrics. See Paper textiles
FOKINE ballet camp. See Dance camps
FOLDING furniture. See Furniture
FOLDS, Thomas McKey
Web of meanings. Redbook 130:62-3+ D '67

FOLEY, Connie
Boom... Am For 73:4+ Mr '67
Washington's petrified forest on the Mall. Am For 73:22-3+ D '67
FOLGER, D. W. and others
Opal phytoliths in a North Atlantic dust fall. bibliog Science 155:1243-4 Mr 10 '67
FOLIC acid
Antimalarial activity of tetrahydrohomopteroic acid. R. L. Kisliuk and others bibliog il Science 156:1616-17 Je 23 '67
FOLK art
Curandera artist; bark paper pictures, once used in religious rites. S. Battist. il Américas 19:36-40 My '67
Folk art of Nepal. S. Peterson. il Craft Horiz 27:36-9 Mr '67
Folk arts of Peru. F. L. Phelps. il Américas 19:18-25 Jl '67
Honey in the honeycomb; exhibition of beehive paintings, in Yugoslavia. il Time 90:46 Jl 28 '67
Living treasures of Japan. R. Beardwood. il Fortune 76:130-5 N '67
Showcase in Spain; Institute of Hispanic culture, Madrid. N. López Pellón. il Américas 19:32-5 N '67
FOLK dance festivals. See Dance festivals
FOLK dancing
From the grass roots; director of Ecuador's ballet folklorico encourages village dance groups. J. Anderson. il Dance Mag 41:14-16+ Ag '67
In the light of a kindred humanity; LA's international folk dance festival. V. H. Swisher. il Dance Mag 41:46-9 Mr '67
FOLK lore. See Folklore
FOLK museums
See also
Shelburne museum, Shelburne, Vt.
FOLK music, American
Nashville the sounds and the symbols; country and western scene. G. Lees. il Hi Fi 17: 57-61 Ap '67
FOLK singers. See Singers
FOLK singing. See Singing
FOLK songs, American
Arlo Guthrie; interview. A. Guthrie. New Yorker 43:18-21 Ja 6 '68
Doc Watson: musicmaker from Appalachia. C. S. Wren. il Look 32:M6-8 Ja 23 '68
FOLK songs, Jewish
Only kid; Had Gadya's origin and interpretations. C. Roth. Commentary 43:82-5 Ap '67
Sholom Aleichem in the park; performance of Yiddish folk songs in Central park. S. Bernard. Nation 205:124-5 Ag 14 '67
FOLK songs, Yiddish. See Folk songs, Jewish
FOLKLORE
Folklore, fakelore, and poplore. M. Fishwick. il Sat R 50:20-1+ Ag 26 '67
Seeing is deceiving; facts disputing traditional beliefs in folk customs and science. L. Rosten. Look 31:10 My 2 '67
Italy
Visit from La Befana. L. D'Angelo. Sat R 50:8+ D 16 '67
FOLKLORE of paper. See Paper in religion, folklore, etc.
FOLKLORE of the sea
See also
St Elmo's fire
FOLKMAN, Judah. See Winsey. H. S. jt. auth.
FOLLEY, Zora
Zora Folley ranks Muhammad Ali as no. 1; ed. by M. Sharnik. Sports Illus 26:32 Ap 10 '67
about
After Muhammad, a graveyard. M. Kram. il por Sports Illus 26:28-9 Ap 3 '67
Book fighter who may change Ali's style. M. Kram. il pors Sports Illus 26:71-2 Mr 20 '67
FOLLIARD, Edward T.
Washington front. See occasional issues of America
FOLLIES (architecture)
Follies at Stowe; the grotto. E. Gaines. il Antiques 91:240+ F '67
FOLLOW Through from Head Start. See Project Head Start
FOLLOW Through program. See Project Head Start
FOLSOM, Michael Brewster
Masses: working-class dreams. Nation 204: 277-9 F 27 '67
FOLSOM, Priscilla L.
Trailing arbutus; poem. Horn Bk 43:322 Je '67

La FONDA del sol. See New York (city)—
Hotels, restaurants, etc.
FONDILLER, Harvey V.
Film notes. See issues of Popular photography
FONDUES. See Cookery
FONTAINE, André
Mass media: a need for greatness. Ann Am
Acad 371:72-84 My '67
FONTAINE, Robert
Graduation address; drama. Plays 26:91-2 My
'67
FONTEYN, Dame Margot
From Paradise lost to a Frisco jail; with
reports by J. Fincher and J. Hicks. il pors
Life 63:83-4 Jl 21 '67
Woman for all seasons. G. Steinem. il por
McCalls 94:86-7+ My '67
World of dance; last appearance in New
York? W. Terry. Sat R 50:46 Je 17 '67
FONTINELL, Eugene
In defense of institutions. America 116:314-16
Mr 4 '67
FONVILLE, Jean L.
Put the grain to work. Sch Arts 67:16-17
O '67
FOOD
Authors & editors; wild food ideas of E.
Gibbons. Pub W 192:25-7 S 11 '67
Educated eater's Baedeker. H. Sutton. Sat R
50:30-1 Jl 1 '67
Foods for tomorrow from the new American
larder. H. McCully. il House B 109:172-3+
S '67
How to transport food in summer. il Good H
165:167 Ag '67
Lyric to a thrush pâté; poor cookbooks vs.
good food. J. H. Plumb. Sat R 50:29-30
O 28 '67
Plenty of the land. H. Borland. il Audubon
69:30-5 N '67
    See also
Cookery
Diet
Dinners and dining
Fasting
Meals
Meat substitutes
Nutrition
Oils and fats, Edible
Packaged foods
Proteins
Sandwiches
United States—Army—Commissariat
Vitamins
    Marketing
    See also
United States—National commission on food
marketing
    New sources
    See Food supply—New sources
    Prices
Day of cheap food is ending. Farm J 91:90
My '67; Excerpt. U S News 62:40 My 15 '67
Food; cut costs but maintain quality. il Good
H 164:199-200 Ap '67
High cost of eating. B. B. Seligman. Com-
mentary 44:48-52 Jl '67; Discussion. 44:6+
O '67
Housewives wrong? food really a bargain? il
U S News 63:68-70 Jl 24 '67
How much do you spend for groceries? il
Changing T 22:39-47 Ja '68
How to beat the high cost of eating; with
recipes. il McCalls 95:84-92+ Ja '68
How to save money on food. J. Roper. il
Redbook 128:66-7+ Mr '67
Paying more for being poor. il Time 90:16 D
1 '67
To market we go; with editorial comment.
E. Dowling. New Repub 156:9, 19-24 Ja 28
'67
When middlemen are in the middle. il Bsns W
p26-7 Ag 26 '67
Who's getting the food dollar now. il U S
News 64:48 Ja 15 '68
    See also subhead Prices under names of
foods, e.g. Milk—Prices

    Quotations, maxims, etc.
Read well before eating; or, A smorgasbord
of opinion for the season of holiday feasts,
comp. by E. Murphy. il N Y Times Mag
p 119-20 N 26 '67

    Ready-to-cook food
From the larder or freezer; with recipes.
V. T. Habeeb. il Am Home 70:102-3+ Mr
'67
No time to cook. il McCalls 94:54 Ap; 42
My; 36 Je '67

Shortcuts to the classics; with recipes. V. T.
Habeeb. il Am Home 70:100-4+ Mr '67
Work wonders with packaged potato prod-
ucts. il Ladies Home J 84:118+ Ap '67

    Storage
How to store foods. Am Home 70:119 Mr '67
Prefab walk-in coolers and freezers meet
changing demands for food storage. G. M.
Prince. il Arch Rec 141:201-2 Je '67

    Terminology
Dining out in French. Am Home 70:108 Ja '67

    Testing
Enzymatic identification of fish products. A.
C. Wilson and others. bibliog il Science
157:82-3 Jl 7 '67
FOOD, Cost of. See Food—Prices
FOOD, drug and cosmetics law. See Food
laws and legislation
FOOD, Effect of radiation on
Building a hotter fire under irradiated foods;
preserving food by using radioisotopes or
electronics under AEC contract. il Bsns W
p90-1 Ap 8 '67
FOOD, Frozen
A la carte dinners on ice; with freezing in-
structions and recipes. il McCalls 94:88-9+
Je '67
Food & freezer deals; how to spot the gyps.
il Changing T 21:43-4 F; 15-16 O '67
From the larder or freezer; with recipes.
V. T. Habeeb. il Am Home 70:102-3+ Mr
'67
Frozen dinners. il Consumer Rep 32:521-5 O
'67
Frozen in suburbia. E. Halston. il Look 31:
92-3 My 16 '67
Just reach in the freezer for one. il Sunset
139:88-9 Ag '67
When your freezer stops freezing; keep the
freezer door shut. il Consumer Bul 50:40
Ag '67
    See also
Freezers
Freezing of food
Ice cream, ices, etc.
Oregon freeze dry foods, incorporated
Potatoes, Frozen
FOOD, Irradiated. See Food, Effect of radiation
on
FOOD, Raw
Steak tartare: beef rarer than rare for the
cocktail hour; with recipes. E. Alston. il
Look 31:82-3 S 19 '67
FOOD, Synthetic. See Food substitutes
FOOD, Wild. See Food
FOOD additives
Healthy coffee breaks. Sci Digest 62:69 D '67
FOOD adulteration and inspection
Dietary intake of pesticide chemicals. R. E.
Duggan and J. R. Weatherwax. bibliog il
Science 157:1006-10 S 1 '67
    See also
Meat inspection
United States—Food and drug administration
FOOD and agriculture organization of the
United Nations
Plankton, sardinella, and the monsoon. R.
L. Tobin. Sat R 50:16 S 2 '67
FOOD as carrier of infection. See Food poison-
ing
FOOD as gifts
Good-enough-to-eat gifts. il Bet Hom & Gard
45:68-70 D '67
Priceless gifts of food; with recipes. il Ladies
Home J 84:120-1+ N '67
FOOD buying. See Purchasing, Household
FOOD chain stores. See Chain stores
FOOD chemistry
    See also
Food additives
FOOD decoration. See Cookery, Ornamental
FOOD fads
Doctor explodes some health-food myths; in-
terview, ed. by C. Phillips. F. Stare. Vogue
149:120-1+ Je '67
Health foods: are they nutritional quackery?
Good H 165:189 S '67
Who's to blame for nutrition nonsense? R. M.
Deutsch. Todays Health 45:66-7 My '67
FOOD fallacies. See Errors, Popular
FOOD for children. See Children—Nutrition
FOOD for peace program. See Food relief
FOOD freezers. See Freezers
FOOD habits
Naturalist at large; man's food relations. M.
Bates. Natur Hist 76:18+ Ag '67

FOOD In packages. See Packaged foods

FOOD industry and trade
Business and the war on hunger. America 116:867-8 Je 24 '67
To market we go; with editorial comment. E. Dowling. New Repub 156:9, 19-24 Ja 28 '67
See also
Beatrice foods company
Food, Frozen
Fruit industry
Heinz, H. J., company
Pet, incorporated
Weston, George, limited

FOOD Inspection. See Food adulteration and inspection

FOOD intake. See Eating

FOOD laws and legislation
Calories author guilty; faces jail and fine. Pub W 191:40 My 22 '67
See also
United States—Food and drug administration

FOOD mixes
Look what you can do with cake mix! il Am Home 70:120-1+ O '67

FOOD names
How some foods got their names. Good H 164:194 My '67

FOOD of love; story. See Tibber, R.

FOOD packaging. See Packaging

FOOD plants. See Plants, Food

FOOD poisoning
Angiostrongylus cantonensis: proof of direct transmission with its epidemiological implications. D. Heyneman and B. L. Lim. bibliog il Science 158:1057-8 N 24 '67
Few pesticides in dinner. Sci Digest 62:29 D '67
Food-borne diseases. Sci N 92:202 Ag 26 '67

FOOD preferences
Food of love; favorite foods of operatic composers, tr. by F. Merkling. H. Schraemli. Opera N 32:6-7 D 30 '67

FOOD preservation and preservatives
Food and what happens to it. Consumer Bul 50:36-40 N '67
Inhibition of banana polyphenoloxidase by 2-mercaptobenzothiazole. J. K. Palmer and J. B. Roberts. bibliog il Science 157:200-1 Jl 14 '67
See also
Food, Effect of radiation on
Freezing of food

FOOD production. See Food supply

FOOD relief
Closing the world food gap. L. Soth. Bul Atomic Sci 23:40-2 N '67
Crusade on hunger; address, May 11, 1967. A. N. McFarlane. Vital Speeches 33:659-61 Ag 15 '67
Hunger is the big story. R. L. Tobin. Cath World 205:26-30 Ap '67
Hunger; the Stennis bill on federal food programs. Reporter 37:16 N 2 '67
It isn't true that nobody starves in America. R. Sherrill. il N Y Times Mag p22-3+ Je 4 '67; Discussion. p4 Jl 16; 7+ Jl 30 '67
Know this about food stamps! J. Volk. Farm J 91:17 Ap '67
Malthus, Marx and the North American breadbasket. O. L. Freeman. il For Affairs 45:579-93 Jl '67; Excerpts. U S News 63: 40-4 Jl 3 '67
On the prongs; shortcomings of federal food programs. Time 90:14-15 Jl 14 '67
President reports to Congress on food aid programs; letter, November 6, 1967. L. B. Johnson. Dept State Bul 57:762-3 D 4 '67
Starving on the installment plan; malnutrition and food for peace. il Sr Schol 91:6-7 N 9 '67
They don't have to starve; private enterprise, blueprint for feeding the world's hungry. W. T. Brady. il Nations Bsns 55:88-90+ Mr '67
Timid war against hunger; excerpts from remarks. G. McGovern. Bul Atomic Sci 23: 38-9 F '67
War on hunger: food for India; text of message, February 2, 1967. L. B. Johnson. Dept State Bul 56:295-301 F 20 '67
We are losing the race against hunger. G. McGovern. il Look 31:86+ Mr 7 '67

India
Editor comments: CBS TV program on American wheat-for-India operation. Bul Atomic Sci 23:3+ F '67
President authorizes additional wheat shipments to India; statement, September 1, 1967. L. B. Johnson. Dept State Bul 57: 430-1 O 2 '67

President signs joint resolution on food assistance to India; statement, April 1, 1967; with text of congressional resolution. L. B. Johnson. Dept State Bul 56:700-1 My 1 '67
War on hunger: food for India; text of message, February 2, 1967. L. B. Johnson. Dept State Bul 56:295-301 F 20 '67

Underdeveloped areas
On helping the hungry. R. M. Fagley. Christian Cent 84:811-13 Je 21 '67
Question of food aid in the perspective of the problems of the developing countries; statement, July 24, 1967. A. E. Goldschmidt. Dept State Bul 57:304-8 S 4 '67

FOOD stamp plan. See Food relief

FOOD stores
See also
Chain stores
Supermarkets

FOOD substitutes
New foods for fighting famine. il Newsweek 69:87-8+ F 27 '67
Orthodox and unorthodox methods of meeting world food needs. N. W. Pirie. il Sci Am 216:27-35 F '67
They're after your market; threat from new food products, substitutes and imitations. Farm J 91:58 Jl '67
See also
Meat substitutes

FOOD supply
Closing the world food gap. L. Soth. Bul Atomic Sci 23:40-2 N '67
Famine, 1975! by W. Paddock, and P. Paddock. Review
Am For 73:27+ Jl '67. M. Bush
Final volume of comprehensive study of world food problem published. Dept State Bul 57:874 D 25 '67
Food for the future. M. Jones. il Américas 19:30-3 Jl '67
Harvest of hope. Time 90:20-1 D 22 '67
Human food from ocean and land. K. O. Emery and C. O'D. Iselin. bibliog il Science 157:1279-81 S 15 '67; Reply. R. G. S. Bidwell. 158:1136-7 D 1 '67
Malthus, Marx and the North American breadbasket. O. L. Freeman. il For Affairs 45:579-93 Jl '67; Excerpts. U S News 63: 40-4 Jl 3 '67
Meeting world food needs. P. H. Abelson. Science 158:865 N 17 '67
Population and food supply; excerpts from papers submitted to the United Nations world population conference. C. Taeuber. bibliog f il Ann Am Acad 369:73-83 Ja '67
Poulation, natural resources, and technology. E. A. Ackerman. bibliog f il Ann Am Acad 369:84-97 Ja '67
Report on food needs; United Nations Secretary-General. UN Mo Chron 4:68-9 Ag '67
War on hunger; address, September 8, 1967. D. H. Jacobson. Vital Speeches 33:763-6 O 1 '67
White House panel completes study of World food problem. Dept State Bul 57: 76-8 Jl 17 '67
World food programme: new form of aid for development. C. Mackenzie. il UNESCO Courier 20:30-2 O '67
World food supply faces twenty-year deadline. il Sci N 92:3 Jl 1 '67
World food supply: PSAC panel warns of impending famine. L. J. Carter. Science 156:1578-9 Je 23 '67
World outlook for conventional agriculture. L. R. Brown. bibliog il Science 158:604-11 N 3 '67
See also
Famines
Fisheries

New sources
Agrobiology: specialization or systems analysis? N. F. Jensen. bibliog Science 157: 1405-9 S 22 '67
Comeback for the sea turtle; breeding and raising. W. Hartley and E. Hartley. il Sci Digest 62:33-7 S '67
Engineered foods. J. Harvey. il Suc Farm 65:36-7+ O; 38-9 N '67
Food from the sea. N. L. Brown. Sci N 91: 154+ F 18 '67
Food proteins: new sources from seeds; address, December 26, 1966. A. M. Altschul. bibliog il Science 158:221-6 O 13 '67
Food value of red tide (gonyaulax polyedra) S. Patton and others. bibliog il Science 158: 789-90 N 10 '67
Growth of a thermophilic bacterium on hydrocarbons: a new source of single-cell protein. R. I. Mateles and others. bibliog il Science 157:1322-3 S 15 '67; Reply. L. R. Pomeroy. 158:579 N 3 '67

FOOD supply—New sources—*Continued*
Human food from ocean and land. K. O.
Emery and C. O'D. Iselin. bibliog il Science
157:1279-81 S 15 '67; Reply. R. G. S. Bidwell. 158:1136-7 D 1 '67
Malnutrition and national development. A.
D. Berg. For Affairs 46:126-36 O '67
New arms for war on hunger; development
of single cell protein. il Bsns W D 160 O
21 '67
New foods for fighting famine. il Newsweek
69:87-8+ F 27 '67
Orthodox and unorthodox methods of meeting world food needs. N. W. Pirie. il Sci
Am 216:27-35 F '67
Plankton, sardinella, and the monsoon; FAO
Plankton project. R. L. Tobin. Sat R 50:16
S 2 '67
Protein gap. Sci Am 217:41 Jl '67
World food supply; problems and prospects.
L. J. Carter; discussion. Science 156:168
Ap 14 '67
See also
Algae as food
Fish flour

Africa, West
Instant fu-fu for West Africa. Sci N 91:430-1
My 6 '67

India
Another kind of hunger; problem of protein
starvation. il Time 90:39+ O 27 '67
Fight for food. M. Zim. il Fortune 75:71-2+
F '67
See also
Famines—India

Underdeveloped areas
Agribusiness approach: problems and opportunities; address, September 11, 1967. L. B.
Lundborg. Vital Speeches 33:756-9 O 1 '67
Agricultural production in the developing
countries. G. F. Sprague. il Science 157:
774-8 Ag 18 '67
Business and the war on hunger. America 116:
867-8 Je 24 '67
Combustibility of humans; how to avoid world
famine and population crisis. H. Brown.
Sat R 50:14-17+ Je 24 '67
Hunger is the big story. R. L. Tobin. Cath
World 205:26-30 Ap '67
Importance of agricultural development in our
strategy for peace; address, May 10, 1967.
E. V. Rostow. Dept State Bul 56:856-65 Je
5 '67
On helping the hungry. R. M. Fagley. Christian Cent 84:811-13 Je 21 '67
Orthodox and unorthodox methods of meeting world food needs. N. W. Pirie. il Sci
Am 216:27-35 F '67
Question of food aid in the perspective of the
problems of the developing countries;
statement. July 24, 1967. A. E. Goldschmidt. Dept State Bul 57:304-8 S 4 '67

United States
Were farmers suckered? Farm J 91:74 N '67
FOOD values
All-time best reducing diets for you, for
him, for the whole family. il Good H 164:
97-108 My '67
Let's talk about food; ed. by P. L. White.
See issues of Today's health
See also
Diet
FOOL hen. See Grouse
FOONER, Michael
Crime & affluence: case of the culpable victim. Nation 204:307-8 Mr 6 '67
FOOSE, Richard M.
Sinkhole formation by groundwater withdrawal: Far West Rand, South Africa. bibliog Science 157:1045-8 S 1 '67
FOOT
See also
Shoes
Care and hygiene
Five myths about your feet. H. L. DuVries.
il Todays Health 45:49-51 Ag '67
Walking happy. il Mlle 64:144 F '67
Your feet deserve it. il Redbook 128:90-1 Mr
'67
FOOT-and-mouth disease
Detergent-solubilized RNA polymerase from
cells infected with foot-and-mouth disease
virus. R. B. Arlinghaus and J. Polatnick.
bibliog il Science 158:1320-2 D 8 '67
Foot-and-mouth alert! test of defenses
against the world's costliest animal disease. J. A. Rohlf. il Farm J 91:25-7+ My
'67

Foot-and-mouth disease: Britain strives to
curb epidemic. J. Walsh. Science 158:1435-7
D 15 '67
Grounds for slaughter; British livestock. Sci
N 92:558-9 D 9 '67
In Britain a plague's grim pileup; foot-and-mouth epidemic. il Life 64:26-9 Ja 5 '68
Letter from London. M. Panter-Downes. New
Yorker 43:52-3 D 23 '67
Modern plague; worst animal epidemic in
British history. il Time 90:40 D 15 '67
New crisis in Britain: deadly cattle disease.
U S News 63:14 D 18 '67
Plague; Britain's current out-break. il Newsweek 70:53 D 18 '67
Politics and disease. J. Ludwigson. il Sci N
92:300-1 S 23 '67
Protection for sheep, cattle in the face of
threat; preventing the disease from entering Australia. Sci N 93:76-7 Ja 20 '68
Virus fells British meat trade. il Bsns W
p76-8 D 9 '67
FOOTBALL
All the way with O.J; USC vs UCLA. D.
Jenkins. il Sports Illus 27:16-21 N 27 '67
A.R.V.N. can fight! M. Novak. Christian
Cent 84:1310 O 18 '67
Blood on the ivy; Ivy league teams. il Time
90:86 N 24 '67
Blue power wins a bowl game; Yale vs Harvard in Yale bowl. D. Jenkins. il Sports
Illus 27:32-3 D 4 '67
Bottoms up; disastrous early season. il Time
90:42+ O 20 '67
Bulldogs looked for trouble and found it;
Georgia Bulldogs vs Clemson. J. Jares. il
Sports Illus 27:46 O 9 '67
Chant at Purdue is give it to Leroy. T. C.
Brody. il Sports Illus 27:52+ N 27 '67
College football forecast. G. Astor. il Look
31:76-80 S 19 '67
College football 1967. D. Jenkins. il Sports
Illus 27:28-52+ S 11 '67
Finally Tennessee state didn't have a prayer;
San Diego state the best small-college team.
G. Ronberg. il Sports Illus 27:51-2 S '67
Football. See issues of New Yorker published
during football season
Football's way-out season; assessment of
autumn just past. D. Jenkins. il Sports Illus 27:44-9 D 25 '67
Football's week. M. Hyman. See issues of
Sports illustrated published during football
season
Grand street fight in disappointment alley;
Miami and Notre Dame in Florida. J. Underwood. il Sports Illus 27:84-5 D 4 '67
Great one confronts O.J; USC vs UCLA.
D. Jenkins. il Sports Illus 27:32-4+ N 20 '67
Houston blasts off. il Newsweek 70:65 O 9
'67
If at first you don't succeed; Dartmouth defeats Harvard. P. Axthelm. il Sports Illus
27:24-5 N 6 '67
Impossible dream; Indiana university Hoosiers. il Newsweek 70:82-3 N 6 '67
In a boneyard for favorites; Army-Navy
game. J. Underwood. il Sports Illus 27:65-
7 D 11 '67
Lot from the leftovers; Waynesburg Yellow
Jackets and the Westminster Titans. il
Time 90:70 N 10 '67
Man in motion beats Texas; Texas vs. USC,
and J. McKay. J. Underwood. il Sports
Illus 27:22-4+ O 2 '67
Man to watch is the middle linebacker. J. K.
Sale. il N Y Times Mag p34-5+ D 10 '67
Necessity is the mother of the forward pass;
Texas vs Rice. D. Jenkins. il Sports Illus
27:46+ N 6 '67
No place for stars to shine; All-stars face
Green Bay. D. Jenkins. il Sports Illus 27:
16-17 Ag 14 '67
Notre Dame: we're number one! J. Bowers.
il Sat Eve Post 240:85-9 O 7 '67
Oklahoma sticks it right to their mustache;
Sooners under J. Mackenzie. G. Ronberg.
il Sports Illus 27:64-5 N 13 '67
One more great play; UCLA vs Tennessee.
D. Jenkins. il Sports Illus 27:14-19 S 25 '67
One way to dam the tide; Tennessee swamps
Bear Bryant's Alabama; with account by
J. Underwood. il Sports Illus 27:12-17 O
30 '67
Orange juice won a poll bowl; USC winner
at South Bend. D. Jenkins. il Sports Illus
27:24-7 O 23 '67
Paper lion, by G. Plimpton. Review
Commentary 44:114+ O '67 B. Glanville;
Discussion. 44:26+ D '67
Punt, John, punt! undefeated Hoosiers. D.
Jenkins. il Sports Illus 27:28-31 N 13 '67

FOOTBALL—*Continued*

Purdue does a no. 1 job against no. 1. G. Ronberg. il Sports Illus 27:20-3 O 9 '67

Rah! club! rah! college-club football. Newsweek 70:82 N 6 '67

Say it isn't so, Woody; passing of football era at Ohio state. R. Cantwell. il Sports Illus 27:98-104+ S 11 '67

So there, Socrates; last day of college football season. il Time 91:35-6 Ja 12 '68

Some kool kyoties get kicked down by a foot; North Carolina state loses to Penn state. P. Axthelm. il Sports Illus 27:44-5 N 20 '67

Some old grads get a hazing; Notre Dame alumni vs varsity. J. Underwood. il Sports Illus 26:26-7 My 15 '67

Spartans get stabbed by Mac the Knife; University of Houston vs Michigan state. D. Jenkins. il Sports Illus 27:54-6 O 2 '67

Spoilers; U.C.L.A. against Southern Cal. Time 90:86 N 24 '67

Stars fell on Alabama; comparison with Nebraska, Notre Dame and Michigan State. H. L. Masin. Sr Schol 90:20 Mr 3 '67

Team that is loved with a purple passion; Kansas state football. W. Johnson. il Sports Illus 27:44-5 O 30 '67

Tom Cahill; Army's accidental coach. T. Cohane. il Look 31:116-19+ N 28 '67

Trojan horses; Southern California's team. il Time 90:68 O 27 '67

Two goats and three flankers make a winner; Syracuse beaten by Navy. J. Jares. il Sports Illus 27:48-9 O 23 '67

Wild card in the West; University of Wyoming Cowboys. H. Peterson. il Sports Illus 27:61-2 O 16 '67

Win one for aunt Mary Margaret! Michigan state against Notre Dame. G. Holland. il Sat Eve Post 240:84-7 N 4 '67

Yale's Mr Quarterback. Newsweek 70:65 N 13 '67

Yes sir; no bowl game for the Army team. Sports Illus 27:11 N 27 '67

See also
Football players
Rugby football
Soccer
Touch football

Accidents and injuries

Break, a wrench and a march of new quarterbacks; Miami Dolphins' J. Stofa with broken ankle and a sprained knee. E. Shrake. il Sports Illus 27:69-72+ S 25 '67

Scientifically dirty. Time 90:46 D 1 '67

Should boys play football? E. C. Scott. il Parents Mag 42:84-6+ N '67

You've got to have some O; W. McVea injured, Houston's Cougars lose. D. Jenkins. il Sports Illus 27:40-2+ O 16 '67

Anecdotes, facetiae, satire, etc.

Pigskin ecumenism; Protestant-Catholic viewpoint. R. M. Brown and M. Novak. Commonweal 85:555-6 F 17 '67

Caricatures and cartoons

Ups and downs of the Bowls. Sports Illus 28:22-3 Ja 8 '68

FOOTBALL, Photography of. See Photography of sports

FOOTBALL accidents. See Football—Accidents and injuries

FOOTBALL clubs

Almost all alone at the top; Houston Oilers the surprise team of AFL. E. Shrake. il Sports Illus 27:16-17 D 25 '67

Almost too good to play; D. Reeves of the Dallas Cowboys. T. Maule. il Sports Illus 27:28-30+ N 6 '67

Always leave those monsters laughing. F. Tarkenton and J. Olsen. il Sports Illus 27:38-45 Ag 7 '67

AFL has a taste of glory; Kansas City's slaughter of the Chicago Bears. M. Mulvoy. il Sports Illus 27:12-15 S 4 '67

And now the Super bowl; Green Bay Packers and Oakland Raiders. il Time 91:35 Ja 12 '68

And still champions; Super bowl game. il Time 89:38 Ja 27 '67

Another old pro kicks for sixteen; Oakland Raiders' first American football league championship. E. Shrake. il Sports Illus 28:14-17 Ja 8 '68

Aura of destiny; Packers lose to Baltimore Colts. T. Maule. il Sports Illus 27:20-3 N 13 '67

Better to scramble than lose. F. Tarkenton and J. Olsen. il Sports Illus 27:74-80 Jl 17 '67 (to be cont)

Big raid that really paid off; Oakland got D. Lamonica from the Bills professional football draft. E. Shrake. il Sports Illus 27:74-5 N 13 '67

Bread-and-butter Packers; turn Super bowl into super upset. T. Maule. il Sports Illus 26:10-17 Ja 23 '67

Break, a wrench and a march of new quarterbacks; Miami Dolphins' J. Stofa with broken ankle and a sprained knee. E. Shrake. il Sports Illus 27:69-72+ S 25 '67

Collective trouble. Sports Illus 27:7 Ag 14 '67

Dear Norm: I cannot return. F. Tarkenton and J. Olsen. il Sports Illus 27:36-42 Jl 31 '67

Defense: the only way the Raiders might win; NFL championship game, Oakland Raiders vs Green Bay Packers. E. Shrake. il Sports Illus 28:14-15 Ja 15 '68

Flaring tempers on wild exhibition; Philadelphia Eagles vs New York Jets. M. Mulvoy. il Sports Illus 27:24-5 Ag 28 '67

For Babe, a week to forget; Boston quarterback, Parilli. E. Shrake. Sports Illus 27:30-1 S 18 '67

Game for madmen; Green Bay Packers. V. Lombardi and W. C. Heinz. il Look 31:85-90 S 5 '67

Giants grow up; New York Giants football players. M. Mulvoy. il Sports Illus 27:26-9 D 4 '67

Green Bay's coach reveals his secrets of winning football. V. Lombardi and W. C. Heinz. il Look 31:70-5 S 19 '67

In Dallas, spytalk and a rout; Los Angeles Rams. T. Maule. il Sports Illus 27:24-5 O 9 '67

It's Johnny U. again; J. Unitas of Baltimore Colts. T. Maule. il Sports Illus 27:14-17 O 2 '67

Just too sophisticated to win; to Washington Redskins. T. Maule. il Sports Illus 27:22-3 N 20 '67

Kansas City's Mike Garrett; big little chief. G. Astor. il Look 31:112-18+ N 14 '67

Long live the king; San Francisco 49ers quarterback, J. Brodie. H. Wilner. il Sat Eve Post 240:85-9 N 18 '67

Marching in; New Orleans Saints. Sports Illus 27:8 D 25 '67

Maximum of crunch; Green Bay-Dallas game. Time 90:40 S 8 '67

NFL CBS football guide 1967, by F. Gifford. Review
Life 63:22 O 27 '67. J. R. McDermott

Oakland's angry men. il Newsweek 71:56 Ja 1 '68

Old pro goes in for six; Green Bay in the Super bowl. T. Maule. il Sports Illus 28:10-15 Ja 8 '68

One title down, two to go; Oakland whips San Diego and wins California state championship of the AFL. E. Shrake. il Sports Illus 27:28-9 D 11 '67

Pair fit to be tied; Colts and the Rams. T. Maule. il Sports Illus 27:18-21 O 23 '67

Patsies no more; NFL vs AFL. il Newsweek 70:68 S 4 '67

Peach fuzz with a difference; quarterback J. Hart of the Cardinals. M. Mulvoy. il Sports Illus 27:30-2+ N 27 '67

Picking on the Packers. il Time 90:68 O 27 '67

Plays go for the new Joe; New York Jets vs Oakland Raiders. E. Shrake. il Sports Illus 27:34-7 O 16 '67

Pro football forecast '67. G. Astor. il Look 31:82-3 S 5 '67

Pro football 1967; scouting reports; National football league, American football league. T. Maule. il Sports Illus 27:48-85 S 18 '67

Pro rookie's ups and downs. F. Tarkenton and J. Olsen. il Sports Illus 27:22-7 Jl 24 '67

Real wowser for the Rams; defeat of Green Bay. T. Maule. il Sports Illus 27:12-17 D 18 '67

Right between the ears; New York Giants get F. Tarkenton. il Time 89:44+ Mr 17 '67

Romp for the pack; Green Bay vs Oakland Raiders in Orange bowl in Miami. T. Maule. il Sports Illus 28:12-15 Ja 15 '68

Roughing it in the football bushes; minor leagues. L. L. King. Harper 235:33-8 Ag '67

Rumor is scotched and a Starr revived; Green Bay Packers and quarterback Starr invulnerable. E. Shrake. il Sports Illus 27:24-5 O 30 '67

Slow bus to Bushville; Westchester Bulls, New York Giants farm team. J. Flaherty. il N Y Times Mag p 100+ N 19 '67

Some new saints in the NFL temple. T. Maule. il Sports Illus 27:30-3 Ag 14 '67

FOOTBALL clubs—*Continued*

Sporting scene; defeat of Kansas City Chiefs by Green Bay Packers in Los Angeles. H. W. Wind. New Yorker 42:102+ F 4 '67

Still a long, rough road ahead for the AFL; Super bowl proved that AFL is far behind NFL. E. Shrake. il Sports Illus 26:34-6 Ja 30 '67

Super bowl preview; Oakland Raiders meet the Green Bay Packers. il Newsweek 71: 80 Ja 15 '68

Two for the football show: the swinger and the square; Namath and Tarkenton. J. Lake. il N Y Times Mag p40-1+ N 5 '67

Unions call the signals; NFL and AFL players plan to register with the National labor relations board as a bona fide union. il Bsns W p26 Ja 13 '68

Year of the Ram; Rams demolish previously undefeated Baltimore Colts. T. Maule. il Sports Illus 27:12-15 D 25 '67

See also
American football league
National football league

FOOTBALL clubs, Professional. See Football clubs

FOOTBALL coaches. See Coaches (athletics)

FOOTBALL fans. See Sports fans

FOOTBALL players

Always leave those monsters laughing. F. Tarkenton and J. Olsen. il Sports Illus 27:38-45 Ag 7 '67

Better to scramble than lose. F. Tarkenton and J. Olsen. il Sports Illus 27:74-80+ Jl 17 '67 (to be cont)

Big ones scouts are watching; G. Halsell, Texas; R. Saul, Michigan state; V. Opalsky, Miami; D. Abbey, Penn state; J. Tasby, Idaho. il Sports Illus 27:82-3 S 11 '67

Bread-and-butter Packers; turn Super bowl into super upset. T. Maule. il Sports Illus 26:10-17 Ja 23 '67

College football 1967. D. Jenkins. il Sports Illus 27:28-52+ S 11 '67

Dear Norm: I cannot return. F. Tarkenton and J. Olsen. il Sports Illus 27:36-42 Jl 31 '67

Football players' fads. il Sci Digest 62:58-9 N '67

Football's hit records. H. L. Masin. il Sr Schol 91:24 N 9 '67

Football's week. M. Hyman. See issues of Sports illustrated published during football season

For openers. Newsweek 70:77 Ag 14 '67

Four at the heart; linemen. il Time 90:44-5 D 29 '67

Game for madmen; Green Bay Packers. V. Lombardi and W. C. Heinz. il Look 31:85-90 S 5 '67

Game without the ball; tackle M. Olsen of Los Angeles Rams. R. Kahn. il Sat Eve Post 240:79-83 D 16 '67

Giants grow up; New York Giants football players. M. Mulvoy. il Sports Illus 27:26-9 D 4 '67

Green Bay's coach reveals his secrets of winning football. V. Lombardi and W. C. Heinz. il Look 31:70-5 S 19 '67

How the pro scouts vote; balloting for Time's annual pro-picked All-America. il Time 90: 55-6 D 15 '67

Little men in the sport of giants. il Ebony 23:99-102+ N '67

Look 1967 All America. G. Astor. il pors Look 31:116-20 D 12 '67

Merry-go-rounds; NFL and AFL common draft of college players. il Time 89:43 Mr 24 '67

Mites for openers; I. Perez and J. Levias of SMU. il Time 90:61-2 S 29 '67

New football stars in the old South; color bars topple. L. Robinson. il Ebony 23: 25-8+ D '67

1966 All-American H.S. football squad. H. L. Masin. Sr Schol 90:25 F 17 '67

No place for stars to shine; All-stars face Green Bay. D. Jenkins. il Sports Illus 27: 16-17 Ag 14 '67

Old pro goes in for six; Green Bay in the Super bowl. T. Maule. il Sports Illus 28:10-15 Ja 8 '68

On the tee: an error and a fumble; football and baseball players at Astrojet classic. D. Jenkins. il Sports Illus 26:16-19 F 27 '67

Pro football 1967; scouting reports; National football league, American football league. T. Maule. il Sports Illus 27:48-85 S 18 '67

Pro rookie's ups and downs. F. Tarkenton and J. Olsen. il Sports Illus 27:22-7 Jl 24 '67

Real draft beef; NFL and AFL draft college players. Newsweek 69:89 Mr 27 '67

Rookies in the line-up. il Time 90:46 D 1 '67

Roughing it in the football bushes; minor leagues. L. L. King. Harper 235:33-8 Ag '67

Slow bus to Bushville; Westchester Bulls, New York Giants farm team. J. Flaherty. il N Y Times Mag p 100+ N 19 '67

Some new Saints in the NFL temple. T. Maule. il Sports Illus 27:30-3 Ag 14 '67

Unions call the signals; NFL and AFL players plan to register with the National labor relations board as a bona fide union. il Bsns W p26 Ja 13 '68

Who these men are, really; the fearsome foursome of the L. A. Rams. il Life 63:99-100B O 13 '67

See also names of football players, e.g. G. Beban

Recruiting

Expo of a different kind; U.S. coaches in Canada. T. C. Brody. il Sports Illus 27:48-9 Jl 3 '67

100 yards and sixty minutes of black power. G. Frazier, IV. il Esquire 68:95-6+ O '67

Pro football's player mutiny; ed. by E. Linn. B. Parrish. il Look 31:66+ Ag 22 '67

FOOTBALL scouting

Big ones scouts are watching. il Sports Illus 27:82-3 S 11 '67

Pro football 1967; scouting reports; National football league, American football league. T. Maule. il Sports Illus 27:48-85 S 18 '67

FOOTBALL trophies. See Trophies, Sport

FOOTE, Emerson, incorporated
Reincarnation. Time 89:86 Mr 10 '67

FOR whom the bell doesn't toll; story. See Meehan, T.

FORAGE crops. See Forage plants

FORAGE plants

Annuals aren't miracle forage. Suc Farm 65: 54F S '67

Successful farming's new eight-star high-yield forage system. C. E. Sommers. il Suc Farm 65:36-9 My '67

See also
Alfalfa
Legumes
Sorghum
Sudan grass

FORAKER, J. D.
Beetle named Tarzan. Parents Mag 42:46-7+ Jl '67

FORAMINIFERA

Planktonic foraminifera: field experiment on production rate. W. H. Berger and A. Soutar. bibliog il Science 156:1495-7 Je 16 '67

Secondary calcification in the foraminiferal genus globorotalia. W. N. Orr. bibliog il Science 157:1554-5 S 29 '67

FORAMINIFERAL ooze. See Sedimentation and deposition

FORBES, Elizabeth
(ed) See Britten, B. Communicator

FORBES, Robert, and Wire, H. R.
Road to Taipei. Am Ed 3:5-7 N '67

FORBES, Robert H.
Highways in the sky. Am For 73:16-18+ Je '67

FORBIS, William
Latin-American common market makes common sense, for U.S. business too. Fortune 75:55-6 Je 1 '67

FORCE (violence) See Violence

FORCE of destiny; opera. See Verdi, G.

FORCED air heating. See Heating

FORCED landings. See Airplanes—Landing

FORCING (plants)

Great aids for seed starting. B. C. Kilvert, jr. il Flower Grower 54:36-7 Ja '67

Perfect child-sized project: hyacinths for Christmas. il Home Gard 54:44-5 N '67

FORD, Corey

Journey among barbarians; condensation of Where the sea breaks its back. Audubon 69:24-31 Mr '67

Lower forty. See issues of Field & stream

One and only W. C. Fields; excerpt from The time of laughter, a sentimental chronicle of the twenties. Harper 235:65-8 O '67

Pleasure to recall. Read Digest 91:205-6 D '67

Son of October. Field & S 72:70-1 O '67

W. C. Fields, the one and only; excerpt from The time of laughter. Read Digest 91:158-62 N '67

When they really knew how to laugh. McCalls 95:82-3+ N '67

FORD, Carey—*Continued*

about

Matter of mood. E. Weeks. Atlan 220:134
N '67

FORD, Del
Leather-stocking trails. Travel 127:45-9 Mr
'67

FORD, Edsel
About grampa, who died poor; poem. Mlle
66:78 D '67

FORD, Edward Charles. See Ford, W.

FORD, Eileen
Eileen Ford's book of model beauty; excerpts.
Ladies Home J 85:30-1, 68-71 Ja '68

FORD, Ford Madox
Five-book shelf. W. Stafford. Poetry 111:186-7
D '67

FORD, Gena
Lines for a hard time; poem. Poetry 110:96
My '67

FORD, Gerald R.
State of the Union; a Republican appraisal;
address, January 19, 1967. Vital Speeches
33:260-4 F 15 '67; Excerpts. U S News 62:
73 Ja 30 '67

about

He wants to be speaker of the House. D.
Oberdorfer. il pors N Y Times Mag p34-
5+ Ap 30 '67
Johnson's war on crime. por U S News 62:48
F 20 '67
90th GOP style; Republican State of the
Union message. il por Newsweek 69:19-20
Ja 30 '67
No consensus; G.O.P. State of the Union
message. il por Time 89:18 Ja 27 '67

FORD, Henry, 1863-1947
How Leland lost Lincoln to Ford. G. Borgeson. il por Motor T 19:19:58-62+ F '67

FORD, Henry, 1917-
Why car prices will rise; Henry Ford gives
reasons; statements. por U S News 62:22
My 29 '67

FORD, Hobart
Commodore buys a boat; interview, ed. by
W. H. deFontaine. Yachting 122:60-1+ D
'67

FORD, Jesse Hill
Act of self-defense; story. Atlan 219:72-6
Ap '67
Savage sound; story. Atlan 220:41-4 Jl '67
Winterkill; story. Esquire 68:112-13 S '67

FORD, John
'Tis pity she's a whore. Criticism
Newsweek 70:92 O 30 '67

FORD, Maurice
Dow at Harvard. New Repub 157:11-13 N 11
'67

FORD, Norman D.
America's retirement islands. Travel 128:
56-8+ D '67

FORD, Whitey
Wave from Whitey; retirement. il por Time
89:82 Je 9 '67

FORD foundation
Action intellectuals; reserve bank for big
ideas, little ideas and oddball ideas. T. H.
White. Life 62:64+ Je 9 '67
Breaking new ground; Ford foundation grant
to establish Negro ensemble company.
Newsweek 69:90 My 29 '67
Cutting back at Ford. Time 89:65 Mr 31 '67
ETV's historic opportunity; Ford founda-
tion's proposal for a new structure to
finance noncommercial television vs. the
Carnegie plan. R. L. Shayon. Sat R 50:71
F 18 '67
Exchange program with eastern Europe. Sch
& Soc 95:345-6 O 14 '67
Ford grants for international studies. Sch &
Soc 94:479 D 24 '66
Ford grants to intellectual and philosophical
projects. Sch & Soc 95:485-6 D 9 '67
Ford proposes satellites to serve educational
TV. Library J 92:279 Ja 15 '67
Look who's talking; investment performance.
il Fortune 76:176 Ag '67
Mac's knife; annual report. Newsweek 69:111
Mr 27 '67
More brainpower for every buck; new presi-
dent. M. Bundy. il Bsns W p46-8+ Ja 6 '68
New ground for giving; three grants to Negro
groups. Sat R 50:62 Ag 19 '67
Promotion of Far-Eastern studies. Sch &
Soc 95:488+ D 9 '67
Public TV: a wasteland oasis. Life 62:4 F
17 '67
Strengthening Negro colleges. Sch & Soc 95:
411+ N 11 '67
Support for work-study projects. Sch & Soc
95:512 D 23 '67

Headquarters
Core of light. il Time 91:50-1 Ja 5 '68
Ford's ir. its heaven. Newsweek 70:68 N 27
'67
Home to work in. New Yorker 43:23-5 D 30
'67

FORD motor company
Auto strike. Nat R 19:1002 S 19 '67
Auto strike talks go into gear. il Newsweek
70:77-8 O 23 '67
Driving down to Rio; Ford buys majority
interest in Willys-Overland do Brasil. Time
90:79 Ag 4 '67
Everyone was lined up, ready for a Ford
shutdown. il Life 63:36-9 S 22 '67
Everything is on ice. Newsweek 70:82 S 25
'67
Ford accord. Sr Schol 91:14 N 9 '67
Ford strike. New Repub 157:7-8 S 23 '67
Ford takes the blow. il Bsns W p35-6 S 9 '67
Going multinational; Ford sets up European-
based subsidiary. Time 89:69 Je 30 '67
Guaranteed wage catches on; the way it will
work. U S News 6384+ N 6 '67
Gut issues start to pain Detroit; auto con-
tract talks approach. il Bsns W p 138+
My 27 '67
Mood is adamant; neither Ford nor UAW is
ready to bargain. il Bsns W p37-8 S 16 '67
Now Ford tries harder; the no. 2 auto maker.
il Bsns W p50-4 S 2 '67
Pressures on Reuther, and Ford. il Newsweek
70:71-4+ S 18 '67
Public interest and the Ford strike. S. Lens.
Commonweal 86:598-9 S 29 '67
Reuther nears showdown; UAW votes to re-
plenish strike fund. Bsns W p 150 O 14
'67
Science puts Ford in the future. il Bsns W
p84-8 Ag 5 '67
Someone up there said, let's race, and lo
. . . Ford came flying. B. Ottum. il Sports
Illus 27:26-32 D 25 '67
Squeeze, squeeze, squeeze. il Time 90:91 N
3 '67
Starting to talk. & sell. il Time 90:94 O 20
'67
Strike at Ford: record losses. U S News 63:
87 N 13 '67
Strike woes multiply. il Bsns W p35-6 O 7
'67
Thinker (Detroit style) Time 89:94 Ap 21 '67
Toll: losses during 1967's third quarter. Time
90:93 N 10 '67
Watch the commercial go by; longest ad-
vertisement in TV history preceding the
Easter showing of The robe. il Bsns W
p82+ Mr 25 '67
Why auto-union demands will be hard to
meet, a company view; excerpts from address, May 5, 1967. M. L. Denise. il U S
News 62:82+ My 22 '67

**FORD motor company, limited, Dagenham,
England**
Cortina takes the crown. il Time 90:109-10
O 6 '67
Pacer from Ford's British stable; compact
Cortina. il Bsns W p98+ N 25 '67

FORDHAM university
Fordham is trying to be Catholic with a small
c. T. J. Fleming. il N Y Times Mag p32-
3+ D 10 '67; Discussion. p22+ Ja 7 '68
Fordham university: renaissance in the
Bronx. J. Cass. il Sat R 50:52-4+ Je 17
'67; Reply. D. Klein. Seventeen 26:158-60
O '67
Pay any price? break any mold? M. Heffron;
W. J. Richardson. il America 116:624-9+
Ap 29 '67
To make a university great. F. Canavan.
America 117:57-60 Jl 15 '67; Discussion.
117:141-2, 230+ Ag 12, S 9 '67

FORD'S theater. See Washington, D.C.—
Theater

FORECASTS
Around the world: prospects for '68. il U S
News 64:50-2 Ja 8 '68
Art of conjecture, by B. de Jouvenel. Review
Bul Atomic Sci 23:33-4 N '67.   P. C.
Ritterbush
Decades ahead from a publisher's view; ex-
cerpts from address, June 22, 1967. E. E.
Booher. Science 158:882-4 N 17 '67
Education in the 1980's. Sch & Soc 95:206+
Ap 1 '67
Forecasting future developments. P. H. Abel-
son. Science 157:995 S 1 '67
In your future: robot slaves, instant knowl-
edge, sea farms. il U S News 62:112-13 Ap
10 '67
Isi does it; Proud Clarion to win Derby.
Sports Illus 26:11 My 22 '67

FOREIGN students in the United States—*Cont.*

Statistics
Annual educational exchange statistics. S. K. Gorney. il Sch & Soc 95:234-7 Ap 1 '67

FOREIGN study
All students aboard! (a compendium of opportunities) A. L. Zeigler. Sat R 50:57-8+ F 18 '67
American scholarship: global affair. il Sat R 50:62 Jl 15 '67
On the evils of a foreign education; attitudes of the eighteenth and nineteenth centuries on sending American youth to Europe for education. H. S. Commager. il Sat R 50: 83-4+ F 18 '67
See also
American institute for foreign study

FOREIGN subsidiaries. See Corporations—Foreign subsidiaries

FOREIGN teachers in the United States
Volunteers to America program gets underway. Dept State Bul 56:244 F 13 '67

FOREIGN trade. See Commerce; *also* subhead Commerce under names of countries, e.g. United States—Commerce

FOREIGN trade promotion. See Trade missions

FOREIGN trade regulation
Beggar thy neighbor; from the allies, cautious reassurance. il Newsweek 71:73+ Ja 22 '68
How Europe applies its border taxes. Bsns W p 19 Ja 13 '68
Non-tariff tricks. il Time 91:55 Ja 12 '68
Payments plan wins backers abroad. Bsns W p21-2 Ja 13 '68

FOREIGN visitors in Africa
Africa revisited. A. Adams. il Hi Fi 17: MA26-7 Ag '67

FOREIGN visitors in Armenia
Armenian diary; L. Chookasian visits the land of her forebears. G. Gavejian. il Opera N 32:14-16 D 23 '67

FOREIGN visitors in Canada
Beard phobia; Calgary police harass San Francisco Mime troupe. Nation 204:485-6 Ap 17 '67
Nova Scotia: where the good times are. E. Logan. il Sr Schol 90:sup20-1 Ap 7 '67

FOREIGN visitors in China
Morley Safer's sojourn. R. L. Shayon. Sat R 50:61 S 16 '67
Orbit of China, by H. E. Salisbury. Review Sat R 50:51 My 6 '67. M. Kalb
Who knows the truth about red China? interview. F. Pardinas. Cath World 205:36-41 Ap '67

FOREIGN visitors in Cuba
Cuban diary: bringing up Castro's new man. J. Reston. il N Y Times Mag p 11-13+ Ag 13 '67
Faces of Fidelismo. L. Eder. il Nation 205: 173-7 S 4 '67

FOREIGN visitors in Egypt
Shark of Araby. C. Gammon. il Sports Illus 27:88-91+ O 16 '67

FOREIGN visitors in Europe
Baby-sitter's bonanza: two months in Europe, including five-week cruise of Adriatic and Aegean aboard chartered yacht. L. Gross. il Look 31:85-6+ Mr 21 '67
Booked for travel; dangers for the traveler in eastern Europe. H. Sutton. Sat R 50: 49-50 Mr 4 '67
Bookman's Baedeker to Europe. A. Plotnik. bibliog il Library J 92:2889-97 S 1 '67
Dark at the top of the stacks; how not to visit the libraries of Europe. A. Plotnik. il Library J 92:1122-5 Mr 15 '67
European odds and ends. J. C. Evans. Christian Cent 84:958 Jl 26 '67
See also
Tourist trade—Europe

Anecdotes, facetiae, satire, etc.
You, too, can be anti-American. R. Baker. il N Y Times Mag p36-7+ Ap 23 '67

FOREIGN visitors in Finland
Northern exposure: visit of Senior scholastic's associate editor. D. Chu. il Sr Schol 90:14-15 My 19 '67

FOREIGN visitors in France
Lucien, Octave, Victoire, Emile; Americans at family reunion in south of France. F. Du Plessix. New Yorker 43:26-34 Jl 29 '67
Missing out on Paris. A. Waugh. il Nat R 19:966 S 5 '67

FOREIGN visitors in Germany
Conundrums for the ausländer. J. C. Evans. Christian Cent 84:167 F 8 '67; Reply. R. Reitz. 84:722 My 31 '67

German journey. S. Kauffmann. New Repub 156:24+ F 18 '67
More from Germany. S. Kauffmann. New Repub 156:24+ F 25 '67

FOREIGN visitors in Greece
Invitation to Greece. S. Kauffmann. New Repub 157:22+ Jl 1 '67
Troika and the tourists. T. L. Christie. il Sat R 50:44-6 O 14 '67

FOREIGN visitors in Ireland
International incident in Cork; French hunting party in Ireland. C. Gammon. il Sports Illus 27:42-4+ N 27 '67
Nearest faraway place. S. Alexander. Life 63:13 S 8 '67

FOREIGN visitors in Israel
Reporter at large. E. Wilson. New Yorker 43:38-40+ Ag 19 '67
Victorious Israel's look and mood. L. J. Walinsky. New Repub 157:9-10 Jl 8 '67

FOREIGN visitors in Italy
Italian enigma. J. C. Evans. Christian Cent 84:710-11 My 31 '67

FOREIGN visitors in Japan
Golden village; Crow Boy and the making of a film. G. L. Johnson. il Horn Bk 43: 183-91 Ap '67

FOREIGN visitors in Jordan
Reporter at large. E. Wilson. New Yorker 43:40+ Ag 19 '67

FOREIGN visitors in Portugal
At home abroad: Portugal. H. Downs. il Travel 128:42-4 D '67

FOREIGN visitors in Russia
Minneapolis to Moscow; mission of business and industry leaders. Christian Cent 84:677 My 24 '67
Report from Russia; three weeks of travel, under auspices of the Citizen exchange corps. J. Gorelick. il Seventeen 26:154-7+ My '67
Russia today; symposium. il Look 31:29-42+ O 3 '67
Russian revolution: fifty years after; questions and answers. J. Brownell. il Sr Schol 91:15-18 O 26; 11-13+ N 2 '67
Ten Glassboro women in Russia. il McCalls 95:84-5+ O '67

FOREIGN visitors in the Middle East
Taming touch of the peaceful invaders. E. Kern. il Life 63:72-86 O 13 '67

FOREIGN visitors in the United States
As others see us, some eye-openers; fifteen foreign newsmen to study the United States. A. H. Sypher. il Nations Bsns 55: 41-2 O '67
Different kind of shortage: foreign visitors. il U S News 62:98-9 F 27 '67
Executive sweets; south Vietnamese businesswomen. il Time 90:70 Jl 21 '67
Guide to the U.S.A. for Frenchmen only. P. Daninos. il Read Digest 91:25-6+ O '67
Huge diamond becomes family's best friend; New York trip for Africans. il Ebony 23:110-15 Ja '68
Journey to understanding; Association for world travel exchange. T. F. Mofford. il Sr Schol 90:sup 16 My 5 '67
Play host to foreign visitors. S. Schuler. Am Home 70:48+ N '67
Reporter at large; American diary by visitor from Warsaw. L. Tyrmand. New Yorker 43:67-8+ N 11 '67
Through darkest America with camera and checkbook. A. Carthew. il N Y Times Mag p30-1+ Ag 27 '67; Discussion. p22+ S 24 '67
To all the world, welcome! Sioux City's foreign visitor program; with report by D. J. Hamblin. il Life 63:46-53 S 1 '67

FOREIGN visitors in Vietnam (Democratic Republic)
Journey to North Vietnam. D. Schoenbrun. il Sat Eve Post 240:21-5+ D 16 '67
North Vietnam under siege; with report by L. Lockwood. il Life 62:33-44D Ap 7 '67
Other side, by S. Lynd and T. Hayden. Review
New Repub 156:27-9 Ap 8 '67. R. Steel
Report from North Vietnam. J. Gerassi. New Repub 156:13-15 Mr 4 '67

FOREIGN visitors in Vietnam (Republic)
Filipino in Vietnam. America 117:446 O 21 '67
Letter from abroad. E. Steinbeck. il McCalls 94:42+ Je '67
Librarian in Vietnam. M. Boaz. il Wilson Lib Bul 41:962-7 My '67
Other Vietnam: behind battlefronts and headlines. J. Bingham. Mlle 65:179+ O '67
Visit to Vietnam; volunteer assistant to Dr Pierce; president of World vision. A. Ives. il Seventeen 26:150-1+ F '67

FOREIGN words and phrases. See subhead
Foreign words and phrases under name of
language, e.g. French language—Foreign
words and phrases

FOREMAN, Fred
Spring dairy feeding tips. Suc Farm 65:49
My '67

FOREMAN, Kenneth J.
Unique memorial for K. J. Foreman; his
own sermon. C. Thielman. Christian Cent
84:414+ Mr 29 '67

FOREMAN, Percy
Bitter Candy. il por Time 89:64 Ap 7 '67

FOREMAN, Robert L.
Me, David Susskind and the greatest man in
the world. Esquire 68:69+ S '67

FORENSIC medicine. See Medical jurisprudence

FORENSIC psychiatry
Gag for psychiatrists; testimony of state-
employed psychiatrists. Time 90:48 Ag 25
'67
Mind of a murderer; excerpt from Born to
raise hell. J. Altman and M. Ziporyn. il
Sat Eve Post 240:27-31+ Jl 1; 38-40+
Jl 15 '67
Rouse case. New Repub 157:5 Jl 1 '67
Who's fit to be free? confinement of C. C.
Rouse in John Howard pavilion of St
Elizabeth's hospital. J. Ridgeway. New
Repub 156:24-6 F 4 '67; Discussion. 156:
35-6 F 18 '67

FORER, Lois G.
Is legislation the answer? Parks & Rec 2:
17 Ap '67

FOREST conservation
November 1, 1967; Senate defeats Anderson-
Ellender amendment of Redwood Park
package. J. B. Craig. Am For 73:10 D '67
Trees, for business or pleasure? L. C. Walk-
er. il Am For 73:16-17+ My '67
See also
Forest fire protection

FOREST fire protection
Eruption in the Northwest. J. C. Hunt. il Am
For 73:22-5+ N '67
New success in fighting fires by making it
rain; cloud-seeding. U S News 63:10 Jl
31 '67

Anecdotes, facetiae, satire, etc.
Smoky years. J. C. Hunt. il Am For 73:30-1+
My '67

FOREST fires
Blitz of fire in the western forests. il U S
News 63:10 S 18 '67
Eruption in the Northwest. J. C. Hunt. il Am
For 73:22-5+ N '67
Fighting future fires. il Time 90:60 S 15 '67
Fire! fires in Northwest. il Newsweek 70:84+
S 11 '67
Forest fires, why? il Am For 73:64 O '67
Million-acre bomb; fires in Northwestern
states. Time 90:17 S 1 '67
Ordeal by forest fire; Pacific Northwest's
worst blazes in fifty years. il Bsns W p46+
S 9 '67
Profiles; Pine Barrens. J. McPhee. New
Yorker 43:92+ D 2 '67

FOREST Lawn memorial park. See Los Angeles—Cemeteries

FOREST management
Aesthetic forests for urban areas. W. T.
Plass and S. G. Boyce. il Parks & Rec 2:
42+ O '67
Call for resources statesmanship. E. F.
Heacox. il Am For 73:14-17+ Ag '67
Forest practices and watershed management
in California; address. W. S. Shannon. il
Am For 73:6-7+ My '67
How to sell multiple use without half trying;
Clearwater River country, Idaho. V.
Fischer. il Am For 73:34-5+ Ag '67
Mike Frome; questioning the future of woods
in a rapidly changing land. M. Frome. Am
For 73:5+ My '67
No wilderness wasted; Turkey point developed
by Florida power & light co. M. Smith.
Parks & Rec 2:20+ Je '67
Recreation land management and the new for-
estry. L. C. Merriam, jr. bibliog il Nat
Parks Mag 41:14-18 Je '67

FOREST products laboratory. See United
Statets—Forest products laboratory

FOREST research. See Forestry research

FORESTERS
Wake up foresters, you're needed! J. J. Sho-
mon. il Am For 73:12-15+ My '67
See also
Women as foresters

FORESTRY, Industrial. See Forest management

FORESTRY exhibits
Seaboard safari; Seaboard railroad's annual
Cooperative field forestry program, Hoffman, N.C. W. E. Towell. il Am For 73:
34-5+ S '67

FORESTRY research
Forestry research in West Virginia. R. C.
Byrd. il Am For 73:8-9+ D '67

FORESTRY schools and education
Our forestry schools. K. A. Argow. il Am For
73:28-9 Ap '67

FORESTRY societies
See also
American forestry association

FORESTS, National. See National forests

FORESTS, State
Adirondacks: forever wild? with editorial
comment. J. T. Cunningham. Audubon 69:4,
38-43 Mr '67

FORESTS and forestry
See also
Forest fires
Forestry exhibits
Lumbering
Tree breeding

Illinois
Aesthetic forests for urban areas. W. T.
Plass and S. G. Boyce. il Parks & Rec 2:
42+ O '67

Kentucky
Lilly's wood. H. M. Caudill. il Audubon 69:
24-7 My '67

Massachusetts
See also
Harvard university—Harvard forest, Peter-
sham, Mass.

Nebraska
Nebraska's man-made forest; Nebraska na-
tional forest. O. A. Clement. il Nat Parks
Mag 41:18-19 N '67

North Borneo
Forests of Sabah. H. S. Kernan. il Am For
73:16-17+ F '67

Peru
Eucalyptus in Peru. K. A. Herath. il Am
For 73:20-2 Ap '67

Switzerland
Forest that pays the taxes; Juriens, village
in foothills of Jura Mountains. P. C. Fraley.
Am For 73:25+ Ja '67

United States
Forestry appropriations; fiscal year ending
June 30, 1968, compared with 1967. Am For
73:8 Ag '67
Forestry in the federal budget (cont) il Am
For 73:10 Mr '67
Washington lookout. A. G. Hall. See issues of
American forests
See also
Forest conservation

Washington (state)
Cascades' green mantle. W. F. Heald. il
Am For 73:12-15+ Ap '67

FORESTS in literature
German forest; photographs. Opera N 32:6-9
D 23 '67

FORGERIES, Art. See Forgery of works of
art

FORGERY
See also
Counterfeits and counterfeiting
Forgery of works of art

FORGERY of antiques. See Antiques, Forged

FORGERY of works of art
Buyers, sellers, and forgers. M. Esterow.
Harper 234:83-6 Je '67
Dealing from Park avenue; David Stein
charged with counterfeiting and grand lar-
ceny. Time 89:75 My 26 '67
Fake or jake? frauds in Meadows's collec-
tion. il Newsweek 69:110 My 22 '67
Fakes, forgeries, foolishness. F. Getlein. New
Repub 156:32-4 My 27 '67
How art swindlers duped a virtuous million-
aire. W. A. McWhirter. il Life 63:52-4+
Jl 7 '67
Let the buyer beware. il Newsweek 69:112-
14 Je 19 '67
Meadows' luck; millionaire's collection large-
ly fakes. il Time 89:94+ My 19 '67
Monet & the phony pony. il Time 90:84 D 15
'67
Of a different color; Met's 15-inch bronze
horse revealed as fake. il Newsweek 70:94
D 18 '67

FORGERY of works of art—*Continued*
Personal business; con men frame naive collectors. Bsns W p 165-6 My 20 '67
Sargent in combat. Newsweek 70:88 O 2 '67
True or false? New York's Graham galleries show called Art: authentic and fake. il Newsweek 69:106 My 15 '67
See also
Art—Expertising

FORGET, Bernard G. and Weissman, S. M.
Nucleotide sequence of KB cell 5S RNA. bibliog Science 158:1695-9 D 29 '67

FORGET it ever happened; story. See Amft, M. J.

FORGETTING. See Memory

FORGING
Atlas F silo will be converted to high energy impaction unit. Aviation W 86:81-3 Ja 30 '67
Forging, press highlight Russian metalworking advances. M. L. Yaffee. il Aviation W 87:70-9 Jl 10 '67
See also
Forging machinery

FORGING machinery
Forge conversion deemed breakthrough; high velocity precision machine. J. F. Judge. il Aero Tech 21:27-9+ D 4 '67
Raising the pressure fourfold. il Bsns W p 126-8 F 18 '67

FORGING presses. See Presses

FORGIVENESS
Sin and forgiveness. V. P. McCorry. America 117:inside back cover S 16 '67

FORK in the road; story. See Trueblood, H. P.

FORMAL gardening. See Landscape gardening

FORMAN, Milos
Chill wind on the new wave. Sat R 50:10-11+ D 23 '67
about
Movers. A. Sarris. por Sat R 50:10 D 23 '67

FORMAN, Sidney, and Collins, R. L.
Paperbound bound? book lists. Sr Schol 89:sup28 Ja 20 '67

FORMER priests. See Ex-priests, nuns, etc.

FORMOSA. See Taiwan

FORNEY, James S.
New wave in image-making; holograms tell it like it really was. Pop Phot 61:120-3+ N '67

FORREST, Hugh S. See Harris, S. E. jt. auth.

FORRESTAL, Michael Vincent
New man at the helm. F. Merkling. por Opera N 31:16-17 Je 10 '67

FORRESTAL fire. See Aircraft carriers—Fires and fire protection

FORSDALE, Louis
Cartridge loop; 8mm made easy. por Library J 92:2002-4 My 15 '67

FORSTER, John
Australasian character. bibliog f Ann Am Acad 370:156-63 Mr '67

FORSYTH, E. B.
When I pushed the starter nothing happened. Motor B 119:34-5+ My '67

FORSYTH, George A.
Don't let them ride over us. G. M. Heinzman. il por Am Heritage 18:44-7+ F '67

FORSYTH garden club. See Garden clubs

FORT, William S.
Justice for children. por Parents Mag 42:50+ O '67

FORT LAUDERDALE, Fla.
Description
Fort Lauderdale. F. Holtun. Mlle 64:194+ Ap '67
Street traffic
Digital computer designed to control traffic only. F. E. May. il Am City 82:100+ Ja '67

FORT MCMURRAY, Canada
From an icy quagmire, half the world's oil. il Newsweek 70:78-80 O 2 '67

FORT SILL, Okla. See Military training camps

FORT WORTH, Tex.
Police
Good communications can cut crime response time. il Am City 82:100-1 Ag '67

FORT WORTH, Tex, public library
Five branches for Fort Worth. W. Jones and R. A. McKinney. il Library J 92:4370-2 D 1 '67

FORT WORTH ballet association
Classic of mischief in Texas. J. Anderson. il Dance Mag 41:59-62 Ap '67

FORT WORTH opera association
Fort Worth; Saint-Saëns' Samson and Delilah. J. Ardoin. Opera N 31:28 Mr 4 '67
Report: Fort Worth; production of Verdi's Aida. L. Eureka. il Opera N 32:29 Ja 13 '68

FORTAS, Abe
Many-sided Justice Fortas. F. P. Graham. il pors N Y Times Mag p26-7+ Je 4 '67

FORTIFICATION
Oh, what a lovely war; shore battery ruins of World war II. il Arch Forum 127:58-63 N '67

FORTS. See Fortification

FORTUNE (periodical)
Henry R. Luce and American business. M. Ways. Fortune 75:115-16+ Ap '67

FORTUNE and men's eyes; drama. See Herbert, J.

FORTUNE telling
Do-it-yourself guide to fortune telling. il McCalls 94:66-73 Jl '67
Seer through a third eye; M. Woodruff. J. Howard. il Life 62:91-2+ Je 16 '67
See also
Astrology

49ers (football club) See Football clubs

FORUMS (discussion and debate)
Listening to youth; Dorothy Gordon youth forums. D. Gordon. il Wilson Lib Bul 42:194-8 O '67
Who leads today's youth? round table discussion from 1967 student burgesses at Williamsburg. il Sr Schol 90:4-9+ Ap 14 '67
See also
Center for the study of democratic institutions, Santa Barbara, Calif.

La FORZA del destino; opera. See Verdi, G.

FOSS, Lukas
Many lives of Lukas Foss. E. Salzman. il pors Sat R 50:73-4+ F 25 '67
Pffhonk! world premiere of concert for cello and orchestra in Carnegie Hall. il por Time 89:70 Mr 17 '67

FOSSIL animals. See Paleontology

FOSSIL ants, Fossil apes; etc. See Ants, Fossil; Apes, Fossil; etc.

FOSSIL fuels. See Fuel

FOSSIL microorganisms. See Micropaleontology

FOSSIL plants. See Paleobotany

FOSTER, Claude R. Jr
Wartburg: symbol of a synthesis? Christian Cent 84:1358+ O 25 '67

FOSTER, Edward J.
How we judge tape recorders. Hi Fi 17:47-51 Ag '67

FOSTER, John Stuart, 1922-
Academic research; Foster defends DoD support in universities; statement, November 2, 1968. por Science 158:1032-4 N 24 '67
Technology-gap debate; excerpts from address. Aviation W 86:11 My 22 '67
about
Man under the gun in military research. il por Bsns W p60-2+ D 16 '67

FOSTER, Malin F.
High Uintas. il Liv Wildn 30:11-13 Wint '66

FOSTER, Neichen
Christmas tree; poem. Horn Bk 43:778 D '67

FOSTER, William C.
Ambassador Foster discusses nonproliferation treaty; transcript of a press conference. August 11, 1967. Dept State Bul 57:291-4 S 4 '67
Draft treaty on nonproliferation of nuclear weapons submitted to Geneva disarmament conference; statement, August 24, 1967. Dept State Bul 57:315-18 S 11 '67

FOSTER, Woodbridge
Hormone-mediated nutritional control of sexual behavior in male dung flies. bibliog Science 158:1596-7 D 22 '67

FOSTER CITY, Calif.
Built to be seen; storm-drainage pump station. D. W. Klar. il Am City 82:96-7 My '67
Life in the instant cities. T. Roszak. il Nation 204:336-40+ Mr 13 '67

FOSTER day care
Concerning day care. L. W. Sauer. il PTA Mag 62:29-30 D '67
Someone to mind the baby. M. Pines. il N Y Times Mag p71+ Ja 7 '68
Urgently needed: more day care centers. K. B. Oettinger. Parents Mag 42:58 N '67
When a mother goes to work. B. Spock. il Redbook 129:20+ Je '67
When mothers work; need for child care facilities il Newsweek 70:73 Ag 28 '67

FOXX, Redd
Redd Foxx, prince of clowns. L. Robinson.
il pors Ebony 22:91-2+ Ap '67
FOY, Fred Calvert
New philosophy at Koppers. R. Levy. por
Duns R 89:48-9+ Mr '67
FOY, Rena
Personal responsibility or education; excerpt
from The world of education. Sch & Soc 95:
521-3 D 23 '67
FOYERS. See Halls
FOYT, Anthony Joseph, 1935?-
A.J. again. il por Newsweek 70:68 D 11 '67
A.J. in the afternoon. E. Dahlquist. il pors Hot
Rod 20:52-4 D '67
Gentlemen, junk your engines. B. Ottum. il
por Sports Illus 26:30-3 Je 12 '67
Glorious double. B. Ottum. il por Sports Illus
26:14-17 Je 19 '67
Joy ride: Le Mans race. Newsweek 69:64 Je
26 '67
There's a turbine in their future. il por Time
89:78 Je 9 '67
FOZZARD, Harry A. and Kipnis, D. M.
Regulation of intracellular sodium concentra-
tions in rat diaphragm muscle. bibliog Sci-
ence 156:1257-60 Je 2 '67
FRACTURE of solids
Fundamental phenomena in the materials sci-
ences; report on fourth annual sym-
posium. L. J. Bonis and J. J. Duga. Sci-
ence 155:357-9+ Ja 20 '67
FRACTURES
First aid; ankle fracture. C. J. Potthoff. To-
days Health 45:74 N '67
FRADIN, Morris
Washington's Rhine? Am For 73:22-5+ My '67
FRADY, Marshall
Governor and Mister Wallace. Atlan 220:35-40
Ag '67
Infamous Mr Bond. Sat Eve Post 240:94-6+
My 6 '67
It is a joyous thing to be a Kirk Republican!
Sat Eve Post 240:75-9 Jl 29 '67
You reckon they thought I was a nut? Sat
Eve Post 240:27-9+ Ap 22 '67
FRAENKEL, Jack R. and Gross, R. E.
Team teaching. bibliog NEA J 56:16-17 Ap '67
FRAGER, Malcolm
Lively arts; interview, ed. by R. Hemming.
por Sr Schol 90:21-2 Ap 14 '67
Recordings. M. Mayer. Esquire 68:57 N '67
FRAGMENTS; drama. See Schisgal, M.
FRAGONARD, Jean Honoré
Young girl reading. A. Saarinen. il McCalls
94:52-4 Je '67
FRAIBERG, Selma
Origins of human bonds. Commentary 44:47-57
D '67
FRAKES, Margaret
Church women united. Christian Cent 84:990-1
Ag 2 '67
How come? Christian Cent 84:345 Mr 15 '67
FRALEY, Pierre C.
Forest that pays the taxes. Am For 73:25+
Ja '67
FRALICK, Richard F.
Social unrest. Parks & Rec 2:26-8+ N '67
FRAME, Robert
Robust painting of Robert Frame. J. Lovoos.
il por Am Artist 31:52-7+ Ap '67
FRAMES for pictures. See Picture frames
FRANC, Helen M.
Editorial: for CRIA. Art N 65:29+ Ja '67
FRANCE, Pierre Mendès-. See Mendès-France,
P.
FRANCE
European notebook. H. Brandon. Sat R 50:
11 S 23 '67
See also
Aerospace industries—France
Agriculture—France
Airlines—France
Airplane industry and trade—France
Airplanes, Military—France
Aluminum industry and trade—France
Americans in France
Architecture, Domestic—France
Astronomical observatories—France
Booksellers and bookselling—France
Brittany
Carcassonne
Children—France
Clothing industry—France
Corsica
Elections—France
Electronic apparatus industry and trade—
France
Government ownership—France
Grenoble
Hotels, taverns, etc.—France
Industrial management and organization—
France

Labor party (Great Britain)
Land tenure—France
Law—France
Lyons
Moving pictures—France
Music—France
Newspapers—France
Paper money—France
Political campaigns—France
Postal service—France
Provence
Public opinion—France
Publishers and publishing—France
Restaurants—France
Royan
Science—France
Skis and skiing—France
Space research—France
Television broadcasting—France
Tourist trade—France
Trials—France
Unemployment—France
Wages—France
Women—France

Army

When the French army mutinied. D. Johnson. il N Y Times Mag p26-7+ My 28 '67

Cabinet

Captive cabinet beguiled by Charles de Gaulle.
il Life 63:44B D 8 '67

Colonies

See also
French Guiana
New Caledonia
Saint Pierre and Miquelon (islands)
Somaliland, French

Commerce

French publishers view the U.S. as export
market. H. R. Lottman. il Pub W 191:20-3
My 15 '67

Defenses

Maturing force: nuclear *force de frappe.* il
Time 90:40 N 17 '67

Economic conditions

For de Gaulle, troubles piling up at home,
too. il U S News 63:78 Ag 14 '67
French people's message to Charles de
Gaulle. il U S News 62:52-3 Mr 27 '67
Troubled economy. Time 89:94 Je 23 '67
Truth about today's France: no base for
grandeur. il U S News 63:59-61 D 25 '67
See also
Unemployment—France

Economic policy

De Gaulle's economic reforms. E. Taylor.
Reporter 37:24-6 N 2 '67
Fighting the invaders; concerning The Amer-
ican challenge. Newsweek 70:88+ N 20 '67
Gaullists call the shots in business, too. il
Bsns W p96+ Ja 14 '67
Progress, independence & peace; address,
August 10, 1967. C. de Gaulle. Vital Speeches
33:677-8 S 1 '67

Economic relations

Charlie against the tide. Fortune 75:77 Je 1 '67
Letter from Paris; fall of the pound sterling.
Genêt. New Yorker 43:95-6+ D 9 '67

Foreign opinion

One man's revolt; Chevrolet dealer's anti-
Gaullist campaign. Newsweek 71:66 Ja 15 '68

American
What to do about de Gaulle? il Time 90:11-12
D 29 '67

Foreign relations

After the vote: where de Gaulle is headed. il
U S News 62:35-6 Mr 20 '67
Anger in Paris; criticism of de Gaulle's
conduct of French foreign policy. il News-
week 70:33-4 Jl 24 '67
Biggest victory for de Gaulle? U S News 63:
19-20 D 4 '67
Buried meaning of a crisis. E. J. Hughes.
Newsweek 69:23 Je 12 '67
De Gaulle speaks; summary of news confer-
ence, November 27, 1967. C. de Gaulle. Sr
Schol 91:15-16 D 14 '67
De Gaulle: wrecker or leader? appraisal of
French president. il U S News 62:66-70 F
20 '67
De Gaulle's great plan. E. M. von Kuehnelt-
Leddihn. Nat R 19:897 Ag 22 '67
France still says 'non'; de Gaulle's anti-
Americanism. il Bsns W p37 D 2 '67

FRANCE—Foreign relations—*Continued*
Grandeur diminished. H. Brandon. Sat R 50:6+ Jl 29 '67
Progress, independence & peace; address, August 10, 1967. C. de Gaulle. Vital Speeches 33:677-8 S 1 '67
Rush to judgement. Nat R 19:1312 N 28 '67
Sad twilight for de Gaulle. Life 63:4 Ag 11 '67
Seeking alternatives to de Gaulle. Life 62: 4 F 10 '67
View from the pique. Time 89:27 Je 30 '67

Canada

Always like that; de Gaulle explains policy to Cabinet. il Time 90:22 Ag 11 '67
French business smiles at Canada; French-owned companies in Canada. il Bsns W p24-6 Jl 22 '67
Le grand faux pas of le grand Charles. M. Clark. il Life 63:44B-44C Ag 4 '67
Incident in Canada. E. Taylor. Reporter 37: 10-11 Ag 10 '67
Second round; cabinet communiqué to justify attitude. Newsweek 70:38+ Ag 14 '67

Germany (Federal Republic)

Quo vadis, Charles de Gaulle? concern with German foreign relations. il Newsweek 70: 32-3 Jl 24 '67

Great Britain

De Gaulle and Britain; same old stand. il Newsweek 69:34+ My 29 '67
Exercise in persuasion; Wilson, de Gaulle & Brown. il Time 89:26+ F 3 '67
Standoff in Paris; British entry into Common market. il Newsweek 69:50+ F 6 '67

Middle East

39,999,999 Frenchmen? Nat R 19:782+ Jl 25 '67

United States

DeGaulle's cold war on the U.S. A. De Borchgrave. il Newsweek 71:36-8 Ja 22 '68
Letter from Paris; excerpt from article Amica America, from Figaro; ed. by Genêt. A. François-Poncet. New Yorker 43:181-3 Ap 15 '67
Seeing de Gaulle plain; Harold Kaplan's article in New leader. Time 91:21 Ja 12 '68
Who needs an enemy? move toward total disengagement from the U.S. il Newsweek 70: 54 D 18 '67
See also
France and the United States

History

Peace, empire, and world government; introduction to Major peace treaties of modern history, 1648-1966. ed. by F. L. Israel. A. Toynbee. Sat R 50:17-21 Ap 29 '67
See also
Franco-German war, 1870-1871

Bibliography

Articles and other books received; comp. by B. F. Hyslop. See issues of American historical review

Revolution

Class in the French revolution; a discussion; with reply by E. L. Eisenstein. J. Kaplow; G. Shapiro. bibliog f Am Hist R 72:497-522 Ja '67
Great human option; concerning books by G. Rudé. E. T. Gargan. Nation 204:216-20 F 13 '67
Noncapitalist wealth and the origins of the French revolution; excerpts from address, December 30, 1965. G. V. Taylor. bibliog f il Am Hist R 72:469-96 Ja '67

Revolution 1789-1799—Drama

Scarlet Pimpernel; dramatization of novel by E. Orczy. M. T. Leech. Plays 26:93-108 My '67

European war, 1914-1918
See European war, 1914-1918—France

Industries

Big yogurt binge; Société Danone leads French yogurt market. Time 90:80 Ag 4 '67
I wasn't created to lose money; business of S. Floirat. il Time 89:84 Mr 31 '67
Merging to survive; in France. il Fortune 75:74+ F '67
Report from Grenoble; fast-growing provincial town points France's future in high-technology industries. J. Davenport. il Fortune 75:69-70+ Mr '67
See also
Computer industry—France
Industrial management and organization—France
Wine trade

Parliament

Letter from Paris; opening of third legislative session of de Gaulle fifth republic. Genêt. New Yorker 43:175 Ap 15 '67

Politics and government

Bad dream for Charles. Newsweek 69:57 Ap 17 '67
Counterattack; de Gaulle silences critics in Independent republican party. Newsweek 70:46-7 S 4 '67
De Gaulle again, or a new popular front? H. Peyre. New Repub 156:10-11 Mr 4 '67
De Gaulle under fire; his tenure threatened? U S News 63:17 Ag 21 '67
De Gaulle: wrecker or leader? appraisal of French president. il U S News 62:66-70 F 20 '67
Flanking movement; no censure on request for emergency powers. il Newsweek 69:36 My 29 '67
France: fading hero. il Newsweek 70:30-2+ Ag 28 '67
Future of Gaullism. il Time 89:28-9 Mr 3 '67
Getting de Gaulle down; Gaullists defeat in local elections. il Newsweek 70:43 O 16 '67
Let's understand the French. F. Morley. il Nations Bsns 55:27-8 My '67
Letter from Paris; concerning F. Mitterrand's opposition address. Genêt. New Yorker 43:170-2 Ap 29 '67
Letter from Paris; excerpts from press conference. C. de Gaulle. New Yorker 43:98 D 9 '67
Letter from Paris; workers political strike for purely political reasons. Genêt. New Yorker 43:126-7 My 27 '67
No extras; plan to legislate by decree. Newsweek 69:54 My 8 '67
Our only real ally; with editorial comment. S. Alsop. il Sat Eve Post 240:16, 84 Jl 1 '67; Same abr. without editorial comment. Read Digest 91:43-5 S '67
Pompon & *les godillots* Time 90:31 D 8 '67
Re-enter: Mendès-France, hoping. S. de Gramont. il N Y Times Mag p25+ Ap 16 '67
Reform by decree. il Time 89:29 My 5 '67
Squeaking through. Newsweek 70:68 O 23 '67
Struggle of après-de Gaulle has begun. F. Lewis. il N Y Times Mag p26-7+ My 14 '67
Temporary victory for de Gaulle. E. Taylor. il Reporter 36:27-8+ Je 15 '67
See also
Communist party (France)
Elections—France
France—Parliament
Political campaigns—France
Political parties—France
Presidents—France

Population

Halfway mark. il Newsweek 70:48 N 13 '67

Religious institutions and affairs

World around us (cont) Christian Cent 84: 445+ Ap 5 '67

Social history

Courtesans: the demi-mode in nineteenth-century France, by J. Richardson. Review Sat R 50:30-1 D 23 '67. L. LeSage
Many lives of Georges Lefebvre. G. Shapiro. bibliog f Am Hist R 72:502-14 Ja '67
Noncapitalist wealth and the origins of the French revolution; excerpts from address, December 30, 1965. G. V. Taylor. bibliog f il Am Hist R 72:469-96 Ja '67
On Who intervened in 1788? J. Kaplow. bibliog f Am Hist R 72:497-502 Ja '67

Social policy

Looking backward; demands to renovate. il Newsweek 69:47 Ap 3 '67
FRANCE (ship) See Ocean liners
FRANCE and the United States
Galled by de Gaulle; consumer backlash against things French. il Bsns W p22 D 30 '67
How to hurt a Frenchman. H. Moffett. il Life 64:34-34B Ja 19 '68
See also
Americans in France
United States—Foreign opinion—French
FRANCEKEVICH, Al
In the darkroom. See issues of Popular photography
FRANCES, Sister Marian. See Marian Frances, Sister

FRANCES, Phoebe
Samuel Frances, revolutionary, patriot and citizen-extraordinary; excerpt from address, August 16, 1966. J. W. Davis. Negro Hist Bul 30:11 N '67

FRANCES, Samuel
Samuel Frances, revolutionary, patriot and citizen-extraordinary; excerpt from address, August 16, 1966. J. W. Davis. Negro Hist Bul 30:11 N '67

FRANCHISE system. See Exclusive agencies

FRANCIS Joseph II, prince of Liechtenstein
124 rooms, twenty baths, elevators, central heating, fit for a prince. J. Wechsberg. il por Esquire 68:217-21+ D '67

FRANCIS, Devon
Come ride on rails at 100 m.p.h! Pop Sci 191:106-9 N '67

FRANCIS, Dick
Authors & editors. por Pub W 193:27-8 Ja 8 '68

FRANCIS, Emile
Francis forges an up team in a down town; Rangers routing the champion Montreal Canadiens. P. Axthelm. il por Sports Illus 26:25-7 Ja 30 '67
Rangers don't have no inferiority complex no more. B. Surface. il pors N Y Times Mag p46-7+ Mr 12 '67

FRANCIS, Sam
Cloud busters in Houston. Time 90:61+ N 3 '67

FRANCISCANS
California's first gardeners. L. E. Hoffman. Horticulture 45:45 D '67

FRANCISCO, Don
SEMA and you. Hot Rod 20:120-1 D '67

FRANCK, Frederick
Will the Dutch change Catholicism in America? excerpts from Exploding church. Look 32:17-21 Ja 23 '68

FRANCK, Kaj
Anonymity. Craft Horiz 27:34-5 Mr '67

FRANCO, Francisco
Franco's reforms: fact or façade? Christian Cent 84:195-6 F 15 '67
Ruler stalks the salmon; with report by B. Wise. il pors Life 63:101-4 D 8 '67
Spain: the vital years, by L. Bolin. Review Nat R 19:1081 O 3 '67. A. Lunn

FRANCO, Marjorie
Eye of love; story. Redbook 129:72-3 Ag '67
I am a gentle, peaceful man; story. Redbook 129:70-1 Je '67

FRANCO-GERMAN war, 1870-1871
American in Paris; B. Washburne, ambassador during Franco-Prussian war. S. Hess. il Am Heritage 18:18-27+ F '67

FRANCO-PRUSSIAN war. See Franco-German war, 1870-1871

FRANÇOIS-PONCET, André
Letter from Paris; excerpt from article Amica America, from Figaro; ed. by Genêt. New Yorker 43:181-3 Ap 15 '67

FRANCONIA NOTCH
See also
Profile Mountain

FRANIC, Frane, bp
Agreement between the Holy See and Yugoslavia; tr. by Z. Damjanov. Cath World 205:353-7 S '67

FRANK, Anne
Living legacy of Anne Frank. O. Frank. il por Ladies Home J 84:87+ S '67
White-gloved killers. por Newsweek 69:48 Ja 30 '67

FRANK, France
(ed) See Del Pierre, F. Francine Del Pierre

FRANK, Gretchen
Cammie; condensation. Read Digest 92:209-12+ Ja '68

FRANK, Isaiah
New perspectives on trade and development. For Affairs 45:520-40 Ap '67

FRANK, Jeffrey
Admissions; story; excerpt from The creep. Mlle 66:84-5 Ja '68

FRANK, Otto
Living legacy of Anne Frank. por Ladies Home J 84:87+ S '67

FRANK, Stanley
Life-or-death decision with a happy ending. Good H 165:48+ O '67
Most delicate problem in marriage. Good H 164:87+ Mr '67
Patricia Neal: suddenly I wanted to live! Good H 165:70-1+ Jl '67

FRANK, Waldo David
Obituary
Nation 204:101 Ja 23 '67
Pub W 191:92 Ja 30 '67

FRANKEL, Charles
Foreign policy for the future: address, May 1967. PTA Mag 62:2-4 S; 10-12 O '67
Some thoughts on education for world responsibility; adaptation of address, June 16, 1966. Sch & Soc 95:219-23 Ap 1 '67

about
International programs: Frankel resigns from State. D. S. Greenberg. por Science 158:1436 D 15 '67

FRANKEL, Haskel
On the fringe (cont) Sat R 50:22-3 S 2; 36-7 N 25 '67
(ed) See Kazan, E. Son of the oven-maker

FRANKEL, Jonathan
Communist rabbi: Moses Hess. bibliog f Commentary 41:77-81 Je '66; 43:23 Ja '67

FRANKEL, Max
Can we end the cold war? N Y Times Mag p20-1+ Ja 29; 37 F 26 '67
How long will it last? N Y Times Mag p28-9+ Ap 30 '67
Why the gap between L.B.J. and the Nation. N Y Times Mag p26-7+ Ja 7 '68

FRANKEL, Tobia
Parent and child. N Y Times Mag p93-6 My 7 '67

FRANKENHEIMER, John
Hollywood in Budapest. H. Alpert. il por Sat R 50:20-1+ D 23 '67

FRANKENSTEIN, Alfred
Chavez: the six splendid symphonies. Hi Fi 17:73 Ag '67
Electronic music with nary a blurp or a whine or a krontch. Hi Fi 17:75-6 D '67
Revivals reign in the Bay area. Hi Fi 17:MA22-3+ D '67
Visitation, home produced. Hi Fi 18:MA18-19 Ja '68

FRANKENTHALER, Helen
People are talking about... il por Vogue 149:190-1+ My '67

FRANKFORT book fair. See Book fairs

FRANKFORT ON THE MAIN
U.S. business pays tribute to Frankfurt; revival of Piper's court. il Bsns W p 110-12 S 9 '67

FRANKFURTER, Felix
FF and FDR. por Newsweek 71:73 Ja 15 '68

FRANKFURTERS
See also
Cookery—Meat

FRANKLIN, Adele
Christmas records for the young, 1967. Sat R 50:52-4 D 9 '67

FRANKLIN, Aretha
Aretha Franklin, sister soul. P. Garland. il pors Ebony 22:47-8+ O '67
Bringing it all together. il por Time 91:48 Ja 5 '68
Over the rainbow. P. D. Zimmerman. por Newsweek 70:70 Ag 21 '67

FRANKLIN, Benjamin
No mere dabbler, he. P. W. Schmidtchen. il pors Hobbies 72:104+ Ag '67
Souvenirs du grand Franklin. R. Davidson. Antiques 91:524 Ap '67

FRANKLIN, Dorothea Zucker-. See Zucker-Franklin, D.

FRANKLIN, Frederic
Capital surprise. H. Saal. il Newsweek 69:107-8 Ap 10 '67

FRANKLIN, Hardy
Reaching the nonuser. Wilson Lib Bul 41:943-6 My '67

FRANKLIN, Ron
Keeping house on the Kissimmee. Motor B 120:32-3 O '67

FRANKLIN, Rosalind
Double helix; the discovery of the structure of DNA; excerpts, with editorial comment. J. D. Watson. il Atlan 221:76-94+ Ja '68 (to be cont)

FRANKLIN, Viola L.
How I almost became a midwife in Africa. por Redbook 129:74-5+ O '67

FRANKLIN Delano Roosevelt memorial. See Washington, D.C.—Monuments, statues, etc.

FRANKLIN PARK, Ill.
Playground equipment. W. C. Kouns. il Parks & Rec 2:20 My '67

FRANKLIN stoves. See Stoves, Franklin

FRANKS, David
Six books by seven poets. R. Vas Dias. Poetry 110:189-90 Je '67

FRANTZ, John C.
Year of library change reported by Brooklyn; summary of annual report. Library J 92:3584+ O 15 '67

FRANZ Joseph II, prince of Liechtenstein. See Francis Joseph II

FRANZ, Dorothy
Festive breads cook book. House & Gard 131: 163+ My '67

FRANZBLAU, Abraham N.
Psychiatrist looks at The homecoming. Sat R 50:58 Ap 2 '67

FRANZEN, Ulrich
Complexity and contradiction in the work of Ulrich Franzen. il Arch Rec 142:133-44 O '67

FRAREY, Carlyle J.
Placement picture: 1966. por Library J 92: 2131-6, 2487 Je 1, Jl '67

FRASER, Charles E.
Charlie Fraser's island paradise. A. J. Reichley. il por Fortune 76:171+ O '67

FRASER, Charles H.
Mumps: fact and fallacy. Todays Health 45:8+ Ap '67

FRASER, Donald M.
Excerpt from address, April 28, 1966. Cong Digest 46:84+ Mr '67

FRASER, Dorothy M.
New social studies. NEA J 56:24-6 N '67

FRASER, Kathleen
Five poets. D. W. Baker. Poetry 111:198-200 D '67

FRATER, Alexander
Autumn sortie; story. New Yorker 43:52-6 O 21 '67
Practitioner; story. New Yorker 43:42-5 Ap 1 '67

FRATERNAL insurance. See Benefit societies

FRATERNITIES. See College fraternities

FRATTI, Mario
Eleonora Duse. Criticism
Sat R 50:22 Ag 5 '67

Die FRAU ohne schatten; opera. See Strauss, R.

FRAUD
Beware search for lost heirs! mailings based on name only. A. Peters. il Ebony 22:94-6+ Jl '67
Beware the highway's bad samaritans. J. Joseph. Motor T 19:83-4+ Jl '67
Case of the disloyal executive. T. J. Murray. Duns R 90:35-7+ D '67
Charge! gang defrauds Diners club. Time 90: 80 N 24 '67
Common thieves; swindlers collect illegal subsidies; EEC scandal. Newsweek 69:78 F 20 '67
Confidence man revisted. L. J. Averill. Christian Cent 84:277-8 Mr 1 '67
Consumer frauds; these schemes can cost you money. il Good H 164:208 Ap '67
Counterfeit prescriptions; traffic in substandard drugs. il Time 89:30 Je 2 '67
Dead men tell no tales; investigating the price rigging of eight stocks. il Newsweek 69:83 My 8 '67
Don't fall for home-repair gyps. il Changing T 21:13-16 My '67
Five common frauds, and how to avoid them. D. Wharton. Read Digest 91:69-72 D '67
Mafia: shadow of evil on an island in the sun. B. Davidson. il Sat Eve Post 240:27-37 F 25 '67
Post office protects consumers against fraud. Consumer Bul 50:19-20 N '67
Scandal in the Bahamas. R. Oulahan and W. Lambert. il Life 62:58-66+ F 3 '67
Scheme of the year; missing-heir dodge. Time 90:83 N 24 '67
Shysters, moochers, and gyp artists are exploiting our students! G. E. Shattuck. NEA J 56:66-7 D '67
Son of Billie Sol. il Newsweek 69:30+ Mr 20 '67
South Vietnam exists. D. Warner. il Reporter 37:18-20 S 21 '67
$3,000,000 sham. D. Nevin. il Life 62:82-6+ Ap 7 '67
Trying no. 2. Newsweek 70:63 S 25 '67
Unwelcome attention. Time 90:29 S 22 '67
Wall Street's own watchdogs; compliance men to prevent stock frauds. il Bsns W p90-2+ Jl 29 '67
Warning: land frauds are flourishing. Changing T 21:6 My '67
Watch out for fire alarm gyps! Consumer Bul 50:18 S '67
See also
Advertising, Fraudulent
Antiques, Forged
Commercial crimes
Counterfeits and counterfeiting
Forgery of works of art
Impostors and imposture
Politics, Corruption in
Quacks and quackery

FRAUDULENT conveyances
FBI warns about: the Christmas trade no business wants; planned bankruptcy. J. E. Hoover. il Nations Bsns 55:44-6+ N '67

FRAUMENI, Joseph F. Jr, and Miller, R. W.
Leukemia mortality: downturn rates in the United States. bibliog Science 155:1126-8 Mr 3 '67

FRAYN, Michael
Russell and Wittgenstein. Commentary 43: 68-75 My '67

FRAZER, John E. and Friggens, Paul
Must India starve? Read Digest 91:117-21 Jl '67

FRAZER, Oliver
Oliver Frazer, early Kentucky portrait painter. M. M. Bridwell. il Antiques 92:718-21 N '67

FRAZIER, George, 4th
If you behave yourself they might serve you a drink. Esquire 68:150-3 N '67
100 yards and sixty minutes of black power. Esquire 68:95-6+ O '67
Sense of style. Esquire 67:31-2+ Ap: 68:62+ S: 70+ N '67

FRAZIER, Joe
Bull market. il por Time 90:70 Jl 28 '67
Have a piece of Georgie boy. M. Kram. il Sports Illus 27:26-8 Jl 31 '67
He scowls like a champ. D. Wolf. il pors Life 63:33-4 Jl 14 '67
Heavyweight Joe Frazier: a stockholder's dream. il pors Ebony 23:136-42 N '67
Heavyweight market. il por Newsweek 70:50 Jl 31 '67
Sad farewell, a glad hello. M. Kram. il por Sports Illus 26:44+ Mr 6 '67
Will Joe Frazier be the next champ? B. J. Friedman. il pors Sat Eve Post 240:97-101 S 23 '67

FRAZIER, Julian
New giraffe house for Denver. Parks & Rec 2:32+ Mr '67

FRAZIER, Willard
Table for two; story. Good H 164:66-7 Ja '67

FREAS, Ralph
Big boom in tiny tape. Pop Mech 129:140-3+ Ja '68
What to look for in color TV sets. Am Home 70:38+ Mr '67
What's new in sight and sound. Am Home 70:50+ O '67

FREBERG, Stan
Fearful sell. Newsweek 69:83-4 My 8 '67
Kooky creator of antic advertising. il pors Bsns W p76+ Je 10 '67

FRED Hoskins fund. See Memorial funds

FREDERICK, John T.
Notes on natural history; poem. Poetry 111: 169-70 D '67

FREDERICK A. Praeger, incorporated. See Praeger, Frederick A, incorporated

FREDERICK Chusid and company. See Chusid, Frederick and company

FREDLAND, John Roger
Master of the job well done. Sat R 50:33+ D 16 '67

FREDRICKSON, Donald T.
Beauty checkout. Vogue 151:30 Ja 1 '68
King-size problem. G. Ace. Sat R 50:7 D 2 '67

FREDRICKSON, Olive A.
I had to have moose. Outdoor Life 139:70-3+ My '67
Wolves were the worst. Outdoor Life 139: 60-1+ Je '67

FREDRIKSON, Karin
Great Scandinavian cook book; excerpts. ed. by J. A. Ellison. Ladies Home J 84:88-9+ Je '67

FREE African societies. See Negroes in the United States—Societies

FREE enterprise
Advertising: let's stop tampering with the machinery; address, February 8, 1967. C. L. Gould. Vital Speeches 33:434-8 My 1 '67
Freedom's last frontier; business; address, November 17, 1966. L. H. Rogers, 2d. Vital Speeches 33:333-9 Mr 15 '67
Myths that keep people hungry. M. Friedman. Harper 234:16+ Ap '67
Role of private enterprise; adaptation of address, May 3, 1967. F. Keppel. il Library J 92:3807-11 O 15 '67
What people should know about our business system. il Nations Bsns 55:46-8+ My '67 (to be cont)
See also
Profit

FREE-lance writers. See Authors
FREE-lance writing. See Authorship
FREE library of Philadelphia. See Philadelphia
  —Free library
FREE press. See Freedom of the press
FREE radicals. See Radicals (chemistry)
FREE speech
  But can you do that? banning of anti-Vietnam
    war posters judged unconstitutional. H. F.
    Pilpel. Pub W 192:24-5 N 27 '67
  Free speech: some limits set by High court.
    il U S News 63:51 D 4 '67
  Glossary; dissent, the right to sing the blues.
    M. Greenfield. Reporter 36:42 Je 15 '67
  Holy human empire; or, Whatever happened
    to the secular city? M. Novak. Christian
    Cent 85:37-8 Ja 10 '68
  Let's forget the First amendment. il Sat Eve
    Post 240:90 Je 17 '67
  Patriotism and Vietnam; concerning W. C.
    Westmoreland's speech against critics of
    U.S. policy. N. Cousins. Sat R 50:26+ My
    13 '67
  Pest of glory; concerning polemics of W. G.
    Sumner. E. J. Hughes. Newsweek 70:13
    Ag 21 '67
  Philadelphia story; the Joe McGinniss col-
    umn. New Repub 157:10-11 S 30 '67
  Prohibited speech. NEA J 56:54-5 Ap '67
  Requiem for the FSM; Free speech movement.
    Newsweek 70:48 Jl 3 '67
  Responsible for the abuse of that liberty;
    First amendment. R. L. Tobin. Sat R 51:
    107-8 Ja 13 '68
  Right to answer dissent Life 62:4 My 12 '67
  Right to disent & the duty to answer; Time
    essay. Time 89:23 My 12 '67
  Self-corrective process; freedom of dissent.
    il Time 89:17-18 My 12 '67
  Sneak attacks on American freedom; proposed
    bills to stifle criticism of Vietnam war.
    Christian Cent 84:1515-16 N 29 '67
    See also
  Libel and slander
FREE trade and protection
  Completing the work of the Kennedy round;
    address, October 5, 1967. W. M. Roth. Dept
    State Bul 57:574-8 O 30 '67
  Holding back on foreign trade. Bsns W p83-4
    S 2 '67
  Last protectionist charge. Reporter 37:10-11
    D 14 '67
  Price of protectionism; statements, with text
    of letter, October 18, 1967. Dept State Bul
    57:634-52 N 13 '67
  Protectionism, a policy of retreat; address,
    October 30, 1967. N. D. Katzenbach. Dept
    State Bul 57:686-9 N 20 '67; Same. Vital
    Speeches 34:119-21 D 1 '67
  Rich scent of protectionism in the air. il
    Newsweek 70:77-9 O 30 '67
  Road test for auto trade accord; U.S.-Canada
    pact. il Bsns W p55-6 Je 17 '67
  Trade backlash? protectionism revived. Sr
    Schol 91:13-14 N 9 '67
    See also
  Import quotas
  Tariff
FREE trade area, Latin American. See Latin
  American free trade association
FREE universities
  Do-it-yourself college; Free university,
    Seattle. America 116:576 Ap 22 '67
  On campus; free university: chaos or a new
    establishment? college board members re-
    port. Mlle 65:55-7+ My '67
  Teaching teachers; the free universities. R.
    Keyes. Nation 205:294-9 O 2 '67
    See also
  Institute for the study of nonviolence
FREE university of Berlin. See Colleges and
  universities—Germany (Federal Republic)
FREE will and determinism
  Evolutionary science and the dilemma of
    freedom and determinism. L. Gilkey. Chris-
    tian Cent 84:339-43 Mr 15 '67; Discussion.
    84:592, 755-7 My 3, Je 7 '67
FREED, Melvyn N.
  Regional education laboratories: bane or ben-
    efit? Sch & Soc 95:492 D 9 '67
FREED, Richard
  Colors we hear. House B 109:140+ My '67
  Farewell to Feuerfest. Sat R 50:74 S 30 '67
  Leslie Haydn-Jones. Sat R 50:78 Mr 25 '67
  Vintage Strauss. Sat R 50:88 F 25 '67
  (comp) Year's best recordings. Sat R 50:91-5
    N 25 '67
FREEDMAN, Daniel G.
  Evolutionary view emerges. Sci N 93:6-7 Ja 6
    '68
FREEDMAN, Florence B.
  New English. PTA Mag 62:6-8 bibliog(p34)
    Ja '68

FREEDMAN, Frances
  Religious libraries and reading rooms. Wilson
    Lib Bul 42:318-21 N '67
FREEDMAN, Michael L. and others
  Membranes in polyribosome formation by
    rabbit reticulocytes. bibliog Science 157:323-5
    Jl 21 '67
FREEDMAN, Richard
  Dorothy Richardson in limbo. Nation 205:280-1
    S 25 '67
FREEDMAN, Samuel J.
  They go in smiling; interview. New Yorker
    42:26-7 F 4 '67
FREEDOM. See Liberty
FREEDOM, Integration, God, honor, today
  (organization) See Civil rights organiza-
  tions
FREEDOM, Intellectual. See Intellectual liberty
FREEDOM in science. See Science, Freedom of
FREEDOM of information. See Information,
  Freedom of
FREEDOM of religion. See Religious liberty
FREEDOM of speech. See Free speech
FREEDOM of the press
  Corrupt church; concerning editorial in New
    blackfriars. Commonweal 85:612 Mr 3 '67
  Freedom is everybody's business; address,
    February 27, 1967. S. Smith. Vital Speeches
    33:361-4 Ap 1 '67
  Jersey justice and LeRoi Jones. R. H. Smith.
    Pub W 193:66 Ja 15 '68
  Less than half the world; University of
    Missouri survey findings. R. L. Tobin.
    Sat R 50:47-8 Jl 8 '67
  Right to privacy. M. Mead. Redbook 128:30+
    Ap '67
  Strange coincidence; concerning editorial
    freedom in the Catholic press. S. J. Adamo.
    America 116:322-3 Mr 4 '67
    See also
  Censorship
  Free speech
  Government and the press
  Libel and slander
FREEDOM of the seas
    See also
  Territorial waters
FREEDOM of the will. See Free will and de-
  terminism
FREEDOM of thought. See Intellectual liberty
FREEDOM studies center
  Military seminars; the mongers return. R.
    Dudman. il Nation 204:101-5 Ja 23 '67
FREEDOM to know. See Information, Freedom
  of
FREEDOM to read. See Intellectual liberty
FREEDOM to travel. See Travel regulations
FREEHAFER, Edward G.
  Ten wonders of NYPL selected by Freehafer.
    Library J 92:954 Mr 1 '67
FREELING, Nicolas
  Authors & editors. por Pub W 191:25 My 29 '67
FREEMAN, A. D.
  Flowers; poem. Sat R 50:31 My 20 '67
FREEMAN, Alan R. See Brandt, P. W. jt.
  auth.
FREEMAN, Anne Hobson
  Long and short of it. McCalls 95:68+ O '67
FREEMAN, Arthur
  Transistors; poem. New Yorker 43:106 D 16 '67
    about
  Seven poets. R. Tillinghast. Poetry 110:261-3
    Jl '67
FREEMAN, C.
  Research comparisons. bibliog Science 158:
    463-8 O 27 '67
FREEMAN, Fulton
  Latin American nations conclude nuclear
    free zone treaty; statement, February 13,
    1967. Dept State Bul 56:436 Mr 13 '67
FREEMAN, Jim
  Best ways to hunt rabbits East to West. Field
    & S 72:46-7+ Ja '68
FREEMAN, John W.
  Drawn from within. Opera N 31:24-5 Ap 1
    '67
  Maestro in Riverdale. Sat R 50:60-1 Mr 25 '67
  Spaceship to nowhere Opera N 31:14-15 My
    13 '67
FREEMAN, Maurice
  Blue chips represent good value; interview.
    por U S News 63:38-40 D '67
FREEMAN, Neal B.
  Men around Nixon. Nat R 19:1118-19+ O 17
    '67
  Muted thunder. Nat R 19:530-1 My 16 '67
  V-day in Omaha. Nat R 19:747 Jl 11 '67

FREEMAN, Orville Lothrop
Agriculture; address, January 20, 1967. Vital Speeches 33:290-4 Mr 1 '67
Agricuiture's stake in the Kennedy round; address, July 7, 1967. Dept State Bul 57:132-6 Jl 31 '67
Freeman answers cheap food charges. Farm J 91:35-6 Ag '67
Malthus, Marx and the North American breadbasket. For Affairs 45:579-93 Jl '67; Excerpts. por U S News 63:40-4 Jl 3 '67
Mr Freeman looks ahead. por Am For 73:10-11+ Ap '67
Price of protectionism; statement, October 18, 1967. Dept State Bul 57:642-5 N 13 '67

about
Mr Freeman's response to reorganization. J. B. Craig. Am For 73:11+ D '67
On the prongs. Time 90:14-15 Jl 14 '67

FREEMAN, Richard, family
Talent for living: sleeping beauty awakened, old iron-balconied house in New Orleans' old French Quarter. il House & Gard 132:164-9 S '67

FREEMAN, Roger A.
What makes Ivan run? Nat R 19:246-9, 961-2+ Mr 7, S 5 '67

FREEPORT sulphur company
Freeport says it with sulfur. il Bsns W p72-6 N 4 '67
Squeeze on sulfur. Bsns W p54 Mr 25 '67

FREEWAYS. See Express highways

FREEZE, Mrs Alys
Get rich quick scheme in the American West. por Wilson Lib Bul 41:603-5 F '67

FREEZER food plans. See Food, Frozen

FREEZERS
Are you getting the most out of your freezer? Bet Hom & Gard 45:121 Ap '67
Choose the right food freezer for your farm home. J. LemMon. il Suc Farm 65:54-5 Je '67
Prefab walk-in coolers and freezers meet changing demands for food storage. G. M. Prince. il Arch Rec 141:201-2 Je '67
Refrigerator-freezer report; with questions and answers. il Good H 164:154+ Ap '67
Side-by-side combination refrigerator freezers. il Consumer Bul 50:9-16 Jl '67
Something new in home refrigerators: Food-life preserver. il Consumer Bul 51:30-1 Ja '68
What to do if your freezer stops working. Good H 164:154 F '67

FREEZING
Amateur scientist; on equipment to study freezing. E. M. Little. il Sci Am 218:128-31 Ja '68
Dimethyl sulfoxide protects tightly coupled mitochondria from freezing damage. D. B. Dickinson and others. bibliog il Science 156:1738-9 Je 30 '67
See also
Frostbite
Ice

FREEZING (therapy)   See Cold—Therapeutic applications

FREEZING of food
Farm home freezing guide. il Suc Farm 65:50+ Je '67
Freeze ahead now for the unexpected. il Sunset 138:202+ Ap '67
Sweets to store. il McCalls 95:118-20+ N '67
See also
Food, Frozen

FREGIA, Theresa
Well drillers save trapped girl; Votaw, Tex. il por Am City 82:95 My '67

FREI, Eduardo
Bid for control. por Time 91:25 Ja 19 '68
Caught in the middle. Time 91:36 Ja 5 '68
Classic blunder. Newsweek 69:64 Ap 17 '67
Eduardo Frei is trying a revolution without the execution wall. B. Collier. il por N Y Times Mag p30-1+ F 19 '67
Frei's visit vetoed. il Sr Schol 90:16-17 F 10 '67
How free is Frei? D. D. Ranstead. Commonweal 85:549-50 F 17 '67
Last, best hope, by L. Gross. Review
New Repub 157:30-1 D 23 '67. J. A. Page
President Frei of Chile to visit the United States; statement, December 20, 1966. L. B. Johnson. Dept State Bul 56:71 Ja 9 '67
President regrets. por Newsweek 69:53 Ja 30 '67
Setback for Frei. Time 89:49 Ap 14 '67
Stalemate in Chile. G. W. Grayson, jr. New Repub 156:14 F 4 '67
Travel ban. Time 89:36 Ja 27 '67

FREIBURG, E. R. von, pseud.
Half & half equals two. Nation 204:502-6 Ap 17 '67

FREIDENBERG, Edgar Z.
Irreverent dissection of libraries; excerpts from address, June 23, 1967, ed. by G. Dusheck. Wilson Lib Bul 42:180 O '67

FREIDIN, Seymour
Whatever happened to Europe? Sat R 50:22-4 My 13 '67

FREIGHT airplanes. See Airplanes, Freight

FREIGHT and freightage
See also
Air freight service
Railroads—Freight service
Railroads—Rates
Trucking

FREIGHT cars. See Railroads—Freight cars

FREIGHT handling
Airline freight handling deficiencies cited. R. G. O'Lone. Aviation W 87:33 Jl 31 '67
Airlines get ready for new VIP; air freight terminal. il Bsns W p 116-18+ My 13 '67
Braniff automates for full-scale move into cargo market. E. J. Bulban. il Aviation W 87:30-2 Jl 31 '67
Major shift seen in blocked-space policy; combination airlines to sell blocked freight space. J. W. Carter. Aviation W 87:41 O 9 '67
Protests anticipated in forwarder ruling; three trucking companies to enter air-freight forwarding. Aviation W 87:33 O 2 '67
Test set for safer helicopter cargo plan; testing army's cargo helicopters in Vietnam. D. A. Brown. il Aviation W 86:85-6 My 22 '67
Tighter security on cargo sought.   R. F. Coburn. Aviation W 87:26-9 S 4 '67
See also
Container system (freight handling)
Containers for shipping
Loading and unloading
Merchant marine

FREIGHT rates. See Railroads—Rates

FREIGHT vessels
Speeding the schedule of seagoing cargo; the Lash and the Seabee. il Bsns W p 124+ Ag 26 '67

FREISER, Leonard H.
Civilized network; adaptation of address, May 30, 1967. por Library J 92:3001-3 S 15 '67
Viewpoint. por Library J 93:166-7 Ja 15 '68

FREITAG, George H.
Old man and his hat; story. Harper 234:96-7 Je '67

FREMANTLE, Anne
Micawber sahib. Reporter 36:46 My 4 '67

FRENAYE, Frances
(tr) See Rosselli, A.   Descent from the hill

FRENCH, Bevan M.
Sudbury structure, Ontario: some petrographic evidence for origin by meteorite impact. bibliog Science 156:1094-8 My 26 '67

FRENCH, Charles
Coin quiz. See issues of Hobbies
Numismatics. See issues of Hobbies

FRENCH, David S.
Does the U.S. exploit the developing nations? Commonweal 86:257-9 My 19 '67

FRENCH, Herb
Travel notes. Holiday 41:4+ Ap; 6+ My; 4+ Je '67

FRENCH, William
Canadian culture. Christian Cent 84:906-10 Jl 12 '67

FRENCH, William Marshall
New federally supported Ciceronianism. Sch & Soc 95:349-50 O 14 '67

FRENCH
French national character in the twentieth century. R. Virtanen. bibliog f Ann Am Acad 370:82-92 Mr '67
See also
Parisians

FRENCH academy
Le mot juste; dictionary to bar foreign immigrant-words. F. C. Livingstone. Sci N 92:21 Jl 1 '67

FRENCH academy of science
Never on Mars. A. Glasser. il Sci Digest 61:81-3 F '67

FRENCH architecture. See Architecture, French

FRENCH artificial satellites. See Artificial satellites, French

FRENCH athletes. See Athletes

FRENCH authors. See Authors, French

FRENCH automobiles. See Automobiles, Foreign

FRENCH CANADA. See Quebec (province)

FRENCH CANADIANS
Hark to the elder institutions! letters. L.
Kerwin; E. O. Dodson. Science 155:256 Ja
20 '67
Push for autonomy picks up in Quebec;
demands for constitutional reform. il
Bsns W p 146+ Ag 19 '67
See also
Quebec (province)
FRENCH caves. See Caves
FRENCH cookery. See Cookery, French
FRENCH exiles. See Exiles
FRENCH furniture. See Furniture, French
FRENCH GUIANA
Faithful daughters. M. J. Kubic. il News-
week 69:63-4 Mr 13 '67
FRENCH language

Foreign words and phrases
Le mot juste; dictionary to bar foreign immigrant-words. F. C. Livingstone. Sci N
92:21 Jl 1 '67

Study and teaching
Happenings in education; teaching spoken
French to children in England. W. D. Bout-
well. PTA Mag 62:9-10 D '67
It helps if you know both of the languages;
English-speaking Canadians flocking to
French classes. il Bsns W p96-7 N 25 '67
FRENCH line. See Steamship lines
FRENCH literary prizes. See Literary prizes
FRENCH literature
French literary prizes, 1967. H. R. Lottman.
il Pub W 192:25-8 D 25 '67
FRENCH military assistance. See Military as-
sistance, French
FRENCH national lotteries. See Lotteries
FRENCH novelists. See Novelists, French
FRENCH painting. See Painting, French
FRENCH poetry
French chronicle. P. Zweig. Poetry 111:124-9
N '67
FRENCH portraits. See Portraits, French
FRENCH pottery. See Pottery, French
FRENCH revolution. See France—History—
Revolution
FRENCH RIVIERA. See Riviera
FRENCH SOMALILAND. See Somaliland,
French
FRENCH visitors in Ireland. See Foreign visi-
tors in Ireland
FRENCH visitors in the United States. See
Foreign visitors in the United States
FRENCH WEST AFRICA
See also
Cotonou, Dahomey
FRENCH women. See Women—France
FRENCHBORO, Me.
Island that borrows its children. J. Skow. il
Sat Eve Post 240:87-91 Mr 25 '67; Same abr.
Read Digest 90:79-83 Je '67
FRENEAU, Philip Morin
Philip Freneau, by J. Axelrad. Review
Sat R 50:23-9 Je 24 '67. R. L. Tobin
FRENZEL, Louis E. Jr.
Digital plotting techniques. Electr World 77:
47-50+ Mr '67
FREONS
Chill of death; cocktail glass chillers. News-
week 70:60 O 16 '67
Trips that kill; fumes from cocktail-glass
chiller. il Time 90:77 O 13 '67
FREQUENCY, Radio. See Radio frequency
FREQUENCY allocation, Radio. See Radio
frequency allocation
FREQUENCY curves
Extended resonance curves. D. E. Lancaster.
il Electr World 78:36 N '67
FREQUENCY measurements
Digital U.H.F. frequency measurements. W.
Barden. il Electr World 78:48-50 N '67
Frequency measurements with the electronic
counter. A. W. Edwards. il Electr World
77:84 Ja '67
FREQUENCY meters
Build direct readout IC freq meter. D. Lan-
caster. il Pop Electr 27:53-6+ O '67
Build the electronic frequency meter. W.
Henry. il Pop Electr 26:73-7 My '67
FREQUENCY modulation. See Radio frequency
modulation
FREQUENCY modulation receivers. See Radio
receivers—Frequency modulation receivers
FREQUENCY modulation transmitters. See
Radio transmitters—Frequency modulation
transmitters

FREQUENCY standards
Selecting frequency and time standards. I.
Math. il Electr World 77:40-1+ My '67
FRERICHS, Allen H. See Mueller, R. J. jt.
auth.
FRESCOES
Important discoveries of renaissance art in
Florence. M. Meiss. il Art N 66:26-7+ Sum
'67
In Florence, new troubles and new treasures.
il Life 62:54-9 Je 30 '67
FRESE, Paul F.
Decorate with material from your garden.
Horticulture 45:16-23 D '67
Iris for every garden. Horticulture 45:38-40
My '67
Put color highlights in your summer garden.
Pop Gard 18:32-5+ Ag '67
There's variety in tulips. Pop Gard 18:48-51
D '67
Treat yourself to a riot of color in your
spring garden. Pop Gard 18:52-3 My '67
FRESH air charity
How to give a child a rare vacation. S.
Schuler. Am Home 70:54+ Je '67
They went out men and women; they have
come back children. E. F. Hunter. Chris-
tian Cent 84:720-2 My 31 '67
FRESH water flora. See Aquatic plants
FRESHMEN. See College students
FRESHWATER limpet. See Limpets
FRESNO COUNTY, Calif.
Floodlighting a courthouse. C. D. Beery. il
Am City 82:118 Ag '67
FRESNOITE
Fresnoite: unusual titanium coordination. P.
B. Moore and J. Louisnathan. bibliog il
Science 156:1361-2 Je 9 '67
FREUD, Sigmund
Books. G. Steiner. New Yorker 42:111-14+
Ja 21 '67
Bullitt to Wilson. R. Coles. New Repub 156:
27-30 Ja 28 '67
Can history use Freud? the case of Woodrow
Wilson. B. W. Tuchman. Atlan 219:39-44
F '67
Freud and his own patients. D. M. Kaplan.
Harper 235:99-100+ D '67
Freudian analysis founders on Wilson book.
P. McBroom. il por Sci N 91:88-9 Ja 28 '67
Freudianism. R. L. Zimmerman. Commentary
43:75-9 Je '67; Discussion. 44:24+ O '67
FREUDISM. See Psychoanalysis
FREUND, Rudolf
On a piece of chalk: illustrations for Thomas
Huxley. il Pub W 191:104+ Mr 6 '67
FREUNDLICH, Martin
Valyl-transfer RNA: role in repression of
the isoleucine-valine enzymes in escherichia
coli. bibliog Science 157:823-5 Ag 18 '67
FREY, Donald Nelson
Thinker (Detroit style) por Time 89:94 Ap
21 '67
FREY, Peter W. and Polidora, V. J.
Magnesium pemoline: effect on avoidance
conditioning in rats. bibliog Science 155:
1281-2 Mr 10 '67
FREYER, Grattan
Retrospect on O'Faolain. New Repub 156:28-
30 F 25 '67
FREYMAN, Leonard
Thriving youth theater. NEA J 57:26-7 Ja '68
FREYRE, Gilberto
Brazilian national character in the twentieth
century. bibliog f Ann Am Acad 370:57-62
Mr '67
FRIBOURG, Switzerland
Your own Swiss discovery. il Sunset 138:45-6
My '67
FRICK, Helen Clay
Authors & editors. Pub W 191:176-7 Ja 23 '67
Essay; filial piety and the First amendment.
O. Jensen. il por Am Heritage 18:2-4 O '67
Final arguments heard in Frick-Stevens
libel case. il Pub W 191:222-6 Ja 23 '67
Frick-Stevens battle enters new phase. Pub
W 192:44 Ag 21 '67
High court denies Stevens' plea. Pub W 191:
43 My 29 '67
History and privacy; dismissal of Frick law-
suit. America 116:848 Je 17 '67
History, warts and all. il por Newsweek 69:
64-5 Je 5 '67
Pitt vs. Frick. Newsweek 69:101 F 20 '67
Stevens asks High court to enjoin Miss
Frick. Pub W 191:37 Ap 17 '67
Stevens' book vindicated by Pennsylvania
court; judge terms book true and excellent
history; with editorial comment. Pub W 191:
144+, 152 Je 5 '67

FRICK, Helen Clay—*Continued*
U.S. Court of appeals denies Stevens' motion for injunction restraining Helen Frick. Pub W 191:52 F 13 '67
Victory for historians. il Time 89:55 Je 2 '67

FRICK, Henry Clay
Essay: filial piety and the First amendment. O. Jensen. il por Am Heritage 18:2-4 O '67

FRICKER, John
Americans are coming! Flying 80:44-7 Je '67
Blue ribbon entry. Flying 80:118-21 Mr '67
Foreign accent. See issues of Flying
Handley Page Jetstream. Flying 81:68-70 Jl '67
Well-tempered Hansa jet. Flying 81:46-51 O '67

FRICTION
See also
Bearings (machinery)

FRIEBERT, Stuart
Fishing off France, summer 1962; poem. Cath World 205:164 Je '67

FRIED, Barbara
Middle-age crisis. McCalls 94:88-9+ Mr '67

FRIED, George H. and others
Alpha-glycerophosphate dehydrogenase and glucose-6-phosphate dehydrogenase in tissues of the Weddell seal. bibliog Science 155:1560-1 Mr 24 '67

FRIED, Lawrence
Lawrence Fried's live color. il Pop Phot 60:100-5+ F '67

FRIED, Morton H.
Emperor's conversion. Sat R 50:50-1 F 25 '67
Those mad Chinese. Nation 204:262-4 F 27 '67

FRIEDBERG, Maurice
Computerized humanity. Sat R 50:31 D 23 '67
Siberia: reality was tragic. Sat R 50:35-6 O 7 '67

FRIEDEBERG, Pedro
Two young rebels in Mexican painting. A. de Neuvillate. il por Américas 19:8-16 Mr '67

FRIEDEL, Ludwig
How to see a picture in color. il Mod Phot 31:84-9+ F '67

FRIEDEN, Earl. See Flores, G. jt. auth.

FRIEDEN-stag; opera. See Strauss, R.

FRIEDENBERG, Edgar Z.
Doctor Edgar Friedenberg: our most devastating critic; statements; ed. by C. Brossard. por Look 31:73-5 My 30 '67
Hooked on law enforcement. Nation 205:360-5 O 16 '67
Requiem for the urban school. Sat R 50:77-9+ N 18 '67
about
Education's romantic critics. P. Schrag. por Sat R 50:80-2+ F 18 '67

FRIEDENSOHN, Elias
Anatomy of an assassination. il por Time 90:96 S 29 '67
Who killed McKinley? F. Getlein. Commonweal 87:301+ D 1 '67

FRIEDLANDER, Paul J. C.
Twenty years of travel writing: Michelin, Baedeker, or bust. Sat R 50:40+ Ap 22 '67

FRIEDLANDER, Peter H. and others
Can you use rail rapid transit? Am City 82:120-2 Ap '67

FRIEDMAN, Bruce Jay
Adam Powell at the end of the world. Sat Eve Post 240:26-9 My 20 '67
Arrested by detectives Valesares and Sullivan, charge: murder. Sat Eve Post 240:38-42+ Ap 22 '67
Pledges; story. Esquire 68:133 S '67
Scientist; story. Esquire 67:105 Ap '67
Will Joe Frazier be the next champ? Sat Eve Post 240:97-101 S 23 '67
about
Bruce Jay Friedman is hanging by his thumbs. J. Greenfeld. il por N Y Times Mag p30-2+ Ja 14 '68
Scuba duba. Criticism
America 117:486-7 O 28 '67
Commentary 44:84 D '67
Life il 63:119-20+ N 17 '67
Nation 205:438-9+ O 30 '67
New Repub 157:31-3 O 28 '67
N Y Times Mag il p30-2+ Ja 14 '68
New Yorker 43:82+ O 21 '67
Newsweek il 70:113+ O 23 '67
Time il 90:82+ O 20 '67

FRIEDMAN, Gilbert B.
High flying fares. New Repub 156:19-21 Mr 4 '67

FRIEDMAN, Harvey Martin
I just thought faster. por Newsweek 70:53 O 2 '67
Nineteen-year-old professor teaches philosophy at Stanford university. il pors Life 63:111-12 O 27 '67

FRIEDMAN, Herbert, and Byram, E. T.
X-rays from sources 3C 273 and M 87. bibliog Science 158:257-9 O 13 '67
—and others
Distribution and variability of cosmic X-ray sources. bibliog Science 156:374-8 Ap 21 '67

FRIEDMAN, L. and Irsa, A. P.
Variations in the isotopic composition of carbon in urban atmospheric carbon dioxide. bibliog Science 158:263-4 O 13 '67

FRIEDMAN, Lillian
World of books. Writer 80:5-6 N; 10 D '67; 81:4+ Ja '68

FRIEDMAN, Martin
Carpenter Gothic. Art N 66:30-1+ Mr '67

FRIEDMAN, Milton
Alleviation of poverty; excerpt from Capitalism and freedom. Nat R 19:240-1 Mr 7 '67
Case for abolishing the draft, and substituting for it an all-volunteer army. N Y Times Mag p23+ My 14 '67
Case for the negative income tax. Nat R 19:239-40 Mr 7 '67
[Column on economic questions] See issues of Newsweek
Excerpt from address, December 9, 1966. Cong Digest 46:240+ O '67
Myths that keep people hungry. Harper 234:16+ Ap '67
about
Radical economics of Milton Friedman. J. Davenport. por Fortune 75:130-2+ Je 1 '67
What happens when Fed changes its tune? il por Bsns W p 188+ Ap 15 '67

FRIEDMAN, Richard N.
Society; poem. Negro Hist Bul 30:7 My '67

FRIEDMAN, Robert M.
Interferon binding: the first step in establishment of antiviral activity. bibliog Science 156:1760-1 Je 30 '67

FRIEDMAN, Saul
Focus on Cleveland. Nat R 19:1335-6 N 28 '67
Riots, violence & civil rights. Nat R 19:898-904+ Ag 22 '67
Successor to Adam Powell? New Repub 156:12-13 F 4 '67
Two Vietnams, one there, the other here; reprint. U S News 63:25 Ag 14 '67

FRIEDMAN, Stanley
Trehalose regulation of glucose-6-phosphate hydrolysis in blowfly extracts. bibliog Science 159:110-11 Ja 5 '68

FRIEDRICH, Otto
Grave of Alice B. Toklas. Esquire 69:98-103+ Ja '68

FRIEDRICHS, G. Shelby, jr
Buddy Friedrichs on Dragon slaying. por Yachting 122:30-1+ Ag; 54+ S '67

FRIEND, Charlotte. See Reem, G. H. jt. auth.

FRIEND leukemia viruses. See Leukemia viruses

FRIENDLY, Alfred
In Turkey, everything comes up roses. Harper 234:85-9 F '67

FRIENDLY, Fred W.
Great sellout to soap opera; excerpt from Due to circumstances beyond our control. por Life 62:84+ Mr 17 '67
Need for public television; summary of address, March 7, 1967. Pub W 191:35 Mr 20 '67
Retrieving a lost rocket; excerpt from Due to circumstances beyond our control . . . pors Life 62:70-2+ Mr 24 '67
Television fiasco; interview. por U S News 62:58-62 Je 12 '67
about
Behind the screens at CBS. R. J. Landry. por Sat R 50:30-1 Ap 1 '67
Books. M. Muggeridge. Esquire 68:8+ Ag '67
Due to circumstances beyond our control . . . por Life 62:82-3 Mr 17 '67
Fred Friendly and Friendlyvision. H. Swados. il pors N Y Times Mag p30-1+ Ap 23 '67
Friendly persuasion. R. L. Shayon. Sat R 50:71 Ap 8 '67
Friendly persuasion. por Newsweek 69:92 Mr 27 '67
Moose & the moneymen. por Time 89:46+ Ap 7 '67
Saving the world every week; See it now series and CBS reports. E. Weeks. Atlan 219:124-6 My '67
Television. J. Horn. Nation 204:476-7 Ap 10 '67

FRIENDLY ISLANDS. See Tonga (islands)

FRIENDS, Society of
Are Quakers going denominational? Christian Cent 84:1060-1 Ag 23 '67; Reply. W. Hubben. 84:1290 O 11 '67
Hanoi and the trek of the Phoenix. C. P Zietlow. Christian Cent 84:1004-6 Ag 2 '67
Have the Quakers a message? J. B. Sheerin. Cath World 206:2-3 O '67
Mercy crosses the Peace bridge; Quakers sending medical aid to civilians in Vietnam. Christian Cent 84:493 Ap 19 '67
Pray for the Phoenix; medical supplies consigned to the Red cross society of North Vietnam for the relief of civilian suffering. Christian Cent 84:366 Mr 22 '67
Quaker underground; sending of medicines to war victims in North and South Vietnam. New Repub 156:7-8 Ja 28 '67
Quaker witness at the Peace bridge. C. E. Fager. Christian Cent 84:602-4 My 3 '67
Quakers of the world confer; fourth Friends world conference. D. V. Steere. Christian Cent 84:1140-2 S 6 '67; Reply. R. M. Jones. 84:1290 O 11 '67
Questioning Quakers; first formal seminary proposed. il Newsweek 69:113 My 8 '67
Singing friends. il Time 90:41 Ag 11 '67
Troubling voyage to North Vietnam; Quakers aboard Phoenix with medical supplies, ed. by W. Hedgepeth. I. Massar. il Look 31:17-21 Je 27 '67
See also
American Friends service committee

FRIENDS of French opera, incorporated
Le jongleur returns; Massenet's opera at St George's church in New York. W. Brockway. il Opera N 31:6-7 Ap 15 '67
Musical events; performance of Massenet's Le jongleur de Notre Dame in St George's church. W. Sargeant. New Yorker 43:157 My 6 '67

FRIENDS of the library
Statewide friends group formed in New Jersey. Library J 92:4457 D 15 '67

FRIENDS service committee, American. See American Friends service committee

FRIENDS world institute, New York
Idea of a world university, by M. Zweig. Review
Bul Atomic Sci 23:34-5 O '67. E. U. Condon
Newest campus: the world. R. Connable. il Mlle 65:180-1+ O '67

FRIENDSHIP
In my opinion: a friend is not a jury. V. Riba. Seventeen 26:192 Je '67
Speaking out; we've lost the art of friendship. H. Calisher. il Sat Eve Post 240:10+ Ag 26 '67
What ever happened to friendship? questions and answers. A. Wood. Seventeen 26:184+ S '67
What teenage friendships are all about. E. G. Neisser. il Parents Mag 42:48-50+ Jl '67
See also
Love

FRIESEN, Abram J. D. and others
Calcium-induced activation of phosphorylase in rat hearts. bibliog Science 155:1108-9 Mr 3 '67

FRIESWYK, Siebolt H.
Federal grants for cultural recreation. Parks & Rec 2:22+ F '67

FRIGATE birds
Skyway robbery! with photographs by F. B. Peck. Audubon 69:58-60 My '67

FRIGATES, Atomic powered. See Warships, Atomic powered

FRIGGENS, Paul
Case for enlightened sex education. Read Digest 90:73-7 My '67
Royal revolution in Iran. Read Digest 91:127-31 O '67
Shameful neglect of sex education. PTA Mag 61:4-7 bibliog(p37) My '67; Same abr. with title Case for enlightened sex education. Read Digest 90:73-7 My '67
—See Frazer, J. E. jt. auth.

FRINGE benefits. See Non-wage payments

FRINK, James
Entomography. il Pop Phot 60:96-7 Je '67

FRISBY, Terence
There's a girl in my soup. Criticism
America 117:623-4 N 18 '67
Life 63:20 D 8 '67
Vogue 150:172 D '67

FRISCH, Bruce H.
Our moving continents. Sci Digest 63:46-8+ Ja '68

FRISCH, Karl von
Honeybees: do they use direction and distance information provided by their dancers? bibliog Science 158:1072-6 N 24 '67

FRISCH, O. R.
Books. Sci Am 216:145-8+ Je '67

FRISSELL, Sidney S. jr
Educating recreational professionals. Parks & Rec 2:30+ Ap '67

FRISSELL, Toni
Midsummer dream; photographs. Vogue 149:152-7+ Je '67
About
Toni Frissell, in her fashion; retrospective at New York's Hallmark gallery. M. R. Weiss. il Sat R 50:48-9 O 21 '67

FRITCHEY, Clayton
'68 is not like '12 or '32. N Y Times Mag p25-7+ D 17 '67
Washington insight. See issues of Harper's magazine

FRITZ, David H.
Packaged insurance plan. Parks & Rec 2:41-2 D '67
Skeet shooting scores a bull's-eye. Am City 82:94 Jl '67

FRITZ, Jean
Catch a falling star; story. Seventeen 26:90-1 D '67
On writing historical fiction. Horn Bk 43:565-70 O '67
Season of renewal; story. McCalls 95:126-7 D '67

FRITZ, Paul J.
Rabbit lactate dehydrogenase isozymes: effect of pH on activity. bibliog Science 156:82-3 Ap 7 '67

FROEHLICH, Doris A.
How to dry flowers. House & Gard 131:30+ My '67

FROESE, Leonhard
Soviet higher education: ideal and reality; excerpts from book. Sch & Soc 95:455-8 N 25 '67

FROG cerebellum. See Cerebellum

FROG men. See United States—Navy—Underwater demolition teams

FROGHOPPERS
Insect that spits its nest; photographs. Sci Digest 62:28-9 Jl '67

FROGS
Cerebellar Purkinje cell projection to the peripheral vestibular organ in the frog. R. Llinás and others. bibliog il Science 158:1328-30 D 8 '67
Cocoon surrounding desert-dwelling frogs. A. K. Lee and E. H. Mercer. bibliog il Science 157:87-8 Jl 7 '67
Fast potential spike of frog skin generated at the outer surface of the epithelium. B. Lindemann and U. Thorns. bibliog il Science 158:1473-7 D 15 '67
Frog comes to Hawaii; importing dendrobates auratus from Panama. H. L. Ullman. il Natur Hist 76:36-7 My '67
In quest of the world's largest frog. P. A. Zahl. il Nat Geog Mag 132:146-52 Jl '67
Night and the iguana; experimental rain forest. M. Bates. Natur Hist 76:22-5 D '67
Ornithine-urea cycle activity in xenopus laevis: adaptation in saline. R. L. McBean and L. Goldstein. bibliog il Science 157:931-2 Ag 25 '67
Toxicity of Panamanian poison frogs (dendrobates): some biological and chemical aspects. J. W. Daly and C. W. Myers. bibliog il Science 156:970-3 My 19 '67

FROM one day to the next; opera. See Schönberg. A.

FROME, Michael
Camping guide to the U.S: the Midwest. Holiday 41:145-52 My '67
Mike Frome. See issues of American forests
Politics of conservation. Holiday. 41:78-9+ F '67
Predators, prejudice, & politics. Field & S 72:24-6+ D '67
Wilderness ignored: the Aleutian Islands. Audubon 69:28-40 Ja '67

FROMM, Erich
Do we still love life? McCalls 94:57+ Ag '67

FROMME, Allan
You don't have to be lonely. J. E. Gibson. il Sci Digest 62:33-6 N '67

FRONDEL, Judith W.
X-ray diffraction study of some fossil and modern resins. Science 155:1411-13 Mr 17 '67

FRONT doors. See Doors

FRONT drive automobiles. See Automobiles—Front wheel drive

FRONT yards. See Home grounds

FRONTIER airlines, Incorporated
Hustle on the frontier. il Time 90:75-6 Ag 4 '67

FRONTIER and pioneer life

Australia
Outback. D. Moser. il Life 63:56-69+ D 22 '67

United States
Gallery of dudes, by M. Sprague. Review
Atlan 219:136 Mr '67. E. Weeks
Sat R il 50:43 F 11 '67. B. Garfield
Last frontier marshal; condensation. F. Miller. il Read Digest 90:201-4+ Je '67
Old settlers. R. Kirk. Nat R 19:641 Je 13 '67
See also
Ranches

FROOK, John
Hepburn comes back big, bringing a niece who calls her Aunt Kat. Life 64:60-5 Ja 5 '68

FROSCHER, Wingate
Surrey with fringe benefits. PTA Mag 61:14-16 Je '67

FROST, George E.
Patent system proposals: how practical? bibliog f Harvard Bsns R 45:111-22 S '67

FROST, Isabel (Moodie)
Agitated heart: adaptation of address. T. Morrison. Atlan 220:74-5 Jl '67

FROST, John
Amateur scientist. Sci Am 216:142-3 My '67

FROST, Lesley
Swinger of birches; interview. ed. by M. Maxwell. Sr Schol 91:sup 10-11 O 19 '67

FROST, Robert
Agitated heart; adaptation of address. R. Morrison. por Atlan 220:72-9 Jl '67
First love. L. Thompson. il Read Digest 91:55-8 Ag '67
Robert Frost: the early years, by L. Thompson. Review
Nation 204:182-4 F 6 '67. Q. Anderson
Poetry 110:425-6 S '67. B. Howes
Swinger of birches; interview. ed. by M. Maxwell. L. Frost. il por Sr Schol 91:sup 10-11 O 19 '67

FROST
See also
Ice

FROSTBITE
Treating burns, frostbite. F. Marley. il Sci N 91:362-3 Ap 15 '67
What you should know about winter health care. il Pop Gard 18:50-1 Mr '67

FROZEN desserts. See Desserts; Ice cream, ices, etc.

FROZEN dinners; Frozen meat; etc. See Food, Frozen; Meat, Frozen; etc.

FROZEN food cabinets. See Freezers

FRUIT
See also
Cookery—Fruit
Preservation
See also
Canning and preserving

FRUIT cake. See Cake

FRUIT culture
Apple fruit-set: evidence for a specific role of seeds. F. G. Dennis, jr. bibliog il Science 156:71-3 Ap 7 '67
Instead of a full-rigged ship, why not a pear in the bottle? il Sunset 138:92-3 My '67
New fruits and vegetables. il Farm J 92:49 Ja '68
See also
Strawberries

FRUIT desserts. See Desserts

FRUIT drinks. See Beverages

FRUIT flies
Florida crops threatened; Caribbean fruit fly. Sci N 92:103 Jl 29 '67
Fruit fly furor; Florida. il Sci N 92:252-3 S 9 '67

FRUIT industry
Year the bees got grounded. Time 90:96 N 10 '67
See also
Citrus fruit industry
United fruit company

FRUIT juices
See also
Orange juice

FRUIT juices, Frozen
Orange juice: frozen, canned or bottled. il Consumer Rep 32:394-7 Jl '67; Correction. 33:5-6 Ja '68

FRUIT trees
Fruits for Florida. P. Dempsey. il Horticulture 45:30-1+ D '67
See also
Persimmons

Care
For top quality fruit follow a regular spray program. il Pop Gard 18:78-9+ My '67

Diseases and pests
See also
Fire blight

FRUIT trees, Dwarf
Dwarf citrus. il Sunset 138:98-9 My '67
Dwarf fruit trees. B. A. Davis. Home Gard 54:16+ F '67
Grow dwarf fruit trees. Am Home 70:34 Mr '67
Growing dwarf fruit trees. il Good H 164:189 My '67

FRUIT trees, Training of
After fifteen years, Sunset's lemon fence is doing nicely. il Sunset 139:122-3 Ag '67

FRUSTRATION
Drugs: flying high or low. R. Coles. Yale R 57:38-46 O '67

FRUTKIN, Arnold W.
Recent advances in international cooperation in space; statement, August 29, 1967. Dept State Bul 57:401-3 S 25 '67

FRY, Edward F.
Issue of innovation. Art N 66:40-3+ O '67
Poons: a clean and balanced world? Art N 65:34-5+ F '67

FRY, Miles
Of people and poplars. Farm J 91:A2-38A Je '67

FRY, Ray MacNairn
LSB reorganization due; Fry appointed director. Library J 92:175 Ja 15 '67
New team at the top. por Library J 93:43-8 Ja 1 '68
—and Carl, H. A.
Washington report: from the Library services branch. ALA Bul 61:803-4 Jl '67

FRYE, John
Electronics and aphasia. por Electr World 78:54-5 D '67
Radiation and the technician. por Electr World 78:52+ N '67

FRYING
French way with french fries; summary, with recipes; ed. by E. Alston. R. Randall. il Look 31:111-12 O 17 '67

FRYING pans. See Skillets

FRYXELL, Paul A. and Lukefahr, M. J.
Hampea Schlecht: possible primary host of the cotton boll weevil. bibliog Science 155:1568-9 Mr 24 '67

FUBINI, Eugene Ghiron
Fubini cites second thoughts on tactical weaponry needs. Aviation W 87:19 S 4 '67

FUCHS, Estelle
Learning to be Navaho-Americans: innovation at Rough Rock. Sat R 50:82-4+ S 16 '67

FUCHS, G. L.
Cordoba (Argentina) takes noise abatement by the horns UNESCO Courier 20:21-2 Jl '67

FUCHS, Louis H.
Stanfieldite: a new phosphate mineral from stony-iron meteorites. bibliog Science 158:910-11 N 17 '67

FUCHSIAS
How to hybridize fuchsias. il Sunset 139:162-4 S '67

FUEL
Combustion without pollution: generating power indirectly from fossil fuels, ammonia. Sci Am 217:39-40 Ag '67
Exotic fuels will power tomorrow. M. J. Schultz. il Sci Digest 62:45-52 O '67
Industrial emissions of carbon dioxide in the United States: a projection; use of fossil fuels. F. A. Rohrman and others. bibliog il Science 156:931-2 My 19 '67
See also
Gas, Natural
also subhead Fuel under various subjects. e.g. Airplane engines—Fuel

FUEL cells
Allis-Chalmers pushes fuel cell efforts. R. D. Hibben. il Aviation W 86:65+ Ja 23 '67
Anodic oxidation and molecular structure: influence on performance of normal saturated hydrocarbons in fuel cells. E. J. Cairns. bibliog il Science 155:1245-6 Mr 10 '67
DSSP prepares for new fuel cell effort. Aero Tech 21:37 S 25 '67
Exotic fuels will power tomorrow. M. J. Schultz. il Sci Digest 62:45-52 O '67
Fuel cell; new primary power source for power and sail. E. Slepian. il Motor B 119:38-40+ My '67
Gas fuel cell to challenge power industry. W. S. Beller. il Tech W 20:15 F 13 '67

FUEL cells—*Continued*
How to make an electrochemical cell; ed. by C. L. Stong. il Sci Am 217:131-2+ N '67
Hydrazine-air fuel cells. G. E. Evans and K. V. Kordesch. bibliog il Science 158: 1148-52 D 1 '67
P&W designing 500-w. fuel cell for army. R. D. Hibben. il Aviation W 86:85-6 Mr 13 '67
Report on fuel-cell technology. Nat Parks Mag 41:20 F '67
Significance of new developments to industry, business, professions. Sci Digest 62:53 O '67

FUEL injection systems. See Automobile engines—Fuel feeding

FUEL oil. See Oil fuel

FUEL pumps
How to troubleshoot and rebuild your fuel pump. M. Schultz. il Pop Mech 128:144-7+ O '67

FUEL-range computer. See Aeronautic instruments

FUEL tanks, Airplane. See Airplanes—Fuel tanks

FUERST, Rita M.
Grandparents are to love. Parents Mag 42: 38-9+ Ag '67

FUHRMAN, Frederick A.
Tetrodotoxin. Sci Am 217:60-2+ Ag '67

FUJICHROME films. See Photography—Films

FUJIMA, Rankei
Rankei Fujima; 92nd street Y. M. Marks. Dance Mag 42:22 Ja '68

FUJIMOTO, M. and others
Paramagnetic resonance spectra of methyl radicals on porous glass surfaces. bibliog Science 156:1105-6 My 26 '67

FUJIOKA, Sharon
Curl up & read. Seventeen 26:138 D '67

FUJITA, S. Neil
Design as a public relations tool. por Wilson Lib Bul 42:293-4 N '67

FUKAMI, Jun-ichi, and others
Metabolism of rotenone in vitro by tissue homogenates from mammals and insects. bibliog Science 155:713-16 F 10 '67

FUKUYAMA, Betty Adkins
In favor of the nonstatistician; poem. Christian Cent 84:683 My 24 '67

FULBRIGHT, James William
Fulbright's proposals for peace; excerpt from Arrogance of power. Christian Cent 84:132 F 1 '67
Great society is a sick society. N Y Times Mag p30-1+ Ag 20 '67
Point of view; address, December 13, 1967. Science 158:1555 D 22 '67
Price of empire; address, August 8, 1967. bibliog Vital Speeches 33:678-82 S 1 '67; Excerpts. U S News 63:16 Ag 21 '67
We must not fight fire with fire. por N Y Times Mag p27+ Ap 23 '67

about
Comedy of errors. il Newsweek 69:32-4 Ap 17 '67
Debate and disquiet. il Newsweek 69:35-6 F 6 '67
Fulbright on riots. K. Crawford. Newsweek 70:28 Ag 21 '67
Fulbright versus Taylor. A. Campbell. New Repub 156:26-7 F 25 '67
Fulbright's dilemma. il por Newsweek 70:18-19 Ag 28 '67
Fulbright's prospects. J. Witcover. New Repub 156:4-5 Je 10 '67
Rethinking the unthinkable. Reporter 37:14+ S 21 '67
Senate spectacular. New Repub 156:6 F 4 '67
We put him in; Ky. K. Crawford. Newsweek 69:42 F 6 '67

FULBRIGHT international exchange program. See Educational exchanges

FULGURITES
Nature note; petrified lightning. il Sci N 91:276 Mr 25 '67

FULL employment. See Employment

FULLER, Blair, family
Streak in San Francisco. il pors Vogue 150: 154-5 Ag 15 '67

FULLER, Buckminster. See Fuller, R. B.

FULLER, Charles Edward
Radio preacher. Newsweek 69:88-9 Ap 24 '67

FULLER, J. F. C.
Pacification primer. A. Brynes. il New Repub 156:39-41 Ap 8 '67

FULLER, John G.
A communication concerning the UFOs. Sat R 50:70-2 F 4 '67

FULLER, John L.
Experiential deprivation and later behavior. bibliog Science 158:1645-52 D 29 '67

FULLER, M. See Smith, R. W. jt. auth.

FULLER, R. C. See Nugent, N. A. jt. auth

FULLER, Richard Buckminster
Man with a Chronofile. il Sat R 50:14-18 Ap 1 '67
Report on the geosocial revolution. Sat R 50:31-3+ S 16 '67

about
Expo named Buckminster Fuller. D. Jacobs. il pors N Y Times Mag p32-3+ Ap 23 '67
Utilized energy potential; a moneyless utopia. D. J. Leary. Cath World 204:335-40 Mr '67

FULLMER, J. Z.
Davy's biographers: notes on scientific biography. bibliog Science 155:285-91 Ja 20 '67

FULTON, George P. See Shepro, D. jt. auth.

FULTON, Robert
Negro child and public education. bibliog f Sch & Soc 95:109-10+ F 18 '67

FUMES, Lead. See Lead fumes

FUNCTIONALISM
Art of human use. N. Silver. Nation 204: 629-31 My 15 '67

FUNCTIONS
See also
Calculus

FUND for the Republic
See also
Center for the study of democratic institutions

FUND raising
Academic philanthropy: the art of getting. G. R. Hawes. Sat R 50:65-7+ D 16 '67
Accent the fun in giving a fund-raising block party. il Seventeen 26:74-7+ Jl '67
Americans rally round to get money to Israel. il Bsns W p34-5 Je 17 '67
Arab DPs and their needs; U.S. NEED project. Life 63:4 O 6 '67
Art of fund-raising. H. N. Weiner. Wilson Lib Bul 42:289-92 N '67
Fund raising: Yale launches marathon campaign. R. J. Samuelson. Science 158:1658-9 D 29 '67
Give as you never gave. il Newsweek 69:35-6 Je 19 '67
Higher education: scrambling for the philanthropic dollar. L. J. Carter. Science 156: 494-6 Ap 28 '67
How to ask your friends for money. il Changing T 21:35-7 Ap '67
Million a minute; support for Israel. Time 89:17-18 Je 16 '67
See also
Campaign funds

FUNDAMENTALISM
Fundamentalism. C. Henry; J. Opie, jr. Cath World 205:145-56 Je '67

FUNDULUS heteroclitus. See Killifishes

FUNDY NATIONAL PARK. See National parks and reserves—Canada

FUNERAL rites and ceremonies
Death in Chamula. P. Menget. il Natur Hist 77:48-57 Ja '68
For the heroes, salute and farewell; burial services for V. Grissom and R. Chaffee. il Life 62:20-1+ F 10 '67
Honored son returns to West Point; military burial of E. White. il Life 62:22-3 F 10 '67
How the Vikings buried their dead. il Life 63:54+ S 15 '67
To honor Der Alte; state funeral of K. Adenauer. il Life 62:34-8 My 5 '67
See also
Kennedy, J. F.—Funeral rites and ceremonies

FUNGI
Fungal morphogenesis ring formation and closure by arthrobotrys dactyloides. M. L. Higgins and D. Pramer. bibliog il Science 155:345-6 Ja 20 '67
Fungus gardens of insects. S. W. T. Batra and L. R. Batra. il Sci Am 217:112-20 bibliog(p 156) N '67
Glucans of oomycete cell walls. J. M. Aronson and others. bibliog il Science 155:332-5 Ja 20 '67
Zeatin and zeatin riboside from a mycorrhizal fungus. C. O. Miller. bibliog Science 157:1055-7 S 1 '67
See also
Lichens
Truffles

FUNGI—*Continued*

Culture media

Blastomyces dermatitidis: production of the sexual stage. E. S. McDonough and A. L. Lewis. bibliog il Science 156:528-9 Ap 28 '67
Muscarine: isolation from cultures of clitocybe rivulosa. M. L. Swenberg and others. bibliog Science 155:1259 Mr 10 '67

Migration

See Plants—Migration

FUNGI, Pathogenic
Blastomyces dermatitidis: production of the sexual stage. E. S. McDonough and A. L. Lewis. bibliog il Science 156:528-9 Ap 28 '67
Elastase: production by ringworm fungi. J. W. Rippon. bibliog Science 157:947 Ag 25 '67
Nobiletin is main fungistat in tangerines resistant to mal secco. A. Ben-Aziz. bibliog il Science 155:1026-7 F 24 '67

FUNGICIDES

Physiological effects

Fungicide danger; captan's genetic effect. il Sci N 91:568 Je 17 '67

FUNGISTATS. See Growth inhibiting substances (fungi)

FUNK, Casimir
Death of the vitamin pioneer. il por Time 90:44 D 1 '67

FUNK, Peter
It pays to increase your word power. See issues of Reader's digest

FUNNIES on Capitol hill. See Comics (books, strips, etc)

FUNSTON, George Keith
Close-up of today's stock market; interview. por U S News 63:62-5 Jl 3 '67
Investment future of America; address. May 1, 1967. Vital Speeches 33:554-9 Jl 1 '67

about

To the letter. Time 89:90 F 10 '67

FUNT, Allen
Smile! por Time 89:63 Mr 3 '67

FUR
Brand-new horror for harried husbands. D. Connelly. il Sports Illus 27:64+ N 27 '67
Lady and the marten; fur ornaments of 16th-century H. A. LaFarge. il Art N 66:40-1 N '67

FUR, Artificial
Facts on fake furs. il Good H 165:152 D '67

FUR bearing animals
See also
Sea otters

FUR coats, wraps, etc.
Fun furs; danger of extermination, in the interests of fashion, of spotted cats. New Yorker 43:32-3 My 20 '67
On furs, look for that label! Consumer Bul 50:16 O '67
Year for fur; youth-oriented mink. il Time 90:50 D 15 '67

FUR trade
Fun furs; danger of extermination, in the interests of fashion, of spotted cats. New Yorker 43:32-3 My 20 '67

FURLAN, Luis Ricardo
Letter to Rubén Dario; poem, with English translation. Américas 19:19-21 D '67

FURLONG, William Barry
Dove versus a dogcatcher. N Y Times Mag p6-7+ Je 25 '67
How faith helped Charles Percy's family face tragedy. Good H 164:78-81+ F '67
How to watch football on TV. Pop Mech 128:87-9+ O '67
It's a long way from the birds and bees. N Y Times Mag p24-5+ Je 11 '67
Percy: everybody's second-best man. Harper 235:41-7 S '67
Re-entry problem of the Vietvets. N Y Times Mag p23+ My 7 '67
What you can do about those obscene telephone calls. Good H 165:82-3+ S '67
(ed) See Stevenson, A. E. 3d. Let's muffle the sound of guns

FURLOUGHS
My son comes home from Vietnam. H. H. Martin. il Sat Eve Post 240:76+ Ap 8 '67

FURNACES
How to troubleshoot furnace failure. S. J. Howard. il Pop Mech 129:192-5+ Ja '68
See also
Heating

FURNESS, Betty
Nation's new icebox-watcher; interview; ed. by deR. Morrissey. pors Life 62:49-50+ Ap 7 '67

about

And now, for the consumer, Miss Betty Furness! A. Chamberlin. il pors Sat Eve Post 240:26-7 Je 17 '67
Betty Furness. New Repub 156:8-9 Mr 18 '67
Betty opens a new door. pors Newsweek 69:92+ Mr 20 '67
Betty's blockbuster. Newsweek 71:57 Ja 8 '68
Can Betty Furness help the consumer? il por Consumer Rep 32:256-8 My '67
How much federal protection do consumers want? Consumer Bul 50:28 My '67
Lady with a sympathetic ear. por Bsns W p63+ S 23 '67
New shopper for LBJ; Betty Furness gets tough job. il por U S News 62:21 Mr 20 '67
100 days of Betty Furness. New Repub 157:10 Ag 5 '67
Opening the door. por Newsweek 69:26 My 15 '67
Packaging peas and Betty Bird Furness. N. K. Herzfeld. Commonweal 86:384-5 Je 23 '67

FURNISHINGS, Household. See Household furnishings

FURNITURE
American modern: freewheeling in all directions! il Bet Hom & Gard 45:64-5 My '67
American traditional: an inheritance from many lands. il Bet Hom & Gard 45:58-9 My '67
Decorating with modern. il Am Home 70:82-3 O '67
Delights of leisure at home. il House & Gard 131:150-9 Ap '67
Don't just sit there. B. Plumb. il N Y Times Mag p66-7 Ja 14 '68
Fold-away counter. il Consumer Rep 32:296 Je '67
Furniture finds: new, snappy, and under $50. il House & Gard 131:156-7 My '67
How to create a new look. il House & Gard 131:144-7 My '67
How to recognize quality in furniture. Parents Mag 42:53-6+ Ja '67
It's a great year for new furniture! il Good H 164:104-11 Je '67
Look again, it's the new modern! il Am Home 70:44 My '67
Next moves in furniture. il House B 109:150-5 S '67
100 good buys under $100; ed. by P. Doherty. il House B 109:96-101 Jl '67
100 ideas under $100 (cont) il Bet Hom & Gard 45:38+ Jl '67
Period rooms updated. il McCalls 94:90-5 My '67
Steel and glass elegance at easy prices; steel-framed furniture. il House & Gard 132:270-1 O '67
See also
Buffets (furniture)
Chairs
House decoration
Tables

Care

Spruce up your outdoor furniture. M. E. Dowd. Am Home 70:94-5 Je '67
Your guide to furniture finish repairs. J. LemMon. Suc Farm 65:93-4 Ap '67
See also
Furniture polishes

Collectors and collecting

Robb collection of American furniture. E. Gaines. il Antiques 92:322-8 S '67

Design

Designs of our time. B. Plumb. il N Y Times Mag p90-1 S 17 '67; Reply. A. Drexler. p22 O 1 '67
Exotica out of Expo. B. Plumb. il N Y Times Mag p36-7 S 3 '67
Eye-fooling furniture. il Life 62:111-12+ Je 9 '67
Good new summertime; outdoor furniture equally good inside. B. Plumb. il N Y Times Mag p64-5 My 28 '67
House beautiful's market notebook: notes and sketches made at the recent showings. H. Morrison. il House B 109:223-30 O '67
International furniture style. R. Davidson. il Antiques 91:652+ My '67
New design, U.S.A. B. Plumb. il N Y Times Mag p 110-12 Ap 23 '67
Pop goes the plastic; transparent furniture. il Time 90:62 O 27 '67
Special report from London: young design revolution. M. Gilliatt. il House B 109:68-73 Jl '67

FURNITURE—*Continued*

Exhibitions

Furniture market gets new polish; Southern furniture exposition. il Bsns W p38-40 Ap 22 '67

Memorial exhibit in Richmond; loan exhibition of American and English furniture at the Valentine museum. B. C. Coons and F. C. Guy. il Antiques 92:542-5 O '67

Finishing

Three easy recipes for finishing furniture with wax. il Pop Mech 128:174-5 O '67

Leasing

When renting furniture is an advantage. il Good H 165:204 O '67

Manufacture

See also
Southern furniture manufacturers association

Purchasing

How to buy summer furniture. Am Home 70: 16 My '67

Ins and outs of buying upholstered furniture. il Good H 165:188+ O '67

Terminology

What does it mean? commode? credenza? lowboy? highboy? il Am Home 70:18 Mr '67

FURNITURE, American

American antiques in the collection of Mr and Mrs Charles L. Bybee. J. L. Fairbanks. il Antiques 92:832-9 D '67 (to be cont)

American modern: freewheeling in all directions! il Bet Hom & Gard 45:64-5 My '67

American traditional: an inheritance from many lands. il Bet Hom & Gard 45:58-9 My '67

Distinctive character of Connecticut furniture. J. T. Kirk. il Antiques 92:524-9 O '67

Furniture in Savannah. Mrs C. M. Theus. il Antiques 91:364-9 Mr '67

History in houses: East, the Bush-Holley house, Cos Cob, Conn. S. H. Lowitz and A. C. Lowitz. il Antiques 91:772-6 Je '67

History in houses: West, the Old Indian agency house. P. M. Stone. il Antiques 91: 768-71 Je '67

Interim report from Washington, D.C. diplomatic reception rooms in the Department of state's building. E. P. Birk. il Antiques 91:724+ Je '67

Memorial exhibit in Richmond; loan exhibition of American and English furniture at the Valentine museum. B. C. Coons and F. C. Guy. il Antiques 92:542-5 O '67

New England furniture. R. Davidson. il Antiques 91:374 Mr '67

Rejuvenation at Blair House. il House & Gard 133:106-7+ Ja '68

Robb collection of American furniture. E. Gaines. il Antiques 92:322-8 S '67

See also
House decoration, American

Collectors and collecting

Rhode Island furniture at Chipstone. S. Stone. il Antiques 91:207-13, 508-13 F, Ap '67

History

American habitat; excerpts from Taste in America. I. Ross. il House B 109:200-2 Ap '67

FURNITURE, Arrangement of

Art of fooling the eye. il Am Home 70:60-1 S '67

Furniture for the instant eclectic. F. Heard. il House B 109:292-5 N '67

Put quality where it counts. V. D. Hahn. il Am Home 70:70-3 Ja '67

Significance of scale. il Am Home 70:58-9 S '67

FURNITURE, Bentwood

Twig was bent. B. Plumb. il N Y Times Mag p 106-7 N 26 '67

FURNITURE, Built in

Any room has space for good built-ins. il Bet Hom & Gard 45:18 My '67

Built-ins set the scene. B. Plumb. il N Y Times Mag p56-8+ Ja 29 '67

Desks for difficult rooms. il Bet Hom & Gard 45:118 F '67

How to build a built-in. D. Jordan. il Bet Hom & Gard 45:42-3+ Ap '67

FURNITURE, Canadian

Canadian furniture in the English taste, 1790-1840. J. Minhinnick. il Antiques 92: 84-90 Jl '67

Early French Canadian furniture. E. McLean. il Antiques 92:72-7 Jl '67

FURNITURE, Childrens

Children's furniture that's here to stay. il Bet Hom & Gard 45:136 O '67

For the child's world, a sculptor creates play furniture. il House B 109:110-11 Jl '67

They are box blocks. il Sunset 139:54-7 D '67

FURNITURE, Chinese

Chinese domestic furniture. R. Davidson. il Antiques 92:732+ N '67

East Side Oriental; R. Ellsworth's collection of Ming furniture. B. Plumb. il N Y Times Mag p98-9 My 7 '67

Oldest house in San Francisco adopts the 20th century. F. Heard. il House B 109: 142-5 Je '67

Oriental: black lacquer, fretwork, concise design. il Bet Hom & Gard 45:54-5 My '67

FURNITURE, English

Adam revolution in furniture. E. Stillinger. il Antiques 91:218-22 F '67

Classic tradition in Georgian and early Victorian furniture. J. Gloag. il Antiques 91: 754-9 Je '67

Elegant as always: 18th-century English. il Good H 164:106-7 Je '67

English: the golden age of cabinetry. il Bet Hom & Gard 45:48-9 My '67

Memorial exhibit in Richmond; loan exhibition of American and English furniture at the Valentine museum. B. C. Coons and F. C. Guy. il Antiques 92:542-5 O '67

Special report from London: young design revolution. M. Gilliatt. il House B 109:68-73 Jl '67

FURNITURE, French

Among the brilliant new choices: furniture in the French tradition. il Good H 164:104-5 Je '67

French: the ultimate in decorative furniture. il Bet Hom & Gard 45:50-1 My '67

Instant antiques; Ateliers d'art A. Mailfert Amos, manufacturers of French furniture. il Newsweek 69:60 My 15 '67

New again: French country furniture; the Norman tradition. il House & Gard 132: 220-3 O '67

Nothing like creatures for creature comfort. B. Wise. il Life 62:76-9 F 3 '67

Wrightsman collection, by F. J. B. Watson. Review
Antiques il 91:620-7 My '67. R. Davidson

FURNITURE, German

German: man-made materials and an emphasis on function. il Bet Hom & Gard 45:60-1 My '67

FURNITURE, Italian

Italian: classic columns, molding, painted woods. il Bet Hom & Gard 45:52-3 My '67

FURNITURE, Modern. See Furniture

FURNITURE, Outdoor

Cast-iron furniture. J. Mebane. il Bet Hom & Gard 45:128 F '67

Exciting summer furniture, food, projects, equipment. D. Popplestone. il Bet Hom & Gard 45:46-65+ Je '67

Spruce up your outdoor furniture. M. E. Dowd. Am Home 70:94-5 Je '67

Sun-drenched summer furniture. il House B 109:160-5 My '67

Two lawn aids you can build. il Pop Sci 190:176-7 Ap '67

See also
Flower pot holders
Furniture, Rustic
Furniture, Summer

FURNITURE, Renaissance. See Furniture, Italian

FURNITURE, Rustic

Chain-saw furniture: attractive, durable, and outdoor flavored. il Field & S 71:64-5+ Mr '67

FURNITURE, Scandinavian

Scandinavian: a natural approach with natural woods. il Bet Hom & Gard 45:62-3 My '67

FURNITURE, Spanish

Spanish: massive design plus iron, leather, heavy carving. il Bet Hom & Gard 45: 56-7 My '67

FURNITURE, Summer

All summer is a holiday, at home! il Good H 165:98-101+ Jl '67

How to buy summer furniture. Am Home 70: 16 My '67

FURNITURE design. See Furniture—Design

FURNITURE designers

Special report from London: young design revolution. M. Gilliatt. il House B 109:68-73 Jl '67

FURNITURE industry and trade
5,350 companies—a mixed-up furniture industry. T. O'Hanlon. il Fortune 75:144-9+ F '67
Flaws in furniture. R. Wyant. il Duns R 89:13 My '67
FURNITURE makers. See Cabinetmakers
FURNITURE polishes
Furniture polishes. il Consumer Rep 32:317-19 Je '67
FURR, William, Jr
Killing of Billy Furr, caught in the act of looting beer. D. Wittner. il pors Life 63: 20-2 Jl 28 '67
FURST, S. Dale, Jr
VD: a major health problem. Parents Mag 42:104 N '67
FURUYA, Yasuo
Japanese view of religion in the U.S. H. Shimmi. Christian Cent 85:61-2 Ja 10 '68
FUSCHETTO, Anthony, family
Baby she'd always wanted. A. Levy. il Good H 164:48+ F '67
FUSCO, Art
Flies with flash. por Outdoor Life 140:52-5+ S '67
FUSELAGE of airplanes. See Airplanes—Fuselage
FUSION, Nuclear. See Nuclear fusion
FUSION reaction. See Nuclear fusion
FUSION reactors. See Nuclear reactors
FUTRELL, Darryl
Some notes on tektites. il Sky & Tel 33: 272-5 My '67
FUTURE
Bringing the future into focus. Nations Bsns 55:82-3+ D '67
Future: still cloudy; Washington conference on the next fifty years. Sci N 92:368-9 O 14 '67
Glimpse of the home of tomorrow. il U S News 63:88-90 Jl 3 '67
How to predict your future. H. MacLean. il Ladies Home J 84:78 Mr '67
Inquiry into a disarmed world. il UNESCO Courier 20:5-9 Ag '67
Intellectuals and the future. E. Shils. Bul Atomic Sci 23:7-14 O '67
Look at world population the day after tomorrow; excerpt from Three comments on the near future of mankind. J. Fourastié. bibliog f il UNESCO Courier 20:10-13+ F '67
100-year life expectancy predicted for 2000 A.D. Todays Health 46:57 Ja '68
Preparing your children for tomorrow's world; with discussion program. C. A. Cerami. il Parents Mag 43:15, 35-8+ Ja '68
Report on the geosocial revolution. B. Fuller. Sat R 50:31-3+ S 16 '67
This is what a baby can look forward to. R. M. Scammon. il Life 63:28-9 D 1 '67
Twenty-first century: the world you'll live in. W. Cronkite. il Pop Sci 190:98-101 Ap '67
See also
Forecasts
Nineteen hundred and eighty-nine
Nineteen hundred and ninety-seven
Prophecies
Two thousand (year)
FUTURE homemakers of America
Future homemakers of America. il Am Ed 3:13 My '67
FUTURE life
Abusing the kingdom; excerpt from Thy kingdom come. J. E. Hines. Christian Cent 84:227 F 22 '67
See also
Eschatology
Spiritualism
FUTURES. See Exchanges; Speculation
FUZ, George C.
Justice denied. Nation 205:386 O 23 '67

G

GAO. See United States—General accounting office
GAR. See Grand army of the Republic
GATT. See General agreement on tariffs and trade
GE. See General electric company
GE letterwriter. See Recording instruments
GI Joe dolls. See Dolls
GM. See General motors corporation

GNP. See Gross national product
GOP. See Republican party
GPO. See United States—Government printing office
GPU. See Secret service—Russia
GABLIK, Suzi
(ed) See Oldenburg, C. Take a cigarette butt and make it heroic
About
Content as combination. J. Russell. il Art N 66:52-3+ O '67
GABO, Naum
Gallery for young people. C. B. Johnson. il Sch Arts 66:52 F '67
GABON
See also
Lambaréné
GABRIEL, Astrik Ladislas
Papal honor to medievalist. il por Sch & Soc 95:72-3 F 4 '67
GABRIEL, Bill
Fool hen of the Rockies. il Nat Parks Mag 41:8-9 Ag '67
GABRIELSON, Catherine
Silly questions? J. Durniak. il Pop Phot 60: 53-6 F '67
GADGETS
Inventive inventory; products of Inventa products corporation. il Newsweek 70:62-3 D 25 '67
Mini wonder-workers. il House & Gard 132: 62 N '67
Pop goes the gadget, or how to get a cherry stoned. il House & Gard 131:146-7+ Ap '67
GADGETS, Garden. See Garden tools, equipment and supplies
GADSDEN, Christopher
Colonial gadfly. T. D. Clark. Sat R 50:48-9 Je 10 '67
GADSKI, Johanna
Historical records. A. Favia-Artsay. por Hobbies 72:34 Ag '67
GAFFNEY, Edward M.
(ed) See Murray, J. C. Religious liberty and development of doctrine
GAGARIN, Iurii Alekseevich
Gagarin helps fight false Soyuz rumors. Aviation W 86:66+ Je 19 '67
GAGE, Peter W. and Eisenberg, R. S.
Action potentials without contraction in frog skeletal muscle fibers with disrupted transverse tubules. bibliog Science 158:1702-3 D 29 '67
—See Eisenberg, R. S. jt. auth.
GAGEN, Joseph F.
Invisible poor of the Garden state. Commonweal 86:540-1 S 8 '67
GAGES
Gauge to measure tiny changes in gas pressure. W. R. Debler. il Sci Am 217:110-11 Ag '67
Gauges. B. Lang. il Hot Rod 20:76 My '67
GAGLIARDO, Ruth
Books for children. PTA Mag 62:29-30 Ja '68
GAGNON, John H. See Simon, W. jt. auth.
GAGNON, Patricia A. and Pollack, J. H.
How safe is your driving? quiz. Ladies Home J 84:180 N '67
GAHVA, Maria
On the gypsy circuit. W. Como. por Dance Mag 41:20 Ap '67
GAINES, Bob
You and your sleep. See issues of Ladies' home journal
GAINES, Charles
Recruitment; story. Harper 235:92-8 D '67
GAINES, Diana
Legacy; story. Redbook 128:167-89 Mr '67
Rules to write by. Writer 80:14-15 Ja '67
GAINES, Edith
(ed) Collectors' notes. See issues of Antiques
More by, and about Pitts of the epergnes. Antiques 91:748-53 Je '67
Robb collection of American furniture. Antiques 92:322-8 S '67
GAINES, Ervin J.
Crucial error in censorship; reprint. por Library J 92:3377-9 O 1 '67
Library bill of rights: reasons for revision. por Library J 92:984-5 Mr 1 '67; Same. ALA Bul 61:409-10 Ap '67
about
Gaines' loss. G. K. Schenk. Library J 92:712 F 15 '67; Reply. A. Curley. 92:1391 Ap 1 '67
GAINS tax. See Income tax—Capital gains tax
GAJDUSEK, D. Carleton, and others
Transmission and passage of experimental kuru to chimpanzees. bibliog Science 155: 212-14 Ja 13 '67

GALACTIC clusters. See Stars—Clusters

GALACTIC systems
Deep-sky wonders. W. S. Houston. See issues of Sky and telescope
Fragments of galaxies. G. S. Mumford. Sky & Tel 33:354 Je '67
Galactic core revealed. Sci Am 216:52+ Je '67
Galaxies and quasars at Prague. T. L. Page. il Sky & Tel 34:372-6; 35:16-20 D '67, Ja '68 (to be cont)
Galaxies as gravitational lenses. D. Sadeh. bibliog il Science 158:1176-8 D 1 '67
NGC 4038-39; an exploding galaxy? G. S. Mumford. il Sky & Tel 33:95 F '67
Observations of the andromeda galaxy at 11-centimeter wavelength. R. C. Cooley and others. bibliog il Science 156:1087-8 My 26 '67
Origin of galaxies. G. S. Mumford. Sky & Tel 34:289 N '67
Over the edge of the universe. I. Asimov. Harper 234:97-8+ Mr '67
Quasi-stellar objects: possible local origin. J. Terrell; reply with rejoinder. J. M. Barnothy. bibliog Science 156:264-5 Ap 14 '67
Spiral patterns in galaxies. B. T. Lynds. il Sky & Tel 33:343-6; 34:18-21 Je-Jl '67

Radiation
Distribution and variability of cosmic X-ray sources. H. Friedman and others. bibliog il Science 156:374-8 Ap 21 '67

Spectra
New ideas on the red shift. T. D. Nicholson. il Natur Hist 76:34-6 F '67

GALACTOSYL diglycerides. See Glycerides

GALAMBOS, Robert. See Klivington, K. A. jt. auth.

GALANOPOULOS, A. G.
Atlantis hypothesis. Sat R 49:93 D 3 '66; 50:56 Ap 1 '67

GALANOS, James
Galanos runs a good gamut. il Life 62:105-6 Mr 10 '67

GALANTAY, Ervin
Architecture (cont) Nation 204:283-5, 473-4+ F 27, Ap 10 '67
Expo 67: space/time in Montreal. Nation 204:557-62 My 1 '67

GALAPAGOS ISLANDS
Galapagos; eerie cradle of new species. R. T. Peterson. il Nat Geog Mag 131:540-85 Ap '67

GALAPAGOS rift zone. See Ocean bottom

GALAX, Va.
Galax, Va. turns out to hail the sergeant. il Life 62:80-1 F 3 '67

GALAXIES. See Galactic systems

GALAXY (Milky way) See Milky way

GALBRAITH, Alan F.
Teton impressions; poem. Liv Wildn 30:35 Wint '66

GALBRAITH, Georgie Starbuck
Too good to be true; poem. McCalls 94:128 Ap '67

GALBRAITH, John Kenneth
Art, diplomacy and vice versa. Esquire 67:112-19+ Mr '67
Capitalism, socialism, and the future of the industrial state; excerpts from The new industrial state. Atlan 219:61-7 Je '67
Galbraith plan to end the war. N Y Times Mag p29-30+ N 12 '67
Market planning and the role of government; excerpt from The new industrial state. por Atlan 219:69-72+ My '67
New industrial state; excerpt. Atlan 219:51-7 Ap '67

about
Al Capp on the hippie economics. A. Capp. il Nations Bsns 55:64-7 S '67
Fine Irish hand? Nat R 19:1309-10 N 28 '67
Galbraith, P. A. Samuelson. Newsweek 70:68 Jl 3 '67
Galbraith dimension. il pors Newsweek 70:24+ O 2 '67
Galbraith speaks; summary of address. il por Pub W 191:25-6 My 22 '67
Importance of being Galbraith. D. Halberstam. il pors Harper 235:47-54 N '67
New, blue, cheerless Galbraith. Life 63:4 Jl 7 '67
Non-debate. K. Crawford. Newsweek 69:46 Ap 17 '67
Signs of erosion. por Newsweek 69:32 Ap 10 '67
Too big for antitrust to handle? il por Bsns W p70-2 Jl 8 '67

GALBRAITH, William E.
To teach the unknowing; address, August 31, 1967. Vital Speeches 34:11-13 O 15 '67

GALE, Don
Tiny tots a go-go. Parks & Rec 2:26-7+ Ag '67

GALE, J. and Poljakoff-Mayber, A.
Plastic films on plants as antitranspirants. bibliog Science 156:650-2 My 5 '67

GALE, Kathryn B.
Abundance of the prairie. Horticulture 45:34-5 Ag '67

GALENA, Ill.
It's great to be in Galena at Christmas. R. Bissell. il Holiday 42:26+ D '67

GALILEO; drama. See Brecht, B.

GALILEO; drama. See Leech, M. T.

GALL, Norman
Legacy of Che Guevara. bibliog f Commentary 44:31-44 D '67
Peru's misfired guerrilla campaign. Reporter 36:36-8 Ja 26 '67

GALLAGHER, Buell G.
Speaking out. Sat Eve Post 240:8+ My 6 '67

GALLAGHER, Francis J.
Biography (cont) America 116:693+ My 6 '67

GALLAGHER, Patrick
Games Malinowski played. New Repub 156:24-6 Je 17 '67

GALLAGHER, Robert S.
Wrecker, spare that frieze! Am Heritage 18:60-4+ Ag '67
(ed) See Catlin, G. Tragic prescience of George Catlin

GALLAGHER, Thomas
Body snatchers; excerpts from The doctors' story. Am Heritage 18:64-73 Je '67

GALLAGHER, Wes
Newsman: society's lonesome end; excerpt from address. Sat R 51:114-15 Ja 13 '68

GALLAMINE triethiodide
Flaxedil gallamine triethiodide: evidence for a central action. L. M. Halpern and R. G. Black. bibliog il Science 155:1685-7 Mr 31 '67

GALLANT, Mavis
Accident; story. New Yorker 43:55-9 O 28 '67
End of the world; story. New Yorker 43:36-9 Je 10 '67
Sunday after Christmas; story. New Yorker 43:35-6 D 30 '67

GALLATIN national forest, Mont. See National forests

GALLEGOS, E. S. See Kenshalo, D. R. jt. auth.

GALLER, David
Graceful reticence. Poetry 110:123-5 My '67
Self-deceptions; poem. New Yorker 43:41 Je 3 '67
Seneca; poem. New Yorker 43:58 D 2 '67
Suitor; poem. Yale R 57:99-100 O '67
Three recent volumes. Poetry 110:267-8 Jl '67
To Nessus; poem. Reporter 37:46 N 2 '67

GALLERIES and museums. See Art—Galleries and museums

GALLEY, Robert
France: first the bomb, then the Plan Calcul. J. Walsh. Science 156:767-70 My 12 '67

GALLICO, Paul William
Aim for the heart. Writer 80:11-12+ S '67
Tale of an ancient mariner. Sports Illus 27:76-8+ S 25 '67

GALLIGAN, Edward
Soldier with a camera. U S Camera 30:44-9+ Je '67

GALLIMARD editions. See Publishers and publishing—France

GALLI-OLIVIER, Carlos
Pediplain in northern Chile and the Andean uplift. bibliog Science 158:653-5 N 3 '67

GALLIUM arsenide diodes. See Diodes

GALLO, Fortune
Fortunes of Gallo. F. Robinson. il Sat R 51:101 +Ja 13 '68

GALLO, Frank
Epoxy playmates. il Time 90:64+ N 24 '67

GALLOWAY, John
Mr Jones goes to Washington. Commonweal 87:374-5 D 22 '67

GALLOZZI, Charles
New hope for the handicapped. bibliog por Library J 92:1417-20 Ap 1 '67

GALLUP polls. See Public opinion polls

GALO LEORO, F.
Sovereignty and Latin American integration. Américas 19:28-33 S '67

GALPIN, Frank S.
How to buck the trend in autos. il Bsns W p 132-3 Mr 18 '67

GALSTON, Arthur W.
Herbicides in Vietnam. New Repub 157:19-21 N 25 '67
—See Siegel, B. Z. jt. auth.

GALTON, Lawrence
Aquiculture is more than a dream. N Y Times Mag p 12-14+ Je 18 '67
LSD, the other side of the story. Pop Sci 190:93-5+ Ja '67
Pain is cruel, but disease is cruel, too. N Y Times Mag p30-1+ F 26 '67
Science works on your headache. Pop Sci 192:70-3+ Ja '68
Surprising new facts about your muscles. Pop Sci 191:54-7+ Jl '67
What your dreams do for you. Pop Sci 191: 98-100+ S '67
Your teeth can last a lifetime. Pop Sci 191: 76-8+ N '67

GALVANIC corrosion. See Corrosion and anti-corrosives

GALVANIZED steel. See Steel. Galvanized

GALVESTON
Street traffic
Good signs reflect a city's image. J. Impey. il Am City 82:156-7 S '67

GALVESTON BAY
Dredging up a Texas squabble; oyster shells from Galveston Bay. E. Shrake. il Sports Illus 27:43-8 Ag 14 '67

GALVIN, Robert W.
Big boom in profit sharing; what's back of it; interview. por U S News 63:64-6 Ag 28 '67

about
Sparks from the campus. por Newsweek 69: 79+ Ap 3 '67

GAMBLERS; story. See Lamott, K.

GAMBLING
Crooked shake; Lake Tahoe hotel casino closed. il Time 90:62 O 27 '67
Editor's report: Las Vegas. M. M. Davis. il Travel 128:36-9 N '67
Fun and games; cheating at Beverly Hills Friars club. il Newsweek 70:44-5 S 18 '67
Grace through gambling. J. Richardson. il Esquire 67:142-4+ Ap '67
How gambling saved me from a misspent life. J. Richardson. Esquire 68:139-41+ N '67
Public attitudes toward gambling and corruption. J. A. Gardiner. bibliog f il Ann Am Acad 374:123-34 N '67
$7 billion from illegal bets and a blight on sports; Cosa nostra involvement. il Life 63:92-3 S 8 '67
Sporting life; sports pages services for gambling. il Newsweek 70:60 O 9 '67
Teacher opinion poll; financing public education by legalized gambling. NEA J 57:2 Ja '68
Why people gamble (and should they?) Time essay. Time 90:26-7 Jl 21 '67
See also
Book making (betting)
Horse race betting
Lotteries
Probabilities

Bahama Islands
Mafia: shadow of evil on an island in the sun. B. Davidson. il Sat Eve Post 240:27-37 F 25 '67
Scandal in the Bahamas. R. Oulahan and W. Lambert. il Life 62:58-66+ F 3 '67

Europe, Eastern
Red roulette. il Time 90:108+ D 1 '67

GAME
See also
Cookery—Game

GAME, Dressing of
How to field dress a deer. N. Smith. il Field & S 72:52-3+ O '67

GAME birds
Big horn of birds. P. Czura. il Field & S 72:104-6+ D '67
Game birds can be garden birds. M. D. Hodgins. il Home Gard 54:40+ F '67
Wingshooting in Saskatchewan. M. Ellis. il Field & S 72:56-7+ Ag '67
See also names of game birds, e.g. Pheasants

GAME calls. See Animal calling

GAME fisheries. See Fisheries

GAME laws
Alaska cracks down. J. Rearden. il Outdoor Life 140:39-41+ O '67
Do residents control resident game? W. E. Towell. il Am For 73:20-1+ Jl '67
Hunting seasons (cont) Outdoor Life 140:12+ S '67
See also
Poaching

GAME preserves
Into the Cabeza Prieta Range. il Sunset 139: 27+ N '67

Natural world; East Africa. O. Prescott. il Sat R 50:42-3 S 2 '67
Reporter at large; exploring Organ Pipe Cactus National Monument and Cabeza Prieta game range, proposed combination for Sonoran Desert National Park. B. Roueché. New Yorker 43:76+ Ag 12 '67

GAME protection
See also
Game wardens
Wildlife conservation

GAME simulation. See Management games

GAME wardens
Cassius Austin: warden; in Maine wilderness. L. Dietz. Field & S 72:44-5+ N '67
Death of a warden; Bob Markle. D. Duffey. il Outdoor Life 139:41-3+ F '67

GAMES
Are you game? il Seventeen 26:242-3 Ap '67
Fun for the mind: science kits and travel games. il Consumer Bul 51:37 Ja '68
Games are to grow on. C. Levine. il Parents Mag 42:44-5+ D '67
Games in the classroom. E. Carlson. il Sat R 50:62-4+ Ap 15 '67
Games in the classroom; symposium; ed. by J. S. Coleman. il Sr Schol 91:sup3+ N 9 '67
Games people play: propaganda, hostility and credibility gap. Newsweek 70:44 D 18 '67
Games to please a crowd. E. D. Craster. il Bet Hom & Gard 45:31-2 Mr '67
Magnetic game. H. Slutz. il Pop Mech 127: 175 F '67
Making ticktacktoe tough. il Life 63:99-100 D 1 '67
Name is the game. M. Mulvey. Good H 165: 227 D '67
New games add fun and wit. E. Kinard. il House B 109:298-9 N '67
Political party games; Credibility gap and others. D. Sanford. New Repub 157:7-8 D 16 '67
Sporting life at sea; pari-mutuels on the Queen Elizabeth. J. Olsen. il Sports Illus 26:54-60 F 27 '67
Toys and games. il Consumer Bul 50:33-6 D '67
Walk the ball. M. H. Slutz. il Pop Mech 128: 142-3 D '67
Where monopoly is not a dirty word: Parker bros. il Bsns W p 180-2+ Mr 25 '67
See also
Badminton (game)
Croquet
Go (game)
Play
School athletics
Shuffleboard

GAMES, Theory of
Escape from paradox. A. Rapoport. il Sci Am 217:50-6 bibliog(p 134) Jl '67

GAMETOPHYTES
Gametophytes of four tropical fern genera reproducing independently of their sporophytes in the southern Appalachians. D. R. Farrar. bibliog Science 155:1266-7 Mr 10 '67

GAMMA globulin
Deficient complement fixation by aggregated gamma globulin from hypogammaglobulinemic patients. R. J. Pickering and others. bibliog il Science 157:454-5 Jl 28 '67
Gamma globulins: structure and control of biosynthesis. F. W. Putnam. Science 158: 813-14 N 10 '67
Limited heterogeneity of gamma globulin in hypogammaglobulinemia. R. Hong and R. A. Good. bibliog il Science 156:1102-3 My 26 '67

GAMMA rays
Radiative-capture studies of the giant dipole resonance. R. E. Segel. bibliog il Science 158:723-30 N 10 '67
Science in search of itself; gamma-ray astronomy. A. Ewing. il Sci N 92:117 Jl 29 '67
See also
Mossbauer effect

GAMMON, Clive
International incident in Cork. Sports Illus 27:42-4+ N 27 '67
Shark of Araby. Sports Illus 27:88-91+ O 16 '67

GAMOW, George
History of the universe; with letters. bibliog Science 158:766-9 N 10 '67

GANDHI, Indira (Nehru)
Crown of thorns. il por Newsweek 69:65-6 Mr 27 '67
Daughter of India. H. Bruno. il por Newsweek 70:76 Jl 31 '67

GANDHI, Indira (Nehru)—*Continued*
Faltering India of Indira Gandhi. U S News 62:22 Mr 27 '67
Gandhi caps are in trouble in India. J. A. Lukas. il por N Y Times Mag p28-9+ F 19 '67
India campaigns: cows, corruption & demonstrations. L. I. Rudolph and S. H. Rudolph. il por Nation 204:138-43 Ja 30 '67
Leadership jolted. il Sr Schol 90:16-17 Mr 10 '67
Mrs Gandhi's headaches. N. J. Nanporia. New Repub 157:8-9 S 16 '67
Plea for the tree; campaign for national elections. il por Time 89:34 Ja 27 '67
Strength in weakness. il Time 89:35-6 Mr 10 '67
Sympathy vote; fractured nose. il por Newsweek 69:57 F 20 '67
Target of sympathy; nose broken. por Time 89:29 F 17 '67

GANGES RIVER
Slowly down the Ganges, by E. Newby. Review
Newsweek il 70:84+ Ag 14 '67. S. Maloff

GANGLIONIC nervous system. See Nervous system, Sympathetic

GANGLIOSIDES. See Sialic acids

GANGS
Gang phenomenon: big city headache; Negro youth gangs. P. Garland. il Ebony 22:96-8+ Ag '67
Hell's Angels, by H. S. Thompson. Review
Nation 204:441-2 Ap 3 '67. E. Bendiner
New Repub 156:30-2+ F 25 '67. R. M. Elman
Newsweek il 69:91+ Mr 6 '67. S. K. Oberbeck
Sat R 50:40 F 18 '67. W. Hogan
Organization men: Blackstone Rangers of Chicago gang, renounces violence. il Newsweek 69:34 Je 5 '67
She didn't scream; motorcycle gang crucify girl. il Newsweek 70:33 D 11 '67

GANGSTER; story. See O'Hara, J.

GANGSTER films. See Moving pictures—Crime films

GANGSTERS. See Crime and criminals—United States

GANN, Ernest Kellogg
Swashbuckler with a message. Sat R 50:28 O 14 '67
about
Aviation's articulate man. E. M. Miller. il pors Flying 80:58-63 Je '67

GANNETS
Nature note. il Sci N 91:204 Mr 4 '67

GANNON, Robert
I drove through a flood in a car that swims. por Pop Sci 191:76-9+ Ag '67
I spent ninety minutes in hell. por Pop Sci 191:66-9 Jl '67
Mystery of the firefly. Read Digest 91:94-7 Jl '67
Only one wheel to a customer! pors Pop Sci 190:86-9+ Je '67
Sailing the hardwater at eighty m.p.h. por Pop Sci 192:134-7 Ja '68
They dropped me in the middle of the ocean and left me there. por Pop Sci 191:90-3+ O '67
—and Fales, E. D. Jr
Dogsled derby: hills, chills, spills, thrills. Pop Sci 190:106-9 F '67
—See Walsh, J. jt. auth.

GANNON, Thomas M.
Can religion prevent delinquency? America 116:755-7 My 20 '67

GANS, Carl
Chameleon; with biographical sketch. Natur Hist 76:6, 52-9 Ap '67

GANS, Henry, and others
Selective phagocytosis: a new concept in protein catabolism. bibliog Science 159:107-10 Ja 5 '68

GANS, Herbert J.
White exodus to suburbia steps up. N Y Times Mag p24-5+ Ja 7 '68

GANTT, William Horsley
Building on Pavlov. P. McBroom. il por Sci N 91:498-9 My 27 '67

GAOLS. See Prisons

GARAGE doors
Four tamperproof ways to operate your garage door. R. M. Benrey. il Pop Sci 191:126-9 N '67

GARAGES
House planned for cars as well as people. il Arch Rec 141:143-6 F '67
In an old garage-laundry an architect finds space for his family to grow. il House B 109:126-31 Je '67

Need space? you can live in a carport. D. Shiner. il Pop Sci 191:138-43 S '67
When it's the garage, or else. il Pop Mech 128:126-9+ S '67
Workshop and a garden shop, within a two-car garage. il Sunset 138:94-7 Mr '67

GARAGES (service stations) See Automobile service stations

GARAGES, Municipal
Melt the snow on underground parking ramps; Washington, D.C. il Am City 82:52 Ag '67
Satellite service centers; Phoenix, Ariz. F. Glendening. il Am City 82:102-4 My '67
Waterproofing a parking garage; Mount Vernon, N.Y. P. Brienza. il Am City 82:142-3 S '67

GARAVANI, Valentino
New chic. il por Newsweek 70:80 Jl 31 '67

GARBAGE. See Refuse and refuse disposal

GARBAGE can. See Refuse receptacles

GARBAGE collection and disposal. See Refuse and refuse disposal

GARBAGE trucks. See Refuse collection trucks

GARCIA, Andrew
Graves and grizzles; excerpt from Tough trip through paradise; ed. by B. H. Stein. Am Heritage 18:36-9+ Je '67

GARCIA, J. and others
Conditioning with delayed vitamin injections. bibliog Science 155:716-18 F 10 '67

GARCIA, Manuel, 1805-1906
Singing voice: magic. R. Rushmore. il por Opera N 31:24-6 Ja 28 '67

GARCIA, Primitivo
Citizen Primitivo. por Time 90:28 D 8 '67

GARD, Wayne
Painter of the old West; Joe Grandee. Am Artist 31:56-7+ Je '67

GARDEN, A. Newell
Decade of marine electronics. Yachting 121:80-2+ Ja '67

GARDEN, Mary
Lyric opera and Mary Garden's shadow. R. C. Marsh. il Hi Fi 17:MA19+ F '67
Mary Garden, February 20, 1874-January 3, 1967. V. Sheean. por Opera N 31:6-7 F 4 '67

GARDEN barrows. See Wheelbarrows

GARDEN borders
Border plants with blue foliage. E. L. Sculthorp. il House B 109:64+ O '67

GARDEN carts. See Carts

GARDEN catalogs. See Catalogs, Seed and plant

GARDEN chemicals. See Agricultural chemicals

GARDEN clubs
To beautify America: turning a shambles into a park; Forsyth, Mont. R. Dalby. Home Gard 54:50 S '67

GARDEN contests. See Gardening—Competitions

GARDEN design
Color of white. il Home Gard 54:40-1 Ap '67
Create a carefree garden. E. Kondonellis. il Am Home 71:64-7 Ja '68
Gardens to live in. E. Kondonellis. il Am Home 70:70-3 Je '67
Here is a garden that began with a plan. H. V. Wilson. il Home Gard 54:32-4 Mr '67
How a bare ledge became a spring bulb garden. il House & Gard 132:232-4 S '67
Mini-garden acts big. E. Kondonellis. il Am Home 70:64-5 S '67
Planting island. J. R. Orlando. Home Gard 54:65 Mr '67
Through the looking glass; garden views. il Sunset 139:82-5 N '67
See also
Gardening—Planting plans and tables

GARDEN equipment. See Garden tools, equipment and supplies

GARDEN furniture. See Furniture, Outdoor

GARDEN gates. See Gates

GARDEN GROVE, Calif.
Centralized duplicating. G. Wiesner. il Am City 82:98-9 F '67

GARDEN hose
Buying a garden hose. il Changing T 21:34 Jl '67
Good answer for deck gardeners. il Sunset 138:219 Je '67
What you should know about garden hose. il Consumer Bul 50:25-8 Je '67

GARDEN houses, shelters, etc.
Build yourself a screen house. W. C. Leckey. il Pop Mech 127:103-7+ Mr '67
Garden house idea: it adds shelter and so it expands outdoor living. il Sunset 138:66-71 Je '67

GARDEN houses, shelters, etc.—*Continued*
Just for fun! H. Mason and others. il Bet
Hom & Gard 45:68-9 Ap '67
Outbuilding is in and the sauna is very in.
il Pop Gard 18:52-5 Mr '67
Two garden shelters. il Pop Mech 128:130-1
S '67
See also
Sheds
Trellises

GARDEN lighting. See Gardens—Lighting

GARDEN ornaments
Add faucets with a flair. W. Radcliffe. il
Pop Gard 18:6-7 Ag '67
At home in the garden. il Home Gard 54:38-9
D '67
Pebbled concrete in the garden. il Sunset 139:
128 N '67
See also
Sundials

GARDEN pests. See Insects, Injurious and
beneficial

GARDEN pools
Exposed lead membrane for reflecting pools.
il Arch Rec 142:161-2 D '67
Make a miniature water garden. D. W.
Weinsheimer. il Home Gard 54:22+ F '67
Simple pool is a wooden box. il Sunset 139:
101-2 S '67

GARDEN rooms. See Rooms

GARDEN sculpture. See Garden ornaments

GARDEN shelters. See Garden houses, shelters,
etc.

GARDEN soils. See Gardening—Soil preparation

GARDEN steps
Ups and downs in the garden. il Sunset 139:
134-5 O '67

GARDEN supplies. See Garden tools, equipment and supplies

GARDEN tools, equipment and supplies
Clip tips. il Pop Gard 18:88 Ag '67
Equipment, the extra hand that helps you;
excerpt from Vegetables for today's gardens.
R. M. Carleton. il Home Gard 54:58-9+ Mr
'67
Facts on hand tools. R. M. Hill. il Flower
Grower 54:65-9 Ja '67
Garden time-savers. il Bet Hom & Gard 45:
135+ Je '67
Gift ideas, to please a weeder, and even to
start a non-weeder off on weeding. il Sunset
139:162+ D '67
Have you heard. See issues of Flower grower,
the home garden (cont as) Home garden
& flower grower
How to make your own lawn spiker. P.
Scott. il Pop Sci 191:131 Jl '67
Machines that rake the leaves. Changing T
21:36 O '67
New gadgets to use in the yard. il Changing
T 21:21-3 F '67
On garden gear; a collection of brief and
poignant essays. il Home Gard 54:45-52
Ap '67
Report from the National hardware show.
Home Gard 54:26 D '67
Twelve days of Christmas. il House & Gard
132:190-1 D '67
See also
Garden hose
Lawn sweepers
Tractors
Care
Mostly for men. il Home Gard 54:41 N '67
Storage
Great ideas for storage space. il Pop Gard
18:40-7 D '67
Workshop and a garden shop, within a two-
car garage. il Sunset 138:94-7 Mr '67

GARDEN tours
Blazing Oregon trail; native color, azaleas and
rhododendrons. R. Friedman. il Home Gard
54:45 Je '67
Garden-hopping in the Caribbean. M. Perry.
il Home Gard 54:22-5 D '67
Garden tour of Venice by gondola. il Sunset
138:198+ Je '67

GARDEN tractors. See Tractors

GARDEN walls
Landscape ideas from Arizona. J. Fanning.
il Pop Gard 18:32-3 Mr '67

GARDENA, Calif.
Clubs
Lowball in a time capsule; poker addicts. D.
Miles. il Sports Illus 26:110-13+ Ap 17 '67

GARDENERS
Friend or foe? J. Fanning. Horticulture 45:
34-5+ O '67

Anecdotes, facetiae, satire, etc.
Block that thrip! spring and the garden expert. D. Williamson. Sat R 50:8-9 Ap 1 '67

GARDENING
Clip tips. il Pop Gard 18:86-7 Mr; 80 My '67
Doctor and his garden. W. Radcliffe. il Pop
Gard 18:69-71 D '67
For gardeners in the West, a new bookful
of answers; Sunset western garden book.
il Sunset 138:74-81 My '67
For the love of peat. J. L. O'Neill. Am
Home 70:36 My '67
Growing up in a garden. L. Bell. il House
B 109:49-51 S '67
H&G's gardener's month. See issues of House
& garden incorporating Living for young
homemakers
How to ease a guilty conscience; or, Things
you can do in July. il Sunset 139:122-3 Jl '67
How to transplant a green thumb; a gardener
adjusts to various environments. T. Hunt.
House B 109:48+ Mr '67
[Month] gardening where you live! H. Per-
kins. See issues of Better homes and gar-
dens
[Month] in your garden. See issues of Sunset
Plant the right way this spring. il Pop Gard
18:96-7 My '67
Quick and easy tips. See issues of Popular
gardening & living outdoors
Regional gardening. See issues of Popular
gardening & living outdoors
Regional report:
  Cedar Rapids, Iowa. Home Gard 54:76
  My '67
  Eugene, Oregon. Home Gard 54:78 My
  '67
  Fulton, Ill. T. Abbott. Home Gard 54:50
  Jl '67
  Jacksonville, Florida. Home Gard 54:74
  My '67
  La Crosse, Wis. P. Shedesky. il Home
  Gard 54:58-9 Ag '67
  Los Angeles, Calif. R. E. Atkinson. Home
  Gard 54:55 S '67
  Pownal, Vermont. Home Gard 54:51-2 Je
  '67
  Roanoke, Indiana. Home Gard 54:53 Je '67
  Spring Valley, N.Y. V. M. Quist. Home
  Gard 54:51 Jl '67
  Springfield, Mass. C. O. Dean. Home Gard
  54:54 S '67
  West Hatfield, Mass. B. Brinhart. il
  Home Gard 54:52-3 N '67
  Westport, Connecticut. Home Gard 54:82
  My '67
Spring planting! il Bet Hom & Gard 45:134+
My '67
Summer garden work. E. F. Steffek. Horti-
culture 45:14+ Je '67
Thirty seven good ideas for your garden. D.
Barrows. il Home Gard 54:27-34 S '67
This fall, don't desert your garden. G.
Schultz. il Pop Gard 18:6-7+ D '67
Today and tomorrow; reports on current re-
search of interest to gardeners and home-
owners. Pop Gard 18:21 Mr; 22 My; 16 Ag
'67
What makes a gardener dig. J. Barthel. il
N Y Times Mag p28-30+ Mr 5 '67
What to do in [month] See issues of Horti-
culture
What you can do now to begin your spring
garden. il Home Gard 54:34-7 Ap '67
See also
Childrens gardens
Gardeners
Mulching
Vegetable gardening
Winter gardening

Bibliography
Books: pleasures of gardening. K. Fredrick.
il House B 109:42+ Ap '67
From seeds to stately gardens. H. S. Witty.
Sat R 50:48-9 N 25 '67
Full-length portrait of H&G's basic garden
library. il House & Gard 132:292-4+ N '67
Onward and upward in the garden. K. S.
White. New Yorker 43:113-14+ D 16 '67

Competitions
Contest rules for garden club yearbooks.
Horticulture 45:44+ O '67

Equipment and supplies
See Garden tools, equipment and supplies

Planting plans and tables
Home garden guide for reluctant gardeners.
il Home Gard 54:20-1 Je; 38-9 Jl; 42-3 Ag;
24-5 S; 36-7 O; 46-7 N; 40-1 D '67

GARDENING—*Continued*

How to make big splashes in little gardens. il House & Gard 131:140-3 My '67

Plant your color. Mrs A. J. Cole. il House B 109:174-5 My '67

Story of a baseball garden; April's opening to October's World series. il Sunset 138:90-5 Ap '67

See also
Garden design

Soil preparation

Making light of heavy soil. R. M. Hill. il Home Gard 54:63-4 F '67

Study and teaching

They're going to gardening class; Los Angeles children's gardening project. il Sunset 139:174 D '67

GARDENING, indoor. See Greenhouses

GARDENING, Landscape. See Landscape gardening

GARDENING, Organic. See Organic gardening

GARDENING, Vegetable. See Vegetable gardening

GARDENS

Doctor and his garden. W. Radcliffe. il Pop Gard 18:69-71 D '67

Golden days in grandpa's garden. M. Holmes. il Todays Health 45:48-51 Je '67

Growing up in a garden. L. Bell. il House B 109:49-51 S '67

Plan a garden oasis. E. Kondonellis. il Am Home 70:58-9 Jl '67

Vest-pocket gardens. il Am Home 70:98-9 O '67

See also
Childrens gardens
City gardens
Gardening
Roof gardens

Color

Border plants with blue foliage. E. L. Sculthorp. il House B 109:64+ O '67

Bountiful gift of summer color. il Home Gard 54:42-4 Je '67

Color of white. il Home Gard 54:40-1 Ap '67

Companion plants with lilies. V. Howie. il Horticulture 45:26-9+ My '67

Flowers of blue for cool accents all season long. A. Murphy. il Home Gard 54:38-9 My '67

Garden is color. il Am Home 70:88 Mr '67

Gardener's calendar of color:
Spring. H. Mason. il Bet Hom & Gard 46:48-53 Ja '68

Instant color, or color soon, with plants you put into your garden now. il Sunset 138:104-7 My '67

Late-blooming perennials. E. S. Henderson. il Horticulture 45:12-15+ S '67

Plant them now for summer color in the shade. il Sunset 138:254+ My '67

Plant two months of spring color now. H. Mason and R. O'Harra. il Bet Hom & Gard 45:64-7 S '67

Plant your color. Mrs A. J. Cole. il House B 109:174-5 My '67

Put color highlights in your summer garden. P. F. Frese. il Pop Gard 18:32-5+ Ag '67

Rainbow of tulip color. il Home Gard 54:20-1 S '67

Snows of spring, fresh with fragrance. L. Bell. il Home Gard 54:38-9 Ap '67

They both give you cool blue. il Sunset 139:154+ S '67

Treat yourself to a riot of color in your spring garden. P. F. Frese. il Pop Gard 18:52-3 My '67

Winter color in your coldframe. M. Helleiner. il Horticulture 45:26-7 N '67

Cost

Ways to trim garden expenses. Am Home 70:118-19 Ja '67

History

Eight great women in the garden world. C. S. Langdon. Home Gard 54:59-60 My '67

Lighting

And on into the night. H. Mason and others. il Bet Hom & Gard 45:74-5+ Ap '67

Glow that only garden lights can give. B. C. Kilvert, jr. il Home Gard 54:20-1 D '67

Plug in on the low voltage circuit. B. Powell. il Pop Gard 18:8-15 D '67

Unusual lights in the garden. il Sunset 139:153+ O '67

Alabama

Bellingrath gardens, colorful remembrance of times past. C. Carter. il Home Gard 54:23-5 N '67

Arizona

Landscape ideas from Arizona. J. Fanning. il Pop Gard 18:32-3 Mr '67

Arkansas

We won the rock fight. A. Daniel. il Home Gard 54:62-3 Mr '67

California

Garden high on a woodsy hill around a circular swimming pool. il Sunset 139:118-19 Ag '67

It's Australia come to California, an almost all-eucalyptus garden. il Sunset 138:190+ Je '67

Landscape ideas from California. J. Fanning. il Pop Gard 18:30-1 Mr '67

This garden almost takes care of itself. il Sunset 139:242-3 O '67

Canada

Canada's garden of wonders; Butchart gardens. D. MacDonald. il Read Digest 90:145-50+ Je '67

One of the great treats of your visit to Victoria, a walk in Butchart gardens. il Sunset 139:46-7 Ag '67

Caribbean Region

Garden-hopping in the Caribbean. M. Perry. il Home Gard 54:22-5 D '67

Connecticut

Here is a garden that began with a plan. H. V. Wilson. il Home Gard 54:32-4 Mr '67

Landscape ideas from Connecticut. J. Fanning. il Pop Gard 18:26-7 Mr '67

Delaware

Delaware delights. D. Seibert. il Travel 127:46-7 Ap '67

Winterthur, the gardens of Mr and Mrs Henry Francis du Pont. C. G. Tyrrell. il Horticulture 45:36-7+ My '67

England

Ancient manor garden; Albury park, one of England's treasures. M. Perry. il Home Gard 54:50-1 My '67

See also
Kent, England—Gardens

Europe, Western

Many facets of Europe. M. Perry. il Home Gard 54:58-61 Ap '67

Florida

Shades of a lath house, and carpets of color. C. Calkins. il House B 109:88-9 Ja '67

Georgia

Touring Georgia. il Home Gard 54:66-7 My '67

Italy

Garden tour of Venice by gondola. il Sunset 138:198+ Je '67

Water gardens of Italy's Villa d'Este. M. J. Dietz. il Home Gard 54:58-9 Ap '67

Japan

Lilliputian world of the bonsai; K. Murata's Garden of the nine mists, Omiya. N. F. Busch. il Read Digest 91:182-6+ S '67

Simplicity is the keynote in Japanese gardening. A. R. Roalman. il Pop Gard 18:18-21+ D '67

Madeira

People and plants of Madeira. J. V. Watkins. il Horticulture 45:42-3 Je '67

Massachusetts

See also
Boston—Gardens
Shelburne Falls, Mass.—Gardens

Mexico

Gardens of Mexico, intriguing alchemy of tradition and imagination. C. M. Zapata. il Home Gard 54:48-9 S '67

Michigan

Island is a place apart. R. B. Alford. Home Gard 54:52-3 Jl '67

Netherlands

Holland's great spring bulb show. il Sunset 138:31-2 My '67

New England

Dooryard garden. C. B. Lees. il Horticulture 45:32-7+ Mr '67

GARDENS—*Continued*

New York (state)

Photographer's paradise. il U S Camera 30:16 N '67

Oregon

Landscape ideas from Oregon. J. Fanning. il Pop Gard 18:34-9 Mr '67

Pennsylvania

Delaware delights. D. Seibert. il Travel 127: 46-7 Ag '67
Longwood gardens; near Kennett Square. il Home Gard 54:44-5 Ag '67

Portugal

Portugal, land of gardeners. J. V. Watkins. il Horticulture 45:36-7+ O '67

Sicily

Garden of the heart; Countess Bismarck's garden. V. Lawford. il Vogue 149:182-7+ Ap 1 '67

South America

Gardener goes to South America. R. Bailey. il House & Gard 132:168-9+ D '67

Texas

Landscape ideas from Texas. J. Fanning. il Pop Gard 18:28-9 Mr '67

Virginia

Virginia welcomes the spring season. il Home Gard 54:14-15 Mr '67
Virginia's historic gardens. C. Massie. il Travel 127:48-9 Ap '67

Washington (state)

Why not golf right at home? il Sunset 138: 112-14+ My '67

GARDENS, Childrens. See Childrens gardens

GARDENS, City. See City gardens

GARDENS, Indoor
Garden for all seasons. B. Plumb. il N Y Times Mag p52-3 Je 18 '67
Indoor flower garden; kitchen garden. Vogue 150:333-5 S 1 '67
Living with plants. M. Adams. il Horticulture 45:34-5+ S '67
Mounting greenery. il Newsweek 70:88 O 23 '67
Shades of a lath house, and carpets of color. C. Calkins. il House B 109:88-9 Ja '67
Wagener house, Boulder, Colorado. il Arch Rec 141:104-7 mid-My '67

GARDENS, Italian
See also
Gardens—Italy

GARDENS, Japanese
For a different look borrow from the East. il Pop Gard 18:44-9 Ag '67
This fifty-year-old Japanese garden south of San Francisco is welcoming visitors. il Sunset 139:42 N '67
See also
Gardens—Japan

GARDENS, Oriental
Add a touch of the Orient. J. Fanning. il Pop Gard 18:16-17 D '67

GARDENS, Rock
Starting a rock garden. R. Murfitt. il Horticulture 45:24-5+ Ap '67

GARDENS, Roof. See Roof gardens

GARDENS, Seaside
Gardening by the sea. G. Taloumis. il Pop Gard 18:24-9+ Ag '67
Native plants for seaside gardens. G. Jenkins. il Horticulture 45:34-7+ Jl '67

GARDENS, Sunken
Charm of a sunken garden. il Pop Gard 18: 42-3 My '67

GARDENS, Vegetable. See Vegetable gardening

GARDENS, Watering of. See Watering of gardens, lawns, etc.

GARDINER, David E.
(comp) Articles and other books received; Africa. See issues of American historical review

GARDINER, Gilbert
(tr) See Turgenev, I. S. Turgenev's Traviata

GARDINER, John A.
Public attitudes toward gambling and corruption. bibliog f Ann Am Acad 374:123-34 N '67

GARDINER, Leslie
Bergamot country. Atlan 220:104-5 Jl '67

GARDINER, Robert David Lion
Two millionaires, East and West. il por Sat Eve Post 240:24-5 D 30 '67

GARDINER, Sprague H.
Postpartum depression. Redbook 129:31+ O '67

GARDNER, Ava
Ava: life in the afternoon. R. Reed. por Esquire 67:102-3+ My '67

GARDNER, Donald W.
Woolpacks and wonders in New Brunswick. Motor B 119:24-7+ Ap '67

GARDNER, Erle Stanley
Can new non-lethal weapons control riots? por Pop Sci 191:48-52 D '67
I love camping, my way. por Pop Sci 190:161+ My '67

GARDNER, Evelyn
My brother Evelyn; excerpts from My brother Evelyn and other literary portraits. A. Waugh. Atlan 219:57-60 Je '67

GARDNER, Herb
Who is Harry Kellerman and why is he saying those terrible things about me? story. Sat Eve Post 240:54-6 Mr 11 '67

GARDNER, Isabella
Who spilled the salt? poem. Atlan 220:111 S '67

GARDNER, John W.
Abused child. McCalls 94:96-7+ S '67
But what of the dream? excerpt from address, October 12, 1967. Read Digest 92:37-41 Ja '68
Century of cooperation. NEA J 56:61 S '67
Fancy gothic fiction; adaptation of remarks, December 2, 1966. Library J 92:1896-7 My 15 '67
Integrating America, the problems; interview. por U S News 62:64-9 My 8 '67
Ten commitments. por Sat R 50:39-40 Jl 1 '67
U.S. domestic crisis? excerpts from address, December 27, 1967. por US News 64:12 Ja 8 '68

about

Well done, Gardner! Reporter 36:10 Je 1 '67
Wooing critics the LBJ way. por U S News 62:20 My 22 '67

GARDNER, Martha
Co-op murals of the past and present. Sch Arts 66:18-19 Mr '67

GARDNER, Martin
Casey at the bat; excerpts from The annotated Casey at the bat. Am Heritage 18: 64-8 O 67
It's more probable than you think. Read Digest 91:107-10 N '67
Mathematical games. See issues of Scientific American
Short but wild history of spirit photography. Pop Phot 61:65 O '67

GARFIELD, Brian
He signposted the Santa Fe trail. Sat R 50:52 Je 10 '67
When Custer guided a coxcomb. Sat R 50:43 F 11 '67

GARFIELD, Eugene
Information retrieval. Science 156:1398+ Je 9 '67

GARFUNKEL, Art
Simon & Garfunkel; interview. New Yorker 43:24-7 S 2 '67
We talk to; interview by Mademoiselle's guest editors. por Mlle 65:326 Ag '67

about

People are talking about... por Vogue 149: 110-11 Je '67
Simon & Garfunkel in action. M. Ames. il pors Hi Fi 17:62-6 N '67
Syncopated times. por Newsweek 69:98+ F 6 '67
Two fine rockers roll their own. S. Kanfer. Life 62:18 Ap 21 '67

GARGA, Bhagwan D.
India's ancient heroes on celluloid. UNESCO Courier 20:43+ D '67

GARGAN, Edward T.
Great human option. Nation 204:216-20 F 13 '67
No right to be wrong. Nation 206:22-4 Ja 1 '68

GARIBALDI, Carole
Movie report. See issues of Good housekeeping

GARIBALDI provincial park. See British Columbia—Parks and reserves

GARIS, Robert
Art-movie style. Commentary 44:77-9 Ag '67
Persona. Commentary 44:80-2 D '67
Watching Antonioni. Commentary 43:86-9 Ap; 44:15-17 Ag '67

GARLAND, Judy
Garland phenomenon. B. Korall. por Sat R 50:66 S 30 '67
Judy Garland at home at the Palace. T. Lewis. America 117:208-inside back cover Ag 26 '67
Plot against Judy Garland. por Ladies Home J 84:64-5+ Ag '67
Séance at the Palace. il Time 90:40 Ag 18 '67

GARLAND, Phyllis
Aretha Franklin, sister soul. Ebony 22:47-8+ O '67
Child is a child, is a child. Ebony 22:44-6+ Ap '67
Gang phenomenon; big city headache. Ebony 22:96-8+ Ag '67
In groups of the big beat. Ebony 22:38+ Je '67
Requiem for 'Trane. Ebony 23:66-8+ N '67

GARLIC
Garlic for garlic's sake; with recipes. E. Alston. il Look 31:44 Je 13 '67
Great garlic surprise; aïoli sauce. il Sunset 138:88-9 Ap '67
Kitchen nosegay of garlic. il Sunset 139:98 Jl '67

GARLITS, Don
Gran papa. J. McFarland. il pors Hot Rod 20: 78-80 D '67

GARMENT trades. See Clothing industry

GARMENT workers
See also
Amalgamated clothing workers of America
Clothing industry—Wages and hours
International ladies garment workers' union

GARNER, H. F.
Rivers in the making; with biographical sketch. Sci Am 216:14, 84-8+ Ap '67

GARNER, John Nance
Cactus Jack. il por Newsweek 70:71-2 N 20 '67
Chairman of the board. il por Time 90:32 N 17 '67
One of the last of the frontier politicians. il pors U S News 63:18 N 20 '67

GARNER, Louis E. jr
Music à la theremin. Pop Electr 27:29-33+ N '67
Solid state. See issues of Popular electronics

GARNETT, William A.
America begins in New England; photographs. Life 62:50-65 Mr 3 '67

GARNISHES
Garnishing cook book. D. R. Pace. il House & Gard 132:133-8 Ag '67
Sumptuous art of garnishing. il House & Gard 132:128-30+ Ag '67

GAROZZO, Benito
Bridge. por Sports Illus 26:50+ Ja 23 '67

GARRETS. See Attics

GARRETT, Mike
Kansas City's Mike Garrett: big little chief. G. Astor. il pors Look 31:112-18+ N 14 '67

GARRETT, W. G. See Walker, G. F. jt. auth.

GARRETT, Wendell D.
Antiques and United States tariff legislation, 1816-1966. Antiques 92:546-51 O '67
Living with antiques. Antiques 92:203-7 Ag '67
—See Parsons, S. jt. auth.

GARRIDO, Salvador Sampayo
Portugal and the new republics. Américas 19: 24-9 Ap '67

GARRIGUE, Jean
Dominant house; poem. New Yorker 43:30 Jl 29 '67
Estates of the Loire; poem. New Yorker 43:30 Ag 19 '67
Flux of autumn: Consecration piece; Little ballad; poems. Poetry 110:359-64 S '67
Those summer guests; poem. Nation 205:157-8 Ag 28 '67

GARRISON, Jim
Bourbon street rococo. por Time 89:26 Mr 3 '67
Carnival in New Orleans. il por Newsweek 69:32+ Mr 6 '67
Case of Jim Garrison and Lee Oswald. G. Roberts. il pors N Y Times Mag p32-5+ My 21 '67
Closing in. Time 90:17 Jl 7 '67
From a governor and a D.A. an offer of resignation. S. Smith. il por Life 63:34-6 S 29 '67
Is Garrison faking? F. Powledge. New Repub 156:13-18 Je 17 '67
JFK conspiracy. H. Aynesworth. il por Newsweek 69:36+ My 15 '67
JFK death: a new investigation, but—. por U S News 62:16 Mr 13 '67
Law unto himself. il por Newsweek 71:25-6 Ja 8 '68

More on the Kennedy assassination charges; concerning his TV broadcast. il por U S News 62:55-6 Je 12 '67
New Orleans: act I. J. Cohen and N. C. Chriss. il Reporter 36:17-20 Ap 6 '67
Odd company. il Time 89:24 Mr 10 '67
Plot to kill Kennedy? rush to judgment in New Orleans. J. Phelan. il por Sat Eve Post 240:21-5 My 6 '67
Something of a shambles. Time 89:42 Je 30 '67
Taste for conspiracy. il Newsweek 69:76 Mr 20 '67
Theory of an Oswald conspiracy. por Life 62:33 Mr 3 '67

GARRISON, Lloyd
Ibos got it alone. N Y Times Mag p30-2+ Je 11 '67
On location with Richard and Elizabeth (& 145 friends) N Y Times Mag p30-1+ My 7 '67

GARRISON, Louis E. See Emery, K. O. jt. auth.

GARRISON, R. Benjamin
Dim view of a bright prospect: the proposed United Methodist church. Christian Cent 84:314-16 Mr 8 '67

GARRISON, Roger H.
Unique problems of junior colleges; excerpts from address. NEA J 56:30-2 N '67

GARSON, Barbara
MacBird! Criticism
Am Rec G 33:974-6 Je '67
Christian Cent 84:725-6 My 31 '67
Commentary 43:88-9 Mr '67
Life 62:16 Mr 17 '67
Nat R 19:702-3 Je 27 '67
Nation 204:348-9 Mr 13 '67
New Repub 156:30-2 Mr 11 '67; Reply with rejoinder. N. Plotkin. 156:41-2 Ap 8 '67
New Yorker 43:127 Mr 11 '67
Newsweek 69:99 F 27 '67
Newsweek il 69:79 Mr 6 '67
Sat R 50:30 Mr 11 '67
Time il 89:52 Mr 3 '67
Vogue 149:48 Ap 15 '67
Much ado about Mac. por Newsweek 69:99 F 27 '67

GARSON, John R. See Berman, H. J. jt. auth.

GARSTANG, R. H.
Joint institute for laboratory astrophysics. Sky & Tel 33:150-2 Mr '67

GART, Murray
Report from Manila. Fortune 76:69+ D '67

GARTH, Midi
Midi Garth dance theatre, Village theatre. J. Anderson. Dance Mag 41:39+ My '67

GARTNER, John
Deschutes steelhead. Field & S 72:40-1+ Jl '67

GARTNER, Louis J.
Going places, finding things on Elba. House & Gard 132:30-1+ N '67

GARVER, Juliet
Father hits the jackpot; drama. Plays 26: 64-72 My '67

GARVEY, Albert
Houseboats of Sausalito. Arch Forum 126:48-53 Mr '67

GARVEY, Ernest, pseud.
White House aborts the riots commission. Commonweal 87:429-30 Ja 12 '68

GARVEY, William D. and Griffith, B. C.
Scientific communication as a social system; excerpt from address, November 22, 1966. bibliog Science 157:1011-16 S 1 '67
—See Compton, B. E. jt. auth.

GARWIN, R. L.
MIRV and the offensive missile race; letter. Bul Atomic Sci 23:21 D '67

GARWOOD, John D.
Teaching, research, and academic freedom. Sch & Soc 95:413-14 N 11 '67

GARWOOD, Margaret
Trojan women. Criticism
Opera N 32:28 D 23 '67

GARY, Romain
Dear elephant, sir. Life 63:126-39 D 22 '67
Flamboyant Guadeloupe. Holiday 42:54-9+ Ag '67

GARY, Ind.

Elections
Black power at the polls; Stokes, Hatcher victories. C. L. Sanders; A. Poinsett. il Ebony 23:23-6+ Ja '68
Cleveland and Gary. Newsweek 70:66-7 N 20 '67
Real black power. il Time 90:23-7 N 17 '67
Victory over prejudice and corruption. il Life 63:38-9 N 17 '67

GARY, Ind.—*Continued*

Negroes

Report. C. Stone. Atlan 220:28-30+ O '67
Vote power; Gary's Negroes nominate R. Hatcher as Democratic mayorial candidate. il Time 89:21-2 My 12 '67

Politics and government

Gary's next mayor; white, pink, or black? H. Higdon. Reporter 37:41-2 N 2 '67
Lawyer takes on a corrupt steel town's machine. il Life 63:38-9 O 13 '67
Plea from Gary. Time 90:24 S 15 '67
Report; mayoral election. C. Stone. Atlan 220:28-30+ O '67
   See also
Gary, Ind.—Elections

Water supply

Our honeymoon with automation. H. D. Harman. il Am City 82:112-13 Je '67

GAS, Interstellar. See Matter, Interstellar

GAS, Natural
Britain's bonanza at the bottom of the sea. J. H. Winchester. il Read Digest 91:138-43 Ag '67
Old fuel gives a new lift to world's power supply. il U S News 63:92+ O 23 '67
Project Gasbuggy. N. Carlisle and J. Carlisle. il Pop Mech 128:102-5+ S '67

Liquefaction

Liquid natural gas. N. De Nevers. il Sci Am 217:30-7 bibliog(p156) O '67
Where natural gas behaves like a genie. il Bsns W p 144-6+ Ja 21 '67

Pipe lines
   See also
Trancontinental gas pipe line corporation

Storage

Where natural gas behaves like a genie. il Bsns W p 144-6+ Ja 21 '67

GAS and oil engines
   See also
Airplane engines
Automobile engines
Marine engines

GAS and oil engines, Inboard
1968 inboard engines. il Motor B 121:140-4 Ja '68

GAS and oil engines, Outboard
Evinrude's 100-S: good-natured speed demon. J. Roe. il Pop Sci 190:132-4 Ap '67
New outboard engines, 1968. E. H. Nabb. il Yachting 122:44-6+ O '67
New power for fishermen. F. M. Paulson. il Field & S 72:90-3 D '67
1968 outboard motors. il Motor B 121:168-71 Ja '68
1968 outboard preview. Outdoor Life 140:8+ O '67
Now Honda's got an outboard and PM tests it. A. Mikesell. il Pop Mech 127:146-8+ Mr '67
Outboard power for '68. J. Gribbins. il Motor B 120:118-20 O '67
Outboard the Bahamas. F. M. Paulson. il Field & S 72:68-71 My '67
'68 outboards are here! J. Roe. il Pop Sci 191:126-30+ O '67
'68 outboards: from 19-pound minipack to a 125-hp powerhorse. A. Mikesell. il Pop Mech 128:90-3+ O '67
Which type of power? J. A. Emmett. il Outdoor Life 140:76-9 Jl '67

Care

Don't leave it alone! interview, ed. by M. Crook. L. Eppel. il Yachting 121:90-1 Je '67
How to get more out of your outboard. H. B. Notrom. il Pop Mech 128:144-7 Jl '67
Starting a stubborn outboard. H. B. Notrom. il Pop Mech 127:134-7 Je '67
Troubleshooting your outboard by ear. H. B. Notrom. il Pop Mech 128:144-7+ Ag '67

Fuel

Flexible fuel system for your outboard. F. C. Clark, jr. il Pop Sci 190:135-7 Ap '67

Ignition

Convert your outboard to electronic ignition. H. B. Notrom. il Pop Mech 127:172-5+ Ap '67
Those new black box ignitions. H. B. Notrom. il Pop Mech 127:158-60+ F '67

Testing

Testing the biggest and the littlest outboards. J. Roe. il Pop Sci 192:116-19 Ja '68

GAS as fuel
   See also
Gas, Natural
Gas heating
Gas stoves

GAS-centrifuge process. See Foundry practice

GAS centrifuges. See Centrifuges

GAS chromatography. See Chromatographic analysis

GAS companies
   See also
Pacific gas and electric company

GAS fuel cells. See Fuel cells

GAS heating
Home-heating battle gets still warmer. il Bsns W p76-7 Ag 12 '67

GAS lasers. See Lasers

GAS stoves
Kitchen ranges. il Consumer Rep 32:12-24 D '67
Newest gas ranges work without pilots! il Good H 165:176 S '67

GAS turbines
In a spin over research; examining turbulent airflow in working model of gas turbine compressor. il Sci N 91:234 Mr 11 '67
Jet turbine for Jacksonville, Ill. il Am City 82:18 S '67

GAS turbines, Aircraft
Allison plans series of small turboprops. M. L. Yaffee. il Aviation W 87:83+ N 27 '67
French engine companies strong, growing. il Aviation W 86:265+ My 29 '67
HP-137 Jetstream aimed at new markets. il Aviation W 86:345+ My 29 '67
Leading international gas turbines; specifications (cont) Aviation W 86:193-4 Mr 6 '67
Leading turbine-powered business aircraft; specifications (cont) Aviation W 86:208 Mr 6 '67
NASA evaluates bids to study lift-engine exhaust ingestion. G. S. Hunter. Aviation W 86:87+ Je 19 '67
New crop. il Flying 80:32-9 F '67
1967 delivery is C-5 flight engine goal. il Aviation W 87:207+ N 20 '67
Pilot report:
   Centurion. A. Trammell. il Flying 81:47-9+ D '67
   Turbo Viking. R. B. Weeghman. il Flying 81:54-5 D '67
Pilot report: Commander Turbo II. R. B. Weeghman. il Flying 81:52-4 O '67
Pilot report: King Air. A. Trammell. il Flying 81:42-6 N '67
Pilot report: Turbo Baron. A. Trammell. il Flying 82:68-71 Ja '68
Pilot report: Volpar Turboliner. R. Blodget. il Flying 81:58-60 O '67
Reduced noise, more flexibility offered in Trent RB.203 engine. Aviation W 86:39 F 6 '67
Rolls stressing airbus engine technology. il Aviation W 86:273+ My 29 '67
Soviets add two new versions to growing An-24 family; twin-turboprop transport. W. H. Gregory. il Aviation W 87:54-5+ Jl 10 '67
Soviets break tradition in Yak-40 design; three-engine, short-haul transport using turbofan engines. W. H. Gregory. il Aviation W 86:30-2 Je 19 '67
Sweden builds powerful military turbofan. il Aviation W 86:278-81 My 29 '67
Thrust growth stressed for 747 engine. M. L. Yaffee. il Aviation W 87:79-81+ N 20 '67
Transall proposed as cargo feederliner; twin-turboprop transport. il Aviation W 86:34 Je 19 '67
Turbines. A. Trammell. il Flying 81:98-102 O '67
U.S. gas turbine engines; specifications (cont) Aviation W 86:191-2 Mr 6 '67
   See also
Helicopter engines

Care

Separators tested to cut engine erosion. R. F. Coburn. il Aviation W 86:55+ My 22 '67

Design

Lycoming expands turbine engine family. M. L. Yaffee. il Aviation W 87:59+ D 18 '67
Maintainability gains as design criteria. J. F. Judge. il Aero Tech 21:55-7+ Jl 17 '67

Fuel

P&W tests thickened fuel in turbojet. il Aviation W 86:71 Ap 17 '67

GAS turbines, Aircraft—*Continued*

Maintenance and repair

Maintainability gains as design criteria. J. F. Judge. il Aero Tech 21:55-7+ Jl 17 '67

Materials

New bonding process may cut titanium engine blade weight. Aviation W 86:37 Ap 3 '67

Statistics

Turbojet aircraft 1966 operations; traffic statistics; table. Aviation W 86:54-5+ Ap 3 '67

Turbojet, turbofan aircraft 1966 operating costs; table. Aviation W 86:46 My 15 '67

Turbojet, turbofan aircraft 1966 operating expense; table. Aviation W 86:49+ My 15 '67

Turbojet, turbofan aircraft operating expense; tables. Aviation W 87:56-7 N 13 '67

Turboprop aircraft 1966 operating costs; table. Aviation W 86:34 My 22 '67

Turboprop aircraft 1966 operating expense, dollars per total aircraft hour; table. Aviation W 86:32-3 My 22 '67

Turboprop aircraft 1966 operations and traffic statistics; table. Aviation W 86:52-3 Ap 3 '67

Turboprop aircraft operating expense; tables. Aviation W 87:50 O 23 '67

Superchargers

See Airplane engines—Superchargers

Testing

Rolls emphasizing composites to cut costs in airbus engine. H. J. Coleman. il Aviation W 87:38-9+ N 6 '67

GAS turbines, Automotive

Big engine that almost did. B. Kilpatrick. il Pop Mech 128:69-71 Ag '67

Equality and fraternity; turbine car. Sports Illus 26:8 Je 19 '67

Gentlemen, junk your engines. B. Ottum. il Sports Illus 26:30-3 Je 12 '67

Rufus and the turbine. J. McFarland. il Hot Rod 20:40-2 N '67

Silence is not always golden; Indy 500. J. Ethridge. il Motor T 19:42-9 Ag '67

Will this turbine change Indy? J. McFarland. il Hot Rod 20:86-8 My '67

GAS turbines, Marine

Is there a marine turbine in your future? V. Debiasi. il Motor B 120:27-30 D '67

GAS warfare. See Gases in warfare

GAS wells. See Gas, Natural

GASBUGGY project. See Atomic blasting

GASES

See also

Space vehicles—Cabin atmospheres

Liquefaction

See also

Gas, Natural—Liquefaction

GASES, Rare

Isotopic analysis of rare gases with a laser microprobe. G. H. Megrue. bibliog il Science 157:1555-6 S 29 '67

Primordial rare gases in unequilibrated ordinary chondrites. D. Heymann and E. Mazor. bibliog Science 155:701-2 F 10 '67

GASES in warfare

Gas warfare; proof of Egyptian poison-gas attacks in Yemen. Newsweek 70:45 Ag 7 '67

How Nasser used poison gas; statements and medical report. R. Janin; W. Brutschin; D. E. Lauppi. U S News 63:60 Jl 3 '67

In new detail, Nasser's gas war; use in Yemen. il U S News 63:9 Jl 10 '67

Nasser's poison gas. Reporter 36:12+ Je 15 '67

See also

Chemical warfare

GASKETS

Sealing watchers. J. McFarland. il Hot Rod 20:92-5 Mr '67

Silicone gaskets lengthen luminaire life. R. R. Long. il Am City 82:113 Jl '67

GASKILL, Gordon

Everything's better in Kyoto. Read Digest 92:166-70+ Ja '68

Never underestimate the power of a pocket piano. Read Digest 91:191-2+ Jl '67

GASOLINE

Additives

Platformate illusion by courtesy of Shell's advertising men. il Consumer Bul 51:26 Ja '68

What can PFA 55MB do for you? alcohol blend eliminates fuel icing problems. A. Trammell. il Flying 80:44-5+ F '67

Prices

Esso goes to war; Britain's gasoline war. il Time 89:97-8 Mr 17 '67

Gasoline's penny rise raises federal hackles; companies march to Washington to debate increase. il Bsns W p40-1 F 18 '67

Not as fast, not as fierce. Time 89:90 F 17 '67

Oilmen get the word on prices. Bsns W p42 F 25 '67

GASOLINE credit cards. See Credit cards

GASPÉ peninsula

Grand loop drive around French Canada's lovely Gaspé. il Sunset 138:50-2+ Ap '67

GASS, Oscar

China, Russia & the U.S. bibliog f Commentary 43:65-73 Mr; 39-46 Ap '67

GASSER, Henry

From pencil note to painting. Design 69:20-4 Wint '67

Illustrations of Steven Kidd. Am Artist 31:38-43+ Je '67

GASTON, Suzanne, and Menaker, Michael

Photoperiodic control of hamster tests. bibliog Science 158:925-8 N 17 '67

GASTRIN antibodies. See Antigens and antibodies

GASTRONOMY. See Eating; Food

GASTROPODS

Gastropod urosalpinx: pH of accessory boring organ while boring. M. R. Carriker and others. bibliog il Science 157:920-2 N 17 '67

Heliacus, gastropoda: architectonicidae, symbiotic with zoanthiniaria, coelenterata. R. Robertson. bibliog il Science 156:246-8 Ap 14 '67

Littorina littorea: occurrence in a northern Newfoundland beach terrace, predating Norse settlements. J. B. Bird. Science 159:114 Ja 5 '68

GASTROVASCULAR system. See Vascular system

GATE; story. See Elizalde, F. de

GATES, Arthur I.

Talks to teachers. NEA J 56:34-5 O '67

GATES, David M.

Missouri botanical garden. Horticulture 45:32-3+ Je '67

GATES, Gary Paul

Chicago after dark. Holiday 41:70-3+ Mr '67

GATES, Gerald F.

Reach to the bottom of the barrel. Sch Arts 67:24-6 O '67

GATES

Look to the east. il Pop Gard 18:17 Ag '67

GATEWAY arch. See St Louis—Monuments, statues, etc.

GATTMANN, Eric, and others

College? man, you must be kidding! NEA J 56:8-10 S '67

GAUCHIE, Robert

Man who refused to die. L. Elliott. il Read Digest 91:73-80 N '67

GAUD, William Steen, 1907-

AID report on Viet-Nam commodity programs submitted to President Johnson; letter of transmittal, January 9, 1967. Dept State Bul 56:200-1 F 6 '67

CENTO economic committee meets at Washington; statement, March 14, 1967. Dept State Bul 56:668-70 Ap 24 '67

New opportunities in Asia; address, October 4, 1967. Dept State Bul 57:579-84 O 30 '67

GAUGES. See Gages

GAULLE, Charles de

De Gaulle speaks; summary of news conference, November 27, 1967. Sr School 91:15-16 D 14 '67

European common market; address, May 16, 1967. Vital Speeches 33:495-7 Je 1 '67

Letter from Paris; excerpts from press conference. New Yorker 43:98 D 9 '67

Progress, independence & peace; address, August 10, 1967. Vital Speeches 33:677-8 S 1 '67

about

After the vote; where de Gaulle is headed. il por U S News 62:35-6 Mr 20 '67

Always like that. il por Time 90:22 Ag 11 '67

Anger in Paris. J. Blocker. il Newsweek 70:33-4 Jl 24 '67

Biggest victory for de Gaulle? por U S News 63:19-20 D 4 '67

Black president for France? position of G. Monnerville. il pors Ebony 23:88-90+ N '67

British question hangs fire. il por Bsns W p38 Je 3 '67

But first, a message. Newsweek 70:50 N 27 '67

Can de Gaulle break the dollar? with interviews with J. Rueff and E. Despres. il U S News 63:54-6+ D 11 '67

GAULLE, Charles de —About—*Continued*
Charles le vieux. il Time 90:45 Ag 4 '67
Charlie against the tide. Fortune 75:77 Je 1 '67
Counterattack. Newsweek 70:46-7 S 4 '67
De Gaulle and the Jews. Newsweek 70:47 D 11 '67
De Gaulle has spoken. Nat R 19:544-5 My 30 '67
De Gaulle on America. Nat R 19:1106+ O 17 '67
De Gaulle surveys the damage. E. Taylor. Reporter 36:29-30 Ap 6 '67
De Gaulle under fire; his tenure threatened? por U S News 63:17 Ag 21 '67
De Gaulle: wrecker or leader? appraisal of French president. il pors U S News 62:66-70 F 20 '67
De Gaulle's cold war on the U.S. A. De Borchgrave. il por Newsweek 71:36-8 Ja 22 '68
De Gaulle's great plan. E. M. von Kuehnelt-Leddihn. Nat R 19:897 Ag 22 '67
De Gaulle's second veto. il Newsweek 71:30+ Ja 1 '68
Europe minus America. New Repub 157:7-8 O 21 '67
For de Gaulle, troubles piling up at home, too. il U S News 63:78 Ag 14 '67
France: fading hero. il por Newsweek 70:30-2+ Ag 28 '67
France still says 'non' il por Bsns W p37 D 2 '67
Free Quebec: how serious a threat? il U S News 63:50 S 11 '67
French business smiles at Canada. il por Bsns W p24-6 Jl 22 '67
French people's message to Charles de Gaulle. il U S News 62:52-3 Mr 27 '67
General attacks: target everyone. il Newsweek 70:42+ D 11 '67
Le grand faux pas of le grand Charles M. Clark. il por Life 63:44B-44C Ag 4 '67
Grandeur diminished. H. Brandon. Sat R 50:6+ Jl 29 '67
Le grim Charles? Sr Schol 90:18-19 Mr 31 '67
How far will de Gaulle unbend? por Bsns W p44 Mr 18 '67
How to hurt a Frenchman. H. Moffett. il por Life 64:34-34B Ja 19 '68
Kind of Europe de Gaulle will allow. il por U S News 62:22 My 29 '67
Letter from Paris (cont) Genêt. New Yorker 42:80+ Ja 28; 43:110+ F 25; 151-4 Mr 11; 172-4 Mr 25; 175 Ap 15; 170-2 Ap 29; 170+ My 13; 124+ My 27; 84+ Je 24 '67
Luxembourg versus de Gaulle. J. Ross-Skinner. il Duns R 90:41-2 Jl '67
No doubts; falling popularity. Time 90:28 Ag 18 '67
Old madnesses in different dress. Christian Cent 84:1620-1 D 20 '67
Old soldier fading? with editorial comment. il por Bsns W p32, 132 Ag 5 '67
On allies and enemies. M. Ascoli. Reporter 36:12 Je 1 '67
Only a man. por Newsweek 70:48+ N 13 '67
Quebec's liberty, de Gaulle keeps pushing. por U S News 63:16 Ag 14 '67
Quo vadis, Charles de Gaulle? il por Newsweek 70:32-3 Jl 24 '67
Running scared. il Newsweek 69:64 Mr 13 '67
Rush to judgement. Nat R 19:1312 N 28 '67
Sad twilight for de Gaulle. Life 63:4 Ag 11 '67
Second round. Newsweek 70:38+ Ag 14 '67
Seeing de Gaulle plain. Time 91:21 Ja 12 '68
Seeking alternatives to de Gaulle. Life 62:4 F 10 '67
Shooting at Europe. il por Bsns W p37-8 Ja 28 '67
Sic transit Charlie. Nation 205:100 Ag 14 '67
Signs of a break in U.S.-British ties. il por U S News 62:14 F 6 '67
Struggle of après-de Gaulle has begun. F. Lewis. il pors N Y Times Mag p26-7+ My 14 '67
Surpassing himself. pors Time 90:30-1 D 8 '67
Temporary victory for de Gaulle. E. Taylor. il Reporter 36:27-8+ Je 15 '67
39,999,999 Frenchmen? Nat R 19:782+ Jl 25 '67
Thoughts of chairman de Gaulle. Nat R 19:1364 D 12 '67
Truth about today's France: no base for grandeur. il por U S News 63:59-61 D 25 '67
Uneasy lies the head. Newsweek 70:32-3 Ag 21 '67
View from the pique. Time 89:27 Je 30 '67
Vulnerable emperor. il por Time 90:36 Jl 21 '67

Visit to Andorra, 1967
Day the prince came. il por Time 90:30 N 3 '67
Two in one. il por Newsweek 70:48 N 6 '67

Visit to Canada, 1967
L'affaire de Gaulle. Sr Schol 91:21 S 21 '67
De Gaulle's Canadian fiasco. il por Newsweek 70:38-9 Ag 7 '67
De Gaulle's insult to Canada: even his backers were shocked. il por U S News 63:15-16 Ag 7 '67
DeGaulle's "royal tour" of Canada. il U S News 63:39 Jl 24 '67
Incident in Canada. E. Taylor. Reporter 37:10-11 Ag 10 '67
Spoiler. il por Time 90:22 Ag 4 '67
Welcome worn thin. il por Bsns W p27 Jl 29 '67

Anecdotes, facetiae, satire, etc.
Chuck. G. Ace. Sat R 50:8 Ag 19 '67

Visit to Poland, 1967
And now a visit to Poland. il por Newsweek 70:46+ S 18 '67
Grand tour: from Quebec to Warsaw. M. Mestrovic. Commonweal 86:599-600 S 29 '67
No sale. Newsweek 70:48 S 25 '67
Report. D. R. Shanor. Atlan 220:43-4 D '67
What Poland got from a de Gaulle visit. U S News 63:13 S 18 '67

GAULT, Gerald
Kids and kangaroos. il por Newsweek 69:25 My 29 '67

GAULT, Henri, and Millau, Christian
Some salty observations on the way we do things here; excerpts from the Guide Julliard de New York. Life 63:136 S 15 '67

about
Two brightly breezy arbiters. il pors Life 63:129-30+ S 15 '67

GAUSE, G. F. and others
Induction of mutants with altered DNA composition: effect of ultraviolet on bacterium paracoli 5099. bibliog Science 157:1196-7 S 8 '67

GAUTHIER, Simonne
(ed) See Picasso, J. Picasso: the ninth decade

GAVEJIAN, George
Armenian diary. Opera N 32:14-16 D 23 '67

GAVER, Mary Virginia
School library: an intellectual force? adaptation of address, March 1967. por Library J 92:1989-91 My 15 '67

GAVIN, Sister Helen, and O'Hara, Sister Kevin
Is feminine psychology justified? Cath World 205:282-5 Ag '67

GAVIN, James M.
General in arms; interview, ed. by E. J. Hughes. por Newsweek 70:28-9 O 16 '67

about
Captive critic. por Newsweek 70:44 N 13 '67
Elusive General Gavin. R. J. Whalen. Harper 235:107-8+ N '67
General attacks. por Newsweek 70:22-3 Ag 14 '67
Three-star civilian with big ideas. il pors Bsns W p78-80+ O 14 '67
Voices of doubt. Nation 205:548 N 27 '67

GAY, Carlo T. E.
Oldest paintings of the New World: with biographical sketch. Natur Hist 76:7, 28-35 Ap '67

GAY, Ernest
Skiing the Sierras. Todays Health 45:28-33+ N '67

GAY, Peter
Books. New Yorker 43:100-2+ Je 24 '67

GAY Head, pseud.
Talking it over with Gay Head; questions and answers. See issues of Senior scholastic

GAYLE, Addison, Jr
Dialectic of The fire next time. Negro Hist Bul 30:15-16 Ap '67

GAYNES, Martin J.
Excerpt from statement before Communications subcommittee, October 13, 1967. Cong Digest 46:309+ D '67

GAYNOR, Mitzi
On the gypsy circuit. W. Como. il por Dance Mag 41:20-1 F '67

GAYNOR, William Jay
Tammany picked an honest man; excerpts. L. Thomas. il pors Am Heritage 18:34-9+ F '67; Discussion. 18:50 O '67

GAZA
Digging in to stay. il Time 90:20-1 Ag 11 '67
Gaza strip. M. Gellhorn. Commonweal 87:
299-300 D 1 '67; Reply. J. H. Davis. 87:459+
Ja 19 '68
Sabbath in the Sinai for Israeli tourists.
B. Wise. il Life 63:30-30A Ag 11 '67

GAZIS, Denos C.
Mathematical theory of automobile traffic.
bibliog Science 157:273-81 Jl 21 '67

GAZZANIGA, Michael S.
Split brain in man. Sci Am 217:24-9 Ag '67

GEAGAN, Bill
Escape to discovery. Field & S 72:42-3+ D
'67
Last of the axmen. Field & S 71:60-1+ Mr
'67

GEARING. See Automobiles—Gearing

GEBER, William F.
Congenital malformations induced by mescaline, lysergic acid diethylamide, and bromolysergic acid in the hamster. bibliog Science
158:265-7 O 13 '67

GEBHART, Lee
Plague of toads. Sci N 92:38-9 Jl 8 '67
Tuna slaughter. Sci N 91:597 Je 24 '67

GECKS. See Lizards

GEDDES, Andrew
Library automation. ALA Bul 61:642-6 Je '67

GEDDES, Donald Porter
University approach; reprint. Sat R 50:24+
Je 10 '67

GEERING, L. G.
Heresy trial. M. W. Wilson. Christian Cent
84:1575-6 D 6 '67

GEESE, Wild
Late-season snows. L. Green. il Field & S
72:44-5+ D '67

GEESEY, Titus
Toys for Christmas. C. B. Simmons. il Antiques 92:848-9 D '67

GEHMAN, Richard
Around the world with Flo. Holiday 42:30+
S '67
Eddie. Sat R 50:55-6 Ap 15 '67
Muggsy. Sat R 50:117+ Mr 11 '67
Random notes on article writing; excerpts
from How to write and sell magazine arti-
cles. Writer 80:25-30 Je '67
Wild Bill. Sat R 50:69+ Ag 26 '67

GEIB, M. Eugenia
Cosi gehen vous? Opera N 31:6-7 F 25 '67

GEIGER, H. Jack
Rural health: OEO launches bold Mississippi
project. L. J. Carter. por Science 156:
1466-8 Je 16 '67

GEIS, Bernard, associates
Sex & the singular Geis. il Time 90:105 O 27
'67
Shoes off, everyone; six partners withdraw.
il Newsweek 70:89 S 18 '67
Six Geis associates pull out; distribution
plans uncertain. Pub W 192:45 S 18 '67
Susann sues to break contract with publisher.
Pub W 191:143-4 Je 5 '67

GEIS, Gilbert
Crime and politics. Nation 205:115-16 Ag 14
'67
Violence in American society. Cur Hist 52:
354-8+ Je '67

GEISEL, Theodor Seuss
Logical insanity of Dr Seuss. il por Time 90:
58-9 Ag 11 '67

GEIST, Valerius
Consequence of togetherness; with biographical sketch. Natur Hist 76:4,24-31 O '67

GEKKONID lizards. See Lizards

GELABERT, Edgar
In the name of love. il Pop Phot 61:59-62 Jl
'67

GELATIN
Perfect fruited gelatin mold. il Good H
164:157 Je '67

GELATIN salads. See Salads

GELATT, Dorothy S.
Kidbirds, cinemates, and seeing-eye children.
Pop Phot 62:100-3+ Ja '68
Picture stations. Pop Phot 61:120-1+ D '67

GELATT, Roland
Armchair opera. Reporter 36:44+ Ap 6 '67
Decca/London on a mission westward. il Hi
Fi 17:18+ Jl '67
Disappearing art. Reporter 36:38-9 My 4 '67
Imperfect and nonpareil. Reporter 37:39-40 D
28 '67
Melodious Albion. Reporter 37:47-8 O 5 '67
Music for all seasons. Reporter 37:59-60 Jl
13 '67
Once and future Bernstein. Reporter 36:49-
51 F 23 '67

Polish musician for our time. Reporter 37:53-4
N 2 '67
Russians are coming. Reporter 36:44+ Je 1
'67
La Scala has the last word. Hi Fi 17:MA24-
5 D '67
Stuff of legend. Reporter 37:45 S 7 '67
Telemania. Reporter 36:46+ Ja 26 '67

GELB, Bruce S.
New York Gelbs. por Fortune 75:120 F '67

GELB, Lawrence M.
New York Gelbs. por Fortune 75:120 F '67

GELBER, Lionel
American role and world order. Yale R 56:
524-36 Je '67

GELBOIN. H. V. See Alfred, L. J. jt. auth.

GELDER, Jan Gerrit van
Labors of Hercules Seghers. Art N 66:26-9+
S '67

GELL, Elizabeth. See Zakroff, P. S. jt. auth.

GELLER, S.
Crystal structure of the solid electrolyte,
RbAg₄I₅. bibliog Science 157:310-12 Jl 21 '67

GELLHORN, Martha
Arab coffee break. Nation 205:395-7 O 23 '67
Gaza strip. Commonweal 87:299-300 D '67
Israeli secret weapon. Vogue 150:192-3+ O 1
'67
Lowest trees have tops; story. Ladies Home J
84:43-50 Ag '67

GELL-MANN, Murray
Macro meets micro. por Sci N 91:160 F 18
'67
Two men in search of the quark. L. Edson.
il por N Y Times Mag p54-6+ O 8 '67

GELPERIN, Alan
Stretch receptors in the foregut of the blowfly. bibliog Science 157:208-10 Jl 14 '67

GELPI, Donald
Canon. America 116:783 My 27 '67

GELTMAN, Max
Decline of the anti-Communist left. Nat R
19:79-83 Ja 24 '67
Electronic anthropology. Nat R 19:426-8 Ap
18 '67
Enemy is the same. Nat R 19:748 Jl 11 '67
New left & the old right. Nat R 19:632-5 Je
13 '67
Religion in Russia: the status of Jews. Nat
R 19:1170-3 O 31 '67
What's wrong with Israel? Nat R 19:568-9
My 30 '67

GELZAYD, Eugene A. and others
Immunoglobulin A: localization in rectal
mucosal epithelial cells. bibliog Science 157:
930-1 Ag 25 '67

GEM cutting. See Lapidary work

GEM stones. See Precious stones

GEMINIANI, Francesco
From Nonesuch, a Geminianian revelation;
The enchanted forest. J. W. Barker. Am
Rec G 33:776 My '67

GEMMILL, Henry
Scavengers of the press. Nation 205:580 D 4 '67

GEMS
See also
Diamonds
Jewelry

GEMSBOK hunting. See Antelope hunting

GENAILLE, Richard A.
Ferrite coil and crystal sideband filter. Electr
World 77:46-7+ Je '67

GENAUER, Emily
Coming to terms with the new art. House B
109:183+ Ap '67

GENDEL, Milton
Rome. Art N 66:61 Mr: 58+ My '67
Venice preserved. Art N 66:54-7+ S '67

GENEALOGY
Try climbing your family tree. J. J. Stewart.
Read Digest 91:103-7 S '67

GENEEN, Harold Sydney
Double the profits, double the pride. il pors
Time 90:86-8+ S 8 '67

GENERAL (locomotive) See Locomotives

GENERAL acceptance corporation
General acceptance; looking around for trouble. il Fortune 75:152-4+ F '67

GENERAL accounting office. See United States
—General accounting office

**GENERAL advisory committee on foreign as-
sistance programs.** See United States—
President's advisory committee on foreign
assistance programs

GENERAL agreement on tariffs and trade
End of the Round. New Repub 156:7 My 27
'67
Future work program of GATT; statement,
November 23, 1967. W. M. Roth. Dept State
Bul 58:13-15 Ja 1 '68

GENERAL agreement on tariffs and trade
—*Continued*
GATT contracting parties hold 24th session. Dept State Bul 57:725 N 27 '67
How big a market for you in Europe? with editorial comment. C. P. Streeter. Farm J 91:81-2+, 138 Mr '67
Improving export earnings of developing countries; statement, January 18, 1967. W. M. Blumenthal. Dept State Bul 56:430-6 Mr 13 '67
It is high noon in Geneva; closing minutes of the Kennedy round. Life 62:4 Ap 14 '67
Kennedy round: a hard task well done. Life 62:4 My 26 '67
Kennedy round agreements signed at Geneva. Dept State Bul 57:95-101 Jl 24 '67
Kennedy round holds promise of free-world economic growth; statements. May 16, 23, 1967. L. B. Johnson; W. M. Roth. Dept State Bul 56:879-80 Je 12 '67
New push for protection; senators asking special-interest protection. il Bsns W p 124-5+ O 21 '67
United States achieves removal of foreign import restrictions. Dept State Bul 56:245-6 F 13 '67

GENERAL assembly of the United Nations. See United Nations—General assembly

GENERAL aviation. See Aviation

GENERAL biological supply house, incorporated
Crowell Collier to buy science materials firm. Pub W 191:37 Ap 17 '67

GENERAL dynamics corporation
F-111 dodges the flak; General dynamics makes the controversial supersonic fighter formerly called the TFX. il Bsns W p52 N 11 '67
Notes that sank a business. Bsns W p 161-2 Je 24 '67

GENERAL education. See Liberal education

GENERAL electric company
For better pictures in your family album. M. B. Keiser. il Parents Mag 42:17-18 Ja '67
GE expands its top echelon; stress on decentralized management. Bsns W p46 N 25 '67
GE learns a lesson in France; spiraling costs force slow down of computer making. Bsns W p74+ Ja 21 '67
GE prepares major shifts. Aviation W 87:33 D 4 '67
G.E.'s $200-million ticket to France. G. H. Wierzynski. il Fortune 75:92-5+ Je 1 '67
How it paid to put an idea to the test; market testing of GE letter writer. il Bsns W p 176-8+ O 14 '67
How Mr Housewares woos his customers; W. H. Sahloff. il Bsns W p98-100+ Jl 1 '67
More cash for Bull. Time 89:106 Je 9 '67
Owners of GE color TV sets take note; sets may emit excessive X-radiation. Consumer Rep 32:349 Jl '67
Rickover tells GE to weight anchor. Bsns W p 105+ Je 24 '67
SST program responsibility shifts; with editorial comment. H. D. Watkins. il Aviation W 86:11, 28-9 My 8 '67
TV that can bite; color sets emit mild X-ray beam. Bsns W p61 My 27 '67
See also
General learning corporation

GENERAL electric letterwriter. See Recording instruments

GENERAL information tests. See Information tests

GENERAL learning corporation
Family squabble. Newsweek 69:84+ Mr 13 '67

GENERAL mills, incorporated
Health, wealth & Wheaties; success of sports image. il Time 89:85 Je 16 '67

GENERAL motors corporation
Again, talk of breaking up GM. il U S News 63:69 N 13 '67
Bonus plan where performance counts; pie that GM's managers share. il Bsns W p58+ My 13 '67
Competitive innovation, key to progress; excerpts from address, July 13, 1967. F. G. Donner. Nations Bsns 55:68-9 S '67
Does a General motors agreement mean full speed ahead for autos? U S News 63:68 D 25 '67
Face of the future at General motors. M. Sullivan. il Fortune 76:84-6 Jl '67
GM in '68: a sleeker Chevelle. Bsns W p53 S 2 '67

GM: test for a new team. il Newsweek 70:83 N 13 '67
GM.'s new line-up. il Time 90:93 N 10 '67
Giant GM splits its big problems. il Bsns W p 134-6+ N 4 '67
Heirs apparent; executive vice presidents. il Time 90:101 O 6 '67
If General motors is struck. U S News 63:91 O 2 '67
Labor peace in '68?. il Bsns W p 17-18 D 23 '67
Latest on auto-contract talks; General motors makes demands. U S News 63:75-6 Ag 14 '67
Nader affair. J. Ridgeway and D. Sanford. New Repub 156:16-18 F 18 '67
Nader again. Newsweek 69:85-6 F 20 '67
New leaders for a mammoth corporation. il U S News 63:19 N 13 '67
News on wheels; proving ground. M. Spiegel. il Sr Schol 91:38-9 S 28 '67
Now the showdown at General motors: what a strike would do. U S News 63:95-6 N 20 '67
Putting the brake on GM; settling the Euclid case with Justice dept. Bsns W p33 Ag 12 '67
Refreshing candor from General motors; recalls Pontiacs because of possible misalignment in the steering shaft. Consumer Rep 32:65 F '67
Reuther escalates his war on auto companies. il U S News 63:85-6 N 13 '67
Roche team at G.M. il Fortune 76:51 D '67
UAW's new target: GM. il Bsns W p50 N 11 '67
When GM sliced its advertising pie. Bsns W p96 Je 3 '67
When union members defy their top leaders. il U S News 62:84-5 Mr 20 '67
Will General motors and union settle without a strike? il U S News 63:76-7 D 4 '67

AC electronics division
AC Carousel chosen as 747 nav system. P. J. Klass. il Aviation W 86:68-71+ F 20 '67
Boeing award means $100 million for AC. il Tech W 20:38-9 F 6 '67

Detroit diesel engine division
Diesel engines step up power. il Bsns W p64-6 Je 3 '67

GENERAL shale products corporation
Brick kiln builds up its speed; first automated plant. il Bsns W p72-4 Jl 15 '67

GENERAL telephone and electronics company
New growth circuit at GT&E. J. Poindexter. il Duns R 90:42-4+ N '67

GENERAL time corporation
Company on the uptick. S. Margetts. il Duns R 90:85-6 O '67

GENERAL tire and rubber company
Suit hits two-way buying; Justice dept. vs General tire & rubber co. Bsns W p 162+ Mr 11 '67

GENERALIĆ, Ivan
Generalić, a Croatian peasant painter. A. Werner. il por Am Artist 31:40-5+ F '67

GENERALS
Almost all generals are almost always wrong about all wars. S. Alsop. Sat Eve Post 240:14 Ag 26 '67

GENERATION gap. See Youth-adult relationship

GENERATIVE organs
Antiandrogen implanted in brain stimulates male reproductive system. G. J. Bloch and J. M. Davidson. bibliog il Science 155:593-5 F 3 '67
Body functions: what to know about ovulation, menstruation, menopause. il Good H 164:136 Ja '67
See also
Gonads
Oviducts

Surgery
Transsexual operation. T. Buckley. Esquire 67:111-15+ Ap '67

GENERATORS. See Pulse generators

GENERATORS, Electric. See Electric generators

GENERATORS, Signal. See Signal generators

GENEROSITY
How children learn the joy of giving. B. Spock. il Redbook 129:41-3+ S '67
See also
Giving

GENES
Amino acid transport: evidence for genetic control of two types in human kidney. C. R. Scriver and O. H. Wilson. bibliog il Science 155:1428-30 Mr 17 '67

GENES—*Continued*
Autosomal linkage between the albumin and Gc loci in humans. E. Kaarsalo and others. bibliog il Science 158:123-5 O 6 '67
Biology of isolated chromatin. J. Bonner and others. bibliog il Science 159:47-56 Ja 5 '68
Building a bacterial virus. W. B. Wood and R. S. Edgar. il Sci Am 217:60-6+ Jl '67
Direction of translation in bacteriophage S13. I. Tessman and others. bibliog il Science 158:267-8 O 13 '67
Gene activation without histone acetylation in drosophila melanogaster. E. G. Ellgaard. bibliog il Science 157:1070-2 S 1 '67
Gene structure and protein structure. C. Yanofsky. il Sci Am 216:80-2+ bibliog(p 167) My '67
Genetics manipulates life. B. Frisch. il Sci Digest 61:49-51 Mr '67
Phage lambda mutants deficient in rII exclusion. B. D. Howard. bibliog il Science 158:1588-9 D 22 '67
Phosphorylase b kinase inheritance in mice. J. B. Lyon, jr. and others. bibliog il Science 155:1550-1 Mr 24 '67
R factors mediate resistance to mercury, nickel, and cobalt. D. H. Smith. bibliog il Science 156:1114-16 My 26 '67
Regulation of the lac operon. J. R. Beckwith. bibliog il Science 156:597-604 My 5 '67
Ribonuclease activity in normal and opaque-2 mutant endosperm of maize. C. M. Wilson and D. E. Alexander. bibliog il Science 155:1575-6 Mr 24 '67
See also
Cholinesterase
GENESCO, incorporated
Genesco: the high style in management. J. B. Weiner. il Duns R 89:36-9+ Je '67
GENÊT, pseud. See Flanner, J.
GENÊT, Jean
Exaltation of evil. T. F. Driver. por Sat R 50:36-7+ Mr 11 '67
GENETIC research
Biochemical genetics of oxidative phosphorylation. L. Kováč and others. bibliog il Science 158:1564-7 D 22 '67
Cerumen in American Indians: genetic implications of sticky and dry types. N. L. Petrakis and others. bibliog il Science 158:1192-3 D 1 '67
Common code. Sci Am 216:48-50 Ap '67
Good genes for bad. Newsweek 69:92 Je 19 '67
Immunological time scale for hominid evolution. V. M. Sarich and A. C. Wilson. bibliog il Science 158:1200-3 D 1 '67
In vitro synthesis of DNA: a perspective on research. M. F. Singer. il Science 158:1550-1 D 22 '67
Predicting tomorrow's children; genetic counseling. D. C. Davis. il Todays Health 46:32-7+ Ja '68
Protein polices genes. Sci N 91:569 Je 17 '67
Public confrontation of Hermann J. Muller. T. T. Balio. Bul Atomic Sci 23:8-12 N '67
Radiation chimeras and genetics of somatic cells. A. Lengerová. bibliog il Science 155:529-35 F 3 '67
Soviet genetics: first Russion visit since 1930's offers a glimpse. E. Langer. il Science 157:1153 S 8 '67; Reply. T. Dobzhansky. 158:577 N 3 '67
Turned-off genes. Sci Am 216:52 Je '67
Turned-off genes; repressor substances. Time 89:51+ Ap 28 '67
Watching a new species develop? experimenting with drosophila paulistorum. il Time 89:37 Ap '67
GENETICS
Eine kleine carbon copy. F. V. Grunfeld. il Reporter 36:44-5 Ja 26 '67
Evolution: implications for religion. T. Dobzhansky. Christian Cent 84:936-41 Jl 19 '67
Experimental genetics and human evolution. J. Lederberg; reply with rejoinder. L. Ornstein. Bul Atomic Sci 23:57-61 Je '67
Familial mental retardation: a continuing dilemma. E. Zigler. bibliog il Science 155:292-8 Ja 20 '67; Discussion. 155:1442; 157:576-9 Mr 17, Ag 4 '67
Genetic control of lactate dehydrogenase formation in the hagfish eptatretus stoutii. S. Ohno and others. bibliog il Science 156:96-8 Ap 7 '67
Genetic counseling. M. W. Thompson. il PTA Mag 61:12-15 F '67
Genetic mapping of phenylalanyl-sRNA synthetase in escherichia coli. A. Böck and F. C. Neidhardt. bibliog il Science 157:78-9 Jl 7 '67

Genetic recombination in escherichia coli: clone heterogeneity and the kinetics of segregation. T. H. Wood. bibliog il Science 157:319-21 Jl 21 '67
Inheritance; report on International seminar on medical genetics. W. H. Finley and S. C. Finley. Science 156:1519 Je 16 '67
Transferrin polymorphism and population differences in the genetic variability of chimpanzees. M. Goodman and others. bibliog il Science 156:98-100 Ap 7 '67
What man can make of man; genetic programming; competence of biologists to determine the optimal genotype. K. H. Hertz. Christian Cent 84:807-10 Je 21 '67
See also
Chromosomes
Crossing over (genetics)

Research
See Genetic research
GENEVA, Switzerland

Description
Geneva stares down the future. R. Condon. il Holiday 42:28+ O '67

Music
Geneva; Grand théâtre's Simon Boccanegra. D. A. Mackinnon. il Opera N 31:32 Ja 28 '67

Religious institutions and affairs
World around us. Christian Cent 84:1001 Ag 2 '67
GENEVA disarmament conference. See Conference of the Eighteen-nation committee on disarmament, Geneva, 1962-
GENIUS
See also
Great men
GENNÉ, Elizabeth, and Genné, William
Interfaith marriages. PTA Mag 62:16-18 Ja '68
GENNÉ, William. See Genné, E. jt. auth.
GENOA
Harbor
Stirrings in *la superba*. il Time 89:86+ Mr 24 '67
GENOCIDE
Holocaust: myths and facts. L. Harap. Nation 205:21-3 Jl 3 '67
Why American jews are disillusioned. D. Polish. Christian Cent 84:965-7 Jl 26 '67
GÉNOISE. See Cake
GENOVÉS, Juan
Through a giant lens. il Time 89:75 Mr 3 '67
GENOVESE, Eugene D.
Past reconstructed. Nation 204:758-61 Je 12 '67
GENSERT, R. M.
Prestressed foundation resists roof thrusts. Arch Rec 142:173-6 N '67
GENTLE soul; story. See Lavin, M.
GENTRY, Bobbie
Bobbie and Billy. il por Newsweek 70:81-2 Ag 28 '67
Bobbie's Billie's bundle. il por Time 90:50-1 S 1 '67
Down home with Bobbie Gentry. il pors Life 63:99-100+ N 10 '67
GENUS ictalurus. See Bullheads
GEOCHEMISTRY
Isoprenoid and dicarboxylic acids isolated from Colorado Green River shale (Eocene) P. Haug and others. bibliog il Science 158:772-3 N 10 '67
GEOCHRONOLOGY. See Geological time
GEODESY
SAO standard earth. R. N. Watts, jr. Sky & Tel 34:89-90 Ag '67
See also
Artificial satellites—Mapping applications
Azimuth
GEODETIC satellites. See Artificial satellites—Mapping applications
GEODETIC survey. See United States—Coast and geodetic survey
GEOGRAPHICAL distribution of animals and plants
See also
Plants—Migration
GEOGRAPHICAL myths
Small world of the toy novel. S. Morse. Sat R 50:23+ O 21 '67
GEOGRAPHICAL names. See Names, Geographical
GEOGRAPHICAL society, American. See American geographical society

GEOGRAPHY
See also
Anthropogeography
Atlases
Man—Influence of environment

Study and teaching
New geography course planned. Sr Schol 90:
sup5+ My 5 '67
Problems approach to geography. M. J.
Bradbury. il NEA J 56:39-40 Ap '67
Sounds and shadows; blind student on geography camping trip; Montgomery Blair H.S,
Silver Springs, Md. P. L. Jones. il Sr Schol
90:sup 19 My 5 '67
See also
National council for geographic education

GEOGRAPHY, Historical

Maps
See also
Maps, Early

GEOLOGICAL chemistry. See Geochemistry
GEOLOGICAL survey (United States) See
United States—Geological survey
GEOLOGICAL time
Kiaman magnetic interval in the western
United States. B. E. McMahon and D. W.
Strangway. bibliog il Science 155:1012-13
F 24 '67
Magnetic clues help date the past. K. F.
Weaver. il Nat Geog Mag 131:696-701 My
'67
Signs test applied to Caribbean deep-sea core
A 172-6. R. Yalkovsky. bibliog il Science 155:
1408-9 Mr 17 '67
Tektites are terrestrial. H. Faul; reply. C.
M. Botley and A. Dauvillier. bibliog Science
156:837 My 12 '67
Unraveling the age of earth and man. E. L.
Simons. il Natur Hist 76:52-9 F '67
See also
Earth—Age
Radioactive dating

GEOLOGY
Geology along the North Atlantic: Gander
conference; report on international conference. H. P. Woodward. Science 158:1368+
D 8 '67
See also
Earth
Faults (geology)
Glacial geology
Ocean bottom
Ore deposits
Volcanoes

California
Sierra Nevada batholith. P. C. Bateman and
J. P. Eaton. bibliog il Science 158:1407-17
D 15 '67

Chile
Pediplain in northern Chile and the Andean
uplift. C. Galli-Oliver. bibliog il Science 158:
653-5 N 3 '67

Florida
Drought or sinkholes. il Sci N 91:520 Je 3
'67

Georgia
Pleistocene shoreline sediments in coastal
Georgia: deposition and modification. J. H.
Hoyt and J. R. Hails. bibliog il Science 155:
1541-3 Mr 24 '67

Grand Canyon
Canyon and the river. W. J. Breed. il Natur
Hist 76:50-1 N '67

Kenya
Hydrous sodium silicates from Lake Magadi,
Kenya: precursors of bedded chert. H. P.
Eugster. bibliog il Science 157:1177-80 S 8 '67

Massachusetts
Cape Cod. B. B. Chamberlain. il Natur Hist
76:24-33 bibliog (p67) My '67

Mexico
Paleozoic sedimentary rocks in Oaxaca, Mexico. J. Pantoja-Alor and R. A. Robison.
bibliog il Science 157:1033-5 S 1 '67

Northwest Territories, Canada
Algal stromatolites: use in stratigraphic correlation and paleocurrent determination. P.
Hoffman. bibliog il Science 157:1043-5 S 1 '67

South Africa
Carbon isotope composition of carbonaceous
matter from the Precambrian of the Witwatersrand system. J. Hoefs and M. Schidlowski. bibliog il Science 155:1096-7 Mr 3
'67

Utah
Arch in the southern Sierra; Arch Rock. il
Sunset 139:20 S '67

GEOLOGY, Stratigraphic
Antarctic rediolaria, magnetic reversals, and
climatic change. J. D. Hays and N. D. Opdyke. bibliog il Science 158:1001-11 N 24 '67

Eocene
New frontier: the tar sands; Athabaska oil
sands. J. Lear. il Sat R 50:57 S 2 '67

Miocene
Carbon-13, rich diagenetic carbonates in miocene formations of California and Oregon.
K. J. Murata and others. bibliog il Science
156:1484-6 Je 16 '67

Paleozoic
Paleozoic sedimentary rocks in Oaxaca, Mexico. J. Pantoja-Alor and R. A. Robison.
bibliog il Science 157:1033-5 S 1 '67

Pleistocene
Coccoliths as paleoclimatic indicators of
pleistocene glaciation. A. McIntyre. bibliog
il Science 158:1314-17 D 8 '67
Pleistocene shoreline sediments in coastal
Georgia: deposition and modification. J. H.
Hoyt and J. R. Hails. bibliog il Science
155:1541-3 Mr 24 '67
Zonation of uplifted pleistocene coral reefs
on Barbados, West Indies. K. J. Mesolella.
bibliog il Science 156:638-40 My 5 '67

Precambrian
Algal stromatolites: use in stratigraphic correlation and paleocurrent determination. P.
Hoffman. bibliog il Science 157:1043-5 S 1
'67
Carbon isotope composition of carbonaceous
matter from the Precambrian of the Witwatersrand system. J. Hoefs and M. Schidlowski. bibliog il Science 155:1096-7 Mr 3
'67
Chromium and nickel in the fig tree shale
from South Africa. R. V. Danchin. bibliog
il Science 158:261-2 O 13 '67

Tertiary
Pediplain in northern Chile and the Andean
uplift C. Galli-Olivier. bibliog il Science
158:653-5 N 3 '67

GEOLOGY, Structural
Advice for the Establishment; excerpt from
address. J. T. Wilson. Sat R 50:50-1 S
2 '67
See also
Faults (geology)
Sinkholes

GEOMAGNETISM. See Magnetism, Terrestrial
GEOMETRY
Non-Cantorian set theory; analogy with non-
Euclidean geometry. P. J. Cohen and R.
Hersh. il Sci Am 217:104-6+ bibliog (p 160)
D '67
GEOPHYSICS
Implications for geophysics of the precise
measurement of the earth's rotation. G.
J. F. MacDonald. bibliog Science 157:304-5
Jl 21 '67
See also
Auroras
Earth—Internal structure
GEORGAKAKIS, Evanghelos
Losing winner. pro Time 89:38 Mr 3 '67
GEORGE VI, king of Great Britain
Greetin's, cousin George; 1939 visit to the
United States. P. L. Cantelon. il pors Am
Heritage 19:6-11+ D '67
**GEORGE, David Lloyd, 1st earl Lloyd George
of Dwyfor.** See Lloyd George of Dwyfor, D.
L. G.
GEORGE, Jean
Crazy, mixed-up adolescents of the wild. Read
Digest 92:159-62+ Ja '68
Wackiest orchestra on earth. Read Digest
91:173-4+ Ag '67
**GEORGE Allen and Unwin, limited. See Allen,
George and Unwin, limited**
GEORGE Eastman house of photography. See
Photography—Galleries and museums
GEORGE Jean Nathan award
Bentley award. Nation 204:229 F 20 '67
GEORGE Weston, limited. See Weston, George,
limited
GEORGES Enesco festival. See Music festivals
—Rumania
GEORGETOWN. See Washington, D.C.

GEORGETOWN university, Washington, D.C.

School of law

Courtroom classrooms. il Time 89:45 Ja 27 '67

GEORGIA
See also
Architecture, Domestic—Georgia
Booksellers and bookselling—Georgia
Crime and criminals—Georgia
Fishing—Georgia
Gardens—Georgia
Geology—Georgia
Hunting—Georgia
Prisons—Georgia

Historic houses, etc.

Living with antiques; Wormsloe the home of Mrs Craig Barrow. L. Giffen. il Antiques 91:370-3 Mr '67
See also
Brunswick, Ga.—Historic houses, etc.

Legislature

Infamous Mr Bond. M. Frady. il Sat Eve Post 240:94-6+ My 6 '67

Parks and reserves

State parks of Georgia. M. Hunn. il Travel 128:36-9+ S '67

Politics and government

Lester Maddox; Puritan in the Statehouse. J. H. Baird. Reporter 37:19-22 O 5 '67
Little governor; Maddox innovations short-lived palliatives. il Time 90:25 S 22 '67
Strange decorum of Lester Maddox. R. G. Sherrill. il Nation 204:553-6 My 1 '67
You reckon they thought I was a nut? M. Frady. il Sat Eve Post 240:27-9+ Ap 22 '67

GEORGIA state college, Atlanta
Teaching private enterprise. S. G. Slappey. Nations Bsns 55:87 D '67

GEORGIA. University, Athens

Law school

From the bottom of nothing. il Time 90:51 D 1 '67

GEORGIADES, William
Team teaching. bibliog NEA J 56:14-15 Ap '67

GEORGIAN architecture. See Architecture, Georgian

GEORGIAN furniture. See Furniture, English

GEOS (satellite) See Artificial satellites—Mapping applications

GEOTHERMAL energy. See Steam, Natural

GEOTHERMAL power plants. See Steam power-er plants

GERACIMOS, Ann
Recipes for success. Sat Eve Post 241:28-9 Ja 27 '68

GERANIUMS
New for 1967, five pelargoniums. Sunset 138:295 My '67
Patricia Andrea geranium. il Horticulture 45:11 Je '67
Pink, white, and cool. il Sunset 138:246 Ap '67

GERARD, Robert D. and Worzel, J. L.
Condensation of atmospheric moisture from tropical maritime air masses as a fresh-water resource. bibliog Science 57:1300-2 S 15 '67

GERARDI, Donald F.
Books in the field; historiography. bibliog por Wilson Lib Bul 42:484-96 Ja '68

GERASIMOV, Sergei
Reflections on Soviet culture. UNESCO Courier 20:21+ N '67

GERASSI, John
Report from North Vietnam. New Repub 156:13-15 Mr 4 '67

GERBER, Alex
After victory, what? Bul Atomic Sci 23:27 Mr '67

GERBER, Israel J.
God is not enough? Christian Cent 84:684-7, 1524-5 My 24, N 29 '67

GERBER, Merrill Joan
Stork is a wonderful bird; story. Redbook 128:84-5 F '67

GERBIE, Albert B.
What happens during labor? Redbook 129:33-4 My '67

GERBILS
Animals suited to epileptic research. D. G. Robinson, jr il Sci N 93:16-18 Ja 6 '68
Gerbil, the new pet. Good H 165:188 S '67
Pet news. J. Kuh. il Ladies Home J 84:31 Jl '67

GERDTS, William H.
Americans in faraway places. Antiques 91:647-9 My '67

GEREZ, Toni de
Books for Miguel. bibliog Library J 92:4587-9+ D 15 '67
Way of Quetzalcóatl. Horn Bk 43:171-5 bibliog(p 132) Ap '67

GERGELY, John
Evolution: criticism unfounded. Christian Cent 84:694+ My 24 '67

GERHARDT, Lillian N. and others
(ed) Book review. Library J 92:327-53, 871-96+, 1309-33, 1723-8+, 2013-45, 2443-6+, 2643-8+, 3175-87+, 3837-70, 4241-72, 4601-15+; 93:281-313 Ja 15, F 15, Mr 15, Ap 15, My 15, Je 15-Jl, S 15, O 15, N 15, D 15 '67, Ja 15 '68

GERLACH, Rex R.
Boom in steelheads. Outdoor Life 139:40-3+ Je '67

GERLICH, J. W.
Better than the pilot model. Am City 82:94-6 O '67

GERM warfare. See Biological warfare

GERMAN airways. See Airways

GERMAN architecture. See Architecture, German

GERMAN artists. See Artists, German

GERMAN atrocities. See World war, 1939-1945 —Atrocities

GERMAN castles. See Castles

GERMAN cookery. See Cookery, German

GERMAN furniture. See Furniture, German

GERMAN glass. See Glassware

GERMAN language
Semantics of separatism; East German dictionary. Time 90:34 Ag 25 '67

Gender

He, she, it. J. Gould. Atlan 220:91 Ag '67

GERMAN literature
Half & half equals two. E. R. von Freiburg. Nation 204:502-6 Ap 17 '67

Translations into English

Authors & editors. Pub W 192:9-10 O 30 '67

GERMAN measles. See Rubella

GERMAN philosophy. See Philosophy, German

GERMAN poetry

Translations into English

Four ballads of Wolf Biermann: Ballad on the poet Francois Villon; Brigitte; Early morning; Ballad of the man; tr. by E. Bentley. W. Biermann. Nation 205:532-3 N 20 '67
O the night of the weeping children! poem; tr. by M. Hamburger. N. Sachs. Harper 235:68 Jl '67
Reiteration of a feeling; tr. by J. Simon. E. Kästner. Mlle 65:42 Jl '67
Ten poems: Agony, metronome of an alien star; Chorus of the unborn; When day grows empty; Earth, old man of the planets; And we who move away; Landscape of screams; How many; Sleepwalker; You in the night; Vainly. N. Sachs. New Yorker 43:30-1 Ag 5 '67
Two poems: The other; The end of the owls; tr. by M. Hamburger. H. M. Enzensberger. Mlle 65:122 My '67

GERMAN pottery. See Pottery, German

GERMAN reunification question. See Germany —Union (proposed)

GERMAN students
Festival in Berlin; demonstrations. J. Maguire. Sat R 50:75+ N 11 '67
Germany 1967. D. Trilling. Atlan 219:46-7 My '67
Letter from Berlin. C. Amery. Nation 205:80-1 Jl 31 '67
Letter from Berlin; West Berlin's free university. J. Wechsberg. New Yorker 43:165-6+ N 18 '67
Student movement, German style; Socialist student union of the Free university of Berlin. H. Brandon. Sat R 50:10+ S 9 '67

GERMAN war criminals. See World war, 1939-1945- —War criminals

GERMANN, Frank
Unforgettable Father Murray. Read Digest 90:113-17 F '67

GERMANS
Germans: analysis of a defamation. G. Krodel. Christian Cent 84:1653-6 D 27 '67
Germany 1967; impressions gathered by American writers and editors; symposium. Atlan 219:41-56 My '67

GERMANY
See also
Airplanes, Military—Germany
Atomic research—Germany
Concentration camps—Germany
Fascism—Germany
Germans
World war, 1939-1945—Germany

Diplomatic and consular services
Wraith of the Reich; case of fictitious diplomat Edmund F. Draecker. Newsweek 70: 48+ O 16 '67

Foreign relations
United States
Swastika and the eagle, by J. V. Compton. Review
  Atlan 220:100 Ag '67. O. Handlin

History
See also
Franco-German war, 1870-1871

Bibliography
Articles and other books received; comp. by A. H. Price. See issues of American historical review

Errors, inventions, etc.
Wraith of the Reich; case of fictitious diplomat Edmund F. Draecker. Newsweek 70: 48+ O 16 '67

Intellectual life
See also
German literature

National socialist movement
See Fascism—Germany

Politics and government
See also
Fascism—Germany

Union (proposed)
After two world wars; address, October 6, 1967. W. Brandt. Vital Speeches 34:106-11 D 1 '67
Bitter letter. Newsweek 70:39-40 O 2 '67
Look in the mirror and over the wall. C. Wilpert. Commonweal 86:224-5 My 12 '67
Secretary Rusk discusses European affairs and Viet-Nam in interview for German television; transcript of interview, February 10, 1967. D. Rusk. Dept State Bul 56:358-65 Mr 6 '67
Signs that two Germanies are slyly inching closer. H. Moffett. Life 62:54+ Ap 28 '67
Special delivery in Berlin; first proposal for high-level talks. il Time 90:39 O 6 '67
Will there always be two Germanys? the odds. il U S News 63:51-2 S 11 '67

GERMANY (Democratic Republic)
End of a concept; citizen of the G.D.R. no longer shares a common nationality with his brothers in West Germany. Time 89: 37 Mr 3 '67
Journey through a haunted land, by A. Elon. Review
  New Repub 156:20+ Mr 11 '67. S. Kauffmann
Profile of East Germany. L. Muray. New Repub 156:6-8 Ap 1 '67
Unpleasant reality. il Time 89:24-6 Ap 7 '67
See also
Berlin (East Berlin)
Music festivals—Germany (Democratic Republic)
Youth—Germany (Democratic Republic)

Art
Old masters and crafts, new performing arts as well. il Life 62:64-5 My 26 '67

Civilization
Separate, and equal; with report by B. Van Voorst. Newsweek 69:56+ Mr 13 '67

Economic conditions
East Germany: the plan collapses. G. Bailey. il Reporter 36:19-24 Ap 20 '67; Reply with rejoinder. J. E. Smith. 36:8 Je 1 '67

Foreign relations
Littler Germany. Reporter 36:14+ F 9 '67

Industries
East Germany: the plan collapses. G. Bailey. il Reporter 36:19-24 Ap 20 '67; Reply with rejoinder. J. E. Smith. 36:8 Je 1 '67
East side of the wall; with report by M. Mok. il Life 62:58-63+ My 26 '67

Poltics and government
Men and politics in East Germany. H. A. Schmitt. bibliog f il Cur Hist 52:232-7 Ap '67
Red Prussianism of the German Democratic Republic. J. E. Smith. bibliog Bul Atomic Sci 23:24-30 My '67
See also
Berlin question, 1945-

Religious institutions and affairs
Angry anniversary; celebration of the 450th anniversary of the Reformation in Wittenberg. il Newsweek 70:60 N 13 '67
East Germany celebrates reformation; 450th anniversary. Christian Cent 84:1062 Ag 23 '67
News from East Germany. Christian Cent 84:1372+ O 25 '67
Requiem for the reformer; Reformation day observances at Wittenberg. il Time 90:75 N 10 '67
Wartburg: symbol of a synthesis? Christianity and Marxism in East Germany. C. R. Foster, jr. Christian Cent 84:1358+ O 25 '67
Wittenberg 1967. C. R. Foster, jr. Christian Cent 84:1538-41 N 29 '67
World around us (cont) Christian Cent 84: 389-90, 480-2, 669-70, 790+, 1536-8 Mr 22, Ap 12, My 17, Je 14, N 29 '67

Riots
Alas, poor Bertolt Brecht; concerning G. Grass's play around 1953 uprising. F. Ewen. Nation 204:213-14 F 13 '67

Social conditions
East side of the wall; with report by M. Mok. il Life 62:58-63+ My 26 '67

GERMANY (Federal Republic)
Journey through a haunted land, by A. Elon. Review
  New Repub 156:20+ Mr 11 '67. S. Kauffmann
See also
Aerospace industries—Germany (Federal Republic)
Airplane industry and trade—Germany (Federal Republic)
Airplanes, Military—Germany (Federal Republic)
Astronomical observatories—Germany (Federal Republic)
Atomic power—Germany (Federal Republic)
Automobile industry and trade—Germany (Federal Republic)
Banks and banking—Germany (Federal Republic)
Berchtesgaden
Berlin (West Berlin)
Bonn
Book industries and trade—Germany (Federal Republic)
Budget—Germany (Federal Republic)
Chemical industries—Germany (Federal Republic)
Church and state in Germany (Federal Republic)
Colleges and universities—Germany (Federal Republic)
Duisburg
Düsseldorf, Germany—Music
Education—Germany (Federal Republic)
Elections—Germany (Federal Republic)
Foreign visitors in Germany
Hamburg
Moselle River
Münster, Germany
Opera—Germany (Federal Republic)
Political parties—Germany (Federal Republic)
Public opinion—Germany (Federal Republic)
Publishers and publishing—Germany (Federal Republic)
Religious thought—Germany (Federal Republic)
Rites and ceremonies—Germany (Federal Republic)
Rothenburg
Steel industry and trade—Germany (Federal Republic)
Taxation—Germany (Federal Republic)
Television broadcasting—Germany (Federal Republic)
Transportation—Germany (Federal Republic)
Women—Germany (Federal Republic)

Air force
Politics alter German air force plans. D. E. Fink. Aviation W 86:35-6 Ap 3 '67

Armed forces
Don't sell it; throw it away; manpower cuts. C. Amery. Nation 205:133-4 Ag 28 '67
Siege of the Pentabonn; projected cuts in defense budget. il Time 90:27-8 Jl 28 '67

GERMANY (Federal, Republic)—*Continued*

Army

On account of the schingderassa; *marschlieder* training. F. V. Grunfeld. il Reporter 36:43-4 Je 15 '67

Equipment and supplies

See also
Tanks, Military

Commerce

Germany and the East. C. McWilliams. Nation 205:138-41 Ag 28 '67

Defenses

Politics alter German air force plans. D. E. Fink. Aviation W 86:35-6 Ap 3 '67

Description and travel

Following the Moselle. J. Aumente. il Travel 127:34-6 Je '67
German journey. S. Kauffmann. New Repub 156:24+ F 18 '67
More from Germany. S. Kauffmann. New Repub 156:24+ F 25 '67
Travel's picture portfolio. Travel 127:54-9 Ap '67

Economic conditions

Hamlet under the elms; cuts in spending. il Newsweek 70:33 Jl 17 '67
Struggle in the valley; tax increases and cuts in welfare spending to fight recession. Time 90:85 Jl 14 '67
Time for a new economic miracle; Germany's recession. il Bsns W p78-80+ Jl 8 '67
Watering the horses; economic slowdown. Newsweek 70:58 Ag 7 '67
Why bloom is off the boom in bustling West Germany. il U S News 62:106-8 Je 19 '67

Economic relations

United States

Breaking the impasse; Bonn to buy medium-term U.S. Treasury bonds to offset balance of payments. Newsweek 69:60 Mr 27 '67

Foreign opinion

American

Germany 1967; impressions gathered by American writers and editors; symposium. Atlan 219:41-56 My '67

Foreign relations

After two world wars; address, October 6, 1967. W. Brandt. Vital Speeches 34:106-11 D 1 '67
Boon changes course. T. Sommer. For Affairs 45:477-91 Ap '67
President Johnson meets with German chancellor; exchange of greetings, statements and exchange of toasts, August 15; with joint statement, August 16, 1967. K. G. Kiesinger; L. B. Johnson. Dept State Bul 57:325-30 S 11 '67
Quo vadis, Charles de Gaulle? concern with German foreign relations. il Newsweek 70:32-3 Jl 24 '67

Europe, Eastern

Berlin again? Newsweek 71:31 Ja 8 '68
Bitter letter. Newsweek 70:39-40 O 2 '67
Bridge building. Newsweek 69:59 F 6 '67
Crack in the ice? Sr Schol 90:17 F 10 '67
Littler Germany. Reporter 36:14+ F 9 '67
Opening toward the East. il Time 89:27 Ja 27 '67
Successful drive. Time 89:26 F 3 '67
Turning East. Newsweek 69:52 F 13 '67

Germany (Democratic Republic)

Esteemed Mr Chairman; Bonn's policy toward East Germany altered. il Newsweek 69:47 Je 26 '67
Special delivery in Berlin; first proposal for high-level talks. il Time 90:39 O 6 '67

United States

American era ends in Germany. C. W. Thayer. il Look 31:25-9 My 2 '67
Building a bridge to Bonn; discussions concerning nuclear nonproliferation, the Kennedy round, and monetary reform. il Bsns W p35-6 Ap 29 '67
Burying Der Alte. and an era. il Newsweek 69:50-1+ My 8 '67
Dialogue with Bonn; some suggestions for what might. but won't be said at the Kiesinger-Johnson meeting in Washington. T. C. Sorensen. Sat R 50:28-9 My 20 '67

How West German leader sees U.S. role in Europe; interview, ed. by R. A. Haeger. K. G. Kiesinger. U S News 63:52-4 Jl 10 '67
Is West Germany pulling away from the United States? il U S News 62:46 Ap 3 '67
Maiden comes of age. il Time 89:18 F 17 '67
President Johnson attends funeral of Konrad Adenauer; exchange of remarks, April 26, statement, and message, April 19, 1967, K. G. Kiesinger; L. B. Johnson. Dept State Bul 56:751-2 My 15 '67
Repairing the alliance. il Time 90:16-17 Ag 25 '67
Setting a new course. il por Newsweek 69·44 Mr 20 '67
Why Adenauer turned against U.S. il U S News 62:89 My 15 '67

Industries

Personal business; guide to Europe's business centers; West Germany. Bsns W p 113-14 Ag 12 '67
See also
Chemical industries—Germany (Federal Republic)
Krupp works. Essen

Intellectual life

Germany 1967. S. Kauffmann. Atlan 219:55-6 My '67

Military policy

West Germany to stress R&D spending. W. C. Wetmore. Aviation W 87:44-5 D 25 '67

Nationalism

Bonn is not Weimar; reflections on the radical right in Germany. W. Laqueur. Commentary 43:33-42 Mr '67
Shaky legs in Bonn. D. Schorr. Sat R 50:28-30 D 16 '67

Politics and government

American era ends in Germany. C. W. Thayer. il Look 31:25-9 My 2 '67
Bonn changes course. T. Sommer. For Affairs 45:477-91 Ap '67
First 100 days. il Time 89:38+ Mr 17 '67
Fox and the bear are cautious partners; K. Kiesinger and W. Brandt. P. Shabecoff. il N Y Times Mag p20-1+ F 5 '67
Future of Germany, by K. Jaspers. Review New Repub 157:30-2 N 11 '67. T. Prittie
Germany, from destruction to democracy; address, June 15, 1967. H. G. Heymann. Vital Speeches 33:666-9 Ag 15 '67
His Germany is now on its own; with report by H. Moffett. il Life 62:47-8+ Ap 28 '67
Judgment at Nuremberg; National democratic party convention cancelled. Newsweek 69:52 My 22 '67
Letter from Bonn. R. H. Rovere. New Yorker 43:136+ F 25 '67
New chancellor of the new Germany. E. Hughes. Read Digest 91:145-9 N '67
Setting a new course. il Newsweek 69:44 Mr 20 '67
Shaky legs in Bonn. D. Schorr. Sat R 50:28-30 D 16 '67
Strange bedfellows in Bonn; coalition of Christian and Social democrats. W. Long. Look 31:78 F 7 '67
Winter of discontent. C. Amery. Nation 204:165 F 6 '67
See also
Berlin question, 1945-
Elections—Germany (Federal Republic)
Fascism—Germany (Federal Republic)
Political parties—Germany (Federal Republic)

Religious institutions and affairs

See also
Catholic church in Germany (Federal Republic)

Riots

Case of *kulturkrankheit*; West Germany's students. Time 89:28 Je 30 '67

GERMANY and Israel. See Israel and Germany

GERMINATION
Ethylene and carbon dioxide; mediation of hypocotyl hook-opening response. B. G. Kang and others. bibliog il Science 156:958-9 My 19 '67
Old seeds; 10,000 year-old lupine. Sci Am 217:55 D '67
Ribonuclease activity in the developing seeds of normal and opaque-2 maize. A. Dalby and I. ab I. Davies. bibliog il Science 155:1573-5 Mr 24 '67

GERNREICH, Rudi
My first trip. McCalls 94:142 My '67
Redbook dialogue. pors Redbook 129:58-9+ My '67

GERNREICH, Rudi—*Continued*
about
Up, up & away. il pors Time 90:70-8+ D 1 '67
GERONTOLOGY. See Aging
GERSONI, Diane. See Putnam, J. jt. comp.
GERVASI, Frank
Authors & editors. Pub W 192:13-14 N 6 '67
GESCHEIDT, Alfred
Alfred Gescheidt; psychedelicate wit. K. Poli.
il Pop Phot 61:84-5 Jl '67
GERSCHENFELD, H. M. See Chiarandini, D.
J. jt. auth.
GERSHENSON, Doris Fisher
Living with antiques. Antiques 91:637-41 My
'67
GERSHON-COHEN, Jacob
Medical thermography; with biographical
sketch. Sci Am 216:22, 94-102 bibliog(p 148)
F '67
GERSTEN, Jerome W. See Sexton, A. W. jt.
auth.
GERTIE, the greeting card girl; drama. See
Huff, B. T.
GESNERIACEAE
See also
Kohlerias
GESSELL, John M.
Riots and our national response. Christian
Cent 84:1063-5 Ag 23 '67
GESSOW, Alfred
Changing helicopter; with biographical
sketch. Sci Am 216:14, 38-46 bibliog(p 146)
Ap '67
GESTIDO, Oscar Daniel
U.S. extends sympathy on death of President
Gestido of Uruguay; statement, December
6, 1967. L. B. Johnson. Dept State Bul 58:5
Ja 1 '68
GETHMAN, M. C.
Hunting for the millions. Field & S 72:60-1+
S '67
Masterpieces in metal. Field & S 72:48-9+
D '67
GETHSEMANE
Scandal and the splendor. V. P. McCorry.
America 116:358 Mr 11 '67
GETLEIN, Frank
Art. Commonweal 87:301+ D 1 '67
Art. See issues of New republic
GETLER, Michael
Editorial. See issues of Technology week in-
cluding Missiles and rockets (cont as)
Aerospace technology, June 26, 1967-
about
Memo from the publisher. A. C. Boughton.
por Tech W 20:11 Mr 6 '67
GETTING even; story. See Talese, G.
GETTING to know Julie; story. See McNevin,
M.
GETTLEMAN, Marvin E. and Silverman, S. L.
(comps) Bookmarks: Vietnam guide. Nation
205:215-17 S 11 '67
GETTY, Jean Paul
Car fare; excerpts from Britain's Automobile
association-published magazine Drive. il
por Time 89:95 My 5 '67
J. Paul Getty's changed plans. J. McDon-
ald. il Fortune 76:108-13+ D '67
GETZ, Stan
Lively arts; interview, ed. by R. Hemming.
por Sr Schol 90:24 Mr 10 '67
GEYER, Georgie Anne
Latin America; rise of a new non-Communist
left. Sat R 50:22-3+ Jl 22 '67
Report: Peru's Inca renaissance. Atlan 220:
28+ N '67
GEYER, Richard E.
How to make more money farming. Suc Farm
65:46A Mr '67
GEZARI, Temima
Pint-size Picassos. Parents Mag 42:52-3+ Mr
'67
GHANA
Ghana after Nkrumah. K. Irvine. bibliog f
Cur Hist 52:149-53+ Mr '67
Tale of two nations; work to recreate basic
science organizations. C. Weiss, jr. Sci N
91:460-1 My 13 '67

Foreign relations
Africa in back and white; concerning K.
Nkrumah's book Challenge of the Congo.
C. Miller. il Sat R 50:28-30 Mr 25 '67
General Ankrah of Ghana visits the United
States; exchange of toasts, October 10, 1967.
L. B. Johnson; J. A. Ankrah. Dept State
Bul 57:571-3 O 30 '67

Politics and government
Amateur day; unsuccessful coup. Newsweek
69:38+ My 1 '67
Guest or prisoner? Nkrumah a millionaire,
but—. U S News 62:16 Ja 30 '67
New start. il Time 91:22+ Ja 12 '68
Problems of dekwamification. il Time 89:
34 F 10 '67
Rise and fall of Kwame Nkrumah, by H. L.
Bretton. Review
Nation 204:309-11 Mr 6 '67. C. C. O'Brien
GHEDINI, Francesco
Sophia Loren talks about the sorrow of los-
ing her baby. Ladies Home J 84:68+ S '67
GHELDERODE, Michel de
Pantagleize; tr. by G. Hauger. Criticism
Commonweal 87:470 Ja 19 '68
Nation 205:669-70 D 18 '67
New Repub 158:41 Ja 6 '68
New Yorker 43:93 D 9 '67
Newsweek il 70:97 D 11 '67
Reporter 38:36-7 Ja 11 '68
Sat R 51:26 Ja 6 '68
Time 90:96-7 D 8 '67
GHENT, Victor H.
Surveyor: an old career has a new look;
Cross & Ghent, certified land surveyors,
Alexandria, Va. il Changing T 21:42-4 Je '67
GHEORGHIU, Mihnea
Young faces, young hearts. Sat R 50:16-17
D 23 '67
GHIBERTI, Lorenzo
Gates of paradise; five panels out of ten ripped
off. il UNESCO Courier 20:18-20 Ja '67
GHILAN, Maxim
Exposing international secrets. il por Time
89:48 Mr 10 '67
GHOST ranch conference center, Abiquiu,
N.Mex. See Ranches
GHOST towns. See Abandoned towns
GHOST writing. See Authorship—Collaboration
GHOSTS
Day I gave up the ghost. J. Hyams. il Sat
Eve Post 240:92-4 Je 3 '67
I don't believe in ghosts, but; experience at
the George and dragon inn, West Wy-
combe, England. J. Robbins. il Read Digest
91:105-9 Jl '67
Photographer's ghost. A. Grant. il Sat Eve
Post 240:95 Je 3 '67
GHUYSEN, Jean Marie. See Strominger, J. L.
jt. auth.
GIACCONI, Riccardo
X-ray stars; with biographical sketch. Sci
Am 217:14, 36-46 bibliog(p 158) D '67
GIACOMETTI, L. and Montagna, W.
Langerhans cells: uptake of tritiated thy-
midine. bibliog Science 157:439-40 Jl 28 '67
GIACOMIN, Eddie
Spread out and puckered up for the new
Rangers; photographs by T. Triolo, with
account by P. Axthelm. Sports Illus 26:
20-7 Ja 30 '67
GIACOMO Joyce; story. See Joyce, J.
GIACOSA, Giuseppe
Act Puccini never wrote: Act III, the court-
yard of La Bohème; text. R. Fellner. Opera
N 31:24-7 F 4 '67
GIANCANA, Momo Salvatore
Fix. S. Smith. il por Life 63:42B-44 S 1 '67
GIANCANA, Sam. See Giancana, M. S.
GIANNI Schicchi; opera. See Puccini, G.
GIANNINI, Vittorio
Servant of two masters. Criticism
Hi Fi 17:MA8-9 Je '67
New Yorker 43:124 Mr 18 '67
Opera N il 31:26 Ap 15 '67
Sat R 50:44 Mr 25 '67
GIAP, Vo-nguyen-. See Vo-nguyen-Giap
GIARCHI, George
Of many things. T. N. Davis. America 117:
425 O 21 '67
GIBB, Jack R.
Dynamics of leadership; address, March 7,
1967. Vital Speeches 33:375-80 Ap 1 '67
GIBBERELLIC acid
Gibberellin delays ripening of tomatoes. H. C.
Dostal and A. C. Leopold. bibliog il Science
158:1579-80 D 22 '67
GIBBERELLINS
Growth substances in plants. E. Pinto. il Sci
Am 217:111-14 Ag '67
GIBBON, Amelia Frances Howard-. See
Howard-Gibbon, A. F.
GIBBON, Edward
Decline and fall. K. Rexroth. Sat R 51:92
Ja 6 '68
GIBBONS, Euell
Authors & editors. por Pub W 192:25-7 S
11 '67

GIBBONS, J. H. and Macklin, R. L.
Neutron capture and stellar synthesis of heavy elements. bibliog Science 156:1039-49 My 26 '67

GIBBONS
Hemoglobin polymorphism in chimpanzees and gibbons. H. A. Hoffman and others. bibliog il Science 156:944 My 19 '67

GIBBS, Ronald J.
Amazon River: environmental factors that control its dissolved and suspended load. bibliog Science 156:1734-7 Je 30 '67

GIBBS, Tony
Cruising with the very young. Motor B 119: 24-7+ Je '67
Flags and you. Motor B 121:83-5+ Ja '68
Rig for night running. Motor B 120:26-9+ Jl '67

GIBBSITE
Transformation of gibbsite to chlorite in ocean bottom sediments. L. D. Swindale and P.-F. Fan. bibliog il Science 157:799-800 Ag 18 '67

GIBNEY, Frank
Intelligentsia in Nippon. Sat R 50:29-30 S 9 '67

GIBOR, Aharon
Phenotypic variations among chloroplasts of a single cell. bibliog Science 155:327-9 Ja 20 '67

GIBRALTAR
End of the road for the Rock? il U S News 62:56 My 22 '67
Gibraltar. A. Burgess. il Holiday 41:70-1+ F '67
99.2 per cent solid; referendum. il Time 90: 31 S 22 '67
Queen's men. il Newsweek 70:48 S 25 '67
See also
United Nations—Gibraltar

History
Stub on the toe of the lion. P. Crumpet. Nat R 19:361-3 Ap 4 '67

GIBRALTAR referendum. See Referendum

GIBSON, Bob
Iceman cometh. il por Newsweek 70:93 O 23 '67

GIBSON, John E.
How well do you understand people? Todays Health 45:28-9+ Mr '67
You don't have to be lonely. Sci Digest 62: 33-6 N '67

GIBSON, John S.
Federal support for the social studies; excerpts from New frontiers in the social studies; action and analysis. Sr Schol 90: sup9+ F 24 '67
about
Subject: human rights. J. H. Sofokidis. il Am Ed 4:12-14 D '67

GIBSON, Nathan R.
Deuces wild. pors Outdoor Life 139:62-3+ F '67

GIBSON, Ronald
Fantastic world of Wagner. House & Gard 132:22-3 D '67
Looking and listening. House & Gard 132: 42+ O; 32+ N '67

GIELGUD, Sir John
Theater. H. Hewes. Sat R 50:51 F 11 '67

GIERKE, David
Simple-minded Maggie. Pop Electr 26:31-4+ Je '67

GIESY, Margaret
Twice (and more!)-told tales. Writer 80:29-30+ My '67

GIFFEN, Lee
Living with antiques. Antiques 91:370-3 Mr '67

GIFFORD, Henry. See Tomlinson, C. jt. auth.

GIFFORD, Walter Sherman
Lessons of history. L. L. L. Golden. Sat R 50:62 Jl 8 '67

GIFT for Hans Brinker; drama. See Thane, A.

GIFT wrappings. See Wrapping of packages

GIFTED children. See Children, Gifted

GIFTS
China return. R. H. Solomon. Yale R 57: 148-60 O '67
Fragrance for father. il Seventeen 26:146+ Je '67
Gifts for an old favorite: for dad on Father's day! il Seventeen 26:166-7 Je '67
Hostile gifts. Sci Am 217:62 O '67
Leather gifts for dads and grads. il Good H 164:186 Je '67

Lost your heart? better find it before February 13! il Seventeen 26:244 F '67
Small enchantments for your hostess. il House & Gard 132:230-1 S '67
See also
Christmas gifts
Colleges and universities—Gifts, legacies, etc.
Food as gifts
Giving
Land as gifts
Wedding gifts
Wine as gifts

Anecdotes, facetiae, satire, etc.
I can't give you anything but. W. K. Zinsser. il Sat Eve Post 240:20 F 11 '67

Taxation
Estates, gifts being eyed for tax raises. U S News 62:107-8 Ap 10 '67

GIFTS for children
Making money grow for your children. M. Feeley. Am Home 70:20-1 Mr '67
See also
Christmas gifts for children

GIFTS for the sick. See Sick, The

GIFTS in business
Corporate gift giving made easy. N. S. Hazelton. Nat R 19:964-5+ S 5 '67

GIJSBERS, Karel J. and Melzack, Ronald
Oxygen tension changes evoked in the brain by visual stimulation. bibliog Science 156: 1392-3 Je 9 '67

GILA national forest. See National forests

GILBERT, Al
Tap for young children (title varies) (cont) Dance Mag 41:74-5 F '67 (to be cont)
Variations in riffs. Dance Mag 41:84-5 Ap '67 (to be cont)

GILBERT, Arthur N.
Intern program for college teachers. Sch & Soc 95:417-20 N 11 '67

GILBERT, Bil
Call of the not-so-wild. Sports Illus 27:40-2+ D 18 '67
Close look at wildlife in America. Sat Eve Post 240:32-6+ S 9 '67
Diving for wolves in ice water. Sports Illus 26:62-6+ F 20 '67
Nature. Sports Illus 26:46+ Je 19 '67
Speaking out. por Sat Eve Post 240:10+ O 21 '67
Why dawgs are better than dogs. Esquire 67:112-15+ Je '67

GILBERT, George
Asphalt documentary. U S Camera 30:70-1 Ag '67
Make sure the screen is right. U S Camera 30:60-1+ Je '67
Super 8 boom. U S Camera 30:63-7+ S '67
Teenage stuntmen. U S Camera 30:24+ Mr '67

GILBERT, Mrs I. M. M.
Strange celebration. McCalls 95:38+ D '67

GILBERT, James
Flying photographer. Flying 80:62-3 Mr; 56-7 Ap '67

GILBERT, John
Personalist view of marriage. Cath World 205:365-70 S '67

GILBERT, Sir William Schwenck, and Sullivan, A. S.
Pirates of Penzance. Criticism
Newsweek il 70:64 Ag 21 '67

GILBERT systems, incorporated
Trucker tries for something extra; nationwide hauling of garments-on-hangers. il Bsns W p 112-14+ Mr 4 '67

GILBRETH, Edward S.
Making book on Mr Daley. Nation 204:395-8 Mr 27 '67

GILDEA, Ray Y. Jr
Haiti. bibliog il Focus 17:1-6 My '67

GILDING
How to turn everything into gold. il House & Gard 132:224-5+ O '67

GILDNER, Gary
Shy roofer; poem. Nation 204:317 Mr 6 '67

GILES, Carl H.
Earthquake lake. il Nat Parks Mag 41:7 N '67
Sentinel of the swamp. il Nat Parks Mag 41:9 My '67

GILES, Henry. See Zapf, F. jt. auth.

GILES, John Warren
Superstitions of the sea. Motor B 119:116-20 F '67

GILES, Robert H.
How to become a target city. Reporter 36: 38-41 Je 15 '67

GILKEY, Langdon
 Evolutionary science and the dilemma of
 freedom and determinism. Christian Cent
 84:339-43 Mr 15 '67
 Standing on the promises. Christian Cent 84:
 1630-2 D 20 '67
GILL, Brendan
 Current cinema. See issues of New Yorker
 to January 6, 1968
 Theatre. New Yorker 43:57 Ja 13 '68
GILL, Robert T.
 Hollow tree. America 116:837 Je 10 '67
GILL, Artificial. See Respiratory apparatus
GILLELAN, G. Howard
 Archery. See issues of Outdoor life
GILLEN, Vincent
 Nader affair. J. Ridgeway and D. Sanford.
 New Repub 156:16-18 F 18 '67
 Nader again. Newsweek 69:85-6 F 20 '67
GILLESPIE, Alfred
 Sheep killer; story. Sat Eve Post 240:56-60
 D 16 '67
 Witness; story. Sat Eve Post 240:42-4 Ag 12
 '67
GILLESPIE, John Freund
 Portable swimming pools. il Parks & Rec
 2:22 My '67
GILLETT, Charles A.
 Profile of a forester. H. Clepper. por Am For
 73:31+ Jl '67
GILLETTE, King Camp
 How many things like corks are there? R.
 Levy. il Duns R 89:44 Ap '67
 Simple idea cuts a wide swath. por Bsns W
 p60 Ap 1 '67
GILLETTE company
 How Gillette has put on a new face; diver-
 sified product line. il Bsns W p58-60+ Ap
 1 '67
 Sharp edge of Gillette. R. Levy. il Duns R
 89:43-4+ Ap '67
GILLHAM, C. E.
 Man and the dog. Field & S 72:116-17 Ag '67
GILLIAM, Harold
 Beating back the bulldozers. Sat R 50:67-
 9 S 23 '67
 San Francisco. Wilson Lib Bul 41:1046-9 Je '67
GILLIAM, Lila Williamson
 Artist with a welding torch. Farm J 91:105
 Mr '67
 Company specialties. Farm J 91:66 O '67
GILLIATT, Mary
 Special report from London: young design
 revolution. House B 109:68-73 Jl '67
GILLIATT, Penelope
 Come back if it doesn't get better; story.
 New Yorker 43:57-62 O 21 '67
 Current cinema. New Yorker 43:92+ Je 17;
 74+ Je 24; 54+ Jl 1; 52+ Jl 8; 100-1 Jl 15;
 70+ Jl 22; 70+ Jl 29; 64+ Ag 5; 72+ Ag 12;
 77-9 Ag 19; 76-9 Ag 26; 74-6 S 2; 109-10+
 S 9 '67
 Life movie review. Life 62:12 Ap 21 '67
GILLINGHAM, Evan S. jr
 Sailing by Chance. il Motor B 119:88-90+ Ap
 '67
GILLIOM, Lyle
 Build yourself a minibike. Pop Mech 127:
 160-4+ Je '67
GILLMAN, Peter A. See Starr, V. P. jt. auth.
GILLMOR, C. Stewart
 New Soviet observatory at Shemakha, Azer-
 baijan. il Sky & Tel 34:215 O '67
GILMAN, John J.
 Nature of ceramics; with biographical sketch.
 Sci Am 217:48, 112-18+ S '67
GILMAN, Richard
 British theater: a sense of destiny. News-
 week 69:85-7 Ap 3 '67
 Doors McLuhan opens. New Repub 157:34-6+
 N 18 '67
 Films. New Repub 157:27-9 N 4; 32-5 N 25 '67
 Theatre. New Repub 157:36-8 O 21; 31-3 O
 28; 35-7 D 2 '67; 158:41-2 Ja 6 '68
GILMONT, Herbert
 Sampling air; interview. New Yorker 43:44-6
 Mr 11 '67
GILMORE, C. P.
 How you'll drive the amazing Urmobile. Pop
 Sci 191:75-8+ O '67
 I used a real computer at home, and so will
 you. pors Pop Sci 190:90-4+ My '67
 Oil for your car. Pop Sci 191:67-71+ S '67
 These codes cost you money. Read Digest 91:
 91-5 D '67
 Things you never knew about beer. Pop Sci
 191:58-61+ Ag '67
 Twenty-one good questions about light bulbs.
 Pop Sci 190:188+ F '67
 Wen's single-post soldering gun. Pop Sci 191:
 126-8+ Ag '67
 What about the new electric car? Read
 Digest 90:84-7 Ap '67

GILMORE, Grant
 Teacher in out of the cold. por Time 91:29
 Ja 12 '68
GILMORE, Woody
 Woody carves a chassis. J. Thawley. il pors
 Hot Rod 20:70-2 Mr '67
GILMOUR, L. P. and O'Brien, R. D.
 Psilocybin: reaction with a fraction of rat
 brain. bibliog Science 155:207-8 Ja 13 '67
GILPATRIC, Roswell L.
 Atomic arms race, a mad momentum may be
 under way. N Y Times Mag p54-5+ D 3 '67
 We should encourage the doves in the Krem-
 lin. N Y Times Mag p9+ Jl 30 '67
GILROY, Frank Daniel
 That summer, that fall. Criticism
 Commonweal 86:153-4 Ap 21 '67
 Newsweek 69:110 Mr 27 '67
 Sat R 50:42 Ap 1 '67
 Time 89:69 Mr 24 '67
GILSDORF, Richard W.
 Next step: an American council. America
 116:277-9 F 25 '67
GILSVICK, Bob
 Catch the red fox napping. pors Outdoor
 Life 140:60-1+ N '67
GIMBEL, Armin F.
 Load-equalizing trailer hitch you can make.
 Pop Sci 191:127-30 Jl '67
GIMBEL, Bernard Feustman
 My most unforgettable character. G. Tun-
 ney. por Read Digest 90:75-80 Ap '67
GIN
 Gin, the original Dutch courage. Consumer
 Rep 32:381-2, 384-5 Jl '67
GINASTERA, Alberto
 Bomarzo. Criticism
 Américas il por 19:34-7 Jl '67
 Hi Fi il 17:MA12-13+ Ag '67
 New Repub 156:28-9 Je 10 '67
 Newsweek 69:90 My 29 '67
 Opera N il 31:21 Je 10 '67
 Sat R il 50:59+ Je 24 '67
 Time il 89:77 My 26 '67
 Don Rodrigo. Criticism
 New Yorker 42:144+ F 18 '67
 Sat R 50:59+ Je 24 '67
GINGER (spice)
 Try something different with ginger! il Bet
 Hom & Gard 45:104-5 Je '67
GINGERBREAD
 Bride makes gingerbread men; with recipe.
 il McCalls 95:37 D '67
GINGERICH, Owen
 Laboratory exercises in astronomy, variable
 stars in M15. Sky & Tel 34:239-42 O '67
 What is an English mounting? il Sky & Tel
 34:293-5 N '67
GINGKO. See Ginkgo
GINGRICH, Arnold
 Publisher's page. See issues of Esquire
GINKGO
 Ginkgo, the most ancient living tree. R. T.
 Major. bibliog il Science 157:1270-3 S 15 '67
 Ginkgo wins in Salzburg. il Sunset 139:8 N
 '67
GINSBERG, Allen
 Open letter to Allen Ginsberg. H. Cox. Com-
 monweal 86:147-9 Ap 21 '67
GINSBURG, Mirra
 Rights and wrongs of advertising and transla-
 tion; letter. Pub W 193:45-6 Ja 15 '68
 (tr) See Singer, I. B. Slaughterer
GINSBURG, Robert N.
 Stromatolites. Science 157:339-40 Jl 21 '67
GINSENG
 Great ginseng trade. D. J. Anderson. il Field
 & S 72:52-3+ N '67
GINZBERG, Eli
 Advice to the Urban coalition. Reporter 37:
 18-20 S 7 '67
 Manpower problem. Reporter 37:23-4+ N 16
 '67
 What is manpower? excerpt from Manpower
 agenda for America. bibliog Wilson Lib Bul
 41:794-9 Ap '67
GINZBURG, Evgeniia Semenovna
 Reader's choice. O. Handlin. Atlan 220:136+
 N '67
 Through rose-colored glasses darkly. A. C.
 Schmidt. Reporter 38:44+ Ja 11 '68
GINZBURG, Ralph
 Ginzburg's conviction upheld by U.S. Court
 of appeals. Pub W 191:39 Mr 20 '67
 Obscenity cases. A. M. Bickel. New Repub
 156:15-17 My 27 '67
La GIOCONDA; opera. See Ponchielli, A.
GIORDANO, Umberto
 Milan. F. P. Hoffer. Opera N 31:31 Ap 1 '67
GIORGI, Elsie A.
 Miracle in Charcoal alley. il por Time 90:57-
 8+ N 17 '67

GIPSIES
Gypsies. by J. Yoors. Review
  Newsweek il 69:93 Ja 30 '67. S. K. Oberbeck
Gypsies; living satire on civilization; with photographs by I. Penn. W. J. Burke. Look 31:58-63 Ag 8 '67
Margaret Mead reviews The gypsies. M. Mead. Redbook 129:52+ S '67

GIPSIES in the United States
Last holdouts. P. Lynden. il Atlan 220:42-6 Ag '67

GIRAFFES
New giraffe house for Denver. J. Frazier. il Parks & Rec 2:32+ Mr '67

GIRARD, Alexander
Alexander Girard invites you to dine at the Compound. il Arch Forum 126:60-3 Je '67

GIRARDIN, Ray
Speaking out. por Sat Eve Post 240:10+ S 23 '67

GIRAUDOUX, Jean
Tiger or disciple. Criticism
  America 116:880 Je 24 '67

GIRL athletes. See Women as athletes

GIRL in the Freudian slip; drama. See Brown, W. F.

GIRL scouts
Girl scouts pitch in. E. W. Brice. il Am Ed 3:32 Jl '67
Teen travel talk; Expo trip by Champlain, Richelieu River and St. Lawrence Seaway. il Seventeen 26:370 Ag '67

GIRL watcher; story. See Madocs, R.

GIRL who took risks; story. See Taylor, T.

GIRL with fifteen speeds; story. See Savage, J.

GIRL with love in her eyes; story. See Soman, F. J.

GIRL with the hometown look; story. See Williams, L.

GIRLING, J. L. S.
Northeast Thailand: tomorrow's Viet Nam? For Affairs 46:388-97 Ja '68

GIRLS
Good place to grow up; Sara Jane Straight of Kendall, Fla. il Look 31:43-9 My 16 '67
How different are they? excerpt from Development of sex differences, ed. by E. E. Maccoby. S. F. Yolles. il N Y Times Mag p64-5+ F 5 '67
Journal miss. M. Kadison. See issues of Ladies' home journal
Junior journal; a monthly report from, by, and for the younger journal set (title varies) (cont) M. Kadison. il Ladies Home J 84:68 Mr '67
Our dancing daughters. R. Cowley. il Horizon 9:98-9 Aut '67
Young living; questions and answers. A. Wood. See issues of Seventeen
  See also
Adolescence
Daughters
High school students
Runaway boys and girls
Young women

GIRLS across the water; story. See Savage, J.

GIRLS as authors. See Women as authors

GIRLS in sports. See Sports for women

GIRSON, Rochelle
Books for spring reading. Sat R 50:46-7+ F 25 '67
Covered with Old Glory. Sat R 50:48-50 My 6 '67
One with the world. E. Kimbrough. il Sat R 50:34 Ap 29 '67
Trade winds. J. Beatty, jr. Sat R 50:13 Ap 22 '67

GISCARD D'ESTAING, Valéry
Gaullists get restive. il por Bsns W p37 My 13 '67
Letter from Paris. Genêt. New Yorker 42:80+ Ja 28 '67

GITA. See Mahabharata—Bhagavadgita

GITLER, Robert L.
Meditations on research. bibliog Wilson Lib Bul 41:904-8 My '67

GITLIN, Irving
Obituary
  Nation 206:60 Ja 8 '68

GIULIO Cesare; opera. See Händel, G. F.

GIVE-away games. See Lotteries

GIVE my heart ease; story. See Katkov, N.

GIVEN names. See Names, Personal

GIVENS, Johnnie
Austin Peay: aesthetics and flexibility. Library J 92:4360-2 D 1 '67

GIVING
Gift of love; offerings of time, compassion and self. il Ladies Home J 84:36+ D '67
Resonance of charity. L. Wainwright. Life 62:21 F 24 '67
  See also
Charities
Christmas gifts
Church finance

GLACIAL epochs
Causes of the ice ages. W. L. Donn. il Sky & Tel 33:221-5 Ap '67

GLACIAL geology
Fossil actinomycetes in middle Precambrian glacial varves. T. A. Jackson. bibliog il Science 155:1003-5 F 24 '67
Fossiliferous bauxite in glacial drift. Martha's Vineyard, Massachusetts. C. A. Kaye. bibliog il Science 157:1035-7 S 1 '67
  See also
Geology, Stratigraphic—Pleistocene

GLACIER BAY NATIONAL MONUMENT
Alaska adventure, a visit to Glacier Bay il Sunset 139:30+ Jl '67
Alaska's Glacier Bay National Monument. D. Lambert. il Nat Parks Mag 41:4-9 S '67
Traveler's choice. M. E. Toof. Travel 127:9 My '67

GLACIER NATIONAL PARK
Glacier: a trail park and its users. L. C. Merriam, jr. il Nat Parks Mag 41:4-8 Ap '67
Oh, my God, I'm dead! deaths from bear attacks. Newsweek 70:26 Ag 28 '67

GLACIER PEAK wilderness area. See Wilderness areas

GLACIERS
Alaska 67: year of ice. H. E. McLean. il Am For 73:6-9 Ja '67
Alaska's mighty rivers of ice; new clues to our climate. M. M. Miller. il Nat Geog Mag 131:194-217 F '67
Spectacular glacier surge; Bering glacier. il Sci Digest 61:29 F '67

GLADIOLUS
Prize-winning gladiolus for 1967. il Flower Grower 54:8 Ja '67

GLADSTONE, Bernard
How the third wire protects you. Am Home 70:82+ N '67
Patching concrete and masonry. Am Home 70:150 O '67

GLADSTONE, William Ewart
Dangerous statesman. J. F. Goldberg. New Repub 156:28-32 Ap 15 '67

GLAMOR. See Beauty, Personal

GLANDS
Calcitonin from ultimobranchial glands of dogfish and chickens. D. H. Copp and others. bibliog il Science 158:924-5 N 17 '67
  See also
Mammary glands
Prostate gland
Thyroid gland

Diseases
Man's disease every woman should know about; prostatic disease. J. Lentz. Todays Health 45:66-8 Mr '67

GLANDS, Ductless
Hormones and endocrine glands of fishes. H. A. Bern. bibliog il Science 158:455-62 O 27 '67
  See also
Thyroid gland

GLANDS, Sexual
  See also
Gonads

GLANVILLE, Brian
Brutal sport. Commentary 44:114+ O; 28 D '67

GLASER, Daniel
National goals and indicators for the reduction of crime and delinquency. bibliog f Ann Am Acad 371:104-26 My '67

GLASER, Milton
We talk to; interview by Mademoiselle's guest editors. por Mlle 65:326 Ag '67

GLASER, Robert
Changes in instructional psychology; summary of address, December 5, 1967. Pub W 193:36 Ja 8 '68

GLASGOW, Betsy
In my opinion. por Seventeen 26:266 S '67

GLASS, Bentley
What man can be; excerpts from address. NEA J 56:11-14 S '67

GLASS, Billy P.
—and Heezen, B. C.
Tektites and geomagnetic reversals; with biographical sketches. Sci Am 217:10, 32-8 Jl '67

GLASS, Billy P.—*Continued*

about

Were comets the midwives at the birth of man? J. Lear. il por Sat R 50:59-62 My 6 '67; Discussion. 50:52-6 Ag 5 '67

GLASS, Carter, 1919-
City v. the publisher. por Time 89:78 My 5 '67
When city bites newspaper, that's news. Life 62:4 My 12 '67

GLASS, Herbert
Un ballo in maschera. Am Rec G 33:904-5 Je '67
Deutsche Grammophon's Die Walküre. Am Rec G 33:734-6 My '67
Don Giovanni. Am Rec G 33:562-4 Mr '67
Fischer-Dieskau's Don. Am Rec G 34:18-21 S '67
Gennady Rozhdestvensky conducts three performances of Prokofiev ballet music, including Cinderella. Am Rec G 34:96-9 O '67
Growth of Istvan Kertesz. Am Rec G 33:1006-7 Jl '67
Very difficult to resist: Schubert by Wunderlich. por Am Rec G 33:634-5 Ap '67

GLASS
Clear facts about glass. J. D. Enney. il Pop Mech 128:156-7 S '67
Look what they're doing with glass. M. J. Schultz. il Sci Digest 62:44-7+ Jl '67
Look what's happening to glass! R. Brady. Read Digest 91:175-6+ D '67
Nature of glasses. R. J. Charles. il Sci Am 217:126-30+ S '67
See also
Tektites

Joining to metal
How to sputter thin films of metal onto glass and experiment with them; ed. by C. L. Stong. N. Steiner. il Sci Am 217:134+ O '67

GLASS, Colored
Blue thumbprint. il Hobbies 72:98S N '67

GLASS, Decorated. See Glass, Ornamental

GLASS, Effect of radiation on
Irradiation effects in glasses: suppression by synthesis under high-pressure hydrogen. S. P. Faile and others. bibliog Science 156:1593-5 Je 23 '67

GLASS, Ornamental
Documenting some Mt. Washington art glass. K. M. Wilson. il Antiques 92:367-71 S '67
See also
Glass, Colored

GLASS, Stained. See Glass painting and staining

GLASS, Structural
Engineering approach to designing glass for wind. il Arch Rec 141:163-6 F '67
See also
Glass construction

GLASS blowing and working
Bertil Vallien: gentle fantasies done with daring and delight. D. Smith. il Craft Horiz 27:8-13+ S '67

GLASS construction
Biggest mirror ever; Bell laboratories, Holmdel, N.J. il Arch Forum 126:33-41 Ap '67
Cleveland arcade; reprint. M.-P. Schofield. il Arch Forum 127:60-5 S '67
Glass house that's fine in winter too. A. C. Borg. il Am Home 70:60-3 D '67
Showcase for sculpture; Lehmbruck museum, Duisburg, Germany. il Arch Forum 126:31-7 Mr '67

GLASS electrodes. See Electrodes, Glass

GLASS etching
Easy way to etch on glass. il Design 68:16 Sum '67

GLASS fabrics
See also
Glass fibers

GLASS fibers
Breezing in: blithe prints new-blown. il House B 109:138-9 My '67
Fiber glass fabrics: a drapery favorite. Good H 165:6 S '67
Resins in the mines. E. S. Gruzinov. Sci N 92:213 Ag 26 '67
Solvent contamination from volatile components of a fiberglass glove box. J. V. Rodricks and others. Science 156:1648 Je 23 '67
See also
Owens-Corning fiberglass corporation
Plastics, Glass reinforced

GLASS Industry
Jefferson glass co. and the Krys-tol trademark. A. G. Peterson. il Hobbies 72:98N-98O O '67

Look what they're doing with glass. M. J. Schultz. il Sci Digest 62:44-7+ Jl '67
U.S. tariff & trade policies: failure to consult industry; address, July 11, 1967. R. G. Wingerter. Vital Speeches 34:28-32 O 15 '67
See also
Pilkington brothers, limited
Pittsburgh plate glass company

GLASS manufacture
George Ravenscroft and his contribution to English glassmaking. J. P. Hudson. bibliog il Antiques 92:822-3 D '67

GLASS menagerie; drama. See Williams, T.

GLASS painting and staining
Decorative glass of Roger Darricarrere. J. Lovoos. il Am Artist 31:48-53+ My '67
Look behind the stained glass; Judson studios, Los Angeles il Sunset 139:72 O '67
Stone, iron, wood, poverty, truth; how windows of A. Winternitz unite with other mediums of sacred art. C. Rodríguez Saavedra. il Américas 19:20-6 My '67
Thousands of stained-glass windows from medieval times; an unparalleled international survey. bibliog il UNESCO Courier 20:18-23 Ap '67

GLASS prints
Pseudo-etchings. W. S. Rice. il Design 68:27 Sum '67

GLASS reinforced plastics. See Plastics, Glass reinforced

GLASS walls. See Walls, Glass

GLASSBORO, N.J.
Chief like near to fell out of his chair. il Newsweek 70:17 Jl 3 '67

GLASSBORO conference, 1967
Aftermath of the summit. U S News 63:27 Jl 17 '67
At the summit and after. il U S News 63:29-31 Jl 3 '67
Beyond the summit. H. Brandon. Sat R 50:14-15 Jl 15 '67
Company came to Hollybush; summit conference. T. E. Robinson. il NEA J 56:20-1 S '67
Down from the summit. il Bsns W p 13-15 Jl 1 '67
Eye to eye at Holly Bush. H. Sidey. il Life 63:26B Jl 7 '67
Glassboro summit. Sr Schol 91:20 S 21 '67
Glassboro summit. il Newsweek 70:14-16+ Jl 3 '67
It was important that we understand; values of the fifth postwar U.S.-Soviet summit. il Newsweek 70:94-6 Jl 10 '67
Johnson after Glassboro. W. V. Shannon. Commonweal 86:439-40 Jl 14 '67
Life at the summit. il Sat Eve Post 240:80 Jl 29 '67
Meet comrade Kosygin. Nat R 19:722 Jl 11 '67
President Johnson and Premier Kosygin discuss international problems; text of toast, June 23, statements, June 23, 25 and report to the Nation, June 25, 1967. L. B. Johnson; A. N. Kosygin. Dept State Bul 57:35-8 Jl 10 '67
Spirit of Hollybush; excerpt from remarks, June 23, 1967. L. B. Johnson. Dept State Bul 57:38-40 Jl 10 '67
Summit at Glassboro. America 117:26 Jl 8 '67
Summit get-together: the big drama in small town, U.S.A. il U S News 63:10 Jl 3 '67
Summit in smalltown. il Time 89:10-16 Je 30 '67
Surprise summit, and the world comes to Glassboro; L. B. Johnson-A. Kosygin talks. il Life 62:32B-32F Je 30 '67
World of reason? D. Lawrence. U S News 63:84 Jl 10 '67

GLASSER, Allen
Never on Mars. Sci Digest 61:81-3 F '67

GLASSER, William
California's gift to psychotherapy. J. Langguth. Harper 234:52-6 Je '67

GLASSES for the eyes. See Eyeglasses

GLASSMAN, William
Brief biography. S. Goodman. pors Dance Mag 41:68-9 My '67

GLASSWARE
Documenting some Mt. Washington art glass. K. M. Wilson. il Antiques 92:367-71 S '67
Fostoria's Valencia, Verona and Ruby patterns. A. G. Peterson. il Hobbies 72:98F-98G S '67
George Ravenscroft and his contribution to English glassmaking. J. P. Hudson. bibliog il Antiques 92:822-3 D '67
Glassware oddities of the 1880s. A. G. Peterson. il Hobbies 72:72 Ag '67

GLASSWARE—*Continued*
Glassware oddities of the 1870s. A. G. Peterson. il Hobbies 72:84 Jl '67
Glass-ware oddities of the 1860s. A. G. Peterson. il Hobbies 72:72 My '67
How to buy glassware Am Home 70:60 O '67
In the museums. R. Davidson. il Antiques 91:784+ Je '67
McKee's Germanic pattern, McKinley mug, and three water-bottles. A. G. Peterson. il Hobbies 72:98U N '67
Marvelous sorcery of the invisible. E. Sverbeyeff. il House B 109:92-5 Jl '67
Mt Washington glass company. R. Grover and L. Grover. il Hobbies 72:74-5+ Ap '67
Richardson glass. H. Wakefield. il Antiques 91:632-6 My '67
Trademarks on glass. A. G. Peterson. il Hobbies 72:90-1 D '67
See also
Corning glass center, Corning, N.Y.

Collectors and collecting
American blown glass in the Seigfred collection. J. Rose. il Antiques 91:744-7 Je '67
Gift of Lion pattern glass; H. H. Whitlow collection. il Hobbies 72:84 Ja '68

Exhibitions
German and English glass; famous Beinecke collection at the Corning museum of glass. E. P. Birk. il Antiques 92:302+ S '67

GLASSWARE industry. See Glass industry

GLAZE, Eleanor
Success story; story. McCalls 94:98-9 My '67
Telephone; story. Redbook 130:88-9 N '67

GLAZER, Nathan
Glazer explains. Harper 235:8+ Ag '67
One kind of life. Commentary 43:83-5 F '67

GLAZER, Sidney
(comp) Articles and other books received; Near East. See issues of American historical review

GLEASON, Jackie
Jackie Gleason: anything I can't lick appeals to me. B. Davidson. il pors Sat Eve Post 240:30-7 F 11 '67
King of Miami. il por Newsweek 69:104+ F 13 '67

GLEASON, Philip
Our new age of romanticism. America 117:372-5 O 7 '67

GLEASON, William P.
Designer's corner. S. Salter. Pub W 191:110 F 6 '67

GLEN ALLAN, Miss.
Struggle that changed Glen Allan; formation of Child development group in Mississippi. D. Nevin. il Life 63:108+ S 29 '67

GLEN CANYON
Gunkholing the Glens. F. C. Clark, jr. il Yachting 122:48-50+ Ag '67

GLEN ECHO amusement park
Washington's Rhine? M. Fradin. il Am For 73:22-5+ My '67

GLENDALE, Calif.
Public buildings
Municipal building that breaks with tradition. il Am City 82:92-3 Jl '67

GLENDAY, Alice
Exit, pursued by pancakes; story. Redbook 130:82-3 N '67
So dark a night; story. Ladies Home J 84:72-3 Je '67

GLENDENING, Fred
Satellite service centers. Am City 82:102-4 My '67

GLENVILLE, Peter
Peter Glenville talks about the Burtons. Vogue 150:282-5+ S 1 '67

GLIADIN
Reversible aggregation of α-gliadin to fibrils. D. D. Kasarda and others. bibliog il Science 155:203-5 Ja 13 '67

GLIAL cells. See Nerve cells

GLIDER pilots. See Air pilots

GLIDERS (aeronautics)
Aqua glider: a great new sportscraft you can build. W. W. Wyper. il Pop Sci 191:50-3 Ag '67
Blue ribbon entry. J. Fricker. il Flying 80:118-21 Mr '67
Powered Bede-2 readied to circle globe; Project Love flight. il Aviation W 86:109 Ap 3 '67
See also
Gliding and soaring

GLIDING and soaring
Sky is their limit. R. N. Buck. Read Digest 90:68-72 Ap '67

GLINKIANA; ballet. See Ballets—Criticisms

GLINN, Burt
Heroes of a harsh land; photographs. Holiday 42:76-83 D '67

GLIXON, David M.
People are looking up. Sat R 50:46-50+ My 20 '67
Semiannual reference book roundup. Sat R 50:38-43 N 18 '67
—See Winterich, J. T. jt. ed.

GLOAG, John
Classic tradition in Georgian and early Victorian furniture. Antiques 91:754-9 Je '67

GLOBAL meteorological experiment. See Weather research

GLOBAL satellite communications systems. See Communications satellites—International aspects

GLOBES
Decorative globes. il House & Gard 131:36-7 F '67

GLOBES, Astronomical
Decorative globes. il House & Gard 131:36-7 F '67

GLOBIGERINA oozes. See Sedimentation and deposition

GLOBINS. See Proteins

GLOBOROTALIA. See Foraminifera

GLOBULINEMIA
Limited heterogeneity of gamma globulin in hypogammaglobulinemia. R. Hong and R. A. Good. bibliog il Science 156:1102-3 My 26 '67

GLOBULINS
Heterologous antilymphocyte globulin: studies in vitro. L. J. Humphrey and others. bibliog il Science 157:441 Jl 28 '67
Ultrastructure of gamma M immunoglobulin and alpha macroglobulin: electron-microscopic study. S. E. Svehag and others. bibliog il Science 158:933-6 N 17 '67
See also
Concanavalin

GLOBULINS in the blood. See Serum globulins

GLOBUS, Albert, and Scheibel, A. B.
Synaptic loci on parietal cortical neurons: terminations of corpus callosum fibers. bibliog Science 156:1127-9 My 26 '67

GLOMERIDA. See Millipeds

GLOMERULONEPHRITIS. See Kidneys—Diseases

GLORIA, Sister
Man is known by his friends; poem. America 116:378 Mr 18 '67
Two brothers; poem. America 117:225 S 2 '67

GLORIOUS whitewasher; drama. See Hackett, W.

GLORY bowers
Indoors, it will bloom and bloom. il Sunset 139:246 O '67

GLORY of the snow
Glory of the snow. R. C. Hands. Horticulture 45:12 F '67

GLORYBOWER. See Glory bowers

GLOSSY ibises. See Ibises

GLOVES, Rubber
Household waterproof gloves. il Consumer Rep 32:165-7 Mr '67

GLOWACKI, Barbara
Gunkholing! Travel 128:40-4 N '67
Michigan's inland waterway. Travel 128:48-51+ S '67

GLUBB, Sir John Bagot
Glubb pasha sizes up the Middle East. il pors Newsweek 69:18 Je 19 '67

GLUCAN
Glucans of oomycete cell walls. J. M. Aronson and others. bibliog il Science 155:332-5 Ja 20 '67

GLUCK, Christoph Willibald
Music to my ears; concert performance of Orfeo ed Euridice. I. Kolodin. Sat R 50:82+ Ap 22 '67
New York; Orfeo ed Euridice. F. Merkling. Opera N 31:28 My 13 '67
Orfeo ed Euridice. P. L. Miller. il Am Rec G 33:558-9 Mr '67
Orfeo out of Orphée. H. Weinstock. Sat R 50:81 F 25 '67
Records:
Orfeo ed Euridice. Opera N 31:34 F 18 '67

GLUCK, Louise
Early December in Croton-On-Hudson; poem. Atlan 220:115 D '67
Edge; poem. Atlan 219:90 Je '67
Grandmother in the garden; The egg; poems. Poetry 109:382-4 Mr '67
Inlet; poem. Mlle 65:94 Je '67
Islander; poem. Nation 204:510 Ap 17 '67
Late snow; poem. New Yorker 43:189 Mr 25 '67

GLUCK, Louise—*Continued*
Letter from Provence; poem. New Yorker 43: 26 Ag 5 '67
My cousin in April; poem. Yale R 56:553 Je '67
Racer's widow; poem. New Yorker 43:83 Je 24 '67

GLUCKSBERG, Sam, and King, L. J.
Motivated forgetting mediated by implicit verbal chaining: a laboratory analog of repression. Science 158:517-19 O 27 '67

GLUCOCORTICOIDS. See Corticosteroids

GLUCOSE
D-Glucose: preferential binding to brush borders disrupted with tris hydroxymethyl aminomethane. R. G. Faust and others. bibliog il Science 155:1261-3 Mr 10 '67
Hexokinase isoenzymes in liver and adipose tissue of man and dog. J. Brown and others. bibliog il Science 155:205-7 Ja 13 '67
Reagentless substrate analysis with immobilized enzymes. S. J. Updike and G. P. Hicks. bibliog il Science 158:270-2 O 13 '67

GLUCOSE phosphate. See Phosphates

GLUCOSE phosphate dehydrogenase. See Dehydrogenases

GLUE
New glue needs no clamps. il Pop Sci 190:150 Mr '67
Nine good gluing tricks. H. Wicks. il Pop Sci 191:146-7 N '67

GLUING. See Glue

GLUTAMINE
Enzyme induction by corticosteroids in embryonic cells: steroid structure and inductive effect. A. A. Moscona and R. Piddington. bibliog il Science 158:496-7 O 27 '67

GLUTARALDEHYDE. See Aldehydes

GLUTATHIONE
Glutathione deficiency in sheep erythrocytes. J. E. Smith and B. I. Osburn. bibliog il Science 158:374-5 O 20 '67

GLUTATHIONE reductase. See Enzymes

GLYCERALDEHYDE phosphate dehydrogenase. See Dehydrogenases

GLYCERIDES
Ethanolamine phosphoglycerides: effect on the properties of myelinoid lecithin water systems. P. G. Fast. bibliog il Science 155: 1680-1 Mr 31 '67
Galactosyl diglycerides: their possible function in euglena chloroplasts. A. Rosenberg. bibliog il Science 157:1191-6 S 8 '67

GLYCERIN
Glycerol excretion by symbiotic algae from corals and tridacna and its control by the host. L. Muscatine. bibliog il Science 156: 516-19 Ap 28 '67

GLYCEROL. See Glycerin

GLYCOGEN
Glycogen synthetase activity in liver: regulation by the autonomic nerves. T. Shimazu. bibliog il Science 156:1256-7 Je 2 '67

GLYCOLS
Want to save a stump? polyethylene glycol treatment. il Pop Sci 190:175 My '67

GLYNDEBOURNE festival. See Music festivals —England

GLYOXAL
Keto-aldehydes and cell division. A. Szent-Györgyi and others. bibliog Science 155: 539-41 F 3 '67

GNOSSIENNES; ballet. See Ballets—Criticisms

GO, Janet Grace
Traveler's choice. Travel 128:9 D '67

GO (game)
Go; Oriental game. J. A. M. Graham. il Horizon 9:100-3 Aut '67

GO buggies. See Motor vehicles

GO-go girls. See Dancers

GO-go gophers; drama. See Martens, A. C.

GO-karts. See Karts (midget cars)

GOA
But not gone. il Time 89:35 Ja 27 '67

GOAL values. See Value (psychology)

GOALBY, Bob
No tranquilizer like victory. A. Wright. il por Sports Illus 26:20-1 Ja 23 '67

GOALKEEPER. See Hockey players

GOALS, National. See United States

GOARD, Dotty
Culls; poem. Christian Cent 84:1490 N 22 '67

GOAT hunting
See also
Rocky Mountain goat hunting

GOBBI, Tito
Recordings. M. Mayer. Esquire 68:16+ O '67

GOBEN, Ronald D.
Fight for integrated schools goes on. Parents Mag 42:58-9+ Je '67

GOBERMAN, Max
Columbia's Odyssey label starts a propitious voyage. S. Fleming. por Hi Fi 17:75-6 Ap '67
Odyssey. M. N. Kanny. Am Rec G 33:638 Ap '67

GOBLE, Emerson
Behind the record. See issues of Architectural record
about
Emerson Goble won't like this a bit, but . . . W. F. Wagner, jr. Arch Rec 142:9 D '67

GOCHMAN, Alice Sabina
Timely sculpture for the garden, and the ancient art of dialing. Home Gard 54:26-7 Ag '67

GOD
Credibility gap in theology. F. Kirschenmann. Christian Cent 84:498-500 Ap 19 '67; Discussion. 84:757 Je 7 '67
'Gimme' is dead? M. Novak. Commonweal 86:174-5 Ap 28 '67; Discussion. 86:379+ Je 23 '67
God and evil. R. H. Luecke. Christian Cent 84:377-8 Mr 22 '67
God; Commonweal paper; symposium. Commonweal 85:498-519+ F 10 '67; Discussion. 85:498, 636 F 10, Mr 10 '67
God: love or death? R. Goetz. Christian Cent 84:1487-90 N 22 '67
Is there a God? M. Muggeridge. Ladies Home J 84:67+ Je '67
Mystery and majesty. V. P. McCorry. America 116:766, inside back cover My 20 '67
To know the pain of being a person; address. H. K. Zeller. Vital Speeches 33:328-30 Mr 15 '67
See also
Atheism
Christianity
Death of God theology
Holy Spirit
Love (theology)
Theology
Biblical teaching
God of history. L. Dupré. Commonweal 85: 516-19+ F 10 '67
God of the Bible. B. Vawter. Commonweal 85:504-7 F 10 '67

GOD is dead (theology) See Death of God

GODDARD, James Lee
Are you wasting money on worthless health aids? interview, ed. by J. C. G. Conniff. por Pop Sci 190:92-3+ Ap '67
How dangerous is marijuana? a top official sparks new debate; excerpts from statements. por U S News 63:20 O 30 '67
about
Goddard: revolution comes hard. B. J. Culliton. por Sci N 91:91 Ja 28 '67
No martyr to marijuana. New Repub 157:6 D 2 '67
Pot & Goddard. por Time 90:54 O 27 '67

GODDARD space flight center. See United States—National aeronautics and space administration—Goddard space flight center

GODFREY, Daniel
Right for the first time. Flying 80:73 Mr '67

GODFREY, P. J. See Billings, W. D. jt. auth.

GODKIN, Edwin Lawrence
Gloom, gloom, gloom, and scarce one ray of light; excerpts from The anti-imperialists: twelve against empire, 1898-1900. R. L. Beisner. por Am Heritage 18:65-71 Ag '67

GODSELL, Geoffrey
Echoes from Sinai. Sat R 50:29+ Ag 26 '67
In the wake of the Boer war. Sat R 50:41 Je 10 '67

GOEHR, Alexander
Britain's avant-garde. P. L. Miller. Am Rec G 33:623 Ap '67

GOEN, Richard L.
How fast is too fast? T. Stimson. il Pop Mech 128:71-4+ S '67
How young is too young? T. Stimson. il Pop Mech 128:132-5+ O '67

GOERNER, Fred G.
Lady vanished. C. Dreher. Nation 204:374-6 Mr 20 '67

GOETHITE
Stable magnetic remanence in antiferromagnetic goethite. D. W. Strangway and others. bibliog il Science 158:785-7 N 10 '67

GOETZ, Ronald
God: love or death? Christian Cent 84:1487-90 N 22 '67
Modernity demythologized. Christian Cent 84: 691-2+ My 24 '67

GOFF, Frederick R.
Bibliographical soufflé, so to speak. por Wilson Lib Bul 41:576-9 F '67

GOGH, Vincent van
Electricity in water. il por Time 90:78-9 N 10 '67
White roses. A. Saarinen. il McCalls 94:132-5 Jl '67

GOGOL', Nikolai Vasil'evich
Government inspector. Criticism
Life 63:12 Ag 4 '67

GOGORZA, Emilio Edoardo de. See De Gogorza, E. E.

GOHEEN, Robert F.
Time to serve; adaptation of address, September 18, 1966. Sch & Soc 95:296-8 Sum '67

GOITER
Sherpa goiter studied. D. A. Ehrlich. Sci N 92:277 S 16 '67

GOLAKAI, V. K. See Schlesinger, M. jt. auth.

GOLBECK, Bernard J.
Slide switches and their ganged arrays. por Electr World 78:44-6 O '67

GOLD, Arthur R.
Exodus as autobiography. Commentary 43:46-51 My '67

GOLD, Herbert
Artist in pursuit of butterflies. Sat Eve Post 240:81-5 F 11 '67
Jerusalem; the holiest city. Holiday 42:84-9+ D '67
Risks and pleasures of fantasy. Holiday 42: 6+ Ag '67
Selfish story; story. Harper 234:88-92 My '67
Where money has more fun. Sat Eve Post 240:64-7 D 30 '67

about
Authors & editors. por Pub W 191:25 Mr 27 '67
Each generation had its own dream. G. Hicks. Sat R 50:25-6 Mr 25 '67
Moving chronicle of life with father. W. Schott. Life 62:17 Ap 7 '67

GOLD, Samuel
Each generation had its own dream. G. Hicks. Sat R 50:25-6 Mr 25 '67
Moving chronicle of life with father. W. Schott. Life 62:17 Ap 7 '67

GOLD, Thomas
Radio method for the precise measurement of the rotation period of the earth. bibliog Science 157:302-4 Jl 21 '67

GOLD, Victor
Cliché expert testifies as a liberal. Nat R 19:690-1 Je 27 '67
Rush to Philippi. Nat R 19:1206-7 O 31 '67

GOLD
Meeting needs for heavy elements. P. H. Abelson. Science 159:37 Ja 5 '68
Where the glitter is. H. French. Holiday 41:6+ My '67

History
To the planets for gold; reprint. G. Allen. il Sci Digest 62:39-44 O '67

Prices
No holds are barred for dollar's defense; effect of British devaluation on U.S. money markets. il Bsns W p38-9 N 25 '67
Price of gold. M. Friedman. Newsweek 71:51 Ja 1 '68

GOLD as money
Ailing dollar: a touch of Midas. Newsweek 70:53 D 25 '67
Another money problem: vanishing gold; address, October 17, 1967. J. P. Koszul. il U S News 63:46-8 D 4 '67
As the Nation's gold keeps melting away. il U S News 62:99-100 My 1 '67
Barriers up & down; France and the U.S. il Time 89:95 F 10 '67
Bullion battle; moves to assure orderly trading on the London gold market. Time 90:71 D 22 '67
Can de Gaulle break the dollar? with interviews with J. Rueff and E. Despres. il U S News 63:54-6+ D 11 '67
Dollar is a dollar. M. Friedman. Newsweek 69:86 My 15 '67
Dollar is not as bad as gold; Time essay. Time 91:16-17 Ja 12 '68
Dollar passes a crucial test; with editorial comment. il Bsns W p 11-13, 88 D 23 '67

Game without winners. Newsweek 69:86 Ap 24 '67
Gold and the dollar. W. F. Butler and J. V. Deaver. For Affairs 46:181-92 O '67
Gold buyers back off; Bucking the gold rush. il Bsns W p33-6 D 2 '67
Gold rush: defending the dollar. il Newsweek 70:68-70+ D 4 '67
Gold, taxes, inflation & co. Nat R 19:1052-3 O 3 '67
Great gold flap: compounding confusion. il Bsns W p 196+ Ap 22 '67
How golden is the dollar? J. K. Jessup. il Life 63:66-8+ Ag 25 '67
In wake of attack on dollar: another side of the gold story. il U S News 63:29-31 D 25 '67
Monetary alchemy; address, January 23, 1967. D. H. McLaughlin. Vital Speeches 33:438-43 My 1 '67
One reason gold is scarce. il U S News 63:80 O 2 '67
Plea to stem dollar flow. Bsns W p 108 Ag 5 '67
Rush for gold: who bought it, and why. il U S New 63:12 D 11 '67
Sanguine & somber. Time 90:97 D 15 '67
Still looking for the Midas touch. il Bsns W p 112-14 Ja 13 '68
Stormy weathr for the dollar; with panel discussion by H. Wallich; P. A. Samuelson; M. Friedman. il Newsweek 69:86-8+ Ap 17 '67
Trying to guard the gold; world's dwindling gold stock. il Bsns W p34-5 D 16 '67
U.S. balance of payments: can we plug the gold drain? il Sr Schol 91:8-11 D 7 '67
Wrong way to solve the gold problem. Bsns W p 174 Ap 29 '67

GOLD country classic race. See Automobile racing
GOLD dollar. See Money—United States
GOLD-headed cane; story. See Crossman, P. R.
GOLD mines and mining
Scientific gold rush; gold-bearing rock, Jackson Hole area of northwest Wyoming. Sci Digest 62:29 Ag '67

History
To the planets for gold; reprint. G. Allen. il Sci Digest 62:39-44 O '67

South Africa
Down to the deeps for gold. J. D. Ratcliff. il Read Digest 91:201-2+ Jl '67
One reason gold is scarce. il U S News 63:80 O 2 '67

United States
Gold rush diary, by E. D. Perkins. Review Sat R 50:27-8 My 27 '67. J. K. Hutchens
Gold rush of '67? Cortez, Nev. and Jackson Hole, Wyo. strikes. Newsweek 69:92 Mr 20 '67
Last gold rush; Old Homestake mine, S.D. N. Willatt. il Duns R 90:41-3+ S '67

GOLD panning
Three ways to find gold. C. Fischer. il Field & S 72:56-7 Jl '67
Trying your luck with a gold pan. il Sunset 138:68+ Mr '67

GOLD reserves. See Gold as money
GOLD rush of 1849. See Gold mines and mining —United States
GOLD standard. See Gold as money
GOLDBERG, Art
Negro self-help. New Repub 156:6 Je 10 '67
GOLDBERG, Arthur Joseph
Ambassador Goldberg reports on his trip to Asia; transcripts of news conferences, March 6, 8, 1967. Dept State Bul 56:505-14 Mr 27 '67
Ambassador on the war. por Newsweek 70:56 Jl 10 '67
Excerpt from statement in the Security council of the United Nations, December 12, 1966. Cong Digest 46:76+ Mr '67
Fifth emergency special session of U.N. General assembly adjourns; statement, July 21, 1967. Dept State Bul 57:216-18 Ag 14 '67
Human rights conventions; statement, February 23, 1967. Dept State Bul 56:524-9 Mr 27 '67
International law in the United Nations; address, December 29, 1966. Dept State Bul 56:140-5 Ja 23 '67; Same with title International law. Vital Speeches 33:234-8 F 1 '67
Letter June 29, 1967. Dept State Bul 57:65 Jl 17 '67
Middle East crisis; address, June 20, 1967. Vital Speeches 33:603-5 Jl 15 '67

GOLDBERG, Arthur Joseph—*Continued*
Outer space treaty signed by sixty nations at White House ceremony; text of statement, January 27, 1967. Dept State Bul 56: 267-8 F 20 '67
Persevering for peace; address, May 12, 1967. Dept State Bul 56:838-44 Je 5 '67
Public diplomacy at the United Nations; address, July 27, 1967. Dept. State Bul 57: 262-5 Ag 28 '67
Report on North Korean violations of DMZ transmitted to U.N; letter. Dept State Bul 57:692 N 20 '67
Responsibility of the United Nations in the search for peace in Viet-Nam; statement, November 2, 1967. Dept State Bul 57:667-72 N 20 '67
Secretary Rusk and Ambassador Goldberg urge Senate approval of outer space treaty; statement, March 7, 1967. Dept State Bul 56:602-12 Ap 10 '67
Security council affirms principles for peace in the Middle East; requests Secretary-General to send special representative; statements. Dept State Bul 57:834-43 D 18 '67
Security council votes mandatory sanctions against Southern Rhodesia; statement, December 12, 1966. Dept State Bul 56:73-7 Ja 9 '67
Southern Yemen admitted to United Nations; statement, December 12, 1967. Dept State Bul 58:65 Ja 8 '68
U.N. adopts resolutions on aid to refugees and status of Jerusalem; rejects other resolutions dealing with the Middle East crisis; statements, July 3, 4, 1967. Dept State Bul 57:108-12 Jl 24 '67
U.N. condemns violations of Middle East cease-fire; statements, October 24, 25, 1967. Dept State Bul 57:690-2 N 20 '67
United Nations force in Cyprus extended through June 1967; statement, December 15, 1966. Dept State Bul 56:179-81 Ja 30 '67
U.N. General assembly endorses outer space treaty; statements, December 17, 19, 1966. Dept State Bul 56:78-83 Ja 9 '67
U.N. General assembly holds fifth emergency session; United States offers proposals for peace in the Middle East; statements, June 17, 19 and 20, 1967. Dept State Bul 57:47-52 Jl 10 '67
U.N. Security council continues consideration of the crisis in the Near East; statements, May 29-31, 1967. Dept State Bul 56:920-9 Je 19 '67
U.N. Security council continues debate on Near East; Soviet proposal condemning Israel rejected; statements, June 10, 13 and 14, with text of letter, June 9, 1967. Dept State Bul 57:3-11 Jl 3 '67
U.N. Security council demands a cease-fire in the Near East; statements, June 6, 8 and 9, 1967. Dept State Bul 56:934-47 Je 26 '67
U.S. abstains on U.N. resolution on Jerusalem; urges steps toward durable peace in Near East; statement, July 14, 1967. Dept State Bul 57:148-51 Jl 13 '67
U.S. asks U.N. Secretary-General for help in seeking peace; text of letter, December 19, 1966. Dept State Bul 56:63-4 Ja 9 '67
United States calls for restraint in the Near East; statement, May 24, 1967. Dept State Bul 56:871-3 Je 12 '67
U.S. calls for U.N. committee to develop principles for cooperative exploration and use of ocean floor; statement, November 8, 1967. Dept State Bul 57:723-5 N 27 '67
U.S. does not concur in request for U.N. General assembly session; text of letter, June 15, 1967. Dept State Bul 57:12-13 Jl 3 '67
United States peace aims in Viet-Nam; address, February 10, 1967. Dept State Bul 56:310-16 F 27 '67
U.S. reaffirms desire for peace in Viet-Nam; exchange of letters with U Thant, December 31, 1966. Dept State Bul 56:137-8 Ja 23 '67
U.S. recapitulates basic principles for U.N. peacekeeping functions; statement, March 22, 1967. Dept State Bul 56:636-41 Ap 17 '67
United States, the United Nations, and southern Africa; address, January 27, 1967. Dept State Bul 56:289-94 F 20 '67
United States urges agreement on peacekeeping question; statement, May 22, 1967. Dept State Bul 56:894-7 Je 12 '67
United States urges dialog regarding South West Africa; statements, April 26 and May 19, 1967. Dept State Bul 56:888-93 Je 12 '67
U.S. viewpoint on four current world problems; statement, September 21, 1967. Dept State Bul 57:483-9 O 16 '67

What the Ambassador said. New Repub 156: 28-9 Ap 1 '67
Work of the 21st session of the U.N. General assembly; statement, December 21, 1966. Dept State Bul 56:98-102 Ja 16 '67

about

RSVP. Nat R 19:554 My 30 '67
Why Goldberg opts out. por Bsns W p40-1 D 16 '67

GOLDBERG, Bertrand
Giving the past a future. H. Meeker. il Arch Forum 126:56-61 My '67
GOLDBERG, Herbert S. See Benarde, M. A. jt. auth.
GOLDBERG, James F.
Dangerous statesman. New Repub 156:28-32 Ap 15 '67
GOLDBERG, Maxwell H.
Humanities and the alienated adolescent. bibliog f Sch & Soc 95:257-61 Ap 15 '67
Religious education as a humanity. Sch & Soc 95:123-4 F 18 '67
GOLDBERG, Milton
Help, my child has taken poison! E. M. Wylie. Good H 164:77+ Je '67; Same abr. il Read Digest 91:133-7 Ag '67
GOLDBERG, Norman
Shop talk. See issues of Popular photography
GOLDBERG, Rube
Our Rube Goldberg tax system. H. S. Reuss. Commonweal 86:280-1 My 26 '67
GOLDBLOOM, Maurice J.
How the military rules 8 million Greeks. N Y Times Mag p26-7+ S 24 '67
What happened in Greece. Commentary 44:68-74 D '67
GOLDEN, Hal
Press relations for nonprofit institutions: a perspective. Wilson Lib Bul 42:280-3 N '67
GOLDEN, Harry
Greetings to a living legend. Life 36:14 Jl 21 '67
How to live with a chair you hate. por Sat R 50:14-17 Je 17 '67
Meaning of Israel. Holiday 42:58-63+ D '67
GOLDEN, L. L. L.
Public relations. See issues of Saturday review
GOLDEN, Linda
Golden is our valley; interview, ed. by K. Davis. Farm J 91:50-1 N '67
GOLDEN, Ruth I.
Speaking the same language. NEA J 56:40+ Mr '67
GOLDEN, William T.
Walter Orr Roberts, president- elect. Science 155:853-4 F 17 '67
GOLDEN age; ballet. See Ballets—Criticisms
GOLDEN door resort. See Health resorts, watering places, etc.
GOLDEN eagle awards. See National recreation and park association
GOLDEN eagles. See Eagles
GOLDEN Gate park. See San Francisco—Parks and playgrounds
GOLDEN needle; story. See Sullivan, E.
GOLDEN passport. See Recreation—Fees
GOLDEN press, incorporated
Golden BooKit package solves processing problem. Library J 92:2346-7 Je 15 '67
Golden press initiates non-returnable policy on books at longer discount; seller has option. Pub W 191:31 My 1 '67
GOLDEN screw; revue. See Musical comedies, revues, etc.—Criticisms, plots, etc.
GOLDEN weddings. See Wedding anniversaries
GOLDFARB, Clare R.
Never too young for music. Parents Mag 42: 52-3+ My '67
GOLDFARB, Ronald L.
Being left alone. New Repub 157:28-9 S 30 '67
GOLDFINE, Bernard
Vicuña man. por Newsweek 70:29 O 2 '67
GOLDFINGER, Myron Henry
Takrouna. Arch Forum 127:98-106 Jl '67
GOLDFISH
Reward and learning in the goldfish. G. Lowes and M. E. Bitterman. bibliog il Science 157: 455-7 Jl 28 '67
GOLDFISH, Experiments on. See Animal experimentation
GOLDHAMMER, Keith
Hottest spot in town; excerpt from Issues and problems in contemporary educational administration. Am Ed 3:2-4 O '67
GOLDIN, Amy
Antihierarchical American. Art N 66:48-50+ S '67
Art in a hairshirt. Art N 65:26+ F '67
Duchamp-Villon: the cubist core. Art N 66: 34-7+ O '67

GOLDING, William
Delphi: the oracle revealed. Holiday 42:60-
1+ Ag '67
GOLDMAN, Albert
Books (cont) Vogue 149:114 F 1; 96 Ap 1;
150:35 Jl '67; 151:58 Ja 1 '68
Boy-man schlemiel: Jewish humor? Common-
weal 86:605-8 S 29 '67
GOLDMAN, L. See Binstock, L. jt. auth.
GOLDMAN, Marshall I.
Soviet economic growth since the revolution.
bibliog f Cur Hist 53:230-5+ O '67
GOLDMAN, Michael
Inventing the American heart. Nation 204:
529-30 Ap 24 '67
Visitor; poem. New Yorker 43:54 S 23 '67
GOLDMAN, Nathan
Social breakdown. bibliog f Ann Am Acad
373:156-79 S '67
GOLDMAN, William
Temple of Goldman. R. A. Schroth. America
117:250 S 9 '67
GOLDMARK, Peter Carl
Lone inventor with a genie complex. L. Ed-
son. il pors N Y Times Mag p28-9+ D 17 '67
GOLDONI, Carlo
Servant of two masters. Criticism
Nation 204:636-8 My 15 '67
Son of nature. P. Weiss. Opera N 31:26-7
Mr 11 '67
GOLDREICH, Peter, and Schubert, Gerald
Rotation of the sun. bibliog Science 156:1101-2
My 26 '67
GOLDSACK, Jack
Change of pace techniques. J. Scully. il Mod
Phot 31:84-7 Je '67
GOLDSACK, José
Why a Christian democratic labor organiza-
tion. America 116:154-6 Ja 28 '67
GOLDSCHLAGER, Seth S.
Interns' dissent. New Repub 157:16 Ag 19 '67
GOLDSCHMIDT, Arthur E.
Question of food aid in the perspective of the
problems of the developing countries; state-
ment, July 24, 1967. Dept State Bul 57:304-
8 S 4 '67

GOLDSMITH, Arthur
Camera shutters: will electronics take over?
Pop Sci 191:120-2+ S '67
Color negative: the one film that does every-
thing. Pop Sci 190:126-9 Ap '67
Inside Photokina; way-out cameras make
news. por Pop Sci 190:134-7 Ja '67
Shooting with the Noctilux and Hologon. il
U S Camera 30:56-7+ F '67
Truth, myth, fallacy, humbug, etcetera. Pop
Phot 62:75+ Ja '68
GOLDSMITH, Harris
Chopin's mazurkas: a new miraculous read-
ing from Rubinstein. Hi Fi 17:73-4 Ap '67
Ormandy and Steinberg complete their Bee-
thoven nine. Hi Fi 17:84-5 Ja '67
GOLDSMITH, Harry
Hemorrheology. Science 155:1443-4 Mr 17 '67
GOLDSMITH, John R.
Carbon monoxide. Science 157:842-4 Ag 18 '67
—and Hexter, A. C.
Respiratory exposure to lead: epidemiological
and experimental dose-response relation-
ships. bibliog Science 158:132-4 O 6 '67
GOLDSMITH, Martin M.
ADF credibility gap. Flying 80:67+ Je '67
GOLDSMITH, Mary Helen M.
Separation of transit of auxin from uptake:
average velocity and reversible inhibition by
anaerobic conditions. bibliog Science 156:
661-3 My 5 '67
GOLDSMITHING
Goldworkers and lapidaries; excerpt from the
16th century Aztec manuscript; tr. by C. E.
Dibble and A. J. O. Anderson. B. de Saha-
gún. il Craft Horiz 27:16-21 S '67
GOLDSTEIN, Abraham S.
Advising the Court. Commentary 44:103-7 S
'67
Preliminary verdict. Commentary 43:96-9 Ap
'67
GOLDSTEIN, Harold
Fahrenheit 902: library research could be
hotter. Wilson Lib Bul 41:901-4 My '67
GOLDSTEIN, Joel
For a growing campus. Pub W 192:56-8 S 18
'67
GOLDSTEIN, Joseph I. See Short, J. M. jt.
auth.
GOLDSTEIN, Leon, and others
Lungfish neoceratodus forsteri: activities of
ornithine-urea cycle and enzymes. bibliog
Science 157:316-17 Jl 21 '67
—See McBean, R. L. jt. auth.
GOLDSTEIN, Lester. See Prescott, D. M. jt.
auth.

GOLDSTEIN, Margaret A. See Philpott, C. W.
jt. auth.
GOLDSTEIN, Richard
Letter from eastern Europe. Holiday 42:20+
N '67
Paupers arrive. Vogue 151:54 Ja 1 '68
GOLDSTEIN, Walter
Books. Bul Atomic Sci 23:30-2 O '67
Dynamic new policy toward the new Europe.
Bul Atomic Sci 23:17-22 Ap '67
GOLDSTONE, Richard H.
Old age inaugural. Sat R 50:27-8 Ap 1 '67
GOLDWATER, Barry Morris
Barry Goldwater speaks out; interview. por
Nat R 20:27-8 Ja 16 '68
Senator and the reporter; interview, ed. by
R. Peterson. pors Flying 81:56-61 S '67
Shine Smith: Navajo friend. por(p96) Mc-
Calls 95:168-9 D '67

about

Bearing Barry; views on Republican chances
in 1968. Time 89:25 Mr 3 '67
Expert advice. il por Newsweek 70:29 Jl 3
'67
Goldwater in South Africa. S. Uys. New
Repub 158:15-17 Ja 6 '67
Goldwater will have his say. S. Alsop. por
Sat Eve Post 240:16 Ap 8 '67
In a cause that will triumph, by K. Hess.
Review
Nat R 19:310+ Mr 21 '67. W. A. Rusher
New Repub 156:28-30 F 11 '67. A. Kopkind
Mr Conservative bows out. por Time 91:28
Ja 12 '68
Speaking out. por Sat Eve Post 240:10+ F
11 '67
Suite 3505: the story of the draft Goldwater
movement, by F. C. White. Review
Nat R il 19:596-7 My 30 '67. M. S. Evans
What is freedom all about? W. F. Buckley,
jr. Nat R 19:184 F 21 '67
GOLDWATER, Robert
Franz Kline: darkness visible. Art N 66:
38-43+ Mr '67
GOLEMON, Harry A.
Office management. Arch Rec 141:93-4 F;
93-4 Mr '67
GOLF
Borrowing a secret from another Player;
Gary Player. J. Nicklaus. il Sports Illus
28:48 Ja 15 '68
Golf is too easy: physical fitness for middle-
aged men. il Sci Digest 62:76 Jl '67
How to beat your husband at golf. A. Palmer.
il McCalls 94:44+ My '67
Instant golf; photographs. Esquire 67:145-8
Ap '67
My friend Arnold Palmer. M. H. McCor-
mack. il Sports Illus 26:56-66 Mr 6; 32-6+
Mr 13; 54-6+ Mr 20; 36-40+ Mr 27 '67
Numbers game for the tour; IBM sports in-
formation service. A. Wright. il Sports
Illus 27:76-8 N 13 '67
Personal business: Gene Sarazen's tips for
senior golfers. Bsns W p 157-8 Je 17 '67
Top man on the laugh tour; P. Hahn, king
of trick-shot artists. M. Cope. il Sports
Illus 27:34-6+ O 30 '67
Trap shot that saves you strokes, but not in
a trap. J. Nicklaus. il Sports Illus 27:60 N
20 '67
Where headwork means more than the swing.
J. Nicklaus. il Sports Illus 26:66 My 1 '67
Zero on the tour. G. Plimpton. il Sports Illus
26:46-56 Ja 30; 28-34 F 6; 36-8+ F 13 '67
See also
Golf courses
Putting (golf)
Swing (golf)

Anecdotes, facetiae, satire, etc.

How to improve your lie. il Esquire 67:150-1
Ap '67
Now that I understand golf. G. Porter. il Read
Digest 91:86-8 Jl '67

Study and teaching

Dauntless Dave; D. Williams, golf coach for
University of Houston. J. Underwood. il
Sports Illus 26:64-9+ Je 19 '67

Tournaments

Augusta had a new look; reflections about the
Masters. A. Wright. il Sports Illus 26:36-8+
Ap 24 '67
Bearding the lion: Arnold Palmer loses Las
Vegas tournament to Frank Beard. News-
week 69:92 My 22 '67
Beating seventeen greens and a brown: B.
Casper wins Canadian Open. A. Wright. il
Sports Illus 27:46-7 Jl 10 '67

GOLF—Tournaments—*Continued*

Ben & Arnie liven up the weekend; Ryder cup matches A. Wright. il Sports Illus 27: 56+ O 30 '67

But papa, I played like a clod; Ladies' PGA. M. Mulvoy. il Sports Illus 27:24-5 Jl 10 '67

Calm before the storm; 26th Bing Crosby national pro-am tournament. il Newsweek 69:91 F 6 '67

Companies tee off to win more friends; tournaments under corporate sponsorship. il Bsns W p28 S 2 '67

Crossed-up golf at Houston; Houston champions international golf tournament. M. Mulvoy. il Sports Illus 26:28-9 My 15 '67

Daughter of Crocodile; C. Lacoste wins U.S. women's Open. il Time 90:50+ Jl 14 '67

Delightful brawl in a gentleman's game; Piccadilly world match play tournament. G. S. Brown. Sports Illus 27:64-5 O 23 '67

Different game; Sahara invitational won by Nicklaus. il Time 90:70 N 10 '67

Doug tames a pink pussycat; winner of Doral open in Miami. M. Mulvoy. il Sports Illus 26:22-3 Mr 13 '67

Eye on the Masters; CBS at the 1966 Masters, Augusta, Ga. D. Jenkins. il Sports Illus 26: 90-2+ Ap 10 '67

From rabbit to real pro; endless summer golf tour. E. Asinof. il N Y Times Mag p54-5+ S 10 '67

Gay's green jacket; Masters tournament. Newsweek 69:70 Ap 24 '67

Glory day for Gay; winner of Masters tournament. D. Jenkins. il Sports Illus 26:22-7 Ap 17 '67

How to hit golf's best shot; ed. by M. Mulvoy. G. Brewer. il Sports Illus 27:30-7 Ag 7 '67

Impossible dreamer; Westchester golf classic. il Time 90:38 S 8 '67

Jack delivers the crusher; wins U.S. Open. A. Wright. il Sports Illus 26:22-7 Je 26 '67

King of the Kelloggs; Doral Open in Miami. Time 89:44 Mr 17 '67

Masters sends an invitation to remember. A. Wright. il Sports Illus 26:51-4+ Ap 10 '67

Mod golf strikes at old St Andrews. G. S. Brown. il Sports Illus 27:32-3 O 16 '67

New year's resolution; Bing Crosby national. il Time 89:60 F 3 '67

1967 U.S. Open; symposium. il Sports Illus 26: 40-2+ Je 12 '67

No tranquilizer like victory; success of B. Goalby. il Sports Illus 26:20-1 Ja 23 '67

Nothing flew right for the home side; Walker cup matches at Royal St George's. B. Wright. il Sports Illus 26:59-60+ My 29 '67

Old story but a new Jack; J. Nicklaus wins Bing Crosby national pro-amateur championship. A. Wright. il Sports Illus 26:16-17 Ja 30 '67

On the tee: an error and a fumble; football and baseball players at Astrojet classic. D. Jenkins. il Sports Illus 26:16-19 F 27 '67

One man's game; Nicklaus wins second U.S. Open victory. il Time 89:54 Je 30 '67

Out of trouble to win a double; R. Dickson wins U.S. and British amateur championship. A. Wright. Sports Illus 27:94-5 S 11 '67

Par busters. il Time 89:58 Ap 7 '67

Positively; Masters tournament. il Time 89: 57-8 Ap 21 '67

Rarefied golf; Professional golfers association tournament. Newsweek 70:82 Ag 7 '67

Soft sell on the links; Shell oil's Wonderful world of golf. il Bsns W p62-7 Ja 6 '68

Sporting scene; master of Baltusrol. H. W. Wind. New Yorker 43:56-8+ Jl 8 '67

Sporting scene; Masters tournament at Augusta, Ga. H. W. Wind. New Yorker 43: 138+ Ap 29 '67

Sprightly boppers and a cool golden swinger; ladies' professional golf team. P. Ryan. il Sports Illus 27:30-5 Jl 3 '67

They all love a Latin; R. de Vicenzo, winner of the British Open at Royal Liverpool. G. S. Brown. il Sports Illus 27:12-15 Jl 24 '67

Tune out, drop in; Jack Nicklaus wins U.S. Open. il Newsweek 70:70+ Jl 3 '67

Two Dons in quest of a title; January and Massengale. A. Wright. il Sports Illus 27: 18-21 Jl 31 '67

Very good start for Egypt; very good finish for the U.S. A. Wright. il Sports Illus 27: 24-5 N 20 '67

What's wrong with Nicklaus? winner of U.S. Open at Baltusrol. J. Nicklaus. il Sports Illus 27:20-2+ Jl 3 '67

Zero on the tour. G. Plimpton. il Sports Illus 26:46-56 Ja 30; 28-34 F 6; 36-8+ F 13 '67

Caricatures and cartoons

That doggone Crosby; Bing Crosby national pro-am. C. Schulz. Sports Illus 28:28-33 Ja 8 '68

GOLF, indoor

Who needs all that fresh air? computer golf; Golf-O-Tron and Golfomat games. J. McDermott. Life 62:9 Mr 24 '67

GOLF and business

Companies tee off to win more friends; tournaments under corporate sponsorship. il Bsns W p28 S 2 '67

GOLF balls

Golf: what it costs to get started. il Changing T 21:17-18 My '67

GOLF clubs. See Sports clubs

GOLF clubs (sticks)

Blow for esthetics; croquet style of putting outlawed. P. Ryan. il Sports Illus 26:28-9 Je 5 '67

Golf: what it costs to get started. il Changing T 21:17-18 My '67

Make mine aluminum il Time 90:42 D 8 '67

Putter flutter; croquet-style putter banned. Newsweek 69:66 Je 5 '67

Trap shot that saves you strokes, but not in a trap. J. Nicklaus. il Sports Illus 27:60 N 20 '67

GOLF courses

Augusta had a new look; reflections about the Masters. A. Wright. il Sports Illus 26:36-8+ Ap 24 '67

Beauty and the bogeyman. Fortune 75:160+ F '67

Completely automated watering systems; Edina, Minn. D. G. Brauer. il Am City 82:96-7 Mr '67

Country club look for public golf courses. G. S. Cornish and W. G. Robinson. il Parks & Rec 2:28-9+ My '67

Day the girls come out to play; Dick Mulvaine: golf pro from Sierra Estrella golf course, Maricopa County, Ariz. L. Botto. il Look 31:M16+ My 16 '67

In search of winter golf. C. Price. il Holiday 42:119-24 N '67

Instead of open terror, a subtle pleasure; lower course at Baltusrol. J. Nicklaus. il Sports Illus 26:59-62+ Je 12 '67

New twists for an old art; golf-course architect D. Muirhead. G. S. Brown. il Sports Illus 26:52-3 F 20 '67

Now they invest in golf! executives owning their own courses. T. J. Murray. il Duns R 89:38-40+ Mr '67

Siren song of Sotogrande; photographs by E. Haas; with account by L. Smith. Sports Illus 26:34-41 Mr 6 '67

Sporting scene; Masters tournament at Augusta, Ga. H. W. Wind. New Yorker 43:138+ Ap 29 '67

Where the shocker is routine; Olympic club. il Sports Illus 26:50-7 Je 12 '67

See also
Putting greens

GOLF resorts. See Winter resorts

GOLFERS

Augusta had a new look; reflections about the Masters. A. Wright. il Sports Illus 26:36-8+ Ap 24 '67

Bigtime golf: Pete Brown hurls his challenge. il Ebony 22:130-2+ My '67

But papa, I played like a clod; Ladies' PGA. M. Mulvoy. il Sports Illus 27:24-5 Jl 10 '67

Day the girls come out to play; Dick Mulvaine: golf pro from Sierra Estrella golf course, Maricopa County, Ariz. L. Botto. il Look 31:M16+ My 16 '67

Delightful brawl in a gentleman's game; Piccadilly world match play tournament. G. S. Brown. Sports Illus 27:64-5 O 23 '67

Dynasty Lacoste; French family of champion golfers. J. Olsen. il Sports Illus 27:68-74+ D 18 '67

Essential suggestion. il Esquire 67:149 Ap '67

From rabbit to real pro; endless summer golf tour. E. Asinof. il N Y Times Mag p54-5+ S 10 '67

How to tell if everything is under control. J. Nicklaus. il Sports Illus 26:48 F 6 '67

It isn't a game of inches. J. Nicklaus. il Sports Illus 26:62 My 8 '67

Miss Avis against Miss Hertz; ladies' golf professional tournaments. M. Mulvoy. il Sports Illus 27:62-3 N 27 '67

Mod golf strikes at old St Andrews. G. S. Brown. il Sports Illus 27:32-3 O 16 '67

Nothing flew right for the home side; Walker cup matches at Royal St George's. B. Wright. il Sports Illus 26:59-60+ My 29 '67

GOLFERS—*Continued*
Numbers game for the tour; IBM sports information service. A. Wright. il Sports Illus 27:76-8 N 13 '67
Paean to the pied piper of golf. A. Gingrich. Esquire 67:6 Ap '67
Seven men who control golf. il Esquire 67: 152-3+ Ap '67
Sprightly boppers and a cool golden swinger; ladies' professional golf team. P. Ryan. il Sports Illus 27:30-5 Jl 3 '67
Very good start for Egypt; very good finish for U.S. A. Wright. il Sports Illus 27:24-5 N 20 '67
Week when the world comes to Augusta; foreign golfers at Masters tournament; photographs. Sports Illus 26:44-50 Ap 10 '67
Who's who & where's Jack? Frank Beard and Jack Nicklaus. il Time 89:83+ My 19 '67
Zero on the tour. G. Plimpton. il Sports Illus 26:46-56 Ja 30; 28-34 F 6; 36-8+ F 13 '67
See also names of golfers. e.g. F. Beard
GOLFERS, Height of. See Golfers
GOLFOMAT. See Golf, Indoor
GOLF-O-TRON. See Golf, Indoor
GOLIATH frogs. See Frogs
GOLLANCZ, Sir Victor
Obituary
Pub W 191:124+ F 20 '67
GOLLIN, Jane
Nolde: art without audience. Art N 65:48-9+ F '67
GOLODNER, Jack
Librarian and the union. por Wilson Lib Bul 42:387-90 D '67
GOLOMSKI, William A.
Are you selling quality short? Nations Bsns 55:72-4 D '67
GOLOVIN, Igor
Father of the Soviet bomb; condensation of book. Bul Atomic Sci 23:13-18 D '67
GOLSCHMANN, Vladimir
Pros & cons of the Golschmann era. A. Young. Hi Fi 17:MA18 Jl '67
GOLTZ, Gene. See Serrin, W. jt. auth.
GOLUB, Cyril N. See Lacy, E. A. jt. auth.
GOMBROWICZ, Witold
Sweet violence. H. Junker. por Newsweek 69: 94+ My 29 '67
GÓMEZ-SICRE, José
Dolores Del Río; excerpts. Américas 19:8-17 N '67
GOMUŁKA, Władysław
Poland's slow road to the promised freedom. il por U S News 63:43-4 O 16 '67
Polish church and Communist state. H. H. Ward. Christian Cent 84:288+ Mr 1 '67
GONADS
Starfish gonad: action and chemical identification of spawning inhibitor. S. Ikegami and others. bibliog il Science 158:1052-3 N 24 '67
Zona pellucida of rhesus monkey ovum after gonadotropin stimulation. C. A. Maruffo. bibliog il Science 157:1313-14 S 15 '67
GONDWANALAND. See Continental drift
GONICK, C. W.
Resentful partner: Canada fights its orbit. Nation 204:489-94 Ap 17 '67
GONZAGA university, Spokane, Wash.
Welcome voices in a wilderness. America 116: 617 Ap 29 '67
GONZALES, Bennie M. family
In the desert, a hacienda for 1967; with account by J. Bonfante. il Life 62:84-7+ F 10 '67
GONZALEZ, R. C. and others
Reversal learning and forgetting in bird and fish. bibliog Science 158:519-21 O 27 '67
GOOCH, Bob
Good day on Mechunk creek. Outdoor Life 140:68-9+ O '67
GOOD, Paul
Draftees who say no: laying freedom on the line. Nation 204:365-70 Mr 20 '67
Kentucky's coal beds of sedition. Nation 205: 166-9 S 4 '67
Nothing worth saving. Nation 205:101-2 Ag 14 '67
Odyssey of a man, and a movement. N Y Times Mag p5+ Je 25 '67
On the march again: New York. Nation 204: 550-2 My 1 '67
Political tour of Harlem. N Y Times Mag p34-6+ O 29 '67
GOOD, Robert A. See Hong, R. jt. auth.
GOOD, Robert E. See Cox, D. F. jt. auth.
GOOD and evil
God and evil. R. H. Luecke. Christian Cent 84:377-8 Mr 22 '67
See also
Sin

GOOD-bye sweet summer, good-bye; story. See Munson, G.
GOOD humor man; story. See Morris, R.
GOOD man, bad man; story. See Weidman, J.
GOOD morning, dear Elizabeth; story. See Kernan, M.
GOOD taste. See Aesthetics
GOOD time to be alive; story. See Stanton, W.
GOOD will (ethics)
You have to be taught to hate. J. M. Eagan. il Parents Mag 42:32+ F '67
GOOD works (theology) See Reward (theology)
GOODALE, Thomas L.
Fallacy of our programs. Parks & Rec 2:39-40+ N '67
GOODALL, Kenneth
Opening the unions to Negro craftsmen. Reporter 37:56+ N 2 '67
GOODE, William J.
Librarian: from occupation to profession; reprint. bibliog por ALA Bul 61:544-55 My '67
GOODELL, H. G. See Watkins, N. D. jt. auth.
GOODENOUGH, Ward H.
Componential analysis. bibliog Science 156: 1203-9 Je 2 '67
GOODING, Judson
Report from Alaska. Fortune 76:49+ S 1 '67
GOODMAN, Benny
Still playing what he feels. il por Time 89: 54 Je 23 '67
GOODMAN, Elizabeth, and Ferber, Ellen
She won't be back. Am Ed 3:6-8 O '67
GOODMAN, Frederick L.
School information center. NEA J 56:20-2 F '67
GOODMAN, George J. W.
Tahiti. Holiday 41:46-63+ F '67
GOODMAN, George W.
Lonely youth in the rural South. Ebony 22: 70-2+ Ag '67
GOODMAN, Grace Ann
End of the apartment house ministry. Christian Cent 84:615-17 My 10 '67
GOODMAN, Joel W.
Convention at Long Beach. il Sky & Tel 34: 223-4 O '67
GOODMAN, Julian
Excerpt from statement before Communications subcommittee, October 9, 1967. Cong Digest 46:303+ D '67
GOODMAN, Marie White
Eggs are our dish. Parents Mag 42:62-3 Mr '67
GOODMAN, Mitchell
Island-hopping off the coast of New England. Redbook 129:35-8 Jl '67
GOODMAN, Morris, and others
Transferrin polymorphism and population differences in the genetic variability of chimpanzees. bibliog Science 156:98-100 Ap 7 '67
GOODMAN, Paul
Empty society; excerpts from Massey lectures. Commentary 42:53-60 N '66; 43:30 Mr '67
Liberal anti-communism revisited. Commentary 44:41-3 S '67
On civil disobedience, 1967. N Y Times Mag p 122+ N 26 '67
Two issues in planning. excerpt from address. Commentary 44:75-7 Ag '67

about
Desires and disappointments. N. Sayre. Reporter 36:48-50 Ja 26 '67
Education's romantic critics. P. Schrag. por Sat R 50:80-2+ F 18 '67
Exile from paradise, a garland for Paul Goodman. W. Hamilton. Christian Cent 84:1046-8 Ag 16 '67
Paul Goodman's pain. R. A. Schroth. America 117:86 Jl 22 '67
Public & private. P. Cowan. Commentary 44:89+ Jl '67
Reforming the universities. P. Clecak. Nation 204:407-11 Mr 27 '67
GOODMAN, Richard E. See Cadman, J. D. jt. auth.
GOODMAN, Ryah Tumarkin
Ribbons of rhyme; poem. Horn Bk 43:453 Ag '67
GOODMAN, Saul
Brief biographies. See issues of Dance magazine
GOODMAN, Stanley J. See Podvoll, E. M. jt. auth.
GOODMAN, Thomas G.
Heitkamp planetarium. por Sky & Tel 33: 141-2 Mr '67

GOODMAN, Walter
Black comic years before his time. Life 62:10 Ja 27 '67
Doctors must experiment on humans. N Y Times Mag p 12-13+ Jl 2 '67
New sex education. Redbook 129:62-3+ S '67
War in the peace camp; liberals vs. radicals. N Y Times Mag p48-9+ D 3 '67
When black power runs the new left. N Y Times Mag p28-9+ S 24 '67
Why don't we save these mothers and babies? Redbook 128:68-9+ Ap '67

GOODRICH, B. F, company
Run faster, jump higher. R. Levy. Duns R 90:78-81 O '67
This war is being brought you by; War in the skies and B. F. Goodrich company. C. W. Morton. il Atlan 220:92 Jl '67

GOODRICH, David L.
Just for laughs. Look 31:M24 My 2 '67

GOODRICH, Frederick W. jr
Classes to prepare you for childbirth. Redbook 129:26+ Je '67

GOODRICH, Wells
What makes a marriage succeed or fail? ed. by S. S. Rosenberg. Parents Mag 42: 60-2+ Je '67

GOODSELL, James Nelson
Balaguer's Dominican Republic. bibliog f Cur Hist 53:298-302+ N '67
From Bogotá to B.A. Sat R 50:37 Jl 15 '67

GOODSELL, Jane
Doesn't anything fit like a glove? Read Digest 91:143-4 N '67
Nobody knows the quandaries I've seen; excerpt from I've only got two hands, and I'm busy wringing them. Read Digest 91: 211-12 Jl '67

GOODWIN, Craufurd D. W.
Canada at a century. bibliog f Cur Hist 52: 282-8+ My '67

GOODWIN, David G.
State of New Jersey sets pace; provides board of recreation examiners. Parks & Rec 2:16+ F '67

GOODWIN, Jonathan H. and Surdam, R. C.
Zeolitization of tuffaceous rocks of the Green River formation, Wyoming. bibliog Science 157:307-8 Jl 21 '67

GOODWIN, Richard Naradof
Our stake in a big awakening. Life 62:66-8+ Ap 14 '67
Shape of American politics. Commentary 43: 25-40 Je '67; Reply. Nat R 19:728-9 Jl 11 '67

about
Natives are stirring. Nat R 19:728-9 Jl 11 '67
Speechwriter for two presidents. G. P. Hunt. por Life 62:3 Ap 14 '67

GOODYEAR tire and rubber company
Good year for Goodyear. Newsweek 69:71-2 Je 12 '67
Running ahead. il Time 91:86+ Ja 19 '68

GOOSSEN, E. C.
O'Keeffe. Vogue 149:174-9+ Mr 1 '67

GORDEY, Michel
Svetlana. New Repub 157:17-21 Jl 1 '67

GORDIMER, Nadine
Bride of Christ; story. Atlan 220:58-64 Ag '67
Color of want. Nation 204:313-15 Mr 6 '67
Out of the walls; story. New Yorker 42:34-7 F 11 '67
Path and not the goal. Nation 204:822-3 Je 26 '67
Satisfactory settlement; story. Atlan 221:54-8 Ja '68

GORDIS, Robert
Negroes are anti-Semitic because they want a scapegoat. N Y Times Mag p28-9+ Ap 23 '67

GORDON, Arnold L.
Geostrophic transport through the Drake Passage. bibliog Science 156:1732-4 Je 30 '67

GORDON, Arthur
Secret of self-renewal. Read Digest 90:103-6 F '67
Throw out the textbooks. Am Ed 3:5-7 S '67
Two words to avoid, two to remember. Read Digest 92:53-6 Ja '68
Way of acceptance. Read Digest 90:136-9 My '67

GORDON, Charles George
Mystic hero met a tragic end in the death-trap of Khartoum. E. Kern. il pors Life 63:66-7 O 6 '67

GORDON, David James
Style of anxiety. Nation 204:730-1 Je 5 '67

GORDON, Dorothy
Listening to youth. pors Wilson Lib Bul 42: 194-8 O '67

GORDON, Ernest
New case for chastity. Read Digest 92:81-5 Ja '68

GORDON, Ethel Edison
Make me no match; story. il McCalls 94:80-1 My '67
Where did the summer go? story. Redbook 129:131-57 Jl '67

GORDON, Gordon, and Gordon, Mildred
Fine art of eavesdropping. Writer 80:16-17+ S '67

GORDON, Harry
Loneliness of the long-distance sailor. N Y Times Mag p30-2+ Ja 22 '67
Mineral boom in the lucky country. N Y Times Mag p38-9+ N 12 '67
When a Texas-style diplomat hits Australia. N Y Times Mag p48-9+ O 8 '67

GORDON, Lincoln
Punta del Este revisited. bibliog f For Affairs 45:624-38 Jl '67

About
Academic democracy. il por Time 89:60-1 Ja 27 '67

GORDON, Lou
Maintaining the public welfare. por Time 90: 51 S 22 '67

GORDON, Malcolm S.
Oxygen consumption of red and white muscles from tuna fishes. bibliog Science 159:87-90 Ja 5 '68

GORDON, Max
My most unforgettable character. Read Digest 90:174-8+ Mr '67
Two Vietnams or one? letter. New Repub 157:36-7 Jl 22 '67

GORDON, Mildred. See Gordon, G. jt. auth.

GORDON, Robert
Bad bridgework. Sat R 50:4+ S 16 '67

GORDON, Ruth
Litany at an elevator file; poem. Christian Cent 84:750 Je 7 '67

GORDON, Shirley
Way back for troubled youngsters. Parents Mag 42:66-7+ N '67

GORDON, Theodore J.
Corporation; address, April 20, 1967. Vital Speeches 33:500-5 Je 1 '67

GORDON research conferences
Calcified tissues; report. G. Nichols, jr. Science 157:961-2 Ag 25 '67
Gordon research conferences; program for 1967. W. G. Parks. Science 155:1290-302+ Mr 10 '67
Gordon research conferences: winter program, 1968. W. G. Parks. Science 158:1086-8 N 24 '67

GORDY, Berry, jr
Heavyweight featherweight. il por Time 90: 80 S 8 '67
Motown sound of money. S. H. Brown. il por Fortune 76:102-5+ S 1 '67

GORE RANGE-EAGLE NEST primitive area.
See Wilderness areas—Colorado

GORELICK, Jamie
Report from Russia. por Seventeen 26:154-7+ My '67

GOREN, Charles Henry
Bridge. See issues of Sports illustrated

GORENSTEIN, Shirley
Museo nacional de antropología de México: with biographical sketch. Natur Hist 76:6, 34-45 Ag '67

GORER, Geoffrey
English character in the twentieth century. bibliog f Ann Am Acad 370:74-81 Mr '67
What's the matter with Britain? N Y Times Mag p 10-11+ D 31 '67

GORES, Harold B.
New look in schools. Parents Mag 42:48-51+ Ja '67
Schoolhouse in the city; address, July 11, 1967. Vital Speeches 33:743-6 O 1 '67

GOREWITZ, Rubin
Financial record-keeping simplified. Dance Mag 41:78-9 S; 90-3 O; 90-2 N '67; 42:88-90 Ja '68
Tax man cometh. Dance Mag 41:26-7 Ag '67

GORGENYI, Imre
Build a MALF. Pop Electr 27:67-9+ S '67

GORILLA queen; musical comedy. See Musical comedies, revues, etc.—Criticisms, plots, etc.

GORILLAS
Life among the gorillas; condensation of The year of the gorilla. G. B. Schaller. il Sci Digest 62:6-13 Jl '67
Snowflake; the world's first white gorilla. A. J. Riopelle. il Nat Geog Mag 131:442-8 Mr '67
Unique in all gorilladom; Roman Luera Carbo's Snowflake. il Life 62:69-70+ Mr 31 '67

GORINI, Luigi, and others
Phenotypic masking and streptomycin dependence. bibliog Science 157:1314-17 S 15 '67
GORIS, James W.
Dog's day. Motor B 120:42-3+ Jl '67
GORKA, Paul
Artistic personality in the making. H. C. Pitz. il por Am Artist 31:50-5 Je '67
GORKY, Arshile
Unknown Gorky. K. Mooradian. il Art N 66:52-3+ S '67
GORMAN, Thomas Kiely, bp
Plea for intramural dialogue. B. Hasbrouck. America 117:38-9 Jl 8 '67
GORNEY, Sondra K.
Annual educational exchange statistics. Sch & Soc 95:234-7 Ap 1 '67
GOROVE, Stephen
Inspection and control in Euratom. Bul Atomic Sci 23:41-6 Mr '67
Outer space treaty. Bul Atomic Sci 23:44-5 D '67
GORSUCH, Jo
Experiment in sex education. Read Digest 91:138-42 N '67
GORTON, Carl E.
Bircher library trustee charged with assault. Library J 92:2986 S 15 '67
Dime-store Paul Revere. E. Moon; K. Nyren. il por Library J 92:3353, 3380-4 O 1 '67
GORTON, John Grey
His own man. il por Time 91:22+ Ja 19 '68
New pilot. il por Newsweek 71:43+ Ja 22 '68
GOSNELL, Charles F.
Copyright grab bag, II. bibliog por ALA Bul 61:707-12 Je '67
GOSS, Bert C.
Public relations; address, April 5, 1967. Vital Speeches 33:426-9 My 1 '67
GOSS, Richard J.
New light on mystery of antlers. por Outdoor Life 139:54-5+ Mr '67
GOSSAGE, Howard
Adman who plays with paper airplanes. il pors Bsns W p74-6+ F 11 '67
GOSSELINK, James G. and Standifer, L. C.
Diurnal rhythm of sensitivity of cotton seedlings to herbicides. bibliog Science 158:120-1 O 6 '67
GOSSETT, Ed
Will we elect the president we vote for in 1968? Read Digest 91:211-14+ N '67
GOSSIP
In defense of gossip. J. Brothers. Good H 165:72+ O '67
In defense of gossip. M. Lerner. il McCalls 94:83+ Mr '67
GOSWAMY, B. N.
Epics in the art of south Asia. UNESCO Courier 20:18-29+ D '67
GÖTEBORG
Gardens
Göteborg's horticultural society gardens. W. O. Hultgren. il Horticulture 45:34-6 N '67
Music
Göteborg; production of Rossini's Comte Ory. O. Walgren. il Opera N 32:31-2 Ja 13 '68
GOTHENBURG. See Göteborg
GOTHIC art. See Art, Gothic
GOTHIC language
Gothic ABC. B. Byfield. il Atlan 219:62-8 Mr '67
GOTHIC romances
Writing the Gothic novel. P. A. Whitney. Writer 80:9-13+ F '67
GOTT, Edwin Hays
Bigger job at big steel. por Bsns W p37 Je 3 '67
It's Gott to be good. por Time 89:102 Je 9 '67
New boss at the Corporation. il por Bsns W p 140-2+ Jl 8 '67
GOTT, Richard
Guevara, Debray and the CIA. Nation 205:521-30 N 20 '67
GOTTEHRER, Barry
Urban conditions; New York city. bibliog f Ann Am Acad 371:141-58 My '67
GOTTHOLD, Beatrice B.
New hope for city schools. Parents Mag 42:68-70+ S '67
GOTTLIEB, Anna
First Pamina. A. M. Lingg. il por Opera N 32:6 Ja 6 '68
GOTTLIEB, Linda
Song that took a city. Read Digest 91:112-15 D '67
Traveling with Mlle: Europe on the cheap. Mlle 64:165-72+ F '67
GOTTLIEB, Robert J.
Cars and the law. See issues of Motor trend to October, 1967

GOTTSCHALK, Louis
Sailing vessel comes into its own. UNESCO Courier 20:16-17 My '67
GOTTWALD, Floyd Dewey
Winner by a knockout. R. Levy. por Duns R 89:42-4 Ja '67
GOTTWALD, Norman Karol
Hippies, political radicals and the church. Christian Cent 84:1043-5 Ag 16 '67
GOUGH, Marion
How to leave home and like it. See issues of House beautiful
Well worth the trip. House B 109:96+ F '67
GOULANDRIS, Dolly
Greece. por Vogue 149:144-5+ Ap 1 '67
GOULART, Ron
Computer, spare that physician. Sat R 50:4 Jl 29 '67
GOULD, Charles L.
Advertising; address, February 8, 1967. Vital Speeches 33:434-8 My 1 '67
Challenges & opportunities; address, December 1, 1966. Vital Speeches 33:217-23 Ja 15 '67
GOULD, George K.
Report on the boating habits of the adult American male. Motor B 121:113-15+ Ja '68
GOULD, Glenn
Search for Petula Clark. Hi Fi 17:67-71 N '67
about
Glenn Gould variations. R. Kostelanetz. por Esquire 68:142-5+ N '67
GOULD, Gordon, Jr. See Luten, D. B. jt. auth.
GOULD, Jay Dennis
Drop-in. Newsweek 71:24 Ja 15 '68
GOULD, Joan
Nine intrepid men. Esquire 67:108-10+ Ap '67
GOULD, John
Wonderful Franklin stove. Field & S 71:52-3+ Mr '67
GOULD, John Thomas
He, she, it. Atlan 220:91 Ag '67
GOULD, Samuel B.
Modern university; concerns for the future. Science 155:1511-14 Mr 24 '67
National research goals and university policies. Sch & Soc 95:347-9 O 14 '67
about
Giant that nobody knows. il pors Time 91:43-8 Ja 12 '68
Profiles. C. Tomkins. por New Yorker 43:67-8+ N 13 '67
GOULDER, Grace
Take a bow: Anne Udin. il Pub W 191:54-5 My 8 '67
GOULDING, Phil G.
A father speaks to the President in behalf of a son killed in Vietnam; letter. U S News 62:46-7 My 8 '67
GOULDING, Ray. See Elliott, B. jt. auth.
GOULDNER, Helen P.
Test tube children: a new kind of orphan; reprint. Sci Digest 62:16-22 Jl '67
GOUNOD, Charles François
All-star Faust: Sutherland, Corelli, Ghiaurov. G. Movshon. por Hi Fi 17:70+ Mr '67
Perhaps the most nearly complete performance we shall ever hear: London's Faust. P. L. Miller. il Am Rec G 33:620-2 Ap '67
Records:
Faust. Opera N 31:34 Mr 11 '67
Romeo and Juliet. Criticism
Dance Mag 41:27+ O '67
Hi Fi il 17:MA6-7 D '67
Hi Fi 18:MA4 Ja '68
New Yorker 43:84+ S 30 '67
Sat R 50:49-50 O 7 '67
GOURDINE, Meredith
Science pacemaker. P. Pierce. il pors Ebony 22:52-4+ Ap '67
GOURMAN, Jack
Measuring colleges qualitatively. R. Kirk. Nat R 19:695 Je 27 '67
GOURMETS. See Eating
GOUSHA, Richard P. and Row, H. E.
Constructive criticism of the guidelines. NEA J 56:44-6 Mr '67
GOUT
End, at last, to gout? A. Q. Maisel. Read Digest 90:113-17 Je '67
Good news about gout. A. Hamilton. il Todays Health 45:16-18 D '67
GOUX, Marvin
Taste of that not-so-old college spirit. J. Underwood. Sports Illus 27:20-1 N 27 '67
GOVER, Robert
Culture comes to Indianapolis. N Y Times Mag p6-7+ D 24 '67

GOVERNMENT. See Federal government; Nations; Political science
GOVERNMENT. Resistance to
Fearsome five; conspiracy charge against Benjamin Spock and others. New Repub 158:7-8 Ja 20 '68
Henry David Thoreau; was he an insurrectionist or a patriot? R. J. Roth. America 117:761-3 D 23 '67
Revolution or reform on the black left. M. Miles. New Repub 157:9-10 Ag 19 '67
See also
Lawlessness
Passive resistance to government
Revolutions
GOVERNMENT agencies. See United States—Executive departments
GOVERNMENT aid. See Grants-in-aid
GOVERNMENT aid to business
See also
Industry and state
GOVERNMENT and art. See Art and state
GOVERNMENT and labor. See Labor laws and legislation
GOVERNMENT and science. See Science and state
GOVERNMENT and the press
Backgrounder; off-the-record information being opposed. Newsweek 69:71 My 22 '67
But don't tell anyone I told you; private briefings of Pentagon press corps by top officials. S. M. Hersh. New Repub 157:13-14 D 9 '67
Compleat Johnson man; Press secretary G. Christian. il Time 89:74-5 Je 16 '67
Credibility gap; L. B. Johnson and the White House press corps. Nation 204:484 Ap 17 '67
Credibility gap: who's to blame, the government or the public? discussion. Sr Schol 91:8-10 O 19 '67
Cutting the red tape; Freedom of information act. Newsweek 70:88 S 18 '67
Does the Washington press lie? S. Alsop. Sat Eve Post 240:16 Jl 15 '67
For attribution; Washington post challenges "background only" government information. Time 89:56 My 19 '67
Gap prone; need for government information on bombing policy. K. Crawford. Newsweek 70:39 S 25 '67
Government has the right to lie. A. Sylvester. Sat Eve Post 240:10+ N 18 '67
Partisan attack on research. P. H. Abelson. Science 156:1315 Je 9 '67; Discussion. 157:368 Jl 28 '67
Pentagon gazette. M. Getler. Aero Tech 21:136 Jl 31 '67
Plaguing fictions of politics. E. J. Hughes. Newsweek 70:15 Jl 24 '67
Public television now, public newspapers later? D. Lawrence. U S News 63:116 N 27 '67
Sketches in the sand, by J. Reston. Review Sat R 50:32+ N 11 '67. R. D. Heffner
Winners & sinners. Nat R 19:626-7 Je 13 '67
GOVERNMENT appropriations and expenditures
See also
Budget
also subhead Appropriations and expenditures under names of countries, e.g. United States—Appropriations and expenditures
GOVERNMENT bonds. See Bonds, Government
GOVERNMENT budgets. See Budget
GOVERNMENT contracts See Contracts, Government
GOVERNMENT cookbooks. See Government publications
GOVERNMENT credit. See Credit
GOVERNMENT documents. See Government publications
GOVERNMENT employees
Federal jobs vary widely. il Ebony 22:86 Je '67
Nine unknowns who influence your business. il Nations Bsns 55:62-6+ Ap '67
Rights in conflict. Reporter 37:10+ O 19 '67
Where unions have most growth potential. il Bsns W p76-8 O 21 '67
See also
Bureaucracy
Civil service
Municipal employees
Nepotism
Public officers
Public service
State employees
Strikes—United States—Government employees

Anecdotes, facetiae, satire, etc.
Portrait of a bureaucrat. J. Zola. il Nat R 19:410-12 Ap 18 '67

Appointment, qualifications, tenure, etc.
U.S. civil service: Washington's bland bondage. F. G. Sherrill. Nation 204:239-42 F 20 '67; Reply with rejoinder. J. W. Macy, jr. 204:418+ Ap 3 '67

Dismissal
U.S. civil service: rebels on the Potomac. R. G. Sherrill. Nation 204:265-8 F 27 '67

Salaries, allowances, etc.
Closing the gap in salaries. il Bsns W p60+ N 4 '67
Federal pay scales cause empty labs. il Sci N 91:375 Ap 22 '67
Government pay on the way up again. il U S News 62:8+ Ap 17 '67
More pay for military and federal workers. il U S News 63:17 D 11 '67
Postage and federal pay: both going up? U S News 63:16 O 23 '67
What a federal job is worth now. il U S News 63:38 D 25 '67
Who gets a raise? C. Fritchey. Harper 235:40 O '67

GOVERNMENT entertaining
An evening at the de Gaulles'; gala reception during the official visit to France of the King of Nepal. P. Feldkamp. Atlan 219:114-18 My '67
Evening at the White House. il U S News 62:58-9 Ja 30 '67
Full evening of brotherliness; President's annual party for the Chief Justice, the Speaker of the House and the Vice President. H. Sidey. il Life 62:30D Ja 27 '67
Ghost hostess: B. Abell. il Newsweek 69:33-4 F 20 '67
Operation Big daddy; C. Channing at first White House dinner of 1967. il Time 89:19-20 Ja 27 '67
White House's able Mrs Abell. G. Astor. il Look 31:74-7 Je 27 '67
See also
Washington, D.C.—Social life and customs
GOVERNMENT ethics. See Political ethics
GOVERNMENT finance. See Finance
GOVERNMENT guaranty of employment. See Employment—Government guaranty
GOVERNMENT housing projects. See Housing projects, Government
GOVERNMENT inspector; drama. See Gogol, N.
GOVERNMENT investigations
Congressional ethics: who watches the watchdog? Sr Schol 90:12-13 F 24 '67
Curbing the diet pills; Senate subcommittee plans hearings on the rainbow pills. Newsweek 71:44 Ja 8 '68
How to succeed on the Potomac: be an investigator. R. Sherrill. il N Y Times Mag p44-5+ O 8 '67
Should paid witnesses say so? witnesses at congressional hearings paid by tobacco industry. il Bsns W p 168+ S 9 '67
There ought to be a law. New Repub 157:4 N 11 '67
See also
Loyalty investigations
United States—President's commission to investigate the assassination of President Kennedy

American telephone and telegraph company
Good news for AT&T in a federal ruling. U S News 63:20 S 25 '67

Drug trade
Drug on the market. D. Sanford. New Repub 157:13-15 Jl 22 '67
Merchant doctors. J. Randal. Reporter 36:29-30 My 4 '67
New headache for drug makers; hearings on Capitol hill. Bsns W p39 My 20 '67

Foundations
Checking the foundations. New Repub 157:8 N 11 '67

Government contracts
Honeywell's $60-million question; why IBM won air force contract. Bsns W p40 Je 3 '67

Government funded research
NIH: Fountain committee issues bitter attack on programs. D. S. Greenberg. Science 158:611-14 N 3 '67

GOVERNMENT investigations—*Continued*

Helicopter industry and trade

LOH hearing may spur tighter bid rules. D. C. Winston. il Aviation W 86:87+ Mr 13 '67

International union of electrical, radio and machine workers

Will scandal blow the fuse at IUE? alleged financial irregularities in District 3. Bsns W p 121 Je 17 '67

Newspaper publishing

Antitrust immunity and the press. R. L. Tobin. Sat R 50:47-8 S 9 '67

When is a failure? Time 90:66-7 Jl 28 '67

Powell case

Adam & Yvette. Time 89:18 F 24 '67

Big issue now in the Powell case. U S News 62:18 F 20 '67

Congress and the question of ethics. Bsns W p204 F 18 '67

Down to 434th. Time 89:22 Mr 3 '67

Et tu, Manny? committee chosen. Time 89: 20 Ja 27 '67

Into Powell's trap. Nat R 19:124 F 7 '67

Judgment on Powell. il Newsweek 69:27-8 Mr 6 '67

Keeping the faith. Newsweek 69:34+ F 20 '67

Ladies' day. il Newsweek 69:28+ F 27 '67

Silence of Mr Terrific. il Time 89:24 F 17 '67

Successor to Adam Powell? J. Conyers of Detroit. S. Friedman. New Repub 156:12-13 F 4 '67

Unprecedented punishment for Powell? U S News 62:16 Mr 6 '67

When Mrs Adam Clayton Powell took the stand. il U S News 62:10 F 27 '67

Riots

Hearing it like it is. il Newsweek 70:23-4+ S 4 '67

Poverty of politics in 1967. J. N. Eller. America 117:170 Ag 19 '67

Search starts for cause of riots in U.S. cities. il U S News 63:53-4 N 13 '67

Seeds of riot. il Newsweek 70:33-4 N 13 '67

T.R.B. from Washington; Kerner commission to investigate riots. New Repub 157:6 Ag 19 '67

Rubber industry and trade

Rubber hears from antitrust; five companies get subpoenas from Justice dept. Bsns W p40 My 13 '67

Stock exchange

Why the government is worried about the stock market; interview. H. F. Owens. U S News 63:65-7 N 20 '67

Brazil

Time-Life caper: Brazil's Yankee network; infiltration of communications media. E. Blum. il Nation 204:678-81 My 29 '67

GOVERNMENT lawyers. See Lawyers

GOVERNMENT liability

Who pays for riots? Time 90:68+ Ag 4 '67

GOVERNMENT officials. See Public officers

GOVERNMENT ownership

Governments in business. Fortune 76:182 S 15 '67

See also

Industry and state

Socialism

Congo (capital Kinshasa)

What goes on in the Congo? nationalization of Union minière. Nation 204:196 F 13 '67

Dominican Republic

Balaguer's burden: the Trujillo holdings; agriculture and industry. N. Raymond and W. P. Carty. Reporter 37:26-8 N 30 '67

France

Bumpy flight toward *la gloire*; Air France management shake-up. il Bsns W p 153-4 My 27 '67

Great Britain

Britain creates its own big steel; nationalization of fourteen companies. Bsns W p30-1 Ag 5 '67

British steel braces for nationalization. il Bsns W p80+ F 4 '67

Costly shibboleth: nationalization of Britain's steel industry. Time 89:31 F 3 '67

GOVERNMENT printing office. See United States—Government printing office

GOVERNMENT procurement, Commission on. See United States—Government procurement, Commission on (proposed)

GOVERNMENT publications

Biggest job shop in the world. W. Sullivan. il Sat R 50:124-5+ O 14 '67

Cookery à la Uncle Sam; inexpensive government cookbooks. il Changing T 21:38 Ag '67

Reprint pitfalls; letter to the editor. R. E. Kirkwood. Library J 92:1095 Mr 15 '67

Uncle Sam's brainwashing machine. il Nations Bsns 55:50-4 Jl '67

See also

Congressional record

Libraries, Depository

Bibliography

Congressional documents relating to foreign policy. See issues of Department of state bulletin

Publications of the Department of state. See issues of Department of state bulletin

Source material; comp. by D. Wasson. See issues of Foreign affairs

GOVERNMENT publicity

See also

Government and the press

GOVERNMENT records. See Records

GOVERNMENT regulation of industry. See Industry and state

GOVERNMENT research

Case for secret research. il Time 90:54+ N 10 '67

Project Hindsight; a Defense department study of the utility of research. C. W. Sherwin and R. S. Isenson. bibliog il Science 156:1571-7 Je 23 '67

Signs read slow for R&D; funds short of last year's appropriations. il Bsns W p70-2 F 4 '67

GOVERNMENT security regulations. See Security classification (government documents)

GOVERNMENT service. See Civil service; Public officers; Public service

GOVERNMENT spending policy

Atlantic report: Washington; too many programs. E. B. Drew. Atlan 219:6+ Mr '67

Congressional outlook; will they get control of spending? il Nations Bsns 55:40-1 D '67

Deadlock on taxes; no cut in spending, on 10 per cent surcharge. Bsns W p39 S 30 '67

$40-billion the budget leaves out. il Bsns W p55-6+ F 25 '67

From business, a grudging acceptance. Bsns W p27 Ag 12 '67

Getting the budget under control; stalemate over spending and taxation. Bsns W p 190 O 14 '67

Great society's wondrous war budget. C. Stevenson. Read Digest 90:49-54 Ap '67

High officials argue over taxes, spending, inflation; excerpts from hearing before the House ways and means committee, November 30, 1967. il U S News 63:90-2 D 18 '67

How Johnson lost his tax bill, for now. Bsns W p42 N 11 '67

If LBJ is right about his spending. il U S News 63:30 Ag 21 '67

If spending is cut 7 billions—. il U S News 63:31-3 O 23 '67

Latest on the taxing and spending squabble. U S News 63:96-7 O 30 '67

McNamara-style budget bureau. Bsns W p 129+ S 23 '67

Our Rube Goldberg tax system; exorcising the deficit demon. H. S. Reuss. Commonweal 86:280-1 My 26 '67

Raise taxes or cut spending. America 116:803 Je 3 '67

Red ink to flood government's books? il U S News 62:31-3 My 29 '67

Spend and spend and spend; why Congress balks. il U S News 64:15-17 Ja 1 '68

Spending crisis for LBJ? a rebellion in Congress; use of federal debt ceiling to force cut. U S News 62:95-6 Je 26 '67

Spending of billions; Johnson's ace? il U S News 62:48 Je 12 '67

Tax troubles; letter. L. H. Keyserling. New Repub 157:39-40 O 21 '67

Taxes and expenditures; address, November 20, 1967. W. D. Mills. Vital Speeches 34: 130-2 D 15 '67

Vital public spending. P. A. Samuelson. Newsweek 70:84 N 27 '67

Wartime controls on the way? il U S News 64:32-4 Ja 15 '68

Way out of the spending crisis; interview. W. Mills. Nations Bsns 55:48-9 O '67

What taxes and spending do to the economy. il Nations Bsns 55:50-2+ N '67

See also

United States—Economic policy

GOVERNORS
Design for daydreaming; Republican party governors. il Time 90:17 Jl 14 '67
From defiance to détente. il Time 89:22 Ja 27 '67
Governors get role in federal largesse; Washington promises funds. il Bsns W p46-7 Mr 25 '67
Republicans stay on the fence for '68; GOP governors conference. il Bsns W p36-7 D 16 '67
Wooing the governors; LBJ style; assignment for F. Bryant. il U S News 62:19 Mr 20 '67
   See also
Southern governors conference

Inaugurations
   See Inaugurations

Protection
Safety first. il Newsweek 70:24 D 25 '67

GOVERNORS conference, 1967
All at sea with the governors; with report by R. B. Stolley. il Life 63:77-9 O 27 '67
Governors' cruise. il Sr Schol 91:17-18 N 2 '67
In unpath'd waters. il Time 90:31-2 O 27 '67
Shakedown cruise. il Newsweek 70:22-3+ O 30 '67
Ship of pols. Newsweek 70:31 O 23 '67
Shipload of doomed men. J. Fischer. Harper 236:9-12 Ja '68

GOVERNORS mansions
Next, a White House? California governor's mansion. il Newsweek 69:36 F 13 '67

GOVERNORS wives
California's stylish first lady, size 6. il Life 62:55-6+ My 19 '67
New style in the G.O.P. spotlight. il Ladies Home J 84:67-9 Ag '67
   See also
Reagan, N. D.

GOW, J. Steele, Jr, and Thompson, Margery
Change, in concert with society. NEA J 56: 22-3 D '67

GOWEN, Emmett
Expedition holy book. Américas 19:1-7 S '67

GOWING, Lawrence
Object-lessons in object-love. Art N 66:24-7+ O '67

GOWLAND, Peter
Gowland's L.A. scene. See issues of Popular photography

GOYA Y LUCIENTES, Francisco José de
Share in the bacchanal. il Time 90:46 D 22 '67
Visions of depravity. H. Cohen. Reporter 36: 39-40+ My 4 '67

GRABAGE dunp; story. See Elkin, S.

GRABHORN press
Grabhorns: their methods and best books. P. A. Bennett. il Pub W 191:96+ Mr 6 '67

GRACE Patricia, consort of Rainier III, prince of Monaco
Jamaica holiday for Princess Grace. H. Ehrlich. il pors Look 31:38-40+ Ap 4 '67
Our life together; excerpts from a prince's story. Rainier III. il Good H 164:100-10 Mr '67

GRACE, J. Peter
Peripatetics of J. Peter Grace. il por Duns R 90:24 Jl '67

GRACE, W. R, and company
Changing face of W. R. Grace. R. Levy. il Duns R 90:22-4+ Jl '67

GRACE line, Incorporated
   See also
Grace, W. R, and company

GRADING and marking (students)
Child's world of marks. M. A. White and A. E. Boehm. il NEA J 57:12-13 Ja '68
Grade expectations; teachers' expectations influence how well pupils learn. Newsweek 70:43 Ag 21 '67
Grading by teachers called harmful. S. Holzman. Sr Schol 91:sup4 N 30 '67
Haverford's new policy. Sch & Soc 95:340-2 O 14 '67
Revolt in the ranks; opposition to class ranking. il Newsweek 69:69 Ap 17 '67
Taking the stress off grades; with study-discussion program, by C. Smallenburg and H. Smallenburg. P. C. Lange. il PTA Mag 62:19-21, 34-5 O '67
To grade or not to grade; with study-discussion program, by E. Harris and D. Harris. F. R. Link. bibliog PTA Mag 62:10-12, 35 N '67
Who's on top? Columbia ends ranking. Sr Schol 90:16 Ap 21 '67
   See also
Ability grouping in education

GRADUATE business schools. See Business education

GRADUATE school of business administration. See Harvard university—Graduate school of business administration

GRADUATE schools. See Colleges and universities—Graduate work

GRADUATE students
Draft: graduate schools fear effect of new law. R. J. Samuelson. Science 158:757-8 N 10 '67
Draft ruffles the ivy; end of blanket deferments for graduate study. il Bsns W p42+ D 16 '67
Gloom in grad schools; graduate students to be called up. Time 90:88 N 24 '67
Good-by, grad school? draft deferments only to graduate students in four fields. Newsweek 70:68 D 18 '67
Higher education and the war machine. Christian Cent 84:1645 D 27 '67

GRADUATES, College. See College graduates; College graduates, Women

GRADUATES, High school. See High school graduates

GRADUATION address; drama. See Fontaine, R.

GRADUATION addresses. See Baccalaureate addresses

GRAEBE, Jan E.
Isoprenoid biosynthesis in a cell-free system from pea shoots. bibliog Science 157:73-5 Jl 7 '67

GRAF, Rudolf F.
Add 1-2-3 turn signals to your car. Pop Sci 190:128-30 Ja '67
Call timer for your telephone. Pop Sci 192: 112-13 Ja '68

GRAFF, M. M.
What makes a gardener dig. J. Barthel. il pors N Y Times Mag p28-30+ Mr 5 '67

GRAFFITI
Graffiti to print. J. Brackman. il N Y Times Mag p97-9 F 12 '67

GRAFFMAN, Gary
Busy eclectic. il por Time 90:51 D 29 '67

GRAFSTEIN, Bernice
Transport of protein by goldfish optic nerve fibers. bibliog Science 157:196-8 Jl 14 '67

GRAFT. See Politics, Corruption in

GRAFTING
Enjoy the satisfaction of successful plant grafting. R. G. Coggeshall. il Horticulture 45:24-5+ Mr '67
Grafting cacti. A. B. Greenberg. il Horticulture 45:40-2 D '67

GRAFTON, Samuel
Young marriages; what happens when parents pay the bills? McCalls 94:67+ Ap '67

GRAHAM, Augusta
Dreams & nightmares. PTA Mag 62:24-6 bibliog(p33) O '67
Farewell to babyhood. PTA Mag 61:25-7 bibliog(p35) My '67

GRAHAM, Billy
Billy Graham's plea to President Johnson; reprint from Washington star and Congressional record, July 21, 1966. D. Lawrence. U S News 63:92 Ag 7 '67
Billy's Communist rally. il Newsweek 70:71 Jl 24 '67
Bowl us no googlies. Christian Cent 84:163-4 F 8 '67
Graham denounces dissenters. Christian Cent 84:645 My 17 '67; Discussion. 84:839-40 Je 28 '67
Graham meets communism. il por Time 90: 60-1 Jl 21 '67

GRAHAM, David
Lucky Bird. New Repub 157:9-10 D 23 '67

GRAHAM, Dominick
Graduated response fallacy. Yale R 57:90-8 O '67

GRAHAM, Don
Road to significance. U S Camera 30:28-9+ Mr '67

GRAHAM, E. R. and Telle, Paul
Zinc retention in rabbits; effect of previous diet. bibliog Science 155:691-2 F 10 '67

GRAHAM, Earl C.
Public library services to the handicapped; address, October 1966. por ALA Bul 61:170-9 F '67

GRAHAM, Frank, 1925-
Gathering storm over DDT. New Repub 156: 15-17 Je 24 '67
Pesticides, politics and the public. Audubon 69:54-62 Jl '67
Taking polluters to court. New Repub 158: 8-9 Ja 13 '68
Uncertain defenders. Audubon 69:28-37 My '67

GRAHAM, Frank—*Continued*
What trails for America? Audubon 69:46-52 N '67
When baseball went to war. Sports Illus 26: 78-82+ Ap 17 '67

GRAHAM, Fred P.
Cops right (?) to stop and frisk. N Y Times Mag p44-5+ D 10 '67
Low-key and liberal. N Y Times Mag p30-1+ Ap 2 '67
Many-sided Justice Fortas. **N Y Times Mag** p26-7+ Je 4 '67
Supreme court: what can business expect? Duns R 90:29-31+ S '67

GRAHAM, James A. Maxtone
Chromosomes and crime. Sci Digest 62:38-40 D '67
Go. Horizon 9:100-3 Aut '67
Mary, 1,000 crossings later. N Y Times Mag p 10-11+ S 3 '67; Same abr. with title Requiem for an ocean queen. Read Digest 91:196-7+ D '67
—and Cross, Wilbur
There's no place like home, somebody else's. Read Digest 91:49-50+ Jl '67

GRAHAM, James J.
Acquittal for Oswald. Commonweal 86:149-51 Ap 21 '67
Ghetto lawyer. Commonweal 87:198-201 N 17 '67

GRAHAM, Janet
Cover girl. Good H 165:26+ Ag '67
Those astonishing Redgraves. Good H 166:16+ Ja '68
To beat the blues. Read Digest 90:39-40+ Ap '67
(ed) See Travers, P. L. Cup of sorrow in every woman's life

GRAHAM, Katharine (Meyer)
Power behind the Post. il pors Bsns W D 158-60+ My 27 '67

GRAHAM, Martha
Martha Graham. C. Barnes. por Vogue 149: 186-7 My '67
Martha Graham: moralist in the theater. **R.** Kotlowitz. por Harper 234:122-4 My '67
What sorrow is there that is not mine? a review of Martha and dance company; Mark Hellinger theatre. D. Hering. il Dance Mag 41:55-8 My '67

GRAHAM, O. D.
Tobogganing in your shirtsleeves. Parks & Rec 2:23+ My '67

GRAHAM, Richard
Brazil's dilemma. bibliog f Cur Hist 53:291-7+ N '67

GRAHAM, Robert A.
Jacques Maritain on aggiornamento. America 116:348-9 Mr 11 '67

GRAHAM, Robert John
Dig to antiquity in your own back yard. por Sci Digest 62:55-9 Jl '67

GRAHAM, Sylvester
Americans not everybody knows. C. W. Ferguson. por PTA Mag 61:14-16 Mr '67

GRAHAM, W. S.
Beast in the space; poem. Poetry 110:1 Ap '67

GRAHAM bread. See Bread

GRAHAME, Arthur
Gun owners should switch to the offense; reprint from November 1963 issue. Outdoor Life 140:33-4 O '67

GRAIG, Frank A. and Smith, J. C.
Creatine phosphokinase in thyroid: isoenzyme composition compared with other tissues. bibliog Science 156:254-5 Ap 14 '67

GRAIN
See also
Feeding and feeding stuffs—Grain
also names of cereal plants, e.g. Corn

Prices
Who will hold grain stocks? D. Hanson. Suc Farm 65:6 Ja '67

Storage
What's happening to farm grain handling. P. B. Jones. il Suc Farm 65:37 Jl '67
Who should store your grain? Suc Farm 65: 36 Jl '67
See also
Corn—Storage

GRAIN in photography. See Photography—Grain

GRAM-negative bacteria. See Bacteria

GRAMBLING college, Grambling, La.
Grumbling at Grambling. il Time 90:46 D 15 '67
100 yards and sixty minutes of black power; Grambling college Tigers. G. Frazier, IV. il Esquire 68:95-6+ O '67

GRAMMAR, English. See English language—Grammar

GRAMONT, Sanche de. See De Gramont, S.

GRAMSCI, Antonio
Antonio Gramsci and the origins of Italian communism, by J. M. Commett. Review Nation 205:249-51 S 18 '67. E. Hobsbaum

GRANADA, Spain
Gardens of Moorish yesterdays. D. A. Nesbett. Sat R 50:52+ Ja 28 '67

GRANADOS, Enrique
Convincing and compelling. Alicia de Larrocha. S. Sell. Am Rec G 33:777 My '67
From Epic, certainly one of the greatest piano recordings ever made. W. Botsford. il Am Rec G 34:222 N '67
Goya of music. A. de Larrocha. il por Opera N 32:6-7 D 9 '67
Granados; ed. by E. Haines. A. de Larrocha. Hi Fi 17:56-8 D '67
Records:
Seventeen songs. Opera N 31:34 F 25 '67

GRAND, Gordon, 1917-
Olin's grand designer. W. Berry. por Duns R 89:50-2 My '67

GRAND army of the Republic
Of fifes and drums and the grand old men. M. Kantor. il Read Digest 90:84-8 Je '67

GRAND BAHAMA ISLAND
Diver's dream come true; Underwater explorers club. C. Phinizy. il Sports Illus 26:38-41 F 6 '67

GRAND BAHAMA underwater explorers club. See Camera clubs

GRAND CANYON
Arizona water project blocked. il Sci N 92: 55-6 Jl 15 '67
Canyon controversy: second round. il Sci N 91:302-3 Ap 1 '67
Canyon dams: dissents from Arizona scientists. L. J. Carter. Science 157:46 Jl 7 '67
Don't flood our Grand Canyon; dam builders vs conservationists. J. Bird. il Sat Eve Post 240:24-9+ Ag 12 '67
Good news on the Grand Canyon; no damming. A. W. Smith. Nat Parks Mag 41:2+ Mr '67
Grand Canyon: dam it or not? pro and con discussion. il Sr Schol 90:6-7 F 3 '67
Grand Canyon still threatened; letter. W. C. Bradley. Science 156:451 Ap 28 '67
Grand Canyon; with photographs by P. Caulfield. B. Atkinson. Natur Hist 76:38-49 N '67
No dams! il Am For 73:8 Mr '67
Shift of signals on Grand Canyon dams. U S News 62:16 F 13 '67
See also
Geology—Grand Canyon

GRAND CANYON dams. See Dams

GRAND CANYON NATIONAL PARK
Jogging down into the Grand Canyon. L. P. Bell. Redbook 130:42 N '67

GRAND CAYMAN (island)
Grand Cayman. il Holiday 43:94-5 Ja '68

GRAND COULEE power and reclamation project
Grand Coulee project stirs up a tempest; Russia's request to be allowed to bid. il Bsns W p59 Ap 15 '67

GRAND jury
Criminal justice revolution; address, May 16, 1967. J. E. Lumbard. Vital Speeches 33: 527-31 Je 15 '67
People vs. some persons. R. Lynes. il Harper 234:28+ Ap '67

GRAND LAKE yacht club. See Yacht clubs

GRAND national steeplechase. See Horse racing

GRAND opera. See Opera

GRAND piano. See Piano

GRAND prix of endurance races. See Automobile racing

GRAND prix of Le Mans. See Automobile racing

GRAND prix races. See Automobile racing

GRAND TETON NATIONAL PARK
On policing a lakeshore; clean-up of the shores of Jackson Lake, Grand Teton National Park. M. W. Payne. il Nat Parks Mag 41:19 Je '67
Trails of the Grand Teton. L. C. Huser. il Nat Parks Mag 41:10-14 My '67

GRAND tour. See Europe—Description and travel

GRANDE, Luke M.
Keep the faith, baby! poem. Christian Cent 84:207 F 15 '67

GRANDEE, Joe Ruiz
Painter of the old West. W. Gard. il por **Am Artist** 31:56-7+ Je '67
GRANDFATHERS. See Grandparents
GRANDMOTHERS. See Grandparents
GRANDPARENTS
Grandma is a swinger. E. J. LeShan. il N Y Times Mag p92+ Ap 23 '67
Grandparents are to love. R. M. Fuerst. il Parents Mag 42:38-9+ Ag '67
Very special grandfather: Joe Dekle. C. Mangel. il Look 31:M21-4 Je 13 '67
What a grandmother is. P. Gray. PTA Mag 61:26 Je '67
Why my grandchildren like me. B. Beck. Farm J 91:51 Jl '67
Les GRANDS ballets canadiens. See Ballet—Canada
GRANDSTAFF, Marvin
Power, freedom and educational revolution. Sch & Soc 95:387-90 O 28 '67
Secrecy, sanity, and the schools. Sch & Soc 95:142-4 Mr 4 '67
GRANFIELD, Patrick
(ed) See Congar, Y. M. J. Interview with Yves Congar
GRANIT, Ragnar
Good beginning. il por Time 90:56 O 27 '67
Nobel prize: three named for medicine, physiology award. F. Ratliff. por Science 158:469-71 O 27 '67
Nobel prize winners. por Sci N 92:437-9 N 4 '67
Nobel work. il por Newsweek 70:82-3 O 30 '67
GRANITE CITY steel company
Top brass takes to the road to sell steel. il Bsns W p90-1 Ja 28 '67
GRANRUD, Carl Frithjof
Unfraternal takeover. Bsns W p 177 S 30 '67
GRANT, Allan
Photographer's ghost. il Sat Eve Post 240:95 Je 3 '67
GRANT, Annette
After graduation. Mlle 65:144-5+ Je '67
Jobscope. Mlle 65:170-1 Je '67
Talk about teaching. Mlle 64:148-9+ Mr '67
You can make it only if it sells. Mlle 65:122-4+ S '67
Zoo's who. Mlle 65:167+ My '67
GRANT, Cary
Until wealth do us part. G. Ace. Sat R 50:10 S 23 '67
GRANT, Donald
Professor Fedorenko lectures at the U.N. N Y Times Mag p 10-11+ Jl 16 '67
GRANT, Ellsworth S.
Main stream of New England. Am Heritage 18:46-59+ Ap '67
Pollution in the East. Am For 73:4-7+ Jl '67
GRANT, F. Blake. See Pickford, G. E. jt. auth.
GRANT, Gerald
Courts take the initiative. Sat R 50:65 Jl 15 '67
Generation gap. Sat R 50:61 Mr 18 '67
GRANT, Lori Lee
Baby who was born twice. T. Morris. por Redbook 129:64-5+ Je '67
GRANT, Mary Kent
Mystery, detective and suspense. See first issue of each month of Library journal
GRANT, Nigel
Problems and developments in teacher education in the U.S.S.R. bibliog f Sch & Soc 95:451-5 N 25 '67
GRANT, Philip A. Jr.
Ferment on the campus. Cath World 205:293-7 Ag '67
GRANT, W. Vance
Back to school. Am Ed 3:8-9 S '67
GRANT, Zalin B.
Training, equipping the Latin American military. New Repub 157:13-14 D 16 '67
GRANTS-In-aid
Should Uncle share the wealth? il Nations Bsns 55:35-7+ Ap '67
States look to federal dividends; idea of unrestricted grants gaining favor among governors and economists. il Bsns W p 156-8 Ja 21 '67
Subsidy or windfall; federal revenue sharing. R. Moley. Newsweek 70:100 O 2 '67
What's wrong with the way we raise revenues. F. Morley. il Nations Bsns 55:27-8 Je '67
See also
Economic assistance, Domestic
GRANTS to colleges and universities. See Colleges and universities—Gifts, legacies, etc.
GRANULOMA
Leukocyte oxidase; defective activity in chronic granulomatous disease. R. L. Baehner and D. G. Nathan. bibliog il Science 155:835-6 F 17 '67

GRANZ, Norman
Granz rides again. S. Dance. Sat R 50:57 Ap 15 '67
Jazz concerts; Jazz at the Philharmonic on JATP Easter Sunday, at Carnegie Hall. W. Balliett. New Yorker 43:163-4 Ap 8 '67
GRAPE industry. See Viticulture
GRAPES
Four-day outing from New York; up-state vineyards and winemakers. W. Clifford. Atlan 219:114-16+ Je '67
Grapes for the Southwest. F. B. Widmoyer and D. T. Sullivan. il Horticulture 45:22-5 S '67
Home with the winos; vineyards in California. H. Sutton. il Sat R 50:44-5 Ag 12 '67
Wines of the Rhine and the Moselle. H. Johnson. House & Gard 133:126+ Ja '68
GRAPHIC arts
Expo 67: winning experiment in systemic graphics. il Pub W 192:76-8 Ag 7 '67
Father of modern print-making; J. Villon's early work, at the International galleries, Chicago. L. Campbell. il Art N 66:38-9+ D '67
Graphic art of corporate image. il Fortune 76:127-8+ Jl '67
Nouveau Frisco. il Time 89:66-7+ Ap 7 '67
See also
American institute of graphic arts
Printing

Exhibitions
British creative talent; show of British design in New York city. il Pub W 193:65 Ja 1 '68
Hewers of woodcuts and drawers of watercolors; Yugoslavia's International graphics exposition. Time 90:34 Ag 4 '67

Study and teaching
Union, management set up school in St Louis. Pub W 191:118 F 6 '67
GRAPHIC arts research and engineering council. See Research and engineering council of the graphic arts industry, incorporated
GRAPHIC arts technical foundation
Technology: demise of hot metal? report of forum. Pub W 192:66+ N 6 '67
GRAPHIC methods
See also
Economics—Graphic methods
GRAPHITE
See also
Cliftonite
GRAPHOLOGY
Doctors of letters. il Newsweek 70:90+ D 11 '67
Graphology: out or in? Sci Digest 63:22-3 Ja '68
GRASS, Günter
Gunter Grass's open letter to Kurt Kiesinger. Nation 204:214 F 13 '67

about
Plebeians rehearse the uprising; tr. by R. Manheim. Criticism
   Nation 204:213-14 F 13 '67
Wicked cooks. Criticism
   Commonweal 85:567 F 17 '67
   New Yorker 42:93-4 F 4 '67
   Newsweek il 69:106 F 6 '67
GRASS, Artificial. See Turf, Artificial
GRASS diseases. See Cows—Diseases and pests
GRASS seed. See Grasses—Seed
GRASS sickness. See Cows—Diseases and pests
GRASSES
Apomixis: seasonal and population differences in a grass. R. B. Knox. bibliog il Science 157:325-6 Jl 21 '67
Decorative use for mondo grass. il Pop Gard 18:89 Ag '67
Dramatic garden grasses. il House & Gard 132:110-11 Ag '67
How to use garden grasses. W. H. Frederick, jr. il House & Gard 132:146-7+ Ag '67
It takes all kinds. il Home Gard 54:42-4 Ap '67
Underground activity supports above-ground action; turf at Busch memorial stadium, St Louis. il Am City 82:129+ S '67
See also
Bamboo
Sod
Sorghum

Diseases and pests
See also
Lawns—Diseases and pests

Seed
How to buy lawn seed. Bet Hom & Gard 45:142-3 Ap '67

GRASSHOPPERS
Phase polymorphism in the grasshopper melanoplus differentialis. H. Dingle and J. B. Haskell. bibliog il Science 155:590-2 F 3 '67
GRAU, Shirley Ann
Sea change; story. Atlan 220:105-9 N '67
GRAUMAN, Lawrence, Jr
Goals of dissent. Nation 205:617-21 D 11 '67
Louisville happening. Nation 204:689-92 My 29 '67
GRAVÉ, Eric V.
Chaos chaos; with biographical sketch. il Natur Hist 76:4, 48-9 O '67
GRAVEL
Gravel did it! B. Christian. il Home Gard 54:68-9 F '67
GRAVER, Lawrence
Daftness falls from the air. New Repub 156:35-7 F 4 '67
GRAVES, Eleanor
Great dinners. See issues of Life
Life restaurant review. Life 62:14 My 5 '67
GRAVES, Elizabeth Minot
Selected list of children's books (cont) Commonweal 86:293-303 My 26 '67
GRAVES, Ralph
See how they run. Life 63:51-2+ Jl 21 '67
GRAVES, Robert
Fact of the act; poem. Atlan 220:71 Ag '67
Six poems: Brief withdrawal; Perfectionists; Bites and kisses; Like owls; Word; Blackening sky. New Yorker 43:32 Jl 8 '67
Song: one in many; poem. Atlan 220:66 D '67
Wigs and beards; poem. Atlan 219:60 Je '67
Wild cyclamen; poem. Ladies Home J 84:139 Ap '67

about

Graves: a ghost and a skeleton key. D. Hoffman. Poetry 110:409-12 S '67
White goddess alone. D. Schiller. Commentary 43:85-8 F '67
GRAVES, William
Rhine; Europe's river of legend. Nat Geog Mag 131:449-99 Ap '67
GRAVES. See Tombs
GRAVESTONES. See Sepulchral monuments
GRAVIMETERS
Bell gravity meter performance praised. R. W. Niblock. il Tech W 20:38-9 Mr 20 '67
GRAVITATION
Einstein under siege. C. Behrens. il Sci N 91:144 F 11 '67
Gravitation collapse. K. S. Thorne. il Sci Am 217:88-92+ bibliog(p 154+) N '67
Gravity increase at the South Pole. J. C. Behrendt. bibliog il Science 155:1015-17 F 24 '67
New method for the detection of light deflection by solar gravity. I. I. Shapiro. bibliog Science 157:806-8 Ag 18 '67
Precision measurement of the acceleration of gravity. J. E. Faller. bibliog il Science 158:60-7 O 6 '67
Was Einstein wrong? reprint. W. Sullivan. il Sci Digest 61:75-8 Ap '67
See also
Gravimeters
Pendulum
Plants. Effect of gravitation on
Weightlessness
GRAVITY free state. See Weightlessness
GRAVITY meters. See Gravimeters
GRAVITY simulators. See Simulators
GRAY, Arthur H.
AAUP: computer-aided composition; summary of address, June 12, 1967. por Pub W 192:78+ Jl 3 '67
GRAY, Cleve
Gray's Ceres series. K. Levin. il por Art N 66:52-3+ N '67
GRAY, Francine du Plessix. See Du Plessix, F.
GRAY, Irwin
Defense expenditures in depressed areas. Mo Labor R 90:34-5 Mr '67
GRAY, Jenny
Discipline problems; excerpts from The teacher's survival guide. NEA J 56:62-3 D '67
GRAY, Jesse
Unpolished nigger. M. Renek. New Repub 157:7 S 9 '67
GRAY, John D.
Creativity in business. Duns R 89:26+ Mr '67
GRAY, Joseph H.
Notes of the fall show. Hobbies 72:118+ Ja '68
Notes of the spring show. Hobbies 72:111 Ag '67
GRAY, Nancy C.
Come to brunch! Am Home 70:58-9 N '67
House that says summer. Am Home 70:62-5 Jl '67

GRAY, Patsy
What a grandmother is. PTA Mag 61:26 Je '67
GRAY, Ruth
My first six months as a mother. Redbook 129:66-7 S '67
GRAY, T. R. G.
Stereoscan electron microscopy of soil microorganisms. bibliog Science 155:1668-70 Mr 31 '67
GRAY, Warren D.
Million dollar copycats. il pors Ebony 23:74-6+ Ja '68
GRAY, William R, and others
Mechanism of antibody synthesis: size differences between mouse kappa chains. bibliog Science 155:465-7 Ja 27 '67
GRAY, Wood
(comp) Articles and other books received; United States. See issues of American historical review
GRAYLING fishing
Fishing light is never out. E. Park. il Outdoor Life 140:46-9+ Ag '67
GRAYSON, George W. Jr
Stalemate in Chile. New Repub 156:14 F 4 '67
Tijerina; with interview. Commonweal 86:464-6 Jl 28 '67
Tijerina's Republic of San Joaquin del Rio de Chama. New Repub 157:10-11 Jl 1 '67
GRAYSON, Julie
Affair of the heart. Good H 164:33-4+ Ap '67
GRAYWACKE
Composition of the ancient North American crust. K. C. Condie. bibliog il Science 155:1013-15 F 24 '67
GREASED samba; story. See Deck, J.
GREAT Atlantic and Pacific tea company
Does A&P really care? il Newsweek 70:78 O 16 '67
GREAT auk, a bird now extinct; story. See Heineman, N.
GREAT BARRIER REEF
End of the Great Barrier Reef? il Sci Digest 63:31-2 Ja '68
Wonderland of Australia's Great Barrier Reef. F. Drake and K. Drake. il Read Digest 90:162-4+ Mr '67
GREAT BARRINGTON, Mass.
Never on Tuesday; filming of She let him continue. R. Lynes. il Harper 236:13-16 Ja '68
GREAT blue herons. See Herons
GREAT BRITAIN
Britain entering Europe. W. Lippmann. Newsweek 69:23 My 22 '67
British take stock. A. Campbell. New Repub 156:3-5 Je 17 '67
See also
Aerospace industries—Great Britain
Airports—Great Britain
Atomic power—Great Britain
Atomic research—Great Britain
Aviation—Great Britain
Ballet—Great Britain
Booksellers and bookselling—Great Britain
Budget—Great Britain
Canals—Great Britain
Cattle industry and trade—Great Britain
Civil rights—Great Britain
Coal industry—Great Britain
Colleges and universities—Great Britain
Commonwealth of nations
Contracts, Government—Great Britain
Costume—Great Britain
Education—Great Britain
Education and state in Great Britain
Foreign students in Great Britain
Government ownership—Great Britain
Immigration and emigration—Great Britain
Justice. Administration of—Great Britain
Labor and laboring classes—Great Britain
Meat industry and trade—Great Britain
Money—Great Britain
Morale, National—Great Britain
Moving pictures—Great Britain
Newspapers—Great Britain
Phonograph record industry—Great Britain
Postal service—Great Britain
Public health—Great Britain
Public opinion—Great Britain
Radio broadcasting—Great Britain
Railroads—Great Britain
Science—Great Britain
Seaside resorts—Great Britain
Secret service—Great Britain
Shopping and shoppers—Great Britain
Space research—Great Britain
Strikes—Great Britain
Television broadcasting—Great Britain
Trade unions—Great Britain
Trials—Great Britain
Wages—Great Britain
World war, 1939-1945—Great Britain
Youth—Great Britain

GREAT BRITAIN—*Continued*

Antiquities

Dig we must! teen-ager's summer job at archeological excavations in England. J. Shumsky. il Seventeen 26:146-7+ S '67

See also
Stonehenge

Appropriations and expenditures

See also
Budget—Great Britain

Armed forces

Britain to stress NATO role, mobility in military deployment. Aviation W 87:28 Jl 24 '67

Forces in Aden

Aden is a little Vietnam for Britain. H. Smith. il N Y Times Mag p 12-14+ Jl 23 '67
Aden: keeping the peace, and tempers. il Life 62:36-7 Ap 14 '67
Desert feud that's explosive. il U S News 62:65-6 Ap 17 '67
Storm in the Crater; week of violence in Aden. il Newsweek 70:38+ Jl 3 '67

Forces in Germany

That old hand McCloy; agreement with London and Bonn on proposed reduction of U.S. and British troops in West Germany. Reporter 36:8+ My 18 '67
U.S., U.K., and Germany conclude trilateral talks; U.S. government statement, May 2, 1967. Dept State Bul 56:788-9 My 22 '67

Forces in the Far East

Britain draws back again, where that leaves U.S. il U S News 63:64-5 Jl 31 '67
Recessional; withdrawal of all troops from Singapore and Malaysia by the mid-1970s. Time 90:22 Jl 28 '67
Ringing down the curtain. Time 91:19 Ja 19 '68
Sunset east of Suez. il Newsweek 70:33 Jl 31 '67
White paper, black news; Far East withdrawal. D. Warner. Reporter 37:11 Ag 10 '67

Forces in the Middle East

Changing of the guard in the Middle East. H. L. Hoskins. Cur Hist 52:65-6+ F '67

Procurement

Ministry, engine firm criticized in excess-profit investigation; Parliamentary committee. Aviation W 87:19 Jl 31 '67

British airports authority

U.K. airports group reports earnings. Aviation W 87:55 S 18 '67

Cabinet

Can Cabinet shake-up cure Britain's ills? U S News 63:36 S 11 '67
Facing facts; Wilson takes charge of Department of economic affairs. Newsweek 70:40+ S 11 '67
Moment of daring; Wilsons cabinet reshuffle. il Time 90:23 S 8 '67

Colonies

Triumphant empire, by L. H. Gipson. Review Sat R 50:32 Je 17 '67. R. B. Morris
See also
Hong Kong

Commerce

Briton tells what's wrong with his country. R. M. Bowker. il U S News 62:70-2 F 27 '67
Cordial dislike; before Britain's talks with European common market. Nat R 19:945 S 5 '67
Is U.S. losing Britain as its no. 1 ally? Britain's entry into the Common market. il U S News 62:52-3 My 15 '67
Letter from London: question of membership in the Common market. M. Panter-Downes. New Yorker 42:145 F 11 '67
Man from Lion & unicorn; marketing company to aid British exports to U.S. il Time 90:61 S 1 '67
Where does Britain go from here? il U S News 63:63-4 O 9 '67
See also
European economic community

Defenses

Britain in the western alliance. A. C. Turner. bibliog f il Cur Hist 52:257-63+ My '67

Britain to stress NATO role, mobility in military deployment. Aviation W 87:28 Jl 24 '67
Devaluation will bring U.K. defense cuts. H. J. Coleman. Aviation W 87:21 N 27 '67
Healey's procurement policy under fire; joint Anglo-French variable-geometry aircraft program. H. J. Coleman. Aviation W 86:20-1 F 20 '67
$730 million R&D in UK defense bid. Tech W 20:39 Mr 6 '67
U.K. defense plan tied to NATO decision. H. J. Coleman. Aviation W 86:23-4 F 27 '67

Diplomatic and consular service

Jacobean diplomatic service. M. Lee, jr. bibliog f Am Hist R 72:1264-82 Jl '67
Sacking an embassy, Red guard style. il U S News 63:8 S 4 '67
Squeeze: in Peking and Hong Kong. il Newsweek 70:41-2 S 4 '67

Economic conditions

After the fall. Time 90:23-4 D 1 '67
Britain's endless troubles: a close look at the causes. il U S News 63:64-6 D 18 '67
Britain's sad plight. Time 90:26-7 D 22 '67
British economy: world trade; address, November 6, 1967. P. Dean. Vital Speeches 34:150-3 D 15 '67
Briton tells what's wrong with his country. R. M. Bowker. il U S News 62:70-2 F 27 '67
Can England make it? N. Macrae. Harper 234:12+ F '67
Devaluing the pound, and labour. G. Bailey. Reporter 37:20-2 D 14 '67
In Britain the walls keep closing in. B. Wenham. New Repub 157:9 S 2 '67
International outlook; new round of difficulties. Bsns W p 131 Je 24 '67
Japan and Britain: a study in contrasts. Read Digest 90:213-14+ Ap '67
Loose upper lip? call for fundamental changes. Newsweek 69:59 Je 26 '67
Patient is getting restless; Britain after 2½ years of the Wilson treatment. B. Wenham. New Repub 156:7-9 Ap 22 '67
Suffering. Time 90:93 O 13 '67
Where does Britain go from here? il U S News 63:63-4 O 9 '67
See also
Budget—Great Britain
Labor and laboring classes—Great Britain
Money—Great Britain
Wages—Great Britain

Economic history

What's the matter with Britain? G. Gorer. il N Y Times Mag p 10-11+ D 31 '67

Economic policy

All at sea. Nat R 19:838+ Ag 8 '67
Atlantic report. Atlan 219:22+ F '67
Britain's retrenchment; disengagement in order to achieve economic solvency. H. Brandon. Sat R 50:10-11 My 6 '67
Britain's wage freeze: a success, but what comes later? il U S News 63:72 Jl 17 '67
British economy. A. D. Monroe. Cur Hist 52:270-5+ My '67
Can Harold Wilson make it work? B. Wenham. New Repub 157:11-12 D 9 '67
Common market: its effect on Britain; address, May 8, 1967. H. Wilson. Vital Speeches 33:482-94 Je 1 '67
International trade and investment; address, March 7, 1967. P. Chambers. Vital Speeches 33:371-5 Ap 1 '67
Labor's dilemma in Britain. P. Crane. America 117:409 O 14 '67
Report from London; devaluation of sterling and the British economy. H. Luce, 3d. il Fortune 77:109+ Ja '68
Waiting for word from France. il Newsweek 69:51 My 22 '67
Wilson tries to wrest victory from retreat; steps after devaluation. il Bsns W p34-7 N 25 '67

Economic relations

British alternatives; if EEC negotiations fail. G. Lichtheim. Commentary 43:47-51 Ap '67

Europe, Western

Britain wants in; no choice but the Common market. S. A. Scheingold. Commonweal 86:84-6 Ap 7 '67
British question hangs fire il Bsns W p 38 Je 3 '67
De Gaulle and Britain: same old stand. il Newsweek 69:34+ My 29 '67
De Gaulle dampens British bid; second move to join Common market. il Bsns W p37 My 20 '67

GREAT BRITAIN—Economic relations—Europe, Western—*Continued*
European common market: the entry of Britain; address, May 16, 1967. C. de Gaulle. Vital Speeches 33:495-7 Je 1 '67
Her Majesty's government decides; Britain's application to join Common market. Newsweek 69:49 My 15 '67
Report; implications of bid to join the Common market. D. Cook. Atlan 219:24+ My '67

United States
Latest idea for Britain: a common market; with U.S. il U S News 64:46-7 Ja 1 '68

Exchequer
Man for all sacrifices; new chancellor. il Time 90:32 D 8 '67

Foreign office
Tough cheese; investigating compensation fund for British victims. Newsweek 71:32 Ja 8 '68

Foreign opinion
French
Britain and France build a common market of youth. S. De Gramont. il N Y Times Mag p7+ Jl 16 '67

Indian
Night train to Chittagong. D. W. David. il Read Digest 91:95-9 O '67

Foreign relations
Travail of Britain. W. Lippmann. Newsweek 70:23 D 4 '67
See also
Great Britain—Diplomatic and consular service

Africa
Britain's influence in Africa. D. J. Murray. bibliog f Cur Hist 52:276-81 My '67

China (People's Republic)
Mao's bullies get a bit of their own medicine. il Life 63:28-28A S 8 '67
Red China vs. Britain; what's ahead now? il U S News 63:10 S 11 '67
Sacking an embassy, Red guard style. il U S News 63:8 S 4 '67
Squeeze; in Peking and Hong Kong. il Newsweek 70:41-2 S 4 '67
Ultimatum & anarchy; Peking's behavior to British and other diplomats. Time 90:20 S 1 '67
See also
Hong Kong—Boundaries

Egypt
When the sun set . . . G. A. Craig. Reporter 37:37-8 N 30 '67
See also
Sudan

Europe, Western
Scurrying in the wings. il Time 89:26 Ja 27 '67

Germany (Federal Republic)
Dismal diplomacy. il Time 89:30 F 24 '67
Six-movement symphony. Newsweek 69:38+ F 27 '67

Middle East
Changing of the guard in the Middle East. H. L. Hoskins. Cur Hist 52:65-6+ F '67
Middle East crisis; address, June 21, 1967. G. Brown. Vital Speeches 33:586-9 Jl 15 '67

Rhodesia
Incredible envoy. Newsweek 70:44 Jl 3 '67
Leave us alone to solve our own affairs; interview, ed. by A. J. Meyers. I. Smith. il U S News 63:76-8 D 18 '67

South Africa
U.K. rejects South Africa defense order. H. J. Coleman. Aviation W 87:20 D 25 '67

Spain
End of the road for the Rock? il U S News 62:56 My 22 '67

United States
Is U.S. losing Britain as its no. 1 ally? Britain's entry into the Common market. il U S News 62:52-3 My 15 '67
LBJ-Wilson talks; end of grand alliance? il U S News 62:20 Je 5 '67
Nineteen seventy-five; crucial year. G. Lichtheim. Commentary 44:62-7 Jl '67
Our only real ally; with editorial comment. S. Alsop. il Sat Eve Post 240:16, 84 Jl 1 '67; Same abr. without editorial comment. Read Digest 91:43-5 S '67

President Johnson confers with British Prime Minister; remarks, June 2, 1967. L. B. Johnson; H. Wilson. Dept State Bul 56: 963-4 Je 26 '67
Suez crisis; a footnote to history. W. W. Aldrich. For Affairs 45:541-52 Ap '67

Historic houses, etc.
Literary past: a view from the tour bus. A. Netboy. il Sat R 50:46-7+ Mr 11 '67

History
Bibliography
Articles and other books received; comp. by L. H. Carlson. See issues of American historical review

17th century
Marquess of Halifax: eloquent paradox. J. Valenti. Sat R 50:22-3+ N 4 '67

Stuarts, 1603-1714
Jacobean diplomatic service. M. Lee, jr. bibliog f Am Hist R 72:1264-82 Jl '67

18th century
Triumphant empire, by L. H. Gipson. Review Sat R 50:32 Je 17 '67. R. B. Morris

1741-1837
See also
United States—History—Revolution

1760-1789
See also
United States—History—Revolution

Victorian period, 1837-1901
In the days of the bric-a-brac queen. L. Kronenberger. Atlan 220:88-91 Jl '67

House of lords
See Great Britain—Parliament—House of lords

Industries
Britain's cult of bigness; government-sponsored mergers. Time 90:93-4 O 27 '67
Can England make it? N. Macrae. Harper 234:12+ F '67
Great tissue war; England. R. Ross-Skinner. Duns R 89:47 F '67
See also
Airplane industry and trade—Great Britain
Candy industry and trade
Clothing industry—Great Britain
Coal industry—Great Britain
Electric apparatus industry
Great Britain—Commerce
Imperial chemical industries, limited
Pilkington brothers, limited
Shipbuilding
Steel industry and trade—Great Britain
Textile industry—Great Britain

Intellectual life
Memories, 1898-1939, by C. M. Bowra. Review New Repub 157:25-8 N 18 '67. J. Wain

Medical research council
See Medical research council (Great Britain)

Military policy
Britain draws back again, where that leaves U.S. il U S News 63:64-5 Jl 31 '67
Britain's retrenchment; disengagement in order to achieve economic solvency. H. Brandon. Sat R 50:10-1 My 6 '67
White paper, black news; Far East withdrawal. D. Warner. Reporter 37:11 Ag 10 '67

Moral conditions
Frankness in the air. il Time 90:22+ Jl 28 '67

National coal board
Terrifying ineptitude; blamed for disaster at Aberfan. Wales Sci N 92:204 Ag 26 '67

National health service
Crisis in Britain's health plan; with interview with F. A. Jones. L. Gross. il Look 31:47-53 Mr 21 '67

National institute for medical research
See Medical research council (Great Britain)

Navy
See also
Warships—Great Britain

Nobility
See Great Britain—Peerage

GREAT BRITAIN—*Continued*

Parliament

House of lords
Blow to the lords. il Time 90:42 N 10 '67
Letter from London; debate on Middle East situation. M. Panter-Downes. New Yorker 43:96+ Je 17 '67
Lords to lose. il Sr Schol 91:22-3 N 16 '67

Peerage
Department of amplification. A. Lewis. New Yorker 43:131-2+ O 21 '67; Reply. N. Bliven. 43:235 N 25 '67
England's second family. L. B. Smith. il Horizon 9:68-79 Aut '67
See also
Great Britain—Parliament—House of lords

Politics and government
After the fall. Time 90:23-4 D 1 '67
After the fall. il Newsweek 70:44+ D 4 '67
British alternatives; if EEC negotiations fail. G. Lichtheim. Commentary 43:47-51 Ap '67
Can Cabinet shake-up cure Britain's ills? U S News 63:36 S 11 '67
Fast shuffle at 10 Downing. C. Brogan. il Nat R 19:1065-6 O 3 '67
Letter from London (cont) M. Panter-Downes. New Yorker 43:226-8+ N 11 '67
One of those weeks. il Newsweek 70:50-1 N 13 '67
Problem of political change in Great Britain. R. Rose. bibliog f Cur Hist 52:264-9+ My '67
We unhappy few. A. Lejeune. Nat R 19:1120 O 17 '67
See also
Conservative party (Great Britain)
Elections—Great Britain
Great Britain—Cabinet
Labor party (Great Britain)
Liberal party (Great Britain)
Socialism—Great Britain

Protectorates
Persian Gulf. M. Page. il Atlan 219:38+ Ap '67
See also
Aden

Race problems
As racial trouble builds up in Britain. il U S News 62:54-5 Ap 3 '67
Benefiting from U.S. race errors. C. Northcott. Christian Cent 84:1037 Ag 16 '67
Coming to grips with the color bar in Britain. B. Wenham. New Repub 156:14-15 Ja 28 '67
John Bull and Jim Crow; Political and economic planning report findings. Newsweek 69:37 My 1 '67
Race report. il Time 89:38 Ap 28 '67

Religious institutions and affairs
See also
Catholic church in Great Britain
Church unity—Great Britain

Royal air force
RAF may increase F-4 order. Aviation W 86:25 Mr 20 '67

Royal family
Family reunion. il Newsweek 69:54 Je 19 '67
Queen Elizabeth and Philip: the good life they share after twenty years. A. Levy. il Good H 165:88-9+ N '67
Return of Britain's prodigal prince. il U S News 62:23 Je 19 '67

Social conditions
All-time high; drug situation in Britain. B. Wenham. New Repub 157:13 Ag 19 '67
Shame is enough; House of commons reforms Britain's criminal statutes against homosexuality. Time 90:30 Jl 14 '67
See also
Social and economic security—Great Britain

Social history
In the days of the bric-a-brac queen. L. Kronenberger. Atlan 220:88-91 Jl '67

Social life and customs
See also
Great Britain—Peerage

GREAT Canadian oil sands, limited
From an icy quagmire, half the world's oil; Fort McMurray plant. il Newsweek 70:78-80 O 2 '67
Unlocking oil from Canada's tar sands; Athabasca sands; reprint. J. H. Carmical. il Sci Digest 61:56-9 Je '67
GREAT contest; drama. See Huff, B. T.
GREAT exhibition of the works of industry of all nations, 1851. See London—Great exhibition of the works of industry of all nations, 1851
GREAT Gulf wilderness area. See Wilderness areas—New Hampshire
GREAT horned owls. See Owls
GREAT KAROO
Plains of Camdeboo, by E. Palmer. Review New Yorker 43:189-90+ Mr 18 '67. N. Bliven

GREAT LAKES
Natural displacement of pollution from the Great Lakes. R. H. Rainey. il Science 155:1242-3 Mr 10 '67; Reply. H. C. Curl, jr. 156:1179 Je 2 '67
Prize catch for the cruising man. J. Roe. il Yachting 121:74-6+ My '67
Salvaging the Lakes; Great Lakes pollution. Time 89:60 Ap 21 '67
GREAT LAKES REGION
See also
Fishing—Great Lakes Region
GREAT LAKES—St Lawrence waterway. See St Lawrence Seaway
GREAT LAKES shipping. See Shipping—United States
GREAT Marsh, Va. See Marshes
GREAT men
Americans not everybody knows. C. W. Ferguson. See issues of PTA magazine
Great men, great events (cont) il UNESCO Courier 20:27-9 O '67
Heroes of a harsh land. il Holiday 42:76-83 D '67
Profiles of great Americans born in February. Negro Hist Bul 30:4-5 F '67
Variety of men, by C. P. Snow. Review Life 62:10 My 5 '67. M. Maddocks New Repub 156:25-6+ My 27 '67. J. Wain
See also
Celebrities
Leadership
GREAT PLAINS
At the grass roots: peace and plenty. il U S News 63:57 Ag 14 '67
GREAT powers
Beginnings of world war III? J. V. Schall. America 117:14-17 Jl 1 '67
How not to be a world power. H. S. Commager. il N Y Times Mag p28-9+ Mr 12 '67
Recalcitrant world; the two superpowers and the U.N. Nation 205:34-5 Jl 17 '67
Some bigs are bigger. J. Burnham. Nat R 19:788 Jl 25 '67
GREAT SALT LAKE
Life in a dead sea, Great Salt Lake. P. A. Zahl. il Nat Geog Mag 132:252-63 Ag '67
GREAT SLAVE LAKE railway
Slow train to Great Slave. H. B. Comstock. il Pop Mech 128:110-13 Jl '67
GREAT SMOKY MOUNTAINS NATIONAL PARK
High horizons. M. B. Mellinger. il Nat Parks Mag 41:10-11 Je '67
Smokies, hike to discovery. C. Brewer. il Liv Wild 30:3-8 Aut '66
Strangers in high places: the story of the Great Smoky Mountains, by M. Frome. Review
Liv Wildn 30:29-30 Aut '66. R. A. Shields
GREAT society. See United States—Social policy
GREAT Soviet encyclopedia. See Encyclopedias
GREAT STONE FACE. See Profile Mountain
GREAT SWAMP national wildlife refuge. See Wildlife sanctuaries
GREAT white hope; drama. See Sackler, H.
GREAT women. See Women, Famous
GREBANIER, Bernard
Venetian Don Juan. Sat R 50:38-9 O 21 '67
GRECHKO, Andrei Antonovich
May day; address, May 1, 1967. Vital Speeches 33:508-9 Je 1 '67
about
Hard-liner moves up. por U S News 62:24 Ap 24 '67
One for the marshals. Newsweek 69:50 Ap 24 '67
Two new men. por Time 89:45 Ap 21 '67

El GRECO
Anatomy of a masterpiece: the burial of Count Orgaz. R. McMullen. il Horizon 9: 48-61 Aut '67

GREECE, Ancient

History

See also
Alexander the Great

GREECE, Modern

See also
Aegean islands
Anti-Communist movements—Greece, Modern
Architecture, Domestic—Greece, Modern
Censorship—Greece, Modern
Delphi
Foreign visitors in Greece
Prisons—Greece, Modern
Tourist trade—Greece, Modern
Trials—Greece, Modern

Cabinet

Report; post coup appointments. S. Hempstone. il Atlan 220:21 Jl '67

Constitution

Greek against Greek; proposals for new constitution. New Repub 157:8 O 28 '67

Description and travel

Greece. D. Goulandris. il Vogue 149:144-5+ Ap 1 '67
Greece; symposium. il Sat R 50:44-8+ O 14 '67

Economic conditions

Greek tragedy. P. A. Samuelson. Newsweek 69:89 My 22 '67
Strange interlude in Athens. G. Bailey. il Reporter 37:36-7 Ag 10 '67

Foreign opinion
American

Invitation to Greece. S. Kauffmann. New Repub 157:22+ Jl 1 '67

Foreign relations

Cyprus: no change. B. Cornwall. New Repub 158:10 Ja 13 '68
Out of the past; Cyprus on the brink. il Newsweek 70:37-8 D 4 '67
Shadows of war; threat of invasion of Cyprus. il Time 90:22-3 D 1 '67
Still ticking; situation in Cyprus; Paradise lost. il Newsweek 70:48-9 D 11 '67
See also
Cyprus

Industries

Litton takes charge; Greek government asks for plan to develop western Peloponnesus and Crete. Time 89:93-4 Je 23 '67

Politics and government

Amnesty & uncertainty. il Time 91:32 Ja 5 '68
Barbs of defiance. il Time 90:36+ O 6 '67
Besieged king; military takeover. il Time 89: 28:31 Ap 28 '67
Checking the king. il Newsweek 69:58 Je 5 '67
Cleanup time; junta begins to run the government. Newsweek 69:54 My 22 '67
Colonels change clothes. il Time 90:17-18 D 29 '67
Colonels endure. Nation 204:740 Je 12 '67
Comings and goings. Newsweek 71:36 Ja 22 '68
Constantine and the colonels: on the eve of civil war. R. C. Macridis. Nation 206:8-11 Ja 1 '68
Coup that collapsed. il Time 90:24-5 D 22 '67
Criticize Greek leaders? excerpts from letter to The Washington post. D. Acheson. U S News 64:11 Ja 1 '68
Democracy under siege; plan to reshape and purify Greek life and policies. il Time 89: 30-1 My 12 '67
Eggs and omens; Greece living under military rule. il Newsweek 69:50-2 My 15 '67
Elections or coup? deadlock in Greece; personalities and events from 1964. S. Rousseas. Nation 204:390-5 Mr 27 '67
First 100 days. il Time 90:29-30 Ag 4 '67
Getting acquainted with the coup. il Time 89: 29-31 My 5 '67
Greece: a tragic hour. il Newsweek 69:34+ My 1 '67
Greece: oldest democracy, newest police state. M. J. Goldbloom. Christian Cent 84:946-9 Jl 19 '67
Greece: the colonels' dictatorship. A. de Borchgrave. il Newsweek 70:42+ S 25 '67
Greece: this winter of discontent. D. Holden. il Sat Eve Post 240:80-2 D 2 '67

Greece: under the knife. il Newsweek 69:48+ My 8 '67
Greek comedy, plus tragedy; latest decrees. Life 63:4 Jl 21 '67
Greek coup. Nation 204:581 My 8 '67
Greek coup seen from a window; with reports by F. Grehan and M. Mok. il Life 62:26-31 My 5 '67
Greek drama; army coup interrupts the festival of Greece; interview, ed. by Q. Eaton. D. Yannopoulos. il Opera N 32:14-15 D 30 '67
Greek tragedy? E. M. von Kuehnelt-Leddihn. Nat R 19:586 My 30 '67
Greek vs. Greek; the U.S. stake. il U S News 63:28 D 25 '67
Gulliver in Greece. T. Sage. Nat R 19:1112-13 O 17 '67
How the military rules 8 million Greeks. M. Goldbloom. il N Y Times Mag p26-7+ S 24 '67; Reply. A. Michalopoulos. p40+ O 15 '67
I am the boss; Papadopoulos' power. Time 90:39 S 15 '67
I was born Greek, I will die Greek, interview, ed. by O. Fallaci. M. Mercouri. il Look 31:72-6 S 5 '67
Irreverent phenomenon. il Time 89:44-5 Ap 14 '67
It's neat in Greece. R. F. McDonald. New Repub 157:15-17 Jl 22 '67
King and junta: the coup that failed. M. J. Goldbloom. Commonweal 87:397-8 D 29 '67
King on the spot? il Sr Schol 90:18 My 12 '67
King tells how his coup failed. Constantine II. Life 64:52-4 Ja 5 '68
King's move: end game? il Newsweek 70:27-9 D 25 '67
Letter to a tyrant. S. W. Rousseas and R. Clements. Nation 205:550-1 N 27 '67
New Greek goals. il Sr Schol 91:34 S 28 '67
Notes and comment. New Yorker 43:25 My 27 '67
Opening performance for a Greek tragedy. M. M. Mestrovic. Commonweal 86:222-3 My 12 '67
Our tragedy in Greece. Nation 204:643-4 My 22 '67
Puritan revolt in Greece. G. Bailey. il Reporter 36:19-23 My 18 '67
Question of terms. il Newsweek 71:30 Ja 1 '68
Report; revolutionary regime and the cause and effects of the coup. S. Hempstone. il Atlan 220:20-3 Jl '67
Saving Greece from the Greeks; background to military coup. B. D. Nossiter. New Repub 156:9-10 My 20 '67
Signs of a showdown; attack on Greece's military rulers by former Premier Karamanlis. Time 90:38-9 D 15 '67
Strange interlude in Athens. G. Bailey. il Reporter 37:34-7 Ag 10 '67
Strong man who hates communism. U S News 64:11 Ja 1 '68
Talk with General Pattakos; interview, ed. by A. Tillier. S. Pattakos. Newsweek 69: 51 My 15 '67
That tragic land. Reporter 37:8+ D 28 '67
Trouble for Athens? il Sr Schol 91:12-13 O 19 '67
U.S. reviews situation in Greece following military takeover; statement, April 28, 1967. D. Rusk. Dept State Bul 56:750 My 15 '67
What happened in Greece; 1947 to 1967. M. Goldbloom. Commentary 44:68-74 D '67
Why the army took over in Greece. il U S News 62:14 My 1 '67
See also
Greece, Modern—Cabinet

Religious institutions and affairs

Onward, Christian soldiers; government dismisses twelve bishops and primate. Time 89:37 My 19 '67
See also
Orthodox Eastern church

Social conditions

Greece; the colonels' dictatorship. A. de Borchgrave. il Newsweek 70:42+ S 25 '67

GREEFF, Edward R.
Beware the big ones! Yachting 121:70-1+ Mr '67

GREEK archipelago. See Aegean Islands
GREEK architecture. See Architecture, Greek
GREEK art. See Art, Greek
GREEK cookery. See Cookery, Greek
GREEK drama
House of Atreus: a point of view. J. Lewin. il Cath World 206:118-20 D '67

GREEK drama—*Continued*

Production, Modern

Theatre; Tyrone Guthrie's production of The house of Atreus. J. Novick. Nation 205:252-4 S 18 '67

GREEK language

Study and teaching

Living Latin and Greek. Sch & Soc 95:290-2 Sum '67

GREEK literature
See also
Greek poetry
GREEK music. See Music, Greek
GREEK Orthodox church. See Orthodox Eastern church
GREEK philosophy. See Philosophy, Greek
GREEK poetry
Greek Anthology. K. Rexroth. Sat R 50:20 Jl 29 '67

Translations into English

Odyssey of Homer; tr. by R. Lattimore. Review
New Repub 157:30-1+ D 9 '67. R. Humphries

GREEK political prisoners. See Political prisoners
GREEK revival architecture. See Architecture, American
GREELEY, Andrew M.
Laicization of Catholic colleges. Christian Cent 84:372-5 Mr 22 '67
Myths and fads in Catholic higher education. America 117:542-5 N 11 '67
Wonderful town. Reporter 36:53-4 Ap 20 '67
GREELEY, Dana McLean
Spry downgrader of divinity; interview, ed. by C. Altman. pors Life 63:31-2+ Jl 28 '67
GREELEY, Horace
Go-West man who didn't. por Sr Schol 90: 1 F 3 '67
Life and death of a great newspaper. F. C. Shapiro. il pors Am Heritage 18:97-112 O '67
GREEN, Alexander, pseud. See Grinevskii, A. S.
GREEN, Arnold W.
What do the intellectuals want? Nat R 19: 203-4 F 21 '67
GREEN, E. J. and Carritt, D. E.
Oxygen solubility in sea water: thermodynamic influence of sea salt. bibliog Science 157:191-3 Jl 14 '67
GREEN, Edith
Friends and enemies. Newsweek 69:30 Je 5 '67
GREEN, Gerald
Old stones. Holiday 42:8+ S '67
GREEN, H. W. 2d
Quartz: extreme preferred orientation produced by annealing. bibliog Science 157: 1444-7 S 22 '67
GREEN, Harold P.
AEC proposals, a threat to scientific freedom. Bul Atomic Sci 23:15-17 O '67
New technological era: a view from the law. Bul Atomic Sci 23:12-18 N '67
GREEN, John d
Guide to some special birds; photographs. Life 63:79-81+ N 24 '67
GREEN, Julian
Frenchman from Savannah. F. Biddle. New Repub 157:26-30 N 11 '67
GREEN, Larry
Deadly bait for bass. Outdoor Life 139:52-3+ Je '67
Late-season snows. Field & S 72:44-5+ D '67
Lures with glows on. Field & S 71:70-1+ F '67
Oh shad, poor shad. Field & S 72:52-5+ My '67
Stripers saw pink. pors Outdoor Life 139:78-80+ Ap '67
GREEN, Leon, Jr
Energy needs versus environmental pollution: a reconciliation? bibliog Science 156:1448-50 Je 16 '67
GREEN, Louis C.
Fourth Texas symposium. Sky & Tel 34:84-8, 153-6 Ag-S '67
GREEN, Merle
There's the rub. il por Newsweek 70:87 O 2 '67
GREEN, Morris B. Jr
Tin can arc welding. Sch Arts 67:6-9 N '67
GREEN, Paul B. and Stanton, F. W.
Turgor pressure: direct manometric measurement in single cells of nitella. bibliog Science 155:1675-6 Mr 31 '67
GREEN, Samuel Adams
Four most likely to succeed. L. Lerman. por Mlle 65:156-7 S '67

GREEN, Stanley
New Russian hit parade. Sat R 50:66 Ag 26 '67
GREEN, Teddy
Self-made Lazarus. il por Time 90:58+ O 13 '67
GREEN algae. See Algae
GREEN BAY Packers (football club) See Football clubs
GREEN Beret force. See United States—Army —Special forces
GREEN glass ball; drama. See Corson, H. W.
GREEN turtles. See Turtles, Green
GREEN valley school, I hate you! story. See Bartholomew, C.
GREENBAUM, Everett
Fine piece of machinery; story. Sat Eve Post 240:62-4 Mr 25 '67
GREENBERG, A. Byron
Grafting cacti. Horticulture 45:40-2 D '67
GREENBERG, Clement
Jackson Pollock: inspiration, vision, intuitive decision. Vogue 149:158-61 Ap 1 '67
Where is the avant-garde? Vogue 149:112-13+ Je '67
GREENBERG, Dan
Paint your wagon. N. Willatt. il Duns R 89: 59+ Mr '67
GREENBERG, Daniel S.
It's time for science to act its political age; excerpts from address, December 1966. Bul Atomic Sci 23:36-7 O '67
Politics of pure science. por Sat R 50:62-9 N 4 '67
Swinging with owl one; adaptation of address; reprint. Sat R 50:50-1 Ap 1 '67
GREENBERG, J. Mayo
Interstellar grains; with biographical sketch. Sci Am 217:19, 106-12+ bibliog(p 156) O '67
GREENBERG, Joanne
Cry of silence; story. Good H 164:88-9 Mr '67
GREENBERG, Ken
Build the electric tic tac toe. Pop Electr 26: 74-5 Ap '67
GREENBERG, Pearl
Woven jewelry. Sch Arts 66:28-30 Ap '67
GREENBERG, Sid
Paint your wagon. N. Willatt. il Duns R 89: 59+ Mr '67
GREENBERG, Syd
Cool it! il U S Camera 30:52-3 My '67
Honeycombs. U S Camera 30:16 D '67

about

There was a time. E. Galligan. il U S Camera 30:48-9 Jl '67
GREENBLATT, Augusta
College student's disease. McCalls 94:42+ S '67
GREENBURG, Dan
How to be a Jewish mother; dramatization. See Vail, S.
GREENE, Bob
Hodaka. Hot Rod 20:86-7 F '67
Hot on the trail. Hot Rod 20:94-5 My '67
Up on two wheels. See issues of Hot rod
GREENE, Carroll
From riots to responsibility. Sat R 50:26-7 Ag 12 '67
GREENE, Charlie
Dashing personality. il por Newsweek 69:91 F 6 '67
Learning to care. Newsweek 69:64 Je 26 '67
That last E is for easy, baby! T. C. Brody. il por Sports Illus 26:51-4 Mr 6 '67
GREENE, Felix
Enemy land at war: North Vietnam; photographs. Look 31:45-51 Jl 25 '67
GREENE, Gael
California woman. Ladies Home J 84:62+ Jl '67
My life with the grape (nut) Sat Eve Post 240:16 Mr 11 '67
Take a surfer out of the surf and what have you got? Ladies Home J 84:172-4+ O '67
Woman who lost $780,000 in jewels but still has everything. Ladies Home J 84:108-9+ N '67
GREENE, H. D. 3d
Our stock control system is invaluable. Pub W 191:35-7 My 15 '67
GREENE, Laura
Stay in shape and love it. il pors Ebony 23: 107-8+ D '67
GREENE, Lorenzo J.
Negro manuscript collections in libraries. Negro Hist Bul 30:20 Mr; 14-15 O '67

GREENE, Maxine
Humanity of desegregation. Sat R 50:66-7 Je 17 '67
Visibility of Harold Hewe: some notes towards a profile. Sch & Soc 95:45-8 Ja 21 '67

GREENE, Nancy
Cup for Canada. il Time 89:60 Ap 7 '67
Little tiger takes the cup. B. Ottum. il por Sports Illus 26:22-3 Ap 3 '67
Sudden streak for Nancy. D. Jenkins. il por Sports Illus 26:10-13 Ja 30 '67

GREENE, Wade
Helping the poor find justice. Reporter 36:16-18 My 18 '67

GREENE, Wallace Martin, 1907-
Generals vs. Vietnam strategy; excerpt from testimony before Senate preparedness investigating subcommittee. U S News 63:114 N 6 '67
Vietnam; address, April 24, 1967. Vital Speeches 33:509-12 Je 1 '67

GREENE rifles. See Rifles

GREENEWALT, Crawford H.
U.S. camera achievement award. por U S Camera 30:41 N '67

GREENFELD, Josh
Bruce Jay Friedman is hanging by his thumb. N Y Times Mag p30-2+ Ja 14 '68
Their hearts belong to La Mama. N Y Times Mag p 10-11+ Jl 9 '67
Treblinka: heroism or fantastic apology? Life 62:3+ My 19 '67

GREENFIELD, Edward
Bennett's A penny for a song. Hi Fi 18:MA24+ Ja '68
Boom in Berlioz. Hi Fi 17:MA26+ Ap '67
Britten and the Aldeburgh miracle. Hi Fi 17:MA24-6 S '67
Notes from our correspondents. See issues of High fidelity incorporating Musical America
Proms, hail and farewell to Sir Malcolm. Hi Fi 17:MA30-1 D '67
Violins of St Jacques. Hi Fi 17:MA26-MA27 F '67

GREENFIELD, Jeff
Selective C.O. New Repub 157:15-16 Jl 1 '67

GREENFIELD, Meg
. . .But do as we say. Reporter 37:14-16 S 7 '67
Glossary. Reporter 36:35 Je 1; 42 Je 15; 37:37 S 7 '67
Kiss and tell memoirs. Reporter 37:14-19 N 30 '67
My generation is missing. Reporter 36:35-6 My 4 '67
Story of forty-eight hours. Reporter 36:19-23 Je 15 '67
What is racial balance in the schools? Reporter 36:20-6 Mr 23 '67

GREENHOUSE plants
Plants in the livable greenhouse. il House & Gard 131:206-8+ Mr '67

GREENHOUSES
Greenhouse enclosed, and a basement finished. il House B 109:152-3 Je '67
Greenhouse of your own. J. Eaton. il Home Gard 54:26-34 N '67
Home greenhouse. J. Eaton. See issues of Flower grower, the home garden (cont as) Home garden & flower grower
Livable greenhouse. il House & Gard 131:170-3+ Mr '67
Naturalist at large. M. Bates. il Natur Hist 76:13-15 Mr '67
Now's the time to build a kit greenhouse. il Pop Mech 127:156-9+ My '67
Plan your greenhouse. C. H. Potter. il Horticulture 45:24-5+ F '67
Push out a wall pull in a view. il Pop Gard 18:6-7 Mr '67
See also
Cold frames
Sun rooms

Heating and ventilation
How to heat your greenhouse. C. H. Potter. il Horticulture 45:32-3+ O '67

GREENHOUSES, Miniature
Amateur scientist; two kinds of apparatus for growing plants in a controlled environment. F. C. Hall. il Sci Am 216:130-2+ Mr '67

GREENLAND
Antiquities
Leif Ericsson and his relatives; skulls excavated from Viking graveyard; with report by M. Steinmann. il Life 63:53-4+ S 15 '67

Climate
Catastrophic climate. H. J. Barnes. Sci N 92:427 O 28 '67

Description and travel
First woman across Greenland's ice. M. Simpson. il Nat Geog Mag 132:264-79 Ag '67

GREENLEAF, W. T.
Walls come tumbling down. Am Ed 3:22 Mr '67

GREENLEE, Lyman E.
Build the 2+2 remote volume control. Pop Electr 27:40 O '67
Solid-state line-operated audio amplifier. Pop Electr 26:40-2 Je '67

GREENLEIGH project. See Reading—Study and teaching

GREENOUGH, Horatio
American sculpture in wood and stone. R. Davidson. il Antiques 92:480+ O '67

GREENOUGH, Richard
Orphanage for wild animals. il UNESCO Courier 20:27-9 Ap '67

GREENSBORO, Ala.
After the agitators left Greensboro. J. K. Batten. il Reporter 37:31-3 Ag 10 '67

GREENSPAN, Jack A. and Owen, Tobias
Jupiter's atmosphere: its structure and composition. bibliog Science 156:1489-94 Je 16 '67

GREENVILLE, S.C.
New city complex combines function with aesthetics. il Am City 82:90 N '67

GREENWALD, Frank L.
Light up your house number. Pop Sci 190:152-3 F '67
Make this copier. Pop Mech 127:182-5+ F '67
Spray booth for a workshop window. Pop Sci 190:168-9 Mr '67
Storage wall for a family room. Pop Sci 190:145-8 F '67

GREENWICH, Conn.
Education
Meaningful fare for terminal students: program built around paperback books and films. H. R. Finch. Sr Schol 91:sup 10-11 N 30 '67

Historic houses, etc.
History in houses: East. the Bush-Holley house. S. H. Lowitz and A. C. Lowitz. il Antiques 91:772-6 Je '67

GREENWICH VILLAGE, New York. See New York (city)—Greenwich Village

GREENWOOD, William Rucker
Deformation lamellae parallel to 1013 and 0001 in quartz of the Coeur d'Alene district, Idaho. bibliog Science 158:1180 D 1 '67

GREENWOOD press
Greenwood press, new publisher, formed. Pub W 192:36-7 Jl 24 '67

GREER, Barbara
Barbara Greer; Judson memorial church. J. Maskey. Dance Mag 41:31 D '67

GREER, Herb
I-A in London. Nation 205:487-8 N 13 '67

GREETING cards
Writing for the greeting card market. L. Hardt. Writer 80:28-9 Mr '67
See also
Christmas cards
Post cards

GREGER, Debora
Curl up and read. Seventeen 26:208 My '67

GREGERSEN, Magnus I. and others
Flow characteristics of human erythrocytes through polycarbonate sieves. bibliog Science 157:825-7 Ag 18 '67

GREGG, Duane L.
Cars in your family. See issues of Better homes and gardens

GREGG, James R.
You can't beat canoe camping. Field & S 71:46-7+ Mr '67

GREGOR, Arthur
Floats; poem. Nation 204:733 Je 5 '67
Gentle lamb; poem. New Yorker 42:78 Ja 28 '67
Likeness; poem. New Yorker 42:134 F 18 '67
Unworldliness that he creates; poem. Poetry 111:175-83 D '67
about
Mystical candor. H. Carruth. Nation 205:473-4 N 6 '67

GREGORY, Cynthia
Child's inhumanity to child. PTA Mag 62:22-5 bibliog(p35) D '67

GREGORY, Cynthia, 1947?-
New stars. W. Terry. il pors Sat R 50:24+ Je 3 '67

GREGORY, Dick
You gits a little uppity and you lands in jail. R. Lipsyte. por Esquire 68:72-5 Ag '67

GREGORY, Jacquelyn
  On the boards. W. Como. por Dance Mag
  41:16 Jl '67
GREGORY, John R.
  Movie Q's and A's. See issues of U.S. camera
  & travel
GREHAN, Farrell
  Greek coup seen from a window; photographs
  and report. Life 62:26-31 My 5 '67
GREINER, Larry E.
  Patterns of organization change; excerpts
  from study. Harvard Bsns R 45:119-22+
  My '67
GRELL, E. H.
  Electrophoretic variants of α-glycerophos-
  phate dehydrogenase in drosophila melano-
  gaster. bibliog Science 158:1319-20 D 8 '67
GRENADINES (islands)
  Dash of Grenadines. il Motor B 119:22-4 F '67
  See also
  Bequia (island)
GRENIER, Cynthia
  (ed) See Luc Dominique. Singing nun's story
GRENNAN, Jacqueline
  Age of the person. Seventeen 26:94-5+ D '67
           about
  American women: the doers. por Vogue 149:
  188 My '67
  Crisis in Catholic education. D. Callahan. il
  pors N Y Times Mag p34-5+ Ap 23 '67
  Grennan affair. V. P. McCorry. America 116:
  149-50 Ja 28 '67; Discussion. 116:138, 298
  Ja 28, Mr 4 '67
  Jacqueline Grennan: ex-nun. R. B. Kaiser.
  il pors Look 31:106-10 My 30 '67
  Real world of Jacqueline Grennan. J. P.
  Doyle. il pors Sat R 50:58-9+ Jl 15 '67
  Webster college. Commonweal 85:442 Ja 27
  '67
GRENNAN, Jim
  Help, my child has taken poison! E. M. Wylie.
  Good H 164:77+ Je '67; Same abr. il Read
  Digest 91:133-7 Ag '67
GRENNAN, Michael Dennis
  Eleven ideas from the CBS dream darkroom.
  il Pop Phot 61:124-7+ D '67
  Face-lifting for cameras. Pop Phot 60:76-7+
  Mr '67
  Think small. Pop Phot 61:48+ Ag '67
GRENOBLE, France
  France, a go-go place for the games; photog-
  raphs by E. Haas; with account by F. R.
  Smith. il Sports Illus 27:46-62 N 13 '67
  Oh what a marvelous place to break a leg. R.
  Joseph. il Esquire 68:146-8+ N '67
  Report from Grenoble; fast-growing pro-
  vincial town points France's future in
  high-technology industries. J. Davenport.
  il Fortune 75:69-70+ Mr '67
  Shook-up town's great shape-up; getting
  ready for 1968 winter Olympics. J. Olsen.
  il Sports Illus 27:80-2+ N 13 '67
GREPP, John
  Saturday high school art classes. Sch Arts
  66:5-8 Ja '67
GRESHAM, Grits
  Best quail hunting in the South? Field & S 72:
  34-5+ N '67
  Dixie's model lake. Field & S 72:56-7+ D '67
  How to hunt fish by plane. Field & S 72:42-
  3+ Je '67
  I have the last gobble. Outdoor Life 139:58-
  9+ Ap '67
  Where Mr Inbetween grew up. Field & S
  71:164-7+ Mr '67
  —See Gresham, M. jt. auth.
GRESHAM, Mary, and Gresham, Grits
  Pickup and go. Field & S 71:54-5+ Mr '67
GREVILLEA
  It works just about anywhere. il Sunset 139:
  238 O '67
GREW, Joseph Clark
  American ambassador, by W. H. Heinrichs.
  Review
    Sat R por 50:47-8 F 4 '67. J. A. Allison
GREWING, M. See Pfleiderer, J. jt. auth.
GREY, Howard M. See Abel, C. A. jt. auth.
GREY, Jerry
  Greyrad building market in heat transfer mea-
  surement. J. F. Judge. il Aero Tech 21:25-6
  Ja 1 '68
GREY, Joel
  Looking for crummies; interview. New
  Yorker 43:34-6 Mr 4 '67
           about
  Apparition of success. il por Time 89:57 Ja
  27 '67
GREY, Zane
  Down an unknown jungle river. Field & S
  72:44-5+ S; 60-1+ O; 42-3+ N '67

GREYHOUND corporation
  Greyhound's new route. il Time 89:89 My
  26 '67
GREYRAD corporation
  Greyrad building market in heat transfer mea-
  surement; probes for taking measurements
  in extremely high-temperature environ-
  ments. J. F. Judge. il Aero Tech 21:25-6 Ja
  1 '68
GREYSER, Stephen A. See Bauer, R. A. jt.
  auth.
GRIBBINS, Joseph
  What's new. See issues of Motor boating
GRIDDLE cakes
  Art of cooking crepes. V. T. Habeeb. il Am
  Home 71:84-5+ Ja '68
  Dessert pancakes. R. Hanna. il Suc Farm
  65:106-7 Ja '67
  Pancakes for every mood. G. Maddox. il To-
  days Health 45:60-5 My '67
  Present from a pear tree. C. Claiborne. il
  N Y Times Mag p22 D 31 '67
  Want to try oven pancakes? Sunset 138:200
  Mr '67
GRIECO, D. Marie
  Communications: the undiscovered country;
  adaptation of address, 1966. bibliog Library
  J 92:845-8 F 15 '67
GRIEF. See Bereavement; Sorrow
GRIER, J. Brown, and others
  Prenatal auditory imprinting in chickens. bib-
  liog Science 155:1692-3 Mr 31 '67
GRIEVANCE man, Official. See Ombudsman
GRIEVANCE procedures
  Maturation of the two movements; labor and
  civil rights movements. R. B. McKersie. Mo
  Labor R 90:36-8 Jl '67
GRIEVE, Christopher Murray
  Cattle show; poem. Nation 204:728 Je 5 '67
           about
  MacDiarmid: Highland red. S. Cronin. Na-
  tion 204:728-30 Je 5 '67
GRIFFEN, Jeff
  Breeding your hunting dog. Field & S 72:178-
  9+ My '67
  Christmas puppy. Field & S 72:106+ Ja '68
  Clinic for the problem hunting dog. Field &
  S 72:144-5+ S '67
  Do-it-yourself dog house. Field & S 71:156-8+
  F '67
  Hound world. Field & S 72:114-16+ D '67
  How to pick a puppy. Field & S 72:114+ Jl '67
  Kenneling your hunting dog. Field & S 72:
  144-5+ Je '67
GRIFFIN, C. W. Jr
  Getting nowhere. Reporter 36:56-8 Mr 23 '67
  Northeast corridor. Reporter 37:49-50 O 5;
  11 N 2 '67
  TranSmogrified city. Reporter 36:44-5 My
  4 '67
GRIFFIN, Charles D.
  Now Russia builds up power in the Mediter-
  ranean; excerpts from address, November
  17, 1967. por U S News 63:46+ D 11 '67
GRIFFIN, Gary A. and Devlin, Joseph
  Teacher evaluates innovations. NEA J 56:26-8
  D '67
GRIFFIN, James B.
  Eastern North American archaeology: a sum-
  mary. bibliog Science 156:175-91 Ap 14 '67
GRIFFIN, John
  Philippines. Holiday 42:36-47+ Jl '67
GRIFFIN, M. J. See Carubelli, R. jt. auth.
GRIFFIN, Stuart
  Brain drain touches lightly. Sci N 91:480-1
  My 20 '67
  Japan's unknown side. Travel 128:45-8 N '67
  New shipbuilding techniques. Sci N 91:580-1
  Je 17 '67
  Oriental psychiatry veering West. Sci N 92:
  254-5 S 9 '67
  Skyline changes. Sci N 92:85 Jl 22 '67
GRIFFIN, Tom
  Our plows had to stop plowing. Am City 82:
  75-7 N '67
GRIFFIN, William D.
  Creative copying. U S Camera 30:40-1+ S '67
GRIFFITH, Belver C. See Garvey, W. D. jt.
  auth.
GRIFFITH, David Wark
  Rights and permissions. P. Nathan. Pub W
  192:71 N 13 '67
GRIFFITH, Emile
  Arrivederci, Nino Benvenuti. T. Maule. il por
  Sports Illus 26:20-3 My 1 '67
  Most unusual champion. C. Brossard. il pors
  Look 31:54-6+ Ap 18 '67
  Repeat for the best negative fighter around.
  M. Kram. il por Sports Illus 26:44-6 F 6
  '67

GRIFFITH, F. H.
  Old mechanical banks. See issues of Hobbies
GRIFFITH, Samuel B. 2d
  I believe the army will be kept off center
    stage; interview. por U S News 62:50+ Ja
    30 '67
GRIFFITH, Thomas
  Election fiesta in Ultra; story. Atlan 219:80-6
    F '67
GRIFFITHS, Bede
  Sacred cow. Commonweal 85:483-4 F 3 '67
GRIFFITHS, D. W. Jr
  University inaugurates turf management pro-
    gram. Parks & Rec 2:35+ Ap '67
GRIGGS, Lee
  Olympics. Sports Illus 26:70+ My 22 '67
  Report from Cairo. Fortune 75:69-70+ My
    '67
GRILLEY, Robert
  Painter's personal testimony. il por Am Art-
    ist 31:46-51+ Mr '67
GRILLS, Barbecue. See Barbecue grills
GRILLS, Picnic. See Camp stoves
GRIMES, Andrew J. See Lombardi, V. jt. auth.
GRIMES, Burleigh
  Grimes tells how he threw it. pors Sports
    Illus 27:16-17 Jl 31 '67
GRIMKÉ, John, family
  Family divided. J. Stevenson. il Am Heritage
    18:4-25+ Ap '67
GRIMM brothers
  Brothers Grimm and their famous law for
    linguists. A. Burgess. il pors Horizon 10:
    66-72 Wint '68
GRIMM'S law. See Language and languages
GRIMOND, Joseph
  Grimond to Thorpe. Nat R 19:126 F 7 '67
  Liberals change command. il por Newsweek
    69:44+ Ja 30 '67
GRIN, Aleksandr, pseud. See Grinevskiǐ, A. S.
GRINDELL, Judd
  How it feels to die. Outdoor Life 140:29-31+
    N '67
GRINDLE, C. R.
  Who really are your best employees? Na-
    tions Bsns 55:106-8+ My '67
GRINEVSKIǏ, Aleksandr Stepanovich
  Russian storyteller: Alexander Green. T. P.
    Whitney. Horn Bk 43:551-60 O '67
GRIS, Charles Édouard Jeanneret-. See Le
  Corbusier
GRISEZ, Germain G.
  Rational ethics says no. Commonweal 86:122-5
    Ap 14 '67
GRISSOM, Virgil I.
  Astronauts' vacation house. il por Pop Mech
    127:142-5 Ap '67
  Fire in the spacecraft! il pors Newsweek 69:
    25-9 F 6 '67
  For the heroes, salute and farewell. il Life
    62:20-1+ F 10 '67
  Grissom. il pors Life 62:24-5 F 3 '67
  To strive, to seek, to find and not to yield.
    il por Time 89:13-16 F 3 '67
  We knew that someday... Sci N 91:112 F
    4 '67
GRISWOLD, Wesley S.
  Dam that talks back: Oroville Dam. Pop Sci
    190:86-8 F '67
  (ed) See Miller, J. S. Classic toys test your
    physics know-how
GRIZZLY bear hunting. See Bear hunting
GRIZZLY bears. See Bears
GROBMAN, Arnold B.
  Science education today, public policy to-
    morrow. NEA J 56:8-10 Mr '67
GROCERY stores
  See also
  Pierce, S. S, company
  Supermarkets
GROCERY trade
  High cost of eating. B. B. Seligman. Com-
    mentary 44:48-52 Jl '67; Discussion. 44:6+
    O '67
  See also
  Independent grocers' alliance of America
GROGAN, Ewart Scott
  All for the love of a lady. B. O'Brien. il
    Field & S 72:32-3+ Ja '68
GROLLMAN, Arthur P.
  Structural basis for the inhibition of pro-
    tein biosynthesis: mode of action of tubulo-
    sine. bibliog Science 157:84-5 Jl 7 '67
GRONOUSKI, John Austin
  Intellectual and American foreign policy; ad-
    dress, August 8, 1967. Dept State Bul 57:
    432-5 O 2 '67
GROOMING. See Beauty, Personal
GROOMS, Charles Rogers. See Grooms, R.

GROOMS, Red
  Art world: exhibition at the Tibor De Nagy
    gallery. H. Rosenberg. New Yorker 43:100+
    F 25 '67
  People painter. J. Kroll. il por Newsweek
    69:98 Ja 30 '67
GROPPI, James Edward
  Groppi's army. Time 90:25 S 15 '67
  Groppi's war on Milwaukee. P. J. Weber.
    America 117:342-3 S 30 '67; Discussion. 117:
    456-7 O 28 '67
  Impossible ideal. S. J. Adamo. America 117:
    359-60 S 30 '67
  Long fight in Milwaukee. il por Bsns W p64+
    O 14 '67
  Miracle in Milwaukee. D. Llorens. il pors
    Ebony 23:29-32+ N '67
  Support for Ajax. il por Time 90:84 S 22 '67
  Synod of bishops and dissent. J. B. Sheerin.
    Cath World 206:98-9 D '67
  Target for hate. il por Newsweek 70:67 O 2
    '67
  Too far to stop. il por Newsweek 70:32+ S
    18 '67
  Where a white priest led Negro defiance. il
    por U S News 63:16 S 11 '67
  Why a racial explosion threatens Milwaukee.
    il U S News 63:24 S 25 '67
GROSCH, Daniel S.
  Poisoning with DDT: effect on reproductive
    performance of artemia. Science 155:592-3
    F 3 '67
GROSKINSKY, Henry
  Where kids perform like pros; photographs.
    Life 64:32-43 Ja 5 '68

                    about
  There's no school like it anywhere. G. P.
    Hunt. por Life 64:3 Ja 12 '68
GROSS, Alfred
  Meeting the competition of giants. Harvard
    Bsns R 45:172-4+ My '67
GROSS, Bertram M.
  (ed) Social goals and indicators for Ameri-
    can society. bibliog f Ann Am Acad 371:1-
    177 My; 373:1-218 S '67
  —and Springer, Michael
  New goals for social information. bibliog f
    Ann Am Acad 373:208-18 S '67
  New orientation in American government.
    bibliog f Ann Am Acad 371:1-19 My '67
GROSS, Earl
  Earl Gross discusses polymer color in depth;
    with biographical sketch. il por Am Artist
    31:28-9+ My '67
GROSS, Elizabeth H.
  Teaching of children's literature. bibliog por
    Wilson Lib Bul 42:199-205 O '67
GROSS, Ernest Arnold
  Where are they now? il por Newsweek 69:14
    F 27 '67
GROSS, Franklin S.
  Canada: an exciting teaching opportunity. Sr
    Schol 90:sup 16 F 10 '67
  Past and present: the twain shall meet. Sr
    Schol 91:sup 13 O 5 '67
GROSS, H. R.
  Excerpt from remarks, May 2, 1966. Cong
    Digest 46:85+ Mr '67
GROSS, M.
  Semiconductor test set. Electr World 78:
    74-6 N '67
GROSS, Marthe
  Meet the raccoon. Parents Mag 42:46-7+
    F '67
  Our outdated adoption laws. Parents Mag
    42:64-5+ N '67
  Teenagers who take but don't give. Good H
    164:66+ Mr '67
GROSS, Martin L.
  Personality tests and invasion of privacy.
    NEA J 56:50-1 N '67
GROSS, Paul R.
  Cellular dynamics. Science 157:727-8 Ag 11 '67
GROSS, Reuben E.
  Relationship of church and state. Wilson Lib
    Bul 41:714-18 Mr '67
GROSS, Richard E. See Fraenkel, J. R. jt.
  auth.
GROSS, Robert A.
  To Mr Potter. Harper 235:50-1 O '67
GROSS, Robert Ellsworth
  New look at Lockheed. il por Newsweek 69:
    78 F 20 '67
GROSS, Ronald
  One brief, shining moment; pop poetry; inter-
    view, ed. by H. Frankel. Sat R 50:22-3 S 2
    '67

                    about
  Authors & editors. Pub W 192:20-1 Ag 7 '67

GROSS, Stu
Footnotes and headlines. Christian Cent 84:
1497 N 22 '67
GROSS, Theodore L.
Nathaniel Hawthorne. Yale R 57:182-95 D '67
GROSS leukemia viruses. See Leukemia viruses
GROSS national product
Capacity of America. America 116:138-9 Ja
28 '67
Goals, priorities, and dollars, by L. Lecht.
Review
Science 155:647 F 10 '67. D. Wolfle
How much should a corporation earn? J. J.
Scanlon. il Harvard Bsns R 45:4-6+ Ja '67
How we measure our wealth. il Nations Bsns
55:78-82 Ag '67
Pause that refreshed. il Bsns W p35 Ap
15 '67
Secret of national economic growth. il Sr
Schol 91:14-16+ N 16 '67
Uncounted product. Fortune 76:66 Ag '67
GROSSE, Aristid V.
Efflux time of soap bubbles and liquid
spheres. bibliog Science 156:1220-2 Je 2 '67
GROSSER, Maurice
Art. Nation 204:634-6; 206:60-2 My 15 '67, Ja
8 '68
GROSSET and Dunlap, incorporated
C.I.T. financial corp. to buy Grosset & Dun-
lap. Pub W 192:32 O 2 '67
GROSSLING, Bernardo F.
What price beauty? Am For 73:43 Je '67
GROSSMAN, Edward
Ascent to Zion. New Repub 157:30-2 N 18 '67
Jewish state. Commentary 43:88-9 F '67
Rough cure for adolescence. Harper 234:69-72
My '67
GROSSMAN, Harold J.
State of the American cocktail. House B 109:
196-7 Ap '67
GROSSO, Gerald H.
Cave life on the Palouse; with biographical
sketch. Natur Hist 76:5, 38-43 F '67
GROSVENOR, Melville Bell
Journey into the living world of the Bible.
Nat Geog Mag 132:494-507 O '67
White Mist cruises to wreck-haunted St
Pierre and Miquelon. Nat Geog Mag 132:
378-419 S '67
Your society offers four new books. Nat
Geog Mag 131:868-75 Je '67
GROSVENOR, Robert
Cantilevered rainbow. D. Bourdon. il Art N
66:28-31+ Sum '67
GROTH, John
Artist and the camera-John Groth. il U S
Camera 30:62-5 N '67
GROTHMANN, Carl
Japanese Wankel-powered car. Pop Sci 190:
81-4 Ap '67
GROTZ, George
How not to buy an early American dry sink.
Time 89:76-7 Ja 27 '67
GROUND communications. See Radio communi-
cation, Underground
GROUND control approach system. See Air-
ports—Traffic control
GROUND covers. See Cover plants
GROUND effect machines
Bell expanding air cushion vehicle effort. M.
L. Yaffee. il Aviation W 86:61+ Mr 20 '67
DOT to build air cushion research vehicle.
H. Taylor. Aero Tech 21:17-18 O 23 '67
Flying saucer from earth. il Sci N 91:453
My 13 '67
Hovering closer to success; hovercraft. il Time
89:42-3 Je 2 '67
Leading international ground effect machines;
specifications (cont) Aviation W 86:215 Mr
6 '67
Skip 1 air cushion vehicle undergoes tests;
skimmer investigation platform . D. A.
Brown. il Aviation W 86:60-1+ My 15 '67
Tiger sharks strike in the Vietnam swamps.
W. Cloud. il Pop Mech 128:131-4+ N '67
Whither hovercraft? il Sci N 92:176 Ag 19
'67
GROUND schools. See Aviation schools
GROUND support equipment. See Ground sup-
port systems (space flight)
GROUND support systems (space flight)
New range instrumentation system opera-
tional soon; air force eastern test range
il Tech W 20:34 My 22 '67
GROUND transportation, High speed. See
Transportation, High speed
GROUND water. See Water, Underground
GROUNDCOVERS. See Cover plants
GROUNDING (electricity) See Electric currents
—Grounding

GROUP conflict. See Social conflict
GROUP psychotherapy
How California is licking drug addiction. I.
Ross. Read Digest 91:138-42 S '67
In my opinion; maybe you should have your
head examined. M. Halas. Seventeen 26:22
Ap '67
Reporter at large. R. Adler. New Yorker
43:55-8+ Ap 15 '67
Tell your troubles to the group. F. R.
Schreiber and M. Herman. il Sci Digest 61:
60-4 My '67
Therapy for families. Sci N 91:246 Mr 11 '67
A way out for homosexuals. S. B. Hadden.
Harper 234:107-8+ Mr '67; Discussion. 234:
4+ My '67
See also
Family psychotherapy
GROUP reading. See Books and reading—Read-
ing aloud
GROUPING by ability. See Ability grouping
in education
GROUPS (sociology)
See also
Age groups
GROUPS, Age. See Age groups
GROUSE
Dawn rendezvous on the lek. P. A. Johns-
gard. il Natur Hist 76:16-21 Mr '67
Enjoying nature; a date with the drum-m-
m-e-r-r. H. S. Buyukmihci. il Audubon 69:
83-7 Mr '67
Fool hen of the Rockies. B. Gabriel. il Nat
Parks Mag 41:8-9 Ag '67
Grouse oddities. B. L. Spiller. il Field & S
72:46-7+ N '67
See also
Prairie chickens
GROUSE shooting
And don't never count your shells. T. Janes.
il Outdoor Life 140:52-3+ O '67
Rough ruffs. D. N. Keller. il Field & S 72:
138-41 O '67
GROUTT, John
On being single in South Bend. Commonweal
86:600-1 S 29 '67
GROVE, Noel
New grain you may be growing. Farm J 91:
44P+ S '67
GROVE, Richard
Museums come alive. Am Ed 3:9-10 Ap '67
GROVE press
Bootleg Secret life draws Grove suit. Pub W
191:80 F 27 '67
Grove, Harper both issue Russian novel, Oct.
4. Pub W 192:45-6 S 18 '67
Master and Margarita; the implicit contro-
versy. Pub W 192:33-4 O 2 '67
Sex in the syllabus. J. H. Plumb. Sat R 50:
27-8 Mr 25 '67; Reply. B. Rosset. 50:26 Ap 29
'67
GROVER, Lee. See Grover, R. jt. auth.
GROVER, Ray, and Grover, Lee
Mt Washington glass company. Hobbies 72:
74-5+ Ap '67
GROVES, Brenton R.
Computer-generated motion pictures. Science
155:1662-3 Mr 31 '67
GROVES, Mary
Open letter to the father of a boy who won't
get his hair cut. Good H 165:62+ N '67
GROVES, William E. and Kempner, E. S.
Amino acid coding in sarcina lutea and
saccharomyces cerevisiae. bibliog Science
156:387-90 Ap 21 '67
GROWTH
See also
Children—Growth and development
Maturity
Regeneration (biology)
Stature
GROWTH (plants)
Isoprenoid biosynthesis in a cell-free system
from pea shoots. J. E. Graebe. bibliog il
Science 157:73-5 Jl 7 '67
Phycomyces sporangiophores; fungal stretch
receptors. D. S. Dennison and C. C. Roth.
il Science 156:1386-8 Je 9 '67
See also
Differentiation (botany)
Growth promoting substances (plants)
Tree rings
GROWTH, Economic. See Economic develop-
ment
GROWTH hormones. See Hormones
GROWTH inhibiting substances (animals)
Human fibroblasts infected with rubella virus
produce a growth inhibitor. S. A. Plotkin
and A. Vaheri. bibliog il Science 156:659-61
My 5 '67

GROWTH inhibiting substances (fungi)
Nobiletin is main fungistat in tangerines resistant to mal secco. A. Ben-Aziz. bibliog il Science 155:1026-7 F 24 '67
GROWTH inhibiting substances (insects)
Conversion of beta sitosterol to cholesterol blocked in an insect by hypocholesterolemic agents. J. A. Svoboda and W. E. Robbins. bibliog il Science 156:1637-8 Je 23 '67
GROWTH inhibiting substances (plants)
Dormin (abscisin II) inhibitor of plant DNA synthesis? J. van Overbeek and others. bibliog il Science 156:1497-9 Je 16 '67
See also
Trichlorophenoxyacetic acid
GROWTH of children. See Children—Growth and development
GROWTH of cities and towns. See Cities and towns—Growth
GROWTH promoting substances (plants)
Growth regulators, how they work for you. C. E. Sommers. il Suc Farm 65:44 Je '67
Plant growth regulation; report on seminar. A. Lang. Science 157:589-92 Ag 4 '67
See also
Colchicine
Trichlorophenoxyacetic acid
GRUBAR, Francis
Gentlemanly genre. Art N 66:32-5 My '67
GRUBER, Murray. See Bartimole. R. S. jt. auth.
GRUBER, Ruth
Heroism of Staszek Jackowski. Sat R 50:19-21+ Ap 15 '67
GRUEN, John
Where is new Bohemia going? Vogue 150:101+ Ag 1 '67
GRUENIG, D. E. See Craigie, J. S. jt. auth.
GRUENINGER, Walter F.
Phonograph records. See issues of Consumer bulletin
GRUENWALD, Andrew
Drinking water from sewage? Am City 82:92-3 Mr '67
GRUMBACH, Doris
Silent singers. Commonweal 87:468-70 Ja 19 '68
GRÜMMER, Elisabeth
Black sheep; interview, ed. by A. M. Lingg. por Opera N 31:27 Mr 25 '67
GRUNDFEST, Harry. See Ozeki, M. jt. auth.
GRUNDY, Kenneth W.
Africa in the world arena. bibliog f Cur Hist 52:129-35+ Mr '67
GRUNER, Wayne R.
Graduate student stipends; excerpts from seminar, May 1965. Science 157:1530-3 S 29 '67
GRUNFELD, Frederic V.
Eine kleine carbon copy. Reporter 36:44-5 Ja 26 '67
Family of twang. Reporter 36:39-40+ Ap 20 '67
Guitar. Horizon 9:80-9 Sum '67
On account of the schingderassa. Reporter 36:43-4 Je 15 '67
Some place to hide. Reporter 37:32-4 N 30 '67
GSCHEIDLE, Gertrude Elizabeth
Shakeup in Chicago: Gscheidle resigns. Library J 92:2698 Ag '67
GUADALAJARA, Mexico
Business shakes up a lotus land. il Bsns W p88-90+ Ja 13 '68
It's a great day in Guadalajara; Revolution day. il Sunset 139:36 N '67
Most Mexican city, Guadalajara! B. McDowell. il Nat Geog Mag 131:412-41 Mr '67
GUADALUPE MOUNTAINS NATIONAL PARK
New Guadalupe Mountains National Park. N. N. Dodge. il Nat Parks Mag 41:4-7 F '67
GUADELOUPE (island)
Flamboyant Guadeloupe. R. Gary. il Holiday 42:54-9+ Ag '67
Looping Guadeloupe. E. T. Juckett. il Travel 127:50-3+ Ap '67
GUAM
Guam. M. Herr. il Holiday 42:56-61+ Jl '67
See also
Birds—Guam
GUAM conference, 1967
B-52's move to Thai bases; from Guam to Thailand. il Sr Schol 90:17-18 Ap 7 '67
Jet extension of the oval office. H. Sidey. il Life 62:28D Mr 31 '67
Ky stole the show. Nation 204:418 Ap 3 '67
Mr Johnson goes to Guam. il Newsweek 69:27-30 Mr 27 '67
No letup in Vietnam: strategy after Guam. il U S News 62:25-8 Ap 3 '67
Pulling together. il Time 89:17-18 Mr 31 '67
Strictly business. il Time 89:13-14 Mr 24 '67
Trip to Guam, and a no from Ho. il Newsweek 69:25-8 Ap 3 '67

U.S. and Vietnamese leaders confer at Guam; remarks, statements, exchange of toasts; with joint communique, March 20-21, 1967. L. B. Johnson; Nguyen-van-Thieu; M. F. L. Guerrero. Dept State Bul 56:586-94 Ap 10 '67
GUAMBIAN Indians. See Indians of South America—Colombia
GUANAJUATO, Mexico
Mexican classic; Teatro Juarez. C. Bailey. il Opera N 31:6 F 18 '67
GUANINE
Crystal structure of the 1 : 1 complex of 5-fluorouracil and 9-ethylhypoxanthine. S. H. Kim and A. Rich. bibliog il Science 158:1046-8 N 24 '67
Guanine nucleotide associated with the protein of the outer fibers of flagella and cilia. R. E. Stevens and others. bibliog il Science 156:1606-8 Je 23 '67
GUARANTEE of wages. See Wages—Dismissal wage
GUARANTEED income. See Income
GUARANTEED wages. See Wages—Annual wage
GUARANTEES. See Guaranty of goods
GUARANTY. See Warranty
GUARANTY of earnings. See Wages—Annual wage
GUARANTY of goods
How good is that guarantee? C. B. Hicks. il Pop Mech 127:128-30+ F '67
Lifetime guarantees, gift or gimmick? M. A. Brice. il Duns R 90:65-6 N '67
They guarantee confusion at least; Maspeth, N.Y., store of Strauss stores corporation. Consumer Rep 32:351 Jl '67
GUARD rails. See Roads—Safety guards
GUARDIAN and ward
Who will look out for the kids if something happens to you? il Changing T 21:37-8 My '67
GUATEMALA
See also
Guerrillas—Guatemala

Description and travel
Fortnight in Guatemala. J. Egan. Atlan 219:128-32 Ap '67
If you like traveling south of the border, Guatemala is a new and different experience. il Sunset 139:32-4+ O '67

Politics and government
Viet Nam in the Americas? S. G. Slappey. il Nations Bsns 55:35-7+ My '67
GUATEMALA CITY
Guatemala's M&M; municipal and marimba; ed. by P. D. Eimon. il Am City 82:136+ My '67
GUBERNATORIAL campaigns. See Political campaigns
GUBERNATORIAL candidates. See Candidates, Political
GUENZI, W. D. and Beard, W. E.
Anaerobic biodegradation of DDT to DDD in soil. bibliog Science 156:1116-17 My 26 '67
GUERNSEY, John
Small school, big curriculum. Am Ed 3:11+ O '67
Teens sound off. Am Ed 3:24-6+ S '67
GUÉRON, J.
Lessons to be learned from Euratom. Bul Atomic Sci 23:38-41 Mr '67
La GUERRA; opera. See Rossellini, R.
GUERRILLA warfare
Military appraisal of the threat to U.S. cities. R. B. Rigg. U S News 64:68-71 Ja 15 '68
GUERRILLAS
Africa
Africa's guerrillas extend their fight. A. Delius. il Reporter 37:38-40 O 5 '67

Asia, Southeastern
Greater S.E. Asia guerrilla activity seen. C. Brownlow. Aviation W 86:39 Ja 30 '67

Bolivia
Case of Régis Debray. Newsweek 70:47-8 Ag 7 '67
Case of Régis Debray. il Time 90:24 S 1 '67
Convincing the cynics; campaign to flush out Communist guerrillas. il Newsweek 69:43-4 Ap 24 '67
Debray convicted. il Sr Schol 91:20 D 7 '67
Guerrillas without Guevara. R. Peter. Nat R 19:1332 N 28 '67
Guevara, Debray and the CIA. R. Gott. il Nation 205:521-30 N 20 '67

GUERRILLAS—Bolivia—*Continued*
Guevara: new martyr, or a symbol of Communist failure? il U S News 63:20 O 23 '67
Latin America: how many Vietnams? D. James. Nat R 19:949-51 S 5 '67
Legacy of Che Guevara. N. Gall. bibliog f Commentary 44:31-5 D '67
Moral of Bolivia. Nat R 19:1158+ O 31 '67
Operation Cynthia. il Time 90:29-30 Jl 28 '67
Unwitting betrayal. il Time 90:33-4 N 24 '67
What 100 Castro-type guerrillas can do. il U S News 62:84-5 Je 26 '67

Guatemala
Viet Nam in the Americas? S. G. Slappey. il Nations Bsns 55:35-7+ My '67

Latin America
Castro's targets; Fidel Castro attempting to export his revolution to other Latin American countries. il Time 89:36 My 19 '67
Cracking down on Castro; OAS resolutions. Nation 205:324-5 O 9 '67
Havana: fanning the guerrilla flames; meeting of the Organization for Latin American solidarity. il Newsweek 70:33-4 Ag 14 '67
Hot potato; Debray captured by government forces in Bolivia. Newsweek 69:61 My 8 '67
Latin lyricism at the foreign ministers meeting. N. Miller. New Repub 157:12 O 7 '67
Legacy of Che Guevara. N. Gall. bibliog f Commentary 44:31-44 D '67
Report: Latin-American guerrillas. B. Lando. Atlan 220:26+ D '67
What Castro is plotting: the fight for a hemisphere. il U S News 63:42-3 O 9 '67
Wild cry from Havana: more revolutions; Latin American solidarity organization conference. il Life 63:30-1 Ag 18 '67

Middle East
Unusual occupation; activities in occupied lands. il Time 90:19 D 29 '67

Nicaragua
Sandino affair, by N. Macaulay. Review Bul Atomic Sci 23:56-7 Je '67. W. F. Barber

Thailand
How the guerrillas came to Koh Noi. P. Braestrup. il N Y Times Mag p30-1+ D 10 '67
Northeast Thailand: tomorrow's Viet Nam? J. L. S. Girling. For Affairs 46:388-97 Ja '68
Slap against the reds. Time 90:37 S 15 '67

Venezuela
Cuban intervention cited in report. Américas 19:45 S '67
Father and son. il Newsweek 69:59 Ap 10 '67

Vietnam (Democratic Republic)
See also
Vietnamese war, 1957—Guerrillas

GUERRY, Alex, 1918-
Guide to decision-making. Duns R 90:53+ N '67

GUEST, Anthony Haden-. See Haden-Guest, A.

GUEST, Winston Frederick Churchill
Caught short. il por Time 90:49 D 8 '67

GUEST houses
Multipurpose guest houses. il House & Gard 132:92-5 Jl '67

GUEST ranches. See Ranches

GUEST rooms
Branch library for your guest room. M. M. Hemingway. il House & Gard 131:185-6 My '67
Instant guestroom. E. Kinard. il House B 109:106-7+ Ag '67

GUEST speakers. See Public speaking

GUESTS
Having houseguests in summer. Am Home 70:116-17 Jl '67
See also
Entertaining

GUESTS, Government. See Government entertaining

GUEVARA, Ernesto
Bidding for Che; publishers bid for diary. Time 90:58+ D 15 '67
Bolivian pictures of missing Che Guevara. il pors Life 63:32 O 6 '67
Ché Guevara: the best way to die. J. Yglesias. Nation 205:463-5 N 6 '67
Che Guevara: the end of a revolutionary. il pors Newsweek 70:64+ O 23 '67

Ché slain. il por Sr Schol 91:20 O 26 '67
Death in the jungle. Nation 205:390 O 23 '67
Death of a dreamer. Commonweal 87:103 O 27 '67
Death of Ché Guevara. B. Kumm. New Repub 157:13-15 N 11 '67
Elusive guerrilla. il pors Time 90:32 S 29 '67
End of a legend. il pors Time 90:26-7 O 20 '67
Geurrillas without Guevara. R. Peter. Nat R 19:1332 N 28 '67
Guevara, Debray and the CIA. R. Gott. il Nation 205:521-30 N 20 '67
Guevara: new martyr, or a symbol of Communist failure. il pors U S News 63:20 O 23 '67
Is Ché Guevara in Bolivia? il por Sr Schol 91:6 O 12 '67
Latin America: how many Vietnams? D. James. Nat R 19:949-51 S 5 '67
Legacy of Che Guevara. N. Gall. bibliog f Commentary 44:31-44 D '67
Mystery man Guevara, bearded or beardless? dead or alive? pors U S News 62:24 My 1 '67
Where's Che? il por Newsweek 70:46 O 2 '67
Where's Guevara? U S News 63:14 Jl 17 '67

GUGGENHEIM, Solomon R, museum, New York. See Solomon R. Guggenheim museum, New York

GUIANA, FRENCH. See French Guiana

GUIDANCE. See Personnel service in education; Vocational guidance

GUIDE books. See Guidebooks

GUIDE Michellin. See Guidebooks

GUIDEBOOKS
America: stars and gripes; Guide Julliard to American restaurants and hostelries. il Newsweek 69:53-4 My 22 '67
Breadwinner on tour; guidebooks for the business man. H. Sutton. Sat R 50:42-3 Jl 15 '67
Coordinated production for Expo 67 guide book. il Pub W 191:99-101 My 1 '67
Educated eater's Baedeker. H. Sutton. Sat R 50:30-1 Jl 1 '67
Fault is in the stars; Guide Michelin. A. C. Schmidt. il Reporter 37:46+ S 7 '67
Four for the road. H. Sutton. Sat R 50:66+ My 20 '67
Guidebooks for Mexico travelers. Sunset 139:41 O '67
Here are books for Sierra enthusiasts. Sunset 138:38+ Je '67
It's a bargain at $1.95; travel guides as research aids. J. A. Sainsbury. Writer 80:26+ N '67
London dossier, by L. Deighton. Review Life 63:13 Jl 28 '67. J. Hicks
Michelin whose inn? who's out? Travel 127:16-17 F '67
On tour with the overprivileged. H. Sutton. il Sat R 50:46-7 Je 24 '67
Profiles: T. H. Fielding. J. McPhee. New Yorker 43:32-4+ Ja 6 '68
Some salty observations on the way we do things here; excerpts from the Guide Julliard de New York. H. Gault and C. Millau. Life 63:136 S 15 '67
Twenty years of travel writing; Michelin, Baedeker, or bust. P. J. C. Friedlander. il Sat R 50:40+ Ap 22 '67
Two brightly breezy arbiters; Guide Julliard de Paris. il Life 63:129-30+ S 15 '67
Vacation guide to Washington, D.C; excerpts from Washington, the New York times' guide to the Nation's capital. B. Dubivsky. il Seventeen 26:130-1+ Ap '67
View the local architectural marvels. il Changing T 21:20-1 Je '67

Bibliography
Travel, bound. S. Robinson. il McCalls 94:40+ F '67

GUIDED missile industries
Europe pushing low-altitude anti-aircraft capabilities; surface-to-air weapons. il Aviation W 87:48-9+ Jl 3 '67

GUIDED missiles
Annual world aerospace encyclopedia 1967. il Aero Tech 21:21-32+ Jl 31 '67
Arms: is U.S. lead shrinking? il U S News 63:61 S 25 '67
Army studies funding request for Dragon missile production. Aviation W 87:81 Ag 21 '67
Astrolog; current status of U.S. missile and space programs. il Aero Tech 21:39+ Ja 1 '68
China; missile program. Time 91:34+ Ja 5 '68

GUIDED missiles—Defenses—*Continued*
New missile race? importance of U.S. and the Soviet Union seeking a moratorium on ABM defense systems. H. Brandon. Sat R 50:14+ Ja 28 '67
New shape of Armageddon. il Bsns W p56-8+ F 11 '67
New U.S. ICBM would cost $10 billion. M. Getler. Tech W 20:14 Ap 3 '67
New view on missiles. U S News 62:15 Ap 3 '67
Nike-X contracts expected by early 1968; anti-Chinese missile defense deployment. il Aviation W 87:16-18 S 25 '67
Nike-X system gets off the pad. il Bsns W p35-7 S 23 '67
Notes and comment; anti-ballistic-missile, or ABM, system. New Yorker 43:33-5 S 30 '67
On walking softly. W. J. Coughlin. Tech W 20:58 My 15 '67
Pastore's ABM plea; excerpts from remarks. J. O. Pastore. Aviation W 87:21 S 18 '67
Perplexing ABM problem. R. Hotz. Aviation W 87:21 O 23 '67
Powerhouse behind the atom: Joint committee's latest goal: development of U.S. antiballistic missile system. il Bsns W p 160-2 S 16 '67
Proposals due on Seaborne ABM system. il Aviation W 87:43+ Jl 17 '67
Raytheon gets nod on Sam-D development. W. Andrews. Tech W 20:18-19 My 29 '67
RFP's due soon from DOD on missile interceptor stage. Tech W 20:15 Ap 24 '67
Scientists differ on use of ABM system. B. M. Elson. Aviation W 88:79+ Ja 8 '68
Secretary McNamara comments on risks of anti-ballistic-missile system; interview, ed. by J. Mossman, February 15, 1967. R. S. McNamara. Dept State Bul 56:442-7 Mr 20 '67
Senate group to evaluate Nike-X decision. Aviation W 87:18-19 S 25 '67
Service secretaries support area defense Nike-X ABM. Tech W 20:15 My 8 '67
Shifting equation of nuclear defense. R. J. Whalen. il Fortune 75:84-7+ Je 1 '67
Shotgun missile: how it affects U.S.-Soviet balance of terror. U S News 64:8 Ja 8 '68
Soviets prepare space weapon for 1968; with editorial comment. C. Brownlow. il Aviation W 87:21. 30-1 N 13 '67
Spartan anti-MIRV capabilities under study. W. Andrews. il Aero Tech 21:15-16 O 9 '67
Special report: ballistic missile defense; symposium. il Aviation W 87:51-7+ O 23 '67
Strategic sophistry; administration's decision to deploy a thin anti-ballistic missile defense system. Nat R 19:1051-2 O 3 '67
Strengthened U.S. ICBM forces to offset Soviet missile defense. P. J. Klass. Aviation W 86:27-8 F 6 '67
SAM-D fiscal 1968 funds slashed again. Aero Tech 21:10 N 6 '67
SAM-D will have advanced guidance. il Aero Tech 21:11 O 23 '67
Terror unbalanced? Sci Am 217:52 N '67
Thin or thick ABMs for U.S? Sr Schol 91: 38 O 5 '67
$30-billion Nike-X debate; special report. il Bsns W p76-80+ Ja 14 '67
Timing China's bombs; fuel to anti-missile debate. Bsns W p31 Ag 5 '67
Tipping the balance of terror? U.S. to deploy anti-ballistic-missile defenses. il Newsweek 70:19-21 O 2 '67
U.S. ABM would imperil test ban treaty. R. Pay. Tech W 20:14-15 Mr 20 '67
USAF, industry studying ABM concepts. Aviation W 86:84-5+ My 15 '67
U.S. discusses effect of ABM deployment on arms control efforts; statements, September 19, 1967. A. S. Fisher. Dept State Bul 57:543-5 O 23 '67
U.S. may revise timing on ABM. D. C. Winston. Aviation W 86:22-3 My 15 '67
U.S. nuclear strategy; address, September 18, 1967. R. S. McNamara. Vital Speeches 33: 738-43 O 1 '67; Same with title Dynamics of nuclear strategy. Dept State Bul 57:443-51 O 9 '67; Same with discussion. Bul Atomic Sci 23:18-31 D '67
U.S. takes stock of its arsenal; aftermath of decision to build a Nike-X system. il Bsns W p36-7 S 30 '67
U.S.'s trump in missile defense; ballisticglide reentry vehicle. il Bsns W p40 N 25 '67
Weapons and world stability; excerpts from address. H. Agnew. Aviation W 86:11 Mr 27 '67

Who rules aerospaces. J. Burnham. Nat R 19:1317 N 28 '67
X-rays, missiles and anti-missiles. Nat R 19: 557 My 30 '67

Electronic equipment
CDC readies Phoenix computer production; fire-control computer for air-to-air missile system. C. D. LaFond. il Tech W 20:24-5 My 8 '67
Improved Sergeant missile electronics ready for test. il Aero Tech 21:51-2 Jl 17 '67
Nike-X advances microcircuit technology. il Aviation W 87:130-1+ O 23 '67

Equipment
Lanyard system dominates $50 million umbilical market. Aero Tech 21:36-7 O 23 '67
Lockheed, navy ready Polaris logistic support streamlining. R. Lindsey. Aero Tech 21:42 S 11 '67

Launching
Research cannon facing financial troubles; Project HARP. R. Barnhart. il Tech W 20:38 Mr 6 '67
Soviet Sandal launch shown in sequence. il Aviation W 88:65 Ja 15 '68
Supersonic Martlet/Scramjet set for first flight in Canada; Project HARP research program to gather atmospheric data. R. Barnhart. il Tech W 20:22-3 My 8 '67

Launching from airplanes
Cathode ray display speeds SRAM data; USAF short-range attack missile. R. G. O'Lone. il Aviation W 86:74-5+ Mr 13 '67
CDC readies Phoenix computer production; fire-control computer for air-to-air missile system. C. D. LaFond. il Tech W 20:24-5 My 8 '67
DOD may use metric system for Maverick; air force's air-to-ground missile program. W. Andrews. Tech W 21:14-15 Jl 3 '67
Navy studies F-111B offensive missions. D. C. Winston. Aviation W 87:29 O 23 '67
Phoenix F-111B test scheduled by navy. Aviation W 88:18 Ja 1 '68
Plans for four new missiles pace expected funding climb. H. Taylor and others. il Tech W 20:101-2+ Mr 27 '67
Services' tactical missile budget requests detailed: development of Condor missile system. Tech W 20:18 F 6 '67

Launching from ships
ASMS proposal requests due in August. W. Andrews. Tech W 20:14-15 Je 12 '67
NATO group working on memorandum for sea sparrow; system for point defense of ships. Aero Tech 21:15 Ja 1 '68

Launching from submarine boats
Lockheed, navy ready Polaris logistic support streamlining. R. Lindsey. Aero Tech 21:42 S 11 '67
Poseidon, new chapter in missilery. H. W. Baldwin. il Read Digest 92:120-4 Ja '68
Withdraw missile submarines? E. W. Crawford. Bul Atomic Sci 23:39 N '67

Launching pads
Atlas F silo will be converted to high energy impaction unit. Aviation W 86:81-3 Ja 30 '67

Manufacture
DOD may use metric system for Maverick; air force's air-to-ground missile program. W. Andrews. Tech W 21:14-15 Jl 3 '67
Second sourcing set for ABM components. Aero Tech 21:10 O 23 '67

Materials
Cheap, simple motor case method shown. J. F. Judge. il Tech W 20:22 Mr 20 '67
Filament methods called best for missiles. J. F. Judge. il Tech W 20:34-6 Ap 10 '67

Names
Awakening Olympus. M. Roshwald. il Nation 204:147-8 Ja 30 '67

Propulsion
Filament methods called best for missiles. J. F. Judge. il Tech W 20:34-6 Ap 10 '67

Protective measures
See also
Guided missiles—Shielding (heat)
Guided missiles—Shielding (radiation)

Shielding (heat)
New Melpar system protects missile hardware from heat. il Tech W 21:31 Jl 3 '67

GUIDED missiles—*Continued*

Shielding (radiation)

Two new tactical weapons taking shape; air-to-ground missile and anti-radiation weapon. W. Andrews. il Aero Tech 21:14-15 Jl 17 '67

Terminology

Fighting a nuclear war of the words; Strangelovisms. il Newsweek 69:47 Mr 27 '67

Testing

China's missile threat; closer than expected. il U S News 63:8 Ag 14 '67

Cosmos flights seen ICBM aids. P. J. Klass. Aviation W 87:26-7 O 16 '67

Crucial testing phase nears for Phoenix. B. Miller. il Aviation W 87:59-60+ S 11 '67

Nike-X system to be tested at Kwajalein Aviation W 87:77 O 23 '67

Sandia designs centrifuge for 100-lb. units. W. E. Wilks. il Aero Tech 21:45 Ag 28 '67

Shillelagh passes rigorous service tests. R. Pay. il Tech W 20:28-30 My 8 '67

GUIDED missiles, Atomic powered

Testing

Is Peking putting missiles on its subs? il Bsns W p 13 D 30 '67

GUIDES

Face to face with a north woods guide; ed. by T. Merkert. B. Rom. il Seventeen 26: 58 Jl '67

On renting a French aristocrat; Hôtesses internationales. il Time 89:50 My 19 '67

GUIGNARD, Jaqueline De Maeyer-. See De Maeyer-Guignard, J.

GUILES, Fred Lawrence

Norma Jean; excerpt. Ladies Home J 84: 171-6 N '67

GUILFORD, Joan S.

Hidden habits of women. C. B. Hicks. il Todays Health 45:28-31+ D '67

GUILLÉN, Jorge

Hispanic chronicle. W. Barnstone. Poetry 111: 46-55 O '67

GUILLOU, Claudine

Twelve-minute makeup. il pors Mlle 64:156-9 Mr '67

GUIMARRA, Joseph

Cesar Chavez's biggest battle. D. Adair. Nation 205:627-8 D 11 '67

GUIMPES and saddles; drama. See Molloy, E. A.

GUINEA

Politics and government

Guinea. R. J. H. Church. bibliog il Focus 17:1-6 Mr '67

GUINN, John W.

Back from the dead. il por Newsweek 70:31A D 4 '67

Johnny redivivus. il por Time 90:16 D 1 '67

GUINNESS, Desmond

Georgian. New Yorker 43:41-2 O 7 '67

GUITAR, Mary Anne

Seven sisters: is the ivy overgrown? Mlle 65:268-9+ Ag '67

Tomorrow's stars: on campus today. Mlle 66: 158-9+ N '67

Why settle for less? Am Home 70:52-3+ S '67

GUITAR

Guitar. F. V. Grunfeld. il Horizon 9:80-9 Sum '67

GUITAR, Electronic. See Musical instruments, Electronic

GUITAR music

See also

Phonograph records—Guitar music

GUITARISTS

Guitar. F. V. Grunfeld. il Horizon 9:80-9 Sum '67

See also

Bream, J.

Farlow, T.

GUITHER, Harold. See Mueller, A. G; Wilken, D. F. jt. auths.

GUITTON, Jean

(ed) See Paul VI, pope. Conversations with Pope Paul VI

GULDA, Friedrich

Musical matchmaker. il por Time 90:42+ Ag 18 '67

GULF American land corporation

Selling land in Florida. J. Hunter. New Repub 157:21-3 S 2 '67

GULF and Western Industries, Incorporated

Cecil B. DeBluhdorn?; new owner of Paramount pictures. il Newsweek 69:82 My 29 '67

G&W loves Lucy. il Newsweek 69:70 F 27 '67

Into new territory; takeover of Desilu. il Time 89:86 F 24 '67

Multimillion reach of Wall Street's mad Austrian. C. Welles. il Life 62:43-4+ Mr 10 '67

GULF oil corporation

Are we being en-gulfed? investment in Reston, Va. W. Von Eckardt. New Repub 157: 21-3 D 9 '67; Reply. F. Flaxman. 157:36 D 23 '67

Can new towns meet a budget? ouster of R. E. Simon. il Bsns W p 103-4 N 18 '67

Gulf buys itself a new town; Reston, Va. Bsns W p50 S 9 '67

GULF states

Description and travel

New Orleans and the Gulf states. il Bet Hom & Gard 45:82-3 Mr '67

GULF STREAM

Capsule history of the Gulf Stream. T. H. Lineaweaver, 3d. Holiday 42:91-2+ N '67

GULICK, Luther

Joseph Prendergast leaves NRPA. Parks & Rec 2:30 Jl '67

GULLS

Visual isolation in gulls. N. G. Smith. il Sci Am 217:94-102 O '67

GUMAER, Harry T.

School librarian shortage in New Jersey. por ALA Bul 61:555-7 My '67

GUMMERE, Richard M. Jr

Toward a new breed of librarians. Wilson Lib Bul 41:810-13 Ap '67

GUMPERZ, John J.

Language and communication. bibliog f Ann Am Acad 373:219-31 S '67

GUMS (anatomy)

Diseases

See also

Periodontia

GUMS and resins

X-ray diffraction study of some fossil and modern resins. J. W. Frondel. il Science 155:1411-13 Mr 17 '67

GUN cabinets. See Cabinets (furniture)

GUN control legislation. See Firearms—Laws and regulations

GUN magazines. See Periodicals—United States

GUN sights. See Firearms—Sights

GUN stocks. See Gunstock

GUNBOAT and Madge; story. See O'Hara, J.

GUNCHEON, June

To make people listen. Nations Bsns 55:96+ O '67

GUNDER, Robert J.

Caribbean vacation on a budget. Redbook 128:48+ Mr '67

GUNDERSHEIMER, Werner L.

Dark deeds and evil books. Reporter 36:39-40 My 18 '67

Journey to synthesis. Reporter 36:58-9 Mr 9 '67

Way to savagery. Reporter 36:44+ Je 29 '67

GUNNERY

Flinching and flinchers. J. O'Connor. il Outdoor Life 140:72+ Ag '67

GUNNISON RIVER

See also

Black Canyon of the Gunnison National Monument

GUNS (ordnance) See Machine guns

GUNS (small arms) See Firearms; Pistols; Revolvers; Shotguns

GUNS, Naval. See Ordnance, Naval

GUNSHIPS. See Airplanes, Military—Armaments

GUNSTOCKS

Checker your own gunstock. W. C. Lammey. il Pop Mech 127:176-80+ Mr '67

GUNTER, Elder

Ex-city manager named HUD deputy for housing assistance. Am City 82:47 D '67

GUNTER, Pete A.

Farewell to Texas; review. Liv Wildn 31: 48-9 Spr '67

GUNTHER, John

Inside Brazil; excerpt from Inside South America. Read Digest 90:119-24 My '67

Inside London. Harper 235:48-54 Jl; 79-82 Ag '67; Same abr. Read Digest 91:169-72+ O '67

about

Behind the lines. por Read Digest 90:25-6 My '67

GUNTHER, Max
American scientist: man or superman? Sat Eve Post 240:30-6+ D 16 '67
Building a framework for an article. Writer 80:14-16+ Ag '67
How to find article ideas. Writer 80:24-7 Ap '67
How we feel about our money. Sat Eve Post 240:72-5 D 30 '67
Why children commit suicide. Sat Eve Post 240:86-9 Je 17 '67

GUNTHER, Walter
Man for the aged. Newsweek 69:56+ Je 5 '67
Successful fraud. il por Time 89:54 Je 9 '67

GUREVITZ, Bernard H.
Framing makes the difference. Design 68:36-8 Mr '67

GURLEY, Henry T.
Why does your gas mileage drop in the winter? Pop Sci 190:168-9 F '67

GURNEY, Dan
Drivin' with Dan; questions and answers. See issues of Popular mechanics

about
Apple pie, mom and Mr Gurney. B. Ottum. por Sports Illus 26:28-9 Je 26 '67
Glorious double. B. Ottum. il Sports Illus 26: 14-17 Je 19 '67

GURNEY, Roy
AAUP: short-run production for books and journals; summary of address, June 12, 1967. por Pub W 192:66-7+ Jl 3 '67

GUROFF, Gordon, and others
Hydroxylation-induced migration: the NIH shift. bibliog Science 157:1524-30 S 29 '67

GUSTAFSON, John Kyle
Last gold rush. N. Willatt. il por Duns R 90:41-3+ S '67

GUSTAITIS, Rasa
Columbia's neighbors: the slums of academe. Reporter 37:34-8 O 5 '67
Private industry's factory classrooms. Reporter 37:23-4 S 7 '67
Twenty-first century comes to Montreal. Reporter 36:36-40 F 9 '67

GUSTAVUS VI, king of Sweden
H.M. King Gustaf VI Adolf of Sweden. il por Vogue 150:86-7 Ag 1 '67

GUTENBERG, Johann
Master of the playing-cards. D. Powills. il Hobbies 72:124-5+ Mr '67

GUTHEIM, Frederick
Urban condition modified. New Repub 157: 32-4 S 2 '67

GUTHMAN, Patricia R.
Castleford pottery for the American trade. Antiques 92:552-5 O '67

GUTHRIE, A. B. Jr
Loco; story. Esquire 68:122-3 N '67

GUTHRIE, Arlo
Arlo Guthrie; interview. New Yorker 43:18-21 Ja 6 '68
Woody's boy. il por Time 91:50 Ja 12 '68

GUTHRIE, Sir Giles
Brickbats at BOAC. il por Time 89:88 Mr 24 '67

GUTHRIE, Helen A.
How to feed your baby. Farm J 91:76 My '67

GUTHRIE, John R.
Single-handed fit out. il por Motor B 119: 84-5+ Mr '67

GUTHRIE, Sir Tyrone
Out of touch. por Opera N 31:8-11 F 11 '67

about
Guthrie's Shakespeare. G. Rogoff. New Repub 156:32-3 Mr 11 '67
Return of Peter Grimes. I. Kolodin. Sat R 50:57 F 4 '67

GUTHRIE, Woodrow Wilson. See Guthrie, Woody

GUTHRIE, Woody
So long, Woody, it's been good to know ya. P. Seeger. Life 63:8 N 10 '67

GUTIERREZ, Rose Mary, and Hnilica, L. S.
Tissue specificity of histone phosphorylation. bibliog Science 157:1324-5 S 15 '67

GUTKNECHT, John
Membranes of valonia ventricosa: apparent absence of water-filled pores. bibliog Science 158:787-8 N 10 '67

GUTNICK, D. L. and others
Cis-trans isomerism in naphthoquinones: interconversion and participation in oxidative phosphorylation. bibliog Science 158:1469-71 D 15 '67

GUTTER cleaners, Cattle. See Barns and stables—Equipment

GUTTERS
Try a flush gutter for large paved areas. il Am City 82:26 N '67

GUTTERS (roof)
How to maintain gutters and downspouts. M. E. Dowd. Am Home 70:146+ O '67

GUTTMANN, Allen
Deviants and Puritans. Nation 205:316-17 O 2 '67

GUTZ, Herbert
Twin meiosis and other ambivalences in the life cycle of schizosaccharomyces pombe. bibliog Science 158:796-8 N 10 '67

GUY, Frances Claiborne. See Coons, B. C. jt. auth.

GUYANA
Jungle road in Guyana. America 117:165 Ag 19 '67
See also
Birds—Guyana

Politics and government
Profile of a prime minister. E. B. Thompson. il Ebony 22:124-8+ Ap '67

GUYER, Robert A. See Bertman, B. jt. auth.

GUZMAN, Anna Emilie
Never on Mars. A. Glasser. il Sci Digest 61: 81-3 F '67

GUZZARDI, Walter, jr
Hitler's tenfold revenge. Sat R 50:42-3 F 4 '67
Management of the war: a tale of two capitals. Fortune 75:134-9+ Ap '67
Olivetti's crisis of identity. Fortune 76:92-7+ Jl '67
Washing the hate away. Sat R 50:39 Ag 5 '67

GUZZWELL, John
Dream into Treasure. Yachting 121:78-80+ Mr '67

GVISHIANI, Liūdmila Alekseevna
Ladies' day: the womenfolk at Glassboro. Time 89:17 Je 30 '67
Sudden guests at the seashore. E. S. Hughes. il McCalls 94:80-1+ S '67

GWINN, William P.
Gwinn of United aircraft. il por Fortune 77: 41 Ja '68

GWYNNE JONES, Arthur, baron Chalfont. See Chalfont, A. G. J.

GYMNASIUMS
Gym initiates master plan to expand an old school; Washington & Lee high school gymnasium, Montross, Va. il Arch Rec 142:186-7 O '67

GYMNASTICS
Gymnastics for the retarded. T. J. Denman. il Parks & Rec 2:44+ Mr '67
Winning ways of Winnipeg. J. Underwood. il Sports Illus 27:20-5 Ag 7 '67
See also
Exercise

GYMNOPÉDIES; ballet. See Ballets—Criticisms

GYMNOSPERMS
See also
Welwitschia

GYNANDROMORPHISM
Gynogenesis and triploidy in the viviparous fish poeciliopsis. R. J. Schultz. bibliog il Science 157:1564-7 S 29 '67

GYÖRGYI, Albert Szent-. See Szent-Györgyi, A.

GYPSIES. See Gipsies

GYPSIES in the United States. See Gipsies in the United States

GYPSIES' secret; drama. See Huff, B. T.

GYPSY student; story. See Schwartz, J.

GYRO compass
Gyrocompass azimuth finders challenge astronomy methods. il Tech W 20:40 Mr 20 '67
Where do you think you're going? slaved gyro compass system. A. A. Macdonald. il Flying 81:79-80 O '67

GYROCOMPASS. See Gyro compass

GYROPLANES. See Autogiros

GYROSCOPES
High-performance gyros seen from radioisotope techniques; utilizing the radioisotope field support principle. R. Pay. il Tech W 20:40-1 My 22 '67
Kearfott developing hybrid two-axis gyro for missiles. Aero Tech 21:43 D 4 '67
100-ft.-lb.-sec. momentum produced by 65-lb. CMG. il Aero Tech 21:40-1 Ag 28 '67
Toy that became a steering machine. E. A. Zadig. il Pop Sci 192:82-5+ Ja '68

GYROSCOPIC instruments
Rate gyros stablize miniature platform. P. J. Klass. il Aviation W 87:118-19+ O 9 '67
See also
Inertial guidance systems

H

H & R Block, incorporated. See Block, H. & R, incorporated
H-bombs. See Hydrogen bombs
HARP (high altitude research project) See Atmospheric research
HELP (highway emergency locating plan) See Radio communication—Emergency applications
HEW. See United States—Health, education and welfare, Department of
H. J. Heinz company. See Heinz, H. J, company
HSGT (high speed ground transport) systems. See Transportation, High speed
HUAC. See United States—Congress—House of representatives—Un-American   activities committee
HUD. See United States—Housing and urban development, Department of
H. W. Wilson company. See Wilson, H. W, company
HAACK, Robert W.
New president; interview. New Yorker 43:49 N 4 '67
about
Big board lists a chief. por Bsns W p 134 Ap 29 '67
Big board's choice. por Newsweek 69:70 My 1 '67
Changing the guard. Newsweek 70:94+ S 25 '67
Haack of the big board. il por Fortune 75:39 Je 1 '67
New no, 1 salesman. por Time 89:95 Ap 28 '67
Problems of plenty pinch the big board. il por Bsns W p 102-4+ Ag 26 '67
HAAR, Charles M.
How HUD helps mass transportation to mold our cities. por Am City 82:113-14 N '67
HAAS, Ernst
France, a go-go place for the games; photographs. Sports Illus 27:46-58 N 13 '67
HAAS, Hans G. See Narahashi, T. jt. auth.
HAAS, Joseph
Keeping out of debt to society. Sat R 50:28 Jl 8 '67
HAAST, William E.
Most snake-bitten man in the world. W. Hartley and E. Hartley .il pors Sci Digest 62:13-17 O '67
HAATAJA, Bob
Bear to be thankful for; ed. by B. East. pors Outdoor Life 140:32-5+ S '67
HABENARIAS. See Orchids
HABER, Paul
Showdown on 92nd street. B. Ottum. il por Sports Illus 27:46-7 Jl 31 '67
HABIT
Making habits work for you; excerpt from Psychology: briefer course; reprint. W. James. Read Digest 91:81-4 Ag '67
HABITABLE worlds. See Life on other planets
HABITS of animals. See Animals—Habits and behavior
HABSBURG, Otto von. See Otto, archduke of Austria
HACILAR excavations. See Turkey—Antiquities
HACK, Margherita
Latetype stars. il por Sky & Tel 33:74-6, 153-5 F-Mr '67
RU camelopardalis, a unique cepheid variable. Sky & Tel 33:350-4 Je '67
HACKER, Andrew
Blaine amendment, yes or no? N Y Times Mag p27-9+ O 1 '67
Eight questions for 1968. Sat R 51:102-3 Ja 6 '68
GOP prospects. Commentary 44:91-2 D '67
Making of a corporation president. N Y Times Mag p26-7+ Ap 2 '67
Salesman, philosopher, riot preventer. N Y Times Mag p26-7+ My 7 '67
When big business makes gifts, tax-deductible. N Y Times Mag p34-5+ N 12 '67
HACKETT, Alice Payne
Hardcover best sellers of 1966 in the U.S. book trade. Pub W 191:40-2 Ja 30 '67
HACKETT, Bobby
Jazz records. W. Balliett. New Yorker 43: 221-2+ N 25 '67
HACKETT, Walter
Christmas carol; dramatization of story by C. Dickens. Plays 27:81-90 D '67
Glorious whitewasher; dramatization of The adventures of Tom Sawyer, by Mark Twain. Plays 27:55-60 Ja '68

HACKMAN, Arthur F.
Switches: a guide to selection & application. Electr World 78:47-50+ S '67
HACKSAWS. See Saws
HADDAD, William F.
Back to the dance. Commonweal 86:332-3 Je 9 '67
HADDEN, Briton
He ran the course. il Time 89:28-33 Mr 10 '67
HADDEN, Samuel B.
A way out for homosexuals. Harper 234: 107-8+ Mr '67
HADDING, Ulrich, and Müller-Eberhard, H. J.
Complement: substitution of the terminal component in immune hemolysis by 1,10-phenanthroline. bibliog Science 157:442-3 Jl 28 '67
HADDOCK, Howard
Resourceful director provides special events program. por Parks & Rec 2:84-6 O '67
HADDON, William, Jr
Danger on the highways; interview. por U S News 63:66-9 O 16 '67
about
Horsetrading? car safety deadline. il Sr Schol 89:16-17 Ja 20 '67
LBJ's safety boss: babe in bureaucracy's jungle. A. Rothenberg. por Look 31:101-3 My 30 '67
HADEN-GUEST, Anthony
Life-styles: royalty in our time. Esquire 69: 88-91+ Ja '68
HADLOCK, Calvin F.
Build a firing-range timer. Pop Electr 26:37-9 Je '67
HADSEL, Fred L.
Africa and the world: nonalignment reconsidered; address, April 1967, with questions and answers. Ann Am Acad 372:93-104 Jl '67
HAENICHEN, Jack
Diffused transistors. por Electr World 78:41-4 Jl '67
HAESE, Günter
Balancing act. il por Time 91:57 Ja 19 '68
Günter Haese's clockworks. il por Horizon 9:62-3 Sum '67
HAFNER, E. M.
Galactic signals; excerpt from address. Bul Atomic Sci 23:50-2 Je '67
HAFSTAD, George E.
Dutch elm disease and you. Am For 73:26-7+ Je '67
Why city folks need trees. Am For 73:18-21 Ag '67
HAGAN, Charles B.
Changing face of Australia. Cur Hist 52: 295-301 My '67
HAGEDORN, George G.
Excerpt from testimony before Joint economic committee of U.S. Congress, February 20, 1967. Cong Digest 46:119+ Ap '67
HÄGER, Bengt
Music in China today. Hi Fi 17:93-8 O '67
HAGER, Philip
California's still choking. New Repub 156: 10-11 F 11 '67
HAGER house. See Hagerstown, Md.—Historic houses, etc.
HAGERSTOWN, Md.
Maps tell us where the lights are. R. E. Roulette. il Am City 82:116 Jl '67

Historic houses, etc.
Museum is opened at Maryland's historic Hager house. il Nat Parks Mag 41:21 Jl '67
HAGFISH
Genetic control of lactate dehydrogenase formation in the hagfish eptatretus stoutii. S. Ohno and others. bibliog il Science 156:96-8 Ap 7 '67
Molecular size of hagfish muscle lactate dehydrogenase. N. Arnheim, jr. and others. bibliog il Science 157:568-9 Ag 4 '67
HAGGADAH. See Passover
HAGGERTY, Patrick Eugene
Texas instruments: all systems go. J. B. Weiner. il por Duns R 89:28-31+ Ja '67
HAGGIN, Bernard H.
New records in review. See issues of Yale review
Records. Commonweal 87:86-7, 206, 383-4 O 20, N 17, D 22 '67
Toscanini reissues, a tribute at last honorably paid. Hi Fi 17:71-2 Ag '67
Toscanini treasury of historic broadcasts. Hi Fi 17:73-5 Je '67
about
Prince Uncharming. por Time 90:59 Jl 21 '67

HAGGIN memorial museum. See Stockton, Calif.—Galleries and museums

HAGINS, W. A. and McGaughy, R. E.
Molecular and thermal origins of fast photo-electric effects in the squid retina. bibliog Science 157:813-16 Ag 18 '67

HAGIOGRAPHY. See Saints

HAGIST, Barbara, and Neighbors, Fred
Fine arts festival in Tulsa. Wilson Lib Bul 42:309-11 N '67

HAGIWARA, T. and Rikitake, T.
Japanese program on earthquake prediction. bibliog Science 157:761-8 Ag 18 '67

HAGLE, Alfred D.
Large print revolution. bibliog por Library J 92:3008-10 S 15 '67

HAGLUND, Tredway
Remote areas can challenge moviemakers. Travel 128:63 D '67

HAHN, Emily
Christmas with the Walkers. New Yorker 43: 152+ My 20 '67
Pawpaw pie. New Yorker 43:47-54 Ap 15 '67
Reporter at large. New Yorker 43:38-40+ S 2; 96+ S 23; 117-18+ S 30; 170+ O 14 '67

HAHN, Eric W. and Ward, W. F.
Increased litter size in the rat X-irradiated during the estrous cycle before mating. bibliog Science 157:956-7 Ag 25 '67

HAHN, Fred E. See Ciak, J. jt. auth.

HAHN, Jan
Adrift and alone. il Yachting 122:44-6+ D '67; 123:94-5+ Ja '68

HAHN, Otto
Autobiographical notes; excerpt from A scientific autobiography. por Bul Atomic Sci 23:19-24 Mr; 22-8 Ap '67

HAHN, Paul
Top man on the laugh tour. M. Cope. il pors Sports Illus 27:34-6+ O 30 '67

HAHN, Vera D.
Decorating newsletter. See issues of American home

HAIDER, Michael Lawrence
Long-term view from the 29th floor. il por Time 90:56-9+ D 29 '67

HAIG-BROWN, Roderick
Winter steels and the fly. por Outdoor Life 140:36-9+ N '67

HAIL
Firing back at hail; suppression by antiaircraft shells. Time 90:89 O 13 '67

HAILE Selassie I, emperor of Ethiopia
Emperor of Ethiopia visits the United States; exchange of greetings, February 13, 1967; exchange of toasts, February 14, 1967. Dept State Bul 56:425-8 Mr 13 '67

about
Aging lion of Judah. C. Sterling. il Reporter 36:28-30 F 9 '67
Lonely emperor. por Time 89:37 F 24 '67
Wise man of Africa. America 116:300 Mr 4 '67

HAILEY, Oliver
Who's happy now? Criticism
Time por 90:49-50 N 17 '67

HAILS, John R. See Hoyt, J. H. jt. auth.

HAINES, Aubrey B.
Edward John Carnell: an evaluation. Christian Cent 84:751 Je 7 '67

HAINES, Edmund
Catalan spice and a new young orchestra. Hi Fi 17:MA24-5+ Ja '67
Notes from our correspondents. Hi Fi 17:18+ Ap '67
Orchestra revamped, a season in full swing. Hi Fi 17:MA24-5 Ag '67
Point of maturity. Hi Fi 17:MA24-5 Je '67
(ed) See Larrocha, A. de. Granados

HAINES, John
Red house; poem. Nation 204:438 Ap 3 '67
Wreck; poem. Nation 204:527 Ap 24 '67
about
Messages in a bottle. P. Zweig. Nation 204: 281-3 F 27 '67

HAIR
Activation analysis of soluble and fixed sodium in mammalian hair. G. S. Kennington. bibliog il Science 155:588-9 F 3 '67
Morphological changes in human scalp hair roots during deprivation of protein. R. B. Bradfield and others. bibliog il Science 157: 438-9 Jl 28 '67
Red at the top; redhead. S. Harney. il Ladies Home J 84:100-3 S '67
See also
Baldness
Hairdressing
Mustaches
Wigs

Anecdotes, facetiae, satire, etc.
Footnotes to the hair explosion. M. Macht. Sat R 50:4 S 16 '67

Care
For prettier hair. V. S. Stitt. Parents Mag 42:40 O '67
Taming the raging mane. il Mlle 65:140-1 S '67

Dyeing and bleaching
How to change your hair color without turning a hair. il Mlle 64:188-9 Ap '67
What color did you say your hair was? il Redbook 129:70-1+ S '67

HAIR curlers
Flammability test of new hair curlers; Quick hair setting rollers. il Consumer Bul 50:17 S '67
What you should know about instant hairdos; hairdo appliances. il Seventeen 26:340 Ag '67

HAIR dressing. See Hairdressing

HAIR dryers
Electric hair dryers. Consumer Rep 32:240-4 D '67
Hair dryers. il Consumer Rep 32:464-9 S '67
What you should know about hair dryers. Seventeen 26:142 D '67

HAIR; musical comedy. See Musical comedies, revues, etc.—Criticisms, plots, etc.

HAIR pieces. See Wigs

HAIR preparations
For that straight-hair look; hair-straightening products. L. Allen. Todays Health 45: 11-12 N '67

HAIR rinses and shampoos. See Shampoos

HAIR rollers. See Hair curlers

HAIR straighteners. See Hair preparations

HAIRBRUSHES. See Brushes

HAIRCUT; story. See Walker, T.

HAIRCUTTING
Name of the game is trim; childrens haircutting. il Redbook 129:72-7 Jl '67
Open letter to the father of a boy who won't get his hair cut. M. Groves. Good H 165:62+ N '67
See also
Barbers and barber shops

Anecdotes, facetiae, satire, etc.
Boy who had his haircut. A. Buchwald. il Ladies Home J 84:52 Je '67
No haircut for Tony. E. J. Kahn, jr. il Parents Mag 43:48-9 Ja '68

HAIRDOS. See Hairdressing

HAIRDRESSING
Beauty life. il Mlle 65:128-39 O '67
Beauty life: the naked nape. il Mlle 65:124-5 Je '67
Big brush-out. il McCalls 94:96-9+ Mr '67
Changing hairdos of Princess Margaret. L. MacNish. il Good H 164:30-1 Ja '67
Cross-country short cuts. S. Harney. il Ladies Home J 84:114-17 Mr '67
Curls and boys. il Mlle 65:72-3 Jl '67
Eye spy hairdos. il McCalls 95:172-3 D '67
For great-looking hair, take a lesson from the experts. il Good H 166:100-1 Ja '68
Glamorous hairdos for women on the go. il McCalls 95:24+ Ja '68
Hairdos of the month. See issues of Seventeen
Hairpiece. E. G. Smith. Atlan 219:119-20 Mr '67
If you love short hair; if you love long hair. il Seventeen 26:258-61+ Ag '67
Long, short, straight, curly; fashionable headliners for fall. il McCalls 95:94-5+ O '67
Longer hair is not necessarily hippie; Time essay. Time 90:46 O 27 '67
Mini/maxi hair. il Mlle 65:248-9 Ag '67
Natural hair, new symbol of race pride. D. Llorens. il Ebony 23:139-44 D '67
New wave in hair styles. il Redbook 128: 70-5+ Ap '67
News at the top. il Vogue 150:202-7 N 1 '67
Notes and comment; male hair length and Puritan conscience. New Yorker 43:29 Je 10 '67
Project: you. il Ladies Home J 84:54 F '67
Project: you; three styles by Kenneth. il Ladies Home J 84:38 Mr '67
Return of the ringlet. il Seventeen 26:132-3+ N '67
Round-the-world beauty news. il Good H 165:104-15+ O '67
Short classic curls. G. Plaut. il Look 31:M12-14 Ap 18 '67

HAIRDRESSING—*Continued*
Some bristly thoughts on victory through hair power; barbers, beards and bangs. W. Zinsser. Life 64:10 Ja 19 '68
Summer-proof hairdos that start perky, stay put. il Good H 164:112-15+ Je '67
Trouble with hair. Am Home 70:72 O '67
Turn problem hair into pretty hair. il Good H 164:98-9+ F '67
Vogue's eye view; journey to the light; coiffures designed by Veruschka for Strega. il Vogue 149:113 Ap 1 '67
Wash & wear hair. il McCalls 94:39-40+ Jl '67
What the new hair action is all about. Vogue 149:114-17 Ja 15 '67
What they say about hair; Paris, London, Rome, New York. Vogue 150:132 S 15 '67
What's the new action at the top of the silhouette? Vogue 149:18 F 1 '67
Young-as-springtime hairdos. il Good H 164: 108-11 Ap '67

HAIRPIECES. See Wigs

HAITI
Birthday blowout; celebrations for F. Duvalier. il Time 89:43 Ap 28 '67
Come to Haiti and meet Papa Doc's police. H. Rosenhouse. New Repub 156:10 Mr 11 '67
Haiti. R. Y. Gildea, jr. bibliog il Focus 17: 1-6 My '67
See also
Civil rights—Haiti

Description and travel
Editor's report; Haitian limbo. M. M. Davis. il Travel 127:45-9 F '67

Politics and government
Come to Haiti and meet Papa Doc's police. H. Rosenhouse. New Repub 156:10 Mr 11 '67
Coming to a boil. Time 90:34 Ag 25 '67
Dictator on a tightrope. il U S News 63:44 Ag 28 '67
Haiti, next mess in the Caribbean? R. D. Heinl, jr Atlan 220:83-4+ N '67
Memo from Haiti; ten years of Papa Doc. E. Dunbar. il Look 31:124 N 28 '67
Plot against Papa Doc. R. K. Brown. Nat R 19:91-2 Ja 24 '67
That old black magic. Reporter 37:11 D 14 '67

HAITINK, Bernard
Diffident Dutchman. il por Time 89:71 My 12 '67

HALABY, Najeeb
Will Russia win the SST race? interview, ed. by B. Kocivar. por Look 31:72+ F 7 '67

HALACY, Dan
Biological radio, ESP. Pop Electr 26:53-8+ '67

HALAS, Mary
In my opinion. por Seventeen 26:22 Ap '67

HALASZ, Nicholas A. See Tai, C. jt. auth.

HALASZ, Piri
Authors & editors. il por(p51) Pub W 191:4i Je 19 '67

HALBERSTAM, David
Importance of being Galbraith. Harper 235: 47-54 N '67
One very hot day; excerpt from novel. Sat Eve Post 241:40-54 Ja 13 '68
Return to Vietnam. Harper 235:47-58 D '67

HALBERSTAM, Michael Joseph
Doctor's diagnosis of medicare. N Y Times Mag p 14-15+ Ag 13 '67
Patients who make the doctor feverish. N Y Times Mag p 18-19+ F 5 '67

HALBEY, Hans
Bookbinding by Kurt Londenberg. Craft Horiz 27:30-3 Ja '67

HALBREICH, Harry
Notes from our correspondents. Hi Fi 18:12+ Ja '68

HALDANE, Bernard
Are you making the most of yourself? Pop Sci 190:76-8 Je '67

HALDEMAN, John S.
We use TV for more than inspection. Am City 82:112-13+ Mr '67

HALE, Dennis
Blaine and secular man. Commonweal 87:105-6 O 27 '67

HALE, Nancy
What haunts thee in fond shapes. il New Yorker 43:27-9 Ag 5 '67

HALE, Nathan
Patriot. J. C. Lobdell. il Read Digest 91: 35-6 O '67

HALE, Thomas
What's wrong with American hospitals? a doctor's opinion. Sat R 50:62-5 F 4; 47 Ap 1 '67

HALE telescope. See Telescope

HALEVY, E. and Payne, B. R.
Deuterium and oxygen-18 in natural waters; analyses compared. Science 156:669 My 5 '67

HALEVY, Ludovic. See Meilhac, H. jt. auth.

HALEY, Charles E.
Make street signs big enough to read. Am City 82:133-4 F '67

HALFORD, Robert G. and Weeghman, R. B.
Expo 67. Flying 80:38-42+ My '67

HALFWAY up the tree; drama. See Ustinov, P.

HALIFAX, George Savile, 1st marquis of
Marquess of Halifax: eloquent paradox. J. Valenti. il por Sat R 50:22-3+ N 4 '67

HALIFAX, Nova Scotia
Biggest blast before the A-bomb; excerpts from The town that died. M. J. Bird. il Pop Mech 128:81-3 D '67

HALL, Albert G.
Washington lookout. See issues of American forests

HALL, Burton
Painters' union. il Nation 205:81-4 Jl 31 '67

HALL, Clarence W.
Sing out, America! Read Digest 90:49-54 My '67
They're out to remake the world; condensation. Read Digest 92:145-56+ Ja '68
Where religion and psychiatry join hands. Read Digest 90:122-6 Mr '67

HALL, D. M.
Wax microchannels in the epidermis of white clover. bibliog Science 158:505 O 27 '67

HALL, Donald
Waters; poem. Nation 206:30 Ja 1 '68

HALL, Edward T.
E. T. Hall and the human space bubble. W. Kloman. il Horizon 9:42-7 Aut '67

HALL, Fernau
Swinging London has its critics. Dance Mag 41:50-3+ O '67

HALL, Floyd D.
Money from the sky; interview, ed. by F. Merkling. por Opera N 32:14 N 25 '67
Transportation; address, June 26, 1967. Vital Speeches 33:656-9 Ag 15 '67
about
What makes a natural leader? por Duns R 88:29 D '66

HALL, Frances
Dessert for a holiday; poem. America 117: 415 O 14 '67
Tisane for bedtime; poem. America 116:587 Ap 22 '67

HALL, Francis C.
Amateur scientist. Sci Am 216:130-2+ Mr '67

HALL, Harry R.
We had better be better! address, October 16, 1967. Vital Speeches 34:125-8 D 1 '67

HALL, James B.
Racer in a far-out country. C. Phinizy. il por Sports Illus 26:30-2+ My 1 '67

HALL, James Baker
Kind of savage; story. Sat Eve Post 240:60-7 F 11 '67

HALL, John
John Hall, a busy man in Baltimore. R. C. Smith. il Antiques 92:360-6 S '67

HALL, John Whitney. See Wright, A. F. jt. auth.

HALL, Joseph G.
White tails and yellow pines. il Nat Parks Mag 41:9-11 Ap '67

HALL, Lawrence S.
Perils of planned prettiness. Life 62:20 My 12 '67

HALL, Lee
In Bolivia, captured Marxist becomes a cause célèbre. Life 63:32-4 Ag 18 '67

HALL, Marie Boas
Robert Boyle. Sci Am 217:96-102 Ag '67

HALL, Marie-Françoise. See Taylor, C. E. jt. auth.

HALL, Mary S.
Remaking Blake. Christian Cent 84:1070 Ag 23 '67

HALL, Norman
Shadow of light by Bill Brandt. Pop Phot 61:102+ S '67

HALL, Ramsey W.
How much force? il por Time 89:58 Mr 24 '67

HALL, Robert
Excerpt from statement before Communications subcommittee, October 16, 1967. Cong Digest 46:310+ D '67

HALL, Ross H. and others
Cytokinins in the soluble RNA of plant tissues. bibliog Science 156:69-71 Ap 7 '67

HALL, William T. and others
Virus particles and murine leukemia virus complement-fixing antigen in neoplastic and nonneoplastic cell lines. bibliog Science 156:85-8 Ap 7 '67

HALL of fame, Baseball. See National baseball hall of fame and museum

HALLBERG, Clarice L.
Building aesthetic qualities in the school art program. Sch Arts 67:19-20 S '67

HALLE, Louis J.
Overestimating the power of power. New Repub 156:15-17 Je 10 '67

HALLE Handel festival. See Music festivals—Germany (Democratic Republic)

HALLECK, Seymour L.
Are parents to blame for student behavior? excerpts from address, May 11, 1967. U S News 62:74-5 My 29 '67
Roots of student despair; reprint. Sci Digest 62:65-70 S '67

HALLELUJAH, baby! musical comedy. See Musical comedies, revues, etc.—Crticisms, plots, etc.

HALLER, Henry
Cool Swiss at the stove of state. pors Life 63:35-6+ Jl 21 '67

Les HALLES market. See Paris—Markets

HALLEY'S comet
Lockheed study shows probe to Halley's comet is feasible. il Aero Tech 21:56 Ag 28 '67
Return of Halley's comet; 1985. R. S. Richardson. il Sci Digest 62:70-5 N '67

HALLIDAY, E. M.
Low blow for the working girl. Am Heritage 18:98-9 Ap '67
Rasputin reconsidered. Horizon 9:80-7 Aut '67

HALLIDAY, Patrick
Bias compensation for transistor output stages. Electr World 78:76-8 Ag '67
New radiotelephone modulation method. Electr World 77:78-9 Ja '67

HALLIDAY lithograph corporation
Halliday lithograph plans new soft cover bindery. Pub W 191:113 F 6 '67

HALLINAN, Paul John, abp
Time to create. Commonweal 87:47-9 O 13 '67

about
Archbishop Hallinan experiments. Christian Cent 84:932 Jl 19 '67
Second Selma. Christian Cent 84:301 Mr 8 '67

HALLIWELL, David, and Calderisi, David
Experiment. Criticism
New Yorker 43:138 My 20 '67

HALLIWELL, Kenneth
Death of a playwright. il por Time 90:40 S 15 '67

HALLMARK cards, incorporated
Hallmark to publish gift books. Pub W 191:35-6 My 1 '67

HALLOWEEN
Anyone for Halloween? J. L. O'Neill. Am Home 70:68 O '67
Halloween: its history and legends. il Good H 165:205 N '67
Spooky but tasty gingerbread house for Halloween; with recipes. il Sunset 139:164+ O '67
Trick of treating; with recipes. il Ladies Home J 84:114+ O '67

Anecdotes, facetiae, satire, etc.
Just say, trick or treat-o-mat. R. Lasson and D. Eynon. il McCalls 95:64 O '67

Drama
House is haunted. M. Hark and N. McQueen. Plays 27:50-6 O '67

HALLOWEEN cookery. See Cookery, Ornamental

HALLOWEEN parties. See Childrens parties

HALLOWELL, John
In Hollywood she walks the other way. Life 63:144 S 29 '67
Show must go on, but not too long. Life 63:41-2 Jl 21 '67

HALLS
Adding a new entry. il Am Home 70:86 Jl '67
Decorating wrongs made right; foyer. il Bet Hom & Gard 45:26 S '67
Hall, and that's not all. il Bet Hom & Gard 45:50 Mr '67

HALLS of fame
See also
Michigan. University, Ann Arbor—Business hall of fame (proposed)

HALLUCINOGENIC drugs
Beyond LSD. il Time 89:84-5 F 10 '67
2,5-Dimethoxy-4-methyl-amphetamine, STP: a new hallucinogenic drug. S. H. Snyder and others. bibliog il Science 158:669-70 N 3 '67
Drugs, behavior, and crime. R. H. Blum. Ann Am Acad 374:135-46 N '67
Hippies. il Time 90:18-22 Jl 7 '67; Same abr. Read Digest 91:70-4 O '67
Love needs care; clinic devoted exclusively to helping hippies with health problems. il Newsweek 70:98 Jl 17 '67
Non-communications; concerning Northwestern university's symposium. P. Michelson. New Repub 156:35-8 Mr 4 '67
Parnassus revisited; letter. A. Cherkin. Science 155:266+ Ja 20 '67
Real STP. Sci N 92:80-1 Jl 22 '67
You can't even step in the same river once. J. Lettvin. il Natur Hist 76:6-12+ O '67; Discussion. 76:106 D '67
See also
Lygersic acid diethylamide
Psilocybin

HALOID company. See Xerox corporation

HALPER, Sam
Bone-bred rebel from Biran. Sat R 50:27-8 Jl 29 '67

HALPERIN, Samuel
First year of title II; summary of address. por Pub W 192:24-6 N 20 '67

HALPERN, Lawrence M. and Black, R. G.
Flaxedil gallamine trithiodide; evidence for a central action. bibliog Science 155:1685-7 Mr 31 '67

HALSMAN, Philippe
Astonish me Sunday; a sermon. pors Pop Phot 60:69-71+ Mr '67

about
How much their eyes tell us! C. Burger. il Pop Phot 60:106-7+ F '67

HALTON, Kathleen
Pinter, funny and moving and frightening. Vogue 150:194-5+ O 1 '67
Tom Stoppard. Vogue 150:112-13 O 15 '67

HALVERSON, Marvin
Tribute. J. Garrett. Christian Cent 84:444 Ap 5 '67

HAM
See also
Cookery—Meat

HAM carving. See Carving (meat, etc)

HAM radio stations. See Radio stations, Amateur

HAMANI, Diori
President Johnson meets with President of Niger; exchange of greetings and exchange of toasts, September 26, 1967. Dept State Bul 57:541-3 O 23 '67

HAMBLEN, John W.
Smart way to check a camera shutter: use your TV. Pop Sci 191:106-7+ D '67

HAMBLETONIAN diet. See Diet

HAMBLETONIAN race. See Harness racing

HAMBLIN, Dora Jane
Cult of angry Ayn Rand. Life 62:92-4+ Ap 7 '67
Immodest perhaps, but I looked handsomer than my sister. Life 63:29-31 O 6 '67
Nobody bothers about protocol, they just get acquainted. Life 63:50-3 S 1 '67
Penn's deed and Washington's lost knife. Life 63:56 Ag 25 '67
Strange quest of James Kidd. Life 62:76-8+ Mr 3 '67

HAMBRECHT, Margaret
Lesson; poem. Mlle 65:208 Ag '67

HAMBRO, Edvard
Voice. New Yorker 43:24-5 Jl 8 '67

HAMBURG, Martin D.
Retrograde amnesia produced by intraperitoneal injection of physostigmine. bibliog Science 156:973-4 My 19 '67

HAMBURG, Morris, and Atkins, R. J.
Computer model for new product demand. Harvard Bsns R 45:107-10+ Mr '67

HAMBURG
Wicked cities of the world. G. Feifer. il Holiday 43:72-83 Ja '68

Harbor
Pragmatic portsmanship. il Time 89:93 Mr 3 '67

Music
Hamburg; Janácek's Jenufa. J. H. Sutcliffe. il Opera N 31:33 F 11 '67
Hamburg; production of Stravinsky's Rake's progress. J. H. Sutcliffe. Opera N 31:27 Je 10 '67

HAMBURG—Music—*Continued*
Hanover, Hamburg. J. H. Sutcliffe. il Opera N 31:28-9 Mr 18 '67
Swinging Staatsoper. P. Moor. il Hi Fi 17:52-5 Je '67

Parks and playgrounds
Reporter at large; Hagenbeck family zoo. E. Hahn. New Yorker 43:128+ S 30 '67

HAMBURG state opera company
Hamburg opera makes U.S. debut. C. L. Osborne. il Hi Fi 17:MA8-11+ S '67
Hamburger heaven; productions in New York. R. Evett. New Repub 157:30-2 Jl 15 '67
How to hear ahead; performances at Manhattan's Lincoln Center. il Time 90:42 Jl 7 '67
Lively arts; Hamburg state opera; interview, ed. by R. Hemming. R. Liebermann. il Sr Schol 90:30 My 19 '67
Music; performances at the Metropolitan opera house. B. Boretz. Nation 204:445-6; 205:157-8 Ap 3, Ag 28 '67
Musical events; performances at the Metropolitan opera house. W. Sargeant. New Yorker 43:63-4 Jl 1; 102+ Jl 15 '67
No small roles. R. Liebermann. il Opera N 32:8-10 S 23 '67
Rare Hamburgers. H. Saal. il Newsweek 70:80-1 Jl 3 '67
What they did to Berg's Lulu. G. Perle. il Sat R 50:43-5 D 30 '67

HAMBURG state opera house. See Opera houses
HAMBURGER, Michael
(tr) See Enzensberger. H. M. Two poems; The other; The end of the owls
(tr) See Sachs, N. O the night of the weeping children

HAMBURGER, Philip
Contemporary writers VI: an interview with Grip Sands. New Yorker 43:24-5 Jl 29 '67
Diaries and letters of Sir Gerald Woolton. New Yorker 43:52-3 O 28 '67
How to get into college. New Yorker 43:36-7 My 20 '67

HAMBURGER steak. See Cookery—Meat
HAMED, J. Arkani-. See Arkani-Hamed, J.
HAMER, Elizabeth E. and McCormick, Adoreen
Washington report: from the Library of Congress. See issues of ALA bulletin

HAMERQUIST, Donald
Marxist from Multnomah. Time 90:30 O 13 '67

HAMERSTROM, Frances
Owls, eagles and prairie chicanery. H. Peterson. il por Sports Illus 26:46-8+ My 29 '67

HAMERSTROM, Frederick Nathan
Owls, eagles and prairie chicanery. H. Peterson. il por Sports Illus 26:46-8+ My 29 '67

HAMILL, Pete
New roughneck breed of ladies' men. Good H 165:94-5+ O '67
Suddenly, without warning or reason, it happens. Good H 164:98-9+ Ap '67

HAMILTON, Andrew
Talk of a Greek solution for Vietnam. New Repub 157:10-11 S 23 '67
Vietnam, fencing in the North. New Repub 157:19-21 Jl 8 '67
Westmoreland's Progress report. New Repub 157:15-18 D 16 '67

HAMILTON, Andrew Jackson
Good news about gout. Todays Health 45:16-18 D '67
No more overhead wires! Read Digest 91:33-4+ N '67
Oldest living thing in the world. Sci Digest 62:37-8 O '67
So your neighbor has fleas? Todays Health 45:59-61 O '67
Victory over epilepsy. Sci Digest 62:26-30 N '67
What plastic surgery can do for you. Sci Digest 61:60-4 Je '67

HAMILTON, Bus. See Dixon, E. jt. auth.
HAMILTON, Charles, 1913-
Record prices mark Charles Hamilton's 1966-67 auctions. K. V. Hostick. il Hobbies 72:108-9 D '67

HAMILTON, Charles. See Carmichael, S. jt. auth.

HAMILTON, Clive, pseud. See Lewis, C. S.
HAMILTON, David
Book reviews. Hi Fi 17:MA28-30 Ap '67
Britten and the bard, a new Midsummer night. Hi Fi 17:128-9 O '67
Dvorak's symphonies: the canonical five plus the early four. Hi Fi 17:64-5 Jl '67
Stravinsky and the microphone. Hi Fi 17:56-60 Je '67

Three new discs continue Columbia's Stravinsky canon. Hi Fi 17:69-70 Ag '67
Time-Life's Story of great music. Hi Fi 17:59-62 D '67

HAMILTON, George Heard
Of art and anti-art. Sat R 50:38+ N 25 '67

HAMILTON, Kenneth
Are you running with me, Jesus? poem. Christian Cent 84:813 Je 21 '67
John Updike: chronicler of the time of the death of God. Christian Cent 84:745-8 Je 7 '67
Situation ethics; poem. Christian Cent 84:905 Jl 12 '67
Warp torn from woof. Christian Cent 84:473 Ap 12 '67

HAMILTON, Mary G. See Sager, R. jt. auth.
HAMILTON, Richard J. See Eglinton, G. jt. auth.

HAMILTON, W. D.
Extraordinary sex ratios. bibliog Science 156:477-88 Ap 28 '67

HAMILTON, William
Exile from paradise, a garland for Paul Goodman. Christian Cent 84:1046-8 Ag 16 '67
Funny thing happened on the way to the library. Christian Cent 84:469-70 Ap 12 '67
Good-by Chalcedon. hello what? Commonweal 87:275-6+ N 24 '67

HAMILTON, William J. 3d, and Heppner, Frank
Radiant solar energy and the function of black homeotherm pigmentation: an hypothesis. bibliog Science 155:196-7; 158:1341 Ja 13, D 8 '67

HAMILTON standard division. See United aircraft corporation—Hamilton standard division

HAMLET; ballet. See Ballets—Criticisms
HAMLET; drama. See Shakespeare, W.—Plays
HAMLET; opera. See Thomas, A.

HAMLIN, Arthur T.
Libraries of Florence, November 1966. por ALA Bul 61:141-50 F '67
Library crisis in Italy. por Library J 92:2516-22 Jl '67

HAMMARSKJÖLD, Dag
Dag Hammarskjöld, by H. P. Van Dusen. Review
Sat R 50:66-7 Ap 8 '67. J. Pelikan
Time 89:77-8 F 3 '67

HAMMEL, H. T. and others
Regulation of body temperature in the blue-tongued lizard. bibliog Science 156:1260-2 Je 2 '67

HAMMEL, Lisa
Home. N Y Times Mag p24-5 Jl 2; 70-1 Ag 20 '67

HAMMER, Armand
Hammer strikes again. por Newsweek 69:83-5 My 29 '67

HAMMERS
Two soft hammers you can make. M. L. Nutting. il Pop Sci 190:159 Mr '67

HAMMERSTEIN, Oscar, 1847-1919
Oscar the first. F. Stevenson. il pors Opera N 31:8-13 Mr 18 '67
Oscar the first, two for operaphiles. R. Zarbock. por Am Rec G 33:861-2 My '67

HAMMOND, John S. 3d
Better decisions with preference theory. bibliog f Harvard Bsns R 45:123-41 N '67

HAMMOND, Philip C.
Desert waterworks of the ancient Nabataeans; with biographical sketch. Natur Hist 76:4, 36-43 Je '67

HAMNER, W. M. See Enright, J. T. jt. auth.
HAMOSH, M. and others
Enhanced protein synthesis in a cell-free system from hypertrophied skeletal muscle. bibliog Science 157:935-7 Ag 25 '67

HAMP; drama. See Wilson, J.
HAMPEA (tree)
Hampea Schlecht: possible primary host of the cotton boll weevil. P. A. Fryxell and M. J. Lukefahr. bibliog Science 155:1568-9 Mr 24 '67

HAMPERS, Clothes. See Clothes hampers
HAMPLE, Stuart. See Marshall, E. jt. comp.
HAMPTON, Duane
Chez Mlle. See issues of Mademoiselle

HAMPTON, Max
Flackery in the Levant; excerpt from Throw away the key. Sat R 50:47-9+ Ap 15 '67

HAMS (radio) See Radio operators, Amateur
HAMSUN, Knut
Books. J. Updike. New Yorker 43:223-4+ D 2 '67
Knut Hamsun: the beginning and the end. R. Coles. New Repub 157:21-4 S 23 '67

HANAWALT, Philip C. and Haynes, R. H.
Repair of DNA; with biographical sketches.
Sci Am 216:22. 36-43 bibliog(p 146) F '67
—See Brunk. C. F. jt. auth.

HANCKE, Bill. See Hancke, C. jt. auth.

HANCKE, Carol, and Hancke, Bill
Interrupted cruise. il pors Yachting 122:44-5+
Ag '67

HANCOCK, Vera
I'll never live among strangers again. por
McCalls 94:20+ S '67

HAND, Jackson
Here come the electric mowers! Pop Sci 190:
154-8 F '67
Smart tricks for finishing fir plywood. Pop
Sci 190:164-7+ F '67

HAND
Beauty life: sleights of hand. il Mlle 65:66-7
Jl '67
Luxury look. il Redbook 128:86-9 Mr '67
Show of hands; hand care. il McCalls 94:
104-5+ F '67

HAND ball
Laughter in the wings, murder on the court.
T. C. Brody. Sports Illus 26:90+ Ap 17 '67
Showdown on 92nd street; P. Haber vs J.
Jacobs. B. Ottum. il Sports Illus 27:46-7 Ji
31 '67

HAND care. See Hand
HAND kissing. See Kissing
HAND lotions. See Cosmetics
HAND luggage. See Luggage
HAND puppets. See Puppets and puppet plays
HAND shaking
Hands down; German handshake. il Time 89:
33 F 17 '67

HAND weaving. See Weaving
HANDBALL. See Hand ball
HANDBOOKS
See also subhead Handbooks manuals,
etc. under various subjects, e.g. Business
—Handbooks, manuals, etc.

HANDEDNESS. See Left- and right-handedness

HÄNDEL, Georg Friedrich
For Handel's organ works. Archive thinks of
everything. N. Broder. il Hi Fi 17:78C-78D
F '67
George Frideric Handel, by P. H. Lang. Re-
view
Hi Fi 17:MA28-9 Ja '67. P. J. Smith
New Yorker 43:146-8 Je 10 '67. W. Sar-
geant
Giulio Cesare. Criticism
Hi Fi 18:MA7 Ja '68
Giulio Cesare the operatic genius of Handel
made plain. C. L. Osborne. il Hi Fi 18:63-5
Ja '68
Handel operas. S. Sadie. il Hi Fi 17:69-72
F '67
Messiah. J. Diether. Am Rec G 33:630-3 Ap
'67
Messiah by Mackerras. R. Weinstock. Sat R
50:70 Ap 29 '67
Music to my ears: performance of Giulio
Cesare. I. Kolodin. Sat R 50:55 Ap 8 '67
New York; Giulio Cesare, at Carnegie Hall.
R. D. Daniels. Opera N 31:28 My 13 '67
Opera production of Handel's Julius Caesar.
S. Lincoln. il Am Rec G 34:268-72 D '67
RCA Victor, Handel's Hercules. J. W. Barker.
il Am Rec G 34:184-7 N '67
Records:
Handel: Giulio Cesare. Opera N 32:34 Ja
20 '68
Hercules. Opera N 32:34 D 30 '67
Messiah. Opera N 31:32 Mr 18 '67
Messiah. Opera N 32:34 D 23 '67

HANDEL festival. See Music festivals—Ger-
man (Democratic Republic)
HANDGUNS. See Pistols
HANDICAPPED
Don't ban handicapped from our buildings.
T. P. Mangelsdorf. Todays Health 45:88 D
'67
Girl who wouldn't give up. il Ebony 23:113-
14+ D '67
New hope for the handicapped; Division for
the blind and physically handicapped at
the Library of Congress. C. Gallozzi. bibliog
il Library J 92:1417-20 Ap 1 '67
See also
Blind
Children, Handicapped
Libraries—Work with the handicapped
Recreation for the handicapped

Apparatus and appliances
Publisher's memo; battery-powered vehicles
for cerebral palsy victims. R. Brock. il Hot
Rod 21:6 Ja '68

Rehabilitation
See Rehabilitation
HANDICRAFT
Money, money, money; start a boutique. il
Seventeen 26:70-1+ Jl '67
See also
Arts and crafts
Christmas projects
Patchwork

HANDLER, Philip
Academic science and the federal government.
Science 157:1140-6 S 8 '67
Federal science policy; excerpts from ad-
dress, December 30, 1966. Science 155:1063-
6 Mr 3 '67
Handler statement on Smale case. Science 157:
1411 S 22 '67

HANDLIN, Oscar
Reader's choice. See issues of Atlantic
HANDLING of animals. See Animals—Treat-
ment
HANDLING of feed. See Feed handling
HANDMADE paper. See Paper making and
trade
HANDSHAKING. See Hand shaking
HANDWRITING. See Penmanship
HANDWRITING analysis. See Graphology
HANDY and Harman (firm)
Stepping out of a silvery past. il Bsns W
p 144-6 N 25 '67

HANEY, Marilyn
Worried ones; poem. Christian Cent 84:1629
D 20 '67

HANG-up; story. See Weyer, S.
HANGARS
Plane in every garage. J. Roe. il House B
109:34+ S '67
HANGEN, Welles
Last trip to Ravensbrück. Holiday 41:70-1+
Ap '67
HANKER, Jacob S. and others
Coordination polymers of osmium: the nature
of osmium black. bibliog Science 156:1737-8
Je 30 '67
HANLEY, Richard H. J.
Obituary
America 116:inside cover Ap 15 '67. T. N.
Davis
HANLEY, T. Edward, collection. See Art—
Private collections
HANNA, Katharine M.
November Sunday; poem. Mlle 66:124 N '67
HANNA, M. G. jr, and others
Serum alpha globulin fraction: survival-and-
recovery effect in irradiated mice. bibliog
Science 157:1458-61 S 22 '67
HANNA, Nancy W.
How to use professional periodicals. NEA J
56:63-4 F '67
HANNAH, John Alfred
Enough food, enough wealth, enough time;
address, June 11, 1967. Vital Speeches 33:
684-6 S 1 '67
about
Megaversity's struggle with itself; running
Michigan state. D. Norton-Taylor. il por
Fortune 75:160-5+ My '67
HANNAH, William
Integrated circuits used in new hi-fi AM/FM
receiver. Electr World 77:34-5+ Ja '67
HANNAN, Cecil J.
Assistant executive secretary for professional
development and Welfare Cecil J. Hannan.
M. O. Donley, jr. por NEA J 56:49 N '67
HANNEMAN, R. E. and others
Hexagonal diamonds in meteorites: implica-
tions. bibliog Science 155:995-7 F 24 '67
HANNIGAN, Ed
Don't flood it, filter it. U S Camera 30:18+
Ag '67
Fun of it all. U S Camera 31:18+ Ja '68
Movie techniques are worth copying. U S
Camera 30:28+ S '67
One photographer's ESP. U S Camera 30:16+
My '67
Photographer as historian. U S Camera 30:
16+ Ap '67
Pointers on print making. U S Camera 30:24+
D '67
Shopping the used camera market. U S
Camera 30:16+ Jl '67
Time to capture gold on silver. U S Camera
30:78-9 N '67
You too can make page one. U S Camera
30:18+ O '67
HANNOCH house, Verplanck's Landing. See
New York (state)—Historic houses, etc.
HANNUM, Alex
Waiting made it sweeter. F. Deford. il por
Sports Illus 26:54-6 My 8 '67

HARDYCK, Curtis D. and others
Feedback of speech muscle activity during silent reading; rapid extinction. Science 154:1467-8; 157:581 D 16 '66, Ag 4 '67
HARE, Denise
Craftsman's guide to Expo '67. Craft Horiz 27:30-3+ Jl '67
HARE, Humphrey
(tr) See Druon, M. Tistou of the green fingers
HARE, Nathan
Behind the black college student revolt. por Ebony 22:58-61 Ag '67
Black power; its goals and methods; interview. por US News 62:64-6+ My 22 '67
HARE lip. See Harelip
HARELIP
Cleft lip and cleft palate; report on meeeting. F. C. Fraser. Science 158:1603-6 D 22 '67
HAREWOOD, George Henry Hubert Lascelles, 7th earl of
Wedding in New Canaan. il por Time 90:42 Ag 11 '67
HARFORD theater association
Bel Air, Maryland; productions of operas and operettas. F. C. Smith. Opera N 32:21 S 23 '67
HÄRING, Bernard
Christian maturity. America 117:240-1 S 9 '67
HARING, Douglas Gilbert
Japanese character in the twentieth century. bibliog f Ann Am Acad 370:133-42 Mr '67
HARINGTON, Donald
Down in the dumps; story. Esquire 67:106-7 F '67
HARJES, Joan Blake
How to manage your money; excerpts from The hardship of accounting. Seventeen 26:236+ My '67
HARJUNPAA, Toivo
Lutheran view of Mariology. America 117:436-7+ O 21 '67
HARK, Mildred, and McQueen, Noel
Christmas shopping early; drama. Plays 27:49-58, 65 D '67
Date with Washington; drama. Plays 26:33-42, 58 F '67
House is haunted; drama. Plays 27:50-6 O '67
Princess and the rose-colored glasses; drama. Plays 26:75-82 Ap '67
When do we eat? drama. Plays 26:45-53 Mr '67
HARKISON, Judith
Middle-class revolutionaries are home. Mlle 66:104-5+ Ja '68
HARKNESS, Georgia
De senectute. Christian Cent 84:1318-19 O 18 '67
HARKNESS, Rebekah
America's ballet royalty. W. Terry. il por Sat R 50:44-5 O 28 '67
Harkness comes home. H. Saal. il por Newsweek 70:100 N 13 '67
HARKNESS ballet
America's ballet royalty. W. Terry. il Sat R 50:44-5 O 28 '67
Countdown begins; preparation for first New York season. B. MacDonald. il Dance Mag 41:38-45 O '67
Harkness comes home. H. Saal. il Newsweek 70:100 N 13 '67
Lady bountiful's bounty; first Manhattan engagement. il Time 90:49 N 17 '67
Musical events; first New York appearance. W. Sargeant. New Yorker 43:234-5 N 11 '67
Musical events; performance of Golden age. W. Sargeant. New Yorker 43:220 N 25 '67
Passions revisited; New York debut. D. Herring. il Dance Mag 42:44-7+ Ja '68
Very special jewel; New York debut. W. Terry. il Sat R 50:72-3 N 25 '67
World of the dance; Broadway season and dancers. W. Terry. il Sat R 50:46-7 D 9 '67
HARL, Nell E.
Ways to lower the tax bite when you sell a farm. Suc Farm 65:60+ Mr '67
HARLAKENDEN family
Harlakenden coat-of-arms. H. K. Eilers. il Hobbies 72:118-19 Je '67
HARLAN, Leonard M. See Hayes, S. L. 3d, jt. auth
HARLAN, Robert D.
Bookmaking around the Bay. por Library J 92:2369-71 Je 15 '67
HARLANDER, Dave
Fire at sea! Yachting 121:197-9 My '67
HARLEM. See New York (city)—Harlem
HARLEM youth opportunities unlimited, incorporated
Black youth in rebellion. C. H. King and others. il Wilson Lib Bul 42:166-72 O '67
Statistic named Mary; Haryou's program for unwed mothers. G. Samuels. il N Y Times Mag p24-5+ Mr 5 '67

HARLEY, Rufus
Skirling the blues. H. Saal. il por Newsweek 69:97-8 Ja 30 '67
HARLOW, Francis H. and Shannon, J. P.
Distortion of a splashing liquid drop. bibliog Science 157:547-50 Ag 4 '67
HARLOW, Lewis A.
Chinese say it how-how. Travel 127:60-2+ Mr '67
How says itself in Russian? Travel 127:61-2+ Ja '67
How to conduct an interview with a tape recorder. Pop Electr 25:63-4 D '66
Parlor game. Pop Electr 25:65 D '66
PEMOHT; the Russian radio, TV serviceman. Pop Electr 27:57-8+ Ag '67
HARLOW, William Morehouse
Patterns of life. Am For 73:4-7+ F '67
Patterns of life; photographs. Audubon 69:58-63 Mr '67
HARLOWE, Marie
Sojourner Truth, the first sit-in. por Negro Hist Bul 29:173-4 Fall '66
HARM, Ray
Ray Harm; the other side of the window. il House B 109:164-5+ Mr '67
HARMAN, Harry D.
Our honeymoon with automation. Am City 82:112-13 Je '67
HARMETZ, Aljean
Johnson comes to town. New Repub 157:7-8 Jl 8 '67
HARMONICAS
Never underestimate the power of a pocket piano. G. Gaskill. il Read Digest 91:191-2+ Jl '67
Seeking a mark; L. Adler. il Time 89:48-9 Je 30 '67
HARMONY (aesthetics)
Design of cities, by E. N. Bacon. Review
New Repub 157:32-4 S 2 '67. F. Gutheim
HARMONY of the spheres
Vibrating string of the Pythagoreans; relation between music and mathematics. E. E. Helm. il Sci Am 217:92-8+ bibliog(p 158) D '67
HARNACK, Curtis
Week of the angry artist. Nation 204:245-8, 350 F 20, Mr 13 '67
HARNESS racing
Classic sort of catastrophe; trotting's Triple crown at Yonkers raceway. P. Axthelm Sports Illus 27:48-9 Jl 31 '67
Classicist from Pekin; F. Ervin, the 1966 Hambletonian winner. W. Leggett. il Sports Illus 26:24-6+ F 27 '67
Dancer has a Hambo parlay. P. Axthelm. il Sports Illus 27:68+ Jl 17 '67
Face to face with a girl who trains racing horses. il Seventeen 26:88 F '67
K.D. figures out the formula; the Hambletonian trotting race at Du Quoin state fair. P. Axthelm. il Sports Illus 27:26-7 S 11 '67
Lady curbed her temper and took the men; Speed Model, winner of Kentucky futurity. P. Axthelm. il Sports Illus 27:72-3 O 16 '67
Pace-setter; International pace, won by Romeo Hanover. il Newsweek 69:58 Je 12 '67
Putting the flimflam on the slickers from the city; Little brown jug at Delaware, Ohio. P. Axthelm. il Sports Illus 27:64+ O 2 '67
Romulus chose the occasion to behave; winner of Messenger stakes at Roosevelt raceway. P. Axthelm. il Sports Illus 26:26-7 My 22 '67
Victorious French trotted out a blockade; Roquepine winner of Roosevelt international. P. Axthelm. il Sports Illus 27:60+ Ag 28 '67
HARNEY, Malachi L.
U.S. bureau of narcotics. bibliog f Cur Hist 53:23-30+ Jl '67
HARNONCOURT, Nikolaus
New performances on old instruments. E. Helm. il por Hi Fi 17:42-6 My '67
HARP seals. See Seals (animals)
HARPER, J. Russell
Painting in Canada, 1604-1867. Antiques 92:66-71 Jl '67
(ed) Canada exposed: the look of the young nation; excerpts from Portrait of a period: a collection of Notman photographs. Am Heritage 18:13-25 Je '67
HARPER, John Dickson
Growing with an organization; interview. pors Nations Bsns 55:64-8 D '67

about

Alcoa's man of mettle. R. Levy. por Duns R 89:50-2 Je '67

HARPER, Marion, 1916-
Changing the format. por Bsns W p42 D 2
'67
Interpublic story. por Newsweek 70:86+ D
11 '67

HARPER and Row, publishers, Incorporated
Catching the 4:52; new chairman. il News-
week 70:69-70 Jl 24 '67
Grove, Harper both issue Russian novel. Oct.
4. Pub W 192:45-6 S 18 '67
Harper's sesquicentennial; adaptation of ad-
dress. A. Nevins. Sat R 50:58-9+ Jl 8 '67
House of Harper. C. B. Grannis. il Pub W
192:23-6 N 6 '67
Master and Margarita: the implicit con-
troversy. Pub W 192:33-4 O 2 '67
Mrs Kennedy reaches accord with Harper &
Row and William Manchester. Pub W 191:
222 Ja 23 '67
Rights and permissions: exhibition at New
York's Pierpont Morgan library commem-
orating 150th anniv. P. Nathan. il Pub W
192:44 Ag 7 '67
Svetlana's book due Oct. 16 from Harper.
Pub W 191:31 My 1 '67

HARPER'S bazaar
100 years in a candy store. Time 89:40+ F
24 '67

HARPERS FERRY, W.Va.
Building for the National park service: de-
signed to respect an historic site. il Arch
Rec 142:136-9 O '67
Interpretive facilities center. R. C. Byrd. il
Parks & Rec 2:23-4+ D '67
Quotes from John Brown; address, October
16, 1966. A. M. Daniel. Negro Hist Bul
30:6-7 My '67

John Brown raid, 1859
John Brown, fanatic or precursor of freedom?
Negro Hist Bul 30:4-5 My '67
Verdicts of history: trial of John Brown. T. J.
Fleming. bibliog il Am Heritage 18:28-33+
Ag '67

HARPER'S magazine
Announcing some changes. J. Fischer. Harper
235:24+ Jl '67
Reflections on reaching the age of 150. C.
Canfield. Harper 234:14+ Je '67
Spur for Harper's. Newsweek 69:68+ My 22
'67
Status report; progress in events and issues
reported in Harper's. Harper 235:34+ S;
70-1 N '67
Youth for Harper's; new editor. il Time 89:
56 My 19 '67

HARRIGAN, Anthony
Where the war might start. Nat R 19:566-7
My 30 '67

HARRIMAN, William Averell
From Stalin to Kosygin: the myths and the
realities. pors Look 31:55-6+ O 3 '67
Marshall plan: from the reconstruction to the
construction of Europe; address, June 6,
1967. Dept State Bul 57:17-18 Jl 3 '67
United States and eastern Europe in perspective; address, April 29, 1967. Dept State
Bul 56:815-21 My 29 '67

about
From Trotsky to Vietnam, Averell Harriman is still very much the Ambassador
at large. H. Brandon. il pors N Y Times
Mag p22-3+ Mr 5 '67
13th annual Mr Travel award. il por Travel
128:42-4+ Jl '67

HARRINGTON, Michael
Liberal anti-communism revisited Commentary 44:43-4 S '67
Liberalism according to Galbraith. Commentary 44:77-83 O '67
Social-industrial complex. Harper 235:55-60 N
'67

HARRIS, Aubrey
Semiconductor switching of low-power circuits. Electr World 77:33-5 Je '67

HARRIS, Brayton
From farm to the Antarctic. Sat R 50:37 D
16 '67

HARRIS, Charles S. See Rock, I. jt. auth.

HARRIS, Christina Phelps
New Egypt after 1952. bibliog f Cur Hist
52:90-7+ F '67

HARRIS, D. H.
Martian relief and the coming opposition.
bibliog Science 155:1100-1 Mr 3 '67

HARRIS, Dale
Nothing but facts (about Mozart) Am Rec G
33:839-40 My '67

HARRIS, David
Watched: the new student president. G. Berriault. por Esquire 68:93+ S '67

HARRIS, Eleanor
How would you like your daughter to marry
William F. Buckley, jr? Look 31:112+ Mr
7 '67
What is Nancy Reagan really, really like?
Look 31:40+ O 31 '67
What now, Jack Paar? Look 31:66-9+ D 12
'67

HARRIS, Elizabeth
Elizabeth Harris, Henry st settlement playhouse. J. Anderson. Dance Mag 41:38 My '67

HARRIS, Fred R.
Case for a national social science foundation; address, May 6, 1967. por Science
157:507-9 Ag 4 '67

HARRIS, Frederick Brown
Blade of a righteous sword; reprint. U S
News 62:120 Ap 24 '67

HARRIS, Henry
Caulking Rx for leaky seams. il Yachting
121:50-2+ F '67

HARRIS, Janette Hoston
Freedom; poem. Negro Hist Bul 30:10 N '67
Reason for violence; poem. Negro Hist Bul
30:13 O '67

HARRIS, Joe
Gypsy Joe: fire and music and miniculture.
M. Kram. il Sports Illus 26:77-9 Ap 10 '67
You sweeter than wine, Joe. M. Kram. il pors
Sports Illus 26:32-4+ Je 19 '67

HARRIS, LaDonna
Warpaint for the senator's wife. C. Mangel.
il pors Look 31:24-9 Ap 4 '67

HARRIS, Leon
Rector, a church and the hippies. L. Kinsolving. Christian Cent 84:667-8 My 17 '67

HARRIS, Louis
How the U.S. public now feels about Vietnam. Newsweek 69:24-5 F 27 '67
Unbelievable explosion; adaptation of address. Sat R 51:43-4+ Ja 6 '68

HARRIS, Mark
Accuser and the accused. Sat R 50:34-5 F 11
'67
Flowering of the hippies. Atlan 220:63-72 S
'67
Max Rafferty of California. Atlan 220:95-101
D '67

HARRIS, Marvin
Books in review. Natur Hist 76:72+ Ag '67
Myth of the sacred cow; with biographical
sketch. Natur Hist 76:4B, 6-8+ Mr '67

HARRIS, Michael
Property tax scandals: bad laws & crafty
assessors. Nation 204:210-12 F 13 '67

HARRIS, Patricia R.
U.N. adopts international covenants on
human rights; statement, December 12,
1966. Dept State Bul 56:104-7 Ja 16 '67

HARRIS, Rex F.
New approach to breadboarding. Electr World
77:82-3 Ja '67

HARRIS, Richard
Reporter at large. New Yorker 43:48-50+ Ap
8 '67

HARRIS, Richard, 1933-
Limerick lad in Arthur's court. J. Borgzinner.
il pors Life 63:76+ S 22 '67

HARRIS, Stephen E. and Forrest, H. S.
RNA and DNA synthesis in developing eggs
of the milkweed bug, oncopeltus fasciatus
(Dallas) bibliog Science 156:1613-15 Je 23 '67

HARRIS, Sydney J.
Simple life. Read Digest 91:24B Ag '67

HARRIS, T. George
What makes Romney run? excerpt from
Romney's way. Look 31:92-4+ D 12 '67

HARRIS, Upham and company
You've got to be optimistic in this business;
Kansas City branch. S. Brown. il Sat Eve
Post 240:68-71 D 30 '67

HARRIS-Intertype corporation
Harris-Intertype introduces electronic-controlled press. il Pub W 192:84 N 6 '67

HARRIS polls. See Public opinion polls

HARRISON, Ernest
Church-without-God minister without
church. Christian Cent 84:334 Mr 15 '67

HARRISON, George
Ravi Shankar and George Beatles. C. Reid.
il pors N Y Times Mag p28-9+ My 7 '67

HARRISON, Gilbert A.
Alice B. Toklas. New Repub 156:24+ Mr 18
'67
Kennedy up-to-date. New Repub 157:29-30+
D 2 '67
Richard Nixon's return engagement. New
Repub 157:11-12 N 4 '67
Vietnam: how to win the war. New Repub
157:13-15 N 18 '67

HARRISON, Halstead, and Schoen, R. I.
Evaporation of ice in space: Saturn's rings.
bibliog Science 157:1175-6 S 8 '67

HARRISON, James O.
Riddle of Costa Rica's jungle spheres; reprint. por Sci Digest 61:14-16 Je '67
HARRISON, Jim
Suite to fathers; poem. Poetry 109:321-4 F '67
HARRISON, Lorena
For Bill, missing in a light plane over Stampede Pass; poem. Mlle 64:97 F '67
HARRISON, Mildred
Mildred Harrison's Viet Nam ordeal. P. Avery. il pors Ebony 22:88-90+ My '67
HARR'SON, Rex
Why Rex Harrison is Dr Dolittle. L. Russ. por Pub W 192:22 D 11 '67
HARRISON, Richard Edes
Friends: new organization called Friends of Central park. New Yorker 42:24-5 F 4 '67
HARRISON, Selig S.
Hiroshima plus twenty-seven. New Repub 156:26+ Mr 11 '67
Reischauer's Asia. New Repub 157:23-6 N 25 '67
HARRISON, Thomas Harnett
Asian diary. J. Mander. Commentary 44:92-3 O '67
HARRISON, William
Pinball machines; story. Sat Eve Post 240:64-8 Ap 22 '67
Snooker shark; story. Sat Eve Post 240:56-8 Jl 29 '67
HARRISS, Joseph
Algerian socialism's slow leak. New Repub 156:19 My 6 '67
HARRISVILLE, Roy A.
On the teeter-totter. Christian Cent 84:1323-4 O 18 '67
HARROD, Sir Roy
Why Britain froze wages. por Duns R 88:32-3+ D '66
HARRODS. See London—Stores
HARSTER, Wilhelm
White-gloved killers. por Newsweek 69:48 Ja 30 '67
HARSY, Mary Jo
Prayer on a line of Teilhard; poem. Cath World 205:176 Je '67
HART, Benjamin L.
Testosterone regulation of sexual reflexes in spinal male rats. bibliog Science 155:1283-4 Mr 10 '67
HART, Charles J.
Collect twice the leaves with the same crew. Am City 82:116-17 Ap '67
HART, Jeffrey
John Dos Passos. Nat R 19:93+ Ja 24 '67
Literature and politics. Nat R 19:809+ Jl 25 '67
Little old professors in tennis shoes. Nat R 19:635+ Je 13 '67
Local guru. Nat R 19:912 Ag 22 '67
Relevance of Burke. Nat R 19:1022-3 S 19 '67
HART, Jerry
Proof of the pudding. il Yachting 121:91+ Ap '67
Safeguard your passage. Yachting 122:47 D '67
HART, Jim
Peach fuzz with a difference. M. Mulvoy. il por Sports Illus 27:30-2+ 27 '67
HART, Philip
Four concertos from Szeryng mark a new star status. Hi Fi 17:78D-79 F '67
Young opera singers, their care and training. Hi Fi 17:MA24-5 O '67
HART, Philip A.
Discount on gorgeous. Nation 205:400-1 O 23 '67
HART, Stanley R. and Aldrich, L. T.
Fractionation of potassium/rubidium by amphiboles: implications regarding mantle composition. bibliog Science 155:325-7 Ja 20 '67
HARTACK, Bill
Hard ride all the way; ed. by W. Tower. pors Sports Illus 26:60-4+ Mr 27; 30-2+ Ap 3; 58-62+ Ap 10 '67
HARTE, Robert A.
International federation for documentation. ALA Bul 61:986-8 S '67
HARTER, M. Russell, and White, C. T.
Perceived number and evoked cortical potentials. bibliog Science 156:406-8 Ap 21 '67
HARTFORD, Bill
Two-way radios you can tuck anywhere. Pop Mech 128:170-2+ Jl '67
You fly this car with a stick. Pop Mech 127:87-9+ Ap '67
HARTFORD, Huntington
Does A&P really care? il por Newsweek 70:78 O 16 '67

HARTFORD, Conn.
Theater
Theatre; Hartford stage company, production of The servant of two masters. J. Novick. Nation 204:636-8 My 15 '67
HARTFORD Insurance group
Story behind the trademark. Changing T 21:32 S '67
HARTFORD stage company. See Hartford, Conn.—Theater
HARTGEN, Vincent A.
Vincent A. Hartgen defends the middle ground of the semi-abstract. il por Am Artist 31:22-3+ S '67
HARTKE, Vance
Make way for drop-ins. NEA J 56:22-3 N '67
Speaking out. por Sat Eve Post 240:10+ Ap 22 '67
HARTLEY, Ellen. See Hartley, W. jt. auth.
HARTLEY, Fred Lloyd
Fred Hartley and his well-oiled multiplying machine. T. O'Hanlon. il por Fortune 75:156-61+ Ap '67
HARTLEY, Russell
You are always somewhere, hopefully. Dance Mag 41:62-5 S '67
HARTLEY, William, and Hartley, Ellen
Comeback for the sea turtle. Sci Digest 62:33-7 S '67
Endurance limits in space. Sci Digest 61:40-7 Ap '67
Most snake-bitten man in the world. Sci Digest 62:13-17 O '67
Rescuing sunken history. Sci Digest 63:24-30 Ja '68
Shark! overrated demon or genuine scourge? Sci Digest 61:6-13 Je '67
HARTLINE, Haldan Keffer
Good beginning. il por Time 90:56 O 27 '67
Nobel prize: three named for medicine, physiology award. F. Ratliff. por Science 158:471-3 O 27 '67
Nobel prize winners. por Sci N 92:437-8 N 4 '67
Nobel work. il por Newsweek 70:82-3 O 30 '67
HARTMAN, Elizabeth
Ex-waif pops up as a sexpot. il pors Life 62:43-4+ Mr 24 '67
HARTNETT, Vincent
Blacklisted! story of J. H. Faulk; condensation of The jury returns. L. Nizer. il Read Digest 90:204+ Mr '67
HARTRIDGE, Walter Charlton
Andrew Low's house. Antiques 91:350-2 Mr '67
Architectural trends in Savannah. Antiques 91:324-8 Mr '67
HARTSELL, Horace C.
Teacher and the instructional materials center. Sr Schol 90:sup 13 F 3 '67
HARTSHORNE, Nathaniel
Carrie's war against the clutch. Good H 164:42+ Mr '67
Just for laughs. Look 31:M8 My 30 '67
HARTUNG, Philip T.
Screen. See issues of Commonweal
HARTWICK, H. A.
Dream; excerpts. Ladies Home J 84:81+ Ap '67
HARVAN, George
Amish portfolio. il Pop Phot 61:98-101+ S '67
HARVARD business school. See Harvard university—Graduate school of business administration
HARVARD coop bookstore. See College bookstores
HARVARD forest, Petersham, Mass. See Harvard forest. Petersham, Mass.
HARVARD square. See Cambridge, Mass.
HARVARD university
Dow at Harvard: the right to recruit on college campuses. M. Ford. New Repub 157:11-13 N 11 '67
Fascism and Harvard. Nat R 19:337 Ap 4 '67
Harvard: beginning to worry about maintaining its faculty. B. Nelson. Science 156:922-5 My 19 '67
Harvard completes a course in urban design. D. Canty. il Arch Forum 126:64-77 Ja '67
Master of Eliot. il Newsweek 69:102 My 29 '67
Mr Leavitt comes to Harvard. G. Ross. Nation 205:654-8 D 18 '67
Upping the ante; fund-raising drive to improve undergraduate science programs. Time 90:81 N 17 '67
War on campus: what happened when Dow recruited at Harvard. R. J. Samuelson. il Science 158:1289-94 D 8 '67
See also
Radcliffe college, Cambridge, Mass.

HARVARD university—*Continued*

Graduate school of business administration

Action intellectuals; on the Charles River, the seedbed of the new elite. T. H. White. Life 62:70+ Je 9 '67

Big men on campus; Advanced management program. il Newsweek 69:74-6 F 27 '67

Top students sell business short; undergraduates internship program by Harvard B-school. il Bsns W p 134-6+ S 9 '67

Wooing the disenchanted. Newsweek 69:76+ Je 19 '67

Graduate school of education

AASA attacks assessment; Harvard groups protest. Library J 92:829-30 F 15 '67

Harvard forest, Petersham, Mass.

Ivy league forest. C. E. Randall. il Am For 73:24-7+ Ap '67

Institute of politics

Institute for activists. Time 89:42-3 F 3 '67

U.S. selective service. T. C. Schelling and others. Bul Atomic Sci 23:38-40 O '67

John Fitzgerald Kennedy school of government

Harvard: power base for the Kennedy's? reprint from Sunday telegraph, January 15, 1967; with excerpts from reply by D. K. Price. H. Fairlie. il U S News 62:37-40 Ja 30 '67

Kennedy stud farm. Nat R 19:124+ F 7 '67

See also

Harvard university—Institute of politics

Law school

Harvard at 150. il Time 90:75-6 O 6 '67

Law at Harvard. il Newsweek 70:53-4 O 2 '67

HARVESTING machinery

Harvest earlier, with less help. il Farm J 91:30-1 S '67

Mechanical harvesting. C. F. Kelly. il Sci Am 217:50-9 Ag '67

Orange terror in our wheatfields; All-Crop combine. G. Logsdon. il Farm J 91:24 O '67

Self-propelled convenience at lower cost? P. B. Jones. il Suc Farm 65:36-7 N '67

HARVEY, Fred

Purveyor to the West. L. Beebe. il por Am Heritage 18:28-31+ F '67

HARVEY, Fred, system

Purveyor to the West. L. Beebe. il Am Heritage 18:28-31+ F '67

HARVEY, James

Stage. Commonweal 86:152-4, 342-5 Ap 21, Je 9 '67

HARVEY, Mary L.

Dial A for attention. Read Digest 91:24B O '67

HARVEY aluminum, incorporated

New processes at Harvey help firm's market drive. J. F. Judge. il Aero Tech 21:44-5 Ag 14 '67

HARWOOD, Richard

And the moral of the Baker case is... New Repub 156:17-19 F 4 '67

Politics for the unpolitical. New Repub 156: 24-5 My 6 '67

HARYOU. See Harlem youth opportunities unlimited, incorporated

HASBROUCK, Beverly

To be perfectly frank. America 117:38-9 Jl 8 '67

HASEK, Joseph A.

Made in the shade. Sch Arts 67:10-11 D '67

HASELDEN, Kyle

Concerned and committed. Christian Cent 84: 197-8 F 15 '67

HASELKORN, Robert

Editorial introduction. Bul Atomic Sci 23:2-3 Mr '67

HASHMAN, Judy Devlin

Judy takes a final curtain call. K. Chapin. il por Sports Illus 26:65-7 Ap 24 '67

HASIDISM

Extreme Jews. I. B. Singer. il Harper 234: 55-62 Ap '67

HASKELL, Jean B. See Dingle. H. jt. auth.

HASKINS, Sam

Haskins makes it up. H. Keppler. il Mod Phot 31:80-91 N '67

HASKINS laboratories

Haskins laboratories: research on human communication, marine ecology, and the biochemistry of protozoa. F. S. Cooper. il Science 158:1213-15 D 1 '67

HASLAM, E. Henley

Louisiana experiment. Dance Mag 41:32+ O '67

HASLER, Arthur D. and Swenson, M. E.

Eutrophication. Science 158:278+ O 13 '67

HASSAN II, king of Morocco

King Hassan II of Morocco visits the United States; exchange of greetings and exchange of toasts, February 9, 1967. Dept State Bul 56:328-31 F 27 '67

about

Potentate with potential. il por Time 89:34+ F 17 '67

Token of esteem. il por Newsweek 69:55 F 20 '67

HASSAN, Ihab

Books in the field: anticriticism. bibliog Wilson Lib Bul 42:477-83 Ja '68

HASSAN, Lorne

Lights, camera, blam! il Newsweek 71:46 Ja 8 '68

HASSENGER, Robert

Price tags for Catholic education. Commonweal 86:223-4 My 12 '67

HASTINGS, Jerry E.

CATV: past, present & future. Electr World 78:23-6+ Ag '67

HASZ, Jim

Virginia City. Parks & Rec 2:24-5+ Ap '67

HATCH, C. Richard

Columbia, pleonexia on the acropolis. Arch Forum 127:68-75 Jl '67

Museum of modern art discovers Harlem. Arch Forum 126:38-47 Mr '67

HATCH, Frank W.

Trial by testing. Dance Mag 41:49-50 Ag '67

HATCH, John

Rhodesia: sanctions on trial. Nation 204:166-9 F 6 '67

HATCH, Robert

Editorial shaping. Nation 205:408-9 O 23 '67

Films. See issues of Nation

San Francisco Mime. Nation 205:637 D 11 '67

Valentino and Hitchcock. Harper 235:121-3 D '67

HATCHER, Harlan Henthorne

Communication with our outdoor heritage; address, November 1, 1966. Am For 73:14-17+ Ja '67

HATCHER, Harry G.

Why you need a safety program; excerpts from address. Am City 82:103-5 Ag '67

HATCHER, Richard Gordon

Backlash, backstab. il por Newsweek 70:25-6 S 11 '67

Black power at the polls. A. Poinsett. il pors Ebony 23:23-5+ Ja '68

Gary's next mayor: white, pink, or black? H. Higdon. Reporter 37:41-2 N 2 '67

Lawyer takes on a corrupt steel town's machine. il pors Life 63:38-9 O 13 '67

Plea from Gary. por Time 90:24 S 15 '67

Real black power. il por Time 90:23-7 N 17 '67

Victory over prejudice and corruption. il por Life 63:38-9 N 17 '67

Vote power. il por Time 89:21-2 My 12 '67

HATFIELD, Antoinette (Kuzmanich)

Women worth watching. por(p30) McCalls 95:103-4 Ja '68

HATFIELD, Mark Odom

Hatfield on LBJ. New Repub 156:18 My 6 '67

Speaking out. por Sat Eve Post 240:12+ Jl 1 '67

United Nations; address, September 19, 1967. Vital Speeches 34:7-10 O 15 '67

Vietnam: charted on a distorted map. Sat R 50:20-2+ Jl 1 '67

about

Hatfield: the Oregon enigma. R. G. Sherrill. por Nation 205:38-44 Jl 17 '67

Prayerful Oregonian. T. S. Stimmel. New Repub 156:17-18 My 6 '67

Social concern in the S.B.C. Christian Cent 84:805 Je 21 '67

HATHAWAY, Mildred L. See Spock, B. jt. auth.

HATHERTON, Trevor. See Dickinson, W. R. jt. auth.

HATHORN, Paul A.

To Texas, by ICW. Motor B 120:52-5 O '67 (to be cont)

HATS

Hats on. il Time 90:49 N 3 '67

Pixie hat for tots 'n' teens. C. Houck. il Parents Mag 42:72 Je '67

Surinam's language of the hat. il Ebony 22: 36-8 My '67

HATTERSLEY, Ralph

Shadow of light by Bill Brandt. Pop Phot 61:103+ S '67

HATTERY, Glenn S.
Get out of the dumps. Am City 82:100-1 Je '67
HAUG, Pat, and others
Isoprenoid and dicarboxylic acids isolated from Colorado Green River shale (Eocene) bibliog Science 158:772-3 N 10 '67
HAUGAARD, Erik Christian
Writer comments. Horn Bk 43:444-6 Ag '67
HAUGAARD, Kay
Book jacket of the month club. Sat R 50:3 Jl 8 '67
HAUGEN, Richard K.
Tree ring indices: a circumpolar comparison. bibliog Science 158:773-5 N 10 '67
HAUGER, George
(tr) See Ghelderode, M. de. Pantagleize
HAUGHEY, John
What is the meaning of the people of Israel? America 117:218-20 S 2 '67
HAUGHTON, Daniel Jeremiah
Businessmen in the news. por Fortune 75: 47 Mr '67
Lockheed tries a new pilot. por Bsns W p34 F 11 '67
HAUGHTON, Rosemary
Faith or works? por Cath World 205:263-7 Ag '67
Open experiments, openly arrived at; with editorial comment. Commonweal 86:507, 511-13 Ag 25 '67
HAUNTED bookshop; drama. See Nicholson, J.
HAUNTED houses. See Ghosts
HAUPT, Hellmut Lehmann-. See Lehmann-Haupt, H.
HAUPT, Terri
Terri Haupt: Thistle crew. E. Horan. il por Yachting 121:47 My '67
HAUPTMANN, Gerhart Johann Robert
Walk with Gerhart Hauptmann. F. Kormendi. il Reporter 37:47-50 N 2 '67
HAURY, Emil W.
First masters of the American desert; the Hohokam. Nat Geog Mag 131:670-95 My '67
HAUSAS
Odyssey of Charles Wayo; Ghanaian boy walks Sahara and Europe in fantastic quest of American education. C. L. Sanders. il Ebony 22:27-30+ F '67
HAUSER, Alfred H.
False alarm in CDs? Duns R 88:43-4+ D '66
HAUSER, Ernest O.
Albrecht Dürer, he painted all creation. Read Digest 90:146-50 Mr '67
John the Baptist: voice in the wilderness. Read Digest 91:118-22 S '67
Miracle of the Twelve. Read Digest 91:85-90 D '67
Peter, prince of apostles. Read Digest 90: 194-5+ Ap '67
HÄUSERMANN, Pascal
Eggs are coming. il por Time 89:53 Je 16 '67
HAUSMAN, G. A.
Tecolote; poem. Liv Wildn 31:19 Spr '67
HAUSMAN, Louis
ABC's of CAI. Am Ed 3:15 N '67
HAVANA conference, 1966. See Tricontinental conference, Havana, 1966
HAVASU LAKE
See also
Lake Havasu City, Ariz.
HAVELOCK, Eric A.
Living Latin and Greek. por Sch & Soc 95: 290-2 Sum '67
HAVENFIELD corporation
Old hand breaks with tradition. Bsns W p 145-6 My 20 '67
HAVENS, Richie
One beautiful guy. il por Newsweek 70:91-2 Ag 14 '67
HAVERFORD college, Haverford, Pa.
Haverford policy on drug use. Sch & Soc 95:250+ Ap 15 '67
Haverford's new policy. Sch & Soc 95:340-2 O 14 '67
HAVIGHURST, Robert J.
Educational changes: their implications for the library. por ALA Bul 61:537-43 My '67
HAWAII
Trees of Hawaii. S. M. Jepsen. il Am For 73: 18-21+ D '67
See also
Birds—Hawaii
Honolulu—City planning
Kauai (island)
Kilauea (crater)
Maui (island)
Molokai (island)
Prisons—Hawaii
Tourist trade—Hawaii
Yachts and yachting—Hawaii
Zoology—Hawaii

Description and travel
Hawaii shows its age. L. Barry. il Pop Phot 60:26+ Mr '67
Hawaii's unknown isles. Travel 127:26 Je '67
Here lived the very first Hawaiians. il Sunset 139:41 S '67
Outer islands of Hawaii. K. Lamott. il Holiday 42:62-9+ Jl '67
HAWAII. University

East-West center
Year of the students: eastern and western grantees of the East-West center. H. Sutton. Sat R 50:50+ F 18 '67
HAWES, Evelyn
Madras-type jacket: story. Redbook 129:155 Je '67
HAWES, Gene R.
Academic philanthropy: the art of getting. Sat R 50:65-7+ D 16 '67
HAWKEN rifles. See Rifles
HAWKES, Jacquetta
Birth of wheat and maize farming. UNESCO Courier 20:6-7 My '67
Early domestication of animals. UNESCO Courier 20:7-8 My '67
HAWKING. See Falconry
HAWKINS, Donald E.
Guaranteed income. Parks & Rec 2:45-6+ Mr '67
Trends at a glance. Parks & Rec 2:21+ Jl '67
HAWKINS, Erick
Erick Hawkins addresses a new-to-dance audience. pors Dance Mag 41:40-4 Je '67
HAWKINS, Joseph E. Jr. See Johnsson, L.-G. jt. auth.
HAWKINS, Micah
Saw-Mill. Criticism
Opera N por 31:6-7 Ap 1 '67
HAWKS
Eagles over Hawk Mountain; excerpt from Flashing wings. J. K. Terres. il Audubon 69:28-33 Jl '67
Hawk and eagle numbers in decline. Nat Parks Mag 41:20 Ja '67
Hawks of southern North America; paintings; with biographical sketch. G. Coheleach. il Audubon 69:41-6 Ja '67
See also
Falcons
Kites (birds)
Ospreys
HAWTHORN books, incorporated
Stone is new president of Hawthorn books. Pub W 191:67 Ap 24 '67
HAWTHORNE, Frances E.
Safety first for the bike brigade. Parents Mag 42:50-1+ Ag '67
HAWTHORNE, Nathaniel
My kinsman, Major Molineux; dramatization. See Lowell, R. Old Glory

about
Nathaniel Hawthorne: the absurdity of heroism. T. L. Gross. Yale R 57:182-95 D '67
HAWTHORNS
Raphiolepis is a good one to push around. il Sunset 139:121 Je '67
HAY, Jacob
Annapolis: commuters, midshipmen and colonial charm. Holiday 42:68-73+ O '67
Cities: what will they be like? Parents Mag 43:44-5+ Ja '68
HAY handling
Six good ways to spoil haylage. N. Reeder. il Farm J 91:46R My '67
HAY making machinery
New hay tools. P. B. Jones. il Suc Farm 65:50D Ap '67
HAYCRAFT, Howard
Wilson company changes. Wilson Lib Bul 41:661-2 Mr '67
HAYDEN, Carl
Hayden moves. New Repub 157:8 O 14 '67
Hayden's rough rider. Time 90:16 O 20 '67
Influence of age. pors Newsweek 69:29 Je 5 '67
Living bond. por Time 89:22 My 5 '67
HAYDEN, Mike
Fishing the Klamath Loop. por Outdoor Life 140:36-9+ S '67
HAYDEN, Robert Earl
Three recent volumes. D. Galler. Poetry 110: 268 Jl '67
HAYDEN, Tom
Coming and going. Newsweek 70:24 N 27 '67
HAYDN, Franz Joseph
Orfeo ed Euridice. Criticism
Time il 89:58 Je 2 '67
Records:
Creation. Opera N 31:34 Mr 25 '67
Haydn: Mass in time of war, and Lord Nelson mass. Opera N 32:34 Ja 20 '68

HAYES, Bartlett Harding, 1904–
How much rubbed off? il por Time 89:76+
Je 16 '67
HAYES, Charles J.
Catholic schools and brotherhood. Cath World
206:165-6 Ja '68
HAYES, Dennis E. See Heirtzler, J. R. jt. auth.
HAYES, Elvin
Big E. H. L. Masin. por Sr Schol 89:20 Ja 20
'67
HAYES, Helen
Childhood in New York. por McCalls 95:97+
D '67
HAYES, Jim
First report: newest fishing in Pennsylvania.
por Field & S 71:50-1+ Ap '67
Midsummer night rainbows. Field & S 72:94-
7+ Ja '68
Some like it cold. Field & S 72:46-7+ D '67
—See Asper, K. jt. auth.
HAYES, John D.
Palomares bomb. Reporter 36:50+ Je 15 '67
HAYES, Nelson
Shoal water secrets of South Andros. il Motor
B 120:32-5 D '67
HAYES, Philip T.
Stubborn old lady; story. Redbook 129:70-1
Ag '67
HAYES, Robert D.
Foundations as easy as ABC. por Time 91:
46 Ja 5 '68
HAYES, Robert M.
Data processing in the library school cur-
riculum. bibliog ALA Bul 61:662-9 Je '67
HAYES, Samuel L. 3d, and Harlan, L. M.
Real estate as a corporate investment.
Harvard Bsns R 45:144-152+ Jl '67
—and Taussig, R. A.
Tactics of cash takeover bids. Harvard
Bsns R 45:135-48 Mr '67
HAYES, Thomas L.
Abortion: a biological view. Commonweal 85:
676-9 Mr 17 '67
HAYES, Warren Billingsley
Changing horses, and streams. il por Bsns
W p 137-8+ Ap 1 '67
HAYFLICK, Leonard. See Perkins, F. T. jt.
auth.
HAYLEY, William
New Blake letter. F. W. Hilles. Yale R 57:
85-9 O '67
HAYLOCK, E. F.
London's international boat show. Motor B
119:130+ Mr '67
HAYMAN, Jane
Journey of a lady, on horseback and, later,
by water; poem. New Yorker 43:28 Je 17
'67
HAYMAN, Leroy. See Mersand, J. L. jt. auth.
HAYNES, Robert H. See Hanawalt, P. C. jt.
auth.
HAYNES, Thomas
Inn sign revived. il pors Am Artist 31:61-5 N
'67
HAYNES, Ulric St Clair, Jr
He finds major minority talent. il por Bsns W
p68+ O 7 '67
HAYS, David
Interview, ed. by A. Fatt. por Dance Mag
41:47 F '67
HAYS, Helen
Adaptive ibis; with biographical sketch. Natur
Hist 76:6, 32-3 Ag '67
HAYS, James D. and Opdyke, N. D.
Antarctic radiolaria, magnetic reversals,
climatic change. bibliog Science 158:1001-11
N 24 '67
HAYS, Jill
Through the eyes of children. U S Camera
30:58-9+ O '67
HAYWARD, James N. See Baker, M. A. jt.
auth.
HAYWARD, Max
Russian anti-Semitism. Commentary 43:91-2
Mr '67
(tr) See Stalina, S. L. To Boris Leonidovich
Pasternak
(tr) See Voznesenskiĭ, A. Two poems: Strip-
tease on strike; Winter at the track
HAYWOOD, Fred
Times came for two teens. K. Chapin. il
Sports Illus 26:97-9 Ap 17 '67
HAYWOOD, William Dudley
Here come the Wobblies! B. A. Weisberger. il
por Am Heritage 18:30-5+ Je '67
HAZELTON, Nika Standen
Delectations. See issues of National review
Winter vegetable cook book. House & Gard
131:149+ F '67
HAZELTON, Roger
Bothersome bishop. New Repub 157:32-3+
O 7 '67
C. S. Lewis: no further than Gethsemane.
New Repub 156:25-7 F 18 '67

How real is reality? New Repub 158:36-7 Ja
6 '68
Tillich's questions and answers. New Repub
157:36-8 Ag 5 '67
Wars of religion. New Repub 156:25-6+ My 6
'67
HAZELWOOD, Jim
Electronic eyes for the blind. Sci N 91:456-7
My 13 '67
HAZLITT, Henry
Coming crisis in welfare. Nat R 19:416-18
Ap 18 '67
Excerpt from address, December 9, 1966. Cong
Digest 46:249+ O '67
HAZO, Robert G.
Between effort and effect. Nation 205:634-6 D
11 '67
Pitiful caricature. Nation 205:537-8 N 20 '67
HAZO, Samuel
End; poem. Sat R 50:65 Mr 11 '67
Nijinsky in St Moritz; poem. Sat R 50:34
F 18 '67
HAZZARD, Shirley
Canton more far. New Yorker 43:42-9 D 16 '67
Everlasting delight; story. New Yorker 43:
32-7 Ag 19 '67
Official life; story. New Yorker 43:24-30 Je
24 '67
Sense of mission; story. New Yorker 43:40-6
Mr 4 '67
Separation of Dinah Delbanco; story. New
Yorker 43:31-4 Jl 22 '67
Story of Miss Sadie Graine; story. New Yorker
43:82 Je 10 '67
Surprise, surprise. Mlle 65:98+ Je '67
Swoboda's tragedy; story. New Yorker 43:39-
48 My 20 '67
HEACOX, E. F.
Call for resources statesmanship. Am For 73:
14-17+ Ag '67
HEAD, Ann
End of innocence; story. Good H 165:92-3 O
'67
Requiem for a bachelor; story. McCalls 94:
82-3 Je '67
HEAD, Barry
Is there a life after marriage? Mlle 66:91+ Ja
'68
HEAD, Douglas M.
Election, USA. R. Lemon. il pors Sat Eve
Post 240:36-40+ N 18 '67
HEAD, Matthew, pseud. See Canaday, J.
HEAD Start, Project. See Project Head Start
HEADACHE
Headache the commonest human complaint.
A. F. Benjamin. Am Home 70:52 O '67
Induced migraines. Sci N 91:497 My 27 '67
Is migraine your headache? E. Maxwell. To-
days Health 45:77 D '67
Science works on your headache. L. Galton.
il Pop Sci 192:70-3+ Ja '68
HEADERS (automobile) See Automobile parts
HEADLEY, Jacqueline
Do I have a daddy? por Redbook 130:10+ D
'67
HEADMASTERS. See Educators
HEADPHONES. See Earphones
HEADS (engine) See Automobile engines
HEADS of state
Key world figures as Khrushchev rates them;
excerpts from NBC documentary, Khru-
shchev in exile. N. S. Khrushchev. il U S
News 63:12-13 Jl 24 '67
Who's who around the world (cont) Sr Schol
91:16-20 O 5 '67
HEALD, Weldon Fairbanks
Cascades' green mantle. il Am For 73:12-15+
Ap '67
about
Obituary
Nat Parks Mag 41:21 S '67
HEALTH
Americans not everybody knows; Sylvester
Graham; first notable health lecturer. C.
W. Ferguson. PTA Mag 61:14-16 Mr '67
Health in the home. A. F. Benjamin. See
issues of American home
Plain talk about family health. See issues of
Better homes and gardens
Today's health news. A. L. Blakeslee. See
issues of Today's health
We're smarter about health. Sci Digest 62:
80 Ag '67
Whatever became of physical fitness? F.
Knebel. il Look 31:94 Mr 7 '67
See also
Children—Care and hygiene
Diet
Exercise
Men—Health and hygiene
Nutrition
Sleep
Women—Health and hygiene

HEALTH, Mental. See Mental hygiene

HEALTH agencies, Voluntary
Cigarette issue; failure to support FCC rule. R. L. Shayon. Sat R 50:58 O 21 '67

HEALTH and aviation. See Aviation—Physiological aspects

HEALTH centers
Doctors meet the people; Neighborhood health center, of Montefiore hospital. M. K. Sanders. Harper 236:56-62 Ja '68
Miracle in Charcoal alley; Watts health center. il Time 90:57-8+ N 17 '67
New kind of care; neighborhood health center, Denver. R. H. Berg. il Look 31:36-40 Mr 21 '67
See also
Health clinics
Medical centers
Mental health centers

HEALTH clinics
Drugs, uses and abuses; D. Smith's Haight-Ashbury medical clinic. J. Luce. il Look 31:28 Ag 8 '67
Love needs care; clinic devoted exclusively to helping hippies with health problems. il Newsweek 70:98 Jl 17 '67
Vulnerable mothers, infants aided by pilot program; Chicago board of health's high-risk clinic. il Todays Health 46:45 Ja '68
Why don't we save these mothers and babies? W. Goodman. il Redbook 128:68-9+ Ap '67

HEALTH costs. See Medical service, Cost of

HEALTH departments
See also
New York (city)—Health, Department of

HEALTH education
Let's improve health education. W. A. Wesley. Todays Health 45:88 S '67
What do children ask the doctor? M. A. Wessel. il Parents Mag 42:61-3+ N '67
See also
Moving pictures in health education
Nutrition education
Physical education and training

HEALTH, education and welfare, Department of. See United States—Health, education and welfare, Department of

HEALTH examinations. See Physical examinations

HEALTH foods. See Food fads

HEALTH insurance. See Insurance, Health

HEALTH lobbyists. See Lobbyists

HEALTH resorts, watering places, etc.
Eating it up at a famous spa; Golden door, Escondido, Calif. Vogue 150:339-41 S 1 '67
Travel well; Spanish spas. E. N. Dye. Travel 128:61-2+ D '67

HEALTH service. See Medical service

HEALTH workers
Technological developments and their effects upon health manpower. H. M. Sturm. il Mo Labor R 90:1-8 Ja '67

Training
Health careers (cont) il Todays Health 45:36-41+ F; 50-5+ Mr; 52-5+ Ap; 54-5+ My; 24-9+ Je '67

HEALY, Paul F.
Seven sitting doves. New Repub 156:8-10 Je 3 '67

HEARD, Frances
Architect's choice: carriage house converted. House B 109:136-9+ F '67

HEARING
Hearing & the heart. il Time 89:47 Je 30 '67
Visual and auditory information processing in children and adults. E. C. Carterette and M. H. Jones. bibliog il Science 156:986-8 My 19 '67
See also
Deafness
Echolocation (physiology)

Testing
Hunt to catch a handicap; volunteers spot hearing defects in newborns. M. P. Downs. il Todays Health 46:46-51 Ja '68

HEARING aids
Aids for the hard-of-hearing. il Consumer Bul 50:26-32 Ag '67

HEARING in animals
Visual and nonvisual auditory systems in mammals. J. M. Harrison and R. Irving; reply with rejoinder. B. Masterton and I. T. Diamond. bibliog il Science 155:1696-7 Mr 31 '67

HEARING in reptiles
Frequency sensitivity of single auditory neurons in the gecko coleonyx variegatus. N. Suga and H. W. Campbell. bibliog il Science 157:88-90 Jl 7 '67

HEARNES, Warren E.
What worries governors; interview. por U S News 62:31-3 Ja 30 '67

HEARST, George Randolph, 1927-
Putting on the pressure. il Newsweek 71:47-8 Ja 8 '68

HEARST, James
It was like this; poem. Commonweal 86:445 Jl 14 '67
Revival; poem. Reporter 37:35 N 30 '67

HEARST, Phoebe (Apperson)
Keeping pace with the PTA. W. R. Hearst, jr. il PTA Mag 61:17-18 My '67

HEARST, William Randolph, 1908-
Keeping pace with the PTA. por PTA Mag 61:17-18 My '67

HEARST corporation
Hearst lives. il Newsweek 71:52+ Ja 22 '68

HEART
Calcium-induced activation of phosphorylase in rat hearts. A. J. D. Friesen and others. bibliog il Science 155:1108-9 Mr 3 '67
Corridors of the heart; with photographs by L. Nilsson. Life 64:22-31 Ja 19 '68
Magnetic fields around the torso; production by electrical activity of the human heart. D. Cohen. bibliog il Science 156:652-4 My 5 '67
Reserpine: effect on structure of heart muscle. D. E. L. Wilcken and others. bibliog il Science 157:1332-4 S 15 '67
See also
Blood—Circulation
Heart beat

Abnormalities and deformities
See also
Heart—Surgery

Diseases
Cardiac neurotics. Newsweek 70:110 S 18 '67
Cardiomyopathies; report on international conference. E. Bajusz and F. Homburger. Science 156:1649-50+ Je 23 '67
Coronary disease in spawning steelhead trout salmo gairdnerii. R. L. Van Citters and N. W. Watson. bibliog il Science 159:105-7 Ja 5 '68
Diet & the heart. Time 89:47 Je 30 '67
Doctor's heart attack; case of I. H. Page. il Time 90:52 N 3 '67
Hearing & the heart. il Time 89:47 Je 30 '67
Heart diseases in children. L. W. Sauer. il PTA Mag 62:29-30 N '67
I am Joe's heart; how to minimize risk of heart disease. J. D. Ratcliff. Read Digest 90:59-62 Ap '67
Mending hearts at home. R. T. Bugg. il Todays Health 45:52-5 N '67
Puzzling particles in the heart; idiopathic cardiomyopathy Time 89:75-6 F 17 '67
Run for your life. A. J. Snider. il Sci Digest 61:80-2 My '67
Science finally caught up; recovery from congenital heart disease due to development of Gibbon heart-lung machine. M. Mushro. il Mlle 65:76+ Ag '67
Scientists hear of new hopes to cut heart toll; highlights of AHA's annual meeting. il Bsns W p88-90 O 28 '67
Search for a way to curb heart disease. U S News 63:12 Jl 3 '67
Shedding new light on heart disease. il Bsns W p 110+ Je 24 '67
They're mending hearts with exercise. R. Bugg. il Todays Health 45:50-5 O '67
20,000 lives a year; emergency service for heart attack and stroke victims. D. A. Ehrlich. Sci N 92:405 O 21 '67

Diagnosis
Does your child have hidden heart trouble? the PhonoCardioScan. P. Deutsch and R. Deutsch. Read Digest 90:92-6 My '67
Early-warning system; studies of patients at Levine cardiac center, Peter Bent Brigham hospital. il Newsweek 69:62 Ja 30 '67
Heart attacks that aren't. S. M. Linde. il Todays Health 45:20-3 F '67

Surgery
And now for golf; mixed-up heart rebuilt. il Time 89:76 F 24 '67
Daring deed in the heart. il Time 89:46 Mr 24 '67
Footnote on the heart; open-heart surgery. il Sat R 50:50 Jl 1 '67
Frozen heart valves replace plastic ones. Sci N 92:358 O 7 '67
New heart for Susan; valve replacement surgery. il Ebony 23:57-8+ N '67
Open heart of Dr Amosoff; Russian surgeon and novelist. L. Gross. il Look 31:122-3+ O 3 '67

HEART—Surgery—*Continued*
Science finally caught up; recovery from congenital heart disease due to development of Gibbon heart-lung machine. M. Mushro. il Mlle 65:76+ Ag '67
Scientists hear of new hopes to cut heart toll; highlights of AHA's annual meeting. il Bsns W p88-90 O 28 '67
Too many & too soon? corrective measures for heart disease in its earlier stages. il Time 91:51 Ja 19 '68
Trial balloon in the aorta. il Time 90:52-3 Ag 25 '67
See also
Transplantation of organs, tissues, etc.

HEART beat
Heart strain greater in landing on carrier than bombing. C. M. Plattner. il Aviation W 86:60-1+ Mr 13 '67
Heart's pacemaker. E. F. Adolph. il Sci Am 216:32-7 bibliog(p 150) Mr '67
State as a determinant of infants' heart rate response to stimulation. M. Lewis and others. bibliog il Science 155:486-8 Ja 27 '67
See also
Pacemaker, Artificial (heart)

HEART disease. See Heart—Diseases
HEART-lung machines. See Hearts, Artificial
HEART of Christ, Devotion to. See Sacred Heart, Devotion to
HEART of the family; story. See Conger, L.
HEART pump. See Hearts, Artificial
HEART rate. See Heart beat
HEART transplants. See Transplantation of organs, tissues, etc.
HEART valves, Artificial. See Heart—Surgery
HEARTS, Artificial
Immediate counterattack; Belfast's mobile heart unit. il Time 90:32 S 1 '67
Lindbergh still pioneers. Sci N 92:177 Ag 19 '67
Mechanical heart being readied for human use. il Todays Health 45:74-5 S '67
Pumps to give the heart a rest; projects by Kantrowitz brothers. il Bsns W p 110-12 O 14 '67
Science finally caught up; recovery from congenital heart disease. M. Mushro. il Mlle 65:76+ Ag '67

HEAT
See also
High temperatures
Hot weather
Temperature
Thermodynamics

Physiological effects
Don't let the sun make you sick! A. F. Benjamin. Am Home 70:39 Jl '67
Heat inactivation of the relaxing site of actomyosin: prevention and reversal with dithiothreitol. H. M. Levy and E. M. Ryan. bibliog il Science 156:73-4 Ap 7 '67
Life at high temperatures. T. D. Brock. bibliog il Science 158:1012-19 N 24 '67
Sporulation mutations induced by heat in bacillus subtilis. J. Northrop and R. A. Slepecky. bibliog il Science 155:838-9 F 17 '67

Radiation and absorption
Kirchhoff-Planck radiation law. J. Agassi. bibliog Science 156:30-7 Ap 7 '67

HEAT conductivity
Thermal properties of materials. J. Ziman. il Sci Am 217:180-8 S '67

HEAT radiation. See Heat—Radiation and absorption
HEATERS
High-low heater. C. Conley. il Field & S 71:155 Mr '67
See also
Electric heaters

HEATH, Aloise Buckley
Thoughts on surveying a host of Heaths; poem. Nat R 19:1421 D 26 '67
(ed) See Heath, P. and others. True sprit of Christmas
about
Aloise B. Heath. RIP. W. F. Buckley, jr. and P. L. Buckley. il por Nat R 19:140-4 F 7 '67

HEATH, Dwight B.
Bolivia under Barrientos. bibliog f Cur Hist 53:275-82+ N '67

HEATH, Edward Richard George
Letter from London (cont) M. Panter-Downes. New Yorker 43:227-8+ N 11 '67

HEATH, Joel
Roadside bargain. Consumer Bul 50:18-19 Jl '67

HEATH, Pam, and others
True sprit of Christmas; ed. by A. B. Heath. Nat R 19:1420-1 D 26 '67

HEATH, Robert Galbraith
Schizophrenic split. por Time 89:56 F 3 '67

HEATHERS
Heaths & heathers for all-season bloom. H. Copeland. il Home Gard 54:76-8 Mr '67

HEATHROW international airport. See London —Airports

HEATHS (plants)
Cape heaths reward you, but they're touchy. il Sunset 139:203-4 N '67
Heaths & heathers for all-season bloom. H. Copeland. il Home Gard 54:76-8 Mr '67

HEATING
How to shop for year-round heating comfort. Bet Hom & Gard 45:12+ N '67
See also
Electric heating
Oil heating
also subhead Heating and ventilation under various subjects, e.g. Boats—Heating and ventilation

Control
Cold drafts and hot flashes? il Pop Mech 128: 178-81 O '67

Costs
Last chance to cut your heat bills. Changing T 21:42 D '67

Terminology
Glossary of heating and air conditioning terms. Arch Rec 142:158 Jl '67

HEATING, infrared
Infrared heat extends recreation season. W. R. Stephens. il Parks & Rec 2:31+ Ja '67

HEATING equipment
Wipe windows with warmth; system for an indoor-outdoor swimming pool. il Am City 82:104-5 Je '67
See also
Electric heaters

HEATING oil. See Oil fuel

HEATWOLE, Thelma C.
Public information service. Science 155:869-70 F 17 '67

HEAVY water. See Deuterium oxide
HEAVYWEIGHT boxers. See Boxers

HEBBLETHWAITE, Peter
What is an anonymous Christian? Cath World 205:90-4 My '67
Why missions? Cath World 205:335-9 S '67

HÉBERT, F. Edward
National guardsmen. New Repub 157:5-6 S 9 '67

HEBERTON, George
Join the in-group and look to the stars. Pop Gard 18:50-3+ Ag '67

HEBREW authors
See also
Agnon, S. J.

HEBREW day schools. See Jews—Education
HEBREW fables. See Fables
HEBREW language
Hebrew language. M. Pei. il Holiday 42:74-5+ D '67

HEBREW literature
See also
Jewish literature

HECHINGER, Fred Michael
What Sputnik did to our schools. McCalls 95:106-7+ O '67

HECHT, Nancy A.
Know your architecture. Am Home 70:24 Mr '67

HECHT, Roger
Poetry in pamphlets. Poetry 110:112-19 My '67
about
Five poets. D. W. Baker. Poetry 109:403 Mr '67

HECKMAN, Donald
Aiming high, the Jazz masters. Am Rec G 33:828+ My '67
In the pop bag. Am Rec G 33:893, 1056-7; 34:80-1, 168-9, 256-7, 342-3 My, Jl, S-D '67
Month's jazz. See issues of American record guide

HECKSCHER, August
New commissioner; interview. New Yorker 43:32-3 Mr 4 '67
Scandinavia observed. House B 110:88-9 Ja '68
Scholar in a nowhere world. Yale R 57:47-55 O '67

HEDDLE, John A. and others
Distribution of chromatids at mitosis. bibliog Science 158:929-31 N 17 '67

HEDGECOCK, Laurie
Eighth grade rebel. NEA J 56:19 S '67
HEDGEPETH, William
Inside the hippie revolution. Look 31:58-61+
Ag 22 '67
about
Behind the scenes. D. Chapman. il por Look
31:M1 Ag 22 '67
HEDGES, William D.
Will we recognize tomorrow's elementary
school? NEA J 56:9-12 D '67
HEDGES
Grow evergreens for privacy. Am Home 70:
120+ N '67
HEDJAZ campaign. See European war, 1914-
1918—Arabia
HEDLEY, John H.
Moscow's new look in western Europe. Yale
R 56:390-6 Mr '67
HEDONISM
Happiness: new light on an old subject;
interview. J. K. Lagemann. Read Digest
91:117-20 O '67
HEESCHEN, D. S.
Radio astronomy: a large antenna array.
bibliog Science 158:75-8 O 6 '67
HEEZEN, Bruce C.
Were comets the midwives at the birth of
man? J. Lear. il por Sat R 50:59-62 My
6 '67
Were comets the midwives at the birth of
man? J. Lear. il por Sat R 50:59-62 My 6
'67; Discussion. 50:52-6 Ag 5 '67
—See Glass, B. P.; Lowrie, A. jr, jt. auths.
HEFFNER, Richard D.
Rush to open-mindedness. Sat R 50:32+ N
11 '67
(ed) See Clark, G. Legacy of a great Ameri-
can
(ed) See Ward, B. Interview with Barbara
Ward
HEFFRON, Michael
Pay any price? break any mold? America
116:624-5 Ap 29 '67
HEFNER, Hugh Marston
Think clean. il pors Time 89:76-8+ Mr 3 '67
HEFNER, Philip
Churches and evolution. Christian Cent 84:651-
6 My 17 '67
HEGEL, Georg Wilhelm Friedrich
Meaning of Karl Marx. G. Morel. America
117:464-8 O 28 '67
HEGG, Eric A.
Off to the Klondike; photographs. Am Herit-
age 18:34-49+ Ag '67
HEGLAND, Maxine
Pin money for paperbacks. Library J 92:2000-
1 My 15 '67
HEIDELBERGER, Charles, and lype, P. T.
Malignant transformation in vitro by
carcinogenic hydrocarbons. bibliog Science
155:214-17 Ja 13 '67
HEIDELBERGER, James Fennell
Take a bow. il Pub W 191:43 Mr 27 '67
HEIDI; drama. See Thane, A.
HEIDT, Ann
Classroom cathedral. Sch Arts 66:11 Je '67
Dental floss and the area rug. Design 68:
18-19 Sum '67
HEIGHT of buildings. See Buildings—Height
HEIGHT of man. See Stature
HEILBRONER, Robert L.
Counterrevolutionary America; adaptation of
address. Commentary 43:31-8 Ap; 44:18+
Jl '67
HEILBRUN, Carolyn
Plea to publishers from a peripatetic parent.
Pub W 192:116-18 Jl 10 '67
HEIMOWITZ, Jack
And the world stopped, waiting. NEA J 56:
21-3 O '67; Same abr. with title Incident
in room 301. Read Digest 92:173-4+ Ja '68
HEIN, A. and Held, Richard
Dissociation of the visual placing response
into elicited and guided components. bib-
liog Science 158:390-2 O 20 '67
HEIN, Fred V.
Why some boys should stay off the team.
Todays Health 45:72+ Ag '67
HEIN, Piet
Piet Hein: a good egg. H. Lundbergh. House
B 110:8+ Ja '68
Piet Hein and his 7000 grooks. J Hicks. il
por Read Digest 90:193-4+ Mr '67
HEINE, Heinrich
Poet as music critic. R. Berges. por Am Rec
G 33:692-6+ My '67
HEINEMAN, Ben Walter
Looking for new ways to welfare. Bsns W
p26 Ja 6 '68

HEINEMAN, Nancy
Great auk, a bird now extinct; story. Sat Eve
Post 241:46-9 Ja 27 '68
HEINER, Lou
Alternator, a generator turned inside out.
Yachting 122:55-7+ D '67
Ignition breakthrough. Yachting 121:82-3+ Mr
'67
That mysterious little black box. Yachting
123:96-7+ Ja '68
HEINITZ, Thomas
Other side. See occasional issues of Saturday
review
HEINL, Robert Debs, Jr
Haiti, next mess in the Caribbean? Atlan
220:83-4+ N '67
HEINOLD, George
Salt water. See issues of Outdoor life
Tidal rivers never sleep. pors Outdoor Life
139:74-5+ My '67
HEINOLD, Laura
Salt water (cont) por Outdoor Life 139:46-7
Ap '67
HEINS, Paul
Ave atque vale. M. E. Manthorne. Horn Bk
43:706 D '67
HEINZ, H. J, company
H. J. Heinz pours it on in products and
profits. il Bsns W p 146-8+ N 11 '67
HEINZ, W. C.
Last campaign of boxing's last angry man.
Sat Eve Post 240:38-42+ F 11 '67
Maybe tomorrow, maybe the next day. Sat
Eve Post 241:65-9 Ja 27 '68
—See Lombardi, V. jt. auth.
HEINZMAN, George
Gobblers get their wings. Outdoor Life 139:
56-9+ F '67
HEINZMAN, George M.
Don't let them ride over us. Am Heritage
18:44-7+ F '67
HEIRS. See Inheritance
HEIRTZLER, James R. and Hayes, D. E.
Magnetic boundaries in the North Atlantic
Ocean. bibliog Science 157:185-7 Jl 14 '67
—See Herron, E. M. jt. auth.
HEISE, J. Arthur
Why the cadets cheat. Nation 204:622-6; 205:
2-L My 15, Jl 3 '67
HEISERMAN, David L.
Calculation of potentiometer linearity and
power dissipation. Electr World 78:59 Ag
'67
Gunn oscillators. Electr World 78:42-3 S '67
Light-emitting diodes. Electr World 79:36-7+
Ja '68
HEISMAN trophy. See Trophies, Sport
HEISS, Wolf Dieter, and Milne, D. C.
Single fibers of cat optic nerve: thresholds
to light. bibliog Science 155:1571-2 Mr 24 '67
HEITKAMP planetarium. See Planetariums
HEITMAN, Sidney
Rasputin and Romanov fall. Sat R 50:34-5
O 7 '67
HEKIMIAN, James S. and Jones, C. H.
Put people on your balance sheet. bibliog f
Harvard Bsns R 45:105-13 Ja '67
HELA cells. See Cells
HELD, John, 1889-1958
John Held's mad world. R. Lynes. il Harper
235:24+ N '67
HELD, Leo A.
Leo's last trip. il Newsweek 70:36-7 N 6 '67
Revolt of Leo Held. il Time 90:21-2 N 3 '67
HELD, Richard, and Bauer, J. A. Jr
Visually guided reaching in infant monkeys
after restricted rearing. bibliog Science 155:
718-20 F 10 '67
—See Hein, A. jt. auth.
HELE, Desmond King-. See King-Hele, D.
HELEN Gavin, Sister. See Gavin, H.
HELIACUS. See Gastropods
HELICOPTER airlines
Operation cost cited in helicopter case. Avia-
tion W 87:33 D 18 '67
HELICOPTER blades. See Helicopters—Blades
HELICOPTER engines
Technique developed to extend helicopter en-
gine-out range. il Aviation W 86:89 My 22
'67
HELICOPTER freight service
Test set for safer helicopter cargo plan; test-
ing army's cargo helicopters in Vietnam.
D. A. Brown. il Aviation W 86:85-6 My 22 '67
HELICOPTER industry and trade

Europe, Western
Europe stressing quick helicopter sales. il
Aviation W 86:322-3+ My 29 '67

HELICOPTER industry and trade—*Continued*
United States
Helicopters showing strong rise in corporate sales. D. A. Brown. il Aviation W 86:306-11 Mr 6 '67
New crop. il Flying 80:32-9 F '67
See also
Government investigations—Helicopter industry and trade
HELICOPTER pilots
Union seeks to organize helicopter pilots. R. F. Coburn. Aviation W 86:93-5 Mr 13 '67
HELICOPTER rotors. See Rotors (helicopters)
HELICOPTER schools. See Aviation schools
HELICOPTER taxi service. See Air taxi service
HELICOPTERS
Brantly 305; Lear jet corporation's piston-powered helicopter. il Flying 80:34-5 F '67
Fairchild-Hiller FH-1100. il Flying 80:39 F '67
Gone flying to Arkansas; Brantly 305. A. Trammell. il Flying 80:64-5 Je '67
Leading international rotary-wing aircraft; specifications (cont) Aviation W 86:213 Mr 6 '67
Pilot report: the rigid rotor; Lockheed's equal-opportunity helicopter. R. Blodget. il Flying 81:61-3 O '67
U.K. Irish market penetration sought for Hughes model 500. il Aviation W 86:113 Ja 23 '67
U.S. rotary-wing aircraft; specifications (cont) Aviation W 86:211-12 Mr 6 '67
See also
Autogiros
Rotors (helicopters)

Armaments
AH-56A sight tracks during maneuvers. il Aviation W 87:50+ O 30 '67

Blades
Tower will test helicopter blades by simulating hovering. il Tech W 20:40 Ap 24 '67

Design
Changing helicopter. A. Gessow. il Sci Am 216:38-46 bibliog(p 146) Ap '67
Helicopter specifications held unrealistic. D. A. Brown. Aviation W 87:103+ D 4 '67
Lockheed's flying gyroscope. il Time 89:88+ My 12 '67

Equipment
See also
Aeronautic instruments

Landing on ships
New helicopter ship landing aid built. K. J. Stein. il Aviation W 87:93-4+ S 25 '67

Military applications
AH-56A set to move to production phase. Aviation W 88:40-1 Ja 15 '68
Advanced avionics used widely in AH-56A. C. M. Plattner. il Aviation W 86:28-31 My 15 '67
ASW helicopter control system tested. K. J. Stein. il Aviation W 87:86+ Ag 28 '67
Army to bolster air strength in Vietnam. C. Brownlow. il Aviation W 86:28-30+ Mr 20 '67
Army to request bids on new LOH orders. D. C. Winston. Aviation W 87:18-19 Jl 31 '67
C-5A logistics spur helicopter proposal. C. Brownlow. il Aviation W 87:53+ N 27 '67
Cheyenne bows in. il Newsweek 70:54 D 25 '67
Cheyenne warrior; Lockheed's combination helicopter and fixed-wing plane. il Time 90:71 D 22 '67
Death by starlight; U.S. night operations in Vietnam carried out by teams of helicopters. Time 90:31 Jl 21 '67
Digging out the V.C. U.S. 1st Cavalry airmobile. il Time 90:38 S 29 '67
Funding problems cloud AH-56A debut. Aviation W 87:20-1 D 18 '67
Germany approves order for 110 Transalls; may reduce helicopter buy. W. C. Wetmore. Aviation W 87:31-2 S 18 '67
Golden Hawks; army's first aviation brigade. il Newsweek 70:32-3 O 2 '67
HH-53B readied for southeast Asia role as interim CARA; combat aircrew rescue aircraft. C. Brownlow. il Aviation W 87:64-5+ Jl 3 '67
Helicopters in Vietnam. K. V. Brown. il Pop Mech 127:107-11+ F '67

HueyCobra praised for Vietnam action. Aviation W 88:33 Ja 15 '68
Israelis relied on helicopters for movement of troops, logistics support, pilot rescue. W. C. Wetmore. il Aviation W 87:90-1+ Ag 7 '67
LOH hearing may spur tighter bid rules. D. C. Winston. il Aviation W 86:87+ Mr 13 '67
Lockheed unveils rigid-rotor AH-56A. il Aviation W 86:25-6 My 8 '67
Probing Pentagon's buying practices; buying in, deliberate bidding at a known loss. il Bsns W p 121-2 Mr 18 '67
S-61 extends Danish rescue unit's reach. D. E. Fink. il Aviation W 87:67-8+ D 4 '67
Weapons for present & future; Hueycobra. il Time 90:21 O 20 '67
Wide use of QH-50 demonstrated. il Aviation W 87:96-7 Ag 14 '67

Piloting
Stiff competition marks helicopter show; Paris flying display. il Aviation W 86:35-6 Je 12 '67

Refueling
USAF HH-3s make record helicopter Atlantic flight; photographs. Aviation W 86:38-9 Je 12 '67

Rotors
See Rotors (helicopters)

Testing
ASW helicopter control system tested. K. J. Stein. il Aviation W 87:86+ Ag 28 '67
FH-1100. M. Paquette and R. B. Weeghman. il Flying 81:48-52 N '67
Pilot report:
Hughes 500; light turbine-powered helicopters. R. Blodget. il Flying 80:32-3+ F '67

Transatlantic flights
See Aviation—Transatlantic flights
HELICOPTERS, Ambulance
See also
Helicopters in medical service
HELICOPTERS, Business
Helicopters showing strong rise in corporate sales. D. A. Brown. il Aviation W 86:306-11 Mr 6 '67
HELICOPTERS, Jet propelled
Testing
Pilot report: the Bell jet ranger. R. B. Weeghman. il Flying 80:34-7 F '67
HELICOPTERS, Military. See Helicopters—Military applications
HELICOPTERS in agriculture
Big birds help the bees. G. C. Lorang. il Farm J 91:39 My '67
HELICOPTERS in building
Union seeks to organize helicopter pilots. R. F. Coburn. Aviation W 86:93-5 Mr 13 '67
HELICOPTERS in freight service. See Helicopter freight service
HELICOPTERS in medical service
Operating under pressure; schoolboy suffering gas gangrene flown by helicopter to Mount Sinai hospital's hyperbaric chamber. il Newsweek 70:52-3 Ag 7 '67
HELICOPTERS in photography
Fred Ward's $25,000 tripod; interview. ed. by J. Neubauer. F. Ward. il Pop Phot 60:69 Je '67
HELICOPTERS in police work
Cheese it, the copters. T. Stimson. il Pop Mech 127:74-7+ Je '67
Project Sky Knight; Los Angeles County. il Am City 82:33 Ag '67
HELICOPTERS in rescue work
Coast guard's Christmas carol; baby born on a Russian fishing ship. W. R. Brantley and J. R. Butler. il Pop Mech 128:76-80+ D '67
HH-53B readied for southeast Asia role as interim CARA; combat aircrew rescue aircraft. C. Brownlow. il Aviation W 87:64-5+ Jl 3 '67
S-61 extends Danish rescue unit's reach. D. E. Fink. il Aviation W 87:67-8+ D 4 '67
See also
United States—Air force—Air rescue service
HELICOPTERS in traffic regulation
How copters can solve traffic jams. D. Francis. il Pop Sci 190:94-7 Ap '67
Somebody up there likes you drivers; WOR's aerial traffic reporter. P. O'Neil. il Life 63:54-54B+ Ag 4 '67
HELIOGRAPH
Scopes for solar study; taking the first radio moving pictures of the sun; experiments at Culgoora, Australia. il Sci N 91:222 Mr 4 '67

HELIOMETER. See Astronomical instruments

HÉLION, Jean
Cool and concrete from the 'thirties. S. Burton. il Art N 66:34-5+ Ap '67

HELIPORTS
Flying downtown; New York city plan for new in-city landing facilities. il Time 91:27 Ja 12 '68
Will it never stop? proposal to put heliports in New York's parks. Parks & Rec 2:19 Ja '67

HELIUM
Animals at very high pressures of helium and neon. K. W. Miller and others. bibliog Science 157:97-8 Jl 7 '67
Elemental centenary. M. J. Walker. il Sci N 92:284-5 S 16 '67
Helium near zero. Sci N 91:424 My 6 '67
Study shows helium increases fire hazards. H. M. David. il Tech W 20:22-3 Mr 13 '67

HELLA, U. W.
Managing human use of natural parks. Parks & Rec 2:34-5+ Ja '67

HELLEGERS, Andre E.
Law and the common good. Commonweal 86: 418-23 Je 30 '67

HELLEINER, Mary
Winter color in your coldframe. Horticulture 45:26-7 N '67

HELLENISM
See also
Classicism

HELLER, Austin N.
Do your city planners know about air pollution? Am City 82:91-4 Ap '67

about

New York's clean-air man. F. J. Cook. il pors N Y Times Mag p44-5+ Mr 5 '67

HELLER, H. F.
To talk of many things; address, April 5, 1967. Vital Speeches 33:697-700 S 1 '67

HELLER, Joseph
Catch-22 revisited. Holiday 41:44-61+ Ap '67
How I found James Bond. Holiday 41:123-5+ Je '67

about

We bombed in New Haven. Criticism
Life 64:14 Ja 12 '68
Nation 206:26-7 Ja 1 '68
Newsweek il 70:96 D 18 '67
Time 90:87 D 15 '67

HELLER, Suzanne
Misery loves company; excerpts. Good H 164: 98-9 Je '67

HELLER, Walter Wolfgang
Excerpt from testimony before Joint economic committee of U.S. Congress, February 15, 1967. Cong Digest 46:124+ Ap '67

about

Walter Heller's federalist papers. M. Nolan. il Reporter 36:13-17 Je 1 '67

HELLMAN, Hal
New look at the UFO enigma; ball lightning, excerpt from Light and electricity in the atmosphere. Sci Digest 62:9-15 N '67

HELLMAN, Lillian
Interlude in Budapest. Holiday 42:60-1 N '67

about

Little foxes. Criticism
America 117:723 D 9 '67
Commonweal 87:304-5 D 1 '67
New Yorker 43:162 N 4 '67
Newsweek il 70:86 N 6 '67
Reporter 38:36 Ja 11 '68
Sat R 50:26 N 11 '67
Time il 90:64+ N 3 '67

HELLO, Dolly! musical comedy. See Musical comedies, revues. etc.—Criticisms, plots, etc.

HELL'S Angels. See Gangs

HELL'S CANYON
Farewell to Hells Canyon; taming Snake River by a new dam. J. Skow. il Sat Eve Post 240:76-83 Jl 1 '67

HELLSTRÖM, I. and Hellström, K. E.
Cell-bound immunity to autologous and syngeneic mouse tumors induced by methylcholanthrene and plastic discs. bibliog Science 156:981-3 My 19 '67

HELLSTRÖM, K. E. See Hellström, I. jt. auth.

HELM, Ann
In my opinion. por Seventeen 26:254 N '67

HELM, E. Eugene
Vibrating string of the Pythagoreans: with biographical sketch. Sci Am 217:14, 92-8+ bibliog(p 158) D '67

HELM, Everett
Biennale 1967. Hi Fi 17:MA28+ Ag '67
Holland festival, 1967. Hi Fi 17:MA26 O '67
New performances on old instruments. por Hi Fi 17:42-6 My '67
Notes from our correspondents (cont) Hi Fi 17:25-6 Ag '67
Opera on an even keel. Hi Fi 17:MA38-9 My '67

HELMER, Olaf
New intellectual climate; address, April 20, 1967. Vital Speeches 33:497-9 Je 1 '67

HELMS, Harvey
Best treatment I've found for baby pig scours. Farm J 91:H14+ Ap '67
How to tell when to call a vet. Farm J 91:H4 Je '67
Tips on preventing baby pig scours. Farm J 91:H16-17 F '67

HELMS, J. Lynn
Space program; address, September 13, 1967. Vital Speeches 34:176-81 Ja 1 '68

HELMS, Richard McGarrah
Silent service. il por Time 89:13-17 F 24 '67

HELOISE, pseud. See Cruse, H.

HELP! or something; story. See Sagan, F.

HELP, the newsboy hollered; story. See Saroyan, W.

HELPMANN, Robert Murray
Royal pair. H. Saal. il Newsweek 69:83-4 My 1 '67

HEMATITE
Alpha-hematite: stable remanence and memory. R. W. Smith and M. Fuller. bibliog il Science 156:1130-3 My 26 '67

HEMATURIA
Hematuria following administration of ethanol. J. M. Orten and others. bibliog Science 157:72-3 Jl 7 '67

HEME
Heme and globin synthesis control: observations in vivo in beta thalassemia. M. Kreimer-Birnbaum and R. M. Bannerman. bibliog il Science 155:1116-18 Mr 3 '67; Reply with rejoinder. T. G. Gabuzda and others. 157:1079 S 1 '67

HEMEROCALLIS. See Day lilies

HEMICHORDATE worms. See Balanoglossus

HEMINGWAY, Ernest
Before and after papa. S. Kauffmann. New Repub 156:18+ Je 10 '67
Captain Hemingway. E. Weeks. Atlan 220: 109-10 Jl '67
Farewell to arms. S. Maloff. il por Newsweek 69:102 Je 5 '67
Hanging up on Hemingway. J. Beatty, jr. Esquire 67:116 F '67
Hemingway's Spain. M. Hemingway. il por Sat R 50:48-9+ Mr 11 '67
Hero as celebrity. por Time 89:133+ My 19 '67
Novelist as newspaperman. G. Hicks. Sat R 50:23-4 My 27 '67
Papa and the parricides. M. Cowley. il Esquire 67:100-1+ Je '67

HEMINGWAY, Mary (Welsh)
Hemingway's Spain. Sat R 50:48-9+ Mr 11 '67

HEMINGWAY, Mary Moon
Branch library for your guest room. House & Gard 131:185-6 My '67
How to transplant your home. House & Gard 131:148-9+ Ap '67
Notes for the hostess. See issues of House & garden incorporating Living for young homemakers

HEMISFAIR. See San Antonio, Tex.—Hemisfair, 1968

HEMLEY, Cecil
Spring beyond the spring. M. McCloskey. Poetry 110:427-8 S '67

HEMLEY, J. J. and others
Sulfide solubilities in alteration-controlled systems. bibliog Science 158:1580-2 D 22 '67

HEMMING, Roy, and others
DIScussions. See issues of Senior scholastic

HEMMINGS, David
It doesn't come easy; ed. by E. Miller. pors Seventeen 26:152-3+ My '67

about

People are talking about . . . il por Vogue 149:94-5 F 15 '67

HEMOCYANIN
Radiation of hemocyanin: inactivation and reactivation of oxygen-carrying capacity. J. Schubert and E. R. White. bibliog il Science 155:1000-3 F 24 '67

HEMOGLOBIN
Globin composition and synthesis of hemoglobins in developing fetal mice erythroid cells. A. Fantoni and others. bibliog il Science 157:1327-9 S 15 '67

HEMOGLOBIN—*Continued*
Heme and globin synthesis control: observations in vivo in beta thalassemia. M. Kreimer-Birnbaum and R. M. Bannerman. bibliog il Science 155:1116-18 Mr 3 '67; Reply with rejoinder. T. G. Gabuzda and others. 157:1079 S 1 '67
Hemoglobin $\alpha_2\beta_2^{121 \ Lys}$ chemical identification in an Egyptian family. K. A. Kamel and others. bibliog il Science 156:397-8 Ap 21 '67
Hemoglobin and its reaction with ligands. E. Antonini. bibliog il Science 158:1417-25 D 15 '67
Hemoglobin gun hill: deletion of five amino acid residues and impaired hemoglobin binding. T. B. Bradley, jr. and others. bibliog il Science 157:1581-3 S 29 '67
Hemoglobin Portland 1: a new human hemoglobin unique in structure. G. L. Capp and others. bibliog il Science 157:65-6 Jl 7 '67
Hemoglobin variants in Koreans: hemoglobin G Taegu. R. Q. Blackwell and others. bibliog Science 158:1056-7 N 24 '67
Hexokinase isoenzymes in human erythrocytes: association of type II with fetal hemoglobin. E. W. Holmes, jr. and others. bibliog il Science 156:646-8 My 5 '67
Induction and survival of hemoglobin-less and erythrocyte-less tadpoles and young bullfrogs. G. Flores and E. Frieden. bibliog il Science 159:101-3 Ja 5 '68
Oxygenation properties of snake hemoglobin. B. Sullivan. bibliog il Science 157:1308-10 S 15 '67
Polymerization of hemoglobins of mouse and man: structural basis. J. Bonaventura and A. Riggs. bibliog il Science 158:800-2 N 10 '67
Rabbit hemoglobin biosynthesis: use of human hemoglobin chains to study molecule completion. J. R. Shaeffer and others. bibliog il Science 158:488-90 O 27 '67
Thick blood disease; risk of clot-caused strokes high among people with elevated-hemoglobin levels. Newsweek 70:65 N 6 '67
HEMOGLOBIN polymorphism. See Polymorphism (biology)
HEMOLYTIC anemia. See Anemia
HEMOPHILIA
Antihemophilic factor release by perfused liver and spleen: relationship to hemophilia. J. C. Norman and others. bibliog il Science 158:1060-1 N 24 '67
Man with 586 blood brothers. il Ebony 22:56-8+ F '67
One man's fight against hemophilia. P. Deutsch and R. Deutsch. il Todays Health 45:40-3 Ag '67; Same abr. with title Doctor Thelin's fight against hemophilia. Read Digest 91:90-4 Ag '67
Overprotected bleeders. Time 89:75 Ja 27 '67
HEMORRHAGE
Viral hemorrhagic encephalopathy of rats. A. H. ElDadah and others. bibliog il Science 156:392-4 Ap 21 '67
HEMORRHAGIC fever
Great Bolivian fever mystery; ed. by D. S. Stroetzel. T. Armbrister. il Read Digest 90:165-6+ F '67
HEMORRHEOLOGY. See Blood—Circulation
HEMPSTEAD, N.Y.

Sanitary affairs
Cleanest incinerator stack gases. L. S. Wegman. il Am City 82:89-91+ My '67
Incinerators can meet tougher standards. H. Mandelbaum. il Am City 82:97-8 Ag '67
HEMPSTEAD, N.Y. public library
Center of foreign language materials. Wilson Lib Bul 41:880 My '67
HEMPSTONE, Smith
Report: Greece. Atlan 220:20-3 Jl '67
HEMSLEY, Stuart
Doctors report that spiders spin slower after a morphine dose; poem. Atlan 219:120 Ap '67
HENAHAN, John F.
Of trains, air, and Eire. Sat R 50:4+ N 25 '67
Poorest of the poor. Sat R 50:4+ Jl 29 '67
Still life in the ould turf. Sat R 50:4 S 23 '67
HÉNARD, Engène
First modern urbanist. P. Wolf. il Arch Forum 127:50-5 O '67
HENDERSON, Arthur, baron Rowley. See Rowley, A. H.
HENDERSON, Bruce D.
Brinkmanship in business. Harvard Bsns R 45:49-55 Mr '67
HENDERSON, Everett S.
Late-blooming perennials. Horticulture 45:12-15+ S '67

Oriental dogwood. Horticulture 45:26-7+ Ap '67
Plant some spectacular poppies. Horticulture 45:18-19+ My '67
Sourwood. Horticulture 45:33 N '67
HENDERSON, Florence
My kids are the real stars. G. M. Laudau. il pors Parents Mag 42:42-5+ Ag '67
HENDERSON, Florence Black
Obituary
Negro Hist Bul 30:20 F '67. J. E. Allen
HENDERSON, Robert
Avizandum; story. New Yorker 43:28-32 S 2 '67
Community spirit; story. New Yorker 43:28-30 Jl 22 '67
Fipple flute; story. New Yorker 43:44-7 Ap 22 '67
HENDLER, Raymond
Two for May: Dunn, Hendler. S. Burton. Art N 66:55+ My '67
HENDRICKS, Bici
Hui Ka Kwong. Craft Horiz 27:40-3+ My '67
HENDRICKSON, Robert
Melville revisited. Sat R 50:43-4 Ag 5 '67
HENDRICKSON, Walter B, Jr
Rescue from the deep! Pop Mech 129:124-6+ Ja '68
HENDRIX, Jimi
Voice of experience. il por Newsweek 70:90+ O 9 '67
HENDRYSON, Elizabeth S.
President's message. See issues of PTA magazine
HENEGAR, Leah
Cued speech. A. C. Miles. il pors Am Ed 3:26-8 N '67
HENEHAN, Anne
Hippies: creative dropouts or escapist copouts? Sr Schol 91:17-19+ N 16 '67
HENEQUEN. See Sisal hemp
HENIZE, Karl G. and others
Ultraviolet stellar spectroscopy on Gemini 11. bibliog Science 155:1407-8 Mr 17 '67
HENKELL, Marjorie
Apple to Mrs Henkell; report. Am Ed 3:21-2 Ap '67
HENLE, Faye
Does it pay for a wife to work? Am Home 70:44-5+ S '67
HENLE, Werner, and others
Herpes-type virus and chromosome marker in normal leukocytes after growth with irradiated Burkitt cells. bibliog Science 157:1064-5 S 1 '67
HENLEY, Fred M.
Boston, 1770. America 117:150-1+ Ag 12 '67
HENN, William D. See Buchsbaum, W. H. jt. auth.
HENNE, Frances
Media standards probed at N.Y. state A/V conference; summary of address, November 1967. Library J 93:253-4 Ja 15 '68
HENNEPIN, Ill.
Helping a small town cope with prosperity; Jones & Laughlin's new steel plant. il Bsns W p184-6+ S 23 '67
HENNESEY, Joanne
Twenty feet can go a long way. Yachting 122:48-9+ N '67
HENNESSEY, Mike
Notes from our correspondents. Hi Fi 17:20+ My '67
HENRY, Benjamin Tyler
B. Tyler Henry. C. G. Worman. il Hobbies 71:124-5 F '67
HENRY, Carl
Fundamentalists and the faith. Cath World 205:145-50 Je '67
Mr Inside. por Newsweek 71:71-2 Ja 15 '68
HENRY, Joseph
Henry papers: works of Joseph Henry to be collected; for publication at the Smithsonian institution. K. Sperry. il por Science 157:908 Ag 25 '67
HENRY, Jules
Education's romantic critics. P. Schrag. por Sat R 50:80-2+ F 18 '67
HENRY, Kenneth
Perspective on public relations. bibliog f Harvard Bsns R 45:14-16+ Jl '67
HENRY, Kenneth R.
Audiogenic seizure susceptibility induced in C57B1/6J mice by prior auditory exposure. bibliog Science 158:938-40 N 17 '67
HENRY, Walt
Build the electronic frequency meter. Pop Electr 26:73-7 My '67
HENRY, sweet Henry; musical comedy. See Musical comedies, revues, etc.—Criticisms, plots, etc.

HENRY E. Huntington library and art gallery, San Marino, Calif.
Understanding Anglo-American civilization. J. Thorpe. il Wilson Lib Bul 41:580-5 F '67

HENRY Francis Du Pont Winterthur museum
Delaware delights. D. Seibert. il Travel 127: 46-7 Ap '67

HENRY S. Borneman fraktur schriften collection. See Philadelphia—Free library

HENRY 3; story. See Krumgold, J.

HENSHAW, Marie
Conversion sampler. por Library J 92:3964-6 N 1 '67

HENSHAW family
At the sign of the crest. H. K. Eilers. il Hobbies 71:120-1 F '67

HENSLEY, William L.
Electric power aplenty for the small boat. Pop Sci 191:86-8 D '67

HENTOFF, Nat
A. J. Muste: 1885—1967. Sat R 50:35 Ap 8 '67
Books (cont) New Yorker 43:154+ Mr 4 '67
Fiction for teen-agers. Atlan 220:136+ D '67
Murderous pleasures of tennis. Atlan 219:98-100 Ap '67
Profiles; J. Lindsay. New Yorker 43:58-60+ O 7; 61-4+ O 14 '67

HENZE, Calvin R.
Plan before you put a computer to work. Am City 82:100-1 Mr '67

HENZE, Hans Werner
Instinct for style; interview, ed. by J. W. Freeman. por Opera N 31:13 F 18 '67

about
Boulevard solitude. Criticism
Hi Fi 17:MA21 O '67
Sat R 50:38 Ag 26 '67
Diddlidong at Dartmouth. il por Time 90:38 Jl 28 '67
Henze at Hanover: the creative experience. B. Jacobson. il por Hi Fi 17:MA18-19 O '67
Lively arts. R. Hemming. por Sr Schol 91:24 S 21 '67
Young lord. Criticism
Hi Fi il 17:MA26-7+ My '67
Opera N il 31:31 Mr 25 '67

HEPATIC pathology. See Liver—Diseases

HEPATICAE. See Liverworts

HEPATITIS
Is hepatitis about to strike again? Changing T 21:13-15 D '67

HEPATOMAS. See Tumors

HEPBURN, Audrey
Audrey Hepburn makes the scene. L. Dowty. il pors Good H 165:84-6 Ag '67

HEPBURN, Katharine
Last visit with two undimmed stars; interview, ed. by J. Hamilton. pors Look 31: 26-30+ Jl 11 '67

about
Hepburn comes back big, bringing a niece who calls her Aunt Kat. J. Frook. il pors Life 64:60-5 Ja 5 '68
Katharine Hepburn. R. Newquist. por McCalls 94:64-5+ Jl '67
Last of the honest-to-God ladies. L. Israel. por Esquire 68:114-16+ N '67

HEPPEL, Leon A.
Selective release of enzymes from bacteria. bibliog Science 156:1451-5 Je 16 '67

HEPPNER, Frank
Science proves it, the robin sees the worm. Audubon 69:86-8+ S '67
—See Hamilton, W. J. 3d, jt. auth.

HERAKLES; drama. See MacLeish, A.

HERALD, Earl S. and others
Impact of homo sapiens upon an alligator wishing well. Parks & Rec 2:30+ S '67

HERALD tribune, New York. See New York herald tribune

HERALDRY
At the sign of the crest. H. K. Eilers. See issues of Hobbies
Fifteen year index; At the sign of the crest. column. H. K. Eilers. Hobbies 72:116 D '67
Name of the game is names; Boston's Sanson institute of heraldry. il Bsns W p 114-15 Je 10 '67

HERATH, Kent A.
Chile's regional universities. Américas 19: 18-20 N '67
Eucalyptus in Peru. Am For 73:20-2 Ap '67

HERB teas. See Tea

HERBARIUMS
Electronic herbarium; National university of Mexico. E. Zubryn. il Sci N 92:161 Ag 12 '67

HERBERG, L. J. and Blundell, J. E.
Lateral hypothalamus: hoarding behavior elicited by electrical stimulation. bibliog Science 155:349-50 Ja 20 '67

HERBERG, Will
Tyrant necessity. Sat R 50:50-1 F 4 '67
Who are the hippies? Nat R 19:844-6+ Ag 8 '67

HERBERS, John
Occupation: farmer; avocation: Senator. N Y Times Mag p24-5+ Ja 29 '67

HERBERT, John
Fortune and men's eyes. Criticism
America 116:510 Ap 1 '67
Commonweal 86:321-3 Je 2 '67
Nation 204:412-13 Mr 27 '67
New Yorker 43:134 Mr 4 '67

HERBICIDES
Diphenamid metabolism in plants. C. D. Kesner and S. K. Ries. bibliog il Science 155:210-11 Ja 13 '67
Herbicide mixtures, should you use them? Suc Farm 65:96 Mr '67
Herbicides in Vietnam. A. W. Galston. New Repub 157:19-21 N 25 '67
Make herbicides work better. Suc Farm 65: 93 Mr '67
Preemergence weed control for corn. Suc Farm 65:100 Mr '67
See also
Dicamba
Weeds—Chemical control

Cost
What does it cost to use a preemergence herbicide? Suc Farm 65:88 Ap '67

Injurious effects
Diurnal rhythm of sensitivity of cotton seedlings to herbicides. J. G. Gosselink and L. C. Standifer. bibliog il Science 158: 120-1 O 6 '67

Residues
How to avoid a herbicide residue problem. Suc Farm 65:56 Ap '67

HERBIG, George H.
Youngest stars. Sci Am 217:30-6 Ag '67

HERBS
Fun and fancy of growing herbs; legend, lore, and practical use. H. S. Witty. il Home Gard 54:40-8 My '67
Grow some of the easy herbs. M. W. Bear. il Horticulture 45:24-5+ My '67
How to dry herbs. J. Sheridan. Horticulture 45:18 S '67
See also
Garlic
Ginseng

HERDER and Herder, incorporated
Herder & Herder and Burns & Oates in merger. Pub W 191:91 Ja 30 '67

HEREDITY
Heredity-environment problem. F. S. Meyer. Nat R 19:1074 O 3 '67
Heritability of plasma cholinesterase activity in inbred mouse strains. C. R. Angel and others. bibliog il Science 156:529-30 Ap 28 '67
Racial studies: Academy states position on call for new research; statement of National academy of sciences. Science 158:892-3 N 17 '67
See also
Eugenics
Evolution
Genes
Genetics
Natural selection

HEREDITY of disease
Chances of a defective child. il Time 89:57 Mr 3 '67
Enzyme defect associated with a sex-linked human neurological disorder and excessive purine synthesis. J. E. Seegmiller and others. bibliog il Science 155:1682-4 Mr 31 '67
Genetic counseling. M. W. Thompson. il PTA Mag 61:12-15 F '67
Genetics cures hereditary diseases. B. Frisch. il Sci Digest 61:44-7 Mr '67
Hereditary renal disease in a mutant strain of rats. B. B. Lozzio and others. bibliog il Science 156:1742-4 Je 30 '67
Inherited diseases: on the way out. B. J. Culliton. il Sci N 92:184-5 Ag 19 '67
Mutant enzymatic and cytological phenotypes in cultured human fibroblasts. J. G. Leroy and R. I. DeMars. bibliog il Science 157:804-6 Ag 18 '67
Predicting tomorrow's children; genetic counseling. D. C. Davis. il Todays Health 46:32-7+ Ja '68

HERESY
Death of dialogue; Episcopal committee dismissing heresy charges against Bishop Pike. W. H. DuBay. Christian Cent 84:1192 S 20 '67; Reply. R. R. Winkelmann. 84:1530 N 29 '67
End to heresy? report by committee on theological freedom and social responsibilities of Episcopal church. Time 90:39 Ag 25 '67
Heresy: an anchronism? America 117:215-16 S 2 '67
In defense of heresy. A. Towne; discussion. Christian Cent 84:211-13 F 15 '67
Is heresy dead? report by Episcopal committee. il Newsweek 70:56 Ag 28 '67

HERING, Doris
Regional ballet, U.S.A. See issues of Dance magazine

HERING, Leroy J.
Is vegetable gardening profitable? Horticulture 45:38-9+ Mr '67

HERMAN, E. P.
What is color? Design 68:7-9 Ja '67

HERMAN, M. Justin
Changes needed to improve low-income housing. Am City 82:22 O '67

HERMAN, Melvin. See Schreiber, F. R. jt. auth.

Las **HERMANAS:** ballet. See Ballets—Criticisms

HERMAPHRODITISM
See also
Gynandromorphism

HERMIT crabs. See Crabs

HERNANDARIAS
Hernandarias. V. Carreño. il por Américas 19:27-35 My '67

HERNANDEZ, Amalia
World of dance. W. Terry. il por Sat R 50:45-6 Je 17 '67

HERNANDEZ, Camila
Curandera artist. S. Battist. il Américas 19:36-40 My '67

HERNON, Joseph M.
High noon at Catholic U. M. I. Urofsky. Nation 205:303-5 O 2 '67

HERO tales. See Epic literature

HERODOTUS
Works of Herodotus K. Rexroth. Sat R 50:23 D 2 '67

HEROES
Nine heroes. il Esquire 68:119-24 S '67
See also
Great men
Vietnamese war, 1957- —Heroes

HEROES in fiction. See Characters in literature

HEROIC tenor. See Voice

HEROIN
Heroin cure works; testing methadone. Sci N 91:116 F 4 '67
Methadone. fighting fire with fire. G. Samuels. il N Y Times Mag p44-5+ O 15 '67; Discussion. p81-2+ N 5; 22+ N 12 '67

HEROINES in literature. See Characters in literature

HEROISM
See also
Courage

HERONS
Ardea's world; excerpts from World of the great white heron: a saga of the Florida Keys. M. B. Sanger. il Audubon 69:54-65 Ja '67
Heronry in the house. G. B. Schaller. il Audubon 69:66-7 Jl '67

HERPES-like viruses. See Viruses

HERPES simplex virus
Recurrent herpes in the rabbit and man. H. E. Kaufman and others. bibliog il Science 156:1628-9 Je 23 '67

HERR, Michael
Expo 67. Holiday 41:72-9+ Ap '67
Guam. Holiday 42:56-61+ Jl '67

HERRERA, Philip
Instant city. Fortune 75:135-8 Je 1 '67
Megalopolis comes to the Northwest. Fortune 76:118-23+ D '67
That Manhattan exodus. Fortune 75:106-9+ Je 1 '67

HERRESHOFF, L. Francis
Designer's comments. Yachting 122:53+ O '67

HERRICK, John
How to start a campaign against disease on your farm. Suc Farm 65:60 O '67
Tell age of cattle by their teeth. Suc Farm 65:50H Ap '67

HERRIN, Moses Reese
My conflict with East German reds; ed. by C. L. Sanders. pors Ebony 22:94-6+ Je '67

HERRON, Ellen M. and Heirtzier, J. R.
Sea-floor spreading near the Galapagos. bibliog Science 158:775-80 N 10 '67

HERRON, Michael M.
How to snap a cat. Pop Mech 127:182-3 Ap '67

HERSEY, Jean
Consider the blessing of a shady place. Home Gard 54:40-1 Ag '67

HERSEY, M. Leonard
Control points. See issues of Yachting
Predicted loggers keep rolling along. Yachting 121:86-7+ Ap '67

HERSH, Reuben. See Cohen, P. J. jt. auth.

HERSH, Seymour M.
But don't tell anyone I told you. New Repub 157:13-14 D 9 '67
Gas and germ warfare. New Repub 157:12-14 Jl 1 '67
Just a drop can kill. New Repub 156:11-15 My 6 '67

HERSHEY, Lenore
Sight and sound. See issues of McCall's

HERSHEY, Lewis Blaine
Changes in the draft: what to expect; interview. por US News 62:68-70 Mr 20 '67

about
Anything but bingo. por Time 90:19 D 22 '67
Bar Hershey. New Repub 157:9 D 23 '67
Crackdown on draft protesters? por U S News 63:6 N 20 '67
Draft crackdown? il Sr Schol 91:18-19 D 7 '67
Draft statements stir controversy. K. Sperry. Science 158:1434 D 15 '67
General Hershey: under fire. but still firm and serene. il por U S News 63:10 D 25 '67
Hershey and the draft. New Repub 157:7 D 2 '67
Hershey assault. Christian Cent 85:3-4 Ja 3 '68
Many thanks, General. Nation 205:642-3 D 18 '67
Super-General Hershey. R. J. Neuhaus. Commonweal 87:465-7 Ja 19 '68
What teeth does the draft law have? il por U S News 63:22-3 D 25 '67

HERSHEY chocolate corporation
Sweet smell of success. R. Levy. il Duns R 90:54-5+ N '67

HERSHON, Robert
Responses; poem. Nation 204:798 Je 19 '67

HERSHORN, Shel
Long day in a boy's world; photographs. Sports Illus 27:30-5 Ag 21 '67

HERST, Herman, Jr
Stamps. See issues of Hobbies

HERTER, Christian Archibald, 1895-1966
President Johnson, Secretary Rusk mourn death of Christian Herter; statements, December 31, 1966. L. B. Johnson; D. Rusk. Dept State Bul 56:147 Ja 23 '67

HERTZ, Gustav Crane
Fight to make the Vietcong let him go; with report by R. B. Stolley. il pors Life 63:22-9 Jl 21 '67
Sequel to Gus Hertz's story, he's alive. G. P. Hunt. por Life 63:3 Ag 11 '67

HERTZ, Karl H.
What man can make of man. Christian Cent 84:807-10 Je 21 '67

HERTZ, Solange Strong
Tomorrow's wife and mother. America 116:718-22 My 13 '67

HERTZ corporation
Avis vs. Hertz: Madison avenue's favorite feud. M. Mayer. Harper 236:40-4 Ja '68
Dear friends; Avis and Hertz, truce or ruse? il Newsweek 69:88 F 13 '67
Is no. 2 really trying harder? basketball series in Pittsburgh between Hertz and Avis. il Bsns W p38-9 F 18 '67
Why they are doing all that. il Time 91:71-2 Ja 5 '68

HERTZBERG, Arthur
Israel and American Jewry. Commentary 44:69-73 Ag '67

HERTZBERG, Robert
Shortwave, have you listened to it lately? Pop Mech 128:170-2+ Ag '67

HERTZIAN resonances. See Magnetic resonance

HERTZSPRUNG, Ejnar
Ejnar Hertzsprung. measurer of stars. A. V. Nielsen. il pors Sky & Tel 35:4-6 Ja '68
Hertzsprung's enigmatic object. J. Ashbrook. il Sky & Tel 34:382-3 D '67

HERTZSPRUNG-Russell diagram. See Astronomy—Charts, diagrams, etc.

HERZ, Hildegard
Eva. child of joy and sorrow. Redbook 128:37-44 F '67

HERZFELD, Norma Krause
Blow-up at Catholic U; with editorial comment. Commonweal 86:187-91 My 5 '67
H.H.H. vote-getter or scapegoat? Commonweal 86:489-92 Ag 11 '67
One-man, one-vote shakes up Maryland. Commonweal 86:142-3 Ap 21 '67
Packaging peas and Betty Bird Furness. Commonweal 86:384-5 Je 23 '67
Problem of Catholic U. Commonweal 86:39-41 Mr 31 '67

HESS, Dame Myra
Myrenes and their friends. I. Kolodin. il Sat R 50:74-5+ N 11 '67

HESS, Eckhard H.
Admen try eye-spy to read buyer's mind. il por Bsns W p 142-4 Ag 19 '67
Not-so-private eye. il Life 62:80A-80B Ap 21 '67

HESS, M. Whitcomb
Alpha and omega; poem. Cath World 204:308 F '67

HESS, Moses
Communist rabbi: Moses Hess. J. Frankel; reply with rejoinder. M. Schulman. Commentary 43:20+ Ja '67

HESS, Rudolf
Two prisoners. Reporter 38:11-12 Ja 11 '68

HESS, Stephen
American in Paris. Am Heritage 18:18-27+ F '67
—and Broder, D. S.
Available Mr Percy; excerpt from The Republican establishment. Atlan 220:87-95 S '67; Same abr. Read Digest 91:102-6 N '67
What keeps Nixon running; excerpt from The Republican establishment. Harper 235:56-8+ Ag '67

HESS, Walter R.
Causality, consciousness and cerebral organization. bibliog Science 158:1279-83 D 8 '67

HESSE, Hermann
Tolkien & Hesse: top of the pops. R. Sklar. Nation 204:598-601 My 8 '67

HESTER, Elizabeth
Generation of illiterates. R. Kirk. Nat R 19:588 My 30 '67

HESTER, James M.
People are talking about... il por Vogue 149:96 F 15 '67

HESTON, Charlton
Charlton Heston stays in great shape and tells how. il pors Vogue 151:67 Ja 1 '68

HETEROSIS (biology)
Heterosis: complementation. by mitochondria. R. G. McDaniel and I. V. Sarkissian; discussion. Science 155:722; 156:263 F 10, Ap 14 '67

HETHERINGTON, Alastair
Who guards the Guardian? Nat R 19:558 My 30 '67

HETTLINGER, Richard F.
Father speaks out on sex. Parents Mag 42:44-5+ Je '67

HEUMANN, Sylvain M.
Amateur scientist. Sci Am 216:122-8 F '67

HEUTTE, Frederic
Uncommon broadleaved evergreens. Horticulture 45:20-1+ Jl '67

HEUVEL, Albert Hendrik van den
Secular ecumenism and the teaching of the faith; excerpt from address, November 22, 1966. Cath World 205:14-19 Ap '67

HEWES, Henry
La Jolla's hourglass stage. Sat R 50:38-9 S 23 '67
Theater. See issues of Saturday review

HEWITT, Jean
Food (cont) N Y Times Mag p60 Ja 22; 99 Mr 5; 107+ Ap 2; 58 Ag 6; 49 Ag 13; 66 Ag 27; 90 O 29; 110+ D 10 '67

HEXOKINASES
Hexokinase isoenzymes in human erythrocytes: association of type II with fetal hemoglobin. E. W. Holmes, jr. and others. bibliog il Science 156:646-8 My 5 '67
Testis-specific and sex-associated hexokinases in drosophila melanogaster. R. F. Murray, jr. and J. A. Ball. bibliog il Science 156:81-2 Ap 7 '67

HEXTER, Alfred C. See Goldsmith, J. R. jt. auth.

HEYEN, William
Kamikaze; poem. Poetry 110:27 Ap '67

HEYERDAHL, Thor
In search of the sun god. il pors Newsweek 70:11 Ag 7 '67

HEYMAN, Ken
Breaking the three-foot barrier. il Pop Phot 60:61-4 Ag '67

HEYMAN, Wayne
Learn to water-ski the instant way. Motor B 120:32-3+ Jl' 67

HEYMANN, Dieter, and Mazor, Emanuel
Primordial rare gases in unequilibrated ordinary chondrites. bibliog Science 155:701-2 F 10 '67

HEYMANN, Hans G.
Germany; address, June 15, 1967. Vital Speeches 33:666-9 Ag 15 '67

HEYNEMAN, Donald, and Lim, B. L.
Angiostrongylus cantonensis: proof of direct transmission with its epidemiological implications. bibliog Science 158:57-8 N 24 '67

HI-FI systems. See High fidelity sound systems

HIATT, Peter
Cry for library research, eloquent but unheeded. Wilson Lib Bul 41:920-3 My '67

HIBBELN, Phyllis. See Aston, R. jt. auth.

HIBBERT, Christopher
Early, miserable life of Charles Dickens; excerpt from The making of Charles Dickens. Horizon 9:90-7 Aut '67

HIBBS, Albert R.
Surface of the moon; with biographical sketch. Sci Am 216:19, 60-72+ bibliog(p 150) Mr '67

HIBBS, Ben
Treasure house on the prairie. Read Digest 90:146-52 My '67

HIBERNATION
Disruption of hibernation caused by hypothalamic lesions. E. Satinoff. bibliog il Science 155:1031-3 F 24 '67

HIBERNATION, Human
Human hibernation; brain research, hypothalamus. P. McBroom. il Sci N 92:447 N 4 '67

HIBISCUS
More new Chinese hibiscus. il Sunset 138:262+ My '67

HICCOUGHS. See Hiccups

HICCUPS
Hiccups, or hiccoughs. E. Maxwell. Todays Health 45:77-8 S '67
Interrupted impulses; new cure. il Time 89:54 Je 9 '67

HICKENLOOPER, Bourke Blakemore
Resignation & a race. por Time 91:25 Ja 5 '68

HICKEY, Robert
Dogs in his trailer. M. Hunn. il por Design 69:4-6 Fall '67

HICKLIN, Ralph
Beautiful dances and cruel swans. Dance Mag 41:30-1 My '67
View from the road. Dance Mag 41:24-7+ Mr '67

HICKMAN, C. Addison
College faculty participation in academic governance. NEA J 56:46-8 O '67

HICKMAN, Ernest E.
Power-tool workbench. Pop Sci 190:178-83+ Ap '67

HICKORY
All about hickory. J. Aughanbauch. il Am For 73:28-30+ Jl '67

HICKS, Clifford B.
Dentistry's exciting new look. Todays Health 45:24-9+ Je '67
Hidden habits of women. Todays Health 45:28-31+ D '67

HICKS, G. P. See Updike, S. J. jt. auth.

HICKS, Granville
Literary horizons. See issues of Saturday review

HICKS, Jim
Frighten them and you're all right. Life 64:76 Ja 19 '68
From hippies to Margot's mum, an uproar across the globe. Life 63:84 Jl 21 '67
Huge slick, spreading with tide and current. Life 62:33-5 Ap 14 '67
Piet Hein and his 7000 grooks. Read Digest 90:193-4+ Mr '67

HICKS, John F. G.
Structure of silica glass. bibliog Science 155:459-61 Ja 27 '67

HICKS, John J. and others
Clear-air turbulence: simultaneous observations by radar and aircraft. bibliog Science 157:808-9 Ag 18 '67

HICKS, Louise (Day)
Athenian democracy. il por Newsweek 70:28+ O 9 '67
Backlash in Boston, and across the U.S. il por Newsweek 70:29-30+ N 6 '67
Balancing act in Boston. E. Sigel. il Reporter 36:22-4 My 4 '67; Reply with rejoinder. J. Lee. 36:10-11 Je 15 '67
Every little breeze. il por Newsweek 70:37+ S 18 '67
Hicks in Boston. New Repub 157:10-11 O 28 '67

HICKS, Louise (Day)—*Continued*
In Cleveland and Boston, the issue is race. B. Rice. il por N Y Times Mag p31+ N 5 '67
Louise Day Hicks gets out the vote. M. Nolan. il por Reporter 37:22-4 O 19 '67
Round one was a breeze for Louise. J. Howard. il pors Life 63:89-90+ O 13 '67
Southies' comfort. il por Time 90:23 O 6 '67

HIDALGO, Francisco
Impact. il U S Camera 31:40-3 Ja '68

HIDE, Raymond
Motions of the earth's core and mantle, and variations of the main geomagnetic field. bibliog Science 157:55-6 Jl 7 '67

HIDES and skins
See also
Fur

HIGDON, Hal
Gary's next mayor: white, pink, or black? Reporter 37:41-2 N 2 '67
Plays tennis like a man, speaks out like. Billie Jean King. N Y Times Mag p28-9+ Ag 27 '67
What you should know about saunas. Todays Health 45:20-3 Mr '67
—See Higdon, R. jt. auth.

HIGDON, Rose, and Higdon, Hal
What sports for girls? Todays Health 45: 20-3+ O '67

HIGGINS, Alice
Horse shows (cont) Sports Illus 26:69 Mr 13; 60-1 My 1; 27:69-70 N 6; 66 N 20 '67
Leaky-roof circuit. Sports Illus 27:50-2+ Jl 3 '67
Modern pentathlon. Sports Illus 27:58 Ag 28 '67

HIGGINS, G. T. See Brett, R. jt. auth.

HIGGINS, John
Notes from our correspondents. Hi Fi 17:16+ Je '67
Where Karajan is king. Hi Fi 17:MA26-7+ N '67

HIGGINS, Judith
Only people; story. Atlan 219:96-8 Je '67

HIGGINS, M. L. and Pramer, David
Fungal morphogenesis ring formation and closure by arthrobotrys dactyloides. bibliog Science 155:345-6 Ja 20 '67

HIGGINS, Pattillo
Americans not everybody knows. C. W. Ferguson. il PTA Mag 62:16-18 O '67

HIGGINS, Thomas Edison
Battery additives: AID's chagrin. D. S. Greenberg. Science 156:627 My 5 '67

HIGGINSON, Thomas Wentworth
Magic prison. A. MacLeish. por Sat R 50: 21-3 O 28 '67

HIGGS, John Wayne
Wilderness in the Nation's capital. Am For 73:34-7 Ja '67

HIGH altitude, Influence of. See Altitude, Influence of

HIGH commissioner for human rights. See United Nations—High commissioner for human rights (proposed)

HIGH commissioner for refugees. See United Nations—High commissioner for refugees

HIGH energy impact forging. See Forging

HIGH energy particles. See Particles (nuclear physics)

HIGH energy physics. See Nuclear physics

HIGH-energy scattering. See Scattering (physics)

HIGH fidelity amplifiers. See Amplifiers

HIGH fidelity music shows. See Audio fairs

HIGH fidelity shows. See Audio fairs

HIGH fidelity sound systems
Equipment in the news. See issues of High fidelity incorporating Musical America
Hi-fi. I. B. Berger. Esquire 67:36+ Mr '67
High fidelity equipment reports. See issues of High fidelity incorporating Musical America
How high the hi-fi sights. I. Berger. Sat R 50:73+ Ap 29 '67
Princess Cinderella. D. B. Weems. il Pop Electr 27:38-40 Jl '67
Rating race, an open letter to the high fidelity industry. il Hi Fi 17:75-6 N '67
What price stereo? a shopper's guide to high fidelity pricing. L. Marcus. Hi Fi 17:68 F '67
See also
Phonograph—High fidelity sound systems
Stereophonic sound systems

Bibliography
Stereo bookshelf. N. Eisenberg. il Hi Fi 18:51-2 Ja '68

Control
Noiseless switching for hi-fi; photocell device permits remote control of volume. B. B. Neiger. il Electr World 77:58-9 Ja '67

Repairing
Sound advice. H. Keppler. Mod Phot 31:122+ Je '67

Tuning
Buying a hi-fi tuner? L. Feldman. Electr World 77:34+ Mr '67
Hi-fi tuner and receiver directory. il Electr World 77:35-7 Mr '67

HIGH fidelity speakers. See Loud speaking apparatus

HIGH-frequency radio waves. See Radio waves

HIGH MOUNTAIN SHEEP DAM (proposed) See Dams

HIGH POINT, N.C.
Good street-sign program. R. V. Moss. il Am City 82:156 O '67

HIGH pressure oxygenation. See Hyperbaric oxygenation

HIGH-rise apartment houses. See Apartment houses

HIGH school annuals
Turn the yearbook back to the students. C. Steers. NEA J 56:74 F '67

Caricatures and cartoons
1967 yearbook. Stevenson. New Yorker 43: 34-7 My 27 '67

HIGH school athletes. See Athletes

HIGH school boys. See Boys

HIGH school counselors. See Personnel service in education

HIGH school debating. See Debates and debating

HIGH school dropouts. See Dropouts

HIGH school football players. See Football players

HIGH school girls. See Girls

HIGH school graduates
Employment of high school graduates and dropouts in 1966. E. Waldman. il Mo Labor R 90:15-21 Jl '67

HIGH school journalism. See College and school journalism

HIGH school libraries
Conant cites unique role of U.S. high school library; excerpts from Comprehensive high school. J. B. Conant. Library J 92:3098+ S 15 '67
See also
Knapp school libraries project

Microfilm collections
See Libraries—Microfilm collections

Paperback books
See School libraries—Paperback books

HIGH school of performing arts. See New York (city)—Education

HIGH school students
American adolescent, a bewildering amalgam. T. R. Leidy and A. R. Starry. il NEA J 56:8-12 O '67
Crime against a generation? overwork of high school students. Time 89:64 F 17 '67
Evolution of the high school student. D. Travers. Cath World 205:139-44 Je '67
I passed as a teenager; excerpts. L. Tornabene. il Ladies Home J 84:113-18 Je '67
Secondary sources; high-school students' judgments about the Vietnamese war. il Newsweek 70:88+ Jl 10 '67
Talking it over with Gay Head; questions and answers. Gay Head. See issues of Senior scholastic
See also
Student achievements
Student demonstrations

Adjustment
Overheard in suburbia: principal. C. S. Wren. Look 31:88 My 16 '67

Anecdotes, facetiae, satire, etc.
Please don't strike the teacher. B. Breisky. il Sat Eve Post 240:21 D 2 '67

Clothing
See Clothing and dress

Dating
See Dating

Employment
See Student employment

HIGH school students—*Continued*

Rating

Minds of high school seniors; impressions gathered from reactions to essay on the open mind. F. B. Maynard. New Repub 156:11-12 My 20 '67

Smoking

See Smoking

HIGH school students, Interchange of. See Students, Interchange of

HIGH school students, Married

What kind of mates will our teen-agers be? T. Irwin. il Todays Health 45:20-3 S '67
When teen-agers talk of marriage. B. Spock. Redbook 129:26+ Ag '67

HIGH school students, Mentally inferior

Alienation in the low-ability classroom. R. J. Mueller and A. H. Frerichs. bibliog f Sch & Soc 95:254-6 Ap 15 '67

HIGH school students, mentally superior

Colgate's high school high ability seminars. J. E. Rexine. il Sch & Soc 95:316-18 Sum '67
New hope for Harlem's bright youth; preparation for prep school class. New York's Wadleigh intermediate school. il Ebony 22: 27-30+ My '67
Presidential scholars; what shapes their talent? W. A. Coyne. il Am Ed 3:27-8 Je '67
Reaching and teaching the gifted. E. M. Drews. il NEA J 56:8-11+ N '67
Special programs give a taste of culture; projects in the South. il Life 63:104-5 S 29 '67

HIGH school students, Negro. See Negro students

HIGH schools

Equalizing opportunity. Time 89:58 Mr 10 '67
High school education news roundup. il Sr Schol 90:sup38 F 17; sup7 Mr 10; sup8 Ap 7; sup7 My 19 '67
New super high school, wave of future for big cities? il U S News 63:58-9 Jl 10 '67
What's going on in schools & colleges. See issues of Changing times
See also
Education, Secondary

Curriculum

Art and a high school humanities program. J. Warwick. il Sch Arts 66:5-8 Je '67
Comprehensive high school; television interview. J. B. Conant. Sr Schol 90:sup 18-19 My 19 '67
Special programs give a taste of culture; projects in the South. il Life 63:104-5 S 29 '67
What Sputnik did to our schools. F. M. Hechinger. il McCalls 95:106-7+ O '67
Where no bells ring; Troy high. Newsweek 69:96+ My 8 '67
Which way to a curriculum for adolescents? F. T. Wilhelms. il NEA J 56:12-15 D '67

Personnel service

See Personnel service in education

Summer sessions

See Summer schools

HIGH seas, Jurisdiction over. See Maritime law

HIGH society. See Upper classes

HIGH speed ground transport systems. See Transportation, High speed

HIGH speed ground transportation, Office of. See United States—Transportation, Department of

HIGH speed railroads. See Railroads—Train speed

HIGH speed trains. See Railroads—Train speed

HIGH speed transportation. See Transportation, High speed

HIGH temperature molecules. See Molecules

HIGH temperatures

Radiation damage at high temperatures. J. R. Weir, jr. bibliog il Science 156:1689-95 Je 30 '67
Stellar and other high-temperature molecules. W. Weltner, jr. bibliog il Science 155:155-64 Ja 13 '67

HIGH velocity forging machine. See Forging machinery

HIGH voltage power lines. See Electric lines

HIGHER education. See College education; Colleges and universities

HIGHER education. See Junior colleges

HIGHET, Gilbert

Where is the bridegroom? Horizon 9:112-15 Spr '67

HIGHET, Keith

South West Africa cases. bibliog f Cur Hist 52:154-61 Mr '67

HIGHLAND PARK, Ill.

Packaged insurance plan. D. H. Fritz. Parks & Rec 2:41-2 D '67
Skeet shooting scores a bull's-eye. D. Fritz. il Am City 82:94 Jl '67

HIGHSMITH, Patricia

Block, failure, and depression. Writer 80:23-6 O '67
Snails; story. Sat Eve Post 240:44-5 Je 17 '67

HIGHWAY, Pan American. See Pan American highway

HIGHWAY beautification. See Roadside improvement

HIGHWAY emergency locating plan. See Radio communication—Emergency applications

HIGHWAY engineering

Building roads without disrupting the city; Baltimore design concept team. il Bsns W p 108+ N 18 '67
Street construction & maintenance. See issues of American city
See also
Roads—Safety guards

HIGHWAY finance. See Roads—Finance

HIGHWAY law

See also
Traffic courts

HIGHWAY location. See Roads—Location

HIGHWAY safety. See Roads—Safety devices
HIGH school students, Mentally superior and measures; Traffic safety

HIGHWAY trust fund, Federal. See Roads—Finance

HIGHWAYS. See Roads

HIGLEY, John R.

River of forgotten trout. pors Outdoor Life 139:60-1+ F '67

HIJACKING. See Robberies and assaults

HIKING. See Walking

HIKING boots. See Shoes

HILBERRY, Conrad

Fundies, infidels, and free inquiry. Mlle 65: 160-1+ My '67

HILDEBRAND, Ruth

Just one; poem. Farm J 91:109 Mr '67

HILDEBRANDT, Franz

Drew professors resign in protest. T. S. Cooper. Christian Cent 85:92-4 Ja 17 '68

HILDER, Rowland

On composition in landscape; excerpts from Starting with watercolor. il Am Artist 31: 42-7 My '67

HILDRETH, Barbara Parsons

Thought for Thanksgiving; poem. Read Digest 91:117 N '67

HILF, Russell

Milk-like fluid in a mammary adenocarcinoma: biochemical characterization. bibliog Science 155:826-7 F 17 '67

HILGER, Sister Mary Inez

Japan's sky people, the vanishing Ainu. pors Nat Geog Mag 131:268-96 F '67

HILL, Albert Fay

Reverend Fay Hill and his lace pants mob. G. Astor. il pors Look 31:71-6 O 31 '67

HILL, Arthur

Lunar walking staff design under way. Tech W 20:24 Mr 6 '67
MSC defining AAP land recovery ideas. Tech W 20:22 My 1 '67
New missions seen dictating tracking system changes. Tech W 20:16 Ap 3 '67
Sixteen experiments contend for 1st AAP flight. Tech W 20:37 My 29 '67
Voyager, manned fly-by may be combined. Tech W 20:20 Mr 13 '67

HILL, Birkbeck. See Hill, G. B. N.

HILL, Elizabeth Starr

Dusk, the magic hour. Read Digest 91:128-30 N '67
Hurray! it's raining! Read Digest 90:55-8 Ap '67
Make room for the simple things. Read Digest 90:203-4+ F '67
Someone missing at the manger; story. Good H 165:108-9 D '67

HILL, Elton

I am the Negro; poem. Negro Hist Bul 30:14 N '67

HILL, George Birkbeck Norman

Books. M. Muggeridge. Esquire 68:80+ O '67

HILL, Goeran

Listen to the engine. Flying 81:87 O '67

HILL, Herbert

Sewing machines & union machines. Nation 205:18-19 Jl 3 '67

HILL, J. Eldred, jr
Excerpt from testimony, July 15, 1966. Cong Digest 46:27+ Ja '67

HILL, J. Newton
Bombs and suburbs. N. C. Mills. Nation 204: 817 Je 26 '67

HILL, James, family
Supreme court extends press freedoms in overruling Desperate hours verdict. Pub W 191:221 Ja 23 '67

HILL, James T., jr
Challenge of human aspirations. Duns R 89: 23-4+ Ja '67

HILL, John J.
Priests' associations go regional. Commonweal 87:69-70 O 20 '67

HILL, Lister
NIH: Lister Hill criticizes LBJ budget. E. Langer. Science 156:1471 Je 16 '67

HILL, Ralph Nading
Curtis and Dunning, clockmakers. Antiques 91:214-17 F '67

HILL, Richard N. and Yunis, J. J.
Mammalian X-chromosomes: change in patterns of DNA replication during embryogenesis. bibliog Science 155:1120-1 Mr 3 '67

HILL, Roland M.
Facts on hand tools. Flower Grower 54:65-9 Ja '67

HILL, Rowland M.
Making light of heavy soil. Home Gard 54: 63-4 F '67

HILL, Samuel A. jr
War in the Bible belt? il Newsweek 69:91 Mr 27 '67

HILL, Sarah Althea. See Terry, S. A. H.

HILL, Thomas T.
1967 film-developer roundup. Mod Phot 31: 98-103 N '67

HILL, William B.
Fiction (cont) America 116:700-2 My 6 '67

HILL and Knowlton, incorporated
Hill & Knowlton's world of images. T. A. Wise. il Fortune 76:98-101+ S 1 '67

HILLBILLY blues; drama. See Huff, B.

HILLEBRAND, Harry
Warm and clear. P. Jordan. New Yorker 43: 42-4 S 23 '67

HILLENBRAND, Barry
Our man in Ethiopia. Commonweal 85:670-1 Mr 17 '67

HILLENBRAND, Bernard F.
Second battle of Antietam; or, The fight to save our parks. Parks & Rec 2:18-19+ N '67

HILLES, Frederick W.
New Blake letter. Yale R 57:85-9 O '67

HILLIARD, R. L.
Steward observatory's new 90-inch reflector. Sky & Tel 34:79-81 Ag '67

HILLIS, Anne
Florida autumn; poem. Horn Bk 43:575 O '67

HILLIS, Burton
Man next door. See issues of Better homes and gardens

HILLMAN, Nina, and Hillman, Ralph
Competent chick ectoderm: nonspecific response to RNA. bibliog Science 155:1563-5 Mr 24 '67

HILLMAN, Ralph. See Hillman, N. jt. auth.

HILLS, B. A.
Distribution of circulation rates within a single tissue type. bibliog Science 157: 942-3 Ag 25 '67

HILLS, G. J. See Hitchborn, J. H. jt. auth.

HILLSDALE, N. J.
Are you paying too much for sewer contractors' guesswork; soil-engineering survey. R. R. Fleming. il Am City 82:112-14 O '67

HILLSIDE architecture
Community mental health center exploits a sloping site for strong identity; Resthaven community mental health center, Los Angeles. il Arch Rec 141:160-1 F '67
Escape to the Mediterranean; a three-room grotto. il House B 109:102-5 Ja '67
Farmhouse for a lively family. il House & Gard 132:182-7 S '67
Future-minded hillside house. il House B 109: 88-91 Jl '67
Illusion of doubled space. il House & Gard 131:134-5 My '67
Inventive shapes of present and future. M. Gough. il House B 109:158-61 S '67
Karas house, Monterey, California. il Arch Rec 141:112-14 mid-My '67
New slant on space. il Am Home 70:54-7 S '67
Newmyer house, Washington, D.C. il Arch Rec 141:82-5 mid-My '67

River house revisited. il Am Home 70:82-3 Je '67
Small wood-and-stone house relates well to a mountain site. il Arch Rec 141:181-4 Ap '67
Takrouna. M. H. Goldfinger. il Arch Forum 127:98-106 Jl '67
Their new pool is in the tree-tops. il Sunset 138:108-9 My '67
Three-level house on stilts. il Am Home 70: 66-7 Ja '67
Three projects by Philip Johnson, each designed for a hill. il Arch Rec 141:139-50 Je '67
Timber treehouse, oriental serenity. J. De Long. il House B 109:160-4 Ap '67
Twin schools on three levels; Stuttgart. il Arch Forum 126:80-6 Ap '67
Woo house, Los Angeles. il Arch Rec 141:92-3 mid-My '67

HILSMAN, Roger
Secret battle over Vietnam; excerpts from To move a nation. por U S News 62:71 Je 19 '67

about

Double the effort & square the error. M. W. Browne. Nation 204:726-8 Je 5 '67
He wouldn't fly with the hawks. H. H. Ransom. Sat R 50:33-4 O 21 '67
JFK's foreign policy. J. C. Thomson, jr. New Repub 157:23-6 Jl 15 '67
Kiss and tell memoirs. M. Greenfield. Reporter 37:14-19 N 30 '67

HILTON, Conrad Nicholson
Men who made the world move. H. Bigart. por Sat R 50:54 Ap 22 '67

HILTON, Ronald
Is there a Latin America? Nation 204:457-63 Ap 10 '67
Yanqui universities. Nation 205:145-8 Ag 28 '67

HILTON, T. E.
Mali. bibliog Focus 18:1-6 S '67

HILTON hotels corporation
Remember the Hilton; Tokyo Hilton hotel take-over. Newsweek 69:84-5 My 8 '67

HILTON International company
Hilton's fortunes ride on the jets; TWA's new partner, Hilton international. il Bsns W p50-4+ Jl 1 '67
Places to put them; preliminary merger agreement between Hilton international and TWA. Time 89:67 Ja 27 '67
TWA Hilton. Newsweek 69:78 Ja 30 '67

HILTS, Edward L.
Sure, you can radio-navigate yourself home. Pop Sci 191:112-14 S '67

HILTUNEN, Eila Wilhelmina
Finland's memorial to Jean Sibelius. C. Willard. il pors Look 31:M16+ O 17 '67

HIMALAYA MOUNTAINS
Ordeal above Tesi Lapcha; three U.S. college students in Himalayas. S. R. McCarthy. il Sports Illus 26:68-70+ My 1 '67

HIMBER, Charlotte
Parent and child (cont) N Y Times Mag p 114+ N 19 '67

HIMEL, Chester M. and Moore, A. D.
Spruce budworm mortality as a function of aerial spray droplet size. bibliog Science 156: 1250-1 Je 2 '67

HIMMELFARB, Milton
In the community (cont) Commentary 43:67-72 Ap; 44:53-61 Jl; 53-61 O '67

HINCHMAN, Jane
Clue of daffodils; story. Redbook 129:62-3 O '67

HINCKLEY, Helen
Where do plots start? Writer 80:19-20+ F '67

HINDEMITH, Paul
Cardillac Criticism.
Hi Fi 17:MA21 O '67
Time 90:64 Ag 4 '67
Mathis der maler (Mathis the painter) Criticism
New Repub 157:31 Jl 15 '67
New Yorker 43:63-4 Jl 1 '67
Sat R 50:32 Jl 8 '67

HINDI poetry
From the East. R. E. Teele. Poetry 109:274 Ja '67

HINDU dancing. See Dancing, Indian (East Indian)

HINDU literature
See also
Mahabharata

HINDU medicine. See Medicine, Hindu

HINDU painting. See Painting, Indian (East Indian)

HINDUISM
Sacred cow. B. Griffiths. Commonweal 85: 483-4 F 3 '67
See also
Mysticism—Hinduism
Sadhus
HINE, Al
Bocce, Italy's favorite pastime. Holiday 43:56-7+ Ja '68
HINE, Daryl
Clôture annuelle; poem. Atlan 220:64 Ag '67
Noon; poem. Atlan 220:86 S '67
HINELINE, Philip N. See Rachlin, H. jt. auth.
HINES, Earl
Golden autumn of Fatha Hines. E. Larrabee. il por Harper 235:97-9 Ag '67
HINES, Jim
Inefficient but fast. il por Time 89:78+ Je 9 '67
Learning to care. Newsweek 69:64 Je 26 '67
Love and hate and a very fast hundred. P. Axthelm. il por Sports Illus 26:66+ Je 5 '67
Two guys named Jim had the same idea. T. C. Brody. il por Sports Illus 26:34-5 Je 12 '67
HINES, John Elbridge, bp
To right a wrong. por Newsweek 70:116 S 25 '67
HINES, William
NASA: the image misfires. Nation 204:517-19 Ap 24 '67
HINKLE, J. E. and McCoy, R. A. Jr
Sewerage program wins by 10-1 vote. Am City 82:74-5 Jl '67
HINSHELWOOD, Sir Cyril
Science and scientists; excerpts from address, September 1, 1965. Bul Atomic Sci 23: 31-6 Je '67
HINTERREITER, H. Gilda
Arthur Lismer, artist and art-educator: a reflection on his life, work and philosophy. Sch Arts 66:21-8 Ja '67
HINTON, Susie
Face to face with a teen-age novelist. por Seventeen 26:133 O '67; Correction. 26:20 N '67

HIPPIES
Al Capp on the hippie economics; J. K. Galbraith and L. Abolafia. A. Capp il Nations Bsns 55:64-7 S '67
California notebook; decline of hippies. H. Brandon. Sat R 50:11 Je 3 '67
Challenge to the hippies. America 117:216 S 2 '67
Christian and the hippie. J. Hitchcock. Christian Cent 84:1040-2 Ag 16 '67
Creator. il Newsweek 71:26-7 Ja 8 '68
De mortuis; passing of the hippie movement. Christian Cent 84:1479 N 15 '67
Death of a flower baby; mother kills child. il Time 90:18 D 1 '67
Dropouts with a mission; the hippies; with report by H. Hertzberg. il Newsweek 69:92-5 F 6 '67
Family: is it out with the go-go generation. il Sr Schol 91:2-7+ O 19 '67
Flowering of the hippies; Haight-Ashbury scene, San Francisco. M. Harris. il Atlan 220:63-72 S '67
Free store. New Yorker 43:49-51 O 14 '67
From a hippie's soul; WNEW's A child again broadcast. R. L. Shayon. Sat R 50:46 D 16 '67
Hashbury is the capital of the hippies; San Francisco's Haight-Ashbury district. H. S. Thompson. il N Y Times Mag p28-9+ My 14 '67
Hippie business. D. Sanford. New Repub 156: 7-8 Je 10 '67
Hippie generation; slouching towards Bethlehem. J. Didion. il Sat Eve Post 240:25-31+ S 23 '67
Hippies. il Time 90:18-22 Jl 7 '67
Hippies. il Time 90:18-22 Jl 7 '67; Same abr. Read Digest 91:70-4 O '67
Hippies; a passing fad? il U S News 63:42-4 O 23 '67
Hippies and their future, a look ahead; interview. J. Masserman. il U S News 63:58-61 Jl 17 '67
Hippies are coming. il Newsweek 69:28-9 Je 12 '67
Hippies: creative dropouts or escapist copouts? A. Henehan. il Sr Schol 91:17-19+ N 16 '67
Hippies of Hashberry. il Ebony 22:116-20 Ag '67
Hippies, political radicals and the church. N. K. Gottwald. Christian Cent 84:1043-5 Ag 16 '67
I'm not on your trip. E. L. Horwitz. il McCalls 94:66-9+ S '67

Incredibles. G. B. Leonard and J. Luce. il Look 32:51-8 Ja 9 '68
Inside the hippie revolution. W. Hedgepeth. il Look 31:58-61+ Ag 22 '67
Intelligent square's guide to hippieland. J. Bingham. il N Y Times Mag p25+ S 24 '67; Discussion. p 16+ O 15 '67
It's love, love, love! Be-ins. il Ebony 22:100-1 Jl '67
Last word on the hippies. H. Toch. il Nation 205:582-8 D 4 '67
Linda's last trip; double murders in New York's East Village. il Newsweek 70:33-4 O 23 '67
Love hippies. W. K. Zinsser. il Look 31:4 Ap 18 '67
Love is dead. E. Shorris. il N Y Times Mag p26-7+ O 29 '67
Love, mysticism, and the hippies. K. Von Meier. il Vogue 150:84-6+ N 15 '67
Love needs care; clinic devoted exclusively to helping hippies with health problems. il Newsweek 70:98 Jl 17 '67
One cheer for the hippies. J. Newfield. il Nation 204:809-10 Je 26 '67
100 years later, a double rediscovery; with report by R. Richman. il Life 63:60-1+ D 1 '67
Opinion: on the hippie put-on. M. Ackerman. Mlle 65:40+ S '67
Personal business; rebels around your home. Bsns W p 135-6 N 25 '67
Rector, a church and the hippies; All Saints Episcopal church in San Francisco's Haight-Ashbury district. L. Kinsolving. Christian Cent 84:667-8 My 17 '67
Reporter at large; Sunset Strip. R. Adler. New Yorker 43:116+ F 25 '67
Speed kills; hippies murdered in New York. il Time 90:23 O 20 '67
Splendid desire for nothing; concerning hippies in the Haight-Ashbury district of San Francisco. America 116:746-7 My 20 '67
Spotlight on hippies. il U S News 62:61-3 My 8 '67
Summer days in psychedelphia; touring the Haight-Ashbury district. H. Sutton. il Sat R 50:36+ Ag 19 '67
Trouble in hippieland. il Newsweek 70:84-90 O 30 '67; Same abr. Read Digest 92:59-63 Ja '68
Where have all the flowers gone? il Time 90:30-1 O 13 '67
Who are the hippies? W. Herberg. il Nat R 19:844-6+ Ag 8 '67
Who killed the hippies? Nat R 19:1250 N 14 '67
Within the tribe; wedding of hippies. il Time 90:46 Ag 25 '67
You can't even step in the same river once. J. Lettvin. il Natur Hist 76:6-12+ O '67; Discussion. 76:106 D '67

Anecdotes, facetiae, satire, etc.
Human comedy: the love wave. C. Tomkins. il Sat Eve Post 240:16 S 9 '67

Caricatures and cartoons
Event. Saxon. New Yorker 43:31-5 Ag 12 '67

Religion
Doctrines of the dropouts. il Time 91:62 Ja 5 '68

HIPPOCAMPUS. See Cerebral cortex
HIPPOPOTAMUS
Herman the hippo. il Newsweek 69:39-40 Ap 10 '67
HIRABAYASHI, Kazuko
Kazuko Hirabayashi & company, 92nd street Y. M. Marks. Dance Mag 41:80 Mr '67
HIRAM Scott college, Scottsbluff, Neb.
Where businessmen gave their community a future. il Nations Bsns 55:92-4+ F '67
HIRANO, M. and others
Murine lymphoma: augmented growth in mice with pertussis vaccine-induced lymphocytosis. bibliog Science 158:1061-4 N 24 '67
HIRED men. See Farm labor
HIROHITO, emperor of Japan
Collector on Sagami Bay; letter. T. Komai. Science 157:488+ Ag 4 '67
Hirohito, emperor of Japan. N. F. Busch. por Read Digest 91:102-6 D '67
HIROSHIGE. 1797-1858
Tokaido; reproductions of wood engravings. Holiday 41:34-45 Je '67

about
Gift from Hiroshige. D. Powills. il Hobbies 72:114-15+ D '67; 110-11+ Ja '68

HIROSHIMA
Fall of Japan; excerpt. W. Craig. il Sat Eve Post 240:36-8+ Ag 26 '67
Hiroshima, Vietnam: sisters in sorrow. B. Reynolds. Christian Cent 84:636-8 My 10 '67
Postscript from Hiroshima, by R. Steinberg. Review
New Repub 156:26+ Mr 11 '67. S. S. Harrison

HIRSCH, Julian D.
EW lab tests of new solid-state stereo receivers. Electr World 78:25-9+ D '67

HIRSCH, Phil
Punchcard snoopers. il Nation 205:369-72, 610+ O 16, D 11 '67

HIRSCHFELD, Robert A.
Integrated circuits and the automobile. Electr World 77:31-3+ F '67
IC engine tachometer and red line indicator. Electr World 77:37-9 My '67

HIRSCHMAN, Susan
Backing our backlist. Pub W 192:120-1 Jl 10 '67

HIRSHEN, Sanford
House of many parts. il Arch Forum 127: 78-81 N '67

HISCOCK, Eric
Bahamas to Maine. il Yachting 122:50-1+ Jl '67
Islands down wind. il Yachting 121:58-60+ F '67
Southward from Maine. il Yachting 122:58-9+ D '67 (to be cont)

HISPANIC AMERICAN history. See Latin America—History

HISPANIOLA
See also
Haiti

HISS, Alger
Friendship and fratricide, by M. A. Zeligs. Review
Atlan por 220:54-7 Ag '67. G. Rees; Reply with rejoinder. M. A. Zeligs. 220:47-8 D '67
Nat R 19:295-8+ Mr 21 '67. E. Van Den Haag
Nation 204:373-4 Mr 20 '67. D. Cort
Sat R por 50:34-5 F 11 '67. M. Harris
Time por 89:102+ F 10 '67

HISS, Anthony
Boss Jones of Tammany Hall. N Y Times Mag p32-3+ F 19 '67

HISS, Philip H.
What ever happened to Sarasota? Arch Forum 126:66-73 Je '67

HISTIDINE
Catalysis of ester hydrolysis by mixed micelles containing N-α-myristol-L- histidine. A. Ochoa-Solano and others. bibliog il Science 156:1243-4 Je 2 '67

HISTOCHEMISTRY
See also
Molecular biology

HISTOIRE du soldat; opera. See Stravinsky, I. F.

HISTONES
Gene activation without histone acetylation in drosophila melanogaster. E. G. Ellgaard. bibliog il Science 157:1070-2 S 1 '67
Histones in the wild-type and the anucleolate mutant of xenopus laevis. L. Berlowitz and M. L. Birnstiel. bibliog il Science 156: 78-80 Ap 7 '67
Tissue specificity of histone phosphorylation. R. M. Gutierrez and L. S. Hnilica. bibliog il Science 157:1324-5 S 15 '67

HISTORIANS
Crisis and comparison. J. Ratté. America 117: 35-7 Jl 8 '67
Historian's opportunity. B. W. Tuchman. Sat R 50:27-31+ F 25 '67
New age of the journalist-historian. Q. Howe. Sat R 50:25-7+ My 20 '67
On the writing of contemporary history; excerpt from address. A. Schlesinger, jr. Atlan 219:69-74 Mr '67

HISTORIANS, Catholic. See Catholic historians

HISTORIANS, English
See also
Namier, L. B.

HISTORIANS, Greek
See also
Herodotus

HISTORIANS, Latin American
Bolivia, Ecuador, Paraguay: historians. E. Uzcátegui. il Américas 19:19-28 F '67

HISTORIC house museums
Antique treasure, modern workings; Mulford-Baker house, East Hampton, L.I. il House B 109:170-7 Ap '67
House museums in Canada. Antiques 92:110 Jl '67

HISTORIC houses, etc.
Historic houses, landmarks, and museums. See issues of Antiques
See also
Literary landmarks
also subhead Historic houses, etc. under names of countries, states, cities, etc. e.g. Virginia—Historic houses, etc.

Conservation and restoration
See Architecture—Conservation and restoration

HISTORIC prints. See Prints

HISTORIC Savannah foundation, incorporated
Historic Savannah foundation, inc. L. Adler. 2d. il Antiques 91:334-8 Mr '67

HISTORIC trails. See Trails

HISTORIC trees. See Trees, Historic

HISTORICAL art. See History in art

HISTORICAL criticism. See History—Historiography

HISTORICAL exhibits
Independence Hall reconstruction sound system; Knott's berry farm, Calif. J. P. Nelson. il Electr World 78:32-3 Jl '67

HISTORICAL fiction
On writing historical fiction. J. Fritz. Horn Bk 43:565-70 O '67
See also
Fiction—Technique

HISTORICAL films. See Moving pictures—Historical films

HISTORICAL libraries
See also
Presidential libraries

HISTORICAL literature
Infusing data with life. Z. Sutherland. il Sat R 50:42 O 21 '67
Scottish history tales. S. N. Leodhas. Horn Bk 43:323-7 Je '67
Timely histories for the holidays. P. Kresh. Sat R 50:28-9 D 2 '67

HISTORICAL museums
Kaintuck territory. il Travel 128:10 O '67
Little journeys to the way we used to live. M. Gough. il House B 109:148+ Ap '67
Somebody shoulda told me . . ; visitor services to interpret natural and historical scenes. D. B. Huyck. il Am For 73:12-15+ Jl '67
Warp's pioneer village traces America's growth. il Hobbies 72:113+ N '67

HISTORICAL research
Guillaume Budé and the first historical school of law. D. R. Kelley. bibliog f Am Hist R 72:807-34 Ap '67

HISTORICAL villages. See Historical museums

HISTORIOGRAPHY. See History—Historiography

HISTORY
Crisis and comparison. J. Ratté. America 117: 35-7 Jl 8 '67
Yesterday, interpreter of human experience. J. H. Plumb. Sat R 50:27-8 Ag 26 '67
See also
Explorations
Folklore
Historians
Historical research
Oral history
also subheads Antiquities; History; Politics and government under names of countries, states, etc e.g. Spain—History;
also subhead History under various subjects, e.g. Education—History

Bibliography
History. C. L. Hohl, jr. America 116:696 My 6 '67
Reading, writing, and history. B. Catton. il Am Heritage 18:82-3 Ap; 56-7+ Je; 80-2 O '67

Errors, inventions, etc.
Norman blood mystery. M. Kempton. New Repub 157:33-8 D 9 '67

Historiography
Books in the field: historiography. D. F. Gerardi. bibliog il Wilson Lib Bul 42:484-96 Ja '68
Essay: what is important in history? M. Bishop. il Am Heritage 19:2-3 D '67
See also
Africa—History—Historiography
China—History—Historiography
Historians
United States—History—Historiography

HISTORY—*Continued*

Philosophy

History in a self-governing culture; address, December 29, 1966. R. F. Nichols. Am Hist R 72:411-24 Ja '67

Sources

Norman blood mystery. M. Kempton. New Repub 157:33-8 D 9 '67

See also
Oral history

Study and teaching

History courses come to life; New York city and Princeton university. Sr Schol 91:sup7 O 5 '67
ST reports: how history is taught in Scotland. R. A. Page. Sr Schol 91:sup 14 O 5 '67
Teaching the newest history. W. W. Brickman. Sch & Soc 95:409 N 11 '67

See also
United States—History—Study and teaching

HISTORY, Ancient
See also
Numismatics, Ancient

Bibliography

Articles and other books received; comp. by T. R. S. Broughton. See issues of American historical review

HISTORY, Medieval. See Middle ages—History

HISTORY, Modern
New age of the journalist-historian. Q. Howe. Sat R 50:25-7+ My 20 '67
On the writing of contemporary history; excerpt from address. A. Schlesinger, jr. Atlan 219:69-74 Mr '67
Peace, empire, and world government; introduction to Major peace treaties of modern history, 1648-1966, ed. by F. L. Israel. A. Toynbee. Sat R 50:17-21 Ap 29 '67

HISTORY, Natural. See Natural history

HISTORY and science. See Science and civilization

HISTORY in art
Canadian chronology in brief, 1605-1867. A. Winchester. il Antiques 92:62-5 Jl '67
Diorama depicting scene of Battle of Monmouth. L. E. Eben. il Sch Arts 66:31-2 F '67

HISTORY lesson; story. See Woiwode, L.

HIT-and-run drivers. See Automobile drivers

HITCH, Charles Johnston
California draws a blank. H. Draper. Nation 205:682-5 D 25 '67
Coordinator for Cal. il por Time 90:64 S 29 '67
Hitch in time? por Newsweek 71:37-8 Ja 1 '68
Hitch succeeds Kerr at U.C. J. Walsh. por Science 157:1538 S 29 '67
Manager for Cal. por Newsweek 70:53 O 2 '67

HITCHBORN, J. H. and Hills, G. J.
Tubular structures associated with turnip yellow mosaic virus in vivo. bibliog Science 157:705-6 Ag 11 '67

HITCHCOCK, Alfred Joseph
Fear and laughter. O. Handlin. Atlan 221:116+ Ja '68
Hitchcock, by F. Truffaut. Review
Harper 235:121-3 D '67. R. Hatch
Newsweek il por 71:59+ Ja 1 '68. J. Morgenstern

HITCHCOCK, James
Christian and the hippie. Christian Cent 84:1040-2 Ag 16 '67
Romantic rebel on the campus. Yale R 57:31-7 O '67

HITCHCOCK, Verna
Works of art from skulls and eggshells. F. Martin. il pors Design 68:10-11 Mr '67

HITCHENS, Gordon
Movie maker's guide to foreign film festivals. Pop Phot 61:130+ D '67

HITCHES. See Knots and splices

HITCHES (automobile) See Automobiles—Equipment

HITE, Cass
On some names in Natural Bridges National Monument. N. M. Judd. bibliog il por Nat Parks Mag 41:16-19 O '67

HITLER, Adolf
Conversion of myths into political power: the case of the Nazi party, 1925-1926. D. Orlow. bibliog f Am Hist R 72:906-24 Ap '67
Hitler's jaw was in her handbag. L. Rosten. il por Look 31:6 Ap 4 '67

HIXSON, Joseph R.
Forecasts from the womb. McCalls 94:60+ F '67

HJORTH, Flemming
Augusta Bournonville: a life in Paris, 1846. Dance Mag 41:59-61 Je '67

HNILICA, Lubomir S. See Gutierrez, R. M. jt. auth.

HO, Don
Trader Ho. por Time 90:60 Ag 25 '67

HOAG, Arthur A. See Ball, W. F. jt. auth.

HOAG, M. De Koning
Liar, liar; story. Seventeen 26:154-5 N '67
Summer hang-up; story. Seventeen 26:92-3 Je '67

HOARD, Floyd
Death of a dogged man. il por Newsweek 70:26-7 Ag 21 '67

HOARDING by animals. See Animals—Habits and behavior

HOAXES
See also
Literary forgeries and mystifications

HOBART, Alice Tisdale (Nourse)
Obituary
Pub W 191:39 Mr 27 '67

HOBBIES
See also
Collectors and collecting
Handicraft
Woodworking—Projects

HOBBIES (periodical)
Fifteen year index; At the sign of the crest, column. H. K. Eilers. Hobbies 72:116 D '67
Hobbies guide 1939-1966; alphabetical index of topics. D. Powills. il Hobbies 72:122-3 Je '67
Hobbies guide, 1939-1966; themes of Playing cards. D. Powills. il Hobbies 72:122-3 My '67

HOBBS, Cecil
(comp) Articles and other books received; south Asia. See issues of American historical review

HOBBS, Horace P. Jr
Old rock dams on the Potomac River. Nat Parks Mag 41:14-19 Ag '67

HOBBS, P. V. and Kezweeny, A. J.
Splashing of a water drop. bibliog Science 155:1112-14 Mr 3 '67
—and Osheroff, T.
Splashing of drops on shallow liquids. bibliog Science 158:1184-6 D 1 '67

HOBBS, R. W. and Hollinger, J. P.
Search for 21-centimeter radiation near cosmic X-ray sources. bibliog Science 155:448-9 Ja 27 '67

HOBBY rooms. See Rooms

HOBSBAWM, Eric
Introduction to Gramsci. Nation 205:249-51 S 18 '67

HOBSON, Thayer
Obituary
Pub W 192:30 O 30 '67

HOCH, William C. Jr
Floodlighting projects a city's image. Am City 82:118-19 Ap '67

HOCHHUTH, Rolf
Playwright who drops political blockbusters. M. Esslin. il por N Y Times Mag p48-9+ N 19 '67
Soldiers Criticism
Nation 205:700-1 D 25 '67
N Y Times Mag il por p48-9+ N 19 '67
Sat R 50:27+ D 2 '67
Time il 90:82 O 20 '67
Wars of Private Hochhuth. C. Amery. Nation 205:700-1 D 25 '67

HO-chi-Minh
Bid for peace, and a rebuff; reply to President Johnson's letter, February 15, 1967. por U S News 62:27 Ap 3 '67
Interview with Ho Chi Minh, 1923; ed. by O. Mandelstam. Commentary 44:80-1 Ag '67
President Johnson's proposal for negotiation on Viet-Nam rejected by Ho Chi Minh; letter, February 15, 1967. Dept State Bul 56:596-7 Ap 10 '67
Talk with Ho Chi Minh; interview, ed. by W. C. Baggs. pors Sat Eve Post 240:26-7 D 16 '67

about
Chances for peace. il por Newsweek 69:25-31 F 20 '67
Ho Chi Minh, like it or not. B. Fall. il Esquire 68:120-1+ N '67
Trials of Ho. il por Time 90:37 N 24 '67
Where the real obstacles to peace are. Bsns W p 146 Ap 1 '67

HOCHMAN, Baruch
Jewish vogue. Commentary 44:107-8+ S '67

HOCHMAN, Sandra
Above sea level; poem. Nation 204:824 Je 26
'67
Goldfish wife; poem. New Yorker 43:128 O 21
'67
Love singer; poem. Nation 204:503 Ap 17 '67
Marianne Moore's magic. Nation 204:602 My 8
'67
Spy; Living without treasures; poems. Poetry
110:157-8 Je '67
This afternoon; poem. New Yorker 43:87 Ag
26 '67

HOCHMUTH, Bruno Arthur
Death of a general. por Newsweek 70:44 N 27
'67
Fallen stars. il por Time 90:27 N 24 '67

HOCHSTEIN, Philip
Abrasive position. il por Newsweek 69:73 Ap
17 '67

HOCHSTEIN, Rollie
Candy Bergen, golden girl. Good H 164:34+
My '67
Mary Tyler Moore bounces back. Good H
164:61-2+ Ap '67
Pound of peas. Good H 164:64+ Je '67
—See Sugarman, D. A. jt. auth.

HOCKEY
As slick as the pros; Russia wins world
amateur championships. Newsweek 69:88 Ap
10 '67
Beware the watchdogs at old folks home;
Toronto Maple Leafs' Stanley cup triumph.
P. Axthelm. il Sports Illus 26:61-4 My 15
'67
Keep your eye on an exciting game; ed. by
M. Mulvoy. H. Blake. il Sports Illus 27:38-
45 N 6 '67
No Red guard in Vienna; 34th world ice
hockey championship. E. Whitehead. Sports
Illus 26:80-2 Ap 10 '67
    See also
National hockey league

HOCKEY players
Hockey 1967-1968. il Sports Illus 27:34-45 N 6
'67
No foldo in Chicago; Black Hawks NHL
champions. P. Axthelm. il Sports Illus 26:
34-6+ Mr 20 '67
Sporting scene; Rangers this season at
Garden. R. Angell. New Yorker 43:128+
Mr 25 '67
Spread out and puckered up for the new
Rangers; New York's E. Giacomin; photo-
graphs by T. Triolo, with account by P.
Axthelm. il Sports Illus 26:20-7 Ja 30 '67
Winning one for the Rocket; New York
Rangers and Montreal Canadiens at Stan-
ley cup playoffs. P. Axthelm. il Sports Illus
26:32-5 Ap 24 '67
    See also names of hockey players, e.g.
B. Hull

HOCKEY teams
Bad start for Black Hawks; Chicago Black
Hawks, NHL champions now in the league
cellar. P. Axthelm. il Sports Illus 27:26-7
N 13 '67
Beware the watchdogs at old folks home;
Toronto Maple Leafs' Stanley cup triumph.
P. Axthelm. il Sports Illus 26:61-4 My 15
'67
Big bad Bruins; leaders in the National
hockey league. il Time 91:43 Ja 5 '68
Deadeye dude of the North; Y. Cournoyer of
the Montreal Canadiens. P. Axthelm. il
Sports Illus 26:43-5 Ap 3 '67
Fine-feathered Forum for the Jack Kent
Kings. P. Axthelm. il Sports Illus 28:40-1 Ja
8 '68
Hobbling off with the cup; Toronto Maple
Leafs. Time 89:66+ My 12 '67
Hockey 1967-1968. il Sports Illus 27:34-45 N
6 '67
No foldo in Chicago; Black Hawks NHL
champions. P. Axthelm. il Sports Illus 26:
34-6+ Mr 20 '67
Old Andy still has the noggin and the shot;
Pittsburgh Penguins vs St Louis Blues. M.
Mulvoy. il Sports Illus 27:63-4 N 20 '67
Old pros; Stanley cup, won by Maple Leafs.
Newsweek 69:68 My 15 '67
Rangers don't have no inferiority complex no
more; National hockey league's biggest sur-
prise. B. Surface. il N Y Times Mag p46-7+
Mr 12 '67
Sporting scene; Rangers this season at
Garden. R. Angell. New Yorker 43:128+
Mr 25 '67
Spread out and puckered up for the new
Rangers; New York's E. Giacomin; photo-
graphs by T. Triolo, with account by P.
Axthelm. Sports Illus 26:20-7 Ja 30 '67
We're doing the pushing; Boston Bruins. il
Newsweek 70:92 D 18 '67

Winning one for the Rocket; New York
Rangers and Montreal Canadiens at Stan-
ley cup playoffs. P. Axthelm. il Sports Illus
26:32-5 Ap 24 '67
You gotta have sock; Boston Bruins. P.
Axthelm. il Sports Illus 27:22-7 D 11 '67

HODGES, C. Walter
On writing about King Alfred. il Horn Bk
43:178-82 Ap '67

HODGES, Elizabeth Jamison
Magic of serendipity. Horn Bk 43:370-4 Je '67

HODGINS, Maibelle Dickey
Bird worth waiting for. il Home Gard 54:
64-5 My '67
Game birds can be garden birds. Home Gard
54:40+ F '67
Thanksgiving for birds. Home Gard 54:43 N
'67

HODGKIN'S disease
Incurable ill responds. Sci N 91:190 F 25 '67

HODGSON, Alice Doan
Living with antiques. Antiques 92:182-6 Ag
'67

HODGSON, Harold R.
When I plant a tree. Am For 73:26-7+ Ja '67

HODSON, James Lansdale
Hamp; dramatization. See Wilson, J.

HOEBEL, E. Adamson
Anthropological perspectives on national
character. bibliog f Ann Am Acad 370:1-7
Mr '67

HOEFS, Jochen, and Schidlowski, Manfred
Carbon isotope composition of carbonaceous
matter from the Precambrian of Witwatersrand system. bibliog Science 155:1096-7 Mr
3 '67

HOELDERLIN, Friedrich. See Hölderlin, F.

HOFFA, James Riddle
What Hoffa wants now to keep trucks rolling
on highways; summary of address, January 17, 1967. por U S News 62:84 Ja 30 '67

        about
Fix. S. Smith. il por Life 63:22 S 1 '67
Hoffa; can he ever make a comeback? por
U S News 62:21 Mr 20 '67
Hoffa goes to jail. por Sr Schol 90:18 Mr 31 '67
Hoffa's gone, but not forgotten. il por Bsns
W p44-5 Mr 11 '67
Hoffa's last stand. por Newsweek 69:83 Mr 13
'67
Imprisoned Hoffa asks no favors. por Bsns W
p 154 My 20 '67
Inmate 33298-NE; James Riddle Hoffa; with
report by S. McBee. il pors Life 62:30-5 Mr
17 '67
Jimmy's nemesis. il por Time 89:25 Mr 17 '67
No more string. il por Time 89:20 Mr 10 '67
Prisoner no. 33298-NE. il por Newsweek 69:
29 Mr 20 '67
Strange help-Hoffa campaign of the U.S.
senator from Missouri. W. Lambert. il por
Life 62:26-31+ My 26 '67
Taps, bugs & spies; anything to get Hoffa.
F. J. Cook. il por Nation 204:230-6 F 20 '67
Tough haul with Hoffa. Bsns W p 114 Ja 28
'67
Why not Hoffa? Department of justice's dis-
closures of illegal wire taps. Nation 204:132
Ja 30 '67
Without Hoffa; truck strike? U S News 62:
110 Mr 13 '67

HOFFER, Eric
Docker of philosophy; interview, ed. by J.
Fincher. pors Life 62:35-6+ Mr 24 '67

        about
Americans not everybody knows. C. W. Fer-
guson. il por PTA Mag 61:4-7 Je '67
From the waterfront. pors Time 90:66 N 17
'67
Hoffer as historian. J. Featherstone. New
Repub 156:30-2 Je 3 '67
Passionate believer. K. Crawford. Newsweek
70:38 O 16 '67

HOFFMAN, Daniel
Breathing purely; poem. Reporter 37:58 Jl 13
'67
Graves; a ghost and a skeleton key. Poetry
110:409-12 S '67
Old Ez and Uncle William. Reporter 37:59-
62 N 2 '67
Two ladies of legend. Reporter 37:41-3 D 28
'67

HOFFMAN, Donald A.
Burns refuse without a flame. Am City 82:
102-4 F '67

HOFFMAN, Dustin
I plummeted to stardom. pors Newsweek 71:
86 Ja 22 '68
Movies. D. Zeitlin. il pors Life 63:111-12+ N
24 '67

HOLIDAYS—*Continued*
New long weekends; re-arrangement plans for some national holidays. Life 63:4 S 1 '67
100 days of summer. L. Lerman. il Mlle 65: 125-7 My '67
Two leftovers for Congress; Smathers bill proposals. America 117:195 Ag 26 '67
See also
Vacations
    also names of holidays. e.g. Memorial day

HOLLAND, Barbara
Backward heart; story. McCalls 95:82-3 Ja '68

HOLLAND, C. L.
Brain workers: suburbia's rising class. T. G. Harris. il pors Look 31:M22+ My 16 '67

HOLLAND, D. J. See Simmons, E. R. jt. auth.

HOLLAND, Gerald
Win one for aunt Mary Margaret! Sat Eve Post 240:84-7 N 4 '67

HOLLAND, Spessard Lindsey
Excerpt from address, May 9, 1967. Cong Digest 46:269+ N '67

HOLLAND, Vyvyan Beresford
Second visit; interview. New Yorker 43:41-2 Ap 15 '67

HOLLAND, Mich.

Parks and playgrounds
Windmill Island. H. H. Holt. il Am For 73: 24-6+ D '67

HOLLAND. See Netherlands

HOLLAND festival. See Music festivals—Netherlands

HOLLANDER, John
Auden at sixty. Atlan 220:84-7 Jl '67
State of nature; poem. Harper 234:16 Je '67

HOLLETT, Grace
On Beacon hill. Horticulture 45:13 N '67

HOLLEY, Myle J. Jr. See Hansen, R J. jt. auth.

HOLLEY, W. D.
Make your cut flowers last. Horticulture 45: 22-3 Je '67

HOLLIDAYSBURG, Pa.
Lighting puts a final touch on a downtown renewal. J. M. Mitchell. il Am City 82:110 Ag '67

HOLLINGER, J. P. See Hobbs, R. W. jt. auth.

HOLLINGSWORTH, Leslie
Silent night; drama. Plays 27:91-6 D '67

HOLLIS, Charles A. See Tepper, H. B. jt. auth.

HOLLISTER, Lincoln S. and Bence, A. E.
Staurolite; sectoral compositional variations. bibliog Science 158:1053-6 N 24 '67

HOLLO, Anselm
Days: air; Journey; poems. Poetry 110:24-6 Ap '67

about
Poetry chronicle. T. Clark. Poetry 110:106 My '67

HOLLOMON, John Herbert
Literate engineering. por Sat R 50:40-1 Jl 1 '67
Standards and the public interest; address, February 13, 1967. Vital Speeches 33:364-8 Ap 1 '67
U.S. patent system; with biographical sketch. Sci Am 216:14, 19-27 Je '67

about
Creation of quality. il por Time 89:44 Je 2 '67
Hollomon leaving science post for presidency at Oklahoma. B. Nelson. por Science 156: 1074 My 26 '67

HOLLOSZY, John O. and Narahara, H. T.
Nitrate ions: potentiation of increased permeability to sugar associated with muscle contraction. bibliog Science 155:573-5 F 3 '67

HOLLOWAY, Bill
Teenage stuntmen. G. Gilbert. il U S Camera 30:24+ Mr '67

HOLLOWAY, R. L. Jr
Human aggression: the need for a species-specific framework. Natur Hist 76:40-4 bibliog(p69) D '67

HOLLOWAY, Trevor
England's Lilliputian towns. Travel 128:58-63 N '67

HOLLY, Roy G. and Meilach, D. Z.
Expectant mother. Redbook 128:31+ F '67

HOLLY
Some good plants. R. C. Hands. Horticulture 45:56 F '67

HOLLY sugar corporation
Fire that stirred Holly sugar to action; unsuccessful corporate take-over by International systems & controls corp. il Bsns W p 151-2+ N 18 '67

HOLLYWOOD, Calif.
Eucalyptic dream. A. Knight. il Sat R 50:70-1+ S 23 '67
Quo Hollywood? W. K. Zinsser. il Look 31: 14 Jl 11 '67

Anecdotes, facetiae, satire, etc.
Billy Brown shoes in west Hollywood. F. P. Tullius. New Yorker 43:31-3 My 27 '67

Social life and customs
Hollywood's night shift; private discothèque clubs. il Newsweek 70:98 O 16 '67
Snob's guide to Hollywood. M. Fessier, jr. il McCalls 94:70-3 Ap '67

HOLLYWOOD gold cup race. See Horse racing

HOLM, Bernard J.
(comp) Articles and other books received; medieval. See issues of American historical review

HOLM, Celeste
Friends: new organization called Friends of Central park. New Yorker 42:24-5 F 4 '67

HOLMAN, C. Hugh
Thomas Wolfe's Berlin. Sat R 50:66+ Mr 11 '67

HOLMAN, Edwin J.
Take your medical complaint to the doctors. Todays Health 45:72+ Jl '67

HOLMAN, Wayne J. 3d
Problems of the sciences. Nat R 19:645+ Je 13 '67

HOLMDEL, N.J.
Biggest mirror ever; Bell laboratories. il Arch Forum 126:33-41 Ap '67

HOLMER, Paul L.
Evolution and being faithful. Christian Cent 84:1491-4 N 22 '67

HOLMES, Donald J.
When child psychiatry is wasted money. Ladies Home J 84:62+ O '67

HOLMES, Doris
Poet's workshop (cont) Writer 80:30-3+ Ja; 23-7 Mr; 24-8+ My; 24-8+ Jl '67
Vision and revision. Writer 80:39-42 Ap '67

HOLMES, Edward W. Jr, and others
Hexokinase isoenzymes in human erythrocytes: association of type II with fetal hemoglobin. bibliog Science 156:646-8 My 5 '67

HOLMES, John Clellon
On the road. S. K. Oberbeck. il por Newsweek 60:112+ Mr 13 '67

HOLMES, John W.
Growing independence in Canadian-American relations. For Affairs 46:151-66 O '67

HOLMES, Karen Tweedy-. See Tweedy-Holmes, K.

HOLMES, Marjorie
All doors led to the kitchen. Todays Health 45:44-5+ N '67
Creative article. Writer 80:16-19 D '67
Days of movie magic. Todays Health 45: 38-41 O '67
Every child was king, in a swing. Todays Health 45:24-7+ Ag '67
Give me an old-fashioned peddler. Todays Health 45:68-70 My '67
Golden days in grandpa's garden. Todays Health 45:48-51 Je '67
What does an apron mean? Todays Health 45:62-3 F '67
Winter is my memory season. Todays Health 45:24-7+ D '67
Yes, we do marry our in-laws! Todays Health 45:38-41 Mr '67

HOLMES, Theodore
Four poets. H. Carruth. Poetry 111:43-5 O '67

HOLOFCENER, Lawrence
Before you go. Criticism
Time 91:67 Ja 19 '68

HOLOGRAMS. See Holography

HOLOGRAPHY
Amateur scientist; how to make holograms and experiment with them. S. M. Heumann. il Sci Am 216:122-8 F '67
Holography by sound. Sci Am 218:46 Ja '68
Making 3-D pictures with sound; acoustical holography. il Time 90:64+ N 10 '67
New random-access memory utilizes lasers and holograms. P. J. Klass. il Aviation W 87:81+ Ag 7 '67
New wave in image-making; holograms tell it like it really was. J. Forney. il Pop Phot 61:120-3+ N '67
25c holograms. Sci Digest 61:31 Ap '67
Vibration analysis finds a tool. il Sci N 93:19-20 Ja 6 '68

HOME ownership—*Continued*
How to sell your home for the best price. R. Beamish. House B 109:24-6 D '67
Let your house cut your tax bill. il Changing T 21:39-41 O '67
Should you buy, build, or rent now? M. Colean. House B 109:122+ F '67
Should you own a home, or rent? il Changing T 21:15-18 N '67
What went wrong in dreamland? Larkdale, Ill. B. Remsberg and C. Remsberg. il Good H 164:74-5+ F '67
Why people don't buy houses. W. McQuade. il Fortune 76:153-5 D '67
See also
Apartment houses—Cooperative ownership
House buying
House selling
Mortgages
HOME safety devices and measures. See Safety devices and measures
HOME savings and loan association of Los Angeles
Emperor in private. il Time 90:96+ N 10 '67
Millionaire, California style; I've never added it all up. il Newsweek 70:84-5 D 11 '67
HOME service industries. See Service industries
HOME sewing. See Sewing
HOME sites. See Building sites
HOME storage. See Storage in the home
HOME study
What about homework? E. H. Hanson. il NEA J 57:32-4 Ja '68
HOME study courses. See Correspondence schools and courses
HOME-swapping vacation. See Vacations
HOME towns. See Birthplaces
HOME workshops. See Workshops
HOMECOMING; drama. See Pinter, H.
HOMEMADE cigarettes. See Cigarette-making machines
HOMEMAKING. See Home economics
HOMEOTHERMY. See Temperature, Animal and human
HOMEOWNER policies. See Insurance—All risk policies
HOMER
Man of many ways. R. Humphries. New Repub 157:30-1+ D 9 '67
Odyssey. P. W. Schmidtchen. il por Hobbies 72:104-5+ Ap '67
Story within a story; Iliad. P. W. Schmidtchen. il Hobbies 71:104-5 F '67
HOMER, Page. See Pemberton, P. jt. auth.
HOMER, Sidney
Homer: bard of the bond market. il pors Bsns W p 116-18+ S 23 '67
HOMES, Institutional
See also
Pestalozzi children's village
HOMESICKNESS. See Nostalgia
HOMICIDE
See also
Murder
HOMING Instinct. See Orientation
HOMING pigeons. See Pigeons
HOMMEL, Martha Hill
Tin collecting. Hobbies 72:98DD-98EE N '67
HOMOSEXUALITY
Civil rights and the homosexual. W. Schott. il N Y Times Mag p44-5+ N 12 '67; Discussion. p 12+ D 3; 40+ D 10 '67
Equality for homosexuals? Christian Cent 84: 1587 D 13 '67
God and the homosexual; views of Protestant ministers in San Francisco area. il Newsweek 69:63 F 13 '67
Homosexual wedding; special mass in Rotterdam. Newsweek 70:59 Jl 17 '67
Shame is enough; House of commons reforms Britain's criminal statutes against homosexuality. Time 90:30 Jl 14 '67
A way out for homosexuals. S. B. Hadden. Harper 234:107-8+ Mr '67; Discussion. 234: 4+ My '67
Wicked and the weak. America 116:802-3 Je 3 '67
HONAN, William H.
Doctor Jonathan Miller operates on Alice. N Y Times Mag p24-7+ Ja 22 '67
New sound of radio. N Y Times Mag p56-8+ D 3 '67
They live in the year 2000. N Y Times Mag p56-7+ Ap 9 '67
Would-be candidate for this season. N Y Times Mag p27+ D 10 '67

HONDA, Soichiro
Big boss of the thunder herd; with report by M. Parker. il pors Life 62:47-8+ My 19 '67
HONESTY
See also
Business ethics
Truthfulness
HONESTY (plant)
One of its names is honesty. il Sunset 138: 271 Ap '67
HONEY bees. See Bees
HONEY bread. See Bread
HONEYCOMB construction. See Sandwich construction
HONEYMOONERS (television program) See Television broadcasting—Humor
HONEYWELL, Incorporated
International VP: man on the run; Honeywell's E. Spencer. il Bsns W p48+ Ag 26 '67
HONG, Richard, and Good, R. A.
Limited heterogeneity of gamma globulin in hypogammaglobulinemia. bibliog Science 156:1102-3 My 26 '67
HONG, Suk Ki, and Rahn, Hermann
Diving women of Korea and Japan; with biographical sketches. Sci Am 216:21, 34-43 My '67
HONG KONG
Canton more far. S. Hazzard. New Yorker 43:42-9 D 16 '67
Hong Kong; the running siege. il Newsweek 70:30-4 Jl 31 '67
Storm, the calm, and the colony. B. Kalb. il Sat R 50:74+ O 14 '67
Will Hong Kong become Peking duck? R. Terrill. New Repub 157:14-15 S 2 '67
See also
Children—Hong Kong
Communism—Hong Kong
Communist party (Hong Kong)
Electronic apparatus industry and trade—Hong Kong
Tourist trade—Hong Kong

Boundaries
Bridge at Lo Wu. C. Lucas. il Sat R 50: 82+ O 14 '67
Commerce
As usual. Time 90:84 Ag 18 '67
Description
Letter from Hong Kong. J. Y. Dickinson. Holiday 42:24+ S '67
Economic conditions
On China's doorstep: has Hong Kong a future? il U S News 63:40 O 16 '67
Volcano's edge; effect of riots on economic health. il Newsweek 69:78-9 Je 12 '67
Harbor
Hong Kong: fragrant harbor of the Orient. N. F. Busch. il Read Digest 90:182-4+ Je '67
Industries
See also
Electronic apparatus industry and trade—Hong Kong
Politics and government
Climate of fear. M. London. Nat R 19:1275 N 14 '67
Riots
Battle on the border; mainland Chinese converge on British police garrison. Newsweek 70:36+ Jl 17 '67
Bell for round two. il Time 90:32+ Jl 21 '67
Flower-factory riot. il Newsweek 69:62 My 22 '67
Flowers from Fu Manchu. il Newsweek 70: 38 Jl 24 '67
Hong Kong writhes in Maoist riots. il Life 62:34 Je 2 '67
Mao-think v. the stiff upper lip. il Time 89:30+ My 26 '67
Red China turns on Britain; with interview with D. Trench. il U S News 62:36-7 My 29 '67
Seeing it through. il Newsweek 69:48 Je 5 '67
Standing firm; anti-British demonstrations. il Newsweek 69:42+ My 29 '67
HONICKER, Dolph
Fallen idol. Sat R 50:4 O 14 '67
HONIG, Edwin
November through a giant copper beech; poem. New Yorker 43:58 N 11 '67
Second son day; poem. Sat R 50:75 D 9 '67

HONOLULU
City planning
Diamond in the rough. il Newsweek 71:29 Ja 22 '68
Plight of Diamond Head. K. Lamott. il Holiday 42:115-16 Jl '67

Description
Bleachies, beachies and blasters on a summer-in at Waikiki; chicks and good guys from the mainland. D. Jenkins. il Sports Illus 27: 48-54 Jl 24 '67

Historic houses, etc.
Honolulu's walk-it-yourself Monarchy promenade. il Sunset 139:56+ N '67

Music
Honolulu; production of La Bohème. W. Aguiar, jr. Opera N 31:31-2 Mr 25 '67

HONOR system. See Self government in education

HONORARY degrees. See Degrees, Honorary

HONRATH, Jean
Girl from V.I.S.T.A. F. Powledge. il por Redbook 129:80-1+ Jl '67

HONWANA, Luis Bernado
Hands of the blacks. N Y Times Mag p26-7 Ap 30 '67

HOOD, Frederick E.
Profiles. A. Bailey. por New Yorker 43:34-6+ Ag 26 '67

HOOD, Robert
Death comes to Robert Capa; excerpt from Twelve at war. Pop Phot 60:84-6+ Je '67

HOOD, Warwick
Yachting interviews. B. Robinson. il por Yachting 122:75+ S '67

HOOF-and-mouth disease. See Foot-and-mouth disease

HOOFT, Willem Adolf Visser't. See Visser't Hooft, W. A.

HOOK, Sidney
Does philosophy have a future? Sat R 50: 21-3+ N 11 '67
Liberal anti-communism revisited. Commentary 44:44-8 S '67
On civil disobedience, 1967. N Y Times Mag p 124+ N 26 '67

HOOKER DAM (proposed) See Dams

HOOKWORMS
Sick worms: well child. Sci N 92:250-1 S 9 '67

HOOLAULEA. See Cookery, Polynesian

HOOPER, Bayard
Problems of having too much to choose from. Life 62:73-4+ Ap 21 '67
Tourist at the Vietnam war. Life 63:14 Jl 7 '67
about
Franchise of human affairs. G. P. Hunt. il por Life 62:3 Mr 31 '67

HOOPER, Bill R.
New Presbyterian bookstore serves the whole person. Pub W 192:90-1 S 25 '67

HOOVER, Herbert Clark
Herbert Hoover and education. R. H. Muessig. bibliog f il pors Sch & Soc 95:309-13 Sum '67

HOOVER, Herbert William, 1918-
Filling a power vacuum at Hoover. il por Bsns W p84-6+ O 21 '67

HOOVER, John Edgar
FBI warns about: the Christmas trade no business wants. por Nations Bsns 55:44-6+ N '67
Now: instant crime control in your town. por Pop Sci 190:67-9+ Ja '67
about
Anti-missive missive. il por Newsweek 69:32 F 6 '67
Clearing it with Hoover. New Repub 156:9 F 4 '67
Matter of mutual advantage. Time 89:19-20 F 3 '67

HOOVER, Mary Bidgood
Are we spoiling our kids? Parents Mag 42: 46-7+ Ja '67

HOOVER company
Filling a power vacuum at Hoover; new management. il Bsns W p84-6+ O 21 '67

HOPE, A. Guy. See Cortada, J. N. jt. auth.

HOPE, Bob
Bob Hope hits the road he never left. B. Rollin. il pors Look 32:44-8 Ja 23 '68
Christmas in Vietnam: Bob Hope style. il pors U S News 64:8 Ja 1 '68
Comedian as hero. il pors Time 90:58-62 D 22 '67

HOPE, Marjorie
No to the draft? Christian Cent 84:715-16 My 31 '67

HOPE
Standing on the promises; Theology of hope. L. Gilkey. Christian Cent 84:1630-2 D 20 '67
Theology of hope; theories of German theologians. il Newsweek 70:92+ D 11 '67
What hope for hope? L. J. Putnam. Christian Cent 84:1519-21 N 29 '67

HOPE (ship) See Hospital ships

HOPEDALE medical complex. See Medical centers

HOPKINS, Donald R.
Negro youth in the now generation. por Ebony 22:110-12+ Ag '67

HOPKINS, Ernest J.
(ed) See Bierce, A. Ambrose Bierce's devilish definitions

HOPKINS, Joseph Martin
I'm sorry you came! Christian Cent 85:14-15 Ja 3 '68

HOPKINS, Lee Bennett
1965 and 1966: happy new years for nonfiction books about the Negro. Negro Hist Bul 30:15-17 N '67

HOPKINS center. See Dartmouth college, Hanover, N.H.—Hopkins center

HOPKIRK, Paddy
Road rallies: agony and ecstasy. Pop Sci 190:74 Mr '67

HOPPER, DeWolf
Casey at the bat; excerpts from The annotated Casey at the bat. M. Gardner. il por Am Heritage 18:64-8 O '67

HOPPER, Edward
Certain alienated majesty. il por Time 89:72 My 26 '67
I want to paint sunlight. J. Kroll. il por Newsweek 69:88 My 29 '67
Obituary
Life il por 62:36A My 26 '67

HOPPER, William DeWolf. See Hopper, D.

HORAN, Ellen
Special time in Maine. bibliog il Yachting 122: 54-6+ Ag '67
With the racing classes. See issues of Yachting

HORAN, Hubert
Missionary's predicament: how far to adapt? America 117:197-200 Ag 26 '67

HORCHLER, Richard
Books. Commonweal 86:473-4 Jl 28 '67

HORIUCHI, Kensuke, and Zinder, N. D.
Azure mutants: a type of host-dependent mutant of the bacteriophage f2. bibliog Science 156:1618-23 Je 23 '67

HORMONES
Cellular dynamics: hormones; report on conference. L. D. Peachey. Science 155:226+ Ja 13 '67
Chemistry of fatness; controlling weight with hormones. Newsweek 69:82 My 1 '67
Enterogastrone inhibits eating by fasted mice. A. V. Schally and others. bibliog il Science 157:210-11 Jl 14 '67
Hormone-dependent differentiation of immature mouse mammary gland in vitro. A. E. Voytovich and Y. J. Topper. bibliog il Science 158:1326-7 D 8 '67
Hormone-dependent differentiation of mammary gland: sequence of action of hormones in relation to cell cycle. D. H. Lockwood and others. bibliog il Science 156:945-6 My 19 '67
Hormones and endocrine glands of fishes. H. A. Bern. bibliog il Science 158:455-62 O 27 '67
Human growth hormone and placental lactogen: structural similarity. K. J. Catt and others. bibliog Science 157:321 Jl 21 '67
Inhibition of lipolytic action of growth hormone and glucocorticoid by ultraviolet and X-radiation. J. N. Fain. bibliog il Science 157:1062-4 S 1 '67
Loused-up lice. Sci Am 217:104 S '67
Many uses of hormones. il Good H 166:166 Ja '68
Messenger RNA patterns in rat liver nuclei before and after treatment with growth hormone. J. Drews and G. Brawerman. bibliog il Science 156:1385-6 Je 9 '67
New hormone class: discovery of sialogen, brain hormone. Sci N 91:400 Ap 29 '67
Nonhormonal basis of maternal behavior in the rat. J. S. Rosenblatt. bibliog il Science 156:1512-14 Je 16 '67
See also
Calcitonin
Ecdysone
Toxohormone

HORMONES, Plant
Insect hormones: alpha ecdysone and 20-hydroxyecdysone in bracken fern. J. N. Kaplanis and others. bibliog il Science 157: 1436-8 S 22 '67
Role of enzymatic wall-softening in plant morphogenesis: hormonal induction in achlya. D. des S. Thomas and J. T. Mullins. bibliog il Science 156:84 Ap 7 '67
See also
Auxins

HORMONES, Sex
Luteinizing hormone activity in plasma during the menstrual cycle. G. T. Ross and others. bibliog il Science 155:1679-80 Mr 31 '67
Ribonucleic acid: control of steroid synthesis in endocrine tissue. D. B. Villee. bibliog il Science 158:652-3 N 3 '67
What hormones have to do with pregnancy. R. W. Kistner. Redbook 129:22+ Ag '67
See also
Estrogens

HORN, Daniel
Smoke signs: the signal remains red; excerpts from address. PTA Mag 62:25 S '67

HORN, George F.
On art in the schools. Sch Arts 67:6-18 S '67

HORN, John
Television. Nation 204:476-7, 570-1, 667-8; 205: 414, 477-8, 574, 638, 702 Ap 10, My 1, 22, O 23, N 6, 27, D 11, 25 '67

HORN, William A. See Winnick, P. jt. auth.

HORN-D'ARTURO, Guido
Italian astronomer. L. Jacchia. Sky & Tel 34:93 Ag '67

HORN book magazine
Ave atque vale. M. E. Manthorne. Horn Bk 43:706 D '67
How do you say good-by? editor retires. R. H. Viguers. Horn Bk 43:549 O '67
Selections from Horn book editorials. B. M. Miller. Horn Bk 43:155-8 Ap '67

HORN tableware. See Tableware, Horn

HORNADAY, Fred Eugene
Wood sunburst: symphony in wood. il pors Am For 73:36-8 Ap '67

HORNBY, Lesley. See Twiggy (model)

HORNBY, Mrs Nel
My girl Twiggy. por Mlle 65:122-3+ Je '67

HORNED owls. See Owls

HORNER, Marian B.
Tree of Christmas; poem. Am For 73:27 D '67

HORNIG, Donald Frederick
Hornig on research policy: public understanding essential to scientific progress; excerpts from address, April 26, 1967. Science 156:628-9 My 5 '67

about
Advisory unit drops war protestor. D. S. Greenberg. Science 157:409 Jl 28 '67

HORNOS, Axel
Frosty days in the land of fire. Sat R 50:67-70 N 11 '67

HOROSCOPES. See Astrology

HOROWITZ, Al
Chess corner. See issues of Saturday review

HOROWITZ, Milton W.
IFR and the single man. Flying 80:73-9 Ap '67
—See Flexman, R. jt. auth

HOROWITZ, N. H. and others
Planetary contamination I: the problem and the agreements. bibliog il Science 155:1501-5; 156:1436; 157:583 Mr 24, Je 16, Ag 4 '67

HOROWITZ, Vladimir
Horowitz live (and otherwise). R. Kammerer. Am Rec G 33:1005 Jl '67
Musical events; recital in Carnegie Hall. W. Sargeant. New Yorker 43:227 D 9 '67
Variations on a tape by Vladimir: the Horowitz concerts. S. Kanfer. Life 62:13 Je 23 '67

HORROCKS, Norman
(ed) Down Under: opportunity beckons. por Library J 92:4107-9 N 15 '67

HORROR films. See Moving pictures—Horror films

HORS d'oeuvres. See Appetizers

HORSE breeding
Best racehorses in all the world: Argentine thoroughbred racehorses. W. Tower. il Sports Illus 26:52-5 My 1 '67
Building an empire on horses ready to run; entrepreneur O'Farrell. P. Axthelm. il Sports Illus 26:45-8 Ja 23 '67
How to stay in the money; champion thoroughbreds for beeding purposes. il Bsns W p96 Jl 1 '67
Personal business; breeding thoroughbred racehorses. Bsns W p 133-4 O 28 '67

HORSE power. See Horsepower (mechanics)

HORSE race betting
Booking Bugged bets brings a Balding bonanza. W. Tower. Sports Illus 27:68+ N 27 '67
When the real McGuire stood up; John a devoted horseplayer. P. Axthelm. il Sports Illus 26:74-8+ Mr 20 '67

HORSE racing
Best from the Derby and some new faces, too; 92nd running of the Preakness at Pimlico. W. Tower. Sports Illus 26:60 My 22 '67
Big balk at the Big A; horse owners refuse to run their horses at Aqueduct. il Time 89:65-6+ Ap 14 '67
Booking Bugged bets brings a Balding bonanza. W. Tower. Sports Illus 27:68+ N 27 '67
Champ was really loaded; Quick Pitch the best hurdler. W. Tower. il Sports Illus 27: 24-5 S 25 '67
Clarion call; Kentucky Derby won by Proud Clarion. Time 89:66 My 12 '67
Clarion call: $62.20! third highest payoff in Derby history. W. Tower. il Sports Illus 26:20-5 My 15 '67
Clarion victory; winner of the Kentucky Derby. Newsweek 69:68 My 15 '67
Crab cakes and tall timber; Maryland hunt cup race. L. Smith. il Sports Illus 26:52-9 Ap 24 '67
Damascus against the world; America's horse of the year. W. Tower. Sports Illus 27:64 N 6 '67
Damascus by a mile; Woodward stakes. W. Tower. il Sports Illus 27:16-19 O 9 '67
Derby in the air. Time 89:76 Ap 28 '67
Disaster at a thorny barricade; Grand national at Aintree. W. Tower. il Sports Illus 26:32-4+ Ap 17 '67
Fastest run in the West; Argentine champion Forli at Hollywood park. W. Tower. Sports Illus 26:70 My 29 '67
Fillies may be better than the colts. W. Tower. Sports Illus 26:54 F 20 '67
Go to the races. W. Johnson. il Sports Illus 27:102-4+ D 4 '67
Governor talks of sport. A. Wright. il Sports Illus 26:40-3 Je 26 '67
Happy return of the native; Native Diver, winner of Hollywood gold cup. W. Tower. il Sports Illus 27:16-17 Jl 24 '67
Hard ride all the way; ed. by W. Tower. B. Hartack. il Sports Illus 26:60-4+ Mr 27; 30-2+ Ap 3; 58-62+ Ap 10 '67
Hopeful time for all; photographs by J. Cooke and others; with account by W. Tower and D. Jenkins. Sports Illus 27: 16-21 S 4 '67
In Reality shows that he's for real; Florida derby winner. W. Tower. il Sports Illus 26:83-5 Ap 10 '67
Invader is there; Ruken, Kentucky Derby contender. W. Tower. il Sports Illus 26:16-19 My 1 '67
Kentucky Derby; paintings by P. Davis; with account by W. Tower. Sports Illus 26:36-41 My 8 '67
Noisy chase Discreetly done; at Miami's Flagler track. R. Boyle. il Sports Illus 26: 44-7 Mr 20 '67
Now the uncontested champ; Damascus. W. Tower. Sports Illus 27:66-7 Ag 28 '67
One tough little guy; S. Silberman, owner of Tropical Park racetrack, Miami. J. Underwood. il Sports Illus 26:54-62 F 6 '67
Painful prognosis for the good Dr Fager; Kentucky Derby favorites. W. Tower. il Sports Illus 26:74-8 Ap 24 '67
Race track. A. Minor. See issues of New Yorker
Revere at the raceway; observance of one-hundred-and-ninety-second anniversary of midnight ride at Roosevelt raceway, Westbury. New Yorker 43:34 Ap 29 '67
Rushing out of the barn and into the picture; Damascus, Bay Shore stakes winner. W. Tower. il Sports Illus 26:54-5 Ap 3 '67
Setting up the race of the decade, maybe; Buckpasser, Dr Fager and Damascus in the Woodward at Aqueduct. W. Tower. il Sports Illus 27:91-2+ S 18 '67
Shades of Silky! Reflected Glory and Ruken, Flamingo and Santa Anita derby winners. W. Tower. il Sports Illus 26:18-21 Mr 13 '67
Steel from Damascus; Woodward stakes. il Time 90:56-7 O 13 '67
Sunshine wins in the mud. W. Tower. Sports Illus 26:33 Ja 30 '67
Suzy's sleeper at Longchamp even fooled the French. W. Tower. Sports Illus 27:84+ O 16 '67

HORSE racing—*Continued*
They're off! Phu tho hippodrome, Saigon's race track. il Newsweek 69:44 Ap 10 '67
Thoroughbred classic; Woodward stakes. Newsweek 70:65-6 O 9 '67
Toe that stopped a show; Santa Anita's big race won by Howard Keck's Drin. W. Tower. il Sports Illus 26:52-3 F 6 '67
Turf tangle; Grand national, Aintree winner; New York's Aqueduct strike. Newsweek 69:74 Ap 17 '67
Two toffs, a lady and a horse; the Epsom derby; excerpt from The pocket Venus. H. Blyth. il Sports Illus 26:66-70+ My 8 '67
Winner but not yet king; Damascus winner of Belmont stakes. W. Tower. il Sports Illus 26:26-9 Je 12 '67
With an assist from pal Duffy; Damascus at Pimlico. W. Tower. il Sports Illus 26:26-9 My 29 '67
Wrong American; Damascus lost the International at Laurel to Fort Marcy. W. Tower. il Sports Illus 27:18-21 N 20 '67
    See also
    Harness racing
    Jockeys
    Race tracks

HORSE serum. See Serum

HORSE shows
Leaky-roof circuit; county-fair shows. A. Higgins. il Sports Illus 27:50-2+ Jl 3 '67
Long run in the blues. A. Higgins. Sports Illus 27:69-70 N 6 '67
Rafe, the tomboy terror of Texas; Fort Sam Houston and San Antonio charity show. A. Higgins. Sports Illus 26:60-1 My 1 '67
Sunny sociable shows of summer; Middlesex County affair at New Brunswick, N.J. il Sports Illus 26:38-43 Je 19 '67
Sunshine circuit goes into eclipse; collapse of Florida's Sunshine circuit. A. Higgins. Sports Illus 26:69 Mr 13 '67

HORSE training
Chicagoan makes horse sense pay off; C. Scott. il Ebony 23:130-2+ D '67
Face to face with a girl who trains racing horses; harness racing. il Seventeen 26:88 F '67
Golden touch. D. Parker. il Sat Eve Post 240:100-5 My 6 '67
    See also
    Horse racing

HORSEBACK riding. See Horsemanship

HORSEMANSHIP
Riding the back country. C. Nansen. il Field & S 71:48-51+ Mr '67

    Anecdotes, facetiae, satire, etc.
Tall in the saddle; western transportation. C. Ford. il Field & S 72:6+ Ag '67

HORSEMINT
Time to plant monarda; for people, bees and hummingbirds. H. Guzelis. il Home Gard 54:49 My '67

HORSEPOWER (mechanics)
Isky's wailin' street Chevy. E. Rickman. il Hot Rod 20:48-51 S '67

HORSERADISH
Here's tears in your eyes. il Sunset 139:208 O '67

HORSES
All my life I've loved horses. D. K. Rodewald. il Seventeen 26:92-3+ Jl '67
Arabian horses, a new surge in America. il Vogue 150:198-203 D '67
Back in the saddle; pleasure horses. W. D. Osborne. il Fortune 76:110-17 S 1 '67
Leaky-roof circuit; county-fair shows. A. Higgins. il Sports Illus 27:50-2+ Jl 3 '67
Nature note; Przewalski's horse. Sci N 91:149 F 11 '67
Pleasure horses in the parks. E. Bowman. il Nat Parks Mag 41:4-6 N '67
    See also
    Horse breeding
    Horse shows
    Race horses

    Anecdotes, facetiae, satire, etc.
Stallion's odyssey; or, How to ship a horse from Piraeus to Patmos. O. Edwards. Holiday 42:110+ S '67

    Photographs
    See Animals—Photographs

    Stories
One last time, amigo. W. J. Buchanan. il Read Digest 90:61-5 My '67

    Training
    See Horse training

HORSES, Fossil
    See also
    Eohippus

HORSES, Photography of. See Photography of animals

HORSES in art
Arabian horses, a new surge in America. il Vogue 150:198-203 D '67
Drawings by Charlotte Daley. C, Daley. il Sch Arts 66:9-12 F '67
Horses in the Queen's gallery. O. Millar. il Antiques 91:628-31 My '67

HORSESHOE crabs. See King crabs

HORSFALL, Frank, Jr. See Webb, R. E. jt. auth.

HORST
Garden of American history: at the White House; photographs. Vogue 149:160-5 F 1 '67

HORTA, Anderson Braga
Marvário; poem; excerpts, with English translation. Américas 19:23 D '67

HORTICULTURAL societies
Goteborg's horticultural society gardens. W. O. Hultgren. il Horticulture 45:34-6 N '67
Members' news. See issues of Horticulture

HORTICULTURAL society gardens, Göteborg. See Göteborg—Gardens

HORTICULTURE

    Bibliography
Books and reviews. See issues of Horticulture

HORTICULTURE (periodical)
Garden club yearbook contest rules. Horticulture 45:12-14 My '67
Garden club yearbook winners (cont) Horticulture 45:16 Ap '67

HORTON, Carolyn
Saving the libraries of Florence. Wilson Lib Bul 41:1034-43 Je '67

    about
Cleaning and preserving bindings and related materials. il Consumer Bul 51:32 Ja '68

HORWICH, Frances R.
Play materials for many moods. PTA Mag 62: 16-18 bibliog(p34-5) D '67

HORWITZ, Elinor Lander
I'm not on your trip. McCalls 94:66-9+ S '67

HORWITZ, Silom
Temperature monitor. Electr World 78:58 N '67

HOSE, Garden. See Garden hose

HOSIERY
Good news about 50¢ nylon stockings. Consumer Rep 32:185 Ap '67
Holy socks! C. R. Tighe. Outdoor Life 140: 83 Jl '67
Hosiery wear and care. il Good H 165:150 D '67
Hot socks; Lectra-Sox. C. Conley. il Field & S 72:99 D '67
Young, wild, wonderful. il Redbook 129:84-7+ O '67

HOSKIN, F. C. G. and Rosenberg, Philip
Penetration of an organophosphorous compound into squid axon and its effects on metabolism and function. bibliog Science 156:966-7 My 19 '67

HOSKINS, Halford L.
Changing of the guard in the Middle East. Cur Hist 52:65-6+ F '67

HOSKINS, Katherine
Five-book shelf. W. Stafford. Poetry 111: 185-6 D '67

HOSMER, Craig
Can U.S. survive red H-bombs? por U S News 63:60 Jl 31 '67

HOSPITAL attendants. See Hospitals—Staff

HOSPITAL care
Hospital of the future? remodeling plans for Georgetown hospital, Washington, D.C. W. R. Young. il Read Digest 90:161-3+ My '67
With a life at stake; struggle to cut through medical confusion and hospital red tape. E. M. Brecher. McCalls 95:96-7+ O '67
    See also
    Hospitals—Family centered maternity care

    Cost
Hospitals try to cure a high-cost syndrome. il Bsns W p 128-30+ Jl 15 '67

HOSPITAL libraries. See Libraries, Hospital

HOSPITAL nursing. See Nurses and nursing

HOSPITAL patients. See Sick, The

HOSPITAL service, Cost of. See Medical service, Cost of

HOSPITAL ships
Seven years of Hope. R. L. Tobin. Sat R 50:24 Jl 15 '67

HOSPITAL training-schools. See Nursing schools

HOSPITALITY
Inviting house sparkling with color and gaiety. il House & Gard 132:98-103 Jl '67

Anecdotes, facetiae, satire, etc.
How to be inhospitable without really trying. R. Warfield. House & Gard 132:88-9 Jl '67

HOSPITALIZATION Insurance. See Insurance, Hospitalization

HOSPITALS
  See also
Children—Hospitals
Hospital ships
Medical centers
Medical service. Cost of
Missions, Medical
Nursing homes

Administration
  See Hospitals—Management and regulation

Architecture
Building types study. il Arch Rec 142:189-204 S '67
Hospital building potential stronger than ever. J. E. Carlson. Arch Rec 142:88 N '67
Hospital of the future? remodeling plans for Georgetown hospital. Washington. D.C. W. R. Young. il Read Digest 90:161-3+ My '67
Tomorrow's hospitals of today. C. Carner. il Todays Health 45:30-7 Mr '67

Automation
$6 million hospital saving claimed for systems method. il Tech W 20:24-5 Je 26 '67

Emergency services
Emergency! what Alexandria hospital, Washington, D.C. is doing. T. Irwin. il Todays Health 45:34-9 Ap '67
Instant appendectomy? portable emergency surgery room. il Sci Digest 62:28 D '67
What are your chances in a medical emergency? C. Remsberg and B. Remsberg. il Good H 165:100-1+ N '67

Employees
  See Hospitals—Staff

Family centered maternity care
Father gets to hold the baby. L. Marek. il Parents Mag 42:56-7+ Je '67

Federal aid
Hospital segregation; Civil rights act of 1964 flouted by Riverside hospital, Newport News, Va. New Repub 156:7 Mr 25 '67

Finance
Needed: new perspective on health services. W. E. Landgraf. Harvard Bsns R 45:75-83 S '67

Home care programs
673-square-mile hospital; Rochester and surrounding Monroe County, N.Y. T. Irwin. il Todays Health 45:52-4+ D '67

Management and regulation
$6 million hospital saving claimed for systems method. il Tech W 20:24-5 Je 26 '67

Nurses
  See Hospitals—Staff

Staff
What's wrong with American hospitals? would a stewardess help? L. Christman. il Sat R 50:65-7 F 4 '67

Peru
Theodor Binder: Peru's Albert Schweitzer. A. J. Carley. il Américas 19:1-7 Mr '67

Sweden
Hospitals in crisis: too many hospitals, too few doctors. Sci N 92:610 D 23 '67

United States
America's ten best hospitals. R. Tunley. Ladies Home J 84:34+ F '67
Down the up escalator; hospital costs. Sci N 92:442 N 4 '67
Future of the Catholic hospital. America 118:4 Ja 6 '68

Growing hospital crisis: big changes coming, the reasons. il U S News 62:66-9 My 29 '67
Making hospitals more efficient, and proficient. D. C. Carner. Todays Health 45:88+ Mr '67
Tomorrow's hospitals of today. C. Carner. il Todays Health 45:30-7 Mr '67
What's wrong with American hospitals? symposium. Sat R 50:59-60+ F 4 '67; Discussion. 50:60-2 Mr 4 '67
  See also subhead Hospitals under names of cities, e.g. New York (city)—Hospitals

Vietnam (Democratic Republic)
Samaritans to Hanoi; German International relief project. A. Schalk. Commonweal 86: 542-4 S 8 '67

Vietnam (Republic)
Civilian count; new hospitals for civilian war casualties. Nation 204:676 My 29 '67
Pat Smith's special war in Vietnam; at the Catholic mission hospital in Kontum. F. Chinnock. il Read Digest 90:195-6+ Je '67
Vietnam, a doctor's journal; U.S. military public health assistance program at Camau hospital. J. J. Weiss. Commentary 43:55-8 My '67

HOSPITALS, Military
W.I.A: facilities for Vietnam war casualties. R. Nessen. il Todays Health 45:20-7 Ap '67

HOSPITALS, Psychiatric
Banned in Massachusetts: Titicut follies. Time 91:65 Ja 19 '68
Building types study; mental health facilities. il Arch Rec 141:147-62 F '67
Coming: better mental care for less. il Changing T 21:21-3 Ap '67
Stripped bare at the follies; documentary on Bridgewater state hospital. R. Coles. New Repub 158:18+ Ja 20 '68
Tempest in a snakepit; Massachusetts seeking permanent injunction against showing of Titicut follies. il Newsweek 70:109 D 4 '67
Titicut follies; case against F. Wiseman for exposé on the State hospital for the criminally insane at Bridgewater, Mass. America 117:539 N 11 '67
Treating mental illness; Bronx State hospital. J. Ridgeway. New Repub 156:13-15 Je 10 '67
Two-way outrage; state charges Titicut follies invaded privacy of inmates. il Time 90: 52 D 1 '67

HOSPITALS, Rural
Rural patient gets a break; Hopedale medical complex. T. Berland. il Todays Health 45: 62-7 O '67

HOSPITALS, Traveling
Mobile hospital; Japanese operating room on wheels. Sci N 91:435 My 6 '67
  See also
Hospitals, Military

HOSTELS. See Youth hostels

HOSTESSES, Air. See Airlines—Hostesses

HOSTESSES gifts. See Gifts

HOSTETLER, Paul B. and others
Activity coefficients of aqueous potassium chloride measured with a potassium-sensitive glass electrode. bibliog Science 155: 1537-9 Mr 24 '67

HOSTICK, King V.
Autographs. See issues of Hobbies

HOSTOS, Eugenio María de
Hostos' Caribbean vision. J. A. Mora. por Américas 19:1-2 D '67

HOT-air balloons. See Balloons

HOT crayon painting. See Encaustic painting

HOT drinks. See Beverages

HOT line (Washington and Moscow)
Hot-line diplomacy; use of link between Washington and Moscow. il Time 89:15-17 Je 16 '67
Lines: hot, cold, tepid. Sci N 92:82 Jl 22 '67
Night the hot line went up. Look 31:31 D 12 '67
Now, a crisis role for the hot line. il U S News 62:12 Je 19 '67
Over the hot line, the Middle East: first official use. H. Sidey. Life 62:24B Je 16 '67
T.R.B. from Washington; hope of the hot line. New Repub 156:2 Je 24 '67

HOT rod (periodical)
Hot rod twentieth anniversary; scrapbook, 1948-1968. J. McFarland. il Hot Rod 21:28-39 Ja '68

HOT rod magazine championship drags. See Automobile racing

HOT rod racing. See Automobile racing

HOT weather
Better ways to beat the heat. J. Lentz. il
 Todays Health 45:45-7 Jl '67
Dog days. Sci N 92:189 Ag 19 '67
Thirty-five ways to cope with hot weather.
 Good H 165:152-3 Jl '67
HOTBEDS
 See also
 Cold frames
HOTCHIN, John. See Baker, F. D. jt. auth.
HOTCHNER, Geraldine. See West, R. jt. auth.
HOTEL architecture. See Hotels, taverns, etc.
HOTELS, taverns, etc.
 Architecture for the new itinerants. G. Nel-
 son. il Sat R 50:30-1+ Ap 22 '67
 Great hotels. R. Beardwood. il Fortune 76:
 162-9 N '67
 Hotel headliners. See issues of Travel
 Three greatest hotels in the world. R. Joseph.
 Esquire 68:205-8+ D '67
 Travel notes; some hotels not included in
 list of twenty-nine greatest. R. Joseph.
 Esquire 68:36+ D '67
 See also
 Hilton hotels corporation
 Hilton international company
 Motels
 Restaurants
 Sheraton corporation of America
 also subhead Hotels, restaurants, etc.
 under names of cities, e.g. Santa Fe, N.
 Mex.—Hotels, restaurants, etc.

 Anecdotes, facetiae, satire, etc.
 Pleasures and miseries of hotels. A. Brien.
 il Holiday 43:10+ Ja '68

 Designs and plans
 Hotel that's all razzle-dazzle; Regency Hyatt
 house, Atlanta. il Life 63:78-80 Jl 21 '67

 Europe, Western
 Aristocrats of the Continent; great old resort
 hotels. il Time 90:68 Jl 14 '67

 Fiji
 They left Pan Am for riches in Fiji. il Bsns
 W p82-3+ S 16 '67

 France
 Ballad of the sad cafés. il Time 89:33 Mr 31
 '67
 Bon appétit! Auberge de l'Ill. il Newsweek
 69:62-3 Ap 3 '67
 Fault is in the stars; Guide Michelin ratings.
 A. C. Schmidt. il Reporter 37:46+ S 7 '67
 Oh what a marvelous place to break a leg;
 Grenoble. R. Joseph. il Esquire 68:146-8+
 N '67

 Ireland
 Our highwayman in Ireland. H. Sutton. Sat R
 50:38+ D 9 '67

 Lebanon
 See also
 Beirut—Hotels, restaurants, etc.

 Nepal
 Who knows where the forks are? Boris. J.
 Howard. il Life 63:52+ Ag 11 '67

 United States
 Celebrity service. il Newsweek 69:82+ F 27
 '67
 Four-day outing from New York; old inns
 in New York state. W. Clifford. Atlan 219:
 114-16+ Je '67
 Inn sign revived. T. Haynes. il Am Artist 31:
 61-5 N '67
 Last resort; singles weekend scene at Cats-
 kills hotels. il Newsweek 71:52-3 Ja 15 '68
 Three little words to mistrust. S. Alexander.
 Life 62:23 Mr 3 '67
 Vacation guide. Ebony 22:142+ Je '67
HOTTENTOTS HOLLAND MOUNTAINS
 From an ancient desert relict to more ele-
 gant floral rarities. W. Tijmens. il Natur
 Hist 76:38-43 Ap '67
HOTTINGER, Arnold
 Silence of the moderates. New Repub 156:7-8
 Je 24 '67
HOUCK, Carter
 Parents' magazine's sewing circle. See issues
 of Parents' magazine and better home-
 making
HOUCK, Gladden B. Jr
 Common slide rule for reactance calculations.
 Electr World 78:93 S '67
HOUGHTON, H. Seymour
 Lessons from experience. Motor B 119:36-7+
 My '67

HOUGHTON, Katharine
 Hepburn comes back big, bringing a niece
 who calls her Aunt Kat. J. Frook. il pors
 Life 64:60-5 Ja 5 '68
HOUGHTON Mifflin company
 Houghton public stock offering due in May.
 Pub W 191:35 Ap 17 '67
HOULE, Cyril O.
 Role of continuing education in current pro-
 fessional development; address, January 11,
 1967. bibliog por ALA Bul 61:259-67 Mr '67
HOUNDS
 Hound world. J. Griffen. il Field & S 72:114-
 16+ D '67
HOUPHOUET-BOIGNY, Félix
 President Johnson holds meeting with pres-
 ident of Ivory Coast; exchange of toasts,
 August 17, 1967. Dept State Bul 57:330-2 S
 11 '67
HOURGLASSES
 Rustic hourglass. A. R. Christensen. il Pop
 Sci 192:172-3+ Ja '68
HOURS of business. See Business hours
HOURS of labor
 Earnings and hours; tables. See issues of
 Monthly labor review
 Growing trend: shorter workweek. U S
 News 62:96 F 20 '67
 Impact of change on work and leisure; ex-
 cerpts from address. H. L. Wilensky. Mo
 Labor R 90:21-2 S '67
 New five-day workweek in the Soviet Union.
 E. Nash. bibliog Mo Labor R 90:18-19 Ag 67
 See also
 Overtime
 Part time employment
 also subhead Wages and hours under
 names of industries, e.g. Railroads—Wages
 and hours
HOUSE armed services committee. See United
 States—Congress—House of representatives
 —Armed services committee
HOUSE boats
 America's houseboat fleet. il Motor B 121:
 105-6 Ja '68
 Escape to the River Po; thatched houseboat.
 il House B 109:91-3 Ja '67
 Houseboat sleeps six. il Travel 127:71 Ap '67
 Houseboating is a family affair; Kentucky
 admirals' picnic and parade. W. Belvin and
 A. Klein. il Motor B 121:102-4 Ja '68
 Houseboats of Sausalito. A. Garvey. il Arch
 Forum 126:48-53 Mr '67
 Keeping house on the Kissimmee. R. Frank-
 lin. il Motor B 120:32-3 O '67
 Look at the latest in houseboats! Z. Taylor.
 il Read Digest 91:145-8 Jl '67
 No weeds on the front lawn; shipboard liv-
 ing. B. Gilbert. il Sports Illus 26:80-2+ Ap
 24 '67
 Our cruising houseboat. M. Clark. il Yacht-
 ing 121:80-1+ Ap '67
 Powerhouseboat! nimble, silky-smooth, 500
 horses strong. J. Roe. il Pop Sci 191:90-2
 D '67
 Split-level home in the waves. M. Simons.
 il Look 31:84-6 Je 13 '67

 Exhibitions
 1968 houseboats. il Motor B 121:158-9 Ja '68
HOUSE building. See Building
HOUSE buying
 Are you financially ready to move? Am Home
 70:40+ O '67
 Becoming your own landlord. H. B. Winsor.
 il PTA Mag 62:24-6 Ja '68
 Buying and selling a home. J. D. Bierman.
 Parents Mag 42:28+ Ap '67
 Deeds: a guide for home buyers. Changing
 T 21:33-5 D '67
 Look, don't leap, before you buy your place
 in the country. J. C. Keeley. il Pop Gard
 18:30-1+ Ag '67
 Mistakes to avoid when buying a house. il
 Good H 164:151 F '67
 Science of sizing up a house; check list to
 follow in house shopping. il Changing T
 21:43-6 Ap '67
 This can be a good time to buy a house. N.
 Strunk. Am Home 70:30+ Mr '67
 See also
 Mortgages
HOUSE cleaning
 Easier housecleaning; when small children are
 around. Redbook 129:44+ My '67
 Is spring-cleaning passé? Am Home 70:128
 My '67
 Spring cleaning year round. il Ladies Home
 J 84:110-11 Ap '67
 Thirty new ways to escape household
 drudgery. D. X. Manners. il House B 109:
 128-30 Ja '67
 See also
 Vacuum cleaning

HOUSE cleaning—*Continued*

Anecdotes, facetiae, satire, etc.

Springtime classic; home accidents during spring cleaning. W. Stanton. Look 31:14 Ap 18 '67

HOUSE committee on un-American activities. See United States—Congress—House of representatives—Un-American activities committee

HOUSE decoration

Actress Lee Remick's second talent: decorating! il Good H 164:100-4+ Ja '67

Apartment with a view to the future. il Good H 164:144-51 Mr '67

Art of fooling the eye. il Am Home 70:60-1 S '67

Be authentic with traditional; 18th-century Massachusetts farmhouse. il Am Home 70:84-7 O '67

Big effects with instant needlepoint. E. Kinard. il House B 109:216-17+ O '67

Big-saver, your own imagination. il Am Home 70:74-7 Ja '67

Bold green look indoors. L. Burgess. il Home Gard 54:38-9 F '67

Bride furnishes her first house, and writes us about it; letter. S. Prost. il House B 109:105-9 F '67

Budget ideas worth copying. il Am Home 70:110+ O '67

Clever remodeling and building ideas. W. C. Leckey. il Pop Mech 128:142-5 S '67

Comforts of home, and more. il House & Gard 132:78-87 Jl '67

Creature comforts. il McCalls 94:94-9 Ap '67

Decorating clinic; questions and answers. See issues of American home

Decorating newsletter. V. D. Hahn. See issues of American home

Decorating with modern. il Am Home 70:82-3 O '67

Decorating with traditional. il Am Home 70:88-9 O '67

Decorative ways with walls. il Good H 165:116-21 O '67

Decorators' secrets: little outlay, great effects. E. Kinard. House B 109:110+ F '67

Discoveries at Expo. A. Stagg. il House & Gard 132:192-7 S '67

Eight rooms designed for looking and listening. E. McDonald. il House B 109:288-91+ N '67

Flight from the cliché. il House B 109:106-7 Ja '67

For the new horizon: a sculptured profile. E. Sverbeyeff. il House B 109:140-5 S '67

Fresh bright look. il House & Gard 132:194-201 O '67

Fresh new looks to live with. M. White. il Ladies Home J 85:56-7 Ja '68

Fun of instant decorating. V. D. Hahn. il Am Home 71:45-59 Ja '68

Give your living room a social life. V. D. Hahn. il Am Home 70:62-5 N '67

Gotham Greek. B. Plumb. il N Y Times Mag p72-3 D 17 '67

Great unlooked-fors; refreshing new roles for an old familiar friend-fabric. il House & Gard 132:250-5 N '67

Great ways to use the room you have. il Good H 164:133-41 My '67

Historic house: today's way; home of the James Scheuers in Washington, D.C. M. White. il Ladies Home J 84:104-9 Mr '67

House in the life of a playwright; Edward Albee's Greenwich Village carriage house. A. Stagg. il House & Gard 132:160-3+ D '67

House that says summer. N. C. Gray. il Am Home 70:62-5 Jl '67

How to create a new look. il House & Gard 131:144-7 My '67

How to create your own personal style; people who have done it state their cases. il House & Gard 131:115-23 My '67

How to delight your guests; visiting the Talbots of Washington, Conn. A. Stagg. il House & Gard 132:65-71 Jl '67

How you can correct ten common farm home decorating mistakes. J. LemMon. il Suc Farm 65:112-15 Mr '67

Ideas for summer. Am Home 70:128 Jl '67

Imaginative details can make all the difference. il House & Gard 131:99-109 F '67

In his own house, a noted architect plays games. il House & Gard 133:110-15 Ja '68

Inside Habitat. B. Plumb. il N Y Times Mag p46-8+ Jl 30 '67

Inviting house sparkling with color and gaiety. il House & Gard 132:98-103 Jl '67

Joy of improving what you have; symposium. il Am Home 70:77-99+ My '67

Joy of interesting spaces. il Am Home 70:66-71 S '67

Let yourself grow. L. Sloane. Am Home 70:74 O '67

Look of a garden, five floors up; apartment of J. Bennett. il House & Gard 132:100-3 Ag '67

Manhattan apartment, country-house charm. F. Heard. il House B 109:126-9 Mr '67

Many-splendored rooms: the art of decorative mixing. il McCalls 95:98-103 O '67

Modern updated. B. Plumb. il N Y Times Mag p20-1 D 31 '67

Most-asked questions about decorating. Am Home 70:89 Ja '67

New kind of counterpoint. il House & Gard 132:122-7 Ag '67

Old rooms with new labels. il House & Gard 132:210-17 O '67

Put quality where it counts. V. D. Hahn. il Am Home 70:70-3 Ja '67

Redbook guide for brides. M. S. Welch. il Redbook 129:98-106 My '67

Serene house: unexpected detail. il House & Gard 131:110-15 F '67

Six new looks in the ascendant. il House & Gard 133:74-83 Ja '68

Spirited decorating. P. Rumely and N. Cordts. il Bet Hom & Gard 45:50-61 S '67

Street signs hit home; indoor and outdoor decor. J. Peter. il Look 31:M30+ N 28 '67

Super décor. il House B 109:195-207 O '67

Surprise is the theme. il House & Gard 131:160-5 Mr '67

Ten lessons from a superb house. A. C. Borg. il Am Home 70:82-7 Mr '67

Their own ideas brought to bloom. il House B 109:146-9 Mr '67

Thousand and one patterns: a new decorative delight worthy of Scheherazade. il House & Gard 132:104-9 Ag '67

To a man's taste; Luis Barragan's home in suburban Mexico city. B. Plumb. il N Y Times Mag p 110-11 Ap 2 '67

Use ideas instead of money. il Am Home 70:50+ Ja '67

Variations on a brownstone; home of Mrs Jacob M. Kaplan. B. Plumb. il N Y Times Mag p 128-9 N 19 '67

What's new for decorating; six ways to keep your rooms from showing their age. il House & Gard 132:202-9 O '67

Where once the alarm sounded; firehouse is home, studio, and office. E. Sverbeyeff. il House B 109:160-3 Mr '67

Window wizardry. il House & Gard 131:128-39+ Mr '67

Word is eclectic. L. Hammel. il N Y Times Mag p70-1 Ag 20 '67

Zest house; Mrs O. Phipps' Palm Beach house. V. Lawford. il Vogue 149:138-43 F 15 '67

See also
Antiques
Apartments
Art in the home
Basements and cellars
Bathroom fixtures
Bathrooms
Bedrooms
Christmas decorations
Color in house decoration
Decoration and ornament, Architectural
Floor coverings
Furniture
Furniture, Arrangement of
Hardware
Household furnishings
Kitchens
Living rooms
Music rooms and equipment
Plants in house decoration
Wall coverings
Wallpaper
Windows

Anecdotes, facetiae, satire, etc.

Chez Mlle: Mary Quant at home; excerpts from interview, ed. by E. Blair. M. Quant. il Mlle 65:82-4+ S '67

Does your eye lack the nerve for a change? R. Warfield. House & Gard 132:218-19 O '67

HOUSE decoration, American

Philadelphia documentary. R. Reif. il N Y Times Mag p 134-5 O 8 '67

See also
Furniture, American

HOUSE decoration, Greek

Gotham Greek. B. Plumb. il N Y Times Mag p72-3 D 17 '67

HOUSES, Remodeled—*Continued*

Joy of improving what you have; symposium. il Am Home 70:77-99+ My '67

Joy of interesting spaces. il Am Home 70:66-71 S '67

Knowing designer transforms an ordinary house; Elaine Lustig Cohen's New York brownstone. il House & Gard 131:160-7 Ap '67

Magic of levels. il Am Home 70:62-3 S '67

Need space? you can live in a carport. D. Shiner. il Pop Sci 191:138-43 S '67

Neo-neo-classic; home of Antonio de Almeida in Paris. R. Reif. il N Y Times Mag p64-5 F 19 '67

Personal remodeling. il Am Home 70:70-1 N '67

Quick-change act for your home. il Am Home 71:60-1 Ja '68

Remodeling that's more than an inside job. E. Gilrain. il Bet Hom & Gard 45:28 S '67

Remodeling your house; how to begin. il Good H 164:148+ My '67

Seven myths of remodeling. J. H. Ingersoll. House B 109:34+ Je '67

Seven subdivision houses, how they grew. J. A. Hufnagel. il Bet Home & Gard 45:82-3+ N '67

Spacemaking; how to get more from the house you have. N. Seney. il Bet Hom & Gard 45:56-63 Ag '67

Talent for living sleeping beauty awakened, old iron-balconied house in New Orleans' old French Quarter. il House & Gard 132:164-9 S '67

Thoroughly modern manor; Flemish farmhouse. B. Plumb. il N Y Times Mag p 134-5 D 3 '67

Twice the house for half the cost. A. C. Borg. il Am Home 70:60-3 Ja '67

Two basic rooms you can add to any house. C. T. Sigman. il Pop Sci 190:162-8 Ap '67

Updating a vacation house. il Am Home 70:84 Jl '67

Very well-planned addition; living room-studio-home office. il Bet Hom & Gard 45:34+ Mr '67

When it's the garage, or else. il Pop Mech 128:126-9+ S '67

Which remodelings pay off best when you sell? P. Lindberg. il Bet Hom & Gard 45:6+ My '67

Years-ago kitchens go young; with remodeling plans. M. Davidson. il Ladies Home J 85:58-61 Ja '68

See also

Apartment houses, Remodeled

HOUSES, Round. See Buildings, Round

HOUSES, Seashore. See Beach architecture

HOUSES, Toy. See Doll houses

HOUSES, Tree. See Tree houses

HOUSEWARES. See Household appliances

HOUSEWIVES

Bored housewife. L. Tornabene; discussion. Ladies Home J 84:8 F '67

Finally: a sure cure for housewife fatigue. W. E. O'Donnell. il Ladies Home J 84:74+ Ap '67

HOUSEWORK. See Home economics

HOUSING

See also

Discrimination in housing

Costs

House beautiful presents five great-value houses; architect-designed homes under $30,000. J. De Long. il House B 109:111-21 F '67

Sellers rule the roost. il Bsns W p41-2 Je 24 '67

Trying to house the have-littles and have-nothings. Bsns W p 104 My 6 '67

Desegregation

Desegregated housing. F. F. Piven and R. A. Cloward; discussion. New Repub 156:44 Ja 7; 44-5 Ja 14; 36-7 Ja 28 '67

Negro in the suburbs; Park Forest, Ill; with painting by N. Rockwell. J. Star. Look 31:51:3+ My 16 '67

Federal aid

Congress reviews low-income housing plans. Arch Rec 142:81-2 O '67

Facts about FHA: low income housing; address, August 23, 1967. R. C. Weaver. Vital Speeches 33:734-6 S 15 '67

Homes for whom? Percy-Mondale scheme. New Repub 157:7 O 14 '67; Reply. W. F. Mondale. 157:45 N 11 '67

Igloo renewal; Alaska housing. Reporter 37:11-12 O 5 '67

Rents & rats; model-cities and rent-supplement bills. Time 90:25 S 29 '67

Slum planners; C. H. Percy-R. F. Kennedy housing plans for the poor. R. B. Semple, jr. New Repub 157:8-10 Jl 22 '67

Which plan for slum renewal? plans sponsored by Senators Percy and Kennedy, or the new Administration plan. Bsns W p77-8 Ag 26 '67

Finance

See Housing finance

Slum clearance

See Slums

Social aspects

Trouble is the ghetto? or let's take another look. E. Goble. Arch Rec 142:9 S '67

Alaska

Igloo renewal. Reporter 37:11-12 O 5 '67

California

California's fair-housing follies. G. V. Kennard. America 117:204-6 Ag 26 '67

Fair housing showdown in the West. G. V. Kennard. America 116:142-6 Ja 28 '67

House of many parts; kit house designed for use in rural and urban fringe areas. il Arch Forum 127:78-81 N '67

Saying no to Proposition 14; California supreme court decision upheld by U.S. Supreme court. il Time 89:75 Je 9 '67

Underdeveloped areas

Profiles; C. Abrams. B. Taper. New Yorker 42:38-42+ F 4 '67

United States

All of a sudden, houses are getting scarce. il U S News 63:48-9 O 9 '67

Changes needed to improve low-income housing. Am City 82:22 O '67

Civil rights at Weston and beyond. Sci N 92:56 Jl 15 '67

Congress and the crisis in our cities. J. Bailey. Arch Forum 127:54-7 S '67

Desegregated housing. F. F. Piven and R. A. Cloward; discussion. New Repub 156:44 Ja 7; 44-5 Ja 14; 36-7 Ja 28 '67

Immobile and mundane; monotonous, mediocre quality. Newsweek 69:84 F 27 '67

McNamara's Negroes; Pentagon's dilatory efforts to end off-base housing segregation. New Repub 156:6 My 6 '67

Slums: cancer in the heart of our cities. il Sr Schol 90:8-12 F 3 '67

That coming boom in housing. M. Cohen. il Fortune 75:134-7+ My '67

Urban housing design for new towns and old neighborhoods. il Arch Rec 142:133-52 Jl '67

Why people don't buy houses. W. McQuade. il Fortune 76:153-5 D '67

See also

Housing—Federal aid

Housing laws and legislation—United States

Housing projects

Housing projects, Government

Negroes in the United States—Housing

United States—Federal housing administration

United States—Housing and urban development, Department of

also subhead Housing under names of cities, e.g. New York (city)—Housing

HOUSING, Discrimination in. See Discrimination in housing

HOUSING, Prefabricated

Finally: a low-cost component system for housing that really works; Techcrete. il Arch Rec 141:187-94 Mr '67

HOUSING administration, Federal. See United States—Federal housing administration

HOUSING and urban development, Department of. See United States—Housing and urban development, Department of

HOUSING construction. See Building industry

HOUSING finance

Financing a house. Consumer Rep 32:398-401 D '67

From blight to light; housing bill. Time 89:22 Ap 28 '67

How to sell your home for the best price. R. Beamish. House B 109:24-6 D '67

Partners for piggyback; materials-making companies form Home capital funds, inc. Time 89:82 Mr 24 '67

Rebound in housing. il Fortune 75:40+ Ap '67

See also

Mortgages

United States—Federal housing administration

HOUSING laws and legislation

United States

Century of no progress? G. R. Metcalf. il Reporter 37:31-2 N 16 '67
Congress reviews low-income housing plans. Arch Rec 142:81-2 O '67
Making a mockery of Title VI; defeat of fair housing bill in Illinois. Christian Cent 84: 886 Jl 12 '67

HOUSING projects
Church as landlord. Newsweek 70:70+ O 16 '67
Double-decked village; Kingsbury green, London. il Arch Forum 126:46-51 Ap '67
Pre-fab housing and the church in Detroit. H. H. Ward. Commonweal 86:602-3 S 29 '67
She makes the city a place for living; town-house projects of C. W. Smith. il Bsns W p76-8+ Je 3 '67
See also
Apartment houses
Levitt and sons, incorporated

Site planning

Lure of living in clustered houses; California's Sea Ranch and Virginia's Reston. il House & Gard 131:124-31 My '67
New town that conserves the landscape; Stafford Harbor, Va. il Arch Rec 141:151-8 Ap '67
Planned unit development means better communities. M. C. Huntoon, jr. il Am Home 70:124+ Mr '67

HOUSING projects, Government
How to clean up the Nation's slums? il Newsweek 70:64-5+ Ag 28 '67
Low income programs; address, August 7, 1967. E. W. Brooke. Vital Speeches 33:719-22 S 15 '67

HOUSING research
Housing: Defense department starts new research program. D. S. Greenberg. Science 158:1432-4 D 15 '67

HOUSING subsidies. See Housing—Federal aid

HOUSTON, Jack
It's a waiting game for squirrels. Field & S 72:68-9+ O '67

HOUSTON, James D.
View from Santa Cruz. Holiday 41:18+ My '67

HOUSTON, Walter Scott
Deep-sky wonders. See issues of Sky and telescope

HOUSTON, Tex.
Houston, prairie dynamo. S. E. Jones. il Nat Geog Mag 132:338-77 S '67

Anti-poverty program

Semper paratus; investigation of anti-poverty team order for seven telescopic rifle sights. Newsweek 70:25-6 Ag 28 '67

Music

See also
Houston grand opera association

Newspapers

See also
Houston chronicle

Riots

Black power explodes again; policeman slain; riot at Texas southern university. il U S News 62:10 My 29 '67
Hate in Houston; riot at Texas southern university. Time 89:21 My 26 '67
Love and hate and a very fast hundred. P. Axthelm. il Sports Illus 26:66+ Je 5 '67
Stokely generation; riots at Texas southern university. il Newsweek 69:24-5 My 29 '67

Sanitary affairs

Composting works in Houston. E. F. Spitzer. il Am City 82:97-9 O '67

Stores

New enclosed-mall shopping center is designed as a small commercial city. il Arch Rec 141:142-3 Mr '67

HOUSTON Astros (baseball) See Baseball clubs

HOUSTON chronicle
Freedom to travel. il Newsweek 69:54 F 27 '67

HOUSTON grand opera association
Houston; performance of La Traviata. A. Holmes. Opera N 31:32 F 25 '67
Houston; production of The magic flute. A. Holmes. il Opera N 31:30 Ja 28 '67
Report: Houston; production of Carmen. A. Holmes. Opera N 32:30 D 16 '67
Report: Houston; production of Hans Werner Henze's Young lord. A. Holmes. Opera N 32:28 Ja 13 '68

HOUSTON Oilers (football club) See Football clubs

HOUSTON tournament. See Golf—Tournaments

HOUSTON. University, Houston, Tex.
Dauntless Dave; D. Williams, golf coach. J. Underwood. il Sports Illus 26:64-9+ Je 19 '67

HOVERCRAFT. See Ground effect machines

HOVING, Thomas Pearsall Field
How to make a city come alive. Parents Mag 42:50-1+ Ap '67
We talk to; interview by Mademoiselle's guest editors. por Mlle 65:324 Ag '67

about

Here comes Hoving! M. Cohen. il por Read Digest 91:98-102 S '67
Kings' ransom. il por Newsweek 69:93 My 1 '67
New Yorker who shook up Central park. J. Peter. il pors Look 31:80+ My 2 '67
People are talking about... il por Vogue 149:140-1 Ap 1 '67
Profiles. J. McPhee. por New Yorker 43:49-50+ My 20 '67

HOW much land does a man need? drama. See Leech, M. T.

HOW now, Dow Jones; musical comedy. See Musical comedies, revues, etc.—Criticisms, plots, etc.

HOW old, how young; story. See O'Hara, J.

HOW to be a Jewish mother; drama. See Vall, S.

HOW to choose a boy; drama. See Boiko, C.

HOW will I know my true love? story. See Bode, E.

HOW you play the game; story. See Tyner, P.

HOWARD, Anthony
At the White House, intellectual-in-residence. N Y Times Mag p34-5+ Mr 12 '67

HOWARD, Bruce D.
Phage lambda mutants deficient in rII exclusion. bibliog Science 158:1588-9 D 22 '67

HOWARD, C. L.
Make your own fishing spoons. Pop Mech 127:112-14 My '67

HOWARD, Elston
Baseball's grand old man. Read Digest 91: 185-8+ O '67

HOWARD, Frances
Off-hours in convention city. Wilson Lib Bul 41:1050-4 Je '67

HOWARD, Gordon E.
Children must understand the past to create a better future. por Parents Mag 42:38+ Mr '67

HOWARD, Harry N.
U.S. in the 1967 Middle East crisis. Cur Hist 53:337-40+ D '67

HOWARD, Jane
Actors and townspeople felt squirrely. Life 62:104A-104B My 12 '67
Girls who have everything are not supposed to do anything. Life 63:52F+ Jl 14 '67
Heloise, the most-headed housewife. Life 62:39+ Ap 21 '67
Round one was a breeze for Louise. Life 63:89-90+ O 13 '67
Seer through a third eye. Life 62:91-2+ Je 16 '67
Whisky and ink, whisky and ink. Life 63: 67-8+ Jl 21 '67
Who knows where the forks are? Boris. Life 63:52+ Ag 11 '67

HOWARD, Jimmie Earl
Motherly sergeant. por Newsweek 70:32 S 4 '67

HOWARD, John A.
Another three Rs; address, September 13, 1967. Vital Speeches 34:18-22 O 15 '67
Necessary separation of education; address, January 24, 1967. Vital Speeches 33:313-16 Mr 1 '67

HOWARD, Richard
British chronicle. Poetry 110:195-203 Je '67
Crepuscular; Secular games; poems. Poetry 109:245-9 Ja '67
Diabolic craft of Alfonso Ossorio. Craft Horiz 27:34-7 Ja '67
Fuel on the fire. Poetry 110:413-15 S '67
Tireless conscience. Poetry 111:39-40 O '67

HOWARD, Robert
Budapest symposium on solar active regions. Sky & Tel 34:296 N '67

HOWARD, Robin
Meet Robin Howard. J. Percival. por Dance Mag 41:22-3+ Mr '67

HOWARD, Steven J.
How to repair aluminum storms. Pop Mech 128:170-2 N '67
How to troubleshoot furnace failure. Pop Mech 129:192-5+ Ja '68
New paint wonder; water-thinned enamel. Pop Mech 128:99-101 Ag '67
Picking the right paint remover. Pop Mech 128:164-6 Jl '67
Repairing drywalls: Rx for popped nails, cracks and holes. Pop Mech 128:154-7 O '67
Stupid questions about bag mixes. Pop Mech 127:178-80 Ap '67

HOWARD, Thomas E.
Rapid excavation; with biographical sketch. Sci Am 217:20, 74-6+ bibliog(p 154) N '67

HOWARD-GIBBON, Amelia Frances
Second thoughts about Victorian children's fare. J. St John. il Wilson Lib Bul 41:590-2 F '67

HOWARD university, Washington, D.C.
Black power threatens a leading Negro college. il U S News 63:38-9 Jl 31 '67
Centennial of Howard U. P. N. Mathless. il NEA J 56:11-13 Mr '67
Colonialism on the black campus; Howard administration. M. Miles. New Repub 157: 15-16 Ag 5 '67
Nabrit and the militants. Sat R 50:62 Ag 19 '67

HOWARD Zahniser memorial fund
Howard Zahniser memorial fund. M. Nadel. Liv Wildn 31:2 Spr '67

HOWE, Diana Carter
Fun on wheels. Parents Mag 42:52-3+ Ap '67

HOWE, Florence
(ed) See Lessing, D. Talk with Doris Lessing

HOWE, Harold, 2d
Century of cooperation. NEA J 56:62 S '67
Changing the pecking order: a credential society; address, October 24, 1967. Vital Speeches 34:70-3 N 15 '67
Closing the gap. por Parents Mag 42:50+ S '67
End the grading system? education chief urges change; excerpts from address, August 22, 1967. por U S News 63:14 S 4 '67
On libraries and learning; interview, ed. with introd. by E. Geller. pors Library J 92:841-4 F 15 '67
Paying for American education. PTA Mag 62: 5-8 S '67
Realities of the learning market; address, August 9, 1966. por(cover) Library J 92: 297-301 Ja 15 '67
Washington report: happy 100th to USOE, ESEA accomplishments; summary of address, March 2, 1967, ed. by J. Lloyd. por Sr Schol 90:sup6 Ap 14 '67
We shouldn't back into the future; observations on the education scene. pors Life 62:42+ F 10 '67

about
Tough, blunt master of U.S. schools. il pors Life 62:37-8+ F 10 '67
Visibility of Harold Howe: some notes towards a profile. M. Greene. Sch & Soc 95:45-3 Ja 21 '67

HOWE, Irving
Beliefs of the masters. New Repub 157:19-20+ S 16 '67
Culture of modernism. Commentary 44:48-59 N '67
Henry James' return to America. New Repub 157:23-6 S 30 '67
Liberal anti-communism revisited. Commentary 44:48-52 S '67
New books. Harper 236:69-70+ Ja '68

HOWE, Leroy T.
Radical theology and the death of discourse. Christian Cent 84:583-6 My 3 '67

HOWE, Mark DeWolfe
Obituary
Pub W 191:42 Mr 20 '67

HOWE, Norma
How I beat my kids. por Redbook 129:10+ Je '67

HOWE, Quincy
New age of the journalist-historian. Sat R 50:25-7+ My 20 '67

HOWE, Russell Warren
Nigeria's civil war. New Repub 157:16 S 16 '67
Report from the Congo: war-drum days ahead. Look 31:106 O 31 '67

HOWELL, Wayne
Agents for change: producer or consumer? por Library J 92:3812-14 O 15 '67

HOWELLS, William Dean
Fame at the end was fickle. G. Hicks. Sat R 50:83-4 Ap 22 '67

HOWELLS, William W. See Patterson, B. jt. auth.

HOWES, Barbara
For an old friend; poem. New Yorker 43:139 S 9 '67
Into strained relation. Poetry 110:425-6 S '67
Viet napalm; poem. New Repub 157:24 S 9 '67

about
Sidesaddle on the ocean. W. Stafford. Poetry 109:270-1 Ja '67

HOWIE, Virginia
Companion plants with lilies. Horticulture 45:26-9+ My '67

HOWLAND, A. W.
Freedom; poem. Negro Hist Bul 30:7 Mr '67

HOWLAND, Richard H.
Journey to Ethiopia's past. UNESCO Courier 20:39-41 N '67

HOWLAND, Stella M.
Easy adventure: East Africa. Travel 128:30-5 N '67

HOWLETT, L. E.
International basis for uniform measurement. Science 158:72-4 O 6 '67

HOWMET corporation
Howmet races to test its mettle. il Bsns W p80+ N 18 '67

HOWORKA, Herb, jr
Small tape recorders. Pop Electr 25:52-3+ D '66

HOY, C. J.
How ALA selects a conference site. ALA Bul 61:423-5 Ap '67

HOY, Ronald R. and others
Regeneration in crustacean motoneurons: evidence for axonal fusion. bibliog Science 156:251-2 Ap 14 '67

HOYA carnosa. See Wax plants

HOYER, Linda Grace
Predator; story. New Yorker 43:53 My 13 '67

HOYLE, Fred
Theoretical astronomy: new institute in Cambridge. J. Walsh. Science 157:1286-8 S 15 '67

HOYT, Charles Alva
Books. Commonweal 87:453-4 Ja 12 '68

HOYT, John H. and Halls, J. R.
Pleistocene shoreline sediments in coastal Georgia: deposition and modification. bibliog Science 155:1541-3 Mr 24 '67

HOYT, Norris D.
Boating (cont) Sports Illus 26:100+ Ap 17 '67

HOYT LAKES, Minn.
This stage goes where the action is. A. Lohmann. Am City 82:38 Mr '67

HRUSKA, Roman Lee
Excerpt from address, March 14, 1967. Cong Digest 46:177+ Je '67

HSIAO, Sigmund. See Nichols, J. R. jt. auth.

HSIEH, S. T.
Macao's surrender to red China. Nat R 19: 746+ Jl 11 '67

HSU, Kai-yu
Chou En-lai New Repub 156:21-5 Ap 8 '67

HU, C. T.
Chinese university: target of the cultural revolution. Sat R 50:52-4+ Ag 19 '67
War nobody wants. Sat R 50:45 S 30 '67

HUAND, W. H. and Walker, R. M.
Fossil alpha-particle recoil tracks: a new method of age determination. bibliog Science 155:1103-6 Mr 3 '67

HUANG, Al
Al and I spend a year in Taiwan. il por Dance Mag 41:47+ N '67

HUANG, C. C. See Sussman, M. V. jt. auth.

HUANG, Su-shu
Origin of binary stars. bibliog Sky & Tel 34: 368-70 D '67

HUARI, Peru
Wari-Willka; shrine of Wankas. R. Matos Mendieta. il Américas 19:9-17 Ja '67

HUBBARD, Dixon D.
How to make more money growing out cattle. por Farm J 91:B14 Mr '67

HUBBARD, J. I. and others
Origin of synaptic noise. bibliog Science 157: 330-1 Jl 21 '67

HUBBARD, Orville Liscum
Hubbard's hotel. por Newsweek 70:80A-80B D 4 '67

HUBBARD, Ruth, and Kropf, Allen
Molecular isomers in vision; with biographical sketches. Sci Am 216:14, 64-70+ bibliog(p 155) Je '67

HUBBELL, John G.
Arizona: the ship that became a shrine. Read Digest 91:64-8 D '67
Courage of Karla Little. Read Digest 91: 149-54 Jl '67

HUBBELL, John G.—_Continued_
Our magicians of limited war. Read Digest 90:181-2+ My '67
Supercommandos of the wetlands. Read Digest 90:49-54 Je '67

HUBER, Kathleen
Very Narcissus; story. Seventeen 26:158-9 My '67

HUBERT, Dick
Pill and the girl next door. Mlle 64:162-3+ Mr '67

HUBIAK, Metro
This city yard is neighborly. Am City 82:114-15 Je '67

HUCK, Susan
Santo Domingo revisited. Nat R 19:471-2 My 2 '67

HUCKLEBERRY Finn (literary character) See Characters in literature

HUDSON, Charles Lowell
Looking ahead; address, January 30, 1967. Vital Speeches 33:465-8 My 15 '67

HUDSON, Helen
Strange fare; story. Reporter 37:41-4+ Ag 10 '67

HUDSON, J. Paul
George Ravenscroft and his contribution to English glassmaking. bibliog Antiques 92: 822-31 D '67
Knight's tombstone at Jamestown, Virginia. Antiques 91:760-1 Je '67

HUDSON, James E. jr. See Schlichting, H. E. jr. jt. auth.

HUDSON, Leonard C. See Batten, J. jt. auth.

HUDSON, Marylin
Tomato sauce primer. Am Home 70:108 N '67

HUDSON, Peggy
Look and listen. See issues of Senior scholastic
Looking & listening. See issues of Senior scholastic

HUDSON, Ralph
Oklahoma state librarian fired. Library J 92: 3579 O 15 '67

HUDSON, Richard
Kunoyama and the saga of the Lucky Dragon; reprint, adaptation of The voyage of the Lucky Dragon, by R. E. Lapp. UNESCO Courier 20:40-5 Ag '67

HUDSON canyon. See Ocean bottom

HUDSON RIVER
Clean up the Hudson. J. A. Clay. il Am For 73:12-15 Je '67
Great northeast cruise; East by West's voyage. J. West and C. West. il Motor B 121:77-82 Ja '68
Hudson River heritage cruise. P. Smyth. il Motor B 120:21-6+ S '67

HUDSON RIVER VALLEY commission. See New York (state)—Hudson River Valley commission

HUEBSCH, Elmer F.
How to succeed, but lose money. il por Bsns W p 149-50 Mr 18 '67

HUETER, Theodor F.
Challenge of inner space; address, May 15, 1967. Vital Speeches 33:551-4 Jl 1 '67

HUEY, Ben M.
Commericial Christmas trees. Am For 73:12-15+ D '67

HUFF, Betty Tracy
Flora of the flower shop; drama. Plays 26: 23-32 F '67
Gertie, the greeting card girl; drama. Plays 26:37-48 My '67
Great contest; drama. Plays 26:15-27 Ap '67
Gypsies' secret; drama. Plays 27:23-32 D '67
Hillbilly blues; drama. Plays 27:1-10, 36 Ja '68
Way, way off Broadway; drama. Plays 27: 29-42 O '67

HUFF, Darrell
How to pour a fireplace. Pop Sci 191:132-5+ N '67
How you can build a Scandinavian fliptop table. Pop Sci 190:144-7+ Je '67
Patio that a painting inspired. Pop Sci 191: 146-9 Ag '67
You can afford your dream house, just build it yourself. Pop Sci 192:63-7+ Ja '68

HUFF, William H. See Brown, N. B. jt. auth.

HUFFMAN, John M.
How to get the most out of local educational resources. Sr Schol 90:sup 16 F 3 '67

HUGGER and the hugged; story. See Luria, J.

HUGGINS, Charles Brenton
Endocrine-induced regression of cancers; address, December 13, 1966. bibliog Science 156:1050-4 My 26 '67

about
Nobelist from Acadia. F. Marley. por Sci N 91:237 Mr 11 '67

HUGGINS, Charles E.
In cold blood. il por Newsweek 69:82 My 1 '67

HUGHES, Catharine R.
Birthday party. America 118:10-12 Ja 6 '68
Theatre goes to war. America 116:759-61 My 20 '67
Two worlds of Isaac Singer. America 117:611-13 N 18 '67

HUGHES, Dimsdale McQuinn
Another young 'un for Aunt Kancie's 100th. il pors Life 63:30-1 D 1 '67

HUGHES, Edward
New chancellor of the new Germany. Read Digest 91:145-9 N '67

HUGHES, Elizabeth (Sullivan)
Sudden guests at the seashore. McCalls 94: 80-1+ S '67

HUGHES, Emmet John
[Current events column] See issues of Newsweek

HUGHES, Harold Everett
Governor from Ida Grove. V. Bourjaily. il pors N Y Times Mag p34-5+ F 26 '67

HUGHES, Howard Robard
Action in Las Vegas. Time 90:101 S 22 '67
Howard Hughes puzzle. il pors Newsweek 71: 25-7+ Ja 15 '68
Howard Hughes underground. J. Didion. Sat Eve Post 240:22-3 S 23 '67
Hughes gambles on Las Vegas. il por Bsns W p80-2+ S 30 '67
Hughes's buying binge. il Newsweek 70:66 Ag 7 '67
Render unto Caesars. il Newsweek 70:32 S 25 '67
Saga of the Spruce Goose. il Newsweek 69:39 F 13 '67
U.S. Supreme court refuses to block Howard Hughes book. Pub W 191:221 Ja 23 '67
Why is Howard Hughes buying up Las Vegas? J. Star. il pors Look 32:69-71+ Ja 23 '68

HUGHES, James J.
Rehearsal for World war II. D. Perry. il por Am Heritage 18:40-5+ Ap '67

HUGHES, Jo
She mothers us all. il por Newsweek 70:62 N 6 '67

HUGHES, John
Report: Indonesia. Atlan 220:20+ D '67

HUGHES, Josephine Blair. See Hughes, Jo

HUGHES, Judith Coolidge
Labels of John Elliott jr. Antiques 91:514-17 Ap '67

HUGHES, Langston
Ballad of Negro history. Negro Hist Bul 30: 17 O '67
When I worked for Dr Woodson. Negro Hist Bul 30:17 O '67

about
Death of simple. S. Maloff. por Newsweek 69:104 Je 5 '67
Hughes at Columbia. New Yorker 43:21-3 D 30 '67
Langston Hughes dies at sixty-five; reprint. por Negro Hist Bul 30:16 O '67
Man who created Simple. K. Kinnamon. Nation 205:599-601 D 4 '67
Obituary
Nation 205:7 Jl 3 '67. G. Brooks
Pub W 191:37 Je 12 '67

HUGHES, Richard Joseph
Excerpt from testimony, August 1, 1967. Cong Digest 46:222 Ag '67
Lessons of New Jersey's race riots; interview. por U S News 63:32-6 Jl 31 '67

about
Of many things. R. A. Schroth. America 117: inside cover Jl 29 '67

HUGHES, Spike
Afternoon at Sant'Agata. Opera N 32:8-13 D 30 '67
Gift of surprise. Opera N 31:24-5 Mr 4 '67
Verdi's fathers. Opera N 31:24-5 Ap 8 '67

HUGHES, Ted
Four poems: Small events; You drive in a circle; Thaw; Fern. New Yorker 43:48 Mr 18 '67
Second glance at a jaguar; poem. New Yorker 43:52 Mr 25 '67

HUGHES, Thomas L.
Relativity in foreign policy. For Affairs 45: 670-82 Jl '67

HUGHES aircraft company
U.K. Irish market penetration sought for Hughes model 500. il Aviation W 86:113 Ja 23 '67

HUGHES tool company
Aircraft division
Procurement policy questions stem from Hughes LOH bid. H. M. David. Tech W 20:19 Mr 6 '67

HUI, Ka-kwong
Dialogue in a museum. Craft Horiz 27:18-22+ Jl '67

about
Hui Ka Kwong. B. Hendricks. il por Craft Horiz 27:40-3+ My '67

HUIE, William Bradford
Authors & editors. Pub W 191:45 Je 19 '67

HUIZINGA, J. H.
Can Hussein survive? Reporter 37:34-6 S 7 '67
European's view of the Vietnam war. Reporter 36:30+ Mr 9 '67
Palestine refugees: perennial source of trouble. Reporter 36:33-5 My 18 '67

HUKBALAHAPS
Again the Huks. New Repub 157:7-8 S 9 '67
Huks again. il Newsweek 69:59-60+ My 22 '67
Return of the Huks. il Time 89:26+ Mr 24 '67

HULET, Ervin Kenneth
Heaviest atom. il por Time 90:59 S 22 '67
—and others
Mendelevium: divalency and other chemical properties. bibliog Science 158:486-8 O 27 '67

HULETT, Gertrude
Clara's reverse psychology; story. NEA J 56:33-4 F '67

HULL, Bobby
Bobby Hull, golden boy of hockey. D. MacDonald. il Read Digest 90:41-2+ Mr '67
Dynamic duo. il por Newsweek 69:62 Mr 20 '67

HULL, E. W. Seabrook
Political ocean. For Affairs 45:492-502 Ap '67

HULL, Roger, jr
Cursing of the fig tree. Christian Cent 84:1429-31 N 8 '67

HULL, William E.
Changing mind. Christian Cent 84:920-1 Jl 12 '67

HULLABALOO teen-age dance clubs. See Clubs

HULLS (naval architecture)
Aerospace techniques eyed for naval use: glass-reinforced plastic composites for navy's surface and submersible craft. J. F. Judge. Tech W 20:42-4 My 15 '67
First plastic underwater hull big enough for men readied. Tech W 20:39-40 My 8 '67
Hull detail, Black Watch. il Yachting 121:210-11 Mr '67
Keeping in trim; the effect of trim tabs in deep-vee hull performance. M. Crook. il Yachting 121:76-7 Je '67
Know the hull shapes. J. A. Emmett. il Outdoor Life 139:25-6+ F '67
Special hull check points. il Motor B 119:28 Mr '67

HULME, Denis
Crowned king of the road. K. Chapin. il por Sports Illus 27:53-4 O 30 '67

HULTGREN, William O.
Goteborg's horticultural society gardens. il Horticulture 45:34-6 N '67

HUMAN aggression. See Fighting (psychology)
HUMAN behavior. See Behavior (psychology)
HUMAN beings. See Man
HUMAN ecology
See also
Man—Influence of environment
Man—Influence on nature

HUMAN figure in art
Letter from Paris; Ingres exhibition at Petit Palais. Genêt. New Yorker 43:96+ Ja 13 '68
Out on a limb; A. Jones' leg paintings. il Newsweek 70:97 S 11 '67
Painting a nude in an alla prima technique; excerpt from Painting the nude. J. De Ruth. il Am Artist 31:44-9+ Je '67
Return to the challenge. il Time 91:30-1 Ja 12 '68
Way of all flesh; S. A. Campbell's paintings of burlesque queens. il Newsweek 70:115 S 25 '67

See also
Nude in art

HUMAN figure in photography
Everything must go! il Esquire 67:95-9 Je '67
Human form. il U S Camera 30:42-3 Ap '67
Never ending joy of shooting women. M. P. R. Thomas. il U S Camera 30:52 F '67
Non-nude nudes. il Pop Phot 60:65-8 Je '67
Two women. M. Orovan. il U S Camera 30:46-7 Mr '67

HUMAN genetics. See Genetics
HUMAN geography. See Anthropogeography
HUMAN hibernation. See Hibernation, Human
HUMAN nature
How well do you understand people? questions and answers. J. E. Gibson. il Todays Health 45:28-9+ Mr '67
Human relations and the nature of man. H. P. Knowles and B. O. Saxberg. bibliog f Harvard Bsns R 45:22-4+ Mr '67
Nature of human nature, by A. Comfort. Review
New Repub 157:22-5 O 14 '67. T. Solotaroff

HUMAN relations
Adept in the world's ways; excerpt from The greatest of these is love. A. A. van Ruler. Christian Cent 84:163 F 8 '67
Alienated vs. society; symposium. bibliog f il Sch & Soc 95:252-68 Ap 15 '67
Brotherhood; address, December 11, 1966. J. M. Roche. Vital Speeches 33:285-8 F 15 '67
Cause of optimism for mankind. F. Morley. il Nations Bsns 55:29-30 D '67
Games analysis adds flavor to psychiatry; transactional analysis. P. McBroom. il Sci N 91:308-9 Ap 1 '67
Human relations. J. H. Starie. NEA J 56:46 Ap '67
Human relations and the nature of man. H. P. Knowles and B. O. Saxberg. bibliog f Harvard Bsns R 45:22-4+ Mr '67
Interview with Barbara Ward; ed. by R. D. Heffner. B. Ward. McCalls 94:48+ Je '67
Origins of human bonds. S. Fraiberg. Commentary 44:47-57 D '67
Theology of conflict. J. J. Lally. Commonweal 87:355-8 D 15 '67
To our Negro brothers. M. Ascoli. Reporter 37:12 Ag 10 '67
Whatever happened to the great simplicities? importance of simple ideas. H. Read. Sat R 50:21-3+ F 18 '67

See also
Conversation
Friendship
Good will (ethics)
Loneliness
Love
Marriage
Sex relations
Sympathy

Study and teaching
See also
Esalen institute. Calif.

HUMAN rights. See Civil rights
HUMAN rights, Universal declaration of. See Universal declaration of human rights
HUMAN rights commission. See United Nations—Commission on human rights
HUMAN rights conference. See International conference on human rights (proposed)
HUMAN rights day and week
Human rights day 10 December 1967; texts of messages. C. Manescu; Thant. UN Mo Chron 4:i-iv D '67
Human rights week and Human rights year; proclamation. L. B. Johnson. Dept State Bul 57:660 N 13 '67

HUMAN rights year. See International human rights year
HUMAN sacrifice. See Sacrifice, Human
HUMAN voice. See Voice
HUMAN welfare, Southern conference for. See Southern conference for human welfare
HUMANE treatment of animals. See Animals—Treatment
HUMANISM
Future for humanism; adaptation of address, December 5, 1966. J. Orne. Library J 92:1893-5 My 15 '67
What is an anonymous Christian? P. Hebblethwaite. Cath World 205:90-4 My '67

HUMANITIES
Humanities and the alienated adolescent. M. H. Goldberg. bibliog f Sch & Soc 95:257-61 Ap 15 '67
Links between the humanities and the literature of the human sciences. I. Bry and L. Afflerbach. Wilson Lib Bul 42:510-25 Ja '68

See also
Science and the humanities

Study and teaching
Curriculum breakthrough in the humanities; Bangor Me, H.S. L. C. Comeau and others. il Sr Schol 90:sup 13-14 Ap 7 '67
Interdisciplinary humanities courses. C. R. Keller. NEA J 57:19-20 Ja '68

HUMANITIES—Study and teaching—*Continued*
Religious education as a humanity. M. H.
Goldberg. Sch & Soc 95:123-4 F 18 '67
Saving the humanities. E. Larrabee; discussion. Commentary 43:20+ Mr '67
HUMANITY (mankind) See Man
HUMBLE oil and refining company
Humble enlarges its pie; agreement to buy
the Signal oil co. div. of Standard oil co.
of California. Bsns W p41 F 18 '67
Into new territory; takeover of Signal oil
service stations. Time 89:86 F 24 '67
HUME, Ivor Noël. See Noël Hume, I.
HUME, Paul
Opera is born. Américas 19:34-7 Jl '67
HUMIC acids
Sodium humate solution studied with small-
angle X-ray scattering. R. L. Wershaw and
others. bibliog il Science 157:1429-31 S 22 '67
HUMILITY
Confidence and arrogance. V. P. McCorry.
America 117:100-inside back cover Jl 22 '67
HUMMINGBIRDS
Naturalist at large. M. Bates. il Natur Hist
76:13-15 Mr; 14+ My '67
HUMOR
Laugh a day; excerpt from Treasury of med-
ical wit and humor. B. Adler. il Todays
Health 45:40-1 Ap '67
Onward and upward with the arts; the put-
on. J. Brackman. New Yorker 43:34-6+ Je
24 '67
Turning on the light; art and craft of
light verse. R. Armour. Writer 80:33-5+
Ap '67
See also
Anecdotes
Comedy
Limericks
Satire
Television broadcasting—Humor
also subhead Anecodotes, facetiae,
satire, etc. under various subjects, e.g.
Shooting—Anecdotes, facetiae, satire, etc.
HUMOR, American
Truly funny play in a most unfunny time. A.
Gingrich. Esquire 68:6 Ag '67
With the bark on, comp. by J. Q. Anderson.
Review
Sat R 50:54 Je 10 '67. P. Flowers
HUMOR, Catholic
Dispatches from the brave new world; or,
Far afield with the Catholic press. P. J.
Laux. America 117:550-3+ N 11 '67
HUMOR, Jewish
Boy-man schlemiel: Jewish humor? A. Gold-
man. Commonweal 86:605-8 S 29 '67
HUMOR, Negro. See Negro humor
HUMOR, Pictorial
Funny thing happened. il U S Camera 30:68-9
N '67
See also
Caricatures and cartoons
Comics (books, strips, etc)
HUMORAL factor. See Body fluids
HUMORISTS
See also
Comedians
Negro comedians
HUMOROUS poetry. See Poetry
HUMPERDINCK, Engelbert
Dreamer. H. Bailey. por Opera N 32:24-5 D
23 '67
Hansel and Gretel. Criticism
Hi Fi 18:MA6+ Ja '68
New Yorker 43:219 N 18 '67
Opera N il 32:17-19 D 23 '67
Opera N por 32:24-5 D 23 '67
Sat R 50:74 N 25 '67
HUMPHREY, Hal
Capsule case history of TV. Holiday 42:54-5
O '67
HUMPHREY, Hubert Horatio, 1911-
Father's role in today's society. por Parents
Mag 42:38 Je '67
From the halls of government. PTA Mag
61:11 F '67
From the iron curtain to the open door; ad-
dress, March 5, 1967. Dept State Bul 56:486-
90 Mr 27 '67; Same with title New engage-
ment. Vital Speeches 33:386-9 Ap 15 '67;
Excerpts. por U S News 62:22 Mr 13 '67
International cooperation for development of
the oceans; address, July 29, 1967. Dept
State Bul 57:227-9 Ag 21 '67
Joy of being Boppa. por McCalls 94:74-5+ Je
'67
Message from Vice President Humphrey. por
Tech W 20:21 Je 5 '67
Needed, two million jobs; letter. por Am
For 73:8 Je '67

One million dropouts. por Am Ed 3:32 S '67
Open letter to employers; plea for summer
jobs. por U S News 62:79 Je 12 '67
Our common commitment; excerpts from ad-
dress, September 18, 1967. por Américas
19:1-4 N '67
Recreation's vital role. por Parks & Rec 2:13
Je '67
Technological revolution and the world of the
1970's; address, December 6, 1966. Dept State
Bul 56:164-8 Ja 30 '67
To America's PTA leaders a message from the
Vice-President of the United States. PTA
Mag 61:19 Je '67
Tribute to Pablo Casals. por Hi Fi 17:MA4
Ap '67
Unrest and revolt, Humphrey's views; ex-
cerpts from address, July 31, 1967. por U S
News 63:10 Ag 14 '67
Vice President Humphrey returns from trip
to Europe; remarks, April 10 and addresses,
April 6, 7, 1967. Dept State Bul 56:679-85
My 1 '67
Vice President Humphrey visits Viet-Nam,
Malaysia, and Indonesia; remarks, toast,
and joint communique, October 30-Novem-
ber 6, 1967. Dept State Bul 57:789-92 D 11
'67
about
Dissenting from the dissenters. il por News-
week 70:25-6 N 6 '67
Goodwill tour II; Atlanta visit. il por News-
week 69:26 Ap 24 '67
Hubert Humphrey's scientific role: from
ocean depths to outer space. B. Nelson.
il por Science 155:981-3 F 24 '67
H.H.H. vote-getter or scapegoat? N. K.
Herzfeld. Commonweal 86:489-92 Ag 11 '67
Humphrey's spurious logic on Vietnam war.
Christian Cent 84:1212-13 S 27 '67
Letter from Stanford. J. Neugeboren. New
Repub 156:32-5 Mr 18 '67
L.B.J.'s ombudsman for the cities. H. Sidey.
il pors Life 63:36 O 6 '67
Nervous cheerleader. Nation 205:674 D 25 '67
Old scoutmaster in action. il pors Life 62:77-
8 Je 16 '67
Report; new relationship with L. B. Johnson.
D. Kiker. Atlan 219:6+ Je '67
Right track. Newsweek 69:39 My 8 '67
Students and the war; Humphrey at Stanford.
M. Novak. Commonweal 86:7-8 Mr 24 '67
Veep lives his convictions. R. Lantz. il pors
Ebony 22:75-8+ My '67
Vice-President; appearance on J. Carson's
Tonight show and meeting with partici-
pants of Double discovery. New Yorker 43:
23-5 Ag 12 '67
View of H.H.H. E.Roper. il por Sat R 50:18-
19 Je 17 '67
Walkout, newsbreak mar National book
awards. Library J 92:1397 Ap 1 '67
Warm but worried. por Newsweek 71:46 Ja
22 '68
When students heckled Mr Humphrey. il por
U S News 62:8 Mr 6 '67
Why it will be a Johnson-Humphrey ticket
again in '68. por U S News 62:40-3 F 13
'67
Visit to Africa, 1967-1968
H.H.H.'s ebullient expedition to Africa. il
pors Life 64:32-3 Ja 19 '68
Veep on the wing. il por Time 91:12 Ja 12
'68
We are your partners. il por Newsweek 71:33
Ja 15 '68
Visit to Europe, 1967
Europe revisited. il por Time 89:15-16 Ap
7 '67
Humphrey and science. Sci N 91:401-2 Ap 29
'67
Humphrey meets the European critics. Bsns
W p200 Ap 15 '67
Humphrey on tour; what he hopes to gain.
por U S News 62:15 Ap 3 '67
Humphrey's mission. W. Lippmann. News-
week 69:23 Ap 24 '67
London paper scolds Europe for attacks on
U.S; reprint. il U S News 62:98 Ap 24 '67
Making the rounds with HHH. il pors News-
week 69:56-7 Ap 17 '67
Roving tranquilizer. Newsweek 69:47-8 Ap 10
'67
Telling and hearing. K. Crawford. Newsweek
69:37 Ap 24 '67
Vice President Humphrey returns from trip
to Europe; remarks, April 10 and addresses,
April 6, 7, 1967. H. H. Humphrey and L.
B. Johnson. Dept State Bul 56:678-85 My 1
'67
What Humphrey gained for U.S. in Europe.
il pors U S News 62:19 Ap 17 '67

HUMPHREY, Hubert Horatio—*Continued*

Visit to Southeast Asia, 1967

Fistful of frangipani; visit to Indonesia. Newsweek 70:79 N 20 '67

Northwest's passage. il por Time 90:26 N 10 '67

Stumping in Saigon. il por Newsweek 70:32-3 N 13 '67

Thieu sworn in. il Sr Schol 91:22 N 16 '67

What Humphrey told Saigon. U S News 63:20 N 13 '67

HUMPHREY, Hubert Horatio, family
Joy of being Boppa. H. H. Humphrey. il pors McCalls 94:74-5+ Je '67

HUMPHREY, Loren J. and others
Heterologous antilymphocyte globulin; studies in vitro. bibliog Science 157:441 Jl 28 '67

HUMPHREY, Richard
Can we stave off radio-frequency super-saturation? Pop Electr 27:71-3+ O '67

New Q-band marine radar. Electr World 77:32-3 Ap '67

Report on annual assembly. Electr World 78:46+ S '67

Report on single sideband radio telephony. Motor B 121:118-19+ Ja '68 (to be cont)

HUMPHREY, William
Rainmaker; story. Sat Eve Post 240:62-4 D 2 '67

HUMPHRIES, D. A. and Driver, P. M.
Erratic display as a device against predators. bibliog Science 156:1767-8 Je 30 '67

HUMPHRIES, Lynn
Businessmen's expectations (cont) Duns R 88:13 D '66; 89:13 Mr; 13 Je; 90:15 S '67

HUMPHRIES, Rolfe
Man of many ways. New Repub 157:30-1+ D 9 '67

Tall-tale Americana. Nation 205:153-7 Ag 28 '67

HUNCHES. See Intuition

HUNGARIAN cookery. See Cookery, Hungarian

HUNGARIAN poetry

Translations into English

Five late poems; tr. by S. Polgar and others. M. Radnoti. Nation 205:440 O 30 '67

HUNGARY
See also
Collective farms—Hungary
Communism—Hungary

Economic conditions

Hungary: the mechanism and the marionettes. C. Sterling. Reporter 36:25-7 My 4 '67

Politics and government

Balkan kaleidoscope. A. Z. Rubinstein. Cur Hist 52:220-2 Ap '67

Toward liberalization. Time 89:45 Ap 21 '67

Religious institutions and affairs
See also
Catholics in Hungary

HUNGER
Food intake controlled by a blood factor. J. D. Davis and others. bibliog il Science 156:1247-8 Je 2 '67

Human hunger as a policy determinant; address, November 3, 1967. H. J. Waters. Dept State Bul 57:764-8 D 4 '67

Hunger is the big story. R. L. Tobin. Cath World 205:26-30 Ap '67

Neural correlates of food and water intake in the rat. J. N. Coury. bibliog il Science 156:1763-5 Je 30 '67

See also
Famines

HUNN, Max
Clark Hill, southern water playground. por Motor B 120:40-1+ Jl '67

Dogs in his trailer. Design 69:4-6 Fall '67

State parks of Georgia. Travel 128:36-9+ S '67

HUNT, Graham R. See Salisbury, J. W. jt. auth.

HUNT, Haroldson Lafayette
Success story. New Repub 156:2 My 27 '67

HUNT, Irene
Books and the learning process; address, June 27, 1967. Horn Bk 43:424-9 Ag '67

about

Aunt Irene. W. B. Beem. il por Horn Bk 43:429-33 Ag '67

Irene Hunt. E. Meeks. Library J 92:1297 Mr 15 '67

Newbery and Caldecott award winners. por ALA Bul 61:358 Ap '67

Newbery and Caldecott winners: Irene Hunt, Evaline Ness. il por Pub W 191:34-5 Mr 13 '67

Newbery-Caldecott winners. por Wilson Lib Bul 41:783 Ap '67

HUNT, Janet
Dumplings are delightful. Parents Mag 42:66-7 Ap '67

Sauces make the difference. Parents Mag 42:64-5+ Mr '67

HUNT, John Clark
Eruption in the Northwest. Am For 73:22-5+ N '67

Smoky years. Am For 73:30-1+ My '67

HUNT, John M. and others
Red Sea: detailed survey of hot-brine areas. bibliog Science 156:514-16 Ap 28 '67

HUNT, Morton M.
Don't trust anyone over thirty. Redbook 129:59-61+ Je '67

Neurosis is just a bad habit. N Y Times Mag p38-9+ Je 4 '67

Social life of married couples: its pleasures and problems. McCalls 94:67-9+ My '67

HUNT, Reed Oliver
Paper profits. il por Time 89:88+ My 5 '67

HUNT, Richard
Stuffed moose & stacked tibias. il por Time 90:96+ D 1 '67

HUNT, Ronald D. and others
Vitamins D₂ and D₃ in New World primates: influence on calcium absorption. bibliog Science 157:943-5 Ag 25 '67

HUNT, Todd
How to transplant a green thumb. House B 109:48+ Mr '67

HUNT, William
Exclusion of the stars; poem. Poetry 110:95 My '67

HUNT foods and industries, incorporated
Changes amid rumors. Time 90:94 N 17 '67

Simon's new recipe. il Bsns W p 180 N 18 '67

HUNTER, Anna C.
Bay: Savannah's water front. Antiques 91:332-3 Mr '67

HUNTER, Caroline
Why healthy mothers need prenatal care; interview, ed. by E. M. Stern. Redbook 128:57+ Ap '67

HUNTER, Dard, paper museum. See Dard Hunter paper museum, Appleton, Wis.

HUNTER, David R.
Case against school prayer. Good H 164:30 Mr '67

HUNTER, Edith Fisher
Grand opening that didn't. Read Digest 90:118-20 Je '67

They went out men and women; they have come back children. Christian Cent 84:720-2 My 31 '67

You used to say you'd marry me. Redbook 129:59+ Ag '67

HUNTER, Evalee S.
You can refreeze meat. Farm J 91:109 F '67

HUNTER, Gerald R.
Family secrets from an old-time machine shop. por Pop Sci 190:160-3 Ja '67

HUNTER, J. Jr. See Wesselink, A. J. jt. auth.

HUNTER, Jenny
You are always somewhere, hopefully. R. Hartley. il pors Dance Mag 41:62-5 S '67

HUNTER, John
Selling land in Florida. New Repub 157:21-3 S 2 '67

HUNTER, John, 1728-1793
John Hunter, brash genius of pathology; excerpt from The great doctors. R. Silverberg. il Todays Health 45:44-5+ F '67

HUNTER, John M.
Latin American integration and the Alliance. bibliog f Cur Hist 53:257-62+ N '67

HUNTER, Madeline C.
Agony and the ecstasy of teaching. NEA J 56:36-8 F '67

HUNTER, Ross
Happy producers make happy movies. H. Alpert. Sat R 50:45 Ap 15 '67

HUNTER, W. Russell, and others
Interpopulation variations in calcium metabolism in the stream limpet, Ferrissia rivularis (Say) bibliog Science 155:338-40 Ja 20 '67

HUNTER, William James D.
A father speaks to the President in behalf of a son killed in Vietnam; letters. U S News 62:46-7 My 8 '67

HUNTER, William W.
Salmon for everyone. Field & S 71:58-9+ Mr '67

HUNTER college, New York
Tomorrow's baroque; staff of practicing artists. il Time 89:66 Ap 7 '67

HUNTER-farmer relations. See Farmer-hunter
  relations
HUNTERS
  Old buck is still around. B. Milek. il Field
    & S 72:54-5+ O '67
  Speaking out; hunting is a dirty business.
    B. Gilbert. Sat Eve Post 240:10+ O 21 '67
HUNTING
  Gist of it; digest of the outdoor news; ed.
    by H. Moore. See issues of Outdoor life
  How to be a failure at hunting. J. B. Scott.
    il Field & S 72:62-3+ My '67
  Sportsman's notebook. H. G. Tapply. See is-
    sues of Field & stream
  Test your hunting know-how; questions and
    answers. G. B. Evans. il Field & S 72:66-7
    My '67
  Vision and the hunter. R. V. McCormick. il
    Field & S 72:54-5+ S '67
  Where to go fishing, vacationing, hunting;
    ed. by V. T. Sparano. See issues of Out-
    door life
    See also
  Hunting with bow and arrow
  Indians of North America—Hunting
  Poaching
    also Deer hunting; Wolf hunting; and
  similar headings

          Anecdotes, facetiae, satire, etc.
  Field & stream guide to the hunting scene.
    il Field & S 72:48-51 S '67

                    Africa
  Pack hunt with camels. L. E. Tassell. il Out-
    door Life 139:46-9+ Je '67
  The .270 in Africa. J. O'Connor. il Outdoor
    Life 139:118-22 Mr '67
  With only a bow and bold belief. W. Negley.
    il Sports Illus 27:50-6+ Jl 31 '67

                  Africa, East
  Africa: safari. C. Bergen. il Vogue 149:146-
    7+ Ap 1 '67

                    Alabama
  Launching pad for doves. C. Sawyer. il Out-
    door Life 140:50-1+ S '67

                    Alaska
  Alaska cracks down. J. Rearden. il Outdoor
    Life 140:39-41+ O '67
  Alaskan arms. W. Page. il Field & S 72:60-4
    Ja '68
  Backpack sheep hunt; ed. by M. Miller. D.
    Schmiege. il Field & S 71:44-5+ Mr '67
  Many bears pass. W. Page. il Field & S
    71:70-1+ Mr '67
  1967 Canada-Alaska hunting forecast. Field &
    S 72:102-3 Ag '67

                    Arizona
  Cochise choice; mule deer and whitetail, too.
    W. A. Cartier. il Outdoor Life 140:48-51+
    O '67
  Hunt in the North Kaibab. V. Kraft. il
    Sports Illus 27:54-7 N 20 '67
  I didn't fire a shot on my greatest hunt. E.
    Meyer. il Outdoor Life 140:54-5+ Ag '67
  Rabbit hunt, Indian style. J. Downs. il Out-
    door Life 139:54-5+ Je '67

                    Arkansas
  I have the last gobble. G. Gresham. il Out-
    door Life 139:58-9+ Ap '67

                Atlantic states
  Best ways to hunt rabbits East to West.
    J. Bashline. il Field & S 72:46-7+ Ja '68

                    Australia
  Old hunter rounds up brumbies on a motor-
    cycle; with report by D. Moser. il Life 63:
    68-9+ D 22 '67

                  Bechuanaland
  Indestructible buffalo. J. O'Connor. il Out-
    door Life 139:52-5+ Ap '67

                    Brazil
  Cat man returns. S. Siemel. il Outdoor Life
    139:46-9+ My '67

                  California
  Buck wore black. J. Mears. Outdoor Life
    139:10 My '67
  First bear in the Yolla Bollys. B. Behme. il
    Field & S 72:56-9 N '67
  Go to beat the bandtails. B. Behme. il Field &
    S 72:62-5 Je '67
  Late-season snows. L. Green. il Field & S
    72:44-5+ D '67
  Something peculiar at Tulelake. N. Riley. il
    Outdoor Life 140:62-4+ N '67

                    Canada
  Campfire inside. D. Brown. il Outdoor Life
    140:50-3+ D '67
  Deuces wild; Yukon hunt. N. R. Gibson. il
    Outdoor Life 139:62-3+ F '67
  Dogs for the prairies. D. M. Duffey. il Out-
    door Life 139:178-83 Ap '67
  Footrace with a caribou. D. Cape. il Outdoor
    Life 140:48-9+ S '67
  Grizzly scalped me. E. Dixon and B. Hamil-
    ton. il Outdoor Life 139:76-7+ Ap '67
  Hound man's dream; cougar hunting. D. D.
    Ellis. il Outdoor Life 140:50-3+ N '67
  I had to have moose. O. A. Fredrickson. il
    Outdoor Life 139:70-3+ My '67
  Instant record; majestic Newfoundland bull.
    B. Knutson. il Outdoor Life 140:20-3+ Jl
    '67
  Man who feeds the trumpeters. J. Turner. il
    Outdoor Life 139:64-7+ F '67
  Moose a mile; Clark-Beaupre region of Sas-
    katchewan. H. Bradshaw. il Field & S 72:
    36-7+ Ag '67
  1967 Canada-Alaska hunting forecast. Field &
    S 72:102-3 Ag '67
  Silent hunter. J. Lesowski. il Outdoor Life
    140:44-7+ Jl '67
  Special-extra moose hunt. H. J. Samuels. il
    Outdoor Life 140:32-5+ N '67
  Stubble-field bird hunt. N. Riley. il Field & S
    72:64-5+ O '67
  Wingshooting in Saskatchewan. M. Ellis. il
    Field & S 72:56-7+ Ag '67
  Wolves were the worst. O. A. Fredrickson.
    il Outdoor Life 139:60-1+ Je '67
  World's biggest grizzly? J. Turner. il Outdoor
    Life 139:41-3+ Mr '67

                    Colorado
  Hard-luck elk. B. Myers. il Field & S 72:
    44-5+ Ag '67
  Rage of a bear. W. L. Cave. il Outdoor Life
    140:26-9+ Ag '67

                    Florida
  Christmas on a houseboat. E. A. Bauer. il
    Outdoor Life 140:42-5+ D '67

                    Georgia
  Muzzle-loader deer hunt. C. Elliott. il Outdoor
    Life 139:48-51+ Mr '67

                    Idaho
  Memory for muleys. C. Conley. il Field & S
    72:38-9+ Ag '67

                    Ireland
  International incident in Cork; French hunt-
    ing party in Ireland. C. Gammon. il Sports
    Illus 27:42-4+ N 27 '67

                    Kansas
  Best duck bargain. P. Czura. il Outdoor Life
    140:62-5 O '67
  Kansas quail renaissance. P. Curtis. il Field
    & S 72:58-9+ O '67
  Varmint shooter's paradise. J. Olt. il Outdoor
    Life 139:62-5+ My '67

                    Maine
  Bear of the decade. B. Degenhardt. il Out-
    door Life 140:36-9+ Jl '67
  Jackpot hunt for $48. B. Holden. il Outdoor
    Life 140:56-9+ S '67
  Nine natives and the hard buck. L. Dietz. il
    Field & S 71:54-5+ Ap '67

                    Mexico
  Crane hunting in Mexico. W. Page. il Field
    & S 72:36-7+ N '67
  Down an unknown jungle river. Z. Grey. il
    Field & S 72:44-5+ S; 60-1+ O; 42-3+ N
    '67

                    Michigan
  Bear to be thankful for; ed. by B. East. B.
    Haataja. il Outdoor Life 140:32-5+ S '67
  Bowhunter's paradise; North Manitou Island.
    G. H. Gillelan. il Outdoor Life 139:20+
    F '67
  I was the dog; ed. by B. East. F Beebe. il
    Outdoor Life 140:68-9+ D '67

                Middle western states
  Best ways to hunt rabbits East to West. C.
    Carpenter. il Field & S 72:46-7+ Ja '68

                    Minnesota
  Catch the red fox napping. B. Gilsvik. il
    Outdoor Life 140:60-1+ N '67

                    Mississippi
  Best quail hunting in the South. G. Gresham.
    il Field & S 72:34-5+ N '67

HUNTING——*Continued*

Montana

Football knee. L. J. Smith. il Outdoor Life 140:42-3+ O '67

Frosting on the cake. B. Kuhn. il Outdoor Life 139:36-9+ Je '67

Old Bruie's last visit; ed. by V. W. Binkley. M. McDonald. il Outdoor Life 140:60-1+ O '67

Morocco

Snipe safari. E. Zern. il Field & S 72:120-3 N '67

Nevada

Jarbidge deer hunt. B. Behme. il Field & S 72:50-1+ O '67

Scarface. R. V. Broadbent. il Outdoor Life 140:66+ D '67

New Hampshire

And don't never count your shells. T. Janes. il Outdoor Life 140:52-3+ O '67

New Jersey

Hardest bird hunting in Jersey. P. McLain. il Field & S 72:36-9+ D '67

New Mexico

Three bucks for the book. E. Morgan. il Outdoor Life 140:54-5+ N '67

New York (state)

Buck picked me. T. Janes. il Outdoor Life 140:40-1+ N '67

Cuyler hill monster. S. Mawson. il Outdoor Life 139:56-7+ My '67

Ohio

Great coon hunt. E. A. Bauer. il Outdoor Life 140:48-9+ N '67

Rough ruffs. D. N. Keller. il Field & S 72:138-41 O '67

Who says hunting's finished around here? E. A. Bauer. il Outdoor Life 140:38-41+ Ag '67

Oregon

Our varmints were trophies. E. Park. il Outdoor Life 139:72-3+ F '67

Tallyho, the bobcat. L. Miracle. il Outdoor Life 140:70-3+ O '67

Pennsylvania

Bear by the square mile. L. J. Bashline. il Field & S 72:42-3+ Ag '67

Brainy black duck. R. Beck. il Outdoor Life 140:42-3+ N '67

Cottontails are tough critters. D. V. Anderson. il Field & S 72:56-7+ S '67

Scotland

Safari to the dour moors of Scotland. D. Barnes. il Sports Illus 26:60-1 F 13 '67

South Africa

Gemsbok in the Kalahari. J. O'Connor. il Outdoor Life 140:28-9+ Jl '67

See also
Hunting—Bechuanaland

South Dakota

Deer drive; Black Hills and Whitetails. H. Bradshaw. il Outdoor Life 139:52-3+ F '67

What happens to pheasants? B. East. il Outdoor Life 140:34-5+ Ag '67

Southwestern states

Buffalo hunt; excerpt from Blessed McGill. E. Shrake. il Sports Illus 27:60-70 D 25 '67

Whitetails along the border. W. Page. il Field & S 72:46-7+ O '67

Tanzania

Old Shugulli. A. Landreth. il Outdoor Life 139:48-51+ F '67

Tennessee

How to stump the ducks; ed. by D. D. Dickey. F. Moses. il Outdoor Life 140:62-5 D '67

Texas

Bad day for crows. B. W. Dalrymple. il Outdoor Life 139:64-5+ Mr '67

First Aransas deer hunt. G. H. Gillelan. il Outdoor Life 139:106-8+ Ap '67

Imp of southern Texas; scaled quail. V. Kraft. Sports Illus 26:41-2+ Ja 30 '67

United States

Field & stream phone forecast of hunting, 1967. Field & S 72:18+ S '67

How much should you charge hunters? B. Dalrymple. Farm J 91:90-1 F '67

Hunting for the millions. M. C. Gethman. il Field & S 72:60-1+ S '67

Hunting will never be the same. W. Page. Field & S 72:62-3+ S '67

No end of game; fall season. il Time 90:61 S 29 '67

Utah

Meet me on the Green. J. S. Flannery. il Outdoor Life 140:50-3+ Ag '67

Runway rabbit hunt. J. S. Flannery. il Outdoor Life 139:74-6 Mr '67

Vermont

Luck of the Willeys. H. Willey, jr. il Outdoor Life 140:56-7+ D '67

Vietnam

Oriental pig tale. H. J. Samuels. il Outdoor Life 139:68-71+ Mr '67

Washington (state)

Luck beats the odds. E. Park. il Outdoor Life 140:40-1+ S '67

Western states

Best ways to hunt rabbits East to West. J. Freeman. il Field & S 72:46-7+ Ja '68

Big-game hunting for everyone. G. Dovel. il Field & S 72:52-3+ S '67

Hunting the ridge runners. C. F. Waterman. il Field & S 72:44-5+ O '67

Wisconsin

Deer hunt I'll never forget. F. McKinley. il Field & S 72:60-1+ Je '67

Errant Eric. M. Ellis. il Field & S 72:38-9+ N '67

Wyoming

Big horn of birds. P. Czura. il Field & S 72:104-6+ D '67

Long, long trail. E. Park. il Outdoor Life 140:46-7+ D '67

Old Ephraim country. C. Elliott. il Outdoor Life 140:58-61+ D '67

We wanted a western hunt. J. O. Cartier. il Outdoor Life 140:29-31+ S '67

Wyoming antelope. B. Milek. il Field & S 72:40-1+ Ag '67

HUNTING clothes. See Clothing and dress—Sports clothes

HUNTING dogs

Christmas puppy. J. Griffen. il Field & S 72:106+ Ja '68

Clinic for the problem hunting dog. J. Griffen. il Field & S 72:144-5+ S '67

Dog Argentine. J. Parry. il Field & S 72:130-1+ N '67

Dogs. D. M. Duffey. See issues of Outdoor life

Dogs for the prairies. D. M. Duffey. il Outdoor Life 139:178-83 Ap '67

Hounds to trail ghosts! D. J. Anderson. il Field & S 72:48-9+ O '67

Sam the potlicker. D. J. Anderson. il Field & S 72:54-5+ Ag '67

See also
Bird dogs
Hounds
Setters

HUNTING knives. See Knives

HUNTING laws. See Game laws

HUNTING lodges. See Lodges (architecture)

HUNTING preserves. See Game preserves

HUNTING with bow and arrow

Archery. G. H. Gillelan. See issues of Outdoor life

Archery hunting in 1925. S. Pope. Field & S 72:45+ Ja '68

Bear of the decade. B. Degenhardt. il Outdoor Life 140:36-9+ Jl '67

Birds and bows. B. Dalrymple. il Field & S 72:42-5+ Jl '67

Bowhunting on Uncle Sam. G. H. Gillelan. il Outdoor Life 139:28+ Je '67

First Aransas deer hunt. G. H. Gillelan. il Outdoor Life 139:106-8+ Ap '67

Footrace with a caribou. D. Cape. il Outdoor Life 140:48-9+ S '67

Mountain sheep and the bow; reprint. A. Young. il Field & S 72:44-5+ Ja '68

Prepare now for deer. G. H. Gillelan. il Outdoor Life 140:60+ Jl '67

With only a bow and bold belief. W. Negley. il Sports Illus 27:50-6+ Jl 31 '67

HUNTINGTON, E. G.
Katey darling; story. Redbook 129:66-7 O '67

HUNTINGTON, Francis Cleaveland
Wall Street priest. il por Newsweek 70:58 O 30 '67

HUNTINGTON, Roger
Supercharging by jet. Hot Rod 20:42-4 Jl '67
What's new from Detroit? a preview of 1968
cars. Consumer Bul 50:20-6 O '67
HUNTINGTON, N.Y.
Patch it right the first time. J. J. Walsh.
il Am City 82:118-19 Mr '67
HUNTINGTON botanical gardens, San Marino,
Calif. See Botanical gardens
HUNTINGTON library and art gallery, San
Marino, Calif. See Henry E. Huntington
library and art gallery, San Marino, Calif.
HUNTON, George K.
Obituary
America 117:631 N 25 '67
HUNTOON, Maxwell C. Jr
Build a basement that's easy to remodel. Am
Home 70:141 O '67
How to get your money's worth in an older
house. Am Home 70:90+ Mr '67
Planned unit development means better com-
munities. Am Home 70:124+ Mr '67
Quality vacation house on a limited budget.
Am Home 70:46+ Jl '67
Simple ways to sound-condition your home.
Am Home 70:110 My '67
HUNTOON, R. D.
Concept of a national measurement system.
bibliog Science 158:67-71 O 6 '67
HUNTSVILLE, Ala.
Huntsville: Alabama cotton town takes off
into space age. L. J. Carter. il Science 155:
1224-9 Mr 10 '67
HUNTSVILLE, Ala, public library
Huntsville public library rocked by Mailer
book. Library J 93:138 Ja 15 '68
HUNTZINGER, Robert
Robert Huntzinger: follow the fire in your
gut. H. M. Kinzer. il por Pop Phot 61:82-91
S '67 V
HUPÉ, Robert Strausz-. See Strausz-Hupé, R.
HURDLE racing
Fleming with a flair; G. Roelants. T. Maule.
il Sports Illus 27:36-43 Jl 17 '67
HURLEY, Jack
Last campaign of boxing's last angry man.
W. C. Heinz. il pors Sat Eve Post 240:38-
42+ F 11 '67
HURLEY, Joseph Patrick, abp
Archbishop Joseph P. Hurley. RIP. Nat R
19:1251 N 14 '67
HURLEY, Neil P.
First decade of the noösphere. America 117:
171-3 Ag 19 '67
Marshall McLuhan: communications explorer.
America 116:241-3 F 18 '67
HURLEY, P. M. and others
Test of continental drift by comparison of
radiometric ages. bibliog Science 157:495-
500 Ag 4 '67
HURLING (game)
Gentle Irish; colorful sport. J. Carroll. il
Sports Illus 27:40-6+ Ag 28 '67
HUROK, Sol
Dance magazine's annual awards 1966. il por
Dance Mag 41:42-3+ Mr '67
HURON, LAKE
See also
Manitoulin Island
HURRICANES
Baleful toll of hurricane Beulah. il Life 63:
34-5 O 6 '67
Big Beulah. il Newsweek 70:31 O 2 '67
Characteristics of hurricanes. B. I. Miller.
bibliog il Science 157:1389-99 S 22 '67
Essa v. Beulah. il Time 90:27 S 29 '67
Fury named Beulah. L. M. Rhodes. il Todays
Health 45:36-41+ D '67
How to outwit a hurricane! Z. Taylor. il
Motor B 120:46-7+ Ag '67
Hurricane Beulah, one of the big ones. il
U S News 63:10 O 2 '67
Now, more action to tame hurricanes. U S
News 63:10 Ag 21 '67
Storm stalkers get jump on hurricanes; U.S.
weather team at Miami. il Bsns W p 106-8
Jl 15 '67
Sweeping disaster along the Rio Grande;
hurricane Beulah. il U S News 63:8 O 9 '67
Wild one; Beulah brings worst floods in
Texas' history. il Time 90:29 O 6 '67
HURT, John Smith
Mississippi John Hurt: 1892-1966; with dis-
cography. L. Cohn. por Sat R 50:90 F 25
'67
HURTIG, Mel G.
Canadian bookseller expands into publishing.
Pub W 192:53 N 13 '67
HURWITZ, Al
Cutting edge of curriculum. Sch Arts 67:9-12
O '67
Very small happening at Forty Mile Bend.
NEA J 56:71-2 S '67

HURWITZ, Howard L.
High school principal looks Up the down
staircase. Sr Schol 91:sup 16-17 O 5 '67
New books of American history (cont) Sr
Schol 90:sup 10 F 17 '67
Teaching about the Russian revolution. bib-
liog Sr Schol 91:sup8-9 N 30 '67
(ed) What's new in social studies; summaries
of articles and reports (cont) Sr Schol 90:
sup 19 Mr 10 '67
HURWITZ, Sidney
My woodcut technique. il por Am Artist 31:
30-5+ My '67
HUSAIN, Zakir
Victory for good sense. il por Time 89:35 My
19 '67
HUSBAND, Helen
Regional report. Home Gard 54:53 Je '67
HUSBAND and wife. See Husbands; Mar-
riage; Marriage counseling
HUSBANDS
For husbands only. B. Kunkel. Farm J 91:66F
Mr '67
How important is the color of a man's
collar? il Good H 165:20+ N '67
In praise of older men; ed. by H. Ehrlich.
R. West and G. Hotchner. il Look 31:80-5
N 28 '67
Perfect husband. S. Blum. il McCalls 94:60-
1+ Ag '67; Same abr. with title What
makes the perfect husband? Read Digest
92:140-3 Ja '68
Summer bachelors. il Newsweek 70:97 Jl 17
'67
Why so many husbands feel inadequate. R. J.
Levin. il Redbook 129:61+ S '67
Why some good husbands run away. D. Mer-
son and B. Merson. il Good H 166:92-3+
Ja '68
See also
Marriage
Wives
HUSER, Laverne C.
Trails of the Grand Teton. Nat Parks Mag
41:10-14 My '67
HUSS, Glenn I. See Nininger, H. H. jt. auth.
HUSSAR, Bruno
How to break down walls. America 117:145
Ag 12 '67
HUSSEIN, king of Jordan
Middle East crisis; address. June 26, 1967.
Vital Speeches 33:610-12 Ag 1 '67
Statement to Life. Life 63:117 S 29 '67

about

Can Hussein survive? J. H. Huizinga. il por
Reporter 37:35-6 S 7 '67
His majesty, the leadfoot. V. Kraft. il pors
Sports Illus 26:42-8 My 8 '67
Imperial non-tool. il por Newsweek 70:48
O 16 '67
In Jordan, a defeated King Hussein keeps his
dignity. il pors Life 62:66-7 Je 23 '67
King Hussein's dilemma: take aid from Rus-
sia, or U.S? il por U S News 63:20 O 16 '67
King pleads the Arab case. il por Life 63:
24-5 Jl 7 '67
Least unreasonable Arab. il por Time 90:
22-3+ Jl 14 '67
HUSSEY, Olivia
New Romeo and Juliet. M. Simons. il pors
Look 31:52-5+ O 17 '67
People are talking about... por Vogue 150:
88-9 Ag 1 '67
HUSSLER, Georg
Samaritans to Hanoi. A. Schalk. Common-
weal 86:542-4 S 8 '67
HUSTON, H. V.
How to build a coffee-table music center.
Pop Sci 191:129-33+ Ag '67
HUTCHENS, John K.
Heritage of the frontier. Sat R 50:34-5+ S
23 '67
One thing and another (cont) Sat R 50:35-6
Ja 28; 42-4 F 25; 25-6+ Mr 18; 27-8 My 27;
28-9+ Je 10; 30-1 O 28; 27-8 D 16 '67
HUTCHESON, Dorothy
Easy-to-prepare rice dishes. Am Home 70:108
S '67
HUTCHINS, Carleen Maley
Physics for the queen. J. Eberhart. il Sci N
91:212-13 Mr 4 '67
HUTCHINS, Robert Maynard
University; address. March 17, 1967. Vital
Speeches 33:475-8 My 15 '67
University and the multiversity; adaptation
of address. New Repub 156:15-17 Ap 1 '67

about

Computer and the chancellor. J. Shera. Wilson Lib Bul 41:837+ Ap '67

HUTCHINSON, Arthur
Open letter: jobs in Europe, anyone? Dance Mag 41:18-20 Jl '67
HUTCHINSON, Karen
Conqueror of the classics. il pors Ebony 23: 38-40+ N '67
HUTCHINSON, Patrick Synge-. See Synge-Hutchinson, P.
HUTCHINSON, Thomas C. See Du Mond, F. V. jt. auth.
HUTCHISON, Bruce
Canada and the United States, a centennial restrospective. Am Heritage 18:6-12+ Je '67
HUTCHISON, G. Scott
Reaction to the Latent lobby. Harvard Bsns R 45:166-8+ Jl '67
HUTCHISON, Ira J. Jr
Promoting functional play patterns. Parks & Rec 2:29+ S '67
HUTH, Hans
Russian lacquer. Antiques 92:843-7 D '67
HUTT, Arthur P.
American alligator. Nat Parks Mag 41:14-17 D '67
HUTTON, E. F, and company
Where traders upstage the stocks in glamour; E. F. Hutton office in MCA's Universal city. il Bsns W p 160-2 S 9 '67
HUXLEY, Aldous
Devils of Loudun; dramatization. See Whiting, J. Devils
HUXLEY, Elspeth
African affairs (cont) por Nat R 19:466-7, 896+ My 2, Ag 22 '67
Blundering into danger. Nat R 19:1339-40 N 28 '67
Letter from Africa. por Nat R 20:33+ Ja 16 '68
HUXLEY, Sir Julian
Beast-watching. Holiday 42:36-43+ S '67
HUXTABLE, Ada Louise (Landman)
Building the Soviet society; excerpts from The Soviet Union, the fifty years. Arch Forum 127:34-41 N '67

about

Civic consciences. por Time 89:66+ Mr 31 '67
HUYCK, Dorothy Boyle
Hoge Veluwe National Park. Am For 73: 22-5+ F '67
Somebody shoulda told me. . Am For 73:12-15+ Jl '67
HYACINTHS
Perfect child-sized project: hyacinths for Christmas. il Home Gard 54:44-5 N '67
You plant now for spring rewards. il Sunset 139:208 N '67
HYALURONIDASE
Histocampatibility antigen transfer in utero: tolerance in progeny and sensitization in mother. C. Tai and N. A. Halasz. bibliog il Science 158:125-6 O 6 '67
HYAMS, Joe
Day I gave up the ghost. Sat Eve Post 240: 92-4 Je 3 '67
HYATT, Herbert, family
Tragedy that wouldn't end. A. Levy. il pors Good H 165:42+ Jl '67
HYBRID cells. See Cells
HYBRID peonies. See Peonies
HYBRID rockets. See Rockets
HYBRIDIZATION
Cells of mice and men. Sci Am 218:51 Ja '68
Have you tried the F1 hybrids? Sunset 138:264 Ap '67
How to hybridize fuchsias. il Sunset 139: 162-4 S '67
See also
Triticale
also subhead Hybrids under various subjects, e.g. Sorghum—Hybrids
HYDE, Arnout, jr
On the go, by plane. il U S Camera 30:44-5+ My '67
HYDE, H. Montgomery
Stalin loved Lucy, the greatest spy of all. Life 62:8 My 12 '67
HYDE, James Hazen
New York to Lakewood in style. por Am Heritage 18:22 O '67
HYDE, Philip
Navaho country; photographs. Audubon 69: 22-7 Ja '67
HYDRA (island)
Hydra adio, Hydra hello. P. Seymour. il Sat R 50:56+ O 14 '67
HYDRA (zoology)
Bud movement in hydra. S. Shostak. bibliog il Science 155:1567-8 Mr 24 '67
Transepithelial potentials in hydra. R. K. Josephson and M. Macklin. bibliog il Science 156:1629-31 Je 23 '67

HYDRATED amines. See Amines
HYDRATED electrons. See Electrons
HYDRAULIC control
Control power with fluid. M. Schultz. il Pop Mech 128:114-17+ Jl '67; Same with title Next household word, fluidics. Sci Digest 62:26-30 S '67
Fluidic systems. C. J. Miller. il Electr World 77:23-5+ Je '67
Fluidics' drive gains momentum; control devices that work on gases and liquids. il Bsns W p 152-4 Ap 29 '67
Fluidics: how they've taught a stream of air to think. R. M. Benrey. il Pop Sci 190:118-21+ Je '67
Fluidics is muscling in. C. Behrens. il Sci N 91:69-70 Ja 21 '67
Fluidics; with report by W. Bradbury. il Life 62:110-13+ My 19 '67
HYDRAULIC engineering
See also
Dams

History

Desert waterworks of the ancient Nabataens. P. C. Hammond. il Natur Hist 76:36-43 Je '67
HYDRAULIC equipment for airplanes. See Airplanes—Hydraulic equipment
HYDROCARBONS
Anodic oxidation and molecular structure: influence on performance of normal saturated hydrocarbons in fuel cells. E. J. Cairns. bibliog il Science 155:1245-6 Mr 10 '67
Benzpyrene hydroxylase induction by polycyclic hydrocarbons in hamster embryonic cells grown in vitro. L. J. Alfred and H. V. Gelboin. bibliog il Science 157:75-6 Jl 7 '67
Gaseous hydrocarbons in sea water: determination. J. W. Swinnerton and V. J. Linnenbom. bibliog il Science 156:1119-20 My 26 '67
Growth of a thermophilic bacterium on hydrocarbons: a new source of single-cell protein. R. I. Mateles and others. bibliog il Science 157:1322-3 S 15 '67; Reply. L. R. Pomeroy. 158:579 N 3 '67
Growth of microbial cells on hydrocarbons. M. J. Johnson. bibliog il Science 155:1515-19 Mr 24 '67
Hydrocarbons in digestive tract and liver o1 a basking shark. M. Blumer. il Science 156: 390-1 Ap 21 '67
Malignant transformation in vitro by carcinogenic hydrocarbons. C. Heidelberger and P. T. Iype. bibliog il Science 155:214-17 Ja 13 '67
Photooxidation of hydrocarbons in the presence of aliphatic aldehydes. A. P. Altshuler and others. bibliog il Science 156:937-9 My 19 '67
HYDROCEPHALUS
Virus-induced hydrocephalus: development of aqueductal stenosis in hamsters after mumps infection. R. T. Johnson and others. bibliog il Science 157:1066-7 S 1 '67
HYDROCORTISONE
Sialic acid in HeLa cells: effect of hydrocortisone. R. Carubelli and M. J. Griffin. bibliog il Science 157:693-4 Ag 11 '67
HYDRODYNAMICS
Distortion of a splashing liquid drop. F. H. Harlow and J. P. Shannon. bibliog il Science 157:547-50 Ag 4 '67
Momentum transport in turbulent flow between concentric rotating cylinders. J. B. Southard. bibliog il Science 156:1725-7 Je 30 '67
Natural displacement of pollution from the Great Lakes. R. H. Rainey. il Science 155: 1242-3 Mr 10 '67
Splashing of a water drop. P. V. Hobbs and A. J. Kezweeny. bibliog il Science 155: 1112-14 Mr 3 '67
Tornadoes: mechanism and control. S. A. Colgate. bibliog il Science 157:1431-4 S 22 '67
Wake collapse in a stratified fluid. A. H. Schooley. il Science 157:421-3 Jl 28 '67
HYDROFOILS
New look for the navy; hydrofoil gunboat. Sci Digest 62:24 S '67
HYDROGEN
Irradiation effects in glasses: suppression by synthesis under high-pressure hydrogen. S. P. Faile and others. bibliog Science 156: 1593-5 Je 23 '67
New lines in the radio spectrum of hydrogen. G. S. Mumford. Sky & Tel 33:284 My '67

Isotopes

Transition-state models and hydrogen-isotope effects. R. E. Weston, jr. bibliog il Science 158:332-42 O 20 '67

HYDROGEN bombs
Bombs of Palomares, by T. Szulc. Review
Nation 204:763 Je 12 '67. M. C. O'Brien
New Repub 156:36-7 My 20 '67. W. K.
Wyant, jr.
China's thermonuclear bomb. Sci Am 217:38
Ag '67
Chinese H-bomb. Nation 205:4 Jl 3 '67
Day H-bombs fell on Palomares. L. Azancot.
il Sat R 50:21-7+ Ja 28 '67
Day they lost the H-bomb, by C. Morris.
Review
Sat R 50:40 Ja 28 '67. O. R. Reid
H-bomb, now: red China. Sr Schol 91:32+ S
28 '67
H-bomb warnings. Commonweal 86:435-6 Jl
14 '67
Joining the H-bomb club; China. il News-
week 69:45 Je 26 '67
One of our H-bombs is missing, by F.
Lewis. Review
Sat R 50:39 Ja 28 '67. O. R. Reid
Palomares bomb. J. D. Hayes. Reporter 36:
50+ Je 15 '67
Peking adds potent punch to its arsenal. il
Bsns W p36-7 Je 24 '67
Peking's big blast. Time 89:27-8 Je 23 '67
Shock wave out of China. Newsweek 70:47-8
Jl 3 '67

Anecdotes, facetiae, satire, etc.
What happened when Albie Watkins got the
bomb. R. Lemon. il Sat Eve Post 240:20 Jl
1 '67
Testing
See Atomic bombs—Testing
HYDROGEN sulfide
Desert in the sea; putrid sediment giving
off gas in Cape Lookout Bight. Sci N 91:
115 F 4 '67
HYDROGRAPHIC ships. See Ships, Research
HYDROGRAPHIC surveying
Mystique of messages in bottles. F. A. Mont-
gomery, jr. il Motor B 120:48-9 D '67
World's newest hydrographic ship; USNS
Kane. F. J. Sweeney. il Motor B 120:25-6+
D '67
See also
United States—Coast and geodetic survey
HYDROGRAPHY
See also
Rivers
HYDROIDEA. See Hydromedusa
HYDROLOGIC research
Hydrologic bench marks in the national
parks. H. C. Riggs. il Nat Parks Mag 41:
17-19 Ja '67
HYDROMECHANICS
Splashing of drops on shallow liquids. P. V.
Hobbs and T. Osheroff. bibliog il Science
158:1184-6 D 1 '67
HYDROMEDUSA
Collector on Sagami Bay; letter. T. Komai.
Science 157:488+ Ag 4 '67
Gastrovascular system of small hydromedusae:
mechanisms of circulation. E. C. Roosen-
Runge. bibliog il Science 156:74-6 Ap 7 '67
HYDROPLANE racing. See Motor boat racing
HYDROPLANES
New unlimiteds. J. Schmale. il Motor B
119:100+ F '67
HYDROXAMIC acids. See Peptides
HYDROXYECDYSONE. See Hormones, Plant
HYDROXYETHYL starch. See Starch
HYDROXYL
Ion signals across space. Sci N 92:251-2 S
9 '67
Is mysterium the message? emission lines
produced by the hydroxyl radical. Sci Am
217:50 O '67
HYDROXYLATION
Hydroxylation-induced migration: the NIH
shift. G. Guroff and others. bibliog il Sci-
ence 157:1524-30 S 29 '67
Introcellular pool of unhydroxylated polypep-
tide precursors of collagen. R. S. Bhatnagar
and others. bibliog il Science 158:492-4 O 27
'67
Tryptophan hydroxylation: measurement in
pineal gland, brainstem, and carcinoid
tumor. W. Lovenberg and others. bibliog
il Science 155:217-19 Ja 13 '67
HYDROXYTRYPTAMINE. See Serotonin
HYERS, M. Conrad
Television. Christian Cent 84:1322-3 O 18 '67
HYGIENE
See also
Men—Health and hygiene

HYMAN, Mervin
Basketball's week. Sports Illus 27:98-9 D 11
'67
Football's week. See issues of Sports illus-
trated published during football season
HYMAN, Ray, and Anderson, Barry
Teach your mind to think. Read Digest 90:
107-10 Mr '67
—and Vogt, E. Z.
Psychologists examine the secrets of water
witching. Sci Digest 63:39-45 Ja '68
HYMAN, Stanley Edgar
Darwin sidelight: the shape of the young
man's nose. Atlan 220:96-100+ N '67
HYNEK, Josef Allen
Flying saucers, are they real? Read Digest
90:61-5 Mr '67
HYNES, H. B. N.
Man-made lakes. Science 156:990-1 My 19 '67
HYPERBARIC oxygenation
Operating under pressure; schoolboy suffering
gas gangrene flown by helicopter to Mount
Sinai hospital's hyperbaric chamber. il
Newsweek 70:52-3 Ag 7 '67
HYPERSENSITIVITY. See Allergy
HYPERSONIC airplanes. See Airplanes, Super-
sonic
HYPERSUSCEPTIBILITY. See Anaphylaxis
HYPERTENSION
Blood pressure on demand. il Sci N 91:365
Ap 15 '67
Renal hypertension; report on meeting. J. W.
McCubbin and F. M. Bumpus. Science 155:
1445 Mr 17 '67
HYPERTENSION control device. See Medical
instruments and apparatus
HYPERTROPHY
Enhanced protein synthesis in a cell-free sys-
tem from hypertrophied skeletal muscle. M.
Hamosh and others. bibliog il Science 157:
935-7 Ag 25 '67
HYPERURICEMIA
Urinary metabolites in congenital hyperurico-
suria. M. E. Balis and others. bibliog il
Science 156:1122-3 My 26 '67
HYPNOTISM
Pain. Sci N 91:423-4 My 6 '67
HYPOCRISY
Hand and heart. V. P. McCorry. America
117:inside back cover S 2 '67
HYPODERMIC syringes. See Syringes
HYPOGAMMAGLOBULINEMIA. See Globulin-
emia
HYPOTHALAMUS
Anatomical connections between medical and
lateral regions of the hypothalamus con-
cerned with food intake. E. A. Arees and
J. Mayer. bibliog il Science 157:1574-5 S
29 '67
Disruption of hibernation caused by hypo-
thalamic lesions. E. Satinoff. bibliog il Sci-
ence 155:1031-3 F 24 '67
Food and water intake after intrahypotha-
lamic injections of carbachol in the rabbit.
S. R. Sommer and others. bibliog il Science
156:983-4 My 19 '67
Human hibernation; brain research. P. Mc-
Broom. il Sci N 92:447 N 4 '67
Lateral hypothalamic stimulation in satiated
rats: the rewarding effects of self-induced
drinking. J. Mendelson. il Science 157:1077-9
S 1 '67
Lateral hypothalamus: hoarding behavior
elicited by electrical stimulation. L. J.
Herberg and J. E. Blundell. bibliog il
Science 155:349-50 Ja 20 '67
Localization of the adrenergic feeding sys-
tem in the rat diencephalon. D. A. Booth.
bibliog il Science 158:515-17 O 27 '67
Olfactory input to the hypothalamus: electro-
physiological evidence. J. W. Scott and C.
Pfaffmann. bibliog il Science 158:1592-4 D
22 '67
Reserpine: inhibition of olfactory blockage of
pregnancy in mice. C. J. Dominic; discussion. bibliog Science 155:851-2 F 17 '67
Somatosensory thalamic neurons: effects of
cortical depression. H. J. Waller and S. M.
Feldman. bibliog il Science 157:1074-7 S
1 '67
Steroid-sensitive single neurons in rat hypothalamus and midbrain: identification by
microelectrophoresis. K. Ruf and F. A.
Steiner. bibliog il Science 156:667-9 My 5
'67
HYPOXANTHINE. See Guanine
HYSLOP, Beatrice F.
(comp) Articles and other books received;
France. See issues of American historical
review

HYSTERECTOMY. See Uterus—Surgery
HYSTERIA (social psychology)
Epidemic hysteria; cases at a girl's school in Blackburn, Lancashire. Sci Am 216:58 F '67
HYUM, Walter
What's a picture agency? U S Camera 30:52-3+ Ap '67

I

IACC. See Inter-American cultural council
IAEA. See International atomic energy agency
IA-ECOSOC. See Inter-American economic and social council
IAF. See International astronautical federation
IAM. See International association of machinists
I am a gentle, peaceful man; story. See Franco, M.
I am an axolotl; story. See Cortázar, J.
IASI. See Inter-American statistical institute
IATA. See International air transport association
IAU. See International astronomical union
IBEC. See International basic economy corporation
IBM (intercontinental ballistic missiles) See Guided missiles
IBM. See International business machines corporation
IBM contract investigation. See Government investigations—Government contracts
IBP (International biological program) See Biological research
IBT. See International brotherhood of teamsters, chauffeurs, warehousemen and helpers of America
IC. See Illinois central railroad company
ICAO. See International civil aviation organization
ICBM (intercontinental ballistic missiles) See Guided missiles
ICC. See United States—Interstate commerce commission
I-CNI (integrated communications-navigation-identification system) See Radio apparatus on aircraft
ICO. See International coffee organization
ICY. See International cooperation year
IDA. See Institute for defense analyses
IDB. See Inter-American development bank
I do! I do! musical comedy. See Musical comedies, revues, etc.—Criticisms, plots, etc.
IDS. See Investors diversified services, incorporated
IESC. See International executive service corps
IFI (Instituto finanziario industriale) See Italy—Industries
IFLA. See International federation of library associations
IFOR. See International fellowship of reconciliation
IFYE. See International farm youth exchange program
IGA. See Independent grocers' alliance of America
IHAS (integrated helicopter avionics systems) See Aeronautic instruments
IIE. See Institute of international education
IISI. See International iron and steel institute
ILA. See Illinois library association; International longshoremen's association
ILAAS (integrated light attack avionics system) See Aeronautic instruments
ILC. See United Nations—International law commission
ILGWU. See International ladies' garment workers' union
ILO. See International labor organization
ILS (instrument landing system) See Airplanes—Landing
IMC. See Instructional materials centers; International minerals and chemical corporation
IMCO. See Intergovernmental maritime consultative organization
IMF. See International monetary fund
IMP (interplanetary monitoring platform) See Artificial satellites—Use in research

I must be talking to my friends (dramatic reading) See Dramatic readings
I never thought of you as Henry; story. See Madocs, R.
INSEA. See International society for education through art
IOS. See Investors overseas services, limited
IPA. See International police academy
IPPF. See International planned parenthood federation
IQSY. See International years of the quiet sun
IRA. See International reading association; International recreation association
IRATE (interim remote area terminal equipment) See Airplanes—Landing
IRI (Istituto per la ricostruzione industriale) See Italy—Industries
IRO. See American library association—International relations office
I remember Beau Geste; story. See Álvarez, A. J.
IRRA. See Industrial relations research association
IRS. See United States—Internal revenue service
ISO. See International standards organization
IT and T. See International telephone and telegraph corporation
ITA (initial teaching alphabet) See Alphabet
ITU. See International telecommunication union; International typographical union
ITY. See International tourist year, 1967
IVS. See International voluntary services
I want to smoke pot; story. See Skow, J.
IWFA. See International women's fishing association
IWIU. See Insurance workers international union
IWW. See Industrial workers of the world
IYRU. See International yacht racing union
IAKOVLEV, Aleksandr Sergeevich
Yakovlev faults U.S. display at Paris air show. Aviation W 87:44 Jl 24 '67
IAN, Janis
I am society's child. il pors Life 63:53-4+ O 27 '67
Too young to cry. H. Saal. il por Newsweek 69:114 Je 19 '67
IANNI, Francis A. J.
Cultivating the arts of poverty. Sat R 50:60-2+ Je 17 '67
Teaching violence as a means towards social justice. Cath World 206:160-4 Ja '68
IBA, Hank
Man who said control the ball. T. C. Brody. il por Sports Illus 27:36-43 D 4 '67
IBA, Henry Payne. See Iba, H.
IBAÑEZ, Carlos
Carlos Ibanez company; Carnegie recital hall. J. Maskey. Dance Mag 41:82 My '67
IBEN, Icko, jr
Stellar evolution: comparison of theory with observation. bibliog Science 155:785-96 F 17 '67
IBISES
Adaptive ibis. H. Hays. il Natur Hist 76:32-3 Ag '67
New scarlet bird in Florida skies. P. A. Zahl. il Nat Geog Mag 132:874-82 D '67
IBO tribe. See Nigeria—Native races
IBSEN, Henrik
Theatre. H. Clurman. Nation 204:156-7 Ja 30 '67
Wild duck; tr. by E. Le Gallienne. Criticism
America 116:265 F 18 '67
Nation 204:156-7 Ja 30 '67
New Yorker 42:69 Ja 21 '67
Sat R 50:48 Ja 28 '67
IBUKA, Masaru
Horatio Alger story, with a Japanese twist. J. L. Schecter. il por N Y Times Mag p56-7+ S 10 '67
ICARUS (asteroid) See Asteroids
ICE
Artistry of ice; with photographs by B. Ratcliffe. H. Borland. il Audubon 69:50-3 Ja '67
Ice nuclei from direct reaction of iodine vapor with vapors from leaded gasoline. A. W. Hogan. Science 158:800 N 10 '67
Metastable superheated ice in liquid-water inclusions under high negative pressure. E. Roedder. bibliog il Science 155:1413-17 Mr 17 '67
Sea ice. il Sci N 92:597 D 16 '67
Temperature-dependence of the polarity of electrical charges on ice crystals. F. K. Odencrantz and R. W. Buecher. bibliog il Science 158:256-7 O 13 '67
See also
Freezing

ICE—*Continued*

Polar Regions

Aluminum-26 and beryllium-10 in Greenland ice. R. McCorkell and others. bibliog il Science 158:1690-2 D 29 '67

Gravity increase at the South Pole. J. C. Behrendt. bibliog il Science 155:1015-17 F 24 '67

Ship of ice; T-3 ice island supports research programs. il Newsweek 70:60 Jl 17 '67

ICE age. See Glacial epochs

ICE boats and ice boating
Build a sail-powered winter skater; summer scooter. il Pop Mech 128:152-3 N '67
Sailing the hardwater at eighty m.p.h. R. Gannon. il Pop Sci 192:134-7 Ja '68

ICE breaking vessels
Arctic trip frozen out; coast guard ships attempting first circumnavigation of the Arctic Ocean. il Sci N 92:273-4 S 16 '67

ICE buckets. See Buckets (pails)

ICE cream, ices, etc.
Fresh-strawberry frost. V. V. Voboril. il Good H 165:124 Ag '67
Fruit sherbets, on the side; with recipes. Sunset 139:109 Jl '67
Ginger ice cream, shakes, sundaes; recipes. Sunset 139:92 Jl '67
Her pleasure is a fruitsicle; with recipes. il Sunset 139:122 S '67
Ice cream fills the pineapple shells; with recipe. il Sunset 138:191 F '67
Ice cream made merry; with recipes. il McCalls 95:130-1+ D '67
Ice creams and ices, homemade and handmade. H. McCully. il House B 109:116-17+ Ag '67
Just add sherbet; with recipes. il Seventeen 26:310-11+ Ag '67
Phony spumoni! il Bet Hom & Gard 45:90 F '67
Playing it cool! il Bet Hom & Gard 45:96-7 Je '67
Prize parfaits. il Bet Hom & Gard 45:89-90 Je '67
Quenching crystals; granite. S. V. Thompson. Vogue 151:151-3+ Ja 1 '68
What's nicer than an ice? J. Hewitt. il N Y Times Mag p58 Ag 6 '67

ICE cubes
Cool comfort. il House & Gard 132:104-5 Jl '67

ICE fishing. See Fishing, Winter

ICE hazards in aviation. See Airplanes—Ice protection

ICE islands. See Ice—Polar Regions

ICE navigation. See Ice breaking vessels

ICE skating. See Skating

ICEBOATS. See Ice boats and ice boating

ICEBREAKERS. See Ice breaking vessels

ICELAND
Civilization
Origin of the Icelanders, by B. Guthmundsson. Review
Sat R 50:41+ Je 10 '67. H. Lundbergh

ICELAND and the United States
President Johnson confers with president of Iceland; exchange of toasts. July 18, 1967. Dept State Bul 57:201-2 Ag 14 '67

ICELANDERS
Origin of the Icelanders, by B. Guthmundsson Review
Sat R 50:41+ Je 10 '67. H. Lundbergh

IDAHO
See also
Camping—Idaho
Fishing—Idaho
Hell's Canyon
Skis and skiing—Idaho
Wilderness areas—Idaho

Description and travel
Idaho's lake country. il Sunset 138:58-63 Je '67

Politics and government
Dove versus a dogcatcher; petition to recall Church. W. B. Furlong. il N Y Times Mag p6-7+ Je 25 '67
Fighting dove; F. Church campaigns against drive for recall election. il Newsweek 69:28-9 Je 5 '67

IDEA files. See Fiction—Technique

IDEALISM
See also
Spirituality

IDEAS
Whatever happened to the great simplicities? importance of simple ideas. H. Read. Sat R 50:21-3+ F 18 '67

IDENTIFICATION
Back from the dead; case of J. Guinn. il Newsweek 70:31A D 4 '67
Cop art. J. Wilson. il Esquire 83:87-9 Jl '67
I hunted twenty years to find my father's killer. W. Lee and B. Lindeman. il Sat Eve Post 240:74-9 Ag 26 '67
Johnny redivivus; confusion over identity of dead soldier. il Time 90:16 D 1 '67
See also
Voiceprints

IDENTIFICATION cards, certificates, etc.
Instant ID cards for tighter security; Clearwater, Fla. J. Stewart. il Am City 82:151 O '67

IDENTIFICATION tags, bracelets, etc.
Correct collar. C. Nansen. il Field & S 72:150-2+ O '67

IDEOLOGY
Ideology and faith: a confrontation. H. Conteris. Christian Cent 84:995-7 Ag 2 '67

IDIOT lights. See Automobiles—Safety devices and measures

IDLEMAN, Peter
America's ski book. Consumer Bul 50:43 D '67
Book review. Consumer Bul 50:18 N '67

IDYLL, C. P.
Pearls of Margarita; reprint. Américas 19:8-14 Ag '67

IERARDI, Gordon S.
Designer's corner. S. Salter. Pub W 191:110+ F 6 '67

IERONYMOS, abp
New primate of Greece. America 116:769-70 My 27 '67
Royal reformation; installed as primate. il por Time 89:80 My 26 '67

IFFT, Edward M.
Science students at Moscow U. Bul Atomic Sci 23:37-40 Ap '67

IGLESIAS, Manuel E.
Night patrol in Brazil. America 116:873-4 Je 24 '67

IGNATOW, David
Exchange; poem. Nation 204:444 Ap 3 '67
For nobody else; poem. Poetry 110:178-9 Je '67
Past reordered. Nation 204:531-2 Ap 24 '67

IGNEOUS rocks. See Rocks, Igneous

IGNITION devices. See Automobile engines—Ignition; Marine engines—Ignition

IGO, John
Books for the new breed; adaptation of address. 1966. Library J 92:1704-5 Ap 15 '67

IGUANAS
Night and the iguana. M. Bates. Natur Hist 76:22-5 D '67
Thermoregulation in the desert iguana dipsosaurus dorsalis. S. M. McGinnis and L. L. Dickson. bibliog il Science 156:1757-9 Je 30 '67; Reply with rejoinder. C. B. DeWitt. 158:809-10 N 10 '67

IGUANODON. See Dinosaurs

IKARD, Frank N.
Speak up to your congressman. Nations Bsns 55:38-9 D '67

IKARIS, Nicholas
Nicholas Ikaris; letter to the editor. F. Deutschendorf. il Américas 19:48 S '67

IKEDA, Masuo
Crazy-quilt composer. por Time 90:64+ Jl 14 '67

IKEGAMI, S. and others
Starfish gonad: action and chemical identification of spawning inhibitor. bibliog Science 158:1052-3 N 24 '67

IKEYA, Kaoru
Another for the amateurs. il por Time 91:37 Ja 12 '68

ILE DU LEVANT (nudist colony) See Nudism

ILEX. See Holly

ILIAD. See Homer

ILLEGAL radio broadcasting stations. See Radio stations, Illegal

ILLEGITIMACY
Abandoned; plight of Negro mixed bloods. il Newsweek 69:50 F 13 '67
Children America forgot; illegitimate children fathered and abandoned by U.S. servicemen in Asia. P. S. Buck. Read Digest 91:108-10 S '67
Japan's rejected; teen-agers fathered by Negro soldiers. E. B. Thompson. il Ebony 22:42-4+ S '67
New group of human beings; Amerasians; mixed-blood children, *konketsuji*. R. Trumbull. il N Y Times Mag p 112-14 Ap 30 '67
Startling story of illegitimate children in U.S. il U S News 63:84-5 O 2 '67
Too many children on relief rolls? U S News 64:7 Ja 1 '68
See also
Mothers, Unmarried

ILLICA, Luigi
Act Puccini never wrote; Act III, the court-yard of La Bohème; text. R. Fellner. Opera N 31:24-7 F 4 '67
ILLINOIS
See also
Architecture, Domestic—Illinois
Booksellers and bookselling—Illinois
Forests and forestry—Illinois
Libraries—Illinois

Description and travel
Illinois: the city and the plain. R. P. Jordan. il Nat Geog Mag 131:745-97 Je '67

Politics and government
Quiet campaign: one state's story. P. Simon. Sat R 50:20 Jl 15 '67

Race problems
200-bev accelerator: moving into a WASP's nest? B. Nelson. il Science 156:1713-16 Je 30 '67
ILLINOIS central railroad company
IC streamlines at the top. il Bsns W p70-2+ O 14 '67
ILLINOIS library association
Dynamic association; letter to the editor. A. Ladenson. Library J 92:507 F 1 '67
ILLINOIS state historical library
Illinois state historical library's collection. R. L. Brubaker. Hobbies 72:109+ Mr '67
ILLINOIS, University
Dance division, University of Illinois; 92nd street Y. D. Hering. Dance Mag 41:66 F '67
Fighting Illini; slush fund for football and basketball players. D. Jenkins. il Sports Illus 26:16-19 Mr 6 '67
Slipping in slush; use of alumni-financed slush fund to support needy athletes. il Time 89:78 Mr 10 '67

Graduate school of library science
Illinois library research center reports trends. Library J 92:3952 N 1 '67
ILLITERACY
Illiteracy: hunger's twin. R. L. Tobin. Sat R 50:16 D 30 '67
Literacy and Ecuador's national development plan. R. Mathias. Sch & Soc 95:84-6 F 4 '67
Literacy programs in Colombia; Books for the people fund, inc. and Laubach literacy, inc; adaptation of report. M. D. Shepard. il Wilson Lib Bul 41:829-33 Ap '67
Third of the world's children; UNESCO chief describes crisis; excerpts from address, October 1967. R. Maheu. Library J 92:4205-6 N 15 '67
Why Juan can read; Mexico's campaign against illiteracy. il Time 90:62 S 8 '67
You're reading, Mr Mitchell! Greenleigh project to test reading systems for adult illiterates. M. W. Clark. NEA J 56:16-19 My '67

ILLUMINATED ceilings. See Ceilings
ILLUMITRAN copying machine. See Photography—Apparatus and supplies
ILLUSIONARY art. See Modernism (art)
ILLUSIONS and hallucinations
See also
Flying saucers
ILLUSTRATED books
Look books. J. H. Plumb. Sat R 50:35-6 N 25 '67
Picture books. J. Low. il Horn Bk 43:715-20 D '67
ILLUSTRATION of books and periodicals
Artist speaks out; with editorial comment. R. J. Lee. il Am Artist 32:38-43+ Ja '68
Aubrey Beardsley master of the line block. il Pub W 191:82-4 Mr 6 '67
Book illustration since 1937. H. C. Pitz. il Am Artist 31:64-71+ Ap '67
Creation of book illustrations; panel discussion. Pub W 191:65-6+ Ap 3 '67
Humor & satire of Susan Perl. J. H. Michel. il Am Artist 32:44-9+ Ja '68
Illustrations of Steven Kidd. H. Gasser. il Am Artist 31:31-43+ Je '67
Illustrator in America; introduction to, and illustrations from book by Walt Reed. N. Rockwell. il Am Artist 31:38-45 Mr '67
In memory of my feelings; illustrations of F. O'Hara's poems. J. Ashbery. Art N 66:50-1+ Ja '68
Letter to an aspiring illustrator. S. Salter. Pub W 191:86 Ap 3 '67

My approach to children's books. A. Dobrin. il Am Artist 31:30-5 Mr '67
On a piece of chalk; illustrations for Thomas Huxley. R. Freund. il Pub W 191:104+ Mr 6 '67
Recollections of an Old West illustrator. L. Bjorklund. il Pub W 192:76-8+ N 6 '67
Sheilah Beckett: classicist. N. Kent. il Am Artist 31:38-44+ Ap '67
Whimsey of Don Madden, a children's book illustrator. J. H. Michel. il Am Artist 31:24-9+ S '67
See also
Newspapers—Illustrations
Picture books for children
ILLUSTRATORS
See also
Beardsley, A. V.
Beckett, S.
Bowler, J.
Erté
Kidd, S R.
Kredel, F
Ness, E.
Rackham, A.
Society of illustrators
ILLYA darling; musical comedy. See Musical comedies, revues, etc.—Criticisms, plots, etc.
I'M in great shape; story. See Fox, W. P.
IMAGINATION
Wondrous reach of imagination; excerpt from address, May 25, 1966. J. Bronowski. Read Digest 91:128-31 S '67
See also
Creation (literary, artistic, etc)
Creative ability
Daydreams
Fairy tales
Fantasy
IMIDAZOLE
Imidazole: fungitoxic derivatives. H. Tolkmith and others. bibliog il Science 158:1462-3 D 15 '67
IMIDES
Chemical modification of yeast alanine-tRNA with a radioactive carbodiimide. S. W. Brostoff and V. M. Ingram. bibliog il Science 158:666-9 N 3 '67
IMINES. See Amines
IMLACH, George
Icy welcome to the NHL. P. Axthem. il Sports Illus 26:22-3 Je 19 '67
IMLER, William A.
Financial aid for the theological student. Christian Cent 84:568+ Ap 26 '67
IMMIGRANTS in Australia
Their shining Eldorado, by E. Huxley. Review
Sat R il 50:30-1 S 9 '67. O. Prescott
What to expect if you emigrate to Australia. il U S News 63:76-7 Jl 17 '67
IMMIGRANTS in Israel
American Jews in Israel, by H. R. Isaacs. Review
New Repub 157:30-2 N 18 '67. E. Grossman
IMMIGRANTS in the United States
Brain drain: foreign aid for U.S; why scientists, engineers, technicians and doctors come here. il U S News 62:78-81 My 22 '67
Brains across the sea. R. Schiller. Read Digest 90:72-6 Mr '67
Cost of the brain drain. W. F. Mondale. Atlan 220:67-9 D '67
See also
Deportation
Italians in the United States
Jews in the United States
IMMIGRATION and emigration
See also
Immigrants in the United States

Australia
See also
Immigrants in Australia

Canada
Boys without a country; U.S. draft dodgers in Canada. O. Clausen. il N Y Times Mag p25+ My 21 '67; Reply with rejoinder. M. Satin. p2 Jl 2 '67
Canada's brain drain eases; skilled craftsman emigration to the U.S. Bsns W p 110 Ap 29 '67
Our draft dodgers in Canada. J. Star. il Look 31:31-3 Mr 7 '67

Cuba
Voyage to doom; excerpts from While six million died. A. D. Morse. il Look 31:59-62+ N 28 '67

IMMIGRATION and emigration—*Continued*

Great Britain

Coming to grips with the color bar in Britain. B. Wenham. New Repub 156:14-15 Ja 28 '67

Italy

See also
Italians in the United States

South Africa

Another vile Vatican plot; Catholic immigrants to South Africa. America 116:713 My 13 '67
New worry for Afrikaners. America 116:171 F 4 '67

Underdeveloped areas

Cost of the brain drain. W. F. Mondale. Atlan 220:67-9 D '67

United States

Brain drain; the sound and the fury. il Sci N 91:255-6 Mr 18 '67
Early dimensions of the new immigration. Mo Labor R 90:III-IV Ap '67
Fewer brains hear U.S.A.'s siren song. il Bsns W p 100+ My 27 '67
Foreign talent heads where the action is. il Bsns W p 196+ S 9 '67
Voyage to doom; excerpts from While six million died. A. D. Morse il Look 31:59-62+ N 28 '67
Wealth attracts talent; taking creative talent from growing societies. R. Jorrin. Nation 204:425-7 Ap 3 '67

See also
Ellis Island

IMMIGRATION and emigration law
New law curtails brain drain. Sci N 92:610 D 23 '67

IMMORAL literature and pictures
Case for pornography is the case for censorship and vice versa. E. Van Den Haag. Esquire 67:134-5 My '67
High court reverses three obscenity convictions, important issue of scienter goes undecided. Pub W 191:41-2 My 22 '67
Landmark decision in the war on pornography; Polly King case in Cincinnati. O. K. Armstrong. Read Digest 91:93-7 S '67
Pause, now, and consider some tentative conclusions about porno-violence. T. Wolfe. Esquire 68:59+ Jl '67
Pornography and violence. I. Younger. Nation 205:120-1+ Ag 14 '67
Public custody of the high pornography; reprint. K Molz. il Library J 92:3373-6 O 1 '67
Smut traffic. il Newsweek 69:29-30 Ap 24 '67
Victory over the smut peddlers; Supreme court ruling. O. K. Armstrong. Read Digest 90:147-8+ F '67
Vom elend der literatur, by W. S. Schlamm. Review
Nat R 19:208-10 F 21 '67. S. J. Tonsor

See also
Obscenity (law)
Sex in literature

Anecdotes, facetiae, satire, etc.

Lament for good old-fashioned smut. J. H. Doolittle. Esquire 67:32+ F '67

IMMORTALITY
Cryonics and the purpose of life. R. C. W. Ettinger. Christian Cent 84:1250-3 O 4 '67; Discussion. 84:1656-8 D 27 '67

See also
Eschatology

IMMUNITY
Immunology: research at Mill Hill institute. N. Calder. Science 157:177-9 Jl 14 '67
Intrinsic immunological tolerance in allophenic mice. B. Mintz and W. K. Silvers. bibliog il Science 158:1484-7 D 15 '67
Mechanism of delayed reactions. S. Leskowitz. bibliog il Science 155:350-2 Ja 20 '67
Solid-phase radioimmunoassay in antibody-coated tubes. K. Catt and G. W. Tregear. bibliog il Science 158:1570-2 D 22 '67

See also
Antigens and antibodies

IMMUNITY, Congressional. See United States—Congress—Privileges and immunities

IMMUNOGLOBULINS. See Serum globulins

IMMUNOLOGY
Cancer and immunology. B. J. Culliton. il Sci N 91:310 Ap 1 '67

IMPERIAL chemical industries, limited
Sirs Paul and Peter. il Time 90:94+ N 17 '67

IMPERIAL hotel. See Tokyo—Hotels, restaurants, etc.

IMPERIAL Russian bonds. See Bonds, Government—Russia

IMPERIALISM
Gloom, gloom, gloom, and scarce one ray of light; excerpts from The anti-imperialists: twelve against empire, 1898-1900. R. L. Beisner. il Am Heritage 18:65-71 Ag '67

IMPLANT biotelemetry. See Biotelemetry

IMPLEMENTS, utensils, etc.
See also
Household appliances
Kitchen utensils
Toilet articles

IMPORT and export controls. See Foreign trade regulation

IMPORT quotas
Department opposes elimination of import quotas on extra long staple cotton; statement, July 12, 1967. E. V. Rostow. Dept State Bul 57:236-9 Ag 21 '67
Misguided protectionism. Life 63:4 N 3 '67
New push for protection; senators asking special-interest protection. il Bsns W p 124-5+ O 21 '67
Price of protectionism; statements, with text of letter, October 18, 1967. Dept State Bul 57:634-52 N 13 '67
Progress achieved in reducing nontariff barriers to trade. Dept State Bul 57:860-1 D 25 '67
Protectionism, a policy of retreat; address, October 30, 1967. N. D. Katzenbach. Dept State Bul 57:686-9 N 20 '67; Same. Vital Speeches 34:119-21 D 1 '67
Trade warriors; Trade expansion act and import quota bills. New Repub 157:5-7 N 11 '67
Uproar over growing imports; a new drive for controls. il U S News 63:56-7 N 13 '67

IMPORT tax. See Tariff

IMPORTS. See Commerce; *also* subhead Commerce under names of countries, e.g. United States—Commerce

IMPOSTORS and imposture
Adult spy goes to high school; L. Tornabene's masquerade to make survey on teenagers. il Life 62:97-8 My 5 '67
Beloved impostor M.D. gives up his practice; F. M. Brant in Groveton, Tex. il Life 64:32-3 Ja 12 '68
Drop-in; parole violator imitates high school student. Newsweek 71:24 Ja 15 '68
Man for the aged; trial of medical director of Berlin's geriatric clinic for imposture. Newsweek 69:56+ Je 5 '67
Médecin malgré lui; case of F. Brant. il Newsweek 70:24-5 D 25 '67
Successful fraud; director of geriatrics clinic in Berlin. il Time 89:54 Je 9 '67

See also
Forgery of works of art
Fraud
Quacks and quackery

IMPRESSIONISM (art)
Impressionist eye; acquisition of C. Monet's La Terrasse. H. Kramer. il N Y Times Mag p28-31 Ja 7 '68
Mark Fisher: an American impressionist. I. M. G. Quimby. il Antiques 91:780-3 Je '67

IMPRIMATUR. See Catholic church—Discipline

IN circles; musical comedy. See Musical comedies, revues, etc.—Criticisms, plots, etc.

IN-flight refueling of helicopters. See Helicopters—Refueling

IN pious memory; story. See Sharp, M.

IN-service teacher education. See Teachers—Education in service

IN Spain there is a saying; story. See Lyons, R.

IN the nick of time; musical comedy. See Musical comedies, revues, etc.—Criticisms, plots, etc.

IN the summer of the valve trombone; story. See Bourjaily, V.

IN transit; story. See Mountzoures, H. L.

INAUGURATIONS
Notes and comment; gubernatorial inaugurations. New Yorker 42:19 Ja 21 '67
Showmanship at Sacramento; California governor's inauguration. Nation 204:100 Ja 23 '67
Time to change the presidential system; months between election day and inauguration. D. Lawrence. U S News 62:124 Mr 13 '67

INBOARD motor boats. See Motor boats

INBOARD-outboard motors. See Marine engines

INCAS
Lost city of the Incas. L. S. De Camp. il Sci Digest 62:68-72 Ag '67

INCAS—*Continued*
Report: Peru's Inca renaissance. G. A. Geyer. Atlan 220:28+ N '67
Visits to vanished cultures. R. Silverberg. Sat R 50:58 N 25 '67

See also
Huari, Peru
Pajaten, Peru

INCENTIVE pay. See Incentives in industry

INCENTIVE taxation. See Taxation—United States

INCENTIVES in industry
Western influences on the U.S.S.R.'s new incentives system. E. Nash. bibliog f Mo Labor R 90:37-40 Ap '67

See also
Profit sharing

INCH, Bert, and Selby, Don
Cape Mendocino crisis. Yachting 122:60+ N '67

INCIDENT at Billy Springs; story. See Moore, H.

INCINERATORS. See Refuse incinerators; Sewage incinerators

INCLINOMETERS. See Measuring instruments

INCOME
Being positive about the negative; negative income tax. il Time 90:99 D 8 '67
Canadian economy and incomes policy; excerpt from Prices, productivity and employment. Mo Labor R 90:55-7 Ap '67
Case for the negative income tax. M. Friedman. Nat R 19:239-40 Mr 7 '67
Coming crisis in welfare; objections to Milton Friedman's negative income tax. H. Hazlitt. Nat R 19:416-18 Ap 18 '67
Diverse $10,000-and-over masses. L. A. Mayer. il Fortune 76:114-17+ D '67
Goal of full employment; excerpt from The guaranteed income. R. Theobald. New Repub 156:15-18 Mr 11 '67
Guaranteed annual incomes; concerning Robert Theobald's views. L. H. Keyserling. New Repub 156:20-3 Mr 18 '67
Guaranteed income; address, March 2, 1967. M. A. Wright. Vital Speeches 33:368-71 Ap 1 '67
Guaranteed income; pro and con. D. E. Hawkins. Parks & Rec 2:45-6+ Mr '67
How to live on an irregular income. L. Lane. Farm J 92:61+ Ja '68
Human values in the computer age: the negative income tax; address, November 30, 1967. A. Miller. Vital Speeches 34:190-2 Ja 1 '68
Income guarantees: a spectrum of opinion. Mo Labor R 90:III-IV F '67
Incomes inch up in 1967; with tables. Bsns W p71-3 Ja 6 '68
Living income, the name of the game. B. L. Masse. America 118:7 Ja 6 '68
Low earners and their incomes. V. C. Perella. il Mo Labor R 90:35-40 My '67
Measure of personal income (title varies) tables. See issues of Business week
Next: equality of incomes? D. Lawrence. U S News 63:96 Jl 3 '67
Pitfalls of guaranteed income. S. A. Levitan. il Reporter 36:12-15 My 18 '67; Reply. L. H. Keyserling. 36:10 Je 15 '67
Push for blue-collar salaries; negotiations for status and security through guaranteed annual wage. il Bsns W p 135-6+ F 25 '67
Should there be a guaranteed annual income for all? pro and con discussion. Sr Schol 91:10-11+ O 26 '67
This month's feature: question of guaranteed annual incomes. Cong Digest 46:225-56 O '67

See also
Gross national product
Retirement income
Royalties
Wages
Wealth, Distribution of

INCOME tax
Why, all other things being equal, it's better to live in Peking than in Reykjavik; mathematical comparison of income-tax laws in forty cities around the world; chart, comp. by A. Wortham. il Esquire 67:110-11 Mr '67

Auditing
See Tax auditing

Capital gains tax
Capital gains provisions may save tax dollars. F. Bailey, jr. Suc Farm 65:31+ Ja '67
Shedding new light on capital gains; IRS study. il Bsns W p90-1 F 11 '67
Surtax: effect on capital gains. U S News 63:96 Ag 21 '67

Collection
See Withholding tax

Deductions
Before you sign your 1967 tax return; common oversights of farm reporting. Farm J 92:56 Ja '68
Family money management. P. Lindberg. Bet Hom & Gard 45:6+ Mr '67
Get ready for the big form 1040 tax battle. P. Lindberg. il Bet Hom & Gard 45:6+ F '67
How trucks and cars may reduce your income tax bill. B. Brantley. Suc Farm 65:70+ Ja '67
Income taxes and children: what parents should know. il Good H 164:202 Mr '67
Income taxes are unfair to us single people. il Changing T 21:13-16 Ag '67; Discussion. 21:31-3 N '67
Income taxes; dont' overlook these deductions. il Good H 164:206 Ap '67
Let your house cut your tax bill. il Changing T 21:39-41 O '67
Money-saving list of tax deductions. B. Brantley. Suc Farm 65:56+ F '67
New tax-free way to invest for your future. Farm J 91:19 F '67
One way to feather the nest; Keogh retirement plan. il Bsns W p 145 N 11 '67
Personal business. Bsns W p 169-70 Mr 18 '67
Personal business; how to save more pay for your pocket. Bsns W p 141-2 Ja 21 '67
Tax break for parents of students? il U S News 62:68 My 1 '67
Tax breaks when you retire. il Changing T 21:27-8 Je '67
Tax credit for donating old clothes. il Good H 165:184 S '67
Tax hints on drought-forced livestock sales. Suc Farm 65:97 F '67
Tax time is coming. get ready. il Changing T 22:17-18 Ja '68
Taxman loseth: value of a triptych donated to the Houston museum of fine arts by Mrs S. C. Blaffer. il Time 89:49 Mr 3 '67
Tips to save you tax trouble. il Changing T 21:24-6 Ap '67
Ways to lower the tax bite when you sell a farm. N. E. Harl. Suc Farm 65:60+ Mr '67
Ways to save on your taxes; steps you can take now. il U S News 63:106-8 N 27 '67
Your friendly Internal revenue service invites you to live it up in Europe, almost free; business travel is tax deductible. R. Joseph. Esquire 69:106-7+ Ja '68
Your income tax. il Changing T 21:21-3 Mr '67
Your income tax; questions and answers. il Changing T 21:13-15 F '67

See also
Amortization deductions
Expense accounts (business)
Tax planning

Anecdotes, facetiae, satire, etc.
Fringe benefits. W. K. Zinsser. il Horizon 9:120 Spr '67

Expenses
Tax man cometh; dancers' income tax. R. Gorewitz. il Dance Mag 41:26-7 Ag '67

Forms
See Tax forms

Returns
See Tax returns

United States
Alleviation of poverty; excerpt from Capitalism and freedom. M. Friedman. Nat R 19:240-1 Mr 7 '67
Coming in 1968: biggest pension boost ever? il U S News 63:113-14+ N 20 '67
Coming in strong for a tax hike; need for surcharge. il Bsns W p 16-17 Jl 1 '67
Fiscal trickery: effect of proposed tax. M. Friedman. il Newsweek 70:71 Ag 28 '67
LBJ tax plan that is going unnoticed; social security pensions. il U S News 62:84-5 F 13 '67
LBJ's tax dilemma. E. L. Dale, jr. New Repub 156:8-10 Ap 1 '67
New plan for a tax increase. il U S News 63:78-80 Jl 10 '67
Newest plan to boost pensions and payroll taxes; social security pensions. il U S News 63:84-6 Ag 14 '67
Outlook for a boost in pensions, and in taxes to pay them. U S News 63:111 N 13 '67

INCOME tax—United States—*Continued*
   Senators speed investment credit; vote to restore 7 per cent tax allowance but question the 6 per cent surtax. il Bsns W p48+ Mr 25 '67
   Should we raise the income tax? Nat R 19: 1156 O 31 '67
   That tax boost, a reprieve? il Newsweek 70: 60+ Ag 28 '67
   Tighter squeeze ahead on middle incomes. il U S News 63:29-31 Ag 28 '67
   To tax and to please; address, December 15, 1966. S. S. Cohen. Vital Speeches 33:268-72 F 15 '67
   Tug-of-war ties up the tax bill; Ways & means halts 10 per cent tax surcharge. Bsns W p46 O 7 '67
   Unfair tax rates. R. Moley. Newsweek 69: 108 F 6 '67
   What the taxpayers say. U S News 63:31 O 16 '67
   Why LBJ tax plan is in trouble. il U S News 63:86-7 Ag 28 '67
     See also
   Tax evasion
L'INCORONAZIONE di Poppea; opera. See Monteverdi, C.
INCORPORATED farms. See Farms, Incorporated
INCREASE of population. See Population, Increase of
INDANEDIONE
   2-Dicyanomethylene-1,3-indanedione: a new electron acceptor. S. Chatterjee. bibliog il Science 157:314-16 Jl 21 '67
INDECENT assault
   Crucible case; teacher exonerated of molesting charge. Newsweek 70:33 S 25 '67
   Drama at Baldwin high; investigation of teacher charged with molesting girl. il Newsweek 70:65-6 S 18 '67
   Question of conduct; accusations of molestation against teacher. il Time 90:52 S 15 '67
INDECENT exposure
   Bare majority; decisions on obscenity and indecent exposure. il Newsweek 69:42+ My 22 '67
INDEPENDENT grocers' alliance of America
   Supermarket gives the women an inning; ladies fairs, sponsored by Wetterau foods, inc, in Ark. and Mo. il Bsns W p66-8 Ap 29 '67
INDEPENDENT moving picture producers. See Moving picture production and direction
INDEPENDENT regulatory commissions
   Regulating federal regulators: agencies face increasingly complex decisions. il Bsns W p24-5 Ja 13 '68
INDEPENDENT television authority. See Television broadcasting—Great Britain
INDEX numbers
   Measurements of sampling error in the CPI. M. Wilkerson. il Mo Labor R 90:47-8 N '67
INDEXES
   Making of an index; how to reminisce while name-dropping. J. O'Brien. Sat R 50:126-7 O 14 '67
   Trade winds; lack of uniformity in reference book indexes. H. R. Mayes. il Sat R 50: 10+ Ap 29 '67
     See also
   Education index
   Science citation index
INDIA
   Two decades of independence. il Time 90:26+ Ag 25 '67
     See also
   Agricultural administration—India
   Airlines—India
   Americans in India
   Atomic research—India
   Bihar
   Birth control—India
   Bombay
   Childrens literature—India
   Costume—India
   Education—India
   Elections—India
   English in India
   Famines—India
   Festivals—India
   Food relief—India
   Food supply—India
   Foreign investments (by India)
   Kashmir
   Missions—India
   Moving pictures—India
   Ootacamund
   Political campaigns—India
   Political crimes and offenses—India
   Prohibition—India
   Rites and ceremonies
   Science—India
   Sikkim
   Taj Mahal
   Youth—India

Architecture
   See also
Taj Mahal

Cabinet
   Mrs Gandhi's headaches. N. J. Nanporia. New Repub 157:8-9 S 16 '67

Civilization
   Vivid variety of India. L. Van Der Post. il Holiday 42:82-3+ N '67

Description and travel
   Ageless mosaic of India. L. Van Der Post. il Holiday 42:38-47+ O '67
   Reporter at large. V. Mehta. New Yorker 43: 50-2+ S 9 '67
   South India. E. R. Mayhew. il Travel 128: 39-41 D '67

Economic conditions
   Accent on pragmatics. Time 89:25 Mr 24 '67
   India adrift. K. Bhatia. For Affairs 45:652-61 Jl '67
   New hope for India, but: still a nation on the brink. il U S News 63:74-6 S 4 '67
     See also
   Famines—India

Economic policy
   India's gigantic effort at modernization. R. L. Strout. New Repub 157:12 D 23 '67

Foreign relations
   Indian-Pakistani relations. R. N. Berkes. bibliog il Cur Hist 52:289-94+ My '67

     China (People's Republic)
   Delegation of donkeys; diplomats expelled from Peking and New Delhi. R. Ramanujam. il Newsweek 70:44 Jl 3 '67

     Middle East
   Out of balance; criticism of government's pro-Arab stand. il Newsweek 69:46 Je 26 '67

Hindu-Muslim relations
   See also
   Cows in religion, folklore, etc.

History
   Its beauty veils a Mogul's ruthless whim. W. A. McWhirter. il Life 63:60+ N 3 '67

Industries
   Gold in the hills; sacrificial hair used for wigmaking. il Newsweek 69:62 Je 26 '67

Languages
   Tower of Babel; Foreign minister resigns over language policy. Newsweek 70:53 S 18 '67

Native races
   Profiles; Todas of Ootacamund. M. Panter-Downes. il New Yorker 43:48-50+ Mr 4 '67

Native states
   India's opposition scents power. S. Rajan. il Reporter 36:35-8 Ap 20 '67
   Opposition maneuvers. Time 89:40 Ap 21 '67
   Steady decline of New Delhi's authority; dissidents form coalition governments. S. Rajan. il Reporter 37:30-3 O 19 '67

Nobility
   End of the maharajas; post-1947 scene. F. Levine. Atlan 219:112-14+ Ap '67
   It's beauty veils a Mogul's ruthless whim. W. A. McWhirter. il Life 63:60+ N 3 '67
   Princes or paupers? Newsweek 70:45 S 4 '67

Politics and government
   Battle royal; in Madhya Pradesh. il Time 90: 21-2 Jl 28 '67
   Communist Brahmin; Communist government in Kerala. E. Behr. Newsweek 69:54 Mr 20 '67
   Crown of thorns. il Newsweek 69:65-6 Mr 27 '67
   Defeat for astrology; Zakir Husain elected president. Newsweek 69:59 My 22 '67
   Faltering India of Indira Gandhi. U S News 62:22 Mr 27 '67
   India adrift. K. Bhatia. For Affairs 45:652-61 Jl '67
   India campaigns: cows, corruption & demonstrations. L. I. Rudolph and S. H. Rudolph. il Nation 204:138-43 Ja 30 '67
   India's post-election fury; with report by D. Moser. il Life 62:22-9 Mr 24 '67
   Karma of Morarji Desai. J. Lelyveld. il N Y Times Mag p30-1+ S 24 '67

INDIA—Politics and government—*Continued*
Me-tooism, here, too. P. C. Jain. Nat R 19: 129+ F 7 '67
New hope for India, but: still a nation on the brink. il U S News 63:74-6 S 4 '67
Perils of India. H. Brandon. Sat R 50:56 N 4 '67
Plague of unrest. il Time 90:36 D 8 '67
Temporary triumph; Mrs Gandhi's choice of a presidential candidate. Newsweek 69:52 Ap 24 '67
Victory for good sense; Moslem elected for first time to the presidency. il Time 89:35 My 19 '67
Victory for Indira. Time 89:31 Mr 17 '67
See also
Elections—India
India—Cabinet
India—Hindu-Muslim relations
India—Native states
Political parties—India

Population
See also
Birth control—India

Religious institutions and affairs
World around us (cont) Christian Cent 84: 1202-3, 1635-6 S 20, D 20 '67
See also
Catholics in India
Missions—India
Sadhus

Riots
India's post-election fury; with report by D. Moser. il Life 62:22-9 Mr 24 '67

Social conditions
Indian national character in the twentieth century. D. Narain. bibliog f il Ann Am Acad 370:124-32 Mr '67
Too many people, is India facing disaster? interview. S. Chandrasekhar. il U S News 62:90-3 Ap 3 '67
See also
Women—India

Social history
Living prehistory in India. D. D. Kosambi. il Sci Am 216:104-12+ F '67

Social life and customs
Reporter at large. V. Mehta. New Yorker 43: 50-2+ S 9 '67
See also
Women—India
INDIA and Great Britain
See also
Great Britain—Foreign opinion—Indian
INDIA hawthorn. See Hawthorns
INDIA-Pakistan dispute. See Kashmir
INDIAN agencies. See Indians of North America—Reservations
INDIAN art (East Indian) See Art, Indian (East Indian)
INDIAN baskets. See Indians of North America—Basket making
INDIAN citizen; story. See Jhabvala, R. P.
INDIAN cookery (East Indian) See Cookery, Indian (East Indian)
INDIAN dancing (East Indian)   See Dancing, Indian (East Indian)
INDIAN elephants. See Elephants
INDIAN Head, Incorporated
Medicine man at Indian Head: R. W. Lear. il Bsns W p84+ Ag 19 '67
INDIAN music (East Indian) See Music, Indian (East Indian)
INDIAN musicians (East Indian) See Musicians, Indian (East Indian)
INDIAN OCEAN
Now a new ocean for U.S. to defend. il U S News 63:32-3 Ag 28 '67
Sunset; power vacuum of the Indian Ocean. J. Burnham. Nat R 19:843 Ag 8 '67
See also
International Indian Ocean expedition

Maps
Science explores the monsoon sea. S. W. Matthews. il Nat Geog Mag 132:554-75, sup (folded map) O '67
INDIAN painting (East Indian) See Painting, Indian (East Indian)
INDIAN pipes (plants)
Nature note; Indian pipe. il Sci N 91:243 Mr 11 '67

INDIAN poetry (East Indian)
Translations into English
Exile of Rama; excerpt, tr. by C. Rajagopalachari. Kamban. il UNESCO Courier 20: 30-1+ D '67
INDIAN relics. See Indians of North America—Antiquities
INDIAN reservations. See Indians of North America—Reservations
INDIAN rice. See Wild rice
INDIAN RIVER
River that isn't a river. K. Ferguson. il Motor B 120:34+ O '67
INDIAN schools. See Indians of North America—Education
INDIAN traders
Indian takes a look at the white man, and is not impressed. il Life 63:56-7 D 1 '67
INDIAN turnip. See Jack-in-the-pulpits
INDIAN weddings (East Indian) See Marriage customs and rites
INDIAN women. See Indians of North America—Women
INDIANA
See also
Fishing—Indiana
Libraries—Indiana

Description and travel
Overlooked Indiana. D. E. Steinmeier. il Travel 127:28-33 Je '67
INDIANA tornado. See Tornadoes
INDIANA. University, Bloomington
Punt, John, punt! undefeated Hoosiers. D. Jenkins. il Sports Illus 27:28-31 N 13 '67
Who says college kids have changed? G. Moore. il Life 62:90-90B+ My 19 '67
INDIANAPOLIS

Clowes memorial hall for the performing arts
Culture comes to Indianapolis. R. Gover. il N Y Times Mag p6-7+ D 24 '67

Music
Indianapolis; Sarah Caldwell and American national opera company opened at Clowes Hall. R. D. Daniels. il Opera N 32:22-3 O 14 '67

Newspapers
Crusading in Indianapolis; News editor leads Anti-crime crusade. il Time 89:38+ Je 23 '67
INDIANAPOLIS automobile races. See Automobile racing
INDIANAPOLIS public library
Indianapolis p.l. report; county expansion works. Library J 93:140 Ja 15 '68
INDIANS
Art
See also
Indians of North America—Art
Totem poles
Education
See also
Indians of North America—Education
INDIANS (of India) See East Indians
INDIANS in art
Bright vignettes of a lost world; paintings of N. Point. Life 63:52-9 D 1 '67
INDIANS of Brazil. See Indians of South America—Brazil
INDIANS of Canada.   See Indians of North America—Canada
INDIANS of Central America

Antiquities
Costa Rica
Riddle of Costa Rica's jungle spheres; reprint. J. O. Harrison. il Sci Digest 61:14-16 Je '67
INDIANS of Mexico
Chamula life. N. Modiano. il Natur Hist 77: 58-63 Ja '68
Oldest paintings in the Americas; Juxtlahuaca cave discoveries by C. E. T. Gay and G. Griffin. il Life 62:107-8+ My 12 '67
See also
Mayas

Antiquities
Ancient apartments; buildings of three stories at Arcelia. E. Zubryn. Sci N 92:106 Jl 29 '67
Indium as an impurity in ancient western Mexican tin and bronze artifacts and in local tin ore. E. R. Caley and D. T. Easby, jr. bibliog Science 155:686-7 F 10 '67

INDIANS of Mexico—Antiquities—*Continued*
Oldest paintings of the New World; Juxtlahuaca cave, Mexico. C. T. E. Gay. il Natur Hist 76:28-35 Ap '67
Olmec civilization, Veracruz, Mexico: dating of the San Lorenzo phase. M. D. Coe and others. bibliog il Science 155:1399-401 Mr 17 '67
Secrets of the people of the jaguar; first great civilization in the Americas, the Olmecs. J. Reinert. il Sci Digest 62:6-12 S '67
See also
Mayas
Sculpture, Pre-Columbian
Teotihuacán, Mexico

Art

Oldest paintings in the Americas; Juxtlahuaca cave discoveries by C. E. T. Gay and G. Griffin. il Life 62:107-8+ My 12 '67

Culture

Farming systems and political growth in ancient Oaxaca. K. V. Flannery and others. bibliog il Science 158:445-54 O 27 '67

Social life and customs

Death in Chamula. P. Menget. il Natur Hist 77:48-57 Ja '68

INDIANS of North America
Cerumen in American Indians: genetic implications of sticky and dry types. N. L. Petrakis and others. bibliog il Science 158: 1192-3 D 1 '67
See also
Association on American Indian affairs, incorporated
Comanche Indians
Cree Indians
Crow Indians
Dakota Indians
Eskimos
Iroquois Indians
Kiowa Indians
Mandan Indians
Navaho Indians
Nez Percé Indians
Seminole Indians
Taos Indians

Antiquities

Eastern North American archaeology: a summary. J. B. Griffin. bibliog il Science 156: 175-91 Ap 14 '67
Eastern woodland culture area. C. Miles. il Hobbies 72:112-13+ Ag; 110+ S '67
Salvage archeology in the Missouri River basin. W. R. Wedel. bibliog il Science 156: 589-97 My 5 '67

Alaska

Alaska's vanishing art (cont) K. Kuh. Sat R 50:23+ Mr 25 '67

Arizona

Boom... C. Foley. il Am For 73:4+ Mr '67
See also
Hohokam culture

California

Indian mound is excavated by high school archaeologists; ed. by C. L. Stong. T. J. O'Neil. il Sci Am 217:134-8 D '67

New York (state)

Dig to antiquity in your own back yard. R. J. Graham. il Sci Digest 62:55-9 Jl '67

Art

Alaska's vanishing art (cont) K. Kuh. Sat R 50:23+ Mr 25 '67
Indian takes a look at the white man, and is not impressed. il Life 63:56-7 D 1 '67
See also
Institute of American Indian art, Santa Fe

Basket making

Indian basketry. C. Miles. Hobbies 72:112-13 Ja '68

Boats

Native American water craft. C. Miles. il Hobbies 72:109-11 O '67

Culture

Bright vignettes of a lost world; with report by R. Richman. il Life 63:52-66+ D 1 '67
California culture areas. C. Miles. il Hobbies 72:112-13+ Ap; 112-13+ My; 112-14+ Je '67
Eastern North American archaeology: a summary. J. B. Griffin. bibliog il Science 156: 175-91 Ap 14 '67

Record of the vanished West. D. McNickle. il Nation 205:692-3 D 25 '67
Southwest Indian culture area. C. Miles. il Hobbies 71:112-14 F; 72:112-13 Mr '67
See also
Hohokam culture

Dances

Adventure into a celestial sphere; Santo Domingo Indians annual corn dance. W. Terry. il Sat R 50:40-1 S 2 '67
Four moons; Oklahoma Indian ballerina festival. W. Terry. il Sat R 50:60-1+ N 18 '67
With old ritual and modern dance, a heritage comes to life. il Life 63:62-5 D 1 '67
See also
Indians of North America—Rites and ceremonies

Dwellings

See also
Cliff dwellers and cliff dwellings

Economic conditions

Forgotten American is aiding himself; antipoverty programs on the Rosebud Sioux reservation. il U S News 63:66-7 O 2 '67
Indian uprising for civil rights. H. Bims. il Ebony 22:64-5+ F '67

Education

Fifteen little Indians: Westinghouse computer project on Menominee reservation, Wisconsin. New Repub 156:6 Je 17 '67; Reply. A. C. Turner. 157:34-5 Jl 1 '67
Good day at Rough Rock; Navajo demonstration school. P. Conklin. il Am Ed 3:4-9 F '67
Indian education. Sci N 91:520 Je 3 '67
Indian education: ferment. P. McBroom. il Sci N 92:13 Jl 1 '67
Learning to be Navaho-Americans: innovation at Rough Rock; demonstration school E. Fuchs. il Sat R 50:82-4+ S 16 '67
Very small happening at Forty Mile Bend; Fla. A. Hurwitz. il NEA J 56:71-2 S '67
See also
Institute of American Indian art, Santa Fe

Government relations

Dead horse walks again; report of pending legislation. D. McNickle. Nation 205:677-8 D 25 '67
Dispatch from Wounded Knee; Pine Ridge reservation, S.D. C. Kentfield. il N Y Times Mag p28-31+ O 15 '67
Indian and the law. il Sr Schol 90:5 F 17 '67
Indian uprising for civil rights. H. Bims. il Ebony 22:64-5+ F '67
They talk about freedom; ed. by E. Miller. B. Sainte-Marie. il Seventeen 26:150-1+ Ap '67
See also
Indians of North America—Land tenure
Indians of North America—Reservations
United States—Indian affairs, Bureau of

Hunting

Poor animals! what a slaughter! poor Indians! il Life 63:58-9 D 1 '67

Implements

See also
Arrowheads

Industries

See also
Indians of North America—Basket making

Land tenure

National council champions Taos Pueblo Indians; restoration of land to Indians. Christian Cent 84:932 Jl 19 '67

Legal status, laws, etc.

See Indians of North America—Government relations

Missions

See also
Jesuits—Missions

Religion and mythology

Deity and the Indians. C. Miles. Hobbies 72:112-13 Jl '67

Reservations

Deadly windfall; Navajo tribe suffers from snowfall. il Time 91:23 Ja 5 '68
Dispatch from Wounded Knee; Pine Ridge reservation, S.D. C. Kentfield. il N Y Times Mag p28-31+ O 15 '67
Forgotten American is aiding himself; antipoverty programs on the Rosebud Sioux reservation. il U S News 63:66-7 O 2 '67

INDIANS of North America—Reservations—
Continued
Reporter at large; wild rice harvest at Lower
Rice Lake, in the White Earth Chippewa
Indian reservation. Minn. B. Roueché. il
New Yorker 43:34-8+ D 23 '67
Reservations please! motels and lodges for
paleface visitors. G. S. Wells. il Travel 127:
32-7 Mr '67
Swim in a pool, sleep in a teepee; Warm
Springs reservation, Oregon. il Sunset 138:
34+ Je '67

Rites and ceremonies
O-kee-pa; excerpts, with editorial comment.
G. Catlin. il Am Heritage 18:30-7+ O '67
Two Leggings: the making of a Crow war-
rior, by P. Nabokov. Review
  Am Heritage 18:80-2 O '67. B. Catton
See also
Indians of North America—Dances

Social conditions
American Indian today: out in the cold? il
Sr Schol 90:3-6+ F 17 '67
Changing world of the Cree. N. A. Chance.
il Natur Hist 76:16-23 My '67
Indian—America's unfinished business, comp.
by W. A. Brophy and S. D. Aberle. Review
  Commonweal 86:182 Ap 28 '67. L. T.
  King; Reply with rejoinder. M. L. Wax.
  86:307+ Je 2 '67
Warpaint for the senator's wife; L. Harris
of Oklahoma. C. Mangel. il Look 31:24-9
Ap 4 '67

Social life and customs
See also
Indians of North America—Dances

Trading posts
Navajos have traded here for ninety-one
years; Hubbell trading post national historic site. il Sunset 139:26 O '67

Transportation
See also
Indians of North America—Boats

Wars
See also
Beecher Island, Battle of, 1868
Little Big Horn, Battle of the, 1876
Wounded Knee Creek, Battle of, 1890

Women
Moon maidens; five part Indian ballerinas. il
Newsweek 70:101-2 N 6 '67

Canada
Changing world of the Cree; Algonquian-
speaking Cree Indians of the Mistassini and
Waswanipi bands. N. A. Chance. il Natur
Hist 76:16-23 My '67
Northern education program; pre-university
education system for residents of the
Northwest territories and Eskimos in
northern Quebec. il Sch & Soc 95:104-5
F 18 '67

INDIANS of South America
Yanomamö social organization and warfare.
N. A. Chagnon. il Natur Hist 76:44-8
bibliog (p69) D '67

Antiquities
Early man in South America. E. P. Lan-
ning and T. C. Patterson. il Sci Am 217:
44-50 bibliog(p 154) N '67
Visits to vanished cultures. R. Silverberg.
Sat R 50:58 N 25 '67
See also
Sculpture, Pre-Columbian

Ecuador
Did Japanese fishermen bring the art of
pottery making to Ecuador 5,000 years ago?
similarity of patterns between Jomon and
Valdivia pottery. B. J. Meggers. il UNESCO
Courier 20:12-13 My '67

Peru
Quishqui Puncu: a preceramic site in highland Peru. T. F. Lynch. bibliog il Science
158:780-3 N 10 '67

Brazil
Dawn people; Kalapalo Indians. il Life 63:40-
46D D 22 '67

Colombia
Andean Indian programme in Colombia;
photographs. UN Mo Chron 4:77-84 My '67
INDIC poetry. See Indian poetry (East Indian)

INDICATORS
Sensitive low-cost indicators. J. L. Beiswen-
ger. il Pop Electr 27:49-50+ Jl '67
INDIGESTION. See Digestive system—Dis-
eases
INDIUM
Indium variations in a petrologic suite of
L-group chondrites. S. N. Tandon and J. T.
Wasson. bibliog il Science 158:259-61 O 13
'67
INDIVIDUAL and society
Another three Rs: the development of the
individual; address, September 13, 1967. J.
A. Howard. Vital Speeches 34:18-22 O 15
'67
Challenge for free men in a mass society;
with report by B. Hooper. il Life 62:60-74+
Ap 21 '67
Company president is a Berkeley student. H.
J. Leavitt. Harvard Bsns R 45:152-4+ N
'67
Frustrating warfare of business; with report
by C. Argyris. il Life 62:40-53+ My 5 '67
Individual and the good technological socie-
ty; address, June 9, 1967. S. Ramo. Vital
Speeches 33:646-8 Ag 15 '67
Search for purpose. il Life 62:66-79 Ap 28 '67
To talk of many things; address, April 5.
1967. H. F. Heller. Vital Speeches 33:697-
700 S 1 '67
Toward a communal society. D. Bell. il Life
62:112-14+ My 12 '67
Where is biology taking us? excerpts from
address, October 1966. R. S. Morison.
Science 155:429-33 Ja 27 '67; Discussion. 156:
11 Ap 7 '67
INDIVIDUAL and state
Deciding careers with the club of induction.
A. V. Krebs, jr. Commonweal 86:468-9 Jl 28
'67
End of the social contract. N. Cousins. Sat R
50:24 O 28 '67
Policy and the people. N. A. Rockefeller. For
Affairs 46:231-41 Ja '68
Political illusion. by J. Ellul. Review
  Nat R 19:755-7 Jl 11 '67. A. Lejeune
  Sat R 50:27-8 Ap 29 '67. S. K. Padover
Power in America, by D. T. Bazelon. Review
  Harper 234:112-13 My '67. E. Larrabee
  Sat R 50:28-9 Ap 29 '67. H. Kohn
Responsibilities of national greatness; a citi-
zen's obligations and the bepuzzlements of
identification. K. Burke. il Nation 205:46-50
Jl 17 '67
What ails America? withering away of the
public's trust in government. H. J.
Morgenthau. New Repub 157:17-21 O 28 '67
INDIVIDUAL differences
See also
Sex differences
INDIVIDUAL instruction
Sophocles and the sixth graders. D. Broden.
NEA J 56:15 N '67
INDIVIDUAL liberty. See Liberty
INDIVIDUALISM
Case for individual man in the educational
environment. J. Van Patten. Sch & Soc 95:
231-2 Ap 1 '67
Hang-loose ethic; excerpts from It's happen-
ing. J. L. Simmons and B. Winograd. NEA
J 56:18-20+ O '67
Limits of individualism. A. Nevins. Sat R
50:25-7+ N 25 '67
See also
Conformity
Individual and state
INDIVIDUALITY
See also
Personality
INDOCHINA, FRENCH

History
Civil war, 1946-1954
Hell in a very small place: the siege of Dien
Bien Phu. by B. Fall. Review
  Sat R 50:31-3 F 18 '67. D. Schoenbrun
War that might not have been: possible out-
come of American help at Dienbienphu in
1954. il Time 89:17 F 10 '67

Civil war, 1946-1954—Peace
and mediation
See also
Council of foreign ministers, Geneva, 1954
INDOCTRINATION
See also
Brainwashing
Propaganda in the schools
INDOLEACETIC acid
Indoleacetic acid oxidase activity of apoper-
oxidase. B. Z. Siegel and A. W. Galston.
bibliog il Science 157:1557-9 S 29 '67

INDOLEACETIC acid—*Continued*
Separation of transit of auxin from uptake:
average velocity and reversible inhibition
by anaerobic conditions. M. H. M. Gold-
smith. bibliog il Science 156:661-3 My 5 '67
INDONESIA
Indonesia: poor people in a rich land; first-
hand report. J. N. Wallace. il U S News 63:
50-4 D 25 '67
See also
Bali
Chinese in Indonesia
Justice, Administration of—Indonesia
Missions—Indonesia
Zoology—Indonesia

Economic conditions
Firmer hand. il Time 90:36 O 20 '67
Indonesia after Sukarno. D. Warner. il Re-
porter 36:34-7 Je 15 '67

Foreign population
See also
Chinese in Indonesia

Politics and government
As the trap closes on Indonesia's Sukarno.
U S News 62:20 F 27 '67
Blossoming of Pak Harto. il Time 90:39 N 17
'67
Building pressure. Time 89:26 F 24 '67
Bung Karno at bay. D. Warner. il Reporter
36:41-4 F 9 '67
End in view; Sukarno signs over all govern-
mental authority to General Suharto. il
Newsweek 69:48-9 Mr 6 '67
End of the line for Sukarno? il Sr Schol 90:16
Mr 10 '67
Fall of Sukarno, by T. Vittachi. Review
Nation 205:217-19 S 11 '67. A. Josey
Indonesia after Sukarno. D. Warner. il Re-
porter 36:34-7 Je 15 '67
Indonesia wobbles toward recovery. G. R.
Packard, 3d. il N Y Times Mag p34-5+ O 1
'67
New order. il Time 89:25-6 Mr 24 '67
Now he's going, now he isn't. Time 89:31-2
Mr 3 '67
On trial. M. Parker. il Newsweek 70:44-5 Ag
28 '67
Promise in Indonesia. A. Malik. For Affairs
46:292-303 Ja '68
Report. J. Hughes. Atlan 220:20+ D '67
Strong-man Suharto's job: to rebuild the
nation that Sukarno wrecked. il U S News
62:14+ Mr 6 '67
Thousand cuts. il Newsweek 69:65 Mr 27 '67
Toward a new order in Indonesia. G. J.
Pauker. For Affairs 45:503-19 Ap '67
See also
Anti-Communist movements—Indonesia
Presidents—Indonesia

Religious institutions and affairs
World around us. Christian Cent 84:449-50
Ap 5 '67
Social life and customs
Villages in Indonesia, ed. by Koentjaranin
grat. Review
Sat R 50:39 Ag 5 '67. W. Guzzardi, ji
INDOOR archery. See Archery
INDOOR games. See Games
INDOOR gardening. See House plants; Window
gardening
INDOOR gardens. See Gardens, Indoor
INDOOR golf. See Golf, Indoor
INDOOR greenhouses. See Greenhouses, Minia-
ture
INDOOR track. See Track athletics
INDULGENCES
Indulgent about indulgences. Christian Cent
84:524-5 Ap 26 '67
INDUSTRIAL arts
See also
Ironwork
INDUSTRIAL buildings
Building types study. il Arch Rec 141:151-66
Ja '67
Four buildings for business. il Arch Rec 141:
165-70 Je '67
Industrial-commercial building: survey indi-
cates '68 gain. G. A. Christie. il Arch Rec
142:83 D '67
See also
Factories
INDUSTRIAL chaplains. See Chaplains, In-
dustrial
INDUSTRIAL clothing. See Clothing and dress
—Work clothes

INDUSTRIAL conferences. See Business con-
ferences
INDUSTRIAL control. See Industry and state
INDUSTRIAL cooperation
East-West business cooperation; a new
approach to Communist Europe. E. Benoit.
New Repub 156:21-3 F 18 '67
Timidity slowing technological decisions;
European aerospace cooperative programs.
H. J. Coleman. il Aviation W 86:94-5+ My
29 '67
INDUSTRIAL design. See Design, Industrial
INDUSTRIAL designers. See Designers
INDUSTRIAL development bonds. See Bonds,
Industrial development
INDUSTRIAL diamonds. See Diamonds, Indus-
trial
INDUSTRIAL diseases. See Diseases, Indus-
trial
INDUSTRIAL diversification. See Diversifica-
tion in industry
INDUSTRIAL education
Our obsolete welfare state; address, October
29, 1967. G. Champion. Vital Speeches 34:
113-14 D 1 '67
See also
Apprentices
Employees—Training
Trade schools
INDUSTRIAL efficiency. See Efficiency, Indus-
trial
INDUSTRIAL employment. See Employment
INDUSTRIAL espionage. See Spies, Industrial
INDUSTRIAL expansion
New world of industry. il Fortune 76:118-27
S 15 '67
See also
Capital investments
INDUSTRIAL forecasting. See Business fore-
casting
INDUSTRIAL forestry. See Forest management
INDUSTRIAL hygiene
Industry doctors try new approach; environ-
mental health. il Bsns W p80-2+ My 13 '67
INDUSTRIAL hygienists. See Health workers
INDUSTRIAL location. See Location in business
and industry
INDUSTRIAL management and organization
Business bites down on its inventories; Busi-
ness week survey of top purchasing agents.
il Bsns W p30-1 Ja 21 '67
Competitive innovation, key to progress; ex-
cerpts from address, July 13, 1967. F. G.
Donner. Nations Bsns 55:68-9 S '67
How a publisher can help improve manu-
facturing. L. Shatzkin. Pub W 192:68+ Ag
7 '67
Manuals of press set-up and work; charts and
procedure guides for university presses. Pub
W 192:29-30 Jl 3 '67
Production planning: a publisher speaks. L.
Shatzkin. Pub W 191:84+ My 1 '67
See also
Business intelligence
Business management and organization
Collective bargaining
Efficiency, Industrial
Factory management
Grievance procedures
Industrial relations
Inventories
Labor productivity
Personnel management

Study and teaching
See also
Harvard university—Graduate school of busi-
ness administration

Czechoslovakia
Rickety Czech new model. C. Sterling. il Reporter 36:22-4 Je 1 '67

Europe, Western
Management gap in Europe. Life 63:4 N 24 '67

France
Profit sharing for France. America 117:106 Jl
29 '67

Russia
Ivan looks to western ways; economy to adopt
capitalistic techniques. il Bsns W p86+
Ap 29 '67
New slogan for bosses: profit or perish. il
Life 63:60-1+ N 10 '67
INDUSTRIAL materials. See Materials
INDUSTRIAL mobilization
Industry passes the ammunition. il Bsns W
p66-8+ Je 24 '67

INDUSTRIAL organization. See Industrial management and organization

INDUSTRIAL photography. See Photography in industry

INDUSTRIAL plants. See Factories

INDUSTRIAL products. See Commercial products

INDUSTRIAL psychology. See Psychology, Industrial

INDUSTRIAL publicity
What is littature? A. C. Van Dine. Sat R 50:4+ Ap 22 '67

INDUSTRIAL recreation
Industrial recreation. D. L. Neer. Parks & Rec 2:79 Ap '67
Small industry provides summer recreation. J. R. Coffey and R. Renaux. il Parks & Rec 2:33-4 Je '67

INDUSTRIAL relations
Big business, big labor and big government; and still growing. il Sr Schol 90:4-8+ Ap 7 '67
Comparison of industrial and race conflict. I. Bernstein. Mo Labor R 90:39-40 Jl '67
Development of labor law in 1966. G. C. Smith. Mo Labor R 90:12-17 F '67
Developments in industrial relations. See issues of Monthly labor review
Gap in labor-management relations; interview, ed. by T. J. Murray. H. Van Arsdale. il Duns R 90:29-30+ Jl '67
Labor crisis. T. J. Murray. il Duns R 89:42-4+ Je '67
Labor management relations in the public service. Mo Labor R 90:III-IV Jl '67
Labor-management relations; the management point of view; address, February 8, 1967. V. B. Day. Vital Speeches 33:309-13 Mr 1 '67
Labor's middle-class revolt. A. H. Raskin. il Reporter 36:24-7 Je 15 '67
Law firm helps shape southern unionism; Cooper, Mitch & Crawford, Birmingham labor law firm. il Bsns W p 154+ S 30 '67
Manpower facts in labor-management negotiations. S. Swerdloff. il Mo Labor R 90:9-14 Ja '67
Maturation of the two movements; labor and civil rights movements. R. B. McKersie. Mo Labor R 90:36-8 Jl '67
R. Conrad Cooper speaks his mind; blames union misuse of power. il Bsns W p 152+ O 7 '67
Reflections on professional organization; excerpt from address. P. C. Briant. Mo Labor R 90:22-5 S '67
Significant decisions in labor cases. See issues of Monthly labor review
'67 trend: employers getting tougher with unions. il U S News 62:87-8 Je 19 '67
We must make work worthwhile. C. Argyris. Life 62:56+ My 5 '67
What's ahead for labor-management relations. L. Sherman; V. B. Day; A. H. Raskin. Mo Labor R 90:44-7 Ap '67
See also
Church and labor
Collective bargaining
Communication in management
Employees
Featherbedding (industrial relations)
Strikes
Trade agreements
United States—National labor relations board

INDUSTRIAL relations research association
Papers from the IRRA annual meeting; excerpts. Mo Labor R 90:23-31 F; 25-6 Mr '67
Papers from the IRRA spring meeting; excerpts. R. B. McKersie; I. Bernstein; H. R. Northrup. Mo Labor R 90:36-43 Jl '67

INDUSTRIAL research
Europe and America: partners in technology; address, November 10, 1966. G. C. McGhee. Dept State Bul 56:148-53 Ja 23 '67
Molecular biology: drug firm to establish new research center. D. S. Greenberg. Science 157:408-9 Jl 28 '67
Philips: international company cultivates basic research. J. Walsh. Science 157:1409-12 S 22 '67
R&D looms big in fiscal budgets; McGraw-Hill survey. il Bsns W p68-9+ My 13 '67
Science puts Ford in the future. il Bsns W p84-8 Ag 5 '67
Strategies for a technology-based business. H. I. Ansoff and J. M. Stewart. il Harvard Bsns R 45:71-83 N '67
See also
Aeronautic research
Products, New
Research laboratories

INDUSTRIAL revenue bonds. See Municipal bonds

INDUSTRIAL revolution
See also
Social revolution

INDUSTRIAL robots. See Automatons

INDUSTRIAL secrets. See Trade secrets

INDUSTRIAL security measures. See Industry—Security measures

INDUSTRIAL sociology. See Sociology, Industrial

INDUSTRIAL spies. See Spies, Industrial

INDUSTRIAL standards. See Labor standards

INDUSTRIAL statistics
See also
Employment—Statistics

INDUSTRIAL tours
Fifty-one vacation stop-offs that will add real excitement to your trip; attractions in the United States. R. Dunlop. il Pop Mech 127:100-3+ Ap '67

INDUSTRIAL trusts. See Trusts, Industrial

INDUSTRIAL waste. See Trade waste

INDUSTRIAL welfare work. See Welfare work in industry

INDUSTRIAL workers of the world
Here come the Wobblies! B. A. Weisberger. il Am Heritage 18:30-5+ Je '67
Labor melts a link with its fiery past; Smelter workers merger into the USW ends an era. il Bsns W p 109-10+ Ja 28 '67
Wobblies, by P. Renshaw. Review Time il 90:84+ Jl 7 '67

INDUSTRIALIZATION
Industrial development survey. UN Mo Chron 4:98 D '67
International symposium on industrial development. UN Mo Chron 4:91-2 D '67
Technology in China. G. Uchida; reply with rejoinder. P. F. Drucker. Sci Am 216:8-9 F '67
See also
Economic development

INDUSTRIES, Service. See Service industries

INDUSTRY
See also
Cities and towns—Industries
Industrial mobilization
Interindustry economics
Inventions
Location in business and industry
Production

Charitable contributions
See Corporations—Charitable contributions

Location
See Location in business and industry

Security measures
How to steal $4 billion. il Newsweek 69:76-8 My 1 '67
Kirk's private police; Wackenhut corp. New Repub 156:10 Ja 28 '67

Social aspects
See Sociology, Industrial

INDUSTRY, Nationalization. See Government ownership

INDUSTRY and art. See Art and industry

INDUSTRY and education. See Business and education

INDUSTRY and state
Adam Smitović on the Sava. G. Burck. il Fortune 75:128-33+ My '67
Agricultural extension for industry begins; federal-state program to disseminate information on technology. Tech W 20:40-1 F 13 '67
AEC centrifuge ban puts industry in spin. il Bsns W p99-100 Je 10 '67
Big business, big labor and big government; and still growing. il Sr Schol 90:4-8+ Ap 7 '67
Business and the big cleanup; need for business initiative in reshaping country's environment. Fortune 75:101-2 Mr '67
Business and the 90th Congress. G. R. Rosen. il Duns R 89:34-6+ Ap '67
Businessman and his government; address. J. M. Patterson. Vital Speeches 33:209-13 Ja 15 '67
Capitalism, socialism, and the future of the industrial state; excerpts from The new industrial state. J. K. Galbraith. Atlan 219:61-7 Je '67
Capitalists & managers in Communist China. B. M. Richman. Harvard Bsns R 45:57-78 Ja '67

INDUSTRY and state—*Continued*
Creative competition. G. Champion. bibliog f Harvard Bsns R 45:61-7 My '67
Delicate balance. F. D. Murphy. Sat R 51:74+ Ja 13 '68
Dialogue that never happens; marketing and its critics. R. A. Bauer and S. A. Greyser. bibliog f Harvard Bsns R 45:2-4+ N '67
Freedom's last frontier: business; address, November 17, 1966. L. H. Rogers, 2d. Vital Speeches 33:333-9 Mr 15 '67
Gaullists call the shots in business, too. il Bsns W p96+ Ja 14 '67
Great power robbery. J. D. Snyder. il Nations Bsns 55:96-7+ Mr '67
How a city took care of itself; reaction to closure of armory. il Nations Bsns 55:48-51 S '67
Is the gap technological? gap between Europe and the United States. J. Diebold. For Affairs 46:276-91 Ja '68
Johnson treatment. T. Levitt. il Harvard Bsns R 45:114-18+ Ja '67
Lions and the lambs; Food and drug administration and the drug industry. Sci N 92:250 S 9 '67
Market planning and the role of government; excerpt from The new industrial state. J. K. Galbraith. Atlan 219:69-72+ My '67
Message for industry; excerpts from address. R. H. Charles. Aviation W 86:11 Mr 13 '67
Multinational enterprise & national sovereignty. R. Vernon. Harvard Bsns R 45:156-8+ Mr '67
New industrial state, by J. K. Galbraith. Review
  Bsns W p77 Jl 8 '67
  Bul Atomic Sci 23:30-2 N '67. R. Eisner
  Commentary 44:77-83 O '67. M. Harrington
  Fortune 76:90-1+ Jl '67. I. Kristol
  Nation 205:246-8 S 18 '67. H. Magdoff
  New Repub 157:26-8 Jl 8 '67. A. S. Miller
  New Yorker 43:85-6+ Ja 6 '68. N. Bliven
  Newsweek 69:75C+ Je 26 '67. S. Maloff
  Sat R 50:29-30 Je 24 '67. A. A. Berle
  Time 89:74 Je 30 '67
New industrial state; excerpt. J. K. Galbraith. Atlan 219:51-7 Ap '67
News lines. See issues of U.S. news & World report
Nine unknowns who influence your business. il Nations Bsns 55:62-6+ Ap '67
Overcharge, by L. Metcalf and V. Reinemer. Review
  Science 155:676-8 F 10 '67. L. J. Carter
Patent problem: who owns the rights? W. W. Eaton. Harvard Bsns R 45:101-10 Jl '67
Portents of trouble. il Time 90:93 N 17 '67
Private responsibility for public management. F. B. Morse. bibliog f Harvard Bsns R 45:6-8+ Mr '67
Profitable and the profligate. A. H. Sypher. il Nations Bsns 55:31-2 F '67
Public interest. New Repub 157:5-6 D 2 '67
Radiation hazards: Senate bill would provide federal regulation. K. Sperry. Science 157:1292-3 S 15 '67; Discussion. 158:1397-8 D 15 '67
Radon daughters and the federal government. M. Viorst and J. V. Reistrup. Bul Atomic Sci 23:25-9 O '67
Robert Kennedy on: government injustice to business. R. F. Kennedy. Nations Bsns 55:70-2+ Je '67
Senate to probe federal role in technology transfer. Tech W 20:23 Je 12 '67
Senators, the funds, and the law. il Fortune 75:152-3 My '67
Should Dow be making napalm? rights and responsibilities of business in relation to government. Bsns W p 160 D 16 '67; Discussion. p5 D 30 '67
Social-industrial complex. M. Harrington. Harper 235:55-60 N '67; Discussion. 236:4 Ja '68
Supreme court: what can business expect? F. P. Graham. il Duns R 90:29-31+ S '67
Technology and politics meet: nuclear ship Savannah to remain afloat. il Sci N 91:591 Je 24 '67
$30 billion for whom? politics, profits and the anti-missile missile. F. W. Collins. New Repub 156:13-15 Mr 11 '67
Too big for antitrust to handle? il Bsns W p70-2 Jl 8 '67
U.S. tariff & trade policies: failure to consult industry; address, July 11, 1967. R. G. Wingerter. Vital Speeches 34:28-32 O 15 '67
Urban redoubt. W. H. Dougherty, jr; J. A. Norton. il Sat R 51:34+ Ja 13 '68

Washington desk. J. R. Slevin. See issues of Dun's review
What LBJ thinks about businessmen now. Nations Bsns 55:46-9 D '67
  See also
Free enterprise
Government ownership
Industrial mobilization
Insurance companies—Regulation
Labor laws and legislation
Price regulation by government
Research—Federal aid
Right to labor
Strikes—United States—Government intervention
Sweden—Labor policy
Trusts, Industrial
United States—Federal power commission
INDUSTRY and war. See War—Economic aspects
INDUSTRY wide collective bargaining. See Collective bargaining, Industry wide
INEQUALITY. See Equality
INERTIAL guidance systems
AC carousel chosen as 747 nav system. P. J. Klass. il Aviation W 86:68-71+ F 20 '67
Boeing award means $100 million for AC; Carousel inertial navigation system. il Tech W 20:38-9 F 6 '67
France has inertial systems competence. il Aviation W 86:310-13 My 29 '67
Navy to test autonavigator on carrier; ship's inertial navigation systems. C. D. LaFond. il Tech W 20:28-9 Mr 13 '67
Pan Am cancels inertial contract. Aviation W 87:47 Jl 17 '67
Pan Am termination could retard inertial introduction. B. Miller. il Aviation W 87:70-5 Jl 31 '67
Prototype work set on new nav system. Aviation W 87:83-5 O 2 '67
747 to set inertial pattern for airlines. B. Miller. il Aviation W 87:89-91+ N 20 '67
  Testing
BOAC to flight test Carousel 4 navaid. B. Miller. il Aviation W 87:93+ N 6 '67
INFALLIBILITY. See Catholic church—Infallibility
INFALLIBILITY, Papal. See Popes—Infallibility
INFANT celebrities. See Celebrities
INFANT feeding. See Infants—Nutrition
INFANT mortality
Declining decline in infant deaths. il Time 90:32 D 29 '67
Health-care cooperation saves babies; National conference on infant mortality. H. S. Morgan. Todays Health 46:88 Ja '68
How doctors are solving the mystery of crib deaths. Good H 165:197-9 N '67
No time to get sick; difference between U.S. and Swedish rates. E. T. Chase. New Repub 157:24-5 N 11 '67
Tenth child; crib deaths. il Newsweek 71:50 Ja 15 '68
INFANT psychology. See Child study
INFANTS
Protecting the infant; symposium. il Todays Health 46:29-57+ Ja '68
  Care and hygiene
Babies make good teachers. J. Whitbread. il Parents Mag 42:33-5+ Jl '67
Bringing up baby for a million mothers; interview, ed. by S. O'Quin. L. Smith. il Life 64:38-9+ Ja 19 '68
Caring for a sick baby. K. Cruzic. il Parents Mag 42:44-5+ Mr '67
My first six months as a mother. R. Gray. il Redbook 129:66-7+ S '67
What to do when a baby is ill. J. T. Burns and A. P. Riker. il Parents Mag 42:36-7+ Ag '67
  See also
Colic
Health clinics
Infant mortality
Infants, Premature
  Clothing
Waterproof baby pants. il Consumer Rep 32:491-3 S '67
  See also
Diapers, Infants
  Food
  See Infants—Nutrition
  Growth and development
All-important first year. H. Caldwell. il Parents Mag 42:38-9+ F '67

INFANTS—Growth and development—*Continued*
Babies love to learn; excerpt from How to raise a brighter child. J. Beck. il Parents Mag 42:58-9+ S '67
Baby's mind; the crucial first months; excerpt from The crucial years. M. Pines. il McCalls 94:74-5+ Ap '67
Infant vocalizations and their relationship to mature intelligence. J. Cameron and others. bibliog il Science 157:331-3 Jl 21 '67
Unlocking early learning's secrets. il Life 62:40-7 Mr 31 '67
What we're learning about learning. R. Kramer. il N Y Times Mag p65-6+ Je 11 '67
Where self begins. B. Bettelheim. il N Y Times Mag p65+ F 12 '67

Management and training
See Children—Management and training

Names
See Names, Personal

Nutrition
Feed baby fashionably; breast feeding. Sci Digest 62:70-1 D '67
How breast-feeding can get you out of practically anything you don't want to do; excerpt from Most of us are mainly mothers. C. Bartholomew. Ladies Home J 84:36 O '67
How to avoid feeding problems. J. Mendels. il Parents Mag 42:38-9+ D '67
How to feed your baby. H. A. Guthrie. Farm J 91:76 My '67

INFANTS, Deformed. See Deformities
INFANTS, Disciplining of. See Discipline
INFANTS, Newborn
First hours. B. Spock. il Redbook 130:65-71+ N '67
High-risk care saves lives and minds; critical hours after birth. T. Irwin. il Todays Health 46:42-4+ Ja '68
Hunt to catch a handicap; volunteers spot hearing defects in newborns. M. P. Downs. il Todays Health 46:46-51 Ja '68
In most newborn babies: brain damage can be prevented; Neonatal intensive care unit, Babies hospital. T. Irwin. il Look 31:61-7+ S 5 '67
Of miracles and medicine; Apgar test for newborn infants. il Todays Health 46:30-1 Ja '68

Surgery
Rescuing newborns with minisurgery. J. H. Winchester. il Todays Health 46:52-6 Ja '68

INFANTS, Photography of. See Photography of children
INFANTS, Premature
As frail as a sparrow. C. S. Shade. il McCalls 94:74+ Mr '67
Coast guard's Christmas carol; baby born on a Russian fishing ship. W. R. Brantley and J. R. Butler. il Pop Mech 128:76-80+ D '67

INFANTS shoes. See Shoes
INFECTION
Arbovirus infections of laboratory workers. R. P. Hanson and others. bibliog il Science 158:1283-6 D 8 '67
Biohazards symbol: development of a biological hazards warning signal. C. L. Baldwin and R. S. Runkle. il Science 158:264-5 O 13 '67

INFECTIOUS disease research. See Medical research
INFECTIOUS diseases. See Communicable diseases
INFECTIOUS mononucleosis. See Mononucleosis, Infectious
INFELD, Leopold
Maria Sklodowska: the dreamer in Warsaw. UNESCO Courier 20:20-2 O '67
INFERTILITY. See Sterility
INFLAMMABLE materials
Some burning questions. J. Daugherty and M. Daugherty. il Sci Digest 61:90-2 Je '67

Laws and regulations
Fire, firewater and labels; federal requirements for flammability labeling. il Consumer Rep 33:22 Ja '68

INFLAMMABLE textile fabrics. See Textile fabrics, Flammable
INFLAMMATION
What causes inflammation, and why it occurs; International inflammation club's first symposium. il Time 89:60+ Je 16 '67
INFLATION (finance)
Accord at Ford, a slippery road. il Newsweek 70:69 O 30 '67

Business feels inflation fever. il Bsns W p41-2 O 21 '67
Canada tries to cool it; efforts to dampen inflation. Bsns W p46 N 18 '67
Does inflation pay? what workers find. il U S News 64:18-19 Ja 1 '68
For a people's lobby; anti-inflation group. America 117:633 N 25 '67
Gold, taxes, inflation & co. Nat R 19:1052-3 O 3 '67
How Americans have weathered twenty-five years of inflation. il U S News 62:32-4 Mr 13 '67
Inflation ahead: what it means to you; based on interview. A. M. Ross. il U S News 63:75 N 13 '67
Inflation and prudent investment. P. A. Samuelson. Vogue 151:58 Ja 1 '68
Inflation on the march. il Newsweek 69:71 Je 5 '67
Labor woes cloud outlook for economy; impact of strikes. il Bsns W p 38-9 O 14 '67
Moribund surtax; need for higher taxes to curb inflation. il Time 90:21-2 S 22 '67
Next: new threat of inflation? impact of auto-wage hike. U S News 63:39-41 N 6 '67
Open letter to Wilbur Mills. P. A. Samuelson. Newsweek 70:81 N 6 '67
Passing the inflated buck. Newsweek 70:75 D 18 '67
Pay vs. profit: where the Nation's money really goes; interview, ed. by A. N. Booth. J. Q. Jennings. Read Digest 90:177-80 F '67
Price of tax delay; more inflation and higher interest rates. il Bsns W p41-3 N 11 '67
Real ripsnorter? il Newsweek 70:81 S 18 '67
Specter & the substance. Time 90:87 S 29 '67
Throwing inflation a tricky curve; Phillips curve to gauge what must be given up in price stability for a cut in unemployment. il Bsns W p62+ Ag 19 '67
Tighter money an official signal; given by the Federal reserve board. U S News 64:86-7 Ja 8 '68
Unturned stones; alternatives to tax increase for stopping inflation. H. C. Wallich. Newsweek 69:80 Je 19 '67
Why bloom is off the boom in bustling West Germany. il U S News 62:106-8 Je 19 '67
Words of warning about inflation in the U.S; excerpts from address, November 15, 1967. W. M. Martin, jr. U S News 63:16 N 27 '67
See also
Currency question

INFLIGHT motion pictures, incorporated
Onward & upward with Inflight; movies on planes. R. Levy. il Duns R 89:55-6 F '67
INFLUENCE of altitude. See Altitude, Influence of
INFLUENCE of literature. See Literature, Influence of
INFLUENCE of music. See Music, Influence of
INFLUENZA
Asian flu on the rise: how big a threat? U S News 64:6 Ja 1 '68
Flu in the East. Time 91:39 Ja 12 '68
Flu time again; widespread outbreaks in the U.S. il Newsweek 71:43 Ja 8 '68
Killer on the rampage: the great flu epidemic. L. M. Rhodes. il Todays Health 45:24-7+ O '67

Vaccines
Flu shots, who needs 'em? Newsweek 70:83 O 30 '67
Get vaccinated against flu this year? Consumer Rep 32:551 O '67

INFLUENZA virus
Breakthrough by Du Pont: a drug that blocks viruses. A. Rosenfeld. il Life 62:60A-61 F 10 '67
INFORMATION. See Knowledge
INFORMATION, Freedom of
Cronkite's alarm. Nation 204:260-1 F 27 '67
Free-for-all in the files. il Bsns W p30-1 Jl 8 '67
Free press & fancy packages. A. Q. Mowbray. Nation 205:621-3 D 11 '67
Freedom of what? Freedom of information act and agency refusals to divulge. New Repub 157:7 S 16 '67
One-sided candor; oil companies file suit against Bureau of land management. Nation 205:293-4 O 2 '67
Suppression business: similarity between J. Kennedy and H. C. Frick. R. H. Smith. Pub W 191:93 Ja 30 '67
See also
Freedom of the press
Government and the press
Journalistic ethics

INFORMATION agency (United States) See
United States—Information agency

INFORMATION display systems
Saturn V automatic checkout uses multiple-media displays. il Aero Tech 21:41-2 D 4 '67
Solid-state flashers for light displays. A. A. Adem. il Electr World 78:83-4 Ag '67
Solid-state ring counters and chasers for light displays. A. A. Adem. il Electr World 78:84-5 S '67

See also
Computers—Input-output equipment

INFORMATION media guaranty program. See
United States—Information agency

INFORMATION science and automation division. See American library association—Information science and automation division

INFORMATION services
Best things in life are free, or almost; camping information. M. Gough. il House B 109:124 Jl '67
Booked for travel, by computer. il Bsns W p 181-2 S 9 '67
Federal info. centers reported thriving. Library J 92:3950 N 1 '67
Somebody shoulda told me. . ; visitor services to interpret natural and historical scenes. D. B. Huyck. il Am For 73:12-15+ Jl '67
Travel the U.S.A. and Canada this summer. Am Home 70:40 My '67
Uncle Sam's brainwashing machine. il Nations Bsns 55:50-4 Jl '67

INFORMATION storage and retrieval systems
Ampex makes a play for the home market; Videofile system. il Bsns W p 170+ Je 17 '67
Coping with the information explosion. P. H. Abelson; discussion. Science 155:398+, 776+; 157:1123 Ja 27, F 17, S 8 '67
Data transfer; explosion and remedies; ABPC conference at Arden house. il Pub W 191:35-41 Ap 10 '67
Economics of information retrieval; adaptation of address, November 22, 1965. W. E. Batten. Library J 92:974-5 Mr 1 '67
Information retrieval; report on symposium. E. Garfield. Science 156:1398+ Je 9 '67
International cooperation: the new ICSU program on critical data; excerpts from address, December 29, 1966. H. Brown. Science 156:751-4 My 12 '67
Laser-recorded digital memory; UNICON mass memory reels. il Electr World 77:76 Mr '67
Leach claiming data packing improvements of at least 18:1. C. D. LaFond. il Tech W 20:34 My 29 '67
M.I.T. gets research grant for remote access library. Pub W 191:59 Ap 10 '67
National standard reference data system. E. L. Brady and M. B. Wallenstein. bibliog il Science 156:754-62 My 12 '67
New Motorola data system aimed at jumbo jet market; aircraft integrated data system. C. D. LaFond. il Tech W 20:20-1 My 22 '67
New random-access memory utilizes lasers and holograms. P. J. Klass. il Aviation W 87:81+ Ag 7 '67
Quick-access pool for world data; Washington study urges system for scientific and engineering information. Bsns W p78+ Je 17 '67
Societal feedback. R. A. Bauer. bibliog f Ann Am Acad 373:180-92 S '67
Systems approach; processing school information. R. A. Van Dusseldorp. il NEA J 56:24-6 F '67
Texas firm adopts micro-records storage and retrieval. il Arch Rec 142:93-4 O '67

See also
Electronic data processing
Libraries—Automation
Microfilms
Programming (computers)
Punched card systems
School libraries—Automation

INFORMATION tests
Are you as good as the forty winners of Westinghouse science competition. Sci N 91:124-5 F 4 '67
Baffling quiz; speaker enclosure designs. R. P. Balin. il Pop Electr 28:60+ Ja '68
Changing times quiz (cont) Changing T 21:42 Ap; 47 Ag; 22 D '67
Color code quiz. R. P. Balin. il Pop Electr 27:70+ N '67
Electronic angle quiz. R. P. Balin. il Pop Electr 27:55+ S '67
Electronic measurements quiz. R. P. Balin. il Pop Electr 27:96+ Ag '67

Electronic switching quiz. R. P. Balin. il Pop Electr 27:52+ O '67
Family quiz game. I. Buchanan. See issues of Parents' magazine and better homemaking
Fooling with light; quiz. J. Daugherty and M. Daugherty. il Sci Digest 61:93-6 F '67
How safe is your driving? quiz. P. A. Gagnon and J. H. Pollack. Ladies Home J 84:180 N '67
International electronics quiz. R. P. Balin. il Pop Electr 27:46+ Jl '67
Lions? elephants? hyenas? how much do you know that isn't so? il Pop Mech 128:92-3 S '67
Mediquiz; questions and answers (title varies) J. Lentz. il Todays Health 45:17-19 Ap; 12+ My; 16-18 S; 75 N '67
1967 contemporary affairs test. Sr Schol 91:39-40 S 21 '67
Quiz. J. Daugherty and M. Daugherty. See issues of Science digest
Senior scholastic end-term review test (cont) Sr Schol 90:39-40 My 12 '67
Take our automotive quiz. W. J. Toth. Am Home 71:30-1 Ja '68
Your literary I.Q; ed. by J. T. Winterich and D. M. Glixon. See issues of Saturday review

See also
Vocabulary tests

INFORMERS (law)
Patriots on the campus; FBI's activities at Duke university. J. Ridgeway. New Repub 156:12-13 Mr 25 '67
Spies, J.G; campus-spy game. il Newsweek 69:112 Mr 27 '67
Vital informers; question of the secret informer. Time 89:73 Mr 31 '67

INFRARED photography. See Photography, Infrared

INFRARED rays
Exploring the universe in infrared. A. Ewing. il Sci N 91:384-5 Ap 22 '67
Far-infrared surveys of the sky. W. F. Hoffmann and others. bibliog il Science 157:187-9 Jl 14 '67

See also
Photography, Infrared

Military applications
SAT supplies infrared systems; Societe anonyme de telecommunications France's only supplier of military infrared systems. il Aviation W 86:320-1 My 29 '67

INFRARED spectrometers. See Spectrometers

INFRARED thermography. See Photography, Infrared

INFRASONIC waves. See Sound waves

INGATE, Margaret Rose
Mobile ironwork. Antiques 92:354-9 S '67

INGENUE (periodical)
Writing for Ingenue. S. Reice. Writer 80:27 D '67

INGER, Morton. See Crain, R. L. jt. auth.

INGERSOLL, John H.
Happenings in paint. House B 109:166+ My '67
Lease and quiet. House B 109:122-4 Ag '67
They made a camper out of a Greyhound. Pop Mech 127:128-31 My '67
Well-built, well-kept house. House B 109:36+ O; 38+ N; 12 D '67

INGERSOLL-Rand company
Dig we must, and faster. il Bsns W p 135-6 F 11 '67

INGLIS, David R.
Anti-missile drag-race. Sat R 50:36+ F 25 '67
Missile defense, nuclear spread, and Vietnam. Bul Atomic Sci 23:49-52 My '67
—and Sandler, C. L.
Special report on Plowshare. Bul Atomic Sci 23:46-53 D '67

INGRAM, Vernon M. See Brostoff, S. W. jt. auth.
—See Lee, J. C. jt. auth.

INGRAMS, Richard, and Wells, John
Mrs Wilson's diary. Criticism
New Yorker 43:228+ N 11 '67

INGRAO, Hector C. and Kasparian, Elaine
Photographic star atlases. bibliog Sky & Tel 34:284-7 N '67

INGRES, Jean Auguste Dominique
Ingres; return of an artist's artist. D. L. Shirey. il Newsweek 70:87-8 D 4 '67
Letter from Paris; exhibit at Petit Palais. Genêt. New Yorker 43:96+ Ja 13 '68
M. Ingres, the indispensable gorilla; exhibition at the Petit Palais, Paris. J. Russell. il Art N 66:30-1+ D '67
Master of line. il Time 89:72-3 F 17 '67

INGWERSEN, John
Poem: To the north. Poetry 109:378-9 Mr '67
INHERITANCE
Beware search for lost heirs! mailings based on name only. A. Peters. il Ebony 22:94-6+ Jl '67
Scheme of the year; missing-heir dodge. Time 90:83 N 24 '67
What happens if a husband and wife die in a common disaster? Bet Hom & Gard 45:8+ Ap '67
See also
Estate planning
Probate law and practice
Wills
INHERITANCE of disease.   See Heredity of disease
INHERITANCE tax
Estates, gifts being eyed for tax raises. U S News 62:107-8 Ap 10 '67
Giveaways of property; a growing boom. il U S News 64:96-8 Ja 15 '68
Should you own property jointly? some pitfalls to guard against. il U S News 64:60-3 Ja 15 '68
INITIAL teaching alphabet. See Alphabet
INJECTIONS
See also
Inoculation
INJURED party; story. See Amft, M. J.
INJURIES. See First aid in illness and injury
INJURIES (law) See Damages
INJURIES, Self inflicted. See Self mutilation
INJURIOUS birds. See Birds, Injurious and beneficial
INKSTER, Tom H.
North to adventure. Travel 127:41-5 Je '67
INLAND navigation
Kayak odyssey from the Inland Sea to Tokyo. D. Dimancescu. il Nat Geog Mag 132:295-337 S '67
Ride round the rivers; Cumberland, Ohio and Tennessee rivers. C. Noe. il Travel 128:38-41 Ag '67
Teen travel talk; girl scouts Expo trip by Champlain, Richelius River and St Lawrence Seaway. il Seventeen 26:370 Ag '67
See also
River trips
Waterways—United States
INLAND steel company
Block bows out. Newsweek 70:80-1 N 6 '67
Maverick steps out. il Time 90:94+ N 3 '67
INLAND water transportation
See also
Ferries
INLAND waterways. See Waterways—United States
INN signs. See Signs and signboards
INNER MONGOLIA. See Mongolia
INNOVATION, Technological. See Technological change
INNSBRUCK, Austria
Alpenzoo
See Zoological gardens
INOCULATION
Summer checkup for school beginners. M. McKinlock. il Parents Mag 42:40-1+ Ag '67
See also
Rabies—Preventive inoculation
INORGANIC phosphates. See Phosphates
INPUT-output analysis. See Interindustry economics
INPUT-output equipment. See Computers—Input-output equipment
INQUIRER, Philadelphia. See Philadelphia inquirer
INQUIRY, Commissions of. See Commissions of inquiry, International
INSANE
Legal status, laws, etc.
See Mental health laws
INSANE, Criminal and dangerous
See also
Forensic psychiatry
INSANITY
See also
Psychiatry
Schizophrenia
Jurisprudence
Courtroom crack-up; case of H. Weinberg. il Time 90:108 N 17 '67
Of course, I'm no psychiatrist; Alabama commitment statute and cases of B. Porter and I. Pruitt. R. Reisig and R. Rapoport. New Repub 156:13-15 Je 24 '67; Reply. E. Opton, jr. 157:34-5 Jl 15 '67

Quick cure for a killer; Raymond Sledge freed. Time 90:38 D 29 '67
Two states of mind; insanity pleas. il Time 90:50 N 3 '67
Whiff of innocence; boy found not guilty of murder after sniffing glue. Time 90:51 Ag 25 '67
See also
Forensic psychiatry
INSCRIPTIONS, Cuneiform. See Cuneiform inscriptions
INSECT baits and repellants
Automobile paint effective as an insect attractant. O. K. Jantz and others. bibliog il Science 156:946-7 My 19 '67
How to beat the bugs. C. B. Colby. il Outdoor Life 140:14+ Ag '67
What to do about bug bites. il Changing T 21:47-8 Jl '67
INSECT bites and stings
First aid: tick bites. C. J. Potthoff. Todays Health 45:66 Je '67
How to beat the bugs. C. B. Colby. il Outdoor Life 140:14+ Ag '67
Sneaky brown spider a hazard to travelers. il Todays Health 45:18 Jl '67
Warm weather hazards; insect stings. A. F. Benjamin. Am Home 70:38 Je '67
What to do about bug bites. il Changing T 21:47-8 Jl '67
INSECT camouflage. See Mimicry (biology)
INSECT control. See Insects, Injurious and beneficial—Control
INSECT foggers. See Spraying apparatus
INSECT hormones. See Hormones
INSECT intelligence. See Insects—Habits and behavior
INSECT mating behavior.   See Courtship of insects
INSECT repellents. See Insect baits and repellents
INSECT resistance. See Plants—Disease and pest resistance
INSECT sex attractants
Sex attractant of the black carpet beetle. R. M. Silverstein and others. bibliog il Science 157:85-7 Jl 7 '67
Sex attractants in frass from bark beetles; with reply by D. L. Wood and others. J. P. Vité. bibliog Science 156:105 Ap 7 '67
Trans-2-hexenal; mating stimulant for polyphemus moths. L. M. Riddiford. bibliog il Science 158:139-41 O 6 '67
INSECT sounds
Ant stridulations and their synchronization with abdominal movement. H. G. Spangler. bibliog il Science 155:1687-9 Mr 31 '67
Evolution of bee language. H. Esch. il Sci Am 216:96-102+ bibliog(p 148) Ap '67
Wackiest orchestra on earth. J. George. il Read Digest 91:173-4+ Ag '67
INSECT-spraying machines. See Spraying apparatus
INSECTICIDES
How to control corn insects. Suc Farm 65:90+ Mr '67
Quick, Henry, the fogger! A. M. Watkins. il Pop Sci 191:138-40+ Ag '67
See also
DDT (insecticide)
Pesticides
Rotenone
Spraying and dusting
Injurious effects
Do you really need this insecticide? No-pest strip insecticide. Consumer Rep 32:408-9 Ag '67
Metabolism of rotenone in vitro by tissue homogenates from mammals and insects. J. Fukami and others. bibliog il Science 155:713-16 F 10 '67
Popular insecticides potential cause of cancer. Consumer Bul 51:38-40 Ja '68
Residues
Persistence of chlorinated hydrocarbon insecticides in soils. R. G. Nash and E. A. Woolson. bibliog il Science 157:924-7 Ag 25 '67
See also
DDT (insecticide)—Residues
INSECTIVOROUS plants
See also
Pitcher plants
Sundew
INSECTS
See also
Embryology—Insects
Growth inhibiting substances (insects)
Insect sounds
Photography of insects
Respiratory organs—Insects
also names of insects, e.g. Fireflies

INSECTS—*Continued*

Anatomy

See also
Antennae

Collection and preservation

With net in hand. C. L. Hogue. il Natur Hist 76:6-8+ My '67

Control

See Insects, Injurious and beneficial

Culture media

Diets for rearing the ambrosia beetle xyleborus ferrugineus (fabricius) in vitro. J. L. Saunders and J. K. Knoke. bibliog il Science 157:460+ Jl 28 '67

Development

River of insecticide; Rio Negro contains plant and tree substances similar to insect hormones. il Time 90:76 Ag 25 '67

Ecology

Fungus gardens of insects. S. W. T. Batra and L. R. Batra. il Sci Am 217:112-20 bibliog(p 156) N '67

Eyes

See Eye (insects)

Flight

Radar observations of insects in free flight. K. M. Glover and others; reply. R. C. Rainey. bibliog Science 157:98 Jl 7 '67

Food

Diets for rearing the ambrosia beetle xyleborus ferrugineus (fabricius) in vitro. J. L. Saunders and J. K. Knoke. bibliog il Science 157:460+ Jl 28 '67

Hormone-mediated nutritional control of sexual behavior in male dung flies. W. Foster. bibliog Science 158:1596-7 D 22 '67

Symbiosis: effects of a mutualistic fungus upon the growth and reproduction of xyleborus ferrugineus. D. M. Norris and J. K. Baker. bibliog Science 156:1120-2 My 26 '67

Habits and behavior

Alarm, defense, and construction behavior relationships in termites isoptera. A. M. Stuart. bibliog il Science 156:1123-5 My 26 '67

Cryptic moths: effects on background selections of painting the circumocular scales. T. D. Sargent. bibliog il Science 159:100-1 Ja 5 '68

Foundress associations in polistine wasps: dominance hierarchies and the evolution of social behavior. M. J. West. bibliog Science 157:1584-5 S 29 '67

Honey bees: do they use the direction information contained in their dance maneuver? D. L. Johnson. bibliog il Science 155:844-5 F 17 '67

Honey bees: do they use the distance information contained in their dance maneuver? A. M. Wenner. bibliog il Science 155:847-9 F 17 '67

Living doors; phragmosis in ants. W. S. Creighton. il Natur Hist 76:71-3 bibliog (p 105) D '67

Natural history; the insect society. Hobbies 72:119 S '67

See also
Courtship of insects
Sex behavior

Physiology

Control of spiracles in silk moths by oxygen and carbon dioxide. B. N. Burkett and H. A. Schneiderman. bibliog il Science 156:1604-6 Je 23 '67

Protein uptake in multivesicular bodies in the molt-intermolt cycle of an insect. M. Locke and J. V. Collins. bibliog il Science 155:467-9 Ja 27 '67

Stretch receptors in the foregut of the blowfly. A. Gelperin. bibliog il Science 157:208-10 Jl 14 '67

Protective equipment

See Defense mechanisms (biology)

INSECTS, Effect of radiation on. See Insects, Injurious and beneficial—Control

INSECTS, Injurious and beneficial

April's quiet intruders and how to do them in. il Sunset 138:254-5 Ap '67

Eaten any good film lately? Mod Phot 31:54 Ap '67

See also names of insects, e.g. Cockroaches

Control

Beneficial insects? H. E. Barké. il Horticulture 45:34-5+ F '67

Hormone insecticide. Sci N 91:329 Ap 8 '67

How to control corn insects. Suc Farm 65::90+ Mr '67

How to control soybean insects. Suc Farm 65:46+ My '67

Insect pests: microbial control; report on seminar. G. R. Stairs. Science 157:464+ Jl 28 '67

Mismating season; fruit-fly experiment in Capri. Newsweek 69:70 My 1 '67

Nature note: weevil killer. il Sci N 91:564 Je 17 '67

River of insecticide; Rio Negro contains plant and tree substances similar to insect hormones. il Time 90:76 Ag 25 '67

Screwworms sneak back; sterilization campaign in Texas. F. Sartwell. il Sci N 91::238-9 Mr 11 '67

Silent spring quiz. J. Daugherty and M. Daugherty. il Sci Digest 62:88-90 O '67

Spruce budworm mortality as a function of aerial spray droplet size. C. M. Himel and A. D. Moore. bibliog il Science 156:1250-1 Je 2 '67

Third-generation pesticides. C. M. Williams. il Sci Am 217:13-17 Jl '67

This month's cover story; insecticide fogger. D. Malena. il Suc Farm 65:65 Ag '67

See also
Mosquitoes—Extermination
Pesticides

INSECTS, Sound production by. See Insect sounds

INSECTS as carriers of infection

See also
Mosquitoes as carriers of infection

INSEMINATION, Artificial. See Artificial insemination, Human

INSHORE naval boats. See United States—Navy—Boats

INSIDE PASSAGE

Passage to the Yukon. K. Lamott. il Holiday 41:68-9+ My '67

INSIDERS; story. See Morrow, S.

INSOLVENCY. See Bankruptcy

INSOMNIA

Long day's journey into the insomniac's night. E. Diamond. il N Y Times Mag p30-1+ O 1 '67; Same abr. with title Inside insomnia. Read Digest 92:131-4 Ja '68; Same with title Insomniac's nightmare, sleep. Sci Digest 63:62-7 Ja '68

Reassuring report for women who have trouble sleeping. G. G. Luce and J. Segal. il McCalls 94:102-3+ F '67

Why you can't sleep. Sci Digest 61:36 F '67

See also
Sleep

INSPIRATION

At what temperature do books burn? reprint. R. Bradbury. Writer 80:18-20 Jl '67

Attention, attention. . . A. Dobrin. il Horn Bk 43:27-30 F '67

INSPIRATION of the Bible. See Bible—Inspiration

INSTALMENT contracts

Before you sign an instalment contract; regulations that protect servicemen. il Changing T 21:19-21 Ag '67

INSTALMENT plan

Buying on credit. J. D. Bierman. Parents Mag 42:20+ Jl '67

Fewer go into hock; consumers hold back. il Bsns W p42+ F 18 '67

Going shopping with lady luck; Brazil's unusual installment buying plans, consortium. il Bsns W p 152+ D 16 '67

See also
Credit

INSTAMATIC cameras. See Cameras

INSTANT coffee. See Coffee

INSTANT sculpture. See Sculpture

INSTINCT

See also
Animals—Habits and behavior
Fighting (psychology)

INSTITUTE for advanced study. See Princeton, N.J.—Institute for advanced study

INSTITUTE for biomedical research. See American medical association—Institute for biomedical research

INSTITUTE for defense analyses

Battle for brainpower; difficulty to recruit first-rate scientists and engineers. Bsns W p78 F 25 '67

INSTITUTE for educational development
Two million dollars to fund materials evaluation project; Educational projects information exchange. Library J 92:279+ Ja 15 '67
INSTITUTE for research in animal behavior
Behavioral research, New York zoological park. R. Penney. il Science 158:144-5 O 6 '67
INSTITUTE for the study of nonviolence
Non-violent soldier; interview. J. Baez. New Yorker 43:44-6 O 7 '67
INSTITUTE of American Indian art, Santa Fe
Our far-flung correspondents. R. M. Coates. il New Yorker 43:102+ Je 17 '67
With old ritual and modern dance, a heritage comes to life. il Life 63:62-5 D 1 '67
INSTITUTE of current world affairs
New waterbird for Egypt: a robot shadoof. J. Lear. il Sat R 50:50 Je 3 '67
INSTITUTE of electrical and electronics engineers
Engineers find ocean formidable. Sci N 91:304 Ap 1 '67
INSTITUTE of international education
Annual educational exchange statistics. S. K. Gorney. il Sch & Soc 95:234-7 Ap 1 '67
INSTITUTE of navigation
Institute of navigation meets. E. S. Maloney. Motor B 120:90-1 S '67
INSTITUTE of paper chemistry, Appleton, Wis.
See also
Dard Hunter paper museum, Appleton, Wis.
INSTITUTE of student opinion. See Scholastic research center
INSTITUTES, Library. See Library institutes and workshops
INSTITUTES, Religious. See Religious institutes and workshops
INSTITUTIONS, Non-profit
See also
Urban America, incorporated

Taxation
Tax threat to nonprofits; Internal revenue proposes to tax publications of nonprofit organizations. Bsns W p 131 My 6 '67
INSTITUTIONS, Social. See Social institutions
INSTITUTIONS, State. See State institutions
INSTRUCTIONAL materials. See Teaching—Aids and devices
INSTRUCTIONAL materials centers
Instructional materials center: innovation, motivation, cooperation. R. H. Burgert. Sr Schol 90:sup4 F 3 '67
McGraw-Hill grant backs USC media project; National information center for educational media. Pub W 191:53 F 13 '67
Media standards probed at N.Y. state A/V conference; summary of address, November 1967. F. Henne. Library J 93:253-4 Ja 15 '68
Teacher and the instructional materials center. H. C. Hartsell. il Sr Schol 90:sup 13 F 3 '67
Teachers know the score in Nassau County; new Social studies planning service center. W. A. Zeralsky and E. Schester. il Sr Schol 91:sup 17-20 O 26 '67
Tiptoe in technology; transforming library into educational materials center, through ESEA Title II and III, at Burnt Hills-Ballston Lakes junior high school, N.Y. M. J. Egan. il Library J 92:1711-13 Ap 15 '67
INSTRUCTORS, Aviation. See Air pilots—Training
INSTRUMENT flying. See Aviation—Instrument flying
INSTRUMENT landing. See Airplanes—Landing
INSTRUMENTAL ensembles
New performances on old instruments; Concentus musicus ensemble. E. Helm. il Hi Fi 17:42-6 My '67
INSTRUMENTAL music
See also
Concertos
INSTRUMENTATION tape recorder. See Magnetic recorders and recording
INSTRUMENTS
See also
Aeronautic instruments
Musical instruments
INSTRUMENTS, Testing. See Testing instruments
INSULIN
Insulin shocker; W. Archerd accused of using insulin as a murder weapon. il Newsweek 70:25-6 D 25 '67
One coincidence too many; W. Archerd accused of insulin murder. il Time 90:18-19 Ag 11 '67

INSULIN biosynthesis. See Biosynthesis
INSURANCE
Best of all possible worlds? insurance management; address, September 13, 1967. J. C. Bateman. Vital Speeches 34:144-6 D 15 '67
Do your increasing needs demand increased protection? Am Home 70:36+ Ja '67
Just how does insurance work? M. Mayer. Bet Hom & Gard 45:36 Ap '67
Packaged insurance plan; Highland Park, Ill. D. H. Fritz. Parks & Rec 2:41-2 D '67
See also subhead Insurance aspects under various subjects, e.g. Electric apparatus and appliances—Insurance aspects

All risk policies
How to understand your home insurance. C. Bakal. House B 109:123+ F '67
Seven tips on insuring your home. D. Wharton. Read Digest 91:77-80 Ag '67

Risks
Writing a policy for the ghetto. il Bsns W p 118+ S 9 '67
INSURANCE, Accident
Insuring children against school accidents. il Good H 164:160 F '67
See also
Insurance, Liability
INSURANCE, Agricultural
New security for your '67 crops. Farm J 91:74A Mr '67
INSURANCE, Automobile
About auto insurance. Sr Schol 90:40 Ap 21 '67
Ahead: auto-insurance crisis. il U S News 62:68-71 Ap 17 '67
Auto insurance. T. Bird. Motor T 19:50+ My '67
Auto insurance. il Consumer Rep 32:404-8 D '67
Auto insurance: a ready target. il Newsweek 70:54-6 Ag 21 '67
Auto insurance: big blow-up ahead. il Changing T 21:7-12 F '67
Auto insurance: congressional investigation requested. New Repub 157:9 Jl 15 '67
Auto insurance: crack-up ahead. R. E. Keeton and J. O'Connell. il Nation 204:498-500 Ap 17 '67
Auto insurance has no friends; Keeton-O'Connell plan. Life 63:4 N 17 '67
Auto insurance reform; basic protection plan. il Consumer Rep 33:9-15 Ja '68
Automobile insurance; practices of insurance underwriters. G. D. Randels. New Repub 156:38 F 4 '67
Car insurance. New Repub 157:4 S 30 '67
Car insurance: is there any way but up? P. Lindberg. il Bet Hom & Gard 45:7-8 S '67
Changes ahead for auto insurance? il U S News 63:49-51 O 2 '67
Check insurance before traveling. Suc Farm 65:52 Ag '67
Controversy over car insurance. il Good H 165:204 N '67
Cost of casualties; demands for changes in auto insurance system. il Time 89:63 Je 2 '67
Facts you should know about auto insurance; interview, ed. by E. D. Fales, jr. M. D. Saldino. Read Digest 91:65-8 Jl '67
Making insurance on beetles pay; Volkswagen insurance. il Bsns W p 119-20+ O 14 '67
New approach to auto insurance; basic protection plan. J. O'Connell. il America 116:830-1+ Je 10 '67; Discussion. 117:25 Jl 8 '67
New road for auto insurance: non-fault insurance. R. Sheehan. il Fortune 76:170-2+ N '67
Next: a new auto insurance policy. D. P. Moynihan. il N Y Times Mag p26-7+ Ag 27 '67; Same with title Let's have a new auto insurance policy. Pop Mech 129:104-7+ Ja '68; Discussion. N Y Times Mag p22+ S 17; 36+ S 24 '67
Personal business; auto theft. Bsns W p 129-30 Jl 22 '67
Settling the claim without the blame; Basic protection plan. il Bsns W p 168+ N 11 '67
'68 buyer's guide; the dealer & the deal. il Motor T 19:24+ N '67
Unusual system for insuring autos; Saskatchewan plan. U S News 63:51 O 2 '67
INSURANCE, Aviation
High claims spur rise in insurance rates. Aviation W 87:107+ Jl 10 '67
Rental pilots, beware. D. H. Scott. Flying 81:63-4 S '67

INSURANCE, Aviation—*Continued*
Tighter security on cargo sought. R. F. Coburn. Aviation W 87:26-9 S 4 '67
U.S. stand on liability draws more fire; fatal accident. Aviation W 87:30 S 4 '67

INSURANCE, Burglary
See also
Insurance, Automobile

INSURANCE, Fraternal. See Benefit societies

INSURANCE, Health
See also
Insurance, Hospitalization

Great Britain
See also
Great Britain—National health service

United States
Personal business; doctor bills. Bsns W p 133-4 Ap 1 '67
What kind of health insurance should you have? il Changing T 21:7-9 My '67
See also
Medicaid program
Medicare program

INSURANCE, Hospitalization
Medicare runs a fever; patients and hospitals complain of red tape and delays. Bsns W p37 F 18 '67
Personal business; doctor bills. Bsns W p 133-4 Ap 1 '67
Why not compulsory hospital insurance? R. Tunley. Sat R 50:12-14 Jl 8 '67

INSURANCE, Liability
Have you insured this summer? M. Feeley. Am Home 70:16+ Jl '67
See also
Insurance, Automobile

INSURANCE, Life
How much life insurance do you need to protect your family? P. Lindberg. Bet Hom & Gard 45:7+ Jl '67
Life insurance selecting the right protection for a family. Good H 164:202-3 Ap '67
NEA life insurance program. NEA J 56:42 O '67
Ten most misunderstood facts about life insurance. G. Bush. Bet Hom & Gard 45:29-30 My '67
See also
Annuities

Credit aspects
Congress attacks loan insurance. il Bsns W p 110+ D 9 '67

Investments
See Insurance companies—Investments

Policies
How to buy life insurance (cont) il Consumer Rep 32:100-7, 156-64 F-Mr '67
Life insurance. Consumer Rep 32:312-16 Je '67
Picking the beneficiary for your life insurance. il Changing T 21:11-13 N '67

Policy loans
Borrowing on your life insurance; not too smart. il Changing T 21:19-20 Ap '67

Premiums
See Insurance, Life—Rates and tables

Rates and tables
Prices, options, and reading the fine print. Consumer Rep 32:156-64 Mr '67

War risks
See also
Insurance, Soldiers and sailors

INSURANCE, Machinery
How to insure farm machinery. B. Brantley. Suc Farm 65:92+ Ja '67

INSURANCE, Marine
In the oily wake of a tragedy at sea. il U S News 62:18 Ap 10 '67
In the wake of the Torrey Canyon. Time 89:98+ Ap 14 '67

Anecdotes, facetiae, satire, etc.
Fallen oak. G. Crandall. il Motor B 119:44-5+ Ap '67

INSURANCE, Medical. See Insurance, Health

INSURANCE, Medical expense
Insurance that pays for drugs. Good H 166:172 Ja '68

INSURANCE, Military. See Insurance, Soldiers and sailors

INSURANCE, Property
After the riots. il Time 90:69-70 Ag 25 '67
Better check that property insurance. Changing T 21:36 S '67

Detroit's economic disaster. il Newsweek 70:57 Ag 7 '67
How to buy property insurance. J. D. Bierman. Parents Mag 42:18+ My '67
Insurers tot up riot tab. il Bsns W p26-7 Jl 29 '67
What riots are doing to business. il U S News 63:44-5 Ag 14 '67
Who pays for riots? Time 90:68+ Ag 4 '67
Writing a policy for the ghetto. il Bsns W p 118+ S 9 '67

INSURANCE, Social

United States
As social security benefits and taxes go up. il U S News 63:109-10 D 18 '67
Boosting the benefits; how social security taxes might go up. il Bsns W p28 Ag 12 '67
Dangerous ground for social security. Bsns W p 128 Ag 26 '67
High-priced spread; proposed series of social-security increases. il Newsweek 69:31-2 F 6 '67
How secure is your social security? C. Stevenson. Read Digest 91:75-80 O '67; Reply. America 117:591 N 18 '67
Is social security still a bargain? il U S News 63:62-4 Ag 14 '67
Is social security to get out of hand? il U S News 62:42-5 Ja 30 '67
Know your social security balance. il Good H 165:202 O '67
Social security. M. Friedman. Newsweek 69:81 Ap 3 '67
Social security; address, September 25, 1967. A. Shivers. Vital Speeches 34:92-4 N 15 '67
Supports automatic social security for ministers; House bill introduced by George M. Rhodes. Christian Cent 84:398 Mr 29 '67
They sure know how to spread it around. A. H. Sypher. il Nations Bsns 55:31-2 Ap '67
Welfare crossroads. New Repub 156:6 F 4 '67
What the elderly can hope to get. il Bsns W p34-5 Ja 28 '67
Will Washington ruin your pension plan? il Nations Bsns 55:40-1+ Ap '67
See also
Insurance, Health—United States
Old age pensions—United States
Social security act, 1935
Social security act amendments

INSURANCE, Soldiers and sailors
Vietnam sparks a family war; heavy losses from military policies. Bsns W p 150 O 21 '67

INSURANCE, Strike
Divide and conquer isn't so easy. Bsns W p59-60 Je 10 '67

INSURANCE, Teachers. See Teachers—Insurance

INSURANCE, Travelers
Intelligent woman traveler. F. Koltun. Mlle 64:207 Mr '67

INSURANCE, Unemployment

United States
Lockout, the other dimension. W. A. Lewis. bibliog f Mo Labor R 90:1-7 Ag '67
New evidence on problems of reemployment. S. O. Schweitzer. bibliog f il Mo Labor R 90:12-14 Ag '67
Railroad unemployment insurance. M. F. Riche. bibliog f il Mo Labor R 90:9-18 N '67
This month's feature: Congress & unemployment compensation. Cong Digest 46:1-32 Ja '67

INSURANCE agents
New frontiers in insurance. il Ebony 22:123-4+ F '67

INSURANCE companies
Best of all possible worlds? insurance management; address, September 13, 1967. J. C. Bateman. Vital Speeches 34:144-6 D 15 '67
Change in standings. Time 89:86 Mr 10 '67
Feeling is Mutual; life-insurance industry plunges into fund business. Newsweek 70:54 D 25 '67
Hitting the top. Newsweek 69:77 Mr 13 '67
Life companies fight back at mutual funds; pushing variable annuity plans. il Bsns W p 122+ My 13 '67
Mutual interest; life-insurance companies in the mutual-fund business. Time 91:87-8 Ja 19 '68
When insurance firms and mutual funds unite forces. US News 63:75 D 25 '67
See also names of insurance companies, e.g. Rio Grande national life insurance company

INSURANCE companies—*Continued*

Employees
Salaries in life insurance offices, late 1966. C. E. Scott, jr. il Mo Labor R 90:59-60 S '67

Investments
Bankrolling the slum clearance job. il Bsns W p58+ O 14 '67

Big first step; life insurance industry to invest $1 billion in the slums. Time 90:23-4 S 22 '67

Billion dollar bubble; insurance companies to invest in slum areas. Commonweal 86:598 S 29 '67

Insurance in the slums. New Repub 157:7-8 S 30 '67

Mortgages for the slums. W. McQuade. Fortune 77:162-3 Ja '68

$1-billion plunge to rebuild slums; insurance industry pledge for mortgage loans. Bsns W p46 S 16 '67

Slum housing: a billion-dollar baby; life-insurance companies to invest in slum redevelopment. il Newsweek 70:81 S 25 '67

Regulation
Note on mail-order insurance. Consumer Bul 50:39 Ag '67

Securities
Insurance racks up a rebound; boom in earnings of fire and casualty insurance stocks. il Bsns W p92 F 11 '67

INSURANCE company of North America
Case of the isolated executive. B. Smith, jr. Duns R 89:34-5+ Ja '67

INSURANCE law
See also
Insurance companies—Regulation

INSURANCE workers international union
Organizing gains among insurance agents. Mo Labor R 90:III-IV My '67

INSURRECTIONS. See Revolutions

INTEGRATED circuits. See Electronic circuits—Integrated circuits

INTEGRATED communications-navigation-identification system. See Radio apparatus on aircraft

INTEGRATION in industry. See Business management and organization

INTEGRATION of libraries. See Libraries and Negroes

INTEGRATION of public schools. See Public schools—Desegregation

INTEGRITY
See also
Truthfulness

INTELLECT
Vintage mind; excerpts from The new years. A. W. Simon. il McCalls 95:75+ Ja '68
See also
Reason

INTELLECTUAL cooperation
See also
Educational exchanges
United States—Cultural relations

INTELLECTUAL liberty
Crucial error in censorship; reprint. E. J. Gaines. il Library J 92:3377-9 O 1 '67

Students' rights; they should have more, establishment agrees. E. Langer. Science 157: 524-6 Ag 4 '67

Svetlana era; Soviet intellectuals swear never again. J. Laber. Commonweal 86:390-2 Je 23 '67
See also
Academic freedom
American library association—Intellectual freedom committee

INTELLECTUAL life
Citizen of the republic of letters; address, November 30, 1967. W. H. Auden. Library J 92:4508-9 D 15 '67

Our new age of romanticism. P. Gleason. America 117:372-5 O 7 '67
See also
Books and reading
also subhead Intellectual life under names of countries, states, cities, e.g. Canada—Intellectual life

INTELLECTUAL workers. See Professional workers

INTELLECTUALS
Action-intellectuals; chartmakers for our demanding future. T. H. White. il Life 62:76-8+ Je 23 '67

Action-intellectuals; history of academic penetration in American politics. T. H. White. il Life 62:44-56+ Je 16 '67

Action intellectuals; idea men in American politics; with biographical sketches. T. H. White. il Life 62:43-58+ Je 9 '67

American intellectuals and foreign policy. I. Kristol. For Affairs 45:594-609 Jl '67

Communication gap; LBJ's monologue with the intellectuals. B. Nelson. il Science 157: 173-6 Jl 14 '67

Elite of the aliented. L. S. Feuer. il N Y Times Mag p22-3+ Mr 26 '67

Highbrow, lowbrow, middlebrow reconsidered. R. Lynes. il Harper 235:16-20 Ag '67

Intellectual and American foreign policy; address, August 8, 1967. J. A. Gronouski. Dept State Bul 57:432-5 O 2 '67

Intellectuals and the presidency. M. Ways. il Fortune 75:146-9+ Ap '67

LBJ and the intellectuals. il Newsweek 69: 27-8 Je 5 '67

Responsibility of the intellectual; address, April 8, 1964. R. Squirru. il Américas 19:17-22 Je '67

Trials of the intellectuals. America 116:139 Ja 28 '67

Unpossessed. M. Ascoli. Reporter 37:15 D 28 '67

Weakness for causes. Time 90:45-6 S 8 '67
See also
Negro intellectuals
also subhead Intellectual life under particular classes of people, e.g. Catholics—Intellectual life

INTELLIGENCE
See also
Intellect

INTELLIGENCE levels
Case of the wandering IQs; study findings of H. M. Skeels and M. Skodak. B. Asbell. il Redbook 129:31+ Ag '67

Creative elite in America, by N. Weyl. Review Nat R 19:531-2 My 16 '67. G. Tullock

Infant vocalizations and their relationship to mature intelligence. J. Cameron and others. bibliog il Science 157:331-3 Jl 21 '67

Negroes
Racial studies; Academy states position on call for new research; statement of National academy of sciences. Science 158:892-3 N 17 '67

INTELLIGENCE service. See Secret service

INTELLIGENCE tests
Chitling test; the Dove counterbalance intelligence test. New Repub 157:7 D 16 '67

Infant vocalizations and their relationship to mature intelligence. J. Cameron and others. bibliog il Science 157:331-3 Jl 21 '67

Intelligence testing; storybook playhouse, Mount Vernon, N.Y. Sr Schol 91:sup4 O 5 '67
See also
Aptitude tests
Colleges and universities—Entrance requirements

INTELSAT. See International telecommunications satellite consortium

INTERAMA exposition. See Architecture—Exhibitions

INTER-AMERICAN commission on human rights
Commission on human rights; sixteenth period of sessions. G. Meek. Américas 19:46 Jl '67

Human rights in Haiti. Américas 19:45 S '67

INTER-AMERICAN committee on the Alliance for progress. See Alliance for progress

INTER-AMERICAN conferences
Alliance for urgency; Punta del Este conference of hemisphere chiefs. il Time 89: 28-9 Ap 21 '67

American chiefs of state meet at Punta del Este; statements, April 11-14, 1967; with text of Declaration of the presidents of America. L. B. Johnson. Dept State Bul 56:706-21 My 8 '67

American chiefs, shoulder to shoulder; hemispheric summit meeting in Punta del Este, Uruguay. il Life 62:36-36A Ap 21 '67

Benefactor sealed off from the benefited; summit conference in Punta del Este. H. Sidey. il Life 62:36B Ap 21 '67

Charter amendments; final preparations for third special Inter-American conference. G. Meek. Américas 19:44 Mr '67

Date in April. Newsweek 69:48 F 27 '67

Dialogue on the Alliance; meeting of American chiefs of state. A. Morales-Carrión. Américas 19:inside cover Jl '67

Example of the Americas; meeting at Punta del Este, Uruguay of American chiefs of state. G. de Zéndegui. Américas 19:inside cover My '67

INTER-AMERICAN conferences—*Continued*
Fact-finding committee prepares report: twelfth meeting of consultation of ministers of foreign affairs. G. Meek. Américas 19:45 Ag '67
Foreign ministers condemn Cuba; twelfth meeting of consultation of ministers of foreign affairs. G. Meek. il Américas 19:43-4 N '67
Foreign ministers of the American republics meet at Buenos Aires; statement, February 21, 1967, with resolution of meeting of foreign ministers, February 26, 1967. E. Bunker. Dept State Bul 56:472-6 Mr 20 '67
Latin America: now the action? conference at Punta del Este. Sr Schol 90:21 Ap 28 '67
Latin American summit meeting; message to Congress, March 13, 1967. L. B. Johnson. Dept State Bul 56:540-5 Ap 3 '67
Latin lyricism at the foreign ministers meeting. N. Miller. New Repub 157:12 O 7 '67
Life with the long-distance runners; Punta del Este summit talks. il Newsweek 69:25 Ap 24 '67
L.B.J.'s diplomatic foray into South America; Punta del Este preview. H. Sidey. il Life 62:38B Ap 14 '67
L.B.J.'s gamble; conference with the presidents of nineteen Latin American republics. il Time 89:38-9 Ap 14 '67
New milestones in the inter-American system. G. Meek. il Américas 19:1-8 Ap '67
Optimism and obstacles; Punta del Este summit. il Newsweek 69:42-3 Ap 24 '67
Punta del Este revisited. L. Gordon. bibliog f For Affairs 45:624-38 Jl '67
Ready to meet; hemispheric summit conference in April. Time 89:38 Mr 3 '67
Reflections on the Inter-American conference of Chiefs of state; excerpts from address, April 21, 1967. S. M. Linowitz. Dept State Bul 56:729-31 My 8 '67
Secretary Rusk and Secretary McNamara discuss developments in Latin America and Viet-Nam; statements, with questions and answers, February 28, 1967. D. Rusk; R. S. McNamara. Dept State Bul 56:464-6 Mr 20 '67
Secretary Rusk discusses the Punta del Este conference and Viet-Nam on Meet the press; transcript of interview, April 16, 1967. D. Rusk. Dept State Bul 56:722-8 My 8 '67
Summit meeting; eleventh meeting of consultation of ministers of foreign affairs. G. Meek. Américas 19:45 My '67
Summit meeting; eleventh meeting of consultation of ministers of foreign affairs. il Américas 19:1-6 Je '67
What Punta del Este lacked. Bsns W p200 Ap 22 '67
INTER-AMERICAN cooperation. See Inter-American relations
INTER-AMERICAN cultural council
Presidential decisions to be implemented; second special meeting. G. Meek. Américas 19:43 Jl '67
Regional program; group of experts on science and technology to plan Regional scientific and technological development program. Américas 19:46 S '67
INTER-AMERICAN defense board. See Organization of American states—Inter-American defense board
INTER-AMERICAN development bank
President Johnson signs IDB authorization bill; remarks, September 22, 1967. L. B. Johnson. Dept State Bul 57:499-500 O 16 '67
INTER-AMERICAN economic and social council
Action plan of Viña del Mar; fifth annual meeting. G. Meek. Américas 19:46 Ag '67
INTER-AMERICAN highway. See Pan American highway; Roads—Latin America
INTER-AMERICAN relations
Alberdi, Pan Americanist. P. F. Lavin. il Américas 19:30-4 Ap '67
L.B.J.'s diplomatic foray into South America. H. Sidey. il Life 62:38B Ap 14 '67
Our common commitment; excerpts from address, September 18, 1967. H. H. Humphrev. il Américas 19:1-4 N '67
Pan Americanism: on the up and up? Sr Schol 90:3+ Ap 14 '67
Two Americas. J. I. Rasco. il Américas 19:12-17 Jl '67
See also
Alliance for progress
Latin America and the United States
Organization of American states
Pan American day and week

INTER-AMERICAN statistical institute
Industrial statistics; first session of Committee on improvement of national statistics (COINS) G. Meek. Américas 19:47 Jl '67
INTER-AMERICANISM. See Inter-American relations
INTERARMCO, limited
Arms merchant to the world. S. De Gramont. il N Y Times Mag p38-9+ S 24 '67
INTERCEPTOR planes. See Airplanes, Military
INTERCHANGE of students. See Students, Interchange of
INTERCHANGE of teachers. See Teachers, Interchange of
INTERCITY cooperation. See Intercommunity cooperation
INTERCITY transportation. See Transportation —United States
INTERCOLLEGIATE football. See Football
INTERCOMMUNITY cooperation
Auspicious crane: model of castle on exhibit for New York city's Japan week celebration; interview, tr. by J. Kawai. K. Komoda. New Yorker 43:43-4 Mr 11 '67
INTERCONTINENTAL ballistic missiles. See Guided missiles
INTERCONTINENTAL hotels corporation
To end uncertain comforts. il Time 89:74 F 3 '67
INTERCROPPING. See Companion crops
INTERCULTURAL relations. See Cultural relations
INTERDENOMINATIONAL churches. See Community churches
INTER design 2000. See Household furnishings —Exhibitions
INTEREST
Bonds vs. stocks: growing dilemma. il U S News 63:87-9 D 18 '67
Borrowing costs: up, and up. U S News 63:112+ D 11 '67
Business borrowers may get another break; lower lending rates. il Bsns W p22-3 Ap 1 '67
Cheaper money: trend goes on. U S News 62:92 F 6 '67
Cost of money adds to case for a tax boost. il Bsns W p40-1 Je 24 '67
Crucial bond rates. il Fortune 75:40+ My '67
Defensive boost; Bank of England raises discount rate. Newsweek 70:69-70 O 30 '67
Down or up, what's that buzzing? Newsweek 69:67 Ap 3 '67
Easy money. H. C. Wallich. Newsweek 69:79 F 27 '67
Economy: a boost and a blow; Federal reserve board slashes discount rate. Newsweek 69:79 Ap 17 '67
Far-out interest rates. C. J. Loomis. il Fortune 76:215-16 D '67
Fed tries a tricky act on the tightrope; economy in danger of overheating. il Bsns W p 145-6 O 21 '67
Financial powers agree to try for easier money; U.S. British, French, German and Italian ministers meeting at Chequers. il Bsns W p36-7 Ja 28 '67
Finding the true interest rate. Sr Schol 90:14 Mr 3 '67
How cool is too cool? Time 89:78 Mr 31 '67
How much can your savings earn? il Changing T 21:12-13 Mr '67
Interest rates continue climb. U S News 63:80 Jl 10 '67
Interest rates edge up again. U S News 63:88 Jl 31 '67
Is another big squeeze on money in offing? il Bsns W p 130-2 Je 3 '67
Latest move toward easier money. U S News 62:111 Ap 17 '67
Living off the interest. J. B. Mosley. il Read Digest 91:118-21 D '67
Loan costs go up again; back of the increase. U S News 62:92-3 My 29 '67
Lower interest, maybe. il Time 90:67 Ag 11 '67
Markets run scared as tax bill falters. il Bsns W p30-1 N 4 '67
Money easier to borrow; what it means. il U S News 62:44-6 F 13 '67
Money market loosens up. B. Brantley. Suc Farm 65:35 Ap '67
Nervous scramble. Time 90:90+ O 27 '67
New break for nation's borrowers. U S News 62:85 Ap 3 '67
No stampede to easier money. Bsns W p30 F 4 '67
Now there's plenty of money; Federal reserve board reduces discount rate. Time 89:95 Ap 14 '67
Paradox for money managers: easy credit at high rates. il U S News 63:90-1 O 16 '67

INTERNATIONAL astronautical federation
Soviets emphasize manned space stations at IAF. R. van Osten. Aero Tech 21:43-4+ O 9 '67
World unity urged on space program; 18th congress. D. E. Fink. Aviation W 87:21-2 O 2 '67
Yugoslavs angered by snub from U.S. Aviation W 87:30 O 9 '67

INTERNATIONAL astronomical union
Astronomical notes from Prague; 13th general assembly. il Sky & Tel 34:297-9 N '67
Budapest symposium on solar active regions. R. Howard. il Sky & Tel 34:296 N '67
IAU at Prague. il Sky & Tel 34:209-12 O '67
International astronomical union; thirteenth general assembly of the International astronomical union. il Sci N 92:226-7 S 2 '67
Planetary and lunar notes from Prague. il Sky & Tel 35:7-9 Ja '68

INTERNATIONAL atomic energy agency
Atomic energy; address, August 31, 1967. G. T. Seaborg. Vital Speeches 33:752-6 O 1 '67; Excerpts. Science 158:226-30 O 13 '67
Can peaceful nuclear power be kept out of bombs? interview. S. Eklund. U S News 62:93-4 Ap 17 '67
Counting the plutonium; IAEA inspection of nuclear facilities. Sci N 92:584 D 16 '67
Getting set to police the treaty; nuclear nonproliferation treaty. il Bsns W p36 My 6 '67
Hopes run high for limiting nuclear club. Bsns W p35-6 My 6 '67
Is the nuclear nonproliferation treaty enough? G. H. Quester. Bul Atomic Sci 23:35-7 N '67
More war or real progress in Mideast. il U S News 63:58-60 Ag 7 '67
United States reviews problems of control of peaceful uses of atomic energy; statement, December 5, 1967. J. J. Sisco. Dept State Bul 58:63-5 Ja 8 '68

INTERNATIONAL automobile show. See Automobiles—Exhibitions

INTERNATIONAL Bach society
Tureck talks Bach. S. Fleming. il Hi Fi 17:MA9+ O '67

INTERNATIONAL balance of payments. See Balance of payments

INTERNATIONAL bank for reconstruction and development
Shaking the money tree at Rio. Bsns W p41-2 S 23 '67
See also
International center for settlement of investment disputes

INTERNATIONAL basic economy corporation
It takes twenty years to learn the ropes; IBEC set up by Nelson Rockefeller in 1947 to encourage private enterprise in underdeveloped lands. il Bsns W p74-6+ F 4 '67

INTERNATIONAL biennial of tapestry. See Tapestry—Exhibitions

INTERNATIONAL bill of human rights. See Universal declaration of human rights

INTERNATIONAL biological program. See Biological research

INTERNATIONAL boat show. See Boats—Exhibitions

INTERNATIONAL book programs. See Books and reading—International aspects

INTERNATIONAL boy scout jamboree. See Boy scouts

INTERNATIONAL brain research organization. See Brain

INTERNATIONAL brotherhood of teamsters, chauffeurs, warehousemen, and helpers of America
DRIVE: teamsters in politics: Democrat Republican independent voter education. T. E. Tornek; reply with rejoinder. B. Weissman. Nation 204:194 F 13 '67
Hoffa's gone, but not forgotten; trucking industry negotiations affected. il Bsns W p44-5 Mr 11 '67
One-man rule ends for the teamsters; back to the old procedures. Bsns W p 152+ My 20 '67
Playing out Hoffa's hand; successor F. Fitzsimmons negotiating with tough demands. Bsns W p81 Mr 18 '67
Teamsters start to slip bridle; steel haulers' strike. il Bsns W p 113-14 O 28 '67
Tough haul with Hoffa; IBT vs. TEI. Bsns W p 114 Ja 28 '67
Tough man ties up the teamsters; E. Fenner, head of independent drivers' union. Bsns W p 158+ My 6 '67

What Hoffa wants now to keep trucks rolling on highways; summary of address, January 17, 1967. J. R. Hoffa. U S News 62:84 Ja 30 '67
Why I am a teamster. U S News 63:105 O 9 '67
Without Hoffa: truck strike? U S News 62:110 Mr 13 '67

INTERNATIONAL business machines corporation
Eye on IBM. il Newsweek 69:81 F 13 '67
For the Yankee dollar; Earl of Cromer becomes chairman of United Kingdom holdings. Time 90:92 S 29 '67
Frustrating warfare of business; interplant problems met by J. Dammeyer during efforts to introduce master plan. il Life 62:40-53 My 5 '67
Honeywell's $60-million question; why IBM won air force contract. Bsns W p40 Je 3 '67
IBM comes under antitrusters' gaze; complaints from competitors. il Bsns W p34 Ja 14 '67
IBM planning to enter photocomposition field. Pub W 191:114-15 Mr 6 '67

INTERNATIONAL cartels. See Trusts, Industrial—International trusts

INTERNATIONAL center for settlement of investment disputes
President names U.S. members to investment disputes panels. Dept State Bul 57:475-6 O 9 '67

INTERNATIONAL chess tournament, Tunisia. See Chess

INTERNATIONAL children's emergency fund. See United Nations children's fund

INTERNATIONAL Christian university. See Colleges and universities—Japan

INTERNATIONAL circus clowns club. See Clowns

INTERNATIONAL city bank and trust company. See New Orleans—Banks

INTERNATIONAL civil aviation organization
Airport, facilities charges seen growing. W. H. Gregory. Aviation W 86:40-1 Ap 24 '67
Spurt seen in European general aviation. il Aviation W 86:342-5 My 29 '67

INTERNATIONAL coffee council
Awful lot of coffee in the bin. Time 90:61 S 1 '67
U.S. and Brazil discuss extension of international coffee agreement; joint statement, November 18, 1967. Dept State Bul 57:799-800 D 11 '67

INTERNATIONAL coffee organization
Coffee crisis. Américas 19:43 Mr '67
Cure for coffee. il Time 89:75 F 3 '67

INTERNATIONAL commercial bank
Multinational venture; five banks open jointly owned bank in London. Time 90:70-1 Jl 21 '67

INTERNATIONAL commissions of inquiry. See Commissions of inquiry, International

INTERNATIONAL conciliation. See Arbitration, International

INTERNATIONAL conference on abortion. See Abortion

INTERNATIONAL conference on human rights (proposed)
International conference on human rights: Preparatory committee, second series. UN Mo Chron 4:40-1 Mr '67
Preparatory committee: third series of meetings. UN Mo Chron 4:47-9 My '67

INTERNATIONAL conference on magnetics
INTERMAG; report. R. F. Elfant. Science 157:1080 S 1 '67

INTERNATIONAL conference on public education
Higher worldwide education budget Sch & Soc 95:410 N 11 '67

INTERNATIONAL conference on water for peace
Commentary on the recent International conference on water for peace. J. H. Cover. Nat Parks Mag 41:22 Ag '67
Desalting dominates international water conference. il Am City 82:82-3 Ag '67
Humanity's greatest need; addresses, May 23, 31, 1967, with Department announcement. L. B. Johnson; D. Rusk. Dept State Bul 56:902-7 Je 19 '67
Reverse osmosis techniques star at water conference. J. F. Judge. il Tech W 20:21-2 My 29 '67
Water for peace. il Sci N 91:519 Je 3 '67
Water international. J. Ludwigson. il Sci N 91:502-3 My 27 '67

INTERNATIONAL conferences
Calendar of international conferences. See issues of Department of state bulletin
Cuba: Organization of Latin American solidarity meeting. L. Bergquist. il Look 31:32-40+ D 12 '67

INTERNATIONAL conferences—*Continued*
Information functions of an international meeting. B. E. Compton and W. D. Garvey. Science 155:1648-50 Mr 31 '67
No short cuts to peace; U.S.-Soviet summit conferences. Bsns W p 120 Jl 1 '67
Seven Asian and Pacific nations consult on efforts in Viet-Nam; text of communique, April 21, 1967. Dept State Bul 56:747-9 My 15 '67
Split-level subversion; Conference on Latin American solidarity. Time 90:26+ Ag 4 '67
See also
Inter-American conferences
Peace conferences
also names of international conferences, e.g. Glassboro conference, 1967

INTERNATIONAL congress of mathematicians
Mathematics: International congress; report on quadrennial session. L. Lorch. Science 155:1038-9 F 24 '67

INTERNATIONAL congress of psychology
Information functions of an international meeting. B. E. Compton and W. D. Garvey. Science 155:1648-50 Mr 31 '67

INTERNATIONAL congress of the petroleum industry. See World petroleum congress

INTERNATIONAL congress on religion, architecture and the visual arts
Congress on religion, architecture and the visual arts. B. Thompson. Christian Cent 84:1296-7 O 11 '67
Kinesthetic happening: art or atrocity? presentation at Judson memorial church. H. Cox. Commonweal 87:44-5 O 13 '67
Miss Bouchard protests; exhibition at Contemporary Christian art gallery. T. W. Moore. Christian Cent 84:1288-90 O 11 '67
Report on the first International congress of religion, architecture and the visual arts; with comments by artist-exhibitors. D. Smith. Craft Horiz 27:34-7+ N '67
Turning point. T. F. Mathews. America 117:393-6 O 7 '67

INTERNATIONAL convention of Christian churches. See Disciples of Christ

INTERNATIONAL cookery. See Cookery, International

INTERNATIONAL cooperation
East-West business cooperation; a new approach to Communist Europe. E. Benoit. New Repub 156:21-3 F 18 '67
Is the gap technological? gap between Europe and the United States. J. Diebold. For Affairs 46:276-91 Ja '68
Japan's new bid for leadership. J. L. Schecter. Reporter 36:31-3 My 18 '67
New opportunities in Asia; address, October 4, 1967. W. S. Gaud. Dept State Bul 57:579-84 O 30 '67
Partnership in east Asia and the Pacific; address, July 28, 1967. W. P. Bundy. Dept State Bul 57:195-200 Ag 14 '67
Political-economic web: crisis in development; text of address. H. Brown. il Bul Atomic Sci 23:2-7 D '67
Progress in a generation of peril; address, October 23, 1967. L. B. Johnson. Dept State Bul 57:631-3 N 13 '67
Regional groupings: islands of hope; economic groupings; Time essay. il Time 89:22-3 F 3 '67
UN and the have-nots: alternatives to explosion. J. Boyd. Nation 204:562-4 My 1 '67
See also
Antarctic treaty, 1959
Colleges and universities—International cooperation
Cultural relations
Economic assistance
Inter-American relations
Patents—International aspects
Science—International aspects
United Nations
United States book exchange

INTERNATIONAL cooperation year
President reviews action taken on ICY recommendations; statement, April 3, 1967. L. B. Johnson. Dept State Bul 56:658-60 Ap 24 '67
Report of committee approved. UN Mo Chron 4:79 Ja '67

INTERNATIONAL copyright. See Copyright

INTERNATIONAL corporations. See Corporations, International

INTERNATIONAL council of community churches
Community churches' annual conference. R. H. Taylor. Christian Cent 84:1138-40 S 6 '67

INTERNATIONAL council of scientific unions
Committee on data for science and technology
International cooperation: the new ICSU program on critical data; excerpts from address, December 29, 1966. H. Brown. Science 156:751-4 My 12 '67

Committee on space research
JPL scientists challenge sterilization goals. H. M. David. Tech W 20:32-3 My 1 '67

INTERNATIONAL court of justice, The Hague
South West Africa cases. K. Highet. bibliog f il Cur Hist 52:154-61 Mr '67

INTERNATIONAL covenant on civil and political rights
Human rights; International covenant and optional protocol; texts. UN Mo Chron 4:38-72 F '67
Resolutions adopted by the General assembly. UN Mo Chron 4:115-17 Ja '67
U.N. adopts international covenants on human rights; statement, December 12, 1966; with text of covenant. P. R. Harris. Dept State Bul 56:104-21 Ja 16 '67

INTERNATIONAL covenant on economic, social and cultural rights
Human rights; text. UN Mo Chron 4:38-72 F '67
Resolutions adopted by the General assembly. UN Mo Chron 4:115-17 Ja '67
U.N. adopts international covenants on human rights; statement, December 12, 1966; with text of covenant. P. R. Harris. Dept State Bul 56:104-21 Ja 16 '67

INTERNATIONAL criminal police organization
Global beat. il Time 89:76 Je 9 '67

INTERNATIONAL documents
See also
International federation for documentation

INTERNATIONAL economic integration
Burst of togetherness. W. S. Rukeyser. il Fortune 76:174+ S 15 '67
Regionalism and world order; address, June 12, 1967. W. W. Rostow. Dept State Bul 57:66-9 Jl 17 '67
World is the problem. H. Wheeler. Nation 205:358-60 O 16 '67

INTERNATIONAL education
Ford grants for international studies. Sch & Soc 94:479 D 24 '66
Some thoughts on education for world responsibility; adaptation of address, June 16, 1966. C. Frankel. Sch & Soc 95:219-23 Ap 1 '67
U.S. Office of education's century of service to international education. W. W. Brickman. Sch & Soc 95:136-7 Mr 4 '67
See also
American institute for foreign study
Experiment in international living (organization)
Students, Interchange of
Teachers, Interchange of
Travel study courses
United Nations educational, scientific and cultural organization

INTERNATIONAL educational exchanges. See Educational exchanges

INTERNATIONAL exchanges, Literary and scientific. See Exchanges, Literary and scientific

INTERNATIONAL executives service corps
Executives out to pasture find greener fields. il Nations Bsns 55:68-9+ Ag '67
Those retired management missionaries. R. Sheehan. il Fortune 76:106-9+ S 1 '67

INTERNATIONAL expositions. See Exhibitions

INTERNATIONAL FALLS, Minn.
Speaking of weather: some like it cold. J. P. Blank. il Look 31:44+ Mr 7 '67

INTERNATIONAL farm youth exchange program
Joys of an IFYE mother. Mrs H. Johnson. il Suc Farm 65:73+ S '67

INTERNATIONAL fashion festival, Moscow. See Fashion shows

INTERNATIONAL federation for documentation
International federation for documentation. R. A. Harte. ALA Bul 61:986-8 S '67

INTERNATIONAL federation of Catholic universities
Catholic university of today; text of statement with introd. by N. G. McCluskey. America 117:154-6 Ag 12 '67

INTERNATIONAL federation of library associations
IFLA/FIAB report. K. Molz. Wilson Lib Bul 42:313-16 N '67

INTERNATIONAL federation of library associa-
tions—*Continued*
IFLA: International federation of library
associations. F. E. Mohrhardt. ALA Bul
61:187-8 F '67
Memo to members; preliminary plans and in-
formation on 1967 meeting; ed. by D. H.
Clift. F. E. Mohrhardt. ALA Bul 61:376-7
Ap '67
T. P. Sevensma prize; announcement. ALA
Bul 61:188-90 F '67
INTERNATIONAL fellowship of reconciliation
I.F.O.R; chrysalis and catalyst. C. Chat-
field. Christian Cent 84:1203-5 S 20 '67
INTERNATIONAL festival of music and drama,
Edinburgh
High camp, straight Bach & Stravinsky. W.
Blevins. Hi Fi 17:MA24-5+ N '67
INTERNATIONAL film festival, Cannes. See
Cannes international film festival
INTERNATIONAL finance. See Finance, Inter-
national
INTERNATIONAL finance corporation
Successful development effort; address. No-
vember 7, 1967. M. M. Rosen. Vital Speeches
34:153-7 D 15 '67
INTERNATIONAL government. See Interna-
tional organization
INTERNATIONAL grains arrangement
President Johnson announces signing of
grains arrangement; statement, November
8, 1967. L. B. Johnson. Dept State Bul 57:
716-17 N 27 '67
INTERNATIONAL graphics exposition. See
Graphic arts—Exhibitions
INTERNATIONAL human rights year
1968: year of human rights. America 118:2
Ja 6 '68
INTERNATIONAL hydrological decade
Water paradox; concerning Water for peace
conference. Sci N 91:447 My 13 '67
INTERNATIONAL Indian Ocean expedition
Indian Ocean; report on symposium. S. Bur-
man. Science 157:962-3+ Ag 25 '67
INTERNATIONAL inventors and new products
exhibition. See Inventions—Exhibitions
INTERNATIONAL iron and steel institute
World steelmen meet but don't quite weld;
IISI first annual meeting in Brussels. il
Bsns W p44+ N 18 '67
INTERNATIONAL joint commission (United
States and Canada)
U.S, Canada request IJC study of American
Falls at Niagara; letter, March 3, 1967. G.
S. Springsteen. Dept State Bul 56:634-5
Ap 17 '67
INTERNATIONAL June festival. See Music
festivals—Switzerland
INTERNATIONAL labor organization
1967 international labor conference. H. M.
Douty. bibliog f Mo Labor R 90:6-11 O '67
South Africa's wasted manpower; excerpts
from report of survey of developments in
connexion with apartheid policy. il UNESCO
Courier 20:30-1 Mr '67
INTERNATIONAL ladies' garment workers'
union
Sewing machines & union machines. H. Hill.
il Nation 205:18-19 Jl 3 '67
INTERNATIONAL law
International law; address, December 29,
1966. A. J. Goldberg. Vital Speeches 33:234-
8 F 1 '67
International law in the United Nations; ad-
dress, December 29, 1966. A. J. Goldberg.
Dept State Bul 56:140-5 Ja 23 '67
Programme of assistance in international
law; General assembly adopted resolution.
UN Mo Chron 4:138-9 Ja '67
U.S. discusses draft articles on the law of
treaties; statement, October 20, 1967. R. D.
Kearney Dept State Bul 57:719-22 N 27 '67
See also
Aggression (international law)
Maritime law
Rule of law
Sanctions (international law)
Territorial waters
Treaties
United Nations—International law commission
United Nations—Legal committee
United Nations—Special committee on princi-
ples of international law concerning friend-
ly relations and co-operation among states
War
Study and teaching
Programme of assistance in international law:
Sixth committee recommendations. UN Mo
Chron 4:110-11 D '67
INTERNATIONAL law commission. See United
Nations—International law commission

INTERNATIONAL loans. See Loans, Foreign
INTERNATIONAL longshoremen's association
New front man on the mob-run piers. S.
Smith. il Life 63:102+ S 8 '67
INTERNATIONAL minerals and chemical cor-
poration
Bonanza in the desert; Spanish government
and IMC mine phosphate deposits in Span-
ish Sahara. il Time 89:64-5 Je 2 '67
INTERNATIONAL monetary fund
All about the SDR. Nat R 19:1109 O 17 '67
Approaching crisis in world money. il Sr
Schol 91:10-12 D 14 '67
Bumpy road; special drawing rights. il News-
week 70:81 O 9 '67
Conjuring a reserve asset out of thin air. il
Bsns W p22-4 S 2 '67
Group of ten agrees on plan for creation of
new international monetary reserve asset;
excerpts from statements, August 28, 29;
with text of communique, August 26, 1967.
L. B. Johnson; H. H. Fowler. Dept State
Bul 57:392-6 S 25 '67
Make way for the SDRs; artificial reserves.
il Time 90:94 S 8 '67
Monetary reform; special drawing rights. P.
A. Samuelson. Newsweek 70:96 S 25 '67
New world money; the way it will work. il
U S News 63:96-8 S 11 '67
On to Rio; preliminary agreement on inter-
national monetary reform. Newsweek 70:
71 Jl 31 '67
Paper gold? Special drawing right. il News-
week 70:69 S 11 '67
Paper solution. il Time 90:109 O 6 '67
Power play in IMF; Common market nations
want a louder voice. il Bsns W p31-3 S 30
'67
Price of money reform; IMF agrees to special
drawing rights plan. il Bsns W p42+ O 7
'67
Report of Council of economic advisers. il
Dept State Bul 56:348-50 F 27 '67
Roosa pats dollar's new friend; drawing
right scheme. Bsns W p 155-6+ S 9 '67
Secretary Fowler's crusade for monetary re-
form. R. C. Albrook. il Fortune 76:78-80+
Ag '67
Shaking the money tree at Rio. Bsns W p41-
2 S 23 '67
U.S. pounds the desk on monetary reform. il
Bsns W p 132+ Ap 29 '67
U.S. reaffirms international monetary co-
operation; statements, November 18, 19,
1967. L. B. Johnson; H. H. Fowler. Dept
State Bul 57:793 D 11 '67
World monetary reform; key to the West's
future prosperity? il Sr Schol 89:13-15 Ja 20
'67
INTERNATIONAL music council
International music weeks; Paris report. J.
Maguire. Hi Fi 17:MA28 F '67
INTERNATIONAL narcotics control board. See
United Nations—International narcotics con-
trol board
INTERNATIONAL nickel company of Canada
Nickel dollars. il Time 91:86 Ja 19 '68
INTERNATIONAL officials and employees
See also
United Nations—Secretariat
INTERNATIONAL Olympic committee. See
Olympic games
INTERNATIONAL operating engineers union
Union seeks to organize helicopter pilots. R.
F. Coburn. Aviation W 86:93-5 Mr 13 '67
INTERNATIONAL organization
International structures for a nuclear age. H.
Burgelin. Christian Cent 84:748-50 Je 7 '67
Peace, empire, and world government; in-
troduction to Major peace treaties of mod-
ern history, 1648-1966. ed. by F. L. Israel.
A. Toynbee. Sat R 50:17-21 Ap 29 '67
Reinhold Niebuhr plays Hamlet; possibility
of world government. J. P. Speer. Christian
Cent 84:336-9 Mr 15 '67; Discussion. 84:591-
2 My 3 '67
See also
United world federalists
World association of world federalists
INTERNATIONAL organizations, Regional
See also
Atlantic union (proposed)
Organization of American states
INTERNATIONAL PEN club. See PEN club
INTERNATIONAL planned parenthood federa-
tion
Number one problem; population control.
Christian Cent 84:259-60 Mr 1 '67
Pills, coils and abortion; planned parenthood
world conference. W. V. D'Antonio. Com-
monweal 86:193-4 My 5 '67
Toward a world of wanted children; with
highlights from conference. L. M. Miller.
Read Digest 91:89-94 O '67

INTERNATIONAL police academy. See Police
—Training
INTERNATIONAL pop festival. See Music fes-
tivals—California
INTERNATIONAL printing and paper fair. See
Exhibitions
INTERNATIONAL printing pressmen's and as-
sistants' union of North America
Last press run for union home; Tennessee re-
treat to be sold. il Bsns W p66+ S 9 '67
INTERNATIONAL professional pilots associa-
tion
NPA meets in Bahamas. Flying 80:15 Je '67
INTERNATIONAL reading association
Meeting, 1967. D. L. Burleson. Sr Schol 91:
sup 10 S 21 '67
INTERNATIONAL recreation association
Recreation in the war zone. T. E. Rivers. il
Parks & Rec 2:26-7 Mr '67
INTERNATIONAL relations
Active defense and international order. O. R.
Young. bibliog Bul Atomic Sci 23:35-42
My '67
Address to Assembly; summary, November 6,
1967. Mahendra. UN Mo Chron 4:62-3 D '67
Appeasement never pays. D. Lawrence. U S
News 63:116 N 13 '67
Can our fractured world be mended? R. W.
King. Bul Atomic Sci 23:31-2 Ja '67
Easier on the heart; meeting of Big four
foreign ministers at U.N. headquarters. il
Newsweek 70:36+ O 9 '67
Europe's elder statesman sizes up today's
world; summary of interview, ed. by K.
Lachmann. K. Adenauer. U S News 62:63
F 13 '67
Fireballs, matzohballs & Nike-X. M. Getler.
Tech W 20:50 Je 26 '67
Foreign affairs. W. Pfaff. See occasional issues
of Commonweal
General assembly adopts resolution; inter-
vention in the domestic affairs of states;
with text. UN Mo Chron 4:46-51 Ja '67
Golden rule of consultation; address, June 20,
1967. H. Cleveland. Dept State Bul 57:141-6
Jl 31 '67
H-bomb warnings. Commonweal 86:435-6 Jl
14 '67
It's an ill wind; Middle East crisis. D. Law-
rence. U S News 62:112 Je 19 '67
It's time to negotiate. W. S. Ellis. Christian
Cent 84:590-1 My 3 '67
Modern international negotiations, principles
and practice, by A. Lall. Review
Bul Atomic Sci 23:32-4 O '67. Q. Wright
New Year's thoughts 1967. E. Rabinowitch.
Bul Atomic Sci 23:2-3 Ja '67
Nineteen seventy-five; crucial year. G. Lich-
theim. Commentary 44:62-7 Jl '67
1967, a progress report; address, December 6,
1967. D. Rusk. Dept State Bul 58:1-5 Ja 1
'68
Our crisis in perspective. C. E. Osgood. Bul
Atomic Sci 23:12-16 F '67
Parting of the ways. J. O'Gara. Commonweal
85:618 Mr 3 '67
Political future of the family of man; ad-
dress, November 14, 1967. D. Rusk. Dept
State Bul 57:735-41 D 4 '67
Race wars in the making. G. Lichtheim. Com-
mentary 43:62-6 Ja '67; Discussion. 44:6+
Ag '67
Realignments in the Communist and western
world; symposium, ed. by J. C. Charles-
worth. bibliog f il Ann Am Acad 372:1-123
Jl '67
Road to a third world war; appeasement.
D. Lawrence. U S News 63:120 O 9 '67;
Same abr. Read Digest 92:19-20 Ja '68
Role of the United States in world affairs;
address, May 1, 1967. D. Rusk. Dept State
Bul 56:770-3 My 22 '67
Secretary Rusk's news conference; July 19,
1967. D. Rusk. Dept State Bul 57:159-67 Ag
7 '67
Secretary Rusk's news conference of Septem-
ber 8, 1967. D. Rusk. Dept State Bul 57:
383-90 S 25 '67
Special political committee adjourns debate;
peaceful settlement of disputes. UN Mo
Chron 4:104-5 Ja '67
U.S. and world affairs annual; 1967-68 edition,
symposium, ed. by E. Sparn and others. il
Sr Schol 91:2-41 O 5 '67
What is sauce for the goose is sauce for the
gander. E. Rabinowitch. Bul Atomic Sci
23:41-3 S '67
When nobody can dominate the world. F.
Morley. il Nations Bsns 55:23-4 Ag '67
Where U.S. stands in a troubled world; views
of top officials. U S News 62:40-2 Je 12 '67

Which isolationism is your isolationism? J.
Burnham. Nat R 20:22 Ja 16 '68
Why are we in Vietnam? possibilities and
perils of withdrawal. R. Christopher. il
Newsweek 70:36+ N 27 '67
See also
Agriculture—International aspects
Ambassadors
Arbitration, International
Atlantic community
Balance of power
Diplomatic and consular service
Disarmament
Great powers
International cooperation
International law
International organization
International security
Intervention
Pacific countries
Peace
Race problems
Sea power
Tariff
United Nations
War
War, Declaration of
War, Prevention of
also Foreign relations under names of
countries, e.g. France—Foreign relations

Anecdotes, facetiae, satire, etc.
Human comedy: the love wave. C. Tomkins.
il Sat Eve Post 240:16 S 9 '67

Bibliography
Recent books on international relations;
comp. by H. L. Roberts. See issues of
Foreign affairs
Source material; comp. by D. Wasson. See is-
sues of Foreign affairs
World scene (cont) V. S. Kearney. America
116:686+ My 6 '67

Psychological aspects
Psychiatry and international affairs; excerpts
from address, October 12, 1966. B. Wedge.
bibliog Science 157:281-5 Jl 21 '67; Reply.
R. M. Barr. 157:1261 S 15 '67
INTERNATIONAL relations office. See American library association—International relations office
INTERNATIONAL science fair. See Science
fairs
INTERNATIONAL scientific and technological
affairs, Office of. See United States—State,
Department of—International scientific and
technological affairs, Office of
INTERNATIONAL security
Madness and Armageddon. N. Cousins. Sat R
50:24 N 11 '67
Suddenly Congress balks at policing the
earth. il U S News 63:27 Jl 24 '67
U.S. recapitulates basic principles for U.N.
peacekeeping functions; statement, March
22, 1967. A. J. Goldberg. Dept State Bul
56:636-41 Ap 17 '67
See also
Aggression (international law)
Arbitration, International
Disarmament
International organization
International relations
United Nations—Security council
War, Prevention of
INTERNATIONAL seminars. See Seminars
INTERNATIONAL society for education
through art
18th INSEA world congress in Prague, Czech-
oslovakia. M. F. Andrews. il Sch Arts 66:
32-7 Mr '67
INTERNATIONAL standards organization
International standards group meets in Mos-
cow; eleventh plenary session. Library J
92:3356+ O 1 '67
INTERNATIONAL sunfish regatta. See Regattas
INTERNATIONAL telecommunication union
Sizing up satellite systems; group meets in
Mexico city. Bsns W p46+ O 28 '67
INTERNATIONAL telecommunications satellite
consortium
Communications policy; message to Congress.
L. B. Johnson. Dept State Bul 57:296-301
S 4 '67
Comsat faces U.S. overseas challenge. K.
Johnsen. il Aviation W 86:165+ Mr 6 '67
Comsat reveals advanced satellite plans. K.
Johnsen. Aviation W 87:21 N 6 '67
Comsat seeks to broaden types of satellite
services. Aviation W 87:29 O 16 '67

INTERNATIONAL telecommunications satellite consortium—*Continued*
Europe unifying policy for Intelsat talks. D. E. Fink. Aviation W 87:69-70 N 27 '67
France backs UN Intelsat control. K. Johnsen. Aviation W 86:26-7 F 13 '67
Intelsat vote expected for new satellite. K. Johnsen. Aviation W 86:33 Ja 23 '67
Italy seeking Intelsat networks operation. Aviation W 87:21 Jl 31 '67
New monitor on communications; study of nation's communications policy. Bsns W p40 Ag 19 '67
Program decision faces Intelsat. Aviation W 87:18 N 27 '67
U.S. dominance seen hindering Intelsat. R. G. O'Lone. Aviation W 87:31 Ag 28 '67
U.S. will fight for Intelsat preservation. K. Johnsen. Aviation W 87:18 Ag 21 '67
INTERNATIONAL telephone and telegraph–American broadcasting company merger. See Business consolidations and mergers
INTERNATIONAL telephone and telegraph corporation
ABC-ITT merger. America 117:759 D 23 '67
Appetite for more; ITT buys Levitt & sons. il Time 90:74-5 Ag 4 '67
Broken engagement for ITT and ABC; corporate marriage ended. Bsns W p24 Ja 6 '68
Double the profits, double the pride. il Time 90:86-8+ S 8 '67
Geneen's machine; ITT's appetite for acquisitions. il Newsweek 70:66-8 Ag 7 '67
How ITT tightens its spreading net. il Bsns W p58-60+ Je 24 '67
ITT Sheraton. Newsweek 70:72 N 6 '67
ITT's press relations; concerning James Mackey investigation of J. Ridgeway. New Repub 157:6-7 S 16 '67; Reply. M. F. Donnelly. 157:36 S 30 '67
Levitt's secret is change; merger with ITT. il Bsns W p46-8+ Jl 29 '67
Room at the inns; ITT buys Sheraton corp. Time 90:94 N 3 '67
Voice of ITT. J. Ridgeway. New Repub 157: 17-19 Jl 8 '67
INTERNATIONAL tourist year, 1967
Greatest go year. H. French. Holiday 41:4+ Je '67
International tourist year. UN Mo Chron 4:81 F '67
There are no aliens. N. Cousins. Sat R 50: 28+ Mr 11 '67
INTERNATIONAL trade. See Commerce
INTERNATIONAL trade regulation. See Foreign trade regulation
INTERNATIONAL travel regulations. See Travel regulations
INTERNATIONAL trusteeships
See also
Trust Territory of the Pacific Islands
United Nations—Trusteeship council
INTERNATIONAL typographical union
Settlement on New York papers confirms big-raise trend of '67. U S News 63:75 Jl 3 '67
INTERNATIONAL union of electrical, radio and machine workers
See also
Government investigations—International union of electrical, radio and machine workers
INTERNATIONAL union of mine, mill and smelter workers
Merger toughens metal unions; MMSW merger into USW. Bsns W p 104 Ja 28 '67
INTERNATIONAL union of mine, mill and smelter workers-United steelworkers of America merger. See Trade unions—Consolidations and mergers
INTERNATIONAL university of social studies
Environment of language; study under way at Pro Deo university, Rome. N. Cousins. Sat R 50:36 Ap 8 '67
INTERNATIONAL voluntary services (organization)
Do-gooders with a difference. Il Time 89:18-19 Ap 7 '67
End this war; IVS workers withdraw; from Vietnam. Nation 205:322-3 O 9 '67
Toughest question. il Newsweek 70:32 O 2 '67
Unrequited love; resignation of four top I.V.S. officials. Time 90:39 S 29 '67
Viet aides quit. il Sr Schol 91:39-40 O 5 '67
INTERNATIONAL volunteer service. See Volunteer service, International
INTERNATIONAL Webern festival. See Music festivals—New York (state)
INTERNATIONAL whaling commission
Whales: decline continues despite limitations on catch. J. Walsh. il Science 157:1024-5 S 1 '67
INTERNATIONAL wheat agreement. See International grains arrangement

INTERNATIONAL women's fishing association
Scourge of the seven seas. V. Kraft. il Sports Illus 27:39-43 Jl 10 '67
INTERNATIONAL yacht racing union
IYRU meetings; some progress, some reversals; Shillalah and Soling. R. N. Bavier, jr. Yachting 121:410-12+ Ja '67
INTERNATIONAL years of the quiet sun
Comets and the IQSY. F. C. Livingstone. Sci N 92:160 Ag 12 '67
Ionosphere after IQSY: London meetings review findings. N. Calder. Science 157:666-8 Ag 11 '67
INTERNATIONAL young operatic singers competition, Sofia. See Singing—Competitions
INTERNATIONAL youth service of solidarity and friendship. See Volunteer service, International
INTERNATIONALISM
See also
International education
INTERNISTS. See Physicians
INTERNMENT camps

United States
See also
Japanese in the United States
INTERNS (civil service)
Interns' dissent; congressional interns sign anti-Vietnam letter. S. S. Goldschlager. New Repub 157:16 Ag 19 '67
Mother government's helpers; summer internship programs. J. Steinberg. il Mlle 66:138-9+ D '67
INTERNS, Congressional. See Interns (civil service)
INTEROCEANIC canal commission. See United States—Interoceanic canal commission
INTERPLANETARY communication
Galactic signals; excerpt from address. E. M. Hafner. Bul Atomic Sci 23:50-2 Je '67
INTERPLANETARY flight. See Space flight
INTERPLANETARY monitoring platform. See Artificial satellites—Use in research
INTERPLANETARY navigation. See Navigation (space flight)
INTERPOL. See International criminal police organization
INTERPRETATION, Oral. See Books and reading—Reading aloud
INTERPUBLIC group of companies, Incorporated
Ax at Interpublic. Time 90:101 D 15 '67
Changing the format. Bsns W p42 D 2 '67
Interpublic story. Newsweek 70:86+ D 11 '67
INTERRACIAL adoption. See Adoption
INTERRACIAL attitudes. See Attitudes
INTERRACIAL cooperation
Negro in the suburbs; Park Forest, Ill; with painting by N. Rockwell. J. Star. Look 31: 51-3+ My 16 '67
Operation friendship; Chicago's Preadolescent enrichment program of the American friends service committee. S. Olds. il Parents Mag 42:56-7+ Ap '67
Summer we learned that kids are kids. S. Lloyd. il Redbook 129:6+ Jl '67
INTERRACIAL marriages. See Intermarriage of races
INTERRACIAL relations. See Race relations
INTERSCHOLASTIC athletics. See School athletics
INTERSTATE commerce commission. See United States—Interstate commerce commission
INTERSTATE highway system. See Express highways
INTERSTELLAR matter. See Matter, Interstellar
INTERSTELLAR navigation. See Navigation (space flight)
INTERVENTION (international law)
General assembly adopts resolution; intervention in the domestic affairs of states; with text. UN Mo Chron 4:46-51 Ja '67
Noninterventionism, 1967 style. D. Oberdorfer. il N Y Times Mag p28-31+ S 17 '67
To intervene or not to intervene. H. J. Morgenthau. For Affairs 45:425-36 Ap '67
INTERVIEWING
After graduation, a job in New York? A. Grant. il Mlle 65:144-5+ Je '67
How to conduct an interview with a tape recorder. L. A. Harlow. il Pop Electr 25:63-4 D '66
I see, no kidding; disc jockeys provide questions for prerecorded interviews. Newsweek 70:82 Jl 3 '67
Where praise is due; the TV sports interview. C. W. Morton. Atlan 220:122 O '67
See also
Applications for positions

INTESTINES
Diseases
Disaccharidase: localization in hamster intestine brush borders. C. F. Johnson. bibliog il Science 155:1670-2 Mr 31 '67
Lysine transport in human kidney; evidence for two systems. L. E. Rosenberg and others. bibliog il Science 155:1426-8 Mr 17 '67
See also
Appendicitis
Surgery
Living with an ostomy. J. F. Montague. Todays Health 45:71 Ap '67
INTO the cone of cold; story. See Elliott, G. P.
INTOLERANCE. See Prejudice
INTOURIST. See Travel agencies
INTRACOASTAL WATERWAY
To Texas, by ICW. P. A. Hathorn. il Motor B 120:52-5 O '67 (to be cont)
INTRA-UTERINE contraceptive devices. See Contraceptives
INTREX (information transfer experiments) See Information storage and retrieval systems
INTRODUCTIONS. See Etiquette
INTROVERSION and extroversion
See also
Autism
INTUITION
Role of intuition. R. L. Wilder. bibliog Science 156:605-10 My 5 '67
INVENTA products corporation
Inventive inventory. il Newsweek 70:62-3 D 25 '67
INVENTIONS
About simultaneous discovery. I. Asimov. Sci Digest 62:88-9 S '67
Inventions for hire, but not for sale; Sibany mfg. corp. il Bsns W p 136-7+ Mr 25 '67
Is the little man more inventive? federal government asked to aid inventors. il Bsns W p 173-4+ Mr 4 '67
Mousetrap school of engineering. N. Goldberg. il Pop Phot 61:114-15 D '67
New ideas from the inventors. See issues of Popular science monthly
Our magicians of limited war; U.S. army scientists produce deadly weapons of warfare. J. G. Hubbell. Read Digest 90:181-2+ My '67
Technology and change, by D. A. Schon. Review
New Repub 157:32-4 Jl 22 '67. R. Nader
Unique patents; process for extracting metal from living bodies. il Pop Electr 28:56 Ja '68
Where inventors have a friend; Regional development laboratory, Philadelphia. il Bsns W p 184+ Je 10 '67
See also
Patent laws and legislation
Patents
Exhibitions
International inventors' show 1967. il Sci Digest 62:85-7 S '67
International showcase for inventors; International inventors exhibition. D. Scott. il Pop Sci 191:74-5 Ag '67
Our Goldbergs covers a Rube Goldberg show; third annual International inventors and new products exposition. N. Goldberg. il Pop Phot 62:45+ Ja '68
Out of the basement; International inventors and new products exposition. Newsweek 70:102 S 25 '67
World's biggest bunch of bright ideas; mechanical creations at New York's Inventors show. S. M. Gallager. il Pop Mech 128:109-17 S '67
World's largest inventors' show lures 1,600 hopefuls. il Pop Sci 191:96-7 S '67
Models
See Inventors models
Study and teaching
Who said you can't teach inventing? course at Purdue university. J. F. Pearson. il Pop Mech 127:140-3+ Mr '67
INVENTORIES
Business bites down on its inventories; Business week survey of top purchasing agents. il Bsns W p30-1 Ja 21 '67
Business slims down for action. il Bsns W p28-9 My 27 '67
Coming inventory slump. il Fortune 75:36+ F '67
Inventories tell too sad a story; with charts. Bsns W p70-2 Ap 8 '67

Inventory cutback. il Fortune 75:36+ My '67
Liquidating inventories. il Fortune 76:16+ Ag '67
Warning signals; inventory stockpile forcing manufacturers to cut production. Time 89: 84+ F 24 '67
INVENTORS
Inventions on demand; K. Kroyer. il Time 90: 96+ S 15 '67
Where inventors have a friend; Regional development laboratory, Philadelphia. il Bsns W p 184+ Je 10 '67
See also
Inventions
Ruben, S.
Wood, G.
INVENTORS models
New home for old inventions; patent museum in Plymouth, N.H. L. Aigner. il Pop Mech 128:102-5 Ag '67
INVENTORY control. See Inventories
INVERTEBRATES
See also
Arthropods
INVESTIGATIONS, Government. See Government investigations
INVESTMENT. See Investments
INVESTMENT advisory services. See Investments—Advisers
INVESTMENT banking
Accent on youth; L. M. Rosenthal & co. Time 90:97 N 3 '67
Investment bankers look ahead. il U S News 63:108-10+ D 11 '67
See also
Havenfield corporation
Kleiner, Bell and company
INVESTMENT clubs
Field day for the little guys. il Bsns W p 104-6 N 25 '67
Vanishing breed; cattle clubs assets missing. Bsns W p40 Jl 15 '67
INVESTMENT companies. See Investment trusts
INVESTMENT counselors. See Investments—Advisers
INVESTMENT credit. See Amortization deductions
INVESTMENT tax credit
Boost for business; restoration of the 7 per cent investment tax credit. il Bsns W p33-4 Mr 18 '67
Business lifts the lid on spending. Bsns W p36-7 Je 17 '67
Company spirits perk up again; proposal to restore the 7 per cent investment credit. il Bsns W p34-6 Mr 18 '67
Down or up, what's that buzzing? Newsweek 69:67 Ap 3 '67
Filling the bill; irrelevant amendment. Newsweek 69:24+ My 1 '67
Fine print in the tax law can save you money. F. Bailey, jr. Suc Farm 65:23 D '67
Foul-up over the investment tax credit; Senate fights compaign fund rider. Bsns W p 174 Ap 29 '67
How business may save on its taxes. Bsns W p50 Mr 25 '67
How cool is too cool? Time 89:78 Mr 31 '67
Investment tax credit. G. Champion. Duns R 89:17+ Ap '67
Losing his cool; President requests Congress to reinstate investment-tax credit. il Time 89:91 Mr 17 '67
LBJ brings back the tax credit for industry. il Newsweek 69:85 Mr 20 '67
More realism in fiscal policy. Bsns W p 196 Mr 18 '67
New plan on business-tax aid. U S News 62:103 Je 5 '67
Now: first aid for business; request to reinstate tax credit and fast-depreciation rules. il U S News 62:53 Mr 20 '67
Rail car makers bank on tax credit; reinstatement of the 7 per cent write-off on capital investment. il Bsns W p 175-6+ Mr 25 '67
Senators speed investment credit; vote to restore 7 per cent tax allowance but question the 6 per cent surtax. il Bsns W p48+ Mr 25 '67
Survey: new incentive to spend. il Newsweek 69:75-6 Mr 27 '67
Tax bill emerges. Bsns W p40 My 27 '67
Tax credit bill weathers Senate. Bsns W p36 My 13 '67
Where the tax bill bogged down. Bsns W p35 Ap 22 '67
INVESTMENT trusts
Big buyers of stock; institutions; including mutual funds, pension funds. U S News 62:87 F 13 '67

INVESTMENTS, Foreign—*Continued*
Foreign stocks yield a fast buck; buying foreign stocks abroad and selling them in the U.S. il Bsns W p 117-18 Jl 15 '67
How the United States protects South Africa. J. Lelyveld. Atlan 219:77-9 Ap '67
Not much pain for big business; borrowing money overseas to finance continued investments. il Bsns W p 16-17 Ja 6 '68
Overseas surge; surveys. Newsweek 69:78 Ap 3 '67
Political decay of foreign aid. J. D. Montgomery. Yale R 57:1-15 O '67
Politics of private foreign investment. L. Model. il For Affairs 45:639-51 Jl '67
Promise of the multinational corporation; excerpts from address. G. W. Ball. Fortune 75:80 Je 1 '67
Pulling back abroad. Newsweek 69:72 Je 12 '67
Shorter strides for the giants? problems of U.S.'s multinational companies. il Bsns W p40-2 D 30 '67
Spending overseas holds to rapid pace; McGraw-Hill survey; with editorial comment. il Bsns W p 104-5, 132 Ag 5 '67
What U.S. companies are doing abroad. See issues of U.S. news & World report
Where business gets the answers on foreign investment; Office of foreign direct investments. Bsns W p20 Ja 13 '68
   See also
Banks and banking—Foreign subsidiaries
Business—Foreign expansion
Corporations—Foreign subsidiaries
International center for settlement of investment disputes

   Taxation
President modifies rates of interest equalization tax; executive order, August 28, 1967. L. B. Johnson. Dept State Bul 57:396-7 S 25 '67

INVESTMENTS, Foreign (by India)
Mr Jolly comes to town; plant to manufacture hardboard, Nova Scotia. il Duns R 90:57-8 S '67

INVESTMENTS, Foreign (by Japan)
Japan's new idea for co-prosperity sphere. il U S News 63:90-1 Jl 24 '67
Japan's powerful push overseas. il Bsns W p92-4+ Ag 19 '67
Report from Alaska; Japanese investors. J. Gooding. il Fortune 76:49+ S 1 '67

INVESTMENTS, Foreign (in Australia)
Linkletter Down Under. il Newsweek 69:76-7 F 6 '67

INVESTMENTS, Foreign (in Belgium)
Belgians wheel, deal for foreign investment. il Bsns W p 139-40 O 28 '67

INVESTMENTS, Foreign (in Canada)
Is Canada for sale? Canadian attitudes toward U.S. control of Canadian industry. Christian Cent 84:134-5 F 1 '67

INVESTMENTS, Foreign (in Communist countries)
Capitalizing on communism. A. De Borchgrave. il Newsweek 70:30-2 D 25 '67

INVESTMENTS, Foreign (in Europe)
Dollar invades Europe. J. D. Phillips. Nation 205:242-5 S 18 '67
Europe's obsession with U.S. economic power. E. Taylor. il Reporter 37:25-7 D 28 '67
First real international bankers; American banks. J. Main. il Fortune 76:143-6+ D '67
Great American purchase; massive and continuing penetration. A. de Borchgrave. il Newsweek 69:36-8 F 27 '67
How U.S. industry is penetrating Europe. il U S News 62:44-6+ F 6 '67
Invasion stirs a cry for action; ideas of J. Servan-Schreiber on American industry in Europe. Bsns W p42 D 30 '67
U.S. business taking over Europe? excerpts from American challenge. J. J. Servan-Schreiber. il U S News 63:103-4 N 20 '67
Why the climate is changing for U.S. investment. W. Guzzardi, jr il Fortune 76:112-17+ S 15 '67

INVESTMENTS, Foreign (in Indonesia)
Back to business. il Time 89:68 Ja 27 '67
Indonesia waits. il Time 90:96 N 10 '67

INVESTMENTS, Foreign (in Japan)
Crack in the door; U.S. investment in Japan aided by liberalization program. Newsweek 69:78 Je 19 '67
Grudging go-ahead; relaxed restrictions on foreign investments. Time 89:67 Je 30 '67
Japan opens wider for capital from West. Bsns W p 143-4 Je 10 '67
President modifies rates of interest equalization tax; executive order, August 28, 1967. L. B. Johnson. Dept State Bul 57:396-7 S 25 '67

INVESTMENTS, Foreign (in Kenya)
Business makes a Kenya safari. il Bsns W p 108+ S 2 '67

INVESTMENTS, Foreign (in Korea)
U.S. businessmen to visit Korea for investment, trade studies. Dept State Bul 56:69 Ja 9 '67

INVESTMENTS, Foreign (in Latin America)
Latin-American common market makes common sense, for U.S. business too. W. Forbis. il Fortune 75:55-6 Je 1 '67
Road from Punta del Este; address, May 1, 1967. S. M. Linowitz. Dept State Bul 56:822-5 My 29 '67

INVESTMENTS, Foreign (in Mexico)
Business shakes up a lotus land. il Bsns W p88-90+ Ja 13 '68
Mexico's success story. il U S News 63:53-6 O 2 '67

INVESTMENTS, Foreign (in Puerto Rico)
Boost for Puerto Rico's boom; overwhelming preference for commonwealth status. il Bsns W p68-70+ Jl 29 '67

INVESTMENTS, Foreign (in South Africa)
Foreign investment in South Africa; U.N, Department of political and Security council affairs report. UN Mo Chron 4:50-1 Je '67

INVESTMENTS, Foreign (in the Caribbean Region)
Caribbean: vacation spots, new investment boom. il U S News 62:88-9 F 27 '67

INVESTMENTS, Foreign (in underdeveloped areas)
Agribusiness approach: problems and opportunities; address, September 11, 1967. L. B. Lundborg. Vital Speeches 33:756-9 O 1 '67
Charting new seas for U.S. capital; new AID program of extended risk guarantees. Bsns W p 130 Ap 8 '67
Does the U.S. exploit the developing nations? D. S. French. Commonweal 86:257-9 My 19 '67
Importance of agricultural development in our strategy for peace; address, May 10, 1967. E. V. Rostow. Dept State Bul 56:856-65 Je 5 '67
Promotion of private foreign investment; report by UN Department of economic and social affairs. UN Mo Chron 4:51-2 Ap '67

INVESTMENTS, Foreign (in United States)
Glamour stocks lure foreigners; overseas investors buying computer, electronics, and aerospace issue. il Bsns W p 127-8 N 25 '67
Wall Street: long view from abroad. C. Morgello. Newsweek 70:81 D 18 '67

INVESTMENTS, Foreign (in Yugoslavia)
Capital proposition; precedent-breaking foreign-investment code. Time 89:94 Ap 7 '67

INVESTORS. See Stockholders

INVESTORS diversified services, Incorporated
IDS men, the feeling is mutual. il Bsns W p68-70+ Ag 26 '67

INVESTORS overseas services, limited
Empire at Bernie-Voltaire. il Time 90:110-11 O 6 '67
Strategic retreat; SEC forces IOS out of U.S. securities market. Newsweek 69:72 Je 5 '67

INVITATIONS
Drop-of-a-hat invitations. il House & Gard 132:106-11 Jl '67

INVOICES. See Billing

IN-WHO-LISE (Nez Perce Indian)
Graves and grizzlies; excerpt from Tough trip through paradise; ed. by B. H. Stein. A. Garcia. il Am Heritage 18: 36-9+ Je '67

IOACHIM, Harry L.
Neoplastic transformation of rat thymic cells induced in vitro by Gross leukemia virus. bibliog Science 155:585-7 F 3 '67

IODIDES
Iodide abundance in oilfield brines in Oklahoma. A. G. Collins and G. C. Egleson. bibliog il Science 156:934-5 My 19 '67
Iodide transport; inhibition by agents reacting at the membrane. P. R. Larsen and J. Wolff. bibliog il Science 155:335-6 Ja 20 '67

IODINE
Ice nuclei from direct reaction of iodine vapor with vapors from leaded gasoline. A. W. Hogan. Science 158:800 N 10 '67

IODINE in the body
Iodine determined in purified thyrocalcitonin. P. Blanquet and others. bibliog il Science 158:381-3 O 20 '67

ION engines
New EOS vacuum chamber tests complete ion engines. il Tech W 20:33 My 29 '67

ION exchange
Chemical exfoliation of vermiculite and the production of colloidal dispersions. G. F. Walker and W. G. Garrett. bibliog il Science 156:385-7 Ap 21 '67
Membrane structure and ion permeation. G. Eisenman and others. bibliog il Science 155:965-74 F 24 '67

ION rockets. See Ion engines

IONESCO, Eugène
Exit the king (Le roi se meurt) tr. by D. Watson. Criticism
Newsweek il 71:96 Ja 22 '68
Time il 91:67 Ja 19 '68

IONIAN ISLANDS
See also
Cephalonia (island)
Corfu (island)

IONIUM dating. See Radioactive dating

IONIZED air. See Air, Ionized

IONOSPHERE. See Atmosphere, Upper

IONOSPHERIC research. See Atmospheric research

IONS
Atmospheric ions and germination of uredospores of puccinia striiformis. E. L. Sharp. bibliog il Science 156:1359-60 Je 9 '67
Ion pairing of magnesium sulfate in seawater: determined by ultrasonic absorption. F. H. Fisher. bibliog Science 157:823 Ag 18 '67
Ionic mechanism of cholinergic inhibition in molluscan neurons. D. J. Chiarandini and H. M. Gerschenfeld. bibliog il Science 156:1595-6 Je 23 '67
Ionic mechanisms of cholinergic excitation in molluscan neurons. D. J. Chiarandini and others. bibliog il Science 156:1597-9 Je 23 '67
Renal erythropoietic factor: role of ions and vasoactive agents in erythropoietin formation. E. D. Zanjani and others. bibliog il Science 156:1367-8 Je 9 '67
See also
Plasma (ionized gases)

IOWA
See also
Conservation of resources—Iowa

Historic houses, etc.
See also
Council Bluffs, Iowa—Historic houses, etc.

Politics and government
Governor from Ida Grove. V. Bourjaily. il N Y Times Mag p34-5+ F 26 '67

IOWA state university of science and technology, Ames
Bearded, sockless radical of Moo U; D. Smith, president of the Government of the student body. W. C. Murray. il N Y Times Mag p25+ Ap 9 '67; Discussion. p 12+ Ap 23 '67
Shaking up Moo U; new student-body president. Newsweek 69:97 Mr 6 '67

IPATIEFF, Vladimir
Ipatieff: man and scientist. H. Pines. por Science 157:166-70 Jl 14 '67

IPHIGENIA in Aulis; drama. See Euripides

IPSWICH, Mass.

Historic houses, etc.
Thanksgiving in Ipswich, circa 1640. P. Hyde and J. L. Hendrix. il House B 109:264-5 N '67

IQUITOS, Peru
Greenstreet, green hell and me. R. Atcheson. Holiday 42:20+ Ag '67

IRAN
Iran: a king crowns himself, and his queen. il Newsweek 70:44-7 N 6 '67
Proud as a peacock. il Time 89:28 Mr 31 '67
Revolution from the throne. il Time 90:32-4 O 6 '67
Royal revolution in Iran. P. Friggens. Read Digest 91:127-31 O '67
See also
Airlines—Iran
Airplanes, Military—Iran
Libraries—Iran
Libraries, Childrens—Iran
Music festivals—Iran

Antiquities
Beyond the Shah's palace. A. Netboy. il Sat R 50:64+ O 14 '67

Defenses
Neutral Iran will add F-4Ds to strengthen air defense. H. D. Watkins. il Aviation W 87:50-1+ Ag 7 '67

Description and travel
Beyond the Shah's palace. A. Netboy. il Sat R 50:64+ O 14 '67

Economic conditions
President Johnson and the Shah of Iran hold talks at Washington: exchange of remarks and exchange of toasts, August 22, with joint statement, August 23, 1967. L. B. Johnson; Mohammed Reza Pahlevi. Dept State Bul 57:358-62 S 18 '67
Spreading the wealth; White revolution. S. G. Slappey. il Nations Bsns 55:86-9 S '67

Royal family
In Iran a crown well earned. il Life 63:28-33 N 10 '67

Social conditions
President Johnson and the Shah of Iran hold talks at Washington; exchange of remarks and exchange of toasts, August 22, with joint statement, August 23, 1967. L. B. Johnson; Mohammed Reza Pahlevi. Dept State Bul 57:358-62 S 18 '67

IRAN national airlines. See Airlines—Iran

IRANIAN cookery. See Cookery, Iranian

IRAQ
See also
Petroleum industry and trade—Iraq

Antiquities
Custodian for the Fertile Crescent. il Time 89:86-9 Mr 31 '67

Politics and government
Political trends in Iraq and Kuwait. M. Khadduri. Cur Hist 52:84-9+ F '67

IRAQ museum. See Baghdad—Galleries and museums

IRAQ petroleum company. See Petroleum industry and trade—Iraq

IRELAND, Charles Thomas, 1921-
Corporate marine. por Time 91:71 Ja 5 '68

IRELAND, Douglas
Ready, willing and able. Commonweal 87:375-6 D 22 '67
Vietnam: labor's love lost. Commonweal 87:292-3 D 1 '67

IRELAND
See also
Airports—Ireland
Architecture—Ireland
Arts and crafts—Ireland
Censorship—Ireland
Colleges and universities—Ireland
Festivals—Ireland
Foreign visitors in Ireland
Hotels, taverns, etc.—Ireland
Hunting—Ireland
Libraries—Ireland
Music festivals—Ireland
Prisons—Ireland
Railroads—Ireland
Tourist trade—Ireland

Anecdotes, facetiae, satire, etc.
Innocent abroad. W. P. Fox. il Holiday 42:68-73 S '67

Description and travel
Nearest faraway place. S. Alexander. Life 63:13 S 8 '67
Personal business; little bit of heaven. Bsns W p 129-30 Jl 8 '67
Travel notes. R. Joseph. Esquire 67:20+ Ap '67
Travel's picture portfolio. Travel 127:50-5 Ja '67

Historic houses, etc.
Georgian: D. Guinness of Irish Georgian society. New Yorker 43:41-2 O 7 '67

History
Constance De Markievicz; in the cause of Ireland, by J. Van Voris. Review
Nation 206:20-1 Ja 1 '68. S. Cronin
See also
Catholic church in Ireland

Bibliography
Articles and other books received; comp. by L. H. Carlson. See issues of American historical review

Sinn Fein rebellion, 1916
Kilmainham gaol: monument to the rising. V. S. Pritchett. il Atlan 219:100-1 F '67

IRELAND—*Continued*

Industries

Distribution point called Ireland. R. Brady. il Duns R 90:44-6+ O '67

First harvest from Ireland's brilliant new design workshop, Kilkenny. M. Gough and J. Hendrix. il House B 109:242-5 O '67

Religious institutions and affairs

World around us (cont) Christian Cent 84: 287-8, 1028+ Mr 1, Ag 9 '67

See also

Catholic church in Ireland

Social conditions

Still life in the ould turf. J. F. Henahan. Sat R 50:4 S 23 '67

IRION, Mary Jean

Libido allegro; poem. Christian Cent 85:74 Ja 17 '68

November first; poem. Christian Cent 84:1396 N 1 '67

IRIS; opera. See Mascagni, P.

IRISES

Dividing and planting bearded iris. il Home Gard 54:19 Je '67

Dwarf iris; add a new dimension to your garden. W. Welch. il Horticulture 45:26-7+ S '67

Five iris of the year: 1968. Home Gard 54:57 Je '67

For more color than a rainbow plant more iris. C. Kendall. il Pop Gard 18:74-5 Ag '67

If you are ready for iris. il Sunset 139:158-9 S '67

Iris color show. il Sunset 139:68-9 S '67

Iris for every garden. P. F. Frese. il Horticulture 45:38-40 My '67

Iris have changed. G. Douglas il Horticulture 45:30-3+ F '67

It's time to plant the Japanse iris. Home Gard 54:53 Ag '67

Magnificent American iris. H. Randall. il Home Gard 54:16-19 Je '67

Not too tall and not too small. il Sunset 138: 248-9 Mr '67

Prelude to spring. I. D. Jolly. il Pop Gard 18:93 Mr '67

Siberian iris. F. W. Cassebeer. il Horticulture 45:22-5+ Jl '67

IRISH art. See Art, Irish

IRISH Georgian architecture. See Architecture, Georgian

IRISH in the United States

Opinion: on writing about America. F. O'Connor. Mlle 64:148+ Ap '67

IRISH literature

Short history of Irish literature, by F. O'Connor. Review

Nation 205:149-50 Ag 28 '67. K. Sullivan

IRISH missionaries. See Missionaries

IRISH revolt See Ireland—History—Sinn Fein rebellion, 1916

IRISH stew. See Stew

IRIZARRY, Carmen

Fátima: reflections after the fact. Christian Cent 84:1016-19 Ag 9 '67

IRON

Equilibration temperatures of iron and magnesium in chondritic meteorites. W. R. Van Schmus and D. M. Koffman. bibliog il Science 155:1009-11 F 24 '67

Mössbauer analysis of iron in clay minerals. C. E. Weaver and others. bibliog il Science 156:504-8 Ap 28 '67

See also

Cliftonite

IRON curtain. See Europe, Eastern

IRON metabolism

Hydroxamic acids in nature. J. B. Neilands. bibliog il Science 156:1443-7 Je 16 '67

IRON metallurgy

Beneficiation of iron ores. M. M. Fine. il Sci Am 218:28-35 Ja '68

IRON meteorites. See Meteorites

IRON mines and mining

See also

Iron ores

Australia

Australia bankrolls its iron. Bsns W p135-6 Ap 15 '67

IRON ores

Beneficiation of iron ores. M. M. Fine. il Sci Am 218:28-35 Ja '68

Expert group on iron ore; methods for updating survey of world iron ore resources. UN Mo Chron 4:126 Ja '67

See also

Taconite

IRON work. See Ironwork

IRONCLADS. See Armored vessels

IRONING board covers

Better material for ironing-board covers. Consumer Rep 32:409 Ag '67

IRONWORK

Architectural ironwork; Savannah, Ga. il Antiques 91:329-30 Mr '67

Filigrees & forgings; Rouen's Musée Le Secq des Tournelles. il Time 89:70-1 Je 16 '67

Mobile ironwork. M. R. Ingate. il Antiques 92:354-9 S '67

Robert Bourdon, blacksmith in wrought iron; a contemporary craftsman. D. J. Willcox. il Am Artist 32:32-7 Ja '68

IROQUOIS Indians

Dilemma of the Iroquois. R. D. Corwin. il Natur Hist 76:6-7+ Je '67

IRRADIATED food. See Food, Effect of radiation on

IRRADIATION

See also

Radioactivation analysis

IRRIGATION

Don't go wild on irrigation! P. B. Jones. Suc Farm 65:52-3 F '67

Egypt

Research frontier; mechanical substitute for the shadoof found? R. B. Murrow. il Sat R 50:51-5 Je 3 '67

Israel

Salt-water agriculture. H. Boyko. il Sci Am 216:89-94+ Mr '67

IRRIGATION farming

From sagebrush to crops; as water rescues arid land; Northwestern states to the Southwest. il U S News 63:123-4+ D 11 '67

IRRIGATION machinery

Research frontier; mechanical model waterlifter devised from drinking bird toy. R. B. Murrow. il Sat R 50:51-5 Je 3 '67

IRSA, A. P. See Friedman, L. jt. auth.

IRVIN, Bob

Detroit listening post. See issues of Popular mechanics

'68 cars: how new will they be? Pop Mech 127:59-62+ Je '67

IRVIN, Robert W.

Automakers focus on Detroit's jobless. Reporter 37:29-30 D 28 '67

Nader takes potshots at the '67s. Motor T 19:79-81 Mr '67

Sports-personal cars: what lies ahead? Motor T 20:21-3 Ja '68

IRVINE, Keith

Ghana after Nkrumah. bibliog f Cur Hist 52:149-53+ Mr '67

IRVINE, Calif.

Homes on the range; Irvine ranch's Fashion island near Los Angeles. il Time 90:94+ S 22 '67

Making of a city. M. Roberts. il Sat R 50: 72-4 S 23 '67

New town rises back at the ranch; south of Los Angeles. il Bsns W p 176-8+ S 23 '67

IRVINE company

New town rises back at the ranch; south of Los Angeles. il Bsns W p 176-8+ S 23 '67

IRVING, Don

Form determinants. Sch Arts 66:12-17 Je '67

IRVING P. Krick associates

Weather preview for sportsmen. il Field & S 72:22+ N '67; 50-1+ Ja '68

Your weather. See issues of Farm journal

IRVING, Tex.

Irving Center for the arts. B. Waldo. il Parks & Rec 2:17+ Je '67

IRWIN, Ray

Close, but no cigar. New Yorker 42:86+ Ja 21 '67

Here we go gathering Nichols and May. Atlan 219:114 F '67

IRWIN, Samuel, and Egozcue, Jose

Chromosomal abnormalities in leukocytes from LSD-25 users. bibliog Science 157: 313-14 Jl 21 '67

IRWIN, Theodore

Children and the law. Parents Mag 42:68-71+ O '67

Emergency! Todays Health 45:34-9 Ap '67

Financing home improvements. Am Home 70:87+ My '67

Forecasting your future health. Todays Health 45:25-9 My '67

High-risk care saves lives and minds. Todays Health 46:42-4+ Ja '68

In most newborn babies: brain damage can be prevented. Look 31:61-7+ S 5 '67

IRWIN, Theodore—*Continued*
Lively Lindsay: mayor on the move. Todays
Health 45:40-3 Je '67
Money management. Am Home 71:10+ Ja '68
673-square-mile hospital. Todays Health 45:
52-4+ D '67
Teenagers speak out about codes of conduct.
Parents Mag 42:43-5+ Ap '67
What kind of mates will our teen-agers be?
Todays Health 45:20-3 S '67

ISAAC, Erich
Enigma of circumcision. Commentary 43:51-5
Ja; 30-2 My '67
Jewish knowledge. Commentary 43:99-101 Ap
'67
Mystical humanism. Commentary 43:99-101
My '67

ISAACS, John D. and others
Satellite elongation into a true Sky-Hook.
bibliog Science 151:682-3; 158:947 F 11 '66,
N 17 '67

ISBELL, Harold
Susan; poem. Commonweal 86:289 My 26 '67

ISELIN, Columbus O'Donnell. See Emery, K. O.
jt. auth.

ISEMAN, Marjorie F.
Sex education. McCalls 95:36-7+ Ja '68

ISENBERG, Robert M.
Education comes alive outdoors. NEA J 56:
34-5 Ap '67

ISENSON, Raymond S. See Sherwin, C. W. jt.
auth.

ISLA DE PASCUA. See Easter Island

ISLAM
Arabia decpeta: a people self-deluded; Time
essay. Time 90:24-5 Jl 14 '67

ISLAM and Christianity. See Christianity and
other religions

ISLAND life. See Islands

ISLAND of Eve; story. Cave, H.

ISLAND of Hydra. See Hydra (island)

ISLAND of pearls. See Margarita Island

ISLANDS
America's retirement islands. N. D. Ford.
il Travel 128:56-8+ D '67
How to buy an island. E. Kinard. il House B
109:124-5+ Ja '67
Island in the sound, by H. Heckman. Re-
view
Sat R 50:64+ Je 10 '67. M. L. Coit
Islands for your next vacation. S. Mix. il
Todays Health 45:42-7+ My; 34-9+ Je '67
My Maine islands. J. T. Starr. il Am For
73:38-41+ F '67

ISLANDS of the Pacific
Enchanted islands. B. L. Burman. il Read
Digest 91:164-6+ D '67
Maugham's Pacific. W. Menard. il Sat R
50:77-8+ Mr 11 '67
Melanesia with a French accent. M. Peter-
sen. il Motor B 119:52+ Ap '67
Powerboating in paradise. B. Robinson. il
Yachting 122:42-3+ Jl '67
See also
Cook Islands
Guam
Micronesia
Oceania
Trust Territory of the Pacific Islands

ISLE OF MAN. See Man, Isle of

ISLE ROYALE NATIONAL PARK
Isle Royale wilderness hearing. Nat Parks
Mag 41:20 Ja '67
Wilderness plan for Isle Royale National Park
and the surrounding region. il Nat Parks
Mag 41:18-19 Mr '67

ISLIP, N.Y.
Something rotten in Islip. Time 91:57 Ja
5 '68

ISOANTIGENS. See Antigens and antibodies

ISOENZYMES. See Enzymes

ISOLATION, Social. See Social isolation

ISOLATIONISM (United States) See United
States—Foreign relations

ISOPRENOID acids. See Acids, Organic

ISOPRENOID biosynthesis. See Biosynthesis

ISOPTERA. See Termites

ISOTOPES
Isotope separation by carrier diffusion. H.
Craig. bibliog il Science 159:93-6 Ja 5 '68
Isotopic analysis of rare gases with a laser
microprobe. G. H. Megrue. bibliog il Sci-
ence 157:1555-6 S 29 '67
See also
Radioisotopes
also subhead Isotopes under names of
chemical elements, e.g. Oxygen—Isotopes

ISOZYMES. See Enzymes

ISRAEL, Adrian C.
Old hand breaks with tradition. por Bsns W
p 145-6 My 20 '67

ISRAEL, Gordon
Biography of a hired gun. R. Bach. il por
Flying 80:40-3 Ap '67

ISRAEL, Lee
Last of the honest-to-God ladies. Esquire 68:
114-16+ N '67
Rise and fall and rise of Elizabeth Taylor.
Esquire 67:96-9+ Mr '67

ISRAEL
Aryanization of the Jewish state, by M.
Selzer. Review
Commentary 44:92-4+ D '67. S. Avineri
Atlantic report. Atlan 219:14+ Mr '67
Coping with victory. il Time 89:22-3+ Je
23 '67
Economics of triumph; post-war economic,
political, and security headaches. A. Rosen-
feld. il Reporter 37:22-5 Jl 13 '67
End of the Jewish people? by G. Friedmann.
Review
Newsweek il 70:91 Jl 17 '67. S. Maloff
Fin du peuple juif? by G. Friedmann. Review
Commentary 43:75-80 Mr '67. R. Alter
In Israel: after the triumph. A. Kazin. il
Harper 235:72-8+ N '67
Israel: a special issue; symposium. il Holiday
42:57-99+ D '67
Israel after victory. D. J. Simpson. Cur Hist
53:341-5+ D '67
Israel: nation too young to die. J. A.
Michener. il Look 31:64-8+ Ag 8 '67
Israel: the unrelenting battle. D. J. Simp-
son. Cur Hist 52:78-83+ F '67
Matter of survival. C. Sterling. il Reporter
36:16-17 Je 29 '67
Nation under siege. il Time 89:38-42 Je 9 '67
Troubles for Israel in hostile Mideast; inter-
view. L. Eshkol. U S News 62:75-7 Ap 17
'67
Victors. il Newsweek 69:21-3 Je 26 '67
What is Israel? Christian Cent 84:1091-2 Ag
30 '67; Discussion. 84:1320-1 O 18 '67
See also
Advertising—Israel
Aeronautics, Military—Israel
Agriculture—Israel
Airplane industry and trade—Israel
Airplanes, Military—Israel
Americans in Israel
Arabs in Israel
Christmas—Israel
Holy Land
Immigrants in Israel
Irrigation—Israel
Jerusalem
Jordan River
Masada (fortress) Israel
Morale, National—Israel
Music—Israel
Political parties—Israel
Public opinion—Israel
Publishers and publishing—Israel
Ramat ha Shofet
Secret service—Israel
Tourist trade—Israel
United Nations—Israel
Water supply—Israel
Women—Israel
Zionism

Air force
Effective airpower. R. Hotz. Aviation W 86:
11 Je 26 '67
History's most outstanding air battle. il U S
News 62:36 Je 19 '67
Israelis' air punch major factor in war. W.
C. Wetmore. il Aviation W 87:18-23 Jl 3 '67
Massive resupply narrows Israeli margin in
air power. il Aviation W 86:16-19 Je 19 '67

Antiquities
Digging for the facts. il Sr Schol 91:13 D 14
'67
Good show; exhibition of Masada rebellion
and the Yadin dig at the Jewish museum.
New Yorker 43:42-4 O 7 '67
In the footsteps of the past. A. Menen. il
Holiday 42:90-1+ D '67
Masada revisited; exhibition in Manhattan's
Jewish museum. M. R. Weiss. il Sat R 50:
24-5 N 4 '67
Museum exhibit tells the Masada story. J. A.
Sanders. Christian Cent 85:89-90 Ja 17 '68

Armed forces
Israel in time of crisis: a report from the
scene. W. MacDougall. il U S News 62:40-1
Je 5 '67
Israel's swift sword. B. W. Tuchman. Atlan
220:56-62 S '67
Report from Israel. A. Campbell. New Repub
156:8-10 Je 10 '67

ISRAEL—*Continued*

Army

Israeli secret weapon. M. Gellhorn. Vogue 150:192-3+ O 1 '67

Major's long ride to a short war. R. Lurie. il Life 62:60A-60B Je 30 '67

Those Israeli troops. B. Mauldin. New Repub 156:5-6 Je 24 '67

Commercial treaties and agreements

U.S. and Israel conclude new cotton textile agreement; Department announcement: with text of U.S. note, January 27, 1967. il Dept State Bul 56:389-92 Mr 6 '67

United States and Israel sign new cotton textile agreement; Department announcement, with text of U.S. note. Dept State Bul 57:243-5 Ag 21 '67

Defenses

Poised fist. il Time 89:35-6 Ja 27 '67

Description and travel

Country comes of age. E. J. Kahn, jr. il Holiday 42:64-5+ D '67

Short story of a short war: the aftermath. H. Black. Nat R 19:1255-6 N 14 '67

Tourist in the wake of war. J. Berke. il Sat R 50:40-1+ O 14 '67

Traveler, consider my Israel; ed. by R. Joseph. D. Ben-Gurion. il Esquire 68:94-5+ Jl '67

Travel's picture portfolio. Travel 128:52-7 S '67

Economic conditions

Atlantic report. Atlan 219:14+ Mr '67

Israel on top: can it survive? il U S News 62:40-2 Je 19 '67

Israel's will to survive. P. Ben. New Repub 156:12-13 Ap 15 '67

Manpower problem. E. Ginzberg. il Reporter 37:23-4+ N 16 '67

Meanwhile, back in Jerusalem. . . Bsns W p 116 Je 17 '67

Recession in Israel; is the success story over? il U S News 62:73-4 Ap 17 '67

When Israel looks ahead. il U S News 62:26-8 Je 26 '67

Economic policy

Long step back. il Time 89:94 Ap 7 '67

Foreign opinion

American Left and Israel. M. Peretz. bibliog f Commentary 44:27-34 N '67

Israel & the intellectuals; American Jewish intellectuals response to victory. R. Alter. Commentary 44:46-52 O '67

Foreign relations

Escalation in Galilee; Israeli-Syrian border. il Newsweek 69:54 Ja 30 '67

Eshkol sticks to his guns. J. Feron. il N Y Times Mag p34-5+ Ja 7 '68

Exploding conflict in the Mideast. il U S News 62:8 My 29 '67

Flare-up jars Mideast truce; sinking of Israeli destroyer Elath and destruction of Egyptian oil installations. il Sr Schol 91:12-13 N 9 '67

Israel on top; can it survive? il U S News 62:40-2 Je 19 '67

Israel's tough stand on captured territories. A. Perlmutter. New Repub 158:12-14 Ja 13 '68

Limited options; L. Eshkol's prognosis for the Middle East in 1968. Newsweek 71:32+ Ja 8 '68

Middle East: Cassandra was right; return to violence. il Newsweek 70:42+ N 6 '67

Poised fist; Syria. il Time 89:35-6 Ja 27 '67

Sound & fury; troubles on Israeli frontiers. il Time 89:26+ My 26 '67

Tension in Jerusalem; Israel's decision to hold military parade in streets of Jerusalem. il Newsweek 69:54+ My 22 '67

Today in Tel Aviv. S. Wolpert. Nation 205:7-8 Jl 3 '67

U.N. censure of Israel; text of resolution. Cur Hist 52:113 F '67

U.N. condemns violations of Middle East cease-fire; statements, October 24, 25, 1967. A. J. Goldberg. Dept State Bul 57:690-2 N 20 '67

United States

Mutual aid. il Newsweek 71:38 Ja 22 '68

History

Arab-Israeli dispute in perspective. N. Safran. il Cur Hist 53:321-30+ D '67

Birth of a nation, roots of the hatred. il Life 62:80-4+ Je 16 '67

Exodus as autobiography. A. R. Gold. Commentary 43:46-51 My '67

Father and hero. Y. Dayan. il Look 31:15-19 Ag 22 '67

Israel, by R. Sanders. Review
  Commentary 43:88-9 F '67. E. Grossman

Meaning of Israel. H. Golden. il Holiday 42:58-63+ D '67

On facing the reality of Israel; Time essay. il Time 89:24-5 Je 23 '67

Storm center on the new map Israel. E. Kern. il Life 63:60-2 O 20 '67

Photographs

Face of a varied land. Holiday 42:92-9 D '67

Politics and government

After the victory. New Repub 156:3-4 Je 24 '67

Hopeful truths of the new reality. M. Dayan. il Life 63:120-120B S 29 '67

In Jerusalem: a new outlook. il Newsweek 70:36+ S 11 '67

Moshe and the mukhtars. il Newsweek 70:37-8 Jl 3 '67

Pairing off the generals. Time 90:42 O 27 '67

Political cross fire; growing struggle for leadership. il Newsweek 70:31+ Jl 17 '67

What's wrong with Israel? M. Geltman. Nat R 19:568-9 My 30 '67

See also
Political parties—Israel

Popular culture

Country comes of age. E. J. Kahn, jr. il Holiday 42:64-5+ D '67

Social conditions

Israeli identity: problems in the development of the collective identity of an ideological society. S. N. Eisenstadt. Ann Am Acad 370:116-23 Mr '67

Territorial expansion

Christians and the Mideast crisis. W. G. Oxtoby. Christian Cent 84:961-5 Jl 26 '67; Reply. D. Lieber. 84:1193-4 S 20 '67

Digging in to stay. il Time 90:20-1 Ag 11 '67

Israel and Nasser. P. Ben. New Repub 157:20-2 S 9 '67

Israeli notebook. H. Brandon. Sat R 50:20 S 30 '67

Israel's administration and Arab refugees. D. Peretz. For Affairs 46:336-46 Ja '68

Israel's strategy for the future. il U S News 63:40-2 D 18 '67

What can and can't be done. P. Ben. New Repub 156:6-7 Je 24 '67

ISRAEL aircraft industries. See Airplane industry and trade—Israel

ISRAEL and Germany

Symbolic atonement in Israel. D. Wigode. Mlle 64:130-1+ F '67

ISRAEL and the United States

Israel and American Jewry. A. Hertzberg. Commentary 44:69-73 Ag '67; Discussion. 44:22+ D '67

ISRAEL philharmonic orchestra

Very special effort. il Newsweek 70:91 Ag 14 '67

ISRAELI-Arab relations. See Jewish-Arab relations

ISRAELI-Arab war, 1948-1949

Birth of a nation, roots of the hatred. il Life 62:80-4+ Je 16 '67

ISRAELI-Arab war, 1967

After the victory. New Repub 156:3-4 Je 24 '67

Again, silence in the churches. A. R. Eckardt and A. L. Eckhardt. Christian Cent 84:992-5 Ag 2 '67

Arab-Israeli war. C. W. Yost; B. Lewis; D. Peretz. For Affairs 46:304-46 Ja '68

Arab-Israeli war and Catholic-Jewish dialogue. J. B. Sheerin. Cath World 205:260-2 Ag '67

Arabs, 1967. J. S. Badeau. Atlan 220:102-4+ D '67

Argument indeed: Soviet attack, Israeli retort; with excerpts from addresses. A. Kosygin; A. Eban. il Life 62:24-5 Je 30 '67

Armor churns up the Syrian hills. T. H White. il Life 62:20-24C Je 23 '67

Back from the brink; with editorial comment. il Bsns W p35-6, 192 Je 10 '67

Backlash of defeat roils Arab world. il Bsns W p 112-14 Je 17 '67

Backlash of Mideast war: Libya turns on the U.S; Wheelus field at stake. il U S News 63:48 Ag 21 '67

Battle and the war. J. Burnham. Nat R 19:680 Je 27 '67

Battle for Jerusalem. S. De Gramont. il Sat Eve Post 240:70-5 Ag 12 '67

ISRAELI-Arab war, 1967—*Continued*
Battle of Jerusalem. M. Elkins. il Newsweek 69:29-31 Je 19 '67
Biggest pie-throwing contest ever? emergency session of the U.N. General assembly. il Newsweek 69:18-20 Je 26 '67
Cairo diary: by a Times correspondent. E. Pace. il N Y Times Mag p7+ Jl 2 '67
Cairo diary of U.S. humiliation. T. Thompson. il Life 62:70+ Je 23 '67
Campaign for the books; battle of Syria's Golan Heights. il Time 90:22-3 S 1 '67
Cold war is still with us. America 116:847 Je 17 '67
Coping with victory. il Time 89:22-3+ Je 23 '67
Crisis; interviews. Thant; F. Y. Chai; R. Bunche. New Yorker 43:19-23 Jl 29 '67
Customers are fighting. W. J. Coughlin. Tech W 20:50 Je 12 '67
Diplomatic counterpoint. il Newsweek 69:31-4 Je 19 '67
Double-think, Egyptian style. A. Carthew. il N Y Times Mag p 19-21+ Ag 20 '67
Economics of triumph; post-war economic, poltical, and security headaches. A. Rosenfeld. il Reporter 37:22-5 Jl 13 '67
Effective airpower. R. Hotz. Aviation W 86:11 Je 26 '67
Efficient conquerors. il Time 89:24+ Je 30 '67
Error of war; and U.S. seamen die. il U S News 62:10 Je 19 '67
European leaders meet with President Johnson; exchange of toasts, June 22, 1967. L. B. Johnson; O. J. Krag. Dept State Bul 57:40-1 Jl 10 '67
Exhilarating crucible of crisis. H. Sidey. il Life 62:32B Je 23 '67
Facing the jihad. Commonweal 86:357 Je 16 '67
Father and hero. Y. Dayan. il Look 31:15-19 Ag 22 '67
Finis; Navy court of inquiry reviews Israeli assault against Liberty. il Newsweek 70:24 Jl 3 '67
Foreign policy: a study in contrasts; US and USSR. Bsns W p 182 Je 24 '67
Fortunate failure; triumph of Israel, also a victory for the U.S. K. Crawford. Newsweek 69:45 Je 19 '67
Found: Paul Schutzer's final twenty-three frames; with photographs. Life 62:30-32A Je 23 '67
Glubb pasha sizes up the Middle East. il Newsweek 69:18 Je 19 '67
Great de-mythification. A. Weill-Tuckerman. Nation 204:770-1 Je 19 '67
Hand of Russia. W. Laqueur. il Reporter 36:18-20 Je 29 '67
Hawk of Israel: M. Dayan. C. G. Pepper. il N Y Times Mag p5+ Jl 9 '67
Hot-line diplomacy; use of link between Washington and Moscow. il Time 89:15-17 Je 16 '67
How the Israelis really did it. L. Rosten. Look 31:10 Jl 25 '67
If the Arabs had won. M. Samuel. il Look 31:80-2 Jl 25 '67
In Jordan, a defeated King Hussein keeps his dignity. il Life 62:66-7 Je 23 '67
In sixty hours a new Middle East. Life 62:4 Je 16 '67
Inquest for Liberty. il Time 90:15 Jl 7 '67
Israel and world politics. T. Draper. bibliog Commentary 44:19-48 Ag '67; Discussion. 44:6+ N; 12+ D '67
Israel to the rescue of the U.S. W. F. Buckley, jr. Nat R 19:679 Je 27 '67
Israeli thrust, the astounding sixty hours; with report by M. Mok. il Life 26-33D+ Je 16 '67
Israeli victory. New Repub 156:1-2 Je 17 '67
Israelis rout Arabs. il Sr Schol 91:19 S 21 '67
Israel's Dayan: mastermind of victory. U S News 62:21 Je 19 '67
Israel's surprise weapon: envoy Eban. il U S News 63:20 Jl 3 '67
Israel's swift sword. B. W. Tuchman. Atlan 220:56-62 S '67
Jam we are in. S. Alsop. il Sat Eve Post 240:14 Jl 29 '67
June 8, at 1400 hours; story of USS Liberty. J. J. Kilpatrick. il Nat R 19:952-8 S 5 '67
King pleads the Arab case. il Life 63:24-5 Jl 7 '67
Last-gasp strafing, then into the compound for PW's. il Life 62:68-9 Je 23 '67
Letter from Cairo. T. Armbrister. il Sat Eve Post 240:62-3 Jl 29 '67
Letter from Israel. R. Adler. New Yorker 43:114+ Je 17 '67

Letter from Paris. Genêt. New Yorker 43:84+ Je 24 '67
Letter from Washington. R. H. Rovere. New Yorker 43:90+ Je 24 '67
Liberty signals: misrouted, misread. U S News 63:7 Jl 10 '67
Lightning in the desert: story of the Israeli victory. W. MacDougall. il U S News 62:62-3 Je 19 '67
Losers; victors. il Newsweek 69:20-3 Je 26 '67
Major's long ride to a short war. R. Lurie. il Life 62:60A-60B Je 30 '67
Middle East aftermath. H. Brandon. Sat R 50:8 Jl 1 '67
Middle East conflict; symposium. Christian Cent 84:959-73 Jl 26 '67
Middle East crisis: a trial balance. L. Binder. il Bul Atomic Sci 23:2-7+ S '67
Middle East crisis; symposium. Vital Speeches 33:578-605 Jl 15; 610-21 Ag 1 '67
Middle East; guidelines for policy. N. Safran and S. Hoffmann. Nation 204:806-8 Je 26 '67
Middle East outcome. K. Crawford. Newsweek 70:27 Jl 17 '67
Mideast war's effect on U.S. business. il U S News 62:48-9 Je 19 '67
Mystery of attack on U.S.S. Liberty. il U S News 62:33 Je 26 '67
National council position on Middle East. Christian Cent 84:804 Je 21 '67
New Arab world. W. Rogers. il Look 31:31-3 O 17 '67
New deal for the Middle East; responsibility of USSR and US. Nation 204:802-3 Je 26 '67
Next battlefield: the U.N. il Bsns W p29-30 Je 17 '67
One step backward; two steps forward. F. Utley. Nat R 19:848+ Ag 8 '67
Over the hot line, the Middle East. H. Sidey. Life 62:24B Je 16 '67
Peace of reconciliation? Commonweal 86:379-80 Je 23 '67
Picking up the pieces. Nat R 19:671-3 Je 27 '67
Plunging into the Mideast crisis. il Bsns W p30-2 Je 17 '67
Politics. D. Macdonald. Esquire 68:44-6 S '67
Principles for peace in the Middle East; address, June 19, 1967. L. B. Johnson. Dept State Bul 57:31-4 Jl 10 '67
Psychedelic debate; General assembly Mideast debate. il Time 89:22 Je 30 '67
Quickest war. il Time 89:22-8+ Je 16 '67
Real cost to Israel on the battlefield; with chart. il U S News 62:11 Je 26 '67
Real news on the hot line. Fortune 76:71-2 Jl '67
Reconfirmations. J. Burnham. Nat R 19:788 Jl 25 '67
Report from the U.N. General assembly. C. M. Eichelberger. Sat R 50:16-17 Ag 12 '67
Report from three battlefronts. G. Bailey. il Reporter 36:13-15 Je 29 '67
Reporter at large. F. Lewis. New Yorker 43:36-42+ Jl 1 '67
Roots of anguish: west bank of the River Jordan. M. J. Kubic. Newsweek 70:31-2 Jl 24 '67
Running from defeat. il Time 89:26-7 Je 23 '67
Russia real loser in Mideast war? il U S News 62:38-9 Je 19 '67
Russian gifts gone to waste; prisoners; refugees. il Life 62:26-32A Je 30 '67
Scope and hazard of victory. il Life 62:24D-27 Je 23 '67
Short story of a short war: the aftermath. H. Black. Nat R 19:1255-6 N 14 '67
Short war and the long war. E. Stillman. il N Y Times Mag p7+ Je 18 '67
Sinai diary: by an Israeli solider. A. Rubinstein. il N Y Times Mag p6+ Jl 2 '67
Situation in the Near East; White House releases, June 5-8, 1967. Dept State Bul 56:949-52 Je 26 '67
Six day war, by R. S. Churchill and W. S. Churchill. Review
  Sat R 50:45-6 N 4 '67. L. Roberts
Skirmishes & minisummits. il Time 90:31-2 Jl 21 '67
Soviet blunder that led to Mideast war: the inside story. il U S News 63:6 Jl 17 '67
Soviet posture in the Middle East. B. Shwadran. Cur Hist 53:331-6+ D '67
T.R.B. from Washington: hope of the hot line. New Repub 156:2 Je 24 '67
Terrible swift sword; How the war was won. il Newsweek 69:24-9 Je 19 '67
There is no false courage left in Egypt. A. Carthew. il N Y Times Mag p45-7+ D 3 '67
Three-day blitz from Gaza to Suez; with military appraisal by M. S. Johnson. il U S News 62:33-7 Je 19 '67
Toll. il Newsweek 69:24+ Je 26 '67

ISRAELI-Arab war, 1967—*Continued*
Unexplained casualty: U.S.S. Liberty. il Life 62:28-9 Je 23 '67
Unfinished war. M. Ascoli. Reporter 36:12 Je 29 '67
U.N. debate unfolds. il Newsweek 70:18-21 Jl 3 '67
Victorious Israel's look and mood. L. J. Walinsky. New Repub 157:9-10 Jl 8 '67
Victory without peace? D. Lawrence. U S News 62:98 Je 26 '67
Waiting for a compromise. P. Ben. New Repub 157:9-10 Jl 1 '67
War in the Middle East: has anyone learned anything? il Sat Eve Post 240:76 Jl 15 '67
War that never was; American press corps in Cairo. G. Montgomery. Sat R 50:54-6 Ag 12 '67
We will kill you Americans, too! Americans in Cairo. J. Law. il U S News 62:30-1 Je 26 '67
What have we learned? N. Cousins. Sat R 50:20+ Je 24 '67
What not to expect from the U.N. Life 62:4 Je 30 '67
See also
Arab states—Foreign relations
Jordan—Israeli occupation, 1967-

Aerial operations
Israeli airlines mobilized for Mideast war. W. C. Wetmore. Aviation W 87:26-8 Jl 31 '67
Israeli mirage pilot describes MiG kills. W. C. Wetmore. il Aviation W 87:76-7+ Jl 17 '67
Israelis' air punch major factor in war. W. C. Wetmore. il Aviation W 87:18-23 Jl 3 '67
Massive resupply narrows Israeli margin in air power. il Aviation W 86:16-19 Je 19 '67
Mock dogfights sharpened Israeli pilots. il Aviation W 87:24-7 Jl 3 '67
Noratlases flew patrol, supply missions. il Aviation W 87:89-91+ Jl 17 '67

Diplomatic history
Consequences of defeat. B. Lewis. For Affairs 46:321-35 Ja '68

Moral and religious aspects
Arabs, Israelis. Christians; letters to editors on the Middle East crisis. Christian Cent 84:1128-30 S 6 '67
Did Christians fail Israel? R. L. Rubenstein. Commonweal 87:297-8 D 1 '67; Discussion. 87:420-1+ D 29 '67
Israel and the Christian dilemma. Christian Cent 84:883-4 Jl 12 '67; Discussion. 84:1022 Ag 9 '67
Messianic times? J. C. Evans. Christian Cent 84:1149-51 S 13 '67
Urbis and orbis: Jerusalem today. J. A. Sanders. Christian Cent 84:967-70 Jl 26 '67

Peace and mediation
After the blitz, can Israel win the peace? il U S News 63:82-3 Ag 14 '67
As new flare-ups broke Mideast truce. il U S News 63:15 S 18 '67
Consequences of defeat. B. Lewis. For Affairs 46:321-35 Ja '68
General assembly debate. P. Ben. New Repub 157:15-16 S 30 '67
Israel's finest future. C. Northcott. Christian Cent 84:1062 Ag 23 '67
Least unreasonable Arab: King Hussein. il Time 90:22-3+ Jl 14 '67
Letter from Israel. D. Lang. New Yorker 43:37-8+ D 30 '67
Mideast: hail the conquered hero. il Newsweek 70:34-6 S 11 '67
Mideast needs less rigidity. Life 63:4 Jl 21 '67
Mideast peace hopes: seeds in the desert. A. De Borchgrave. il Newsweek 70:32 Jl 17 '67
No kibitzers wanted; Yugoslav peace proposals fail. il Newsweek 70:40 Ag 28 '67
No mood for accommodation. il Time 90:21 S 1 '67
No sign of compromise; Marshal Tito's plan for settlement. il Newsweek 70:29 Ag 21 '67
Puzzling portents. Newsweek 70:51-2 N 13 '67
Rebuilding peace in the Middle East. America 117:51 Jl 15 '67
Still a fever; Yugoslav compromise proposal fails. il Time 90:32 Ag 25 '67
Tone v. substance; King Hussein seeks U.S. support for softening Israel's terms for peace. il Time 90:37 N 17 '67
Tougher terms for peace. Time 90:40+ N 10 '67
What Israel wants. Nat R 19:1313-14 N 28 '67

What's next for Israel; interview, ed. by W. MacDougall. L. Eshkol. il U S News 63:29-31 Jl 10 '67
Why Israel holds on to Arab lands. il U S News 63:80 N 13 '67

Anecdotes, facetiae, satire, etc.
Peace is hell. G. Ace. Sat R 50:7 Ag 5 '67

Personal narratives
Echoes from Sinai. G. Godsell. Sat R 50:29+ Ag 26 '67
Eyewitness to war in the Holy Land. C. Harbutt. il Nat Geog Mag 132:782-95 D '67
Letter from the Sinai front. A. Elon. Commentary 44:60-8 Ag '67
Report. M. Lerner. il Atlan 220:24+ S '67

Propaganda
Christians and the Mideast crisis. W. G. Oxtoby. Christian Cent 84:961-5 Jl 26 '67; Reply. D. Lieber. 84:1193-4 S 20 '67

Public opinion
American Left and Israel. M. Peretz. bibliog Commentary 44:27-34 N '67
Israel & the intellectuals; American Jewish intellectuals response to victory. R. Alter. Commentary 44:46-52 O '67
Israel, the Arabs, and world opinion. W. Laqueur. Commentary 44:49-59 Ag '67

Songs and music
Song that took a city: Jerusalem of gold. L. Gottlieb. Read Digest 91:112-15 D '67

Women and the war
Girls who fought for Israel. L. Uris. il Ladies Home J 84:83-6 S '67
When my mother, Rachel, went down to Jericho. R. Dayan. McCalls 94:24+ S '67
ISRAELI-Arab war and literature. See War and literature
ISRAELI occupation of Jordan, 1967. See Jordan—Israeli occupation, 1967-
ISRAELIS
Girls who fought for Israel. L. Uris. il Ladies Home J 84:83-6 S '67
Impassioned Israelis. D. Bar-Illan. il Hi Fi 17:47-50 Jl '67
Isaac and Ishmael: 1967. N. B. McLeod. Christian Cent 84:959-61 Jl 26 '67
Israeli identity: problems in the development of the collective identity of an ideological society. S. N. Eisenstadt. Ann Am Acad 370:116-23 Mr '67
Matter of survival. C. Sterling. il Reporter 36:16-17 Je 29 '67
Messianic times? J. C. Evans. Christan Cent 84:1149-51 S 13 '67
People of a proud land. il Holiday 42:66-73 D '67
Sabbath in the Sinai for Israeli tourists. B. Wise. il Life 63:30-30A Ag 11 '67
ISSEI. See Japanese Americans
ISTHMUS of Tehuantepec. See Tehuantepec, Isthmus of
ISTITUTO per la ricostruzione industriale. See Italy—Industries
ISTOCK, Conrad
U.S. deaths in Vietnam: a definition of escalation. Bul Atomic Sci 23:62-3 Je '67
ITALIAN American anti-defamation league. See American Italian anti-defamation league
ITALIAN art. See Art, Italian
ITALIAN artificial satellites. See Artificial satellites, Italian
ITALIAN automobiles. See Automobiles, Foreign
ITALIAN castles. See Castles
ITALIAN cookery. See Cookery, Italian
ITALIAN drama
See also
Theater—Italy
ITALIAN furniture. See Furniture, Italian
ITALIAN literature
Old and new trends in contemporary Italian literature. J. Tusiani. Cath World 205:112-15 My '67
ITALIAN majolica. See Majolica
ITALIAN manuscripts. See Manuscripts, Italian
ITALIAN painting. See Painting, Italian
ITALIAN RIVIERA. See Riviera
ITALIAN violinist; story. See Pattison, J.
ITALIANS
In Rome they call it *il miracolo italiano*. A. Menen. il N Y Times Mag p6-7+ Jl 9 '67; Reply with rejoinder. M. Stein. p5 Ag 6 '67
Italian enigma. J. C. Evans. Christian Cent 84:710-11 My 31 '67

ITALIANS in the United States
Italians, American style. M. Puzo. il N Y
Times Mag p7+ Ag 6 '67; Discussion. p 12+
Ag 20; 12 Ag 27; 62+ S 10 '67
See also
Tampa, Fla.—Ybor City
ITALO-AMERICANS. See Italians in the United States
ITALY
See also
Airlines—Italy
Architecture, Domestic—Italy
Assisi
Automobile industry and trade—Italy
Banks and banking—Italy
Calabria
Capri
Censorship—Italy
Colleges and universities—Italy
Communism—Italy
Elba (island)
Festivals—Italy
Florence
Folklore—Italy
Gardens—Italy
Genoa
Music festivals—Italy
Negroes in Italy
Opera—Italy
Petroleum industry and trade—Italy
Phonograph record industry—Italy
Publishers and publishing—Italy
Rome (city)
Science—Italy
Shopping and shoppers—Italy
Space research—Italy
Taranto
Technical assistance in Italy
Theater—Italy
Tourist trade—Italy
Turin, Italy
Tyrol
World war, 1939-1945—Italy
Zingonia

Antiquities
Art: Taranto museum. M. Grosser. Nation
206:60-2 Ja 8 '68
See also
Pompeii

Central institute of restoration
See Art—Conservation and restoration

Description and travel
Catch-22 revisited. J. Heller. il Holiday 41:
55-60+ Ap '67
Editor's report: Amalfi excursion. M. M.
Davis. il Travel 127:64-6+ Ap '67
Going places, finding things on the Italian
Riviera. M. Roche. il House & Gard 132:58-
9+ S '67
See also
Gardens—Italy

Economic conditions
In Rome they call it *il miracolo italiano.* A.
Menen. il N Y Times Mag p6-7+ Jl 9 '67;
Reply with rejoinder. M. Stein. p5 Ag 6 '67
Italy's new boom: solid and sober. il Bsns
W p31 D 23 '67
Report from Milan. W. Wynn. il Fortune 76:
39+ Jl '67

Economic relations
Ideology & practice; Russia. il Time 89:31
F 3 '67

Education
See also
Florence—Education

Foreign relations
United States
President Saragat of Italy visits the United
States; exchange of greetings, September
18, exchange of toasts, and joint state-
ment, September 19, 1967. L. B. Johnson;
G. Saragat. Dept State Bul 57:500-3 O 16 '67

History
Bibliography
Articles and other books received; comp. by
E. P. Noether. See issues of American
historical review

Industries
Bergamot country; Reggio. L. Gardiner. Atlan
220:104-5 Jl '67
In Italy, Agnelli is the man to see. il Bsns W
p 128-9+ My 13 '67
Italy exports its building knowhow: Italian
construction companies working around the
globe. il Bsns W p91-2+ N 18 '67

Tentacles of IRI. Fortune 76:196 S 15 '67
Two Italys: tug-of-war between the bureau-
crats and technocrats. P. Ben. New Repub
156:11-12 F 25 '67
See also
Electric apparatus industry
Olivetti

Literary landmarks
See Literary landmarks

Politics and government
Two Italys: tug-of-war between the bureau-
crats and technocrats. P. Ben. New Repub
156:11-12 F 25 '67
See also
Communist party (Italy)
Tyrol

Religious institutions and affairs
World around us (cont) Christian Cent 84:
1266-7 O 4 '67
ITHACA, N.Y.
Education
Community service; tuition-free Ithaca neigh-
borhood college. Time 90:82 N 17 '67
IT'S the duty of the young to be happy; story
See Farrell, P.
IUSUPOV, Feliks Feliksovich, kniaz'
Final accounting. il por Newsweek 70:27-8
O 9 '67
IVERSON, Warren P.
Disulfur monoxide: production by desulfovi-
brio. bibliog Science 156:1112-14 My 26 '67
IVES, Alexander
Visit to Vietnam. por Seventeen 26:150-1+
F '67
IVES, Burl
Traveler, consider my Bahamas. . .; inter-
view. ed. by R. Joseph. por Esquire 67:120-
1+ Mr '67
IVES, Charles Edward
Ives's holidays: a glorious fourth, and no
anticlimax. W. Shirley. il Hi Fi 17:79-80
S '67
IVES, Ronald L.
Electronics technician shortage. Pop Electr
27:56-61+ S '67
IVORY-billed woodpeckers. See Woodpeckers
IVORY COAST
Foreign relations
President Johnson holds meeting with presi-
dent of Ivory Coast; exchange of toasts,
August 17, 1967. F. Houphouet-Boigny; L.
B. Johnson. Dept State Bul 57:330-2 S 11 '67
IVY poisoning. See Poison ivy
IXORAS
Hybrid ixoras. P. Swedroe. il Horticulture
45:44 Ap '67
IYPE, P. T. See Heidelberger, C. jt. auth.

J

J. Walter Thompson company. See Thompson,
J. Walter, company
J. B. Lippincott company. See Lippincott, J. B.
company
J. C. Penney company. See Penney, J. C, com-
pany
JCS. See United States—Joint chiefs of staff
J. P. Stevens and company. See Stevens, J. P,
and company
JABONSKI, John R.
Man, culture, evolution and environment.
Christian Cent 84:495-8 Ap 19 '67
JACCHIA, Luigi
Italian astronomer. Sky & Tel 34:93 Ag '67
JACK, Homer A.
ENDC at the General assembly. Bul Atomic
Sci 23:30-3 F '67
Geneva conference, five years later; excerpt
from report. Bul Atomic Sci 23:38-42 Ja '67
JACK Driscoll's revenge; story. See Fox, W. P.
JACK-in-the-pulpits
Nature note. il Sci N 91:444 My 13 '67
JACKLET, Jon W. and Cohen, M. J.
Nerve regeneration: correlation of electrical,
histological, and behavioral events. bibliog
Science 156:1640-3 Je 23 '67
Synaptic connections between a transplanted
insect ganglion and muscles of the host.
bibliog Science 156:1638-40 Je 23 '67
JACKOWSKI, Staszek
Heroism of Staszek Jackowski. R. Gruber.
il por Sat R 50:19-21+ Ap 15 '67

JACKRABBIT hunting. See Rabbit hunting
JACKSON, Barbara (Ward) lady. See Ward, B.
JACKSON, Bruce
Battle of the Pentagon. Atlan 221:35-42 Ja
'68
Blackballing the Fiedlers. New Repub 157:
13-14 S 9 '67
JACKSON, Charles Reginald
Trade winds. J. Beatty, jr. Sat R 50:7 S 2
'67
JACKSON, Clarence
Luck of Clarence Jackson. il por Time 90:
64 S 1 '67
JACKSON, Donald
Brash newcomer to the ranks of great de-
fenders. Life 62:45-6+ F 17 '67
JACKSON, Faith
Who am I? why do I dance? Dance Mag
41:54-7+ S '67
JACKSON, Gene L.
Wide-range electronic timer. Electr World
78:56-7 N '67
JACKSON, Harry
Death on the range; paintings. D. G. Lowe.
Am Heritage 18:48-9+ O '67
JACKSON, Henry Martin
National security; address, October 11, 1967.
Vital Speeches 34:34-7 N 1 '67
JACKSON, Howard E.
Unique new teaching tool. Design 69:29-31
Fall '67
JACKSON, James P.
Strange world of Reelfoot. il Am For 73:38-9+
Mr '67
Trees across the plains. il Am For 73:34-5+ N
'67
JACKSON, Jesse
Apostle of economics. D. Llorens. il pors
Ebony 22:78-80+ Ag '67
JACKSON, Katherine Gauss
Books in brief. See issues of Harper's maga-
zine
JACKSON, Livingston
Tennessee rebels. New Repub 157:9-10 S 9
'67
JACKSON, Mahalia
Jazz concerts; recital at Philharmonic Hall.
W. Balliett. New Yorker 43:164-5 Ap 8 '67
JACKSON, Milt
Jazz and the vibraphone. M. Williams. il por
Sat R 50:78-9 N 11 '67
JACKSON, Norman
Before marriage; poem. Sat R 50:63 S 16 '67
Bird hunt; poem. Sat R 50:57 S 30 '67
Confessional; poem. Reporter 36:46 Je 29 '67
Hawk; Talk to me now; poems. Reporter
37:40, 48 O 19 '67
Realism; poem. Reporter 37:55 N 2 '67
JACKSON, Robert L.
Accepted or rejected? interview, ed. by D.
Klein. por Seventeen 26:134-5+ Mr '67
JACKSON, Sidney L.
Bumpy road in libraryland. Wilson Lib Bul
41:909-11 My '67
JACKSON, Togwell A.
Fossil actinomycetes in middle Precambrian
glacial varves. bibliog Science 155:1003-5
F 24 '67
JACKSON, W. E. and Wohlers, H. C.
You need an air-pollution inventory. Am City
82:119-20 O '67
JACKSON, William E. Jr
Defense: the missile nobody needs. New
Repub 157:13-16 O 28 '67
JACKSON, Miss.
City hall blossoms at night. B. Horne. il Am
City 82:160 O '67

Negroes
Prevalence of scapegoats: Negro anti-Semitism. Nation 206:5 Ja 1 '68

Riots
Hot spring; riot at Jackson state college. il
Newsweek 69:36-7 My 22 '67

Water supply
Dixie's model lake; Ross Barnett reservoir.
G. Gresham. il Field & S 72:56-7+ D '67
JACKSON laboratory. See Biological labora-
tories
JACKSON state college, Jackson, Miss.
Mississippi's beehive college. C. Parsons and
W. B. Welch. il Am Ed 4:19-22+ D '67
JACKSONVILLE, Ill.
Jet turbine for Jacksonville, Ill. il Am City
82-18 S '67
JACOBI, Lotte
Lotte Jacobi: photographic psychedelics. J.
Deschin. il por Pop Phot 61:38+ Jl '67

JACOBS, Arthur P.
How a new film maker made it in Hollywood.
il pors Bsns W p 188-90+ S 16 '67
JACOBS, David
Expo named Buckminster Fuller. N Y Times
Mag p32-3+ Ap 23 '67
Rudolph style: unpredictable. N Y Times Mag
p46-7+ Mr 26 '67
What it's like to live in an experiment. por
N Y Times Mag p50-1+ Je 4 '67
JACOBS, Hayes B.
Here's to education! Atlan 220:114-15 S '67
Just for laughs. Look 31:M24 O 17 '67
JACOBS, Herbert A.
Perils of crowd counting. il por Time 89:44
Ap 7 '67
JACOBS, Jay
Back to the Casbah. Reporter 37:52 N 2 '67
In hot water. Reporter 38:38 Ja 11 '68
JACOBS, Jimmy
Laughter in the wings, murder on the court.
T. C. Brody. Sports Illus 26:90+ Ap 17 '67
Showdown on 92nd street. B. Ottum. il por
Sports Illus 27:46-7 Jl 31 '67
JACOBS, Joe
I care; excerpts from letters. por Time 89:18-
19 Mr 31 '67
JACOBS, Paul
How it is, getting on welfare; excerpt from
Prologue to riots. Harper 235:74-5 O '67
JACOBS, Walter Darnell
Dream-world treaties. Nat R 19:913 Ag 22 '67
Second place in the arms race. Nat R 19:
186-9 F 21 '67
about
Overstated case. J. Burnham. Nat R 19:185
F 21 '67
JACOBS, William Jay
John R. Tunis: a commitment to values.
Horn Bk 43:48-54 F '67
JACOB'S Pillow dance festival. See Dance
festivals
JACOBSEN, Josephine
Art in transition. L. Lieberman. Poetry 109:
398 Mr '67
JACOBSON, Alma Frank
Who feeds the golden goose? address, Feb-
ruary 1, 1967. Vital Speeches 33:306-9 Mr
1 '67
JACOBSON, Bernard
English tone poems: the minor graces, and
some major ones. Hi Fi 17:69-70 My '67
Mahler symphonies on records. Hi Fi 17:55-
9 S '67
Monteverdi's Vespers: two versions that make
a lovely sound. Hi Fi 17:61-2 Jl '67
Mozart month at Philharmonic Hall. Hi Fi 17:
MA8-9+ N '67
Music of Shakespeare's time. Hi Fi 17:63
D '67
Nielsen symphonies. Hi Fi 17:54-6 Ap '67
Penderecki, a mighty voice from Poland. Hi
Fi 17:74-5 Ap '67
Russians have arrived, thanks to Melodiya/
Angel. Hi Fi 17:67-8 Mr '67
Visiting orchestras: Suisse Romande & Bath.
Hi Fi 17:MA16-17 S '67
(ed) See Brusilow, A. And we quote
(ed) See Josephs, W. And we quote
(ed) See Penderecki, K. And we quote
(ed) See Szeryng, H. And we quote
JACOBSON, Dan
Lost world? Commentary 43:81-3 Je '67
JACOBSON, Dorothy H.
War on hunger; address, September 8, 1967.
Vital Speeches 33:763-6 O 1 '67
JACOBSON, Marcus
Retinal ganglion cells: specification of central
connections in larval xenopus laevis. bibliog
Science 155:1106-8 Mr 3 '67
JACOBSON, Martin. See Jones, W. A. jt. auth.
JACOBSON, Robert
Britten's Dream of Shakespeare. Sat R 50:85
N 25 '67
Butterfly by Barbirolli. Sat R 50:56-7+ O
28 '67
Capital Ginastera in Washington. Sat R 50:
59+ Je 24 '67
Cosi nearly complete. Sat R 50:85 F 25 '67
Monteverdi for moderns. Sat R 50:44 Jl 29 '67
Record makers. Sat R 50:67-9 Ag 26 '67
(comp) Toscanini bibliography. Sat R 50:
64-5 Mr 25 '67
JACOBY, Oswald
Masterful show of the wizardry of Ozzie. C.
Goren. il Sports Illus 27:61 O 30 '67
JACOBY, Susan, and Lavigne, Richard
Tune in the kids with records and films. Sr
Schol 91:sup9 D 7 '67
JACOBY, Susan L.
National monument to failure. Sat R 50:71-
3+ N 18 '67

JACQUELINE Grennan, Sister. See Grennan, J.

JADE
Monterey nephrite. H. D. Brown. il Hobbies 72:124 Ja '68

JAFFE, Joseph
Blocks behind our words. Sat R 50:32 Ag 19 '67

JAFFE, Leonard. See Newell, H. E. jt. auth.

JAFFRY, Jacques
Meet our master chef. V. T. Habeeb. il por Am Home 70:104-5+ Jl '67

JAGIELLO, Georgiana
Streptonigrin: effect on the first meiotic metaphase of the mouse egg. bibliog Science 157:453-4 Jl 28 '67

JAGUAR hunting
Cat man returns. S. Siemel. il Outdoor Life 139:46-9+ My '67
Down an unknown jungle river. Z. Grey. il Field & S 72:44-5+ S; 60-1+ O '67 (to be cont)

JAHN, Mike
After Sgt Pepper. Sat R 50:55 D 30 '67

JAHODA, Gloria
Gulf Coast of Florida. Holiday 41:70-8+ My '67

JAIL libraries. See Prison libraries

JAILS. See Prisons

JAIN, Prakash C.
Me-tooism, here. too. Nat R 19:129+ F 7 '67

JAM. See Jelly, jam, etc.

JAMAICA
Jamaica goes it alone. J. Cerruti. il Nat Geog Mag 132:842-73 D '67
New tenants in government house. E. B. Thompson. il Ebony 22:80-1 O '67
United States and Jamaica sign new cotton textile agreement. il Dept State Bul 57:622-4 N 6 '67
See also
Architecture, Domestic—Jamaica
Elections—Jamaica
Port Royal
Water supply—Jamaica

Politics and government
His own man. Time 89:38 Mr 3 '67

JAMES I, king of Great Britain
Jacobean diplomatic service. M. Lee, jr. bibliog f Am Hist R 72:1264-82 Jl '67

JAMES, Daniel
Latin America: how many Vietnams? Nat R 19:949-51 S 5 '67

JAMES, F. Cyril
Culture in the making. UNESCO Courier 20:4-9+ Ap '67

JAMES, Henry
Henry James' return to America. I. Howe. New Repub 157:23-6 S 30 '67
House of the seven ushers and how they grew: a look at Jamesian Gothicism. M. Banta. Yale R 57:56-65 O '67

JAMES, Jesse. See Shepard, G. H. jt. auth.

JAMES, Jessie
James gang rides again. il por Time 90:31 O 13 '67

JAMES, L. Eldon
Excerpt from testimony before House committee on armed services, June 29, 1966. Cong Digest 46:155+ My '67

JAMES, Orlando
New hope for brain-damaged children? Parents Mag 42:72-5+ N '67

JAMES, Ronald
Profile in juvenile decency. il pors Ebony 22:122-6 Ag '67

JAMES, Stuart
Anyone can climb a mountain. Pop Mech 127:112-15+ F '67
Four-wheel safari test in the rugged Rockies. Pop Mech 127:119-22+ My '67

JAMES, William
Making habits work for you; excerpt from Psychology: briefer course; reprint. Read Digest 91:81-4 Ag '67
Talks to teachers on psychology and to students on some of life's ideals; excerpts, with comments by A. I. Gates. NEA J 56:34-5 O '67
about
William James, by G. W. Allen. Review
Atlan 219:129-31 My '67. O. Handlin
Reporter 37:48+ Ag 10 '67. R. Sklar
Sat R 50:31-2 Ag 12 '67. W. Kaufmann
William James as sage. J. Featherstone. New Repub 157:18-21 O 14 '67

JAMES Bond (literary character) See Spies in literature

JAMES E. Murphy Jr. dance company. See Dance companies

JAMESTOWN, Va.
Jamestown, exposition. B. Finnegan. il Hobbies 72:114-15 Ap '67
Knight's tombstone at Jamestown, Virginia. J. P. Hudson. il Antiques 91:760-1 Je '67

JAMIESON, George L.
He knows where to drill for water. G. L. Morris. il por Pop Mech 128:124-6+ O '67

JAMIESON, James B.
Park bond issues. Parks & Rec 2:22+ N '67

JAN Holcman collection. See Phonograph records—Collectors and collecting

JANÁČEK, Leoš
From the house of the dead. R. Jones. il Am Rec G 33:992-6 Jl '67
Janáček on Dostoevsky. H. Weinstock. Sat R 50:63 My 27 '67
Janáček's House of the dead: the problem of sung drama. C. L. Osborne. il Hi Fi 17:75-6 Je '67
Makropulos case. Criticism
Hi Fi il 17:MA20-MA21 F '67
On four records from two labels, seven works by Janáček. R. Jones; A. Cohn. il Am Rec G 33:378-84 Ja '67
Records:
From the house of the dead, and The Makropoulos case. Opera N 32:34 D 16 '67

JANCAUSKAS, Raymond C.
Educational loans. America 116:440-1+ Mr 25 '67

JANDOLI, Russell J.
I edited and indexed thirty years of home movies. U S Camera 30:70-1+ Ap '67

JANE Eyre; drama. See Olfson, L.

JANER, Victor Frederick Christ-. See Christ-Janer, V. F.

JANES, Ted
And don't never count your shells. Outdoor Life 140:52-3+ O '67
Buck picked me. por Outdoor Life 140:40-1+ N '67
Down by the old smelt stream. pors Outdoor Life 140:48-9+ D '67
Flag is up! pors Outdoor Life 139:74-5+ F '67
Ponds upon ponds of bass. por Outdoor Life 139:66-7+ My '67
(comp) That's where I want to fish. Outdoor Life 139:81-4 Ap '67

JANEWAY, Elizabeth (Hall)
Nabokov the magician. Atlan 220:66-71 Jl '67

JANEWAY, Michael C.
Lyndon Johnson's other wars. Atlan 220:73-5 S '67
Report; Washington. Atlan 221:4+ Ja '68
Who is Doris Grumbach? Atlan 220:90-1 Ag '67

JANIS, Jack Harold
Authors & editors. Pub W 192:19-20 N 13 '67

JANIS, Rosamond, and others
Synovial cell synthesis of a substance immunologically like cartilage proteinpolysaccharide. bibliog Science 158:1464-7 D 15 '67

JANOV, Ellen
Ellen Janov; photographs. Vogue 149:160-1 My '67

JANOWITZ, Gundula
Karajan's choice; interview, ed. by J. Wechsberg. pors Opera N 32:15 S 9 '67

JANSEN, Guenter
Matter of reputation. K. Nyren. Library J 92:173 Ja 15 '67

JANSSEN, Horst
Wild one. il por Newsweek 69:98 Ap 3 '67

JANSSEN, Peter A.
NEA: the reluctant dragon. Sat R 50:56-7+ Je 17 '67
Union response to academic mass production. Sat R 50:64-6+ O 21 '67

JANTZ, Orlo K. and others
Automobile paint effective as an insect attractant. bibliog Science 156:946-7 My 19 '67

JANUARY, Don
Two Dons in quest of a title. A. Wright. il por Sports Illus 27:18-21 Jl 31 '67

JANUS (satellite) See Satellites

JAPAN
Japanese notebook. H. Brandon. Sat R 51:20+ Ja 13 '68
Japan's switch to metrics. il Sci N 91:288-9 Mr 25 '67

JAPAN—*Continued*
Report; concern over lack of U.S. news coverage. J. M. Truitt. Atlan 219:12+ Je '67
Right eye of Daruma. il Time 89:24-8 F 10 '67

See also
Air travel—Japan
Airlines—Japan
American school in Japan
Americans in Japan
Architecture—Japan
Arts and crafts—Japan
Automobile industry and trade—Japan
Birds—Japan
Birth control—Japan
Bonin Islands
Children—Japan
Colleges and universities—Japan
Earthquakes—Japan
Education—Japan
Elections—Japan
Electronic apparatus industry and trade—Japan
Gardens—Japan
Hiroshima
Investments, Foreign (by Japan)
Investments, Foreign (in Japan)
Kyoto
Kyushu
Mikura-jima (island)
Music—Japan
Music festivals—Japan
Okinawa
Railroads—Japan
Reporters and reporting—Japan
Research—Japan
Rites and ceremonies—Japan
Space research—Japan
Strikes—Japan
Television broadcasting—Japan
World war, 1939-1945—Japan

Bibliography
Highly adaptable package. M. S. Plank and J. B. Scholl. il Library J 92:1716-17+ Ap 15 '67

Commerce
Chestnuts and jellyfish; Canton trade fair wins trade for Japan. Newsweek 69:72 Je 5 '67

See also
Japan—Industries
Joint United States-Japan committee on trade and economic affairs

Description and travel
Henri Cartier-Bresson's Japan. il Look 31:28-33 F 7 '67
Japan's unknown side; from Shimonoseki to Aomori. S. Griffin. il Travel 128:45-8 N '67
Kayak odyssey from the Inland Sea to Tokyo. D. Dimancescu. il Nat Geog Mag 132:295-337 S '67
Tokaido; photographs and reproductions of wood engravings. D. Stock; Hiroshige. Holiday 41:34-45 Je '67

Economic conditions
Japan and Britain: a study in contrasts. Read Digest 90:213-14+ Ap '67
Why Japan's growth is different. M. Ways. il Fortune 76:126-9+ N '67
See also
Japan—Industries
Wages—Japan

Economic policy
MITI: Japan's economic watchdog; Ministry of international trade & industry. Bsns W p 102 Ag 19 '67

Economic relations
Changing images. il Newsweek 70:36 O 9 '67
Crack in the door: U.S. investment in Japan aided by liberalization program. Newsweek 69:78 Je 19 '67
Grand tour, Japanese style; emergence as a world power. il Newsweek 70:36-8 O 2 '67
Japan's new bid for leadership. J. L. Schecter. Reporter 36:31-3 My 18 '67
Japan's new idea for co-prosperity sphere. il U S News 63:90-1 Jl 24 '67
Japan's quiet war against Mao. L. Velie. Read Digest 91:116-20 Ag '67
See also
Joint United States-Japan committee on trade and economic affairs

Emperors and empresses
See also
Hirohito, emperor of Japan

Foreign relations
Changing images. il Newsweek 70:36 O 9 '67
Grand tour, Japanese style; emergence as a world power. il Newsweek 70:36-8 O 2 '67
Role for Japan to live up to. Life 63:4 D 8 '67
Year of Japan's emergence. Nation 206:68-9 Ja 15 '68

Asia, Southeastern
Japan in Asia's future. W. M. Ball. Nation 206:82-4 Ja 15 '68

United States
Complete meeting of the minds. il Newsweek 70:49-50 N 27 '67
Something for the hat. il Time 90:24 N 24 '67
U.S. and Japan reaffirm common objectives and pledge continued cooperation; exchange of greetings and toasts, November 14, with joint communique, November 15, 1967. L. B. Johnson; E. Sato. Dept State Bul 57:742-7 D 4 '67
What U.S. is giving back to Japan. il U S News 63:54 N 27 '67
See also
Panay (gunboat) incident

History
Bibliography
Chinese and Japanese historiography: some trends, 1961-1966. A. F. Wright and J. W. Hall. bibliog f Ann Am Acad 371:178-93 My '67

Historiography
Chinese and Japanese historiography: some trends, 1961-1966. A. F. Wright and J. W. Hall. bibliog f Ann Am Acad 371:178-93 My '67

Industries
Horatio Alger story, with a Japanese twist; Sony corporation. J. L. Schecter. il N Y Times Mag p56-7+ S 10 '67
Japan's powerful push overseas. il Bsns W p92-4+ Ag 19 '67
New spark at the GE of Japan; Toshiba electric. il Bsns W p 123-6+ F 11 '67
Ubiquitous Mitsui. il Time 89:93 F 17 '67
Why Japan's growth is different. M. Ways. il Fortune 76:126-9+ N '67
See also
Automobile industry and trade—Japan
Electronic apparatus industry and trade—Japan
Shipbuilding

Intellectual life
Conversations in Japan, by D. Riesman and E. T. Riesman. Review
Sat R 50:29-30 S 9 '67. F. Gibney

Military policy
Japan in Asia's future. W. M. Ball. Nation 206:82-4 Ja 15 '68

Nationalism
Switzerland East? Newsweek 70:45-6 Ag 28 '67

Native races
Japan's sky people, the vanishing Ainu. M. I. Hilger. il Nat Geog Mag 131:268-96 F '67

Politics and government
Living with the real Japan. G. R. Packard, 3d. For Affairs 46:193-204 O '67
Marchers of Tokyo. A. Axelbank. il Nation 206:41-3 Ja 8 '68
See also
Elections—Japan
Japan—Nationalism

Race problems
Abandoned; plight of Negro mixed bloods. il Newsweek 69:50 F 13 '67
Japan's rejected; teen-agers fathered by Negro soldiers. E. B. Thompson. il Ebony 22:42-4+ S '67
New group of human beings: Amerasians; mixed-blood children, *konketsuji*. R. Trumbull. il N Y Times Mag p 112-14 Ap 30 '67

Religious institutions and affairs
Rush hour of the gods, by H. N. McFarland. Review
Christian Cent 84:691 My 24 '67. R. H. Drummond
World around us (cont) Christian Cent 84:123-4, 286, 384-7, 513-14, 632-4, 760+, 981-2, 1136+ Ja 25, Mr 1, 22, Ap 19, My 10, Je 7, Jl 26, S 6 '67

JAPAN—*Continued*

Social life and customs

Japanese character in the twentieth century. D. G. Haring. bibliog f Ann Am Acad 370:133-42 Mr '67

Japan's sky people, the vanishing Ainu. M. I. Hilger. il Nat Geog Mag 131:268-96 F '67

Teahouse in the sky; William Johnstones' Japanese tearoom. UN plaza. J. Peter. il Look 31:M28+ D 26 '67

Study and teaching

Highly adaptable package; homemade media kit to provide unit on Japan, in Pennsylvania department of public instruction. M. S. Plank and J. B. Scholl. il Library J 92:1714-17+ Ap 15 '67

Treaties

Okinawa's future and Far-East security; hope of reversion of 1951 peace treaties. M. E. Weinstein. Reporter 37:39-40 N 2 '67

JAPAN air lines. See Airlines—Japan

JAPAN and the United States

Living with the real Japan. G. R. Packard, 3d. For Affairs 46:193-204 O '67

Marchers of Tokyo. A. Axelbank. il Nation 206:41-3 Ja 8 '68

President Johnson greets Japanese governors; remarks, May 24, 1967. L. B. Johnson. Dept State Bul 56:917-18 Je 19 '67

Report; concern over lack of U.S. news coverage. J. M. Truitt. Atlan 219:12+ Je '67

JAPAN overseas cooperation volunteers. See Volunteer service, International

JAPAN-United States committee on scientific cooperation. See Joint United States-Japan committee on scientific cooperation

JAPAN-United States cooperative science program. See Science—International aspects

JAPANESE

Golden village; Crow Boy and the making of a film. G. L. Johnson. il Horn Bk 43:183-91 Ap '67

Henri Cartier-Bresson's Japan. il Look 31: 28-33 F 7 '67

Japanese character in the twentieth century. D. G. Haring. bibliog f Ann Am Acad 370: 133-42 Mr '67

JAPANESE-American exchanges. See Educational exchanges

JAPANESE AMERICANS

America's concentration camps, by A. R. Bosworth. Review
Christian Cent 84:409-10 Mr 29 '67. M. Polner
Sat R 50:29 Mr 18 '67. H. Mitgang
Time il 89:100+ F 17 '67

Authors & editors; forthcoming book on America's concentration camps. Pub W 191:39 F 6 '67

Epilogue to a sorry drama; Supreme court decision on U.S. debt owed to Japanese-Americans. Life 62:4 Ap 28 '67

Issei and Nisei, by D. Kitagawa. Review
Sat R 51:89 Ja 13 '68. L. Katcher

Supreme court orders repayment to Japanese Americans. Christian Cent 84:525 Ap 26 '67

Wrong partially righted; settlement of Japanese-Americans' claims for seizure of property during World war II. il Time 89: 25 Ap 21 '67

JAPANESE architecture. See Architecture, Japanese

JAPANESE automobiles. See Automobiles, Foreign

JAPANESE carpentry. See Carpentry

JAPANESE cookery. See Cookery, Japanese

JAPANESE dancing. See Dancing, Japanese

JAPANESE drama
See also
Nō (Japanese drama and theater)

JAPANESE economic assistance. See Economic assistance, Japanese

JAPANESE engineers. See Engineers, Japanese

JAPANESE flowering dogwood. See Dogwood

JAPANESE folk art. See Folk art

JAPANESE gardens. See Gardens, Japanese

JAPANESE in the United States
See also
Japanese Americans

JAPANESE irises. See Irises

JAPANESE language
Advanced Japanese for beginners. M. Berry. Sat R 50:54-5 Ja 28 '67

JAPANESE literature
See also
Japanese poetry

JAPANESE musicians. See Musicians, Japanese

JAPANESE newspapers. See Newspapers—Japan

JAPANESE poetry
Japanese poetry. K. Rexroth. Sat R 50:44 S 2 '67

JAPANESE pottery. See Pottery, Japanese

JAPANESE prints. See Prints

JAPANESE quails. See Quails

JAPANESE scientists. See Scientists, Japanese

JAPONICAS. See Camellias

JAQUITH, Lawrence C.
Building costs; trends and analysis. See issues of Architectural record

JARASHOW, Barbara
Dieters' clipboard; letters (cont) Seventeen 26:207 F '67

JARES, Joe
Baseball (cont) Sports Illus 26:66-8+ My 15; 64-6 Je 26 '67
Basketball. Sports Illus 26:56-7 F 13 '67
College football. Sports Illus 27:46 O 9 '67

JARGON
Jargon, past and present. W. McQuade. il Arch Forum 127:92 S '67
See also
Slang

JARMUL, Ruth
Curl up and read. Seventeen 26:38 Jl '67

JARRELL, Mary Eloise Von Schrader
Group of two; a memoir of a marriage; excerpt from Randall Jarrell, 1914-1965. Harper 234:73-8 Ap '67

JARRELL, Randall
Man meets a woman in the street; poem. Harper 234:79 Ap '67
Player piano; poem. Harper 234:72 F '67
Say good-bye to big daddy; poem. Atlan 220:99 S '67

about

Group of two; a memoir of a marriage; excerpt from Randall Jarrell, 1914-1965. M. E. V. Jarrell. il Harper 234:73-8 Ap '67

Randall Jarrell, ed. by R. Lowell and others. Review
Sat R 50:26 S 2 '67. R. Whittemore
Time por 90:102 S 15 '67

Randall Jarrell; excerpt from Randall Jarrell, 1914-1965. M. Moore. por Atlan 220:96-8 S '67

JARRETT, Edith Moore
Secret cupboards I have known. Pop Sci 190: 160-2 F '67

JARRY, Alfred
French chronicle. P. Zweig. Poetry 111:124-9 N '67

JARS, Insulated. See Thermos containers

JARVIS, Lucy
Mission: impossible. il por Time 91:52 Ja 12 '68

JARVIS, Porter Maxwell
Hog butcher for the world. R. Levy. il por Duns R 89:36-8 F '67

JASPERS, Karl
Delusion of perfection. por Time 90:119 D 8 '67

JASTROW, Robert
Cosmic evolution; with biographical sketch. Natur Hist 77:4, 32-9 bibliog(p76) Ja '68

JASZI, George
Building a base for forecasters. il pors Bsns W p 117-19 Je 10 '67

JAVAN, Ali
Optical properties of materials; with biographical sketch. Sci Am 217:54, 238-42+ S '67

JAVITS, Jacob Koppel
Last chance for a common market. For Affairs 45:449-62 Ap '67

about

No longer a hot subject. il por Time 90:16 Jl 28 '67

Vice-President? President? Sen. Javits' biggest gamble. W. Rogers. il pors Look 31: M14-19 F 21 '67

JAY, Antony
Six types of bad executives; excerpts from Management and Machiavelli. Duns R 90: 53-4 D '67

JAY, Donald
Long distance trailing. Yachting 122:62-3+ D '67

JAYNE, Gerald A.
On the Snake River lavas; with biographical sketch. il Natur Hist 76:4, 44-7 O '67

JAYROE, Jane Anne
Miss America does her bit in Vietnam. il por Life 63:26 S 1 '67

JAZZ
Jazz. W. Balliett. New Yorker 43:130-2 Mr
18 '67
JAZZ bands. See Bands (music)
JAZZ festivals. See Music festivals
JAZZ music
Beat me daddy, twenty-seven to the bar. il
Time 89:76-7 My 26 '67
Dolphins on a wave; C. Lloyd, prophet of
new wave jazz. il Time 89:38 F 3 '67
Granz rides again; Jazz at the Philharmonic
concerts at Carnegie Hall. S. Dance. Sat R
50:57 Ap 15 '67
Has jazz a place in the church? H. Dance.
il Sat R 50:46-7 Jl 15 '67
Jazz. W. Balliett. New Yorker 43:130-2 Mr
18; 96 Ag 12; 86 Ag 19; 74 Ag 26 '67
Jazz concerts (cont) W. Balliett. New Yorker
42:109-11 Ja 28; 43:125-6 Mr 25; 163-5 Ap 8;
80 Ag 5 '67
Lively arts; interview, ed. by R. Hemming.
S. Getz. Sr Schol 90:24 Mr 10 '67
Making a lady of jazz. F. Bowers. House &
Gard 131:24+ Ap '67
New surge for a tired old idiom: Charles
Lloyd and jazz. R. Saltonstall, jr. Life
62:15 Je 9 '67
Reporter at large; jazz in Bombay. V. Mehta.
New Yorker 43:209-10+ D 9 '67
Secular music; soul music. R. Christgau.
Esquire 68:54+ O '67
Sing all songs to God. J. DeMuth. Christian
Cent 84:833-9 Je 28 '67
Skirling the blues; R. Harley. il Newsweek
69:97-8 Ja 30 '67
Turkish tycoons of "soul". il Time 90:43 Jl 28
'67
Way out of the muddle; rock music influ-
ence on jazz idiom. il Time 90:36 Ag 11 '67
See also
Phonograph records—Jazz music
Rock 'n' roll music

Bibliography
Seven jazz books. S. Dance. il Sat R 50:61+
F 11 '67
Russia
Sound of music; Music—U.S.A. most popular
radio program in eastern Europe. il News-
week 69:50+ Je 5 '67
JAZZ musicians
Aiming high, the jazz masters. D. Heckman.
Am Rec G 33:828+ My '67
Billy Mo: the Satchmo of Germany. H. J.
Massaquoi. il Ebony 22:68-73 Jl '67
Four lives in the bebop business, by A. B.
Spellman. Review
Vogue 149:114 F 1 '67. A. Goldman
Jazz concerts; Spirituals to swing—1967. W.
Balliett. New Yorker 42:109-11 Ja 28 '67
Powell, pianists, and saxophones. M. Wil-
liams. Sat R 50:75 Ap 29 '67
Vibe tribe; vibraharp players. il Newsweek
69:105 My 15 '67
See also
Armstrong, L.
Coltrane, J.
Davison, W. E.
Kellaway, R.
Lloyd, C.
Rich, B.
JAZZ orchestras. See Orchestras
JAZZMEN. See Musicians, American
JEANETTE Marie. Sister
Come to the Father; a new catechetical
program. Cath World 205:47-51 Ap '67
JEANNERET, Marsh
Needs and obligations. Sat R 50:15-17 Je 10
'67
JEANNERET-GRIS, Charles Édouard. See Le
Corbusier
JEDELE, D. G.
Quality concrete floor stops foot problems.
Farm J 91:H17 O '67
JEEPS. See Automobiles
JEEPSTERS. See Automobiles
JEFFERSON, Louis
Conversation with Dulles. Nat R 19:681-2 Je
27 '67
JEFFERSON, Thomas
Consensus politics, 1800-1805. L. W. Koenig.
il por Am Heritage 18:4-7+ F '67
Verdicts of history. T. J. Fleming. il por
Am Heritage 19:22-7+ D '67
JEFFERSON glass company. See Glass in-
dustry
JEFFERSON national expansion memorial. See
St Louis—Monuments, statues, etc.
JEFFREY, G. A. and others
Clathrate hydrates of some amines. bibliog
Science 155:689-91 D 10 '67

JEHOVAH'S Witnesses
More barbarism in Spain; humiliation of con-
scientious objectors. Christian Cent 84:933
Jl 19 '67
JELKE, Minot Frazier, 1930?-
Jelke? Jelke? wasn't he the guy who. .? N.
Randolph. il por Esquire 67:136-9+ Ap '67
JELLEMA, Dirk
Easter song. Christian Cent 84:374 Mr 22 '67
JELLICO, John
John Zahourek, draughtsman. Am Artist 31:
36-41+ S '67
JELLIED salads. See Salads
JELLINEK, George
(comp) Ten years of recordings. Sat R 50:50-
60 Ag 26 '67
JELLINEK, Hedy D.
(comp) Guide to European music festivals,
1967. Sat R 50:52-3 Ap 15 '67
(comp) Music festivals U.S.A. summer 1967.
Sat R 50:86-9 Je 10 '67
JELLY, jam, etc.
Best preserves and jams. K. Schaller. il Farm
J 91:48-50 Ag '67
Four unusual preserve recipes. Sunset 139:128
S '67
Have you tried fresh kumquat lately? il
Bet Hom & Gard 45:114 Mr '67
Jams, jellies, pickles, and relishes. il Suc
Farm 65:60-1 Ag '67
Jelly, jam or what? Bet Hom & Gard 45:117
Je '67
Making citrus marmalades; with recipes. Sun-
set 138:160 F '67
Successful recipes, any-season jams and
jellies. il Suc Farm 65:69-70 My '67
See also
Canning and preserving
JELLYFISH
Sea wasp, the deadliest jellyfish. il Sci Digest
61:25 Je '67
JENCKS, Christopher
Limits of the new left. New Repub 157:19-21
O 21; 29 N 4 '67
Negotiations now? reflections on a meeting
with the enemy. New Repub 157:19-23 O 7
'67
JENKINS, Dan
Bleachies, beachies and blasters on a sum-
mer-in at Waikiki. Sports Illus 27:48-54 Jl
24 '67
College football (cont) Sports Illus 27:54-6
O 2; 46+ N 6 '67
Eye on the Masters. Sports Illus 26:90-2+
Ap 10 '67
JENKINS, F. A. Jr. See Crompton, A. W. jt.
auth.
JENKINS, Gladys
Native plants for seaside gardens. Horticul-
ture 45:34-7+ Jl '67
JENKINS, Jean Foster
Masks. Sch Arts 67:38-9 N '67
JENKINS, Ray
Queen of Alabama and the prince consort.
N Y Times Mag p26-7+ My 21 '67
JENKINS, Roy Harris
What the British are doing to crack down on
crime; interview. por U S News 62:86 F 6 '67
about
Letter from London. M. Panter-Downes. New
Yorker 43:49-50 D 23 '67
Man for all sacrifices. il por Time 90:32 D 8 '67
Paying the price. por Newsweek 70:47-8 D 11
'67
JENKINS, Speight, Jr
Flashes of lightning. Opera N 32:24-5 Ja 20
'68
Ring East and West. Opera N 32:15-17 N 25
'67
(ed) See Vickers, J. Postscript on Vickers
JENKINS, Trefor, and others
Cholinesterase in plasma: first reported ab-
cence in the Bantu: half-life determination.
bibliog Science 156:1748-50 Je 30 '67
JENNINGS, Frank G.
Carpe diem. por Library J 92:531-6 F 1 '67
How plain is English? Sat R 50:73 D 16 '67
Jean Piaget: notes on learning. Sat R 50:81-3
My 20 '67
Revolution in education: it didn't start with
Sputnik. Sat R 50:77-9+ S 16 '67
Schaefer memorandum. Sat R 50:66-7 Mr 18
'67
JENNINGS, Gary
Empty seats in the cockpit. Read Digest 90:
127-31 Je '67
Opera's first step was a stumble. Opera N
31:6-7 F 11 '67
JENNINGS, John Q.
Pay vs. profit: where the Nation's money
really goes; interview, ed. by A. N. Booth.
Read Digest 90:177-80 F '67

JENNINGS, Paul
Will scandal blow the fuse at IUE? por
Bsns W p 121 Je 17 '67
JENNINGS, William H.
Stewardship and social action. Christian Cent
84:1593-5 D 13 '67
JENNISON, M. Harry
Little relief in sight. por Todays Health 45:65
S '67
JENSEN, Eileen
Touch of magic; story. Good H 165:98-9 N '67
JENSEN, Elwood V. and others
Sulfhydryl groups and estradiol-receptor in-
teraction. bibliog Science 158:385-7 O 20 '67
JENSEN, Eric
Treasure finders: do they really work? Pop
Mech 128:112-14+ Ag '67
JENSEN, F. See Defendi, V. jt. auth.
JENSEN, George M.
Let's try year-round schools. Parents Mag 42:
60-1+ S '67
JENSEN, Joerg
Anaphylatoxin in its relation to the comple-
ment system. bibliog Science 155:1122-3 Mr
3 '67
JENSEN, Marilyn A.
Computer ogre or tool? Parks & Rec 2:22+
S '67
JENSEN, Neal F.
Agrobiology: specialization or systems analy-
sis? bibliog Science 157:1405-9 S 22 '67
JENSEN, Neal P. and Burawa, A. W.
Magnetic reed switch. Pop Electr 27:47-9 S '67
Make your own reed switch-relay. Pop Electr
27:49-51 S '67
JENSEN, Oliver
Essay: filial piety and the First amendment.
Am Heritage 18:2-4 O '67
JENSEN, Paul. See Corliss, R. jt. auth.
JENSEN, Russell. See Abbott, R. T. jt. auth.
JENSEN, Wallace N. and others
Microincision of sickled erythrocytes by a
laser beam. bibliog Science 155:704-7 F 10 '67
JENT, H. Clay
Inverse plagiarism. Sch & Soc 95:314-16 Sum
'67
JEPSEN, Stanley M.
Trees of Hawaii. Am For 73:18-21+ D '67
JEROME, Judson
Chromatic; poem. Harper 236:52 Ja '68
From the desk of; poem. Harper 235:108 O
'67
JERSEY central railroad. See Central railroad
company of New Jersey
JERSEY CITY, N.J.

Negroes

Mayor tells how firmness stopped riots; interview. T. J. Whelan. il U S News 63:40-2 Ag
14 '67; Same abr. with title How to stop
riots. Read Digest 91:132-5 O '67

Police

Mayor tells how firmness stopped riots; inter-
view. T. J. Whelan. il U S News 63:40-2 Ag
14 '67; Same abr. with title How to stop
riots. Read Digest 91:132-5 O '67
JERSEY meadows. See New Jersey meadows
JERUSALEM
Battle for Jerusalem. S. De Gramont. il Sat
Eve Post 240:70-5 Ag 12 '67
Capture of the old Holy City. il Life 62:38A-
38C Je 16 '67
Future of Jerusalem: bonanza for Israel? il
U S News 62:10 Je 26 '67
Israel annexes old Jerusalem. Christian Cent
84:884-5 Jl 12 '67
Jerusalem: experiment in coexistence. S. De
Gramont. il N Y Times Mag p 14-18+ Jl 30
'67
Jerusalem; proposal for international control
of sacred places. New Repub 157:4 Jl 1 '67
Jerusalem's holy places; question of interna-
tionalizing the city. America 117:26 Jl 8 '67
Letter from Israel. D. Lang. New Yorker
43:44-5 D 30 '67
Refugees; Jerusalem reunified. il Time 90:25-6
Jl 7 '67
Reporter at large. E. Wilson. New Yorker 43:
38-40+ Ag 19 '67
Return to Jerusalem. N. Kotker. il Reporter
37:29-40+ Jl 13 '67
Should the Temple be rebuilt? il Time 89:56
Je 30 '67
Situation in the Middle East: report on Jeru-
salem; General assembly and Security
council. UN Mo Chron 4:11-13 O '67
Tension in Jerusalem; Israel's decision to
hold military parade in streets of Jerusalem.
il Newsweek 69:54+ My 22 '67

U.S. abstains on U.N. resolution on Jerusa-
lem; urges steps toward durable peace in
Near East; statement, July 14, 1967, with
text of resolution. A. J. Goldberg. Dept
State Bul 57:148-51 Jl 31 '67
United States reiterates policy on status of
Jerusalem; statements, June 28, 1967. Dept
State Bul 57:60 Jl 17 '67
Urbis and orbis: Jerusalem today. J. A.
Sanders. Christian Cent 84:967-70 Jl 26 '67
See also
Holy places

Antiquities

True path lies buried under stone and myth.
D. Seiberling. il Life 62:60+ Mr 24 '67

Church of the Holy Sepulcher

True path lies buried under stone and myth.
D. Seiberling. il Life 62:60+ Mr 24 '67

Description

As you walk in Jerusalem. il Sunset 138:63
F '67
Jerusalem; the holiest city. H. Gold. il Holi-
day 42:84-9+ D '67

History

City of war & worship. il Time 90:46-54 Ag 4
'67
Return to Jerusalem. N. Kotker. il Reporter
37:29-30+ Jl 13 '67

Parades

Spectacle of Easter in Jerusalem; in art
and life, the jarring contrasts of the pas-
sion; with report by D. Seiberling. il Life
62:50-60+ Mr 24 '67
JERUSALEM, Battle of, 1967. See Israeli-Arab
war, 1967
JESSUP, John K.
Henry R. Luce: the values that shaped his
work. Life 62:30-1 Mr 10 '67
How golden is the dollar? Life 63:66-8+ Ag
25 '67
JESSUP, Philip Caryl
Where are they now? il por Newsweek 69:14
F 27 '67
JESUIT universities. See Catholic church—Edu-
cation
JESUITS
Black pope; Father Arrupe superior general
of the Society of Jesus. J. Kobler. il Sat
Eve Post 240:30-4+ Mr 11 '67
Jesuit general and race; directives for Ameri-
can Jesuits. America 117:592 N 18 '67
Jesuit grass-roots renewal; meeting at St
Mary's college, St Marys, Kan. D. E.
Campion. America 116:286 F 25 '67
Jesuits face the future; report on the decrees
of the recent General congregation of the
Society of Jesus. E. J. Sponga. America
116:208-11+ F 11 '67
Of many things; concerning Bishop Pike's
statistics about the economic wealth of
the Jesuits. T. N. Davis. America 16:608
Ap 29 '67
Tomorrow's Jesuit. C. J. McNaspy. America
117:222-4 S 2 '67

Education

See also
Gonzaga university, Spokane, Wash.

Missions

Bright vignettes of a lost world; journals of
N. Point. il Life 63:52-9 D 1 '67
JESUS CHRIST
Christ today. D. S. Moore. il Cath World
206:109-10 D '67
Human God; Jesus. J. S. Dunne. Common-
weal 85:508-11 F 10 '67; Reply with re-
joinder. R. Ruether. 85:636-7+ Mr 10 '67
Jesus; Commonweal paper; symposium. bibliog
Commonweal 87:224-50+ N 24 '67
Patient teacher. V. P. McCorry. il America
117:inside back cover N 18 '67
Person and Lord. V. P. McCorry. America
117:inside back cover O 28 '67
Question from youth. America 117:7 Jl 1
'67
Was Jesus an outsider? Newsweek 70:83 Ag
7 '67
Where Jesus walked; visit to the Holy Land.
H. LaFay. il Nat Geog Mag 132:739-81 D '67
See also
Sacred Heart, Devotion to
Salvation

Agony

See Gethsemane

Appearances

Gospel of encounter. V. P. McCorry. America
116:569-70 Ap 15 '67

JESUS CHRIST—*Continued*

Art

Mystical Nativity. A. Saarinen. il McCalls 95:78-9 D '67
Spectacle of Easter in Jerusalem; in art and life, the jarring contrasts of the passion; with report by D. Seiberling. il Life 62:50-60+ Mr 24 '67
When Jesus was born in Bethlehem of Judaea. M. Mulvey. il Good H 165:77-81 D '67

Crucifixion

Notes on a death. V. P. McCorry. America 116:389-90 Mr 18 '67

Divinity

Gospel of the only-begotten Son. V. P. McCorry. America 116:662 Ap 29 '67

Humanity

Humanity of Jesus. T. E. Clarke. Commonweal 87:237-41 N 24 '67

Miracles

Gospel of encounter. V. P. McCorry. America 116:569-70 Ap 15 '67
Other air we breathe. V. P. McCorry. America 118:inside back cover Ja 13 '68

Mystical body

Invitation requires answer. V. P. McCorry. America 117:331-2 S 23 '67

Nativity

See also
Christmas
Christmas cribs
Magi

Parables

Cursing of the fig tree. R. Hull, jr. Christian Cent 84:1429-31 N 8 '67

Passion

Spectacle of Easter in Jerusalem; in art and life, the jarring contrasts of the passion; with report by D. Seiberling. il Life 62:50-60+ Mr 24 '67

Resurrection and ascension

All is well. V. P. McCorry. America 116:484+ Mr 25 '67
Empty tomb; excerpt from The resurrection. G. W. H. Lampe and D. M. MacKinnon. Christian Cent 84:363 Mr 22 '67
Gospel of triumph. V. P. McCorry. America 116:705-6 My 6 '67
Resurrection and biblical criticism. R. E. Brown. Commonweal 87:232-6 N 24 '67

Trial

Attempt to save Jesus? theories of Haim Cohn. il Time 90:76 N 10 '67

JET airplane engines

First Concorde engines delivered early. Aviation W 87:31 D 18 '67
Longer FB-111 with AMSA engines studied; advanced manned strategic aircraft. M. Getler. Tech W 20:14 F 20 '67
NASA engine work keyed to components. M. L. Yaffee. il Aviation W 87:64-5+ S 4 '67
NASA planning to test AiResearch ramjet in X-15A-2. I. Stone. il Aviation W 86:74-5+ Ja 30 '67
P&W keys airbus engine work to JT9D. I. Stone. Aviation W 87:45 Jl 10 '67

Design

GE sets airbus engine design, cost. M. L. Yaffee. il Aviation W 87:28-30 S 25 '67
NASA seeks quiet aircraft engine design. W. S. Beller. il Tech W 20:20-1 Je 19 '67
New engine aimed at use in small jets. il Aviation W 87:96-7 O 9 '67
P&W bases airbus powerplant on JT9D. M. L. Yaffee. il Aviation W 87:43+ O 9 '67

Fuel

Bullet strike gels treated fuel; Safuel. Aviation W 87:106 Jl 10 '67

Testing

GE accumulating SST engine test time. il Tech W 20:28-9 Ap 3 '67
Olympus 593 200 hr. ahead of schedule. il Aviation W 86:206-7+ My 29 '67

JET airplane fares. See Airlines—Fares
JET business planes. See Airplanes, Business
JET propelled airplanes. See Airplanes, Jet propelled

JET propulsion laboratory

JPL scientists challenge sterilization goals. H. M. David. Tech W 20:32-3 My 1 '67
JPL seeking prime role on Mariner/Mars '71 probe. H. Taylor. Tech W 20:15 My 22 '67
JPL story. H. L. Nieburg; reply with rejoinder. L. A. DuBridge. Bul Atomic Sci 23:28 F '67

JETS (football club) See Football clubs

JETT, Stephen C.

Navajo country; excerpts from Navajo wildlands. Audubon 69:22-7 Ja '67

JEUX; ballet. See Ballets—Criticisms
JEWEL thefts. See Burglary and burglars

JEWELL, Derek

When Lilli went to war, for both sides. N Y Times Mag p52-3+ N 19 '67

JEWELRY

Charcoal casting; jewelry-making on high school level. S. S. Madeja. il Sch Arts 67:26-9 S '67
Enamel on clay. O. Johnson. il Sch Arts 67:32-5 N '67
First you make a silver hairpin. il Sunset 139:98+ N '67
Gems in a hurry. il Design 69:28-30 Wint '67
Jewelry by Sepp Schmölzer. I. Brynner. il Craft Horiz 27:14-15 S '67
Lady and the marten; fur ornaments of 16th-century. H. A. LaFarge. il Art N 66:40-1 N '67
Masterpieces in metal; three-dimensional wildlife ornaments. M. C. Gethman. il Field & S 72:48-9+ D '67
Stunning jewelry to make in minutes. il Good H 165:158 D '67
Woven jewelry. P. Greenberg il Sch Arts 66:28-30 Ap '67
See also
Brooches
Earrings

Cleaning

Hints for cleaning jewelry. Consumer Bul 50:36 Ap '67

Exhibitions

American jewelry today; Everhart museum's biennial national show. J. Skoogfors. il Craft Horiz 27:26-7 N '67
Jewelry by contemporary painters and sculptors; traveling exhibit organized by New York's Museum of modern art. il Craft Horiz 27:32-9 My '67

Terminology

Glossary of jewelry terms. il Good H 165:192 D '67

JEWELRY trade

King of colored gems; H. Stern's jewelry business. S. Seegers and K. Seegers. il Read Digest 92:203-8 Ja '68

JEWELS; ballet. See Ballets—Criticisms

JEWETT, Paul K.

Can we learn from Mariology? Christian Cent 84:1019-21 Ag 9 '67

JEWISH Americans in Israel See Americans in Israel
JEWISH antiques. See Antiques

JEWISH-Arab relations

ABC's of Israeli-Arab conflict; the U.S. role. il U S News 62:44-6 Je 19 '67
Again, silence in the churches. A. R. Eckardt and A. L. Eckardt. Christian Cent 84:992-5 Ag 2 '67
Arab-Israeli dispute in perspective. N. Safran. il Cur Hist 53:321-30+ D '67
Arab refugees: relentless hate. J. Law. il U S News 63:62-3 Jl 31 '67
Arab world girds for second round against Israel. J. Law. il U S News 63:27-8 Jl 10 '67
Arabs, Israelis, Christians; letters to editors on the Middle East crisis. Christian Cent 84:1128-30 S 6 '67
Arabs-Israelis muzzle to muzzle. il Life 62:30-1 Je 2 '67
Arabs, 1967. J. S. Badeau. Atlan 220:102-4+ D '67
Arabs vs. Israel: twenty years of crisis. il Newsweek 69:43 Je 5 '67
Bitter exchange; Israeli destroyer sunk and Egyptian refinery shelled. il Time 90:23 N 3 '67
But what do we do about the Arabs? D. Cordtz. il Fortune 76:74-9+ S 1 '67
Eshkol sticks to his guns. J. Feron. il N Y Times Mag p34-5+ Ja 7 '68
Futility in the Middle East. W. V. Shannon. Commonweal 86:406-7 Je 30 '67

JEWISH-Arab relations—*Continued*
Hopeful truths of the new reality. M. Dayan.
il Life 63:120-120B S 29 '67
Is peace in the Middle East possible? W.
Laqueur. il N Y Times Mag p38-9+ Ag 27
'67; Reply. D. Sharma. p 123 S 24 '67
Israel after victory. D. J. Simpson. Cur Hist
53:341-5+ D '67
Israel and Nasser. P. Ben. New Repub 157:
20-2 S 9 '67
Israel: nation too young to die. J. A. Mich-
ener. il Look 31:64-8+ Ag 8 '67
Israel's new burden. Christian Cent 84:804
Je 21 '67
Jerusalem. New Repub 157:4 Jl 1 '67
King Hussein's new offensive. Christian Cent
84:1485 N 22 '67
Letter from Israel. D. Lang. New Yorker 43:
37-8+ D 30 '67
Messiah in motion; Algerian president calls
for guerrilla war against Israel. News-
week 70:37-8 Jl 31 '67
Middle East conflict; symposium. Christian
Cent 84:959-73 Jl 26 '67
Middle East in crisis. W. Pfaff. Common-
weal 86:382-3 Je 23 '67
Middle ground in the Middle East? N. S.
Booth, jr. il Christian Cent 84:1188-92 S 20
'67; Discussion. 84:1528+ N 29 '67
Multiproblems in the Middle East. J. C.
Evans. Christian Cent 84:1183-4 S 20 '67
Not too fast. Nat R 19:620-2 Je 13 '67
Object lesson in the Middle East. America
116:867 Je 24 '67
On facing the reality of Israel; Time essay.
il Time 89:24-5 Je 23 '67
Onslaught of rigidity. Time 90:28 Jl 28 '67
Palestine refugees: perennial source of
trouble; Palestine liberation organization.
J. H. Huizinga. il Reporter 36:33-5 My 18 '67
Report: after the Arab defeat. Atlan 220:38+
O '67
Rights of large nations. J. Burnham. Nat R
19:730 Jl 11 '67
Storm center on the new map: Israel. E.
Kern. il Life 63:60-2+ O 20 '67
U.S. viewpoint on four current world prob-
lems; statement, September 21, 1967. A. J.
Goldberg. Dept State Bul 57:486-7 O 16 '67
Waiting game; Yugoslav proposals for peace.
il Time 90:27-8 Ag 18 '67
Water vs. hatred; Lewis Strauss scheme.
C. L. Sulzberger. Read Digest 91:144+ O
'67
West bank waits for an answer. A. Rosenfeld.
Reporter 37:31-4 O 5 '67
What can and can't be done. P. Ben. New
Repub 156:6-7 Je 24 '67
When Israel looks ahead. il U S News 62:26-8
Je 26 '67
Where the war might start. A. Harrigan.
Nat R 19:566-7 My 30 '67
Wise men in the Middle East. Christian
Cent 84:955-6 Jl 26 '67
See also
Middle East crisis, 1967
JEWISH-Arab war, 1948-1949. See Israeli-Arab
war, 1948-1949
JEWISH art and symbolism
Contemporary synagogue art, by A. Kampf.
Review
Commentary 44:88-90 Ag '67. C. Roth
JEWISH athletes
Encyclopedia of Jews in sports, by B. Postal
and others. Review
Commentary 43:79-81 F '67. M. Liben
JEWISH cantors. See Cantors, Jewish
JEWISH daily forward
Greetings to a living legend: seventy for
the Forward. H. Golden. Life 63:14 Jl 21
'67
JEWISH day schools. See Jews—Education
JEWISH fiction
Bernard Malamud. J. Featherstone. Atlan
219:95-8 Mr '67
Jewish vogue. B. Hochman. Commentary
44:107-8+ S '67
JEWISH folk songs. See Folk songs, Jewish
JEWISH humor. See Humor, Jewish
JEWISH language. See Hebrew language
JEWISH literature
Sabbatai Zevi and the Jewish imagination.
R. Alter. Commentary 43:66-71 Je '67
JEWISH literature (American)
Jewish vogue. B. Hochman. Commentary
44:107-8+ S '67
JEWISH museum, New York
Exhibiting the Lower East side. R. Alter.
Commentary 43:67-71 Ja '67
JEWISH names. See Names, Jewish

JEWISH patient begins his analysis; story. See
Roth, P.
JEWISH question. See Anti-Semitism
JEWISH refugees. See Refugees, Jewish
JEWISH sects
See also
Hasidism
Sabbathaians
Zealots (Jewish party)
JEWISH theological seminary of America, New
York
Operation Booklift. D. Dempsey. il Sat R
50:39-41 Ap 15 '67
JEWISON, Norman
Improvise! films are made of whimsy. J.
Lipscomb. il por Life 63:86-8+ N 10 '67
JEWS
End of the Jewish people? by G. Friedmann.
Review
Newsweek il 70:91 Jl 17 '67. S. Maloff
Extreme Jews. I. B. Singer. il Harper 234:
55-62 Ap '67
Fin du peuple juif? by G. Friedmann. Re-
view
Commentary 43:75-80 Mr '67. R. Alter
In the light of Israel's victory. M. Himmel-
farb. Commentary 44:53-61 O '67
Jerusalem: experiment in coexistence. S. De
Gramont. il N Y Times Mag p 14-18+
Jl 30 '67; Discussion. p 12+ Ag 27; 70+
S 10 '67
Jews among the nations, by E. Kahler.
Review
Sat R 50:33 Jl 22 '67. A. Montagu
Varieties of Jewish experience. M. Him-
melfarb. Commentary 44:53-61 O '67
With status came perplexity. A. L. Sachar.
Sat R 50:36+ O 28 '67
See also
Anti-Semitism
Catholic church—Relations—Jews
Israel
Maranos
Names, Jewish
Zionism

Education

Statistics on Jewish day schools. Sch & Soc
95:26-7 Ja 7 '67

History

Battle of the scrolls: the Dead Sea discoveries
reconsidered. C. Raphael. il Atlan 219:88-
92+ My '67
Christian education and the Jewish people;
address before American academy of religion. L. D. Streiker. Christian Cent 84:168-
71 F 8 '67; Reply. J. E. Krueger. 84:348
Mr 15 '67

Rebellion, 66-73

Chip of history from Masada; with report by
M. Steinmann. il Life 63:120-2+ D 8 '67

Liturgy and ritual

See also
Passover

Persecutions

Holocaust: myths and facts. L. Harap. Na-
tion 205:21-3 Jl 3 '67
Warrant for genocide, by N. Cohn. Review
Commentary 44:80-4 Jl '67. W. Laqueur;
Reply. N. Cohn. 44:14+ N '67
Reporter 36:44+ Je 29 '67. W. L. Gunder-
sheimer

Political and social conditions

Absurdity of the Jewish condition. D.
Joravsky. Nation 204:661-3 My 22 '67
Jews and Germans; excerpt from address at
World Jewish congress, 1966; tr. by W. J.
Dannhauser. G. Scholem; discussion. Com-
mentary 43:15-16+ Mr '67
See also
Jews—Persecutions
Protocols of the wise men of Zion

Psychology

Lester Drentluss, a Jewish boy from Baltimore, attempts to make it through the summer of 1967. C. Trillin. Atlan 221:43-5 Ja
'68

Religion

See Judaism

Rites and ceremonies

Escalating bar mitzvahs. il Newsweek 69:94
Ap 17 '67
See also
Mikveh

Sports

Encyclopedia of Jews in sports, by B. Postal
and others. Review
Commentary 43:79-81 F '67. M. Liben

JEWS and Catholics. See Catholic church—Relations—Jews

JEWS and Christians. See Christianity and other religions

JEWS and Germans
Jews and Germans; excerpt from address at World Jewish congress, 1966; tr. by W. J. Dannhauser. G. Scholem; discussion. Commentary 43:15-16+ Mr '67

JEWS and Negroes
Black racists attack Jews. Christian Cent 84:1211 S 27 '67
Facts and fallacies: Negro anti-Semitism. G. T. Marx. Nation 206:11-13 Ja 1 '68
For better communication; American Judaism to step up communications with Christianity and the Negro ghettos. Time 90:72 N 24 '67
Gentile beast. Christian Cent 84:299-300 Mr 8 '67
Letters. R. Ellison; N. Podhoretz. Harper 235:4+ Jl '67; Discussion. 235:6+ Ag '67
Native sons. R. Robbins. Cath World 206: 81-6 N '67
Negroes are anti-Semitic because they want a scapegoat. R. Gordis. il N Y Times Mag p28-9+ Ap 23 '67; Discussion. p 12+ My 21 '67
Negroes are anti-Semitic because they're anti-white. J. Baldwin. il N Y Times Mag p26-7+ Ap 9 '67; Discussion. p 12+ My 21 '67
SNCC and the Jews. il Newsweek 70:22 Ag 28 '67

JEWS and the world war. See World war, 1939-1945—Jews

JEWS in Arab states
Exodus; flight from native Arab lands. il Newsweek 70:57-8 N 27 '67

JEWS in Czechoslovakia
Protest in Prague; author charges anti-Semitism. Newsweek 70:36 Ag 28 '67

JEWS in Denmark
Test of a democracy, by L. Yahil. Review
Commentary 44:97-8+ O '67. E. Livneh

JEWS in eastern Europe. See Jews in Europe

JEWS in Europe
Golden tradition, ed. by L. S. Dawidowicz. Review
Commentary 43:81-3 Je '67. D. Jacobson

JEWS in France
Letter from Paris; prayers for peace and for Israel. Genêt. New Yorker 43:138 Je 10 '67

JEWS in Germany
Jews and Germans; excerpt from address at World Jewish congress, 1966; tr. by W. J. Dannhauser. G. Scholem; discussion. Commentary 43:15-16+ Mr '67

JEWS in literature
Two worlds of Isaac Singer. C. R. Hughes. America 117:611-13 N 18 '67

JEWS in Palestine
Why American Jews are disillusioned. D. Polish. Christian Cent 84:965-7 Jl 26 '67

JEWS in Poland
Jewish question. il Time 90:28-9 Ag 18 '67
Poland's anti-Semitic Maoist underground. S. L. Shneiderman. il Reporter 36:21-3 Ja 26 '67
Ugly story; anti-Israel posture. Newsweek 70:40 Ag 7 '67

JEWS in Portugal
Last Marranos. A. Novinsky and A. Paulo. Commentary 43:76-81 My '67; Reply. S. J. Maslin. 44:20+ O '67

JEWS in Russia
Absurdity of the Jewish condition. D. Joravsky. Nation 204:661-3 My 22 '67
Between hammer and sickle, by B. Ami. Review
Sat R il 50:35 S 2 '67. R. I. Rubin
Fred Yusfin: the Jew who had never heard of Yom Kippur. il Look 31:82 O 3 '67
Jews of silence. D. Stern. Commonweal 86: 232-4 My 12 '67
Jews of silence, by E. Wiesel. Review
Commentary 43:91-2 Mr '67 M. Hayward
Reporter 36:60-2 Mr 9 '67. A. Brumberg
Open road caution light. America 116:170 F 4 '67
Pains of prayer in Russia. Time 89:69-70 Ap 21 '67
Playing with fire; change of propaganda target from Israel to Zionism and world Jewry. Newsweek 70:30-1 Ag 21 '67
Religion in Russia; the status of Jews. M. Geltman. il Nat R 19:1170-3 O 31 '67
Will Soviet Jewry survive? E. Wiesel. Commentary 43:47-52 F '67

JEWS in the United States
Are Jews still liberals? how they voted on the Civilian review board issue. M. Himmelfarb. Commentary 43:67-72 Ap 67; Discussion. 44:6+ S '67

Exhibiting the Lower East side; exhibition at Jewish museum. R. Alter. Commentary 43:67-71 Ja '67
Give as you never gave. il Newsweek 69:35-6 Je 19 '67
Israel and American Jewry. A. Hertzberg. Commentary 44:69-73 Ag '67; Discussion. 44:22+ D '67
Million a minute; support for Israel. Time 89:17-18 Je 16 '67
Our crowd, by S. Birmingham. Review
Atlan 221:112-13 Ja '68. E. Weeks
Commonweal 87:208-9 N 17 '67. S. Zoll
Life 63:6 Jl 14 '67. P. Lyon
Our crowd; excerpt. S. Birmingham. il Ladies Home J 84:165-70 N '67
See also
Union of American Hebrew congregations

JHABVALA, R. Prawer
Indian citizen; story. New Yorker 43:38-46 S 30 '67
Passion; story. New Yorker 43:56-64 D 2 '67

JIGS
Rip-fence stop jig. R. J. De Cristoforo. il Pop Sci 190:140-1 F '67

JIGSAWS
Getting the most from your zippy little jigsaw. J. Burroughs. il Pop Mech 128:186-90 N '67
Metalworking tricks on a jigsaw. W. Thomas. il Pop Sci 190:154-6 Je '67

JILLSON, Willard Rouse
Teddy Roosevelt and the boy from Syracuse. K. V. Hostick. Hobbies 71:109+ F '67

JILTING; story. See Delman, D.

JIREŠ, Jaromil
Movers, A. Sarris. por Sat R 50:38 D 23 '67

JIU-Jitsu
See also
Judo

JOACHIM, Sister Mary
To lovers; poem. Cath World 205:275 Ag '67

JOB corps. See United States—Job corps

JOB instruction training. See Employees—Training

JOB interviews. See Interviewing

JOB mobility. See Occupational mobility

JOB performance. See Employees—Rating

JOB quitting. See Labor turnover

JOB satisfaction
Got the itch to change jobs? il Changing T 21:31-2 F '67
We must make work worthwhile. C. Argyris. Life 62:56+ My 5 '67

JOB training. See Employees—Training

JOBIM, Antonio Carlos
Lyric impulse. B. Korall. Sat R 50:58 D 2 '67

JOBS. See Employment; Occupations

JÖBSIS, Frans F. and Duffield, J. C.
Force, shortening, and work in muscular contraction; relative contributions to over-all energy utilization. bibliog Science 156: 1388-92 Je 9 '67

JOCKEYS
Latin jockeys. Newsweek 70:62 D 4 '67
See also
Davidson, J.
Horse racing
Kusner, K.
Ussery, B.
Velásquez, J.
Ycaza, C. M. de

JOEL, Lawrence
Dixie town fetes war hero. R. Lantz. il pors Ebony 22:27-8+ Je '67
Soldier does his job. il Newsweek 69:30 Mr 20 '67

JOFFE, Lydia
La Péri: 1912. Dance Mag 41:40-2 Ap '67

JOFFREY ballet. See City Center Joffrey ballet

JOGGING. See Running

JOGGLING boards
Old-time joggling board bounces back. il Sunset 139:56-7 Jl '67

JOHANN, Robert O.
Philosopher's notebook (cont) America 116: 506; 117:61, 614 Ap 1, Jl 15, N 18 '67

JOHANNESBURG
Music
Johannesburg. S. R. Karnovsky. il Opera N 35:25 S 9 '67

JOHANOS, Donald
Lively arts; interview, ed. by R. Hemming, por Sr Schol 90:24 My 5 '67

JOHANSEN, John M.
New town. Arch Forum 127:44-53 S '67

JOHN, Saint, the Baptist
Evangelical V.I.P. V. P. McCorry. America 117:699-inside back cover D 2 '67
John the Baptist: voice in the wilderness. E. O. Hauser. il Read Digest 91:118-22 S '67
Strange friendship. V. P. McCorry. America 117:751-2 D 16 '67
Task: preparation. V. P. McCorry. America 117:inside back cover D 9 '67

JOHN, Amelia
Correcting the image. PTA Mag 62:13 S 67

JOHN, E. Roy, and others
Effects of visual form on the evoked response. bibliog Science 155:1439-42 Mr 17 '67

JOHN, Gospel of. See Bible—New Testament—John

JOHN Bates Clark medal. See American economic association

JOHN Birch society
Cinematic big lie: propaganda film. Anarchy, U.S.A. Christian Cent 84:860-1 Jl 5 '67
Mutiny in the Birch society. J. Phelan. il Sat Eve Post 240:21-5 Ap 8 '67

JOHN Brown raid, 1859. See Harpers Ferry, W.Va.—John Brown raid, 1859

JOHN Cotton Dana publicity awards
Dana publicity awards announced at ALA. Library J 92:2506 Jl '67

JOHN F. Kennedy airport. See New York (city)—Airports

JOHN LaFarge institute
Of many things. T. N. Davis. America 117:588 N 18 '67

JOHN of Leiden
Holy terrors of Munster. E. Stillman. il Horizon 9:90-5 Sum '67

JOHN S. Roberts junior high school. See New York (city)—Education

JOHNCOCK, Gordon
Gordon Johncock tests AMC's Javelin. pors Pop Mech 128:128-30+ N '67
Gordon Johncock tests the new Corvette. Pop Mech 129:108-10+ Ja '68

JOHNNYCAKE. See Bread

JOHNS Hopkins book center. See College bookstores

JOHNS Hopkins university
Academic democracy. il Time 89:60-1 Ja 27 '67
New man at Hopkins. Newsweek 69:88 Ja 30 '67

JOHNS ISLAND
Tree of life. W. K. Zinsser. il Look 31:18 Je 13 '67

JOHNSGARD, Paul A.
Dawn rendezvous on the lek; with biographical sketch. Natur Hist 76:4B, 16-21 Mr '67

JOHNSON, A. M.
New paving materials benefit St Louis parks. Parks & Rec 2:32-3 D '67

JOHNSON, Avery
Watercolor page: with biographical sketch. il por Am Artist 31:34-5+ O '67

JOHNSON, B. Lennart
Tetraploid wheats: seed protein electrophoretic patterns of the emmer and timopheevi groups. bibliog Science 158:131-2 O 6 '67

JOHNSON, B. Thomas, and others
Conversion of DDT to DDD by pathogenic and saprophytic bacteria associated with plants. bibliog Science 157:560-1 Ag 4 '67

JOHNSON, Barry
Seminarian in the resistance. Christian Cent 85:15-17 Ja 3 '68

JOHNSON, Bonnie E.
Sandcasting. Sch Arts 66:18-20 Je '67

JOHNSON, Charles E. See Powell, L. D. jt. auth.

JOHNSON, Charles F.
Disaccharidase: localization in hamster intestine brush borders. bibliog Science 155:1670-2 Mr 31 '67

JOHNSON, Charlotte Buel
Gallery for young people. See issues of School arts to May, 1967

JOHNSON, Chester
All the world's a toy. Nation 204:506-7 Ap 17 '67

JOHNSON, Clarence Leonard
Ten urgent aeronautical tasks. por Tech W 20:66-7 Ja 23 '67

JOHNSON, Claudia Alta (Taylor)
Rockefeller home designated historic landmark; address. Parks & Rec 2:23+ Ag '67
Talk with the First lady; interview, ed. by H. Brandon. pors N Y Times Mag p47-9+ S 10 '67

about

AFA's Distinguished service award for 1967, Mrs Lyndon B. Johnson. il por Am For 73:76 N '67

Back to the land? il por Time 90:26-7 S 29 '67
Ladies' day; the womenfolk at Glassboro. Time 89:17 Je 30 '67
Ladybird on tour, politicking whirlwind. il pors U S News 63:21 O 2 '67
Mrs Johnson's private White House world. H. Sidey. por Life 63:42 S 15 '67
Mrs LBJ: saleslady for Great society. il por U S News 62:22 Mr 27 '67
Sudden guests at the seashore. E. S. Hughes. il McCalls 94:80-1+ S '67

JOHNSON, David
When the French army mutinied. N Y Times Mag p26-7+ My 28 '67

JOHNSON, Dennis L.
Honey bees: do they use the direction information contained in their dance maneuver? bibliog Science 155:844-7 F 17 '67
—See Wenner, A. M. jt. auth.

JOHNSON, Donovan A.
Instructional materials in the mathematics classroom. NEA J 56:39-40 My '67

JOHNSON, Edgar
Christmas carol; excerpt from introduction to A Christmas carol in two Christmas classics. Sat R 50:13+ D 30 '67

JOHNSON, Eric Folke
AWWA taps Eric Johnson to succeed Ray Faust. por Am City 82:96+ Ag '67

JOHNSON, F. M. See Burns, J. M. jt. auth.

JOHNSON, Frank J.
Nuclear plateau psychology. Nat R 19:1387-8 D 12 '67

JOHNSON, Frank Minis, 1918-
Demons in Alabama. Time 89:50 My 5 '67
Interpreter in the front line. il por Time 89:72-4+ My 12 '67

JOHNSON, Frederick
Radiocarbon dating and archeology in North America. bibliog Science 155:165-9 Ja 13 '67

JOHNSON, Fridolf
Henry Morris: papermaker & printer. Am Artist 31:56-61+ O '67

JOHNSON, George, and Russell, John
Corn yields: are you aiming high enough? Farm J 91:40-1+ Mr '67

JOHNSON, George M.
Badlands and Teddy's park. Liv Wildn 31:20-7 Spr '67

JOHNSON, Georgia Douglas
Interrracial; poem. Negro Hist Bul 30:18 My '67

JOHNSON, Gerald W.
American power politics. New Repub 156:31-2 Mr 25 '67
Chief Justice. New Repub 157:34-5 Ag 5 '67
Guide to politics. New Repub 156:28-9 Mr 11 '67
Laugh, Casca, laugh! Sat R 50:16+ D 2 '67
Onward and upward. New Repub 156:26+ Je 10 '67
Pulitzer's progress. New Repub 157:29+ S 30 '67
Taps for FDR. New Repub 156:25-6 F 25 '67

JOHNSON, Glenn L.
Golden village. Horn Bk 43:183-91 Ap '67

JOHNSON, Harold K.
End of Vietnam war in sight? interview. pors U S News 63:44-8 S 11 '67
Generals vs. Vietnam strategy; excerpt from testimony before Senate preparedness investigating subcommittee. U S News 63:114 N 6 '67
Vietnam; address, November 7, 1967. Vital Speeches 34:168-71 Ja 1 '68

JOHNSON, Harold L.
Infrared stars. bibliog Science 157:635-8 Ag 11 '67

JOHNSON, Haynes
Life in the Nation's capital, where crime and despair rule; reprint from the Washington star, week of January 16, 1967. U S News 62:76-8 Ja 30 '67

JOHNSON, Mrs Herbert
Joys of an IFYE mother. por Suc Farm 65:73+ S '67

JOHNSON, Hugh
Corkscrew: offbeat wines for dinner for two. House & Gard 131:172+ Ap '67
Going places, finding things in Alaska. House & Gard 131:40-4+ My '67
Going places, finding things in the Monterey Peninsula. House & Gard 132:23-4+ Jl '67
No debate: the wines of California. Vogue 150:32+ Ag 15 '67
Sherry. House & Gard 131:148+ F '67
Smart way to buy wine; excerpts from Wine. House & Gard 132:202+ S '67
Wines of the Rhine and the Moselle. House & Gard 133:126+ Ja '68

JOHNSON, Irving M.
Getting unstuck. Yachting 123:84-5+ Ja '68

JOHNSON, Lyndon Baines—*Continued*

President Johnson announces signing of grains arrangement; statement, November 8, 1967. Dept State Bul 57:716-17 N 27 '67

President Johnson attends funeral of Konrad Adenauer; statement, April 19, 1967. Dept State Bul 56:751-2 My 15 '67

President Johnson confers with British Prime Minister; remarks, June 2, 1967. Dept State Bul 56:963 Je 26 '67

President Johnson confers with Canadian Prime Minister; remarks, May 25, 1967. Dept State Bul 56:908-9 Je 19 '67

President Johnson expresses sorrow at death of Lord Attlee; statement, October 8, 1967. Dept State Bul 57:568 O 30 '67

President Johnson greets Japanese governors; remarks, May 24, 1967. Dept State Bul 56:917-18 Je 19 '67

President Johnson holds meeting with president of Ivory Coast; exchange of toasts, August 17, 1967. Dept State Bul 57:330-2 S 11 '67

President Johnson holds talks with Australian Prime Minister; remarks, June 1, 1967. Dept State Bul 56:960-1 Je 26 '67

President Johnson invites Hanoi to shipboard peace talks; remarks, November 11, 1967. Dept State Bul 57:747-8 D 4 '67

President Johnson meets with German chancellor; exchange of greetings, statements and exchange of toasts, August 15; with joint statement, August 16, 1967. Dept State Bul 57:325-30 S 11 '67

President Johnson meets with President of Niger; exchange of greetings and exchange of toasts, September 26, 1967. Dept State Bul 57:541-3 O 23 '67

President Johnson reaffirms support for free flow of trade; statement, October 12, 1967. Dept State Bul 57:573 O 30 '67

President Johnson renews call for nonproliferation treaty; message, February 21, 1967. Dept State Bul 56:447-8 Mr 20 '67

President Johnson sets goal of substantial export increase; remarks, May 23, 1967. Dept State Bul 56:886-7 Je 12 '67

President Johnson signs IDB authorization bill; remarks, September 22, 1967. Dept State Bul 57:499-500 O 16 '67

President Johnson visits Expo 67 at Montreal; remarks, May 25, 1967. Dept State Bul 56:907-8 Je 19 '67

President Johnson welcomes Crown Prince of Laos; toast, November 9, 1967. Dept State Bul 57:752 D 4 '67

President Johnson welcomes OAS foreign ministers; toast, September 22, 1967. Dept State Bul 57:498-90 O 16 '67

President Johnson's press conference of November 17; excerpts. Dept State Bul 57:775-80 D 11 '67

President Johnson's proposal for negotiation on Viet-Nam rejected by Ho Chi Minh; letter, February 8, 1967. Dept State Bul 56:595-6 Ap 10 '67

President Johnson's special message to Congress; children and youth. PTA Mag 61:20-2 Mr; 12-14+ Ap '67

President of Cameroon visits the United States; exchange of toasts, October 24, 1967. Dept State Bul 57:654-5 N 13 '67

President of Malawi visits the United States; exchange of toasts, June 8, 1967. Dept State Bul 57:42-4 Jl 10 '67

President reaffirms U.S. desire for peace in Viet-Nam; text of message to Pope Paul VI, February 8, 1967. Dept State Bul 56:319 F 27 '67

President recommends ratification of OAS charter amendments; message, June 12, 1967. Dept State Bul 57:78-9 Jl 17 '67

President reports to Congress on food aid programs; letter, November 6, 1967. Dept State Bul 57:762-3 D 4 '67

President reviews action taken on ICY recommendations; statement, April 3, 1967. Dept State Bul 56:658-60 Ap 24 '67

President reviews U.S. position on bombing of North Viet-Nam; text of letter, March 1, 1967. Dept State Bul 56:514-16 Mr 27 '67

President Saragat of Italy visits the United States; exchange of greetings, September 18, exchange of toasts, and joint statement, September 19, 1967. Dept State Bul 57:500-3 O 16 '67

President sends congratulations to Vietnamese chief of state; text of message, September 10, 1967. Dept State Bul 57:421 O 2 '67

President signs joint resolution of food assistance to India; statement, April 1, 1967. Dept State Bul 56:700 My 1 '67

President transmits fifth annual report of Peace corps to Congress. Dept State Bul 56:529 Mr 27 '67

President transmits Kennedy round trade agreement to the Congress; message, November 27, 1967. Dept State Bul 57:883-5 D 25 '67

President urges action on funds for southeast Asia operations; text of letter to Speaker of the House; January 24, 1967. Dept State Bul 56:236-7 F 13 '67

President urges ratification of Consular pact with U.S.S.R; statement,, February 2, 1967. Dept State Bul 56:287-8 F 20 '67

President urges study of future of Pacific Islands Trust Territory; text of letter, August 21, 1967. Dept State Bul 57:363 S 18 '67

President's education proposals sent to Congress; summary, ed. by G. Krettek and E. D. Cooke. Wilson Lib Bul 41:849 Ap '67

Prime Minister of Afghanistan visits the United States; exchange of greetings, exchange of toasts, and joint statement, March 28, 1967. Dept State Bul 56:627-32 Ap 17 '67

Prime Minister of Singapore visits the United States; exchange of greetings and toast, October 17, with joint statement, October 18, 1967. Dept State Bul 57:612-15 N 6 '67

Prince Souvanna Phouma of Laos meets with President Johnson; exchange of toasts and statement, October 20, 1967. Dept State Bul 57:653 N 13 '67

Principles for peace in the Middle East; address, June 19, 1967. Dept State Bul 57:31-4 Jl 10 '67

Problem is not with this government. . ; excerpts from press conference. Time 89:22 Mr 17 '67

Progress in a generation of peril; address, October 23, 1967. Dept State Bul 57:631-3 N 13 '67

Report on educational and cultural exchange sent to Congress; letter of transmittal, August 14, 1967. Dept State Bul 57:303 S 4 '67

Sacrifices in Viet-Nam marked in Memorial day messages; May 30, 1967. Dept State Bul 56:917 Je 19 '67

Situation in the Near East; statement, June 7, and exchange of letters, June 8, 1967. Dept State Bul 56:951-2 Je 26 '67

Sixth anniversary of the Alliance for progress; remarks, August 17, 1967. Dept State Bul 57:287-8 S 4 67

Spirit of Hollybush; excerpt from remarks, June 23, 1967. Dept State Bul 57:38-40 Jl 10 '67

State of the budget and the economy; excerpts from message to the Congress, August 3, 1967. Dept State Bul 57:266-8 Ag 28 '67

State of the Union; address, January 10, 1967. Vital Speeches 33:226-34 F 1 '67; Excerpts. Dept State Bul 56:158-63 Ja 30 '67; Cur Hist 52:238-40+ Ap '67

Tariff commission to report on textile and apparel industries; statement, October 4, 1967. Dept State Bul 57:529 O 23 '67

Turkey and the United States reaffirm bonds of friendship and cooperation; exchange of greetings and exchange of toasts, April 3, 1967, with joint communique. Dept State Bul 56:652-7 Ap 24 '67

20th anniversary of the Truman doctrine; text of letter and messages. Dept State Bul 56:546-7 Ap 3 '67

U.S. and Japan reaffirm common objectives and pledge continued cooperation; exchange of greetings and toasts, November 14, with joint communique, November 15, 1967. Dept State Bul 57:742-7 D 4 '67

U.S. and Korea pledge continued friendship and cooperation; exchange of greetings, exchange of toasts, with joint statement, March 14, 1967. Dept State Bul 56:548-53 Ap 3 '67

United States and Thailand pledge to continue close cooperation to promote peace; exchange of greetings and exchange of toasts, June 27, with joint statement, June 29, 1967. Dept State Bul 57:61-4 Jl 17 '67

U.S. and Vietnamese leaders confer at Guam; responses, remarks, and statements, March 20-21, 1967. Dept State Bul 56:586-94 Ap 10 '67

United States calls for restraint in the Near East; statement, May 23, 1967. Dept State Bul 56:870-1 Je 12 '67

United States commemorates closing of successful AID mission to Iran; message, November 29, 1967. Dept State Bul 57:827 D 18 '67

JOHNSSON, Lars-Göran, and Hawkins, J. E.
Jr
  Otolithic membranes of the saccule and
  utricle in man. bibliog Science 157:1454-6
  S 22 '67
JOHNSTON, Don Porter
  Johnston decade. por Am For 73:19+ S '67
JOHNSTON, George
  Country of champs. Vogue 150:164-6+ S 15
  '67
JOHNSTON, Gladys
  Two rebels with a lovely cause. C. Phinizy.
  il pors Sports Illus 26:42-6 F 27 '67
JOHNSTON, Harry
  Obituary
    Time por 89:15 F 17 '67
JOHNSTON, J. A. Jr. See Baker, W. R. jr. jt.
  auth.
JOHNSTON, Thomas
  Two rebels with a lovely cause. C. Phinizy.
  il pors Sports Illus 26:42-6 F 27 '67
JOHNSTONE, B. M. and Boyle, A. J. F.
  Basilar membrane vibration examined with
  the Mössbauer technique. bibliog Science
  158:389-90 O 20 '67
JOHNSTONE, William C.
  Political commitment in southeast Asia. bib-
  liog f Cur Hist 54:1-6 Ja '68
JOHNTZ, William F.
  Googol! J. Benet. il por Am Ed 39-10 O '67
JOINER, Charles A.
  Politics in South Vietnam. bibliog f Cur
  Hist 54:35-41+ Ja '68
JOINT adventures
  North American, Mobil oil agree to pool
  technology. il Tech W 20:30+ F 13 '67
JOINT apprenticeship program. See Appren-
  tices
JOINT Dominican Republic-Puerto Rican eco-
  nomic commission
  Dominican Republic-Puerto Rican economic
  commission announced; joint statement.
  Dept State Bul 57:620 N 6 '67
JOINT economic committee. See United States
  —Congress—Joint economic committee
JOINT tenancy
  Joint tenancy: can it work for you? M. T.
  Bloom. Read Digest 91:163+ O '67
  Should you own property jointly? some pit-
  falls to guard against. il U S News 64:60-3
  Ja 15 '68
JOINT United States-Canadian committee on
  trade and economic affairs
  U.S.-Canada economic committee concludes
  eleventh meeting; text of communique,
  June 22, 1967. Dept State Bul 57:44-6 Jl
  10 '67
JOINT United States-Japan committee on
  scientific cooperation
  Endoplasmic reticulum: United States-Japan
  cooperative science program; report on symposium. G. Palade and K. Porter. Science
  156:106-10 Ap 7 '67
  Paleomagnetism: United States-Japan com-
  mittee on scientific cooperation. A. Cox
  and N. Kawai. Science 155:724 F 10 '67
JOINT United States-Japan committee on trade
  and economic affairs
  U.S.-Japan joint economic committee holds
  sixth meeting; statement, September 13,
  with joint communique and news confer-
  ence, September 15, 1967. D. Rusk; T. Miki.
  Dept State Bul 57:451-9 O 9 '67
JOINTS
                  Diseases
      See also
  Arthritis
JOINTS (carpentry)
  How to cut rabbet-miter joints. R. J. De
  Cristoforo. il Pop Sci 190:151-5 My '67
JOKES. See Humor
JOLLY, Ovid R.
  Mr Jolly comes to town. il por Duns R 90:
  57-8 S '67
JOMON pottery. See Pottery, Japanese
JONAS, Charles Raper
  Excerpt from address, January 31, 1967. Cong
  Digest 46:113+ Ap '67
JONAS, Gerald
  Another trip down highway 1040; poem. New
  Yorker 43:44 Ap 8 '67
  Cattle of the king; poem. Atlan 220:115 S '67
  Day the T.V. broke; poem. Sat R 50:51 F 25
  '67
  How-to-do-it song for today; poem. New
  Repub 157:22 S 23 '67
  Line at Radio City music hall. N Y Times
  Mag p 114+ N 12 '67
  Love; poem. Nation 204:381 Mr 20 '67
JONAS, Hans
  Judaism, Christianity, and the western tradi-
  tion. Commentary 44:61-8 N '67

JONAS, Stephen
  Six books by seven poets. R. Vas Dias.
  Poetry 110:186-9 Je '67
JONATHAN Logan, incorporated. See Logan,
  Jonathan, incorporated
JONCKHEERE, Lucy
  Chesapeake; colonial haven. il Sr Schol 91:
  sup 14-16+ S 28 '67
JONES, Alan Pryce-. See Pryce-Jones, A.
JONES, Allen
  Out on a limb. il Newsweek 70:97 S 11 '67
JONES, Alma L.
  Private park for rockhounds. Nat Parks Mag
  41:15 My '67
JONES, Antony Charles Robert Armstrong-,
  1st earl of Snowdon. See Snowdon, A. C.
  R. A.-J.
JONES, Arthur Gwynne, baron Chalfont. See
  Chalfont, A. G. J.
JONES, Bartlett F.
  Fine arts. America 117:329-31 S 23 '67
  From S.F. and L.A. America 116:841 Je 10 '67
JONES, Blair F. and others
  Silica in alkaline brines. bibliog Science 158:
  1310-14 D 8 '67
JONES, Casey
  Life and death of Casey Jones. T. Mahoney.
  il Read Digest 90:25-6+ Ap '67
JONES, Cranston
  Breuer: the last modern architect. Horizon
  9:32-41 Sum '67
JONES, Curtis H. See Hekimian, J. S. jt. auth.
JONES, David
  Monkee talk; interview, ed. by E. Miller. por
  Seventeen 26:302+ Ag '67
JONES, Doug
  Sad farewell, a glad hello. M. Kram. il por
  Sports Illus 26:44+ Mr 6 '67
JONES, Edward V.
  Owens-Thomas house. Antiques 91:342-6 Mr
  '67
JONES, Elvin
  Jazz. W. Balliett. New Yorker 43:74 Ag 26
  '67
JONES, Francis Avery
  Doctor views nineteen years of socialized
  medicine; interview, ed. by L. Gross. il
  pors Look 31:48-53 Mr 21 '67
JONES, George W.
  Compensatory education for the disadvan-
  taged. bibliog NEA J 56:21-3 Ap '67
JONES, Homer
  Homer the bomb. il Newsweek 70:93 O 23 '67
JONES, Inigo
  Masked & bared. il Time 89:82 Ap 14 '67
JONES, J. Raymond
  Boss Jones of Tammany Hall. A. Hiss. il
  pors N Y Times Mag p32-3+ F 19 '67
JONES, James
  Aging heavy of the Paris expatriates. H.
  Moffett. il pors Life 63:30-2+ Ag 4 '67
  Jones boy forever. W. Sheed. por Atlan 219:
  68-72 Je '67
JONES, James C.
  Romney: still blooper-prone, but very much
  alive. Newsweek 70:26 O 9 '67
JONES, Jenkin Lloyd
  Excerpt from program, Weep for the in-
  nocent, televised on April 3, 1967. Cong
  Digest 46:213+ Ag '67
JONES, Joela
  Hand that touched Brahms's touched mine!
  ed. by E. Miller. pors Seventeen 26:156-7+
  S '67
JONES, Johnathan Luther. See Jones, Casey
JONES, Jon
  Painting with smoke. Design 69:36-7 Fall '67
JONES, Joseph Lee
  Mr Jones goes to Washington. J. Galloway.
  Commonweal 87:374-5 D 22 '67
JONES, K. P.
  Roses; selecting, cutting, preparing for shows.
  Horticulture 45:26-9+ Je '67
JONES, Kenneth Glyn
  Some new notes on Messier's catalogue. Sky
  & Tel 33:156-8 Mr '67
JONES, Kenneth T.
  Island millionaire. il por Time 90:103 D 15
  '67
JONES, Larry R.
  Backpacking with Joe. por Liv Wildn 30:24-6
  Aut '66
JONES, LeRoi
  Brave new words. H. S. Resnik. Sat R 50:28-9
  D 9 '67
  Curtains for LeRoi. il por Time 91:14 Ja 12
  '68
  Jersey justice and LeRoi Jones. R. H. Smith.
  Pub W 193:66 Ja 15 '68
  Poetic justice. il por Newsweek 71:24 Ja 15
  '68

JONES, Leslie
Leslie Haydn-Jones. R. Freed. Sat R 50:78
Mr 25 '67
JONES, Margaret Hubbard. See Carterette, E.
C. jt. auth.
JONES, Merriam
Food for the future. Américas 19:30-3 Jl '67
JONES, Parnelli
Javelin SST: an exciting new sportster for
'68. pors Pop Sci 191:76-9 S '67

about

Gentlemen, junk your engines. B. Ottum.
il por Sports Illus 26:30-3 Je 12 '67
Rufus and the turbine. J. McFarland. il pors
Hot Rod 20:40-2 N '67
JONES, Phil B.
What's new (cont) Suc Farm 65:74 Ja; 76
F; 8 Ap; 15 O '67
JONES, Phillip L.
Sounds and shadows. Sr Schol 90:sup 19
My 5 '67
JONES, Robert
From the house of the dead. Am Rec G
33:992-6 Jl '67
On four records from two labels, seven works
by Janáček. Am Rec G 33:378+ Ja '67
JONES, Robert Trent
Beauty and the bogeyman. por Fortune 75:
160+ F '67
JONES, Rufus Parnelli. See Jones, P.
JONES, Samellyn
Traveling with Mlle: we conquistadoras. Mlle
65:327-32 Ag '67
JONES, Stacy V.
Mechanical calf. Sci Digest 61:74 My '67
Power from a bottled thunderstorm. Sci
Digest 61:27 Ap '67
Safer landings. Sci Digest 61:80 Je '67
Soluble basting thread. Sci Digest 62:80-1
Jl '67
JONES, Stuart E.
Houston, prairie dynamo. Nat Geog Mag
132:338-77 S '67
JONES, Virginia Lacy
Delicate area for research. Wilson Lib Bul
41:913-14 My '67
JONES, William A. and Jacobson, Martin
Isolation of N,N-diethyl-m-toluamide, deet.
from female pink bollworm moths. bibliog
Science 159:99-100 Ja 5 '68
JONES, William R.
Sheepherder versus the geologist. Audubon
69:47-9 Ja '67
JONES, Wyman H. and McKinney, R. A.
Five branches for Fort Worth. Library J 92:
4370-2 D 1 '67
JONES, Wyman L.
April thoughts; poem. Wilson Lib Bul 41:835
Ap '67
JONES and Laughlin steel corporation
Helping a small town cope with prosperity;
new steel plant at Hennepin, Ill. il Bsns W
p 184-6+ S 23 '67
JONKER, Ingrid
Black butterflies. J. Cope. por Mlle 64:167+
Mr '67
JONSSON, John Erik
Troubled cities, and their mayors. il por
Newsweek 69:40-2 Mr 13 '67
JORAVSKY, David
Absurdity of the Jewish condition. Nation
204:661-3 My 22 '67
Communist dreams and Soviet reality. Nation
206:85-6 Ja 15 '68
JORDAN, Charles H.
Death in Prague. por Newsweek 70:43 S 4 '67
JORDAN, Eileen Herbert
Man who stopped the square dance; story.
Ladies Home J 84:70-1 Ag '67
JORDAN, Harry Edward
Obituary
Am City 82:46 F '67
JORDAN, Hope Dahle
Elusive secret. Writer 80:24-6 D '67
JORDAN, Lloyd F.
Coordinated planning for science in Com-
munist Europe. bibliog Science 155:796-802
F 17 '67
JORDAN, Paul
Warm and clear; interview. New Yorker
43:42-4 S 23 '67
JORDAN, Robert Paul
Illinois: the city and the plain. Nat Geog Mag
131:745-97 Je '67
JORDAN, Robert T.
Home-delivery library service. Wilson Lib Bul
42:403-5 D '67
Libraries of the future for the liberal arts
college. por Library J 92:537-9 F 1 '67

JORDAN
Tone v. substance. il Time 90:37 N 17 '67
See also
Bethlehem
Foreign visitors in Jordan
Holy Land
Jerusalem
Petra
Qalqilah
Tourist trade—Jordan

Antiquities
What's left after the tornado? T. L. Christie.
Sat R 50:41 O 14 '67

Description and travel
Tourist in the wake of war; touring the
newly occupied territories. J. Berke. il Sat R
50:40-1+ O 14 '67

Foreign relations
Roots of anguish; west bank of the River
Jordan. M. J. Kubic. Newsweek 70:31-2
Jl 24 '67

Industries
Jordan. P. P. Vouras. bibliog il Focus 17:1-6
F '67

Israeli occupation, 1967-
West bank waits for an answer. A. Rosenfeld.
Reporter 37:31-4 O 5 '67

Politics and government
Can Hussein survive? J. H. Huizinga. il Re-
porter 37:34-6 S 7 '67
JORDAN high school. See Los Angeles—Edu-
cation
JORDAN RIVER
To resume river diversion. M. Dean. il Sci N
92:203 Ag 26 '67
JORGENSEN, William E.
Carpeting in libraries. por Library J 92:4344
D 1 '67
JORRIN, Ruth
Wealth attracts talent. Nation 204:425-7 Ap
3 '67
JOSELYN, Bob
Three high spots for a hobby room. Pop
Mech 128:136-41 Jl '67
JOSEPH, Helen
Lady at home. por Newsweek 70:35-6 D 25
'67
JOSEPH, James
Beware the highway's bad samaritans. Mo-
tor T 19:83-4+ Jl '67
Cars of the stars. Motor T 19:89-92 Jl '67
Piecework mechanic caper. Motor T 19:52-3+
Ag '67
Sex and the single car. Motor T 19:44-7 Ap
'67
Shop the glitter lots. Motor T 19:41-2 Je '67
JOSEPH, Richard
San Francisco for nobs and no-nobs. Esquire
67:116-23 Je '67
Travel notes. See issues of Esquire
(ed) See Donleavy, J. P. Traveler, consider
my Dublin
(ed) See Ives. B. Traveler, consider my
Bahamas
JOSEPH Magnin company. See Magnin, Joseph,
company
JOSEPH Magnin store. See Los Angeles—Stores
JOSEPHS, Wilfred
And we quote; ed. by B. Jacobson. por Hi Fi
16:MA17 Ja '67

about

Music to my ears; performance of Requiem
by Cincinnati symphony at Carnegie Hall.
I. Kolodin. Sat R 50:58 F 11 '67
Musical events; performance of his Requiem,
Opus 39, by Cincinnati symphony orchestra
in Carnegie Hall. W. Sargeant. New Yorker
42:116+ F 4 '67
No more molars. por Time 89:38 F 3 '67
JOSEPHSON, Larry
Larry Josephson; interview. New Yorker
43:25-6 Je 17 '67
JOSEPHSON, Matthew
Depression made lively. R. Wohlforth. Na-
tion 205:474-6 N 6 '67
JOSEPHSON, Robert K. and Macklin, Martin
Transepithelial potentials in hydra. bibliog
Science 156:1629-31 Je 23 '67
JOSEY, Alex
Guru and the coup. Nation 205:217-19 S 11
'67
JOSEY, E. J.
Reading is what's happening; address, April
21, 1967. Negro Hist Bul 30:14-17 My '67

JOSHI, P. C. and Noggle, G. R.
Growth of isolated mesophyll cells of arachis hypogaea in simple defined medium in vitro. bibliog Science 158:1575-7 D 22 '67

JOURNALISM
New age of the journalist-historian. Q. Howe. Sat R 50:25-7+ My 20 '67
New candor. il Newsweek 70:51 Jl 31 '67
See also
Editors and editing
Libel and slander
News
Newspaper court reporting
Reporters and reporting

Anecdotes, facetiae, satire, etc.
Adversaria (cont) il Esquire 67:95 Mr; 130 Je '67

Study and teaching
So you want to teach journalism. M. L. Stein. Sat R 51:112-13+ Ja 13 '68
What happens to J-school graduates; job squeeze in the U.S, western Europe and the United Kingdom. J. Tebbel. Sat R 50:126-7+ Mr 11 '67
Where the action is; Urban journalism center. Newsweek 70:58-9 Ag 14 '67

Great Britain
See also
Newspapers—Great Britain

Japan
See also
Newspapers—Japan

United States
An opinion: on the new journalism. R. Reed. Mlle 66:64+ N '67
Press: how clear is its mirror on our world? il Sr Schol 90:6-12 Ap 28 '67
Viscous circle. Reporter 36:12+ Mr 9 '67
See also
Catholic press
Newspapers—United States

JOURNALISTIC ethics
Harry the muckracker. il Time 89:84+ Ap 21 '67
Integrity of the U.S. press; concerning an article in the Wall Street journal of July 25, 1967. America 117:148 Ag 12 '67
Intruders: Unesco's Director-General looks at ethics in the mass media. R. Maheu. UNESCO Courier 20:23-4 F '67
Reporter; Philadelphia magazine's exposé of Karafin affair. S. J. Adamo. America 116:822 Je 3 '67: Discussion. 117:101 Jl 29 '67
Should reporters buy news? B. Surface. Sat R 50:85-6 My 13 '67
See also
Crime and the press

JOURNALISTIC photography. See Photography, Journalistic

JOURNALISTS
New age of the journalist-historian. Q. Howe. Sat R 50:25-7+ My 20 '67
Newsman: society's lonesome end; excerpt from address. W. Gallagher. il Sat R 51:114-15 Ja 13 '68
What happens to J-school graduates; job squeeze in the U.S, western Europe and the United Kingdom. J. Tebbel. Sat R 50:126-7+ Mr 11 '67
See also
Foreign correspondents
Sigma delta chi
United States—History—Civil war—Journalists
Women as journalists

JOURNALS. See Periodicals

JOURNALS, Personal. See Diaries

JOURNET, Marcel
Marcel Journet. A. Favia-Artsay. por Hobbies 72:36 My '67

JOUVET, Michel
States of sleep; with biographical sketch. Sci Am 216:22, 62-8+ bibliog (p 146) F '67

JOVANOVICH, William
Information as a property; address, 1967. por Wilson Lib Bul 42:46-55 S '67
My illusions and yours. Harper 235:56-60 O '67

JOY, James H.
Of teachers and transparencies. Sr Schol 90: sup 17 F 3 '67

JOY manufacturing company
Joy calls in a new team. Bsns W p 136 Mr 11 '67

JOYCE, Brice
Nigger priest. il por Newsweek 69:64 F 20 '67

JOYCE, Charles
Choosing a circulation control system. Library J 93:162-5 Ja 15 '68
Goals, myths, and realities. por Library J 92:3385-8 O 1 '67

JOYCE, Donald V.
New look at playstreets. Parks & Rec 2:28-9+ Jl '67
Playstreets add novel pastimes. Am City 82:83-5 Jl '67

JOYCE, James
Dublin where James Joyce lived; excerpts from Ulysses. Look 31:34-40 Ap 18 '67
Finnegans wake; dramatization. See Erdman, J. Coach with the six insides
Giacomo Joyce; story; excerpts. Harper 236:27-30 Ja '68
Letters of James Joyce, ed. by R. Ellmann. Review
Nat R 19:968-9 S 5 '67. H. Kenner
Stephen D; dramatization. See Leonard, H.

about
HCE's chaste ecstasy. J. M. Morse. Yale R 56:397-405 Mr '67
It will keep the professors busy for centuries: Ulysses. J. Roddy. il Look 31:42 Ap 18 '67
Joyce's Ireland. C. O'Brien. il pors Sat R 50:56-7+ Mr 11 '67
Joyce's letters. B. McCabe. Commonweal 85:587-90 F 24 '67
Simplicity behind the disguises. K. Sullivan. Nation 204:341-3 Mr 13 '67
Tenor of James Joyce. R. Rushmore. il pors Opera N 32:8-12 D 9 '67
Ulysses in the reel world. B. McCabe. il Cath World 204:346-51 Mr '67

JOYCE, James Avery
SEATO: false alibi. Christian Cent 84:1424-9 N 8 '67

JOYFUL noise; musical comedy. See Musical comedies, revues, etc.—Criticisms, plots, etc.

JUAN de Flandes
Pictures for praying. il Time 91:52 Ja 19 '68

JUAN FERNÁNDEZ ISLANDS
Crusoe's island. P. Quennell. il Horizon 9:66-83 Spr '67

JUÁREZ, Benito Pablo
Mexico. A. Zambrano and M. Zambrano. Christian Cent 84:820 Je 21 '67

JUÁREZ, Carlos T. Torrealba. See Torrealba Juárez, C. T.

JUAREZ, Mexico
Cleaning up Juarez. W. Eastlake. Nation 205:300-3 O 2 '67

JUCKETT, Eunice Telfer
Looping Guadeloupe. Travel 127:50-3+ Ap '67

JUDAISM
After Auschwitz, by R. L. Rubenstein. Review
Commonweal 87:209-10 N 17 '67. M. D. Zeik
Franz Rosenzweig: a voice for today. H. E. Schaalman. Christian Cent 84:233-6 F 22 '67
Judaism and the Christian predicament, by B. Z. Bokser. Review
New Repub 156:25-6+ My 6 '67. R. Hazelton
Justifying man's way to man. B. Mandelbaum. Sat R 50:57-8 F 25 '67
Orthodoxy's new look; world conference of Orthodox Jewry. il Time 91:58 Ja 19 '68
Should the Temple be rebuilt? il Time 89:56 Je 30 '67
Varieties of Jewish experience. M. Himmelfarb. Commentary 44:53-61 Jl '67
What is the meaning of the people of Israel? J. Haughey. America 117:218-20 S 2 '67
See also
Church and state in Israel
Converts from Judaism
Passover
Union of American Hebrew congregations

JUDAISM and Christianity. See Christianity and other religions

JUDAISM and philosophy. See Philosophy and religion

JUDD, Donald
Antihierarchical American. A. Goldin. il Art N 66:48-50+ S '67

JUDD, Neil M.
On some names in Natural Bridges National Monument. bibliog il por Nat Parks Mag 41:16-19 O '67

JUDEA
See also
Holy Land

JUDGE, Joseph
Florence rises from the flood. Nat Geog Mag 132:1-43 Jl '67
New grandeur for flowering Washington. Nat Geog Mag 131:500-39 Ap '67

JUDGES
All in the family; R. Clark and T. C. Clark. il Time 89:22 Mr 10 '67
Are judges remaking America? il U S News 63:36-8 D 18 '67
Interpreter in the front line; F. M. Johnson, district judge for Alabama's southeastern counties. il Time 89:72-4+ My 12 '67
Judge and the agitator; cases of D. E. Metzger and A. Felicani. Nation 204:613 My 15 '67
Judges' party; given for those in New York for series of seminars. New Yorker 43:20-1 Ag 26 '67
Juridical chairs; R. Clark appointment; T. Clark retirement. il Newsweek 69:36-7 Mr 13 '67
LBJ's turn to change the Court. il U S News 62:70 Mr 13 '67
U.S. Supreme court. pors Sr Schol 91:36-7 O 5 '67
With Mr Marshall on the Supreme court. il U S News 62:12-13 Je 26 '67
See also
Fortas, A.
Negro judges

Appointments, qualifications, tenure, etc.
Discrimination in reverse? D. Lawrence. U S News 63:88 S 4 '67
Term's end; T. Marshall appointment to Supreme court. J. J. Kilpatrick. il Nat R 19:804-5 Jl 25 '67

JUDGES wives
See also
Douglas, C.

JUDICIAL review
Supreme court review, 1966; ed. by P. B. Kurland. Review
Commentary 44:103-7 S '67. A. S. Goldstein

JUDICIARY. See Judges

JUDINE, Sister M. See M. Judine, Sister

JUDO
Confessions of a judo roll-out. J. Bruce. il Sports Illus 26:74-6+ My 22 '67; Same abr. Read Digest 91:89-92 S '67
Judo black belt queen. il Ebony 22:107-8+ Ap '67

JUDSON dance theatre. See Dance companies

JUDSON memorial church. See New York (city)—Churches

JUILLIARD dance ensemble
Juilliard dance ensemble; Juilliard concert hall. M. Marks. Dance Mag 41:36 Je '67

JUILLIARD school of music, New York
Musical events; performance of L. Berio's Passaggio and C. Monteverdi's Il combatimento di Tancredi e Clorinda. W. Sargeant. New Yorker 42:105 Ja 21 '67
New York. F. Markling. il Opera N 31:31 F 11 '67

JUILLIARD string quartet. See String quartets

JULESZ, Bela, and Spivack, G. J.
Stereopsis based on vernier acuity cues alone. bibliog Science 157:563-5 Ag 4 '67

JULIETTE Gordon Low birthplace. See Savannah, Ga.—Historic houses, etc.

JULIN, Gosta
Judges are everywhere. Nation 204:712-14 Je 5 '67

JUMBO jets. See Airplanes, Jet propelled

JUNEBUG graduates tonight! drama. See Shepp, A.

JUNIOR colleges
Coming: community colleges for everyone? R. C. Davids. il Farm J 91:32-3+ My '67
Experimental junior college; National conference on the experimental junior college. B. L. Johnson. Sch & Soc 95:427-8 N 11 '67
How good are the junior colleges? R. Lynes; discussion. Harper 234:4+ F '67
Instant campus; a remedy for junior college growing pains. J. H. Sofokidis. il Am Ed 3:15-19 S '67
Junior colleges are blooming in the sunshine state. B. Carter. il NEA J 56:22-4 My '67
Nine community colleges. il Arch Rec 142:155-71 N '67
Recreation education in selected junior or community colleges. W. M. Bartholomew. il Parks & Rec 2:25-6+ Ja '67
Rise in enrollments. Sch & Soc 95:344 O 14 '67

Summer research subsidies; letter. C. G. Danforth. Science 155:781 F 17 '67
There is nothing junior about the junior college. P. J. Verhoven. Parks & Rec 2:43-4 O '67
Unique problems of junior colleges; excerpts from address. R. H. Garrison. il NEA J 56:30-2 N '67
Universal community college education. Sch & Soc 95:139-40 Mr 4 '67

JUNIOR colleges, Catholic. See Catholic church—Education

JUNIOR museums. See Childrens museums

JUNIPER
Shore junipers for a ground carpet. Sunset 138:203 Je '67
Trim a juniper to make a miniature Christmas tree. il Sunset 139:156 D '67

JUNK
Don't throw it away too soon; junk in your barnyard. G. Logsdon. il Farm J 91:74B+ Mr '67
Room on the other side; furnishing a living room for $200. il Esquire 67:101-3 Mr '67

JUNK sculpture. See Metal sculpture

JUNKER, Howard
Electronic music, wiggy. Newsweek 69:98-98B+ My 22 '67
Underground channels. New Repub 157:33-4 S 9 '67

JUPITER (planet)

Atmosphere
Jupiter's atmosphere: its structure and composition. J. A. Greenspan and T. Owen. bibliog il Science 156:1489-94 Je 16 '67
NASA tests boost Jupiter life possibility. Tech W 20:28 Ap 24 '67
Pre-life on Jupiter? il Sci N 91:376 Ap 22 '67

Radiation
Jupiter: gravitational energy. il Sci N 91:134 F 11 '67

Surface
Jupiter's Great red spot and three white ovals. E. J. Reese. il Sky & Tel 34:185-6 S '67

JURASSIC period. See Paleontology—Jurassic

JURISPRUDENCE
Juridical perspectives on national character. J. Lazar. bibliog f Ann Am Acad 370:16-22 Mr '67

JURY
All deliberate, little speed; selecting jurors for trial of R. Speck. Time 89:60 Mr 24 '67
American jury, by H. Kalven, jr. and others. Review
Commentary 43:96-9 Ap '67. A. S. Goldstein
Art of voir dire; search for twelve jurors for Speck trial. il Time 89:63-4 Ap 7 '67
What every trial juror should know. G. G. Coughlin. il Read Digest 91:145-9 Ag '67
See also
Grand jury

JUST a simple bride; story. See Shyer, M. F.

JUSTICE
Search for a nexus. Vietnam and the Negroes. W. F. Buckley, jr. Nat R 19:894 Ag 22 '67
Task is more than personal; young people and social problems. B. L. Masse. America 117:8 Jl 1 '67

JUSTICE, Administration of
See also
Criminal law
Criminal procedure
Due process of law
Judges
Legal aid
Punishment
Speedy trial

Alabama
Justice under law: Hugo L. Black. P. W. Romero. Negro Hist Bul 30:12-14 F '67

California
Los Angeles: western justice. P. Kerby. Nation 205:104-5 Ag 14 '67

Great Britain
Diluted doubt; unanimity requirement is about to be abandoned. Time 89:91 My 19 '67

Indonesia
Lost Chevrolet. Newsweek 71:46 Ja 22 '68

Mississippi
First step in a long journey; conspiracy trial verdicts. Nation 205:451-2 N 6 '67
Justice turns a corner in Mississippi; verdict on 1964 killings of civil rights workers. America 117:495 N 4 '67

JUSTICE, Administration of—*Continued*

South Africa

Illegal trial in South Africa. Christian Cent 84:1549 D 6 '67
Law as a bludgeon. Commonweal 87:290-1 D 1 '67

Southern states

Justice on the bench in Mississippi. B. H. Bagdikian. New Repub 156:12-13 F 18 '67
See also
Courts—Southern states
Justice, Administration of—Alabama

United States

Broken promise to juveniles; worry about juvenile justice. Life 62:4 My 5 '67
Case of the debatable Brooklyn D. A. T. J. Fleming. il N Y Times Mag p32-3+ Mr 19 '67
Challenge of crime in a free society. Report by the President's commission on law enforcement and administration of justice. Review
New Repub 156:38-40 My 20 '67. F. Remington
Courts: pyramid of U.S. justice. il Sr Schol 91:18-20 N 30 '67
Crisis of overcriminalization. S. H. Kadish. bibliog f Ann Am Acad 374:157-70 N '67
Interrogation and the criminal process. A. J. Reiss, jr. and D. J. Black. bibliog f Ann Am Acad 374:47-57 N '67
Obscenity cases; Supreme court decision triggers R. Ginzburg appeal. A. M. Bickel. New Repub 156:15-17 My 27 '67
Trial by headline. L. Nizer. il McCalls 94:93+ F '67
U.S. courts and criminal justice. W. M. Beaney. bibliog f Cur Hist 53:65-9+ Ag '67
White man's justice. Christian Cent 84:708 My 31 '67
See also
Courts—United States
Jury
Sacco-Vanzetti case
Trials
United States—Justice, Department of

Virginia

Crime of interracial marriage; Loving case. America 116:522-3 Ap 8 '67
JUSTICE, Department of. See United States—Justice, Department of
JUSTICES. See Judges
JUSTMAN, Joseph
Government and the schools. Sch & Soc 95:75-8 F 4 '67
JUVENILE courts
Broken promise to juveniles. Life 62:4 My 5 '67
Challenges of delinquency. Commonweal 86:331-2 Je 9 '67
Children and the law; with editorial comment. T. Irwin. il Parents Mag 42:50+, 68-71+ O '67
Delinquent, without doubt; constitutional rights of juveniles. il Time 91:47 Ja 5 '68
Justice for juveniles; with case histories; adaptation of address. D. L. Bazelon. New Repub 156:13-16 Ap 22 '67; Discussion. 156:35-6 My 6 '67
Kids and kangaroos; Supreme court reverses decision against G. Gault. il Newsweek 69:25 My 29 '67
Living with Gault; juvenile court judges attend summer college. il Time 90:68 Ag 4 '67
Parents and juvenile courts. America 116:775 My 27 '67
Reforming juvenile justice; first review of juvenile court case. Time 89:69 My 26 '67
Role of juvenile courts. M. G. Paulsen. bibliog f Cur Hist 53:70-5 Ag '67
Supreme court rules: treat juvenile offenders like adults. U S News 62:12 My 29 '67
See also
Juvenile delinquency
JUVENILE delinquency
Boy killer; eight year-old pushes boys off roofs. il Newsweek 69:26 My 29 '67
Explosion in teen-age crimes. U S News 63:74 O 9 '67
In the matter of Gault; excerpts from United States Supreme court decision and from the dissent, May 15, 1967. Cur Hist 53:112-13+ Ag '67
Juvenile delinquency. S. M. Robison. bibliog f Cur Hist 52:341-8 Je '67
Kids in trouble; Detroit suburbs. G. Astor. il Look 31:34-6 My 16 '67
Persistence of juvenile delinquency and crime. W. W. Brickman. Sch & Soc 95:375 O 28 '67

Recent trends: deviant behavior and social control. D. J. Bordua. bibliog f Ann Am Acad 369:156-63 Ja '67
Teenagers outside the law: should their names be published? pro and con discussion. Sr Schol 91:14-15+ S 28 '67
We burned a bum Friday night and we're going to burn another one tonight. N. Pileggi. il Esquire 68:48-50+ Jl '67
Youth and crime; Washington, D.C. Sr Schol 90:9 F 17 '67
See also
Discipline
Gangs
Juvenile courts
Police services for juveniles
Problem children
Reformatories
Rehabilitation of juvenile delinquents

Prevention

Can religion prevent delinquency? T. M. Gannon. America 116:755-7 My 20 '67
Community and the juvenile. H. Ohmart. bibliog f Cur Hist 53:94-101 Ag '67
Delinquency: fresh wind; Juvenile delinquency act of 1967 pending in Congress. Sci N 91:568-9 Je 17 '67
James gang rides again; Mission rebels in action of San Francisco. il Time 90:31 O 13 '67
National goals and indicators for the reduction of crime and delinquency. D. Glaser. bibliog f il Ann Am Acad 371:104-26 My '67
Police; do they belong in the schools? G. H. Shepard and J. James. il Am Ed 3:2-4 S '67
Prevention and control of delinquency, by R. M. MacIver. Review
Sat R 50:39+ Mr 11 '67. G. Samuels
Real Great society; New York slum kids team up to fight poverty. R. Vaughan. il Life 63:76+ S 15 '67
Small awakening; Chicago's Better boys foundation. il Ebony 22:154-5 Je '67
JUVENILE hormones. See Hormones
JUVENILE libraries. See Libraries, Childrens
JUVENILE literature. See Childrens literature
JUXTLAHUACA cave. See Caves

K

KCL. See Kern County land company
KGB. See Secret service—Russia
KKK. See Ku Klux klan
KQED-TV. See Television stations, Educational
KRLA (radio station) See Radio stations
KAARSALO, E. and others
Autosomal linkage between the albumin and Gc loci in humans. bibliog Science 158:123-5 O 6 '67
KAAT, Jim
Kaat on a hot tin roof. H. L. Masin. por Sr Schol 90:18 Ap 21 '67
KABALIN, Fedor
Over twenty-one. Opera N 31:8-12 F 18 '67
KADAR, János
Hungary: the mechanism and the marionettes. C. Sterling. Reporter 36:25-7 My 4 '67
KADISH, Sanford H.
Crisis of overcriminalization. bibliog f Ann Am Acad 374:157-70 N '67
KADISON, Margaret
Journal miss. See Issues of Ladies' home journal
Junior journal (title varies) (cont) Ladies Home J 84:68 Mr '67
KAEL, Pauline
Current cinema. New Yorker 43:90+ Ja 13 '68
Movies. See Issues of New republic
Onward and upward with the arts. New Yorker 43:120+ Je 3; 147-8+ O 21 '67
KAFKA, Barbara
Woven structures of Alice Adams. Craft Horiz 27:14-17 Mr '67
KAFRI, Rachel
Rachel Kafri & dance company. Judson Hall. M. Marks. Dance Mag 41:79 Mr '67
Rachel Kafri and John Herbert McDowell; Judson memorial church. M. Marks. Dance Mag 41:32+ D '67
Rachel Kafri: Judson Hall. J. Maskey. Dance Mag 41:66 F '67
KAGE, Manfred
Take a close look. M. Laurance. il U S Camera 31:38-9 Ja '68

KAHIN, George McT.
NLF's terms for peace. New Repub 157:13-17 O 14 '67
—and Lewis, J. W.
Escalation and East Asia; excerpt from The United States in Vietnam. Bul Atomic Sci 23:20-4 Ja '67
KAHLENBERG, Arthur, and others
Sodium-potassium adenosine triphosphatase: acyl phosphate intermediate shown to be L-glutamyl-y-phosphate. bibliog Science 157:434-6 Jl 28 '67
KAHN, Ely Jacques, 1916-
Country comes of age. Holiday 42:64-5+ D '67
No haircut for Tony. Parents Mag 43:48-9 Ja '68
Our far-flung correspondents. New Yorker 43:119-26+ Je 10 '67
KAHN, Herman
Herman Kahn's thinkable future. il por Bsns W p 114-16+ Mr 11 '67
Visit with the great Kahn. S. Paradise. Christian Cent 84:1556-8 D 6 '67
—See Wiener, A. J. jt. auth.
KAHN, Lothar
Books: S. Y. Agnon: Nobel laureate. Cath World 205:245-7 Jl '67
KAHN, Louis I.
Summer architecture. W. McQuade. il Arch Forum 126:86 Je '67
KAHN, Roger
Game without the ball. Sat Eve Post 240: 79-83 D 16 '67
KAHNEMAN, Daniel, and others
Perceptual deficit during a mental task. bibliog Science 157:218-19 Jl 14 '67
KAIBAB squirrels. See Squirrels
KAIN, John F.
Some factors affecting housing density and auto ownership; excerpt from Postwar metropolitan development: housing preferences and auto ownership. Mo Labor R 90:45-6 Mr '67
KAISER, Henry John
Man who always hurried. il pors Time 90:60 S 1 '67
Master builder. il pors Newsweek 70:59 S 4 '67
KAISER, Robert Blair
Jacqueline Grennan: ex-nun. Look 31:106-10 My 30 '67
Lessons from revolution. America 117:469+ O 28 '67
Nuns that quit. Ladies Home J 84:82-3+ Ap '67
KAISER steel corporation
New slices for Kaiser's melon? Kaiser steel-United steelworkers long-range sharing plan. il Bsns W p 149-50 Mr 4 '67
KALAMAZOO, Mich.

Art
Culture kick in Kalamazoo. G. Zimmermann. il Look 32:26-9 Ja 9 '68

Music
Culture kick in Kalamazoo. G. Zimmermann. il Look 32:26-9 Ja 9 '68

Street traffic
Disposable stencils cut marking costs. R. B. Carroll. il Am City 82:98 Ja '67

Theater
Culture kick in Kalamazoo. G. Zimmermann. il Look 32:26-9 Ja 9 '68
KALAMAZOO, Mich, public library
From abacus to zoos. S. Miller. il Library J 92:4477-9 D 15 '67
KALAMAZOO college, Kalamazoo, Mich.
Thinking on one's knees; dice game to teach logic. il Sch & Soc 95:210-12 Ap 1 '67
KALAMAZOO nature center. See Nature centers
KALAPALO Indians. See Indians of South America—Brazil
KALB, Bernard
Storm, the calm, and the colony. Sat R 50: 74+ O 14 '67
KALB, Marvin
Doves, hawks and flutterers in the Foreign relations committee. N Y Times Mag p56-8+ N 19 '67
Pasternak's Russia. Sat R 50:70+ Mr 11 '67
Russian record of Nazi terror. Sat R 50:37+ Mr 11 '67
Russian who dared. Sat R 50:53-4 N 18 '67
Watcher along the border. Sat R 50:51 My 6 '67
KALER, Grace
Old metals. See issues of Hobbies
KALEVALA (epic poem) See Finnish poetry

KALINE, Al
Those big Tiger muscles. W. Leggett. il por Sports Illus 26:24-7 Je 5 '67
Tiger at the plate. il por Newsweek 69:68 My 15 '67
KALITTA, Conrad
Kalittascope; interview, ed. by J. McFarland. pors Hot Rod 20:56-8 My '67
KALMAN, Paul
Play safe with sunburn. Field & S 71:72-4+ F '67
KALS, William S.
How far the horizon? Motor B 119:38-9+ Je '67
Polynesian navigation. Sky & Tel 33:358-60 Je '67
KAMAGRAPHY. See Reproduction of works of art
KAMBAN
Exile of Rama; excerpt, tr. by C. Rajagopalachari. UNESCO Courier 20:30-1+ D '67
KAMEL, K. A. and others
Hemoglobin $\alpha_2\beta_2^{-121}$ L^{y} chemical identification in an Egyptian family. bibliog Science 156:397-8 Ap 21 '67
KAMENTSKY, Louis A. and Melamed, M. R.
Spectrophotometric cell sorter. bibliog Science 156:1364-5 Je 9 '67
KAMINETSKY, Joseph
Dialogue between public and nonpublic educators. Sch & Soc 95:425-6 N 11 '67
KAMINETZKY, Harold A. and Meilach, D. Z.
When another baby is on the way. Parents Mag 42:38-9+ Ja '67
KAMISAR, Yale
Citizen on trial: the new confession rules. bibliog f Cur Hist 53:76-81+ Ag '67
KAMMERER, Rafael
Josef Hofmann, memorable Chopin. Am Rec G 33:556-7 Mr '67
Massive documentary release, the Everest archive of piano music. Am Rec G 33:728-31 My '67
KAMPF, Louis
Riots: schools for revolution? Nation 205: 117-18 Ag 14 '67
Scandal of literary scholarship; excerpt from The dissenting academy, ed. by T. Roszak. Harper 235:86-91 D '67
Upper case conservatism. Nation 205:535-7 N 20 '67
KANDEL, Eric R. and others
Opposite synaptic actions mediated by different branches of an identifiable interneuron in aplysia. bibliog Science 155:346-9 Ja 20 '67
—See Wachtel, H. jt. auth.
KANDEL, Lenore
Love in California. A. V. Krebs, jr. Commonweal 86:360-1 Je 16 '67
KANE, James
New books. Cath World 205:251 Jl '67
KANE, Julian
Surtsey; with biographical sketch. Natur Hist 76:5, 22-7 Mr '67
KANE, Rita
Future lies ahead. bibliog por Library J 92: 3971-3 N 1 '67
KANFER, Allen
Something about territory; poem. Harper 236:70 Ja '68
KANFER, Stefan
Life music review. Life 62:18 Ap 21; 13 Je 23; 63:12 N 3 '67
Tristan without technology. Life 62:22 F 17 '67
KANG, Bin G. and others
Ethylene and carbon dioxide: mediation of hypocotyl hook-opening response. bibliog Science 156:958-9 My 19 '67
KANNY, Mark N.
First complete recording of the Brahms trios and other chamber works. Am Rec G 34:208-10+ N '67
Szell's complete Brahms symphonies. Am Rec G 33:912-14 Je '67
Two views of the nine Beethoven symphonies. Am Rec G 33:646-8 Ap '67
Way Beethoven's amanuensis heard him. Am Rec G 33:830+ My '67
KANSAS
Reporter at large; effects of Vietnamese war. C. Trillin. New Yorker 43:56-8+ Ap 22 '67
See also
Architecture, Domestic—Kansas
Hunting—Kansas
KANSAS CITY, Mo.
Out of ledger limbo; publicity by tri-rama slide presentations. il Am City 82:158+ S '67

Banks
Kempers of Kansas City. J. Main. il Fortune 75:170-2+ Ap '67

KANSAS CITY, Mo.—*Continued*

City planning

Why everything is up to date in Kansas City; businessmen and civic pride. il Bsns W p 102-6 Ap 8 '67

Crime

Citizen Primitivo; Mexican killed protecting naturalization teacher. Time 90:28 D 8 '67

Description

Return to Kansas City. E. Dahlberg. il Holiday 41:16+ Je '67

Education

What makes a good junior high art program? C. Mulford. il NEA J 56:14-17 Mr '67

Fire department

To train a firefighter. C. Campbell. il Am City 82:102-3 Mr '67

Industries

Cavemen in Kansas City. il Newsweek 69: 78-80 My 1 '67

Lighting

More light to grow by. C. F. Sharpe. il Am City 82:120 D '67

Music

Kansas City; Performing arts foundation. J. Haskins. il Opera N 32:21 S 9 '67

Parks and playgrounds

Higher standard of maintenance. G. Eib. il Am City 82:100-1 F '67

KANSAS CITY American Royal (horse show) See Horse shows

KANSAS CITY Athletics (baseball) See Baseball clubs

KANSAS CITY Chiefs (football club) See Football clubs

KANSAS CITY lyric theater
Kansas City (cont) J. Haskins. Opera N 32: 22 N 4 '67

KANSAS university press
University press of Kansas opens. Pub W 193: 43 Ja 8 '68

KANT, Immanuel
Sage of Königsburg. P. A. Schilpp. Sat R 50: 35 Ag 5 '67

KANTOR, MacKinlay
Of fifes and drums and the grand old men. Read Digest 90:84-8 Je '67

KANTROWITZ, Adrian
Brainy brother act to heal the heart. il pors Life 62:35-6+ Ja 27 '67
Pumps to give the heart a rest. il por Bsns W p 110-12 O 14 '67

KANTROWITZ, Arthur
Proposal for an institution for scientific judgment; excerpts from report to U.S. Senate, March 16, 1967. Science 156:763-4 My 12 '67

about

Brainy brother act to heal the heart. il pors Life 62:35-6+ Ja 27 '67
Pumps to give the heart a rest. il por Bsns W p 110-12 O 14 '67

KANTROWITZ, Barbara
It was a long, hot summer. Seventeen 26:114-15+ Je '67

KAPLAN, Allan
Ave Maria; poem. Nation 205:437 O 30 '67
New York times weather map; poem. Nation 205:22 Jl 3 '67
Tonight; poem. Nation 205-286 S 25 '67

KAPLAN, Boche
Bookmaking exhibition on developing a picture book. il Pub W 191:98 F 6 '67

KAPLAN, Donald M.
Freud and his own patients. Harper 235:99-100+ D '67
Psychoanalysis: the decline of a golden craft. Harper 234:41-6 F '67

KAPLAN, Ethel
Were you the oldest child? Sci Digest 61:72-6 F '67

KAPLAN, Harold
Asian perspectives; address, July 11, 1967. Dept State Bul 57:230-5 Ag 21 '67
Class of '67: the gentle desperadoes. Nation 204:775-6 Je 19 '67

KAPLAN, Jacques
Salesmanship: fun fur division; interview, ed. by W. H. Manville. por(p51) Sat Eve Post 240:53 D 30 '67

about

Skin game. il por Newsweek 69:111 My 22 '67

KAPLAN, Justin
Lives: heroic, psychotic, and shabby. Harper 235:108+ D '67

KAPLAN, Kivie
Honor guard of the NAACP. il pors Ebony 22:53-4+ Mr '67

KAPLAN, Maurice S.
Designer's corner. S. Salter. Pub W 191:110 F 6 '67

KAPLAN, Morton A.
Books. Bul Atomic Sci 23:32-3 D '67

KAPLAN, Robert M.
Credit risks & opportunities. Harvard Bsns R 45:83-8 Mr '67

KAPLANIS, J. N. and others
Insect hormones: alpha ecdysone and 20-hydroxyecdysone in bracken fern. bibliog Science 157:1436-8 S 22 '67

KAPLOW, Jeffry J.
18th-century man. Nation 204:220-1 F 13 '67
From Algeria to Vietnam. Commonweal 86: 260-2 My 19 '67
On Who intervened in 1788? bibliog f Am Hist R 72:497-502 Ja '67

KAPPEL, Frederick R.
Individual views of Mr Kappel. Mo Labor R 90:46 N '67

about

Kappel and Romnes of A.T.&T. por Fortune 75:53 F '67

KAPPLER, Frank
Heigh ho! soft sell at the fair: U.S. pavilion. Life 62:13 Je 16 '67
Mixed media, communication that puzzles, excites and involves. Life 63:28C Jl 14 '67
Not a home but a happening. il Life 62:89-90 Mr 24 '67

KAPROW, Allan
Pinpointing happenings. por Art N 66:46-7+ O '67

about

Art. M. Kozloff. Nation 205:27-9 Jl 3 '67

KAPSTEIN, Jonathan
Uncle Dan's feud with the Albany newspapers. Reporter 36:37-40 Mr 9 '67

KARAFIN, Harry J.
Harry the muckraker. il por Time 89:84+ Ap 21 '67
How did he do it? por Newsweek 69:64-5 My 1 '67
Reporter. S. J. Adamo. America 116:822 Je 3 '67

KARAJAN, Herbert von
Carry on, Karajan. il Time 89:74 Mr 31 '67
Karajan at La Scala. I. Kolodin. Sat R 50:22 Je 24 '67
Karajan's Ring. H. Saal. il Newsweek 70:112 D 4 '67
Maestro von Karajan is always turned on. M. Mayer. il pors N Y Times Mag p50-1+ D 3 '67
Music to my ears; Bach programs in Carnegie Hall. I. Kolodin. Sat R 50:38-9 D 16 '67
Musical events; conductor of Metropolitan opera and Berlin philharmonic. W. Sargeant. New Yorker 43:225-6 D 9 '67
Musical events; performance of Verdi's Requiem by orchestra and chorus of La Scala. W. Sargeant. New Yorker 43:107+ O 28 '67
Total conductor. il por Time 90:116 D 1 '67
Von Karajan at the Met. New Yorker 43:54-5 N 25 '67
Von Karajan's Easter festival. P. Moor. il Hi Fi 17:MA21+ Je '67
Where Karajan is king. J. Higgins. il Hi Fi 17:MA26-7+ N '67

KARAMANLIS, Constantine
Signs of a showdown. por Time 90:38-9 D 15 '67

KARAS, Nicholas
Easy camping in the Canadian bush. Field & S 71:62-3+ Mr '67
Oneida, fishiest lake of them all. Field & S 72:98-105 Jl '67

KARASZ, Mariska
Sand dollars. D. Van Dommelen. il Sch Arts 66:24 My '67

KARG, Elissa Jane
How to be a nonconformist; excerpts. Seventeen 26:383+ Ag '67

KARIEL, Henry S.
At the dead center. Nation 204:827-8 Je 26 '67

KARIM al Hussaini Shah. See Aga Khan IV

KARINSKA, Barbara
Costumes by Karinska; reprint. J. A. Rubin. il pors Dance Mag 41:49-51+ Je '67

KARL, Frederick R.
Picaresque and the American experience. Yale R 57:196-212 D '67

KARL, Jean
Children's editor looks at excellence in children's literature. Horn Bk 43:31-41 F '67

KARLEN, Arno
Antioch college. Holiday 41:46-9+ Je '67
New Chicago. Holiday 41:46-53 Mr '67
O'er Ramparts we watch. Holiday 41:147-9+ Ap '67

KARNOW, Stanley
How revolutions die. New Repub 156:24+ Je 10 '67

KAROO. See Great Karoo

KARP, David
Look back into the tube. N Y Times Mag p50-1+ N 19 '67

KARP, Harvey L.
On the run. por Time 90:101 O 13 '67

KARP, Ivan C.
Wrecker, spare that frieze. R. S. Gallagher. il Am Heritage 18:60-4+ Ag '67

KARP, Tony
Tony Karp on 35mm. See issues of Modern photography

KARP, Walter
Leonardo's Ginevra. Horizon 9:24-9 Aut '67
Posters. Horizon 9:104-12 Aut '67

KARROO. See Great Karoo

KARSH, Yousuf
Karsh '67. il U S Camera 30:56-7 Jl '67
Karsh's one-man show at Expo 67: centennial salute. M. R. Weiss. il por Sat R 50:54-7 Ap 29 '67

KARTH, Joseph E.
Karth: practical benefits needed to buoy space science; ed. by W. S. Beller. por Tech W 20:18-19 Ap 3 '67

KARTS (midget cars)
Glassy, klassy kart. D. C. Fales. il Pop Mech 127:104-5 F '67
Karts with rocket power. J. E. Boykin. il Pop Mech 127:120-1 Mr '67

KARTUZ, Michael J.
Grow a colorful kohleria. Horticulture 45:20-1 N '67

KARUME, Abeid Amani
Spinning in. J. Barnes. il por Newsweek 70:51 D 4 '67

KASAI, Zenzaburo. See Shimokawa, K. jt. auth.

KASARDA, Donald D. and others
Reversible aggregation of α-gliadin to fibrils. bibliog Science 155:203-5 Ja 13 '67

KASER, David
Dispelling hunches, intuition, and that professional mystique. Wilson Lib Bul 41:923-5 My '67

KASH, Don E.
Tyranny of realism. Bul Atomic Sci 23:16-20 F '67

KASHMIR
Indian-Pakistani relations. R. N. Berkes bibliog f il Cur Hist 52:289-92 My '67
Lion on the loose. il Newsweek 71:38 Ja 15 '68

KASOS (island)
Feasts of memory, by E. Kulukundis. Review Sat R 50:31 S 9 '67. H. M. Petrakis

KASPARIAN, Elaine. See Ingrao, H. C. jt. auth.

KASPER, Hirschel
Britain devalues the pound. Commonweal 87:325-6 D 8 '67
Tithing for war. Commonweal 87:50-2 O 13 '67

KASPERAK, Michael
Michael Kasperak. il por Time 91:50-1 Ja 19 '68

KASSALOW, E. M.
National wage policies in Europe and the U.S. Mo Labor R 90:36-7 Mr '67

KASSEBAUM, John Philip
Italian majolica. Antiques 91:202-6 F '67

KASSMAN, Deborah N.
What's in a pen name? Writer 80:19-23 My '67

KASTENMEIER, Robert William
Advice to congressmen. Nation 205:5-6 Jl 3 '67

KASTLE, Leonard
Deseret. Criticism
    Opera N il 31:30 Ap 8 '67

KASTLER, Alfred
Optical methods for studying Hertzian resonances; tr. of address, December 12, 1966. bibliog Science 158:214-21 O 13 '67

about
Laser's grandfather. G. M. Spruch. il Sat R 50:56-9 Mr 4 '67

KÄSTNER, Erich
Reiteration of a feeling; poem, tr. by J. Simon. Mlle 65:42 Jl '67

KASTOR Foote Hilton and Atherton, Incorporated. See Foote, Emerson, incorporated

KASTRUP airport. See Copenhagen—Airports

KAT
East Africa turns on with khat. L. Fellows. il N Y Times Mag p22-3+ Jl 9 '67

KATAHN, Martin
Alleviating the college student's anxiety. NEA J 57:17-18 Ja '68

KATAN, Roger
Compact urban gateway. il Arch Forum 126:72-3 Ap '67

KATAOKA, K. and others
Prostaglandins: localization in subcellular particles of rat cerebral cortex. bibliog Science 157:1187-9 S 8 '67

KATCHER, Leo
Virus of hate. Sat R 51:89 Ja 13 '68

KATEY darling; story. See Huntington, E. G.

KATHREN, Ronald L.
Radiation protection. Science 156:544-6+ Ap 28 '67

KATIMS, Milton
Toscanini as mentor and teacher. Sat R 50:55-7 Mr 25 '67

KATKOV, Norman
Give my heart ease; story. Good H 164:86-7 My '67

KATONA, George
Changing mood of the American buying public; interview. por U S News 63:39-40 Jl 17 '67

KATONA, Peter Mario
(ed) See Souzay, G. Mystery of performing

KATZ, Arnold M. See Rubin, B. B. jt. auth.

KATZ, Bernard
Second version of Lucy Terry's early ballad. por Negro Hist Bul 29:183-4 Fall '66

KATZ, Bill
(ed) Magazines. See issues of Library journal

KATZ, Herbert, and Katz, Marjorie
Trial marriage with art. House B 109:30+ F '67

KATZ, Joseph J. See Uphaus, R. A. jt. auth.

KATZ, Marjorie. See Katz, H. jt. auth.

KATZ, Menke
On the birthday of a forgotten poet. Atlan 219:79 F '67

KATZ, Morris
Morris Katz story. B. Finnegan. il por Hobbies 72:120-1+ Jl '67

KATZ, Robert
Death in Rome focuses new controversy on Vatican. por Pub W 191:47-8 F 6 '67

KATZ, William Loren
Africa and slave trade in the classroom. Negro Hist Bul 30:11 O '67
Courage beyond the call of duty. Sat R 50:30-1 Je 17 '67

KATZENBACH, Nicholas deBelleville
America and Africa: the New World and the newer world; address, May 26, 1967. Dept State Bul 56:954-9 Je 26 '67; Same. Vital Speeches 33:622-5 Ag 1 '67
America's role in world affairs: reflections on a year of anniversaries; address, November 27, 1967. Dept State Bul 57:815-20 D 18 '67
Comparative roles of the President and the Congress in foreign affairs; statement, August 17, 1967. Dept State Bul 57:333-6 S 11 '67
Complex and difficult problems in Viet-Nam; excerpt from address, October 17, 1967. Dept State Bul 57:602-4 N 6 '67
Crime; interview, ed. by W. Rogers. Look 31:101-4+ Mr 7 '67
Department seeks criminal penalties on travel to restricted areas; letter, December 11, 1967. Dept State Bul 58:53-4 Ja 8 '68
Foreign aid: an essential element of U.S. foreign policy; address, September 30, 1967. Dept State Bul 57:530-4 O 23 '67
President urges accession to 1961 single convention on narcotics; text of report. Dept State Bul 56:672-3 Ap 24 '67
Protectionism, a policy of retreat; address, October 30, 1967. Dept State Bul 57:686-9 N 20 '67; Same. Vital Speeches 34:119-21 D 1 '67
U.S. arms for the developing world; dilemmas of foreign policy; address, November 17, 1967. Dept State Bul 57:794-8 D 11 '67
United States relations with the Soviet Union; address, April 21, 1967. Dept State Bul 56:753-6 My 15 '67

KATZENBACH, Nicholas deBelleville—_Cont._

about

No. 2 man at State is a cooler-downer. V. S. Navasky. il pors N Y Times Mag p3+ D 24 '67

Under Secretary Katzenbach visits eleven African countries. Dept State Bul 56:756 My 15 '67

KATZENBERG, Jeffrey
Face to face with a boy who loves politics; ed. by A. Eiseman. por Seventeen 26:111 Je '67

KAUAI (island)
Kauai National Park. R. Wenkham. il Nat Parks Mag 41:4-8 Mr '67

KAUAI NATIONAL PARK (proposed) See National parks and reserves—United States

KAUFFMAN, Ewing Marion
M as in money. il por Time 90:110+ D 1 '67
Percentage player makes his pitch for K.C. T. O'Leary. por Sports Illus 28:42-3 Ja 8 '68

KAUFFMAN, Joseph F.
Needed: heroic examples for the young; excerpts from address. NEA J 56:16-17 O '67

KAUFFMAN, Kenneth M. and Stalson, Helena
U.S. assistance to less developed countries, 1956-65. For Affairs 45:715-25 Jl '67

KAUFFMAN, Ray
Owner's comments. Yachting 121:121-2 Je '67

KAUFFMANN, Stanley
[Column] See issues of New republic
Enroute to the future; reprint. Negro Hist Bul 30:13 Ap '67
Germany 1967. Atlan 219:55-6 My '67
Stanley Kauffmann on films. New Repub 157: 20+ D 2; 19+ D 16; 22+ D 23 '67; 158:22+ Ja 13 '68

KAUFMAN, Bel
Anyone you know? ed. by E. Miller. por Seventeen 26:119 Je '67

KAUFMAN, George S.
My most unforgettable character. M. Gordon. por Read Digest 90:174-8+ Mr '67
—and Ferber, Edna
Dinner at eight. Criticism
Christian Cent 84:144 F 1 '67
Nat R 19:99 Ja 24 '67

KAUFMAN, Glen
Glen Kaufman. F. Schwartz. il Craft Horiz 27:14-16 Ja '67

KAUFMAN, Herbert E. and others
Recurrent herpes in the rabbit and man. bibliog Science 156:1628-9 Je 23 '67

KAUFMAN, I. Charles, and Rosenblum, L. A.
Depression in infant monkeys separated from their mothers bibliog Science 155:1030-1 F 24 '67

KAUFMAN, Lynne
To find my heart again; story. Good H 165: 65-9 Ag '67
Wild nights; story. Ladies Home J 84:148-53 O '67

KAUFMAN, Murray
Pop goes Murray. il por Newsweek 70:100+ O 16 '67

KAUFMAN, Zenn
Textbook considerations, merchandising. Pub W 191:29-30 My 22 '67

KAUFMANN, Edgar, Jr
Canada's new turn in architecture. Harper 234:62-8 My '67

KAUFMANN, R. J.
Class of '67: the gentle desperadoes. Nation 204:777-8 Je 19 '67

KAUFMANN, Walter
Philosopher for the tender-minded. Sat R 50:31-2 Ag 12 '67

KAVA
Kava drug a sleeper; Piper methysticum. Sci N 91:138 F 11 '67

KAVANAGH, Patrick
Baggot street bard. S. Cronin. Commonweal 87:447-8 Ja 12 '68
Notes and comment. New Yorker 43:51-2 D 9 '67

KAVANAU, J. Lee
Behavior of captive white-footed mice. bibliog Science 155:1623-39 Mr 31 '67

KAVANAUGH, James J.
Modern priest looks at his outdated church; excerpts. por Look 31:54-8+ Je 13 '67
Speaking out. por Sat Eve Post 240:10+ D 16 '67

about

Anger of a rebel. por Time 90:50 Jl 7 '67
Arrogant, smug, angry. K. L. Woodward. por Newsweek 69:69 Je 26 '67
Ex-priests on the attack. il por Time 90:70+ O 27 '67

High octane. C. M. Smith. Christian Cent 84:999 Ag 2 '67
Modern church, outdated priest? T. E. Clarke. America 116:758 My 20 '67
Reverend James Kavanaugh, broadcaster. J. McLaughlin. America 117:42-4 Jl 8 '67

KAWAI, June
(tr) See Komoda, K. Auspicious crane

KAWAI, Naoto. See Cox, A. jt. auth.

KAWAI, Nobufumi. See Yamamoto, C. jt. auth.

KAWAKAMI, Thomas G. and others
C-type viral particles in plasma of cats with feline leukemia. bibliog Science 158:1049-50 N 24 '67

KAY, Jane H.
Newest ancient art. Américas 19:9-16 Ap '67

KAYE, Clifford A.
Fossiliferous bauxite in glacial drift, Martha's Vineyard, Massachusetts. bibliog Science 157:1035-7 S 1 '67

KAYE, Danny
Danny Kaye's own story: if I can learn to fly, you can learn to fly. pors Pop Sci 190:76-9+ Ja '67

KAZAN, Elia
Son of the oven-maker; excerpts from interview; ed. by H. Frankel. por Sat R 50: 26-7 Mr 4 '67

KAZAN, Lainie
Lively arts; interview, ed. by R. Hemming. por Sr Schol 91:30 N 16 '67

about

Pitching curves. H. Saal. por Newsweek 69: 117 Ap 17 '67

KAZAN-KOMAREK, Vladimir
Booked for travel; dangers for the traveler in eastern Europe. H. Sutton. Sat R 50: 49-50 Mr 4 '67
Dubious detour. Time 89:33-4 F 10 '67
Overpriced revenge. Newsweek 69:52+ F 13 '67

KAZANTZAKIS, Nikos
A cross in Heraklion. F. Riley. pors Sat R 50: 57-8+ O 14 '67

KAZICKAS, Jurate
Opinion: on men at war. Mlle 64:124+ Mr '67

KAZIN, Alfred
Art on trial. Harper 235:51-5 O '67
Books. Vogue 149:144 My; 150:173 D '67
Edmund Wilson: his life and books. Atlan 220:80-3 Jl '67
In Israel: after the triumph. Harper 235:72-8+ N '67
Solitary expert. Atlan 221:59-60+ Ja '68

KEARNEY, Paul W.
How you can be an expert night driver. Pop Sci 190:82-5 Mr '67
Radial-plies: a dramatic advance in tires. Read Digest 90:129-32 Mr '67
What you should know about sunglasses. Read Digest 90:68-71 Je '67

KEARNEY, Richard D.
U.S. discusses draft articles on the law of treaties; statement. October 20, 1967. Dept State Bul 57:719-22 N 27 '67

KEARNEY, Vincent S.
Mao Tse-tung's last revolution. America 116: 215-17 F 11 '67
Of many things. America 116:inside cover Ap 8 '67
World scene (cont) America 116:686+ My 6 '67
(ed) See McCarthy, E. J. Interview with McCarthy

KEARNS, Doris, and Levinson, Sanford
How to remove LBJ in 1968. New Repub 156:13 My 13 '67

KEARNS, Francis E.
Meredith's one-night stand. Commonweal 86: 78-9 Ap 7 '67
Splitting over Adam: the liberal-Negro breach. Commonweal 85:443 Ja 27 '67

KEARTON, Sir Frank
Wry look at Americans. Duns R 89:27 F '67

KEATING, Edward M.
Fall of the archangel. por Time 89:77-8 My 5 '67

KEATING, James W.
Educational research and the hidden author. Sch & Soc 95:350-1 O 14 '67

KEATING, Michael F.
TV editorials: How brave & free? V. H. Bernstein. por Nation 205:170-3 S 4 '67; Reply with rejoinder. D. J. Trageser. 205: 290+ O 2 '67

KEATING, Rex
Plight of the Florentine artisans. UNESCO Courier 20:12-13 Ja '67

KEATING, Stephen F.
What makes a good manager? Duns R 89:28-9+ F '67

KELNER, Joseph
Highway murder. New Repub 157:13 S 2 '67
KELSALL, Margaret A.
Chromosomes and leukocytes. Science 155:
1039-40 F 24 '67
KELSEY, Everett Newton
Fast-moving banker abroad. il pors Ebony
23:41-2+ D '67
KELTON, Richard
Cruising to the Garden of the Hesperides.
Motor B 119:28-9+ My '67
KEMBLE, Edwin C.
Physicist replies to Langdon Gilkey. Chris-
tian Cent 84:755-7 Je 7 '67
KEMMERER, Jack B.
Cats that swim. Field & S 72:30-1+ Jl '67
KEMP, F. Roy
Manhole cover artist. Design 68:36-7 Ja '67
KEMP, Gérald van der
Versailles, its persuasive curator. V. Law-
ford. il por Vogue 150:126+ Ag 1 '67
KEMPER, Robert Graham
Drama (cont) Christian Cent 84:144, 276-7,
596-7, 657-8, 725-6, 1048-9, 1131, 1561; 85:26+;
87 F 1, Mr 1, My 3, 17, 31, Ag 16, S 6, D 6
'67, Ja 3, 17 '68
KEMPER, William T, family
Kempers of Kansas City. J. Main. il pors
Fortune 75:170-2+ Ap '67
KEMPLER, Joseph
How to select magnetic sound recording
tapes. Electr World 78:27-31+ Ag '67
KEMPNER, Ellis S. See Groves, W. E. jt.
auth.
KEMPNER, Mary Jean
New life for the river that isn't a river. N Y
Times Mag p32-4+ Ag 6 '67
KEMPTON, Murray
Liberal anti-communism revisited. Commen-
tary 44:52-4 S '67
Machiavelli the idealist. New Repub 156:21-4
Mr 11 '67
Norman blood mystery. New Repub 157:33-8
D 9 '67
Rage greater than grief. Atlan 219:98-100 My
'67
Underestimation of Dwight D. Eisenhower.
Esquire 68:108-9+ S '67
KENAI national moose range. See Wildlife
sanctuaries
KENDALL, Elaine
Negro press. Holiday 41:82-4 My '67
KENDALL, N. J.
Computerized water system. Am City 82:99-
100 S '67
KENDALL, Parker H.
No greater reward. Atlan 219:113 F '67
KENDALL, Raymond
Many-splendored sound of Los Angeles. Sat
R 50:46+ S 23 '67
KENDALL, Virginia
Catholic world of books for Lent. Cath World
204:288-9 F '67
KENDALL, William H.
New Gulf coast ICW link. Motor B 119:49
F '67
KENDALL, Willmoore
Willmoore Kendall, RIP. Nat R 19:786 Jl 25
'67
KENDALL, Fla.
Good place to grow up; Sara Jane Straight.
il Look 31:43-9 My 16 '67
KENDREW, John Cowdery
Books. Sci Am 216:141+ Mr '67
KENNAN, George Frost
Russian revolution; its nature and conse-
quences. For Affairs 46:1-21 O '67
U.S. policy in Asia: as two ex-envoys see
it; excerpts from testimony. por U S
News 62:19-20 F 13 '67

about

Between effort and effect. R. G. Hazo. Na-
tion 205:634-6 D 11 '67
Books. R. H. Rovere. New Yorker 43:238+
N 11 '67
Clarity of hindsight; US policy in Vietnam.
K. Crawford. Newsweek 69:40 F 13 '67
Containment has won, but... E. Stillman. il
por N Y Times Mag p23+ My 28 '67
Kennan looks back. G. A. Craig. Reporter
37:45-6+ D 14 '67
Making of a geopolitician. J. Lukacs. New
Repub 157:28-31 O 28 '67
Professional diplomat. O. Handlin. Atlan 220:
146+ D '67
Prophet without a cause. W. S. Schlamm.
Nat R 19:1431-2 D 26 '67
Real Mr X. F. Y. Blumenfeld. por Newsweek
70:100+ O 30 '67
Solitary expert. A. Kazin. Atlan 221:59-60+
Ja '68

Swing of the pendulum. por Time 90:104+ N 3
'67
Why stay in Vietnam? New Repub 156:9 F 11
'67
Winter term. il por Newsweek 69:35 F 13 '67
KENNARD, G. V.
California's fair-housing follies. America 117:
204-6 Ag 26 '67
Fair housing showdown in the West. Amer-
ica 116:142-6 Ja 28 '67
KENNECOTT copper corporation
Copper company vs. the North Cascades. P.
Brooks. il Harper 235:48-50 S '67
Miners ridge threatened; Glacier Peak wilder-
ness area. Liv Wildn 31:60 Spr '67
North Cascades National Park: copper mining
vs. conservation. K. Sperry. il Science 157:
1021-4 S 1 '67; Discussion. 158:205; 159:31-2+
O 13 '67, Ja 5 '68
KENNEDY, Caroline
Mini trend setter. por Time 90:43 Ag 11 '67
KENNEDY, Cora Wright
Tools & techniques. See issues of Popular
photography
KENNEDY, Donald
Small systems of nerve cells; with biograph-
ical sketch. Sci Am 216:21, 44-52 bibliog
(p 167) My '67
KENNEDY, Duff
I would be a little cautious; interview. por
U S News 63:40-2 D 4 '67
KENNEDY, Edward Moore
Ellis Island. Esquire 67:118-21 Ap '67
Excerpt from address, February 23, 1967.
Cong Digest 46:146+ My '67
Excerpt from address, April 2. 1967. Cong
Digest 46:218-19 Ag '67
Plan of action. por Sat Eve Post 240:28-9
F 11 '67

about

Home for Ted. por Time 90:15 D 1 '67
Kennedy backs NSF. Sci N 92:489-90 N 18
'67
KENNEDY, Edward Moore, family
Kennedy children; photographs. McCalls 94:
101 F '67
KENNEDY, Eugene C.
Quiet Catholic question. America 116:147-8
Ja 28 '67
Speaking out. por Sat Eve Post 241:8+ Ja 27
'68
KENNEDY, Jacqueline Lee (Bouvier)
Real Robert F. Kennedy. Ladies Home J
84:75 F '67

about

Death of a President, by W. Manchester.
Review
Reporter 36:37-9 My 18 '67. R. West
Feud over Death of a President intensi-
fies as Manchester attacks Kennedy family
and aides. Pub W 191:88-9 Ja 30 '67
Frangipani & bafflegab. il por Time 90:29 N
10 '67
How Jacqueline Kennedy influences the way
you look. M. Bender. por Redbook 129:52+
Ag '67
How the remarkable Auchincloss family
shaped the Jacqueline Kennedy style. S.
Birmingham. il pors Ladies Home J 84:
91-3+ Mr '67
How to lose a war; long-running row over
Manchester's book. Newsweek 69:34-5 F 6
'67
In the hours after Dallas: the book and the
testimony; concerning The death of a
President by W. Manchester. il pors U S
News 62:51-2 F 20 '67
Jackie exclusive; concerning interview in New
York world journal tribune. il por Time 89:
63-4 Mr 24 '67
Jackie Kennedy: a view from the crowd.
A. Levy. il pors Sat Eve Post 240:19-23
Mr 11 '67
Jackie Kennedy: what people close to her
think about her now. H. Dudar. il por
Good H 165:90-1+ O '67
Jackie's next trip: Cambodia visit on again.
il por U S News 63:20 O 16 '67
Jacqueline Kennedy: the magic and the
myth. J. Brothers. Good H 164:60+ Mr '67
Jacqueline Kennedy's years in the White
House; excerpts. M. V. Thayer. il pors Mc-
Calls 95:12-15+ D '67; 8-9+ Ja '68
(to be cont)
Living theater. il por Newsweek 70:57-8 N 13
'67
Manchester book: despite flaws & errors, a
story that is larger than life or death.
Time 89:22-3 Ap 7 '67
Mrs John F. Kennedy; photographs. Vogue
149:176-7 My '67

KENNEDY, Jacqueline Lee (Bouvier)—about
—*Continued*
Mrs Kennedy reaches accord with Harper & Row and William Manchester. Pub W 191:222 Ja 23 '67
Now that Jackie Kennedy has visited Cambodia. il pors U S News 63:20 N 13 '67
Perils of overexposure. Nation 204:164 F 6 '67
Rage greater than grief. M. Kempton. Atlan 219:98-100 My '67
Suppression business. R. H. Smith. Pub W 191:93 Ja 30 '67
To help you keep the record straight about that book; concerning The death of a President, by W. Manchester. por U S News 62:66-7 F 6 '67
To see ancient Cambodia. il pors Life 63:97-100+ N 17 '67
Travels of Jackie. il pors Newsweek 70:76-7 N 20 '67
Trials of government-in-exile; graceless battle between the Kennedy family and W. Manchester. E. J. Hughes. Newsweek 69:20 F 6 '67
Truth as private property. A. Gingrich. Esquire 67:6+ Mr '67
Two Mrs Kennedys. Nat R 19:335-6 Ap 4 '67
Very special tourist. il pors Time 90:40-1 N 17 '67
William Manchester's own story. W. Manchester. Look 31:62-6+ Ap 4 '67; Reply with rejoinder. P. Salinger. 31:8 My 16 '67

KENNEDY, John Fitzgerald, 1917-1963
Camera and JFK. J. Neubauer. il pors Pop Phot 61:88-103+ N '67
How Kennedy's concern for Negroes led to his death. C. T. Rowan. il pors Ebony 22:27-30+ Ap '67
John F. Kennedy and American Catholicism, by L. H. Fuchs. Review
 America 116:507-8 Ap 1 '67. J. T. Ellis
 Commentary 44:105-8 N '67. J. O'Gara
May 29, 1967 would have been John Kennedy's 50th birthday. T. C. Sorensen. McCalls 94:58-9 Je '67
More light on a JFK ailment. U S News 63:9 Jl 24 '67
My visit with John F. Kennedy. C. Clemens. Hobbies 72:109+ Ap '67
Nov. 22, 1963, Dallas: photos by nine bystanders. Life 63:87-97 N 24 '67
Pathologist-sleuth reopens Kennedy controversy; suggests J. F. Kennedy suffered from Addison's disease. por Sci N 92:79-80 Jl 22 '67
Postmortem on JFK. por Newsweek 70:54 Jl 24 '67
To move a nation, by R. Hilsman. Review
 Reporter 37:14-19 N 30 '67. M. Greenfield
U.S.S. John F. Kennedy, remarks, May 27, 1967. L. B. Johnson. Dept State Bul 56:959-60 Je 26 '67
Why Adenauer turned against U.S. por U S News 62:89 My 15 '67
Why Kennedy went to Texas. J. Connally. il por Life 63:86A-86B+ N 24 '67

Assassination

Agony relived; second Look installment of The death of a President. il Time 89:58 Ja 27 '67
Assassination, a new medical opinion. A. J. Snider. il Sci Digest 61:35-6 F '67
Back to Dallas; theories of J. Thompson and J. Connally. Time 90:54-5 N 24 '67
Book; W. Manchester's Death of a President. il Newsweek 69:34-5 Ap 10 '67
Bourbon street rococo; J. Garrison's investigation. Time 89:26 Mr 3 '67
Carnival in New Orleans; J. Garrison's investigation. il Newsweek 69:32+ Mr 6 '67
Case of Jim Garrison and Lee Oswald. G. Roberts. il N Y Times Mag p32-5+ My 21 '67
Chapter II; excerpts from The death of a President. W. Manchester. il Newsweek 69:22-4 Ja 30 '67
Charge of conspiracy. Newsweek 69:36-7 Ap 3 '67
Closing in; Garrison's unofficial chief investigator quits. Time 90:17 Jl 7 '67
Cross fire that killed President Kennedy; excerpt from Six seconds in Dallas. J. Thompson. il por(cover) Sat Eve Post 240:27-31+ D 2 '67
Death of a President, by W. Manchester. Review
 Nat R 19:591-2 My 30 '67. G. Wills
 New Yorker 43:172-6 Ap 8 '67. R. H. Rovere
 Reporter 36:37-9 My 18 '67. R. West
 Sat R por 50:30-1 Ap 15 '67. M. L. Coit

Death of a President; excerpts (cont) W. Manchester. il Look 31:40-6+ F 7; 42-8+ F 21; 50-66 Mr 7 '67
Death of a President; review of the reviews. P. K. Cuneo. America 116:684-5 My 6 '67
D.A. wins a round; Jim Garrison's investigation. Time 89:17-18 Mr 24 '67
He was my brother; excerpts from Lee. R. L. Oswald and others. il Look 31:62-6+ O 17 '67
History or headlines? New Orleans investigation. il Newsweek 69:44+ Mr 13 '67
If they've found another assassin, let them name names and produce their evidence. J. Berendt. il Esquire 68:80-2+ Ag '67
In the hours after Dallas: the book and the testimony; concerning The death of a President by W. Manchester. il U S News 62:51-2 F 20 '67
Inconceivable connivance. Time 91:14 Ja 12 '68
Is Garrison faking? F. Powledge. New Repub 156:13-18 Je 17 '67
JFK and LBJ: more untold stories; concerning The death of a President by W. Manchester. il por U S News 62:36 Ja 30 '67
JFK conspiracy; J. Garrison's investigation of a plot to kill J. F. Kennedy. H. Aynesworth. il Newsweek 69:36+ My 15 '67
JFK death: a new investigation, but—. U S News 62:16 Mr 13 '67
Kennedy assassination: something rotten... por Sat Eve Post 240:88 D 2 '67
Life sues to enjoin book on assassination of Kennedy. Pub W 192:32 D 25 '67
Manchester affair, by J. Corry. Review
 Sat R 50:61 S 9 '67. S. W. Little
Manchester book: despite flaws & errors, a story that is larger than life or death. Time 89:22-3 Ap 7 '67
Manchester unexpurgated; from Death of Lancer to The death of a President; comparative study of successive versions of book. E. J. Epstein. bibliog f Commentary 44:25-31 Jl '67
More on the Kennedy assassination charges; concerning J. Garrison's TV broadcast. il U S News 62:55-6 Je 12 '67
Mystery makers; J. Sparrow's evaluation of the Warren commission report and its critics. il Time 90:21 D 22 '67
New assassination theory; theory of J. Thompson. il Newsweek 70:29-30+ N 27 '67
New light on second assassin theory. il U S News 62:14 My 29 '67
New Orleans: act I. J. Cohen and N. C. Chriss. il Reporter 36:17-20 Ap 6 '67
New Orleans plot? Sr Schol 90:18-19 Ap 14 '67
Notes and comment; other substanceless witnesses. New Yorker 43:51 D 9 '67
Nov. 22, 1963, Dallas: photos by nine bystanders. Life 63:87-97 N 24 '67
Odd company. il Time 89:24 Mr 10 '67
Outdoor life and The death of a President; W. Manchester charges Outdoor life with hard-boiled callousness toward a national tragedy. Outdoor Life 140:32-3 O '67
Plot to kill Kennedy? rush to judgment in New Orleans. J. Phelan. il por(cover) Sat Eve Post 240:21-5 My 6 '67
Rage greater than grief; evaluation of and excerpts from W. Manchester's The death of a President. M. Kempton. Atlan 219:98-100 My '67
Reporter at large; the buffs. C. Trillin. New Yorker 43:41-6+ Je 10 '67
Return to Dallas. A. M. Bickel. New Repub 157:34 D 23 '67
Scene of the crime. il Newsweek 70:31B-32+ D 4 '67
Second primer of assassination theories. il Esquire 67:104-7 My '67
Shadow on a grassy knoll; photographic-analysis shows no new evidence. Time 89:21 My 26 '67
Sifting fact from fantasy; use of truth drugs in Jim Garrison's investigation. il Time 89:41 Mr 31 '67
Sleight of hand; Jim Garrison's assassination investigation extended to FBI and CIA. Newsweek 69:40+ My 22 '67
Taste for conspiracy; European newsmen are leery of Garrison's investigation. il Newsweek 69:76 Mr 20 '67
Theory of an Oswald conspiracy. Life 62:33 Mr 3 '67
Thickening the plot; judges support. J. Garrison plot theory. Newsweek 69:37 Mr 27 '67
To help you keep the record straight about that book; concerning The death of a President, by W. Manchester. il U S News 62:66-7 F 6 '67

KENNEDY, Robert Francis, family
Kennedy children; photographs. McCalls 94:
96-100 F '67
Robert F. Kennedy: at home with the heir
apparent. R. S. Bird. il pors Sat Eve Post
240:28-35 Ag 26 '67
What it takes to be a Kennedy. G. Cameron.
il pors Ladies Home J 84:76-7+ F '67
KENNEDY, Rose (Fitzgerald)
Rose Kennedy at 76. America 117:595 N 18 '67
KENNEDY, Ted. See Kennedy, E. M.
KENNEDY, Thelma T. See Crill, W. E. jt.
auth.
KENNEDY, William V.
How much force? America 117:278-80 S 16
'67
Who shall serve? America 116:854-5 Je 17 '67
KENNEDY, X. J.
Poets; poem. Atlan 221:101 Ja '68
KENNEDY, CAPE
Alligator on the pad! L. B. Taylor, jr. il
Sci Digest 62:53-7 D '67
Cape Kennedy. P. Blake. il Arch Forum
126:50-9 Ja '67
Space-age sights; USA. L. M. Rhodes. il
Todays Health 46:24-6 Ja '68
KENNELS
Do-it-yourself dog house. J. Griffen. il Field
& S 71:156-8+ F '67
Kenneling your hunting dog. J. Griffen. il
Field & S 72:144-5+ Je '67
Space-age doghouse. C. Conley. il Field & S
72:151 My '67
KENNER, Hugh
Artemis and harlequin. Nat R 19:1432-3 D 26
'67
Barbarous English; excerpts from letter to
William F. Buckley, jr. Commonweal 87:
371+ D 22 '67
Movies. Nat R 19:599-600 My 30 '67
Never a boast or a see-here. Nat R 19:1217-
18 O 31 '67
Of notes and horses. Poetry 111:112-21 N '67
Stan, Ollie, and the universe. Nat R 19:
1277-8 N 14 '67
Tone of a terrible century. Nat R 19:147+
F 7 '67
Understanding Expo. Nat R 19:1070-3+ O 3
'67
World; gritty, particular. Nat R 19:968-9 S
5 '67
KENNEY, Ann D.
(ed) Family movie guide. See issues of Par-
ents' magazine and better homemaking
KENNEY, Francis T.
Turnover of rat liver tyrosine transaminase:
stabilization after inhibition of protein syn-
thesis. bibliog Science 156:525-8 Ap 28 '67
KENNEY, Herbert A.
Metric goad; poem. Nat R 20:39-40 Ja 16 '68
KENNEY, Nathaniel T.
Big Bend jewel in the Texas desert. Nat
Geog Mag 133:104-33 Ja '68
KENNINGTON, Garth S.
Activation analysis of soluble and fixed so-
dium in mammalian hair. bibliog Science
155:588-9; 156:1397 F 3, Je 9 '67
KENNY, Clare G.
No-work flower beds. Suc Farm 65:111+ Mr
'67
KENNY, Herbert A.
Litany in an old boat; poem. Cath World
205:111 My '67
KENNY, Sean
Wild Irishman's space journey, with its vol-
canic splashdown. T. Prideaux. il por Life
62:38-9 Ap 28 '67
KENOSHA, Wis.
Combustibles cost double. Am City 82:39 N '67
KENSHALO, Dan R. and Gallegos, E. S.
Multiple temperature-sensitive spots inner-
vated by single nerve fibers. bibliog Sci-
ence 158:1064-5 N 24 '67
KENSINGTON, Md.
Luaus in the library; or, The curriculum
that wasn't; Rock Creek Palisades elemen-
tary school. M. Murray. il Library J 92:
1708-10 Ap 15 '67
KENT, Douglas R.
History in houses. Antiques 92:187-93 Ag '67
KENT, John L.
Wild new flying machines. Sci Digest 61:64-8
F '67
KENT, Sister Mary Corita
Footnotes and headlines. S. Gross. Christian
Cent 84:1497 N 22 '67
Joyous revolutionary. il por Time 90:82 S
8 '67
Nun; a joyous revolution. il pors Newsweek
70:45-8 D 25 '67
Painting nun. il por Newsweek 70:88-9 D 4
'67

KENT, Norman
Drawings of Richard Welling. Am Artist
31:52-9 F '67
Paintings of Betty Warren. Am Artist 31:
36-41+ My '67
Sheilah Beckett: classicist. Am Artist 31:38-
44+ Ap '67
KENT, Thomas
Clandestine broadcasters. Pop Electr 27:49-52
N '67
KENT, England
Gardens
Churchill's Chartwell; Sir Winston Chur-
chill's garden in Kent. M. Perry. il Flower
Grower 54:46-7+ Ja '67
KENTFIELD, Calvin
Dispatch from Wounded Knee. N Y Times
Mag p28-31+ O 15 '67
Incident in Rio Arriba. N Y Times Mag p20-
1+ Jl 16 '67
Two kinds of tankers, clean and dirty. N Y
Times Mag p24-5+ My 14 '67
KENTUCKY
See also
Cumberland Plateau
Fishing—Kentucky
Forests and forestry—Kentucky
Libraries—Kentucky
Mammoth Cave National Park

Commerce, Department of
How Katie makes Kentucky grow. il Bsns W
p 184-6+ S 9 '67

Elections
See Kentucky—Politics and government

Historic houses, etc.
History in houses: Locust Grove, near Louisville, Kentucky. S. W. Thomas. il Antiques
91:223-7 F '67

Politics and government
Focus on Kentucky; the loser was LBJ. P.
Ardery, jr. Nat R 19:1318 N 28 '67
Kentucky's coal beds of sedition. P. Good. il
Nation 205:136-9 S 4 '67
Nothing grand; campaign for governor. Time
90:20 N 3 '67
Sedition in Kentucky. J. Ridgeway. New
Repub 157:10 S 2 '67
Winners & sinners. Nat R 19:626-7 Je 13 '67
KENTUCKY Derby. See Horse racing
KENTUCKY fried chicken corporation. See
Restaurants—United States
KENTUCKY long rifle. See Rifles
KENTUCKY Southern college, Louisville
Dream with a deadline. Time 90:110 D 8 '67
KENWORTHY, E. W.
Eugene McCarthy hits the road. New Repub
157:11-13 N 25 '67
KENWORTHY, Eldon
Argentina: the politics of late industrializa-
tion. For Affairs 45:463-76 Ap '67
Black-white at home. North-South abroad.
Yale R 57:161-81 D '67
Peace politics: calculus for '68. Nation 206:
46-50 Ja 8 '63
KENYA
See also
Geology—Kenya
Investments, Foreign (in Kenya)
Mau Mau
Nairobi National Park
Tourist trade—Kenya
Women—Kenya

Economic conditions
Business makes a Kenya safari. il Bsns W
p 108+ S 2 '67

Race problems
Shifta revolt; insurrection by Somali seces-
sionists. il Newsweek 70:46+ S 11 '67
Success at pacification; Somali guerrillas in
revolt. Time 90:26 S 8 '67
See also
Mau Mau
KENYON review
Writing for The Kenyon review. G. Lanning.
Writer 80:31-2 O '67
KEPPEL, Francis
Role of private enterprise: adaptation of ad-
dress, May 3, 1967. por Library J 92:3807-11
O 15 '67
KEPPLER, Herbert
Assignment #1. il Mod Phot 31:58-65 F '67
Keppler on the SLR. See issues of Modern
photography

KERALA, India
Communism, Kerala style. J. Lelyveld. il N Y Times Mag p30-1+ Ap 30 '67
Communist Brahmin. E. Behr. Newsweek 69:54 Mr 20 '67

KERALA election. See Elections—India

KERBY, Phil
Abortion: laws and attitudes. Nation 204: 754-6 Je 12 '67
Los Angeles: western justice. Nation 205: 104-5 Ag 14 '67
Most likely to succeed. Nation 206:80-2 Ja 15 '68
Revolt against the poor. Nation 205:262-7 S 25 '67

KERENSKII, Aleksandr Fedorovich. See Kerensky, A.

KERENSKY, Alexander
Fifty years after: communism has failed, it is being destroyed by life itself; interview. por U S News 62:66-9 Mr 13 '67
Freedom on the way for Soviet people? statement, 1917. por U S News 63:16 N 20 '67

about
Lost revolution. il pors Time 89:32-3 Mr 17 '67

KERLEY, Ellis R. and Bass, W. M.
Paleopathology: meeting ground for many disciplines. bibliog Science 157:638-44 Ag 11 '67

KERMAN, R. and others
Altered response to pneumococcal polysaccharide in offspring of immunologically paralyzed mice. bibliog Science 156:1514-16 Je 16 '67

KERN, Edward
[Middle East; last 100 years] Life 63:52-70+ O 6; 72-86 O 13; 48-62+ O 20 '67

about
Scholarly nomad in the Ottoman empire. G. P. Hunt. por Life 63:3 O 6 '67

KERN COUNTY land company
Hammer strikes again. Newsweek 69:83-5 My 29 '67
Tenneco lands Kern County. il Bsns W p96-8+ Jl 22 '67

KERNAN, Henry S.
Forests of Sabah. Am For 73:16-17+ F '67

KERNAN, Michael
Good morning, dear Elizabeth; story. Ladies Home J 84:100-1 N '67

KERNER, Ben
Fast start for Ben's Hawks. F. Deford. il por Sports Illus 27:24-5 N 13 '67

KERNODLE, John R.
Help to needy grows through medicaid. Todays Health 45:88+ N '67

KEROUAC, Jack
Vanity on the gridiron; story; excerpts from Vanity of Duluoz. Sports Illus 28:44-8 Ja 8 '68

KERR, Alix
What's new in medicine. See issues of McCall's

KERR, Chester
Period of youthful aging. Sat R 50:34 Je 10 '67

KERR, Clark
Clark Kerr calls it the exaggerated generation. por N Y Times Mag p28-9+ Je 4 '67
Clark Kerr tells his story; interview, ed. by W. Flynn and J. M. Russin. por Newsweek 69:64-5 F 6 '67
Turmoil in higher education; interview, ed. by G. B. Leonard and T. G. Harris. por Look 31:17-21 Ap 18 '67

about
Angry aftermath at Cal. il Time 89:42 F 3 '67
Berkeley story; facts on a big university. il por U S News 62:54-5 F 6 '67
Cal's Kerr ousted. Sr Schol 90:13-14 F 17 '67
Clark Kerr heads study of U.S. higher education. Pub W 191:47 F 6 '67
Dismissal of President Kerr. Sch & Soc 95: 280 Sum '67
Failure of a peacemaker. il Time 89:60 Ja 27 '67
Kerr affair. H. Brandon. Sat R 50:13 F 11 '67
Public money; private control. Sci N 93:34 Ja 13 '67
Reagan uses his broom. Bsns W p38 Ja 28 '67
Reagan's lesson. Nation 204:166 F 6 '67
Tragedy at Cal: a fiscal & presidential crisis. il Time 89:44-5 F 24 '67

What Reagan hath wrought. J. Duscha. New Repub 156:10-12 F 4 '67
Wounded are many. il por Newsweek 69:87-8 Ja 30 '67

KERR, Frederick H.
Two unusual solid-waste solutions. Am City 82:114-15 Ap '67

KERR, Frederick W. L.
Function of the dorsal motor nucleus of the vagus. bibliog Science 157:451-2 Jl 28 '67

KERR, Jean
As I was saying to a geranium. Ladies Home J 84:84-5 Ap '67
I saw mommy kicking Santa Claus. McCalls 95:89+ D '67
Twiggy who? McCalls 94:62-3+ Jl '67

KERR, Robert Samuel
Dead men tell no tales; Bobby Baker trial. por Time 89:22-3 Ja 27 '67
Friend in need. Newsweek 69:29 Ja 30 '67

KERR, Russell
Stage band. Opera N 31:24-5 F 25 '67

KERR, Walter
Negro actor asks himself: am I a Negro or am I an actor? N Y Times Mag p34-5+ O 15 '67
Theater is the victim of a plot. N Y Times Mag p 10-11+ Je 25 '67

about
Amiable springboard. M. Gussow. Newsweek 70:96+ D 18 '67
Critic earns his laurels: Walter Kerr on the drama. T. Prideaux. Life 62:18 My 19 '67
End of one-man's opinion. Time 89:51 Mr 17 '67

KERR, Walter B.
House of Pravda. Sat R 50:60-1 D 9 '67

KERRIGAN, Anthony
Windmills in the head. Nat R 19:102 S 19 '67

KERSH, Gerald
Literary sea chest. Sat R 50:30 Ag 26 '67
Second time around. Sat R 50:23 Jl 1 '67
Trip out on Red Lizzie; story. Sat Eve Post 241:50-2 Ja 27 '68

KERSHNER, William K.
Rule of thumb for power settings. Flying 80:98 Ap '67

KERSTA, Lawrence G.
Valuable clues from sounds made visible. il Life 63:56A-56B Jl 21 '67

KERTESZ, Istvan
Growth of Istvan Kertesz. H. Glass. Am Rec G 33:1006-7 Jl '67
Music to my ears. I. Kolodin. Sat R 50:58 F 11 '67

KESLER, Earl M. See Patton, S. jt. auth.

KESNER, C. D. and Ries, S. K.
Diphenamid metabolism in plants. bibliog Science 155:210-11 Ja 13 '67

KESSEL, David, and others
Transport and phosphorylation as factors in the antitumor action of cytosine arabinoside. bibliog Science 156:1240-1 Je 2 '67

KESSLER, A. E.
New Hampshire's White Mountain huts. Travel 127:37-40 Je '67

KESSLER, Dagmar
Brief biography. S. Goodman. pors Dance Mag 41:54-5 N '67

KESSLER, Edward
Granary; poem. Sat R 50:38 Jl 29 '67
Snob; poem. Sat R 51:90 Ja 6 '68

KESSLER, Harry H.
Mona Lisa's mustache. Sports Illus 26:11 F 20 '67

KESSLER, Jascha
Little Ivy league; poem. Sat R 50:39 Mr 4 '67

KESSLER, Stephen
High ground. Newsweek 70:37 N 6 '67
Two states of mind. il por Time 90:50 N 3 '67

KESSLER, the inside man; story. See Fox, G.

KESTER, Bernard
California arts commission. Craft Horiz 27: 24-7+ Mr '67

KETCHUM, Richard M.
Faces from the past (cont) Am Heritage 18: 26-7 Ag; 18-19 O '67

KETENE
Biosynthesis of polyketides and related compounds; excerpts from address, June 28, 1966. A. J. Birch. bibliog il Science 156:202-6 Ap 14 '67

KETO-aldehydes. See Glyoxal

KETY, Seymour S. See Schildkraut, J. J. jt. auth.

KEVIN O'Hara, Sister. See O'Hara, K.

KEY, Philip Barton
Verdicts of history: husband's revenge; Daniel E. Sickles case. T. J. Fleming. il por Am Heritage 18:65-75 Ap '67
KEY WEST, Fla.
Key West. N. Brower. il Travel 128:24-9 D '67
Like no other water works; desalting plant. W. S. Foster. il Am City 82:91-3 O '67

Water supply
Drinkable sea water. Time 90:17 Jl 28 '67
Water, water everywhere, and now to drink. il Newsweek 70:69-70 Jl 31 '67
KEY WEST bridge. See Bridges
KEYERS, Code. See Radio telegraph
KEYES, Allan
Sanity at Pittsburgh. Nat R 19:1056-8 O 3 '67
KEYES, Frances Parkinson
Minority report. Travel 127:58-9+ Mr '67
KEYES, Leroy
Chant at Purdue is give it to Leroy. T. C. Brody. il Sports Illus 27:52+ N 27 '67
Three for the trophy. il Newsweek 70:94 N 27 '67
KEYES, Marvin Leroy. See Keyes, L.
KEYES, Ralph
Free universities. Nation 205:294-9 O 2 '67
KEYSERLING, Leon H.
Employment and the new economics. Ann Am Acad 373:102-19 S '67
Guaranteed annual incomes. New Repub 156:20-3 Mr 18 '67
Guaranteed income. Reporter 36:10 Je 15 '67
Sharing revenue with the states. New Repub 156:14-18 Mr 25 '67
Supporting the poor; letter. New Repub 156:33-4 Je 10 '67
Tax troubles; letter. New Repub 157:39-40 O 21 '67
KEZWEENY, A. J. See Hobbs, P. V. jt. auth.
KEZYS, Algimantas
Dramatic photos from ordinary scenes. J. Scully. il Mod Phot 31:64-9 Je '67
KHADDURI, Majid
Political trends in Iraq and Kuwait. Cur Hist 52:84-9+ F '67
KHAN, Ali Akbar
Rock, raga and the cop-out. G. Lees. il por Hi Fi 17:82-3 Jl '67
KHAT. See Kat
KHEEL, Theodore Woodrow
Mr Kheel's defense of strikes. B. L. Masse. America 117:431 O 21 '67
KHOSLA, Mahesh C. and others
Apparatus for solid-phase peptide synthesis. bibliog Science 156:253-4 Ap 14 '67
KHOTSO
Khotso's millions. J. Cope. Reporter 37:41-4 D 14 '67
KHRUSHCHEV, Nikita Sergeevich
Key world figures as Khrushchev rates them; excerpts from NBC documentary. Khrushchev in exile. pors U S News 63:12-13 Jl 24 '67

about
Good old whatzisname; concerning a NBC TV program. Nat R 19:782 Jl 25 '67
Harmless deception? R. L. Shayon. Sat R 50:42 Ag 5 '67
Khrushchev, by M. Frankland. Review
Nation 204:790-2 Je 19 '67 A. Werth
Sat R il por 50:36 S 2 '67 L. Fischer
Khrushchev's vision of the future Soviet school. W. W. Brickman. bibliog f il Sch & Soc 95:461-74 N 25 '67
Nikita in exile. il por Newsweek 70:100 Jl 17 '67
Senior citizen Khrushchev. il por Time 90:71 Jl 7 '67
KIBBUTZIM. See Collective settlements—Israel
KIDD, James
Strange quest of James Kidd. D. J. Hamblin. il por Life 62:76-8+ Mr 3 '67
KIDD, Steven R.
Illustrations of Steven Kidd. H. Gasser. il por Am Artist 31:38-43+ Je '67
KIDDE, Walter, and company
Litton's "children": Kidde and Teledyne. Fortune 75:321-2 Je 15 '67
KIDNAPPING
Fight to make the Vietcong let him go; case of G. C. Hertz; with report by R. B. Stolley. il Life 63:22-9 Jl 21 '67
Merchandise; Kenneth Young case. il Newsweek 69:44 Ap 17 '67
Merchandise returned; return of Kenneth Young. il Time 89:37 Ap 14 '67

Moise Tshombe on the way to his kidnaping. il Life 63:28D-30 Jl 14 '67
Sequel to Gus Hertz's story, he's alive. G. P. Hunt. Life 63:3 Ag 11 '67
Wood wizard; tracking down Lindbergh kidnapper by wood analysis. J. B. Craig. il Am For 73:28-30+ O '67
KIDNEY beans. See Beans
KIDNEY stones. See Calculi, Urinary
KIDNEYS
Amino acid transport: evidence for genetic control of two types in human kidney. C. R. Scriver and O. H. Wilson. bibliog il Science 155:1428-30 Mr 17 '67
Lysine transport in human kidney: evidence for two systems. L. E. Rosenberg and others. bibliog il Science 155:1426-8 Mr 17 '67

Diseases
Autologous immune-complex pathogenesis of experimental allergic glomerulonephritis. T. S. Edgington and others. bibliog il Science 155:1432-4 Mr 17 '67
Dangers of analgesics. il Time 89:74+ F 24 '67
Polycystic renal disease: a new experimental model. D. Y. E. Perey and others. bibliog il Science 158:494-6 O 27 '67
Slow virus kidney disease of mice. F. D. Baker and J. Hotchin. bibliog il Science 158:502-4 O 27 '67
See also
Nephritis
KIDNEYS, Artificial
Artificial kidneys: where we stand. B. T. Burton. il Todays Health 45:26-9+ Jl '67
Do-it-yourself for kidney patients. il Bsns W p72-3 F 4 '67
Lymphatic kidney? Sci Am 216:58 My '67
Rest are simply left to die; nephritis victims. J. Robbins and J. Robbins. Redbook 130-80-1+ N '67
KIDNEYS, Transplantation of. See Transplantation of organs, tissues, etc.
KIENHOLZ, Edward
Art; exhibition at Washington gallery of modern art. M. Kozloff. Nation 206:29-30 Ja 1 '68
KIENZ, Ethel T.
Living in a mobile home in Florida. Consumer Bul 50:35-6 Ag '67
KIENZL, Wilhelm
Records:
Der evangelimann. Opera N 31:34 Ja 7 '67
KIESINGER, Kurt Georg
How West German leader sees U.S. role in Europe; interview, ed. by R. A. Haeger. por U S News 63:52-4 Jl 10 '67
President Johnson attends funeral of Konrad Adenauer; exchange of remarks, April 26, 1967. Dept State Bul 56:751 My 15 '67
President Johnson meets with German chancellor; exchange of greetings, statements and exchange of toasts, August 15; with joint statement, August 16, 1967. Dept State Bul 57:325-30 S 11 '67

about
Dialogue with Bonn; some suggestions for what might, but won't be said at the Kiesinger-Johnson meeting in Washington. T. C. Sorensen. Sat R 50:28-9 My 20 '67
First 100 days. il por Time 89:38+ Mr 17 '67
Fox and the bear are cautious partners. P. Shabecoff. il pors N Y Times Mag p20-1+ F 5 '67
Gathering at the grave. il Time 89:29 My 5 '67
Grinder ground. Newsweek 69:54 Je 19 '67
Gunter Grass's open letter to Kurt Kiesinger. G. Grass. Nation 204:214 F 13 '67
His Germany is now on its own; with report by H. Moffett. il pors Life 62:47-8+ Ap 28 '67
Letter from Bonn. R. H. Rovere. New Yorker 43:142-4 F 25 '67
Making the grand coalition work. il por Time 89:27 Je 2 '67
New chancellor of the new Germany. E. Hughes. por Read Digest 91:145-9 N '67
Problem for LBJ; feud between top Germans. U S News 63:16 Ag 21 '67
Setting a new course. il por Newsweek 69:44 Mr 20 '67
Taming the pros. il por Newsweek 69:56 Je 5 '67
KIESTER, Edwin, Jr. See Miel, A. jt. auth.
KIEV, Russia
Dina Mironovna Pronichev remembers Babi Yar; excerpt from novel, Babi Yar. A. Kuznetsov; reply. E. Litvin. il N Y Times Mag p 121+ Ap 30 '67

KIGOSHI, Kunihiko
Ionium dating of igneous rocks. bibliog Science 156:932-4 My 19 '67

KIKER, Douglas
Atlantic report. Atlan 219:4+ F '67
Education of Robert McNamara. Atlan 219: 49-55 Mr '67
Report: Washington (cont of) Atlantic report: Washington. See issues of Atlantic

KILAUEA (crater)
Balloon bursts, more to come. il Sci N 92:487 N 18 '67

KILGORE, Bernard
Read Kilgore. por Newsweek 70:88 N 27 '67
Wall Street publishing giant. J. Tebbel. Sat R 51:110-11+ Ja 13 '68

KILGOUR, Martha Jane
Where ocean birds climb island trees. Audubon 69:70-7 Jl '67

KILKENNY design workshops, limited. See Ireland—Industries

KILL three; story. See Shulman, M.

KILLIAN, James R. 1904-
Doctor Killian notes progress in Latin American science program. Dept State Bul 57: 717 N 27 '67

KILLIFISHES
Sodium- and potassium-activated adenosine triphosphatase of gills: role in adaptation of teleosts to salt water. F. H. Epstein and others. bibliog il Science 156:1245-7 Je 2 '67
Toughness of species; research in the Everglades. L. Gebhart. Sci N 92:355 O 7 '67

KILLING, Mercy. See Euthanasia

KILLING of Sister George; drama. See Marcus. F.

KILLINGSWORTH, Mark R.
To Mr Jovanovich. Harper 235:60+ O '67

KILLY, Jean Claude
Fastest man on any mountain. D. Jenkins. il por Sports Illus 26:18-21 Mr 27 '67
Lafayette, they are back; photographs by M. E. Newman; with account by D. Jenkins. Sports Illus 26:20-5 Mr 20 '67
Le Superman. por Newsweek 69:83 Mr 6 '67
Trouble with being no. 1. Time 91:33 Ja 19 '68
World's greatest skier; with report by M. Durham. il pors Life 62:57-8+ F 24 '67

KILMAINHAM gaol. See Prisons—Ireland

KILNS
Wood-burning raku kiln. L. Lipke. il Sch Arts 66:36-8 Ja '67
See also
Brickmaking
Cement kilns

KILPATRICK, James Jackson
All they need to know and more. Sat R 50:42-3 S 16 '67
Crisis seven. Nat R 19:1263-74 N 14 '67
Romney: salesman on the move. Nat R 19: 1372-83+ D 12 '67
Term's end. Nat R 19:789-93+ Jl 25 '67
Walls have eyes and ears. Sat R 50:31-2 Ap 1 '67
What makes Wallace run? Nat R 19:400-9 Ap 18 '67
—and others
Rhodesia: a case history. Nat R 19:512-26 My 16 '67

KILSDONK, Henrica Marcella Maria. See Rikki

KILTS
Kilt kick. il Newsweek 70:59 Ag 21 '67

KILVERT, B. Cory, Jr
Glow that only garden lights can give. Home Gard 54:20-1 D '67
Home garden notebook. Home Gard 54:61-2 My: 45-6 S; 45-6 O '67

KIM, Ki-han, and others
Thyroxine interaction with actinomycin D and possible biological implications. bibliog Science 156:245-6 Ap 14 '67

KIM, Sung-hou, and Rich, Alexander
Crystal structure of the 1 : 1 complex of 5-fluorouracil and 9-ethylhypoxanthine. bibliog Science 158:1046-8 N 24 '67

KIM, Willa
Interview, ed. by A. Fatt. por Dance Mag 41:46 F '67

KIMBALL, Penn
Can we communicate with Europe? Sat R 50: 54-5 Jl 8 '67

KIMBALL, Ruth
NYPL denies Ebony charge of Schomburg neglect. Library J 92:4455 D 15 '67

KIMBALL, Thomas L.
Facts about a Redwoods National Park. por Am For 73:20-3+ Mr '67
Wilderness and public lands. Liv Wildn 30: 14-17 Wint '66

KIMBERLY corporation
Wardrobes for the wastebasket. R. Levy. il Duns R 89:59 Je '67

KIMBLE, Daniel P. See Beach, G. jt. auth.

KIMBROUGH, Emily
One with the world. Sat R 50:34 Ap 29 '67

KIMELDORF, Donald J. See Carroll, H. W. jt. auth.

KIMMEL, Walter S.
Mystiques and techniques of conducting. Am Rec G 33:853-5 My '67
Sainsbury revisited, 142 years later. Am Rec G 33:847 My '67

KINARD, Epsie
Address book. See issues of House beautiful
Decorators' secrets: little outlay, great effects. House B 109:110+ F '67
New techniques and equipment for home moviemaking. House B 109:158-9+ Je '67
Safe at home. House B 109:30+ Ap '67
Tomorrow's designers. House B 109:52-3 S '67

KIND, Joshua
Chicago. Art N 65:27+ Ja; 66:59+ Mr; 61 Sum '67

KIND of savage; story. See Hall, J. B.

KINDERGARTEN
160-acre kindergarten; school on a farm, Accokeek, Md. N. M. Wagner. il NEA J 56: 41-2 F '67
Should Johnny read in kindergarten? a report on the Denver experiment; with comment by K. D. Wann. J. E. Brzeinski and others. il NEA J 56:23-6 Mr '67
See also
Montessori method of education
Nursery schools

KINDIG, David A. and Kirsten, W. H.
Virus-like particles in established murine cell lines: electron-microscopic observations. bibliog Science 155:1543-5 Mr 24 '67

KINDNESS
See also
Charity

KINDREGAN, Charles P.
Life control and the Christian. America 117: 406-8 O 14 '67

KINETIC art. See Art in motion

KING, Bettina
Junior high that's like a college. J. Kozol. il N Y Times Mag p32-3+ O 29 '67; Discussion. p24+ N 19 '67

KING, Billie Jean Moffitt
King-size tennis. Newsweek 70:53 Jl 17 '67
Plays tennis like a man, speaks out like, Billie Jean King. H. Higdon. il pors N Y Times Mag p28-9+ Ag 27 '67; Reply. J. C. Smith. p97 O 1 '67
Some beer for Newk, a waltz for Billie. F. Deford. il por Sports Illus 27:22-5 Jl 17 '67
Two who didn't stay away. K. Chapin. il por Sports Illus 27:97-8+ S 18 '67
U.S. men are losers. B. Bruns. il pors Life 63:109+ S 22 '67
Wimbledon à la King. il por Time 90:53 Jl 21 '67

KING, Bruce
Dance in our schools: how long before the issue is faced? por Dance Mag 41:62-6+ D '67

KING, Charles H. and others
Black youth in rebellion. Wilson Lib Bul 42:166-72 O '67

KING, Jill
After the desert; poem. Harper 234:51 Je '67
Child's answers; poem. Atlan 220:71 Jl '67

KING, Kenneth
On the move. Dance Mag 41:56-8 Je '67
about
Kenneth King; Film-makers' cinematheque. J. Anderson. Dance Mag 41:80 Ap '67

KING, Larry L.
Another warning to whitey. New Repub 158: 21-3 Ja 20 '68
Battle of Popcorn Bay. Harper 234:50-4 My '67
Dear congressman: is Doddism dead? N Y Times Mag p26-7+ Ap 16 '67
Everybody's Louie. Harper 235:61-9 N '67
God, man, and William F. Buckley. Harper 234:53-61 Mr '67
Speaking out. por Sat Eve Post 240:10+ Ap 8 '67

KING, Lawrence T.
Books. Commonweal 86:182, 327 Ap 28, Je 2 '67
Unjolly green giant. Commonweal 86:461 Jl 28 '67

KING, Lloyd J. See Glucksberg, S. jt. auth.

KING, Martin Luther, 1929-1968
International evening: Martin Luther King; summary of address. por Pub W 191:52 Je 19 '67
Martin Luther King defines black power. por N Y Times Mag p26-7+ Je 11 '67
New Negro threat: mass disobedience; excerpts from address, August 15, 1967. por U S News 63:10 Ag 28 '67

about

Birmingham revisited. Time 90:28 N 10 '67
Cities in '68. New Repub 157:5-7 D 16 '67
Court v. King. Time 89:20 Je 23 '67
Curse of confusion. E. J. Hughes. Newsweek 69:17 My 1 '67
Doctor King's boycott. il por Sr Schol 90: 15-16 Ap 21 '67
Doctor King's crusade: how he hopes to end the war. U S News 62:14 My 8 '67
Doctor King's disservice to his cause. Life 62:4 Ap 21 '67
King speaks for peace. Christian Cent 84: 492-3 Ap 19 '67
Lord of the doves. Newsweek 69:44+ Ap 17 '67
Martin Luther King's tragic decision. C. T. Rowan. por Read Digest 91:37-42 S '67
MLK's tropic interlude. il pors Ebony 22:112- 14+ Je '67
Memo to Martin Luther King. Nat R 19:1368 D 12 '67
Non-debate. K. Crawford. Newsweek 69:46 Ap 17 '67
Principles & heresies. F. S. Meyer. Nat R 20:36 Ja 16 '68
Second coming of Martin Luther King. D. Halberstam. il por Harper 235:39-51 Ag '67
Signs of erosion. por Newsweek 69:32 Ap 10 '67
Which way for the Negro? il por Newsweek 69:27-8+ My 15 '67
With but one voice. Nation 204:515-16 Ap 24 '67

KING, Robert W.
Can our fractured world be mended? Bul Atomic Sci 23:31-2 Ja '67
KING-HELE, Desmond
Shape of the earth: with biographical sketch. Sci Am 217:19, 67-72+ O '67
KING COUNTY, Wash.
New idea in landfill operation. H. Evans, jr. il Am City 82:114-15 Mr '67
KING crabs
Crab that isn't. R. Rood. il Audubon 69:38-43 My '67
Resource comes out of its shell in Alaska. il Bsns W p 132-4 O 7 '67
Tetrodotoxin blocks a graded sensory response in the eye of limulus. R. M. Benolken and C. J. Russell. bibliog il Science 155:1576-7 Mr 24 '67; Reply with rejoinder. H. Grundfest. 156:1771 Je 30 '67
See also
Wakefield seafoods, incorporated
KING of the castle; story. See Holt, V.
KING Thrushbeard; drama. See Thane, A.
KINGDOM of earth; drama. See Williams, T.
KINGMAN, Dong
What makes an object interesting? Design 68:20-1 Ja '67
KINGS and rulers
See also
Coronations
Europe—Kings and rulers
Heads of state
KINGS (hockey team) See Hockey teams
KINGS CANYON NATIONAL PARK
Pictograph cave in Kings Canyon National Park. C. W. Stouffer. il Nat Parks Mag 41: 16-17 My '67
Preliminary wilderness plan for Sequoia-Kings Canyon National Parks and the surrounding region. il Nat Parks Mag 41:9-13 Ja '67
KINGSLEY, Ione T.
Yachting two miles up. Yachting 122:50-1+ D '67
KINGSPORT, Tenn.

Labor and laboring classes

Kingsport press four years later, an assessment. il Pub W 191:62-3+ My 1 '67
KINGSPORT press, incorporated
Anti-union vote at Kingsport certified by NLRB and U.S. Court of appeals: four-year strike near end. Pub W 192:47 Jl 17 '67
Kingsport press four years later, an assessment. il Pub W 191:62-3+ My 1 '67

Quasi-boycott of Kingsport press in Detroit. Pub W 191:89 Ja 30 '67
Two unions decertified in Kingsport election. Pub W 191:226+ Ja 23 '67
Unions lose in Kingsport election; votes impounded. Pub W 191:37 My 8 '67
KINN, Barry
Look of longing. il U S Camera 30:52-3 Jl '67
KINNAMON, Keneth
Man who created Simple. Nation 205:599-601 D 4 '67
KINNARD, H. W. O.
U.S. weapons in Vietnam; are they good enough? interview. por U S News 62:68-71 F 6 '67
KINNELL, Galway
In the Anse Galet valley; In the farmhouse; How many nights; poems. Poetry 110:406-8 S '67
KINROSS, John Patrick Douglas Belfour, 3d baron
Total recoil of the first Edwardian. Life 63:10 Ag 4 '67
KINSELLA, Thomas
Ritual of departure; poem. Poetry 110:98-9 My '67
KINSHIP

Terminology

Componential analysis; kinship studies in cultural anthropology. W. H. Goodenough. bibliog il Science 156:1203-9 Je 2 '67
KINSOLVING, Lester
Coup that impends: Episcopal extremism. Nation 204:105-9 Ja 23 '67

about

Restless clergy. G. Zimmermann. il por Look 31:27 F 7 '67
KINTNER, Robert Edmonds
Fade-out. por Newsweek 69:38+ Je 26 '67
KINTREA, Frank
When the coachman was a millionaire. Am Heritage 18:20-5+ O '67
KINZEL, Augustus B.
Engineering, civilization, and society; excerpts from address, November 8, 1966. Science 156:1343-5 Je 9 '67
KINZER, Stephen
Mr Pierson's brainstorm. Pop Phot 61:132+ D '67
KIOWA Indians
Way to Rainy Mountain. N. S. Momaday. il Reporter 36:41-3 Ja 26 '67
KIPLING, Rudyard
Rudyard Kipling, by B. Dobrée. Review Sat R 50:31 Ag 26 '67. O. Prescott
KIPLINGER, Walter M. jr
Press conference pointers. por Parks & Rec 2:29 Mr '67
KIPLINGER, Willard Monroe
It started with Kip. por Newsweek 70:62-3 Ag 21 '67
KIPNIS, David M. See Fozzard, H. A. jt. auth.
KIPPY'S steak and lobster palace. See New York (city)—Hotels, restaurants. etc.
KIPUKA Puaulu bird park. See Bird sanctuaries
KIRBY, G. W.
Biosynthesis of the morphine alkaloids. bibliog Science 155:170-3 Ja 13 '67
KIRCHOFF radiation law. See Heat—Radiation and absorption
KIRK, Claude Roy, jr
Power not to tax; address, October 30, 1967. Vital Speeches 34:141-4 D 15 '67

about

Affairs of state. il por Newsweek 69:24+ Ja 30 '67
Governor Kirk's not-so-secret police. F. Murray. il Reporter 36:27-30 Mr 23 '67
Governor Kirk's private eyes. F. J. Cook. il Nation 204:616-22 My 15 '67
I, Claudius. por Newsweek 69:36 Ap 10 '67
I, Claudius. il por Time 90:26 D 15 '67
It is a joyous thing to be a Kirk Republican! M. Frady. il pors Sat Eve Post 240:75-9 Jl 29 '67
Kirk's private police. New Repub 156:10 Ja 28 '67
New way of operating. il por Time 89:19-20 Ap 7 '67
Political happening named Claude Kirk. R. Sherrill. il pors N Y Times Mag p34-5+ N 26 '67
Two for a monologue: Governor Kirk interrupts speech by H. R. Brown. il por Time 90:21-2 Ag 18 '67
When a state opens its own war on crime. il por U S News 62:61-2 My 22 '67

KIRK, Dudley
Prospects for reducing natality in the underdeveloped world. bibliog f Ann Am Acad 369:48-60 Ja '67

KIRK, Grayson
Crisis in financing; excerpt from address. por U S News 63:88 Jl 17 '67

KIRK, John T.
Distinctive character of Connecticut furniture. Antiques 92:524-9 O '67

KIRK, Russell
From the academy. See issues of National review

KIRK, Ruth
Bogachiel reverie; with photographs. Liv Wildn 30:10-15 Aut '66
From Tulelake to Death Valley; the unknown California. Redbook 130:37-9 N '67

KIRK, Stanley
What makes Stanley run? R. Levy. por Duns R 89:42-4 Ja '67

KIRKLAND, Douglas
Lincoln park; photographs. Holiday 41:74-83 Mr '67

KIRKLAND, Richard
All together now, a big whompf for Norfolk state. C. Kirkpatrick. il Sports Illus 28:20 Ja 8 '68

KIRKLAND, Sally
Girls of Budapest. Life 63:82+ D 8 '67
In a swinging resort the star is Merle Oberon. Life 62:62A Ja 27 '67

KIRKPATRICK, Curry
Baseball. Sports Illus 27:42-3 Jl 24 '67
Baseball's week. Sports Illus 27:73 Ag 21; 81 Ag 28 '67
Softball. Sports Illus 27:92-3 S 11 '67

KIRKPATRICK, Evron Maurice
Professor & the CIA. R. G. Sherrill. Nation 204:253-60 F 27 '67; Reply. R. B. Luce. 204:386 Mr 27 '67

KIRKWOOD, Mo.
Lend-a-hand plan. R. G. Reim. il Am City 82:98-9 Mr '67

KIRSCHENMANN, Fred
Credibility gap in theology. Christian Cent 84:498-500 Ap 19 '67

KIRSCHKE, Jack
Dolce vita, Rivo Alto style. il por Time 89: 20 Je 23 '67
That's it, Jack. por Newsweek 71:29 Ja 22 '68

KIRSTEIN, Lincoln
Dancer's bookshelf. J. Anderson. Dance Mag 41:18+ N '67
Three recent volumes. D. Galler. Poetry 110: 267-8 Jl '67
White House happening. Criticism Newsweek il 70:64 Ag 21 '67

KIRSTEN, W. H. See Kindig, D. A. jt. auth.

KIRTLEY, David W.
Reef builders; with biographical sketch. Natur Hist 77:4, 40-5 Ja '68

KIRWAN, John D.
One man's Newark. Nat R 19:847 Ag 8 '67

KIRWAN, Michael Joseph
Mike Kirwan's big ditch. W. Schulz. Read Digest 90:59-64 Je '67

KISHIDA, Keiko, and Naka, K. I.
Amino acids and the spikes from the retinal ganglion cells. bibliog Science 156:648-50 My 5 '67

KISICH, Margaret Cochran (Shedd) See Shedd, M. C.

KISLIUK, R. L. and others
Antimalarial activity of tetrahydrohomopteroic acid. bibliog Science 156:1616-17 Je 23 '67

KISSIMMEE RIVER
Keeping house on the Kissimmee. R. Franklin. il Motor B 120:32-3 O '67

KISSIN, Benjamin
Marijuana causes psychic dependence, says physician. Todays Health 45:13 S '67

KISSING
Gentle art of handkissing. L. Crawford. il Ebony 22:91-2+ O '67

KISSING disease. See Mononucleosis, Infectious

KISTER, Daniel A.
Universa Laus Spain, August, 1967. America 117:522-3 N 4 '67

KISTNER, Robert W.
What hormones have to do with pregnancy. Redbook 129:22+ Ag '67

KIT amplifiers. See Amplifiers

KIT automobiles. See Automobiles

KIT building
Five kits you can build just for fun; stereo hi-fi, TV set and a shortwave radio. il Pop Sci 191:92-5 Jl '67

KIT greenhouses. See Greenhouses

KIT radio receivers. See Radio receivers, Short wave

KIT tape recorders. See Magnetic recorders and recording

KIT television sets. See Television receivers

KITCHEN cabinets
Build your own kitchen cabinets. W. C. Leckey. il Pop Mech 128:146-55+ S '67

KITCHEN entrances. See Doorways

KITCHEN furniture
Big, bright and beautiful. il Good H 165:88-91 Jl '67
Five ideas for your kitchen. il Pop Sci 190: 164-5 Ja '67
Island gives this big kitchen compact work areas. R. Martens. il Farm J 91:68-9 O '67
Kitchen planning: outdoor division. il Good H 164:102-3+ Je '67
See also
Snack bars

KITCHEN gardening. See Vegetable gardening

KITCHEN ranges. See Stoves

KITCHEN storage. See Storage in the home

KITCHEN utensils
Buyer's guide to cookware. il Am Home 70: 86 N '67
Colorful new cookware. V. T. Habeeb. il Am Home 70:72-3 N '67
Cooking with company. il Seventeen 26:212 S '67
Culinary cornucopia. il House & Gard 132:65-6 N '67
Decorative dividend for the kitchen. il House & Gard 132:290-1 N '67
Exciting summer furniture, food, projects, equipment. D. Popplestone. il Bet Hom & Gard 45:46-65+ Je '67
Good utensils make good cooks. il House & Gard 132:226-7 S; 254-5 O; 286-7 N '67
Great little gadgets. il Redbook 120:26+ Jl '67
Kitchen planning: outdoor division. il Good H 164:102-3+ Je '67
Little things mean a lot. Am Home 70:98-9 Mr '67
Plain and Teflon-coated cookware. il Consumer Rep 32:534-41 O '67
Pots and pans. il Redbook 129:88-91+ Je '67
Right pots and pans. H. Dawson. il Bet Hom & Gard 45:124-6 Je '67
Western kitchen. See issues of Sunset
When you buy cookware. il House B 109:136+ Ap '67
You can surprise her with one: tortilla press. il Sunset 138:117 F '67
See also
Cookery—Measurements

Care
Care and safekeeping of cookware. House & Gard 131:38+ Mr '67

KITCHEN ware. See Cooking utensils

KITCHENER, Horatio Herbert, 1st earl
Kitchener of Khartoum. See Kitchener of Khartoum, H. H. K.

KITCHENER of Khartoum, Horatio Herbert Kitchener, 1st earl
Carnage in the Sudan settled old scores for the British. E. Kern. il por Life 63:68-9 O 6 '67

KITCHENS
All doors led to the kitchen. M. Holmes. il Todays Health 45:44-5+ N '67
Apartment kitchens of two bachelors: big plans in snug space. N. Craig. il House B 109:118-19 Ag '67
Beautiful kitchen in every way! H. A. Dawson and G. V. Young. il Bet Hom & Gard 45:90-1+ N '67
Big ideas for tiny kitchens. il Bet Hom & Gard 45:45 Je '67
Black and white and red all over. il Am Home 70:94 Mr '67
Brand-new kitchen in an old farm home. J. LemMon. il Suc Farm 65:104-5 Ja '67
Center of action: expanded kitchen. J. Gillies. il Farm J 91:62-3+ S '67
Compact kitchen with country charm. il Good H 165:120-1+ S '67
Cooking for extras is easier in her remodeled kitchen. J. Gillies. il Farm J 91: 66-7 My '67
Good housekeeping designs a kitchen, family style. il Good H 164:140-3 Mr '67
Great comeback for an old kitchen. M. Davidson. il Ladies Home J 84:112-13+ My '67

KITCHENS—*Continued*
Here's a kitchen to live in. J. Gillies. il Farm J 91:75+ Ja '67
How a little old kitchen became a big success. il Bet Hom & Gard 45:88 Jl '67
How to add a kitchen to a camper. A. S. Ryan. il Pop Sci 190:160-2 Je '67
How to make the best of a bad kitchen. il Redbook 129:78-9+ O '67
I designed my own kitchen. B. Wason. il Parents Mag 42:85-9 O '67
Island gives this big kitchen compact work areas. R. Martens. il Farm J 91:68-9 O '67
Island is partly for traffic control. il Sunset 138:156 My '67
Key to kitchen traffic problems: move the back entrance. J. Gillies. il Farm J 92:66 Ja '68
Kitchen for all seasons. V. T. Habeeb. il Am Home 70:90 Jl '67
Kitchen long on efficiency. il Bet Hom & Gard 45:128 S '67
Kitchens take new shapes. il House & Gard 133:118-23 Ja '68
Lots from little. il Am Home 70:134 O '67
Make your farm kitchen a time-and-work-saver. J. LemMon. il Suc Farm 65:69-73 O '67
New farm kitchen. J. Gillies. il Farm J 91:57 Je '67
New party scene: the kitchen. il House & Gard 132:234-7 O '67
One counter now is seven feet of maple. il Sunset 138:109 F '67
Open kitchen. il Sunset 138:80-1 Je '67
Organization in the kitchen. il Am Home 70:72-3 S '67
Packable kitchen, that you can take with you when you move. il House & Gard 131:136-9 My '67
Remodeled on a shoestring. il Am Home 70:111 Ja '67
Remodeling for warmth and workability. K. Russeth. il Bet Hom & Gard 45:134 F '67
Sea-foam for a Philadelphia suburb. il House B 109:159 My '67
Step-by-step to a better kitchen in the same space! il Bet Hom & Gard 45:56-63 Mr '67
Sunshine for a Manhattan apartment. il House B 109:158 My '67
Terrace kitchen. il House & Gard 131:124-5 Je '67
This farm family dared to try new ideas: Bavarian-flavored kitchen. J. LemMon. il Suc Farm 65:54-5 Jl '67
Three super kitchens. N. Craig. il House B 109:300-5 N '67
Today everyone is cooking; seven kitchens and how they grew. il House & Gard 132:89-99 Ag '67
Today's old-fashioned kitchen. Am Home 70:66-7 N '67
Turnabout in the kitchen. V. T. Habeeb. il Am Home 70:98-9 My '67
What a difference a new kitchen makes! R. Charles. il Parents Mag 42:55-8+ Ag '67
Where the action is. V. T. Habeeb. il Am Home 70:84-5 Je '67
Where the family meets, and cooks. N. Craig. il House B 109:150-1 Je '67
Years-ago kitchens go young; with remodeling plans. M. Davidson. il Ladies Home J 85:58-61 Ja '68

Safety devices and measures
Key rules about kitchen safety. il Good H 164:194-5 Mr '67

KITCHENS, Outdoor
It's their outdoor kitchen. il Sunset 139:69 Jl '67

KITCHINER, William
Harem of telescopes. J. Ashbrook. il Sky & Tel 33:346+ Je '67

KITCHING, John
Why do mergers miscarry? Harvard Bsns R 45:84-101 N '67

KITES
Build your own reentry kite. W. Yolen. il Pop Sci 191:112-14 Jl '67
Prize-winning kites; annual kite carnival at Brooklyn's Pratt institute. A. Lees. il Pop Mech 127:108-11 Mr '67
Secrets of the kite. B. Farrell. Life 63:25 D 1 '67

Safety devices and measures
Kite safety rules. il Good H 164:191 My '67

KITES (birds)
Kites of Europe. W. Condry. il Natur Hist 76:46-51 bibliog(p67) My '67
Sunset of the snail kite. E. A. Bauer. il Field & S 72:58-60 Ag '67

KITT PEAK national observatory. See Astronomical observatories

KITTLEMAN, L. R. See Morris, R. W. jt. auth.

KITZHABER, Albert R.
New Oregon rhetoric curriculum. por Sr Schol 90:sup 13-14 My 12 '67

KIVITT, Ted
World of dance. W. Terry. il por Sat R 50:45 Je 24 '67

KJELGAARD, Betty
Too bad, so sad; story. Ladies Home J 84:88-9 S '67

KLAGES, John W.
How to make owl stones. Design 68:18-19 Ja '67

KLAMATH MOUNTAINS
Blessed Trinities; Trinity Alps. H. D. Bishop. il Am For 73:36-7+ O '67
Hike up Canyon Creek in the Trinity Alps. il Sunset 139:22+ S '67

KLAR, Daniel W.
Built to be seen. Am City 82:96-7 My '67

KLAW, Spencer
Two for the money and nothing shows. Sat Eve Post 240:22 Jl 15 '67

KLEE, Paul
Art world; exhibition at the Guggenheim museum. H. Rosenberg. New Yorker 43:179-80+ Mr 25 '67
From S.F. and L.A.; retrospective exhibit. B. F. Jones. America 116:841 Je 10 '67
Invisible made visible; Guggenheim museum show. A. Werner. il Reporter 36:46+ Mr 23 '67
Klee's world. Newsweek 69:79 Mr 6 '67
Paul Klee: a dissenting opinion. J. Perreault. il Art N 66:42-3+ My '67
Perverse child into master. J. Canaday. il N Y Times Mag p38-9 F 19 '67

KLEEMAN, J. D. and Lovering, J. F.
Uranium distribution in rocks by fission-track registration in Lexan plastic. bibliog Science 156:512-13 Ap 28 '67

KLEIN, Art. See Belvin, W. jt. auth.

KLEIN, David
College & careers. See issues of Seventeen
How much does your father's job affect you? Seventeen 26:130-1+ O '67
What makes freshman year so dangerous? Seventeen 26:158-9+ S '67
Where is the ivy greenest? Seventeen 26:152-3+ N '67
Which personality succeeds in college? Seventeen 26:148-9+ My '67
(ed) See Clough, B. M. Accepted or rejected?
(ed) See Jackson, R. L. Accepted or rejected?
(ed) See Vroman, C. Accepted or rejected?

KLEIN, Deanne Arkus
Still unique, Schmitz on Debussy's piano works. Am Rec G 33:855 My '67

KLEIN, Edmund
Apply-it-yourself salve for skin cancer. il por Life 62:87-8 Mr 3 '67

KLEIN, Herbert E.
Expanding world of membranes. Duns R 89:41+ Ja '67

KLEIN, Marcus
Books in the field: American fiction. por Wilson Lib Bul 42:467-76 Ja '68
Homilies of Horatio. Reporter 37:53-4 S 7 '67

KLEIN, Martin J.
Thermodynamics in Einstein's thought. bibliog Science 157:509-16 Ag 4 '67

KLEIN, Norma
Magic; story. Mlle 64:180-1 Ap '67

KLEIN, Oskar
Antimatter and cosmology. H. Alfvén. il Sci Am 216:106-12+ Ap '67

KLEIN, Stanley
Literature program of engineering societies. Science 155:1698-9 Mr 31 '67

KLEIN, William
CERN's human computer. D. A. Ehrlich. il por Sci N 93:72-3 Ja 20 '68

KLEIN, Woody
Beginnings of wisdom. Nation 205:112-15 Ag 14 '67
What's good for the cities. Reporter 37:43-4 D 28 '67

KLEIN, Yves
Art world; exhibition of all-blue paintings at Jewish museum. H. Rosenberg. New Yorker 43:99-100+ F 25 '67
Blue boy. J. Kroll. il pors Newsweek 69:105 F 6 '67
Blues for Yves Klein. L. Rivers. il por Art N 65:32-3+ F '67

KLEINER, Burt
When investing is like show biz. il pors Bsns W p96-7+ O 28 '67

KLEINER, Bell and company
When investing is like show biz; flamboyant approach to investment banking. il Bsns W p96-7+ O 28 '67

KLEIST, Lucille
Heartglow; poem. Farm J 91:113 Mr '67

KLEMPERER, Otto
Conductor Otto Klemperer; giant on the podium. H. C. Schonberg. il por House B 109:138-9+ Mr '67

KLEPPER, Max
New York to Lakewood in style; watercolors. Am Heritage 18:22-5 O '67

KLIGLER, David
Q's and A's about colic. Parents Mag 42:44-5+ My '67

KLINE, Franz Josef
Franz Kline: darkness visible. R. Goldwater. il por Art N 66:38-43+ Mr '67

KLING, Joseph W.
Books behind the bars. Library J 92:1424-5 Ap 1 '67

KLIVINGTON, Kenneth A. and Galambos, Robert
Resistance shifts accompanying the evoked cortical response in the cat. bibliog Science 157:211-13 Jl 14 '67

KLOCKO, Richard Phillp
U.S. air force; address, May 24, 1967. Vital Speeches 33:648-51 Ag 15 '67

KLOMAN, William
Can the forces of virtue defeat John Barleycorn? Sat Eve Post 240:85-9 Mr 11 '67
E. T. Hall and the human space bubble. Horizon 9:42-7 Aut '67
Just call us super group. Sat Eve Post 240: 36-41 Mr 25 '67
Meet Gloria Stavers. Sat Eve Post 240:80+ N 4 '67

KLONDIKE gold fields
Frozen El Dorado. J. Lotz. il Américas 19: 21-7 N '67
Lure of the Klondike. A. M. Lingg. il Opera N 31:6-7 My 13 '67
Off to the Klondike! excerpts from One man's gold rush; a Klondike album; with photographs by E. A. Hegg. M. Morgan. Am Heritage 18:34-49+ Ag '67

KLOPFER, F. D. See Schalock, R. L. jt. auth.

KLOPFER, Peter H.
Stimulus preferences and imprinting. bibliog Science 156:1394-6 Je 9 '67

about
Out of legal limbo. Time 89:58+ Mr 24 '67

KLOSSOWSKI, Balthus. See Balthus

KLOTZ, Irving M.
Protein subunits; a table. bibliog Science 155:697-8 F 10 '67

KLUTZNICK, Philip M.
Debate is over. Sat R 51:54+ Ja 13 '68

KNAP, Thaddeus L.
George Wallace maps his way to the White House. New Repub 156:7-9 Ap 29 '67

KNAPIK, Harold
Man talks turkey. E. Alston. il por Look 31: 98-9 Mr 7 '67

KNAPP, Sy
Clean the snow off the parking lots first. Am City 82:86-7 Ag '67

KNAPP, T. R.
Lighting gets more people in the swim. por Am City 82:130+ Je '67

KNAPP foundation
School library manpower project wins $1.1 million grant. Library J 93:249 Ja 15 '68

KNAPP school libraries project
Changing attitudes toward the library and the librarian; survey results from two high schools. J. L. Walker. il ALA Bul 61:977-81 S '67

KNEBEL, Fletcher
Whatever became of physical fitness? Look 31:94 Mr 7 '67

KNEE
Knee by any other name. S. Auerbach. il Atlan 220:123-4 O '67

KNEELAND, Douglas E.
Pigs are not a funny business. N Y Times Mag p30-1+ My 14 '67

KNEZEVICH, Stephen J.
Administrator and EDP. NEA J 56:18-19 F '67

KNICKERBOCKER, Suzy, pseud. See Mehle, A.

KNIGHT, Arthur
Bright spring, the bleak winter. Sat R 50:12-13 D 23 '67
Eucalyptic dream. Sat R 50:70-1+ S 23 '67
He raised Cain and Columbia. Sat R 50:30 Mr 18 '67
SR goes to the movies. See issues of Saturday review

KNIGHT, C. S.
Classical recordings at budget prices. Am Home 71:12+ Ja '68

KNIGHT, David M.
What happened at Catholic U. America 116: 723-5 My 13 '67

KNIGHT, Doug
Wilderness lake cutthroat. Field & S 71: 36-7+ Ap '67

KNIGHT, Douglas Maitland
Interview with Douglas M. Knight; ed. by K. Molz. por Wilson Lib Bul 42:56-64 S '67

KNIGHT, Elaine
Essenes; poem. Christian Cent 84:750 Je 7 '67

KNIGHT, Max
Authors & editors. Pub W 192:9-10 O 30 '67

KNIGHT, Pamela
Food. Sports Illus 27:80-3 O 16 '67

KNIGHT, Russell
Spoon sculpture. Design 68:20-2 Sum '67

KNIGHT in unshining armor; story. See Briskin, J.

KNIGHTS of labor
Southern Negro and the Knights of labor. I. M. Marcus. bibliog Negro Hist Bul 30: 5-7 Mr '67

KNITTING needles
Big stitch; one inch needles. il Time 90:74 O 13 '67

KNIVES
Anatomy of a knife. il House & Gard 132: 50+ S '67
Chef's knife. il House & Gard 132:39+ N '67
Electric knives. il Consumer Bul 51:15-19 Ja '68
Electric knives. il Consumer Rep 32:267-72 My '67
Multi-point, multi-purpose knife. Consumer Bul 50:40 O '67
Versatile scalloped-edge knife. il House & Gard 132:258+ O '67
Which knife? T. Trueblood. il Field & S 71: 20+ Mr '67

KNOEPFLE, John
Generation at the noonday; poem. Nation 204: 760 Je 12 '67

KNOKE, J. K. See Saunders, J. L. jt. auth.

KNOPF, Alfred A. incorporated
Three S&S vice-presidents to join Knopf in March. il Pub W 193:61 Ja 15 '68

KNORPP, C. T. and others
Hydroxyethyl starch: extracellular cryophylactic agent for erythrocytes. bibliog Science 157:1312-13 S 15 '67

KNOTS, Macramé. See Macramé

KNOTS and splices
Making fast. G. S. Smith. il Motor B 119:122 My '67
Safety-pin snell knot. R. C. Yahnke. il Outdoor Life 139:34 My '67
Short splice. G. S. Smith. il Motor B 120:38 D '67
There's a hitch to it. G. S. Smith. il Motor B 119:52 Je '67

KNOTT, Walter
Tory and old Whig fun. R. Kirk. Nat R 19:911 Ag 22 '67

KNOTT'S berry farm. See Amusement parks

KNOWLEDGE
Re: information; symposium. bibliog il Wilson Lib Bul 42:32-79 S '67
See also
Intellect
Intuition

KNOWLEDGE, Theory of
Cognitive capacity of very young children. J. Mehler and T. G. Bever. bibliog il Science 158:141-2 O 6 '67
It's the idea of the thing; address, December 5, 1966. L. W. Norris. bibliog f Vital Speeches 33:468-72 My '67
Why we don't really know. I. Asimov. Sci Digest 62:85-6 Ag '67
See also
Education—Philosophy

KNOWLES, Everett
Success story. il pors Newsweek 69:33-4 Je 12 '67

KNOWLES, Henry P. and Saxberg, B. O.
Human relations and the nature of man. bibliog f Harvard Bsns R 45:22-4+ Mr '67

KNOWLTON, Robert A.
Country of the heart; story. Good H 164:58-9 Ja '67
Man in the mirror; story. Ladies Home J 84:86-7 Ap '67
Second honeymoon; story. Good H 165:86-7 Jl '67
Sense of balance. Writer 80:17-19+ Ap '67

KNOWLTON, Robert A.—*Continued*
Two wishes for Christmas; story. Good H
165:86-7 D '67
Wrong way home; story. Redbook 129:82-3
Jl '67
KNOX, R. B.
Apomixis: seasonal and population differences in a grass. bibliog Science 157:325-6
Jl 21 '67
KNOX, Thomas Wallace
Generals and the news spy. T. L. Christie.
Sat R 50:60-1+ Jl 8 '67
KNUTSON, Bob
Instant record. por Outdoor Life 140:20-3+
Jl '67
KNUTSON, L. V. and others
Calcareous septa formed in snail shells by
larvae of snail-killing flies. bibliog Science
156:522-3 Ap 28 '67
KO, W. H. and Neuman, M. R.
Implant biotelemetry and microelectronics.
bibliog Science 156:351-60 Ap 21 '67
KOALAS
Children find koala ranges. Sci N 92:563 D 9
'67
KOBLER, John
Black pope. Sat Eve Post 240:30-4+ Mr 11
'67
—and Wyden, Peter
Real Svetlana Stalin story. Ladies Home J
84:59-63+ Ag '67
KOCH, Arthur L. See Ehrenfeld, D. W. jt.
auth.
KOCH, Herman William
Electron beams: National bureau of standards and the new technology. bibliog Science 156:321-8 Ap 21 '67
KOCH, Ilse
Best years of her life. il pors Newsweek
70:51 S 18 '67
KOCH, Kenneth
Poetry chronicle. T. Clark. Poetry 110:108-9
My '67
KOCH, Stephen
Performance without a net. Nation 204:524-6
Ap 24 '67
Surrealist Quixote. Nation 204:120-1 Ja 23
'67
KOCHI, Jay K.
Mechanisms of organic oxidation and reduction by metal complexes. bibliog Science
155:415-24 Ja 27 '67
KODA, Arthur J.
Mercury-wetted relays. por Electr World
77:56-7 Ap '67
KODACHROME films. See Photography—Films
KODAKS. See Cameras
KODÁLY, Zoltán
Apostle of the mother tongue. por Time 89:
70 Mr 17 '67
Obituary
Opera N por 31:30 Ap 15 '67
KOEHLER, Arthur
Wood wizard. il por Am For 73:28-30+ O '67
KOELLE, George B. See Nichols, C. W. jt.
auth.
KOELLE, Heinz Hermann
World unity urged on space programs. D. E.
Fink. Aviation W 87:21-2 O 2 '67
KOENIG, H. P.
Victorian New Jersey. Travel 128:42-5+ S '67
KOENIG, Louis W.
Consensus politics, 1800-1805. Am Heritage
18:4-7+ F '67
Junior senator from New York. Sat R 50:36
My 27 '67
KOERNER, James D.
EDC: general motors of curriculum reform.
Sat R 50:56-8+ Ag 19 '67
KOETHE, John
Process: Your day; poems. Poetry 110:28-9
Ap '67
KOFFMAN, D. M. See Van Schmus, W. R. jt.
auth.
KOGEN, J. H.
Measuring tracking ability of phono cartridges. Electr World 77:26-8+ Je '67
KOHAV, Hava
Hava Kohav and company, 92nd street Y. M.
Marks. Dance Mag 41:34-6 Mr '67
KOHEN, Charles
Sallie and Charles Kohen; donors deluxe. K.
V. Hostick. Hobbies 72:108-9+ My '67
KOHEN, Sallie
Sallie and Charles Kohen; donors deluxe. K.
V. Hostick. Hobbies 72:108-9+ My '67
KOHL, Douglas A.
Amateur scientist. Sci Am 216:135-6+ Je '67
KOHL, Herbert
How to get through. por Time 91:34+ Ja
19 '68

Requiem for the urban school. E. Z. Friedenberg. il Sat R 50:77-9+ N 18 '67
Thirty-six children. il por Newsweek 71:70
Ja 15 '68
KOHL, Schuyler G.
Is pregnancy the time to think about spacing
children? Redbook 130:29+ N '67
KOHLER, Foy David
Constructive initiatives in East-West relations; address, February 17, 1967. Dept
State Bul 56:406-13 Mr 13 '67
East-West relations; address, December 11,
1966. Vital Speeches 33:196-200 Ja 15 '67
KOHLERIAS
Grow a colorful kohleria. M. J. Kartuz. il
Horticulture 45:20-1 N '67
KOHN, Hans
E pluribus unum? Sat R 50:43 Je 10 '67
His chips are on the brainy. Sat R 50:28-9
Ap 29 '67
Spectacles of fanaticism. Sat R 50:30 D 16 '67
Three goals for Prussia. Sat R 50:28 Ag 19
'67
KOHNER, Susan
High cost of making the scene. J. Krantz.
il pors Ladies Home J 84:106-7+ S '67
KOK, Bessel, and Varner, J. E.
Extraterrestrial life detection based on
oxygen isotope exchange reactions. bibliog
Science 155:1110-12 Mr 3 '67
KOKANEE. See Salmon
KOLACHE. See Buns
KOLAR, O. See Ciembroniewicz, J. jt. auth.
KOLB, Allen
Idle millions. S. Pelletiere. Nation 205:401-3
O 23 '67
KOLB, Claudia
Remarkable Debbie and Claudia. il pors Life
63:66-7 S 1 '67
KOLB, Philip
Three friends of Proust. Vogue 149:186-91
Mr 15 '67
KOLKO, Gabriel
Universities and the Pentagon. Nation 205:
328-32 O 9 '67
Untangling the alliances. Nation 205:645-8 D
18 '67
KOLLIAS, Constantine
Comings and goings. Newsweek 71:36 Ja 22
'68
KOLODIN, Irving
Britten at Aldeburgh. Sat R 50:41-3 Jl 29 '67
Competitive, cooperative, and communal. Sat
R 50:40-1 S 23 '67
Genesis of the inexplicable. Sat R 50:62-3 Mr
25 '67
Man and his musical world at Expo 67. Sat R
50:61-2 Ap 29 '67
Music to my ears. See issues of Saturday
review
Myrenes and their friends. Sat R 50:74-5+ N
11 '67
Recordings in review. See issues of Saturday
review
Recordings reports: miscellaneous LPs. See
issues of Saturday review
Recordings reports: orchestral LPs See issues of Saturday review
Stereo evolution. Sat R 50:47+ Ag 26 '67
KOLTUN, Frances
Adventurous young Parisians. Mlle 65:151-4
Je '67
Intelligent woman traveler; excerpts from
Complete guide for the intelligent woman
traveler. Mlle 64:203-8 Mr '67
KOMAIKO, Jean R.
Children in crisis. Parents Mag 42:35-7+
F '67
KOMAN, Bill
Tell-tale heart. H. L. Masin. por Sr Schol
91:28 O 12 '67
KOMAREK, Vladimir Kazan-. See Kazan-Komarek, V.
KOMAROV, Vladimir
Correcting the fatal flaws. il por Newsweek
69:64-5+ My 8 '67
Death of a cosmonaut. por Time 89:45-6 My
5 '67
Shadow on Soviet moon race. Bsns W p42-3
Ap 29 '67
See also
Space flight—Manned flights—Komarov flight,
1967
KOMATSU, H. See Tolansky, S. jt. auth.
KOMEITO party. See Political parties—Japan
KOMER, Robert W.
Economic situation in Viet-Nam. Dept State
Bul 56:469-71 Mr 20 '67

KOMER, Robert W.—*Continued*
about
Quartet at the top. il por Time 89:14 Mr 24
'67
Vietnam: those computer reports. W. J.
Lederer. New Repub 157:13-14 D 23 '67
KOMODA, Kimio
Auspicious crane; interview, tr. by J. Kawai.
New Yorker 43:43-4 Mr 11 '67
KOMORNY, Annie
How to be very, very popular; poem. McCalls
94:118 S '67
KOMSOMOL. See Youth—Russia
KONDONELLIS, Evanthia
Invest in a fine garden. Am Home 70:78-9 Ja
'67
KONER, Pauline
Making cultural exchange a real exchange.
il pors Dance Mag 41:21-3 O '67
KONIGSBERG, Harold
Talk tactics. il Time 89:76+ Ap 21 '67
KONKETSUJI. See Illegitimacy
KONNER, Harold
One man's revolt. Newsweek 71:66 Ja 15 '68
KONTARSKY, Aloys
Contents of Kontarsky. O. Daniel. por Sat R
50:47+ D 30 '67
KONTOS, C. William
Books. Bul Atomic Sci 23:53-4 Je '67
KONVITZ, Milton R.
Civil liberties. bibliog f Ann Am Acad 371:
38-58 My '67
Power for the poor. Sat R 50:29-30 Jl 8 '67
Road sign for the Negro. Sat R 50:41-2
Ap 8 '67
KOOB, C. A. and Shaw, Russell
Planning for change. Cath World 206:23-6 O
'67
KOONTZ, Donald R.
Ice skating, Whitemarsh style. Parks &
Rec 2:27 Ja '67
KOOSER, Ted
Official entry form; poem. Reporter 37:42 D
28 '67
Rooming house; Gas station; poems. Reporter
36:40 My 4 '67
KOOTA, Aaron Edward
Case of the debatable Brooklyn D.A. T. J.
Fleming. il por N Y Times Mag p32-3+
Mr 19 '67
KOPAL, Z.
Lunar photography at Pic du Midi observatory. Sky & Tel 33:216-19 Ap '67
KOPKIND, Andrew
Future-planners. New Repub 156:19-23 F 25
'67
Meredith: the ambiguous heroes of Harlem:
Powell. Life 62:32-32A Mr 24 '67
Poverty politics in California. New Repub
156:19-20 F 18 '67
Reagan, ex-radical. New Repub 157:17-21 Jl
15 '67
—See Ridgeway, J. jt. auth.
KOPPEL, Ted
Wham! Nation 204:812-13 Je 26 '67
KOPPERS company
New philosophy at Koppers. R. Levy. Duns R
89:48-9+ Mr '67
KORALL, Burt
Garland phenomenon. Sat R 50:66 S 30 '67
Jazz orchestra. Sat R 50:116-17+ Mr 11 '67
King of the Savoy. Sat R 50:51+ D 30 '67
Lyric impulse. Sat R 50:58 D 2 '67
McRae, Maye, and Lee. Sat R 50:76-7 Ap 29
'67
Of times that are a-changin. Sat R 50:76-7
Ag 26 '67
Portrait of Buddy. Sat R 50:64-5 My 27 '67
Strayhorn and the Duke. Sat R 50:71-2 S
16 '67
Who is Roger Kellaway? Sat R 50:66-7 O 28
'67
KORDA, Michael V.
Cartier-Bresson today. Pop Phot 60:140-2 My
'67
KORDESCH, Karl V. See Evans, G. E. jt. auth.
KOREA
See also
Botany—Korea
United Nations—Korea
KOREA (People's Democratic Republic)
Case of frustration; provocations divert
thoughts from deepening economic troubles.
Time 89:23-4 Je 2 '67
Report on North Korean violations of DMZ
transmitted to U.N; letter. with text of
report. A. J. Goldberg. il Dept State Bul
57:692-4 N 20 '67
Why I fled from Communist North Korea;
interview. ed. by K. M. Chrysler. S. K.
Lee. il U S News 62:60-1 My 29 '67

Army
Creating a crisis; infiltration and ambush by
North Koreans. il Newsweek 69:45 F 27 '67
KOREA (Republic)
See also
Birth rate—Korea (Republic)
Children—Korea (Republic)
Economic assistance in Korea (Republic)
Elections—Korea (Republic)
Investments, Foreign (in Korea)
Music—Korea (Republic)
Public health—Korea (Republic)
Trials—Korea (Republic)

Army
Creating a crisis; infiltration and ambush by
North Koreans. il Newsweek 69:45 F 27 '67
Why Korean troops are so effective in Vietnam. U S News 63:10 O 2 '67

Commerce
See also
Korea (Republic)—Industries

Economic conditions
Growing girl's problems. Newsweek 70:34+
Jl 31 '67
Korea: tenacity pays off. E. Chapin. Reporter 37:25-6+ D 14 '67
Korea's comeback, what Humphrey found.
U S News 63:13 Jl 10 '67
See also
Korea (Republic)—Industries

Foreign relations
U.S. and Korea pledge continued friendship
and cooperation; exchange of greetings,
exchange of toasts, with joint statement,
March 14, 1967. I. K. Chung; L. B. Johnson. Dept State Bul 56:548-53 Ap 3 '67

Industries
B. C. Lee's world; Korea fertilizer co. il
Time 89:98 Ap 28 '67

Politics and government
Korea: tenacity pays off. E. Chapin. Reporter
37:25-6+ D 14 '67
On the eve of balloting in South Korea: why
the reelection of Park is practically certain. A. Axelbank. New Repub 156:9-11 Ap
29 '67

Religious institutions and affairs
World around us (cont) Christian Cent 84:
484-6, 796-8 Ap 12, Je 14 '67

Social conditions
Hope in the hermit kingdom. il Time 89:40-1
Mr 10 '67
KOREA, NORTHERN. See Korea (People's
Democratic Republic)
KOREA and the United States
See also
Korean war, 1950-1953—American participation
KOREAN poetry
From the East. R. E. Teele. Poetry 109:
273-4 Ja '67
KOREAN pottery. See Pottery, Korean
KOREAN war, 1950-1953
Korean war, by M. B. Ridgway. Review
Sat R 50:43 N 4 '67. J. M. Allison

American participation
Mr Katzenbach's puzzle. C. Ogburn, jr. New
Repub 157:13-14 N 4 '67; Reply with rejoinder. C. T. McGuire. 157:15-18 D 2 '67
Reflections; difference between Vietnam and
Korea. R. H. Rovere. New Yorker 43:60-4+
O 28 '67

Chinese participation
Danger of miscalculation: when did China
decide to enter the Korean war? J. Osborne. New Repub 156:3-4 Je 3 '67; Reply
with rejoinder. P. H. Tannenbaum. 156:32+
Je 24 '67

Personal narratives
Korean war, by M. B. Ridgway. Review
Life 63:12 N 17 '67. H. Moffett

Strategy
Korean war, by M. B. Ridgway. Review
Newsweek il 70:112+ N 20 '67. S. Maloff

War correspondents
Mouthpiece for reds: the strange role of Wilfred Burchett. il U S News 62:19-20 F 27
'67

KOREANS
Hemoglobin variants in Koreans: hemoglobin G Taegu. R. Q. Blackwell and others. bibliog Science 158:1056-7 N 24 '67
KOREY, William
Global ombudsman. Sat R 50:20 Ag 12 '67
Human rights treaties: why is the U.S. stalling? For Affairs 45:414-24 Ap '67
KORMENDI, Ferenc
Walk with Gerhart Hauptmann. Reporter 37: 47-50 N 2 '67
KORN, Pearl
Offbeat Corsica. il U S Camera 30:58-9+ S '67
Rain, don't let it stop you. U S Camera 30:44-5+ Mr '67
KORN, Peter Jona
Diary of a young man of fashion. Hi Fi 17: 60-3 S '67
KORNBERG, Arthur
Lab creates life in a test tube. il por Bsns W p58 D 23 '67
Synthesis of DNA: how they spread the good news. D. S. Greenberg. il por Science 158: 1548-50 D 22 '67
Viable synthetic DNA; with editorial comment. il Sci N 92:629-30 D 30 '67
KORNFELD, Rosemary
Impressions from a Caribbean tour. Sch Arts 67:29 N '67
KORR, I. M. and others
Axonal delivery of neuroplasmic components to muscle cells. bibliog Science 155:342-5 Ja 20 '67
KORSAKOV, Nikolai Andreevich Rimskii-. See Rimskii-Korsakov, N. A.
KÖRTE, Sister Mary Norbert
At very early dawn on the first day of the week; poem. America 116:378 Mr 18 '67
Reason; poem. America 117:765 D 23 '67
KORTENDICK, James J.
Continuing education and library administration; address, January 11, 1967. por ALA Bul 61:268-72 Mr '67
KORTKAMP, Richard, and O'Keefe, Patricia
Family pet. Am Home 70:56 My '67
KORVETTE, E. J. incorporated
Discounter on 34th street. il Time 90:94+ N 10 '67
KOSAMBI, D. D.
Living prehistory in India; with biographical sketch. Sci Am 216:22, 104-12+ F '67
KOSKIMIES, O. See Rapola, J. jt. auth.
KOSMOVSKA, Irina
I go to the studio and try out my dreams. V. H. Swisher. il pors Dance Mag 42:64-7 Ja '68
KOSTELANETZ, Richard
Glenn Gould variations. Esquire 68:142-5+ N '67
New sound for a plugged-in age. Look 32:45 Ja 9 '68
Understanding McLuhan (in part) N Y Times Mag p 18-19+ Ja 29 '67
KOSTROWISKY, Guillaume Apollinaire de. See Apollinaire, G. pseud.
KOSYGIN, Aleksei Nikolaevich
Argument indeed: Soviet attack, Israeli retort; excerpt from address. por Life 62: 24 Je 30 '67
Middle East crisis; address, June 19, 1967. Vital Speeches 33:581-6 Jl 15 '67
President Johnson and Premier Kosygin discuss international problems; statements, June 23, 25, 1967. Dept State Bul 57:36-8 Jl 10 '67

about

Aleksei Kosygin: the compleat apparatchik. il por Time 89:13 Je 30 '67
Chief aim of Kosygin's British trip. il por U S News 62:22 F 20 '67
Communist at Claridge's. il pors Newsweek 69:48-9 F 20 '67
Decision-making in the Kremlin. F. B. Stevens. il por U S News 63:24-5 Jl 10 '67
Foreign policy: a study in contrasts. Bsns W p 182 Je 24 '67
Kosygin in Britain: the peace almost within our grasp. por Life 62:32-32A F 24 '67
Kosygin in Paris; differences within amity. A. Werth; reply with rejoinder. P. Baum. Nation 204:162+ F 6 '67
Kosygin's aim at U.N: victory in a propaganda carnival. il por U S News 62:6 Je 26 '67
Over the hot line, the Middle East. H. Sidey. Life 62:24B Je 16 '67
Unsmiling comrade. il por Time 89:28 F 17 '67

See also
Glassboro conference. 1967

KOSZUL, Julien Pierre
Another money problem: vanishing gold; address, October 17, 1967. por U S News 63: 46-8 D 4 '67
Reserve currencies; address, April 14, 1967. Vital Speeches 33:682-4 S 1 '67

KOTKER, Norman
Literary road to Rome. Horizon 9:16-31 Sum '67
Return to Jerusalem. Reporter 37:29-30+ Jl 13 '67
KOTLER, Neil G.
Ethiopia: the over-present Americans. Nation 204:236-9 F 20 '67
KOTLER, Philip
Operations research in marketing. bibliog f Harvard Bsns R 45:30-4+ Ja '67
KOTLOWITZ, Robert
Performing arts. See issues of Harper's magazine
KOTSONIS, Jerome. See Ieronymos, abp
KOTZ, Nick
Meat inspection: the new jungle. Nation 205:230-3 S 18 '67

about
Jungle revisited. Nation 206:2 Ja 1 '68

KOUFAX, Sandy
Great holdout. B. Bavasi and J. Olsen. il por Sports Illus 26:78-82+ My 15 '67
Koufax the incomparable. M. Richler; discussion. Commentary 43:43-6+ F '67
KOUNS, William C.
Playground equipment. Parks & Rec 2:20 My '67
KOUNTZ, John C.
Charting a course in charaymak: a didactic tale with overtones. ALA Bul 61:396-408 Ap '67
KOUSSEVITZKY, Serge
Koussevitzky returns, and the lesson is of passion lavishly spent. L. Marcus. por Hi Fi 17:79-80 F '67
Last years of Serge Koussevitzky. R. Sabin. por Am Rec G 34:22-3 S '67
KOVÁC, L. and others
Biochemical genetics of oxidative phosphorylation. bibliog Science 158:1564-7 D 22 '67
KOVACH, Bill
Some lessons of reapportionment. Reporter 37:26+ S 21 '67
—and Caldwell, Nat
Atom's challenge to the coal industry. Reporter 36:39-41 F 23 '67
KOVACH, Joseph K.
Maternal behavior in the domestic cock under the influence of alcohol. bibliog Science 156: 835-7 My 12 '67
KOVACH, Robert L. See Breiner, S. jt. auth.
KOVAL, Patricia
Women in a contraceptive culture. Commonweal 87:381-2 D 22 '67
KOVALEVSKY, J.
Great French astronomer. Sky & Tel 33:347-9 Je '67
KOVEN, Stanley
Seville; poem. New Yorker 43:46 My 13 '67
KOVNER, Milton
Soviet aid and trade. bibliog f Cur Hist 53: 217-23+ O '67
KOWALSKI, Julius M. See Czura, P. jt. auth.
KOZIARA, Karen Shallcross
Agricultural minimum wage: a preliminary look. bibliog f Mo Labor R 90:26-9 S '67
KOZINTSEV, Grigorii Mikhailovich
New film-makers. Sat R 50:15+ D 23 '67
KOZLICK, Joseph C.
Favorite harbors of the Caribbean. il Motor B 121:97-101+ Ja '68
Leisurely cruise around St John. Motor B 120: 38-9+ O '67
KOZLOFF, Max
Art. See issues of Nation
Collage of indignation. Nation 204:248-51 F 20 '67
Photography. Nation 204:571-3 My 1 '67
Sickert's unsentimental journey. Art N 66: 50-3+ Ap '67
KOZOL, Jonathan
Death at an early age; excerpts. Atlan 220: 49-55, 107-10 S, O '67
Department of lower learning. New Repub 156:33-5 My 20 '67
How to keep your mouth shut. New Repub 157:32+ S 30 '67
Junior high that's like a college. N Y Times Mag p32-3+ O 29 '67
Pioneer book about children. Life 63:12 D 15 '67

About
Children are dying. J. R. Lowe. McCalls 95: 4-5 Ja '68
Instant expert. il por Time 90:56 N 10 '67
Requiem for the urban school. E. Z. Friedenberg. il Sat R 50:77-9+ N 18 '67
Spokesmen for the Blacks. J. Meyer. Nation 205:598-9 D 4 '67
Whipping boys. il por Newsweek 70:94 O 16 '67

KRAFT, Ivor
Classroom struggle. Nation 205:54-7 Jl 17 '67
Retreat to separate but equal. Nation 205:
552-5 N 27 '67
KRAFT, R. Wayne
Controlled   eutectics;   with   biographical
sketch. Sci Am 216:22, 86-92 bibliog (p
146+) F '67
KRAFT, Virginia
Belle of the mushers. pors Sports Illus 26:54-
63 Ja 23 '67
Dogs. Sports Illus 27:49-50+ Ag 7 '67
Fishing. Sports Illus 27:53-4+ D 18 '67
Hunting. Sports Illus 26:41-2+ Ja 30; 60+ Je
5: 27:58-62 N 6 '67
KRAG, Jens Otto
European leaders meet with President John-
son; exchange of toasts, June 22, 1967.
Dept State Bul 57:41 Jl 10 '67
KRAM, Mark
Boxing   (cont)   Sports   Illus   26:44-6   F   6;
44+ Mr 6; 71-2 Mr 20; 77-9 Ap 10; 27:48-50
Jl 10 '67
KRAMARICH, Irene
Obituary
Opera N 32:28 S 23 '67
KRAMER, Arthur
Kramer's korner. por Mod Phot 31:52+ N:
151-2 D '67; 32:62-3 Ja '68
KRAMER, Henry H. See Wahl, W. H. jt. auth.
KRAMER, Hilton
Impressionist eye. N Y Times Mag p28-31 Ja
7 '68
Young Picasso. New Repub 157:32+ O 21 '67
KRAMER, Jack
How and where to buy orchids. Horticulture
45:46-7+ Mr '67
How to grow orchids for all-season bloom. il
Home Gard 54:42-5 D '67
KRAMER, Karl
Loudspeakers for electronic musical instru-
ments. Electr World 77:32 Je '67
KRAMER, Matt, and Sheppard, Roger
Smoke cooking; excerpts from Smoke cook-
ing. Ladies Home J 84:90-1+ Jl '67
KRAMER, Rita
Parent and child (cont) N Y Times Mag
p 107+ Ap 9; 65-6+ Je 11; 80+ S 17; 87+
N 5; 109-10+ N 26 '67
KRAMER, Robert L. and Livingston, W. P.
Cashing in on the checkless society. bib-
liog f Harvard Bsns R 45:141-9 S '67
KRAMER, Sam
Gems in a hurry. il Design 69:28-30 Wint '67
KRAMER, Stanley
He could wither you with a glance. pors Life
62:69-70+ Je 30 '67
KRANCE, John
New sounds of brass. woodwind, and percus-
sion. House B 109:46+ Ap '67
KRANE, Stephen M. and others
Collagen-like fragments: excretion in urine of
patients with Paget's disease of bone. bib-
liog Science 157:713-16 Ag 11 '67
KRANNERT, Herman C.
Experience; address, July 27, 1967. Vital
Speeches 33:651-4 Ag 15 '67
KRANTZ, Judith
High cost of making the scene. Ladies Home
J 84:106-7+ S '67
KRANTZ, Ray
Kakki M. Yachting 123:116+ Ja '68
KRASLOW, David
Coplon case dismissed. New Repub 156:10-11
F 18 '67
Four years after the Kennedy assassination:
could it happen again? Pop Sci 191:70-3+
N '67
KRAUS, Alfredo
Man from the Islands; interview, ed. by F.
Stevenson. il por Opera N 31:15 Ja 28 '67
KRAUS, Arthur James Israel
Is there a statute of limitations on justice?
J. Chamberlain. Nat R 19:1257-8 N 14 '67
KRAUS, Bertram S. and Oka, S. W.
Wrinkling of molar crowns: new evidence.
bibliog Science 157:328-9 Jl 21 '67
KRAUS, Hans
Don't let tension push you around. C.
Mitchell. il Pop Sci 191:79-82+ O '67
KRAUS, Henry
Cathedrals as living drama. il Time 90:88+
N 17 '67
KRAUS, Joseph H.
Obituary
Sci N por 92:148 Ag 12 '67
KRAUS, Lili
And we quote; ed. by S. Fleming. por Hi Fi
17:MA21 Mr '67
KRAUS, Michael
He pleaded the Quaker cause. Sat R 50:48
Je 10 '67
KRAUS periodicals, incorporated
Postmark, Liechtenstein. il Pub W 191:49 F
13 '67

KRAUS reprint corporation
Postmark, Liechtenstein. il Pub W 191:49 F
13 '67
KRAUSE, Tom
Finn for Figaro; interview, ed. by S. Jen-
kins. jr. por Opera N 32:18 D 9 '67
KRAUSZ, N. G. P.
Nine questions to ask before you make a will;
with answers. Farm J 91:92-3 Mr '67
KRAVITZ, Herbert
Discovery. J. Scully. il Mod Phot 32:78-9+
Ja '68
KRAWETZ, Michael
Cameras and combat. U S Camera 30:68+
Jl '67
KREBBS, Margaret
Paintings of Mildred Lapson Stevens. il Am
Artist 31:44-9+ S '67
KREBS, A. V. jr
Deciding careers with the club of induction.
Commonweal 86:468-9 Jl 28 '67
Love in California. Commonweal 86:359-61 Je
16 '67
National war park. Commonweal 87:161 N 10
'67
Paulists depart, but tensions linger in Dallas.
Commonweal 87:68-9 O 20 '67
KREDEL, Fritz
Kredel: renaissance man among illustrators.
P. Standard. il Pub W 192:68-9+ S 4 '67
KREFETZ, Gerald, and Marossi, Ruth
Shrewdest man in the money market; ex-
cerpt from The money managers. Harper
235:43-7 Jl '67
KREH, William
Most dangerous job in Vietnam. Pop Mech
127:81-3+ My '67
What causes those giant killer waves. Pop
Mech 129:98-101+ Ja '68
KREIMER, Evered. See Mallas, J. H. jt. auth.
KREIMER-BIRNBAUM, Martha, and Banner-
man, R. M.
Heme and globin synthesis control: observa-
tions in vivo in beta thalassemia. bibliog
Science 155:1116-18; 157:1079 Mr 3, S 1 '67
KREINHEDER, Arthur Carl
Only Lutheran monk. il por Newsweek 70:84-
5 D 4 '67
KREITLOW, Burton W.
Reorganization really makes a difference. NEA
J 56:44-5 My '67
KREMEN, Bennett
East Harlem. Nation 205:107+ Ag 14 '67
Playing it by ear. Nation 204:378-9 Mr 20 '67
KRENOV, James
Wood: the friendly mystery. Craft Horiz 27:
28-9+ Mr '67
KRESH, Paul
Timely histories for the holidays. Sat R 50:
28-9 D 2 '67
KRETTEK, Germaine, and Cooke, E. D.
ALA Washington notes. See issues of Wilson
library bulletin
Washington report: from the ALA Washing-
ton office. See issues of ALA bulletin
KRETZ, Thomas
Café au lait; poem. Christian Cent 84:174 F
8 '67
Determination; poem. Christian Cent 84:167
F 8 '67
Time of flesh; poem. Christian Cent 84:1284
O 11 '67
KREUGER, Miles
Collector, insatiable lusts. Am Rec G 33:536-
7 F '67
Gorgeous contrast. Am Rec G 33:612-13 Mr
'67
In the limelight. See issues of American record
guide
KREY, P. W.
Atmospheric burnup of a plutonium-238 gen-
erator. bibliog Science 158:769-71 N 10 '67
KRICK, Irving P.
Good summer rains for the Midwest. Farm
J 91:22 Ap '67
KRICK, Irving P, associates. See Irving P.
Krick associates
KRIEGE, Dorothy T. and Krieger, H. P.
Circadian pattern of plasma 17-hydroxycorti-
costeroid: alteration   by   anticholinergic
agents. bibliog Science 155:1421-2 Mr 17 '67
KRIEGEL, Annie
Blum phenomenon. Commentary 44:108-12 N
'67
KRIEGEL, Leonard
Art and the book reviewer. Nation 204:732-3
Je 5 '67
Education up a tree: the plight of City col-
lege. Commonweal 87:137-8 N 3 '67
KRIEGER, Howard P. See Krieger, D. T. jt.
auth.
KRIEGSMAN, Alan M.
Fact and fantasy. Reporter 36:47-8 Je 15 '67
KRIENDLER, Irving Robert
Book collecting, anyone? J. T. Winterich. por
Sat R 50:129-30+ Mr 11 '67

KUNISHI, Alice T. See Lieberman, M. jt. auth.

KUNITZ, Stanley
Other country inside Russia. por N Y Times Mag p24-5+ Ag 20 '67
(tr) See Akhmatova, A. Reading Hamlet; July 1914; Heart's memory of sun
(tr) See Voznesenskii, A. Call of the lake
(tr) See Voznesenskii, A. To Bela Akhmadulina; Lament for two unborn poems; Self-portrait; Note to E. Yanitskaya, formerly typist to Mayakovsky; Lieutenant Zagorin

KUNKEL, Betty
For husbands only. Farm J 91:66F Mr '67

KUPFERBERG, Herbert
Conducted tour of conductors. Life 63:24 S 15 '67
Music: record reviews. See issues of Atlantic

KUPFERMAN, Theodore Roosevelt
When Uncle Sam takes his bite. Sat R 50: 38 Mr 4 '67

KURALT, Charles
Into the heartland. il por Newsweek 71:54 Ja 1 '68
Travels with Charley. il por Time 91:44+ Ja 19 '68

KURCHATOV, Igor' Vasil'evich
Igor Kurchatov, 1903-1960. E. Rabinowitch; A. P. Alexandrov; I. Golovin. por Bul Atomic Sci 23:8-18 D '67

KURENKO, Maria
Historical records. A. Favia-Artsay. il por Hobbies 72:35 Jl '67
Records:
Maria Kurenko. Opera N 31:34 My 13 '67

KURILIK, Norman A.
Memory; poem. New Repub 157:24 S 30 '67

KURKA, Robert
Music to my ears; concert performance of the Good soldier Schweik by the Chamber symphony of Philadelphia. I. Kolodin. Sat R 50:38 D 16 '67
Report: New York. J. W. Freeman. Opera N 32:31 D 30 '67

KURTZ, Madalynne R.
Night of the full moon; story. Sat Eve Post 240:54-6 Jl 1 '67

KURTZ, Russell E.
Maintenance tips for harried park officials. Am City 82:98-9 My '67

KURU. See Nervous system—Diseases

KUSANO, K. and others
Tetraethylammonium ions: effect of pre-synaptic injection on synaptic transmission. bibliog Science 155:1257-9 Mr 10 '67

KUSNER, Kathy
She has a passion. por Newsweek 70:59+ D 4 '67

KUSS, Henry J. 1922?-
Arms trafficker. New Repub 156:4 F 25 '67

KUST, Leonard E.
Way out of the tax thicket? Nations Bsns 55:82-4 F '67

KUTLER, Stanley I.
Ex parte McCarle: judicial impotency? the Supreme court and Reconstruction reconsidered. bibliog f Am Hist R 72:835-51 Ap '67

KUTSUZAWA, Asaji
Last hope of an ancient tradition; photographs by T. Tanuma; with account by J. Schecter. pors Sports Illus 26:48-53 Mr 20 '67

KUWAIT
Desert democracy. Time 89:33 F 3 '67
One shoe off; effects of Israeli-Arab war M. J. Kubic. il Newsweek 70:30 Ag 21 '67
Political trends in Iraq and Kuwait. M. Khadduri. Cur Hist 52:84-9+ F '67

KUZNETSOV, Anatolii
Destruction of differences. T. S. Szasz. New Repub 156:21-3 Je 10 '67
Russian record of Nazi terror. M. Kalb. Sat R 50:37+ Mr 11 '67

KWARTIN, Paul
Art of the cantor. Sat R 50:91 F 25 '67

KY, Nguyen-cao-. See Nguyen-cao-Ky

KYANITE
Electron microprobe and optical absorption study of colored kyanites. E. W. White and W. B. White. bibliog il Science 158: 915-17 N 17 '67

KYLE, Jim
Communicating with computers. Electr World 77:50-2+ F '67

KYLE, Keith
Plot and counter-plot. New Repub 157:13-16 S 16 '67

KYLSTRA, J. A. and others
Hydraulic compression of mice to 166 atmospheres. bibliog Science 158:793-4 N 10 '67

KYODAN. See United church of Christ in Japan

KYOTO, Japan
Everything's better in Kyoto. G. Caskill. il Read Digest 92:166-70+ Ja '68

KYUSHU, Japan
Kyushu. S. Clark. il Travel 127:46-9+ Je '67

L

LAFTA. See Latin American free trade association

LAPL. See Los Angeles public library

LC (Library of Congress) headings. See Subject headings

LCDC. See Lawyers constitutional defense committee

LNG (liquefied natural gas) See Gas, Natural —Liquefaction

LORAS (low-range airspeed system) See Aeronautic instruments

LSA (limited space charge accumulation) diodes. See Diodes

LSCA (Library services and construction act) See Library laws and legislation

LSD. See Lysergic acid diethylamide

LTV. See Ling-Temco-Vought, incorporated

LABARGE, L.
Confetti coating for countertops and floors. Pop Mech 129:168-70 Ja '68

LABELS
Biohazards symbol: development of a biological hazards warning signal. C. L. Baldwin and R. S. Runkle. il Science 158:264-5 O 13 '67; Reply. W. Schiff. 158:1398 D 15 '67
Candy-labeled candleholder caper; Vogels edible candy cake decorations. Consumer Rep 33:7-8 Ja '68
Look for that label! Textile fiber products identification act. Consumer Bul 50:27 S '67
Looking glasses and labels. E. Gaines. il Antiques 92:563-5 O '67
Prominently and conspicuously labeled? il Consumer Bul 51:8 Ja '68
Step right up and guess the weight of the turkey: U.S. Department of agriculture style, that is! il Consumer Bul 51:33-4 Ja '68

Law
See Packaging—Laws and regulations

LABER, Jeri L.
Svetlana era. Commonweal 86:390-2 Je 23 '67

LABOR (obstetrics) See Childbirth

LABOR, Department of. See United States— Labor, Department of

LABOR, Farm. See Farm labor

LABOR, Migrant. See Migrant labor

LABOR, Skilled. See Skilled labor

LABOR absenteeism. See Absenteeism

LABOR and laboring classes
Foreign labor briefs. See issues of Monthly labor review
Labor standards and job training in foreign countries. H. Hilaski. Mo Labor R 90:36-41 S '67
See also
Apprentices
Farm labor
Industrial relations
Right to labor
Trade unions

Bibliography
Book reviews and notes. See issues of Monthly labor review

Education
Education and manpower. H. J. Noah and R. Blandy. il Wilson Lib Bul 41:814-19 Ap '67
Educational attainment of workers, March 1966. H. R. Hamel. il Mo Labor R 90:39-47 Je '67
Full employment and workers' education. E. Hardin il Mo Labor R 90:21-5 My '67
Private industry's factory classrooms. R. Gustaitis. il Reporter 37:23-4 S 7 '67

Non-wage payments
See Non-wage payments

Statistics
Current labor statistics. See issues of Monthly labor review

LABOR and laboring classes—*Continued*

Canada
See also
Labor laws and legislation—Canada
Strikes—Canada
Trade unions—Canada
Wages—Canada

Europe, Eastern
Nonworkers of the world, unite! Time 89:28
Je 2 '67

Europe, Western
Is Europe's low-cost labor really a myth? il
Bsns W p88+ Mr 11 '67

Florida
And magnolia. D. Y. Meader. New Yorker
43:40-7 Ap 8 '67

France
See also
Strikes—France
Trade unions—France
Wages—France

Great Britain
British idea: work without pay. U S News
64:80 Ja 15 '68
Instant heroines; Back Britain movement.
il Time 91:20 Ja 12 '68
Typists' rebellion; I'm backing Britain cam-
paign. il Newsweek 71:67-8 Ja 15 '68
What's the matter with Britain? G. Gorer. il
N Y Times Mag p 10-11+ D 31 '67; Reply.
R. Beardwood. p 12 Ja 14 '68
See also
Immigration and emigration—Great Britain
Labor party (Great Britain)
Strikes—Great Britain
Trade unions—Great Britain

Japan
See also
Trade unions—Japan
Wages—Japan

Latin America
See also
Trade unions—Latin America

New York (state)
See also
Labor laws and legislation—New York (state)

Russia
Domestic crisis; shortage of maids in Rus-
sia. Newsweek 70:57 N 27 '67
New five-day workweek in the Soviet Union.
E. Nash. bibliog Mo Labor R 90:18-19 Ag
'67
Western influences. on the U.S.S.R.'s new in-
centives system. E. Nash. bibliog f Mo
Labor R 90:37-40 Ap '67

South Africa
Colour makes the job; excerpts from Unesco
report on apartheid. il UNESCO Courier
20:18-19 Mr '67

Spain
See also
Trade unions—Spain

Sweden
How Sweden keeps them working. il Bsns W
p 100-2 Jl 15 '67

United States
Chronology of recent labor events. See issues
of Monthly labor review
Labor month in review. See issues of Month-
ly labor review
Labor's ominous week. il Newsweek 70:59-60
Jl 24 '67
Labor's stake in the Kennedy round; ad-
dress, July 7, 1967. J. J. Reynolds. Dept
State Bul 57:137-40 Jl 31 '67
Special labor force report. See issues of
Monthly labor review
Strikes by public employees. A. H. Raskin.
Atlan 221:46-51 Ja '68
See also
American federation of labor and Congress
of industrial organizations
Arbitration, Industrial—United States
Industrial workers of the world
Labor laws and legislation—United States
Labor supply—United States
Migrant labor
Negroes in the United States—Economic
conditions
Negroes in the United States—Employment
Poor—United States
Strikes—United States

Trade unions—United States
Unemployment—United States
United States—Labor, Department of
Wages—United States
   also subhead Labor and laboring classes
under names of cities, e.g. New York (city)
—Labor and laboring classes

Political activities
See Trade unions—Political activities

Vietnam (Republic)
Vietnamese labor force in transition. M. B.
Zuzik. Mo Labor R 90:32-5 N '67

LABOR boards
See also
United States—National labor relations board

LABOR camps
Oak Glen, a training camp for youth. J. R.
Chapman. Mo Labor R 90:27-30 Ja '67

LABOR conferences
See also
International labor organization

LABOR cost
Is Europe's low-cost labor really a myth? il
Bsns W p88+ Mr 11 '61
Productivity in manufacturing. M. Ziegler.
il Mo Labor R 90:1-5 O '67
Recent developments in productivity and unit
labor costs. J. A. Mark and M. Ziegler. il
Mo Labor R 90:26-9 My '67

LABOR courts
Better way to handle strikes. S. I. Rosenman. Read Digest 91:106-10 O '67

LABOR discipline
Dismissal for off-the-job criminal behavior.
J. W. Leonard. bibliog f Mo Labor R 90:
21-6 N '67
How garnisheed workers fare under arbitration. R. W. Fisher. bibliog f Mo Labor R
90:1-6 My '67

LABOR displacement. See Unemployment,
Technological

LABOR disputes
As strike crisis grows: new talk of controlling
unions. il U S News 62:72-3 My 8 '67
Mediation in civil rights disputes. J. T.
Barrett. Mo Labor R 90:44-6 Jl '67
Report of the special railroad board; issued
September 15, 1967. Mo Labor R 90:43-6 N
'67
Unions mass for copper showdown; rubber
walkout is stalemated. Bsns W p 156+ My
20 '67
See also
Grievance procedures
Strikes
United States—Federal mediation and con-
ciliation service
United States—National labor relations board

LABOR ethics
Trade winds; unyielding bargaining table ap-
proach of a Bertram Powers. H. R. Mayes.
Sat R 50:11-12 My 27 '67

LABOR in politics. See Trade unions—Political
activities

LABOR laws and legislation
Any real answer to big strikes? il U S News
62:39-41 Ap 24 '67
See also
Labor courts
Lockouts

Canada
Canada turns to laws to end strikes. U S
News 63:88 N 6 '67

New York (state)
Antistrike law: upheld, but-. U S News 63:
67 D 25 '67
Can new state law end public worker strikes?
Condon-Wadlin act replaced with heavy
fines on organizations. il Bsns W p98 Ap 8
'67
Enforcing one injunction, at least; ruling
against UFT. il Time 90:58 O 13 '67
Substitute for Condon-Wadlin. America 116:
547-8 Ap 15 '67

Sweden
See also
Sweden—Labor policy

United States
Antistrike legislation. H. C. Wallich. News-
week 70:71 Jl 31 '67
As strike crisis grows: new talk of controlling
unions; proposals for a permanent ban on
crippling work stoppages. il U S News 62:
72-3 My 8 '67
As strike crises pile up for LBJ: new push
for new law. U S News 62:97 Ap 17 '67
Avco strike heats up pressure for a law. il
Bsns W p 114 Jl 1 '67
Bargaining's bite hits small business; unions
pressing hard at all levels. Bsns W p 154+
My 6 '67

LABOR laws and legislation—United States—
Continued
Better way to handle strikes. S. I. Rosenman. Read Digest 91:106-10 O '67
Can the unions block LBJ's plan to prevent a railroad strike? U S News 62:114 My 15 '67
Critique of cost-benefit analyses of training; excerpt from Training the poor. D. O. Sewell. bibliog f Mo Labor R 90:45-51 S '67
Development of labor law in 1966. G. C. Smith. Mo Labor R 90:12-17 F '67
Euphemism of postponement; new anti-strike plan insufficient. Time 89:19 My 12 '67
Extent of coverage under FLSA as amended in 1966. E. C. Martin. il Mo Labor R 90:21-4 Ap '67
Frustrating bargaining laws. Life 62:4 My 19 '67
How labor laws could be reformed. W. Wingo. il Nations Bsns 55:104+ O '67
How to avoid strikes that hurt the Nation. Bsns W p200 Ap 22 '67
Ineffective injunctions; public employees' strikes. il Time 90:77 S 29 '67
Ingenious answers to crisis strikes. B. L. Masse. America 116:749 My 20 '67
It's definite now: no permanent law to stop big strikes. U S News 63:66-8 Jl 31 '67
Justice too long deferred. B. L. Masse. America 117:238 S 9 '67
Labor crisis. T. J. Murray. il Duns R 89:42-4+ Je '67
Labor's middle-class revolt. A. H. Raskin. il Reporter 36:24-7 Je 15 '67
More strikes, more inflation: collision course on the labor front. A. H. Raskin. Sat R 50:32-5+ F 25 '67
Railroad peace plan. Sr Schol 90:26-7 My 19 '67
Right to want; Oil, chemical and atomic workers research department's right to work study findings. Nation 205:132 Ag 28 '67
Significant decisions in labor cases. See issues of Monthly labor review
Strike law may go broad image; impasse on anti-strike legislation. Bsns W p 148+ Je 24 '67
Strikes force the issue in Congress; tough, wide-ranging legislation against strikes. il Bsns W p44+ Ap 29 '67
Tough test for labor; congressional pressure for laws to curb transportation tie-ups. il Bsns W p33-5 Ap 15 '67
When the president steps in. il Bsns W p 122-4 Je 17 '67
Where unions are getting help from the courts. il U S News 62:76-7 Je 26 '67
Why the House rejected LBJ's plan to head off rail strike. U S News 62:77 Je 26 '67
Why union affection for Johnson has cooled; but AFL-CIO leaders trying to avoid a break. Bsns W p 142+ My 27 '67
Worry over strikes. B. L. Masse. America 116:207, 276 F 11. 25 '67
See also
Arbitration, Industrial—United States
Boycott
Minimum wage—United States

Taft-Hartley law
After twenty years of Taft-Hartley. U S News 63:72 S 4 '67
Labor and the law. Sr Schol 90:7 Ap 7 '67
Situs picketing nears a showdown; trades unions pushing hard for bipartisan backing of Taft-Hartley amendment. Bsns W p 158 Ap 15 '67
Testing Taft-Hartley anew. Bsns W p86 Mr 11 '67
LABOR lawyers. See Lawyers
LABOR leaders. See Trade unions—Officials
LABOR-management relations. See Industrial relations
LABOR market. See Labor supply
LABOR mobility. See Occupational mobility
LABOR officials. See Trade unions—Officials
LABOR output. See Labor productivity
LABOR party (Great Britain)
Bitter aftertaste; squabbling within the party. il Time 90:18 D 29 '67
Clobbering of Harold Wilson. P. Crane. America 116:683 My 6 '67
Craving for substance. Newsweek 69:46-7 Ap 3 '67
Devaluing the pound, and labour. G. Bailey. Reporter 37:20-2 D 14 '67
From defeat to disaster. T. J. Spinner, jr. Nation 204:588-9 My 8 '67
I am what I am; annual convention. il Newsweek 70:46+ O 16 '67
Letter from London. M. Panter-Downes. New Yorker 43:80+ Ag 19 '67

Maid servant. Nation 205:578 D 4 '67
Outbluffing the outraged; annual conference. Time 90:36-7 O 13 '67
Sea of troubles; Wilson lashes rebels. Newsweek 69:56 Mr 13 '67
Why Labor government is slipping in Britain. U S News 63:16 O 2 '67
Wilson barks back. Time 89:36 Mr 10 '67
LABOR productivity
Cost pressures add their heat. il Bsns W p 19-21 S 2 '67
Is Europe's low-cost labor really a myth? il Bsns W p88+ Mr 11 '67
Productivity in manufacturing. M. Ziegler. il Mo Labor R 90:1-5 O '67
Recent developments in productivity and unit labor costs. J. A. Mark and M. Ziegler. il Mo Labor R 90:26-9 My '67
What makes Ivan run? R. A. Freeman. Nat R 19:246-9 Mr 7 '67; Reply with rejoinder. E. Lyons. Nat R 19:960-2+ S 5 '67
LABOR relations. See Industrial relations
LABOR relations board, National. See United States—National labor relations board
LABOR saving devices
Five idea centers. N. Craig. il House B 109:108-9 Jl '67
Take it easy. J. Polshek. See issues of House beautiful
See also
Automatons
LABOR shortage. See Labor supply
LABOR standards
Fair labor standards for world trade. R. B. Schwenger. Mo Labor R 90:27-31 N '67
LABOR supply
Brain drain: a U.S. dilemma. H. G. Grubel; discussion. Science 155:1495-7 Mr 24 '67
See also
Unemployment

Europe
Guest workers. E. M. von Kuehnelt-Leddihn. Nat R 19:476 My 2 '67

South Africa
South Africa's wasted manpower; excerpts from report of International labor organization survey of developments in connexion with apartheid policy. il UNESCO Courier 20:30-1 Mr '67

Underdeveloped areas
Labor supply and employment in less developed countries. J. L. Sadie. bibliog f il Ann Am Acad 369:121-30 Ja '67

United States
Adult men not in the labor force; special labor force report. S. S. Holland. il Mo Labor R 90:5-15 Mr '67
Labor force. G. B. McNally. Mo Labor R 90:5-8 F '67
Manpower and the library profession; symposium. bibliog il Wilson Lib Bul 41:792-827+ Ap '67
Manpower planning; address, May 9, 1967. F. H. Cassell. Vital Speeches 33:559-65 Jl 1 '67
People and jobs. J. Tebbel. il Sat R 50:8-12+ D 30 '67
Reasons for nonparticipation in the labor force. R. L. Stein. il Mo Labor R 90:22-7 Jl '67
Recent influences on the supply of labor. J. Mincer. Mo Labor R 90:30-1 F '67
See also
Education and manpower
LABOR turnover
Got the itch to change jobs? il Changing T 21:31-2 F '67
Labor turnover; tables. See issues of Monthly labor review
See also
Occupational mobility
LABOR unions. See Trade unions
LABOR vote. See Trade unions—Political activities
LABORATORIES
See also
Biological laboratories
Medical laboratories
Research laboratories
Testing laboratories
Underwater laboratories

Architecture
Biggest mirror ever; Bell laboratories, Holmdel, N.J. il Arch Forum 126:33-41 Ap '67
Building designed for scenic effect; National center for atmospheric research. J. Barnett. il Arch Rec 142:145-54 O '67

LABORATORIES—Architecture—*Continued*
Pool and fountains shield offices from labs; Donaldson co, Bloomington, Minn. il Arch Rec 144:163 Ja '67
Towers in the sky; National center for atmospheric research. P. Blake. il Arch Forum 127:31-43 O '67

Equipment

How to sputter thin films of metal onto glass and experiment with them; ed. by C. L. Stong. N. Steiner. il Sci Am 217:134+ O '67

LABORATORY animals
Animal care: voluntary accreditation; letters. B. J. Cohen; B. J. Powell. Science 158:1621-2 D 29 '67
Behavior of captive white-footed mice. J. L. Kavanau. bibliog il Science 155:1623-39 Mr 31 '67
Jackson: a lab that links mice and men. il Bsns W p 192-4 S 9 '67
Mongrels for progress; Ventura County dog fanciers association. Sports Illus 26:7 Ja 23 '67
Pain is cruel, but disease is cruel, too. L. Galton. il N Y Times Mag p30-1+ F 26 '67; Discussion. p21+ Mr 19 '67
Pint-sized porker goes to the lab. il Bsns W p 104-5 My 27 '67
Sharper bite for lab animals; federal law regulating treatment. il Bsns W p 132+ F 18 '67
Toxicity of antibiotics in laboratory rodents. V. A. A. Killby and P. H. Silverman. Science 156:264 Ap 14 '67; Reply with rejoinder. R. Donovick. 157:338 Jl 21 '67
See also
Animal experimentation
LABORATORY infection. See Infection
LABORATORY labels. See Labels
LABORATORY technicians
See also
Medical workers

Training

Medical training costs too much; excerpt from Case studies in change. B. Asbell. il Am Ed 3:5-6 Mr '67
LABORDE Ellis P.
Unique utilization of surroundings. Parks & Rec 2:25+ N '67
LABORDE DE MONPEZAT, Henri, comte de
Princess and the diplomat. C. Plimmer and D. Plimmer. il por Redbook 129:47-9+ Je '67
LABRADOR retriever trials. See Field trials (dogs)
LACASSAGNE, A. and others
5-Oxo-5H-benzo[e]isochromeno-[4,3-b] indole, a new type of highly sarcomagenic lactone. bibliog Science 158:387-8 O 20 '67
LACCHINI, Giovanni Battista
Italian astronomer dies. por Sky & Tel 33: 149 Mr '67
LACE and lace making
See also
Macramé
LACOSTE, Catherine
But papa, I played like a clod. M. Mulvoy. il por Sports Illus 27:24-5 Jl 10 '67
Daughter of Crocodile. il por Time 90:50+ Jl 14 '67
Sportsman of the year, and two to remember. il por Sports Illus 27:24-5 D 25 '67
LACOSTE, René
Le crocodile. il pors Time 90:62 S 1 '67
LACOSTE, René, family
Dynasty Lacoste. J. Olsen. il pors Sports Illus 27:68-74+ D 18 '67
LACQUER and lacquering
Best finishes for wood; now everyone can use lacquers. J. Hand. il Pop Sci 190:151-3+ Mr '67
Russian lacquer. H. Huth. il Antiques 92: 843-7 D '67
LACROSSE
Game on the eastern shore; photographs by R. Meek; with account by R. M. Mechem. il Sports Illus 26:30-5 Mr 27 '67
Jays turned into eagles; Hopkins Blue Jays vs United States naval academy. G. Ronberg. il Sports Illus 26:28-9 My 22 '67
LACTIC dehydrogenases. See Dehydrogenases
LACTONES
Lactones as inhibitors of the fibrinolytic system. W. Auerswald and W. Doleschel. bibliog il Science 156:1244-5 Je 2 '67
5-Oxo-5H-benzo[e]isochromeno-[4,3-b] indole, a new type of highly sarcomagenic lactone. A. Lacassagne and others. bibliog il Science 158:387-8 O 20 '67
LACTOSE
Regulation of the lac operon. J. R. Beckwith. bibliog il Science 156:597-604 My 5 '67

LACY, Dan
National commission's task described by Dan Lacy; summary of address, May 25, 1967. Library J 92:2494 Jl '67
Printing week; summary of address. Pub W 191:105 F 6 '67
LACY, Edward A.
For whom does the system toll? Pop Electr 26:64-7 Je '67
Radar signature analysis. Electr World 77: 23-5+ F '67
Static electricity; the space age's billion-year-old gremlin. Electr World 78:21-3+ Jl '67
—and Golub, C. N.
Measuring missile explosions. Electr World 78:23-6 S '67
LADA, Ed
Human form. il U S Camera 30:42-3 Ap '67
LADA-MOCARSKI, Polly
Flex binding: its uses in hand bookbinding. Pub W 192:82 Ag 7 '67
LA DANY, L.
Downfall of red China? interview. por U S News 62:35-7 F 27 '67
Mao's China: the decline of a dynasty. For Affairs 45:610-23 Jl '67
LADBROKE and company
Making book on a sure thing. il Time 90:94 S 29 '67
LADD, Harry S. and others
Drilling on Midway atoll, Hawaii. bibliog Science 156:1088-94 My 26 '67
LADDERS
Get more use from your stepladder. W. Swallow. il Am Home 70:126 N '67
Safe use of ladders; excerpt from Ladders, their selection, care and safe use. il Consumer Bul 50:31-4 S '67
What's helpful and what's safe; as up the ladder you go. il Sunset 139:83-6 S '67
LADENSON, Alex
Legislative roundup. por Library J 93:41-2 Ja 1 '68
LADIES' home journal
Freckled superwoman; concerning report on California women. Time 90:67 Jl 28 '67
LADIZINSKY, Gideon, and Zohary, Daniel
Avena ventricosa: possible diploid contributor to hexaploid oats. bibliog Science 155:1553-4 Mr 24 '67
LADY and the lifeguard; story. See Mackey, E.
LADY Moon and the thief; drama. See Boiko, C.
LADY with the lute; story. See Toddie, J.
LAESTAR, Carl H. and Laestar, M. E.
Mail order pointers; how to handle returns; excerpt from Successful selling of antiques by mail. Hobbies 72:117 My '67
LAESTAR, Martha E. See Laestar, C. H. jt. auth.
LA FARGE, Henry A.
Baltimore bounty. Art N 66:44-7+ Mr '67
Noble Metropolitan visitors. Art N 65:27-31+ F '67
LAFARGE, John, institute. See John LaFarge institute
LAFARGE, Phyllis
I want to go home. Redbook 129:59+ O '67
LAFAY, Howard
St Lawrence River: key to Canada. Nat Geog Mag 131:622-67 My '67
Where Jesus walked. Nat Geog Mag 132:739-81 D '67
LAFAYETTE, La.
Deep-hole method extends landfill use. G. Hernandez. il Am City 82:17 Mr '67
LAFEBER, Walter
America's long dream in Asia. Nation 205: 456-9 N 6 '67
LA FOLLETTE, Robert Marion
Action intellectuals. T. H. White. Life 62:56 Je 16 '67
LA FONTAINE, Barbara
Motor sports. Sports Illus 27:92+ D 4 '67
Today's trivia, tomorrow's..? N Y Times Mag p82+ D 3 '67
LAGASSE, Alfred Bazil, 1922-
Change in NRPA staff, Al LaGasse resigns. L. B. Houston. por Parks & Rec 2:28 Ag '67
LAGEMANN, John Kord
Don't be afraid of your feelings. Read Digest 91:137-40 Jl '67
Happiness: new light on an old subject; interview. Read Digest 91:117-20 O '67
How much space does a man need? Read Digest 91:72-6 Ag '67
How to get more work done. Read Digest 90:85-7 My '67
LAGGTARTA. See Cake
LAGOE, Ron
Pint-sized Surveyor. Sci Digest 62:30-1 Ag '67

LAGOONS, Manure. See Manure lagoons
LAGOONS, Sewage. See Sewage lagoons
LA GORCE medal. See National geographic society
LAGUNA BEACH, Calif.

Music
Laguna Beach, Cal. (cont) W. Aguiar, jr. Opera N 32:21-2 N 4 '67
LAHR, Bert
Notes and comment. New Yorker 43:37 D 16 '67
LAINEZ, Manuel Mujica. See Mujica Lainez, M.
LAING, Alexander
Bright Heraclitus; poem. Sat R 50:42 Ap 8 '67
LAING, Dilys
Meters of wisdom and innocence. L. Untermeyer. Sat R 50:31 D 2 '67
LAING, Ronald David
Life's madness. R. Coles. New Repub 156:24-8+ My 13 '67
Schizophrenic split. por Time 89:56 F 3 '67
LAIRD, Bailey, pseud.
Political fiction. New Yorker 43:42-6 S 16 '67
Who is Bailey Laird? Newsweek 70:96+ O 23 '67
LAIRD, Melvin R.
Wooden army. E. J. Hughes. Newsweek 70: 13 D 25 '67
LAISE, Caroline Clendening
Mr & Mrs Ambassador. il pors Life 62:118-19 Je 9 '67
LAITY
Hierarchy and laity; verticality as a theological category. J. W. Dixon, jr. il Christian Cent 84:1353-6+ O 25 '67
Parishfield community. G. Winter. Christian Cent 84:776-8 Je 14 '67
Today's layman: an uncertain Catholic. D. J. Thorman; discussion. America 116: 231-2 F 18 '67

Catholic church
Chicago conference. Commonweal 86:109 Ap 14 '67
Democracy in the church; will it work? W. L. Doty. America 117:76-8 Jl 22 '67
Hearings on renewal; Chicago conference of laymen. Commonweal 86:460 Jl 28 '67
NAL or never for laity; National association of laymen. P. Lally. Commonweal 86:437-8 Jl 14 '67
Plea for intramural dialogue; removal of Paulist fathers challenged by laymen in Richardson, Tex. B. Hasbrouck. America 117:38-9 Jl 8 '67
Silent singers. D. Grumbach. Commonweal 87:468-70 Ja 19 '68
Specter of the lay trustee; laymen in the American Catholic church. J. J. McCadden. America 117:133-6 Ag 5 '67
See also
World congress for the lay apostolate
LA JOLLA, Calif.
La Jolla's hourglass stage. H. Hewes. il Sat R 50:38-9 S 23 '67
LAKE, Alice
And then there was one. Good H. 164:90-1+ Mr '67
Drop those prejudices against women doctors. Good H 164:88-9+ My '67
How to get sick on pills and capsules. Seventeen 26:312+ Ag '67
How you can beat fatigue. Seventeen 26: 112-13+ Je '67
Pill, McCalls 95:96-7+ N '67; Same abr. with title How safe is the pill? Read Digest 92: 48-52 Ja '68
Redbook guide to the health problems of young women. Redbook 129:21-8 S '67
Teen-agers and sex: a student report. Seventeen 26:88-9+ Jl '67
This is the way a girl grows. Seventeen 26: 156-7+ Ap '67
What happens behind the doctor's door. Seventeen 26:102-3+ D '67
What makes boys so different. Seventeen 26:108-9+ O '67
Why you need a doctor of your own. Seventeen 26:146-7+ F '67
LAKE, J. A. and Beeman, W. W.
Yeast transfer RNA: a small-angle X-ray study. bibliog Science 156:1371-3 Je 9 '67
LAKE, John
Two for the football show: the swinger and the square. N Y Times Mag p40-1+ N 5 '67
LAKE, WHISKEYTOWN. See Whiskeytown Lake
LAKE BAYKAL NATIONAL PARK (proposed)
See National parks and reserves—Russia
LAKE cruises. See Cruising
LAKE DISTRICT, England
English lakes. J. T. Starr. il Am For 73:28-30+ D '67

LAKE ERIE college, Painesville, Ohio
Lake Erie, constituent imagery determines campus design. V. Christ-Janer. il Arch Forum 127:62-7 Jl '67
LAKE GENEVA, Wis.
Teen-ager rampage on glorious Fourth. il U S News 63:10 Jl 17 '67
LAKE GEORGE opera festival. See Music festivals—New York (state)
LAKE HAVASU CITY, Ariz.
Instant city. il Time 89:97 Ap 14 '67
LAKE MEAD national recreation area
Lake Mead national recreation area, outstanding success story. il Am For 73: 38 Ag '67
LAKE MICHIGAN. See Michigan, Lake
LAKE pollution. See Water pollution
LAKE POWELL. See Lakes, Artificial
LAKE RICE. See Rice Lake, Minn.
LAKE TAHOE. See Tahoe, Lake
LAKE TOTA. See Tota, Lake
LAKE trout fishing. See Trout fishing
LAKE vegetation. See Aquatic plants
LAKES
Idaho's lake country. il Sunset 138:58-63 Je '67
Ohio's new lakes; Tappan, Atwood, Leesville, Clendening, Piedmont and Seneca lakes. G. Lindsey. Travel 127:41 My '67
See also
Great Lakes
LAKES, Artificial
Builders fish profits from man-made lakes; booming market for second homes on artificial lakes. il Bsns W p 186-8 Mr 4 '67
Clark Hill, southern water playground. M. Hunn. il Motor B 120:40-1+ Jl '67
Gunkholing the Glens. F. C Clark, jr. il Yachting 122:48-50+ Ag '67
Lake Powell: waterway to desert wonders. W. M. Edwards. il Nat Geog Mag 132:44-75 Jl '67
Man-made lakes; report on an international symposium. H. B. N. Hynes. Science 156: 990-1 My 19 '67
Rear-guard ecology: man-made lakes create new problems in West and Central Africa. C. Weiss. il Sci N 91:595 Je 24 '67
See also
Reservoirs
LAKESIDE building. See Building sites
LAKESIDE center. See Nature centers
LALANDE, Michel de
Do not miss this gem of a baroque release. J. W. Barker. Am Rec G 34:42 S '67
LALANNE, Claude
Marvellous trickery; tr. by A. Foulke. J. Cau. il por Vogue 149:140-1+ Ap 15 '67
LALANNE, François Xavier
Marvellous trickery; tr. by A. Foulke. J. Cau. il por Vogue 149:140-1+ Ap 15 '67
Nothing like creatures for creature comfort. B. Wise. il por Life 62:76-9 F 3 '67
LALL, Arthur S.
Books. Bul Atomic Sci 23:33-4 D '67
Neutralization in southeast Asia. Bul Atomic Sci 23:29-32 Ap '67
LALL, Betty Goetz
American attitudes on U.S.-Soviet relations. Bul Atomic Sci 23:34-8 Ja '67
ABM decision. Commonweal 86:144-7 Ap 21 '67
Congress debates the ABM. Bul Atomic Sci 23:28-33 S '67
Gaps in the ABM debate. Bul Atomic Sci 23: 45-6 Ap '67
Race to split U-235. Sat R 50:29+ Je 3 '67
Superiority and innovation in U.S. defense forces. Bul Atomic Sci 23:11-13 Mr '67
U.S.-European relations: appraisal and future policy. Bul Atomic Sci 23:45-7 Je '67
LALLY, John J.
Theology of conflict. Commonweal 87:355-8 D 15 '67
LALLY, Patrick
NAL or never for laity. Commonweal 86: 437-8 Jl 14 '67
LALLY, Vincent E.
Trial balloons in the southern hemisphere. Science 155:456-9 Ja 27 '67
LA MAMA ETC (Experimental theater club)
See New York (city)—Theater
LAMANTIA, Philip
Poetry chronicle. T. Clark. Poetry 110:105-6 My '67
LA MARCHINA, Robert
Robert La Marchina to Honolulu. por Hi Fi 17:MA2 S '67
LAMB, Edward
Country fair. Nation 204:435-6 Ap 3 '67
LAMB, Elisabeth Searle
Thirteen readings from a double compass: Petén Itzá; Quetzal; Tropical storm warning; poems. Américas 19:22 D '67

LAMB, W. Kaye
Canada: the National library. Library J 92: 4383-5 D 1 '67
LAMB (meat) See Cookery—Meat
LAMBARÉNÉ, Gabon
Lambaréné since Schweitzer. H. Bowser. Sat R 50:30 N 25 '67
Young doctor at Lambaréné. G. N. Marshall. Christian Cent 84:1636-8 D 20 '67
LAMBDA polypeptides. See Peptides
LAMBERT, Darwin
Alaska's Glacier Bay National Monument. Nat Parks Mag 41:4-9 S '67
Facets of wilderness. il Liv Wildn 31:10-18 Spr '67
National park experience. Nat Parks Mag 41:4-8 My '67
LAMBERT, Sam M.
NEA and the real world of education; excerpts from address, October 20, 1967. NEA J 56:34-6 D '67

about

Executive secretary Sam M. Lambert. M. B. Tucker. por NEA J 56:30-3 S '67
Sam Lambert, executive secretary, NEA. por Sch & Soc 95:342-3 O 14 '67
LAMBERT, William
Deeper debt of gratitude to the mob. Life 63:38-38B N 10 '67
Strange help-Hoffa campaign of the U.S. senator from Missouri. Life 62:26-31+ My 26 '67
—See Oulahan, R; Smith, S. jt. auths.
LAMBETH, Edmund B.
Prodigious satellites: Comsat, ma Bell and ETV. Nation 204:109-12 Ja 23 '67
LAMBORGHINI, Ferruccio
Car to fugit in. il Newsweek 69:102+ Ap 17 '67
LAMBORGHINI company. See Automobile industry and trade—Italy
LAMBRAKIS, Christos
Elections or coup? deadlock in Greece. S. Rousseas. Nation 204:392-5 Mr 27 '67
LAMBS
Three lamb crops every two years. Farm J 91:64A F '67
LAMENTS
See also
Phonograph records—Laments
LAMINATED construction. See Sandwich construction
LAMINATED plastics. See Plastics, Laminated
LAMM, Michael
Hamming it up at a stock car race. Pop Mech 128:88-9 Jl '67
Hooray for the human spirit, human spirit, human spirit. Esquire 68:142-3 D '67
Secrets of a car thief. Motor T 19:68+ F '67
LAMMEY, W. Clyde
Build this butterfly-trestle table. Pop Mech 127:172-4 F '67
Checker your own gunstock. Pop Mech 127:176-80+ Mr '67
Homeowners' clinic; questions and answers. See issues of Popular mechanics
How to get started in metal turning (cont) Pop Mech 127:176-9+ F; 170-3 Mr '67 (to be cont)
LAMONICA, Daryle
Big raid that really paid off. E. Shrake. il por Sports Illus 27:74-5 N 13 '67
LAMONT, Lansing
Oppie: the troubled Pied Piper of Los Alamos. Life 62:34B Mr 3 '67
LAMONT geological observatory. See Columbia university—Lamont geological observatory
LAMOTT, Kenneth
Dawks and the hoves. Nation 205:564-5 N 27 '67
Gamblers; story. Sat Eve Post 240:54-8 D 30 '67
Outer islands of Hawaii. Holiday 42:62-9+ Jl '67
Passage to the Yukon. Holiday 41:68-9+ My '67
Plight of Diamond Head. Holiday 42:115-16 Jl '67
LAMP shades
Make your own Tiffany shade. L. C. Vierno. il Pop Mech 128:166-9 Ag '67
LAMPMAN, Ben Hur
In defense of bait fishing. Field & S 71:52-3 Ap '67
LAMPORT, Felicia
Get that chipmunk off your boulder; poem. Harper 234:56 Je '67
LAMPS
Best light for reading. D. X. Manners. House B 109:64-5+ My '67
High-intensity plus. il House B 109:132-4 Ap '67

LANAHAN, Scottie
Group and I. McCalls 94:59+ Jl '67
LANCASTER, Clay
Prospect park; interview. New Yorker 43:48-50 O 28 '67
LANCASTER, Donald E.
Audio integrated circuits, what's available? Electr World 78:34-6 O '67
Build an IC Testone. Pop Electr 28:27-9 Ja '68
Build direct readout IC freq meter. Pop Electr 27:53-6+ O '67
Build the amligner. Pop Electr 26:60-1+ F '67
Build the supertrol. Pop Electr 26:41-4+ Mr '67
Experimenter's professional power supply. Pop Electr 27:71-3+ N '67
Extended resonance curves. Electr World 78:36 N '67
Logic demon. Pop Electr 25:41-5+ D '66
Operational amplifier; circuits & applications. Electr World 78:49-52+ Ag '67
Using the new constant-current diodes. Electr World 78:30-1+ O '67
Want to build an integrated circuit binary counter? Pop Electr 25:57-61+ D '66
LANCASTER, Osbert
Matter of mood. E. Weeks. Atlan 220:135 N '67
LANCASTER, Pa.
Further probe into housing rehabilitation. Am City 82:44+ N '67
LANCE (guided missile) See Guided missiles
LANCOUR, Harold
Lancour hits parochialism in world library education; excerpts from address, May 20, 1967. Library J 92:2326+ Je 15 '67
LAND, Edwin Herbert
Men who made the world move. H. Bigart. por Sat R 50:64 Ap 22 '67
LAND, Frances
What every young father should know about mutual funds. Parents Mag 42:52+ Ja '67
LAND, Thomas
Conscientious AWOLs. Nation 205:488-91 N 13 '67
LAND
See also
Eminent domain
Real property

Prices

See Land values

California

Forest practices and watershed management in California; address. W. S. Shannon. il Am For 73:6-7+ My '67

Florida

Selling land in Florida. J. Hunter. New Repub 157:21-3 S 2 '67

Kentucky

These murdered old mountains; effects of strip mining operations in Kentucky. D. Nevin. il Life 64:54-60+ Ja 12 '68

Maryland

Second battle of Antietam; opposition to line towers of Potomac Edison company. Life 62:4 Je 23 '67

New York (state)

Catskills of New York: past, present, potential. S. S. Chase. il Am For 73:22-5+ Ag '67
LAND as gifts
Gift of land. D. MacDonald. il House B 109:162+ D '67
LAND between the lakes national recreation area. See Wilderness areas
LAND clearing. See Clearing of land
LAND crabs. See Crabs
LAND fills. See Municipal dumps
LAND leases. See Leases
LAND management, Bureau of. See United States—Land management, Bureau of
LAND mines. See Mines, Military
LAND planning. See Land utilization
LAND Rover (automobile) See Automobiles, Foreign
LAND sailboats. See Sand yachts
LAND sinking. See Subsidences (earth movements)
LAND slides. See Landslides
LAND subsidence. See Subsidences (earth movements)
LAND surveying. See Surveying

LAND tenure
Brazil
Lust for territory; foreign land owners. il Time 90:33-4 D 22 '67
Chile
Bitter victory; land-reform program passed after two years. Newsweek 70:43-4 Jl 31 '67
France
Noncapitalist wealth and the origins of the French revolution; excerpts from address, December 30, 1965. G. V. Taylor. bibliog f il Am Hist R 72:469-96 Ja '67

Underdeveloped areas
Who owns the land? C. Bowles. Read Digest 91:143-4 O '67

United States
Incident in Rio Arriba; attempt by small band of Spanish-Americans to seize land in N.Mex. C. Kentfield. il N Y Times Mag p20-1+ Jl 16 '67
Indian givers; Federal claims court upholds 1964 verdict. Newsweek 69:43-4 Je 26 '67
Tijerina brass; attempt to reclaim ancestral land leads to shootings. il Newsweek 69:37-8 Je 19 '67
Tijerina's Republic of San Joaquin del Rio de Chama. G. W. Grayson, jr. New Repub 157:10-11 Jl 1 '67

Vietnam (Republic)
Is land reform enough? Nat R 19:1160 O 31 '67
LAND utilization
Can we save our open space? Parks & Rec 2:23 Mr '67
Catskills of New York: past, present, potential. S. S. Chase. il Am For 73:22-5+ Ag '67
County parks and open space planning. A. C. Stelling and N. D. Mitchell. il Parks & Rec 2:28-9+ Ap '67
Drain it, or lease it to hunters? Farm J 91:80B Mr '67
Ending a fiefdom; homeowners ask for legislation giving them permanent possessory use of public land. K. B. Pomeroy. Am For 73:5+ Ag '67
Forest practices and watershed management in California; address. W. S. Shannon. il Am For 73:6-7+ My '67
Ground water to bolster river flow and prevent the use of valuable land for reservoirs; Britain's Thames conservancy. C. E. Tiffen. il Am City 82:139+ S '67
Land: an American dream in crisis. R. Starr. il Horizon 10:22-9 Wint '68
Let's save the most important open space, now! D. F. Rettie. il Parks & Rec 2:30-1+ My '67
Look who's voting to cut your taxes! farmers are gaining new tax relief. J. Carlson. il Farm J 91:30-1+ Ja '67
Mike Frome; mining interests enjoy special privileges in use of natural resources. M. Frome. Am For 73:3+ S '67
$1 billion mistake; holders of special use permits on the Stanislaus national forest in California demand permanent rights. K. B. Pomeroy. Am For 73:23+ Ap '67
Open spaces get wider, cities grow denser. il U S News 63:47 D 18 '67
Philanthropic funds. Parks & Rec 2:13 N '67
Profiles; C. Abrams. B. Taper. New Yorker 42:39-42+ F 4 '67
Recreation land management and the new forestry. L. C. Merriam, jr. bibliog il Nat Parks Mag 41:14-18 Je '67
Skylands of New Jersey; conservation environmental renewal program. R. A. Roe. il Parks & Rec 2:17+ S '67
Sustained yield and balanced use. W. E. Towell. Am For 73:11 S '67
We switched from cows to roller skates. E. M. Pearson. Farm J 91:60D Mr '67
You rent an acre to city folks. R. C. Davids. Farm J 91:48B Ja '67
See also
City planning
LAND values
Forty-seven places in America to buy land and make money. W. H. Robbins. il Esquire 68:141-4+ O '67
Land: an American dream in crisis. R. Starr. il Horizon 10:22-9 Wint '68
Warning: land frauds are flourishing. Changing T 21:6 My '67
What is happening to the big boom in land. il U S News 63:94-5 Jl 24 '67
Why land boom has slowed; interview. R. Wenzlick. il U S News 63:95-6 Jl 24 '67
See also
Assessment

LAND yachts. See Sand yachts
LANDAU, Lev Davidovich
He died four times. il por Newsweek 71:7 Ja 15 '68
LANDER, Toni
Pas de deux, marital style. W. Terry. il pors Sat R 50:41-2 Ag 5 '67
LANDFILLS. See Municipal dumps
LANDGRAF, Walter E.
Needed: new perspective on health services. Harvard Bsns R 45:75-83 S '67
LANDING fees, Airport. See Airports—Finance
LANDING gear, Airplane. See Airplanes—Landing gear
LANDING of airplanes. See Airplanes—Landing
LANDLORD and tenant
Rent strike; proposals for disrupting the slum system in New York. F. F. Piven and R. A. Cloward. New Repub 157:11-15 D 2 '67; Reply. E. Spannaus. 158:45-6 Ja 6 '68
Tenant unions seek to put an end to slums. S. Olds. Christian Cent 84:1579-82 D 6 '67
See also
Farm tenancy
LANDMAN, Hedy Backlin-. See Backlin-Landman, H.
LANDMARKS, Literary. See Literary landmarks
LANDO, Barry
Report: Latin-American guerrillas. Atlan 220:26+ D '67
LANDON, Alfred Mossman
Republicans' affable old radical. H. H. Martin. il pors Sat Eve Post 240:42+ Mr 25 '67
LANDRETH, Alice
Old Shuguli. pors Outdoor Life 139:48-51+ F '67
LANDRETH, Harry
Creeping capitalism in the Soviet Union? excerpts from address, 1967. bibliog f Harvard Bsns R 45:133-40 S '67
LANDRETH, Hobart F. and Ferguson, D. E.
Newts: sun-compass orientation. bibliog f Science 158:1459-61 D 15 '67
LANDRUM, Phillip Mitchell
Where poverty program is doing poorly; interview. por Nations Bsns 55:52+ O '67
LANDRY, Lionel
Behind Asia's headlines. Sat R 50:38 Ag 5 '67
LANDRY, Robert J.
Behind the screens at CBS. Sat R 50:30-1 Ap 1 '67
Business trends. Duns R 90:11 Ag '67
LANDS, Public. See Public lands
LANDSBERG, Hans
Aid problem. Reporter 36:54-6 Je 15 '67
LANDSCAPE
To beautify America; turning a shambles into a park; Forsyth, Mont. R. Dalby. Home Gard 54:50 S '67
See also
Color in landscape
LANDSCAPE architecture
Happy blend of garden and house. E. Kondonellis. il Am Home 70:90-1 O '67
Quality environment. A. C. Borg. il Am Home 70:92-7 O '67
LANDSCAPE design. See Landscape architecture
LANDSCAPE gardening
ABC's of fence gardening. il Pop Gard 18:38-41 My '67
Beauty of a long-range plan. H. V. Wilson. il Home Gard 54:56-8 My '67
Companion plants with lilies. V. Howie. il Horticulture 45:26-9+ My '67
Here's help in choosing plants for specific landscape uses. il Sunset 138:208+ F '67
House in my head; excerpts. D. Rodgers. il House B 109:124-30+ S; 208-15+ O; 70+ N '67
How to be your own landscape designer. J. R. Rebhan. il Home Gard 54:52-4 Mr '67
How to build excitement into the simplest garden. il House & Gard 131:128-31 F '67
How to plan your landscape. E. Kondonellis. il Am Home 70:96-7+ My '67
Invest in a fine garden. E. Kondonellis. il Am Home 70:78-9 Ja '67
Islands of plants. il Home Gard 54:52-5 My '67
Keep your cool in a pool. Am Home 70:51-3 Jl '67
Landscape ideas U.S.A. J. Fanning. il Pop Gard 18:24-39 Mr '67
Landscaping the new Oakland museum. il Parks & Rec 2:18-19 S '67
Landscaping with evergreens. H. Mason and R. O'Harra. il Bet Hom & Gard 45:58-63 O '67
Native plants for seaside gardens. G. Jenkins. il Horticulture 45:34-7+ Jl '67

LANDSCAPE gardening—*Continued*
Planned garden has a great future. il Pop
Gard 18:16-17 Mr '67
Serene facade conceals pools, fountains and
spatial excitement. il Arch Rec 142:185-8 S
'67
Steep front garden and the steep back garden.
il Sunset 139:94-7 O '67
Terraces and trees. il Home Gard 54:53-6+
Ap '67
This garden almost takes care of itself. il
Sunset 139:242-3 O '67
Thomas D. Church; the influence of 2,000
gardens. C. Calkins. il House B 109:140-5
Mr '67
Three tricks with trees. il Pop Gard 18:10
My '67
Two Newport Beach neighbors decide to co-
ordinate their front landscaping. il Sunset
138:100-1 My '67
Vines for privacy and vines for shade. il
Sunset 139:150-2 S '67
We landscape everything, even the vegetable
garden. B. Pearson. il Farm J 91:102-3 Ap
'67
Wild flowers for natural beauty, when the
builder leaves trees. il Home Gard 54:52-3
F '67
See also
Airports—Landscape gardening
City gardens
Garden design
Gardens, Japanese
Golf courses
Home grounds
Landscape architecture
Outdoor rooms
Topiary work
LANDSCAPE improvement
Golden is our valley; interview, ed. by K.
Davis. L. Golden. il Farm J 91:50-1 N '67
Here's LBJ's grand design to change the
face of America. il U S News 62:72-4 F
13 '67
Rockefeller home designated historic land-
mark; address. C. A. T. Johnson. il Parks
& Rec 2:23+ Ag '67
To beautify America. Home Gard 54:16 My;
48 Je; 10 Jl; 10+ Ag; 50 S; 51 O; 57 N '67
Transmission lines; the placement of power
lines and the preservation of aesthetic
value. L. C. White. Parks & Rec 2:19+ D
'67
See also
White House youth conference on natural
beauty and conservation
LANDSCAPE in poetry. See Nature in poetry
LANDSCAPE painting
American debut; landscapes of the Norwich
school; exhibition at the Cummer gallery of
art, Jacksonville, Fla. E. P. Birk. il An-
tiques 91:276+ Mr '67
Jasper F. Cropsey, child of the Hudson
River school. W. S. Talbot. il Antiques 92:
713-7 N '67
Magnificent eccentrics; Chinese paintings on
exhibition at New York's Asia house. il
Newsweek 69:99 Ap 3 '67
Mark Fisher; an American impressionist. I.
M. G. Quimby. il Antiques 91:780-3 Je '67
Notes on composition for the young land-
scape painter. P. L. Martin. il Am Artist
31:50-5 S '67
On composition in landscape; excerpts from
Starting with watercolor. R. Hilder. il Am
Artist 31:42-7 My '67
Sumer is icumen in. N. Kent. Am Artist
31:3+ Je '67
William H. Bartlett and his imitators; ex-
cerpts. M.-E. Earl. il Antiques 92:772-5 N
'67
LANDSCAPE photography. See Photography—
Landscapes
LANDSCAPE protection
Holiday awards for a beautiful America. il
Holiday 41:39-40 My '67
Is it good-bye green earth? symposium. il
Pop Gard 18:22-39 D '67
Is legislation the answer? Parks & Rec 2:17
Ap '67
Let's save the most important open space,
now! D. F. Rettie. il Parks & Rec 2:30-1+
My '67
Litterbugs not wanted in the country. Con-
sumer Bul 50:27-8 Ap '67
Mike Frome; Tellico Dam across the Little
Tennessee River. M. Frome. Am For 73:7+
Mr '67
Preservation of natural beauty in England. A.
Nethoy. il Am For 73:16-19+ Mr '67
See also
Conservation of resources
LANDSLIDES
Landslide noise. J. D. Cadman and R. E.
Goodman. bibliog il Science 158:1182-4 D 1
'67

Landslides in the *favelas* of Rio. il UNESCO
Courier 20:18-19 F '67
Rates of surficial rock creep on hillslopes in
western Colorado. S. A. Schumm. bibliog
il Science 155:560-2 F 3 '67
LANDY, Dick
Pair of dandy's. E. Dahlquist. il por Hot Rod
21:54-6 Ja '68
LANDY, Marc
Family farmer fights back. Commonweal 87:
431-2 Ja 12 '68
LANE, E. A. See Mavrides, C. jt. auth.
LANE, Laurence William
Obituary
Sunset por 138:31 Ap '67
LANE, Mark
Acquittal for Oswald. J. J. Graham. Common-
weal 86:149-51 Ap 21 '67
Rush to Philippi. V. Gold. Nat R 19:1206-7
O 31 '67
LANE, Will
Vagabond camera. See issues of Travel
LANE, Willard R. and others
Historical context of educational adminis-
tration; excerpt from Foundations of edu-
cational administration: a behavioral an-
alysis. bibliog f Sch & Soc 94:482-92+ D
24 '66
LANE cake. See Cake
LANEY college, Oakland, Calif.
Laney college, an urban campus for a center
city site. il Arch Rec 142:156 N '67
LANG, Anton
Plant growth regulation. Science 157:589-92
Ag 4 '67
LANG, Barbara
Instant football. McCalls 95:44+ O '67
LANG, Daniel
Letter from Geneva (cont) New Yorker 43:
70+ Ag 5 '67
Letter from Israel. New Yorker 43:37-8+
D 30 '67
LANG, Eugene M.
Foreign scout for the small man. il por Bsns
W p 131-2+ O 21 '67
LANG, Janet
Do you love Mao? por Newsweek 69:46-8 F 27
'67
LANG, Pearl
Pearl Lang and dance company, Hunter
playhouse. J. Maskey. Dance Mag 41:29 Jl
'67
LANGDON, John E.
Form and ornament in early Canadian silver.
Antiques 92:78-83 Jl '67
LANGE, Phil C.
Taking the stress off grades. PTA Mag 62:
19-21 bibliog(p35) O '67
LANGE, Walter F.
Amateur radio for CB'ers. Pop Electr 26:51-8
My 59-63 Je '67
LANGER, Don
Eleventh birthday party is a once-in-a-life-
time movie happening. il Pop Phot 61:112-
13+ S '67
LANGER, Henry C. Jr
Man and his boat. Yachting 121:71-3+ Ja '67
LANGER, Susanne Katherina (Knauth)
Books; mind over matter. W. Sargeant. New
Yorker 43:98+ Ag 12 '67
LANGERHANS cells. See Cells
LANGERMAN, Stephen
Seven ways to see a chair. M. Orovan. il
U S Camera 30:62-3 F '67
LANGEWIESCHE, Wolfgang
Here comes the mini-airliner. Read Digest
92:189-93+ Ja '68
Look at America's new towns! Read Digest
90:140-5 Mr '67
Now you can double your learning power.
Read Digest 90:112-16 Ap '67
LANGFORD, Thomas A.
Campus turmoil: a religious dimension.
Christian Cent 84:172-4 F 8 '67
LANGGUTH, Jack
California's gift to psychotherapy. Harper
234:52-6 Je '67
Yorty has his eye on the big apple. N Y
Times Mag p32-3+ S 17 '67
LANGHAM, Michael
La Jolla's hourglass stage. H. Hewes. Sat R
50:39 S 23 '67
LANGLEY research center. See United States
—National aeronautics and space admin-
istration—Langley research center
LANGMYHR, George J.
How safe is the pill? Parents Mag 42:58-9+
O '67
LANGSNER, Jules
Los Angeles. See issues of Art news
LANGTON, Daniel J.
Popcorn; poem. Atlan 220:101 Jl '67
LANGUAGE, Psychology of. See Language and
languages—Psychology

LANGUAGE and languages
Brothers Grimm and their famous law for linguists. A. Burgess. il Horizon 10:66-72 Wint '68
Environment of language; study under way at Pro Deo university, Rome. N. Cousins. Sat R 50:36 Ap 8 '67
Language and communication. J. J. Gumperz. bibliog f Ann Am Acad 373:219-31 S '67
See also
Alphabet
Bilingualism
Chinese language
Communication
English language
Jargon
Onomatopoeia
Semantics
Style, Literary
Vocabulary
Words

Etymology
No strings attached. P. W. Schmidtchen. il Hobbies 72:104+ N '67

Psychology
Subconscious language, by T. Thass-Thienemann. Review
Sat R 50:32 Ag 19 '67. J. Jaffe
LANGUAGE and thought. See Thought and language
LANGUAGE of animals. See Animal communication
LANGUAGES. See Language and languages
LANGUAGES, Modern

Conversation and phrase books
English: how she is talked; a kook's tour of conversation, Italian-style. H. A. Smith. il Read Digest 91:109-11 D '67

Study and teaching
Brainwashing to teach; Berlitz schools' Total immersion course. il Time 89:63-4 F 17 '67
FLES programs; foreign language in the elementary school. F. P. Del Olmo and G. Del Olmo. il NEA J 56:42-3 My '67
If FLES is to succeed; foreign languages in the elementary school. L. S. Adams. NEA J 56:72 D '67
Impact on foreign language teaching. Sch & Soc 95:482 D 9 '67
Language requirements for the Ph.D; letter. S. Ross and C. W. Shilling; discussion. Science 154:1603; 155:1492 D 30 '66, Mr 24 '67
Parlez-vous-français? poor quality college foreign-language training. Newsweek 71:66 Ja 8 '68
Personal business; U.S. companies pushing language study. Bsns W p 169-70 Mr 4 '67
When should youngsters begin a second language? B. Eisenpreis. il Parents Mag 42:66-7+ S '67
See also
Berlitz schools of languages
English language—Study and teaching

Anecdotes, facetiae, satire, etc.
Why learn the language? D. M. Doren. Atlan 221:102-3 Ja '68
LANIER, Edmond
Keeping French glory afloat. il por Bsns W p90-2+ Ja 14 '67
LANJARÓN, Spain
Travel well; Spanish spas. E. N. Dye. Travel 128:61-2+ D '67
LANKENAU hospital. See Philadelphia—Hospitals
LANKFORD, Grace Ward
Music; certificate. il por Américas 19:42-3 F '67
LANNIE, Vincent P.
Samuel Lewis and the people's colleges. bibliog f Sch & Soc 95:493-8 D 9 '67
LANNING, Edward P. and Patterson, T. C.
Early man in South America; with biographical sketches. Sci Am 217:20, 44-50 bibliog (p 154) N '67
LANNING, George
Writing for The Kenyon review. Writer 80:31-2 O '67
LANNING, James W.
Farm boy's thoughts in Vietnam; letter. Farm J 91:50N+ O '67
LANOUE, George R.
Public library principles and Title II. bibliog Wilson Lib Bul 41:700-7 Mr '67
LANSCHE, Bob
Compact darkroom. Pop Sci 192:128-9 Ja '68

LANSING, Mich.
Education
Lansing, Michigan's 8mm film workshop. L. Steen. il Sr Schol 91:sup8-9 O 26 '67
Role playing in the library; Reo and Michigan avenue schools. P. Anderson. Library J 93:267 Ja 15 '68
LANSING, Mich. diocese. See Catholic church —Dioceses
LANSKY, Meyer
Mob town, U.S.A. il Newsweek 69:38 F 13 '67
LANTERN projection
Post cards in 3-D. B. Finnegan. il Hobbies 72:114-15 My '67
LANTERNS
These are ice lights; Mexican tin lanterns. il Sunset 139:62-3 D '67
LANTZ, Ragni
Dixie town fetes war hero. Ebony 22:27-8+ Je '67
Hello, Dolly. Ebony 23:83-9 Ja '68
Veep lives his convictions. Ebony 22:75-8+ My '67
LAOS
Princely sum-ups. il Time 89:39 Ap 14 '67
See also
Communism—Laos
Economic assistance in Laos
Medicine—Laos

Foreign relations
In hot pursuit; reactions to U.S. pursuit of North Vietnamese inside borders. A. Campbell. New Repub 158:19-21 Ja 13 '68
President Johnson welcomes Crown Prince of Laos; toast, November 9, 1967. L. B. Johnson. Dept State Bul 57:752 D 4 '67
Prince Souvanna Phouma of Laos meets with President Johnson; exchange of toasts and statement, October 20, 1967. L. B. Johnson; Souvanna Phouma. Dept State Bul 57:653-4 N 13 '67
Wider war in southeast Asia? Communists use neighboring countries as sanctuaries. il Bsns W p20-1 Ja 6 '68

Neutrality
Special war; operations against Ho Chi Minh trial. il Time 89:34 My 19 '67

Politics and government
Report. P. Braestrup. Atlan 220:10+ Ag '67
LAPHAM, Lewis H.
Old money, new money. Sat Eve Post 240:22-3 D 30 '67
LAPIDARY work
Gems in a hurry. il Design 69:28-30 Wint '67
Goldworkers and lapidaries; excerpt from the 16th century Aztec manuscript; tr. by C. E. Dibble and A. J. O. Anderson. B. de Sahagún. il Craft Horiz 27:16-21 S '67
LAPIERRE, Dominique. See Collins, L. jt. auth.
LAPIN, Sergei Georgievich
Two new men. por Time 89:45 Ap 21 '67
LAPLAND
See also
Rovaniemi

Description and travel
Points North. P. L. Adams. il Atlan 219:99-100+ Mr '67
LAPP, Ralph E.
Useless secrecy and the world bomb balance. por Sci N 92:31 Jl 8 '67
LAPSON, Mildred
Paintings of Mildred Lapson Stevens. M. Krebbs. il por Am Artist 31:44-9+ S '67
LAQUEUR, Walter
Anti-Semitism. Commentary 44:80-4 Jl; 14+ N '67
Bonn is not Weimar; reflections on the radical right in Germany. Commentary 43:33-42 Mr '67
Hand of Russia. Reporter 36:18-20 Je 29 '67
Is peace in the Middle East possible? N Y Times Mag p38-9+ Ag 27 '67
Israel, the Arabs, and world opinion. Commentary 44:49-59 Ag '67
LARA-BRAUD, Jorge
Latin America; the crisis and signs of hope. Cath World 204:290-5 F '67
Our Spanish-American neighbors. Christian Cent 85:43-5 Ja 10 '68
(tr) See Maldonado-Denis, M. Situation of Cuba's intellectuals
LARDNER, Godfrey E. A.
Science and technology in Africa. Bul Atomic Sci 23:36-9 Je '67
LARDNER, Rex
Baseball is the waiting game. N Y Times Mag p30-2+ Jl 30 '67
Sporting life. Holiday 41:28+ Mr '67

LARDNER, Susan
Family portrait; story. Seventeen 26:106-7 D '67
LARGE families. See Family, Size of
LARGE print books. See Printing—Legibility
LARGE scale cookery. See Cookery
LARGEMOUTH bass fishing. See Bass fishing
LARGENT, Frank D. and May, J. W.
Swim'st thou in wealth. Am Ed 3:12-13 Je '67
LARKIN, Emmet
Economic growth, capital investment, and the Roman Catholic church in nineteenth-century Ireland. bibliog f Am Hist R 72:852-84 Ap '67
LARKIN, Mrs Peter
American westerns, 1967. il pors Vogue 149:242-3 My '67
LARNER, Jeremy
He's a stubborn idealist with a romantic streak. Life 64:57-8 Ja 19 '68
How Goliath, typecast to lose, finally didn't. Life 62:84+ Ap 21 '67
LARRABEE, Eric
Bazelon view of America. Harper 234:112-13 My '67
Performing arts: the state of jazz. Harper 234:116-18 F; 235:97-9 Ag '67
LARRAMENDI, L. M. H. and others
Synaptic vesicles of inhibitory and excitatory terminals in the cerebellum. bibliog Science 156:967-9 My 19 '67
LARREY, Martin F.
Jesuit university. Commonweal 86:43-5 Mr 31 '67
LARRICK, Nancy
Baby dolls are gone. bibliog por Library J 92:3815-17 O 15 '67
LARROCHA, Alicia de
Goya of music. Opera N 32:6-7 D 9 '67
Granados; ed. by E. Haines. por Hi Fi 17:56-8 D '67

About
In the blood. il por Time 90:94 D 15 '67
Music to my ears; recital in Carnegie Hall. I. Kolodin. Sat R 50:34 D 23 '67
Musical events; recital in Carnegie Hall. W. Sargeant. New Yorker 43:154 D 16 '67
LARSEN, Jack Lenor
Jack Lenor Larsen. il Craft Horiz 27:22-5 S '67
LARSEN, P. Reed, and Wolff, J.
Iodide transport: inhibition by agents reacting at the membrane. bibliog Science 155:335-6 Ja 20 '67
LARSON, Arthur
Last chance on nuclear nonproliferation? Sat R 50:21-4 O 7 '67
Real nature of the world revoluton. Sat R 50:15-18 Je 3 '67
LARVAE
Calcareous septa formed in snail shells by larvae of snail-killing flies. L. V. Knutson and others. bibliog il Science 156:522-3 Ap 28 '67
See also
Caterpillars
LARYNX
Singing voice: magic. R. Rushmore. il Opera N 31:24-6 Ja 28 '67

Surgery
Hope for cancer victims. Sci N 91:86 Ja 28 '67
Marine speaks again. il Time 89:75 Ja 27 '67
LARYNX, Artificial
Marine speaks again. il Time 89:75 Ja 27 '67
Rebuilt larynx. Sci Digest 61:57 Ap '67
LASANSKY, Mauricio
Art: drawings from hell; Nazi drawings. C. Willard. il Look 31:78+ F 21 '67
Nameless evil; Nazi drawings on exhibit at Manhattan's Whitney museum. il Time 89:86 Mr 31 '67
Visions of depravity. H. Cohen. Reporter 36:39-40+ My 4 '67
LA SCALA opera company. See Opera—Italy
LASCELLES, George Henry Hubert, 7th earl of Harewood. See Harewood, G. H. H. L.
LASCH, Christopher
Cold war, revisited and re-visioned. N Y Times Mag p26-7+ Ja 14 '68
Cultural cold war; excerpt from Towards a new past. Nation 205:198-212, 309 S 11, O 2 '67
LASER altimeters. See Altimeters
LASER communication systems. See Light communication systems
LASER computers. See Computers
LASER-holography. See Holography

LASER interferometers. See Interferometers
LASER modulators. See Modulators
LASER photography. See Lasers—Photographic applications
LASERS
Burning questions on lasers; injuries stir concern about health hazard. Bsns W p44 Je 3 '67
CO_2 lasers tested for deep space use. il Aero Tech 21:31 O 23 '67
Dangers of the laser miracle ray; reprint. W. J. Perkinson. il Sci Digest 62:62-4 N '67
French firm pushing laser research. Aviation W 86:94-5+ Je 5 '67
High pulse rate neodymium, CW CO_2 lasers developed. il Aero Tech 21:37-8 N 6 '67
Isotopic analysis of rare gases with a laser microprobe. G. H. Megrue. bibliog il Science 157:1555-6 S 29 '67
Laser delay line seen aid to design of future radars; gas laser with quartz bar. il Aero Tech 21:34 O 9 '67
Laser modulation. Sci N 91:233 Mr 11 '67
Laser-recorded digital memory; UNICON mass memory reels. il Electr World 77:76 Mr '67
Laser, the light fantastic. T. Meloy. il Read Digest 90:107-11 Ap '67
Laser's grandfather; a Kastler's optical pumping technique. G. M. Spruch. il Sat R 50:56-9 Mr 4 '67
Light-emitting semiconductors. F. F. Morehead, jr. il Sci Am 216:108-13+ bibliog(p 168) My '67
Liquid lasers. A. Lempicki and H. Samelson. il Sci Am 216:80-7+ bibliog(p 155) Je '67
Miracle ray grows up. J. H. McElroy. il Sci Digest 61:8-13 My '67
Principles of a laser. I. Asimov. Sci Digest 62:87 Ag '67
Self-induced transparency. Sci Am 216:57 Je '67
Students make laser breakthrough; hard rock crumbled by laser beam. il Sci Digest 61:25 F '67
Tracking ships to use lasers for accuracy; flexure monitor system. Aero Tech 21:54 N 6 '67
Tuning laser beams. Sci Am 216:56 My '67
Ultrashort light pulses. A. J. DeMaria and others. bibliog il Science 156:1557-68 Je 23 '67
Wonderworld of lasers. Changing T 21:17-19 F '67

Military applications
U.S. plan to accelerate laser development spurs market. B. Miller. il Aviation W 87:92-3+ Ag 21 '67

Photographic applications
Explosion photographed. il Sci N 91:279 Mr 25 '67

Use in research
Selective laser photocatalysis of bromine reactions. W. B. Tiffany and others. bibliog il Science 157:40-3 Jl 7 '67
LASHER, Mrs Milton T. Jr
Cold wax batik. Sch Arts 67:40 D '67
LASKER, Albert and Mary foundation. See Albert and Mary Lasker foundation
LASKER, Mary (Woodard)
Great persuader. V. Lawford. il pors Vogue 149:194-7+ My '67
Health syndicate. E. B. Drew. Atlan 220:75-82 D '67
LASKER awards. See Albert Lasker awards
LASKI, Michael I.
Comrade Laski, CPUSA (M-L) J. Didion. Sat Eve Post 240:24+ N 18 '67
LASSITER, Luther
Shooting out the lights with Wimpy; ed. by B. Ottum. pors Sports Illus 27:50-9 O 16 '67
LASSON, Robert
Just for laughs. Look 31:113 Je 13 '67
Three networks in search of a dollar. Esquire 69:46 Ja '68
—and Eynon, David
Just for laughs. Look 31:M8 Jl 25 '67
Just say, trick or treat-o-mat. McCalls 95:64 O '67
Shoprite tours. Atlan 220:102+ Jl '67
LASSWELL, Harold D.
Do we need social observatories? Sat R 50:49-52 Ag 5 '67
about
Harold Lasswell: a memoir. L. Rosten. por Sat R 50:65-7 Ap 15 '67
LAS VEGAS, Nev.
Hughes gambles on Las Vegas. il Bsns W p80-2+ S 30 '67
Marrying absurd. J. Didion. Sat Eve Post 240:18 D 16 '67

LAS VEGAS, Nev.—*Continued*
Why is Howard Hughes buying up Las Vegas?
J. Star. il Look 32:69-71+ Ja 23 '68
You're going on a spree in 1973; city selected
for ALA conference. J. Shera. Wilson Lib
Bul 41:723+ Mr '67; Reply. H. G. More-
house. 41:887 My '67

Description
Editor's report: Las Vegas. M. M. Davis.
il Travel 128:36-9 N '67
Las Vegas: where anything is forgivable
except restraint. C. Stinnett. il Holiday
41:32+ My '67

LAS VEGAS, N.Mex.
That other Las Vegas. L. W. Beck. il Travel
128:36-8 D '67

LAS VEGAS tournament of champions. See
Golf—Tournaments

LASZLO, Erno
Svengali of the skin; with report by D. Lurie.
il pors Life 62:35-6+ Je 23 '67

LA TANA, Teresita
Teresita La Tana & Spanish dance co; 92nd
street Y. M. Marks. Dance Mag 41:70
Jl '67

LATENT heterosexual; drama. See Chayefsky,
P.

LATEX paint. See Paint

LATIL, Pierre de
TV programme girdling the world. UNESCO
Courier 20:38 N '67

LATIMER, Robert A.
Truly Nolen: exterminator of classics?
Motor T 19:84-6+ My '67

LATIMERIA. See Coelacanths

LATIN AMERICA
Focus on a few Latin American hangups.
L. Hayman. Sr Schol 91:9 O 5 '67
Is there a Latin America. R. Hilton. il Na-
tion 204:457-63 Ap 10 '67
Latin America, 1967; symposium. bibliog f
il Cur Hist 53:257-302+ N '67
Latin America today; symposium. Christian
Cent 85:69-83+ Ja 17 '68
South America's onrush to mañana; with re-
port by R. N. Goodwin. il Life 62:42-55+
Ap 14 '67
See also
Agriculture—Latin America
Anti-Communist movements—Latin America
Arts and crafts—Latin America
Catholic church in Latin America
Childrens literature—Latin America
Churches—Latin America
Cities and towns—Latin America
Colleges and universities—Latin America
Communism—Latin America
Community development—Latin America
Disarmament—Latin America
Economic assistance in Latin America
Education—Latin America
Guerrillas—Latin America
Investments, Foreign (in Latin America)
Missions—Latin America
Political parties—Latin America
Public health—Latin America
Roads—Latin America
Science—Latin America
Social classes—Latin America
Technical assistance in Latin America
Trade unions—Latin America
United Nations—Latin America
United States—Armed forces—Forces in Latin
America
Waterways—Latin America
Women—Latin America

Antiquities
See also
Indians of South America—Antiquities

Bibliography
Latin America's sociopolitical scene; checklist of pertinent paperbacks. Christian Cent
85:85 Ja 17 '68

Commerce
Goods for export. Américas 19:45 Je '67
Punta del Este revisited. L. Gordon. bibliog
f For Affairs 45:624-38 Jl '67
See also
Latin America—Economic integration
Latin American free trade association

Defenses
Arms to the Latins. New Repub 157:7 N 4 '67
Where a new arms race threatens. il U S
News 63:16 O 30 '67

Description and travel
From Bogotá to B.A; two nineteenth-century
travel books. J. N. Goodsell. Sat R 50:37
Jl 15 '67

Discovery and exploration
Dante discovers America. P. A. Cuadra. il
Américas 19:32-9 F '67
Raleigh and El Dorado of Guiana. H. T.
Sturcken. il Américas 19:15-21 Ag '67
South from the Spanish Main, ed. by E. P.
Hanson. Review
Sat R 50:41-2 O 7 '67. R. E. Crist

Economic conditions
Alliance that lost its way. E. F. Montalva.
For Affairs 45:436-48 Ap '67
Impasse in Latin America. A. H. Whiteford.
Christian Cent 85:71-4 Ja 17 '68
Latin America LBJ will not see. il U S News
62:35-7 Ap 17 '67
Problems and progress in Latin America; a
look ahead; interview. J. N. Wallace. il U S
News 63:70-2+ S 18 '67
South America's onrush to mañana; with re-
port by R. N. Goodwin. il Life 62:42-55+ Ap
14 '67
See also
United Nations—Economic commission for
Latin America

Economic integration
American Chiefs of state meet at Punta
del Este; statements, April 11-14, 1967;
with text of Declaration of the presidents
of America. L. B. Johnson. Dept State
Bul 56:706-21 My 8 '67
Economic integration of Latin America; ad-
dress, September 29, 1967. A. M. Solomon.
Dept State Bul 57:534-40 O 23 '67
Foreign ministers of the American republics
meet at Buenos Aires; statement, February
21, 1967, with resolution of meeting of for-
eign ministers, February 26, 1967. E. Bunker.
Dept State Bul 56:472-6 Mr 20 '67
Last chance for a common market. J. K.
Javits. For Affairs 45:449-62 Ap '67
Latin America LBJ will not see. il U S Nws
62:35-7 Ap 17 '67
Latin America now ready to get moving? il
U S News 62:52-4+ Ap 24 '67
Latin-American common market makes com-
mon sense for U.S. business too. W. Forbis
il Fortune 75:55-6 Je 1 '67
Latin American integration and the Alliance.
J. M. Hunter. bibliog f il Cur Hist 53:257-
62+ N '67
Latins try togetherness; Latin American Com-
mon market. il Bsns W p 104-5+ Ap 15 '67
Prologue to a common effort. Life 62:4 Ap 28
'67
Punta del Este revisited. L. Gordon. bib-
liog f For Affairs 45:624-38 Jl '67
Reflections on the Inter-American conference
of Chiefs of state; excerpts from address,
April 21, 1967. S. M. Linowitz. Dept State
Bul 56:729-31 My 8 '67
Road from Punta del Este; address, May 1,
1967. S. M. Linowitz. Dept State Bul 56:
822-5 My 29 '67
Secretary Rusk discusses the Punta del Este
conference on Viet-Nam on Meet the
press; transcript of interview, April 16, 1967.
D. Rusk. Dept State Bul 56:722-8 My 8 '67
Sovereignty and Latin American integration;
1967 constitution of Ecuador. F. Galo Leoro.
il Américas 19:28-33 S '67
Summit benefits. Time 89:38+ Ap 28 '67
Uncommon common market. S. Lens. Commonweal 86:387-9 Je 23 '67

Economic policy
Business advisory council of the OAS; annual
meeting. G. Meek. il Américas 19:40-1 D '67

Economic relations
United States
Can Sol Linowitz make it work? U.S. new
Latin American policy. il Bsns W p62+ F
18 '67
Latin America now ready to get moving? il
U S News 62:52-4+ Ap 24 '67
Latins try togetherness; Latin American Com-
mon market. il Bsns W p 104-5+ Ap 15 '67
Uncommon common market. S. Lens. Com-
monweal 86:387-9 Je 23 '67

Foreign relations
Cuba
Foreign ministers condemn Cuba; twelfth
meeting of consultation of ministers of for-
eign affairs. G. Meek. il Américas 19:43-4 N
'67
United States
See also
Inter-American conferences

History
Hernandarias; upper Peru to the Plate River.
V. Carreño. il Américas 19:27-35 My '67

LAUNDRIES, Commercial
    Wages and hours
    Earnings in laundry and cleaning services. J.
        C. Bush. bibliog f il Mo Labor R 90:52-4 Ap
        '67
LAUNDRY
    Care and safekeeping of table linens; how to
        keep them spot-free and crisply laundered.
        House & Gard 131:216+ Ap '67
    It all comes out in the wash. M. Davidson.
        il Ladies Home J 84:52+ S '67
    Laundry conference sets communication pat-
        tern. il Consumer Bul 50:30-1 F '67
    Removing rust from water and wash. E. Tay-
        lor. il Good H 165:187 Ag '67
LAUNDRY equipment
    Forty per cent of those laundry equipment
        services charges could be avoided. R.
        Charles. Parents Mag 42:71+ Jl '67
        See also
    Clothes dryers
    Washing machines
LAUNDRY workers
        See also
    Laundries, Commercial—Wages and hours
LAURANCE, Mike
    High speed Ektachrome; how far will it push?
        U S Camera 31:36-7+ Ja '68
    Nikon Photomic Tn. U S Camera 30:66-7 Jl
        '67
LAUREL and Hardy films. See Moving pic-
        tures—Comedy
LAUREL international. See Horse racing
LAUREL-Langley agreement. See Philippines—
        Commercial treaties and agreements
LAUREN, Carol, and Conn, F. G.
    Teenage ambassadors abroad. Parents Mag
        42:54-7+ My '67
LAURENCE, John
    Air; C.B.S. news show about Con Thien.
        M. J. Arlen. New Yorker 43:161-4+ S 30 '67
LAURENS, Henri
    Gallery for young people. C. B. Johnson. il
        Sch Arts 66:48 Mr '67
    Mirror of the moderns. il Time 90:40 S 1 '67
LAURENT, Pierre Henri
    (comp) Articles and other books; Low coun-
        tries. Am Hist R 72:1545 Jl '67
LAURENTS, Gene
    Shoot projected color. M. A. Matzkin. il Mod
        Phot 31:74-5+ Je '67
LAURINO, Agnes McEvoy
    Obituary
        Sr Schol por 91:sup3 O 19 '67
LAUX, P. J.
    Awful confessions of an anti-organization
        Catholic. America 117:108-10 Jl 29 '67
    Dispatches from the brave new world; or,
        Far afield with the Catholic press. America
        117:550-3+ N 11 '67
    Get thee to a nunnery, Ophelia de Sade!
        America 116:420-2 Mr 25 '67
        about
    Of many things; concerning Purple nuns of
        the divine retribution. T. N. Davis. America
        116:739 My 20 '67
LAUZON, June
    City kids take to the farm. Parents Mag 42:
        50-1+ D '67
LAVA
    Pahoehoe. il Sci N 92:223 S 2 '67
    Primary oxidation variation and distribution
        of uranium and thorium in a lava flow.
        N. D. Watkins and others. bibliog il Sci-
        ence 155:579-81 F 3 '67
        See also
    Volcanoes
LAVENDER, David
    How to make it to the White House without
        really trying. Am Heritage 18:26-7+ Je '67
LAVENDER
    It is fragrant, it is lavender. Sunset 139:139
        Jl '67
LAVER, James
    In the days of the bric-a-brac queen. L.
        Kronenberger. Atlan 220:88-91 Jl '67
LAVEY, Anton
    Ping is the thing. S. Alexander. Life 62:31
        F 17 '67
LAVIGNE, Richard. See Jacoby, S. jt. auth.
LAVIN, Henry St. C.
    Pictures at an Expo. America 117:344 S 30
        '67
LAVIN, Mary
    Gentle soul; story. Atlan 219:80-7 My '67
LAVIN, Pablo F.
    Alberdi, Pan Americanist. Américas 19:30-4
        Ap '67
LAVRENT'EV, Mikhail Alekseevich
    700,000 scientists in the U.S.S.R. in 1967.
        UNESCO Courier 20:31-2+ N '67

        about
    Man behind Science city. il pors UNESCO
        Courier 20:36 N '67
    Siberia's oasis for scientists. il por Bsns W
        p74-6+ Jl 22 '67
LAW, G. R. J.
    Alkaline phosphatase and leucine amino-
        peptidase association in plasma of the
        chicken. bibliog Science 156:1106-7; 157:721
        My 26, Ag 11 '67
LAW, John
    Eyewitness story; journey into a forgotten
        war. il U S News 62:58-60 Ap 3 '67
LAW
        See also
    Confession (law)
    Copyright
    Inheritance
    International law
    Judges
    Juvenile courts
    Lawyers
    Libel and slander
    Marriage
    Probate law and practice
    Roman law
    Trespass
    Wills
        also special branches of law e.g. Crim-
        inal law; also law on special subjects, e.g.
        Boats and boating—Laws and regulations

        History
        See also
    Roman law
        Study and teaching
    Course change in law school. il Sch & Soc
        95:103-4 F 18 '67
    New law vs. tradition. il Newsweek 69:104+
        Je 19 '67
        See also
    Law schools
        Alabama
    Interpreter in the front line; F. M. Johnson,
        district judge for Alabama's southeastern
        counties. il Time 89:72-4+ My 12 '67
        Argentina
        See also
    Legislation—Argentina
        Arkansas
    Hypocrisy in Arkansas; law makes it a
        felony to serve wine to minors during com-
        munion service. Christian Cent 84:365 Mr
        22 '67
        California
    California's law on Negro history. Negro Hist
        Bul 30:21-2 F '67
        See also
    Justice, Administration of—California
        Colorado
    Report from Colorado; we'll be the abortion
        mecca for the nation. J. Star. Look 31:67-9
        Jl 11 '67
        Denmark
    Transplants suspended; Danish nurses refuse
        assistance in kidney operations. H. J.
        Barnes. Sci N 92:60 Jl 15 '67
        France
    Floriot loses one. il Time 90:72-3 Jl 28 '67
        Great Britain
        See also
    Automobile laws and regulations—Great
        Britain
        Maryland
    One-man, one-vote shakes up Maryland. N.
        K. Herzfeld. Commonweal 86:142-3 Ap 21
        '67
        Massachusetts
        Anecdotes, facetiae, satire, etc.
    Open letter to the junior senator from
        Massachusetts; problem of getting a pool
        dug in North Egremont. R. Lynes. Harper
        234:28+ Mr '67
        North Carolina
    North Carolina High court denies pastoral
        immunity. Christian Cent 84:166 F 8 '67
        United States
        See also
    Courts—United States
    Justice, Administration of—United States
    Law enforcement
    Service men—Laws and legislation
    United States—Constitution

LAW, Maritime. See Maritime law
LAW, Roman. See Roman law
LAW, Usury. See Usury laws
LAW and mental illness. See Mental health laws
LAW and society. See Jurisprudence
LAW and technology. See Technology and law
LAW enforcement
Billy Graham's plea to President Johnson; reprint from Washington star and Congressional record, July 21, 1966. D. Lawrence. U S News 63:92 Ag 7 '67
Combating crime; symposium, ed. by L. E. Ohlin and H. S. Ruth, jr. bibliog f il Ann Am Acad 374:1-184 N '67
Cops, courts and Congress; effects of Supreme court decisions. J. O. Newman. New Repub 156:16-20 Mr 18 '67; Discussion. 156: 24-6 Ap 1; 44-5 Ap 8 '67
Hooked on law enforcement. E. Z. Friedenberg. il Nation 205:360-5 O 16 '67
Is it wrong to handcuff the police? W. J. Dempsey, jr Cath World 204:264-9 F '67
Medieval commune and internal violence; police power and public safety in Siena, 1287-1355. W. M. Bowsky. bibliog f Am Hist R 73:1-17 O '67
Recent trends: deviant behavior and social control. D. J. Bordua. bibliog f Ann Am Acad 369:149-63 Ja '67
Rising crime and the courts; state justices take a stand; text of resolution. U S News 63:53 Ag 28 '67
This month's feature: Congress & the national crime problem. Cong Digest 46:193-224 Ag '67
U.S. crime and law enforcement; symposium. bibliog f Cur Hist 53:1-42+ Jl '67
    See also
Police
LAW libraries
    See also
American association of law libraries
LAW of nations. See International law
LAW of relativity. See Relativity (physics)
LAW offenders. See Crime and criminals
LAW schools
Law schools: the thinking man's bastion; excerpts from The lawyers and the law. M. Mayer. Harper 234:70-4+ Je '67
New law vs. tradition. il Newsweek 69:104+ Je 19 '67
    See also
Association of American law schools
LAWFORD, Valentine
At Schloss Fasanerie. Vogue 150:142-9+ O 15 '67
Fresh wind through Versailles. Vogue 150: 124+ Ag 1 '67
Garden of American history; at the White House. Vogue 149:166-7+ F 1 '67
Garden of the heart. Vogue 149:182-7+ Ap 1 '67
Great persuader. Vogue 149:194-7+ My '67
Rococo getaway for Donna Marella Agnelli, in Italy. Vogue 150:218-25 O 1 '67
Zest house. Vogue 149:138-43 F 15 '67
LAWHEAD, C. Richard
Rubbermaid takes its turn at wheel. il por Bsns W p 124+ Ja 28 '67
LAWLER, Justus George
No time to leave. Commonweal 86:87-92 Ap 7 '67
LAWLESSNESS
Anarchy growing threat to big cities? il U S News 63:28-30 Ag 7 '67
Appeal by four Negro leaders: mob law, let's end it now! il U S News 63:11 Ag 7 '67
Civil disobedience: prelude to revolution? address, October 5, 1967. L. F. Powell, jr. il U S News 63:66-9 O 30 '67
Dissent or destruction? E. Sevareid. Look 31: 21-3 S 5 '67
Explosion in the cities; with editorial comment. il Bsns W p21-3, 124 Jl 29 '67
If you have any doubts Rap Brown inciting riots; excerpts from news conference, July 27, 1967. H. R. Brown. il U S News 63:8 Ag 7 '67
Is U.S. able to govern itself? il U S News 63:25-9 Jl 31 '67
Is U.S. fed up with lawlessness? excerpts from address, November 14, 1967. R. B. Morris. U S News 63:10 N 27 '67
It's time for courageous leadership. D. Lawrence. U S News 63:112 D 4 '67
LBJ's ideas on how to stop riots in the Nation's cities; address, July 27, 1967. L. B. Johnson. il U S News 63:56-7 Ag 7 '67; Same with title Rioting in the cities. Vital Speeches 33:642-4 Ag 15 '67

New Johnson makes his debut; excerpts from news conference, November 17, 1967. L. B. Johnson. il U S News 63:21-2 N 27 '67. Same with title LBJ fights back at critics. Sr Schol 91:21 N 30 '67
New Negro threat: mass disobedience; excerpts from address, August 15, 1967. M. L. King. U S News 63:10 Ag 28 '67
Our disordered society. D. Lawrence. U S News 63:88 Ag 14 '67
Patriot and protester: can a man be both? History behind the headlines. il Sr Schol 91:8-12+ S 21 '67
Politics as usual; Republican coordinating committee statement. Nation 205:99-100 Ag 14 '67
Racial violence inevitable or preventable? il Sr Schol 91:8-13 O 13 '67
Respect for the law: breaking down all over? excerpts from address, 1967. G. B. McClellan. U S News 63:17 Ag 21 '67
Riot forecast: more violence in new year. il U S News 64:62 Ja 8 '68
Riots and mob spirit: America's greatest danger; excerpts from address, January 27, 1838. A. Lincoln. U S News 63:92+ Ag 28 '67
Speech that touched a tender nerve in Congress; excerpts from address, July 25, 1967. T. G. Abernethy. U S News 63:33 Ag 7 '67
We should be ashamed. D. D. Eisenhower. Read Digest 91:67-71 Ag '67
What has happened to America? R. M. Nixon. Read Digest 91:49-54 O '67
White House aborts the riots commission. E. Garvey. Commonweal 87:429-30 Ja 12 '68
Why organized crime thrives. H. S. Ruth, jr. bibliog f Ann Am Acad 374:113-22 N '67
LAWN bowling. See Bowling
LAWN edgers. See Lawn mowers
LAWN mowers
Case for buying a reel mower. J. Hand. il Pop Sci 190:154-8 Mr '67
Do you need a lawn edger? A. Whittier. il Pop Sci 191:124-6+ Jl '67
Gasoline mowers. Consumer Rep 32:189-95 D '67
Here come the electric mowers! J. Hand. il Pop Sci 190:154-8 F '67
Is your lawn mower ready for a trade-in? J. Liston. il Pop Gard 18:60-7 Ag '67
Lawn edgers. il Consumer Rep 32:386-9 Jl '67
Mowing the lawn by electricity. il Consumer Bul 50:20-1 Jl '67
Power explosion. il House & Gard 131:200-3 Ap '67
Riding mower or tractor, which for you? J. Hand. il Pop Sci 190:144-7 Ap '67
Rivals join Sunbeam's lawn party. il Bsns W p 184-5 My 6 '67
Your power mower, friend and foe. Am Home 70:138 Mr '67
    Care
Winterizing your power mower. R. J. Berger. Am Home 70:142+ O '67
LAWN seeds. See Grasses—Seed
LAWN spikers. See Garden tools, equipment and supplies
LAWN sprinklers. See Sprinklers
LAWN sweepers
What's become of the leaf rake? J. Raymond. il Pop Gard 18:76-81 D '67
LAWN tennis. See Tennis
LAWNS
Build a weed free lawn. Pop Gard 18:65 My '67
Early spring lawn care; your questions answered. R. W. Schery. Home Gard 54: 72-4 Mr '67
Establishing a new lawn. Pop Gard 18:62 My '67
Good lawns; from coast to coast. il Home Gard 54:35-6 My '67
Instant lawn from sod. Am Home 71:110 Ja '68
Instant lawn: sodding. il Sunset 139:62-3 S '67
Now you can have a perfect lawn. il Pop Gard 18:60-1+ My '67
Perfect lawn. il Home Gard 54:50-1 Mr '67
Seeding a lawn. il Bet Hom & Gard 45:10+ S '67
Sod, just unroll a new lawn. il Changing T 21:30 Ap '67
Time of decision (again) il Home Gard 54:22-3 S '67
Twenty steps to a perfect lawn. M. C. Shurtleff. il Pop Gard 18:68-9+ Ag '67
University inaugurates turf management program. D. W. Griffiths, jr. il Parks & Rec 2:35+ Ap '67
When the lawn becomes a playground. R. Engel. il Home Gard 54:47 Je '67
    See also
Sprinklers

LAWNS—*Continued*

Diseases and pests

Lawn pests, the grass invaders. Am Home 70:64 My '67
Out, browned spot! out, I say! il Home Gard 54:54-5 Ag '67
What's causing those brown spots? il Sunset 138:186+ Je '67

LAWNS, Artificial. See Turf, Artificial

LAWNS, Watering of. See Watering of gardens, lawns, etc.

LAWRENCE, David
Road to a third world war. U S News 63:120 O 9 '67; Same abr. Read Digest 92:19-20 Ja '68

LAWRENCE, David Herbert
D. H. Lawrence in Taos. P. S. Beagle. Holiday 42:44-5+ S '67

LAWRENCE, Gertrude
Julie plays Gertie. J. A. Zill. il Look 31:63-8 S 19 '67

LAWRENCE, L. George
Electronics for speech and hearing therapy. Electr World 78:44-5+ S '67
Microwave ETV system planning & installation. Electr World 77:34-6 My '67

LAWRENCE, Paul R. and Lorsch, J. W.
New management job: the integrator. Harvard Bsns R 45:142-51 N '67

LAWRENCE, Robert
Freni-Gedda Elisir. Sat R 50:56 O 28 '67
London Faust. Sat R 50:61-2 Je 24 '67
Orchestra in opera. Opera N 32:14-17 D 9; 13-16 D 16; 10-13 D 23; 26-9 D 30 '67; 26-9 Ja 6 '68
Treasury of Toscanini broadcasts. Sat R 50:61 My 27 '67

LAWRENCE, Samuel A.
Lawrence to head marine commission. S. Montgomery. Tech W 20:40 My 15 '67

LAWRENCE, Sheree Gayle
Two women. M. Orovan. il U S Camera 30:46-7 Mr '67

LAWRENCE, Thomas Edward
Desert revolt urged on by a legendary Englishman. E. Kern. il por Life 63:54-5 O 20 '67

LAWRENCE memorial award. See Ernest Orlando Lawrence memorial awards

LAWRENSON, Helen
Mirror, mirror, on the ceiling: how'm I doin'? Esquire 68:72-4+ Jl '67
Who is the world's foremost actor? Esquire 68:180-3+ D '67

LAWS of thermodynamics. See Thermodynamics

LAWSON, R. B. and Mount, D. C.
Minimum condition for stereopsis and anomalous contour. bibliog Science 158:804-6 N 10 '67

LAWSON, Ruth C.
New regime in Turkey. Cur Hist 52:105-10+ F '67

LAWSON company
Lawson constructing new plant in Canada. Pub W 191:115 F 6 '67

LAWSUITS. See Actions and defenses

LAWYERS
Bailey for the defense. il Newsweek 69:35-6+ Ap 17 '67
Brash newcomer to the ranks of great defenders: F. L. Bailey. D. Jackson. il Life 62:45-6+ F 17 '67
Clients against lawyers. D. T. Bazelon. Harper 235:104+ S '67
Few words about lawyers. M. Mayer. il Esquire 67:124-7+ Ap '67
Gadflies who put the bite on business; plaintiffs' lawyers. il Bsns W p 124-6+ O 14 '67
Ghetto lawyer; free legal services to indigents. J. J. Graham. Commonweal 87:198-201 N 17 '67
Handbook of success, chapter III; F. L. Bailey. il Time 89:91 My 19 '67
Law firm helps shape southern unionism; Cooper, Mitch & Crawford, Birmingham labor law firm. il Bsns W p 154+ S 30 '67
Lawyers, by M. Mayer. Review
  Commentary 44:102+ D '67. D. T. Bazelon
  New Repub 157:24-5 S 23 '67. A. M. Bickel
Legal checkup your family may need. Good H 164:156 F '67
Losing winner; blind and crippled lawyer in Greece. Time 89:38 Mr 3 '67
Special breed: three others; Ed Williams; Percy Foreman; Melvin Belli. il Newsweek 69:42 Ap 17 '67
Why law is a growth industry. il Bsns W p78-9 Ja 13 '68
Winning loser: E. B. Williams loses case of Bobby Baker. il Time 89:66+ F 10 '67
  See also
American bar association
Legal aid

Salaries, fees, etc.
See Cost (law)

Training
See Law—Study and teaching

LAWYERS constitutional defense committee
Civil-rights setback in southern courts; efforts to deny northern lawyers right to practice. G. B. Driesen. il Reporter 36:18-22 F 23 '67

LAY-off compensation. See Wages—Dismissal wage

LAY professors See College professors and instructors

LAYCOCK, George
Camping the calendar highway. Field & S 71:40-3 Mr '67
Dam the Big Hole, full speed ahead. Field & S 72:12-16+ My '67
Tow your boat to a northern wilderness. Field & S 72:158-61+ My '67
Troubled alligator. Field & S 71:49+ Ap '67

LAYMEN. See Laity

LAYTON, Winifred Heiskell
Oldest living thing; poem. Am For 73:51 Jl '67
Silence; poem. Liv Wildn 30:35 Wint '66

LAZAR, Joseph
Juridical perspectives on national character. bibliog f Ann Am Acad 370:16-22 Mr '67

LAZARD, Naomi
Ever since Greencastle; poem. Sat R 50:35 F 11 '67

LAZARUS, A. L.
Children's matinee; poem. Christian Cent 84:198 F 15 '67
Grandfather; poem. Commonweal 87:111 O 27 '67

LAZARUS, Fred, family
Shuffling the Lazari. il por Time 90:90 S 29 '67
Who's watching the store. Newsweek 70:81+ O 2 '67

LAZARUS, George
Madison avenue. Sat R 50:128 Mr 11; 94-5 My 13; 103-5 Je 10; 58-9 S 9; 93-4 N 11; 64 D 9 '67

LAZARUS, Ralph
Federated, and the consumer comeback. J. Poindexter. il por Duns R 90:38-42+ D '67

LAZARUS, Simon
Black power? New Repub 158:27-8+ Ja 13 '68

LAZEGA, Max
Aftermath of war in the Middle East. Cath World 206:155-9 Ja '68

LEACH corporation
Leach claiming data packing improvements of at least 18:1. C. D. LaFond. il Tech W 20:34 My 29 '67

LEAD
Exposed lead membrane for reflecting pools. il Arch Rec 142:161-2 D '67

Isotopes
Oceanic basalt leads: a new interpretation and an independent age for the earth. T. J. Ulrych. bibliog il Science 158:252-6 O 13 '67

LEAD fumes
Ice nuclei from direct reaction of iodine vapor with vapors from leaded gasoline. A. W. Hogan. Science 158:800 N 10 '67

LEAD in the body
Lead hazard discounted. D. A. Ehrlich. Sci N 92:278 S 16 '67

LEAD poisoning
Lead poisoning. Consumer Bul 50:37-40 F '67
Respiratory exposure to lead: epidemiological and experimental dose-response relationships. J. R. Goldsmith and A. C. Hexter. bibliog il Science 158:132-4 O 6 '67

LEADABRAND, Russ
What about Mineral King? Am For 73:18-20+ F '67

LEADERSHIP
Dynamics of leadership; address, March 7, 1967. J. R. Gibb. Vital Speeches 33:375-80 Ap 1 '67
From a coach of champions: advice to businessmen on how to lead; excerpts from address, February 8, 1967. V. Lombardi. U S News 62:14 F 20 '67
If we are to be leaders... R. M. McClure and O. Sand. NEA J 56:28-31 D '67
Management of disappointment. A. Zaleznik. bibliog f Harvard Bsns R 45:59-70 N '67
Missing element, moral courage. B. W. Tuchman. McCalls 94:28+ Je '67
What it takes to be a leader; excerpt from address. M. W. Clark. Read Digest 91:160-2 Jl '67
Who leads today's youth? round table discussion from 1967 student burgesses at Williamsburg. il Sr Schol 90:4-9+ Ap 14 '67

LEADVILLE, Colo.
There may be joy in Leadville, if silver pans
  out. il Bsns W p 128-30 D 2 '67
LEAF blowers. See Lawn sweepers
LEAF cookery. See Cookery—Vegetables
LEAF gatherers
Collect twice the leaves with the same crew;
  Massapequa Park, N.Y.   C. J. Hart. il
  Am City 82:116-17 Ap '67
Low-cost leaf collection without special equip-
  ment; West Allis, Wis. R. E. Hahn. il Am
  City 82:54 Ap '67
  See also
  Lawn sweepers
**LEAF pulverizers. See Garden tools, equip-
  ment and supplies**
LEAF-spring switches. See Electric switches
LEAFLETS. See Pamphlets
LEAGUE of Nations
U.N. vs. League of Nations. il U S News
  63:29 Jl 24 '67
LEAGUE of New York theatres, incorporated
Theatre bus; East side service. New Yorker
  43:37-8 My 6 '67
**LEAGUE of women voters of the United
  States**
  Overseas education fund
Women as citizens; conferences. C. F. Ware.
  il Américas 19:26-30 D '67
LEAHY, William
Friction in Philadelphia. A. Swidler. Common-
  weal 87:463-4 Ja 19 '68
LEAKE, Chauncey D.
Drug information. Science 158:161-3 O 6 '67
LEAKEY, Louis Seymour Bazett
Ascent of man. B. Tufty. il por Sci N 91:
  188-9 F 25 '67
Bones of contention. Newsweek 69:102+ F 13
  '67
Searching for the common link. il por Time
  89:64-5 F 3 '67
LEAMER, Laurence
Out West with candidate Wallace. New Repub
  157:11-13 D 16 '67
**LEANING tower of Pisa. See Pisa—Campanile
  (leaning tower)**
LEAR, Evelyn
Eye on tomorrow; interview, ed. by R. D.
  Daniels. por Opera N 31:16 Mr 18 '67
Operatic jet set. pors Hi Fi 17:53-6 Mr '67
  about
Lively arts; interview, ed. by R. Hemming.
  il por Sr Schol 91:27-8 O 26 '67
LEAR, John
Research in America. See issues of Saturday
  review
Science and the peace adventure. Sat R 50:
  64-5+ S 23 '67
  about
A communication concerning the UFOs. J. G.
  Fuller. Sat R 50:70-2 F 4 '67
LEAR, Martha Weinman
Caine mutiny. McCalls 94:86-7+ Mr '67
Her name is Barbra. Redbook 130:54-5+
  Ja '68
LEAR, Robert W.
Medicine man at Indian Head. il por Bsns W
  p84+ Ag 19 '67
LEAR Jet corporation
Biography of a hired gun. R. Bach. il Flying
  80:40-3 Ap '67
LEAR Siegler, incorporated
Building muscle with outside help. il Bsns W
  p93-4+ S 16 '67
LEARNED, Stanley
How they won the West, and more. il por
  Bsns W p 178-80+ Ja 28 '67
LEARNED journals. See Priodicals
LEARNING, Maze. See Maze tests
LEARNING, Psychology of
Changes in instructional psychology; sum-
  mary of address, December 5, 1967. R. Glas-
  er. Pub W 193:36 Ja 8 '68
Discrimination learning and inhibition. H. S.
  Terrace; reply with rejoinder. J. A. Deutsch.
  Science 156:988-9 My 19 '67
Early learners; excerpt from Revolution in
  learning. M. Pines. il McCalls 95:74+ Ja '68
Education comes alive outdoors. R. M. Isen-
  ber. il NEA J 56:34-5 Ap '67
Effects of magnesium pemoline and dextro-
  amphetamine on human learning. J. T.
  Burns and others. bibliog il Science 155:
  849-51 F 17 '67
Fear of being wrong; theories of J. Holt. il
  Time 90:37 S 1 '67
Formulas for learning. il Sci N 91:406-7 Ap 29
  '67

Freeing pupils from the sit-look-listen syndrome. H. W. Ray. il NEA J 56:8-10 Ap '67
Hand them a *frobish*; learning through the
  five senses. R. M. Bilenker. il NEA J 56:
  30-1+ O '67
Help your child learn more, better, faster. M.
  Mayer. Bet Hom & Gard 45:18+ S '67
How children learn, by J. Holt. Review
  Life 63:12 D 15 '67. J. Kozol
Jean Piaget: notes on learning; with excerpts
  from addresses. F. G. Jennings. il Sat R
  50:81-3 My 20 '67
Learning-set formation by mink, ferrets,
  skunks, and cats. B. A. Doty and others.
  bibliog il Science 155:1579-80 Mr 24 '67
Nervous habits are assets. A. J. Snider. il
  Sci Digest 62:68 D '67
Self-fulfilling prophecies. Sci Am 217:54+ N
  '67
Total luminous flux: a possible response de-
  terminant for the normal monkey. P. Schil-
  der and others. bibliog il Science 158:806-9
  N 10 '67
Unlocking early learning's secrets. il Life
  62:40-7 Mr 31 '67
Visual and auditory information processing in
  children and adults. E. C. Carterette and
  M. H. Jones. bibliog il Science 156:986-8
  My 19 '67
What we're learning about learning. R.
  Kramer. il N Y Times Mag p65-6+ Je 11 '67
You get what you expect. Sr Schol 91:sup4
  O 5 '67
  See also
  Ability
  Attention
  Conditioned response
  Psychology, Educational
  Readiness for learning
LEARNING ability. See Ability
LEARNING and scholarship
  See also
  Humanism
  Intellectuals
  Knowledge
LEARNING centers. See Childrens rooms
**LEARNING materials. See Teaching—Aids and
  devices**
LEARY, Daniel J.
Book of the month. Cath World 205:177-8 Je
  '67
Cinema of the absurd. Cath World 204:301-6
  F '67
Evolution; poem. Cath World 205:115 My '67
New books. Cath World 205:54+ Ap '67
Theater of dislike. Cath World 205:217-22
  Jl '67
Under twenty-five. Cath World 206:121-4 D '67
Utilized energy potential: a moneyless utopia.
  Cath World 204:335-40 Mr '67
LEARY, Francis
Tower of London. Horizon 10:73-81 Wint '68
LEARY, Howard R.
Crime in the city; address, June 5, 1967.
  Vital Speeches 34:22-4 O 15 '67
LEARY, John P.
Catholic college education; address, June 11,
  1967. Vital Speeches 33:635-8 Ag 1 '67
Layman in Catholic higher education. Amer-
  ica 116:251-3 F 18 '67
LEARY, Mary Ellen
Emancipation comes to the Pribilofs. Re-
  porter 36:25-9 Mr 9 '67
LEARY, Timothy
Drugs and mysticism: visions of Saint Tim.
  J. W. Flagler. il pors Look 31:18+ Ag 8
  '67
Giants. por Esquire 68:138 O '67
Leary under the glass. D. McDonagh. Nat R
  19:360+ Ap 4 '67
LEASES
Guidelines to cash farm leasing. R. J. Fee.
  il Suc Farm 65:31+ O '67
If you rent your home for the summer. il
  Good H 164:196 My '67
More interest in renting land. B. Brantley.
  Suc Farm 65:74 Ap '67
What's a fair lease for irrigated lamb? B.
  Brantley. Suc Farm 65:22C My '67
**LEASING of equipment. See Agricultural ma-
  chinery—Leasing**
LEATHAM, Nyle
Pilot report: Lark 95. Flying 80:44-8 Mr '67
LEATHER gifts. See Gifts
LEATHER industry and trade
  See also
  Mark Cross company
LEATHER substitutes
Du Pont stubs its toe. J. Ross-Skinner. il
  Duns R 89:61 Je '67
Footrace in synthetics; man-made shoe ma-
  terials called poromerics. il Bsns W p40
  F 25 '67

LEATHERBEE, Mary
Brave ghosts, gallant dancers. Life 62:72+ F 17 '67
Fresh bread, a secret agent and a lock-keeper's cactus. Life 62:63+ Je 23 '67
Lively night on river of the dead. por Life 63:88A-88B S 8 '67

LEAVENS, Peter A.
Space astronomy at Expo 67. Sky & Tel 34: 72-8 Ag '67

LEAVES
How to cope with leaves that fall. D. Barrows. Home Gard 54:47 O '67
Leaf epicuticular waxes. G. Eglinton and R. J. Hamilton. bibliog il Science 156:1322-35 Je 9 '67

LEAVES of absence. See College professors ond instructors—Leaves of absence

LEAVITT, Frederick
Mr Leavitt comes to Harvard. G. Ross. Nation 205:654-8 D 18 '67

LEAVITT, Harold J.
Company president is a Berkeley student. Harvard Bsns R 45:152-4+ N '67

LEAVITT, Helen
Washington fights creeping concrete. Reporter 36:39-41 Ja 26; 12 F 23 '67

LEAVITT, Hunt
Ten safety tips for outboard racing. Motor B 120:36-7+ Jl '67

LEBANESE in Brazil
Sons of the Phoenicians. Newsweek 71:39-40 Ja 8 '68

LEBANON
See also
Banks and banking—Lebanon

Description and travel
Lebanon's coastal salt farms. il Sunset 139: 19 D '67
Travel's picture portfolio. Travel 128:50-5 O '67

Economic conditions
Bystander country in Mideast, it was hurt, too. il U S News 63:56 Ag 28 '67

Politics and government
Cairo's meddler at it again. America 116:615 Ap 29 '67

LEBEL, Jean Jacques
Other culture. B. Farrell. il por Life 62:88+ F 17 '67

LEBER, Georg
Blitzing trucks off the highway. il por Bsns W p 104-6+ N 11 '67

LEBHERZ, Herbert G. and Rutter, W. J.
Glyceraldehyde-3-phosphate dehydrogenase variants in phyletically diverse organisms. bibliog Science 157:1198-200 S 8 '67

LE BLANC, Jerry
(ed) See Mitchell, A. Killing me solves nothing

LEBRUN, Charles, family
Life-or-death decision with a happy ending. S. Frank. il Good H 165:48+ O '67

LEBRUN, Marie Louise Elisabeth Vigée-. See Vigée-Lebrun, M. L. E.

LEC, Stanislaw J.
More unkempt thought; poem. Holiday 41: 118p F '67

LECHLITNER, Ruth
Drawing by Ronnie C, grade one; poem. Sat R 50:39 Jl 15 '67

LECHT, Charles T.
No nonsense; interview. New Yorker 43:25-7 Ag 19 '67

LECITHIN
Forces between lecithin bimolecular leaflets are due to a disordered surface layer. V. A. Parsegian. bibliog il Science 156:939-42 My 19 '67

LECLERCQ, Tanaquil
Who's cooking? excerpts from The ballet cook book. pors Dance Mag 41:58-9+ N '67

LE CORBEILLER, Jean
About the author. Natur Hist 76:20 Je '67

LE CORBUSIER
Centre Le Corbusier. U. Roth. il Arch Forum 127:82-7 S '67
Homage to Corbu. il Time 90:72 S 15 '67

LECTURES and lecturing

Copyright
See Copyright—Lectures, sermons, etc.

LEDDIHN, Erik Maria, ritter von Kuehnelt-. See Kuehnelt-Leddihn, E. M. von

LEDDY, John M.
NATO on the eve of its 20th anniversary; address, November 13, 1967. Dept State Bul 57:759-62 D 4 '67

LEDERBERG, Joshua
Eutechnics, motif for new technology. por Tech W 20:49-50+ Ja 23 '67

Experimental genetics and human evolution. Bul Atomic Sci 22:4-11 O '66; 23:60-1 Je '67
Some problems of instant medicine. por Sat R 50:66-70 My 6 '67

LEDERER, Muriel
Perspiration, everybody's problem. Todays Health 45:12-14 Ag '67

LEDERER, William J.
Vietnam: those computer reports. New Repub 157:13-14 D 23 '67

LEE, Ann
It is Christ who dwells in me. D. Martin. Life 62:68+ Mr 17 '67

LEE, Anthony K. and Mercer, E. H.
Cocoon surrounding desert-dwelling frogs. bibliog Science 157:87-8 Jl 7 '67
—See MacMillen, R. E. jt. auth.

LEE, Bud
Soldier with a camera. E. Galligan. il U S Camera 30:44-9+ Je '67

LEE, Byung Chull
B. C. Lee's world. il por Time 89:98 Ap 28 '67

LEE, David
Serial rights. Art N 66:42-5+ D '67

LEE, Deborah
Works by Joseph Cino, Deborah Lee, Charles Stanley & James Waring, Judson memorial church. J. Anderson. Dance Mag 41:37+ Mr '67

LEE, Gordon
Data processing can save money. Pub W 191:52-4 Mr 20 '67

LEE, Jessica
Island of pearls. Travel 128:45-9 D '67

LEE, Joe B.
Angelo state designs for growth. Library J 92: 4358-9 D 1 '67

LEE, John C. and Ingram, V. M.
Erythrocyte transfer RNA: change during chick development. bibliog Science 158:1330-2 D 8 '67

LEE, Josie
Face to face with a Vietnamese girl in New York. por Seventeen 26:161 My '67

LEE, Kuan-yew
Prime Minister of Singapore visits the United States; exchange of greetings, October 17, with joint statement, October 18, 1967. Dept State Bul 57:612-15 N 6 '67
about
Asian diary J. Mander. Commentary 44:92 O '67
Lee Kuan Yew's fight for survival. D. Warner. Reporter 37:36-8 N 2 '67
Rugged society. il por Time 89:38+ Ap 21 '67
Two Asian leaders who support U.S. role in Vietnam. por U S News 63:22 O 30 '67

LEE, Laurie
Charm. Mlle 65:152+ My '67; Same abr. with title Essence of charm. Read Digest 91: 181-2+ Ag '67
Village that lost its children. Redbook 130: 58-60+ Ja '68

LEE, Marjorie
Be honest with me; story. Redbook 128:80-1 Ap '67

LEE, Maurice, jr
Jacobean diplomatic service. bibliog f Am Hist R 72:1264-82 Jl '67

LEE, Oliver M.
Myth of Chinese aggression. Nation 205:459-63 N 6 '67

LEE, Patricia Ann
Printing with a soap eraser. Sch Arts 67:28-9 O '67

LEE, Peggy
Parsimonious Peggy. por Time 90:46+ N 3 '67

LEE, Philip R.
Health and well-being. bibliog f Ann Am Acad 373:193-207 S '67

LEE, Richard B.
Trance cure of the Kung Bushmen. il Natur Hist 76:30-7 N '67

LEE, Richard Charles
Dick Lee discovers how much is not enough. B. Asbell. il por N Y Times Mag p6-7+ S 3 '67
Mayor's game, by A. R. Talbot. Review Reporter 37:46-8 O 19 '67. R. D. Masters
Troubled cities, and their mayors. il por Newsweek 69:38-41 Mr 13 '67

LEE, Robert J.
Artist speaks out. il Am Artist 32:38-43+ Ja '68

LEE, Robert W.
Baltimore bookman fights against KKK terrorism. Pub W 191:35-6 Mr 27 '67

LEE, Su Kun
Why I fled from Communist North Korea; interview, ed. by K. M. Chrysler. por U S News 62:60-1 My 29 '67

LEE, Sung, and Aronoff, S.
Boron in plants: a biochemical role. bibliog Science 158:798-9 N 10 '67

LEE, Welby, and Lindeman, Bard
I hunted twenty years to find my father's killer. pors Sat Eve Post 240:74-9 Ag 26 '67

LEE, William Storrs
Stone walls do not a prison make. Am Heritage 18:40-3+ F '67

LEECH, Michael T.
Emperor and the nightingale; dramatization of story by H. C. Andersen. Plays 26:49-54 Ap '67
Galileo; drama. Plays 27:13-27 O '67
How much land does a man need? dramatization of story by L. Tolstoy. Plays 27:75-86 Ja '68
Scarlet Pimpernel; dramatization of novel by E. Orczy. Plays 26:93-108 My '67
Snow queen; dramatization of a story by H. C. Andersen. Plays 26:69-74, 96 F '67
Story of Gilbert and Sullivan; drama. Plays 27:83-96 N '67

LEEDHAM, Charles
Handwriting on the air terminal wall. N Y Times Mag p28-9+ My 21 '67

LEEK, Sybil
Horoscopes. See issues of Ladies' home journal
Horoscopes for mothers. Ladies Home J 84:12+ My '67

LEEN, Nina
To see America: photographs. Life 63:44-55 Ag 25 '67

LEES, Al
Now you can lay a Spanish tile floor. Pop Mech 127:106-9+ Je '67
Prize-winning kites. Pop Mech 127:108-11 Mr '67

LEES, Bob
It's a bird! it's a plane! it's industrials! W. Como. il por Dance Mag 41:24-5 Je '67

LEES, Gene
Beatles. op. 15. Hi Fi 17:94 Ag '67
Folk music. Hi Fi 17:118 S '67
From spirituals to swing, 1967. Hi Fi 17:MA7+ Ap '67
Johnny Mercer, master lyricist. Hi Fi 17:61-3 Je '67
Lees side. See issues of High fidelity incorporating Musical America
Nashville the sounds and the symbols. Hi Fi 17:57-61 Ap '67
New sound on the soundtracks. Hi Fi 17:58-61 Ag '67
Newport revisited. Hi Fi 17:MA20-3 S '67
Oscar Peterson playing. Holiday 41:152+ Ap '67
Rock. Hi Fi 17:57-61 N '67

LEES, Hannah
How to be happy though incompatible; reprint; excerpt from Help your husband stay alive. Read Digest 90:138-40 Ap '67

LEEWARD ISLANDS
See also
Guadeloupe (islands)

LEFEBVRE, Georges
Many lives of Georges Lefebvre. G. Shapiro. bibliog f Am Hist R 72:502-14 Ja '67

LEFEVER, Ernest W.
Church and politics: the Protestant debate. Reporter 38:39-40+ Ja 11 '68
Rhodesia's case. Reporter 37:45 O 19 '67
Vietnam: joining the issues. Cath World 205:72-7 My '67

LEFEVRE, Paul G.
Imine-bonding in membrane transport of monosaccharides: invalidity of kinetic evidence. bibliog Science 158:274-5 O 13 '67

LEFF, J. and Krinsky, N. I.
Mutagenic effect of visible light mediated by endogenous pigments in euglena gracilis. bibliog Science 158:1332-5 D 8 '67

LEFFERTS, Barney
Chief guru of the western world. N Y Times Mag p44-5+ D 17 '67

LEFKOWITZ, Bernard. See Carlinsky, D. jt. auth.

LEFT and right (political science) See Right and left (political science)

LEFT- and right-handedness
Evoked cortical potentials: relation to visual field and handedness. R. G. Eason and others. bibliog il Science 156:1643-6 Je 23 '67
Left-handers. il Newsweek 69:72 F 13 '67
Lefties, a maligned minority. H. J. Massaquoi. il Ebony 22:63-4+ My '67
New Year's plea: the right to be left-handed. P. Farber. il U S Camera 31:24+ Ja '68

LEFT wing (politics) See Right and left (political science)

LEFTOVERS. See Cookery—Leftovers

LEG
Legs swollen? find the cause. Todays Health 45:76-8+ F '67

LEG braces. See Orthopedic apparatus

LEGACIES
See also
Wills

LEGACY; story. See Gaines, D.

LEGAL aid
Champion of the rural poor; California rural legal assistance agency. Time 90:75 D 15 '67
Courtroom classrooms; Georgetown students. il Time 89:45 Ja 27 '67
Ghetto lawyer; free legal services to indigents. J. J. Graham. Commonweal 87:198-201 N 17 '67
Helping the poor find justice; Legal services program of the OEO. W. Greene. il Reporter 36:16-18 My 18 '67
Lawyers for the poor; legal services program. New Repub 157:9-10 N 11 '67
U.S. letter: McFarland; California rural legal assistance program. C. Trillin. New Yorker 43:173-4+ N 4 '67
Why Reagan's mad; California rural legal assistance program. New Repub 157:13-14 O 21 '67

LEGAL confession. See Confession (law)

LEGAL education. See Law—Study and teaching; Law schools

LEGAL ethics
Ghetto lawyer; free legal services to indigents. J. J. Graham. Commonweal 87:198-201 N 17 '67

LEGAL profession. See Lawyers

LE GALLIENNE, Eva
(tr) See Ibsen, H. Wild duck

LEGEND of the invisible city of Kitezh; opera. See Rimskiĭ-Korsakov, N. A.

LEGENDS
Legends of gem stones. Good H 165:195 O '67
See also
Folklore

LÉGER, Alexis Saint-Léger
Perse in flight. K. G. Chapin. New Repub 157:26-8 S 23 '67
Poetry of abstraction. H. Carruth. Poetry 110:184-6 Je '67

LÉGER, Fernand
Léger legacy. M. Pleynet. il Art N 65:42-3+ F '67

LEGER, Paul Emile, cardinal
Cardinal for a leper colony. por Time 90:87 N 17 '67
Cardinal resigns. C. De Mestral. Christian Cent 84:1606 D 13 '67
Sense of mission. il por Newsweek 70:122 N 20 '67

LEGERDEMAIN. See Conjuring

LEGEROS, Racquel Z. and others
Apatite crystallites: effects of carbonate on morphology. bibliog Science 155:1409-11 Mr 17 '67

LEGG, Jean
Open-door policy for state libraries? por Library J 92:207-9 Ja 15 '67

LEGGE, Bill
English-language broadcasts to North America. See issues of Popular electronics

LEGGE, Robert
Foreign-language broadcasts to North America. Pop Electr 27:74 N '67

LEGGE, Roger
Let's listen to Central and South America. Pop Electr 28:80 Ja '68

LEGGETT, John
Little flames of genius; story. Mlle 65:138-9 Je '67

LEGGETT, William
Baseball (cont) Sports Illus 26:66+ Mr 20; 65-8 My 22; 58+ Je 19; 27:61-3 O 23 '67
—See Stanky, E. jt. auth.

LEGIBILITY of printing. See Printing—Legibility

LEGISLATION
Argentina
Is Bormann in Argentina? Nation 205:229 S 18 '67
New York (state)
Alimony for men? New York bill for alimony reform. Newsweek 71:58 Ja 8 '68
See also
Labor laws and legislation—New York (state)

United States
Congress puts off the tough decisions. Bsns W p38-40 D 16 '67
GOP digs in its heels; proposals; prospects. Bsns W p42+ Je 24 '67
How Johnson fared with an unhappy Congress. il U S News 63:18-20 D 25 '67
Laundry list; legislative proposals. Newsweek 69:32+ Mr 27 '67

LEGISLATION—United States—*Continued*
Monkey business. il Newsweek 69:33+ Ap 24 '67
President's program. Newsweek 69:32 Mr 27 '67
See also
Judicial review
Library laws and legislation
Lobbying
Social legislation—United States
United States—Congress
United States—Supreme court

LEGISLATIVE bodies
United States
See also
State legislatures
United States—Congress

LEGISLATURES, State. See State legislatures

LEGLER, Philip
Bedstraw; poem. Poetry 110:390 S '67
O yellow eye. Poetry 110:125-7 My '67
Three poets. Poetry 109:411-15 Mr '67

LEGO building toys. See Toys

LEGUMES
Legume revolutionizes beef output; northern Australia. W. A. Scholes. Sci N 92:563 D 9 '67

LEHMAN, Edward W. See Etzioni, A. jt. auth.

LEHMAN, Leo
East wind. Criticism
America 116:355-6 Mr 11 '67
Commonweal 85:681-2 Mr 17 '67
New Yorker 42:132 F 18 '67
Newsweek 69:102 F 20 '67
Sat R 50:59 F 25 '67
Time 89:70 F 17 '67

LEHMAN, Robert A.
Close-up photography for gardeners. Horticulture 45:28-9+ Ap '67

LEHMAN CAVES NATIONAL MONUMENT
Sharing monument facilities National park service and U.S. forest service. Nat Parks Mag 41:20 Ag '67

LEHMANN, Gunther
Noise and health. UNESCO Courier 20:26-7+ Jl '67

LEHMANN-HAUPT, Hellmut
Sampling of rare books; introductory remarks. Wilson Lib Bul 41:566-8 F '67

LEHMBRUCK, Wilhelm
Showcase for sculpture: Lehmbruck museum, Duisburg, Germany. il Arch Forum 126:31-7 Mr '67

LEHNDORFF, Vera Gottlieb, gräfin von. See Veruschka

LEHNER, Francis
Year was nudging December; poem. Cath World 206:108 D '67

LEHRBAUMMER, Andrew L.
Hows and whys of bidding. Am City 82:168+ O '67
Petty cash fund handles small-order purchases. Am City 82:95-6 Jl '67

LEHRER, Tom
Laughing matter? por Newsweek 69:55 My 29 '67

LEICA cameras. See Cameras

LEICAFLEX cameras. See Cameras

LEIDER, Frida
Frida Leider: a great Wagnerienne looks back. P. L. Miller. por Am Rec G 33:848-9 My '67
Lady of Berlin. J. H. Sutcliffe. il por Opera N 31:28-9 Ja 28 '67

LEIDER, Philip
Gallery '68: high art and low art. Look 32:14-21 Ja 9 '68

LEIDY, Thomas R. and Starry, A. R.
American adolescent, a bewildering amalgam. NEA J 56:8-12 O '67

LEIF Ericsson
Leif Ericsson and his relatives; with report by M. Steinmann. il Life 63:53-4+ S 15 '67

LEIFER, Neil
Stadiums of the '60s; photographs. Sports Illus 27:30-7 Jl 10 '67

LEIGH, Carma Russell
Measuring our achievements. Wilson Lib Bul 41:933-6 My '67
about
New ALA officer. M. E. Reynolds. por ALA Bul 61:869-70 Jl '67

LEIGHTON, Joseph, and others
Collagen-coated cellulose sponge: three-dimensional matrix for tissue culture of Walker tumor 256. bibliog Science 155:1259-61 Mr 10 '67

LEIMBACH, Patricia P.
Bum steer. Farm J 91:45+ Ag '67
Not by bread alone... por Farm J 91:101+ Mr '67

LEINSDORF, Erich
Faithful to Fidelio; original score conducted at Tanglewood. Time 90:42 Ag 18 '67

LEINSTER, Colin
Two wars of General Lew Walt. Life 62:77-80+ My 26 '67

LEIPZIG trade fair. See Exhibitions

LEISURE
Impact of change on work and leisure; excerpt from address. H. L. Wilensky. Mo Labor R 90:21-2 S '67
Invitation to serenity; recollection of childhood. S. Rama Rau. Redbook 128:65+ F '67
Riddle for tomorrow's world; how to lead a good life; excerpts from address. E. F. Zeigler. Parks & Rec 2:28+ S '67
Sociologist discusses the new meaning of recreative use of leisure. W. L. Stone. bibliog Parks & Rec 2:22+ Ap '67
Working more, sleeping less. Time 90:61 S 8 '67

LEISURE World, Seal Beach, Calif. See Aged—Housing

LEITH, Emmett N.
U.S. camera achievement award. por U S Camera 30:42 N '67

LEITNER, Irving A.
Excitement at the circus; drama. Plays 27:79-82 N '67

LEJEUNE, Anthony
Confrontation. Nat R 20:37+ Ja 16 '68
Defects of the body politic. Nat R 19:755-7 Jl 11 '67
Gentleman of the old school. Nat R 19:529-30 My 16 '67
Letter from London (cont) Nat R 19:473-4, 637+, 1120, 1384 My 2. Je 13. O 17. D 12 '67
Somber seer. Nat R 19:1079-80 O 3 '67

LEK ceremonies. See Courtship of birds

LEKACHMAN, Robert
Death of a slogan: the Great society 1967. Commentary 43:56-61 Ja; 18 My '67
Economy. por Duns R 90:11 N; 11 D '67
Sounding the alarm. Commentary 44:86-8 Ag '67

LELAND, Dorothy E.
Books for boys and girls. See issues of Parents' magazine and better homemaking

LELAND, Henry Martyn
How Leland lost Lincoln to Ford. G. Borgeson. il por Motor T 19:58-62+ F '67

LELYVELD, Joseph
But Marcos is a persistent man. N Y Times Mag p28-9+ F 26 '67
Communism, Kerala style. N Y Times Mag p30-1+ Ap 30 '67
How the United States protects South Africa. Atlan 219:77-9 Ap '67
It's God's will; why interfere? N Y Times Mag p28-9+ Ja 14 '68
Karma of Morarji Desai. N Y Times Mag p30-1+ S 24 '67

LE MANS Grand prix. See Automobile racing

LEMAY, Curtis E.
General LeMay's god. Christian Cent 84:229 F 22 '67

LEMBO, Diana
Screenings; filmstrips. por Library J 92:3133-4, 4236-8; 93:276-7 S 15, N 15 '67, Ja 15 '68
Stepchild comes of age. por Library J 92:3122-3 S 15 '67

LEMIRE, Clement M.
Senior citizens bowling. Parks & Rec 2:33+ My '67

LEMMON, Jack
Jack Lemmon: most serious funnyman in the flicks; interview, ed. by C. Brossard. pors Look 31:66-71 F 7 '67
Redbook dialogue. por Redbook 130:50-1+ D '67

LEMMON, Lawrence C.
New directions in design for D.C. department. Parks & Rec 2:24-5+ My '67

LEMNITZ, Tiana
Perennial Pamina; interview, ed. by J. Fleetwood. por Opera N 31:26 Mr 4 '67

LEMON, Richard
Election, USA. por Sat Eve Post 240:36-40+ N 18 '67
Father-by-himself cookbook. Sat Eve Post 240:14 Ag 12 '67
Is this any way to run an airline? (don't ask me) Sat Eve Post 240:24 Ap 22 '67
What happened when Albie Watkins got the bomb. Sat Eve Post 240:20 Jl 1 '67

LEMONE, Evelyn
Records for teachers. See issues of Dance magazine

LEMONS
See also
Cookery—Fruit

LEMPICKI, Alexander, and Samelson, Harold
Liquid lasers; with biographical sketches. Sci Am 216:14, 80-7+ bibliog(p 155) Je '67

LEONARDO da Vinci
Cover; portrait of Ginevra de' Benci. il Am
    Artist 31:4 My '67
Enhanced beauty; Ginevra dei Benci on dis-
    play. il Time 89:66-7 Mr 24 '67
$5 million gets the U.S. its first Leonardo. il
    Life 62:32-3 Mr 3 '67
$5.8 million lady: Ginevra de' Benci. il News-
    week 69:39 Mr 6 '67
Flight of the bird; portrait of Ginevra dei
    Benci. il Time 89:72 Mr 3 '67
Leonardo il magnifico. il por Sr Schol 90:20
    Mr 10 '67
Leonardo's Ginevra. W. Karp. il Horizon 9:
    24-9 Aut '67
Leonardo's lost notebooks. il por Life 62:24-31
    Mr 3 '67
Lost Leonardos. il Newsweek 69:97 F 27 '67
Notes and comment. New Yorker 43:39 Mr 25
    '67

LEONCAVALLO, Ruggiero
Pagliacci. Criticism
    Dance Mag il 41:26 D '67
    New Yorker 43:178 O 7 '67

LEONE, Sergio
Hi-ho, denaro! il por Time 90:56-7 Ag 4 '67

LEONIAN, Phillip
Silent world. il U S Camera 30:46-7+ F '67

LEONTIEF, Wassily
Planners put big picture on a grid. il Bsns
    W p62+ S 23 '67

LEOPOLD, A. C. See Dostal, H. C. jt. auth.

LEOPOLD, A. Starker
Dr A. Starker Leopold named NPS chief
    scientist. Nat Parks Mag 41:21-2 Ag '67

about
A. Starker Leopold Audubon medalist, 1966.
    C. W. Buchheister. por Audubon 69:20-1
    Ja '67

LEORO, F. Galo. See Galo Leoro, F.

LE PARC, Julio
Julio Le Parc: the craft of light. E. Benson.
    il Craft Horiz 27:26-9 Jl '67
Labyrinthine fun house; exhibition at Man-
    hattan's Howard Wise gallery. il por Time
    89:66 Mr 24 '67

LEPERS. See Leprosy and lepers

LEPIDOCROCITE. See Apatite

LEPORE, Michael J.
Secret of caring for the patient; ed. by
    W. S. Ross. pors Todays Health 45:38-42+
    N '67

LEPROSY and lepers
Latin campaign. il Sci N 92:59 Jl 15 '67
Science cleanses the leper. F. Marley. il
    Sci N 92:110-11 Jl 29 '67

LEPROSY research
Leprosy vaccine. Sci N 91:521 Je 3 '67

LERMAN, Leo
Catch up with. See issues of Mademoiselle
Four most likely to succeed. Mlle 65:156-9 S
    '67
International movie report; photographs. Mlle
    64:116-19 F '67
Something to talk about (cont) Mlle 64:186-
    7 Mr; 182 Ap '67

LERNER, Judith
Brief biography. S. Goodman. pors Dance
    Mag 41:56-7 Jl '67

LERNER, Max
Are the experts destroying our judgment?
    McCalls 95:26+ N '67
In defense of gossip. McCalls 94:83+ Mr '67
Literature vs. trash: where can we draw the
    line? Redbook 129:60-1+ Ag '67

LERNER, Michael
Report: Israel. Atlan 220:24+ S '67

LEROY, Catherine
Up Hill 881 with the marines; photographs.
    Life 62:40-44A My 19 '67
Gnat of Hill 881. il por Time 89:42 My 12 '67

LEROY, Jules G. and DeMars, R. I.
Mutant enzymatic and cytological phenotypes
    in cultured human fibroblasts. bibliog Sci-
    ence 157:804-6 Ag 18 '67

LESAGE, Laurent
When love was never free. Sat R 50:30-1
    D 23 '67

LESHAN, Eda J.
Abolishing childhood; excerpts. Todays Health
    45:57 S '67
Are you afraid of your children? PTA Mag
    62:2-5 bibliog(p35-6) D '67
Parent and child (cont) N Y Times Mag
    p92+ Ap 23; 63-4+ Ap 27 '67
What children learn when they play; excerpt
    from Conspiracy against childhood. Red-
    book 129:66-7+ Jl '67

LESHER, John M.
City-school cooperation builds a park two
    years sooner. Am City 82:80-1 N '67

LESKOWITZ, Sidney
Mechanism of delayed reactions. bibliog Sci-
    ence 155:350-2 Ja 20 '67

LESLIE, Alfred
Return to the challenge. il pors Time 91:30-1
    Ja 12 '68

LESLIE, Elsie
To a dear child... J. Douglass Horn Bk 43:
    571-5 O '67

LESLIE, Sir Shane
Holmes' Doyle. Nat R 19:915-16 Ag 22 '67
Mayfair in its last throes. Nat R 19:480-2 My
    2 '67
Reminiscence. Nat R 19:1392-3 D 12 '67

about
Gentleman of the old school. A. Lejeune. Nat
    R 19:529-30 My 16 '67

LESOTHO
Africa: new nations and new alignments. N.
    Mostert. il Reporter 36:27-31 Je 29 '67

LESOTHO diamond. See Diamonds

LESOWSKI, John
Silent hunter. por Outdoor Life 140:44-7+ Jl
    '67

L'ESPERANCE, Phil
Man who didn't come to dinner; interview,
    ed. by C. West. por Yachting 121:65+ Mr
    '67

LESSEPS, Ferdinand Marie, vicomte de
Frenchman took on an old idea and began
    to dig. E. Kern. il por Life 63:56-61 O 6
    '67

LESSER, Arthur J.
Equalizing opportunity for family planning.
    PTA Mag 61:20-2 Ap '67

LESSER ANTILLES. See West Indies

LESSING, Doris May
Gray princess; excerpts from Particularly
    cats. McCalls 94:110-11+ Mr '67
Talk with Doris Lessing; excerpts from in-
    terview; ed. by F. Howe. Nation 204:311-13
    Mr 6 '67

LESSING, Lawrence
Ever magnifying wonders of the optics in-
    dustry. Fortune 75:150-5+ Ap '67
Revolt against the internal-combustion engine.
    Fortune 76:78-83+ Jl '67

LESTER, Elenore
Shaking the world with an 8-mm. camera.
    N Y Times Mag p44-5+ N 26 '67

LESTER, Richard
Richard Lester; interview. New Yorker 43:
    50-1 O 28 '67

about
Minute that took fifteen hours. C. Schwal-
    berg. il pors U S Camera 30:66-7+ O '67
Vaudeville of the absurd. il por Time 90:105
    N 17 '67

LESTER associates, incoporated
Bringing the world down to scale. il Bsns W
    p 112-17 Jl 29 '67

LESURE, Thomas B.
U.S. music festivals. Travel 127:34-9+ Ja '67

LETCHER, John S. Jr
On avoiding collisions. Yachting 121:72-3+
    Mr '67

LET'S just say I've been around; story.
See Adarkar, V.

LETTER boxes. See Mailboxes

LETTER paper. See Stationery

LETTER to a colleague; story. See Ravitch.
M. M.

LETTER writer; story. See Singer, I. B.

LETTER writing
When you query, write it right! L. Olfson.
    Writer 80:14-15+ Mr '67

Anecdotes, facetiae, satire, etc.
Do forget to write. J. Brown. il Holiday 41:
    80-1 Ap '67
Where is my pen? R. Warfield. House &
    Gard 132:240-1 N '67

LETTER writing machines. See Recording instruments

LETTERING
In search of type. K. Butler and G. Like-
    ness. il Design 68:25-9 Mr '67

LETTERS
Around the world with stamps; contents of
    old letters. H. Herst, jr. Hobbies 72:99 My
    '67
Joyce's letters. B. McCabe. Commonweal 85:
    587-90 F 24 '67
Surprises of the mail. S. Alexander. Life 62:
    20 Je 30 '67
See also
Chain letters
Love letters

LETTERS by children
Children's letters to God; excerpts, comp. by E. Marshall and S. Hample. il Read Digest 90:97-9 Mr '67
What children think of God. Time 91:62 Ja 5 '68

LETTERS from servicemen
I died a soldier. H. D. Strickland. Read Digest 90:103 My '67
Mail from the front. O. Prescott. Sat R 50:35 Ap 29 '67
Voice of a soldier in Vietnam. D. E. Capurro, U S News 62:112 Je 5 '67

LETTERS of application. See Applications for positions

LETTERS of the alphabet. See Alphabet

LETTERS to congressmen. See Lobbying

LETTERS to editors. See Newspapers—Letters to editors; Periodicals—Letters to editors

LETTERWRITER, Electric. See Recording instruments

LETTVIN, Jerome
You can't even step in the same river once; with biographical sketch. Natur Hist 76:4, 6-12+ O '67

LEUCINE
Alkaline phosphatase and leucine aminopeptidase association in plasma of the chicken. G. R. J. Law. bibliog il Science 156:1106-7 My 26 '67; Reply with rejoinder. M. E. Etzler. 157:721 Ag 11 '67
Lack of end-product inhibition and repression of leucine synthesis in a strain of salmonella typhimurium. R. A. Calvo and J. M. Calvo. bibliog il Science 156:1107-9 My 26 '67

LEUCOCYTES
Chromosomal damage in human leukocytes induced by lysergic acid diethylamide. M. M. Cohen and others. bibliog il Science 155:1417-19 Mr 17 '67
Chromosomes and leukocytes; report on conference. M. A. Kelsall. bibliog Science 155:1039-40 F 24 '67
Herpes-type virus and chromosome marker in normal leukocytes after growth with irradiated Burkitt cells. W. Henle and others. bibliog il Science 157:1064-5 S 1 '67
Human polymorphonuclear leukocytes: demonstration of microtubules and effect of colchicine. S. E. Malawista and K. G. Bensch. bibliog il Science 156:521-2 Ap 28 '67
Increased cystine in leukocytes from individuals homozygous and heterozygous for cystinosis. J. A. Schneider and others. bibliog il Science 157:1321-2 S 15 '67
Lactic dehydrogenase and metabolism of human leukocytes in vitro. A. D. Bloom and others. bibliog il Science 156:979-81 My 19 '67
Leukocyte oxidase: defective activity in chronic granulomatous disease. R. L. Baehner and D. G. Nathan. bibliog il Science 155:835-6 F 17 '67
Mixed leukocyte reactions and histocompatibility in rates. W. K. Silvers and others. bibliog il Science 155:703-4 F 10 '67
Release of slow-reacting substance of anaphylaxis in the rat: polymorphonuclear leukocyte. R. P. Orange and others. bibliog il Science 157:318-19 Jl 21 '67
See also
Eosinophils

LEUKEMIA
Advance against leukemia. il Time 90:70+ S 29 '67
L-Asparaginase: toxicity to normal and leukemic human lymphocytes. R. Schrek and others. bibliog il Science 155:329-30 Ja 20 '67
Chromosome abnormality in rat leukemia induced by 7,12-dimethylbenz[a]anthracene. T. Sugiyama and others. bibliog il Science 158:1058-9 N 24 '67
Closing in on leukemia; drugs to fight acute lymphocytic leukemia. il Bsns W p87-8 O 7 '67
Crystallization of human lysozyme. E. F. Osserman. bibliog il Science 155:1536-7 Mr 24 '67
Depression of circulating interferon response in Balb/c mice after urethan treatment. J. De Maeyer-Guignard and E. De Maeyer. bibliog il Science 155:482-4 Ja 27 '67
Doctors turn leukemia tide. Bsns W p 110 Mr 11 '67
Enzyme v. leukemia; L-asparaginase. Time 90:67 Jl 7 '67
House of cancer? possibility that leukemia is contagious. il Newsweek 69:86 Je 12 '67
Leukemia and tumors. L. W. Sauer. PTA Mag 61:33-4+ My '67
Leukemia mortality; downturn rates in the United States. J. F. Fraumeni and R. W. Miller. bibliog il Science 155:1126-8 Mr 3 '67

Leukocytes of humans exposed to lysergic acid diethylamide; lack of chromosomal damage. W. D. Loughman and others. bibliog il Science 158:508-11 O 27 '67
Tragic secret. Good H 164:14+ Ap '67
Transport and phosphorylation as factors in the antitumor action of cytosine arabinoside. D. Kessel and others. bibliog il Science 156:1240-1 Je 2 '67

LEUKEMIA viruses
Assault on viral leukemia. il Sci N 91:174-5 F 18 '67
C-type viral particles in plasma of cats with feline leukemia. T. G. Kawakami and others. bibliog il Science 158:1049-50 N 24 '67
Leukemogenic activity of ether-extracted Rauscher leukemia virus. G. P. Shibley and others. bibliog il Science 156:1610-13 Je 23 '67
Neoplastic transformation of rat thymic cells induced in vitro by Gross leukemia virus. H. L. Ioachim. bibliog il Science 155:585-7 F 3 '67
Phosphoribosylamidotransferase: regulation of activity in virus-induced murine leukemia by purine nucleotides. G. H. Reem and C. Friend. bibliog il Science 157:1203-4 S 8 '67
Susceptibility to two strains of Friend leukemia virus in mice. F. Lilly. bibliog il Science 155:461-2 Ja 27 '67
Virus particles and murine leukemia virus complement-fixing antigen in neoplastic and nonneoplastic cell lines. W. T. Hall and others. bibliog il Science 156:85-8 Ap 7 '67

LEUKOCYTES. See Leucocytes

LEV, Donald
Operation slaughterhouse; poem. Christian Cent 85:77 Ja 17 '68

LEVEL indicators
See also
Liquid level indicators

LEVENSON, Dorothy
Mothers bring their skills to school. Parents Mag 42:48-9+ F '67

LEVENSON, Rosaline
Fringe benefits, what they can cost. Am City 82:182-3 S '67

LEVENSON, Sam
Everything but money; condensation. Read Digest 90:219-22+ My '67

LEVENTRITT award
Cookie & Pinky come through; winners of Leventritt award. il Time 89:78 My 26 '67

LEVER brothers and associates, limited
Lowering the suds; Britain's Board of trade orders company to de-escalate. Time 89:94+ My 12 '67

LEVER brothers and Unilever, limited
Split personalities. Fortune 76:200 S 15 '67

LEVERTOV, Denise
Advent 1966; poem. Nation 204:246 F 20 '67
A vision; poem. Poetry 109:357-8 Mr '67

LÉVESQUE, René
Case for a free Quebec; interview. por U S News 64:44-6 Ja 15 '68

LEVEY, Seymour
Are we driving teachers out of ghetto schools? Am Ed 3:2-4 My '67

LEVI, Edward Hirsch
Chicago names new president. R. J. Samuelson. por Science 157:1415 S 22 '67
Happy marriage in Chicago. por Time 90:44+ S 22 '67
Local boy makes good. por Newsweek 70:75-6 S 25 '67

LEVI, Stephen
Daphne in cottage D. Criticism Newsweek il 70:92 O 30 '67

LEVI CASTILLO, Vicente
Dynamite man. Time 89:39+ Je 16 '67

LÉVI-STRAUSS, Claude
Man's new dialogue with man; Time essay. por Time 89:34-5 Je 30 '67

LEVIANT, Curt
Moral cats and religious bears. Sat R 50:40 F 11 '67

LEVIN, Bernard
Bertrand Russell: prosecutor, judge and jury. N Y Times Mag p24-5+ F 19; 144 Ap 16 '67

LEVIN, Dan
Real American life. Nation 204:184-6 F 6 '67

LEVIN, Ira
Authors & editors. por Pub W 191:19 My 22 '67
Dr Cook's garden. Criticism New Yorker 43:131 O 7 '67

LEVIN, Kim
In and out of time. Art N 65:40-1+ F '67

LEVIN, Martin
(ed) Phoenix nest. See issues of Saturday review

LEVIN, Philip Jerome
Fight in the lion's den. il por Time 89:87
Mr 3 '67
Senators, the funds, and the law. il Fortune
75:152-3 My '67
LEVIN, Phyllis Lee
Stewart covers up. Sat Eve Post 240:35 Je
3 '67
LEVIN, Robert J.
Why so many husbands feel inadequate. Red-
book 129:61+ S '67
LEVINE, Carol
Games are to grow on. Parents Mag 42:44-
5+ D '67
When father's a traveling man. Parents Mag
42:54-5+ Je '67
LEVINE, Faye
Atlantic report. Atlan 219:24+ Mr '67
End of the maharajas. Atlan 219:112-14+ Ap
'67
Report: India's holy men. Atlan 220:18+ O
'67
LEVINE, Joel S.
Astronomy for juniors in Brooklyn. Sky &
Tel 34:291-2 N '67
LEVINE, Joseph E.
Power of cash; interview, ed. by W. H.
Manville. por Sat Eve Post 240:50 D 30 '67
about
Profiles. C. Tomkins. por New Yorker 43:55-
6+ S 16 '67
LEVINE, Les
Tiptoe through the silver. il por Time 89:60E
My 5 '67
LEVINE, Louis
Unforgettable Thornton W. Burgess. Read
Digest 91:100-5 O '67
LEVINE, Morton H.
Basques; with biographical sketch. Natur
Hist 76:6, 44-51 Ap '67
LEVINE, Philip
Spanish lesson; poem. Poetry 111:167-8 D
'67
LEVINE, Philip, 1900-, and Celano, M. J.
Agglutinating specificity for LW factor in
guinea pig and rabbit anti-Rh serums.
bibliog Science 156:1744-6 Je 30 '67
LEVINE, Richard H.
Learn a lito Englich. Am Ed 4:24-5 D '67
LEVINE, Seymour
Allergic adenohypophysitis: new experimental
disease of the pituitary gland. bibliog Sci-
ence 158:1190-1 D 1 '67
Maternal and environmental influences on the
adrenocortical response to stress in wean-
ling rats. bibliog Science 156:258-60 Ap 14
'67
LEVINSON, Robert E.
Seven sure-fire weapons for trouble shooters;
excerpts from The knack of developing and
using management savvy. Nations Bsns 55:
80-2+ S '67
LEVINSON, Sanford. See Kearns, D. jt. auth.
LEVITAN, Sar A.
Operational problems of the job corps. Mo
Labor R 90:27 F '67
Pitfalls of guaranteed income. Reporter 36:
12-15 My 18 '67
—and Mangum, G. L.
Programs and priorities. Reporter 37:20-2 S
7 '67
LEVITAS, Mitchel
Present and future of Kingman Brewster.
N Y Times Mag p30-1+ F 12 '67
LEVITIN, Sonia
Why children are crazy about nursery school.
Parents Mag 42:52-4+ Ag '67
LEVITT, Helen
Way of seeing. J. Scully. il Mod Phot 31:78
9 Mr '67
LEVITT, Leonard
Illustrated in black & white. Nation 205:569-70
N 27 '67
LEVITT, Morton. See Rubenstein, B. jt. auth.
LEVITT, Robert A. and Fisher, A. E.
Anticholinergic blockade of centrally induced
thirst. bibliog Science 154:520-2; 157:839-41
O 28 '66, Ag 18 '67
LEVITT, Theodore
Johnson treatment. Harvard Bsns R 45:114-
18+ Ja '67
about
What business are you really in? il pors
Bsns W p 178-80+ Mr 11 '67
LEVITT, William Jaird
Revolutionizing an industry; interview. por
Nations Bsns 55:54-6+ F '67
about
After the Levittowns. il por Time 89:118 My
19 '67

LEVITT and sons, Incorporated
After the Levittowns. il Time 89:118 My 19
'67
Appetite for more; ITT buys Levitt & sons.
il Time 90:74-5 Ag 4 '67
Levitt's secret is change; merger with ITT.
il Bsns W p46-8+ Jl 29 '67
LEVITTOWN, N.Y.
Don't say it's not worthwhile to plant a tree.
il Hom Gard 54:38-9 N '67
Social life and customs
Levittowners, by H. J. Gans. Review
Nation 205:57-8 Jl 17 '67. E. Bendiner
LEVY, Alan
Baby she'd always wanted. Good H 164:48+
F '67
Friendship really is the best medicine. Good
H. 166:46+ Ja '68
Jackie Kennedy; a view from the crowd. por
Sat Eve Post 240:19-23 Mr 11 '67
Queen Elizabeth and Philip: the good life
they share after twenty years. Good H
165:88-9+ N '67
Tragedy that wouldn't end. Good H 165:42+
Jl '67
Up at Yale, way off off off Broadway. N Y
Times Mag p30-1+ My 21 '67
LEVY, Harvey M. and Ryan, E. M.
Heat inactivation of the relaxing site of
actomyosin: prevention and reversal with
dithiothreitol. bibliog Science 156:73-4 Ap 7
'67
LEVY, Hilton B. See Carter, W. A. jt. auth.
LEVY, Howard Brett
Back to business. il por Newsweek 69:30+
Je 5 '67
Conviction of Captain Levy. N. Von Hoffman.
New Repub 156:9-11 Je 17 '67
Court-martial of Captain Levy: medical ethics
v. military law. E. Langer. il por Science
156:1346-50 Je 9 '67; Discussion. 157:140
Jl 14 '67
Doctors' dilemma. Nation 204:676-7 My 29 '67
Guilty as charged. il por Time 89:33 Je 9 '67
Men at war. Time 89:15-16 Je 2 '67
Nuremberg revisited. il por Newsweek 69:23-4
My 29 '67
Nürnberg & Viet Nam. il por Time 89:20 My
26 '67
To the stockade. Newsweek 69:33 Je 12 '67
LEVY, Leon
Investment manager looks at stocks; inter-
view. il por Duns R 90:44-5+ S '67
LEVY, Mark
Putting the poor out of business. Nation 204:
750-3 Je 12 '67
LEVY, Marvin David
And we quote; ed. by P. G. Davis. por Hi Fi
17:MA20 Mr '67
about
Drawn from within. J. W. Freeman. il Opera
N 31:24-5 Ap 1 '67
Mourning becomes Electra. Criticism
Hi Fi il 17:MA6-7 Je '67
New Yorker 43:120+ Mr 25 '67
Newsweek il 69:109-10 Mr 27 '67
Opera N 31:15-16 Ap 1 '67
Opera N il 31:17-20 Ap 1 '67
Opera N il 31:24-5 Ap 1 '67
Sat R 50:24+ Ap 1 '67
Time il 89:74 Mr 31 '67
LEWENTHAL, Raymond
Masters of the piano, in recordings of rare
provenance. Hi Fi 18:65-7 Ja '68
LEWIN, John
House of Atreus: a point of view. Cath
World 206:118-20 D '67
House of Atreus; adaptation of Oresteia, by
Aeschylus. Criticism
Nation 205:252-4 S 18 '67
Sat R 50:24 S 9 '67
LEWIN, Leonard C.
Peace games. por Time 90:44 N 17 '67
LEWIS, Alfred Henry
Tall-tale Americana. R. Humphries. Nation
205:153-7 Ag 28 '67
LEWIS, Ann L. See McDonough, E. S. jt. auth
LEWIS, Anthony
Department of amplification. New Yorker
43:131-2+ O 21 '67
LEWIS, Bernard
Consequences of defeat. For Affairs 46:321-35
Ja '68
LEWIS, Bobby
Chapel Hill's tobacco rogues. F. Deford. il
pors Sports Illus 26:24-6+ F 20 '67
LEWIS, Cecil Day-. See Day-Lewis, C.
LEWIS, Clive Staples
C. S. Lewis: no further than Gethsemane.
R. Hazelton. New Repub 156:25-7 F 18 '67
Ghostly wisdom. G. Wills. Nat R 19:369-71 Ap
4 '67

LEWIS, Cotesworth Pinckney
Daffy datelines for a critical sermon. H.
Sidey. il por Life 63:38B N 24 '67
Prickly sermon for LBJ. il por Newsweek
70:93 N 27 '67
LEWIS, D. O. See Caspi, E. jt. auth.
LEWIS, Faye C.
Patients who want to be sick; excerpt from
Patients. doctors and families. por Todays
Health 46:20-3 Ja '68
LEWIS, Flora
No revolution for the woman of Algiers. N Y
Times Mag p28-9+ O 29 '67
Reporter at large. New Yorker 43:36-42+
Jl 1 '67
Struggle of après-de Gaulle has begun. N Y
Times Mag p26-7+ My 14 '67
Tragedy of Bertrand Russell. Look 31:30-2+
Ap 4; 14 Je 27 '67
LEWIS, Frank W.
Challenges to American education. Cath
World 206:11-13 O '67
LEWIS, Griselda
Some makers of Pratt ware. Antiques 91:
762-7 Je '67
LEWIS, Henry
Maestro on the rise. il pors Ebony 22:112-
14+ My '67
LEWIS, Hunter
Capitol hill's ugliness club. Atlan 219:60-6 F
'67
LEWIS, Joan
Our happy underachiever. Parents Mag 42:
48-9+ Ap '67
LEWIS, John
Odyssey of a man, and a movement. P.
Good. il por N Y Times Mag p5+ Je 25 '67
LEWIS, John, and company, limited. See Chain
stores
LEWIS, John W.
Chinese bureaucrat. New Repub 157:23-5 D
16 '67
—See Kahin, G. M. jt. auth.
LEWIS, Leon
Letting off steam. il por Newsweek 69:114
My 8 '67
LEWIS, Merrick
It's all in the family. L. J. Kennedy. il por
Motor B 119:46-7+ My '67
LEWIS, Michael, and others
State as a determinant of infants' heart rate
response to stimulation. bibliog Science 155:
486-8 Ja 27 '67
LEWIS, Odell
Wild dash to sea. B. Ottum. il Sports Illus
26:20-5 My 22 '67
LEWIS, Oscar
Redbook dialogue. por Redbook 129:74-5+ S
'67
LEWIS, Richard
(ed) Bringing poetry out of hiding. NEA J
56:12-14 F '67
Place for poetry. Pub W 192:119-20 Jl 10 '67
LEWIS, Richard S.
Goal and no goal: a new policy in space.
Bul Atomic Sci 23:17-20 My '67
Pennant on Venus. Bul Atomic Sci 23:19-24
N '67
Science and space policy. Bul Atomic Sci
23:9-10 Ap '67
LEWIS, Richard Warren
Sudden stardom of Raquel Welch. Sat Eve
Post 240:32-5 N 18 '67
LEWIS, Samuel
Samuel Lewis and the people's colleges. V.
P. Lannie. bibliog f por Sch & Soc 95:493-
8 D 9 '67
LEWIS, Ted
More Blondin, less Lincoln. il Time 90:58 D
15 '67
LEWIS, Theophilus
Theatre. See issues of America
LEWIS, Willard A.
Lockout, the other dimension. bibliog f Mo
Labor R 90:1-7 Ag '67
LEWIS, Willard M.
From Buttermilk to Gum Log. Am Ed 3:8-11
Je '67
LEWIS, William H.
Trends in north Africa. Cur Hist 52:136-41+
Mr '67
LEWIS, Wilmarth Sheldon
Walpole in Farmington. E. Weeks. Atlan 220:
135-6 O '67
LEWIS, Wyndham
Apes of God invade U.S; excerpts from The
apes of God, ed. by T. B. Hess. Art N 66:
25 Mr '67
LEWIS research center. See United States—
National aeronautics and space administra-
tion—Lewis research center
LEWISTON, Idaho
Air pollution: the feds move to abate Idaho
pulp mill stench. B. Nelson. il Science 157:
1018-21 S 1 '67

LEWITZKY, Bella
Bella Lewitzky: dance is my window of life.
V. H. Swisher. il pors Dance Mag 41:70-5
Ap; 32+ My '67
LEWY, Guenter
Questions of complicity. Commentary 44:100-
5 N '67
LE-xuan-Chuyen
Why I defected from the Vietcong; interview,
ed. by N. Turner. por Read Digest 91:91-6
N '67
LEY, Ronald
Why anglers really angle. Field & S 71:63+
F '67
LEY, Willy
Next five years in space. Pop Mech 127:93-7+
F '67
LEYDET, François
Down the Colorado. Holiday 41:50-5+ Je '67
L'HEUREUX, John
Bargain; poem. Atlan 220:55 Jl '67
Brother Jordan's fox; poem. Atlan 220:96 O
'67
Canon. America 116:782 My 27 '67
Conquest; poem. Cath World 205:370 S '67
God, dying; poem. America 117:83 Jl 22 '67
about
Book review. J. Moffitt. America 117:480+ O
28 '67
LIABILITY (law)
Auto insurance reform; basic protection
plan. il Consumer Rep 33:9-15 Ja '68
Intellectuals and the future. E. Shils. Bul
Atomic Sci 23:7-14 O '67
Legal liabilities of executives. M. Feuer. il
Duns R 89:48-9+ My; 48-9+ Je '67
Lengthening reach of liability; damage suits
against the manufacturers. il Bsns W
p100+ S 16 '67
Responsible at any speed? driver sues General
motors. il Time 90:48 Ag 25 '67
See also
Damages
Government liability
LIABILITY insurance. See Insurance, Liability
LIABILITY of the state. See Government
liability
LIACOURAS, Marina
Rain; poem. Horn Bk 43:239 Ap '67
LIAR, liar; story. See Hoag, M. D.
LIBBY, Steve
Hidden state park. Travel 128:11+ N '67
LIBBY, William Charles
Offset lithography as a fine art. il por Am
Artist 31:24-9+ Mr '67
LIBEL and slander
Actual malice, test of libel of a public figure.
H. F. Pilpel. Pub W 193:22-3 Ja 1 '68
But can you do that? trio of libel cases. H.
F. Pilpel. Pub W 191:32-4 Mr 27 '67
Can directors be sued personally for libel?
H. F. Pilpel. Pub W 191:87 Ja 30 '67
History, warts and all; suit against Stevens
book rejected. il Newsweek 69:64-5 Je 5 '67
Irksome quirk; train robber Goody awarded
£2 in damages. Time 90:41 Jl 14 '67
Libel and the P.M. Newsweek 71:47 Ja 15 '68
Libel, by R. H. Phelps and E. D. Hamilton.
Review
Sat R 50:137 Mr 11 '67. A. Balk
Libel case involving alleged obscenity. H. F.
Pilpel. Pub W 191:28-30 My 1 '67
Libel liability; test for public figures. il Time
89:46+ Je 23 '67
Limits of libel; Supreme court extends rights
of press. il Newsweek 69:76-7 Je 26 '67
Pearson vs. Reagan; editors wonder about
limits of libel. Newsweek 70:88 N 27 '67
Prime minister sues; H. Wilson sues Interna-
tional herald tribune. Time 91:28 Ja 12 '68
Toward free and responsible speech. Nat R
19:673-4 Je 27 '67
U.S. Court of appeals denies Stevens' motion
for injunction restraining Helen Frick. Pub
W 191:52 F 13 '67
Victory for historians; Stevens book on Henry
Clay Frick protected as free speech. il Time
89:55 Je 2 '67
See also
Trials (libel)
LIBEN, Meyer
Athletic Jews. Commentary 43:79-81 F '67
Ball of fire; story. Commentary 43:57-62 Mr
'67
about
Authentic voice. T. Solotaroff. Commentary
43:91-2 My '67
LIBERAL arts colleges. See Colleges and uni-
versities
LIBERAL education
Education of wombats. P. West. Common-
weal 87:143-6 N 3 '67

LIBERAL education—*Continued*
General education after twenty years. Sch &
Soc 94:472+ D 24 '66
Reed college: hunting for money, a president,
and a mission. B. Nelson. il Science 157:
1282-4+ S 15 '67; Discussion. 158:1398+ D
15 '67
See also
Humanities
LIBERAL party (Canada)
Bowing out; L. Pearson to retire from office.
Newsweek 70:36 D 25 '67
Pearson's retreat; L. Pearson resigns. Time
90:34 D 22 '67
LIBERAL party (Great Britain)
Grimond to Thorpe. Nat R 19:126 F 7 '67
Liberals change command. il Newsweek 69:
44+ Ja 30 '67
LIBERAL party (United States)
Liberal crisis. W. Pfaff. Commonweal 87:462-
3 Ja 19 '68
LIBERALISM
Alienated; liberal disenchantment with big
government. H. C. Wallich. Newsweek 70:
89 N 13 '67
Coalition for victory in '68: will LBJ get
Republican votes? H. Paolucci. Nat R 19:
630-1 Je 13 '67
Darts to the heart; excerpts from address.
D. P. Moynihan. Time 90:27-8 O 6 '67
Heredity-environment problem. F. S. Meyer.
Nat R 19:1074 O 3 '67
Lecture for liberals from a liberal; address,
1967. D. P. Moynihan. U S News 63:22 O 9
'67
Liberal-Conservatives; address, August 11,
1967. R. M. Roelfs. Vital Speeches 33:746-
9 O 1 '67
Liberal crisis. W. Pfaff. Commonweal 87:462-
3 Ja 19 '68
Moynihan at the ADA. W. F. Buckley, jr.
Nat R 19:1110 O 17 '67
See also
Right and left (political science)
LIBERATOR (periodical)
Black anti-Semitism. Time 89:51 Mr 17 '67
LIBERIA
Politics and government
Resilient uncle. Time 91:35 Ja 5 '68
LIBERMAN, Alexander
Alexander Liberman in orbit. il por Art N
66:40-1+ Ap '67
LIBERMAN, Evsei Grigor'evich
Soviet economic reform. For Affairs 46:53-63
O '67
LIBERTY
Be like me! be free! J. G. Milhaven. America
116:584-6 Ap 22 '67; Discussion. 116:784-90
My 27 '67
General and the refugee. E. J. Hughes. News-
week 69:23 My 15 '67
Our free world. Commonweal 86:308 Je 2 '67
Power, freedom, and educational revolution.
M. Grandstaff. Sch & Soc 95:387-90 O 28
'67
Revolution. D. Lawrence. U S News 62:116
My 22 '67
Wanting what we want. R. O. Johann.
America 117:614 N 18 '67
World Presbyterian area meeting. D. H.
Rayner. Christian Cent 84:250+ F 22 '67
See also
Anarchism and anarchists
Civil rights
Democracy
Free speech
Intellectual liberty
Religious liberty
LIBERTY (periodical)
Life, Liberty and the flight of happiness. il
Esquire 68:108-9 O '67
LIBERTY (ship) See Warships—United States
LIBERTY broadcasting system
New Russian hit parade; V. Duke series on
the American musical theater. S. Green.
Sat R 50:66 Ag 26 '67
LIBERTY of speech. See Free speech
LIBERTY of the press. See Freedom of the
press
LIBET, Benjamin
Short reactions stay unconscious. Sci N 92:
631-2 D 30 '67
—and others
Responses of human somatosensory cortex to
stimuli below threshold for conscious sen-
sation. bibliog Science 158:1597-600 D 22 '67
LIBRARIANS
Librarian in today's society; excerpts from
address, November 7, 1966. D. M. Broderick.
il Library J 92:1413-16 Ap 1 '67; Discussion.
92:1875, 2312 My 15, Je 15 '67
Libraries unlimited; address, July 1, 1967.
F. E. Mohrhardt. bibliog ALA Bul 61:811-
19 Jl '67

Quo vadis: librarian's role in a democratic
culture; adaptation of address, February 6,
1967. R. R. Shaw. il Library J 92:2881-4
S 1 '67
Stress and strain in academic librarianship;
adaptation of address, October 1967. G. R.
Lyle. bibliog Library J 93:158-61 Ja 15 '68
Tiparillos and hacksaws; librarian's image.
E. Moon. Library J 92:1879 My 15 '67; Dis-
cussion. 92:2488 Jl '67
Toward a new breed of librarians; college
library work. R. M. Gummere, jr. il Wilson
Lib Bul 41:810-13 Ap '67
See also
Librarianship
Library assistants
Library staffs
School librarians

Anecdotes, facetiae, satire, etc.
Nothing like a dame: NLW plan for Miss
Library universe of 1968; with editorial
comment. P. S. Dunkin. Library J 92:1591
Ap 15 '67

Education
See Library schools and education

Placement
See Librarians—Selection and appointment

Political activities
Voices on Vietnam? what of librarians? E.
Moon. Library J 92:3577 O 15 '67; Discus-
sion. 92:4305-6+ D 1 '67

Recruiting
Manpower blueprint; reprint. P. Wasserman
and M. L. Bundy. il Library J 92:197-200
Ja 15 '67
Manpower shortages in sparsely settled areas.
G. K. Schenk. Wilson Lib Bul 41:853 Ap '67
Recruitment in action. H. Richmond. il Wil-
son Lib Bul 41:824-7 Ap '67
Show-me state recruits; cooperation between
Missouri library association recruitment
committee and Missouri state library. S.
Shinn. ALA Bul 61:205-7 F '67
See also
School librarians—Recruiting

Salaries
Cash and the common man; professionalism.
P. S. Dunkin. Library J 92:3015+ S 15 '67;
Discussion. 92:4083, 4448 N 15, D 15 '67
Federal library survey aims to up salaries.
Library J 93:136 Ja 15 '68
Placement picture: 1966. C. J. Frarey. il
Library J 92:2131-6 Je 1 '67; Correction. 92:
2487 Jl '67
Placement situation 1965 (with a preview of
1966) D. E. Strout and R. B. Strout; reply.
R. L. Waters. Library J 92:1550 Ap 15 '67
Talking of minimums; questions and an-
swers. E. Moon Library J 92:2979 S 15 '67
Terre Haute library pay scale ties salaries
to school rates: New York state: librarians
surging ahead of local teaching pay scales.
Library J 92:958 Mr 1 '67

Selection and appointment
Placement picture: 1966. C. J. Frarey. il
Library J 92:2131-6 Je 1 '67; Correction.
92:2487 Jl '67
Placement situation 1965 (with a preview of
1966) D. E. Strout and R. B. Strout; reply.
R. L. Waters. Library J 92:1550 Ap 15 '67
See also
School librarians—Selection and appointment

Supply and demand
ALA manpower film now available. Library
J 92:3355 O 1 '67
ALA meets in San Francisco: theme: Crisis
in library manpower: myth and reality.
Wilson Lib Bul 41:1044-5 Je '67
Crisis in library manpower: myth and reality;
symposium. bibliog il ALA Bul 61:527-57 My
'67
[Crisis: library manpower problem; sympo-
sium] Library J 92:1795-801 My 1 '67; Dis-
cussion. 92:1781, 2311, 2855 My 1, Je 15, S
1 '67
Helping hands. K. Nyren. Library J 92:2101
Je 1 '67
Library manpower; address, June 1967. H. T.
Drennan and S. R. Reed. bibliog il ALA
Bul 61:957-65 S '67
Major manpower project funded at U. of
Maryland. Library J 92:2867+ S 1 '67
Manpower; ALA program meetings. ALA Bul
61:836-40 Jl '67
Manpower and the library profession; sym-
posium. bibliog il Wilson Lib Bul 41:792-
827+ Ap '67
Manpower shortages in sparsely settled areas.
G. K. Schenk. Wilson Lib Bul 41:853 Ap '67

LIBRARIANS—Supply and demand—*Continued*
Manpower: the big show; ALA conference.
S. Havens. il Library J 92:2713-19 Ag '67
Myths and realities; ALA conference theme;
Crisis in library manpower. E. Moon. Library
J 92:2319 Je 15 '67

Trade unions

See Librarians unions

LIBRARIANS, Professional ethics for
Discussion in Dallas. T. M. Bogie. il Library
J 92:2127-30 Je 1 '67
In search of ourselves; address, June 1967,
with editorial comment. S. Rothstein. Li-
brary J 93:131, 156-7 Ja 15 '68
Wagon full of maize; code of ethics. P. S.
Dunkin. Library J 92:215 Ja 15 '67
LIBRARIANS, Reference. See College libraries
—Reference work
LIBRARIANS, Retired
Arrivederci, trauma! retiring to a small pub-
lic library; Martha Canfield free memorial
library, Arlington, Vt. G. Raftery. il
Library J 92:4475-6 D 15 '67
LIBRARIANS unions
Brooklyn gambit; decision by professional
librarians to join AFL-CIO American feder-
ation of state, county, and municipal em-
ployees. K. Nyren; discussion. Library J
92:508+ F 1 '67
Brooklyn library staff pickets in protest. il
Library J 92:2493 Jl '67
Brooklyn trustees and union approve con-
tract. Library J 92:2981-3 S 15 '67; Reply.
L. Brandwein. 92:3935 N 1 '67
Librarian and the union. J. Golodner. Wilson
Lib Bul 42:387-90 D '67
Libraries and labor unions. K. Nyren. il Li-
brary J 92:2115-21 Je 1 '67
Queens borough trustees refuse union negotia-
tion. Library J 92:722 F 15 '67
Strike threat cancelled at Chicago public li-
brary. Library J 92:1398-9 Ap 1 '67
LIBRARIANSHIP
ALA goals for action, 1967; with statement
by N. Cousins. ALA Bul 61:951-4 S '67
Bugles at credibility gap. K. Nyren. Library
J 92:1555 Ap 15 '67
Calling the commission; symposium. il Library
J 92:1802-7, 1901-5 My 1-15 '67
.Carpe diem; libraries in an age of change.
F. G. Jennings. il Library J 92:531-6 F 1 '67
Circulation fetish; public service vs. circula-
tion statistics; letter to the editor. M. L.
Bob. Library J 92:3936 N 1 '67
Civilized network: development of public li-
brary as instrument for education; adapta-
tion of address, May 30, 1967. L. H. Freiser.
il Library J 92:3001-3 S 15 '67
Current topics: a new year's roundup of
some of librarianship's problems; symposium
(cont) Library J 92:206 Ja 15 '67; Reply. A.
Ladenson. 92:507 F 1 '67
Disgruntled student; letter. Library J 92:711-
12 F 15 '67
For a new theory of the leisure class. J.
Shera. Wilson Lib Bul 42:423+ D '67
Future for humanism; adaptation of address,
December 5, 1966. J. Orne. Library J 92:
1893-5 My 15 '67
Goals, myths, and realities. C. Joyce. il Li-
brary J 92:3385-8 O 1 '67
Helping hands. K. Nyren. Library J 92:2101
Je 1 '67
Invisible librarian. D. Klein. il Seventeen
26:28+ Jl '67
Kaleidoscopic view of library research; sym-
posium. bibliog il Wilson Lib Bul 41:896-
949 My '67; Discussion. 42:23 S '67
Librarian in today's society; excerpts from
address, November 7, 1966. D. M. Broderick.
il Library J 92:1413-16 Ap 1 '67; Discussion.
92:1875, 2312 My 15, Je 15 '67
Librarians against machines. J. H. Shera.
bibliog Science 156:746-50 My 12 '67
Libraries unlimited; address, July 1, 1967.
F. E. Mohrhardt. bibliog ALA Bul 61:811-
19 Jl '67
Manpower blueprint; reprint. P. Wasserman
and M. L. Bundy. il Library J 92:197-200
Ja 15 '67
Meditation for April 1. P. S. Dunkin. Library J 92:1131 Mr 15 '67
National library day. P. S. Dunkin. Library J
92:3615+ O 15 '67
Office of the librarian; address June 28, 1967.
F. E. Mohrhardt. bibliog Wilson Lib Bul
42:391-6 D '67
Playgirl of the western world; ALA member-
ship. J. Shera. Wilson Lib Bul 42:529+ Ja
'68

Quo vadis: librarian's role in a democratic
culture; adaptation of address, February 6,
1967. R. R. Shaw. il Library J 92:2881-4
S 1 '67

Re: information; symposium. bibliog il Wil-
son Lib Bul 42:32-79 S '67
Research mind in library education and
practice; relating to the improvement of
libraries. R. H. Muller. bibliog Library J
92:1126-9 Mr 15 '67
Research, planning, coordination. H. T. Drennan. ALA Bul 61:1062-5 O '67
Stress and strain in academic librarianship;
adaptation of address, October 1967. G. R.
Lyle. bibliog Library J 93:158-61 Ja 15 '68
What is a librarian? letter to the editor. A.
Stein. Wilson Lib Bul 41:781 Ap '67
What is past is prologue: beyond 1984. J. H.
Shera; reply. R. R. Shaw. ALA Bul 61:231-
2 Mr '67
Wit to win; dealing with expansion of knowl-
edge; address, 1966. R. J. Blakely. bibliog f
il ALA Bul 61:152-4+ F '67

Anecdotes, facetiae, satire, etc.

Notables of 1967. E. Moon. Library J 92:4453
D 15 '67

International aspects

Why comparative librarianship? L. Shores;
reply. A. Turner. Wilson Lib Bul 41:559 F
'67

LIBRARIANSHIP as a profession
Cash and the common man; professionalism.
P. S. Dunkin. Library J 92:3015+ S 15 '67;
Discussion. 92:4083, 4448 N 15, D 15 '67
Fine art of abdicating responsibility; adapta-
tion of address, June 23, 1967. R. Dillon. il
Library J 92:2885-8 S 1 '67
Librarian: from occupation to profession;
reprint. W. J. Goode. bibliog ALA Bul 61:
544-55 My '67
Library technicians; instant librarians? ex-
cerpts from address, May 28, 1967. S. Sass.
bibliog Library J 92:2123-6 Je 1 '67; Discus-
sion. 92:2685, 3571 Ag. O 15 '67
Medium is the victim? L. H. Freiser. Library
J 93:166-7 Ja 15 '68
Try to remember: autumn beginning of a
great career. J. Shera. Wilson Lib Bul 42:
215+ O '67
LIBRARIES
Carpe diem; libraries in an age of change.
F. G. Jennings. il Library J 92:531-6 F 1 '67
See also
Bookbinding
Books and reading
College libraries
Prison libraries
School libraries

Acquisitions

Federal funds for materials and services.
ALA Bul 61:1057+ O '67
Libraries make a noise; suits over setting
net prices for specially bound library editions. Bsns W p39 My 6 '67

Administration

See Library administration

Advertising

See Library publicity

Architecture

See Library architecture

Audio-visual materials

See Libraries and audio-visual materials

Automation

Call for research: computerized circulation
control systems in libraries and informa-
tion centers; letter to the editor. C. D. Gull.
ALA Bul 61:903-4 S '67
Computer and the chancellor. J. Shera. Wil-
son Lib Bul 41:837+ Ap '67
Computerized library system to index books
in depth; SUNY. Library J 92:3360+ O 1 '67
Data processing in the library; symposium;
reply. R. Daehler. Wilson Lib Bul 41:559
F '67
DOD mechanization spotty says Booz-Allen
report. Library J 92:956 Mr 1 '67
Few building changes like from new tech-
nology. Library J 92:4322+ D 1 '67
For a new theory of the leisure class. J.
Shera. Wilson Lib Bul 42:423+ D '67
Librarians against machines. J. H. Shera.
bibliog Science 156:746-50 My 12 '67; Same.
Wilson Lib Bul 42:65-73 S '67
Library automation papers sought by collo-
quium. Library J 92:3953 N 1 '67
Library automation: tomorrow becomes today;
symposium, ed. by S. R. Salmon. bibliog
il ALA Bul 61:635-75+ Je '67
Not a shared system; computer operation de-
signed for library use at the University of
Missouri. R. H. Parker. il Library J 92:3967-
70 N 1 '67

LIBRARIES—Automation—*Continued*
Science libraries: prospects and problems. C. F. J. Overhage. Science 155:802-6 F 17 '67
What is past is prologue: beyond 1984. J. H. Shera; reply. R. R. Shaw. ALA Bul 61: 231-2 Mr '67
See also
College libraries—Automation
Information storage and retrieval systems
School libraries—Automation
United States—Library of Congress—Automation

Anecdotes, facetiae, satire, etc.
Fire and pill: solutions to book and population explosions as opposed to machine to make books and people smaller. P. S. Dunkin. Library J 92:1907 My 15 '67
Look to the closet, friend. P. S. Dunkin. Library J 92:2539 Jl '67

Bibliography
Bibliography of library automation. L. C. McCune and S. R. Salmon. ALA Bul 61:674-5+ Je '67

Book selection
See Book selection

Branches and stations
Charting a course in charaymak: a didactic tale with overtones. J. C. Kountz. il ALA Bul 61:396-408 Ap '67

Censorship
Crucial error in censorship; reprint. E. J. Gaines. il Library J 92:3377-9 O 1 '67
Dime-store Paul Revere; C. Gorton, trustee of Farmingdale public library, N.Y. E. Moon; K. Nyren. il Library J 92:3353, 3380-4 O 1 '67
Intellectual freedom and the teenager; preconference sponsored by Intellectual freedom committee, Young adult services division, and American association of school librarians. ALA Bul 61:833 Jl '67
Intellectual freedom: intellectual? free? J. Shera. Wilson Lib Bul 42:323+ N '67; Discussion. 42:458-9 Ja '68
Intellectual freedom preconference: sponsored by Intellectual freedom committee and YASD and AASL. Wilson Lib Bul 42:14+ S '67
Librarians and Fahrenheit 451. R. Kirk. Nat R 19:1124 O 17 '67
Library bill of rights: reasons for revision; with present text, proposed text. E. J. Gaines. Library J 92:984-5 Mr 1 '67; Same. ALA Bul 61:409-10 Ap '67; Reply. Z. Horn. Library J 92:1875-6 My 15 '67
Lips will move again; pre-conference on Intellectual freedom and the teenager. E. Moon. Library J 92:1980 My 15 '67
Other side: hardest of all things to come by; reply to E. Z. Freidenberg; address, June 27, 1967. M. Rafferty. il Wilson Lib Bul 42: 181-6 O '67
Public custody of the high pornography; reprint. K. Molz. il Library J 92:3373-6 O 1 '67
Publisher retaliates for book banning; Stein and Day offer free copies of Kazan book to Mount Pleasant, Iowa. Library J 92:2103 Je 1 '67
Teaching a commitment to intellectual freedom; adaptation of address, January 14, 1967. D. K. Berninghausen. il Library J 92: 3601-5 O 15 '67
Trustee responsibility; letter to the editor. J. Smith. Library J 92:4083-4 N 15 '67
Two cheers for liberty; ALA preconference on intellectual freedom and the teenager, sponsored by YASD and AASL. E. Geller. il Library J 92:3095, 3109-13 S 15 '67; Reply. P. S. Jacobstein. 92:4551-2 D 15 '67
See also
American library association—Intellectual freedom committee
School libraries—Censorship

Charging systems
Choosing a circulation control system. C. Joyce. il Library J 93:162-5 Ja 15 '68

Childrens rooms
See Libraries, Childrens

Circulation, loans, etc.
Call for research: computerized circulation control systems in libraries and information centers; letter to the editor. C. D. Gull. ALA Bul 61:903-4 S '67
Police-check on overdues; Roswell public library. N.Mex; letter to the editor. G. McShean. Library J 92:2096+ Je 1 '67

What is happening to public library circulation? E. Moon; discussion. Library J 91: 5504+; 92:710, 1776 N 15 '66, F 15, My 1 '67
See also
Libraries—Delivery service
Libraries, Childrens—Circulation, loans, etc.

Classification
See Classification

Cooperation service
See Library cooperation

Delivery service
Home-delivery library service. R. T. Jordan. Wilson Lib Bul 42:403-5 D '67

Equipment and supplies
See Library furniture and equipment

Extension work
See Library extension

Federal aid
See Libraries and state

Film strips
Frozen image: filmstrips in the school library; with list. D. Bardsley. il Library J 92:856-7+ F 15 '67

Finance
Determining the cost of library automation. P. J. Fasana. il ALA Bul 61:656-61 Je '67
Habits and attitudes; role of money in establishing rigidity. W. Brahm. Library J 92:1804-5 My 1 '67
Reading is the key; understanding of public budgeting. K. Schenk. Wilson Lib Bul 41: 637 F '67
See also
Libraries—Statistics
Libraries and state
School libraries—Finance

Fines
Bookworm turns; Chicago's amnesty on fines for overdue books. Newsweek 71:32 Ja 15 '68

Foreign language collections
See also
College libraries—Foreign language collections
School libraries—Foreign language collections

Furniture
See Library furniture and equipment

Heating and ventilation
Lighting and ventilation; adaptation of address, May 16, 1966. E. Mason. il Library J 92:201-6 Ja 15 '67

Information service
See Libraries—Reference work

Instruction in use
Introducing the library through film; list of films and filmstrips. H. Wheeler. Wilson Lib Bul 41:197-9 O '66; Correction. 41:559 F '67
Orientation of the out-of-school adult to the use of public libraries; preconference workshop sponsored by the Adult services division, Reference services division, with cooperation of Public library association. M. C. Hannigan. ALA Bul 61:829-30 Jl '67
Role playing in the library; Reo and Michigan avenue schools, Lansing, Mich. P. Anderson. Library J 93:267 Ja 15 '68
Student-built halls of fame; library lesson to familiarize students with biographical reference materials; Alexander Hamilton H.S, Los Angeles. S. Cochell. il Sr Schol 90:sup28 F 17 '67

Intermediate departments
See also
Libraries—Work with young people

International aspects
Government directives issued on int'l book programs. Library J 92:724 F 15 '67
International exchange (cont) il Wilson Lib Bul 41:829-33, 962-7 1055-61; 42:209-13, 313-16, 417-21 Ap-Je. O-D '67
National policy statement on international book and library activities; text. Library J 92:515 F 1 '67; Same. ALA Bul 61:186 F '67
U.S. sets policy on int'l. book programs. Pub W 191:90 Ja 30 '67
Why comparative librarianship? L. Shores; reply. A. Turner. Wilson Lib Bul 41:559 F '67

Layout
See Library architecture

LIBRARIES—*Continued*

Legislation

See Library laws and legislation

Lighting

Lighting and ventilation; adaptation of address, May 16, 1966. E. Mason. il Library J 92:201-6 Ja 15 '67

Location

Public library and the planning agency. L. M. Bewley. bibliog ALA Bul 61:968-74 S '67

Management

See Library administration

Manuscript collections

Negro manuscript collections in libraries. L. J. Greene. Negro Hist Bul 30:20 Mr; 14-15 O '67
Sampling of rare books; symposium. il Wilson Lib Bul 41:566-607+ F '67

Map collections

Map librarianship. W. W. Ristow. bibliog il Library J 92:3610-14 O 15 '67

Microfilm collections

Microfilm: a must in the high school library. R. Erbes. il Sr Schol 90:sup 18 Ap 14 '67
Reproduction vs. preservation; excerpt from Care and preservation of books. J. Alden; reply. J. B. Blake. Library J 92:507-8 F 1 '67

Anecdotes, facetiae, satire, etc.

Fire and pill: solutions to book and population explosions as opposed to machine to make books and people smaller. P. S. Dunkin. Library J 92:1907 My 15 '67

Moving picture collections

8mm revolution. J. L. Limbacher; reply. G. H. Tubbs. Library J 92:1267 Mr 15 '67
See also
College libraries—Moving picture collections
United States—Library of Congress—Moving picture collections

Oral history collections

Oral history colloquium points new directions. Library J 93:28 Ja 1 '68

Organization

See Library administration

Pamphlet collections

From abacus to zoos; Kalamazoo public library, Mich. S. Miller. il Library J 92:4477-9 D 15 '67

Paperback books

Paperback wearability; evaluation at Bloomington public and Monroe County library, Ind. E. N. Howard; reply. F. Lewis. Library J 92:2096 Je 1 '67

Phonograph and phonograph records

Composer and his music on record: conducting or playing his own works; with discography. J. R. Douglas. il Library J 92:1117-21 Mr 15 '67
New beat for the teen: library rock; with discography. C. Clark. il Library J 92:1706-7 Ap 15 '67

Public relations

It's the latest, it's the greatest, it's the i-ber-ee. P. Winnick. il Am Ed 3:5-7 Je '67
Public relations and the library: symposium. il Wilson Lib Bul 42:278-311+ N '67
See also
Adult education—Library participation

Reference departments

Farmer Jones's information network; Seven Rivers library system. N. Neafie. il Library J 92:1586-7 Ap 15 '67
Library education and reference performance. C. A. Bunge. Library J 92:1578-81 Ap 15 '67
Reference roundup; developments in communications, resources, cooperation, personnel, research, computers, and financing. K. Nyren. il Library J 92:1582-5 Ap 15 '67; Correction. 92:2488 Jl '67
See also
Reference books

Religious collections

Common ministry: aspects of librarianship as it relates to religion in America; letter to the editor. R. J. Callanan. Library J 92:1776 My 1 '67

Science collections

Books and libraries in the scientific age; adaptation of address, January 9, 1967. H. Wooster. bibliog il Library J 92:2511-15 Ji '67
See also
College libraries—Science collections

Special collections

Sampling of rare books; symposium. il Wilson Lib Bul 41:566-607+ F '67
See also
Libraries—Manuscript collections
Libraries—Map collections
Libraries—Moving picture collections
United States—Library of Congress—Moving picture collections

Standards

Public library standards; ALA meeting, letter to the editor. P. Hiatt. Library J 92:3349 O 1 '67

Statistics

Charting a course in charaymak: a didactic tale with overtones. J. C. Kountz. il ALA Bul 61:396-408 Ap '67
Circulation fetish; public service vs. circulation statistics; letter to the editor. M. L. Bob. Library J 92:3936 N 1 '67
Indexes of American public library statistics. ALA Bul 61:557 My '67
Library buildings study gives new statistics. Library J 92:2694+ Ag '67
Library manpower; address, June 1967. H. T. Drennan and S. R. Reed. bibliog il ALA Bul 61:957-65 S '67
What is happening to public library circulation? E. Moon; discussion. Library J 91: 5504+; 92:710, 1776 N 15 '66, F 15, My 1 '67

Technical processes

Integrate major programs, advises N.Y. study; A. D Little report. Library J 92: 4089-90+ N 15 '67

Trustees, boards, committees, etc.

Dime-store Paul Revere; C. Gorton, trustee of Farmingdale public library, N.Y. E. Moon; K. Nyren. il Library J 92:3353, 3380-4 O 1 '67
Ex New Orleans librarian blasts board, friends; excerpts from letter. J. Cushman. Library J 92:1403 Ap 1 '67
Library boards outmoded, Calif. study suggests. Library J 92:3946+ N 1 '67
Misuse of librarians; letter to the editor. W. Deakyne. Library J 92:1094 Mr 15 '67
N.Y. trustee disqualified after eight years service; Mid-Hudson library system. Library J 93:22 Ja 1 '68
Trustee responsibility; intellectual freedom vs. censorship; letter to the editor. J. Smith. Library J 92:4083-4 N 15 '67

Ventilation

See Libraries—Heating and ventilation

Work with blind

New accreditation body for service to blind. Library J 92:3948 N 1 '67
Public library services to the handicapped; two new programs; address, October 1966. E. C. Graham. il ALA Bul 61:170-9 F '67
See also
United States—Library of Congress—Division for the blind and physically handicapped

Work with children

See also
Libraries, Childrens

Work with churches

Common ministry: aspects of librarianship as it relates to religion in America; letter to the editor. R. J. Callanan. Library J 92: 1776 My 1 '67

Work with handicapped

Library services to the disadvantaged and handicapped. P. Winnick and H. H. Lyman. bibliog f il ALA Bul 61:1065-74 O '67
Physically handicapped observance Oct. 1-7. Library J 92:2986+ S 15 '67
Public library services to the handicapped; two new programs; address, October 1966. E. C. Graham. il ALA Bul 61:170-9 F '67
See also
United States—Library of Congress—Division for the blind and physically handicapped

Work with schools

See Libraries and schools

LIBRARIES—*Continued*

Work with young people

Books for the new breed; adaptation of address, 1966. J. Igo. il Library J 92:1704-5 Ap 15 '67; Reply. R. Wyndham. 92:3781-2 O 15 '67

Intellectual freedom and the teenager; preconference sponsored by Intellectual freedom committee, Young adult services division, and American association of school librarians. ALA Bul 61:833 Jl '67

Intellectual freedom preconference sponsored by Intellectual freedom committee and YASD and AASL. Wilson Lib Bul 42:14+ S '67

Lips will move again; pre-conference on Intellectual freedom and the teenager. E. Moon. Library J 92:1980 My 15 '67

New goals for teen service proposed at Albany meeting; with editorial comment. il Library J 92:4555, 4557-8+ D 15 '67

Other side: hardest of all things to come by; reply to E. Z. Freidenberg; address, June 27, 1967. M. Rafferty. il Wilson Lib Bul 42: 181-6 O '67

Two cheers for liberty; ALA preconference on intellectual freedom and the teenager, sponsored by YASD and AASL. E. Geller. il Library J 92:3095, 3109-13 S 15 '67; Reply. P. S. Jacobstein. 92:4551-2 D 15 '67

See also
Libraries and students

Alabama
See also
Huntsville, Ala. public library

Arkansas
See also
Arkansas River Valley regional library, Dardanelle, Ark.

Australia
Down Under: opportunity beckons; symposium, ed. with introd. by N. Horrocks and with editorial comment. il Library J 92:4087, 4107-26+ N 15 '67

California
California public libraries: few gains in library use. Library J 92:4457 D 15 '67
Library boards outmoded, Calif. study suggests. Library J 92:3946+ N 1 '67
See also
Henry E. Huntington library and art gallery, San Marino
Los Angeles public library
Mill Valley, Calif. public library
San Francisco—Libraries
San Francisco public library
Santa Rosa-Sonoma County free public library, Santa Rosa

California, Lower
Trade winds; Good neighbor bilingual public library, La Paz, Baja California. J. Beatty, jr. Sat R 50:13 Ap 22 '67

Canada
See also
Canada—National library
Canadian library association
Toronto public library

Colorado
See also
Denver public library

England
See also
Birmingham, England, public library

Europe
Bookman's Baedeker to Europe. A. Plotnik. bibliog il Library J 92:2889-97 S 1 '67

Europe, Western
Dark at the top of the stacks; how not to visit the libraries of Europe. A. Plotnik. il Library J 92:1122-5 Mr 15 '67

Florida
Florida: not all sunshine. V. Nistendirk. il Library J 92:1898-900 My 15 '67
See also
Clewiston, Fla. public library
Orlando, Fla. public library

Illinois
Public library development in Illinois. L. L. Stoffel. il Library J 92:210-13 Ja 15 '67
See also
Chicago public library
Illinois state historical library

Indiana
Eight library bills passed in Indiana. Library J 92:2342 Je 15 '67
See also
Bloomington public and Monroe County library
Indianapolis public library

Iowa
See also
Mount Pleasant, Iowa, public library
Seven Rivers library system

Iran
Libraries for the children of Iran. L. J. Arjomand. il Wilson Lib Bul 41:1055-61 Je '67

Ireland
Bring in the whiskey now. Mary. F. O'Connor. New Yorker 43:36-40+ Ag 12 '67

Italy
See also
Florence—Libraries
Vatican—Library

Kansas
See also
Wichita, Kan. public library

Kentucky
Report from Pikeville, Kentucky; with testimony by R. Caudill. K. Molz. il Wilson Lib Bul 42:397-402+ D '67
Spirit of Pikeville. K. Nyren. il Library J 92:4465-70 D 15 '67

Louisiana
See also
New Orleans public library

Maryland
High John; experiment in Fairmount Heights. E. Moon. il Library J 93:147-55 Ja 15 '68
Metropolitan public library use. M. L. Bundy. bibliog il Wilson Lib Bul 41:950-61 My '67
Politicians eye libraries in Oklahoma and Maryland. Library J 92:1104 Mr 15 '67
Public library development in Maryland. K. F. Duchac. il Library J 92:1113-16 Mr 15 '67
See also
Prince Georges County memorial library, Hyattsville

Mexico
See also
Libraries—California, Lower

Michigan
LSCA grants awarded to Mich. projects. Library J 92:3582+ O 15 '67
Michigan: opening up resources. G. M. Casey. il Library J 92:2523-5 Jl '67
See also
Detroit public library
Kalamazoo, Mich. public library

Minnesota
See also
Minneapolis public library

Missouri
Missouri increases funds for aid to public libraries. Library J 92:3364 O 1 '67
See also
Missouri state library, Jefferson City

New England
New England survey pegs library ills. Library J 92:3946 N 1 '67

New Jersey
Statewide friends group formed in New Jersey. Library J 92:4457 D 15 '67

New Mexico
See also
Roswell, N.Mex. public library

New York (state)
Experiment in a rural system; consolidation of public relations programs of Four county, Chemung-Southern Tier and the Finger Lakes library systems. M. A. Wright. Wilson Lib Bul 42:301-3 N '67
Facsimile transmission project set for NY state. Library J 92:952 Mr 1 '67
Integrate major programs, advises N.Y. study; A. D. Little report. Library J 92: 4089-90+ N 15 '67
Library development group appointed in New York. Library J 93:27 Ja 1 '68
New goals for teen service proposed at Albany meeting; with editorial comment. il Library J 92:4555, 4557-8+ D 15 '67

LIBRARIES—New York (state)—*Continued*
N.Y. state aid bill dies in committee. Library
  J 92:1886+ My 15 '67
N.Y. trustee disqualified after eight years service; Mid-Hudson library system. Library
  J 93:22 Ja 1 '68
      See also
Farmingdale, N.Y. public library
Hempstead, N.Y. public library
Nassau library system
New York public library
Rochester, N.Y. public library

Ohio
      See also
Cincinnati and Hamilton County, Ohio, public library
Cleveland public library
Ohio state library, Columbus

Oklahoma
Politicians eye libraries in Oklahoma and
  Maryland. Library J 92:1104 Mr 15 '67
      See also
Oklahoma state library, Oklahoma City

Ontario
      See also
Toronto public library

Oregon
      See also
Portland, Ore.—Libraries

Pennsylvania
      See also
Pennsylvania state library, Harrisburg

South Carolina
State aid in S. Carolina; letter to the editor.
  E. P. Walker. Library J 92:2487 Jl '67

Tennessee
      See also
Memphis, Tenn, public library

Texas
Medical libraries unite in Texas. Library J
  92:1105 Mr 15 '67
      See also
Dallas public library
Fort Worth, Tex, public library

United States
Comments on public library research; symposium. il Wilson Lib Bul 41:928-47 My '67
Community library: its search for a vital
  purpose. W. R. Monat. bibliog il ALA Bul
  61:1301-10 D '67
Factors influencing public library use. M. L.
  Bundy. il Wilson Lib Bul 42:371-82 D '67
Here and there: comparison with Australia.
  E. Moon. Library J 92:4087 N 15 '67
Hustle-bustle in the library. Changing T 21:6
  F '67
It's the latest, it's the greatest, it's the li-ber-
  ee. P. Winnick. il Am Ed 3:5-7 Je '67
Legislative roundup. A. Ladenson. Library J
  93:41-2 Ja 1 '68
1967: year of growth and second thoughts. K.
  Nyren. il Library J 93:33-40 Ja 1 '68
Small library faces the future. R. H. Parker.
  ALA Bul 61:669-71 Je '67
View of the American library; statement. N.
  Cousins. ALA Bul 61:953 S '67
      See also
Council on library resources, incorporated
Libraries—Statistics
Libraries, County
Library surveys
National library week
Presidential libraries
Special libraries association
  also subhead Libraries under names of
  cities, e.g. Chicago—Libraries

Vermont
      See also
Martha Canfield free memorial library,
  Arlington

Vietnam (Republic)
Librarian in Vietnam. M. Boaz. il Wilson
  Lib Bul 41:962-7 My '67

Washington (state)
      See also
North central regional library, Wentachee
Seattle public library
LIBRARIES (rooms)
To get away at home: escape rooms. il House
  B 109:108-12 Ja '67
LIBRARIES, Business
Manager training facility relies on library;
  Donald W. Mitchell memorial library,
  Hamilton, N.Y. Library J 92:3580+ O 15 '67

LIBRARIES, Childrens
Children's library; Rye free reading room,
  Rye, N.Y. Horn Bk 43:55 F '67
Children's library scene; Australia. M. Trask.
  bibliog il Library J 92:4222-4 N 15 '67
How many blocks to New York? hobby club
  at Venice branch of Los Angeles public li-
  brary. S. Benjamin. il Library J 93:265-6 Ja
  15 '68
Joy on wheels. L. Conger. Writer 80:7+ D '67
Libraries for the children of Iran. L. J.
  Arjomand. il Wilson Lib Bul 41:1055-61 Je
  '67
Library services to children in the mosaic
  of administration; address, July 1967. R.
  Warncke. il ALA Bul 61:1324-7 D '67
Open access for children at Rochester proves
  successful. Library J 93:255 Ja 15 '68
      See also
Book week
Story telling

Book selection
  See Book selection

Circulation, loans, etc.
LAPL commission orders study of juvenile
  circulation drop. Library J 93:252-3 Ja 15
  '68

Iran
Report from Iran. M. Schindel. il Horn Bk
  43:726-9 D '67
LIBRARIES, Church
      See also
Church and synagogue library association
LIBRARIES, College. See College libraries
LIBRARIES, County
City-county library in a business district. il
  Arch Rec 142:178-9 S '67
Experiment in a rural system; consolidation
  of public relations programs of Four county,
  Chemung-Southern Tier and the Finger
  Lakes library systems. M. A. Wright. Wil-
  son Lib Bul 42:301-3 N '67
LIBRARIES, Depository
Future lies ahead; documents depository li-
  brary of tomorrow. R. Kane. bibliog Li-
  brary J 92:3971-3 N 1 '67
LIBRARIES, High school. See High school li-
  braries
LIBRARIES, Hospital
Out of isolation; adaptation of address, April
  20, 1966. C. E. Lucioli. bibliog il Library J
  92:1421-3 Ap 1 '67
LIBRARIES, Institution
Goals for state library service to state
  agencies and state institutions. S. G. Pren-
  tiss. il ALA Bul 61:387-92 Ap '67
Patient and the inmate; program meetings of
  Association of hospital and institution li-
  braries and American association of state
  libraries. P. Goldie. ALA Bul 61:843-4 Jl
  '67
      See also
Prison libraries
LIBRARIES, Instruction in use of. See Li-
  braries—Instruction in use
LIBRARIES, Medical. See Medical libraries
LIBRARIES, Prison. See Prison libraries
LIBRARIES, Private
Branch library for your guest room. M. M.
  Hemingway. il House & Gard 131:185-6
  My '67
      See also
Book collecting
LIBRARIES, Regional
      See also
Arkansas River Valley regional library, Dar-
  danelle, Ark.
LIBRARIES, Religious
Religious libraries and reading rooms; two
  in Boston: Christian Science reading room
  and Catholic information center. F. Freed-
  man. il Wilson Lib Bul 42:318-21 N '67
      See also
Church and synagogue library association
LIBRARIES, School. See School libraries
LIBRARIES, Special
      See also
Special libraries association
LIBRARIES, State
Goals for state library service to state
  agencies and state institutions. S. G.
  Prentiss. il ALA Bul 61:387-92 Ap '67
Open-door policy for state libraries? J. Legg.
  il Library J 92:207-9 Ja 15 '67
Where the action is. E. Moon. Library J 92:
  1395 Ap 1 '67
      See also
Ohio state library, Columbus
Pennsylvania state library, Harrisburg
LIBRARIES, Theological. See Theological li-
  braries

LIBRARIES, Traveling
See also
Bookmobiles
LIBRARIES, University. See College libraries
LIBRARIES and adult education. See Adult
education—Library participation
LIBRARIES and art
Art in libraries; report. R. McClarren. il
Library J 92:4337-40 D 1 '67
Chicago public library bans art again. Library J 92:1783 My 1 '67
LIBRARIES and audio-visual materials
Film librarians form independent organization. Library J 92:2498+ Jl '67
See also
School libraries and audio-visual materials
LIBRARIES and booksellers
Developing a reading public, Ivan Ludington, sr. at work; schools get free paperback books. il Pub W 192:46-7 S 4 '67
See also
Bookselling in libraries
LIBRARIES and communication. See Communication
LIBRARIES and film strips
Any old irons. or filmstrips? using Title II as excuse for unloading old inventories; letter to the editor. D. Bardsley. Library J 92:273 Ja 15 '67
LIBRARIES and moving pictures
See also
Libraries—Moving picture collections
Libraries and audio-visual materials
School libraries and audio-visual materials
LIBRARIES and Negroes
Harlem project granted six-month extension; North Manhattan project in Countee Cullen and the adjacent Schomburg collection. Library J 92:1690-1 Ap 15 '67
Reading is what's happening; address. April 21. 1967. E. J. Josey. il Negro Hist Bul 30:14-17 My '67
Struggle doth avail; ed. by G. K. Schenk. Wilson Lib Bul 41:1073 Je '67
LIBRARIES and politics
Politicians eye libraries in Oklahoma and Maryland. Library J 92:1104 Mr 15 '67
LIBRARIES and publishers
Relations with libraries; summary of reports at AAUP annual meeting. Pub W 192:26-7 Jl 3 '67
Reprint pitfalls. E. Moon. Library J 92:4311 D 1 '67
LIBRARIES and readers
Comments on public library research; symposium. il Wilson Lib Bul 41:928-47 My '67
Community library; its search for a vital purpose. W. R. Monat. bibliog il ALA Bul 61:1301-10 D '67
Factors influencing public library use. M. L. Bundy. il Wilson Lib Bul 42:371-82 D '67
Goals, myths, and realities. C. Joyce. il Library J 92:3385-8 O 1 '67
Goin' down the road feelin' bad; whatever happened to the Carnegie buildings? P. T. Barkey. Library J 92:3389 O 1 '67
LIBRARIES and research
Information access; equality of access for the advanced student and scholar. M. J. Voigt. Library J 92:1802 My 1 '67
Library and information science research program. P. P. Price and H. A. Carl. ALA Bul 61:246 Mr '67
Research papers and the small college library. I. H. Smith. il Library J 92:544-5 F 1 '67
LIBRARIES and schools
Bookmobile service to schools. G. K. Schenk. Wilson Lib Bul 41:853+ Ap '67
Church-state issue in federal aid to education; symposium. bibliog il Wilson Lib Bul 41:682-718 Mr '67; Discussion. 41:884-5. 1014-16; 42-20+. 273+ My-S. N '67
Civilized network; development of public library as instrument for education; adaptation of address. May 30, 1967. L. H. Freiser. il Library J 92:3001-3 S 15 '67
Liaison librarian; public library-school relations project. P. Winnick and W. A. Horn. il Am Ed 4:26-7 D '67
New goals for teen service proposed at Albany meeting; with editorial comment. il Library J 92:4555. 4557-8+ D 15 '67
Plus ça change; classic patterns in public/school library relations. D. M. Broderick. bibliog Library J 92:1995-7 My 15 '67
LIBRARIES and social and economic problems
Baby dolls are gone; effect of TV on children's reading. N. Larrick. bibliog il Library J 92:3815-17 O 15 '67
Books for adults beginning to read. Wilson Lib Bul 41:83-7 S '66; Correction. 41:671 Mr '67
Child-concerned world; symposium. bibliog il Wilson Lib Bul 42:164-205+ O '67

Comics scene; magazines in the library, ed. by B. Katz. A. E. Prentice. Library J 93:59 Ja 1 '68
Community library; its search for a vital purpose. W. R. Monat. bibliog il ALA Bul 61:1301-10 D '67
Delicate area for research. V. L. Jones. Wilson Lib Bul 41:913-14 My '67
Disadvantaged and the public library. J. G. Sutton. Wilson Lib Bul 41:946-7 My '67
Greater role in education seen for public libraries; summary of statement, May 15, 1967. H. W. Tucker. Library J 92:2322+ Je 15 '67
Harlem and Bronx projects set for coming year. Library J 92:3586+ O 15 '67
Harlem project granted six-month extension; North Manhattan project in Countee Cullen and the adjacent Schomburg collection. Library J 92:1690-1 Ap 15 '67
High John; experiment in Fairmount Heights, Md. E. Moon. il Library J 93:147-55 Ja 15 '68
How many blocks to New York? hobby club at Venice branch of Los Angeles public library. S. Benjamin. il Library J 93:265-6 Ja 15 '68
Library services to the disadvantaged and handicapped. P. Winnick and H. H. Lyman. bibliog f il ALA Bul 61:1065-74 O '67
Limited adult reader; Cleveland public library's Reading centers program. T. E. Barensfeld. il Library J 92:3004-7 S 15 '67
Nervous Nellies on race relations? school libraries. A. G. Mims. bibliog Library J 92:1291-3+ Mr 15 '67
Reaching the nonuser. H. Franklin. Wilson Lib Bul 41:943-6 My '67
Role of the library in the study of social and urban problems. J. F. Anderson. Wilson Lib Bul 41:942-3 My '67
This is my beat; D. Roberts of Venice branch of Los Angeles public library. E. Geller. il Library J 93:259-64 Ja 15 '68
Wit to win; dealing with expansion of knowledge; address, 1966. R. J. Blakely. bibliog f il ALA Bul 61:152-4+ F '67
LIBRARIES and state
ALA Washington notes; opening days of the first session of the 90th Congress. G. Krettek and E. D. Cooke. Wilson Lib Bul 41:743+ Mr '67
Budget for 1968 proposes changes. Library J 92:721 F 15 '67
Calling the commission; symposium. il Library J 92:1802-7. 1901-5 My 1-15 '67
Federal aid going up; allotments to the states for public library construction and services. Sch & Soc 95:289-90 Sum '67
Federal library legislation. programs. and services; symposium with introd. by G. Venn, ed. by H. Drennan. il ALA Bul 61:1049-57+ O '67
Hit the deck; running! concerning HUD's Model neighborhoods under the Demonstration cities act. and Program guide. K. Nyren. Library J 92:715 F 15 '67; Discussion. 92:1549-50. 2312+ Ap 15. Je 15 '67
How a library won an election; Minneapolis public library. K. C. Busch and E. J. Gaines; reply. G. K. Schenk. Library J 92:712 F 15 '67
Integrate major programs. advises N.Y. study; A. D. Little report. Library J 92:4089-90+ N 15 '67
It's a date; don't be late; opportunity to communicate our convictions about American librarianship to National advisory commission on libraries. E. Moon. Library J 92:949 Mr 1 '67
Library related programs get federal budget figures. Library J 92:4317 D 1 '67
Library research committee sets guidelines for grants; Advisory committee on library research and training. Library J 92:516-17 F 1 '67
Missouri increases funds for aid to public libraries. Library J 92:3364 O 1 '67
Money for 1968 library-education activities. G. Krettek and E. Cooke. ALA Bul 61:921-3 S '67
N.Y. state aid bill dies in committee. Library J 92:1886+ My 15 '67
1967; year of growth and second thoughts. K. Nyren. il Library J 93:33-40 Ja 1 '68
President to sign 1968 HEW appropriations act. G. Krettek and E. D. Cooke. ALA Bul 61:1293 D '67
Public library and the planning agency. L. M. Bewley. bibliog ALA Bul 61:968-74 S '67
State aid in S. Carolina; letter to the editor. E. P. Walker. Library J 92:2487 Jl '67
State library agency and metropolitan library service; adaptation of address. S. G. Prentiss. il Library J 92:546-9 F 1 '67

LIBRARIES and state—*Continued*
Tiptoe in technology; transforming library into educational materials center, through ESEA Titles II and III, at Burnt Hills-Ballston Lake junior high school, N.Y. M. J. Egan. il Library J 92:1711-13 Ap 15 '67
Union protests Title II practice; library committee of UFT in New York city schools. Library J 92:1688+ Ap 15 '67
Vocational education act offers technician aid in '69. Library J 93:136 Ja 15 '68
See also
College libraries and state
School libraries and state

LIBRARIES and students
Chicago area librarians score use by outsiders. Library J 92:1558+ Ap 15 '67; Discussion. 92:2095-6 Je 1 '67
Greater role in education seen for public libraries; summary of statement, May 15, 1967. H. W. Tucker. Library J 92:2322+ Je 15 '67
Plus ça change: classic patterns in public/school library relations. D. M. Broderick. bibliog Library J 92:1995-7 My 15 '67
See also
Libraries—Work with young people

LIBRARIES and the public. See Libraries—Public relations

LIBRARY administration
Bugbear of school library education; results of ESEA. J. Rowell; reply. M. Cheeseman. Library J 92:1681 Ap 15 '67
Charting a course in charaymak: a didactic tale with overtones. J. C. Kountz. il ALA Bul 61:396-408 Ap '67
Continuing education and library administration; address, January 11, 1967. J .J. Kortendick. ALA Bul 61:268-72 Mr '67
Courses for adminstrators; letter to the editor. E. A. Temkin. Library J 92:510 F 1 '67
Hints to the harried. P. S. Dunkin. Library J 92:2738-9 Ag '67
Library services to children in the mosaic of administration; address, July 1967. R. Warncke. il ALA Bul 61:1324-7 D '67
Management training advocated; letter to the editor. J. J. Oliva; discussion. ALA Bul 61:368-9, 904-5 Ap, S '67
Office of the librarian: address, June 28, 1967. F. E. Mohrhardt. bibliog Wilson Lib Bul 42:391-6 D '67
Personnel problems studied at Indianapolis institute. M. A. Gray. Library J 92:1557-8 Ap 15 '67
See also
Librarians—Selection and appointment
Libraries—Trustees, boards, committees, etc.

Anecdotes facetiae, satire, etc.
Trial by computer; excerpts from address. April 1967. B. Stuart-Stubbs. il Library J 92:4471-4 D 15 '67

Study and teaching
Administrators' development program. H. L. Tosi. il Wilson Lib Bul 42:406-10 D '67

LIBRARY advertising. See Library publicity

LIBRARY architecture
Addition to the Boston public library. il Arch Rec 142:110-11 D '67
Architectural issue (cont) il Library J 92:4337-85+ D 1 '67
Bricks and mortar. See occasional issues of Library journal
Bright new use, and new form, for the monitor skylight; new library; Institute for advanced study, Princeton, N.J. il Arch Rec 141:151-4 My '67
Courtyard unifies varied elements and spaces; four-level library. il Arch Rec 141:155-8 My '67
Federal funds for facilities. H. T. Drennan. il ALA Bul 61:1054-7 O '67
Four public libraries. il Arch Rec 142:177-84 S '67
Goin' down the road feelin' bad; whatever happened to the Carnegie buildings? P. T. Barkey. Library J 92:3389 O 1 '67
Instant college libraries; California's new campuses at Santa Cruz and Irvine; interview, ed. by J. Cushman. D. T. Clark; J. E. Smith. il Library J 92:240-3 F 1 '67
Johansen's Orlando library: compatible colony of varied forms. il Arch Rec 141:151-6 Je '67
Johnson plugs monumentality for library buildings; excerpts from address, May 18, 1967. P. Johnson. Library J 92:2324+ Je 15 '67
Lake Erie, constituent imagery determines campus design. V. Christ-Janer. il Arch Forum 127:62-7 Jl '67

Library buildings study gives new statistics. Library J 92:2694+ Ag '67
Library which affirms an old style, and dormitories which establish a newer one. il Arch Rec 141:207-9 Ap '67
Magic box; Trinity college library, Dublin. J. Donat. il Arch Forum 127:78-85 O '67
New library buildings in the San Francisco Bay area. C. Coolidge and N. Coolidge. ALA Bul 61:738-9 Je '67
Seminary library sets a high architectural standard for the archdiocese of Boston; St John's seminary. il Arch Rec 142:101-4 Ag '67
University of California at Santa Cruz: university library. il Arch Rec 141:202-5 Ap '67

LIBRARY assistants

Education
Canadian L.A. committee releases technician plan. Library J 92:3360 O 1 '67
Library technicians: instant librarians? excerpts from address, May 28, 1967. S. Sass. bibliog Library J 92:2123-6 Je 1 '67; Discussion. 92:2685, 3571 Ag, O 15 '67

LIBRARY association of Australia
Man's world. J. Whyte. bibliog il Library J 92:4120-2 N 15 '67

LIBRARY associations
Aslib for America: solution to problem of proliferation of specialized organizations and their overlapping membership. J. Shera. Wilson Lib Bul 41:1063-4 Je '67
Cooperation between ALA and state library associations; address, September 1966. R. Warnecke. ALA Bul 61:191-6 F '67
National library council proposed by committee. Library J 92:2104+ Je 1 '67
See also
Film library information council
Friends of the library

LIBRARY bill of rights
Library bill of rights: reasons for revision; with present text, proposed text. E. J. Gaines. Library J 92:984-5 Mr 1 '67; Same. ALA Bul 61:409-10 Ap '67

LIBRARY boards. See Libraries—Trustees, boards, committees, etc.

LIBRARY book postage. See Postal rates—United States

LIBRARY bookbinding. See Bookbinding

LIBRARY buildings. See Library architecture

LIBRARY carpets. See Library furniture and equipment

LIBRARY censorship. See Libraries—Censorship

LIBRARY classification. See Classification

LIBRARY company of Philadelphia
Cultural relic of colonial America; J. Logan's quest for Ptolemy's Almagest. E. Wolf, 2d. il Wilson Lib Bul 41:569-72 F '67

LIBRARY conferences
Calendar. See issues of Library journal
Conference report; meeting in Atlanta to discuss library education in the South, sponsored by Atlanta university's School of library service. H. Richmand and N. Kirin. Wilson Lib Bul 41:1009+ Je '67
Geneseo conference probes library education. Library J 92:1403-4 Ap 1 '67
International conference on library education set; Univ. of Illinois, host. Library J 92:177 Ja 15 '67
Manpower: a dialogue; Washington, D.C. conference report. S. Havens. il Library J 92:1799-801 My 1 '67
Manpower: a proposal; Philadelphia conference report. K. F. Duchac. Library J 92:1797-8 My 1 '67; Reply. K. Parke. 92:2855 S 1 '67
Meetings, courses, associations, etc. See issues of Wilson library bulletin
Report on manpower conference. K. Molz. Wilson Lib Bul 41:820-3+ Ap '67
See also
American library association—Meetings

LIBRARY consultants
Inept library consultants attacked by Shaffer; excerpts from address, October 5, 1967. K. R. Shaffer. Library J 92:3946 N 1 '67

LIBRARY cooperation
Eleven college groups form National council for foreign area materials. Library J 92:2106 Je 1 '67
Experiment in a rural system: consolidation of public relations programs of Four county, Chemung-Southern Tier and the Finger Lakes library systems. M. A. Wright. Wilson Lib Bul 42:301-3 N '67
Implications of cooperation. D. Sinclair. il Wilson Lib Bul 41:939-42 My '67
Leader in cooperation; Australian national library. J. Balnaves. bibliog il Library J 92:4117-19 N 15 '67

LIBRARY cooperation—*Continued*
Library cooperation; ALA program meetings. ALA Bul 61:840-1 Jl '67
N.Y. library cooperation moves ahead with METRO. Library J 92:952+ Mr 1 '67
Seamless web: the systems approach to library service, address, November 1966. ALA Bul 61:180-5 F '67
States report progress in LSCA title III pans. Library J 92:2866 S 1 '67
See also
Interlibrary loans
LIBRARY deposit stations. See Libraries—Branches and stations
LIBRARY discipline. See Library administration
LIBRARY education. See Library schools and education
LIBRARY employees. See Library assistants
LIBRARY equipment. See Library furniture and equipment
LIBRARY exhibits
Bulletin board displays. il Wilson Lib Bul 42:86-7 S '67
Displays: the book as art; Dallas public library. il Wilson Lib Bul 42:334-5 N '67
Exhibitors oppose plan for ALA midwinter exhibits. Library J 92:722 F 15 '67
LIBRARY extension
Extending library service; ed. by G. K. Schenk. See issues of Wilson library bulletin to June 1967
See also
Bookmobiles
Libraries, County
LIBRARY finance. See Libraries—Finance
LIBRARY furniture and equipment
Buyers' guide; ed. by T. W. McConkey. See usually first issue of each month of Library journal
Carpeting in libraries. W. E. Jorgensen. Library J 92:4344 D 1 '67
Gifts for bookworms. il Am Home 70:26 D '67
Goods and gadgets. See issues of ALA bulletin
Library shelving firms pay antitrust damages; Oregon and California. Library J 92:1403 Ap 1 '67
Library technology. G. T. Piez. See issues of ALA bulletin to October 1967
Purchasing guide 1967; ed. by T. W. McConkey. Library J 92:1433-5+ Ap 1 '67
Well-wrought interior design; adaptation of address, May 16, 1966. E. Mason. il Library J 92:743-7 F 15 '67
LIBRARY institutes and workshops
Meetings, courses, associations, etc. See issues of Wilson library bulletin
Personnel problems studied at Indianapolis institute. M. A. Gray. Library J 92:1557-8 Ap 15 '67
LIBRARY instruction. See Libraries—Instruction in use
LIBRARY Journal
More Podunk plodders: letter to the editor, with editorial comment. C. Joyce. Library J 93:127-8 Ja 15 '68
Those current topics. Library J 92:206 Ja 15 '67
LIBRARY laws and legislation
ALA Washington notes. G. Krettek and E. D. Cooke. See issues of Wilson library bulletin
Eight library bills passed in Indiana. Library J 92:2342 Je 15 '67
Legislative roundup. A. Ladenson. Library J 93:41-2 Ja 1 '68
New hope for the handicapped; Division for the blind and physically handicapped. C. Gallozzi. bibliog il Library J 92:1417-20 Ap 1 '67
Public library services to the handicapped; two new programs; address, October 1966. E. C. Graham. il ALA Bul 61:170-9 F '67
States report progress in LSCA title III plans. Library J 92:2866 S 1 '67
Washington report: from the ALA Washington office. G. Krettek and E. D. Cooke. See issues of ALA bulletin
LIBRARY loans. See Libraries—Circulation, loans, etc.
LIBRARY management. See Library administration
LIBRARY of Congress. See United States—Library of Congress
LIBRARY of Congress catalog cards. See Catalog cards
LIBRARY of Congress subject headings. See Subject headings
LIBRARY of presidential papers, New York. See Presidential libraries
LIBRARY orientation. See Libraries—Instruction in use

LIBRARY patrons. See Libraries and readers
LIBRARY personnel. See Library assistants; Library staffs
LIBRARY publicity
How a library won an election; Minneapolis public library. K. C. Busch and E. J. Gaines; reply. G. K. Schenk. Library J 92: 712 F 15 '67
It's the latest, it's the greatest, it's the li-ber-ee. P. Winnick. il Am Ed 3:5-7 Je '67
Library lunch: NYPL Neighbors lunches to make services of the Central research library better known. New Yorker 43:18-19 Ja 6 '68
Library newspaper column: its format and function. V. Leonard. ALA Bul 61:412-14 Ap '67
Public relations and the library: symposium. il Wilson Lib Bul 42:278-311+ N '67
See also
National library week
LIBRARY research. See Library science—Research
LIBRARY schools, Association of American. See Association of American library schools
LIBRARY schools and education
Accredited library schools. ALA Bul 61:1233-4 N '67
Bugbear of school library education; results of ESEA. J. Rowell; reply. M. Cheeseman. Library J 92:1681 Ap 15 '67
Conference report; meeting in Atlanta to discuss library education in the South, sponsored by Atlanta university's School of library service. H. Richmond and N. Kirin. Wilson Lib Bul 41:1009+ Je '67
[Continuing education for librarians; symposium] bibliog ALA Bul 61:259-81+ Mr '67
Courses for administrators; letter to the editor. E. A. Temkin. Library J 92:510 F 1 '67
[Crisis: library manpower problem; symposium] Library J 92:1795-801 My 1 '67; Discussion. 92:1781, 2311, 2855 My 1, Je 15, S 1 '67
Data processing in the library school curriculum. R. H. Hayes. bibliog il ALA Bul 61:662-9 Je '67
Disgruntled student; letter. Library J 92: 711-12 F 15 '67
Federal government and library education. S. R. Reed. ALA Bul 61:1050-4 O '67
Geneseo conference probes library education. Library J 92:1403-4 Ap 1 '67
International conference on library education set; Univ. of Illinois, host. Library J 92:177 Ja 15 '67
Lancour hits parochialism in world library education; excerpts from address, May 20, 1967. H. Lancour. Library J 92:2326+ Je 15 '67
Library education and reference performance. C. A. Bunge. Library J 92:1578-81 Ap 15 '67
Library education and the shortage of both manpower and talent; symposium, ed. by D. Bendix with editorial comment; discussion. Library J 91:6020+; 92:170 D 15 '66, Ja 15 '67
Library manpower; address, June 1967. H. T. Drennan and S. R. Reed. bibliog il ALA Bul 61:957-65 S '67
Library training expansion charted by OE for 1967-68. Library J 92:951 Mr 1 '67
Management training advocated; letter to the editor. J. J. Oliva; discussion. ALA Bul 61:368-9, 904-5 Ap, S '67
Manpower; ALA program meetings. ALA Bul 61:836-40 Jl '67
Manpower: the big show; ALA conference. S. Havens. il Library J 92:2713-19 Ag '67
Meetings, courses, associations, etc. See issues of Wilson library bulletin
Midwinter for the masses; program without precedent: Continuing education for librarians. ALA midwinter report. S. Havens. il Library J 92:738-42 F 15 '67
Myths and realities: ALA conference theme: Crisis in library manpower. E. Moon. Library J 92:2319 Je 15 '67
On library education; letter to the editor. A. W. Russell. Library J 92:4199-200 N 15 '67
Research mind in library education and practice; relating to the improvement of libraries. R. H. Muller. bibliog Library J 92:1126-9 Mr 15 '67
Teaching a commitment to intellectual freedom; adaptation of address, January 14, 1967. D. K. Berninghausen. il Library J 92:3601-5 O 15 '67
To kill a whooping crane: fresh approach to the problem of educating librarians. P. Sexton; discussion. Library J 92:1775 My 1 '67

LIBRARY schools and education—*Continued*
Trading stamp mentality; British instructor's opinion of American library education; adaptation of addresses, 1966. R. Stokes. il Library J 92:3595-600 O 15 '67
Try to remember: autumn, beginning of a great career. J. Shera. Wilson Lib Bul 42:215+ O '67
What is a librarian? letter to the editor. A. Stein. Wilson Lib Bul 41:781 Ap '67
Which SLJ do you read? letter to the editor. A. H. Stein. Library J 92:3091 S 15 '67
See also
American library association—Commission on a national plan for library education
Association of American library schools
Cataloging—Study and teaching
Library assistants—Education
also names of library schools, e.g. Illinois. University—Graduate school of library science

Australia
Man's world. J. Whyte. bibliog il Library J 92:4120-2 N 15 '67

Canada
Technician courses boom in Canada. Library J 92:2870+ S 1 '67

LIBRARY science
See also
Bibliography
Librarianship

Bibliography
Professional reading. See issues of Library journal

Periodicals
See also
Library journal

Research
Call for research: computerized circulation control systems in libraries and information centers; letter to the editor. C. D. Gull. ALA Bul 61:903-4 S '67
Clearinghouse for library science. W. Simonton. il Wilson Lib Bul 42:383-5 D '67
Kaleidoscopic view of library research; symposium. bibliog il Wilson Lib Bul 41:896-949 My '67; Discussion. 42:23 S '67
Library research due for $3.5 million boost. Library J 92:2691-2+ Ag '67; Reply. P. S. Dunkin. 92:4127 N 15 '67
Research mind in library education and practice; relating to the improvement of libraries. R. H. Muller. bibliog Library J 92:1126-9 Mr 15 '67
Research, planning, coordination. H. T. Drennan. ALA Bul 61:1062-5 O '67
Writing research proposals. J. F. Krug. bibliog ALA Bul 61:1314-18 D '67

Scholarships and fellowships
Fellowships for librarians to be quadrupled in 1967. Library J 92:2332+ Je 15 '67

Study and teaching
See Library schools and education
LIBRARY science as a profession. See Librarianship as a profession
LIBRARY services and construction act. See Library laws and legislation
LIBRARY services and educational facilities, Division of. See United States—Education, Office of—Library services and educational facilities, Division of
LIBRARY services branch. See United States—Education, Office of—Library services and educational facilities, Division of; United States—Education, Office of—Library services branch
LIBRARY shelving. See Library furniture and equipment
LIBRARY sites. See Libraries—Location
LIBRARY staffs
Library education and reference performance. C. A. Bunge. Library J 92:1578-81 Ap 15 '67
See also
Librarians unions
LIBRARY standards. See Libraries—Standards
LIBRARY statistics. See Libraries—Statistics
LIBRARY surveys
Art in libraries; report. R. McClarren. il Library J 92:4337-40 D 1 '67
Examination of methods used in a study of decision-making; science library materials. M. B. Snyder. il ALA Bul 61:1319-23 D '67
Factors influencing public library use. M. L. Bundy. il Wilson Lib Bul 42:371-82 D '67
Federal library survey aims to up salaries. Library J 93:136 Ja 15 '68

Inept library consultants attacked by Shaffer; excerpts from address, October 5, 1967. K. R. Shaffer. Library J 92:3946 N 1 '67
Library education and reference performance. C. A. Bunge. Library J 92:1578-81 Ap 15 '67
Metropolitan public library use; Maryland. M. L. Bundy. bibliog il Wilson Lib Bul 41:950-61 My '67
New England survey pegs library ills. Library J 92:3946 N 1 '67
Placement picture: 1966. C. J. Frarey. il Library J 92:2131-6 Je 1 '67; Correction. 92:2487 Jl '67
Placement situation 1965 (with a preview of 1966) D. E. Strout and R. B. Strout; reply. R. L. Waters. Library J 92:1550 Ap 15 '67
See also
School library surveys
LIBRARY technology program. See American library association—Library technology program
LIBRARY trustees. See Libraries—Trustees, boards, committees, etc.
LIBRARY week. See National library week
LIBRARY workers. See Library assistants
LIBRARY workshops. See Library institutes and workshops
LIBRATION of the moon. See Moon—Libration
LIBRETTISTS
See also
Libretto
LIBRETTO
Act Puccini never wrote; Act III, the courtyard of La Bohème. R. Fellner. Opera N 31:24-7 F 4 '67
Measure of greatness. H. Taubman. il Opera N 31:8-13 Ap 1 '67
LIBRIUM. See Tranquilizing drugs
LIBYA
See also
Newspapers—Libya
Petroleum industry and trade—Libya
LICATA, Anthony
Doubleheader for George. il por Time 89:15 Je 2 '67
To the rescue. Newsweek 69:33 Je 5 '67
LICE
Loused-up lice. Sci Am 217:104 S '67
LICENSED merchandise. See Merchandising
LICENSES
See also
Air pilots—Licenses
Automobile drivers—Licenses
LICENSING corporation of America
And the tennis racket; Manhattan's licensing corp. il Time 89:94+ Ap 21 '67
LICENSING of patents. See Patents—Licensing
LICHENS
Habitat selection by chemically differentiated races of lichens. W. L. Culberson and C. F. Culberson. bibliog il Science 158:1195-7 D 1 '67
LICHINE, Alexis
Gospel of the grape. il por Newsweek 69:98+ My 29 '67
LICHT, Fred
For Florence, from Florence. Art N 66:44-7+ My '67
LICHTBLAU, John H.
Politics of petroleum. Reporter 37:26-8 Jl 13 '67
LICHTENSTEIN, Roy F.
Kidding everybody. il por Time 89:72-3 Je 23 '67
Remarkable commonplace. D. Waldman. il por Art N 66:28-31+ O '67
LICHTHEIM, George
Birth of a philosopher. Commentary 43:86+ Je '67
Public affairs (cont) Commentary 43:62-6 Ja; 47-51 Ap; 44:62-7 Jl; bibliog f 62-7 O '67
What is left of communism? For Affairs 46:78-94 O '67
About
No right to be wrong. E. T. Gargan. Nation 206:22-4 Ja 1 '68
LICODIA EUBEA, Sicily
Ties; Sicilian barbers in New York. New Yorker 43:38-9 S 9 '67
LIDOCAINE hydrochloride
Circadian periodicity in susceptibility to lidocaine hydrochloride. E. F. Lutsch and R. W. Morris. bibliog il Science 156:100-2 Ap 7 '67

LIE; drama. See Sarraute, N.
LIEB, Charles H.
Computer and copyright: the next five years. Pub W 192:40-2 S 18 '67
LIEBER, David
Jewish-Christian concerns. Christian Cent 84: 1193-4 S 20 '67
LIEBERMAN, Edward M. and others
Bioelectric phenomena related to protein-fixed charge in a crab nerve fiber. bibliog Science 156:240-2 Ap 14 '67
LIEBERMAN, Elias
Quatrain for moderns. Cath World 205:30 Ap '67
LIEBERMAN, Laurence
Art in transition. Poetry 109:395-9 Mr '67
Skin song; House skin; poems. Poetry 110: 236-8 Jl '67
Transvestite; poem. New Yorker 43:61 D 30 '67
Unblinding; poem. New Yorker 43:59 N 25 '67
LIEBERMAN, Morris, and Kunishi, A. T.
Propanal may be a precursor of ethylene in metabolism. bibliog Science 158:938 N 17 '67
LIEBERMANN, Robert C. and Pomeroy, P. W.
Excitation of surface waves by events in southern Algeria. bibliog Science 156:1098-100 My 26 '67
LIEBERMANN, Rolf
Lively arts; interview, ed. by R. Hemming. por Sr Schol 90:30 My 19 '67
No small roles. Opera N 32:8-10 S 23 '67
LIEBERSON, Goddard
What happened since LP. Sat R 50:61-3 Ag 26 '67
about
He makes music pay at CBS. il pors Bsns W p 106-7+ O 7 '67
LIEBERT, Herman W.
Single, simple leaf of papyrus. por Wilson Lib Bul 41:606-7+ F '67
LIEBMAN, Marvin
(ed) They also serve. por Nat R 19:1327-31 N 28 '67
LIECHTENSTEIN
124 rooms, twenty baths, elevators, central heating, fit for a prince. J. Wechsberg. il Esquire 68:217-21+ D '67
Scaling the Alps for tax havens. il Bsns W p66-7+ O 21 '67
LIECHTENSTEIN collection. See Art—Private collections
Das LIED von der erde; ballet. See Ballets— Criticisms
LIEDER, Ruth
Sporting look. Sports Illus 27:45 Jl 31 '67
LIFE
Are you present? J. B. Mosley. Read Digest 91:131-2 Ag '67
Cryonics and the purpose of life. R. C. W. Ettinger. Christian Cent 84:1250-3 O 4 '67; Discussion. 84:1656-8 D 27 '67
Do we still love life? E. Fromm. il McCalls 94:57+ Ag '67
Greatest gift of all. M. MacWilliams. McCalls 94:38+ Je '67
To know the pain of being a person; address. H. K. Zeller. Vital Speeches 33:328-30 Mr 15 '67
See also
Conduct of life
LIFE (biology)
See also
Genetics
Origin
In the beginning. I. Asimov. Sci Digest 62: 82-4 O '67
Life three billion years ago. il Sci Digest 63: 19 Ja '68
LIFE (periodical)
Conflict of values: news and privacy; Hill vs. Life. Sr Schol 90:18 F 10 '67
Franchise of human affairs. G. P. Hunt. il Life 62:3 Mr 31 '67
Life sues to enjoin book on assassination of Kennedy. Pub W 192:32 D 25 '67
Life vs. photography. J. Durniak. Pop Phot 60:68 Ap '67
Luce raised the level of photographic art. P. Stackpole. U S Camera 30:14+ Je '67
Special double issue; wild world. il Life 63:4+ D 22 '67
296 stringers help us cover the world. G. P. Hunt. Life 62:5 F 24 '67
U.S. camera achievement award. U S Camera 30:45 N '67
Word man for Life; three-way editorial shift. Newsweek 70:98 D 11 '67

LIFE cycle costing. See Contracts, Government—Accounting
LIFE expectancy. See Longevity
LIFE extension society
Will we freeze ourselves into the future? B. H. Frisch. il Sci Digest 61:17-21+ Je '67
LIFE insurance. See Insurance, Life
LIFE insurance companies. See Insurance companies
LIFE insurance premium rates. See Insurance, Life—Rates and tables
LIFE jackets. See Life preservers
LIFE line movement. See Telephone—Religious applications
LIFE on other planets
Better life spies for space. il Sci Digest 62:37 D '67
Extraterrestrial life detection based on oxygen isotope exchange reactions. B. Kok and J. E. Varner. bibliog il Science 155:1110-12 Mr 3 '67
Flying saucers, are they real? J. A. Hynek. Read Digest 90:61-5 Mr '67
Gasbags of Venus. il Time 90:60 O 20 '67
Have we been visited by spacemen? D. Cohen. il Sci Digest 61:84-5 F '67
Life in the clouds; conditions on Venus. Sci N 92:320 S 30 '67
Little men from Mars. Sci Digest 62:37 N '67
Lust for life; search for life on other worlds. Sci N 93:29-31 Ja 13 '68
Martian wolf trap in action; soil samples to be examined for evidence of living organisms. il Sci Digest 61:72-3 Je '67
Maser here. Hello there! radiation waves from hydroxyl clouds. Newsweek 70:84 S 11 '67
NASA tests boost Jupiter life possibility. Tech W 20:28 Ap 24 '67
New life detection methods studied by Martin's RIAS. Tech W 20:44 My 15 '67
Prevention of protein denaturation during exposure to sterilization temperatures. E. W. Chappelle and others. bibliog il Science 155: 1287-8 Mr 10 '67
Search for extraterrestrial life; adaptation of address, October 13, 1965. N. H. Horowitz; reply. W. B. Smith. bibliog Science 155:852 F 17 '67
LIFE preservers
New look at life jackets. Z. Taylor. il Motor B 119:45-6+ F '67
See also
Life-saving equipment
LIFE saving. See Rescue work
LIFE-saving equipment
Abandon-ship bubble; Brucker survival capsule. il Life 63:55-6 S 29 '67
LIFE span. See Longevity
LIFE support systems (space environment)
Can we keep our astronauts alive in space? K. V. Brown. il Pop Mech 128:82-5+ Ag '67
Orbiting rescue vehicle proposed by GPI. K. Voss. il Tech W 20:32-3 Ap 10 '67
Regenerative system sought for long-flight life support; advanced integrated life support system. I. Stone. Aviation W 87:25 O 2 '67
Sewage treatment in space. il Sci Digest 61: 37 Ap '67
Space suit and life support projects escape trimming. il Aero Tech 21:100-5 N 20 '67
See also
Space vehicles—Cabin atmospheres
LIFE support systems (submarine environment)
CAVE study sets future life support goals. H. M. David. il Aero Tech 21:37+ S 25 '67
LIFEBOATS
See also
Life-saving equipment
LIFEBOATS, Unsinkable
Abandon-ship bubble; Brucker survival capsule. il Life 63:55-6 S 29 '67
LIFETIME sports foundation
Dade County's Lifetime sports program holds community and individual interests. il Parks & Rec 2:46+ O '67
Dallas benefits from Lifetime sports program. W. Keeling. il Parks & Rec 2:20+ Jl '67
Lifetime sports camps. il Parks & Rec 2: 24+ F '67
Lifetime sports recreation project to be expanded. il Parks & Rec 2:24 Ja '67
1967 Lifetime sports programs kick off with gusto. il Parks & Rec 2:28+ Je '67
Participants in 1967 Lifetime sports recreation project. Parks & Rec 2:39+ Ap '67
Public consensus. il Parks & Rec 2:23-4 N '67
LIFLAND, William T.
Banking and the antitrust laws. bibliog f Harvard Bsns R 45:138-44 My '67

LIKENESS, George. See Butler, K. jt. auth.

LIKENS, G. E. See Bormann, F. H. jt. auth.

LILEY, Margaret, and Day, Beth
Doctor's guide to a healthy pregnancy; excerpt from Infant world. Parents Mag 42: 46-7+ Ap '67

LILIEN, Jack E. and Moscona, A. A.
Cell aggregation: its enhancement by a supernatant from cultures of homologus cells. bibliog Science 157:70-2 Jl 7 '67

LILIENTHAL, David Eli
Economic situation in Viet-Nam. Dept State Bul 56:467-9 Mr 20 '67
Mr Lilienthal discusses Viet-Nam's economic development program; news briefing, December 6, 1967. Dept State Bul 57:864-7 D 25 '67

about
Mr Lilienthal to head U.S team studying Vietnamese development. Dept State Bul 56:69 Ja 9 '67
Selling self-help at a profit. il por Bsns W p54-6+ Ag 12 '67

LILIES
Companion plants with lilies. V. Howie. il Horticulture 45:26-9+ My '67
Lilies for every clime. J. De Graaff. il Home Gard 54:39 Ag '67
See also
Calla lilies
Day lilies

LILLARD, Richard G.
Soil beneath the blacktop. Nation 204:206-10 F 13 '67

LILLEHEI, Clarence Walton
Fertile seedbed of transplant surgery. por Bsns W p98-100 Ja 6 '68

LILLIPUTIAN villages. See Models of cities, towns, etc.

LILLY, Frank
Susceptibility to two strains of Friend leukemia virus in mice. bibliog Science 155: 461-2 Ja 27 '67

LIM, Boo-liat. See Heyneman, D. jt. auth.

LIMBACHER, James L.
On the record: Words. See issues of Library journal
Recordings (cont of) Recordings for young people. See second issue of each month of Library journal

LIMERICKS
Lure of the limerick, by W. S. Baring-Gould. Review
Time 90:106+ S 22 '67

LIMITATION of armaments. See Disarmament

LIMITED editions. See Publishers and publishing—Limited editions

LIMITED war. See War

LIMITED war laboratory. See United States —Army research office

LIMÓN, José
José and others. D. Hering. il Dance Mag 41:33 O '67

LIMPETS
Interpopulation variations in calcium metabolism in the stream limpet, ferrissia rivularis (Say) W. R. Hunter and others. bibliog il Science 155:338-40 Ja 20 '67

LIMULUS. See King crabs

LIMULUS eye. See Eye (crustacea)

LIN, Norman
Role differentiation in copulating cicada killer wasps. bibliog Science 157:1334-5 S 15 '67

LIN, Piao
Long march of Lin Piao. L. Fessler. il pors N Y Times Mag p64-5+ S 10 '67
We're not sure what will happen next. il por Newsweek 69:43 Ap 3 '67
What's really going on now in red China; symposium. il U S News 62:46-50+ Ja 30 '67
Writhing dragon. Nat R 19:70+ Ja 24 '67

LINCOLN, Abraham
Riots and mob spirit: America's greatest danger; excerpts from address, January 27, 1838. U S News 63:92+ Ag 28 '67

about
Mexican war dove. H. Mitgang. New Repub 156:23-4 F 11 '67

Assassination
Another assassination, another widow, another embattled book; excerpts from Behind the scenes, ed. by M. Wefer. E. Keckley. il Am Heritage 18:79-88 Ag '67

Bibliography
Lincolniana in 1966. B. E. Wheeler. il Hobbies 71:35+ F; 72:114-15+ Mr '67

Drama
Young Abe's destiny. C. Boiko. Plays 26:43-8 F '67

LINCOLN, Alexander, Jr
Facts on the redwoods. Am For 73:40-1+ N '67

LINCOLN, C. Eric
Handbook on the struggle. Sat R 50:28 Ag 5 '67
Theological and ethical implications of the black ghetto. Christian Cent 84:264-7 Mr 1 '67

LINCOLN, Marshall
Watch it, speeders! Pop Mech 128:61-3+ Ag '67

LINCOLN, Mary (Todd)
Another assassination, another widow, another embattled book; excerpts from Behind the scenes, ed. by M. Wefer. E. Keckley. il por Am Heritage 18:79-88 Ag '67

LINCOLN, Robert Todd
Another assassination, another widow, another embattled book; excerpts from Behind the scenes, ed. by M. Wefer. E. Keckley. il por Am Heritage 18:79-88 Ag '67

LINCOLN, Neb.
Streets
How to promote sidewalk construction; excerpts from report. R. Holsinger. il Am City 82:80-2 Jl '67

LINCOLN Center for the performing arts, New York
If you must build a cultural center. R. Kotlowitz. il Harper 235:96-8 Jl '67
Lincoln Center festival '67. L. Lerman. Mlle 65:96 My '67
Opera house
Architecture. E. Galantay. Nation 204:473-4+ Ap 10 '67
New house (cont) F. Stevenson. il Opera N 31:30-1 Ja 7 '67

Vivian Beaumont theater
Saturn eats his children. R. Brustein. New Repub 156:34-5 Ja 28 '67

LINCOLN Center fund for education and artistic advancement
It's fun to yell bravo; Lincoln Center's student program. L. Rich. il Am Ed 3:15-20+ Je '67

LINCOLN Center repertory theater company
Saturn eats his children. R. Brustein. New Repub 156:34-5 Ja 28 '67
Scene shifting. Newsweek 69:106-7 F 6 '67

LINCOLN Filene center for citizenship and public affairs. See Tufts university, Medford, Mass.—Lincoln Filene center for citizenship and public affairs

LINCOLN hospital. See New York (city)—Hospitals

LINCOLN park. See Chicago—Parks and playgrounds

LINDBECK, George A.
Secular ecumenism in action; excerpt from address, November 20, 1966. Cath World 205:7-13 Ap '67

LINDBERGH, Anne (Morrow)
Charles and Anne Morrow Lindbergh: America's most remarkable parents; excerpts from The last hero; Charles A. Lindbergh. W. S. Ross. il por Ladies Home J 85:43-6+ Ja '68

LINDBERGH, Charles Augustus
Wisdom of wildness. por Life 63:8-10 D 22 '67

About
Aloof Lone Eagle; Lindy shuns air show. il por U S News 62:24 My 1 '67
Charles and Anne Morrow Lindbergh: America's most remarkable parents; excerpts from The last hero; Charles A. Lindbergh. W. S. Ross. il por Ladies Home J 85:43-6+ Ja '68
Flight that tied the world together. K. V. Brown. il pors Pop Mech 127:84-7 My '67
Lindbergh: the way of a hero; Time essay. Time 89:22-3 My 26 '67
Lucky Lindy's luckiest day. il por Sr Schol 90:16 My 19 '67
Picture post card. B. Finnegan. il pors Hobbies 72:120-1+ O '67
Weekend pilot. F. K. Smith. Flying 80:126 My '67
Where are they now? il pors Newsweek 69: 22 My 8 '67

LINDBERGH, Jon M.
  Whale. Life 63:48-50+ D 22 '67
LINDBERGH case. See Kidnapping
LINDBERGH flight.   See Aviation—Trans-
    atlantic flights
LINDBERGH pump. See Hearts, Artificial
LINDBOM, Torsten H.
  Robots; interview. New Yorker 43:20-2 Je
    24 '67
LINDE, Jed
  Past and present. New Repub 157:40-2 S 2 '67
LINDE, Shirley Motter
  Heart attacks that aren't. Todays Health
    45:20-3 F '67
  What we know about children's convulsions.
    Todays Health 45:56-7 O '67
  —See McGovern, J. P. jt. auth.
LINDEMAN, Bard. See Lee, W. jt. auth.
LINDEMANN, B. and Thorns, U.
  Fast potential spike of frog skin generated
    at the outer surface of the epithelium.
    bibliog Science 158:1473-7 D 15 '67
LINDENBLAD, Nils E.
  Amateur scientist. Sci Am 216:124-8 Ap '67
LINDER, Ronald L.
  Mountain climbing not limited to experts.
    Parks & Rec 2:30-1+ Mr '67
LINDGREN, Gerry
  Joyous night for a pixie. G. S. Brown. il
    por Sports Illus 26:48-50 F 27 '67
LINDHEIMER astronomical research center.
    See Astronomical observatories
LINDNER, Richard
  Baal booster. il por Time 89:44 F 3 '67
  Venus in vinyl. J. Perreault. il por Art N
    65:46-8+ Ja '67
LINDOW, Lester W.
  Excerpt from statement before Communica-
    tions subcommittee, October 13, 1967. Cong
    Digest 46:307+ D '67
LINDSAY, Cynthia
  Case of the tense lobsters; excerpt from
    Home is where you hang yourself. Read
    Digest 91:12B S '67
LINDSAY, Howard
  If a body... Sat R 50:8+ Ap 8 '67
  Silence is not always golden. Sat R 50:6 S 30
    '67
LINDSAY, John Vliet
  Our precious right to be unheard. Life 63:19
    O 6 '67
  Violence in the cities; address, July 31, 1967.
    Vital Speeches 33:674-7 S 1 '67
  What's ahead for New York city; interview.
    por U S News 62:56-60+ Ap 10 '67

          about
According to John. Time 90:28 O 13 '67
Fellow citizens. Newsweek 70:75 D 25 '67
Handsome is as handsome does. G. Ace. Sat R
    50:8 Je 17 '67
High-minded man ponders an old and bitter
    lesson. S. Smith and W. Lambert. il pors
    Life 64:50-1 Ja 5 '68
John Lindsay: ringmaster of fun city. G.
    Astor. il pors Look 31:22-6+ Mr 21 '67
Lindsay inner circle. M. Arnold. il N Y Times
    Mag p32-3+ O 15 '67
Lindsay therapy. Nation 205:131-2 Ag 28 '67
Lively Lindsay: mayor on the move. T. Irwin.
    il pors Todays Health 45:40-3 Je '67
Mayor Lindsay's goal: the White House? por
    U S News 63:28 N 6 '67
Mayor's human touch as he walks, listens.
    il pors Life 63:32-3 Ag 25 '67
One for the money? il por Newsweek 70:28-
    9 N 27 '67
People are talking about. il por Vogue 150:
    104-5 N 15 '67
Profiles. N. Hentoff. New Yorker 43:58-60+
    O 7; 61-4+ O 14 '67
R for a long, hot summer: a long, cool mayor.
    il pors Newsweek 70:21 Ag 28 '67
Report. Atlan 219:25-6+ Je '67
Rockefeller-Lindsay feud. G. Pressman. Na-
    tion 205:591-3 D 4 '67
Very tall client. W. McQaude. il por Arch
    Forum 126:92 My '67
Walks on the wild side. il por Time 90:18
    Ag 25 '67
Young easterner with style. il por Time 90:
    25-6 N 24 '67
LINDSAY, Mary (Harrison)
  New style in the G.O.P. spotlight. il por
    Ladies Home J 84:66 Ag '67
LINDSAY, Merrill
  Wear gloves before firing. Esquire 68:100-3
    O '67
LINDSAY, Tomlin K.
  Plugging profit leaks in small-order pur-
    chases. Am City 82:135-7 N '67

LINDSEY, George
  Ohio's new lakes. Travel 127:41 My '67
LINDSEY, Robert
  Future of ESRO hinges on July meeting.
    Tech W 20:22+ Ap 3 '67
  Improved Agena to increase launch vehicle
    payload 25 per cent. Tech W 20:29-30 My 29
    '67
LINE of balance control. See Production con-
    trol
LINE ISLANDS experiment. See National cen-
    ter for atmospheric research
LINEAR accelerators. See Accelerators (elec-
    trons, etc)
LINEAR programming
      See also
    Interindustry economics
LINEAWEAVER, Thomas H. 3d
  Capsule history of the Gulf Stream. Holiday
    42:91-2+ N '67
  Our catch-as-catch-can fisheries. Reporter 37:
    38-40 S 7 '67
LINEN, Household
  Durable-press sheets & pillowcases. il Con-
    sumer Rep 32:264-6 My '67
  How to buy bed linens. Am Home 70:24 Jl
    '67
  Lively linen: color and new design excite-
    ment. il Newsweek 69:87+ Mr 6 '67
  Pleasure of beautiful linens. il Good H 164:
    116-23 F '67
  Treasure of new linens for bedroom & bath.
    il Good H 166:94-9 Ja '68
      See also
    Sheets
LINEN closets. See Closets
LINERS. See Ocean liners
LINEWEAVER, Marion
  Map of the shore; poem. Ladies Home J 84:149
    Mr '67
LING, James Joseph
  Hidden appeal of Allis-Chalmers. S. H.
    Brown. il por Fortune 76:155-7+ N '67
  LTV blitzes its way into ranks of giants. il
    pors Bsns W p 178-80+ Mr 18 '67
  Ling the merger king. il pors Newsweek 70:
    71-4+ O 9 '67
LING-Temco-Vought, incorporated
  In a single stroke; acquiring Wilson & co.
    il Time 89:94 Mr 17 '67
  Ling raises the ante; attempt to acquire
    Allis-Chalmers. Bsns W p36 Ag 19 '67
  LTV blitzes its way into ranks of giants;
    take-over of Chicago-based Wilson & co. il
    Bsns W p 178-80+ Mr 18 '67
  Ling the merger king. il Newsweek 70:71-4+
    O 9 '67
  LTV maps two giant deals; Greatamerica
    corp. and Allis-Chalmers mfg. co. Bsns W
    p40 Ag 12 '67
  Ling's latest; proposal to buy Greatamerica
    corp. Newsweek 70:72+ Ag 14 '67
  Teaching Ling a thing; takeover offer re-
    fused by Allis-Chalmers. il Time 90:68-9
    Ag 25 '67
LINGARD, Joan
  Ontario's historic cruiseway. Yachting 121:
    73-5+ Je '67
LINGEMAN, Richard R.
  Understanding our cultural revolution. N Y
    Times Mag p6+ My 14 '67
LINGG, Ann M.
  Angelic choir. Opera N 32:26-7 D 23 '67
  City of firsts. Opera N 32:16-19 N 4 '67
  Cost of opera. Opera N 31:14-15 Mr 25 '67
  Council surprises. Opera N 32:13 D 9 '67
  First Don. Opera N 31:16-17 Ja 28 '67
  First Pamina. Opera N 32:6 Ja 6 '68
  Lure of the Klondike. Opera N 31:6-7 My 13
    '67
  Metropolitan family. Opera N 31:6-7 Mr 11 '67
  Whose English? Opera N 31:28-9 Ja 7 '67
LININGTON, Elizabeth
  Writing the police-routine novel. Writer 80:
    11-13+ Mr '67
LINK, Arthur S.
  Case for Woodrow Wilson. Harper 234:85-8+
    Ap '67
LINK, Edwin A.
  Our first ferry to the bottom of the sea. Pop
    Sci 191:47-9+ Jl '67
LINK, Frances R.
  To grade or not to grade. PTA Mag 62:10-
    12 bibliog(p35) N '67
LINK, Ruth
  Those new Swedish abortion pills. Ladies
    Home J 84:42+ Je '67
LINK trainers. See Flight simulators
LINKLETTER, Art
  My first trip. McCalls 94:142 My '67
  No one slept with mom while you were gone,
    dad! excerpts from Oops! or life's awful
    moments. por Ladies Home J 84:36+ Ag '67

LINKLETTER, Art—*Continued*
About
Linkletter Down Under. il por Newsweek 69:76-7 F 6 '67
LINN, Anita Bensing
Folk music. Am Rec G 33:882-3 My '67
LINN, Edward
(ed) See Coppolino, M. Mary Coppolino's own story
(ed) See Parrish, B. Pro football's player mutiny
LINNAEUS, Carl. See Linné, C. von
LINNÉ, Carl von
Carl Linnaeus. May 1707-Jan 1778; symposium. il Home Gard 54:34-6 My '67
LINNENBOM, V. J. See Swinnerton, J. W. jt. auth.
LINOLEUM
Linoleum and roto vinyl floor coverings. il Consumer Rep 32:78-81 F '67
LINOLEUM block printing
Block printing calendars. L. J. Miller. il Design 69:9 Wint '67
Block to block. S. Sturtz. il Sch Arts 67:18-21 O '67
LINOLEUM cuts. See Linoleum block printing
LINOTRON. See Phototypesetting
LINOWITZ, Sol Myron
Alliance for progress: dramatic start and hopeful future; address, August 21, 1967. Dept State Bul 57:321-4 S 11 '67
Hemisphere cooperation through the Alliance for progress; address, October 19, 1967. Dept State Bul 57:616-20 N 6 '67
Reflections on the Inter-American conference of Chiefs of state; excerpts from address, April 21, 1967. Dept State Bul 56:729-31 My 8 '67
Road from Punta del Este; address, May 1, 1967. Dept State Bul 56:822-5 My 29 '67

about
Can Sol Linowitz make it work? il por Bsns W p62+ F 18 '67
LINSKENS, H. F. See Stanley, R. G. jt. auth.
LINSKY, Jack
King of the staplers. R. Levy. il por Duns R 89:47-8 Ja '67
LINZ, Werner
Linz urges joint action to aid Catholic bookselling; summary of talk. Pub W 191:78 F 27 '67
LIONS, Mountain. See Pumas
LIP-reading. See Deaf—Means of communication
LIPIDES
Cholinergic binding capacity of proteolipids from isolated nerve-ending membranes. E. D. P. de Robertis and others. bibliog il Science 158:928-9 N 17 '67
Ethanolamine phosphoglycerides: effect on the properties of myelinoid lecithin water systems. P. G. Fast. bibliog il Science 155:1680-1 Mr 31 '67
Euglena gracilis: a novel lipid energy reserve and arachidonic acid enrichment during fasting. A. Rosenberg. bibliog il Science 157:1189-91 S 8 '67
LIPKE, Lynn
Wood-burning raku kiln. Sch Arts 66:36-8 Ja '67
LIPKIN, John P.
Education's integrative movement. bibliog f Sch & Soc 95:490-1 D 9 '67
LIPKING, Lawrence
Class of '67: the gentle desperadoes. Nation 204:780 Je 19 '67
LIPOPROTEINS. See Proteins
LIPP, A. E. Grant. See Ballard, L. A. T. jt. auth.
LIPPINCOTT, J. B. company
J. B. Lippincott company, at 175, looks ahead. il Pub W 192:27-30 Jl 31 '67
Thoughts on getting older. D. Dempsey. Sat R 50:41 S 16 '67
LIPPITT, Gordon L. and Schmidt, W. H.
Crises in a developing organization. Harvard Bsns R 45:102-12 N '67
LIPPMAN, Paul
We camped Europe. Field & S 72:52-5+ Je '67
LIPPMANN, Walter
[Current events column] See issues of Newsweek
New leader for the orchestra; interview. New Repub 157:18-21 D 9 '67
What we offer. Harper 235:45-6 O '67

about
Lippmann in new form. por Newsweek 69:64 Je 5 '67
Oval office vs. the attic. H. Sidey. por Life 62:44B My 19 '67
LIPSCOMB, Glenard P.
East-West trade; address, March 8, 1967. bibliog f Vital Speeches 33:389-94 Ap 15 '67
Excerpt from statement, March 13, 1967. Cong Digest 46:187+ Je '67
LIPSCOMB, James
Getting the elbow is a pain. Sports Illus 26:38-40+ Je 5 '67
Improvise! films are made of whimsy. Life 63:86-8+ N 10 '67
LIPSTICK
New lipsticks. S. Harney. il Ladies Home J 84:106-7 My '67
LIPSYTE, Robert
I'm free to be who I want. N Y Times Mag p28-9+ My 28 '67
You gits a little uppity and you lands in jail. Esquire 68:72-5 Ag '67
LIPTON, Morris A. and others
p-Chlorophenylalanine-induced chemical manifestations of phenylketonuria in rats. bibliog Science 156:248-50 Ap 14 '67
LIQUEFIED natural gas. See Gas, Natural—Liquefaction
LIQUEURS
Cordials and liqueurs, most luxurious of drinks. R. A. De Groot. il House B 109:262+ N '67
Drinks to serve after dinner. P. S. Brown. House & Gard 132:242+ O '67
How to make the perfect pousse-café. R. A. De Groot. House B 109:80 N '67
Smooth chasers; with recipes. E. Alston. il Look 32:50-1 Ja 23 '68
LIQUID carbonic division. See General dynamics corporation
LIQUID crystals
Chameleon chemical. Life 64:40-5 Ja 12 '68
LIQUID detergents. See Detergents
LIQUID fertilizers. See Fertilizers and manures
LIQUID ion exchanger. See Biological apparatus and supplies
LIQUID level indicators
Liquid level indicator for the blind; electronic device. T. V. Cranmer. il Pop Electr 26:59-60 My '67
LIQUID nitrogen. See Nitrogen, Liquid
LIQUID plant foods. See Plants—Nutrition
LIQUID propellant rockets
AF opens new liquid engine competition. H. Taylor. il Tech W 20:18-19 Mr 13 '67
LIQUID supplements (feeding stuffs) See Feeding and feeding stuffs
LIQUIDITY (economics)
Easier times for money? il Fortune 76:26+ S 1 '67
LIQUIDITY, International
Liquidity by the drop. H. C. Wallich. Newsweek 70:78 S 11 '67
LIQUIDS
Intermolecular forces and the nature of the liquid state; address, April 1966. B. Widom. bibliog il Science 157:375-82 Jl 28 '67
See also
Fluids
Soap bubbles and films
LIQUOR habit. See Alcoholism
LIQUOR industry
Price ferment stirs liquor industry; New York's law putting ceiling on prices. il Bsns W p86-8+ F 18 '67
Scotch with a soul; Soul brands ltd. il Newsweek 70:77+ N 6 '67

Advertising
For the ladies. il Time 90:99 N 3 '67
LIQUOR laws and regulations

New Zealand
Liquor laws. M. W. Wilson. Christian Cent 84:1414 N 1 '67
LIQUOR problem
See also
Alcoholism

United States
Alcohol in perspective. Consumer Rep 32:97-9 F '67
Drinking & pot parties; with study-discussion program, by C. Smallenburg and H. Smallenburg. M. G. Rector. bibliog il PTA Mag 61:4-7, 35-6 Mr '67

LIQUOR problem—United States—*Continued*
GH poll: question of a uniform drinking age for young people throughout the United States? with readers opinions. G. L. Maddox. Good H 164:8+ Ja '67
Little family cheer. il Newsweek 70:92 O 23 '67
Teaching high school students about C₂H₅OH. F. C. Weed. Sr Schol 91:sup20 N 16 '67

LIQUOR traffic
United States
See also
Bars and barrooms
Bootlegging

LIQUORS
Aquavit and beer. R. J. Misch. il House B 110:124+ Ja '68
Entertaining people; party ideas from everywhere. il McCalls 94:14+ My '67
Salubrious drinks for the holiday season. P. S. Brown. House & Gard 132:172+ D '67
Too hot not to cool down. il Esquire 68:75-82 Jl '67
Traveler's guide to the native drinks and wines of Italy. R. Neville. House & Gard 131:178+ Mr '67
Vodkas, gins and rums. il Consumer Rep 32:380-5 Jl '67
Wine, women & so on. P. Cannon. Ladies Home J 84:60 O '67

See also
Beer
Brandy
Cocktails
Liqueurs
Tequila
Whiskey

Prices
Price ferment stirs liquor industry; New York's law putting ceiling on prices. il Bsns W p86-8+ F 18 '67

LIRIODENDRON tulipifera. See Tulip trees

LISAGOR, Peter
Trends: Washington mood. See issues of Nation's business

LISBON, Portugal
Music
Lisbon. F. Teixeira Direito. Opera N 31:30 Mr 4 '67
Lisbon; production of Gluck's Orfeo ed Euridice. F. Teixeira Direito. Opera N 31:28 Ap 15 '67

LISCO, Hermann, and Conard. R. A.
Chromosome studies on Marshall islanders exposed to fallout radiation. bibliog Science 157:445-7 Jl 28 '67

LISMER, Arthur
Arthur Lismer, artist and art-educator: a reflection on his life, work and philosophy. H. G. Hinterreiter. il por Sch Arts 66:21-8 Ja '67

LISSANEVITCH, Boris
Who knows where the forks are? Boris. J. Howard. il pors Life 63:52+ Ag 11 '67

LISTENER (periodical)
Listener into talker. Newsweek 70:66 S 25 '67

LISTENING. See Attention

LISTENING devices, Electronic. See Electronics in criminal investigation, espionage, etc.

LISTER, Merle
Merle Lister & dance company; Sloane house YMCA. M. Marks. Dance Mag 41:32 S '67

LISTER, R. P.
Devil will shake. Atlan 219:122+ Ap '67
How useful was my paperweight. Atlan 220:118-19 N '67

LISTON, James
Is your lawn mower ready for a trade-in? Pop Gard 18:60-7 Ag '67

LISTON, Joseph
Who said you can't teach inventing? J. F. Pearson. il por Pop Mech 127:140-3+ Mr '67

LISZT, Franz
Collage of genius, the hexameron. R. Kammerer. Am Rec G 33:950-1 Je '67
Cziffra: the virtuoso recital of the century? R. Kammerer. Am Rec G 33:790 My '67

LITCHFIELD PARK, Ariz.
New town takes form. il Am City 82:109 O '67
Planned pathways bring leisure and safety. A. E. Patterson. il Parks & Rec 2:22-3 Je '67

LITERACY. See Illiteracy

LITERARY agents
Literary agents. J. O. Brown. Writer 80:15-17 Jl '67

LITERARY and scientific exchanges. See Exchanges, Literary and scientific

LITERARY censorship. See Censorship

LITERARY characters. See Characters in literature

LITERARY clubs
See also
PEN club

LITERARY correspondence. See Letters

LITERARY criticism
Art lost in analysis; the New criticism. G. Hicks. Sat R 50:29-30 My 13 '67
Attitudes toward literature. F. Lentricchia, jr. Poetry 110:119-23 My '67
Books in the field: anticriticism. I. Hassan. bibliog il Wilson Lib Bul 42:477-83 Ja '68
Language and silence, by G. Steiner. Review New Repub 156:21-2+ My 13 '67. T. Solotaroff
T. S. Eliot and the literature of waste. R. Poirier. New Repub 156:19-25 My 20 '67
See also
Book reviews
Critics

LITERARY fantasies. See Fantasies, Literary

LITERARY forgeries and mystifications
Snouters, by Harald Stümpke. G. Steiner. il Natur Hist 76:8-13 Ap '67
See also
Germany—History—Errors, inventions, etc.

LITERARY inspiration. See Inspiration

LITERARY journeys
A cross in Heraklion. F. Riley. il Sat R 50:47-8+ O 14 '67

LITERARY landmarks
Afternoon at Sant'Agata; Verdi's villa. S. Hughes. il Opera N 32:8 O '67
European literary scene; Palma de Mallorca. R. J. Clements. il Sat R 50:32 O 7 '67
In the writer's place; symposium. il Sat R 50:45-51+ Mr 11 '67
Melville revisited; Seaman's bethel; Herman Melville's Whaleman's chapel, New Bedford, Mass. R. Hendrickson. Sat R 50:43-4 Ag 5 '67
See also
Literary journeys

LITERARY periodicals. See Literature—Periodicals

LITERARY prizes
French literary prizes, 1967. H. R. Lottman. il Pub W 192:25-8 D 25 '67
Prizes authors seek. G. Hicks. Sat R 50:35-6 My 20 '67
See also
Faulkner award

LITERARY property. See Copyright

LITERARY research
It's a bargain at $1.95; travel guides as research aids. J. A. Sainsbury. Writer 80:26+ N '67
Magic of serendipity. E. J. Hodges. Horn Bk 43:370-4 Je '67

LITERARY societies
See also
Library company of Philadelphia

LITERARY style. See Style, Literary

LITERARY topics. See Literature—Themes

LITERATURE
Literary vanguard: why the avante-garde has died. G. P. Elliott. Commentary 43:93-6 Je '67
Must writers hate the universe? the literary avant-garde; its emphasis on violence, perversion, and nihilism. J. W. Krutch. Sat R 50:19-21+ My 6 '67
Your literary IQ; ed. by J. T. Winterich and D. M. Glixon. See issues of Saturday review

See also
Best sellers
Biography
Books and reading
Characters in literature
Childrens literature
Devil in literature
Erotic literature
Fiction
Folklore
Immoral literature and pictures
Literary criticism
Modernism (literature)
Nature literature
Plagiarism
Quotations
Romanticism
Style, Literary
Symbolism in literature
Totalitarianism and literature
Travel literature
also American literature; Italian literature; etc.

LITERATURE—*Continued*

Appreciation and interpretation

Uses of literature. F. J. Hoffman. Poetry 111: 203-5 D '67

Competitions

And the world stopped, waiting; first prize! Teachers writing competition. J. Heimowitz. NEA J 56:21-3 O '67; Same abr. with title Incident in room 301. il Read Digest 92:173-4+ Ja '68

See also
Fiction—Competitions
Poetry—Competitions

History

Great men, great events (cont) il UNESCO Courier 20:27-9 O '67

Periodicals

Life among the littles. D. Dempsey. New Repub 157:22+ Jl 8 '67; Reply. R. Whittemore. 157:38 Jl 22 '67

See also
New American review

Philosophy

Literature of exhaustion. J. Barth. Atlan 220: 29-34 Ag '67
Real world; excerpt from address. W. H. Auden. New Repub 157:25-7 D 9 '67

Prizes

See Literary prizes

Study and teaching

Art lost in analysis; the New criticism; it's effect on teaching. G. Hicks. Sat R 50:29-30 My 13 '67
Scandal of literary scholarship; excerpt from The dissenting academy, ed. by T. Roszak. L. Kampf. Harper 235:86-91 D '67

Technique

Literature of exhaustion. J. Barth. Atlan 220: 29-34 Ag '67

See also
Characterization
Fiction—Technique

Themes

Generation of the assassination. G. Hicks. Sat R 50:35-6 F 4 '67
House of the seven ushers and how they grew; a look at Jamesian Gothicism. M. Banta. Yale R 57:56-65 O '67
John Updike: chronicler of the time of the death of God. K. Hamilton. Christian Cent 84:745-8 Je 7 '67
Lachrymose ladies; address, September 15, 1966. J. Manthorne. bibliog Horn Bk 43: 275-84, 501-13, 622-30 Je-Ag, O '67
Magic of serendipity. E. J. Hodges. Horn Bk 43:370-4 Je '67
Mann, Yeats, and the truth of art. L. Conversi. Yale R 56:506-23 Je '67
Must writers hate the universe? the literary avant-garde; its emphasis on violence, perversion, and nihilism. J. W. Krutch. Sat R 50:19-21+ My 6 '67
Off the cuff; on writing seasonal stuff. L. Conger. Writer 80:7-8 F '67
Pause, now, and consider some tentative conclusions about porno-violence. T. Wolfe. Esquire 68:59+ Jl '67
Pop goes America; absurdity in literature. P. Michelson. New Repub 157:23-6+ S 9 '67
Prejudice and hope; reprint. V. Peterson. Writer 80:21-4 F '67
Uses of literature. F. J. Hoffman. Poetry 111: 203-5 D '67
When we are gods; despair in literature. A. MacLeish. Sat R 50:22 O 14 '67

See also
Drama—Themes
Gothic romances
Love in literature
Negroes in literature
Sex in literature
Social problems in literature
Sports in literature
War in literature

LITERATURE, Childrens. See Childrens literature

LITERATURE, Didactic. See Didactic literature

LITERATURE, Immoral. See Immoral literature and pictures

LITERATURE, Influence of
How to raise a bookworm. M. Nash. il Redbook 128:63+ Mr '67

Influence of Emerson, Thoreau, and Whitman on the early American naturalists John Muir and John Burroughs. M. C. Davis. bibliog il Liv Wildn 30:18-23 Wint '66
It was that damned book: The stranger by Albert Camus. B. Davidson. il Sat Eve Post 240:81-9 Ap 8 '67
On iniquity, by P. H. Johnson. Review Reporter 36:39-40 My 18 '67. W. L. Gundersheimer
Persistence of the sacred; novels which have become college and high school fads. D. J. Dwyer. Cath World 205:298-302 Ag '67

See also
Childrens literature, Influence of

LITERATURE, Mathematical. See Mathematical literature

LITERATURE and morals
See also
Didactic literature

LITERATURE and religion. See Religion and literature

LITERATURE and science
See also
Science fiction

LITERATURE and social problems. See Social problems in literature

LITERATURE and society
Creative writer today. C. Quigley. Cath World 206:111-17 D '67

LITERATURE and war. See War and literature

LITERATURE as a profession. See Authorship

LITHIUM
Lithium in old stars. G. S. Mumford. Sky & Tel 33:94 F '67

LITHIUM carbonate
Lithium vs manic-depression. P. McBroom. il(p561) Sci N 91:575 Je 17 '67

LITHOGRAPHY
Bringing stones to Manhattan; new Atelier Mourlot in Greenwich Village. il Time 90: 96 D 1 '67
Lithography and the artist; work of H. Simon. S. Salter. Pub W 191:106-7 Mr 6 '67
Offset lithography as a fine art. W. C. Libby. il Am Artist 31:24-9+ Mr '67

See also
Printing, Offset

LITHOPS. See Flowering stones

LITHUANIA
Baltic states. J. Bowen. il Travel 127:37-40 My '67

LITIGATION. See Actions and defenses

LITTELTON, Joanna
Oxford's Ashmolean. House & Gard 131:12+ Je '67

LITTER. See Refuse and refuse disposal

LITTER (bedding)
See also
Poultry houses—Litter

LITTLE, John B. and Radford, E. P. Jr
Polonium-210 in bronchial epithelium of cigarette smokers. bibliog Science 155:606 F 3 '67

LITTLE, Karla
Courage of Karla Little. J. G. Hubbell. il Read Digest 91:149-54 Jl '67

LITTLE, Malcolm. See Malcolm X

LITTLE, Robert T.
Shooting stars. K. Poli. il Pop Phot 61:96-7+ S '67

LITTLE, Stuart W.
Books in communications. Sat R 50:106-7 Je 10; 66 Ag 12; 61 S 9; 128-9 O 14; 94-5 N 11; 68 D 9 '67; 51:117 Ja 13 '68

LITTLE BIG HORN, Battle of the, 1876
After seventy-eight years: Custer's aide is cleared. il U S News 62:16 Je 12 '67
Reno's last stand; case for exonerating. il Newsweek 69:35 My 15 '67
Reno's last stand; grandnephew asks army to exonerate Major M. Reno. il Time 89:22 My 12 '67

LITTLE flames of genius; story. See Leggett, J.

LITTLE foxes; drama. See Hellman, L.

LITTLE girls. See Girls

LITTLE leagues
Giants of tomorrow; Mountain View, Calif. M. Butler. il Parks & Rec 2:30-1+ Je '67
How dangerous is little league baseball? il Good H 164:188 My '67

LITTLE learning; story. See Amft, M. J.

LITTLE murders; drama. See Feiffer, J.

LITTLE orchestra society, New York
Musical events; concert performance of Ferruccio Busoni's Turandot. W. Sargeant. New Yorker 43:201-2 O 21 '67

LITTLE orchestra society, New York—*Cont.*
Musical events; concert performance of Leoš
Janáček's The Makropulos case. W. Sar-
geant. New Yorker 43:55-6 D 23 '67
Musical events; concert performance of R.
Strauss' Die Aegyptische Helena. W. Sar-
geant. New Yorker 43:176 Ap 22 '67
Report: New York; church performance of
Benjamin Britten's Curlew River. Q. Eaton.
Opera N 32:31 D 30 '67
Report: New York; performance of Busoni's
Turandot. F. Merkling. Opera N 32:23-4
N 25 '67
Report: New York; presentation of The
Makropulos case in Philharmonic Hall. F.
Merkling. Opera N 32:29 Ja 13 '68

LITTLE ROCK, Ark.

Education

Decade of desegregation. Time 89:63 F 17 '67
Little Rock ten years later. J. Egerton. il Sat
R 50:60-1 D 16 '67
Revolution since Little Rock; Central high
school. il Life 63:92-7 S 29 '67

LITTLECOTT, Lorna C. See Pomeroy, K. B. jt.
auth.

LITTLEFIELD, Edward W.
Changing forest preserve. por Am For 73:12-
15+ Mr '67
Forever wild upheld: anatomy of a convention. Am For 73:36-7+ N '67

LITTLEJOHN, David
Doom-haunted prodigy. Commonweal 87:113+
O 27 '67

LITTON industries, incorporated
Litton, American book sign merger plan.
Pub W 191:229 Ja 23 '67
Litton: B-school for conglomerates. il Bsns W
p88-90 D 2 '67
Litton drawing on space role to develop
underwater suit. S. Montgomery. il Tech W
20:39-41 My 29 '67
Litton looks for corner in the kitchen; pro-
poses Stouffer merger. Bsns W p58 Ap 8
'67
Litton proposing off-the-shelf sub design. C.
D LaFond. il Tech W 20:30-1+ Mr 6 '67
Litton radio relay/beacon tested for jungle
air drops. C. D. LaFond. il Tech W 20:34-5
Je 19 '67
Litton takes charge; Greek government asks
for plan to develop western Peloponnesus
and Crete. Time 89:93-4 Je 23 '67
Litton to run $830 million Greek development
program; plans revealed at Paris air show.
H. Taylor. il Tech W 20:17-19 Je 12 '67
Litton's Belgian unit to manage Greek pact.
R. van Osten. Tech W 20:32 Je 26 '67
Out at the ballpark; Stouffer foods corp, ap-
proves Litton industries' buy-out offer. il
Time 89:94 Ap 21 '67
Voice-controlled computer is teachable; Lit-
ton's Mellonics div. system. R. Lindsey.
Aero Tech 21:52-3 O 9 '67

LITTON-Stouffer merger. See Business consolidations and mergers

LITURGICAL language
First mass in English. America 116:866 Je
24 '67
Living language for the liturgy. America
116:670 My 6 '67
Name of the game: mother, may I? J. B.
Mannion. Commonweal 86:76-7 Ap 7 '67
See also
Liturgics

LITURGICAL movement

Catholic church

Name of the game: mother, may I? J. B.
Mannion. Commonweal 86:76-7 Ap 7 '67

LITURGICAL music. See Church music

LITURGICAL symbolism. See Christian art and
symbolism

LITURGICAL week
Bishops' loyal opposition. R. J. Neuhaus.
Commonweal 86:565-7 S 22 '67

LITURGICS
New face on the scene: Societas liturgica.
E. S. Brown, jr. Christian Cent 84:1080-2
Ag 23 '67

LITURGIES
See also
Catholic church—Liturgy and ritual

LITVINOV, Ivy
Farewell to the dacha; story. New Yorker
43:47-54 S 16 '67

LITVINOV, Pavel Mikhailovich
Chain reaction. il Newsweek 71:29-31 Ja 8 '68

LITWAK, Leo E.
Joy is the prize: a trip to Esalen institute.
N Y Times Mag p8-9+ D 31 '67

LITZ, Katherine
Katherine Litz; interview, ed. by O. Maynard. pors Dance Mag 41:56-60+ F '67

about

Katherine Litz and company in Continuum,
Hunter playhouse. D. Hering. Dance Mag
41:78 Ap '67

LITZEL, Otto
Foto facts. P. Faber. U S Camera 30:30+ S
'67

LIU, B. Alfred
Population growth and educational development. Ann Am Acad 369:109-20 Ja '67

LIU, Shao-chi
Funeral in Peking. il por Newsweek 69:65
Ap 17 '67
Into the dustbin! onto the garbage heap!
por Time 89:40+ Ap 14 '67
Making it official. Time 90:26+ Jl 7 '67
Mao vs. Liu: who holds the guns? il U S News
63:13 Ag 28 '67
Survival of a scapegoat. por Newsweek 70:
48 S 11 '67
Target is Liu. por Newsweek 69:52 Ap 24 '67
What the villain did. il Newsweek 69:43 My
1 '67

LIU, Sidney C. See Elegant, R. S. jt. auth.

LIU, Wu-chi
Wise men of the Chou dynasty. Sat R 50:61
Je 10 '67

LIUNI, Mary
They asked us to give up our child. Ladies
Home J 84:92-3+ Ap '67

about

Adoption laws. L. F. Aarons. New Repub
156:10-11 Ja 28 '67

LIUNI, Michael
Adoption laws. L. F. Aarons. New Repub
156:10-11 Ja 28 '67

LIVADAS, Dorothy
FIGHT-Kodak fight. Nat R 19:683 Je 27 '67

LIVE bait. See Bait

LIVER
Circadian rhythms of liver enzymes and
their relationship to enzyme induction. M.
Civen and others. bibliog il Science 157:
1563-4 S 29 '67
Liver, seat of the soul, is a busy organ.
Todays Health 45:72 S '67
Messenger RNA patterns in rat liver nuclei
before and after treatment with growth
hormone. J. Drews and G. Brawerman.
bibliog il Science 156:1385-6 Je 9 '67
Urea and its formation in coelacanth liver.
G. W. Brown, jr. and S. G. Brown. bibliog
il Science 155:570-3 F 3 '67

Diseases

Virus-induced peliosis hepatis in rats. V. V.
Bergs and T. M. Scotti. bibliog il Science
158:377-8 O 20 '67
See also
Hepatitis

Surgery

Four little girls stave off death with liver
transplants. il Life 63:28-31 D 15 '67

LIVER cells. See Cells

LIVER enzymes. See Enzymes

LIVER membranes. See Membranes (biology)

LIVER microsomes. See Microsomes

LIVER transplants. See Transplantation of organs, tissues, etc.

LIVER tyrosine. See Tyrosine

LIVERNASH, E. Robert
Trends in employer manpower policies. Mo
Labor R 90:28-9 F '67

LIVERPOOL

Cathedral of Christ The King

Crown is consecrated; Liverpool's new Metro-
politan cathedral of Christ the King. il
Time 89:72-3+ My 26 '67
Liverpudlians' cathedral; new Cathedral of
Christ the King. America 116:799 Je 3 '67

Street traffic

Computer to control tunnel traffic. il Am City
82:130-1 Mr '67

LIVERWORTS
Liverwort lady's bonanza. Sci Digest 62:67
Ag '67

LIVESTOCK
News. See issues of Farm journal

LIVESTOCK—*Continued*
Diseases and pests
How to start a campaign against disease on your farm. J. Herrick. Suc Farm 65:60 O '67
Let's get rid of these diseases! Bang's, TB, cholera, scabies. il Suc Farm 65:45 F '67
Successful farming's ten-point disease-prevention program. il Suc Farm 65:49-51+ O '67
Veterinary helps. J. W. Bailey. See issues of Successful farming
What you should know about disease. Suc Farm 65:65 O '67
Why animals are sold subject or condemned. J. W. Bailey. Suc Farm 65:46I Mr '67

See also
Bloating
Cattle—Diseases and pests
Foot-and-mouth disease
Screwworms
Marketing

Now, livestock credit cards. R. C. Black. Farm J 91:B12+ S '67
Prices
Cows and sows; marketing pregnant cows and sows for slaughter. Newsweek 69:70+ Mr 6 '67

LIVESTOCK, Cooling of
Hot weather cuts hog profits. J. Harvey. il Suc Farm 65:42F Jl '67
Summer cattle coolers. il Suc Farm 65:42B Jl '67

LIVESTOCK breeding. See Breeding
LIVESTOCK credit cards. See Credit cards
LIVING. See Conduct of life
LIVING, Cost of. See Cost of living
LIVING, Standard of. See Standard of living
LIVING conditions. See Standard of living
LIVING rocks. See Flowering stones
LIVING rooms
Expansive living in one room. il House & Gard 131:90-1 Je '67
Fabulous family room on a lower level. J. LemMon. il Suc Farm 65:106-7 F '67
Fresh new face to the street and a spacious new bay-windowed living room. il Sunset 139:78-9 Ag '67
Give your living room a social life. V. D. Hahn. il Am Home 70:62-5 N '67
Ideas for your family room. il Am Home 70:106+ My '67
Kitchen satellite: family room/hideaway sewing center. S. Kaiser. il Farm J 91:60-1 S '67
Need space? you can live in a carport. D. Shiner. il Pop Sci 191:138-43 S '67
New book wall and window seat. il Sunset 139:104 S '67
Room on the other side; furnishing a living room for $200. il Esquire 67:101-3 Mr '67
Tiffany touch: home of board chairman Walter Hoving. J. Peter. il Look 31:79 Je 27 '67
Where the family meets, and cooks. N. Craig. il House B 109:150-1 Je '67

LIVING rooms, Outdoor. See Outdoor rooms
LIVING theater group. See Theater—Europe
LIVINGSTON, Albert L.
Little wolves. por Outdoor Life 140:38-41+ D '67
LIVINGSTON, Alan Wendell
Capitol gains. il por Newsweek 69:76+ F 27 '67
LIVINGSTON, J. A.
Unpaid arm of the press. Sat R 51:30 Ja 13 '68
LIVINGSTON, W. Putnam. See Kramer, R. L. jt. auth.
LIVINGSTON, William C. See Orville, R. E. jt. auth.
LIVINGSTONE, F. C.
Computer diagnosis. Sci N 91:558 Je 10 '67
Le mot juste. Sci N 92:21 Jl 1 '67
Steelmaking in midair. Sci N 91:454-5 My 13 '67
LIVINGSTONE, Frank B.
Effects of warfare on the biology of the human species. Natur Hist 76:61-5 biblliog(p70) D '67
LIVNEH, Eliezer
Saving the Jews. Commentary 44:97-8+ O '67
LIZARD brain. See Brain

LIZARDS
Ecological significance of sexual dimorphism in size in the lizard anolis conspersus. T. W. Schoener. bibliog il Science 155:474-7 Ja 27 '67
Frequency sensitivity of single auditory neurons in the gecko coleonyx variegatus. N. Suga and H. W. Campbell. bibliog il Science 157:88-90 Jl 7 '67
Gekkonid lizards adapt fat storage to desert environments. H. R. Bustard. bibliog Science 158:1197-8 D 1 '67
Regulation of body temperature in the blue-tongued lizard. H. T. Hammel and others. bibliog il Science 156:1260-2 Je 2 '67
Sex chromosomes in lizards. C. J. Cole and others. bibliog il Science 155:1028-9 F 24 '67
Side-blotched lizard; uta stansburiana. il Sci N 92:508 N 25 '67
Voluntary hypothermia in reptiles. P. J. Regal. bibliog il Science 155:1551-3 Mr 24 '67

See also
Chameleons
Iguanas
LIZZIE Borden: opera. See Beeson, J.
LLERAS RESTREPO, Carlos
Taking a stand. il por Time 89:39 F 17 '67
LLINAS, Rodolfo, and Bloedel, J. R.
Frog cerebellum: absence of long-term inhibition upon Purkinje cells. bibliog Science 155:601-3 F 3 '67
—and others
Cerebellar Purkinje cell projection to the peripheral vestibular organ in the frog. bibliog Science 158:1328-30 D 8 '67
LLORENS, David
Apostle of economics. Ebony 22:78-80+ Ag '67
Baseball's gentle iron man. Ebony 22:50-2+ Jl '67
He makes decisions after twenty years behind bars. Ebony 23:44-6+ Ja '68
Miracle in Milwaukee. Ebony 23:29-32+ N '67
New life for an old man. Ebony 22:100-2+ O '67
LLOYD, Charles
Charles Lloyd: at home in a new universe. E. Larrabee. por Harper 234:116-18 F '67
Dolphins on a wave. il por Time 89:38 F 3 '67
Incident at Tallinn. J. Roddy. il pors Look 31:50 O 3 '67
New surge for a tired old idiom. R. Saltonstall, jr. Life 62:15 Je 9 '67
LLOYD, Harvey
Harvey Lloyd. il por Pop Phot 61:90-9 Ag '67
Operatic Paris; photographs. Opera N 31:13-17 F 4 '67
LLOYD, J. W. F. See Silverman, S. M. jt. auth.
LLOYD, John
Getting into the acts, continued. Sr Schol 90:sup4-5 Mr 10 '67
Washington report. See issues of Senior scholastic
LLOYD, R. Michael
Oxygen-18 composition of oceanic sulfate. bibliog Science 156:1228-31 Je 2 '67
LLOYD, Susan
Summer we learned that kids are kids. Redbook 129:6+ Jl '67
LLOYD GEORGE, David, 1st earl Lloyd George of Dwyfor. See Lloyd George of Dwyfor, D. L. G.
LLOYD GEORGE of Dwyfor, David Lloyd George, 1st earl
Lloyd George: Britain's great radical; excerpt from Variety of men. C. P. Snow. por Atlan 219:68-70+ F '67
LOADING and unloading
S-64 demonstrates ability to unload ship; photographs. Aviation W 86:48-9 F 20 '67
See also
Freight handling
LOAN associations. See Finance companies
LOANS
Borrowing money for new home furnishings. M. Feeley. Am Home 70:16 Je '67
See also
Credit
Insurance, Life—Policy loans
Interest
Mortgages
Student loans
Usury laws
LOANS, Bank
Beleaguered bankers. il Fortune 75:81-2+ Je 15 '67
Business borrowers may get another break; lower lending rates. il Bsns W p22-3 Ap 1 '67
Fewer go into hock; consumers hold back. il Bsns W p42+ F 18 '67

LOANS, Foreign
Eurobonds get a young brother; European bank for medium term credit. Bsns W p 156+ S 23 '67
  See also
Export-import bank of Washington
LOANS, Interlibrary. See Interlibrary loans
LOANS, Mortgage. See Mortgages
LOANS, Student. See Student loans
LOB (line of balance control) See Production control
LOBBYING
Case of the Latent lobby. D. H. Fenn, jr. Harvard Bsns R 45:22-4+ Ja '67; Discussion. 45:166-8+ Jl '67
Caveat vendor: R. Nader. Time 90:28-9 D 15 '67
Congress jittery as public mood shifts. il U S News 63:26-8 Ag 28 '67
Industry still has something to learn about Congress. J. Main. il Fortune 75:128-9+ F '67
Letter power; letters to congressmen. il Ebony 22:72-3 My '67
Overhaul for Congress; control over lobbyists. Bsns W p45 Mr 11 '67
Speak up to your congressman. F. N. Ikard. Nations Bsns 55:38-9 D '67
Tax laws; conservationists must step gingerly on Capitol hill. L. J. Carter. Science 155:179-81 Ja 13 '67
Why the scenic route can't be seen; lobby works to weaken billboard control legislation. il Bsns W p 106-8 Je 17 '67
LOBBYISTS
For a people's lobby; anti-inflation group. America 117:633 N 25 '67
Health syndicate; the Lasker group of health lobbyists. E. B. Drew. Atlan 220:75-82 D '67
Up the up staircase; educational lobbyists. il Newsweek 69:70 My 15 '67
  See also
Lobbying
LOBDELL, Jared C.
Patriot. Read Digest 91:35-6 O '67
LO BELLO, Susan
I fell in love with kibbutzniks. Seventeen 26:136-7+ Mr '67
LOBSENZ, Norman M.
Innocent game that disrupts marriage. Redbook 128:64-5+ Ap '67; Same abr. with title Innocent game that can disrupt marriage. Read Digest 91:122-4 Jl '67
—See Bernard, J. jt. auth.
LOBSTERS
Case of the tense lobsters; excerpt from Home is where you hang yourself. C. Lindsay. Read Digest 91:12B S '67
Computerizing lobsters. il Sci Digest 62:25 D '67
  See also
Cookery—Shellfish
LOBUGLIO, Albert F. and others
Red cells coated with immunoglobulin G: binding and sphering by mononuclear cells in man. bibliog Science 158:1582-5 D 22 '67
LOCAL educational associations. See Educational associations
LOCAL employees. See Municipal employees
LOCAL government
  See also
Metropolitan areas
Metropolitan government
Municipal government

United States
Can local government be saved? J. N. Miller. Read Digest 90:140-5 My '67
Local governments; 90,000 other governments. il Sr Schol 91:14-15+ N 30 '67
Speaking out; local government is a farce. F. H. Ornstein. il Sat Eve Post 240:10+ D 2 '67
  See also
State and local relations
LOCAL government officers. See Public officers
LOCAL service airlines
American gains in shuttle market battle; New York-Washington commuter market. J. W. Carter. Aviation W 87:35-6 S 11 '67
CAB will tighten route case procedures. J. W. Carter. Aviation W 87:38-9 O 23 '67
Firms urged to monitor air taxi service; supplemental air transportation. Aviation W 86:99+ Je 5 '67
Here comes the mini-airliner; short haul airlines. W. Langewiesche. Read Digest 92:189-93+ Ja '68

Long-term inclusive tour plans clouded. H. D. Watkins. Aviation W 87:29 Jl 31 '67
More outside firms buy supplementals. Aviation W 87:34 Ag 7 '67
New authority urged for two local airlines. Aviation W 87:37 O 23 '67
New procedure set to strengthen locals. Aviation W 87:40-1 O 16 '67
New routes awarded three local airlines. Aviation W 87:41 S 18 '67
Puddle-jump airlines struggle with jets; new routes, mergers, longer hauls. il Bsns W p 151+ O 28 '67
Russians to use Be-30 as micro-airbus. il Aviation W 87:30-1 N 6 '67
Supplementals mount drive for routes. H. D. Watkins. Aviation W 87:26-7 D 25 '67
  See also
Allegheny commuter airlines
Commuter airlines (company)
Frontier airlines, incorporated
Pacific airline
    Federal aid
Board shifts policy on subsidies. il Aviation W 86:36-7 Ap 10 '67
CAB proposes local service subsidy cuts. Aviation W 86:75 My 29 '67
LOCAL taxation
State and local taxes; up almost 10 per cent, but cities ask more. U S News 62:110 My 1 '67
Where state & local taxes go. il Changing T 21:24-5 O '67
LOCANTHI, B. N.
Operational amplifier circuit for hi-fi. Electr World 77:39-41 Ja '67
LOCATION in business and industry
Accidental village; Senate authorizes location of AEC atom smasher. Newsweek 70:27-8 Jl 24 '67
Building on the border; U.S. manufacturers building plants in north Mexico. il Time 89:106+ Je 9 '67
Companies hark to Coral Gables' Spanish accent; base for directing Latin American operations. il Bsns W p 123-4+ Ap 22 '67
Huntsville; Alabama cotton town takes off into the space age. L. J. Carter. il Science 155:1224-9 Mr 10 '67
Mini-megalopolis rises along the Mississippi; thriving Quad-cities of Iowa and Illinois. il Bsns W p 168-70 F 25 '67
Pepsi leaving the bright lights; New York losing fight to stem corporate departures. il Bsns W p44 F 18 '67
Surveying a city's labor market: Newburyport, Mass. E. F. Cook. il Am City 82:155 Je '67
That Manhattan exodus. P. Herrera. il Fortune 75:106-9+ Je 1 '67
Wooing white collars to suburbia; office parks. il Bsns W p96-8 Jl 8 '67
  See also
Cities and towns—Industries
LOCATION of airports. See Airports—Location
LOCATION of metals. See Metal detectors
LOCATIONS, Moving picture. See Moving pictures—Setting and scenery
LOCH NESS, Scotland. See Ness, Loch, Scotland
LOCH NESS monster
Closing in on the Loch Ness monster. D. Scott. il Read Digest 90:86-90 F '67
Modern monsters, some are real some are not. D. Cohen. il Sci Digest 61:14-20 My '67
LOCHER, Ralph Sidney
Troubled cities, and their mayors. il por Newsweek 69:41 Mr 13 '67
LOCKE, David M.
Drug racket exposé. Sat R 50:39-40 My 20 '67
LOCKE, Edward Gibson
Tribute to Dr Locke. il por Am For 73:28-9+ F '67
LOCKE, Eugene Murphy
New team for the U.S. in Vietnam. por U S News 62:20 Mr 27 '67
Quartet at the top. il por Time 89:14 Mr 24 '67
LOCKE, Jeannine
When a parent drinks too much. Parents Mag 42:44-5+ Jl '67
LOCKE, Kay
Sleeping Chinese beauty; drama. Plays 26:81-4 My '67
LOCKE, Michael, and Collins, J. V.
Protein uptake in multivesicular bodies in the molt-intermolt cycle of an insect. bibliog Science 155:467-9 Ja 27 '67
LOCKER, Arthur R.
Santa Barbara's miracle. Parks & Rec 2:42+ N '67

LOCKHEED aircraft corporation
Brain workers: suburbia's rising class; C. L. Holland, human factors engineer at Lockheed-Georgia co. T. G. Harris. il Look 31:M22+ My 16 '67
Cheyenne bows in. il Newsweek 70:54 D 25 '67
Cheyenne warrior; Lockheed's combination helicopter and fixed-wing plane. il Time 90: 71 D 22 '67
Defense gravy train. Nation 205:549 N 27 '67
Here comes the bus. il Time 90:96 S 22 '67
Lock step at Lockheed. il Time 89:86 F 17 '67
Lockheed tries a new pilot; D. J. Haughton. Bsns W p34 F 11 '67
Lockheed's airbus. Newsweek 70:76 S 18 '67
New look at Lockheed. Newsweek 69:78 F 20 '67
U.S. firms pushing trade-off studies of medium-range jet. Aviation W 86:29 Mr 13 '67
LOCKHEED-Georgia company. See Lockheed aircraft corporation
LOCKHEED propulsion company
Low-cost sled motor offers versatility; solid-propellant unit is reusable. M. L. Yaffee. il Aviation W 86:50-2 F 20 '67
LOCKJAW. See Tetanus
LOCKMAN, Ronald
Damned fool. Nation 205:357 O 16 '67
Two who stayed home. Time 90:28 N 24 '67
LOCKOUTS
Bigger guns for bargaining wars: coordinated multi-group teams vs offensive lockouts. Bsns W p49-50 Ag 12 '67
Guns of April; nationwide lockout by trucking firms. il Time 89:35 Ap 14 '67
Lockout, the other dimension. W. A. Lewis. bibliog f Mo Labor R 90:1-7 Ag '67
When lockout of union is legal. U S News 63:71 Jl 17 '67
LOCKWOOD, Dean H. and others
Hormone-dependent differentiation of mammary gland: sequence of action of hormones in relation to cell cycle. bibliog Science 156: 945-6 My 19 '67
LOCKWOOD, Gary
You get what you go after; ed. by E. Miller. por Seventeen 26:142-3+ F '67
LOCKWOOD, Lee
Recollections of four weeks with the enemy. Life 62:44B-44D Ap 7 '67
(ed) See Nguyen-van-Tien. Revealing highlights from two interviews with enemy leaders
(ed) See Pham-van-Dong. Revealing highlights from two interviews with enemy leaders
U.S. prisoners and an eerie puppet show. Life 62:44-44A Ap 7 '67

about

Authors & editors. il por Pub W 191:21 My 1 '67
LOCO; story. See Guthrie, A. B. jr
LOCOMOTION
See also
Walking
LOCOMOTIVES
Chattanooga choo-choo; mayor hijacks The General. il Newsweek 70:33 S 25 '67
LOCOMOTIVES, Gas turbine
Turbine train test slips five months. il Aviation W 87:55 Ag 28 '67
LOCUST GROVE (historic house) See Kentucky—Historic houses, etc.
LODEN, Barbara
Women worth watching. por McCalls 95:30+ Ja '68
LODGE, Henry Cabot 1902-
Ambassador Lodge discusses Viet-Nam in interview on Meet the press; September 17, 1967. Dept State Bul 57:464-9 O 9 '67
Ambassador Lodge discusses Viet-Nam in New York times interview. Dept State Bul 56:795-800 My 22 '67
American group to observe elections in Viet-Nam; press interview, August 28, 1967. Dept State Bul 57:349-51 S 18 '67
Speaking out; we're winning in Vietnam. por Sat Eve Post 240:6+ Jl 29 '67

about

Changing the guard. il por Newsweek 69:26 Mr 20 '67
Henry Cabot Lodge, by W. J. Miller. Review
Sat R 50:25-6 D 9 '67. M. L. Colt
Man & his country. por Time 90:68 S 1 '67
New faces, new mood? por Sr Schol 90:19 Mr 31 '67
Rare sort of man. Bsns W p204 Mr 25 '67

LODGES (architecture)
Family hunting lodge; in woods of Norway. il House B 110:100-1 Ja '68
Resort designed to fit a scenic site; Salishan lodge, Gleneden Beach, Ore. il Arch Rec 141:145-50 Ja '67
Skylit rocket in the Rockies; conical lodge, Colorado. il House B 109:30+ S '67
LOEB, Leonard B.
Tornadoes: puzzling phenomena and photographs. Science 155:1037 F 24 '67
LOENGARD, John
Inspired renaissance in Indiana; photographs. Life 63:74-84+ N 17 '67
To see America, from a city window; photographs. Life 62:58-69 Mr 10 '67
LOFT buildings
Larry Rivers' living room; block-deep floor in Manhattan loft building. M. Simons. il Look 31:M20+ Mr 21 '67
LOFTING, Christopher
Who me fly? pors Flying 81:34-41 N '67

about

Dolittle explosion. R. A. Sokolov. il por Newsweek 71:58 Ja 1 '68
LOFTING, Colin
Cowboy and the Comanche. Flying 81:82-6 D '67
LOFTING, Hugh
Dolittle explosion. R. A. Sokolov. il por Newsweek 71:58 Ja 1 '68
LOFTS, Norah
Ticket to Timbuktu. Writer 80:11-13 Je '67
LOGAN, Andy
JFK: the stained-glass image. Am Heritage 18:4-7+ Ag '67
LOGAN, Cynthia D.
The rival; poem. Yale R 56:434 Mr '67
LOGAN, Edgar
Hands across the border. Sr Schol 90:sup7 F 10 '67
Nova Scotia: where the good times are. Sr Schol 90:sup20-1 Ap 7 '67
Pied Piper of paperbacks. Sr Schol 89:sup 17 Ja 20 '67
ST reports: Detroit's extended school program. Sr Schol 90:sup7 Ap 28 '67
Turn turtle: carry your house on your back. por Sr Schol 90:sup20 My 12 '67
LOGAN, James
Cultural relic of colonial America; quest for Ptolemy's Almagest. E. Wolf, 2d. il Wilson Lib Bul 41:569-72 F '67
LOGAN, John
Carmel: Point Lobos: Big Sur: Partington Cove; poems. Poetry 109:388-94 Mr '67
Interior and exterior worlds. Nation 204:541-2 Ap 24 '67
Spun on a thread. Nation 205:601-2 D 4 '67
LOGAN, Jonathan, incorporated
Young man & the women. il Time 90:83 Ag 18 '67
LOGAN, Milla Z.
Terrazzo; story. Reporter 36:41-6 Mr 23 '67
LOGGING. See Lumbering
LOGIC
See also
Fallacies (logic)
Probabilities
LOGIC, Symbolic and mathematical
Digital computer logic; what the symbols mean. E. Bukstein. il Electr World 78:46-7 Ag '67
See also
Algebra, Boolean
LOGIC of mathematics. See Mathematics—Philosophy
LOGINOV, fUrii
Man of the world. Newsweek 70:56 S 25 '67
LOGISTICS
C-5A logistics spur helicopter proposal. C. Brownlow. il Aviation W 87:53+ N 27 '67
Illusions of distance. A. Wohlstetter. bibliog f For Affairs 46:242-55 Ja '68
Lockheed, navy ready Polaris logistic support streamlining. R. Lindsey. Aero Tech 21:42 S 11 '67
LOGORECI, Anton
Albania and China: the incongruous alliance. bibliog f Cur Hist 52:227-31+ Ap '67
LOGSDON, Gene
Dog hunters. Farm J 91:72Q F '67
Don't throw it away too soon. Farm J 91: 74B+ Mr '67
Pitfalls of family partnerships. Farm J 91: 30-1+ D '67
What's new in mulching? Farm J 91:66N Mr '67
Young tigers in farming. Farm J 91:29-31+ Ap '67

LOHENGRIN; opera. See Wagner, R.
LOMA, Point, Calif
  See also
Cabrillo National Monument
LOMASK, Milton
  Benedict Arnold: the aftermath of treason.
  bibliog Am Heritage 18:16-17+ O '67
LOMBARDI, Vince
  From a coach of champions: advice to busi-
  nessmen on how to lead; excerpts from ad-
  dress, February 8, 1967. por U S News 62:
  14 F 20 '67
  —and Heinz, W. C.
  Game for madmen. pors Look 31:85-90 S 5 '67
  Green Bay's coach reveals his secrets of
  winning football. por Look 31:70-5 S 19 '67
  about
  Toughest man in pro football. L. Shecter.
  por Esquire 69:68-71+ Ja '68
LOMBARDI, Vincent, and Grimes, A. J.
  Primer for a theory of white-collar unioniza-
  tion. bibliog f Mo Labor R 90:46-9 My '67
LOMBARDO, Kathleen
  On being pregnant and having an imagina-
  tion; poem. Sat R 50:46 N 4 '67
LONBORG, Jim
  Don't dig in on gentleman Jim. W. Craig.
  il pors Sat Eve Post 240:70-3 S 9 '67
LONDENBERG, Kurt
  Bookbinding by Kurt Londenberg. H. Halbey.
  il Craft Horiz 27:30-3 Ja '67
LONDON, George
  World of Wieland Wagner. por Sat R 50:
  59-60+ Ja 28 '67
  about
  Recital by London. I. Kolodin. Sat R 50:28
  My 13 '67
LONDON, Maria
  China: stories from the inside. Nat R 19:
  744-6 Jl 11 '67
  Letter from Hong Kong. Nat R 19:1275 N
  14 '67
LONDON
  Flowered ways of Chelsea. W. Marchant. il
  Holiday 43:58-61+ Ja '68
  Inside London. J. Gunther. il Harper 235:48-54
  Jl; 79-82 Ag '67; Same abr. Read Digest
  91:169-72+ O '67
  Travel notes. R. Joseph. Esquire 67:12+ F '67
  Air raids
  When dynamite rains from the sky. R. L.
  Tobin. Sat R 50:18-19 Ag 5 '67
  Airports
  High-speed Heathrow cargo complex set.
  H. J. Coleman. il Aviation W 86:43+ Ja 23
  '67
  Art
  London. J. Russell. See issues of Art news
  British museum
  See British museum
  Clubs
  Dark days in clubland; men's clubs. News-
  week 69:69 Ja 30 '67
  Great clubs of the world; the Portland of
  London. il Esquire 67:104-5 Je '67
  Covent Garden
  London; Berlioz' Benvenuto Cellini. F.
  Aprahamian. il Opera N 31:32 F 4 '67
  Description
  London. P. Coffin. il Look 31:52-9 My 2 '67
  London dossier. by L. Deighton. Review
  Life 63:13 Jl 28 '67. J. Hicks
  My London; interview, ed. by S. Robinson.
  J. Andrews. il McCalls 94:46+ Ap '67
  T. S. Eliot's London. S. Spender. il Sat R
  50:58-9+ Mr 11 '67
  Teen travel talk. il Seventeen 26:206 Ap '67
  Galleries and museums
  See also
  British museum
  Tate gallery
  Great exhibition of the works of
  industry of all nations, 1851
  Expo 51; with chromolithograph by C. T. Rod-
  gers. il Am Heritage 18:23-5 Ag '67
  Hotels, restaurants, etc.
  Aftermath. L. Saalburg. Esquire 67:62+ My
  '67

  Housing
  Double-decked village, Kingsbury green. il
  Arch Forum 126:46-51 Ap '67
  Libraries
  See also
  British museum
  Lighting
  London will try high pressure sodium light-
  ing. Am City 82:120+ Ag '67
  Music
  Bennett's A penny for a song. E. Greenfield.
  il Hi Fi 18:MA24+ Ja '68
  Boom in Berlioz. E. Greenfield. Hi Fi 17:
  MA26+ Ap '67
  London; Sadler's Well's performance of Verdi's
  Ernani. F. Aprahamian. Opera N 31:30 My
  13 '67
  London; Visconti production of Verdi's
  Traviata. F. Aprahamian. il Opera N 31:25
  Je 10 '67
  New concert hall, Moore's farewell. T. Heinitz.
  il Sat R 50:76-7+ Mr 25 '67
  New halls under way. E. Greenfield. il Hi Fi
  17:MA22-3 Je '67
  Notes from our correspondents. J. Diether.
  Hi Fi 17:24+ S '67
  Notes from our correspondents. E. Greenfield.
  See issues of High fidelity incorporating
  Musical America
  Other side. T. Heintz. Sat R 50:71 Ap 29 '67
  Proms, hail and farewell to Sir Malcolm. E.
  Greenfield. il Hi Fi 17:MA30-1 D '67
  Report: London; world premieres at Sadler's
  Wells theatre. F. G. Barker. il Opera N
  32:32 Ja 20 '68
  Violins of St Jacques. E. Greenfield. il Hi Fi
  17:MA26-MA27 F '67
  See also
  Covent Garden opera company
  Newspapers
  See also
  Times, London
  Politics and government
  Letter from London; elections for the Greater
  London council and county councils. M.
  Panter-Downes. New Yorker 43:177-9 My
  6 '67
  St Paul's cathedral
  Preacher for the empire's parish: dean of
  St Paul's. Time 89:63-4 Je 23 '67
  Social life and customs
  Beautiful pacesetter of the London whirl;
  with account by D. Lurie. il Life 62:48-
  51+ F 10 '67
  London, a man's city. A. Waugh. Nat R
  19:1337 N 28 '67
  Travel notes; hip set. R. Joseph. Esquire
  69:14+ Ja '68
  Stores
  London for sale. K. Simon. il Holiday 42:91-6
  Ag '67
  Venerable store begins to swing; Harrods of
  London bidding for young mods. il Bsns W
  p74-6+ S 9 '67
  Theater
  Funny side up. H. Hewes. Sat R 50:40 Jl 8
  '67
  Importance of writing good plays; four of
  Wilde's plays revived. J. Rosselli. il Re-
  porter 36:44+ My 18 '67
  London. P. P. Witonski. Nat R 19:265-6 Mr
  7 '67
  Men without women; all-male version of As
  you like it staged by National theater
  company. il Time 90:72 O 13 '67
  Theatre in Europe. H. Clurman. Nation 205:
  29-30 Jl 3 '67
  Theatre in Europe; productions of Strindberg's
  The dance of death, and T. Stoppard's
  Rosencrantz and Guildenstern are dead. H.
  Clurman. Nation 204:797-8 Je 19 '67
LONDON, Tower of. See Tower of London
LONDON Economist. See Economist (London)
LONDON records, incorporated
  McGraw-Hill & London records announce
  affiliation. Library J 92:4456 D 15 '67
LONDON school of economics and political
  science
  Daffodils, unite! issues of the sit-in. R. Rosen-
  blatt and D. Schechter. New Repub 156:
  13-14 Ap 15 '67
  London school of economics & Berkeley. A.
  Lejeune. Nat R 19:473-4 My 2 '67

LONDON symphony orchestra
Music to my ears; Carnegie Hall concert. I.
Kolodin. Sat R 50:44 Mr 25 '67
Pffhonk! world première of L. Foss's con-
cert for cello and orchestra in Carnegie Hall.
il Time 89:70 Mr 17 '67

LONDON Times. See Times, London

LONDON university
See also
London school of economics and political
science

LONDONERS
Beautiful pacesetter of the London whirl;
with account by D. Lurie. il Life 62:48-51+
F 10 '67

LONELINESS
You don't have to be lonely. J. E. Gibson.
il Sci Digest 62:33-6 N '67

LONG, Barbara
Joe Namath. Vogue 149:156-7+ F 1 '67
Theatre. Vogue 149:94 Ap 1 '67

LONG, Delois
Lonely youth in the rural South. G. Goodman.
il pors Ebony 22:70-2+ Ag '67

LONG, Edward Vaughan
Are you safe from electronic snoopers? excerpt from The intruders. pors Pop Sci
190:144-8+ My '67
Excerpt from address before Indiana civil
liberties union, April 1, 1967. Cong Digest
46:204+ Ag '67

about

Deeper debt of gratitude to the mob. W.
Lambert. il pors Life 63:38-38B N 10 '67
$48,000 question; payments linked with Hoffa
case. por Newsweek 69:29-30 Je 5 '67
Hoffa taint. D. L. Spitzer. New Repub 156:5
Je 10 '67
Long account. por Newsweek 70:35-6 N 6 '67
Nothing but the facts. Time 90:18-19 N 3 '67
Other Long; investigations of political and
financial interests. il por Time 89:13-14 Je
2 '67
Senator cleared of misconduct charges. U S
News 63:18 N 6 '67
Strange help-Hoffa campaign of the U.S.
senator from Missouri. W. Lambert. il pors
Life 62:26-31+ My 26 '67

LONG, Eula (Kennedy)
Brazil's Methodists celebrate centennial.
Christian Cent 84:1298-300 O 11 '67
Priests with pricked consciences. Christian
Cent 85:82-3 Ja 17 '68

LONG, F. A.
Peter Debye, an appreciation. Science 155:
979-80 F 24 '67
Scientists in foreign affairs: where do we go
now? adaptation of address, April 1966.
Bul Atomic Sci 23:14-18 Mr '67

LONG, Nat G.
Excuses that keep people from church. Farm
J 91:72E F '67
Things that make a preacher laugh. Farm J
91:38I Je '67

LONG, Richard R.
Silicone gaskets lengthen luminaire life. Am
City 82:113 Jl '67

LONG, Russell Billiu
Excerpt from debate, August 4, 1966. Cong
Digest 46:14+ Ja '67
Lesson in practical politics; reprint. por U S
News 63:61 Jl 3 '67

about

But for the grace of Dodd. por Newsweek
69:37 Je 26 '67
By Long possessed. Newsweek 69:26 My 15 '67
Demeaning indulgence. por Time 89:19-20 My
12 '67
Filibuster repeat. New Repub 156:4 My 13 '67
Senate's rising star loses bid for power. por
Bsns W p35-6 My 13 '67
Washington. D. Kiker. Atlan 220:4+ Ag '67
Whip's lash; Senate's majority whip. por
Newsweek 69:27 Je 12 '67

LONG, Walter K.
Glutathione reductase in red blood cells: variant associated with gout. bibliog Science
155:712-13 F 10 '67

LONG, Wellington
Memo from Berlin: the new threat from
within. Look 31:110 D 12 '67
Report from Germany. Look 31:78 F 7 '67

LONG BEACH, Calif.
Decorating the derricks; oil drilling finances
improvements. il Time 90:49 S 15 '67

LONG division. See Division

LONG ISLAND, N.Y.
Problem: the Long Island expressway; solu-
tion: close down Long Island. J. McCarthy.
il N Y Times Mag p34-6+ Mr 19 '67
See also
Architecture, Domestic—Long Island, N.Y.
Nassau County, N.Y.

Photographs
Long Island lens. R. Strovnik. U S Camera
30:72-3 N '67

LONG ISLAND agricultural and technical
institute, Farmingdale. See New York state
university—Agricultural and technical institute, Farmingdale

LONG ISLAND festival. See Music festivals—
New York (state)

LONG ISLAND kennel club show. See Dog
shows

LONG ISLAND SOUND
Who's afraid of L.I. Sound? M. Rosenblad.
il Yachting 121:61+ F '67

LONG ISLAND university, Brooklyn, N.Y.
Behind the scenes at Long Island U. J.
Ridgeway. New Repub 156:10-11 Ap 15 '67
Duel at LIU. Newsweek 69:68+ Ap 10 '67

LONG playing records. See Phonograph records

LONGCHAMPS restaurants. See New York
(city)—Hotels, restaurants, etc.

LONGEVITY
Secret of long life; claims of extreme age. il
Time 90:70 Jl 14 '67
We won't live longer; potential advances.
Sci Digest 62:57-8 N '67
See also
Aging

LONGFELLOW, Henry Wadsworth
Poet or poetaster? L. Untermeyer. Sat R 50:
27 Jl 1 '67

LONGINELLI, A. and Craig, H.
Oxygen-18 variations in sulfate ions in sea
water and saline lakes. bibliog Science
156:56-9 Ap 7 '67

LONGLEAT (estate) See Country estates—
England

LONGSHOREMEN
See also
International longshoremen's association

LONGWOOD gardens. See Gardens—Pennsylvania

LONGWORTH, Alice (Roosevelt)
Talk with an eighty-three-year-old enfant
terrible; ed. by H. Brandon. pors N Y Times
Mag p8-9+ Ag 6 '67

LØNNING, Per
Theological basis of the Geneva conference.
Christian Cent 84:270-1 Mr 1 '67

LOOK (periodical)
Agony relived; second installment of The
death of a President. il Time 89:58 Ja 27
'67
Look, Manchester sue N.Y. World Journal
tribune. Pub W 191:53 F 13 '67
Manchester story. Newsweek 69:95 Mr 27 '67
Missouri state library advertises in Look. Li-
brary J 92:2700-1 Ag '67
Roger Tenney: teacher of the year. C. Mangel.
il Look 31:64-9 My 2 '67
See also
All-America cities

LOOKING glass murder; drama. See Murray, J.

LOOKING glasses. See Mirrors

LOOMER, Alice
Do you play fair with your kids? Parents
Mag 43:50-1+ Ja '68
Myth of the only child. Parents Mag 42:54-5+
' '67

LOOMIS, Alfred F.
Around the rock. Yachting 123:78-9+ Ja '68

LOOMIS, W. Farnsworth
Skin-pigment regulation of vitamin-D biosynthesis in man. bibliog Science 157:501-6;
158:579-80 Ag 4, N 3 '67

LOOMS
See also
Weaving

LOOS, Anita
My first trip. McCalls 94:142 My '67

LOOTING. See Pillage

LOPATA, Walter
Hope for cancer victims. Sci N 91:86 Ja 28
'67
Marine speaks again. il Time 89:75 Ja 27 '67

LOPEZ, Enrique Hank
Late late lovers. Atlan 220:95+ Jl '67

LÓPEZ PELLÓN, Nivio
Return of the viceroys. Américas 19:35-41 Ap
'67
Showcase in Spain. Américas 19:32-5 N '67

LOPEZ TIJERINA, Reies. See Tijerina, R. L.
LOQUATS
See also
Cookery—Fruit
LORANG, Glenn C.
Big birds help the bees. Farm J 91:39 My '67
LORCH, Lee
Mathematics: International congress. Science 155:1038-9 F 24 '67
LORD, Walter
Midway; excerpts from Incredible victory. Look 31:32-8+ Ag 8; 32-6+ Ag 22 '67
LORDS prayer
And forgive us our sins; United church of Christ adopts modernized rendering. Time 90:50 Jl 7 '67
One text for our common prayers. Christian Cent 84:1518 N 29 '67
LORDS Supper
Sign still signifies; mystery of the eucharist. V. P. McCorry. America 116:inside back cover My 27 '67
See also
Catholic church—Eucharist
Mass
LOREN, Sophia
Sophia Loren talks to women who want to be beautiful; interview. por Redbook 129: 68-9+ Je '67
about
Sophia Loren talks about the sorrow of losing her baby. F. Ghedini. por Ladies Home J 84:68+ S '67
Sophia, Sophia, Sophia. J. Cheever. il pors Sat Eve Post 240:32-5 O 21 '67
LORENGAR, Pilar
And we quote; interview. ed. by C. L. Osborne. por Hi Fi 17:M18 D '67
Long way home; interview. ed. by G. Fitzgerald. por Opera N 31:14 Ja 28 '67
LORENZ, James Douglas
Champion of the rural poor. por Time 90:75 D 15 '67
LORENZ, Konrad Zacharias
Konrad Lorenz. E. Stillman. il por Horizon 9:60-5 Spr '67
Naturalist at large. M. Bates. Natur Hist 75:14+ Ap '67
LORETTO-Hilton center of the performing arts. See Webster college. Webster Groves, Mo.
LORILLARD, P, company
Schenley highball. il Newsweek 69:82 Mr 27 '67
To the package store; plan to acquire Schenley industries. il Time 89:84 Mr 24 '67
LORR, John S.
Let's arrange a counterchange. Design 68:4-6 Ja '67
LORSCH, Jay W. See Lawrence, P. R. jt. auth.
LORTZING, Albert
Records:
Zar und zimmermann. Opera N 32:30 S 23 '67
LOS ALAMOS, N.Mex.
Space-age sights; USA. L. M. Rhodes. il Todays Health 46:27-8 Ja '68
LOS ANGELES
Dateline Watts; from the ashes, a solution. A. Nevins. il Sat R 50:79 S 23 '67

Airports
Can airports cope with the jet age? Los Angeles' way. il Bsns W p64+ Jl 22 '67
Los Angeles moves to meet traffic gain. G. S. Hunter. il Aviation W 87:55+ Jl 17 '67
One city's airport of the future; plans for International airport. il U S News 62:16 My 8 '67
United opens new LA air-freight facility. il Aviation W 86:57 Ja 30 '67

Anti-poverty program
Message from Watts to Newark. S. Alexander. Life 63:14B Jl 28 '67
Other pacification, to cool U.S. cities; Watts summer festival. il Life 63:30-1 Ag 25 '67

Art
Los Angeles. J. Langsner. See issues of Art news

Cemeteries
Commercial undertaking; Forest Lawn memorial-park, commercials on radio. Newsweek 70:92 D 11 '67
De mortuis; concerning Forest Lawn. J. H. Plumb. il Horizon 9:40-1 Spr '67

Center for the performing arts
From S.F. and L.A. C. J. McNaspy. America 116:840 Je 10 '67
Go west, go. il Newsweek 69:107-8 Ap 24 '67
Three in the West; Music center of Los Angeles County. il Time 89:88 Ap 21 '67

City planning
Expediters. Nation 204:740-1 Je 12 '67
Nose for corruption. Nation 205:452-3 N 6 '67

Clubs
Fun and games; cheating at Beverly Hills Friars club. il Newsweek 70:44-5 S 18 '67

Economic conditions
Learn, baby, learn; economic stagnation in Watts. il Newsweek 69:76+ Ap 10 '67

Education
Different view of Watts; follow-up report. L. B. Work. Harper 234:38 My '67
In a class by themselves; Tele-class program; reprint. C. E. Cassidy. il Sr Schol 90:sup 10-11 Ap 14 '67
Sixth graders make terrific tutors; remedial reading program at Haynes street school. V. Bartel. il Parents Mag 42:56-7+ S '67
Student-built halls of fame; library lesson to familiarize students with biographical reference materials. Alexander Hamilton H.S. S. Cochell. il Sr Schol 90:sup28 F 17 '67
Where school taxes sparked a revolt. il U S News 62:64 F 27 '67

Galleries and museums
See also
Los Angeles County museum of art

Hospitals
Miracle in Charcoal alley; Watts health center. il Time 90:57-8+ N 17 '67

Hotels, restaurants, etc.
Los Angeles for visitors. D. Messinesi. Vogue 150:78-9 Ag 15 '67

Industries
Where the people are; Watts manufacturing co. to employ Negroes. il Newsweek 70:84 S 18 '67

Intellectual life
Creators in a creative society. H. Temianka. il Sat R 50:30+ S 23 '67

Libraries
See also
Los Angeles public library

Municipal officers
See Los Angeles—Officials and employees

Music
Copland at the Bowl. Samuel at Cabrillo. I. Kolodin. Sat R 50:45 S 9 '67
Does L.A. want opera? H. Stevens. il Hi Fi 17:MA22+ F '67
Los Angeles; first American performance of Friedenstag. A. Goldberg. Opera N 31:24 Je 10 '67
Many-splendored sound of Los Angeles. R. Kendall. il Sat R 50:46+ S 23 '67
New York city opera goes to Los Angeles. il Opera N 32:19-21 N 25 '67
Notes from our correspondents. R. Gelatt. il Hi Fi 17:18+ Jl '67
Notes from our correspondents. E. Tiegel. il Hi Fi 17:18+ Ag '67
Report; Los Angeles; performances of New York city opera. A. Goldberg. Opera N 32: 30-1 Ja 6 '68
Search for novelty. H. Stevens. Hi Fi 17: MA19 Jl '67
World of dance; presentations at the Music center. W. Terry. Sat R 50:38 Ag 26 '67
See also
Los Angeles—Center for the performing arts
Los Angeles philharmonic orchestra

Negroes
Different view of Watts; follow-up report. L. B. Work. Harper 234:38 My '67
Insider's Watts; Mafundi institute's movie project. il Newsweek 69:84+ My 1 '67
Mighty, mighty Watts. Time 90:11 S 1 '67
Prelude to riot, by P. Jacobs. Review
New Repub 158:21-3 Ja 20 '68. L. L. King
Report from Watts. il Newsweek 70:32-3 Ag 7 '67

LOS ANGELES—Negroes—*Continued*
Self-help program stirs a Negro slum; Operation Bootstrap. il Bsns W p67-8+ Mr 25 '67
Watts: facing the problems of minority ghettos in today's cities. A. Henehan. il Sr Schol 89:9-12 Ja 20 '67
What to do about slums, riots, city ills; interview. S. Yorty. il U S News 63:72-6 Ag 21 '67
  See also
Compton, Calif.—Negroes

Newspapers
  See also
Los Angeles herald-examiner

Officials and employees
Sam's hard Times; indictment against four commissioners. Time 91:15 Ja 19 '68

Police
Johnson comes to town; actions against peace marchers. A. Harmetz. New Repub 157:7-8 Jl 8 '67
Nightstick politics; inquiry into the violence during President Johnson's visit. Nation 205:435 O 30 '67
Was this violence necessary? actions against anti-Vietnam war demonstrators. Nation 205:36 Jl 17 '67
Western justice. P. Kirby. Nation 205:104-5 Ag 14 '67

Police department
L.A. police: as seen from Olympus. B. Vaccariello. Nat R 19:77 Ja 24 '67
Optimist for Los Angeles; Reddin as deputy chief. Time 89:50 F 17 '67

Public library
  See Los Angeles public library

Recreation
Surf safety school. M. C. Cronin. il Parks & Rec 2:16-17+ Jl '67

Riots
Voices from burning slums. E. M. Yoder, jr. Sat R 50:28-9 Ag 26 '67
Watts: facing the problems of minority ghettos in today's cities. A. Henehan. il Sr Schol 89:9-12 Ja 20 '67
What to do about slums, riots, city ills; interview. S. Yorty. il U S News 63:72-6 Ag 21 '67
Who are the rioters? a study of two cities. il U S News 63:40-1 S 11 '67

Social conditions
Los Angeles, by C. Rand. Review
  Reporter 36:44-5 My 4 '67. C. W. Griffin, jr
New American woman; the L.A. woman. il Esquire 67:57-62+ F '67
  See also
Los Angeles—Anti-poverty program

Stores
Graphic design and allied arts play important role in the design of West coast store. il Arch Rec 141:184-5 My '67
Learn, baby, learn; new White Front store opens in Watts. il Newsweek 69:76+ Ap 10 '67

Streets
Reporter at large; Sunset Strip. R. Adler. New Yorker 43:116+ F 25 '67

Theater
Go west, go; controversy over John Whiting's Devils. il Newsweek 69:107-8 Ap 24 '67
Gregorian chance; Inner city repertory company and the New theatre for now series. Sat R 50:28 O 7 '67
Incline of the West; Ahmanson theatre and the Mark Taper forum. H. Hewes. il Sat R 50:50 Ap 15 '67

Transportation
Watts, his line; Negro owned Blue and White bus co. il Newsweek 71:50-1 Ja 1 '68

Water supply
Filter backwash gets special treatment. L. Streicher. il Am City 82:94-5 N '67
LOS ANGELES COUNTY, Calif.
Signs $6.4 million contract for new voting system. Am City 82:50 N '67

Police
Cheese it, the copters! T. Stimson. il Pop Mech 127:74-7+ Je '67
Project Sky Knight. il Am City 82:33 Ag '67

Social welfare, Department of
Way back for troubled youngsters; mental health volunteers in Los Angeles County help former psychiatric patients. S. Gordon. il Parents Mag 42:66-7+ N '67
LOS ANGELES COUNTY museum of art
From S.F. and L.A. C. J. McNaspy. America 116:840 Je 10 '67
Statuary for an Adam house; stucco figures made for Croome court. R. Davidson. il Antiques 91:186 F '67
Third dimension; exhibition at Los Angeles County museum of art's special exhibit building. il Newsweek 69:92-4 My 8 '67
White wings in the sunlight; exhibition of American sculpture of the sixties. il Time 89:80-3 My 12 '67
LOS ANGELES COUNTY music center. See Los Angeles—Center for the performing arts
LOS ANGELES Dodgers (baseball) See Baseball clubs
LOS ANGELES herald-examiner
Putting on the pressure; strike. il Newsweek 71:47-8 Ja 8 '68
LOS ANGELES International airport. See Los Angeles—Airports
LOS ANGELES Junior ballet. See Ballet companies
LOS ANGELES philharmonic orchestra
Musical events; concert in Carnegie Hall; conducted by Z. Mehta. W. Sargeant. New Yorker 43:164+ My 13 '67
LOS ANGELES public library
L.A. library's bond issue endorsed by Cal. publishers. Pub W 191:38 Ap 17 '67
LAPL commission orders study of juvenile circulation drop. Library J 93:252-3 Ja 15 '68

Branches
How many blocks to New York? hobby club at Venice branch. S. Benjamin. il Library J 93:265-6 Ja 15 '68
This is my beat; D. Roberts of Venice branch. E. Geller. il Library J 93:259-64 Ja 15 '68
LOS ANGELES Rams (football club) See Football clubs
LOS ANGELES times
Defining monopoly. Newsweek 70:96 O 23 '67
Most likely to succeed. P. Kerby. Nation 206:80-2 Ja 15 '68
New winds in the South, new splash in the North. W. L. Rivers. il Sat R 50:75-6+ S 23 '67
Nose for corruption; exposé on City harbor commission contract. Nation 205:452-3 N 6 '67
Question of competition; ordered to divest itself of the San Bernardino sun and telegram. Time 90:58 O 20 '67
LOSEY, George S. Jr. See Rosenblatt, R. H. jt. auth.
LOS GATOS, Calif.
Distinguished civic center for a small town. il Arch Rec 141:159-64 Ap '67
LOSINSKI, Julia
Looking ahead; summer reading potpourri. Sr Schol 90:sup 17 Ap 28 '67
LOST children. See Missing persons
LOST cities. See Cities and towns, Ruined, extinct, etc.
LOST city of the Incas. See Machu Picchu, Peru
LOST continent. See Atlantis
LOST in the funhouse; story. See Barth, J.
LOST wax process
Make your own metal castings. C. W. Westrick. il Pop Mech 128:162-5 Ag '67
LOTS, Building. See Building sites
LOTSPEICH, William D.
Healing diplomacy. Sat R 50:45-6 Jl 1 '67
Metabolic aspects of acid-base change. bibliog Science 155:1066-75 Mr 3 '67
LOTTERIES
Facts about give-away games. il Good H 165:202-3 N '67
Frankie Carlin, the bookie. J. Flaherty. il N Y Times Mag p28-9+ Ap 2 '67
How to play a lottery; French national lottery. S. de Gramont. il N Y Times Mag p24-5+ My 7 '67
Longest shot; New York's state lottery. Time 89:21 Je 23 '67

LOTTERIES—*Continued*
Motes and beams in Albany. Sports Illus 26:
6 F 6 '67
New York gambles and loses. Christian Cent
84:1245 O 4 '67
Notes and comment; New York state lottery
ticket. New Yorker 43:19 Je 24 '67
Numbers, the game that only the mobsters
win. T. R. Brooks. Read Digest 91:79-82
S '67
Prize dopes; Americans going ga-ga over
giveaways. R. P. Sessions. Christian Cent
84:306-9 Mr 8 '67
Where legal gambling doesn't pay—enough;
New Hampshire and New York. il U S
News 63:80-1 Ag 28 '67
Winners and losers; New York state lottery.
Newsweek 70:35-6 Ag 7 '67
Wriggling and smarting; savings banks'
reaction to selling lottery tickets issued by
New York state. New Yorker 43:29-30 Je
10 '67

LOTTMAN, Herbert R.
Calabrian days with Norman Douglas. Sat R
50:61+ Mr 11 '67
Direct mail bookselling threatened in France.
Pub W 191:30-2 Mr 27 '67
Editions Arthaud and the Syndicat des
editeurs. Pub W 192:30-2 O 23 '67
Editions Flammarion's new look. Pub W 191:
43-5 F 6 '67
France's great big personal publisher. Pub W
192:29-32 S 4 '67
French literary prizes, 1967. Pub W 192:25-8
D 25 '67
French publishers view the U.S. as export
market. Pub W 191:20-3 My 15 '67
Gallimard: synonymous with French litera-
ture. Pub W 193:55-9 Ja 15 '68
Grasset: the firm that won the prizes. Pub W
191:42-4 Mr 6 '67
Italy: *il* boom in paperbacks slows down.
Pub W 191:31-4 Ap 17 '67
Laffont: most American publisher in France.
Pub W 192:29-31 Ag 7 '67
Literary life in Paris. Pub W 192:21-3 N 27
'67
Stockholm is host for Berne copyright re-
vision. Pub W 192:31-2 Jl 31 '67

LOTZ, Jim
Frozen El Dorado. Américas 19:21-7 N '67

LOUCHHEIM, Katie (Scofield)
Commencement; poem. McCalls 94:141 Jl '67
Computer people's Christmas; poem. Mc-
Calls 95:155 D '67
For the man on my right; poem. Harper 235:
70 Ag '67
about
State department's poetic powerhouse. H.
Ehrlich. il pors Look 31:118+ O 17 '67

LOUD speaking apparatus
Alert system that blankets a borough; Red
Bank, N.J. F. E. Brower, jr. il Am City
82:30 My '67
Build the mixed twelve speaker system. D.
B. Weems. il Pop Electr 26:74-7+ Mr '67
Hi-fi speakers for small rooms. il Pop Electr
27:34-5 N '67
Independence Hall reconstruction sound sys-
tem; Knott's berry farm, Calif. J. P. Nel-
son. il Electr World 78:32-3 Jl '67
Loudspeakers for electronic musical instru-
ments. K. Kramer. Electr World 77:32 Je '67
Mortal coil. A. Sterling. il Hi Fi 17:50-1 Je '67
Outdoor listening; weather-resistant speaker
system. R. Angus. il Hi Fi 17:47-9 Je '67
Princess Cinderella. D. B. Weems. il Pop
Electr 27:38-40 Jl '67
Problems of matching speakers to solid-state
amplifiers. V. Brociner. il Electr World
77:23-6+ Ja '67
Shop for speakers by ear. N. Eisenberg. il
Hi Fi 17:43-6 Je '67
Three-corner space saver. D. B. Weems. il
Pop Electr 27:57-61 O '67

Cabinets
Build this fine-furniture hi-fi control console.
B. Hartford. il Pop Mech 128:177-80 S '67
Danish decor goes stereo; photographs by E.
Svensson; with editorial comment. Hi Fi
17:45, 46-53 Ap '67
Instant non-fat speaker enclosure; plastic
milk containers. D. B. Weems. il Pop Electr
27:53-4 N '67
Three-corner space saver. D. B. Weems. il
Pop Electr 27:57-61 O '67

LOUDERBACK, Lew
Speaking out. por Sat Eve Post 240:10+ N
4 '67

LOUGHARY, John W.
Computer-assisted counselor. NEA J 56:22-4
F '67

LOUGHLIN, Richard L.
Friendly grasp of hand to junior college
transferees. bibliog f Sch & Soc 95:352 O 14
'67

LOUGHMAN, William D. and others
Leukocytes of humans exposed to lysergic
acid diethylamide; lack of chromosomal
damage. bibliog Science 158:508-11 O 27 '67

LOUIS XIV, king of France
Twilight princess and the Sun King. J. Barry.
il por Horizon 9:106-11 Spr '67

LOUIS, Father. See Merton, T.

LOUIS, Arthur M.
Computer-leasing stocks. Fortune 76:167-8+
Jl '67
Investing in the 500. Fortune 75:305-6+ Je 15
'67
Mutual funds have the votes. Fortune 75:150-
3+ My '67

LOUIS, E. G.
Brute-70. Pop Electr 26:41-6+ F '67

LOUIS, Morris
Art; Aleph series, 1960; on view at the Emmerich gallery. M. Kozloff. Nation 204:379-
81 Mr 20 '67
Unfurled banners; retrospective exhibition at
Boston museum of fine arts. il Time 89:72-
3 Ap 21 '67

LOUIS, Murray
Murray Louis and co; Henry street settlement
playhouse. M. Marks. Dance Mag 41:34 F '67

LOUIS, Victor
Boy has to hustle. Newsweek 70:66 S 25 '67
Who is Victor Louis? il por Newsweek 70:
62 Ag 21 '67

LOUISIANA
See also
Crime and criminals—Louisiana
Fishing—Louisiana
Petroleum industry and trade—Louisiana

History
Get rich quick scheme in the American West;
concerning French manuscript, Memoire
sur La Louisiane in Denver public library.
Mrs A. Freeze. il Wilson Lib Bul 41:603-5
F '67

Politics and government
Constitutional disenfranchisement of the Ne-
gro in Louisiana (cont) G. E. Cunningham.
Negro Hist Bul 29:174+ Fall '66

Race problems
Constitutional disenfranchisement of the Ne-
gro in Louisiana (cont) G. E. Cunningham.
Negro Hist Bul 29:174+ Fall '66

LOUISIANA state university, Baton Rouge, La.
Man in the fish fry parlor; T. Marshall's
registration of dozen Negro students. W.
Rogers. Look 31:115 O 17 '67

LOUISNATHAN, John. See Moore, P. B. jt.
auth.

LOUISVILLE

Hotels, restaurants, etc.
Dining in/out with Esquire; The old house.
Esquire 68:299-30 D '67

Housing
Louisville happening; Derby runs scared; open
housing issue. L. Grauman, jr. il Nation
204:689-92 My 29 '67
Louisville's race; Derby bogs down. W. H.
Poore. Christian Cent 84:817-18 Je 21 '67
Open housing; ordinance outlawing racial discrimination. W. Peeples. New Repub 158:
9-10 Ja 13 '68

Negroes
Louisville's race; Derby bogs down. W. H.
Poore. Christian Cent 84:817-18 Je 21 '67

Riots
Whose Kentucky home? il Newsweek 69:27-8
My 1 '67

LOURIA, Donald Bruce
Cool talk about hot drugs. N Y Times Mag
p 12-13+ Ag 6 '67; Same abr. Read Digest
91:111-17 N '67
LSD, a medical overview. Sat R 50:91-2 Ap
22 '67

LOUVERS
Louver to shade a west wall. il Sunset 138:
118 Ap '67

LOVDJIEFF, Crist
Guru of San Quentin. E. Cleaver. Esquire
67:88+ Ap '67

LOVE, Rose Leary
George Washington Carver; a boy who wished to know why. Negro Hist Bul 30:13-15 Ja; 15-18 F; 15-19 Mr '67

LOVE
Casanova, junior grade. G. Porter. il Read Digest 90:81-3 Ap '67
Do we still love life? E. Fromm. il McCalls 94:57+ Ag '67
Love in America; discussion. Sat Eve Post 239:78 D 31 '66; Christian Cent 84:438-9 Ap 5 '67
Man talk; by love possessed; flower children and real love. D. Newman and R. Benton. il Mlle 66:76 D '67
Quiet Catholic question; unpublicized Pentecost. E. C. Kennedy. America 116:147-8 Ja 28 '67
Speaking out; we overrate love. W. Sheed. Sat Eve Post 240:10 +Mr 25 '67
Venus and you. A. Star. il Seventeen 26:144-5 S '67
See also
Marriage

Anecdotes, facetiae, satire, etc.
Of human bondage. T. Meehan. il Sat Eve Post 240:22 Je 3 '67

LOVE (charity) See Charity
LOVE (theology)
In defense of love. Christian Cent 84:886 Jl 12 '67
Of many things. V. R. Yanitelli. America 116:394 Mr 25 '67
Quiet Catholic question; unpublicized Pentecost. E. C. Kennedy. America 116:147-8 Ja 28 '67
Two commandments; love of neighbor and love of God. V. P. McCorry. America 117: inside back cover Ag 5 '67
LOVE, Maternal
See also
Mothers
LOVE and let love; musical comedy. See Musical comedies, revues, etc.—Criticisms, plots, etc.
LOVE in literature
Temple of Goldman. R. A. Schroth. America 117:250 S 9 '67
LOVE letters
Prelude to love; three letters; excerpts from Soul on ice. E. Cleaver. Mlle 65:170+ S '67
LOVE object; story. See O'Brien, E.
LOVELACE, William Randolph, 1907-
CAB accident investigation report: Beechcraft crash in box canyon kills NASA official, two others. Aviation W 86:93 Mr 27 '67
LOVELL, Sir Bernard
Conversation about Venus. J. Lear. Sat R 50: 60-1 N 4 '67
Science versus spectaculars. Nation 204:612 My 15 '67
LOVELL, Merle B.
Working farm within the city. por Parks & Rec 2:40-1 Ja '67
LOVEMAN, Amy, national award. See Amy Loveman national award
LOVENBERG, Walter, and others
Tryptophan hydroxylation: measurement in pineal gland, brainstem, and carcinoid tumor. bibliog Science 155:217-19 Ja 13 '67
LOVERING, J. F. See Kleeman, J. D. jt. auth.
LOVER'S mask; story. See Bourjaily, V.
LOVI, George
Sky and telescope's new star charts. Sky & Tel 35:34-6 Ja '68
LOVING, Graham
Young millionaires of finance. por Bsns W p76-9 D 30 '67
LOVING, Richard Perry, family
Couple that rocked courts. S. Booker. il Ebony 22:78-80+ S '67
LOVITT, George
Lovitt's advice to publishers at NABE meeting: summary of address. Pub W 192:31-2 N 20 '67
LOVSTUHAGEN, Knut
ESRANGE being expanded for Skylark. Tech W 20:40-1 F 6 '67
LOW, Joseph
Picture books. Horn Bk 43:715-20 D '67
LOW, Robert B. and Wool, I. G.
Mammalian ribosomal protein: analysis by electrophoresis on polyacrylamide gel. bibliog Science 155:330-2 Ja 20 '67
LOW-level counting. See Statistical methods
LOW-protein diets. See Diet
LOW-range airspeed system. See Aeronautic instruments

LOW temperature cameras. See Cameras
LOW temperature research
Lowest temperature yet. il Sci N 92:32 Jl 8 '67
Not-so-common cold. il Time 90:74-6 O 27 '67
LOW temperatures
Aquanauts get liquid air; cryogenic breathing units. J. Eberhart. il Sci N 92:138-9 Ag 5 '67
Cold way to new life; body of J. H. Bedford frozen shortly after death. L. Wainwright. Life 62:16 Ja 27 '67
Cryogenic scuba; liquid air rig. il Time 89: 53 Je 16 '67
Cryogenic underground. B. H. Frisch. il Sci Digest 61:22-3 Je '67
Never say die; body of J. H. Bedford frozen. il Time 89:57 F 3 '67
Photoinduced DNA-protein cross-links and bacterial killing: a correlation at low temperatures. K. C. Smith and M. E. O'Leary. bibliog il Science 155:1024-6 F 24 '67
Super-cold; the hottest thing in science. J. Lentz. il Todays Health 45:18-19+ F '67
Wider use of cryogenic quenching seen. M. L. Yaffee. il Aviation W 86:81+ Ap 10 '67
Will we freeze ourselves into the future? B. H. Frisch. il Sci Digest 61:17-21+ Je '67
LOWE, A. J.
Build the sound sync'er. Pop Electr 26:59-60 Ap '67
Slave driver. Pop Electr 28:65-7 Ja '68
LOWE, Charles H. and others
Natural free-running period in vertebrate animal populations. bibliog Science 156:531-4 Ap 28 '67
LOWE, David G.
Death on the range. Am Heritage 18:48-9+ O '67
England, the melting pot. Horizon 9:56-9 Spr '67
LOWE, Steven
Boulez as composer, conductor, hero. Hi Fi 17:MA18-19 Ag '67
Ivan the Terrible. Prokofiev's music towers grandly alone. Hi Fi 17:80-1 S '67
Shelving the problem. Hi Fi 17:68-71 S '67
LOWELL, James Russell
James Russell Lowell, by M. Duberman. Review
Nation 204:442-3 Ap 3 '67. C. Bedient
LOWELL, Robert
Liberal anti-communism revisited. Commentary 44:54 S '67
about
Difficulties of being major. P. Davison. por Atlan 220:116-21 O '67
Fuel on the fire. R. Howard. Poetry 110:413-15 S '67
Murderous solvent. P. Zweig. Nation 204:536-8 Ap 24 '67
Old Glory; dramatization of stories by N. Hawthorne and H. Melville. Criticism
Reporter 36:44-6 Je 15 '67
Poet as folk hero, wounded but game. W. Schott. Life 62:17 F 17 '67
Prometheus bound; adaptation of play by Aeschylus. Criticism
Nation 204:829-30 Je 26 '67
Newsweek il 69:109 My 22 '67
Reporter 36:44-6 Je 15 '67
Sat R 50:49 My 27 '67
Second chance. il pors Time 89:67-74 Je 2 '67
LOWELL family
Lowell coat-of-arms. H. K. Eilers. il Hobbies 72:120-1 Mr '67
LOWEN, Janice. See Walker, M. J. jt. auth.
LOWENKOPF, Martin
Upheaval in Kenya. New Repub 156:34-5 F 25 '67
LOWENSTAM, H. A.
Lepidocrocite, an apatite mineral, and magnetite in teeth of chitons polyplacophora. bibliog Science 156:1373-5 Je 9 '67
LOWER, Elmer W.
Racial stress and the mass media; address, September 21, 1967. Vital Speeches 34:53-9 N 1 '67
LOWER, Richard
Spate of heart transplant. il Sci N 93:59-60 Ja 20 '68
LOWER MONUMENT DAM. See Dams
LOWER RICE LAKE. See Rice Lake, Minn.
LOWES, Gillian, and Bitterman, M. E.
Reward and learning in the goldfish. bibliog Science 157:455-7 Jl 28 '67
LOWEST trees have tops; story. See Gellhorn, M.

LOWITZ, Anson C. See Lowitz, S. H. jt. auth.
LOWITZ, Sadyebeth H. and Lowitz, A. C.
History in houses: East. Antiques 91:772-6 Je '67
LOWN, Bernard
Early-warning system. il por Newsweek 69: 62 Ja 30 '67
LOWRIE, Allen, jr, and Heezen, B. C.
Knoll and sediment drift near Hudson canyon. bibliog Science 157:1552-3 S 29 '67
LOWRY, Bates
New man at MOMA. por Newsweek 69:110 My 22 '67
New man at MOMA. il por Time 89:94 My 19 '67
LOWRY, Betty
In the pine scented morning; poem. America 117:415 O 14 '67
LOWRY, Malcolm
Lowry/Aiken symbiosis. R. H. Costa. Nation 204:823-6 Je 26 '67
LOWRY, Warren M.
Two-way contracting. Harvard Bsns R 45: 131-7 My '67
LOWRY, William P.
Climate of cities. Sci Am 217:15-23 Ag '67
LOYALTY
Draft-age dilemma. G. Wilson; O. S. Johnson. McCalls 94:34+ Ag '67
See also
Patriotism
LOYALTY, Oaths of
California oath controversy, by D. P. Gardner. Review
Nation 204:795-6 Je 19 '67. G. R. Stewart
Sat R 50:80 O 21 '67. F. Fertig
Feinberg law, 6-3, 4-5; loyalty oaths declared unconstitutional. America 116:200-1 F 11 '67
Loyalty laws: Supreme court upholds academic freedom. L. J. Carter. Science 155: 987 F 24 '67
Self-reversal: Feinberg law. Time 89:47 F 3 '67
Whither loyalty oaths? ACLU leads drive. Sr Schol 90:sup4 Mr 3 '67
LOYALTY investigations
Privacy: how much need you tell a visiting federal investigator? B. Nelson. Science 157:1539-41 S 29 '67
LOYD, Clay
Remembering forgotten Americans. NEA J 56:58-9 D '67
LOZZIO, Bismarck B. and others
Hereditary renal disease in a mutant strain of rats. bibliog Science 156:1742-4 Je 30 '67
LUARD, Nicholas
Warm and golden war; story. Mlle 65:93-114 Jl '67
LUBAROFF, David M. and Waksman, B. H.
Delayed hypersensitivity: bone marrow as the source of cells in delayed skin reactions. bibliog Science 157:322-3 Jl 21 '67
LUBOLD, Joyce Kissock
Why mothers don't get sick. Read Digest 90: 51-4 F '67
LUBRICATION and lubricants
Pick the right engine oil. Suc Farm 65:62 Ja '67
See also
Airplanes, Supersonic—Lubrication
Automobiles—Lubrication
LUC Dominique
Singing nun's story; interview, ed. by C. Grenier. il pors McCalls 94:64+ My '67
LUC Gabrielle, Sister. See Luc Dominique
LUCAS, Christopher
Bridge at Lo Wu. Sat R 50:82+ O 14 '67
Possibility of paradise. Atlan 220:120+ N '67
LUCAS, Frank Laurence
Obituary
Yale R 57:317-20 D '67. B. Blanshard
LUCAS, Joseph W. and Miner, Mae
Small craft sailing program in San Diego. Parks & Rec 2:25+ Ag '67
LUCAS, Zoltan J.
Pyrimidine nucleotide synthesis: regulatory control during transformation of lymphocytes in vitro. bibliog Science 156:1237-40 Je 2 '67
LUCCOCK, Halford Edward
Powell in the pulpit: excerpts from Marching off the map. D. Poling. Sat R 50:89-90 Ap 22 '67
LUCE, Charles Franklin
Case of Con Edison. L. L. L. Golden. Sat R 50:96 My 13 '67
Luce of Con Edison. por Fortune 75:51 My '67
LUCE, Clare (Boothe)
Without portfolio. See issues of McCall's
LUCE, Donald
No way home: Vietnam's refugees. Christian Cent 84:1279-81 O 11 '67

about
End this war. Nation 204:322-3 O 9 '67
Toughest question. il por Newsweek 70:32 O 2 '67
LUCE, Gay Gaer, and Segal, Julius
Reassuring report for women who have trouble sleeping. McCalls 94:102-3+ F '67
LUCE, Henry, 1925-
Report from London. Fortune 77:109+ Ja '68
LUCE, Henry Robinson
[Address at centennial convention of the AIA, May 16, 1957] por Arch Forum 126:38-9 Je '67
H.R.L. on his country; sampling of speeches, memos and editorial musings about America. Time 89:27 Mr 10 '67
His warm remembrances of how it all began; excerpts from addresses. por Life 62:38B-38D Mr 10 '67
On business; On peace through law; On personalities & people. Time 89:29-30+ Mr 10 '67

about
He ran the course. il pors Time 89:28-33 Mr 10 '67
Henry Luce and his time. J. Epstein. bibliog f Commentary 44:35-47 N '67
Henry Luce: founder of publishing empire. por U S News 62:24 Mr 13 '67
Henry R. Luce. H. R. Mayes. por Sat R 50: 16-17 Mr 18 '67
H.R.L: an appreciation. E. J. Hughes. Newsweek 69:71 Mr 13 '67
Henry R. Luce and American business. M. Ways. por Fortune 75:115-16+ Ap '67
Henry R. Luce: end of a pilgrimage. il por Time 89:26-8 Mr 10 '67
Henry R. Luce: his Time and Life. il pors Newsweek 69:68-70+ Mr 13 '67
Henry R. Luce: the values that shaped his work. J. K. Jessup. Life 62:30-1 Mr 10 '67
Journalist: the title he proudly claimed. il pors Life 62:32-38A Mr 10 '67
Last testament. Time 89:51 Mr 17 '67
Letter from the staff. il pors Time 89:10-11 Mr 10 '67
Luce raised the level of photographic art. P. Stackpole. U S Camera 30:14+ Je '67
Obituary
Nat R por 19:291-3 Mr 21 '67. W. S. Schlamm
New Yorker 43:187-8 Mr 18 '67. M. J. Arlen
Pub W por 191:41 Mr 13 '67
Sr Schol por 90:19 Mr 17 '67
Old China hands. N. Wales. New Repub 156: 13-15 Ap 1 '67
Quintessential Harry. Nation 204:358 Mr 20 '67
Recollections of Henry R. Luce. Fortune 75: 121-2 Ap '67
Roper remembers Luce; letter. E. Roper. Sat R 50:23+ Ap 29 '67
Stop and think what you really love. G. P. Hunt. Life 62:3 Mr 10 '67
Taking up where Luce left off. por Bsns W p38 Mr 4 '67
Tall, balding, dead Henry R. Luce. T. S. Matthews. Esquire 68:131-2+ S '67
LUCE, Phillip Abbott
What the new left did to me. por Read Digest 90:93-7 F '67
LUCEY, William L.
Home scene (cont) America 116:690+ My 6 '67
LUCI, Michel
Ten dogs know all about you; reprint. Seventeen 26:138-9+ Mr '67
LUCIA di Lammermoor; opera. See Donizetti, G.
LUCIENTES, Francisco José de Goya y. See Goya y Lucientes, F. J. de
LUCIOLI, Clara E.
Out of isolation; adaptation of address, April 20, 1966. bibliog por Library J 92: 1421-3 Ap 1 '67
LUCK, James Murray
Training for engineering and technology in Switzerland; excerpt from Science in Switzerland. bibliog f Sch & Soc 94:499-502 D 24 '66
LUCKMAN, Charles
Our uncommon profession; address, May 16, 1967. Arch Rec 141:93-4 Je; 142:93-4 Jl '67

about
Better break for the fans. il por Time 91:68 Ja 5 '68
He sells architecture the way he sold soap. il pors Bsns W p74-6+ O 28 '67
LUCRETIUS CARUS, Titus
Poetry of Lucretius. K. Rexroth. Sat R 50: 56 D 9 '67

LUDGIN, Chester
All American; interview, ed. by F. Stevenson. pors Opera N 32:13 O 14 '67
LUDINGTON, Ivan
Developing a reading public. Ivan Ludington, sr. at work. il por Pub W 192:46-7 S 4 '67
LUDWIG, Christa
Happy scrappers. il por Time 89:72 F 10 '67
LUDWIG, Donald
Finding relay operate and release times. Electr World 77:48 Ap '67
LUDWIG, John H. See McCormick, R. A. jt. auth.
LUDWIGSON, John
Elms for the future. Sci N 92:256-7 S 9 '67
LUECKE, Richard H.
God and evil. Christian Cent 84:377-8 Mr 22 '67
LUEKING, F. Dean
Mission histories. Christian Cent 84:176 F 8 '67
LUGER pistol. See Pistols
LUGGAGE
Checklist of luggage gifts. Good H 165:180 D '67
Color covers the continent. il Seventeen 26:98-9 Je '67
Garment-bag luggage. il Consumer Rep 32:584-8 N '67
Go-go safari! il Seventeen 26:162-3 F '67
Happy wanderers. il Seventeen 26:209 N '67
How safe is your baggage when you travel? Bet Hom & Gard 45:93 Ap '67
When I pack for school. il Seventeen 26:278-9 Ag '67
See also
Packing of luggage
LUGGAGE handling, Airlines. See Airlines—Passenger service
LUIGI
Luigi: East & West. W. Como. il por Dance Mag 41:21 Jl '67
LUKACS, John Adalbert
Dissenting view of the day that shook the world. N Y Times Mag p32-3+ O 22 '67; 113 Ja 7 '68
Making of a geopolitician. New Repub 157:28-31 O 28 '67
Memories of England's finest hour. Sat R 50:27-8 Je 17 '67
LUKAS, J. Anthony
Gandhi caps are in trouble in India. N Y Times Mag p28-9+ F 19 '67
Maybe somebody else can learn from it. Read Digest 91:96-101 D '67
Whitey hasn't got the message. N Y Times Mag p24-5+ Ag 27 '67
LUKASZEWSKI, Jerzy
Western integration and the people's democracies. For Affairs 46:377-87 Ja '68
LUKE, David Lincoln, 1923-
New gospel at Westvaco. R. Levy. por Duns R 89:48-50+ Mr '67
LUKEFAHR, M. J. See Fryxell, P. A. jt. auth.
LULU; opera. See Berg, A.
LUMBARD, J. Edward
Criminal justice revolution; address, May 16, 1967. Vital Speeches 33:527-31 Je 15 '67
LUMBER
How to buy a board. il Bet Hom & Gard 45:130-1 S '67
Why is it called a 2x4? il Pop Mech 127:177 My '67
See also
Sawmills
LUMBER Industry and trade
Boom in log exports raises knotty problems. il Bsns W p68+ D 23 '67
Meet Miss Connie; log buyer in England. J. Doussard. il Am For 73:31+ D '67
LUMBERING
Airlift for logs. il Fortune 75:150-1 F '67
Doomed by destiny; great river log drives. H. E. McLean. il Am For 73:36-9+ Je '67
See also
Balloons in lumbering
Lumberjacks
LUMBERJACKS
Hell and high water; excerpts from Tall trees, tough men. R. E. Pike. il Am Heritage 18:64-70 F '67
LUMINAL art. See Electric lamps in art
LUMINESCENCE
Thermoluminescence of geological materials; report on first International symposium on applications of thermoluminescence to geological problems. D. J. McDougall. Science 156:1137 My 26 '67

See also
Electroluminescence
Phosphors
LUMINOUS ceilings. See Ceilings
LUMLEY, Kathryn
Reading is fun in Washington. por Sr Schol 90:sup 1-2 Mr 31 '67
LUNAR bases
After Apollo, a colony on the moon. I. Asimov. il N Y Times Mag p30-2+ My 28 '67; Same. Sci Digest 62:44-8+ S '67
See also
Moon—Exploration

Anecdotes, facetiae, satire, etc.
Moon ghetto; religious bickering in space chapel. Christian Cent 85:31 Ja 3 '68
LUNAR eclipses. See Eclipses, Lunar
LUNAR exploration. See Moon—Exploration
LUNAR landing systems. See Space vehicles—Landing systems—Moon
LUNAR magnetic fields. See Magnetic fields (cosmic physics)
LUNAR modules. See Space vehicles—Landing systems—Moon
LUNAR photography See Astronomical photography
LUNAR probes
Planetary probes are long-term goals. Aviation W 86:138-9 Mr 6 '67
LUNAR radiation
Radioactivity of lunar rocks. G. S. Mumford. Sky & Tel 33:354 Je '67
LUNAR receiving laboratory. See United States—National aeronautics and space administration—Manned spacecraft center
LUNAR research. See Moon
LUNAR simulators. See Simulators
LUNAR vehicles
Getting along on the moon; moon hoppers and other moonmobiles. il Sci N 91:269-71 Mr 18 '67

Equipment
Lunar walking staff design under way. A. Hill. il Tech W 20:24 Mr 6 '67

Launching
First lunar module launch now planned for late 1967. Tech W 20:19 Je 19 '67
LUNCHEONS
Company's coming to luncheon before bridge. Am Home 70:126 My '67
Company's coming to luncheon; with recipes. Am Home 70:116 Mr '67
Fresh-thinking luncheon tray. il Bet Hom & Gard 45:84 Je '67
Gourmet luncheon in the marvelous kitchen of a famous cook. il House & Gard 132:154-5 D '67
Lazy-day luncheon; with recipes. il Bet Hom & Gard 45:80-1+ Jl '67
Luncheon in a one-time church. il House & Gard 132:226-7 N '67
Sudden guests at the seashore; luncheon for First ladies of two great nations. E. S. Hughes. il McCalls 94:80-1+ S '67
See also
Brunches
LUNCHES
Field meals and lunches that hit the spot. B. L. Henry. il Farm J 91:52-3 Je '67
Lunches kids like. B. B. Smith. See issues of Parents' magazine and better homemaking
LUND, Kenneth W.
Aid to education; planning is the key; excerpts from testimony, March 17, 1967; ed. by R. H. Smith. Pub W 191:40 Mr 27 '67
LUNDBERGH, Holger
Piet Hein: a good egg. House B 110:8+ Ja '68
LUNDBORG, Louis B.
Agribusiness approach; address, September 11, 1967. Vital Speeches 33:756-9 O 1 '67
LUNGFISHES
Lungfish neoceratodus forsteri: activities of ornithine-urea cycle and enzymes. L. Goldstein and others. bibliog il Science 157:316-17 Jl 21 '67
Lungfish park; Bundaberg, Queensland, Australia. il Sci Digest 62:24-5 S '67
Most interesting fish in the world. il Sci Digest 61:38-9 Ap '67
LUNGS
Bronchiolar and large alveolar cell in pulmonary phospholipid metabolism. A. H. Niden. bibliog il Science 158:1323-4 D 8 '67

LYNCH, William F.
Counterrevolution in the movies. Commonweal 87:77-9+ O 20 '67
Psychological man. America 117:635-7 N 25 '67

LYNCHBURG, Va.

Newspapers

City v. the publisher; abuse of Negroes. Time 89:78 My 5 '67
Lynchburg's daily shame; papers' treatment of Negroes. Newsweek 69:88 My 8 '67
When city bites newspaper, that's news; white community reacts to racist policies of the News and Daily advance. Life 62:4 My 12 '67

LYNCHING
See also
Mob violence

LYND, Staughton
Radical speaks in defense of S.N.C.C. N Y Times Mag p50-1+ S 10 '67

about

Dissent threshold. il por Newsweek 70:46-7 Jl 31 '67

LYNDEN, Patricia
Last holdouts. Atlan 220:42-6 Ag '67

LYNDS, Beverly T.
Spiral patterns in galaxies. Sky & Tel 33:343-6; 34:18-21 Je-Jl '67

LYNES, Russell
After hours. See issues of Harper's magazine
Cool cheer for middle age. Look 31:45+ O 17 '67

LYNN, Conrad J.
Whistling in a very lively graveyard. M. Renek. New Repub 156:14-15 My 13 '67

LYNN, Kenneth S.
And middle-class daydreams. Nation 204:279-81 F 27 '67

LYNXES
See also
Bobcats

LYON, Danny
Graphics are crucial! so is emotional impact! J. Scully. il Mod Phot 31:52-61+ My '67

LYON, David L.
Ecologist's view of the population problem. Liv Wildn 31:31-5 Spr '67

LYON, Harold C. Jr
Introduction to success. Am Ed 3:5-6+ My '67

LYON, John B. Jr, and others
Phosphorylase b kinase inheritance in mice. bibliog Science 155:1550-1 Mr 24 '67

LYON, Peter
Tale of real rags to real riches. Life 63:6 Jl 14 '67

LYONS, Augusta Wallace
All the lovely possibilities; story, excerpt from Manhattan geishas. Redbook 130:143-69 D '67

LYONS, Daniel
Diverted by infanticide. Sat R 50:34 Ap 15 '67

LYONS, Eugene
Russia before the revolution; excerpts from Workers paradise lost. Nat R 19:1166-9 O 31 '67
Vietnam: the charges and the facts. Read Digest 91:57-63 O '67
Workers' paradise lost; condensation. Read Digest 91:233-7+ N '67

about

Behind the lines. por Read Digest 91:9-10 N '67
Consumers in the US vs. the USSR. Consumer Bul 51:25-6 Ja '68

LYONS, Leonard
Grape peelers and other famous food kooks. Vogue 150:22+ O 15 '67

LYONS, Linda Brody. See Zinder, N. D. jt. auth.

LYONS, Ruth
In Spain there is a saying; story. Redbook 130:56-7 Ja '68

LYONS, Sylvia R.
New grandmother's prayer. McCalls 94:70 F '67

LYONS, France

Music

Lyons: production of Schoenberg's Erwartung and Bartók's Bluebeard's castle. D. Stevens. Opera N 31:29 Mr 18 '67

LYRIC opera of Chicago
Lyric opera and Mary Garden's shadow. R. C. Marsh. il Hi Fi 17:MA19+ F '67
Lyric opera wins by a Chicago margin. C. Cassidy. il Sat R 51:100-1 Ja 13 '68

LYSENKO, Trofim Denisovich
Soviet genetics: first Russian visit since 1930's offers a glimpse. E. Langer. il Science 157:1153 S 8 '67; Reply. T. Dobzhansky. 158:577 N 3 '67

LYSERGIC acid diethylamide
Broken chromosomes: some evidence. Sci N 92:465 N 11 '67
Cell damage from LSD. il Time 89:46+ Mr 24 '67
Chromosomal abnormalities in leukocytes from LSD-25 users. S. Irwin and J. Egozcue. bibliog il Science 157:313-14 Jl 21 '67
Chromosomal damage in human leukocytes induced by lysergic acid diethylamide. M. M. Cohen and others. bibliog il Science 155:1417-19 Mr 17 '67
Cool talk about hot drugs; misconceptions about heroin, LSD and marijuana. D. B. Louria. il N Y Times Mag p 12-13+ Ag 6 '67; Same abr. Read Digest 91:111-17 N '67; Discussion. N Y Times Mag p 14+ Ag 27 '67
Creator. il Newsweek 71:26-7 Ja 8 '68
Curbing the drug traffic in Britain; plans to change prescription system. B. Wenham. New Repub 156:9-10 Mr 18 '67
Donna's long trip; effects of LSD trip accidentally taken by a five-year old. il Newsweek 70:98 S 25 '67
Drug abuse and the value crisis. L. G. Richards. il Sr Schol 91:sup 13-14 N 16 '67
Drugs, a personal LSD experience. J. Shepherd. Look 31:23 Ag 8 '67
Drugs & chromosomes. Time 90:84-5 S 15 '67
Drugs and mysticism: visions of Saint Tim. J. M. Flagler. il Look 31:18-22 Ag 8 '67
Drugs, narcotics, and the flight from reality; with interview and press comments. il Sr Schol 90:4-12 F 10 '67
Drugs on the campus. J. Shepherd. il Look 31:14-17 Ag 8 '67
Hidden evils of LSD; genetic damage. B. Davidson. il Sat Eve Post 240:19-23 Ag 12 '67
Leukocytes of humans exposed to lysergic acid diethylamide: lack of chromosomal damage. W. D. Loughman and others. bibliog il Science 158:508-11 O 27 '67
LSD, a creativity bust. Sci Digest 62:71-2 O '67
LSD, a medical overview. D. B. Louria. Sat R 50:91-2 Ap 22 '67
LSD and the unborn. il Newsweek 70:110 S 18 '67
LSD & the unborn. il Time 90:60 Ag 11 '67
LSD: danger to unborn babies. E. M. Brecher. McCalls 94:70-1+ S '67
Lysergic acid diethylamide: effect on embryos. R. Auerbach and J. A. Rugowski. bibliog il Science 157:1325-6 S 15 '67
LSD for sociopaths. Sci N 91:352 Ap 15 '67
LSD: growing menace to teenagers; with study discussion program. W. W. Zeller. Parents Mag 42:49-50. 70-1+ N '67
LSD harms cells. Sci N 91:518 Je 3 '67
LSD: injection early in pregnancy produces abnormalities in offspring of rats. G. J. Alexander and others. bibliog il Science 157:459-60 Jl 28 '67; Reply with rejoinder. J. A. DiPaolo. 158:522 O 27 '67
LSD, one way trip for alcoholics. F. R. Schreiber and M. Herman. il Sci Digest 62:60-4 Jl '67
LSD syndrome. F. S. Meyer. Nat R 19:301 Mr 21 '67
LSD, the other side of the story. L. Galton. Pop Sci 190:93-5+ Ja '67
My LSD trip; non-cop, non-hippie report. R. Gannon. il Pop Sci 191:60-5+ D '67
My son is on LSD. M. Roberts. il Ladies Home J 85:38+ Ja '68
New light on LSD. Sr Schol 91:22+ S 28 '67
New report on LSD: threat to unborn children. il U S News 63:66 O 9 '67
New reports on rising problem; use of LSD. U S News 62:12 Ap 10 '67
Psychedelic experience. L. Bieberman. New Repub 157:17-19 Ag 5 '67
Serotonin release from brain slices by electrical stimulation: regional differences and effect of LSD. T. N. Chase and others. bibliog il Science 157:1461-3 S 22 '67
Should we have laws banning the use of LSD? M. Mead. Redbook 130:30+ Ja '68

LYSIN
Lysine transport in human kidney: evidence for two systems. L. E. Rosenberg and others. bibliog il Science 155:1426-8 Mr 17 '67

LYSIS (bacteriology) See Bacteriolysis
LYSOSOMES
Lysosomal enzyme inhibition by trypan blue;
a theory of teratogenesis. F. Beck and
others. bibliog il Science 157:1180-2 S 8 '67
Lysosomes and disease. A. Allison. il Sci
Am 217:62-72 N '67
What causes inflammation, and why it oc-
curs; International inflammation club first
symposium. il Time 89:60+ Je 16 '67
Why arthritis hurts. Newsweek 69:32 Je 19 '67
LYSOZYME
Crystallization of human lysozyme. E. F. Os-
serman. bibliog il Science 155:1536-7 Mr 24
'67
LYTTON, Bart
Leeching Lytton back to health. por Bsns W
p 130+ N 11 '67

M

M-16 rifle. See Rifles
MAC. See United States—Military airlift com-
mand
MARS (multiple artillery rocket system) See
Weapons systems
MBT (main battle tank) See Tanks, Military
METCO (metropolitan council for educational
opportunity) See Boston—Education
MHD. See Magnetohydrodynamics
MHMA. See Mobile home manufacturers asso-
ciation
MIFS (multiplex interferometric Fourier spec-
trometer) See Spectrometers
MILPHAP (United States military public
health assistance program) See United
States—Agency for international develop-
ment
MIT. See Massachusetts institute of technol-
ogy, Cambridge
MLA. See Modern language association of
America
MMSW. See International union of mine, mill
and smelter workers
MOL (manned orbiting laboratory) See Space
stations
MRP (Mouvement republicain populaire) See
Political parties—France
MSU. See Michigan state university, East
Lansing
MUST (medical unit self-contained, transport-
able) See Hospitals, Military
MA, Sitson. See Ma, S. T.
MA, Ssu-tsung
Cruelty and insanity made me a fugitive. pors
Life 62:24-9+ Je 2 '67
We are slaves who have been betrayed. por
Life 63:64-6+ Jl 14 '67

about

Of devils & demons. il por Time 89:40 Ap 21
'67
Terror at the hands of the Red guards. il por
Life 62:22-3 Je 2 '67
MAARANEN, Steve
Racing through dairyland. H. Peterson. il
Sports Illus 27:20-1 Ag 21 '67
MAAS, Peter
Rescuer. Sat Eve Post 240:36-40+ S 23 '67
Sport of stings. Holiday 42:50-3+ O '67
MAAZEL, Lorin
Recordings. M. Mayer. Esquire 67:74+ My '67
MACACA nemestrina. See Monkeys
MCADAMS, Thomas
Riding the 44-footer through hell and high
water; interview, ed. by G. Silk. por Life
63:44-5+ Jl 7 '67
MCALISTER, Edgar R.
Survey shows truth about lending. Nations
Bsns 55:116-20 My '67
MCALLISTER, Jane Ellen
Mississippi's beehive college. C. Parsons and
W. B. Welch. il por Am Ed 4:19-22+ D '67
MACAO
Gunboat diplomacy. Newsweek 69:42+ Ja 30
'67
Macao's Communists challenge Catholics.
R. W. Fox. Christian Cent 85:54 Ja 10 '68
Macao's surrender to red China. S. T.
Hsieh. Nat R 19:746+ Jl 11 '67
Report; Chinese turn tables against the
Portuguese. Atlan 219:14+ My '67
Shadow and substance. Newsweek 69:49 F 13
'67

MACAQUES. See Monkeys
MCARDLE, Alma
Charles Dickens would have loved this house.
Am Home 70:48-9 D '67
MACARONI
Pasta by the sea. C. Claiborne. il N Y Times
Mag p 110 O 5 '67
Pasta, glorious pasta. N. S. Hazelton. il
Nat R 19:807 Jl 25 '67
Spaghetti with a flair; with recipes from A
snob in the kitchen, by S. Fabiani. il Red-
book 128:96-8+ Mr '67
Spoonable spaghetti; SpaghettiOs. B. J. Sane-
holtz. il Parents Mag 43:22+ Ja '68
See also
Noodles
MACARTHUR, Douglas, 1880-1964
Korean war, by M. B. Ridgway. Review
Life 63:12 N 17 '67. H. Moffett
MCAULAY, John D.
Reaching the nonreaders. NEA J 56:15 S '67
MACAULAY, Pauline
Astrakhan coat. Criticism
New Yorker 42:69 Ja 21 '67
MCBAIN, L. Doward
A.B.C. president supports negotiation in Viet-
nam. Christian Cent 84:772 Je 14 '67
MCBEAN, Ralph L. and Goldstein, Leon
Ornithine-urea cycle activity in xenopus
laevis; adaptation in saline. bibliog Science
157:931-2 Ag 25 '67
MCBEE, Susanna
New fish; first days in a tough school. Life
62:34B Mr 17 '67
$300,000 payroll for Catfish. Life 63:34 Ag 25
'67
MACBETH, Norman
Question: Darwinism revisited. Yale R 56:
616-31 Je '67
MACBIRDI drama. See Garson, B.
MCBRIDE, C. H.
Upstairs at El Morocco. Esquire 67:116-17 Ap
'67
MCBRIDE, R. A. See Schierman, L. W. jt.
auth.
MCBROOM, Patricia
Man and his science. Sci N 91:498-9 My 27 '67
MCCABE, Bernard
Joyce's letters. Commonweal 85:587-90 F 24
'67
Ulysses in the reel world. Cath World 204:
346-51 Mr '67
MCCABE, Edward James
Bowker lecture; subscription books; address,
May 18, 1967. Pub W 191:36-40 My 29 '67
MCCABE, Herbert
Corrupt church; concerning editorial in New
Blackfriars. Commonweal 85:612 Mr 3 '67;
Reply. T. F. Mader. 86:3+ Mr 24 '67
Letter from London. R. Williams. Nation
205:51 Jl 17 '67
McCabe affair; with editorial comment. J. M.
Cameron. Commonweal 85:653-5 Mr 10 '67
Strange coincidence. S. J. Adamo. America
116:322-3 Mr 4 '67
MCCABE, Thomas B.
Enriching life by broad experience; interview.
por Nations Bsns 55:52-3+ Je '67
MCCADDEN, Joseph J.
Specter of the lay trustee. America 117:133-6
Ag 5 '67
MCCAFFERTY, Phil
Concrete can be colorful. Pop Sci 190:184-8
Ap '67
Heat gun for home use. Pop Sci 190:158-9 Ja
'67
Power hacksaw comes in $18.95 kit. Pop Sci
192:160-3 Ja '68
Rattle-free case for car tools. Pop Sci 191:
130-1 N '67
Sixteen ways to get better travel pictures.
Pop Sci 190:112-15+ Je '67
MCCAFFREY, Austin J.
Creating a home-study center. Parents Mag
42:42-3+ Ja '67
MCCAFFREY, Neil
Best of the dance bands. Nat R 19:1082-5 O 3
'67
MCCAMIS, Marvin J. See Trumbull, J. V. A.
jt. auth.
MCCARRAN act. See Communism—United
States—Anti-Communist measures
MCCARRY, Charles
Hot actor for a cool time. Sat Eve Post 240:
94-7 My 20 '67
MCCARTEN, John
Theatre. See issues of New Yorker to De-
cember 23, 1967
MCCARTHY, Eugene Joseph
Arms and the man who sells them; excerpt
from The limits of power. Atlan 220:82-6
O '67
Interview with McCarthy; ed. by V. S.
Kearney and H. J. Sievers. America 117:
734-9 D 16 '67

MCCARTHY, Eugene Joseph—*Continued*

about

ADA's options. New Repub 157:6-7 D 23 '67
As LBJ's political troubles mount. por U S
News 63:8 N 20 '67
Broadcasting and impartiality. America 118:
26-7 Ja 13 '68
Dream is of peace. H. J. Sievers. America
117:705 D 9 '67
Eugene McCarthy hits the road. E. W. Ken-
worthy. New Repub 157:11-13 N 25 '67
Eugene McCarthy's mission. W. Lippmann.
por Newsweek 70:25 D 18 '67
Eugene who? P. Wieck. New Repub 158:14-15
Ja 13 '68
Faith of Eugene McCarthy. R. G. Sherrill.
Nation 205:589-91 D 4 '67
Fate of McCarthyism. Nat R 19:1415-17 D 26
'67
Gene McCarthy. New Repub 157:7-8 N 18 '67
Hedging, waffling and straddling. S. Alsop.
por Sat Eve Post 241:14 Ja 27 '68
Is it really McCarthy? Reporter 37:10 D 14 '67
Letter from Washington. R. H. Rovere. New
Yorker 43:154-5 D 9 '67
Limited candidate. por Time 90:30 N 17 '67
McCarthy bomb. K. Crawford Newsweek 70.
32 D 4 '67
McCarthy candidacy. Christian Cent 84:1620
D 20 '67
McCarthy candidacy. Commonweal 87:193-4
N 17 '67
McCarthy: critic or challenger? Nation 206:
5-6 Ja 1 '68
McCarthy in Chicago. P. R. Wieck. New Re-
pub 157:9-11 D 16 '67
McCarthy or McCoy? por Newsweek 70:30 D
11 '67
McCarthy style. New Repub 157:8 D 23 '67
Man for this season? J. Newfield. Common-
weal 87:400-1 D 29 '67
Motives for McCarthy's move. M. McGrory.
America 117:760 D 23 '67
Move to dump Johnson il pors Newsweek
70:25-8 N 27 '67
New rallying point for dissent. il pors Life
63:38-38A N 24 '67
Now is the time. New Repub 157:7-8 D 9 '67
Oh come all ye true doves. il por Time 90:18-
19 D 22 '67
Ready, willing and able. D. Ireland. Common-
weal 87:375-6 D 22 '67
Report; Washington. M. C. Janeway. Atlan
221:4+ Ja '68
Scientists and engineers for McCarthy. P.
M. Boffey. Science 158:1554 D 22 '67
Spirit of McCarthy. K. Crawford. Newsweek
70:44 D 18 '67
They all love Gene until he takes the stump.
G. Moore. il pors Life 64:50B-54 Ja 19 '68
Voice for dissent. por Time 90:21-2 D 8 '67
Warming up. Newsweek 71:17 Ja 15 '68
Whose stalking horse? Newsweek 70:32 D 18
'67
Why McCarthy challenges LBJ in primaries.
por U S News 63:24 D 11 '67
Would-be candidate for this season. W. H.
Honan. il pors N Y Times Mag p27+ D 10
'67

MCCARTHY, Glenn
Texas poor. J. G. Dunne. Sat Eve Post 240:14
D 30 '67

MCCARTHY, Joe
Problem: the Long Island expressway; solu-
tion: close down Long Island. N Y Times
Mag p34-6+ Mr 19 '67

MCCARTHY, Joseph Raymond
Most gifted and successful demagogue this
country has ever known. R. H. Rovere. il
pors N Y Times Mag p23+ Ap 30 '67

MCCARTHY, Mary
Mary in the big PX. il por Newsweek 69:72-
3 Ap 17 '67

MCCARTHY, Stephen R.
Ordeal above Tesi Lapcha. Sports Illus 26:
68-70+ My 1 '67

MCCARTHY, Tom
Tom McCarthy tries the fish-eye everybody
can afford. il Pop Phot 60:78-81+ Ap '67

MCCARTHY, James E. and Williams, Ralph
Just like putting a foreman in the cab. por
Am City 82:94-5 Mr '67

MCCAULEY, T. J.
Theatrical opener. Writer 80:26-8 F '67

MCCAW, John E.
American church? America 117:498-501 N 4
'67

MCCLANE, A. J.
Big three of cold-water sport fishing: trout,
char, salmon. Field & S 72:43-9+ My '67
(ed) Fishing. See issues of Field & stream

How to pop your cork and enjoy it. Field
& S 72:28-9 Jl '67
Where do we go from here? Field & S 71:
10-12+ F '67

MCCLARREN, Robert R.
Art in libraries. por Library J 92:4337-40 D 1
'67

MCCLELLAN, Gary
Aah-chooo! not another pepper? Pop Electr
27:60-1 Jl '67

MCCLELLAN, George B.
Respect for the law: breaking down all over?
excerpts from address, 1967. por U S News
63:17 Ag 21 '67

MCCLELLAN, John Little
Excerpt from addresses, January 25 and April
17, 1967. Cong Digest 46:211+ Ag '67

MCCLELLAND, David C.
Want to be a success? reprint. Sci Digest
61:69-74 Ap '67

MCCLENDON, Robertine K.
Juliette Gordon Low birthplace. Antiques 91:
360-3 Mr '67

MCCLISH, Gerald F.
Bahamas bearings. Motor B 119:172 Ap; 179
My; 148-50 Je; 120:141-3 Ag '67
Story of Ona. Motor B 121:93-6+ Ja '68

MCCLOSKEY, Mark
Insurance agent; Our kingdom; Meetings,
departures; Stars; poems. Poetry 111:15-18
O '67
Spring beyond the spring. Poetry 110:427-8
S '67

MCCLOSKEY, Michael
Why worry about the redwoods? Sat R 50:18-
19 Je 3 '67

MCCLOSKEY, Paul N. Jr
Black out. New Repub 157:7 N 25 '67
Man nobody knows. New Repub 157:11-12
O 21 '67

MCCLOSKEY, Paul W.
CAIP what is its future? Commonweal 87:
194-5 N 17 '67

MCCLOSKEY, Robert
To America, with daughters: in search of
Robert McCloskey. R. Stokes. il Horn Bk
43:419-23 Ag '67

MCCLOSKEY, Robert James
U.S. releases selected arms items to Israel
and certain Arab states; excerpt from press
and radio news briefing, October 24, 1967.
Dept State Bul 57:652 N 13 '67

MCCLOUGHAN, Kent
Witness for the defense. H. L. Masin. por Sr
Schol 91:54 S 28 '67

MCCLOY, John J.
That old hand McCloy. Reporter 36:8+ My
18 '67

MCCLURE, Charles
African potato printing. Sch Arts 66:32-3 Ap
'67

MCCLURE, Ken
Arizona's Turquoise triangle. Travel 128:41-
3+ O '67

MCCLURE, Michael
Beard. Criticism
Christian Cent 85:87 Ja 17 '68
Nation 205:508 N 13 '67
New Repub 157:35-7 D 2 '67
Newsweek il 70:86+ N 6 '67
Sat R 50:26 N 11 '67
Time 90:69 N 3 '67

MCCLURE, Robert M. and Sand, Ole
If we are to be leaders. . . NEA J 56:28-31
D '67

MCCLUSKEY, Neil G.
Financial crisis in Catholic colleges. America
117:298-304 S 23 '67
New Catholic college. America 116:414-17
Mr 25 '67

MACCOBY, Michael
On Mexican national character. bibliog f
Ann Am Acad 370:63-73 Mr '67

MCCOID, Ann
Curl up & read. Seventeen 26:32 N '67

MCCOLLUM, L. F.
Spurring growth with imagination; interview.
por Nations Bsns 55:46-7+ Ap '67

MCCONKEY, Thomas W.
(ed) Buyers' guide. See usually first issue of
each month of Library Journal
(ed) Purchasing guide 1967. Library J 92:
1433-5+ Ap 1 '67

MCCONNELL, John Paul
Airpower over North Vietnam; excerpts from
statement. Aviation W 87:21 Ag 28 '67
If U.S. hadn't pulled its punch; excerpts
from testimony, August 1967. por U S News
63:10 O 16 '67
More of the same. por Time 90:27 O 13 '67

MCCORD, David
I like all fishermen if; poem. Holiday 42:
43 Ag '67

MCCORKELL, R. and others
Aluminum-26 and beryllium-10 in Greenland ice. bibliog Science 158:1690-2 D 29 '67
MCCORMACK, John William
Bolling is right. New Repub 157:8-9 N 11 '67
Old Jawn. por Newsweek 69:28 Mr 6 '67
Speaking out on the Speaker. Time 89:20 Ja 27 '67
MCCORMACK, Mark H.
My friend Arnold Palmer. Sports Illus 26:56-66 Mr 6; 32-6+ Mr 13; 54-6+ Mr 20; 36-40+ Mr 27 '67

about

I remember this strong-looking guy. il por Sports Illus 26:59 Mr 6 '67
MCCORMACK, Thelma
Styles in educated females. Nation 204:117-18 Ja 23 '67
MCCORMICK, Adoreen. See Hamer, E. E. jt. auth.
MCCORMICK, Carolyn
Thank you, Wadi Botts! Reporter 37:41-4+ O 5 '67
MCCORMICK, James G. See Ridgway, S. H. jt. auth.
MCCORMICK, Jo Mary
Camera cat: Pippy the poster cat. il U S Camera 31:80-1 Ja '68
MCCORMICK, John
Ten toreros in need of a bull. Sports Illus 27:34-9 Jl 24 '67
MCCORMICK, Katharine (Dexter)
American women: the changers. por Vogue 149:184 My '67
MCCORMICK, Richard A.
Aspects of the moral question. America 117:716-19 D 9 '67
MCCORMICK, Ricky
Tricky Ricky. H. L. Masin. il por Sr Schol 90:32 Ap 14 '67
MCCORMICK, Robert A. and Ludwig, J. H.
Climate modification by atmospheric aerosols. bibliog Science 156:1358-9 Je 9 '67
MCCORMICK, Robert V.
Vision and the hunter. Field & S 72:54-5+ S '67
MCCORMICK Place, Chicago. See Chicago—McCormick Place
MCCORMICK Place fire. See Fires
MCCORRY, Vincent P.
Grennan affair. America 116:149-50 Ja 28 '67
No laughing matter. America 116:218-19 F 11 '67
Word. See issues of America
MCCOY, Charles Brelsford
Du Pont McCoy. il por Time 90:63 D 29 '67
Outsider. il por Newsweek 71:45-6 Ja 1 '68
MCCOY, D. B.
Mentor marsh. il Nat Parks Mag 41:12-13 Jl '67
MCCOY, Paul S.
Miss fix-it; drama. Plays 26:37-48 Ap '67
MCCOY, Russel A. Jr. See Hinkle, J. E. jt. auth.
MACCRACKEN, Brooks W.
Althea and the judges. Am Heritage 18:60-3+ Je '67
MCCRACKEN, Jack
Put your boat in business. R. P. Murdock. il por Motor B 120:40+ O '67
MCCRACKEN, Rachel
December sonnet. Cath World 206:131 D '67
MCCRACKEN, Robert James
McCracken resigns. Christian Cent 84:644 My 17 '67
Preaching from the heights. il por Time 89:82+ My 5 '67
MCCRAY, E. Ward
Great hatch. Outdoor Life 140:24-7+ Jl '67
MCCREA, W. H.
Quasars: rapid light fluctuations. bibliog Science 157:400-2 Jl 28 '67
MCCRORY corporation
Meshulam Riklis: how to build an empire without cash; acquisition of Manhattan's Lerner stores. il Duns R 90:21 Jl '67
MCCUBBIN, James W. and Bumpus, F. M.
Renal hypertension. Science 155:1445 Mr 17 '67
MCCUE, George
Civic consciences. por Time 89:66+ Mr 31 '67
MCCULLERS, Carson (Smith)
Hospital Christmas eve. por McCalls 95:96-7 D '67
March; story. Redbook 128:64-5 Mr '67

about

Carson McCullers: 1917-1967. R. McGill. por Sat R 50:31+ O 21 '67
Lonely heart of Carson McCullers. R. Drake. Christian Cent 85:50-1 Ja 10 '68

MCCULLOCH, Frank
Farewell assessment of Vietnam. Life 63:34-34A D 15 '67
From Vietnam to Washington. G. P. Hunt. por Life 63:3 D 15 '67
MCCULLOUGH, David G.
Oak Bluffs. Am Heritage 18:38-47 O '67
MCCULLOUGH, M. E.
How to squeeze more milk from your feed. por Farm J 91:D10-11 Ap '67
MCCULLY, Helen
Nobody ever tells you these things; questions and answers. See issues of House beautiful
Sunday-night soups. House B 109:152+ F '67
When the chefs cook for themselves. House B 109:174-6+ Mr '67
—and others
Other half of the egg; excerpt. Ladies Home J 84:114-15+ S '67
MCCUNE, Lois C. and Salmon, S. R.
Bibliography of library automation. ALA Bul 61:674-5+ Je '67
MCDANIEL, A. H.
Calf mortality takes a licking. Farm J 91:D12-13 Ag '67
MCDERMOTT, Geoffrey
James Bond could have learned from Philby. N Y Times Mag p36-7+ N 12 '67
MCDERMOTT, John
Vietnam is no mistake. Nation 204:203-6 F 13 '67
MCDERMOTT, John F. Jr
Parent and child. N Y Times Mag p99+ O 22 '67
MCDERMOTT, John R.
He can't remember a time when he wasn't talking. Life 62:106-8+ Ap 7 '67
How about at your place? said the colonel. Life 63:65 Ag 4 '67
Praise or boo him, but in Dallas call Don Meredith Dandy. Life 63:73.4+ D 1 '67
MCDERMOTT, Walsh
NAS establishes Board on medicine. por Science 158:891 N 17 '67
MCDIARMID, Hugh, pseud. See Grieve, C. M.
MCDONAGH, Don
Leary under the glass. Nat R 19:360+ Ap 4 '67
MACDONALD, Angus A.
Where do you think you're going? Flying 81:79-80 O '67
MCDONALD, B. E. and Dicke, R. H.
Solar oblateness and fluid spin-down. bibliog Science 158:1562-4 D 22 '67
MACDONALD, Brian
Countdown begins; with biographical note. por Dance Mag 41:38-45, 82 O '67
MACDONALD, Charles
Coming of age party. Library J 92:2731-3 Ag '67
Hot precoated aggregate eliminates sealcoat dust. Am City 82:110-12 F '67
MACDONALD, David
Bobby Hull, golden boy of hockey. Read Digest 90:41-2+ Mr '67
Canada's garden of wonders. Read Digest 90:145-50+ Je '67
Expo 67: Canada's billion-dollar birthday party. Read Digest 90:184-6+ Ap '67
Quo vadis: R for the nursing shortage. Read Digest 91:15-16+ S '67
MACDONALD, Don
Auto news makers. Motor T 19:30 Ap; 62 My; 8 Je; 98 Jl '67
Way we see it. See issues of Motor trend
What you should know about buying tires. Motor T 20:47-51 Ja '68
MACDONALD, Duncan
Scene from here. See issues of House beautiful
MACDONALD, Dwight
Liberal anti-communism revisited. Commentary 44:54-6 S '67
On civil disobedience, 1967. N Y Times Mag p 130 N 26 '67
Politics. See issues of Esquire
MCDONALD, Elvin
(ed) See Miller, T. P. Medieval flowers for today's gardens
MACDONALD, George
Afterword. W. H. Auden. Horn Bk 43:176-7 Ap '67
MACDONALD, Gordon J. F.
Implications for geophysics of the precise measurement of the earth's rotation. bibliog Science 157:304-5 Jl 21 '67
Science and space policy. Bul Atomic Sci 23:2-9 My '67
MCDONALD, John
How they minted the new Penney. Fortune 76:110-13+ Jl '67

MCDONALD, John—*Continued*
J. Paul Getty's changed plans. Fortune 76:
108-13+ D '67
Why Evans products co. had a bad year. For-
tune 75:138-41+ My '67
MCDONALD, Katherine (Griffith)
At home with the sea. Opera N 31:24-5 F 11
'67
Champagne sec. Opera N 31:24-5 Ja 7 '67
MCDONALD, Marguerite
Old Bruie's last visit; ed. by V. W. Binkley.
pors Outdoor Life 140:60-1+ O '67
MACDONALD, Michael C. D.
Documentary films. New Repub 156:32-4 My
13 '67
MACDONALD, Ray Woodward
Things are adding up again at Burroughs.
il pors Bsns W p 192-4+ Mr 11 '67
MACDONALD, Robert David
(tr) See Neumann, A. and others. War and
peace
MCDONALD, Robert F.
It's neat in Greece. New Repub 157:15-17 Jl
22 '67
MCDONALD, William Joseph, bp
Urge to retire. por Time 90:57 Jl 21 '67
MACDONALD, William W.
Luther and Catholic historians. America 117:
434-6 O 21 '67

MCDONNELL, Helen M.
Aiding unwilling readers: paperbacks do the
trick. Sr Schol 90:sup21-2 Mr 31 '67
New paperbacks on reading. Sr Schol 90:sup
24 Ap 28 '67
Paperbacks for slow readers. Sr Schol 89:
sup27 Ja 20 '67
MCDONNELL, James Smith
McDonnell moves in. Bsns W p36 Ja 21 '67
Mr Mac & his team. il por Time 89:79-83
Mr 31 '67
MCDONNELL, Thomas P.
Light in a dark journey. America 116:729-31
My 13 '67
**MCDONNELL company-Douglas aircraft com-
pany merger.** See Airplane industry and
trade—Consolidations and mergers
MCDONNELL Douglas corporation
Bright future seen for McDonnell Douglas.
Tech W 20:31 Ap 24 '67
DC-8, DC-9 deliveries below forecasts. C. M.
Plattner. il Aviation W 87:33 Jl 3 '67
McDonnell and Douglas holders approve
merger. Aviation W 86:35 Ap 24 '67
McDonnell Douglas shows six month loss.
Aviation W 87:23 Jl 31 '67
Mr Mac & his team. il Time 89:79-83 Mr
31 '67
Under the umbrella: executive placements. il
Time 89:70 F 3 '67
MCDONOUGH, E. S. and Lewis, A. L.
Blastomyces dermatitidis: production of the
sexual stage. bibliog Science 156:528-9 Ap
28 '67
MCDONOUGH, Roger Henry
ALA committee appointments. ALA Bul 61:
909 S '67

about
New ALA officer. J. E. Bryan. por ALA Bul
61:868+ Jl '67
MCDOUGALL, David J.
Thermoluminescence of geological materials.
Science 156:1137 My 26 '67
MACDOUGAL, Gary E.
Investing in a dividend boost. Harvard Bsns
R 45:87-92 Jl '67
MACDOUGALL, John S.
Low-cost semiconductors for the consumer
market. Electr World 78:37-9 S '67
MCDOWELL, Bart
Most Mexican city, Guadalajara! Nat Geog
Mag 131:412-41 Mr '67
MCDOWELL, Charles, Jr
Report: New Hampshire. Atlan 220:4+ D '67
MCDOWELL, John Herbert
Joan Baker and John Herbert McDowell. Jud-
son memorial church. J. Anderson. Dance
Mag 41:78-9 Mr '67
Rachel Kafri and John Herbert McDowell;
Judson memorial church. M. Marks. Dance
Mag 41:32+ D '67
MACE, David R.
How to be a good wife. Parents Mag 42:44-
5+ F '67
MACEDONIA
History, Ancient
In the footsteps of Alexander the Great. H.
Schreider and F. Schreider. il Nat Geog
Mag 133:1-65 Ja '68
MCELROY, George
Romance with reality. Opera N 31:8-12 F 4 '67

MCELROY, James Dennis
Real, live superman. P. Wyche. il pors Ebony
22:97-8+ S '67
MCELROY, John H.
Miracle ray grows up. Sci Digest 61:8-13
My '67
MCELROY, W. D. and others
Molecular uniformity in biological catalyses.
bibliog Science 157:150-60 Jl 14 '67
MCELWAIN, Franklin R.
For social studies teachers. Sr Schol 91:sup27
S 28 '67
MACEOIN, Gary
Bishops' synod. Commonweal 86:546-8 S 8 '67
Reform, but not yet, Lord. Commonweal 86:
515-18 Ag 25 '67
MCEVILLY, William G.
Save street surfaces the easy way. Am City
82:106-7 Je '67
MCFARLAND, Elizabeth
Seasonal; poem. Ladies Home J 84:172 Mr '67
MCFARLAND, Jim
Shop talk. See issues of Hot rod
MCFARLAND, William N. and Moss. S. A.
Internal behavior in fish schools. bibliog
Science 156:260-2 Ap 14 '67
MCFARLANE, Alexander Nelson
Crusade on hunger; address, May 11, 1967.
Vital Speeches 33:659-61 Ag 15 '67
MCFEGGAN, James
Why we began plowing sidewalks. Am City
82:70-1 Ja '67
MCGAHERN, John
Irish censorship: the case of John McGahern.
B. Cook. Cath World 206:176-9 Ja '68
**MCGAUGH, James L. See Luttges, M. W. jt.
auth.**
**MCGAUGHY, R. E. See Hagins, W. A. jt.
auth.**
MCGEE, David
Family affair. Reporter 36:43-8 Mr 9 '67
MCGEE, Gale W.
Family affair. D. McGee. il Reporter 36:43-8
Mr 9 '67
MCGEE, Max E. See Wujek, J. H. jr, jt. auth.
MCGEE, R. T.
On behalf of art. NEA J 57:36-7 Ja '68
MCGEHEE, Helen
Helen McGehee: 92nd street Y. M. Marks.
Dance Mag 42:80 Ja '68
MCGHEE, George C.
Europe and America: partners in technology;
address, November 10, 1966. Dept State
Bul 56:148-53 Ja 23 '67
MCGHEE, Michael Anthony
Colonel second. Time 89:48 Mr 10 '67
MCGILL, Ralph
Carson McCullers: 1917-1967. Sat R 50:31+
O 21 '67
MCGINLEY, Phyllis
Good companions. Mlle 66:122-3+ D '67
Night after Christmas; poem. McCalls 95:
42 D '67
MCGINNETY, J. A. and others
Structural aspects of reversible molecular
oxygen uptake. bibliog Science 155:709-10
F 10 '67
MCGINNIS, Lila Sprague
Secrets of a clock watcher; story. Good H
164:94-5 Mr '67
MCGINNIS, Samuel M. and Dickson, L. L.
Thermoregulation in the desert iguana
dipsosaurus dorsalis. bibliog Science 156:
1757-9; 158:810 Je 30, N 10 '67
MCGLOTHLIN, James
Angel. por Time 90:50 Jl 14 '67
MCGONAGLE, William Loren
June 8, at 1400 hours. J. J. Kilpatrick. il por
Nat R 19:952-8 S 5 '67
MCGOUG, Roger
Two poems: 2; 13. Mlle 65:118 O '67
MCGOVERN, George Stanley
Timid war against hunger; excerpts from re-
marks. Bul Atomic Sci 23:38-9 F '67
Vietnam and the birds; letter. New Repub
157:28 S 23 '67
We are losing the race against hunger. Look
31:86+ Mr 7 '67
Why don't you speak out, senator? New Re-
pub 156:10-11 Mr 18 '67

about
Speaking out; concerning speech of April 25,
1967. Nation 204:578-9 My 8 '67
MCGOVERN, John P. and Linde, S. M.
Why Johnny can't breathe, allergy? Todays
Health 45:11-13+ Mr '67
—See Barkin, G. D. jt. auth.
MCGOVERN, Robert
To a friend; poem. Christian Cent 84:1513
N 29 '67
To my new niece, who shares my blood and
name; poem. Christian Cent 84:896 Jl 12 '67

MCGRATH, Glen W.
State-local cooperative purchasing. Am City 82:120+ Mr '67

MCGRATH, Lawrence H.
School libraries: waiting in the wings. bibliog por Library J 92:4225-7 N 15 '67

MCGRATH, Thomas
All the dead soldiers; End of the line; Restless night; poems. Poetry 109:385-7 Mr '67

MCGRAW-Hill, incorporated
McGraw-Hill & London records announce affiliation. Library J 92:4456 D 15 '67
McGraw-Hill offers packaged science program. il Library J 92:1286 Mr 15 '67
McGraw-Hill opens second bookstore, in New Jersey. il Pub W 191:50 Je 12 '67

MCGRAW-Hill publishing company. See McGraw-Hill, incorporated

MCGRORY, Mary
Pope Paul speaks for the have-nots. America 116:552 Ap 15 '67
Washington front. See occasional issues of America

MCGUCKIN, Floyd, and Payne, Jack
Redwood canoe. . .a beauty you can build. Pop Sci 190:171-5+ Mr '67

MCGUFFEY, William Holmes
Americans not everyone knows. C. W. Ferguson il por PTA Mag 62:6-8 N '67

MCGUIGAN, R. A.
Harmful physically and mentally. por Todays Health 45:62-3 S '67

MCGUIRE, Frank C.
Vr-o-o-m with a view. Am For 73:42-3+ Ja '67

MCGUIRE, John
When the real McGuire stood up. P. Axthelm. il pors Sports Illus 26:74-8+ Mr 20 '67

MCGUIRE, Marie C.
Marie C. McGuire housing expert honored by NAHRO. Am City 82:28+ Ap '67

MCHALE, John
Science, technology, and change. bibliog f Ann Am Acad 373:120-40 S '67

MACHIAVELLI, Niccolò
Dastardly Florentine. P. W. Schmidtchen. il por Hobbies 72:104-5+ Je '67
Machiavelli, by G. Prezzolini. Review
  New Repub 156:21-4 Mr 11 '67. M. Kempton

MACHINE age
  See also
Technology and civilization

MACHINE Bull manufactures. See Electronic apparatus industry and trade—France

MACHINE embroidery. See Embroidery

MACHINE guns
100-bullet-a-second machine gun. J. Crane. il Pop Sci 190:86-7 Ap '67

MACHINE tool industry and trade
Europe's tool makers take on the world; European machine tool exhibition, Hanover, Germany. il Bsns W p90-2 O 7 '67

MACHINE tools
Shop talk. R. P. Stevenson. See issues of Popular science monthly
  See also
Drilling and boring machinery
      Exhibitions
Europe's tool makers take on the world; European machine tool exhibition, Hanover, Germany. il Bsns W p90-2 O 7 '67

MACHINE translators. See Translating machines

MACHINE works
      Employees
  See also
Machinery industry—Wages and hours

MACHINERY
Machines that make money for you. H. Shuldiner. il Pop Sci 191:62-4 Jl '67
  See also machinery used in particular industries or for special purposes, e.g. Bookbinding machinery

MACHINERY, Automatic
From design to finished product; automated metalworking factory. il Bsns W p88-90 D 30 '67
What robots do now for industry. il Bsns W p 114-16 My 20 '67
  See also
Automation

MACHINERY in agriculture. See Agricultural machinery

MACHINERY industry
      Wages and hours
Earnings in the machinery industries, mid-1966. F. L. Bauer. il Mo Labor R 90:52-5 Ag '67

MACHINERY insurance. See Insurance, Machinery

MACHINISTS union. See International association of machinists

MACHIS, Alfred
What third-stage sewage treatment means. Am City 82:110+ S '67

MACHT, Murray
Footnotes to the hair explosion. Sat R 50:4 S 16 '67

MACHU PICCHU, Peru
Lost city of the Incas. L. S. De Camp. il Sci Digest 62:68-72 Ag '67

MCHUGH, Simon F. jr
How to succeed. il por Newsweek 70:21 Jl 31 '67
Way to get a big federal job? il por U S News 63:10 Jl 31 '67

MCILVANNEY, Hugh
Fierce holy war in a violent city. Sports Illus 28:40-3 Ja 15 '68
Knees-up for the hot Spurs. Sports Illus 26: 32-4+ Je 5 '67

MCINERNY, Ralph
Addressee unknown: story. Redbook 128:76-7 Mr '67
Breaking free; story. Redbook 129:76-7 S '67
Make me chased, Lord; story. Redbook 128: 62-3 Ap '67
Season of endings; story. Redbook 129:159 Ag '67
Two hearts, vulnerable; story. Redbook 130: 76-7 N '67
When a girl is twenty-five; story. Good H 165:96-7 O '67

MACINNIS, Donald E.
Maoism: the religious analogy. Christian Cent 85:39-42 Ja 10 '68

MCINTIRE, Carl
Hatemongers and the people's ether; radio station WXUR. Christian Cent 84:1451-2 N 15 '67

MCINTYRE, Andrew
Coccoliths as paleoclimatic indicators of pleistocene glaciation. bibliog Science 158: 1314-17 D 8 '67

MCINTYRE, James Francis, cardinal
New voices from the convent. Nation 205:677 D 25 '67

MCINTYRE, Jennie
Public attitudes toward crime and law enforcement. bibliog f Ann Am Acad 374:34-46 N '67

MCJENKIN, Virginia
Continuing education for school librarians; address, January 11, 1967. bibliog por ALA Bul 61:272-5 Mr '67

MACK, Gordon
Nora. Criticism
  Opera N 31:31 Mr 11 '67

MACK trucks, incorporated
Mack strikes oil in Signal deal. Bsns W p60 My 13 '67

MCKAY, John
Man in motion beats Texas. J. Underwood. il pors Sports Illus 27:22-4+ O 2 '67

MACKAY, Ralph Stuart
Radio pill: symbol of a new science. Todays Health 45:16+ Ap '67

MACKAYE, Benton
Benton Mackaye's message. Liv Wildn 30:9 Aut '66

MCKAYLE, Donald
Black new world by Donald McKayle; 92nd street Y. D. Hering. Dance Mag 41:34+ Ap '67

MCKEAN, Charles M. and others
Aminoacidemias: effects on maze performance and cerebral serotonin. bibliog Science 157:213-15 Jl 14 '67

MCKEE, Alexander
Defeat and death of General Rommel. N Y Times Mag p44-5+ O 22 '67

MCKEITHEN, John Julian
From a governor and a D.A. an offer of resignation. S. Smith. il por Life 63:34-6 S 29 '67

MCKENNA, Kenneth
Money matters. Parents Mag 42:22+ Mr '67

MCKENNA, Richard
Sons of Martha; story. Harper 234:64-72 F '67

MCKENNY, Betsy
Curl up and read (cont) Seventeen 26:150 Je '67

MACKENZIE, Colin
World food programme: new form of aid for development. UNESCO Courier 20:30-2 O '67

MCKENZIE, Dave
Over the hills and far ahead. T. C. Brody. por Sports Illus 26:62-2+ My 1 '67

MACKENZIE, Donald
Who is your hero? Writer 81:18-19 Ja '68
MACKENZIE, Fred T. and others
Silica in sea water; control by silica minerals.
bibliog Science 155:1404-5 Mr 17 '67
MACKENZIE, Gordon N.
Process of innovation. NEA J 56:27-31 My '67
MACKENZIE, Jim
Oklahoma sticks it right to their mustache.
G. Ronberg. il Sports Illus 27:64-5 N 13
'67
MCKENZIE, John Lawrence
Sophisticating the catechism. Commonweal
87:201-2 N 17 '67
MACKENZIE, John P.
Compromise report on crime. New Repub 156:
15-16 F 4 '67
MCKENZIE, Kenneth G.
Ostracod living fossils: new finds in the
Pacific. bibliog Science 155:1005 F 24 '67
MCKERNAN, Louis F.
Aggiornamento. See issues of Catholic world
MCKERSIE, Robert B.
Maturation of the two movements. Mo Labor
R 90:36-8 Jl '67
MACKEY, Ernan
Lady and the lifeguard; story. Redbook 129:
42 Ag '67
MCKIBBIN, Eugene F.
Touching base with our youth. Sch & Soc
95:424-5 N 11 '67
MCKIE, Ronald
Bali. Holiday 42:48-53+ Jl '67
Persistence of Singapore. Holiday 42:32-41+
Ag '67
MCKIERNAN, Joseph
Night flight; poem. America 116:247 F 18
'67
MACKIN, Theodore
Vatican II, contraception and Christian mar-
riage. America 117:54-7 Jl 15 '67
MCKINLEY, David
Greens of spring. Audubon 69:74 Mr '67
MCKINLEY, Fred
Deer hunt I'll never forget. Field & S 72:60-
1+ Je '67
MCKINLEY, William
Presidential leadership in foreign affairs:
William McKinley and the Turpie-Foraker
amendment. P. S. Holbo. bibliog f Am Hist
R 72:1321-35 Jl '67
MCKINLEY, MOUNT
Denali strikes back; seven men die in storm.
il Time 90:19 Ag 11 '67
MCKINLEY NATIONAL PARK. See Mount
McKinley National Park
MCKINLOCK, Muriel
Summer checkup for school beginners. Parents
Mag 42:40-1+ Ag '67
MCKINNEY, Don
What are we looking for? Writer 80:14-16+
N '67
MCKINNEY, George W. Jr
Should the President set tax rates? Duns R
90:33-4 Jl '67
MCKINNEY, Ruth Ann. See Jones, W. H. jt.
auth.
MACKINNON, Edward
Truth of belief. America 116:553-6 Ap 15 '67
MCKINNON, Ethelyn Nightingale
Davenport house. Antiques 91:339-41 Mr '67
MCKINSEY, William R.
Excerpt from statement before Communica-
tions subcommittee, October 16, 1967. Cong
Digest 46:306+ D '67
MCKINSEY and company
How McKinsey minds its business. il Bsns W
p 175-6+ N 18 '67
MCKISSICK, Floyd B.
Successor to Floyd McKissick may not be so
reasonable. F. C. Shapiro. il pors N Y Times
Mag p32-3+ O 1 '67
Which way for the Negro? il por Newsweek
69:27-8+ My 15 '67
MACKLIN, Martin. See Josephson, R. K. jt.
auth.
MACKLIN, R. L. See Gibbons, J. H. jt. auth.
MCKNIGHT, Felix R.
Year that was; address, December 28, 1966.
Vital Speeches 33:282-5 F 15 '67
MCKNIGHT, John G.
Biasing in magnetic tape recording. Electr
World 78:34-6+ Ag '67
MCKUSICK, Victor A. and Rimoin, D. L.
General Tom Thumb and other midgets; with
biographical sketches. Sci Am 217:10, 102-
6+ bibliog(p 136) Jl '67
MCLAIN, Pete
Hardest bird hunting in Jersey. Field & S
72:36-9+ D '67
Summer tide-marsh stripers. Field & S 72:60-
1+ My '67

MCLANAHAN, David
Diary of an American medical intern in Viet-
nam. Sat R 50:18-21+ Mr 25 '67
MCLANE, James C. Jr, and others
Lunar receiving laboratory. bibliog Science
155:525-9 F 3 '67
MCLAREN, A. D. See Skujins, J. J. jt. auth.
MCLAREN, Bruce
Why I like sports-car racing. por Pop Sci
190:72 Mr '67
MCLAUGHLIN, Bernie
McLean vs. the McLaughlins: feud. il por
Life 62:26-7 F 24 '67
MCLAUGHLIN, Donald H.
Monetary alchemy; address, January 23, 1967.
Vital Speeches 33:438-43 My 1 '67
MCLAUGHLIN, George
McLean vs. the McLaughlins: feud. il Life
62:26-7 F 24 '67
MCLAUGHLIN, John
Book reviews. America 116:564 Ap 15 '67
Communications. America 117:488, 621-2, 771-2
O 28, N 18, D 23 '67
Public broadcasting corporation. America 117:
9-14 Jl 1 '67
TV and radio. America 116:567 Ap 15; 841-3
Je 10; 117:42-4 Jl 8; 140-inside back cover
Ag 5; 227-inside back cover S 2; 326-7+ S
23 '67
MCLAUGHLIN, Leo
Fordham is trying to be Catholic with a
small c. T. J. Fleming. il pors N Y Times
Mag p32-3+ D 10 '67
MCLAUGHLIN, Mignon
(ed) See Bailey, F. L. F. Lee Bailey: a
new breed of hero
MCLEAN, Buddy
McLean vs. the McLaughlins: feud. il por
Life 62:26-7 F 24 '67
MCLEAN, Eric
Early French Canadian furniture. Antiques
92:72-7 Jl '67
MACLEAN, Harriet
How to predict your future. Ladies Home J
84:78 Mr '67
MCLEAN, Herbert E.
Alaska, '67: year of ice. Am For 73:6-9 Ja '67
Alaska's beach bounty. por Am For 73:28-31+
Je '67
Alaska's boating centennial. il Motor B 119:
25-7+ F '67
Doomed by destiny. Am For 73:36-9+ Je '67
On top of Mount Timp. Am For 73:26-9 N '67
MCLEAN, Jackie
Four lives in the bebop business, by A. B.
Spellman. Review
Nation 204:378-9 Mr 20 '67. B. Kremen
MCLEAN, Malcom P.
Let's take our ships out of the bottle. L.
Velie. Read Digest 90:132-6 F '67
MACLEISH, Archibald
Magic prison. Sat R 50:21-3 O 28 '67
When we are gods. Sat R 50:22 O 14 '67
Where a poet's from; poem. Sat R 50:21 D 2
'67
about
Herakles. Criticism
New Repub 157:25-6+ Jl 22 '67
MACLEISH, Kenneth
Taxi for the deep frontier. Nat Geog Mag 133:
138-50 Ja '68
MACLEISH, Rod
How to cover wars. R. L. Shayon. Sat R
50:22 Ag 12 '67
MCLELLAN, David S.
Changing nature of Soviet and American
relations with western Europe; address,
April 1967, with questions and answers.
bibliog f Ann Am Acad 372:16-32 Jl '67
MCLELLAN, Joseph
Harangues and hurrahs in Boston. Common-
weal 86:405-6 Je 30 '67
MCLELLAND, Joseph C.
Symbol of hope for Man and his world.
Christian Cent 84:893-6 Jl 12 '67
MCLENDON, Gordon
Socking it to 'em. Time 89:53 My 26 '67
MACLEOD, Charlotte
Mine to love; story. Good H 164:86-7 F '67
MCLEOD, N. Bruce
Isaac and Ishmael: 1967. Christian Cent 84:
959-61 Jl 26 '67
MCLOUGHLIN, William G.
(comp) Trade cards. Am Heritage 18:48-63
F '67
MCLUHAN, Herbert Marshall
Architecture in the electronic age; interview,
ed. by J. Barnett. Arch Rec 141:151-2
Mr '67

MCLUHAN, Herbert Marshall—*Continued*
Medium is the message; excerpts from Understanding media. NEA J 56:24-7 O '67
Santa Claus gets the message. por McCalls 95:97+ D '67
—and Leonard, G. B.
Future of education: the class of 1989. Look 31:23-5 F 21 '67
Future of sex. Look 31:56-60+ Jl 25 '67
—See McLuhan, H. M. jt. auth

about
Air. M. J. Arlen. New Yorker 43:135-8 Ap 1 '67
Book of the month. D. J. Leary. Cath World 205:177-8 Je '67
Graphics convey message in Medium is the massage; interview, with excerpts from the book. Q. Fiore. il Pub W 191:62-4 Ap 3 '67
McLuhan hot and cool, ed. by G. E. Stern. Review
New Repub 157:34-6+ N 18 '67. R. Gilman
McLuhan montage. il Library J 92:1701-3 Ap 15 '67
Marshall McLuhan: communications explorer. N. P. Hurley. America 116:241-3 F 18 '67
Medium is the medium. F. S. Meyer. Nat R 19:419 Ap 18 '67
Message of Marshall McLuhan. il pors Newsweek 69:53-7 Mr 6 '67
Not-so-cool medium. R. L. Shayon. Sat R 50:46 Ap 15 '67
Schoolman's guide to Marshall McLuhan. J. M. Culkin. il por Sat R 50:51-3+ Mr 18 '67
Understanding McLuhan (in part) R. Kostelanetz. il por N Y Times Mag p 18-19+ Ja 29 '67; Discussion. p 12+ F 12 '67
Understanding Marshall McLuhan; or, Will TV put a zombie in your future? il por Sr Schol 90:13-16 Ap 28 '67

MCMAHAN, Ida, and Whitehorn, Ethel
Motion picture previews. See issues of PTA magazine

MCMAHON, Beverly E. and Strangway, D. W.
Kiaman magnetic interval in the western United States. bibliog Science 155:1012-13 F 24 '67

MCMAHON, Franklin
Partridge of the Don Quixote country; reproductions of paintings. Sports Illus 27:40-5 O 2 '67

MCMANUS, Irene
Nation of waterhogs? Am For 73:43-4 Mr '67

MCMATH, Sidney Sanders
Fulbright's prospects. J. Witcover. New Repub 156:4-5 Je 10 '67

MCMELLON, Arthur N.
No ordinary man. H. A. Mulligan. il por Read Digest 91:127-31 Jl '67

MCMICKING, Joseph Ralph
Siren song of Sotogrande; photographs by E. Haas; with account by L. Smith. Sports Illus 26:34-41 Mr 6 '67

MCMILLAN, Gene, and Stryker, Evelyn
How to survive a field trip. NEA J 56:58 O '67

MACMILLAN, Harold
Churchill's gillie. il pors Time 91:76 Ja 5 '68
Gents of the disestablishment. G. Dangerfield. Nation 204:437-8 Ap 3 '67
MacMillan: a study in ambiguity, by A. Sampson. Review
Newsweek pors 70:99 N 27 '67. F. Y. Blumenfeld

MACMILLAN, Viola
Queen Bee gets stung. Time 89:98 Mr 17 '67

MACMILLAN and company, limited
Backing our backlist: children's books. S. Hirschman. il Pub W 192:120-1 Jl 10 '67
Postmark: Pall Mall; debate over agreements made with African nations. G. R. Davies. Pub W 191:23-4 My 15 '67

MACMILLEN, Richard E. and Lee, A. K.
Australian desert mice: independence of exogenous water. bibliog Science 158:383-5 O 20 '67

MCMORROW, Fred
And be a good boy; story. Good H 164:82-3 F '67
Confession; story. Sat Eve Post 240:72-4 O 21 '67

MCMORROW, Tom, and Farkas, H. M.
Danger in the woods! Travel 128:56-8 Ag '67

MCMULLEN, Roy
Anatomy of a masterpiece: the burial of Count Orgaz. Horizon 9:48-61 Aut '67

MCMULLIN, Margery D. and Clarke, Margaret
Weekends at the seashore for physically disabled persons and their families. Parks & Rec 2:24+ Je '67

MCMURRAY, Joseph P.
Plan for financing higher education. Sch & Soc 95:489-90 D 9 '67

MCMURRY, Robert N.
Who riots and why. Nations Bsns 55:72-5 O '67

MCNABB, Harold S. Jr
Dutch elm disease roundup. Bet Hom & Gard 45:38+ My '67

MCNALLY, Robert E.
Religious poverty: a virtue? America 117:200-1 Ag 26 '67

MCNALLY, Tom
Troublesome tarpon. Outdoor Life 139:72-3+ Mr '67

MCNAMARA, Eugene
Heart surprised: a poem for my fourth child. Horn Bk 43:500 Ag '67

MCNAMARA, John J. jr
Dark sky over Tara; excerpt from White sails, black clouds. Sports Illus 27:54-62 Ag 7 '67
We came for the gold; except from White sails, black clouds. Yachting 122:42-3+ D '67

MCNAMARA, Margaret (Craig)
Mrs McNamara's crusade. H. Brandon. Sat R 50:9-10 Je 17 '67

MCNAMARA, Robert J.
Seminary education: separate and unequal. America 116:533-6 Ag 8 '67

MCNAMARA, Robert Strange
Airpower over North Vietnam; excerpts from statements. Aviation W 87:11 S 4 '67
Decision on ABM; excerpts from address. Aviation W 87:11 S 25 '67
Defense fantasy now come true; interview, ed. by R. B. Stolley. por Life 63:28-28C S 29 '67
Keep the faith baby; excerpts from addresses, February 1, 1963 to July 21, 1967. New Repub 157:8-9 Ag 5 '67
McNamara explains limited missile defense for U.S; text of address, September 18, 1967. por U S News 63:106-11 O 2 '67
McNamara on bombing the North; excerpts from report. Time 90:19 S 1 '67
McNamara's plan for defending the U.S. in a nuclear age; statement, January 26, 1967. por U S News 62:38-9 F 6 '67
NATO nuclear planning group holds first ministers meeting; statement, April 3, 1967. Dept State Bul 56:686-7 My 1 '67
Reports on nine Vietnam visits, the record. U S News 63:23 Jl 24 '67
Secretary McNamara comments on risks of anti-ballistic-missile system; interview, ed. by J. Mossman, February 15, 1967. Dept State Bul 56:442-7 Mr 20 '67
Secretary McNamara discusses the situation in Viet-Nam; statement, July 12, 1967. Dept State Bul 57:167-70 Ag 7 '67
Secretary Rusk and Secretary McNamara discuss developments in Latin America and Viet-Nam; statement. with questions and answers, February 28, 1967. Dept State Bul 56:465-6 Mr 20 '67
Sino-Soviet threat; testimony. Aviation W 86:11 F 27 '67
Social inequities; address, November 7, 1967. Vital Speeches 34:98-103 D 1 '67
Three gaps; address, February 24, 1967. Vital Speeches 33:357-61 Ap 1 '67
U.S. nuclear strategy; address, September 18, 1967. Vital Speeches 33:738-43 O 1 '67; Same with title Dynamics of nuclear strategy. Dept State Bul 57:443-51 O 9 '67; Same. Bul Atomic Sci 23:26-31 D '67
U.S. Secretary of defense testifies; excerpts from address, January 23, 1967. Bul Atomic Sci 23:21-4 Je '67
Why war declaration seems undesirable, the official view; excerpts from statement, February 24, 1966. por U S News 62:33 My 22 '67

about
Better job for McNamara. Nation 204:675 My 29 '67
Big shoes for the U.S. to fill; with report by H. Sidey. il pors Life 63:34-41 D 8 '67
Brainwashing furor Romney set off. U S News 63:22 S 18 '67
Close-up of McNamara's fence: how it works, why it's disputed. il U S News 64:24-5 Ja 1 '68
Departure of a titan. il por Time 90:22-5 D 8 '67
Education of Robert McNamara. D. Kiker. Atlan 219:49-55 Mr '67
Exit McNamara. Nation 205:610-11 D 11 '67
Exit McNamara. New Repub 157:6 D 9 '67

MCSHEA, William P.
On being born black but not beautiful: the Nativity in Harlem; poem. Christian Cent 84:1627 D 20 '67
MCSHEAN, Gordon
Roswell librarian resigns; charges smear campaign. il por Library J 92:3943 N 1 '67
MCSHERRY, Nona R. See Mangos, J. A. jt. auth.
MCSORLEY, Harry J.
Why Catholics want to dialogue with Lutherans. Cath World 206:71+ N '67
MCSTALLWORTH, Paul
Monthly report on Africa. Negro Hist Bul 30:19-20 Ja '67
MCVEA, Warren
Spartans get stabbed by Mac the Knife. D. Jenkins. il Sports Illus 27:54-6 O 2 '67
You've got to have some O. D. Jenkins. il por Sports Illus 27:40-2+ O 16 '67
MACWEENEY, Alen
Alen MacWeeney; an Irish poet with the camera. M. Orovan. il por U S Camera 30: 36-9 Ap '67
MCWHINNEY, Edgar L.
Vanishing breed; cattle clubs assets missing. Bsns W p40 Jl 15 '67
MCWHIRTER, William A.
How art swindlers duped a virtuous millionaire. Life 63:52-4+ Jl 7 '67
Its beauty veils a Mogul's ruthless whim. Life 63:60+ N 3 '67
National guard, awake or asleep? por Life 63: 85-6+ O 27 '67
MCWILLIAMS, Carey
Germany and the East. Nation 205:138-41 Ag 28 '67
Protest, power and the future of politics. Nation 206:71-7 Ja 15 '68
MACWILLIAMS, Margaret
Greatest gift of all. por McCalls 94:38+ Je '67
MCWILLIAMS, Wilson Carey
C.I.A. and the students. Commonweal 85:613- 14 Mr 3 '67
Will China intervene? Commonweal 85:553-5 F 17 '67
MAD (periodical)
Mad morality: an exposé. V. Eller. Christian Cent 84:1647-9 D 27 '67
MADAGASCAR. See Malagasy
MADAME Butterfly; opera. See Puccini, G.
MADAR, Olga M.
UAW structure emphasizes recreation, leisuretime activities and conservation. por Parks & Rec 2:31+ N '67
MADARIAGA, Salvador de
Dangerous lure of parrotland. por Sat R 50: 17-19+ Ap 22 '67
MADDEN, Don
Whimsey of Don Madden, a children's book illustrator. J. H. Michel. il Am Artist 31: 24-9+ S '67
MADDOCKS, Melvin
Behind the scenes at Snow's powerama. Life 62:10 My 5 '67
Brilliant hobbyist of modern infernos; P. Bowles. Life 63:8 Jl 21 '67
Knuckle-hard code of the barrio. Life 62:8 Je 9 '67
MADDOX, Gaynor
[Monthly column on cookery] See issues of Today's health
MADDOX, George L.
GH poll; question of a uniform drinking age for young people throughout the United States? Good H 164:8+ Ja '67
MADDOX, Lester
Gone fishing. il por Newsweek 70:34+ S 25 '67
Lester Maddox as a leader of men. R. Reed. il por Esquire 68:120-3+ O '67
Lester Maddox: Puritan in the Statehouse. J. H. Baird. Reporter 37:19-22 O 5 '67
Lester's itching jaw. Newsweek 70:30 S 4 '67
Little governor. il Time 90:25 S 22 '67
Maddox of Georgia. R. Coles. New Repub 157:19-22 Ag 5 '67
Meaning of Lester Maddox. por Sat Eve Post 240:96 Ap 22 '67
People's choice. il por Newsweek 71:24 Ja 8 '68
Strange decorum of Lester Maddox. R. G. Sherrill. il por Nation 204:553-6 My 1 '67
You reckon they thought L was a nut? M. Frady. il pors Sat Eve Post 240:27-9+ Ap 22 '67
MADEIRA
See also
Gardens—Madeira
MADEJA, Stanley S.
Charcoal casting. Sch Arts 67:26-9 S '67

MADEMOISELLE (periodical)
Mademoiselle merit awards 1967. il Mlle 66:49- 54 Ja '68
Mademoiselle's college competitions. Mlle 66: 47 N '67
Mlle's guest editors: 1967. M. Scarbrough. il Mlle 65:222-3 Ag '67
MADISON, Wis.
Churches
When the U.W. peace crowd came to church; First Congregational church. H. M. Shetler. Christian Cent 84:420-2 Mr 29 '67
Police
On Wisconsin; activities against campus demonstrators. J. Ridgeway. New Repub 157: 8-10 N 4 '67
MADISON Square Garden. See New York (city) —Madison Square Garden
MADNESS in the family; story. See Saroyan, W.
MADNESS of us alone; story. See Donis, M.
MADOCS, Rita
Best regards to Mr Cary Grant; story. McCalls 94:62-3 Ag '67
Girl watcher; story. McCalls 94:68-9 Ap '67
I never thought of you as Henry; story. Redbook 128:74-5 F '67
Trouble with marriage; story. McCalls 94:94-5 S '67
MADRAS-type jacket; story. See Hawes, E.
MADRID
Galleries and museums
Return of the viceroys; Museum of the new world. N. L. Pellón. il Américas 19:35-41 Ap '67
Showcase in Spain; Institute of Hispanic culture. N. López Pellón. il Américas 19:32-5 N '67
See also
Prado museum
Historic houses, etc.
Travel notes. R. Joseph. Esquire 67:10+ F '67
Music
Notes from our correspondents. E. Haines. Hi Fi 17:18+ Ap '67
Point of maturity. E. Haines. il Hi Fi 17: MA24-5 Je '67
National library
Leonardo's lost notebooks. il Life 62:24-31 Mr 3 '67
MADRID. University. See Colleges and universities—Spain
MADSEN, Edna
Stitchery for the young child. Sch Arts 67:12- 13 D '67
MAFIA
Crime in the suburbs. il Newsweek 70:24 Jl 31 '67
From a governor and a D.A. an offer of resignation; reactions to articles concerning Cosa nostra's empire in Louisiana. S. Smith. il Life 63:34-6 S 29 '67
Hood's who; Chicago crime commission's directory. Time 90:21 N 3 '67
Mafia: how it bleeds New England. B. Davidson. il Sat Eve Post 240:27-31 N 18 '67
Mafia: shadow of evil on an island in the sun. B. Davidson. il Sat Eve Post 240:27- 37 F 25 '67
Methodological problems in the study of organized crime as a social problem. D. R. Cressey. bibliog f Ann Am Acad 374:101-12 N '67
Mob; empire of organized crime, its power, structure, tactics; with report by S. Smith. il Life 63:15-23+ S 1; 91-102+ S 8 '67
Mob; how the Mafia penetrates respectable segments of our society; with account by S. Smith and W. Lambert. il Life 64:44-51 Ja 5 '68
We can break the grip of the mob. Life 63:4 S 8 '67
Your land is hoodland; Costa nostra families. il Life 63:20-1 S 1 '67
MAGARSHACK, David
Introduction to the Pasternak letters. Vogue 151:104 Ja 1 '68
(tr) See Pasternak, B. Intimate letters of Pasternak
MAGAZINE articles. See Periodical literature
MAGAZINE fiction. See Fiction in periodicals and newspapers

MAGNETIC resonance—*Continued*
Optical methods for studying Hertzian resonances; tr. of address, December 12, 1966. A. Kastler. bibliog il Science 158:214-21 O 13 '67

MAGNETIC resonance, Nuclear. See Nuclear magnetic resonance

MAGNETIC shielding. See Shielding (electricity)

MAGNETIC stars. See Magnetism, Stellar

MAGNETIC surveys. See Magnetism, Terrestrial

MAGNETIC tape
Automatic transports; at New York's Consumer electronics show. I. Berger. Sat R 50:51 Jl 29 '67
Biasing in magnetic tape recording. J. G. McKnight. il Electr World 78:34-6+ Ag '67
Big boom in tiny tape. R. Freas. il Pop Mech 129:140-3+ Ja '68
DuPont goes on record with a magnetic tape; Crolyn. il Bsns W p 172 Je 24 '67
How to select magnetic sound recording tapes. J. Kempler. il Electr World 78:27-31+ Ag '67
Innovations on the threshold but not past the door; Crolyn, a new tape coating. N. Eisenberg. Hi Fi 18:36 Ja '68
New pop-in tape cartridge. R. Gibson. House & Gard 132:42+ O '67
Poured vs. laminated striping. J. Wesson. U S Camera 30:32 S '67
Right tape for the job. J. Rahm. il Hi Fi 17:52-5 Ag '67
Tape cartridges, a progress report. Hi Fi 17: 38 Ag '67
  See also
Tape recordings

MAGNETIC tape players
Automatic transports; at New York's Consumer electronics show. I. Berger. Sat R 50:51 Jl 29 '67

MAGNETISM
Domain walls in computers of the future. A. Ewing. il Sci N 91:436-7 My 6 '67
Ferrites in GI series. Sci N 92:299 S 23 '67
Magnetic properties of materials. F. Keffer. il Sci Am 217:222-4+ S '67
Stable magnetic remanence in antiferromagnetic goethite. D. W. Strangway and others. bibliog il Science 158:785-7 N 10 '67
  See also
International conference on magnetics
Magnets
Thermomagnetism

MAGNETISM, Lunar
  See also
Magnetic fields (cosmic physics)

MAGNETISM, Stellar
Planetary magnetic fields and rotation. R. T. Brown. bibliog Science 158:674 N 3 '67

MAGNETISM, Terrestrial
Aftermath of a cataclysm; reversal of the earth's magnetic field. il Time 89:44 My 12 '67
Alpha-hematite; stable remanence and memory. R. W. Smith and M. Fuller. bibliog il Science 156:1130-3 My 26 '67
Antarctic radiolaria, magnetic reversals, and climate change. J. D. Hays and N. D. Opdyke. bibliog il Science 158:1001-11 N 24 '67
Canada's unappreciated role as scientific innovator; magnetic surveys and the theory of convection in the earth's mantle; theories of J. T. Wilson and L. W. Morley. J. Lear. il Sat R 50:45-50 S 2 '67
Earth is viewed as dc. generator. Aviation W 87:19 N 27 '67
Earth's magnetic field & color TV. Electr World 77:71 Ja '67
Geomagnetic polarity change and faunal extinction in the southern ocean. N. D. Watkins and H. G. Goodell. bibliog il Science 156:1083-7 My 26 '67
Kiaman magnetic interval in the western United States. B. E. McMahon and D. W. Strangway. bibliog il Science 155:1012-13 F 24 '67
Local geomagnetic events associated with displacements on the San Andreas fault. S. Breiner and R. L. Kovach. bibliog il Science 158:116-18 O 6 '67
Magnetic anomalies over the mid-Atlantic ridge near 27°N. J. D. Phillips. bibliog il Science 157:920-3 Ag 25 '67
Magnetic boundaries in the North Atlantic Ocean. J. R. Heirtzler and D. E. Hayes. bibliog il Science 157:185-7 Jl 14 '67
Magnetic clues help date the past. K. F. Weaver. il Nat Geog Mag 131:696-701 My '67

Motions of the earth's core and mantle, and variations of the main geomagnetic field. R. Hide. bibliog Science 157:55-6 Jl 7 '67
Paleomagnetic field reversals and cosmic radiation. C. J. Waddington. bibliog Science 158:913-15 N 17 '67
Paleomagnetism: United States-Japan committee on scientific cooperation. A. Cox and N. Kawai. Science 155:724 F 10 '67
Reversals of the earth's magnetic field. A. Cox and others. il Sci Am 216:44-54 bibliog (p 146) F '67
Tektites and geomagnetic reversals. B. P. Glass and B. C. Heezen. il Sci Am 217:32-8 Jl '67
Tertiary sediment from the East Pacific rise. L. H. Burckle and others. bibliog il Science 157:537-40 Ag 4 '67
Under the spreading sea floor. Sci Am 217: 40+ Ag '67
  See also
Van Allen radiation belts

MAGNETITE
Lepidocrocite, an apatite mineral, and magnetite in teeth of chitons, polyplacophora. H. A. Lowenstam. bibliog il Science 156: 1373-5 Je 9 '67

MAGNETIZED plastics. See Plastics, Magnetized

MAGNETOHYDRODYNAMIC generators. See Electric generators

MAGNETOHYDRODYNAMICS
Army studies hybrid rocket MHD power for lasers. R. Lindsey. il Aero Tech 21:48-9 Ag 14 '67
MHD: a cloudy future. il Sci N 93:5-6 Ja 6 '68

MAGNETOMETERS
He knows where to drill for water. G. L. Morris. il Pop Mech 128:124-6+ O '67

MAGNETS
Advances in superconducting magnets. W. B. Sampson and others. il Sci Am 216:114-23 bibliog(p 152) Mr '67
Glassy magnets. Sci Am 217:42+ Jl '67
Superconducting magnets in high-energy physics. M. Derrick. bibliog il Science 155: 325-31 O 20 '67

MAGNIN, Joseph, company
Swinger. il Newsweek 70:84 O 23 '67

MAGNITUDES of stars. See Stars—Magnitudes

MAGNUSON, Warren Grant
Excerpt from address before World affairs council, March 6, 1967. Cong Digest 46:176+ Je '67

MAGRAW, Daniel B. See Magraw, R. M. jt. auth.

MAGRAW, Richard M. and Magraw, D. B.
Automating medicine; excerpt from Ferment in medicine. Sat R 50:66-9 O 7 '67

MAGUIRE, Francis
Ménage à trois; poem. America 117:616 N 18 '67

MAGUIRE, Jan
Contemporary music at full tilt. Hi Fi 17: MA24-5+ Ap '67
Festival in Berlin. Sat R 50:75+ N 11 '67
Iannis Xenakis; formula for new music. Sat R 50:51-3 Je 24 '67
International music weeks. Hi Fi 17:MA28 F '67
Munch and the Orchestre de Paris. Sat R 50: 46-7 D 30 '67
Out of decay, an operatic prophet. Hi Fi 17: MA28-9+ Mr '67
30th biennale. Sat R 50:108-9 O 14 '67

MAGUIRE, Richard
Surgeon to a dead patient; poem. Sat R 50:58 Ap 1 '67

MAHABHARATA
Ramayana and the Mahabharata; symposium, with excerpt from poems and with paintings. bibliog il UNESCO Courier 20:4-45 D '67
  Bhagavadgita
Mahabharata. K. Rexroth. Sat R 50:24+ S 30 '67

MAHAN, Larry
Cowboy and the Comanche. C. Lofting. il pors Flying 81:82-6 D '67
Grey flannel cowboy. il por Time 89:49 Mr 31 '67
Roughest rides to richest. T. C. Brody. il pors Sports Illus 27:20-2+ D 18 '67

MAHARAJAS. See India—Nobility

MAHARISHI Mahesh (Indian yogi) See Mahesh

el MAHDI, Sayed Sadik
Tolerant young man. Time 89:40 Mr 17 '67

MAHENDRA, king of Nepal
Address to Assembly; summary, November 6, 1967. UN Mo Chron 4:62-3 D '67
King Mahendra of Nepal visits the United States: exchange of greetings and toasts, with joint communique, November 1, 1967. Dept State Bul 57:707-9 N 27 '67

about

An evening at the de Gaulles'. P. Feldkamp. Atlan 219:114-18 My '67

MAHER, Arthur J.
Mainly for men. Am Home 70:32+ Ja; 44+ Mr; 30+ My; 30 Je '67

MAHESH (Indian yogi)
Chief guru of the western world. B. Lefferts. il pors N Y Times Mag p44-5+ D 17 '67
Guru. il Newsweek 70:67 D 18 '67
Invitation to instant bliss. L. Wainwright. Life 63:26 N 10 '67
Soothsayer for everyman. il por Time 90:86 O 20 '67

MAHEU, René
For Florence and Venice. UNESCO Courier 20:4-5 Ja '67
Intruders. UNESCO Courier 20:23-4 F '67
Third of the world's children; UNESCO chief describes crisis; excerpts from address, October 1967. Library J 92:4205-6 N 15 '67
To build a new order in the world; reply to encyclical On the development of peoples by Pope Paul VI. por UNESCO Courier 20: 36-9 Ag '67

MAHLER, Fritz
Japan and Korea. Hi Fi 17:MA29 Ag '67

MAHLER, Gustav
Bernstein's Mahler: a prophecy fulfilled. M. N. Kanny. il por Am Rec G 34:278-81 D '67
Bernstein's majestic Mahler 8th. i. Kolodin. il Sat R 50:65 Ja 28 '67
Georg Solti's Mahler Second. J. Diether. Am Rec G 34:46-8 S '67
Gustav Mahler, by N. Cardus. Review
Am Rec G por 33:834+ My '67. J. Diether
Leinsdorf's Mahler Third. J. Diether. il Am Rec G 34:100-2 O '67
Leonard Bernstein is not a man to pass up such a challenge. Mahler's Symphony of a thousand. D. Newlin. por Am Rec G 33: 416-17 Ja '67
Das lied von der erde, three new sets and three perspectives. M. Malloch. por Hi Fi 17:69-70 Mr '67
Mahler: his time has come. L. Bernstein. por Hi Fi 17:51-4 S '67
Mahler symphonies on records. B. Jacobson. Hi Fi 17:55-9 S '67
Man who speaks to a high-strung generation. por Time 89:54+ Je 23 '67
Music to my ears; unofficial Mahler week. I. Kolodin. Sat R 50:28 My 13 '67
Polished and quite beautiful Mahler Third. J. Diether. Am Rec G 33:791-3 My '67
Recordings. M. Mayer. Esquire 68:28+ D '67
Records:
Des knaben wunderhorn. Opera N 31:34 Mr 11 '67
Das lied von der erde. Opera N 31:34 Ap 8 '67
Second and Third symphonies. Opera N 32:30 O 14 '67
Symphony No. 8. Opera N 31:34 My 13 '67
Three at once: Das lied. J. Diether. il por Am Rec G 33:722-7 My '67
Triumph by Lenny and Mahler. S. Kanfer Life 63:12 N 3 '67

MAHLER, Victor C.
Miniature megastructure. Arch Forum 127: 35-43 S '67

MAHLMANN, Ernest R.
Panegyric for Panay. il por Am Heritage 18: 51 O '67

MAHON, George Herman
Is Congress neglecting the poor? excerpts from address, July 31, 1967. U S News 63: 46 Ag 14 '67

about

George Mahon wields a powerful ax. il por Bsns W p 110-12+ F 18 '67
Mahon's stacked deck. Reporter 37:17 S 7 '67

MAHONEY, David Joseph, 1923-
New ginger at Canada dry. il por Bsns W p58-60+ Ag 5 '67

MAHONEY, Mary Reeves
Children's pageant; poem. Christian Cent 84: 1590 D 13 '67

MAHONEY, Stephen
After 116 years, a plump little Dutch prince. Life 62:46-46A My 12 '67

How a ready-made can work out. Life 63: 113-14 S 8 '67
Nature does most of the work. Life 62:85-6 Je 30 '67

MAHONEY, Tom
Life and death of Casey Jones. Read Digest 90:25-6+ Ap '67

MAHONEY, William E.
Bird watcher; poem. Nat Parks Mag 41:15 O '67

MAIDENHAIR tree. See Ginkgo

MAIDS (servants) See Household employees

MAIER, William
Young biddy; story. McCalls 94:84-5 Mr '67

MAIL advertising. See Advertising, Direct mail

MAIL boxes. See Mailboxes

MAIL cars. See Railway mail service—Cars

MAIL censorship. See Postal censorship

MAIL fraud. See Fraud

MAIL handling
Post office seeks proposals on $23 million package. Tech W 20:35 Mr 20 '67

MAIL order advertising. See Books—Advertising

MAIL order business
Bang! bang! you're dead; mail order guns. C. Bakal. il Esquire 68:44-5 Jl '67
Europeans take fancy to buying by the book; catalogue houses. il Bsns W p86-7+ Je 3 '67
Mail order pointers: how to handle returns; excerpt from Successful selling of antiques by mail. C. H. Laestar and M. E. Laestar. Hobbies 72:117 My '67
Note on mail-order insurance. Consumer Bul 50:39 Ag '67
Selected products to order by mail with confidence. N. Pierce. il Parents Mag 42:96-7 Ja '67
Twelve suggestions for successful antique buying by mail order; excerpt from Successful selling of antiques by mail. Hobbies 72:80-1+ Ag '67
What records you must keep; excerpt from Successful selling of antiques by mail. Hobbies 72:120-1 S '67
You too can buy by mail; the publisher and the mail-order market. D. Dempsey. Sat R 50:30+ Jl 15 '67
See also
Montgomery Ward and company

Taxation

Mail order wins a round; states have no power to tax out-of-state merchandisers. Bsns W p44 My 13 '67

MAIL robberies. See Robberies and assaults

MAIL service. See Postal service

MAIL service, Air. See Air mail service

MAILBOXES
Beats requirement for curbside mail boxes. Am City 82:38+ F '67
First-class home for a mailbox. il Pop Sci 191:148-9 S '67
How to be nice to your mailman, all delivery-men, and also to first time quests. il Sunset 133:96-7 Ap '67
Rear-windows mailbox saves you steps. A. Winn. il Pop Mech 128:171 D '67

MAILER, Norman
Some dirt in the talk: a candid history of an existential movie called Wild 90. por Esquire 68:190-4+ D '67

about

Bullfight. W. D. Patterson. Sat R 51:105 Ja 13 '68
Deer park; dramatization of novel. Criticism
Commonweal 85:657-8 Mr 10 '67
Life 62:8 F 24 '67
Nation 204:252-3 F 20 '67
New Yorker 42:116 F 11 '67
Newsweek 69:109+ F 13 '67
Reporter 36:47-8 Ap 6 '67
Sat R 50:45 Mr 4 '67
Time il 89:58 F 10 '67
Vogue 149:94 Ap 1 '67
Huntsville public library rocked by Mailer book. Library J 93:138 Ja 15 '68
Lark in race for presidency. G. Hicks. Sat R 50:39-40 S 16 '67
Mailer writes dirty about aurora borealis. W. Schott. Life 63:8 S 15 '67
Norman Mailer today. J. Toback. Commentary 44:68-76 O '67

MAIN, Jeremy
Computer time-sharing, everyman at the console. Fortune 76:88-91+ Ag '67

MAIN, Jeremy—*Continued*
First real international bankers. Fortune 76:143-6+ D '67
Industry still has something to learn about Congress. Fortune 75:128-9+ F '67
Kempers of Kansas City. Fortune 75:170-2+ Ap '67
Slow getaway for the auto market. Fortune 75:110-15+ Je 1 '67
Stocks of the 200. Fortune 76:151-2+ S 15 '67

MAIN battle tank. See Tanks, Military

MAINAU ISLAND
Mike Frome; culture of the landscape. M. Frome. Am For 73:3+ Ag '67

MAINE
My Maine islands. J. T. Starr. il Am For 73:38-41+ F '67
See also
Architecture, Domestic—Maine
Education—Maine
Hunting—Maine
Wilderness areas—Maine

Description and travel
Discover the many moods of Maine. il Home Gard 54:42-3 Jl '67
Special time in Maine. E. Horan. bibliog il Yachting 122:54-6+ Ag '67

MAINO, Jeannette
Game; poem. Ladies Home J 84:168 My '67

MAINTENANCE of prices. See Price maintenance by industry

MAISEL, Albert Q.
End, at last, to gout? Read Digest 90:113-17 Je '67

MAIWANDWAL, Mohammed Hashim
Prime Minister of Afghanistan visits the United States; exchange of greetings, exchange of toasts, and joint statement, March 28, 1967. Dept State Bul 56:627-32 Ap 17 '67

MAIZE. See Corn

MAJOLICA
Italian majolica; a summary based on an American collection. J. P. Kassebaum. il Antiques 91:202-6 F '67

MAJOR, Randolph T.
Ginkgo, the most ancient living tree. bibliog Science 157:1270-3 S 15 '67

MAKAPUU Point lighthouse. See Lighthouses

MAKARENKO, Anton Semenovich
What the Soviet Spock taught. T. Frankel. il por N Y Times Mag p93-6 My 7 67

MAKAVEJEV, Dusan
Movers. A. Sarris. por Sat R 50:16 D 23 '67

MAKE me chased, Lord; story. See McInerny, R.

MAKE me no match; story. See Gordon, E. E.

MAKE-up
Beauty bulletin. il Vogue 150:132-5 S 15 '67
Beauty life. il Mlle 64:132-5 F '67
Beauty life: making up for men. il Mlle 65:68-9 Jl '67
Close-up on three G.E. makeovers. il Mlle 65:254-9 Ag '67
Eileen Ford's book of model beauty; excerpts. E. Ford. il Ladies Home J 85:30-1, 68-71 Ja '68
Eye spy. il McCalls 95:114-19 D '67
Focus on your eyes. V. S. Stitt. il Parents Mag 42:54 N '67
For every girl on your Christmas list. il Seventeen 26:118-19 D '67
Great new beauty opportunities. il Vogue 150:196-203 O 1 '67
Holiday eyes. il Seventeen 26:104-5 D '67
Letting George do it; how G. Masters made up Lynda Bird Johnson. il Newsweek 70:31 D 18 '67
Makeup shades for costume colors. McCalls 94:161 Ap '67
Makeup today is subtle, natural. Farm J 91:58-9 Ag '67
More life to your face. A. Thompson. Am Home 70:26 Mr '67
Party face put-on. il Look 31:52-5 N 28 '67
Princess and the paper lash. il Life 62:63-4 Mr 31 '67
Project: you. il Ladies Home J 84:54 F '67
Round-the-world beauty news. il Good H 165:104-15+ O '67
Summer make-up: a light touch. il Seventeen 26:80-1 Jl '67
Twelve-minute makeup. il Mlle 64:156-9 Mr '67
Twiggy. il Seventeen 26:116-19 Mr '67
Twiggy talks about the Twiggy look. Twiggy. Ladies Home J 84:62 Je '67

Watch the shadows, the gleam; eye make-up. il Vogue. 149:116-17 Ap 15 '67
What to do when your looks go wrong; twenty-five good-looking women's recipes. il Vogue 149:128-31+ Ap 15 '67
See also
Beauty, Personal

MAKE-up, Theatrical
Makeup: the reality of illusion; performer becomes what he is not. F. Bowers. il Opera N 31:8-12 Mr 11 '67
Million dollars worth of make-up obliterates some famous faces. il Life 63:82-3 Ag 18 '67

Anecdotes, facetiae, satire, etc.
Dab of powder, a dab of paint; TV make-up for R. Nixon. G. Ace. Sat R 50:6 D 16 '67
Frog week at the 7-11, near West Hollywood. F. P. Tullius. New Yorker 43:40-2 S 9 '67

MAKOW, David
Brain scans by ultrasound. il Sci N 91:62 Ja 21 '67

MAKOW brain scanner. See Medical instruments and apparatus

MAKROPULOS case; opera. See Janáček, L.

MAL secco disease of citrus
Nobiletin is main fungistat in tangerines resistant to mal secco. A. Ben-Aziz. bibliog il Science 155:1026-7 F 24 '67

MALAGASY

Description and travel
Madagascar, island at the end of the earth. L. Marden. il Nat Geog Mag 132:443-87 O '67

MALAMUD, Bernard
Bernard Malamud. J. Featherstone. por Atlan 219:95-8 Mr '67

MALAMUD, Daniel I.
Do child psychologists make good parents? Redbook 130:47+ Ja '68

MALANGA, Gerard
Human sunlight: a sonnet; Nice things; Coming up for air; poems. Poetry 109:327-9 F '67

MALANIA, Fae E.
Rejoice and be glad; excerpt from The quantity of a hazelnut. Redbook 130:35-42 Ja '68

MALARIA
Eperythrozoon coccoides: influence on course of infection of plasmodium chabaudi in mouse. K. J. Ott and L. A. Stauber. bibliog il Science 155:1546-8 Mr 24 '67
Sickle-cell trait in human biological and cultural evolution; excerpt from address, January 1967. S. L. Wiesenfeld. bibliog il Science 157:1134-40 S 8 '67
Tiny enemy in Vietnam; falciparum strain. il Life 63:53-4+ N 24 '67

Prevention and control
Antimalarial activity of tetrahydrohomopteroic acid. R. L. Kisliuk and others. bibliog il Science 156:1616-17 Je 23 '67
SPQ against malaria. Time 89:56 F 3 '67
See also
Quinine

MALAWI
Heroes or Neros? il Time 89:46 Ap 14 '67
See also
Economic assistance in Malawi

MALAWISTA, Stephen E. and Bensch, K. G.
Human polymorphonuclear leukocytes: demonstration of microtubules and effect of colchicine. bibliog Science 156:521-2 Ap 28 '67

MALAYSIA
Malaysia after confrontation. D. Warner. Reporter 36:33-5 Ja 26 '67
Ten fruitful years. Time 90:20 S 8 '67
Tunku Abdul Rahman's Malaysian miracle. D. Reed. Read Digest 90:139-44 F '67
See also
Kuala Lumpur

MALCOLM X
Malcolm X is alive. R. A. Schroth. America 116:594 Ap 22 '67
Minister Malcolm; orator profundo. N. H. Boulware. por Negro Hist Bul 30:12-14 N '67
Redemption of Malcolm X. R. A. Schroth. Cath World 205:346-52 S '67

MALCOLM, Donald
Department of amplification. New Yorker 42:101-3 Ja 28 '67

MALCOLM, Janet
Books (cont) New Yorker 43:157-60+ D 16 '67

MALDONADO-DENIS, Manuel
Situation of Cuba's intellectuals; tr. by J. Lara-Braud. Christian Cent 85:78-80 Ja 17 '68

MALE birth control drug. See Contraceptives
MALE coiffure. See Hairdressing
MALE cosmetics. See Cosmetics for men
MALE sterility. See Sterility
MALECELA, John W. S.
United Nations and the decolonization of non-self-governing territories. UN Mo Chron 4:84-96 Ag '67
MALFORMATIONS. See Deformities
MALI (Republic)
Industries
Mali. T. E. Hilton. bibliog il Focus 18:1-6 S '67
MALIC dehydrogenases. See Dehydrogenases
MALIGNANT tumors. See Cancer
MALIK, Adam
Promise in Indonesia. For Affairs 46:292-303 Ja '68
MALIK, Charles Habib
Domestic public affairs; address, April 20, 1967. Vital Speeches 33:538-41 Je 15 '67
MALINA, Mylan M. See Webb, R. B. jt. auth.
MALINOVSKII, Rodion fAkovlevich
Hard-liner moves up. U S News 62:24 Ap 24 '67
MALINOWSKI, Bronislaw
Diary of an anthropologist. M. Harris. Natur Hist 76:72+ Ag '67
Games Malinowski played. P. Gallagher. New Repub 156:24-6 Je 17 '67
Melancholy in Melanesia. J. Middleton. por Sat R 50:65 Ap 8 '67
MALKIN, Audree
(comp) Business books of 1966. Library J 92:976-8 Mr 1 '67
MALKIN, Lawrence
Looking backward. Commentary 44:84-9 Jl '67
MALLAN, Lloyd
It's not safe to read. M. Mintz. New Repub 156:28-30 Mr 25 '67
MALLARD (airplane) See Airplanes, Amphibious
MALLARD multi-nation communications system. See Communications, Military
MALLAS, John H. and Kreimer, Evered
Messier album. See issues of Sky and telescope
MALLÉ, Luigi
Barons and beggars of Giacomo Ceruti. Art N 66:26-9+ Mr '67
MALLEA, Eduardo
Inner silence of Eduardo Mallea. M. Belloni. il Américas 19:20-7 O '67
MALLOCH, William
Das lied von der erde, three new sets and three perspectives. Hi Fi 17:69-70 Mr '67
MALLORY battery company
Where tiny cells power big sales. il Bsns W p60-2+ Ja 14 '67
MALMö, Sweden
Music
Report: Malmo; production of Mozart's Nozze di Figaro. S. A. K. Roewade. Opera N 32:32 Ja 6 '68
MALMSTADT, Howard
Electronics training for all. W. A. Stocklin. Electr World 78:6 D '67
MALNUTRITION. See Children—Nutrition; Diet, Deficient
MALOFF, Saul
House that lost its head; Pentagon besieged. Commonweal 87:135-6 N 3 '67
Negro's inheritance; a culture of poverty. Commonweal 87:449-50 Ja 12 '68
MALONE, Mike
On the boards. W. Como. por Dance Mag 41:18 D '67
MALONE, Thomas F.
Weather modification; implications of the new horizons in research; excerpts from address, December 28, 1966. bibliog Science 156:897-901 My 19 '67
MALONEY, Elbert S.
Auto pilot, able assistant for the skipper. Motor B 120:42-5 D '67
Boat handling with the seasoned skipper. Motor B 120:46-7+ S '67
FCC proposals for single sideband and VHF radiophones hit by delegates from other nations at RTCM meeting. Motor B 120:93-5 Jl '67
Language of electronics. Motor B 120:30-3 S '67
New charts. See issues of Motor boating
MALONEY, George A.
Orthodox church in Greece today. America 116:340-5 Mr 11 '67

MALONEY, Joseph A.
Gadfly with a sting. il por Time 89:40 Je 23 '67
MALONEY, Ralph
No man on Ocracoke. Atlan 219:122+ Mr '67
What I need don't come in suitcases; story. Atlan 220:113-15 O '67
MALLS, Shopping. See Business districts
MALPASS, Eric
By the light of the moon; story. Redbook 129:145-71 S '67
Speed the parting guest; story. Redbook 130: 52-3 Ja '68
You can't win with Gaylord; story. Redbook 128:72-3 Mr '67
MALPIGHI, Marcello
Marcello Malpighi and the evolution of embryology, by H. B. Adelmann. Review Sci Am 216:135-6+ Ap '67. M. T. Braverman; Reply. W. Montagna. 217:6-7 Jl '67
MALRAUX, André
Letter from Paris. Genêt. New Yorker 43: 188+ N 11 '67
Malraux's fate. il por Newsweek 70:60 S 11 '67
Mandarin's anti-memoirs. por Time 90:24 S 8 '67
MALTA
Malta, the unique. V. Cowles. Vogue 149: 99+ F 1 '67
Painful decision; British base to phase out. Newsweek 69:54+ F 13 '67
Tenant moves out; Great Britain plans to remove garrison. Time 89:36 F 17 '67
MALTÊTE, René
Funny thing happened. il U S Camera 30:68-9 N '67
MALTSEV, Vladimir, family
On location in Rostov: filming the new revolution. D. Smith. il Nation 204:268-72 F 27 '67
MALTZ, Albert
Going to the baths; letter. New Repub 157: 34+ S 30 '67
MALVESTA, Daniel, and Ronayne, E. L.
Cops in the classroom. NEA J 56:71 D '67
MALVILLE, J. McKim
Coronal studies at the eclipse in Bolivia. por Sky & Tel 33:136-9 Mr '67
MAMA, La. See New York (city)—Theater
MAMAS and the Papas (singers) See Singers
MAMEY
Mammea: excerpt from The mamey. J. F. Morton. il Horticulture 45:32-3 D '67
MAMMALIAN cells. See Cells
MAMMALS
American Jurassic symmetrodonts and Rhaetic pantotheres. A. W. Crompton and F. A. Jenkins, jr. bibliog il Science 155:1006-9 F 24 '67
Visual and nonvisual auditory systems in mammals. J. M. Harrison and R. Irving; reply with rejoinder. B. Masterton and I. T. Diamond. bibliog il Science 155:1696-7 Mr 31 '67
See also
Carnivora
Cetacea
Embryology—Mammals
Whales

Anecdotes, facetiae, satire, etc.
Snouters, by Harald Stümpke. G. Steiner. il Natur Hist 76:8-13 Ap '67
MAMMARY cancer. See Cancer
MAMMARY glands
Colostral immunoglobulin-A: synthesis in vitro of T-chain by rabbit mammary gland. R. Asofsky and P. A. Small, jr. bibliog il Science 158:932-3 N 17 '67
Hormone-dependent differentiation of immature mouse mammary gland in vitro. A. E. Voytovich and Y. J. Topper. bibliog il Science 158:1326-7 D 8 '67
Hormone-dependent differentiation of mammary gland: sequence of action of hormones in relation to cell cycle. D. H. Lockwood and others. bibliog il Science 156: 945-6 My 19 '67
MAMMEA americana. See Mamey
MAMMOTH CAVE NATIONAL PARK
Some problems and opportunities at Mammoth Cave National Park. P. M. Smith. il Nat Parks Mag 41:14-19 F '67
MAN
Can we survive nihilism? J. Milton's Satan and A. Camus's Sisyphus. T. Merton. Sat R 50:16-19 Ap 15 '67
Cryonics and the purpose of life. R. C. W. Ettinger. Christian Cent 84:1250-3 O 4 '67; Discussion. 84:1656-8 D 27 '67

MAN—*Continued*
Difference of man and the **difference** it
makes, by M. J. Adler. Review
Sat R 50:30-1 N 18 '67. H. Read
Time 91:60+ Ja 12 '68
End of the beginning. R. Shinsheimer. Bul
Atomic Sci 23:8-12 F '67
Love's body, by N. O. Brown. Review
Commentary 43:71-5 F '67. H. Marcuse;
Reply. N. O. Brown. 43:83-4 Mr '67
Nation 204:405-7 Mr 27 '67. K. Burke
Man's new dialogue with man; Time essay.
Time 89:34-5 Je 30 '67
Naked ape; excerpt. D. Morris. il Life 63:
94D-98+ D 22 '67
Politics and the sacred; man's ambivalent
concept of the sacred. T. Eagleton. Com-
monweal 87:402-6 D 29 '67
Unpalatable man. Time 89:46 F 24 '67
See also
Anthropology
Civilization
Evolution
History
Human nature
Human relations
Humanism
Man, Primitive
Race problems

Attitude and movement
Antiquity of human walking. J. Napier. il
Sci Am 216:56-66 Ap '67

Constitution
What man can make of man; genetic programming; competence of biologists to determine the optimal genotype. K. H. Hertz.
Christian Cent 84:807-10 Je 21 '67

Food habits
See Food habits

Influence of environment
Can man survive life in big cities? interview.
R. Dubos. il U S News 62:64-7 My 1 '67
Coming era of ecumenopolis. C. A. Doxiadis.
Sat R 50:11-14 Mr 18 '67
Environment for man, ed. by W. R. Ewald,
jr. Review
Sat R 50:23-4 Jl 29 '67. J. H. Plumb
Heredity-environment problem. F. S. Meyer.
Nat R 19:1074 O 3 '67
National character in the perspective of cul-
tural geography. J. O. M. Broek. bibliog f
Ann Am Acad 370:8-15 Mr '67
Racial studies: Academy states position on
call for new research; statement of National
academy of sciences. Science 158:892-3 N
17 '67
World around us: toward an architecture of
joy and human sensibility. B. Thompson.
il Arch Rec 142:153-8 S '67

Influence on nature
Captives and cultigens. M. Bates. il Natur
Hist 77:22+ Ja '68
Communication with our outdoor heritage;
address, November 1, 1966. H. Hatcher. il
Am For 73:14-17+ Ja '67
Economic development and its long-run en-
vironmental implications. J. H. Cumber-
land. il Nat Parks Mag 41:11-13 N '67
Geotechnology objectives demand imaginative
planning. A. F. Spilhaus. il Tech W 20:68-
71 Ja 28 '67
Historical roots of our ecologic crisis; ad-
dress, December 26, 1966. L. T. White, jr.
Science 155:1203-7 Mr 10 '67; Same with
title What hath man wrought? il Américas
19:11-19 My '67; Same with title Saint
Francis and the ecologic backlash. il Horizon
9:42-7 Sum '67
Man, culture, evolution and environment.
J. R. Jablonski. Christian Cent 84:495-8 Ap
19 '67
Mike Frome; culture of the landscape at
Mainau Island. M. Frome. Am For 73:3+
Ag '67
Naturalist at large; environmental deteriora-
tion. M. Bates. il Natur Hist 76:8+ Je '67
Needed now: a department of environment.
R. Starnes. Field & S 72:14+ Ag '67
Now we have tools to break nature's sys-
tem. il Pop Gard 18:30-1 D '67
Oxygen crisis. Newsweek 71:45 Ja 8 '68
We have a nonsystem approach to our en-
vironment. il Pop Gard 18:22 D '67
When I plant a tree. H. R. Hodgson. il Am
For 73:26-7+ Ja '67
Why worry about nature? R. L. Means. Sat R
50:13-15 D 2 '67

Origin and antiquity
Cerumen in American Indians: genetic im-
plications of sticky and dry types. N. L.
Petrakis and others. bibliog il Science 158:
1192-3 D 1 '67
Early man in South America. E. P. Lanning
and T. C. Patterson. il Sci Am 217:44-50
bibliog(p 154) N '67
Face is familiar; concerning The naked ape.
Newsweek 71:80-1 Ja 22 '68
God seen everywhere; letter to the editor.
R. G. Schipf. Am For 73:4-5+ Ja '67
Man and pre-man: new finds. il Sci N 91:83
Ja 28 '67
See also
Apes, Fossil
Evolution
Man, Prehistoric
Stone age

Periodicity
See Periodicity
MAN, Effect of altitude on. See Altitude, In-
fluence of
MAN, Erect position of. See Man—Attitude
and movement
MAN, ISLE OF
Little places. il Newsweek 70:39 Ag 21 '67
MAN, Prehistoric
Ancient remains; discovery at Old Crow
flats, Yukon. Sci N 91:510 My 27 '67
Ascent of man. B. Tufty. il Sci N 91:188-9
F 25 '67
Bones of contention; two bench marks on evo-
lutionary path revised. Newsweek 69:102+
F 13 '67
Earliest New World men. Sci Am 216:57 Je
'67
40,000-year-old Americans. Sci Digest 62:66
Ag '67
Hominid humeral fragment from early pleis-
tocene of northwestern Kenya. B. Patter-
son and W. W Howells. bibliog il Science
156:64-6 Ap 7 '67
Man and pre-man: new finds. il Sci N 91:83
Ja 28 '67
Naturalist at large; man's food relations. M.
Bates. Natur Hist 76:18+ Ag '67
New World man; find at Valsequillo gravels,
Mexico. il Sci N 91:447 My 13 '67
Older and older? discovery of bone in Kenya,
Africa. il Sr Schol 90:17-18 F 10 '67
Oldest australopithecus. Sci Am 216:52 Mr '67
Overkill, not overchill; theories of Paul
Martin. il Time 90:94 D 8 '67
Peking man refound. B. Tufty. il Sci N 92:
592-3 D 16 '67
Pleistocene overkill; extinction of North
America's large mammals. P. S. Martin.
il Natur Hist 76:32-8 bibliog(p 105) D '67;
Reply with rejoinder. L. S. B. Leakey. 77:
73-5 Ja '68
Searching for the common link; manlike crea-
ture 20 million years ago. il Time 89:64-5
F 3 '67
Unraveling the age of earth and man. E. L.
Simons. il Natur Hist 76:52-9 F '67
See also
Man—Origin and antiquity
MAN, Primitive
Savage mind, by C. Lévi-Strauss. Review
Reporter 36:52 Ap 6 '67. R. Sklar
MAN, Size of. See Body size
MAN and nature. See Man—Influence on nature
MAN in the glass booth; drama. See Shaw, R.
MAN in the mirror; story. See Knowlton, R.
MAN-made lakes. See Lakes, Artificial
MAN of war birds. See Frigate birds
MAN on the corner; story. See Wallace, M.
MAN who stopped the square dance; story. See
Jordan, E. H.
MAN who washed his hands; drama. See
Thompson, W. C.
MANAGEMENT, Business. See Business man-
agement and organization
MANAGEMENT, Industrial. See Industrial
management and organization
MANAGEMENT consultants. See Business con-
sultants
MANAGEMENT costs. See Cost
MANAGEMENT games
Fun with the Future; Kaiser game called
Future. Duns R 89:38 Ja '67
Games executives play; community land use
game and other simulation games. il News-
week 70:86 N 27 '67

MANAGEMENT games—*Continued*
Profits set score at B-school tournament; Emory university's annual Intercollegiate business game. il Bsns W p 156-8 Mr 13 '67
Social problem-solvers; games devised by Abt associates. J. Ridgeway. New Repub 156: 18-20 Ap 8 '67

MANAGEMENT is not responsible; story. See Clay, G. R.

MANAGEMENT of children. See Children— Management and training

MANAGEMENT research, American foundation for. See American foundation for management research, incorporated

MANAGEMENT resources corporation. See Employment agencies

MANAGERS. See Executives

MANAGERS, Baseball. See Baseball managers

MANAGERS, Concert. See Concert managers

MANATEE COUNTY, Fla.
County water system proved best. P. A. Cessna. il Am City 82:105-7+ F '67
Fight air pollution before it starts. F. L. Cross, jr. and R. Ross. il Am City 82:101-3 S '67

MANATEES
Manatees, living lawn mowers. il Sci Digest 62:33-5 Ag '67

MANCHESTER, Harland
Two-way stretch in space. Pop Mech 127: 136-9 Ap '67
What you should know about flammable fabrics. Read Digest 90:37-8+ My '67

MANCHESTER, William
Chapter II; excerpts from The death of a President. Newsweek 69:22-4 Ja 30 '67
Death of a President; excerpts (cont) Look 31:40-6+ F 7: 42-8+ F 21: 50-66 Mr 7 '67
Manchester's own story; interview, ed. by J. M. Cannon and E. Kosner. por Newsweek 69:21-2 Ja 30 '67
William Manchester's own story. por Look 31:62-6+ Ap 4; 8 My 16 '67

about
Book. il por Newsweek 69:34-5 Ap 10 '67
Can it hit 1-million? Bsns W p28 Ap 1 '67
Chinoiserie. Reporter 36:14 F 9 '67
Death of a President: review of the reviews. P. K. Cuneo. America 116:684-5 My 6 '67
Death of Lancer; concerning first draft manuscript of Death of a President. por Newsweek 70:25 Jl 17 '67
Feud over Death of a President intensifies as Manchester attacks Kennedy family and aides. por Pub W 191:88-9 Ja 30 '67
Full record; L.B.J.'s inaugural oath after assassination; with photographs. Time 89: 19-21 F 24 '67
In the hours after Dallas: the book and the testimony; concerning The death of a President. il U S News 62:51-2 F 20 '67
JFK and LBJ: more untold stories; concerning his The death of a President. il U S News 62:36 Ja 30 '67
Look, Manchester sue N.Y. World journal tribune. Pub W 191:53 F 13 '67
Manchester affair, by J. Corry. Review Sat R 50:61 S 9 '67. S. W. Little
Manchester book: despite flaws & errors, a story that is larger than life or death. Time 89:22-3 Ap 7 '67
Manchester papers. J. Corry. il Esquire 67: 83:91+ Je '67
Manchester unexpurgated: from Death of Lancer to The death of a President; comparative study of successive versions of book. E. J. Epstein. bibliog f Commentary 44:25-31 Jl '67
Manchester story. Newsweek 69:95 Mr 27 '67
Mrs Kennedy reaches accord with Harper & Row and William Manchester. Pub W 191:222 Ja 23 '67
Outdoor life and The death of a President. Outdoor Life 140:32-3 O '67
Rage greater than grief; evaluation of and excerpts from The death of a President. M. Kempton. Atlan 219:98-100 My '67
Real villains of the William Manchester book. J. Crist. il Ladies Home J 84:60 Ap '67
Right to privacy. M. Mead. Redbook 128: 30+ Ap '67
To help you keep the record straight about that book; concerning his The death of a President. por U S News 62:66-7 F 6 '67
Trials of government-in-exile; graceless battle between the Kennedy family and W. Manchester. E. J. Hughes. Newsweek 69:20 F 6 '67
Truth as private property. A. Gingrich. Esquire 67:6+ Mr '67

Verdict on Manchester. Newsweek 69:90+ Ap 24 '67
Where was O'Donnell? Johnson's swearing-in after assassination. il Time 89:78 F 17 '67

MANCINI, Henry
Lively arts; interview, ed. by R. Hemming. por Sr Schol 90:17 F 3 '67

MANCUSO, Ben
One on the aisle. il U S Camera 30:54-5 Ag '67

MANDA, Robert F.
Hoyas. Horticulture 45:24-5+ Je '67

MANDAN Indians
O-kee-pa; excerpts, with editorial comment. G. Catlin. il Am Heritage 18:30-7+ O '67

MANDARIN porcelain. See Pottery, Chinese

MANDEL, H. George
Cancer dissemination. Science 158:958-60 N 17 '67

MANDELBAUM, Bernard
Justifying man's ways to man. Sat R 50:57-8 F 25 '67

MANDELBAUM, Edward
Nonphotographer looks at the medium; interview, ed. by J. Deschin. por Pop Phot 60: 22+ Je '67

MANDELBAUM, Ellen
Figure in the center. Art N 66:58-9+ S '67

MANDELBAUM, Herbert
Incinerators can meet tougher standards. Am City 82:97-8 Ag '67

MANDELBROT, Benoit
How long is the coast of Britain? statistical self-similarity and fractional dimension. bibliog Science 156:636-8 My 5 '67

MANDEL'SHTAM, Osip Emil'evich
(ed) See Ho-chi-Minh. Interview with Ho Chi Minh, 1923

about
Observations. C. Brown. Commentary 44:80 Ag '67

MANDER, John
Asian diary. Commentary 44:90-5 O '67

MANER, William
More than memory; story. Good H 164:96-7 Ap '67

MANESCU, Corneliu
Human rights day 10 December 1967; message. UN Mo Chron 4:i-iii D '67
United Nations day 1967; message. UN Mo Chron 4:i-ii O '67

about
Comrade president. il por Newsweek 70:38-9 O 2 '67
Now: a Communist in a key U.N. spot. il por U S News 63:22 O 2 '67

MANEUVERS, Naval. See Naval maneuvers

MANGANESE
Beryllium-10 in a manganese nodule. B. L. K. Somayajulu. bibliog il Science 156:1219-20 Je 2 '67
Brazil's magic mountain: Serra do Navio in Amapá. K. Seegers and S. Seegers. il Américas 19:20-7 Mr '67
Manganese and related elements in the interstitial water of marine sediments. B. J. Presley and others. bibliog il Science 158: 906-10 N 17 '67

MANGELSDORF, T. P.
Don't ban handicapped from our buildings. Todays Health 45:88 D '67

MANGER groups. See Christmas cribs

MANGIERI, A. A.
Solderless breadboard. Pop Electr 25:54 D '66
Who's afraid of the SCR? Pop Electr 28:53-5+ Ja '68

MANGIN, William
Squatter settlements; with biographical sketch. Sci Am 217:19, 21-9 bibliog(p 156) O '67

MANGOS, John A. and McSherry, N. R.
Sodium transport: inhibitory factor in sweat of patients with cystic fibrosis. bibliog Science 158:135-6 O 6 '67

MANGUM, Garth L. See Levitan, S. A. jt. auth.

MANHATTAN college, New York
Teaching peace; conference for the study of peace. Nation 204:564 My 1 '67

MANHATTAN festival ballet
In search of new talent: Manhattan festival ballet productions. W. Terry. il Sat R 50:43-9 N 4 '67
Manhattan festival ballet, Theatre 80 St Marks. D. Hering. Dance Mag 41:32+ N '67
Manhattan festival ballet, Theatre 80 St Marks place. D. Hering. Dance Mag 41:32 Ap '67

MANUFACTURERS, National association of.
See National association of manufacturers
MANUFACTURERS and traders trust company
of Buffalo. See Buffalo, N.Y.—Banks
MANUFACTURES
Labor turnover; tables. See issues of Monthly labor review
  See also
Products, New
Statistics
Ratios of manufacturing; with table (cont) Duns R 90:78-81 N '67
MANURE handling. See Fertilizers and manures—Preservation and storage
MANURE lagoons
How to handle feedlot runoff. O. Bay. Farm J 91:44R-44S S '67
MANURES. See Fertilizers and manures
MANUSCRIPT division. See United States—Library of Congress—Manuscript division
MANUSCRIPTS
  See also
Dead Sea scrolls
Music—Manuscripts

Collection and preservation
  See also
Libraries—Manuscript collections

Conservation and restoration
Painting hospital in the lemon grove. H. J. Plenderleith. il UNESCO Courier 20:24-34 Ja '67
MANUSCRIPTS, Italian
Leonardo's lost notebooks. il Life 62:24-31 Mr 3 '67
MANVILLE, W. H.
Does this Mother know best? Sat Eve Post 241:56-7 Ja 13 '68
Who are you, Joan? Sat Eve Post 240:67-8 Jl 1 '67
MANZELLA, David
Too good to teach? Sch Arts 66:12-13 Mr '67
MAO, Tse-tung
Antimémoires, by A. Malraux. Review New Yorker 43:190-4 N 11 '67. Genêt
Backward, march! il Newsweek 69:43 Mr 6 '67
China—a smell of madness. S. Alsop. il por Sat Eve Post 240:14 F 11 '67
China puzzle: old man in a hurry. C. P. Fitzgerald. por Nation 204:326-9 Mr 13 '67
Chou takes the reins. il por Bsns W p39 Mr 11 '67
Do you love Mao? Australian and New Zealand students tour red China. J. Lang. il por Newsweek 69:46-8 F 27 '67
Downfall of red China? interview. L. La Dany. il por U S News 62:35-7 F 27 '67
Lessons through the barrel of a gun. G. Woodcock. il Commonweal 86:81-4 Ap 7 '67
Mao and the Paris commune. il Newsweek 69:46-7 F 27 '67
Mao and the struggle for China. il pors Newsweek 69:32-9+ Ja 30 '67
Mao at seventy-four: a strange kind of victory. por Newsweek 71:29 Ja 8 '68
Mao power. il Newsweek 70:48-50 N 6 '67
Mao Tse-tung's last revolution. V. S. Kearney. America 116:215-17 F 11 '67
Mao vs. Liu: who holds the guns? il por U S News 63:13 Ag 28 '67
Mao's revolution. J. R. Townsend. il Nation 204:781-6 Je 19 '67
Mao's worst crisis. M. Omori. New Repub 156:17-19 Ja 28 '67
Mind of China. Time 89:28-9 Mr 17 '67
Out of chaos: end of an era for red China. il por U S News 62:36 F 13 '67
Stiffening opposition to Mao? il Sr Schol 90:13-14 F 3 '67
There's no future in Maoism. Life 62:4 Ja 27 '67
Understanding Mao; or, look back to Stalin. H. R. Trevor-Roper. il por N Y Times Mag p28-9+ F 12 '67
Upheaval in Communist China; Mao vs. anti-Maoists. Sr Schol 89:16 Ja 20 '67
What's really going on now in red China; symposium. il U S News 62:46-50+ Ja 30 '67
Writhing dragon. Nat R 19:70+ Ja 24 '67
MAO, Tse-tung, Mme
Public fury no. 1. por Time 89:31-2 F 10 '67
MAOISM. See Communism—China (People's Republic)
MAP making. See Cartography
MAPLE
America's sweetest tree: sugar maple. C. E. Randall. il Am For 73:16-18+ Ap '67

MAPLE syrup
America's sweetest tree: sugar maple. C. E. Randall. il Am For 73:16-18+ Ap '67
Maple syrup: what consumers ought to know about it; with editorial comment. W. R. Wells. Am For 73:28-9+ Ja '67
MAPLEWOOD, Mo.
Minimum lighting not good enough. Am City 82:122 D '67
MAPLEWOOD, N.Y. See Albany, N.Y.
MAPPING, Aerial
IR mapping system readied for market. C. D. LaFond. il Tech W 20:30+ F 27 '67

Equipment
New process cuts aerial mapping time; universal automatic map compilation equipment. il Aero Tech 21:36+ S 11 '67
MAPS
  See also
Atlases
Libraries—Map collections
World maps
  also subhead Maps under names of countries, states, etc. e.g. Middle East—Maps
MAPS, Biblical. See Bible—Geography
MAPS, Cataloging of. See Cataloging
MAPS, Early
Maps that whetted the world. P. W. Schmidtchen. il Hobbies 72:104-5+ D '67
MAPS, Military
  See also
Military topography
MAPS, Pictorial
Great gold rush. il Sat Eve Post 240:28-9 D 30 '67
MAPS, Soil. See Soil surveys
MAQUET, Jacques
Quest for beauty in Dahomey. Vogue 150:218-27+ D '67
MARAN, Stephen P.
Telescopes and automation. bibliog Science 158:867-71 N 17 '67
—and Cameron, A. G. W.
Relativistic astrophysics. bibliog Science 157:1517-24 S 29 '67
MARANOS
Last Marranos. A. Novinsky and A. Paulo. Commentary 43:76-81 My '67; Reply. S. J. Maslin. 44:20+ O '67
MARATHON races. See Running
MARAVICH, Pete
Coach's dream. il por Newsweek 71:56 Ja 1 '68
Guy named Pete. il por Time 91:33 Ja 19 '68
MARBELLA, Spain
Princely resorts. il Holiday 43:38-55 Ja '68
MARBLEHEAD-Halifax race. See Yacht racing
MARCA-RELLI, Corrado
Action from the gluepot; exhibition at Manhattan's Whitney museum. il Time 90:76-7 O 20 '67
Figure in the center. E. Mandelbaum. il Art N 66:58-9+ S '67
MARCELLO, Carlos
Carlos Marcello: king thug of Louisiana. il por Life 63:94-7 S 8 '67
From a governor and a D.A. an offer of resignation. S. Smith. il por Life 63:34-6 S 29 '67
MARCH, Judith
Not a case history, not a statistic: our daughter. McCalls 94:76-7+ Ag '67
MARCH; story. See McCullers, C.
MARCH on Washington, 1968 (proposed) See Civil rights demonstrations
MARCHANT, William
Flowered ways of Chelsea. Holiday 43:58-61+ Ja '68
MARCKER, Kjeld A. See Clark, B. F. C. jt. auth.
MARCOS, Ferdinand E.
Atlantic report. Atlan 219:12 F '67
Bothered archipelago. il Time 89:24+ Je 2 '67
But Marcos is a persistent man. J. Lelyveld. il pors N Y Times Mag p28-9+ F 26 '67
Report from Manila. M. Gart. il por Fortune 76:69+ D '67
Victory for the non-candidate. Time 90:38+ N 24 '67
MARCUS, Frank
Killing of Sister George. Criticism Nat R 19:100 Ja 24 '67
MARCUS, Irvin M.
Southern Negro and the Knights of labor. bibliog Negro Hist Bul 30:5-7 Mr '67

MARCUS, James Lewis
How to clean a big reservoir. por Am City 82:69-71 N '67

about

Mafia scandal: new trouble for Lindsay. U S News 64:10 Ja 1 '68
Mob finds a patsy in a mayor's inner circle. S. Smith and W. Lambert. il pors Life 64: 46-51 Ja 5 '68
Murk from the reservoir. il por Time 90:14 D 29 '67

MARCUS, Joel
Discipline problems. NEA J 56:60-1 D '67

MARCUS, Judith R. and Cohen, Gerald
Riddle of the dangerous bean. Harper 234: 98-102 Je '67

MARCUS, Leonard
FM: the reluctant independent. Hi Fi 17:39-42 Jl '67
Koussevitzky returns, and the lesson is of passion lavishly spent. Hi Fi 17:79-80 F '67
What price stereo? a shopper's guide to high fidelity pricing. Hi Fi 17:68 F '67

MARCUS, Ruth
Small wonders. See issues of Good housekeeping

MARCUS, Stanley
Dissertation on beards, and other hairy recollections. E. Whitehead. por Bsns W p9 D 2 '67
Merchant prince of Dallas. il pors Bsns W p 114-16+ O 21 '67

MARCUSE, Herbert
Love mystified: a critique of Norman O. Brown. Commentary 43:71-5 F '67

about

Resistance and technology D. Callahan. Commonweal 87:377-81 D 22 '67

MARCUSE, Peter
Crop allotments. Nation 206:43-6 Ja 8 '68

MARCY, Carol
Carol Marcy; Judson memorial church. M. Marks. Dance Mag 41:31 D '67

MARDEN, Brice
Total and complex. H. Rosenstein. il por Art N 66:52-4+ My '67

MARDEN, Luis
Madagascar, island at the end of the earth. il Nat Geog Mag 132:443-87 O '67
Sailing oystermen of Chesapeake Bay. Nat Geog Mag 132:798-819 D '67

MAREK, George R.
Appointment in Milan. Hi Fi 17:42-7 Mr '67
Records, circa 1987. Sat R 50:64-5+ Ag 26 '67
Springtime of life. Opera N 31:24-6 Mr 25 '67
Strauss as musician and man. Opera N 31: 8-12 Ap 8 '67
Swallow returns. Opera N 31:14-15 Mr 18 '67
Toscanini celebration, Italian style. Hi Fi 17: MA26-7 Je '67

MAREK, Lois
Father gets to hold the baby. Parents Mag 42:56-7+ Je '67

MARES, Vaclav E.
Czechoslovakia's half century. bibliog f Cur Hist 52:200-7 Ap '67

MARGARET, princess of Great Britain
Changing hairdos of Princess Margaret. L. MacNish. il pors Good H 164:30-1 Ja '67
Life-styles: royalty in our time. A. Haden-Guest. il por Esquire 69:88-91+ Ja '68

MARGARITA ISLAND
Island of pearls. J. Lee. il Travel 128:45-9 D '67
Pearls of Margarita; reprint. C. P. Idyll. il Américas 19:8-14 Ag '67
Venezuela's offshore island resort. il Sunset 138:66+ My '67

MARGGRAF, Martin
Covey of spies is flushed in Germany. M. Durham and J. Cook. il por Life 63:65-6+ N 3 '67

MARGIN requirements, Stock. See Stock exchange—Regulation

MARGINAL forest highway. See Roads—Latin America

MARGOLIASH, Emanuel. See Fitch, W. M. jt. auth.

MARGOLIN, Joseph B.
Technology: a tower of Babel? Am Ed 3: 22-3 N '67

MARGOLIS, Howard
UFO phenomenon. Bul Atomic Sci 23:40-2 Je '67

MARGOLIS, J.
Citation indexing and evaluation of scientific papers. bibliog Science 155:1213-19 Mr 10 '67

MARGRAVE, John L. See Thompson, J. C. jt. auth.

MARGRETHE, crown princess of Denmark
Heiress to a friendly throne; interview, ed. by P. Dragadze. pors Life 64:35-8 Ja 12 '68

about

Princess and the diplomat. C. Plimmer and D. Plimmer. il por Redbook 129:47-9+ Je '67

MARIAN Frances, Sister
On the Nativity; poem. Christian Cent 84:1622 D 20 '67

MARIANA ISLANDS
Marianas turkey shoot; excerpt from Carrier admiral. J. J. Clark. il Am Heritage 18: 26-9+ O '67
New defense line in Pacific. il U S News 63:52-4 Ag 7 '67

MARIANISM. See Mary, Virgin—Theology

MARICHAL, Juan
Always they want more, more, more. A. Stump. il pors Sat Eve Post 240:68-71 Jl 29 '67

MARIE, Sister Alfreda. See Alfreda Marie, Sister

MARIE Adélaïde de Savoie, duchess of Burgundy
Twilight princess and the Sun King. J. Barry. il por Horizon 9:106-11 Spr '67

MARIE Antoinette, consort of Louis XVI, king of France
Vigée-Lebrun and the women of the French court. I. Bischoff. il pors Antiques 92:706-12 N '67

MARIE Clarence, Sister
Burlap bags and boys. Sch Arts 67:36-7 D '67

MARIER, John. See Rose, R. jt. auth.

MARIETTA college, Marietta, Ohio
Another Marietta mud puddle; third annual Mid-America regatta on Ohio River. H. Peterson. il Sports Illus 26:30-1 My 15 '67

MARIJUANA
Case of the pot-smoking school principal; Mrs G. Brennan of Nicasio, Calif. S. Alexander. Life 63:25 N 17 '67
Confessions of a campus pot dealer. Ric. il Esquire 68:100-1+ S '67
Confusion over effects. Sci N 92:345-6 O 7 '67
Crime of marijuana. New Repub 157:9-10 O 7 '67
Dream farm; field of marijuana destroyed by narcotic agents. il Time 90:17-18 S 8 '67
Drugs on the campus. J. Shepherd. il Look 31:14-17 Ag 8 '67
Fiedler affair; Buffalo university group aims to legalize marijuana. il Newsweek 69:29 Je 12 '67
Getting tough with pot; marijuana smokers discovered at New Jersey's Hun preparatory school. Time 90:110 D 8 '67
Going to pot in Washington; a hippie party. U S News 62:63 My 8 '67
How dangerous is marijuana? a top official sparks new debate; excerpts from statements. J. L. Goddard. U S News 63:20 O 30 '67
It's up to the young to solve the problem. C. E. Wyzanski, jr. New Repub 157:15-16 O 21 '67
Keep off the grass? New Repub 156:5-6 Je 17 '67
Marijuana before the bench. il Time 90: 77+ S 29 '67
Marijuana causes psychic dependence, says physician. Todays Health 45:13 S '67
Marijuana: dangerous as alcohol. New Repub 157:7-8 O 28 '67
Marijuana is still illegal; Massachusetts ruling. J. Oteri. Time 90:38+ D 29 '67
Marijuana: millions of turned-on users; with report by A. Rosenfeld. il Life 63:16-23 Jl 7 '67
Marijuana problem; symposium. il Newsweek 70:46-50+ Jl 24 '67
Mary Jane in action; GI's arrested in Vietnam on charges of smoking pot. J. Donnelly. Newsweek 70:40 N 6 '67
No martyr to marijuana; new Goddard line. New Repub 157:6 D 2 '67
Pot & Goddard. Time 90:54 O 27 '67
Pot boils. P. McBroom. il(cover) Sci N 92: 500-1 N 18 '67
Pot bust at Cornell. D. Sanford. New Repub 156:17-20 Ap 15 '67
Pot's luck; Massachusetts, ban. Newsweek 71:14 Ja 1 '68
Potted ivy; alienated students smoking marihuana. il Time 89:98+ My 19 '67

MARIJUANA—*Continued*
Risks of marijuana. D. Sanford. New Repub 156:11-12 Ap 22 '67
Standard marijuana. Sci N 91:461 My 13 '67
What's wrong with pot? Newsweek 70:30 O 2 '67

MARIN, Luis Muñoz. See Muñoz Marin, L.

MARIN COUNTY, Calif.
Where money has more fun. H. Gold. il Sat Eve Post 240:64-7 D 30 '67

MARINA CAY (island) See British Virgin Islands

MARINARO, Vincent C.
Big fly; big trout. Outdoor Life 139:56-9+ Mr '67

MARINAS
High rise on the low lands. P. M. Wilson. il Motor B 121:110-12 Ja '68
Kansas launches marina development. il Parks & Rec 2:29+ Je '67

MARINATOS, Spyridon
Promise of Thera. E. Vermeule. il Atlan 220:90-4 D '67

MARINE algae. See Algae

MARINE aquariums. See Aquariums

MARINE biological laboratories. See Biological laboratories

MARINE biological laboratory, Woods Hole. See Woods Hole, Mass, marine biological laboratory

MARINE biology
See also
Marine resources
Spawning

Research

Naples station: crisis Italian style at marine biology center. J. Walsh. il Science 156:1066-71 My 26 '67

Study and teaching

From the log of the Te Vega. R. L. Bolin. il Natur Hist 76:24-31 Ag '67

MARINE cookery. See Cookery, Marine

MARINE corps. See United States—Marine corps

MARINE deposits. See Deep sea deposits

MARINE ecology
Ecological studies during Project Sealab II. T. A. Clarke and others. bibliog il Science 157:1381-9 S 22 '67
Toughness of species: research in the Everglades. L. Gebhart. Sci N 92:355 O 7 '67
Vertical diurnal migration and endogenous rhythmicity. J. T. Enright and W. M. Hamner. bibliog il Science 157:937-41 Ag 25 '67

MARINE engines
Experts talk about marine power; symposium, ed. by J. Roe. il Pop Sci 190:132-6 F '67
400 hp. from an eighty-pound rotary engine. W. S. Bacon. il Pop Sci 190:110-11+ Je '67
Inboard-outdrives; the stern-drive engine. F. M. Paulson. il Field & S 71:130-5 Ap '67
Powerhouseboat! nimble, silky-smooth, 500 horses strong. J. Roe. il Pop Sci 191:90-2 D '67
Stern drives. il Motor B 121:144-7 Ja '68
Tomorrow's marine engines are running today. E. H. Nabb. il Pop Mech 127:128-32+ Je '67
Yachting's boat show. il Yachting 121:123-6+ Ja '67; 123:120-2+ Ja '68
See also
Gas and oil engines, Outboard

Care

Consider the systems. il Motor B 119:29-30 Mr '67
Tune that engine. il Motor B 119:38-9 Ap '67
What makes for peak performance? F. M. Paulson. il Field & S 72:114-17 S '67
Winter wrap-up for your stern drive. H. B. Notrom. il Pop Mech 128:164-7+ N '67

Ignition

Ignition breakthrough. L. Heiner. il Yachting 121:82-3+ Mr '67

Repairing

Troubleshooting tactics. A. P. Smith. il Motor B 119:30-2 Je '67

MARINE fauna
Ecological studies during Project Sealab II. T. A. Clarke and others. bibliog il Science 157:1381-9 S 22 '67
Geomagnetic polarity change and faunal extinction in the southern ocean. N. D. Watkins and H. G. Goodell. bibliog il Science 156:1083-7 My 26 '67

Life in a dead sea, Great Salt Lake. P. A. Zahl. il Nat Geog Mag 132:252-63 Ag '67
Noisy chorus of the sea. W. N. Tavolga. il Natur Hist 76:20-7 Ap '67
Wonderland of Australia's Great Barrier Reef. F. Drake and K. Drake. il Read Digest 90:162-4+ Mr '67
See also
Cetacea
Sea anemones

MARINE flora
See also
Diatoms

MARINE geology
See also
Ocean bottom

MARINE insurance. See Insurance, Marine

MARINE laboratories
Labs: Osborn laboratories of marine sciences, Coney Island. New Yorker 43:48 N 4 '67
New York aquarium and Osborn laboratories of marine sciences. G. D. Ruggieri. il Science 158:675-6 N 3 '67
Sea-going penthouse. il Sci Digest 62:34-5 O '67

MARINE painting
Down to the sea; paintings by E. Moran, with quotations by nineteenth century American authors. Am Heritage 18:40-55 Je '67
Planning and painting a seascape; excerpts from Painting sea and shore. H. R. Ballinger. il Design 68:4-9 Mr '67

MARINE photography. See Photography—Marines

MARINE radar. See Radar in navigation

MARINE radiophone. See Radio telephone on ships, boats, etc.

MARINE resources
Aquiculture is more than a dream. L. Galton. il N Y Times Mag p 12-14+ Je 18 '67
Drugs from the oceans. il Sci N 92:249-50 S 9 '67
Human food from ocean and land. K. O. Emery and C. O'D. Iselin. bibliog il Science 157:1279-81 S 15 '67; Reply. R. G. S. Bidwell. 158:1136-7 D 1 '67
Marine science and technology. P. H. Abelson. Science 155:1621 Mr 31 '67
Oceans becoming everybody's business; corporations recognizing potentials R. W. Irelan. il Nations Bsns 55:40-6 S '67
Political ocean. E. W. S. Hull. For Affairs 45:492-502 Ap '67
Russia dives for the sea bottom. A. Parry. il Sci Digest 62:60-4 S '67
Sea talk; conference titled Materials: key to effective use of the sea. New Yorker 43:48-9 O 14 '67
Secrets of sunken lands; studies off the Atlantic coast reveal history and wealth of the shelf. B. Tufty. il Sci N 91:77-9 Ja 21 '67
U.S. sets priorities for tapping the sea. Bsns W p 112 Mr 18 '67
See also
Fisheries
United States—National council on marine sciences and engineering development

Anecdotes, facetiae, satire, etc.

Sea-green pastures. R. G. G. Price. Atlan 220:111+ S '67

International aspects

Bar association probes UN undersea role. R. W. Niblock. Tech W 20:39-40 Je 19 '67
International cooperation for development of the oceans; address, July 29, 1967. H. H. Humphrey. Dept State Bul 57:227-9 Ag 21 '67
Law of the sea; University of Rhode Island first summer conference. G. Pontecorvo. Bul Atomic Sci 23:46-8 Ap '67
U.N. and the sea; General assembly debate. C. M. Eichelberger. Sat R 50:22+ O 14 '67
U.S. calls for U.N. committee to develop principles for cooperative exploration and use of ocean floor; statement, November 8, 1967. A. J. Goldberg. Dept State Bul 57:723-5 N 27 '67

MARINE sciences council. See United States—National council on marine sciences and engineering development

MARINE sediments. See Sedimentation and deposition

MARINE structures
New town; Grand Isle, prefabricated mining town in the Gulf of Mexico. J. Johansen. il Arch Forum 127:44-53 S '67

MARINE surveying. See Hydrographic surveying

MARINE water. See Sea water

MARLAR, Mary A.
Lights are on. Am Ed 3:21-4 My '67
MARLER, Peter
Animal communication signals. bibliog Science 157:769-74 Ag 18 '67
MARLEY, Faye
Man and his science. Sci N 91:237 Mr 11 '67
MARLIN fishing
Some new battles are boiling in the Coral Sea. V. Kraft. il Sports Illus 27:53-4+ D 18 '67
Strange ways for striped marlin. J. Hardie. il Field & S 71:66-9+ Mr '67
MARMALADE. See Jelly, jam, etc.
MARMEIN, Phyllis
Report from Boston. Dance Mag 41:20+ S '67
MAROSSI, Ruth. See Krefetz. G. jt. auth.
MAROTTA, Anthony
You got to be a hero. R. Crichton. il pors Sat Eve Post 240:30-2+ D 30 '67
MAROTTA'S Italian hero sandwich shop. See New York (city)—Hotels, restaurants, etc.
MAROWITZ, Charles
Pinterism is maximum tension through minimum information. N Y Times Mag p36-7+ O 1 '67
MARQUÉS, René
Ox cart. Criticism
America 116:161 Ja 28 '67
America 117:inside back cover Ag 26 '67
MARR, Dave
From rabbit to real pro. E. Asinof. il pors N Y Times Mag p54-5+ S 10 '67
MARRANOS. See Maranos
MARRIAGE
California woman: ten reasons why her marriage goes wrong. P. Popenoe and D. C. Disney. Ladies Home J 84:62 Jl '67
Can this marriage be saved? ed. by D. C. Disney. See issues of Ladies' home journal
Gaps and gains in matrimony. Sci Digest 62:36 O '67
Growing together or apart. B. W. Overstreet. il PTA Mag 62:6-8 D '67
He loved me: fixations or crushes and love; excerpts from The winner's notebook. T. I. Rubin. McCalls 95:48+ O '67
How to be a good wife; with discussion group program, by E. G. Neisser. D. R. Mace. il Parents Mag 42:24+, 44-5+ F '67
How to be happy though incompatible: reprint; excerpt from Help your husband stay alive. H. Lees. Read Digest 90:138-40 Ap '67
How to keep your marriage from slowing down. il Farm J 91:51+ Je '67
Husband hunting? the chances. U S News 63:68 O 2 '67
I, John, take thee, Mary, for the next five years. Christian Cent 84:1182 S 20 '67
I, Sharon, take thee, Jay . . . J. Robbins and J. Robbins. il McCalls 94:108-9+ Mr '67
Innocent game that disrupts marriage. N. M. Lobsenz. il Redbook 128:64-5+ Ap '67; Same abr. with title Innocent game that can disrupt marriage. Read Digest 91:122-4 Jl '67
Is marriage dying, too? excerpt from Sex is dead and other postmortems. E. H. Brill. Christian Cent 84:268-70 Mr 1 '67
Is there a life after marriage? B. Head. Mlle 66:91+ Ja '68
Let's be sexumenical: marriage in three parts. R. Kirk. Nat R 19:1430 D 26 '67
Lutheran clergyman looks at marriage; reply. R. Moynihan. Cath World 205:2-3 Ap '67
Making marriage work; with study discussion program. P. Popenoe. il Parents Mag 42:46-7+, 73 D '67
Man talk; doll's house. D. Newman and R. Benton. il Mlle 66:30 Ja '68
Marriage in the modern world; address. July 1966. D. Burke. Cath World 205:101-6 My '67
Married life, for better or worse. G. D. Hanson. il PTA Mag 62:14-17 N '67
Marrying absurd; weddings in Las Vegas. J. Didion. Sat Eve Post 240:18 D 16 '67
Model-railroad marriage therapy: Interpersonal behavior game-test. il Life 63:93-4+ O 6 '67
Most delicate problem in marriage. S. Frank. il Good H 164:87+ Mr '67
Most unexpected threat to a good marriage; effect of children. V. Cadden. il McCalls 94:94-5+ Jl '67
My pride was shattered. P. Mitchell. McCalls 94:24+ Jl '67
Now that you are married, do not always expect the lover; letter, February 6, 1838. C. L. Preston. il Am Heritage 19:34-5 D '67
Of many things. P. Weber. America 117: inside cover Jl 15 '67

Personalist view of marriage. J. Gilbert. Cath World 205:365-70 S '67
Rational ethics says no. G. G. Grisez. Commonweal 86:122-5 Ap 14 '67
Social life of married couples: its pleasures and problems; survey findings. M. M. Hunt. il McCalls 94:67-9+ My '67
Students' views on marriage. Sr Schol 90: sup8 Ap 21 '67
Testing of a marriage. McCalls 95:18+ Ja '68
What a man really wants in a woman. J. Brothers. Good H 164:58+ F '67
What makes a marriage succeed or fail? National institute of mental health study; ed. by S. S. Rosenberg. W. Goodrich. il Parents Mag 42:60-2+ Je '67
Why husbands and wives remain strangers. J. Bernard and N. M. Lobsenz. il Redbook 129:60-1+ O '67
You can make yourself sick. F. R. Schreiber and M. Herman. Sci Digest 61:24-5 Ap '67
Young wife's world. H. Valentine. See issues of Good housekeeping
See also
Alimony
Celibacy
Divorce
Family
High school students. Married
Husbands
Intermarriage of races
Love
Remarriage
Sex relations
Sexual ethics
Wives

Anecdotes, facetiae, satire, etc.
Let me count the ways. . . J. F. Swan. Farm J 91:97 F '67
Man talk. D. Newman and R. Benton. il Mlle 65:68+ My '67

Saudi Arabia
On being a sheik's wife. A. Shammout. il Sat R 50:71-2+ O 14 '67

United States
See Marriage
MARRIAGE, Common law
Althea and the judges. B. W. Maccracken. il Am Heritage 18:60-3+ Je '67
Detroit's marry-in. Newsweek 70:61 S 18 '67
MARRIAGE counseling
Can this marriage be saved? ed. by D. C. Disney. See issues of Ladies' home journal
Making marriage work; with study discussion program. P. Popenoe. il Parents Mag 42:46-7+, 73 D '67
Shocking facts about fake marriage counselors. D. Robinson. Good H 165:74-5+ Jl '67
MARRIAGE customs and rites
Bride wore red; marriage Indian style. J. Baer. il Seventeen 26:139 F '67
MARRIAGE law
See also
Adultery
MARRIAGE of Figaro; opera. See Mozart, J. C. W. A.
MARRIAGES, Interracial. See Intermarriage of races
MARRIAGES, Mixed
Catholic-Orthodox marriages. America 116:334 Mr 11 '67
Interfaith marriages. E. Genné and W. Genné. il PTA Mag 62:16-18 Ja '68
Mixed marriages; religious education of the children. L. M. Örsy. America 117:242-5 S 9 '67; Discussion. 117:398, 589 O 14, N 18 '67
More than guests. D. McCabe. Christian Cent 84:1291 O 11 '67
My parents are so narrow-minded! questions and answers. A. Wood. Seventeen 26:164+ Mr '67
MARRIED women
See also
Wives
Employment
Do women really want the freedom they've won? G. Samuels. il Redbook 129:54-5+ My '67
Does it pay for a wife to work? F. Henle. Am Home 70:44-5+ S '67
How much should a working wife spend on herself? P. Lindberg. Bet Hom & Gard 45:6+ Ag '67
Marital and family characteristics of workers, March 1966. E. Waldman. bibliog f il Mo Labor R 90:29-36 Ap '67

MARRIED women—Employment—*Continued*
So your mother is going to work. N. E. Scofield. il Seventeen 26:362+ Ag '67
Someone to mind the baby. M. Pines. il N Y Times Mag p71+ Ja 7 '68
Tomorrow's wife and mother. S. Hertz. America 116:718-22 My 13 '67; Discussion. 116:875-7 Je 24 '67
When a mother goes to work. B. Spock. il Redbook 129:20+ Je '67
Why job figures jump. il Bsns W p37 N 18 '67

MARRIOTT, Dana P.
When Christmas was banned in Boston. Am Heritage 19:107-11 D '67

MARRIOTT, Ron
Showing off The show-offs. V. H. Swisher. il pors Dance Mag 41:24-5+ My '67

MARROW
Delayed hypersensitivity. bone marrow as the source of cells in delayed skin reactions. D. M. Lubaroff and B. H. Waksman. bibliog il Science 157:322-3 Jl 21 '67

MARS, Forrest E.
Sweet, secret world of Forrest Mars. H. B. Meyers. il pors Fortune 75:154-7+ My '67

MARS (planet)
Mars: a new world to explore. C. Sagan. il Nat Geog Mag 132:820-41 D '67
Mars and the moon at comparable resolutions. T. Pope. il Sky & Tel 33:119-20 F '67
Observing Mars in 1967. C. F. Capen. il Sky & Tel 33:208-10 Ap '67
See also
Space flight to Mars

Atmosphere
Little men from Mars. Sci Digest 62:37 N '67
Martian ionosphere: a component due to solar protons. C. Sagan and J. Veverka. bibliog il Science 158:110-12 O 6 '67

Contamination
JPL scientists challenge sterilization goals. H. M. David. Tech W 20:32-3 My 1 '67
Planetary contamination I: the problem and the agreements. N. H. Horowitz and others. bibliog Science 155:1501-5 Mr 24 '67; Discussion. 156:1436; 157:582-3 Je 16, Ag 4 '67
Planetary contamination II: Soviet and U.S. practices and policies. B. C. Murray and others. bibliog il Science 155:1505-11 Mr 24 '67; Discussion. 157:487 Ag 4 '67

Surface
Frost phenomena on Mars. D. M. Anderson and others. bibliog il Science 155:319-22 Ja 20 '67
Mars data refined. Sci N 91:198 F 25 '67
Mars: influence of topography on formation of temporary bright patches. B. T. O'Leary and D. G. Rea. bibliog il Science 155:317-19 Ja 20 '67
Martian relief and the coming opposition. D. H. Harris. bibliog il Science 155:1100-1 Mr 3 '67
Martian surface. E. J. Öpik; reply with rejoinder. R. A. Wells and G. Fielder. bibliog Science 155:354-6 Ja 20 '67

Temperature
Frost phenomena on Mars. D. M. Anderson and others. bibliog il Science 155:319-22 Ja 20 '67

MARS probe. See Space probes

MARSDEN, Brian G.
One hundred periodic comets. bibliog Science 155:1207-13 Mr 10 '67

MARSDEN, Sullivan S. Jr, and Davis, S. N.
Geological subsidence; with biographical sketches. Sci Am 216:14, 93-100 Je '67

MARSEILLES, France

Antiquities
New battle of Marseille; excavation of fortifications. il Time 90:60+ S 15 '67

MARSH, Albert W.
Turfgrass irrigation. Parks & Rec 2:43-4+ Ja '67

MARSH, George Perkins
Rockefeller home designated historic landmark; address. C. A. T. Johnson. il Parks & Rec 2:23+ Ag '67

MARSH, John O. 1926-
Mahon's stacked deck. Reporter 37:17 S 7 '67

MARSH, Ngaio
Stratford-on-Avon. Atlan 219:116+ F '67

MARSH, Robert C.
Auditorium reborn. Hi Fi 18:MA22+ Ja '68
Grandiose musical muddle. Hi Fi 17:MA20+ Ag '67
Lyric opera and Mary Garden's shadow. Hi Fi 17:MA19+ F '67
Orchestra hall remodeled; the eye is pleased, but... Hi Fi 17:MA20-1 Ja '67
Reunion at Orchestra Hall. Hi Fi 17:MA25 My '67
Toscanini and the recording machine. Sat R 50:59-60+ Mr 25 '67

MARSH, Tracy H.
Unique salt and pepper shaker. Hobbies 72:84 My '67

MARSH plants. See Bog vegetation

MARSHALL, Catherine
How I'm raising my second family. por Good H 166:76-7+ Ja '68

MARSHALL, Charles
Next move is ours. Sat R 51:52+ Ja 13 '68

MARSHALL, Charles Burton
Limits of power. Nat R 19:1279 N 14 '67

MARSHALL, E. M.
Catch your vacation costs! Travel 128:46-7 S '67

MARSHALL, Eric, and Hample, Stuart
(comps) Children's letters to God; excerpts. Read Digest 90:97-9 Mr '67

MARSHALL, George Catlett
George C. Marshall, by F. C. Pogue. Review
Atlan 219:136-7 Mr '67. E. Weeks.
Nat R 19:256-7 Mr 7 '67. G. F. Eliot

MARSHALL, Herbert
(tr) See Evtushenko, E. A. Babi Yar

MARSHALL, Jack
Bearings; poem. New Yorker 43:56 Mr 18 '67
Setting out; poem. New Yorker 43:96 Ap 1 '67

MARSHALL, Jon Clark
Problems of high school students in relation to grade achievement. bibliog f Sch & Soc 95:237-8 Ap 1 '67

MARSHALL, Lenore
Tourist's Great Britain; poem. Sat R 50:17 Mr 18 '67

MARSHALL, Lynn L.
Strange stillbirth of the Whig party. bibliog f Am Hist R 72:445-68 Ja '67

MARSHALL, Richard
Literature and religion in Russia today; interview, ed. by C. L. Palms. Cath World 204:362-7 Mr '67
New books. Cath World 205:57-60, 248-9 Ap, Jl '67

MARSHALL, Richard E. and others
Fine structure of RNA codewords recognized by bacterial, amphibian and mammalian transfer RNA. bibliog Science 155:820-6 F 17 '67

MARSHALL, Thurgood
Bar exam. por Newsweek 70:22-3 S 11 '67
First Negro justice. Sr Schol 91:20 S 21 '67
First Negro justice. Time 90:16 S 8 '67
Good Court gets better. Christian Cent 84:827-8 Je 28 '67
High court hints a softer tone. por Bsns W p40 Je 17 '67
Ignore Earl Warren? Newsweek 70:30 O 16 '67
Kite flying & other games. Time 90:16 Jl 28 '67
Man in the fish fry parlor. W. Rogers. por Look 31:115 O 17 '67
Mr Justice Marshall. il por Newsweek 69:34-6 Je 26 '67
Negro justice. il por Time 89:18 Je 23 '67
Supreme court justice Thurgood Marshall. por Negro Hist Bul 30:4-5 O '67
Term's end. J. J. Kilpatrick. il Nat R 19:804-5 Jl 25 '67
Thurgood Marshall. New Repub 156:9 Je 24 '67
With another liberal on High court. por U S News 63:21 S 11 '67
With Mr Marshall on the Supreme court; with excerpts from address by A. H. Kelly. il por U S News 62:12-13 Je 26 '67

MARSHALL committee. See United States—President's committee on selective service

MARSHALL plan. See Economic assistance in Europe

MARSHES
Fuel of the future; fill and garbage destruction of wetlands. il Newsweek 69:59 F 20 '67
Great swamp and the good life; Great swamp of New Jersey vs. jetport. il Audubon 69:5 Mr '67
Great swamp is good for nothing, but life, knowledge, peace and hope; Morris County, N.J. B. Atkinson. il N Y Times Mag p32-6+ F 12 '67; Discussion. p 14+ Mr 5 '67

MARSHES—*Continued*
Great Swamp of New Jersey: jetports and progress; statement before Fish and wildlife service hearing. T. M. Edison. Nat Parks Mag 41:18 My '67
Mentor marsh. D. B. McCoy. il Nat Parks Mag 41:12-13 Jl '67
Mike Frome; Great Swamp, N.J. and Great Marsh. Va. M. Frome. Am For 73:3+ Ap '67

See also
Bog vegetation
Bogs
Peat bogs

Reclamation
See also
New Jersey meadows
MARSHES, Salt. See Salt marshes
MARSICANO, Merle
Merle Marsicano & dance co, Village theatre. J. Anderson. Dance Mag 41:75+ Je '67
MARSTON, Red
Changing West coast. Yachting 122:40-1+ N '67
MARSUPIAL moles
Two for extinction. il Sci Digest 61:22-4 F '67
MARSUPIALS
See also
Anteaters
Marsupial moles
MARTELL, Charles B.
On the record; interview. por Aero Tech 21:42-3 N 6 '67
MARTENHOFF, Jim
Pocket yacht. Yachting 123:104-5+ Ja '68
MARTENS, Anne Coulter
Costume caper; drama. Plays 27:1-12 O '67
Fit to be tied; drama. Plays 27:1-11 N '67
Go-go gophers; drama. Plays 26:1-12, 96 Mr '67
MARTHA; opera. See Flotow, F. von
MARTHA Canfield free memorial library, Arlington, Vt.
Arrivederci, trauma! retiring to a small public library. G. Raftery. il Library J 92:4475-6 D 15 '67
MARTHA Washington's spy; drama. See Dias, E. J.
MARTHA'S VINEYARD
See also
Oak Bluffs, Mass.
MARTI, José
Rebel without hatred. J. A. Del Regato. il por Américas 19:29-35 Ja '67
MARTIN, Allie Beth
Focus on ALA-PLA membership. por ALA Bul 61:1095-101 O '67
MARTIN, David Thomas
Excerpt from debate, October 13, 1966. Cong Digest 46:51+ F '67
It is Christ who dwells in me. Life 62:68+ Mr 17 '67
MARTIN, Dean
Dean Martin talks about: his drinking, the Mafia, Frank Sinatra, women, Bobby Kennedy; interview, ed. by O. Fallaci. pors Look 31:78-85+ D 26 '67

about
Dino's breezy way to easy money: Dean Martin show. B. Williamson. Life 62:18 My 26 '67
Funny-side up. il pors Newsweek 69:97+ Mr 20 '67
Is there a real Dean Martin? B. Thomas. il por Good H 165:96-7+ N '67
MARTIN, Dean, family
TV Christmas with the Martins and the Sinatras. il pors Look 31:76-7 D 26 '67
MARTIN, Edwin M.
Edwin M. Martin elected chairman. Development assistance committee. Dept State Bul 57:808 D 11 '67
MARTIN, Everett G.
Vietnam: last chance? por Newsweek 70:64-5 S 25 '67

about
Under a cloud in Saigon. por Time 91:28 Ja 12 '68
Why Saigon ousted Everett Martin. por Newsweek 71:3 Ja 22 '68
MARTIN, Frank
Works of art from skulls and eggshells. Design 68:10-11 Mr '67
MARTIN, George, 1925?-
Mix-master to the Beatles. il por Time 89:67 Je 16 '67

MARTIN, George, 1926-
Santa Fe in flames. Opera N 32:12-14 S 9 '67
(ed) See Zorina, V. Practical streak
MARTIN, Graham
Thailand and southeast Asia; address. January 18, 1967. Dept State Bul 56:193-9 F 6 '67
United States and Thailand; address, May 3, 1967. Dept State Bul 56:851-5 Je 5 '67
MARTIN, Harold H.
Diving for treasure in the pirate city. Sat Eve Post 240:63-7 Ag 12 '67
My son comes home from Vietnam. Sat Eve Post 240:76+ Ap 8 '67
Republicans' affable old radical. Sat Eve Post 240:42+ Mr 25 '67
Well, ma, I'm still here. Sat Eve Post 240:67a N 18 '67
MARTIN, Jay
Adding up the double. Nation 205:24-6 Jl 3 '67
MARTIN, Jim
Beaver state bonus. Field & S 72:50-1+ D '67
Fishing a floating island. Outdoor Life 140:42-3+ Jl '67
Sundown stripers. Field & S 72:52-3+ Jl '67
MARTIN, John
John Martin at school. E. Rothschild. il pors Dance Mag 42:38-40 Ja '68
MARTIN, John Bartlow
Meaning in a disordered university. Harper 234:107-8 Ap '67
My Chicago. Holiday 41:54-7+ Mr '67

about
Liberals in wonderland. R. Shereff. Commonweal 86:198-9+ My 5 '67
MARTIN, John Henry
Good grades, green grass. Sat R 50:89 My 20 '67
MARTIN, Joy Logee
Winter-flowering begonias. Home Gard 54:20-1 O '67
MARTIN, Laurence W.
Ballistic missile defense and Europe. Bul Atomic Sci 23:42-6 My '67
MARTIN, Lawrence, and Martin, Sylvia
How grand it was! excerpts from Europe: the grand tour. Sat R 50:41-3 My 27 '67
MARTIN, Linda Grant
Angels of Viet Nam. Todays Health 45:16-23 Ag '67
Keeping up with the Tran Quan Lacs. N Y Times Mag p22-3+ Ag 20 '67
Thirty-seven year war of the village of Tananhoi. N Y Times Mag p30-1+ O 29 '67
MARTIN, Oliver, jr
Champion on wheels. il pors Ebony 22:108+ S '67
MARTIN, Paul
Canada; address, November 13, 1967. Vital Speeches 34:133-5 D 15 '67
MARTIN, Paul S.
Pleistocene overkill; with biographical sketch. por Natur Hist 76:4, 32-8 bibliog(p 105) D '67; 77:74-5 Ja '68
MARTIN, Philip L.
Notes on composition for the young landscape painter. Am Artist 31:50-5 S '67
MARTIN, Preston
California's doctor for ailing S&Ls. por Bsns W p77-8+ Ap 1 '67
MARTIN, Robert W. jr
Message from the publisher (cont) Aviation W 86:11 F 20 '67
MARTIN, Sylvia. See Martin, L. jt. auth.
MARTIN, Victoria (Claflin) Woodhull
First teeny-bopper. S. Maloff. il Newsweek 69:101-101A+ Ap 10 '67
MARTIN, William C.
Shepherds vs. flocks. Atlan 220:53-9 D '67
MARTIN, William McChesney, 1906-
Experts say of '67: a good year; excerpts from testimony. U S News 62:116 F 20 '67
High officials argue over taxes, spending, inflation; excerpts from hearing before the House ways and means committee, November 30, 1967. por U S News 63:90-2 D 18 '67
If taxes aren't raised: one view; excerpts from testimony, September 14, 1967. U S News 63:125 S 25 '67
Mr Martin's view; excerpts from address, May 16, 1967. U S News 62:58 My 29 '67
Words of warning about inflation in the U.S; excerpts from address, November 15, 1967. por U S News 63:16 N 27 '67

about
Back at the bank. il por Time 89:87 Ap 7 '67

MARTIN, William McChesney—about—*Cont.*
Billion-dollar decision. il por Time 89:81
 Mr 24 '67
Dilemma for Johnson: who is to manage
 dollar. il por U S News 62:72 Mr 13 '67
Inflation's arch-enemy at the Fed. por Bsns
 W p72-3+ Ap 22 '67
Keeping the Fed on middle ground. il por
 Bsns W p36-7 F 25 '67
LBJ's $1 billion Fed appointment. il por
 Newsweek 69:75 Ap 10 '67
Martin stays on as top U.S. money man.
 por Bsns W p21 Ap 1 '67
Oracle views the economy. il por Newsweek
 69:77 F 20 '67
Why the President renamed Martin as head
 of the Fed. por U S News 62:23 Ap 10 '67
MARTIN-VISCOUNT, Bill
Brief biography. S. Goodman. pors Dance Mag
 41:54-5 Ag '67
MARTIN company
Martin withdraws as SST subcontractor.
 Aviation W 87:23 S 25 '67
MARTINDALE, Don
(ed) National character in the perspective
 of the social sciences. bibliog f Ann Am
 Acad 370:1-163 Mr '67
Sociology of national character. bibliog f Ann
 Am Acad 370:30-5 Mr '67
MARTINE, Jean Kinkead
Homecoming. por McCalls 95:68+ N '67
MARTINEZ MONTERO, Homero
Historical roots of Latin American integra-
 tion. Américas 19:17-23 Ap '67
October 12, 1492. Américas 19:1-4 O '67
MARTINON, Jean
Lively arts; new direction in Chicago? inter-
 view, ed. by R. Hemming. por Sr Schol 90:
 22 F 10 '67
 about
Recordings. M. Mayer. Esquire 68:26 Ag '67
MARTINU, Bohuslav
Bohuslav Martinu. C. J. Luten. il por Am
 Rec G 33:916-17 Je '67
MARTIS, Joseph
Lighting expert with other talents. G. P.
 Hunt. por Life 63:7 S 22 '67
MARTY, Martin E.
Eye opener on Latin America. Christian Cent
 84:261-3 Mr 1 '67
Prophetic visage. Christian Cent 84:440 Ap 5
 '67
Records. Christian Cent 84:1562 D 6 '67
MARTYN, Howe
Old worlds to conquer. Nation 204:427-9 Ap
 3 '67
MARTZ, Louis L.
Varieties of criticism. Poetry 110:254-7 Jl '67
MARTZLOFF, Thomas H.
Large firm and its corporate plan. por Pub
 W 191:28-30 My 8 '67
MARUFFO, Cesar A.
Zona pellucida of rhesus monkey ovum after
 gonadotropin stimulation. bibliog Science
 157:1313-14 S 15 '67
MARUSI, Augustine Raymond
Chemical reaction at Borden. por Bsns W
 p200 F 18 '67
MARVIN, Lee
Redbook dialogue. por Redbook 130:74-5+ N
 '67
MARX, Anne
Small fortune; poem. Good H 164:181 Je '67
MARX, Gary T.
Negro anti-Semitism. Nation 206:11-13 Ja 1
 '68
MARX, Groucho
Epistles of Groucho. P. D. Zimmerman. il por
 Newsweek 69:93A+ Ap 3 '67
Marxisms. M. Nolan. Reporter 37:61-2 Jl 13 '67
MARX, Karl
Cursing the carbuncles. il Time 90:35 S 22
 '67
Karl Marx was all wet. il Nations Bsns 55:
 100-2+ N '67
Lessons from revolution. R. B. Kaiser. Amer-
 ica 117:469+ O 28 '67
Marx's Das kapital. P. A. Samuelson. News-
 week 70:87 O 16 '67
Meaning of Karl Marx. G. Morel. America
 117:464-8 O 28 '67
MARX, Wilhelm, family
Brazil's Marx brothers. il pors Time 90:50
 Jl 21 '67
MARXISM. See Communism; Socialism
MARY, Virgin

Apparitions and miracles (modern)

Fátima: reflections after the fact: 50th anniversary of the famous apparitions. C. Irizarry. Christian Cent 84:1016-19 Ag 9 '67
Pope's pilgrimage; spiritual mission to
 Fatima. il Newsweek 69:66-7 My 22 '67

Assumption

Reward and promise. V. P. McCorry. America
 117:inside back cover Ag 12 '67

Theology

Can we learn from Mariology? P. K. Jewett.
 Christian Cent 84:1019-21 Ag 9 '67
Fátima and Populorum progressio; ecumenical
 setback. R. J. Mollar. Christian Cent 84:
 1025-6 Ag 9 '67
Fátima: reflections after the fact; 50th anni-
 versary of the famous apparitions. C. Iriz-
 arry. Christian Cent 84:1016-19 Ag 9 '67
Letter signum magnum; Pope Paul's promised
 message on devotion to the Mother of Christ.
 America 116:798-9 Je 3 '67
Lutheran view of Mariology. T. Harjunpaa.
 America 117:436-7+ O 21 '67
More than one myth. R. S. Ellwood. Chris-
 tian Cent 84:1258 O 4 '67
Pope's pilgrimage; spiritual mission to
 Fatima. il Newsweek 69:66-7 My 22 '67
M. Angelica Seng, Sister. See Seng, M. A.
M. Angelique, Sister
Poetry, prayer and cosmic reality. por Cath
 World 205:237-44 Jl '67
MARY Anthony, Mother
Route; poem. Commonweal 87:385 D 22 '67
M. Baylon Zamboni, Sister. See Zamboni,
 M. B.
MARY Briant, Sister. See Briant, M.
MARY Corita Kent, Sister. See Kent, M. C.
MARY Ellen, Sister
Recall; poem. Commonweal 87:148 N 3 '67
MARY Faith, Sister
Of many things. America 116:230 F 18 '67
MARY Inez Hilger, Sister. See Hilger, M. I.
MARY Joachim, Sister. See Joachim, M.
M. Judine, Sister
Chiaroscuro, at the grave of an artist-nun;
 poem. Commonweal 85:462 Ja 27 '67
MARY Katharine Drexel, Mother. See Drexel,
 M. K.
MARY Norbert Körte, Sister. See Körte, M. N.
M. Simplicia, Sister
To an exceptional child; Anniversary; poems.
 Commonweal 85:489 F 3 '67
M. Stanislaus, Sister. See Stanislaus, M.
MARY Teresa Joseph Murphy, Sister. See
 Murphy, M. T. J.
MARY Thérèse, Sister
Configurations; poem. America 117:225 S 2 '67
Manhattan evening; poem. Sat R 50:22 Ap 22
 '67
MARY Verona Murray, Sister. See Murray,
 M. V.
MARYLAND
 See also
 Architecture, Domestic—Maryland
 Booksellers and bookselling—Maryland
 Chesapeake Bay
 Education—Maryland
 Land—Maryland
 Law—Maryland
 Libraries—Maryland
 Public welfare—Maryland

Constitution

New model. Newsweek 71:23-4 Ja 22 '68

Description and travel

Just across a bridge. M. Wallace. Sat R 50:
 37+ Je 17 '67

Historic houses, etc.

Washington's Rhine? M. Fradin. il Am For
 73:22-5+ My '67
 See also
 Baltimore—Historic houses, etc.
 Hagerstown, Md.—Historic houses, etc.

History

Maryland, their Maryland; with paintings. W.
 E. Wilson. Am Heritage 18:8-19+ Ag '67

Parks and reserves

 See also
 Glen Echo amusement park

Politics and government

Athenian touch. Time 89:20 Ap 7 '67
MARYLAND academy of sciences, Baltimore
Events of 1968 in the Graphic time table.
 Sky & Tel 35:31-3 Ja '68
MARYLAND cup corporation
Neat feat for nepotism; quadrupled sales. il
 Time 89:64 Je 30 '67
MARYLAND hunt cup race. See Horse racing
MARYLAND-National capital park and plan-
 ning commission
Revenue facilities and services by lease; ad-
 dress. F. F. Rubini. Parks & Rec 2:45-6 Ja;
 36+ Mr '67

MARYLAND. University, College Park
Bureau of economic and business research
What input-output tells industry; University of Maryland's computerized model of the economy. il Bsns W p88-90+ D 9 '67

School of library and information services
Administrator's development program. H. L. Tosi. il Wilson Lib Bul 42:406-10 D '67
Major manpower project funded at U. of Maryland. Library J 92:2867+ S 1 '67
Poverty project underway at Maryland univ. Library J 92:2702 Ag '67

MARZLUFT, J. M. and South, Kent
Streamlined purchasing. Am City 82:119-20+ My '67

MÁS A TIERRA. See Juan Fernández Islands

MASADA (fortress) Israel
Chip of history from Masada; with report by M. Steinmann. il Life 63:120-2+ D 8 '67
Digging for the facts. il Sr Schol 91:13 D 14 '67
Good show; exhibition of Masada rebellion and the Yadin dig at the Jewish museum. New Yorker 43:42-4 O 7 '67
Masada revisited; exhibition in Manhattan's Jewish museum. M. R. Weiss. il Sat R 50:24-5 N 4 '67
Museum exhibit tells the Masada story. J. A. Sanders. Christian Cent 85:89-90 Ja 17 '68
Volunteers at Masada; Manhattan's Jewish museum display of models. il Time 90:88-9 O 13 '67

MASAI (native race) See Africa—Native races

MASCAGNI, Pietro
Cavalleria rusticana. *Criticism*
Dance Mag il 41:26 D '67
New Yorker 43:173 O 7 '67
Iris. *Criticism*
Opera N 32:24 N 25 '67

MASEFIELD, John
Obituary
Newsweek por 69:52 My 22 '67
Pub W 191:46 My 22 '67
Time por 89:37-8 My 19 '67

MASERS
See also
Lasers

MASHECK, Joseph
Guernica as art history. Art N 66:32-5+ D '67

MASIN, Herman L.
Sports. See issues of Senior scholastic

MASKA, Karl
Men of third squad, second platoon, C company, third battalion. T. Buckley. il pors N Y Times Mag p34-5+ N 5 '67

MASKED ball; opera. See Verdi, G.

MASKS (for the face)
How to make festive, whimsical masks. il House & Gard 132:248-9 N '67
Masks. J. F. Jenkins. il Sch Arts 67:38-9 N '67

MASKS, Oxygen. See Oxygen apparatus

MASOCHISM
Perverted piety; mortification of the flesh. Christian Cent 84:428 Ap 5 '67

MASON, Edith
All pepper; ed. by M. J. Matz. por Opera N 31:26-7 Mr 18 '67

MASON, Edward S.
Coming events. Commentary 43:92-5 Ja '67

MASON, Edwin A.
What are the best bird houses? Horticulture 45:22-3+ Mr '67

MASON, Ellsworth
Lighting and ventilation; adaptation of address, May 16, 1966. Library J 92:201-6 Ja 15 '67
Well-wrought interior design; adaptation of address, May 16, 1966. Library J 92:743-7 F 15 '67

MASON, George
George Mason country. H. D. Crawford. il por Am For 73:18-21+ N '67

MASON, James A.
New dimensions in music lessons. House B 109:150-1+ F '67

MASON, John F.
Whom the gods love. Reporter 37:21-5 S 21 '67

MASON NECK, Va. See Wildlife sanctuaries

MASONRY
How to pick the right masonry paint. J. P. Schenley. il Pop Mech 128:168-70+ O '67
Patching concrete and masonry. B. Gladstone. Am Home 70:150 O '67

MASS
First mass in English. America 116:866 Je 24 '67
How U.S. Catholics view their rites. Newsweek 69:70 Mr 20 '67
In search of an author; Roman canon of the mass. C. J. McNaspy. America 117:667-8 N 25 '67
Let the children come to me; children's mass. America 117:164 Ag 19 '67
New canons for the mass. C. J. McNaspy; J. L'Heureux; D. Gelpi. America 116:781-3 My 27 '67
Non-Latin mass. W. F. Buckley, jr. Commonweal 87:167-9 N 10 '67; Discussion. 87:318-19 D 1 '67
Sometimes on Saturday. Time 89:69 Ap 21 '67
Student involvement in the liturgy; survey findings of attitudes of Catholic college freshmen toward the mass. W. J. Farrell. il Cath World 205:199-204 Jl '67
To the rear, march; Rome's move to discourage profane music in the mass. J. O'Gara. Commonweal 85:552 F 17 '67
See also
Liturgical language

MASS (music)
Mass production; Misa Criolla sung in Spanish. Newsweek 70:98 S 11 '67
See also
Phonograph records—Mass

Anecdotes, facetiae, satire, etc.
New mass to be celebrated. P. J. Laux. il America 117:550 N 11 '67

MASS communication. See Mass media

MASS for the present time; ballet. See Ballets—Criticisms

MASS media
Can we communicate with Europe? P. Kimball. Sat R 50:54-5 Jl 8 '67
Communications: mass without meaning; address, March 1, 1967. A. R. Murphy, jr. Vital Speeches 33:573-6 Jl 1 '67
Communications technology: a social force; address, October 10, 1967. R. W. Sarnoff. Vital Speeches 34:94-6 N 15 '67
Crisis coverage; conference on the mass media and race relations at Columbia university. Newsweek 70:60+ O 30 '67
Debt of thanks; concerning salutatorian address by F. S. Murray. S. Kauffmann. New Repub 157:24+ Jl 22 '67
Great media impact war; concerning Roper and other survey findings. J. Tebbel. il Sat R 50:96-7 Je 10 '67
Intruders; Unesco's Director-General looks at ethics in the mass media. R. Maheu. UNESCO Courier 20:23-4 F '67
Is Babbitt dead? survey reveals what real estate people think of their reflected images. L. S. Burns. bibliog f Harvard Bsns R 45:14-16+ S '67
Kidbirds, cinemates, and seeing-eye children. D. S. Gelatt. il Pop Phot 62:100-3+ Ja '68
Mass media; a need for greatness. A. Fontaine. Ann Am Acad 371:72-84 My '67
Medium is the victim? new media and the library profession. L. H. Freiser. Library J 93:166-7 Ja 15 '68
New reformation and the myth of media objectivity. J. D. Callaway. Christian Cent 84:1349-52 O 25 '67
Press: how clear is its mirror on our world? il Sr Schol 90:6-12 Ap 28 '67

Brazil
Time-Life caper: Brazil's Yankee network; infiltration of communications media. E. Blum. il Nation 204:678-81 My 29 '67

China (People's Republic)
Writing on the wall; posters and other sources of news. il Newsweek 70:40-2 Jl 17 '67

MASS transit. See Rapid transit

MASSACHUSETTS
See also
Architecture, Domestic—Massachusetts
Fishing—Massachusetts
Geology—Massachusetts
Law—Massachusetts
Trials—Massachusetts

MASSACHUSETTS college of art, Boston
Saturday high school art classes. J. Grepp. il Sch Arts 66:5-8 Ja '67

MASSACHUSETTS institute of technology, Cambridge
Action intellectuals: on the Charles River, the seedbed of the new elite. T. H. White. Life 62:70+ Je 9 '67

MASSACHUSETTS Institute of technology, Cambridge—*Continued*
Avoiding an asteroid; MIT engineering students solve problem. il Time 89:54-5 Je 16 '67
New center at M.I.T; Education research center. Sch & Soc 95:375-6 O 28 '67
Oceanography: Woods Hole and MIT pool their resources. L. J. Carter. il Science 157:1154-7 S 8 '67
University information system: projects MAC and INTREX; summary of address at ABPC conference. C. Overhage. Pub W 191:37-8 Ap 10 '67

MASSACHUSETTS. University, Amherst
Mass. committee raps university. Library J 93:142 Ja 15 '68
Mass. univ. wins court fight against librarian. Library J 92:2496 Jl '67
Matter of reputation. K. Nyren. Library J 92:173 Ja 15 '67
Montgomery case goes to court. Library J 92:1557 Ap 15 '67

MASSACRES (World war, 1939-1945) See World war, 1939-1945—Atrocities

MASSAPEQUA PARK, N.Y.
Collect twice the leaves with the same crew. C. J. Hart. il Am City 82:116-17 Ap '67

MASSAQUOI, Hans J.
Billy Mo: the Satchmo of Germany. Ebony 22:68-73 Jl '67
Lefties, a maligned minority. Ebony 22:63-4+ My '67

MASSAR, Ivan
Troubling voyage to North Vietnam; ed. by W. Hedgepeth. por Look 31:17-21 Je 27 '67

MASSE, Benjamin Louis
Mergers are changing the landscape. America 117:107 Jl 29 '67
Pope's plea for poor nations. America 117:129-32 Ag 5 '67
Social front. See occasional issues of America
Sputtering war on poverty. America 116:346-8 Mr 11 '67

MASSEE, May
Books, children and women. R. H. Viguers. Horn Bk 43:152-3 Ap '67
Homage to May Massee. C. H. Bishop. il Commonweal 87:173-4 N 10 '67
To May Massee. R. Sawyer. Horn Bk 43:229-32 Ap '67
Young man remembers May Massee. A. Bell. por Pub W 191:84-5 F 20 '67

MASSENET, Jules
Le jongleur returns. W. Brockway. il Opera N 31:6-7 Ap 15 '67
Records:
Thaïs (excerpts) Opera N 31:34 F 25 '67

MASSENGALE, Don
Two Dons in quest of a title. A. Wright. il por Sports Illus 27:18-21 Jl 31 '67

MASSERMAN, Jules
Hippies and their future, a new look ahead; interview. por U S News 63:58-61 Jl 17 '67

MASSES (periodical)
Echoes of revolt, ed. by W. L. O'Neill. Review
Nation 204:277-9 F 27 '67. M. B. Folsom

MASSIE, Charlotte
Virginia's historic gardens. Travel 127:48-9 Ap '67

MASSIE, Robert K.
Authors & editors. por Pub W 192:39 S 18 '67

MASTAI, Marie-Louise
Antiques of tomorrow. Am Home 70:112 N '67

MASTER E S
Mystery of the master E S. il Life 63:87-8+ O 6 '67

MASTER photo dealers and finishers association annual trade show. See Photography—Exhibitions

MASTERS, George
Letting George do it. L. Howard. il por Newsweek 70:31 D 18 '67

MASTERS, Roger D.
Leemanship. Reporter 37:46-8 O 19 '67
NATO: the ailing alliance. Harper 234:126+ Mr '67

MASTERS, William Howell, and Johnson, V. E.
Sex and sexuality: the crucial difference. Read Digest 90:123-6 F '67

MASTERS golf tournament. See Golf—Tournaments

MASTITIS
Do milking machines really cause mastitis? Farm J 91:34F Ag '67
Read this before you milk. D. Braun. il Farm J 91:D6+ O '67

MASTS and rigging
Question of rake. A. Ellis. il Yachting 122:29+ Jl '67
Roller furling jibs. N. Nadel. il Yachting 122:54-5+ N '67
See also
Sails

MATCH (periodical) See Periodicals—France
MATCH for a princess; story. See Singer, I. B.
MATCH-making by computers. See Computers—Social applications

MATCHAN, Leonard Joseph
Conglomerate, London-style. il por Time 90:96 O 13 '67
Socialist tycoon. il por Newsweek 70:85 O 16 '67
Takeover tycoon: I win because I intend to win. por Duns R 90:35 S '67

MATCHES
Hazards of playing with matches; likely explanation for potassium flare stars. G. S. Mumford. il Sky & Tel 34:380 D '67
Hazards of smoking; likely explanation for potassium flare stars. Sci Am 217:60-1 N '67

MATELES, R. I. and others
Growth of a thermophilic bacterium on hydrocarbons: a new source of single-cell protein. bibliog Science 157:1322-3 S 15 '67

MATERIALS
Composite materials growth barrier cited. Aviation W 86:32 Ap 10 '67
Composites reaching production stage; plastic and metal composites. J. F. Judge. il Aero Tech 21:26-30 O 23 '67
Electronic properties of amorphous materials. J. Tauc. bibliog il Science 158:1543-8 D 22 '67
Expanding aerospace usage looms for woven components. W. E. Wilks. il Tech W 20:24-51+ Je 12 '67
Materials; symposium. bibliog il Sci Am 217:67-100+ S '67
New processes at Harvey help firm's market drive. J. F. Judge. il Aero Tech 21:44-5 Ag 14 '67
Strength of a whisker; composite materials. Newsweek 69:84-5 Je 5 '67
Textile engineering seen as spur to composite market: astrocarb, laminated fabric for aerospace use. il Tech W 20:29 Je 12 '67

Bibliography
Bibliography. Sci Am 217:312+ S '67

Cost
Competition of materials. W. O. Alexander. il Sci Am 217:254-6+ S '67

Deterioration
See also
Erosion of metals

Fatigue
See also
Fracture of solids

History
Materials. C. S. Smith. il Sci Am 217:68-79 S '67
Testing
See Testing

MATERIALS, Artists. See Artists materials
MATERIALS, Flammable. See Inflammable materials
MATERIALS centers. See Instructional materials centers
MATERIALS handling
See also
Freight handling
MATERIALS of instruction. See Teaching—Aids and devices
MATERIALS research
Concern mounts over long-term support; technological base for space programs. il Aero Tech 21:66-70 N 20 '67
MATERNAL behavior. See Mothers
MATERNAL deprivation
Depression in infant monkeys separated from their mothers. I C. Kaufman and L. A. Rosenblum. bibliog il Science 155:1030-1 F 24 '67
Experiential deprivation and later behavior. J. L. Fuller. bibliog il Science 158:1645-52 D 29 '67
MATERNAL effect. See Prenatal influences
MATH, Irwin
Selecting frequency and time standards. Electr World 77:40-1+ My '67
MATHEMATICAL biology. See Biomathematics
MATHEMATICAL economics. See Economics, Mathematical
MATHEMATICAL formulas. See Mathematics—Formulae
MATHEMATICAL literature
Books in the field: mathematics. R. L. Davis. bibliog il Wilson Lib Bul 42:497-509 Ja '68

MATHEMATICAL physics
New math of physics. Sci Am 217:59 N '67
MATHEMATICAL recreation
Mathematical games. M. Gardner. See issues of Scientific American
MATHEMATICAL research
Role of intuition. R. L. Wilder. bibliog Science 156:605-10 My 5 '67; Reply. G. L. Kesteven. 157:1376-7 S 22 '67
MATHEMATICAL societies
See also
International congress of mathematicians
MATHEMATICIANS
See also
International congress of mathematicians
MATHEMATICS
See also
Calculus
Economics, Mathematical
Games, Theory of
Numerals
Probabilities

Bibliography
See also
Mathematical literature

Formulae
Rodder 'rithmetic. J. McFarland. Hot Rod 20:94-7 Ap '67
To avoid long division, use this short-cut table. A. P. Armagnac. Pop Sci 190:124-5 Mr '67

Philosophy
Yes, we have no foundations. Sci Am 216:52 Ap '67

Problems, exercises, etc.
High-speed math short cuts. A. P. Armagnac. il Pop Sci 190:119-26 Mr '67

Study and teaching
College math for 11-year-olds; letter. E. H. Lehman, jr. Science 157:367 Jl 28 '67
How children learn; British primary school method. J. Featherstone. New Repub 157:18-21 S 2 '67
Instructional materials in the mathematics classroom. D. A. Johnson. NEA J 56:39-40 My '67
International study of achievement in mathematics, ed. by T. Husén. Review
Sat R il 50:68-9 Jl 15 '67. M. Beberman
Is our math inferior? global project tests the schools. G. S. Carnett. il Am Ed 3:1-3 Mr '67
Poor marks in math for U.S. pupils, but--. U S News 62:12 Mr 20 '67
Price of mathophobia; survey showing American 13-year-olds lag behind in math. il Time 89:60 Mr 17 '67
Primary mathematics; Nuffield series. J. Featherstone. New Repub 157:34-5+ N 11 '67
Role of intuition. R. L. Wilder. bibliog Science 156:605-10 My 5 '67; Reply. G. L. Kesteven. 157:1376-7 S 22 '67
Several revolutions in elementary school mathematics. F. J. Mueller. NEA J 57:53-4 Ja '68
U.S. ranks low in math survey. Sr Schol 90:sup4 Ap 14 '67
Upgrading mathematics education. Sch & Soc 95:410-11 N 11 '67
Who's afraid of the new math? A. Van Dine. il Parents Mag 42:62-3+ S '67
Why Johnny can't add; results of tests given students in different countries. Newsweek 69:117 Mr 13 '67

MATHEMATICS, Logic of. See Mathematics—Philosophy
MATHEMATICS and music. See Music—Theory
MATHER, Berkely
Diamond watch; story. Sat Eve Post 240:64-70 Ap 8 '67
MATHEWS, Carol
What makes a glamour stock? Duns R 90:36-7+ O '67
Which way for stocks in '68? Duns R 90:36-7+ N '67
MATHEWS, Thomas F.
New city, new church. Commonweal 86:518-20+ Ag 25 '67
Turning point: International congress on religion, architecture and the visual arts. America 117:393-6 O 7 '67
MATHEWSON, Franklin D.
Films and filmstrips for PTA committee chairmen. PTA Mag 61:30-2 My; 30-1 Je; 62:37 S '67
MATHEWSON, Joseph
Griselda, doge of Venice, by Pollo Cacciatore (1820-1881) Opera N 31:16 Ap 15 '67
Just for laughs. Look 31:M14 N 14 '67

MATHIAS, Bob
Olympic golden boy in Congress. il pors Life 63:39-40+ O 20 '67
MATHIAS, Robert
Literacy and Ecuador's national development plan. Sch & Soc 95:84-6 F 4 '67
MATHIS der maler; opera. See Hindemith, P.
MATING behavior. See Sex behavior
MATING behavior (insects) See Courtship of insects
MATKOVICH, Diane
Pioneer daze. H. L. Masin. il por Sr Schol 91:20 N 2 '67
MATOS, Huber
Terms of trade. il por Newsweek 71:43 Ja 15 '68
Unusual prisoner. por Time 91:25 Ja 12 '68
MATOS MENDIETA, Ramiro
Wari-Willka. por Américas 19:9-17 Ja '67
MATRANGA, Frances Carfi
Tips for artists (cont) Design 68:38 Ja '67
MATRIMONY. See Marriage
MATSON, Randy
Now two wizards of oomph. T. C. Brody. il por Sports Illus 26:58-9 F 13 '67
One man's meet. il por Time 89:58 Ap 21 '67
MATSUMURA, F. and Boush, G. M.
Dieldrin: degradation by soil microorganisms. bibliog Science 156:959-61 My 19 '67
MATTEO
Matteo and Indo-American dance company; 92nd street Y. D. Hering. Dance Mag 42:79 Ja '68
MATTER
Ordinary matter. G. Feinberg il Sci Am 216:126-30+ My '67
See also
Matter, Interstellar
Particles (nuclear physics)
MATTER, Interstellar
Aluminum-26 in Pacific sediment; implications. J. T. Wasson and others. bibliog il Science 155:446-8 Ja 27 '67
Antimatter and cosmology. H. Alfvén. il Sci Am 216:106-12+ Ap '67
Antimatter and creation. A. Ewing il Sci N 91:64+ Ja 21 '67
Interstellar grains. J. M. Greenberg. il Sci Am 217:106-12+ bibliog(p 156) O '67
Where do stars come from? I. Asimov. il Sci Digest 61:80-1 Mr '67
Zodiacal dust and deep-sea sediments. S. F. Singer. bibliog il Science 156:1080-3 My 26 '67
MATTER of living; story. See Williams, L.
MATTHAU, Walter
Unmasking the great putty face; interview, ed. by G. Moore. pors Life 62:37-8+ Mr 3 '67
MATTHEWS, Fred
My conflict with East German reds; ed. by C. L. Sanders. M. R. Herrin. il pors Ebony 22:94-6+ Je '67
MATTHEWS, Herbert Lionel
Castro and the Times. il por Newsweek 70:60-1 S 11 '67
History and Herbert Matthews. Nat R 19:1004-5 S 19 '67
MATTHEWS, Howard A.
Tomorrow is now. Am Ed 3:21-2 Je '67
MATTHEWS, Jack
Five poets. E. Blum. Poetry 109:343 F '67
MATTHEWS, James L. and others
Giant-cell centrioles. bibliog Science 155:1423-4 Mr 17 '67
MATTHEWS, L. D
Back country go-around. Flying 80:91 F '67
MATTHEWS, S. W.
Recreation demand in Miami Beach. Parks & Rec 2:23+ Jl '67
MATTHEWS, Samuel W.
Science explores the monsoon sea. Nat Geog Mag 132:554-75 O '67
MATTHEWS, T. S.
How to work the London telephone, think of Allah. Mlle 64:208-10 Mr '67
Tall, balding, dead Henry R. Luce. Esquire 68:131-2+ S '67
Why so gloomy? poem. Atlan 219:132 Ap '67
MATTHEWS, Tanya
Chess. Sports Illus 27:69-70+ N 20 '67
MATTHEWS, William B. Jr
Chesapeake log. See issues of Motor boating
In the wake of the skipjacks. Motor B 119:32-3+ Ap '67
MATTHIAS, B. T. and others
Superconductivity at 20 degrees Kelvin. bibliog Science 156:645-6 My 5 '67
MATTHIESSEN, Peter
Last great strand: Corkscrew swamp sanctuary. Audubon 69:64-71 Mr '67
Reporter at large. New Yorker 43:40-4+ My 27; 42-4+ Je 3; 120+ O 28 '67

MATTLAGE, Louise
Dance vacation. Dance Mag 41:27-8+ Jl '67
MATTRESSES
How to buy a mattress. Bet Hom & Gard 45: 43-4+ O '67
MATURITY
Age of the person. J. Grennan. il Seventeen 26:94-5+ D '67
How to handle a crisis. D. A. Sugarman and R. Hochstein. Seventeen 26:150-1+ S '67
One and only you? excerpt from The Seventeen guide to knowing yourself. D. A. Sugarman and R. Hochstein. il Seventeen 26: 300-1+ Ag '67
So your mother is going to work. N. E. Scofield. il Seventeen 26:362+ Ag '67
To be or not to be mature. F. R. Schreiber and M. Herman. il Sci Digest 63:68-71 Ja '68
MATURITY, Sexual. See Puberty
MATZ, Mary Jane
First ladies of the Puccini premieres. Opera N 32:6-7 Ja 13 '68
MATZKE, Edwin B.
New botanical classic. Natur Hist 76:18-19+ F '67
MATZKIN, Myron A.
Matzkin on movies. See issues of Modern photography
MAU MAU
Myth of Mau Mau, by C. G. Rosberg and J. Nottingham. Review
  New Repub 156:34-5 F 25 '67. M. Lowenkopf
MAUCHER, Arnold
Fashion head. il U S Camera 31:64-7 Ja '68
MAUGHAM, William Somerset
Maugham's Pacific. W. Menard. il por Sat R 50:77-8+ Mr 11 '67
MAUI (island)
Traveler's choice. J. G. Go. Travel 128:9 D '67
MAULDIN, Bill
Those Israeli troops. New Repub 156:5-6 Je 24 '67
MAULDIN, William Henry. See Mauldin, B.
MAULE, Tex
In Dallas, spytalk and a rout. Sports Illus 27:24-5 O 9 '67
Soccer. Sports Illus 26:68+ Ap 24 '67
—See Dundee, A. jt. auth.
MAURA, Sister
Christmas star; poem. Cath World 206:159 Ja '68
MAURITIUS
Little places. il Newsweek 70:39 Ag 21 '67
Prospect of independence. Time 90:30+ Ag 18 '67
MAURO, F. and Elkind, M. M.
Sulfur mustard and X-rays: differences in expression of lethal damage. bibliog Science 155:1561-3 Mr 24 '67
MAUROIS, André
My debt to Romain Rolland. Sat R 50:21+ D 16 '67
about
Immortal. por Newsweek 70:110+ O 23 '67
Obituary
  Pub W 192:36 O 23 '67
MAURY, Philippe
Philippe Maury, 1916-1967. B. Thompson. Christian Cent 84:806 Je 21 '67
MAUSOLEUMS. See Tombs
MAUTNER, Henry G. See Rosenberg, P. jt. auth.
MAVERICK (missile) See Guided missiles
MAVOR, James W.
Don't believe all they dig up. B. Boothroyd. Atlan 219:111-12 Je '67
MAVRIDES, C. and Lane, E. A.
Failure of cycloheximide to induce tyrosine transaminase in the anesthetized rat. bibliog Science 156:1376-8; 157:1591 Je 9, S 29 '67
MAWSON, Sidney
Cuyler hill monster. por Outdoor Life 139: 56-7+ My '67
MAX Planck institute for physiology of behavior
Konrad Lorenz. E. Stillman. il Horizon 9: 60-5 Spr '67
MAXIE, E. C. and Crane, J. C.
2,4,5-Trichlorophenoxyacetic acid: effect on ethylene production by fruits and leaves of fig tree. bibliog Science 155:1548-50 Mr 24 '67
MAXIMS
See also
Aphorisms and apothegms
MAXON, John
J. L. David's portrait of the Marquise de Pastoret. Art N 66:44-6 N '67

MAXWELL, G. Edward
Rehabilitation, the fight back. Todays Health 45:62-7 D '67
MAXWELL, J. C.
One trillion passenger miles; excerpts from address. Aviation W 87:21 Jl 10 '67
MAXWELL, Margaret
(ed) See Frost, L. Swinger of birches
MAXWELL, Mary
Mary Maxwell reclines to paint her watercolors. il por Am Artist 31:28-31+ Je '67
MAXWELL, William
Books. New Yorker 43:156-9 F 25; 63-4+ D 23 '67
MAXWELL'S equations
Can you please give an explanation of the unified field theory? I. Asimov. Sci Digest 61:86 F '67
Maxwell's demon. W. Ehrenberg. il Sci Am 217:103-10 bibliog(p 156) N '67
Toward nuclear truth. il Sci N 91:287 Mr 25 '67
MAY, Don
Sweetheart of Dayton place. H. L. Masin. il por Sr Schol 91:18 D 14 '67
MAY, Elaine
Not enough rope; drama. Mlle 66:152-3+ N '67
about
Whatever happened to Elaine May? T. Thompson. il pors Life 63:54-54B+ Jl 28 '67
MAY, Francis E.
Digital computer designed to control traffic only. Am City 82:100+ Ja '67
MAY, J. William. See Largent, F. D. jt. auth.
MAY, Rollo
Frontiers of being human. Sat R 50:37-9 My 20 '67
MAY festival, Cincinnati. See Music festivals—Ohio
MAYA, Mario
Holiday bounty. W. Terry. il por Sat R 51: 36+ Ja 6 '68
MAYAS
Expedition holy book; holy book, CEDAM, at Chumpon. E. Gowen. il Américas 19:1-7 S '67
Fugue in varied tempos; ruins at Palengue. R. H. Buck. il Sr Schol 90:sup 14-15 My 5 '67
There's the rub; rubbings of Palenque sarcophagus. il Newsweek 70:87 O 2 '67
MAYBE later it will come back to my mind; story. See Faessler, S.
MAYBER, A. Poljakoff-. See Poljakoff-Mayber, A.
MAYE, Marilyn
Two for the show. por Time 89:63-4 Mr 3 '67
MAYER, Christian
Don't sell it; throw it away. Nation 205:133-4 Ag 28 '67
Letter from Berlin. Nation 205:80-1 Jl 31 '67
Letter from Munich. Nation 205:368-9 O 16 '67
Uneasy alliance. Commonweal 87:45-6 O 13 '67
Wars of Private Hochhuth. Nation 205:700-1 D 25 '67
Winter of discontent. Nation 204:165 F 6 '67
MAYER, George Louis
Beatrice di Tenda. Am Rec G 34:180-2 N '67
Purcell omnibus: Dido & Aeneas, and The Indian queen. Am Rec G 33:464-6 F '67
Thoughtful history of singing. Am Rec G 33:864+ My '67
Two about Bayreuth. Am Rec G 33:1120-1 Ag '67
MAYER, Jean, and Thomas, D. W.
Regulation of food intake and obesity. bibliog Science 156:328-37 Ap 21 '67
—See Arees, E. A. jt. auth.
MAYER, Lawrence A.
Diverse $10,000-and-over masses. Fortune 76: 114-17+ D '67
Home goods: but what will they think of next? Fortune 76:114-18+ Ag '67
Why the U.S. population isn't exploding. Fortune 75:162-6+ Ap '67
MAYER, Martin
Avis vs. Hertz: Madison avenue's favorite feud. Harper 236:40-4 Ja '68
Blinding facility of Leonard Bernstein. Esquire 67:66-8+ F '67
Criminal and the law; excerpts from Lawyers and laws. Sat Eve Post 240:25-7+ F 11 '67
Few words about lawyers. Esquire 67:124-7+ Ap '67
Help your child learn more, better, faster. Bet Hom & Gard 45:18+ S '67
Hogan's office is a kind of ministry of justice. N Y Times Mag p7+ Jl 23; 9 Ag 13 '67

MAYER, Martin—*Continued*
Horizon, with clouds. Opera N 32:8-11 S 9 '67
How courts decide the value of a husband's life. Redbook 129:72-3+ Je '67
Law schools: the thinking man's bastion; excerpts from The lawyers and the law. Harper 234:70-4+ Je '67
Maestro von Karajan is always turned on. N Y Times Mag p50-1+ D 3 '67
Met's new Peter Grimes. Hi Fi 17:MA8-9 Ap '67
Recordings. See issues of Esquire
Understanding and using economics (cont) Bet Hom & Gard 45:42 F; 28 Mr; 36 Ap; 84 My; 128 Je '67
What's wrong with our big-city schools. Sat Eve Post 240:21-3+ S 9 '67

MAYER, Milton
Life of Professor Riley. Harper 235:88-9 O '67
Much better mousetrap. Harper 234:77-80 F '67

MAYER, Philip F.
Venture in cultural anthropology. por Negro Hist Bul 29:179-80+ Fall '66

MAYER, Ralph
Ralph Mayer's technical question & answer page. See issues of American artist

MAYER, Robert E.
Look at it another way. il U S Camera 30: 46-7+ Ap '67

MAYES, Herbert R.
Henry R. Luce. Sat R 50:16-17 Mr 18 '67
Trade winds. See issues of Saturday review

MAYFIELD, Catfish
Pride, inc: D.C.'s cool answer to hot summers. il pors Ebony 23:82-4+ D '67
$300,000 payroll for Catfish. S. McBee. il por Life 63:34 Ag 25 '67

MAYFIELD, Harold
Shed few tears. Audubon 69:61-5 My '67

MAYFIELD, Rufus. See Mayfield, C.

MAYHEW, Eleanor R.
South India. Travel 128:39-41 D '67

MAYHEW, Lewis B.
What's ahead for higher education? NEA J 56:16-18 D '67

MAYNARD, Elden C.
Build the pulse command responder. Pop Electr 27:33-7 Jl '67
Remote commander. Pop Electr 27:42-6+ Ag '67

MAYNARD, Fredelle Bruser
Dream vacation. Good H 165:48+ Ag '67
Housewives' crime, and what makes them do it? Good H 165:98-9+ O '67
Karen and the facts of life. Good H 164:37-9 F '67
Minds of high school seniors. New Repub 156:11-12 My 20 '67
Red dress; story. Sat Eve Post 240:58-62 Je 17 '67
Teacher gap, and how to close it. Read Digest 91:50-4 Ag '67

MAYNARD, Olga
(ed) See Litz, K. Katherine Litz

MAYNARD, Theodore E.
He makes utilities blow fuses. por Bsns W p54+ Je 3 '67

MAYNARD, Walter
Stock market outlook. Duns R 89:17+ F '67

MAYO, E. L.
On growing invisible: Substance; At the odds; Sparrows; poems. Poetry 111:28-30 O '67

MAYOR, Alfred
Behind the fun at the fairs. Holiday 42:30+ N '67
Club Méditerranée. Holiday 42:62-7+ Ag '67

MAYORAL candidates. See Candidates, Political

MAYORS
Troubled cities, and their mayors. il Newsweek 69:38-43 Mr 13 '67
With the mayors. Nat R 19:1248-50 N 14 '67
See also subhead Mayors under names of cities, e.g. Chicago—Mayors

MAYORS, Negro. See Negro municipal officers

MAYORS wives
See also
Lindsay, M. H.

MAYS, Billy Wayne
Hustle of Texas Billy. G. Rogin. il pors Sports Illus 27:58-64+ S 4 '67

MAYS, Willie
Fun and games with Willie Mays. il pors Ebony 22:37-8+ Mr '67
Say hey no more. M. Mulvoy. il pors Sports Illus 27:26-9 Ag 7 '67

MAZE tests
Aminoacidemias: effects on maze performance and cerebral serotonin. C. M. McKean and others. bibliog il Science 157:213-15 Jl 14 '67

Reminiscence in the cold flour beetle, tenebrio molitor. T. M. Alloway and A. Routtenberg. bibliog il Science 158:1066-7 N 24 '67

MAZOR, Emanuel. See Heymann, D. jt. auth.

MAZURKAS
See also
Phonograph records—Mazurkas

MAZZONE, Jay
Boy who wouldn't give up. E. Keiffer. il pors Good H 165:56+ S '67

MBA, Léon
Obituary
UN Mo Chron 4:112 D '67

MEACHEM, William L.
New bulb culture research. Horticulture 45: 22-3 O '67

MEAD, Jere, and others
Pulmonary ventilation measured from body surface movements. bibliog Science 156:1383-4 Je 9 '67

MEAD, Loren B.
Seminary community: a critique. Christian Cent 84:563+ Ap 26 '67

MEAD, Margaret
Alternatives to war. Natur Hist 76:65-9 bibliog(p70) D '67
And children shall lead the way. por Redbook 128:46+ F '67
Are the natives friendly? por Redbook 128: 31+ Mr '67
Books for Christmas: an anthropologist's choice. por Redbook 130:22+ D '67
Changing world of living; address. Sci Digest 62:38-43 S '67
Letter from the field: return to New Guinea. por Redbook 130:20+ N '67
Margaret Mead answers questions (title varies) (cont) por Redbook 129:36+ Je; 38+ O '67; 130:30+ Ja '68

MEAD, Matthew
(tr) See Sachs, N. O the homeless colours; In this amethyst

MEAD, Robert G. Jr
Maze of the unreal and real. Sat R 50:44-5 My 13 '67
Myth for mankind. Sat R 50:32 N 4 '67

MEAD, Ruth
(tr) See Sachs, N. O the homeless colours; In this amethyst

MEAD, LAKE
See also
Lake Mead national recreation area

MEAD corporation
Mead papers making stock a revolutionary way. il Pub W 191:72 My 1 '67

MEADE, J. E.
Rates of population growth and standards of living; excerpt from address, June 1967. Mo Labor R 90:55-8 S '67

MEADOW rues
Dusty meadow-rue. il Home Gard 54:57 Ap '67

MEADOWBROOK Junior high school. See Newton, Mass.—Education

MEADOWLANDS of New Jersey. See New Jersey—Meadowlands

MEADOWS, Algur Hurtle
Back to market. il Time 89:84 Je 9 '67
How art swindlers duped a virtuous millionaire. W. A. McWhirter. il pors Life 63:52-4+ Jl 7 '67
Meadows' luck. il por Time 89:94+ My 19 '67

MEALS
Feeding young children can be easy and fun; with recipes. M. C. Newsom. il Parents Mag 42:62-5+ My '67
Meals that take the simmer out of summer; with recipes. R. Holmberg. il Bet Hom & Gard 45:76-7+ Jl '67
Month of marvelous meals; menus, with recipes. il McCalls 94:102-12+ My '67
Mood food; with recipes. il Seventeen 26: 142-5+ O '67
Quick meal beginnings and endings. Bet Hom & Gard 45:87 S '67
See also
Breakfasts
Christmas meals
Cookery
Diet
Dinners and dining
Luncheons
Lunches
Outdoor meals
Snacks
Suppers
Thanksgiving dinners

MEANING of life. See Life

MEANING of words. See Semantics

MEANS, Richard L.
Why worry about nature? Sat R 50:13-15 D 2 '67

MEANY, George
Excerpt from testimony. July 21, 1966. Cong Digest 46:20+ Ja '67

about

Bone in Meany's throat. H. Rowen. New Repub 156:9-10 My 6 '67; Correction. 156:42 Je 3 '67

Inside story of the Reuther-Meany fight. por U S News 62:93-5 F 20 '67

Labor in the bag. S. Lens. Commonweal 87: 432-3 Ja 12 '68

Labor's newest split: the price of a Reuther walkout. U S News 62:76-8 F 27 '67

Open door. por Time 89:24 Mr 3 '67

Reuther vs. Meany: background to labor's showdown. B. J. Widick. Nation 204:614-16 My 15 '67

Reuther vs. Meany. S. Lens. Commonweal 85:557-9 F 17 '67

Split in labor. W. V. Shannon. Commonweal 85:584-5 F 24 '67

Split labor faces a big year. il por Newsweek 69:82-5 F 20 '67

MEARS, Joe
Buck wore black. Outdoor Life 139:10 My '67
—and Miracle, Leonard
(comp) That's where I want to fish. Outdoor Life 139:93-6 Ap '67

MEASLES
Goal for '67: no more measles. L. Boston. Todays Health 45:48-51 My '67

Vaccination
Good-by to measles. il Newsweek 69:67 Mr 20 '67
Out, red spot; drive to eradicate measles from the U.S. il Time 89:67 Mr 17 '67

Vaccines
Can measles be eradicated? letter. R. M. Albrecht. Science 156:1029 My 26 '67; Reply. J. Stokes, jr. bibliog 157:626+ Ag 11 '67
Cheaper measles vaccine still only a promise. Sci N 93:76 Ja 20 '68
Measles: the disease that needn't exist. Consumer Rep 32:398-9 Jl '67

MEASLES, German. See Rubella
MEASURE for measure; drama. See Shakespeare, W.—Plays
MEASUREMENT
Concept of a national measurement system. R. D. Huntoon. bibliog il Science 158:67-71 O 6 '67
Doesn't anything fit like a glove? J. Goodsell. il Read Digest 91:143-4 N '67
International basis for uniform measurement. L. E. Howlett. Science 158:72-4 O 6 '67
Precision measurement of the acceleration of gravity. J. E. Faller. bibliog il Science 158:60-7 O 6 '67
See also
Cookery—Measurements
Distances—Measurement
Frequency measurement
Geodesy
MEASUREMENT, Mental. See Psychometrics
MEASURING instruments
Greyrad building market in heat transfer measurement; probes for taking measurements in extremely high-temperature environments. J. F. Judge. il Aero Tech 21:25-6 Ja 1 '68
Instruments: lab to shop; submillimeter instrument measuring. D. Fishlock. Sci N 92:137+ Ag 5 '67
Make an inclinometer, and get those angles straight! W. Burton. il Pop Mech 128:176-9 D '67
Make this handy indicator for your shop. W. E. Burton. il Pop Mech 129:196-9 Ja '68
Precision measurement of the acceleration of gravity. J. E. Faller. bibliog il Science 158:60-7 O 6 '67
MEASURING utensils, Household. See Cookery —Measurements
MEAT
See also
Cookery—Meat
Meat inspection

Grading and standardization
New look in meat; excerpt from address. M. E. Brunk. Farm J 91:54N Ap '67

Marketing
Cattlemen map bold plan to push up beef prices. R. C. Black. il Farm J 91:B4-5 Mr '67
Five risks of selling on the hook. R. C. Black. il Farm J 91:B4-6 Ja '67
New ways to hedge with futures. R. C. Black. il Farm J 91:B8-9 Ja '67

Prices
Can cattlemen be price makers? il Farm J 91:66L Mr '67
Cattlemen have a case. Farm J 91:66 Ag '67
Cattlemen map bold plan to push up beef prices. R. C. Black. il Farm J 91:B4-5 Mr '67
More pork crimps prices. il Farm J 91:H19 F '67
New ways to hedge with futures. R. C. Black. il Farm J 91:B8-9 Ja '67
Pricecast. See issues of Farm journal
Slump, how come, how long? il Farm J 91: B15 Ja '67
We aren't out of the woods yet. il Farm J 91:B15 Jl '67
What happened to beef demand? il Farm J 92:B15 Ja '68
Where are they all coming from? il Farm J 91:B19 Mr '67

MEAT, Dried
Making and using Mexico's *carne seca;* with recipe. il Sunset 138:189 F '67

MEAT, Frozen
Work wonders with canned and frozen poultry products. il Ladies Home J 84:101+ F '67
You can refreeze meat. E. S. Hunter. Farm J 91:109 F '67

MEAT industry and trade
Are we producing what the housewife wants? D. Malena. il Suc Farm 65:33+ N '67
Hogmen vote for check-off. Farm J 91:22 Ja '67
New ways they're selling your beef. il Farm J 91:B6+ Mr '67
See also
Meat inspection
Rath packing company
Swift and company

Great Britain
Virus fells British meat trade. il Bsns W p76-8 D 9 '67

MEAT inspection
Inroads in the meat jungle; proposed extension of federal controls. Sci N 92:129 Ag 5 '67
Jungle revisited. Nation 206:2 Ja 1 '68
Meat fit to eat; bill calling for federal inspection of all meat sold for human consumption. Time 90:96 N 24 '67
Meat inspection: the new jungle. N. Kotz. il Nation 205:230-3 S 18 '67
One man's meat; bill to improve intrastate inspection. Newsweek 70:29-30 D 4 '67
Watch that hamburger; need for bill to bring all intrastate plants under federal meat inspection service. R. Nader. New Repub 157:15-16 Ag 19 '67
We're still in the jungle; proposed amendments to the meat inspection act. R. Nader. New Repub 157:11-12 Jl 15 '67

MEAT substitutes
Meatless meats. J. Harvey. il Suc Farm 65: 36-7+ O; 38-9 N '67

MEBANE, John
Fashion periodicals. Bet Hom & Gard 45: 12+ Mr '67
Treasure hunt. See issues of Better homes and gardens

MECHANICAL aids in education. See Teaching —Aids and devices
MECHANICAL aptitude tests. See Aptitude tests
MECHANICAL developments, incorporated
Big gamble of Lillord Cobb. il Ebony 22:63- 4+ O '67
MECHANICAL devices
See also
Automatons
MECHANICAL dolls. See Dolls
MECHANICAL drawing
See also
Drawing instruments
MECHANICAL equipment of buildings
Budget shifts reflect need for new design approach. L. C. Jaquith. il Arch Rec 141:87 Ap '67
Elevated flooring permits impossible time schedule and great flexibility. il Arch Rec 141:227-8 Ap '67

MECHANICAL harvesting. See Harvesting machinery
MECHANICAL hearts. See Hearts, Artificial
MECHANICAL horsepower. See Horsepower (mechanics)
MECHANICAL inventions. See Inventions
MECHANICAL models
Classic toys test your physics know-how; interview. ed. by W. S. Griswold. J. S. Miller. il Pop Sci 190:116-21+ Ap '67
How do they do it? the tricky mouse on the Ed Sullivan show. H. Shuldiner. il Pop Sci 190:68-70 F '67
Research frontier; mechanical model water-lifter devised from drinking bird toy. R. B. Murrow. il Sat R 50:51-5 Je 3 '67
See also
Automatons
MECHANICAL translating. See Translating machines
MECHANICS
See also
Pendulum
Perpetual motion
MECHANICS (persons)
See also
Airplane mechanics
Automobile mechanics (persons)
MECHANISM (philosophy)
See also
Cybernetics
MECHANICS, Household
See also
Repairing
MECHANIZATION in agriculture. See Agricultural machinery
MECHEM, James
Dear Paulina, tenting tonight; story. Américas 19:32-7 Ag '67
MECKLIN, John
$4-billion machine that reshapes geography. Fortune 75:113-16+ F '67
Jim Webb's earthy management of space. Fortune 76:82-7+ Ag '67
Prescriptions and palliatives. Reporter 37:48+ D 14 '67
Rockwells take off for outer space. Fortune 75:100-4+ Je 1 '67
Struggle to rescue the people. Fortune 75:126-33+ Ap '67
MECOSTA, Mich.
Old settlers. R. Kirk. Nat R 19:641 Je 13 '67
MEDAL of honor (United States)
Courage beyond the call of duty. W. L. Katz. il Sat R 50:30-1 Je 17 '67
Dixie town fetes war hero: Medal of honor winner Lawrence Joel is hailed by Winston-Salem. R. Lantz. il Ebony 22:27-8+ Je '67
Soldier does his job: L. Joel. il Newsweek 69:30 Mr 20 '67
MEDALS
Centennial exposition medals: United States centennial exposition. C. French. Hobbies 72:102 Jl '67
Decoration day; craze in West Germany. il Newsweek 69:49-50 Mr 6 '67
Medal that started the wars; collecting medals. C. French. Hobbies 71:102 F '67
See also
Decorations of honor
also names of medals, e.g. Caldecott medal
MEDDERS, Ernest
Son of Billie Sol. il por Newsweek 69:30+ Mr 20 '67
$3,000,000 sham. D. Nevin. il pors Life 62:82-6+ Ap 7 '67
MEDDERS, Margaret
$3,000,000 sham. D. Nevin. il pors Life 62:82-6+ Ap 7 '67
MEDEA; opera. See Cherubini, L.
MEDELMAN, John
Cancer is bad for you. Esquire 68:111+ N '67
Immense journey of Loren Eiseley. Esquire 67:92-4+ Mr '67
Why I am not a psychiatrist. Harper 234:46-9 F; 11 Ap '67
MEDIATION, Industrial. See Arbitration, Industrial
MEDIATION, International. See Arbitration, International
MEDICAID program
Crisis in medicine. E. T. Chase. Commonweal 85:650-2 Mr 10 '67
Doctors' bonanza. E. T. Chase. New Repub 156:15-17 Ap 15 '67
End of the handout? what Congress plans. il U S News 63:46 D 25 '67
Help to needy grows through medicaid. J. R. Kernodle. Todays Health 45:88+ N '67
Medicaid in the billions; getting out of hand? il U S News 63:32-4 O 16 '67

Medicare: expensive & successful, medicaid: chaotic but irrevocable. il Time 90:96+ O 6 '67
State medicine in trouble in U.S. il U S News 62:75-6 My 22 '67
Why not compulsory hospital insurance? R. Tunley. Sat R 50:12-14 Jl 8 '67
MEDICAL assistants. See Medical workers
MEDICAL care. See Medical service
MEDICAL centers
Cologne's drive-in hospital: traffic in three dimensions; University medical center. il Arch Rec 142:190-3 S '67
Rural patient gets a break; Hopedale medical complex. T. Berland. il Todays Health 45:62-7 O '67
U.C.L.A.'s 20-year plan for health science. il Arch Rec 142:198-201 S '67
Western Reserve university: three schools on one base. il Arch Rec 142:202-3 S '67
See also
Health centers
New York (city)—Columbia-Presbyterian medical center
MEDICAL clinics. See Health clinics
MEDICAL colleges
Healing diplomacy; proposal for a cooperative center for graduate training in sub-Sahara Africa. W. D. Lotspeich. Sat R 50:45-6 Jl 1 '67
See also
Association of American medical colleges
Columbia university—College of physicians and surgeons
Medical centers
Medical education
New York medical college

Entrance requirements
Admission to medical school. Sch & Soc 95:25-6 Ja 7 '67
MEDICAL delusions
Common health frauds to avoid. il Good H 165:155 Jl '67
MEDICAL education
Future of medical education. O. Cope. Harper 235:98-9+ O '67; Discussion. 236:6-8 Ja '68
Medical education and the AMA. M. O. Rouse. Todays Health 45:88 O '67
Mt Sinai: how a hospital builds a medical school. R. J. Samuelson. il Science 158:614-18 N 3 '67
Quality versus quantity in American medical education. G. Williams; discussion. Science 154:723+; 155:642+ N 11 '66; F 10 '67
See also
Medical centers
Medical colleges
Medical research
Medicine—Study and teaching
MEDICAL electronics
Electric limbs; implanted electronic pickup. F. C. Livingstone. Sci N 92:495 N 18 '67
Electronics and aphasia; teaching stroke victims to talk. J. Frye. Electr World 78:54-5 D '67
Medical electronics takes a deeper look; $170-million-a-year industry's fast-growing arsenal of weapons for combating disease. il Bsns W p86+ F 25 '67
Medical instrumentation systems. J. H. Wujek, jr. il Electr World 79:46-7+ Ja '68
New medical tool; electron linear accelerator. Electr World 79:93 Ja '68
Wired for living. G. G. Keeping. Read Digest 91:110-12 Jl '67
See also
Telemeter (physiological apparatus)
MEDICAL engineering. See Biomedical engineering
MEDICAL ethics
Authors & editors; corruption in a certain segment of American medicine, as presented in The healers. Pub W 191:40 F 13 '67
Coup de grâce. M. M. Shideler; discussion. Christian Cent 84:20, 82-3, 272-3, 471 Ja 4, 18, Mr 1, Ap 12 '67
Court-martial of Captain Levy: medical ethics v. military law. E. Langer. il Science 156:1346-50 Je 9 '67; Discussion. 157:140 Jl 14 '67
Ethical issues in research with human subjects. W. Wolfensberger; discussion. Science 155:1617-18 Mr 31 '67
Healers, by Anonymous. M. D. pseud. Review
Sat R 50:38 Mr 11 '67. M. Clark
Merchant doctors. J. Randal. Reporter 36:29-30 My 4 '67

MEDICAL examinations. See Physical examinations

MEDICAL fakers. See Quacks and quackery

MEDICAL fees. See Medical service, Cost of

MEDICAL fog. See Fog, Artificial

MEDICAL hypnosis. See Hypnotism

MEDICAL information. See Communication in medicine

MEDICAL instruments and apparatus
Blood pressure on demand; hypertension control device. il Sci N 91:365 Ap 15 '67
Brain scans by ultrasound; Makow scanner. il Sci N 91:62 Ja 21 '67
Does your child have hidden heart trouble? the PhonoCardioScan. P. Deutsch and R. Deutsch. Read Digest 90:92-6 My '67
Electronic stethoscope and cardiac rate meter. A. L. Dunn and others. il Electr World 78: 30+ Jl '67
Medical miracles in South Vietnam. J. H. Winchester. il Pop Sci 191:70-3+ Jl '67
New medicine and its weapons. il Newsweek 69:60-8 Ap 24 '67
Pacemakers move ahead. il Sci N 91:294-5 Mr 25 '67
Radio pill: symbol of a new science; R. S. Mackay's radio telemetry. Todays Health 45:16+ Ap '67
Relieving pressure & pain; use of decompression unit. il Time 90:36 D 22 '67
See also
Respiratory apparatus

MEDICAL jurisprudence
Where laughter flees; forensic pathologists. il Newsweek 69:90 My 8 '67
See also
Insanity—Jurisprudence

MEDICAL laboratories
In the lab: too many defective tests. il Time 89:75 F 17 '67
Medicine under fire. Sci N 91:161 F 18 '67

MEDICAL libraries
Medical libraries unite in Texas. Library J 92:1105 Mr 15 '67
See also
United States—National library of medicine

MEDICAL library association
Barefoot in Bal Harbour; annual conference. R. T. Esterquest. il Library J 92:2734-6 Ag '67

MEDICAL literature
Information systems in medicine; summary of addresses at ABPC conference. G. O. Barnett; R. L. Hayne. Pub W 191:40-1 Ap 10 '67

MEDICAL literature analysis and retrieval system. See Information storage and retrieval systems

MEDICAL microscopy. See Microscopy, Medical

MEDICAL missions. See Missions, Medical

MEDICAL photography. See Photography, Medical

MEDICAL practice. See Medicine—Practice

MEDICAL profession. See Medicine—Practice; Physicians

MEDICAL relief work

Vietnam (Democratic Republic)
News and views; medical aid for civilian needy of North Vietnam. J. Deedy. Commonweal 87:134 N 3 '67
U.S. says no; move to block Americans from sending medical supplies to civilian war victims in North Vietnam. Commonweal 86: 37-8 Mr 31 '67

Vietnam (Republic)
Bac si from Iowa: W. Owen. il Life 62:78A-80+ F 17 '67
Diary of an American medical intern in Vietnam. D. McLanahan. il Sat R 50:18-21+ Mr 25 '67
Pat Smith's special war in Vietnam; at the Catholic mission hospital in Kontum. F. Chinnock. il Read Digest 90:195-6+ Je '67
Visit to Vietnam; volunteer assistant to Dr Pierce; president of World vision. A. Ives. il Seventeen 26:150-1+ F '67
See also
Committee of responsibility to save war-burned and war-injured Vietnamese children

MEDICAL research
Better health for all babies; Collaborative perinatal project, U.S. Public health service. T. C. Wilson and K. Niehans. Parents Mag 42:68-9+ N '67

Biohazards symbol: development of a biological hazards warning signal. C. L. Baldwin and R. S. Runkle. il Science 158:264-5 O 13 '67; Reply. W. Schiff. 158:1398 D 15 '67
Comparative medicine; report on workshop conference. W. I. Gay. Science 158:1220+ D 1 '67
Engineers' talents aid medical research; employees at Western electric's Hawthorne works. il Todays Health 45:76 S '67
Health research: a small start for an international center. J. Walsh. Science 155: 1088-90 Mr 3 '67
Immunology: research at Mill Hill institute. N. Calder. Science 157:177-9 Jl 14 '67
LBJ at NIH: President offers kind words for basic research. E. Langer. il Science 157:403-5 Jl 28 '67
Medical research: new disoveries that may save your life. il Changing T 21:29-33 Jl '67
Medicine: for a healthier future. J. Whitbread. il Parents Mag 43:42-3+ Ja '68
More problems of instant medicine; dangers of premature practical application of research findings. J. D. Cooper. il Sat R 50: 56-61 Je 3 '67
Most snake-bitten man in the world. W. Hartley and E. Hartley. il Sci Digest 62: 13-17 O '67
Progress in medicine: latest findings. U S News 62:12 My 22 '67
Sherpa goiter studied. D. A. Ehrlich. Sci N 92:277 S 16 '67
Some problems of instant medicine. J. Lederberg. il Sat R 50:67-70 My 6 '67
Tetrodotoxin; possible model for new local anesthetics. F. A. Fuhrman. il Sci Am 217: 60-2+ Ag '67
Uses of biomedical research. Sci N 91:231 Mr 11 '67
See also
American medical association—Institute for biomedical research
Animal experimentation
Computers—Medical applications
Dental research
Drugs, Experimental
Laboratory animals
Laboratory technicians
Salk institute for biological studies, San Diego, Calif.
United States—National institutes of health

Experimentation on man
Consent: it's the law. B. J. Culliton. il Sci N 92:88-9 Jl 22 '67
Doctors must experiment on humans; but, what are the patient's rights? W. Goodman. il N Y Times Mag p 12-13+ Jl 2 '67; Reply. I. D. J. Bross. p4 Jl 23 '67
Ethical guidelines for clinical investigation. Todays Health 45:70 Ap '67
Ethical issues in research with human subjects. W. Wolfensberger; discussion. Science 155:1617-18 Mr 31 '67
Experiments on man. Newsweek 69:84 Mr 6 '67
Medical experiments on humans; new guidelines. M. Alderman; reply. I. Shapiro. New Repub 156:37-8 Ja 28 '67
Somebody had to be first pioneer patients and treatments. R. Winter. il Todays Health 45: 66-9 Ap '67

Federal aid
Achievement and management. D. Wolfle. Science 158:721 N 10 '67; Discussion. 158: 995, 1621 N 24, D 29 '67
Collaboration for accelerating progress in medical research; excerpts from Senate committee testimony, March 16, 1967. A. B. Sabin. Science 156:1568-71 Je 23 '67
Medical research: NIH wants divorce from PHS. L. J. Carter. il Science 156:45-8 Ap 7 '67
Policing the consequences of science. J. Lear. Sat R 50:65-7 D 2 '67; Discussion. 51:104-5 Ja 6 '68
Science vs. democracy; NIH blanket grant to Sloan-Kettering institute and HSAA award. J. Lear. Sat R 50:57-61 N 4 '67
Some problems of instant medicine. J. Lederberg. il Sat R 50:66-70 My 6 '67

MEDICAL research council (Great Britain)
Immunology: research at Mill Hill institute. N. Calder. Science 157:177-9 Jl 14 '67

MEDICAL schools. See Medical colleges

MEDICAL service
Crisis of organization. il Time 90:43 D 1 '67
Health and well-being. P. R. Lee. bibliog f il Ann Am Acad 373:193-207 S '67

MEDICAL service—*Continued*
National campaign to prevent catastrophes; glaring inadequacies in health care. Sci N 92:535-6 D 2 '67
No time to get sick. E. T. Chase. New Repub 157:24-6 N 11 '67
Patients come first; Student health organization's patient advocacy system brings health care to ghettos. il Newsweek 70:70-1 Ag 21 '67
Tomorrow's hospitals of today. C. Carner. il Todays Health 45:30-7 Mr '67
Why don't we save these mothers and babies? W. Goodman. il Redbook 128:68-9+ Ap '67
See also
Helicopters in medical service
Physicians
Radio in medicine
United States—National advisory commission on health manpower

Asia, Southeastern
Floating clinic for Mekong River launched by Dooley foundation. il Todays Health 45: 72 O '67

Sweden
Hospitals in crisis; too many hospitals, too few doctors. Sci N 92:610 D 23 '67

Underdeveloped areas
Reverse foreign aid; problem of medical brain drain from developing countries. il Sci N 91:75 Ja 21 '67

MEDICAL service, Cost of
AMA: some doctors are in revolt, but revolution is not in sight. E. Langer. Science 157:285-8 Jl 21 '67; Discussion. 157:1261-3 S 15 '67
Bad case of inflation; HEW report to President Johnson. Bsns W p35 Mr 4 '67
Doctors' bonanza; inflationary effects of medicare and medicaid. E. T. Chase. New Repub 156:15-17 Ap 15 '67; Discussion. 156:36 My 6 '67
Hospitals try to cure a high-cost syndrome. il Bsns W p 128-30+ Jl 15 '67
How medical costs in the U.S. have shot up. il U S News 62:105 Mr 13 '67
If you think hospital costs are high now—. il U S News 62:77 My 22 '67
Lavish happening. Sci N 92:31 Jl 8 '67
Looking ahead in medicare and business; address, January 30, 1967. C. L. Hudson. Vital Speeches 33:465-8 My 15 '67
Medical costs: rapid rise causing government concern. E. Langer. Science 155:1519-21 Mr 24 '67
Medical expenses; key ways to reduce them. Good H 164:200 Ap '67
Medicare's birthday. New Repub 157:5 Jl 8 '67
National headache. New Repub 158:4 Ja 13 '68
Needed; new perspective on health services. W. E. Landgraf. Harvard Bsns R 45:75-83 S '67
Plot against the patient, by F. J. Cook. Review
Sat R 50:40-1 My 20 '67. M. Clark
Revolution in medicine: United States, Britain; symposium. il Look 31:35-42+ Mr 21 '67
Up, up, up. il Time 90:36 Jl 28 '67
What should be done about the high cost of medical care? Good housekeeping readers poll. Good H 165:12+ Jl '67
MEDICAL service, Industrial
See also
Industrial hygiene
MEDICAL service, Radio. See Radio in medicine
MEDICAL service, State
AMA: some doctors are in revolt, but revolution is not in sight. E. Langer. Science 157:285-8 Jl 21 '67; Discussion. 157:1261-3 S 15 '67
Governor no; R. Reagan to defend cutbacks of medical aid. Reporter 37:12-13 O 19 '67
Hospitals, doctors reveal: medicare's maladies. il Nations Bsns 55:44-6+ Mr '67
LBJ's message on youth: pointing a new path for medical practice. B. Nelson. Science 155:811-12 F 17 '67
Medicaid: a big headache in some areas. U S News 62:10 Ap 17 '67
Medicine and politics: a fresh look at the British experience. J. Walsh. Science 155: 671-2 F 10 '67
Revolution in medicine: United States, Britain; symposium. il Look 31:35-42+ Mr 21 '67

Why don't we save these mothers and babies? W. Goodman. il Redbook 128:68-9+ Ap '67
See also
Medicaid program
Medicare program
MEDICAL social work
Doctors meet the people; Neighborhood health center, of Montefiore hospital. M. K. Sanders. Harper 236:56-62 Ja '68
MEDICAL social workers. See Social workers
MEDICAL societies
See also names of medical societies, e.g. American medical association
MEDICAL students
Patients come first; Student health organization's patient advocacy system brings health care to ghettos. il Newsweek 70:70-1 Ag 21 '67
MEDICAL supplies
Medical supplies. Consumer Rep 32:219-22 D '67
MEDICAL technicians. See Medical workers
MEDICAL ultrasonics. See Ultrasonic waves—Medical applications
MEDICAL workers
Arbovirus infections of laboratory workers. R. P. Hanson and others. bibliog il Science 158:1283-6 D 8 '67
Brain drain: a bargaining point; British heart-lung machine technicians threaten mass emigration. Sci N 91:510 My 27 '67
Groups cooperate to steer vets into health careers. Todays Health 45:15 N '67
Tests that fail. Newsweek 69:62 F 20 '67

Training
Health careers (cont) il Todays Health 45: 36-41+ F; 50-5+ Mr; 52-5+ Ap; 54-5+ My; 24-9+ Je '67
Medical training costs too much; excerpt from Case studies in change. B. Asbell. il Am Ed 3:5-6 Mr '67
MEDICARE program
Coming changes in medicare; good and bad of medicare: a sampling of views and experiences. il U S News 63:52-3 Jl 31 '67
Crisis in medicine; impact of medicare and medicaid. E. T. Chase. Commonweal 85: 650-2 Mr 10 '67; Reply with rejoinder. J. A. Fabro. 86:251+ My 19 '67
Doctors' bonanza; inflationary effects of medicare and medicaid. E. T. Chase. New Repub 156:15-17 Ap 15 '67; Discussion. 156: 36 My 6 '67
Doctor's diagnosis of medicare. M. J. Halberstam. il N Y Times Mag p 14-15+ Ag 13 '67
Eight tips on collecting medicare. il Changing T 21:31-2 Ag '67
For us, the big change is now! medicare, medicaid, preventicare. R. H. Berg. Look 31:41-2 Mr 21 '67
Happy, healthy birthday. il Newsweek 70: 50-1 Jl 3 '67
Hospitals, doctors reveal: medicare's maladies. il Nations Bsns 55:44-6+ Mr '67
Looking ahead in medicare and business; address, January 30, 1967. C. L. Hudson. Vital Speeches 33:465-8 My 15 '67
Medicare: expensive & successful, medicaid: chaotic but irrevocable. il Time 90:96+ O 6 '67
Medicare: foretaste of 1984? W. H. Chamberlin. Nat R 19:413 Ap 18 '67
Medicare: headache or cure-all? S. M. Spencer. il Sat Eve Post 240:21-5 My 20 '67
Medicare runs a fever; patients and hospitals complain of red tape and delays. Bsns W p37 F 18 '67
Medicare's birthday; costs up. New Repub 157:5 Jl 8 '67
Medicare's woes: skyrocketing prices and a snarl of red tape. il U S News 62:10 Mr 20 '67
R for medicare; should medicare cover the cost of prescription drugs? Newsweek 69: 86 Je 12 '67
State medicine in trouble in U.S. il U S News 62:75-6 My 22 '67
MEDICI, Marino de
Cost of eight years of Castro. Read Digest 91:89-93 Jl '67
MEDICINAL plants. See Botany, Medical
MEDICINE
Keep up with medicine. B. Yuncker. See issues of Good housekeeping
Medical sciences notes. See issues of Science news
Medicine today; ed. by V. Cohn. P. Wright. See issues of Ladies' home journal
Mediquiz; questions and answers. J. Lentz. il Todays Health 45:17-19 Ap; 12+ My '67

MEDICINE—*Continued*
News from the world of medicine. See issues of Reader's digest
Tommorow's medical miracles. A. J. Snider. il Sci Digest 62:72-4 Jl '67
What's new in medicine. A. Kerr. See issues of McCall's
See also
Biomedical engineering
Communication in medicine
Drugs
Medical research
Pharmacology
Prescriptions
Quacks and quackery

Anecdotes, facetiae, satire, etc.
Apple a day keeps the flexowriter away. W. K. Zinsser. Horizon 9:120 Aut '67
Laugh a day; excerpts from Treasury of medical wit and humor. B. Adler. il Todays Health 45:40-1 Ap; 52-3 My '67

Bibliography
Books to come; ed. by J. Putnam. Library J 92:1037-62+, 2611-41, 4033-63 Mr 1, Jl, N 1 '67

History
See also
Medical research

Practice
Man for the aged; trial of medical director of Berlin's geriatric clinic for imposture. Newsweek 69:56+ Je 5 '67
Saying ah (cont) J. Miller. Vogue 149:149-51 Mr 15 '67
Successful fraud; director of geriatrics clinic in Berlin. il Time 89:54 Je 9 '67
See also
Medical ethics
Medical service
Physicians
Physicians and patients
Quacks and quackery

Study and teaching
Almost man: the doctor trainer. C. Carner. il Todays Health 45:16-18 My '67
New approaches to medical studies. Sch & Soc 95:74+ F 4 '67
See also
Medical colleges
Medical education

Laos
Blunder in Laos; how USAID disrupted one of the most successful programs for co-operation between Asian nations. M. A. Bernad. America 117:766-9 D 23 '67

Russia
Open heart of Dr Amosoff. L. Gross. il Look 31:122-3+ O 3 '67

United States
Advances in medicine: doctors' reports; American medical association's convention. il U S News 63:21 D 11 '67
Crisis in health: will it get even worse? U S News 63:14 D 4 '67
Doctors report: what's new in medicine; annual convention of American medical association. U S News 63:12 Jl 3 '67
Healers, by Anonymous. M. D, pseud. Review
Sat R 50:33 Mr 11 '67. M. Clark

History
Revolutionary doctor, by C. Binger. Review
Sat R 50:52 F 25 '67. M. M. Brown

Vietnam (Republic)
See also
Medical relief work—Vietnam (Republic)
MEDICINE, Clinical
Two faces of medicine, by C. Binger. Review
Sat R 50:32+ Ag 12 '67. D. Woods
MEDICINE, Experimental. See Medical research
MEDICINE, Hindu
Letter from abroad: marvelous medicine of Malabar; Ayurvedic practitioners. S. Rama Rau. McCalls 94:40+ My '67
MEDICINE, Military
See also
Hospitals, Military
United States—Army—Medical corps
Vietnamese war, 1957- —Medical and sanitary affairs
MEDICINE, Primitive
See also
Medicine men

MEDICINE men
Trance cure of the Kung Bushmen. R. B. Lee. il Natur Hist 76:30-7 N '67
MEDICINES. See Drugs
MEDICINES, Patent, proprietary, etc.
Are you wasting money on worthless health aids? Interview, ed. by J. C. G. Conniff. J. L. Goddard. Pop Sci 190:92-3+ Ap '67
Those leftovers in the medicine chest. il Changing T 21:42 O '67
When sniffles can be beautiful; Contac, cold remedy by Menley & James division of Smith, Kline & French. il Bsns W p69-70+ Ja 14 '67
MEDIEVAL art. See Art, Medieval
MEDIEVAL music. See Music, Medieval
MEDIEVAL poetry. See Poetry, Medieval
MEDINA, Harold R.
Press in the jury box? por Time 89:96+ Mr 10 '67
MEDINA-SIDONIA, duchess of
Red Duchess. Newsweek 69:46 Ja 30 '67
MEDITATION
Chief guru of the western world. B. Lefferts. il N Y Times Mag p44-5+ D 17 '67
Invitation to instant bliss. L. Wainwright. Life 63:26 N 10 '67
MEDITERRANEAN anemia. See Anemia
MEDITERRANEAN REGION
Where war threatens next: the Mediterranean and beyond. il U S News 63:44-6 D 11 '67
See also
Middle East
MEDITERRANEAN resorts. See Summer resorts
MEDITERRANEAN SEA
Now Russia builds up power in the Mediterranean; excerpts from address, November 17, 1967. C. D. Griffin. il U S News 63:46+ D 11 '67
Soviet fleet in the Mediterranean. C. Sterling. il Reporter 37:14-18 D 14 '67
See also
Aegean Islands
Corsica
Suez Canal
MEDIUMS
See also
Spiritualism
MEDLARS (medical literature analysis and retrieval system) See Information storage and retrieval systems
MEDLIN, Faith
Owl and the artist; excerpt from Centuries of owls, with biographical sketch. Natur Hist 76:4, 32-9 O '67
MEEHAN, Thomas
America: a nation in utter confusion. Sat Eve Post 240:16 My 6 '67
For whom the bell doesn't toll; story. New Yorker 43:47-9 Mr 18 '67
Of human bondage. Sat Eve Post 240:22 Je 3 '67
Otto the Terrible. Sat Eve Post 240:26-31 Ap 8 '67
Portrait of a babe. Sat Eve Post 240:22 Mr 25 '67
Il talento mysterioso; story. New Yorker 43:27-8 Je 17 '67
MEEK, George
Expo 67. Américas 19:34-40 S '67
New milestones in the inter-American system. Américas 19:1-8 Ap '67
OAS in action. See issues of Américas
MEEKER, Hubert
Giving the past a future. Arch Forum 126:56-61 My '67
MEEKER, Leonard C.
Viet-Nam and the international law of self-defense; address, December 13, 1966. Dept State Bul 56:54-63 Ja 9 '67
MEEKS, Esther
Irene Hunt. por Library J 92:1297 Mr 15 '67
MEEMAN, Edward J.
Mike Frome. M. Frome. Am For 73:3+ F '67; Reply. Mrs W. W. Deupree. 73:35 Ap '67
MEENAN, Daniel F. X.
Of many things. America 117:670 D 2 '67
MEETINGS
See also
Conventions
Public meetings
Stockholders meetings
MEGALITHIC monuments
See also
Stonehenge, England
MEGGERS, Betty J.
Did Japanese fishermen bring the art of pottery making to Ecuador 5,000 years ago? UNESCO Courier 20:12-13 My '67

MEGRUE, G. H.
Isotopic analysis of rare gases with a laser microprobe. bibliog Science 157:1555-6 S 29 '67

MEHLE, Aileen
Husband stealer. American style. por Vogue 149:192-3+ My '67
(ed) See Farrow, M. Mia

about

Trilling from a new tree. por Time 89:42 Je 30 '67

MEHLER, Alan H. and Cusic, M. E. Jr
Aldolase reaction with sugar diphosphates. bibliog Science 155:1101-3 Mr 3 '67

MEHLER, Jacques, and Bever, T. G.
Cognitive capacity of very young children. bibliog Science 158:141-2 O 6 '67

MEHTA, Ved
Reporter at large. New Yorker 43:50-2+ S 9; 159-60+ D 9 '67

MEHTA, Zubin
Gypsy boy. il pors Time 91:76-80 Ja 19 '68
Musical events; concert in Carnegie Hall by Los Angeles philharmonic. W. Sargeant. New Yorker 43:164+ My 13 '67
Musical events; conducting of Verdi's Otello at Metropolitan opera house. W. Sargeant. New Yorker 43:155-6 Mr 11 '67
Profiles. W. Sargeant. por New Yorker 43:53-4+ D 16 '67

MEILACH, Dona Z. See Holly, R. G; Kaminetzky, H. A; Southam, A. L. jt. auths.

MEILHAC, Henry, and Halévy, Ludovic
La Cigale; excerpts. Art N 65:55 Ja '67

MEINEL, A. B. and Meinel, M. P.
Volcanic sunset-glow stratum; origin. bibliog Science 155:189 Ja 13 '67

MEINEL, M. P. See Meinel, A. B. jt. auth.

MEINKE, Peter
John Dove; poem. Christian Cent 84:810 Je 21 '67
Sonnet on Christmas morning. Ladies Home J 84:117 D '67

MEIOSIS. See Cell division (biology)

MEISLER, Stanley
Breakup in Nigeria. Nation 205:334-6 O 9 '67
Mercenaries change sides. Nation 205:689-91 D 25 '67

MEISS, Millard
Important discoveries of renaissance art in Florence. Art N 66:26-7+ Sum '67

MEISSEN china. See Pottery, German

Die **MEISTERSINGER** von Nürnberg; opera. See Wagner, R.

MEIXNER, Mary
Fashion illustrating. Design 68:22-4 Ja '67

MEKONG RIVER
Mekong discussions. UN Mo Chron 4:97-8 D '67

MELADY, Thomas Patrick
Dialogue with the third world. Sat R 50:64 Ap 8 '67
Vatican and the third world. America 117:641-3 N 25 '67

MELAMED, Myron R. See Kamentsky, L. A. jt. auth.

MELAMID, Alexander
Eastern Arabia. bibliog Focus 18:1-6 N '67

MELANCHOLIA
See also
Depression, Mental

MELANESIA. See Islands of the Pacific

MELANOMA
Tyrosinase inhibition: its role in suntanning and in albinian. L. T. Y. Chian and G. F. Wilgram. bibliog il Science 155:198-200 Ja 13 '67

MELANOPLUS differentialis. See Grasshoppers

MELATONIN
Visual pathway mediating pineal response to environmental light. R. Y. Moore and others. bibliog il Science 155:220-3 Ja 13 '67

MELBOURNE, Australia

Description

Melbourne: green, spired, good for shopping. D. Messinesi. Vogue 150:78 S 15 '67

MELCHER, Daniel
Net pricing and the salesman. Library J 92:1979-80 My 15 '67
Proposed standards for library bindings. Pub W 192:18-20 D 11 '67

MELCHER, Peggy (Zimmerman)
Obituary
Library J il pors 92:1273 Mr 15 '67. E. Geller and E. Moon

MELCHETT, Julian Edward Alfred Mond, 3d baron
Lord of steel. il por Time 90:70 Ag 11 '67
Melchett of British steel. por Fortune 76:37 S 1 '67

MELE, Sabath A. See Mele, S.

MELE, Sam
Magic manager. Newsweek 70:76-7 S 25 '67
Poor Sam, what a weird week. J. Jares. il por Sports Illus 26:24-6+ My 1 '67

MELFI, Leonard
Wry and healthy humanist. J. Simon. Life 63:23 O 13 '67

MELGES, Bud
They sail to win. por Yachting 121:56+ Ap '67

MELIOIDOSIS
Viet Nam's time bomb. Time 89:84 F 10 '67

MELIS, Carmen
Historical records. A. Favia-Artsay. por Hobbies 72:33-4 Ag '67

MELKITES. See Catholic church—Byzantine rite

MELLAART, James
Strange case of James Mellaart; with editorial comment by J. J. Thorndike. K. Pearson and P. Connor. il por Horizon 9:2-3, 4-15 Sum '67

MELLINGER, Glen D. See Manheimer, D. I. jt. auth.

MELLINGER, Marie B.
High horizons. il Nat Parks Mag 41:10-11 Je '67

MELLON, Paul
In quest of beauty. Nat Geog Mag 131:372-85 Mr '67

MELLON, Paul collection. See Art—Private collections

MELLON family
Mellons of Pittsburgh. C. J. V. Murphy. il pors Fortune 76:120-9+ O; 158-61+ N; 132-4+ D '67

MELLONICS division. See Litton industries, incorporated

MELLONIE, David B.
100,000 miles for pay and pleasure. por Motor B 120:31+ D '67

MELMAN, Seymour
Small wars: the peril escalates. Nation 204:774-5 Je 19 '67

MELO, Francisco de Assis Chateaubriand Bandeira de. See Assis Chateaubriand Bandeira de Melo, F. de

MELONS
Melons and; meat with melon as appetizer. il Sunset 139:60-1 S '67

MELOY, Thomas
Laser, the light fantastic. Read Digest 90:107-11 Ap '67

MELSON, William G. and others
St Peter and St Paul Rocks; a high-temperature, mantle-derived intrusion. bibliog Science 155:1532-5 Mr 24 '67

MELVILLE, Herman
Benito Cereno; dramatization. See Lowell, R. Old Glory

about

Tragedy of justice in Billy Budd. C. A. Reich. Yale R 56:368-89 Mr '67

MELVIN, A. Gordon
Natural history. See issues of Hobbies

MELZACK, Louis
Selling books at Expo 67. Pub W 192:44-5 O 23 '67

about

Prescription for success: hard work, imagination; reprint. M. Ballantyne. Pub W 191:49-50 Ap 17 '67

MELZACK, Ronald. See Gijsbers, K. J. jt. auth.

MEMBRANES (biology)
Cholinergic binding capacity of proteolipids from isolated nerve-ending membranes. D. P. de Robertis and others. bibliog il Science 158:928-9 N 17 '67
Collagen-derived membrane: corneal implantation. M. W. Dunn and others. bibliog Science 157:1329-30 S 15 '67
Ethanolamine phosphoglycerides: effect on the properties of myelinoid lecithin water systems. P. G. Fast. bibliog il Science 155:1680-1 Mr 31 '67
Fracture planes in an ice-bilayer model membrane system. D. W. Deamer and D. Branton. bibliog il Science 158:655-7 N 3 '67
Giant axon of myxicola: some membrane properties as observed under voltage clamp. L. Binstock and L. Goldman. bibliog il Science 158:1467-9 D 15 '67
Imine-bonding in membrane transport of monosaccharides: invalidity of kinetic evidence. P. G. LeFevre. bibliog il Science 158:274-5 O 13 '67

MEMBRANES (biology)—*Continued*
Iodide transport; inhibition by agents reacting at the membrane. P. R. Larsen and J. Wolff. bibliog il Science 155:335-6 Ja 20 '67
Membrane structure and function; report on biochemical conference. J. H. Quastel. Science 158:146+ O 6 '67
Membrane structure and ion permeation. G. Eisenman and others. bibliog il Science 155: 965-74 F 24 '67
Membranes in polyribosome formation by rabbit reticulocytes. M. L. Freedman and others. bibliog il Science 157:323-5 Jl 21 '67
Membranes of valonia ventricosa: apparent absence of water-filled pores. J. Gutknecht. bibliog il Science 158:787-8 N 10 '67
Otolithic membranes of the saccule and utricle in man. L.-G. Johnsson and J. E. Hawkins, jr. bibliog il Science 157:1454-6 S 22 '67
Plasma membranes of rat liver: isolation of lipoprotein macromolecules. M. Barclay and others. bibliog il Science 156:665-7 My 5 '67
Plasma membrane: substructural changes correlated with electrical resistance and pinocytosis. P. W. Brandt and A. R. Freeman. bibliog il Science 155:582-5 F 3 '67
See also
Epithelium

MEMBRANES (technology)
Detergents in membrane filters. R. D. Cahn. bibliog il Science 155:195-6 Ja 13 '67
Expanding world of membranes. H. E. Klein. il Duns R 89:41+ Ja '67

MEMENTOS. See Keepsakes

MEMO minders. See Electronic apparatus and appliances

MEMORABILIA. See Keepsakes

MEMORANDUMS
Build your own memo minder. R. Persing. il Pop Electr 27:49-51+ O '67

MEMORIAL cultural center, Atlanta. See Concert halls

MEMORIAL day
Memorial day. C. Davis. il Holiday 41:60-1+ My '67
Prayer for peace, Memorial day, 1967; proclamation. L. B. Johnson. Dept State Bul 56: 873 Je 12 '67

MEMORIAL funds
Announcement; Fred Hoskins fund established at Yale university. Christian Cent 84:462 Ap 12 '67

MEMORIALS
See also
War memorials

MEMORY
Actinomycin D blocks formation of memory of shock-avoidance in goldfish. B. W. Agranoff and others. bibliog il Science 158: 1600-1 D 22 '67
Can you improve your memory? il Good H 165:202-3 N '67
Decay of visual information from a single letter. M. I. Posner and S. W. Keele. bibliog il Science 158:137-9 O 6 '67
Interference theory of forgetting. J. Ceraso. il Sci Am 217:117-21+ bibliog(p 156) O '67
Memory and protein synthesis. B. W. Agranoff. il Sci Am 216:115-22 Je '67
Memory in mice analyzed with antibiotics. L. B. Flexner and others. bibliog il Science 155:1377-83 Mr 17 '67
Memory pills: new route to brain power. B. H. Frisch. il Sci Digest 62:37-43 Jl '67
Puromycin and retention in the goldfish. A. Potts and M. E. Bitterman. bibliog il Science 158:1594-6 D 22 '67
Puromycin effect on memory may be due to occult seizures. H. D. Cohen and S. H. Barondes. bibliog il Science 157:333-4 Jl 21 '67
Recovery of memory after amnesia induced by electroconvulsive shock. S. Zinkin and A. J. Miller; reply with rejoinder. M. J. Herz and H. V. S. Peeke. Science 156: 1396-7 Je 9 '67
Short-term memory, parsing, and the primate frontal cortex. K. H. Pribram and W. E. Tubbs. bibliog il Science 156:1765-7 Je 30 '67
See also
Maze tests
Reminiscence

Quotations, maxims, etc.
Fine art of memory; comp. by R. Block. il N Y Times Mag p32 Ja 7 '68

MEMORY, Loss of. See Amnesia

MEMORY devices (computers)
See also
Magnetic memory (computers)

MEMORY pills. See Magnesium pemoline

MEMOS. See Memorandums

MEMPHIS, Tenn.
Plan before you put a computer to work. C. R. Henze. il Am City 82:100-1 Mr '67

MEMPHIS, Tenn, public library
Memphis: a seven branch salvo. C. L. Wallis. il Library J 92:4373-6 D 1 '67

MEN
Masculinity: real and put on. H. Rosenberg. Vogue 150:106-7+ N 15 '67
See also
Boys
Cookery by men
Great men
Husbands
Mustaches
Sex differences
Young men

Clothing
See Clothing and dress—Men

Health and hygiene
Charlton Heston stays in great shape and tells how. il Vogue 151:67 Ja 1 '68
Field & stream six-week conditioning program for sportsmen. P. Czura and J. M. Kowalski. il Field & S 72:47-53 Ag '67
Fitness can also be a state of mind. A. H. Sypher. il Nations Bsns 55:27-8 Ag '67
Golf is too easy; physical fitness for middle-aged men. il Sci Digest 62:76 Jl '67
How to live five years longer; interview. F. J. Stare. il Nations Bsns 55:78-81 D '67
I am Joe's heart; how to minimize risk of heart disease. J. D. Ratcliff. Read Digest 90:59-62 Ap '67
Keeping dad healthy. D. J. Lauer. il Parents Mag 42:46-7+ Je '67
Personal business; checkup with a psychiatrist. Bsns W p 167-8 My 6 '67
Personal business; daily exercise to build stronger heart. Bsns W p95-6 Ja 6 '68
Work limitations and chronic health problems. C. Rosenfeld and E. Waldman. il Mo Labor R 90:38-41 Ja '67

Psychology
Girl's guide to men-on-the-make. J. Brown. Mlle 66:120-1+ D '67
Sexual roles being reversed, says psychiatrist; theories of Ralph R. Greenson. Todays Health 45:85 Ap '67
Twilight of the he-man. C. W. Morton. il Atlan 219:111 F '67
What's in a face? the mind of the man behind it. A. Brien. il Holiday 42:10+ D '67
Why so many husbands feel inadequate. R. J. Levin. il Redbook 129:61+ S '67

MEN, Short. See Stature

MEN and women. See Women and men

MEN teachers. See Teachers

MENAGERIES. See Zoological gardens

MENAKER, Michael, and Eskin, Arnold
Circadian clock in photoperiodic time measurement: a test of the Bünning hypothesis. bibliog Science 157:1182-5 S 8 '67
—See Gaston, S. jt. auth.

MENARD, H. W.
Sea floor spreading, topography, and the second layer. bibliog Science 157:923-4 Ag 25 '67

MENARD, Wilmon
Maugham's Pacific. Sat R 50:77-8+ Mr 11 '67

MENCKEN, August
August. H. A. Smith. Sat R 50:6 Je 24 '67

MENDELEVIUM
Heaviest atom; mendelevium 258. il Time 90:59 S 22 '67
Mendelevium: divalency and other chemical properties. E. K. Hulet and others. bibliog il Science 158:486-8 O 27 '67

MENDELS, Joe
How to avoid feeding problems. Parents Mag 42:38-9+ D '67
How to help the child who wets his bed. Parents Mag 42:38-9+ Jl '67

MENDELSON, Joseph
Lateral hypothalamic stimulation in satiated rats: the rewarding effects of self-induced drinking. Science 157:1077-9 S 1 '67

MENDELSSOHN, Felix
Prime Casals from Marlboro. M. N. Kanny. Am Rec G 33:489 F '67
What prodigies are made of. Discus. il Harper 234:118+ Ap '67

MENDENHALL, Ralph F.
Sports ambassadors. por Parks & Rec 2:20-1+ F '67

MENDÈS-FRANCE, Pierre
Phoenix. il por Newsweek 69:50+ F 20 '67
Re-enter: Mendès-France, hoping. S. de Gramont. il pors N Y Times Mag p25+ Ap 16 '67

MENDIETA, Ramiro Matos. See Matos Mendieta. R.

MENDOZA FERNÁNDEZ, José
Mendoza the builder. il por Time 90:98 O 13 '67

MENEN, Aubrey
Bold, brave bathroom. House & Gard 131: 118-19 Je '67
In Rome they call it *il miracolo italiano.* N Y Times Mag p6-7+ Jl 9; 5 Ag 6 '67
In the footsteps of the past. Holiday 42:90-1+ D '67

MENGEL, Robert M.
Talent of Robert Verity Clem. Audubon 69: 56-61 S '67

MENGER, Carl Simone
Three-sided figure. R. Levy. por Duns R 90: 48-9+ S '67

MENGET, Patrick
Death in Chamula; with biographical sketch. Natur Hist 77:4, 48-57 Ja '68

MENGO virus. See Viruses

MENHADEN fishing
Where did the menhaden go? il Time 89:87 Je 16 '67

MENINGIOMA cells. See Cells

MENINGOENCEPHALITIS. See Encephalitis

MENNINGER, Edwin A.
Colorful new shrub. Horticulture 45:43 D '67

MENNINGER, Roy W.
Our troubled youth; address, August 18, 1967. Vital Speeches 34:121-5 D 1 '67

MENNONITES
Amish, Black Muslims and Catholics. America 116:550 Ap 15 '67
Educational freedom for the Amish. il Sch & Soc 95:486-8 D 9 '67
Unyielding Amish; we want to be left alone; Old Order Amish. J. Bird. il Sat Eve Post 240:28-36 Je 17 '67
World's Mennonites meet in Amsterdam M. Shelly. Christian Cent 84:1109-10 Ag 30 '67

MENOPAUSE
Change of life. il Good H 165:10+ S '67
Feminine forever; R. A. Wilson and others' theories on estrogen therapy. il Newsweek 69:55 Ap 3 '67
Menopause: is there a cure? B. Davidson. il Sat Eve Post 240:70-2 Ag 26 '67
Sex and the older woman; hormones to prolong femininity. F. Marley. il Sci N 91: 413 Ap 29 '67

MENS clothes. See Clothing and dress—Men

MEN'S shirts. See Shirts

MEN'S socks. See Hosiery

MEN'S underwear. See Underwear

MENSCH, Ralph
Diesel dollars and sense. Yachting 123:98-9+ Ja '68

le **MENSONGE drama.** See Sarraute, N.

MENSTRUATION
For husbands only. B. Kunkel. Farm J 91: 66F Mr '67
Hygiene: what to do for personal problems. Good H 164:146 Ja '67
Luteinizing hormone activity in plasma during the menstrual cycle. G. T. Ross and others. bibliog il Science 155:1679-80 Mr 31 '67
Pill: early breakthroughs; letters. S. R. M. Reynolds; S. H. Sturgis. Science 155:1361 Mr 17 '67
Premenstrual tension an ancient and entirely normal problem. Todays Health 45:80 S '67

Disorders
Pain your doctor can help you avoid; cramps. A. Kerr. McCalls 94:30-1 Je '67

MENTAL ability. See Ability

MENTAL arithmetic. See Arithmetic, Mental

MENTAL depression. See Depression, Mental

MENTAL development of children. See Children—Growth and development

MENTAL development of infants. See Infants—Growth and development

MENTAL healing
See also
Psychoanalysis

MENTAL health centers
Community-based volunteers; in Illinois mental health therapy. P. Douglass and others. Parks & Rec 2:26+ Ap '67

New building type takes shape: the community health center. il Arch Rec 141:157-9 F '67
Treating mental illness; community and family therapy programs of the Albert Einstein college. J. Ridgeway. New Repub 156:13-15 Je 10 '67

MENTAL health laws
Of course, I'm no psychiatrist; Alabama commitment statute and cases of B. Porter and I. Pruitt. R. Reisig and R. Rapoport. New Repub 156:13-15 Je 24 '67; Reply. E. Opton, jr. 157:34-5 Jl 15 '67

MENTAL health literature. See Psychological literature

MENTAL hospitals. See Hospitals, Psychiatric

MENTAL hygiene
American woman: her breaking point. F. F. Flach. Vogue 149:248+ My '67
How can drugs affect mental health? Good H 166:171 Ja '68
How to drive your family crazy. F. R. Schreiber and M. Herman. il Sci Digest 62:65-9 N '67
My escape from worry. il Farm J 91:20+ F '67
New town blues. F. R. Schrieber and M. Herman. il Sci Digest 62:61-2 D '67
Psychiatrist's notebook; questions and answers. T. I. Rubin. See issues of McCall's to September 1967
Test yourself on mental health. F. R. Schreiber and M. Herman. Sci Digest 62:56-60 Ag '67
They're all against me! il Good H 164:12+ Mr '67
You can make yourself sick. F. R. Schrieber and M. Herman. Sci Digest 61:24-5 Ap '67
See also
Adjustment. Social
Children—Management and training
College students—Health and hygiene
Maturity
Psychiatry

MENTAL illness
Suddenly, without warning or reason, it happens. P. Hamill. Good H 164:98-9+ Ap '67
See also
Nervous system—Diseases
Neuroses
Schizophrenia

Therapy
See also
Psychotherapy

MENTAL illness and law. See Mental health laws

MENTAL processes. See Thought and thinking

MENTAL telepathy. See Telepathy

MENTALLY handicapped
Drugs and poisons in mental retardation; report on meeting. G. M. McKhann and S. J. Yaffe. Science 156:266+ Ap 14 '67
Familial mental retardation: a continuing dilemma. E. Zigler. bibliog il Science 155: 292-8 Ja 20 '67; Discussion. 155:1442; 157: 576-9 Mr 17, Ag 4 '67

MENTALLY handicapped children
Cammie; condensation. G. Frank. il Read Digest 92:209-12+ Ja '68
Eva, child of joy and sorrow. H. Herz. il Redbook 128:37-44 F '67
Poverty and mental retardation. Sci Am 217: 50 D '67
Some children are special; grandchild of Vice President and Mrs Hubert Humphrey. R. Kramer. il N Y Times Mag p87+ N 5 '67; Discussion. p42+ N 26; 42 D 10 '67
Survival despite autosome lack; retardation due to missing autosome. il Sci N 92:393 O 21 '67
Tragedy and hope of retarded children; experiment at Seaside regional center, Conn. B. Blatt and C. Mangel. il Look 31:96-9+ O 31 '67
What's being done for the mildly retarded child? L. W. Sauer. il PTA Mag 62:31-2 O '67
See also
Slow learning children

Education
Mentally retarded children aren't all alike. B. Banks and A. Warkentin. il Parents Mag 42:56-8+ Mr '67
No child is hopeless here; Little City residential training and treatment center, Palatine. Ill. H. G. Earl. il Todays Health 45:71-5 My '67
See also
Slow learning children—Education
Special classes and special schools

MENTALLY ill

Care and treatment
Coming: better mental care for less. il Changing T 21:21-3 Ap '67
Schizophrenic day camp. Sci Digest 62:63 D '67
Therapeutic farm hands; psychotherapy. in Czechoslovakia. Sci Digest 62:65 D '67
See also
Hospitals, Psychiatric

Legal status, laws, etc.
See Mental health laws

Rehabilitation
Friendship really is the best medicine; Operation Homecoming in Springfield, Ill. A. Levy. il Good H 166:46+ Ja '68

MENTALLY ill children
World without I; University of Chicago's Orthogenic school for autistic children. il Newsweek 69:70-1 Mr 27 '67

Care and treatment
Way back for troubled youngsters; mental health volunteers in Los Angeles County help former psychiatric patients. S. Gordon. il Parents Mag 42:66-7+ N '67

Education
Equity for the emotionally ill; Ohio law. il PTA Mag 62:26 D '67

MENTALLY retarded children. See Mentally handicapped children

MENTALLY superior college students. See College students, Mentally superior

MENTALLY superior high school students. See High school students, Mentally superior

MENTOR marsh. See Marshes

MENUS
Deluxe menu for holiday meals. il Good H 165:130-44+ N '67
Dinner's ready in only an hour, or less. il Good H 165:130-45 O '67
Last-minute meals that busy women can prepare and serve in less than an hour; with recipes. il Redbook 129:90-4+ S '67
Meal a day. P. Cannon. See issues of Ladies' home journal
Menus in the making; with recipes. H. McCully. il House B 109:194-5+ Ap '67
[Month] menus; with recipes. See issues of Sunset
Plan dinner by the week. Bet Hom & Gard 45:86 S '67
You and your diet. il Good H 164:178+ Ap '67
See also
Breakfasts
Buffet meals
Dinners and dining
Meals

MENZEL, Jiri
Movers. A. Sarris. por Sat R 50:41 D 23 '67

MEPROBAMATES
FDA gets Miltown ruling. Sci N 91:184 F 25 '67

MERAS, Phyllis L.
Author. Sat R 50:36 Jl 22; 30 O 7 '67

MERCANTILE bank of Canada. See Banks and banking—Canada

MERCAPTO group
Inhibition of banana polyphenoloxidase by 2-mercaptobenzothiazole. J. K. Palmer and J. B. Roberts. bibliog il Science 157:200-1 Jl 14 '67
Sulfhydryl groups and estradiol-receptor interaction. E. V. Jensen and others. bibliog il Science 158:385-7 O 20 '67

MERCENARIES (soldiers) See Mercenary troops

MERCENARY troops
Last stand; Red cross plans to evacuate rebels from Bukavu. il Newsweek 70:50+ N 6 '67
Mercenaries change sides. S. Meisler. il Nation 205:689-91 D 25 '67
Mercenaries; participation in the Vietnam war. Nation 206:37 Ja 8 '68
Second front; white mercenaries and black rebels in Katanga. il Newsweek 70:51 N 13 '67
Shrinking giants; white mercenaries willing to call off revolt in exchange for amnesty and safe conduct from Congo. Time 90:24 S 1 '67
Terrible ones; Congo mercenaries. il Time 90:28 Ag 11 '67
U.N. condemns use of Angola as base for Congo mercenaries; statement, November 8, 1967; with text of resolution. W. B. Buffum. Dept State Bul 57:807-8 D 11 '67

U.N. security council condemns recruitment of mercenaries; statements, July 6, 10, 1967, with text of resolution. W. B. Buffum. Dept State Bul 57:151 Jl 31 '67
Vanishing breed. il Newsweek 70:34+ Ag 21 '67

MERCER, E. H. See Lee, A. K. jt. auth.

MERCER, Harry E.
Fantasyland finds. Travel 128:59-60+ D '67
Fun in Fiji. Travel 127:60-4 F '67

MERCER, Johnny
Johnny Mercer, master lyricist. G. Lees. pors Hi Fi 17:61-3 Je '67

MERCER, Ruby
Flags from Canada. Opera N 31:8-13 My 13 '67

MERCER ISLAND, Wash.
Gulf between parents. R. Vaughan. Life 63:104A-104B+ N 17 '67

MERCERSBURG theology
Mercersburg theology, ed. by J. H. Nichols. Review
Christian Cent 84:312 Mr 8 '67. K. Penzel

MERCHANDISE thefts. See Stealing

MERCHANDISING
And the tennis racket; Manhattan's licensing corp. il Time 89:94+ Ap 21 '67

MERCHANT, Jane
Thursday book review; poem. McCalls 94:143 Mr '67

MERCHANT, Larry
Lady-killer. Sports Illus 26:9 Ap 3 '67

MERCHANT, Vivien
Mrs Pinter. il por Time 89:78+ F 10 '67

MERCHANT marine

Russia
Titan unbound; Russian seapower. R. Moley. Newsweek 70:84 Ag 7 '67

United States
Let's take our ships out of the bottle. L. Velie. Read Digest 90:132-6 F '67
Merchant marine; address, February 13, 1967. T. N. Downing. Vital Speeches 33:478-80 My 15 '67
New chart for shipping. Bsns W p37 Mr 4 '67
Revolution in shipping: can it save U.S. merchant marine? il U S News 62:116-17 My 15 '67
Sink the Savannah? il Newsweek 69:80 F 6 '67
Swabbing down the merchant fleet. il Bsns W p 173-4+ Mr 18 '67
Technology and politics meet; nuclear ship Savannah to remain afloat. il Sci N 91:591 Je 24 '67
Unshipshape industry. il Newsweek 69:76-8 Je 12 '67
White House at bay; maritime unions attack on administration policy. Bsns W p 124+ Je 3 '67
See also
National maritime union of America

History
Pride of the seas; merchant navy; with portfolio of paintings. C. B. Mitchell. bibliog il Am Heritage 19:64-88 D '67

MERCHANT of new desires; story. See Elkin, S.

MERCIER, Vivian
Swift conviviality. Nation 205:151-3 Ag 28 '67

MERCOURI, Melina
I was born Greek, I will die Greek; interview, ed. by O. Fallaci. pors Look 31:72-6 S 5 '67

about
Melina. pors Life 62:48-51 Je 30 '67
View from the road; dances of Illya darling. R. Hicklin. il pors Dance Mag 41:24-7+ Mr '67

MERCURY

Prices
Quotations in quicksilver. il Time 89:65 Ja 27 '67

MERCURY (planet)
Temperature of Mercury. Sky & Tel 33:225 Ap '67

Photographs, maps, etc.
Mercury's rotation and visual observations. D. P. Cruikshank and C. R. Chapman. Sky & Tel 34:24-6 Jl '67

Radiation
Mercury: observations of the 3.4-millimeter radio emission. E. E. Epstein and others. bibliog il Science 157:1550-2 S 29 '67

MERCURY (planet)—*Continued*

Rotation

Mercury's double dawn. Time 89:56 Mr 10 '67

Mercury's rotation and visual observations. D. P. Cruikshank and C. R. Chapman. il Sky & Tel 34:24-6 Jl '67

Spectra

Mercury: new observations of the infrared bands of carbon dioxide. A. B. Binder and D. P. Cruikshank. bibliog Science 155: 1135 Mr 3 '67

MERCURY turbines
Turbo-alternator power units pass tests for AEC at TRW. W. S. Beller. il Tech W 20:36-7 My 29 '67

MERCY killing. See Euthanasia

MÉRÉ, Andrée Brossin de. See Brossin de Méré, A.

MEREDITH, Donald
Praise or boo him, but in Dallas call Don Meredith Dandy. J. R. McDermott. il pors Life 63:73-4+ D 1 '67

MEREDITH, James Howard
Blacklash in Harlem. il por Newsweek 69: 27-8 Mr 20 '67
Hometown advice. Newsweek 69:39-40 Mr 27 '67
Loner. Reporter 36:17 Mr 23 '67
Loner & the shaman. il por Time 89:23-4 Mr 17 '67
Meredith: the ambiguous heroes of Harlem; Powell. A. Kopkind. il por Life 62:32-32A Mr 24 '67
Meredith vs. Powell: how solid is the Negro vote? por U S News 62:52 Mr 20 '67
Meredith's one-night stand. F. E. Kearns. Commonweal 86:78-9 Ap 7 '67
Why Meredith quit the race with Powell. U S News 62:16 Mr 27 '67

MEREDITH, William
Winter verse for my sister. New Yorker 42:38 Ja 28 '67

MERGERS. See Business consolidations and mergers; Trusts, Industrial

MERICK, Wendell S.
Way out for U.S. in Vietnam war? report from the scene. U S News 63:28-32 Jl 17 '67

MERINGUE
Sculpture with meringue; with recipes. il Sunset 139:178-80 O '67

MERIT (Christianity) See Reward (theology)

MERIT rating of employees. See Employees— Rating

MERKERT, Tilde
(ed) See Rom, B. Face to face with a north woods guide

MERKINGER, Perry
All things visual. il U S Camera 31:46-7 Ja '68

MERKSON, Laverne, family
Negro; three families. J. A. Williams. il Holiday 41:58-61+ Mr '67

MERLIS, George
Why our paper died. Nat R 19:572-3+ My 30 '67

MERRIAM, Eve
Brotherhood, or Some of my best friends are Martin Luther King, jr; poem. Negro Hist Bul 30:23 Ap '67

MERRIAM, Lawrence C. Jr
Glacier; a trail park and its users. bibliog Nat Parks Mag 41:4-8 Ap '67
Recreation land management and the new forestry. bibliog Nat Parks Mag 41:14-18 Je '67

MERRICK, David
Philadelphian frolics. L. D. Streiker. Christian Cent 84:815-16 Je 21 '67

MERRILL, Charles
Negroes in the private schools. Atlan 220:37-40 Jl '67

MERRILL, Charles E, books, incorporated
Merrill to be acquired by Bell & Howell company. Pub W 191:122 F 20 '67

MERRILL, Grayson
Bahamian fortnight. Motor B 120:41-3+ O '67

MERRILL, James
Last words; poem. Atlan 219:76 Ap '67
More enterprise; Kitchen knight; poems. Nation 204:532 Ap 24 '67
Trellis; poem. New Yorker 43:59 D 28 '67

MERRIMAN, Nan
Singer's view of Toscanini. Sat R 50:53+ Mr 25 '67

MERRITT, LeRoy C.
Censorship in schools rising, says Merritt; summary of statement, 1967. Library J 92: 4318+ D 1 '67

MERRITT-Chapman and Scott corporation
Hauling down the horse flag? il Time 89:87 Mr 10 '67
Striking the flag. Newsweek 69:83-4 Mr 13 '67

MERRITT college, Oakland, Calif.
Merritt college, a compact campus to crown a hill site. il Arch Rec 142:157 N '67

MERRY mix-up; drama. See Watts, F. B.

MERRY Tyll and the three rogues; drama. See Thane, A.

MERSAND, Joseph L.
For English teachers. Sr Schol 91:sup26 S 28 '67
New books for teaching drama. Sr Schol 90: sup 18-19 Mr 17 '67
—and Hayman, Leroy
Professional bookshelf. Sr Schol 90:sup 18 Ap 28 '67

MERSON, Ben
Husbands with more than one wife. Ladies Home J 84:78-9+ Je '67
One man's impossible triumph. Good H 165: 74-5+ Ag '67
—See Merson, D. jt. auth.

MERSON, Dorothy, and Merson, Ben
Why some good husbands run away. Good H 166:92-3+ Ja '68

MERTON, Robert K.
Matthew effect in science; address, August 1967. bibliog Science 159:56-63 Ja 5 '68

MERTON, Thomas
Beyond the sacred; letter. Commonweal 87: 479 Ja 19 '68
Can we survive nihilism? Sat R 50:16-19 Ap 15 '67
Teilhard's gamble. Commonweal 87:109-11 O 27 '67

MERWIN, W. S.
Animula; poem. Nation 205:694 D 25 '67
Come back; poem. New Yorker 43:50 My 6 '67
Dry stonemason; poem. New Yorker 42:78 Ja 21 '67
Fly; poem. Atlan 219:62 My '67
How we are spared; Dream again; Death of a favorite bird; Provision; Dragonfly; poems. Poetry 109:235-6 Ja '67
Hydra; Is that what you are; End in spring; Divinities; poems. Poetry 110:100-2 My '67
In the winter of my thirty-eighth year; poem. Atlan 219:98 Mr '67
Looking for mushrooms at sunrise; poem. New Yorker 43:32 My 27 '67
Peasant; poem. New Yorker 43:44 Je 10 '67
Plane; poem. New Yorker 43:34 Ja 13 '68

MERYMAN, Richard
Boat journey down a moving adversary. Life 63:122+ D 22 '67
(ed) See Chaplin, C. Ageless master's anatomy of comedy

MESA VERDE NATIONAL PARK
Climate and tree rings in Mesa Verde. D. O'Bryan. il Nat Parks Mag 41:17-19 Ap '67

MESCALINE
Private sea: LSD & the search for God, by W. Braden. Review
Sat R 50:90-1 Ap 22 '67. N. W. Ross

MESENCHYMA. See Embryonic tissues

MESILLA, N.Mex.
On the streets of Mesilla. C. Stinnett. Holiday 41:26+ F '67

MESOLELLA, Kenneth J.
Zonation of uplifted pleistocene coral reefs on Barbados, West Indies. bibliog Science 156:638-40 My 5 '67

MESONS
Bioscience from nuclear particles; pi meson may be useful for cancer treatment. Sci N 91:85 Ja 28 '67
Meson factory on order. Sci N 91:231 Mr 11 '67

MESOPOTAMIA
History
Early Mesopotamian constitutional development. N. Bailkey. bibliog f Am Hist R 72: 1211-36 Jl '67

MESROP, Robert B.
Robert B. Mesrop prefers painting indoors. il por Am Artist 31:38-9+ F '67

MESSAGES, Bottle. See Bottle messages

MESSER, Alfred A.
Parent and child. N Y Times Mag p 123+ Mr 19 '67

MESSERLY, Wayne
How to select the right corn hybrid. Suc Farm 65:78 F '67

MESSERSCHMITT airplanes. See Airplanes, Military—Germany

MESSIAEN, Olivier
Backward revolutionary. il por Time 89:73 Ap 14 '67
Letter from Paris; concert in the Théâtre national populaire. Genêt. New Yorker 42:126+ F 11 '67
On CBS, Argo, and Music guild: Messiaen, slow-motion romanticism. A. Cohn. por Am Rec G 34:229-30+ N '67

MESSIER catalog. See Stars—Catalogs

MESSINA, Antonello da. See Antonello da Messina

MESSINESI, Despina
Travel. See occasional issues of Vogue

MESTA machine company
USW signs holdout. Bsns W p66 Je 10 '67

MESTRE Noza
Mestre Noza; with engravings. S. Biderman. Américas 19:5-7 N '67

MESTROVIC, Matthew M.
Grand tour: from Quebec to Warsaw. Commonweal 86:599-600 S 29 '67
Opening performance for a Greek tragedy. Commonweal 86:222-3 My 12 '67
Tito the liberal, Tito the Stalinist. Commonweal 85:477-8 F 3 '67

METABOLISM
First in-flight studies of metabolism. Sci N 91:159 F 18 '67
Lactic dehydrogenase and metabolism of human leukocytes in vitro. A. D. Bloom and others. bibliog il Science 156:979-81 My 19 '67
Metabolic aspects of acid-base change. W. D. Lotspeich. bibliog il Science 155:1066-75 Mr 3 '67
Regulation of the lac operon. J. R. Beckwith. bibliog il Science 156:597-604 My 5 '67
Tetrodotoxin: effects on brain metabolism in vitro. S. L. Chan and J. H. Quastel. bibliog il Science 156:1752-3 Je 30 '67
Urinary metabolites in congenital hyperuricosuria. M. E. Balis and others. bibliog il Science 156:1122-3 My 26 '67
See also
Bacteria—Metabolism
Calcium metabolism
Iron metabolism
Plants—Metabolism
Protein metabolism

METABOLISM, Disorders of
Thyrocalcitonin: evidence for release in a spontaneous hypocalcemic disorder. C. C. Capen and D. M. Young. bibliog il Science 157:205-6 Jl 14 '67

METACHROMATIC leukodystrophy. See Nervous system—Diseases

METAL, Scrap. See Scrap metal

METAL bonding
Diffusion bonding techniques changing aerospace industry. J. F. Judge. il Tech W 20:28-31 My 1 '67

METAL box company
Knock at metal box; challenge by American can. Time 89:94 Je 23 '67

METAL coating
Hard faces. Sci Am 217:106 S '67
Wide application expected for new coating technique; metalliding process. Aviation W 87:55 Jl 3 '67

METAL crystals
Perfect blade; single-crystal blade. Sci Am 216:58+ F '67

METAL cutting
See also
Electrochemical cutting

METAL detectors
Build the Beachcomber. D. Meyer. il Pop Electr 27:27-32+ Jl '67

METAL etching
Equipment
To write your name on metal; electro-chemical etching. il Consumer Rep 32:460 S '67

METAL finishing
Paints that won't peel on galvanized steel. Farm J 91:48 Ap '67

METAL-glass bonding. See Glass—Joining to metal

METAL locators. See Metal detectors

METAL match. See Fire making

METAL protection. See Corrosion and anticorrosives

METAL sculpture
Artist with a welding torch. L. W. Gilliam. il Farm J 91:105 Mr '67
Di Suvero: the pressures of reality. H. Rosenstein. il Art N 65:36-9+ F '67
Infinity in eight minutes; J. de Rivera's sculpture piece in front of Smithsonian institution's new Museum of history and technology. il Time 89:66 Ap 7 '67

Picasso in the steelworks; sculpture piece for Chicago's civic center. il Fortune 76:111-13 Ag '67
Stuffed moose & stacked tibias; welded metal sculptures of R. Hunt. il Time 90:96+ D 1 '67
Tin can arc welding. M. B. Morris, jr. il Sch Arts 67:6-9 N '67
Welded giants; sculpture garden of Lippincott environmental arts, inc. North Haven, Conn. il Arch Forum 126:52-7 Ap '67

METAL work
See also
Art metal work
Forging
Ironwork
Tinware

Projects
Family secrets from an old-time machine shop. G. R. Hunter. il Pop Sci 190:160-3 Ja '67
See also
Barbecue grills

METAL working industries
Hygienic aspects
Small companies are the big problem in today's occupational health care. il Bsns W p82 My 13 '67

METALLIDING process. See Metal coating

METALLURGY
See also
Extrusion process
Iron metallurgy
Steel metallurgy
Zone refining

History
Indium as an impurity in ancient western Mexican tin and bronze artifacts and in local tin ore. E. R. Caley and D. T. Easby, jr. bibliog Science 155:686-7 F 10 '67

METALS
Mechanisms of organic oxidation and reduction by metal complexes. J. K. Kochi. bibliog il Science 155:415-24 Ja 27 '67
Meeting needs for heavy elements. P. H. Abelson. Science 159:37 Ja 5 '68
Nature of metals. A. H. Cottell. il Sci Am 217:90-100 S '67
R factors mediate resistance to mercury, nickel, and cobalt. D. H. Smith. bibliog il Science 156:1114-16 My 26 '67
See also
Ore deposits
Transition metals
also names of metals, e.g. Iron

Coatings
See Metal coating

Detection
See Metal detectors

Erosion
See Erosion of metals

Prices
Commodity outlook: healthy now. Bsns W p41 Je 10 '67
Metal price bandwagon picks up more riders; aluminum and molybdenum follow copper and steel price increases. Bsns W p34+ Ja 21 '67

Quenching
See Quenching

Strength
Aerojet metal strengthening process. il Aero Tech 21:22 N 6 '67

METALS, Effect of temperature on
Stable magnetic remanence in antiferromagnetic goethite. D. W. Strangway and others. bibliog il Science 158:785-7 N 10 '67

METAMORPHIC rocks. See Rocks

METAMORPHISM
Geochemical evidence of present-day serpentinization. I. Barnes and others. bibliog il Science 156:830-2 My 12 '67
Quartz: extreme preferred orientation produced by annealing. H. W. Green, 2d. bibliog il Science 157:1444-7 S 22 '67
Sulfide solubilities in alteration-controlled systems. J. J. Hemley and others. bibliog il Science 158:1580-2 D 22 '67
Zeolitization of tuffaceous rocks of the Green River formation, Wyoming. J. H. Goodwin and R. C. Surdam. bibliog il Science 157:307-8 Jl 21 '67

METCALF, George R.
Century of no progress? Reporter 37:31-2 N
16 '67

METCALF, Robert L. See Williamson, R. L.
jt. auth.

METEORITE craters
Meteorite field studies at Campo del Cielo.
W. A. Cassidy. il Sky & Tel 34:4-10 Jl '67
Shock effects in certain rock-forming min-
erals. E. C. T. Chao. bibliog il Science
156:192-202 Ap 14 '67
Sudbury structure, Ontario: some petrographic
evidence for origin by meteorite impact.
B. M. French. bibliog il Science 156:1094-8
My 26 '67

METEORITES
Amphibole: first occurrence in a meteorite.
E. Olsen. bibliog il Science 156:61-2 Ap 7
'67
Chondritic meteorites and the lunar surface.
J. A. O'Keefe and R. F. Scott. bibliog
il Science 158:1174-6 D 1 '67
Cliftonite in meteorites: a proposed origin.
R. Brett and G. T. Higgins. bibliog il Sci-
ence 156:819-20 My 12 '67
Farmington meteorite: cristobalite xenoliths
and blackening. R. A. Binns. bibliog il
Science 156:1222-6 Je 2 '67
Fireballs associated with the Barwell meteo-
rite. H. Miles. il Sky & Tel 33:73 F '67
Hexagonal diamonds in meteorites. Sci N
91:226 Mr 11 '67
Hexagonal diamonds in meteorites: implica-
tions. R. E. Hanneman and others. bib-
liog il Science 155:995-7 F 24 '67
Indium variations in a petrologic suite of
L-group chondrites. S. N. Tandon and J.
T. Wasson. bibliog il Science 158:259-61
O 13 '67
Irons scrutinized; iron meteorites. il Sky
& Tel 35:24 Ja '68
Niningerite: a new meteoritic sulfide. K. Keil
and K. G. Snetsinger. bibliog il Science 155:
451-3 Ja 27 '67
Potassium:argon dating of iron meteorites.
L. Rancitelli and others. bibliog il Science
155:999-1000 F 24 '67
Primordial rare gases in unequilibrated ordi-
nary chondrites. D. Heymann and E. Mazor.
bibliog Science 155:701-2 F 10 '67
Shock-wave compression and X-ray studies
of titanium dioxide. R. G. McQueen and
others. bibliog il Science 155:1401-4 Mr 17
'67
Stanfieldite: a new phosphate mineral from
stony-iron meteorites. L. H. Fuchs. bibliog
il Science 158:910-11 N 17 '67
Stone meteorites: time of fall and origin. G.
W. Wetherill. bibliog il Science 159:79-82 Ja
5 '68
Western Australia's Mundrabilla meteorite.
R. B. Wilson and A. M. Cooney. il Sky &
Tel 33:72-3 F '67
Xenon-iodine dating: sharp isochronism in
chondrites. C. M. Hohenberg and others.
bibliog il Science 156:233-6 Ap 14 '67
See also
Tektites

Temperature and radiation
Equilibration temperatures of iron and mag-
nesium in chondritic meteorites. W. R. Van
Schmus and D. M. Koffman. bibliog il
Science 155:1009-11 F 24 '67
Rapid methods of determining cooling rates
of iron and stony iron meteorites. J. M.
Short and J. I. Goldstein. bibliog il Sci-
ence 156:59-61 Ap 7 '67

METEOROLOGICAL instruments
Taking the weather at home. il House B 109:
22+ N '67
See also
Thermometers and thermometry

METEOROLOGICAL models. See Weather
models

METEOROLOGICAL optics
See also
Airglow
Rainbow

METEOROLOGICAL research
Competition to balloons seen from reusable
solid rockets. W. E. Wilks. il Tech W 20:
25+ Je 19 '67
See also
Artificial satellites—Meteorological applica-
tions
National center for atmospheric research
Rockets—Use in research
Weather control
Weather research

METEOROLOGY
See also
Auroras
Climate
Computers—Meteorological applications
Droughts
Electronics in meteorology
Evaporation
Fog
Hail
Micrometeorology
Rain and rainfall
Rainbow
Thunderstorms
Tornadoes
Weather
Weather forecasts
Winds
World meteorological organization

METEOROLOGY, Aeronautic
Automated weather forecasting urged. Aviation W 87:55 O 30 '67
Clear-air turbulence: simultaneous observations by radar and aircraft. J. J. Hicks
and others. bibliog il Science 157:808-9 Ag
18 '67
Pilots' weather outlook. R. Blodget. il Flying
81:38-43 Ag; 53-5 S '67
That puzzling problem for space launches:
weather. W. Von Braun. il Pop Sci 191:
102-4 S '67

METEORS
Amateurs observe many summer meteors. T.
Sato. il Sky & Tel 34:264-7 O '67
Fireballs associated with the Barwell meteo-
rite. H. Miles. il Sky & Tel 33:73 F '67
Great bolide of April 25, 1966. C. P. Olivier.
il Sky & Tel 33:83-4 F '67
Shooting stars. Hobbies 72:119 O '67

METEORS, Photography of. See Astronomical
photography

METERS
See also
Dwell meters
Exposure meters
Frequency meters
Parking meters
Radiometers
Voltmeters

METHADONE
Heroin cure works. Sci N 91:116 F 4 '67
Methadone, fighting fire with fire; controver-
sial program to combat heroin addiction.
G. Samuels. il N Y Times Mag p44-5+ O
15 '67; Discussion. p81-2+ N 5; 22+ N 12 '67

METHEDRINE. See Amphetamines

METHERD, Carol
Death of a flower baby. il por Time 90:18
D 1 '67

METHODIST church

Board of missions
Methodist missions: money and witness. B.
Thompson. Christian Cent 84:218+ F 15 '67

METHODIST church in Brazil
Brazil's Methodists celebrate centennial. E.
K. Long. Christian Cent 84:1298-300 O 11
'67

METHODIST church in England
Britain's Methodists go Episcopal. C. Northcott. Christian Cent 84:613-14 My 10 '67

METHODIST church in Latin America
Latin America's Methodist women. N. Barber. Christian Cent 84:247-8 F 22 '67

METHODIST church in the United States
Dim view of a bright prospect: the proposed
United Methodist church; E.U.B.-Method-
ist merger. R. B. Garrison. Christian Cent
84:314-16 Mr 8 '67; Discussion. 84:501 Ap
19 '67
Loosening the cork; Oregon Methodist
churches repeal non-drinking laws. Newsweek 69:69 Je 26 '67
Methodist women as peace disturbers. B.
Thompson. Christian Cent 84:1205-6 S 20
'67

METHODIST monasteries. See Monasteries

METHOTREXATE
Apply-it-yourself salve for skin cancer. il Life
62:87-8 Mr 3 '67

METHVIN, Eugene H.
Is the Supreme court really supreme? Read
Digest 91:80-5 Jl '67

METHYL radicals. See Radicals (chemistry)

METHYL sulfoxide
Blackout on DMSO; Food and drug administration restricts testing. il Time 89:70+ My
5 '67
Dimethyl sulfoxide: lens changes in dogs during oral administration. L. F. Rubin and
P. A. Mattis; discussion. Science 154:543;
155:404 O 28 '66, Ja 27 '67

METHYL sulfoxide—*Continued*
Dimethyl sulfoxide protects tightly coupled mitochondria from freezing damage. D. B. Dickinson and others. bibliog il Science 156: 1738-9 Je 30 '67
Pemoline levels in brain; enhancement by dimethyl sulfoxide. J. J. Brink and D. G. Stein. bibliog il Science 158:1479-80 D 15 '67

METHYLAMINES
D-Glucose: preferential binding to brush borders disrupted with tris hydroxymethyl aminomethane. R. G. Faust and others. bibliog il Science 155:1261-3 Mr 10 '67

METRIC system
Centimeters inch up. Sci N 91:87 Ja 28 '67
DOD may use metric system for Maverick; air force's air-to-ground missile program. W. Andrews. Tech W 21:14-15 Jl 3 '67
Japan's switch to metrics. il Sci N 91:288-9 Mr 25 '67
Metric missile: Maverick. Sci N 92:320 S 30 '67
NSF, metric bills advance. Sci N 91:208 Mr 4 '67

METRO-Goldwyn-Mayer, incorporated
Back to work? Time 89:94 Mr 17 '67
Box office movie belle makes its third debut; Gone with the wind. il Bsns W p40-1 O 14 '67
End of a lion hunt; P. J. Levin sells shares. Newsweek 70:59 S 4 '67
Fight in the lion's den. il Time 89:87 Mr 3 '67
Fight over M-G-M: money grabs movies. il Newsweek 69:68-70 Mr 6 '67
MGM's own drama: the great proxy war; attempt by Levin group to oust O'Brien management. il Bsns W p 126-8 Mr 4 '67
Newest life of Leo the lion; proxy battles for MGM. Time 90:59-60 S 1 '67

METROMEDIA, incorporated
Select list for advertisers; Metromail group. Bsns W p92 My 27 '67

METROPOLITAN areas
Decentralization of jobs. D. K. Newman. bibliog f il Mo Labor R 90:7-13 My '67
Harvest of sour grapes. J. O'Hara. il Holiday 41:20+ Mr '67
Mini-megalopolis rises along the Mississippi; thriving Quad-cities of Iowa and Illinois. il Bsns W p 168-70 F 25 '67
Rise of a new political force. il Nations Bsns 55:72-4+ F '67
Some factors affecting housing density and auto ownership; excerpt from Postwar metropolitan development: housing preferences and auto ownershsip. J. F. Kain. Mo Labor R 90:45-6 Mr '67
Wages and supplementary benefits in metropolitan areas. K. J. Hoffmann. il Mo Labor R 90:48-54 Je '67
See also
City planning
Metropolitan government
Regional planning
Urban renewal

METROPOLITAN council for educational opportunity. See Boston—Education

METROPOLITAN government
Black control of cities. F. F. Piven and R. A. Cloward. New Repub 157:19-21 S 30; 15-19 O 7 '67

METROPOLITAN life insurance company
Rock at the top. Fortune 75:262 Je 15 '67

METROPOLITAN museum of art, New York
Collecting American art for the Metropolitan: 1961-1966. J. Biddle. il Antiques 91:481-6 Ap '67
Defrosting Canova; acquisition of Perseus. il Newsweek 70:90 S 18 '67
Impressionist eye; acquisition of C. Monet's La Terrasse. H. Kramer. il N Y Times Mag p28-31 Ja 7 '68
Kings' ransom; In the presence of kings exhibition. il Newsweek 69:93 My 1 '67
Marble for the Met; Canova's Perseus. il Time 90:77 S 15 '67
Million-dollar Monet. il Newsweek 70:42-3 D 25 '67
Monet & the phony pony. il Time 90:84 D 15 '67
New Yorker who shook up Central park. J. Peter. il Look 31:80+ My 2 '67
Noble Metropolitan visitors: old masters loaned to the Met from private collections in America and abroad. H. A. La Farge. il Art N 65:27-31+ F '67
Of a different color; Met's 15-inch bronze horse revealed as fake. il Newsweek 70:94 D 18 '67

Pleasing to the eye and ear alike; rare and beautiful musical instruments. E. P. Birk. il Antiques 92:434 O '67
Profiles; T. P. F. Hoving. J. McPhee. New Yorker 43:55-6+ My 20 '67
Some rare American prints in the Middendorf collection. W. J. Shadwell. il Antiques 92:558-62 O '67
Temple on Fifth avenue; Metropolitan museum acquires Temple of Dendur. il Time 89:80 My 12 '67
Under wraps, the Met's newest star; Perseus holding the head of Medusa. il Life 63:125-6 S 15 '67

Cloisters
Medieval flowers for today's gardens; ed. by E. McDonald. T. P. Miller. il House B 109: 158-61 D '67

METROPOLITAN national company. See Metropolitan opera national company

METROPOLITAN opera association
The line; a report on a changing institution. J. Weber. il Opera N 32:6-7 N 25 '67
People and their feelings; Lincoln Center student program. R. A. Tuggle. il Opera N 31:8-13 Mr 4 '67

Finance
Money from the sky; interview. ed. by F. Merkling. F. D. Hall. Opera N 32:14 N 25 '67

METROPOLITAN opera auditions. See Singing —Competitions

METROPOLITAN opera ballet
Metropolitan opera ballet; La ventana; Hansel and Gretel. J. Maskey. Dance Mag 42:30 Ja '68

METROPOLITAN opera company
At the Met; new Elektra and old friends. P. G. Davis. il Hi Fi 17:MA9+ Ja '67
How to run a festival. il Time 90:50 S 1 '67
Met outdoors (and in) Verdi festival at Newport. G. Movshon. il Hi Fi 17:MA12-13+ N '67
Metropolitan opera. il Hi Fi 17:MA6-8 D '67; 18:MA4-6+ Ja '68
Metropolitan opera repertory 1967-68 and roster. il Opera N 32:16-17 S 23 '67
Met's Flute: apotheosis of Chagall? P. J. Smith. il Hi Fi 17:MA10-11 My '67
Met's new Peter Grimes. M. Mayer. il Hi Fi 17:MA8-9 Ap '67
New Met at mid-point. G. Movshon. il Hi Fi 17:MA12-13 Mr '67
Verdi in Newport; Metropolitan opera festival. H. Saal. il Newsweek 70:81 Ag 28 '67
Von Karajan at the Met; rehearsal for American début with a new production of Wagner's Die Walküre. New Yorker 43:54-5 N 25 '67
See also
Radio broadcasting—Opera

METROPOLITAN opera guild
Metropolitan family; annual evening for supporting members. A. M. Lingg. il Opera N 31:6-7 Mr 11 '67
New man at the helm. F. Merkling. Opera N 31:16-17 Je 10 '67
Tea and glamor; Guild's lecture-teas at Colony club. il Opera N 32:13 Ja 6 '68
See also
Metropolitan opera studio

METROPOLITAN opera house, New York
End of Diamond horseshoe. continuation of a bitter argument. il Life 62:30A Ja 27 '67
Last look; photographs. Opera N 31:28 Je 10 '67

METROPOLITAN opera national company
Chances to be heard; Metropolitan opera regional auditions. R. Eyer. Opera N 32:14-15 Ja 6 '68
Council surprises. A. M. Lingg. il Opera N 32:13 D 9 '67
Met touring company canceled. Hi Fi 17: MA2 Mr '67
Music to my ears; production of Figaro, at New York city center. I. Kolodin. Sat R 50:46 F 18 '67
Musical events; performance of Mozart's Marriage of Figaro. W. Sargeant. New Yorker 42:158 F 11 '67
New York. R. D. Daniels. Opera N 31:31-2 F 11 '67
Newport; opera in town; photographs. Opera N 31:18-20 Je 10 '67
On the road. Newsweek 69:76 Mr 6 '67
On the road with the Met national company. A. Darack. il Hi Fi 17:MA18+ Ja '67
People and their feelings; Lincoln Center student program. R. A. Tuggle. il Opera N 31:8-13 Mr 4 '67
Spotlight on Britten. F. Merkling. il Opera N 31:12-13 Ja 7 '67

METROPOLITAN opera on the air. See Radio broadcasting—Opera

METROPOLITAN opera studio
Opera for hire. A. M. Lingg. il Opera N 32: 6-7 N 4 '67

METROPOLITAN Washington council of governments. See Washington, D.C.—Politics and government

METS (baseball) See Baseball clubs

METZGER, Delbert Everner
Judge and the agitator. Nation 204:613 My 15 '67

MEXICAN AMERICAN students in the United States
See also
Spanish speaking students

MEXICAN AMERICANS
Help for Spanish-speaking youngsters. J. Stocker. il Am Ed 3:17-18+ My '67
Mexican-Americans make themselves heard. M. Alisky. Reporter 36:45-6+ F 9 '67
Minority nobody knows. H. Rowan. Atlan 219:47-52 Je '67
Pocho's progress; nation's second largest disadvantaged minority. il Time 89:24-5 Ap 28 '67
See also
United States—Cabinet committee on Mexican Americans

Education
Tucson's tale of two cultures. NEA J 56: 62+ F '67

MEXICAN authors. See Authors, Mexican

MEXICAN caves. See Caves

MEXICAN cookery. See Cookery, Mexican

MEXICAN economic assistance. See Economic assistance, Mexican

MEXICAN folk art. See Folk art

MEXICAN Grand prix. See Automobile racing

MEXICAN literature
Literary life south of the Rio Grande. J. K. Hutchens. il Sat R 50:42-4 F 25 '67; Discussion. 50:26 Mr 25 '67
See also
Aztec literature

MEXICAN war, 1845-1848. See United States—History—War with Mexico, 1845-1848

MEXICANS
Late late lovers. E. H. Lopez. Atlan 220:95+ Jl '67
On Mexican national character. M. Maccoby. bibliog f Ann Am Acad 370:63-73 Mr '67

MEXICANS in the United States
See also
Mexican Americans

MEXICO
See also
Acapulco
Astronomical observatories—Mexico
Aviation—Mexico
Crime and criminals—Mexico
Cuernavaca
Ensenada
Fishing—Mexico
Gardens—Mexico
Geology—Mexico
Guadalajara
Hunting—Mexico
Juarez
Oaxaca (state)
Pátzcuaro
Poor—Mexico
Rural schools—Mexico
Sulfur mines and mining—Mexico
Taxco
Teotihuacán
Tourist trade—Mexico
Trade unions—Mexico

Antiquities
See Indians of Mexico—Antiquities

Boundaries
Amigos reunited. Diaz Ordaz and LBJ. il U S News 63:28 N 6 '67
Ceremonies at U.S.-Mexican border; remarks, October 28, 1967; with Declaration of the Presidents. L. B. Johnson. Dept State Bul 57:683-4 N 20 '67
Chamizal to Mexico. il Sr Schol 91:15 N 9 '67
Out of the thicket; U.S.-Mexican border dispute settled. Time 90:19 N 3 '67
U.S. and Mexico complete Chamizal settlement; statement, October 27, 1967, with White House announcement. D. Rusk. Dept State Bul 57:684-5 N 20 '67

Commerce
Industrial export expansion; Mexico's exports to western Europe. UN Mo Chron 4:41-2 Mr '67

Mexican-U.S. trade committee holds second meeting; joint communique, December 21, 1966. Dept State Bul 56:70-1 Ja 9 '67
See also
United States—Commerce—Mexico

Description and travel
Mexico. M. H. Bearns, 3d. il Flying 80:44-7 Ap '67
Mexico. M.-P. De Cicco. il Vogue 149:145+ Ap 1 '67
Mines of Mexico. il U S Camera 30:62-3+ Je '67
Photocade 1967: Mexico. L. Barry. il Pop Phot 60:20+ My '67
Wise ways to enjoy Mexico. P. Raymond. il Todays Health 45:42-7+ O '67

Economic conditions
Mexico: an economy comes of age. il Newsweek 70:60-6 Ag 7 '67
Now, for Mexico: a new revolution? il U S News 62:92-4 Je 5 '67

Economic policy
Mexico's success story. il U S News 63:53-6 O 2 '67
See also
American property in Mexico

Foreign relations
Mexican president honored; excerpts from address, October 26, 1967, ed. by G. Meek. G. Díaz Ordaz. il Américas 19:40 D '67
U.S. and Mexico conclude fisheries agreement. Dept State Bul 57:685 N 20 '67
United States and Mexico reaffirm friendship and good will: exchange of toasts, statements, October 26-28, 1967, with joint communique, Presidents' action program, and ceremonies at U.S.-Mexican border. L. B. Johnson; G. Díaz Ordaz. Dept State Bul 57: 673-84 N 20 '67
Why Mexico stays on the sidelines; relations with Cuba. U S News 63:43 O 9 '67

Industries
Incubating industry in Mexico; B. Quintana's Industria del Hierro. il Bsns W p86-8 Je 24 '67
Mendoza the builder; Bufete industrial. il Time 90:98 O 13 '67
Mexico: an economy comes of age. il Newsweek 70:60-6 Ag 7 '67

Intellectual life
Literary life south of the Rio Grande. J. K. Hutchens. il Sat R 50:42-4 F 25 '67; Discussion. 50:26 Mr 25 '67
See also
Mexico (city)—Intellectual life

Politics and government
No cause to hedge; Institutional revolutionary party suffers troubles. Time 90:32 Jl 14 '67
Now, for Mexico: a new revolution? il U S News 62:92-4 Je 5 '67

Religious institutions and affairs
Churchmen discover border problems. A. Zambrano and M. Zambrano. Christian Cent 84:248-50 F 22 '67
World around us (cont) Christian Cent 84: 220, 1407-10 F 15, N 1 '67
See also
Protestants in Mexico

Social conditions
No cause to hedge; Institutional revolutionary party suffers troubles. Time 90:32 Jl 14 '67
See also
Poor—Mexico

Social life and customs
See also
Indians of Mexico—Social life and customs

MEXICO (city)
City planning
Bully buildup in old Mexico; preparations for 19th Olympic games. B. Ottum. il Sports Illus 27:20-3 O 30 '67

Description
Letter from Mexico city. D. Gold. Holiday 42:16+ O '67

Galleries and museums
Museo nacional de antropología de México. S. Gorenstein. il Natur Hist 76:34-45 Ag '67

MEXICO (city)—*Continued*

Hotels, restaurants, etc.
Travel notes. R. Joseph. Esquire 68:60+ N '67

Intellectual life
Past and present. J. Linde. New Repub 157:40-2 S 2 '67

Music
Mexico city. L. Frick. Opera N 32:26 N 4 '67
Report: Mexico city; operatic productions. L. Frick. Opera N 32:31-2 D 16 '67

MEXICO and the United States
Agreement to solve Rio Grande salinity problem approved; statement, February 10, 1967. L. B. Johnson. Dept State Bul 56:428 Mr 13 '67
Building on the border; U.S. manufacturers building plants in north Mexico. il Time 89:106+ Je 9 '67
United States and Mexico reaffirm friendship and good will; exchange of toasts, statements, October 26-28, 1967, with joint communique. Presidents' action program, and ceremonies at U.S.-Mexican border. L. B. Johnson; G. Diaz Ordaz. Dept State Bul 57:673-84 N 20 '67

MEYER, Daniel
Build an electronic reverb-b-b adapter. Pop Electr 28:41-4 Ja '68
Build CB audio leveler. Pop Electr 26:55-8+ F '67
Build the Beachcomber. Pop Electr 27:27-32+ Jl '67
Build the mini-verb. Pop Electr 26:41-6 My '67
Build the mule box. Pop Electr 26:45-50+ Mr '67
Build the two-by-two stereo preamplifier. Pop Electr 26:69-73+ Mr '67
Getting the most from your CB rig. Pop Electr 26:72-3+ Ap '67

MEYER, David B. See Singh, R. P. jt. auth.

MEYER, Debbie
Remarkable Debbie and Claudia. il pors Life 63:66-7 S 1 '67

MEYER, Dorothy V. See Ellis, P. A. jt. auth.

MEYER, Elwood
I didn't fire a shot on my greatest hunt. Outdoor Life 140:54-5+ Ag '67

MEYER, Frank S.
Principles and heresies. See issues of National review

MEYER, Harry H.
Snap-action switches and their ganged arrays. por Electr World 78:53-6 O '67

MEYER, John Robert
Outgrowing the business cycle. il por Bsns W p 119-20 My 6 '67

MEYER, June
Spokesmen for the Blacks. Nation 205:597-9 D 4 '67

MEYER, Nicholas A.
New trends in colored paper; reprint. Am Artist 31:12+ O '67

MEYER, William
Phoebe Neville and William Meyer; Judson memorial church. M. Marks. Dance Mag 41:33 Ag '67

MEYERS, Sister Bertrande
Raise your voice; address, May 27, 1967. Vital Speeches 33:661-4 Ag 15 '67

MEYERS, Edward
Meyers on technique. See issues of Modern photography

MEYERS, Gilbert L.
Generals vs. Vietnam strategy; excerpt from testimony before Senate preparedness investigating subcommittee. U S News 63:114 N 6 '67
Meyers deplores Viet air war gradualism; testimony before the Senate Armed services preparedness investigating subcommittee. por Aviation W 87:55+ N 6 '67

about
Tactical air power curtailment seen causing excessive losses; with editorial comment. D. C. Winston. Aviation W 87:11, 17-18 O 30 '67

MEYERS, Harold B.
Sweet, secret world of Forrest Mars. Fortune 75:154-7+ My '67
Toughest best year ever. Fortune 75:170-3+ Je 15 '67

MEYERS, William
Sequatchie; story. Esquire 68:67-71 Jl '67

MEYERSON, Martin
Price of admission into the defense business. Harvard Bsns R 45:111-23 Jl '67

MIAMI, Fla.

Crime
Mob town, U.S.A. il Newsweek 69:38 F 13 '67
Murf the Surf and his jewel-studded jinx. K. Wheeler and S. Smith. il Life 62:92-4+ Ap 21 '67

Music
Miami; first U.S. production of Mozart's Oca del Cairo. D. Reno. Opera N 31:23 Je 10 '67
Miami; Greater Miami's new Tosca. D. Reno. il Opera N 31:29 Mr 4 '67
Miami; production of A. Thomas's Mignon. D. Reno. il Opera N 31:29 Ap 8 '67

Sanitary affairs
Super street litter needs a special hauler; junked cars. il Am City 82:56 O '67
Time-tested maintenance tips. D. P. Backmeyer. il Am City 82:96-100 Ap '67

MIAMI BEACH, Fla.

History
Recent history of 1967 congress site. il Parks & Rec 2:27+ Ap '67

Hotels, restaurants, etc.
Why Miami's visitors sign up for the year. il Bsns W p 169-70+ O 14 '67

Parks and playgrounds
Recreation demand in Miami Beach. S. W. Matthews. il Parks & Rec 2:23+ Jl '67

Recreation
Entertainment world of Miami Beach. il Parks & Rec 2:20-1+ N '67

MIAMI-Dade junior college, Miami, Fla.
Miami-Dade County's South campus, compact urban college in an as yet undeveloped area. il Arch Rec 142:164-5 N '67

North campus
Miami-Dade County's North campus, one of two campuses for expressway commuters. il Arch Rec 142:162-3 N '67

MIAMI Dolphins (football club) See Football clubs

MIAMI-KEY WEST race. See Motor boat racing

MIAMI RIVER
Short trip up the river. J. Wilson. il Motor B 120:35-7 O '67

MICA
Mica. il Sci N 92:272 S 16 '67
See also
Biotite

MICE
Australian desert mice: independence of exogenous water. R. E. MacMillen and A. K. Lee. bibliog il Science 158:383-5 O 20 '67
Circadian periodicity in susceptibility to lidocaine hydrochloride. E. F. Lutsch and R. W. Morris. bibliog il Science 156:100-2 Ap 7 '67
Endrin resistance in the pine mouse. R. E. Webb and F. Horsfall, jr. bibliog il Science 156:1762 Je 30 '67
Mice: individual recognition by olfactory cues. J. M. Bowers and B. K. Alexander. bibliog il Science 158:1208-10 D 1 '67

MICE, Mechanical. See Mechanical models

MICE, White footed
Behavior of captive white-footed mice. J. L. Kavanau. bibliog il Science 155:1623-39 Mr 31 '67

MICE as laboratory animals. See Laboratory animals

MICHAEL, Franz
Moscow and the current Chinese crisis. bibliog f Cur Hist 53:141-7+ S '67

MICHAELIAN, Al
Autorandom. See issues of Motor trend

MICHEAELS, Gregory J.
Low-rise in suburbia. Christian Cent 84:871-2 Jl 5 '67

MICHEL, Aloys A.
Pakistan. Focus 17:1-6 Ja '67

MICHEL, Joan Hess
Evaline Ness, the Caldecott medalist for 1967. Am Artist 31:32-7+ Je '67
Whimsey of Don Madden, a children's book illustrator. Am Artist 31:24-9+ S '67

MICHELANGELO Buonarroti
Nureyev. il Vogue 150:210-15 D '67

MICHELIN guide. See Guidebooks

MICHELS, Joseph W.
Archeology and dating by hydration of obsidian. bibliog Science 158:211-14 O 13 '67

MICHELSON, Annette
Light, silence, and space. Vogue 149:142-3+
Mr 15 '67
MICHELSON, Peter
Non-communications. New Repub 156:35-8
Mr 4 '67
Pop goes America. New Repub 157:25-8 S 2;
23-6+ S 9 '67
MICHENER, James Albert
Christmas present. Read Digest 91:60-3 D '67
Israel: nation too young to die. Look 31:
64-8+ Ag 8 '67
MICHENER, Martin C. and Walcott, Charles
Navigation of single homing pigeons; air-
plane observations by radio tracking. bib-
liog Science 154:410-13; 155:1136 O 21 '66,
Mr 3 '67
MICHIGAN
    See also
Architecture, Domestic—Michigan
Banks and banking—Michigan
Beaver Island
Booksellers and bookselling—Michigan
Fishing—Michigan
Gardens—Michigan
Hunting—Michigan
Libraries—Michigan
Unemployment—Michigan
Water supply—Michigan

Description and travel
Michigan's inland waterway. B. Glowacki. il
Travel 128:48-51+ S '67

Legislature
Referendum row; Michigan petition suspends
anti-daylight saving law. Time 90:47 Jl 7
'67

Politics and government
Michigan's Negro mayors. il Ebony 22:74-6+
Jl '67
Romney: stresses private effort. il U S News
63:57-60 O 30 '67
MICHIGAN, LAKE
Dead fish by the ton. il Sci N 92:9-10 Jl 1
'67
Dying Lake Michigan. Newsweek 70:110A+
N 13 '67
Watery grave for Lake Michigan? result of
industrial waste. il Bsns W p 103-4+ O 21
'67
MICHIGAN education association
Michigan adopts unification. M. Zemke. il
NEA J 56:43-4 O '67
MICHIGAN national guard. See United States—
National guard
MICHIGAN state university, East Lansing
Megaversity's struggle with itself; running
Michigan state. D. Norton-Taylor. il For-
tune 75:160-5+ My '67
MICHIGAN, University, Ann Arbor
Action intellectuals: elm-lined campus chang-
ing the Nation's standards. T. H. White.
Life 62:68+ Je 9 '67
Bilingualism and language learning; FLICS
project. Sch & Soc 95:294 Sum '67
Confessions of a campus pot dealer. Ric.
il Esquire 68:100-1+ S '67
Growing pains of the multiversity. W. Will-
cox. Atlan 220:45-7 Jl '67
In defense of the multiversity. R. Rapoport.
Atlan 219:73-4 Je '67
Mediator for Michigan. Newsweek 69:68 Ap
10 '67
Mediator for Michigan: new president. il
Time 89:39 Ap 7 '67
Michigan: ruckus over race has relevance to
other universities. B. Nelson. Science 156:
1209-12 Je 2 '67
Pedestrian mall links housing clusters to
form a community at University of Mich-
igan. il Arch Rec 141:147 Mr '67

Business hall of fame (proposed)
Bizneyland. Nation 204:293 Mr 6 '67

Clements library of
American history
Your excellency most obedient...servant;
concerning letter from J. André to Sir H.
Clinton. H. H. Peckham. Wilson Lib Bul
41:586-9 F '67
MICROBIOLOGY
Capillary-tube scanner for mechanized micro-
biology. R. L. Bowman and others. bibliog
il Science 158:78-83 O 6 '67
MICROBIOLOGY, Soil. See Soil microbiology
MICROELECTRODES. See Electrodes
MICROELECTRONICS. See Miniature electron-
ic equipment

MICROELECTROPHORESIS. See Electrophore-
sis
MICROFILMS
Industry starts a run on microfilm banks. il
Bsns W p66+ Je 17 '67
Microfilm and the need for standards; report
of second International congress on re-
prography, Cologne. F. B. Myrick. Pub W
192:75 D 4 '67
    See also
Libraries—Microfilm collections
MICROMANOMETERS. See Manometers
MICROMETEOROLOGY
Amateur scientist; sensitive electronic ther-
mometer used for making a study in micro-
meteorology. D. A. Kohl. il Sci Am 216:
135-6+ Je '67
MICROMETERS
Winners see frontiers during lab visits. Sci
N 91:259 Mr 18 '67
MICRONESIA
Micronesia; photographs. C. Purcell. Holiday
42:70-5 Jl '67
Micronesia: the Americanization of Eden. D.
S. Boyer. il Nat Geog Mag 131:702-44 My
'67
    See also
Airlines—Micronesia
Trust Territory of the Pacific Islands
MICROORGANISMS
Disinfection by electrohydraulic treatment.
M. Allen and K. Soike. il Science 156:524-5
Ap 28 '67
Hydroxamic acids in nature. J. B. Neilands.
bibliog il Science 156:1443-7 Je 16 '67
Relatives on Jupiter; microorganism grown
in hostile ammoniac atmosphere resembles
microfossils. il Time 90:62-3 Jl 21 '67
Scanning electron microscope: potentials in
the morphology of microorganisms. G. A.
Bartlett. bibliog il Science 158:1318-19 D 8
'67
Virus-like organism. Sci N 91:430 My 6 '67
    See also
Soil microbiology

Culture media
Capillary-tube scanner for mechanized mi-
crobiology. R. L. Bowman and others. bibliog il Science 158:78-83 O 6 '67
Growth of microbial cells on hydrocarbons.
M. J. Johnson. bibliog il Science 155:1515-
19 Mr 24 '67
Induced rapid release and uptake of phos-
phate by microorganisms. J. Shapiro. bib-
liog il Science 155:1269-71 Mr 10 '67
MICROORGANISMS, Pathogenic
Recommendations on nomenclature of the
order mycoplasmatales; subcommittee on
the taxonomy of mycoplasmatales. bibliog
Science 155:1694-6 Mr 31 '67
Strain of mycoplasma associated with human
reproductive failure. R. B. Kundsin and
others. bibliog il Science 157:1573-4 S 29 '67
MICROPALEONTCLOGY
Alga-like fossils from the early Precambrian
of South Africa. J. W. Schopf and E. S.
Barghoorn. bibliog il Science 156:508-12 Ap
28 '67
Fossil actinomycetes in middle Precambrian
glacial varves. T. A. Jackson. bibliog il
Science 155:1003-5 F 24 '67
Living relative of the microfossil kakabekia.
S. M. Siegel and others. bibliog il Science
156:1231-4 Je 2 '67
Primitive microfossils or not? M. N. Bram-
lette. il Science 158:673-4 N 3 '67
Radiolarian evidence consistent with spread-
ing of the Pacific floor. W. R. Riedel. bib-
liog il Science 157:540-2 Ag 4 '67
MICROPHONE amplifiers. See Amplifiers
MICROPHONES
Hi-fi product report; Electro-voice RE-15
microphone. il Electr World 79:12+ Ja '68
Microphones. H. Fantel. Opera N 32:33 Ja 20
'68
Microphones make the difference. il Hi Fi
17:55-62 F '67
MICROPHONES in criminal investigation, es-
pionage, etc. See Electronics in criminal
investigation, espionage, etc.
MICROPHOTOGRAPHY
    See also
Microfilms
MICROSCOPE and microscopy
New reflected-light microscope for viewing
unstained brain and ganglion cells. M. D.
Egger and M. Petran. bibliog il Science
157:305-7 Jl 21 '67
    See also
Electron microcsope and microscopy
Field ion microscope
Microscopy, Medical
Photomicrography

MICROSCOPE and microscopy—*Continued*

Exhibitions

Microbes: ninetieth annual exhibition of the New York microscopical society. New Yorker 43:26-8 Je 3 '67

MICROSCOPY. See Microscope and microscopy

MICROSCOPY, Medical
New view of the brain cell; new light microscope. Sci N 92:128 Ag 5 '67

MICROSOMES
Induction of drug-metabolizing enzymes in liver microsomes of mice and rats by softwood bedding. E. S. Vesell. bibliog il Science 157:1057-8 S 1 '67

MICROTUBULES. See Plant cells and tissues

MICROWAVE communications, Incorporated
New jolt for Ma Bell and friends. Bsns W p91 Ag 19 '67

MICROWAVE radio. See Radio communication, Short wave

MICROWAVE tactical landing system. See Aeronautic instruments

MICROWAVES
Microwave ETV system planning & installation. L. G. Lawrence. il Electr World 77:34-6 My '67
Millimeter-wave communication through the atmosphere. D. C. Hogg. bibliog il Science 159:39-46 Ja 5 '68
New wave; microwave technology. Time 89:64 Ap 21 '67

Industrial applications

Microwave dryer; experimental microwave machine for rapid drying of paper, photographic prints and leather. T. Weissmann. Sci N 91:582 Je 17 '67

MID-AMERICA regatta. See Regattas

MID-ATLANTIC ridge. See Ocean bottom

MIDBRAIN. See Brain

MIDDENDORF, J. William, 2d
Collecting American nineteenth-century art. Antiques 92:680-8 N '67

MIDDLE age
Cool cheer for middle age. R. Lynes. Look 31:45+ O 17 '67
Halfway home. J. G. Dunne. Sat Eve Post 240:20-1 Jl 15 '67
Middle-age crisis. B. Fried. il McCalls 94:88-9+ Mr '67

Anecdotes, facetiae, satire, etc.

Antacid trip with the tweeny-boppers. R. Price. il Sat Eve Post 240:22 N 18 '67

MIDDLE ages
Medieval studies; new program; Pennsylvania state university. Sch & Soc 95:73-4 F 4 '67

History

Birth of Europe, by R. S. Lopez. Review New Yorker 43:100-2+ Je 24 '67. P. Gay

Bibliography

Articles and other books received; comp. by B. J. Holm. See issues of American historical review

MIDDLE ATLANTIC states. See Atlantic states

MIDDLE classes
Growing success of Negroes in the U.S. il U S News 63:54-7 Jl 3 '67

MIDDLE EAST
Fact sheet on the Middle East. Sr Schol 91:10 O 5 '67
In the wake of war; time and reality in the Middle East. B. W. Tuchman. Atlan 220:62-9 N '67
Middle East today; symposium. bibliog f il Cur Hist 52:65-110+ F '67
Where war threatens next: the Mediterranean and beyond. il U S News 63:44-6 D 11 '67

See also
Americans in the Middle East
Arab states
Arabia
Arabs
Central treaty organization
Communism—Middle East
Foreign visitors in the Middle East
Petroleum—Middle East
Petroleum industry and trade—Middle East
Slavery—Middle East
Suez Canal
Tourist trade—Middle East
United Nations—Armed forces—Forces in the Middle East
United Nations—Middle East
Water supply—Middle East

Commerce

Mideast war's effect on U.S. business. il U S News 62:48-9 Je 19 '67

Defenses

Soviet Mideast buildup shows tactic shift. D. C. Winston. Aviation W 87:19-20 N 6 '67

Description and travel

Holy Land; symposium. il Sat R 50:38-41+ O 14 '67

Economic conditions

Middle East: analyzing social change. W. R. Polk. il Bul Atomic Sci 23:12-19 Ja '67
Picking up the pieces. Time 90:24-5 Jl 7 '67

History

ABC's of Middle East crisis; Arabs and Israel: the case for each side. il U S News 63:90-5 O 30 '67
[Middle East; last 100 years] E. Kern. il Life 63:52-70+ O 6; 72-86 O 13; 48-62+ O 20 '67

Bibliography

Articles and other books received; comp. by S. Glazer. See issues of American historical review

Industries

Imported machine age and first oil finds. E. Kern. il Life 63:82-3 O 3 '67

Maps

Lands of the Bible today. Nat Geog Mag 132:796-7, sup(folded map) D '67
Map of the Middle East (cont) Sr Schol 91:23 O 5 '67
Middle East: a broad view. Cur Hist 52:67 F '67

Politics

Aftermath of war in the Middle East. M. Lazega. il Cath World 206:155-9 Ja '68
Anyone for cribbage? two U.S. foreign-aid officials arrested in Yemen. Newsweek 69:52 My 15 '67
But what do we do about the Arabs? D. Cordtz. il Fortune 76:74-9+ S 1 '67
Consequences of defeat; Arab-Israeli war. B. Lewis. For Affairs 46:321-35 Ja '68
Exploding conflict in the Mideast. il U S News 62:8 My 29 '67
Explosive triangle. J. Burnham. Nat R 19:561 My 30 '67
Focus changes. il Newsweek 69:50+ F 13 '67
Futility in the Middle East. W. V. Shannon. Commonweal 86:406-7 Je 30 '67
Incurable arsonist; Nasser's fight to win absolute control over the Arab world. il Time 89:36 My 12 '67
Is peace in the Middle East possible? W. Laqueur. il N Y Times Mag p38-9+ Ag 27 '67; Reply. D. Sharma. p 123 S 24 '67
Is peace possible? address, March 12, 1967. F. B. Morse. Vital Speeches 33:452-5 My 15 '67
Israel and world politics. T. Draper. bibliog Commentary 44:19-48 Ag '67; Discussion. 44:6+ N; 12+ D '67
Israel's will to survive. P. Ben. New Repub 156:12-13 Ap 15 '67
King's plight; state visit of Saudi Arabia's King Feisal to Britain. il Time 89:38 My 19 '67
Limited options; L. Eshkol's prognosis for the Middle East in 1968. Newsweek 71:32+ Ja 8 '68
Middle East crisis and beyond; address, December 8, 1967. E. V. Rostow. Dept State Bul 58:41-8 Ja 8 '68
Middle East in crisis. W. Pfaff. Commonweal 86:382-3 Je 23 '67
Middle East in crisis; symposium. bibliog f il Cur Hist 53:321-58+ D '67
Mideast juggle. Commonweal 87:461-2 Ja 19 '68
Mideast stalemate. il Newsweek 70:73 N 20 '67
Misguided monarch; ex-King Saud visit to Yemen. il Time 89:37 My 5 '67
Mission impossible; reactions to Gunnar V. Jarring's arrival. Newsweek 71:33-4 Ja 1 '68
New power play? il Newsweek 69:63 Ap 17 '67
Razor's edge. il Newsweek 69:40+ My 29 '67
Real Mideast crisis. Nat R 19:1361-2 D 12 '67
Reports: after the Arab defeat. Atlan 220:38+ O '67
Return to Etzion. Sr Schol 91:22 O 26 '67
Revolt within a war; Yemen. il Time 89:36+ F 17 '67

MIDDLE EAST—Politics—*Continued*
Security council affirms principles for peace in the Middle East; requests Secretary-General to send special representative; statements with text of resolution. A. J. Goldberg. Dept State Bul 57:834-44 D 18 '67
Sound & fury; troubles on Israeli frontiers. il Time 89:26+ My 26 '67
Struggle for power; US-USSR influences. H. Brandon. Sat R 50:11 Ag 12 '67
T.R.B. from Washington; this is the Middle East. New Repub 156:inside cover Je 17 '67
Tunisia and Egypt. il Atlan 219:28+ Ap '67
Unsettlement is the Middle East prospect. P. Ben. New Repub 157:10-11 N 25 '67
See also
Arab states—Politics
Israeli-Arab war, 1967
Jewish-Arab relations
Middle East crisis, 1967

Relief work
U.S. to join in emergency relief programs for the Middle East; statement, June 27, and letter, June 29, 1967. L. B. Johnson; A. J. Goldberg. Dept State Bul 57:64-5 Jl 17 '67

Religious institutions and affairs
World around us (cont) Christian Cent 84: 1574 D 6 '67

Social conditions
Middle East: analyzing social change. W. R. Polk. il Bul Atomic Sci 23:12-19 Ja '67
MIDDLE EAST crisis, 1967
Back from the brink? U S News 62:30 Je 5 '67
Buried meaning of a crisis. E. J. Hughes. Newsweek 69:23 Je 12 '67
Commitment to Israel. America 116:802 Je 3 '67
Continuing cold war. K. Crawford. Newsweek 69:34 Je 12 '67
Cooling the Mideast; White House role. il U S News 62:8 Je 12 '67
Countdown in the Middle East; symposium. il Nat R 19:562+ My 30 '67
Did U Thant bungle the Middle-East crisis? U S News 62:19 Je 5 '67
Hatreds, tensions and theatrics. Life 62:4 Je 9 '67
If Egypt does fight Israel: who wins? il U S News 62:32-5 Je 12 '67
In the Middle East, blockade and face-off. il Life 62:40-1 Je 9 '67
Intermission: too late and too early. il Newsweek 69:38+ Je 12 '67
Israel in time of crisis: a report from the scene. W. MacDougall. il U S News 62:40-1 Je 5 '67
It's an ill wind. D. Lawrence. U S News 62:112 Je 19 '67
Letter from London; House of lords debate. M. Panter-Downes. New Yorker 43:96+ Je 17 '67
Middle East crisis. Bsns W p 164 Je 3 '67
Middle East: the scent of war. il Newsweek 69:40+ Je 5 '67
Mideast fuse still sputters. il Bsns W p29-30 Je 3 '67
Nasser and Israel. New Repub 156:1-3 Je 3 '67; Discussion. 156:34 Je 24 '67
Nasser lights fuse. il Bsns W p25-6 My 27 '67
Nasser the troublemaker; what he is up to now. U S News 62:19-20 Je 5 '67
Nation under siege. il Time 89:38-42 Je 9 '67
Region slipping to Russia, and U.S. has a big stake. J. Law. il U S News 62:32-5 Je 5 '67
Report from Israel. A. Campbell. New Repub 156:8-10 Je 10 '67
Staving off a second front. il Time 89:11-12 Je 2 '67
Story of forty-eight hours; U Thant's part in UNEF withdrawal. M. Greenfield. il Reporter 36:19-23 Je 15 '67
Strait that pinches big powers. il Newsweek 69:25-6 Je 12 '67
Test of patience & resolve. il Time 89:29-30 Je 9 '67
Third front. A. Weill-Tuckerman. Nation 204:706-7 Je 5 '67
Thunder over Sinai. Christian Cent 84:708 My 31 '67
U.N. Security council continues consideration of the crisis in the Near East; statements, May 29-31, 1967. A. J. Goldberg. Dept State Bul 56:920-9 Je 19 '67
U.S. absence. M. Ascoli. Reporter 36:18 Je 15 '67

United States calls for restraint in the Near East, statements, May 23, 24, 1967. L. B. Johnson; A. J. Goldberg. Dept State Bul 56: 870-3 Je 12 '67
Week when talk broke out. il Time 89:20-2 Je 2 '67
What Nasser has won by his threats. J. Law. il U S News 62:35-6 Je 12 '67
Where next big war can strike. il U S News 62:29-31 Je 5 '67
See also
Israeli-Arab war, 1967
MIDDLE EAST crisis and literature. See War and literature
MIDDLE EAST treaty organization
See also
Central treaty organization
MIDDLE EASTERN cookery. See Cookery, Middle Eastern
MIDDLE schools. See Education—United States
MIDDLE WEST
See also
Camping—Middle western states
Fishing—Middle western states
Great Plains
Hunting—Middle western states

Description and travel
Camping guide to the U.S; the Midwest. M. Frome. il Holiday 41:145-52 My '67
See also
Automobile touring—Middle western states

Tornadoes
See Tornadoes
MIDDLEHURST, Barbara M. and Moore, P. A.
Lunar transient phenomena; topographical distribution. Science 155:449-51 Ja 27 '67
MIDDLETON, C. J.
How to set up a project organization. Harvard & Bsns R 45:73-82 Mr '67
MIDDLETON, John
Melancholy in Melanesia. Sat R 50:65 Ap 8 '67
MIDDLETON, John T.
Automobile internal-combustion engine and the interests of the American people are on a collision course. por Pop Sci 190:96-9+ My '67
MIDDLETON, Robert G.
Notes on Protestant self-loathing. Christian Cent 84:304-6 Mr 8 '67
MIDGET automobiles. See Karts (midget cars)
MIDGETS. See Dwarfs
MIDGETTE, Willard F.
Philip Pearlstein: the naked truth. Art N 66:54-5+ O '67
MID-HUDSON library system, Poughkeepsie, N. Y. See Libraries—New York (state)
MIDNIGHT watch; story. See Potter, D.
MIDWAY (Islands)
Drilling on Midway atoll, Hawaii. H. S. Ladd and others. bibliog il Science 156:1088-94 My 26 '67
MIDWAY, Battle of, 1942
Incredible victory, by W. Lord. Review
Atlan 220:125-6 S '67. E. Weeks
Sat R 50:23-4 S 2 '67. R. L. Tobin
Midway; excerpts from Incredible victory. W. Lord. il Look 31:32-8+ Ag 8; 32-6+ Ag 22 '67
MIDWAY airport. See Chicago—Airports
MIDWEST. See Middle West
MIDWEST fall book festival. See Book fairs
MIDWIVES
Sudan's donkey-back midwives; with photos by Paul Almasy. Todays Health 46:16-18 Ja '68
MIDWOOD, Barton
Automotive immortality; story. Esquire 68: 110 O '67
Sheriff; story. Esquire 68:149 N '67
MIEL, Alice
Shortchanged in suburbia; excerpts from Shortchanged children of suburbia. Sr Schol 90:sup4 My 12 '67
—and Kiester, Edwin, Jr
Parent and child. N Y Times Mag p99-100+ Ap 16 '67
MIELZINER, Jo
Interview, ed. by A. Fatt. por Dance Mag 41:50 F '67
MIGDOLL, Herbert
Dance; photographs. Horizon 9:96-105 Sum '67
MIGRAINE. See Headache
MIGRAINE workers; story. See Petry, A.

MIGRANT labor
American farm labor displaces braceros. Christian Cent 84:133 F 1 '67; Discussion. 84:316 Mr 8 '67
Charity ends at home; proposal to improve living conditions in south Jersey stalemated. New Repub 156:9 F 18 '67
Effects of ending bracero program. America 116:546 Ap 15 '67
Invisible poor of the Garden state; conditions in New Jersey. J. F. Gagen. Commonweal 86:540-1 S 8 '67
Migrant workers to be trained for aircraft production jobs. Aviation W 87:127-8 Ag 14 '67
New grapes; el Teatro campesino (the Farm workers' theater) performs for migrant workers. il Newsweek 70:79 Jl 31 '67
See also
Children of migrant laborers
National farm workers' association

MIGRATION, internal
Growing problem for big cities. il U S News 62:115 Ap 24 '67
Here today, but where tomorrow? E. S. Oshin. il N Y Times Mag p89-90+ Mr 5 '67
Memoirs of a recent migrant. H. Brucker. il Sat R 50:20-1+ S 23 '67
White exodus to suburbia steps up. H. J. Gans. il N Y Times Mag p24-5+ Ja 7 '68
See also
Negroes in the United States—Migration

MIGRATION from cities. See Migration, Internal

MIGRATION of Negroes. See Negroes in the United States—Migration

MIGRATORY workers. See Migrant labor

MIHAJLOV, Mihajlo
Matter of definition. il por Newsweek 69:38 My 1 '67
Religious freedom in Yugoslavia; yes and no. M. Bourdeaux. Christian Cent 84:1228+ S 27 '67

MIJAL, Kazimierz
Poland's anti-Semitic Maoist underground. S. L. Shneiderman. il Reporter 36:21-3 Ja 26 '67

MIKE Douglas show. See Television broadcasting—Programs

MIKESELL, Art
Art Mikesell tests Starcraft's Super Sport-V. pors Pop Mech 128:160-2+ N '67

MIKHAILOV, Nikolai
U.S.S.R. today. UNESCO Courier 20:4-10 N '67

MIKI, Takeo
U.S.-Japan joint economic committee holds sixth meeting; news conference, September 15, 1967. Dept State Bul 57:455-9 O 9 '67

MIKITA, Stan
Dynamic duo. il por Newsweek 69:62 Mr 20 '67
Good Gvoth! il por Time 89:57 F 24 '67

MIKURA-jima (island)
Where ocean birds climb island trees. M. J. Kilgour. il Audubon 69:70-7 Jl '67

MIKVEH
Moving the mikveh; dispute in Wilkes-Barre, Pa. S. J. Ungar. Commentary 44:89-91 S '67; Discussion. 44:10+ D '67

MILAN, Italy
Music
Appointment in Milan; Toscanini's postwar return to La Scala. G. R. Marek. il Hi Fi 17:42-7 Mr '67
Milan; La Scala's production of Giordano's Madame Sans-Gêne. F. P. Hoffer. Opera N 31:31 Ap 1 '67
Milan; performance of Mussorgsky's Khovanshchina. F. P. Hoffer. Opera N 31:26 Je 10 '67

MILANESE cookery. See Cookery, Italian

MILAS, Suzanne
Why I believe in sex before marriage. Redbook 130:10+ N '67

MILDENBERGER, Karl
Bean-can bout in Frankfurt. M. Kram. il Sports Illus 27:20-3 S 25 '67

MILEAGE indicators. See Odometers

MILEK, Bob
Growing crisis on our public land. Field & S 72:10-11+ Ja '68
Old buck is still around. Field & S 72:54-5+ O '67
Pain-in-the-neck pack trip. Field & S 72:50-1+ My '67
Wyoming antelope. Field & S 72:40-1+ Ag '67

MILES, Arthur Curtis
Cued speech. Am Ed 3:26-8 N '67

MILES, Charles
Indian relics. See issues of Hobbies

MILES, Dick
Lowball in a time capsule. Sports Illus 26:110-13+ Ap 17 '67
Table tennis. Sports Illus 26:59 My 1 '67

MILES, Howard
Fireballs associated with the Barwell meteorite. il Sky & Tel 33:73 F '67

MILES, Joseph E.
Tax speedups & corporate liquidity. Harvard Bsns R 45:2-4+ Jl '67

MILES, Josephine
Hampton institute album; National parks; poems. Poetry 110:365-6 S '67

MILES, Marvin
Where were you, Marvin? W. J. Coughlin. Tech W 20:50 Mr 13 '67

MILES, Michael
Colonialism on the black campus. New Repub 157:15-16 Ag 5 '67
Politics of consortium. New Repub 157:11-13 S 9 '67
Revolution or reform on the black left. New Repub 157:9-10 Ag 19 '67
Tactics of disruption. New Repub 157:10 N 4 '67

MILES college, Birmingham, Ala.
Act of involvement; new director of freshman studies. il Time 89:60 Mr 17 '67
Dean Monro's enormous reward. Nation 204:389 Mr 27 '67
Monro's choice. Newsweek 69:61 Mr 20 '67

MILETUS, Turkey
City as an act of will; excerpt from Design of cities. E. N. Bacon. il Arch Rec 141:120-1 Ja '67

MILFOIL. See Yarrows

MILHAVEN, John G.
To be perfectly frank. America 116:584-6, 788-90 Ap 22, My 27 '67

MILITARISM
Nigeria in crisis; three military coups. W. A. E. Skurnik. Cur Hist 52:142-8+ Mr '67

MILITARY administration
African affairs; a confusion of colonels. E. Huxley. Nat R 19:466-7 My 2 '67

MILITARY air traffic control. See Air traffic control

MILITARY airlift command. See United States—Military airlift command

MILITARY airplanes. See Airplanes, Military—United States

MILITARY art and science
Reformation of war, by J. F. C. Fuller. Review
New Repub il 156:39-41 Ap 8 '67. A. Brynes
Robert McNamara and the process of military decision. G. F. Eliot. Nat R 19:189+ F 21 '67
See also
Chemical warfare
Firearms
Military research
Strategy
War

MILITARY assistance
Gun-peddling; US-USSR. New Repub 157:6 Jl 8 '67
New deal for the Middle East; USSR and US aid to Arab states. Nation 204:802-3 Je 26 '67

MILITARY assistance, American
America's foreign aid program; reappraising its relevancy; address, January 14, 1967. J. S. Clark. Vital Speeches 33:299-303 Mr 1 '67
Arms and the man who sells them; excerpt from The limits of power. E. J. McCarthy. Atlan 220:82-6 O '67
Arms export credit funds face Congress conference showdown. Aviation W 87:23 S 4 '67
Arms sales and foreign policy; excerpts from Arms sales and foreign policy, January 25, 1967. Bul Atomic Sci 23:44-8 S '67
Arms to the Latins. New Repub 157:7 N 4 '67
As others see us, some eye-openers; fifteen foreign newsmen to study the United States. A. H. Sypher. il Nations Bsns 55:41-2 O '67
Blunt business; request that U.S. supply arms for moderate Arab states. il Time 90:13 S 1 '67
Case of Greece. Nation 205:195-6 S 11 '67
Congo and the Senate. New Repub 157:6-7 Jl 22 '67
DOD plan would separate civil, military aid requests. D. C. Winston. Aviation W 87:17-18 D 25 '67
Foreign aid; an essential element of U.S. foreign policy; address, September 30, 1967. N. D. Katzenbach. Dept State Bul 57:530-4 O 23 '67

MILITARY research—*Continued*

Economic aspects

Man under the gun in military research; Pentagon research chief. il Bsns W p60-2+ D 16 '67

MILITARY schools

Girls before the mast: Culver military academy, Summer naval school. B. Kocivar. il Look 31:89-91 Je 13 '67

New curriculum for citizenship education; Culver military academy. L. K. Moore. il Sr Schol 90:sup 14-15 My 19 '67

MILITARY service

Careers in the military, pro & con. il Changing T 21:41-4 Ag '67

See also

Conscientious objectors

Soldiers

MILITARY service, Compulsory

Deciding careers with the club of induction. A. V. Krebs, jr. Commonweal 86:468-9 Jl 28 '67

Higher education and the war machine. Christian Cent 84:1645 D 27 '67

Deferments and exemptions

Beating General Marsbars; draft-counseling and resistance centers il Time 90:15 S 8 '67

Congress draws up battle lines over draft; with editorial comment. il Bsns W p42-3, 200 Mr 11 '67

Dissenting champion; case of C. Clay. Nat R 19:504-6 My 16 '67

Good-by, grad school? draft deferments only to graduate students in four fields. Newsweek 70:68 D 18 '67

Reprieving students; Senate armed services committee's draft bill. New Repub 156:6 My 27 '67

Sad young men; graduate deferments to end. New Repub 157:10 D 9 '67

Science deferments. Sci N 91:546 Je 10 '67

Selective service and student deferment; statement, April 25, 1967. Sch & Soc 95: 428-30 N 11 '67

Should ministers be draft-exempt? il Time 89:70+ Ap 7 '67

Students still deferred. Sci N 92:33 Jl 8 '67

Twenty questions about draft answered. il U S News 63:36-7 Jl 10 '67

Who shall serve? W. V. Kennedy. America 116:854-5 Je 17 '67

Australia

Australia's deep divisions; Vietnam and the draft. N. Brennan. Commonweal 86:79-80 Ap 7 '67

Russia

Soviets overhaul draft policies. il Sr Schol 91:19 O 26 '67

United States

About the draft. il Nat R 19:556 My 30 '67

Academic rank and the draft. Sch & Soc 95:43-4 Ja 21 '67

After protesters burned a U.S. flag. il U S News 62:12+ My 1 '67

All's fair; Lyndon Johnson's message. Newsweek 69:43-4 Mr 13 '67

Ambivalence on draft resistance. L. Kinsolving. Christian Cent 85:57-8 Ja 10 '68

American fantasy; Stop the draft week. S. Maloff. Commonweal 87:399-400 D 29 '67

Among Vietnam's victims: the draft. il Newsweek 70:42-3 Jl 10 '67

Antidraft movement. J. Burnham. Nat R 19: 629 Je 13 '67

Anything but bingo; advice to induct draft-deferred protesters. Time 90:19 D 22 '67

As the judge threw the book at Muhammad; sentence of C. Clay. il Sports Illus 27:18-19 Jl 3 '67

Bar Hershey; recommendations to call up anti-Vietnam demonstrators. New Repub 157:9 D 23 '67

Big draft shake-up. Sr Schol 90:20 Mr 31 '67

Boys without a country; U.S. draft dodgers in Canada. O. Clausen. il N Y Times Mag p25+ My 21 '67; Reply with rejoinder. M. Satin. p2 Jl 2 '67

Broadening the base; recommendation by Armed services committee. Time 89:19 My 12 '67

Burning words, yes; burning cards, no; case of D. J. Miller. Time 89:51-2 F 24 '67

By the numbers? L. B. Johnson's proposals. Newsweek 69:29-30 Mr 20 '67

Case for abolishing the draft, and substituting for it an all-volunteer army. M. Friedman. il N Y Times Mag p23+ My 14 '67; Discussion. p 12+ Je 4 '67

Caught in the draft; Mark Clark amendments signed into law. New Repub 157:4-5 Jl 8 '67

Champ in the jug? Muhammad Ali prefers jail to army duty. R. H. Boyle. il Sports Illus 26:30-3 Ap 10 '67

Changes in draft law; what to expect. U S News 62:16 My 15 '67

Changes in the draft: what to expect; interview. L. B. Hershey. U S News 62: 68-70 Mr 20 '67

Class, race and the draft. Sci Am 216:54 My '67

Clay vs. draft. Sr Schol 90:19-20 My 12 '67

Congress draws up battle lines over draft; with editorial comment. il Bsns W p42-3, 200 Mr 11 '67

Conscience and the war. New Repub 156:7-8 Ap 15 '67

Crackdown on draft protesters. U S News 63:6 N 20 '67

Disputation defused. il Time 89:23 Mr 17 '67

Doing their thing; Stop the draft week. il Newsweek 70:41 D 18 '67

DO's drafted with MD's. Sci N 91:135 F 11 '67

Draft-age dilemma. G. Wilson; O. S. Johnson. McCalls 94:34+ Ag '67

Draft and conscience. Commonweal 86:139-41 Ap 21 '67

Draft crackdown? il Sr Schol 91:18-19 D 7 '67

Draft: graduate schools fear effect of new law. R. J. Samuelson. Science 158:757-8 N 10 '67

Draft is no answer to dissent; General Hershey's directive. Life 63:4 N 24 '67

Draft law changes. Commonweal 86:5 Mr 24 '67

Draft may not be used to silence dissent. il Time 89:66 F 10 '67

Draft outlook under the new law. il U S News 62:70 Je 19 '67

Draft: protest, debate, renewal. il Newsweek 69:25-6 My 22 '67

Draft reform. Time 89:31 Je 9 '67

Draft revolt: how far it has gone. U S News 62:14 My 22 '67

Draft ruffles the ivy; end of blanket deferments for graduate study. il Bsns W p42+ D 16 '67

Draft statements stir controversy; suit against L. B. Hershey. K. Sperry. Science 158:1434 D 15 '67

Draft the clergy too; World alliance of reformed churches proposal. Christian Cent 84:133-4 F 1 '67

Draft uncertain. Sci N 91:470 My 20 '67

Draft: who, when, why? il Sr Schol 91:8-13 S 28 '67

Draftees who say no: laying freedom on the line. P. Good. il Nation 204:365-70 Mr 20 '67

Drive for big changes in draft; here is the latest plan. il U S News 62:44-6 Mr 13 '67

Dubious privilege; draft boards and others who interfere with the draft. Time 90:27 D 15 '67

FAIR shake? fair and impartial random selection. Time 89:23 Mr 10 '67

Forgotten history of the draft. D. J. Fliegel. il Nation 204:454-6 Ap 10 '67

Gaseous Cassius; refusal to be inducted into the army. Time 89:23-4 My 5 '67

General Hershey: under fire, but still firm and serene. il U S News 63:10 D 25 '67

Gloom in grad schools; graduate students to be called up. Time 90:88 N 24 '67

Government's round; C. Clay receives sentence. il Newsweek 70:24+ Jl 3 '67

Hell, no, we won't go. B. Davidson. il Sat Eve Post 241:21-6 Ja 27 '68

Hershey and the draft; recommends revoking deferments of dissenters. New Repub 157:7 D 2 '67

Higher draft calls ahead. il U S News 63:54 D 4 '67

I am not worried about Ali; ed. by T. Maule. B. Russell. il Sports Illus 26:18-21 Je 19 '67

I'm free to be who I want. R. Lipsyte. il N Y Times Mag p28-9+ My 28 '67

Into the fiery furnace; Clay resists draft. il Newsweek 69:72 My 8 '67

Keeping square with the draft board. il Changing T 21:12 My '67

K.O. for Cass. il Time 89:20 Je 30 '67

Latest draft plan: who would be taken. il U S News 62:12 F 20 '67

Let the Negro do it; antiwar whites exploit Negro dilemma. K. Crawford. Newsweek 69:46 My 8 '67

MILITARY service, Compulsory—United States
—*Continued*
Life with father; draft boards could not punish protesters. Newsweek 69:40 F 13 '67
Making the draft more equitable. America 116:366 Mr 18 '67
Many thanks, General; reactions to L. B. Hershey's proposal. Nation 205:642-3 D 18 '67
More protests, growing lawlessness: how far will it go? il U S News 63:6+ D 18 '67
Need for selective service policy. D. Wolfle. Science 157:1515 S 29 '67
Negro and Vietnam. Nation 205:37-8 Jl 17 '67
Nineteen-year-olds first. Sr Schol 90:25 My 19 '67
No to the draft? M. Hope. Christian Cent 84:715-16 My 31 '67
1-A or 2-S, the draft and the student. C. D. B. Bryan. il N Y Times Mag p26-7+ Mr 19 '67; Discussion. p22+ Ap 9 '67
Our draft dodgers in Canada. J. Star. il Look 31:31-3 Mr 7 '67
Overhauling the draft system: hard times for the reformers. R. J. Samuelson. Science 157:290-4 Jl 21 '67; Reply. J. D. Alden. 157:1511 S 29 '67
Personal business; what to do about the draft. Bsns W p 171 Mr 25 '67
Plan for an equitable draft; L. B. Johnson's recommendations. Life 62:4 Mr 17 '67
Prospects now for changing draft rules. U S News 62:6+ Mr 6 '67
Real story on draft dodging: a survey shows this. il U S News 63:53-4 D 4 '67
Redrafting the draft. Reporter 36:8 Ap 6 '67
Reform the draft. New Repub 156:8 Mr 11 '67
Reprieving students; Senate armed services committee's draft bill. New Repub 156:6 My 27 '67
Retaliation barred; dissent and the draft. Sr Schol 90:15-16 F 17 '67
Rising pressure to end draft deferments. U S News 62:8-9 Ap 3 '67
Rout of the reformers; new Selective service bill. Newsweek 69:36 Je 26 '67
Science deferments. Sci N 91:546 Je 10 '67
Science deferments under the gun. Sci N 91:256 Mr 18 '67
Selective objection and the public interest; present law is unconstitutional. W. Arnold. Christian Cent 84:1218-21 S 27 '67
Selective service changes. D. Wolfle. Science 155:1499 Mr 24 '67
Selective service solution. D. Wolfle. Science 158:1271 D 8 '67
Seminarian in the resistance. B. Johnson. Christian Cent 85:15-17 Ja 3 '68
Shaping up youth; Senate draft hearings. Sr Schol 90:19-20 Ap 7 '67
Should there be a draft? Nation 204:354 Mr 20 '67
Show goes on; case of David J. Miller. il Time 89:79 Ap 14 '67
Speaking out: the draft should be abolished. M. O. Hatfield. Sat Eve Post 240:12+ Jl 1 '67
Students and the draft: when not all serve. J. Cass. Sat R 50:59-60 Ap 15 '67
Super-General Hershey. R. J. Neuhaus. Commonweal 87:465-7 Ja 19 '68
Support for a lottery; Kennedy subcommittee hearings. il Newsweek 69:33 Ap 3 '67
Surprised 1A: Henry Braun reclassified for violating draft card law. Time 90:11 D 29 '67
Taps for the champ; with editorial comment. E. Shrake. il Sports Illus 26:11, 19-25 My 8 '67
Thanks, but no thanks; draft dodgers granted a second chance. Time 89:27 Mr 3 '67
This month's feature: new moves to revise Selective service. Cong Digest 46:131-60 My '67
Turmoil over draft: effect of LBJ's plan. il U S News 62:33-4 Mr 20 '67
Twenty-five years of conscription; subordination of the individual to the state. J. M. Swomley, jr. Christian Cent 84:465-8 Ap 12 '67
Twenty questions about draft answered. il U S News 63:36-7 Jl 10 '67
U.S. selective service. T. C. Schelling and others. Bul Atomic Sci 23:38-40 O '67
War and the draft. S. Tax. il Natur Hist 76:54-8 bibliog(p70) D '67
What kind of draft? Christian Cent 84:333 Mr 15 '67
What teeth does the draft law have? il U S News 63:22-3 D 25 '67

When baseball went to war; World war II. F. Graham, jr. il Sports Illus 26:78-82+ Ap 17 '67
Where blows the draft? Nat R 19:286+ Mr 21 '67
Who shall serve? W. V. Kennedy. America 116:854-5 Je 17 '67
Why not abolish the draft? B. K. Chapman. Nat R 19:303-5 Mr 21 '67
See also
Conscientious objectors
MILITARY service, Voluntary
Case for abolishing the draft, and substituting for it an all-volunteer army. M. Friedman. il N Y Times Mag p23+ My 14 '67; Discussion. p 12+ Je 4 '67
Dose of boot camp; three days military training feature of personnel-training in Japan. il Time 89:106 Je 9 '67
Principles & heresies; Council for a volunteer military. F. S. Meyer. Nat R 19:749 Jl 11 '67
MILITARY strategy. See Strategy
MILITARY supplies
Industry passes the ammunition. il Bsns W p66-8+ Je 24 '67
See also
Vietnamese war, 1957- —Equipment and supplies
Maintenance and repair
Avionics to feel life-cycle-cost impact. P. J. Klass. il Aviation W 86:261-3+ Mr 6 '67
MILITARY tanks. See Tanks, Military
MILITARY topography
Computers cut topographic survey costs. C. D. LaFond. il Tech W 20:20-1 F 20 '67
MILITARY training camps
Preparing for the worst; prisoner-of-war course at Fort Sill, Okla. il Time 90:15 S 1 '67
MILITARY transport airplanes. See Airplanes, Military transport
MILITARY trials. See Courts martial
MILK
Fat content
Stop the premium for butterfat? D. Braun. Farm J 92:44B Ja '68
Marketing
First Class I base plan. G. Lorang. Farm J 91:D6P Je '67
Will nine giant co-ops sell most of the milk? N. Reeder. il Farm J 91:24-5+ Je '67
See also
Marketing, Cooperative
Prices
Crackdown; NFO injunction. il Newsweek 69:76 Ap 10 '67
Curds & woe. il Time 89:22 Mr 31 '67
Dairymen rebel. il Sr Schol 90:18 Ap 14 '67
Dairymen vote on first class I plan; milk pricing in federal marketing orders. G. Lorang. Farm J 91:44B S '67
Discontent in dairyland. il Newsweek 69:44+ My 8 '67
First Class I base plan. G. Lorang. Farm J 91:D6+ Je '67
Keeping milk off the market; what NFO is seeking. P. Wieck. New Repub 156:9-10 Ap 22 '67
Milk bargaining hits first snag. D. Seim and N. Reeder. Farm J 92:44D Ja '68
Milking the public? price fixing in New York. Newsweek 67:71-2 Je 5 '67
NFO milk dumping, what did it do? N. Reeder. il Farm J 91:28-9+ My '67
New way to protect your milk prices. N. Reeder. Farm J 91:59 F '67
Should states set retail milk prices? D. Braun. Farm J 91:21-2 Mr '67
Spilled milk. Nation 204:453 Ap 10 '67
Spilled milk. il Newsweek 69:68 Ap 3 '67
Would higher prices cause a milk surplus? D. Braun. il Farm J 91:35+ F '67

Production
Five ways to make more milk from fewer cows. G. Lorang. il Farm J 91:D8 O '67
How to squeeze more milk from your feed. M. E. McCullough. il Farm J 91:D10-11 Ap '67
Predict a cow's production. Suc Farm 65:65 Jl '67
MILK, Acidophilus
See also
Yogurt
MILK, Dried
How to save money on milk; use of instant nonfat dry milk. J. Daniel. Read Digest 90:79-82 Mr '67

MILK contamination
This disposal system eats milk. E. Welch.
il Farm J 91:D15 F '67
MILK drinks. See Beverages
MILK industry and trade
See also
Borden company
Milk—Marketing
MILK production. See Milk—Production
MILK substitutes
We can beat those milk substitutes; symposium. il Farm J 91:D4-5 Ap '67
MILKING
Cows ride while you milk. il Farm J 91:D4+ D '67
MILKING machines
Do milking machines really cause mastitis? Farm J 91:34F Ag '67
MILKING parlors
Borrow ideas from this dairy setup. J. R. Borcherding. il Suc Farm 65:42-3+ Ag '67
Milking parlor ideas. J. R. Borcherding. il Suc Farm 65:30F N '67
MILKY way
Galactic nucleus. Sky & Tel 33:203 Ap '67
Milky way: old. il Sci N 91:496 My 27 '67
MILL, John Stuart
John Stuart Mill on intemperate discussion. Commonweal 87:379 D 22 '67

about

John Stuart Mill: independent radical. W. H. Chamberlin. por Sat R 50:30-1 My 20 '67
MILL VALLEY, Calif. public library
Library in a city park with unusual assets. il Arch Rec 142:180-1 S '67
MILLAIS, Sir John Everett
Letter from London; exhibition at the Walker art gallery, Liverpool. M. Panter-Downes. New Yorker 42:148+ F 11 '67
Spiteful fairy. il Newsweek 69:105-6 F 6 '67
Success that failed. J. Russell. il Art N 65:58-61 Ja '67
MILLAR, Oliver
Horses in the Queen's gallery. Antiques 91:628-31 My '67
MILLAU, Christian
—See Gault, H. jt. auth.

about

Two brightly breezy arbiters. il pors Life 63:129-30+ S 15 '67
MILLENDER, Dharathula H.
Through a glass, darkly. bibliog Library J 92:4571-6 D 15 '67
MILLER, A. J. See Zinkin, S. jt. auth.
MILLER, Ak
Horsing around with the Mustang six. por Hot Rod 20:91-3 Je; 48-50 Jl '67
MILLER, Alan R. and others
Fission-fragment synthesis of a new nitrogen-fluorine compound. bibliog Science 155:688 F 10 '67
MILLER, Arjay
Human values in the computer age; address, November 30, 1967. Vital Speeches 34:190-2 Ja 1 '68
MILLER, Arthur
Notes and comment; concerning article in the Times. New Yorker 43:19 Ja 13 '68
MILLER, Arthur R.
National data center and personal privacy. Atlan 220:53-7 N '67
MILLER, Arthur Selwyn
Government and the corporations. New Repub 157:26-8 Jl 8 '67
MILLER, Banner I.
Characteristics of hurricanes. bibliog Science 157:1389-99 S 22 '67
MILLER, Bertha E. (Mahony)
Selections from Horn book editorials. Horn Bk 43:155-8 Ap '67

about

Books, children, and women. R. H. Viguers. Horn Bk 43:152-3 Ap '67
Medals and magic. R. H. Viguers. Horn Bk 43:24-5 F '67
MILLER, C. J.
Fluidic systems. Electr World 77:23-5+ Je '67
MILLER, Carlos O.
Zeatin and zeatin riboside from a mycorrhizal fungus. bibliog Science 157:1055-7 S 1 '67
MILLER, Charles
Africa in black and white. Sat R 50:28-30+ Mr 25 '67
Their cargo was human. Sat R 50:39-41 Je 10 '67

MILLER, Clem O.
Toxicology: use of nonhuman primates. Science 156:1772-3 Je 30 '67
MILLER, Conrad
Propulsion efficiency starts at the prop. Motor B 121:87-92 Ja '68 (to be cont)
MILLER, David
Burning words, yes; burning cards, no. Time 89:51-2 F 24 '67
MILLER, Don Hugo
How to succeed in business by really trying; address, May 3, 1967. Vital Speeches 33:531-5 Je 15 '67
MILLER, Dulcy B.
Nursing home setting. Parks & Rec 2:38-9+ Ja '67
MILLER, Edwin
Spotlight! See issues of Seventeen
MILLER, Elva
Most unlikely lark. J. Bonfante. il pors Life 63:117-18+ S 22 '67
MILLER, Floyd
Last frontier marshal; condensation. Read Digest 90:201-4+ Je '67
MILLER, George Paul
Ghost vote. Nation 205:37 Jl 17 '67
MILLER, Gloria Bley
Thousand recipe Chinese cookbook; excerpt. Ladies Home J 84:124-5+ Mr '67
MILLER, Helen Louise
Circus daze; drama. Plays 26:49-57 My '67
Missing Linc; drama. Plays 26:13-22 F '67
New shoes; drama. Plays 26:85-9 My '67
Return of Bobby Shafto; drama. Plays 27:69-76 O '67
Simple Simon's reward; drama. Plays 27:65-74 N '67
Thanks to butter-fingers; drama. Plays 27:35-44 N '67
Tomboy and the dragon; drama. Plays 27:73-86 D '67
Trial of Mother Goose; drama. Plays 26:65-72 Ap '67
Vanishing Easter egg; drama. Plays 26:27-36 Mr '67
MILLER, Henry, 1827-1916
King of ranchers. B. Taper. il por Am Heritage 18:20-3+ Ag '67
MILLER, J. Irwin
How Columbus started building two landmarks per year. M. Wellemeyer. il Life 63:86+ N 17 '67
Is it too late for a man of honesty, high purpose and intelligence to be elected president of the United States in 1968? with editorial comment. S. V. Roberts. il pors Esquire 68:6+, 89-93+ O '67
SR's businessman of the year. W. D. Patterson. por Sat R 51:67-8+ Ja 13 '68
Secular magazine nominates churchman for presidency. Christian Cent 84:1212 S 27 '67
MILLER, James L. Jr
Southern regional education board: continuity and change. Sch & Soc 95:184-5 Mr 18 '67

about

Expanding southern universities. por Sch & Soc 95:408-10 N 11 '67
MILLER, James Nathan
Can local government be saved? Read Digest 90:140-5 My '67
City pulls itself together. Read Digest 91:132-6 Jl '67
Metro: Toronto's answer to urban sprawl. Read Digest 91:85-9 Ag '67
Selective enforcement: R to prevent auto accidents. Read Digest 91:147-51 D '67
To stay alive on the highways. Read Digest 90:128-31 Ap '67
MILLER, Jane E.
Illustration: an art form. Design 69:12-13 Fall '67
MILLER, John B.
Shotguns. Consumer Bul 50:31-7 O '67
Shotguns, parts and accessories. Consumer Bul 50:21-4 N '67
Travel trailer hauling and necessary auxiliary equipment. Consumer Bul 50:21-4 F '67
MILLER, Jonathan
I won't pay for the trip. Vogue 150:286-7+ S 1 '67; Same abr. Read Digest 91:132-4 D '67
Saying ah (cont) Vogue 149:149-51 Mr 15 '67

about

Doctor Jonathan Miller operates on Alice. W. H. Honan. il por N Y Times Mag p24-7+ Ja 22 '67
MILLER, Julius Sumner
Classic toys test your physics know-how; interview, ed. by W. S. Griswold. pors Pop Sci 190:116-21+ Ap '67

MILLER, K. W. and others
Animals at very high pressures of helium and neon. bibliog Science 157:97-8 Jl 7 '67
MILLER, Larry
Chapel Hill's tobacco rogues. F. Deford. il pors Sports Illus 26:24-6+ F 20 '67
MILLER, Laurence E. jr
(ed) Teens talk about religion. Seventeen 26:146-7+ Ap '67
MILLER, Lloyd Eldon, jr
Classic case of false evidence. por Time 89:52-3 F 24 '67
Immunity of prosecutors. il por Time 89:72 Mr 31 '67
MILLER, Lois Mattox
Toward a world of wanted children. Read Digest 91:89-94 O '67
MILLER, Louis J.
Block printing calendars. Design 69:9 Wint '67
Cubism as a class project. Design 69:36-7 Wint '67
Relief printing from cardboard. Sch Arts 66: 21-3 Je '67
MILLER, Mary Britton
Again perfection. V. Peterson. Reporter 36: 50-2 Ja 26 '67
MILLER, Maynard M.
Alaska's mighty rivers of ice. Nat Geog Mag 131:194-217 F '67
MILLER, Michael
Marble stockpile; poem. Commonweal 86:366 Je 16 '67
MILLER, Mike
Next door to Siberia. Travel 128:31-7 Ag '67
(ed) See Schmiege, D. Backpack sheep hunt
MILLER, Nathan
Alliance without progress. New Repub 157:8-9 S 9 '67
Latin Americans teach the Greeks. New Repub 157:17 Jl 22 '67
Latin lyricism at the foreign ministers meeting. New Repub 157:12 O 7 '67
MILLER, Newton
Trouble in Wayne. il por Newsweek 69:80 F 27 '67
MILLER, Paul A.
Editor interviews Paul A. Miller on International education act; ed. by M. S. Fenner. pors NEA J 56:63-4 Ap '67
MILLER, Philip L.
Frida Leider: a great Wagnerienne looks back. Am Rec G 33:848-9 My '67
Montserrat Caballé in La Traviata. Am Rec G 34:194-5 N '67
On London, the first recording of Rossini's Semiramide. Am Rec G 33:372-5 Ja '67
On the record: Music. See issues of Library journal
Orfeo ed Euridice. Am Rec G 33:558-9 Mr '67
Perhaps the most nearly complete performance we shall ever hear: London's Faust. Am Rec G 33:620-2 Ap '67
Sergei Prokofiev: simultaneously, his last three operas. Am Rec G 33:468-70+ F '67
MILLER, Ralph
On buying a photo gift. U S Camera 30: 42-3+ D '67
MILLER, Robert B.
You'd better count me out. America 116: 590-3 Ap 22 '67
MILLER, Robert G.
Sojourn on the Susquehanna. Motor B 119: 183-4+ Mr '67
MILLER, Robert W. See Fraumeni, J. F. jr. jt. auth.
MILLER, S. M. and others
Poverty, inequality, and conflict. bibliog f Ann Am Acad 373:16-52 S '67
MILLER, Shirley
From abacus to zoos. por Library J 92:4477-9 D 15 '67
MILLER, Thomas Pelham
Medieval flowers for today's gardens; ed. by E. McDonald. House B 109:158-61 D '67
MILLER, Wayne
Focus on: Wayne Miller. C. Schwalberg. il pors Pop Phot 60:88-9+ Mr '67
MILLER, William C.
Sharper eye on the sky. il Sci Digest 61:61-2 Ap '67
MILLER, William Edward
Where is Bill Miller? D. Schaap. Harper 235: 68-72 D '67
MILLER, William K.
New international rules for passengership safety. Dept State Bul 56:173-8 Ja 30 '67
MILLER, William Lee
Moynihan revisited. Reporter 37:46-8 Ag 10 '67
MILLER, William Robert
Mind of his own. Christian Cent 84:177-8 F 8 '67

MILLET, Mona
Face to face with a busy boutique-owner. por Seventeen 26:145 Mr '67
MILLIAMMETERS. See Ammeters
MILLIMETER wavelengths. See Microwaves
MILLION guitars; story. See Boles, P. D.
MILLIONAIRES
Negro millionaire's advice to his race; interview, ed. by F. X. Tolbert. H. T. Taylor U S News 63:68-9 S 4 '67
New look in lady millionaires. M. Abramson. il Good H 165:86-9 S '67
Two millionaires, East and West. il Sat Eve Post 240:24-7 D 30 '67
MILLIPEDS
Mongoose throwing and smashing millipedes. T. Eisner and J. A. Davis. bibliog il Science 155:577-9 F 3 '67
MILLÖCKER, Karl
Records:
Gasparone. Opera N 31:34 Ja 7 '67
MILLON, René
Teotihuacán; with biographical sketch. Sci Am 216:14, 38-48 bibliog(p 155) Je '67
MILLONES, Peter
Light on our light bills. New Repub 156:32+ F 4 '67
MILLS, Edward D.
Operation anti-disaster. UNESCO Courier 20: 16-17+ F '67
MILLS, Ernest M.
Trapping mammals about the home. Consumer Bul 50:24-6 Jl '67
MILLS, Hayley
Hayley at twenty-one. il por Time 90:51-3 Jl 28 '67
MILLS, Jesse C.
Catalog of misfortunes. por Library J 92: 4341-3 D 1 '67
MILLS, Joan
Let the screen door slam. Read Digest 91: 57-9 Jl '67
See mother run! story Read Digest 91:61-2 S '67
MILLS, Nicolaus C.
Bombs and suburbs. Nation 204:817 Je 26 '67
Workers on the farms. New Repub 157:9 S 23 '67
MILLS, Ralph J. jr
Five anthologies. Poetry 109:345-50 F '67
Herbert Read as poet. Poetry 110:45-7 Ap '67
MILLS, Wilbur Daigh
High officials argue over taxes, spending, inflation; excerpts from hearing before the House ways and means committee, November 30, 1967. por U S News 63:90-2 D 18 '67
Tax rise? Wilbur Mills is the key man; excerpts from statements. por U S News 63: 29 S 25 '67
Taxes and expenditures; address, November 20, 1967. Vital Speeches 34:130-2 D 15; Excerpts. U S News 63:102 D 4 '67
Way out of the spending crisis; interview. pors Nations Bsns 55:48-9 O '67
Will Congress raise taxes? interview. por U S News 63:52-5 O 9 '67

about

Cautious eye on the tax package. por Bsns W p 124-5 F 4 '67
Chairman Mills, he wouldn't budge when LBJ pushed. por U S News 63:19 D 4 '67
Man who is calling the signals on a tax rise. por U S News 63:12 Ag 28 '67
Mills takes his time on tax rise. il Bsns W p31 Ag 19 '67
Paying the store. Time 89:17 Je 30 '67
Surtax scrimmage. W. V. Shannon. Commonweal 87:108 O 27 '67
Tax hike still has a chance. il por Bsns W p35-6 O 14 '67
Tax rise blocked again, how and why it happened. por U S News 63:8 D 11 '67
MILLS
See also
Sawmills
Windmills
MILLS college, Oakland, Calif.
Search for distinction. il Time 90:61 O 27 '67
MILLS in art. See Architecture in art
MILLSPAUGH, Frank
Black power: five shades of gray. Mlle 66:94+ Ja '68
MILNE, David C. See Heiss. W. D. jt. auth.
MILNE, Lorus, and Milne, Margery
They conquered earth; excerpts from Living plants of the world. Audubon 69:58-69 N '67

MILNE, Margery. See Milne, L. jt. auth.

MILNE, Robert Scott
To Moosonee by Polar bear express. Atlan 219:118-20 Je '67

MILO
Feed your grain wet? C. E. Ball. il Farm J 92:B6-8 Ja '68

MILON, Dennis
Russell W. Porter exhibit. Sky & Tel 34:226-8 O '67

MILPITAS, Calif.
Rapid-bloc system accelerates treatment. R. E. Boone. il Am City 82:80-3 Ja '67

MILTON, Alec
Take special care of your equipment. Am City 82:108-9 S '67

MILTON, John, 1608-1674
Can we survive nihilism? T. Merton. Sat R 50:16-19 Ap 15 '67

MILTONIAS. See Orchids

MILWAUKEE
Why you need a safety program; excerpts from address. H. G. Hatcher. il Am City 82:103-5 Ag '67

Finance
Petty cash fund handles small-order purchases. A. L. Lehrbaummer. il Am City 82:95-6 Jl '67

Housing
Fair housing splits Catholics in Milwaukee. B. L. Masse. America 117:368 O 7 '67
Our integrated Milwaukee neighborhood; activities of the Committee for fair housing legislation and education. R. Thielke. America 117:566-7 N 11 '67

Music
Milwaukee; Florentine opera company ends season with Offenbach's Perichole. J. Joslyn. Opera N 31:24 Je 10 '67

Negroes
And other notables. America 117:166 Ag 19 '67
Black Christmas. Newsweek 70:42+ D 18 '67
Groppi's army. Time 90:25 S 15 '67
Groppi's war on Milwaukee. P. J. Weber. America 117:342-3 S 30 '67; Discussion. 117: 456-7 O 28 '67
Long fight in Milwaukee; issue is open housing. il Bsns W p64+ O 14 '67
Miracle in Milwaukee. D. Llorens. il Ebony 23:29-32+ N '67
Our integrated Milwauke neighborhood; activities of the Committee for fair housing legislation and education. R. Thielke. America 117:566-7 N 11 '67
Target for hate; Father J. E. Groppi. il Newsweek 70:67 O 2 '67
Too far to stop. il Newsweek 70:32+ S 18 '67

Parks and playgrounds
Maintenance tips for harried park officials. R. E. Kurtz. il Am City 82:98-9 My '67

Public works, Department of
Street records that work. L. A. DeMers. il Am City 82:130-2 O '67

Recreation
Snowmobiles for winter fun. il Am City 82:21 S '67

Riots
Cage and the curfew. il Newsweek 70:18-20 Ag 14 '67
Why a racial explosion threatens Milwaukee. il U S News 63:24 S 25 '67

Sanitary affairs
Refuse sacks perform indoors. il Am City 82:39 N '67

Theater
Brewing with yeast; activities of Milwaukee repertory theatre and Theater for tomorrow studio series. H. Hewes. Sat R 50:47 Mr 25 '67

MILWAUKEE art center
Mod in Milwaukee. il Newsweek 70:115 S 25 '67

MILWAUKEE COUNTY, Wis.
Milwaukee County park commission plans recreation complex. il Parks & Rec 2:35+ My '67

MILWAUKEE repertory theater. See Milwaukee—Theater

MIMA mounds. See Physical geography—Washington (state)

MIME
Dialogue between mime and skeptic. J. Anderson. Dance Mag 41:20-1 Ag '67

MIMICRY (biology)
Mimicry; the deceptive way of life. M. Rothschild. il Natur Hist 76:44-51 F '67

MIMS, A. Grace
Nervous Nellies on race relations? bibliog por Library J 92:1291-3+ Mr 15 '67

MINCEMEAT
Work wonders with mincemeat. il Ladies Home J 84:129+ N '67

MINCER, Jacob
Recent influences on the supply of labor. Mo Labor R 90:30-1 F '67

MIND. See Intellect

MIND-altering drugs. See Hallucinogenic drugs

MIND and body
Mind: an essay on human feeling, by S. K. Langer. Review
New Yorker 43:98+ Ag 12 '67. W. Sargeant
School for the senses; body-awareness classes at Esalen institute. il Time 90:69 S 29 '67
See also
Psychology, Physiological

MIND reading. See Telepathy

MINDSZENTY, Jozsef, cardinal
Cardinal's move. il por Newsweek 70:37-8 O 30 '67
Two prisoners. Reporter 38:11-12 Ja 11 '68

MINE to love; story. See MacLeod, C.

MINER, Francis M.
Children garden at the Brooklyn botanic garden. Horticulture 45:34-8 Ap '67

MINER, Mae. See Lucas, J. W. jt. auth.

MINERAL exhibits
Mineral show; opening at American museum of natural history. New Yorker 43:53-4 N 11 '67

MINERAL fertilizers. See Fertilizers and manures

MINERAL KING, Calif.
After 700 road curves, there's old Mineral King, your destination or jumping-off place. il Sunset 138:42-4+ Je '67

MINERAL KING recreation area (proposed)
See Recreation areas

MINERAL resources. See Mines and mineral resources

MINERAL resources in submerged lands
Red Sea's treasure; reprint. W. J. Perkinson. Sci Digest 62:22-4 D '67

MINERALOGY
Shock effects in certain rock-forming minerals. E. C. T. Chao. bibliog il Science 156: 192-202 Ap 14 '67
See also
Concretions

MINERALS. See Mineralogy; Mines and mineral resources

MINERALS in soils. See Soils—Mineral content

MINERS asthma
Miner's asthma. Sci N 91:521 Je 3 '67

MINES, Military
Most dangerous job in Vietnam; disarming Vietcong bombs and booby traps. W. Kreh. il Pop Mech 127:81-3+ My '67
Secret weapons: Viet Cong booby traps. il Newsweek 69:36 Je 12 '67
Ten favorite, and deadly: booby traps of the Viet Cong. il U S News 62:40-1 Mr 13 '67

MINES and mineral resources
See also
Mica
Ore deposits

Australia
Australia strikes it rich. il U S News 62: 74-7 My 1 '67
Mineral boom in the lucky country. H. Gordon. il N Y Times Mag p38-9+ N 12 '67

Brazil
Brazil's magic mountain: Serra do Navio in Amapá. K. Seegers and S. Seegers. il Américas 19:20-7 Mr '67

Mexico
See also
Sulfur mines and mining—Mexico

Russia
Resins in the mines. E. S. Gruzinov. Sci N 92:213 Ag 26 '67

South Africa
See also
Gold mines and mining—South Africa

United States
Mike Frome: mining interests enjoy special privileges in use of natural resources. M. Frome. Am For 73:3+ S '67

MINES and mineral resources—United States
—*Continued*
Mineral opportunities go begging. H. D.
Brown. Hobbies 71:122-3 F '67
See also
Copper
Oil shales
Sulfur mines and mining—United States
Uranium mines and mining—United States
MING furniture. See Furniture, Chinese
MINGO COUNTY, W. Va.
Rougher road of Russell Hicks. I. Mothner.
il Look 31:29-33 Je 13 '67
MINH, Ho-chi-. See Ho-chi-Minh
MINHINNICK, Jeanne
Canadian furniture in the English taste,
1790-1840. Antiques 92:84-90 Jl '67
MINIATURE cameras. See Cameras
MINIATURE electronic equipment
Implant biotelemetry and microelectronics.
W. H. Ko and M. R. Neuman. bibliog il
Science 156:351-60 Ap 21 '67
Microelectronic unit readied for Saturn IU;
advanced control signal processor. il Aero
Tech 21:40 O 23 '67
MINIATURE houses. See House models
MINIATURE objects
Madame Schlumberger's miniatures. S. A.
Parvin. il Hobbies 72:110-11 Ap; 110-11+
My; 109-11+ Je '67
See also
Doll houses
Exhibitions
Notes of the fall show. J. H. Gray. Hobbies
72:118+ Ja '68
Notes of the spring show. J. H. Gray. Hob-
bies 72:111 Ag '67
MINIATURE roses. See Roses
MINIATURE switches. See Electric switches
MINIBIKES. See Motor scooters
MINIBUSES. See Motor buses—Small size
MINIMUM wage
United States
Agricultural minimum wage: a preliminary
look. K. S. Koziara. bibliog f Mo Labor R
90:26-9 S '67
Basic provisions of the 1966 FLSA amend-
ments. S. Kocin. il Mo Labor R 90:1-4 Mr
'67
Economic effects of the 1966 changes in the
FLSA. J. I. Karlin. il Mo Labor R 90:21-5
Je '67
Extent of coverage under FLSA as amended
in 1966. E. C. Martin. il Mo Labor R 90:
21-4 Ap '67
Jobs that were lost when minimum wage
went up. il U S News 63:71-3 Jl 10 '67
New minimum wage: price rises, squeeze on
jobs and profits. il U S News 62:72-3 Mr 6
'67
Now an added billion in pay. U S News 62:89
F 6 '67
MINING industry and finance
Congo (capital Kinshasa)
Talent for survival; Union minière. Fortune
76:187 S 15 '67
MINISTERS of the gospel. See Clergy
MINK, Ken
Big Tumbling creek. Outdoor Life 139:62-5
Je '67
MINK, Walter D. and others
Neurons in paradoxical sleep and motivated
behavior. bibliog Science 158:1335-7 D 8 '67
MINK coats, etc. See Fur coats, wraps, etc.
MINNAERT, M.
Relief effect on looking at lunar photographs.
Sky & Tel 33:90-1 F '67
MINNEAPOLIS
Business at work in the Twin Cities. P.
Herrera. il Fortune 76:123-4+ Ag '67
Banks
Little bank with big connections: National
city bank of Minneapolis. il Bsns W p49-50
F 4 '67
City planning
Mall-transitway constructed by force account;
Nicollet mall. H. Erickson. il Am City 82:
134-6 S '67
Galleries and museums
Minneapolis is mega-town. R. Lynes. il
Harper 235:28-31 Jl '67
Libraries
See also
Minneapolis public library

Music
Minneapolis; productions at the Tyrone
Guthrie theater. A. B. Cutts. il Opera N
31:32-3 Mr 25 '67
Mischievous opera at the Tyrone Guthrie.
J. K. Sherman. il Hi Fi 17:MA21+ Ap '67
See also
Minneapolis symphony orchestra

Politics and government
Metro: Toronto's answer to urban sprawl;
Minneapolis-St Paul federation. J. N. Mil-
ler. Read Digest 91:85-9 Ag '67

Theater
Regional crucible; fifth season at Tyrone
Guthrie theatre of Minnesota theatre com-
pany. il Time 89:59 Je 16 '67
Renovating the house; Tyrone Guthrie's
production of The house of Atreus. H.
Hewes. Sat R 50:24 S 9 '67
Theatre; Tyrone Guthrie's production of The
house of Atreus. J. Novick. Nation 205:252-4
S 18 '67
MINNEAPOLIS public library
How a library won an election. K. C. Busch
and E. J. Gaines; discussion. Library J
92:712, 1391 F 15, Ap 1 '67
MINNEAPOLIS symphony orchestra
Big five plus one? Time 90:84-5 N 10 '67
Lively arts; interview, ed. by R. Hemming.
S. Skrowaczewski. Sr Schol 90:21 Mr 17 '67
MINNEN, Dina van
On the boards. W. Como. por Dance Mag 41:
24 O '67
MINNESOTA
See also
Architecture, Domestic—Minnesota
Booksellers and bookselling—Minnesota
Fishing—Minnesota
Hunting—Minnesota
Rice Lake
Climate
Speaking of weather: some like it cold; In-
ternational Falls. J. P. Blank. il Look
31:44+ Mr 7 '67
Industries
Billion-dollar comeback; iron-range country
of northeastern Minnesota. il Nations Bsns
55:38-41 Ag '67
See also
Minnesota mining and manufacturing com-
pany
Parks and reserves
Hidden state park. S. Libby. il Travel 128:11+
N '67
Managing human use of natural parks. U. W.
Hella. Parks & Rec 2:34-5+ Ja '67
MINNESOTA mining and manufacturing com-
pany
3M: management, marketing and momen-
tum. J. B. Weiner. il Duns R 89:32-5+ Mr
'67
MINNESOTA multiphasic personality inven-
tory. See Personality tests
MINNESOTA theatre company. See Minneapolis
—Theater
MINNESOTA Twins (baseball) See Baseball
clubs
MINNESOTA, University, Minneapolis
Campus guns widen their range; Technology
utilization program. il Bsns W p58+ N 25
'67
Library school
Clearinghouse for library science. W. Simon-
ton. il Wilson Lib Bul 42:383-5 D '67
Library clearinghouse set for Minnesota. Li-
brary J 92:2872+ S 1 '67
MINOAN civilization. See Civilization, Minoan
MINOFF, Lee, and Price, Stanley
Come live with me. Criticism
Commonweal 85:567-8 F 17 '67
New Yorker 42:93 F 4 '67
Sat R 50:51 F 11 '67
MINOR, Audax, pseud.
Race track. See issues of New Yorker
MINOR, Delores
Summer study tour of New York and New
England. Sr Schol 90:sup21 Mr 3 '67
MINOR, Pearl
Imminence; poem. Christian Cent 84:1313 O
18 '67
MINOR league baseball. See Baseball
MINOR planets. See Asteroids
MINORITIES
Trade books surpass texts in treatment of
minorities. Library J 92:1284-5 Mr 15 '67

MINORITIES—*Continued*
Treatment of minorities in textbooks. Sch & Soc 95:323-4 Sum '67
See also
Race discimination
United Nations—Sub-commission on prevention of discrimination and protection of minorities

MINOT, Stephen
Crossings; story. Redbook 128:70-1 F '67

MINTURN, Leigh
Children's views of foreign peoples. por Wilson Lib Bul 42:187-93 O '67

MINTZ, Beatrice, and Silvers, W. K.
Intrinsic immunological tolerance in allophenic mice. bibliog Science 158:1484-7 D 15 '67

MINTZ, Morton
It's not safe to read. New Repub 156:28-30 Mr 25 '67

MINUDRI, Regina. See Trahan, M. jt. ed.

MINUJIN, Marta
Number is 581-4570, but don't call it, let it call you. il por Time 90:58 Jl 7 '67

MINUTEMAN (guided missile) See Guided missiles

MINUTEMAN (launch vehicle) See Space vehicles—Propulsion systems

MIOCENE period. See Geology, Stratigraphic —Miocene

MIQUELON. See Saint Pierre and Miquelon (islands)

MIRACLE, Leonard
Tallyho, the bobcat. Outdoor Life 140:70-3+ O '67
—See Mears, J. jt auth.

MIRACLE; story. See Drury, M.

MIRACLES
Gospel of signs. V. P. McCorry. America 116: 605-6 Ap 22 '67
See also
Jesus Christ—Miracles

MIRAGE; story. See O'Donnell, M. K.

MIRAND, E. A.
Virus-induced erythropoiesis in hypertransfused-polycythemic mice. bibliog Science 156:832-3 My 12 '67

MIRANDA, Ernesto
Catching up with Miranda. Time 89:49 Mr 3 '67
Crime, confessions and the Supreme court. G. L. Chamberlain. America 117:32-4 Jl 8 '67

MIRANDA, Francisco de
Francisco de Miranda; a vindication. C. Valdovinos. bibliog il pors Américas 19: 28-35 Mr '67

MIRIAM; story. See Capote, T.

MIRIAM; story. See Sullivan, P. W.

MIRÓ, Joan
What does Miro do with what he sees? J. Alvard. il Art N 66:32-3+ N '67

MIRRORS
Looking glasses and labels. E. Gaines. il Antiques 92:563-5 O '67
Mirros are magic. E. Bowen. House & Gard 132:112-13 Ag '67

MIRRORS for cameras
Techniques tomorrow; all metal mirrors. B. Sherman. Mod Phot 32:106+ Ja '68

MIRRORS for telescopes
Composite mirror under study for future orbiting telescope. il Aviation W 87:111 O 16 '67
Corning fabricating mirror for European observatory. il Tech W 20:36-7 Mr 6 '67
Lightweight aluminum mirrors. il Sky & Tel 34:213 O '67
144-inch mirror blank cast and a 23-foot aluminum mirror. G. S. Mumford. il Sky & Tel 33:283-4 My '67
Steward observatory's new 90-inch reflector; at Kitt Peak. R. L. Hilliard. il Sky & Tel 34:79-81 Ag '67
Techniques tomorrow. B. Sherman. Mod Phot 31:32+ Ap '67

MIRSKY, Jonathan
Conversation with a monk. Nation 205:678-81 D 25 '67
Forms of modern Sinology. Nation 204:468-70+ Ap 10 '67
Hanoi and the front. Nation 205:86+ Jl 31 '67
Too blind stupid to see. Nation 205:397-400 O 23 '67
Unmaking a village. Nation 206:55-6 Ja 8 '68

MISCEGENATION. See Intermarriage of races

MISCH, Robert Jay
Aquavit and beer. House B 110:124+ Ja '68
Six oysters, six ales, peace. Esquire 67:54-5+ F '67
Who says it won't grow here? House B 109: 140+ Ap '67

MISCONDUCT in office
Mob finds a patsy in a mayor's inner circle; Commissioner Marcus. S. Smith and W. Lambert. il Life 64:46-51 Ja 5 '68
Tragedy of Thomas Dodd; excerpt from Above the law. J. Boyd. il Sat Eve Post 241:19-25 Ja 13; 58-62+ Ja 27 '68 (to be cont)

MISHAN, E. J.
Spill-over: the costs of growth. Nation 205: 558-61 N 27 '67

MISHKIN, Leo
Mishkin. Opera N 32:12-15 Ja 20 '68

MISPRONUNCIATION. See English language— Pronunciation

MISS fix-it; drama. See McCoy, P. S.

MISS Millard; story. See West, A.

MISSILES, Guided. See Guided missiles

MISSING Linc; drama. See Miller, H. L.

MISSING persons
Little girl is lost; case of Debbie Smith. J. Robbins and J. Robbins. il Good H 165: 12+ Ag '67

MISSION BAY yacht club. See Yacht clubs

MISSION hospital, Kontum. See Hospitals— Vietnam (Republic)

MISSIONARIES
Ecumenical breakthrough in the South Pacific. H. P. Van Dusen. Christian Cent 84:730 My 31 '67
Irish missionary dispersion. Christian Cent 84:1061 Ag 23 '67
Missionary's predicament: how far to adapt? H. Horan. America 117:197-200 Ag 26 '67
Old China hands. N. Wales. New Repub 156: 13-15 Ap 1 '67
See also
Missions

MISSIONARY order of St Paul the apostle. See Paulist fathers

MISSIONS
Changing mission scene. E. C. Parker. Christian Cent 84:1590 D 13 '67
Mission histories. F. D. Lueking. Christian Cent 84:176 F 8 '67
See also
Catholic church—Missions
Jesuits—Missions
Missionaries

Africa
Africanization or exile. il Time 89:56 F 17 '67
See also
Catholic church—Missions

Congo (capital Kinshasa)
See also
Catholic church—Missions

India
Vietnam and the Christian mission: perspective from India. J. A. Bergquist. Christian Cent 84:764-6 Je 7 '67

Indonesia
Conversion in Indonesia; evangelical revival. Time 89:56 Je 16 '67

Latin America
Ecumenical tangle. J. G. Chamberlin. Christian Cent 85:75-7 Ja 17 '68

United States
Our Spanish American neighbors; domestic mission programs of U.S. Protestant churches. J. Lara-Braud. Christian Cent 85: 43-5 Ja 10 '68

MISSIONS, Medical
Pat Smith's special war in Vietnam: at the Catholic mission hospital in Kontum. F. Chinnock. il Read Digest 90:195-6+ Je '67

MISSIONS, Military. See Military missions

MISSISSIPPI
See also
Education—Mississippi
Hunting—Mississippi
Prisons—Mississippi
Public welfare—Mississippi
Trials—Mississippi

Anti-poverty program
Grudge fight; L. B. Johnson rejects emergency food rations proposals. Nation 204:644-5 My 22 '67
Struggle that changed Glen Allan; formation of Child development group in Mississippi. D. Nevin. il Life 63:108+ S 29 '67

Economic conditions
Darkness on the Delta. F. Davis. Reporter 37: 35-7 S 21 '67

MISSISSIPPI—*Continued*

Legislature

Last citadel. il Newsweek 71:23 Ja 15 '68

Politics and government

Black polling power. Newsweek 70:26 Ag 21 '67

Like old times; Negro candidates fail to win election. il Newsweek 70:24 S 11 '67

More toward moderation; Republican gubernatorial campaign. Time 90:29 O 13 '67

New note or two; campaign for Democratic gubernatorial nomination. Time 90:21 Ag 4 '67

They voted; success of Negro candidates. il Time 90:22 Ag 18 '67

Vote for the past; Negro candidates defeated. il Time 90:17 S 8 '67

Race problems

Act of savagery; killing of Wharlest Jackson in Natchez. il Time 89:25 Mr 10 '67

For us, the living; excerpts. ed. by W. Peters. M. B. Evers. il McCalls 94:86-7+ Jl; 88-9+ Ag '67

Gamble in Natchez; killing of Wharlest Jackson. il Newsweek 69:47-8 Mr 13 '67

I learned to feel black. J. Smith. Redbook 129:64-5+ Ag '67

In darkest America; Delta ministry programs. V. Ullman. Nation 205:177-80 S 4 '67

Stranger at the gates, by T. Sugarman. Review

New Repub 156:28+ F 4 '67. E. Sutherland

Social conditions

Outsiders; doctors report on health of rural children. New Repub 157:4 Jl 15 '67

Poverty: the hungry world of Teresa Pilgrim; Yazoo City. W. Hedgepeth. il Look 31:40-4 D 26 '67

When you look for starvation in the South. il U S News 63:44 Jl 31 '67

MISSISSIPPI RIVER

Wisconsin's river road. T. S. Wettach. il Travel 127:58-61 My '67

Discovery and exploration

Passion of Hernando de Soto; excerpt from Explorers of the Mississippi. T. Severin. il Am Heritage 18:26-31+ Ap '67

Preposterous pathfinder; excerpt from Explorers of the Mississippi. T. Severin. il Am Heritage 19:56-63 D '67

MISSISSIPPI test facility. See Proving grounds

MISSOURI

See also

Architecture, Domestic—Missouri

Booksellers and bookselling—Missouri

Libraries—Missouri

Music festivals—Missouri

Paleontology—Missouri

Prisons—Missouri

Description and travel

St Louis and heartland USA. il Bet Hom & Gard 45:74-5 My '67

Historic houses, etc.

See also

Sainte Genevieve, Mo.—Historic houses, etc.

Politics and government

What worries governors; interview. W. E. Hearnes. U S News 62:31-3 Ja 30 '67

MISSOURI. University, Columbia

Not a shared system; computer operation designed for library use. R. H. Parker. il Library J 92:3967-70 N 1 '67

MISSOURI botanical garden

Missouri botanical garden. D. M. Gates. il Horticulture 45:32-3+ Je '67

MISSOURI library association

Show-me state recruits. S. Shinn. ALA Bul 61:205-7 F '67

MISSOURI RIVER

Proposed Lewis and Clark national river; National park service proposes to conserve certain sections of the Missouri. il Parks & Rec 2:22+ Ag '67

Salvage archeology in the Missouri River basin. W. R. Wedel. bibliog il Science 156: 589-97 My 5 '67

MISSOURI state library, Jefferson City, Mo.

Missouri state library advertises in Look. Library J 92:2700-1 Ag '67

Show-me state recruits. S. Shinn. ALA Bul 61:205-7 F '67

MISSPELLING. See Spelling

MIST. See Fog

MIST propagation. See Plant propagation

MISTAKEN identity. See Identification

MISTAKES. See Blunders

MR Catesby brings it off; story. See Moore, J.

MR Keogh; story. See West, A.

MR Travel award

13th annual Mr Travel award: W. Averell Harriman. il Travel 128:42-4+ Jl '67

MRS Billingsby's wine; story. See Taylor, P.

MRS Wilson's diary; drama. See Ingrams, R. and Wells, J.

MITCHELL, Aaron

Killing me solves nothing; interview. ed. by J. Le Blanc. pors Ebony 22:121-2+ Je '67

MITCHELL, C. Bradford

Pride of the seas. bibliog Am Heritage 19: 64-88 D '67

What price concrete? Am Heritage 18:112 Ag '67

MITCHELL, Carleton

French Riviera, storied playground on the Azure coast. Nat Geog Mag 131:798-835 Je '67

More of sea than of land: the Bahamas. Nat Geog Mag 131:218-67 F '67

New twelve and three also-rans. Sports Il-lus 27:26-8+ Ag 28 '67

Our Virgin Islands, fifty years under the flag. por Nat Geog Mag 133:66-103 Ja '68

MITCHELL, Clarence

Excerpt from statement, July 19, 1966. Cong Digest 46:26+ Ja '67

Excerpt from testimony before Subcommittee on constitutional amendments, May 18, 1967. Cong Digest 46:284+ N '67

MITCHELL, Curtis

Don't let tension push you around. Pop Sci 191:79-82+ O '67

MITCHELL, Eileen

Audubon cause. il Audubon 69:92-3 S '67

MITCHELL, Emerson Blackhorse

Horse thief and the historian. M. Brown. Sat R 50:36-7 S 9 '67

MITCHELL, Fred

Architectural art in Germany. Craft Horiz 27:10-13 Ja '67

MITCHELL, Henry H.

Key term in theological education for the Negro; compensatory. Christian Cent 84:530-3 Ap 26 '67

MITCHELL, J. McD.

Lighting puts a final touch on a downtown renewal. Am City 82:110 Ag '67

MITCHELL, Margaret

First of the month. C. Amory. Sat R 50:2+ Ag 5 '67

MITCHELL, Maria

Faces from the past. R. M. Ketchum. il Am Heritage 18:26-7 Ag '67

MITCHELL, Newell D. See Stelling, A. C. jt. auth.

MITCHELL, P. M.

Sweet suffering in Iceland. Sat R 50:58 N 11 '67

MITCHELL, Pam

My pride was shattered. por McCalls 94:24+ Jl '67

MITCHELL, Richard S.

Tridymite pseudomorphs after wood in Virginian lower cretaceous sediments. bibliog Science 158:905-6 N 17 '67

MITCHELL, Roy

Is radar worthwhile? Motor B 120:38-9+ S '67

MITCHELL, Shiela C. and Woodside, G. L.

Virus etiology of congenital malformations. Science 157:1337-8 S 15 '67

MITCHELL, W. P.

Turn indicator flasher unit. Pop Electr 27:66 O '67

MITCHELL, Wanda B.

Speech education in the secondary school. NEA J 56:35-6 Mr '67

MITCHELL, William

Upstart prophet. S. K. Oberbeck. il por Newsweek 69:98+ Je 19 '67

MITCHELL, William, 1925?-

Instant sculpture. T. Conway. il Design 69: 31-3 Wint '67

MITCHELL, William R.

Aboriginal sin; poem. Christian Cent 84:1345 O 25 '67

MITER boxes

Case for buying a good miter box. R. J. De Cristoforo. il Pop Sci 190:154-7 Ja '67

MITFORD, Nancy

Life book review. Life 62:10 Ap 28 '67

MITGANG, Herbert
Accent. Atlan 220:116+ D '67
Carl Sandburg: 1878-1967. Sat R 50:18-19 Ag 12 '67
Mexican war dove. New Repub 156:23-4 F 11 '67
Relocated in land of the free. Sat R 50: 29 Mr 18 '67
Squalls in the Windy city. Sat R 50:36-7 Ja 28 '67
MITOCHONDRIA
Adenosine 3',5'-cyclic phosphate: stimulation of steroidogenesis in sonically disrupted adrenal mitochondria. S. Roberts and others. bibliog il Science 158:372-4 O 20 '67
Dimethyl sulfoxide protects tightly coupled mitochondria from freezing damage. D. B. Dickinson and others. bibliog il Science 156:1738-9 Je 30 '67
Heterosis: complementation by mitochondria. R. G. McDaniel and I. V. Sarkissian; discussion. Science 155:722; 156:263 F 10, Ap 14 '67
Interlocked DNA. Sci Am 218:46+ Ja '68
Mitochondrial malate dehydrogenase: a new genetic polymorphism in man. R. G. Davidson and J. A. Cortner. bibliog il Science 157:1569-71 S 29 '67
Mitochondrial-satellite and circular DNA filaments in yeast. J. H. Sinclair and others. bibliog il Science 156:1234-7 Je 2 '67
Passive transport of 5,5-dimethyl-2,4-oxazolidinedione into beef heart mitochondria. S. Addanki and others. bibliog il Science 155: 1678-9 Mr 31 '67
Psilocybin: reaction with a fraction of rat brain. L. P. Gilmour and R. D. O'Brien. bibliog il Science 155:207-8 Ja 13 '67
MITOSIS. See Cell division (biology)
MITROPOULOS, Dimitri, international music competition. See Music—Competitions
MITSUI trading company. See Japan—Industries
MITTERRAND, François
Letter from Paris; concerning opposition address. Genêt. New Yorker 43:170-2 Ap 29 '67
MIWOK Indians. See Indians of North America
MIX, Sheldon A.
Islands for your next vacation. Todays Health 45:42-7+ My; 34-9+ Je '67
MIXED marriages. See Marriages, Mixed
MIXES, Food. See Food mixes
MIXING utensils
    See also
Electric apparatus and appliances, Domestic
MIZER, Jean E.
Giving faces to the faceless. NEA J 57:6-8 Ja '68
MŇAČKO, Ladislav
Author! author! il Time 89:33-4 Mr 17 '67
Protest in Prague. por Newsweek 70:36 Ag 28 '67
MO, Billy
Billy Mo: the Satchmo of Germany. H. J. Massaquoi. il pors Ebony 22:68-73 Jl '67
MOB violence
Riots and mob spirit: America's greatest danger; excerpts from address, January 27, 1838. A. Lincoln. U S News 63:92+ Ag 28 '67
MOBIL oil company
Mobil oil squarely in the middle; search for new fields. T. O'Hanlon. il Fortune 76:86-9+ S 1 '67
North American, Mobil oil agree to pool technology. il Tech W 20:30+ F 13 '67
MOBILE, Ala.
    Historic houses, etc.
Mobile ironwork. M. R. Ingate. il Antiques 92:354-9 S '67
MOBILE home manufacturers association
Modules gain ground in housing landscape; modular construction turning into assembly-line industry. il Bsns W p78-81 Ja 6 '68
MOBILE homes. See Automobile trailers; Campers and coaches, Truck
MOBILE hospitals. See Hospitals, Traveling
MOBILE libraries. See Bookmobiles
MOBILE radio telephone. See Radio telephone, Portable
MOBILES
3-D woven forms. L. Campbell. il Sch Arts 66:17-18 My '67
MOBILIZATION, Industrial. See Industrial mobilization
MOBILIZATION for youth, Incorporated
Is it just for jobs? Dance project of the M.F.Y. R. A. Rodgers. il Dance Mag 41: 26-8 Ap '67

MOBS
    See also
Mob violence
MOBUTU, Joseph Désiré
Cause for optimism. por Time 90:30 D 1 '67
Confrontation in the Congo. E. Bustin. Cur Hist 52:168-74 Mr '67
Misfortunes of Mobutu. il Newsweek 70:44 Ag 28 '67
Plot and counter-plot. K. Kyle. New Repub 157:13-16 S 16 '67
Question of price. il por Newsweek 70:44 Ag 14 '67
MOCARSKI, Polly Lada-. See Lada-Mocarski, P.
MODEL, Leo
Politics of private foreign investment. For Affairs 45:639-51 Jl '67
MODEL making. See Models and modelmaking
MODEL of a sage man; story. See Coleman, E.
MODELL, Walter
Mass drug catastrophes and the roles of science and technology. bibliog Science 156: 346-51 Ap 21 '67
MODELMAKING. See Models and modelmaking
MODELS
    See also
Dioramas
MODELS (persons)
Awesome Aussies are amazing. P. Gowland. il Pop Phot 61:36+ O '67
New body: more woman than you'd think; Courrèges dancing mannequins. il Vogue 150:137-9 N 15 '67
To be a beauty; all me and nobody else; symposium. il Seventeen 26:90-5 O '67
    See also
Angle, L.
Tree, P.
Twiggy
Veruschka
MODELS, Anatomical. See Anatomical models
MODELS, Rocket. See Rocket models
MODELS and modelmaking
Bringing the world down to scale. il Bsns W p112-17 Jl 29 '67
Cliff dwelling model. P. S. Zakroff and E. Gell. il Design 69:6-8 Wint '67
MODELS of cities, towns, etc.
England's Lilliputian towns. T. Holloway. il Travel 128:58-63 N '67
MODERN architecture. See Architecture, Modern
MODERN art museum, New York. See Museum of modern art, New York
MODERN civilization. See Civilization
MODERN dance. See Dancing
MODERN design. See Design
MODERN drama. See Drama
MODERN furniture. See Furniture
MODERN history. See History, Modern
MODERN language association of America
Refurbishing American authors: Center for editions of American authors launches five-year program. D. Dempsey. Sat R 50:30+ Je 10 '67
MODERN music. See Music
MODERN pentathlon. See Pentathlon
MODERN sculpture. See Sculpture
MODERNISM
Crisis and comparison. J. Ratté. America 117:35-7 Jl 8 '67
Triumph of modernism. il Time 90:64-5 Jl 28 '67
MODERNISM (art)
Aid for artists: but is it really art? il U S News 63:11 Ag 28 '67
Anarchy of art. J. H. Plumb. il Horizon 9:106-7 Sum '67
Art; attitudes of C. Oldenburg and A. Kaprow. M. Kozloff. Nation 205:27-9 Jl 3 '67
Art; boxes of J. Cornell. M. Kozloff. Nation 204:701-2 My 29 '67
Art is light; electronic art. D. L. Shirey. il Newsweek 69:101 F 20 '67
Art world; Chicago museum of contemporary art opening exhibition: Pictures to be read/ Poetry to be seen. H. Rosenberg. New Yorker 43:225-8+ N 18 '67
Art world; current exhibitions. H. Rosenberg. New Yorker 43:99-100+ Jl 25 '67
Art world; environmental art. H. Rosenberg. New Yorker 43:189-92+ O 21 '67
Art world; exhibition at the Museum of modern art of drip paintings by J. Pollock. H. Rosenberg. New Yorker 43:162+ My 6 '67

MODERNISM (art)—*Continued*
Art world; exhibition at the Museum of modern art: The 1960s. H. Rosenberg. New Yorker 43:76+ Jl 29 '67
Art world; exhibitions of boxes and collages by J. Cornell and of sculptures and drawings by C. Oldenburg. H. Rosenberg. New Yorker 43:112+ Je 3 '67
Avant the avant-garde. il Esquire 68:134-5 S '67
Cornell: the cube root of dreams; show of boxes and collages at the Guggenheim. J. Ashbery. il Art N 66:56-9+ Sum '67
Fate worse than; present-day pop art. N. Kent. Am Artist 31:5 N '67
Gallery '68; high art and low art. P. Leider. il Look 32:14-21 Ja 9 '68
Heritage of pop. R. Berenson. Nat R 19:1028+ S 19 '67
History by contact. F. C. Castle. Art N 66: 48-51+ O '67
Homage to Hans Hofmann; contemporary art scene. H. Rosenberg. il Art N 65:49+ Ja '67
In the art world: the young crowd. L. Alloway. House B 109:118-20 Jl '67
Jackson Pollock in retrospect, he broke the ice. V. Raynor. il pors N Y Times Mag p50-1+ Ap 2 '67
Kidding everybody; pop paintings of Lichtenstein. il Time 89:72-3 Je 23 '67
Krushenick's blazing blazons. J. Perreault. il Art N 66:34-5+ Mr '67
Master of the minimal; with account by D. Bourdon. il Life 62:45-51 F 3 '67
Master of the monumentalists. il Time 90:80-6 O 13 '67
New art selection process. I. Fleminger. Art N 65:56-7+ Ja '67
Number is 581-4570, but don't call it, let it call you; environmental telephone booth. il Time 90:58 Jl 7 '67
Opinion: a defense of fad. D. M. Davis. Mlle 65:50+ O '67
Paradise regained; exhibition of boxes at New York's Guggenheim museum. J. Kroll. il Newsweek 69:86 Je 5 '67
Serial rights: concepts and feelings behind the new serial art first showing at Finch college. D. Lee. il Art N 66:42-5+ D '67
Shape of art for some time to come; primary structures. il Life 63:38-43+ Jl 28 '67
Skin game; Kaplan uses furs in art. il Newsweek 69:111 My 22 '67
Take a cigarette butt and make it heroic; interview, ed. by S. Gablik. C. Oldenburg. il Art N 66:30-1+ My '67
Tiptoe through the silver; environmental school of art. il Time 89:60E My 5 '67
Total weapon; Marta Minujin's computerized telephone booth at the Howard Wise gallery, N.Y. W. K. Zinsser. il Look 31:24 N 14 '67
2½ dimension; constructions. il Time 89:84-5 Je 9 '67
Visitors to a Pistoletto show get right into his paintings. il Horizon 9:84-5 Spr '67
Washington mannerists, or the foresight to look backward; F. Wright, G. Wartofsky, D. Spadaro and W. Woodward. R. Squirru. il Américas 19:18-26 Ja '67
What is art today? Time essay. Time 89: 24-5 Ja 27 '67
Who killed McKinley? pop art painting by E. Friedensohn. F. Getlein. Commonweal 87:301+ D 1 '67
See also
Architecture, Modern
Cubism
Electric lamps in art
Happenings (art)

Anecdotes, facetiae, satire, etc.
Genius scene. D. Goodrich. Look 31:M24 My 2 '67

MODERNISM (literature)
Culture of modernism. I. Howe. Commentary 44:48-59 N '67
MODERNISM in music. See Music
MODERNIZATION. See Social change
MODERNIZATION of houses. See Houses, Remodeled
MODIANO, Nancy
Chamula life; with biographical sketch. Natur Hist 77:4, 58-63 Ja '68
MODIFIED airplanes. See Airplanes, Remodeled
MODULAR coordination (architecture)
Building-block houses. il House & Gard 133: 90-1 Ja '68

Centre Le Corbusier; Zurich. U. Roth. il Arch Forum 127:82-7 S '67
Habitat and after; with account by R. Boyd and J. Bailey. il Arch Forum 126:34-51 My '67
Megastructure for renewal. il Arch Forum 126:58-9 Je '67
Modules gain ground in housing landscape; modular construction turning into assembly-line industry. il Bsns W p78-81 Ja 6 '68
Serene facade conceals pools, fountains and spatial excitement. il Arch Rec 142:185-8 S '67
Tomorrow's Pueblo: Expo 67's controversial Habitat. il Life 62:74-5+ Mr 31 '67
What it's like to live in an experiment; Habitat of Expo 67. D. Jacobs. il N Y Times Mag p50-1+ Je 4 '67
Will Habitat cast new mold for housing? il Bsns W p 164-6+ Je 24 '67
MODULAR design. See Modular coordination (architecture)
MODULATION (electronics)
Percent modulation nomogram. M. H. Applebaum. il Electr World 77:31 Ja '67
Stereo mods. N. Eisenberg. il Hi Fi 17:62-5 Ja '67
MODULATORS
Laser modulators. il Electr World 77:82-3 Ap '67
MOE, Mrs D. J.
Miniatures are big in our family. Hobbies 72:109-110 Ag '67
MOECKEL, Fred
Evangelist; poem. Christian Cent 84:683 My 24 '67
MOEHLE, John H.
Good American; address, May 20, 1967. Vital Speeches 33:567-9 Jl 1 '67
MOFFAT, David
On the boards. W. Como. por Dance Mag 41:21 N '67
MOFFAT, Lorna
Colours of passion in Pátzcuaro. Vogue 149: 49-53 F 15 '67
MOFFATT, Dorothy
Christmas eve; poem. Ladies Home J 84:119 D '67
MOFFETT, Hugh
Aging heavy of the Paris expatriates. Life 63:30-2+ Ag 4 '67
How to hurt a Frenchman. Life 64:34-34B Ja 19 '68
Signs that two Germanies are slyly inching closer. Life 62:54+ Ap 28 '67
MOFFITT, John
Of many things. America 116:359 Mr 18 '67
Wherever I speed; poem. Commonweal 86: 394 Je 23 '67
MOFFORD, Thomas F.
Journey to understanding; Sr Schol 90:sup 16 My 5 '67
MOGENSON, Paul
Total and complex. H. Rosenstein. il por Art N 66:52-4+ My '67
MOHAMMED Reza Pahlevi, shah of Iran
President Johnson and the Shah of Iran hold talks at Washington; exchange of remarks and exchange of toasts, August 22, with joint statement, August 23, 1967. Dept State Bul 57:358-62 S 18 '67

about
Case of Iran. Nation 205:196 S 11 '67
Proud as a peacock. il por Time 89:28 Mr 31 '67
Revolution from the throne. il por Time 90: 32-4 O 6 '67
Royal revolution in Iran. P. Friggens. por Read Digest 91:127-31 O '67

Coronation
Crowning the shadow of God. il por Time 90: 29-30 N 3 '67
In Iran a crown well earned. il Life 63:28-33 N 10 '67
Iran: a king crowns himself, and his queen. il pors Newsweek 70:44-7 N 6 '67
MOHAMMEDANISM. See Islam
MOHIEDDIN, Zakarya
What the West can expect after Nasser. por U S News 62:23 Je 19 '67
MOHIT, Behzad, and Sato, G. H.
Improved in vitro survival of normal, functional spleen cells. bibliog Science 157:449-51 Jl 28 '67
MOHLER, Harold Shaeffer
Sweet smell of success. R. Levy. il Duns R 90:54-5+ N '67
MOHOLE project
Oil companies to use Mohole technology. R. W. Niblock. il Tech W 20:24-5 Ap 17 '67

MOHR, Shemuel
Exposing international secrets. il por Time 89:48 Mr 10 '67

MOHRHARDT, Foster E.
IFLA: International federation of library associations. ALA Bul 61:187-8 F '67
Libraries unlimited; address, July 1, 1967. bibliog por ALA Bul 61:811-19 Jl '67
Memo to members; ed. by D. H. Clift. ALA Bul 61:376-7 Ap '67
Office of the librarian; address, June 28, 1967. bibliog por Wilson Lib Bul 42:391-6 D '67

MOISTURE condensation. See Condensation

MOK, Michael
Photographer's death, his last photographs. Life 62:34 Je 16 '67
Soldiers, tanks and business as usual. Life 62:29 My 5 '67
Still three years to wait for a car. Life 62:70-2 My 26 '67
SHAPE takes shape. Life 62:105-6+ Je 9 '67

MOLAJOLI, Bruno
Years to repair the damage. UNESCO Courier 20:6-11 Ja '67

MOLBACH, Irving
Do they believe; poem. Cath World 205:352 S '67
Dylan Thomas; poem. Cath World 205:309 Ag '67

MOLDS (botany)
Role of enzymatic wall-softening in plant morphogenesis: hormonal induction in achlya. D. des S. Thomas and J. T. Mullins. bibliog il Science 156:84 Ap 7 '67

See also
Microorganisms
Phycomyces

MOLDS (for casting)
Charcoal casting; jewelry-making on high school level. S. S. Madeja. il Sch Arts 67:26-9 S '67
Ingot mold maker casts new horoscope; Valley mould & iron corp. il Bsns W p74-6+ Ag 5 '67

MOLÉ, Paul
Profiles. W. Whitworth. por New Yorker 43:63-4+ O 21 '67

MOLECULAR beams
Molecular beams with energies above one electron volt. N. Abuaf and others. bibliog il Science 155:997-9 F 24 '67

MOLECULAR biology
Antireductionism and molecular biology. K. F. Schaffner. bibliog Science 157:644-7 Ag 11 '67; Discussion. 158:857+ N 17 '67
End of the beginning. R. Shinsheimer. Bul Atomic Sci 23:8-12 F '67
Molecular biology: European laboratory still in limbo. J. Walsh. Science 156:1213 Je 2 '67
Molecular biology: U.S. and Italy to establish new graduate school. J. Walsh. il Science 156:1582-3 Je 23 '67
Molecular isomers in vision. R. Hubbard and A. Kropf. il Sci Am 216:64-70+ bibliog(p 155) Je '67
Phage and the origins of molecular biology, ed. by J. Cairns and others. Review Sci Am 216:141+ Mr '67. J. C. Kendrew
Toward a biology CERN. D. A. Ehrlich. Sci N 91:451 My 13 '67
Ultrastructure and cytochemistry of the synaptic region. E. D. P. de Robertis. bibliog il Science 156:907-14 My 19 '67

MOLECULAR seives. See Adsorbents

MOLECULES
Absorption of intact protein molecules across the pulmonary air-tissue barrier. K. G. Bensch and others. bibliog il Science 157:1204-6 S 8 '67
Anodic oxidation and molecular structure: influence on performance of normal saturated hydrocarbons in fuel cells. E. J. Cairns. bibliog il Science 155:1245-6 Mr 10 '67
Anomeric bond-character in the pyranose sugars. H. M. Berman and others. bibliog il Science 157:1576-7 S 29 '67
Biomacromolecules: views and models; report on symposium. S. S. Breese, jr. Science 157:727 Ag 11 '67
Catalysis of ester hydrolysis by mixed micelles containing N-α-myristoyl-L-histidine. A. Ochoa-Solano and others. bibliog il Science 156:1243-4 Je 2 '67
Comparative X-ray and neutron diffraction study of bonding effects in s-triazine. P. Coppens. bibliog il Science 158:1577-9 D 22 '67
Destruction of molecules by nuclear transformations. S. Wexler. bibliog il Science 156:901-7 My 19 '67

Field ion microscopical imaging of biomolecules. E. W. Müller and K. D. Rendulic. bibliog il Science 156:961-3 My 19 '67
Forces between lecithin biomolecular leaflets are due to a disordered surface layer. V. A. Parsegian. bibliog il Science 156:939-42 My 19 '67
Intermolecular forces and the nature of the liquid state; address, April 1966. B. Widom. bibliog il Science 157:375-82 Jl 28 '67
Molecular aspects of lens cell differentiation. J. Papaconstantinou. bibliog il Science 156:338-46 Ap 21 '67
Molecular biology; British groups push enzyme-structure studies. N. Calder. Science 156:367-9 Ap 21 '67
Molecular pathology and carcinogenesis; report on first New Zealand international symposium. J. H. Weisburger and C. M. Goodall. Science 159:115-16 Ja 5 '68
Molecular uniformity in biological catalyses. W. D. McElroy and others. bibliog il Science 157:150-60 Jl 14 '67
Nature of glasses. R. J. Charles. il Sc⁴ Am 217:126-30+ S '67
Nature of polymeric materials. H. F. Mark. il Sci Am 217:148-54+ S '67
Plasma membranes of rat liver: isolation of lipoprotein macromolecules. M. Barclay and others. bibliog il Science 156:665-7 My 5 '67
Selective laser photocatalysis of bromine reactions. W. B. Tiffany and others. bibliog il Science 157:40-3 Jl 7 '67
Smallest copy; selection pressure favored the molecular species. Sci Am 217:103 S '67
Spectroscopy, molecular orbitals, and chemical bonding; address, December 12, 1966. R. S. Mulliken. bibliog il Science 157:13-24 Jl 7 '67
Stellar and other high-temperature molecules. W. Weltner, jr. bibliog il Science 155:155-64 Ja 13 '67
Structural aspects of reversible molecular oxygen uptake. J. A. McGinnety and others. bibliog il Science 155:709-10 F 10 '67
Transforming activity in both complementary strands of bacillus subtilis DNA. M.-D. Chilton. bibliog il Science 157:817-19 Ag 18 '67
Transition-state models and hydrogen-isotope effects. R. E. Weston, jr. bibliog il Science 158:332-42 O 20 '67

See also
Atoms
Polymers

MOLES (dermatology)
Common sense about moles. J. M. Snyder and A. Rostenberg, jr. Todays Health 46:74-5 Ja '68

MOLEY, Raymond
Perspective. See issues of Newsweek

MOLIÈRE, Jean Baptiste Poquelin
Dom Juan, or The feast of the statue. Criticism
New Yorker 43:149-51 Mr 11 '67
Les femmes savantes. Criticism
Nation 204:285-6 F 27 '67
Tartuffe. Criticism
Sat R 50:28 O 7 '67

MOLINA, José
Jose Molina bailes espanoles, Brooklyn academy of music. J. Maskey. Dance Mag 41:36 Mr '67

MOLINAR, Demostines
Modern argonauts. V. D. Smith. il pors Ebony 22:99-102+ Mr '67

MOLINE, Ill.
Mini-megalopolis rises along the Mississippi; thriving Quad-cities of Iowa and Illinois. il Bsns W p 168-70 F 25 '67

MOLL, Richard W.
Foreign study, perils and possibilities. Sat R 50:85-7+ F 18 '67

MOLLER, Paul
Flying saucer from earth. il por Sci N 91:453 My 13 '67

MOLLOY, Edward A.
Guimpes and saddles. Criticism
America 114:422+ O 14 '67

MOLLUSKS
Collectors; xenophora the carrier shell. P. Villiard. il Audubon 69:85-7 My '67
Molluscan faunal changes around Bermuda. R. T. Abbott and R. Jensen. bibliog Science 155:687-8 F 10 '67

See also
Embryology—Mollusks
Nervous system—Mollusks

MOLNAR, Thomas
Book of the month. Cath World 204:307-8 F '67

MOLNAR, THOMAS—*Continued*
Christian socialism's day. Nat R 19:348-9 Ap 4 '67
Letter from Europe. Nat R 19:1285+ N 14 '67
Maritain's message at eighty. Cath World 204:368-71 Mr '67
Old rebels in modern dress. Nat R 19:863-4 Ag 8 '67

MOLNIYA (satellites) See Communications satellites, Russian

MOLOKAI (island)
Molokai: the Hawaiian island nobody knows. R. Joseph. il Esquire 67:132-3 My '67

MOLSINK chamber. See Testing laboratories

MOLTING
Protein uptake in multivesicular bodies in the molt-intermolt cycle of an insect. M. Locke and J. V. Collins. bibliog il Science 155:467-9 Ja 27 '67

MOLTON, Warren Lane
And after three days; poem. Christian Cent 84:367 Mr 22 '67
Birth of a sea child; poem. Christian Cent 84:1066 Ag 23 '67

MOLZ, Kathleen
Public custody of the high pornography; reprint. por Library J 92:3373-6 O 1 '67

MOMADAY, N. Scott
Way to Rainy Mountain. Reporter 36:41-3 Ja 26 '67

MOMSEN, Charles Bowers
Rescuer. P. Maas. il pors Sat Eve Post 240:36-40+ S 23 '67

MOMYER, William Wallace
Rolling the thunder. il por Time 90:23 D 29 '67

MONACO
Royal family
Jamaica holiday for Princess Grace. H. Ehrlich. il Look 31:38-40+ Ap 4 '67
Our life together; excerpts from A prince's story. Rainier III. il Good H 164:100-10 Mr '67

MONAGHAN, Charles
Stage. Commonweal 86:472-3 Jl 28 '67

MONARDA. See Horsemint

MONASTERIES
Community and privacy for Benedictines. il Arch Rec 142:138-42 N '67
Methodist monasteries. America 116:137 Ja 28 '67

MONASTICISM
Only Lutheran monk. il Newsweek 70:84-5 D 4 '67
Psychoanalysis causes a break; monks of the Benedictine monastery at Cuernavaca renouncing their vows. America 117:5 Jl 1 '67
See also
Trappists

MONAT, William R.
Community library: its search for a vital purpose. bibliog por ALA Bul 61:1301-10 D '67

MONBOUQUETTE, Bill
Humiliation of a hero. L. Shecter. il por Sports Illus 26:66-71 Je 12 '67

MONCRIEFF, Donald
We all men die in pieces; Poem. America 117:225 S 2 '67

MOND, Julian Edward Alfred, 3d baron Melchett. See Melchett, J. E. A. M.

MONDALE, Walter Frederick
Brain drain: how poor nations give to the rich. Sat R 50:24-6 Mr 11 '67
Cost of the brain drain. Atlan 220:67-9 D '67
Housing for whom? New Repub 157:45 N 11 '67

about
Council of social advisers: new approach to welfare priorities? R. J. Samuelson. por Science 157:49-50 Jl 7 '67

MONDAY child; story. See O'Connell, J. S.

MONDAY holiday movement. See Holidays

Le MONDE. See Paris—Newspapers

MONDO grass. See Grasses

MONEGAL, Emir Rodriguez-. See Rodriguez-Monegal, E.

MONET, Claude
Impressionist eye. H. Kramer. il por N Y Times Mag p28-31 Ja 7 '68
Million-dollar Monet. il Newsweek 70:42-3 D 25 '67
Misunderstanding Monet. J. Rewald. Art N 66:25+ Ja '68

MONETARY fund. See International monetary fund

MONETARY policy
Current monetary policy. M. Friedman. il Newsweek 70:80 O 30 '67
Fed sticks to its course. il Bsns W p36-7 Ap 15 '67
Fed uses new tools to sharpen policy. Bsns W p 168 F 18 '67
Magic numbers; proposals for money supply increase rate. H. C. Wallich. Newsweek 69:82 Ap 10 '67
New worries for the budget makers. Bsns W p 164 Je 3 '67
What the Fed watchers watch. il Bsns W p 158+ Mr 25 '67
Why your dollar is sound; interview. H. H. Fowler. il U S News 63:74-9 O 2 '67
See also
Currency question

MONEY
First prize for the quetzal; international depreciation. il Time 90:86 Jl 14 '67
How we feel about our money; Roper research survey findings; with test and editorial comment. M. Gunther. il Sat Eve Post 240:72-5 D 30 '67
I just don't understand these kids; attitude toward money. E. Weston. McCalls 95:8 D '67
Inflation around the world. U S News 63:92 Jl 17 '67
Money goes electronic in the 1970s; checkless, cashless society. il Bsns W p54-6+ Ja 13 '68
Of money and its makers. L. Kronenberger. il Atlan 220:100+ S '67
The rich have beards, and the poor walk droopy; thirteen children look at money. A. Bayer. il Sat Eve Post 240:12+ D 30 '67
Sex and money: the modern equation. A. Brien. il Holiday 42:12+ O '67
Soon you'll never see money at all; cashless, checkless society. il Changing T 21:7-11 O '67
See also
Checks
Coins
Credit
Finance
Gold as money
Inflation (finance)
Interest
Investments
Paper money

International aspects
All about the SDR. Nat R 19:1109 O 17 '67
Bumpy road; special drawing rights. il Newsweek 70:81 O 9 '67
Coming to the crunch: London meeting of finance ministers. Bsns W p36+ Ag 12 '67
Conjuring a reserve asset out of thin air; special drawing right. il Bsns W p22-4 S 2 '67
Devaluation parable. P. A. Samuelson. Newsweek 70:85 D 18 '67
Fowler's formula; reform. Newsweek 69:82-3 Mr 27 '67
How paper gold could work; concerning ideas of R. V. Roosa. Fortune 76:81+ Ag '67
Improving the international monetary mechanism; statement, September 26, with text of resolution, September 29, 1967. H. H. Fowler. Dept State Bul 57:523-9 O 23 '67
Paper solution; special drawing rights. il Time 90:109 O 6 '67
Secretary Fowler's crusade for monetary reform. R. C. Albrook. il Fortune 76:78-80+ Ag '67
Shaking the money tree at Rio. Bsns W p41-2 S 23 '67
Stormy weather for the dollar; with panel discussion by H Wallich; P. A. Samuelson; M. Friedman. il Newsweek 69:86-8+ Ap 17 '67
U.S. pounds the desk on monetary reform. il Bsns W p 132+ Ap 29 '67
Why did it happen and what will it do to the U.S? C. Welles. il Life 63:36-7 D 1 '67
World and the mini-pound. il Newsweek 70:73-4 D 4 '67
See also
Currency question
Finance, International
Gold as money
International monetary fund

Psychological aspects
Speaking of money: interviews, ed. by W. H. Manville. il Sat Eve Post 240:50-3 D 30 '67

England
See Money—Great Britain

MONEY—*Continued*

Europe

Guide to European currencies. Holiday 43:114+ Ja '68

Finland

Trimming the finnmark. Time 90:92 O 27 '67

Germany

Multiple talers sought by collectors. C. French. Hobbies 72:102 Ja '68

Great Britain

Agony of the pound. il Time 90:29-32 N 24 '67

Britain devalues the pound. H. Kasper. Commonweal 87:325-6 D 8 '67

Britain devalues the pound. il Sr Schol 91: 17-18 D 7 '67

British business does its sums; devaluation of sterling. Bsns W p 124+ D 2 '67

British government to adopt decimal system in 1971. C. French. Hobbies 72:102 Ap '67

Craving for substance; decimal currency in 1971. Newsweek 69:46-7 Ap 3 '67

Devaluation: crisis of the mini-pound; with report by C. Welles. il Life 63:34-7 D 1 '67

Devaluation will bring U.K. defense cuts. H. J. Coleman. Aviation W 87:21 N 27 '67

Foreign operations weather storm; U.S. companies with overseas operations. Bsns W p 122 N 25 '67

From crisis to convalescence; British pound shows signs of returning health. Time 89:98 Mr 17 '67

High price of socialism. A. Lejeune. Nat R 19:1384 D 12 '67

How markets acted when pound fell. il U S News 63:37 D 4 '67

In the red, by H. Brandon. Review
    Sat R 50:37 Mr 4 '67. W. Diebold, jr

Is there to be a money crisis? with interview with R. V. Roosa. il U S News 63: 35-7 N 27 '67

Letter from London: pound devalued. M. Panter-Downes. New Yorker 43:150-3 D 2 '67

Letter from Paris; fall of the pound sterling. Genêt. New Yorker 43:95-6+ D 9 '67

Maneuvering to aid sterling. Bsns W p36 N 25 '67

New money game; devaluation of the British pound. il Bsns W p31-2 N 25 '67

Report from London; devaluation of sterling and the British economy. H. Luce. 3d. il Fortune 77:109+ Ja '68

Weathering the fallout. il Time 90:105-6 D 1 '67

What cheaper pound means to Americans. U S News 63:36 D 4 '67

Wilson devalues the pound, what price the damage? il Newsweek 70:73-4+ N 27 '67

Sweden

Sweden's coinage. C. French. Hobbies 72: 102 My '67

United States

An authority tells: what to do to strengthen the dollar. il U S News 64:53 Ja 1 '68

Blocking the threat to the dollar. Bsns W p 160 N 25 '67

Can de Gaulle break the dollar? with interviews with J. Rueff and E. Despres. il U S News 63:54-6+ D 11 '67

Defending the dollar. il Time 90:13-14 D 1 '67

Dollar is not as bad as gold; Time essay. Time 91:16-17 Ja 12 '68

Dollar passes a crucial test; with editorial comment. il Bsns W p 11-13, 88 D 23 '67

Dollar; what it's worth today. il Good H 164: 207 Ap '67

Gold rush: defending the dollar. il Newsweek 70:68-70+ D 4 '67

How golden is the dollar? J. K. Jessup. il Life 63:66-8+ Ag 25 '67

If the dollar were devalued. il U S News 64:47-8 Ja 8 '68

Is there to be a money crisis? with interview with R. V. Roosa. il U S News 63:35-7 N 27 '67

Money, money, money; symposium. il Sat Eve Post 240:3-4+ D 30 '67

No holds are barred for dollar's defense; effect of British devaluation on U.S. money markets. li Bsns W p38-9 N 25 '67

Return of the prodigal dollar? Nat R 20: 13-14+ Ja 16 '68

Shrewdest man in the money market; excerpt from The money managers. G. Krefetz and R. Marossi. Harper 235:43-7 Jl '87

Speaking of inflation: how dollar stacks up against other currencies. U S News 63:92 Jl 17 '67

Sterling's lesson for the dollar. Life 63:4 D 1 '67

Stormy weather for the dollar; with panel discussion by H. Wallich; P. A. Samuelson; M Friedman. il Newsweek 69:86-8+ Ap 17 '67

Tight money ahead? what it will do to the boom. il U S News 63:109-10 O 23 '67

Tighter money an official signal; given by the Federal reserve board. U S News 64:86-7 Ja 8 '68

U.S. balance of payments: can we plug the gold drain? il Sr Schol 91:8-11 D 7 '67

Wartime controls on the way? il U S News 64:32-4 Ja 15 '68

We can't win a war without it. F. Morley. il Nations Bsns 55:29-30 Mr '67

Why did it happen and what will it do to the U.S? C. Welles. il Life 63:36-7 D 1 '67

Why your dollar is sound; interview. H. H. Fowler. il U S News 63:74-9 O 2 '67

Will the dollar slip, too? il U S News 63: 33-6 D 4 '67
    See also
Paper money—United States
Silver as money

MONEY, Counterfeit. See Counterfeits and counterfeiting

MONEY management. See Budget, Household; Budget, Personal; Domestic finance

MONEY raising campaigns. See Fund raising

MONEY rates. See Interest

MONGAN, Elizabeth
Boucher's lovers in a park. Art N 66:50-1+ Sum '67

MONGOLIA
Nomads of Inner Mongolia. il Natur Hist 76:46-51 Je '67

MONGOLIANS. See Mongols

MONGOLISM
Mongoloid outbreak feared; Victoria, Australia. Sci N 92:563 D 9 '67

MONGOLOIDS. See Mongolism

MONGOLS
Nomads of Inner Mongolia. il Natur Hist 76: 46-51 Je '67

MONGOOSES
In Hawaii, face to face with a mongoose. Sunset 138:8 F '67

Mongoose throwing and smashing millipedes. T. Eisner and J. A. Davis. bibliog il Science 155:577-9 F 3 '67

MONIHAN, William J.
Lessons from revolution. R. B. Kaiser. America 117:469+ O 28 '67

MONK, Meredith
Evening of dance theatre. D. Hering. Dance Mag 41:29 Jl '67

Meredith Monk and company, Judson gallery and Judson memorial church. J. Maskey. Dance Mag 42:23 Ja '68

MONK, Thelonious Sphere
Mostly Monk. M. Williams. Sat R 50:91 Je 10 '67

MONKEES. See Singers

MONKEY trial. See Tennessee evolution controversy

MONKEYPOD trees. See Rain trees

MONKEYS
Behavior of vervet monkeys and other cercopithecines. T. T. Struhsaker. bibliog il Science 156:1197-203 Je 2 '67

Depression in infant monkeys separated from their mothers. I. C. Kaufman and L. A. Rosenblum. bibliog il Science 155:1030-1 F 24 '67

Night and the iguana; experimental rain forest. M. Bates. Natur Hist 76:22-5 D '67

Pinocchio becomes a father; first proboscis monkey born in captivity; with photographs. Sci Digest 61:61-3 F '67

Reporter at large; Japan monkey center at Inuyama. E. Kahn. New Yorker 43:126-33 S 23 '67

Squirrel monkey reproduction: the fatted male phenomenon and seasonal spermatogenesis. F. V. Du Mond and T. C. Hutchinson. bibliog il Science 158:1067-70 N 24 '67

Training without reward: traditional training of pig-tailed macaques as coconut harvesters. M. Bertrand. il Science 155:484-6 Ja 27 '67
    See also
Gibbons

MONKEYS in literature. See Animals in literature

MONKS. See Monasticism

MONNERVILLE, Gaston
Black president for France? il pors Ebony 23:88-90+ N '67

MONOAMINE oxidase
Brain monoamine oxidase in mice after exposure to aggression and defeat. B. E. Eleftheriou and K. W. Boehlke. bibliog il Science 155:1693-4 Mr 31 '67

MONOCYTIC leukemia. See Leukemia

MONOGRAM industries, Incorporated
On the run. Time 90:101 O 13 '67

MONONUCLEOSIS, infectious
College student's disease; International infectious mononucleosis symposium. A. Greenblatt. McCalls 94:42+ S '67
Heterophile reactive antigen in infectious mononucleosis. J. H. Peters. bibliog il Science 157:1200-2 S 8 '67
Kissing disease. Newsweek 69:93-4 Ap 10 '67
Mononucleosis: an updated report. Good H 164:196-7 Je '67
Mononucleosis: separating fact from fancy. S. L. Englebardt. Read Digest 91:154-7 N '67
Zeroing in on mono; relationship between mononucleosis and Burkitt's lymphoma. Newsweek 71:61 Ja 22 '68

MONOPOLIES
Rising corporate power: a national dilemma. il Sr Schol 90:9-11+ Ap 7 '67

MONOPOLY. See Monopolies

MONOPOLY (game) See Games

MONORAIL railroads. See Railroads, Single rail

MONOSACCHARIDES. See Saccharides

MONOTONY
See also
Boredom

MONOTROPA uniflora. See Indian pipes (plants)

MONRO, John Usher
Act of involvement. por Time 89:60 Mr 17 '67
Dean Monro's enormous reward. Nation 204: 389 Mr 27 '67
Monro's choice. Newsweek 69:61 Mr 20 '67

MONROE, Ann D.
British economy. Cur Hist 52:270-5+ My '67

MONROE, E. A. and Monroe, S. E.
Origin of iridescent colors on the indigo snake. bibliog Science 159:97-8 Ja 5 '68

MONROE, Earl
It's Earl, Earl, Earl the pearl. F. Deford. il por Sports Illus 27:18-19 O 30 '67

MONROE, Margaret E.
Variety in continuing education; address, January 11, 1967. por ALA Bul 61:275-8 Mr '67

MONROE, Marilyn
Dear Marilyn; N. Rosten. por McCalls 94:74-5+ Ag '67
Marilyn; peek-preview of Homage to Marilyn Monroe. L. Lerman. il pors Mlle 65:74-5 Jl '67
Norma Jean; excerpt. F. L. Guiles. por Ladies Home J 84:171-6 N '67

MONROE, S. E. See Monroe, E. A. jt. auth.

MONROE, N. C.
Sewerage program wins by 10-1 vote. J. E. Hinkle and R. A. McCoy, jr. il Am City 82: 74-5 Jl '67

MONRONEY, Almer Stillwell Mike
Air safety problems; excerpts from address. Aviation W 87:11 Jl 3 '67

MONSANTO company
What makes a Barbra special. il Bsns W p64-8+ My 20 '67

MONSERRAT, Joseph
Puerto Rican family. Natur Hist 76:70+ Ap '67

MONSTERS
More monsters, please! S. Alexander. Life 63: 30B D 8 '67

MONTAGE
Scissors & paint. il Pop Phot 62:55-8 Ja '68
See also
Collage

MONTAGNA, W. See Giacometti, L. jt. auth.

MONTAGNARDS
Elephants to the rescue; Special forces use elephants hired from Montagnards. R. West. il N Y Times Mag p85-7 Je 11 '67
Winning back the Montagnards. K. Prager. Reporter 36:38-40 Mr 23 '67

MONTAGU, Ashley
Unique global people. Sat R 50:33 Jl 22 '67

MONTAGU, Lady Mary (Pierrepont) Wortley
Ousted by age from old intrigue. R. Alter. Sat R 50:40 O 21 '67

MONTAGUE, Joseph Franklin
Living with an ostomy. Todays Health 45: 71 Ap '67

MONTALE, Eugenio
Montale: the longest glow, the longest shadows. E. Coleman. Poetry 109:268-70 Ja '67

MONTALVA, Eduardo Frei
Alliance that lost its way. For Affairs 45: 437-48 Ap '67

MONTAÑA, Antonio
This cursed fog; story. Américas 19:26-9 Jl '67

MONTANA
See also
Booksellers and bookselling—Montana
Fishing—Montana
Glacier National Park
Hunting—Montana
Wilderness areas—Montana

History
Graves and grizzlies; excerpt from Tough trip through paradise; ed. by B. H. Stein. A. Garcia. il Am Heritage 18:36-9+ Je '67
See also
Little Big Horn, Battle of the, 1876

MONTANA, University, Missoula
Themis: DOD plan to spread the wealth raises questions in academe. E. Langer. Science 156:48-50, 366 Ap 7, 21 '67; Reply. T. E. Phipps, jr. 156:1307 Je 9 '67

MONTE CARLO rally. See Automobile racing

MONTEFIORE hospital, New York. See New York (city)—Hospitals

MONTEREY COUNTY, Calif.
They saved the Big Sur. F. J. Taylor. il Read Digest 91:170-5 N '67

MONTEREY international pop festival. See Music festivals—California

MONTEREY jazz festivals. See Music festivals—California

MONTEREY PENINSULA, Calif.
Going places, finding things in the Monterey Peninsula. H. Johnson. il House & Gard 132:23-4+ Jl '67

MONTERO, Homero Martínez. See Martínez Montero, H.

MONTESSORI method of education
Montessori and traditional American nursery schools, how they are different, how they are alike. B. Spock and M. L. Hathaway. Redbook 128:20+ Mr '67

MONTEVERDI, Claudio
Coronation of Poppea. (L'incoronazione di Poppea) Criticism
Opera N il 32:31 Ja 13 '68
Magnificent achievement: Telefunken's Vespro della Beata Vergine. J. W. Barker. il Am Rec G 33:716-18 My '67
Monteverdi for moderns. R. Jacobson. il por Sat R 50:44 Jl 29 '67
Monteverdi's Poppea, for the first time near perfectly realized. J. Noble. il Hi Fi 17:70-1 My '67
Monteverdi's Vespers: two versions that make a lovely sound. B. Jacobson. il Hi Fi 17:61-2 Jl '67
Music for all seasons. R. Gelatt. Reporter 37: 59-60 Jl 13 '67
Project three. Monteverdi, etc. J. W. Barker. Am Rec G 34:135-6 O '67
Records:
L'incoronazione di Poppea. Opera N 31:30 Je 10 '67

MONTGOMERY, Charlotte
Speaker for the house. See issues of Good housekeeping

MONTGOMERY, Frank A. Jr
Mystique of messages in bottles. Motor B 120:48-9 D '67

MONTGOMERY, George
War that never was. Sat R 50:54-6 Ag 12 '67

MONTGOMERY, Hugh
Mass. univ. wins court fight against librarian. Library J 92:2496 Jl '67
Matter of reputation. K. Nyren. Library J 92:173 Ja 15 '67
Montgomery case goes to court. Library J 92: 1557 Ap 15 '67

MONTGOMERY, J. R. and others
Viral inhibition of lymphocyte response to phytohemagglutinin. bibliog Science 157: 1068-70 S 1 67

MONTGOMERY, John D.
Political decay of foreign aid. Yale R 57:1-15 O '67

MONTGOMERY, Roger
Detroit ends a twenty-year demonstration. Arch Forum 126:82-7 Ja '67

MONTGOMERY, Ruth
My psychic friends; excerpts from A search for the truth. Read Digest 90:151-2+ Ap '67

MONTGOMERY, Stuart
Circe; poem. Poetry 110:304-20 Ag '67
MONTGOMERY, Ala.

Fires

See Fires

Newspapers

Reprieve for the Courier. Newsweek 70:52 Jl 3 '67
MONTGOMERY COUNTY, Md.
Is central processing for you? services for school libraries. R. L. Darling; reply. M. Heglund. Library J 92:1267-8 Mr 15 '67
See also
Maryland-National capital park and planning commission
MONTGOMERY COUNTY, Pa.
High-volume deed recording made easy. J. S. Magill. il Am City 82:90-1 Jl '67
MONTGOMERY place (historic house) See New York (state)—Historic houses, etc.
MONTGOMERY Ward and company
Somebody loves Ward's; merger rumors are flying. Bsns W p34 Ap 1 '67
MONTHS
See also
December
MONTI, Eugenio
Ghostly go for the bobs. B. Ottum. il por Sports Illus 26:16-21 F 20 '67
MONTICELLI, Michel
Success in Canada. il U S Camera 30:50-1 S '67
MONTREAL

Airports

Expo 67: trio of airports to entice yankee pilots. R. G. Halford and R. B. Weeghman. il Flying 80:38-42 My '67

Architecture

Place Bonaventure: a unique urban complex. il Arch Rec 142:139-48 D '67
See also
Montreal—Worlds fair, 1967—Architecture

Churches

Underground and above. C. J. McNaspy. America 116:540+ Ap 8 '67

City planning

Expo 67: space/time in Montreal. E. Galantay. il Nation 204:557-62 My 1 '67
Place Bonaventure: a unique urban complex. il Arch Rec 142:139-48 D '67

Description

Expo 67. M. Herr. il Holiday 41:72-9+ Ap '67
Going places, finding things in Montreal and Toronto. J. Wilson. il House & Gard 132:20+ Ag '67
Sum-noo suur laa bun root poohr Kaybek? H. Sutton. il Sat R 50:68+ My 13 '67
Travel notes. R. Joseph. Esquire 68:34+ Jl '67

Historic houses, etc.

Living with antiques; the Hosmer house in Montreal. E. H. Turner. il Antiques 92:91-5 Jl '67

Hotels, restaurants, etc.

Sum-noo suur laa bun root poohr Kaybek? H. Sutton. il Sat R 50:68+ My 13 '67

Politics and government

Mayor. New Yorker 43:33-4 Ap 29 '67

Subways

Mass transit, today and tomorrow. il Am City 82:84-5 D '67 (to be cont)
Underground and above. C. J. McNaspy. America 116:540+ Ap 8 '67

Worlds fair, 1967

Another U.S.-Russian contest: exhibits at Expo 67. il U S News 62:96-8 My 22 '67
Awaiting big spenders. il Bsns W p24 Jl 1 '67
Best bets at Canada's Expo 67. il U S News 63:11 Jl 3 '67
Biggest fair ever: Canada's Expo 67. J. S. Walsh. il Good H 164:172+ Ap '67
Canada's big Expo 67 opens April 28 in Montreal. il Sunset 138:46+ Ap '67
Canada's centennial. America 116:493-4 Ap 1 '67
Canada's centennial fever. S. Robinson. il McCalls 94:70+ Mr '67
Coordinated production for Expo 67 guide book. il Pub W 191:99-101 My 1 '67
Craftsman's guide to Expo '67. D. Hare. il Craft Horiz 27:30-3+ Jl '67

Discoveries at Expo. A. Stagg. il House & Gard 132:192-7 S '67
Expo 67. C. Walter. il U S Camera 30:24-5+ F '67
Expo 67. G. Meek. il Américas 19:34-40 S '67
Expo 67. H. Sutton; M. R. Weiss; D. Campau. il Sat R 50:51-60 Ap 29 '67
Expo '67. J. Morris. il U S Camera 30:54-5 Jl '67
Expo 67. M. Herr. il Holiday 41:72-9+ Ap '67
Expo 67. N. Compton. Commentary 44:32-9 Jl '67
Expo 67. il Ebony 22:140-1+ Je '67
Expo 67. il Mod Phot 31:46-7+ Ag '67
Expo 67. il UNESCO Courier 20:10-13 Ap '67
Expo '67: a world in a thousand acres. il Sr Schol 90:12-15 Ap 7 '67
Expo 67: Canada's billion-dollar birthday party. D. MacDonald. il Read Digest 90:184-6+ Ap '67
Expo '67, Man and his world. il Sci Digest 61:21-3 My '67
Expo 67 preview. il Travel 127:38-42 Ap '67
Expo 67, preview of the future for audio-video? N. Eisenberg. Hi Fi 17:16 D '67
Expo 67: the big blast up north. A. Chamberlin. il Sat Eve Post 240:30-7 Ap 22 '67
Expo 67: the fairest of all. il Newsweek 69:54-61 My 1 '67
Expo 67: trio of airports to entice yankee pilots. R. G. Halford and R. B. Weeghman. il Flying 80:38-42 My '67
Expo 67: winning experiment in systemic graphics. il Pub W 192:76-8 Ag 7 '67
EXPO 67: world's biggest happening. W. D. Boutwell. il Sr Schol 90:sup 14-15 F 10 '67
First of the month. C. Amory. Sat R 50:4+ S 2 '67
Flags for Canada. R. Mercer. il Opera N 31:8-13 My 13 '67
Go-go debut for Expo. il Bsns W p37 My 6 '67
Goodby Expo, hello Canada. Life 63:4 N 3 '67
Goodbye to Expo. Time 90:49 N 3 '67
Letter from Expo 67. A. Chamberlin. il Sat Eve Post 240:68-9 Ag 26 '67
Man & his world. il Time 89:48-9 My 5 '67
Montreal and Canada's Expo 67; travel information. il Bet Hom & Gard 45:76-7 Mr '67
Montreal greets the world. J. B. Billard. il Nat Geog Mag 131:600-21 My '67
Montreal's Expo 67. H. Ehrlich. il Look 31:48-53 Ap 4 '67
Montreal's spectacular Expo 67, new shapes, art, culture, and hoopla. D. Messinesi. il Vogue 149:140-1+ My '67
Our far-flung correspondents. E. J. Kahn, jr. New Yorker 43:119-26+ Je 10 '67
Personal business. Bsns W p 155-6 F 25 '67; p 149-50 My 27 '67
Photographer's guide to Expo 67. C. Burger. il Pop Phot 60:74-7+ Ap '67
Pictures at an Expo. H. S. Lavin. America 117:344 S 30 '67
Pop fare for a popular fair; Americas vs. Europe track-and-field meet. J. Underwood. il Sports Illus 27:22-4+ Ag 21 '67
President Johnson visits Expo 67 at Montreal; remarks, May 25, 1967. L. B. Johnson. Dept State Bul 56:907-8 Je 19 '67
Preview of Expo 67. C. J. McNaspy. America 116:531-3 Ap 8 '67
Redbook's guide to Canada's fair. M. Cohen. il Redbook 128:19-21 Ap '67
Selling books at Expo 67; British book shop. L. Melzack. il Pub W 192:44-5 O 23 '67
September and October look like the best months for Montreal's Expo 67. il Sunset 139:33+ S '67
Snafus of success. il Time 89:58 My 12 '67
Space astronomy at Expo 67. P. A. Leavens. il Sky & Tel 34:72-8 Ag '67
Success closes its gates. il Bsns W p40-1 O 28 '67
Super '67 vacation: French Canada and a world's fair too. R. Dunlop. il Todays Health 45:24-9+ F '67
Teen travel talk: Canada kicks up its heels with a stupendous attraction named Expo 67. il Seventeen 26:222 F '67
This year it's Montreal. il Pop Gard 18:8-9 Ag '67
Twenty-first century comes to Montreal. R. Gustaitis. il Reporter 36:36-40 F 9 '67
Twenty-three days hath Expo. H. Sutton. Sat R 50:55-6 O 7 '67
Understanding Expo. H. Kenner. il Nat R 19:1070-3+ O 3 '67
Visiting Expo 67 by boat. Yachting 121:220-1 Mr '67

MONTREAL—Worlds fair, 1967—Continued
What's got into our good, gray neighbor? Expo 67. I. Mothner. il Look 31:28-31 Ag 22 '67
What's happening in education? children and Expo '67. W. D. Boutwell. PTA Mag 61:15 Ap '67
World's biggest birthday party; Expo 67. il Bsns W p50-4+ Ap 1 '67
World's fairest. il Newsweek 70:62-3 N 6 '67
Your preview of Expo 67. il Changing T 21: 46-8 Mr '67

Anecdotes, facetiae, satire, etc.

Man and whose world? C. Tomkins. New Yorker 43:24 Ag 26 '67
T.R.B. from Montreal; preview. New Repub 156:6 Ap 15 '67

Architecture

Architecture's leap into the future; with report by T. Prideaux. il Life 62:32-9 Ap 28 '67
Art and its world at Montreal. K. Kuh. il Sat R 50:44-7 My 27 '67
Beauty or the blob; exhibit Habitat 67: revolutionary design for living. il Sr Schol 90:16+ Ap 7 '67
Brilliantly ordered visual world; with account by M. F. Schmertz. il Arch Rec 142:115-26 Jl '67
Building-block houses. il House & Gard 133:90-1 Ja '68
Canada's new turn in architecture. E. Kaufmann, jr. il Harper 234:62-8 My '67
Expo named Buckminster Fuller. D. Jacobs. il N Y Times Mag p32-3+ Ap 23 '67
Expo 67: space/time in Montreal. E. Galantay. il Nation 204:557-62 My 1 '67
Expo 67: the fairest of all. il Newsweek 69: 54-61 My 1 '67
Field day for engineers. H. Comstock. il Pop Mech 127:88-92 My '67
Frei Otto designs 1,864 million cubic feet of air; German pavilion at Expo 67. il Arch Forum 126:58-65 Ap '67
Habitat and after; with account by R. Boyd. il Arch Forum 126:34-44 My '67
Inside Habitat. B. Plumb. il N Y Times Mag p46-8+ Jl 30 '67
Intimations of the future: Expo 67. M. Gough. il House B 109:198-9 Ap '67
Modules gain ground in housing landscape; modular construction turning into assembly-line industry. il Bsns W p78-81 Ja 6 '68
Montreal lights up. H. Sutton. il Sat R 50:51-3 Ap 29 '67
Three cubes; Venezuelan pavilion. il Arch Forum 127:58-9 S '67
Tomorrow's Pueblo: Expo 67's controversial Habitat. il Life 62:74-5+ Mr 31 '67
Twenty-first century comes to Montreal; Habitat 67 and pavilions. R. Gustaitis. il Reporter 36:37-40 F 9 '67
What it's like to live in an experiment; Habitat of Expo 67. D. Jacobs. il N Y Times Mag p50-1+ Je 4 '67
Will Habitat cast new mold for housing? il Bsns W p 164-6+ Je 24 '67

Art

Art and its world at Montreal. K. Kuh. il Sat R 50:44-7 My 27 '67
Playful and the inspired at Expo. F. Getlein. New Repub 157:35-6 Jl 22 '67
Too good to be true; Man and his world art theme of Expo 67. il Time 89:60-60E My 5 '67

Halls of science

Halls of science and exotica. il Life 62:40-1 Ap 28 '67

Moving pictures

Expo movie recaptures childhood fun; Time to play. W. Lane. il Travel 128:69 Jl '67
Expo: the point is pictures. J. Morgenstern. il Newsweek 70:88-90 Jl 17 '67
Film revolution to blitz man's mind; with report by F. Kappler. il Life 63:20-28C Jl 14 '67
Labyrinth: film in a framework. M. R. Weiss. il Sat R 50:51-3+ Jl 8 '67
Life movie review; the fair in retrospect. M. Rapf. Life 63:18 N 24 '67
Magic in Montreal; the films of Expo. il Time 90:80+ Jl 7 '67
Marshaling McLuhanism. A. Knight. il Sat R 50:41-2+ Ag 12 '67
Rights and permissions; future in commercial entertainment field for movie processes. P. Nathan. Pub W 192:95 S 25 '67

Music

Big opera; Bolshoi opera at Expo. H. Saal. il Newsweek 70:69 Ag 21 '67
Bolshoi; thinking big. P. G. Davis. il Hi Fi 17:MA18-19+ N '67
Expo 67, a musical cornucopia. Hi Fi 17:41 My '67
Expo 67 offers unusual treats. Sunset 138:9 Je '67
Highlights of May and June at Expo 67. Sat R 50:64-5 Ap 29 '67
Man and his musical world at Expo 67. I. Kolodin. il Sat R 50:61-2 Ap 29 '67
Montreal. F. Merkling; F. Campbell. il Opera N 32:22 S 9 '67
Montreal; Montreal symphony orchestra's productions at Expo 67. F. Campbell. il il Opera N 32:23-4 S 23 '67
Montreal; performances of Bolshoi opera at Expo 67; symposium. il Opera N 32:24-6 O 14 '67
Moscow in Montreal. H. Weinstock. Sat R 50:64+ S 16 '67
Music at Expo, from Bach to bleeps. S. Fleming. il Hi Fi 17:MA22-3 Jl '67
Music in Montreal; Expo 67. il Hi Fi 17:MA33-5 My '67
Musical events; performances by Moscow's Bolshoi opera at Expo 67. W. Sargeant. New Yorker 43:141-2 S 9 '67
Musical events; performances by Royal opera of Stockholm at Expo 67. W. Sargeant. New Yorker 43:78+ Je 24 '67
Musical events; performances by Vienna opera at Expo 67. W. Sargeant. New Yorker 43: 135-8 S 23 '67
Opera at Expo 67; six opera companies from abroad. il Opera N 31:17-25 My 13 '67
Power of positive vocalizing; La Scala at Expo 67. Time 90:81 O 20 '67
Report: Montreal. J. W. Freeman; S. Jenkins; F. Campbell. il Opera N 32:23-4 N 4 '67
Report: Montreal. R. D. Daniels; F. Campbell. il Opera N 32:26 N 25 '67
La Scala has the last word. R. Gelatt. il Hi Fi 17:MA24-5 D '67
Seeing sounds; electronic music at Expo 67. il Time 90:48+ O 6 '67
Soulful giant; Bolshoi opera at Expo 67. il Time 90:42 Ag 18 '67
Swedes at Expo; performances of Royal opera of Stockholm. G. Movshon. il Hi Fi 17: MA22-3+ Ag '67
Tarnished tradition; Vienna state opera at Expo. il Newsweek 70:91 S 18 '67
Total opera; La Scala at Expo. H. Saal. il Newsweek 70:61-2 O 16 '67
Vienna opera at Expo. G. Movshon. il Hi Fi 17:MA20-1+ N '67

Pavilions

Culture: the new joy; United States pavilion at Expo 67. W. K. Zinsser. Look 32:8 Ja 9 '68
Disaster or masterpiece? U.S. pavilion. il Time 89:47-9 Je 2 '67
Heigh ho! soft sell at the fair; U.S. pavilion. F. Kappler. Life 62:13 Je 16 '67
Labyrinth: film in a framework. M. R. Weiss. il Sat R 50:51-3+ Jl 8 '67
Quebec's shimmering vitrine. P. Blake. il Arch Forum 126:29-37 Je '67

Photography

Expo-graphy 67. H. M. Kinzer. il Pop Phot 61:114-17 O '67
Photography at Expo: a first look. B. Newhall. il Pop Phot 61:61+ S '67

Religious exhibits

Christian shocker at Canada's Expo 67? il U S News 62:14 Ap 17 '67
McLuhanite Christianity at Expo 67; Christian pavilion sponsored by Canadian Catholics and Protestants. H. Cox. Commonweal 86: 277-9 My 26 '67
Quebec; the pavilion, pro and con. C. De Mestral. Christian Cent 84:922+ Jl 12 '67
Symbol of hope for Man and his world. J. C. McLelland. il Christian Cent 84:893-6 Jl 12 '67

Sculpture

Delightful surprises. il Time 90:34-9 Ag 4 '67

MONTREAL Canadiens (hockey team) See Hockey teams
MONTREAL symphony orchestra. See Orchestras
MONTRESOR, Beni
See-a-story game; excerpts from I saw a ship a-sailing. McCalls 95:62-5 D '67

MONTROSS, Va.
Gym initiates master plan to expand an old school; Washington & Lee high school gymnasium. il Arch Rec 142:186–7 O '67

MONUMENTS
Take a cigarette butt and make it heroic; interview, ed. by S. Gablik. C. Oldenburg. il Art N 66:30–1+ My '67
See also
National monuments
War memorials
also subhead Monuments, statues, etc. under names of cities, e.g. Washington, D.C.—Monuments, statues, etc.

MOOD, Alexander M.
Machete in the paper jungle. Am Ed 3:5 O '67
National assessment. Am Ed 3:11–12+ Ap '67
—and others
Reaction to reactions. NEA J 56:28+ S '67

MOODY, G. Joseph
Woven ojos de dios. il Sch Arts 67:8–9 D '67

MOODY, John Wallace
Liturgy and the arts: a unique relationship. Cath World 205:303–9 Ag '67

MOODY, Joyce H.
IMC on wheels. Library J 92:304–5 Ja 15 '67

MOOG, Robert A.
Electronic music, its composition & performance. Electr World 77:42–6+ F '67

MOOLTEN, Frederick L. and Bucher, N. L. R.
Regeneration of rat liver: transfer of humoral agent by cross circulation. bibliog Science 158:272–4 O 13 '67

MOON, Samuel
River; Plane; Man in the landscape; poems. Poetry 111:163–5 D '67

MOON, Sheila
Christmas, 1967; poem. Christian Cent 84:1622 D 20 '67

MOON
Fingerprinting the moon; identifying lunar samples. Sci N 91:376 Ap 22 '67
Footprints on the moon; landing zones. Newsweek 69:70+ Ap 17 '67
Lunarlock-up; lunar receiving laboratory. il Sci N 91:165 F 18 '67
Mars and the moon at comparable resolutions. T. Pope. il Sky & Tel 33:119–20 F '67
New twist for an old theory; genesis of its own existence. il Time 89:64 F 3 '67
Planetary and lunar notes from Prague. il Sky & Tel 35:7–9 Ja '68
Sun, moon, and planets this month. See issues of Sky and telescope
Theory reinforced moon is lifeless. Aviation W 88:52 Ja 8 '68
Water on the moon. Time 89:46 My 5 '67
What's new on the moon. J. Daugherty and M. Daugherty. il Sci Digest 62:76–8 D '67
See also
Earthshine
Eclipses, Lunar
Lunar radiation
Occultations
Space flight to the moon
Space vehicles—Landing systems—Moon

Contamination
NASA sets plan to quarantine returning lunar mission crew. A. Hill. il Aero Tech 21:52–3 Ag 28 '67

Exploration
Alsep array cut for first moon missions. R. D. Hibben. il Aviation W 86:63+ Ap 3 '67
Fourteen Apollo applications experiments picked. Aviation W 86:82 My 1 '67
Lunar walking staff design under way. A. Hill. il Tech W 20:24 Mr 6 '67
Moon exploration: advent of the new engineering. I. Asimov. Tech W 20:46–8 Ja 23 '67
New lunar module versions taking shape. M. Getler. il Tech W 20:28–9+ Je 26 '67
SNAP-27 readied for tests with ALSEP; Apollo lunar surface experiments package. W. S. Beller. il Tech W 20:23–5 My 1 '67

Libration
Strange islands in space; libration centers. T. M. Morse. il Sci Digest 62:30–6 Jl '67

Names
See Names, Lunar

Observations
Lunar transient phenomena: topographical distribution; study of reports covering 400 years. B. M. Middlehurst and P. A. Moore. il Science 155:449–51 Ja 27 '67; Reply with rejoinder. C. R. Chapman. bibliog 157:959–60 Ag 25 '67

Orbit
Lunar latitude fluctuation. Sky & Tel 34:213–14 O '67

Photographs, maps, etc.
Around the lunar edge; Orientale basin photographed by Orbiter 4. Time 89:55 Je 16 '67
Delayed christening. Time 90:37 S 8 '67
In focus. Sky & Tel 33:302–3; 34:22–3 My, Jl '67
Lunar Orbiter 5 takes unusual pictures. R. N. Watts, jr. Sky & Tel 34:216–18 O '67
Lunar Orbiter photographs crater details. Aviation W 86:27 Ap 10 '67
Lunar Orbiter photographs: some fundamental observations. N. J. Trask and L. C. Rowan. bibliog Science 158:1529–35 D 22 '67
Lunar photography at Pic du Midi observatory. Z. Kopal. il Sky & Tel 33:216–19 Ap '67
Lunar surface strength estimate from Orbiter II photograph. A. L. Filice. Science 156:1486–7 Je 16 '67
NASA solving camera system problems on Orbiter 4. Aviation W 86:20–1 My 22 '67
New moon; photographs from Surveyor 3 and Orbiter 4. Time 89:42 Je 2 '67
One step nearer a lunar landing; pictures sent back by Surveyor III. Bsns W p74–6 Ap 29 '67
Orbiter photographs moon landing site. Aviation W 86:72–3 Ja 30 '67
Orbiter sends back pictures of moon's equatorial gap. G. S. Hunter. Aviation W 87:28–30 Ag 14 '67
Orbiter 2 photos used to identify Ranger 8 crater. Aviation W 86:30–1 Ja 23 '67
Orbiter 3 photographs lunar craters. Aviation W 86:70–1 Mr 13 '67
Photographs by Lunar Orbiter 4. R. N. Watts, jr. Sky & Tel 34:27–31 Jl '67
Relief effect in looking at lunar photographs. M. Minnaert. il Sky & Tel 33:90–1 F '67
Sharp eye of Orbiter V. Bsns W p55+ Ag 19 '67
Snapping the hidden face; Orbiter 5 pictures. il Time 90:36 Ag 18 '67
Surveyor I: location and indentification. L. H. Spradley and others. Science 157:681–4 Ag 11 '67
Surveyor 3 indicates firm lunar surface. G. S. Hunter. Aviation W 86:19–21 My 1 '67
Virtuosity on the moon. il Time 89:45 My 5 '67
What's on the other side of the moon. W. Von Braun. Pop Sci 191:82–4 D '67
See also
Space photography

Surface
AF uses IR remote scanning to obtain lunar surface data. J. A. Strasser. il Aero Tech 21:36+ D 4 '67
Alsep array cut for first moon missions; Apollo lunar surface experiments package. R. D. Hibben. il Aviation W 86:63+ Ap 3 '67
Apollo landing site choices. Sci N 91:85 Ja 28 '67
Around the lunar edge; Orientale basin photographed by Orbiter 4. il Time 89:54 Je 16 '67
Astronauts may find moon a bit like home; findings of Surveyor V. il Bsns W p80–2 O 7 '67
Bistatic-radar detection of lunar scattering centers with Lunar Orbiter I. G. L. Tyler and others. il Science 157:193–5 Jl 14 '67
Central peaks of Copernicus. A. K. Herring. il Sky & Tel 33:187 Mr '67
Chemistry of the moon. Sci Am 217:52–3 N '67
Chondritic meteorites and the lunar surface. J. A. O'Keefe and R. F. Scott. bibliog il Science 158:1174–6 D 1 '67
Earthlike moon. Time 90:90–1 O 6 '67
Earthy moon. il Sci N 92:367–8 O 14 '67
Far side lunar spectacular. il Sci Digest 62:20 Ag '67
Feel of the moon. R. F. Scott. il Sci Am 217:34–43 bibliog(p 154) N '67
Feel of the moon; exploration by Surveyor 3. Sci Am 216:50 Je '67
Hard gray moon. il Newsweek 69:84 Je 5 '67
In the lunar highlands. J. Lear. il Sat R 51:95–8 Ja 6 '68
Infrared images of tycho on dark moon. J. W. Salisbury and G. R. Hunt. bibliog il Science 155:1098–100 Mr 3 '67
Last Surveyor to study lunar highlands. G. S. Hunter. il Aviation W 87:40–1 D 25 '67

MOON—Surface—*Continued*
  Lunar controversy. Sci Digest 61:34 Mr '67
  Lunar Orbiter 5 takes unusual pictures;
    Surveyor 5 to test moon's surface com-
    position. R. N. Watts, jr. il Sky & Tel
    34:216-18 O '67
  Lunar Orbiter photographs: some fundamen-
    tal observations. N. J. Trask and L. C.
    Rowan. bibliog il Science 158:1529-35 D 22
    '67
  Lunar ring dikes from Lunar Orbiter 1. J. A.
    O'Keefe and others; discussion. bibliog il
    Science 156:1134; 157:841 My 26, Ag 18 '67
  Lunar surface analyzer studied. il Aviation W
    87:91+ O 2 '67
  Lunar surface: composition inferred from
    optical properties. B. Hapke. bibliog il Sci-
    ence 159:76-9 Ja 5 '68
  Lunar surface strength estimate from Orbiter
    II photograph. A. L. Filice. il Science 156:
    1486-7 Je 16 '67
  Lunar transient phenomena: topographical
    distribution; study of reports covering 400
    years. B. M. Middlehurst and P. A. Moore.
    il Science 155:449-51 Ja 27 '67; Reply with
    rejoinder. C. R. Chapman. bibliog 157:959-
    60 Ag 25 '67
  Moon digger; Surveyor 3 explores lunar sur-
    face. Newsweek 69:69 My 8 '67
  Moon's soil tested. Sr Schol 91:13-14 O 19 '67
  Observing the moon, Herodotus. A. K. Her-
    ring. il Sky & Tel 34:340-1 N '67
  Observing the moon, Linne. A. K. Herring.
    il Sky & Tel 33:259 Ap '67
  Observing the moon, Tobias Mayer. A. K.
    Herring. il Sky & Tel 34:119 Ag '67
  One step nearer a lunar landing; pictures
    sent back by Surveyor III. Bsns W p74-6
    Ap 29 '67
  Orbiter sends back pictures of moon's equa-
    torial gap. G. S. Hunter. il Aviation W
    87:28-30 Ag 14 '67
  Photographs by Lunar Orbiter 4. R. N.
    Watts, jr. il Sky & Tel 34:27-31 Jl '67
  Precise measurements result from Surveyor's
    leap. Sci N 92:536 D 2 '67
  Ranger VIII and gravity scaling of lunar
    craters. R. B. Baldwin. bibliog il Science
    157:546-7 Ag 4 '67
  Relief effect in looking at lunar photo-
    graphs. M. Minnaert. il Sky & Tel 33:90-1
    F '67
  Robot on the moon. il Sci Digest 61:33-4 Mr
    '67
  Scientists now certain of the maria. Sci N
    92:632 D 30 '67
  Scientists study data linking earth, moon. il
    Aviation W 87:29-30 O 9 '67
  Sharp eye of Orbiter V. il Bsns W p55+ Ag
    19 '67
  Soil test indicates clear vision for astro-
    nauts in lunar landing. il Aviation W 87:
    23 N 27 '67
  Space chemistry set tests moon's makeup;
    Surveyor V will help clear way for manned
    Apollo landing. il Bsns W p48 S 16 '67
  Spectrometer will evaluate solar plasma; solar
    wind spectrometer for Apollo lunar surface
    experiments package. G. S. Hunter. il Avi-
    ation W 86:55 F 27 '67
  Surface of the moon. A. R. Hibbs. il Sci Am
    216:60-72+ bibliog(p 150) Mr '67
  Surveyor I: location and identification. L. H.
    Spradley and others. il Science 157:681-4 Ag
    11 '67
  Surveyor 3 indicates firm lunar surface. G.
    S. Hunter. il Aviation W 86:19-21 My 1 '67
  Surveyor 3 on the moon. R. N. Watts, jr. il
    Sky & Tel 33:361-3 Je '67
  Surveyor V experiment links several
    earth/moon elements. il Aero Tech 21:25
    O 9 '67
  Surveyor 5 lunar chemistry data studied. I.
    Stone. il Aviation W 87:28-9 S 18 '67
  Surveyor V; reports. bibliog il Science 158:
    631-52 N 3 '67
  Surveyor 7 investigates lunar highlands. il
    Aviation W 88:32-3 Ja 15 '68
  Surveyor's moon. il Sci N 91:517-18 Je 3 '67
  Trench-digger on the moon; secrets it is un-
    veiling; Surveyor's finding. il U S News 62:
    12 My 8 '67
    Temperature
  Infrared images of tycho on dark moon. J.
    W. Salisbury and G. R. Hunt. bibliog il
    Science 155:1098-100 Mr 3 '67
MOON, Flight to the. See Space flight to the
    moon
MOON, Origin of. See Cosmogony
MOON, Photography of. See Astronomical
    photography; Space photography

MOON bases. See Lunar bases
MOON landing systems. See Space vehicles—
    Landing systems—Moon
MOON settlements. See Lunar bases
MOON vehicles. See Lunar vehicles
MOONEY, Hugh J.
  What the cigarette commercials don't show.
    Read Digest 92:71-4 Ja '68
MOONEY, Joe
  Music has its humor. G. Lees. por Hi Fi 17:
    118 Ja '67
MOONEY aircraft, incorporated
  Mitey Mooney. il Time 90:106+ D 1 '67
MOONEY positive control. See Automatic pilot
    (airplanes)
MOONEY problem check list. See Personality
    tests
MOONLIGHTING. See Supplementary employ-
    ment
MOONMOBILES. See Lunar vehicles
MOOR, Paul
  Festival for the case-hardened veteran. Hi Fi
    17:MA26+ Jl '67
  Festival in a fairy-tale kingdom. Hi Fi 17:
    MA28-9 D '67
  Hit from Hamburg: a U.S. opera. Life 62:11
    Je 30 '67
  Komische oper: near-perfect. Hi Fi 17:MA24-
    MA25 F '67
  Notes from our correspondents. Hi Fi 17:16+
    Mr '67
  Swinging Staatsoper. Hi Fi 17:52-5 Je '67
  Von Karajan's Easter festival. Hi Fi 17:
    MA21+ Je '67
  Wieland Wagner, elaborate mourning, future
    uncertainties. Hi Fi 17:MA3 Ja '67
MOORADIAN, Karlen
  Unknown Gorky. Art N 66:52-3+ S '67
MOORE, A. B. B.
  Ecumenical movement in Canada. Christian
    Cent 84:902-5 Jl 12 '67
MOORE, Alexander
  Emerging self. Cath World 206:180-2 Ja '68
MOORE, Archie
  Archie's ABCs. Sports Illus 27:9 Ag 21 '67
  Excerpt from statement, August 8, 1967;
    reprint. Cong Digest 46:253+ O '67
MOORE, Arthur Dearth
  Amateur scientist. Sci Am 217:118-23 Jl '67
MOORE, Arthur Dudley. See Himel, C. M. jt.
    auth.
MOORE, Betty
  (comp) World as a gift. Sat R 50:36 D 2 '67
MOORE, Bud
  Bud Moore, the man who makes the Mer-
    curys tick. B. Lang. il pors Hot Rod 20:
    44-6 Ap '67
MOORE, Charles Willard
  In his own house, a noted architect plays
    games. il House & Gard 133:110-15 Ja '68
MOORE, Clement Clarke
  Visit from St Nicholas; poem. McCalls 95:
    107 D '67
    about
  Doctor Moore's little masterpiece. C. Fadi-
    man. il McCalls 95:104-6 D '67
MOORE, Dom Sebastian
  Christ today. Cath World 206:109-10 D '67
MOORE, Edward
  Eliminated; one expensive rehandling opera-
    tion. por Am City 82:76-7 Jl '67
MOORE, Frank
  Cardsharp, or vice versa; excerpt from The
    diary of the American revolution, 1775-1781,
    ed. by J. A. Scott. Am Heritage 19:112 D
    '67
MOORE, George Eugene
  We're spending too much. Good H 164:14 Je
    '67
    about
  Major battlefield in war on cancer. il por
    Bsns W p88-9+ Ap 22 '67
MOORE, George Stevens
  Moore and Wriston of First national city. por
    Fortune 76:27 Jl '67
MOORE, Gerald
  From any angle, always different. Life 63:
    122 N 24 '67
  They all love Gene until he takes the stump.
    Life 64:50B-54 Ja 19 '68
  Who says college kids have changed? Life
    62:90-90B+ My 19 '67
MOORE, Gerald, 1899-
  Arrivederci, Gerald. H. Weinstock. il Sat R
    50:62 D 2 '67
  Evening with Gerald Moore and friends. E.
    Greenfield. il por Hi Fi 17:16+ My '67
  Homage rightly and fittingly paid to pianist
    Gerald Moore. C. L. Osborne. il por Hi Fi
    17:125-6 O '67

MOORE, Gerald, 1899-—*Continued*
Long live the king. il por Newsweek 69:75 Mr 6 '67
Moore's farewell to Schubert. I. Kolodin. Sat R 50:50 Ap 8 '67
Other side; farewell recital at Festival hall. T. Heinitz. il por Sat R 50:77 Mr 25 '67
Records:
    Homage to Gerald Moore. Opera N 32:34 Ja 13 '68

MOORE, Gilbert
I hope you enjoyed my movie, and they did. Life 63:42 Ag 25 '67
No one has ever called me a nigger. I have never been bitten by a rat. Life 62:77-8+ Je 30 '67

MOORE, Harold
Incident at Billy Springs; story. Esquire 67: 124-5 My '67

MOORE, Harry T.
She adopted Augustus John. Sat R 50:66 Ap 8 '67

MOORE, Henry
(ed) Gist of it. See issues of Outdoor life

MOORE, Hugh L.
Aligning FM-stereo receivers without a generator. il Electr World 78:33-5+ N '67

MOORE, James
How to get money for vocational education. Am Ed 4:10-11 D '67
Notes from our correspondents. Hi Fi 17:24+ Ja '67

MOORE, John Cecil
Mr Catesby brings it off; story. Ladies Home J 84:82-3 F '67
Novelist and his trade. Writer 80:13-16 O '67
Sword cactus; story. Sat Eve Post 240:50-5 Jl 29 '67

MOORE, John R.
Space; address, October 16, 1967. Vital Speeches 34:76-9 N 15 '67

MOORE, John Travers
Coat; poem. Horn Bk 43:316 Je '67

MOORE, L. Kingsley
New curriculum for citizenship education. por Sr Schol 90:sup 14-15 My 19 '67

MOORE, L. W.
Urban unrest; address, August 25, 1967. Vital Speeches 33:749-52 O 1 '67

MOORE, Lillian
Plainsman and ballerina. Dance Mag 41:46-9 O '67

about
Lillian Moore: a joyous searching. S. J. Cohen. il por Dance Mag 41:34-7 S '67

MOORE, Marianne
Camperdown elm; poem. New Yorker 43:48 S 23 '67
Precepts for poets; excerpt from Tell me, tell me. Writer 80:32 Ap '67
Randall Jarrell; excerpt from Randall Jarrell, 1914-1965. Atlan 220:96-8 S '67

about
Artemis and harlequin. H. Kenner. Nat R 19:1432-3 D 26 '67
Marianne Moore's magic. S. Hochman. Nation 204:602 My 8 '67
Two ladies of legend. D. Hoffman. Reporter 37:41-3 D 28 '67
Urgency and deference. S. P. Zitner. Poetry 110:423-4 S '67

MOORE, Mary Tyler
Mary Tyler Moore bounces back. R. Hochstein. il pors Good H 164:61-2+ Ap '67

MOORE, Mary Virginia, and Ranney, J. B.
Your voice; the most personal thing about you. Todays Health 45:60-1+ D '67

MOORE, Patrick A. See Middlehurst, B. M. jt. auth.

MOORE, Paul B. and Louisnathan, John
Fresnoite; unusual titanium coordination. bibliog Science 156:1361-2 Je 9 '67

MOORE, Richard
Conquest; poem. Mlle 65:42 Jl '67
Hymn to an automatic washer. Harper 234:52 Mr '67

MOORE, Robert Y. and others
Visual pathway mediating pineal response to environmental light. bibliog Science 155: 220-3 Ja 13 '67

MOORE, Rosalie
Death of the story teller; Sea look; Love poem; What he sees; poems. Poetry 110: 222-5 Jl '67

MOORE, Thomas
It's a long way to Alviso Slough. Yachting 123:88-9 Ja '68

MOORE, Trevor Wyatt
Miss Bouchard protests. Christian Cent 84: 1288-90 O 11 '67
Mission of Melchizedek Truepew. Christian Cent 84:1397-8 N 1 '67

MOORE, Virginia Bennett
Virgin Islands National Park. Nat Parks Mag 41:4-8 Ja '67

MOORE corporation
Foreigner is no. 1 in U.S. market; Toronto's Moore corp. largest maker of business forms. il Bsns W p 171-2+ S 23 '67

MOORE COUNTY, N.C.
Nobody wanted school desegregation. D. Cooper. il Am Ed 3:2-4 Je '67

MOORER, Thomas Hinman
U.S. seapower; address, September 28, 1967. Vital Speeches 34:83-5 N 15 '67

about
Comer arrives. il por Time 89:33 Je 9 '67

MOORESTOWN, N.J.
Moorestown builds modern neighborhood center. M. B. Berman. il Parks & Rec 2:36-7 My '67

MOORHEAD, Jennelle
President's message. See issues of PTA magazine
Summer seminar in Ecuador. Sr Schol 90: sup 13-14 Mr 3 '67
What the PTAs are up to now; interview. por Am Ed 3:19-20 My '67

MOORING of boats. See Boats—Mooring

MOORING of canoes. See Boats—Mooring

MOORMAN, Maurice
He roams the range. H. L. Masin. por Sr Schol 91:26 N 16 '67

MOORS (people)
Moorish matter; an incident in North Africa. N. Mostert. il Reporter 37:36-9 N 16 '67

MOOSE FACTORY, Ontario
To Moosonee by Polar bear express. R. S. Milne. Atlan 219:120 Je '67

MOOSE hunting
I had to have moose. O. A. Fredrickson. il Outdoor Life 139:70-3+ My '67
Moose a mile; Clark-Beaupre region of Saskatchewan. H. Bradshaw. il Field & S 72:36-7+ Ag '67
Special-extra moose hunt. H. J. Samuels. il Outdoor Life 140:32-5+ N '67

MOOSEHORN national wildlife refuge. See Wildlife sanctuaries

MOOSONEE, Ontario
To Moosonee by Polar bear express. R. S. Milne. Atlan 219:118-20 Je '67

MORAES, Dom
Three poets. P. Legler. Poetry 109:414 Mr '67

MORAL attitudes
Apollo, the destroyer; moral horror that afflicts our society. D. J. Stewart. New Repub 156:15 F 18 '67
Crisis of overcriminalization. S. H. Kadish. bibliog f Ann Am Acad 374:157-70 N '67
Gilt-edged guilt. New Repub 156:5-6 Mr 11 '67
Missing element, moral courage. B. W. Tuchman. McCalls 94:28+ Je '67
Moral double bookkeeping. Nation 204:546 My 1 '67
Public attitudes toward gambling and corruption. J. A. Gardiner. bibliog f il Ann Am Acad 374:123-34 N '67
Resistance and technology; theory of the new left vs. technological man. D. Callahan. Commonweal 87:377-81 D 22 '67
Why organized crime thrives. H. S. Ruth, jr. bibliog f Ann Am Acad 374:113-22 N '67

Anecdotes, facetiae, satire, etc.
Prescription for pandemonium. R. E. Fitch. Christian Cent 84:1591-2 D 13 '67

MORAL codes. See Ethics

MORAL conditions
See also
Moving pictures—Moral aspects
also subhead Moral conditions under names of countries, etc. e.g. United States —Moral conditions

MORAL education
Helping children to clarify values; excerpts from Values and teaching; working with values in the classroom. L. E. Raths and others. il NEA J 56:12-15 O '67
Needed: heroic examples for the young; excerpts from address. J. F. Kauffman. NEA J 56:16-17 O '67
Teaching ethics and moral values in the schools. W. Fallaw. Christian Cent 84:1153-7 S 13 '67; Reply. L. R. Ward. 84:1498 N 22 '67
Touching base with our youth. E. F. McKibbin. Sch & Soc 95:424-5 N 11 '67

MORAL philosophy. See Ethics
MORAL principles. See Principles
MORAL rearmament
Sing out, America! C. W. Hall. il Read Digest 90:49-54 My '67
They're out to remake the world; condensation. C. W. Hall. Read Digest 92:145-56+ Ja '68
U.S. letter: Chicago; performances of Sing-out. C. Trillin. New Yorker 43:128+ D 16 '67
MORAL sense. See Ethics
MORAL theology. See Christian ethics
MORALE, National
Egypt
There is no false courage left in Egypt. A. Carthew. il N Y Times Mag p45-7+ D 3 '67
Europe, Eastern
Back to normal. F. Y. Blumenfeld. il Newsweek 69:58+ Ap 17 '67
Great Britain
English sickness; state of discontent. D. W. Brogan. Harper 234:57-62 Je '67
Israel
Ebbing of euphoria. H. Weiner. il Reporter 37:16-19 N 16 '67
In Israel: after the triumph. A. Kazin. il Harper 235:72-8+ N '67
Today in Tel Aviv. S. Wolpert. Nation 205:7-8 Jl 3 '67
Victorious Israel's look and mood. L. J. Walinsky. New Repub 157:9-10 Jl 8 '67
United States
American rediscovers America. F. C. Painton. il U S News 63:58-62 S 4 '67
Are we having a nervous breakdown? H. Cox. McCalls 95:6+ Ja '68
As Truman said; excerpt from address. May 18, 1951. H. S. Truman. Reporter 36:8 My 18 '67
Congress jittery as public mood shifts. il U S News 63:26-8 Ag 28 '67
Gilt-edged guilt. New Repub 156:5-6 Mr 11 '67
Good times, but people are unhappy; findings of nationwide survey. il U S News 62:50-5 My 22 '67
Looking out at John Q. Public. H. Sidey. il Life 63:46 S 22 '67
Real story of revolt in Congress, as told by members themselves. il U S News 63:36-9 N 13 '67
Smell of crisis. E. J. Hughes. Newsweek 70:29 N 13 '67
T.R.B. from Washington; growing disillusionment. New Repub 157:6 S 2 '67
Uneasy America; why? what a nationwide survey shows. il U S News 63:42-6+ S 18 '67
Uneasy lie the states; observations of a British visitor. C. Northcott. Christian Cent 84:1213-14 S 27 '67
What ails America? withering away of the public's trust in government. H. J. Morgenthau. New Repub 157:17-21 O 28 '67
What has happened to America? R. M. Nixon. Read Digest 91:49-54 O '67
What the people want. D. Lawrence. U S News 63:100 Ag 21 '67
Vietnam (Republic)
Return to Vietnam; why this bewildering war will not be won. D. Halberstam. il Harper 235:47-58 D '67
Thirty-seven year war of the village of Tananhoi. L. G. Martin. il N Y Times Mag p30-1+ O 29 '67
MORALES-CARRIÓN, Arturo
Dialogue on the Alliance. Américas 19:inside cover Jl '67
University and development. Américas 19:8-13 S '67
MORALITY. See Ethics
MORALS. See Ethics
MORALS and war. See War—Moral aspects
MORAN, Charles McMoran Wilson, 1st baron
Fixed resolve not to quit. F. J. Braceland. il por Sat R 50:37 My 13 '67
MORAN, Edward
Down to the sea; paintings, with quotations by nineteenth century American authors. por Am Heritage 18:40-55 Je '67
MORAN, Gabriel
Failure of structures. Commonweal 86:50+ Mr 31 '67
God of revelation. Commonweal 85:499-503 F 10 '67

MORAN, J. M. and others
Spectral line interferometry with independent time standards at stations separated by 845 kilometers. bibliog Science 157:676-7 Ag 11 '67
MORAN towing and transportation company
Man from Moran. C. Peet. il Pop Mech 128:136-9+ N '67
MORANDA, George E.
Colonel second. Time 89:48 Mr 10 '67
MORANDI, Giorgio
Art; exhibition at the Loeb and Krugier gallery. M. Kozloff. Nation 204:765-6 Je 12 '67
MORAY, Ann
Tom Tinker Ellis; story. Mlle 66:100-1 D '67
MORCA, Teodoro
On the boards. W. Como. il por Dance Mag 41:17 Ag '67
MORE, Sir Thomas, Saint
Thomas More: church, state and ecumenicity. R. C. Marius. Christian Cent 84:934-6 Jl 19 '67
MORE effective schools (program) See Socially handicapped children—Education
MORE stately mansions; drama. See O'Neill, E. G.
MORE than memory; story. See Maner, W.
MOREEN, Howard A.
Continuing education; address, December 16, 1966. Vital Speeches 33:244-7 F 1 '67
MOREHEAD, Frederick F. Jr
Light-emitting semiconductors; with biographical sketch. Sci Am 216:21, 108-13+ bibliog(p 168) My '67
MOREHOUSE college, Atlanta, Ga.
Swimming makes a splash at Morehouse. il Ebony 22:56-8+ My '67
MOREIRA SALLES, Elizinha
China. por Vogue 149:142-4+ Ap 1 '67
MOREL, Georges
Meaning of Karl Marx. America 117:464-8 O 28 '67
about
Lessons from revolution. R. B. Kaiser. America 117:469+ O 28 '67
MORGAN, Berry
Barrand's landing; story. New Yorker 43:54-6 Mr 11 '67
Pepper trick; story. New Yorker 43:53-5 Ap 22 '67
MORGAN, Derek
I want my bloody game back. Sports Illus 27:52-4 Ag 28 '67
Mixed bag from Britain. Reporter 36:50+ Mr 9 '67
These our actors. Reporter 36:46+ F 23 '67
MORGAN, Ed
Three bucks for the book. pors Outdoor Life 140:54-5+ N '67
MORGAN, Harold S.
Health-care cooperation saves babies. Todays Health 46:88 Ja '68
MORGAN, Karl Ziegler
X-ray exposures. R. Nader. New Repub 157:11-12 S 2 '67; Discussion. 157:37-8 S 30 '67
MORGAN, Murray
Off to the Klondike! excerpts from One man's gold rush: a Klondike album. Am Heritage 18:34-49+ Ag '67
MORGAN, Neil
California. Sat R 50:16-19+ S 23 '67
Grandeur of the Great Divide. Holiday 41:42-59+ My '67
MORGAN, Richard Lyon
Let's be honest about the canon. Christian Cent 84:717-19 My 31 '67
MORGAN, Robert P.
Window newly opened: music from Portugal's Golden age. Hi Fi 17:78+ D '67
MORGAN, Robin
Satellite; poem. Yale R 57:256-7 D '67
MORGAN, Thomas B.
Angry playwright in a soft spell. Life 62:90-90B+ My 26 '67
Most happy fella in the White House. Life 63:80-80B+ D 1 '67
MORGAN library. See Pierpont Morgan library
MORGANTE, Odosca, and Shemanchuk, J. A.
Virus of the California encephalitis complex: isolation from culiseta inornata. bibliog Science 157:692-3 Ag 11 '67
MORGENSTERN, Sheldon
Upbeat in the key of youth; interview, ed. by R. Hemming. por Sr Schol 90:20 My 5 '67
MORGENTHAU, Hans J.
New foreign policy for the United States: basic issues. Bul Atomic Sci 23:7-11 Ja '67
To intervene or not to intervene. For Affairs 45:425-36 Ap '67

MORGENTHAU, Hans J.—*Continued*
U.S. misadventure in Vietnam. Cur Hist 54:
29-34 Ja '68
What ails America? New Repub 157:17-21 O
28 '67
MORGENTHAU, Henry, 1891-1967
Henry Morgenthau jr, RIP. Nat R 19:183 F 21
'67
Obituary
Newsweek por 69:73 F 20 '67
Two of a kind. il por Time 89:25 F 17 '67
MORIARTY, James R.
Transitional pre-desert phase in San Diego
County, California. bibliog Science 155:553-6
F 3 '67
MORIARTY, John K.
Policies of delusion. Commonweal 86:574-80
S 22 '67
MORIN, Edward
Good Friday morning; poem. Christian Cent
84:367 Mr 22 '67
MORISON, Robert S.
Where is biology taking us? excerpts from
address, October 1966. Science 155:429-33
Ja 27 '67
MORISON, Stanley
Obituary
Pub W 192:35-6 O 23 '67
MORISSEAU, James J.
Schoolhouse in the city. Sat R 50:58-9 Mr
18 '67
MORITA, Akio
Horatio Alger story, with a Japanese twist.
J. L. Schecter. il por N Y Times Mag p56-
7+ S 10 '67
MORLACCHI, Giuseppina
Plainsman and ballerina. L. Moore. il por
Dance Mag 41:46-9 O '67
MORLEY, Charles
(comp) Articles and other books received;
eastern Europe. See issues of American his-
torical review
MORLEY, Felix
Trends: the state of the Nation. See issues
of Nation's business
What's wrong with the way we raise reve-
nues. Nations Bsns 55:27-8 Je '67
MORLEY, L. W.
Canada's unappreciated role as scientific in-
novator; with excerpt from letter. J. Lear.
il por Sat R 50:46-50 S 2 '67
MORLEY, Robert
Enter, laughing. E. Weeks. Atlan 219:126-7 Je
'67
—and Stokes, Sewell
Backstage with Shakespeare, Morley, and
Bogart; excerpt from Robert Morley: a
reluctant autobiography. Atlan 219:58-62 Ap
'67
MORMONS and Mormonism
For time & eternity; Mormon marriage of
Governor Romney's son. il Time 90:46 S 1
'67
Husbands with more than one wife. B. Mer-
son. il Ladies Home J 84:78-9+ Je '67
Mrs Romney's quandry; concerning Mormon
treatment of Negroes. Christian Cent 84:165
F 8 '67
Mormons and the Negro. il Newsweek 69:80
Mr 6 '67
Orrin Porter Rockwell, by H. Schindler.
Review
Sat R 50:36 F 11 '67. M. Brown
Prosperity & protest; 137th anniversary of
the founding of Mormonism. il Time 89:
104 Ap 14 '67
Spectacular rise of the Mormon church. Read
Digest 90:78-82 F '67
MORNING glories
These are cheery morning glories. il Sunset
138:248 Ap '67
MOROCCAN cookery. See Cookery, Moroccan
MOROCCO
See also
Hunting—Morocco
Moors (people)

Cultural relations
United States and Morocco sign cultural
agreement. Dept State Bul 56:351-2 F 27 '67

Description and travel
Well traveled camera. il Mod Phot 31:97-8
My; 110+ Jl '67

Foreign relations
King Hassan II of Morocco visits the United
States; exchange of greetings and exchange
of toasts, February 9, 1967. Hassan II; L. B.
Johnson. Dept State Bul 56:328-31 F 27 '67

Politics and government
Potentate with potential. il Time 89:34+ F
17 '67
MOROZE, Lewis M.
Lethal indifference. Nation 205:105-7 Ag 14 '67
MORPHINE
Biosynthesis of the morphine alkaloids. G. W.
Kirby. bibliog il Science 155:170-3 Ja 13 '67
MORPHOGENESIS. See Morphology
MORPHOLOGY
Apatite crystallites: effects of carbonate on
morphology. R. Z. LeGeros and others. bib-
liog il Science 155:1409-11 Mr 17 '67
Embryonic morphogenesis: role of fibrous
lattice in the development of feathers and
feather patterns. E. S. Stuart and A. A.
Moscona. bibliog il Science 157:947-8 Ag 25
'67
Fungal morphogenesis ring formation and
closure by arthrobotrys dactyloides. M. L.
Higgins and D. Pramer. bibliog il Science
155:345-6 Ja 20 '67
Morphological changes in human scalp hair
roots during deprivation of protein. R. B.
Bradfield and others. bibliog il Science 157:
438-9 Jl 28 '67
Role of enzymatic wall-softening in plant
morphogenesis: hormonal induction in
achlya. D. des S. Thomas and J. T. Mullins. bibliog il Science 156:84 Ap 7 '67
Scanning electron microscope: potentials in
the morphology of microorganisms. G. A.
Bartlett. bibliog il Science 158:1318-19 D
8 '67
Tribolium castaneum: morphology of aureate
revealed by the scanning electron micro-
scope. A. Sokoloff and others. bibliog il Sci-
ence 157:443-5 Jl 28 '67
MORREL, Marc
Test case for Old Glory; stuffed sculpture
dramatizes the uses and abuses of the flag;
with report by F. Powledge. il por Life 62:
18-19+ Mr 31 '67
MORRILL, Justin Smith
Action intellectuals. T. H. White. por Life 62:
56 Je 16 '67
MORRIS, Austin P.
Of many things. America 118:inside cover
Ja 13 '68
MORRIS, Charles B.
Galax, Va. turns out to hail the sergeant.
il pors Life 62:80-1 F 3 '67
MORRIS, Charles C.
Universal wiring for automotive ignition sys-
tems. Electr World 78:48 Ag '67
MORRIS, Delyte Wesley
Out of nowhere. por Newsweek 69:102-3 Je 12
'67
MORRIS, Desmond
Naked ape: excerpt. Life 63:94D-98+ D 22 '67

about
Face is familiar. Newsweek 71:80-1 Ja 22 '68
MORRIS, Everett B.
America's cup eliminations. Yachting 121:300
Ja '67
Obituary
Motor B por 119:188 Mr '67
Yachting por 121:245-6 Ap '67. J. Rendell
MORRIS, Gitta L.
He knows where to drill for water. Pop Mech
128:124-6+ O '67
MORRIS, Greg
Mission: Impossible's Greg Morris. il pors
Ebony 23:99-100+ D '67
MORRIS, Henry
Henry Morris: papermaker & printer. F.
Johnson. il Am Artist 31:56-61+ O '67
MORRIS, James, 1926-
Ethiopia: the lion-hearted land. Holiday 41:-
58-67+ Je '67
I love America. Read Digest 90:147-8+ Ap
'67
Road to Llanystumdwy. Harper 234:94-7 Ap
'67
Silk road. Horizon 9:4-23 Aut '67
MORRIS, Jesse
Negro self-help. A. Goldberg. New Repub 156:
6 Je 10 '67
MORRIS, Jill
Expo '67. U S Camera 30:54-5 Jl '67
MORRIS, Joe Alex
New York city's multimillion-dollar village
green. Read Digest 91:193-7+ O '67
What the credit bureaus know about you.
Read Digest 91:85-9 N '67
MORRIS, Joe Alex, Jr
South Arabia: Nasser and the sultans. Na-
tion 204:358-61 Mr 20 '67

MORRIS, John N.
Soldiering in innocence. Nation 205:85-6 Jl 31 '67
With the doctor's bill; poem. Nation 204:318 Mr 6 '67

MORRIS, Marnee
Brief biography. S. Goodman. pors Dance Mag 41:54-5 F '67

MORRIS, N. Roland, and others
Magnesium pemoline: failure to affect in vivo synthesis of brain RNA. bibliog Science 155:1125-6 Mr 3 '67

MORRIS, Philip, incorporated
Machine that will sell anything; marketing mechanism geared to low-priced packaged goods. il Bsns W p92-4+ Mr 4 '67

MORRIS, Ralph W. See Lutsch, E. F. jt. auth.

MORRIS, Rebecca
Good humor man; story. New Yorker 43:29-36 Je 17 '67

MORRIS, Richard B.
Is U.S. fed up with lawlessness? excerpts from address, November 14, 1967. por U S News 63:10 N 27 '67

MORRIS, Richard Brandon
Where the sun never set. Sat R 50:32 Je 17 '67

MORRIS, Robert K.
James Purdy and the works. Nation 205:342-4 O 9 '67

MORRIS, Robert W. and Kittleman, L. R.
Piezoelectric property of otoliths. bibliog Science 158:368-70 O 20 '67

MORRIS, Terry
Baby who was born twice. Redbook 129:64-5+ Je '67
Svetlana: a love story. por McCalls 94:74-5+ Jl '67

MORRIS, Thomas D.
Excerpt from testimony before Senate subcommittee on employment, manpower and poverty, March 20, 1967. Cong Digest 46:156+ My '67

MORRIS, Walter
Build this underwater aquaplane. Pop Mech 128:142-3 Jl '67

MORRIS, William
William Morris, his life, work and friends, by P. Henderson. Review
Time il por 90:115-16 D 8 '67
Work of William Morris, by P. Thompson. Review
Nation 205:534-5 N 20 '67. C. Bedient

MORRIS, William J.
Baja California: late cretaceous dinosaurs. bibliog Science 155:1539-41 Mr 24 '67

MORRIS, Willie
Provincial in New York; excerpts from North toward home. Harper 234:43-51 Je; 235:60-8 Jl '67
Yazoo years; excerpt from North toward home. Sat Eve Post 240:38-42+ O 7 '67

about
Authors & editors. por Pub W 192:21-2 O 9 '67
Book reviews. E. P. J. Corbett. America 117:720 D 9 '67
Books. A. Kazin. Vogue 150:173 D '67
Bright boy from Yazoo. J. S. Carroll. New Repub 157:32-4 N 18 '67
Homecoming. P. Schrag. Reporter 37:44+ N 30 '67
How to succeed at an early age. G. Hicks. Sat R 51:77-8+ Ja 13 '68
North by South. il por Time 90:61-2 N 10 '67
Spur for Harper's. por Newsweek 69:68+ My 22 '67
Youth for Harper. il por Time 89:56 My 19 '67

MORRIS, Wright
Huck Finn on a motorcycle. G. Hicks. Sat R 50:29-30 F 18 '67

MORRISON, Allan
Negro humor: an answer to anguish. Ebony 22:99-100+ My '67
New surge in the arts. Ebony 22:134-6+ Ag '67

MORRISON, Gordon
How to get the most out of corn. Horticulture 45:34-5+ My '67
Summer in the vegetable garden. Horticulture 45:26+ Ag '67

MORRISON, Karl R.
Inventive approach. Design 68:23 Sum '67

MORRISON, Philip, and Morrison, Phylis
Books (cont) Sci Am 217:140+ D '67

MORRISON, Phylis. See Morrison, Philip, jt. auth.

MORRISON, Ray
Latin American writer's congress: a dialog tries to fill a void. Pub W 191:18-19 My 15 '67

MORRISON, Theodore
Agitated heart; adaptation of address. Atlan 220:72-9 Jl '67

MORROW, Bruce
Cousin Brucie: balm for adolescence. D. R. Maxey. il pors Look 31:M10-12+ Mr 7 '67

MORROW, Susan
Insiders; story. Good H 164:70-3 F; 98-9 Mr '67

MORS, Walter B. and others
Chemoprophylactic agent in schistosomiasis: 14,15-epoxygeranylgeraniol. bibliog Science 157:950-1 Ag 25 '67

MORSBERGER, Robert E.
Days of the Onitsha ferry; with biographical sketch. Natur Hist 76:7, 62-3+ Ap '67

MORSE, Arthur D.
Nazi murder plot; excerpts from While six million died. Look 31:49-52+ N 14 '67
Voyage to doom; excerpts from While six million died. Look 31:59-62+ N 28 '67

MORSE, F. Bradford
Is peace possible? address, March 12, 1967. Vital Speeches 33:452-5 My 15 '67
Private responsibility for public management. bibliog f por Harvard Bsns R 45:6-8+ Mr '67

MORSE, J. Mitchell
HCE'S chaste ecstasy. Yale R 56:397-405 Mr '67

MORSE, Richard S.
Businessman sizes up Russia; interview. por U S News 63:50-4 Ag 14 '67
Fighting auto fumes; the latest prescription. il por U S News 63:64-5 O 30 '67

MORSE, Stearns
Small world of the toy novel. Sat R 50:23+ O 21 '67

MORSE, Thomas M.
Strange islands in space. Sci Digest 62:30-6 Jl '67

MORSE, W. H. and others
Modulation of elicited behavior by a fixed-interval schedule of electric shock presentation. bibliog Science 157:215-17 Jl 14 '67

MORSE, Wayne
Excerpt from address, February 2, 1967. Cong Digest 46:200+ Ag '67
Guns, butter: must we choose? address, August 4, 1967. Vital Speeches 32:714-17 S 15 '67

about
Morse the mediator, strikebreaker or friend of labor? por U S News 63:13 Jl 31 '67
Reign of Wayne. por Time 91:24 Ja 5 '68

MORSE, William B.
Don't call red alder a weed! Am For 73:38-40+ S '67

MORTALITY
Control of mortality. T. E. Smith. bibliog f il Ann Am Acad 369:16-25 Ja '67
Death in America. Sci Am 216:56 F '67
Leukemia mortality: downturn rates in the United States. J. F. Fraumeni, jr. and R. W. Miller. bibliog il Science 155:1126-8 Mr 3 '67

See also
Infant mortality

MORTAR locators. See Detectors

MORTGAGES
Escalator in your home mortgage rate? Consumer Rep 32:126-7 Mr '67
Going looks rough for home builders. U S News 64:10 Ja 8 '68
Home-loan rates & terms, city by city. Changing T 21:14 S '67
How much your mortgage really costs. il Changing T 21:16-17 Je '67
Lending aid to the mortgage market. Bsns W p 108 My 6 '67
Mortgage men draw purse strings tight. il Bsns W p 154+ O 14 '67
Mortgages; facts every home buyer should know. il Good H 164:205 Ap '67
New plan for helping pay off a mortgage. U S News 62:15 My 1 '67
$1-billion plunge to rebuild slums; insurance industry pledge for mortgage loans. Bsns W p46 S 16 '67
Personal business; housing: rates down, prices up. Bsns W p 173 Ap 15 '67
Props for mortgage market? il Bsns W p95-6+ My 27 '67
Slum planners; C. H. Percy-R. F. Kennedy housing plans for the poor. R. B. Semple, jr. New Repub 157:8-10 Jl 22 '67
Systematic mess. il Time 90:74 Jl 7 '67
Where will all the mortgage money come from? Fortune 75:233 My '67

MORTGAGES—*Continued*
　Why not mortgages with variable payments?
　　il Changing T 21:51-3 Jl '67
　Worst is over in housing; Fed and White
　　House push recovery. il Bsns W p27 Ja
　　21 '67
　　See also
　Federal national mortgage association
MORTON, Charles W.
　Accent. See issues of Atlantic

about

Obituary
　Atlan 220:114 N '67
MORTON, Donald C. See Underhill, A. B. jt
　auth.
MORTON, Julia F.
　Mammea; excerpt from The mamey. il Horti-
　　culture 45:32-3 D '67
MORTON, Marcia Colman
　When Vienna eats, it's cake. Holiday 42:74-
　　6+ S '67
MORTON, Miriam
　Department of amplification and correction.
　　New Yorker 43:166+ Ap 8 '67
　Department of amplification; concerning
　　translation of From two to five. K. I.
　　Chukovskii. New Yorker 42:81-2+ Ja 21 '67
MORTON, Thruston B.
　Excerpt from debate, August 4, 1966. Cong
　　Digest 46:15+ Ja '67
　Excerpt from testimony before Subcommittee
　　on constitutional amendments, July 20,
　　1967. Cong Digest 46:275+ N '67

about

Defection of Senator Morton. Nat R 19:1105
　O 17 '67
Morton the realist. Nation 205:354-5 O 16 '67
New leader for constructive opposition? P.
　Lisagor. por Nations Bsns 55:25-6 S '67
Senator speaks his mind. Nation 205:130 Ag
　28 '67
MOSAICS
　Works of art from skulls and eggshells. F.
　　Martin. il Design 68:10-11 Mr '67
MOSBACHER, Emil, 1922-
　Intrepid gentleman. il pors Time 90:64-8 Ag
　　18 '67
　Two Intrepid men. F. Rohr, jr. il por Motor B
　　120:26-7+ Ag '67
MOSCONA, A. A. and Piddington, R.
　Enzyme induction by corticosteroids in em-
　　bryonic cells; steroid structure and induc-
　　tive effect. bibliog Science 158:496-7 O 27
　　'67
　—See Lilien, J. E.; Stuart E. S. jt. auths.
MOSCOSO, Teodoro
　Shangri-la or hamburger heaven? Sat R 51:
　　53-4+ Ja 6 '68
MOSCOW
　　　　　Architecture
New horizons in Moscow. il UNESCO Courier
　20:22-5 N '67
　　　　　City planning
Bourgeois glamour for Moscow skyline; urban
　renewal program. il Bsns W p 142-3 O 28
　'67
New horizons in Moscow. il UNESCO Courier
　20:22-5 N '67
　　　　　Description
Moscow: of people, poets, places. P. de
　Rothschild. Vogue 149:82-5+ Ja 15 '67
　　　　　Streets
Moscow's snowfighting techniques. il Am City
　82:30 Ja '67
MOSCOW, International fashion festival. See
　Fashion shows
MOSCOW circus. See Circus
MOSCOW university. See Colleges and univer-
　sities—Russia
MOSELEY, Robert F. jr
　Great Gulf wilderness. il Liv Wildn 31:3-9
　Spr '67
MOSELLE RIVER
　Following the Moselle. J. Aumente. il Travel
　127:34-6 Je '67
MOSELY, Philip E.
　Kremlin and the third world. For Affairs 46:
　64-77 O '67
MOSER, Don
　Fire on the hanger deck! Read Digest 90:
　100-5 Mr '67
　Outback. Life 63:56-69+ D 22 '67
　Their mission: defend, befriend. Life 63:24-9+
　Ag 25 '67

U.S. paratroopers in a stepped-up war: bat-
　tle jump. Life 62:72-7 Mr 10 '67
Vietcong cadre of terror. Life 64:19-29 Ja 12
　'68
What staggered the old order. Life 62:27-8
　Mr 24 '67
—and others
By any count it was an act of mass courage.
　Life 63:33 S 15 '67
MOSER, Lida
　Fantasy photography, but will it sell? M.
　Orovan. il U S Camera 30:48-9 Ap '67
MOSES, Anna Mary (Robertson)
　Incredible career of Grandma Moses. D.
　Wharton. il por Read Digest 91:145-50+
　S '67
MOSES, Freddie
　How to stump the ducks; ed. by D. D.
　Dickey. Outdoor Life 140:62-5 D '67
MOSES, Lincoln E. and others
　Scaling data on inter-nation action. bibliog
　Science 156:1054-9 My 26 '67
MOSES, Robert, 1888-
　What the big cities must do to stay alive; in-
　terview. por U S News 64:66-8 Ja 8 '68
MOSES, Wally
　Coach me a little bit. il Newsweek 69:88-92
　Ap 10 '67
MOSES and Aaron; opera. See Schönberg, A.
MOSHER, Lawrence
　Nasser's drive for south Arabia. Reporter
　36:24-7 F 9 '67
MOSIER, Donald E.
　Requirement for two cell types for antibody
　formation in vitro. bibliog Science 158:1573-
　5 D 22 '67
MOSKOS, Charles C. jr
　Sociologist appraises the G.I. N Y Times
　Mag p32-3+ S 24 '67
MOSKOWITZ, Saul
　Visual aspects of trans-stellar space flight.
　Sky & Tel 33:290-4 My '67
MOSLEY, Jean Bell
　Are you present? Read Digest 91:131-2 Ag '67
　I wish you a Merry Christmas! Farm J 91:53
　D '67
　Living off the interest. Read Digest 91:118-21
　D '67
　Question of insight. Read Digest 90:55-8 Je
　'67
MOSPORT park Grand prix. See Automobile
　racing
MOSQUITOES
　Mosquitoes: female monogamy induced by
　male accessory gland substance. G. B.
　Craig, jr. bibliog il Science 156:1499-501 Je
　16 '67
　　　　　Extermination
Swatting mosquitoes with sex. Time 89:66 Je
　23 '67
War on insects; use of sterilized male insects
　il Sci N 91:567 Je 17 '67
MOSQUITOES as carriers of infection
　Virus of the California encephalitis complex:
　isolation from culiseta inornata. O. Mor-
　gante and J. A. Shemanchuk. bibliog il Sci-
　ence 157:692-3 Ag 11 '67
MOSS, Howard
　Another life; poem. New Yorker 43:38 Je 10 '67
　Arsenic; poem. New Yorker 43:38 Ap 8 '67
　Beach glass; poem. New Yorker 43:40 Jl 1 '67
　Books. New Yorker 43:185-9 O 7 '67
　Dune wig; poem. New Yorker 43:30 Ag 12 '67
　Maid's story; poem. Nation 204:286 F 27 '67
　Particular beauties; poem. New Yorker 43:
　188 My 13 '67
　Skaters' waltz; poem. New Yorker 42:26
　Ja 21 '67
　Wars; poem. New Yorker 43:60 N 18 '67
MOSS, Laurence I.
　In search of a subsidy machine: or, Why
　the Grand Canyon must be dammed; ex-
　cerpt from address, March 17, 1967. Bul
　Atomic Sci 23:25-30 Je '67
MOSS, M. J.
　Versatile transistor tester. Electr World 78:
　56-8 Ag '67
MOSS, Norman
　McNamara's ABM policy: a failure of com-
　munications. Reporter 36:34-6 F 23 '67
　Narrow confines of British crime reporting.
　Reporter 37:29-31 N 30 '67
MOSS, Sanford A. See McFarland, W. N. jt.
　auth.
MOSS, Stanley
　Fallen angel. New Repub 156:19-20 Je 10 '67
　Love's edge; poem. Nation 204:532 Ap 24 '67
MOSS, Stirling
　Stirling Moss on racing. See issues of Motor
　trend to June 1967

MOSSBAUER effect
Mössbauer analysis of iron in clay minerals. C. E. Weaver and others. bibliog il Science 156:504-8 Ap 28 '67
Test techniques emerge for chemists. Sci N 92:298 S 23 '67

MOSSES
Theft is the first step in growing moss. il Sunset 138:232+ Mr '67
    See also
Lichens

MOSSMAN, James
(ed) See McNamara, R. S. Secretary McNamara comments on risks of anti-ballistic-missile system

MOST special dragon; drama. See Ferguson, D.

MOSTERT, Noel
Africa: new nations and new alignments. Reporter 36:27-31 Je 29 '67
Creative vision of Europort. Reporter 37:22-4+ D 28 '67
Farewell to the great ships. Reporter 37:38-41 Ag 10 '67
Ghosts of Windhoek. Reporter 37:39-42 S 21 '67
Moorish matter. Reporter 37:36-9 N 16 '67
Slavery: the crime the world ignores. Reporter 38:29-31 Ja 11 '68
Vorster's practical approach. Reporter 36:15-19 My 4 '67

MOTELS
Discount house; Motel 6 chain. il Newsweek 70:85-6 O 9 '67
$6 motel; something new in discounting. N. Willatt. il Duns R 89:61-2+ My '67
Trade winds; sophisticated trend. J. Beatty, jr. Sat R 50:12 Ag 19 '67
    See also
Holiday inns of America, incorporated

MOTHER-child relationship. See Parent-child relationship

MOTHER GOOSE
Family friend of all the world; five of Perrault's Tales of Mother Goose. F. B. Adams, jr. il Wilson Lib Bul 41:573-5 F '67
Matriarch of the nursery. D. Thomas. bibliog il Library J 92:1300-2 Mr 15 '67
Mother Goose; with illustrations by C. Addams; excerpts. Sat Eve Post 240:36-41 O 21 '67
See-a-story game; excerpts from I saw a ship a-sailing. B. Montresor. il McCalls 95:62-5 D '67

Anecdotes, facetiae, satire, etc.

Mother Goose report. J. Roche. il Sat Eve Post 240:22 O 7 '67

MOTHERHOOD. See Mothers

MOTHERS
Don't be surprised by after-baby blues. C. Carner. il Todays Health 45:32-5 D '67
Expectant mother. Redbook 128:57+ Ap; 129:33-4 My '67
Fine art of mothering. N. Shainess. il Parents Mag 43:46-7+ Ja '68
Horoscopes for mothers. S. Leek. Ladies Home J 84:12+ My '67
I was free! trapped housewife. N. E. Sephton. il Redbook 129:10+ O '67
My first six months as a mother. R. Gray. il Redbook 129:66-7+ S '67
Nonhormonal basis of maternal behavior in the rat. J. S. Rosenblatt. bibliog il Science 156:1512-14 Je 16 '67
Suburban Midwest; Nancy Daniel, car-pool mother. M. Simons. il Look 31:77-9 My 16 '67
Tribute to mothers. G. J. Hecht. il Parents Mag 42:38 My '67
Why don't we save these mothers and babies? W. Goodman. il Redbook 128:68-9+ Ap '67
Why mothers don't get sick. J. Lubold. il Read Digest 90:51-4 F '67
You used to say you'd marry me. E. Hunter. Redbook 129:59+ Ag '67
Young mothers answer back: you don't have to feel trapped! letters; with editorial comment. Redbook 129:61, 116-18+ Jl '67
Young mother's story. See issues of Redbook
    See also
Daughters
Stepparents

Anecdotes, facetiae, satire, etc.

Every day is mother's day. M. Brophy. See issues of Good housekeeping

Employment
See Married women—Employment

MOTHERS, Unmarried
Maturity for unwed mothers; educational centers. il Time 89:63+ F 10 '67
New help for pregnant teenagers. J. H. Pollack. il Good H 164:84-5+ My '67
Schools and the pregnant teen-ager. S. Strom. il Sat R 50:80-1+ S 16 '67
She won't be back; Webster girls school, public school for pregnant girls. E. Goodman and E. Ferber. il Am Ed 3:6-8 O '67
Should birth control be available to unmarried women? with discussion. F. C. Wood, jr. Good H 164:12+ F '67
Statistic named Mary; Haryou's program for unwed mothers. G. Samuels. il N Y Times Mag p24-5+ Mar 5 '67; Discussion. p 17+ Mr 26 '67
Where unwed mothers stay in school. J. H. Pollack. il Todays Health 45:24-7 S '67
    See also
Illegitimacy

MOTHERS and daughters. See Parent-child relationship

MOTHERS helpers. See Household employees

MOTHER'S warning; story. See O'Connor, F.

MOTHS
Control of spiracles in silk moths by oxygen and carbon dioxide. B. N. Burkett and H. A. Schneiderman. bibliog il Science 156:1604-6 Je 23 '67
Cryptic moths: effects on background selections of painting the circumocular scales. T. D. Sargent. bibliog il Science 159:100-1 Ja 5 '68
Life on the sticky sundew. T. Eisner. il Natur Hist 76:32-5 Je '67
Trans-2-hexenal: mating stimulant for polyphemus moths. L. M. Riddiford. bibliog il Science 158:139-41 O 6 '67
Volatile principle from oak leaves: role in sex life of the polyphemus moth. L. M. Riddiford and C. M. Williams. bibliog il Science 155:589-90 F 3 '67

MOTION
    See also
Perpetual motion

MOTION in art. See Action in art

MOTION picture association of America
Czar of the movie business; J. Valenti. V. Canby. il N Y Times Mag p38-9+ Ap 23 '67

MOTIVATION (education)
Introduction to success; teenage trainees working with preschool youngsters. H. C. Lyon, jr. il Am Ed 3:5-6+ My '67
What turns kids on? Philadelphia cooperative schools curriculum of concerns program. T. Borton. il Sat R 50:72-4+ Ap 15 '67

MOTIVATION (psychology)
Freudianism. R. L. Zimmerman. Commentary 43:75-9 Je '67; Discussion. 44:24+ O '67
Muddle in management motivation. J. B. Weiner. il Duns R 88:28-31+ D '66
Neurons in paradoxical sleep and motivated behavior. W. D. Mink and others. bibliog il Science 158:1335-7 D 8 '67
Riots: the more there are, the less we understand. R. J. Samuelson. Science 157:663-5 Ag 11 '67; Reply. J. Boeke. 158:577 N 3 '67

Want to be a success? reprint. D. C. McClelland. il Sci Digest 61:69-74 Ap '67

MOTLEY, Constance (Baker)
American women: the changers. por Vogue 149:184-5 My '67

MOTOR boat racing
All-American racing team. M. Crook. il Yachting 121:100-2 Ja '67
Bahamas 500. T. Anable, jr. il Motor B 119:42-3 My '67
Demolition derby; Bahamas 500. Time 89:83 My 19 '67
Fearsome 500 for Mona Lou. F. Rohr. il Motor B 119:112-14 Je '67
First 500 is the hardest. M. Crook. il Yachting 122:22-4+ Jl '67
Great impact; how developments in offshore powerboat racing have been passed down to pleasure boating. E. H. Nabb. il Yachting 123:80-2+ Ja '68
Griffith race, serene but surprising. J. O. Crouse. il Motor B 119:96-8 Ap '67
Growth stocks; Outboard world championships at Lake Havasu. il Time 90:42 D 8 '67
Month in yachting. See issues of Yachting
More power to you. M. Crook. See issues of Yachting
Motorboat racing records. il Motor B 121:315-17 Ja '68

MOTOR boat racing—*Continued*
Offshore powerboat racing, 1966. M. Crook. il Yachting 121:46-7+ F '67
Rewarding race in Detroit; hydro racing. K. Chapin. il Sports Illus 27:22-3 Jl 10 '67
Rooster tales. E. Rickman. See issues of Hot rod
Too fast for the three fastest; outboard racers on Lake Havasu. K. Chapin. Sports Illus 27:96-7 D 4 '67
Wet and wild; National drag boat association's fourth annual National championship. E. Rickman. il Hot Rod 20:92-3 D '67
Wild dash to sea; Bahamas 500 powerboat race. B. Ottum. il Sports Illus 26:20-5 My 22 '67
Wynne becomes world offshore champion; Miami-Key West race. M. Crook. il Yachting 121:54+ Ja '67

Safety devices and measures
Ten safety tips for outboard racing. H. Leavitt. il Motor B 120:36-7+ Jl '67

MOTOR boating (periodical)
First electronic navigation contest for the new Motor boating trophy. il Motor B 119:40-3+ Je '67

MOTOR boats
Boating today: wild, wet, wonderful. C. S. Wren. il Look 31:75-81 Je 13 '67
Customizing the open runabout. F. C. Clark, jr. il Yachting 121:92-3+ Ap '67
How to buy a runabout. J. Seville. il Pop Mech 127:153+ F '67
How to buy a ski boat; How to buy a cruiser. P. Callahn; J. Seville. il Pop Mech 127:155-6+ F '67
Inside the inboard. F. M. Paulson. il Field & S 72:106-8 N '67
It's all in the family. L. J. Kennedy. il Motor B 119:46-7+ My '67
Offshore powerboat racing, 1966. M. Crook. il Yachting 121:46-7+ F '67
Offshore raceboat? B. Ruskauff. il Yachting 121:200-1 My '67
Rooster tales. E. Rickman. See issues of Hot rod
Yachting eyes a boat; Chris-Craft's 28' Corinthian. il Yachting 121:35+ F '67
Yachting eyes a boat; Marauder 27-foot express cruiser. il Yachting 122:58 S '67
Yachting eyes a boat: Wahoo 25. il Yachting 122:27 O '67

Design
Designs. W. H. deFontaine. See issues of Yachting
Most wanted fishing, family, and fun boat. J. Roe. il Pop Sci 191:92-4 Ag '67
What makes Bertram go. F. Rohr. il Motor B 119:44-5+ My '67
Yachting eyes a boat. il Yachting 121:51 My '67
Yachting eyes a boat; Chris-Craft's Cavalier Cutlass. il Yachting 122:31 Jl '67
Yachting eyes a boat; Fairliner 360 space sedan. il Yachting 122:35+ Ag '67

Electric equipment
Push-button boating. R. A. Palmer. il Motor B 120:44-5 Ag '67

Equipment
Customizing the open runabout. F. C. Clark, jr. il Yachting 121:92-3+ Ap '67
Pocket yacht. J. Martenhoff. il Yachting 123:104-5+ Ja '68
Two for your outboard; silent trolling motor, and trailing brace. E. Studinka and J. S. Shreve. il Pop Sci 192:120-1 Ja '68
Yachting's boat show. il Yachting 121:123-6+ Ja '67; 123:120-2+ Ja '68

Exhibitions
Boat show calendar. Yachting 123:119+ Ja 68
1968 inboards. il Motor B 121:126-39+ Ja '68
1968 outboards. il Motor B 121:160-7+ Ja '68

Noise
Down with decibels! G. P. Manning. il Motor B 119:34-8 F; 46-9 Mr '67

Stability and stabilizers
Flopperstoppers for seagoing motorboats. R. Beebe. il Motor B 119:42-4+ F '67

Steering gear
Steering and remote control. J. A. Emmett. il Outdoor Life 139:20+ My '67

Testing
Art Mikesell tests Starcraft's Super Sport-V. A. Mikesell. il Pop Mech 128:160-2+ N '67
Chrysler's five-boat fleet, fast and fancy! J. Roe. il Pop Sci 190:104-8+ Je '67
Dateline: Acapulco, PM tests Glastron's new Swinger. A. Mikesell. il Pop Mech 127:158-61+ Mr '67
Sea Craft 19 bow rider, clean and classic. J. Roe. il Pop Sci 190:137-9 F '67
Tolly serves up a sandwich hull. J. Roe. il Pop Sci 191:108-10+ S '67
Two Jim Roes test the Glasspar. J. Roe and J. Roe, jr. il Pop Sci 191:104-6 Jl '67

MOTOR boats, Outboard
First family boat. B. D. Barker, 3d. il Yachting 121:114-15+ Ja '67

Testing
How to be your own boat tester. J. Roe. il Pop Sci 190:122-6 My '67

MOTOR bus lines
Duo-bus brings luxury to freeway commuting; Alameda-Contra Costa, Calif. transit district. K. F. Hensel. il Am City 82:140+ Mr '67
New buses rid city of red ink; Coral Gables, Fla. T. C. Hall. il Am City 82:37 Ap '67
Watts, his line; Negro owned, Blue and White bus co. il Newsweek 71:50-1 Ja 1 '68
Wizard of Paterson; Inter-City transportation co. bankruptcy. Newsweek 70:72 N 6 '67
See also
Greyhound corporation

Stations
Bus-shelter program woos new riders; Detroit. il Am City 82:138 Je '67

MOTOR bus travel
Leave the driving to us; Vietnam. il Newsweek 69:46 F 6 '67
On the go, by bus. I. Desfor. il U S Camera 30:42-3+ My '67
Teen travel talk; chartered trips. il Seventeen 26:42 S '67

MOTOR buses
Mileage meters cut bus costs; Chicago. il Am City 82:134 My '67

Small size
Small buses restore transit; Rome, N.Y. R. D. McCutchen. il Am City 82:66 F '67
Travel trend: minibuses, monorails. il Travel 128:12 S '67

MOTOR buses on rails
Rail/bus evaluation continues. il Aviation W 87:57 Ag 28 '67

MOTOR cycle racing. See Motorcycle racing
MOTOR cycles. See Motorcycles
MOTOR oils. See Lubrication and lubricants
MOTOR scooters
Baggage bike. S. V. Jones. il Sci Digest 62:78 Ag '67
Build yourself a minibike. L. Gilliom. il Pop Mech 127:160-4+ Je '67
Motorscooters and motorbikes. il Consumer Bul 50:9-14 Ag '67
Vr-o-o-m with a view; trail bikes. F. C. McGuire. il Am For 73:42-3+ Ja '67

MOTOR trend (periodical)
Motor trend contest winners. Motor T 19:100+ N '67

MOTOR trend award
Announcing for 1968: the biggest and most important Motor trend awards program in twelve years. il Motor T 19:70-1 D '67
Motor trend car of the year: Cougar. il Motor T 19:30-8 F '67
Motor trend's special awards; features and accessories. il Motor T 19:42-3 F '67

MOTOR trend-Riverside 500. See Automobile racing

MOTOR truck drivers
See also
International brotherhood of teamsters, chauffeurs, warehousemen and helpers of America
Strikes—United States—Truck drivers

MOTOR truck engines
Brute hauler; engine swap for Chevy pickup. il Hot Rod 20:96+ N '67
Simplified swapping; bigger engines in the family pickup. E. Rickman. il Hot Rod 20:96-7 S '67
See also
Diesel engines, Automotive

MOTOR truck robberies. See Robberies and assaults

MOTOR trucking. See Trucking

MOTOR trucks
Elegant pickups; your next family car? il Pop Sci 191:54-7 Ag '67
New trucks for '68. il Farm J 91:20 O '67
What's new. See issues of Successful farming

Care
See Motor trucks—Maintenance and repair

Engines
See Motor truck engines

Maintenance and repair
How to keep 'em rolling when the going gets tough. M. Smith, jr. il Pop Mech 128:106-9+ Jl '67
Twelve sure ways to cut truck and car expenses. P. B. Jones. il Suc Farm 65:40-1 Je '67

Radio equipment
See also
Radio telephone on motor trucks

MOTOR trucks, Municipal
Mercury lighting adds a plus to rescue operations; Dayton and Montgomery County. Ohio. il Am City 82:69 F '67
See also
Refuse collection trucks

MOTOR vehicle drivers
See also
Automobile drivers

MOTOR vehicles
Four wheel flyers. B. Lang. il Hot Rod 20: 42-4 S '67
Horse of a different color; Dearborn Bronco. R. Barlow. il Field & S 72:82-4 Ja '68
Whoosh, zoom, splash; new machines. il Time 90:49 S 15 '67
See also
Motor scooters
Snowmobiles

MOTOR vehicles, Amphibious
Biggest wheel in Vietnam: the BARC. il Pop Mech 129:120-3 Ja '68
Boy, if it could only fly! tactical articulated swimmable carrier. B. Kilpatrick. il Pop Mech 127:118-19 Mr '67

MOTOR vehicles, Military
Biggest wheel in Vietnam: the BARC. il Pop Mech 129:120-3 Ja '68
See also
Tanks, Military

MOTOR vehicles, Municipal
See also
Tractors, Municipal

MOTORBOATS. See Motor boats

MOTORCYCLE accidents. See Traffic accidents

MOTORCYCLE engines
Go-go engines that power motorcycles. E. H. Arctander. il Pop Sci 191:102-7 Ag '67

MOTORCYCLE racing
Bonneville side-kicks. B. Greene. il Hot Rod 20:86-7 N '67
Fun on a winter day; ice race. B. Greene. il Hot Rod 21:116-17 Ja '68
Please don't die now, baby. K. Chapin. il Sports Illus 27:30-1 O 16 '67
Viva! but hide your women; Italy's G. Agostini, world motorcycle racing champion. B. Ottum. il Sports Illus 26:32-4+ My 15 '67

MOTORCYCLE riding. See Motorcycling

MOTORCYCLES
BSA sporting 441's. B. Greene. il Hot Rod 20:90-2 Ag '67
Bombin' bambino; Aermacchi Harley-Davidson. B. Greene. il Hot Rod 20:96-8 Je '67
Hodaka; the Japanese trail bike the Japanese never see. B. Grene. il Hot Rod 20: 86-7 F '67
Hot on the trail; Yamaha's new electric Trailmaster 100. B. Greene. il Hot Rod 20: 94-5 My '67
Kawasaki; Japanese 250 Scrambler. B. Greene. il Hot Rod 21:88-9 Ja '68
Mighty Avenger; Japanese. B. Greene. il Hot Rod 20:84-6 S '67
Motorscooters and motorbikes. il Consumer Bul 50:9-14 Ag '67
Plight of the cyclists; New York city's Metropolitan cycle association counterattacks parking and tow-away program. Newsweek 69:88-9 Mr 27 '67

Up on two wheels. B. Greene. See issues of Hot rod
Wild thing. B. Greene. il Hot Rod 20:64-6 Jl '67
See also
Motor scooters
Motorcycling

Safety devices and measures
Death rides on two wheels. F. Warshofsky. il Read Digest 91:151-2+ O '67
Your youngster and the motorcycle. H. E. Dark. il Todays Health 45:20-4 My '67

Testing
Baja and back, on a Honda! D. Richmond. il Pop Mech 128:118-20+ N '67
PM tests BSA's 250-cc Starfire. D. Richmond. il Pop Mech 128:116-18 D '67

MOTORCYCLING
Map run. B. Greene. il Hot Rod 20:106-7 D '67
News on wheels. D. Chu. Sr Schol 90:32 Mr 31 '67

Study and teaching
Boy scouts enroll in cycle driving course; program in Los Angeles. il Todays Health 45:13 N '67

MOTORISTS. See Automobile drivers

MOTOROLA semiconductor products, incorporated
TV servicing, the modular approach. W. A. Stocklin. Electr World 79:6 Ja '68

MOTORS. See Electric motors

MOTORS, Outboard. See Gas and oil engines, Outboard

MOTOWN record corporation
Heavyweight featherweight; president of Motown records. il Time 90:80 S 8 '67
Motown sound of money. S. H. Brown. il Fortune 76:102-5+ S 1 '67

MOTT, Charles Stewart
Mr Flint. il por Newsweek 69:29-30 My 1 '67

MOTT, Sir Nevill
Solid state; with biographical sketch. Sci Am 217:48, 80-9 S '67

MOTT, William Penn, Jr
Lake that looked impossible. por Parks & Rec 2:14-15+ F '67

MOULDS, George Henry
Color it black or white; address, February 28, 1967. Vital Speeches 33:380-4 Ap 1 '67

MOUNDS, Mima. See Physical geography—Washington (state)

MOUNDS and mound builders
See also
Earthworks (archeology)

MOUNT, Charles Merrill
Sargent in combat. Newsweek 70:88 O 2 '67

MOUNT, D. C. See Lawson, R. B. jt. auth.

MOUNT, Ferdinand
Ban the boom? Nat R 19:850-4 Ag 8 '67
Bug-happy big brother. Nat R 19:1213-14 O 31 '67
Delectations. Nat R 19:636 Je 13 '67
Dodd and mammon. Nat R 19:731-7 Jl 11 '67
Last night in Detroit city. Nat R 19:905-8 Ag 22 '67
Last of the old school. Nat R 19:859-61 Ag 8 '67
Nobody loves the poor prez. Nat R 20:24-7 Ja 16 '68

MOUNT, Rick
Couple of coming-out parties. J. Jares and C. Kirkpatrick. il por Sports Illus 27:30-3 D 11 '67

MOUNT, William Sidney
Down from the attic. il Time 90:40-1+ S 1 '67

MOUNT ARARAT. See Ararat, Mount

MOUNT MCKINLEY. See McKinley, Mount

MOUNT MCKINLEY NATIONAL PARK
Denali interlude. W. Peterson. il Audubon 69:44-55 My '67

MOUNT PALOMAR observatory. See Astronomical observatories

MOUNT PLEASANT, Iowa, public library
Publisher retaliates for book banning; Stein and Day offer free copies of Kazan book. Library J 92:2103 Je 1 '67

MOUNT SINAI hospital. See New York (city) —Hospitals

MOUNT VERNON, N.Y.
Waterproofing a parking garage. P. Brienza. il Am City 82:142-3 S '67

MOUNT VERNON (historic house)
News from Mount Vernon. R. Davidson. il Antiques 92:176+ Ag '67

MOUNT WASHINGTON art glass. See Glass, Ornamental

MOUNTAIN climbing. See Mountaineering

MOUNTAIN goat hunting. See Rocky Mountain goat hunting

MOUNTAIN lion hunting. See Puma hunting

MOUNTAIN lions. See Pumas

MOUNTAIN lodges. See Lodges (architecture)

MOUNTAIN sheep
Big lift for bighorns; water to Santa Catalina Mountains. T. Foust. il Outdoor Life 139:70-3+ Ap '67
Consequence of togetherness. V. Geist. il Natur Hist 76:24-31 O '67
Duel in the Rockies; bighorn rutting activity. J. S. Crawford. il Outdoor Life 140:54-7+ O '67
Home of the desert bighorn; Desert national wildlife range, Nevada. il Am For 73:8 My '67
News for sheep hunters; transplanting bighorns in Nevada. R. V. Broadbent. il Outdoor Life 140:107 D '67

MOUNTAIN sheep hunting
Backpack sheep hunt; ed. by M. Miller. D. Schmiege. il Field & S 71:44-5+ Mr '67
Campfire inside. D. Brown. il Outdoor Life 140:50-3+ D '67
Mountain sheep and the bow; reprint. A. Young. il Field & S 72:44-5+ Ja '68
Ram fever. W. Page. il Field & S 72:34-5+ Ag '67
Scarface. R. V. Broadbent. il Outdoor Life 140:66+ D '67

MOUNTAIN states. See West

MOUNTAIN VIEW college, Dallas
Mountain View college, first of six new campuses near Dallas. il Arch Rec 142:159 N '67

MOUNTAINEERING
Anyone can climb a mountain. S. James. il Pop Mech 127:112-15+ F '67
Challenge of winter; assault on Alaska's Mount McKinley. il Time 89:44 Mr 17 '67
Climb far, climb high. J. Wing. il Seventeen 26:90-1+ Jl '67
First conquest of Antarctica's highest peaks. N. B. Clinch. il Nat Geog Mag 131:836-63 Je '67
Friendship is climbing a Soviet mountain. C. S. Wren. il Look 31:64 O 3 '67
On top of Mount Timp. H. E. McLean. il Am For 73:26-9 N '67
Ordeal above Tesi Lapcha; three U.S. college students in Himalayas. S. R. McCarthy. il Sports Illus 26:68-70+ My 1 '67
Speaking out: I like to risk my life. A. Alvarez. Sat Eve Post 240:10+ S 9 '67
We take to the hills; climbing with young children. C. W. Casewit. il Parents Mag 42:48-9+ Ag '67

Accidents
Death in a far place; climbing Mount Huntington; excerpt from Mountain of my fear. D. S. Roberts. il Sat Eve Post 241:30-4+ Ja 27 '68
Denali strikes back; seven men die in storm on Mount McKinley. il Time 90:19 Ag 11 '67

Study and teaching
Mountain climbing not limited to experts; beginning mountaineering at Alaska Methodist university in Anchorage. R. L. Linder. il Parks & Rec 2:30-1+ Mr '67

MOUNTAINEERS (southern states)
Girl from V.I.S.T.A; experiences of J. Honrath as a worker in the mountains of eastern Kentucky. F. Powledge. il Redbook 129:80-1+ Jl '67

MOUNTCASTLE, Vernon B. and others
Neural basis of the sense of flutter-vibration. bibliog Science 155:597-600 F 3 '67

MOUNTING (taxidermy) See Taxidermy

MOUNTING of automobile engines. See Automobile engines—Mounting

MOUNTING of fishes. See Fishes—Collection and preservation

MOUNTINGS, Telescope. See Telescope mountings

MOUNTZOURES, H. L.
Empire of things; story. New Yorker 43:46-9 S 23 '67
Fathers; story. New Yorker 42:24-6 Ja 21 '67
In transit; story. New Yorker 43:50-2 D 16 '67
Reunion; story. New Yorker 42:42-4 F 11 '67

MOURNING becomes Electra; opera. See Levy, M. D.

MOURNING dove shooting
Launching pad for doves. C. Sawyer. il Outdoor Life 140:50-1+ S '67

MOURNING doves
See also
Cookery—Game

MOUSETRAPS
Man v. mouse in 2500 B.C. Sci Am 216:60 My '67

Anecdotes, facetiae, satire, etc.
Much better mousetrap. M. Mayer. il Harper 234:77-80 F '67

MOUSSE
See also
Desserts

MOUSSORGSKY, Modest Petrovich. See Musorgskii, M. P.

MOUTH organs. See Harmonicas

MOUTH to mouth resuscitation. See Respiration, Artificial

MOUVEMENT Républicain populaire. See Political parties—France

MOVEMENT, Notation of. See Dance notation

MOVES; ballet. See Ballets—Criticisms

MOVIE shorts. See Moving pictures—Short subject films

MOVING
How to move, from here to there. S. Nirenberg. il House B 109:70+ Ag '67
How to transplant your home; moving abroad. M. M. Hemingway. il House & Gard 131:148-9+ Ap '67
I want to go home. P. LaFarge. il Redbook 129:59+ O '67
Moving? how to manage it. il Changing T 21:33-6 Ag '67
Personal business: tax hints for executives on the move. Bsns W p 137-8 Jl 15 '67
Step-by-step guide to easier moving. il Bet Hom & Gard 45:80 Je '67
What it costs to move. il Good H 165:190 S '67
See also
Moving and storage companies

Anecdotes, facetiae, satire, etc.
Rituals of a long farewell. L. Wainwright. Life 63:20 Ag 18 '67

MOVING and storage companies
Another hot summer for movers. il Bsns W p94-6+ Jl 15 '67
How to move, from here to there. S. Nirenberg. il House B 109:70+ Ag '67
Moving? how to manage it. il Changing T 21:33-6 Ag '67

MOVING objects, Photography of. See Photography of moving objects

MOVING of structures, etc.
Long-winded lady; moving of two-hundred-year-old wooden farmhouse from Seventy-first street and York avenue to Charles and Greenwich streets. New Yorker 43:44-6 Mr 18 '67

MOVING picture actors and actresses
Activism, Hollywood style. il Newsweek 70:74 Ag 28 '67
Alan Arkin talks about what it's like to be a star. B. Weinraub. il N Y Times Mag p30-1+ Mr 12 '67
Burtons in Dahomey. L. Rasponi. il Vogue 149:92-3+ Ap 15 '67
Cars of the stars. J. Joseph. il Motor T 19:89-92 Jl '67
Commercially yours; stars and the ads. J. Crist. Ladies Home J 84:70 Mr '67
Have nymphet, will travel; Romina Power, fifteen-year-old daughter of Linda Christian. il Time 89:49-50 My 12 '67
Hot actor for a cool time; M. Caine. C. McCarry. il Sat Eve Post 240:94-7 My 20 '67
Intermission. il Esquire 67:78-9 Mr '67
International movie report; photographs. L. Lerman. Mlle 64:116-19 F '67
Sexy little me. J. Bowers. il Sat Eve Post 240:26-31 My 6 '67
Snob's guide to Hollywood. M. Fessier, jr. il McCalls 94:70-3 Ap '67
Spotlight! E. Miller. See issues of Seventeen
What's happening. G. Shalit. See issues of Ladies' home journal
When they really knew how to laugh; 1920s revisited. C. Ford. il McCalls 95:82-3+ N '67
Where traders upstage the stocks in glamour; E. F. Hutton office in MCA's Universal city. il Bsns W p 160-2 S 9 '67
See also
Children as actors
Make-up, Theatrical
also names of moving picture actors and actresses, e.g. R. Harris

MOVING picture adaptations. See Film adaptations

MOVING picture agents. See Theatrical agencies

MOVING picture animal actors. See Animals in moving pictures

MOVING picture authorship

Anecdotes, facetiae, satire, etc.

How I found James Bond. J. Heller. il Holiday 41:123-5+ Je '67

MOVING picture cameras

Bolex 150. M. Duitz. il Pop Phot 60:117-19 Mr '67

Matzkin on movies; Bolex 16 pro has new ideas that someday you may find on your super 8 camera. M. A. Matzkin. il Mod Phot 31:48 F '67

Movie cameras. il Consumer Rep 32:338-45 D '67

Movie test reports. See issues of Popular photography

Single 8 movie camera. il Consumer Rep 32:338-9 Je '67

Super 8 boom. G. Gilbert. il U S Camera 30:63-7+ S '67

Super 8 for close-ups. M. A. Matzkin. il Mod Phot 31:78+ S '67

Super 8: more sophisticated. H. V. Fondiller. il Pop Phot 60:106-7 Je '67

Super 8 movie cameras: tests of eight models in the less than $100 price range. il Consumer Bul 51:11-14 Ja '68

Third look at a two-year-old; Super-8. R. Miller. il U S Camera 30:68-9+ Ag '67

Loading

See Cameras—Loading

Sound equipment

Sound: and a bit of fury. J. Wesson. U S Camera 31:26 Ja '68

Testing

Barry Brown tests the Scoopic 16, designed to be held. B. Brown. il Pop Phot 61:138-41 N '67

MOVING picture cameras on space vehicles. See Space vehicles—Equipment

MOVING picture cartoons. See Moving pictures—Animated cartoons

MOVING picture censorship

Joyce unconfined. il Newsweek 69:104+ Ap 17 '67

MOVING picture criticisms. See Moving picture plays—Criticisms, plots, etc.

MOVING picture directors

International movie report. L. Lerman. il Mlle 66:62-5 Ja '68

International movie report; photographs. L. Lerman. Mlle 64:116-19 F '67

Movers. A. Sarris. il Sat R 50:10+ D 23 '67

See also

Antonioni, M.
Hitchcock, A.
Lester, R.

Quotations, maxims, etc.

And for best director. . ; comp. by G. Flatley. N Y Times Mag p 174 Mr 19 '67

MOVING picture editing. See Moving pictures—Editing

MOVING picture exchanges. See Moving pictures—International aspects

MOVING picture festivals

Berlin and Cannes. G. D. Phillips. Cath World 206:87-9 N '67

Czech new wave; Czechoslovak film festival at Museum of modern art. il Time 89:97 Je 23 '67

Festival attraction, side-show action; New York film festival. il Time 90:100-1 S 29 '67

Film festival reception; 1967 New York opening-night. New Yorker 43:37 S 30 '67

Films; New York film festival. H. Clurman. Nation 205:348-9, 381-2 O 9-16 '67

Films; New York film festival. W. Sheed. Esquire 69:24+ Ja '68

How useful are film festivals? H. Alpert. Sat R 50:56-8 Jl 8 '67

Independent, avant-garde, underground, anti-establishment, new American cinema. H. V. Fondiller. il Pop Phot 60:68-70+ F '67

Is this the world we live in? New York film festival. J. Morgenstern. il Newsweek 70: 105-6 O 9 '67

Lively arts; Czechoslovak film festival at the Museum of modern art. R. Hemming and W. Johnson. il Sr Schol 91:26 O 12 '67

Lively arts: living history through the movie lens; New York film festival. W. Johnson. il Sr Schol 91:22 N 2 '67

Movie maker's guide to foreign film festivals. G. Hitchens. il Pop Phot 61:130+ D '67

New films: adultery, murder, and a big revolution; fifth New York film festival. R. Kotlowitz. il Harper 235:130-3 D '67

SR goes to the movies; festival at the Museum of modern art. A. Knight. Sat R 50:44 Jl 15 '67

Screen; Ann Arbor film festival. R. Corliss. Commonweal 86:497-8 Ag 11 '67

Screen; Berlin film festival. P. T. Hartung. Commonweal 86:495-7 Ag 11 '67

Screen; New York film festival. P. T. Hartung. Commonweal 87:87-8 O 20 '67

Unfestive flicks at the festival; New York film festival. J. M. Wall. Christian Cent 84:1432+ N 8 '67

Whose truth? New York festival of documentaries. J. Yglesias. Nation 205:410-12 O 23 '67

World soul on film: the fifth New York film festival. B. Colimore. il Cath World 206: 171-5 Ja '68

See also

Cannes international film festival

MOVING picture film collections

See also

Libraries—Moving picture collections

MOVING picture films

Does the serious amateur need 16mm? E. Wildi. il Mod Phot 31:82-3+ O '67

Now! shoot Super 8 in available light! W. Hanson. il Pop Phot 61:116-17 D '67

History

28mm movies? aw c'mon. L. Morris. il Mod Phot 31:16+ Jl '67

MOVING picture industry

See also

Moving picture production and direction

Finance

Box office movie belle makes its third debut; Gone with the wind. il Bsns W p40-1 O 14 '67

Should American films be subsidized? W. Fadiman. Sat R 50:14-17+ Ag 5 '67

Upsurge for the movies. Time 90:51 Jl 28 '67

Czechoslovakia

Chill wind on the new wave. M. Forman. Sat R 50:10-11+ D 23 '67

Europe, Eastern

Film-making behind the iron curtain; symposium. il Sat R 50:8-17+ D 23 '67

Rumania

Young faces, young hearts. M. Gheorghiu. il Sat R 50:16-17 D 23 '67

Russia

Giant Soviet film factory succeeds with a new soft sell; behind the walls of Mosfilm studio; with report by P. Young. il Life 62:64-77+ Ap 7 '67

Soviet Union. A. Knight; R. Roud; G. Kozintsev il Sat R 50:12-15+ D 23 '67

Spain

Spanish films: paradoxes and hopes. R. Schickel. Harper 235:127-9 S '67

United States

Movie making: another U.S. invasion of Europe. il U S News 62:113-14+ Mr 20 '67

New York, the big set; Mayor Lindsay reduces restrictions on film making. il Newsweek 69:86-7 My 29 '67

Shock of freedom in films. il Time 90:66-8+ D 8 '67

Should American films be subsidized? W. Fadiman. Sat R 50:14-17+ Ag 5 '67

See also

American international pictures (firm)
Embassy pictures corporation
Hollywood, Calif.
Metro-Goldwyn-Mayer, incorporated
Motion picture association of America
Paramount pictures corporation

MOVING picture locations. See Moving pictures—Setting and scenery

MOVING picture make-up. See Make-up, Theatrical

MOVING picture music. See Moving pictures—Music

MOVING picture photography

Classy glassy movies. A. W. Ahlers. il Mod Phot 31:76-7+ Jl '67

MOVING picture photography—*Continued*
Endless summer, a fine example of uncomplicated movie-making technique. M. A. Matzkin. il Mod Phot 31:14 Jl '67
How old are the new screen formats? H. V. Fondiller. il Pop Phot 62:124 Ja '68
Into each movie some rain should fall. W. L. Broecker. Pop Phot 60:125+ Je '67
Matzkin on movies. M. A. Matzkin. See issues of Modern photography
Motion pictures of insects. P. Villiard. il Natur Hist 76:50+ Mr '67
Move in close with super 8. N. Rothschild. il Pop Phot 61:112-14+ Ag '67
Movie Q's and A's. J. R. Gregory. See issues of U.S. camera & travel
Movie techniques are worth copying. E. Hannigan. U S Camera 30:28+ S '67
Moving camera. W. L. Broecker. il Pop Phot 61:122-5+ O '67
Remote areas can challenge moviemakers. W. Lane. il Travel 128:63-4 D '67
What's new in experimental films? C. J. Cook. il U S Camera 30:70-1+ Mr '67

Apparatus and supplies

Classy glassy movies. A. W. Ahlers. il Mod Phot 31:76-7+ Jl '67
Movie Q's and A's. J. R. Gregory. See issues of U.S. camera & travel
Movie test reports. See issues of Popular photography

Films

See Moving picture films

Sports

C. B. DeMille of the pros; filming football games. T. C. Brody. il Sports Illus 27:74-6+ N 20 '67

Study and teaching

From touchdown to take-off. A. Blinderman. il U S Camera 30:70-1+ D '67
Shaking the world with an 8-mm. camera. E. Lester. il N Y Times Mag p44-5+ N 26 '67

MOVING picture photography, Submarine
Underwater movies in a tide pool. P. Villiard. il Natur Hist 76:68+ Ag '67

MOVING picture plays
See also
Film adaptations
Television broadcasting—Moving pictures

Criticisms, plots, etc.

Bell ringers. M. Ronan. Sr Schol 90:sup6 Ap 21 '67
Catch up with. L. Lerman. il Mlle 64:86-7 Ap '67
Current cinema. B. Gill. See issues of New Yorker to January 6, 1968
Current cinema. P. Kael. New Yorker 43:90+ Ja 13 '68
Current cinema; A. Warhol's avant-garde **** B. Gill. New Yorker 43:74 Ja 6 '68
Family movie guide; ed. by A. D. Kenney. See issues of Parents' magazine and better homemaking
Films. M. Walsh. See issues of America
Films. R. Hatch. See issues of Nation
Films. W. Sheed. See issues of Esquire
Following the films. M. Ronan. See issues of Senior scholastic
Goings on about town. See issues of New Yorker
In my opinion; H. Bogart and his fans are for the birds. E. Roseman. Seventeen 26: 268 F '67
Independent, avant-garde, underground, anti-establisment, new American cinema. H. V. Fondiller. il Pop Phot 60:68-70+ F '67
Life movie review. R. Schickel. See issues of Life
Motion picture previews. I. McMahan and E. Whitehorn. See issues of PTA magazine
Movie report. C. Garibaldi. See issues of Good housekeeping
Movies. See issues of Consumer reports
Movies. See issues of National review
Movies. See issues of Vogue
Movies. J. M. Wall. Christian Cent 84:1432+ N 8 '67
Movies. L. Lerman. Mlle 64:64-5 Mr '67
Movies. P. Kael. See issues of New republic
Movies in brief. R. Corliss. Nat R 19:917-19 Ag 22 '67
New film vocabulary. A. Knight. Sat R 50:50 F 11 '67
New movies. F. Somers. See issues of Redbook

Professionals: the year's ten best. A. Knight. Sat R 51:94 Ja 13 '68
Ratings of current motion pictures. See issues of Consumer bulletin
Rigors of criticism. il Time 90:38 D 1 '67
SR goes to the movies. H. Alpert; A. Knight. See issues of Saturday review
Screen. P. T. Hartung. See issues of Commonweal
Screen: ten best. P. T. Hartung. Commonweal 87:446 Ja 12 '68
Show business puts its holiday foot forward. J. Barthel. il Good H 165:54+ D '67
Sight and sound. L. Hershey. See issues of McCall's
Spotlight! E. Miller. See issues of Seventeen
Stanley Kauffmann on films. New Repub 157: 20+ D 2; 19+ D 16; 22+ D 23 '67; 158:22+ Ja 13 '68
Ten at the top. il Newsweek 71:61-2 Ja 8 '68
Time listings. See issues of Time
Year and its best. M. Walsh. America 118:18 Ja 6 '68

Single works

Accident
America 116:821-2 Je 3 '67
Christian Cent 84:754-5 Je 7 '67
Commonweal 86:177-8 Ap 28 '67
Esquire 68:20 Jl '67
Harper 234:110-11 Je '67
Life 62:12 Ap 21 '67
Nation 204:638 My 15 '67
New Repub 156:38-41 Je 3 '67
New Yorker 43:150-1 Ap 22 '67
Newsweek il 69:96+ Ap 24 '67
Sat R 50:47 Ap 29 '67
Time il 89:101+ Ap 21 '67
Vogue 149:77 Je '67
Africa addio
America 116:601-2 Ap 22 '67
Newsweek 69:101 Mr 20 '67
Africa-Texas style!
Commonweal 86:424 Je 30 '67
Time il 90:76 Jl 21 '67
Age of illusions
Esquire 68:16 Jl '67
Newsweek 69:100 Ap 10 '67
Alfi
Christian Cent 84:178-9 F 8 '67
Ambushers
America 118:inside back cover Ja 13 '68
Barefoot in the park
Commonweal 86:369 Je 16 '67
Life 62:12 Je 9 '67
New Yorker 43:72 Je 10 '67
Sat R 50:43 Je 3 '67
Time il 89:111+ Je 9 '67
Battle of Algiers
America 117:521 N 4 '67
Commonweal 87:88 O 20 '67
Esquire 69:32 Ja '68
Harper 235:133 D '67
Life 63:16 O 27 '67
Nation 205:348-9 O 9 '67
New Repub 157:19+ D 16 '67
New Yorker 43:93 S 23 '67
Newsweek il 70:102 O 23 '67
Reporter 37:52 N 2 '67
Sat R 50:75 Ap 22 '67
Time il 90:100-1 S 29 '67
Beach red
America 117:186-7 Ag 19 '67
Time 90:63 Ag 18 '67
Bedazzled
Nation 206:28 Ja 1 '68
New Repub 158:30+ Ja 6 '68
Sat R 51:38 Ja 6 '68
Berserk
Time 91:90 Ja 19 '68
Bible
Nat R 19:428-30 Ap 18 '67
Big city
Life 63:8 Ag 18 '67
New Yorker 43:54 Jl 8 '67
Newsweek 70:75-6 Jl 24 '67
Time il 90:78 Ag 25 '67
Billion dollar brain
America 118:48 Ja 13 '68
Newsweek 71:76+ Ja 15 '68
Sat R 51:38 Ja 6 '68
Time il 91:74 Ja 5 '68
Birds, the bees, and the Italians
America 117:424 O 14 '67
New Yorker 43:74-5 Ag 12 '67
Time 90:63 Ag 18 '67
Blow-up
Christian Cent 84:178 F 8 '67
Commentary 43:86-9 Ap '67; Reply. P. Warshow. 44:14-15 Ag '67
Esquire 67:47-8 Ap '67
Life il 62:62B-65 Ja 27 '67
Nat R 19:482-5 My 2 '67
New Repub 156:30+ F 11 '67
Reporter 36:47-8 Je 15 '67

MOVING picture plays—Criticisms, plots, etc.—
Single works—*Continued*
Bobo
 Life 63:12 S 15 '67
 Newsweek 70:107+ S 25 '67
 Time il 90:107 O 13 '67
Les bonnes femmes
 Nat R 19:814+ Jl 25 '67
Bonnie and Clyde
 America 117:227 S 2 '67
 Christian Cent 84:1326 O 18 '67
 Commonweal 87:170-1 N 10 '67
 Esquire 68:32 N '67
 Esquire 68:46 D '67
 Life 63:16 O 13 '67
 Nation 205:444-5 O 30 '67
 New Repub 157:27-9 N 4 '67
 New Yorker 43:77-9 Ag 19 '67
 New Yorker 43:147-8+ O 21 '67
 Reporter 37:46-7 O 5 '67
 Sat R 50:40 Ag 5 '67
 Sr Schol il 91:25 D 7 '67
 Time il 90:78 Ag 25 '67
 Time il 90:67-8+ D 8 '67
 Vogue 150:68 S 15 '67
Born losers
 New Yorker 43:110+ S 9 '67
 Sat R 50:47 Jl 22 '67
Boudu saved from drowning
 New Repub 156:32-3 Ap 15 '67
 Newsweek 69:109-10 Mr 13 '67
Bullwhip Griffin
 Sr Schol 90:29 Mr 31 '67
Burmese harp
 Sr Schol 90:43 My 19 '67
Camelot
 America 117:582-3 N 11 '67
 Christian Cent 85:52-3 Ja 10 '68
 Commonweal 87:207 N 17 '67
 Harper 236:81-2 Ja '68
 Life il 63:70-5 S 22 '67
 Newsweek il 70:90+ N 6 '67
 Sr Schol il 91:21 D 14 '67
 Time il 90:100 N 3 '67
 Vogue 150:175 D '67
Caprice
 Commonweal 86:392 Je 23 '67
 Newsweek 69:73 Je 26 '67
 Sat R 50:43 Je 3 '67
Les carabiniers
 Esquire 69:24 Ja '68
Casino Royale
 America 116:764 My 20 '67
 Commonweal 86:264 My 19 '67
 Esquire 68:30 Ag '67
 Life il 62:108-10 Ap 21 '67
 New Yorker 43:172 My 6 '67
 Newsweek il 69:94 My 15 '67
 Sat R 50:65 My 20 '67
 Time il 89:100 My 12 '67
 U S Camera il 30:61 Ag '67
Chappaqua
 Nation 205:573-4 N 27 '67
 New Yorker 43:195-6 N 11 '67
 Sat R 50:50 F 11 '67
 Sr Schol il 91:37 N 16 '67
 Time il 90:106 N 17 '67
Chelsea girls
 Esquire 67:48+ Ap '67
Chickamauga
 New Yorker 43:94+ Ap 1 '67
China is near
 New Yorker 43:90+ Ja 13 '68
 Newsweek 71:84 Ja 22 '68
 Time 91:59 Ja 12 '68
Chuka
 Life 63:8 S 29 '67
Chushingura
 Christian Cent 84:240+ F 22 '67
Climax
 America 117:424 O 14 '67
 New Yorker 43:187-8 S 16 '67
 Sat R 50:52 O 7 '67
 Time il 90:105+ S 22 '67
Closely watched trains
 America 117:722 D 9 '67
 Harper 236:82-3 Ja '68
 Life 63:12 N 10 '67
 Nation 205:506 N 13 '67
 Newsweek 70:97 N 27 '67
 Sat R 50:44 D 9 '67
 Time il 90:101-2 S 15 '67
Comedians
 America 117:695 D 2 '67
 Commonweal 87:336-7 D 8 '67
 New Repub 157:20+ D 2 '67
 Newsweek 70:123 N 13 '67
 Sat R 50:26 O 28 '67
 Time il 90:103+ N 3 '67
Cool hand Luke
 America 117:694 D 2 '67
 Commonweal 87:305-6 D 1 '67
 Esquire 68:24+ S '67
 Life 63:10 N 3 '67
 New Yorker 43:196-7 N 11 '67
 Newsweek il 70:123 N 13 '67
 Sat R 50:82 N 11 '67
 Sr Schol il 91:17 N 9 '67

Time il 90:102 N 10 '67
Corrupt ones
 America 116:292 F 25 '67
Countess from Hong Kong
 America 116:511-12 Ap 1 '67
 Commonweal 86:128 Ap 14 '67
 Nat R 19:599-600 My 30 '67
 Newsweek 69:89C+ Ap 3 '67
 Sat R 50:41 Ap 1 '67
 Sr Schol 90:30 My 5 '67
 Time 89:95 Mr 31 '67
Crazy quilt
 Cath World il 204:301-6 F '67
 Sr Schol 90:18 F 3 '67
Cul-de-sac
 Esquire 67:18+ Mr '67
Daisies
 Nation 205:508 N 13 '67
 New Yorker 43:56 Jl 1 '67
 Newsweek il 70:106+ N 20 '67
Day the fish came out
 America 117:668 N 25 '67
 Time il 90:109 O 13 '67
 Vogue 150:68 O 15 '67
Deadlier than the male
 Time il 89:99 Mr 10 '67
Deadly affair
 America 116:194 F 4 '67
 Commonweal 85:566 F 17 '67
 Esquire 67:20 Mr '67
 New Yorker 42:98 F 4 '67
 Newsweek il 69:97 F 6 '67
 Sat R 50:49 Ja 28 '67
 Sr Schol 90:28 Mr 10 '67
 Time il 89:80 Ja 27 '67
Deadly bees
 Commonweal 86:323 Je 2 '67
Le depart
 Time 90:100 S 29 '67
Difficult love
 New Yorker 43:54+ Jl 1 '67
Dirty dozen
 America 117:22-3 Jl 1 '67
 Esquire 68:46+ D '67
 Life 63:10 Jl 21 '67
 New Yorker 43:70+ Jl 22 '67
 Newsweek il 70:78 Jl 3 '67
 Sat R 50:47 Je 17 '67
 Time il 89:70 Je 30 '67
Divorce American style
 America 117:119 Jl 29 '67
 Esquire 68:28+ S '67
 Life 62:6 Je 23 '67
 New Yorker 43:73 Jl 22 '67
 Newsweek il 70:83 Ag 14 '67
 Time il 90:76 Jl 21 '67
Doctor Dolittle
 Commonweal 87:472 Ja 19 '68
 Look 31:86-90 D 12 '67
 Newsweek il 71:64 Ja 1 '68
 Time il 90:54 D 29 '67
Don't make waves
 Commonweal 86:393 Je 23 '67
El Dorado
 Life 63:8 Ag 4 '67
 New Repub 157:41 Ag 5 '67
 Sat R 50:44 Jl 15 '67
 Time il 90:80 Jl 28 '67
Drifter
 Commonweal 86:370 Je 16 '67
Dutchman
 Commonweal 86:19 Mr 24 '67
 Esquire 67:44 Je '67
 New Yorker 43:140+ Mr 4 '67
 Vogue 149:95 Ap 1 '67
Echoes of silence
 New Yorker 43:148 Ap 15 '67
Eight on the lam
 Newsweek 69:104 My 8 '67
 Time 89:100 My 12 '67
Elvira Madigan
 Commonweal 87:384-5 D 22 '67
 Harper 235:130-1 D '67
 Nation 205:542 N 20 '67
 New Repub 157:20 D 2 '67
 New Yorker 43:164+ N 4 '67
 Newsweek 70:108+ N 20 '67
 Sat R 50:57 N 18 '67
Enter laughing
 America 117:254-5 S 9 '67
 Christian Cent 84:1401 N 1 '67
 New Yorker 43:64+ Ag 5 '67
 Newsweek 70:75-6 Ag 7 '67
 Time 90:63 Ag 18 '67
 Vogue 150:42 Ag 1 '67
Eric Soya's '17'
 Commonweal 85:461 Ja 27 '67
Exterminating angel
 Christian Cent 84:1468+ N 15 '67
 Commonweal 86:588 S 22 '67
 Life 63:14 O 6 '67
 New Yorker 43:78-9 Ag 26 '67
 Newsweek il 70:72+ S 4 '67
 Time 90:99-100 S 8 '67

MOVING picture plays—Criticisms, plots, etc.—
  Single works—*Continued*
  Privilege
    America 117:160 Ag 12 '67
    Christian Cent 84:1164 S 13 '67
    Life 63:10 Ag 25 '67
    New Yorker 43:70+ Jl 29 '67
    Newsweek 70:75 Ag 7 '67
    Sat R 50:38 Jl 29 '67
    Sr Schol 91:34 S 21 '67
    Time il 90:72 Ag 11 '67
  Quiller memorandum
    America 116:194 F 4 '67
    Commonweal 85:489 F 3 '67
    Life 62:15 Ja 27 '67
  Rear window
    Nat R 19:482-5 My 2 '67
  Reflections in a golden eye
    New Yorker 43:137-8 O 21 '67
    New Yorker 43:165 O 28 '67
    Newsweek il 70:94 O 30 '67
    Sat R 50:26 O 28 '67
    Time il 90:102+ O 27 '67
  Rise of Louis XIV
    Harper 235:131-2 D '67
  Robbery
    Sr Schol 91:28 N 2 '67
  Romeo and Juliet
    Look 31:52-5+ O 17 '67
  Sailor from Gibraltar
    Commonweal 86:237 My 12 '67
    New Yorker 43:178+ My 13 '67
    Newsweek 69:96 My 15 '67
    Sat R 50:45 My 6 '67
  St Valentine's day massacre
    America 117:283-4 S 16 '67
    Newsweek 70:76 Ag 7 '67
    Sat R 50:40 Ag 5 '67
    Sr Schol 91:46 S 28 '67
    Time 90:73 Ag 4 '67
  Sand pebbles
    Christian Cent 84:313 Mr 8 '67
    Sr Schol 90:24 F 10 '67
  She and he
    Newsweek 69:87 My 1 '67
  Shoot loud, louder, I don't understand
    Reporter 37:39-40+ O 19 '67
  Smashing time
    America 118:48 Ja 13 '68
    Time il 91:74 Ja 5 '68
  Spy with the cold nose
    Commonweal 85:489 F 3 '67
    Sr Schol 90:28 Mr 10 '67
  Star!
    Look il 31:63-8 S 19 '67
  Stranger
    New Repub 158:22 Ja 13 '68
    New Yorker 43:48 D 30 '67
    Newsweek 71:64 Ja 1 '68
    Sat R 51:38 Ja 6 '68
    Time il 90:54-5 D 29 '67
  Sucker
    America 117:451 O 21 '67
  Sweet love, bitter
    New Yorker 42:135 F 11 '67
  Taming of the shrew
    America 116:480+ Mr 25 '67
    Christian Cent 84:597 My 3 '67
    Commonweal 86:19 Mr 24 '67
    Esquire 67:42+ Je '67
    Mlle 65:97 My '67
    Newsweek 69:98 Mr 20 '67
    Sat R 50:40 Mr 18 '67
    Sr Schol 90:27-8 Ap 28 '67
    Time il 89:104+ Mr 17 '67
    Vogue 149:49 Ap 15 '67
  Tender scoundrel
    New Yorker 43:154 D 2 '67
  Thief of Paris
    Life 63:19 S 22 '67
    New Yorker 43:74-6 S 2 '67
    Newsweek 70:83 Ag 28 '67
    Time il 90:65 S 1 '67
    Vogue 150:226 S 1 '67
  This special friendship
    America 117:722-3 D 9 '67
    Commonweal 87:384 D 22 '67
    Time il 90:90 N 24 '67
  Thoroughly modern Millie
    America 116:512-13 Ap 1 '67
    Commonweal 86:127 Ap 14 '67
    Life 62:17 Ap 28 '67
    New Yorker 43:94 Ap 1 '67
    Newsweek il 69:96 Ap 10 '67
    Sat R 50:45 Ap 15 '67
    Sr Schol 90:34 My 12 '67
    Time il 89:95+ Ap 7 '67
  Tiger makes out
    America 117:450 O 21 '67
    Commonweal 87:55 O 13 '67
    New Yorker 43:93+ S 23 '67
    Reporter 37:39-40 O 19 '67
    Sat R 50:36 S 30 '67
    Vogue 150:142 O 1 '67

  Time lost and time remembered. See I was
    happy, above
  To be a crook
    America 116:226 F 11 '67
    Commonweal 85:657 Mr 10 '67
    New Yorker 42:134 F 11 '67
    Newsweek il 69:97 F 6 '67
    Time 89:76 F 3 '67
  To sir, with love
    America 116:880 Je 24 '67
    Christian Cent 84:1198-9 S 20 '67
    Ebony il 22:68-70+ Ap '67
    New Yorker 43:92 Je 17 '67
    Newsweek 69:73 Je 26 '67
    Sat R 50:39 Jl 8 '67
    Sr Schol 90:30 My 5 '67
    Sr Schol il 90:sup6 Ap 7 '67
    Time il 89:70+ Je 30 '67
  Tobruk
    New Yorker 42:143 F 18 '67
  Tonio Kröger
    Time il 91:90 Ja 19 '68
  Tony Rome
    Newsweek 70:109 D 4 '67
    Sat R 50:64 N 25 '67
    Time il 90:90 N 24 '67
  Trip
    New Yorker 43:109-10 S 9 '67
    Newsweek il 70:100 S 11 '67
    Sat R 50:39 S 2 '67
  Triple cross
    Commonweal 86:392 Je 23 '67
    Newsweek 69:90+ Je 12 '67
    Time il 90:80 Jl 28 '67
  25th hour
    America 116:356-7 Mr 11 '67
    Commonweal 85:625-6 Mr 3 '67
  Two for the road
    America 116:794 My 27 '67
    Christian Cent 84:945 Jl 19 '67
    Commonweal 86:236-7 My 12 '67
    Life 62:16 My 12 '67
    New Repub 156:29-30+ My 27 '67
    Newsweek il 69:96+ My 15 '67
    Sat R 50:45 My 6 '67
  2001: a space Odyssey
    Pop Mech 127:106-9+ Ap '67
  Two weeks in September
    Sat R 50:53 D 2 '67
  Ulysses
    America 116:539-40 Ap 8 '67
    Cath World 204:346-51 Mr '67
    Commonweal 86:95 Ap 7 '67
    Esquire 68:16 Jl '67
    Harper 234:112 Je '67
    Life il 62:54-6 Mr 31 '67
    Nation 204:414 Mr 27 '67
    New Repub 156:31-4 My 6 '67
    New Yorker 43:93-4 Ap 1 '67
    Newsweek 69:102B Mr 27 '67
    Reporter 36:37-8 My 4 '67
    Sat R 50:41 Ap 1 '67
    Time il 89:92+ Mr 31 '67
    Vogue 149:143 My '67
  Up the down staircase
    America 117:254 S 9 '67
    Life 63:11 Jl 7 '67
    Look il 31:M10+ Je 27 '67
    New Yorker 43:76 Ag 26 '67
    Newsweek 70:73 Jl 31 '67
    Sat R 50:35 Jl 1 '67
    Sr Schol 90:27 Ap 28 '67
    Sr Schol 91:sup 16-17 O 5 '67
    Time il 90:63 Ag 18 '67
  Valley of the dolls
    Time il 90:78 D 22 '67
  Venetian affair
    Sat R 50:49 Ja 28 '67
  La vie de chateau
    Life 62:14 Je 2 '67
    New Yorker 43:152 Mr 25 '67
  Wait until dark
    America 117:723 D 9 '67
    Newsweek 70:93-4 N 6 '67
    Sr Schol 91:21 O 19 '67
  Wandering
    New Yorker 43:57 Jl 1 '67
  War game
    America 116:703 My 6 '67
    Esquire 68:14 Jl '67
    Esquire 68:52+ N '67
    Life 62:20 Ap 7 '67
    New Repub 156:32-4 My 13 '67
    New Yorker 43:94+ Ap 1 '67
    Newsweek 69:89A Ap 3 '67
  War Italian style
    Newsweek 69:109 Mr 13 '67
  War wagon
    Commonweal 86:424 Je 30 '67
    Life 63:8 Ag 4 '67
    New Repub 157:40-1 Ag 5 '67
    Sat R 50:44 Jl 15 '67
    Time il 89:95 Je 16 '67

MOVING picture theaters

Employees

Earnings in motion picture theater industry. April 1966. C. M. O'Connor. bibliog f il Mo Labor R 90:48-51 Ap '67

MOVING pictures

Art-movie style. R. Garis. Commentary 44: 77-9 Ag '67

Art of light & lunacy: the new underground films. il Time 89:94+ F 17 '67

Counterrevolution in the movies. W. F. Lynch. Commonweal 87:77-9+ O 20 '67

Film notes. H. V. Fondiller. See issues of Popular photography

New cinema: short films, not merely short subjects. il Sr Schol 90:26 Ap 14 '67

Rights and permissions; predictions in 1924 by D. W. Griffith. P. Nathan. Pub W 192: 71 N 13 '67

Up from underground. J. Kroll. il Newsweek 69:117-19 F 13 '67

See also

Academy awards (moving pictures)

Animals in moving pictures

Montreal—Worlds fair, 1967—Moving pictures

Moving picture censorship

Moving picture photography

Moving picture production and direction

Realism in moving pictures

Television broadcasting—Moving pictures

Animated cartoons

Film animation at the Yellow ball workshop. Y. Andersen. il Design 69:7-11 Fall '67

See also

Disney, Walt, productions

Criticisms, plots, etc.

Jungle book
   Life 64:11 Ja 5 '68
   Newsweek il 70:102+ D 11 '67
   Sr Schol 91:17 N 9 '67
   Time il 91:90 Ja 19 '68

Audience rating

What women think of the movies; responses to movie questionnaire. L. Hershey. il McCalls 94:28+ My '67

Bibliography

Word people on film people. R. Sklar. Reporter 37:52+ D 14 '67

Censorship

See Moving picture censorship

Children, Effect on

See Moving pictures and children

Classification

Sick movies, a menace to children. M. C. Smith. Read Digest 91:139-42 D '67

Comedy

Films of Laurel and Hardy, by W. K. Everson. Review
   Nat R il 19:1277-8 N 14 '67. H. Kenner

L. & H. cult; Laurel and Hardy fan club. il Time 90:74 Jl 14 '67

Costume

See Costume, Theatrical

Crime films

Bloody murder. J. Jacobs. Reporter 37:46-7 O 5 '67

Onward and upward with the arts; the case of B. Parker and C. Barrow. P. Kael. New Yorker 43:147-8+ O 21 '67

Dancing

Dancer-Choreographer-show doctor now film director Herb Ross talks shop. L. Joel. il pors Dance Mag 41:42-9+ D '67

Film dance and things to come. G. Compton. il Dance Mag 42:34-7 Ja '68

Distribution

Academy looks abroad; difficulties encountered by non-winning award foreign language films. A. Knight. Sat R 50:75 Ap 22 '67

And selected short subjects; distributors addresses. A. Knight. Sat R 50:73 My 13 '67

Joyce unconfined; distribution of Ulysses. il Newsweek 69:104+ Ap 17 '67

Documentary films

Drugs and tobacco. V. Falconer. il Sr Schol 91:sup 15-16 N 16 '67

Films and filmstrips for sex education. V. M. Falconer. Sr Schol 90:sup25 Ap 28 '67

From touchdown to take-off. A. Blinderman. il U S Camera 30:70-1+ D '67

Lively arts: living history through the movie lens; New York film festival. W. Johnson. il Sr Schol 91:22 N 2 '67

Marshaling McLuhanism; exhibits at Expo 67. A. Knight. il Sat R 50:41-2+ Ag 12 '67

Movies. J. M. Wall. Christian Cent 84:1432+ N 8 '67

Roundup of films and filmstrips on Canada. V. M. Falconer. il Sr Schol 90:sup20-1 F 10 '67

Screenings; 8mm. A. Cohen. Library J 92: 3833-5, 4595-6 O 15, D 15 '67

Whose truth? New York festival of documentaries. J. Yglesias. Nation 205:410-12 O 23 '67

Criticisms, plots, etc.

Anderson platoon
   Nation 206:94 Ja 15 '68
Black Natchez
   New Repub 156:31-4 F 18 '67
Don't look back
   Christian Cent 84:1287-8 O 11 '67
   Life 63:10 Ag 11 '67
   New Yorker 43:116 S 9 '67
   Newsweek il 70:65 Ag 21 '67
   Sat R 50:44 S 9 '67
   Time 90:72 Ag 11 '67
Goal
   New Yorker 42:77 Ja 28 '67
   Sr Schol 90:22 Mr 3 '67
Inside North Vietnam
   Nation 205:701 D 25 '67
   Newsweek 71:63 Ja 1 '68
King's story
   Commonweal 86:291-2 My 26 '67
   New Yorker 43:72+ Je 10 '67
   Newsweek 69:96 Je 5 '67
   Sat R 50:83 Je 10 '67
Lay my burden down
   Time 90:101 S 29 '67
Lenny Bruce
   Esquire 68:14+ Jl '67
Like a beautiful child
   Nation 205:349-50 O 9 '67
Not much to do
   U S Camera 30:70-1 Ag '67
Portrait of Jason
   New Yorker 43:159 O 14 '67
   Sat R 50:44 S 9 '67
Rush to judgment
   Commonweal 86:149-51 Ap 21 '67
   New Yorker 43:95 Je 17 '67
Sons and daughters
   Christian Cent 84:1226 S 27 '67
Strike city
   New Repub 157:41-2+ N 11 '67
Titicut follies
   America 117:539 N 11 '67
   Life 63:12 D 1 '67
   Nation 205:446 O 30 '67
   New Repub 158:18+ Ja 20 '68
   New Yorker 43:166-7 O 28 '67
   Newsweek 70:100+ O 23 '67
   Sat R 50:44 S 9 '67
   Time il 90:101 S 29 '67
Vali
   New Yorker 43:94 Je 17 '67
Warrendale
   Time 90:101 S 29 '67
Wholly communion
   New Yorker 43:92+ Je 17 '67
Year toward tomorrow
   Sat R 50:50 Ap 8 '67

Editing

Matzkin on movies: new Eumig splicing technique. M. A. Matzkin. il Mod Phot 31:28+ My '67

Three missing minutes. A. Knight. Sat R 50: 48+ Ap 8 '67

Educational aspects

See Moving pictures in education

Educational films

See Moving pictures in education

Foreign language films

Academy looks abroad: best foreign language picture. A. Knight. Sat R 50:75 Ap 22 '67

Potpourri. P. T. Hartung. Commonweal 86: 610-11 S 29 '67

Historical films

Lively arts: living history through the movie lens; New York film festival. W. Johnson. il Sr Schol 91:22 N 2 '67

MOVING pictures—*Continued*

History
Days of movie magic. M. Holmes. il Todays Health 45:38-41 O '67

Horror films
Illustrated history of the horror film, by C. Clarens. Review
  Newsweek il 69:95-6 Je 19 '67. P. D. Zimmerman

International aspects
Film-making behind the iron curtain; symposium. il Sat R 50:8-17+ D 23 '67

Marketing
Where film buyers meet sellers. W. A. Berns. Sat R 50:45 D 23 '67

Medical films
See Moving pictures in medicine

Moral aspects
Case of Crowther. H. Alpert. Sat R 50:111 S 23 '67
How old is mature? J. Crist. il Ladies Home J 84:89 My '67
Movies: where anything goes. J. Crist. il Look 32:22-5 Ja 9 '68
Nude morality; or, But, fellows, we don't live in Eden any more! V. Eller. Christian Cent 84:689-91 My 24 '67; Reply with rejoinder. F. B. Stipp. 84:919 Jl 12 '67
Sick movies, a menace to children. M. C. Smith. Read Digest 91:139-42 D '67
Thin red line; violent movies. J. Morgenstern. il Newsweek 70:82-3 Ag 28 '67
Tom, Tom, the peeper's son. P. T. Hartung. Commonweal 85:460-2 Ja 27 '67
  See also
Moving picture censorship
National Catholic office for motion pictures

Music
Lights, camera, music! il Newsweek 70:77-8 Jl 24 '67
New sound on the soundtracks. G. Lees. il Hi Fi 17:58-61 Ag '67
  See also
Phonograph records—Moving picture music

Musical films
Lively arts; Hollywood musicals of 1930's and 1940's. P. Hudson and R. Hemming. il Sr Schol 91:42-3 S 28 '67

News films
See Newsreels

Periodicals
Literature of film. A. Knight. Sat R 50:51+ N 4 '67
Rise and fall and rise of Elizabeth Taylor. L. Israel. il Esquire 67:96-9+ Mr '67

Propaganda films
On the way to 1984; analysis of film Why Vietnam, and arguments against carrying war propaganda into the classroom. H. S. Commager. il Sat R 50:68-9+ Ap 15 '67; Discussion. 50:72 My 20 '67

Psychological aspects
Mixed media, communication that puzzzles, excites and involves; films at Expo 67. F. Kappler. Life 63:28C Jl 14 '67

Setting and scenery
Green shills of Africa; filming of Comedians. il Time 89:55 F 3 '67
Hollywood in Budapest H. Alpert. il Sat R 50:20-1+ D 23 '67
Long-winded lady; movie-making in Algonquin hotel, starring J. Andrews. New Yorker 43: 21-3 Je 17 '67
Many lives of James Bond. il Esquire 67:73-85 Mr '67
Movie making: another U.S. invasion of Europe. il U S News 62:113-14+ Mr 20 '67
Never on Tuesday; filming of She let him continue. R. Lynes. il Harper 236:13-16 Ja '68
New York, the big set; Mayor Lindsay reduces restrictions on film-making. il Newsweek 69:86-7 My 29 '67
Nightmare lived again; filming Truman Capote's In cold blood at murder site; with report by J. Howard. il Life 62:98-101+ My 12 '67
On location in Rostov; filming the new revolution. D. Smith. il Nation 204:268-72 F 27 '67

Truman Capote reports on the filming of In cold blood. T. Capote. il Sat Eve Post 241: 62-5 Ja 13 '68
2001: backstage magic for a trip to Saturn. R. F. Dempewolff. il Pop Mech 127:106-9+ Ap '67
Two unknowns seek movie fame as killers; In cold blood. S. Gordon. il Look 31:114+ Je 13 '67

Short subject films
And selected short subjects. A. Knight. Sat R 50:73 My 13 '67
Films; two evenings of New cinema at Lincoln Center. R. Hatch. Nation 204:157-8 Ja 30 '67

Social aspects
Hollywood Negro; changing image. M. Boyd. Christian Cent 84:1560-1 D 6 '67
Insiders' Watts; Mafundi institute's movie project. il Newsweek 69:84+ My 1 '67

Sound effects
Anecdotes, facetiae, satire, etc.
That old regenerative set of mine. F. E. Ebel. il Pop Electr 28:50-1 Ja '68

Sports films
Filet and football; film presentations of professional football at restaurants. Newsweek 70:62 N 6 '67

Study and teaching
Film club; films made by teenagers on the streets of ghetto neighborhoods. New Yorker 43:19-21 Ja 13 '68
Teaching about the screen arts; place in the school art program. G. S. Wright, jr. il Sch Arts 66:41-3 My '67

Themes
Cinema of the absurd. D. J. Leary. il Cath World 204:301-6 F '67
Don't watch this part, honey, I'll tell you when it's over; violence in movies. il Esquire 68:60-3 Jl '67
Films; violent movies. W. Sheed. Esquire 68:44+ D '67
Happy movies are here again! il Good H 164: 102-5 Ap '67
Thin red line; violent movies. J. Morgenstern. il Newsweek 70:82-3 Ag 28 '67
World soul on film: the fifth New York film festival. B. Colimore. il Cath World 206:171-5 Ja '68

Travel films
New films: focus on Africa. V. M. Falconer. il Sr Schol 91:sup 18-19 O 5 '67

War films
Air; treatment of World war II in movies and on TV. M. J. Arlen. New Yorker 42:75-6+ Ja 21 '67
Battle of Popcorn Bay. L. L. King. il Harper 234:50-4 My '67
John Wayne's Green Beret. Nation 205:614 D 11 '67
Kill Cong; no films on Vietnamese war from Hollywood. Nation 204:453 Ap 10 '67

Westerns
Hi-ho, *denaro!* westerns filmed in Spain by an Italian company. il Time 90:56-7 Ag 4 '67
Saddle sore. P. Kael. New Repub 157:38-41 Ag 5 '67

Canada
See also
Canada—National film board

Czechoslovakia
Current cinema; Czech films at Museum of modern art. P. Gilliatt. New Yorker 43:54 Jl 1 '67
Czech new wave. il Time 89:97 Je 23 '67
Czech sex. H. Alpert. Sat R 50:44 D 9 '67
Here comes a Czech film classic: Closely watched trains. R. Schickel. Life 63:12 N 10 '67
Lively arts. R. Hemming and W. Johnson. il Sr Schol 91:26 O 12 '67
SR goes to the movies; festival at the Museum of modern art. A. Knight. Sat R 50:44 Jl 15 '67
  See also
Moving picture industry—Czechoslovakia
Moving picture industry—Europe, Eastern

Europe, Eastern
See also
Moving picture industry—Europe, Eastern

MOVING pictures—*Continued*

France

Letter from Paris; showing of Jeu de Massacre, Mouchette, and J'ai Tué Raspoutine at Cannes. Genêt. New Yorker 43:127-9 My 27 '67

Great Britain

Bundles from Britain. S. Eimerl. il Reporter 36:40-4 Ap 6 '67
Where it's happening. H. Alpert. Sat R 50:47 Ap 29 '67

India

India's ancient heroes on celluloid. B. D. Garga. il UNESCO Courier 20:43+ D '67
Maestro; current projects and future plans of S. Ray. New Yorker 43:25-7 Jl 22 '67

Rumania

See also
Moving picture industry—Rumania

Russia

From Russia, with love; prize-winning film by Soviet amateur shows universality of Mother's day. H. V. Fondiller. il Pop Phot 61:70-1 Jl '67

See also
Moving picture industry—Russia

United States

See also
American film institute
Disney, Walt, productions
Moving picture industry—United States

MOVING pictures, Amateur
How to make good movies. R. Pinney. il Parents Mag 42:36+ O '67
Matzkin on movies. M. A. Matzkin. Mod Phot 31:82 S '67
New techniques and equipment for home moviemaking. E. Kinard. il House B 109:158-9+ Je '67
Pro movie effects; easy does it. A. W. Ahlers. il Mod Phot 31:86-7+ Ap '67
Teaching about the screen arts; place in the school art program. G. S. Wright. jr. il Sch Arts 66:41-3 My '67
Teenage stuntmen; film production group of Leominster, Mass. G. Gilbert. il U S Camera 30:24+ Mr '67

See also
Moving picture photography

Editing

I edited and indexed thirty years of home movies. R. J. Jandoli. il U S Camera 30:70-1+ Ap '67
Matzkin on movies; movie editor. M. A. Matzkin. Mod Phot 31:14+ Ap '67
Movie editors. il Consumer Rep 32:420-3 Ag '67

Lighting

Matzkin on movies. M. A. Matzkin. il Mod Phot 31:48-9 Ag '67

Sound effects

Sound. J. Wesson. See issues of U.S. camera & travel
Sound for photographers. T. Schwartz. See issues of Popular photography

Sound recording

Coming; home sound movies for everyone. P. Wahl. il Pop Mech 128:74-5 Jl '67
Talking home movies; beam of light writes sound on the film. il Sci Digest 61:24-5 Mr '67

Themes

Asphalt documentary; film made by six Philadelphia boys. G. Gilbert. il U S Camera 30:70-1 Ag '67
Christmas movies can be good. Am Home 70:95 D '67
Eleventh birthday party is a once-in-a-lifetime movie happening. D. Langer. il Pop Phot 61:112-13+ S '67
From Russia, with love; prize-winning film by Soviet amateur shows universality of Mother's day. H. V. Fondiller. il Pop Phot 61:70-1 Jl '67
Make better Christmas movies. J. R. Oswald. il U S Camera 30:62-3+ D '67
Skyrockets, sparklers, and starbursts. N. Rothschild. il Pop Phot 61:94-5+ Jl '67

Titles

Home movies deserve better titles. J. R. Oswald. il U S Camera 30:72-3 Ag '67
Matzkin on movies. M. A. Matzkin. il Mod Phot 31:66 N '67

MOVING pictures, Children. See Moving pictures for children
MOVING pictures, Musical. See Moving pictures—Musical films
MOVING pictures, Realism in. See Realism in moving pictures
MOVING pictures and children
Sick movies, a menace to children. M. C. Smith. Read Digest 91:139-42 D '67
MOVING pictures and morals. See Moving pictures—Moral aspects
MOVING pictures and reading
Meaningful fare for terminal students; program built around paperback books and films; Greenwich, Conn. H. R. Finch. Sr Schol 91:sup 10-11 N 30 '67
MOVING pictures and television
Air; new developments. M. J. Arlen. New Yorker 42:138-40 F 18 '67
MOVING pictures for children
Family movie guide; ed. by A. D. Kenney. See issues of Parents' magazine and better homemaking
What the kids should see. J. Morgenstern. il Newsweek 70:92+ S 18 '67
MOVING pictures in astronomy. See Astronomical photography
MOVING pictures in aviation
FAA and the nouvelle vague. R. Burkhardt. Flying 80:31 Je '67
MOVING pictures in education
Challenge of the rival educators; educational films vs mass media; with list of films. A. Cohen. il Library J 92:853-5 F 15 '67
Curtain of illusion; the odyssey of the Children's caravan; OEO grant, with list of films and filmstrips. J. Poignand and P. Mann. il Library J 92:860-3 F 15 '67
50,000 films for sale; government educational films. J. Morgenstern. il Newsweek 69:88-88A Mr 6 '67
Film happening at Fordham university. J. Foster. Sr Schol 91:sup 11 S 21 '67
Film; the place in the school art program. G. S. Wright. jr. il Sch Arts 66:31-5 Ja '67
Films and filmstrips for PTA committee chairmen. F T. Mathewson. PTA Mag 61:30-2 My; 30-1 Je; 62:37 S '67
How to make single-concept films. H. S. Fisk. Sr Schol 91:sup 12-13 O 12 '67
Lansing, Michigan's 8mm film workshop. L. Steen. il Sr Schol 91:sup8-9 O 26 '67
Mr Pierson's brainstorm; film appreciation at Brookline high, near Boston. S. Kinzer. il Pop Phot 61:132+ D '67
Star billing; university-at-large. Newsweek 70:68 N 27 '67
Teaching art through film making. G. S. Wright, jr. il Sch Arts 66:36-9 Je '67
Tune in the kids with records and films; John Reed middle school, West Redding, Conn. S. Jacoby and R. Lavigne. il Sr Schol 91:sup9 D 7 '67

See also
Moving pictures—Study and teaching
Moving pictures in health education
MOVING pictures in health education
Films of interest (cont) Todays Health 45:85 Mr; 60 Jl '67
MOVING pictures in medicine
Films of interest (cont) Todays Health 45:85 Mr; 60 Jl '67
MOVSHON, George
All-star Faust; Sutherland, Corelli, Ghiaurov. Hi Fi 17:70+ Mr '67
How the gods were caught. Hi Fi 17:18+ D '67
How to improve your off-the-air recordings. Hi Fi 17:72-4 N '67
Met outdoors (and in) Hi Fi 17:MA12-13+ N '67
New Met at mid-point. Hi Fi 17:MA12-13 Mr '67
Puccini's La rondine, the charm of delicate felicities. Hi Fi 17:127-8 O '67
Swedes at Expo. Hi Fi 17:MA22-3+ Ag '67
To mark Canada's centenary, great singers of her past. Hi Fi 17:63 Jl '67
Vienna opera at Expo. Hi Fi 17:MA20-1+ N '67

(ed) See Scovotti, J. And we quote
(ed) See Shirley, G. And we quote
MOW, Joseph B.
Jean-Paul Sartre; Christian theist? Christian Cent 83:1437-9; 84-146+ N 23 '66, F 1 '67
MOWBRAY, A. Q.
Free press & fancy packages. Nation 205:621-3 D 11 '67
MOWRER, Edgar Ansel
Power of arrogance. Nat R 19:367-8 Ap 4 '67

MOWING machines
See also
Lawn mowers
MOXIE company
It's the old Moxie; plans to update the drink and revive the industry. il Bsns W p42 My 20 '67
MOYER, Donald
Devil's relic; Coronation and the funeral; Basin; poems. Poetry 110:93 My '67
MOYERS, Bill D.
American editor's odyssey. Sat R 50:30-1+ N 11 '67
about
Heir for the captain. il por Time 89:43 F 24 '67
Newsday under Moyers. por Newsweek 70:51 Ag 28 '67
MOYNIHAN, Daniel Patrick
Case for a family allowance; excerpt from testimony before a Senate government operations subcommittee on the federal role in urban problems. N Y Times Mag p 13+ F 5 '67
Civic architecture. Arch Rec 142:107 D '67
Darts to the heart; excerpts from address. por Time 90:27-8 O 6 '67
Germany 1967. Atlan 219:43-4 My '67
Lecture for liberals from a liberal; address, 1967. por U S News 63:22 O 9 '67
Moynihan retort. Harper 235:6+ Ag '67
Next: a new auto insurance policy. N Y Times Mag p26-7+ Ag 27 '67; Same with title Let's have a new auto insurance policy. Pop Mech 129:104-7+ Ja '68
President & the Negro: the moment lost. Commentary 43:31-45 F; 22-3 Je '67
Urban conditions: general. bibliog f Ann Am Acad 371:159-77 My '67
about
Great opportunity of 1965. W. F. Buckley, jr. Nat R 19:842 Ag 8 '67
Idea broker in the race crisis. F. Powledge. il pors Life 63:72A-72B+ N 3 '67
Light in the frightening corners. il pors Time 90:10-15 Jl 28 '67
Moynihan and the Negro. America 116:269 F 25 '67
Moynihan at the ADA. W. F. Buckley, jr. Nat R 19:1110 O 17 '67
Riots and Daniel Patrick Moynihan. Am City 82:6+ S '67
MOZAMBIQUE
High cost of historic rights; what the Portuguese face in Africa. P. Ben. New Repub 156:13-14 Ja 28 '67
Portugal in Africa: Angola and Mozambique. A. Voth. il Sat R 50:52+ S 16 '67
MOZART, Johann Chrysostom Wolfgang Amadeus
Don Giovanni. H. Glass. Am Rec G 33:562-4 Mr '67
Don Giovanni. Criticism
New Yorker 43:135-6 S 23 '67
Opera N il 31:18-20 Ja 28 '67
Time il 90:49 Jl 14 '67
First Pamina. A. M. Lingg. il Opera N 32:6 Ja 6 '68
Fischer-Dieskau's Don. H. Glass. il Am Rec G 34:18-21 S '67
Letter from Paris; disappearance of autograph manuscript of Don Giovanni. Genêt. New Yorker 42:130-2 F 11 '67; Correction 43:115 F 25 '67
Magic flute (Die zauberflöte) Criticism
Hi Fi 17:MA7 D '67
Hi Fi 18:MA4 Ja '68
Hi Fi il 17:MA10-11 My '67
New Yorker 43:145-6 Mr 4 '67
New Yorker 43:139-40 S 23 '67
Opera N 32:24-5 Ja 6 '68
Opera N il 31:17-20 Mr 4 '67
Opera N il 31:24-5 Mr 4 '67
Opera N il 32:17-19 Ja 6 '68
Sat R 50:46 Mr 4 '67
Sat R 50:41 Mr 18 '67
Sat R 50:106-7 O 14 '67
Sat R 51:97 Ja 13 '68
Marriage of Figaro (Le nozze di Figaro) Criticism
New Yorker 42:158 F 11 '67
New Yorker 43:136-7 S 23 '67
Opera N il 32:19-21 D 9 '67
Sat R 50:46 F 18 '67
Sat R 50:56 S 30 '67
Sat R 50:50-1 O 28 '67
Sat R 50:59 N 18 '67
Mozart: a documentary biography, by O. E. Deutsch. Review
Am Rec G 33:839-40 My '67. D. Harris

Mozart month at Philharmonic Hall. B. Jacobson. il Hi Fi 17:MA8-9+ N '67
Records:
Concert arias. Opera N 32:30 S 23 '67
Cosi fan tutte. Opera N 31:34 F 4 '67
Die entführung aus dem serail. Opera N 32:38 D 9 '67
Don Giovanni. Opera N 31:32 Mr 4 '67
Le nozze di Figaro; Cosi fan tutte; Don Giovanni; Die Zauberflöte. Opera N 31:34 Ja 28 '67
Le nozze di Figaro. Opera N 32:30 O 14 '67
Il re pastore, and Don Giovanni. Opera N 32:34 Ja 6 '68
Report on a marathon. S. Sell. Am Rec G 33:802+ My '67
Soaring of a great spirit. M. Davenport. il Opera N 32:24-5 Ja 6 '68
Who can understand genius? J. Wechsberg. por Holiday 42:60-1+ S '67
MPHAHLELE, Ezekiel
Trends in present-day Africa literature; excerpts from African literature. por UNESCO Courier 20:22-3+ Je '67
MROŻEK, Sławomir
Tango. Criticism
Newsweek il 71:78 Ja 15 '68
Sat R 50:34 Jl 29 '67
MUDD, S. Harvey, and others
Sulfite oxidase deficiency in man: demonstration of the enzymatic defect. bibliog Science 156:1599-602 Je 23 '67
MUECKE, Berthold, jr
Journey for Muecke. R. Levy. por Duns R 90:56-8 D '67
MUEHLING, A. J.
Lifetime confinement, coming way to manage sows? Suc Farm 65:108 Mr '67
MUEHLING, Arthur
How to get better concrete. Suc Farm 65:48-9 Je '67
MUELLER, A. G. and Guither, Harold
Beans vs. corn, which will net you most in 1967? Suc Farm 65:104 Mr '67
MUELLER, Francis J.
Several revolutions in elementary school mathematics. NEA J 57:53-4 Ja '68
MUELLER, Lisel
Nude by Edward Hopper; Names; Civvilizing the child; Gift of fire; On reading an anthology of postwar German poetry; poems. Poetry 110:226-30 Jl '67
Reading the brothers Grimm to Jenny; poem. New Yorker 43:56 N 4 '67
MUELLER, Richard J. and Frerichs, A. H.
Alienation in the low-ability classroom. bibliog f Sch & Soc 95:254-6 Ap 15 '67
MUELLER, Samuel A.
Relevance, community organization and sociology. Christian Cent 84:1282-4 O 11 '67
MUELLER, Willard Fritz
Antitrust hears a kind word. il por Bsns W p78+ Jl 29 '67
MUENCH, David
Storm in the Tetons; photographs. Am For 73:32-3 N '67
MUESSIG, Raymond H.
Herbert Hoover and education. bibliog f Sch & Soc 95:309-13 Sum '67
MUGGERIDGE, Malcolm
Books. See issues of Esquire
Is there a God? Ladies Home J 84:67+ Je '67
MUHAMMAD Ali. See Clay, C.
MUHLFELD, Edward D.
From the tower (cont of) Publisher's memo. See issues of Flying
Lady AWTAR comes of age. Flying 80:98-100 Je '67
Publisher's memo. See issues of Flying
MUHSAM, B. Feldman-. See Feldman-Muhsam, B.
MUIR, E. A.
Computations after depositing one freshman; poem. Harper 235:50 S '67
MUIR, John
Influence of Emerson, Thoreau, and Whitman on the early American naturalists John Muir and John Burroughs. M. C. Davis. bibliog il por Liv Wildn 30:18-23 Wint '66
Sheepherder versus the geologist. il por Audubon 69:47-9 Ja '67
MUIRHEAD, Desmond
New twists for an old art. G. S. Brown. il Sports Illus 26:52-3 F 20 '67
MUIRHEAD, Peter
College publishers to advise USOE; summary of address. Pub W 191:78+ F 27 '67
MUJICA LAINEZ, Manuel
Bomarzo, si, Rigoletto, no. R. Evett. New Repub 156:28-9 Je 10 '67

MULCHING
How to keep new plants alive; plastic and wood-chip mulching. il Am City 82:30 D '67
Mulches. P. E. Waggoner. Horticulture 45:10+ Ag '67
Plant a rug and forget the weeds. J. Krill. il Pop Mech 127:168 Mr '67
What's new in mulching? G. Logsdon. Farm J 91:66N Mr '67
MULDER, Marie
Teen-ager on a comeback trail. G. S. Brown. il por Sports Illus 26:22-3 F 20 '67
MULDOON, Joseph F. X.
How to rescue America from plumbers, carpenters, and people like that. J. Fischer; discussion. Harper 234:6+ Mr '67
MULE deer hunting. See Deer hunting
MULFORD, Raymon H.
Pluralism redefined. Sat R 51:33-4 Ja 13 '68
MULLER, Charles
Electronic percussion instruments. Electr World 77:36-7 F '67
MULLER, Erwin W. and Rendulic, K. D.
Field ion microscopical imaging of biomolecules. bibliog Science 156:961-3 My 19 '67
MULLER, Hermann J.
Biologists' statement on teaching evolution; text with comment. Bul Atomic Sci 23:39-40 F '67
about
On the pioneering generation. E. Rabinowitch. Bul Atomic Sci 23:2 N '67
Public confrontation of Hermann J. Muller. T. T. Balio. Bul Atomic Sci 23:8-12 N '67
MULLER, Robert H.
Research mind in library education and practice. bibliog por Library J 92:1126-9 Mr 15 '67
MÜLLER-EBERHARD, Hans J. See Hadding, U. jt. auth.
MULLET fishing
Here's how you snag a mullet. il Sunset 138:74+ Ap '67
Make the most of mullet. W. Davis. il Outdoor Life 140:118-21 S '67
MULLICA RIVER
Mullica: river of iron. G. F. Stucker. il Nat Parks Mag 41:10-15 S '67
MULLIGAN, Hugh A.
No ordinary man. Read Digest 91:127-31 Jl '67
MULLIKEN, Robert S.
Spectroscopy, molecular orbitals, and chemical bonding; address, December 12, 1966. bibliog Science 157:13-24 Jl 7 '67
MULLINS, J. T. See Thomas, D. des S. jt. auth.
MULLOY, William
Easter Island; with biographical sketch. por Natur Hist 76:4, 74-81 bibliog(p 105) D '67
MULROW, Patrick J. See Palmore, W. P. jt. auth.
MULTER, Abraham J.
Excerpt from debate, October 13, 1966. Cong Digest 46:60+ F '67
MULTI-market companies. See Diversification in industry
MULTIMETERS. See Voltmeters
MULTINUCLEATED giant cells. See Cells
MULTIPLE access computer. See Computers—Cooperative use
MULTIPLE artillery rocket system. See Weapons systems
MULTIPLE jobholding. See Supplementary employment
MULTIPLE sclerosis. See Sclerosis, Multiple
MULTIPLEX interferometric Fourier spectrometer. See Spectrometers
MULTIPURPOSE furniture. See Furniture, Childrens
MULTIPURPOSE rooms. See Rooms
MULTI-waveform generators. See Signal generators
MULTNOMAH COUNTY library. See Portland. Ore.—Libraries
MULVEHILL, Larry
Man in the orange suit. il U S Camera 30:38-9+ My '67
1200mm. il U S Camera 30:64-5+ F '67
MULVEY, Mina
Name is the game. Good H 165:227 D '67
When Jesus was born in Bethlehem of Judaea. Good H 165:77-81 D '67
MULVOY, Mark
Baseball (cont) Sports Illus 26:53-4 Mr 27 '67
Baseball's week. Sports Illus 27:65 Ag 7 '67
Golf (cont) Sports Illus 27:62-3 N 27 '67
Stadiums. Sports Illus 26:79-81 Je 12 '67

MUMFORD, George S. 3d
News notes. See issues of Sky and telescope
MUMFORD, L. Quincy
Librarian of Congress reports year of growth; summary of report. Library J 92:2497 Jl '67
Library research: looking to the future not the past. Wilson Lib Bul 41:926-7 My '67
MUMFORD, Lewis
Trend is not destiny. Arch Rec 142:131-4 D '67
about
Lewis Mumford at seventy-two. A. Temko. Harper 235:106+ O '67
MUMMIES
Body in the bog; archaeological detective story. G. Bibby. il Horizon 10:44-51 Wint '68
Mummies' teeth; periodontal problems of ancient Egypt. il Sci N 91:280 Mr 25 '67
Ramses had a royal toothache; malocclusion research on Egyptian pharaohs; X-ray study findings. il Life 62:57-8+ Ap 7 '67
MUMPS
Mumps: fact and fallacy. C. H. Fraser. il Todays Health 45:8+ Ap '67
Vaccines
Armed forces eye vaccine. Sci N 93:62 Ja 20 '68
Now, a new vaccine against mumps. U S News 64:13 Ja 15 '68
MUMPS virus
Virus-induced hydrocephalus: development of aqueductal stenosis in hamsters after mumps infection. R. T. Johnson and others. bibliog il Science 157:1066-7 S 1 '67
MUMS. See Chrysanthemums
MUNCEY, Mary Douglas Graham
She sails while he drives; interview, ed. by S. Lowell. pors Motor B 120:44-5+ S '67
MUNCH, Charles
Charles Munch forms Paris orchestra. Hi Fi 17:MA3 S '67
Munch and the Orchestre de Paris. J. Maguire. il por Sat R 50:46-7 D 30 '67
MUNDIS, Jerrold J.
He took the bull by the horns. Am Heritage 19:50-5 D '67
MUNDT, Karl Earl
Aid to our enemies; address, August 27, 1967. Vital Speeches 34:44-8 N 1 '67
Excerpt from address, February 6, 1967. Cong Digest 46:271+ N '67
Excerpt from address, March 10, 1967. Cong Digest 46:173+ Je '67
about
T.R.B. from Washington. New Repub 156:6 F 11 '67
MUNGENAST, John E.
D.C. motor drive for electric cars. Electr World 77:25 My '67
MUNGOS. See Mongooses
MUNI. Paul
Mr Paul Muni. pors Newsweek 70:72 S 4 '67
MUNICH
Music
Munich. E. D. Echols. il Opera N 31:26 Je 10 '67
Opera in trouble. B. Partington. Hi Fi 17 MA23 F '67
Report: Munich: production of Gluck's Orpheus und Eurydike. E. D. Echols. il Opera N 32:31 D 16 '67
MUNICH festival. See Music festivals—Germany (Federal Republic)
MUNICIPAL accounting
See also
Billing
MUNICIPAL advertising
City tells its story; ed. by P. D. Eimon. See issues of American city
Dallas scores; Goals for Dallas program. il Am City 82:130-1+ N '67
Roses by another name, ideas. il Am City 82:124+ D '67
MUNICIPAL and federal relations. See Federal and municipal relations
MUNICIPAL art society of New York
Municipal art society of New York, 1892-1967. B. S. Delaney. il Antiques 91:642-3 My '67
MUNICIPAL bonds
Municipal finance. See issues of American city
Park bond issues; mechanical factors involved to help your bond proposals succeed. J. B. Jamieson. Parks & Rec 2:22+ N '67

MUNICIPAL bonds—*Continued*
Two leftovers for Congress; tax-exempt industrial revenue bonds. America 117:195 Ag 26 '67
Where bond issues won, lost. U S News 63: 11C-17 N 20 '67
See also
Bonds, Revenue

MUNICIPAL buildings
Modern workshop is more efficient; Saginaw, Mich. L. D. Worth. il Am City 82:112+ D '67
Three-step municipal service center; Palo Alto, Calif. il Am City 82:88-9 D '67
See also
Municipal centers

MUNICIPAL centers
Chicago prepares for biggest Picasso of all; 136-ton sculpture to Chicago's new Civic center. il Bsns W p 122-3 My 6 '67
Distinguished civic center for a small town; Los Gatos, Calif. il Arch Rec 141:159-64 Ap '67
New city complex combines function with aesthetics; Greenville, S.C. il Am City 82: 90 N '67
Philadelphia firm wins competition for Birmingham-Jefferson civic center. il Arch Rec 142:40-1 Jl '67
Small-city municipal center; Rock Falls, Ill. il Am City 82:90-1 Ja '67

MUNICIPAL corporations
Legal notes and decisions; prepared by National institute of municipal law officers. See issues of American city

MUNICIPAL dumps
Deep-hole method extends landfill use; Lafayette. La. G. Hernandez. il Am City 82: 17 Mr '67
Get out of the dumps. G. S. Hattery. il Am City 82:100-1 Je '67
New idea in landfill operation; King County, Wash. H. Evans, jr. il Am City 82:114-15 Mr '67
Ninety-four per cent vote aye; disposable refuse-sack system; Barrington, R.I. il Am City 82:78-9 Jl '67
Regional refuse-disposal solution; Sparta, N.J. P. Braun. il Am City 82:96-7 D '67
Ripper chews through frozen clay; Champaign, Ill. J. T. Kearns. il Am City 82:60 F '67
See also
Refuse and refuse disposal

MUNICIPAL elections
Sunflower in the spring; rerun elections in Sunflower and Moorhead, Miss. caused by discrimination against prospective Negro registrants. New Repub 156:10 Ap 8 '67

MUNICIPAL employees
Employment effect of state and local government spending. J. C. Wakefield. il Mo Labor R 90:15-17 Ag '67
How to negotiate with municipal labor unions. Am City 82:50-1 Mr '67
State and local government manpower in 1975. H. V. Stambler. il Mo Labor R 90:13-17 Ap '67
See also
Municipal officers
   also subhead Officials and employees under names of cities, e.g. New York (city) —Officials and employees

Domicile
See Domicile

Salaries
Twenty-four states to test wage-hour law. U S News 62:86 Mr 20 '67

MUNICIPAL engineering
How to dovetail construction projects; Richmond, Va. C. DuVal. il Am City 82:58 D '67

MUNICIPAL equipment
Designed for six major functions; municipal service building in Sheboygan. R. E. Fleischer. il Am City 82:104-7 S '67
New equipment is less costly than old; findings of Tampa, Fla. sanitation department. il Am City 82:114-15+ S '67
Self-contained drill speeds sign-post installation; New Haven, Conn. H. Skinner. il Am City 82:133 Ap '67
See also
Motor trucks, Municipal
Snow removal equipment, Municipal
Street cleaning apparatus
Tractors, Municipal

Repairing
Quit guessing about maintenance costs; Denver, Colo. J. A. Wikgren. in Am City 82: 84-5 Ja '67
Satellite service centers; Phoenix, Ariz. F. Glendening. il Am City 82:102-4 My '67

MUNICIPAL finance
Municipal finance. See issues of American city
Potholes in the road to renewal. il Bsns W p 183 F 18 '67
See also
Local taxation
Municipal bonds

MUNICIPAL garages. See Garages, Municipal

MUNICIPAL government
City tells its story; ed. by P. D. Eimon. See issues of American city
COG, today's urban glamor girl. Am City 82:8 My '67
Future role of the city clerk. W. H. Cape. il Am City 82:174+ S '67
Metro: Toronto's answer to urban sprawl; Minneapolis-St Paul federation. J. N. Miller. Read Digest 91:85-9 Ag '67
Metropolitan government on the way; summary of address. H. F. Wise. Am City 82: 18+ Je '67
Urges less power for metro fractions. Am City 82:44+ Ag '67
See also
Metropolitan government
Police
Suggestion systems

Canada
See also
Toronto—Politics and government

England
See also
London—Politics and government

United States
See also subhead Politics and government under names of cities, e.g. New York (city) —Politics and government

MUNICIPAL improvement
City meets the space age; summer study on science and urban development, Woods Hole, Mass. J. Bailey. Arch Forum 126:60-3+ Ja '67
Clean-up and beautification campaigns. R. R. Fleming. il Am City 82:105-7 My '67
Here's LBJ's grand design to change the face of America. il U S News 62:72-4 F 13 '67
Incredibility gap. Am City 82:7 F '67
Keeping cities cool. il Bsns W p46+ Je 10 '67
Lend-a-hand plan; Kirkwood, Mo. extends the municipal services to Meacham park. R. G. Reim. il Am City 82:98-9 Mr '67
Mall idea. il Sunset 139:70-5 S '67
Streets lights and signs; federal grants. Am City 82:53 D '67
Systems engineering invades the city. L. Lessing. il Fortune 77:154-7+ Ja '68
Urban gardens. A. W. Smith. Nat Parks Mag 41:2 O '67
Why everything is up to date in Kansas City; businessmen and civic pride. il Bsns W p 102-6 Ap 8 '67
See also
City planning
Parks
Refuse and refuse disposal
Trees in cities
Urban renewal
Water fronts

MUNICIPAL incinerators. See Refuse incenerators

MUNICIPAL lighting. See Street lighting

MUNICIPAL markets. See Markets, Municipal

MUNICIPAL officers
Future role of the city clerk. W. H. Cape. il Am City 82:174+ S '67
Personal business; business executives as town officials. Bsns W p 141-2 N 11 '67
See also
Councilmen
Negro municipal officers
   also subhead Officials and employees under names of cities, e.g. Los Angeles—Officials and employees

MUNICIPAL ordinances
Legal notes and decisions; prepared by National institute of municipal law officers. See issues of American city

MUNICIPAL parking facilities. See Automobile parking

MUNICIPAL parks. See Parks

MUNICIPAL publications

Bibliography
Municipal and civic publications. See issues of American city

MUNICIPAL purchasing. See Purchasing, Municipal

MUNICIPAL records
Street records that work; Milwaukee's system.
L. A. DeMers. il Am City 82:130-2 O '67
MUNICIPAL reports
Annual reports, these have it! Tennessee communities; ed. by P. D. Eimon. Am City 82:
148+ Je '67
MUNICIPAL swimming pools. See Swimming
pools, Municipal
MUNICIPAL taxation. See Local taxation
MUNICIPAL tractors. See Tractors, Municipal
MUNICIPAL transportation. See Rapid transit
MUNICIPAL waterworks. See Waterworks
MUNICIPAL workshops. See Municipal buildings
MUNITIONS
Egypt seeks new Soviet missiles. W. C.
Wetmore. Aviation W 87:26 Jl 10 '67
    See also
Projectiles
Weapons
Weapons systems

            Manufacture
Different kind of war for Norris; Norris industries, inc. il Bsns W p 147-8+ Je 3 '67
MUNITIONS industries

            Employees
Worker skills in current defense employment.
M. A. Rutzick. il Mo Labor R 90:17-20 S
'67
            Latin America
Arms siphon. Time 90:30+ N 3 '67

            Sweden
Swedegroup moves to increase exports. il
Aviation W 86:183-4 My 29 '67

            United States
Broad-based drive to increase exports urged
by industry unit. D. C. Winston. Aviation W 87:31-2 Jl 10 '67
Complex-complex; distrust of military-industrial complex. M. Getler. Aero Tech 21:
58 Ja 1 '68
Customers are fighting. W. J. Coughlin. Tech
W 20:50 Je 12 '67
Defense expenditures in depressed areas. I.
Gray. Mo Labor R 90:34-5 Mr '67
Economists debate military-industrial concentration. Sci N 99:33-4 Ja 13 '68
From the U.S.A. to all the world, with love.
F. Church. Esquire 68:83-4+ Jl '67
Industry passes the ammunition. il Bsns W
p66-8+ Je 24 '67
Phrase rediscovered; the military industrial
complex; profiting from defense contracts.
Nation 205:420-1 O 30 '67
MUNITIONS workers
    See also
Munitions industries—Employees
MUNITIONS works
Different kind of war for Norris; Norris
industries, inc. il Bsns W p 147-8+ Je 3
'67
MUNK, Arthur W.
Education and the challenge of the future.
Sch & Soc 95:180-2 Mr 18 '67
MUNK, Walter H. and Zetler, B. D.
Deep-sea tides: a program. Science 158:884-6
N 17 '67
MUÑOZ MARIN, Luis
Puerto Rico. G. T. Nunn. Nation 205:44-6
Jl 17 '67
MUNROE, William
To photography, with love. M. Orovan. il U S
Camera 30:62-3 My '67
MUNSEY, Wallace. See Cleland, D. I. jt. auth.
MUNSINGWEAR, incorporated
Making the turtles move; can turtlenecks replace the button-down shirts. il Bsns W
p 152 N 11 '67
MUNSON, Genevieve
Good-bye, sweet summer, good-bye; story.
Seventeen 26:296-7 Ag '67
That's why I loved Chauncey Meadors; story.
Seventeen 26:108-9 Je '67
MUNSON, Gorham
Workshops for writers (cont) Sat R 50:37-9+
Ap 29 '67
MÜNSTER, Germany
Holy terrors of Munster. E. Stillman. il Horizon 9:90-5 Sum '67
MUNTYAN, Miodrag
What lies ahead? Sat R 50:14-15+ Je 10 '67
MUNTZ, Earl
Return of the madman. il por Newsweek
69:76+ Ap 24 '67

MUNTZ stereo-pak, incorporated
Return of the madman. il Newsweek 69:76+
Ap 24 '67
MUNZ, Walter
Lambaréné since Schweitzer. H. Bowser.
Sat R 50:30 N 25 '67
Young doctor at Lambaréné. G. N. Marshall.
Christian Cent 84:1636-8 D 20 '67
MURAL painting and decoration
Big paint job; murals. A. M. D. Ashley. il
Sch Arts 66:39 My '67
Co-op murals of the past and present. M.
Gardner. il Sch Arts 66:18-19 Mr '67
Operation Sunshine; E. Reinhardt's murals
for children's infirmaries and state hospitals. C. W. Wittman. il Am Artist 31:27-31
F '67
Paint big; mural on side of tenement in Manhattan's East Village. il Time 90:46 Jl 28
'67
    See also
Cave drawings and paintings
Frescoes
MURALS, Photographic. See Photographic
murals
MURAMATSU, Konosuke
Antlers of Nara; photographs. Natur Hist
76:30-3 F '67
MURATA, K. J. and others
Carbon-13, rich diagenetic carbonates in miocene formations of California and Oregon.
bibliog Science 156:1484-6 Je 16 '67
MURATA, Kyuzo
Lilliputian world of the bonsai. N. F. Busch.
il por Read Digest 91:182-6+ S '67
MURAY, Leo
Profile of East Germany. New Repub 156:6-8
Ap 1 '67
Red guard invasion. New Repub 156:15 F 25
'67
Split in Egypt. New Repub 157:22 S 9 '67
Why Nasser is no longer a free agent. New
Repub 157:10-11 D 23 '67
MURCH, Walter Tandy
Silent world. D. L. Shirey. il por Newsweek
71:59 Ja 8 '68
MURDER
Born to raise hell, by J. Altman and M.
Ziporyn. Review
    Newsweek il 70:108+ S 25 '67. S. K.
    Oberbeck
Case for the defense; famous attorneys talk
of famous cases. il Esquire 68:51-4 Jl '67
Cathey, where's Cathey? murder of three
girls by E. Seibold. il Newsweek 70:42+
S 18 '67
Death of a flower baby; mother kills child.
il Time 90:18 D 1 '67
Dolce vita, Rivo Alto style; J. Kirschke indicted on two counts of murder. il Time 89:
20 Je 23 '67
End of the dance; murders of two hippie drug
peddlers. il Time 90:22-3 Ag 18 '67
How faith helped Charles Percy's family
face tragedy. W. B. Furlong. il Good H
164:78-81+ F '67
It was that damned book: The stranger by
Albert Camus. B. Davidson. il Sat Eve
Post 240:81-9 Ap 8 '67
Kind of crucifixion; D. Hoskins admits murder and arson. Newsweek 70:26-7 Ag 28 '67
Leo's last trip; L. Held kills six people. il
Newsweek 70:36-7 N 6 '67
Life without the hangman; murder rate in
Britain drops. Time 90:48 Jl 7 '67
Linda's last trip; double murder in New
York's East Village. il Newsweek 70:33-4 O
23 '67
Maybe somebody else can learn from it:
murder of L. Fitzpatrick. J. A. Lukas.
Read Digest 91:96-101 D '67
Mind of a murderer; excerpt from Born to
raise hell. J. Altman and M. Ziporyn. il Sat
Eve Post 240:27-31+ Jl 1; 38-40+ Jl 15 '67
Modern Medea? A. Crimmins charged with
murder of daughter. il Newsweek 70:34
S 25 '67
One coincidence too many; W. Archerd accused of insulin murder. il Time 90:18-19
Ag 11 '67
Overkill in Boston; fratricide among racketeers. Time 89:21 F 10 '67
Revolt of Leo Held. il Time 90:21-2 N 3 '67
Shocking rise of murder; Chicago's ghetto
and police. J. Star. il Look 31:28-34 S
19 '67
Speed kills; hippies murdered in New York.
il Time 90:23 O 20 '67
Suddenly, without warning or reason, it happens. P. Hamill. Good H 164:98-9+ Ap '67
Time for violence. il Newsweek 70:36+ N 13
'67

MURDER—*Continued*
We burned a bum Friday night and we're going to burn another one tonight. N. Pileggi. il Esquire 68:48-50+ Jl '67
Ye friendly tobacconist; murder of University of Pennsylvania freshman. il Time 90: 28 N 10 '67
See also
Capital punishment
Trials (murder)
MURDER trials. See Trials (murder)
MURDERERS. See Murder
MURDOCK, Richard P.
Put your boat in business. Motor B 120:40+ O '67
MURFITT, Rex
Starting a rock garden. Horticulture 45:24-5+ Ap '67
MURGER, Henri
Romance with reality. G. McElroy. il Opera N 31:8-12 F 4 '67
MURIE, Margaret E.
Alaska's conservation challenge. Liv Wildn 30:31-2 Aut '66
MURINE leukemia virus. See Leukemia viruses
MURINE lymphomas. See Tumors
MURPHY, Arthur R. Jr
Communications; address, March 1, 1967. Vital Speeches 33:573-6 Jl 1 '67
MURPHY, Calvin
Calvinists all. il Newsweek 69:88 Mr 13 '67
Couple of coming-out parties. J. Jares and C. Kirkpatrick. il por Sports Illus 27:30-3 D 11 '67
MURPHY, Charles J. V.
How the battle got turned around. Fortune 75:140-5+ Ap '67
Mellons of Pittsburgh. Fortune 76:120-9+ O; 158-61+ N; 132-4+ D '67
MURPHY, Edward F.
(comp) Be nice! N Y Times Mag p42 Mr 5 '67
(comp) Bookish. N Y Times Mag p37+ Ap 16 '67
(comp) Dogs in review. N Y Times Mag p 128 My 14 '67
(comp) June and weddings. N Y Times Mag p98 Je 4 '67
(comp) Musical notes. N Y Times Mag p40 Ap 23 '67
(comp) Of autos and auto safety. N Y Times Mag p81 Ja 22 '67
(comp) Read well before eating. N Y Times Mag p 119-20 N 26 '67
(comp) Take it easy. N Y Times Mag p6 Ag 27 '67
MURPHY, Franklin D.
Delicate balance. Sat R 51:74+ Ja 13 '68
MURPHY, George Lloyd
George Murphy: the old soft shoe. H. Sutton. il por Sat R 50:25-6 S 23 '67
Senator Murphy digs the facts. Nation 205: 517 N 20 '67
MURPHY, H. C. and others
Avena magna: an important new tetraploid species of oats. bibliog Science 159:103-4 Ja 5 '68
MURPHY, Jack Rolland
Murf the Surf and his jewel-studded jinx. K. Wheeler and S. Smith. il pors Life 62: 92-4+ Ap 21 '67
MURPHY, James E.
Data processing speeds the election process. Am City 82:100 My '67
MURPHY, James E. Jr
James E. Murphy, jr. and dance company, Clark center for the performing arts. J. Maskey. Dance Mag 41:38 My '67
MURPHY, Kenneth W.
Too young to die; interview, ed. by R. W. O'Donnell. Sr Schol 91:sup7-8 N 16 '67
MURPHY, Lawrence P.
Speedup; interview. New Yorker 43:51-2 N 25 '67
MURPHY, Mary Lois
American women: the doers. por Vogue 149: 189 My '67
MURPHY, Sister Mary Teresa Joseph, and others
Perhydro-β-carotene in the Green River shale. bibliog Science 157:1040-2 S 1 '67
MURPHY, Michael
Joy is the prize: a trip to Esalen institute. L. E. Litwak. il pors N Y Times Mag p8-9+ D 31 '67
MURPHY, Robert Cushman
Antarctica. Natur Hist 76:21-31 Je '67
Trumpeter returns from oblivion. Read Digest 90:190-2+ Je '67

about
About the author. J. Le Corbeiller. il por Natur Hist 76:20 Je '67
MURRAY, Anne Wood
Sunshades, parasols, and umbrellas. Antiques 91:492-5 Ap '67
MURRAY, Athol
Unforgettable Father Murray. F. Germann. il Read Digest 90:113-17 F '67
MURRAY, Bain
Blossom center: old dream come true. Hi Fi 17:MA22-3 Ap '67
R. and G, G. and R; interview. New Yorker 43:52 N 4 '67
MURRAY, Bruce C. and others
Planetary contamination II: Soviet and U.S. practices and policies. bibliog Science 155: 1505-11 Mr 24 '67
MURRAY, Catherine
For you; poem. Commonweal 86:151 Ap 21 '67
So soon, another season; poem. Commonweal 86:95 Ap 7 '67
MURRAY, Christopher
New books. Cath World 205:313-14 Ag '67
MURRAY, David J.
Britain's influence in Africa. bibliog f Cur Hist 52:276-81 My '67
MURRAY, F. Scott
Debt of thanks; concerning the salutatorian address. S. Kauffmann. New Repub 157:24+ Jl 22 '67
MURRAY, Frank
Governor Kirk's not-so-secret police. Reporter 36:27-30 Mr 23 '67
MURRAY, Geoffrey
Rationing the Christmas spirit. Christian Cent 84:1634 D 20 '67
MURRAY, Gordon
Miracle surgery case. il por Newsweek 70: 56+ D 11 '67
Rejoining the spinal cord. il Time 90:70 N 24 '67
Repairing the paraplegic. il Newsweek 70:66 N 27 '67
Second thoughts. Newsweek 71:49-50 Ja 15 '68
MURRAY, John
Looking glass murder; drama. Plays 27:11-25 Ja '68
Spies and dolls; drama. Plays 26:13-26 Mr '67
MURRAY, John Courtney
Religious liberty and development of doctrine; interview, ed. by E. Gaffney. por Cath World 204:277-83 F '67

about
John Courtney Murray, RIP. Nat R 19:946+ S 5 '67
Man of the city. por Time 90:38-9 Ag 25 '67
Obituary
America 117:220-1 S 2 '67. J. Cogley
Commonweal 86:540 S 8 '67
Protestants pay tribute to John Courtney Murray. Christian Cent 84:1182 S 20 '67
Tribute to John Courtney Murray. A. Broderick; W. J. Burghardt. por America 117: 246-9 S 9 '67
Voice of reason. il por Newsweek 70:57 Ag 28 '67
MURRAY, Margaret (Lally)
My most unforgettable character. G. M. Keddell. por Read Digest 90:125-9 My '67
MURRAY, Margaret R. and Benitez, H. H.
Deuterium oxide: direct action on sympathetic ganglia isolated in culture. bibliog Science 155:1021-4 F 24 '67
MURRAY, Marguerite
Luaus in the library; or, The curriculum that wasn't. Library J 92:1708-10 Ap 15 '67
MURRAY, Sister Mary Verona
Gift for all seasons. Am Ed 4:5-7 D '67
MURRAY, Robert F. Jr, and Ball, J. A.
Testis-specific and sex-associated hexokinases in drosophila melanogaster. bibliog Science 156:81-2 Ap 7 '67
MURRAY, Spencer
By sea, to see the elephants. Yachting 122: 52-5+ Jl; 46-7+ Ag '67
MURRAY, William
Hanging five. Holiday 42:62-7 S '67
Troubled arts. Holiday 41:62-5+ Mr '67
MURRAY, William Cotter
Bearded, sockless radical of Moo U. N Y Times Mag p25+ Ap 9 '67
MURRAY the K. See Kaufman, M.
MURROW, Edward R.
Behind the screens at CBS. R. J. Landry. Sat R 50:30-1 Ap 1 '67
I can hear it now reissued. R. L. Tobin. Sat R 50:52 D 16 '67

MURROW, Edward R.—*Continued*
Murrow in type. S. W. Little. Sat R 50:106-7 Je 10 '67
News and the newsman. G. Baro. Reporter 37:46+ S 21 '67
Peripatetic reviewer. E. Weeks. por Atlan 220:96-7 Ag '67
Saving the world every week; See it now series and CBS reports. E. Weeks. Atlan 219:124-6 My '67

MURROW, Richard B.
Research frontier. por Sat R 50:51-5 Je 3 '67

MURVILLE, Maurice Couve de. See Couve de Murville, M.

MUS, David
Rain. .; poem. Poetry 109:299-301 F '67

MUSBURGER, Brent
Baseball. Sports Illus 27:50-2 S 4 '67

MUSCARINE
Muscarine: isolation from cultures of clitocybe rivulosa. M. L. Swenberg and others. bibliog Science 155:1259 Mr 10 '67

MUSCATINE, Charles
Muscatine's challenge to universities. por Sch & Soc 95:168 Mr 18 '67

MUSCATINE, Leonard
Glycerol excretion by symbiotic algae from corals and tridacna and its control by the host. bibliog Science 156:516-19 Ap 28 '67

MUSCLE
Action potentials without contraction in frog skeletal muscle fibers with disrupted transverse tubules. P. W. Gage and R. S. Eisenberg. bibliog il Science 158:1702-3 D 29 '67
Crayfish muscle: permeability to sodium induced by calcium depletion. J. P. Reuben and others. bibliog il Science 155:1263-6 Mr 10 '67
Enhanced protein synthesis in a cell-free system from hypertrophied skeletal muscle. M. Hamosh and others. bibliog il Science 157:935-7 Ag 25 '67
Force, shortening, and work in muscular contraction: relative contributions to overall energy utilization. F. F. Jöbsis and J. C. Duffield. bibliog il Science 156:1388-92 Je 9 '67
Frog skeletal muscle fibers: changes in electrical properties after disruption of transverse tubular system. R. S. Eisenberg and P. W. Gage. bibliog il Science 158:1700-1 D 29 '67
Heat inactivation of the relaxing site of actomyosin: prevention and reversal with dithiothreitol. H. M. Levy and E. M. Ryan. bibliog il Science 156:73-4 Ap 7 '67
Isometric tension differences in fibers of red and white muscles. A. W. Seton and J. W. Gersten. bibliog il Science 157:199 Jl 14 '67
Molecular size of hagfish muscle lactate dehydrogenase. N. Arnheim, jr. and others. bibliog il Science 157:568-9 Ag 4 '67
Muscle-spindle histochemistry. B. Nyström. bibliog il Science 155:1424-6 Mr 17 '67
Neuromuscular transmitter substance in insect visceral muscle. B. E. Brown. bibliog il Science 155:595-7 F 3 '67
Nitrate ions: potentiation of increased permeability to sugar associated with muscle contraction. J. O. Holloszy and H. T. Narahara. bibliog il Science 155:573-5 F 3 '67
Regulation of intracellular sodium concentrations in rat diaphragm muscle. H. A. Fozzard and D. M. Kipnis. bibliog il Science 156:1257-60 Je 2 '67
Sarcoplasmic reticulum of striated muscle: localization of potential calcium binding sites. C. W. Philpott and M. A. Goldstein. bibliog il Science 155:1019-21 F 24 '67
Sodium and potassium effects on skeletal muscle microsomal adenosine triphosphatase and calcium uptake. B. B. Rubin and A. M. Katz. bibliog il Science 158:1189-90 D 1 '67
Submaxillary gland of mouse: properties of a purified protein affecting muscle tissue in vitro. D. G. Attardi and others. bibliog il Science 156:1253-5 Je 2 '67

MUSCLES
Surprising new facts about your muscles. L. Galton. il Pop Sci 191:54-7+ Jl '67
See also
Ligaments
Tendons

Diseases
Erythrocyte abnormality in human myopathy. H. D. Brown and others. bibliog il Science 157:1577-8 S 29 '67
Myxoivirus-like structures in a case of human chronic polymyositis. S. M. Chou. bibliog il Science 158:1453-5 D 15 '67

Wounds and injuries
Strains and sprains. A. F. Benjamin. Am Home 70:34 N '67

MUSCULAR power
Real, live superman. P. Wyche. il Ebony 22:97-8+ S '67

MUSÉE Le Secq des Tournelles, Rouen. See Museums

MUSEUM education
See also
Museums—Work with children

MUSEUM exhibits
Museums come alive. R. Grove. il Am Ed 3:9-10 Ap '67

MUSEUM of contemporary art, Chicago
Art. M. Kozloff. Nation 205:571-2 N 27 '67
Art world; opening exhibition: Pictures to be read/Poetry to be seen. H. Rosenberg. New Yorker 43:225-8+ N 18 '67
Chicago modern. il Newsweek 70:114+ N 13 '67
Contemporary in Chicago. il Time 90:60 N 3 '67

MUSEUM of contemporary crafts, New York
Dialogue in a museum. K. K. Hui; J. Crumrine. il Craft Horiz 27:18-22+ Jl '67

MUSEUM of illustration art, New York
New Museum of illustration art chartered. Pub W 192:37 O 16 '67

MUSEUM of modern art, New York
Alfred Barr: modern art's durable crusader; with excerpts from interview. K. Kuh. il Sat R 50:51-3 S 30 '67
Arts of the 1960's; painting and sculpture from Museum's collection on exhibit. C. J. McNaspy. America 117:98 Jl 22 '67
Designs of our time. B. Plumb. il N Y Times Mag p90-1 S 17 '67 O 1 '67
Exciting world of art; special art classes for youngsters and their parents. V. D'Amico. il Parents Mag 42:48-9+ D '67
John Szarkowski: photography as interpreter. J. Deschin. Pop Phot 61:18+ S '67
Mr Barr. il Newsweek 70:77 Jl 31 '67
Modern museum to expand book publishing program. Pub W 193:63 Ja 15 '68
Museum of modern art discovers Harlem; exhibition, The new city: architecture and urban renewal. C. R. Hatch. il Arch Forum 126:38-47 Mr '67
New man at MOMA. Newsweek 69:110 My 22 '67
New man at MOMA. il Time 89:94 My 19 '67

MUSEUM of natural history. See American museum of natural history, New York

MUSEUM of primitive art, New York
Museum of primitive art, New York; editorial. T. B. Hess. Art N 66:27 Ja '68

MUSEUM of science, Boston
Paul Revere's shop in miniature. R. Davidson. il Antiques 92:176 Ag '67

MUSEUM of the new world. See Madrid—Galleries and museums

MUSEUM of the prefecture of police. See Paris—Galleries and museums

MUSEUM shops. See Art—Galleries and museums

MUSEUMS
Filigrees & forgings; Rouen's Musée Le Secq des Tournelles. il Time 89:70-1 Je 16 '67
Museum-publisher marriage. D. Dempsey. Sat R 50:45 F 25 '67
Museum world. J. L. Stoutenburgh. See Issues of Hobbies
New home for old inventions; patent museum in Plymouth, N.H. L. Aigner. il Pop Mech 128:102-5 Ag '67
Science map and guide to the U.S. L. Thomas. il Pop Sci 190:59-63+ Je '67
Visit a favorite sports museum. il Changing T 21:19-20 Je '67
See also
Art—Galleries and museums
College museums
Historical museums
also names of museums, e.g. Shelburne museum, Shelburne, Vt; *also* subhead Galleries and museums under names of cities, e.g. New York (city)—Galleries and museums

Architecture
New art gallery for the Capitol mall, Washington, D.C. il Arch Rec 142:112-15 D '67
Philip Johnson's suburban museum; experiment in Connecticut backyard. J. Peter. il Look 31:60-4 My 16 '67
Showcase for sculpture; Lehmbruck museum, Duisburg, Germany. il Arch Forum 126:31-7 Mr '67
Sunken hillside gallery; Philip Johnson's art gallery. il Arch Rec 141:146-7 Je '67

MUSEUMS—*Continued*

Fires and fire protection

Fire: Guggenheim museum. New Yorker 43: 39-40 Ap 15 '67

Work with children

Museums come alive. R. Grove. il Am Ed 3:9-10 Ap '67

MUSEUMS, Private

Philip Johnson's suburban museum; experiment in Connecticut backyard. J. Peter. il Look 31:60-4 My 16 '67

MUSEUMS and schools

See also

Museums—Work with children

MUSEUMS and women; story. See Updike, J.

MUSHRO, Marie

Science finally caught up. pors Mlle 65:76+ Ag '67

MUSHROOMS

Department of amplification. D. Malcolm. New Yorker 42:101-3 Ja 28 '67

See also

Cookery—Mushrooms

Mycology

Truffles

MUSIAL, Stan

Red and his roomie, and the pennant. J. Brosnan. il pors N Y Times Mag p36-7+ S 17 '67

Stanley, the general manager. W. Leggett. il por Sports Illus 26:66+ Mr 20 '67

MUSIC

About getting here from there; Twentieth century music. J. Ringo. Am Rec G 33:824+ My '67

Artist life. D. J. Soria. See issues of High fidelity incorporating Musical America

Here & there. See issues of High fidelity incorporating Musical America

Music! music! from pop to op. L. Lerman. il Mlle 65:144-5 O '67

Musical events; avant-garde concert at Town Hall. W. Sargeant. New Yorker 43: 133-4 My 27 '67

Musical events; concert of romantic twentieth-century music performed by American symphony orchestra. W. Sargeant. New Yorker 43:232 N 11 '67

Quarter master; concert of quarter-tone music. Time 89:71 My 12 '67

See also

Bands (music)

Church music

Composition (music)

Concertos

Jazz music

Moving pictures—Music

Music, Concrete

Musical instruments

Orchestras

Radio broadcasting—Music

Television broadcasting—Music

Acoustics and physics

Physics for the queen. J. Eberhart. il Sci N 91:212-13 Mr 4 '67

Analysis, interpretation, etc.

Imagery in music. A. Rich. House B 109:164+ Je '67

Mystery of performing; ed. by P. M. Katona, tr. by A. M. Lingg. G. Souzay. il Opera N 32:8-11 N 25 '67

Sign of the storm; cue from the opening tempest. E. Downes. il Opera N 31:24-5 Mr 11 '67

See also

Conducting (music)

Appreciation

Infinite variety of music, by L. Bernstein. Review

Am Rec G 33:856-8 My '67. R. Kennedy

Time-Life's Story of great music. D. Hamilton. il Hi Fi 17:59-62 D '67

What you can learn from Frère Jacques. A. Rich. House B 109:60+ O '67

See also

Music—Philosophy and aesthetics

Bibliography

Book reviews. See issues of American record guide

Da capo, your key to significant out-of-print music publications. Am Rec G 33:835 My '67

Musical events. W. Sargeant. New Yorker 43: 103+ Je 3 '67; 71-3 Ja 6 '68

Competitions

Conductors: fifth annual Dimitri Mitropoulos international competition for conductors; with interview with J. F. M. Vonk. New Yorker 42:28-30 Ja 28 '67

Lively arts: winning the prize is just the beginning, piano competitions; interviews, ed. by R. Hemming. M. Frager; M. Dichter. Sr Schol 90:21-2 Ap 14 '67

Music; certificate to G. W. Lankford, chairman of the Van Cliburn quadrennial international piano competition. il Américas 19: 42-3 F '67

Music to my ears: Dimitri Mitropoulos international competition. I. Kolodin. Sat R 50:58+ F 11 '67

See also

Bands (music)—Competitions

Leventritt award

Singing—Competitions

History and criticism

Drawn from within; O'Neill's Mourning becomes Electra and M. D. Levy's music. J. W. Freeman. il Opera N 31:24-5 Ap 1 '67

Finding your way through modern music. F. Bowers. House & Gard 131:122+ Mr '67

Music that laughs and capers; Falstaff, Verdi's last opera. E. Downes. il Opera N 32:24-5 D 16 '67

Opera's first step was a stumble. G. Jennings. il Opera N 31:6-7 F 11 '67

When Orpheus struck the trembling lyre. L. Pareti. il UNESCO Courier 20:9-11 My '67

See also

Jazz music

Opera—History and criticism

Instruction and study

Sonata for two clarinets; student composers take over. H. W. Arberg and C. S. Carleton. il Am Ed 3:30-2 F '67

Sure, you can still learn music. il Changing T 21:19-20 S '67

See also

Music camps

Opera—Instruction and study

Piano—Instruction and study

Violin—Instruction and study

Jews

See also

Cantors, Jewish

Manuscripts

Letter from Paris; disappearance of Mozart's autograph manuscript of Don Giovanni. Genêt. New Yorker 42:130-2 F 11 '67; Correction. 43:115 F 25 '67

Moving pictures

See Moving pictures—Music

Periodicals

Face to face with the editor of a rock and roll magazine: Crawdaddy! P. Williams. il Seventeen 26:159 Ap '67

Philosophy and aesthetics

Ethos and education in Greek music, by W. D. Anderson. Review

Am Rec G il 33:840-3 My '67. J. W. Barker

Music, the arts, and ideas, by L. B. Meyer. Review

New Yorker 43:51-3 D 30 '67. W. Sargeant

Quotations, maxims, etc.

Musical notes; comments for National music week, comp. by E. F. Murphy. N Y Times Mag p40 Ap 23 '67

Themes, motives, etc.

Verdi's fathers; subject close to composer's heart. S. Hughes. Opera N 31:24-5 Ap 8 '67

Theory

Vibrating string of the Pythagoreans; relation between music and mathematics. E. E. Helm. il Sci Am 217:92-8+ bibliog(p 153) D '67

Argentina

See also

Buenos Aires—Music

Austria

By the blue-chip Danube. Time 90:52 D 8 '67

See also

Opera—Austria

Salzburg festival

Vienna—Music

MUSIC—*Continued*

Canada
See also
Musicians, Canadian

China (People's Republic)
Music in China today. B. Häger. il Hi Fi 17:93-8 O '67

Czechoslovakia
See also
Prague—Music

Denmark
See also
Music, Danish

England
New hall at Snape; notable events in the hall. T. Heinitz. il Sat R 50:49+ Jl 29 '67
See also
Music, English

France
Letter from Paris; concert in Notre Dame. Genêt. New Yorker 43:138 Je 10 '67
Out of decay, an operatic prophet. J. Maguire. Hi Fi 17:MA28-9+ Mr '67
See also
Paris—Music

Germany (Federal Republic)
See also
Hamburg—Music
Hanover, Germany—Music
Munich—Music
Opera—Germany (Federal Republic)
Wiesbaden, Germany—Music

Great Britain
See also
London—Music

Hawaii
See also
Honolulu—Music

Hungary
See also
Budapest—Music

India
See also
Bombay—Music
Music, Indian (East Indian)
Opera—India

Israel
Impassioned Israelis. D. Bar-Illan. il Hi Fi 17:47-50 Jl '67
See also
Israel philharmonic orchestra

Italy
Before and after the deluge. R. Feist. America 116:151-3 Ja 28 '67
See also
Bergamo, Italy—Music
Bologna, Italy—Music
Milan, Italy—Music
Naples—Music
Opera—Italy
Rome (city)—Music
Verona, Italy—Music

Japan
Japan and Korea: appreciation and understanding of western music. F. Mahler. Hi Fi 17:MA29 Ag '67
See also
Musicians, Japanese
Tokyo—Music

Korea (Republic)
Japan and Korea: appreciation and understanding of western music. F. Mahler. Hi Fi 17:MA29 Ag '67

Mexico
Mexican classic; Teatro Juarez, Guanajuato. C. Bailey. il Opera N 31:6 F 18 '67
See also
Mexico (city)—Music

Portugal
See also
Lisbon, Portugal—Music

Russia
New Russian hit parade; V. Duke series on the American musical theater. S. Green. Sat R 50:66 Ag 26 '67
See also
Jazz music—Russia
Opera—Russia

South Africa
See also
Johannesburg—Music

Spain
See also
Barcelona—Music

Switzerland
See also
Opera—Switzerland

United States
California music; symposium. il Sat R 50:40-6+ S 23 '67
See also
Folk songs, American
Jazz music
Music, American
Opera—United States
also subhead Music under names of cities, e.g. New York (city)—Music

Yugoslavia
See also
Zagreb, Yugoslavia—Music

MUSIC, American
Collector's guide to American show music. F. Bowers. House & Gard 132:12+ Ag '67
See also
Folk songs, American
Jazz music
Music—United States
Musicians, American
Opera, American

MUSIC, Asian
Music cultures of the Pacific, the Near East, and Asia, by W. P. Malm. Review
Am Rec G il 33:850-1 My '67. W. L. Purcell

MUSIC, Assyro-Babylonian
Music ages a thousand years. il Sci N 91:400 Ap 29 '67

MUSIC, Austrian
See also
Phonograph records—Austrian music

MUSIC, Babylonian. See Music, Assyro-Babylonian

MUSIC, Baroque
New performances on old instruments; Concentus musicus ensemble. E. Helm. il Hi Fi 17:42-6 My '67

MUSIC, Canadian
See also
Musicians, Canadian
Phonograph records—Canadian music

MUSIC, Church. See Church music

MUSIC, Concrete
Compose concrete music for your compositions. R. White. il Dance Mag 41:58-61 S '67

MUSIC, Czech
See also
Composers, Czech
Phonograph records—Czech music

MUSIC, Danish
Nielsen symphonies. B. Jacobson. Hi Fi 17:54-6 Ap '67
See also
Phonograph records—Danish music

MUSIC, Electronic
Adventure in affinities; Electric Christmas concert in Carneige Hall. il Time 91:48 Ja 5 '68
Dial it yourself. R. Evett. New Repub 156:33-5 Ap 15 '67
Electronic music, its composition & performance. R. A. Moog. il Electr World 77:42-6+ F '67
Electronic music, wiggy. H. Junker. il Newsweek 69:98-98B+ My 22 '67
Electronic Noel; production by The electric circus, inc. in Carnegie Hall. P. Velde. Commonweal 87:471-2 Ja 19 '68
Flashes of a mad logic: K. Stockhausen. il Time 89:73 F 10 '67
New sound for a plugged-in age. R. Kostelanetz. Look 32:45 Ja 9 '68
Seeing sounds; electronic music at Expo 67. il Time 90:48+ O 6 '67
See also
Music, Concrete
Phonograph records—Electronic music

MUSIC, English
English musical renaissance, by F. Howes. Review
Reporter 37:47-8 O 5 '67. R. Gelatt
See also
Phonograph records—English music

MUSIC, French
See also
Phonograph records—French music

MUSIC, Greek
Ethos and education in Greek music, by W. D. Anderson. Review
Am Rec G il 33:840-3 My '67. J. W. Barker
Sound of Greek, by W. B. Stanford. Review
Am Rec G 33:843-4 My '67. J. W. Barker

MUSIC, Hindu
See also
Phonograph records—Hindu music
Shankar, R.

MUSIC, Hungarian
See also
Phonograph records—Hungarian music

MUSIC, Indian (East Indian)
His sitar sound rocks the U.S. J. Borg-zinner. il Life 63:35-6+ Ag 18 '67
Raga is all the rage! ed. by E. Miller. R. Shankar. il Seventeen 26:346+ Ag '67
Reporter at large. V. Mehta. New Yorker 43:159-60+ D 9 '67
See also
Opera—India
Phonograph records—Indian music (East Indian)

MUSIC, Influence of
Who leads today's youth? round table discussion from 1967 student burgesses at Williamsburg. il Sr Schol 90:8-9+ Ap 14 '67

MUSIC, Irish
See also
Phonograph records—Irish music

MUSIC, Italian
See also
Phonograph records—Italian music

MUSIC, Jewish
See also
Phonograph records—Jewish music

MUSIC, Latin American
Music. See issues of *Américas*

MUSIC, Medieval
See also
Phonograph records—Medieval music

MUSIC, Modern. See Music

MUSIC, Oriental
See also
Music, Asian
Opera—India

MUSIC, Polish
See also
Phonograph records—Polish music

MUSIC, Popular (songs, etc)
How not to flop at pop; guide to the new music. H. Smith and J. Newfield. il McCalls 95:78-9+ N '67
In the pop bag. D. Heckman. See issues of American record guide
It's time to start listening. R. Kramer. il N Y Times Mag p80+ S 17 '67
Lively arts; interview, ed. by R. Hemming. H. Mancini. Sr Schol 90:17 F 3 '67
Of times that are a-changin. B. Korall. il Sat R 50:76-7 Ag 26 '67
Pop music: the most? or just a mess? A. G. Aronowitz. il Sat Eve Post 240:70-5 Jl 15 '67
Pop music: what's been happening. R. Corliss. Nat R 19:371-4 Ap 4 '67
Purge; morality campaign against dirty lyrics. Newsweek 69:114 My 8 '67
Simon & Garfunkel in action. M. Ames. il Hi Fi 17:62-6 N '67
Simon & Garfunkel; interview. P. Simon; A. Garfunkel. New Yorker 43:24-7 S 2 '67
Socking it to 'em; G. McLendon's crusade against lyrics. Time 89:53 My 26 '67
Song too big for words: P. Nichols. J. Kornbluth. il Look 31:90+ N 28 '67
Sound of Bob Dylan. E. Willis. Commentary 44:71-8 N '67
Two fine rockers roll their own; Simon and Garfunkel. S. Kanfer. Life 62:18 Ap 21 '67
Words for new songs by Gentry, Simon, Ochs, Arlo Guthrie, and a surprise. il Mlle 66:94-7 D '67
See also
Israeli-Arab war, 1967—Songs and music
Phonograph records—Songs
Songs, American
Vietnamese war, 1957- —Songs and music

Europe, Eastern
In the socialist groove; socialist lyrics to capitalist tunes. Time 89:28-9 Je 30 '67

MUSIC, Portuguese
See also
Phonograph records—Portuguese music

MUSIC, Russian
See also
Phonograph records—Russian music

MUSIC, Wedding. See Wedding music

MUSIC and children
Never too young for music. C. R. Goldfarb. il Parents Mag 42:52-3+ My '67

MUSIC and color
Colors we hear. R. Freed. il House B 109:140+ My '67

MUSIC and mathematics. See Music—Theory

MUSIC and moving pictures. See Moving pictures—Music

MUSIC as recreation
Personal business; carry a tune instead of a tranquilizer. Bsns W p93-4 D 30 '67
Play is the thing! athletes as musicians. H. L. Masin. il Sr Schol 90:32 Ap 28 '67
Symphony for New York's elder population; Sirovich day center, New York city. G. Bamberger. il Parks & Rec 2:32+ My '67

MUSIC camps
Upbeat in the key of youth; Eastern music camp, Greensboro, N.C; interview, ed. by R. Hemming. S. Morgenstern. Sr Schol 90:20 My 5 '67

MUSIC conductors. See Conductors (music)

MUSIC conferences
Universa Laus; Spain, August, 1967; conference on liturgical music. D. A. Kister. America 117:522-3 N 4 '67

MUSIC contests. See Music—Competitions

MUSIC council, international. See International music council

MUSIC criticism. See Music—History and criticism

MUSIC critics. See Critics

MUSIC festivals
Pan American week; piano festival. Américas 19:44 Je '67

Austria
Von Karajan's Easter festival. P. Moor. il Hi Fi 17:MA21+ Je '67
See also
Salzburg festival

California
Anatomy of a love festival; Monterey international pop festival. R. Christgau. il Esquire 69:60-7+ Ja '68
Blow, Europe, blow! Monterey jazz festival. il Newsweek 70:86-7 O 2 '67
Boulez as composer, conductor, hero; Ojai report. S. Lowe. il Hi Fi 17:MA18-19 Ag '67
Competitive, cooperative, and communal. I. Kolodin. il Sat R 50:40-1 S 23 '67
Copland at the Bowl, Samuel at Cabrillo. I. Kolodin. Sat R 50:45 S 9 '67
Monterey's tenth jazz festival. il Sunset 139:42+ S '67
Music at Monterey. W. Conover. Sat R 50:109+ O 14 '67
Pop powwow; Monterey international pop festival. il Newsweek 70:80 Jl 3 '67
Soulin' at Monterey; first International pop festival. il Time 89:48 Je 30 '67
See also
Bach festivals

Colorado
Central City. B. Haddad. il Opera N 32:21-2 S 23 '67

England
Bath, Aldeburgh. T. Urquhart. Opera N 32:27 S 23 '67
Britten and the Aldeburgh miracle; Maltings at Snape. E. Greenfield. il Hi Fi 17:MA24-6 S '67
Glyndebourne. D. Shawe-Taylor. il Opera N 32:23 S 9 '67
Maltings at Snape; old malthouses converted into a concert hall for Aldeburgh music festival. il Arch Forum 127:66-71 N '67

Estonia
Incident at Tallinn; C. Lloyd at Tallinn jazz festival. J. Roddy. il Look 31:50 O 3 '67
Sound of music; Music—U.S.A. most popular radio program in eastern Europe. il Newsweek 69:50+ Je 5 '67

Europe
Guide to European music festivals, 1967; comp. by H. D. Jellinek. Sat R 50:52-3 Ap 15 '67

Europe, Western
Lively arts; festivally, it was an exciting summer. R. Hemming. Sr Schol 91:24 S 21 '67
Summer evenings (cont) Opera N 31:31-2 Ap 15 '67

France
Festival for the case-hardened veteran; Royan's international festival of contemporary art. P. Moor. Hi Fi 17:MA26+ Jl '67
Grand encounters; Touraine festival. il Time 90:49 Jl 14 '67
Strasbourg. M. E. Davies. Opera N 32:27 S 23 '67

MUSIC festivals—*Continued*

Germany (Democratic Republic)

Dresden, Berlin; Festival of the arts. J. H.
Sutcliffe. il Opera N 31:32 Mr 11 '67
Happy Handel festival; Halle report. J. H.
Sutcliffe. il Hi Fi 17:MA28-9+ S '67

Germany (Federal Republic)

Berlin, Hamburg; performances of Die
Walküre, and Otello. J. H. Sutcliffe. il
Opera N 32:26-7 N 25 '67
Festival in Berlin. J. Maguire. Sat R 50:75+
N 11 '67
Munich. E. Davidson; E. D. Echols. Opera N
32:27 O 14 '67
Quick, Karl, the potentiometer! Vacation
courses in new music at Darmstadt. il Time
90:78 S 8 '67
Schwetzingen. W. B. Rios. Opera N 31:27
Je 10 '67
    See also
Bayreuth festival

Greece, Modern

Greek drama; army coup interrupts the festival of Greece; interview, ed. by Q. Eaton.
D. Yannopoulos. il Opera N 32:14-15 D 30
'67

Iran

Festival in a fairy-tale kingdom; Festival of
the arts in Shiraz and Persepolis. P. Moor.
il Hi Fi 17:MA28-9 D '67

Ireland

Report: Wexford; productions of Shakes-
perian double, Rossini's Otello and Gounod's
Roméo et Juliette. M. E. Davies. Opera N
32:31-2 D 23 '67
Wexford. W. H. A. Williams. il Opera N 32:
14-17 O 14 '67

Italy

Donizetti's Pia de' Tolomei; Siena report. W.
Weaver. il Hi Fi 17:MA31 N '67
Florence; thirtieth Maggio musicale. T. Goth.
Opera N 32:24 S 9 '67
Forum for Toscanini; international conference
in Florence. J. W. Freeman. il Opera N 32:
6-7 S 9 '67
Old and new at the Umbrian festival. W.
Weaver. il Hi Fi 17:MA27+ D '67
30th biennale. J. Maguire. il Sat R 50:108-9
O 14 '67
Thirtieth Maggio musicale; Florence report.
W. Weaver. il Hi Fi 17:MA27+ S '67

Japan

In Japan: new Bayreuth productions; Tristan
and Walküre in Osaka. J. Wade. il Hi Fi
17:MA24-5+ Jl '67
Osaka. E. C. Wilkes. Opera N 31:26 Je 10 '67

Massachusetts

    See also
Berkshire symphonic festival

Missouri

Camping on Olympus; festival of 19th century music in Kansas City. il Time 89:70
Je 9 '67

Netherlands

Amsterdam. J. Mindszenthy. Opera N 32:24
S 23 '67
Holland festival, 1967. E. Helm. Hi Fi 17:MA26
O '67

New York (state)

Ambitious six-week repertory; Lake George
opera festival. H. Vincent. il Hi Fi 17:
MA15+ N '67
Burning fiery furnace; Caramoor report. P.
G. Davis. il Hi Fi 17:MA13 S '67
Caramoor; photographs. Opera N 31:14-15 Je
10 '67
Erotic dances in the starlight; presentations
at Caramoor, N.Y. W. Terry. il Sat R 50:
49-50 Jl 22 '67
Evening of dance, Caramoor. M. Marks.
Dance Mag 41:68 Ag '67
International ballet evening; Long Island
festival. J. Anderson. Dance Mag 41:76-7+
S '67
Katonah, N.Y; Burning fiery furnace at Car-
amoor festival. F. Merkling. il Opera N 32:
22 S 23 '67
Lake George; Douglas Moore's Ballad of Baby
Doe at Lake George opera festival. A. M.
Lingg. Opera N 32:23 O 14 '67
Third International Webern festival; Buffalo
report. J. Noble. Hi Fi 17:MA19 Ja '67

Norway

Bergen. F. Stevenson. Opera N 32:25 S 23 '67

Ohio

May festival: ovations and paid bills; Cincinnati report. A. Darack. Hi Fi 17:MA21+
Ag '67

Rhode Island

How to run a festival; Metropolitan opera in
Newport. il Time 90:50 S 1 '67
Met outdoors (and in) Verdi festival at New-
port. G. Movshon. il Hi Fi 17:MA12-13+ N
'67
Metropolitan opera at Newport, R.I. il Hi Fi
17:MA16-17 Ag '67
Music in the mansions; Metropolitan opera's
1967 Verdi festival, Newport. Q. Eaton. il
Opera N 32:6 O 14 '67
Musical events; Newport jazz festival. W.
Balliett. New Yorker 43:74+ Jl 22 '67
Newport; opera in town; photographs. Opera
N 31:18-20 Je 10 '67
Newport revisited. G. Lees. il Hi Fi 17:MA20-3
S '67
Verdi in Newport; Metropolitan opera festi-
val. H. Saal. il Newsweek 70:81 Ag 28 '67

Rumania

Bucharest battle; Georges Enesco festival.
Time 90:48 S 29 '67

Scotland

    See also
International festival of music and drama,
Edinburgh

Switzerland

Zurich; International June festival. E. V. Epstein. il Opera N 32:25 S 9 '67

United States

Lively arts; festivally, it was an exciting
summer. R. Hemming. Sr Schol 91:24 S 21
'67
Music festivals U.S.A, summer 1967; comp.
by H. D. Jellinek. Sat R 50:86-9 Je 10 '67
Special festival and summer study section. il
Am Rec G 33:704-15, 918-29 My-Je '67
Summer evenings (cont) Opera N 31:31-2 Ap
15 '67
Summer festivals in North America; a state-
by-state guide. il Hi Fi 17:MA28-32 My '67
U.S. music festivals. T. B. Lesure. il Travel
127:34-9+ Ja '67

Yugoslavia

Biennale 1967; Zagreb report. E. Helm. Hi Fi
17:MA28+ Ag '67

MUSIC for children
    See also
Phonograph records—Childrens records

MUSIC history. See Music—History and criticism

MUSIC in schools. See School music

MUSIC in the home
Eight rooms designed for looking and listen-
ing. E. McDonald. il House B 109:288-91+
N '67
Make yours a musical family. M. S. Egbert.
il Suc Farm 65:101+ Ja '67
    See also
Music rooms and equipment

MUSIC of the spheres. See Harmony of the
spheres

MUSIC rooms and equipment
Danish decor goes stereo; photographs by E.
Svensson; with editorial comment. Hi Fi
17:45, 46-53 Ap '67
Shelving the problem. S. Lowe. il Hi Fi 17:
68-71 S '67
Stereo alla Toscana. il Hi Fi 17:71-3 Ja '67

MUSIC schools
Special festival and summer study section.
il Am Rec G 33:704-15 My, 918-29 My-Je '67
    See also
Eastman school of music, Rochester, N.Y.
Manhattan school of music

MUSIC titles
Farewell to Feuerfest; concerning translation
of J. Strauss's title. R. Freed. Sat R 50:74
S 30 '67

MUSIC walls. See Music rooms and equipment

MUSICAL appreciation. See Music—Appreciation

MUSICAL arrangement
Farnon of England. G. Lees. il Hi Fi 17:101
Mr '67

MUSICAL careers. See Pianists

MUSICAL comedies, revues, etc.
    See also
Musical comedy, revue, etc.
Phonograph records—Musical comedies, re-
vues, etc.
Television broadcasting—Musical comedies,
revues, etc.

MUSICAL comedies, revues, etc.—*Continued*

Criticisms, plots, etc.

Apple tree
  Christian Cent 84:144 F 1 '67
  Dance Mag 41:22 F '67
Arabian nights
  America 117:139 Ag 5 '67
  Dance Mag 41:24-5 Ag '67
At the drop of another hat
  Commonweal 85:459 Ja 27 '67
By Jupiter
  America 116:264 F 18 '67
  New Yorker 42:46+ Ja 28 '67
Cabaret
  Christian Cent 84:1071-2 Ag 23 '67
  Look il 31:72-4+ Mr 7 '67
  Mlle il 64:186-7 Mr '67
  Reporter 36:49 Mr 9 '67
Carousel
  Dance Mag 41:25 F '67
Dynamite tonite
  Commonweal 86:126 Ap 14 '67
  Commonweal 86:152-4 Ap 21 '67
Finian's rainbow
  Dance Mag 41:26 My '67
Golden screw
  New Yorker 42:116+ F 11 '67
Gorilla queen
  New Repub 156:28-30 My 6 '67
  New Yorker 43:152 My 6 '67
Hair
  Dance Mag il 41:28-9 D '67
  New Repub 157:38-9 N 18 '67
  New Yorker 43:128+ N 11 '67
  Newsweek il 70:124 N 13 '67
  Sat R 51:95 Ja 13 '68
Hallelujah, baby!
  America 116:879 Je 24 '67
  Christian Cent 84:1106 Ag 30 '67
  Commonweal 86:342-5 Je 9 '67
  Dance Mag 41:78-9 Je '67
  Nat R 19:976-7 S 5 '67
  New Yorker 43:150 My 6 '67
  Newsweek il 69:116 My 8 '67
  Sat R 50:66 My 13 '67
  Time il 89:58 My 5 '67
Hello, Dolly!
  America 118:20 Ja 6 '68
  Ebony il 23:83-9 Ja '68
  Life il 63:128-30+ D 8 '67
  Newsweek il 70:105 N 27 '67
  Sat R 50:24 D 2 '67
  Time il 90:56 N 24 '67
Henry, sweet Henry
  America 117:624 N 18 '67
  Newsweek 70:89A N 6 '67
  Sat R 50:26 N 11 '67
How now, Dow Jones
  Nation 206:28 Ja 1 '68
  New Yorker 43:97 D 16 '67
  Newsweek 70:94+ D 18 '67
I do! I do!
  America 116:263 F 18 '67
  Christian Cent 84:144 F 1 '67
Illya darling
  America 116:737-8 My 13 '67
  Commonweal 86:342-5 Je 9 '67
  Dance Mag 41:38 Je '67
  Newsweek il 69:107 Ap 24 '67
  Sat R 50:47 Ap 29 '67
  Time 89:83 Ap 21 '67
In circles
  Nation 205:572 N 27 '67
  New Yorker 43:131-3 N 18 '67
  Newsweek 70:105 N 27 '67
In the nick of time
  Commonweal 86:394 Je 23 '67
Joyful noise
  Dance Mag 41:23 F '67
Love and let love
  New Yorker 43:58-9 Ja 13 '68
Now is the time for all good men
  America 117:421-2 O 14 '67
  New Yorker 43:133-4 O 7 '67
Sherry
  America 116:736-7 My 13 '67
  Christian Cent 84:870-1 Jl 5 '67
  Commonweal 86:208-10 My 5 '67
  Dance Mag 41:27-8 My '67
  New Yorker 43:138 Ap 8 '67
  Newsweek il 69:109 Ap 10 '67
  Vogue 149:142 My '67
Shoemaker's holiday
  New Yorker 43:127-8+ Mr 11 '67
Sound of music
  Dance Mag 41:38+ Je '67
South Pacific
  America 117:63 Jl 15 '67
Walking happy
  America 116:160 Ja 28 '67
Wonderful town
  Dance Mag 41:70-1 Jl '67

You're a good man, Charlie Brown
  Christian Cent 84:1561 D 6 '67
  Nat R 19:976-8 S 5 '67
  Nation 204:444-5 Ap 3 '67
  New Yorker 43:121-3 Mr 18 '67
  Newsweek 69:109 Mr 20 '67
  Sat R 50:42 Ap 1 '67
  Time il 89:62 Mr 17 '67
MUSICAL comedy production. See Theatrical production
MUSICAL comedy, revue, etc.
  Goings on about town. See issues of New Yorker
  It's a bird! it's a plane! it's industrials! W. Como. il Dance Mag 41:24-5 Je '67
  Peripatetic reviewer; composition demands of the new musical theater on Broadway. E. Weeks. Atlan 220:108 Jl '67
MUSICAL composition. See Composition (music)
MUSICAL education
  Key to teaching music; Owatonna, Minn; interview. R. Tenney. il NEA J 56:69-70 D '67
    See also
  Music and children
  Opera—Instruction and study
  Piano—Instruction and study
  School music
MUSICAL festivals. See Music festivals
MUSICAL films. See Moving pictures—Musical films
MUSICAL form
    See also
  Concertos
MUSICAL instruments
  Musical instrument sound chart. il Electr World 78:45 Ag '67
  New performances on old instruments; Concentus musicus ensemble. E. Helm. il Hi Fi 17:42-6 My '67
  Pleasing to the eye and ear alike; rare and beautiful musical instruments at Metropolitan museum of art. E. P. Birk. il Antiques 92:434 O '67
  Siren sounds of harpsichord, virginal, and clavichord, the lute and the recorder. A. Rich. il House B 109:122-3+ Ja '67
  When Orpheus struck the trembling lyre. L. Pareti. il UNESCO Courier 20:9-11 My '67
    See also
  Percussion instruments
  Stringed instruments
    also names of musical instruments, e.g. Harmonicas
MUSICAL instruments, Electronic
  Current scene. Time 90:42 Jl 7 '67
  Design of an electronic guitar system. J. Arndt. il Electr World 77:26-7+ F '67
  Electronic guitars and amplifiers. D. Queen. il Electr World 77:38-41 F '67
  Electronic percussion instruments. C. Muller. il Electr World 77:36-7 F '67
  Guitar-organ; unusual instrument combines electronic guitar and organ. Electr World 77:65 F '67
  Loudspeakers for electronic musical instruments. K. Kramer. Electr World 77:32 Je '67
  So your youngster wants an electric guitar. il Consumer Bul 50:26-30 D '67
  Varitone electronic saxophone. D. Tomcik. il Electr World 77:30+ F '67
    See also
  Theremin
MUSICAL instruments, Hindu
    See also
  Sitar
MUSICAL instruments, Primitive
  Family of twang. F. V. Grunfeld. Reporter 36:39-40+ Ap 20 '67
MUSICAL prodigies. See Children as musicians
MUSICAL societies
    See also
  International Bach society
MUSICAL theory. See Music—Theory
MUSICAL titles. See Music titles
MUSICIANS
  Artist life. D. J. Soria. See issues of High fidelity incorporating Musical America
  Debuts & reappearances; New York concerts. il Hi Fi 17:MA16-21+ My '67
  Here & there. See issues of High fidelity incorporating Musical America
  Music has its humor. G. Lees. Hi Fi 17:118 Ja '67
  Musical whirl; photographs. See issues of High fidelity incorporating Musical America

MUSICIANS—*Continued*
Psychic symphony; typing the man by the instrument he plays. il Time 89:69-70 F 17 '67
Where the big bands are. G. Lees. il Hi Fi 17:100 S '67
See also
Children as musicians
Composers
Conductors (music)
Jazz musicians
Orchestras
Pianists

Bibliography
Book reviews. See issues of American record guide

Dictionaries
Dictionary of musicians from the earliest times, ed. by J. S. Sainsbury. Review
Am Rec G 33:847 My '67. W. S. Kimmel

Salaries
Cost of opera. A. M. Lingg. Opera N 31:14-15 Mr 25 '67
Horizon, with clouds; cultural explosion a boom or a bust? M. Mayer. il Opera N 32:8-11 S 9 '67

Supply and demand
Horizon, with clouds; cultural explosion a boom or a bust? M. Mayer. il Opera N 32:8-11 S 9 '67

MUSICIANS, American
Young excitement in music; three who are making it. A. Rich. il House B 109:102-3+ Jl '67
See also
Bernstein, L.
Coleman, O.
Goodman, B.
Jazz musicians
Porter, C.

MUSICIANS, Austrian
See also
Mozart, J. C. W. A.

MUSICIANS, Canadian
Music and musicians of Canada. P. Ashley. il Sat R 50:66-7 Ap 29 '67

MUSICIANS, Chinese
See also
Ma, S. T.

MUSICIANS, Czech
See also
Martinů, B.

MUSICIANS, French
See also
Fournier, P.

MUSICIANS, Indian (East Indian)
Reporter at large. V. Mehta. New Yorker 43:159-60+ D 9 '67

MUSICIANS, Italian
See also
Toscanini, A.

MUSICIANS, Japanese
Invasion from the Orient. il Time 90:46 N 3 '67

MUSICIANS, Polish
See also
Rubinstein, A.

MUSICIANS, Russian
See also
Rostropovich, M.

MUSICIANS, Spanish
See also
Casals, P.

MUSICIANS of Bremen town; drama. See Roberts, W.

MUSK oxen
Golden shmoo of the barren lands. D. Connelly. il Sports Illus 27:44-7 Jl 17 '67
Return of the musk ox. il Life 63:95-6+ S 15 '67

MUSKA, Rudolph C.
Uncharted future of faith. Sat R 50:34-5+ Jl 22 '67

MUSKEGON, Mich.

Churches
Bold geometric image for a church; St Francis de Sales church. il Arch Rec 142:130-7 N '67

MUSKELLUNGE fishing
Boss of the weed beds. W. Davis. il Outdoor Life 140:114-17+ O '67
Don't bet on a muskie. J. O. Cartier. il Outdoor Life 139:50-1+ Je '67
Some like it cold. J. Hayes. il Field & S 72:46-7+ D '67
Suckers for muskies. F. M. Stephey. il Outdoor Life 139:148 Mr '67

MUSKIE, Edmund Sixtus
Excerpt from debate. August 18, 1966. Cong Digest 46:54+ F '67

about
Air quality act of 1967; a step forward, but don't expect immediate improvement of your air. B. Nelson. il por Science 158:355-7 O 20 '67
Muskie of Maine. M. Nolan. Reporter 37:44-6 Jl 13 '67
Thermal pollution: Senator Muskie tells AEC to cool it. B. Nelson. Science 158:755-6 N 10 '67
Washington. D. Kiker. Atlan 220:4+ Ag '67

MUSKINGUM watershed conservancy district
Ohio's new lakes; Tappan, Atwood, Leesville, Clendening, Piedmont and Seneca lakes. G. Lindsey. Travel 127:41 My '67

MUSKOXEN. See Musk oxen

MUSLIMS (Negro cult) See Black Muslim movement

MUSLIMS in China (People's Republic)
Russia gives China anti-Moslem label. M. Bourdeaux. Christian Cent 84:1108-9 Ag 30 '67

MUSORGSKII, Modest Petrovich
Boris Godunov. Criticism
New Yorker 43:144 S 9 '67
Opera N 32:28 D 16 '67
Sat R 50:64+ S 16 '67

MUSSAENDA erythrophylla
Colorful new shrub; ashanti blood. E. A. Menninger. il Horticulture 45:43 D '67

MUSSELS
Mussels in the pipeline; clogging mollusks. D. A. Ehrlich. Sci N 92:471 N 11 '67

MUSSINI, Emilio, and others
Collagen proline hydroxylase in wound healing, granuloma formation, scurvy, and growth. bibliog Science 157:927-9 Ag 25 '67

MUSTACHES
Mustache is back. il Newsweek 71:81 Ja 22 '68

MUSTARD gas
Sulfur mustard and X-rays: differences in expression of lethal damage. F. Mauro and M. M. Elkind. bibliog il Science 155:1561-3 Mr 24 '67

MUSTE, Abraham John
A.J. T. Roszak. Nation 204:293-4 Mr 6 '67
Abraham Johannes. por Newsweek 69:104+ Mr 20 '67
A. J. Muste: 1885-1967. N. Hentoff. por Sat R 50:35 Ap 8 '67
Grand old man of American pacifism. Christian Cent 84:230 F 22 '67
Moral man. G. Woodcock. Commentary 44:104-6+ O '67
Number one pacifist. N. J. Whitney. Christian Cent 84:622-4 My 10 '67
Obituary
Commonweal 86:14-16 Mr 24 '67

MUSTER, Karl W.
These techniques work for me. NEA J 56:16-18 S '67

MUSTOE, Judy, and Yourke, Electra
We just sailed the Atlantic, said my husband casually. pors Redbook 129:62-3+ Ag '67

MUTAROTASE
Mutarotase in erythrocytes: isolation and properties. W. Sacks. bibliog il Science 158:498-9 O 27 '67

MUTATION (bacteria)
Azure mutants: a type of host dependent mutant of the bacteriophage f2. K. Horiuchi and N. D. Zinder. bibliog il Science 156:1618-23 Je 23 '67
Induction of mutants with altered DNA composition: effect of ultraviolet on bacterium paracoli 5099. G. F. Gause and others. bibliog il Science 157:1196-7 S 8 '67
Mutagenesis by near-visible light. H. E. Kubitschek. bibliog il Science 155:1545-6 Mr 24 '67
Mutagenesis in escherichia coli by visible light. R. B. Webb and M. M. Malina. bibliog il Science 156:1104-5 My 26 '67
Substrate binding properties of mutant and wild-type A proteins of escherichia coli tryptophan synthetase. J. K. Hardman and C. Yanofsky. bibliog il Science 156:1369-71 Je 9 '67
Suppressor selection for amino acid replacements expected on the basis of the genetic code. H. Berger and C. Yanofsky. bibliog il Science 156:394-7 Ap 21 '67

MUTATION (biology)
Athens variant of glucose-6-phosphate dehydrogenase. G. Stamatoyannopoulos and others. bibliog il Science 157:831-3 Ag 18 '67
Chemical production of mutations. C. Auerbach. bibliog Science 158:1141-7 D 1 '67
Hereditary renal disease in a mutant strain of rats. B. B. Lozzio and others. bibliog il Science 156:1742-4 Je 30 '67

NEA. See National education association

NEA mutual fund. See Investment trusts

NERVA (nuclear engine for rocket vehicle application) See Rockets, Atomic powered

NET. See National educational television network

NFL. See National football league

NFO. See National farmers organization

NFWA. See National farm worker's association

NHL. See National hockey league

NICB. See National industrial conference board

NICEM (National information center for educational media) See Southern California university, Los Angeles

NIFA. See National intercollegiate flying association

NIH. See United States—National institutes of health

NLF (national liberation front) See Political parties—Vietnam

NLM. See United States—National library of medicine

NLRB. See United States—National labor relations board

NLW. See National library week

NMU. See National maritime union of America

NPD (National democratic party) See Political parties—Germany (Federal Republic)

NRAO. See National radio astronomy observatory, Green Bank, W.Va.

NRC. See Natural resources council of America

NRMA. See National retail merchants association

NRPA. See National recreation and park association

NSA. See United States national student association

NSC. See United States—National security council

NSF. See United States—National science foundation

NSRDS (national standard reference data system) See Information storage and retrieval systems

NSU-Wankel engines. See Automobile engines

NYPL. See New York public library

NYSE (New York stock exchange) See Stock exchange—New York (city)

NYYC. See New York yacht club

NABATAEANS
Desert waterworks of the ancient Nabataeans. P. C. Hammond. il Natur Hist 76:36-43 Je '67

NABB, Edward H.
Great impact. Yachting 123:80-2+ Ja '68
More power to you. Yachting 122:28 N; 32+ D '67
New outboard engines, 1968. Yachting 122:44-6+ O '67
Tomorrow's marine engines are running today. Pop Mech 127:128-32+ Je '67

NABOKOV, Vladimir
And now, poshlost. por Time 90:118 D 1 '67
Artist in pursuit of butterflies. H. Gold. il pors Sat Eve Post 240:81-5 F 11 '67
Little girl migrates. C. Brown. New Repub 158:19-20 Ja 20 '68
Man of many words. G. Hicks. Sat R 50:31-2 Ja 28 '67; Discussion. 50:30 F 18 '67
Nabokov. by A. Field. Review
Sat R 50:30 Ag 26 '67. G. Kersh
Nabokov the magician. E. Janeway. por Atlan 220:66-71 Jl '67
Virtuoso. S. K. Oberbeck. pors Newsweek 70:74-5 Jl 31 '67

NABORS, Jim
Success is a warm puppy. il por Time 90:88 N 10 '67

NABRIT, James M. Jr
Urge to retire. por Time 90:57 Jl 21 '67

NACE, Raymond L.
Some pertinent comments on water problems: summary of address, May 2, 1967. R. L. Nace. Nat Parks Mag 41:21 Ag '67

NADEL, Michael
Among the books. Liv Wildn 30:30-1 Aut '66

NADEL, Norman
Roller furling jibs. Yachting 122:54-5+ N '67

NADER, Ralph
Business crime. New Repub 157:7-8 Jl 1; 35 S 9 '67
Inventions and their uses. New Repub 157:32-4 Jl 22 '67
Something fishy. New Repub 158:19-21 Ja 6 '68

Watch that hamburger. New Repub 157:15-16 Ag 19 '67
We're still in the jungle. New Repub 157:11-12 Jl 15 '67
X-ray exposures. New Repub 157:11-12 S 2 '67

about

Auto safety; the truth and the hokum. J. Chamberlain. il por Nat R 19:343-6 Ap 4 '67
Caveat vendor. por Time 90:28-9 D 15 '67
Meet Ralph Nader. il por Newsweek 71:65-7+ Ja 22 '68
Nader affair. J. Ridgeway and D. Sanford. New Repub 156:16-18 F 18 '67
Nader again. Newsweek 69:85-6 F 20 '67
Nader takes potshots at the '68s. R. W. Irvin. il Motor T 19:79-81 Mr '67; Discussion. 19:82 Mr; 30 Je '67
Ralph Nader, crusader; or, The rise of a self-appointed lobbyist. P. Anderson. il pors N Y Times Mag p25+ O 29 '67

NAESS, Ragnar
Not worried about stock market; interview. por U S News 63:42-3 D 4 '67

NÄF, Ulrich
Anemia phyllitidis: inducibility of physiological state antagonistic to antheridium formation. bibliog Science 156:1117-19 My 26 '67

NAGASAKI
Fall of Japan; excerpt. W. Craig. il Sat Eve Post 240:36-8+ Ag 26 '67

NAGLE, Darragh E.
Linear accelerators for protons: new developments. bibliog Science 157:145-9 Jl 14 '67

NAGOYA, Japan
Reporter at large: Higashiyama zoo. E. Kahn. New Yorker 43:123-6 S 23 '67

NAHUATL literature. See Aztec literature

NAIL-biting
Nail-biting and thumb-sucking: habit or need? B. Bettelheim. Ladies Home J 84:32 F '67

NAILS (anatomy)
Nails. il Mlle 64:136-7 F '67

NAIPAUL, V. S.
Speaking out. por Sat Eve Post 240:12+ Je 3 '67

NAIR, C. Kunchu
Kathakali and the dance-drama of India. por UNESCO Courier 20:36-42 D '67

NAIROBI NATIONAL PARK
Orphanage for wild animals. R. Greenough. il UNESCO Courier 20:27-9 Ap '67

NAISBITT, John
Education in Vietnam. il Sat R 50:53-5+ Jl 15 '67

NAISMITH, Grace
Operation every woman should understand. Todays Health 45:50-1+ Ap '67

NAJER, Alfred
Why I am for Article XIV. por Am For 73:30-1+ Ag '67

NAKA, K. I. See Kishida, K. jt. auth.

NAKANO, Masayasu. See Braun, W. jt. auth.

NAKEDNESS. See Nudism

NAKIAN, Reuben
Demigods from Stamford. il por Time 89:50-1 Je 30 '67

NAMATH, Joe Willie
Joe Namath. B. Long. il pors Vogue 149:156-7+ F 1 '67
Plays go for the new Joe. E. Shrake. il pors Sports Illus 27:34-7 O 16 '67
Two for the football show: the swinger and the square. J. Lake. il pors N Y Times Mag p40-1+ N 5 '67

NAMBOODIRIPAD, Elankulam Manakkal Sankaran
Communist Brahmin. E. Behr. Newsweek 69:54 Mr 20 '67

NAMES
See also
Corporations—Names

NAMES, Fictitious. See Pseudonyms

NAMES, Geographical
Standardization of geographical names; UN conference. UN Mo Chron 4:35 O '67
See also
Street names

NAMES, Jewish
Jews, by R. Peyrefitte. Review
Newsweek 71:64 Ja 8 '68. S. Maloff

NAMES, Literary. See Characters in literature

NAMES, Lunar
Delayed christening. il Time 90:37 S 8 '67

NAMES, Personal
How to choose the right name for your baby. S. G. Streshinsky. il Parents Mag 42:62-3+ O '67

NARCOTICS, Bureau of. See United States—
Narcotics, Bureau of
NARCOTICS, Control of
Curbing the drug traffic in Britain; plans
to change prescription system. B. Wen-
ham. New Repub 156:9-10 Mr 18 '67
Drugs on campus; undercover agents at
Cornell and Fairleigh Dickinson universi-
ties. il Time 89:36+ Mr 24 '67
Failure of permissiveness: addiction increas-
ing in Great Britain. il Time 89:76 F 17 '67
Permanent central narcotics board; final ses-
sion at Geneva. UN Mo Chron 4:95-6 D '67
Spies, J.G; campus-spy game. il Newsweek
69:112 Mr 27 '67
War on narcotics; illegal fields of marijuana
and amapola in Mexico. J. N. Bell. il Todays
Health 45:48-62 Jl '67
While you weren't looking; Senate ratifies a
new international treaty. New Repub 157:7
Jl 8 '67

See also
Narcotic addicts
United Nations—International narcotics con-
trol board
NASA. See United States—National aeronautics
and space administration
NASA commuter airlines, incorporated
New commuter airline planning MSC-Houston
airport shuttle. Aviation W 87:86 Jl 3 '67
NASH, Manning
American dream and dilemma. Sat R 50:30-1
Jl 8 '67
NASH, Mary
How to raise a bookworm. Redbook 128:63+
Mr '67
NASH, Ogden
God bless the Gideons; poem. New Yorker
43:30 Jl 1 '67
If a boder meet a boder, need a boder cry?
yes; poem. New Yorker 43:58 O 28 '67
If there were no England, Country life could
invent it; poem. New Yorker 43:54 O 14 '67
Ill Met by Zenith; poem. New Yorker 43:40
Ap 1 '67
Mr Judd and his snail; poem. Sat Eve Post
240:18 S 23 '67
My mind is reeling; poem. Holiday 42:42 Ag
'67
Nonbiography of a nobody; poem. Sat R 50:8
Ap 1 '67
Take off with books; poem. Pub W 192:162
Jl 10 '67
Tale of two husbands; poem. Sat R 50:6
Je 24 '67
We're fine, just fine; poem. New Yorker 43:
40 F 25 '67
While Homer nodded: a footnote to the Iliad;
poem. Harper 234:63 F '67
NASH, Ralph G. and Woolson, E. A.
Persistence of chlorinated hydrocarbon in-
secticides in soils. bibliog Science 157:924-
7 Ag 25 '67
NASH, Ray
Genius of Rudloph Ruzicka. Am Artist 31:44-
50+ D '67
NASHVILLE, Tenn.

Education
Teachers reach the children with affection
and new ways; Nashville educational improvement project. il Life 63:102-3+ S 29
'67

Music
Nashville the sounds and the symbols; country
and western scene. G. Lees. il Hi Fi 17:57-61
Ap '67

Police
How much force? il Time 89:58 Mr 24 '67

Politics and government
City pulls itself together; Nashville-Davidson
County merger. J. N. Miller. Read Digest
91:132-6 Jl '67

Riots
Already under way: '67 racial flare-ups. il U S
News 62:10 Ap 24 '67
Go for the honkies; aftermath of S. Car-
michael visit. Newsweek 69:28 Ap 24 '67

Theater
Night at the opry. W. P. Fox, jr. il Holiday
41:99-100+ My '67
NASSAU, Bahama Islands
Let's travel. E. Schoen. il Mlle 65:30+ Jl '67
NASSAU COUNTY, N.Y.
Drinking water from sewage? A. Gruenwald.
il Am City 82:92-3 Mr '67
Teachers know the score in Nassau County;
new social studies planning and service
center. W. A. Zeralzky and E. Schester. il
Sr Schol 91:sup 17-20 O 26 '67

NASSAU library system
Library automation: an essential of service.
A. Geddes. ALA Bul 61:642-6 Je '67
NASSER, Gamal Abdel
Ass in lion's skin. R. Moley. Newsweek 69:80
Je 26 '67
Boss holds out. por Newsweek 70:67 O 23 '67
Double-think, Egyptian style. A. Carthew.
il pors N Y Times Mag p 19-21+ Ag 20
'67
Hatreds, tensions and theatrics. Life 62:4
Je 9 '67
In disaster's wake; resignation refused. il
por Time 89:32+ Je 16 '67
In the wake of war: can Nasser survive? il
por U S News 62:32 Je 26 '67
Incurable arsonist. il Time 89:36 My 12 '67
Intransigence renewed. por Time 90:28+ D 1
'67
Mideast: hail the conquered hero. il por
Newsweek 70:34-6 S 11 '67
Nasser and Israel. New Repub 156:1-3 Je 3
'67; Discussion. 156:34 Je 24 '67
Nasser of Egypt; he has landed on his feet
again. il por U S News 64:32-3 Ja 1 '68
Nasser the troublemaker: what he is up to
now. por U S News 62:19-20 Je 5 '67
Nasser's drive for south Arabia. L. Mosher.
il Reporter 36:24-7 F 9 '67
Night to remember. Newsweek 70:40+ Ag 7
'67
There is no false courage left in Egypt. A.
Carthew. il pors N Y Times Mag p45-7+
D 3 '67
What Nasser has won by his threats. J. Law.
il por U S News 62:35-6 Je 12 '67
What the West can expect after Nasser. il
U S News 62:23 Je 19 '67
Why Nasser is no longer a free agent. L.
Muray. New Repub 157:10-11 D 23 '67
NAT Turner's insurrection. See Southampton
insurrection, 1831
NATCHEZ, Miss.
Natchez, lovely Natchez; concerning the
film, Black Natchez. R. Coles. New Repub
156:31-4 F 18 '67
Natchez, Mississippi. il Bet Hom & Gard
45:26 Ag '67
NATHAN, David G. See Baehner, R. L. jt.
auth.
NATHAN, George Jean award. See George Jean
Nathan award
NATHAN, Paul
Rights and permissions. See issues of Pub-
lishers' weekly
NATHAN, Robert
Heidenleben; poem. Sat R 50:4 Je 10 '67
Single destiny. Sat R 50:4 Mr 18 '67
NATHAN, Simon. See Simon
NATION (periodical)
West coast office; Frontier magazine merger.
Nation 204:259 F 27 '67
NATIONAL academy of engineering
New members of science and engineering
academies. Science 156:630-1 My 5 '67
NATIONAL academy of religion and mental
health. See Academy of religion and mental
health
NATIONAL academy of sciences
Abstracts of papers presented at meetings,
1967. Science 156:535-44; 158:523-38 Ap 28,
O 27 '67
Committee to organize an international book
institute. Pub W 191:31-2 My 1 '67
Membership of the National academy of
sciences as of 1 July 1966. Science 156:224-5
Ap 14 '67
National academy of sciences. D. S. Green-
berg. il Science 156:222-3+, 360-4, 488-93
Ap 14-28 '67; Reply. J. H. Hildebrand. 156:
1177 Je 2 '67
NAS charts goals for applied technology.
J. F. Judge. Tech W 20:36-7 Je 19 '67
NAS notes. Sci N 92:467 N 11 '67
New members of science and engineering
academies. Science 156:630-1 My 5 '67
Oceanography 1966, NAS report. Science 155:
1391 Mr 17 '67
Policing the consequences of science; pro-
posed Committee on biological research, so-
cial behavior, and social policy. J. Lear. Sat
R 50:67 D 2 '67
Racial studies: Academy states position on
call for new research; statement. Science
158:892-3 N 17 '67

Board on medicine
From lab to patient; newly appointed Board
on medicine. Sci N 92:514 N 25 '67
NAS establishes Board on medicine. Science
158:891 N 17 '67

NATIONAL academy of sciences—*Continued*

Committee on potential contamination and interference from satellites
Crack in able; plan for a gigantic mirror to be in orbit and beam sun's rays down to earth. Sci N 91:304 Ap 1 '67

Space science board
Planetary investigations; excerpt from Space research: directions for the future. il Bul Atomic Sci 23:10 My '67

NATIONAL academy of television arts and sciences. See Academy of television arts and sciences

NATIONAL advisory commission on health manpower. See United States—National advisory commission on health manpower

NATIONAL advisory commission on libraries. See United States—National advisory commission on libraries

NATIONAL advisory committee on aeronautics. See United States—National advisory committee on aeronautics

NATIONAL advisory council on the education of disadvantaged children. See United States—National advisory council on the education of disadvantaged children

NATIONAL advisory health council. See United States—National advisory health council

NATIONAL aeronautics and space administration. See United States—National aeronautics and space administration

NATIONAL air taxi conference
Air taxi conference asks CAB for new industry regulations. Aviation W 86:39 Ap 10 '67

NATIONAL airlines incorporated
Booked for travel; new terminal. H. Sutton. Sat R 50:48-9 Mr 4 '67

NATIONAL archery association
Archery for the young. G. H. Gillelan. il Outdoor Life 140:24-7+ N '67

NATIONAL armed forces museum and park (proposed) See Smithsonian institution

NATIONAL art education association
Art educator award, NAEA 1967. Sch Arts 66:4 Je '67

NATIONAL association for pastoral renewal
Challenging celibacy; National association for pastoral renewal's plan. il Newsweek 69:61 Ap 3 '67

NATIONAL association for the advancement of colored people
Blackout; continuation of moderate civil-rights course. Newsweek 70:24+ Jl 24 '67
Green power; National Negro business and professional committee to subsidize the N.A.A.C.P. legal-defense and educational fund. Time 89:21 Mr 31 '67
Honor guard of the NAACP. il Ebony 22:53-4+ Mr '67
NAACP sues to integrate Alabama schools. Library J 92:278 Ja 15 '67
Roy Wilkins, Mr Civil Rights. I. Ross. Read Digest 92:86-91 Ja '68

NATIONAL association of broadcasters
See also
Television information office

NATIONAL association of business economists
Growth has its pains; NABE survey, with editorial comment. il Bsns W p31-3, 188 O 7 '67

NATIONAL association of college stores
ATPI-NACS: problems of order-fulfillment. Pub W 191:31-2 Mr 13 '67
NACS plans for expansion in growing market; annual convention. il Pub W 191:24-39 My 22 '67
1966 in review. Pub W 191:54 Ja 30 '67
To sit down and talk it out. D. Rustin. Pub W 191:47 My 22 '67

NATIONAL association of flight instructors
NAFI: more professionalism. Flying 80:16+ Je '67

NATIONAL association of housing and redevelopment officials
Marie C. McGuire housing expert honored by NAHRO. Am City 82:28+ Ap '67

NATIONAL association of laymen. See Laity—Catholic church

NATIONAL association of manufacturers
New NAM; project aimed at enlisting young executives to help train the jobless and participate in other poverty programs. Newsweek 69:76+ My 15 '67

NATIONAL association of music merchants
Counterattack in Chicago. Hi Fi 17:38 S '67

NATIONAL association of photo-lithographers
Web offset for books: a major NAPL topic. F. B. Myrick. il Pub W 192:62-3+ O 2 '67

NATIONAL association of secondary-school principals
Meeting, 1967. Sr Schol 90:sup2 Mr 17; sup8 Ap 7 '67

NATIONAL association of securities dealers
New no. 1 salesman. Time 89:95 Ap 28 '67

NATIONAL association of social workers
You'd better count me out. R. B. Miller. America 116:590-3 Ap 22 '67

NATIONAL Audubon society
Callison named society's top administrator. Audubon 69:19 Ja '67
Era of great progress. C. W. Buchheister. Audubon 69:4-5 Ja '67
National Audubon society sues to protect the Everglades. C. H. Callison. Audubon 69:56-7 My '67
Sacramento notebook; 62nd convention in Sacramento, Calif. L. Line. il Audubon 69:76-7 Mr '67
See also
Audubon medal

NATIONAL automobile dealers association
Auto dealers fret over '67 performance; confusion over callbacks, credit and Vietnam. il Bsns W p32-3 F 4 '67
Seasonal demand and used car prices. il Mo Labor R 90:12-16 O '67

NATIONAL ballet
Capital surprise. H. Saal. il Newsweek 69:107-8 Ap 10 '67
Getting to know you; a review of the National ballet of Washington; New York city center. M. Marks. il Dance Mag 41:63-5 My '67
Musical events; performance of Homage; Night; La peri; Four temperaments at City Center. W. Sargeant. New Yorker 43:158 Ap 8 '67
National ballet; Whitman auditorium, Brooklyn college. D. Hering. Dance Mag 41:72 D '67
World of dance; program at the Walt Whitman auditorium of Brooklyn college. W. Terry il Sat R 50:80-1 N 11 '67

NATIONAL ballet of Canada
Beautiful dances and cruel swans; Erik Bruhn's new production of Swan lake. R. Hicklin. il Dance Mag 41:30-1 My '67

NATIONAL baseball hall of fame and museum
Thank God for nuts. W. K. Zinsser. il Look 31:4 Ag 8 '67
Time to go to Cooperstown; photographs by J. Drake; with account by W. Leggett. Sports Illus 27:28-33 Jl 24 '67

NATIONAL basketball association
Bay of bigs. Sports Illus 26:17 Je 12 '67

NATIONAL better business bureaus. See Better business bureaus

NATIONAL bicycle championships. See Bicycle racing

NATIONAL biscuit company
Turning men into decision-makers; interview. L. S. Bickmore. Nations Bsns 55:88-90+ O '67

NATIONAL boat show. See Boats—Exhibitions

NATIONAL book awards
Book awards; an eventful week. il Pub W 191:30-3 Mr 20 '67
Contenders listed for National book awards. Pub W 191:46 F 6 '67; Same. Library J 92:764-88+ F 15 '67; Wilson Lib Bul 41:666 Mr '67
Judges for the National book awards. Wilson Lib Bul 42:269 N '67; Same. Library J 92:3948 N 1 '67
Judges named for National book awards. Pub W 192:35 O 16 '67
NBA betting game. J. K. Hutchens. Sat R 50:25-6+ Mr 18 '67
National book awards '67; winners. il Newsweek 69:103+ Mr 20 '67; Same. Wilson Lib Bul 41:783-4 Ap '67; Same. Pub W 191:36-7 Mr 13 '67; Library J 92:1470+ Ap 1 '67
New National book award established for translations. Pub W 191:52-3 F 13 '67
Reading and one's own perspective. J. Foster. il Sr Schol 90:sup20-1 Ap 28 '67
Walkout, newsbreak mar National book awards. Library J 92:1397 Ap 1 '67
Winners. S. Kauffmann. New Repub 156:18+ Ap 1 '67
Wrong symbol; choice of H. H. Humphrey as principal speaker. Nation 204:357 Mr 20 '67

NATIONAL book committee
Book committee charts future programs. il Pub W 192:23-4 D 11 '67
National book committee announces 1968 plans. il Library J 93:21 Ja 1 '68
1966 in review. Pub W 191:54 Ja 30 '67
See also
National medal for literature

NATIONAL broadcasting company
Filtering out the facts; Strickman's damages suit. il Newsweek 71:52 Ja 1 '68
NBC buys golf. il Time 89:85 Mr 10 '67
NATIONAL broadcasting company symphony orchestra. See Radio broadcasting—Music
NATIONAL budget. See Budget—United States
NATIONAL bureau of economic research
Life in the old boom yet; drops in NBER's leading indicators. il Bsns W p39-42 Mr 25 '67
Outgrowing the business cycle. Bsns W p 119-20 My 6 '67
NATIONAL bureau of standards. See United States—Standards, National bureau of
NATIONAL business aircraft association
Annual report to the single-engine stockholders. R. Blodget. il Flying 81:34-7 O '67
Business pilots seek alternates; facilities to help reduce the load at major terminal airports. Aviation W 87:27 S 11 '67
NATIONAL car rental systems, Incorporated
Killing. Newsweek 70:78 O 23 '67
NATIONAL Catholic conference for interracial justice
Lecture the leaders; concerning Robert Kennedy address. Commonweal 86:539 S 8 '67
NATIONAL Catholic educational association
Catholic education in crisis; conference. J. H. Lloyd. Sr Schol 91:sup2 D 7 '67
Meeting, 1967. Sr Schol 90:sup2+ Ap 28 '67
Price tags for Catholic education. R. Hassenger. Commonweal 86:223-4 My 12 '67
NATIONAL Catholic news service
Tomorrow never comes. S. J. Adamo. America 116:704-5 My 6 '67
NATIONAL Catholic office for motion pictures
Double standard. il Time 89:104 Ap 28 '67
No more ratings? G. D. Phillips. America 117:560-1 N 11 '67
NATIONAL Catholic office for radio and television
Danger ahead; NCCM-NCORT tension. Commonweal 87:372-3 D 22 '67
NATIONAL Catholic welfare conference
CRS and the militia; Catholic relief services policy in South Vietnam. America 117:233-4 S 9 '67
Chauvinistic Catholic charity; American Catholic relief services. Commonweal 87:159-60 N 10 '67
Political ocean; cooperative enterprise in African fishing village. America 116:825 Je 10 '67
NATIONAL center for atmospheric research
Closing the weather gap; Line Islands experiment. il Sci N 91:325 Ap 8 '67
Pueblo for highbrows; NCAR complex at Boulder, Colo. il Time 90:78-9 S 22 '67
Towers in the sky. P. Blake. il Arch Forum 127:31-43 O '67
NATIONAL championship custom car show. See Automobiles—Exhibitions
NATIONAL characteristics
American style: our past and our principles. S. Hoffmann. For Affairs 46:362-76 Ja '68
Children's views of foreign peoples, by W. E. Lambert and O. Klineberg. Review
Wilson Lib Bul il 42:187-93 O '67. L. Minturn
National character in the perspective of the social sciences; symposium, ed. by D. Martindale. bibliog f Ann Am Acad 370:1-163 Mr '67
NATIONAL childrens book week. See Book week
NATIONAL Christian council of India
Christians and the rebel areas. V. Koilpillai. Christian Cent 84:1635-6 D 20 '67
NATIONAL city bank. See New York (city)—Banks
NATIONAL city bank of Minneapolis. See Minneapolis—Banks
NATIONAL coal board. See Great Britain—National coal board
NATIONAL collegiate athletic association
NCAA: twenty-two teams after Alcindor. F. Deford. il Sports Illus 26:28-30+ Mr 20 '67
NATIONAL commission on food marketing. See United States—National commission on food marketing
NATIONAL commission on teacher education and professional standards
Have traveled, will teach; Peace corpsmen come home with ideas. M. Bonn. il Am Ed 3:1-3 F '67
NATIONAL committee for a sane nuclear policy
Labor and peace; SANE calls an Assembly for peace. Nation 205:325 O 9 '67

SANE warning. Christian Cent 84:1419-20 N 8 '67; Reply. R. J. Neuhaus. 84:1600 D 13 '67
Vietnam: labor's love lost; National labor leadership assembly for peace. D. Ireland. Commonweal 87:292-3 D 1 '67
NATIONAL communicable disease center, Atlanta. See United States—Communicable disease center
NATIONAL company of the Metropolitan opera. See Metropolitan opera national company
NATIONAL conference of Catholic bishops
Bishops meet. J. O'Gara. Commonweal 86:166 Ap 28 '67
NCCB annual meeting. America 117:674 D 2 '67
Spring meeting of NCCB. America 116:616 Ap 29 '67
NATIONAL conference on state parks
National conference on state parks', Park practice program. il Parks & Rec 2:34 D '67
NATIONAL congress of parents and teachers
Fare well, but not farewell. J. Moorhead. PTA Mag 61:2-3 Je '67
Head start on home-school cooperation; low income communities il PTA Mag 62:26-8 N '67
No smoking! smoking among children and youth. il Am Ed 3:7 My '67
President's message: mountain meditation. E. S. Hendryson. il PTA Mag 62:20-1 S '67
Selected to serve: presidents of state congresses. il PTA Mag 61:16-17 F '67
What the PTAs are up to now; interview. J. Moorhead. Am Ed 3:19-20 My '67
NATIONAL conventions (political)
Shorter conventions and campaigns. R. L. Tobin. Sat R 50:24 Ap 15 '67
See also
Television in politics
NATIONAL conventions, Democratic
And a small plus; integrated seating resolution for August convention. New Repub 158:9 Ja 20 '68
Daley delivers; convention to be held in Chicago. Newsweek 70:32 O 23 '67
Democratic solidarity; National committee's loyalty rule for four-day convention. New Repub 157:12 O 21 '67
How the Young were kept in line; Young Democrats convention, Florida. P. R. Wieck. New Repub 157:9-10 D 2 '67
Inside and out; National committee planning session. Newsweek 71:21 Ja 22 '68
Young Democrats and old pros: College Young Democrats. P. Wieck. New Repub 157:13-15 N 25 '67
Young Democrats; Miami. Boston preview. New Repub 157:7 N 11 '67
NATIONAL conventions, Republican
Road to Miami Beach R. Evans and R. Novak. il Harper 236:21-6 Ja '68
Senator to the young reporter. Nat R 19:1413-15 D 26 '67
Washington; Young Republican national federation. D. Kiker. il Atlan 220:4+ S '67
NATIONAL council for geographic education
Meeting, 1967. L. Hayman. Sr Schol 91:sup9 D 14 '67
NATIONAL council for the social studies
Meeting, 1967. il Sr Schol 91:sup3+ D 14 '67
NATIONAL council of Catholic bishops. See National conference of Catholic bishops
NATIONAL council of Catholic men
Catholic hour loses its magic. America 117:700 D 9 '67; Discussion. 117:753-4, 771-2; 118:99, 242 D 23 '67, Ja 27, F 24 '68
Danger ahead; NCCM-NCORT tension. Commonweal 87:372-3 D 22 '67
Profile of NCCM members; and significant NCCM loss. America 116:203 F 11 '67
NATIONAL council of churches. See National council of the churches of Christ in the United States of America
NATIONAL council of dance teacher organizations
Progress report. R. D. Curry. il Dance Mag 41:64-5 O '67
NATIONAL council of teachers of English
ALA freedom committee awaits NCTE conference. Library J 92:723 F 15 '67
Meeting, 1967. Sr Schol 91:sup4+ D 14 '67
NATIONAL council of the churches of Christ in the United States of America
Consultation on technology and human values. G. M. Schurr. Christian Cent 84:874-6 Jl 5 '67
In darkest America; Delta ministry programs in Mississippi. V. Ullman. Nation 205:177-80 S 4 '67

NATIONAL council of the churches of Christ in the United States of America—*Continued*
N.C.C. holding operation; seventh triennial General assembly. K. Haselden; discussion. Christian Cent 84:81, 144+ Ja 18-25 '67
National council position on Middle East. Christian Cent 84:304 Je 21 '67
New-time religion; modest liberal stance. Newsweek 69:69 Je 26 '67
Sense and psychedelics; United States conference on church and society. K. Haselden. Christian Cent 84:1453-4 N 15 '67
Tithing for the poor; investments in the slums. New Repub 157:8 S 30 '67
    See also
Church women united (organization)
NATIONAL council of the Metropolitan opera association. See Metropolitan opera national council
NATIONAL council on the arts. See United States—National foundation on the arts and the humanities
NATIONAL council on marine resources and engineering development. See United States—National council on marine resources and engineering development
NATIONAL crime commission. See United States—President's commission on law enforcement and administration of justice
NATIONAL crime information center. See United States—Federal bureau of investigation—National crime information center
NATIONAL custom auto fairs. See Automobiles—Exhibitions
NATIONAL data center (proposed) See United States—National data center (proposed)
NATIONAL debt (United States) See Debts, Public—United States
NATIONAL defense
    See also
United States—Defenses
NATIONAL democratic party. See Political parties—Germany (Federal Republic)
NATIONAL education association
Breezes and freshets in the NEA. Mo Labor R 90:III-IV S '67
Century of cooperation. J. W. Gardner; W. G. Carr; H. Howe, 2d. il NEA J 56:61-2 S '67
Commitment to action. B. Alonso. NEA J 56:29 S '67
Computer to help school librarians find jobs. Library J 92:1685 Ap 15 '67
Executive secretary Sam M. Lambert. M. B. Tucker. NEA J 56:30-3 S '67
Legacy of honor; new help from the NEA for teaching about Negro history. S. Dorros. il Negro Hist Bul 30:6-7 Ja '67
Michigan adopts unification. M. Zemke. il NEA J 56:43-4 O '67
NEA and the real world of education; excerpts from address, October 20, 1967. S. M. Lambert. NEA J 56:34-6 D '67
NEA candidates to be voted on in Minneapolis. il NEA J 56:46-7 My '67
NEA conference on minorities in textbooks is prelude to Negro history week. Negro Hist Bul 30:17 Ap '67
NEA search locates teachers and jobs; interview. ed. by J. Lloyd. G. Arnstein. Sr Schol 91:sup4+ O 26 '67
NEA sets new guidelines for textbook purchases. Pub W 192:29-30 N 6 '67
NEA special services. NEA J 57:25 Ja '68
NEA; the reluctant dragon. P. Janssen. il Sat R 50:56-7+ Je 17 '67
NEA's fight for equal opportunity. il NEA J 56:58-61 F '67
New look at NEA. il Newsweek 70:54 Jl 17 '67
On to 2,000,000 members! il NEA J 56:63-9 S '67
President Applegate comments on: the proposed dues increase; development project; Minneapolis meeting, July 2-7, 1967. I. Applegate. NEA J 56:35-8 My '67
Professor and collective negotiations. J. F. Day and W. H. Fisher. bibliog f Sch & Soc 95:226-9 Ap 1 '67
Proposed amendments to NEA bylaws. NEA J 56:56+ Ap '67
Summary financial report to members. il NEA J 56:52 O '67
Teachers getting into politics; NEA citizenship committee. Sr Schol 90:sup8 Ap 14 '67
Treatment of minorities in textbooks; resolutions by NEA. il Negro Hist Bul 30:8-10 Mr '67
Washington report. J. Lloyd. Sr Schol 91: sup20 S 28 '67
Washington report; NEA all-day meeting on Education for the real world. J. Lloyd. G. Arnstein. Sr Schol 91:sup5 N 16 '67
When the votes are counted. . . R. J. Flynn. NEA J 56:48+ My '67
    See also
American association of school administrators

Meeting, 1967
Early look at the convention program. il NEA J 56:11 F '67
NEA convention. J. Lloyd. Sr Schol 91: sup2+ S 21 '67
NEA resolutions. 1967. il NEA J 56:56-60 S '67

Department of audio-visual instruction
New materials at DAVI. Sr Schol 90:sup4 My 5 '67

Department of elementary school principals
Meeting, 1967. Sr Schol 90:sup2 My 5 '67

Division of educational travel
Miniprice tours for budget-minded teachers; NEA tours in capsule. il NEA J 57:50-1 Ja '68

Teach corps
NEA teach corps; six weeks in Sierra Leone. D. Watson. il Sr Schol 90:sup6-7 Mr 3 '67
NATIONAL educational television network
Casting the NET wider; major live events. il Newsweek 69:60 Ja 30 '67
Old power play; suppression of documentary film on Catholic schools to aid repeal of Blaine amendment. Commonweal 87:67-8 O 20 '67
Saving face; series called Your dollar's worth. il Time 90:86 N 3 '67
    See also
Public broadcast laboratory
NATIONAL elections. See Elections—United States
NATIONAL endowment for the arts. See United States—National foundation on the arts and the humanities
NATIONAL farm bureau federalton. See American farm bureau federation
NATIONAL farm workers' association
Delano: the story of the California grape strike, by J. G. Dunne. Review
    New Repub 157:23-6 D 2 '67. M. Duberman; Reply. W. L. Kircher. 158:46 Ja 6 '68
Migrants' directions '67. J. F. Conway. Cath World 205:31-5 Ap '67
Strike! California's grape pickers. J. G. Dunne. il Sat Eve Post 240:32-6+ My 6 '67
NATIONAL farmers organization
Cows and sows; marketing pregnant cows and sows for slaughter. Newsweek 69:70+ Mr 6 '67
Farm bureau, NFO settle on next moves. Farm J 91:37 Ja '67
Farmers union votes to stop buying. Farm J 91:46F My '67
Keeping milk off the market. P. Wieck. New Repub 156:9-10 Ap 22 '67
Labor can do it, why can't you? with editorial comment. C. W. Gifford. Farm J 91:33-5+, 98 O '67
NFO endorses across-the-board holding actions. D. Seim. Farm J 91:50T O '67
NFO milk dumping, what did it do? N. Reeder. il Farm J 91:28-9+ My '67
When dairy farmers went on strike. il U S News 62:53 Ap 3 '67
When middlemen are in the middle. il Bsns W p26-7 Ag 26 '67
NATIONAL field trials. See Field trials (dogs)
NATIONAL film board. See Canada—National film board
NATIONAL football league
Merry-go-rounds; NFL and AFL common draft of college players. il Time 89:43 Mr 24 '67
Pro football's player mutiny; ed. by E. Linn. B. Parrish. Look 31:66+ Ag 22 '67
Real draft beef; NFL and AFL draft college players. Newsweek 69:89 Mr 27 '67
Sporting scene: defeat of Kansas City Chiefs by Green Bay Packers in Los Angeles. H. W. Wind. New Yorker 42:102+ F 4 '67
NATIONAL foreign policy conference for educators, Washington, D.C.
Some thoughts on education for world responsibility; adaptation of address, June 16, 1966. C. Frankel. Sch & Soc 95:219-23 Ap 1 '67
NATIONAL forests
And bust; earthquake. in Gallatin national forest. M. Ericson. il Am For 73:5+ Mr '67
Arch in the southern Sierra; Arch Rock. il Sunset 139:20 S '67
Confrontation in Gila wilderness. Liv Wildn 30:44-5 Aut '66

NATIONAL forests—*Continued*
Ending a fiefdom; homeowners ask for legislation giving them permanent possessory use of public land. K. B. Pomeroy. Am For 73:5+ Ag '67
Fish-watching at Taylor Creek; in Eldorado national forest. il Sunset 139:46+ S '67
Island in the sky; Toiyabe national forest. il Am For 73:23+ Jl '67
Lake that's all your own; Tongass national forest, Alaska. il Sunset 138:27 Je '67
$1 billion mistake; holders of special use permits on the Stanislaus national forest in California demand permanent rights. K. B. Pomeroy. Am For 73:23+ Ap '67
What about Mineral King? R. Leadabrand. il Am For 73:18-20+ F '67
See also
National parks and reserves—United States

Roads
Confrontation in Gila wilderness. Liv Wildn 30:44-5 Aut '66

NATIONAL foundation for the social sciences (proposed)
Social sciences: Harris bill evokes limited support. D. S. Greenberg. Science 155:812-14 F 17 '67

NATIONAL foundation on the arts and the humanities. See United States—National foundation on the arts and the humanities

NATIONAL funeral directors association
Cost of being buried; Justice department's antitrust suit. America 117:703-4 D 9 '67

NATIONAL gallery of art, Washington, D.C.
Enhanced beauty; Ginevra dei Benci on display. il Time 89:66-7 Mr 24 '67
$5 million gets the U.S. its first Leonardo. il Life 62:32-3 Mr 3 '67
$5.8 million lady: Da Vinci's Ginevra de' Benci. il Newsweek 69:39 Mr 6 '67
Leonardo's Ginevra. W. Karp. il Horizon 9:24-9 Aut '67
National gallery after a quarter century. J. Walker. il Nat Geog Mag 131:348-71 Mr '67

NATIONAL geographic magazine
Taxing the Geographic. Newsweek 70:74 D 25 '67

NATIONAL geographic society
Canada marks her first century; a salute. M. B. Grosvenor. il Nat Geog Mag 131:597-9 My '67
First La Gorce medal honors Antarctic expedition. il Nat Geog Mag 131:864-7 Je '67
Life as it is. il Newsweek 70:59 Ag 14 '67
National geographic society trustees elect key executives. il Nat Geog Mag 132:576-90 O '67
World in Geographic filmstrips. M. M. Payne. il Nat Geog Mag 133:134-7 Ja '68
Your society offers four new books. M. B. Grosvenor. il Nat Geog Mag 131:868-75 Je '67

NATIONAL goals. See United States

NATIONAL guard (United States) See United States—National guard

NATIONAL health service (Great Britain) See Great Britain—National health service

NATIONAL hockey league
Crashing into a new ice age; expansion of NHL. P. Axthelm. il Sports Illus 27:34-7 N 6 '67
Expect the unexpected; six new teams. Time 90:74+ N 17 '67
Growing pains. Newsweek 70:65-6 N 13 '67
Icy welcome to the NHL. P. Axthelm. il Sports Illus 26:22-3 Je 19 '67

NATIONAL holidays. See Holidays

NATIONAL industrial conference board
Personnel man wears a bigger hat; highlights of NICB's study. Bsns W p 131 Mr 4 '67
What twelve top forecasters expect for '68; symposium. il U S News 64:32-8 Ja 8 '68

NATIONAL information center for educational media. See Southern California university, Los Angeles

NATIONAL institute of general medical sciences. See United States—National institute of general medical sciences

NATIONAL institute of mental health. See United States—National institute of mental health

NATIONAL institutes of health. See United States—National institutes of health

NATIONAL intercollegiate flying association
Too young to fly? R. B. Parke. il Flying 80:68-71 My '67

NATIONAL labor leadership assembly for peace. See National committee for a sane nuclear policy

NATIONAL labor relations board. See United States—National labor relations board

NATIONAL laboratories. See United States—Atomic energy commission

NATIONAL league of women voters. See League of women voters of the United States

NATIONAL liberation front. See Political parties (Vietnam)

NATIONAL library of Australia
Leader in cooperation; Australian national library. J. Balnaves. bibliog il Library J 92:4117-19 N 15 '67

NATIONAL library of Canada. See Canada—National library

NATIONAL library of Madrid. See Madrid—National library

NATIONAL library of medicine. See United States—National library of medicine

NATIONAL library week
Dates set for the week for next three years. Library J 92:2336 Je 15 '67
National library week: new legislation and read-ins. il Library J 92:1881-2 My 15 '67
1968 NLW materials strike humorous note; National book committee announces 1968 plans. il Library J 93:21 Ja 1 '68
Reading is what's happening; address, April 21, 1967. E. J. Josey. il Negro Hist Bul 30:14-17 My '67
Reading is what's happening. il Wilson Lib Bul 41:556 F '67

Anecdotes, facetiae, satire, etc.
Nothing like a dame: NLW plan for Miss Library universe of 1968; with editorial comment. P. S. Dunkin. Library J 92:1591 Ap 15 '67

Quotations, maxims, etc.
Bookish; comp. by E. F. Murphy. il N Y Times Mag p37+ Ap 16 '67

NATIONAL manufacturers association. See National association of manufacturers

NATIONAL maritime union of America
Curran's NMU; headquarters vs. the men at sea. D. J. Fliegel. il Nation 204:143-7 Ja 30 '67

NATIONAL measurement system. See Measurement

NATIONAL medal for literature
W. H. Auden awarded National medal for literature. Pub W 191:35 My 1 '67
W. H. Auden receives National literature medal. Pub W 192:24 D 4 '67

NATIONAL military establishment. See United States—Defense, Department of

NATIONAL monuments
Preserving an island paradise; Biscayne National Monument in upper Florida Keys. D. B. Fascell. il Am For 73:32-3+ Mr '67
See also names of national monuments. e.g. Glacier Bay National Monument

NATIONAL morale. See Morale, National

NATIONAL municipal league
See also
All-America cities

NATIONAL museum of anthropology, Mexico city. See Mexico (city)—Galleries and museums

NATIONAL museum of Tunisia. See Tunis—Galleries and museums

NATIONAL music camp. Interlochen, Mich.
See also
Interlochen arts academy. Mich.

NATIONAL observer (newspaper)
Wallflower at five. il Newsweek 69:54-5 F 27 '67

NATIONAL oceanographic association
Industry ocean role sought. Tech W 20:41-2 F 27 '67

NATIONAL park service (United States) See United States—National park service

NATIONAL parks and reserves

Roads
Beneficial alternate proposal for a Great Smokies road. E. M. Dickerman. il Liv Wildn 30:42-4 Wint '66
Conference rejects small wilderness in Smokies. Nat Parks Mag 41:20 Jl '67
Mineral King; construction of highway through Sequoia-Kings Canyon National Park. A. W. Smith. Nat Parks Mag 41:2 Jl '67
Mineral King development; Sequoia-Kings Canyon National Parks. Liv Wildn 31:60-1 Spr '67
Proposed alternative to the Great Smokies transmountain road. il Nat Parks Mag 41:19 My '67
Smokies. hike to discovery. C. Brewer. il Liv Wildn 30:3-8 Aut '66

NATIONAL parks and reserves—*Continued*

Trails

National trail system. Nat Parks Mag 41:24 Ap '67

Africa

To save an Eden, wildlife must pay. L. Brown. il Audubon 69:42-9 S '67
See also
Nairobi National Park

Australia

Australia views its parks. Nat Parks Mag 41:21 Mr '67

Canada

East of the border: New Brunswick and Fundy National Park. C. W. White. il Redbook 129:40-1 Jl '67

Netherlands

Hoge Veluwe National Park. D. B. Huyck. il Am For 73:22-5+ F '67

Russia

First Soviet national park; on shores of Lake Baykal in eastern Siberia. P. R. Pryde. bibliog il Nat Parks Mag 41:20-3 Ap '67
U.S.S.R.'s first national park; Lake Baykal. il Am For 73:30-1+ Ja '67

Tanzania

Predators and scavengers; carnivores of Ngorongoro Crater in Africa. R. D. Estes. il Natur Hist 76:20-9 F; 38-47 bibliog(p70) Mr '67

United States

Alarm sounded on new Redwood Park proposal. J. B. Craig. Am For 73:7+ N '67
Battle of the redwoods. R. Wernick. il Sat Eve Post 240:90-5 Ap 22 '67
Conservation docket. See issues of National parks magazine
Deadline for the redwoods. il Newsweek 69:30-3 Ap 24 '67
Facts about a Redwoods National Park. T. L. Kimball. il Am For 73:20-3+ Mr '67; Reply. J. Davis. 73:32-3+ Ag '67
Fight for America's Alps: preserving the North Cascades in Washington. P. Brooks. il Atlan 219:87-90+ F '67; Same abr. Read Digest 90:104-8 My '67
If you plan to visit national parks—. il U S News 62:66-8 Je 19 '67
Kauai National Park. R. Wenkham. il Nat Parks Mag 41:4-8 Mr '67
Last stand; saving the redwoods. il Time 89:18-19 Mr 24 '67
Life and death of a primeval empire; proposed Redwood National Park. il Am Heritage 18:112 F '67
Matter of principle; establishment of a Redwood National Park in California. J. B. Craig. Am For 73:9 Ag '67
Mike Frome; management and use of wilderness and national parks. M. Frome. Am For 73:3+ O '67
National park experience. D. Lambert. il Nat Parks Mag 41:4-8 My '67
National park service proposes a Cumberland Island National Seashore on Georgia coast. il Nat Parks Mag 41:19 D '67
North Cascades. il Nat Parks Mag 41:20-1 Je '67
North Cascades National Park: copper mining vs. conservation. K. Sperry. il Science 157:1021-4 S 1 '67; Discussion. 158:205; 159:31-2+ O 13 '67, Ja 5 '68
November 1, 1967: Senate defeats Anderson-Ellender amendment of Redwood Park package. J. B. Craig. Am For 73:10 D '67
Over-use of the national parks. W. A. Johnson. il Nat Parks Mag 41:4-7 O '67
Park for the North Cascades? meeting the test of national park eligibility. C. F. Brockman; reply. S. F. Arno. Am For 73:3-4 Ja '67
Parks are for people; balancing park use and preservation of resources. W. E. Towell. Am For 73:5+ O '67
Plan for a park for the crowded East; Rockefeller proposal for Adirondacks National Park. Life 63:4 Ag 25 '67
Pleasure horses in the parks. E. Bowman. il Nat Parks Mag 41:4-6 N '67
Proposed Redwood National Park. T. H. Kuchel. il Parks & Rec 2:22+ Jl '67
Quiet revolution in our national parks. J. Peter. il Look 31:34-43 Mr 7 '67
Ransoming the redwoods. J. B. Craig. Am For 73:11 My '67

Redwood National Park. D. F. Anthrop. il Liv Wildn 31:36-47 Spr '67
Redwood Park: squabbling on details delays final agreement. R. J. Samuelson. Science 157:410 Jl 28 '67
Redwoods and the American forestry association: Redwood National Park. J. B. Craig. Am For 73:8-9 Ap '67
Redwoods National Park. Nat Parks Mag 41:19-20 My '67
Report of president and general counsel to the general membership of National parks association, May 25, 1967. A. W. Smith. Nat Parks Mag 41:I-IV Ap '67
Reporter at large; exploring Organ Pipe Cactus National Monument and Cabeza Prieta game range, proposed combination for Sonoran Desert National Park. B. Roueché. New Yorker 43:76+ Ag 12 '67
Road ahead: editorial. A. W. Smith. Nat Parks Mag 41:2 Ja '67
Saving original prairieland; efforts to establish a Prairie National Park. Nat Parks Mag 41:21 Jl '67
Trees, for business or pleasure? L. C. Walker. il Am For 73:16-17+ My '67
Why worry about the redwoods? M. McCloskey. il Sat R 50:18-19 Je 3 '67
Will these redwoods survive? il Life 62:84-7+ Ap 28 '67
See also names of national parks and reserves, e.g. Theodore Roosevelt National Memorial Park

NATIONAL parks association
Report of president and general counsel, May 25, 1967. A. W. Smith. Nat Parks Mag 41:I-IV Ap '67

NATIONAL pilots association. See International professional pilots association

NATIONAL planning
Delicate balance. F. D. Murphy. Sat R 51:74+ Ja 13 '68
Most notorious victory, by B. B. Seligman. Review
    Commentary 44:86-8 Ag '67. R. Lekachman
Toward a communal society. D. Bell. il Life 62:116+ My 12 '67

NATIONAL players company
Theater; revival of Peter Weiss's Marat/de Sade. H. Hewes. Sat R 50:48 Ja 28 '67

NATIONAL professional soccer league
Soccer is simple? il Newsweek 69:70-1 Ap 24 '67

NATIONAL prohibition party. See Prohibition party (United States)

NATIONAL psychology. See National characteristics

NATIONAL radio astronomy observatory, Green Bank, W.Va.
Eavesdroppers; NRAO plans to bring the most distant radio sources 1,000 times closer. il Newsweek 70:73-4 Ag 7 '67
Proposed very large radio telescope array. il Sky & Tel 33:213 Ap '67

NATIONAL railway labor conference
Report of the special railroad board; issued September 15, 1967. Mo Labor R 90:43-6 N '67

NATIONAL recreation and park association
Change in NRPA staff, Al LaGasse resigns. L. B. Houston. Parks & Rec 2:28 Ag '67
Congress program develops. il Parks & Rec 2:29+ Ag '67
Endicott Davison elected new NRPA president. Parks & Rec 2:18+ Jl '67
Federal aid institute to be sponsored by NRPA; with editorial comment. Parks & Rec 2:13, 26 F '67
First NRPA federal assistance institute. il Parks & Rec 2:32-3 Jl '67
Fragmentation a luxury. S. J. Prezioso. Parks & Rec 2:15 S '67
Model cities, $11 million appropriated for planning. Parks & Rec 2:31+ D '67
NRPA board of governors forms, National committee on education and personnel services. Parks & Rec 2:26+ S '67
NRPA boards-commissions branch holds organization meeting. il Parks & Rec 2:32 Je '67
NRPA branch officers. il Parks & Rec 2:28-30 Ja '67
NRPA committee appointments announced. Parks & Rec 2:20 S '67
NRPA news. See issues of Parks & recreation

NATIONAL recreation and park association
—*Continued*
NRPA receives Golden eagle award. il Parks
& Rec 2:41 Ap '67
NRPA, year of decision. Parks & Rec 2:35-6
D '67
New home for a new organization; new
Mills building. il Parks & Rec 2:22-3 Ja
'67
1967, the park and recreation movement in
retrospect. il Parks & Rec 2:39-40+ D '67
Open forum; branch societies discuss
strengthening relationships. il Parks & Rec
2:32-3 N '67
Proposed Adirondack Mountains National
Park. S. J. Prezioso. il Parks & Rec 2:14-
16+ N '67
Revenue sources management school graduates
first class. il Parks & Rec 2:36-7 Ap '67
Trustees name Sal Prezioso NRPA executive
vice president and secretary; with editorial
comment. il Parks & Rec 2:13, 15+ Ag '67

Meetings
State society presidents meet in Washington.
Parks & Rec 2:25+ D '67

Encroachment committee
Encroachment committee plans program im-
plementation. Parks & Rec 2:34+ N '67
NATIONAL repertory theatre foundation, New
York
Theatre; performances of Molière's The
imaginary invalid, O'Neill's A touch of the
poet, and Coward's Tonight at 8:30. J.
McCarten. New Yorker 43:158 My 13 '67
NATIONAL responsibility. See Responsibility
NATIONAL retail merchants association
NRMA issues guidelines for civil disorder
areas. Pub W 192:42 Ag 14 '67
NATIONAL review
God, man, and William F. Buckley. L. L.
King. Harper 234:53-61 Mr '67
NR poll; conservatives' preferences for the
1968 Republican nomination. il Nat R 19:
236-7, 340-1, 456, 559, 678, 786, 893-4, 1007,
1251 Mr 7, Ap 4, My 2, 30, Je 27, Jl 25, Ag
22, S 19, N 14 '67
NR's annual guide to unsatisfactory people;
comp. by C. H. Simonds. il Nat R 19:1428-9
D 26 '67
NATIONAL rifle association
Lobby on target. R. Sherrill. il N Y Times
Mag p27+ O 15 '67; Discussion. p85 N 5 '67
Setback for the NRA. Newsweek 70:35-6 N 13
'67
Win for the gun lobby. Newsweek 70:29-30
S 4 '67
NATIONAL science board. See United States—
National science board
NATIONAL science foundation. See United
States—National science foundation
NATIONAL security. See Internal security
NATIONAL security council. See United States
—National security council
NATIONAL self determination. See Self deter-
mination, National
NATIONAL semiconductor corporation
Fast footwork in an industry talent hunt. il
Bsns W p 132+ Mr 11 '67
NATIONAL severe storms laboratory, Norman,
Okla.
Tornadoes, a mystery. il Sci N 91:422-3 My
6 '67
NATIONAL shooting dog championship. See
Field trials (dogs)
NATIONAL social science foundation (pro-
posed) See United States—National social
science foundation (proposed)
NATIONAL socialism
See also
Fascism—Germany
NATIONAL standard reference data system.
See Information storage and retrieval sys-
tems
NATIONAL stock exchange
Peaceful stock exchange. il Fortune 76:172+
S 1 '67
NATIONAL student association. See United
States national student association
NATIONAL symphony orchestra, Washington,
D.C.
Nation's capital: out on a limb? J. Vinton.
Hi Fi 17:MA24+ Mr '67
NATIONAL teacher corps. See United States
—National teacher corps
NATIONAL theatre, British. See Theater—
Great Britain

NATIONAL theater of the deaf
Pictures in the air. il Time 90:86 O 27 '67
NATIONAL traffic safety agency. See United
States—National traffic safety agency
NATIONAL union catalog. See United States
—Library of Congress—Union catalog
NATIONAL urban league
Other 97 per cent; moderate Negro leaders. il
Time 90:12-17 Ag 11 '67
NATIONAL utility service, Incorporated
He makes utilities blow fuses. Bsns W p54+
Je 3 '67
NATIONAL water commission. See United
States—National water commission
NATIONAL youth conference on natural beauty
and conservation. See White House youth
conference on natural beauty and conserva-
tion
NATIONAL zoological park, Washington, D.C.
Washington national zoological park has star
performers; reprint. J. Arundel. il Parks &
Rec 2:17+ F '67
NATIONALISM
See also
Americanism
Patriotism
Self determination, National

Negro race
American Negro is dead; international sup-
port for black power. W. Worthy. il Es-
quire 68:126-30+ N '67
Black mischief; S. Carmichael's call for in-
ternational black power movement. il News-
week 70:58 N 27 '67
Black power & black pride; Time essay. Time
90:20-1 D 1 '67
Black power and urban unrest, by N. Wright,
jr. Review
Sat R 50:26-7 Ag 12 '67. C. Greene
Black power, by S. Carmichael and C. V.
Hamilton. Review
Sat R 50:55 N 11 '67. S. Stevens
Black power: five shades of gray. F. Mills-
paugh; C. H. Polite. Mlle 66:94-5+ Ja '68
Black power threatens a leading Negro col-
lege. il U S News 63:38-9 Jl 31 '67
Black power: tool for the Communists? il
U S News 64:14 Ja 15 '68
Black revolution, theme in Newark; black
power conference. il U S News 63:8 Jl 31 '67
How red China stirs U.S. racial strife. il
U S News 63:11 S 4 '67
How the white problem spawned black power.
A. F. Poussaint. il Ebony 22:88-90+ Ag '67
Is Castro behind guerrilla war in U.S. cities?
il U S News 63:23-5 Ag 14 '67
Israel for Negroes? Newsweek 70:24-5 S 11
'67
Literature and thought of modern Africa, by
C. Wauthier. Review
Nation 204:822-3 Je 26 '67. N. Gordimer
Memo from the ghetto; the dispirit of '67.
E. Dunbar. Look 31:92 S 19 '67
Natural hair, new symbol of race pride. D.
Llorens. il Ebony 23:139-44 D '67
Newark: post-riot summit for black power.
il Life 63:26-8 Ag 4 '67
Real story of the riots and who's behind
them; excerpts from testimonies. il U S
News 63:64-7 Ag 21 '67
Revolution or slave despair? W. V. Shannon.
Commonweal 86:603-4 S 29 '67
Search for identity. K. B. Clark. il Ebony
22:39-40+ Ag '67
Second look at black nationalism. J. J. Car-
roll. America 117:84-5 Jl 22 '67
Thinking black. il Newsweek 70:37-41 N 20
'67
Voices from burning slums. E. M. Yoder, jr.
Sat R 50:28-9 Ag 26 '67
What black power leaders are demanding. il
U S News 63:31 Ag 7 '67
Wright concept of black power; excerpts from
Black power and urban unrest. N. Wright,
jr. Sat R 50:26-7 Ag 12 '67
NATIONALISM and communism. See Commu-
nism and nationalism
NATIONALITY, Dual. See Citizenship
NATIONALIZATION of industry. See Govern-
ment ownership
NATIONALIZATION of the steel industry. See
Steel industry and trade—Government
ownership
NATIONS
Black-white at home, North-South abroad.
E. Kenworthy. Yale R 57:161-81 D '67
Nations of the world; table (cont) Sr Schol
91:29-33 O 5 '67
See also
States, Small

NATIVE states of India. See India—Native states

NATIVITY, Feast of. See Christmas

NATIVITY groups. See Christmas cribs

NATIVITY of Christ in art. See Jesus Christ—Art

NATKIN, Robert
Natkin: overtones at outskirts. il por Art N 66:48-9+ Mr '67

NATURAL beauty and conservation, White House youth conference. See White House youth conference on natural beauty and conservation

NATURAL BRIDGES NATIONAL MONUMENT
On some names in Natural Bridges National Monument. N. M. Judd. bibliog il Nat Parks Mag 41:16-19 O '67

NATURAL forms
See also
Found objects

NATURAL gas. See Gas, Natural

NATURAL history
Demise of natural history. J. W. Krutch. il Audubon 69:50-5 S '67
Naturalist at large. M. Bates. See issues of Natural history
Nature note. See issues of Science news
See also
Nature
Wildlife conservation

Bibliography
Book essay: the naturalist's library. H. Borland. Natur Hist 77:68-70 Ja '68

Connecticut
Hill country harvest, by H. Borland. Review
Sat R 50:33 S 2 '67. R. L. Perkin

NATURAL history museums
Where the deer and the first bats play; Arizona Sonora desert museum. H. Sutton. il Sat R 50:42-3 Mr 18 '67
See also
American museum of natural history, New York

NATURAL history stamps. See Postage stamps

NATURAL lighting. See Lighting

NATURAL look; drama. See Thuna, L.

NATURAL MONUMENTS
See also
Natural Bridges National Monument

NATURAL resources
Natural resources; world-wide survey proposed. UN Mo Chron 4:49 My '67
Remote sensing of natural resources. R. N. Colwell. il Sci Am 218:54-69 Ja '68
Survey of natural resources; UN ad hoc group. UN Mo Chron 4:39-40 Mr '67
See also
Conservation of resources
Marine resources
Mines and mineral resources
Power resources
Water resources development
Wildlife conservation

Bibliography
Reading about resources. M. Bush. See issues of American forests

Vocational guidance
Outdoor career guide. C. Nansen. il Field & S 71:10-12+ Ap '67

Africa
Destruction of Eden. L. Brown. il Audubon 69:36-53 Jl '67

Alaska
Alaska tries to break the ice. il Bsns W p 150-2+ N 4 '67
Mike Frome: trip in Alaska. M. Frome; reply. R. E. Bell. Am For 73:62-3 Ja '67

Guinea
Guinea. R. J. H. Church. bibliog il Focus 17:1-6 Mr '67

Jordan
Jordan. P. P. Vouras. bibliog il Focus 17:1-6 F '67

Mali (Republic)
Mali. T. E. Hilton. bibliog il Focus 18:1-6 S '67

Pakistan
Pakistan. A. A. Michel. il Focus 17:1-6 Ja '67

Paraguay
Paraguay. R. E. Crist. bibliog il Focus 18:1-6 D '67

Peru
Peru. R. E. Crist and A. Taylor. bibliog il Focus 17:1-6 Ap '67

Russia
Nyet raskhititelyam prirody (no to the plunderers of nature) S. Ostrander and L. Schroeder. il Audubon 69:63-5 Jl '67
U.S.S.R. today; metamorphosis of a continent. N. Mikhailov. il UNESCO Courier 20:4-10 N '67

South Africa
South Africa. D. L. Niddrie. bibliog il Focus 17:1-6 Je '67

Taiwan
Taiwan. il Focus 17:1-6 D '66

United States
Natural environment. J. L. Fisher. il Ann Am Acad 371:127-40 My '67
On destruction. D. Sorgman. Nat Parks Mag 41:15 O '67
Secondhand everything. Sci N 91:162 F 18 '67
Washington lookout. A. G. Hall. See issues of American forests

NATURAL resources council of America
Conservation's grand lodge. H. Clepper. il Am For 73:22-7+ O '67

NATURAL science for youth foundation
Meet the raccoon; new kind of nature museum. M. Gross. il Parents Mag 42:46-7+ F '67

NATURAL selection
Visual isolation in gulls. N. G. Smith. il Sci Am 217:94-102 O '67
See also
Evolution

NATURALISTS
Influence of Emerson, Thoreau, and Whitman on the early American naturalists John Muir and John Burroughs. M. C. Davis. bibliog il Liv Wildn 30:18-23 Wint '66
Naturalist at large. M. Bates. See issues of Natural history

NATURE
Hill country homilies. H. Borland. il Audubon 69:66-77 My '67
Seed of a conscience; excerpt from Manual of outdoor interpretation. P. Brooks. il Audubon 69:36-7 N '67
See also
Man—Influence on nature
Natural history
Wildlife

Bibliography
Books in review. See issues of Natural history incorporating Nature magazine
Naturalist's bookshelf. See issues of Audubon

Philosophy
Wisdom of wildness. C. A. Lindbergh. il Life 63:8-10 D 22 '67

NATURE, Balance of. See Balance of nature

NATURE, Human. See Human nature

NATURE and man. See Man—Influence on nature

NATURE books. See Nature literature

NATURE centers
Nature center with glass-domed hall; Kalamazoo nature center. A. B. Dow. il Arch Rec 142:166-7 S '67
Please don't eat the poison ivy; High Rock nature conservation center, Staten Island. il Am Ed 3:14-19 Jl '67
Private school's campus fulfills community needs; Lakeside school in Spring Valley, N.Y. il Audubon 69:80-1 My '67
Story of Seven Ponds. D. W. Scott. il Audubon 69:82 S '67

NATURE in art
Ray Harm; the other side of the window. il House B 109:164-5+ Mr '67
See also
Birds in art
Landscape painting
Trees in art

NATURE in literature
See also
Forests in literature

NATURE in poetry
Landscape and language. R. Sward. Poetry 109:407-11 Mr '67

NATURE literature
Nature beneath the tree. P. Farb. il Sat R 50:44+ N 25 '67

NATURE museums. See Childrens museums

NATURE of man. See Man

NATURE photography

Art and technique of Eliot Porter; interview, ed. by P. Caulfield. E. Porter. il Natur Hist 76:26-31+ D '67

Eliot Porter: how he works. P. Caulfield. il Mod Phot 31:66-9 S '67

Nature and the camera. P. Caulfield. Natur Hist 76:60-1 O '67

Nature and the camera. P. Villiard. Natur Hist 76:50+ Mr; 68+ Ag '67

There's more to autumn than the leaves on the trees. B. Randall. il U S Camera 30: 38-41+ O '67

Time to capture gold on silver. E. Hannigan. U S Camera 30:78-9 N '67

Uncharted worlds on the face of a tree; with photographs and comments by N. Cousins. C. C. Calkins. Home Gard 54:35-7 N '67

See also
Photography of birds
Photography of flowers, plants, trees, etc.

NATURE study

Beetle named Tarzan. J. D. Foraker. il Parents Mag 42:46-7+ Jl '67

Education come alive outdoors. R. M. Isenberg. il NEA J 56:34-5 Ap '67

Enjoying nature. P. Villiard. See issues of Audubon

Long day in a boy's world; photographs. S. Hershorn. Sports Illus 27:30-5 Ag 21 '67

Tulip poplars and protozoa on the Chopawamsic; educational camping at Prince William Forest park. P. Thomson. il NEA J 56:32-3 O '67

See also
Bird study
Camping—Educational aspects
Childrens gardens
Natural history
Nature
Nature centers

NATURE trails. See Trails

NAUGHTON, Bill

Keep it in the family. Criticism Newsweek 70:108 O 9 '67

NAUGHTON, James M.

In Cleveland and Boston, the issue is race. N Y Times Mag p30+ N 5 '67

NAULT, William H.

Life with an encyclopedist; summary of address. por Pub W 191:86-7 Je 12 '67

NAUMAN, Hilda

How Faulkner went his way and I went mine. Esquire 68:173-5 D '67

NAUR, Robert

Notes from our correspondents. Hi Fi 17:14+ Ap '67

NAURU (island)

Utopia in mid-ocean. Time 89:29 Je 30 '67
See also
United Nations—Nauru (island)

NAUTICAL astronomy

Noon position. A. Piver. il Motor B 119:34-7+ Je '67

NAUTICAL charts

New charts. E. S. Maloney. See issues of Motor boating

Piloting with the seasoned skipper. il Motor B 120:76-9 D '67; 121:310-14+ Ja '68

Prize catch for the cruising man. J. Roe. il Yachting 121:74-6+ My '67

Where to get charts and general cruising information. T. Bowman. Motor B 119:112-14+ Ap '67
See also
United States—Coast and geodetic survey

NAUTICAL instruments

See also
Compass

NAVAHO Indians

Cry for help from the proud Navajo; photographs. R. Crane. Life 64:14-23 Ja 5 '68

Good day at Rough Rock; Navajo demonstration school. P. Conklin. il Am Ed 3:4-9 F '67

Learning to be Navaho-Americans; innovation at Rough Rock; demonstration school. E. Fuchs. il Sat R 50:82-4+ S 16 '67

Rabbit hunt, Indian style. J. Downs. il Outdoor Life 139:54-5+ Je '67

NAVAJO demonstration school. See Indians of North America—Education

NAVAJO Indian reservation. See Indians of North America—Reservations

NAVAJO Indians. See Navaho Indians

NAVAL airplanes. See Airplanes, Military—United States

NAVAL architecture

See also
Hulls (naval architecture)
Warships

NAVAL battles

See also
Midway, Battle of, 1942

NAVAL craft. See United States—Navy—Boats

NAVAL desertion. See United States—Navy—Desertions

NAVAL guns. See Ordnance, Naval

NAVAL maneuvers

Collision course; harassment of U.S. naval vessels conducting exercises on the high seas. Newsweek 69:62 My 22 '67

Game of chicken; Russians harass U.S. naval maneuvers Time 89:35 My 19 '67

Just what are the Russians up to now? Russian harassment of U.S. warship. il U S News 62:8 My 22 '67

Soviet challenge that is growing; effort by Soviet warships to harass U.S. naval units in strategic waters. il U S News 62:15 My 29 '67

NAVAL museums

See also
Mystic seaport museum, Mystic, Conn.

NAVAL offenses

United States

See United States—Navy—Crimes and misdemeanors

NAVAL ordnance. See Ordnance, Naval

NAVAL postgraduate school. See United States naval postgraduate school, Monterey, Calif.

NAVAL power. See Sea power

NAVAL research

Navy will add labs to ship R&D center. R. W. Niblock. il Aero Tech 21:54-5 Ag 28 '67

Sailing yacht research; report on symposium. B. Chance and others. Science 156:411-12 Ap 21 '67

NAVAL ship research and development center. See United States—Naval ship research and development center

NAVASKY, Victor S.

No. 2 man at State is a cooler-downer. N Y Times Mag p3+ D 24 '67

Wrong guy for the wrong post at the wrong time? Sat Eve Post 240:74-5+ D 16 '67

NAVIES

See also
Sea power
also subhead Navy under names of countries, e.g. Russia—Navy

NAVIGATION

Bob Sharp on navigation. B. Sharp. il Yachting 121:81+ Je '67

Finding your way with sounders. J. West. il Yachting 122:47-9+ O '67

Navigation in the South Pacific. S. Pinchot. Yachting 122:112 Jl '67

Who's afraid of L.I. Sound? M. Rosenblad. il Yachting 121:61+ F '67

See also
Artificial satellites—Navigational applications
Azimuth
Collisions at sea
Compass
Inland navigation
Institute of navigation
Nautical astronomy
Pilots and pilotage
Radar in navigation
Sailing
Winds

Competitions

Control points. M. L. Hersey. See issues of Yachting

First electronic navigation contest for the new Motor boating trophy. il Motor B 119:40-3+ Je '67

Predicted loggers keep rolling along. M. L. Hersey. il Yachting 121:86-7+ Ap '67

NAVIGATION (space flight)

Calming a navigator's nightmare; problems of navigating among the stars. A. Ewing. il Sci N 92:448-9 N 4 '67

Incredible flight to the stars, theories of S. Moskowitz. Time 90:94 D 8 '67

NAVIGATION, Aerial

See also
Airplanes—Piloting
Decca navigation
Inertial guidance systems
Tacan

Study and teaching

See also
Air pilots—Training

NAVIGATION, Primitive

Magical stones of the sun; cordierite identified as Viking navigation aid. il Time 90:58 Jl 14 '67

NAVIGATION, Primitive—*Continued*
Navigating by sun stone; Viking aid to navigation. Sci Am 217:44 Jl '67
Polynesian navigation. W. S. Kals. il Sky & Tel 33:358-60 Je '67
NAVIGATION aids
   See also
   Electronics in navigation
NAVROTSKY, Alexandra, and others
Enthalpy of transformation of a high-pressure polymorph of titanium dioxide to the rutile modification. bibliog Science 158:388-9 O 20 '67
NAVY department. See United States—Navy department
NAVY league of the United States
Ocean uses accentuated at Navy league; 10th annual symposium on seapower. R. Niblock. Tech W 20:31 F 20 '67
NAVY space systems activity. See United States—Naval air systems command
NAWAPA. See North American water and power alliance
NAZI war criminals. See World war, 1939-1945—War criminals
NAZISM. See Fascism—Germany; Germany (Federal Republic)
NEA Journal
How to use professional periodicals. N. W. Hanna. NEA J 56:63-4 F '67
NEAFIE, Nelle
Farmer Jones's information network. por Library J 92:1586-7 Ap 15 '67
NEAL, Alfred C.
Economic necessities and Atlantic communities. For Affairs 45:694-705 Jl '67
NEAL, Jay T.
What you should know to grow African-violets. Home Gard 54:41 O '67
NEAL, Patricia
Pat Neal makes a radiant return. B. Farrell. il pors Life 62:119-20 Ap 7 '67
Patricia Neal: suddenly I wanted to live! S. Frank. por Good H 165:70-1+ Jl '67
NEAR EAST. See Middle East
NEAR Eastern and South Asian affairs, Bureau of. See United States—State, Department of—Near Eastern and South Asian affairs, Bureau of
NEARY, John
Head taller than the six-foot drifts. G. P. Hunt. por Life 62:3 F 10 '67
NEBRASKA
Centennial for Nebraska. B. Belford. il Travel 127:32-7 Ap '67
   See also
   Forests and forestry—Nebraska

   Politics and government
New way to spell Nebraska. il Time 89:23 Ap 28 '67
NEBRASKA centennial. See Centennials
NEBRASKA national forest. See Forests and forestry—Nebraska
NEBULAE
Barnard's loop nebula. il Sky & Tel 34:145-6 S '67
Crab nebula in X-rays; radio source mapped. il Sci N 91:330-1 Ap 8 '67
Stellar birthplace. Sci Am 217:60 O '67
NEBULAE, Photography of. See Astronomical photography
NECK
First aid. C. J. Potthoff. Todays Health 45: 74 F '67
NECKLACES
Necklaces from the kitchen. il Sunset 139:83 Jl '67
NECROSIS
Ischemic necrosis: prevention by stress. H. Selye. bibliog il Science 156:1262-3 Je 2 '67
NEDBAILO, Petr
Commission on human rights strongly condemns the policies of apartheid and repressive measures in South Africa. UN Mo Chron 4:59-68 My '67
NEEDHAM, Joseph
Joseph Needham and the science of China. D. J. de S. Price. il por Horizon 10:52-63 Wint '68
NEEDLEPOINT
Big effects with instant needlepoint. E. Kinard. il House B 109:216-17+ O '67
How to get big effects with instant needlepoint. il House B 109:50+ O '67
New directions in needlepoint. il Good H 164:92-3 F '67
NEEDLEWORK
For nimble needles: stitchery kits. il House & Gard 132:32+ D '67

Forty-two gifts they'll be glad you made. il Good H 165:108-13+ N '67
Heirlooms of tomorrow that you can make today. il McCalls 94:90-3 S '67
Mail-order mecca for needleworkers; Nantucket. House & Gard 132:89-90 O '67
Sand dollars; stitchery composition. D. Van Dommelen. il Sch Arts 66:24 My '67
   See also
   Embroidery
   Macramé
   Needlepoint
   Patchwork
   Sewing
NEEDLEWORK pictures. See Pictures
NEER, Don L.
Industrial recreation. Parks & Rec 2:79 Ap '67
NEGATIVE income tax. See Economic assistance, Domestic; Income
NEGATIVES, Photographic. See Photography—Negatives
NEGLEY, William
With only a bow and bold belief. Sports Illus 27:50-6+ Jl 31 '67
NEGLIGENCE
33,000-volt shock wins two award of $½ million. A. Peters. il Ebony 23:112-14+ N '67
NEGOTIABLE instruments
   See also
   Checks
NEGOTIATION, International. See Arbitration, International; International relations
NEGOTIATION now (organization) See Vietnamese war. 1957- —Peace and mediation
NEGRITUDE. See Nationalism—Negro race
NEGRO (term)
What's in a name? Negro vs. Afro-American vs. black. L. Bennett, jr. il Ebony 23:46-8+ N '67; Discussion. 23:10-11 Ja '68
NEGRO actors and actresses
Enroute to the future; Negro actors playing white roles; reprint. S. Kauffmann. Negro Hist Bul 30:13 Ap '67
Hello, Dolly. R. Lantz. Ebony 23:83-9 Ja '68
Leslie Uggams, star in a new galaxy. il Newsweek 70:63-7 Jl 17 '67
Negro actor asks himself: am I a Negro or am I an actor? W. Kerr. il N Y Times Mag p34-5+ O 15 '67
   See also
   Brown, J.
   Greene, L.
   Morris, G.
   Sands, D.
NEGRO ambassadors
Fruitful life of Lady Carter; wife of ambassador of Guyana. il Ebony 22:40-2+ Jl '67
NEGRO American visitors in Africa. See Foreign visitors in Africa
NEGRO Americans in Africa. See Americans in Africa
NEGRO anti-Semitism. See Anti-Semitism; Jews and Negroes
NEGRO art. See Art, Negro (American)
NEGRO artists
American Negro art in progress. L. J. Pierre-Noel. il Negro Hist Bul 30:6-9 O '67
New surge in the arts. A. Morrison. il Ebony 22:134-6+ Ag '67
Wall of respect; artists of Organization of black American culture paint mural in Chicago ghetto. il Ebony 23:48-50 D '67
   See also
   White, C.
NEGRO associations
Wall of respect; artists of Organization of black American culture paint mural in Chicago ghetto. il Ebony 23:48-50 D '67
NEGRO athletes
Cause for alarm; Olympic boycott. Sports Illus 27:11 S 25 '67
Negro Olympics boycott is off target. Life 63:4 D 8 '67
Negro youth in sports. il Ebony 22:130-3 Ag '67
Olympic boycott? il Newsweek 70:59 D 4 '67
Step to an Olympic boycott; Western regional black youth conference. J. Rodgers. il Sports Illus 27:30-1 D 4 '67
Where Negroes have struck it rich. il U S News 63:71 D 11 '67
NEGRO authors
Anger, and beyond, ed. by H. Hill. Review Commentary 43:100-4 Mr '67. J. Anderson
From the ashes: voices of Watts, ed. by B. Schulberg. Review Sat R 50:78 S 23 '67. P. Thomas
New surge in the arts. A. Morrison. il Ebony 22:134-6+ Ag '67
A very stern discipline; interview. R. Ellison. Harper 234:76-80+ Mr '67
   See also
   Abrahams, P.
   Authors, African
   Baldwin, J.
   Hughes, L.

NEGRO bankers
Fast-moving banker abroad; assistant manager, loan officer at Chase Manhattan's Paris bank. il Ebony 23:41-2+ D '67
Negro pioneers in mortgage banking. il Ebony 22:60-1+ Jl '67

NEGRO baseball players. See Baseball players

NEGRO basketball players. See Basketball players

NEGRO businessmen
Made in Italy export house manager. il Ebony 22:75-6+ F '67
World of the wealthy Negro. B. Surface. il N Y Times Mag p 10-11+ Jl 23 '67
  See also
Cobb, L.

NEGRO children
Children must be protected from the harm of race. B. Spock. Negro Hist Bul 30:14 Ap '67
Children of the American ghetto. R. Coles. Harper 235:16+ S '67
Civil rights is also a state of mind. R. Coles. il N Y Times Mag p32-4+ My 7 '67
Ghetto schools: an educational wasteland. A. Poinsett. il Ebony 22:52-7 Ag '67
Negro child and public education. R. Fulton. bibliog f Sch & Soc 95:109-10+ F 18 '67
Summer we learned that kids are kids. S. Lloyd. il Redbook 129:6+ Jl '67
White skins, dark skins, thin skins; middleclass Negro in suburbia. M. Watkins. il N Y Times Mag p 127+ D 3 '67

NEGRO church. See Negroes in the United States—Religion

NEGRO circus performers. See Circus performers

NEGRO civil rights organizations. See Civil rights organizations

NEGRO coeds. See College students, Women

NEGRO college graduates. See College graduates

NEGRO colleges. See Negroes in the United States—Education

NEGRO comedians
Negro humor: an answer to anguish. A. Morrison. il Ebony 22:99-100+ My '67
  See also
Cosby, B.
Foxx, R.
Pryor, R.

NEGRO conductors. See Conductors (music)

NEGRO congressmen
James T. Rapier; congressman from Alabama. N. W. Walton. bibliog f Negro Hist Bul 30:6-10 N '67
Three Negro senators of the United States. il Negro Hist Bul 30:4-5+ Ja '67
  See also
Brooke, E. W.

NEGRO criminals. See Negroes in the United States—Crime

NEGRO dancers
Paris ballet star: Norman de Joie. il Ebony 23:67-8+ D '67

NEGRO diplomats
  See also
Carter, C. C.

NEGRO drama
  See also
Theater, Negro

NEGRO education. See Negroes in the United States—Education

NEGRO educators
Behind the black college student revolt. N. Hare. il Ebony 22:58-61 Ag '67
First Negro president of the D.C. Board of education: Wesley S. Williams. il Negro Hist Bul 29:177-8+ Fall '66

NEGRO entertainers
Cultivating the arts of poverty. F. A. J. Ianni. il Sat R 50:60-2+ Je 17 '67
New surge in the arts. A. Morrison. il Ebony 22:136+ Ag '67
Opportunity please knock; youth gang produces lively show with guidance of O. Brown, jr. il Ebony 22:104-7 Ag '67
Sense of style. G. Frazier. Esquire 68:70+ N '67
  See also
Cambridge, G. M.
Falana, L.

NEGRO executives
Executive Negro. I. Oxaal. Sat R 50:47-8 Jl 1 '67

NEGRO family life. See Negroes in the United States—Social conditions

NEGRO farmers
Crop allotments: power behind the cotton. P. Marcuse. il Nation 206:43-6 Ja 8 '68

NEGRO football players. See Football players

NEGRO gangs. See Gangs

NEGRO hairdressing. See Hairdressing

NEGRO history. See Negroes—History; Negroes in the United States—History

NEGRO history week
NEA-produced exhibit and filmstrip honoring Negro history week. Negro Hist Bul 30:17 Ap '67
Negro history week. C. C. Robinson. bibliog il Library J 93:268-9 Ja 15 '68
Twenty governors proclaim Negro history week in response to the request by Dr J. Rupert Picott. il Negro Hist Bul 30:12-14 Mr '67

NEGRO humor
Negro humor: an answer to anguish. A. Morrison. il Ebony 22:99-100+ My '67

NEGRO insurance agents. See Insurance agents

NEGRO intellectuals
Dialectic of The fire next time. A. Gayle, jr. Negro Hist Bul 30:15-16 Ap '67

NEGRO judges
  See also
Marshall, T.

NEGRO labor. See Negroes in the United States—Employment

NEGRO literature
Anger, and beyond, ed. by H. Hill. Review Commentary 43:100-4 Mr '67. J. Anderson
Ebony book shelf. See issues of Ebony
Prison reading edict raises rights issue. Library J 93:138 Ja 15 '68
Through a glass, darkly, books for children. D. H. Millender. bibliog il Library J 92:4571-6 D 15 '67
  See also
African literature
Negro authors

    Collections
Schomburg's ailing collection. il Ebony 22:55-6+ O '67

NEGRO market
Why the Negro market counts. il Bsns W p64-8+ S 2 '67

NEGRO mayors. See Negro municipal officers

NEGRO middle class. See Middle classes

NEGRO migration. See Negroes in the United States—Migration

NEGRO millionaires. See Millionaires

NEGRO Mormons. See Mormons and Mormonism, Negro

NEGRO municipal officers
Backlash, backstab; appeal for support for Gary mayoralty candidate. il Newsweek 70:25-6 S 11 '67
Elections '67: what clues for '68? with press comments. il Sr Schol 91:21-3 N 30 '67
First mayor of the Nation's capital. il Negro Hist Bul 30:4-5 N '67
Michigan's Negro mayors. il Ebony 22:74-6+ Jl '67
Negro marches toward city hall; C. Stokes wins primary. il Bsns W p36-7 O 7 '67
Off-year vote gives few clues to 1968. il Bsns W p48-9 N 11 '67
Power and responsibility. Nation 205:356-7 O 16 '67
Prospects for more Negro mayors. il U S News 63:49 N 27 '67
Race issue: what city voters say now. il U S News 63:35 O 16 '67
Report: Gary, Ind. C. Stone. Atlan 220:28-30+ O '67
Six his honors already in office. il Life 63:40-1 O 13 '67
U.S. letter: Cleveland; C. Stokes winner of Democratic mayoralty nomination. C. Trillin. New Yorker 43:210-14+ O 14 '67

NEGRO musicians
Lesson of experience; members of Symphony of the New World. il Newsweek 69:102 F 20 '67
  See also
Armstrong, L.
Coleman, O.
Mo, Billy
Negro singers
Smith, W.
Webb, C.

NEGRO newspapers. See Negro press

NEGRO periodicals
How John Johnson made it. A. J. Reichley. il Fortune 77:152-3+ Ja '68
  See also
Liberator (periodical)

NEGRO physicians
Crisis in Negro medicine. il Ebony 23:77-8+ N '67

NEGRO politicians. See Negroes in the United States—Politics and suffrage

NEGRO press
Negro press. E. Kendall. il Holiday 41:82-4 My '67
Playing it cool. il Time 90:66 Jl 28 '67
Reprieve for the Courier. Newsweek 70:52 Jl 3 '67

NEGRO public officers
Money men; three hold high finance posts. il Ebony 22:65-6+ S '67
Negroes move up in government. il U S News 63:57-8 Jl 3 '67
Political tour of Harlem; new breed Democrats. P. Good. il N Y Times Mag p34-6+ O 29 '67; Reply. C. Greitzer. p66+ N 26 '67
Vote power; Gary's Negroes nominate R. Hatcher as Democratic mayorial candidate. il Time 89:21-2 My 12 '67

NEGRO race
Hands of the blacks. L. B. Honwana. il N Y Times Mag p26-7 Ap 30 '67
No one has ever called me a nigger, I have never been bitten by a rat. G. Moore. Life 62:77-8+ Je 30 '67
See also
Nationalism—Negro race

NEGRO radio stations. See Radio stations

NEGRO reporters. See Reporters and reporting

NEGRO schools
Ghetto schools: an educational wasteland. A. Poinsett. il Ebony 22:52-7 Ag '67
Tennessee rebels; Nashville liberation school. L. Jackson. New Repub 157:9-10 S 9 '67

NEGRO scientists
See also
Alexander, B. H.
Crummie, J. H.
Gourdine, M.

NEGRO service men and women
Social inequities; Defense department programs; address, November 7, 1967. R. S. McNamara. Vital Speeches 34:98-103 D 1 '67
See also
United States—Armed forces—Negroes

NEGRO singers
Fifth dimension. il Ebony 22:152-4+ O '67
In groups of the big beat. P. Garland. il Ebony 22:38+ Je '67
See also names of Negro singers, e.g. M. Harrison

NEGRO slum clearance. See Urban renewal

NEGRO societies. See Negroes in the United States—Societies

NEGRO students
Agony at State; problems of San Francisco state college. il Newsweek 71:59 Ja 22 '68
Behind the black college student revolt. N. Hare. il Ebony 22:58-61 Ag '67
Black pride. il Time 90:70 O 6 '67
Black revolt hits the white campus. E. Dunbar. il Look 31:27-31 O 31 '67
How to wreck a campus; violence at San Francisco state college. D. Swanston. il Nation 206:38-41 Ja 8 '68
May queens and effigies; Negroes on southern campuses. il Newsweek 69:98+ Je 5 '67
Negroes in the private schools. C. Merrill. Atlan 220:37-40 Jl '67
Reading is what's happening; address, April 21, 1967. E. J. Josey. il Negro Hist Bul 30:14-17 My '67
Soul brothers and Swahili. il Newsweek 70:59 O 9 '67
Young man on the go; versatile Alaska high schooler. J. Davis. il Ebony 22:56-8+ S '67
See also
Colleges and universities—Desegregation

Aid
See Student aid

NEGRO suffrage. See Negroes in the United States—Politics and suffrage

NEGRO teachers
Negro students' demand: more Negro teachers. U S News 64:16 Ja 15 '68

NEGRO terrorists. See Terrorism

NEGRO theater. See Theater. Negro

NEGRO voters, Registration of. See Voters, Registration of

NEGRO-white intermarriage. See Intermarriage of races

NEGRO-white relations. See Race relations

NEGRO women
Divorce and the Negro woman. P. Pierce. il Ebony 22:84-6+ Jl '67
See also
Single women

Employment
See also
Married women—Employment
Negro women—Occupations

Occupations
Career expectations of Negro women graduates; excerpt from report. J. H. Fichter. bibliog f il Mo Labor R 90:36-42 N '67
Half a hundred eligible girls. il Ebony 22:44-6+ F '67

NEGRO women and politics. See Women and politics

NEGRO women college graduates. See College graduates, Women

NEGRO youth
Black youth in rebellion. C. H. King and others. il Wilson Lib Bul 42:166-72 O '67
I learned my lesson. F. Pickett. il Nations Bsns 55:76+ O '67
Negro youth in America; symposium. il Ebony 22:21+ Ag '67
See also
Negro students

NEGROES
No one has ever called me a nigger, I have never been bitten by a rat. G. Moore. Life 62:77-8+ Je 30 '67

History
Calendar of Negro history. See issues of Negro history bulletin
Current problems of African historiography; address, October 22, 1965. C. G. Contee. bibliog il Negro Hist Bul 30:5-10 Ap '67
See also
Negroes in the United States—History

Psychology
Mr Genocide; views of black power militants. S. Alsop. Sat Eve Post 240:14 S 9 '67
Negro psychiatrist explains the Negro psyche. A. F. Poussaint. il N Y Times Mag p52-3+ Ag 20 '67; Discussion. p 123 S 4 '67
Thinking black. il Newsweek 70:37-41 N 20 '67
Up from hate. T. Slaughter. il Sat R 50:59 D 16 '67
Why Juanita enjoyed the riot. S. Alsop. il Sat Eve Post 240:16 S 23 '67

Religion
See also
Negroes in the United States—Religion

NEGROES, Catholic. See Catholic church—Negroes

NEGROES, Discrimination against. See Race discrimination

NEGROES, Famous. See Great men

NEGROES and Jews. See Jews and Negroes

NEGROES and libraries. See Libraries and Negroes

NEGROES as farmers. See Negro farmers

NEGROES in Africa
Monthly report on Africa. P. McStallworth. Negro Hist Bul 30:19-20 Ja '67
See also
South Africa—Race problems

NEGROES in art
Charles White: portrayer of black dignity. L. Robinson. il Ebony 22:25-8+ Jl '67

NEGROES in business. See Negro businessmen

NEGROES in Canada
Child is a child, is a child. P. Garland. il Ebony 22:44-6+ Ap '67

NEGROES in Italy
Made in Italy export house manager. il Ebony 22:75-6+ F '67

NEGROES in literature
Book reviews. See issues of Negro history bulletin
Ebony book shelf. See issues of Ebony
Nervous Nellies on race relations? school libraries. A. G. Mims. bibliog Library J 92:1291-3+ Mr 15 '67
Role of the book in combating prejudice; concerning third edition of list: We build together. C. Rollins. il Wilson Lib Bul 42:176-9 O '67
Spokesmen for the Blacks. J. Meyer. Nation 205:597-9 D 4 '67
Through a glass, darkly, books for children. D. H. Millender. bibliog il Library J 92:4571-6 D 15 '67
To Mississippi in the interest of children and books: three trips to speak at University of Mississippi on the Negro child in children's books. G. Woods. il Wilson Lib Bul 41:1028-33 Je '67

NEGROES in South Africa
See also
South Africa—Race problems

NEGROES In television. See Television broadcasting—Performers

NEGROES in textbooks. See Textbooks

NEGROES In the United States
Black and white, by W. Brink and L. Harris. Review
   Sat R il 50:28 Ag 5 '67. E. R. Lincoln
Black power and urban unrest, by N. Wright, jr. Review
   Sat R 50:26-7 Ag 12 '67. C. Greene
Black power establishment; comp. by W. Worthy. Esquire 68:131-3 N '67
Black power: its goals and methods; interview. N. Hare. il U S News 62:64-6+ My 22 '67
Black-white at home, North-South abroad. E. Kenworthy. Yale R 57:161-81 D '67
Can money satisfy the black American? S. Lens. Commonweal 86:508-9 Ag 25 '67
Current events and branch news. See issues of Negro history bulletin
Fire this time. il Time 90:13-18 Ag 4 '67
Grasping at chaos. Nation 205:547-8 N 27 '67
Hard-core ghetto mood. il Newsweek 70:20-2+ Ag 21 '67
How long, oh Lord, how long? il Ebony 22:106-7 S '67
How to cool it; measures to avert racial violence in slums. il Time 89:21 Je 30 '67
I learned to feel black. J. Smith. Redbook 129:64-5+ Ag '67
Invasion by armed Black Panthers: Sacramento, Calif; trouble in other spots, too. il U S News 62:12 My 15 '67
Light in the frightening corners. il Time 90:10-15 Jl 28 '67
Maturation of the two movements; labor and civil rights movements. R. B. McKersie. Mo Labor R 90:36-8 Jl '67

Negro in America; effect of views of well-intentioned liberals. M. Friedman. Newsweek 70:89 D 11 '67

Negro in America; what must be done; symposium, with editorial comment. il Newsweek 70:32-42+ N 20 '67
Negro youth in America; symposium. il Ebony 22:21+ Ag '67
New Negro mood; urban Negro attitudes; with editorial comment. R. Beardwood. il Fortune 77:127-8, 146-51+ Ja '68
Other 97 per cent; moderate Negro leaders. il Time 90:12-17 Ag 11 '67
Power of blackness. C. Brown. il Look 31:22-7 Je 27 '67
Profiles of great Americans born in February. Negro Hist Bul 30:4-5 F '67
Progress report 1967. il Ebony 23:118-22 Ja '68
Racial crisis: a consensus. il Newsweek 70:16-17 Ag 21 '67
Riots and root causes. Commonweal 86:483-4 Ag 11 '67
Sense of style. G. Frazier. Esquire 68:70+ N '67
This is my country too: a pessimistic postscript. J. A. Williams. il Holiday 41:8+ Je '67
Time for cooperation. il Ebony 22:150-1 O '67
Time of violence & tragedy. il Time 90:12-13 Ag 4 '67
Tree of life; isolation of Negroes of Johns Island. W. K. Zinsser. il Look 31:18 Je 13 '67
Uneasy calm. il Time 90:18-20 Ag 18 '67
We're going to shoot the cops. U S News 62:10 My 29 '67
What can be done? il Newsweek 70:31-2 Ag 7 '67
Whistling in a very lively graveyard; C. Lynn's ideas on black unrest. M. Renek. New Repub 156:14-15 My 13 '67
White man's justice. Christian Cent 84:708 My 31 '67
   See also
Black Muslim movement
Interracial cooperation
National association for the advancement of colored people
Negro authors
Negro history week
Negro market
United States—Army—Negroes
   also Subhead Negroes under names of cities, e.g. Chicago—Negroes

Bibliography
1965 and 1966: happy new years for non-fiction books about the Negro. L. B. Hopkins. Negro Hist Bul 30:15-17 N '67

Civil rights
After the long, hot summer, where do we go? E. W. Brooke. il Look 31:24-7 S 5 '67
Black power and the American Christ. V. Harding; discussion. Christian Cent 84:214 F 15 '67
Civil rights; we haven't really improved, we may have slipped; excerpts from address, April 13, 1967. R. Clark. il U S News 62:50-1 My 1 '67
Color it black or white; address, February 28, 1967. G. H. Moulds. Vital Speeches 33:380-4 Ap 1 '67
End of the road? Time 90:18 Ag 25 '67
How Kennedy's concern for Negroes led to his death. C. T. Rowan. il Ebony 22:27-30+ Ap '67
Integrating America, the problems; interview. J. W. Gardner. il U S News 62:64-9 My 8 '67
Integration has failed. M. Halsey; discussion. Christian Cent 84:180 F 8 '67
International evening: Martin Luther King; summary of address. M. L. King, jr. il Pub W 191:52 Je 19 '67
Is the race problem insoluble? C. Brown; T. G. Harris. Look 31:28+ Je 27 '67
Logical assumption. il Ebony 23:64-5 N '67
Long, hot century? Time 89:21 Ap 28 '67
Meaning of the Newark riots. J. B. Sheerin. Cath World 205:324-6 S '67
Needed: progress without riots. il Bsns W p20-2 Jl 1 '67
Negro psychiatrist explains the Negro psyche. A. F. Poussaint. il N Y Times Mag p52-3+ Ag 20 '67; Discussion. p 123 S 24 '67
Never glad confident morning again. S. Alsop. Sat Eve Post 240:20 O 7 '67
No access to access. il Ebony 22:110-11 F '67
Package of mischief; why 1966 act was rejected. New Repub 157:4 S 23 '67
Powell row hurts the civil rights movement; dwindling white support. il Bsns W p42 Mr 18 '67
Powell splits the rights movement. il Bsns W p48 Mr 11 '67
Principles & heresies. F. S. Meyer. Nat R 20:36 Ja 16 '68
Representative; interview. J. Bond. New Yorker 43:34-5 Ap 1 '67
Revolution in the civil rights movement; address, February 28, 1967. N. R. Douglas. Vital Speeches 33:443-5 My 1 '67
Second coming of Martin Luther King. D. Halberstam. il Harper 235:39-51 Ag '67
Speaking out: America will burn. D. H. Watts. Sat Eve Post 241:6+ Ja 13 '68
Temper of our time, by E. Hoffer. Review
   Sat R 50:41-2 Ap 8 '67. M. R. Konvitz
Washington report; Conference on Negro history. J. Lloyd. Sr Schol 89:sup6 Ja 20 '67
Way to racial peace in America; interview. R. Wilkins. il U S News 63:80-6 S 25 '67
What price integration? Nat R 19:887-8 Ag 22 '67
When the Negroes in Vietnam come home; with excerpts from interviews. W. M. Young, jr. Harper 234:63-9 Je '67
Where do we go from here, by M. L. King, jr. Review
   Sat R 50:29-30 Jl 8 '67. M. R. Konvitz
Which way for the Negro? il Newsweek 69:27-8+ My 15 '67
With but one voice; reaction to M. L. King's declaration of opposition to the war in Vietnam. Nation 204:515-16 Ap 24 '67
   See also
Civil rights act of 1964
Civil rights demonstrations
Race relations

Anecdotes, facetiae, satire, etc.
Elementary guide to civil rights bird watching. M. Turner. il Ebony 22:68-9+ Mr '67

History
Climbing Jacob's ladder, by P. Watters and R. Cleghorn. Review
   New Repub 157:20-3 D 16 '67. R. Coles
Sojourner Truth, the first sit-in. M. Harlowe. Negro Hist Bul 29:173-4 Fall '66

Crime
Crime and insurrection. Nation 205:68-9 Jl 31 '67
How to start a riot; address, August 2, 1967. E. J. Younger. Vital Speeches 33:759-63 O 1 '67
Planned, mass violations of our laws; address, February 14, 1967. C. E. Whittaker. Vital Speeches 33:322-8 Mr 15 '67
Poverty: phony excuse for riots? yes, says a key senator; excerpt from address, July 17, 1967. R. Byrd. U S News 63:14 Jl 31 '67

NEGROES in the United States—*Continued*

Economic conditions

Apostle of economics; J. Jackson's Operation Breadbasket in Chicago. D. Llorens. il Ebony 22:78-80+ Ag '67

Bigotry's greedy roots; white man's oppression of the Negro. Christian Cent 84:1547-8 D 6 '67

Black poverty. il Newsweek 70:41-2+ N 20 '67

Blow-up in the cities. New Repub 157:5-7 Ag 5 '67

Darkness on the Delta. F. Davis. Reporter 37: 35-7 S 21 '67

For Negroes, the pie cuts too thin; job dilemma virtually unchanged. il Bsns W p26-8 Ag 5 '67

Great opportunity of 1965. W. F. Buckley, jr. Nat R 19:842 Ag 8 '67

How to stop riots. L. Bennett, jr. il Ebony 22:29-32+ O '67

Looters: deprived or in Cadillacs? U S News 63:27 Ag 14 '67

Martin Luther King defines black power. M. L. King, jr. il N Y Times Mag p26-7+ Je 11 '67

Mississippi frontier. R. Coles. New Repub 157: 41-2+ N 11 '67

More dollars and more diplomas; with charts and with editorial comment. E. K. Faltermayer. Fortune 77:127-8, 140-5+ Ja '68

Negro economy. H. C. Wallich. Newsweek 70:64 D 25 '67

Negroes: big gains, but still problems. U S News 63:16 N 13 '67

New idea: mass bankruptcy, and the damage it could do. il U S News 63:124-5 S 25 '67

Off the land; plight of the Negroes in the Mississippi Delta. Nation 204:261 F 27 '67

Socio-economic profile of non-whites. America 117:594 N 18 '67

Taxing situation. il Ebony 23:64-5 D '67

Today's Negroes: better off than yesterday's immigrants? excerpt from A nation of cities. I. Kristol. U S News 63:77-8 N 27 '67

Way out of the exploding ghetto. B. Rustin. il N Y Times Mag p 16-17+ Ag 13 '67

When the southern Negro moves North. R. Coles. il N Y Times Mag p25-7+ S 17 '67

See also

Negroes in the United States—Migration

Education

ABC's of race. il Newsweek 70:52-3 N 20 '67

Academic disaster area; Negro colleges. il Time 89:64 Mr 31 '67

Behind the black college student revolt. N. Hare. il Ebony 22:58-61 Ag '67

Boat rockers; white teachers at Negro colleges in the South. il Newsweek 69:90-1 My 22 '67

Chemical education in Negro colleges. E. O. Woolfolk and L. S. Smith. il Negro Hist Bul 30:7-11 F '67

Children are dying. J. R. Lowe. McCalls 95: 4-5 Ja '68

Death of a dropout. J. Sideman. New Repub 156:11-14 Je 3 '67

Dilemma in the schools; how to improve Negro education. il U S News 63:43-5 D 25 '67

End of the line; Southern regional education board to strengthen Negro colleges. Newsweek 70:81 S 11 '67

Fate of Negro colleges. B. Stretch. il Sat R 50:77 Ap 15 '67

Ghetto schools: an educational wasteland. A. Poinsett. il Ebony 22:52-7 Ag '67

How South hopes to keep Negroes; technical training schools. il U S News 63:42-4 O 2 '67

How to get through: H. Kohl's experience as described in his 36 children. Time 91:34+ Ja 19 '68

Is desegregation impractical? R. Schwartz and others. New Repub 158:27-9 Ja 6 '68

Mississippi's beehive college. C. Parsons and W. B. Welch. il Am Ed 4:19-22+ D '67

Negro child and public education. R. Fulton. bibliog f Sch & Soc 95:109-10+ F 18 '67

Negro graduates: PHS study reports opinions and problems. B. Nelson. Science 158: 99-100 O 6 '67

Negro's place in the American dream. C. T. Rowan. Read Digest 90:63-7 Ap '67

New hope for Harlem's bright youth; preparation for prep school class, New York's Wadleigh intermediate school. il Ebony 22: 27-30+ My '67

No more nonsense about ghetto education! J. Alsop. New Repub 157:18-23 Jl 22 '67; Same abr. with title Can Negro children make the grade? Read Digest 91:81-4 N '67; Discussion. New Repub 157:42-4 S 2; 16-19 S 23; 38-9 O 21; 18-23 N 18 '67

Overhauling Negro colleges. B. Stretch. Sat R 50:86 N 18 '67

Program for overcoming the handicap of dialect. T. R. Temple. New Repub 156:11-12 Mr 25 '67

Reading is what's happening; address, April 21, 1967. E. J. Josey. il Negro Hist Bul 30: 14-17 My '67

Requiem for the urban school; experiences of H. Kohl and J. Kozol in Boston and Harlem. E. Z. Friedenberg. il Sat R 50: 77-9+ N 18 '67

Research scientist lends a hand to capital's poor. Ebony 22:124-6+ Mr '67

Retreat to separate but equal. I. Kraft. Nation 205:552-5 N 27 '67

Schools aren't enough. Commonweal 87:348-9 D 15 '67

Self-help program stirs a Negro slum; Operation Bootstrap in Los Angeles. il Bsns W p67-8+ Mr 25 '67

Strengthening Negro colleges. Sch & Soc 95: 411+ N 11 '67

There are 300 Negroes at the University of Alabama. G. Samuels. il N Y Times Mag p32-3+ My 14 '67

Thirty-six children; concerning H. Kohl's account of teaching in Harlem's P.S. 103. il Newsweek 71:70 Ja 15 '68

Upward bound; educational projects for Negroes. il Fortune 77:164-9 Ja '68

Where ghetto schools fail; excerpt from Death at an early age. J. Kozol. il Atlan 220:107-10 O '67

See also

Allen university, Columbia, S.C.

Colleges and universities—Desegregation

Grambling college, Grambling, La.

Howard university, Washington, D. C.

Miles college, Birmingham, Ala.

Private schools—Desegregation

Public schools—Desegregation

South Carolina state college, Orangeburg

Texas southern university, Houston, Tex.

Employment

Adjustment to plant closure: excerpt from report to the Automation fund committee. J. L. Stern. Mo Labor R 90:42-6 Ja '67

And organized labor gets involved, too. Sr Schol 91:10 N 2 '67

Apostle of economics; J. Jackson's Operation Breadbasket in Chicago. D. Llorens. il Ebony 22:78-80+ Ag '67

Automakers focus on Detroit's jobless. R. W. Irvin. Reporter 37:29-30 D 28 '67

Bars to apprenticeship; Marshall-Briggs study on Negro participation in apprenticeship programs. America 117:538-9 N 11 '67

Bearing down on job bias. Bsns W p 18-19 D 23 '67

Bringing new jobs into the ghettos; companies putting up plants in slum areas. il Bsns W p84-6 D 2 '67

Business: bridge to racial progress. il Nations Bsns 55:62-5 O '67

Case against the unions. T. O'Hanlon. il Fortune 77:170-3+ Ja '68

Changing pattern of Negro employment. A M. Ross. il Ebony 22:38-9 Jl '67

Civil rights: what role for business? C. Marshall; P. M. Klutznick. il Sat R 51:52+ Ja 13 '68

Comparing racial employment. il Sch & Soc 95:340 O 14 '67

Crafts ease their stand on bias. Bsns W p 133-4 D 9 '67

Curing explosive disillusionment: individual initiative; address, October 27, 1967. L. H. Sullivan. Vital Speeches 34:117-19 D 1 '67

Deep South boss who hires ex-cons; with report by R. Busch. il Life 63:38-40+ D 15 '67

Detroit: up from the ashes; New Detroit committee program. il Newsweek 71:48-50 Ja 1 '68

Do it yourself. Newsweek 70:51 N 20 '67

FIGHT-Kodak fight. D. Livadas. Nat R 19: 683 Je 27 '67

Fight that swirls around Eastman Kodak; battle over more jobs for Negroes. il Bsns W p38-41 Ap 29 '67

For Negroes, the pie cuts too thin; job dilemma virtually unchanged. il Bsns W p26-8 Ag 5 '67

NEGROES in the United States—Employment
—*Continued*
He helps the poor help themselves; interview L. H. Sullivan. il Nations Bsns 55:42-4+ Jl '67
How South hopes to keep Negroes; technical training schools. il U S News 63:42-4 O 2 '67
Job program that works; New York city's Joint apprenticeship program. T. R. Brooks. il Reporter 37:28-30 N 16 '67
Kodak and Fight agree to agree; plan for hiring a fixed number of Negroes. Bsns W p22 Jl 1 '67
Luring business into the ghettos. il Newsweek 70:77 O 16 '67
More and better jobs for Negroes: what the latest studies show. il U S News 63:83-4 Ag 21 '67
More dollars and more diplomas; with charts and with editorial comment. E. K. Faltermayer. Fortune 77:127-8, 140-5+ Ja '68
More jobs for Negroes. il Nations Bsns 55: 36-9 S '67
Negro self-help; Poor people's corporation cooperatives. A. Goldberg. New Repub 156:6 Je 10 '67
Negroes go national with demands for jobs; SCLC's Operation Breadbasket. Bsns W p37-8 Ag 19 '67
New business for business: reclaiming human resources. G. Burck. il Fortune 77:158-61+ Ja '68
New threat for employers? what a Negro group seeks from Kodak; FIGHT dispute over hiring agreement. il U S News 62: 74-5 My 8 '67
Opening the record on jobs for Negroes; industry-by-industry survey of minority hiring. il Bsns W p 128+ Ag 12 '67
Pattern of Negro jobs. America 117:166 Ag 19 '67
Racial policies of American industry. H. R. Northrup. Mo Labor R 90:41-3 Jl '67
Solving the Q.N. problem; Opportunities industrialization center, Philadelphia. il Time 89:25-6 Mr 3 '67
Summer's backlash: more job programs. Bsns W p 194+ O 21 '67
Teaching people to hold jobs: the Philadelphia plan; Opportunities industrialization center. il U S News 64:58-9 Ja 1 '68
Technology and the Negro. Sci Am 217:102 S '67
To prevent a chain of super-Watts. A. J. Cervantes. bibliog f Harvard Bsns R 45:55-65 S '67; Excerpts. il U S News 63:108-11 O 9 '67
Two halves; problems of newly hired slum dwellers. Time 90:28 D 8 '67
Unemployment among youth: the explosive statistic! il Ebony 22:127-9 Ag '67
What business is doing: opening up new jobs for Negroes. il U S News 62:62 Mr 6 '67
What the Kodak fracas means: job problems of Negroes. Bsns W p 192 My 6 '67
Where the people are; Watts manufacturing co. to employ Negroes. il Newsweek 70:84 S 18 '67
Will labor feel a backlash? labor's liberal wing campaigns for Negro rights. il Bsns W p69-70 Ag 5 '67
See also
Discrimination in employment
Negroes in the United States—Occupations
United States—President's equal employment opportunity commission

Health and hygiene
Crisis in Negro medicine. il Ebony 23:77-8+ N '67
Outsiders; doctors report on health of rural children in Alabama and Mississippi. New Repub 157:4 Jl 15 '67
Poverty: the hungry world of Teresa Pilgrim; Yazoo City, Miss. W. Hedgepeth. il Look 31:40-4 D 26 '67
Urge for Argo; laundry starch eaten by Negro women causes anemia. il Time 90: 36-7 Jl 28 '67
When you look for starvation in the South. il U S News 63:44 Jl 31 '67

History
American dream and dilemma. M. Nash. Sat R 50:30-1 Jl 8 '67
Calendar of Negro history. See issues of Negro history bulletin
California's law on Negro history. Negro Hist Bul 30:21-2 F '67
Courage beyond the call of duty. W. L. Katz. il Sat R 50:30-1 Je 17 '67
Dynamite; excerpt from Black power; the politics of liberation in America. S. Carmichael and C. Hamilton. il Atlan 220:98-102 O '67

Evolving Negro solidarity; what lies behind the support of Adam Clayton Powell. Christian Cent 84:395-6 Mr 29 '67; Discussion. 84:625 My 10 '67
Legacy of honor; new help from the NEA for teaching about Negro history. S. Dorros. il Negro Hist Bul 30:6-7 Ja '67
Past reconstructed. E. D. Genovese. Nation 204:758-61 Je 12 '67
Social power of the Negro. J. F. Comer. il Sci Am 216:21-7 bibliog(p 146) Ap '67
Washington report; Conference on Negro history. J. Lloyd. Sr Schol 89.sup6 Ja 20 '67
See also
Slavery—United States

Bibliography
Books on the American Negro. J. Foster. il Sr Schol 90:sup29 F 17 '67

Housing
Century of no progress? G. R. Metcalf. il Reporter 37:31-2 N 16 '67
Open housing; ordinance outlawing racial discrimination adopted in Louisville. W. Peeples. New Repub 158:9-10 Ja 13 '68
Open housing: the touchstone. America 116:620 Ap 29 '67
See also
Discrimination in housing
Housing—Desegregation

Migration
Black immigrants. B. H. Bagdikian. il Sat Eve Post 240:25-9+ Jl 15 '67
Can the big cities ever come back? il U S News 63:28-31 S 4 '67
Can the southern Negro exodus be stemmed? P. Clancy. il Reporter 37:27-8+ N 2 '67
Dynamite: excerpt from Black power; the politics of liberation in America. S. Carmichael and C. Hamilton. il Atlan 220:98-9 O '67
Negro problem keeps growing; the reason. il U S News 62:58-62 Mr 6 '67
When the southern Negro moves North. R. Coles. il N Y Times Mag p25-7+ S 17 '67

Occupations
Growing success of Negroes in the U.S. il U S News 63:54-7 Jl 3 '67
Jobs for college grads; with list of occupations, salaries and information sources. il Ebony 22:81-2+ Je '67
Lot has happened; Negroes given high appointments. il Time 90:17 Jl 7 '67
Speaking of people. See issues of Ebony
See also
Negro businessmen

Politics and suffrage
Black control of cities. F. F. Piven and R. A. Cloward. New Repub 157:19-21 S 30; 15-19 O 7 '67
Black polling power; Negro successes in Mississippi. Newsweek 70:26 Ag 21 '67
Black power and coalition politics. B. Rustin; discussion. Commentary 43:6+ Ja '67
Black power at the polls; Stokes, Hatcher victories. C. L. Sanders; A. Poinsett. il Ebony 23:23-6+ Ja '68
Black power, by S. Carmichael and C. V. Hamilton. Review
New Repub 158:27-8+ Ja 13 '68. S. Lazarus
Black-power summit. il Newsweek 70:19-20 Jl 31 '67
Constitutional disenfranchisement of the Negro in Louisiana (cont) G. E. Cunningham. Negro Hist Bul 29:174+ Fall '66
Elections: poor guys finish last. S. V. Roberts. Commonweal 87:291-2 D 1 '67
Far cry. J. H. Plumb. Sat R 50:21+ D 30 '67
From Saigon to Detroit. W. Pfaff. Commonweal 86:567-8 S 22 '67
Impact of Negro votes on southern politics. R. Cleghorn and P. Watters. il Reporter 36:24-5+ Ja 26 '67
In defense of black power. D. Danzig; discussion. Commentary 43:6+ Ja '67
Martin Luther King defines black power. M. L. King, jr. il N Y Times Mag p26-7+ Je 11 '67
Meredith vs. Powell: how solid is the Negro vote? il U S News 62:52 Mr 20 '67
Meredith's one-night stand. F. E. Kearns. Commonweal 86:78-9 Ap 7 '67
Needed: progress without riots. il Bsns W p20-2 Jl 1 '67
New reconstruction. il Ebony 23:52-3 Ja '68
Off-year vote gives few clues to 1968; election of two Negro mayors. il Bsns W p48-9 N 11 '67

NEGROES in the United States—Politics and suffrage—*Continued*
Politics; black power. D. MacDonald. Esquire 68:38+ O '67
Powell and the House; a black power victory? C. E. Fager. Christian Cent 84:175 F 8 '67; Discussion. 84:380 Mr 22 '67
Power and responsibility. Nation 205:356-7 O 16 '67
Protest; involvement of Negro leaders in Vietnam protest in New York city. W. F. Buckley, jr. Nat R 19:470 My 2 '67
Race issue: what city voters say now. il U S News 63:35 O 16 '67
Real black power. il Time 90:23-7 N 17 '67
Report; Gary, Ind. C. Stone. Atlan 220:28-30+ O '67
Revolution or reform on the black left. M. Miles. New Repub 157:9-10 Ag 19 '67
Right use of black power; elections in Gary, Ind. and Cleveland. Life 63:4 N 17 '67
Score one for Stokes, and Negroes up for mayor. il Life 63:36-41 O 13 '67
They voted; success of Negro candidates. il Time 90:22 Ag 18 '67
Three elections under microscope. Christian Cent 84:1483 N 22 '67
What Republican victory means to the Negro. S. Booker. il Ebony 22:88-90+ F '67

Religion
Black prayer; gospel of black nationalism. il Newsweek 71:71 Ja 15 '68
Key term in theological education for the Negro; compensatory. H. H. Mitchell. Christian Cent 84:530-3 Ap 26 '67
Politics of God, by J. Washington. Review Christian Cent 84:594 My 3 '67. V. Harding

Segregation
Children of crisis, by R. Coles. Review
Atlan 219:129 Je '67. O. Handlin
Commentary 44:91-2+ N '67. M. Ellmann
Nation 205:188-9 S 4 '67. R. Belenky
Newsweek 69:96+ Je 12 '67. S. Maloff
Sat R il 50:66-7 Je 17 '67. M. Greene
Dynamite; excerpt from Black power: the politics of liberation in America. S. Carmichael and C. Hamilton. il Atlan 220:93-102 O '67
Letter. N. Podhoretz. Harper 234:11 My '67; Discussion. 235:4+ Jl; 6+ Ag '67
Theological and ethical implications of the black ghetto. C. E. Lincoln. Christian Cent 84:264-7 Mr 1 '67; Discussion. 84:471 Ap 12 '67
What business can do for the Negro; interview. K. B. Clark. il Nations Bsns 55: 66-70 O '67
What price integration? Nat R 19:887-8 Ag 22 '67
White skins, dark skins, thin skins; middle-class Negro in suburbia. M. Watkins. il N Y Times Mag p 127+ D 3 '67
See also
Church and race problems
Public schools—Desegregation
Segregation in education

Segregation, Resistance to
Integration: desirable and possible. Christian Cent 84:459-60 Ap 12 '67
Integration has failed. M. Halsey; discussion. Christian Cent 84:180 F 8 '67
See also
Civil rights workers

Social conditions
After the long, hot summer, where do we go? E. W. Brooke. il Look 31:24-7 S 5 '67
Bill that must be paid. America 117:194 Ag 26 '67
Black ghettos: the American nightmare; symposium. il Atlan 220:97-110 O '67
Can the big cities ever come back? il U S News 63:28-31 S 4 '67
Cities in '68; M. L. King's 1968 plan to march on Washington by poor Negroes. New Repub 157:5-7 D 16 '67
Civil war two? New Repub 157:7-8 Ag 19 '67
Crime and insurrection. Nation 205:68-9 Jl 31 '67
Crisis that won't go away. il Newsweek 70: 17-19 Ag 14 '67
Hallelujah, amen! Nat R 19:1109 O 17 '67
Hard-core ghetto mood. il Newsweek 70:20-2+ Ag 21 '67
Idea broker in the race crisis. F. Powledge. il Life 63:72A-72B+ N 3 '67
Little girl, big burden; with excerpts from interview. il Ebony 22:44-50 Ag '67

Moynihan report and the politics of controversy, by L. Rainwater and W. L. Yancey. Review
Reporter 37:46-8 Ag 10 '67. W. L. Miller
Negro graduates: PHS study reports opinions and problems. B. Nelson. Science 158: 99-100 O 6 '67
Negro problem keeps growing; the reason. il U S News 62:58-62 Mr 6 '67
Negroes: big gains, but still problems. U S News 63:16 N 13 '67
One Negro woman's advice to her people. il U S News 62:68-9 Mr 27 '67
Prelude to riot, by P. Jacobs. Review
New Repub 158:21-3 Ja 20 '68. L. L. King
President & the Negro: the moment lost. D. P. Moynihan. Commentary 43:31-45 F '67; Discussion. 43:6+ Je '67
Psychiatrists seek secrets of the riots. J. H. Pollack. il Todays Health 45:24-7+ N '67
Psychology behind black power; interview; reprint. N. Wright, jr. il Sci Digest 63: 58-61 Ja '68
Riots and Daniel Patrick Moynihan. Am City 82:6+ S '67
Social power of the Negro. J. P. Comer. il Sci Am 216:21-7 bibliog(p 146) Ap '67
Summer riots. New Repub 156:8 Je 24 '67
Talley's corner, by E. Liebow. Review
Commonweal 87:449-50 Ja 12 '68. S. Maloff
Teaching violence as a means towards social justice. F. A. J. Ianni. il Cath World 206: 160-4 Ja '68
Three revolutions. Nation 205:98-9 Ag 14 '67
U.S. letter: Columbia, S.C. C. Trillin. New Yorker 43:208+ N 25 '67
You can't run away. il Newsweek 70:17-18 Jl 31 '67
See also
Alabama—Social conditions
Negroes in the United States—Segregation

Societies
Free African societies. il(p 1) Negro Hist Bul 30:4 Ap '67

Suffrage
See Negroes in the United States—Politics and suffrage

Trade union membership
See Trade unions—Negro membership

North
See also subhead Negroes under names of cities, e.g. Philadelphia—Negroes

South
Can the southern Negro exodus be stemmed? P. Clancy. il Reporter 37:27-8+ N 2 '67
Children of crisis, by R. Coles. Review
Atlan 219:129 Je '67. O. Handlin
Nation 205:188-9 S 4 '67. R. Belenky
Sat R il 50:66-7 Je 17 '67. M. Greene
Climbing Jacob's ladder, by P. Watters and R. Cleghorn. Review
New Repub 157:20-3 D 16 '67. R. Coles
Darkness on the Delta. F. Davis. Reporter 37: 35-7 S 21 '67
Desegregation success stories: Arkansas and Texas. Sr Schol 90:sup2 My 12 '67
I never hit nobody; acquittal for eight white men on trial for violence to Negro schoolchildren. il Time 89:48 Je 16 '67
Interpreter in the front line: F. M. Johnson, district judge for Alabama's southeastern counties. il Time 89:72-4+ My 12 '67
Lonely youth in the rural South. G. Goodman. il Ebony 22:70-2+ Ag '67
Lord, I'm hungry; Senate antipoverty subcommittee tours lands of the Mississippi delta. il Newsweek 70:22-4 Jl 24 '67
Negro mood; new hope in Dixie. Fortune 77: 234 Ja '68
On racial front; a quiet South and a troubled North: why. il U S News 63:76-7 S 25 '67
Southern Negro and the Knights of labor. I. M. Marcus. bibliog Negro Hist Bul 30:5-7 Mr '67
See also
Mississippi—Race problems
also subhead Negroes under names of cities, e.g. Atlanta—Negroes

NEGROES in the United States armed forces. See United States—Armed forces—Negroes
NEGROES in the United States army. See United States—Army—Negroes
NEHRU, Braj Kumar
Nehru memorial museum; letter to the editor. New Repub 156:36 Ja 28 '67

NEHRU, Jawaharlal
Man does not live by politics alone; excerpts from address, April 9, 1950. por UNESCO Courier 20:46-8+ Ag '67

about

Antimémoires, by A. Malraux. Review New Yorker 43:190-2 N 11 '67. Genêt
Nehru memorial museum; letter to the editor. B. K. Nehru. New Repub 156:36 Ja 28 '67

NEIDER, Charles
Major author in a minor key. Sat R 50:34-5 Mr 25 '67

NEIDHARDT, F. C. See Böck, A. jt. auth.

NEIGER, Ben B.
Noiseless switching for hi-fi. Electr World 77:58-9 Ja '67

NEIGHBORHOOD betterment. See Municipal improvement

NEIGHBORHOODS
See also
Community life

NEIGHBORS, Fred. See Hagist, B. jt. auth.

NEILANDS, J. B.
Hydroxamic acids in nature. bibliog Science 156:1443-7 Je 16 '67

NEILL, A. S.
Teacher's case against discipline; excerpts from Freedom, not license! Redbook 128: 61+ Ap '67

NEILL, Stephen Charles, bp
Bishop Neill on bars to unity. C. De Mestral. Christian Cent 84:1606 D 13 '67

NEIMAN, LeRoy
He's the smartest and fastest man that there is/with brushstroke or footwork Muhammad Ali's a whiz. Esquire 68:136-7 S '67

NEIMAN-Marcus stores. See Dallas—Stores; Houston, Tex.—Stores

NEISSER, Edith G.
Goals of discipline. Parents Mag 42:66-7+ O '67
Special world of mothers and daughters; excerpts from Mothers and daughters. Parents Mag 42:41-3+ My '67
What teenage friendships are all about. Parents Mag 42:48-50+ Jl '67

NELLIGAN, J. W.
St Petersburg tapers go back to school. Pop Electr 25:50-1 D '66

NELLIS air force base. See Air bases

NELOY, Eddie
Golden touch. D. Parker. il pors Sat Eve Post 240:100-5 My 6 '67

NELSON, Bruce W.
Sedimentary phosphate method for estimating paleosalinities. bibliog Science 158:917-20 N 17 '67

NELSON, C. A. See Cloud, P. E. jr. jt. auth.

NELSON, Claud D.
Claud Nelson: servant to mankind. Christian Cent 84:1452 N 15 '67

NELSON, Elmer K. jr
Community-based correctional treatment: rationale and problems. bibliog f Ann Am Acad 374:82-91 N '67

NELSON, Eugene, jr
Huelga: new goals for labor. Nation 204:724-5 Je 5 '67

NELSON, Frederic
Girls, or boys, who needs them? Nat R 19: 1067-9 O 3 '67

NELSON, Gaylord Anton
Systems bills in flux. por Sci N 91:147 F 11 '67

NELSON, George
Architecture for the new itinerants. Sat R 50:30-1+ Ap 22 '67
Space and gadgets. Am Home 70:16 S '67

NELSON, J. Peter
Independence Hall reconstruction sound system. Electr World 78:32-3 Jl '67

NELSON, J. Robert
Faith and order goes secular. Christian Cent 84:1092-3 Ag 30 '67
O little town of Phuvinh. Christian Cent 84: 1619 D 20 '67
Vietnam Summer. Christian Cent 84:678-9 My 24 '67

NELSON, Kay Shaw
Dutch & Belgian cook book. House & Gard 132:203+ S '67

NEMATODES
Modified cilia in sensory organs of juvenile stages of a parasitic nematode. M. M. R. Ross. bibliog il Science 156:1494-5 Je 16 '67

NEMEROV, Howard
Presidential address to a party of exiles leaving for the moon; poem. New Yorker 43:92 Ag 12 '67
Projection: poem. Atlan 219:87 My '67
Rope's end; poem. Atlan 220:103 S '67

about

Poet as novelist. M. Van Duyn. Poetry 109: 333-5 F '67

NEMESIA
Nemesia makes a color mantle. il Sunset 139: 251 O '67

NEOLITHIC period. See Stone age

NEON
Animals at very high pressures of helium and neon. K. W. Miller and others. bibliog Science 157:97-8 Jl 7 '67

NEON lamps in art. See Electric lamps in art

NEONATAL surgery. See Infants, Newborn—Surgery

NEPAL
King Mahendra of Nepal visits the United States; exchange of greetings and toasts, with joint communique, November 1, 1967. L. B. Johnson; Mahendra. Dept State Bul 57:706-9 N 27 '67
Neutral cockpit. il Time 90:26+ N 3 '67

See also
Americans in Nepal
Arts and crafts—Nepal
Birds—Nepal
Economic assistance in Nepal
Hotels, taverns, etc.—Nepal

Description and travel

Isolated beauty of Nepal; with report by J. Howard. il Life 63:38-52+ Ag 11 '67
Nepal notebook. H. Brandon. Sat R 50:10+ O 14 '67

NEPHRITE. See Jade

NEPHRITIS
Rest are simply left to die. J. Robbins and J. Robbins. Redbook 130:80-1+ N '67

NEPOTISM
Hiring relatives: new federal rules; anti-nepotism rule. U S News 63:7 D 25 '67

NEPTUNE (planet)

Satellites

See Satellites

NERBER, John
Textbook considerations, merchandising. Pub W 191:29-30 My 22 '67

NERUDA, Pablo
Sonnet XXIX; you come from the destitute South, from the house, tr. by B. Belitt. Nation 205:697 D 25 '67

about

Hispanic chronicle. W. Barnstone. Poetry 111:46-55 O '67
Journey toward rebirth. M. L. Rosenthal. por Sat R 50:25 S 2 '67

NERVE cells
Axonal delivery of neuroplasmic components to muscle cells. I. M. Korr and others. bibliog il Science 155:342-5 Ja 20 '67
Gangliosides in isolated neurons and glial cells. D. M. Derry and L. S. Wolfe. bibliog il Science 158:1450-2 D 15 '67
Inferior olive of the cat: intracellular recording. W. E. Crill and T. T. Kennedy. bibliog il Science 157:716-18 Ag 11 '67
Neurons in paradoxical sleep and motivated behavior. W. D. Mink and others. bibliog il Science 158:1335-7 D 8 '67
Neurosecretory cells in a cestode, hymenolepis diminuta. K. G. Davey and W. R. Breckenridge. bibliog il Science 158:931-2 N 17 '67
Small systems of nerve cells. D. Kennedy. il Sci Am 216:44-52 bibliog(p 167) My '67
Steroid-sensitive single neurons in rat hypothalamus and midbrain: identification by microelectrophoresis. K. Ruf and F. A. Steiner. bibliog il Science 156:667-9 My 5 '67
Transport of protein by goldfish optic nerve fibers. B. Grafstein. bibliog il Science 157: 196-8 Jl 14 '67

NERVE-ending membranes. See Membranes (biology)

NERVE membrane conductance. See Electrophysiology

NERVE regeneration. See Regeneration (biology)

NERVES
Function of the dorsal motor nucleus of the vagus. F. W. L. Kerr. bibliog il Science 157:451-2 Jl 28 '67
Glycogen synthetase activity in liver: regulation by the autonomic nerves. T. Shimazu. bibliog il Science 156:1256-7 Je 2 '67

NERVES—*Continued*
Homology of retractile filaments of vampire squid. R. E. Young. bibliog il Science 156: 1633-4 Je 23 '67
See also
Nerve cells
Synapses
Surgery
See Nervous system—Surgery
NERVOUS breakdown. See Neuroses
NERVOUS habits
See also
Nail-biting
NERVOUS system
Cerebellar Purkinje cell projection to the peripheral vestibular organ in the frog. R. Llinás and others. bibliog il Science 158: 1328-30 D 8 '67
DDT: interaction with nerve membrane conductance changes. T. Narahashi and H. G. Haas. bibliog il Science 157:1438-40 S 22 '67
Evoked potentials: three-dimensional display. S. K. Burns and others. bibliog il Science 157:457-9 Jl 28 '67
Small systems of nerve cells. D. Kennedy. il Sci Am 216:44-52 bibliog(p 167) My '67
See also
Brain
Psychology, Physiological
Shock
Synapses
Diseases
Bluetongue virus infection: pathologic responses of nervous systems in sheep and mice. W. P. C. Richards and D. R. Cordy. bibliog il Science 156:530-1 Ap 28 '67
Disease theory skips DNA; study of kuru and scrapie. F. Marley. il Sci N 91:169-70 F 18 '67
Enzyme defect associated with a sex-linked human neurological disorder and excessive purine synthesis. J. E. Seegmiller and others. bibliog il Science 155:1682-4 Mr 31 '67
Metachromatic leukodystrophy, sulfatide lipidoses, cultured in vitro. H. Cravioto and others. bibliog il Science 156:243-5 Ap 14 '67
10,000-to-1 payoff; Dilantin therapy for emotional disturbance. A. Rosenfeld. il Life 63: 121-2+ S 29 '67
Transmission and passage of experimental kuru to chimpanzees. D. C. Gajdusek and others. bibliog il Science 155:212-14 Ja 13 '67
See also
Neuroses
Refsum's disease
Mollusks
Ionic mechanism of cholinergic inhibition in molluscan neurons. D. J. Chiarandini and H. M. Gerschenfeld. bibliog il Science 156: 1595-6 Je 23 '67
Ionic mechanisms of cholinergic excitation in molluscan neurons. D. J. Chiarandini and others. bibliog il Science 156:1597-9 Je 23 '67
Surgery
Radio pulses to kill pain. il Life 62:97-8 Je 16 '67
See also
Spinal cord—Surgery
NERVOUS system, Sympathetic
Amino acids and the spikes from the retinal ganglion cells. K. Kishida and K. I. Naka. bibliog il Science 156:648-50 My 5 '67
Deuterium oxide: direct action on sympathetic ganglia isolated in culture. M. R. Murray and H. H. Benitez. bibliog il Science 155: 1021-4 F 24 '67
Retinal ganglion cells: specification of central connections in larval xenopus laevis. M. Jacobson. bibliog il Science 155:1106-8 Mr 3 '67
NERVOUS tension. See Stress (physiology)
NESBETT, Daniel A.
Gardens of Moorish yesterdays. Sat R 50:52+ Ja 28 '67
NESBIT, Edith
E. Nesbit. by D. L. Moore. Review
New Yorker 43:156-9 F 25 '67. W. Maxwell
NESBIT, Evelyn
Tired butterfly. il pors Newsweek 69:30-1 Ja 30 '67
NESBITT, Elizabeth
Inheritance of our children. Horn Bk 43:328-35 Je '67

NESMITH, Michael
Monkee talk; interview, ed. by E. Miller. por Seventeen 26:303+ Ag '67
NESS, Evaline
Caldecott acceptance speech; June 27, 1967. Horn Bk 43:434-8 Ag '67
about
Evaline Ness. A. Durell. il Library J 92:1298-9 Mr 15 '67
Evaline Ness. A. Durell. por Horn Bk 43: 438-43 Ag '67
Evaline Ness, the Caldecott medalist for 1967. J. H. Michel. il Am Artist 31:32-7+ Je '67
Newbery and Caldecott award winners. por ALA Bul 61:358 Ap '67
Newbery and Caldecott winners: Irene Hunt, Evaline Ness. il por Pub W 191:34-5 Mr 13 '67
Newbery-Caldecott winners. por Wilson Lib Bul 41:783 Ap '67
NESS, LOCH Scotland
Closing in on the Loch Ness monster. D. Scott. il Read Digest 90:86-90 F '67
NESSEN, Ron
W.I.A. por Todays Health 45:20-7 Ap '67
NESTROY, Johann Nepomuk
Authors & editors. Pub W 192:9-10 O 30 '67
NET book agreement. See Books—Prices
NETBOY, Anthony
Beyond the Shah's palace. Sat R 50:64+ O 14 '67
Literary past: a view from the tour bus. Sat R 50:46-7+ Mr 11 '67
Melancholy fate of salmo salar; with biographical sketch. Natur Hist 76:4, 52-9 bibliog(p74) Je '67
Nuclear power on salmon rivers. Nation 205: 337-9 O 9 '67
Pollution in the West. Am For 73:8-11+ Jl '67
Preservation of natural beauty in England. Am For 73:16-19+ Mr '67
Use of high country in Switzerland. Am For 72:6-7+ O '66; 73:2 Ja '67
NETHERLANDS
See also
Airplane industry and trade—Netherlands
Catholic church in the Netherlands
Delft
Gardens—Netherlands
Music festivals—Netherlands
National parks and reserves—Netherlands
Petroleum industry and trade—Netherlands
Political parties—Netherlands
Youth—Netherlands
Description and travel
Dutch life of Riley; prize-winning photo tour. il Pop Phot 60:50+ My '67
Holland. M. Orovan. il U S Camera 30:66-9+ F '67
Travel's picture portfolio. Travel 128:50-5 Jl '67
Economic conditions
Much-governed Dutch, too, getting tired of rules. il U S News 62:34-5 Ja 30 '67
History
Bibliography
Articles and other books received; comp. by P. Rosenfeld. See issues of American historical review
Industries
See also
Philips of Eindhoven companies
Politics and government
Much-governed Dutch, too, getting tired of rules. il U S News 62:34-5 Ja 30 '67
Religious institutions and affairs
See also
Catholic church in the Netherlands
Royal family
After 116 years, a plump little Dutch prince. S. Mahoney. il Life 62:46-46A My 12 '67
NETHERLANDS office for foreign student relations tours. See Student travel
NETSCHERT, Bruce C. See Stelzer, I. M. jt. auth.
NETTL, J. P.
Soviet achievement; excerpt from The Soviet achievement, 1917-1967. Harper 235:90-4+ O '67
NEUBAUER, John
Camera and JFK. Pop Phot 61:88-103+ N '67
Focus on Stan Wayman: 35-mm for tigers or tankers. Pop Phot 61:106-7+ Ag '67

NEUGEBOREN, Jay
Disobedience now! Commonweal 86:367-9 Je 16 '67
Letter from Stanford. New Repub 156:32-5 Mr 18 '67

NEUHAUS, Richard John
Bishops' loyal opposition. Commonweal 86:565-7 S 22 '67
Dangerous assumptions. Commonweal 86:408-13 Je 30 '67
Liturgy and the politics of the kingdom. Christian Cent 84:1623-7 D 20 '67
Super-General Hershey. Commonweal 87:465-7 Ja 19 '68

NEUMAN, Ilene
Special language. Horn Bk 43:498-500 Ag '67

NEUMAN, M. R. See Ko, W. H. jt. auth.

NEUMANN, Alfred, and others
War and peace; dramatization of novel by L. N. Tolstoi; tr. by R. D. MacDonald. Criticism
America 116:603 Ap 22 '67

NEURATH, Hans, and others
Evolution of structure and function of proteases. bibliog Science 158:1638-44 D 29 '67

NEUROENDOCRINOLOGY
New hormone class. Sci N 91:400 Ap 29 '67

NEURONS. See Nerve cells

NEUROPHYSIOLOGY. See Nervous system

NEUROSECRETORY cells. See Nerve cells

NEUROSECRETORY hormones. See Hormones

NEUROSES
Anatomy of courage, by Lord Moran. Review Sat R il 50:37 My 13 '67. F. J. Braceland
Cardiac neurotics. Newsweek 70:110 S 18 '67
Neurosis is just a bad habit. M. M. Hunt. il N Y Times Mag p38-9+ Je 4 '67
Neurotics assessed; research in England and Wales. Sci N 91:531 Je 3 '67
Psychiatry and war; British treatments of neurotics during World war II; excerpts from The unquiet mind. W. Sargant. Atlan 219:102-9 My '67
See also
Depression, Mental
Nervous system—Diseases

NEUROSURGERY. See Nervous system—Surgery

NEUROTICS. See Neuroses

NEUSCHEL, Robert P.
Physical distribution, forgotten frontier. Harvard Bsns R 45:125-34 Mr '67

NEUTRALITY
Glossary; entangling nonalignments. M. Greenfield. Reporter 37:37 S 7 '67
See also
Europe—Neutrality

NEUTRINOS
Neutrinos: current experiments at CERN. N. Calder. Science 157:411-12 Jl 28 '67
Outer space trap in mountain. il Sci Digest 62:64 O '67

NEUTRON activation analysis. See Radioactivation analysis

NEUVILLATE, Alfonso de
Two young rebels in Mexican painting. Américas 19:8-16 Mr '67

NEVADA
See also
Architecture, Domestic—Nevada
Death Valley National Monument
Hunting—Nevada
Lehman Caves National Monument

Description and travel
Nevada's neglected bonanzaland. T. L. Barbour. il Travel 127:45-9 Ja '67

NEVADA state education association
Approach to professional practices legislation. J. T. Butler. NEA J 56:43-4 F '67

NEVELSON, Louise
Art; exhibition at Whitney museum. M. Kozloff. Nation 204:477-8 Ap 10 '67
Louise Nevelson. D. Smith. il por Craft Horiz 27:44-9+ My '67
Mansions of mystery. il por Time 89:86 Mr 31 '67
She and her shadows; Whitney museum display. il Newsweek 69:110-11 Mr 20 '67

NEVILLE, Phoebe
Phoebe Neville and William Meyer; Judson memorial church. M. Marks. Dance Mag 41:33 Ag '67

NEVILLE, Robert
Traveler's guide to the native drinks and wines of Italy. House & Gard 131:178+ Mr '67

NEVILLE, Robert C.
Book of the month. Cath World 205:371-3 S '67

NEVIN, David
Struggle that changed Glen Allan. Life 63:108+ S 29 '67
These murdered old mountains. Life 64:54-60+ Ja 12 '68
$3,000,000 sham. Life 62:82-6+ Ap 7 '67

about
Deep roots in the new South. G. P. Hunt. por Life 63:3 S 29 '67

NEVINS, Allan
Dateline Watts: from the ashes, a solution. Sat R 50:79 S 23 '67
Goal: eminence. Sat R 50:34+ N 18 '67
Harper's sesquicentennial; adaptation of address. Sat R 50:58-9+ Jl 8 '67
Limits of individualism. por Sat R 50:25-7+ N 25 '67
Treasure house of New York's past. Sat R 50:27 S 2 '67

NEVLING, Floyd M.
Police can make the difference. Parks & Rec 2:33-4 S '67

NEW American review
Authors & editors. Pub W 192:183-5 Ag 28 '67
Escaping cult and coterie. G. Hicks. Sat R 50:25-6 S 9 '67
Needed home for new writing. B. Brower. Life 63:22 S 22 '67
New American review, ed. by T. Solotaroff. Review
Nation 205:408-9 O 23 '67. R. Hatch

NEW BEDFORD, Mass.

Churches
Melville revisited; Seaman's bethel. R. Hendrickson. Sat R 50:43-4 Ag 5 '67

NEW BEDFORD painting. See Painting, American

NEW book of knowledge
Encyclopedias, an adventure in learning. M. B. Keiser. il Parents Mag 42:43+ N '67

NEW books preview. See Book exhibits

NEW BRUNSWICK, Canada
Woolpacks and wonders in New Brunswick. D. W. Gardner. il Motor B 119:24-7+ Ap '67

Description and travel
East of the border: New Brunswick and Fundy National Park. C. W. White. il Redbook 129:40-1 Jl '67

NEW business enterprises. See Business enterprises, New

NEW CALEDONIA
New Caledonia. H. Sutton. il Holiday 42:20+ Jl '67
Nickel squabble rocks Pacific isle. il Bsns W p86-8+ Mr 25 '67

NEW Catholic encyclopedia
Art and the New Catholic encyclopedia. C. J. McNaspy. America 116:387-8 Mr 18 '67
Authors & editors; the making of the new encyclopedia; summary of address. J. P. Whalen. il Pub W 191:45 Ap 24 '67
Encyclopedia for a postconciliar age. C. J. McNaspy. America 116:456+ Mr 25 '67
Modern encyclopedia. Time 89:79 Mr 17 '67
New Catholic encyclopedia. Review
Cath World 205:116-17 My '67. J. B. Sheerin
New Catholic encyclopedia to be launched March 9. Pub W 191:77 F 27 '67

NEW Christian (periodical) See Periodicals—Great Britain

NEW Christians. See Maranos

NEW cities. See New towns

NEW deal. See United States—History—1933-1945

NEW dealers. See Public officers

NEW ENGLAND
To see this land, to see America; photographs by W. Garnett. Life 62:50-65 Mr 3 '67
See also
Arts and crafts—New England
Colleges and universities—New England
Connecticut River
Festivals—New England
Gardens—New England
Libraries—New England
Skis and skiing—New England

Description and travel
Profiles: through the great city. A. Bailey. il New Yorker 43:35-42+ Jl 22 '67
To visit New England's colleges. il Sunset 139:57-8 O '67

History
Colonial period
Far cry. J. H. Plumb. Sat R 50:21+ D 30 '67

NEW ENGLAND book show. See Book exhibits
NEW ENGLAND cookery. See Cookery, American
NEW ENGLAND furniture. See Furniture, American
NEW GUINEA

Native races
Are the natives friendly? M. Mead. Redbook 128:31+ Mr '67
Letter from the field: return to New Guinea; changes in Tambunam. M. Mead. Redbook 130:20+ N '67
NEW HAMPSHIRE
See also
Hunting—New Hampshire

Historic houses, etc.
See also
Orford, N.H.—Historic houses, etc.

Hotels, taverns, etc.
New Hampshire's White Mountain huts. A. E. Kessler. il Travel 127:37-40 Je '67
NEW HAMPSHIRE lottery. See Lotteries
NEW HAMPSHIRE primary. See Primaries
NEW HAMPSHIRE. University, Durham
State university residence hall: spatial complexity on a low budget. il Arch Rec 142: 142-4 O '67
NEW HAVEN, Conn.

Churches
Warm and clear; installation of new organ in the United church on the green; interview. P. Jordan. New Yorker 43:42-4 S 23 '67

Education
Privacy and quiet highlight K-4 school for urban renewal; Timothy Dwight school. il Arch Rec 142:182-3 O '67

Mayors
See also
Lee, R. C.

Politics and government
City where computers will know about everybody; UMIS for Urban management information system. il U S News 62:78-9 My 15 '67
Mayor's game, by A. R. Talbot. Review Reporter 37:46-8 O 19 '67. R. D. Masters

Population
City where computers will know about everybody; UMIS for Urban management information system. il U S News 62:78-9 My 15 '67

Riots
Dick Lee discovers how much is not enough. B. Asbell. il N Y Times Mag p6-7+ S 3 '67
No haven. il Time 90:9 S 1 '67
Why New Haven? il Newsweek 70:23 S 4 '67

Street traffic
Self-contained drill speeds sign-post installation. H. Skinner. il Am City 82:133 Ap '67
NEW HAVEN railroad. See New York, New Haven and Hartford railroad company
NEW HEBRIDES
Ecumenical breakthrough in the South Pacific. H. P. Van Dusen. Christian Cent 84:730 My 31 '67
New Hebrides: archipelago under two flags. M. Petersen. il Motor B 119:41+ Mr '67
NEW HOPE, Pa.
New Hope, Pennsylvania. il Bet Hom & Gard 45:14+ Ag '67

Historic houses, etc.
Christmas in New Hope, circa 1735. P. Hyde and J. L. Hendrix. il House B 109:266-9 N '67
NEW JERSEY
See also
Architecture, Domestic—New Jersey
Booksellers and bookselling—New Jersey
Colleges and universities—New Jersey
Education—New Jersey
Hunting—New Jersey
Libraries—New Jersey
Pine Barrens
Mullica River

Community affairs, Department of
New force focuses on urban ills. il Bsns W p75-6+ Je 24 '67

Parks and reserves
Deserted village; Allaire, part of Allaire state park. H. W. Hoffman. il Sch Arts 66:20-2 Mr '67
Skylands of New Jersey; conservation environmental renewal program. R. A. Roe. il Parks & Rec 2:17+ S '67

Race problems
Lessons of New Jersey's race riots; interview. R. J. Hughes. il U S News 63:32-6 Jl 31 '67
Real tragedy of Newark. il U S News 63:30-1 Jl 31 '67
NEW JERSEY (battleship) See Warships—United States
NEW JERSEY Americans (basketball team) See Basketball teams
NEW JERSEY meadows
Sweetening the meadowlands. Bsns W p76 Je 24 '67
NEW JERSEY symphony orchestra
New Jersey symphony; on the move. E. Palatsky. Hi Fi 17:MA26-7+ Mr '67
NEW left (politics) See Right and left (political science)
NEW man; story. See Roth, P.
NEW mathematics. See Mathematics
NEW Mayfair orchestra. See Bands (music)
NEW MEXICO
See also
Fishing—New Mexico
Hunting—New Mexico
NEW ORLEANS

Banks
Banks that went marching in; International city bank & trust co. of New Orleans. il Bsns W p 143-4+ Jl 15 '67

City planning
Expressway named destruction. P. Dunhill. il Arch Forum 126:54-9 Mr '67

Historic houses, etc.
Bureau of public roads, devastator. R. Kirk. Nat R 19:202 F 21 '67

Libraries
See also
New Orleans public library

Music
See also
New Orleans opera house association

Parks and playgrounds
Unique utilization of surroundings. E. P. Laborde. il Parks & Rec 2:25+ N '67

Sanitary affairs
Heavy pipe on the half shell. il Am City 82: 28 Ag '67

Theater
Theater; production of Ionesco's Victims of duty. H. Hewes. Sat R 50:64 My 20 '67
Theatre; Repertory theatre. J. Novick. Nation 204:509-10 Ap 17 '67
NEW ORLEANS opera house association
New Orleans (cont) J. Belsom. Opera N 31: 27 Ap 15; 24 Je 10 '67
Report: New Orleans; production of Verdi's Macbeth. J. Belsom. Opera N 32:30 D 30 '67
Report: New Orleans; production of Wagner's Fliegende Holländer. J. Belsom. Opera N 32:31 Ja 20 '68
Report: New Orleans; productions of Faust and Madama Butterfly. J. Belsom. Opera N 32:29 D 16 '67
NEW ORLEANS public library
Ex New Orleans librarian blasts board, friends; excerpts from letter. J. Cushman. Library J 92:1403 Ap 1 '67
Matter of reputation. K. Nyren. Library J 92:173 Ja 15 '67
New Orleans librarian reinstated, but penalized. Library J 92:2698 Ag '67
NEW ORLEANS Saints (football club) See Football clubs
NEW politics convention. See Political conventions
NEW products. See Products, New
NEW ROCHELLE, N.Y.

Crime
Reverend Fay Hill and his lace pants mob; anti-crime campaign. G. Astor. il Look 31: 71-6 O 31 '67
NEW school for social research. New York
New school for old students. il Time 89: 45 F 24 '67

NEW shoes; drama. See Miller, H. L.
NEW sources of food supply. See Food supply
—New sources
NEW SOUTH WALES
New South Wales, the state that cradled
Australia. H. Walker. il Nat Geog Mag 132:
591-635 N '67
NEW stars. See Stars, New
NEW states. See States, New
NEW stock issues. See Stocks
NEW Tokaido line. See Railroads—Japan
NEW towns
Auroville: India's international city of Con-
cord. il UNESCO Courier 20:48-51 Ag '67
Britain's new towns: cure for urban sprawl?
il U S News 64:90-2 Ja 15 '68
Coal's boom creates a new kind of town. il
Bsns W p 164+ S 16 '67
Designed for healthier living: America's new
cities. A. R. Roalman il Todays Health 45:
46-9+ F '67
Inside London: the city and the green towns.
J. Gunther. Harper 235:79-82 Ag '67; Same
abr. with title Inside London. Read Digest
91:169-72+ O '67
Instant city; corporate builders of new towns.
P. Herrera. il Fortune 75:135-8 Je 1 '67
Look at America's new towns! W. Lange-
wiesche. il Read Digest 90:140-5 Mr '67
Montgomery Village, a new town within a
corridor city is shaped by new planning
concepts required by improved zoning code.
il Arch Rec 142:134-41 Jl '67
Schools can be interwoven into fabric of new
towns. il Arch Rec 142:190-2 O '67
Thistles in the new towns. il Time 90:87-8
S 29 '67
What's needed for new cities; Urban Amer-
ica meeting. il Am City 82:104+ Ap '67
See also
Columbia, Md.
Irvine, Calif.
Lake Havasu City, Ariz.
Litchfield Park, Ariz.
Reston, Va.
Stafford Harbor, Va.
Valencia, Calif.
Zingonia, Italy
NEW Trier high school. See Chicago—Educa-
tion
NEW words. See Words, New
NEW YEARS eve suppers. See Suppers
NEW YEARS parties. See Entertaining
NEW YEARS resolutions
Great aspirations and dreadful despairs. L.
Conger. Writer 80:8-10 Ja '67
Resolutions for a happy New Year of re-
warding photography. A. Rothstein. U S
Camera 31:14 Ja '68
NEW YORK (city)
After graduation, a job in New York? A.
Grant. il Mlle 65:144-5+ Je '67
Jobscope: knowing New York. A. Grant. Mlle
65:170-1 Je '67
New York, New York: good-bye, good-bye.
H. Rudd. Esquire 68:130-1+ O '67
Rebellion: water-main break and steam ex-
plosion at Seventh avenue and Sixteenth
street. New Yorker 43:22-3 Ja 13 '68
Week of the angry artist. C. Harnack. Na-
tion 204:245-8 F 20 '67; Discussion. 204:322+
Mr 13 '67
What's ahead for New York city; interview.
J. V. Lindsay. il U S News 62:56-60+ Ap
10 '67
See also
Brooklyn
East River
Lincoln Center for the performing arts
Port of New York authority
Staten Island
Air pollution
Powdery air; R. F. Kennedy investigates air
pollution. New Yorker 43:21-3 Jl 15 '67

Air pollution control, Department of
Inspector Deppe and the smoky boiler. New
Yorker 42:32-3 F 11 '67
New York's clean-air man; A. H. Heller,
New York's Air pollution control commis-
sioner. F. J. Cook. il N Y Times Mag p44-
5+ Mr 5 '67
Sampling air; interview. H. Gilmont. New
Yorker 43:44-6 Mr 11 '67

Airports
Airport area housing criticized. Aviation W
87:55-7 N 13 '67

Can airports cope with the jet age? New
York problem. il Bsns W p61-3 Jl 22 '67
Computer will control airport traffic. il Am
City 82:140+ Je '67
Handwriting on the air terminal wall. C.
Leedham. il N Y Times Mag p28-9+ My 21
'67
Jetport tangle. W. Pitkin, jr. New Repub 156:
11-12 My 27 '67
Ordeal of the short distance; shortsighted-
ness in planning John F. Kennedy inter-
national airport. N. Cousins. Sat R 50:28-
9 F 11 '67
PAA operation of two airports aimed at eas-
ing New York jam. Aviation W 87:39 O 2
'67
Pan Am cargo terminal heavily automated,
mechanized; photographs. Aviation W 86:38-
9+ My 22 '67
Possible solutions to improve New York air-
port access cited. F. Cogan. Aviation W
86:33 My 1 '67
Seventy miles from town? Nelson Rockefeller's
Calverton, L.I. proposal. il Newsweek 69:84
Mr 27 '67
See also
Heliports
Anti-poverty program
Fox's folly; summer in the city. il Newsweek
70:82 S 11 '67
Mayor's human touch as he walks, listens.
il Life 63:32-3 Ag 25 '67
Real Great society; New York slum kids team
up to fight poverty. R. Vaughan. il Life 63:
76+ S 15 '67
Reporter at large; summer in the city. J.
Stevenson. New Yorker 43:141-2+ S 16 '67

Architecture
Architectural iron works; excerpts from a
century old building front catalog. il Arch
Forum 126:63-70 My '67
Facility for a religious society: a victory for
neighborhood scale. il Arch Rec 142:140-1
O '67
Home to work in; Ford foundation head-
quarters. New Yorker 43:23-5 D 30 '67
Lost New York, by N. Silver. Review
Nation 205:694-6 D 25 '67. S. Zoll
New Repub 157:22+ Ag 19 '67. S. Kauff-
mann. Reply with rejoinder. N. Silver.
157:28-30 O 14 '67
Nervi's gilded gateway; George Washington
bridge bus terminal. D. Canty. il Arch For-
um 126:68-73 Mr '67
Office boom changes the scene. il Bsns W
p 167-8+ O 7 '67
Tallest: Singer building to come down. New
Yorker 43:37-8 S 9 '67
Very tall client. W. McQuade. il Arch Forum
126:92 My '67
See also
New York (city)—Rockefeller Center

Art
Art world. H. Rosenberg. New Yorker 43:99-
100+ F 25; 179-80+ Mr 25; 162 My 6; 112+
Je 3; 76+ Jl 29; 90+ Ag 26; 145-6+ S 23;
189-92+ O 21; 225-8+ N 18; 138+ D 16 '67
New New York art scene: who makes it? ex-
cerpts from New York: the new art scene.
A. Solomon. il Vogue 150:102-7 Ag 1 '67

Banks
Chase breaks into mutual funds. il Bsns W
p78 D 23 '67
Citibank banks on its economists; First national city bank of New York. il Bsns W
p 142-4+ F 25 '67
Citibank row boils over in Ottawa; Mercan-
tile bank in Canada owned by New York's
First national city bank. Bsns W p 120 Ja
28 '67
David Rockefeller, banker's banker; and
Chase Manhattans role in banking world. il
Newsweek 69:72-4+ Ap 3 '67
No more starched collars; professional public
relations department of Chase Manhattan
bank. L. L. L. Golden. Sat R 50:76 F 11
'67
Plum at First national city; new president.
il Time 89:86-7 Je 16 '67
Why the First national city bank took the
rap in Canada. M. Clark. il Fortune 75:75+
Ap '67

Bookstores
See Booksellers and bookselling—New York
(state)

Buildings
See New York (city)—Architecture

Buses
See New York (city)—Rapid transit

NEW YORK (city)—*Continued*

Churches

Chaplain to the cool world; M. Allen of St Mark's in-the-Bowery. G. Astor. il Look 31:79-84 O 31 '67

Church that turned a corner; Church of the Epiphany. il Arch Forum 127:82-7 N '67

Evening of poetry and dance; Judson memorial church. D. Hering. Dance Mag 41:65-6 F '67

Preaching from the heights; at Riverside church. il Time 89:82+ My 5 '67

See also
New York (city)—St John the Divine, Cathedral of
New York (city)—St Patrick's cathedral

City council

See New York (city)—Council

City planning

Lower Manhattan expressway. R. H. Silver. il Arch Forum 127:66-9 S '67

Museum of modern art discovers Harlem; exhibition, The new city; architecture and urban renewal. C. R. Hatch. il Arch Forum 126:38-47 Mr '67

Profiles; C Abrams. B. Taper. New Yorker 42:45-8+ F 11 '67

Sewage treatment plant designed to enhance a riverfront. il Arch Rec 142:108-9 D '67

City university of New York

See New York (city) City university of New York

Clubs

Anniversary; wreath-laying ceremony conducted by Shakespeare club of New York city. New Yorker 43:35-6 My 6 '67

When the coachman was a millionaire; with watercolors by M. Klepper. F. Kintrea. Am Heritage 18:20-5+ O '67

See also
Explorers club

Columbia-Presbyterian medical center

In most newborn babies: brain damage can be prevented; Neonatal intensive care unit, Babies hospital. T. Irwin. il Look 31:61-7+ S 5 '67

Council

City Councilman John Santucci is a man in a wind tunnel. M. Arnold. il N Y Times Mag p56-7+ Ap 16 '67

Crime

Big city thieves. J. Bowers. Harper 234:50-4 F '67

We burned a bum Friday night and we're going to burn another one tonight. N. Pileggi. il Esquire 68:48-50+ Jl '67

Wild West side. il Newsweek 70:34 D 11 '67

See also
Mafia

Description

Iconography of Manhattan island, 1498-1909, by I. N. P. Stokes. Review
Sat R il 50:27 S 2 '67. A. Nevins

Lower East side: portal to American life; exhibition at the Jewish museum. U S Camera 30:50-1 Mr '67

To see America, from a city window; with photographs by J. Loengard. Life 62:58-69 Mr 10 '67

See also
New York (city)—Streets

District attorneys

Hogan's office is a kind of ministry of justice. M. Mayer. il N Y Times Mag p7+ Jl 23 '67; Reply with rejoinder. K. Fleischmann. p9 Ag 13 '67

Economic conditions

Urban conditions: New York city. B. Gottehrer. bibliog f il Ann Am Acad 371:141-58 My '67

Why the growing flight of business from New York city. il U S News 62:45-6 Mr 6 '67

Education

Academic sickness in New York; mass resignation of teachers from Bronx junior high school 98 and other problems. il Time 89:35-6 Mr 24 '67

Are we driving teachers out of ghetto schools? concerning John S. Roberts junior high school. S. Levey. il Am Ed 3:2-4 My '67

Bundy report. B. Stretch. Sat R 50:70-1 D 16 '67

Can parents run New York's schools? decentralization experiment. T. R. Brooks. il Reporter 38:20-2 Ja 11 '68

Community control of our schools: Bundy report. J. Featherstone. New Repub 158:16-19 Ja 13 '68

Decentralization dilemma; Bundy proposal. il Time 90:31 D 29 '67

Filling the void; Urban league street academies and new school planned. Newsweek 69:101 My 29 '67

Give urban schools back to the people? McGeorge Bundy decentralization proposals. J. Cass. Sat R 50:55 D 16 '67

Help and no help for ghetto children; bussing to white schools. Sci N 92:486 N 18 '67

How to get through; H. Kohl's experience as described in his 36 children. Time 91:34+ Ja 19 '68

Illustrious dance alumni of P.A; School of performing arts. W. Terry. il Sat R 50:32-3 Jl 1 '67

Indian rasa for U.S students. J. Anderson. il Dance Mag 41:28-30 F '67

Media; performances at the School of visual arts. P. Velde. Commonweal 87:334-5 D 8 '67

Mini-school districts; Bundy plan. Reporter 37:8-9 N 30 '67

New hope for city schools; More effective schools. B. B. Gotthold. il Parents Mag 42: 68-70+ S '67

New hope for Harlem's bright youth; preparation for prep school class, Wadleigh intermediate school. il Ebony 22:27-30+ My '67

Parent power; M. Bundy's plan for New York schools. M. R. Berube. Commonweal 87: 349-50 D 15 '67

Puerto Rican pupils and American education; adaptation of address, August 30, 1966. F. M. Cordasco. bibliog f Sch & Soc 95:116-19 F 18 '67

Renovation scheme adapts old school for future; Joseph H. Wade junior high school, Bronx. il Arch Rec 142:188-9 O '67

Requiem for the urban school; experiences of H. Kohl. E. Z. Friedenberg. il Sat R 50:77-9+ N 18 '67

School of performing arts; concert at New York school of printing. J. Maskey. Dance Mag 41:30 Jl '67

Shrewd union leader takes his teachers out. il Life 63:32-5 S 22 '67

Siege at the fortress school. P. Schrag. Sat R 50:82 N 18 '67

Street academies; new way to reach the ghetto dropout; Harlem's Street academy program. P. Pierce. il Ebony 22:158-60+ Ag '67

Talent in the ghetto; New York city's Brownsville section. E. M. Zaslow. il Am Ed 3:24-7 Mr '67

Thirty-six children, by H. Kohl. Review
New Repub 157:23-6+ D 23 '67. J. Featherstone

Thirty-six children; concerning H. Kohl's account of teaching in Harlem's P.S. 103. il Newsweek 71:70 Ja 15 '68

Union protests Title II practice; library committee of UFT in city schools. Library J 92:1688+ Ap 15 '67

What's wrong with our big-city schools. M. Mayer. il Sat Eve Post 240:21-3+ S 9 '67

See also
New York (city) City university of New York
Private schools
Public education association

Education, Board of

No student center for New York city either; letter to the editor. H. R. Sattley. Wilson Lib Bul 42:18-20 S '67

Parents take over; experimental autonomous community school boards. il Newsweek 70: 67-8 D 11 '67

What's wrong with our big-city schools. M. Mayer. il Sat Eve Post 240:21-3+ S 9 '67

Electric power

See also
Consolidated Edison company of New York

Finance

See also
Stock exchange—New York (city)

Fires

See Fires

NEW YORK (city)—*Continued*

Foreign population

Exhibiting the Lower East Side; exhibition at Jewish museum. R. Alter. Commentary 43:67-71 Ja '67

Ties; Sicilian barbers from Licodia Eubea. New Yorker 43:38-9 S 9 '67

See also
Puerto Ricans in the United States

Galleries and museums

Reviews and previews. See issues of Art news
See also
American museum of natural history
Contemporary Christian art, incorporated
Jewish museum
Metropolitan museum of art
Museum of illustration art
Museum of modern art
Museum of primitive art
Solomon R. Guggenheim museum
Whitney museum of American art

Gardens

See also
New York botanical garden

Greenwich Village

Long-winded lady; apartment on Tenth street between Fifth and Sixth. New Yorker 43:54-5 N 11 '67

Long-winded lady; moving of two-hundred-year-old wooden farmhouse from Seventy-first street and York avenue to Charles and Greenwich streets. New Yorker 43:44-6 Mr 18 '67

Maybe somebody else can learn from it; murder of L. Fitzpatrick. J. A. Lukas. Read Digest 91:96-101 D '67

Report from teeny-boppersville. J. K. Sale and B. Apfelbaum. il N Y Times Mag p24-5+ My 28 '67

Runaways. J. Whitbread. il Look 31:26-32 Jl 25 '67

Harlem

Adam's vacuum; district without a congressman. il Time 90:25-6 S 29 '67

Columbia's neighbors; the slums of academe. R. Gustaitis. il Reporter 37:34-8 O 5 '67; Discussion. 37:10 N 2 '67

Filling the void; Urban league street academies and new school planned. Newsweek 69:101 My 29 '67

Harlem's sputtering fuse; disorders flare up in Spanish Harlem. il Newsweek 70:33-4 Ag 7 '67

Lull; demolition of a famous block. New Yorker 43:51-3 N 11 '67

Meredith: the ambiguous heroes of Harlem; Powell. A. Kopkind. il Life 62:32-32A Mr 24 '67

Museum of modern art discovers Harlem; exhibition, The new city: architecture and urban renewal. C. R. Hatch. il Arch Forum 126:38-47 Mr '67

Ned O'Gorman: worker at Harlem library and day care center; interview. N. O'Gorman. New Yorker 43:54-5 D 2 '67

New York's superblock: 114th street. Harlem. B. Bard. Good H 166:134 Ja '68

Notes and comment; sniping and looting in Puerto Rican ghetto of Manhattan. New Yorker 43:19-23 Ag 5 '67

Nothing worth saving. P. Good. Nation 205: 101-2 Ag 14 '67

Political tour of Harlem; new breed Democrats. P. Good. il N Y Times Mag p34-6+ O 29 '67; Reply. C. Greitzer. p66+ N 26 '67

Preservation: private homes in Mount Morris Park section. E. Adair. New Yorker 43:31-3 F 25 '67

Health, Department of

Help, my child has taken poison! Poison control centers. E. M. Wylie. Good H 164:77+ Je '67; Same abr. il Read Digest 91:133-7 Ag '67

Historic houses, etc.

Cottage: A. Austin house and esplanade. Staten Island. New Yorker 43:35-6 S 30 '67

Facility for a religious society: a victory for neighborhood scale. il Arch Rec 142:140-1 O '67

Long-winded lady; moving of two-hundred-year-old wooden farmhouse from Seventy-first street and York avenue to Charles and Greenwich streets. New Yorker 43:44-6 Mr 18 '67

Preservation: private homes in Mount Morris Park section of Harlem; interview. E. Adair. New Yorker 43:31-3 F 25 '67

History

Iconography of Manhattan island, 1498-1909, by I. N. P. Stokes. Review
Sat R il 50:27 S 2 '67. A. Nevins

Hospitals

City should get out of the hospital business. M. Cherkasky. il N Y Times Mag p52-3+ O 8 '67; Reply. Mrs M. Ascoli. p 16 N 12 '67

Doctors meet the people; Neighborhood health center, of Montefiore hospital. M. K. Sanders. Harper 236:56-62 Ja '68

Films; concerning Like a beautiful child, filmed at Mount Sinai hospital. H. Yglesias. Nation 205:349-50 O 9 '67

Mt Sinai: how a hospital builds a medical school. R. J. Samuelson. il Science 158:614-18 N 3 '67

Treating mental illness; Lincoln hospital's mental clinic. J. Ridgeway. New Repub 156: 13-15 Je 10 '67

Hotels, restaurants, etc.

Delmonico's: a century of splendor, by L. Thomas. Review
Newsweek il 71:62B-64 Ja 8 '68. S. Maloff

Dining in/out with Esquire; Act I; Janssen's. Esquire 68:198-9 O '67

Dining in/out with Esquire; Kippy's steak and lobster palace. C. H. McBride. Esquire 67: 190 Je '67

Dining out: rooftop and street level; Tower suite and la Fonda del sol. N. S. Hazelton. Nat R 19:145 F 7 '67

Goings on about town. See issues of New Yorker

La Grenouille: a private view that nobody sees. P. Devlin. il Vogue 151:144-7+ Ja 1 '68

Long-winded lady; episode at Longchamps, Twelfth street and Fifth avenue. New Yorker 43:41-3 Ap 22 '67

Long-winded lady; future demolition of Le steak de Paris, and other buildings on Forty-ninth street, between Sixth and Seventh avenues. New Yorker 43:39-41 S 16 '67

Long-winded lady; movie-making in Algonquin hotel, starring J. Andrews. New Yorker 43:21-3 Je 17 '67

Lunching in New York. il Newsweek 69:60-5 My 15 '67

Paella in a priceless setting: Spanish pavilion. E. Graves. Life 62:14 My 5 '67

Some salty observations on the way we do things here; excerpts from the Guide Julliard de New York. H. Gault and C. Millau. Life 63:136 S 15 '67

You got to be a hero; Marotta's restaurant. R. Crichton. il Sat Eve Post 240:30-2+ D 30 '67

See also
Night clubs

Anecdotes, facetiae, satire, etc.

Craig's life. H. B. Jacobs. Look 31:M24 O 17 '67

Housing

Airport area housing criticized. Aviation W 87:55-7 N 13 '67

Art city; help for space-seeking artists in New York. il Newsweek 70:63 Ag 21 '67

Dropping in, speeding up; rehabilitating slum structure in forty-eight hours. il Time 89: 60 Ap 21 '67

Failure in the slums. W. F. Buckley, jr. Nat R 19:341 Ap 4 '67

Instant rehab not so instant; New York's drop-in kitchen-bathroom core concept. il Arch Rec 141:175-6 Ja '67

Instant renewal; HUD's instant rehabilitation project. il Newsweek 69:84-6 Ap 24 '67

New York's superblock: 114th street. Harlem. B. Bard. Good H 166:134 Ja '68

Out of slums into instant homes in forty-eight hours. il Life 62:57-8+ My 12 '67

Profiles: C. Abrams. B. Taper. New Yorker 42:45-8+ F 11 '67

Profiles: through the great city. A. Bailey. il New Yorker 43:35-8 Jl 29 '67

Rent strike; proposals for disrupting the slum system. F. F. Piven and R. A. Cloward. New Repub 157:11-15 D 2 '67; Reply. E. Spannaus. 158:45-6 Ja 6 '68

Slum landlords. M. Renek. New Repub 156:4-5 Je 3 '67

See also
Citizens housing and planning council of New York, incorporated

Industries

Exodus from fun city. il Time 89:83-4 F 24 '67

NEW YORK (city)—Industries—*Continued*

New York, the big set; Mayor Lindsay reduces restrictions on film-making. il Newsweek 69:36-7 My 29 '67

Nice place to visit. Newsweek 69:69-70 F 27 '67

Sewing machines & union machines; ILGWU and ACWA opposition to federal training in clothing trades. H. Hill. il Nation 205:18-19 Jl 3 '67

Why the growing flight of business from New York city. il U S News 62:45-6 Mr 6 '67

Intellectual life

Marathon for culture; report on New York symposium. Q. Eaton. Opera N 32:30 N 25 '67

Labor and laboring classes

Labor; threatened slowdowns or strikes involving fire department, radio and television networks, and, once again, newspapers. New Yorker 43:31-3 Ap 8 '67

Libraries

N.Y. library cooperation moves ahead with METRO. Library J 92:952+ Mr 1 '67

See also
Brooklyn public library
New York public library
Pierpont Morgan library
Presidential libraries
Queens borough public library

Madison Square Garden

Better break for the fans: mammoth sports palaces. il Time 91:68 Ja 5 '68

Huge new sports center: how the Garden grew. H. Comstock. il Pop Mech 128:140-3+ N '67

New Garden; interview. S. Schneider. New Yorker 42:25-6 F 4 '67

New Garden tries more varied crop. il Bsns W p 126-8 N 11 '67

Sporting scene; Rangers this season. R. Angell. New Yorker 43:128+ Mr 25 '67

Medical and health centers

See also
New   York   (city)—Columbia-Presbyterian medical center

Metropolitan museum of art

See Metropolitan museum of art

Mobilization for youth programs

See Mobilization for youth, incorporated

Monuments, statues, etc.

New York's no more; Philadelphia museum of art keeps statue of Diana. il Time 90:45 S 1 '67

Sylvette; Picasso sculpture for Washington Square center apartments. il Newsweek 70:89 D 4 '67

Moral conditions

Fun city; prostitution increases. Newsweek 70:74 Jl 3 '67

Hooker's market; prostitutes in Manhattan. il Time 90:23 Ag 18 '67

Municipal officers

See New York (city)—Officials and employees

Music

Debuts & reappearances. il Hi Fi 17:MA16-21+ My '67

Eternal and everyday; three concerts in Carnegie Hall. C. J. McNaspy. America 116:292-3 F 25 '67

Fischer-Dieskau & Moore: boffo at the box office. C. L. Osborne. il Hi Fi 17:MA10+ Je '67

From spirituals to swing, 1967. G. Lees. Hi Fi 17:MA7+ Ap '67

Hamburg opera makes U.S. debut. C. L. Osborne. il Hi Fi 17:MA8-11+ S '67

Met on the green. il Opera N 32:16-17 S 9 '67

Mozart month at Philharmonic Hall. B. Jacobson. il Hi Fi 17:MA8-9+ N '67

Music to my ears. I. Kolodin. See issues of Saturday review

Musical events. W. Sargeant. See issues of New Yorker

New sacred music in Carnegie Hall. America 116:237 F 18 '67

New York. F. Merkling. il Opera N 32:18-19 S 9 '67

New York. R. D. Daniels. il Opera N 31:28 Ap 8 '67

New York; revival of Massenet's Jongleur de Notre Dame at St George's church. F. Merkling. il Opera N 31:22 Je 10 '67

Notes and comment; Philharmonic concert in the Sheep meadow of Central park. New Yorker 43:21 Ag 12 '67

Notes from our correspondents. P. G. Davis. See issues of High fidelity incorporating Musical America

Notes from our correspondents. S. Fleming. Hi Fi 17:30+ D '67

Opera and an accolade. C. J. McNaspy. America 116:191-2 F 4 '67

Report: New York; productions in Carnegie Hall. R. D. Daniels. Opera N 32:31 Ja 6 '68

Rostropovich whirlwind. S. Fleming. Hi Fi 17:MA9+ My '67

Visiting orchestras; Suisse Romande & Bath. B. Jacobson. Hi Fi 17:MA16-17 S '67

See also
Lincoln Center for the performing arts
Little orchestra society
Metropolitan opera company
New York city opera company
Philharmonic-symphony society of New York

Newspapers

How to survive in the afternoon. il Time 89:54 My 26 '67

Life in the afternoon; publishers considering new paper. Newsweek 69:58 My 29 '67

New York afternoon. Time 90:102+ O 13 '67

Picking up the pieces. Newsweek 69:66 Je 12 '67

P.M. plunge; attempt to create an afternoon newspaper. il Newsweek 70:83 Jl 17 '67

Settlement on New York papers confirms big-raise trend of '67. U S News 63:75 Jl 3 '67

Signs in the afternoon; publishers investigate field. il Time 90:44 Jl 14 '67

Strike four? Newsweek 69:58 Ap 3 '67

See also
El Diario-la Prensa
New York (periodical)
New York herald tribune
New York post
New York times
World journal tribune

Officials and employees

Great Marcus. il Newsweek 71:12-13 Ja 1 '68

Mafia scandal; new trouble for Lindsay. U S News 64:10 Ja 1 '68

Murk from the reservoir; J. L. Marcus scandal. il Time 90:14 D 29 '67

Parks, Department of

Checked; Check-a-child service. New Yorker 43:23 Jl 15 '67

Parks and playgrounds

Adding to the heritage; polo field & underground stable for Central park. il Time 89:78 F 24 '67

Bike patrol; Central park. New Yorker 43:35-7 S 9 '67

Child's garden of plastic delights. il Life 63:74-6+ Jl 14 '67

Cows in the meadow; Central park sheep meadow to celebrate Greater New York dairy month. New Yorker 43:19-20 Je 24 '67

Friends; new organization called Friends of Central park. C. Holm; R. E. Harrison. New Yorker 42:24-5 F 4 '67

New commissioner; interview. A. Heckscher. New Yorker 43:32-3 Mr 4 '67

New light on the World fair's Unisphere. il Am City 82:122 My '67

New Yorker who shook up Central park. J. Peter. il Look 31:80+ My 2 '67

Notes and comment; need for number of small parks. New Yorker 43:21 Jl 8 '67

Notes and comment; Philharmonic concert in the Sheep meadow of Central park. New Yorker 43:21 Ag 12 '67

Open space design; New York shows how in its park program. A. Rosenblatt. il Arch Rec 142:110-24 Ag '67

The park; problems of a city park system. J. Hope. il Natur Hist 76:8-10+ Ag '67

Place to play; Riis plaza. il Horizon 9:42-9 Spr '67

Profiles; T. P. F. Hoving. J. McPhee. New Yorker 43:88-9+ My 20 '67

Sholom Aleichem in the park; program of Yiddish poetry and folk music in Central park. S. Bernard. Nation 205:124-5 Ag 14 '67

NEW YORK (city)—Parks and playgrounds—
Continued
Will it never stop? proposal to put heliports in New York's parks. Parks & Rec 2:19 Ja '67
Woodsman; trees in Central park; interview. C. O'Shea. New Yorker 43:41-3 Mr 18 '67
See also
New York zoological park

Police

East Harlem: do not cross, flatfoot! Puerto Ricans and the Tactical patrol force. B. Kremen. Nation 205:107+ Ag 14 '67
Justice of sorts; interrogation of suspect. C. P. Crow. Reporter 37:37-41 D 14 '67

Police department

Are Jews still liberals? how they voted on the Civilian review board issue. M. Himmelfarb. Commentary 43:67-72 Ap '67; Discussion. 44:6+ S '67
Backlash in Brooklyn, why the Review board failed. J. J. Graham; discussion. Commonweal 85:384, 495 Ja 6, F 3 '67
He's moving; protecting Premier Kosygin and others attending the emergency session of the United Nations General assembly. New Yorker 43:23-5 Jl 1 '67
Ignition control; method of taking illegally parked cars to the pound without using tow trucks. New Yorker 43:28-9 My 27 '67

Politics and government

Cardinal Spellman and New York politics. J. Corry. Harper 235:74-80+ D '67
John Lindsay: ringmaster of fun city. G. Astor. il Look 31:22-6+ Mr 21 '67
Lower Manhattan expressway. R. H. Silver. il Arch Forum 127:66-9 S '67
Profiles; J. Lindsay. N. Hentoff. New Yorker 43:58-60+ O 7; 61-4+ O 14 '67
Report; problems and achievements of the Lindsay administration. M. Arnold. Atlan 219:22+ Je '67
Rockefeller: operates on big scale. il U S News 63:54-7 O 30 '67
Urban conditions: New York city. B. Gottehrer. bibliog f il Ann Am Acad 371:141-58 My '67
See also
New York (city)—Council
Tammany Hall

Poor

Caseworker and the client. T. R. Brooks. il N Y Times Mag p26-7+ Ja 29 '67
Lindsay therapy. Nation 205:131-2 Ag 28 '67
Reporter at large; summer in the city. J. Stevenson. New Yorker 43:141-2+ S 16 '67
Summer in the city; projects of R. J. Fox. M. Cole. il Cath World 205:223-30 Jl '67

Public officers

Lindsay inner circle. M. Arnold. il N Y Times Mag p32-3+ O 15 '67

Rapid transit

New route out of traffic jams? New York's $2.5-billion transportation bond issue. il Bsns W p 160+ N 4 '67
Theatre bus; East side service sponsored by the League of New York theatres. New Yorker 43:37-8 My 6 '67
See also
New York (city)—Subways

Recreation

Recreation: a chance for innovative urban design; build types study. il Arch Rec 142:109-24 Ag '67
See also
New York (city)—Parks and playgrounds

Religious institutions and affairs

Kind of mecca; Emmaus house in Manhattan's East Harlem. il Newsweek 70:92 N 27 '67
Wall Street priest. il Newsweek 70:58 O 30 '67

Restaurants

See New York (city)—Hotels, restaurants, etc.

Riots

East Harlem: do not cross, flatfoot! Puerto Ricans and the Tactical patrol force. B. Kremen. Nation 205:107+ Ag 14 '67
Harlem's sputtering fuse; disorders flare up in Spanish Harlem. il Newsweek 70:33-4 Ag 7 '67
Nightmare night in *mi barrio.* P. Thomas. il N Y Times Mag p 16-17+ Ag 13 '67
Notes and comment; sniping and looting in Puerto Rican ghetto of Manhattan. New Yorker 43:19-23 Ag 5 '67

Rockefeller Center

New York city's multimillion-dollar village green. J. A. Morris. il Read Digest 91:193-7+ O '67

St John the Divine, Cathedral of

St John the Divine's unfinished symphony. Christian Cent 84:1485-6 N 22 '67

St Patrick's cathedral

Demonstrations during mass. America 116:172 F 4 '67
Fighting travesty with travesty. Christian Cent 84:164 F 8 '67

Sanitary affairs

Big but compact; thirteenth water-pollution-control plant. J. Cunetta. il Am City 82:137-9 O '67
In an emergency, call a contractor to solve a critical sewer-cleaning problem at high speed. M. M. Cohn. il Am City 82:84-5 Ag '67

School board

See New York (city)—Education, Board of

Schools

See New York (city)—Education

Social conditions

Games people play; concerned citizens stage a design-in, in Central park. New Yorker 43:26-8 My 27 '67
Report; problems and achievements of the Lindsay administration. M. Arnold. Atlan 219:22+ Je '67
See also
New York (city)—Harlem
New York (city)—Poor

Social history

Jacksonian aristocracy, by D. T. Miller. Review
New Repub 156:25-6 Ap 29 '67. M. Renek

Social life and customs

Lunching in New York. il Newsweek 69:60-5 My 15 '67
New girl in town, what she seeks & what she finds. J. Paulson. il Ladies Home J 85:62-3+ Ja '68
Provincial in New York; excerpts from North toward home. W. Morris. Harper 234:43-51 Je; 235:60-8 Jl '67
When the coachman was a millionaire; with watercolors by M. Klepper. F. Kintrea. Am Heritage 18:20-5+ O '67
See also
Night clubs

Social work

See also
New York (city)—Welfare, Department of

Stations

Nervi's gilded gateway; George Washington bridge bus terminal. D. Canty. il Arch Forum 126:68-73 Mr '67

Stock exchange

See Stock exchange—New York (city)

Stores

Amelia and YASNY; dancer opens boutique. A. Fatt. il Dance Mag 41:54-5 O '67
Art of selling to the affluent. il Bsns W p32-5 D 23 '67
Bloomingdale's; first the idea, then the merchandise. S. Margetts. il Duns R 90:41 D '67
Does Macy's tell Gimbels? competitors promoting same sort of Mediterranean merchandise. il Newsweek 70:82 S 25 '67
She mothers us all; J. B. Hughes at Bergdorf's. il Newsweek 70:62 N 6 '67
See also
Alexander's department stores, incorporated

Street traffic

Compact urban gateway; R. Katan's gateway to Manhattan plan. il Arch Forum 126:72-3 Ap '67
Handsome is as handsome does; J. V. Lindsay and traffic problem. G. Ace. Sat R 50:8 Je 17 '67
International incident; parking restrictions. Newsweek 69:41 F 6 '67
Plight of the cyclists; Metropolitan cycle association counterattacks parking and tow-away program. Newsweek 69:88-9 Mr 27 '67
Tow-away program a success. il Am City 82:110 Jl '67

NEW YORK (city)—*Continued*

Streets

Long-winded lady; future demolition of Le steak de Paris, and other buildings on Forty-ninth street, between Sixth and Seventh avenues. New Yorker 43:39-41 S 16 '67

Long-winded lady; high-school students' demonstration on Washington place. New Yorker 43:35-7 Ap 29 '67

Long-winded lady; West Forty-eighth street and Broadway. New Yorker 43:50-1 O 21 '67

New look at playstreets. D. V. Joyce. il Parks & Rec 2:28-9+ Jl '67

Notes and comment; obstacle course on the sidewalks due to building construction. New Yorker 43:31 My 20 '67

Playstreets add novel pastimes. D. V. Joyce. il Am City 82:83-5 Jl '67

Two walks: down Broadway at night, up Fifth avenue at noon. New Yorker 43:51 O 14 '67

Winds of Barclay street. J. Ferris. Sat R 50:4+ S 23 '67

See also
New York (city)—City planning

Subways

Notes and comment. New Yorker 42:29 F 11 '67

Notes and comment; concerning leaflet: Rules for the regulation of the use of New York city transit system. New Yorker 43:51 D 2 '67

Of trains, air, and Eire; Atmospheric railway. J. F. Henahan. Sat R 50:4+ N 25 '67

Theater

Amateur nights; National repertory theater on Broadway. il Time 89:84 My 12 '67

Bests of the 1966-67 theater season. H. Hewes. il Sat R 50:18-22 Je 10 '67

Broadway malady. G. Ace. Sat R 50:6 N 11 '67

Curtain rises: a new season. il Newsweek 70:89-90+ S 11 '67

English imports on Broadway. J. Richardson. Commentary 43:73-5 Je '67

Follies of Broadway. J. O'Hara. Holiday 41:23+ F '67

Good portents; new Broadway season. il Time 90:60-1 Ag 25 '67

Making of a theater; New York Shakespeare festival public theater. Newsweek 70:124-5 N 13 '67

New theater season. H. Hewes. Sat R 50:60 S 16 '67

Off-Broadway; Chelsea theatre center group. R. Pasolli. Nation 204:411-13 Mr 27 '67

Off-off-Broadway: it's in. M. Gussow. il Newsweek 69:88+ My 1 '67

Off off-Broadway. New York. A. Croce. Nat R 19:261-5 Mr 7 '67

Rep on Broadway, U.S.A. L. Lerman. il Mlle 64:182 Ap '67

Seven hits, five walks, twenty-five errors. Time 89:41 Je 30 '67

Show must go on, but not too long; Broadway stars balk at lengthy runs. J. Hallowell. il Life 63:41-2 Jl 21 '67

Spotlight! E. Miller. See issues of Seventeen

Theater is the victim of a plot; staleness of new plays. W. Kerr. il N Y Times Mag p 10-11+ Je 25 '67

Theater of dislike; observations on the season's contemporary drama. D. J. Leary. Cath World 205:217-22 Jl '67

Their hearts belong to La Mama; Experimental theater club. J. Greenfeld. il N Y Times Mag p 10-11+ Jl 9 '67

They go in smiling; briefing latecomers at matinée of Don't drink the water; interview. S. J. Freedman. New Yorker 42:26-7 F 4 '67

See also
League of New York theatres, incorporated
Lincoln Center for the performing arts
New York drama critics circle

Traffic problem

See New York (city)—Street traffic

Transportation

Ordeal of the short distance. N. Cousins. Sat R 50:28-9 F 11 '67

See also
New York (city) Rapid transit
New York (city)—Subways

Views

See New York (city)—Description

Water supply

How to clean a big reservoir. J. L. Marcus. il Am City 82:69-71 N '67

New York's forgotten drought. N. Perrin. il Nation 204:721-3 Je 5 '67

Welfare, Department of

Caseworker and the client. T. R. Brooks. il N Y Times Mag p26-7+ Ja 29 '67

Zoological park

See New York zoological park

NEW YORK (city) City university of New York

City college

Education up a tree: the plight of City college. L. Kriegel. Commonweal 87:137-8 N 3 '67

Hunter college

See Hunter college

Libraries

Community college libraries: problems and prospects. D. Peele. il Library J 92:2898-901 S 1 '67

NEW YORK (periodical)

New York rebirth. il Time 90:44 N 17 '67

NEW YORK (state)

From sword to scythe in Champlain country. E. A. Starbird. il Nat Geog Mag 132:153-201 Ag '67

See also
Adirondack Mountains
Architecture, Domestic—New York (state)
Booksellers and bookselling—New York (state)
Catskill Mountains
Divorce—New York (state)
Education—New York (state)
Erie Canal
Fishing—New York (state)
Hudson River
Hunting—New York (state)
Labor laws and legislation—New York (state)
Legislation—New York (state)
Libraries—New York (state)
Music festivals—New York (state)
Nassau County, N.Y.
Public welfare—New York (state)
Roads—New York (state)

Antiquities

See Indians of North America—Antiquities—New York (state)

Capitol

Nineteenth-century sampler. il Fortune 75:174 My '67

Constitution

Blaine amendment, yes or no? A. Hacker. il N Y Times Mag p27-9+ O 1 '67; Discussion. p40+ O 22; 14+ O 29 '67; America 117:399 O 14 '67

Blaine and secular man. D. Hale. Commonweal 87:105-6 O 27 '67

Catholics, liberals and Jews. America 116:578 Ap 22 '67; Reply. Sister Gloria. 116:795 Je 3 '67

Church and state; Blaine amendment. il Newsweek 70:61 N 6 '67

Constitutional crisis in New York. Christian Cent 84:1387-8 N 1 '67

Lefkowitz, McLuhan and Blaine. America 117:340 S 30 '67

Constitutional convention, 1967

Catholics, liberals and Jews. America 116:578 Ap 22 '67; Reply. Sister Gloria. 116:795 Je 3 '67

Church and school; proposed new constitution. L. Pfeffer. Nation 205:389-90 O 23 '67

Con con game. Newsweek 70:33 O 9 '67

Forever wild upheld; anatomy of a convention. E. W. Littlefield. il Am For 73:36-7+ N '67

Other half of the state government; Democratic speaker. A. J. Travia. R. Reeves. il N Y Times Mag p24-5+ Ap 2 '67

Tough to write a good one. il Time 90:49 O 20 '67

Council on the arts

Arts council that works. K Kuh. il Sat R 50:68-9 F 25 '67

Awards. New Yorker 43:26 Je 3 '67

Description and travel

Four-day outing from New York; food and drink expedition. W. Clifford. Atlan 219:114-16+ Je '67

Leather-stocking trails. D. Ford. il Travel 127:45-9 Mr '67

See also
Finger Lakes Region

NEW YORK (state)—*Continued*

Education

Save them young; New York state's pre-kindergarten program. M. P. Berson. il Am Ed 3:5-8 Jl '67

Education, Department of

Even in high school; case of student who cheated on regents exam. il Time 90:41 Jl 14 '67

Elections

See also

New York (state)—Politics and government

Historic houses, etc.

Boscobel; Garrison-on-Hudson. New York. C. Pintchman. il Horticulture 45:36-7+ D '67

Footnotes; painting Hannoch house at Verplanck's Landing. il(cover) Am Artist 31:6 S '67

History in houses; Hyde hall, Otsego County, N.Y. D. R. Kent. il Antiques 92:187-93 Ag '67

Living with antiques; Montgomery place, the home of Major and Mrs John White Delafield. A. Delafield. il Antiques 91:234-9 F '67

Hudson River Valley commission

Profiles; through the great city. A. Bailey. New Yorker 43:38+ Jl 29 '67

Legislature

Criminal justice revolution; address, May 16, 1967. J. E. Lumbard. Vital Speeches 33:527-31 Je 15 '67

Parks and reserves

Is a park for people? Adirondack park. il Newsweek 70:96+ O 9 '67

Proposed Adirondack Mountains National Park. S. J. Prezioso. il Parks & Rec 2:14-16+ N '67

Runouts, kickouts, and popouts at Gilgo beach. New Yorker 43:24 Je 17 '67

Why I am for Article XIV. A. Najer. il Am For 73:30-1+ Ag '67

History

Changing forest preserve. E. W. Littlefield. il Am For 73:12-15+ Mr '67

Politics and government

Other half of the state government; Democratic speaker, A. J. Travia. R. Reeves. il N Y Times Mag p24-5+ Ap 2 '67

Reporter at large; race between O. G. Pike and J. M. Catterson, jr. for seat in House of representatives from First congressional district. R. Harris. New Yorker 43:48-50+ Ap 8 '67

NEW YORK (state) State university

Computerized library system to index books in depth; SUNY. Library J 92:3360+ O 1 '67

Giant that nobody knows. il Time 91:43-8 Ja 12 '68

Profiles; S. B. Gould. C. Tomkins. New Yorker 43:67-8+ N 18 '67

Agricultural and technical institute, Farmingdale

University inaugurates turf management program. D. W. Griffiths, jr. il Parks & Rec 2:35+ Ap '67

Albany campus

Albany: New York state university center on the way up. B. Nelson. il Science 155:1521-5 Mr 24 '67; Reply. R. F. Creegan. 156:893 My 19 '67

Something new in college campuses. il U S News 63:54-6 S 4 '67

University at Buffalo

Fiedler affair; Buffalo university group aims to legalize marijuana. il Newsweek 69:29 Je 12 '67

NEW YORK aquarium. See Aquariums

NEW YORK automobile show. See Automobiles—Exhibitions

NEW YORK botanical garden

Graduation; ceremony for Children's garden-craft classes. New Yorker 43:36 S 30 '67

New York botanical garden, research and education. W. C. Steere. il Science 158:539-41 O 27 '67

NEW YORK central railroad

End of the affair? Twentieth century limited. C. Stinnett. il Holiday 41:40+ Mr '67

Last run; Twentieth Century limited. New Yorker 43:20-3 D 23 '67

NEW YORK central railroad-Pennsylvania merger. See Railroads—Consolidations and mergers

NEW YORK city ballet

Balanchine's latest. I. Kolodin. Sat R 50:24 Ap 29 '67

Early-season report; Nov. 15-Dec. 3, 1967. M. Marks. il Dance Mag 42:41+ Ja '68

Gem dandy; première of Balanchine's untitled work. il Time 89:89 Ap 21 '67

Jewels by Balanchine. H. Saal. il Newsweek 69:105 Ap 24 '67

Let's talk about people; review of season. D. Hering. il Dance Mag 41:56-7+ Mr '67

Movement makers. H. Saal. il Newsweek 70:114-15 D 11 '67

Music to my ears; Jacques d'Amboise's Prologue. I. Kolodin. Sat R 50:73 Ja 28 '67

Musical events; performance of Balanchine's Jewels. W. Sargeant. New Yorker 43:219 N 25 '67

Musical events; performance of George Balanchine's ballet about jewels. W. Sargeant. New Yorker 43:177 Ap 22 '67

Nutcracker, a Christmas gift. W. Terry. il Sat R 50:51-2 D 2 '67

These are my jewels; spring season at New York state theater. D. Hering. il Dance Mag 41:46-8+ Je '67

World of dance; performance of Glinkiana. W. Terry. Sat R 50:79 D 16 '67

NEW YORK city opera company

City opera takes to the baroque; recording of Handel's Julius Caesar. P. G. Davis. Hi Fi 17:20+ Jl '67

City opera's Traviata, Magic flute, Tosca. C. L. Osborne. il Hi Fi 17:MA6-8 Ja '67

Cry at dawn. F. Merkling. il Opera N 32:6-7 S 23 '67

Music to my ears; new season. I. Kolodin. Sat R 50:56 S 30 '67

Musical events; double bill; P. Mascagni's Cavalleria rusticana and R. Leoncavallo's Pagliacci. W. Sargeant. New Yorker 43:178 O 7 '67

Musical events; performance of Giannini's Servant of two masters. W. Sargeant. New Yorker 43:124 Mr 18 '67

Musical events; performance of J. Beeson's Lizzie Borden. W. Sargeant. New Yorker 43:189-90 N 4 '67

Musical events; performance of Puccini's Il trittico: Gianni Schicchi, Il tabarro, Suor Angelica. W. Sargeant. New Yorker 43:147 Mr 4 '67

Musical events; performance of R. Strauss' Der Rosenkavalier. W. Sargeant. New Yorker 43:127 Ap 1 '67

Musical events; performances of Ginastera's Don Rodrigo, and Puccini's La Bohème. W. Sargeant. New Yorker 42:144+ F 18 '67; Correction. 43:94 F 25 '67

Musical events; performances of R. Strauss' Der Rosenkavalier and Verdi's La Traviata. W. Sargeant. New Yorker 43:93-4 F 25 '67

Musical events; performances of Verdi's La Traviata and Mozart's The magic flute. W. Sargeant. New Yorker 43:138-40 S 23 '67

Musical events; Rimski-Korsakov's Le coq d'or. W. Sargeant. New Yorker 43:86+ S 30 '67

New pair at City opera. C. L. Osborne. il Hi Fi 17:MA8-9 Je '67

New York city opera. il Hi Fi 17:MA9-11+ D '67; 18:MA7 Ja '68

New York city opera goes to Los Angeles. il Opera N 32:19-21 N 25 '67

New York; City opera Rosenkavalier. F. Merkling. il Opera N 31:33 Mr 25 '67

New York; revival of Coq d'or and new productions of Cavalleria rusticana and Pagliacci. F. Merkling; R. D. Daniels. il Opera N 32:20-1 N 4 '67

Report: Los Angeles; performances of New York city opera. A. Goldberg. Opera N 32:30-1 Ja 6 '68

Rudel's Rosenkavalier. C. L. Osborne. il Hi Fi 17:MA12-13 My '67

Tale of two Juliuses. H. Kupferberg. Atlan 221:106-7 Ja '68

True story of Beverly Sills. H. Saal. il N Y Times Mag p34-5+ S 17 '67; Discussion. p97 O 1 '67

NEW YORK city transit authority

But can you do that? banning of anti-Vietnam war posters judged unconstitutional. H. F. Pilpel. Pub W 192:24-5 N 27 '67

NEW YORK COUNTY lawyers association

Law group seeks to enjoin How to avoid probate. Pub W 191:36 Ap 17 '67

NEW YORK drama critics circle

Drama critics' voting, 1967. Sat R 50:19 Je 10 '67

NEW YORK film festival. See Moving picture festivals

NEW YORK Giants (football club) See Football clubs

NEW YORK herald tribune
Life and death of a great newspaper. F. C. Shapiro. il Am Heritage 18:97-112 O '67

NEW YORK hi-fi show. See Audio fairs

NEW YORK high fidelity music show. See Audio fairs

NEW YORK Jets (football club) See Football clubs

NEW YORK Knickerbockers (basketball team) See Basketball teams

NEW YORK medical college
Convocation; New York medical college installation of president. D. Denker. New Yorker 43:21-2 Ja 13 '68

NEW YORK Mets (baseball) See Baseball clubs

NEW YORK, New Haven and Hartford railroad company
Down, down, down. Fortune 75:260 Je 15 '67
Suburbia East; Donald Goss executive train commuter. M. Simons. Look 31:25-7 My 16 '67

NEW YORK Philharmonic. See Philharmonic-symphony society of New York

NEW YORK post
Alone in the afternoon. Newsweek 69:68 My 22 '67
New York afternoon. Time 90:102+ O 13 '67

NEW YORK public library
Library lunch; NYPL Neighbors lunches to make services of the Central research library better known. New Yorker 43:18-19 Ja 6 '68
NYPL large print project gets another $21,500 grant. Library J 92:176 Ja 15 '67
Speedup; interlibrary loans by Datafax; interview. L. P. Murphy. New Yorker 43:51-2 N 25 '67
Ten wonders of NYPL selected by Freehafer; service cuts feared as deficit mounts; main building designated as landmark. Library J 92:954 Mr 1 '67

Branches

Harlem and Bronx projects set for coming year. Library J 92:3586+ O 15 '67
Harlem project granted six-month extension; North Manhattan project in Countee Cullen and the adjacent Schomburg collection. Library J 92:1690-1 Ap 15 '67

135th Street branch

Schomburg's ailing collection. il Ebony 22:55-6+ O '67; Reply. Library J 92:4455 D 15 '67

NEW YORK Rangers (hockey team) See Hockey teams

NEW YORK review of books (periodical)
Sharpening the knife. il Time 90:84 D 8 '67

NEW YORK state council on the arts. See New York (state)—Council on the arts

NEW YORK state forest preserve. See Forests, State

NEW YORK state historical association
See also
Farmers' museum, Cooperstown, N.Y.

NEW YORK state lottery. See Lotteries

NEW YORK state university. See New York (state) State university

NEW YORK stock exchange. See Stock exchange—New York (city)

NEW YORK taxicabs. See Taxicabs

NEW YORK theatres, League of. See League of New York theatres, incorporated

NEW YORK times
Amiable springboard; theater critics. M. Gussow. Newsweek 70:96+ D 18 '67
Artillery of the press, by J. Reston. Review New Repub 156:23-4 Ap 29 '67. M. Childs
Credibility and the Times; abandonment of balanced reporting; concerning H. Salisbury dispatches. H. K. Smith. Nat R 19:73-4 Ja 24 '67
Difference in South Vietnam. America 117:263-4 S 16 '67
End of one-man's opinion; two theater critics. il Time 89:51 Mr 17 '67
Enter Clive Barnes. Newsweek 69:109 Mr 20 '67
Just the facts, please. S. J. Adamo. America 116:483 Mr 25 '67
N.Y. times enlarges book and education division. Pub W 191:46 F 6 '67
N.Y. times to buy 51 per cent of Arno press. Pub W 193:61 Ja 15 '68
Public and private wars of Harrison E. Salisbury. G. Talese. Esquire 67:88-90+ My '67

Quiet subversive; humor columnist R. Baker. Time 91:60 Ja 19 '68
Weight lifters. Newsweek 71:54 Ja 22 '68
Winners & sinners. Nat R 19:626-7 Je 13 '67
Youth movement; critical departments. il Newsweek 70:99-99A D 4 '67

NEW YORK times index
New York times index to go on computer. Pub W 193:46 Ja 8 '68

NEW YORK transit authority. See New York city transit authority

NEW YORK university
Talent hunt in the East Village. R. Kotlowitz. Harper 234:141-4 Mr '67

NEW YORK yacht club
Committee is charged, America's cup committee. F. Rohr, jr. il Motor B 120:29 Ag '67

NEW YORK Yankees (baseball) See Baseball clubs

NEW YORK zoological park
Animal world of darkness; pavilion at New York's Bronx zoo. il Sci Digest 62:32-6 D '67

NEW YORK zoological society
See also
Institute for research in animal behavior

NEW YORKER (periodical)
Civilized eye on the jungle; R. Rovere's views. il Time 90:65 D 22 '67
Infallibility of Eustace Tilley; concerning story by Renata Adler on the Chicago convention on New politics; letter to the editor. A. I. Waskow. Nation 205:450+ N 6 '67
MacBlackout; why MacBird was ignored. Newsweek 69:73 Ap 17 '67
New New Yorker. Newsweek 71:53 Ja 1 '68
New Yorker lists at this season some books by its contributors published during the year (cont) New Yorker 43:221 D 2 '67
Sanderson Vanderbilt. New Yorker 42:132 F 4 '67

NEW YORKERS
Images of elegant New York; conversation pieces; portfolio. L. Auchincloss. Am Heritage 17:48-65 O '66; Correction. il 18:76 F '67
Long-winded lady (cont) New Yorker 43:41-3 Ap 22; 35-7 Ap 29; 50-1 O 21; 54-5 N 11 '67
Provincial in New York; excerpts from North toward home. W. Morris. Harper 234:43-51 Je; 235:60-8 Jl '67
River on Fourth street; summer activities. New Yorker 43:22-3 Jl 8 '67
Two walks; down Broadway at night, up Fifth avenue at noon. New Yorker 43:51 O 14 '67

Anecdotes, facetiae, satire, etc.

Genus; waiter; species; New York. L. Rosten. il Look 31:8 N 28 '67

NEW ZEALAND
Across the Tasman to the island continent. M. Petersen. il Motor B 119:50+ Je '67
See also
Atomic power—New Zealand
Birds—New Zealand
Liquor laws and regulations—New Zealand

Description and travel

Aerial sightseeing over New Zealand's South Island. il Sunset 138:56+ F '67
Down Under. J. Durniak. il Pop Phot 61:116-19+ N '67
Way down South where the weather's iffy. M. Petersen. il Motor B 119:52+ My '67

Religious institutions and affairs

World around us. Christian Cent 84:924+ Jl 12 '67
See also
Presbyterian church in New Zealand

Social conditions

Australasian character. J. Forster. bibliog f Ann Am Acad 370:156-63 Mr '67
See also
Social and economic security—New Zealand

NEW ZEALANDERS
Australasian character. J. Forster. bibliog f Ann Am Acad 370:156-63 Mr '67

NEWARK, N.J.
Negroes

Voices of Newark; Central ward conditions. J. Anderson. Commentary 44:85-90 O '67

Police

Lethal indifference. L. M. Moroze. Nation 205:105-7 Ag 14 '67

Riots

Anatomy of a riot. R. Whitehead. Commonweal 86:492-4 Ag 11 '67

NEWARK, N.J.—Riots—*Continued*
Lessons of New Jersey's race riots; interview. R. J. Hughes. il U S News 63:32-6 Jl 31 '67
Lethal indifference. L. M. Moroze. Nation 205:105-7 Ag 14 '67
Meaning of the Newark riots. J. B. Sheerin. Cath World 205:324-6 S '67
Morning after Newark's nightmare; with editorial comment. il Bsns W p22-3, 138 Jl 22 '67
Negro revolt echoes to the ugly crack of sniper fire; with reports by D. Wittner and R. Sackett. il Life 63:16-28A Jl 28 '67
Newark boils over. il Newsweek 70:21-2 Jl 24 '67
Newark race riot: open rebellion, just like wartime. il U S News 63:6 Jl 24 '67
Newark: scarred, scared, but hopeful. Bsns W p25 Jl 29 '67
Notes and comment; actions of police, state troopers, and national guardsmen. New Yorker 43:23-5 Jl 22 '67
One man's Newark. J. D. Kirwan. Nat R 19:847 Ag 8 '67
Real tragedy of Newark. il U S News 63:30-1 Jl 31 '67
Rebellion in Newark, by T. Hayden. Review Sat R 50:41-2 S 30 '67. S. Tepper
Sparks & tinder. il Time 90:15-21 Jl 21 '67
Spirit of Newark, U.S.A. America 117:105 Jl 29 '67

NEWBERY medal
Irene Hunt. E. Meeks. Library J 92:1297 Mr 15 '67
Newbery and Caldecott award winners. ALA Bul 61:358 Ap '67
Newbery and Caldecott winners: Irene Hunt, Evaline Ness. il Pub W 191:34-5 Mr 13 '67
Newbery-Caldecott party. il Pub W 191:38 Mr 27 '67
Newbery-Caldecott winners. il Wilson Lib Bul 41:783 Ap '67

NEWBORN, Isi
Isi does it. Sports Illus 26:11 My 22 '67

NEWBORN infants. See Infants, Newborn

NEWBURGH, N.Y.
Streets
Save street surfaces the easy way; use of slurry seal. W. G. McEvilly. il Am City 82:106-7 Je '67

NEWBURYPORT, Mass.
Surveying a city's labor market. E. F. Cook. il Am City 82:155 Je '67

NEWCOMBE, John
He's old hat to Australians. F. Deford. il por Sports Illus 27:30-3 S 4 '67
Some beer for Newk, a waltz for Billie. F. Deford. il por Sports Illus 27:22-5 Jl 17 '67
Two who didn't stay away. K. Chapin. il Sports Illus 27:97-8+ S 18 '67

NEWELL, Gordon
Common-sense magic of Birch cottage; adaptation. Read Digest 91:223-34+ O '67

NEWELL, Homer E. and Jaffe, Leonard
Impact of space research on science and technology. Science 157:29-39 Jl 7 '67

NEWFIELD, Jack
One cheer for the hippies. Nation 204:809-10 Je 26 '67
—See Smith, H. jt. auth.

NEWFOUNDLAND
See also
Birds—Newfoundland

NEWHALL, Beaumont
Photography at Expo: a first look. Pop Phot 61:61+ S '67
Soon after sunrise; the light is much softer. Pop Phot 61:88-9+ Ag '67
This was 1937. Pop Phot 60:73-5+ My '67

NEWHOUSE, Samuel I.
Plain and fancy dealing. Newsweek 69:78 Mr 13 '67
Why the Newhouse touch is golden. por Bsns W p 138 Mr 11 '67

NEWLEY, Anthony
Anthony Newley: inside out; ed. by E. Miller. pors Seventeen 26:124-5+ O '67

NEWLIN, Dika
Leonard Bernstein is not a man to pass up such a challenge, Mahler's Symphony of a thousand. Am Rec G 33:416-17 Ja '67

NEWLUN, Larry C.
Bull trout testimonial. Field & S 71:56-7+ Ap '67

NEWMAN, Arnold
Meaning of Israel; photographs. Holiday 42:59+ D '67
about
World's greatest pictures: Stravinsky by Newman. J. Scully. il Mod Phot 31:70-1+ My '67

NEWMAN, Barnett
New man in town. T. B. Hess. il Art N 66:27 N '67

NEWMAN, David, and Benton, Robert
Man talk. See issues of Mademoiselle
Now let the festivities proceed. Esquire 68:55-8 Jl '67
Scientific American; parody. Esquire 67:71-5+ F '67
about
Dynamic duo. il por Newsweek 70:84 N 6 '67
Why your parties will never be as good as Truman Capote's. Esquire 68:165 D '67

NEWMAN, Deborah
First Thanksgiving; drama. Plays 27:75-8 N '67
Pride and prejudice; dramatization of novel by J. Austen. Plays 26:83-96 Ap '67
Somebody's valentine; drama. Plays 26:75-8 F '67

NEWMAN, Ed
Newman-at-large. il por Newsweek 69:79 Je 26 '67

NEWMAN, Harold
Porcelain pots for brewing and warming coffee. Antiques 92:329-31 S '67

NEWMAN, Harry Shaw
Obituary
Am Heritage por 18:97 F '67

NEWMAN, John Henry, cardinal
No time to leave. J. G. Lawler. Commonweal 86:87-92 Ap 7 '67

NEWMAN, Jon Ormond
Cops, courts, and Congress. New Repub 156:16-20 Mr 18 '67

NEWMAN, Jonathan U.
Teaching the Bill of rights. PTA Mag 62:2-5 bibliog(p36) N '67

NEWMAN, Leonard Hugh
Like lovely flowers on the wing. House B 109:114-15+ Je '67

NEWMAN, Marvin E.
Marvin Newman in Africa. E. Galligan. il por U S Camera 30:61+ My '67

NEWMAN, Nicholas C.
Wax makers. il Nat Parks Mag 41:14-15 Ja '67

NEWMAN, Paul Baker
Christ, anarchist; poem. Christian Cent 84:494 Ap 19 '67

NEWMARK, Steve
Steve Newmark on Transpac background and characteristics. Yachting 121:79-80 Je '67

NEWPORT, R.I.
Seacoast of despair. J. Didion. Sat Eve Post 240:20+ Jl 29 '67
Description
Newport, Rhode Island. il Bet Hom & Gard 45:10 Ag '67
Historic houses
Fabulous cottages of Newport. R. Deardorff. il Redbook 129:39 Jl '67

NEWPORT, R.I. Verdi festival. See Music Festivals—Rhode Island

NEWPORT Jazz festival. See Music festivals —Rhode Island

NEWPORT NEWS, Va.
Hospitals
Hospital segregation; Civil rights act of 1964 flouted by Riverside hospital. New Repub 156:7 Mr 25 '67

NEWPORT NEWS shipbuilding and dry dock company
Shipbuilding's leader heads into a storm. il Bsns W p 178-80+ O 7 '67

NEWQUIST, Roy
Katharine Hepburn. McCalls 94:64-5+ Jl '67

NEWS
Censorship by boredom. A. Gingrich. Esquire 67:6 Je '67
On trusting the news you read. B. L. Masse. America 116:804 Je 3 '67
Should reporters buy news? B. Surface. Sat R 50:85-6 My 13 '67
See also
Government and the press
Journalism
News letters
Radio broadcasting—News
Reporters and reporting
Television broadcasting—News

NEWS agencies
Abrasive position; Newhouse news service and P. Hochstein. il Newsweek 69:73 Ap 17 '67
Contacts for sale. W. Shelton. il Sat R 50:84-5+ My 13 '67
Under de Gaulle's umbrella; Agence France presse. Time 90:80+ S 15 '67

NEWS agencies—*Continued*
Underground trips; Underground press syndicate. il Newsweek 69:65 My 1 '67
War of the wires; Associated press and Reuters. Newsweek 70:60 O 9 '67
  See also
Novosti
Reuters (news agency)
United press international
NEWS broadcasts. See Radio broadcasting—News
NEWS commentators. See Television broadcasting—News
NEWS films. See Newsreels
NEWS letters
Big news in miniatures. il Am City 82:114+ Ja '67
NEWS magazines. See Periodicals
NEWS photographers
  See also
Salomon, E.
Schutzer, P.
NEWS photography. See Photography, Journalistic
NEWS services. See News agencies
NEWSDAY (newspaper)
Newsday under Moyers. Newsweek 70:51 Ag 28 '67
Something rotten in Islip. Time 91:57 Ja 5 '68
NEWSLETTERS. See News letters
NEWSOM, Margot Copeland
Feeding young children can be easy and fun. Parents Mag 42:62-5+ My '67
NEWSOME, William E.
We open doors for migrant children. NEA J 56:27-8 Ap '67
NEWSPAPER advertising. See Advertising mediums—Newspapers
NEWSPAPER columns. See Newspapers—Sections, columns, etc.
NEWSPAPER correspondents. See Reporters and reporting
NEWSPAPER court reporting
Justice vs. journalism; Speck trial. il Newsweek 69:37 Mr 6 '67
Narrow confines of British crime reporting. N. Moss. il Reporter 37:29-31 N 30 '67
Press & Richard Speck. Time 89:49 Mr 3 '67
Press in the jury box? Time 89:96+ Mr 10 '67
NEWSPAPER editors. See Editors and editing
NEWSPAPER ethics. See Journalistic ethics
NEWSPAPER men. See Journalists
NEWSPAPER publishing
Dead giveaway; afternoon newspapers unpopular. Newsweek 70:92 O 16 '67
It's just bad news. B. H. Bagdikian. Esquire 67:124+ Mr '67
New processes and old stupidity. R. L. Tobin. Sat R 50:93-4 Je 10 '67
Winter of discontent. R. L. Tobin. Sat R 50:123-4 Mr 11 '67
  See also
Government investigations—Newspaper publishing
NEWSPAPER strikes. See Strikes—United States—Newspapers
NEWSPAPERS
Gone and forgotten. S. Kauffmann. New Repub 156:24+ Je 27 '67
How you can be as well-informed as we are. Esquire 68:136-7 N '67
  See also
Editors and editing
Freedom of the press
Journalism
News
News agencies
Photography, Journalistic
Publicity
    Advertising policy
Journalism's two faces; Washington post's policy. New Repub 157:5-6 Jl 1 '67
    Book reviews
  See Book reviews
    Columns
  See Newspapers—Sections, columns, etc.
    Consolidations and mergers
Antitrust immunity and the press. R. L. Tobin. Sat R 50:47-8 S 9 '67
Boston strangle; Traveler merges with morning Herald. Newsweek 70:52 Jl 3 '67
Europe gets a new logotype; Times international merges with the Paris herald tribune-Washington post. Bsns W p48 My 20 '67

Partners in Paris; international editions of the Herald tribune and The New York times. il Newsweek 69:58 My 29 '67
Question of competition; Los Angeles times ordered to divest itself of the San Bernardino sun and telegram. Time 90:58 O 20 '67
Surrender in Paris; Times international merges with Trib-post. Time 89:55 My 26 '67
When is a failure? Time 90:66-7 Jl 28 '67
    Crime reporting
  See Crime and the press
    Employees
  See also
Journalists
    Foreign news
Asian news void. A. Balk. Sat R 50:97 My 13 '67
Battlefield report; foreign reaction to Detroit riots. Newsweek 70:70 Ag 7 '67
Castro and the Times; effect of H. L. Matthews' interview with Castro. il Newsweek 70:60-1 S 11 '67
Covering the crisis; correspondents in Israel. il Newsweek 69:82+ Je 19 '67
On the scene in the Middle East; coverage of war. Time 89:73 Je 16 '67
Report; Japanese news underplayed by U.S. press. J. M. Truitt. Atlan 219:12+ Je '67
    Illustrations
Art with a deadline; newspaper art. J. Waddingham. Am Artist 31:54-62 My '67
    Indexes
Canadian newspaper index announced for 1967. Library J 92:1408-9 Ap 1 '67
  See also
New York times index
    Letters to editors
Letters to the world's editors; comp. by N. G. Balint. Sat R 50:45 Jl 8; 40 S 9; 54 O 7; 64-5 N 11; 51 D 9 '67; 51:99 Ja 13 '68
    Magazine sections
  See also
Parade (periodical)
    Political activities
  See Newspapers and politics
    Political news
Artillery of the press, by J. Reston. Review New Repub 156:23-4 Ap 29 '67. M. Childs
History and Herbert Matthews. Nat R 19:1004-5 S 19 '67
  See also
Government and the press
    Sections, columns, etc.
Heloise, the most-heeded housewife; H. Cruse's Hints from Heloise. J. Howard. il Life 62:39+ Ap 21 '67
Library newspaper columns; its format and function. V. Leonard. ALA Bul 61:412-14 Ap '67
Not just words but action; action columns devoted to helping people solve their problems. il Time 89:58 F 3 '67
Oh, for a good aardvark stampede; feature stories. J. O'Reilly. Sat R 50:90-2 My 13 '67
Opinion shapers; newspaper columinsts. Sr Schol 90:10-11 Ap 28 '67
Responsibility of the mass media; summary of panel sponsored by National book committee. il Pub W 191:36-7 Mr 20 '67
  See also
Newspapers—Advice columns
    Social aspects
Crisis coverage; conference on the mass media and race relations at Columbia university. Newsweek 70:60+ O 30 '67
    Sports news
  See Sports journalism
    Syndicate service
Selling subsidiary rights; syndicated religious features; summary of address. P. Reed. Pub W 191:29 Ap 3 '67
    Tabloid papers
Underground trips; hippie press. il Newsweek 69:65 My 1 '67
    Womens pages
Pages for women. il Time 89:55 My 19 '67

NEWSPAPERS—*Continued*

Alaska

See also
Anchorage, Alaska—Newspapers

France

But first, a message; television commercials to weaken power of press. Newsweek 70:50 N 27 '67
See also
Paris—Newspapers

Great Britain

Britain's chronic press crisis; results of survey made by the Economist intelligence unit. J. Tebbel. Sat R 50:49-50 Jl 8 '67
Britain's press crisis. R. Williams. Nation 204:466-7 Ap 10 '67
D for indefensible? dispute over D-notice. Newsweek 70:83-4 Jl 17 '67
Into Britain's parlor with his hat on; Lord Thomson of Fleet. D. Norton-Taylor. il Fortune 75:136-9+ F '67
Making the British press responsible; British press council. J. Tebbel. Sat R 50:118+ O 14 '67
Narrow confines of British crime reporting. N. Moss. il Reporter 37:29-31 N 30 '67
Self-medication. il Time 89:58-9 Ja 27 '67
Spies every Sunday; Sunday Times and the Observer coverage of Philby case. il Time 90:61 N 10 '67
See also
Times, London

Ireland

We filled page four; Portlaoighise's Leinster express. G. Clark. il Reporter 36:37-40 Ap 6 '67

Japan

Not the right to know, but to know what's right. il Time 90:49 D 29 '67

Libya

Thank you, Wadi Botts! C. McCormick. Reporter 37:41-4+ O 5 '67

Russia

House of Pravda. W. B. Kerr. il Sat R 50:60-1 D 9 '67
Soviet circulation battle. il Time 89:78+ F 17 '67

United States

Alicia and the underground press. J. Didion. Sat Eve Post 241:14 Ja 13 '68
American newspaper is neither record, mirror . . . nor herald of the day's events. B. H. Bagdikian. Esquire 67:124-8+ Mr '67
Crybaby act? Senate antitrust and monopoly subcommittee investigates newspapers. Newsweek 70:70 Jl 24 '67
Does the U.S. need a national press council? R. L. Tobin. Sat R 50:115-16 O 14 '67; Discussion. 50:84 N 11 '67
Help wanted. il Newsweek 69:70-1 Ja 30 '67
How you can be as well-informed as Dwight Macdonald. D. Macdonald. Esquire 68:137-8+ N '67
Integrity of the U.S. press; concerning an article in the Wall Street journal of July 25, 1967. America 117:148 Ag 12 '67
Needling the press; role of the small publication. Nation 204:325 Mr 13 '67
Overheard in suburbia; editor. W. Hedgepeth. Look 31:88 My 16 '67
Seedier media: underground press. D. Sanford. New Repub 157:7-8 D 2 '67
Strength in the afternoon; Lord Thomson buys Brush-More chain. il Time 90:45 S 8 '67
What's wrong with American newspapers? A. H. Raskin. il N Y Times Mag p28-9+ Je 11 '67
Why the Newhouse touch is golden; newspaper magnate draws profits. Bsns W p 138 Mr 11 '67
See also
American newspaper publishers association
Catholic press
Hearst corporation
Negro press
also names of newspapers, e.g. San Francisco chronicle
also subhead Newspapers under names of cities, e.g. Philadelphia—Newspapers

Foreign language press

See also
El Diario-la Prensa
Jewish daily forward

Vietnam (Republic)

Vietnam's not-so-free press. R. Coffey. il Sat R 50:122-3+ O 14 '67

NEWSPAPERS, Publishing of. See Newspaper publishing

NEWSPAPERS, Student. See College and student journalism

NEWSPAPERS and politics
Artillery of the press: its influence on American foreign policy, by J. Reston. Review Nat R 19:530-1 My 16 '67. N. Freeman
Choosing sides; newspapers' attitudes to Negro candidates. il Newsweek 70:94 N 20 '67
Doubts about Vietnam; editorial policies. Newsweek 70:96 O 23 '67
Editorial unease; shift in support of newspapers for President Johnson's policies in Viet Nam. il Time 90:57 O 20 '67
Pearson vs. Reagan; editors wonder about limits of libel. Newsweek 70:88 N 27 '67
Tailored press; R. Reagan's influence on California papers. Nation 205:676 D 25 '67

Anecdotes, facetiae, satire, etc.

Very special edition of The New York times; ed. by C. H. Simonds. il Nat R 19:580-5 My 30 '67

NEWSREELS
Change of screens. il Time 90:35 D 29 '67
Last reel. il Newsweek 71:53 Ja 1 '68

NEWSWEEK (periodical)
Impossible ideal. S. J. Adamo. America 117:359-60 S 30 '67

NEWSWRITERS. See Reporters and reporting

NEWTON, Huey P.
Call of the Black Panthers. S. Stern. il por N Y Times Mag p 10-11+ Ag 6 '67

NEWTON, Sir Isaac
Calculus in high school. Sci N 91:246 Mr 11 '67

NEWTON, Ivor
At the piano; excerpts. Opera N 31:6-7 Je 10 '67

NEWTON, Mass.

Education

Junior high that's like a college; Meadowbrook school. J. Kozol. il N Y Times Mag p32-3+ O 29 '67; Discussion. p24+ N 19 '67

NEWTON'S rings. See Interference (light)

NEWTS
Newts: sun-compass orientation. H. F. Landreth and D. E. Ferguson. bibliog il Science 158:1459-61 D 15 '67

NEYMAN, Jerzy
R. A. Fisher, 1890-1962: an appreciation; address, December 29, 1966. bibliog Science 156:1456-60 Je 16 '67

NEZ Percé Indians
Graves and grizzlies; excerpt from Tough trip through paradise; ed. by B. H. Stein. A. Garcia. il Am Heritage 18:36-9+ Je '67

NGORONGORO CRATER. See National parks and reserves—Tanzania

NGUYEN-al-Quoc. See Ho-chi-Minh

NGUYEN-cao-Ky
Blood on the stars. Newsweek 70:45-6 Jl 17 '67
Flying young man on the Saigon trapeze. K. Beech. il por Read Digest 91:75-9 Jl '67
Ky figure. Newsweek 69:38 Ap 3 '67
Ky stages a coup; Australian visit. il por Newsweek 69:44 Ja 30 '67
Ky stole the show. Nation 204:418 Ap 3 '67
Ky v Buddhists, round two. Tran-van-Dinh. New Repub 156:15-19 My 13 '67
Letter from Saigon (cont) R. Shaplen. New Yorker 43:149-54+ O 7 '67
Low Ky; dismissal of General Co. il por Time 89:32 F 3 '67
Peace moves next in Vietnam? W. S. Merick. il por U S News 63:38-40 S 18 '67
Report; Ky factor; abandoned quest for presidency. Atlan 220:20+ S '67
Thieu victory; divided reaction. il por Sr Schol 91:30+ S 28 '67
Visit Down Under. il por Time 89:33-4 Ja 27 '67
We put him in; J. W. Fulbright's opinion. K. Crawford. Newsweek 69:42 F 6 '67

NGUYEN-chi-Thanh
Wanted: a new commissar. Time 90:21 Jl 14 '67

NGUYEN-duc-Thang
Hatchet man. por Newsweek 70:49 Ag 28 '67

NGUYEN-huu-Co
Cleanup time. Newsweek 69:44 F 6 '67
Low Ky. il por Time 89:32 F 3 '67

NGUYEN-van-Be
Nonheroic non-death. il por Time 90:21 Jl 28 '67

NGUYEN-van-Sam
Vietcong cadre of terror. D. Moser. il Life 64:19-29 Ja 12 '68

NGUYEN-van-Tao
Public sector goes to pot in Saigon; or At sea in a fuming bus; excerpt. Nat R 19: 1006 S 19 '67

NGUYEN-van-Thieu
New president of South Vietnam speaks out; interview, ed. by W. S. Merick. por U S News 63:32-4 O 30 '67
Revealing highlights from two interviews with enemy leaders; ed. by L. Lockwood. Life 62: 44C Ap 7 '67
Sacrifices in Viet-Nam marked in Memorial day messages; May 30, 1967. Dept State Bul 56:917 Je 19 '67

about

Deal on peace talks? por U S News 63:22 O 23 '67
Ky v Buddhists, round two. Tran-van-Dinh. New Repub 156:17-18 My 13 '67
Letter from Saigon. R. Shaplen. New Yorker 43:149-54+ O 7 '67
Peace moves next in Vietnam? W. S. Merick. il por U S News 63:38-40 S 18 '67
Thieu sworn in. il por Sr Schol 91:22 N 16 '67
Thieu victory; divided reaction. il por Sr Schol 91:30+ S 28 '67
Vietnam makes ready for another beginning; with editorial comment. il por Bsns W p42-3, 164 O 28 '67
Vote for the future. il pors Time 90:28-32 S 15 '67

NHAT Hanh
Hiroshima, Vietnam: sisters in sorrow. B. Reynolds. Christian Cent 84:636-8 My 10 '67
Voice for the voiceless. Christian Cent 85:4 Ja 3 '68

NIAGARA FALLS
U.S, Canada request IJC study of American Falls at Niagara; letter, March 31, 1967. G. S. Springsteen. Dept State Bul 56:634-5 Ap 17 '67

NICARAGUA
See also
Guerrillas—Nicaragua

History

Mr Coolidge's jungle war. R. O'Connor. il Am Heritage 19:36-9+ D '67
Sandino affair, by N. Macaulay. Review
Newsweek 69:94-5 Mr 6 '67. P. D. Zimmerman

Politics and government

Challenge to a birthright. il Time 89:34 F 3 '67
Fathers and sons; Aguero's futile power play. il Newsweek 69:60-1 F 6 '67
Friendship's toll. Newsweek 69:56 F 13 '67
One-family rule for thirty-five years; will it continue? il U S News 62:14 F 6 '67
One more Somoza. M. Smith. il Life 62:82 Ap 28 '67
Where a dynasty was extended, but—. U S News 62:22 F 20 '67

NICARAGUAN poets. See Poets, Nicaraguan

NICHOLAS II, emperor of Russia
See also
Romanov, House of

NICHOLAS, George
Protect your family against colds. Suc Farm 65:103+ F '67

NICHOLS, Benjamin David
Taps, bugs & spies: anything to get Hoffa. F. J. Cook. il Nation 204:230-6 F 20 '67

NICHOLS, Bud. See Nichols, B. D.

NICHOLS, Byron John
Automotive safety; address, June 5, 1967. Vital Speeches 33:628-31 Ag 1 '67

NICHOLS, Charles W. and Koelle, G. B.
Acetylcholinesterase: method for demonstration in amacrine cells of rabbit retina. bibliog Science 155:477-8 Ja 27 '67

NICHOLS, Christopher
R&G: a minority report. Nat R 19:1393-5 D 12 '67

NICHOLS, G. Jr
Calcified tissues. Science 157:961-2 Ag 25 '67

NICHOLS, Harvey
Pollen diagrams from sub-Arctic central Canada. bibliog Science 155:1665-8 Mr 31 '67

NICHOLS, Herbie
Four lives in the bebop business, by A. B. Spellman. Review
Nation 204:378-9 Mr 20 '67. B. Kremen

NICHOLS, Jeannette
Bicycle; poem. Harper 236:60 Ja '68
Birthday in the house of the poor; poem. Atlan 219:94 Mr '67

Imaginary companion; poem. Sat R 50:47 My 6 '67
Poem for David 8 & open. Sat R 50:85 F 25 '67
Something about to happen; poem. Sat R 50:88 Mr 11 '67
To my nephew headed everywhere; poem. Sat R 50:97 My 13 '67

NICHOLS, John R. and Hsiao, Sigmund
Addiction liability of albino rats; breeding for quantitative differences in morphine drinking. bibliog Science 157:561-3 Ag 4 '67

NICHOLS, Mike
Whatever happened to Elaine May? T. Thompson. il por Life 63:54-54B Jl 28 '67

NICHOLS, Penny
Song too big for words. J. Kornbluth. il pors Look 31:90+ N 28 '67

NICHOLS, Peter
Day in the death of Joe Egg. Criticism
Life il 63:106+ N 24 '67
New Yorker 43:84 Ag 19 '67
Vogue 150:70 O 15 '67
Making comedy out of a family tragedy; with report by D. Doust. il pors Life 63: 106+ N 24 '67

NICHOLS, Roy F.
History in a self-governing culture; address, December 29, 1966. Am Hist R 72:411-24 Ja '67

NICHOLS, William I.
Sex; address, March 27, 1967. Vital Speeches 33:445-8 My 1 '67

NICHOLSON, Don
What makes Nicholson run. J. Thawley. il pors Hot Rod 20:58-61 F '67

NICHOLSON, Ellen
Song of my heart. Horn Bk 43:515 Ag '67

NICHOLSON, H. Page
Pesticide pollution control. bibliog Science 158:871-6 N 17 '67

NICHOLSON, Jessie
Haunted bookshop; drama. Plays 27:55-64 N '67

NICHOLSON, Margaret
Author's and editor's responsibility; excerpts from A practical style guide for authors and editors. Pub W 191:28-30 Ap 17 '67

NICHOLSON, Thomas D.
Sky reporter. See issues of Natural history incorporating Nature magazine

NICK, Inocêncio da Costa. See Mestre Noza

NICKEL
See also
International nickel company of Canada

NICKEL mines and mining
Nickel squabble rocks Pacific isle; New Caledonia's revolt against French giant's monopoly. il Bsns W p86-8+ Mr 25 '67

NICKERSON, Clarence H.
Regional report. Home Gard 54:51-2 Je '67

NICKERSON, Dorothy M.
Squirrel stopper. Horticulture 45:47 F '67

NICKERSON, Kerry Ann
Seasons of the sea; poem. Horn Bk 43:516 Ag '67

NICKLAUS, Jack
Golf. See issues of Sports illustrated
Instead of open terror, a subtle pleasure. Sports Illus 26:59-62+ Je 12 '67
What's wrong with Nicklaus? pors Sports Illus 27:20-2+ Jl 3 '67

about

Calm before the storm. il por Newsweek 69:91 F 6 '67
Different game. il por Time 90:70 N 10 '67
Jack delivers the crusher. A. Wright. il Sports Illus 26:22-7 Je 26 '67
New year's resolution; Bing Crosby national. por Time 89:60 F 3 '67
Old story but a new Jack. A. Wright. il por Sports Illus 26:16-17 Ja 30 '67
One man's game. il Time 89:54 Je 30 '67
Sporting scene. H. W. Wind. New Yorker 43:142+ Ap 29; 56-8+ Jl 8 '67

NICOLAEFF, Ariadne
(tr) See Arbuzov, A. N. Promise

NICOLL, G. Douglas
Admissions and the private college. Sch & Soc 95:148-9 Mr 4 '67

NICOLSON, Sir Harold
Books. N. Bliven. New Yorker 43:170+ S 9 '67
Curious vanity of a latter-day Pepys. A. Cooke. Life 62:6 Je 30 '67
Diaries and letters of Harold Nicolson, 1930-1939, ed. by N. Nicolson. Review
Nat R 19:480-2 My 2 '67. S. Leslie
Gents of the disestablishment. G. Dangerfield. Nation 204:437 Ap 3 '67

NICOLSON, Sir Harold—*Continued*
Harold Nicolson: the war years 1939-1945, ed. by N. Nicolson. Review
  Sat R por 50:27-8 Je 17 '67. J. Lukacs
Memory lane. S. Kauffmann. New Repub 156: 20+ Je 17 '67
Nicolson II: diarist triumphant. por Time 89: 98+ Je 23 '67
NICOTIANA
Tobaccos that satisfy. E. W. Cox. il Horticulture 45:42-3+ O '67
NICOTINAMIDE adenine dinucleotide. See Diphosphopyridine nucleotide
NIDDRIE, David L.
South Africa. bibliog Focus 17:1-6 Je '67
NIDEN, Albert H.
Bronchiolar and large alveolar cell in pulmonary phospholipid metabolism. bibliog Science 158:1323-4 D 8 '67
NIDETCH, Jean
Weight watchers cook book; excerpts. Ladies Home J 84:114-15+ Ap; 128 My '67

about
Changing lost pounds into dollars. il por Bsns W p 106+ Mr 4 '67
NIEBUHR, Reinhold
Vietnam: study in ironies. New Repub 156: 11-12 Je 24 '67

about
Reinhold Niebuhr plays Hamlet. J. P. Speer. Christian Cent 84:336-9 Mr 15 '67; Discussion. 84:591-2 My 3 '67
NIEBURG, H. L.
JPL story. Bul Atomic Sci 22:35-8 O '66; 23:28 F '67
R&D and the contract state; throwing away the yardstick; excerpt from Science, stagnation, and the contract state. Bul Atomic Sci 22:20-4 Mr '66; 23:29 F '67
NIEDECKER, Lorine
Four poems. Poetry 111:159-60 D '67
NIEHANS, Ken. See Wilson, T. C. jt. auth.
NIELSEN, A. C. company
Nielsen rating for a box of spaghetti. D. D. Trainer. il N Y Times Mag p 12-13+ Jl 30 '67
NIELSEN, Axel V.
Ejnar Hertzsprung, measurer of stars. Sky & Tel 35:4-6 Ja '68
NIELSEN, Carl
Nielsen symphonies. B. Jacobson. por Hi Fi 17:54-6 Ap '67
NIELSEN, Jon
Portfolio of drawings of Vietnam. pors Am Artist 31:58-63 Ap '67
NIELSEN rating system. See Television broadcasting—Program rating
NIEMEYER, Oscar
Two from the first team. il Time 90:90-3 D 8 '67
NIEMÖLLER, Martin
Niemoeller reports on Vietnam; interview, ed. by R. Wuliger. Christian Cent 84:215-16 F 15 '67
NIÉPCE, Janine
Photography family. il U S Camera 30:54-5 O '67
NIERLICH, Donald P.
Radioisotope uptake as a measure of synthesis of messenger RNA. bibliog Science 158:1186-8 D 1 '67
NIETZSCHE, Friedrich Wilhelm
Moral in an amoral world. E. Weber. por Sat R 50:34-5 Ag 5 '67
Musical events; performance of Delius' Mass of life based on Also sprach Zarathustra. W. Sargeant. New Yorker 42:153-4+ F 11 '67
Prophet of modernity. S. J. Tonsor. Nat R 20:41-3 Ja 16 '68
NIGER RIVER
Days of the Onitsha ferry. R. E. Morsberger. il Natur Hist 76:62-3+ Ap '67
NIGERIA
Tale of two nations; work to recreate basic science organizations. C. Weiss, jr Sci N 91:460-1 My 13 '67
  See also
Christians in Nigeria
Petroleum—Nigeria

Economic policy
Planning without facts, by W. F. Stolper. Review
  Bul Atomic Sci 23:53-4 Je '67. C. W. Kontos

Industries
  See also
Petroleum—Nigeria

Native races
Africa's shattered showcase: tribal hatreds wreck a nation. il U S News 62:76-7 My 8 '67
Bloody war in the showplace of black Africa; rebellion of Ibos. A. J. Meyers. il U S News 63:56-8 N 20 '67
Ibos go it alone. L. Garrison. il N Y Times Mag p30-2+ Je 11 '67
Nigeria. S. Thompson. il Atlan 219:16+ Ap '67
Preserving unity by staying apart. il Time 89:36 Ja 27 '67
Self-defeating civil war in Nigeria. C. Sterling. il Reporter 37:23-4+ Ag 10 '67

Politics and government
Africa in black and white; concerning Ian Brook's book One-eyed man is king. C. Miller. Sat R 50:30+ Mr 25 '67
Africa's shattered showcase: tribal hatreds wreck a nation. il U S News 62:76-7 My 8 '67
Anybody's war. Time 90:29-30 Ag 18 '67
Biafra libre? E. Huxley. Nat R 19:896+ Ag 22 '67
Birth of a nation? eastern Nigerian independence. il Newsweek 69:48+ Je 12 '67
Bloody confusion. Newsweek 70:45-6 Ag 7 '67
Bloody escalation; civil war. P. Webb. il Newsweek 71:37-8 Ja 8 '68
Bloody war in the showplace of black Africa. A. J. Meyers. il U S News 63:56-8 N 20 '67
Breakup in Nigeria; roots of the civil war. S. Meisler. il Nation 205:334-6 O 9 '67
Case of nerves, federal government's reaction to Biafran air threat. il Newsweek 70:45-6 S 11 '67
Civil war. il Time 90:19 Jl 14 '67
Declaration of independence; eastern Nigeria secedes. il Time 89:45 Je 9 '67
Determined Ibos. il Time 89:32 Ap 7 '67
Drums of defeat. il Time 90:42 O 6 '67
Fighting in the mist. il Time 90:29 Jl 28 '67
Ibos go it alone. L. Garrison. il N Y Times Mag p30-2+ Je 11 '67
Last hope; civil war spreads. Newsweek 70: 41+ Ag 28 '67
Little country that won't give up; Biafra. Time 90:36-7 D 8 '67
Nigeria. S. Thompson. il Atlan 219:16+ Ap '67
Nigeria in crisis. W. A. E. Skurnik. Cur Hist 52:142-8+ Mr '67
Nigeria vs. Biafra. il Newsweek 70:36 Jl 17 '67
Nigerian breakaway. Nat R 19:625 Je 13 '67
Nigeria's civil war. R. W. Howe. New Repub 157:16 S 16 '67
No place to go. Newsweek 70:68 O 23 '67
One down one to go. Time 90:28 Jl 21 '67
Peace hopes dim. il Sr Schol 91:5-6 O 12 '67
Preserving unity by staying apart. il Time 89:36 Ja 27 '67
Razor's edge; Gowon vows to crush secessionist movement. il Newsweek 69:48-9 Je 26 '67
Right sort of chaps. il Newsweek 70:35+ Jl 24 '67
Search for a sterile scalpel; loss of midwestern region. il Time 90:20-1 S 1 '67
Self-defeating civil war in Nigeria. C. Sterling il Reporter 37:23-4+ Ag 10 '67
Setting sun; federal government gaining upper hand. il Newsweek 70:41-2 O 9 '67
Time for slaughter. il Newsweek 70:38+ Jl 31 '67
Waiting for a miracle; Eastern Region secession threat. J. Barnes. il Newsweek 69:66+ Mr 27 '67
Where turmoil is rising in troubled black Africa; secessionist Republic of Biafra, or eastern region. il U S News 62:6+ Je 12 '67

Race problems
Breakup in Nigeria; roots of the civil war. S. Meisler. il Nation 205:334-6 O 9 '67
NIGERIA and the United States
Technicolored Christian; as Nigerian sees the American. E. G. Dalbey, jr. Christian Cent 84:1158-60 S 13 '67
NIGGERLOVERS; drama. See Tabori, G.
NIGHT airglow. See Airglow
NIGHT animals. See Animals—Habits and behavior
NIGHT blindness. See Night vision
NIGHT boating. See Boats and boating
NIGHT business. See Business hours
NIGHT club dancers. See Dancers
NIGHT clubs
Babes in a turned-on toyland: Rock Flow in East Village. T. Prideaux. Life 62:17 Ap 14 '67

NIGHT clubs—*Continued*
Chicago after dark. G. P. Gates. il Holiday 41:70-3+ Mr '67
Hollywood's night shift; private discothèque clubs. il Newsweek 70:98 O 16 '67
Judy at the Electric circus. J. Brin. il Dance Mag 41:56-7 O '67
Non-toxic psychedelia for squares: Electric circus; New York city discothèque. J. Stickney. Life 63:12 Ag 11 '67
Swinging Europe: in and way-out; survey by British European airways personnel. M. Finn. il Travel 127:30-6 F '67
Upstairs at El Morocco. C. H. McBride. il Esquire 67:116-17 Ap '67
NIGHT driving, Automobile. See Automobile driving
NIGHT face up; story. See Cortázar, J.
NIGHT flight; opera. See Dallapiccola, L.
NIGHT flying. See Aviation—Night flying
NIGHT of the full moon; story. See Kurtz, M. R.
NIGHT vision
Is your night driving in focus? W. J. Toth. Am Home 70:31+ S '67
What sun glare can do to your driving. J. Berry. il Pop Mech 128:78-80+ Jl '67
NIGHTCLUBS. See Night clubs
NIGHTGLOW. See Airglow
NIGHTINGALE, Florence
Tough angel of the battlefield. J. H. Winchester. il Todays Health 45:30-3+ My '67
NIGHTMARES. See Dreams
NIHILISM (philosophy)
Can we survive nihilism? J. Milton's Satan and A. Camus's Sisyphus. T. Merton. Sat R 50:16-19 Ap 15 '67
NIKE-X. See Guided missiles—Defenses
NIKOLAEVA, Alenushka
Study of a space child. J. Lear. il pors Sat R 50:72-3 D 2 '67
NIKOLAIS, Alwin
Imago by Alwin Nikolais; Henry street settlement playhouse. M. Marks. Dance Mag 41:34 Ap '67
Lurch, lean, walk, waddle. J. Kroll. il por Newsweek 69:97 Ap 3 '67
NIKOLAIS, Alwin, dance company. See Dance companies
NILSSON, Lennart
Corridors of the heart; photographs. Life 64: 22-31 Ja 19 '68
about
Fantastic, even frightening scene. L. Wainwright. por Life 64:3 Ja 19 '68
Must he share technique? J. Deschin. il Pop Phot 60:16+ My '67
NIMBUS (satellite) See Artificial satellites—Meteorological applications
NIMMANHEMINDA, Sukich
Chinese threat to world order; address, April 8, 1967. Ann Am Acad 372:59-63 Jl '67
NIMS, John Frederick
D.O.M., A.D. 2167; A.D. 2267; poems. Sat R 50:31 Ap 15 '67
Embroidery at Bayeux; poem. Nation 204:662 My 22 '67
Girl marcher; poem. Sat R 50:69 My 20 '67
Parting; poem. Nation 204:278 F 27 '67
Short poems. Atlan 219:101 My '67
NIN, Anaïs
Id of Dostoevsky. Sat R 50:35+ Je 10 '67
about
Sponge for the world's tears. A. Balakian. Sat R 50:38 Jl 22 '67
NINA of Ashkelon; story. See Amichai, Y.
NINETEEN hundred and eighty
Eight questions for 1968. A. Hacker. Sat R 51:102-3 Ja 6 '68
NINETEEN hundred and eighty-nine
Future of education: the class of 1989. M. McLuhan and G. B. Leonard. il Look 31: 23-5 F 21 '67
NINETEEN hundred and ninety
Wondrous world of 1990; outlook for young people. il U S News 62:62-6 Ja 30 '67
NINETEEN hundred and ninety-seven
David B. Elsendrath's 1997. D. B. Elsendrath. il Pop Phot 60:56+ Je '67
NINETEEN hundred and seventies
What the 1970's will bring. il Changing T 22:6-16 Ja '68
When business really will boom in U.S. il U S News 62:42-6 F 20 '67
NINETEEN hundred and seventy-five
Nineteen seventy-five; crucial year. G. Lichtheim. Commentary 44:62-7 Jl '67

NINETEEN hundred and sixty-eight
Looking ahead through '68: what the trends show. il U S News 64:19-20 Ja 8 '68
1968: no easy answers. Bsns W p 100 D 30 '67
NINETEEN hundred and sixty-seven
As the year ends... Am City 82:6 D '67
Business in 1967, the nervous year. Time 90: 60-1 D 29 '67
Man-made misery and God's promise. Christian Cent 84:1643-5 D 27 '67
Man of the year; L. Johnson. il Time 91: 13-14+ Ja 5 '68
Progress report 1967. il Ebony 23:118-22 Ja '68
Season gone but not forgotten; summer of 1967. il Newsweek 70:19-20 S 11 '67
Seventh annual dubious achievement awards for 1967. il Esquire 69:49-55 Ja '68
Some cartoons of 1967. Nation 206:14-15 Ja 1 '68
Thoughts on a year of strife and trial. B. L. Masse. America 117:733 D 16 '67
NINETEEN hundred and sixty-six
Toughest best year ever. H. B. Meyers. Fortune 75:170-3+ Je 15 '67
Year that was; address, December 28, 1966. F. R. McKnight. Vital Speeches 33:282-5 F 15 '67
NINETEEN hundred and twenties
Babbitts & bohemians, by E. Stevenson. Review
Atlan il 220:110-13 N '67. L. Kronenberger
John Held's mad world. R. Lynes. il Harper 235:24+ N '67
Return to paradise. D. Wakefield. Atlan 219: 102-4+ F '67
NINETY day mistress; drama. See Coyle, J. J.
NINETY-nines International convention. See Aviation conferences
NININGER, H. H. and Huss, G. I.
Tektites that were partially plastic after completion of surface sculpturing. bibliog Science 157:61-2 Jl 7 '67
NININGERITE. See Sulfides
NIPPON electric company. See Electronic apparatus industry and trade—Japan
NIRENBERG, Marshall W.
Will society be prepared? excerpts from address. Science 157:633 Ag 11 '67
NIRENSKA, Pola
How to win friends and influence dancers. por Dance Mag 41:28-9+ Je '67
NISEI. See Japanese Americans
NISONOFF, Alfred, and others
Antibodies to rabbit cytochrome c arising in rabbits. bibliog Science 155:1273-5 Mr 10 '67
NISTENDIRK, Verna
Florida: not all sunshine. por Library J 92: 1898-900 My 15 '67
NITRATES
Nitrate ions: potentiation of increased permeability to sugar associated with muscle contraction. J. O. Holloszy and H. T. Narahara. bibliog il Science 155:573-5 F 3 '67
NITROGEN
Fixation
Biological nitrogen fixation; report on colloquium. W. S. Silver. Science 157:100-2 Jl 7 '67
Nitrogen-fixing plants. W. D. P. Stewart. bibliog il Science 158:1426-32 D 15 '67
NITROGEN, Liquid
Liquid nitrogen used to cut danger from hypergolics. K. Voss. il Tech W 20:30 Je 12 '67
NITROSO rubber. See Rubber, Artificial
NITROUS oxide
Parnassus revisited; letter. A. Cherkin. Science 155:266+ Ja 20 '67
NITZE, Paul Henry
New no. 2. il por Newsweek 69:37 Je 19 '67
New no. 2. por Time 89:17 Je 23 '67
NIVEN, Paul
(ed) See Rusk, D. Conversation with Dean Rusk
NIVOLA, Costantino
Poet in the piazza. il Arch Forum 127:70-5 O '67
NIX, Lucile
Summer reading. PTA Mag 61:22-6 Je '67
NIXON, Julie
That's the ticket. il pors Newsweek 70:31 D 11 '67
NIXON, Richard Milhous
Asia after Vietnam. For Affairs 46:111-25 O '67; Same. por U S News 63:86-91 O 23 '67
Nixon tells how '68 race stands; interview. por U S News 63:74-80 N 20 '67

NIXON, Richard Milhous—*Continued*
Richard Nixon and the locked door; interview, ed. by S. Alsop. Sat Eve Post 240:18 D 2 '67
Unforgettable John Foster Dulles. Read Digest 91:99-104 Jl '67
What has happened to America? Read Digest 91:49-54 O '67

about

Alas, poor Nixon. Nation 205:613 D 11 '67
Around the world, a block away. il por Time 89:29-30 My 19 '67
Crisis seven. J. J. Kilpatrick. il por Nat R 19:1263-74 N 14 '67
Dab of powder, a dab of paint. G. Ace. Sat R 50:6 D 16 '67
Dick's lucky palm. Time 89:15 Je 2 '67
For Nixon, a rosier time in Latin America this trip. il por U S News 62:20 My 22 '67
Forever amber. il por Newsweek 69:31-2 Mr 27 '67
How Nixon plans to bring it off. A. J. Reichley. il por Fortune 76:124-7+ D '67
Letter from Washington. R. H. Rovere. New Yorker 43:153-60 Ap 22 '67
Look beyond the war. R. Moley. Newsweek 70:108 N 27 '67
Men around Nixon. N. B. Freeman. Nat R 19:1118-19+ O 17 '67
Morning line. Newsweek 69:34 Ap 3 '67
My generation is missing. M. Greenfield. Reporter 36:35-6 My 4 '67
Nixon for president in '68? J. Witcover. il pors Sat Eve Post 240:93-7 F 25 '67
Nixon: the reentry program. J. Witcover. New Repub 156:11-12 Je 17 '67
Nixon vs. Rockefeller: choice shaping up. il por U S News 64:38-40 Ja 1 '68
Not right now, please. Nat R 19:178+ F 21 '67
On the rim. Time 89:16 Mr 24 '67
Other fellows. il por Newsweek 71:21 Ja 22 '68
Philosophy of office and the ache of ambition. H. Sidey. por Life 63:30 N 3 '67
Republican choice: now it's Nixon over Romney. il por U S News 62:14 F 20 '67
Richard Nixon's return engagement. G. A. Harrison. New Repub 157:11-12 N 4 '67
Romney and Nixon: each makes gains in polls. il por U S News 63:12-13 Ag 28 '67
See Dick run. il por Newsweek 70:17-18 D 25 '67
War, welfare and Richard Nixon. Nations Bsns 55:61-2+ N '67
What keeps Nixon running; excerpts from The Republican establishment. S. Hess and D. S. Broder. il Harper 235:56-8+ Ag '67

NIZER, Louis
Blacklisted! story of J. H. Faulk; condensation of The jury returns. por Read Digest 90:201-4+ Mr '67
Trial by headline. McCalls 94:93+ F '67

NKOSI, Lewis
Forbidden dialogue. por UNESCO Courier 20:20-2 Mr '67

NKRUMAH, Kwame
Guest or prisoner? Nkrumah a millionaire, but—. por U S News 62:16 Ja 30 '67
Rise and fall of Kwame Nkrumah, by H. L. Bretton. Review
Nation 204:309-11 Mr 6 '67, C. C. O'Brien
Reporter 36:50-2 Ap 6 '67, T. Szamuely
Sat R 50:42 F 25 '67, J. H. Plumb

Nō (Japanese drama and theater)
Getting to know the Noh. N. Uenishi. Mlle 66:144-5+ N '67

NO boy. I'm a girl! story. See Rieth, M.

NO-pest strip insecticide. See Insecticides

NOAH, Harold J. and Blandy, Richard
Education and manpower. Wilson Lib Bul 41:814-19 Ap '67

NOBEL, Alfred Bernhard
Nobel and his prizes. F. C. Livingstone. por Sci N 92:474 N 11 '67

NOBEL prizes
Good beginning; eye cartographers. il Time 90:56 O 27 '67
Nobel and his prizes. F. C. Livingstone. Sci N 92:474 N 11 '67
Nobel prize: three named for medicine, physiology award. J. E. Dowling; F. Ratliff. il Science 158:468-73 O 27 '67
Nobel prize winners; physiology, medicine award. il Sci N 92:437-9 N 4 '67
Nobel prizes. Sci Am 217:48-9 D '67
Nobel prizes: four named for international award. V. F. Weisskopf; H. Eyring; E. M. Eyring. il Science 158:745-8 N 10 '67
Nobel work; prize in physiology and medicine. il Newsweek 70:82-3 O 30 '67
Nobelists in physics and chemistry. il Sci N 92:463-5 N 11 '67

Quick and the cosmic; prizes in physics and chemistry. Newsweek 70:106+ N 13 '67
Sociology of the Nobel prizes. H. Zuckerman. il Sci Am 217:25-33 bibliog(p 154) N '67
Unpredictable Nobel; laureates in physics and chemistry. Time 90:67 N 10 '67
See also
Huggins, C. B.

NOBELIUM
Discovery, undiscovery, rediscovery. il Sci N 92:274-5 S 16 '67

NOBILETIN. See Growth inhibiting substances (fungi)

NOBILITY
See also
Great Britain—Nobility

NOBLE, Hubert C.
British universities confront a dilemma. Christain Cent 84:701 My 24 '67

NOBLE, Jeremy
Monteverdi's Poppea, for the first time near perfectly realized. Hi Fi 17:70-1 My '67
Music in ancient cities, all eloquence and delight. Hi Fi 17:106-7 Ja '67
Third International Webern festival. Hi Fi 17:MA19 Ja '67

NOBLE, Mary
Regional report. Home Gard 54:74 My '67

NOBLE, Ray
Best of the dance bands. N. McCaffrey. Nat R 19:1082-5 O 3 '67

NOBLE metals. See Metals

NOBLETT, Richard A.
New direction. Flying 80:78-80 Je '67

NOCTILUCENT clouds. See Clouds

NODELMAN, Sheldon
Gold age bronze. Art N 66:26-9 D '67

NODULES (geology) See Concretions

NOE, Courtney
Ride round the rivers. Travel 128:38-41 Ag '67

NOEL, Lois Jones Pierre-. See Pierre-Noel, L. J.

NOEL-BAKER, Philip John
Science and disarmament. bibliog f por UNESCO Courier 20:10-21+ Ag '67

NOEL HUME, Ivor
Rhenish gray stonewares in colonial America. Antiques 92:349-53 S '67

NOETHER, Emiliana P.
(comp) Articles and other books received; Italy. See issues of American historical review

NOGGLE, G. R. See Joshi, P. C. jt. auth.

NOGUCHI, Isamu
Interview, ed. by A. Fatt. por Dance Mag 41:44-5 F '67

NOH. See Nō (Japanese drama and theater)

NOISE
All those noises that assail us. Life 62:4 Ja 27 '67
Down with decibels! O. Schenker-Sprüngli. il UNESCO Courier 20:4-7 Jl '67
It's getting noisier. C. Dreher. il Nation 205:238-42 S 18 '67
See also
Apartment houses—Noise

Physiological effects

Noise and health. G. Lehmann. il UNESCO Courier 20:26-7+ Jl '67
Noise: nuisance or health hazard? il Good H 165:199 O '67
Noise pollution: a growing menace. M. Brower. Sat R 50:17-19 My 27 '67
Noise takes toll, say experts. Todays Health 45:87 O '67
That noise you hear may be pollution; scientists fighting noise pollution. il Bsns W p40-1 Ap 22 '67

Psychological effects

Jet noise is getting awful. R. Sherrill. il N Y Times Mag p24-5+ Ja 14 '68
Noise and health. G. Lehmann. il UNESCO Courier 20:26-7+ Jl '67

NOISE control
It's getting noisier. C. Dreher. il Nation 205:238-42 S 18 '67
Noise control in architecture: more engineering than art. il Arch Rec 142:193-203 O '67
Noise pollution: a growing menace. M. Brower. Sat R 50:17-19 My 27 '67
Noise pollution; symposium. bibliog il UNESCO Courier 20:4-31 Jl '67

Laws and legislation

Noise pollution: a growing menace; Kupferman bill; New York city code proposals. M. Brower. Sat R 50:18-19 My 27 '67

NOISE control—*Continued*
Terminology
Glossary of noise control terms. Arch Rec 142:204 O '67
NOISE prevention. See Noise control
NOISE suppressors. See Sound suppressors
NOLAN, Brian
Darling writer. S. Maloff. Newsweek 71: 58+ Ja 1 '68
NOLAN, Martin F.
Belated effort to save our cities. Reporter 37:16-21 D 28 '67
Louise Day Hicks gets out the vote. Reporter 37:22-4 O 19 '67
Marxisms. Reporter 37:61-2 Jl 13 '67
Muskie of Maine. Reporter 37:44-6 Jl 13 '67
One man, one vote, one dollar. Reporter 36:28-9 My 4 '67
Primary primary. Reporter 37:32-4+ S 7 '67
Walter Heller's federalist papers. Reporter 36:13-17 Je 1 '67
NOLAN, Paul T.
Whole city's down below; drama. Plays 27: 12-22 D '67
NOLAND, Kenneth
Art; exhibition at the Emmerich gallery. M. Kozloff. Nation 205:668 D 18 '67
Sky-colored popsicle. A. Brunelle. il por Art N 66:42-3+ N '67
NOLAND company
Rare blending of carrot and stick; annual meeting of the nation's largest independent distributor of plumbing and heating equipment. il Bsns W p 132+ Mr 4 '67
NOLDE, Emil
Emil Nolde's unpainted pictures. il por Horizon 9:64-5 Sum '67
Fulfilling fear; exhibition at Manhattan's Knoedler gallery. il Time 89:76-7 Mr 17 '67
Nolde: art without audience. J. Gollin. il por Art N 65:48-9+ F '67
NOLEN, Truly
Truly Nolen: exterminator of classics? R. A. Latimer. il por Motor T 19:84-6+ My '67
NOLL, Bink
October: dead steer; poem. Nation 205:190 S 4 '67
To the god Morpheus; poem. Yale R 56:550 Je '67
NOLTE, Richard
New waterbird for Egypt: a robot shadoof. J. Lear. il por Sat R 50:49-50 Je 3 '67
NOMAD, Max, pseud.
Heritage of October. Sat R 50:32-5 D 9 '67
They tried to topple the tsar. Sat R 40:38-9+ My 13 '67
NOMADISM
See also
Gipsies
NOMADS
See also
Mongols
NOMINATIONS for office
Hitched to LBJ? case for not renominating L. B. Johnson. New Repub 157:1+ S 30 '67
How Nixon plans to bring it off; campaign for 1968 nomination. A. J. Reichley. il Fortune 76:124-7+ D '67
There ought never to be another presidential nominating convention; excerpts from letter, February 5, 1913. W. Wilson. U S News 63: 124 O 23 '67
NONALIGNMENT. See Neutrality
NONCOMMERCIAL television. See Television broadcasting. Noncommercial
NON-COMMISSIONED officers. See United States—Army—Non-commissioned officers
NONCONFORMITY. See Conformity; Individualism
NONCONFORMITY (religion) See Dissenters. Religious
NONDESTRUCTIVE testing. See Testing
NON-EUCLIDEAN geometry. See Geometry
NONFAT dry milk. See Milk. Dried
NONINTERVENTION. See Intervention
NON-MUSICAL phonograph records. See Phonograph records—Spoken records
NON-OBJECTIVE art. See Art. Abstract
NON-PROFESSIONAL instructional assistance. See Volunteer workers in education
NONPROFIT corporations. See Corporations. Nonprofit
NON-SELF governing territories. See Colonies
NONTE, George C. Jr
Amazing new kind of gun, it's not all hot air. Pop Mech 128:120-2+ O '67
NON-VIOLENCE. See Pacifism
NON-VIOLENT non-cooperation. See Passive resistance to government

NON-WAGE payments
Challenge of human aspirations. J. T. Hill, jr. Duns R 89:23-4+ Ja '67
Employers toot on the horn of plenty. il Bsns W p94+ Ja 28 '67
Fringe benefits, what they can cost. R. Levenson. il Am City 82:182-3 S '67
If pay keeps rising at 6 per cent a year; wages and fringes. il U S News 63:80-1 O 30 '67
Vacations with a premium. Bsns W p 17 Jl 1 '67
Value of fringe benefits. J. D. Bierman. Parents Mag 42:16+ Je '67
Wages and supplementary benefits in metropolitan areas. K. J. Hoffmann. il Mo Labor R 90:48-54 Je '67
See also
Sick leave
NON-WOVEN fabrics. See Textile fabrics
NOODLES
Try these six great noodle recipes, even a dessert! J. McCloskey. il Suc Farm 65:74-5 O '67
NOONAN, John T. Jr
Pope's conscience. Commonweal 85:559-60 F 17 '67
NORA; opera. See Mack, G.
NORDINE, Roy M.
Mist propagation. Horticulture 45:30-1 Jl '67
NORDSTROM, Ursula
Joyful challenge. Sat R 50:39-40 N 11 '67
NOREPINEPHRINE
Adenyl cyclase activity in rat pineal gland: effects of chronic denervation and norepinephrine. B. Weiss and E. Costa. bibliog il Science 156:1750-2 Je 30 '67
Increased turnover of cerebral norepinephrine during rebound of paradoxical sleep in the rat. J. F. Pujol and others. bibliog il Science 159:112-14 Ja 5 '68
Localization of the adrenergic feeding system in the rat diencephalon. D. A. Booth. bibliog il Science 158:515-17 O 27 '67
NORMAN, James
Exciting, yet comfortably intimate. House & Gard 131:126+ Ap '67
NORMAN, John C. and others
Antihemophilic factor release by perfused liver and spleen: relationship to hemophilia. bibliog Science 158:1060-1 N 24 '67
NORMAN, Leonard
Swazis prepare for the inde-pen-dance. Sat R 50:48+ S 30 '67
NORMAN, R. J. See Schapiro, S. jt. auth.
NORMAN furniture. See Furniture, French
NORODOM Sihanouk, king of Cambodia (abdicated 1955)
About, face! Newsweek 71:41 Ja 8 '68
He is the state. Newsweek 69:57 My 15 '67
How Peking doublecrosses a friend. il por U S News 62:26 Ap 24 '67
Letter from Cambodia (cont) R. Shaplen. New Yorker 43:66+ Ja 13 '68
Next, hot pursuit of the Communists? il por U S News 64:6 Ja 8 '68
Prince and US. D. G. Porter. Commonweal 87:442-3 Ja 12 '68
Very special tourist. il pors Time 90:40-1 N 17 '67
NORRIS, Dale M. and Baker, J. K.
Symbiosis: effects of a mutualistic fungus upon the growth and reproduction of xylebo us ferrugineus. bibliog Science 156: 1120-2 My 26 '67
NORRIS, Hoke
Final distance; story. Redbook 129:66-7 Je '67
NORRIS, Leslie
Water; poem. Atlan 220:41 Ag '67
Winter song; poem. Atlan 221:67 Ja '68
NORRIS, Louis William
It's the idea of the thing; address. December 5, 1966. bibliog f Vital Speeches 33:468-72 My 15 '67
NORRIS Industries, Incorporated. See Munitions works
NORRISH, Ronald George Wreyford
Defining sections of the chemical blur. por(p463) Sci N 92:464-5 N 11 '67
Nobel prizes; chemistry. H. Eyring and M. Eyring. por Science 158:746-8 N 10 '67
NORTH AFRICA. See Africa, North
NORTH AMERICA
Antiquities
Radiocarbon dating and archeology in North America. F. Johnson. bibliog Science 155: 165-9 Ja 13 '68
NORTH AMERICAN Indians. See Indians of North America

NORTH AMERICAN Rockwell corporation
Apollo: can do? technology and management improvements. il Newsweek 69:94 My 22 '67
Apollo contractor criticisms, fixes summarized for House committee; text of summary. Aviation W 86:28-9 Ap 24 '67
Apollo project: North American's Achilles' heel. W. S. Rukeyser. Fortune 75:105+ Je 1 '67
Beleaguered giant; Apollo's prime contractor indicted. il Time 89:88 My 12 '67
Declaration of confidence; recovery of the Apollo program. W. J. Coughlin. Tech W 20:58 My 22 '67
Faithless men. Nation 204:547-8 My 1 '67
Into new territory; North American aviation-Rockwell-Standard corp, merger plans. il Time 89:78 Mr 31 '67
NASA ready to add quality control contractors to Apollo team. Tech W 20:10 My 8 '67
NASA to detail Apollo fire impact. D. C. Winston. Aviation W 86:16-17 My 8 '67
North American, Mobil oil agree to pool technology. il Tech W 20:30+ F 13 '67
NAA facing heavy loss of AAP funding. H. Taylor and H. M David. il Tech W 20:19-22 My 15 '67
North American Rockwell; Rockwell-standard corporation and North American aviation merger under way. Newsweek 69:78 Ap 3 '67
North American tries to advance under fire; North American aviation merger move with Rockwell-Standard. il Bsns W p 154-6+ Je 3 '67
Rockwells take off for outer space. J. Mecklin. il Fortune 75:100-4+ Je 1 '67
Shuffle at North American il Newsweek 69:76 My 15 '67
Text of NASA summary of Phillips report; with editorial comment. S. Phillips. Tech W 20:39-40, 50 Ap 24 '67
When a giant stumbles. Newsweek 69:63 My 1 '67

NORTH AMERICAN rowing championships. See Rowing

NORTH AMERICAN water and power alliance
Engineers of prophecy. D. B. Luten and G. Gould, jr. il Nation 205:70-4 Jl 31 '67
Nawpa: a continental water system; symposium. il Bul Atomic Sci 23:8-27 S '67

NORTH ANDEAN highway. See Roads—Latin America

NORTH ATLANTIC council. See North Atlantic treaty organization

NORTH ATLANTIC free trade area (proposed)
Latest idea for Britain: a Common market with U.S. il U S News 64:46-7 Ja 1 '68

NORTH ATLANTIC regional water resources study. See Water resources development

NORTH ATLANTIC treaty organization
Address to North Atlantic council, Paris, April 7, 1967. H. H. Humphrey. Dept State Bul 56:681-3 My 1 '67
Adieu; official departure from France. Time 89:27-8 Ap 7 '67
As U.S. starts a pullback of troops from Europe. U S News 62:10 My 15 '67
Bid requests due in February for NATO Comsat stations. Aviation W 87:22 D 25 '67
Canada; collective security; address, November 13, 1967. P. Martin. Vital Speeches 34:133-5 D 15 '67
Comeback of NATO: a setback for de Gaulle. il U S News 63:57-8 D 25 '67
Concert and conciliation: the next stage of the Atlantic alliance; address, September 11, 1967. E. V. Rostow. Dept State Bul 57:422-30 O 2 '67; Same Vital Speeches 34:13-18 O 15 '67
Does NATO have a future? D. Cook. Read Digest 90:132-7 Ap '67
Europe minus America; de Gaulle plan. New Repub 157:7-8 O 21 '67
Final NADGE designs emerge as system enters detail stage; NATO air defense ground environment. Aviation W 86:315-16 My 29 '67
Future of NATO. A. Buchan. bibliog f Int Concil 565:5-61 N '67
Future of NATO: meaning to U.S; with excerpt from address by H. Cleveland. il U S News 63:60-4 S 11 '67
Golden rule of consultation; address, June 20, 1967. H. Cleveland. Dept State Bul 57:141-6 Jl 31 '67
How not to lead an alliance. B. Brodie. il Reporter 36:18-24 Mr 9 '67
Letter from Paris, excerpt from article Amica America, from Figaro; ed. by Genêt. A. François-Poncet. New Yorker 43:181-3 Ap 15 '67

Looking southward; Soviet buildup in the Mediterranean. il Time 90:27 D 22 '67
North Atlantic council meets at Luxembourg; text of communique, June 14, 1967. Dept State Bul 57:14-16 Jl 3 '67
North Atlantic council meets at Luxembourg; text of final communique; with annex, December 15, 1967. Dept State Bul 58:49-52 Ja 8 '68
North Atlantic council meets at Paris; texts of final communique and three annexes, December 16, 1966; with list of members of US delegation. Dept State Bul 56:49-53 Ja 9 '67
NATO and Europe, by G. A. Beaufre. Review Harper 234:126+ Mr '67. R. D. Masters
NATO move from Paris to shift traffic. Aviation W 86:37-8 Ja 23 '67
NATO nuclear planning group holds first ministers meeting; statement, April 3, 1967; with text of communique, April 7, 1967. R. S. McNamara. Dept State Bul 56:686-8 My 1 '67
NATO on the eve of its 20th anniversary; address, November 13, 1967. J. M. Leddy. Dept State Bul 57:759-62 D 4 '67
NATO ready to act on satellite project. D. E. Fink. Aviation W 86:24 My 1 '67
NATO seeks improved non-nuclear force. D. E. Fink. Aviation W 87:47 D 25 '67
NATO shifts procuring plans to meet military needs. Aviation W 86:94-5 Mr 6 '67
NATO's big powers adjusts to the times. il Bsns W p34 My 6 '67
Paradoxes de la paix, by P. M. Gallois. Review Nat R 19:1125-6 O 17 '67. S. T. Possony
Present viability of NATO, SEATO, and CENTO; address, April 1967, with questions and answers. A. E. P. Duffy. Ann Am Acad 372:33-9 Jl '67
President Johnson meets with German chancellor; exchange of greetings, statements and exchange of toasts, August 15; with joint statement, August 16, 1967. K. G. Kiesinger; L. B. Johnson. Dept State Bul 57:325-30 S 11 '67
Soviet view of NATO; address, April 24, 1967. L. I. Brezhnev. Vital Speeches 33:514-22 Je 15 '67
Studies spur change in NATO posture. Aviation W 86:123+ My 29 '67
Systems development dispute delays NATO Comsat effort. Aviation W 87:28 Ag 7 '67
Timely transfusion; newly defined political role. Newsweek 70:29-30 D 25 '67
Why senators demand a U.S. cutback in Europe; excerpts from address, January 19, 1967. M. Mansfield. U S News 62:33 F 13 '67

See also
Atlantic community

Headquarters
Dangers of détente. il Time 90:34 O 27 '67
New HQ for NATO, and a new role? il Newsweek 70:30 O 30 '67
NATO learns to live in exile from France; new home in Brussels. il Bsns W p46-8 O 21 '67
SHAPE takes shape; new headquarters at Casteau. M. Mok. il Life 62:105-6+ Je 9 '67

Science committee
NATO: a North Atlantic technology organization? J. Walsh. Science 155:985-6+ F 24 '67

NORTH BORNEO
See also
Forests and forestry—North Borneo

NORTH BRENTWOOD, Md.
Lights are on; and the whole family goes to school at night; Operation Reach. M. A. Marlar. il Am Ed 3:21-4 My '67

NORTH CAROLINA
See also
Education—North Carolina
Law—North Carolina
Moore County
Ocracoke Island
Outer Banks (islands)
Prohibition—North Carolina
Wake County

Description and travel
North Carolina: Outer Banks and inner peaks. R. Atcheson. il Holiday 42:16+ S '67

Historic houses, etc.
Corps in the Cradle; Cradle of forestry. K. B. Pomeroy. il Am For 73:20-3 S '67

NORTH CAROLINA school of the arts, Winston Salem
Leisure to learn; dance education. D. Hering. il Dance Mag 41:60-3+ O '67

NORTH CAROLINA. University, Chapel Hill
Chapel Hill's tobacco rogues: L&M kids. B. Lewis and L. Miller. F. Deford. il Sports Illus 26:24-6+ F 20 '67

School of forestry
Our forestry schools. K. A. Argow. il Am For 73:28-9 Ap '67

NORTH CASCADES. See Cascade Range

NORTH CASCADES NATIONAL PARK (proposed) See National parks and reserves—United States

NORTH CASCADES wilderness area (proposed) See Wilderness areas—Washington (state)

NORTH central regional library, Wenatchee, Wash.
Pioneering with the Job corps: camp near Curlew, Wash. J. H. Pardee. il Library J 92:748-9 F 15 '67

NORTH HEMPSTEAD, N.Y. See Hempstead, N.Y.

NORTH KOREA. See Korea (People's Democratic Republic)

NORTH MIAMI, Fla.
Accident-prevention program that works. E. J. Connell. il Am City 82:147+ O '67

NORTH Park college, Chicago
To change North Park. B. Bankson. Christian Cent 84:980-1 Jl 26 '67

NORTH VIETNAM. See Vietnam (Democratic Republic)

NORTHCOTT, Cecil
Dallying on union. Christian Cent 84:1309-10 O 18 '67
Roman thaw. Christian Cent 84:1024 Ag 9 '67
Uneasy lie the states. Christian Cent 84:1213-14 S 27 '67
Why not Presbyterian? Christian Cent 84:1550 D 6 '67

NORTHEAST AFRICA. See Africa, Northeast

NORTHEAST airlines, Incorporated
CAB withdraws subsidy from Northeast. J. W. Carter. Aviation W 88:29 Ja 8 '68
Northeast emphasizing route expansion. Aviation W 87:41+ N 13 '67

NORTHEAST corridor project. See Transportation, High speed

NORTHEAST regional ballet festival. See Dance festivals

NORTHEASTERN states
Northerner's North. B. Brower. il Holiday 41:10+ My '67
Profiles: through the great city. A. Bailey. il New Yorker 43:35-42+ Jl 22; 35-8+ Jl 29; 32-6+ Ag 5 '67
Through the great city, by A. Bailey. Review Reporter 37:49-50 O 5 '67. C. W. Griffin, jr; Reply with rejoinder. A. Bailey. 37:10-11 N 2 '67

NORTHERN IRELAND
    See also
Belfast
Education—Northern Ireland

NORTHERN lights. See Auroras

NORTHERN nations. See Nations

NORTHERNERS
Northerner's North. B. Brower. il Holiday 41:10+ My '67

NORTHMEN
    See also
Vikings

NORTHROP, J. and Siepecky, R. A.
Sporulation mutations induced by heat in bacillus subtilis. bibliog Science 155:838-9 F 17 '67

NORTHROP corporation
European interest sought for Northrop 530 fighter. Aviation W 87:26 Ag 7 '67

NORTHRUP, Herbert R.
Racial policies of American industry. Mo Labor R 90:41-3 Jl '67

NORTHWEST
    See also
Fishing—Northwestern states
Skis and skiing—Northwestern states
Water supply—Northwestern states

Economic conditions
Megalopolis comes to the Northwest. P. Herrera. il Fortune 76:118-23+ D '67

NORTHWEST TERRITORIES, Canada
Canada's Far North; a land on the move. I. Baird. il UNESCO Courier 20:14-17+ Ap '67
    See also
Geology—Northwest Territories, Canada

NORTHWESTERN university, Evanston, Ill.
Course change in law school. il Sch & Soc 95:103-4 F 18 '67

Medill school of journalism
Where the action is; Urban journalism center. Newsweek 70:58-9 Ag 14 '67

Observatory
    See Astronomical observatories

NORTON, Charles Eliot
Gloom, gloom, gloom, and scarce one ray of light; excerpts from The anti-imperialists: twelve against empire, 1898-1900. R. L. Beisner. por Am Heritage 18:65-71 Ag '67

NORTON, James A.
Catalyst or crusader? Sat R 51:40 Ja 13 '68

NORTON, R. Lee
New city hall that borrows from the past. Am City 82:108-9 Ag '67

NORTON, W. W. and company
Norton to publish fifty-book Jewish heritage classics. Pub W 192:53 N 13 '67

NORTON-TAYLOR, Duncan
Into Britain's parlor with his hat on. il Fortune 75:136-9+ F '67
Megaversity's struggle with itself. Fortune 75:160-5+ My '67
Nelson Rockefeller: a record to fit the times. Fortune 75:96-9+ Je 1 '67

NORTON company
Ceramics puts a shield under 'copter crews. il Bsns W p80 D 9 '67

NORWALK, Calif.
Norwalk on record. il Am City 82:118+ Jl '67

NORWAY
    See also
Country estates—Norway
Fishing—Norway
Music festivals—Norway
Publishers and publishing—Norway

Description and travel
Majestic Norse course; auto route from Oslo to Bergen. J. Aumente. il Travel 128:42-4 Ag '67
Over the top of Norway to Bergen. il Sunset 138:78+ My '67

Social life and customs
    See also
Christmas—Norway

NORWEB, R. Henry, Jr
Holden arboretum. Horticulture 45:36-7 S '67

NORWOOD, William R.
Trust Territory of the Pacific Islands; statement, June 8, 1967. Dept State Bul 57:366-75 S 18 '67

NOSE
    See also
Rhinitis

NOSE drops
Do you use nose drops correctly? Good H 164:158 F '67

NOSEK, Thad
Sand, salt and calcium chloride. Am City 82:82-3 D '67

NOSSITER, Bernard D.
Saving Greece from the Greeks. New Repub 156:9-10 My 20 '67

NOSTALGIA
I want to go home. P. LaFarge. il Redbook 129:59+ O '67

NOSTRAND, Foster
Out of a clear blue sky. Yachting 122:42-3+ O '67

NOT a way of life; drama. See Rush J.

NOTABLES. See Celebrities

NOTE paper. See Stationery

NOTE taking
Using tape to teach note-taking. C. G. Woodhouse. NEA J 56:53 D '67

NOTES (money) See Paper money

NOTESTEIN, Frank W.
Population crisis: reasons for hope. For Affairs 46:167-80 O '67

NOTHING to write home about; story. See De Vries, P.

NOTIONS (merchandise)
Notions; National notion association semi-annual show. New Yorker 43:33-4 Mr 4 '67

NOTMAN, William
Canada exposed: the look of the young nation; photographs. por Am Heritage 18:13-25 Je '67

NOTRE DAME, Ind. University
Notre Dame: our first great Catholic university? P. Schrag. Harper 234:41-9 My '67
Notre Dame: we're number one! J. Bowers. il Sat Eve Post 240:85-9 O 7 '67
Notre Dame's anniversary. America 117:730 D 16 '67
Some old grads get a hazing. J. Underwood. il Sports Illus 26:26-7 My 15 '67

NOTROM, Henry B.
Convert your outboard to electronic ignition.
Pop Mech 127:172-5+ Ap '67
How to get more out of your outboard. Pop
Mech 128:144-7 Jl '67
Starting a stubborn outboard. Pop Mech 127:
134-7 Je '67
Those new black box ignitions. Pop Mech
127:158-60+ F '67
Troubleshooting your outboard by ear. Pop
Mech 128:144-7+ Ag '67
Winter wrap-up for your stern drive. Pop
Mech 128:164-7+ N '67

NOURSE, Joan, and Nourse, Philip
Happy faculty. Criticism
America 116:738 My 13 '67

NOURSE, Philip. See Nourse, J. jt. auth.

NOVA SCOTIA
Midwesterner cruises east. J. R. Witmer. il
Yachting 122:52-4+ D '67
See also
Halifax
Sable Island

Description and travel
Nova Scotia: where the good times are. E
Logan. il Sr Schol 90:sup20-1 Ap 7 '67

Industries
Mr Jolly comes to town; plant to manufacture hardboard. il Duns R 90:57-8 S '67

NOVA university, Fort Lauderdale, Fla.
National center encourages use of academic
games. Sr Schol 91:sup3 N 9 '67
Novel ideas at Nova U. il Time 89:58 Je 30 '67

NOVAE. See Stars, New

NOVAK, Franz
New Austria & the old Nazis. P Lendvai.
Commentary 44:81-2 S '67

NOVAK, Michael
A.R.V.N. can fight! Christian Cent 84:1310
O 18 '67
Abortion is not enough. Christian Cent 84:
430-1 Ap 5 '67
Belief and Mr Dewart. Commonweal 85:485-8
F 3 '67
Draft board theology. Commonweal 86:467-8 Jl
28 '67
'Gimme' is dead? Commonweal 86:174-5 Ap 28
'67
Holy human empire; or, Whatever happend
to the secular city? Christian Cent 85:37-8
Ja 10 '68
Numbers game in Vietnam. Commonweal 87:
373-4 D 22 '67
Religion of Paul Tillich. bibliog f Commentary 43:53-65 Ap '67
Revolution of 1976. Commonweal 86:441-3,
552-3 Jl 14, S 8 '67
Students and the war; Humphrey at Stanford.
Commonweal 86:7-8 Mr 24 '67
—See Brown, R. M. jt. auth.

about
New style in Catholicism. P. K. Cuneo. Sat
R 51:34 Ja 6 '68

NOVAK, Robert D.
Republican reasoning. New Repub 157:28+ N
18 '67
—See Evans, R. jt. auth.

NOVELISTS
First novelists; spring 1967; statements by
the writers. ed. by K. McQuade. il Library J 92:600-9 F 1 '67
First novelists; summer-autumn 1967; statements by the writers. il Library J 92:2182-
93, 3452-62 Je 1, O 1 '67
See also
Women as authors

NOVELISTS, American
See also
Fiedler, L. A.
Jones, J.
O'Hara, J.
Purdy, J.
Pynchon, T.
Robbins, H. pseud.
Styron, W.

NOVELISTS, English
Perpetuating the obsolete. P. West. Commonweal 87:203-5 N 17 '67
See also
Richardson, D. M.

NOVELISTS, French
French novelists of today, by H. Peyre. Review
Sat R 50:28 Je 24 '67. T. Bishop

NOVELISTS, Latin American
Into the mainstream: conversations with
Latin American writers. R. Squirru. Américas 19:44 My '67

NOVELISTS, Norwegian
See also
Hamsun, K.

NOVELISTS, Polish
See also
Gombrowicz, W.

NOVELISTS, Russian
See also
Ehrenburg, I.

NOVELS. See Fiction

NOVELS, American. See American fiction

NOVICK, Julius
Theatre (cont) Nation 204:509-10, 636-8, 829-
30; 205:220-2, 252-4, 285-6 Ap 17, My 15, Je
26, S 11-25 '67
Tragic cakewalk. Nation 206:93-4 Ja 15 '68

NOVIE, Raven
How can a girl defend herself? il por Time
89:71 F 10 '67

NOVINSKY, Anita, and Paulo, Amilcar
Last Marranos. Commentary 43:76-81 My '67

NOVOSTI (news agency) See News agencies

NOVOTNY, Antonin
Reason to hope. il por Time 91:19-20 Ja 12
'68
Stalinist at bay. por Newsweek 71:34-5 Ja
1 '68

NOVROS, David
Total and complex. H. Rosenstein. il por
Art N 66:52-4+ My '67

NOW is the time for all good men; musical
comedy. See Musical comedies, revues, etc.
—Criticisms, plots, etc.

NOWELL, Don
Swinging Chevy plan. il Hot Rod 20:90-1 Mr
'67

NOYD, Dale
Countdown on Noyd. D. Sanford. New Repub
157:14-15 O 21 '67

NOYES, Eliot
Continuing study of the window wall. il Arch
Rec 141:173-80 Ap '67

NOYES, Polly
West coast wanderings. See issues of Travel

NOZA, Mestre. See Mestre Noza

Le NOZZE di Figaro; opera. See Mozart, J.
C. W. A.

NUCCIO, Sal
Money and your long-range plans. Am Home
70:57+ Ja '67

NUCLEAR age. See Atomic age

NUCLEAR bombs. See Atomic bombs

NUCLEAR counters. See Counters (electrons,
ions, etc)

NUCLEAR energy. See Atomic power

NUCLEAR excavation. See Atomic blasting

NUCLEAR fission
Autobiographical notes; excerpt from A scientific autobiography. O. Hahn. Bul Atomic
Sci 23:19-24 Mr; 22-8 Ap '67

NUCLEAR fusion
Leakage problem in fusion reactors. F. F.
Chen. il Sci Am 217:76-88 bibliog (p 134+) Jl
'67
Taming the H-bomb for power; generating
electricity from nuclear fusion. il Bsns W p
102-4+ Mr 18 '67

NUCLEAR magnetic resonance
Can science tune out drug side effects? il
Bsns W p94+ D 2 '67
High-resolution nuclear magnetic resonance
spectroscopy. R. C. Ferguson and W. D.
Phillips. bibliog il Science 157:257-67 Jl 21
'67

NUCLEAR physics
Bioscience from nuclear particles; pi meson
may be useful for cancer treatment. Sci N
91:85 Ja 28 '67
Destruction of molecules by nuclear transformations. S. Wexler. bibliog il Science
156:901-7 My 19 '67
New math of physics. Sci Am 217:59 N '67
Optical methods for studying Hertzian
resonances; tr. of address, December 12,
1966. A. Kastler. bibliog il Science 158:
214-21 O 13 '67
Particle physics: new talk of East-West ties.
D. S. Greenberg. Science 156:1069 My 26 '67
Physics expanding; Mexico. Sci N 92:260 S
9 '67
Search for simplicity; high energy physics;
symposium. il Sci N 92:321-9+ S 30 '67
Stoking mechanism of stellar furnaces; H. A.
Bethe. il Sci N 92:463-4 N 11 '67
Superconducting magnets in high-energy
physics. M. Derrick. bibliog il Science 158:
325-31 O 20 '67
See also
Atomic nuclei
Cosmic rays
Mossbauer effect
Nuclear fission
Particles (nuclear physics)
Time reversal

NUCLEAR power plants. See Atomic power plants

NUCLEAR powered airplanes. See Airplanes, Atomic powered

NUCLEAR propulsion. See Rockets, Atomic powered

NUCLEAR reactions
Nuclear changes. J. Daugherty and M. Daugherty. Sci Digest 62:94-6 S '67
Polarized protons as nuclear probes. L. Rosen. bibliog il Science 157:1127-34 S 8 '67
See also
Nuclear fusion

NUCLEAR reactors
AEC cuts reactor off budget; need has evaporated. Bsns W p 116 Mr 18 '67
AEC's fast breeder plan due next month. H. Taylor. Aero Tech 21:20-1 D 18 '67
Europe's nuclear battle. J. Ross Skinner. il Duns R 89:65-6+ Mr '67
Five-year test in one; effect of irradiation on fuel elements and shielding material. il Sci N 92:80 Jl 22 '67
Improving the breeder. Time 91:64 Ja 5 '68
Leakage problem in fusion reactors. F. F. Chen. il Sci Am 217:76-88 bibliog(p 134+) Jl '67
Man with an atomic reactor; Mirzhalil Mirzaev at Uzbek academy of sciences Ulugbek, Uzbekistan. C. S. Wren. il Look 31:M19-22 O 3 '67
More fuel for new-reactor race; fast breeder reactor for commercial power. il Bsns W p46+ Ja 13 '68
Next step is the breeder reactor. il Fortune 75:120-3+ Mr '67
Phoebus 2A set for April; hot flow test. Aero Tech 21:12-13 Ja 1 '68
Radioactive wastes from fusion reactors. F. L. Parker. bibliog il Science 159:83-4 Ja 5 '68
Taming the H-bomb for power; generating electricity from nuclear fusion. il Bsns W p 102-4+ Mr 18 '67
Teller attacks breeder safety; nuclear power reactors, sodium-cooled. il Sci N 92:200+ Ag 26 '67
Thinning the reactor jungle. C. Behrens. il Sci N 91:360-1 Ap 15 '67
Third generation of breeder reactors. T. R. Bump. il Sci Am 216:25-33 My '67
Worldwide nuclear power; progress and problems. G. T. Seaborg. il Dept State Bul 56:90-7 Ja 16 '67

Safety devices and measures
Permit process a bottleneck; AEC licensing of reactors for industry. C. Behrens. il Sci N 92:594 D 16 '67

NUCLEAR research. See Atomic research

NUCLEAR rockets. See Rockets, Atomic powered

NUCLEAR scattering. See Scattering (physics)

NUCLEAR shielding. See Shielding (radiation)

NUCLEAR test ban treaty, 1963
Test ban treaty, by J. H. McBride. Review Nat R 19:913 Ag 22 '67. W. D. Jacobs

NUCLEAR warfare. See Atomic warfare

NUCLEAR weapons. See Atomic weapons

NUCLEI, Atomic. See Atomic nuclei

NUCLEIC acid purines. See Purines

NUCLEIC acids
Assembly of a virus. Sci Am 216:56+ My '67
Chemistry and structure of nucleic acids of bacteriophages. J. A. Cohen. bibliog il Science 158:343-51 O 20 '67
See also
Deoxyribonucleic acid
Ribonucleic acid

NUCLEOPROTEINS
Amino acid coding in sarcina lutea and saccharomyces cerevisiae. W. E. Groves and E. S. Kempner. bibliog il Science 156: 387-90 Ap 21 '67
Brain polysomes: response to environmental stimulation. S. H. Appel and others. bibliog il Science 157:836-8 Ag 18 '67
Crystalline ribosomes. Sci Am 217:104 S '67
Cytoplasmic and chloroplast ribosomes of chlamydomonas: ultracentrifugal characterization. R. Sager and M. G. Hamilton. bibliog il Science 157:709-11 Ag 11 '67
Deoxycytidylate and deoxyguanylate kinase activity in pneumococci after exposure to known polyribonucleotides. W. Firshein and others. bibliog il Science 157:821-2 Ag 18 '67
Functional chloroplast polyribosomes from tobacco leaves. J. L. Chen and S. G. Wildman. bibliog il Science 155:1271-3 Mr 10 '67

Mammalian ribosomal protein: analysis by electrophoresis on polyacrylamide gel. R. B. Low and I. G. Wool. bibliog il Science 155:330-2 Ja 20 '67
Membranes in polyribosome formation by rabbit reticulocytes. M. L. Freedman and others. bibliog il Science 157:323-5 Jl 21 '67
Polyribosomes of growing bacteria. C. P. Flessel and others. bibliog il Science 158: 658-60 N 3 '67
Protein components in the 40S ribonucleoprotein particles in escherichia coli. E. Otaka and others. bibliog il Science 157:1452-4 S 22 '67
Rabbit hemoglobin biosynthesis: use of human hemoglobin chains to study molecule completion. J. R. Shaeffer and others. bibliog il Science 158:488-90 O 27 '67
Reformation of functional liver polyribosomes from ribosome monomers in the absense of RNA synthesis. G. A. Stewart and E. Farber. bibliog il Science 157:67-9 Jl 7 '67
Ribonucleoproteins; report on conference. E. H. McConkey. Science 158:1498-9 D 15 '67
Ribosomes: effect of interferon on their interaction with rapidly labeled cellular and viral RNA's. W. A. Carter and H. B. Levy. bibliog il Science 155:1254-7 Mr 10 '67
See also
Interferon

NUCLEOTIDES
Fine structure of RNA codewords recognized by bacterial, amphibian, and mammalian transfer RNA. R. E. Marshall and others. bibliog il Science 155:820-6 F 17 '67
Guanine nucleotide associated with the protein of the outer fibers of flagella and cilia. R. E. Stevens and others. bibliog il Science 156:1606-8 Je 23 '67
Nucleotide sequence of KB cell 5S RNA. B. G. Forget and S. M. Weissman. bibliog il Science 158:1695-9 D 29 '67
Orientation of nonsense codons on the genetic map of the lac operon. D. Zipser. bibliog il Science 157:1176-7 S 8 '67
Phosphoribosylamidotransferase: regulation of activity in virus-induced murine leukemia by purine nucleotides. G. H. Reem and C. Friend. bibliog il Science 157:1203-4 S 8 '67
Pyrimidine nucleotide synthesis: regulatory control during transformation of lymphocytes in vitro. Z. J. Lucas. bibliog il Science 156: 1237-40 Je 2 '67

NUDE in art
Philip Pearlstein: the naked truth. W. F. Midgette. il Art N 66:54-5+ O '67
See also
Human figure in art

NUDE in photography. See Human figure in photography

NUDIBRANCHS
Nudibranch: snail without a shell. il Sci N 92:548 D 2 '67

NUDISM
No cover, small minimum; Ile du Levant, a rocky island in the Mediterranean. C. Stinnett. il Holiday 41:40+ Ap '67
Nudity. P. O'Neil. Life 63:107-8+ O 13 '67
Pride of body. il Vogue 150:130-1 S 15 '67

NUDIST colonies. See Nudism

NUGENT, Donald
Psalm of Quasimodo, 1967. Cath World 205: 52 Ap '67

NUGENT, Hugh
Laws of probability and bureaucratic style. Atlan 219:118+ Mr '67

NUGENT, James
Our special hell. Sr Schol 90:sup 13 My 19 '67

NUGENT, Jim
Love in the park; excerpt from A gallery of dudes. M. Sprague. il Am Heritage 18: 8-13+ F '67

NUGENT, Luci Baines (Johnson)
I just want to go bubble around people; interview, ed. by deR. Morrissey. por Life 63: 50 Jl 7 '67
about
Full story of Lyndon Johnson's world war III remark. il por U S News 62:21 My 29 '67
In grandfather country. il Newsweek 70:22 Jl 3 '67

NUGENT, N. A. and Fuller, R. C.
Carotenoid biosynthesis in rhodospirillum rubrum; effect of pteridine inhibitor. bibliog Science 158:922-4 N 17 '67

NUGENT, Patrick John
Pat Nugent: growing figure in the expanding Johnson empire. il por U S News 62:19 My 22 '67

NUGENT, Patrick Lyndon
In grandfather country. il Newsweek 70:22 Jl 3 '67

NUGENT, Patrick Lyndon—*Continued*
LBJ and Lyn, official, word-by-word account; excerpt from statement, July 3, 1967. il por U S News 63:8 Jl 17 '67
Patrick Lyndon. Time 89:17 Je 30 '67
Slate-gray eyes, plump and three days old; with report and interview with L. B. Nugent, ed. by deR. Morrissey. il por Life 63:47-50+ Jl 7 '67
Tiny new Texan visits LBJ. W. Hedgepeth. il pors Look 31:32-5 O 31 '67

NUMBATS. See Anteaters

NUMBERS. See Numerals

NUMBERS game. See Lotteries

NUMERALS
Numerals open new mathematical horizons. P. Wolff. il UNESCO Courier 20:11 My '67

NUMERATION
Want to build an integrated circuit binary counter? D. Lancaster. il Pop Electr 25: 57-61+ D '66

NUMERICAL reference data storage. See Information storage and retrieval systems

NUMISMATICS
Coin collecting. il Consumer Bul 51:27-9 Ja '68

NUMISMATICS, Ancient
Coins are collected for beauty and history. C. French. Hobbies 72:102 S '67

NUNLIST, Frank J.
Wanted: executive time power. Dung R 90: 51-2+ O '67

NUNN, Guy T.
Puerto Rico. Nation 205:44-6 Jl 17 '67

NUNN, Jessie Alford
Turquoise trail; story. NEA J 56:20-1 N '67

NUNN, Louie B.
Focus on Kentucky. P. Ardery, jr. Nat R 19:1318 N 28 '67
Nothing grand. Time 90:20 N 3 '67

NUNS. See Sisterhoods

NUNS as teachers. See Sisterhoods

NUORO, Sardinia
Poet in the piazza. il Arch Forum 127:70-5 O '67

NÜRBURGRING speedway. See Speedways

NUREEV, Rudolf
From Paradise lost to a Frisco jail; with reports by J. Fincher and J. Hicks. il pors Life 63:83-4 Jl 21 '67
Nureyev. il Vogue 150:210-15 D '67
Nureyev and Fonteyn; with report by C. Barnes. il pors Life 62:126-8+ My 12 '67
People are talking about... il por Vogue 149:84-5 Mr 15 '67
Report from Vienna: Nureyev stages Don Quixote. L. Zamponi. il Dance Mag 41: 70 F '67
World of dance. W. Terry. il Sat R 50:84-5 Je 10 '67

NUREMBERG

Parades
Nuremberg party rallies, 1923-39, by H. T. Burden. Review
    Sat R il 50:30 D 16 '67. H. Kohn

NUREMBERG trials
Reunion in Warsaw: remembering Nuremberg; meeting of former trial correspondents. V. H. Bernstein. il Nation 204:112-16 Ja 23 '67
Trial of the Germans: Nuremberg 1945-1946, by E. Davidson. Review
    Nat R 19:314-16 Mr 21 '67. W. S. Schlamm
    Sat R 50:44 F 4 '67. L. L. Snyder

NURSERIES, Day. See Day nurseries

NURSERY rhymes
Pudding down the immortals: Little Jack Horner as various English bards might have penned it. D. Raben. il Horizon 10: 120 Wint '68
    See also
Mother Goose

Anecdotes, facetiae, satire, etc.
Nab blonde, 8, as porridge thief. D. Williamson. il Sat Eve Post 240:18 My 20 '67

NURSERY schools
Fun on wheels; mobile unit program of the San Pablo, Calif. recreation department. D. C. Howe. il Parents Mag 42:52-3+ Ap '67
Mama goes to nursery school; Malabar street school, East Los Angeles. il Am Ed 3:10-11 S '67
Matriculating at 3? Jean-Jacques Rousseau creative early childhood day school. K. D. Fishman. il N Y Times Mag p72+ F 26 '67

Montessori and traditional American nursery schools, how they are different, how they are alike. B. Spock and M. L. Hathaway. Redbook 128:20+ Mr '67
Save them young; New York state's prekindergarten program. M. P. Berson. il Am Ed 3:5-8 Jl '67
Should a child go to nursery school? il Good H 165:182-3 S '67
Somebody at your house ready for nursery school? il Changing T 21:35-6 Jl '67
Why children are crazy about nursery school. S. Levitin. il Parents Mag 42:52-4+ Ag '67
    See also
Day nurseries

NURSES and nursing
Angel of mercy is dead; nursing becoming a profession. R. Hoffmann. Mlle 66:134-5+ D '67
Angels of Viet Nam; U.S. military nurses. L. G. Martin. il Todays Health 45:16-23 Ag '67
Jobscope: nonhospital nursing opportunities. bibliog Mlle 66:144-5 D '67
Our flying Nightingales in Vietnam. K. Drake. il Read Digest 91:73-9 D '67
Position of organized nursing. Sat R 50:61-2 F 4 '67: Discussion. 50:60-2 Mr 4 '67
San Francisco Bay area 1966 nurses' negotiations. M. D. Kossoris. Mo Labor R 90:8-12 Je '67
Schooled to save lives; Linda Schmidt's career as a psychiatric nurse. T. Berland. il Todays Health 45:51-5+ Mr '67
What's wrong with American hospitals? a doctor's opinion: nursing shortage. T. Hale. il Sat R 50:62-5 F 4 '67; Discussion. 50:60-2 Mr 4; 47 Ap 1 '67
Where did all the nurses go? Nurse in training. R. H. Berg. il Look 32:26+ Ja 23 '68
Which nurse does what? Good H 164:190 My '67
Why we need more nurses, now. R. Tunley. il Redbook 129:68-9+ Jl '67

History
Tough angel of the battlefield: the real Florence Nightingale. J. H. Winchester. il Todays Health 45:30-3+ My '67

Salaries
Earnings of hospital nurses, July 1966. G. L. Stelluto. il Mo Labor R 90:55-8 Je '67

Study and teaching
Quo vadis: R for the nursing shortage; Toronto project. D. MacDonald. il Read Digest 91:15-16+ S '67

Training
Medical training costs too much; excerpt from Case studies in change. B. Asbell. il Am Ed 3:5-6 Mr '67

NURSING homes
Nursing home setting; Miller center for nursing care, White Plains, N.Y. D. B. Miller. il Parks & Rec 2:38-9+ Ja '67
Nursing homes; design and construction. il Arch Rec 142:169-76 O '67
What to look for in a nursing home. il Todays Health 45:84-6 S '67

NURSING schools
Nurse in training; Joan Meakins at St Vincent's hospital school of nursing, New York. R. H. Berg. il Look 32:30-2 Ja 23 '68
Nursing education facilities. il Arch Rec 141: 159-66 My '67
What's wrong with American hospitals? a doctors opinion; nursing shortage. T. Hale. il Sat R 50:62-5 F 4 '67; Discussion. 50:60-2 Mr 4; 47 Ap 1 '67

NUT; story. See Chase, V.

NUT bread. See Bread

NUTCRACKER; ballet. See Ballets—Criticisms

NUTRITION
Guide to the basic food elements. Good H 165:156-7 Jl '67
Let's talk about food; ed. by P. L. White. See issues of Today's health
More power to you. il Sr Schol 91:27 D 7 '67
Travel well. E. N. Dye. See issues of Travel
    See also
Children—Nutrition
Diet
Food habits
Proteins
Vitamins

Study and teaching
    See Nutrition education

NUTRITION education
Food for thought and vice versa; American medical association nutrition series. J. L. Breeling. il Todays Health 45:14-15 S '67
NUTRITION of plants. See Plants—Nutrition
NUTRITION research
Ecological ectocrines in experimental epidemiology. H. A. Schneider. bibliog il Science 158:597-603 N 3 '67
Polydipsia elicited by the synergistic action of a saccharin and glucose solution. E. S. Valenstein and others. bibliog il Science 157:552-4 Ag 4 '67
Starvation and the brain; permanent brain damage from improper diets. il Sci N 91:307 Ap 1 '67

NUTTALL, Roger
Great Cunard gamble. Duns R 90:51+ N '67

NUTTALL, Thomas
Thomas Nuttall. R. G. Beidleman. por Horticulture 45:36-7+ Je '67
Thomas Nuttall, naturalist, by J. E. Graustein. Review
Sat R 50:28-9 Jl 8 '67. R. L. Perkin

NUTTER, G. Warren
Ahead is change, I don't believe the system can survive; interview. por U S News 63:74-7 N 6 '67

NUTTING, Anthony
When Egypt won and UAR lost. L. Roberts. Sat R 50:44-5 N 4 '67; Reply. 50:24 D 9 '67

NUTTING, Mark L.
Two soft hammers you can make. Pop Sci 190:159 Mr '67

NUVEEN, John
Vietnam: the neglected debate. Christian Cent 84:399-403 Mr 29 '67

NYE, Joseph S. Jr
Central American regional integration. bibliog f Int Concil 562:5-66 Mr '67

NYERERE, Julius Kambarage
Nyerere: Operation bootstrap, or backstep? interview. ed. by P. Webb. por Newsweek 69:47 Mr 6 '67

about

Dog days. il Newsweek 69:46 Mr 6 '67
Follow that car! il por Newsweek 70:45 Ag 7 '67
Paving Tanzania's way with good intentions. A. Delius. Reporter 37:41-3 Jl 13 '67
Report. Atlan 219:32-4+ Je '67
Socialism, tribal style. il por Newsweek 69:55-6 F 20 '67

NYGREN, H. D.
For 160 years, nautical chartmakers for the Nation. Motor B 120:21-4+ D '67

NYLON
Stopping bullets with nylon. Time 90:57 Ag 11 '67

NYLON hosiery. See Hosiery

NYMPHOIDES indicum. See Water snowflake

NYSTRÖM, Bo
Muscle-spindle histochemistry. bibliog Science 155:1424-6 Mr 17 '67

NYSWANDER, Marie
Methadone, fighting fire with fire. G. Samuels. il por N Y Times Mag p44-5+ O 15 '67; Discussion. p22+ N 12 '67

O

OAO (orbiting astronomical observatory) See Artificial satellites—Astronomical applications

OART. See United States—National aeronautics and space administration—Advanced research and technology, Office of

OAS. See Organization of American states

OAU. See Organization of African unity

OECD. See Organization for economic cooperation and development

OEO. See United States—Economic opportunity, Office of

OEP. See United States—Emergency planning, Office of

OGO (orbiting geophysical observatory) See Artificial satellites—Astronomical applications

ORNL. See Oak Ridge national laboratory

OSO (orbiting solar observatory) See Artificial satellites—Astronomical applications

OSSA. See United States—National aeronautics and space administration—Space science and applications, Office of

OST. See United States—Science and technology, Office of

OSTS. See United States—Commerce, Department of—State technical services, Office of

OV (orbital vehicle) See Artificial satellites—Use in research

OAK
Volatile principle from oak leaves: role in sex life of the polyphemus moth. L. M. Riddiford and C. M. Williams. bibliog il Science 155:589-90 F 3 '67

OAK BLUFFS, Mass.
Oak Bluffs. D. G. McCullough. il Am Heritage 18:38-47 O '67

OAK electro-netics corporation
Adventures of Nick Carter. T. J. Murray. il Duns R 89:50-2+ Ap '67

OAK GLEN training camp. See Labor camps

OAK PARK, III.

Education
Million dollar carrels: Oak Park and River Forest, high school library; with report by L. Salinger. G. L. Schwilk. il Library J 92:306-10 Ja 15 '67

OAK RIDGE national laboratory
New force in vaccines; developed at AEC center. Bsns W p 127 Ag 12 '67

OAKHURST, N.J.
Aiding unwilling readers: paperbacks do the trick; Ocean township H.S. H. M. McDonnell. Sr Schol 90:sup21-2 Mr 31 '67

OAKLAND, Calif.

City planning
Oakland presents its case for salvaging a ghetto. J. Bailey. il Arch Forum 126:42-5 Ap '67

Galleries and museums
Landscaping the new Oakland museum. il Parks & Rec 2:18-19 S '67

Police
Reagan on police brutality. Nation 205:453-4 N 6 '67
Tactics of disruption; actions against Stop the draft week demonstration. M. Miles. New Repub 157:10 N 4 '67

Religious institutions and affairs
New type parish in west Oakland. W. E. Golder. Christian Cent 84:188-90 F 8 '67

Sanitary affairs
Just like putting a foreman in the cab; installing recording devices on street sweepers. J. E. McCarthy and R. Williams. il Am City 82:94-5 Mr '67

Taxation
Get the tax bills out on time. E. V. Waring. il Am City 82:110-11 Je '67

Water supply
But it doesn't look like a pumping station. il Am City 82:95 Ap '67

OAKLAND community college, Union Lake, Mich.
Oakland college's Orchard Ridge campus, a unique college with few classrooms. il Arch Rec 142:168-70 N '67

OAKLAND museum. See Oakland, Calif.—Galleries and museums

OAKLAND Oaks (basketball team) See Basketball teams

OAKLAND PARK, Fla.
Eighty tons go into a wet hole. il Am City 82:42 D '67

OAKLAND Raiders (football club) See Football clubs

OARSMANSHIP. See Rowing

OATES, James Franklin, 1899-
Close-up: executives, educators and youth; interview. por Duns R 89:10-11+ Ja '67

OATES, Joyce Carol
Background and foreground in fiction. Writer 80:11-13 Ag '67
Four summers; story. Yale R 56:406-25 Mr '67
Wheel of love; story. Esquire 68:134-7 O '67

OATHS of loyalty. See Loyalty, Oaths of

OATS
Avena ventricosa: possible diploid contributor to hexaploid oats. G. Ladizinsky and D. Zohary. bibliog il Science 155:1553-4 Mr 24 '67
Oats compete with corn? D. F. Wilken and H. Guither. Suc Farm 65:98 F '67

OATS—*Continued*

Disease and pest resistance

Avena magna: an important new tetraploid species of oats. H. C. Murphy and others. bibliog il Science 159:103-4 Ja 5 '68

OAXACA (state) Mexico
Farming systems and political growth in ancient Oaxaca. K. V. Flannery and others. bibliog il Science 158:445-54 O 27 '67

OBEDIENCE
See also
Authoritarianism

OBEDIENCE (canon law)
Case of Camilo Torres: the problem of obedience. C. Sussman and I. Sussman. Cath World 204:356-61 Mr '67

OBER, William B.
It's not safe to read. M. Mintz. New Repub 156:28-30 Mr 25 '67

OBERBECK, S. K.
Upstart prophet. Newsweek 69:98+ Je 19 '67

OBERDORFER, Don
He wants to be speaker of the House. N Y Times Mag p34-5+ Ap 30 '67
Noninterventionism, 1967 style. N Y Times Mag p28-31+ S 17 '67
Wobble on the war on Capitol hill. N Y Times Mag p30-1+ D 17 '67

OBERON, Merle
Travel. Vogue 149:43 Ja 15 '67

about
In a swinging resort the star is Merle Oberon. S. Kirkland. por Life 62:62A Ja 27 '67

OBERWEISER, Gilbert
New look at porky. Field & S 72:46+ Ag '67

OBESITY. See Corpulence

OBEY, Warren
Trials of man from big business. por Life 62:60 My 12 '67

OBITUARIES
I'm no ghoul; Times's chief obituary writer. il Newsweek 70:71 Ag 7 '67

OBJECTIVES in education. See Education—Aims and objectives

OBJECTIVISM
Cult of angry Ayn Rand. D. J. Hamblin. il Life 62:92-4+ Ap 7 '67

OBJECTS, Miniature. See Miniature objects

OBOLENSKY, Serge
Shepherd & his lambs. il por Time 91:41 Ja 19 '68

OBOLER, Eli M.
Ideas and the state university. Sch & Soc 95:78-80 F 4 '67

OBOTE, Milton
Making of a president, Uganda style. E. R. F. Sheehan. il pors N Y Times Mag p36-7+ Ja 22 '67
Tough shepherd. por Time 90:38+ O 13 '67

O'BOYLE, Patrick A. cardinal
Isaiah award and Cardinal O'Boyle. America 117:593 N 18 '67

OBRAZTSOV, Ivan Filippovich
Soviet educator urges engineer rewards; excerpts from Izvestia. Aviation W 87:115+ S 11 '67

O'BRIEN, Brian
All for the love of a lady. Field & S 72:32-3+ Ja '68

O'BRIEN, Conor Cruise
Counter-revolutionary reflex. Commonweal 85:619-21 Mr 3 '67
Joyce's Ireland. Sat R 50:56-7+ Mr 11 '67
Losing our cool, in Ghana. Nation 204:309-11 Mr 6 '67

O'BRIEN, David J.
American Catholics and anti-Semitism in the 1930's. Cath World 204:270-6 F '67

O'BRIEN, Donald K.
Build your ration by the bell. il Farm J 91: B13 S '67
Slats and free stalls, hard to beat. Farm J 91: D4-5 Je '67

O'BRIEN, Edna
Love object; story. New Yorker 43:42-52 My 13 '67

O'BRIEN, Flann, pseud. See Nolan, B.

O'BRIEN, James
Young skippers set a safety record. Motor B 119:32-3+ My '67

O'BRIEN, Justin
Making of an index: how to reminisce while name-dropping. Sat R 50:126-7 O 14 '67

O'BRIEN, Lawrence Francis
How to head off mail crisis; interview. por U S News 62:59-62 Ap 24 '67

New design for the postal service; address, April 3, 1967. Vital Speeches 33:418-21 My 1 '67; Excerpts. por U S News 62:54 Ap 17 '67
Other side of the postal story. por U S News 63:54 D 18 '67

about
Apolitical postmaster. Reporter 36:6+ Ap 20 '67
Is a drastic facelift in store for the mails? por Bsns W p32-3 Ap 8 '67
Mr O'Brien's leviathan. R. Moley. Newsweek 69:96 My 1 '67
Progress above politics. il por Time 89:33 Ap 14 '67

O'BRIEN, Maire Cruise
More callous than we know. Nation 204:763 Je 12 '67

O'BRIEN, Robert
How to save money buying a car. Read Digest 91:69-72 S '67

O'BRIEN, Robert C.
Telepsyche: the meeting of minds. Holiday 41:8+ F '67

O'BRIEN, Robert H.
Fight in the lion's den. il por Time 89:87 Mr 3 '67

O'BRIEN, Robert Yorke
To be perfectly frank. America 116:313 Mr 4 '67

O'BRIEN, William V.
Comments on the Vietnam debate. Cath World 205:169-70 Je '67

O'BRYAN, Deric
Climate and tree rings in Mesa Verde. Nat Parks Mag 41:17-19 Ap '67

OBSCENE literature. See Immoral literature and pictures

OBSCENE telephone calls. See Telephone calls

OBSCENITY (law)
ACLU supports review of Michigan censorship verdict. Pub W 191:226 Ja 23 '67
Bare majority; decisions on obscenity and indecent exposure. il Newsweek 69:42+ My 22 '67
CLEAN down the drain; California league enlisting action now. E. T. Moore; reply. E. Cray. Library J 92:945 Mr 1 '67
Guessing about obscenity. Time 90:50 N 3 '67
High court reverses three obscenity convictions, important issue of scienter goes undecided. Pub W 191:41-2 My 22 '67
High court to weigh N.Y. minor obscenity laws. Pub W 191:51 Je 26 '67
Hint on obscenity; Supreme court reverses three judgments. Time 89:91 My 19 '67
Libel case involving alleged obscenity. H. F. Pilpel. Pub W 191:28-30 My 1 '67
1966 in review; censorship and the freedom to read. Pub W 191:50-2 Ja 30 '67
Obscenity cases; Supreme court decision triggers R. Ginzburg appeal. A. M. Bickel. New Repub 156:15-17 My 27 '67
On the obscene scene. Reporter 36:10 Je 29 '67
President to empanel nat'l obscenity commission. Pub W 192:35 O 16 '67
Smut traffic; law in a muddle. il Newsweek 69:29-30 Ap 24 '67
Victory over the smut peddlers; Supreme court ruling. O. K. Armstrong. Read Digest 90:147-8+ F '67
What is the rule for seizing obscene materials? H. F. Pilpel. Pub W 193:22 Ja 1 '68
See also
Trials (obscenity)

OBSERVATORIES
See also
Astronomical observatories

OBSIDIAN hydration dating. See Archeological research

OBSOLESCENCE
Any old irons, or filmstrips? using Title II as excuse for unloading old inventories; letter to the editor. D. Bardsley. Library J 92:273 Ja 15 '67

OBSTACLE racing. See Hurdle racing

OBSTETRICS
Monitoring childbirth; Yale-New Haven medical center devises new way to monitor heartbeat of babies. il Newsweek 69:84 F 6 '67
See also
Cesarean section
Childbirth

OCALA stud. See Horse breeding

O'CALLAGHAN, Denis
Birth control crisis; reprint. por Cath World 204:326-34 Mr 7 '67

O'CASEY, Sean
O'Casey's benevolent blasts. S. Cronin. Nation 205:315-16 O 2 '67

OCCIDENTAL civilization. See Civilization

OCCIDENTAL petroleum corporation
Hammer strikes again. Newsweek 69:83-5 My 29 '67

OCCULT sciences
See also
Astrology

OCCULTATIONS
Grazing occultation of Antares. D. W. Dunham. il Sky & Tel 35:62 Ja '68
1968 occultation supplement; predictions for the United States and Canada. il Sky & Tel 34:313-20 N '67
Notable occultation of Saturn. D. W. Dunham. il Sky & Tel 34:336-8 N '67
November Saturn occultation. il Sky & Tel 35:58-9 Ja '68
Occultation highlights (cont) D. W. Dunham. il Sky & Tel 33:262; 34:62; 35:63 Ap, Jl '67, Ja '68
Occultations of Mars by Venus. G. S. Mumford. Sky & Tel 33:159 Mr '67
Saturn goes behind the moon in October. il Sky & Tel 34:412 D '67

OCCUPANCY
See also
Squatters

OCCUPATIONAL diseases. See Diseases, Industrial

OCCUPATIONAL education. See Vocational education

OCCUPATIONAL guidance. See Vocational guidance

OCCUPATIONAL mobility
Occupational mobility of employed workers. S. Saben. bibliog f il Mo Labor R 90:31-8 Je '67
Recent influences on the supply of labor. J. Mincer. Mo Labor R 90:30-1 F '67

OCCUPATIONS
Changes in occupational employment over the past decade. P. M. Ryscavage. il Mo Labor R 90:27-30 Ag '67
Education and the labor market; with study-discussion program, by C. Smallenburg and H. Smallenburg. bibliog il PTA Mag 61:24-6, 36-7 Ap '67
How much does your father's job affe t you? D. Klein. il Seventeen 26:130-1+ O '67
Job market for class of '67: more openings, better pay. il U S News 62:77-8 Mr 6 '67
New jobs with a big future. il Changing T 21: 6-10 N '67
Outdoor career guide. C. Nansen. il Field & S 71:10-12+ Ap '67
Surveying a city's labor market; Newburyport, Mass. E. F. Cook. il Am City 82:155 Je '67
What I'd like my son to be; eight famous athletes tell. N. Seitz. il Parents Mag 42: 50-3 Je '67
See also
Negroes in the United States—Occupations
Woman—Occupations

Classification
Occupational classification: an economic approach. Mo Labor R 90:48-52 F '67; Discussion. 90:64-5 Mr '67

Hygienic aspects
See Industrial hygiene

OCCUPATIONS, Choice of. See Occupations; Vocational guidance

OCEAN
Antipodal location of continents and oceans. C. G. A. Harrison; reply with rejoinder. R. Thompson. Science 156:263-4 Ap 14 '67
Ionospherically propagated sea scatter. L. H. Tveten. bibliog il Science 157:1302-4 S 15 '67
See also
Coasts
Indian Ocean
Oceanographic research
Oceanography
Sea water
Tides

Economic aspects
See Marine resources

OCEAN bottom
Advice for the Establishment; excerpt from address. J. T. Wilson. Sat R 50:50-1 S 2 '67
Blake outer ridge: development by gravity tectonics. J. E. Andrews. bibliog il Science 156:642-5 My 5 '67
Canada's unappreciated role as scientific innovator; magnetic surveys and the theory of convection in the earth's mantle; theories of J. T. Wilson and L. W. Morley. J. Lear. il Sat R 50:45-50 S 2 '67

Ecological studies during Project Sealab II. T. A. Clarke and others. bibliog il Science 157:1381-9 S 22 '67
Knoll and sediment drift near Hudson canyon. A. Lowrie, jr. and B. C. Heezen. bibliog il Science 157:1552-3 S 29 '67
Magnetic anomalies over the mid-Atlantic ridge near 27°N. J. D. Phillips. bibliog il Science 157:920-3 Ag 25 '67
Mid-Atlantic fault; earthquake locations under the mid-Atlantic ridge. Sci N 91: 351 Ap 15 '67
Radiolarian evidence consistent with spreading of the Pacific floor. W. R. Riedel. bibliog il Science 157:540-2 Ag 4 '67
Red Sea: detailed survey of hot-brine areas. J. M. Hunt and others. bibliog il Science 156:514-16 Ap 28 '67
Sea-floor spreading near the Galapagos. E. M. Herron and J. R. Heirtzler. bibliog il Science 158:775-80 N 10 '67
Sea floor spreading, topography, and the second layer. H. W. Menard. bibliog il Science 157:923-4 Ag 25 '67
Sediment distribution on the mid-ocean ridges with respect to spreading of the sea floor. J. Ewing and M. Ewing. bibliog il Science 156:1590-2 Je 23 '67
Tertiary sediment from the East Pacific rise. L. H. Burckle and others. bibliog il Science 157:537-40 Ag 4 '67
Transformation of gibbsite to chlorite in ocean bottom sediments. L. D. Swindale and P.-F. Fan. bibliog il Science 157:799-800 Ag 18 '67
Under the spreading sea floor. Sci Am 217: 40+ Ag '67
See also
Continental shelf
Deep sea deposits

International aspects
Deep seabed: who should control it? U.N. asks. L. J. Carter. Science 159:66-8 Ja 5 '68
Recent international developments concerning the ocean and ocean floor; statement, November 29, 1967. J. J. Sisco. Dept State Bul 58:17-19 Ja 1 '68
U.S. calls for U.N. committee to develop principles for cooperative exploration and use of ocean floor; statement. November 8, 1967. A. J. Goldberg. Dept State Bul 57: 723-5 N 27 '67

OCEAN bottom ore deposits. See Ore deposits

OCEAN currents
Geostrophic transport through the Drake Passage. A. L. Gordon. bibliog il Science 156:1732-4 Je 30 '67
See also
Gulf Stream

OCEAN fishing. See Salt water fishing

OCEAN in art
See also
Marine painting

OCEAN life. See Marine biology

OCEAN liners
Caviar and mutiny; Queen Mary's last voyage. il Newsweek 70:42 D 18 '67
Dance wildly, Queen Mary's about to die. A. Chamberlin. il Sat Eve Post 240:72-3 D 16 '67
Death of the Queens. il Time 89:122 My 19 '67
Faded splendor of a royal line. F. Mount. il Nat R 19:636 Je 13 '67
Farewell to the great ships: the Queen Mary and Queen Elizabeth. N. Mostert. il Reporter 37:38-41 Ag 10 '67
Great Cunard gamble. R. Nuttall. il Duns R 90:51+ N '67
Lindsay's ark? offer to buy Queen Mary for school. il Newsweek 70:61-2 Jl 31 '67
Long live the Queen. il Newsweek 70:72 O 2 '67
Long live the Q; Q-4 to be launched. il Time 90:104 S 22 '67
Luxury era fades at sea; plan to scrap Cunard's Queens. il Bsns W p 122-4 My 20 '67
Mary, 1,000 crossings later. J. A. M. Graham. il N Y Times Mag p 10-11+ S 3 '67; Same abr. with title Requiem for an ocean queen. Read Digest 91:196-7+ D '67
Memo from the Mary's last stowaway. T. Barry. il Look 31:122 N 14 '67
Once and future ships. T. L. Christie. il Sat R 51:51-2+ Ja 6 '68
Out to sea and into history; Queen Mary; with report by D. J. Hamblin. il Life 63: 26-31 O 6 '67

OCEAN liners—*Continued*
  Queen bids farewell; another is coming; Queen Mary retiring, Queen Elizabeth II launched. il Bsns W p46 S 30 '67
  Queens in check. il Newsweek 69:78 My 22 '67
  Roamer's ramblings. T. Shane. Travel 127:16-17 Je '67
  Sailing to France; aboard the S.S. France. il Mlle 65:83 Je '67
  Sporting life at sea; pari-mutuels on the Queen Elizabeth. J. Olsen. il Sports Illus 26:54-60 F 27 '67
  Successor to the Queens; Cunard's new luxury liner, Q4. il Pop Mech 128:106-8+ S '67
  Travel notes; Queen Mary. R. Joseph. Esquire 68:74+ O '67
  Why the rule of the ocean Queen is ending. il U S News 62:12-13 My 22 '67
    See also
  Shipwrecks
  Steamship lines

OCEAN science and engineering corporation
  Gulf oil gets research ship. Tech W 20:46-7 My 22 '67

OCEAN sounds
  Noisy chorus of the sea. W. N. Tavolga. il Natur Hist 76:20-7 Ap '67

OCEAN systems, incorporated
  600-ft. dives planned by OSI; Deep Diver, new submersible. Tech W 20:41 My 15 '67

OCEAN systems division. See North American aviation, incorporated—Ocean systems division

OCEAN travel
  Let's travel: Caribbean cruise. B. T. Blackwell. Mlle 65:195-9 My '67
  Once and future ships. T. L. Christie. il Sat R 51:51-2+ Ja 6 '68
  Tang of ocean thoughts. L. Wainwright. Life 63:12 S 1 '67
    See also
  Ocean liners
  Voyages around the world

OCEAN yacht racing. See Yacht racing

OCEANARIUMS. See Aquariums

OCEANIA
  Books in review; Australia and the islands. H. M. Van Deusen. Natur Hist 76:64-9 Mr '67
    See also
  South Sea Islands

OCEANIC basalt. See Basalt

OCEANIC ferromanganese. See Ferromanganese

OCEANOGRAPHIC institution, Woods Hole. See Woods Hole, Mass, oceanographic institution

OCEANOGRAPHIC instruments
  Deep divers at work. Sci Am 217:44 Ag '67
  Electronics in oceanography. J. Althouse. il Electr World 77:44-6+ Mr '66
  New designs may remove need for pressure housing; electronic equipment carried by deep submersibles. W. E. Wilks. il Aero Tech 21:48+ Jl 17 '67
  Oceanology products and processes. il Aero Tech 21:85-7 S 25 '67
  Temperature-depth measurements in the ocean. J. Althouse. il Electr World 78:33-6+ S '67
    See also
  Life support systems (submarine environment)
  Oceanographic research—Equipment

OCEANOGRAPHIC research
  Business takes the deep plunge; U.S. companies to launch subs to explore the sea's possibilities. il Bsns W p74-6 Je 17 '67
  Challenge of inner space; address, May 15, 1967. T. F. Hueter. Vital Speeches 33:551-4 Jl 1 '67
  Deep ocean technology may spur funding. R. W. Niblock and S. Montgomery. il Tech W 20:40-2+ Je 5 '67
  Deep sea exploration. E. Wenk, jr. il Sat R 50:43-4 Jl 1 '67
  Frontiersman of the sea; with interview, ed. by M. Silva. T. A. Pryor. il Life 63:45-6+ O 27 '67
  Litton drawing on space role to develop underwater suit. S. Montgomery. il Tech W 20:39-41 My 29 '67
  Navy intensifies surveys near USSR; antisubmarine warfare-undersea warfare survey project. R. W. Niblock. il Tech W 21:29-30 Jl 3 '67
  Oceanography: will LBJ's new study panel make its mark? L. J. Carter. Science 155:306-7 Ja 20 '67
  Oceanography: Woods Hole and MIT pool their resources. L. J. Carter. il Science 157:1154-7 S 8 '67

Off-the-shelf proposal; exploit the continental shelf. M. Getler. Aero Tech 21:90 S 25 '67
Russia dives for the sea bottom. A. Parry. il Sci Digest 62:60-4 S '67
Science explores the monsoon sea. S. W. Matthews. il Nat Geog Mag 132:554-75, sup (folded map) O '67
Secrets of sunken lands; studies off the Atlantic coast reveal history and wealth of the shelf. B. Tufty. il Sci N 91:77-9 Ja 21 '67
States drive to develop capabilities for ocean work. Tech W 21:27-8 Jl 3 '67
Taxi for the deep frontier, project Man-insea goes mobile. K. MacLeish. il Nat Geog Mag 133:138-50 Ja '68
U.S. sets priorities for tapping the sea. Bsns W p 112 Mr 18 '67
War budget slows national momentum; setbacks to oceanology program. R. W. Niblock and S. Montgomery. il Aero Tech 21:30-2 S 25 '67
Wenk sees U.S. favoring ocean ESRO. S. Montgomery. Tech W 20:25 Ap 24 '67
Westinghouse wins navy DOT award; deep ocean technology development plan. W. E. Wilks. Aero Tech 21:24 O 9 '67
Work beneath the waves. il Time 91:68-75 Ja 19 '68
    See also
Aerospace industries—Oceanographic activities
International Indian Ocean expedition
National oceanographic association
United States—National council on marine resources and engineering development
Woods Hole, Mass, oceanographic institution

Equipment
Deepstar set for Gulf, Atlantic waters; photographs. Tech W 20:41 My 15 '67
First plastic underwater hull big enough for men readied. Tech W 20:39-40 My 8 '67
Marine science and technology. P. H. Abelson. Science 155:1621 Mr 31 '67
Symposium stresses need for unsophisticated ocean tools; symposium on Underwater welding, cutting and hand tools. S. Montgomery. Aero Tech 21:44+ O 23 '67
Undersea hardware still untrustworthy. il Sci N 91:408-9 Ap 29 '67
    See also
Submarine boats
Underwater laboratories

Manufacture
Component manufacturers, subcontractors and suppliers. Aero. Tech 21:72+ S 25 '67

Finance
Industry investing heavily in oceanology. il Aero Tech 21:44+ S 25 '67

International control
Can U.N. parcel out the sea-bed? Maltese proposal. il Bsns W p66-8 N 11 '67
U.S. calls for U.N. committee to develop principles for cooperative exploration and use of ocean floor; statement, November 8, 1967. A. J. Goldberg. Dept State Bul 57:723-5 N 27 '67

OCEANOGRAPHY
  Greater DOD ocean role hinted by Foster; statement revealed at the fourth military symposium on oceanography. R. W. Niblock. Tech W 20:22 My 22 '67
  Lack of organization impedes industry role. R. W. Niblock. il Aero Tech 21:21-2 Jl 17 '67
  Ocean uses accentuated at Navy league; 10th annual symposium on seapower. R. Niblock. Tech W 20:31 F 20 '67
    See also
  Aerospace industries—Oceanographic activities
  Marine resources
  Oceanographic research
  United States naval oceanographic office, Suitland, Md.

Instruments
  See Oceanographic instruments

Study and teaching
  Promise of the sea; doctoral programs in oceanography. il Newsweek 70:56+ Ag 14 '67

OCEANOGRAPHY, Committee on. See National academy of sciences

OCHOA-SOLANO, Armando, and others
  Catalysis of ester hydrolysis by mixed micelles containing N-α-myristoyl-L-histidine. bibliog Science 156:1243-4 Je 2 '67

OCONEE bells
Mystery flower of Carolina. M. Donahue and R. Donahue. il Home Gard 54:68 My '67
O'CONNELL, Adelyn
Coming; poem. America 117:764 D 23 '67
Door; poem. America 117:616 N 18 '67
Literary forms (M,W,F 2:30) poem. America 116:247 F 18 '67
O'CONNELL, Daniel
Uncle Dan's feud with the Albany newspapers. J. Kapstein. il Reporter 36:37-40 Mr 9 '67
O'CONNELL, Jean S.
Monday child; story. McCalls 94:92-3 Ap '67
O'CONNELL, Jeffrey
Look ma, no driver. America 117:638-40 N 25 '67
New approach to auto insurance. America 116:830-1+ Je 10 '67
—See Keeton, R. E. jt. auth.
O'CONNELL, Richard
Small talk; poem. Atlan 219:120 Mr '67
O'CONNELL, Shaun
Styron's Nat Turner. Nation 205:373-4 O 16 '67
O'CONNOR, Daniel R.
Smooth tax collections mean soothed taxpayers. Am City 82:94-5 Ag '67
O'CONNOR, Edwin
Publisher and the pep talk. Writer 80:31-2 Ap '67
O'CONNOR, Flannery
Displaced person; dramatization. See Dawkins, C.
O'CONNOR, Frank
Act of charity; story. New Yorker 43:48-51 My 6 '67
Bring in the whiskey now, Mary. New Yorker 43:36-40+ Ag 12 '67
In dreams: does seven mean conception? Vogue 150:164-5+ N 1 '67
Mother's warning; story. Sat Eve Post 240:54-7 O 7 '67
Opinion: on writing about America. por Mlle 64:148+ Ap '67
about
Listening to Frank O'Connor. H. O'Connor. Nation 205:150-1 Ag 28 '67
O'CONNOR, Gerard
Yes, darling, but who was on third? Sports Illus 26:42-4+ Ap 24 '67
O'CONNOR, Harriet
Listening to Frank O'Connor. Nation 205:150-1 Ag 28 '67
O'CONNOR, Jack
Gemsbok in the Kalahari. por Outdoor Life 140:28-9+ Jl '67
Getting the range. See issues of Outdoor life
Indestructible buffalo. Outdoor Life 139:52-5+ Ap '67
Shooting. See issues of Outdoor life
O'CONNOR, John
Africa's need: African socialism. Cath World 205:358-64 S '67
O'CONNOR, John A.
To be perfectly frank. America 116:180-2 F 4 '67
about
Catholic press troubles. por Newsweek 70:59 Jl 17 '67
Dialog, but blandly; controversy over editorial policy. J. Deedy. Commonweal 86:484-6 Ag 11 '67
News and views. J. Deedy. Commonweal 86:378 Je 23 '67
Too much too soon; resignation of editor of the Delmarva dialog. S. J. Adamo. America 116:860-1 Je 17 '67
O'CONNOR, Richard
Black Jack of the 10th. Am Heritage 18:14-17+ F '67
Mr Coolidge's jungle war. Am Heritage 19:36-9+ D '67
OCRACOKE, N.C.
Ocracoke, North Carolina. il Bet Hom & Gard 45:22+ Ag '67
OCRACOKE ISLAND
No man on Ocracoke. R. Maloney. il Atlan 218:122+ Mr '67
OCTOBER song; story. See Sansom, W.
ODD lot sales. See Stocks—Odd lots
ODEN, Thomas C.
Seminary and preseminary education: analyses of two A.A.T.S. reports. Christian Cent 84:536 Ap 26 '67
ODENCRANTZ, F. Kirk, and Buecher, R. W.
Temperature-dependence of the polarity of electrical charges on ice crystals. bibliog Science 158:256-7 O 13 '67

ODETS, Clifford
Country girl. Criticism
Nat R 19:99 Ja 24 '67
ODHIAMBO, Thomas R.
East Africa: science for development. bibliog Science 158:876-81 N 17 '67
O'DOHERTY, Barbara Novak
Philosopher of the face. Art N 66:42-5+ Sum '67
ODOMETERS
I'll cheat you if you don't watch out; how used-car mileage is faked. il Pop Sci 191:76-9+ D '67
O'DONNELL, Gladys (Berry)
Making of a president. por Time 89:21 My 12 '67
O'DONNELL, Kenneth
Where was O'Donnell? il por Time 89:78 F 17 '67
O'DONNELL, Mary Kathleen
Mirage; story. Atlan 220:87-90 O '67
O'DONNELL, Richard W.
(ed) See Murphy, K. B. Too young to die
O'DONNELL, Walter Edward
Doctor talks sense about physical checkups. por Good H 164:111+ Mr '67
Finally: a sure cure for housewife fatigue. Ladies Home J 84:74+ Ap '67
O'DONOGHUE, Joseph
Those faceless chanceries. Commonweal 86:167-71 Ap 28 '67
ODORI festival of Japan. See Dancing, Japanese
ODORS
How to trace bad odors. Am City 82:144 Je '67
Mice: individual recognition by olfactory cues. J. M. Bowers and B. K. Alexander. bibliog il Science 158:1208-10 D 1 '67
See also
Perfumery
ODYSSEY. See Homer
OEHLERT, Benjamin H. jr
Congress; address, February 7, 1967. Vital Speeches 33:472-5 My 15 '67
OEHSER, Paul H.
From the Thoreauvian well. Liv Wildn 30:27-9 Aut '66
OERKE, Andrew
J.C; poem. Christian Cent 84:367 Mr 22 '67
Lover; poem. Mlle 65:94 Je '67
OERTLE, V. Lee
Hottest lake in Utah. Field & S 71:152-3+ Ap '67
Trailer hitch that's easy on a car. Pop Sci 190:158-9 Je '67
Why it pays to rent a vacation camper. Pop Sci 190:176-80+ My '67
OETTINGER, Katherine Brownell
Urgently needed: more day care centers. por Parents Mag 42:58 N '67
about
Parents' magazine's 1967 awards. il por Parents Mag 42:52+ D '67
OF love remembered; drama. See Sundgaard, A.
O'FAOLAIN, Julia
Pray for grace, poor little sinner; story. Sat Eve Post 240:78-80 F 25 '67
O'FAOLAIN, Seán
Smithsonian: biographer to the world. Holiday 42:44-9+ Ag '67
about
Retrospect on O'Faolain. G. Freyer. New Repub 156:28-30 F 25 '67
O'FARRELL, Joe
Building an empire on horses ready to run. P. Axthelm. il por Sports Illus 26:45-8 Ja 23 '67
OFF-Broadway theater. See New York (city)—Theater
OFF-the-air recording. See Magnetic recorders and recording
OFFENBACH, Jacques
Tales of Hoffmann. Criticism
Opera N il 32:28 Ja 13 '68
OFFERTORIES
Anecdotes, facetiae, satire, etc.
New committee on liturgy named. P. J. Laux. America 117:555 N 11 '67
OFFICE appliances
Turning deaf ear to rich suitors; Acme visible records not for sale. il Bsns W p 148-50 Ja 14 '67
See also
Burroughs corporation
Dictating machines
OFFICE buildings
Building types study. il Arch Rec 141:171-86 Je '67

OFFICE buildings—*Continued*
Office boom changes the scene. il Bsns W p 167-8+ O 7 '67
Two office buildings in Pasadena. il Arch Rec 142:155 D '67
See also
New York (city)—Architecture
New York (city)—Rockefeller Center

Designs and plans
Challenging collaboration for TAC. M. F. Schmertz. il Arch Rec 142:159-64 S '67
Erieview plaza; Cleveland, Ohio. il Arch Rec 141:153-6 Mr '67
Low-rise office buildings. il Arch Rec 141: 157-62 Mr '67
Small office building by Marcel Breuer: sophisticated use of precast concrete; Torrington manufacturing co. il Arch Rec 141: 131-6 F '67

Location
See Location in business and industry

OFFICE decoration
It's the detailing that counts; interview. F. Stanton. il House & Gard 131:132-5 F '67

OFFICE furniture
It's the detailing that counts; interview. F. Stanton. il House & Gard 131:132-5 F '67
Madison avenue was never like this; offices of Papert, Koenig, Lois, inc. J. M. Dixon. il Arch Forum 126:90-5 Ja '67

OFFICE holders. See Public officers

OFFICE management
Network planning: management tool for architects. H. A. Goleman. il Arch Rec 141: 93-4 F; 93-4 Mr '67
So you think you're indispensable. il Nations Bsns 55:56-8+ D '67
See also
Billing

OFFICE parties. See Business entertaining

OFFICE workers
Common paradox: white-collar organization in Britain; excerpt from Trade union growth and recognition. G. S. Bain. bibliog f il Mo Labor R 90:42-7 O '67
Primer for a theory of white-collar unionization. V. Lombardi and A. J. Grimes. bibliog f Mo Labor R 90:46-9 My '67

Salaries
Latest white-collar salaries. il Nations Bsns 55:36-7 Ag '67

Training
From mop to typewriter; pilot clerical training unit at the University of California at Los Angeles. L. A. W. Darling. il NEA J 56:28-9 O '67

OFFICES
Madison avenue was never like this; offices of Papert, Koenig, Lois, inc. J. M. Dixon. il Arch Forum 126:90-5 Ja '67
OFFICES of the United States government. See name of office, inverted under United States. e.g. United States—Science and technology. Office of

OFFICIAL entertaining. See Government entertaining

OFFICIAL grievance man. See Ombudsman

OFFICIAL life; story. See Hazzard, S.

OFFICIAL secrets
See also
Government and the press

OFFSET lithography. See Lithography

OFFSET printing. See Printing, Offset

OFFSHORE boundaries. See Territorial waters

OFFSHORE exploration conference
Aerospace firms prominent at OECON. il Tech W 20:32-3 F 20 '67

OFFSHORE oil well drilling. See Oil well drilling, Submarine

OFFSHORE platforms. See Artificial islands

O'GARA, James
All things considered. See issues of Commonweal
Bishops' synod, a decisive perhaps. Commonweal 87:162-3 N 10 '67
Religion & politics. Commentary 44:105-8 N '67

OGBURN, Charlton, jr
Mr Katzenbach's puzzle. New Repub 157: 13-14 N 4; 17-18 D 2 '67
Yard; story. Harper 235:55-9 Jl '67

OGG, Robert D.
Anchors and anchoring. Yachting 121:79+ Ja '67

OGILVY, David
Men who made the word move. H. Bigart. por Sat R 50:59-60 Ap 22 '67

OGLESBY, Carl
Spanked and the unspanked. Sat R 50:76-7+ My 20 '67
Vietnam: this is Guernica. Nation 204:714-21 Je 5 '67

O'GORMAN, Ned
Blue shutter; poem. Nation 204:522 Ap 24 '67
Harvesters' vase; poem. Nation 204:185 F 6 '67
Ned O'Gorman; interview. New Yorker 43:54-5 D 2 '67
Paralytic; poem. Nation 204:630 My 15 '67
Paulo climbing down through a tree; poem. Nation 204:702 My 29 '67

O'HANLON, Thomas
5,350 companies=a mixed-up furniture industry. Fortune 75:144-9+ F '67
Fred Hartley and his well-oiled multiplying machine. Fortune 75:156-61+ Ap '67
Mobil oil squarely in the middle. Fortune 76: 86-9+ S 1 '67
Odd news about conglomerates. Fortune 75: 174-7 Je 15 '67

O'HARA, Edward
VISTA. Am Ed 3:27-9 S '67

O'HARA, Frank
Cavalier of the open city. il Newsweek 71: 88+ Ja 22 '68
In memory of my feelings. J. Ashbery. il Art N 66:50-1+ Ja '68
Making of In memory of my feelings. G. Williams, jr. il Pub W 193:60+ Ja 1 '68

O'HARA, John
Barred; story. Sat Eve Post 240:60-2 O 7 '67
Celibacy, sacred and profane. Holiday 42:28-9 Ag '67
Gangster; story. Sat Eve Post 240:56-8 N 18 '67
Gunboat and Madge; story. Sat Eve Post 240: 64-6 F 25 '67
How old, how young; story. New Yorker 43: 28-32 Jl 1 '67
Whistle stop. See issues of Holiday

about
Peripatetic reviewer. E. Weeks. il Atlan 220: 130 D '67

O'HARA, Sister Kevin. See Gavin, H. jt. auth.

O'HARE International airport. See Chicago—Airports

O'HARROW, Dennis
Obituary
Am City por 82:22 O '67

O'HEARN, Robert
Interview; ed. by A. Fatt. por Dance Mag 41:55 Ap '67

OHIO
Ohio's new lakes; Tappan, Atwood, Leesville, Clendening, Piedmont and Seneca lakes. G. Lindsey. Travel 127:41 My '67
See also
Architecture, Domestic—Ohio
Booksellers and bookselling—Ohio
Canals—Ohio
Hunting—Ohio
Music festivals—Ohio
Taxation—Ohio

Politics and government
Rhodes at the crossroads: voters defeat Ohio bond commission. M. I. Urofsky. New Repub 156:7-8 My 20 '67

OHIO state library, Columbus
Ohio tackles trail-blazing Books/jobs project. Library J 92:2863 S 1 '67
Say it isn't so, Woody; passing of football era at Ohio state. R. Cantwell. il Sports Illus 27:98-104+ S 11 '67

OHIO state university, Columbus
Two dormitories at Ohio state. il Arch Rec 142:153-4 D '67

OHIO. University, Athens
Introduction to success: teenage trainees working with preschool youngsters. H. C. Lyon, jr. il Am Ed 3:5-6+ My '67
Renaissance in Athens. il Time 89:63 F 10 '67

OHLES, John F.
Watts, the schools, and citizenship education. Sch & Soc 95:256 Ap 15 '67

OHLIN, Lloyd E. and Ruth, H. S. jr
(eds) Combating crime. bibliog f Ann Am Acad 374:1-184 N '67

OHMART, Howard
Community and the juvenile. bibliog f Cur Hist 53:94-101 Ag '67

OHMMETERS
See also
Voltohmmeters

OHNO, Susumu, and others
Genetic control of lactate dehydrogenase formation in the hagfish eptatretus stoutii. bibliog Science 156:96-8 Ap 7 '67

OIEN, Alvin F. family
Please hurry, someone; ordeal after crash in mountains of northern California. H. H. Martin. il pors Sat Eve Post 241:30-2+ Ja 13 '68

OIL. See Petroleum

OIL as fuel. See Oil fuel; Oil heating

OIL changes, Automobile. See Automobiles—Lubrication

OIL companies. See Oil industries; Petroleum industry and trade

OIL field flooding
Geological subsidence. S. S. Marsden, jr. and S. N. Davis. il Sci Am 216:93-100 Je '67

OIL fields, Offshore. See Petroleum in submerged lands

OIL fuel
Cutting down the reek of pollution; residual oil with high sulfur content major contributor to big-city smog. il Bsns W p79-80+ Ja 28 '67

Prices

Northeast frets about fuel oil. il Bsns W p50+ O 21 '67

OIL gages. See Gages

OIL heating
Home-heating battle gets still warmer. il Bsns W p76-7 Ag 12 '67

OIL industries
Aladdin's lamp. New Repub 156:4 F 25 '67
See also
Petroleum industry and trade

Advertising

New keeper for Esso's tiger? Bsns W p48 Ap 22 '67

OIL pollution of coastal waters. See Oil pollution of rivers, harbors, etc.

OIL pollution of rivers, harbors, etc.
Are American beaches in danger, too? il U S News 62:46-7 Ap 17 '67
Battling the blob; effects of oil discharge from tanker aground off British coast. il Newsweek 69:44+ Ap 3 '67
Britain's great, ghastly ooze; fight against oil from the Torrey Canyon shipwreck off the Cornish coast. il Newsweek 69:48-51 Ap 10 '67
Clean-sea code. il Parks & Rec 2:37-8 N '67
Detergents at sea. Newsweek 69:110 Ap 10 '67
Ecological disaster; Torrey Canyon disaster. il Sci Digest 61:26 Je '67
In the oily wake of a tragedy at sea. il U S News 62:18 Ap 10 '67
Letter from London; battle to finish off the Torrey Canyon. M. Panter-Downes. New Yorker 43:158 Ap 15 '67
Letter from Paris; two Brittany departments: Côtes du Nord and Finistère devastated areas, because of wreck of Torrey Canyon. Genêt. New Yorker 43:166+ Ap 29 '67
Mopping up oily oceans. il Time 90:63 Jl 28 '67
Oil around us. R. Rienow and L. T. Rienow. il N Y Times Mag p24-5+ Je 4 '67
Oil globs coat Cornwall; wreck of tanker Torrey Canyon. il Sr Schol 90:17 Ap 14 '67
Oil, oil everywhere; water pollution problem posed by breakup of oil tanker Torrey Canyon. il Sci N 91:328 Ap 8 '67
Oil pollution. P. H. Abelson. Science 156:1037 My 26 '67; Discussion. 157:251, 625 Jl 21, Ag 11 '67
Oily flotsam that fouled fair England; with report by J. Hicks. il Life 62:26-35 Ap 14 '67
One answer shows through the oil slick. il Audubon 69:4-5 N '67
Operation Canute; fighting the oil from tanker Torrey Canyon, aground off Cornish coast. il Time 89:28 Ap 7 '67
Pollution with antipollutants. Sci Am 217: 53-4 N '67
Silicones could have saved sea life; Torrey Canyon disaster. Sci N 92:343-4 O 7 '67
Sunken time bombs full of oil! D. C. Fales. il Pop Mech 128:97-101+ N '67
Tanker's messy wake; wreck of the Torrey Canyon. Bsns W p 128 Ap 1 '67
Tarfoot; great need for international control of oil shipping. New Repub 156:4-5 Ap 29 '67
Time bombs off the Atlantic coast; deep sea pollution by oil. il Sci N 92:369-70 O 14 '67
Tragedy of errors; effect of Torrey Canyon disaster on sea life. J. Fisher and S. Charlton. il Audubon 69:72-85 N '67

Two kinds of tankers, clean and dirty; Torrey Canyon wreck. C. Kentfield. il N Y Times Mag p24-5+ My 14 '67
What is the answer to an oil slick threat? Pop Mech 128:101 N '67

OIL shales
Dependable supplies of hydrocarbons. P. H. Abelson. Science 157:11 Jl 7 '67; Discussion. 157:755 Ag 18 '67
40,000 for you? New Repub 156:2 Ap 29 '67
No more teapot domes; shale oil deposits along the Green River in Colorado, Wyoming and Utah. Am For 73:11 Mr '67
Oil for shale; proposal to lift federal ban on the staking of new oil-shale claims. il Newsweek 69:86-8 My 22 '67
Opening up oil shale. Bsns W p 180+ My 20 '67
Shale oil question. Nat Parks Mag 41:21 Mr '67

OIL tankers. See Tank ships

OIL well drilling, Submarine
Oil companies to use Mohole technology. R. W. Niblock. il Tech W 20:24-5 Ap 17 '67
See also
Artificial islands
Petroleum in submerged lands

OIL wells
Americans not everybody knows: Pattillo Higgins; first geyser of oil. C. W. Ferguson. il PTA Mag 62:16-18 O '67

Flooding
See Oil field flooding

OILERS (football club) See Football clubs

OILS, Lubricating. See Lubrication and lubricants

OILS and fats, Edible
Fat in the foods we eat. il Consumer Bul 50:37-40 Jl '67

OINTMENTS
Treating burns, frostbite; saving lives with sulfonomide-based burn cream. F. Marley. il Sci N 91:362-3 Ap 15'67

OJAI festival. See Music festivals—California

OJHA, Ishwer Chandra
China and North Vietnam: the limits of the alliance. bibliog f Cur Hist 54:42-7 Ja '68
China's cautious American policy. bibliog f Cur Hist 53:135-40+ S '67

OKA, Seishi W. See Kraus, B. S. jt. auth.

OKEECHOBEE WATERWAY. See Waterways—United States

O'KEEFE, John A. and Scott, R. F.
Chondritic meteorites and the lunar surface. bibliog Science 158:1174-6 D 1 '67

O'KEEFE, Patricia
Family pet. See issues of American home
—See KortKamp, R. jt. auth.

O'KEEFFE, Georgia
O'Keeffe. E. C. Goossen. il pors Vogue 149: 174-9+ Mr 1 '67

OKEY, Robert W.
Membranes will cut treatment costs. Am City 82:124 Je '67

OKINAWA
Okinawa; indispensable U.S. bastion in Asia. B. Krisher. il Newsweek 70:50 N 27 '67
Okinawa's future and Far-East security; hope of reversion of 1951 peace treaties. M. E. Weinstein. Reporter 37:39-40 N 2 '67
Something for the hat. il Time 90:24 N 24 '67
What U.S. is giving back to Japan. il U S News 63:54 N 27 '67

OKLAHOMA
See also
Fishing—Oklahoma
Libraries—Oklahoma

OKLAHOMA CITY

Airports
City ordinance regulates private airports. Am City 82:162+ Je '67

City planning
One city's answer to the big-city crisis. il U S News 63:88-9 O 16 '67

Civil defense
See Oklahoma City—Defenses

Defenses
Getting our back-up; Ridgeview PTA forms civil defense auxiliary. il PTA Mag 62:27 S '67

OKLAHOMA Indians. See Indians of North America

OKLAHOMA state library, Oklahoma City
Oklahoma state librarian fired. Library J 92: 3579 O 15 '67

OKLAHOMA. University, Norman
Creation of quality; new president. il Time 89:44 Je 2 '67
OKLAWAHA RIVER
Vanishing waterway; a sentimental pilgrimage to the Oklawaha River system. E. White. il Yachting 122:42-3+ N '67
OKRA
See also
Cookery—Vegetables
OKUN, Arthur M.
Good-by to LBJ's Mr Chips. il por Newsweek 71:57-8 Ja 15 '68
Steady beat at the CEA. por Bsns W p 19 Ja 6 '68
OLD age
The best is yet to be. L. De Veuve. Christian Cent 84:866-7 Jl 5 '67
See also
Aged
Longevity
OLD age homes
See also
Nursing homes
OLD age income. See Retirement income
OLD age pensions
See also
Pensions, Industrial

United States
LBJ tax plan that is going unnoticed; social security pensions. il U S News 62:84-5 F 13 '67
Newest plan to boost pensions and payroll taxes; social security pensions. il U S News 63:84-6 Ag 14 '67
Retirement benefits: pension plans on thin ice. A. Prisendorf. il Nation 204:175-8 F 6 '67
Second thoughts about LBJ's pension plan; social security pensions. il U S News 62:100 Je 19 '67
Soon, it will be easier to build your own pension. il U S News 63:82-3 S 4 '67
Who foots what bill for social security? Congress to pay pensions of the lower-income workers. il Bsns W p 110-11 Ja 13 '68
Wrong road for social security; President Johnson's proposals. Bsns W p 160 Ja 21 '67

OLD farmer's almanac. See Almanacs
OLD Glory. See Flags—United States
OLD Glory; drama. See Lowell, R.
OLD man and his hat; story. See Freitag, G. H.
OLD MAN OF THE MOUNTAIN. See Profile Mountain
OLD Order Amish. See Mennonites
OLD people. See Aged
OLD SALEM village. See Winston-Salem, N.C.
OLDENBURG, Claes
Take a cigarette butt and make it heroic; interview, ed. by S. Gablik. il Art N 66:30-1+ My '67
about
Art. M. Kozloff. Nation 205:27-9 Jl 3 '67
Art world. H. Rosenberg. New Yorker 43:117-18 Je 3 '67
OLDENDORPH, O. F.
California's Anza-Borrego Desert state park. il Nat Parks Mag 41:4-9 D '67
Ground afire. il Nat Parks Mag 41:4-9 Jl '67
OLDS, Greg
LBJ will make it despite a GOP trend. New Repub 158:13-14 Ja 20 '68
OLDS, Robin
War hero comes home, and speaks out; excerpts from news conference. por U S News 63:19 O 16 '67
about
Old man & the MIGs. il por Time 89:16 Je 2 '67
Robin Olds and his battle aces. T. Buckley. il por Esquire 68:117-19 O '67
OLDS, Sally
Operation friendship. Parents Mag 42:56-7+ Ap '67
OLDSTONE, Michael B. A. and Dixon, F. J.
Lymphocytic choriomeningitis: production of antibody by tolerant infected mice. bibliog Science 158:1193-5 D 1 '67
OLEANDERS
Happy oleander. il Sunset 138:250-1 My '67
O'LEARY, B. T. and Rea, D. G.
Mars: influence of topography on formation of temporary bright patches. bibliog Science 155:317-19 Ja 20 '67
O'LEARY, James John
Edie's new mind & manners. Time 89:84 Mr 24 '67

O'LEARY, Mary E. See Smith, K. C. jt. auth.
O'LEARY, Ted
Pool. Sports Illus 27:52-4 Jl 10 '67
OLEASTERS
Russian olive can take it. il Sunset 139:130+ Jl '67
OLEFINS
Chlorination of unsaturated compounds in nonpolar media. M. L. Poutsma. bibliog il Science 157:997-1005 S 1 '67
OLEKSY, Jerry. See Duffy, T. jt. auth.
OLEMBO, Reuben J.
East African academy. Science 155:1581-2+ Mr 24 '67
OLESHA, [urii Karlovich
Computerized humanity. M. Friedberg. Sat R 50:31 D 23 '67
OLFSON, Lewy
Jane Eyre; dramatization of novel by C. Brontë. Plays 27:89-96 O '67
When you query, write it right! Writer 80:14-15+ Mr '67
Wuthering Heights; dramatization of novel by E. Brontë. Plays 27:87-96 Ja '68
OLIN Mathieson chemical corporation
Olin's grand designer; G. Grand. W. Berry. Duns R 89:50-2 My '67
To the letter; G. K. Funston. Time 89:90 F 10 '67
OLITSKI, Jules
Olitski: nothing but color. K. S. Champa. il por Art N 66:36-8+ My '67
OLIVARES, J. and others
Toxohormone from normal tissues. bibliog Science 157:327-8 Jl 21 '67
OLIVE industry and trade
Conference on olive oil to prolong agreement. UN Mo Chron 4:64-5 Ap '67
OLIVER, Andrew
Antiques book preview. Antiques 91:476-80 Ap '67
OLIVER, Covey T.
Alliance for progress moves on: a report on developments since the summit meeting; address, November 14, 1967. Dept State Bul 57:754-8 D 4 '67; Same with title Latin America. Vital Speeches 34:135-8 D 15 '67
Business of development; address, September 13, 1967. Dept State Bul 57:470-5 O 9 '67
Contours of change in the home hemisphere; excerpts from address, December 7, 1967. Dept State Bul 58:8-10 Ja 1 '68
Institution-building and the Alliance for progress; address, June 7, 1967. Dept State Bul 57:102-7 Jl 24 '67
Our continuing commitment in the home hemisphere; address. November 30, 1967. Dept State Bul 57:868-73 D 25 '67
OLIVER, Dixie
Forget TV, children, let's play: creative fun for kids. Life 63:11 S 1 '67
OLIVER, Edith
Off Broadway. See issues of New Yorker
Theatre. New Yorker 42:93-4 F 4; 43:94 Jl 15; 127-8+ N 11; 46 D 30 '67
OLIVER, R. Spencer
How the Young were kept in line. P. R. Wieck. New Repub 157:9-10 D 2 '67
OLIVES
Six rich Mediterranean recipes. E. Alston. il Look 31:64-5+ O 31 '67
OLIVETTI
Olivetti's crisis of identity. W. Guzzardi, jr. il Fortune 76:92-7+ Jl '67
Renaissance. il Time 89:88 F 24 '67
OLIVIER, Carlos Galli-. See Galli-Olivier, C.
OLIVIER, Charles P.
Great bolide of April 25, 1966. Sky & Tel 33:83-4 F '67
OLIVIER, Sir Laurence
Best of breed. il por Time 90:64 N 3 '67
Letter from London; performance in the National theatre production of Strindberg's Dance of death at the Old Vic. M. Panter-Downes. New Yorker 43:158+ Ap 15 '67
Olivier triumphant. H. Hewes. Sat R 50:36 Jl 1 '67
Theatre in Europe. H. Clurman. Nation 204:797-8 Je 19 '67
OLLER, Emma Boehm-. See Boehm-Oller, E.
OLLER, Francisco
Francisco Oller: Puerto Rican impressionist. E. Boehm-Oller. il por Américas 19:22-7 S '67
OLLESTAD, Norman
Trade winds. J. Beatty, jr. Sat R 50:6 Jl 8 '67
OLMECS. See Indians of Mexico
OLQUIN, Leonard
Learn a lito Englich. R. H. Levine. il Am Ed 4:24-5 D '67

OLSEN, Edward G.
Teacher education for the deprived: a new pattern. Sch & Soc 95:232-4 Ap 1 '67
OLSEN, Edward John
Amphibole: first occurence in a meteorite. bibliog Science 156:61-2 Ap 7 '67
OLSEN, Herb
Child portraiture. Design 69:10-13 Wint '67
OLSEN, Jack
Not a park to go barefoot in. Sports Illus 26:58-60+ Ap 3 '67
Off season for izards. Sports Illus 27:70-2+ O 23 '67
Sporting life at sea. Sports Illus 26:54-60 F 27 '67
—See Tarkenton, F. jt. auth.
OLSEN, Leif H.
Citibank banks on its economists. il por Bsns W p 142-4+ F 25 '67
OLSEN, Merlin
Game without the ball. R. Kahn. il pors Sat Eve Post 240:79-83 D 16 '67
OLSON, Bernhard Emmanuel
Answer to Hochhuth. Sat R 50:27-8 S 9 '67
OLSON, Richard Hugo
From outer space to open space. il por Bsns W p98-100 N 11 '67
OLSON, Ted
Meteora; poem. Sat R 50:68 Mr 18 '67
OLT, James R.
Steamboat bull. Field & S 72:62-3+ O '67
Varmint shooter's paradise. Outdoor Life 139: 62-5+ My '67
Ways for fox squirrels. por Outdoor Life 140:62-4+ S '67
OLYMPIA press
Girodias to start publishing in U.S. Pub W 192:44 Ag 21 '67
OLYMPIC country club course. See Golf courses
OLYMPIC games
Last living amateur is still a king among kings; A. Brundage, president of IOC. L. Griggs. il Sports Illus 26:70+ My 22 '67
See also
Pan American games
OLYMPIC games, 1956
Running of the green. R. Delany. il Sports Illus 28:18-23 Ja 15 '68
OLYMPIC games, 1968
Bully buildup in old Mexico; preparations for 19th Olympic games. B. Ottum. il Sports Illus 27:20-3 O 30 '67
Cause for alarm; negro athletes might boycott the games in Mexico. Sports Illus 27:11 S 25 '67
France, a go-go place for the games; photographs by E. Haas; with account by F. R. Smith. il Sports Illus 27:46-62 N 13 '67
Letter from Mexico city. D. Gold. Holiday 42:16+ O '67
Negro Olympics boycott is off target. Life 63:4 D 8 '67
Olympic boycott? il Newsweek 70:59 D 4 '67
Pills and Olympians; doping with amphetamines. Sci N 91:353 Ap 15 '67
Plague of high altitudes. B. J. Culliton. Sci N 92:587 D 16 '67
Shook-up town's great shape-up; Grenoble getting ready for winter Olympics. J. Olsen. il Sports Illus 27:80-2+ N 13 '67
Step to an Olympic boycott; Western regional black youth conference. J. Rodgers. il Sports Illus 27:30-1 D 4 '67
Travel notes. R. Joseph. Esquire 68:60+ N '67
Where Negroes have struck it rich. il U S News 63:71 D 11 '67
OLYMPIC NATIONAL PARK
Bogachiel reverie; with photographs. R. Kirk. Liv Wildn 30:10-15 Aut '66
Olympic rain forest, by R. Kirk. Review Liv Wildn 30:30-1 Aut '66. M. Nadel
Some animals of Olympic Park. S. F. Arno. il Nat Parks Mag 41:10-14 Mr '67
OLYMPIC PENINSULA
Last frontier: the Olympic Peninsula. E. Clark. il Todays Health 45:34-9+ Ag '67
Private park for rockhounds; Agate Beach. A. L. Jones. il Nat Parks Mag 41:15 My '67
OLYMPIC rain forest. See Olympic National Park
OMAHA, Neb.
Hospitals
Archbishop Bergan mercy; growth on a new site. il Arch Rec 142:194-5 S '67
OMBUDSMAN
Corporate ombudsman. I. Silver. bibliog f Harvard Bsns R 45:77-87 My '67

Educational tyranny and the ombudsman; protecting pupils and teachers. R. O. Werner. Sch & Soc 95:391-2 O 28 '67
Protecting the poor. L. Chazen. Commentary 44:93-6 Ag '67
Tough cheese; Britain's first ombudsman. Newsweek 71: 32 Ja 8 '68
OMBUDSMAN; story. See Benchley, N.
O'MEARA, Patrick M.
Church management systems. America 116: 835-7 Je 10 '67
O'MEARA, Thomas F.
Theology: made in U.S.A. Cath World 205: 231-6 Jl '67
OMELETS. See Cookery—Eggs
OMNITRON. See Accelerators (electrons, etc)
OMOHUNDRO, John Burwell
Plainsman and ballerina. L. Moore. il por Dance Mag 41:46-9 O '67
OMORI, Minoru
Can Mao win? New Repub 156:14-16 F 25 '67
Mao's worst crisis. New Repub 156:17-19 Ja 28 '67
ON this day; story. See Woiwode, L.
ON the development of peoples. See Encyclicals
ONCHOCERCIASIS
River blindness afflicts 200,000,000. D. A. Ehrlich. il Sci N 92:16-17 Jl 1 '67
ONCOGENIC virus. See Sarcoma
ONE-act plays. See Dramas—One-act plays
ONE of the family; story. See Turner, C.
ONE-room apartment. See Apartments
ONE unhappy bachelor; story. See Soman, F. J.
ONE very hot day; novel. See Halberstam, D.
O'NEIL, Paul
Nudity. Life 63:107-8+ O 13 '67
Somebody up there likes you drivers. Life 63:54-54B+ Ag 4 '67
Woody. Life 62:92-4+ Ap 28 '67
O'NEIL, Terrence Jay
Indian mound is excavated by high school archaeologists; ed. by C. L. Stong. Sci Am 217:134-8 D '67
O'NEILL, Eugene Gladstone
More stately mansions. Criticism
America 117:622 N 18 '67
Commonweal 87:335-6 D 8 '67
Life il 63:63-4 O 13 '67
Nat R 20:43-4 Ja 15 '68
Nation 205:538-40 N 20 '67
New Yorker 43:127 N 11 '67
Newsweek il 70:125 N 13 '67
Reporter 37:34-5 N 30 '67
Sat R 50:26+ N 18 '67
Time il 90:76-7 S 22 '67
Vogue 151:62 Ja 1 '68
Mourning becomes an opera. F. Stevenson. il Opera N 31:14-16 Ap 1 '67
Old Testament man as American. A. Croce. Nat R 20:43-4 Ja 16 '68
O'NEILL, Jeanne Lamb
Among my un-souvenirs. Am Home 70:25 S '67
Anyone for Halloween? Am Home 70:68 O '67
For the love of peat. Am Home 70:36 My '67
Go away madly. Am Home 70:44 Ja '67
Let George do it, diet, that is. Am Home 70:50-1 Mr '67
Mama's little workshop. Am Home 70:25 D '67
On the street, lane, circle or drive where you live. Am Home 71:40 Ja '68
Please don't move the piano. Am Home 70:44 Jl '67
Sonnets from a porch-ophile. Am Home 70:33 Je '67
Where there's smoke, there's me. Am Home 70:37 N '67
O'NEILL, Michael
Four myths about parochial schools (cont) America 116:183-7 F 4 '67
ONG, Yoke Lin
What is at stake in Vietnam: an Asian view; interview, ed. by C. T. Rowan. por Read Digest 91:118-21 N '67
ONGANIA, Juan Carlos
End of a truce. il por Time 89:40 Mr 17 '67
ONLY child. See Children—Only child problem
ONLY people; story. See Higgins, J.
ONLY son; story. See Banks, L. R.
ONOMATOPOEIA
How did language begin? M. Pei. il Sat R 50:54-5 S 9 '67
ONTARIO
See also
Bruce Peninsula
Canals—Ontario
Manitoulin Island
Paleontology—Ontario

ONTARIO—*Continued*

Description and travel

Discover Ontario's Land O'Lakes. H. L. Brun. il Motor B 119:22-3+ Je '67

Religious institutions and affairs

World around us. Christian Cent 84:187-8, 634-6, 1201-2 F 8, My 10, S 20 '67

ONTHANK, Karl William

Obituary

Nat Parks Mag 41:18-19 D '67

OOMYCETES. See Fungi

OOTACAMUND, India

Profiles. M. Panter-Downes. il New Yorker 43:48-50+ Mr 4; 57-62+ Mr 11 '67

OP art. See Modernism (art)

OPALS

Nature note; opal fires; electron microscope shows spheres. il Sci N 91:79 Ja 21 '67

OPDYKE, Neil D. See Hays, J. D. jt. auth.

OPEN air church services. See Church services

OPEN and closed shop

Legal test of union shop. U S News 63:106-7 O 9 '67

OPEN-end investment trusts. See Investment trusts

OPEN shop. See Open and closed shop

OPEN space program. See Land utilization

OPERA

Handel operas. S. Sadie. il Hi Fi 17:69-72 F '67

Is opera dead? G. Schuller. il Opera N 31: 8-12 Je 10 '67

Orchestra in opera. R. Lawrence. il Opera N 32:14-17 D 9; 13-16 D 16; 10-13 D 23; 26-9 D 30 '67; 26-9 Ja 6 '68

Sisters under the skin; opera and ballet. C. Barnes. il Opera N 31:8-13 Ap 15 '67

See also

Libretto

Anecdotes, facetiae, satire, etc.

Griselda, doge of Venice, by Pollo Cacciatore (1820-1881) J. Mathewson. Opera N 31:16 Ap 15 '67

Benefit performances

Five for the Guild. il Opera N 32:15 S 23 '67

Bibliography

Horn of plenty. S. Jenkins, jr. il Opera N 32:6-7 D 16 '67

History and criticism

At home with the sea. K. McDonald. Opera N 31:24-5 F 11 '67

Champagne sec; Fledermaus concocted from dry wit and sweet melody. K. McDonald. il Opera N 31:24-5 Ja 7 '67

Flashes of lightning; Verdi goes to the heart of his characters. S. Jenkins, jr. il Opera N 32:24-5 Ja 20 '68

Measure of greatness. H. Taubman. il Opera N 31:8-13 Ap 1 '67

Out of touch. T. Guthrie. Opera N 31:8-11 F 11 '67

Springtime of life; Verdi's La Traviata and Dumas's story. G. R. Marek. Opera N 31: 24-6 Mr 25 '67

Why opera? J. Barzun. il Opera N 31:6-10 Ja 28 '67

Instruction and study

Body and song. H. Danziger. il Opera N 32:8-11 Ja 13 '68

Language

Cosi gehen vous? M. E. Geib. Opera N 31:6-7 F 25 '67

Whose English? translated opera. A. M. Lingg. il Opera N 31:28-9 Ja 7 '67

Stage music

See Stage music

Stage scenery

Flowery Flute; sets and costumes for The magic flute by Chagall. il Time 89:43+ Mr 3 '67

Met's Flute; apotheosis of Chagall? P. J. Smith. il Hi Fi 17:MA10-11 My '67

Moses, Mozart, Pinter; interview. ed. by E. Rizzo. J. Bury. Opera N 32:16 Ja 13 '68

Mozart and Chagall; Metropolitan opera's production of The magic flute. il Newsweek 69:75 Mr 6 '67

Set to go. J. Ardoin. il Opera N 31:6-7 Mr 18 '67

Three flutes: new productions of Mozart's Die zauberflöte, designed by Oskar Kokoschka; Beni Montresor; Marc Chagall. il Opera N 31:11-13 Ja 28 '67

Armenia

Armenian diary; L. Chookasian visits the land of her forebears. G. Gavejian. il Opera N 32:14-16 D 23 '67

Austria

Musical events; performances by Vienna opera at Expo '67. W. Sargeant. New Yorker 43: 135-40 S 23 '67

Tarnished tradition; Vienna state opera at Expo. H. Saal. il Newsweek 70:91 S 18 '67

Vienna opera at Expo. G. Movshon. il Hi Fi 17:MA20-1+ N '67

See also

Vienna state opera

Bulgaria

Young opera singers, their care and training. P. Hart. Hi Fi 17:MA24-5 O '67

Europe, Western

Lively arts; interview, ed. by R. Hemming. E. Lear; T. Stewart. Sr Schol 91:27-8 O 26 '67

Germany (Federal Republic)

Essen, Dusseldorf. H. Koegler. il Opera N 31: 31 Mr 4 '67

Munich. E. Davidson; E. D. Echols. Opera N 32:27 O 14 '67

Rhine-Ruhr; new productions. H. Koegler. Opera N 32:28 N 25 '67

See also

Bayreuth festival

Great Britain

Music to my ears; Glyndebourne's La Bohème, Covent Garden's Carmen. I. Kolodin. Sat R 50:78 Je 10 '67

India

Opera and India. H. Schramm. il Opera N 32:8-12 O 14 '67

Italy

After the flood, the operas open. W. Weaver. Hi Fi 17:MA30 Mr '67

Music to my ears; performances of Cavalleria rusticana and Falstaff. I. Kolodin. Sat R 50:22 Je 24 '67

Musical events; performance of Verdi's Requiem by orchestra and chorus of La Scala, conducted by H. von Karajan. W. Sargeant. New Yorker 43:107+ O 28 '67

Power of positive vocalizing; La Scala at Expo 67. Time 90:81 O 20 '67

La Scala has the last word; at Expo 67. R. Gelatt. il Hi Fi 17:MA24-5 D '67

Total opera; La Scala at Expo. H. Saal. il Newsweek 70:61-2 O 16 '67

Verdi and Giordano revived. W. Weaver. il Hi Fi 17:MA36-7 My '67

Verdian Requiem by La Scala. I. Kolodin. Sat R 50:49-50 N 4 '67

Russia

Big opera; Bolshoi opera at Expo. H. Saal. il Newsweek 70:69 Ag 21 '67

Bolshoi; thinking big; performances at Montreal's Expo 67. P. G. Davis. il Hi Fi 17: MA18-19+ N '67

Moscow in Montreal; Bolshoi opera presentations at Expo 67. H. Weinstock. Sat R 50: 64+ S 16 '67

Musical events; performance by Moscow's Bolshoi opera at Expo 67. W. Sargeant. New Yorker 43:141-2 S 9 '67

Soulful giant; Bolshoi opera at Expo 67. il Time 90:42 Ag 18 '67

Switzerland

Opera on an even keel. E. Helm. il Hi Fi 17:MA38-9 My '67

Turkey

Recordings. M. Mayer. Esquire 67:60+ Je '67

United States

Across the land. R. D. Daniels. Opera N 31:32 Ja 7 '67

Lively arts; interview, ed. by R. Hemming. E. Lear; T. Stewart. Sr Schol 91:27-8 O 26 '67

On the road; plans for new American national opera company. Newsweek 69:76 Mr 6 '67

Opera for hire. A. M. Lingg. il Opera N 32:6-7 N 4 '67

OPERA—United States—*Continued*
Report: across the land. R. D. Daniels. Opera N 32:30 D 9 '67
Transcontinental bang; new season opens. il Time 90:48 S 29 '67
U.S. calendar. See issues of Opera news published during opera season
U.S. opera survey: onward and upward. F. Merkling. il Opera N 32:12-13 N 25 '67
What price culture? Nat R 19:627-8 Je 13 '67

See also
American national opera company
American opera society
Associated opera companies of America
Connecticut opera association
Lyric opera of Chicago
Metropolitan opera company
Metropolitan opera guide
New York city opera company
Opera, American
Opera guilds
Philadelphia lyric opera company
Radio broadcasting—Opera
San Carlo opera company
San Francisco opera company

OPERA, American
Hit from Hamburg: a U.S. opera; G. Schullers The visitation. P. Moor. Life 62:11 Je 30 '67
Measure of greatness. H. Taubman. il Opera N 31:8-13 Ap 1 '67
Yankee trick. Q. Eaton. Opera N 31:6-7 Ap 1 '67

OPERA, Swedish
Musical events; performances by Royal opera of Stockholm at Expo 67. W. Sargeant. New Yorker 43:78+ Je 24 '67
Spaceship to nowhere; Aniara, a parable for our time. J. W. Freeman. il Opera N 31:14-15 My 13 '67

OPERA ballet. See Ballet
OPERA broadcasts. See Radio broadcasting—Opera
OPERA company of Boston
At the opera: mod Stravinsky, brilliant Bartók. M. Steinberg. il Hi Fi 17:MA20-1 Jl '67
Boston. H. Rogers. il Opera N 31:30 Ap 1 '67
Boston; Hogarth's Tom Rakewell. H. Rogers. il Opera N 31:28 My 13 '67
OPERA composers. See Composers
OPERA conducting. See Conducting (music)
OPERA festivals. See Music festivals
OPERA guilds
Affiliated guilds report (cont) Opera N 31:6-7 Ap 8 '67
See also
Metropolitan opera guild
OPERA houses
Mexican classic; Teatro Juarez, Guanajuato, Mexico. C. Bailey. il Opera N 31:6 F 18 '67
Swinging Staatsoper. P. Moor. il Hi Fi 17:52-5 Je '67
Sydney opera house, what happened and why. il Arch Rec 141:189-92 My '67

Fires and fire protection
Santa Fe in flames. G. Martin. il Opera N 32:12-14 S 9 '67
OPERA quiz. See Radio broadcasting—Opera
OPERA singers
Also in the cast . . . A. Velis. il Opera N 32:8-12 D 16 '67
At the piano; excerpts. I. Newton. il Opera N 31:6-7 Je 10 '67
Fulbright story; Educational exchange program. R. Eyer. il Opera N 31:8-11 Ja 7 '67
Great singers. by H. Pleasants. Review
Sat R 50:69 Mr 25 '67. H. Weinstock
If the tights fit; women playing men's roles, and vice versa. J. W. Stedman. il Opera N 31:6-7 Ja 7 '67
Metropolitan opera repertory 1967-68 and roster. il Opera N 32:16-17 S 23 '67
No small roles. R. Liebermann. il Opera N 32:8-10 S 23 '67
Operatic jet set. E. Lear. il Hi Fi 17:53-6 Mr '67
Plain case for the golden age. C. L. Osborne. il Hi Fi 17:102-7 O '67
Singing voice: heroes and peach fuzz; operatic tenors. R. Rushmore. il Opera N 31:26-8 F 25 '67
Singing voice: indisposed. R. Rushmore. il Opera N 31:28-30 Mr 25 '67
Singing voice: light and soaring. R. Rushmore. il Opera N 31:28-30 F 4 '67

Singing voice: rarest of all. R. Rushmore. il Opera N 31:28-30 F 11 '67
Singing voice: the lower depths. R. Rushmore. il Opera N 31:28-30 Mr 11 '67
Thelma Votipka featured on LP; American lady singers. A. Favia-Artsay. il Hobbies 71:36+ F '67
To mark Canada's centenary, great singers of her past. G. Movshon. il Hi Fi 17:63 Jl '67
World's greatest tenor; with biographical sketches of eight singers. R. Daley. il Life 63:74-6+ D 15 '67
See also
Singing

Photographs
Mishkin; photographer to the Metropolitan opera. L. Mishkin. Opera N 32:12-15 Ja 20 '68
OPERA society of Washington
Ginastera's Bomarzo. C. L. Osborne. il Hi Fi 17:MA12-13+ Ag '67
Washington; production of A. Ginastera's Bomarzo. F. Merkling. il Opera N 31:21 Je 10 '67
OPERA tickets
The line; a report on a changing institution. J. Weber. il Opera N 32:6-7 N 25 '67
OPERAS
See also
Phonograph records—Operas

Caricatures and cartoons
Another roundup; more broadcast operas. M. Thaler. Opera N 31:14-16 Ap 8 '67
Mad look at Trovatore; with remarks by N. Meglin. M. Drucker. Opera N 31:14-16 F 18 '67
Roundup; broadcast operas to date. M. Thaler. Opera N 31:14-16 Ja 7 '67

Choral singing
Angelic choir; children's chorus in Hansel and Gretel. A. M. Lingg. il Opera N 32:26-7 D 23 '67

Criticisms, plots, etc.
See name of composer for full entry
Aïda. G. Verdi
Aniara. K. B. Blomdahl
Antony and Cleopatra. S. Barber
Un ballo in maschera. See Masked ball, below
La Bohème. G. Puccini
Bomarzo. A. Ginastera
Boris Godunov. M. P. Musorgskiĭ
Boulevard solitude. H. W. Henze
Burning fiery furnace. B. Britten
Cardillac. P. Hindemith
Carmen. G. Bizet
Cavalleria rusticana. P. Mascagni
Le coq d'or. N. A. Rimskiĭ-Korsakov
Coronation of Poppea. C. Monteverdi
Daughter of the regiment. G. Donizetti
Deseret. L. Kastle
Don Giovanni. J. C. W. A. Mozart
Don Rodrigo. A. Ginastera
Dream of Liu-Tung. I. Yun
Ernani. G. Verdi
Falstaff. G. Verdi
Die fledermaus. J. Strauss, jr
Force of destiny. See La forza del destino, below
La forza del destino. G. Verdi
Die frau ohne schatten. See Woman without a shadow, below
Friedenstag. R. Strauss
From one day to the next. A. Schönberg
Gianni Schicchi. G. Puccini
La Gioconda. A. Ponchielli
Giulio Cesare. G. F. Handel
La guerra. R. Rossellini
Hamlet. A. Thomas
Hansel and Gretel. E. Humperdinck
Histoire du soldat. I. F. Stravinsky
L'incoronazione di Poppea. See Coronation of Poppea, above
Iris. P. Mascagni
Legend of the invisible city of Kitezh. N. A. Rimskiĭ-Korsakov
Lizzie Borden. J. Beeson
Lohengrin. R. Wagner
Lucia di Lammermoor. G. Donizetti
Lulu. A. Berg
Madame Butterfly. G. Puccini
Magic flute. J. C. W. A. Mozart
Makropulos case. L. Janácek
Marriage of Figaro. J. C. W. A. Mozart
Martha. F. von Flotow
Masked ball. G. Verdi
Mathis der maler. P. Hindemith
Mathis the painter. See Mathis der maler, above

OPPENHEIMER, Julius Robert—*Continued*
In passing: Dr Oppenheimer. A. Ewing. il
  pors Sci N 91:205+ Mr 4 '67
J. Robert Oppenheimer dies. por Sr Schol 90:
  18-19 Mr 10 '67
J. Robert Oppenheimer, 1904-1967. por Bul
  Atomic Sci 23:2-6 O '67
J. Robert Oppenheimer, RIP. Nat R 19:236
  Mr 7 '67
Notes and comment. New Yorker 43:31-2 Mr
  4 '67
Obituary
  Reporter 36:12 Mr 9 '67
  Science 155:1061 Mr 3 '67. D. K. Price
Oppenheimer: where he was there was al-
  ways life and excitement. H. A. Bethe. il
  pors Science 155:1080-4 Mr 3 '67
Oppie. por Newsweek 69:98 Mr 6 '67
Oppie: the troubled Pied Piper of Los
  Alamos. L. Lamont. il por Life 62:34B Mr
  3 '67
OPPENHEIMER, Monroe
Day of magic; story. Redbook 129:38-9 Ag
  '67
OPPORTUNITIES industrialization center. See
  Negroes in the United States—Employment
OPPORTUNITY, Mont.
Right man in the right place, at last;
  R. Rouse to meet champion Dick Tiger.
  G. Rogin. il Sports Illus 27:32-4+ N 13 '67
OPPOSITION (political science)
Anti-politics in America, by J. H. Bunzel.
  Review
  Nation 204:827-8 Je 26 '67. H. S. Kariel
OPTIC, Oliver, pseud. See Adams, W. T.
OPTICAL communication systems. See Light
  communication systems
OPTICAL masers. See Lasers
OPTICAL modulators. See Modulators
OPTICAL stimulus. See Stimulus and response
OPTICAL test bench. See Photography—Appa-
  ratus and supplies
OPTICAL trade
Ever magnifying wonders of the optics in-
  dustry. L. Lessing. il Fortune 75:105-5+
  Ap '67
OPTICS
Ever magnifying wonders of the optics in-
  dustry. L. Lessing. il Fortune 75:105-5+
  Ap '67
Optical methods for studying Hertzian
  resonances; tr. of address, December 12,
  1966. A. Kastler. bibliog il Science 158:214-
  21 O 13 '67
Optical properties of materials. A. Javan.
  il Sci Am 217:238-42+ S '67
  See also
  Reflection (optics)
OPTICS, Physiological
Optical differentiation of amoebic ectoplasm
  and endoplasmic flow. W. R. Baker, jr.
  and J. A. Johnston, jr. bibliog il Science
  156:825-6 My 12 '67; Discussion. 158:142-3
  O 6 '67
OPTIONS
  See also
  Put and call transactions
OPTIONS, Stock purchase. See Stock pur-
  chase options
OPUS Dei
God's octopus. il Time 89:32+ My 12 '67
ORACLES
Delphi: the oracle revealed. W. Golding. il
  Holiday 42:60-1+ Ag '67
ORAL cancer. See Cancer
ORAL contraceptives. See Contraceptives
ORAL English. See English language—Study
  and teaching
ORAL history
Dimensions of oral history; adaptation of ad-
  dress, September 1966. L. Shores. il Library
  J 92:979-83 Mr 1 '67
Voice as history. A. B. Rollins, jr. Nation
  205:518-21 N 20 '67
ORAL reading. See Books and reading—Read-
  ing aloud
ORANGE, Robert P. and others
Release of slow-reacting substance of ana-
  phylaxis in the rat: polymorphonuclear leu-
  kocyte. bibliog Science 157:318-19 Jl 21 '67
ORANGE juice
Orange juice: frozen, canned or bottled. il
  Consumer Rep 32:394-7 Jl '67; Correction.
  33:5-6 Ja '68
ORANGE juice, Frozen. See Fruit juices,
  Frozen
ORANGES
Orange crush; growers face catastrophe. Time
  89:67 Ja 27 '67
  See also
  Orange juice

ORANGUTANS
Smuggled orangutan seized by U.S. officials.
  Parks & Rec 2:13+ My '67
ORATORIOS
No more molars; W. Joseph's Requiem. Time
  89:38 F 3 '67
  See also
  Phonograph records—Oratorios
ORATORY
  See also
  Public speaking
ORBITAL applications center. See Space sta-
  tions
ORBITING astronomical observatory. See Arti-
  ficial satellites—Astronomical applications
ORBITAL flight. See Space flight
ORBITAL rendezvous (space flight)
Back on the track; Soviet space spectacular.
  il Newsweek 70:105 N 13 '67
Coupling by computer; Russian automatic
  rendezvous. il Time 90:64 N 10 '67
Russia takes the lead; rendezvous and
  docking of two unmanned spacecraft. il
  Bsns W p36 N 4 '67
Russians press earth-orbit goals; with edi-
  torial comment. Aviation W 87:11, 16-17
  N 6 '67
ORBITING geophysical observatory. See Arti-
  ficial satellites—Astronomical applications
ORBITING solar observatory. See Artificial
  satellites—Astronomical applications
ORBITS
  See also
  Moon—Orbits
ORCHESTRA hall, Chicago. See Concert halls
ORCHESTRA musicians. See Musicians
ORCHESTRAL conductors. See Conductors
  (music)
ORCHESTRAL music
  See also
  Phonograph records—Orchestral music
ORCHESTRAS
Debuts & reappearances; New York concerts.
  il Hi Fi 17:MA16-21+ My '67
Jazz orchestra; Thad Jones-Mel Lewis al-
  liance. B. Korall. il Sat R 50:116-17+ Mr
  11 '67
Letter from Paris; Orchestre de Paris début.
  Genêt. New Yorker 43:232-4 N 25 '67
Many-splendored sound of Los Angeles; with
  list of community orchestras in California.
  R. Kendall. il Sat R 50:46+ S 23 '67
Montreal; Montreal symphony orchestra's pro-
  ductions at Expo 67. F. Campbell. il Opera
  N 32:23-4 S 23 '67
Munch and the Orchestre de Paris. J.
  Maguire. il Sat R 50:46-7 D 30 '67
Musical events; concert performed in Car-
  negie Hall by Concertgebouw orchestra of
  Amsterdam. W. Sargeant. New Yorker 43:
  161 My 6 '67
Orchestra in opera. R. Lawrence. il Opera N
  32:14-17 D 9; 13-16 D 16; 10-13 D 23; 26-9
  D 30 '67; 26-9 Ja 6 '68
Together at last; Orchestre de Paris. il Time
  90:106 N 24 '67
Visiting orchestras: Suisse Romande & Bath.
  B. Jacobson. Hi Fi 17:MA16-17 S '67
  See also
  Conducting (music)
  also names of orchestras, e.g. Buffalo
  philharmonic orchestra
ORCHESTRE de Paris. See Orchestras
ORCHIDS
Give her an orchid that grows. il Pop Gard
  18:12-13 Mr '67
Hardy orchids outdoors all year. il Sunset
  138:252-3+ Mr '67
How and where to buy orchids. J. Kramer.
  il Horticulture 45:46-7+ Mr '67
How to grow orchids for all-season bloom.
  J. Kramer. il Home Gard 54:42-5 D '67
Remarkable miltonias. H. R. Sweet. il Horti-
  culture 45:38-9+ Je '67
Want an orchid? grow one at home. I. Ross
  and M. Ross. il Pop Gard 18:82-3+ D '67
Wild orchid worth taming. A. Anthony. il
  Home Gard 54:70 F '67
ORCZY, Emmuska, baroness
Scarlet Pimpernel; dramatization. See Leech,
  M. T.
ORDAZ, Gustavo Díaz. See Díaz Ordaz, G.
ORDNANCE, Naval
Honeywell gun for Vietnam patrol boats.
  C. D. LaFond. il Tech W 20:30 F 6 '67
ORE deposits
Confirmation from afar; hot brines and
  heavy metal deposits in deeps of the Red
  Sea. E. T. Degens and D. A. Ross. il Sat R
  50:52 S 2 '67

OREGON
See also
Architecture, Domestic—Oregon
Birds—Oregon
Columbia River
Coos Bay
Fishing—Oregon
Gardens—Oregon
Hell's Canyon
Prisons—Oregon

Description and travel
Portland and surprising Oregon. il Bet Hom & Gard 45:76-7 My '67

Industries
Oregon graduate center: a new Portland scientific institution. B. Nelson. il Science 157:1151-2+ S 8 '67

Parks and reserves
Oregon offers an autumn treat for boaters and for campers; Cove Palisades State Park. il Sunset 139:20-1 O '67

Religious institutions and affairs
Loosening the cork; Oregon Methodist churches repeal non-drinking laws. Newsweek 69:69 Je 26 '67

OREGON Fairview home, Salem. See Rehabilitation centers

OREGON freeze dry foods, Incorporated
Gourmet C-rations; long range patrol subsistence. Newsweek 70:95 N 13 '67

OREGON graduate center, Portland
Oregon graduate center: a new Portland scientific institution. B. Nelson. il Science 157:1151-2+ S 8 '67

OREGON state university, Corvallis
Saga of the barefoot bag on campus. J. Riley. il Life 62:72A-72B Mr 17 '67

O'REILLY, John
Oh, for a good aardvark stampede. Sat R 50:90-2 My 13 '67

ORES
See also
Iron ores
Ore deposits

ORESTEIA; drama. See Lewin, J.

ORFEO ed Euridice; opera. See Haydn, F. J.

ORFORD, Robert Walpole, 1st earl of
Echoes across the centuries. J. H. Plumb. Sat R 50:34-5 Ja 28 '67

ORFORD, N.H.

Historic houses, etc.
Living with antiques; New Hampshire home of Mr and Mrs John Hodgson. A. D. Hodgson. il Antiques 92:182-6 Ag '67

ORGAN
New electronic organ kit; Heathkit-Thomas Paramount theater organ. il Electr World 79:52-4+ Ja '68
Planning to buy an organ? il Bet Hom & Gard 45:108+ S '67
Two top-notch electronic organs that come in kits. R. M. Benrey. il Pop Sci 192:108-11 Ja '68
Warm and clear; installation of new organ in the United church on the green, New Haven, Conn; interview. P. Jordan. New Yorker 43:42-4 S 23 '67

ORGAN PIPE CACTUS NATIONAL MONUMENT
Reporter at large; exploring this area and Cabeza Prieta game range, proposed combination for Sonoran Desert National Park. B. Roueché. New Yorker 43:76+ Ag 12 '67

ORGANELLES
See also
Lysosomes

ORGANIC compounds
See also
Electroorganic chemistry

ORGANIC evolution. See Evolution

ORGANIC gardening
Truth about organic gardening. R. M. Carleton. il Pop Gard 18:12-13+ My '67

ORGANIZATION charts
Manuals of press set-up and work; charts and procedure guides for university presses. Pub W 192:29-30 Jl 3 '67

ORGANIZATION for economic cooperation and development
Address to OECD council, Paris, April 7, 1967. H. H. Humphrey. Dept State Bul 56:683-5 My 1 '67
Adjusting manpower requirements to constant change. Mo Labor R 90:36-41 O '67

Edwin M. Martin elected chairman, Development assistance committee. Dept State Bul 57:808 D 11 '67
Europe warns America: tighten your belt. U S News 64:10 Ja 8 '68
World monetary system; address, March 17, 1967. H. F. Fowler. Vital Speeches 33:455-62 My 15 '67

ORGANIZATION for European nuclear research. See European organization for nuclear research

ORGANIZATION in industry. See Industrial management and organization

ORGANIZATION of African unity
Address to OAU; summary. Thant. UN Mo Chron 4:26-7 O '67
Africa in the world arena. K. W. Grundy. bibliog f Cur Hist 52:134-5+ Mr '67
Assembly expresses satisfaction; UN and OAU cooperation. UN Mo Chron 4:79-80 Ja '67
Degree of success. il Newsweek 70:56 S 25 '67
Order or oratory? Time 90:30-1 S 22 '67
Reluctant guests; meeting to be held in Congo. il Newsweek 70:52 S 18 '67

ORGANIZATION of American states
Another can of worms. Nation 206:36 Ja 8 '68
Barbados: a small great American nation. G. de Zéndegui. Américas 19:inside cover D '67
CIDEM meeting in Canada; Inter-American music council. il Américas 19:42-4 Je '67
Hemisphere cooperation through the Alliance for progress; address, October 19, 1967. S. M. Linowitz. Dept State Bul 57:616-20 N 6 '67
Is Ché Guevara in Bolivia? il Sr Schol 91:6 O 12 '67
Latin lyricism at the foreign ministers meeting. N. Miller. New Repub 157:12 O 7 '67
New milestones in the inter-American system. G. Meek. il Américas 19:1-8 Ap '67
OAS foreign ministers take steps against Cuban subversion; statements, September 23, 24 with text of final act, September 24, 1967. D. Rusk. Dept State Bul 57:490-8 O 16 '67
OAS in action. G. Meek. See issues of Américas
President recommends ratification of OAS charter amendments; message, June 12, 1967. L. B. Johnson. Dept State Bul 57:78-9 Jl 17 '67
Public opinion and the OAS. G. de Zéndegui. Américas 19:inside cover Je '67
Slow progress in the OAS. America 116:299 Mr 4 '67
What Castro is plotting: the fight for a hemisphere. il U S News 63:42-3 O 9 '67

Inter-American defense board
Defense board anniversary. G. Meek. Américas 19:47-8 My '67

ORGANIZATION of black American culture, Chicago. See Negro associations

ORGANIZATIONS. See Associations

ORGANIZATIONS, Aviation. See Aviation associations

ORGANIZATIONS, Communist. See Communist organizations

ORGANOPHOSPHOROUS compounds. See Phosphorous compounds

ORGANS. See Organ

ORIENT. See Asia

ORIENT express. See Railroads—Europe

ORIENTAL art. See Art, Oriental

ORIENTAL dolls. See Dolls

ORIENTAL game. See Go (game)

ORIENTAL gardens. See Gardens, Oriental

ORIENTAL persimmons. See Persimmons

ORIENTAL poppies. See Poppies

ORIENTAL rugs. See Rugs and carpets, Oriental

ORIENTAL studies
Promotion of Far-Eastern studies. Sch & Soc 95:488+ D 9 '67

ORIENTALS. See Asians

ORIENTATION
Amphibian orientation: an unexpected observation. V. Twitty and others. bibliog il Science 155:352-3 Ja 20 '67
Geomagnetism and animal orientation. J. D. Palmer. il Natur Hist 76:54-7 N '67
Honey bees: do they use the direction information contained in their dance maneuver? D. L. Johnson. bibliog il Science 155:844-7 F 17 '67

ORIENTATION—*Continued*
Honey bees: do they use the distance information contained in their dance maneuver? A. M. Wenner. bibliog il Science 155:847-9 F 17 '67
How birds get home. il Sci Digest 62:22 S '67
Navigation of single homing pigeons; airplane observations by radio tracking. M. C. Michener and C. Walcott; reply with rejoinder. B. G. Murray, jr. Science 155:1135-6 Mr 3 '67
Newts: sun-compass orientation. H. F. Landreth and D. E. Ferguson. bibliog il Science 158:1459-61 D 15 '67
Orientation by taste in fish of the genus ictalurus. J. E. Bardach and others. bibliog il Science 155:1276-8 Mr 10 '67
Radio tracking of homing bats. T. C. Williams and J. M. Williams. bibliog il Science 155:1435-6 Mr 17 '67
See also
Echolocation (physiology)

ORIENTATION (architecture)
Case house, Van Hornesville, New York. il Arch Rec 141:78-81 mid-My '67
Escape to the Atlantic shore; six faces to the sun. J. L. Hendrix. il House B 109:94-9 Ja '67
Gonzales house, Paradise Valley, Arizona. il Arch Rec 141:94-7 mid-My '67
Private residence, Sherman Oaks, California. il Arch Rec 141:86-7 mid-My '67
Rouse house, Clayton, New York. il Arch Rec 141:108-11 mid-My '67
There is always room at the top. il House & Gard 131:148-55 Mr '67
Updating the big old house. il Am Home 70:90-5 My '67

ORIGIN of man. See Man—Origin and antiquity

ORIGINAL sin. See Sin

ORIGINALITY. See Creation (literary, artistic, etc)

ORIGO, Iris
Ignazio Silone. Atlan 219:86-93 Mr '67

ORION (constellation)
Ultraviolet spectra in Orion. il Sky & Tel 33:162 Mr '67

ORION nebula. See Nebulae

ORLANDINI, Pamela
Andean awakening. Travel 127:64-6+ My '67

ORLANDO, 1925-
Orlando. il Pop Phot 60:98-101+ Je '67

ORLANDO, Jacque Reed
Planting island. Home Gard 54:65 Mr '67

ORLANDO, Fla.
Music
Orlando; performances of Rossini's Barber of Seville. M. E. Peltz. Opera N 31:30 Ap 1 '67

ORLANDO, Fla., public library
Johansen's Orlando library: compatible colony of varied forms. il Arch Rec 141:151-6 Je '67
Monolithic concrete in Orlando. C. E. Wendel. il Library J 92:4363-4 D 1 '67

ORLANS, Harold
Developments in federal policy toward university research; adaptation of address, September 29, 1966. bibliog Science 155:665-8 F 10 '67; Excerpt. Sat R 50:45-6 Ap 1 '67

about
Basic science in mission-oriented endeavor. T. L. Campbell. por Science 156:670-2 My 5 '67

ORLEANS, Leo A.
Research and development in Communist China. bibliog Science 157:392-400 Jl 28 '67

ORLOW, Dietrich
Conversion of myths into political power: the case of the Nazi party, 1925-1926. bibliog f Am Hist R 72:906-24 Ap '67

ORME, Frank
Report on TV for children. Parents Mag 42:40-1+ F '67

ORMSBY, Virginia H.
Brad. NEA J 56:20-1 My '67

ORNAMENTAL cookery. See Cookery, Ornamental

ORNAMENTAL design. See Design, Decorative

ORNAMENTAL gardening. See Topiary work

ORNAMENTAL glass. See Glass, Ornamental

ORNAMENTAL onions. See Alliums

ORNAMENTS, Christmas tree. See Christmas decorations

ORNE, Jerrold
Academic library building in 1967. por Library J 92:4345-50 D 1 '67
Future for humanism; adaptation of address, December 5, 1966. por Library J 92:1893-5 My 15 '67

ORNSTEIN, Franklin H.
Speaking out. por Sat Eve Post 240:10+ D 2 '67

O'ROURKE, Gerald G.
Flight in the fabulous Phantom. Atlan 220:57-60 Jl '67

OROVAN, Mary
Alen MacWeeney. U S Camera 30:36-9 Ap '67

OROVILLE DAM. See Dams

ORPHANS and orphan asylums
See also
Pestalozzi children's village
War orphans

ORR, Bobby
Well, Orr right! H. L. Masin. por Sr Schol 90:25 F 3 '67

ORR, W. N.
Secondary calcification in the foraminiferal genus globorotalia. bibliog Science 157:1554-5 S 29 '67

ORSI, Adolfo
Swift cars built in slow motion. il por Bsns W p62-3 Ja 21 '67

ÖRSY, Ladislas M.
Mixed marriages. America 117:242-5 S 9 '67

ORTEGO, Philip Darraugh
Cabinet meeting in El Paso. Nation 205:624-7 D 11 '67

ORTEN, James M. and others
Hematuria following administration of ethanol. bibliog Science 157:72-3 Jl 7 '67

ORTH, Franklin L.
Excerpt from testimony, July 19, 1967. Cong Digest 46:221+ Ag '67

ORTHODONTICS
Orthodontics: why, when, how much? il Changing T 21:33-5 S '67
Ramses had a royal toothache; malocclusion research on Egyptian pharaohs; X-ray study findings. il Life 62:57-8+ Ap 7 '67
When a child's teeth need straightening. D. Bressler. il Parents Mag 42:82-3+ N '67

ORTHODOX Eastern church
Orthodox church in Greece today. G. A. Maloney. America 116:340-5 Mr 11 '67
Royal reformation; Ieronymos Kotsonis installed as primate. il Time 89:80 My 26 '67
See also
Catholic church—Relations—Orthodox Eastern church
Church and state in Greece

ORTHODOX Eastern church, Russian
Orthodox face a crisis at Kirov. M. Bourdeaux. Christian Cent 84:478 Ap 12 '67
Stalin's daughter and the Russian church; opinions from Soviet press. M. Bourdeaux. Christian Cent 84:1330-2 O 18 '67

ORTHODOX Eastern church in Turkey
See also
Church and state in Turkey

ORTHODOX Eastern church in Ukraine
Eastern Catholics in the Ukraine. M. Bourdeaux. America 116:344-5 Mr 11 '67

ORTHOGENIC school. University of Chicago
See Special classes and special schools

ORTHOPEDIC apparatus
Better brace; one-sided leg brace. il Time 90:71 N 24 '67

ORTHOPEDICS. See Walking

ORTHOPTICS
Schooled to save lives; Darleen Radoff's career as an orthoptist. L. Berland. il Todays Health 45:51-5+ Mr '67

ORTHOPTISTS. See Orthoptics

ORTIZ, Carlos
No weighty problems for Carlos. M. Kram. Sports Illus 27:48-50 Jl 10 '67

ORTON, Joe
Death of a playwright. il por Time 90:40 S 15 '67

ORVILLE, Richard E. and Livingston, W. C.
Color through a raindrop; with biographical sketch. Natur Hist 76:5, 44-5 My '67

ORWELL, George, pseud.
Books. M. Muggeridge. Esquire 67:28+ My '67
Crystal spirit, by G. Woodcock. Review Commentary 43:102+ My '67. J. Epstein
George Orwell. A. Powell. por Atlan 220:62-8 O '67

ORYX hunting. See Antelope hunting

OSAKA International festival. See Music festivals—Japan

OSBORN, Anne G. and others
Effects of thiopental sedation on learning and memory. bibliog Science 157:574-6 Ag 4 '67

OSBORN, Robert Chesley
Osborn on the war. il New Repub 156:19-26 Je 3 '67

OSBORNE, Conrad L.
Batch of one-act operas, in both ancient and modern taste. Hi Fi 17:106 F '67
Butterfly that satisfies all round. Hi Fi 17:81-2 S '67
City opera's Traviata, Magic flute, Tosca. Hi Fi 17:MA6-8 Ja '67
Franco Corelli in and out of costume. Hi Fi 17:63-7 F '67
Ginastera's Bomarzo. Hi Fi 17:MA12-13+ Ag '67
Giulio Cesare the operatic genius of Handel made plain. Hi Fi 18:63-5 Ja '68
Hamburg opera makes U.S. debut. Hi Fi 17:MA8-11+ S '67
Karajan's Walkuere and a brave new Ring begins. Hi Fi 17:67-9 My '67
Met's new Lohengrin. Hi Fi 17:MA7+ F '67
New pair at City opera. Hi Fi 17:MA8-9 Je '67
Rudel's Rosenkavalier. Hi Fi 17:MA12-13 My '67
Tchaikovsky's Pique dame: a spine-chiller from today's Bolshoi. Hi Fi 17:87-8 N '67
U.S. premiere: Moses and Aaron. Hi Fi 17:MA8+ F '67
Wagner operas on records (cont) Hi Fi 17:44+ Ja '67
(ed) See Lorengar, P. And we quote
(ed) See Sills, B. And we quote
(ed) See Stewart, T. And we quote
(ed) See Venora, L.   And we quote

OSBORNE, John, 1907-
Danger of miscalculation. New Repub 156:3-4 Je 3; 34 Je 24 '67
Fantasy in Vietnam. New Repub 156:13-15 My 27 '67

OSBORNE, Karl
Mission to Cape Romain. Field & S 72:48-9+ Jl '67
Renaissance at Santee-Cooper. Field & S 72:72-4+ My '67

OSBORNE, Walter D.
Back in the saddle. il Fortune 76:110-17 S 1 '67

OSBURN, Bennie I. See Smith, J. E. jt. auth.

OSCILLATING detectors. See Detectors

OSCILLATORS
Build the emitter dipper. R. N. Tellefsen. il Pop Electr 25:47-9 D '66
Build the incredible VFO. R. L. Winkle-pleck. il Pop Electr 26:69-71 Ap '67
Getting the most from your CB rig; tuning your transmitter. D. Meyer. il Pop Electr 26:72-3+ Ap '67
L'il Richie; harmonic-rich crystal oscillator. D. Lancaster. il Pop Electr 27:70-3 S '67
Selecting frequency and time standards. I. Math. il Electr World 77:40-1+ My '67
See also
Pulse generators

OSCILLOGRAPHS
Laboratory oscilloscope. J. Frye. Electr World 79:62-3 Ja '68
Scope sweep generator; calibrating the horizontal sweep of an oscilloscope. R. G. Teeter. il Electr World 77:80-1 F '67

OSCILLOSCOPES. See Oscillographs

OSGOOD, Charles E.
Our crises in perspective. Bul Atomic Sci 23:12-16 F '67

O'SHEA, Cornelius
Woodsman: interview. New Yorker 43:41-3 Mr 18 '67

OSHEROFF, T. See Hobbs, P. V. jt. auth.

OSHIN, Edith Sonn
Parent and child (cont) N Y Times Mag p89-90+ Mr 5 '67

OSMIUM
Coordination polymers of osmium: the nature of osmium black. J. S. Hanker and others. bibliog Science 156:1737-8 Je 30 '67

OSMOSIS
Reverse osmosis techniques star at water conference. J. F. Judge. il Tech W 20:21-2 My 29 '67

OSMOTIC pressure
Osmotic mechanism and negative pressure. P. F. Scholander. bibliog il Science 156:67-9 Ap 7 '67; Discussion. 158:1210-12 D 1 '67

OSPREYS
Skyway robbery! with photographs by F. B. Peck. Audubon 69:58-60 My '67

OSSERMAN, Elliott F.
Crystallization of human lysozyme. bibliog il Science 155:1536-7 Mr 24 '67

OSSINING, N.Y.

Recreation
Ossining answers teen entertainment turmoil; Cellar discotheque. S. Stenek. il Parks & Rec 2:21+ Ag '67

OSSORIO, Alfonso
Diabolic craft of Alfonso Ossorio. R. Howard. il Craft Horiz 27:34-7 Ja '67

OSTEN, Richard van
Hughes ADGE consoles shown in Belgium. Tech W 21:21 Jl 3 '67
Litton's Belgian unit to manage Greek pact. Tech W 20:32 Je 26 '67

OSTEOARTHRITIS. See Arthritis

OSTEOCLASTS. See Cells

OSTEOPATHS
DO's drafted with MD's. Sci N 91:135 F 11 '67

OSTEOPOROSIS. See Bones—Diseases

OSTERLUND, Steven
Summer telegram: a painting; poem. Nation 204:637 My 15 '67

OSTOMY surgery. See Intestines—Surgery

OSTOS, Jaime
Brave and the beautiful. R. Daley. il pors Vogue 149:114-19+ Je '67

OSTRACODS
Ostracod living fossils: new finds in the Pacific. K. G. McKenzie. bibliog il Science 155:1005 F 24 '67

OSTRANDER, Sheila, and Schroeder, Lynn
Nyet raskhititelyam prirody (no to the plunderers of nature) Audubon 69:63-5 Jl '67

OSTROM, Vincent
Political feasibility. Bul Atomic Sci 23:13-17 S '67

OSTROW, Joanna
Celtic twilight; story. New Yorker 43:41-9 Ap 29 '67

O'SULLIVAN rubber corporation
Why O'Sullivan is kicking up its heels; producer of rubber heels. il Bsns W p 163-4+ F 25 '67

OSWALD, James R.
Home movies deserve better titles. U S Camera 30:72-3 Ag '67
Make better Christmas movies. U S Camera 30:62-3+ D '67
Shoot through the hole. U S Camera 30:68-9 O '67

OSWALD, Lee Harvey
Case of Jim Garrison and Lee Oswald. G. Roberts. il por N Y Times Mag p32-5+ My 21 '67
He was my brother; excerpts from Lee. R. L. Oswald and others. il pors Look 31:62-6+ O 17 '67

OSWALD, Robert L. and others
He was my brother; excerpts from Lee. pors Look 31:62-6+ O 17 '67

OSWALD family
Scene of the crime. il Newsweek 70:31B-32+ D 4 '67

OSWEGO tea. See Horsemint

OTAKA, Eiko, and others
Protein components in the 40S ribonucleo-protein particles in escherichia coli. bibliog Science 157:1452-4 S 22 '67

OTELLO; opera. See Verdi, G.

OTERI, Joseph
Marijuana is still illegal. Time 90:38+ D 29 '67

OTIENO, N. C.
Today's schools prepare tomorrow's African scientists. por UNESCO Courier 20:33-6 Je '67

OTOLITHIC membranes. See Membranes (biology)

O'TOOLE, Peter
New roughneck breed of ladies' men. P. Hamill. por Good H 165:94-5+ O '67

OTT, Karen J. and Stauber, L. A.
Eperythrozoon coccoides: influence on course of infection of plasmodium chabaudi in mouse. bibliog Science 155:1546-8 Mr 24 '67

OTTAVIANI, Alfredo, cardinal
Shake-up in the curia. il por Newsweek 71:78-9 Ja 22 '68

OTTERS
See also
Sea otters

OTTINGER, Richard Lawrence
Requests, advice complicate ATC effort. Aviation W 87:101 O 9 '67

OTTINO, Carlo
Fowl play. Newsweek 69:54+ Mr 20 '67

OTTO, archduke of Austria
Otto and the Austrian psyche. E. v. Kuehnelt Leddihn. Nat R 19:1326 N 28 '67
OTTO, Nikolaus August
Origin of the automobile engine. L. Bryant. il por Sci Am 216:102-10+ bibliog(p 152) Mr '67
OTTOMAN empire. See Turkey
OTTUM, Bob
Boxing. Sports Illus 27:66-8 O 23 '67
Handball. Sports Illus 27:46-7 Jl 31 '67
Motor sports (cont) Sports Illus 27:70-3 O 2; 60+ O 9 '67
OUDES, Bruce J.
Siege of Cicero. Nation 204:398-401 Mr 27 '67
OUELLETTE, Cecil M.
State parks of Washington. Travel 128:45-9 Jl '67
OULAHAN, Richard, and Lambert, William
Scandal in the Bahamas. Life 62:58-66+ F 3 '67
OUT of the walls; story. See Gordimer, N.
OUTBOARD motor boat racing. See Motor boat racing
OUTBOARD motor boats. See Motor boats, Outboard
OUTBOARD motors. See Gas and oil engines, Outboard
OUTBUILDINGS. See Sheds
OUTDOOR advertising. See Advertising, Outdoor
OUTDOOR art fair, Washington, D.C. See Art —Exhibitions
OUTDOOR carpets. See Rugs and carpets, Outdoor
OUTDOOR Christmas decorations. See Christmas decorations, Outdoor
OUTDOOR church services. See Church services
OUTDOOR cookery. See Cookery, Outdoor
OUTDOOR education
See also
Camping—Educational aspects
Outward bound schools
OUTDOOR entertaining. See Entertaining
OUTDOOR fireplaces. See Fireplaces, Outdoor
OUTDOOR furniture. See Furniture, Outdoor
OUTDOOR life
Outdoor living. il Am Home 70:56-7 Jl '67
See also
Camping
Camps
Country life
House boats
Mountaineering
Nature
Outdoor meals
Survival (after airplane accidents, shipwrecks, etc)
Vacations
OUTDOOR life (periodical)
Outdoor life and The death of a President; W. Manchester charges Outdoor life with hard-boiled callousness toward a national tragedy. Outdoor Life 140:32-3 O '67
OUTDOOR lighting. See Lighting, Outdoor
OUTDOOR markets. See Street trades
OUTDOOR meals
Adventures with food on a camping vacation; with recipes. C. Pines. il Parents Mag 42:64-5+ Ap '67
Campers specialties; with recipes. il Ebony 22:164+ Je '67
Exciting summer furniture, food, projects, equipment. D. Popplestone. il Bet Hom & Gard 45:46-65+ Je '67
Four marvelous ways to eat outdoors; with menus and recipes. R. A. De Groot. il Sat Eve Post 240:30-7 Jl 15 '67
Let's have a party just like that! V. D. Hahn. il Am Home 70:62-9+ Je '67
Outdoor parties for cool fall nights. il Pop Gard 18:56-9 D '67
Poolside living. il Sunset 139:48-51 Ag '67
See also
Barbecue cookery
Cookery, Outdoor
Picnics
OUTDOOR photography. See Photography
OUTDOOR restaurants. See Restaurants
OUTDOOR rooms
Art and an open kitchen. il House & Gard 131:132-3 My '67
Choose the right flooring for your patio. il Pop Gard 18:24-31 My '67
Cool off with a covered patio. il Pop Mech 128:126-9 Jl '67

Decks with a difference. il Am Home 70:78-9 Je '67
Escape to the Texas prairie; open-and-shut shelter. J. DeLong. il House B 109:80-1+ Ja '67
Garden house idea: it adds shelter and so it expands outdoor living. il Sunset 138:66-71 Je '67
Gravel did it! B. Christian. il Home Gard 54:68-9 F '67
Happy blend of garden and house. E. Kondonellis. il Am Home 70:90-1 O '67
Jamaican pavilion. il House B 109:116-19 Ja '67
Killingsworth gains spaciousness with garden rooms. il Arch Rec 142:152-4 N '67
Listen to the peace and quiet. H. Mason and others. il Bet Hom & Gard 45:60-1 Ap '67
New entry is a private outdoor room. il Sunset 138:132 Ap '67
New patio for an old house. il Pop Gard 18:60-5 D '67
No longer a billy goat garden. il Sunset 138:76-7 Je '67
Outdoor living, even on a tough lot! il Bet Hom & Gard 45:26 My '67
Outdoor living starts with the patio! H. Mason and others. il Bet Hom & Gard 45:52-3+ Ap '67
Patio that a painting inspired. D. Huff. il Pop Sci 191:146-9 Ag '67
Plan a garden oasis. E. Kondonellis. il Am Home 70:58-9 Jl '67
Pleasures of detail in a thoughtfully planned house. il House & Gard 131:120-7+ F '67
Quick course in exterior decorating. B. R. Earl. il Pop Gard 18:18-23 Ag '67
Screening: so easy to do, so worth its cost. H. Mason. and others. il Bet Hom & Gard 45:56-7 Ap '67
Serene facade conceals pools, fountains and spatial excitement. il Arch Rec 142:185-8 S '67
Shall we go inside? outdoor living room. R. Boellstorff. il Farm J 91:37 Jl '67
Summer sun spots. il Am Home 70:54-5 Jl '67
Terraces and trees. il Home Gard 54:53-6+ Ap '67
They live on a deck, but still they manage to garden in a grand way. il Sunset 139:58-9 S '67
Towers, decks, and a view. A. C. Borg. il Am Home 70:68-71 Jl '67
Welch house, Harvard, Massachusetts. il Arch Rec 141:100-3 mid-My '67
See also
Courtyards
Roof gardens
Care
Keep your deck shipshape. R. A. Henry. il Pop Gard 18:36-9+ Ag '67
OUTDOOR rugs. See Rugs and carpets, Outdoor
OUTDOOR sleeping. See Sleeping, Outdoor
OUTDRIVES. See Marine engines
OUTER BANKS (islands)
No man on Ocracoke. R. Maloney. il Atlan 219:122+ Mr '67
OUTER MONGOLIA. See Mongolia
OUTLER, Albert C.
Ecumenical crisis we face; interview. Cath World 205:20-5 Ap '67
Reformation Roman-style; excerpt from Methodist observer at Vatican II. por Cath World 204:341-5 Mr '67
OUTLINES, syllabi, etc.
One, two, three... L. Conger. Writer 80:7-8 O '67
Study in intense competition: the review book industry. il Pub W 191:40-2 F 6 '67
See also
Workbooks (education)
OUTWARD bound schools
Rough cure for adolescence. E. Grossman. Harper 234:69-72 My '67
Shock treatment for teen-agers. H. N. Ferguson. il Todays Health 45:28-33+ Ap '67
OVEN cleaners. See Cleaning compositions
OVEN dinners. See Dinners and dining
OVER-the-counter market. See Stocks—Marketing
OVERACHIEVEMENT, Student. See Student achievements
OVERDRIVE transmission. See Automobiles—Transmission
OVERDUE books. See Libraries—Circulation, loans, etc; Libraries—Fines
OVERHAGE, Carl F. J.
Science libraries: prospects and problems. Science 155:802-6 F 17 '67
University information system; summary of address. Pub W 191:37-8 Ap 10 '67

OVERHEAD projectors. See Projectors

OVERLAKE golf and country club course. See Golf courses

OVERPOPULATION. See Population—Overpopulation

OVERSEAS dependents schools. See American schools abroad

OVERSEAS education fund. See League of women voters of the United States—Overseas education fund

OVERSEAS forces. See United States—Armed forces—Forces in foreign countries

OVERSEAS spending. See Investments, Foreign

OVERSEAS weekly
Twitting the brass. il Time 90:57-8 O 20 '67

OVERSTREET, Bonaro W.
Growing together or apart. PTA Mag 62:6-8 D '67

OVERTIME
Overtime hours and premium pay. J. R. Wertzel. il Mo Labor R 90:41-5 My '67

OVERWEIGHT. See Corpulence

OVID
Caxton manuscript to remain in Britain: Metamorphoses. il Wilson Lib Bul 41:548 F '67

OVIDUCTS
Mammalian oviduct: international symposium; report. E. S. E. Hafez. Science 158:1606-9 D 22 '67

OVIEDO, Spain
Unspoiled Asturias. V. E. Condon. il Travel 127:58-60 Ja '67

OVUM
Blastokinin: inducer and regulator of blastocyst development in the rabbit uterus. R. S. Krishnan and J. C. Daniel, jr. bibliog il Science 158:490-2 O 27 '67
Zona pellucida of rhesus monkey ovum after gonadotropin stimulation. C. A. Maruffo. bibliog il Science 157:1313-14 S 15 '67

OVUM, Transplantation of. See Transplantation of organs, tissues, etc.

OWEN, Dwight Hall, Jr
Unanswered questions. por Time 90:23 S 15 '67

OWEN, K. D.
K.D. figures out the formula. P. Axthelm. il por Sports Illus 27:26-7 S 11 '67

OWEN, Tobias. See Greenspan, J. A. jt. auth.

OWEN, William E.
Bac si from Iowa. il pors Life 62:78A-80+ F 17 '67

OWENS, Boone B. and Argue, G. R.
High-conductivity solid electrolytes: MAg₄I₅. bibliog Science 157:308-10 Jl 21 '67

OWENS, Hugh F.
Why the government is worried about the stock market; interview. por U S News 63:65-7 N 20 '67

OWENS, Rochelle
Beclch. Criticism
Time il 89:58 F 10 '67

OWENS-Corning fiberglas corporation
Owens-Corning molds an industry. il Bsng W p 120-2+ Mr 4 '67

OWENS-Thomas house. See Savannah, Ga.—Historic houses, etc.

OWL in art. See Birds in art

OWLS
Great horned owl. il Sci N 92:244 S 9 '67
Happening at Hoogdal: an unidentified beeping object; UFO, or, midget saw-whet owl near Sedro-Woolley, Wash. T. Beauchamp. Look 31:42-3 N 14 '67

OWNER builders. See Building

OX cart; drama. See Marques, R.

OXAAL, Ivar
Executive Negro. Sat R 50:47-8 Jl 1 '67

OXAZOLIDINEDIONE
Passive transport of 5,5-dimethyl-2,4-oxazolidinedione into beef heart mitochondria. S. Addanki and others. bibliog il Science 155:1678-9 Mr 31 '67

OXENSTIERNA, Eric
Vikings; with biographical sketch. Sci Am 216:21, 66-78 My '67

OXFORD, England

Galleries and museums
Oxford's Ashmolean. J. Littelton. House & Gard 131:12+ Je '67

OXFORD. University
Memories, 1898-1939, by C. M. Bowra. Review
New Repub 157:25-8 N 18 '67. J. Wain
Oxford: a vote for Latin on the way to reform. J. Walsh. Science 157:47-9 Jl 7 '67

Libraries
Shackleton committee reports academic libraries plight. Library J 92:957 Mr 1 '67

OXIDASES
Sulfite oxidase deficiency in man: demonstration of the enzymatic defect. S. H. Mudd and others. bibliog il Science 156:1599-602 Je 23 '67

OXIDATION, Physiological
Oxygenases; report on colloquium. P. Feigelson. Science 155:609+ F 3 '67
Oxygenation properties of snake hemoglobin. B. Sullivan. bibliog il Science 157:1308-10 S 15 '67
Radiation of hemocyanin: inactivation and reactivation of oxygen-carrying capacity. J. Schubert and E. R. White. bibliog il Science 155:1000-3 F 24 '67

OXIDATION reduction reaction
Extraterrestrial life detection based on oxygen isotope exchange reactions. B. Kok and J. E. Varner. bibliog il Science 155:1110-12 Mr 3 '67
Hydroxamic acids in nature. J. B. Neilands. bibliog il Science 156:1443-7 Je 16 '67
Mechanisms of organic oxidation and reduction by metal complexes. J. K. Kochi. bibliog il Science 155:415-24 Ja 27 '67
Primary oxidation variation and distribution of uranium and thorium in a lava flow. N. D. Watkins and others. bibliog il Science 155:579-81 F 3 '67
Structural aspects of reversible molecular oxygen uptake. J. A. McGinnety and others. bibliog il Science 155:709-10 F 10 '67
Sulfate reduction in soil: effects of redox potential and pH. W. E. Connell and W. H. Patrick, jr. bibliog il Science 159:86-7 Ja 5 '68

OXIDATIVE phosphorylation. See Phosphorylation

OXTOBY, Willard G.
Christians and the Mideast crisis. Christian Cent 84:961-5 Jl 26 '67

OXYDENDRUM arboreum. See Sourwood

OXYGEN
Carbon dioxide, oxygen separation; facilitated transport of carbon dioxide across a liquid film. W. J. Ward, 3d. and W. L. Robb. bibliog il Science 156:1481-4 Je 16 '67
Deuterium and oxygen-18 in natural waters: analyses compared. E. Halevy and B. R. Payne. il Science 156:669 My 5 '67
O₂: a dangerous drug. Sci N 91:280 Mr 25 '67
Oxygen crisis. Newsweek 71:45 Ja 8 '68
Oxygen solubility in sea water: thermodynamic influence of sea salt. E. J. Green and D. E. Carritt. bibliog il Science 157:191-3 Jl 14 '67
See also
Space vehicles—Cabin atmospheres

Isotopes
Isotopic paleotemperatures. C. Emiliani; discussion. Science 156:410; bibliog 157:722-5 Ap 21, Ag 11 '67
Oxygen-18 composition of oceanic sulfate. R. M. Lloyd. bibliog il Science 156:1228-31 Je 2 '67
Oxygen-18 variations in sulfate ions in sea water and saline lakes. A. Longinelli and H. Craig. bibliog il Science 156:56-9 Ap 7 '67
Oxygen isotopes: experimental vapor fractionation and variations in tektites. L. S. Walter and R. N. Clayton. bibliog il Science 156:1357-8 Je 9 '67
Temperature measurements from oxygen isotope ratios of fish otoliths. I. Devereux. il Science 155:1684-5 Mr 31 '67

OXYGEN apparatus
Oxygen; testing new style mask. A. Trammell. il Flying 80:49-53 Mr '67
See also
Respiratory apparatus

OXYGEN in the body
Oxygen consumption of red and white muscles from tuna fishes. M. S. Gordon. bibliog il Science 159:87-90 Ja 5 '68
Oxygen tension changes evoked in the brain by visual stimulation. K. J. Gijsbers and R. Melzack. bibliog il Science 156:1392-3 Je 9 '67

OXYGEN masks. See Oxygen apparatus

OXYGENATION, Hyperbaric. See Hyperbaric oxygenation

OYSTER, Clyde W. and Barlow, H. B.
Direction-selective units in rabbit retina: distribution of preferred directions. bibliog Science 155:841-2 F 17 '67

OYSTER boats. See Fishing boats
OYSTER fisheries. See Shellfish fisheries
OYSTER plates. See Tableware
OYSTER sauce. See Sauces
OYSTER shells
Dredging up a Texas squabble; oyster shells
from Galveston Bay. E. Shrake. il Sports
Illus 27:43-8 Ag 14 '67
OYSTERMEN. See Fishermen
OYSTERS
Le petit bélon; shortage of oysters in Brit-
tany. P. Brown. il Holiday 41:56-7+ Je '67
Six oysters, six ales, peace. R. J. Misch. il
Esquire 67:64-5+ F '67
See also
Cookery—Shellfish
Pearls
OZARK trail. See Trails
OZAWA, Seiji
Music to my ears. I. Kolodin. Sat R 50:82+
Ap 22; 89 N 25 '67
Musical events; concert performed by Phila-
delphia orchestra in Philharmonic Hall. W.
Sargeant. New Yorker 43:156+ Mr 11 '67
Musical events; concert performed by Toronto
symphony in Carnegie Hall. W. Sargeant.
New Yorker 43:169 Ap 15 '67
OZEKI, Masahiro, and Grundfest, Harry
Crayfish muscle fiber: ionic requirements for
depolarizing synaptic electrogenesis. bibliog
Science 155:478-81 Ja 27 '67
ÖZGÜÇ, Tahsin
Ancient Ararat; with biographical sketch.
Sci Am 216:19. 38-46 bibliog(p 150) Mr '67

P

PACE (projects to advance creativity in edu-
cation) See Creative education
PACV (Patrol air cushion vehicle) See Ground
effect machines
PAHO. See Pan American health organization
PAR (precision approach radar) See Radar in
aviation
PARC (predator and rodent control) See United
States—Fish and wildlife service
PAU. See Pan American union
PBL. See Public broadcast laboratory
PCM (pulse code modulation) See Space te-
lemetry
PEBCO. See American library association—
Program evaluation and budget committee
PEN club
PEN in Africa; thirty-fifth congress. A.
Waugh. Nat R 19:1018-19 S 19 '67
PERT (program evaluation review technique)
See Critical path analysis
PGW. See Philadelphia gas works
PIA. See Printing industries of America, in-
corporated
PKI. See Communist party (Indonesia)
PKU. See Phenylketonuria
PLA. See American library association—Public
library association
PLA (People's liberation army) See China
(People's Republic)—Armed forces
PRSA. See Public relations society of Amer-
ica
PSA. See Photographic society of America
PSAC. See United States—President's science
advisory committee
PTA. See Parents and teachers associations
PTA magazine
Recover story. PTA Mag 61:26 Mr '67
PX. See United States—Armed forces—Post
exchanges
PAAR, Jack
What now, Jack Paar? E. Harris. il pors Look
31:66-9+ D 12 '67
PACE, Dorothy R.
Garnishing cook book. House & Gard 132:
133-8 Ag '67
PACE, Eric
Cairo diary: by a Times correspondent. N Y
Times Mag p7+ Jl 2 '67
PACEMAKER, Artificial (heart)
Cable of life; cardiac pacemaker. S. V. Jones.
il Sci Digest 62:87 N '67
PACIFARINS
Ecological ectocrines in experimental epidemi-
ology. H. A. Schneider. bibliog il Science
158:597-603 N 3 '67

PACIFIC air lines
How to make ten from three; merger of
Pacific with Phoenix's Bonanza and
Seattle's West coast. Time 90:59 S 1 '67
Pacific fear of flying drive criticized; execu-
tive resigns. Aviation W 86:30-1 My 8 '67
PACIFIC airways. See Airways
PACIFIC coast
Cruising unlimited; from Olympia, Wash,
northwestward to Alaska. W. Dawson. il
Yachting 121:68-70+ Ja '67
PACIFIC countries
Latest boom in travel. il U S News 63:90-2
O 9 '67
Step right up, folks, to thirty million square
miles of the greatest show on earth! R.
Joseph. il Esquire 68:58-71 Ag '67
Travel notes. R. Joseph. Esquire 68:41-3 Ag
'67
See also
ANZUS council
Tourist trade—Pacific countries
PACIFIC gas and electric company
Growth power on the Pacific; PG&E in Cali-
fornia. il Bsns W p44-6+ S 2 '67
Power push at PG&E. N. Willatt. il Duns R
90:39-40+ Ag '67
PACIFIC ISLANDS. See Islands of the Pacific
PACIFIC ISLANDS, TRUST TERRITORY OF.
See Trust Territory of the Pacific Islands
PACIFIC OCEAN
Pacific panorama; harbors. il Yachting 122:
40-1 Jl '67
See also
Coral Sea
South Sea Islands
PACIFIC Southwest airlines
Pacific Southwest seeks interstate status.
Aviation W 87:32 Ag 21 '67
PACIFIC TRUST TERRITORY. See Trust Ter-
ritory of the Pacific Islands
PACIFIC Western regional ballet festival. See
Dance festivals
PACIFISM
Face to face with a girl who has gone to jail
for what she believes. S. Williams. Seven-
teen 26:153+ S '67
Non-violent Christology. J. W. Douglass.
Commonweal 87:259-64 N 24 '67
Number one pacifist; A. J. Muste. N. J.
Whitney. Christian Cent 84:622-4 My 10 '67
Peace and pacifism; the Pope's call for a day
of peace. Commonweal 87:395-6 D 29 '67
War in the peace camp; liberals vs. radicals.
W. Goodman. il N Y Times Mag p48-9+
D 3 '67; Discussion. p4+ D 31 '67
See also
Conscientious objectors
Passive resistance to government
Peace
Vietnamese war, 1957- —Protests, demonstra-
tions, etc, against
PACIFISTS. See Pacifism
PACINI, Giovanni
Saffo. Criticism
Hi Fi il 17:MA28-9 Je '67
PACK transportation
Riding the back country. C. Nansen. il Field
& S 71:48-51+ Mr '67
PACKAGED foods
No time to cook; menu with recipes. See
issues of McCall's
See also
Reynolds, R. J, foods, incorporated
PACKAGE tours. See Travel
PACKAGED mixes. See Food mixes
PACKAGES, Wrapping of. See Wrapping of
packages
PACKAGING
Out of the frying pan; shock hazard in the
Reddi-bacon package. il Consumer Rep 32:
64 F '67
Packaging wraps up the future. il Fortune
75:122-7 F '67
Sharing the risk in packaging war; Riegel
paper. il Bsns W p 132-4 Jl 8 '67
See also
Advertising mediums—Packaging
Wrapping of packages

Laws and regulations
Consumer: king or vassal of the economy?
il Sr Schol 90:13-15+ F 10 '67
Free press & fancy packages. A. Q. Mowbray.
Nation 205:621-3 D 11 '67
Industry still has something to learn about
Congress. J. Main. il Fortune 75:128-9+
F '67

PACKAGING—Laws and regulations—*Cont.*
Packagers wait for the new rules; Truth-in-packaging bill. il Bsns W p 177-8+ My 13 '67
Packaging peas and Betty Bird Furness; Truth-in-packaging law. N. K. Herzfeld. Commonweal 86:384-5 Je 23 '67
Some truth-in-packaging, but not enough; Fair packaging and labeling act. il Consumer Rep 32:113-15 F '67

PACKARD, David
Maverick of electronics. por Duns R 90:42-4 Ag '67

PACKARD, George R. 3d
Indonesia wobbles toward recovery. N Y Times Mag p34-5+ O 1 '67
Living with the real Japan. For Affairs 46: 193-204 O '67

PACKARD, George V.
It was only a game of touch. Sports Illus 27: 108-10+ S 18 '67

PACKARD, Robert F.
Space diplomacy; excerpts from address. Aviation W 86:17 Mr 20 '67

PACKER, Barbara
Blue eagle; story. Mlle 65:276-7 Ag '67

PACKER, Sir Frank
If at first. il Time 89:58+ Ap 7 '67

PACKER, Leo S.
Can systems research put zip in the mail? Bsns W p94+ Ap 1 '67

PACKING of luggage
How to pack for a trip. Good H 165:196 O '67
Teen travel talk. Seventeen 26:152 Je '67
Travelers' comforts. N. S. Hazelton. Nat R 19:475+ My 2 '67

PACKS
Day pack, rucksack, or packframe with bag, your choice is wide. Sunset 139:34-5 Ag '67

PADDLE tennis
Equality on a platform. il Time 89:59 Mr 3 '67
Paddle tennis; winter sport in Darien, Conn; platform paddle tennis. J. Peter. il Look 31:M20-3 F 21 '67

PADDLE tennis courts
Paddle tennis courts redesigned. il Parks & Rec 2:26+ My '67

PADEV, Michael
Communism's common goal. Read Digest 91: 142-3 Jl '67

PADILLA, Victoria
Bromeliads. Horticulture 45:22-5+ Ag '67

PADOVER, Saul K.
State of man and state. Sat R 50:27-8 Ap 29 '67
This bloodless world war III. Sat R 50:32-3 O 21 '67
Well-off, middle-aged rebels. Sat R 50:30-1 Ag 19 '67

PADRE ISLAND
Treasure of pleasure. P. Crittenden. il Travel 127:41-4 Mr '67

PADREVIA; opera. See Pasatieri, T.

PADS, Rug. See Rug pads

PADUCAH, Ky.
Follow the red line. P. D. Eimon. il Am City 82:144+ Ap '67

PAGE, Irvine Heinly
Clinical investigator, patient, pharmaceutical industry, and federal agencies. Science 157: 143 Jl 14 '67

about
Doctor's heart attack. por Time 90:52 N 3 '67

PAGE, Jerry Dentler
Pentagon crackdown on a critic? por U S News 62:8 F 6 '67

PAGE, Joseph A.
Facade in Brazil. New Repub 157:8 S 9 '67
Report; Northeast Brazil. Atlan 221:20-3 Ja '68
Revolution in liberty. New Repub 157:30-1 D 23 '67

PAGE, Martin
Persian Gulf. Atlan 219:38+ Ap '67

PAGE, Ronald A.
ST reports; how history is taught in Scotland. Sr Schol 91:sup 14 O 5 '67

PAGE, Ruth
We who travel. Dance Mag 41:62+ Je '67

PAGE, Thornton L.
Galaxies and quasars at Prague. Sky & Tel 34:372-6; 35:16-20 D '67, Ja '68 (to be cont)

PAGE, Warren
Crane hunting in Mexico. Field & S 72:36-7+ N '67
First shootoff of the franchises. Field & S 71:12+ Mr '67
Hunting will never be the same. Field & S 72:62-3+ S '67

Many bears pass. Field & S 71:70-1+ Mr '67
Ram fever. Field & S 72:34-5+ Ag '67
Whitetails along the border. Field & S 72: 46-7+ O '67
(ed) Shooting. See issues of Field & stream

PAGE, Wilber Allen
Notes on George W. Williams. Negro Hist Bul 30:12 O '67

PAGEANTS
Letter from Ceylon. M. Connelly. Holiday 42: 51-4 D '67

PAGET'S disease
Collagen-like fragments; excretion in urine of patients with Paget's disease of bone. S. M. Krane and others. bibliog il Science 157:713-16 Ag 11 '67

PAGLIACCI; opera. See Leoncavallo, R.

PAGLIAI, Merle Oberon. See Oberon, M.

PAHLEVI, Mohammed Reza, shah of Iran. See Mohammed Reza Pahlevi

PAHOEHOE. See Lava

PAIN
Pain. Sci N 91:423-4 My 6 '67
Peril of painlessness. A. J. Snider. il Sci Digest 62:79-80 S '67
Sensory coding; report on conference. G. G. Somjen. Science 158:399-400+ O 20 '67
What to do about aches and pains. Bet Hom & Gard 45:24+ O '67
See also
Anesthesia

PAIN killing drugs. See Analgesics

PAINT
Breakthrough! new foolproof water paints you can use anywhere. J. Hand. il Pop Sci 191:108-10+ Jl '67
Happenings in paint. J. H. Ingersoll. il House B 109:166+ My '67
Latex flat interior paints. il Consumer Rep 32:517-20 O '67
New paint wonder; water-thinned enamel. S. J. Howard. il Pop Mech 128:99-101 Ag '67
Painting interior walls. il Consumer Bul 50: 31-4 Ap '67
There's good news about exterior finishes. Pop Gard 18:18-19 My '67
Wild things you can do with paint. il Changing T 21:30 F '67

Removal
Picking the right paint remover. S. J. Howard. il Pop Mech 128:164-6 Jl '67

PAINT, Protective
How to pick the right masonry paint. J. P. Schenley. il Pop Mech 128:168-70+ O '67
Time to switch? Color hit, bus upholstery experiment. E. Rickman. il Hot Rod 20:76 Mr '67

PAINT brushes
Buy the right paintbrush for the job. il Bet Hom & Gard 45:130-1 F '67

PAINT industry and trade
See also
Sherwin-Williams company
Standard brands paint company, Los Angeles

PAINT rollers
Paint roller covers. il Consumer Rep 32:90-3 F '67
What you should know about paint rollers. B. W. Powell. il Pop Mech 128:158-61 O '67

PAINT sprayers. See Spraying apparatus

PAINTER, Harold W.
Mark, I love you! excerpts. pors Good H 164: 93-5+ Ap '67

PAINTER, Mark
Mark, I love you! excerpts. H. Painter. il pors Good H 164:93-5+ Ap '67

PAINTING
See also
Action in art
Animals in art
Artists
Color
Cubism
Flowers in art
Frescoes
Impressionism (art)
Landscape painting
Paintings

Technique
Assembly line for oil paintings. F. Worth. il Design 69:20-2 Fall '67
Hereward Lester Cooke. D. Holden. il Am Artist 31:46-51+ F '67
Painter's personal testimony. R. Grilley. il Am Artist 31:46-51+ Mr '67
Painting a nude in an alla prima technique; excerpt from Painting the nude. J. De Ruth. il Am Artist 31:44-9+ Je '67

PAINTING—Technique—*Continued*
Painting with smoke. J. Jones. il Design 69: 36-7 Fall '67
Some elementary questions; what is technique. M. Feldman. il Art N 66:54-5+ Ap '67

See also
Marine painting
Water color painting
   also names of individual artists, e.g. D. Putman

PAINTING, Abstract. See Art, Abstract

PAINTING, American
American largeness; exhibition at Manhattan's Jewish museum shows mural-size paintings. il Time 90:64 Jl 14 '67
Americans in faraway places; Roderic H. D. Henderson collection. W. H. Gerdts. il Antiques 91:647-9 My '67
Art world; Large scale American paintings exhibition at the Jewish museum. H. Rosenberg. New Yorker 43:90+ Ag 26 '67
Collecting American nineteenth-century art. J. W. Middendorf, 2d. il Antiques 92:680-8 N '67
European and American realists of the late nineteenth century. A. von Saldern. il Antiques 92:694-705 N '67
Founders of the American tradition; exhibition of two hundred years of American painting. H. A. LaFarge. il Art N 66:36-7+ D '67
Immediacy is the message. J. Schuyler. il Art N 66:32-3+ Mr '67
Neck & neck; survey of painting at the Whitney. il Time 90:46-7 D 22 '67
New Bedford artists of the nineteenth century. D. L. Smith. il Antiques 92:689-93 N '67
Visions of innocence; traveling exhibition of 101 American primitive watercolors collected by Edgar and Bernice Chrysler Garbisch. il Time 89:66-7 Mr 10 '67

See also
Albright, I. L.
Arnholm, R.
Artists, American
Beall, C. C.
Benson, H. J.
Bingham, G. C.
Bluhm, N.
Brainard, J.
Chiara, A. R.
Conrad, B.
Cooke, H. L.
Cropsey, J. F.
De Kooning, W.
Dunn, H.
Fisher, M.
Frame, R.
Francis, S.
Frankenthaler, H.
Frazer, O.
Gorka, P.
Gorky, A.
Grandee, J. R.
Gray, C.
Grilley, R.
Grooms, R.
Hendler, R.
Hopper, E.
Jackson, H.
Johnson, A.
Katz, M.
Kienholz, E.
Kline, F. J.
Krushenick, N.
Kuhn, W.
Lapson, M.
Lee, R. J.
Liberman, A.
Lichtenstein, R. F.
Lindner, R.
Louis, M.
McNeil, G.
Marca-Relli, C.
Maxwell, M.
Moses, A. M. R.
Mount, W. S.
Natkin, R.
Noland, K.
O'Keeffe, G.
Olitski, J.
Peale, C. W
Pearlstein, P.
Petlin, I.
Pollet, J.
Pollock, J.
Poons, L.
Porter, F.
Pousette-Dart, R
Putman, D.
Reinhardt, A.
Resika, P.
Rivers, L.

Rose, H.
Shahn, B.
Sloan, J.
Soyer, R.
Stella, F.
Stuart, G.
Stüssy, J.
Tanner, H. O.
Tooker, G.
Walton, H.
Welliver, N.
Whistler, J. A. M.
Woodville, R. C.
Wyeth, A.

PAINTING, Argentine
See also
Celis, P.

PAINTING, Australian
See also
Whiteley, B.

PAINTING, Baroque
Deliberate speed. L. Steinberg. il Art N 66: 42-7+ Ap '67

PAINTING, British
American debut: landscapes of the Norwich school; exhibition at the Cummer gallery of art, Jacksonville, Fla. E. P. Birk. il Antiques 91:276+ Mr '67
Century of exception; British masterpieces, exhibition in Detroit. il Time 91:52-7 Ja 19 '68

See also
Bartlett, W. H.
Beardsley, A. V.
Dunn, A.
Hogarth, W.
Millais, J. E.
Salmon, R.
Sickert, W. R.
Turner, J. M. W.

PAINTING, Canadian
Painting in Canada, 1604-1867. J. R. Harper. il Antiques 92:66-71 Jl '67
See also
Lismer, A.
Murch, W. T.

PAINTING, Childrens. See Childrens art

PAINTING, Chinese
Mad Ming monks and eccentric exiles; exhibition at Asia house, New York. H. Y. Shih. il Art N 66:36-9+ Ap '67
Magnificent eccentrics; exhibition at New York's Asia house. il Newsweek 69:99 Ap 3 '67

PAINTING, Cuban
Fidelism; artists eschew socialist realism. il Newsweek 70:90 S 18 '67

PAINTING, Czech
London; cubist art from Czechoslovakia at the Tate. J. Russell. Art N 66:51 N '67

PAINTING, Dutch
See also
Gogh, V. van
Rembrandt Hermanszoon van Rijn

PAINTING, English. See Painting, British

PAINTING, European
European and American realists of the late nineteenth century. A. von Saldern. il Antiques 92:694-705 N '67

PAINTING, Flemish
See also
Brueghel, P.
Juan de Flandes

PAINTING, Florentine. See Painting, Italian

PAINTING, French
In quest of beauty; collecting 19th- and 20th-century French painting; with reproductions of paintings. P. Mellon. il Nat Geog Mag 131:372-85 Mr '67
Letter from Paris; exhibition of French painting from Swiss collectors at the Orangerie. Genêt. New Yorker 43:141-2+ Je 10 '67

See also
Boucher, F.
David, J. L.
Degas, E.
Derain, A.
Dubuffet, J.
Fragonard, J. H.
Hélion, J.
Ingres, J. A. D.
Klein, Y.
La Tour, M. Q. de
Léger, F.
Monet, C.
Rousseau, H.
Soulages, P.
Vigée-Lebrun, M. L. E.
Villon, J. pseud.

PAINTING, German
See also
Dürer, A.
Elsheimer, A.
Janssen, H.
Nolde, E.
Schönfeld, J. H.

PAINTING, Indian (East Indian)
Art, diplomacy and vice versa: Indian paintings of the sixteenth, seventeenth and eighteenth centuries. J. K. Galbraith. il Esquire 67:112-19+ Mr '67

PAINTING, Industrial and practical
Interior painting: how to get the best job with the least trouble. il Bet Hom & Gard 45:124+ F '67
Look what happened to red barns! color coordinate your buildings. R. Wilmore. il Farm J 91:36-7 Ap '67
Painting interior walls. il Consumer Bul 50: 31-4 Ap '67
See also
Metal finishing

PAINTING, Israeli
See also
Agam, Y.

PAINTING, Italian
For Florence, from Florence; show at Wildenstein, for the Committee to rescue Italian art. F. Licht. il Art N 66:44-7+ My '67
Important discoveries of renaissance art in Florence. M. Meiss. il Art N 66:26-7+ Sum '67
In Florence, new troubles and new treasures. il Life 62:54-9 Je 30 '67
Tapping the mother lode; CRIA Italian Heritage, exhibit at Manhattan's Wildenstein gallery. il Time 90:52-4 Ag 11 '67
See also
Bellotto, B.
Ceruti, G.
Leonardo da Vinci
Morandi, G.
Pistoletto, M.

PAINTING, Landscape. See Landscape painting

PAINTING, Marine. See Marine painting

PAINTING, Mexican
See also
Cuevas, J. L.
Siqueiros, D. A.

PAINTING, Modern. See Modernism (art)

PAINTING, Polish
See also
Balthus (Balthus Klossowski)

PAINTING, Puerto Rican
See also
Oller, F.

PAINTING, Russian
Art world; survey of Russian painting from the fifteenth century to the present at the Gallery of modern art. H. Rosenberg. New Yorker 43:72 Jl 1 '67
Icons and isms; Survey of Russian painting at New York's Gallery of modern art. il Newsweek 70:79 Jl 3 '67
Unrealism in Moscow; display of Russian painting at Manhattan's Gallery of modern art. il Time 89:50 Je 30 '67

PAINTING, Spanish
See also
Goya y Lucientes, F. J. de
Greco
Juan de Flandes
Miró, J.
Picasso, P.

PAINTING, Submarine
Striped bass in canvas chronicle; paintings by S. Meltzoff; with account by D. Barnes. Sports Illus 27:34-9 S 4 '67

PAINTING, Swedish
See also
Fahlström, Ö.

PAINTING, Swiss
See also
Klee, P.

PAINTING, Yugoslav
See also
Generalić, I.

PAINTINGS
Eight colorplates of old and modern masters from the collections of the Albright-Knox art gallery. il Art N 65:39-45 Ja '67
[Fine art reproductions] A. Saarinen. il McCalls 94:52-4 Je; 132-5 Jl; 114-15 Ag; 30-1 S; 95:38-9 O; 42-3 N; 78-9 D '67; 41-2 Ja '68
In the museums: paintings (cont) R. Davidson. il Antiques 91:661+; 92:376+ My, S '67

Masters in the art news. See issues of Art news
Where is it? L. Lerman. il Mlle 65:103-5 Je '67
See also
Art—Expertising
Forgery of works of art
Portraits

Collections
See Art—Private collections

Transportation
See Transportation of works of art

PAINTINGS, Photography of. See Photography of works of art

PAINTINGS, Reproduction of. See Reproduction of works of art

PAINTINGS, Theft of. See Art thefts

PAINTINGS in a paper bag; story. See Bradshaw, G.

PAISLEY, Ian
Another hole in the head. Christian Cent 84: 525 Ap 26 '67

PAISNER, Bruce
Now it's student power. Life 63:91-2 O 20 '67

PAJATÉN, Peru
Lost city of Pajaten. S. Tomkievicz. il Horizon 9:62-7 Aut '67
Pajatén: a lost city found. R. Wood. il Américas 19:7-16 Je '67

PAK, Chung Hi. See Park, C. H.

PAK, William L. and Boes, R. J.
Rhodopsin: responses from transient intermediates formed during its bleaching. biblog Science 155:1131-3 Mr 3 '67

PAKE, George
Basic research and financial crisis in the universities; excerpts from address, March 1967. Science 157:517-20 Ag 4 '67

PAKISTAN
Other celebration; progress since independence. Time 90:31 Ag 25 '67
See also
Airlines—Pakistan
Childrens literature—Pakistan
Communication—Pakistan
Dams—Pakistan
Economic assistance in Pakistan
Kashmir
Natural resources—Pakistan

Commercial treaties and agreements
U.S. and Pakistan conclude new cotton textile agreement; Department announcement and text of U.S. note. il Dept State Bul 57: 114-16 Jl 24 '67

Foreign relations
As a backsliding ally draws closer to Russia. il U S News 63:22 O 9 '67
Indian-Pakistani relations. R. N. Berkes. biblog f il Cur Hist 52:289-94+ My '67

History
Pakistan. A. A. Michel. il Focus 17:1-6 Ja '67

PAKISTAN international airlines corporation. See Airlines—Pakistan

PAKISTAN poetry
From the East. R. E. Teele. Poetry 109:272-5 Ja '67

PAKISTANI cookery. See Cookery, Pakistani

PALACES
See also
Versailles, Palaces of

PALACES, Miniature. See Doll houses

PALADE, G. and Porter, K. R.
Endoplasmic reticulum: United States-Japan cooperative science program. Science 156: 106-10 Ap 7 '67

PALATE, Cleft
Cleft lip and cleft palate; report on meeting. F. C. Fraser. Science 158:1603-6 D 22 '67

PALATINATE
Palatinate, pick of the lot. T. Prittie. il Atlan 220:116-18 S '67

PALATSKY, Eugene
New Jersey symphony: on the move. Hi Fi 17:MA26-7+ Mr '67
These dancers have character. Dance Mag 41:42-6 N '67

PALENQUE. See Mayas

PALEOANTHROPOLOGY. See Man, Prehistoric

PALEOBOTANY
Pollen diagrams from sub-Arctic central Canada. H. Nichols. biblog il Science 155: 1665-8 Mr 31 '67

PALEOBOTANY—*Continued*

Devonian

Seed from the upper Devonian. J. M. Pettitt and C. B. Beck. bibliog il Science 156:1727-9 Je 30 '67

World's first tall tree. Time 89:55 Je 16 '67

Pleistocene

Late pleistocene history of coniferous woodland in the Mohave Desert. P. V. Wells and R. Berger. bibliog il Science 155:1640-7 Mr 31 '67

Lupinus arcticus Wats. grown from seeds of pleistocene age. A. E. Porsild and others. bibliog il Science 158:113-14 O 6 '67

PALEOCLIMATOLOGY

Coccoliths as paleoclimatic indicators of pleistocene glaciation. A. McIntyre. bibliog il Science 158:1314-17 D 8 '67

PALEOMAGNETISM. See Magnetism, Terrestrial

PALEONTOLOGY

Fever chart for fossils; analysis of collagen to calculate temperatures of extinct species. Time 90:32+ S 8 '67

Fossil behavior; some fossils represent the tracks or burrows of ancient animals. A. Seilacher. il Sci Am 217:72-6+ Ag '67

See also
Elephants, Fossil
Man, Prehistoric
Micropaleontology
Paleobotany

Cambrian

Phanerozoic-cryptozoic and related transitions: new evidence. P. E. Cloud, jr. and C. A. Nelson; reply with rejoinder. T. D. Ford. Science 157:957-8 Ag 25 '67

Cretaceous

Baja California: late cretaceous dinosaurs. W. J. Morris. bibliog il Science 155:1539-41 Mr 24 '67

Devonian

Fossilization of an ancient, Devonian, softbodied worm. B. Cameron. bibliog il Science 155:1246-8 Mr 10 '67

Eocene

Middle and late eocene mammal communities: a major discrepancy. C. C. Black. bibliog Science 156:62-4 Ap 7 '67

Jurassic

American Jurassic symmetrodonts and Rhaetic pantotheres. A. W. Crompton and F. A. Jenkins, jr. bibliog il Science 155:1006-9 F 24 '67

Paleozoic

Romeriscus, the oldest known reptile. D. Baird and R. L. Carroll. bibliog il Science 157:56-9 Jl 7 '67

Pliocene

Vertebrate evidence of a low sea level in the middle pliocene. S. D. Webb and N. Tessman. bibliog il Science 156:379 Ap 21 '67

Precambrian

Fossil actinomycetes in middle Precambrian glacial varves. T. A. Jackson. bibliog il Science 155:1003-5 F 24 '67

Precambrian fossils (?) near Elliot Lake, Ontario. H. J. Hofmann. bibliog il Science 156:500-4 Ap 28 '67

California

Phanerozoic-cryptozoic and related transitions: new evidence. P. E. Cloud, jr. and C. A. Nelson; reply with rejoinder. T. D. Ford. bibliog Science 157:957-8 Ag 25 '67

Transitional pre-desert phase in San Diego County, California. J. R. Moriarty. bibliog il Science 155:553-6 F 3 '67

California, Lower

Baja California: late cretaceous dinosaurs. W. J. Morris. bibliog il Science 155:1539-41 Mr 24 '67

Florida

Vertebrate evidence of a low sea level in the middle pliocene. S. D. Webb and N. Tessman. bibliog il Science 156:379 Ap 21 '67

Missouri

Ice-age pigs unearthed. il Sci Digest 62:33-4 O '67

North America

See also
Indians of North America—Antiquities

Ontario

Precambrian fossils (?) near Elliot Lake, Ontario. H. J. Hofmann. bibliog il Science 156:500-4 Ap 28 '67

South Africa

Alga-like fossils from the early Precambrian of South Africa. J. W. Schopf and E. S. Barghoorn. bibliog il Science 156:508-12 Ap 28 '67

South America

See also
Indians of South America—Antiquities

Wyoming

Middle and late eocene mammal communities: a major discrepancy. C. C. Black. bibliog Science 156:62-4 Ap 7 '67

PALEOPATHOLOGY

Paleopathology: meeting ground for many disciplines. E. R. Kerley and W. M. Bass. bibliog il Science 157:638-44 Ag 11 '67

PALEOSALINITIES. See Sedimentation and deposition

PALEOZOIC period. See Geology, Stratigraphic —Paleozoic; Paleontology—Paleozoic

PALESTINE

See also
Israel
Jerusalem

Antiquities

See also
Jordan—Antiquities

Partition

See also
Israeli-Arab war, 1948-1949

PALESTINE refugees. See Refugees, Arab

PALEVSKY, Max

Enter Max Palevsky. il por Time 89:86 F 24 '67

PALEY, Grace

Distance; story. Atlan 220:111-15 D '67

PALEY, Mrs William S.

Mrs William S. Paley; photographs. Vogue 149:164-5 My '67

PALEY, William Samuel

Great sellout to soap opera; excerpt from Due to circumstances beyond our control. F. W. Friendly. il por Life 62:84+ Mr 17 '67

PALM SPRINGS, Calif.

Resourceful director provides special events program. H. Haddock. il Parks & Rec 2:84-6 O '67

PALM Sunday. See Holy week

PALMA DE MALLORCA, Spain

European literary scene. R. J. Clements. il Sat R 50:32 O 7 '67

PALMER, Arnold

How to beat your husband at golf. McCalls 94:44+ My '67

about

Ben & Arnie liven up the weekend. A. Wright. il Sports Illus 27:56+ O 30 '67

My friend Arnold Palmer. M. H. McCormack. il pors Sports Illus 26:56-66 Mr 6; 32-6+ Mr 13; 54-6+ Mr 20; 36-40+ Mr 27 '67

PALMER, Arnold, enterprises, incorporated

Evolution of a golf tycoon. M. H. McCormack. il Sports Illus 26:32-6+ Mr 13 '67

NBC buys golf. il Time 89:85 Mr 10 '67

PALMER, Bill

Don't gripe about a splinter. Seventeen 26:128-9+ O '67

PALMER, Bruce, 1913-

Quartet at the top. il por Time 89:14 Mr 24 '67

PALMER, James K. and Roberts, J. B.

Inhibition of banana polyphenoloxidase by 2-mercaptobenzothiazole. bibliog Science 157:200-1 Jl 14 '67

PALMER, John D.

Euglena and the tides; with biographical sketch. Natur Hist 76:5, 60-4 F '67

Geomagnetism and animal orientation. Natur Hist 76:54-7 N '67

PALMER, Joseph, 1914-

Africa and America; address, March 31, 1967. Dept State Bul 56:646-51 Ap 24 '67

America's understanding of Africa; address, October 21, 1967. Dept State Bul 57:656-60 N 13 '67

New Africa; address, November 9, 1966. Vital Speeches 33:272-8 F 15 '67

Other Africa: the Maghreb; address, May 9, 1967. Vital Speeches 33:522-7 Je 15 '67; Same. Dept State Bul 56:806-14 My 29 '67

Southern Rhodesia: the issue of majority rule. Dept State Bul 56:449-58 Mr 20 '67

PALMER, Leland
Under our eyes. S. Estrada and R. Estrada. il pors Dance Mag 41:38-43+ S '67
PALMER, Raymond A.
Push-button boating. Motor B 120:44-5 Ag '67
PALMIERI, Eddie
New voice from the barrios. R. F. Thompson. il por Sat R 50:53-5+ O 28 '67
PALMORE, William P. and Mulrow, P. J.
Control of aldosterone secretion by the pituitary gland. bibliog Science 158:1482-4 D 15 '67
PALMS, Charles L.
(ed) See Marshall, R. Literature and religion in Russia today
PALMS
Palms in the floor or in the window. il Sunset 138:278+ My '67
PALO ALTO, Calif.
Classic telling; A look at your city government. il Am City 82:144+ Mr '67
Three-step municipal service center. il Am City 82:88-9 D '67

Lighting
Reducing the overhead. G. E. Morgan. il Am City 82:138 F '67
PALOMAR, MOUNT, observatory. See Astronomical observatories
PALOMARES, Spain
Bombs of Palomares, by T. Szulc. Review
Nation 204:763 Je 12 '67. M. C. O'Brien
Day H-bombs fell on Palomares. L. Azancot. il Sat R 50:21-7+ Ja 28 '67
Day they lost the H-bomb, by C. Morris. Review
Sat R 50:40 Ja 28 '67. O. R. Reid
One of our H-bombs is missing, by F. Lewis. Review
Sat R 50:39 Ja 28 '67. O. R. Reid
Palomares bomb. J. D. Hayes. Reporter 36:50+ Je 15 '67
PALOOS Indians
Cave life on the Palouse; salvage archeologists win a race with builders of Lower Monumental Dam on the Snake River. G. H. Grosso. il Natur Hist 76:38-43 F '67
PALOS VERDES, Calif, library district
Jewel for Palos Verdes; Peninsula Center library. W. L. Emerson. il Library J 92:4379-80 D 1 '67
PALOUSE Indians. See Paloos Indians
PALYTHOA. See Sea anemones
PAMPHLETS
Best in booklets. See issues of House & garden incorporating Living for young homemakers
Booklets worth writing for. Good H 164:194 My '67
Books and booklets. See issues of American home
Information unlimited; government booklets. K. Fredrick. House B 109:58 Ap '67
New literature for house planning. Arch Rec 141:26+ mid-My '67
Tell me more. See issues of House beautiful
Things to write for. See issues of Changing times
Write for these. See issues of Wilson library bulletin
See also
Libraries—Pamphlet collections
PANAGRA-Braniff merger. See Airlines—Consolidations and mergers
PANAIEFF, Michel
Franz, otherwise known as Michel Panaieff, tells about his swanildas. V. H. Swisher. il pors Dance Mag 41:56-9+ D '67
PANAMA
See also
Panama Canal
Panama Canal Zone
Zoology—Panama

Description and travel
Picturesque Panama. B. De Holguin. il Travel 127:40-4 Ja '67

Religious institutions and affairs
See also
Panama (city)—Religious institutions and affairs

Treaties
As treaty dispute heats up, terms of U.S.-Panama pacts; reprint. il U S News 63:71 Ag 28 '67

Deal on Panama Canal: rough transit ahead; new treaties. il U S News 63:41 Jl 10 '67
Panama Canal; proposed treaties; address, September 2, 1967. S. Thurmond. Vital Speeches 34:103-6 D 1 '67
Rough sailing ahead; new treaties will recognize Panamanian sovereignty. Nat R 19:724-6 Jl 11 '67
Terms of the new treaty for the Panama Canal. H. Rosenhouse. New Repub 157:10-11 Jl 22 '67
PANAMA (city)

Religious institutions and affairs
Laymen. . . is what it takes! pastoral experiment of San Miguelito, Panama City. F. Bravo. America 116:524-8 Ap 8 '67
PANAMA CANAL
New clothes? new treaties. Sr Schol 91:36 S 28 '67
Uncertain future of the Panama Canal. il U S News 63:70-1 Ag 28 '67
PANAMA CANAL ZONE
Is U.S. facing another crisis over the Panama Canal? il U S News 62:104-5 Mr 27 '67
Speaking softly; U.S. agrees to surrender sovereignty over the Canal Zone. il Newsweek 70:25-6 Jl 17 '67
Terms of the new treaty for the Panama Canal. H. Rosenhouse. New Repub 157:10-11 Jl 22 '67
PANAMANIAN frogs. See Frogs
PAN AMERICAN conferences. See Inter-American conferences
PAN AMERICAN day and week
Pan American day and Pan American week, 1967; proclamation. L. B. Johnson. Dept State Bul 56:632-3 Ap 17 '67
Pan American week; piano festival. Américas 19:44 Je '67
PAN AMERICAN development foundation
Sense of personal commitment. W. Sanders. il Américas 19:1-7 Ag '67
PAN AMERICAN games
And the melody lingered on. B. Ottum. il Sports Illus 27:18-21 Ag 14 '67
Embarrassment of riches? U.S. victories. il Newsweek 70:76 Ag 14 '67
Naiad's triumph; brilliant performances of U.S. swimmers. il Time 90:40 Ag 4 '67
Sporting life. Newsweek 70:81 Ag 7 '67
To Becky with love from all the Harvards; Harvard's victory over Vesper boat club. M. Riley. il Sports Illus 27:44 Jl 10 '67
Winning ways of Winnipeg. J. Underwood. il Sports Illus 27:20-5 Ag 7 '67
PAN AMERICAN health organization
Progress notes; summary of report. G. Meek. Américas 19:46 Ja '67
PAN AMERICAN highway
Alaska to South America by car, when? il U S News 62:108-9 Je 5 '67
PAN AMERICAN union
Art. See issues of Américas
PAN AMERICAN world airways
CAB faces problem in Pan Am route bid. R. G. O'Lone. Aviation W 86:39 My 1 '67
PAA operation of two airports aimed at easing New York jam. Aviation W 87:39 O 2 '67
Pan Am cargo terminal heavily automated, mechanized; photographs. Aviation W 86:38-9+ My 22 '67
Pan Am prepares for next business jet. D. A. Brown. il Aviation W 87:81+ Jl 31 '67
Pan Am termination could retard inertial introduction. B. Miller. il Aviation W 87:70-5 Jl 31 '67
Saigon's squeeze play; refused landing clearance. Time 89:90 Mr 3 '67
Transpacific route case: Pan Am aims to keep top role in Pacific. J. W. Carter. il Aviation W 86:40-1+ Je 19 '67
See also
Intercontinental hotels corporation
PAN AMERICANISM. See Inter-American relations
PANARABISM
See also
Arab states
PANAY (gunboat) incident
Rehearsal for World war II. D. Perry. il Am Heritage 18:40-5+ Ap '67; Reply. 18:51 O '67
PANCAKES. See Griddle cakes
PANCREAS

Diseases
Annals of medicine; pseudocyst of pancreas. B. Roueché. New Yorker 43:110+ My 27 '67

PANELING
How to shop for paneling. Bet Hom & Gard
45:24+ Jl '67
Panels that tame wind and sun. il Pop Gard
18:34-7 My '67
PANGBORN, Cyrus R.
Sex and the single standard. Christian Cent
84:648-50 My 17 '67
PANICS
1929
See also
Stock exchange—Crisis, October 1929
PANNENBERG, Wolfhart
Revelation & history. il por Time 90:61 Jl
14 '67
PANNING (photography) See Photography of
moving objects
PANNING, Gold. See Gold panning
PANOS, Dee
Debt; story. Reporter 38:34-5 Ja 11 '68
PANSY orchids. See Orchids
PANTAGLEIZE; drama. See Ghelderode, M. de
PANTER-DOWNES, Mollie
Letter from London (cont) New Yorker 42:
145-6+ F 11; 158+ Ap 15; 177-80 My 6;
43:96+ Je 17; 80+ Ag 19; 226-8+ N 11; 150-
3 D 2; 49-50+ D 23 '67
Profiles; Ootacamund, India. New Yorker
43:48-50+ Mr 4; 57-62+ Mr 11 '67
PANTINS. See Paper dolls
PANTOJA-ALOR, Jerjes, and Robison, R. A.
Paleozoic sedimentary rocks in Oaxaca,
Mexico. bibliog Science 157:1033-5 S 1 '67
PANTOMIME
See also
Mime
Shadow pantomimes and plays
PANTRIES
There's a pantry with space measured for
bulky items. R. Martens. il Farm J 91:
75 O '67
PAOLUCCI, Henry
Coalition for victory in '68; will LBJ get
Republican votes? Nat R 19:630-1 Je 13 '67
PAPACONSTANTINOU, John
Molecular aspects of lens cell differentiation.
bibliog Science 156:338-46 Ap 21 '67
PAPACY
Christian and the fisherman; proposal to call
pope head of universal church. America
117:6-7 Jl 1 '67
COCU assaulted in its cradle; C. K. Myers
proposal. Christian Cent 84:803-4 Je 21 '67;
Discussion. 84:1073 Ag 23 '67
Pan-Christian papacy? proposal of Bishop
Myers. R. M. Brown. Commonweal 86:446+
Jl 14 '67
Understanding the papacy. Christian Cent 84:
1115-17 S 6 '67
PAPADOPOULOS, George
I am the boss. Time 90:39 S 15 '67
Strong man who hates communism. por U S
News 64:11 Ja 1 '68
PAPAL encyclicals. See Encyclicals
PAPAL infallibility. See Popes—Infallibility
PAPANDREOU, Andreas
Elections or coup? deadlock in Greece. S.
Rousseas. Nation 204:392-5 Mr 27 '67
Gulliver in Greece. T. Sage. Nat R 19:1112-
13 O 17 '67
Letter to a tyrant. S. W. Rousseas and R.
Clements. Nation 205:550-1 N 27 '67
Long view. il por Newsweek 71:37 Ja 8 '68
Strange interlude in Athens. G. Bailey. il
Reporter 37:35-6 Ag 10 '67
PAPANDREOU, George
Elections or coup? deadlock in Greece. S.
Rousseas. Nation 204:390-5 Mr 27 '67
Greece: a tragic hour. il por Newsweek 69:34+
My 1 '67
King on the spot? il Sr Schol 90:18 My 12 '67
Saving Greece from the Greeks. B. D. Nossi-
ter. New Repub 156:9-10 My 20 '67
PAPER
It's only paper. J. Daugherty and M.
Daugherty. il Sci Digest 61:87-9 Mr '67
New trends in colored paper; reprint. N. A.
Meyer. Am Artist 31:12+ O '67
Picking the right paper. il Am Artist 31:
32-3+ O '67
Reverence for paper. N. Kent. Am Artist 31:5
O '67
See also
Paper making and trade

History
Brief history of papermaking. N. Kent. il
Am Artist 31:36-41+ O '67
See also
Dard Hunter paper museum, Appleton, Wis.

PAPER, Handmade. See Paper making and
trade
PAPER airplanes. See Airplane models
PAPER bag puppets. See Puppets and puppet
plays
PAPER bags
High cost of vacuum cleaner bags; for Elec-
trolux canister vacuum cleaner. Consumer
Rep 32:463 S '67
PAPER box industry
See also
Container corporation of America
PAPER clothes. See Clothing and dress
PAPER cups, plates, etc.
See also
Maryland cup corporation
PAPER dolls
Data on the dangerous pantin, paper doll that
dances. S. Aker. il Dance Mag 41:50-3 D '67
PAPER dresses. See Clothing and dress
PAPER fabrics. See Paper textiles
PAPER-hanging
Step by step to successful wallpapering. D.
Jordan. il Bet Hom & Gard 45:124+ Mr '67
PAPER in religion, folklore, etc.
Curandera artist; bark paper pictures, once
used in religious rites. S. Battist. il Amér-
icas 19:36-40 My '67
PAPER making and trade
Annual paper week held in New York.
Pub W 191:114 Mr 6 '67
Brief history of papermaking. N. Kent. il
Am Artist 31:36-41+ O '67
Great tissue war; England. R. Ross-Skinner.
Duns R 89:47 F '67
Henry Morris: papermaker & printer. F.
Johnson. il Am Artist 31:56-61+ O '67
See also
Kimberly corporation
Mead corporation
Paper mills
Papercraft corporation
Scott paper company

Collective bargaining
See Collective bargaining—Paper industry

Wages and hours
See also
Collective bargaining—Paper industry
PAPER mills
Ultimatum in the West; clean up or close
down. Bsns W p 104 O 21 '67
Employees
Crossfire catches paper companies; contract
negotiations held up. il Bsns W p 118+ F
4 '67
PAPER money
France
Letter from Paris; new French five-franc
note. Genêt. New Yorker 43:177-8 Mr 25
'67
United States
Paper currency of the United States. C.
French. Hobbies 72:102 O '67
Playing for coin; silver certificates and rush
on silver. il Newsweek 70:68-70 Ag 28 '67
Silver price calms down; silver certificate
legislation passed. Bsns W p 138 Je 17 '67

History
Confederate currency. C. French. Hobbies 72:
102 Je '67
PAPER products
Big paper caper. B. Plumb. il N Y Times
Mag p 104-5 N 5 '67
Big play in paper. il Life 63:84-6+ N 3 '67
Chez Mlle: the paper pad. D. Hampton. il
Mlle 65:80-1 Je '67
Everything's paper but the doll. V. D. Hahn.
il Am Home 70:66-7 Jl '67
It's a paper world! il Seventeen 26:320+ Ag
'67
Paper power; new ways of using paper. il
House & Gard 133:88-9 Ja '68
Paper wrap-up. il McCalls 94:10+ Ap '67
Summer's dashing toss-aways. il House &
Gard 131:104-11 Je '67
See also
Paper towels
Exhibitions
Paper: events celebrating opening of exhibi-
tion at Museum of contemporary crafts. New
Yorker 43:51-3 D 2 '67
PAPER sculpture
Making paper sculpture. R. Fabri. il Am
Artist 31:42-6 O '67

PAPER textiles
Clothes that glisten; dresses of foil. il Consumer Bul 50:35 N '67
Institute report on paper clothing. il Good H 165:6 Ag '67
It really is paper! N. L. Pouch. il Good H 165:144 Ag '67
Now it's the little paper dress; disposable garments. il Bsns W p 132-4+ Jl 22 '67
Paper caper. A. Chamberlin. il Sat Eve Post 240:32-7 D 2 '67
Paper chase, the boom in disposable clothing. il Consumer Bul 50:4-6 Jl '67

PAPER towels
Paper towels. il Consumer Rep 32:88-9 F '67

PAPER weaving. See Weaving

PAPER work
Cartonnage; creating accessories from corrugated cardboard. il House & Gard 131:138+ Je '67
Sound of paper; collective compositions by Ayo and others. Craft Horiz 27:12a+ N '67

See also
Paper sculpture

Exhibitions

Fantastics made with paper; exhibition at New York's Museum of contemporary crafts. il House & Gard 132:164-7 D '67
Think paper; exhibition at New York's Museum of contemporary crafts. R. Manoff. il Craft Horiz 27:11, 14-19 N '67

PAPERBACK book covers. See Book covers

PAPERBACK books
1966 paperback best sellers in the bookstores. Pub W 191:43-6 Ja 30 '67
Throw out the textbooks. A. Gordon. il Am Ed 3:5-7 S '67

See also
Booksellers and bookselling—Paperback books
Publishers and publishing—Paperback books

Bibliography

Books to come; children's and adult; comp. by J. C. Thomson and J. Putnam. Library J 92:367-403 Ja 15 '67
Books to come; childrens and adult; comp. by M. Philips; J. Putnam; D. Gersoni. Library J 93:320-66 Ja 15 '68
Books to come; children's and adult; comp. by S. Roth and J. Putnam. Library J 92:2053-4+, 3137-73 My 15, S 15 '67
Latin America's sociopolitical scene: checklist of pertinent paperbacks. Christian Cent 85:85 Ja 17 '68
New paperbacks for high school students. Sr Schol 90:sup20 Mr 10 '67
On parade: new paperbacks; symposium. il Sr Schol 89:sup8-9+ Ja 20 '67
Paperback bookshelf. See issues of Changing times
Pick of the paperbacks. R. W. Saal. See issues of Saturday review
Picking out the best in paperbooks. America 117:617-20 N 18 '67

Prices

Price averages, 1966, cited in major categories. il Pub W 191:54-5 F 13 '67

PAPERCRAFT corporation
It's a merry Christmas when the output is torn to shreds. il Time 90:70 Ag 25 '67

PAPERS, Family. See Family records

PAPERWEIGHTS
Old glass paperweights (cont) J. P. Boore. il Hobbies 72:84-5+ Ag '67

Anecdotes, facetiae, satire, etc.

How useful was my paperweight. R. P. Lister. Atlan 220:118-19 N '67

PAPIER-MÂCHÉ
Nativity scene from Roscoe Wilson elementary school, Lubbock, Texas. il Sch Arts 67:48 D '67
New dimensions in sculpture. J. Belik. il Sch Arts 66:9-12 Ja '67
Papier-mâché project. M. W. Sheehan. il Sch Arts 67:16-17 D '67

PAPP, Joseph
Anti-Hamlet of Joseph Papp. R. Brustein. New Repub 158:23+ Ja 20 '68
Hamlet. il Time 91:55 Ja 5 '68
Making of a theater. por Newsweek 70:124-5 N 13 '67
Off Broadway, production of Hamlet. E. Oliver. New Yorker 43:68+ Ja 6 '68
Theatre. H. Clurman. Nation 206:92-3 Ja 15 '68
Theater of shattered focus. H. Hewes. Sat R 51:95 Ja 13 '68

PAPPAS, Marilyn R.
Contemporary craftsman and fabric collage. il Sch Arts 66:11-14 Ap '67

PAPRIKA
Hungarian accent. C. Claiborne. il N Y Times Mag p 102 Ap 16 '67

PAPYRUS
Papyrus. Sci N 92:451 N 4 '67

PAQUETTE, Maurie, and Weegham, R. B.
FH-1100. Flying 81:48-52 N '67

PARABIOSIS
Protection through parabiosis against the lethal effects of exposure to large doses of X-rays. H. W. Carroll and D. J. Kimeldorf. bibliog il Science 156:954-5 My 19 '67; Reply with rejoinder. S. Warren. 157:582 Ag 4 '67

PARABLES
See also
Jesus Christ—Parables

PARACHUTE jumping. See Parachuting

PARACHUTING
Bad trip; parachutists drown in Lake Erie. il Time 90:38 S 8 '67
Best way; skydiving death. Newsweek 70:33 O 9 '67
Case of paracide; suicide of J. Wasik. Time 90:28-9 O 6 '67
High altitude, low opening. il Ebony 22:40-2+ My '67
Last jump; parachutists drown in Lake Erie. il Newsweek 70:25 S 11 '67
Parakiting! K. D. Curtis. il Travel 128:40-1 S '67
Sense of bursting away, utterly free; death of D. Rutledge. H. Suydan. il Life 62:74+ F 10 '67
Washington clipboard; proposed regulation of skydiving. R. Burkhardt. Flying 81:18 D '67

Accidents and injuries

Safety board rules in skydiving deaths. Aviation W 87:26 O 2 '67

PARACHUTING, Cargo
Energy absorber key to free-fall supply. B. K. Thomas, jr. il Aviation W 87:77-8 Jl 3 '67

PARADE (periodical)
Inside stuff; Personality parade of L. Shearer. il Newsweek 69:76 Je 26 '67

PARADES

Safety devices and measures

How to love a parade. A. R. Roalman. il Todays Health 45:20-5+ Jl '67

PARADIS, Marjorie B.
Was her face red! drama. Plays 26:29-36 Ap '67

PARADISE, Scott
Visit with the great Kahn. Christian Cent 84:1556-8 D 6 '67

PARADISE lost; ballet. See Ballets—Criticisms

PARADOX
Escape from paradox. A. Rapoport. il Sci Am 217:50-6 bibliog(p 134) Jl '67

PARADOXICAL sleep. See Sleep

PARAGUAY
See also
Natural resources—Paraguay

History

Paraguay. R. E. Crist. bibliog il Focus 18:1-6 D '67

PARAKITING. See Parachuting

PARALYSIS
Altered response to pneumococcal polysaccharide in offspring of immunologically paralyzed mice. R. Kerman and others. bibliog il Science 156:1514-16 Je 16 '67
Attack on Parkinson's. il Newsweek 69:84 Mr 6 '67
End to Parkinson's. Time 90:68 O 20 '67
Paraplegic cure? Sci Digest 61:29-30 Mr '67
Viral hemorrhagic encephalopathy of rats. A. H. ElDadah and others. bibliog il Science 156:392-4 Ap 21 '67

PARAMECIA
Photoreactivation in vivo of pyrimidine dimers in paramecium DNA. B. M. Sutherland and others. bibliog il Science 158:1699-700 D 29 '67

PARAMETERS
Operate and release times of relays. W. W. Wright. il Electr World 77:54-5 Ap '67
Small-signal high-frequency transistors. T. J. Robe. il Electr World 78:38-40 Jl '67

PARAMETRIC amplifiers. See Amplifiers

PARAMONOV, Albert Mikhailovich
New slogan for bosses: profit or perish. il pors Life 63:60-1+ N 10 '67

PARAMOUNT pictures corporation
Cecil B. DeBluhdorn? Gulf & Western industries new owner of Paramount pictures. il Newsweek 69:82 My 29 '67

PARASITES
See also
Plasmodium (parasite)

Livestock

Eperythrozoon coccoides: influence on course of infection of plasmodium chabaudi in mouse. K. J. Ott and L. A. Stauber. bibliog il Science 155:1546-8 Mr 24 '67

PARASITIC diseases
See also
Ascariasis
Schistosomiasis
Toxoplasmosis

PARASITIC plants
See also
Indian pipes (plants)

PARASOLS. See Umbrellas

PARCEL post rates. See Postal rates—United States

PARDEE, Arthur B.
Crystallization of a sulfate-binding protein (permease) from salmonella typhimurium. bibliog Science 156:1627-8 Je 23 '67

PARDEE, Josephine H.
Pioneering with the Job corps. por Library J 92:748-9 F 15 '67

PARDEE, William D. and Sommers, C. E.
Seed selection, first step to top yields. Suc Farm 65:36-7 Ja '67

PARDINAS, Felipe
Who knows the truth about red China? interview. Cath World 205:36-41 Ap '67

PARENT and child (law)
Mark, I love you! excerpts. H. Painter il Good H 164:93-5+ Ap '67

PARENT-child relationship
Adopted children are different. H. H. Work. il Parents Mag 42:42-3+ F '67
Are parents to blame for student behavior? excerpts from address, May 11, 1967. S. L. Halleck. il U S News 62:74-5 My 29 '67
Are you afraid of your children? with study-discussion program, by C. Smallenburg and H. Smallenburg. E. J. Le Shan. bibliog PTA Mag 62:2-5, 35-6 D '67
Babies make good teachers. J. Whitbread. il Parents Mag 42:33-5+ Jl '67
Back to baby farming? F. R. Schreiber and M. Herman. Sci Digest 61:25-6 Ag '67
Can I practice what I preach? H. J. Burn. McCalls 94:62+ Ap '67
Conversations teens never hear. Seventeen 26:164-5 N '67
Conversations with Katey. A. Birstein. il McCalls 94:22+ Mr '67
Curiosity, wonder, awareness; symposium, ed. by M. Longwell. il Farm J 91:102-3 Mr '67
Do celebrities make good parents? J. Brothers. Good H 165:34+ S '67
Do child psychologists make good parents? D. I. Malamud. il Redbook 130:47+ Ja '68
Do you play fair with your kids? A. Loomer. il Parents Mag 43:50-1+ Ja '68
Getting on talking terms; with study-discussion program by R. Strang. M. G. Brook. bibliog il PTA Mag 62:14-16, 32 S '67
Getting the kids we deserve. E. J. Anthony. il N Y Times Mag p57+ Ja 22 '67
Growing and learning. H. E. Rie and E. D. Rie. Cath World 206:13-16 O '67
Gulf between parents. R. Vaughan. Life 63: 104A-104B+ N 17 '67
Harem in the house; condensation. G. Porter. il Read Digest 91:245-51+ D '67
How much does your father's job affect you? D. Klein. il Seventeen 26:130-1+ O '67
Innocent rebels; friendship between parents and children. J. D. Verdery. il Parents Mag 42:46-7+ Ag '67
Is snooping ever justified? J. Brothers. Good H 164:66+ My '67
My parents are so narrow-minded! questions and answers. A. Wood. Seventeen 26:164+ Mr '67
My parents won't trust me; questions and answers. A. Wood. Seventeen 26:342-3 Ag '67
On being an American parent; Time essay. Time 90:30-1 D 15 '67
One child, one vote; weekly family meetings. J. H. Cohen. il Parents Mag 42:40-1+ Ja '67
Open-letter to the father of a boy who won't get his hair cut. M. Groves. Good H 165: 62+ N '67

Opinion on home truths; with reply by her mother. J. Bingham. Mlle 65:52+ Je '67
Parental nudity. B. Bettelheim. il Ladies Home J 84:56 Ag '67
Pound of peas. R. Hochstein. il Good H 164: 64+ Je '67
Redbook dialogue. L. Marvin; J. Carson. il Redbook 130:74-5+ N '67
Scapegoat child. K. D. Fishman. il N Y Times Mag p86+ S 24 '67
Self-made man as father. A. A. Messer. N Y Times Mag p 123+ Mr 19 '67
Sex, my daughters, and me. M. Decter. Harper 235:27-32 Ag '67
Simple child, doubting parent. D. Callahan. Commonweal 86:287-90 My 26 '67
Special world of mothers and daughters; excerpts from Mothers and daughters. E. G. Neisser. il Parents Mag 42:41-3+ My '67
Take it easy with teen-agers. H. Thomson. il Todays Health 45:33-5 F '67
Teaching styles we parents practice; with study-discussion program, by R. Strang. W. J. Anderson. bibliog il PTA Mag 61:8-10, 34 Mr '67
Teenagers who take but don't give. M. Gross. il Good H 164:66+ Mr '67
A time to every purpose. V. Ebinger. il Redbook 128:8+ Ap '67
What a father's role should be; fathers and sons. B. Spock. il Redbook 128:22+ F '67
What did we do wrong? D. Barr. il N Y Times Mag p36-7+ N 26 '67; Discussion. p22+ D 10: 12+ D 17 '67
See also
Family life
Fathers
Maternal deprivation
Mothers
Youth—Management and training

PARENT education
Father gets to hold the baby. L. Marek. il Parents Mag 42:56-7+ Je '67

PARENT-teacher associations. See Parents and teachers associations

PARENT-teacher cooperation. See School and the home

PARENTHOOD, Training for. See Parent education

PARENTS
Most unexpected threat to a good marriage; effect of children. V. Cadden. il McCalls 94:94-5+ Jl '67
When parents separate; common sins committed by divorced parents. J. H. Pollack. il Todays Health 45:16-19+ Je '67
See also
Daughters
Family life
Fathers
Foster parents
School and the home
Stepparents

PARENTS and teachers associations
Gifts? E. S. Hendryson. PTA Mag 62:15 D '67
Keeping pace with the PTA. See issues of PTA magazine
Membership proclamation. E. Hendryson. PTA Mag 62:5 O '67
PTA, where the action is. il PTA Mag 62:26-8 S '67
People want to know. J. Moorhead. PTA Mag 61:2-3 Mr '67
Poor and the PTA. E. Schindler-Rainman. il PTA Mag 61:4-7 Ap '67
Share the benefits. J. Moorhead. PTA Mag 61:2-3 My '67
Speak up for the PTA! J. Moorehead. il PTA Mag 61:2-3 F '67
See also
National congress of parents and teachers

Student participation

Growing up through the PTA; with study-discussion program, by C. Smallenburg and H. Smallenburg. bibliog il PTA Mag 61: 4-7, 31-2 F '67

PARENTS and teachers conferences. See School and the home

PARENTS attitudes. See Attitudes

PARENTS' magazine
Parents' magazine's 1967 awards. il Parents Mag 42:52+ D '67
See also
Youth group achievement awards

PARENTS school visiting. See School and the home

PARETI, Luigi
When Orpheus struck the trembling lyre. UNESCO Courier 20:9-11 My '67

PARFAITS. See Ice cream, ices, etc.

PARIAH; story. See Williams, J.

PARIBAS. See Banks and banking—France

PARILLI, Babe
For Babe, a week to forget. E. Shrake. por Sports Illus 27:30-1 S 18 '67

PARIS, James D.
APBA action report. See issues of Motorboating

PARIS
Letter from Paris (cont) Genêt. New Yorker 42:124+ F 11 '67

American colony
See Americans in France

Art
From the River Plate to the Seine. D. C. Bayón. il Américas 19:22-7 Ag '67
Paris. J. Alvard. See issues of Art news

City planning
First modern urbanist; E. Hénard. P. Wolf. il Arch Forum 127:50-5 O '67
Letter from Paris; height of new buildings, construction of new Vercingetorix expressway. Genêt. New Yorker 43:172+ My 13 '67

Commune
See Paris—History

Description
Operatic Paris; photographs. H. Lloyd. Opera N 31:13-17 F 4 '67

Education
School that breeds France's business elite; Ecole Polytechnique, Paris. il Bsns W p 184-6+ My 20 '67

Elysée palace
An evening at the de Gaulles'. P. Feldkamp. Atlan 219:114-18 My '67

Galleries and museums
Travel notes. R. Joseph. Esquire 67:10 F '67
Tutankhamania; objects from King Tut's tomb on display at the Petit palais. il Time 89:76 Mr 17 '67

History
Mao and the Paris commune. il Newsweek 69:46-7 F 27 '67

Hotels, restaurants, etc.
Aftermath. L. Saalburg. Esquire 67:62+ My '67
Gourmets' delight is lean on profits; Tour d'argent. il Bsns W p62-4 D 30 '67
Two brightly breezy arbiters; Guide Julliard de Paris. il Life 63:129-30+ S 15 '67

Intellectual life
Literary life in Paris. H. R. Lottman. il Pub W 192:21-3 N 27 '67
Twenties in Montparnasse; lives of young American writers. M. Cowley. il Sat R 50:51+ Mr 11 '67

Markets
Departed glory of Les Halles. J. Flanner. il Life 62:82+ My 12 '67

Monuments, statues, etc.
Arch of triumph. J. Bryan, 3d. il Holiday 43:62-3+ Ja '68

Music
Contemporary music at full tilt. J. Maguire. il Hi Fi 17:MA24-5+ Ap '67
Letter from Paris; Orchestre de Paris début. Genêt. New Yorker 43:232-4 N 25 '67
Notes from our correspondents. J. Moore. il Hi Fi 17:24+ Ja '67
Notes from our correspondents. M. Hennessey. Hi Fi 17:20+ My '67
Paris (cont) D. Stevens. il Opera N 31:32 Ap 8 '67

Newspapers
Le Monde's world. Newsweek 70:98+ D 11 '67

Social life and customs
On renting a French aristocrat; Hôtesses internationales. il Time 89:50 My 19 '67
Paris collections, '67. Mlle 64:16+ Ap '67

Stores
Boutiques of Paris and Rome. E. Sheppard. il Holiday 42:78-80+ N '67
Francs before fondles; Paris' first computerized grocery store. Time 89:98+ Ap 28 '67

Theater
Theatre in Europe. H. Clurman. Nation 205:30 Jl 3 '67

PARIS air and space show. See Aviation—Exhibitions

PARIS air show. See Aviation—Exhibitions

PARIS international air show. See Aviation—Exhibitions

PARIS-match (periodical) See Periodicals—France

PARIS observatory. See Astronomical observatories—France

PARISHES
Bury the parish? B. Barr. Christian Cent 84:199-202 F 15 '67; Discussion. 84:411-12 Mr 29 '67
Laymen. . . is what it takes! pastoral experiment of San Miguelito, Panama City. F. Bravo. America 116:524-8 Ap 8 '67
Parishes in the central city. N. J. Rashford. America 117:381-3 O 7 '67
Tomorrow's parish. America 117:50 Jl 15 '67

PARISHFIELD community. See Laity

PARISIANS
Adventurous young Parisians. F. Koltun. il Mlle 65:151-4 Je '67

PARK, Chung Hee
Growing girl's problems. Newsweek 70:34+ Jl 31 '67
Hope in the hermit kingdom. il por Time 89:40-1 Mr 10 '67
Winner in Korea; a friend of U.S. US News 62:19 My 15 '67

PARK, Ed
Fishing light is never out. Outdoor Life 140:46-9+ Ag '67
Long, long trail. por Outdoor Life 140:46-7+ D '67
Luck beats the odds. pors Outdoor Life 140:40-1+ S '67
Mackinaw on a fly. Field & S 71:42-3+ Ap '67
Our varmints were trophies. por Outdoor Life 139:72-3+ F '67

PARK, Maeva
Call to a stranger; story. Redbook 129:175-88 Ag '67

PARK bonds. See Municipal bonds

PARK FOREST, Ill.
Negro in the suburbs; with painting by N. Rockwell. J. Star. Look 31:51-3+ My 16 '67

PARK maintenance equipment. See Parks—Equipment

PARK RIDGE, Ill.
Big comprehensive high school uses a new 300 plan; Maine township high school south. il Arch Rec 142:180-1 O '67

PARK roads. See National parks and reserves—Roads

PARKE-Bernet galleries, incorporated

History
Classic action at a vintage auction; first auction of automobiles conducted in this country. J. Wilson. il Motor T 19:74-7 Ap '67

PARKER, Ann
Mees, you goin' to be real teacher now, don'cha? Am Ed 3:14-16 My '67; Same abr. with title Worst bunch in school. Read Digest 91:182-4+ Jl '67

PARKER, Bonnie
Onward and upward with the arts. P. Kael. New Yorker 43:147-8+ O 21 '67

PARKER, Don
Golden touch. Sat Eve Post 240:100-5 My 6 '67

PARKER, Dorothy (Rothschild)
Guinevere of the round table. il por Time 89:94 Je 16 '67
Obituary
Pub W 191:64+ Je 19 '67
Queen of the round table. por Newsweek 69:43 Je 19 '67

PARKER, Eugene
How stars are born. Newsweek 71:45 Ja 8 '68

PARKER, Frank L.
Radioactive wastes from fusion reactors. bibliog Science 159:83-4 Ja 5 '68

PARKER, Franklin
Federal influences on the future of American education. Sch & Soc 95:383-7 O 28 '67
1967 as a centennial year in the history of education. Sch & Soc 95:56-7 Ja 21 '67

PARKER, Garland G.
Statistics of attendance in American universities and colleges, 1966-67. por Sch & Soc 95:9-24, 124-5 Ja 7, F 18 '67

PARKER, Harry
Parker's pachyderms. por Time 90:50 Jl 14 '67
Streaking Harvards. il por Newsweek 69:89 Je 19 '67

PARKER, Maynard
Barry works twice as hard because he thinks he was born two steps behind. Life 62:54-5 My 12 '67
He fueled his first motorcycle with crushed pine roots. Life 62:52 My 19 '67
Report: Hong Kong. Atlan 220:14+ N '67

PARKER, Patrick L. and others
Fatty acids in eleven species of blue-green algae: geochemical significance. bibliog Science 155:707-8 F 10 '67

PARKER, Ralph Halstead
Not a shared system. por Library J 92:3967-70 N 1 '67
Significant research; the survival of librarianship. Wilson Lib Bul 41:919-20 My '67
Small library faces the future. ALA Bul 61:669-71 Je '67

PARKER, Sanford S. and others
Business roundup. See issues of Fortune

PARKER brothers, incorporated
Where monopoly is not a dirty word. il Bsns W p 180-2+ Mr 25 '67

PARKING, Automobile. See Automobile parking

PARKING fines. See Fines (penalties)

PARKING lots. See Automobile parking

PARKING meters
Flip-top menace; parking-meter jamming. Time 90:43 Ag 11 '67
Meter collection uses sealed bags; Arlington Heights, Ill. L. A. Hanson. il Am City 82: 126+ F '67

PARKINS, Barbara
Dames in the Valley of the dolls. B. Rollin. il pors Look 31:53-6+ S 5 '67
Helping Barbara Parkins; photographs. Esquire 68:104-7 Ag '67

PARKINSON, C. Northcote
Norman Island. Atlan 220:92-4 Ag '67

PARKINSON'S disease. See Paralysis

PARKLAND hospital. See Dallas—Hospitals

PARKS, Ed
Is it wrong to make pets of wild animals? Sci Digest 62:61-4 Ag '67

PARKS, Edgar L.
From dream to reality (cont) il Motor B 119: 50-2+ F '67
Shook-up shakedown. Motor B 119:50-1+ Ap '67

PARKS, Gordon
Bodyguard of young cats, a bag of equalizers, and a lonely road. Life 62:76B-78+ My 19 '67

PARKS, Joel D.
Need index in park planning. Parks & Rec 2:28+ Mr '67

PARKS, Norman L.
Sovereign state of Bell. Nation 205:430-5 O 30 '67
Who will Bell the colossus? Nation 205:391-3 O 23 '67

PARKS, W. George
Gordon research conferences: program for 1967. Science 155:1290-302+ Mr 10 '67
Gordon research conferences: winter program, 1968. Science 158:1086-8 N 24 '67

PARKS
County parks and open space planning. A. C. Stelling and N. D. Mitchell. il Parks & Rec 2:28-9+ Ap '67
How to make a city come alive. T. P. F. Hoving. il Parents Mag 42:50-1+ Ap '67
Never never land; lifesized fiberglassed storybook characters in Point Defiance park. il Parks & Rec 2:18-19 Je '67
The park; problems of a city park system. J. Hope. il Natur Hist 76:8-10+ Ag '67
Parks and recreation. See issues of American city
Vest-pocket parks. il Newsweek 69:64-5 Je 19 '67

See also
Zoological gardens

Care
Good ground maintenance; address, October 1966. H. S. Conover. Parks & Rec 2:38+ Ap '67
Maintenance tips for harried park officials; Milwaukee. R. E. Kurtz. il Am City 82:98-9 My '67

Equipment
Best in park maintenance. R. R. Fleming. il Am City 82:71-4 D '67
Park and recreation equipment roundup. il Am City 82:153+ N '67

Fees
See Recreation—Fees

Lighting
New light on the World fair's Unisphere. il Am City 82:122 My '67

Maintenance
Best in park maintenance. R. R. Fleming. il Am City 82:71-4 D '67
High-density use, low-maintenance operation; new regional parks in Allegheny County, Pa. G. E. Kelly. il Am City 82:102-4 O '67
Higher standard of maintenance; Kansas City, Mo. G. Eib. il Am City 82:100-1 F '67
Park maintenance tasks expanding; public disregard, vandalism, littering, increase workload. J. A. Reynolds. Parks & Rec 2: 39-40+ O '67
Will a park die in Brooklyn? Brooklyn's Prospect park. J. J. Shomon. il Audubon 69:80-1 Mr '67

Management
Wake up foresters, you're needed! J. J. Shomon. il Am For 73:12-15+ My '67

Canada
See also
British Columbia—Parks and reserves

United States
City-school cooperation builds a park two years sooner; Dixon, Calif. J. M. Lesher. il Am City 82:80-1 N '67
Managing human use of natural parks. U. W. Hella. Parks & Rec 2:34-5+ Ja '67
Somebody shoulda told me..; visitor services to interpret natural and historical scenes. D. B. Huyck. il Am For 73:12-15+ Jl '67
Trustees name Sal Prezioso NRPA executive vice president and secretary; with editorial comment. il Parks & Rec 2:13, 15+ Ag '67
See also
National parks and reserves—United States

History
Trends at a glance; progress of park and recreation services over the past twenty-five years. D. E. Hawkins. il Parks & Rec 2:21+ Jl '67

PARLIAMENTARY practice
Open letter to the ALA council. L. M. Morsch. ALA Bul 61:1276 D '67
Your turn to run the meeting? il Changing T 21:27-8 Jl '67

PARLOR cars. See Railroads—Cars

PARMAR, S. L.
Laissez-faire is not enough. Christian Cent 84:587-9 My 3 '67

PAROCHIAL schools
Dialogue on aid to schools; National commission for Methodist-Catholic dialogue. America 118:4 Ja 6 '68
Financial problems of the parochial school network. L. R. Downey. Sch & Soc 95:305-6 Sum '67
See also
Education and state

Federal aid
See Federal aid to education

PAROCHIAL schools, Catholic
Abandon Catholic elementary grades? Sr Schol 90:sup2 Mr 3 '67
Catholic education in Latin America. F. P. Chamberlain. America 116:750-3 My 20 '67; Discussion. 116:745; 117-1-2 My 20, Jl 1 '67
Financial problems of the parochial school network. L. R. Downey. Sch & Soc 95:305-6 Sum '67
Four myths about parochial schools (cont) M. O'Neill. America 116:183-7 F 4 '67; Discussion. 116:329 Mr 11 '67
Immaculate heart sisters? America 117:629 N 25 '67
Lay leader's view: Catholic schools today; interview, ed. by H. Ravis. J. A. Davitt. Sr Schol 90:sup4 Mr 31 '67
On confession and grade schools; letter to the editor. I. Philip. America 117:397-8 O 14 '67
Parochial pressures. Newsweek 70:122 N 20 '67
PEARL, POAU and prophecies. America 116: 711 My 13 '67
Planning for change. C. A. Koob and R. Shaw. Cath World 206:23-6 O '67
Price tags for Catholic education. R. Hassenger. Commonweal 86:223-4 My 12 '67
Romeo and renewal. J. Syburg. Cath World 206:21-3 O '67

PAROCHIAL schools, Catholic—*Continued*
Shadow of the concordat; Catholic schools and German bishops. C. Wilpert. Commonweal 86:333-4 Je 9 '67
Trouble in the classroom; teacher walkouts in parochial schools. il Time 89:56 Je 2 '67

Federal aid
See Federal aid to education

Finance
Catholic education: why its special problems are increasing. il U S News 63:69 S 11 '67

PARODIES
Death of a President; a dissent. J. Brennan. Nat R 19:415 Ap 18 '67
Portrait of a babe. T. Meehan. il Sat Eve Post 240:22 Mr 25 '67
Scientific American. D. Newman and R. Benton. il Esquire 67:71-5+ F '67

PAROLE
Paroles for sale; corruption on Georgia parole board. il Newsweek 71:15-16 Ja 1 '68

PARONI, Adele
What teachers can do about smoking. Sr Schol 91:sup 18 N 16 '67

PARR, Dorothy W.
Squeezing the orange. Writer 80:25-6 S '67

PARRAVANO, Carlo, and others
Diffusion of water in zeolites. bibliog Science 155:1535-6 Mr 24 '67

PARRISH, Bernie
Pro football's player mutiny; ed. by E. Linn. Look 31:66+ Ag 22 '67

PARRISH, John B.
Is U.S. really filled with poverty? por U S News 63:50-3 S 4 '67

PARRISH, Wayne W.
Letter to our readers. Tech W 21:8 Jl 3 '67

PARROT in art. See Birds in art

PARRY, Albert
Communism's great divide. Reporter 36:29-32 Je 1 '67
Russia dives for the sea bottom. Sci Digest 62:60-4 S '67

PARRY, Jack
Bonefish of the North. Field & S 72:60-1+ D '67
Dog Argentine. Field & S 72:130-1+ N '67

PARRY, Stanley
Great tradition. Nat R 19:423-4 Ap 18 '67

PARSEGHIAN, Ara
Notre Dame: we're number one! J. Bowers. il pors Sat Eve Post 240:85-9 O 7 '67

PARSEGIAN, V. Adrian
Forces between lecithin bimolecular leaflets are due to a disordered surface layer. bibliog Science 156:939-42 My 19 '67

PARSELL, Carl
Police spokesman's views on Detroit; dispatch. U S News 63:25 Ag 7 '67

PARSONAGES and rectories
Rectory: Old St Mary's parish rectory, San Francisco. il Arch Rec 141:137-8 My '67

PARSONS, Betty
Studio by the sea. il House & Gard 131:86-9 Je '67

PARSONS, Cynthia, and Welch, W. B.
Mississippi's beehive college. Am Ed 4:19-22+ D '67

PARSONS, Donald Holcombe
Parsons group. por Time 90:98+ N 17 '67

PARSONS, James J. and Denevan, W. M.
Pre-Columbian ridged fields; with biographical sketches. Sci Am 217:10, 92-100 Jl '67

PARSONS, R. W.
Op goes the easel. il Pop Phot 60:88-9+ F '67

PARSONS, Susan, and Garrett, W. D.
Second Harrison Gray Otis house, Boston. Antiques 92:536-41 O '67

PARSONS, Willard
They went out men and women; they have come back children. E. F. Hunter. Christian Cent 84:720-2 My 31 '67

PARSONS college, Fairfield, Ia.
Flunking of drop-out U. Time 89:74+ Ap 14 '67
Penalizing Parsons. Newsweek 69:69 Ap 17 '67

PART time employment
Short workweeks and underemployment. C. C. Hodge and J. R. Wetzel. bibliog f il Mo Labor R 90:30-5 S '67
See also
Supplementary employment

PARTHASARATHY, R.
Flux density of cassiopeia-A at 3.0 megacycles per second. bibliog Science 158:1449-50 D 15 '67

PARTHENOGENESIS (plants)
Apomixis: seasonal and population differences in a grass. R. B. Knox. bibliog il Science 157:325-6 Jl 21 '67

PARTICIPATIVE management. See Business management and organization

PARTICLE accelerators. See Accelerators (electrons, etc)

PARTICLES (nuclear physics)
And all from fission-track dating. A. Ewing. il Sci N 91:266-7 Mr 18 '67
Antimatter and cosmology. H. Alfvén. il Sci Am 216:106-12+ Ap '67
Hunting of the quark; search for truly elemental particle. il Time 89:124+ My 19 '67
Neutron capture and stellar synthesis of heavy elements. J. H. Gibbons and R. L. Macklin. bibliog il Science 156:1039-49 My 26 '67
No superweak force; study of CP symmetry. Sci Am 216:50 Mr '67
Nucleon-meson cascade and shielding. R. G. Alsmiller, jr. bibliog il Science 157:1399-405 S 22 '67
Plethora of particles. C. Behrens. il Sci N 92:324-6 S 30 '67
Quark hunt; concerning subatomic particle physics. Sci N 91:115 F 4 '67
Radiative-capture studies of the giant dipole resonance. R. E. Segel. bibliog il Science 158:723-30 N 10 '67
Science fictionally speaking. I. Asimov. Sci Digest 63:85-6 Ja '68
Sodium humate solution studied with small-angle X-ray scattering. R. L. Wershaw and others. bibliog il Science 157:1429-31 S 22 '67
Streamer chamber; particle detector at Stanford linear accelerator. D. Yount. il Sci Am 217:38-46 bibliog(p 156) O '67
Toward nuclear truth. il Sci N 91:287 Mr 25 '67
Two men in search of the quark. L. Edson. il N Y Times Mag p54-6+ O 8 '67
Useful tracks; trailing charged particles through solids. Sci Am 216:51-2 Je '67
What is parity? I. Asimov. Sci Digest 61:83-4 Ap '67
See also
Mesons
Protons
Scattering (physics)
Van Allen radiation belts

Detection
Detecting nuclear particles. A. Ewing. il Sci N 92:333-4 S 30 '67

PARTIES. See Childrens parties; Entertaining

PARTIN, Edward Grady
Fix. S. Smith. il por Life 63:22 S 1 '67

PARTINGTON, Bruce
Opera in trouble. Hi Fi 17:MA23 F '67

PARTITIONS
Make this handsome home-office room divider. il Pop Mech 127:102-5+ Je '67

PARTON, Margaret
If only we had spoken. McCalls 95:66+ O '67

PARTRIDGE shooting
Partridge of the Don Quixote country; reproductions of paintings. F. McMahon. Sports Illus 27:40-5 O 2 '67
Stubble-field bird hunt. N. Riley. il Field & S 72:64-5+ O '67

PARTRIDGES
See also
Cookery—Game

PARTY funds. See Campaign funds

PARTY on Greenwich avenue; drama. See Conover, G.

PARVIN, Stuart A.
Miniaturia. See issues of Hobbies

PAS de deesses; ballet. See Ballets—Criticisms

PASADENA, Calif.

Music
See also
Pasadena opera company

Sanitary affairs
Mammoth trucks and mini scooters. F. Zapf and H. Giles. il Am City 82:77-9 Ja '67

PASADENA opera company
Pasadena. A. Goldberg. Opera N 31:27 Ap 15 '67
Pasadena; performance of Rigoletto. W. Arlen. Opera N 31:32 F 25 '67
Pasadena; production of Madama Butterfly. A. Goldberg. Opera N 31:29 Ap 8 '67

PASARELL, Charles, 1943?-
Bomb at Wimbledon. il por Time 90:65 Jl 7 '67
Mental muscle on court. il por Time 89:69-70 Mr 3 '67

PASATIERI, Thomas
Padrevia. Criticism
Opera N il 32:30 D 23 '67

PASCHAL, Billy J.
Goals for space age education. Sch & Soc 95:390-1 O 28 '67
Pound of cure for educational problems. Sch & Soc 95:53-5 Ja 21 '67

PASCHAL, Justin
Creative writers; poem. Commonweal 86:588 S 22 '67

PASHKA. See Cookery, Russian

PASOLLI, Robert
Off-Broadway. Nation 204:411-13 Mr 27 '67
Theatre (cont) Nation 204:573-4; 205:540-1 My 1, N 20 '67

PASSENGER fares. See Airlines—Fares

PASSENGER service on airlines. See Airlines —Passenger service

PASSENGER traffic (railroads) See Railroads —Passenger traffic

PASSENGER trains. See Railroads—Trains

PASSINO, Jacque
Auto news makers. D. MacDonald. por Motor T 19:62 My '67

PASSION; story. See Jhabvala, R. P.

PASSION music
See also
Phonograph records—Passion music

PASSION of Christ. See Jesus Christ—Passion

PASSION of Jesus Christ in art. See Jesus Christ—Art

PASSIVE resistance to government
Because of Vietnam, in conscience, I must break the law; civil disobedience. R. M. Brown. il Look 31:48+ O 31 '67
Change. Nation 204:645 My 22 '67
Disobedience now! the Stanford statement. J. Neugeboren. Commonweal 86:367-9 Je 16 '67; Discussion. 86:443-5 Jl 14 '67
Escalation of dissent; RESIST organization; statement of the Catholic intellectuals. Commonweal 87:102-3 O 27 '67; Reply. P. Garver. 87:193+ N 17 '67
Goals of dissent; evaluation of the Vietnam protest movement. L. Grauman, jr. Nation 205:617-21 D 11 '67
On civil disobedience, 1967; symposium. N Y Times Mag p27-9+ N 26 '67
Resistance and technology; theory of the new left vs. technological man. D. Callahan. Commonweal 87:377-81 D 22 '67
Spurious sacrifice; campaign for tax refusal. Reporter 37:12-13 O 5 '67
Thomas More: conscientious objector; conscience and the civil law, topic at Ecumenical conference on the role of conscience. J. B. Sheerin. Cath World 205:196-8 Jl '67
See also
Dissenters
Tax evasion

PASSOVER
Only kid; Seder service. C. Roth. Commentary 43:82-5 Ap '67

PASSPORTS
U.S. issuing visitors visas with indefinite validity. Dept State Bul 56:695 My 1 '67
See also
Travel regulations

PAST, John. See Marko, M. jt. auth.

PASTA. See Cookery, Italian; Macaroni

PASTERNAK, Boris Leonidovich
Intimate letters of Pasternak; excerpts from Letters to Georgian friends, tr. by D. Magarshack. Vogue 151:105-7 Ja 1 '68
Pasternak writes on Russia; excerpt from Doctor Zhivago. Sat R 50:87 Mr 11 '67

about

Introduction to the Pasternak letters. D. Magarshack. Vogue 151:104 Ja 1 '68
Pasternak's Russia. M. Kalb. il pors Sat R 50:70+ Mr 11 '67

PASTERNAK, Michael
Le deejay. il por Newsweek 69:52 My 1 '67

PASTEUR, Louis
Letter from Paris. Genêt. New Yorker 43:178 Mr 25 '67

PASTOR, José M. F.
Streets and spaces. Américas 19:5-11 O '67

PASTORAL letters
Plaintive letter; bishops' last letter. Newsweek 71:79 Ja 22 '68
U.S. bishops' pastoral; How will it be received? America 118:23 Ja 13 '68

PASTORE, Arthur R. Jr
Bermuda's off-shore isles. Travel 128:35-6 O '67

PASTORE, John O.
Pastore wants accelerator deferred; statement, June 19, 1967. Science 156:1714 Je 30 '67
Pastore's ABM plea; excerpts from remarks. Aviation W 87:21 S 18 '67

PASTRY
Bride makes cream puffs; with recipe. Mc-Calls 94:68 F '67
Christmas pastries from around the world. *U* Good H 165:196 D '67
How to sweeten up a coffee break. il Bet Hom & Gard 45:98-9 Mr '67
Personalized pastry. S. Sarvis. il Farm J 91: 106-7 F '67
Puff pastry, plain and fancy. Bet Hom & Gard 45:84-5+ F '67
Say good-morning in Danish; with recipes. il McCalls 95:114-15+ O '67
Sweets from the pastry cart. il Am Home 70:96+ S '67
This Turkish food makes splendid picnic eating; boerek; with recipes. il Sunset 138:158+ Ap '67
When Vienna eats, it's cake. M. C. Morton. il Holiday 42:74-6+ S '67
See also
Pie
Shortcake
Tarts

PATAGONIA
Park for Patagonia. E. J. Wilhelm, jr. il Am For 73:32-3+ D '67

PATANE, Franco
Music to my ears. I. Kolodin. Sat R 50:114-15 Mr 11 '67

PATCHEN, Kenneth
Our land & our sea & hallelujah. R. Rosehep. Poetry 111:93-5 D '67

PATCHWORK
Art hidden in a bramble patch; patchwork pictures of E. Allen. il Life 63:76-9 Ag 18 '67
Patchwork prophecies; quilt-pictures of E. Allen. il Time 89:53 Je 2 '67

PATENAUDE, J. Z. Léon
Canadian publishing; summery of address. Pub W 192:28-9 Jl 24 '67

PATENT laws and legislation
Inventor's vindication; lawsuits won by widow of FM discoverer. il Newsweek 70: 70 O 30 '67
Lines are drawn for patent law fight; a presidential Commission's report. il Bsns W p56-8+ Ja 28 '67
Patent reform and international commerce; address, September 8, 1967. A. B. Trowbridge. Dept State Bul 57:504-7 O 16 '67
Patent reform slowed. Sci N 91:495 My 27 '67
Patent revision proposed. Sci N 91:208 Mr 4 '67
Patent system proposals: how practical? Presidential commission urges many changes. G. E. Frost. bibliog f Harvard Bsns R 45: 111-22 S '67
U.S. patent system. J. H. Hollomon. il Sci Am 216:19-27 Je '67
See also
Patents—Licensing

PATENT museums. See Museums

PATENT office (United States) See United States—Patent office

PATENT rights. See Patent laws and legislation; Patents

PATENTS
Autogiro flies once again, in the courts; battling helicopter industry over patent rights. il Bsns W p78-80+ My 27 '67
Computers go to court; legal hassle between Honeywell and Sperry Rand over patent licensing. Bsns W p 150 Je 10 '67
Current patents. See issues of Science news
Enough is enough, Tom Edison. A. Chamberlin. il Sat Eve Post 240:91-2 My 20 '67
Patent problem: who owns the rights? W. W. Eaton. Harvard Bsns R 45:101-10 Jl '67
Revised patent system? Sci Am 216:48 Ap '67
Who will profit from new machining ideas? electrochemical machining patent suit between Anocut engineering co. and Cincinnati milling. il Bsns W p 179-80+ Ap 22 '67
See also
Firearms—Patents
Patent laws and legislation
United States—Patent office

International aspects

International patent planning. J. R. Shipman. il Harvard Bsns R 45:56-72 Mr '67
Overdue reform; plan for worldwide patent clearing houses. il Time 90:92 O 20 '67
Patent reform and international commerce; address, September 8, 1967. A. B. Trowbridge. Dept State Bul 57:504-7 O 16 '67
Patent treaty; proposed treaty by United international bureau for the protection of intellectual property. Sci N 91:567-8 Je 17 '67

PATENTS—*Continued*

Licensing

Poke at the power of patent holders; Justice dept. investigating corporate patent holders. Bsns W p36-7 F 18 '67

PATENTS, Government owned
Patent problem: who owns the rights? W. W. Eaton. Harvard Bsns R 45:101-10 Jl '67

PATERNAL love in music. See Music— Themes, motives, etc.

PATERSON, N.J.

Police

Mobile identifier transmits safety signal without words. il Am City 82:20 N '67

PATHOLOGY
John Hunter, brash genius of pathology; excerpt from The great doctors. R. Silverberg. il Todays Health 45:44-5+ F '67
See also
Inflammation
Paleopathology

PATIENTS, Hospital. See Sick, The

PATIENTS and physicians. See Physicians and patients

PATIOS. See Outdoor rooms

PATLER, John
Deadly friendship. D. Rader. New Repub 157: 13-15 S 23 '67

PATMAN, Wright
Excerpt from debate, October 13, 1966. Cong Digest 46:58+ F '67
Federal reserve; address, October 16, 1967. Vital Speeches 34:138-41 D 15 '67
Tight money crisis; address, January 27, 1967. Vital Speeches 33:295-9 Mr 1 '67

PATON, Alan
Called to reconciliation; excerpt from Instrument of thy peace. Christian Cent 84:1628-9 D 20 '67
Challenge of fear. por Sat R 50:19-21+ S 9 '67
Price of segregation. bibliog por UNESCO Courier 20:14-17 Mr '67

PATRIARCA, Raymond
Fix. S. Smith. il por Life 63:44 S 1 '67

PATRICK, Dave
Faster and better and still only no. 2. T. C. Brody. il Sports Illus 26:64-6 Mr 13 '67
First blood of a classic duel. G. S. Brown. il Sports Illus 26:26-7 Mr 20 '67
One, two. il por Newsweek 69:62 Mr 20 '67

PATRICK, W. H. Jr. See Connell, W. E. jt. auth.

PATRICK, William Penn
It's all in the book. il por Newsweek 70:67 Jl 3 '67

PATRIOTISM
Changing patriotism. L. Wainwright. Life 63:18 Jl 14 '67
Inverted truth, subverted dream; discussion. Christian Cent 84:179-80, 381 F 8, Mr 22 '67
Patriot and protester: can a man be both? History behind the headlines. il Sr Schol 91:8-12+ S 21 '67
Patriotism for all seasons. R. Pearson. il Sat R 50:15-17 Ag 19 '67
Whatever happened to patriotism? Time essay. Time 90:30-1 N 10 '67
See also
Americanism
Citizenship
Loyalty

PATRIOTS (football club) See Football clubs

PATROL boats, Navy. See United States— Navy—Boats

PATROLMEN. See Police

PATT, Stevie
Strange struggle of Sy Patt. B. Remsberg and C. Remsberg. il pors Good H 166:88-9+ Ja '68

about
Letter to a tyrant. S. W. Rousseas and R. Clements. Nation 205:550-1 N 27 '67

PATTERN glass. See Glassware

PATTERN in design. See Design, Decorative

PATTERN recognition computers. See Perceptrons

PATTERNS (dress)
How to alter a dress pattern to fit you. J. LemMon. il Suc Farm 65:58-9 Ag '67
Revolutionary news for home sewers who use patterns; new sizing. il Redbook 130: 66+ Ja '68

PATTERSON, A. E.
Planned pathways bring leisure and safety. Parks & Rec 2:22-3 Je '67

PATTERSON, Bryan
Bones of contention. Newsweek 69:102+ F 13 '67
Older and older? il por Sr Schol 90:17-18 F 10 '67
—and Howells, W. W.
Hominid humeral fragment from early pleistocene of northwestern Kenya. bibliog Science 156:64-6 Ap 7 '67

PATTERSON, Charles
Ice-out bluegills. Outdoor Life 139:52-3+ Mr '67

PATTERSON, Floyd
They're still waiting for Jerry. M. Kram. il por Sports Illus 27:20-3 N 6 '67

PATTERSON, George
Yachting interviews; ed. by H. deFontaine. por Yachting 121:107+ Ja '67

PATTERSON, James M.
Businessman and his government; address. Vital Speeches 33:209-13 Ja 15 '67
New deal and the states. bibliog f Am Hist R 73:70-84 O '67

PATTERSON, Thomas C. See Lanning, E. P. jt. auth.

PATTERSON, William D.
Air race into the future. Sat R 50:15 Jl 8 '67
Bullfight. Sat R 51:105 Ja 13 '68
SR's businessman of the year. Sat R 51:67-8+ Ja 13 '68
SR's fifteenth annual advertising awards. Sat R 50:76-83 Ap 8 '67

PATTISON, Jane
Italian violinist; story. Seventeen 26:142-3 Mr '67

PATTON, Arch
Coming scramble for executive talent. bibliog f Harvard Bsns R 45:155-6+ My '67

PATTON, Grant W. Jr, and others
Malic dehydrogenase isozymes: distribution in developing nucleate and anucleate halves of sea urchin eggs. bibliog Science 156:400-1 Ap 21 '67

PATTON, Stuart, and Kesler, E. M.
Saturation in milk and meat fats. bibliog Science 156:1365-6 Je 9 '67
—and others
Food value of red tide (gonyaulax polyedra) bibliog Science 158:789-90 N 10 '67

PÁTZCUARO, Mexico
Colours of passion in Pátzcuaro. L. Moffat. Vogue 149:49-53 F 15 '67

PAUKER, Guy J.
Toward a new order in Indonesia. For Affairs 45:503-19 Ap '67

PAUL, Saint

Teaching

Paul and his opponents. S. G. F. Brandon. il pors Horizon 10:106-11 Wint '68

PAUL VI, pope
Birth control: the Pope's latest views; excerpts from encyclical. por U S News 62: 12 Ap 10 '67
Christmas message; address, December 22, 1966. Vital Speeches 33:194-6 Ja 15 '67
Conversations with Pope Paul VI; excerpt from Dialogues with Paul VI, ed. by J. Guitton. por McCalls 95:92-3+ O '67
Development, new name for peace; excerpt from On the development of peoples. por UNESCO Courier 20:28-36 Ag '67
Message from Pope Paul VI; text of message, September 22, 1967. UN Mo Chron 4:26 O '67

about
Appeals to reason. New Repub 156:7-8 Ap 8 '67
Are we our brothers' keepers? por Sat Eve Post 240:106 My 6 '67
Disappointing Marian development. S. Benko; reply. L. J. White. Christian Cent 84:280 Mr 1 '67
How to belittle the Pope. America 116:204 F 11 '67
How U.S. Catholics view the Pope. il por Newsweek 69:74 Mr 20 '67
Letter from Vatican City (cont) X. Rynne. New Yorker 43:119-20+ S 9 '67
On church and state. M. Ascoli. Reporter 36: 18 Ap 20 '67
Papal economics. M. Friedman. Newsweek 69: 87 Ap 24 '67
Paul VI's secular ecumenism. R. M. Brown. Commonweal 86:262-4 My 19 '67
Pope addresses mother superiors. America 116:491 Ap 1 '67
Pope and Patriarch. America 117:105-6 Jl 29 '67

PAUL VI, pope—about—*Continued*
Pope and peace. Christian Cent 85:3 Ja 3 '68
Pope Paul's alarm. Christian Cent 84:1307-8 O 18 '67
Pope speaks to Africa. America 117:632-3 N 25 '67
Pope speaks to historians. America 117:235 S 9 '67
Pope's illness. Newsweek 70:116 S 25 '67
Pope's worst enemy. J. O'Gara. Commonweal 86:282 My 26 '67
Populorum progressio. Christian Cent 84:460 Ap 12 '67
Populorum progressio. il por Time 89:70 Ap 7 '67
Rome haul; meeting between the President and the Pope at the Vatican. il por Newsweek 71:40 Ja 8 '68
Soviet president at the Vatican. America 116: 202 F 11 '67
Vietnam as a matter of conscience. America 118:5-6 Ja 6 '68
We must make haste; concerning encyclical. il por Newsweek 69:84 Ap 10 '67

Visit to Fátima, 1967
At Mary's feet. il por Time 89:48 My 19 '67
Fátima and Populorum progressio; ecumenical setback. R. J. Mollar. Christian Cent 84: 1025-6 Ag 9 '67
Fátima: reflections after the fact; 50th anniversary of the famous apparitions. C. Irizarry. Christian Cent 84:1016-19 Ag 9 '67
Pilgrimage of Pope Paul; pilgrimage to Fatima, Portugal. America 116:769 My 27 '67
Pope's pilgrimage. il por Newsweek 69:66-7 My 22 '67
Vigil at Fatima on the eve of Pope Paul's visit. il pors Life 62:32-5 My 26 '67

Visit to Turkey, 1967
Historic embrace. il por Newsweek 70:82 Ag 7 '67
Patriarch and Pope meet on the Bosporus. il por Life 63:66-7 Ag 4 '67
Symbolic voyage. il por Time 90:54 Ag 4 '67
Why the Pope visited Turkey. il por U S News 63:14 Ag 7 '67

PAUL, Annette av
Brief biography. S. Goodman. pors Dance Mag 42:62-3 Ja '68

PAUL, Jeremiah
Paul's Washington family in oil on canvas. G. D. Guadagni. il Antiques 91:519+ Ap '67

PAUL, Ken
Electronic culture and the future church; reprint. Cath World 205:157-9 Je '67

PAUL, Peter, Incorporated
Mounds of joy. il Time 90:76+ Ag 18 '67

PAUL, Sherman
Interior order. Nation 204:121-2 Ja 23 '67
Politics of art. Nation 204:792-3 Je 19 '67

PAUL Taylor dance company
Out of the rain; intersection between modern dance and ballet il Time 91:55 Ja 5 '68
Paul Taylor sends Decatur; Harper theatre dance festival, Illinois. A. Barzel. il Dance Mag 42:42-3 Ja '68
So that's what the planets do! Paul Taylor's newest work, Orbs. il Dance Mag 41:32-3 F '67

PAULING, Linus Carl
Peace on earth; the position of the scientists; statement, May 1967. Bul Atomic Sci 23: 46-8 O '67
about
Double helix; the discovery of the structure of DNA; excerpts, with editorial comment. J. D. Watson. il Atlan 221:76-94+ Ja '68 (to be cont)

PAULIST fathers
Paulists and the Dallas affair. J. B. Sheerin. Cath World 205:319-20 Ag '67
Paulists depart, but tensions linger in Dallas. A. V. Krebs, jr. Commonweal 87:68-9 O 20 '67

PAULO, Amilcar. See Novinsky, A. jt. auth.

PAULSEN, Monrad G.
Role of juvenile courts. bibliog f Cur Hist 53:70-5 Ag '67

PAULSEN, Pat
Fantastic face. il por Newsweek 69:84 Je 12 '67

PAULSON, F. M.
(ed) Boating. See issues of Field & stream
Cruising Lake Nipissing. Field & S 71:34-5+ Ap '67
Gold Coast to Gulf coast by boat. Field & S 72:34-7 Ja '68
Outboard the Bahamas. Field & S 72:68-71 My '67

Trailer boating the Bruce Peninsula. Field & S 72:36-9 Jl '67
You can be a boatman for less than you think. Field & S 72:38-9+ Ja '68

PAULSON, Joan
T is for tomatoes. Ladies Home J 84:98 Je '67
Why roommates make the best wives. Ladies Home J 84:171-3 Mr '67; Same abr. Read Digest 91:203-4 O '67

PAVEMENTS
Let's pave more streets. M. D. Calkins. il Am City 82:88-9 Ag '67
More paving, less costs, fewer complaints; deep-lift method of paving; interview. C. Beagle. il Am City 82:124-6 S '67
See also
Sidewalks

Maintenance and repair
City officials favor sawing pavements. il Am City 82:89-90 N '67
See also
Streets—Maintenance and repair

Surface treatment
Asbestos fibers toughen thin overlays; Bayonne. N.J. il Am City 82:66 Je '67
Hot precoated aggregate eliminates sealcoat dust; Phoenix, Ariz. C. McDonald. il Am City 82:110-12 F '67
How to sealcoat a blacktop driveway. il Pop Gard 18:86-8 My '67
New paving materials benefit St Louis parks. A. M. Johnson. il Parks & Rec 2:32-3 D '67
New slurry-seal specs. Am City 82:55 O '67
Patch it right the first time; Huntington, N.Y. J. J. Walsh. il Am City 82:118-19 Mr '67
Quick-set slurry replaces sand seal; Toronto. A. W. Pellegrino. il Am City 82:109-12 Ap '67
Save street surfaces the easy way; use of slurry seal in Newburgh, N.Y. W. G. McEvilly. il Am City 82:106-7 Je '67
Which trees and what street surfacing; regional APWA meeting. E. F. Spitzer. il Am City 82:97+ Jl '67

PAVEMENTS, Brick
Bricks underfoot. il Sunset 138:98-105 Ap '67
New modern base restores the oldest street in America; St Augustine, Fla. S. G. Stepp. il Am City 82:93-4 D '67

PAVEMENTS, Wood
Building a wood-disk patio? treat it right! P. J. Bois. il Am For 73:32-3+ Ap '67

PAVILION, Cleveland. See Concert halls

PAVILION houses. See Architecture, Domestic

PAVILIONS
Centre Le Corbusier; Zurich. U. Roth. il Arch Forum 127:82-7 S '67

PAVING. See Pavements

PAVLOK, Antonin
Development of mouse ova in explanted oviducts: fertilization, cultivation, and transplantation. bibliog Science 157:1457-8 S 22 '67

PAVLOV, Ivan Petrovich
Building on Pavlov. P. McBroom. il Sci N 91:498-9 My 27 '67

PAX Christi movement
Pax Christi council. America 117:729 D 16 '67

PAY-as-you-see television. See Television broadcasting—Subscription programs

PAY differentials. See Wage differentials

PAYMENTS, Balance of. See Balance of payments

PAYNE, B. R. See Halevy, E. jt. auth.

PAYNE, Jack
How to make the cabbage-shredder table. Pop Sci 191:120-1 Jl '67
—See McGuckin, F. jt. auth.

PAYNE, Lee
Beer can regatta. il Yachting 121:76-7 Mr '67

PAYNE, Martin W.
On policing a lakeshore. Nat Parks Mag 41:19 Je '67

PAYNE, W. H.
Visual reaction times on a circle about the fovea. Science 155:481-2 Ja 27 '67

PEABODY, Endicott
Dinner dunner. il por Newsweek 69:38 Je 26 '67

PEABODY, Larry D.
How to fight page fright. Writer 80:25-6 F '67

PEABODY, Sabra
First love. L. Thompson. il Read Digest 91:55-8 Ag '67

PEABODY conservatory of music. See Peabody institute, Baltimore

PEABODY Institute, Baltimore
Baltimore; American premiere of La guerra. A. M. Lingg. Opera N 31:21 Je 10 '67

PEACE
Building a durable peace; address, January 26, 1967. D. Rusk. Dept State Bul 56:269-73 F 20 '67
Christmas message; address, December 22, 1966. Paul VI. Vital Speeches 33:194-6 Ja 15 '67
Do we need peace candidates? T. C. Sorensen; A. I. Waskow. Sat R 50:32-3 F 4 '67
Does man really want peace? N. F. S. Ferre. Sat R 50:10-12 Jl 1 '67
Education of peacemakers; proposals for a peacekeepers academy. A. I. Waskow. Sat R 50:12-15+ Ag 12 '67
Giving peace the bird. il Sr Schol 91:26 S 28 '67
Peace and war, by R. Aron. Review
    New Repub 156:26-8+ Mr 4 '67. S. Hoffmann
Peace is possible, ed. by E. J. Hollins. Review
    Sat R 50:34 Je 24 '67. G. N. Shuster
Peace on earth; the position of the scientists; statement, May 1967. L. Pauling. Bul Atomic Sci 23:46-8 O '67
Pope and peace; appeal against pacifism. Christian Cent 85:3 Ja 3 '68
Prayer for peace, Memorial day, 1967; proclamation. L. B. Johnson. Dept State Bul 56:873 Je 12 '67
Road to a lasting peace; address, July 6, 1967. D. Rusk. Dept State Bul 57:87-91 Jl 24 '67
Spirit of Hollybush; excerpt from remarks, June 23, 1967. L. B. Johnson. Dept State Bul 57:38-40 Jl 10 '67
Unesco in the service of peace. V. De Lipski. il UNESCO Courier 20:28-30 F '67
United States urges agreement on peacekeeping question; statement, May 22, 1967. A. J. Goldberg. Dept State Bul 56:894-7 Je 12 '67
United States urges renewed dedication to U.N. peace and security activities; statement, November 28, 1967. L. H. Fountain. Dept State Bul 58:20-5 Ja 1 '68
War or peace? symposium. bibliog il UNESCO Courier 20:4-66 Ag '67
    See also
Aggression (international law)
Arbitration, International
International relations
International security
Pacifism
Treaties

Anecdotes, facetiae, satire, etc.
Digging at Iron Mountain. Sci N 92:557-8 D 9 '67
Hoax or horror? a book that shook White House; concerning Report from Iron Mountain on the possibility and desirability of peace. il U S News 63:48 N 20 '67
Iron Mountain lies beyond credibility gap. I. Kristol. Fortune 77:185-6 Ja '68
On the possibility and desirability of peace; excerpts from Report from Iron Mountain bibliog f Esquire 68:129-37+ D '67
Peace games; concerning Report from Iron Mountain. Time 90:44 N 17 '67
Peace games, war games; Report from Iron Mountain. Christian Cent 84:1588 D 13 '67
Report from Iron Mountain on the possibility and desirability of peace, with introd. by L. C. Lewin. Review
    Nation 205:633-4 D 11 '67. D. Cort
    Newsweek il 70:103-103B D 4 '67. H. Junker

PEACE (theology)
O little town of Phuvinh; joy and evil at Christmas. J. R. Nelson. Christian Cent 84:1619 D 20 '67

PEACE candidates. See Candidates, Political

PEACE conferences
Address of Secretary-General to convocation of Pacem in terris II; text of address. Thant. UN Mo Chron 4:83-6 Je '67
Ill-starred peace meeting; Pacem in terris convocation in Geneva sponsored by the Center for the study of democratic institutions. M. McGrory. America 116:829 Je 10 '67
Labor and peace; SANE calls an Assembly for peace. Nation 205:325 O 9 '67
Labor meets for peace. B. J. Widick. Nation 205:561-3 N 27 '67
Ladies and gentlemen, do not despair; Pacem in terris conference, Geneva. New Repub 156:19 Je 17 '67

No peace for the righteous; Pacem in terris convocation, in Geneva. Newsweek 69:47 Je 12 '67
Not all of labor agrees with Meany; Labor leadership assembly for peace, Chicago. W. L. Abbott. New Repub 157:15-16 N 25 '67
Of many things; convocation in Geneva sponsored by Center for the study of democratic institutions. H. J. Sievers. America 116:inside cover Je 3 '67
Pacem in terris II. E. M. Bogese. Nation 205:74-9 Jl 31 '67
Peace on earth at Geneva. America 116:845 Je 17 '67
Stockholm conference reveals hard truths; World conference on Vietnam. H. A. Jack. Christian Cent 84:1168+ S 13 '67

PEACE corps. See United States—Peace corps

PEACE corps, Russian. See Volunteer service, International

PEACE movement. See Pacifism

PEACE RIVER
Exploring the Peace River; British Columbia River that cuts through the Rocky Mountains. J. Clark. il Field & S 72:40-1+ Ja '68

PEACE societies
    See also
Catholic association for international peace

PEACE treaties. See Treaties

PEACEFUL coexistence. See World politics, 1945-

PEACEFUL uses of atomic power. See Atomic power—Economic aspects

PEACH aphids. See Plant lice

PEACHES
    See also
Cookery—Fruit

PEACHEY, Lee D.
Cellular dynamics; hormones. Science 155:226+ Ja 13 '67

PEACOCK, Andrew C. and others
Haptoglobin levels in serum of various strains of mice. bibliog Science 158:1703-4 D 29 '67

PEACOCK, F. Edward
F. E. Peacock; new college text publisher. Pub W 191:80 F 27 '67

PEALE, Charles Willson
First family. il por Time 89:68-71 F 24 '67

PEALE, Norman Vincent
Gift from the heart. Read Digest 92:95-8 Ja '68

PEALE family
First family. il pors Time 89:68-71 F 24 '67

PEARCE, Donald
(comp) Out of the mouths of freshmen; excerpts from the writings of freshmen at the University of California, Santa Barbara. Good H 165:102-3 O '67

PEARCE, Jack B.
Thermal addition to the marine environment. Science 157:1080 S 1 '67

PEARCE, Philippa
Writing a book; excerpt from address. Horn Bk 43:317-22 Je '67

PEARL, Milton A.
New look at the public lands. Nat Parks Mag 41:8-12 F '67

PEARL industry and trade
Shell sales drop as hems go up; cultured pearl industry. il Bsns W p 139-40+ N 25 '67

PEARLS
Pearls of Margarita; reprint. C. P. Idyll. il Américas 19:8-14 Ag '67; Correction. 19:48 S '67

PEARLSTEIN, Philip
Philip Pearlstein; the naked truth. W. F. Midgette. il Art N 66:54-5+ O '67
Return to the challenge. il por Time 91:30-1 Ja 12 '68

PEARS, Peter
Disappearing art. R. Gelatt. Reporter 36:38-9 My 4 '67
Music to my ears; performance of Schubert's Die winterreise in the Hunter college playhouse. I. Kolodin. Sat R 50:107 O 14 '67

PEARS
Bradford ornamental pear. W. Ackerman. Horticulture 45:32 N '67

PEARSE, Benjamin H.
Postman is the proctor. Am Ed 3:10-12 F '67

PEARSON, David
My kind of racing, stock cars. por Pop Sci 190:72 Mr '67
    about
David. E. Dahlquist. il por Hot Rod 20:72-4 Je '67

PEARSON, Sir Denning
$15-billion aviation market seen. Aviation W 87:63 O 2 '67

PEARSON, Drew
Pearson the conqueror. Nat R 19:507 My 16 '67
Pearson vs. Reagan. Newsweek 70:88 N 27 '67

PEARSON, Ethelyn M.
We switched from cows to roller skates. Farm J 91:60D Mr '67

PEARSON, Henry
Mima mounds. il Nat Parks Mag 41:13 F '67

PEARSON, John F.
Aboard the navy's newest seagoing laboratory. Pop Mech 127:124-7+ Ap '67
Who said you can't teach inventing? Pop Mech 127:140-3+ Mr '67

PEARSON, Kenneth, and Connor, Patricia
Strange case of James Mellaart. Horizon 9: 4-15 Sum '67

PEARSON, Lester Bowles
President Johnson confers with Canadian Prime Minister; remarks, May 25, 1967. Dept State Bul 56:909 Je 19 '67

about
Bowing out. por Newsweek 70:36 D 25 '67
Pearson's retreat. Time 90:34 D 22 '67

PEARSON, Ralph M.
What is design? Design 68:23-4 Mr '67

PEARSON, Roy
Patriotism for all seasons. Sat R 50:15-17 Ag 19 '67

PEARY, Robert Edwin
Ends of the earth. R. L. Tobin. il Sat R 50:25-6 Jl 1 '67

PEAS
Anecdotes, facetiae, satire, etc.
Pound of peas. R. Hochstein. il Good H 164: 64+ Je '67

PEAS, Frozen. See Vegetables, Frozen

PEASANT art. See Folk art

PEASANTRY

Brazil
Brazil's miserable northeast. H. W. Flannery. Cath World 205:276-81 Ag '67
Report; Northeast Brazil. J. A. Page. Atlan 221:20-3 Ja '68

China
Fanshen, by W. Hinton. Review
Nation 205:184-5 S 4 '67. C. P. Fitz-Gerald

Vietnam (Republic)
Hanoi and the front. J. Mirsky. Nation 205: 88-9 Jl 31 '67
Voice for the voiceless; Buddhist poet-monk Thich Nhat Hanh. Christian Cent 85:4 Ja 3 '68

PEAT bogs
Freshwater peat on the continental shelf. K. O. Emery and others. bibliog il Science 158: 1301-7 D 8 '67

PEAVY, Katherine B.
Traveler's choice. Travel 128:11 S '67

PECHMAN, Joseph A.
Money for the states. New Repub 156:15-17 Ap 8 '67
Soul-searching on taxes. New Repub 157:11-12 S 23 '67

PECK, Franklin B.
Skyway robbery! photographs. Audubon 69: 58-60 My '67

PECK, Paula
Paula Peck's art of good cooking; excerpts. Ladies Home J 84:118-19+ My '67
Risottos and pilafs. House & Gard 133:127-9+ Ja '68

PECK, Robert M.
Needed: more statistical information; summary of address. por Pub W 192:27 N 20 '67

PECKHAM, Howard H.
Your excellencys most obedient. . .servant. por Wilson Lib Bul 41:586-9 F '67

PEDANTRY

Anecdotes, facetiae, satire, etc.
Investigation into the causes of hyperpedantism. C. P. Ridley. Atlan 221:101-2 Ja '68

PEDEN, Katherine Graham
How Katie makes Kentucky grow. il pors Bsns W p 184-6+ S 9 '67

PEDERSEN, Richard F.
U.N. peace force in Cyprus again extended for six months; statement, June 19, 1967. Dept State Bul 57:52-3 Jl 10 '67

PEDESTRIAN accidents. See Traffic accidents

PEDIATRIC research. See Medical research

PEDIATRICIANS
Pediatrics by phone. il Newsweek 71:43-4 Ja 8 '68

PEEBLES, P. J. E. and Wilkinson, D. T.
Primeval fireball; with biographical sketches. Sci Am 216:14, 28-37 bibliog (p 155) Je '67

PEELE, David
Community college libraries: problems and prospects. por Library J 92:2898-901 S 1 '67

PEEPLES, William
Open housing. New Repub 158:9-10 Ja 13 '68

PEERAGE
See also
Great Britain—Peerage

PEERMAN, Dean
Religious liberty: down the drain in Spain. Christian Cent 84:742-4 Je 7 '67

PEET, Creighton
Man from Moran. Pop Mech 128:136-9+ N '67

PEETS, Carl O. and Schwartz, L. J.
Counseling the average child. NEA J 57:14-16 Ja '68

PEGASUS (submarine vehicle) See Submarine vehicles

PEI, Mario
Big mystery in small words. Sat R 50:98-9+ Je 10 '67
Hebrew language. Holiday 42:74-5+ D '67
How did language begin? Sat R 50:54-5 S 9 '67

PEIRCE, Neal R.
Case against the electoral college. New Repub 156:12-13 F 11 '67

PEKING man. See Man, Prehistoric

PELARGONIUMS. See Geraniums

PELIKAN, Jaroslav
He inspired the death of God. Sat R 50:30+ Mr 18 '67
Pantheist or God-intoxicated? Sat R 50:66-7 Ap 8 '67

PELIOSIS hepatis. See Liver—Diseases

PELL, Claiborne
Eastern Europe; address, March 15, 1967. Vital Speeches 33:394-400 Ap 15 '67

PELLEGRENO, Ann Holtgren
I completed Amelia Earhart's flight. por McCalls 95:48+ N '67

PELLEGRINO, A. W.
Quick-set slurry replaces sand seal. Am City 82:109-12 Ap '67

PELLETIER, Gaston
Cricket in academe; address, June 11, 1967. Vital Speeches 34:24-6 O 15 '67

PELLETIER, Wilfrid
Pelly; interview, ed. by J. W. Freeman. por Opera N 31:26-7 My 13 '67

PELLETIERE, Steve
Idle millions. Nation 205:401-3 O 23 '67

PELLÓN, Nivio López. See López Pellón, N.

PELLOWSKI, Anne
Beyond the colonial bias. Library J 92:4228-31+ N 15 '67
Center on children's cultures. bibliog Wilson Lib Bul 42:209-13 O '67

PELLY, Thomas M.
Excerpt from address, April 27, 1967. Cong Digest 46:239+ O '67

PELOMYXA carolinensis. See Ameba

PELZ, Donald C.
Creative tensions in the research and development climate. bibliog Science 157:160-5 Jl 14 '67

PEMBERTON, Prentiss, and Page, Homer
Translating antiwar protest into political power. Christian Cent 85:11-14 Ja 3 '68

PEMOLINE. See Magnesium pemoline

PEN club. See PEN club

PEN drawing
Drawing with ink. il Design 68:30-5 Sum '67

PEN names. See Pseudonyms

PENAL colonies
Island, by A. Chekhov. Review
New Repub 157:26-8+ O 21 '67. C. Brown
Sat R 50:35-6 O 7 '67. M. Friedberg

PENANCE, Sacrament of. See Confession

PENBERTHY, William R.
Computerized voter registration. Am City 82:78-9 N '67

PENCIL drawing. See Drawing

PENDERECKI, Krzysztof
And we quote; interview, ed. by B. Jacobson. por Hi Fi 18:MA20 Ja '68

about
Penderecki, a mighty voice from Poland. B. Jacobson. por Hi Fi 17:74-5 Ap '67

PENDERECKI, Krzysztof—about—*Continued*
Polish musician for our time. R. Gelatt. Reporter 37:53-4 N 2 '67
Polish passion; new recording Passion according to Saint Luke. Discus. Harper 236:84 Ja '68

PENDLETON, Jerry
Jerry Pendleton on the commissary. Yachting 121:125-7 Je '67

PENDLETON, Robert Cecil
Underground A-tests may be making us radioactive. N. Wadsworth. il por Sci Digest 62:13-17 S '67

PENDULUM
Amateur scientist; little pendulums that oscillate like big ones. N. E. Lindenblad. il Sci Am 216:124-8 Ap '67

PENE DU BOIS, Raoul
Interview; ed. by A. Fatt. por Dance Mag 41:56 Ap '67

PENICILLIN
Mechanisms of enzymatic bacteriolysis. J. L. Strominger and J. M. Ghuysen. bibliog il Science 156:213-21 Ap 14 '67
Toward a safer penicillin. Time 89:62 Je 16 '67

PENKOVSKII, Oleg Vladimirovich
Contact on Gorki street; condensation. G. Wynne. il Read Digest 91:185-90+ Ag '67

PENMANSHIP
Improving handwriting skills. E. A. Enstrom and D. C. Enstrom. il Sr Schol 91:sup 10-11 O 12 '67
Is penmanship dead? A. P. Eliasberg. il N Y Times Mag p 109+ D 10 '67
See also
Graphology

PENN, Irving
Gypsies; photographs. Look 31:58-63 Ag 8 '67
Incredibles; photographs. Look 32:51-8 Ja 9 '68

PENN, William
Ancestry of William Penn. H. K. Eilers. il Hobbies 72:118-19+ Jl '67
William Penn, by M. M. Dunn. Review
Sat R 50:48 Je 10 '67. M. Kraus

PENN relays. See Running

PENNANTS. See Flags

PENNEY, J. C. company
How they minted the new Penney. J. McDonald. il Fortune 76:110-13+ Jl '67

PENNEY, Richard
Behavioral research, New York zoological park. Science 158:144-5 O 6 '67

PENNSYLVANIA
See also
Booksellers and bookselling—Pennsylvania
Fishing—Pennsylvania
Gardens—Pennsylvania
Hunting—Pennsylvania
Police—Pennsylvania
Reclamation of land—Pennsylvania

Historic houses, etc.
Living with antiques: Pennsylvania home of Mr and Mrs Charles J. Fox. 2d. E. Stillinger. il Antiques 92:214-17 Ag '67
Living with antiques; Ross house in York County, Pa. W. D. Garrett. il Antiques 92:203-7 Ag '67
To see America: houseful of our history; White Chimneys, near Lancaster; with report by D. J. Hamblin. il Life 63:44-56 Ag 25 '67

Parks and reserves
High-density use, low-maintenance operation; new regional parks in Allegheny County, Pa. G. E. Kelly. il Am City 82:102-4 O '67

Politics and government
Debut of a wallflower. il Time 89:21 My 26 '67

PENNSYLVANIA ballet company
Pennsylvania ballet company, Brooklyn academy of music. D. Hering. il Dance Mag 41:33-4 Mr '67
These dancers have character. E. Palatsky. il Dance Mag 41:42-6 N '67

PENNSYLVANIA Dutch cookery. See Cookery, American

PENNSYLVANIA railroad-New York central merger. See Railroads—Consolidations and mergers

PENNSYLVANIA state library, Harrisburg
Book week on a budget. R. Fink. il Library J 92:3124-5 S 15 '67

PENNSYLVANIA state university
New study-discussion program on human values. Sch & Soc 94:478-9 D 24 '66

PENNSYLVANIA. University, Philadelphia
Universities and the Pentagon. G. Kolko. Nation 205:329-32 O 9 '67

School of dental medicine
New dental course of study. Sch & Soc 95:518-19 D 23 '67

Wharton school of finance and commerce
Cooling off without a chill; Wharton's computer prediction; with editorial comment. il Bsns W p29-30, 190 Mr 4 '67
It's a go-go economy; Wharton school prediction. il Bsns W p21-3 Ag 26 '67

PENNY for a song; opera. See Bennett. R. R.

PENOLOGY. See Punishment

PENROSE, Sir Roland
Picasso as sculptor; excerpt from introduction to The sculpture of Picasso. Atlan 220:69-76 O '67

PENROSE annual
Penrose annual, 1967; ed. by H. Spencer. Review
Pub W il 192:73-4 Ag 7 '67. C. B. Grannis

PENSINGER, Glen
Video tape: mass medium for individualized instruction. Sr Schol 91:sup22-3 O 26 '67

PENSION funds. See Pensions—Finance

PENSIONS
Pensions: unsafe at any age? M. C. Bernstein. il Duns R 89:32-3+ Ja '67
See also
Carnegie foundation for the advancement of teaching
Old age pensions

Finance
Administration of large pension plans. E. K. Goodman. bibliog f il Mo Labor R 90:48-50 O '67
Big buyers of stock: institutions; including mutual funds, pension funds. U S News 62:87 F 13 '67
Coming in 1968: biggest pension boost ever? il U S News 63:113-14+ N 20 '67
Now private pensions are in the line of fire. il U S News 62:67-8 Mr 6 '67
Outlook for a boost in pensions, and in taxes to pay them. U S News 63:111 N 13 '67
Pension advisers play it cool; buying stocks. il Bsns W p 115-16 Ap 1 '67
Pensions may get a watchdog; law for regulating private pension funds. il Bsns W p41 Mr 11 '67
Union investors stick to blue chips. Bsns W p 104+ Ja 13 '68
Will Washington ruin your pension plan? il Nations Bsns 55:40-1+ Ap '67

Laws and regulations
New rules for pensions. Bsns W p41 My 20 '67
Pensions may get a watchdog; law for regulating private pension funds. il Bsns W p41 Mr 11 '67

PENSIONS, Industrial
Administration of large pension plans. E. K. Goodman. bibliog f il Mo Labor R 90:48-50 O '67
Pension plans; suggestion of IRS to put more tax-exempt money into pensions for the lower-paid employees than for higher salaried. New Repub 156:4-5 My 20 '67
Private pension plan coverage of older workers. D. M. Landay. il Mo Labor R 90:47-51 Ag '67
Terminations of pension plans: eleven years' experience. E. H. Beier. il Mo Labor R 90:26-30 Je '67
Union investors stick to blue chips. Bsns W p 104+ Ja 13 '68
See also
Old age pensions
United mine workers welfare and retirement fund

PENTAGON building, Arlington, Va.
Silver for the brass. Newsweek 71:23 Ja 22 '68

PENTAGON press corps. See Reporters and reporting

PENTATHLON
Trials of a busy pentathlete; J. du Pont host to National modern pentathlon championships. A. Higgins. il Sports Illus 27:58 Ag 28 '67

PENTAZOCINE. See Analgesics

PENTECOST
Holy Spirit works today; message from the presidents of the World council of churches. Christian Cent 84:611 My 10 '67
Pentecost and peace. V. P. McCorry. America 116:738-9 My 13 '67

PERELMAN, Sidney Joseph—*Continued*
Paint me a pinion immortal, limner dear.
New Yorker 43:41-3 My 6 '67
10:30, and all quiet on West Forty-fifth
street. New Yorker 43:24-6 D 23 '67

PERENNIALS
Beauty that grows from year to year. H.
Mason and others. il Bet Hom & Gard 45:
70-3 Ap '67
Late-blooming perennials. E. S. Henderson. il
Horticulture 45:12-15+ S '67
Late summer go-togethers. il Home Gard 54:
50-1 F '67
Perennials for every garden. il Home Gard
54:44-9 Mr '67
See also
Peonies
Shasta daisies
Yarrows

PERENTESIS, Mary
Dolls! dolls! dolls! Sch Arts 67:14-15 D '67

PERERA, George Alfred
Admission to medical school. por Sch & Soc
95:25-6 Ja 7 '67

PERETZ, Don
Israel's administration and Arab refugees.
For Affairs 46:336-46 Ja '68

PERETZ, Martin
American Left and Israel. bibliog f Com-
mentary 44:27-34 N '67
Ramparts dropout. por Time 90:38 D 1 '67

PEREY, Daniel Y. E. and others
Polycystic renal disease: a new experimental
model. bibliog Science 158:494-6 O 27 '67

PEREY, Marguerite
Women we called *la patronne*. UNESCO Courier 20:22-4 O '67

PEREZ, Rudy
Elizabeth Keen & Rudy Perez; Judson
memorial church. J. Anderson. Dance Mag
41:76-7 Ap '67

PERFECT punishment; story. See Ferard. N.

PERFORMERS. See Actors and actresses

PERFORMING animals. See Animals—Training

PERFORMING artists, Legal rights of. See
Copyright—Artistic performance

PERFORMING arts
Sound and fury in the arts; symposium; ed.
by A. Hurlburt and P. Coffin. il Look 32:13-
30+ Ja 9 '68
Troubled arts; situation in Chicago. W.
Murray. il Holiday 41:62-5+ Mr '67

Study and teaching
It's fun to yell bravo; Lincoln Center's
student program. L. Rich. il Am Ed 3:
15-20+ Je '67
See also
Interlochen arts academy, Mich.

PERFORMING arts, School of. See New York
(city)—Education

PERFORMING bears. See Bears—Training

PERFORMING dogs. See Dogs—Training

PERFUMERY
For the best brother in the world (yours or
somebody else's) with love at Christmas. il
Seventeen 26:116-17 D '67
Fragrance gifts that give more. il Good H 165:
112-13 D '67
How to choose a perfume. V. S. Stitt. il Par-
ents Mag 42:18 D '67
Patchouli. L. Blanch. il Vogue 150:184-5+
O 1 '67
Whiff of Christmas. il Seventeen 26:158-9 N
'67
See also
Bergamot oil

PERFUMERY for men
Beauty life: hitting the bottle. il Mlle 65:
130-2 Je '67
Fragrance for father. il Seventeen 26:146+
Je '67

PERFUSION pumps (heart) See Hearts, Artificial

PERGAMON press
Chambers's fourth edition promoted in U.S.
market. Pub W 191:38+ Mr 13 '67

PERGOLESI, Giovanni Battista
Records:
La serva padrona. Opera N 31:34 Ja 28
'67

PERHYDRO carotene. See Terpenes

La PÉRI (ballet) See Ballets

PERIOD furniture. See Furniture

PERIODICAL advertising. See Advertising
mediums—Periodicals

PERIODICAL literature
Building a framework for an article. M.
Gunther. Writer 80:14-16+ Ag '67

Changing needs of magazines. R. Stein. Writ-
er 81:14-15 Ja '68
Creative article. M. Holmes. Writer 80:16-19
D '67
How to find article ideas. M. Gunther.
Writer 80:24-7 Ap '67
How to sell to the top religious magazines.
E. H. Pitts. Writer 80:31-3 Je '67
Random notes on article writing; excerpts
from How to write and sell magazine
articles. R. Gehman. Writer 80:25-30 Je '67
Viewing with alarm. T. Curry. Writer 80:29-
30 Jl '67
What are we looking for? Saturday evening
post. D. McKinney. Writer 80:14-16+ N '67
Writing non-fiction. C. M. Curtis. Writer 80:
22-9 Ja '67
See also
Fiction in periodicals and newspapers

PERIODICAL postage rate. See Postal rates—
United States

PERIODICALS
How you can be as well-informed as we are.
Esquire 68:136-7 N '67
Report on the quarterlies. P. P. Witonski.
Nat R 19:431-4 Ap 18 '67
Teen-age and young adult market: editorial
needs and requirements; symposium.
Writer 80:43-5 Ap '67
Youth, it's beautiful; new magazines for
youth market. Newsweek 70:60 S 11 '67
See also
Blind, Periodicals for the
House organs
Journalism
Photography, Journalistic

Bibliography
Magazines; ed. by B. Katz. See issues of
Library journal

Facsimile transmission
See Facsimile transmission

Indexes
See also
Readers' guide to periodical literature

Letters to the editor
How not to write the editor. C. P. Streeter.
Farm J 91:12 F '67

Anecdotes, facetiae, satire, etc.
In place of soft answers. L. Rosten. il Look
32:14 Ja 23 '68

Prices
Price indexes for 1967; U.S. periodicals. H.
M. Welch. il Library J 92:2526-7 Jl '67

Sections, columns, etc.
Responsibility of the mass media; summary
of panel sponsored by National book committee. il Pub W 191:36-7 Mr 20 '67

France
At Paris match all the world's a football
game; France's leading picture weekly. il
Bsns W p74-5+ Mr 25 '67

Germany (Federal Republic)
Death of a famous name; Simplicissimus
ceases publication. il Time 89:36 Je 2 '67
Mirror of Germany; Der Spiegel. il Newsweek 70:99-99A+ O 23 '67

Great Britain
Bowl us no googlies; criticism of Cardinal
Spellman's and Billy Graham's Vietnam
speeches. Christian Cent 84:163-4 F 8 '67
See also
Economist (London)
Encounter (periodical)

Israel
Exposing international secrets; Bul editors
jailed. Time 89:48 Mr 10 '67

Italy
European literary scene; Quindic. R. J.
Clements. il Sat R 50:32 O 7 '67

Russia
In Russia, too, business is news; voice of
Moscow's economic policy Economit-
cheskaya gazetta. il Bsns W p 114-16+
My 27 '67
Launching Sputnik at U.S. readers; Soviet
life as reflected in new Russian maga-
zine. il Bsns W p38-9 F 25 '67

United States
Aiming at the hip; teen publishers. il Time
89:33+ Je 2 '67

PERIODICALS—United States—*Continued*
City magazines are the talk of the town.
il Bsns W p 184+ F 18 '67
Glory of guns; gun magazines campaign
against legal control of gun sales. il Time
90:62-3 Ag 25 '67
How you can be as well-informed as Dwight
Macdonald. D. Macdonald. Esquire 68:137-
8+ N '67
Where to sell manuscripts. See issues of
Writer
Why editors use form rejection slips; dis-
cussion. Writer 80:1 Ja '67
See also
Catholic press
Periodicals for women
also names of periodicals, e.g. Daedalus
(periodical)
PERIODICALS, Comic. See Comics (books,
strips, etc)
PERIODICALS, Immoral. See Immoral litera-
ture and pictures
PERIODICALS, Publishing of
At our corner; Scholastic magazines: from
press, to post office, to you. Sr Schol 90:
sup22 Mr 17 '67
Tax threat to nonprofits; Internal revenue
proposes to tax publications of nonprofit
organizations. Bsns W p 131 My 6 '67
PERIODICALS, Trade. See Trade journals
PERIODICALS for women
Battle of the Amazons. il Newsweek 70:52
Ag 28 '67
Fashion periodicals. J. Mebane. il Bet Hom
& Gard 45:12+ Mr '67
See also
Ladies' home journal
PERIODICITY
Ambiguities in the use of the term circadian.
R. J. Wurtman. bibliog Science 156:104 Ap
7 '67
Body clock's effect on drugs. Sci Digest 61:
58-9 Ap '67
Circadian clock in photoperiodic time meas-
urement: a test of the Bünning hypothesis.
M. Menaker and A. Eskin. bibliog il Sci-
ence 157:1182-5 S 8 '67
Circadian pattern of plasma 17-hydroxy-
corticosteroid: alteration by anticholinergic
agents. D. T. Krieger and H. P. Krieger.
bibliog il Science 155:1421-2 Mr 17 '67
Circadian periodicity in susceptibility to
lidocaine hydrochloride. E. F. Lutsch and
R. W. Morris. bibliog il Science 156:100-2
Ap 7 '67
Circadian rhythms of liver enzymes and their
relationship to enzyme induction. M. Civen
and others. bibliog il Science 157:1563-4
S 29 '67
Daily rhythm in tyrosine concentration in
human plasma; persistence on low-protein
diets. R. J. Wurtman and others. bibliog
il Science 158:660-2 N 3 '67
Diurnal rhythm of sensitivity of cotton seedlings to herbicides. J. G. Gosselink and
L. C. Standifer. bibliog il Science 158:120-1
O 6 '67
Natural free-running period in vertebrate animal populations. C. H. Lowe and others.
bibliog il Science 156:531-4 Ap 28 '67
Second hands for biological clocks; rhythms
regulated by enzyme system. T. W. Hill.
il Sci N 92:380-1 O 14 '67
Squirrel monkey reproduction: the fatted
male phenomenon and seasonal spermatogenesis. F. V. Du Mond and T. C. Hutchinson. bibliog il Science 158:1067-70 N 24 '67
Successiveness discrimination as a two-state,
quantal process. A. B. Kristofferson. bibliog
il Science 158:1337-9 D 8 '67
Temperature compensation in short-duration
time-measurement by an intertidal am-
phipod. J. T. Enright. bibliog il Science
156:1510-12 Je 16 '67
Vertical diurnal migration and endogenous
rhythmicity. J. T. Enright and W. M.
Hamner. bibliog il Science 157:937-41 Ag
25 '67
See also
Tree rings
PERIODONTIA
Mummies' teeth: periodontal problems of an-
cient Egypt. il Sci N 91:280 Mr 25 '67
PERIWINKLES
Perils of periwinkle; smoking dried leaves.
Newsweek 69:68 Je 26 '67
PERJURY
Nader affair. J. Ridgeway and D. Sanford.
New Repub 156:16-18 F 18 '67
Perjury routine: police perjury. I. Younger.
il Nation 204:596-7 My 8 '67
See also
Trials (perjury)

PERKIN, Robert L.
Finder and namer of nature. Sat R 50:28-9 Jl
8 '67
Nature is no sentimentalist. Sat R 50:33 S
2 '67
PERKINS, Carl D.
Washington report. J. Lloyd. Sr Schol 90:
sup8 F 10 '67
PERKINS, Elisha Douglass
Loser on El Dorado trail. J. K Hutchens.
Sat R 50:27-8 My 27 '67
PERKINS, Frank T. and Hayflick, L.
Cell cultures; report on third annual meet-
ing of Committee on cell cultures of the
permanent section on microbiological stand-
ardization of the inter-national association
of microbiological societies. Science 155:723-
4 F 10 '67
PERKINS, Harold Oliver
[Month] gardening where you live! See
issues of Better homes and gardens
You can use vines everywhere. Horticulture
45:18-21 Je '67
PERKINS, John Alanson
Goodbye, academe. por Time 89:90 Je 23 '67
PERKINSON, William J.
Dangers of the laser miracle ray; reprint.
Sci Digest 62:62-4 N '67
Puzzle of Antarctica's desert valleys; reprint.
Sci Digest 61:32-6 Ap '67
Red Sea's treasure; reprint. Sci Digest 62:22-4
D '67
PERL, Lila
Delights of the Ottoman table; excerpt from
Rice, spice, and bitter oranges, Mediter-
ranean foods and festivals. Sat R 50:61-2
O 14 '67
PERL, Susan
Humor & satire of Susan Perl. J. H. Michel.
il por Am Artist 32:44-9+ Ja '68
PERLBERG, Mark
To Dietrich Bonhoeffer; poem. Christian
Cent 84:832 Je 28 '67
PERLE, George
Three views of Wozzeck Sat R 50:54-5 D 2
'67
What they did to Berg's Lulu. Sat R 50:43-5
D 30 '67
PERLMAN, Itzhak
Most auspicious debut. H. Glass. il por Am
Rec G 33:1098 Ag '67
PERLMUTTER, Amos
Israel's tough stand on captured territories.
New Repub 158:12-14 Ja 13 '68
PERMEASE. See Proteins
PERMITS, Building. See Building laws and
regulations
PEROMYSCUS. See Mice, White footed
PEROXIDASES
Indoleacetic acid oxidase activity of apoper-
oxidase. B. Z. Siegel and A. W. Galston.
bibliog il Science 157:1557-9 S 29 '67
Prevention of induced atherosclerosis by
peroxidase. J. Caravaca and others. bibliog
il Science 155:1284-7 Mr 10 '67
PERPETUAL motion
Hooray for the human spirit, human spirit,
human spirit. M. Lamm. il Esquire 68:
142-3 D '67
Perpetual motion machines. S. W. Angrist. il
Sci Am 218:114-22 Ja '68
PERREAULT, John
Krushenick's blazing blazons. Art N 66:34-5+
Mr '67
Paul Klee: a dissenting opinion. Art N 66:
42-3+ My '67
Venus in vinyl. Art N 65:46-8+ Ja '67
about
Landscape and language. R. Sward. Poetry
109:408-10 Mr '67
PERRETT, Patrick
Boat camping. il Yachting 121:84-5+ My '67
PERRIN, Noel
New York's forgotten drought. Nation 204:
721-3 Je 5 '67
Sister's on the other line. New Yorker 43:
150+ N 18 '67
Tell me, pretty billboard. New Yorker 43:
163-4+ Ap 22 '67
PERRIN, Ursula
Promises to keep; story; excerpt from
Ghosts. Ladies Home J 84:151-8 Mr '67
PERROT, Paul N.
Special collection somewhat off the beaten
track. por Wilson Lib Bul 41:593-7 F '67
PERRY, Darby
Rehearsal for World war II. Am Heritage
18:40-5+ Ap '67
PERRY, Farwell, and Perry, Lois
Exploring north of nowhere. pors Field & S
72:46-9+ Je '67

PERRY, Gregg
Video tape in the classroom. Sr Schol 90:sup21
My 12 '67
PERRY, Lois. See Perry, F. jt. auth.
PERRY, Margaret
Churchill's Chartwell. Flower Grower 54:46-
7+ Ja '67
Garden-hopping in the Caribbean. il Home
Gard 54:22-5 D '67
PERRY, Matthew Calbraith
Old Bruin, by S. E. Morison. Review
Atlan 221:114-15 Ja '68. O. Handlin
Life 63:20 N 10 '67. A. B. C. Whipple
Sat R 50:33+ D 16 '67. J. R. Fredland
PERSE, St John, pseud. See Léger, A. S.
PERSECUTION
Façade crumbles; persecution of Muslims
and Buddhists. America 116:331 Mr 11 '67
See also
Genocide
Jews—Persecutions
PERSEIDS. See Meteors
PERSHALL, T. W.
Man and the dog. C. E. Gillham. il por
Field & S 72:116-17 Ag '67
PERSHING, John Joseph
Black Jack of the 10th. R. O'Connor. il por
Am Heritage 18:14-17+ F '67
PERSIA. See Iran
PERSIAN art. See Art, Persian
PERSIAN cookery. See Cookery, Iranian
PERSIAN GULF
Persian Gulf. M. Page. il Atlan 219:38+ Ap
'67
PERSIAN rugs. See Rugs and carpets, Oriental
PERSIMMONS
Trees are good-looking all year, and the
handsome fruit ripens in November. il
Sunset 139:212-13 N '67
PERSING, Robert F.
Build your own memo minder. Pop Electr
27:49-51+ O '67
PERSISTENCE
Persistent child; excerpt adapted from Tem-
perament and behavior disorders in chil-
dren. A. Thomas and others. il Parents
Mag 42:35-7+ D '67
PERSONAL airplanes. See Airplanes—Private
ownership
PERSONAL beauty. See Beauty, Personal
PERSONAL credit. See Credit
PERSONAL finance. See Finance, Personal
PERSONAL injuries
Lengthening reach of liability; damage suits
against the manufacturers. il Bsns W
p 100+ S 16 '67
PERSONAL liability insurance. See Insurance,
Liability
PERSONAL liberty. See Liberty
PERSONAL names. See Names, Personal
PERSONAL opinions. See Attitudes
PERSONAL records
Is there a simple way to organize your
tax records? P. Lindberg. Bet Hom & Gard
45:6 Ap '67
PERSONAL responsibility. See Responsibility
PERSONAL rights. See Civil rights
PERSONALITY
Charm. L. Lee. Mlle 65:152+ My '67; Same
abr. with title Essence of charm. Read
Digest 91:181-2+ Ag '67
Evolutionary view emerges; human person-
ality. Sci N 93:6-7 Ja 6 '68
Which personality succeeds in college? D.
Klein. il Seventeen 26:148-9+ My '67
See also
Attitudes
Character
Human relations
Persistence
PERSONALITY, Disorders of
Girls who cut themselves; slashers in mental
hospitals. Sci N 92:496 N 18 '67
See also
Autism
PERSONALITY tests
Computerized man: cause of privacy; address,
May 20, 1967. W. Douglas. Vital Speeches
33:700-4 S 1 '67
Personality tests and invasion of privacy.
M. L. Gross; J. N. Butcher. NEA J 56:50-
2 N '67
Problems of high school students in relation
to grade achievement; high-average-, and
low-achievers problems analyzed by the
Mooney problem check list. J. C. Marshall.
bibliog f il Sch & Soc 95:237-8 Ap 1 '67

Testing issue: a straw man; Minnesota
multiphasic personality inventory moves
into personnel offices. Sci N 91:350-1 Ap
15 '67
PERSONNEL management
Blueprint to build executives. G. E. Keck.
Duns R 90:45-6+ N '67
Checkers or choice in manpower manage-
ment. T. M. Alfred. bibliog f Harvard
Bsns R 45:157-8+ Ja '67
Confrontation meeting. R. Beckhard. Har-
vard Bsns R 45:149-55 Mr '67
Corporate ombudsman. I. Silver. bibliog f
Harvard Bsns R 45:77-87 My '67
Dismissal for off-the-job criminal behavior.
J. W. Leonard. bibliog f Mo Labor R 90:
21-6 N '67
How garnisheed workers fare under arbitra-
tion. R. W. Fisher. bibliog f Mo Labor R
90:1-6 My '67
Human relations and the nature of man.
H. P. Knowles and B. O. Saxberg. bibliog
f Harvard Bsns R 45:22-4+ Mr '67
Personnel man wears a bigger hat; highlights
of NICB's study. Bsns W p 131 Mr 4 '67
Put people on your balance sheet. J. S.
Hekimian and C. H. Jones. bibliog f il
Harvard Bsns R 45:105-13 Ja '67
Seven sure-fire weapons for trouble shoot-
ers; excerpts from The knack of developing
and using management savvy. R. E. Lev-
inson. il Nations Bsns 55:80-2+ S '67
Who works with whom? D. I. Cleland and
W. Munsey. il Harvard Bsns R 45:84-90
S '67
See also
Bonus system
Communication in management
Employment systems
Industrial relations
Job satisfaction
Leadership
Library administration
Profit sharing
Seniority. Employee
PERSONNEL selection. See Employment sys-
tems
PERSONNEL service in education
Computer-assisted counselor. J. W. Lough-
ary. il NEA J 56:22-4 F '67
Counseling the average child. C. O. Peets and
L. J. Schwartz. il NEA J 57:14-16 Ja '68
Study of educational and job counseling. Sch
& Soc 95:286-8 Sum '67
This way to the counselor; summer guidance
and counseling program, Bismarck, N.D. il
Am Ed 3:25 O '67
Where to get bad advice about college; high
school guidance counselor. J. F. Scott. il
Ladies Home J 84:76+ N '67
PERSPIRATION
Perspiration, everybody's problem. M. Leder-
er. il Todays Health 45:12-14 Ag '67
Sodium transport: inhibitory factor in sweat
of patients with cystic fibrosis. J. A.
Mangos and N. R. McSherry. bibliog il
Science 158:135-6 O 6 '67
PERT. See Critical path analysis
PERU
See also
Amazon River
Arts and crafts—Peru
Forests and forestry—Peru
Hospitals—Peru
Huari
Incas
Iquitos
Machu Picchu
Natural resources—Peru
Pajatén
Roads—Peru
Tourist trade—Peru

Antiquities
See Indians of South America—Antiquities—Peru

Description and travel
Going places, finding things in Lima, Cuzco,
Machu Picchu. J. Wilson. il House & Gard
131:32-5+ F '67
Traveling with Mlle: we conquistadoras. S.
Jones. il Mlle 65:327-32 Ag '67

Economic conditions
Regaining a lost habit; effect of Belaúnde's
Marginal highway. il Time 90:37 D 8 '67

History
Peru. R. E. Crist and A. Taylor. bibliog il
Focus 17:1-6 Ap '67

PERU—*Continued*

Politics and government

Peru's misfired guerrilla campaign. N. Gall. Reporter 36:36-8 Ja 26 '67

Swirl of trouble. il Time 90:32 N 3 '67
See also
Political parties—Peru

Religious institutions and affairs

See also
Catholic church in Peru
Church and state in Peru

Social conditions

Squatter settlements. W. Mangin. il Sci Am 217:21-9 bibliog(p 156) O '67

PERUVIAN folk art. See Folk art

PESTALOZZI children's village

Pestalozzi children's village, Trogen, Switzerland. A. Bill. il Sch & Soc 95:502-3 D 9 '67

PESTICIDES

Any progress toward safer pesticides? il Good H 165:171 Ag '67

Latest report on fertilizer-pesticide mixtures. Suc Farm 65:88 Mr '67

New pesticides are safer, more effective, easier to use. M. C. Shurtleff. il Pop Gard 18:80-1+ Mr '67

Pesticide pollution control. H. P. Nicholson. bibliog il Science 158:871-6 N 17 '67

Taking polluters to court; V. J. Yannacone's control movement. F. Graham, jr. New Repub 158:8-9 Ja 13 '68

Third-generation pesticides, C. M. Williams. il Sci Am 217:13-17 Jl '67

Which chemicals kill which garden pests; with charts. il Changing T 21:45-7 Je '67
See also
Spraying and dusting

Injurious effects

Facts help quiet pesticide fuss. D. Hanson. Suc Farm 65:6 Mr '67

Pesticide plague; possible effects on human mutation. il Newsweek 69:94+ My 22 '67

Pesticide warning; organochlorines apparently cause liver damage. D. A. Ehrlich. Sci N 92:495 N 18 '67

Science predicts a growing danger; Legator-Verrett report on pesticide effects on humans. il Bsns W p42+ My 13 '67

Toxic substances and ecological cycles. G. M. Woodwell. il Sci Am 216:24-31 Mr '67; Discussion. 216:6+ Je '67

Laws and legislation

Pesticides, politics and the public. F. Graham, jr. il Audubon 69:54-62 Jl '67

Residues

Dietary intake of pesticide chemicals. R. E. Duggan and J. R. Weatherwax. bibliog il Science 157:1006-10 S 1 '67

Few pesticides in dinner. Sci Digest 62:29 D '67

Pesticide transformation to aniline and azo compounds in soil. R. Bartha and D. Pramer. bibliog il Science 156:1617-18 Je 23 '67

PET, Incorporated

Pet's playing field. Fortune 75:316 Je 15 '67

PET foods. See Animals—Food

PETER, Saint

Peter, prince of apostles. E. O. Hauser. il Read Digest 90:194-5+ Ap '67

PETER, Robert

Letter from Latin America. Nat R 19:1332 N 28 '67

PETER Bent Brigham hospital. See Boston—Hospitals

PETER Grimes; opera. See Britten, B.

PETER Paul, Incorporated. See Paul, Peter, incorporated

PETER Wolf associates. See Wolf, Peter, associates

PETERS, Art

Beware search for lost heirs! Ebony 22:94-6+ Jl '67

33,000-volt shock wins two award of $1½ million. Ebony 23:112-14+ N '67

PETERS, Doris, pseud.

Change the weather, change the world. Harper 234:98-101 My '67

PETERS, John H.

Heterophile reactive antigen in infectious mononucleosis. bibliog Science 157:1200-2 S 8 '67

PETERS, Roberta

Back to school. L. Gmoser. il pors Opera N 31:16 Mr 4 '67

PETERS, William

Priest who practiced what he preached. Good H 165:82-3+ Ag '67

(ed) See Evers, M. B. For us, the living

PETERSEN, Marjorie

Stornoway progress report. See issues of Motor boating

PETERSON, Arthur G.

Fostoria's Valencia, Verona and Ruby patterns. Hobbies 72:98F-98G S '67

Glassware oddities of the 1880s. Hobbies 72:72 Ag '67

Glassware oddities of the 1870's. Hobbies 72:84 Jl '67

Glass-ware oddities of the 1860s. Hobbies 72:72 My '67

Jefferson glass co. and the Krys-tol trademark. Hobbies 72:98N-98O O '67

PETERSON, Don

Does a tiger wear a necktie? Criticism Sat R 50:45 Mr 4 '67

PETERSON, Esther

Can Betty Furness help the consumer? il por Consumer Rep 32:256-8 My '67

How much federal protection do consumers want? Consumer Bul 50:26-8 My '67

PETERSON, Harold

College football. Sports Illus 27:61-2 O 16 '67

Rowing. Sports Illus 26:58-9 My 22; 60 Je 26 '67

Singing blues in the night. Sports Illus 26:36-8 Je 12 '67

PETERSON, Martha Elizabeth

Barnard looks west. por Time 89:40+ My 26 '67

Healthy type. por Newsweek 69:102 My 29 '67

PETERSON, Oscar

Oscar Peterson playing. G. Lees. il por Holiday 41:152+ Ag '67

PETERSON, Robert

Evening poem; Two sonnets: When you look one way; Mazatlan, an unenclosed system. Poetry 110:21-3 Ap '67

PETERSON, Roger Tory

Birders: a more civilized breed. N Y Times Mag p65+ D 17 '67

Carl W. Buchheister, a tribute. Audubon 69:54-5 Mr '67

Galapagos; eerie cradle of new species. il Nat Geog Mag 131:540-85 Ap '67

PETERSON, Rudolph Arvid

Cooperation or stagnation? address, November 15, 1967. Vital Speeches 34:165-8 Ja 1 '68

Our evolving international strategy; address, April 6, 1967. Vital Speeches 33:429-34 My 1 '67

PETERSON, Russell W.

New venture management in a large company. Harvard Bsns R 45:68-76 My '67

PETERSON, Stanze

Stanze Peterson dance theatre; 92nd street Y. J. Maskey. Dance Mag 41:81 My '67

PETERSON, Susan

Folk art of Nepal. Craft Horiz 27:36-9 Mr '67

PETERSON, Virgil W.

Local and state law enforcement today. bibliog f Cur Hist 53:8-14+ Jl '67

PETERSON, Virgilia

Again perfection. Reporter 36:50-2 Ja 26 '67

Prejudice and hope; reprint. Writer 80:21-4 F '67

PETERSON, William H.

Future & the futurists. bibliog f Harvard Bsns R 45:168-70+ N '67

PETERSON, Willis

Denali interlude. Audubon 69:44-55 My '67

PETIT-four cookies. See Cookies

PETITIONS

Petition syndrome; collective public signature by professors. Time 89:43 F 24 '67

PETLIN, Irving

Art; exhibition at the galleria Odyssia. M. Kozloff. Nation 205:509-10 N 13 '67

PETRA, Jordan

Chasm opens and you are in Petra. il Sunset 138:37+ Ap '67

Desert waterworks of the ancient Nabataeans. P. C. Hammond. il Natur Hist 76:36-43 Je '67

PETRAKIS, Harry Mark

Dream of kings; story; excerpt from novel. Ladies Home J 84:99-100 F '67

Return to Kasos. Sat R 50:31 S 9 '67

PETRAKIS, Nicholas L. and others

Cerumen in American Indians; genetic implications of sticky and dry types. bibliog Science 158:1192-3 D 1 '67

PETRAŇ, Mojmir. See Egger, M. D. jt. auth.

PETRIE, Paul

Suite of children; poem. New Yorker 43:32 Je 17 '67

PETRIFIED FOREST NATIONAL PARK
Wilderness plan for Petrified Forest National Park and the surrounding region. il Nat Parks Mag 41:10-11 Jl '67
PETRIFIED wood. See Trees, Fossil
PETROLEUM
See also
Bituminous sand
Oil shales

Chemistry
Iodide abundance in oilfield brines in Oklahoma. A. G. Collins and G. C. Egleson. bibliog il Science 156:934-5 My 19 '67

International aspects
Boomerang boycott. Time 90:98 S 15 '67
Burdensome boycott. il Time 90:76 Jl 7 '67
De Gaulle wins dividends in oil; agreements with Iraq for new exploration. Bsns W p 126 D 2 '67
France blends politics with a push for oil; trying to steal a march on Anglo-Saxon oil producers in the Middle East. il Bsns W p91-2+ N 11 '67
How Arabs push up oil prices to pay for the war they lost. il U S News 63:98-9 N 6 '67
Oil embargo that isn't. il Bsns W p32-3 Je 17 '67
Oil keeps flowing; Rotterdam transshipping point for Mideastern oil. il Bsns W p32+ Jl 8 '67
Oil: when is a ban not a ban? il Newsweek 69:57+ Je 26 '67
Politics of petroleum. J. H. Lichtblau. il Reporter 37:26-8 Jl 13 '67
Shadow war on the economic front; effect of Arab-Israeli conflict. il Newsweek 69:68-70 Je 19 '67
Shock waves from the Middle East. il Time 89:88 Je 16 '67
Tankers strike it rich; chartering combats Suez Canal closure. il Newsweek 70:70+ Jl 17 '67

Pipe lines
Alpine pipeline. Newsweek 70:83-4 O 23 '67
Subterranean surge; western European crude-oil-carrying network. il Time 89:98+ Ap 21 '67

Prices
Oil prices stay in line. Bsns W p28 Jl 22 '67

Prospecting
Mobil oil squarely in the middle; search for new fields. T. O'Hanlon. il Fortune 76:86-9+ S 1 '67

Transportation
See also
Petroleum—Pipe lines
Tank ships

Alberta
See Petroleum—Canada

Canada
Alberta oil: the cup runneth over; huge finds in Rainbow-Zama region. il Bsns W p68-73 Jl 1 '67
New frontier: the tar sands; Athabaska oil sands. J. Lear. il Sat R 50:57 S 2 '67

Middle East
Eastern Arabia. A. Melamid. bibliog il Focus 18:1-6 N '67
Oil: a new war Nasser is losing. il U S News 63:66 Jl 3 '67

Nigeria
Where oil is an innocent bystander; rival tribes threatening petroleum companies in Nigeria. il Bsns W p62+ My 6 '67
PETROLEUM and war. See Petroleum—International aspects
PETROLEUM congress, World. See World petroleum congress
PETROLEUM in submerged lands
New showdown over offshore oil; Interior dept. vs. state of Louisiana. il Bsns W p 186 Ja 28 '67
North American, Mobil oil agree to pool technology. il Tech W 20:30+ F 13 '67
PETROLEUM industry and trade
See also
Royal Dutch-Shell group
Shell oil company
World petroleum congress

Consolidations and mergers
And they lived happily ever after; merger of Atlantic refining and Richfield oil. il Bsns W p 156-8+ Ap 29 '67

Humble enlarges its pie; agreement to buy the Signal oil co. div. of Standard oil co. of California. Bsns W p41 F 18 '67
J. Paul Getty's changed plans; merger of Tidewater into Getty oil. J. McDonald. il Fortune 76:108-13+ D '67

International aspects
See Petroleum—International aspects

Laws
See Petroleum laws and legislation

Securities
Attraction in weakness. il Duns R 90:87-8 D '67
What's holding back the oils? il Bsns W p 127-8+ Ap 29 '67

Arabia
See Petroleum industry and trade—Middle East

Canada
Now Canada strikes it rich in oil; Athabaska tar sands and Rainbow Lake area, Alberta. il U S News 62:108-10 My 22 '67

France
France blends politics with a push for oil; trying to steal a march on Anglo-Saxon oil producers in the Middle East. il Bsns W p91-2+ N 11 '67

Iraq
De Gaulle wins dividends in oil; agreements with Iraq for new exploration. Bsns W p 126 D 2 '67
Turning the valves. il Time 89:88 Mr 10 '67

Italy
Cefis of E.N.I. Fortune 76:31 Ag '67
Rewards from rivals. Time 89:93 F 17 '67

Libya
Pumping up profits. il Time 89:87 F 24 '67
What a newly rich country does with its oil money. il U S News 64:59-60 Ja 8 '68

Louisiana
Bombs in the bayous; bombing of wells and pipelines. il Newsweek 71:55 Ja 8 '68

Middle East
How Arabs push up oil prices to pay for the war they lost. il U S News 63:98-9 N 6 '67
Just how important is Arab oil? il U S News 62:49-51 Je 19 '67
Lesson of Suez is paying off. il Bsns W p37-8 Je 10 '67
Oil embargo that isn't. il Bsns W p32-3 Je 17 '67
Oil: when is a ban not a ban? il Newsweek 69:57+ Je 26 '67
Politics of petroleum. J. H. Lichtblau. il Reporter 37:26-8 Jl 13 '67
Report from Arabia; Gulf sheikdoms. A. Verrier. il Fortune 76:77+ N '67

Netherlands
Working while waiting; Europoort refineries. il Time 90:71 Ag 11 '67

Texas
Where Texas falls short. Bsns W p32 Jl 29 '67

United States
As oil industry looks away from the uncertain Mideast; interviews. il U S News 63:54-6 Jl 31 '67
Gasoline's penny rise raises federal hackles; companies march to Washington to debate increase. il Bsns W p40-1 F 18 '67
Oil and the Middle East; domestic oil industry asks for special favors. M. Friedman. Newsweek 69:63 Je 26 '67
Price of protectionism; statement, October 18, 1967. S. L. Udall. Dept State Bul 57: 638-42 N 13 '67
Safeguarding tomorrow's growth; address, November 16, 1966. R. G. Dunlop. Vital Speeches 33:252-6 F 1 '67
Tapping world's biggest oil reserve; shales of Colorado, Utah and Wyoming. il U S News 62:110 My 22 '67
When the U.S. oil industry looks ahead. il U S News 64:64-6 Ja 15 '68
See also
Mobil oil company
Union oil company of California

PETROLEUM industry and trade—*Continued*

Venezuela

Jam in Mideast oil could aid Venezuela, but—. il U S News 62:84-5 Je 12 '67

PETROLEUM laws and legislation

Fencing in Esso's brand. Bsns W p98 Ja 21 '67

PETROLEUM pipe lines. See Petroleum—Pipe lines

PETROVICH, Michael B.

United States policy in east Europe. bibliog f Cur Hist 52:193-9+ Ap '67

PETRY, Ann

Migraine workers; story. Redbook 129:66-7 My '67

PETS

Call of the not-so-wild; wild pets. B. Gilbert. il Sports Illus 27:40-2+ D 18 '67

Family pet. P. O'Keefe. See issues of American home

Family pet. R. KortKamp and P. O'Keefe. Am Home 70:56 My '67

If a pet causes an allergy. il Good H 165:170 Ag '67

Is it wrong to make pets of wild animals? E. Parks. il Sci Digest 62:61-4 Ag '67

Pet news. J. Kuh. See issues of Ladies' home journal

Picking a pet for an apartment. il Changing T 21:37-9 Ag '67

See also

Christmas gifts for pets

also names of animal pets, e.g. Dogs

Equipment and supplies

Housing your pet. Am Home 71:34 Ja '68

PETSCHEK, Albert G.

Intensity fluctuations of a relativistically expanding source. bibliog Science 156:239 Ap 14 '67

PETSCHEK, Willa

Betjeman phenomenon. N Y Times Mag p24-5+ Ag 13 '67

PETTINELLA, D. M.

Albergo Santa Teresa; poem. Cath World 206:10 O '67

PETTINGILL, Olin Sewall, jr

New Zealand spring. Audubon 69:6-10+ Ja '67

PETTITT, John M. and Beck, C. B.

Seed from the upper Devonian. bibliog Science 156:1727-9 Je 30 '67

PETTY, Frank

When union members defy their top leaders. il por U S News 62:84-5 Mr 20 '67

PETTY, Richard

Boy with a silver spanner. il por Time 90:58 S 15 '67

Champ with a feel for the rattlesnake. por Sports Illus 26:36-8 F 27 '67

Chip off the old block. il por Newsweek 70:46 Ag 21 '67

Darlington Southern 500. B. Myers. il Motor T 19:66-9 D '67

Easy five-0-0 R. Brock. il Hot Rod 20:64-5 N '67

Stockers: winners and hopefuls. il por Motor T 19:108-11 N '67

PETUNIAS

Pink, white, and cool. il Sunset 138:246 Ag '67

PEW, Thomas W. jr

Yankee station. Nation 205:141-2 Ag 28 '67

PEYRE, Henri

De Gaulle again, or a new popular front? New Repub 156:10-11 Mr 4 '67

PEYSER, Joseph L.

Educational consultant and commercially produced instructional media. bibliog f Sch & Soc 95:301-3 Sum '67

PFAFF, William

Foreign affairs. See occassional issues of Commonweal

PFAFFMANN, Carl. See Scott, J. W. jt. auth.

PFANN, William G.

Zone refining; with biographical sketch. Sci Am 217:14, 62-70+ bibliog(p 158) D '67

PFEFFER, Leo

Church and school. Nation 205:389-90 O 23 '67

PFIZER, Beryl

Poor woman's almanac. Ladies Home J 84:8 Ap; 32 Ag; 74 S; 91 N; 8 D '67

PFLEIDERER, J. and Grewing, M.

Emission-line variability and distance of quasars. bibliog Science 157:544-5 Ag 4 '67

PHAGOCYTES and phagocytosis

Selective phagocytosis: a new concept in protein catabolism. H. Gans and others. bibliog il Science 159:107-10 Ja 5 '68

PHALON, Richard A.

Wall Street under fire. Duns R 89:39-40+ Ap '67

PHAM-van-Dong

Revealing highlights from two interviews with enemy leaders; ed. by L. Lockwood. Life 62:44B Ap 7 '67

PHARMACEUTICAL industry. See Drug trade

PHARMACISTS

What a pharmacist can and cannot do. il Good H 166:168 Ja '68

PHARMACOLOGY

Bridging two disciplines; research of B. Brodie. B. J. Culliton. il Sci N 92:476-7 N 11 '67

Drug makers make a difference. B. J. Culliton. il Sci N 91:382-3 Ap 22 '67

PHARMACY

Pharmacy, serving man and medicine. G. E. Cwalina and others. il Todays Health 45:54-5+ My '67

See also

Prescriptions

PHEASANT shooting

How to hunt smart pheasant. M. Ellis. il Field & S 72:46-7+ S '67

Something peculiar at Tulelake. N. Riley. il Outdoor Life 140:62-4+ N '67

PHEASANTS

What happens to pheasants? B. East. il Outdoor Life 140:34-5+ Ag '67

See also

Cookery—Game

PHEASANTS; story. See Wolwode, L.

PHELAN, James

Democratic disaster area. Reporter 37:18-21 N 2 '67

Mutiny in the Birch society. Sat Eve Post 240:21-5 Ap 8 '67

Plot to kill Kennedy? rush to judgment in New Orleans. Sat Eve Post 240:21-5 My 6 '67

PHELPS, Anthony

Cool milk before you feed it? Farm J 91:D2 O '67

First results with oxidation ditches on the farm. Farm J 91:48L+ Ja '67

PHELPS, Robert

Fine book for children by a secret child: hidden world of Maurice Sandak. il Life 63:8 D 15 '67

PHENACETIN

Pain killers indicted. Sci N 91:116 F 4 '67

PHENANTHROLINES. See Chemical reagents

PHENOLS

Bromophenols from red algae. J. S. Craigie and D. E. Gruenig. bibliog il Science 157:1058-9 S 1 '67

Isolation of 2,6-dibromophenol from the marine hemichordate, balanoglossus biminiensis. R. B. Ashworth and M. J. Cormier. bibliog il Science 155:1558-9 Mr 24 '67; Reply. J. S. Webb. 158:522 O 27 '67

PHENOTHIAZINES

See also

Chlorpromazine

PHENOTYPIC masking. See Drugs—Physiological effects

PHENYLALANINE

Aminoacidemias: effects on maze performance and cerebral serotonin. C. M. McKean and others. bibliog il Science 157:213-15 Jl 14 '67

p-Chlorophenylalanine-induced chemical manifestations of phenylketonuria in rats. M. A. Lipton and others. bibliog il Science 156:248-50 Ap 14 '67

Starving out cancer; low-phenylalanine diet. Newsweek 69:68 Je 26 '67

PHENYLKETONURIA

p-Chlorophenylalanine-induced chemical manifestations of phenylketonuria in rats. M. A. Lipton and others. bibliog il Science 156:248-50 Ap 14 '67

More problems of instant medicine; dangers of premature practical application of research findings. J. D. Cooper. il Sat R 50:56-61 Je 3 '67

Phenylketonuria: enduring behavioral deficits in phenylketonuric rats. R. L. Schalock and F. D. Klopfer. bibliog il Science 155:1033-5 F 24 '67

PHERBELLIA. See Flies

PHIFER, James Cameron

Mother, I do not hate to die. Am Heritage 18:32-3+ F '67

PHIL Berg collection. See Art—Private collections

PHILADELPHIA

Anti-poverty program

Andy Miller moves up; Philadelphia's Opportunities Industrialization center (OIC) I. Mothner. il Look 31:27-8 Je 13 '67

PHILADELPHIA—*Continued*

Architecture

Progressive-traditional style for bank operations; stock exchange building. il Arch Rec 141:182-3 Je '67

Art

Moments for tomorrow; citywide sculpture expedition. il Newsweek 69:97-8 F 27 '67

Centennial exhibition, 1876

Centennial exposition medals; United States centennial exposition. C. French. Hobbies 72:102 Jl '67

City planning

Philadelphia renews renewal. J. Bailey. il Arch Forum 126:64-7 Mr '67
Profiles: through the great city. A. Bailey. il New Yorker 43:32-6+ Ag 5 '67

Description

Step by step through Philadelphia. R. Deardorff. il Travel 128:36-41+ Jl '67

Education

Meanwhile, back in Philadelphia; strike of lay teachers in the diocesan high school system. A. Swidler. Commonweal 86:191-2 My 5 '67
Revolution in Philadelphia. Newsweek 70:70 D 18 '67
What turns kids on? Philadelphia cooperative schools curriculum of concerns program. T. Borton. il Sat R 50:72-4+ Ap 15 '67

Finance

Setting up a small-city purchasing system. O. R. Winter. Am City 82:168+ Je '67

Free library

Potter, pirates, and punctuation; Henry S. Borneman fraktur schriften collection. E. Shaffer. il Wilson Lib Bul 41:598-602 F '67

Historic houses, etc.

New comfort and old grace, or, notes on the Victorian age at times exuberant, often ostentatious; Ebenezer Maxwell mansion. E. P. Birk. il Antiques 92:296+ S '67

Hospitals

What's wrong with American hospitals? asking a computer; mathematical model of Lankenau hospital. J. D. Corbit, jr. and others. il Sat R 50:67-9 F 4 '67

Housing

House on Diamond street. il Am City 82:88-9 Jl '67

Libraries

See also
Library company of Philadelphia

Music

Philadelphia. M. De Schauensee. Opera N 31:24 Je 10 '67
Philadelphia; two Toscas by the Philadelphia lyric and Tristan und Isolde by the Philadelphia grand. M. De Schauensee. Opera N 31:28-9 Mr 4 '67
See also
Philadelphia grand opera company
Philadelphia orchestra

Negroes

Andy Miller moves up; Philadelphia's Opportunities industrialization center (OIC) I. Mothner. il Look 31:27-8 Je 13 '67
How they cool it in Philadelphia; techniques of police commissioner, Frank Rizzo. Bsns W p21 Jl 1 '67
Solving the Q.N. problem; Opportunities industrialization center. il Time 89:25-6 Mr 3 '67
Teaching people to hold jobs; the Philadelphia plan; Opportunities industrialization center. il U S News 64:58-9 Ja 1 '68
You sweeter than wine. Joe. M. Kram. il Sports Illus 26:32-4+ Je 19 '67

Newspapers

See also
Bulletin, Philadelphia
Philadelphia inquirer

Police

How they cool it in Philadelphia; techniques of police commissioner, Frank Rizzo. Bsns W p21 Jl 1 '67

Politics and government

Republican Specter. il Time 89:26-7 Mr 17 '67

Search for an heir; mayorality campaign. Time 90:33 O 27 '67
Threatening Specter; mayorality nomination. il Newsweek 69:31-2 My 29 '67

Race problems

He helps the poor help themselves; interview. L. H. Sullivan. il Nations Bsns 55:42-4+ Jl '67

Theater

Philadelphian frolics. L. D. Streiker. Christian Cent 84:815-16 Je 21 '67

PHILADELPHIA (periodical)
Harry the muckraker. il Time 89:84+ Ap 21 '67
Reporter; Philadelphia magazine's exposé of Karafin affair. S. J. Adamo. America 116:822 Je 3 '67; Discussion. 117:101 Jl 29 '67

PHILADELPHIA bulletin. See Bulletin, Philadelphia

PHILADELPHIA chamber symphony. See Chamber orchestras

PHILADELPHIA evening bulletin. See Bulletin, Philadelphia

PHILADELPHIA free library. See Philadelphia —Free library

PHILADELPHIA gas works
TV and radio; programs sponsored by Philadelphia gas works. R. L. Shayon. Sat R 51:39 Ja 6 '68

PHILADELPHIA grand opera company
Philadelphia. M. De Schauensee. Opera N 31:29 Ap 8 '67
Report; Philadelphia; productions. M. De Schauensee. Opera N 32:31 Ja 6 '68

PHILADELPHIA inquirer
Harry the muckraker. il Time 89:84+ Ap 21 '67
Philadelphia story; the Joe McGinniss column. New Repub 157:10-11 S 30 '67
Reporter; Philadelphia magazine's exposé of Karafin affair. S. J. Adamo. America 116:822 Je 3 '67; Discussion. 117:101 Jl 29 '67

PHILADELPHIA lyric opera company
Philadelphia (cont) M. De Schauensee. Opera N 31:29 Ap 8 '67
Philadelphia; Madama Butterfly. M. De Schauensee. Opera N 31:30 Ja 28 '67
Philadelphia; performance of Bellini's Sonnambula. M. De Schauensee. Opera N 31:32 F 25 '67
Report; Philadelphia. M. De Schauensee. Opera N 32:23 N 25 '67
Rossellini's view. F. Stevenson. il Opera N 32:20-1 O 14 '67
View from the bridge; operatic production of Arthur Miller's View from the bridge. P. J. Smith. il Hi Fi 18:MA23 Ja '68

PHILADELPHIA orchestra
Musical events; concert in Philharmonic Hall, conducted by L. Stokowski. W. Sargeant. New Yorker 43:220-1 N 18 '67
Musical events; concert in Philharmonic Hall, conducted by S. Ozawa. W. Sargeant. New Yorker 43:156+ Mr 11 '67

PHILADELPHIA pepper pot. See Soups

PHILADELPHIA symphony orchestra. See Philadelphia orchestra

PHILANTHROPY. See Charities; Giving

PHILBRICK, Charles
Debuts and encores. Sat R 50:32-4 Je 3 '67

PHILBY, Harold Adrian Russell
Hello, comrade Philby; with excerpts from interview. il por Newsweek 71:32-3 Ja 1 '68

about

Communist in M.I. 6. por Time 90:37-8 O 13 '67
Establishment man. por Newsweek 70:45-6 O 16 '67
James Bond could have learned from Philby. G. McDermott. il pors N Y Times Mag p36-7+ N 12 '67
Lesson of Philby. Nat R 19:1155 O 31 '67
On display. Time 90:20+ D 29 '67
Scandal rocks MI-6. por Sr Schol 91:21 O 26 '67
Spies every Sunday. il Time 90:61 N 10 '67
Stranger than spy fiction: the story of double agent Philby. por U S News 63:19-20 O 16 '67

PHILBY, Kim. See Philby, H. A. R.

PHILCO-Ford corporation
Philco-Ford installing twelve AUTODIN centers; automatic digital network. il Tech W 20:33 F 6 '67
What Vietnam is teaching Philco; transport and warehousing for the military. il Bsns W p 100+ S 9 '67

PHILHARMONIC-symphony society of New York

Birthday; concert at Philharmonic Hall and reception at the New York state theatre. New Yorker 43:19-20 D 23 '67

How to think about Leonard Bernstein. J. Roddy. Look 32:74-7 Ja 9 '68

Lively arts; from Ureli Corelli to Lenny in 125 historic years. R. Hemming. il Sr Schol 91:21-2 D 7 '67

Lively arts; Philharmonic guessing game: who will succeed Bernstein. R. Hemming. il Sr Schol 89:22 Ja 20 '67

Music to my ears; Leonard Bernstein conducts Verdi's Requiem. I. Kolodin. Sat R 50:50+ Ap 8 '67

Musical events:
Concert conducted by assistant conductors: S. Caduff, J. P. Izquierdo, and A. Lombard. W. Sargeant. New Yorker 43:126 Ap 1 '67
Concert in Philharmonic Hall, podium shared by K. Böhm and L. Bernstein. W. Sargeant. New Yorker 43:203-4 O 21 '67
Concerts in Philharmonic Hall (cont) W. Sargeant. New York 42:106 Ja 21 '67; 43:60+ Ja 13 '68
Performance in Philharmonic Hall, of Mendelssohn's Overture and incidental music for Shakespeare's Midsummer night's dream. W. Sargeant. New Yorker 43:159 Ap 8 '67
Performance of Berlioz's The damnation of Faust. W. Sargeant. New Yorker 43:193-4 D 2 '67
Performance of Britten's War requiem. W. Sargeant. New Yorker 43:134+ Ap 29 '67
Performance of Bruckner's Eighth symphony. W. Sargeant. New Yorker 43:170+ Ap 15 '67
Performance of Lukas Foss's Phorion and Mahler's Sixth symphony. W. Sargeant New Yorker 43:158+ My 6 '67

Philharmonic sweepstakes; search for Bernstein's successor. il Newsweek 70:114+ D 18 '67

Philharmonic's 125th. I. Kolodin. Sat R 50:34-5 D 23 '67

Report: New York; performance of La damnation de Faust. F. Merkling. Opera N 32:31 D 30 '67

Revival at the mueum; 125th anniversary. il Time 90:92+ D 15 '67

PHILIP, consort of Elizabeth II, queen of Great Britain

Prince Charles joins the royal men; with report by L. Gross. il pors Look 31:64-7+ Ap 18 '67

Queen Elizabeth and Philip: the good life they share after twenty years. A. Levy. por Good H 165:88-9+ N '67

PHILIP Morris, incorporated. See Morris, Philip, incorporated

PHILIPPINE folk art. See Folk art

PHILIPPINE SEA, Battles of the, 1944

Marianas turkey shoot; excerpt from Carrier admiral. J. J. Clark. il Am Heritage 18:26-9+ O '67

PHILIPPINES

Asian ally of the U.S. that's heading into trouble. il U S News 63:112+ N 13 '67

Atlantic report. Atlan 219:12 F '67

See also
Agriculture—Philippines
Arts and crafts—Philippines
Economic assistance in the Philippines
Education—Philippines
Hukbalahaps
Transportation—Philippines

Commercial treaties and agreements

U.S. and Philippines begin talks on future economic relations; statement, November 20, 1967. E. M. Braderman. Dept State Bul 58:11-12 Ja 1 '68

U.S. Philippines exchange notes on cotton textile arrangements. il Dept State Bul 57:511-14 O 16 '67

Description and travel

Philippines. J. Griffin. il Holiday 42:36-47+ Jl '67

Economic conditions

Report from Manila. M. Gart. il Fortune 76:69+ D '67

U.S.-Philippine relations: where we stand today; address, March 9, 1967. E. M. Braderman. Dept State Bul 56:660-4 Ap 24 '67

Foreign relations

Depth and durability of U.S.-Philippine relations; address, June 29, 1967. W. M. Blair, jr. Dept State Bul 57:203-7 Ag 14 '67

Philippine national policy; the United States and the Socialist countries; address, September 12, 1967. M. S. Enverga. Vital Speeches 34:10-11 O 15 '67

U.S.-Philippine relations: where we stand today; address, March 9, 1967. E. M. Braderman. Dept State Bul 56:660-4 Ap 24 '67

History

Insurrection, 1899-1901

War protest in wartime. J. R. Shirley. New Repub 156:15-16 My 6 '67

Politics and government

Bothered archipelago. il Time 89:24+ Je 2 '67

But Marcos is a persistent man. J. Lelyveld. il N Y Times Mag p28-9+ F 26 '67

Candidates under fire. Time 90:29 N 3 '67

See also
Elections—Philippines

Religious institutions and affairs

World around us (cont) Christian Cent 84:184-5, 450-1, 1269-70, 1576-7 F 8, Ap 5, O 4, D 6 '67

PHILIPS, Melody
(comp) Children's paperbacks. Library J 93:320-4 Ja 15 '68

PHILIPS of Eindhoven companies
Philips & the primitive. R. Ross-Skinner. il(p 47) Duns R 89:48+ F '67
Philips: international company cultivates basic research. J. Walsh. Science 157:1409-12 S 22 '67

PHILLIPS, Cabell
Johnson has the kind of troubles Truman had. N Y Times Mag p34-5+ O 22 '67

PHILLIPS, Carol
(ed) Perfect teeth; how can you have them? Vogue 150:130-1+ O 15 '67
(ed) See Stare, F. Doctor explodes some health-food myths

PHILLIPS, Christopher H.
President hails U.S. council's support of East-West trade; text of letter, March 3, 1967. Dept State Bul 56:696-7 My 1 '67

PHILLIPS, Gene D.
Berlin and Cannes. Cath World 206:87-9 N '67
No more ratings? America 117:560-1 N 11 '67

PHILLIPS, J. D.
Magnetic anomalies over the mid-Atlantic ridge near 27°N. bibliog Science 157:920-3 Ag 25 '67

PHILLIPS, Jackson
Business trends. See issues of Dun's review

PHILLIPS, James
How to find the waterfowl hotspots. Field & S 72:40-1+ N '67

PHILLIPS, John
Styron unlocked. Vogue 150:216-17+ D '67

PHILLIPS, John A.
Radical understanding. Christian Cent 84:869-70 Jl 5 '67

PHILLIPS, John David
Trying to package entrepreneurs. il por Bsns W p 175-6 Ja 28 '67

PHILLIPS, Joseph Dexter
Dollar invades Europe. Nation 205:242-5 S 18 '67

PHILLIPS, Olive
Cardboard star; drama. Plays 27:1-11 D '67

PHILLIPS, Robert Allan
Lasker awards. por Sci N 92:488-9 N 18 '67
Lasker largesse. por Newsweek 70:105A N 20 '67
Lasker lens. il por Time 90:57 N 17 '67

PHILLIPS, Samuel
Text of NASA summary of Phillips report. Tech W 20:39-40 Ap 24 '67

about
Apollo. New Repub 156:6 My 13 '67
Full Phillips report demanded by Rep. Ryan. Tech W 20:19 My 1 '67
Phillips report's tortured trail. Sci N 91:446 My 13 '67

PHILLIPS, Tom
Vietnam blues. N Y Times Mag p 12+ O 8 '67

PHILLIPS, W. D. See Ferguson, R. C. jt. auth.

PHILLIPS, William
Liberal anti-communism revisited. Commentary 44:56-8 S '67

PHILLIPS academy, Andover, Mass. See Private schools

PHILLIPS petroleum company
How they won the West, and more; engaged in at least eighty-five ventures in thirty-three countries. il Bsns W p 178-80+ Ja 28 '67

PHILLIPS screw. See Screws

PHILLIPS screw company
How Phillips fastens onto its profits; Posidriv, the new screw design. il Bsns W p 154+ N 11 '67

PHILODENDRONS
Grow philodendrons in many varieties. K. Berggrav. il Horticulture 45:20-1+ Mr '67

PHILOLAOS
Philolaos. E. Benson. il Craft Horiz 27:32-3+ S '67

PHILOSOPHERS
Basic writings of Mo Tzu, Hsün Tzu, and Han Fei Tzu, tr. by B. Watson. Review Sat R 50:61 Je 10 '67. W. C. Liu

PHILOSOPHY
Christology and contemporary philosophy. F. E. Crowe. Commonweal 87:242-7 N 24 '67
Does philosophy have a future? S. Hook. Sat R 50:21-3+ N 11 '67
Maritain asks some questions. J. Collins. America 118:29-32 Ja 13 '68
Philosophy in the Catholic university. J. Donceel; discussion. America 115:470-1; 116:99+, 580-2 O 22 '66, Ja 21, Ap 22 '67
Russell and Wittgenstein. M. Frayn. Commentary 43:68-75 My '67
  See also
Evolution
Knowledge
Life
Mathematics—Philosophy
Matter
Music—Philosophy and aesthetics
Nihilism (philosophy)
Political philosophy
Theism
Thomism
  Study and teaching
Thinking on one's knees; dice game to teach logic. il Sch & Soc 95:210-12 Ap 1 '67

PHILOSOPHY, American
Theology: made in U.S.A. T. F. O'Meara. Cath World 205:231-6 Jl '67

PHILOSOPHY, Chinese
Basic writings of Mo Tzu, Hsün Tzu, and Han Fei Tzu; tr. by B. Watson. Review Sat R 50:61 Je 10 '67. W. C. Liu

PHILOSOPHY, English
  See also
Russell, B. R.

PHILOSOPHY, German
Kant: philosophical correspondence 1759-1799, tr. by A. Zweig. Review Sat R 50:35 Ag 5 '67. P. A. Schilpp
Will to power, by F. Nietzsche. Review Sat R 50:34-5 Ag 5 '67. E. Weber

PHILOSOPHY, Greek
Jerusalem and Athens; beginning of the Bible and its Greek counterparts. L. Strauss. Commentary 43:45-57 Je '67

PHILOSOPHY, Latin American
  See also
Varona, E. J.

PHILOSOPHY, Moral. See Ethics

PHILOSOPHY, Political. See Political philosophy

PHILOSOPHY and religion
Judaism, Christianity, and the western tradition. H. Jonas. Commentary 44:61-8 N '67
Varieties of Jewish experience. M. Himmelfarb. Commentary 44:53-61 Jl '67
  See also
Faith and reason

PHILOSOPHY of education. See Education—Philosophy

PHILOSOPHY of nature. See Nature—Philosophy

PHILPOTT, Charles W. and Goldstein, M. A.
Sarcoplasmic reticulum of striated muscle: localization of potential calcium binding sites. bibliog Science 155:1019-21 F 24 '67

PHILPOTT, Gladys Oakes
Vietnamese school gongs sound; interview, ed. by R. D. Childs. NEA J 56:22-3 S '67

PHINIZY, Coles
Bora-Bora a paradise on a precipice. Sports Illus 28:24-31 Ja 15 '68

PHIPPS, David
Can Ford beat Ferrari again at Le Mans? Pop Sci 190:100-3 Je '67
—and Wright, J. W.
Indy '67; will new, wild, far-out cars shake Ford's grip? Pop Sci 190:118-21+ My '67

PHIPPS, Diana (Sternberg)
Diana Phipps in her London house. il pors Vogue 149:126-9+ Ja 15 '67

PHIPPS, Lillian (Bostwick)
Zest house. V. Lawford. il pors Vogue 149:138-43 F 15 '67

PHOBIAS
Barber shop phobia. Sci Digest 62:64 D '67

PHOENIX, Ariz.
Satellite service centers. F. Glendening. il Am City 82:102-4 My '67

  Police
Police records get an overhaul. A. L. Pasquan. Am City 82:12 Mr '67

  Sanitary affairs
We're switching to diesel-driven refuse trucks. J. E. Attebery. il Am City 82:79-80 Ag '67

  Street traffic
Make street signs big enough to read. C. E. Haley. il Am City 82:133-4 F '67

  Streets
Hot precoated aggregate eliminates sealcoat dust. C. McDonald. il Am City 82:110-12 F '67

  Water supply
Reservoirs don't have to be eyesores. R. N. Taylor. il Am City 82:71-2 Jl '67

PHOENIX (guided missile) See Guided missiles—Launching from airplanes

PHOENIX steel corporation
What makes Stanley run? R. Levy. Duns R 89:42-4 Ja '67

PHONETIC alphabet. See Alphabet

PHONIC method. See Reading—Study and teaching

PHONOCARDIOSCAN. See Medical instruments and apparatus

PHONOGRAPH
Introduction to audio components. il Consumer Rep 32:276-97 D '67
Sound ideas. L. Zide. See issues of American record guide
  See also
Loud speaking apparatus

  High fidelity sound systems
Affording high fidelity. I. Berger. Sat R 50:62 Je 24 '67

  Pickup
Phono cartridges. il Consumer Rep 32:148-53 Mr '67
Torture tests to check your cartridge. N. Eisenberg. Hi Fi 17:57 Mr '67
  See also
Phonograph—Stereophonic pickup

  Record changers
Automatic record changers. il Consumer Bul 50:29-33 My '67
Automatic transports; at New York's Consumer electronics show. I. Berger. Sat R 50:51 Jl 29 '67

  Stereophonic equipment
Gadgets for your stereo; are they any good? R. M. Benrey. il Pop Sci 190:140-3+ Ap '67
Stereo mods. N. Eisenberg. il Hi Fi 17:62-5 Ja '67

  Stereophonic pickup
Hi-fi product report; Shure M75 stereo phono cartridge. il Electr World 79:12+ Ja '68
New phono cartridge ranks among the best; ADC 10/E. Consumer Rep 33:4 Ja '68
What's new in phono cartridges? R. Angus. il Hi Fi 18:44-7 Ja '68

  Testing
Measuring tracking ability of phono cartridges. J. H. Kogen. il Electr World 77:26-8+ Je '67

  Tone arm
Skating; tone arm to slide toward the center of the turntable. H. Fantel. Opera N 31:33 Ja 7 '67

  Turntables
Best buy turntable changed but still good; AR XA. il Consumer Rep 32:244 My '67

PHONOGRAPH, Automobile. See Automobiles—Phonograph equipment

PHONOGRAPH, Portable
Portable stereo phonographs. il Consumer Rep 32:308-11 Je '67

PHONOGRAPH cabinets
How to build a coffee-table music center. H.
V. Huston. il Pop Sci 191:129-33+ Ag '67
PHONOGRAPH in education
New horizons for records and tapes. C.
Schicke. Sr Schol 90:sup 13 Mr 10 '67
Tune in the kids with records and films;
John Reed middle school, West Redding,
Conn. S. Jacoby and R. Lavigne. il Sr
Schol 91:sup9 D 7 '67
Using records in U.S. history classes; dis-
cography. L. Rappaport. il Sr Schol 91:sup
10 D 7 '67
PHONOGRAPH industry and trade
See also
Phonograph record industry
PHONOGRAPH record industry
Music in your mail box; Longines symphon-
ette mail order house. N. Pierce. il Par-
ents Mag 42:96-7 Ja '67
Record makers. R. Jacobson. il Sat R 50:67-9
Ag 26 '67
Record producers; electronic-age impresa-
rios. P. G. Davis. il Hi Fi 18:38-43 Ja '68
They call them compatible; mono/stereo discs.
N. Eisenberg. il Hi Fi 17:55-6 My '67
View from a record dealer's window. R.
Bialek. Am Rec G 34:92-4 O '67
See also
Atlantic recording corporation
Capitol records, incorporated

Czechoslovakia
Two-way traffic in the record mart. H. Halbreich. Hi Fi 18:20+ Ja '68

Great Britain
Going stereo; EMI's classical issues. T. Hein-
itz. Sat R 50:63 Je 24 '67
See also
London records, incorporated

Italy
RFTM, the new entrepreneurs; recording
from the manuscripts. W. Weaver. Hi Fi
17:26+ S '67

Russia
Russians have arrived, thanks to Melodiya/
Angel. B. Jacobson. Hi Fi 17:67-8 Mr '67
PHONOGRAPH records
Beecham discography. W. Botsford. Am
Rec G 33:745-7, 930-2, 1009-12, 1078-81; 34:
150-1, 244-5 My-Ag, O-N '67
Bullfight: N. Mailer's Book/record album. W.
D. Patterson. Sat R 51:105 Ja 13 '68
Concert records (cont) D. Watt. New Yorker
43:161-2+ Mr 11 '67
Discovering great music; who, what, which;
discography, ed. by R. Hemming. Sr Schol
90:21-3 My 5 '67
DIScussions. R. Hemming and others. See
issues of Senior scholastic
Favorite pioneer recording artists. J. Walsh.
See issues of Hobbies
Historical records. A. Favia-Artsay. See is-
sues of Hobbies
Imperfect and nonpareil; Toscanini record-
ings. R. Gelatt. Reporter 37:39-40 D 28 '67
Lighter side. See issues of High fidelity in-
corporating Musical America
LP as program maker. Hi Fi 17:61 Ja '67
Melodies for merrymaking. il Seventeen 26:
22+ D '67
Mid-month recordings. See issues of Satur-
day review
Music in ancient cities, all eloquence and de-
light: Hanover, Venice. J. Noble. il Hi Fi
17:106-7 Ja '67
Music in the round. Discus. See issues of
Harper's magazine
Music: record reviews. H. Kupferberg. See
issues of Atlantic
New records in review. B. H. Haggin. See
issues of Yale review
On CBS, Argo, and Music guild: Messiaen,
slow-motion romanticism. A. Cohn. Am
Rec G 34:229-30+ N '67
On the record; fine records issued in the last
half of 1967. il Newsweek 71:83-4 Ja 22 '68
On the record: Music. P. L. Miller. See is-
sues of Library journal
Once and future Bernstein; new recordings.
R. Gelatt. Reporter 36:49-51 F 23 '67
Op. 1 from Opus one; Erb: Diversion for
two. J. Diether. Am Rec G 33:497-8 F '67
Opening up the romantic repertoire; works by
Hummel and Spohr. Discus. Harper 235:99-
100 Jl '67
Other reviews, including stereo. See issues
of American record guide
Other side. T. Heinitz. See occasional issues
of Saturday review

Phonograph records. W. F. Grueninger. See
issues of Consumer bulletin
Really new new music from RCA Victrola.
A. Cohn. Am Rec G 34:288-9 D '67
Recommended recordings, Christmas 1967;
comp. by L. Cohn. Sat R 50:49 D 16 '67
Record preview; annual report. Hi Fi 17:64-7
S '67
Record reviews. See issues of Consumer re-
ports
Recordings. M. Mayer. See issues of Esquire
Recordings in review. I. Kolodin. See issues
of Saturday review
Recordings reports: miscellaneous LPs. I.
Kolodin. See issues of Saturday review
Records (cont) B. Boretz. Nation 204:221-2;
205:603-5 F 13, D 4 '67
Records. B. H. Haggin. Commonweal 87:86-7,
206, 383-4 O 20, N 17, D 22 '67
Records. W. F. Rickenbacker. Nat R 19:
866+, 1344-6 Ag 8, N 28 '67
Records 1967. B. Boretz. Nation 205:698-700
D 25 '67
Sight and sound. L. Hershey. See issues of
McCall's
Sir Thomas Beecham: a half century of re-
cordings. W. Botsford. Am Rec G 33:742-5
My '67
Something to remember them by; selection
from the collaboration of H. Dietz and
A. Schwartz. I. Kolodin. il Sat R 50:60
F 11 '67
Spotlight! popular; classical. E. Miller. See
issues of Seventeen
Spring records. B. Boretz. Nation 204:604-6,
669-70 My 8, 22 '67
Ten years of recordings; comp. by G. Jellinek.
Sat R 50:50-60 Ag 26 '67
Three new discs continue Columbia's Stravin-
sky canon; Symphony in E flat, opera
Mavra, Cantata and In memoriam Dylan
Thomas. D. Hamilton. Hi Fi 17:69-70 Ag
'67
Top ten, and how they get there; selections
from Billboard. Hi Fi 17:49 F '67
Twelve tones of Christmas; Columbia's re-
leases of far-out music. il Time 90:52 D 8
'67
Via Nonesuch, a trip to another brave new
world. A. Cohn. il Am Rec G 34:190-1 N '67
View from a record dealer's window. R.
Bialek. Am Rec G 34:92-4 O '67
Year's best recordings; comp. by R. Freed.
Sat R 50:91-5 N 25 '67
See also
Copyright—Phonograph records
Libraries—Phonograph and phonograph
records
Time, incorporated

Arias
Arrivederci, Gerald; Homage to Gerald Moore
discs. H. Weinstock. il Sat R 50:62 D 2 '67
Prima donna: Price. G. L. Mayer. il Am
Rec G 34:188-9 N '67
Records:
Bellini/Donizetti: Duets. Opera N 32:30
N 4 '67
Beniamino Gigli. Opera N 31:34 F 4 '67
Concert arias. Opera N 32:30 S 23 '67
Erika Köth. Opera N 32:34 Ja 6 '68
Five arias from Verdi operas. Opera N
31:34 F 25 '67
Gérard Souzay. Opera N 31:34 Ap 8 '67
Geraint Evans. Opera N 31:30 Je 10 '67
Gwyneth Jones. Opera N 31:34 Ap 8 '67
Jeannette Scovotti. Opera N 31:32 Mr 18 '67
Leontyne Price. Opera N 31:34 F 4 '67
Leontyne Price. Opera N 32:30 N 4 '67
Marcel Journet. Opera N 31:32 Mr 4 '67
Nancy Tatum. Opera N 31:34 F 4 '67
Norman Treigle. Opera N 32:34 D 16 '67
Pilar Lorengar. Opera N 31:32 Mr 4 '67
Sena Jurinac. Opera N 32:30 S 9 '67
Teresa Stich-Randall. Opera N 32:34 D 16
'67
Walter Widdop. Opera N 31:32 Mr 4 '67

Austrian music
Vintage Strauss. R. Freed. Sat R 50:88 F 25
'67

Ballet music
Efrem Kurtz's balletic Tchaikovsky, a subtle
instinct for musical drama; Swan Lake.
G. L. Mayer. Am Rec G 34:240 N '67
Gennady Rozhdestvensky conducts three per-
formances of Prokofiev ballet music, in-
cluding Cinderella. H. Glass. il Am Rec G
34:96-9 O '67
Rite of spring like none other. H. Glass. il
Am Rec G 34:59 S '67

PHONOGRAPH records—*Continued*

Band music
New voice from the barrios; Afro-Latin music of the Eddie Palmieri ensemble. R. F. Thompson. il Sat R 50:53-5+ O 28 '67
Sweet and swinging. F. Reynolds. See issues of American record guide

Blues (music)
See Phonograph records—Negro music

Canadian music
Music and musicians of Canada. P. Ashley. il Sat R 50:66-7 Ap 29 '67
To mark Canada's centenary, great singers of her past. G. Movshon. il Hi Fi 17:63 Jl '67

Cantatas
Bach bargains, nine cantatas on five discs. P. L. Miller. Am Rec G 33:570+ Mr '67
Records:
Hodie. Opera N 32:34 D 23 '67

Catalogs
Early Victor photographs and catalogs. J. Walsh. il Hobbies 72:36+ Ja '68 (to be cont)

Cello music
Elgar's Cello concerto; recorded by Jacqueline Du Pré. J. Diether. Am Rec G 33:550-1 Mr '67

Chamber music
First complete recording of the Brahms trios and other chamber works. M. N. Kanny. il Am Rec G 34:208-10+ N '67
On crossroads, a superb Tchaikovsky serenade. M. N. Kanny. Am Rec G 34:60 S '67

Childrens records
Christmas records for the young, 1967. A. Franklin. Sat R 50:52-4 D 9 '67
On and off the avenue (cont) New Yorker 43:127-8+ D 9 '67
Recordings for young people. J. L. Limbacher. See second issue of each month of Library journal
Recordings (cont of) Recordings for young people. J. L. Limbacher. See second issue of each month of Library journal
Words only; especially for children. S. Potter. Am Rec G 34:330-2+ D '67

Choral music
Gustav Holst; Argo releases. J. Diether. Am Rec G 33:1002-4 Jl '67
In celebration, Stravinsky's 85th. C. J. Luten. Am Rec G 33:1008 Jl '67
Records:
Symphony of psalms. Opera N 32:34 D 30 '67
Telefunken again, and a nomination for the outstanding choral record of the year: Chormusik der gegenwart. A. Cohn. Am Rec G 33:719 My '67

Christmas music
Holiday recordings for family enjoyment. Good H 165:191 D '67
Music in celebration of the Nativity. J. Diether; J. W. Barker. il Am Rec G 34:282+ D '67
Yule, Jul, and Julie. I. Kolodin. Sat R 50:48-9 D 16 '67

Church music
Monteverdi's Vespers; two versions that make a lovely sound. B. Jacobson. il Hi Fi 17:61-2 Jl '67

Collectors and collecting
Collector, insatiable lusts; a discography. M. Kreuger. Am Rec G 33:536-40 F '67
Holcman collection. J. Bowen. il Sat R 50:53-5 My 27 '67
Records:
Historical records. M. De Schauensee. Opera N 32:34 N 25 '67
Suggestions and cautions. M. Kreuger. Am Rec G 33:452+ Ja '67

Concertos
Brahms by Arrau and Giulini, unorthodox, but superbly executed. M. N. Kanny. Am Rec G 34:206 N '67
For Handel's organ works, Archive thinks of everything. N. Broder. il Hi Fi 17:78C-78D F '67
Four concertos from Szeryng mark a new star status. P. Hart. il Hi Fi 17:78D-79 F '67

Neoclassic delights: the music of Vittorio Rieti. A. Cohn. Am Rec G 33:817-18 My '67
Op. 1 from Opus one; Schubel: Insected surfaces. J. Diether. Am Rec G 33:497-8 F '67
Two concerti: Gary Graffman. J. Diether. Am Rec G 33:472-4 F '67

Czech music
From the banks of the Vltava. O. Daniel. Sat R 50:76-7 F 25 '67

Dance music
New voice from the barrios; Afro-Latin music of the Eddie Palmieri ensemble. R. F. Thompson. il Sat R 50:53-5+ O 28 '67
Records for teachers. E. LeMone. See issues of Dance magazine
Sweet and swinging. F. Reynolds. See issues of American record guide
See also
Phonograph records—Ballet music

Danish music
Denmark, post Nielsen. O. Daniel. Sat R 50:52 D 16 '67

Documentary records
Probes, mostly superficial. G. Lees. il Hi Fi 17:102 Ap '67

Educational applications
See Phonograph in education

Electronic music
Electronic music on records: the medium is the message. P. G. Davis. il Hi Fi 17:108-10 O '67
Electronic music with nary a blurp or a whine or a krontch. A. Frankenstein. il Hi Fi 17:75-6 D '67
New sound of music; two discs issued by University of Illinois. O. Daniel. Sat R 50:65 O 28 '67

English music
Britain's avant-garde; new music from Britain. P. L. Miller. Am Rec G 33:623 Ap '67
Britain's musical revival. H. Kupferberg. Atlan 219:135-8 Ap '67
English tone poems: the minor graces, and some major ones. B. Jacobson. Hi Fi 17:69-70 My '67
Music of Shakespeare's time; a sampling of recent discs. B. Jacobson. il Hi Fi 17:63 D '67

Flute music
Three flutists. M. A. Silver. il Am Rec G 34:104-5 O '67

Folk music
Folk music. G. Lees; O. B. Brummell. Hi Fi 17:118 S '67
Folk music. H. Yurchenco. See issues of American record guide
Folk music (cont) O. B. Brummell. Hi Fi 17:112+ Mr; 112+ Ap; 106+ My; 106+ Je; 92 Jl; 110 Ag; 138-9 N; 134 D '67; 18:108-9 Ja '68
Folk music. O. B. Brummell; J. S. Wilson. Hi Fi 17:136 Ja '67
Recordings reports: folk and blues LPs (cont) L. Cohn. Sat R 50:86 F 25; 54 D 30 '67

French music
Stuff of legend; P. Bernac recording of F. Poulenc songs. R. Gelatt. Reporter 37:45 S 7 '67

Guitar music
Master of the solo guitar in music of modern masters. S. Fleming. Hi Fi 17:89 N '67

Harpsichord music
See also
Phonograph records—Concertos

Hindu music
Rock, raga and the cop-out. G. Lees. il Hi Fi 17:82-3 Jl '67

History
Re-coupled Victor records. J. Walsh. il Hobbies 72:37-8+ Je; 36-7 Jl '67
Twenty-four best Columbia records. J. Walsh. il Hobbies 72:37-8 Ap; 37-8 My '67

Hungarian music
Marvelous music of Hungary. O. B. Brummell. il Hi Fi 17:85 Ja '67

PHONOGRAPH records—*Continued*

Indian music (East Indian)

Family of twang; sitar recordings. F. V. Grunfeld. Reporter 36:40 Ap 20 '67
Raves for Ravi & Yehudi. il Time 90:64 Ag 4 '67
Recordings; Yehudi Menuhin and Ravi Shanker. M. Mayer. Esquire 68:84+ S '67

Instrumental music

Recommended recordings. J. Krance. House B 109:52 Ap '67

Irish music

More piper's tunes. R. L. Tobin. Sat R 50: 47 Jl 15 '67
Ring of the Piper's tune. R. L. Tobin. Sat R 50:72-3 Mr 25 '67

Italian music

Music for all seasons; Monteverdi discography. R. Gelatt. Reporter 37:59-60 Jl 13 '67

Jazz music

Bechet the prophet. M. Williams. Sat R 50: 64-5 F 11 '67
Jazz. J. S. Wilson. See issues of High fidelity incorporating Musical America
Jazz and the vibraphone. M. Williams. il Sat R 50:78-9 N 11 '67
Jazz orchestra; Thad Jones-Mel Lewis alliance. B. Korall. il Sat R 50:116-17+ Mr 11 '67
Jazz records (cont) W. Balliett. New Yorker 43:221-2+ N 25 '67
King of the Savoy; C. Webb albums. B. Korall. il Sat R 50:51+ D 30 '67
Month's jazz. D. Heckman. See issues of American record guide
Mostly modernists (cont) M. Williams. Sat R 50:120 Mr 11; 75 Ap 29; 77 My 13; 91 Je 10; 49 Jl 15; 45 Jl 29; 81 Ag 26; 71 S 30; 59 D 2 '67
Portrait of Buddy; B. Rich recordings. B. Korall. Sat R 50:64-5 My 27 '67
Recordings reports: jazz LPs. S. Dance. See issues of Saturday review
Strayhorn and the Duke. B. Korall. Sat R 50:71-2 S 16 '67
Who is Roger Kellaway? B. Korall. Sat R 50:66-7 O 28 '67

Jewish music

Art of the cantor; cantorial recordings. P. Kwartin. Sat R 50:91 F 25 '67

Laments

Polish musician for our time; K. Penderecki's threnody. To the victims of Hiroshima. R. Gelatt. Reporter 37:53-4 N 2 '67

Mass

Records:
Haydn: Mass in time of war, and Lord Nelson mass. Opera N 23:34 Ja 20 '68
Missa solemnis. Opera N 31:34 My 13 '67
Mozart: Coronation mass, and Mass in C minor. Opera N 32:34 Ja 13 '68

Mazurkas

Chopin's mazurkas: a new miraculous reading from Rubinstein. H. Goldsmith. il Hi Fi 17:73-4 Ap '67

Medieval music

Project three, Monteverdi, etc. J. W. Barker. Am Rec G 34:135-6 O '67

Moving picture music

Ivan the Terrible, Prokofiev's music towers grandly alone; landmark in film history. S. Lowe. il Hi Fi 17:80-1 S '67
Jazz at the movies. M. Williams. Sat R 50: 49 Jl 15 '67
Musical souvenir of a famous collaboration. A. Cohn. il Am Rec G 34:196-7 N '67
Recordings reports: stage and screen. R. Sherman. Sat R 50:52 Jl 29; 56 D 2 '67
Words by Shakespeare; music by Roman Vlad; highlights from Castellani's Romeo and Juliet. J. Diether. Am Rec G 33:529 F '67

Musical comedies, revues, etc.

Collector's guide to American show music. F. Bowers. House & Gard 132:12+ Ag '67
Recordings reports: stage and screen. R. Sherman. Sat R 50:52 Jl 29; 56 D 2 '67
Records:
Gasparone. Opera N 31:34 Ja 7 '67

Negro music

Blues and more blues. M. Williams. Sat R 50:59 D 2 '67
Recordings reports: folk and blues LPs (cont) L. Cohn. Sat R 50:86 F 25; 54 D 30 '67

Operas

All-star Faust: Sutherland, Corelli, Ghiaurov. G. Movshon. Hi Fi 17:70+ Mr '67
Armchair opera; Wagner on records. R. Gelatt. Reporter 36:44+ Ap 6 '67
As before, but even better: Katerina Ismailova. G. L. Mayer. Am Rec G 45:14 S '67
Authentic Prince Igor; Queen of spades. H. Weinstock. il Sat R 50:84 N 25 '67
Un ballo in maschera. H. Glass. il Am Rec G 33:904-5 Je '67
Batch of one-act operas, in both ancient and modern taste. C. L. Osborne. Hi Fi 17:106 F '67
Beatrice di Tenda; Joan Sutherland in the title role. G. L. Mayer. il Am Rec G 34: 180-2 N '67
Böhm's Bayreuth Tristan. R. Lawrence. Sat R 50:63 Ja 28 '67
Britten and the bard, a new Midsummer night. D. Hamilton. il Hi Fi 17:128-9 O '67
Britten's Dream of Shakespeare. R. Jacobson. Sat R 50:85 N 25 '67
Butterfly by Barbirolli. R. Jacobson. il Sat R 50:56-7+ O 28 '67
Concert records; Donizetti's Lucrezia Borgia D. Watt. New Yorker 43:161-2+ Mr 11 '67
Così nearly complete; Philips world series's release. R. Jacobson. Sat R 50:85 F 25 '67
Deutsche Grammophon's Die Walküre. H. Glass. Am Rec G 33:734-6 My '67
Don Giovanni. H. Glass. Am Rec G 33:562-4 Mr '67
Donizetti's Daughter, raised by the Bonynges. E. Greenfield. il Hi Fi 17:24+ O '67
Falstaff and Faust. Discus. Harper 234:125-6 My '67
Fantastic world of Wagner. R. Gibson. House & Gard 132:22-3 D '67
Fischer-Dieskau's Don. H. Glass. il Am Rec G 34:18-21 S '67
Freni-Gedda Elisir; new release by Angel. R. Lawrence. Sat R 50:56 O 28 '67
From Butterfly to Wozzeck. H. Kupferberg. il Atlan 220:124+ N '67
From the house of the dead; stereo première. R. Jones. il Am Rec G 33:992-6 Jl '67
Ghost of Semiramide. H. Weinstock. Sat R 50:71 Ja 28 '67
Giulio Cesare the operatic genius of Handel made plain. C. L. Osborne. il Hi Fi 18:63-5 Ja '68
Gustav Holst; Argo releases. J. Diether. Am Rec G 33:1002-4 Jl '67
High emotions, radiant melos, in a first Beatrice di Tenda. P. J. Smith. il Hi Fi 17:76+ D '67
Janáček on Dostoevsky; recording of From the house of the dead. H. Weinstock. Sat R 50:63 My 27 '67
Janacek's House of the dead: the problem of sung drama. C. L. Osborne. il Hi Fi 17: 75-6 Je '67
Karajan's Walküre. I. Kolodin. il Sat R 50: 67+ Mr 25 '67
Karajan's Walkuere and a brave new Ring begins. C. L. Osborne. Hi Fi 17:67-9 My '67
London Faust. R. Lawrence. il Sat R 50:61-2 Je 24 '67
Many facets of Benjamin Britten; Midsummer night's dream. H. Kupferberg. il Atlan 220: 126+ D '67
Monteverdi's Poppea, for the first time near perfectly realized. J. Noble. il Hi Fi 17:70-1 My '67
Montserrat Caballé in La Traviata. P. L. Miller. il Am Rec G 34:194-5 N '67
New flight for La Rondine. I. Kolodin. Sat R 50:69+ S 30 '67
New Handel Hercules. H. Weinstock. Sat R 50:67 S 30 '67
Old operas and real music; bel canto operas and new recording of Tristan und Isolde. Discus. Harper 234:145-6 Mr '67
On London, the first recording of Rossini's Semiramide. P. L. Miller. il Am Rec G 33:372-5 Ja '67
Once around the Ring; London recording. H. Kupferberg. il Atlan 219:119-20 F '67
Opera production of Handel's Julius Caesar. S. Lincoln. il Am Rec G 34:268-72 D '67
Operas: six all-time thrillers. Discus. Harper 235:134+ D '67
Orfero ed Euridice. P. L. Miller. il Am Rec G 33:558-9 Mr '67
Orfeo out of Orphée; Bach guild recording. H. Weinstock. Sat R 50:81 F 25 '67

PHONOGRAPH records—Operas—*Continued*
Perhaps the most nearly complete perform-
ance we shall ever hear: London's Faust.
P. L. Miller. il Am Rec G 33:620-2 Ap '67
Pierre Boulez conducts Wozzeck. A. Sperber.
il Am Rec G 33:1064-6 Ag '67
Puccini's La rondine, the charm of delicate
felicities. G. Movshon. Hi Fi 17:127-8 O '67
Purcell omnibus: Dido & Aeneas, and The
Indian queen. G. L. Mayer. il Am Rec G
33:464-6 F '67
Recordings. M. Mayers. Esquire 67:54+ Mr '67
Records:
   Britten: A midsummer night's dream.
      Opera N 32:34 Ja 13 '68
   Cavalleria rusticana. Opera N 32:30 S 23
      '67
   L'elisir d'amore. Opera N 32:34 D 16 '67
   Die entführung aus dem serail. Opera N
      32:38 D 9 '67
   Der freischütz. Opera N 32:34 D 23 '67
   From the house of the dead, and The
      Makropoulos case. Opera N 32:34 D 16
      '67
   Handel: Giulio Cesare. Opera N 32:34 Ja 20
      '68
   L'incoronazione di Poppea Opera N 31:30
      Je 10 '67
   Katerina Ismailova. Opera N 32:34 N 25
      '67
   Madama Butterfly. Opera N 32:30 O 14
      '67
   Mavra and Les noces; Pulcinella; Oedipus
      Rex; Persephone; Symphony of psalms.
      Opera N 32:34 D 30 '67
   Le nozze di Figaro. Opera N 32:30 O 14
      '67
   Queen of spades. Opera N 32:38 D 9 '67
   Il re pastore, and Don Giovanni. Opera
      N 32:34 Ja 6 '68
   La rondine. Opera N 32:30 S 9 '67
   Der Rosenkavalier. Opera N 32:34 Ja 6 '68
   Tosca. Opera N 32:30 N 4 '67
   La Traviata. Opera N 32:34 N 25 '67
   Wozzeck. Opera N 32:38 D 9 '67
   Zar und zimmermann. Opera N 32:30 S
      23 '67
La rondine: a case that needed presenting.
P. L. Miller. Am Rec G 34:310 D '67
Russians have arrived, thanks to Melodiya/
Angel. B. Jacobson. Hi Fi 17:67-8 Mr '67
Sergei Prokofiev: simultaneously, his last
three operas: The betrothal in a monas-
tery; War and peace; and the story of a
real man. P. L. Miller. il Am Rec G 33:468-
70+ F '67
Sophisticated children's opera: The happy
prince. P. L. Miller. Am Rec G 33:158 F
'67
Tchaikovsky's Pique dame: a spine-chiller
from today's Bolshoi. C. L. Osborne. il
Hi Fi 17:87-8 N '67
Three views of Wozzeck. G. Perle. il Sat R
50:54-5 D 2 '67
Tristan without technology; Deutsche Grammophon recording. S. Kanfer. Life 62:22 F
17 '67
Triumph! London's new Elektra. G. L.
Mayer. il Am Rec G 34:274-7 D '67
Wagner operas on records: a discography
(cont) C. L. Osborne. Hi Fi 17:44+ Ja '67

Oratorios
From Telefunken, a commemorative first rec-
ording of G. P. Telemann's The day of
judgment. P. L. Miller. il Am Rec G 33:
906-7 Je '67
Messiah. J. Diether. Am Rec G 33:630-3 Ap
'67
Messiah by Mackerras. H. Weinstock. Sat R
50:70 Ap 29 '67
RCA Victor, Handel's Hercules. J. W. Bark-
er. il Am Rec G 34:184-7 N '67
Records:
   Creation. Opera N 31:34 Mr 25 '67
   Dream of Gerontius. Opera N 31:34 Ja 7
      '67
   Easter oratorio. Opera N 31:34 Mr 25 '67
   Messiah. Opera N 31:32 Mr 18 '67
   Messiah. Opera N 32:34 D 23 '67

Orchestral music
Dallas rediscovered; Rachmaninoff Symphonic
dances. M. N. Kanny. il Am Rec G 33:1073
Ag '67
Execution of Stepan Razin; Shostakovich
score composed to a Yevtushenko text. il
Am Rec G 34:12-14 S '67
Four Tchaikovsky suites. C. J. Lutten. il Am
Rec G 33:555 Mr '67
Koussevitzky returns, and the lesson is of
passion lavishly spent. L. Marcus. Hi Fi
17:79-80 F '67

Last years of Serge Koussevitzky. R. Sabin.
Am Rec G 34:22-3 S '67
Maestro at 100; Toscanini treasury of his-
toric broadcasts. C. J. Luten. il Am Rec G
33:720-1 My '67
New sound of music; Stockhausen-Pender-
ecki-Brown-Pousseur record. O. Daniel.
Sat R 50:64 O 28 '67
The planets, Sir Adrian's fourth and finest.
J. Diether. Am Rec G 33:785-6 My '67
Recordings reports: orchestral LPs. I. Kolo-
din. See issues of Saturday review
So soon, a classic: Le marteau sans maitre
(The masterless hammer) P. L. Miller. Am
Rec G 33:639 Ap '67
Toscanini reissues. G. J. Luten. Am Rec G
33:998-1000 Jl '67
Toscanini treasury of historic broadcasts.
B. H. Haggin. Hi Fi 17:73-5 Je '67
Treasury of Toscanini broadcasts; NBC sym-
phony orchestra album. R. Lawrence. Sat R
50:61 My 27 '67
Want to feel like a prince? Scheherazade.
M. N. Kanny. Am Rec G 34:52 S '67

Passion music
Penderecki, a mighty voice from Poland; St
Luke passion. B. Jacobson. Hi Fi 17:74-5 Ap
'67
Polish musician for our time: K. Penderecki's
Passion according to St Luke. R. Gelatt.
Reporter 37:53-4 N 2 '67
Polish passion; new recording K. Pender-
ecki's Passion according to Saint Luke.
Discus. Harper 236:84 Ja '68
Real sleeper from Nonesuch; St John passion.
J. W. Barker. Am Rec G 33:492-3 F '67
Records:
   St John passion; St Mark passion.
      Opera N 31:34 Mr 25 '67
   St Matthew passion. Opera N 31:34 Mr
      25 '67

Piano music
Arrivederci, Gerald; Homage to Gerald Moore
discs. H. Weinstock. il Sat R 50:62 D 2
'67
Collage of genius, the hexameron. R. Kam-
merer. Am Rec G 33:950-1 Je '67
Contents of Kontarsky; K. Stockhausen's
Complete piano music. O. Daniel. il Sat R
50:47+ D 30 '67
Convincing and compelling, Alicia de Lar-
rocha. S. Sell. Am Rec G 33:777 My '67
Cziffra: the virtuoso recital of the century?
R. Kammerer. Am Rec G 33:790 My '67
From Epic, certainly one of the greatest
piano recordings ever made: Alicia de Lar-
rocha on piano. W. Botsford. il Am Rec G
34:222 N '67
Gilt-edged aural securities. A. Cohn. Am
Rec G 33:731-2 My '67
Heroic pianists. Discus. Harper 235:138+ N
'67
Horowitz live (and otherwise) R. Kammerer.
Am Rec G 33:1005 Jl '67
Josef Hofmann, memorable Chopin: Piano
concerto no. 2. R. Kammerer. il Am Rec
G 33:556-7 Mr '67
Keyboard music by two dozen (!) Americans.
A. Cohn. Am Rec G 33:733 My '67
Massive documentary release, the Everest
archive of piano music. R. Kammerer. Am
Rec G 33:728-31 My '67
Masters of the piano, in recordings of rare
provenance. R. Lewenthal. il Hi Fi 18:65-7
Ja '68
On four records from two labels, seven works
by Janáček. R. Jones; A. Cohn. il Am
Rec G 33:378-84 Ja '67
Outstanding: Bishop alone: Beethoven's
Piano sonatas. M. N. Kanny. Am Rec G
33:549-50 Mr '67
Peter Serkin: it is what the music does for
him. R. Sabin. il Am Rec G 34:54 S '67
Piano rolls and travesties. Discus. Harper
234:119-21 F '67
Records: Music of Arnold Schoenberg. B.
Boretz. Nation 204:349-50 Mr 13 '67
Report on a marathon: Mozart's Piano con-
certi. S. Sell. Am Rec G 33:802+ My '67
Variations on a tape by Vladimir: the Horo-
witz concerts. S. Kanfer. Life 62:13 Je 23 '67
See also
Phonograph records—Concertos

Polish music
Avant-garde in Russia and Poland. Discus.
Harper 235:130+ S '67
Four works from Poland, one of them a
masterpiece. A. Cohn. il Am Rec G 34:26-
7 S '67

PHONOGRAPH records—*Continued*

Portuguese music

Window newly opened: music from Portugal's Golden age. R. P. Morgan. Hi Fi 17:78+ D '67

Prices

Are records too cheap? G. Lees. Hi Fi 17:95 Je '67

Classical recordings at budget prices. C. S. Knight. Am Home 71:12+ Ja '68

Latest in low-price records. il Changing T 21:31-2 My; 19-20 N '67

Recording

Another imprimatur for Mahler; Das klagende lied. J. Diether. Hi Fi 17:24+ S '67

Best seat. H. Fantel. Opera N 31:33 F 18 '67

Blasts and whispers. H. Fantel. Opera N 31:30 Mr 18 '67

Britten's fiery furnace makes a glorious noise. P. G. Davis. il Hi Fi 17:16+ S '67

Conductor Szell at the keyboard; to record the Mozart piano quartets. S. Fleming. Hi Fi 17:30+ D '67

DGG records Mozart's Don on its native grounds. J. Higgins. il Hi Fi 17:16+ Je '67

Decca/London on a mission westward; recording conductor Zubin Mehta and the Los Angeles philharmonic. R. Gelatt. il Hi Fi 17:18+ Jl '67

Dolby system of recording. L'histoire du soldat conducted by Leopold Stokowski. J. Diether. il Am Rec G 33:624-6 Ap '67

Donizetti's Daughter, raised by the Bonynges. E. Greenfield. il Hi Fi 17:24+ O '67

Enoch light, a different brigade; recording Monteverdi's Scherzi musicali. P. G. Davis. Hi Fi 17:18+ Je '67

Georg Solti's full score; twenty years on record. C. Reid. il Hi Fi 17:66-70 Ja '67

He makes music pay at CBS; G. Lieberson. il Bsns W p 106-7+ O 7 '67

In prospect from Previn, a Vaughan Williams cycle; RCA Victor's project. E. Greenfield. il Hi Fi 17:24+ D '67

In this harem, English spoken; Mozart's Abduction from the harem. E. Greenfield. il Hi Fi 18:12+ Ja '68

Mahler by the Berrys and Bernstein. P. G. Davis. Hi Fi 18:24 Ja '68

Mix-master to the Beatles. il Time 89:67 Je 16 '67

Morals of the microphone. H. Fantel. Opera N 31:32 Ap 1 '67

New ring en route. Karajan's Walkuere. P. Moor. il Hi Fi 17:16+ Mr '67

Nonesuch: more Dolby: ...and a postscript by our sonic specialist. L. Zide. Am Rec G 33:627-8 Ap '67

Open season for opera. W. Weaver. Hi Fi 17:40+ O '67

Pretty Purdie. New Yorker 43:52-6 N 18 '67

Price and Previn form a team. E. Tiegel. il Hi Fi 17:18+ Ag '67

Record producers; electronic-age impresarios. P. G. Davis. il Hi Fi 18:38-43 Ja '68

Recordist Peter Willemoës and other royal Danes; recording Danish music with Royal orchestra. R. Naur. il Hi Fi 17:14+ Ap '67

Ring resounding, by J. Culshaw. Review Am Rec G 34:322+ O '67. C. J. Luten Hi Fi il 17:18+ D '67. G. Movshon

Ring twice and ask for Mario; recording of Tosca at Rome. C. Raeburn. il Hi Fi 17:56-7 Ag '67

Second conductor; man in charge of the immensely technical complexities. H. Fantel. Opera N 31:33 F 4 '67

Simon & Garfunkel in action. M. Ames. il Hi Fi 17:62-6 N '67

Some reflections on recording the Boulez Wozzeck. T. Z. Shepard. il Am Rec G 33:1067-72 Ag '67

Sonic showcase. R. D. Darrell. See issues of High fidelity incorporating Musical America

Stravinsky and the microphone. D. Hamilton. il Hi Fi 17:56-60 Je '67

Szell and company at Abbey road. E. Greenfield. il Hi Fi 17:28+ N '67

Today's stereo sound: how they capture it on records. R. M. Benrey. il Pop Sci 191: 84-8 Ag '67

Two new worlds, the LSO. Kertesz, Ormandy. E. Greenfield. Hi Fi 17:21+ F '67

What happened since LP. G. Lieberson. il Sat R 50:61-3 Ag 26 '67

Young Americans with Russian medals; RCA Victor's roundup. P. G. Davis. Hi Fi 17:20+ Ja '67

Unauthorized recording

Don't be fooled by pirated records. Good H 164:154 F '67

Verdi and the pirates; pirated recordings. G. Fitzgerald. il Opera N 31:14-15 F 25 '67

Reissues

Canadian centennial issue. A. Favia-Artsay. il Hobbies 72:35+ S '67

Collectors' LP of Caruso. A. Favia-Artsay. il Hobbies 72:36 O '67

Columbia's new budget label; Odyssey's sources of reissues. R. Freed. Sat R 50: 74+ Ja 28 '67

Columbia's Odyssey label starts a propitious voyage; Goberman records reissued. S. Fleming. Hi Fi 17:75-6 Ap '67

Historical records; Russian singers of the past. A. Favia-Artsay. il Hobbies 72:35+ Jl '67

Historical records; souvenirs of Italian opera. A. Favia-Artsay. il Hobbies 72:35+ Ja '68

I can hear it now reissued. R. L. Tobin. Sat R 50:52 D 16 '67

Latest in low-price records. il Changing T 21:31-2 My '67

Odyssey; Columbia's new budget line. M. A. Silver. Am Rec G 33:636-8 Ap '67

Piano rolls and travesties. Discus. Harper 234:119-21 F '67

Records:
Golden age, and Canadian centennial. Opera N 31:30 Je 10 '67
Historical reissues. Opera N 32:34 Ja 20 '68

Repeat performance. P. G. Davis. See issues of High fidelity incorporating Musical America

Toscanini reissues. C. J. Luten. Am Rec G 33:998-1000 Jl '67

Toscanini reissues, a tribute at last honorably paid. B. H. Haggin. Hi Fi 17:71-2 Ag '67

Vocal miscellany, including reissues. Am Rec G 33:1109-17 Ag '67

Religious records

Magnificent achievement; Telefunken's Vespro della Beata Vergine. J. W. Barker. il Am Rec G 33:716-18 My '67

Monteverdi for moderns. R. Jacobson. Sat R 50:44 Jl 29 '67

Monteverdi's Vespers of 1610. J. W. Barker. Am Rec G 33:1076-7 Ag '67

Records. M. E. Marty. Christian Cent 84: 1562 D 6 '67

Russian music

Avant-garde in Russia and Poland. Discus. Harper 235:130+ S '67

Rozhdestvensky; vital and exuberant. J. Diether. Am Rec G 33:1103 Ag '67

Russians are coming; Melodiya/Angel releases. R. Gelatt. Reporter 36:44+ Je 1 '67

Stravinsky and Shostakovich. H. Kupferberg. Atlan 219:120-1 My '67

Sonatas

Jacqueline Du Pré and Stephen Bishop; individually and together. M. N. Kanny. il Am Rec G 33:548-9 Mr '67

Nonesuch: more Dolby: Rachmaninoff: Sonata in G minor, and Kodály: Sonata. J. Diether. Am Rec G 33:627 Ap '67

Triumphant Cliburn recital; Mozart and Beethoven. C. J. Luten. il Am Rec G 33:397 Ja '67

Songs

Affectionately recalled: John Charles Thomas. P. L. Miller. Am Rec G 33:635 Ap '67

Ancient Russian rarities. A. Favia-Artsay. il Hobbies 72:35+ D '67

Basic Dylan. il Time 91:50 Ja 12 '68

Collector's records; American male singers. A. Favia-Artsay. il Hobbies 72:35-6 N '67

Disappearing art. R. Gelatt. Reporter 36: 38-9 My 4 '67

Facing the music; the Beatles Sgt. Pepper's lonely hearts club band. P. Schrag. Sat R 50:61 Ag 19 '67

Farewell to all that. A. Sperber. Am Rec G 33:756-7+ My '67

Gorgeous contrast. M. Kreuger. Am Rec G 33:612-13 Mr '67

In the limelight. M. Kreuger. See issues of American record guide

Long-singing singers. H. Kupferberg. il Atlan 219:130-2 Mr '67

Lyric impulse; A. C. Jobim albums. B. Korall. Sat R 50:58 D 2 '67

McRae, Maye, and Lee. B. Korall. il Sat R 50:76-7 Ap 29 '67

PHONOGRAPH records—Songs—*Continued*
New beat for the teen: library rock; with discography. C. Clark. il Library J 92:1706-7 Ap 15 '67
On IRCC, Americans all. P. L. Miller. Am Rec G 33:385 Ja '67
Poulenc and Bernac, French song, with pure pleasure the aim. N. Rorem. il Hi Fi 17:85-6 N '67
Pretty Purdie. New Yorker 43:52-6 N 18 '67
Recital of Purcell songs. G. L. Mayer. Am Rec G 33:466 F '67
Recordings; J. Raskin sings Schubert songs. M. Mayer. Esquire 67:79+ Ap '67
Records:
  Best of Mapleson; LP's from cylinders. M. De Schauensee. Opera N 31:34 My 13 '67
  Eighteen songs. Opera N 32:30 S 9 '67
  Elisabeth Söderström. Opera N 31:32 Mr 18 '67
  Four song cycles. Opera N 31:34 Ja 28 '67
  French song recital: Victoria de los Angeles. Opera N 32:34 Ja 13 '68
  Fritz Wunderlich. Opera N 31:30 Je 10 '67
  Hanne-Lore Kuhse. Opera N 31:30 Je 10 '67
  Joan Sutherland sings Noel Coward. Opera N 31:34 F 11 '67
  John Reardon sings contemporary songs. Opera N 31:34 F 11 '67
  Des knaben wunderhorn. Opera N 31:34 Mr 11 '67
  Maria Kurenko. Opera N 31:34 My 13 '67
  Recent Seraphim releases. Opera N 31:34 F 18 '67
  Seventeen songs. Opera N 31:34 F 25 '67
  Song recitals. Opera N 32:30 N 4 '67
  Twenty songs. Opera N 31:34 F 25 '67
  Winterreise, six songs. Opera N 31:32 Mr 4 '67
Records: Music of Arnold Schoenberg. B. Boretz. Nation 204:349-50 Mr 13 '67
Stars are ageless, aren't they? M. Kreuger. il Am Rec G 33:684-5 Ap '67
Stuff of legend; P. Bernac recording of F. Poulenc songs. R. Gelatt. Reporter 37:45 S 7 '67
Very difficult to resist: Schubert by Wunderlich. H. Glass. Am Rec G 33:634-5 Ap '67
Vocal miscellany, including reissues. Am Rec G 33:1109-17 Ag '67
Wunderlich's Lieder, an artistry almost fully in flower. P. G. Davis. Hi Fi 17:83-4 Ja '67

Spoken records

Dallas: a shrill documentary: The Warren report and the controversy. J. Diether. Am Rec G 33:443 Ja '67
Model documentary, December 7, 1941. Am Rec G 33:605 Mr '67
New records. Sr Schol 91:sup 13-14 D 7 '67
New records and tapes. il Sr Schol 90:sup 16+ Mr 10 '67
On Capitol (Hill) Gallant men told by Senator Everett Dirksen. Am Rec G 33:603 Mr '67
On the record: Words. J. L. Limbacher. See issues of Library journal
Pitfalls of pop's pompous pop-off; an open letter to my teen-age son. W. Zinsser. Life 64:6 Ja 5 '68
Recordings (cont of) Recordings for young people. J. L. Limbacher. See second issue of each month of Library journal
Well, man, that's progress. G. Lees. il Hi Fi 18:96-7 Ja '68
Words only. S. Potter. See issues of American record guide
  See also
Talking books

Stage music

Records:
  Music for the theater. Opera N 31:34 Ap 15 '67

Stereophonic records

Going stereo; EMI's classical issues. T. Heinitz. Sat R 50:63 Je 24 '67
Other reviews, including stereo. See issues of American record guide
Phonograph records. W. F. Grueninger. See issues of Consumer bulletin
Record reviews. See issues of Consumer reports
Stereo evolution. I. Kolodin. il Sat R 50:47+ Ag 26 '67

String quartet music

On four records from two labels, seven works by Janáček. A. Cohn. il Am Rec G 33:379+ Ja '67

Semblance of a resemblance; quartets by E. Bloch and M. Tippett. O. Daniel. Sat R 50:113 O 14 '67
Yale quartet on Cardinal, one of the finest performances ever; Beethoven: quartet no. 15. M. N. Kanny. Am Rec G 34:300 D '67

Symphonies

Again, Schmidt-Isserstedt's great Beethoven; Symphony no. 3 the Eroïca. M. N. Kanny. Am Rec G 33:576-7 Mr '67
Babi Yar; Shostakovich Symphony no. 13. J. Diether. il Am Rec G 34:4-6+ S '67
Beethoven out of Mahler by Steinberg. J. Diether. Am Rec G 33:386-7 Ja '67
Bernstein's Copland Third. C. J. Luten. Am Rec G 33:933 Je '67
Bernstein's Mahler: a prophecy fulfilled. M. N. Kanny. il Am Rec G 34:278-81 D '67
Bernstein's majestic Mahler 8th. I. Kolodin. il Sat R 50:65 Ja 28 '67
Bohuslav Martinu. C. J. Luten. il Am Rec G 33:916-17 Je '67
Bruckner's First: what a symphony! J. Diether. Am Rec G 33:560-1 Mr '67
Chávez symphonies. Américas 19:42 N '67
Chavez: the six splendid symphonies. A. Frankenstein. Hi Fi 17:73 Ag '67
David Oistrakh's Red angel conducting debut; Fifth symphony of Prokofiev. J. Diether. Am Rec G 33:474 F '67
Decca's Brahms Fourth, the cream of the crop. M. N. Kanny. Am Rec G 33:475 F '67
Do not miss this gem of a baroque release; Symphonies pour les soupers du roi. J. W. Barker. Am Rec G 34:42 S '67
Dvorak's symphonies: the canonical five plus the early four. D. Hamilton. Hi Fi 17:64-5 Jl '67
Georg Solti's Mahler Second. J. Diether. Am Rec G 34:46-8 S '67
Growth of Istvan Kertesz; complete Dvořák symphonies. H. Glass. Am Rec G 33:1006-7 Jl '67
Leinsdorf's Mahler Third. J. Diether. il Am Rec G 34:100-2 O '67
Leonard Bernstein is not a man to pass up such a challenge. Mahler's Symphony of a thousand. D. Newlin. por Am Rec G 33:416-17 Ja '67
Leslie Haydn-Jones; Haydn: Symphonies nos. 82-87. R. Freed. Sat R 50:78 Mr 25 '67
Das lied von der erde, three new sets and three perspectives. M. Malloch. Hi Fi 17:69-70 Mr '67
Lorin Maazel's beautiful Sibelius: vibrancy, tension, plasticity. J. Diether. Am Rec G 33:591-2 Mr '67
Mahler symphonies on records; an analysis. B. Jacobson. Hi Fi 17:55-9 S '67
Markevitch's magnificent Manfred. J. Diether. Am Rec G 33:594 Mr '67
Musical aristocrat: I. Fine. R. Sabin. Am Rec G 34:103 O '67
One of the happy composers; nine Dvorák symphonies. Discus. Harper 235:100-1 Ag '67
Ormandy and Steinberg complete their Beethoven nine. H. Goldsmith. Hi Fi 17:84-5 Ja '67
Polished and quite beautiful Mahler Third. J. Diether. Am Rec G 33:791-3 My '67
Prime Casals from Marlboro: Beethoven Eighth and Mendelssohn Italian. M. N. Kanny. Am Rec G 33:489 F '67
Recordings; complete set of Mahler symphonies conducted by Leonard Bernstein. M. Mayer. Esquire 68:28+ D '67
Records:
  Das lied von der erde. Opera N 31:34 Ap 8 '67
  Mahler's Second and Third symphonies. Opera N 32:30 O 14 '67
  Mahler: Symphony No. 8. Opera N 31:34 My 13 '67
Russians have arrived, thanks to Melodiya/Angel. B. Jacobson. Hi Fi 17:67-8 Mr '67
Schmidt-Isserstedt's mastery; Beethoven: symphony no. 4. M. N. Kanny. Am Rec G 34:296 D '67
Szell's complete Brahms symphonies. M. N. Kanny. il Am Rec G 33:912-14 Je '67
Three at once: Das lied. J. Diether. il Am Rec G 33:722-7 My '67
Triumph by Lenny and Mahler; nine Mahler symphonies conducted by Bernstein. S. Kanfer. Life 63:12 N 3 '67
Two new worlds, the LSO, Kertesz, Ormandy. E. Greenfield. Hi Fi 17:21+ F '67
Two views of the nine Beethoven symphonies. M. N. Kanny. Am Rec G 33:646-8 Ap '67
Vaughan Williams: four works, one, a first on records. J. Diether. il Am Rec G 33:552-4 Mr '67

PHONOGRAPH records—*Continued*

Violin music

See also
Phonograph records—Concertos

PHORBOL ester. See Cancer producing substances

PHOSPHATASES
Alkaline phosphatase and leucine aminopeptidase association in plasma of the chicken. G. R. J. Law. bibliog il Science 156:1106-7 My 26 '67; Reply with rejoinder. M. E. Etzler. 157:721 Ag 11 '67
Glutaraldehyde activation of nuclear acid phosphatase in cultured plant cells. D. W. De Jong and others. bibliog il Science 155: 1672-4 Mr 31 '67

See also
Adenosine triphosphatase

PHOSPHATE mines and mining
Bonanza in the desert; Spanish government and IMC mine phosphate deposits in Spanish Sahara. il Time 89:64-5 Je 2 '67

PHOSPHATES
Induced rapid release and uptake of phosphate by microorganisms. J. Shapiro. bibliog il Science 155:1269-71 Mr 10 '67
Phosphorylation with inorganic phosphates at moderate temperatures. A. Beck and others. bibliog il Science 157:952 Ag 25 '67
Sedimentary phosphate method for estimating paleosalinities. B. W. Nelson. bibliog il Science 158:917-20 N 17 '67
Trehalose regulation of glucose-6-phosphate hydrolysis in blowfly extracts. S. Friedman. bibliog il Science 159:110-11 Ja 5 '68

See also
Adenosine phosphates
Apatite
Phosphorylation
Stanfieldite

PHOSPHATES in the body
Aldolase reaction with sugar diphosphates. A. H. Mehler and M. E. Cusic, jr. bibliog il Science 155:1101-3 Mr 3 '67
Sleep: effects on incorporation of inorganic phosphate into brain fractions. P. Reich and others. bibliog il Science 157:336-8 Jl 21 '67

PHOSPHATIDES
Bronchiolar and large alveolar cell in pulmonary phospholipid metabolism. A. H. Niden. bibliog il Science 158:1323-4 D 8 '67

PHOSPHOGLYCERIDES. See Glycerides

PHOSPHOKINASE. See Enzymes

PHOSPHOLIPIDES. See Phosphatides

PHOSPHORESCENCE
See also
Fireflies

PHOSPHOROUS compounds
Penetration of an organophosphorous compound into squid axon and its effects on metabolism and function. F. C. G. Hoskin and P. Rosenberg. bibliog il Science 156: 966-7 My 19 '67

PHOSPHORS
New developments in CRT phosphors. J. R. Collins. il Electr World 77:48-52+ Ja '67

PHOSPHORYLASES
Calcium-induced activation of phosphorylase in rat hearts. A. J. D. Friesen and others. bibliog il Science 155:1108-9 Mr 3 '67
Phosphorylase b kinase inheritance in mice. J. B. Lyon, jr. and others. bibliog il Science 155:1550-1 Mr 24 '67

PHOSPHORYLATION
Biochemical genetics of oxidative phosphorylation. L. Kováč and others. bibliog il Science 158:1564-7 D 22 '67
Cis-trans isomerism in naphthoquinones: interconversion and participation in oxidative phosphorylation. D. L. Gutnick and others. bibliog il Science 158:1469-71 D 15 '67
Oxidative phosphorylation in experimental bilirubin encephalopathy. I. Diamond and R. Schmid. bibliog il Science 155:1288-9 Mr 10 '67
Phosphorylation with inorganic phosphates at moderate temperatures. A. Beck and others. bibliog il Science 157:952 Ag 25 '67
Phosphorylative inactivation of aminoglycosidic antibiotics by escherichia coli carrying R factor. H. Umezawa and others. il Science 157:1559-61 S 29 '67
Salicylanilides: a new group of active uncouplers of oxidative phosphorylation. R. L. Williamson and R. L. Metcalf. bibliog il Science 158:1694-5 D 29 '67
Seed dormancy: breaking by uncouplers and inhibitors of oxidative phosphorylation. L. A. T. Ballard and A. E. G. Lipp. bibliog il Science 156:398-9 Ap 21 '67

Tissue specificity of histone phosphorylation. R. M. Gutierrez and L. S. Hnilica. bibliog il Science 157:1324-5 S 15 '67
Transport and phosphorylation as factors in the antitumor action of cytosine arabinoside. D. Kessel and others. bibliog il Science 156:1240-1 Je 2 '67

PHOTOCHEMISTRY
Photooxidation of hydrycarbons in the presence of aliphatic aldehydes. A. P. Altshuller and others. bibliog il Science 156:937-9 My 19 '67

PHOTOCOMPOSING machines
IBM planning to enter photocomposition field. Pub W 191:114-15 Mr 6 '67

PHOTOCOPYING processes
Nearer to the dust, by G. A. Gipe. Review Sat R 50:63 Jl 8 '67. S. W. Little

PHOTODIODES. See Diodes

PHOTOELECTRON spectroscopy. See Spectrum analysis

PHOTOFLASH electric lamps. See Electric lamps, Photoflash

PHOTOFLASH lamps. See Electric lamps Photoflash

PHOTOGRAMS. See Shadowgrams

PHOTOGRAPHERS
Are your standards high enough? A. Francekevich. Pop Phot 61:8 S '67
Flying photographer. See issues of Flying
For photographers who care: a helping hand; Fund for the concerned photographer. J. Deschin. il Pop Phot 62:40+ Ja '68
Photographer of the year and other winners; University of Missouri school of journalism awards. G. P. Hunt. Life 62:3 Mr 17 '67
Photographer pleads his case; new rates. C. E. Rotkin. il Pub W 191:90-1+ F 6 '67
Road to significance. D. Graham. il U S Camera 30:28-9+ Mr '67
Thunder of shutters; photo festival at Mission Bay, San Diego. il U S Camera 30:58-9 Je '67
Tips for the travelling photographer. A. Rothstein. U S Camera 30:13-14 My '67
To sleep, to see. J. Durniak. Pop Phot 60: 66+ Mr '67
See also
Women as photographers
also names of photographers, e.g. R. Selby

PHOTOGRAPHERS agents
What's a picture agency? W. Hyum. il U S Camera 30:52-3+ Ap '67

PHOTOGRAPHIC albums
Wolfman on printing; how you can store picture books. A. Wolfman. il Mod Phot 31: 18+ My '67

PHOTOGRAPHIC apparatus industry and trade
How to succeed in business when your hobby is photography. E. Hannigan. il U S Camera 30:18+ Je '67
Marriage, European style; Agfa-Gevaert merger. Fortune 76:214 S 15 '67
On buying a photo gift; tips from dealers. R. Miller. il U S Camera 30:42-3+ D '67
Value of the specialty store. W. Clark. U S Camera 30:40 D '67
See also
Eastman Kodak company

Securities
Opportunity's knock. il Duns R 90:63-4 Jl '67

PHOTOGRAPHIC chemistry
Foto facts; a formula for a divided developer. P. Farber; reply. R. J. Starks. U S Camera 30:18 Mr '67
Home cooking; or why you might want to mix your chemicals. D. Vestal. il Pop Phot 61:102-3+ Ag '67

PHOTOGRAPHIC composing machines. See Photocomposing machines

PHOTOGRAPHIC copying. See Photography—Copying

PHOTOGRAPHIC equipment. See Photography—Apparatus and supplies

PHOTOGRAPHIC exhibitions. See Photography—Exhibitions

PHOTOGRAPHIC films. See Photography—Films

PHOTOGRAPHIC filters. See Light filters

PHOTOGRAPHIC finishing
Underexposed slides can be saved; Colorbrite color reducers. A. Francekevich. Pop Phot 60:30 Je '67

PHOTOGRAPHIC humor. See Humor, Pictorial

PHOTOGRAPHIC industry. See Photographic apparatus industry and trade

PHOTOGRAPHIC lenses. See Lenses, Photographic

PHOTOGRAPHIC murals
Giant size prints. M. Schultz. il U S Camera 30:54-5+ Ap '67
PHOTOGRAPHIC paper
How to use the S & M darkroom meter to determine proper paper contrasts for different negatives. A. Wolfman. il Mod Phot 31:14+ O '67
Kramer's korner. A. Kramer. il Mod Phot 31:52+ N '67
P.O.P. revisited; printing-out paper. C. W. Kennedy. il Pop Phot 61:15-16+ O '67
Papers: how the major ones compare; enlarging papers. il Mod Phot 31:68-71 F '67
Print sharp, print bright. J. B. Johnson. il U S Camera 30:50-1 Jl '67
Varilour: Du Pont's paper tiger. P. R. Farber. il U S Camera 30:44-5+ Ag '67
Wolfman on printing; enlarging paper. A. Wolfman. Mod Phot 31:14+ D '67
PHOTOGRAPHIC reproduction. See Photography—Copying
PHOTOGRAPHIC slides. See Transparencies
PHOTOGRAPHIC society of America
PSA judge defects; guidelines of PSA jurists. J. Deschin. il Pop Phot 60:22+ Ap '67
PHOTOGRAPHIC supplies. See Photography—Apparatus and supplies
PHOTOGRAPHIC themes. See Photography—Themes
PHOTOGRAPHS
Freedom to find pictures; portfolio by freelancers. Pop Phot 62:90-9 Ja '68
Instant sketches from photo prints. B. Corley. il Pop Mech 128:156-7 D '67
Putting your pictures to work. W. Clark. U S Camera 30:36 N '67
Quiet picture; portfolio. Pop Phot 61:96-105 O '67
Readers' gallery. il U S Camera 30:64-7 Mr '67
US-camera gallery. il U S Camera 30:58-61 Ap; 44-5 Jl; 46-7 N '67; 31:56-7 Ja '68
See also subhead Photographs under various subjects, e.g. Bridges—Photographs

Collectors and collecting
Photographica. bibliog il Pop Phot 60:94-103+ My '67

Prices
Photographer pleads his case. C. E. Rotkin. il Pub W 191:90-1+ F 6 '67

Storage
Wolfman on printing; storing prints. A. Wolfman. il Mod Phot 31:46+ Mr '67

Trimming, mounting, etc.
Wolfman on printing; filing prints. A. Wolfman. il Mod Phot 31:29+ Ap '67
Wolfman on printing; mounting prints back to back. A. Wolfman. il Mod Phot 31:36+ Ag '67
PHOTOGRAPHS, Judging of. See Photography—Criticism
PHOTOGRAPHY
Ansel Adams. A. Adams. il Pop Phot 61:82-3 Jl '67
Around the world on a camera. A. N. Podell. il U S Camera 30:62-3+ Jl '67
But how do I cool the water? D. Bennett. U S Camera 30:28+ D '67
Camera cues (cont) R. Pinney. il Parents Mag 42:20 Je; 60+ Ag '67
Change of pace techniques. J. Scully. il Mod Phot 31:84-7 Je '67
Color & content! I. Tybel. il Pop Phot 61:111-13+ Jl '67
David B. Eisendrath's 1997. D. B. Eisendrath. il Pop Phot 60:56+ Je '67
Ed Scully on basics; choosing the right color film. E. Scully. Mod Phot 31:12 Ag '67
Expo 70. H. V. Fondiller. il Pop Phot 62:120-3+ Ja '68
Foto facts. P. Farber. See issues of U.S. camera & travel
Good vacation photography. Am Home 70:76 Jl '67
Harvey Lloyd; what he believes about his craft. H. Lloyd. il Pop Phot 61:90-9 Ag '67
Honestly erotic; photography of S. Sannes. J. Deschin. Pop Phot 60:22+ F '67
How to take really fine vacation photos. D. Jordan. il Bet Hom & Gard 45:64-7 Ag '67
Impact; people and motion in F. Hidalgo's pictures. il U S Camera 31:40-3 Ja '68
Improvising camera supports outdoors. C. W. Kennedy. il Pop Phot 60:55-6+ Ap '67
In defense of wasting film. L. Barry. Pop Phot 60:28+ Ap '67

Large camera: top image sharpness. A. Feininger. Mod Phot 31:44-5 Ag '67
Lens lines. W. Clark. See issues of U.S. camera & travel
Modern's shooting guide. E. Scully. il Mod Phot 31:50-65 S '67
Movie techniques are worth copying. E. Hannigan. U S Camera 30:28+ S '67
Must he share technique? L. Nilsson's refusal to discuss his method in public. J. Deschin. il Pop Phot 60:16+ My '67
On learning photography; reprint. C. Rider. il U S Camera 31:61 Ja '68
Paul Strand at seventy-six, interview, ed. by J. Deschin. P. Strand. Pop Phot 60:14+ Mr '67
Photo beat. W. Hanson; N. Rothschild; B. Pierce. See issues of Popular photography
Photo tips. See issues of Popular photography
Photography can work for you. C. Walker. il Parks & Rec 2:24-5+ Jl '67
Premiere; lesson in photography. M. Laurance. il U S Camera 30:56-7 O '67
Rainy day photos. R. Pinney. il Parents Mag 42:32+ My '67
Silly questions? J. Durniak. il Pop Phot 60:53-6 F '67
Sixteen ways to get better travel pictures. P. McCafferty. il Pop Sci 190:112-15+ Je '67
Tools & techniques. C. W. Kennedy. See issues of Popular photography
Travel & camera. See issues of U.S. camera & travel
Truth, myth, fallacy, humbug, etcetera. A. Goldsmith. Pop Phot 62:75+ Ja '68
Vacation tips for all seasons. D. B. Eisendrath, jr. il Pop Phot 61:8+ Ag '67
Vagabond camera. W. Lane. See issues of Travel
When the living is easy. il U S Camera 30:40-1 Jl '67
Which technique for which subject? J. Scully. il Mod Phot 31:56-65 O '67
Worth knowing. il U S Camera 30:49+ Mr '67
See also
Ambrotypes
Astronomical photography
Daguerreotypes
Human figure in photography
Lasers—Photographic applications
Moving picture photography
Photomicrography
Telephotography
Television—Photographic aspects
Tintypes
Vietnamese war, 1957- —Photography

Apparatus and supplies
Basic stuff. A. Francekevich. Pop Phot 60:26+ F '67
Behind the scenes. il Mod Phot 31:14+ Mr '67
Big show? Chicago dealer exhibit. il Mod Phot 31:76-82 Je '67
Bright new aids for better pictures. il Pop Mech 128:166-7 S '67
Christmas shopping guide. il Mod Phot 31:137-40 D '67
Color in the kitchen sink. R. Excell. il U S Camera 30:64-5+ Jl '67
Color room; darkroom equipment. J. M. Zanutto. il Pop Phot 61:118 Jl '67
Down to the seas again. A. Rothstein. U S Camera 30:28+ Ag '67
Fotoval, revisited. P. Farber. U S Camera 30:28-9 Jl '67
Fun of it all. E. Hannigan. U S Camera 31:18+ Ja '68
Help from the outside world; nonphotographic gadgets and appliances. D. B. Eisendrath, jr. Pop Phot 60:16+ Je '67
If I were the camera industry . . . N. Rothschild. il Pop Phot 62:112-13+ Ja '68
In the darkroom; basic stuff; equipment needed to make prints. A. Francekevich. Pop Phot 60:8+ Mr '67
Kodak goes Ektagraphic. il U S Camera 30:54-5 S '67
Meyers on techniques. E. Meyers. Mod Phot 31:22+ Mr '67
Modern tests. See issues of Modern photography
New products. See issues of U.S. camera & travel
New Year's plea: the right to be left-handed. P. Farber. il U S Camera 31:24+ Ja '68
Offbeat. N. Rothschild. Pop Phot 61:58+ D '67; 62:52+ Ja '68
On the go, by bus. I. Desfor. il U S Camera 30:42-3+ My '67
Once over lightly. il Mod Phot 31:46 F '67
One jump behind technology; new products. D. B. Eisendrath, jr. Pop Phot 61:22+ N '67

PHOTOGRAPHY—Apparatus and supplies—
  Continued
Photo beat. W. Hanson; N. Rothschild; B.
  Pierce. See issues of Popular photography
Photo tips. See issues of Popular photography
Rapid copy stand. C. J. Spears. il U S
  Camera 31:50-1+ Ja '68
Resolutions for a happy New Year of rewarding photography. A. Rothstein. U S
  Camera 31:14 Ja '68
Safelights: most are safe, but others? Mod
  Phot 31:77 F '67
Seen in Chicago. il U S Camera 30:41+ Je '67
Seven good ideas for photographers. il Pop
  Sci 191:154-5 N '67
Shop talk. N. Goldberg. il Pop Phot 61:66-7
  Jl; 104-5 Ag '67
Simon says; color film processor. N. Simon.
  Mod Phot 31:28 Jl '67
Six pros in search of a gift; symposium. il
  Pop Phot 61:118-19 D '67
Taking a memo to Neptune; waterproof housing for the camera. L. Barry. il Pop Phot
  60:46+ F '67
Techniques tomorrow; optical bench puzzle.
  B. Sherman. Mod Phot 31:40+ Jl '67
Test reports. See issues of Popular photography
Test strips, plain and fancy. A. Francekevich. il Pop Phot 61:54+ D '67
35mm techniques; photo tips for the man
  who's planning a trip. P. Stackpole. U S
  Camera 31:16+ Ja '68
Tools & techniques. C. W. Kennedy. See issues of Popular photography
Turn off the dark; new safelights. H. Zucker. il Pop Phot 61:92-5+ S '67
2¼ SLR systems compared. D. L. Miller. il
  Mod Phot 31:60-1 Mr '67
Underwater testing for six weeks at Bermuda. P. Stackpole. U S Camera 30:26+
  N '67
U.S. camera & travel test reports. See issues
  of U.S. camera & travel
What can't they can? directory of aerosols
  for photographers. H. Zucker. Pop Phot 60:
  118 My '67
What's what in SLR? D. L. Miller. il Mod
  Phot 31:62-7 My '67
Who took the math out of duping? Illumitran,
  that's who! N. Rothschild. il Pop Phot 61:
  100-3+ Jl '67
Wolfman on printing; contact proofers. A.
  Wolfman. il Mod Phot 31:22+ Jl '67
Worth knowing. il U S Camera 30:49+ Mr '67
You can't judge a tank by its lid. H. Zucker.
  il Pop Phot 60:110-13+ Je '67
    See also
Camera tripods
Cameras
Exposure meters
General electric company
Lenses, Photographic
Mirrors for cameras
View finders
        Storage
And now, ladies & gentlemen, introducing
  the electronic popsicle; keeping batteries
  refrigerated. P. Farber. il U S Camera 30:
  20+ O '67
Caulfield on color; tropical problem. P. Caulfield. Mod Phot 31:12+ S '67

        Testing
Keppler on the SLR. H. Keppler. Mod Phot
  31:22+ My '67

      Bibliography
Addenda to 30 years of books; personal favorites. J. Deschin. il Pop Phot 61:16+ Ag '67
Books in review. See issues of Modern photography
Critics at large. Pop Phot 61:14 Jl '67
New books, in brief. Pop Phot 60:64 F; 48
  Mr; 54 Ap; 61:6 Ag; 60 S '67
Photographic reading. See issues of U.S.
  camera & travel
Thirty years of books that shaped photography. il Pop Phot 60:104-7+ My; 88-9+
  Je '67
      Charts, diagrams, etc.
Photo charts; don't let 'em scare you. E.
  Scully. Mod Phot 31:70-1 Je '67

    Cold weather conditions
Skiing; pack camera, film, longjohns. il U S
  Camera 30:58-9+ Mr '67

        Competitions
Contests & exhibits. See issues of U.S. camera
  & travel
Home garden photography contest il Home
  Gard 54:38-40 O '67

Monthly contest. See issues of Modern photography
1967 Scholastic photography awards. il Sr
  Schol 90:20, 44-6 My 19 '67
Photographer of the year and other winners;
  University of Missouri school of journalism
  awards. G. P. Hunt. Life 62:3 Mr 17 '67
Photography in the front line; Pictures of the
  year award winners. M. R. Weiss. il Sat R
  50:134-5 Mr 11 '67
SR's photo contest; with gallery of winning
  photos and list of winners. M. R. Weiss.
  Sat R 51:64+ Ja 6 '68
Winners at the White House; White House
  news photographers association competition.
  M. R. Weiss. il Sat R 50:88-9 Ap 8 '67
Winners, Scholastic magazine's annual photography contest. il U S Camera 30:66-7 N
  '67
        Composition
  See Composition (photography)

        Copying
High and low cost of slide duping. D. B.
  Eisendrath, jr. Pop Phot 61:20+ O '67
Instant B&W prints from slides. C. W. Kennedy. il Pop Phot 60:136 My '67
Make this copier. F. L. Greenwald. il Pop
  Mech 127:182-5+ F '67
Quickie copying stand from plywood scrap.
  P. Wahl. il Pop Mech 128:128-9 Ag '67
Reproduction vs. preservation; excerpt from
  Care and preservation of books. J Alden;
  reply. J. B. Blake. Library J 92:507-8 F 1
  '67
        Criticism
Critics at large. il Pop Phot 61:14 Jl; 110
  Ag; 61+ S; 144-7 D '67
Critic's choice. See issues of Popular photography
PSA judge defects; guidelines of PSA jurists. J. Deschin. il Pop Phot 60:22+ Ap
  '67
        Darkrooms
  See Photography—Studios and darkrooms

    Developing and developers
ASA 25, 40, 100, 400; eleven minutes develops
  all four. H. Zucker. il Pop Phot 61:74-5+
  Ag '67
Avoid trouble by knowing your developer.
  P. Farber. U S Camera 30:26-7 D '67
Basic stuff. A. Francekevich. Pop Phot
  60:108-11+ F '67
Caulfield on color; developing in daylight. P.
  Caulfield. il Mod Phot 31:48+ Ap '67
Caulfield on color; Tetenal's neofin-color. P.
  Caulfield. Mod Phot 31:14 My '67
Developers; they are similar, but... Mod
  Phot 31:72-3 F '67
E-4 replaces E-2. M. Edelson. il U S Camera
  30:62+ O '67
Ed Scully on basics; film processing. E. Scully. il Mod Phot 31:17-18 N '67
Exposure and development; is there an easy
  system? P. R. Farber. il U S Camera 30:
  42-3+ Je '67
High speed Ektachrome; how far will it
  push? M. Laurance. il U S Camera 31:36-
  7+ Ja '68
Home-made soups grow in number. P. Farber.
  il U S Camera 30:24+ Ap '67
How to get pushy with color. B. Pierce. il
  Pop Phot 61:92-3+ Jl '67
Kramer's korner; film-developer combinations. A. Kramer. Mod Phot 31:151-2 D '67
1967 film-developer roundup. T. T. Hill. Mod
  Phot 31:98-103 N '67
Print making. il Mod Phot 31:68-71 F '67
Simon says; color film processor. N. Simon.
  Mod Phot 31:28 Jl '67
35mm techniques; photo tips for the man
  who's planning a trip. P. Stackpole. U S
  Camera 31:16+ Ja '68
You can't judge a tank by its lid. H. Zucker.
  il Pop Phot 60:110-13+ Je '67
    See also
Photographic chemistry

        Enlarging
Don't squint! make giant contacts; present
  enlarged proofs to editors. H. Zucker. il
  Pop Phot 61:84-7+ Ag '67
How to get the most out of under-$50
  enlarging meters. H. Zucher. il Pop Phot
  60:108-11+ F '67
In the darkroom; focusing an enlarger. A.
  Francekevich. Pop Phot 61:28+ Jl '67
Instant color enlarging without trays. C. W.
  Kennedy. il Pop Phot 60:96-9+ Ap '67
It doesn't make a grain of sense. P. R.
  Farber. il U S Camera 30:46-7+ Jl '67

PHOTOGRAPHY—Enlarging—*Continued*

Meyers on technique; how to make big prints. F. Meyers. Mod Phot 31:44+ D '67

New processor simplifies home printmaking. W. Lane. il Travel 127:72 F '67

Papers: how the major ones compare; enlarging papers. il Mod Phot 31:68-71 F '67

Tele pictures after the fact, enlarge with tiny lenses. E. Meyers. Mod Phot 31:54+ Ag '67

Too little, too much, do this, and voila. D. Becker. il Mod Phot 32:80-1+ Ja '68

Wolfman on printing; enlarging exposure meters. A. Wolfman. il Mod Phot 31:26+ N '67

Equipment

See Photography—Apparatus and supplies

Exhibitions

Big Chicago show: lots of new stuff; Master photo dealers and finishers association trade show. il Pop Phot 60:82-3+ Ap '67

Big show? Chicago dealer exhibit. il Mod Phot 31:76-82 Je '67

California exposed; Eloquent light exhibition by A. Adams at the Boston museum of fine arts. M. R. Weiss. il Sat R 50:50-3 S 23 '67

Chicago '67; symposium. il Pop Phot 60:102-9 Je; 61:114-18 Jl '67

Concerned photographer; exhibition at Riverside museum, N.Y. D. Vestal. il Pop Phot 61:106-13 O '67

Contests & exhibits. See issues of U.S. camera & travel

Do-it-yourself kinetic art; Lights in orbit exhibition. N. Goldberg. il Pop Phot 61:78+ Jl '67

Fads and faces; concerning touring exhibition The Lower East side: portal to American life. R. Lynes. il Harper 235:26+ S '67

Friends of photography get started at Carmel. P. Stackpole. il U S Camera 30:28-9+ O '67

Girl watching; Pepsi-Cola and photographer A. Brooks get together. E. Galligan. il U S Camera 30:48-9 O '67

Instant art; Photography in the fine arts exhibition V at the Metropolitan museum. R. Lynes. il Harper 234:28+ Je '67

John Szarkowski: photography as interpreter. J. Deschin. Pop Phot 61:18+ S '67

Karsh's one-man show at Expo 67: centennial salute. M. R. Weiss. il Sat R 50:54-7 Ap 29 '67

Lens on the locks; Erie Canal sesquicentennial exhibition. M. R. Weiss. il Sat R 50:57-9 Ag 12 '67

Light itself is a picture; Lights in orbit show. H. M. Kinzer. il Pop Phot 61:79-81 Jl '67

Lower East side: portal to American life; exhibition at the Jewish museum. il U S Camera 30:50-1 Mr '67

Mutual concern; Concerned photographer; exhibition at Riverside museum. M. R. Weiss. il Sat R 50:66-7 D 9 '67

PSA judge defects; guidelines of PSA jurists. J. Deschin. il Pop Phot 60:22+ Ap '67

PFA-V: the museum is the message; on view in the Metropolitan museum of art. M. R. Weiss. il Sat R 50:37-44 My 6 '67

Photography: Winogrand-Friedlander-Arbus exhibition. M. Kozloff. Nation 204:571-3 My 1 '67

Salon calendar. See issues of Modern photography

Selection of photographs from Man in sport: exhibition at Baltimore museum of art; excerpts from introduction to catalogue. Am Artist 32:56-9+ Ja '68

Telling it as it is; Museum of modern art's show, New documents. il Newsweek 69:110 Mr 20 '67

35mm in the thirties; photographs by F. J. Scherschel at Modernage headquarters. M. R. Weiss. il Sat R 50:74-5 F 11 '67

Toni Frissell, in her fashion; retrospective at New York's Hallmark gallery. M. R. Weiss. il Sat R 50:48-9 O 21 '67

Viewpoint; Allon Schoener exhibitions. J. Deschin. Pop Phot 61:66+ O '67

Voices on film; Concerned photography exhibition at Riverside museum. R. A. Sokolov. il Newsweek 70:97+ O 30 '67

Exposure

Caulfield on color; high subject lighting contrast. P. Caulfield. il Mod Phot 31:30+ Je '67

Creative color; necessary adjustments for long exposure. A. Rothstein. il U S Camera 30:10+ Ap '67

Exposure. D. Ulffers. U S Camera 30:61+ D '67

Exposure. J. Scully. il Mod Phot 31:62-9 Jl '67

Exposure and development: is there an easy system? P. R Farber. il U S Camera 30:42-3+ Je '67

How to shoot flashy color without a flash. P. Wahl. il Pop Mech 129:160-1+ Ja '68

Keppler on the SLR; behind-the-lens meter systems. H. Keppler. il Mod Phot 31:28+ O '67

Large camera; check list to prevent errors. A. Feininger. Mod Phot 31:46+ N '67

Large camera; swings and tilts. A. Feininger. il Mod Phot 31:103+ O '67

Modern's shooting guide. E. Scully. il Mod Phot 31:62-3 S '67

Reply to the SLR know-it-alls. N. Rothschild. il Pop Phot 60:71-3+ Ap '67

Two kinds of snow jobs. D. B. Eisendrath, jr. Pop Phot 60:16+ F '67

When a meter won't help. D. B. Eisendrath, jr. Pop Phot 61:14+ S '67

Would you use half a meter? P. R. Farber. il U S Camera 30:54-5+ F '67

See also
Exposure meters

Films

ABC's of Bez. il Pop Phot 62:106-7 Ja '68

ASA 25, 40, 100, 400: eleven minutes develops all four. H. Zucker. Pop Phot 61:74-5+ Ag '67

Acufine/Tri-X revisited. C. W. Kennedy. il Pop Phot 61:63-4 Jl '67

Agfachrome. M. Edelson. il U S Camera 30:64-5+ D '67

Amazing Anscochromes. M. Edelson. il U S Camera 30:48-9+ F '67

Anscochrome 500: when do you need it? E. Scully. il Mod Phot 31:78-81 Jl '67

Caulfield on color; how and why to care for film before processing. P. Caulfield. Mod Phot 31:42 Ag '67

Cheap color films: are they worth using? H. Keppler. il Mod Phot 31:66-7+ F '67

Color film for available light; Anscochrome 500. A. Rothstein. U S Camera 30:28+ Je '67

Color; it really started with 35mm Kodachrome in 1936. E. Bennett. il U S Camera 30:58+ My '67

Color negative: the one film that does everything. A. Goldsmith. il Pop Sci 190:126-9 Ap '67

Directory of color films. U S Camera 30:52-3+ S '67

Eaten any good film lately? Mod Phot 31:54 Ap '67

Ed Scully on basics. E. Scully. il Mod Phot 31:90+ My; 28 Je '67

Ed Scully on basics; choosing the right color film. E. Scully. Mod Phot 31:12 Ag '67

Ektacolor print film. R. Fuschetto and M. Orovan. il U S Camera 30:62-3+ Mr '67

Film speed runs amok. J. S. Forney. il Pop Phot 60:82-3+ Je '67

Fujichrome RT50. W. Hanson. il Pop Phot 60:126-7 Je '67

Gee whiz, here's Kodak's super speed but not super film. H. Keppler. il Mod Phot 31:120-1 D '67

High speed color films; Anscochrome 500. il Consumer Bul 50:38-40 O '67

House-brand films are a bargain? N. Rothschild. il Pop Phot 61:88-91+ O '67

How good is Ansco's 500 speed 35-mm color? N. Rothschild. Pop Phot 60:54+ Je '67

How to get the most out of Anscochrome 500. N. Rothschild. il Pop Phot 61:110-13+ D '67

How to get the most out of Dynachrome. N. Rothschild. il Pop Phot 60:88-91+ Ap '67

Is 35-mm dead? is super-35 alive? W. Hanson. Pop Phot 61:73+ Ag '67

Kodachromes and Ektachromes. M. Edelson. il U S Camera 30:40-3+ Ag '67

Large camera: choice of film size. A. Feininger. Mod Phot 32:48+ Ja '68

New: Agfachrome super 8 film, how good is it? W. Hanson. il Pop Phot 61:114 S '67

Screenings; 8mm. A. Cohen. Library J 92:3833-5, 4595-6 O 15, D 15 '67

Should you really switch to Anscochrome 50 or..? H. Keppler. Mod Phot 31:68-9+ Mr '67

Simon says; long, hard look at 220. Simon. Mod Phot 32:107 Ja '68

Soaring price of film. N. Rothschild. Pop Phot 61:52+ N '67

Ten color films: and how they're different! H. Keppler. il Mod Phot 31:72-5+ My '67

PHOTOGRAPHY—Films—*Continued*
Vacation tips for all seasons. D. B. Eisendrath, jr. il Pop Phot 61:8+ Ag '67
Welcome back, Ektachrome EP 120! D. B. Eisendrath, jr. Pop Phot 60:22+ Mr '67
Which Polaroid Land film? N. Rothschild. il Pop Phot 60:86-7+ Mr '67
World's fastest color film; Anscochrome. P. Wahl. il Pop Mech 128:96-8 Ag '67
Wow! Kodak's 1600 speed film. H. Keppler. il Mod Phot 31:72-3+ Jl '67
See also
Moving pictures

Storage
Caulfield on color; tropical problem. P. Caulfield. Mod Phot 31:12+ S '67
Cool it in the refrigerator. C. W. Kennedy. il Pop Phot 61:41-2+ N '67

Testing
Anscochrome D-500. il U S Camera 30:38-9+ Je '67
Caulfield on color; test color transparency films before shooting. P. Caulfield. Mod Phot 31:60+ Jl '67

Fixing
Fixers: some are slow, others fast. Mod Phot 31:74-5 F '67
Stop baths: what they stop and why. Mod Phot 31:74 F '67
Washing: when do you know it's complete? Mod Phot 31:76-7 F '67

Focusing
Breaking the three-foot barrier. il Pop Phot 60:61-4 Ap '67
Ed Scully on basics; depth of field. E. Scully. il Mod Pho 31:33+ O '67
Ed Scully on basics; sharpness problems. E. Scully. Mod Phot 31:20+ S '67
F/stop. R. Arnold. il U S Camera 30:40-1+ Ap '67
Fine art of grabshooting. H. Zucker. il Pop Phot 60:72-5+ Mr '67
Modern's shooting guide. E. Scully. il Mod Phot 31:58-61 S '67
Quick ways to sharper shots. H. Keppler. il Mod Phot 31:96-7 N '67
Soft focus: shoot it or print it? il Mod Phot 31:66-7 O '67
See also
Lenses, Photographic

Galleries and museums
Attention exhibit chairmen! Mod Phot 31:122 Ap '67
U.S. camera achievement award. U S Camera 30:43 N '67

Grain
It doesn't make a grain of sense. P. R. Farber. il U S Camera 30:46-7+ Jl '67

History
Photo heritage; excerpts from U.S. camera world annual, 1968. il U S Camera 30:54-60+ My '67 (to be cont)
Photographica. bibliog il Pop Phot 60:94-103+ My '67
This was 1937. B. Newhall. il Pop Phot 60:73-5+ My '67

Industrial applications
See Photography in industry

Landscapes
To see this land, to see America; New England photographs by W. Garnett. Life 62:50-65 Mr 3 '67

Light
Master of timing, master of light. P. Caulfield. il Mod Phot 31:52-9 Mr '67
Rain, don't let it stop you. P. Korn. il U S Camera 30:44-5+ Mr '67
Seeing red in black & white. H. C. Birnbaum. il U S Camera 30:42-3+ O '67
See also
Photography—Exposure

Lighting
Ed Scully on color; outdoor color portraits. E. Scully. il Mod Phot 32:42+ Ja '68
How to get the most out of a red filter. N. Rothschild. il Pop Phot 62:104-5+ Ja '68
Light and lighting. E. Scully. il Mod Phot 31:64-5 S '67
Lighting by which portraits are made. G. F. Duryea. il U S Camera 30:58-61 F '67
Lighting expert with other talents; J. Martis. G. P. Hunt. Life 63:7 S 22 '67

Lighting for portraits. E. Scully. il Mod Phot 32:72-7 Ja '68
Simple lighting set-ups. D. L. Miller and E. Meyers. il Mod Phot 31:76-7 Mr '67
See also
Photography, Flashlight

Marines
Color slides on the water. D. Rosenfeld. il Yachting 122:56+ Jl '67
Down to the seas again. A. Rothstein. U S Camera 30:28+ Ag '67

Negatives
Anything you can do I can do better; no you can't! T. Karp. il Mod Phot 31:78-81+ F '67
Meyers on technique. E. Meyers. Mod Phot 31:60 Je '67
Techniques tomorrow; photographic images on negatives. B. Sherman. Mod Phot 31:12+ D '67
You-print-'em negatives by famous photographers. il Pop Phot 60:81-2 My '67

News
See Photography, Journalistic

Portraits
ABC's of Bez. il Pop Phot 62:106-7 Ja '68
Birthday party photos. U S Camera 30:52-3 Ag '67
Breaking the three-foot barrier. il Pop Phot 60:61-4 Ap '67
Cartes de visite: rage of the 60's. Pop Phot 60:100+ My '67
Ed Scully on color; outdoor color portraits. E. Scully. il Mod Phot 32:42+ Ja '68
Girl watching; Pepsi-Cola and photographer A. Brooks get together. E. Galligan. il U S Camera 30:48-9 O '67
Gowland's L.A. scene. P. Gowland. See issues of Popular photography
Harvey Lloyd; what he believes about his craft. H. Lloyd. il Pop Phot 61:90-9 Ag '67
How much their eyes tell us! C. Burger. il Pop Phot 60:106-7+ F '67
How to make portraits with warmth, meaning and interest. A. Rothstein. U S Camera 30:14+ F '67
In the name of love. E. Gelabert. il Pop Phot 61:59-62 Jl '67
Karsh '67; exhibit at Expo '67. il U S Camera 30:56-7 Jl '67
Karsh's one-man show at Expo 67; centennial salute. M. R. Weiss. il Sat R 50:54-7 Ap 29 '67
Lighting by which portraits are made. G. F. Duryea. il U S Camera 30:58-61 F '67
Lighting for portraits. E. Scully. il Mod Phot 32:72-7 Ja '68
Look of longing. il U S Camera 30:52-3 Jl '67
Lotte Jacobi: photographic psychedelics. J. Deschin. il Pop Phot 61:38+ Jl '67
Natural color for nature's beauties; photographing beautiful women. A. Rothstein. U S Camera 30:14-15 Jl '67
Orlando. il Pop Phot 60:98-101+ Je '67
Painless, almost carefree, print retouching. P. Farber. il U S Camera 30:52-3+ D '67
Photography family. il U S Camera 30:54-5 O '67
Portraits: long, medium, close-up. Pop Phot 61:102-9 D '67
Powerful portrait. J. Durniak. il Pop Phot 60:100-7 Ap '67
Revealing eye, by N. Muray. Review Atlan 221:113 Ja '68. E. Weeks
Trade cards: graphic giveaways. Pop Phot 60:101+ My '67
Veruschka. F. Rubartelli. il Life 63:45-53 Ag 18 '67
Where there's smoke. . . il U S Camera 30:80-1 O '67
World's greatest pictures: Stravinsky by Newman. J. Scully. il Mod Phot 31:70-1+ My '67
See also
Daguerreotypes

Printing processes
Color in the kitchen sink. R. Excell. il U S Camera 30:64-5+ Jl '67
Color prints by automation: skill or money. P. Stackpole. U S Camera 30:20+ S '67
Colorval. P. R. Farber. il U S Camera 30:44-5+ Ap '67
Create the picture in your darkroom. E. Scully. il Mod Phot 31:62-3 Mr '67
Cutting the cost of color printing. P. Farber. U S Camera 30:20+ My '67

PHOTOGRAPHY—Printing processes—*Cont.*
Darkroom magic, by O. Litzel. Review
  U S Camera il 30:30+ S '67. P. Farber
Drum's little helpers. D. B. Eisendrath, jr.
  Pop Phot 60:14+ Ap '67
First week of color printing. A. Francekevich.
  Pop Phot 61:24 N '67
Meyers on technique. E. Meyers. Mod Phot
  31:26 My; 34+ N '67
Meyers on technique; Colorval, E. Meyers.
  il Mod Phot 31:18+ Ap '67
New instant printer makes pictures right
  before your eyes. il Pop Mech 128:123 D '67
New processor simplifies home printmaking.
  W. Lane. il Travel 127:72 F '67
Photomate heat printing. H. Zucker. il Pop
  Phot 62:108-11 Ja '68
Pointers on print making. E. Hannigan. U S
  Camera 30:24+ D '67
Print making. il Mod Phot 31:68-71 F '67
Print sharp, print bright. J. B. Johnson.
  il U S Camera 30:50-1 Jl '67
P.O.P. revisited; printing-out paper. C. W.
  Kennedy. il Pop Phot 61:15-16+ O '67
Soft focus: shoot it or print it? il Mod Phot
  31:66-7 O '67
Spotless darkroom. D. Richmond. il U S
  Camera 30:64-5+ My '67
Techniques tomorrow; photographic images
  on negatives. B. Sherman. Mod Phot 31:
  12+ D '67
Wolfman on printing. A. Wolfman. See is-
  sues of Modern photography
Wolfman on printing; contact printing. A.
  Wolfman. il Mod Phot 31:38+ Je '67
Wolfman on printing; stabilization proc-
  essing. A. Wolfman. il Mod Phot 31:30+
  F '67
  See also
Solarization

Retouching
Give prints a hand. A. Kramer. il Mod Phot
  32:62-3 Ja '68
Painless, almost carefree, print retouching.
  P. Farber. il U S Camera 30:52-3+ D '67
Who says you can't intensify, bleach,, tone
  Polaroid Land B&W prints? C. W. Kennedy.
  il Pop Phot 60:84-7+ F '67
Wolfman on printing. A. Wolfman. il Mod
  Phot 32:30+ Ja '68

Scientific applications
Evoked potentials: three-dimensional display.
  S. K. Burns and others. bibliog il Science
  157:457-9 Jl 28 '67
Gifts from out there; with photographs by
  H. Sochurek. Esquire 67:92-101 My '67
Moonsnaps: a fabulous new approach to the
  science of photography. J. Lear. il Sat R
  50:45-8 Ag 5 '67

Social aspects
For photographers who care: a helping hand;
  Fund for the concerned photographer. J.
  Deschin. il Pop Phot 62:40+ Ja '68

Still life
Egg and eye. il Pop Phot 61:63-6 Ag '67
How they made our cover. il Pop Phot 60:12
  My '67

Studios and darkrooms
Building your own, from scratch. A. France-
  kevich. il Pop Phot 61:40+ O '67
Compact darkroom. B. Lansche. il Pop Sci
  192:128-9 Ja '68
Eleven ideas from the CBS dream darkroom.
  M. D. Grennan. il Pop Phot 61:124-7+ D
  '67
Happy workplace; importance of a comfortable darkroom. A. Francekevich. Pop Phot
  60:8+ Ap '67
Incredible lab of Aaron Rose. A. Francekevich. il Pop Phot 62:28+ Ja '68
Presto! instant darkroom; apartment bathroom. E. Scully. il Mod Phot 31:83+ Je '67
Spotless darkroom. D. Richmond. il U S
  Camera 30:64-5+ My '67
3½ square. J. Seginski. il U S Camera 30:
  54-5+ Mr '67

Study and teaching
David in Adamsland; photography workshop
  of A. Adams. D. Vestal. il Pop Phot 61:
  90-101+ D '67
Hattersley class. See issues of Popular
  photography
  See also
Moving picture photography—Study and
  teaching
Shadowgrams

Terminology
Twisted terminology. D. P. Blake. U S
  Camera 30:65 Ap '67

Themes
Amish portfolio. G. Harvan. Pop Phot 61:
  98-101+ S '67
And all through the house; Christmas shots.
  E. Galligan. il U S Camera 30:44-5 D '67
Camera takes a trip; capturing the visual
  essence of an LSD trip. M. Laurance. il
  U S Camera 30:48-9 D '67
Cartier-Bresson today. B. Schwalberg; D.
  Vestal; M. Korda. il Pop Phot 60:108-17+
  My '67
Color & content! I. Tybel. il Pop Phot 61:
  106-10 Jl '67
Dramatic photos from ordinary scenes. J. Scul-
  ly. il Mod Phot 31:64-9 Je '67
Graphics are crucial! so is emotional impact!
  J. Scully. il Mod Phot 31:52-61+ My '67
Hate it? shoot it! il Pop Phot 60:43-6 Mr '67
In search of knowledge. il U S Camera 30:
  86-7 O '67
Man from Paris. il U S Camera 30:50-1 Ag
  '67
Photographing King Puck's fair. il U S
  Camera 30:56-7 D '67
Pictures & poetry. il Pop Phot 61:77-80 D
  '67
Pictures that make you wonder. il Pop Phot
  61:108-15 N '67
Sight and insight; excerpts from Look at
  us. W. Saroyan. il U S Camera 30:50-1
  D '67
Theme can turn jumble of slides into story.
  W. Lane. il Travel 127:70 Ap '67
Way of seeing. J. Scully. il Mod Phot 31:78-
  9 Mr '67

PHOTOGRAPHY, Aerial
Flying photographer. See issues of Flying
Fred Ward's $25,000 tripod; interview, ed. by
  J. Neubauer. F. Ward. il Pop Phot 60:69 Je
  '67
Israeli pilot's panoramic souvenir; with aerial
  photographs. Life 63:52B-52C Jl 14 '67
On the go, by plane. A. Hyde, jr. il U S
  Camera 30:44-5+ My '67
So, rent a helicopter! D. S. Gelatt. il Pop
  Phot 60:94-9 F '67
  See also
Mapping, Aerial

PHOTOGRAPHY, Artistic
Abstractions by Aptecker. M. Orovan. il U S
  Camera 30:56-7 Mr '67
Berdoy portfolio. il Craft Horiz 27:17-23 Ja '67
Create the picture in your darkroom. E.
  Scully. il Mod Phot 31:62-3 Mr '67
Discovery. J. Scully. il Mod Phot 31:68-9+
  My '67
Discovery; interview, ed. by P. Caulfield.
  L. Salzmann. il Mod Phot 31:64-5+ Mr '67
Lotte Jacobi; photographic psychedelics. J.
  Deschin. il Pop Phot 61:38+ Jl '67
Non-nude nudes. il Pop Phot 60:65-8 Je '67
Photographer's eye, by J. Szarkowski. Re-
  view
  Américas il 19:41-3 O '67. F. L. Phelps
Rothschild a la carte. N. Rothschild. il Pop
  Phot 60:84-93+ My '67
Sharpen your color eye. K. Poli. il Pop Phot
  61:96-7 Jl '67
Shoot projected color. M. A. Matzkin. il Mod
  Phot 31:74-5+ Je '67
Spreading the word; photography is art. P.
  Stackpole. U S Camera 30:26-7+ Mr '67
Turner; excerpts from address. P. Turner. il
  Pop Phot 60:90-9+ Mr '67

PHOTOGRAPHY, Astronomical. See Astronomical photography

PHOTOGRAPHY, Close-up
Large camera. A. Feininger. il Mod Phot 31:
  118+ Je '67
Move in close with super 8. N. Rothschild.
  il Pop Phot 61:112-14+ Ag '67
Super 8 for close-ups. M. A. Matzkin. il
  Mod Phot 31:78+ S '67
Take critically sharp close-ups with any SLR
  without pain or strain. H. Keppler. il Mod
  Phot 31:66-73 Ap '67

PHOTOGRAPHY, Color. See Color photography

PHOTOGRAPHY, Commercial
Confessions of a horse trader. N. Dean. il
  Pop Phot 61:89+ D '67
Money, pictures. A. Ahlers. il Pop Phot 60:83+
  My; 61:68+ Ag '67
Robert Huntzinger: follow the fire in your
  gut. H. M. Kinzer. il Pop Phot 61:82-91
  S '67
Soldier with a camera. E. Galligan. il U S
  Camera 30:44-9+ Je '67
To photography, with love. M. Orovan. il U S
  Camera 30:62-3 My '67
You too can make page one. E. Hannigan.
  U S Camera 30:18+ O '67
  See also
Photography, Fashion
Photography, Journalistic
Photography in advertising

PHOTOGRAPHY, Documentary
Assignment #1; photographs of American Indians at St Labre Indian mission, Ashland, Mont. H. Keppler. il Mod Phot 31:58-65 F '67
Fads and faces; concerning touring exhibition The Lower East side; portal to American life. R. Lynes. il Harper 235:26+ S '67
Help save our heritage. il Mod Phot 31:80-1+ O '67
Lower East side: portal to American life; exhibition at the Jewish museum. il U S Camera 30:50-1 Mr '67
Paul Strand at seventy-six; interview, ed. by J. Deschin. P. Strand. Pop Phot 60:14+ Mr '67
Photographer as historian. E. Hannigan. il U S Camera 30:16+ Ap '67
Photography. M. Kozloff. Nation 204:571-3 My 1 '67
Shadow of light by Bill Brandt; views from two sides of the ocean. N. Hall; R. Hattersley. il Pop Phot 61:102-3+ S '67
Television: an infinite source for color pictures. A. Rothstein. U S Camera 30:18-19 D '67
Two faces of Berlin. J. Faber. il U S Camera 30:56-7+ Ag '67

PHOTOGRAPHY, Electronic
Computer is now working on a camera like this. What else is coming? first Zeiss electronics symposium. N. Goldberg. il Pop Phot 61:69-73+ S '67
Full automation with accessories? C. W. Kennedy. il Pop Phot 61:28+ Ag '67
Latest electronics in photography; holograms without lasers, 20-second TV prints, microelectric eyes. H. Zucker. il Pop Phot 61:98-9+ Jl '67
Tony Karp on 35mm; photography goes solid-state. T. Karp. il Mod Phot 31:40+ Mr '67

PHOTOGRAPHY, Fashion
Bruce Davidson: my Leica, the movie camera. H. V. Fondiller. il Pop Phot 60:130-3+ My '67
Fashion head. il U S Camera 31:64-7 Ja '68
Reporter at large; Twiggy in New York. T. Whiteside. New Yorker 43:64-6+ N 4 '67

PHOTOGRAPHY, Flashlight
Fill-in flash indoors. C. W. Kennedy. il Pop Phot 60:33+ Je '67
Flash from the medical world. P. Stackpole. U S Camera 30:30+ F '67
Flash; most flash equipment is improperly used. P. R. Farber. il U S Camera 30:48-9+ My '67
Flashbulbs, color them amber. C. W. Kennedy. il Pop Phot 62:64+ Ja '68
Incredible cronoscope. P. R. Farber. il U S Camera 30:42-3+ Mr '67
Use an exposure meter for flash? P. Farber. il U S Camera 30:42-3+ S '67

Apparatus and supplies
Build the sound sync'er. A. J. Lowe. il Pop Electr 26:59-60 Ap '67
Slave driver; light-activated device for amateur photography. A. J. Lowe. il Pop Electr 28:65-7 Ja '68

PHOTOGRAPHY, Industrial. See Photography in industry

PHOTOGRAPHY, Infrared
AF uses IR remote scanning to obtain lunar surface data. J. A. Strasser. il Aero Tech 21:36+ D 4 '67
Infrared: lighting up the invisible. J. R. Berry. il Sci Digest 62:40-7+ N '67
IR mapping system readied for market. C. D. LaFond. il Tech W 20:30+ F 27 '67
Infrared radiometry. J. R. Collins. il Electr World 78:23-7+ O '67
Man in the orange suit. L. Mulvehill. il U S Camera 30:38-9+ My '67
Remote sensing of natural resources. R. N. Colwell. il Sci Am 218:54-69 Ja '68

PHOTOGRAPHY, Journalistic
...And you are there; news photographs of violence. Esquire 68:42-3 Jl '67
Anybody with a camera can be a newsman! D. P. Blake. il Pop Phot 60:81-3+ F '67
Bruce Downes; a critical appraisal. J. Balish. il Pop Phot 61:124-7+ N '67
Don't squint! make giant contacts; present enlarged proofs to editors. H. Zucker. il Pop Phot 61:84-7+ Ag '67
Focus on Stan Wayman; 35-mm for tigers or tankers. J. Neubauer. il Pop Phot 61:106-7+ Ag '67
Lawrence Fried's live color. il Pop Phot 60:100-5+ F '67

Life vs. photography. J. Durniak. Pop Phot 60:68 Ap '67
Luce raised the level of photographic art. P. Stackpole. U S Camera 30:14+ Je '67
One photographer's ESP. E. Hannigan. il U S Camera 30:16+ My '67
Photographer's place among the editors. A. Gingrich. Esquire 67:6+ My '67
Shoot projected color. M. A. Matzkin. il Mod Phot 31:74-5+ Je '67
Success in Canada. il U S Camera 30:50-1 S '67
35mm in the thirties; exhibition of photographs at Modernage headquarters. M. R. Weiss. il Sat R 50:74-5 F 11 '67
Who was Erich Salomon? J. Deschin. Pop Phot 61:36+ N '67
Woman on the run. E. Bennett. il U S Camera 30:44-5+ S '67

PHOTOGRAPHY, Laser. See Lasers—Photographic applications

PHOTOGRAPHY, Marine. See Photography—Marines

PHOTOGRAPHY, Medical
Corridors of the heart; with photographs by L. Nilsson. Life 64:22-31 Ja 19 '68
First film of cancer cells in action; taken by Russell Sherwin. il Life 63:57-8+ N 17 '67
Medical thermography. J. Gershon-Cohen. il Sci Am 216:94-102 bibliog(p 148) F '67

PHOTOGRAPHY, Moving picture. See Moving picture photography

PHOTOGRAPHY, Nature. See Nature photography

PHOTOGRAPHY, Night
How to take pictures at night. il Good H 165:173 Ag '67

PHOTOGRAPHY, Pictorial. See Photography, Artistic

PHOTOGRAPHY, Space. See Space photography

PHOTOGRAPHY, Stereographic. See Stereophotography

PHOTOGRAPHY, Submarine
Do flash & filters improve underwater pictures? B. Slosky. il Mod Phot 31:88-9+ Je '67
Taking a memo to Neptune. L. Barry. il Pop Phot 60:46+ F '67
35mm techniques; underneath the beautiful Bermuda water. P. Stackpole. U S Camera 30:30+ D '67
Underwater testing for six weeks at Bermuda. P. Stackpole. U S Camera 30:26+ N '67
See also
Moving picture photography, Submarine

PHOTOGRAPHY, Theatrical
One on the aisle. il U S Camera 30:54-5 Ag '67

PHOTOGRAPHY, Three dimensional. See Stereophotography

PHOTOGRAPHY, Trick
Alfred Gescheidt psychedelicate wit. K. Poli. il Pop Phot 61:84-5 Jl '67
Anselm M Spring: he has pictures to burn. il Pop Phot 60:94-5 Ap '67
Honeycombs; add the grid glass from a Weston meter to your 35. S. Greenberg. il U S Camera 30:16 D '67
Pseudo-solarizations of Giovanni Rutelli. il Pop Phot 60:92-5 Je '67
Silent world. P. Leonian. il U S Camera 30:46-7+ F '67
Tom McCarthy tries the fish-eye everybody can afford. il Pop Phot 60:78-81+ Ap '67
Weegee unveils his plastic lens. H. V. Fondiller. il Pop Phot 61:115 Ag '67

PHOTOGRAPHY and art. See Art and photography

PHOTOGRAPHY as a profession
Discovery. J. Scully. il Mod Phot 32:78-9+ Ja '68
Focus on: Wayne Miller. C. Schwalberg. il Pop Phot 60:88-9+ Mr '67

PHOTOGRAPHY by children. See Children as photographers

PHOTOGRAPHY clubs. See Camera clubs

PHOTOGRAPHY festivals
Thunder of shutters; photo festival at Mission Bay, San Diego. il U S Camera 30:58-9 Je '67

PHOTOGRAPHY from moving objects
On the go, by car. M. Bernstein. il U S Camera 30:46-7+ My '67

PHOTOGRAPHY in advertising
Advertising photographer. il U S Camera 30:58-9 Ag '67
Assignment Bahamas. il U S Camera 30:56-7 Je '67
Fantasy photography, but will it sell? M. Orovan. il U S Camera 30:48-9 Ap '67
Shooting with couples only. P. Gowland. il Pop Phot 60:30+ Mr '67

PHOTOGRAPHY in industry
Color at work. L. Schugar. il Pop Phot 61:104-5 Jl '67

PHOTOGRAPHY in medicine. See Photography, Medical

PHOTOGRAPHY in science. See Photography—Scientific applications

PHOTOGRAPHY in the fine arts (organization)
Instant art; Photography in the fine arts exhibition V. R. Lynes. il Harper 234:28+ Je '67
PFA-V: the museum is the message; on view in the Metropolitan museum of art. M. R. Weiss. il Sat R 50:37-44 My 6 '67

PHOTOGRAPHY in traffic regulation
Reconnaissance camera focused on traffic; applying aerial photography in Project Sky Count. il Tech W 20:35-6 Ap 3 '67

PHOTOGRAPHY of animals
Camera cat; Pippy the poster cat. il U S Camera 31:80-1 Ja '68
Camera hunting a coyote; photographs. J. Tallon. Field & S 72:40-1 D '67
Family of white wolves; with report by S. Wayman. il Life 62:50-7+ Je 2 '67
How to make a horse say cheese. D. Terrell. il U S Camera 30:64 Ap '67
How to snap a cat. M. M. Herron. il Pop Mech 127:182-3 Ap '67
Marvin Newman in Africa. E. Galligan. il U S Camera 30:61+ My '67
Photographing wild animals   P. Caulfield. Natur Hist 76:60-1 O '67
Safari, anyone? photographic safaris. E. A. Bauer. il Audubon 69:22-7 Jl '67
Wild game in East Africa. K. Sharma. il U S Camera 30:44-7 O '67
    See also
Animals—Photographs

PHOTOGRAPHY of apparitions
Short but wild history of spirit photography. M. Gardner. Pop Phot 61:65 O '67

PHOTOGRAPHY of birds
Photographing birds. P. Caulfield. Natur Hist 77:64+ Ja '68
Rare black eagles on the wing. il Life 62:66B-67 Mr 3 '67

PHOTOGRAPHY of children
Better baby pictures. R. Pinney. il Parents Mag 42:20 Je '67
Candid kids. il U S Camera 30:50-1 My '67
Day at the seashore. R. Pinney. il Parents Mag 42:60+ Ag '67
Family man; W. Smith photographs the things closest to him. M. Orovan. il U S Camera 30:60-1 Mr '67
How to take better children's pictures. Good H 164:191 My '67
Land and the sky. il U S Camera 30:54-5 D '67
Through the eyes of children. J. Hays. il U S Camera 30:58-9+ O '67

PHOTOGRAPHY of emotions
Amazing weekend with the amazing Ted Serios. C. Reynolds; D. B. Eisendrath, jr. il Pop Phot 61:81-7+ O '67; Reply. J. Eisenbud. 61:31-2+ N '67
Concerned photographer; exhibition at Riverside museum, N.Y. D. Vestal. il Pop Phot 61:106-13 O '67
Haskins makes it up; portfolio from November girl. H. Keppler. Mod Phot 31:80-91 N '67
One man's way; with photographs by G. Ward. U S Camera 30:66-7 D '67
Shadow of light by Bill Brandt; views from two sides of the ocean. N. Hall; R. Hattersley. il Pop Phot 61:102-3+ S '67
Thy name is woman. K. Tweedy-Holmes. il Pop Phot 61:69-72 O '67

PHOTOGRAPHY of fireworks
Skyrockets, sparklers, and starbursts. N. Rothschild. il Pop Phot 61:94-5+ Jl '67

PHOTOGRAPHY of flowers, plants, trees, etc.
Close-up photography for gardeners. R. A. Lehman. il Horticulture 45:28-9+ Ap '67
Home garden photography contest. il Home Gard 54:38-40 O '67
Patterns of life. W. M. Harlow. il Am For 73:4-7+ F '67
Patterns of life; excerpts from Patterns of life: the unseen world of plants. W. M. Harlow. il Audubon 69:58-63 Mr '67
Take pictures of trees. il Horticulture 45:26-7 O '67

PHOTOGRAPHY of girls. See Photography—Portraits

PHOTOGRAPHY of infants. See Photography of children

PHOTOGRAPHY of insects
Cool it! S. Greenberg. il U S Camera 30:52-3 My '67
Entomography. il Pop Phot 60:96-7 Je '67
Motion pictures of insects. P. Villiard. il Natur Hist 76:50+ Mr '67

PHOTOGRAPHY of light
Light itself is a picture; Lights in orbit show. H. M. Kinzer. il Pop Phot 61:79-81 Jl '67
Shoot swirling color from a swinging light. W. S. Schenck. il Pop Mech 127:90-1 Je '67

PHOTOGRAPHY of meteors. See Astronomical photography

PHOTOGRAPHY of moving objects
Fine art of grabshooting. H. Zucker. il Pop Phot 60:72-5+ Mr '67
Matzkin on movies; Bilora's motorama. M. A. Matzkin. il Mod Phot 31:24+ Mr '67
Scrambling cycles. D. Richmond. il U S Camera 30:46-7+ Ag '67
Slow down for action. M. Laurance. il U S Camera 30:54-5 Je '67
Where the action is. il U S Camera 30:56-7 S '67

PHOTOGRAPHY of nature. See Nature photography

PHOTOGRAPHY of nebulae. See Astronomical photography

PHOTOGRAPHY of paintings. See Photography of works of art

PHOTOGRAPHY of ships
Rosie remembers, nearly seventy years of America's cup memories. D. Rosenfeld. il Motor B 120:30-3+ Ag '67

PHOTOGRAPHY of snow, ice, etc.
Two kinds of snow jobs. D. B. Eisendrath, jr. Pop Phot 60:16+ F '67

PHOTOGRAPHY of sports
Packer snapper. D. Schreiner. il U S Camera 30:60-1+ N '67
Scrambling cycles. D. Richmond. il U S Camera 30:46-7+ Ag '67
Shooting the bull. L. Sherwood. il U S Camera 30:64-5+ Je '67
Shooting the sports spectacle. il U S Camera 31:54-5 Ja '68
Sports: same old view, or? J. Scully. il Mod Phot 32:52-61 Ja '68
Those great pictures in Grand prix, how they were made. R. Dempewolff. il Pop Mech 127:77-81+ Mr '67
Time to think winter; Quebec winter carnival. L. Barry. il Pop Phot 61:26+ O '67
Where the action is. il U S Camera 30:56-7 S '67
    See also
Baseball—Photographs
Sports—Photographs

PHOTOGRAPHY of the human figure. See Human figure in photography

PHOTOGRAPHY of the sun. See Astronomical photography

PHOTOGRAPHY of works of art
Large camera; making good reproductions. A. Feininger. Mod Phot 31:96+ My '67
Large camera; photographing sculpture. A. Feininger. il Mod Phot 31:100+ Ap '67
Large camera; right equipment for photographing paintings and sculpture. A. Feininger. Mod Phot 31:28+ F '67

PHOTOGRAPHY of yachts. See Photography of ships

PHOTOJOURNALISM. See Photography, Journalistic

PHOTOLITHOGRAPHY
    See also
Printing, Offset

PHOTOMATE heat printing. See Photography—Printing processes

PHOTOMETRY, Astronomical
    See also
Spectrophotometry

PHOTOMICROGRAPHY
Amateur scientist; how to photograph tiny live crustaceans. P. Rowe. il Sci Am 216:143-4+ My '67
Color through a microscope. M. Abramowitz. il Pop Phot 61:86-9+ Jl '67
Patterns of life. W. M. Harlow. il Am For 73:4-7+ F '67
Patterns of life; excerpts from Patterns of life: the unseen world of plants. W. M. Harlow. il Audubon 69:58-63 Mr '67
Take a close look. M. Laurance. il U S Camera 31:38-9 Ja '68
Think small. M. D. Grennan. il Pop Phot 61:48+ Ag '67

PHOTOMONTAGE
Op goes the easel. R. W. Parsons. il Pop Phot 60:88-9+ F '67

PHOTOMURALS. See Photographic murals

PHOTOPERIODISM. See Light—Physiological effects

PHOTOSYNTHESIS
Deuterium isotope effect on carbon isotope fractionation in photosynthesis. R. A. Uphaus and J. J. Katz. bibliog il Science 155:324-5 Ja 20 '67

PHOTOSYNTHESIS—Continued
Photosynthetic system II: racial differentiation in typha latifolia. S. J. McNaughton. bibliog il Science 156:1363 Je 9 '67
Photosynthetic utilization of internal carbon dioxide by hollow-stemmed plants. W. D. Billings and P. J. Godfrey. bibliog il Science 158:121-3 O 6 '67

PHOTOSYNTHETIC bacteria. See Bacteria, Photosynthetic

PHOTOTYPESETTING
Electronic setting on film for ideographic languages. il Pub W 192:90 O 2 '67
Fast type; use of the Linotron at the U.S. government printing office. Sci Am 217:55+ D '67
Printing is turning the page; Videocomp. il Bsns W p 122-4+ S 9 '67
Science publisher looks at phototypesetting. E. J. Hoguet. il Pub W 192:86+ N 6 '67

PHRAGMOSIS. See Insects—Habits and behavior

PHRASES. See English language—Terms and phrases

PHUOC VINH
Thirty-five miles from Saigon. F. Sully. New Repub 157:11-12 Ag 5 '67

PHYCOMYCES
Phycomyces sporangiophores: fungal stretch receptors. D. S. Dennison and C. C. Roth. il Science 156:1386-8 Je 9 '67

PHYLOGENY
Construction of phylogenetic trees. W. M. Fitch and E. Margoliash. bibliog il Science 155:279-84 Ja 20 '67

PHYSICAL astronomy. See Astrophysics

PHYSICAL chemistry. See Chemistry, Physical and theoretical

PHYSICAL directors
See also
Coaches (athletics)

PHYSICAL education and training
Fitness time in Topeka. J. Corcoran. il Am Ed 3:21-3+ S '67
Learning about movement. N. Allenbaugh. il NEA J 56:48+ Mr '67
Sizing your school's phys ed. il Changing T 22:30-2 Ja '68

PHYSICAL education and training of women
What sports for girls? R. Higdon and H. Higdon. il Todays Health 45:20-3+ O '67

PHYSICAL examinations
Doctor talks sense about physical checkups. W. E. O'Donnell. il Good H 164:111+ Mr '67
Forecasting your future health. T. Irwin. il Todays Health 45:25-9 My '67
Physical exams; medical checkups every woman needs. il Good H 164:137 Ja '67
What should a good physical exam tell you? il Bet Hom & Gard 45:30+ Ag '67
What to do about aches and pains. Bet Hom & Gard 45:24+ O '67
Your child's health; periodic health checkups. L. W. Sauer. il PTA Mag 62:31-2 Ja '68
See also
Air pilots—Physical examinations
Children—Care and hygiene

PHYSICAL exercise. See Exercise

PHYSICAL fitness. See Health; Men—Health and hygiene

PHYSICAL geography
See also
Earth
Man—Influence on nature
Ocean bottom
Rivers
Volcanoes
Washington (state)
Mima mounds. H. Pearson. il Nat Parks Mag 41:13 F '67

PHYSICAL geology. See Geology, Structural

PHYSICAL therapists
Professionals who help humanity. T. Berland. il Todays Health 45:52-5+ Ap '67

PHYSICAL training. See Physical education and training

PHYSICALLY handicapped. See Handicapped

PHYSICIANS
Doctors' own diet. P. Wyden and B. Wyden. Ladies Home J 84:61+ F '67
Joys and problems of being a doctor. M. O. Rouse. Todays Health 45:72+ Je '67
MD's as addicts. Sci Digest 62:72-3 O '67
New role for doctors; clinical associates. Sci Digest 62:83 S '67
Why a doctor's orders should be followed. il Good H 166:162-3 Ja '68

With a life at stake; services of an internist. E. M. Brecher. McCalls 95:96-7+ O '67
See also
Medical education
Medical ethics
Medicine—Practice
Osteopaths
Pediatricians
Psychiatrists
Women as physicians

Fees
See Medical service, Cost of

Supply and demand
Again, the doctor shortage. America 117:461-2 O 28 '67
Answers to doctor shortage in U.S. il U S News 63:56-8 O 9 '67
Doctor shortage. Nation 205:372 O 16 '67
Doctors: the supply and demand. Life 63:4 Jl 14 '67
Every tenth doctor a brain drain statistic; conditions in Israel. M. Dean. Sci N 92:155 Ag 12 '67
Foreign-doctor invasion of U.S. il U S News 63:72 Ag 28 '67
How to get a doctor in a farm community. R. H. Sterenborg. il Suc Farm 65:51+ Jl '67
Is there a doctor..? il Newsweek 69:82 Je 5 '67
Reverse foreign aid; problem of medical brain drain from developing countries. il Sci N 91:75 Ja 21 '67
Six-year wonders; accelerated training programs. il Time 90:70+ Jl 14 '67
Too few doctors; an alarming situation. il U S News 63:12 Jl 3 '67

PHYSICIANS and patients
Drop those prejudices against women doctors. A. Lake. Good H 164:88-9+ My '67
Fear of death; patients with fatal diseases. il Newsweek 69:56 F 27 '67
I prescribe... J. D. Wassersug. See issues of Science digest
Oath of secrecy; concerning college psychiatry. Sci N 91:354 Ap 15 '67
Oriental psychiatry veering West; Japan. S. Griffin. il Sci N 92:254-5 S 9 '67
Patients who make the doctor feverish. M. Halberstam. il N Y Times Mag p 18-19+ F 5 '67; Discussion. p6+ F 26 '67
Patients who want to be sick; excerpt from Patients, doctors and families. F. C. Lewis. il Todays Health 46:20-3 Ja '68
Secret of caring for the patient; ed. by W. S. Ross. M. J Lepore il Todays Health 45:38-42+ N '67
Take your medical complaint to the doctors. E. J. Holman. Todays Health 45:72+ Jl '67
What doctors should tell their patients. Good H 165:207 N '67
What happens behind the doctor's door. A. Lake. il Seventeen 26:102-3+ D '67
Why you need a doctor of your own. A. Lake. il Seventeen 26:146-7+ F '67

PHYSICISTS
See also
Einstein, A.

PHYSICS
Six impossible tricks. il Sci Digest 62:30-1 O '67
See also
American institute of physics
American physical society
Astrophysics
Fluids
Mathematical physics
Matter
Music—Acoustics and physics
Pressure

Experiments
Classic toys test your physics know-how; interview, ed. by W. S. Griswold. J. S. Miller. il Pop Sci 190:116-21+ Ap '67
Physics for fun: Bernoulli's paradox. K. Swezey. il Pop Sci 191:88-9+ O '67

History
Michael Faraday and the physics of 100 years ago; excerpts from Michael Faraday, a biography. L. P. Williams. bibliog il Science 156:1335-42 Je 9 '67
Thermodynamics in Einstein's thought. M. J. Klein. bibliog Science 157:509-16 Ag 4 '67

Scholarships and fellowships
Graduate student stipends; excerpts from seminar, May 1965. W. R. Gruner. il Science 157:1530-3 S 29 '67

PHYSICS—*Continued*

Study and teaching

Good enough for Galileo; Harvard Project Physics. P. Boulay. il Am Ed 4:15-18 D '67

PHYSICS, American institute. See American institute of physics

PHYSIOGNOMY

See also

Face

PHYSIOLOGICAL apparatus

Spectrophotometric cell sorter. L. A. Kamentsky and M. R. Melamed. bibliog il Science 156:1364-5 Je 9 '67

See also

Anatomical models

Heart, Artificial

PHYSIOLOGICAL chemistry. See Biochemistry

PHYSIOLOGICAL effects of noise; Physiological effects of X rays; etc. See Noise—Physiological effects; X rays—Physiological effects; etc.

PHYSIOLOGICAL oxidation. See Oxidation, Physiological

PHYSIOLOGICAL psychology. See Psychology, Physiological

PHYSIOLOGICAL research

Globin composition and synthesis of hemoglobins in developing fetal mice erythroid cells. A. Fantoni and others. bibliog il Science 157:1327-9 S 15 '67

How much can your body take? il Sci Digest 61:40-53 Ap '67

See also

Space flight—Physiological aspects

PHYSIOLOGY

See also

Absorption (physiology)

Dehydration (physiology)

Electrophysiology

Man

Metabolism

Nervous system

Psychology, Physiological

Underwater physiology

Vascular system

PHYSOSTIGMINE

Retrograde amnesia produced by intraperitoneal injection of physostigmine. M. D. Hamburg. bibliog il Science 156:973-4 My 19 '67

PHYTOHEMAGGLUTININS. See Agglutinins

PHYTOLACCA dodecandra. See Endod

PI mesons. See Mesons

PIAGET, Jean

Jean Piaget: notes on learning; with excerpts from addresses. F. G. Jennings. il pors Sat R 50:81-3 My 20 '67

PIANISTS

Hand that touched Brahms's touched mine! ed. by E. Miller. J. Jones. il Seventeen 26: 156-7+ S '67

Mood merchants; cocktail pianists. il Time 89:54 Mr 24 '67

See also

Argerich, M.

Barenboim, D.

Frager, M.

Gould, G.

Graffman, G.

Gulda, F.

Horowitz, V.

Larrocha, A. de

Peterson, O.

Rubinstein, A.

Smith, W.

PIANO

How to buy a piano. R. Gibson. House & Gard 132:32+ N '67

How to give your piano the attention it deserves. C. Calkins. House B 109:64+ Mr '67

Keyboard in perspective. G. Benko. Am Rec G 33:870-1 My '67

Question on pianos: vertical or grand? il Consumer Bul 50:7-14 O '67

Right care for your piano. il Good H 164:190 My '67

See also

Pianists

Instruction and study

Hand that touched Brahms's touched mine! ed. by E. Miller. J. Jones. il Seventeen 26: 156-7+ S '67

New dimensions in music lessons; group teaching. J. A. Mason. il House B 109:150-1+ F '67

PIANO competitions. See Music—Competitions

PIANO festivals. See Music festivals

PIANO industry and trade

See also

Aeolian corporation

PIANO music

Keyboard in perspective. G. Benko. Am Rec G 33:870-1 My '67

Piano works of Claude Debussy, by E. R. Schmitz. Review

Am Rec G 33:855 My '67. D. A. Klein

See also

Concertos

Phonograph records—Piano music

PIANO playing

See also

Piano—Instruction and study

PIANO rolls. See Player piano rolls

PIANOFORTE. See Piano

PIC, Roger

Fighting with the Vietcong; photographs. Look 32:62-3 Ja 23 '68

PICARESQUE literature

Picaresque and the American experience. F. R. Kari. Yale R 57:196-212 D '67

PICASSO, Jacqueline (Roque)

Picasso: the ninth decade; interview, ed. by S. Gauthier. Look 31:86-8 N 28 '67

PICASSO, Pablo

Picasso: the ninth decade; interview, ed. by S. Gauthier. por Look 31:86-8 N 28 '67

about

Art; The sculpture of Picasso, at the Museum of modern art. M. Kozloff. Nation 205:441-4 O 30 '67

Chicago prepares for biggest Picasso of all. il Bsns W p 122-3 My 6 '67

Chicago's Picasso. il Life 63:85-6 Ag 25 '67

Desire caught by the tail. Criticism

Time 90:51 Jl 28 '67

Doodles of genius; sculpture il Time 90:76 O 20 '67

Guernica as art history. J. Masheck. il Art N 66:32-5+ D '67

Letter from Paris; G. Stein collection. Genêt. New Yorker 43:174+ Mr 25 '67

Object-lessons in object-love; survey of sculptures. L. Gowing. il Art N 66:24-7+ O '67

Old maestro's magic; sculpture in Chicago's civic center. il Time 90:54-5 Ag 25 '67

Picasso and company, by Brassaï. Review

Nation 204:694-5 My 29 '67. W. Fowlie

Picasso & photography; excerpts from Picasso and company. Brassaï. il por Pop Phot 60: 78-80+ My '67

Picasso as sculptor; excerpt from introduction to The sculpture of Picasso. R. Penrose. il Atlan 220:69-76 O '67

Picasso in the steelworks. il Fortune 76:111-13 Ag '67

Picasso: the blue and rose periods, by P. Daix and G. Boudaille. Review

New Repub 157:32+ O 21 '67. H. Kramer

Picasso the craftsman; exhibition of sculpture at the Museum of modern art. R. Arneson. il Craft Horiz 27:28-33 N '67

Picasso's hidden treasure; Museum of modern art's retrospective exhibition of sculpture. D. L. Shirey. il Newsweek 70:110-11 O 16 '67

Picasso's sculpture. R. Berenson. il Nat R 19:1434-7 D 26 '67

Putting Pablo to the vote. il Time 90:46 D 29 '67

PIC DU MIDI observatory. See Astronomical observatories—France

PICCADILLY world match play tournament. See Golf—Tournaments

PICCUS, Jules

Lost Leonardos. il por Newsweek 69:97 F 27 '67

PICHLER, Joseph A.

Means of adjustment to technological displacement. Mo Labor R 90:32-3 Mr '67

PICK, Edgar, and Feldman, J. D.

Autoradiographic plaques for the detection of antibody formation to soluble proteins by single cells. bibliog Science 156:964-6 My 19 '67

PICK, Franz

Shrewdest man in the money market; excerpt from The money managers. G. Krefetz and R. Marossi. Harper 235:43-7 Jl '67

PICKERING, Jack

Drugs & driving, a deadly mix! Motor T 19: 58-60 My '67

PICKERING, James S.

Backyard astronomer (cont) Natur Hist 76: 54+ Mr; 60+ Ag '67

PICKERING, Richard J. and others

Deficient complement fixation by aggregated gamma globulin from hypogammaglobulinemic patients. bibliog Science 157:454-5 Jl 28 '67

PICKETT, Bill

He took the bull by the horns. J. J. Mundis. il por Am Heritage 19:50-5 D '67

PICKETT, Frank
I learned my lesson. Nations Bsns 55:76+
O '67
PICKFORD, Grace E. and Grant, F. B.
Serum osmolality in the coelacanth, latimeria
chalumnae: urea retention and ion regula-
tion. bibliog Science 155:568-70 F 3 '67
PICKLES and relishes
It's time to make melon pickles; with rec-
ipes. Sunset 139:118 S '67
Jams, jellies, pickles, and relishes. il Suc
Farm 65:60-1 Ag '67
Make these pickle pepper-uppers. il Farm J
91:46-7 Ag '67
Perfect pickles; with recipes. il Bet Hom
& Gard 45:104 S '67
Tips on canning. il Suc Farm 65:55 Ag '67
PICKUP, Phonograph. See Phonograph—Pick-
up
PICKUP campers. See Campers and coaches,
Truck
PICKUP trucks. See Motor trucks
PICKUS, Robert
Liberal anti-communism revisited. Com-
mentary 44:58-62 S '67
PICNIC baskets, boxes, etc.
In time for picnics. N. Craig. il House B
109:6-8 Jl '67
PICNICS
Are picnics necessary? N. S. Hazelton. Nat R
19:694 Je 27 '67
Art of the picnic; with recipes. il Sunset
139:38-45 Ag '67
Come join the fun! you're just in time for
GH's picnic cookbook! il Good H 165:106-
22 Jl '67
End-of-haying picnic. B. L. Henry. il Farm J
91:44-5+ Jl '67
Family food section. B. M. Stover. il Parents
Mag 42:54-9+ Jl '67
Picnic; a bite-size vacation. il House B 109:
116-17+ Jl '67
Tailgate picnic. il Bet Hom & Gard 45:98 Je
'67
Transportable parties. il House & Gard 131:79-
85 Je '67
PICTORIAL display systems, Airborne. See
Aeronautic instruments—Display systems
PICTORIAL humor. See Humor, Pictorial
PICTORIAL maps. See Maps, Pictorial
PICTORIAL photography. See Photography,
Artistic
PICTURE books
Critics at large. il Pop Phot 61:144-7 D '67
Eliot Porter: medication to conservation. J.
Deschin. il Pop Phot 61:70+ D '67
PICTURE books for children
Bookmaking exhibition on developing a pic-
ture book. il Pub W 191:98 F 6 '67
Choosing for our youngest. A. Rusk. il Li-
brary J 92:1294-5 Mr 15 '67
From Aardvark to Zymurgy. D. Thomas.
bibliog il Library J 92:4582-6 D 15 '67
My goals as an illustrator. M. Brown. il Horn
Bk 43:304-16 Je '67
See also
Caldecott medal
PICTURE frames
Fine art for framing. il McCalls 94:51+ Je '67
Framing makes the difference. B. H. Gure-
vitz. il Design 68:36-8 Mr '67
New picture-framing ideas. Good H 165:174
Ag '67
PICTURE post cards. See Post cards
PICTURES
Paint a picture with needle and yarn! il
Good H 164:136-7 Mr '67
See also
Drawings
Paintings
PICTURES, Framing of. See Picture frames
PICTURES, Patchwork. See Patchwork
PICTURES, Theft of. See Art thefts
PICTURES of the year competition. See Pho-
tography—Competitions
PIDDINGTON, R. See Moscona, A. A. jt. auth.
PIE
Bride makes a deep-dish fruit pie; with
recipes. il McCalls 94:42 Ag '67
Down East delicacy; blueberry pie; with
menu and recipes by E. Graves. il Life
63:62-5 Jl 7 '67
Here are four variations on Thanksgiving's
finale, and all are pumpkin. il Sunset 139:
152+ N '67
Just warn them what's coming: chocolate
pies. il Sunset 138:188+ Ap '67
Marmalade but memorable; pie made with
orange liqueur. C. Claiborne. il N Y Times
Mag p59 Mr 26 '67

My mother, the pie maker; with recipes. J.
Agan. il Parents Mag 42:90-3 N '67
Pastry plus. il Bet Hom & Gard 45:112 My
'67
Pies that please in more ways than one!
with recipes. il Good H 165:122-7 S '67
Pleasing autumn pies. il Ebony 22:134+ O '67
Seedless grape pie surprises. il Sunset 139:
98+ Ag '67
Spinach pie? certainly. and also leek, carrot,
and mushroom pies. il Sunset 138:203-4 Mr
'67
Sweet cherry pie as a June surprise; with
recipes. il Sunset 138:64-5 Je '67
Wonderful, wonderful fruit-filled pies. Am
Home 70:126c N '67
PIEPKORN, Arthur C.
Why Lutherans should engage in conversa-
tion with Roman Catholics. Cath World 206:
77-80 N '67
PIERCE, Bill
Photo beat. See issues of Popular photography
PIERCE, Douglas R. See Egner, J. R. jt. auth.
PIERCE, Edith Lovejoy
Espalier fruit; poem. Christian Cent 84:105
Ja 25 '67
Men as trees walking; poem. Christian Cent
84:1281 O 11 '67
PIERCE, Noel
Music in your mail box; Longines symphon-
ette mail order house. Parents Mag 42:96-7
Ja '67
What's new for children. Parents Mag 43:16
Ja '68
PIERCE, Ponchitta
Divorce and the Negro woman. Ebony 22:84-
6+ Jl '67
Science pacemaker. Ebony 22:52-4+ Ap '67
Street academies: new way to reach the
ghetto dropout. Ebony 22:158-60+ Ag '67
PIERCE, Robert Willard
Visit to Vietnam. A. Ives. il Seventeen 26:150-
1+ F '67
PIERCE, Suzanne
Al and I spend a year in Taiwan. il por Dance
Mag 41:47+ N '67
PIERCE, Wendell H.
Administrator speaks out; interview. por Am
Ed 3:27-9 F '67
Education commission of the states. NEA J
56:30-1 Mr '67
PIERCE, William S. See Boretos, J. W. jt.
auth.
PIERCE, S. S, company
Laird of the epicurean manner; company
bought by Laird Industries inc. il Time 89:
88-9 Je 23 '67
PIERCED ear earrings. See Earrings
PIERCY, Esther J.
Obituary
Wilson Lib Bul 41:671 Mr '67. J. H. Shera
Two memorial funds for Esther J. Piercy.
Library J 92:957 Mr 1 '67
PIERPONT Morgan library
Family friend of all the world; five of Per-
rault's Tales of Mother Goose. F. B. Adams,
jr. il Wilson Lib Bul 41:573-5 F '67
PIERRE-NOEL, Lois Jones
American Negro art in progress. il Negro Hist
Bul 30:6-9 O '67
PIERSALL, Glenna
Black marble moat for Fort Campbell. Library
J 92:4381-3 D 1 '67
PIERSALL, Jimmy
Fallen idol. D. Honicker. Sat R 50:4 O 14 '67
PIEZ, Gladys T.
Library technology. See issues of ALA bul-
letin to October 1967
PIGEON shooting
Go to beat the bandtails. B. Behme. il Field &
S 72:62-5 Je '67
PIGEONS
Foolproof control of pigeons and starlings;
Columbia, Mo. M. R. Sanford. il Am City
82:116-17 Mr '67
Lessons from experience; use of a carrier
pigeon in a boating emergency. H. S.
Houghton. il Motor B 119:36-7 My '67
Navigation of single homing pigeons; air-
plane observations by radio tracking. M.
C. Michener and C. Walcott; reply with
rejoinder. B. G. Murray, jr. Science 155:
1135-6 Mr 3 '67
Pigeons walk right into a trap; Hudson, N.Y.
Am City 82:46 N '67
PIGEONS; story. See Singer, I. B.
PIGNATELLI, Luciana, princess
Princess and the paper lash. il por Life
62:63-4 Mr 31 '67
PIGS. See Swine
PIGWEED. See Purslane

PIKE, Frederick B.
Church and state in Peru and Chile since 1840; a study in contrasts. bibliog f Am Hist R 73:30-50 O '67

PIKE, James Albert, bp
Authors & editors. Pub W 191:28-9 Je 26 '67
Bishop Pike catches attention at Richmond. W. B. Gray. Christian Cent 84:221-2 F 15 '67
Bothersome bishop. R. Hazelton. New Repub 157:32-3+ O 7 '67
Death of dialogue. W. H. DuBay. Christian Cent 84:1192 S 20 '67; Reply. R. R. Winkelmann. 84:1530 N 29 '67
Empirical faith. por Time 90:66 S 15 '67
Episcopal report may preclude Pike trial. Christian Cent 84:1147-8 S 13 '67
Four cases in the new morality; excerpts from You and the new morality. por Ladies Home J 84:104-5+ My '67
God is evolving, not dead; with excerpt from If this be heresy. K. S. Latourette. por Sat R 50:45-6 S 16 '67
Heresy trial postponed. Christian Cent 84:134 F 1 '67
In defense of heresy. A. Towne; discussion. Christian Cent 84:211-13, 380-1 F 15, Mr 22 '67
Is heresy dead? il por Newsweek 70:56 Ag 28 '67
Medium's message il por Newsweek 70:57 O 9 '67
Messages through the medium. il por Time 90:55 O 6 '67
Of many things; concerning Bishop Pike's statistics about the economic wealth of the Jesuits. T. N. Davis. America 116:608 Ap 29 '67
Séance in Seattle: ruminations in a ruin. A. Towne. Christian Cent 84:1442-4 N 8 '67

PIKE, Otis G.
Reporter at large. R. Harris. New Yorker 43:48-50+ Ap 8 '67

PIKE, Robert E.
Hell and high water; excerpts from Tall trees, tough men. Am Heritage 18:64-70 F '67

PIKE fishing
Fishing light is never out. E. Park. il Outdoor Life 140:46-9+ Ag '67
Lesson in pints and pounds. M. Ellis. il Field & S 71:46-8+ Ap '67
Very superior pike! R. Dornquast. il Field & S 72:54-5+ D '67
Voyage to wilderness fishing; from Ohio to Ontario. G. Lau. il Outdoor Life 140:17-19+ Jl '67

PIKES PEAK race. See Automobile racing

PILAF. See Cookery—Rice

PILEGGI, Nicholas
Long palm of the law. Esquire 67:132-5+ Ap '67
We burned a bum Friday night and we're going to burn another one tonight. Esquire 68:48-50+ Jl '67

PILFERING. See Stealing

PILGRIMS and pilgrimages
Dialogue in the Near East; pilgrim visiting the Bible lands. C. J. McNaspy. il America 116:726-7 My 13 '67
Oldest, newest and in between. C. J. McNaspy. America 116:765-6 My 20 '67
Spectacle of Easter in Jerusalem; in art and life, the jarring contrasts of the passion; with report by D. Seiberling. il Life 62:50-60+ Mr 24 '67
Vigil at Fatima on the eve of Pope Paul's visit. il Life 62:32-5 My 26 '67

PILIÉ, Roland J. and others
Warm fog suppression in large-scale laboratory experiments. Science 157:1319-20 S 15 '67

PILKINGTON brothers, limited
Pilkington shines again. il Time 90:98+ D 15 '67

PILLAGE
I don't care if I die; report of four days among the Detroit rioters. J. Dotson. il Newsweek 70:26-7 Ag 7 '67
Looters: deprived or in Cadillacs? U S News 63:27 Ag 14 '67

PILLOW cases
Institute reports on. ., new no-iron sheets and pillowcases. il Good H 164:6 F '67

PILLOWS
Cardboard pets and woolly pillows; make a merry menagerie. il Bet Hom & Gard 45:48-50 D '67
Discover the soft life. il Redbook 129:82-3+ Ag '67
It's just a big pillow clock. il Sunset 139:98 D '67

PILLSBURY company
Adjusting the mix at Pillsbury. il Bsns W p 167-8+ S 30 '67

PILOT training. See Air pilots—Training

PILOTING, Airplane. See Airplanes—Piloting

PILOTS and pilotage
Constructing a speed curve. il Motor B 119:102-5 Je '67
Lessons from experience; use of a carrier pigeon in a boating emergency. H. S. Houghton. il Motor B 119:36-7+ My '67

PILOU, Jeannette
Out of Egypt; interview, ed. by R. D. Daniels. por Opera N 32:26 Ja 13 '68

PILPEL, Harriet F.
But can you do that? See occasional issues of Publishers' weekly

PIMLOTT, Douglas H.
Whitecoat in peril. il Audubon 69:76-81 S '67

PINBALL machines; story. See Harrison, W.

PINCHOT, Gifford B.
To the South Seas in Loon. Yachting 122:44-6+ Jl; 42-3+ Ag '67

PINCHOT, Sally
Navigation in the South Pacific. Yachting 122:112 Jl '67

PINDLING, Lynden Oscar
Black vote revolt in the Bahamas. L. Bennett, jr. il pors Ebony 22:68-70+ Je '67
Negro leader takes over; white rule in Bahamas ends. il por U S News 62:16 Ja 30 '67

PINE
Enclosed bark as a pollen trap. D. P. Adam and others. bibliog il Science 157:1067-8 S 1 '67
Helping hand for the Torrey pine. B. Dillon. il Nat Parks Mag 41:16-17 S '67
Oldest living thing in the world; bristlecone pines. A. Hamilton. il Sci Digest 62:37-8 O '67
Utah has its own ancient bristlecones. il Sunset 138:34+ My '67

PINE BARRENS, N.J.
Profiles. J. McPhee. New Yorker 43:67-8+ N 25; 66-8+ D 2 '67

PINE mice. See Mice

PINE RIDGE reservaton, S.D. See Indians of North America—Reservations

PINEAL body
Adenyl cyclase activity in rat pineal gland: effects of chronic denervation and norepinephrine. B. Weiss and E. Costa. bibliog il Science 156:1750-2 Je 30 '67
Avian pineal gland: progonadotropic response in the Japanese quail. A. Sayler and A. Wolfson. bibliog il Science 158:1478-9 D 15 '67
Visual pathway mediating pineal response to environmental light. R. Y. Moore and others. bibliog il Science 155:220-3 Ja 13 '67

PINEAL gland. See Pineal body

PINEAPPLES
How to cope with a pineapple. il Ladies Home J 84:58 Jl '67

PINES, Christine
Adventures with food on a camping vacation. Parents Mag 42:64-5+ Ap '67

PINES, Herman
Ipatieff; man and scientist. Science 157:166-70 Jl 14 '67

PINES, Maya
Baby's mind: the crucial first months; excerpt from The crucial years. McCalls 94:74-5+ Ap '67
Early learners; excerpt from Revolution in learning. McCalls 95:74+ Ja '68
Parent and child. N Y Times Mag p72+ My 21 '67; 73+ Ja 7 '68
Slum children must make up for lost time. N Y Times Mag p66-7+ O 15 '67
Someone to mind the baby. N Y Times Mag p71+ Ja 7 '68

PING pong. See Table tennis

PINHEIRO FERREIRA, Silvestre
Portugal and the new republics. S. S. Garrido. il por Américas 19:24-7 Ap '67

PINK bollworms. See Bollworms, Pink

PINKERTON'S, Incorporated
Agent 26250, where are you? detectives at the Masters, college football games and racetracks. M. Cope. il Sports Illus 27:24-6+ O 2 '67
Public private eye. il Time 89:91 Ap 7 '67

PINNACLES NATIONAL MONUMENT
Pinnacles monument hearing. Nat Parks Mag 41:22 Ja '67

PINNEY, Margaret E.
Miniature roses. Horticulture 45:20-1 S '67

PINNEY, Roy
Camera cues (cont) Parents Mag 42:32+ My; 20 Je; 60+ Ag '67

PINOCYTOSIS
Plasma membrane: substructural changes correlated with electrical resistance and pinocytosis. P. W. Brandt and A. R. Freeman. bibliog il Science 155:582-5 F 3 '67

PINSLY, Samuel M.
Hoot, toot and whistle. por Newsweek 69:85-6 Ja 30 '67

PINSON, Penelope
Books for parents. See issues of Parents magazine and better homemaking

PINTAURO, Joseph
Death of Saint Theresa, Little Flower; poem. Commonweal 87:337 D 8 '67

PINTCHMAN, Charles
Boscobel; Garrison-on-Hudson, New York. Horticulture 45:36-7+ D '67

PINTER, Harold
Probing Pinter's play; interview; ed. by H. Hewes. por Sat R 50:56+ Ap 8 '67
Two people in a room: playwriting; interview. New Yorker 43:34-6 F 25 '67

about

Birthday party. Criticism
America 117:487 O 28 '67
America 118:10-12 Ja 6 '68
Christian Cent 84:1604 D 13 '67
Commonweal 87:122-3 O 27 '67
Nation 205:412-14 O 23 '67
New Repub 157:36-8 O 21 '67
New Yorker 43:151 O 14 '67
Newsweek 70:104+ O 16 '67
Sat R 50:50 O 21 '67
Sat R 50:46-7 O 28 '67
Time il 90:71-2 O 13 '67
Vogue 150:134 N 1 '67
Homecoming. Criticism
America 116:353 Mr 11 '67
Christian Cent 84:276-7 Mr 1 '67
Commentary 43:73-4 Je '67
Commonweal 85:459-60 Ja 27 '67
Life 62:6 Mr 3 '67
Nat R 19:316-17 Mr 21 '67
Nation 204:122-3 Ja 23 '67
New Repub 156:35-6 Ja 28 '67
Reporter 36:46+ F 23 '67
Vogue 149:110 Mr 1 '67
Pinter, funny and moving and frightening. K. Halton. por Vogue 150:194-5+ O 1 '67
Pinterism is maximum tension through minimum information. C. Marowitz. il por N Y Times Mag p36-7+ O 1 '67
Psychiatrist looks at The homecoming. A. N. Franzblau. Sat R 50:58 Ap 8 '67

PINTO, Edmund
Some very special teachers' pets. Sr Schol 90:sup 16 Ap 7 '67

PINTO, Edward
Growth substances in plants. Sci Am 217: 111-14 Ag '67

PIONEER probes. See Space probes

PIOUS fund
United States and Mexico agree on settlement of Pious fund claim; Department announcement. Dept State Bul 57:261 Ag 28 '67

PIPE laying
Unusual pipe-bedding technique; Texas Panhandle. F. E. Dominy. il Am City 82:90-3 F '67 (to be cont)

PIPE lines
See also
Steam pipe lines

Protection
Warning tape protects utility lines; Angleton, Tex. il Am City 82:97 D '67

PIPER methysticum. See Kava

PIPER'S court. See Rites and ceremonies—Germany (Federal Republic)

PIPES
Four weekend projects with pipe. J. Burroughs. il Pop Mech 127:178-83 My '67

PIPES, Water. See Water pipes

PIQUE dame; opera. See Tchaikovsky, P. I.

PIRANDELLO, Luigi
To clothe the naked. Criticism
New Yorker 43:155 My 6 '67
Time 89:58 My 5 '67

PIRATES (baseball) See Baseball clubs

PIRATES of Penzance; opera. See Gilbert, W. S. and Sullivan, A. S.

PIRIE, Norman Wingate
Orthodox and unorthodox methods of meeting world food needs; with biographical sketch. Sci Am 216:22, 27-35 F '67

PISA
Campanile (leaning tower)
Can we save the falling tower? T. Roberts. il Sci Digest 61:57-9 My '67

PISTOLETTO, Michelangelo
Gallery for young people; composition called Sacra conversazione. C. B. Johnson. il Sch Arts 66:44 Ja '67
Visitors to a Pistoletto show get right into his paintings. il Horizon 9:84-5 Spr '67

PISTOLS
Crazy pistols. W. Page. il Field & S 72:82-5 S '67
Luger pistol. C. G. Worman. il Hobbies 72: 122-3 O '67
See also
Colt industries, incorporated
Revolvers

PISTON, Walter
Piston's vice; performance of Variations for cello and orchestra. Time 89:74-5 Mr 10 '67

PISTON rings
Ring making. J. McFarland. il Hot Rod 20: 80 My '67

PISTONS
Button up! persistent piston problems. J. Wright. il Hot Rod 20:54-5 My '67
Pistons for performance. E. Lang. il Hot Rod 20:54-7 F '67

PISTONS (basketball team) See Basketball teams

PITCHER plants
Its leaves are insect traps. il Sunset 139:248-9 O '67

PITCHERS, Baseball. See Baseball players

PITCHING (baseball)
Infamous spitter; illegal but popular spitball. H. Weiskopf. il Sports Illus 27:12-17 Jl 31 '67
Long, wet summer; spitball pitchers. il Time 90:52-3 S 1 '67
Side-door entrance to the major leagues; right-handed pitcher, D. Baldwin of Washington Senators. L. Shecter. il Sports Illus 27:61-2+ Jl 17 '67
Strong-arm tactics. Newsweek 70:69 Jl 24 '67

PITKIN, Walter, Jr
Jetport tangle. New Repub 156:11-12 My 27 '67

PITNEY-BOWES, Incorporated
Studied gamble of Pitney-Bowes. J. Berry. il Duns R 89:30-1+ F '67

PITT, Barrie
Cord to Anglo-American accord. Sat R 50:30 O 14 '67

PITT, Virginia Daniel
My most unforgettable character. Read Digest 91:37-41 Ag '67

PITT, W. Page
My most unforgettable character. V. D. Pitt. por Read Digest 91:37-41 Ag '67

PITTENDRIGH, Colin S.
Biologist in the solar system. Bul Atomic Sci 23:4-10 Mr '67

PITTENGER, Norman
As Advent approaches. Christian Cent 84: 1522-4 N 29 '67
Militant anti-Christianity. Christian Cent 84: 712-14 My 31 '67
Theological students today. Christian Cent 84: 527-9 Ap 26 '67

PITTERMAN flies; story. See Schmidt, A. C.

PITTS, Edward H.
How to sell to the top religious magazines. Writer 80:31-3 Je '67

PITTS, Thomas
More by, and about Pitts of the epergnes. E. Gaines. il Antiques 91:748-53 Je '67

PITTSBURGH
Architecture
Pittsburgh skyscraper achieves breakthrough in steel fireproofing: United States steel corporation. il Arch Rec 141:165-72 Ap '67

Bridges
Bridges of Pittsburgh. W. McQuade. il Fortune 76:95-102 Ag '67

City planning
Pittsburgh goes back to school. J. Bailey. il Arch Forum 126:40-51 Je '67

Education
New super high school, wave of future for big cities? il U S News 63:58-9 Jl 10 '67
Pittsburgh goes back to school. J. Bailey. il Arch Forum 126:40-51 Je '67

Housing
Finding a profit in slum streets; Pittsburgh group called Action-housing. il Bsns W p52-4+ F 4 '67

PITTSBURGH—*Continued*

Music

Pittsburgh; production of Madama Butterfly.
R. J. Croan. Opera N 31:28 Mr 4 '67
Small slice of the moderns. R. Croan. Hi Fi
17:MA20 Je '67
See also
Pittsburgh opera company

Negroes

Television; Thomas H. Allen survey. J. Horn.
Nation 205:638 D 11 '67

Rapid transit

Transit expressway proves a success. il Am
City 82:116 D '67

PITTSBURGH opera company
Pittsburgh; production of Lohengrin. F. A.
York. Opera N 31:22 Je 10 '67
Report: Pittsburgh; productions of Lucia di
Lammermoor and Madame Butterfly. R.
Croan. Opera N 32:29-30 D 16 '67

PITTSBURGH Penguins (hockey team) See
Hockey teams

PITTSBURGH Pirates (baseball) See Baseball
clubs

PITTSBURGH plate glass company
PPG: has it found the formula? J. Poindexter. il Duns R 90:38-9+ S '67

PITTSBURGH steel company
Simon keeps the experts guessing; sale of
Wheeling stock to Pittsburgh steel. Bsns W
p 140+ Ap 29 '67
Where two's company in steel; pact with
Wheeling steel. il Bsns W p38-9 My 6 '67

PITTSBURGH. University
Pitt picks chancellor: agrees that modesty
is the best policy. B. Nelson. il Science
155:541-4 F 3 '67
Pitt vs. Frick Newsweek 69:101 F 20 '67

Airglow observatory

See Astronomical observatories

PITUITARY body
Control of aldosterone secretion by the pituitary gland. W. P. Palmore an P. J.
Mulrow. bibliog il Science 158:1482-4 D 15
'67

Diseases

Allergic adenohypophysitis: new experimental
disease of the pituitary gland. S. Levine.
bibliog il Science 158:1190-1 D 1 '67

PITZ, Henry C.
Artistic personality in the making. Am Artist
31:50-5 Je '67

PITZER, Kenneth S.
How much research? address, April 12, 1967.
Science 157:779-81 Ag 18 '67

PIUS XII, pope
Death in Rome, by R. Katz. Review
Nation 204:663-4 My 22 '67. R. Rothstein
Death in Rome focuses new controversy on
Vatican. Pub W 191:47-8 F 6 '67
Three popes and the Jews, by P. E. Lapide.
Review
Commentary 44:100-5 N '67. G. Lewy

PIVEN, Frances Fox, and Cloward, R. A.
Black control of cities. New Repub 157:19-
21 S 30 ; 15-19 O 7 '67
Rent strike. New Repub 157:11-15 D 2 '67
—See Cloward, R. A. jt. auth.

PIVER, Arthur
Noon position. Motor B 119:34-7+ Je '67

PIZER, Vernon
Helping hand of Jim Redding. Read Digest
90:99-103 Je '67

PIZZA. See Cookery, Italian

PLACE names. See Names, Geographical

PLACEBOS
Value of those drugless pills. Good H 164:
201 Mr '67

PLACEMENT bureaus. See Employment agencies

PLACEMENT of teachers. See Teachers—Selection and appointment

PLACENTA
Human growth hormone and placental lacto-
gen; structural similarity. K. J. Catt and
others. bibliog Science 157:321 Jl 21 '67
Placenta wondrous organ of pregnancy. Good
H 164:195 My '67

PLACES of retirement. See Retirement, Places
of

PLAGEMANN, Bentz
My most unforgettable character. Read Digest
91:127-31 D '67

PLAGIARISM
Inverse plagiarism. H. C. Jent. Sch & Soc
95:314-16 Sum '67

Powell in the pulpit; way A. Powell used
material from works of G. Buttrick and
H. Luccock in Keep the faith, baby! D.
Poling. il Sat R 50:86+ Ap 22 '67
Way with words; A. C. Powell's sermons.
Newsweek 69:28-9 My 1 '67

PLAIN dealer. See Cleveland plain dealer

PLAINFIELD, N.J.
Real tragedy of Newark. il U S News 63:31
Jl 31 '67
Role of criminals in a major race riot. U S
News 63:12 D 18 '67

PLAINS
See also
Great Plains

PLAINTIFFS' lawyers. See Lawyers

PLANEPORTS. See Hangars

PLANETARIUMS
Calgary's planetarium and museum. S. Wie-
ser. il Sky & Tel 34:14-15 Jl '67
Current planetarium activity in Canada. D. A.
Rodger. il Sky & Tel 34:13-14 Jl '67
Heitkamp planetarium; Loras college, Du-
buque, Ia. T. G. Goodman. il Sky & Tel
33:141-2 Mr '67
Planetarium notes (cont) Sky & Tel 34:162-5
S '67
Some college planetariums. M. Briant and
others. il Sky & Tel 34:158-61 S '67

PLANETS
Astronomy. J. Stokley. See issues of Science
news
Planetary and lunar notes from Prague. il
Sky & Tel 35:7-9 Ja '68
Sun, moon, and planets this month. See
issues of Sky and telescope
See also
Earth
Interplanetary communication
Life on other planets
Occultations
also names of planets, e.g. Pluto (planet)

Atmosphere

Radio reflection by free radicals in earth's
atmosphere. J. D. Barry and others. bibliog il Science 156:1730-2 Je 30 '67; Reply
with rejoinder. P. L. Bender. 158:1487-8 D
15 '67

Contamination

Contamination safeguards grow in cost, complexity. Aviation W 87:68+ Ag 7 '67

Radiation

See also
Jupiter (planet)—Radiation

Rotation

Planetary magnetic fields and rotation. R. T.
Brown. bibliog Science 158:674 N 3 '67

PLANETS, Minor. See Asteroids

PLANING machines
Rockwell's rotary planer is a whiz. W. C.
Leckey. il Pop Mech 129:184-5+ Ja '68

PLANK, Marion S. and Scholl, J. B.
Highly adaptable package. bibliog Library J
92:1714-17+ Ap 15 '67

PLANKTON
Food value of red tide (gonyaulax polyedra)
S. Patton and others. bibliog il Science
158:789-90 N 10 '67
Vertical diurnal migration and endogenous
rhythmicity. J. T. Enright and W. M.
Hamner. bibliog il Science 157:937-41 Ag
25 '67
See also
Diatoms

PLANKTONIC foraminifera. See Foraminifera

PLANNING, Business. See Business management and organization

PLANNING, Educational. See Educational
planning

PLANNING, Industrial. See Industrial management and organization

PLANNING, Land. See Land utilization

PLANNING, National. See National planning

PLANNING of cities. See City planning

PLANNING research corporation
Consultants with a flair for math. il Bsns
W p 196-8+ S 16 '67

PLANT alkaloids. See Alkaloids

PLANT breeding
New fruits and vegetables. il Farm J 92:49
Ja '68
See also
Hybridization
Tree breeding

PLANT catalogs. See Catalogs, Seed and plant

PLANT cells and tissues
Cytokinins in the soluble RNA of plant tissues. R. H. Hall and others. bibliog il Science 156:69-71 Ap 7 '67
Glutaraldehyde activation of nuclear acid phosphatase in cultured plant cells. D. W. De Jong and others. bibliog il Science 155: 1672-4 Mr 31 '67
Human polymorphonuclear leukocytes: demonstration of microtubules and effect of colchicine. S. E. Malawista and K. G. Bensch. bibliog il Science 156:521-2 Ap 28 '67
Mitotic reactivation of the terminal bud and cambium of white ash. H. B. Tepper and C. A. Hollis. bibliog il Science 156:1635-6 Je 23 '67
Subcellular structure of endosperm protein in high-lysine and normal corn. M. J. Wolf and others. bibliog il Science 157:556-7 Ag 4 '67
Turgor pressure: direct manometric measurement in single cells of nitella. P. B. Green and F. W. Stanton. bibliog il Science 155:1675-6 Mr 31 '67
See also
Chromosomes (botany)

Culture

Growth of isolated mesophyll cells of arachis hypogaea in simple defined medium in vitro. P. C. Joshi and G. R. Noggle. bibliog il Science 158:1575-7 D 22 '67

PLANT conservation
See also
Cylburn wildflower preserve and garden center, Baltimore, Md.

PLANT diseases. See Plants—Diseases and pests

PLANT evolution. See Plants—Evolution

PLANT foods. See Fertilizers and manures; Plants—Nutrition

PLANT growth. See Growth (plants)

PLANT growth regulators. See Growth promoting substances (plants)

PLANT holders. See Flower boxes, planters, etc.

PLANT hormones. See Hormones, Plant

PLANT introduction
Ernest H. "Chinese" Wilson, the man and his plants. D. S. Manks. il Horticulture 45:28-30 N '67

PLANT lice
Aphids; report on project orientated around the green peach aphid. M. J. Way. Science 156:1401-3 Je 9 '67

PLANT nutrition. See Plants—Nutrition

PLANT pots. See Flower pots

PLANT propagation
Early start for seeds, under fluorescent lights. H. G. Shuman. il Home Gard 54:88-9 Ap '67
Great flowers from little seeds do grow. il Pop Gard 18:92 Mr '67
Grow your own from seed. B. Brinhart. il Home Gard 54:64+ Ap '67
Growing wild flowers from seed. K. S. Taylor. il Horticulture 45:30-3 My '67
How to have more of a good thing; succulents. D. Barrows. il Home Gard 54:32-4 Jl '67
Mist propagation. R. M. Nordine. il Horticulture 45:30-1 Jl '67
Peonies. B. C. Kilvert, jr. il Home Gard 54: 45-6 S '67
Start your garden indoors this spring. Am Home 70:115 Ja '67
See also
Grafting

PLANT proteins
Subcellular structure of endosperm protein in high-lysine and normal corn. M. J. Wolf and others. bibliog il Science 157:556-7 Ag 4 '67
Tetraploid wheats; seed protein electrophoretic patterns of the emmer and timopheevi groups. B. L. Johnson. bibliog il Science 158:131-2 O 6 '67

PLANT viruses. See Viruses, Plant

PLANT waxes. See Botany—Physiology

PLANTERS (farm machines)
It's planter tune-up time. P. B. Jones. il Suc Farm 65:44-5 Ap '67
See also
Seeding machinery

PLANTERS (flower boxes) See Flower boxes, planters, etc.

PLANTING. See Gardening; Plants, Space arrangement of

PLANTING plans and tables. See Gardening—Planting plans and tables

PLANTS
Best plants. Home Gard 54:80 My; 50 Je; 58 Jl; 61 Ag; 18 S '67
Captives and cultigens. M. Bates. il Natur Hist 77:22+ Ja '68
Here's help in choosing plants for specific landscape uses. il Sunset 138:208+ F '67
How to grow container marvels like these. il Sunset 138:224-5 Mr '67
[Month] in your garden. See issues of Sunset
More plants for your garden. il Horticulture 45:40-3 F '67
New plants for the new year. Am Home 70: 120+ Ja '67
Plant a crooked tree. E. L. Sculthorp. il House B 109:38+ My '67
Plants for dry places. G. W. Kelly. il Horticulture 45:32-3 Jl '67
Plants for hillsides; with table. il Sunset 138:210+ F '67
Plants for narrow beds along walks; with table. il Sunset 138:214+ F '67
Plants for shady entries and overhangs; with table. il Sunset 138:220-1 F '67
Plants to spill over a retaining wall; with table. il Sunset 138:219-20 F '67
Put variety into your garden. il Pop Gard 18:58-9 My '67
To giant size in one season. Sunset 138:238+ Ap '67
Today and tomorrow; reports on current research of interest to gardeners and home-owners. Pop Gard 18:21 Mr; 22 My; 16 Ag '67
What you can do now to begin your spring garden. il Home Gard 54:34-7 Ap '67
Who says it won't grow here? R. J. Misch. House B 109:140+ Ap '67
See also
Annuals (plants)
Bulbs
Fertilization of plants
Forcing (plants)
also names of plants, e.g. Pokeweed, and headings beginning Plant

Absorption of water

Cherry trees hoard water. Sci N 91:195 F 25 '67
Plant moisture stress: evaluation by pressure bomb. R. H. Waring and B. D. Cleary. bibliog il Science 155:1248+ Mr 10 '67

All America selections

All-America roses, 1968. il Horticulture 45: 14-15 Jl '67
All-America roses 1967. il Pop Gard 18:56-7 Mr '67
For gardeners: the new ones for 1968. il Am Home 71:20+ Ja '68
Make your garden the talk of the town with the 1967 All-America annuals. il Pop Gard 18:8 Mr '67
New All-Americas; 1968 All-America rose winners. il Home Gard 54:24-5 Jl '67
New roses for next summer. il Am Home 70: 88 Jl '67

Anecdotes, facetiae, satire, etc.

As I was saying to a geranium. J. Kerr. il Ladies Home J 84:84-5 Ap '67

Chemical analysis

Leaf analysis, how to use it. C. E. Sommers. il Suc Farm 65:34-5+ Jl '67

Disease and pest resistance

Insect hormones: alpha ecdysone and 20-hydroxyecdysone in bracken fern. J. N. Kaplanis and others. bibliog il Science 157: 1436-8 S 22 '67

Diseases and pests

H&G's 1967 guide to plant protection. C. Westcott. House & Gard 131:34+ Ap '67

Evolution

Butterflies and plants. P. R. Ehrlich and P. H. Raven. il Sci Am 216:104-11+ Je '67
They conquered earth; excerpts from Living plants of the world. L. Milne and M. Milne. il Audubon 69:58-69 N '67

Fertilization

See Fertilization of plants

Metabolism

Diphenamid metabolism in plants. C. D. Kesner and S. K. Ries. bibliog il Science 155:210-11 Ja 13 '67
Propanal may be a precursor of ethylene in metabolism. M. Lieberman and A. T. Kunishi. bibliog il Science 158:938 N 17 '67

PLANTS—*Continued*

Migration
Atmospheric transfer of carbon-14: a problem in fungus translocation studies. C. P. Reid and F. W Woods. bibliog il Science 157:712-13 Ag 11 '67

Nutrition
Leaf analysis, how to use it. C. E. Sommers. il Suc Farm 65:34-5+ Jl '67
Some new uses for liquid plant foods. G. Abraham Horticulture 45:27 D '67

Physiology
See Botany—Physiology

Potassium content
Light-enhanced potassium absorption by corn leaf tissue. D. W. Rains. bibliog il Science 156:1382-3 Je 9 '67

Reproduction
See also
Gametophytes

Resistance to insects
See Plants—Disease and pest resistance

Respiration
Photosynthetic utilization of internal carbon dioxide by hollow-stemmed plants. W. D. Billings and P. J. Godfrey. bibliog il Science 158:121-3 O 6 '67

Translocation
Plant physiology: translocation in plants; report on symposium. D. S. Fensom. Science 157:728 Ag 11 '67
Wax microchannels in the epidermis of white clover. D. M. Hall. bibliog il Science 158:505 O 27 '67

Transpiration
Membranes of valonia ventricosa: apparent absence of water-filled pores. J. Gutknecht. bibliog il Science 158:787-8 N 10 '67
Osmotic mechanism and negative pressure. P. F. Scholander. bibliog il Science 156:67-9 Ap 7 '67; Discussion. 158:1210-12 D 1 '67
Plastic films on plants as antitranspirants. J. Gale and A. Poljakoff-Mayber. bibliog il Science 156:650-2 My 5 '67

PLANTS, Dwarf
Dwarf bamboos and how to restrain them. il Sunset 138:205 Je '67

PLANTS, Edible. See Plants, Food

PLANTS, Effect of boron on
Boron in plants: a biochemical role. S. Lee and S. Aronoff. bibliog il Science 158:798-9 N 10 '67

PLANTS, Effect of carbon dioxide on
Induction of coiling in tendrils by auxin and carbon dioxide. L. Reinhold. bibliog il Science 158:791-3 N 10 '67

PLANTS, Effect of climate on
Photosynthetic system II: racial differentiation in typha latifolia. S. J. McNaughton. bibliog il Science 156:1363 Je 9 '67

PLANTS, Effect of gravitation on
Plants' growth seen affected by gravity. Aviation W 87:20 N 6 '67

PLANTS, Effect of light on
Apomixis: seasonal and population differences in a grass. R. B. Knox. bibliog il Science 157:325-6 Jl 21 '67
Early start for seeds, under fluorescent lights. H. G. Shuman. il Home Gard 54:88-9 Ap '67
Fast light-evoked potential from leaves. T. G. Ebrey. bibliog il Science 155:1556-7 Mr 24 '67
House plants without daylight. il Pop Gard 18:60-5 Mr '67
Light-enhanced potassium absorption by corn leaf tissue. D. W. Rains. bibliog il Science 156:1382-3 Je 9 '67
Look to the sun before you plan. G. Schultz. il Pop Gard 18:40-5+ Mr '67
Mutagenic effect of visible light mediated by endogenous pigments in euglena gracilis. J. Leff and N. I. Krinsky. bibliog il Science 158:1332-5 D 8 '67

PLANTS, Effect of oxygen on
Oxygen tension as a control mechanism in pollen tube rupture. R. G. Stanley and H. F. Linskens. bibliog il Science 157:833-4 Ag 18 '67

PLANTS, Effect of radiation on
Ecological dosimetry: radiation levels influenced by plant growth. W. C. Ashby and others. bibliog il Science 155:1430-2 Mr 17 '67

Radiation and the patterns of nature; excerpts from address, March 24, 1965. G. M. Woodwell. bibliog il Science 156:461-70 Ap 28 '67

PLANTS, Effect of temperature on
Acropetal movement of auxin: dependence on temperature. G. W. Keitt, jr. and R. A. Baker. bibliog il Science 156:1380-1 Je 9 '67

PLANTS, Food
Greens of spring. D. McKinley. il Audubon 69:74 Mr '67
Pick instead of pack; selection of wild plants, edible and nourishing. B. Angier. il Field & S 72:8+ N '67

PLANTS, Fossil. See Paleobotany
PLANTS, Indoor. See House plants
PLANTS, Poisonous. See Poisonous plants

PLANTS, Potted
Best plants for containers; symposium. il Home Gard 54:27-8 D '67
Flowering plants come indoors for Christmas. il Sunset 139:64-5 D '67
Plants in pots in Spain. il Sunset 138:196 Je '67
Portable topiary. il House & Gard 133:124-5+ Ja '68
See also
Flower boxes, planters, etc.
House plants

PLANTS, Protection of
See also
Mulching

PLANTS, Rock garden
Spring bulbs was a rocky ledge with a sea of color. il House & Gard 132:180-1 S '67

PLANTS, Sex in
See also
Antheridia

PLANTS, Shade
Consider the blessing of a shady place. J. Hersey. il Home Gard 54:40-1 Ag '67
Plant them now for summer color in the shade. il Sunset 138:254+ My '67
Shade for sun-shy flowers. il Am Home 70:32 Jl '67

PLANTS, Space arrangement of
Faster planting in narrow rows. il Farm J 91:34-5+ Ap '67
They went to equal-distance corn spacing. C. E. Sommers. il Suc Farm 65:32-3 Ja '67
What farmers think of 20-inch row corn. C. E. Sommers. il Suc Farm 65:40-1+ Ja '67

PLANTS, Watering of. See Watering of plants

PLANTS as gifts
Gift camellia, in a container. il Sunset 139:158 D '67
Green, growing gifts. il Bet Hom & Gard 45:44-6 D '67
Growing your own Christmas ornaments; bromeliads. il Sunset 139:180 D '67

PLANTS for shady places. See Plants, Shade

PLANTS in art
My paper flower garden. E. Finch. il Home Gard 54:82 Mr '67
Spirit of bamboo; interview. C. Sie. New Yorker 43:36-7 My 6 '67
See also
Flowers in art

PLANTS in house decoration
Connoisseur of art and nature. M. Gough. il House B 109:134-7 Mr '67
Flowers to greet you in every room. il House & Gard 132:96-7 Jl '67
House of fresh-cut color. M. White. il Ladies Home J 84:84-7 F '67

PLAQUES, plaquettes
Constructing a wood relief. R. Barrio. il Design 68:25-9 Ja '67

PLASMA (ionized gases)
Hot plasma studied as antenna possibility. G. S. Hunter. il Aviation W 86:77+ F 20 '67
Leakage problem in fusion reactors. F. F. Chen. il Sci Am 217:76-88 bibliog(p 134+) Jl '67
New look at the UFO enigma; ball lightning, excerpt from Light and electricity in the atmosphere. H. Hellman. il Sci Digest 62:9-15 N '67

PLASMA cells. See Cells
PLASMA membrane. See Membranes (biology)
PLASMIN. See Fibrinolysin

PLASMODIUM (parasite)
Eperythrozoon coccoides: influence on course of infection of plasmodium chabaudi in mouse. K. J. Ott and L. A. Stauber. bibliog il Science 155:1546-8 Mr 24 '67
Stearic acid as plasma replacement for intracellular in vitro culture of plasmodium knowlesi. W. A. Siddiqui and others. bibliog il Science 156:1623-5 Je 23 '67

PLASS, William T. and Boyce, S. G.
Aesthetic forests for urban areas. Parks & Rec 2:42+ O '67

PLASTIC bags
Trash can liners. il Consumer Bul 50:23 Ag '67

PLASTIC boats. See Boats—Materials

PLASTIC bottles. See Bottles

PLASTIC cars. See Automobiles—Materials

PLASTIC containers. See Containers

PLASTIC domes. See Domes

PLASTIC lenses. See Lenses, Plastic

PLASTIC mulch. See Mulching

PLASTIC sculpture
See-through sculpture. S. Burton. il Art N 66:36-7+ Mr '67

PLASTIC surgery. See Surgery, Plastic

PLASTIC wood finishing. See Wood finishing

PLASTIC worms. See Fishing lures, flies, etc.

PLASTICS
Acrylic-latex additives create extra-strength new concretes. il Arch Rec 141:199-200 Mr '67
Encasement lies in wait for all of us. W. McQuade. il Arch Forum 127:92 N '67
Plastics: the raw material for nearly everything. M. J. Schultz. il Sci Digest 62:45-53 Ag '67
Resins in the mines. E. S. Gruzinov. Sci N 92:213 Ag 26 '67
Summer's dashing toss-aways. il House & Gard 131:104-11 Je '67
Tracks of cosmic rays in plastics. R. L. Fleischer and others. bibliog il Science 155: 187-9 Ja 13 '67
Vacuum-sealed silage: how it fed out. il Farm J 91:46L+ My '67
Workshop: expanded polystyrene for ceramic production; International center of ceramics, Rome. N. Caruso. il Craft Horiz 27: 34-5 S '67

PLASTICS, Glass reinforced
Aerospace techniques eyed for naval use; glass-reinforced plastic composites for navy's surface and submersible craft. J. F. Judge. Tech W 20:42-4 My 15 '67
Glass reinforced plastic hull set for delivery soon to DSRV; deep submergence rescue vehicle. il Aero Tech 21:39+ N 6 '67

PLASTICS, Laminated
Working with plastic laminate. il Bet Hom & Gard 45:153-6 O '67

PLASTICS, Magnetized
Magnetic plastics in the offing. Sci N 91:279 Mr 25 '67

PLASTICS, Transparent
Marvelous sorcery of the invisible. E. Sverbeyeff. il House B 109:92-5 Jl '67

PLASTICS industry and trade
Soothing the pains of growing too fast. il Bsns W p 190-2+ F 18 '67

PLATES (dishes) See Tableware

PLATFORM paddle tennis. See Paddle tennis

PLATFORM tennis. See Paddle tennis

PLATFORM tennis courts. See Paddle tennis courts

PLATFORMATE. See Gasoline—Additives

PLATH, Sylvia
Sylvia Plath's last poems. E. R. Taylor. Poetry 109:260-2 Ja '67

PLATYZOMA. See Ferns

PLAY
Parents' guide to child's play; with suggestions by Rowena Shoemaker. O. Schisgall. il N Y Times Mag p 115+ S 10 '67
Play materials for many moods; with study-discussion program, by R. Strang. F. R. Horwich. bibliog il PTA Mag 62:16-18, 34-5 D '67
Promoting functional play patterns. I. J. Hutchison, jr. il Parks & Rec 2:29+ S '67
What children learn when they play; excerpt from Conspiracy against childhood. E. LeShan. il Redbook 129:66-7+ Jl '67
Wonderful world of water play. M. D. Sanger. il PTA Mag 61:20-1 Je '67
See also
Childrens amusements

PLAY apparatus. See Playgrounds—Equipment

PLAY books. See Childrens amusements

PLAY production. See Theatrical production

PLAY schools
See also
Nursery schools

PLAY writing. See Drama—Technique

PLAYBILL (periodical)
Trade winds. J. Beatty, jr. Sat R 50:12 S 30 '67

PLAYBOY (periodical)
Think clean. il Time 89:76-8+ Mr 3 '67

PLAYER piano
Piano roll legacy. G. Benko and W. Santaella. il Hi Fi 17:51-3 Jl '67

PLAYER piano rolls
Piano roll legacy. G. Benko and W. Santaella. il Hi Fi 17:51-3 Jl '67
Piano rolls and travesties. Discus. Harper 234:119-21 F '67
Sound archive for piano rolls; International piano library. P. G. Davis. Hi Fi 17:22 Ap '67

PLAYGROUND; story. See Epstein, L.

PLAYGROUND activities
Experiment with brainstorming; creative playground activities. B. A. Wagner and J. Conley. il Parks & Rec 2:21+ S '67
New look at playstreets. D. V. Joyce. il Parks & Rec 2:28-9+ Jl '67
Playstreets add novel pastimes; New York city. D. V. Joyce. il Am City 82:83-5 Jl '67
Tiny tots a go-go; group adjustment program for four & five year olds; Mountain View, Calif. D. Gale. il Parks & Rec 2: 26-7+ Ag '67

PLAYGROUND apparatus. See Playgrounds—Equipment

PLAYGROUNDS
Parks and recreation. See issues of American city
See also
Parks

Activities
See Playground activities

Equipment
Child's garden of plastic delights. il Life 63: 74-6+ Jl 14 '67
New way to play. il Fortune 75:149-51 Mr '67
Playground equipment; playscape, Franklin Park, Ill. W. C. Kouns. il Parks & Rec 2: 20 My '67
See also
Swings

PLAYGROUNDS, Home

Equipment
All summer is a holiday, at home! il Good H 165:102-3 Jl '67
Free play for imaginations. J. H. Ingersoll. il House B 109:112-13 Jl '67
Old-time joggling board bounces back. il Sunset 139:56-7 Jl '67

PLAYGROUNDS, Roof
Rooftop playground puts our kids in the sun. R. Ruthman. il Pop Sci 190:189 Ap '67

PLAYGROUNDS, School. See School grounds

PLAYHOUSES
Build now, play later. il Am Home 70:78 Jl '67
Just for kids. il Pop Gard 18:54-5 Ag '67
See also
Tree houses

PLAYING cards. See Cards

PLAYSTREETS. See New York (city)—Streets

PLAYWRITING. See Drama—Technique

PLEASANTS, Julian
Morality of consequences. Commonweal 86: 413-16 Je 30 '67

PLEASANTVILLE, N.Y.
Pictures from Pleasantville. il Read Digest 91:158-69 Ag '67

PLEBEIANS rehearse the uprising; drama. See Grass, G.

PLEDGES; story. See Friedman, B. J.

PLEISTOCENE period. See Geology, Stratigraphic—Pleistocene; Paleobotany—Pleistocene

PLENDERLEITH, Harold J.
Painting hospital in the lemon grove. UNESCO Courier 20:24-34 Ja '67

PLEUROPNEUMONIA-like organism. See Microorganisms, Pathogenic

PLEYNET, Marcelin
Léger legacy. Art N 65:42-3+ F '67

PLIER wrench. See Wrenches

PLIMMER, Charlotte, and Plimmer, Denis
Princess and the diplomat. Redbook 129:47-9+ Je '67

PLIMMER, Denis. See Plimmer, C. jt. auth.

PLIMPTON, George
What the deuce is going on? Sports Illus 27: 34-6+ S 18 '67
Zero on the tour. pors Sports Illus 26:46-56 Ja 30; 28-34 F 6; 36-8+ F 13 '67

PLIMPTON, George—*Continued*
about
Swinging Walter Mitty. il por Time 89:40 Ap 7 '67
Winningest born loser; with report by S. Wright. il pors Life 62:35-6+ Je 30 '67

PLIOCENE period. See Paleontology—Pliocene

PLOTKIN, Stanley A. and Vaheri, Antti
Human fibroblasts infected with rubella virus produce a growth inhibitor. bibliog Science 156:659-61 My 5 '67

PLOTNIK, Arthur
Bookman's Baedeker to Europe. bibliog por Library J 92:2889-97 S 1 '67
Dark at the top of the stacks. por Library J 92:1122-5 Mr 15 '67

PLOTS (drama, novel, etc)
How much of a story is real? M. Stolz. Writer 80:9-10+ Mr '67
Probing Pinter's play; The homecoming; with interview with H. Pinter; ed. by H. Hewes. il Sat R 50:56+ Ap 8 '67
Psychiatrist looks at The homecoming. A. N. Franzblau. Sat R 50:58 Ap 8 '67
Stuff of a plot. M. F. Shyer. Writer 80:15-16 My '67
Substance of fiction; excerpts from The story; a critical anthology. M. Schorer. Writer 80:14-18+ Je '67
What the villain did; plot of Hai Jui dismissed from office. by H. Wu. il Newsweek 69:43 My 1 '67
Where do plots start? H. Hinckley. Writer 80:19-20+ F '67
Your plot is contrived. C. Armstrong. Writer 80:17-19 O '67

PLOWING. See Tillage

PLUMB, Barbara
Chez Mlle. See issues of Mademoiselle
Home. See issues of New York times magazine

PLUMB, J. H.
Anarchy of art. Horizon 9:106-7 Sum '67
De mortuis. Horizon 9:40-1 Spr '67
Perspective. See issues of Saturday review
Which age of anxiety? Horizon 9:88-9 Aut '67

PLUMBING
Build a pretty little privy for your weekend retreat. D. Shiner. il Pop Mech 127:156-9+ Ap '67
Domestic water supply systems. il Consumer Bul 50:36-40 Je '67
Facts about all kinds of faucets. G. Daniels. il Pop Sci 191:141-6 D '67
Half-bath is a do-it-yourself job. L. Weaver and G. Daniels. il Pop Sci 191:153-8 S; 155-8 O '67
Home-plumbing know-how. G. Daniels and L. Weaver. il Pop Sci 190:169-74 Ap; 169-73 My; 131-6 Je; 191:133-8 Jl '67
Home-plumbing know-how. L. Weaver and G. Daniels. il Pop Sci 192:151-4 Ja '68
How to open clogged house drains. G. Daniels and L. Weaver. il Pop Sci 190:131-6 Je '67
How to pipe water to your outdoors. G. Daniels and L. Weaver. il Pop Sci 191:113-17 Ag '67
When your plumbing gushes or when it just won't work. il Sunset 139:106+ O '67

PLUMBING fixtures. See Bathroom fixtures

PLUTO (planet)
Enigma of Pluto. T. D. Nicholson. il Natur Hist 76:48-9 Mr '67

PLUTONIUM
Transplutonium elements; report on second International transplutonium symposium. O. L. Keller, jr. Science 156:838-40 My 12 '67

Isotopes
Atmospheric burnup of a plutonium-238 generator. P. W. Krey. bibliog il Science 158:769-71 N 10 '67

PLYMELL, Charles
December; poem. Poetry 110:90-2 My '67

PLYMOUTH, N.H.
New home for old inventions; patent museum. L. Aigner. il Pop Mech 128:102-5 Ag '67

PLYWOOD
New plywood grades you can use. Farm J 91:64R F '67

PLYWOOD floors. See Floors, Plywood

PLYWOOD paneling. See Paneling

PNEUMATIC passenger transportation. See Transportation, High speed

PNEUMOCOCCAL polysaccharide. See Polysaccharides

PNEUMOCOCCI
Choline in the cell wall of a bacterium: novel type of polymer-linked choline in pneumococcus. A. Tomasz. bibliog il Science 157:694-7 Ag 11 '67
Deoxycytidylate and deoxyguanylate kinase activity in pneumococci after exposure to known polyribonucleotides. W. Firshein and others. bibliog il Science 157:821-2 Ag 18 '67

POACHING
Troubled alligator. G. Laycock. il Field & S 71:49+ Ap '67
Will Congress stop commerce in endangered wildlife? C. H. Callison. il Audubon 69:20-1 Jl '67

POAGE, William Robert
Meet the new man behind farm laws; interview. por Farm J 91:47 Je '67

POATS, Rutherford Meil
Post for Poats. Time 89:14 My 26 '67

POCHOS. See Mexican Americans

POCKET billiards. See Billiards

PODELL, Albert N.
Around the world on a camera. U S Camera 30:62-3+ Jl '67

PODGORNYI, Nikolai Viktorovich
Ideology & practice. il por Time 89:31 F 3 '67
Russian in Rome. il por Newsweek 69:52 F 6 '67
Soviet president at the Vatican. America 116:202 F 11 '67

PODHORETZ, Norman
Letter. Harper 234:11 My; 235:18+ Jl '67
Making it; excerpt. Harper 235:59-62+ D '67
about
Climbing the pole. S. Maloff. por Newsweek 71:62+ Ja 8 '68
How I made it to true literary happiness. J. W. Aldridge. Life 64:8 Ja 12 '68
How to succeed at an early age. G. Hicks. Sat R 51:77-8+ Ja 13 '68
Little Norman. por Time 91:94+ Ja 19 '68

PODLESKI, T. and Changeux, J. P.
Electrical phenomena associated with the activity of the membrane-bound acetylcholinesterase. bibliog Science 157:1579-81 S 29 '67

PODVOLL, Edward M. and Goodman, S. J.
Averaged neural electrical activity and arousal. bibliog Science 155:223-5 Ja 13 '67

POECILIOPSIS
Gynogenesis and triploidy in the viviparous fish poeciliopsis. R. J. Schultz. bibliog il Science 157:1564-7 S 29 '67

POETICAL criticism. See Literary criticism

POETICS
Experience of the poem. A. Stanford. Writer 80:20-3 D '67
Poet's workshop. F. Trefethen. Writer 80:21-4 S; 22-5 N '67; 81:27-30 Ja '68
Poet's workshop (cont) D. Holmes. Writer 80:30-3+ Ja; 23-7 Mr; 24-8+ My; 24-8 Jl '67
Precepts for poets; excerpt from Tell me, tell me. M. Moore. Writer 80:32 Ap '67
Time and the poet. P. Davison. Writer 80:20-1 Ag '67
Vision and revision. D. Holmes. Writer 80:39-42 Ap '67
See also
Versification

POETRY
Authors & editors; found poetry and pop poetry. Pub W 192:20-1 Ag 7 '67
Definition implied. H. Behn. Horn Bk 43:561-4 O '67
Found object; found poetry from Books in print, U.S.A. Christian Cent 84:1583 D 6 '67
Higgledy piggledy; double dactyl. il Time 89:108 Mr 3 '67
Manner of speaking; of poetry and sloganeering. J. Ciardi. Sat R 51:14 Ja 6 '68
One brief, shining moment; pop poetry; interview, ed. by H. Frankel. R. Gross. Sat R 50:22-3 S 2 '67
Poetry place. See issues of Mademoiselle
Poets on poetry; symposium. Nation 204:520-32+ Ap 24 '67
Time to rhyme. Good H 164:181 Je '67
Vocation of poetry; address, November 28, 1966. H. Rago. Poetry 110:328-48 Ag '67
See also
Childrens poetry
Christmas poetry
Limericks
Poetics
Poets
Political poetry
also American poetry; Greek poetry; etc.

POETRY—*Continued*
Bibliography
New books of poems. L. Simpson. Harper 235:89-91 Ag '67
New poetry of protest. R. D. Spector. Sat R 50:38-40 F 11 '67
Of laureates and lovers. L. Turco. Sat R 50:31-3+ O 14 '67
Verse. L. Bogan. New Yorker 43:160-2 Mr 4 '67
Collections
See Anthologies
Competitions
Rubén Darío poetry contest. Américas 19: inside cover F '67
Philosophy
Poetry, prayer and cosmic reality. Sister M. Angelique. Cath World 205:237-44 Jl '67
Study and teaching
Special language. I. Neuman. Horn Bk 43: 498-500 Ag '67
Technique
See Poetics
Themes
See Literature—Themes
Translating
Translating César Vallejo. C. Eshleman. Nation 204:540 Ap 24 '67
POETRY (periodical)
Announcement of prize awards for 1967. Poetry 111:130-2 N '67
POETRY, Medieval
Carmina Burana; rise in appreciation of medieval Latin poetry. K. Rexroth. Sat R 50:24 Ap 22 '67
POETRY and religion. See Religion and poetry
POETRY contests. See Poetry—Competitions
POETRY readings
Books; International poetry festival. M. Muggeridge. Esquire 68:34+ N '67
MacDiarmid; Highland red. S. Cronin. Nation 204:728-30 Je 5 '67
Poet at the podium; Y. Yevtushenko's New York recital. S. Bernard. Nation 204:534-6 Ap 24 '67
Poetry, drama in Harlem. S. Bernard. Nation 204:826-7 Je 26 '67
Sholom Aleichem in the park; Yiddish poetry in Central park. S. Bernard. Nation 205: 124-5 Ag 14 '67
POETS
Definition implied. H. Behn. Horn Bk 43: 561-4 O '67
Poet as novelist. M. Van Duyn. Poetry 109: 332-9 F '67
POETS, American
How poets make a living, if any. K. Rexroth. Harper 234:90-2+ F '67
Performance without a net. S. Koch. Nation 204:524-6 Ap 24 '67
See also
Aiken, C.
American poetry
Ammons, A. R.
Bradstreet, A. D.
Dickey, J.
Frost, R.
Gross, R.
Howes, B.
Jarrell, R.
Lowell, R.
Moore, M.
Nemerov, H.
O'Hara, F.
Patchen, K.
Plath, S.
Pound, E.
Riley, J. W.
Roethke, T.
Sandburg, C.
Shapiro, H.
Stafford, W.
Stein, G.
Stevens, W.
Tate, J.
Touster, S.
Zukofsky, L.
POETS, Canadian
See also
Swenson, M.
POETS, Chilean
See also
Neruda, P.

POETS, English
See also
Auden, W. H.
Betjeman, J.
Blake, W.
Browning, R.
Bunting, B.
English poetry
Graves, R.
MacNeice, L.
Masefield, J.
POETS, European
Eastern European poetry. V. Contoski. Poetry 110:52-5 Ap '67
POETS, French
See also
Jarry, A.
Léger, A. S.
POETS, German
See also
Berges, R.
Biermann, W.
Hölderlin, F.
Sachs, N.
POETS, Indian (East Indian)
See also
Ray, T.
POETS, Irish
See also
Kavanagh, P.
Yeats, W. B.
POETS, Italian
See also
Dante Alighieri
Montale, E.
Satta, S.
POETS, Nicaraguan
Eight Nicaraguan poets; with poems. J. E. Arellano. il Américas 19:33-9 O '67
See also
Dario, R.
POETS, Paraguayan
Seven Paraguayan poets; with poems. E. Wiezell de Espínola. il Américas 19:31-6 Je '67
POETS, Roman
See also
Lucretius Carus, T.
POETS, Russian
Poets, red and white. D. Brown. il N Y Times Mag p6+ My 28 '67
See also
Evtushenko, E. A.
Voznesenskii, A.
POETS, South African
See also
Jonker, I.
POETS, Spanish
See also
Vallejo, C.
POETS, Welsh
See also
Thomas, D.
POETS, essayists, novelists club.   See PEN club
POGO sky taxi. See Flying machines
POGROMS
See also
Jews—Persecutions
POIGNAND, John, and Mann, Peggy
Curtain of illusion: the odyssey of the children's caravan. Library J 92:860-3 F 15 '67
POINDEXTER, Joseph
High-octane world of Shell. Duns R 90:40-2+ O '67
PPG: has it found the formula? Duns R 90: 38-9+ S '67
POINSETT, Alex
Black power at the polls. Ebony 23:23-5+ Ja '68
Ghetto schools: an educational wasteland. Ebony 22:52-7 Ag '67
Thirteen years after 1954. Ebony 22:76-7+ Ap '67
POINT, Nicolas
Bright vignettes of a lost world. il Life 63: 52-9 D 1 '67
POINT PLEASANT, W.Va.
Luring the poor out of the hills. il Bsns W p74-6+ Jl 1 '67
POINT REYES NATIONAL SEASHORE
Visit to the West's first national seashore. il Sunset 138:48+ F '67
POINT ROBERTS, Wash.
Washington's Canadian corner. F. M. Appleton. il Travel 127:50-1+ My '67
POIRIER, Richard
T. S. Eliot and the literature of waste. New Repub 156:19-25 My 20 '67

POISON ivy
Beware of the itchy outdoors. B. Gilbert. Sports Illus 26:46+ Je 19 '67
Nature note; three-fingered menace. il Sci N 92:54 Jl 15 '67
Treatment and prevention of poison ivy. Good H 164:192-3 Je '67
Watch out for poison ivy. A. F. Benjamin. Am Home 70:39 My '67

POISONERS
See also
Trials (poisoning)

POISONOUS gases in warfare. See Gases in warfare

POISONOUS plants
Successful farming's guide to poisonous plants. C. E. Sommers. il Suc Farm 65:77-82 Mr '67
See also
Poison ivy

POISONS
Be wary! be wise! keep children alive! I. Sunshine. il PTA Mag 61:17 Mr '67
Drugs and poisons in mental retardation; report on meeting. G. M. McKhann and S. J. Yaffe. Science 156:266+ Ap 14 '67
First-aid for poisoning emergencies. Todays Health 45:86 O '67
Help, my child has taken poison! Poison control centers. E. M. Wylie. Good H 164:77+ Je '67; Same abr. il Read Digest 91:133-7 Ag '67
Poisons & cosmetics: adventures in the skin trade. T. Stabile. Nation 206:16-19 Ja 1 '68
Strychnine caper; poisoning of wolves. S. P. Young. il Am For 73:20-3+ Je '67
Strychnine onslaught. S. P. Young. il Am For 73:32-3+ Jl '67
Victims of varnish; India. K. S. Nayar. Sci N 92:278 S 16 '67
See also
Drugs
Lead poisoning

POISONS, Animal. See Venom

POITIER, Sidney
Admirable Sidney. H. Alpert. Sat R 50:39 Jl 8 '67
From Sidney with love. il por Newsweek 70:101+ D 11 '67
Teacher in slum school; interview, ed. by M. Ronan. E. R. Braithwaite. il Sr Schol 90:sup6 Ap 7 '67
To sir, with love. il pors Ebony 22:68-70+ Ap '67

POKER clubs. See Gardena, Calif.—Clubs

POKER players
Lowball in a time capsule; poker addicts. D. Miles. il Sports Illus 26:110-13+ Ap 17 '67

POKER session; drama. See Leonard, H.

POKEWEED
Poke sallet: spring greens, wild & cultivated. V. A. Croley. Home Gard 54:78+ Ap '67

POKHARA, Nepal
Holiday discovery of the month. il Holiday 42:84-5 S '67

POKORNY, Theodore, jr
Metal-scrap animals. Sch Arts 66:29-30 Mr '67

POLAND
Report. D. R. Shanor. Atlan 220:36+ D '67
See also
Agricultural administration—Poland
Airlines—Poland
Airplane industry and trade—Poland
Colleges and universities—Poland
Communist party (Poland)
Concentration camps—Poland
Jews in Poland
Public opinion—Poland
World war, 1939-1945—Underground movements—Poland

Boundaries
Here to stay; former German territories. J. Dornberg. il Newsweek 70:56+ D 18 '67

Commercial treaties and agreements
United States and Poland sign cotton textile agreement. Dept State Bul 56:612 Ap 10 '67

Description and travel
Poland. A. Berrisford. il Travel 127:56-61 Je '67

Economic conditions
Poland's slow road to the promised freedom. il U S News 63:43-4 O 16 '67

Foreign relations
What Poland got from a de Gaulle visit. U S News 63:13 S 18 '67

Israel
Jewish question. il Time 90:28-9 Ag 18 '67

Intellectual life
Intellectual revolt in Poland. T. Szamuely. il Reporter 36:32-4 Je 1 '67

Politics and government
Hard line in Poland. R. F. Staar. bibliog f Cur Hist 52:208-13+ Ap '67
Polish consensus. R. Terrill. New Repub 156:17-22 My 27 '67
See also
Communist party (Poland)

Religious institutions and affairs
See also
Catholic church in Poland

Social conditions
Love, life, and selling out in Poland. D. Halberstam. il Harper 235:78-81+ Jl '67

POLAR bears. See Bears

POLAR currents. See Ocean currents

POLAR exploration
Ends of the earth. R. L. Tobin. il Sat R 50:25-6 Jl 1 '67
See also
Antarctic exploration
Polar research

POLAR ice. See Ice—Polar Regions

POLAR lights. See Auroras

POLAR REGIONS
See also
Antarctic Regions
Arctic Regions

POLAR research
Antarctic notes; U.S. Antarctic research program. Sci N 92:586 D 16 '67
Massive scientific effort. B. A. Leerburger, jr. il Sci N 92:635-6 D 30 '67
Puzzle of Antarctica's desert valleys; reprint. W. J. Perkinson. il Sci Digest 61:32-6 Ap '67
Ship of ice; T-3 ice island supports research programs. il Newsweek 70:60 Jl 17 '67
Space man's look at Antarctica; tour of McMurdo base. W. Von Braun. il Pop Sci 190:114-16+ My '67
Symbol of good will: the Antarctic treaty. M. Amaro. il Américas 19:1-9 F '67

POLAR zone; story. See Carter, M.

POLARIS missiles. See Guided missiles—Launching from submarine boats

POLARIZING filters. See Light filters

POLAROID Land cameras
Camera from Cambridge. E. Hannigan. il U S Camera 30:57-8+ My '67
Can't tell 'em apart without a scorecard. H. Keppler and E. Scully. il Mod Phot 31:114 Je '67
Important Polaroid patent for 35-mm instant slide camera. N. Goldberg. il Pop Phot 61:50+ S '67
Polaroid cameras. il Consumer Rep 33:45-6 Ja '68
Polaroid's new $50 color camera, and four other new Polaroids. E. H. Ortner. il Pop Sci 190:140-1 My '67
Those new Polaroid Land cameras. il Consumer Bul 50:27-30 N '67
Which Polaroid Land film? N. Rothschild. il Pop Phot 60:86-7+ Mr '67
Worth knowing; five new Polaroid color pack cameras. il U S Camera 30:62 Ap '67

POLATNICK, Jerome. See Arlinghaus, R. B. jt. auth.

POLE beans. See Beans

POLE vaulting. See Vaulting (sport)

POLGAR, Stephen, and others
(tr) See Radnoti, M. Five late poems

POLIAKOV, Léon
Eichmann trial. Commentary 43:86-8+ Ja '67

POLICE
Crossroads toreador. il Ebony 22:64+ Ap '67
How rest of world handles riots. il U S News 63:36-8 Ag 14 '67; Same abr. with title How they do it abroad. Read Digest 91:135-6 O '67
See also
Border patrol
Police questioning
Traffic police

Electronic equipment
See Electronics in criminal investigation, espionage, etc.

Equipment and supplies
Calling Dick Tracy; report recommends scientific research. Newsweek 69:34 Je 12 '67

POLICE—Equipment and supplies—*Continued*
Can new non-lethal weapons control riots?
E. S. Gardner. il Pop Sci 191:48-52 D '67
Disabling without killing. il Time 89:50+ My 5 '67
Gentle persuasion; aerosol bomb. Time 90:10 S 1 '67
Humane policing. E. F. Fennessy, jr. and others. Sat R 50:48 Jl 1 '67
Look at new weapons to cope with riots. il U S News 64:6-7 Ja 1 '68
New nonlethal weapons. il Life 63:76-7 N 24 '67
Poof the magic flagon; new nonlethal arms. Newsweek 70:27 Jl 24 '67
Wanted: weapons that do not kill; chemical mace. A. Sagalyn and J. Coates. il N Y Times Mag p6+ S 17 '67

Public relations
Breaking down the wall; Task force report. Newsweek 69:42+ My 8 '67
Our war was with the police department; San Francisco police department's Community relations unit. E. Carruth. il Fortune 77:195-7 Ja '68
Role of the police. B. J. Terris. bibliog f il Ann Am Acad 374:58-69 N '67
Violence; symposium. il Nation 205:101-7+ Ag 14 '67

Supply and demand
Our alarming police shortage. W. Schulz. Read Digest 92:75-80 Ja '68

Training
Agitators in a fertilizer factory; International police academy. D. Sanford. New Repub 156:16-18 F 11 '67
Breaking down the wall; Task force report. Newsweek 69:42+ My 8 '67
How much force? il Time 89:58 Mr 24 '67

Canada
Beard phobia; Calgary police harass San Francisco Mime troupe. Nation 204:435-6 Ap 17 '67

Florida
Governor Kirk's not-so-secret police; controversy over special investigators to fight crime. F. Murray. il Reporter 36:27-30 Mr 23 '67
Governor Kirk's private eyes; the Wackenhut corporation. F. J. Cook. il Nation 204:616-22 My 15 '67
Great Wackenhut; privately financed police force. Nation 204:292-3 Mr 6 '67
When a state opens its own war on crime. il U S News 62:61-2 My 22 '67

Germany (Federal Republic)
Katzenjammer kops; nationwide drive to round up most wanted criminals. Newsweek 70:54 D 18 '67

Pennsylvania
Police can make the difference; Allegheny County. F. M. Nevling. il Parks & Rec 2:33-4 S '67

Russia
See also
Secret service—Russia

United States
Big blue line: police power vs. human rights, by E. Cray. Review
    Sat R 50:48-9 F 4 '67. F. J. Cook
Bitter world of the policeman. il Nations Bsns 55:84-6 O '67
Cop's right (?) to stop and frisk. F. P. Graham. il N Y Times Mag p44-5+ D 10 '67
Crime; a contemporary responsibility; address, October 16, 1967. H. C. Donnelly. Vital Speeches 34:114-16 D 1 '67
Crime and punishment; action against the spreading epidemic of street violence. il Newsweek 71:24-5 Ja 8 '68
Crime in the city; can it be controlled? address, June 5, 1967. H. R. Leary. Vital Speeches 34:22-4 O 15 '67
Delicate balance; President says local police have responsibility for keeping the peace. il Newsweek 70:30 S 25 '67
Hooked on law enforcement. E. Z. Friedenberg. il Nation 205:360-5 O 16 '67
Is the U.S. coddling criminals? pro and con discussion. Sr Schol 90:11-12 F 17 '67
Local and state law enforcement today. V. W. Peterson. bibliog f Cur Hist 53:8-14+ Jl '67
Long palm of the law. N. Pileggi. il Esquire 67:132-5+ Ap '67
Police. S. Blum. il Redbook 128:76-7+ F '67

Police, judges tell Congress: criminals get the breaks; excerpts from hearings by Senate judiciary committee's sub-committee on criminal laws and procedures. il U S News 62:44-5 Mr 27 '67
Real story of the riots and who's behind them; excerpts from testimonies. il U S News 63:64-7 Ag 21 '67
Riot control. G. M. Chamberlain. il Am City 82:87-9+ F; 107-9 Mr '67
Role of the police. B. J. Terris. bibliog f il Ann Am Acad 374:58-69 N '67
Tough time to be a good cop. L. Wainwright. Life 63:14B Ag 4 '67
See also
Strikes—United States—Police
    also subhead Police under names of cities e.g. Tucson, Ariz.—Police

Vietnam (Republic)
White mice; national police. J. Donnelly. il Newsweek 70:49 Ag 28 '67

POLICE, Private
Private police: are they the answer? il U S News 62:92 Je 12 '67

POLICE, State
Local and state law enforcement today. V. W. Peterson. bibliog f Cur Hist 53:8-14+ Jl '67
    See also subhead Police under names of states, e.g. Texas—Police

POLICE and education. See Police services for juveniles

POLICE automobiles. See Automobiles, Police

POLICE cars. See Automobiles, Police

POLICE communication systems
Good communications can cut crime response time; Fort Worth il Am City 82:100-1 Ag '67
Radio-telephone answers communication lack; Tucson, Ariz. D. W. Richards. il Am City 82:113 Ap '67
    See also
Police radio

POLICE helicopters. See Helicopters in police work

POLICE interrogation. See Police questioning

POLICE patrol
Police can make the difference; Allegheny County, Pa. F. M. Nevling. il Parks & Rec 2:33-4 S '67

POLICE power
Interrogation and the criminal process. A. J. Reiss, jr. and D. J. Black. bibliog f Ann Am Acad 374:47-57 N '67
Medieval commune and internal violence; police power and public safety in Siena, 1287-1355. W. M. Bowsky. bibliog f Am Hist R 73:1-17 O '67

POLICE questioning
Justice of sorts; interrogation of suspect in New York city. C. P. Crow. Reporter 37:37-41 D 14 '67

POLICE radio
Mobile identifier transmits safety signal without words; Paterson, N.J. il Am City 82:20 N '67
Personal touch in police communications. E. Soldan. il Am City 82:36 Je '67

POLICE records
Police records get an overhaul; Phoenix. A. L. Pasquan. Am City 82:12 Mr '67

POLICE services for juveniles
Cops in the classroom. D. Malvesta and E. Ronayne. NEA J 56:71 D '67
Police; do they belong in the schools? G. H. Shepard and J. James. il Am Ed 3:2-4 S '67

POLICE uniforms. See Uniforms, Police

POLICEMEN. See Police

POLIDORA, V. J. See Frey, P. W. jt. auth.

POLING, David
Powell in the pulpit. Sat R 50:86+ Ap 22 '67

POLISH, David
Why American Jews are disillusioned. Christian Cent 84:965-7 Jl 26 '67

POLISH visitors in the United States. See Foreign visitors in the United States

POLISHING materials
    See also
Furniture polishes

POLISTINE wasps. See Wasps

POLITE, Carlene Hatcher
Black power: five shades of gray. Mlle 66:95+ Ja '68
    about
Authors & editors. H. R. Lottmann. por Pub W 191:20-1 Je 12 '67

POLITE, Frank
Dear lady; poem. Reporter 38:37 Ja 11 '68
Mine; poem. New Yorker 43:64 D 2 '67
Outrider; poem. Reporter 36:48 F 23 '67

POLITICAL parties—*Continued*

Australia
His own man; new prime minister. il Time
91:22+ Ja 19 '68

Canada
In Canada, socialism loses: a portent for
U.S? defeat of Cooperative commonwealth
federation (CCF) in Saskatchewan. il U S
News 63:69-70 N 20 '67
See also
Conservative party (Canada)
Liberal party (Canada)

Chile
Bid for control. Time 91:25 Ja 19 '68
Caught in the middle; E. Frei's Christian
democrats. Time 91:36 Ja 5 '68
Chile: open season on President Frei. P. E.
Sigmund. Reporter 37:33-5 S 21 '67
Chilean Christian democracy. W. R. Duncan.
bibliog f Cur Hist 53:263-9+ N '67
Chile's Christian democrats. P. E. Sigmund.
America 117:602-4 N 18 '67
How free is Frei? D. D. Ranstead. Common-
weal 85:549-50 F 17 '67

France
Christian democracy, R.I.P; MRP once the
largest party in France. P. Steinfels. Com-
monweal 87:294-6 D 1 '67
De Gaulle surveys the damage. E. Taylor.
Reporter 36:29-30 Ap 6 '67
End of MRP. Nat R 19:1058 O 3 '67
French vote: why be surprised? A. Werth.
Nation 204:422-4 Ap 3 '67
See also
Communist party (France)

Germany (Federal Republic)
Bonn is not Weimar: reflections on the
radical right in Germany. W. Laqueur.
Commentary 43:33-42 Mr '67
Bothersome opposition; National democratic
party. il Time 91:34 Ja 5 '68
Germans are worrying the world again; neo-
Nazism: National democratic party (NPD)
J. Roddy. il Look 31:17-21 Mr 21 '67
In the back of the train National democratic
party gains. Nation 204:581 My 8 '67
Letter from Munich: Social democrats meet-
ing. C. Amery. Nation 205:368-9 O 16 '67
Making the grand coalition work; Kiesinger
voted chairman of the C.D.U. il Time 89:
27 Je 2 '67
Socialist showdown. il Time 90:32-3 N 24
'67
Strange bedfellows in Bonn; coalition of
Christian and Social democrats. W. Long.
Look 31:78 F 7 '67
Suicide on the right; National democrats re-
form. Newsweek 69:45 Mr 20 '67
Taming the pros; Kiesinger elected party
chairman. il Newsweek 69:56 Je 5 '67
That old feeling; National democratic party.
il Newsweek 70:51 N 27 '67

Great Britain
See also
Conservative party (Great Britain)
Labor party (Great Britain)
Liberal party (Great Britain)

Hong Kong
See also
Communist party (Hong Kong)

India
After the fall, who will lead? with report
by E. Behr. il Newsweek 69:52-4 Mr 13 '67
Before chaos, one last chance; India goes to
the polls. G. Woodcock. Commonweal 86:
109-11 Ap 14 '67
Divisive forces in post-election India. N. J.
Nanporia. New Repub 156:9-10 My 25 '67
Elections cast a pall over India's future;
Congress party's most humiliating defeat.
il Bsns W p 164 Mr 4 '67
Gandhi caps are in trouble in India. J. A.
Lukas. il N Y Times Mag p28-9+ F 19 '67
India campaigns: cows, corruption & demon-
strations. L. I. Rudolph and S. H. Rudolph.
il Nation 204:138-43 Ja 30 '67
India: out of the straitjacket. D. K. Das.
Nat R 19:290-1 Mr 21 '67
India's opposition scents power. S. Rajan. il
Reporter 36:35-8 Ap 20 '67
Mrs Gandhi's headaches; Congress party
unrest. N. J. Nanporia. New Repub 157:
8-9 S 16 '67
Steady decline of New Delhi's authority;
dissidents form coalition governments. S.
Rajan. il Reporter 37:30-3 O 19 '67
Strength in weakness; election setback in
Congress party. il Time 89:35-6 Mr 10 '67

Israel
Coming together; four separate labor parties.
il Time 90:28 D 22 '67

Japan
Soka Gakkai stirs the ashes of nationalism;
Japan's quasi-religious Komeito party. il
Bsns W p 114+ F 11 '67
See also
Communist party (Japan)

Latin America
Latin America: rise of a new non-Communist
left. G. A. Geyer. Sat R 50:22-3+ Jl 22 '67

Netherlands
Nation of splinters. il Newsweek 69:40 F 27
'67

Peru
Report: Peru's Inca renaissance. G. A. Geyer.
Atlan 220:28+ N '67

Poland
Poland's anti-Semitic Maoist underground. S.
L. Shneiderman. il Reporter 36:21-3 Ja 26
'67

Russia
See also
Communist party (Russia)

Turkey
Report; ideas and record of the Justice
party. T. Prittie. il Atlan 220:32+ S '67
Turkey: emerging democracy. A. Yalcin. For
Affairs 45:706-14 Jl '67

United States
American party politics, elections, and voting
behavior. H. A. Bone. bibliog f il Ann
Am Acad 372:124-37 Jl '67
Black power: a third party going nowhere;
national conference on New politics. il U S
News 63:78 S 18 '67
Freak-out in Chicago: the national confer-
ence of New politics. J. Ridgeway. New
Repub 157:9-12 S 16 '67
How to remove LBJ in 1968; question of a
third party. D. Kearns and S. Levinson.
New Repub 156:13 My 13 '67; Reply. D. W.
Crofts. 156:30-2 Je 10 '67
Left, right and center: essays on liberalism
and conservatism in the United States, ed.
by R. A. Goldwin. Review
Nat R 20:37+ Ja 16 '68. A. Lejeune
Letter from the Palmer house; national New
politics convention, Chicago. R. Adler. New
Yorker 43:56-8+ S 23 '67; Discussion. Na-
tion 205:450+. 514+ N 6, 20 '67
Racists' rights; Maryland Court of appeals
rules ten-month ban violates rights of
States' rights party. Time 90:38+ Jl 14 '67
Third party in '68? the George Wallace story;
with interview. il U S News 62:54-8+ Mr
20 '67
See also
Communist party (United States)
Democratic party
Progressive party
Progressivism (United States politics)
Prohibition party (United States)
Republican party
Whig party (United States)

Vietnam
NLF's new program. D. Warner. Reporter
37:23-4+ O 5 '67
Promise vs. performance; new NLF program.
il Newsweek 70:63 S 25 '67
Struggle and the war. F. FitzGerald. il Atlan
220:72-82+ Ag '67
Talk of a Greek solution for Vietnam; Na-
tional liberation front as a party in the
South. A. Hamilton. New Repub 157:10-11
S 23 '67
What role for the NLF? H. Brandon. Sat R
50:5 D 30 '67
See also
Communist party (Vietnam)

POLITICAL philosophy
Gospel according to Ayn Rand. M. S. Evans.
Nat R 19:1059-63 O 3 '67
National character in the perspective of politi-
cal science. J. C. Charlesworth. bibliog f
Ann Am Acad 370:23-9 Mr '67
Personal note; historical cycle in U.S. politics.
R. Moley. Newsweek 70:76 D 25 '67
Reflections; truth and politics. H. Arendt.
New Yorker 43:49-52+ F 25 '67
Socrates and Aristophanes, by L. Strauss. Re-
view
Nat R 19:423-4 Ap 18 '67. S. Parry

POLITICAL philosophy—*Continued*
Whatever happened to the great simplicities? importance of simple ideas. H. Read. Sat R 50:21-3+ F 18 '67
See also
Communism and democracy
Conservatism
Democracy
Liberalism

POLITICAL poetry
On political poetry. R. Bly. Nation 204:522-4 Ap 24 '67
Poetry and politics 1900-1960, by C. M. Bowra. Review
Américas 19:38-9 Ja '67. K. Congdon

POLITICAL power. See Power (political science)

POLITICAL prisoners
Dubious detour; V. Kazan released in Czechoslovakia and four Americans freed in East Germany. Time 89:33-4 F 10 '67
How the military rules 8 million Greeks. M. Goldbloom. il N Y Times Mag p26-7+ S 24 '67; Reply. A. Michalopoulos. p40+ O 15 '67
Lady at home; five year house arrest of H. Joseph. Newsweek 70:35-6 D 25 '67
Long view; release of 300 Greek prisoners. il Newsweek 71:37 Ja 8 '68
My conflict with East German reds; ed. by C. L. Sanders. M. R. Herrin. il Ebony 22:94-6+ Je '67
Overpriced revenge; case of V. Kazan-Komarek. Newsweek 69:52+ F 13 '67
Political detainees in Greece; Greek ambassador replies to U Thant's appeal. UN Mo Chron 4:61 Je '67
Pronouncements on prisoners; Greece. Time 90:39 S 15 '67
Two prisoners; R. Hess and J. Mindszenty. Reporter 38:11-12 Ja 11 '68

POLITICAL reporting. See Reporters and reporting

POLITICAL responsibility. See Responsibility

POLITICAL rights. See Civil rights

POLITICAL science
Social origins of dictatorship and democracy, by B. Moore, jr. Review
Reporter 36:58-9 Mr 9 '67. W. L. Gundersheimer
See also
American political science association
Anarchism and anarchists
Civil rights
Communism
Decision making (political science)
Democracy
Federal government
Liberalism
Nations
Opposition (political science)
Political philosophy
Politics
Power (political science)
Revolutions
Socialism
State governments

Study and teaching
Fascism and Harvard. Nat R 19:337 Ap 4 '67
Group case study method in political education. R. Y. Fluno. il Sch & Soc 95:188-91 Mr 18 '67

POLITICAL scientists
Political science: CIA, ethics stir otherwise placid convention. R. J. Samuelson. Science 157:1414-17 S 22 '67

POLITICAL theory. See Political philosophy

POLITICAL thought
American style: our past and our principles. S. Hoffmann. For Affairs 46:362-76 Ja '68
Momentous question for our future. F. Morley. il Nations Bsns 55:27-8 F '67
Policy and the people. N. A. Rockefeller. For Affairs 46:231-41 Ja '68
Revolution of 1976. M. Novak. Commonweal 86:441-3 Jl 14 '67; Discussion. 86:550-3 S 8 '67

POLITICIANS
Compleat politician. S. Alsop. Sat Eve Post 240:16 F 25 '67
Men around Nixon. N. B. Freeman. Nat R 19:1118-19+ O 17 '67
See also
Statesmen

POLITICS
Politics, by A. Ribicoff and J. O. Newman. Review
New Repub 156:28-9 Mr 11 '67. G. W. Johnson
See also
Conservatism
Economics and politics
Liberalism
Politicians
Scientists—Political activities
Television in politics
Women and politics
also subhead Politics and government under names of countries, states, etc, e.g. France—Politics and government

Terminology
Words in the news. Sr Schol 91:43 O 5 '67

POLITICS, Corruption in
Another crack at the machine; editor fights political machine that rules Conway County. il Time 89:42 Je 30 '67
Corruption in Asia; Time essay. Time 90:24-5 Ag 18 '67; Same abr. with title Is corruption inevitable in Asia? Read Digest 91:163-6 N '67
Corruption in the Senate; excerpt from Hannibal's legacy. A. J. Toynbee. Atlan 220:56 Jl '67
Fix. S. Smith. il Life 63:22-3+ S 1 '67
From a governor and a D.A. an offer of resignation; reactions to articles concerning Cosa nostra's empire in Louisiana. S. Smith. il Life 63:34-6 S 29 '67
Ghost vote; teller vote falsified on NASA budget bill. Nation 205:37 Jl 17 '67
Graft, the ratsbane of politics. J. H. Plumb. il Sat R 50:41-2 F 25 '67
Great Marcus. il Newsweek 71:12-13 Ja 1 '68
Mafia scandal: new trouble for Lindsay. U S News 64:10 Ja 1 '68
Murk from the reservoir; J. L. Marcus scandal. il Time 90:14 D 29 '67
Public attitudes toward gambling and corruption. J. A. Gardiner. bibliog f il Ann Am Acad 374:123-34 N '67
Speaking out; Congress is hypocritical. L. L. King. Sat Eve Post 240:10+ Ap 8 '67
See also
Campaign funds
Misconduct in office

POLITICS and art. See Art and politics

POLITICS and authors. See Authors and politics

POLITICS and business. See Business—Political aspects

POLITICS and Christianity. See Church and politics

POLITICS and industry. See Industry and state

POLITICS and libraries. See Libraries and politics

POLITICS and newspapers. See Newspapers and politics

POLITICS and religion. See Church and politics

POLITICS and science. See Science and state

POLITICS and war
Nonmorality of cruelty and killing. H. A. Bosmajian. Christian Cent 84:1065-7 Ag 23 '67
War and capitalism. H. C. Wallich. Newsweek 70:66 Jl 10 '67
Washington: how L. B. Johnson is exploiting dissent on Vietnam to domestic political advantage. D. Kiker. il Atlan 220:4+ Jl '67
When nobody can dominate the world. F. Morley. il Nations Bsns 55:23-4 Ag '67

POLJAKOFF-MAYBER, A. See Gale, J. jt. auth.

POLK, James Knox
How to make it to the White House without really trying; Z. Taylor in Mexican war. D. Lavender. il por Am Heritage 18:26-7+ Je '67

POLK, William R.
Middle East: analyzing social change. Bul Atomic Sci 23:12-19 Ja '67

POLL of the people. See Referendum

POLLACK, H. N. See Briggs, L. I. jt. auth.

POLLACK, Herman
Science, foreign affairs, and the State department; address, May 17, 1967. Dept State Bul 56:910-17 Je 19 '67

about
Pollack to head State science office. D. S. Greenberg. por Science 157:292 Jl 21 '67

POLLACK, Jack Harrison
New help for pregnant teenagers. Good H 164:84-5+ My '67

POLLACK, Jack Harrison—*Continued*
Psychiatrists seek secrets of the riots. Todays Health 45:24-7+ N '67
Seven mistakes divorced parents make. Parents Mag 42:48-9+ Mr '67
When parents separate. Todays Health 45:16-19+ Je '67
Where unwed mothers stay in school. Todays Health 45:24-7 S '67
—See Gagnon, P. A. jt. auth.

POLLACK, Merrill
Most important questions unpublished writers ask. Writer 80:14-16+ F '67

POLLEN
Oxygen tension as a control mechanism in pollen tube rupture. R. G. Stanley and H. F. Linskens. bibliog il Science 157:833-4 Ag 18 '67

POLLEN, Fossil
Bering land bridge: evidence of spruce in late-Wisconsin times. P. A. Colinvaux. bibliog il Science 156:380-3 Ap 21 '67
Chenopod and amaranth pollen: electronmicroscopic identification. M. Tsukada. bibliog il Science 157:80-2 Jl 7 '67
Enclosed bark as a pollen trap. D. P. Adam and others. bibliog il Science 157:1067-8 S 1 '67
Freshwater peat on the continental shelf. K. O. Emery and others. bibliog il Science 158:1301-7 D 8 '67
Pollen diagrams from sub-Arctic central Canada. H. Nichols. bibliog il Science 155:1665-8 Mr 31 '67

POLLET, Joseph
In and out of time. K. Levin. il por Art N 65:40-1+ F '67

POLLINATION. See Fertilization of plants

POLLOCK, Francis
Peace corps returnees. Nation 205:15-17 Jl 3 '67

POLLOCK, Jackson
Art world; exhibition at the Museum of modern art. H. Rosenberg. New Yorker 43:162+ My 6 '67
God made manifest; show at the Museum of modern art. F. Getlein. New Repub 156:26-7 Ap 22 '67
Jackson Pollock; an artists' symposium; with editorial comment. il pors Art N 66:27, 28-33+ Ap; 26-9+ My '67; Reply. D. Hare. 66:8+ D '67
Jackson Pollock in retrospect, he broke the ice. V. Raynor. il pors N Y Times Mag p50-1+ Ap 2 '67
Jackson Pollock: inspiration, vision, intuitive decision. C. Greenberg. il por Vogue 149:158-61 Ap 1 '67
Jackson Pollock retrospective. B. F. Jones. America 117:329-31 S 23 '67
Magic life. J. Kroll. il por Newsweek 69:96-8 Ap 17 '67
Pollock revisited; exhibition at Manhattan's Museum of modern art. Time 89:85 Ap 14 '67

POLLS, Public opinion. See Public opinion polls
POLLUTION, Air. See Air pollution
POLLUTION, Water. See Water pollution
POLLUTION of lakes. See Water pollution
POLLUTION of streams. See Water pollution

POLNER, Murray
Despicable episode. Christian Cent 84:409-10 Mr 29 '67

POLO, Water. See Water polo

POLONIUM
Polonium-210 in bronchial epithelium of cigarette smokers; with reply by R. B. Holtzman. J. B. Little and E. P. Radford, jr. Science 155:606-7 F 3 '67
Polonium-210: removal from smoke by resin filters. E. W. Bretthauer and S. C. Black. bibliog il Science 156:1375-6 Je 9 '67

POLSHEK, Julie
It's worth mentioning. See issues of House beautiful
Take it easy. See issues of House beautiful

POLTERGEISTS. See Ghosts

POLYADENYLIC acid
Antibody formation: stimulation by polyadenylic and polycytidylic acids. W. Braun and M. Nakano. bibliog il Science 157:819-21 Ag 18 '67
Deoxycytidylate and deoxyguanylate kinase activity in pneumococci after exposure to known polyribonucleotides. W. Firshein and others. bibliog il Science 157:821-2 Ag 18 '67

POLYANTHUS. See Primroses
POLYCHAETA. See Marine worms
POLYCYSTIC renal disease. See Kidneys—Diseases

POLYCYTIDYLIC acid
Antibody formation: stimulation by polyadenylic and polycytidylic acids. W. Braun and M. Nakano. bibliog il Science 157:819-21 Ag 18 '67
Deoxycytidylate and deoxyguanylate kinase activity in pneumococci after exposure to known polyribonucleotides. W. Firshein and others. bibliog il Science 157:821-2 Ag 18 '67

POLYELECTROLYTES. See Electrolytes
POLYETHYLENE glycol. See Glycols
POLYETHYLENE miniboat. See Boats—Materials

POLYGAMY
Husbands with more than one wife. B. Merson. il Ladies Home J 84:78-9+ Je '67

POLYGRAPH
Polygraph. B. M. Smith; discussion. Sci Am 216:6+ Mr '67

POLYKETIDES. See Ketene

POLYKOFF, Shirley
Color her blond. il por Newsweek 69:70 Je 19 '67

POLYMERIZATION
Polymerization of hemoglobins of mouse and man: structural basis. J. Bonaventura and A. Riggs. bibliog il Science 158:800-2 N 10 '67

POLYMERS
Biosynthesis of polyketides and related compounds; excerpts from address, June 28, 1966. A. J. Birch. bibliog il Science 156:202-6 Ap 14 '67
Nature of polymeric materials. H. F. Mark. il Sci Am 217:148-54+ S '67

POLYMORPHISM
Shock-wave compression and X-ray studies of titanium dioxide. R. G. McQueen and others. bibliog il Science 155:1401-4 Mr 17 '67

POLYMORPHISM (biology)
Autosomal phosphogluconic dehydrogenase polymorphism in the cat, felis catus L. H. C. Thuline and others. bibliog il Science 157:431-2 Jl 28 '67
Esterase polymorphism in natural populations of a sulfur butterfly, colias eurytheme. J. M. Burns and F. M. Johnson. bibliog il Science 156:93-6 Ap 7 '67
Hemoglobin polymorphism in chimpanzees and gibbons. H. A. Hoffman and others. bibliog il Science 156:944 My 19 '67
Mitochondrial malate dehydrogenase: a new genetic polymorphism in man. R. G. Davidson and J. A. Cortner. bibliog il Science 157:1569-71 S 29 '67
Phase polymorphism in the grasshopper melanoplus differentialis. H. Dingle and J. B. Haskell. bibliog il Science 155:590-2 F 3 '67
Transferrin polymorphism and population differences in the genetic variability of chimpanzees. M. Goodman and others. bibliog il Science 156:98-100 Ap 7 '67

POLYMORPHONUCLEAR leukocytes. See Leucocytes
POLYMYOSITIS. See Muscles—Diseases
POLYNESIA
See also
Americans in Polynesia
Easter Island

POLYNESIAN cookery. See Cookery, Polynesian
POLYNESIAN sculpture. See Sculpture, Polynesian

POLYNESIANS
Are the natives friendly? M. Mead. Redbook 128:31+ Mr '67
Polynesian navigation. W. S. Kals. il Sky & Tel 33:358-60 Je '67

POLYPEPTIDES. See Peptides
POLYPHEMUS moths. See Moths
POLYRIBONUCLEOTIDES. See Nucleoproteins
POLYRIBOSOMES. See Nucleoproteins

POLYSACCHARIDES
Altered response to pneumococcal polysaccharide in offspring of immunologically paralyzed mice. R. Kerman and others. bibliog il Science 156:1514-16 Je 16 '67
Direction of chain growth in polysaccharide synthesis. P. W. Robbins and others. bibliog il Science 158:1536-42 D 22 '67
Synovial cell synthesis of a substance immunologically like cartilage proteinpolysaccharide. R. Janis and others. bibliog il Science 158:1464-7 D 15 '67

POLYSOMES. See Nucleoproteins
POLYSTYRENE. See Plastics

POLYURETHANE. See Urethans

POMARE, Eleo, dance company. See Dance companies

POMEROY, Kenneth B.
Corps in the Cradle. por Am For 73:20-3 S '67
Ending a fiefdom. Am For 73:5+ Ag '67
New Asiatic invader. Am For 73:22-4+ Ja '67
$1 billion mistake. Am For 73:23+ Ap '67
—and Littlecott, L. C.
Social register: eighty-five new champs. Am For 73:28-33 S '67

POMEROY, Mary Barnas
Saloya. Américas 19:28-33 O '67

POMEROY, Paul W. See Liebermann, R. C. jt. auth.

POMEROY, Ralph
Black Persephone. Art N 66:44-5+ O '67
Going places, finding things in Brussels. House & Gard 132:76+ O '67
Overwhelmed by the moon at the wrong but imperative moment; poem. Poetry 110:243 Jl '67

POMPEII
Last moments of Pompeii. il UNESCO Courier 20:7 O '67

POMPIDOU, Georges
Gaullists get restive. il por Bsns W p37 My 13 '67
Pompon & les godillots. por Time 90:31 D 8 '67

PONCET, André François-. See François-Poncet, A.

PONCHIELLI, Amilcare
La Gioconda. Criticism
Opera N 31:24-5 Ap 15 '67
Opera N il 31:17-20 Ap 15 '67

POND vegetation. See Aquatic plants

PONDS
Building a farm pond. Suc Farm 65:50L Ap '67

PONT, A. D.
Interim report on South Africa libel trial. Christian Cent 84:677 My 24 '67
Justice wins a case in South Africa. Christian Cent 84:828-9 Je 28 '67

PONT, John
Impossible dream. il por Newsweek 70:82-3 N 6 '67

PONTECORVO, Giulio
Books. Bul Atomic Sci 23:55-6 Je '67
Law of the sea. Bul Atomic Sci 23:46-8 Ap '67

PONTIFICAL commission on justice and peace
Toward building a better world. America 116: 773 My 27 '67

POODLES
Most popular dog in America. B. Rice. il N Y Times Mag p50-i+ Ja 7 '68

POOL (game) See Billiards

POOLS. See Garden pools; Swimming pools

POONS, Larry
Art; exhibition at Castelli gallery. M. Kozloff. Nation 204:189-90 F 6 '67
Poons: a clean and balanced world? E. F. Fry. il Art N 65:34-5+ F '67

POOR
See also
Church and social problems
Legal aid
Poverty
Public welfare
Slums

Brazil
Night patrol in Brazil. M. E. Iglesias. America 116:873-4 Je 24 '67
See also
Peasantry—Brazil

Mexico
Cleaning up Juarez. W. Eastlake. Nation 205:300-3 O 2 '67

Puerto Rico
La vida: a Puerto Rican family in the culture of poverty—San Juan and New York, by O. Lewis. Review
Commentary 43:83-5 F '67. N. Glazer
Natur Hist 76:70+ Ap '67. J. Monserrat
New Yorker 43:154+ Mr 4 '67. N. Hentoff

United States
Battle line of welfare: the hungry can't wait. C. I. Schottland. il Nation 204:649-52 My 22 '67
Business zeroes in on poverty. Life 63:4 D 15 '67
Case for a family allowance; excerpt from testimony before a Senate government operations subcommittee on the federal role in urban problems. D. P. Moynihan. il N Y Times Mag p 13+ F 5 '67; Discussion. p 12+ F 26 '67

Dream city (almost) H. Cox; discussion. Commonweal 85:631, 688 Mr 3, 17 '67
Forgotten men: the poor whites. il U S News 63:76 N 27 '67
Is rural poverty a national disgrace? U S News 63:8 D 25 '67
Is U.S. really filled with poverty? J. B. Parrish. il U S News 63:50-3 S 4 '67; Reply. New Repub 157:4 O 7 '67
It can be done! conquering poverty in the US by 1976. J. Tobin. New Repub 156:14-18 Je 3 '67; Reply. L. H. Keyserling. 156:33-4 Je 10 '67
It isn't true that nobody starves in America. R. Sherrill. il N Y Times Mag p22-3+ Je 4 '67; Discussion. p4 Jl 16; 7+ Jl 30 '67
Lord, I'm hungry; Senate antipoverty subcommittee tours lands of the Mississippi delta. il Newsweek 70:22-4 Jl 24 '67
Luring the poor out of the hills; West Virginia's drive to urbanize. il Bsns W p74-6+ Jl 1 '67
New kind of poverty war; improving life of poor on farms and in small towns. il Bsns W p44+ D 16 '67
Not just Negroes; excerpts from address, October 1967. K. G. Myrdal. Sr Schol 91:13 O 19 '67
Poor and the PTA. E. Schindler-Rainman. il PTA Mag 61:4-7 Ap '67
Poor power; National welfare rights movement. Nation 204:228-9 F 20 '67
Poverty in the ghetto. the view from Watts. P. Bullock. Mo Labor R 90:26 F '67
Poverty, inequality, and conflict. S. M. Miller and others. bibliog f il Ann Am Acad 373: 16-52 S '67
Poverty, paternalism and protest. M. A. Sebg. Cath World 204:352-5 Mr '67
Quiet progress in the cities; programs to alleviate poverty. Life 63:4 O 6 '67
Redbook dialogue. R. Kennedy; O. Lewis. il Redbook 129:74-5+ S '67
Riots and our national response. J. M. Gessell. Christian Cent 84:1063-5 Ag 23 '67
Shortchanging the rural poor. America 116: 168-9 F 4 '67
Task Americans are called to; concerning Franz Koenig's statement. America 117:236 S 9 '67
Unions for people on relief? il U S News 63: 36-8 O 30 '67
We've got rights! R. A. Cloward and F. F. Piven. New Repub 157:23-7 Ag 5 '67
Welfare mess. Sat Eve Post 240:90 Ap 8 '67
White Americans in rural poverty; BirdMcCoy report. America 117:704 D 9 '67
See also
Anti-poverty program, 1964-
Church and social problems
Economic assistance, Domestic
Negroes in the United States—Social conditions
  also subhead Poor under names of cities, e.g. New York (city)—Poor

Anecdotes, facetiae, satire, etc.
Poorest of the poor. J. F. Henahan. Sat R 50: 4+ Jl 29 '67

POOR laws
See also
Public welfare—Law

United States
See also
Public welfare—United States

POOR peoples corporation
Negro self-help. A. Goldberg. New Repub 156: 6 Je 10 '67

POOR relief. See Public welfare

POOR whites. See Poor—United States

POORE, William H.
Louisville's race; Derby bogs down. Christian Cent 84:817-18 Je 21 '67

POP art. See Modernism (art)

POP music. See Music, Popular (songs, etc)

POP poetry. See Poetry

POPE, Patricia Mae Moffat
American westerns, 1967. il pors Vogue 149: 246-7 My '67

POPE, Saxton
Archery hunting in 1925. Field & S 72:45+ Ja '68

POPENOE, Paul, and Disney, D. C.
California woman. Ladies Home J 84:62 Jl '67

POPES
See also
Papacy

Election
Suenens supports synodical election of popes; Cardinal Suenens of Belgium. Christian Cent 84:261 Mr 1 '67

POPES—*Continued*

Infallibility

How U.S. Catholics view the Pope. il Newsweek 69:74 Mr 20 '67
Pope as leader of all Christians? U S News 62:15 Je 19 '67

POPKIN, Henry
Theatre. Vogue 150:70-1+ O 15 '67

POPLAR
Of people and poplars. M. Fry. il Farm J 91:A2-38A Je '67

POPLAR forest (historic house) See Virginia—Historic houses, etc.

POPP, Lucia
Hard life; interview, ed. by A. M. Lingg. por Opera N 31:13 Ap 8 '67

POPPER, David H.
China, the United Nations, and the United States; address, March 28, 1967. Dept State Bul 56:689-95 My 1 '67

POPPIES
Plant some spectacular poppies. E. S. Henderson. il Horticulture 45:18-19+ My '67
Shirley poppies. R. C. Hands. il(cover) Horticulture 45:9 Je '67

POPULAR culture
Folklore, fakelore, and poplore. M. Fishwick. il Sat R 50:20-1+ Ag 26 '67
Ins and outs of a mobile age; 1947 and 1967. il Sat R 50:48-9 Ap 22 '67
Questions of passion: turning an audience on. R. Kotlowitz. Harper 235:120-3 O '67
Scholar in a nowhere world. A. Heckscher. Yale R 57:47-55 O '67
See also subhead Popular culture under names of countries, e.g. United States—Popular culture

POPULAR music. See Music, Popular (songs, etc)

POPULAR photography (periodical)
Dutch life of Riley; prize-winning photo tour. il Pop Phot 60:50+ My '67
Nostalgic look at the medium; thirtieth anniversary of Popular photography. D. B. Eisendrath, jr. Pop Phot 60:54+ My '67
Thirty people-years. J. Durniak. Pop Phot 60:64+ My '67

POPULAR republican party. See Political parties—France

POPULAR singers. See Singers

POPULAR songs. See Music, Popular (songs, etc)

POPULATION
But then came man; address, May 4, 1967. S. L. Udall. Vital Speeches 33:569-73 Jl 1 '67
Demographic yearbook 1966. UN Mo Chron 4: 99 D '67
World population; symposium, ed. by J. D. Durand. bibliog f il Ann Am Acad 369:1-140 Ja '67
See also
Birth control
Demography
United Nations—Population commission
also subhead Population under names of countries, states, etc. e.g. Rumania—Population

History

Long-range view of world population growth. J. D. Durand. bibliog f il Ann Am Acad 369:1-8 Ja '67

Overpopulation

Ecologist's view of the population problem. D. L. Lyon il Liv Wildn 31:31-5 Spr '67
Human race has, maybe, thirty-five years left. D. Lyle. il Esquire 68:116-18+ S '67
Malthus, Marx and the North American breadbasket. O. L. Freeman. il For Affairs 45:579-93 Jl '67; Excerpts. U S News 63: 40-4 Jl 3 '67
Our perilous population implosion. S. L. Udall. Sat R 50:10-13 S 2 '67
Overpopulation: threat to survival. W. H. Draper, jr. Parents Mag 42:30 Ag '67
Politics of progress; address, February 20, 1967. E. V. Rostow. Dept State Bul 56:398-405 Mr 13 '67
Population crisis: reasons for hope. F. W. Notestein. For Affairs 46:167-80 O '67
S. R. O; excerpt from Moment in the sun. R. Rienow and L. T. Rienow. il N Y Times Mag p62-3+ My 28 '67
We are losing the race against hunger. G. McGovern. il Look 31:86+ Mr 7 '67
See also
Population, Increase of

Statistics

Population projections for the world, developed and developing regions: 1965-2000. M. A. El-Badry. bibliog f il Ann Am Acad 369:9-15 Ja '67

POPULATION, Distribution of
Rush to the cities eases off: National planning assn. study. il Bsns W p90+ Je 24 '67

POPULATIONS, Fish. See Fish populations

POPULATION, Increase of
Burdened acres, the people question. M. Bush. il Liv Wildn 31:28-31 Spr '67
Effects of population growth on the economic development of developing countries. R. A. Easterlin. bibliog f il Ann Am Acad 369:98-108 Ja '67
Health, population, and economic development. C. E. Taylor and M.-F. Hall. bibliog Science 157:651-7 Ag 11 '67
Impasse in Latin America. A. H. Whiteford. Christian Cent 85:71-4 Ja 17 '68
Look at world population the day after tomorrow; excerpt from Three comments on the near future of mankind. J. Fourastié. bibliog f il UNESCO Courier 20:10-13+ F '67
Putting a brake on runaway birth rates; U.S. to supply developing nations with contraceptives. il Bsns W p76-8 S 23 '67
Rates of population growth and standards of living; excerpt from address, June 1967. J. E. Meade. Mo Labor R 90:55-8 S '67
What explosion? Newsweek 69:55-6 My 8 '67
See also
Population—Overpopulation

POPULATION, Rural. See Population, Distribution of

POPULATION commission. See United Nations—Population commission

POPULATION pressure. See Population—Overpopulation

POPULORUM progressio. See Encyclicals

PORCELAIN. See Pottery

PORCELAIN enamel. See Enamels and enameling

PORCHES
Porch that came in from the cold. il Bet Hom & Gard 45:110 F '67
Remember screened porches? il Am Home 70: 80-1 Je '67
Sonnets from a porch-ophile; in praise of a screened porch. J. L. O'Neill. Am Home 70:33 Je '67
See also
Sun rooms

PORCUPINES
New look at porky. G. Oberweiser. il Field & S 72:46+ Ag '67
See also
Cookery—Game

POREL, Jacques
Three friends of Proust. P. Kolb. il por Vogue 149:88-9 Mr 15 '67

PORK
See also
Cookery—Meat

PORK barrel legislation. See United States—Appropriations and expenditures

PORK industry. See Meat industry and trade

PORNOGRAPHY. See Immoral literature and pictures; Obscenity (law)

POROMERICS. See Leather substitutes

PORPOISES. See Dolphins (mammals)

PORSILD, A. E. and others
Lupinus arcticus Wats. grown from seeds of pleistocene age. bibliog Science 158:113-14 O 6 '67

PORT authority of New York. See Port of New York authority

PORT CHICAGO, Calif.
On the edge of extinction. J. G. Dunne and J. Didion. Sat Eve Post 240:24+ O 7 '67
On the volcano's edge; dangers in loading of ammunition for Vietnam. T. Plate. il Newsweek 70:26 Jl 10 '67

PORT CHICAGO disaster. See Explosions

PORT of New York authority
Reconnaissance camera focused on traffic; applying aerial photography in Project Sky Count. il Tech W 20:35-6 Ap 3 '67

PORT of New York authority bus terminal. See New York (city)—Stations

PORT ROYAL, Jamaica
Diving for treasure in the pirate city. H. H. Martin. il Sat Eve Post 240:63-7 Ag 12 '67

PORTABLE classrooms. See Classrooms

PORTABLE electric tools; Portable phonograph; etc. See Electric tools, Portable; Phonograph, Portable; etc.

PORTABLE typewriters. See Typewriters

PORTER, Bernard
Of course, I'm no psychiatrist. R. Reisig and R. Rapoport. New Repub 156:13-14 Je 24 '67

PORTER, Cole
Life that late he led, by G. Eells. Review Atlan 220:108-9 Jl '67. E. Weeks
Night and day. H. Saal. il por Newsweek 69:101-2 Je 12 '67

PORTER, D. Gareth
Is this a limited war? Commonweal 86:9-11 Mr 24 '67
Prince and US. Commonweal 87:442-3 Ja 12 '68

PORTER, Eliot
Adirondack spring; with photographs. Audubon 69:32-7 Mr '67
Art and technique of Eliot Porter; interview, ed. by P. Caulfield. Natur Hist 76:26-31+ D '67

about
Eliot Porter: how he works. P. Caulfield. il pors Mod Phot 31:66-9 S '67
Eliot Porter: medication to conservation. J. Deschin. il por Pop Phot 61:70+ D '67

PORTER, Fairfield
Immediacy is the message. J. Schuyler. il Art N 66:32-3+ Mr '67

PORTER, George
Defining sections of the chemical blur. por(p463) Sci N 92:464-5 N 11 '67
Nobel prizes; chemistry. H. Eyring and E. M. Eyring. por Science 158:746-8 N 10 '67

PORTER, Graham
Casanova, junior grade. Read Digest 90:81-3 Ap '67
Harem in the house; condensation. Read Digest 91:245-51+ D '67
Now that I understand golf. Read Digest 91:86-8 Jl '67
Paint me a silver lining. Read Digest 90:88-90 Mr '67

PORTER, John
Canadian character in the twentieth century. bibliog f Ann Am Acad 370:48-56 Mr '67

PORTER, Katherine Anne
Christmas story. McCalls 95:90-1+ D '67

PORTER, Keith R. See Palade, G. jt. auth.

PORTER, R. R.
Structure of antibodies; with biographical sketch. Sci Am 217:19, 81-7+ O '67

PORTER, Russell W.
Russell W. Porter exhibit. D. Milon. il por Sky & Tel 34:226-8 O '67

PORTER, Sylvia
Spending your money; questions and answers. See issues of Ladies' home journal

PORTLAND, Me.
Our plows had to stop plowing. T. Griffin. il Am City 82:75-7 N '67

PORTLAND, Ore.

Education
Oregon graduate center; a new Portland scientific institution. B. Nelson. il Science 157:1151-2+ S 8 '67

Libraries
Books behind the bars; prisons and jails served by Multnomah County library. J. W. Kling. il Library J 92:1424-5 Ap 1 '67; Reply. M. H. Vedder. 92:2488 Jl '67

Sanitary affairs
Fine screens for combined sewage. Am City 82:42 D '67

PORTLAND, Ore. zoological garden
I go back to an elephant nursery. S. Alexander. Life 62:31 Ap 7 '67

PORTLAND general electric company
Nuclear power on salmon rivers. A. Netboy. il Nation 205:337-9 O 9 '67

PORTMAN, John Calvin, Jr
Big ideas that give downtown a new look. il pors Bsns W p 100-2+ F 25 '67

PORTRAIT dolls. See Dolls

PORTRAIT painting
Child portraiture. H. Olsen. il Design 69:10-13 Wint '67
Paintings of Betty Warren. N. Kent. il Am Artist 31:36-41+ My '67
See also
Human figure in art

PORTRAIT sculpture
How to portray a martyr? Hawaiian controversy over statue of Father Damien. il Time 89:83 My 12 '67

PORTRAITS
See also
Photography—Portraits

Exhibitions
Philosopher of the face; G. Stuart retrospective at the National gallery. B. N. O'Doherty. il Art N 66:42-5+ Sum '67

PORTRAITS, American
Antiques book preview; people who lived at Dumbarton Oaks. E. Gaines. il Antiques 92:198-202 Ag '67
Antiques book preview: Portraits of John and Abigail Adams: a quest for a likeness. A. Oliver. il Antiques 91:476-80 Ap '67
Group portraits; Ames and Hogarth. I. F. Cortelyou. il Antiques 92:632+ N '67
Images of elegant New York; conversation pieces; portfolio. L. Auchincloss. Am Heritage 17:48-65 O '66; Correction. il 18:76 F '67
Oliver Frazer, early Kentucky portrait painter. M. M. Bridwell. il Antiques 92:718-21 N '67
Portrait of John Bartram? more American portraits. R. Davidson. Antiques 92:376+ S '67
Portraits of Savannah people. L. T. Cheney. il Antiques 91:353-9 Mr '67

PORTRAITS, Egyptian
Myopic tribute; exhibition at Detroit institute of arts. il Time 89:82-3+ Ap 14 '67

PORTRAITS, French
Vigée-Lebrun and the women of the French court. I. Bischoff. il Antiques 92:706-12 N '67

PORTRAITS in a village; story. See Stewart, N.

PORTRAITURE. See Photography—Portraits

PORTS
See also subhead Harbor under names of cities. e.g. Genoa—Harbor

PORTUGAL
See also
Automobile touring—Portugal
Gardens—Portugal
St Paul Rocks
Tourist trade—Portugal
United Nations—Portugal

Colonies
Hernandarias; upper Peru to the Plate River. V. Carreño. il Américas 19:27-35 My '67
Portugal and the new republics. S. S. Garrido. il Américas 19:24-9 Ap '67
See also
Angola
Macao

Commercial treaties and agreements
United States and Portugal amend cotton textile agreement. W. T. Bennett, jr. il Dept State Bul 57:548-9 O 23 '67

Description and travel
Portuguese people and places. L. W. Thieme. il U S Camera 31:74-5 Ja '68
Travel's picture portfolio. Travel 127:50-5 Je '67

History
Bibliography
Articles and other books received; comp. by C. J. Bishko. See issues of American historical review

Moral conditions
Affairs of state; high-society prostitution ring's political implications. Time 90:28 D 22 '67

Politics and government
Affairs of state; high-society prostitution ring's political implications. Time 90:28 D 22 '67

Religious institutions and affairs
See also
Jews in Portugal

PORTUGUESE EAST AFRICA. See Mozambique

PORTUGUESE WEST AFRICA. See Angola

POSITION, Social. See Social status

POSITIONS, Applications for. See Applications for positions

POSNER, Aaron S. See Termine, J. D. jt. auth.

POSNER, David
Dialogue with Norman Douglas; poem. Poetry 110:367-9 S '67
Education; poem. New Yorker 43:148 N 18 '67

POSNER, Michael I. and Keele, S. W.
Decay of visual information from a single letter. bibliog Science 158:137-9 O 6 '67

POSS, Stanley
To the Woolf house. Nation 204:187-8 F 6 '67
POSSER, Fred H.
Value engineering for the electronics industry.
Electr World 78:41-4+ Ag '67
POSSESSION (law)
See also
Real property
POSSONY, Stefan T.
Antidote to brainwashing. Nat R 19:1283-5 N
14 '67
NATO and the nuclear deterrent. Nat R 19:
1125-6 O 17 '67
POST, Marjorie Merriweather
Mumsy the magnificent. il pors Time 89:48-9
F 3 '67
POST, New York. See New York post
POST, Washington. See Washington post and
Times herald
POST cards
Ancient castles. B. Finnegan. il Hobbies 72:
119-21 D '67
Columbian exposition. B. Finnegan. il Hobbies
72:120+ Ag '67
Flower show to feature post cards. B. Fin-
negan. il Hobbies 72:116-17+ Mr '67
Holiday post cards. il Am Heritage 19:18-21
D '67
Our national Capitol. B. Finnegan. il Hobbies
72:115-17 Je '67

Collectors and collecting
Fun, sex & war in the mailbag. il Pop Phot
60:102+ My '67
POST exchanges. See United States—Armed
forces—Post exchanges
POST libraries. See United States—Army—Li-
braries
POST office. See Postal service
POST office department (United States) See
United States—Post office department
POST office inspection service. See United
States—Post office department
POSTAGE stamps
Around the world with stamps; canceled
stamps. H. Herst, jr. Hobbies 72:99+ Ap
'67
Natural world of the post office; natural his-
tory theme on stamps. A. Ross. il Natur
Hist 77:28-31 Ja '68
Philatelic fury; objections to new issues.
il Time 90:23-4 Jl 21 '67
Stamp out stamps! commemorative issues.
Reporter 36:16 Mr 9 '67
Stamps. H. Herst, jr. See issues of Hobbies
Stamps around the world; sizes and shapes.
H. Herst, jr. Hobbies 71:99 F '67
Support the drive for flower stamps. il Horti-
culture 45:32-3 S '67

Catalogs
Around the world with stamps. H. Herst, jr.
Hobbies 72:99 D '67

Collectors and collecting
How to prepare a collection for sale. H. Herst,
jr. Hobbies 72:99+ O '67
Stamps around the world. H. Herst, jr. Hobbies 72:99+ Mr '67

POSTAL censorship
Hearing set on obscene mail. G. Krettek and
E. D. Cooke. ALA Bul 61:466-7 My '67
Mail sex behavior. Reporter 37:12+ N 16 '67
POSTAL rates
United States
ABA and ABPC criticize new postal rate bill.
Pub W 192:29 N 20 '67
Big postal rate increase asked; effect on
schools and libraries. il Sr Schol 90:sup4
My 12 '67
Book rate hikes asked in post office message.
Pub W 191:35 Ap 17 '67
Changes for the mails; postage up, service
down. il U S News 63:76-8 D 11 '67
End of the 5-cent letter? LBJ asks that and
more. il U S News 62:64 F 6 '67
Escalating mail rates; hikes for junk mail
and magazines. il Bsns W p48-9 O 21 '67
Higher postal rates; what's in store. U S
News 63:8 S 4 '67
Licking the postage hike; third-class mailers.
Bsns W p52 D 9 '67
Mail rates: going even higher than ex-
pected? U S News 63:9 Jl 24 '67
Postal and federal pay: both going up? U S
News 63:16 O 23 '67
Postal rate increase proposed. G. Krettek and
E. D. Cooke. ALA Bul 61:466 My '67
Postal rate increases now in effect. Pub W
193:46 Ja 8 '68

Postal rate revision; special rate for fourth
class mail. G. Krettek and E. Cooke. ALA
Bul 61:923 S '67
Postal rates. G. Krettek and E. D. Cooke.
Wilson Lib Bul 42:337 N '67
Press, too, is educational; proposed tax or
surcharge on delivery by mail of publica-
tions distributing more than 500,000 copies
D. Lawrence. U S News 62:108 F 27 '67
Proposed postal rates: costs to be planned
for. C. B. Grannis. Pub W 192:37 O 23 '67
Those alleged postal subsidies. R. Moley.
Newsweek 70:112 O 16 '67
Will a rate hike help to bail out post of-
fice? $1-billion-plus deficit. Bsns W p 152+
Ja 21 '67
With higher postal rates, will the mails im-
prove? il U S News 62:8 Ap 17 '67
POSTAL savings banks
Great uncashed; final close-out of postal sav-
ings. Newsweek 70:66-7 Jl 3 '67
POSTAL service

Laws and regulations
See also
Postal censorship
France
Direct mail bookselling threatened in France.
H. R. Lottman. Pub W 191:30-2 Mr 27 '67

Great Britain
Britain seeks a postal corporation, too. U S
News 62:61 Ap 24 '67

Russia
If you think U.S. mails are in trouble—.
U S News 62:22 Ap 24 '67

United States
Can anything be done about U.S. mail serv-
ice? il U S News 62:56-7 Ap 3 '67
Can systems research put zip in the mail?
Bsns W p94+ Ap 1 '67
Changes for the mails: postage up, service
down. il U S News 63:76-8 D 11 '67
Crisis coming in the mails. U S News 62:58-9
Ap 24 '67
Is a drastic facelift in store for the mails?
take politics out of the postal system.
Bsns W p32-3 Ap 8 '67
Mailmen's woes: snow & rain aren't the half
of it. il Sr Schol 91:12-16 D 7 '67
Other side of the postal story. L. F. O'Brien.
U S News 63:54 D 18 '67
Post office; need for private ventures. M.
Friedman. Newsweek 70:87 O 9 '67
Profitable and the profligate. A. H. Sypher.
il Nations Bsns 55:31-2 F '67
U.S. mail wail. Sr Schol 90:21-2 Ap 28 '67
Will a rate hike help to bail out post office?
$1-billion-plus deficit. Bsns W p 152+
Ja 21 '67
Zip code, new tool for marketers. M. Baier.
Harvard Bsns R 45:136-40 Ja '67
See also
Air mail service
Mailboxes
Postal censorship
Railway mail service
United States—Post office department
POSTCARDS. See Post cards
POSTERS
Coolest things; personality posters and psy-
chedelic posters. il Newsweek 69:87 Mr 6 '67
Great poster wave; with report by J. Borg-
zinne. il Life 63:36-43 S 1 '67
Mrs Johnson inaugurates anti-litter poster
for parks and forests. il Nat Parks Mag
41:20 Jl '67
Nouveau Frisco. il Time 89:66-7+ Ap 7 '67
Posters for all seasons. J. Gollin. il Art N
66:22-4 D '67
Posters: the newest fad in the bookshops.
il Pub W 191:45-7 Ap 3 '67
Posters; with portfolio. W. Karp. Horizon
9:104-12 Aut '67
Six party ideas. il Seventeen 26:228+ F '67
POSTMASTER General. See United States—
Post office department
POSTMORTEMS. See Autopsy
POSTPARTUM depression. See Depression,
Mental
POSTURE
See also
Man—Attitude and movement
POSVAR, Wesley W.
Pitt picks chancellor; agrees that modesty
is the best policy. B. Nelson. por Science
155:541-4 F 3 '67
POT. See Marijuana
POT roasting. See Cookery—Meat

POTASSIUM
Fractionation of potassium/rubidium by amphiboles: implications regarding mantle composition. S. R. Hart and L. T. Aldrich. bibliog il Science 155:325-7 Ja 20 '67

POTASSIUM argon dating. See Radioactive dating

POTASSIUM chloride
Activity coefficients of aqueous potassium chloride measured with a potassium-sensitive glass electrode. P. B. Hostetler and others. bibliog il Science 155:1537-9 Mr 24 '67
Mating behavior: facilitation in the female rat after cortical application of potassium chloride. L. G. Clemens and others. bibliog il Science 157:1208-9 S 8 '67

POTASSIUM in the body
Cochlear function and sodium and potassium activated adenosine triphosphatase. W. Kuijpers and others. bibliog il Science 157:949-50 Ag 25 '67
Sodium and potassium effects on skeletal muscle microsomal adenosine triphosphatase and calcium uptake. B. B. Rubin and A. M. Katz. bibliog il Science 158:1189-90 D 1 '67
Solium-potassium adenosine triphosphatase: acyl phosphate intermediate shown to be L-glutamyl-γ-phosphate. A. Kahlenberg and others. bibliog il Science 157:434-6 Jl 28 '67

POTATO salads. See Salads

POTATO spindle tuber virus. See Viruses, Plant

POTATOES
See also
Cookery—Vegetables

POTATOES, Frozen
Frozen spud; with recipes. Am Home 71:92b Ja '68

POTENTIOMETERS
Calculation of potentiometer linearity and power dissipation. D. L. Heiserman. il Electr World 78:59 Ag '67

POTLATCH forests, incorporated
Air pollution; the Feds move to abate Idaho pulp mill stench. B. Nelson. il Science 157:1018-21 S 1 '67
She's hauling! N. Willatt. Duns R 90:54-5+ N '67

POTLUCK suppers. See Suppers

POTOK, Chaim
Chosen; story; excerpts from novel. Ladies Home J 84:149-56 My '67

about
Authors & editors. por Pub W 191:25 Ap 3 '67

POTOMAC bald eagle refuge (proposed) See Bird sanctuaries

POTOMAC Edison company
Second battle of Antietam; or, The fight to save our parks. B. F. Hillenbrand. Parks & Rec 2:18-19+ N '67
Second battle of Antietam; proposed Potomac Edison transmission lines. M. Frome. Am For 73:36 Jl '67

POTOMAC RIVER
Mess on the Potomac. A. W. Smith. il Nat Parks Mag 41:2+ Ap '67
Old rock dams on the Potomac River. H. P. Hobbs, jr. il Nat Parks Mag 41:14-19 Ag '67
Third Potomac conference. Nat Parks Mag 41:20 Mr '67

POTPOURRI
Old English potpourri. il House B 109:168 Je '67
Sweet smell of potpourri. il Home Gard 54:45 Jl '67

POTS and pans. See Kitchen utensils

POTTED plants. See Plants, Potted

POTTER, Beatrix
Potter, pirates, and punctuation; concerning original manuscript of The tailor of Gloucester. E. Shaffer. il Wilson Lib Bul 41:598-602 F '67

POTTER, Charles H.
How to heat your greenhouse. il Horticulture 45:32-3+ O '67
Plan your greenhouse. Horticulture 45:24-5+ F '67

POTTER, Daniel
Midnight watch; story. McCalls 94:80-1 Je '67

POTTER, Fred H.
New Sather Gate shop thriving despite side-street locale. por Pub W 192:33-4 D 4 '67

POTTER, Nicholas S.
Designer's comments. Yachting 122:61 Jl '67

POTTER, Paul
Future is not inevitable. Harper 235:47-50 O '67

POTTER, Stephen
Two views of MacBird! Am Rec G 33:974-5 Je '67
Words only. See issues of American record guide

POTTER, Willis N.
Academe's cult of innovation. Sch & Soc 95:80-2 F 4 '67

POTTERY
Ceramics photography. J. Schlanger. il Craft Horiz 27:24-9 Ja '67
Clay and fibres: a beginning. H. Riegger. il Sch Arts 66:19-22 Ap '67
Nature of ceramics. J. J. Gilman. il Sci Am 217:112-18+ S '67
Porcelain pots for brewing and warming coffee. H. Newman. il Antiques 92:329-31 S '67
Rhenish gray stonewares in colonial America. I. Noël Hume. il Antiques 92:349-53 S '67
Turn the table on china. il Am Home 70:60-1 N '67

Collectors and collecting
Burnap collection today. R. E. Taggart. il Antiques 92:850-3 D '67

Exhibitions
Hui Ka Kwong; exhibition in New York's Museum of contemporary crafts. B. Hendricks. il Craft Horiz 27:40-3+ My '67

History
Ceramist as educator; excerpts from address, April 15, 1967. F. Schwartz. Craft Horiz 27:16-17+ Jl '67

Study and teaching
Ceramist as educator; excerpts from address, April 15, 1967. F. Schwartz. Craft Horiz 27:16-17+ Jl '67
Summer school for teachers; Herron school of art, Indianapolis. il Design 68:12-15 Sum '67
Working with clay. T. G. Supensky. il Sch Arts 67:16-28 N '67

Technique
For beginners; pinch pottery lamp. il Sunset 138:136+ F '67
Francine Del Pierre; interview, ed. by F. Frank. F. Del Pierre. il Craft Horiz 27:10-13+ Mr '67
Workshop: expanded polystyrene for ceramic production; International center of ceramics, Rome. N. Caruso. il Craft Horiz 27:34-5 S '67

POTTERY, American
Specimens of American porcelain. E. P. Birk. il Antiques 91:154 F '67

POTTERY, Chinese
Hui Ka Kwong: exhibition in New York's Museum of contemporary crafts. B. Hendricks. il Craft Horiz 27:40-3+ My '67
Rose medallion and mandarin patterns in China trade porcelain. C. L. Crossman. il Antiques 92:530-5 O '67

POTTERY, Dutch
See also
Delft ware

POTTERY, English
Burnap collection today. R. E. Taggart. il Antiques 92:850-3 D '67
Castleford pottery for the American trade. P. R. Guthman. il Antiques 92:552-5 O '67
Some English and German porcelain in an English collection. P. Synge-Hutchinson. il Antiques 91:614-19 My '67
Some makers of Pratt ware. G. Lewis. il Antiques 91:762-7 Je '67
See also
Wedgwood, Josiah and sons, limited

POTTERY, French
Francine Del Pierre; interview, ed. by F. Frank. F. Del Pierre. il Craft Horiz 27:10-13+ Mr '67

POTTERY, German
Of Meissen men. il Time 90:92 S 29 '67
Some English and German porcelain in an English collection. P. Synge-Hutchinson. il Antiques 91:614-19 My '67

POTTERY, Japanese
Did Japanese fishermen bring the art of pottery making to Ecuador 5,000 years ago? similarity of patterns between Jomon and Valdivia pottery. B. J. Meggers. il UNESCO Courier 20:12-13 My '67
Wood-burning raku kiln. L. Lipke. il Sch Arts 66:36-8 Ja '67

POTTERY, Korean
Mystery of beauty; address. S. Yanagi. Craft Horiz 27:50+ My '67
POTTERY, Swedish
Bertil Vallien: gentle fantasies done with daring and delight. D. Smith. il Craft Horiz 27:8-13+ S '67
POTTERY kilns. See Kilns
POTTHOFF, Carl J.
First aid. See issues of Today's health
POTTS, Alcine, and Bitterman, M. E.
Puromycin and retention in the goldfish. bibliog Science 158:1594-6 D 22 '67
POULENC, Francis
Poulenc and Bernac, French song, with pure pleasure the aim. N. Rorem. il por Hi Fi 17:85-6 N '67
Records:
Four song cycles. Opera N 31:34 Ja 28 '67
Stuff of legend. R. Gelatt. Reporter 37:45 S 7 '67
POULOS, Constantine
Bugging the press; reprint of dispatch in New York times, March 2, 1967. Nation 204:421 Ap 3 '67
POULTRY
Maternal behavior in the domestic cock under the influence of alcohol. J. K. Kovach. bibliog il Science 156:835-7 My 12 '67
News. See issues of Farm journal
See also
Cookery—Poultry

Breeding
See Poultry breeding
POULTRY, Frozen
Frozen turkeys. il Consumer Rep 32:568-71 N '67
Step right up and guess the weight of the turkey; U.S. Department of agriculture style, that is! il Consumer Bul 51:33-4 Ja '68
Thanksgiving dinner is easier now. il Good H 165:6 N '67
With game hens from your freezer. il Sunset 139:142 D '67
POULTRY breeding
Chickens: cheaper by the million. I. Wolfert. Read Digest 91:97-100 Ag '67
POULTRY houses

Litter
Compost your litter right in place. G. Hinton. il Farm J 91:66A Mr '67
POULTRY industry and trade
Chickens: cheaper by the million. I. Wolfert. Read Digest 91:97-100 Ag '67
POUND, Ezra
Old Ez and Uncle William. D. Hoffman. Reporter 37:59-62 N 2 '67
On a picture of Ezra Pound. H. Carruth. Poetry 110:103-5 My '67
POUND sterling. See Money—Great Britain
POUNDS, Norman J. G.
Fissures in the eastern Europe bloc; address, April 1967, with questions and answers. bibliog f Ann Am Acad 372:40-58 Jl '67
POUSETTE-DART, Richard
Yankee vedanta. J. Perreault. il Art N 66:54-5+ N '67
POUSSAINT, Alvin F.
How the white problem spawned black power. por Ebony 22:88-90+ Ag '67
Negro psychiatrist explains the Negro psyche. N Y Times Mag p52-3+ Ag 20 '67
POUSSE-café. See Liqueurs
POUTSMA, Marvin L.
Chlorination of unsaturated compounds in nonpolar media. bibliog Science 157:997-1005 S 1 '67
POVERTY
Alleviation of poverty; excerpt from Capitalism and freedom. M. Friedman. Nat R 19:240-1 Mr 7 '67
Birth of a movement. R. A. Cloward and F. F. Piven. il Nation 204:532-8 My 8 '67
Justice and international development, a manifesto for American action in the struggle against world poverty. Christian Cent 84:660+ My 17 '67
See also
Anti-poverty program, 1964-
Poor
Public welfare
Slums

United States
See Poor—United States
POVERTY (virtue)
Religious poverty: a virtue? R. E. McNally. America 117:200-1 Ag 26 '67
Religious poverty: fact or fiction? E. J. Ahern. America 116:753-4 My 20 '67; Discussion. 116:844 Je 17 '67

POVERTY, Vow of
Religious poverty: a virtue? R. E. McNally. America 117:200-1 Ag 26 '67
Religious poverty: fact or fiction? E. J. Ahern. America 116:753-4 My 20 '67; Discussion. 116:844 Je 17 '67
POWELL, Adam Clayton, 1908-
Powell in the pulpit; excerpts from Keep the faith, baby! por Sat R 50:86+ Ap 22 '67

about
Adam Clayton Powell; out now, but will he get back? il por U S News 62:12 Mr 13 '67
Adam Clayton Powell; the man behind the controversy. S. Booker. il pors Ebony 22:27-30+ Mr '67
Adam had 'em. Christian Cent 84:363-4 Mr 22 '67; Discussion. 84:593 My 3 '67
Adam Powell at the end of the world. B. J. Friedman. il pors Sat Eve Post 240:26-9 My 20 '67
Adam's vacuum. Time 90:25-6 S 29 '67
Back in circulation. il por Newsweek 71:28 Ja 22 '68
Basic issue. il por Time 89:16 Mr 24 '67
Congressman Powell sits it out; with press comments. Sr Schol 90:14-15 F 3 '67
Dodd and Powell. Nation 204:337-8 Mr 27 '67
Elected again, but Powell still faces problems. por U S News 62:26 Ap 24 '67
Faith that heals; pledge to pay $33,000 against slander judgment. Newsweek 69:34 F 6 '67
Hometown advice. Newsweek 69:39-40 Mr 27 '67
House denies seat to Powell. il por Sr Schol 90:17 Mr 17 '67
If Powell comes in, will 14th amendment go out? D. Lawrence. U S News 62:124 Mr 20 '67
Jig is up, baby. Nat R 19:72 Ja 24 '67
Keeping faith with Adam. Newsweek 69:26 Ap 24 '67
Law and prudence in the Powell case. A. M. Bickel. New Repub 156:9-10 F 25 '67
Letter from Washington. R. H. Rovere. New Yorker 42:103-4 Ja 21 '67
Loner & the shaman. il por Time 89:23-4 Mr 17 '67
Make way for de lawd. por Time 89:20 F 3 '67
Martyred, baby. K. Crawford. Newsweek 69:40 Mr 27 '67
Meredith: the ambiguous heroes of Harlem: Powell. A. Kopkind. il pors Life 62:32-32A Mr 24 '67
Meredith vs. Powell: how solid is the Negro vote? por U S News 62:52 Mr 20 '67
Meredith's one-night stand. F. E. Kearns. Commonweal 86:78-9 Ap 7 '67
My life with Adam. Y. D. Powell. il Ladies Home J 84:91-3+ My '67
No home in the House. il pors Time 89:19-20 Mr 10 '67
Now what? re-election to House seat. Time 89:24 Ap 21 '67
Powell and black bravado. A. Kopkind; reply. J. V. Tunney. New Repub 156:37-8 F 11 '67
Powell and Dodd cases, how they differ. il por U S News 62:35-7 My 1 '67
Powell and the House: a black power victory? C. E. Fager. Christian Cent 84:175 F 8 '67; Discussion. 84:380 Mr 22 '67
Powell case: bungling all around. P. Duke. il Reporter 36:32-5 Ap 20 '67
Powell in the pulpit; use of material from works of G. Buttrick and H. Luccock in Keep the faith, baby! D. Poling. il por Sat R 50:86+ Ap 22 '67
Powell re-elected. Sr Schol 90:23 Ap 28 '67
Powell row hurts the civil rights movement. il por Bsns W p42 Mr 18 '67
Saviors of the Constitution. Reporter 36:16 F 23 '67
Scent of blood. il por Newsweek 69:35-6 Mr 13 '67
Shoo on the other foot. Time 89:37 Ap 14 '67
Sic transit everything, baby. Reporter 36:8+ Ja 26 '67
Sin of Adam. Nat R 19:288-90 Mr 21 '67
Splitting over Adam: the liberal-Negro breach. F. E. Kearns. Commonweal 85:443 Ja 27 '67
Washington report. J. Lloyd. Sr Schol 90:sup8 F 10 '67
Way with words. Newsweek 69:28-9 My 1 '67
Why Meredith quit the race with Powell U S News 62:16 Mr 27 '67
See also
Government investigations—Powell case

POWELL, Anthony
George Orwell. Atlan 220:62-8 O '67

POWELL, Bernard W.
GE's new Traffic topping waterproofs a sun deck. Pop Sci 190:138-41+ Je '67
Plug in on the low voltage circuit. Pop Gard 18:8-15 D '67
What you should know about paint rollers. Pop Mech 128:158-61 O '67

POWELL, John Wesley
Rivermen, rustlers and uranium hunters. R. L. Reynolds. il por Am Heritage 18:52-63 O '67

POWELL, Kathleen V.
Boys like to dance. Dance Mag 41:73 Mr '67

POWELL, Lacy D. and Johnson, C. E.
Clayton County seeks some answers. NEA J 56:36-7 Ap '67

POWELL, Lawrence Clark
Climbing the ladder; excerpt from Fortune and friendship. pors Library J 93:49-53 Ja 1 '68

POWELL, Lewis Franklin, 1907-
Civil disobedience: prelude to revolution? address, October 5, 1967. por U S News 63: 66-9 O 30 '67

POWELL, Richard
Magic of words. Writer 80:20-2+ O '67

POWELL, Robert S.
New light on flying saucers. il U S News 62:16 Mr 20 '67

POWELL, Yvette Diago
My life with Adam. pors Ladies Home J 84: 91-3+ My '67

about
Adam & Yvette. por Time 89:18 F 24 '67
Ladies' day. il por Newsweek 69:28+ F 27 '67
When Mrs Adam Clayton Powell took the stand. il por U S News 62:10 F 27 '67

POWELL, LAKE. See Lakes, Artificial

POWER, Donald Clinton
Power formula for profit. R. Brady. por Duns R 90:44 N '67

POWER, Eugene Barnum
Xerox director named first American Magdalene fellow. Pub W 192:25 D 11 '67

POWER (mechanics)
Energy needs versus environmental pollution: a reconciliation? L. Green, jr. bibliog Science 156:1448-50 Je 16 '67; Reply. R. G. Minet. 157:1373 S 22 '67
Your child can power a paint shaker. W. G. Waggoner. il Pop Sci 190:166-7 Ja '67

POWER (political science)
Arrogance of power, by J. W. Fulbright. Review
Nat R 19:367-8 Ap 4 '67. E. A. Mowrer
Color it black or white; address, February 28, 1967. G. H. Moulds. Vital Speeches 33:380-4 Ap 1 '67
Conversion of myths into political power: the case of the Nazi party, 1925-1926. D. Orlow. bibliog f Am Hist R 72:906-24 Ap '67
Democratic participation. S. Verba. bibliog f il Ann Am Acad 373:53-78 S '67
End to alibis. D. F. Dowd: J. McDermott. il Nation 204:198-206 F 13 '67
Formula for new politics. R. E. Fitch. Christian Cent 84:139-41 F 1 '67; Reply. W. R. Barnhart. 84:347 Mr 15 '67
Galbraith speaks; summary of address. il Pub W 192:5-6 My 22 '67
Intellectuals and the presidency. M. Ways. il Fortune 75:146-9+ Ap '67
Overestimating the power of power. L. J. Halle. New Repub 156:15-17 Je 10 '67
Poverty, paternalism and protest. M. A. Seng. Cath World 204:352-5 Mr '67
Power in America. by D. T. Bazelon. Review
New Repub 156:31-2 Mr 25 '67. G. W. Johnson
Power structure. by A. M. Rose. Review
Fortune 76:269-70 N '67. I. Kristol
Redirecting American power. Nation 204:194 F 13 '67
Saying no to power: conduct of our foreign affairs. Nation 204:420-1 Ap 3 '67
White power; use and abuse. America 117: 127-8 Ag 5 '67
See also
Executive power
Politics and war

POWER (psychology)
Power, freedom and educational revolution. M. Grandstaff. Sch & Soc 95:387-90 O 28 '67

POWER, Muscular. See Muscular power
POWER bicycles. See Motor scooters
POWER boat racing. See Motor boat racing
POWER cartridges
Little bang. il Sci Digest 61:28 Ap '67

POWER commission, Federal. See United States—Federal power commission
POWER failures. See Electric power
POWER industry. See Electric power
POWER lawn mowers. See Lawn mowers
POWER lines. See Electric lines
POWER pills. See Power cartridges
POWER plants
Refuse is the sweetest fuel; pollution-free generation of power in municipal incinerators; report on symposium. il Am City 82: 116-18 My '67
See also
Atomic power plants
POWER politics. See Power (political science)
POWER pools. See Electric plants—Interconnection
POWER resources
Atom's challenge to the coal industry. B. Kovach and N. Caldwell. Reporter 36:39-41 F 23 '67
Hot war in the energy industry. I. M. Stelzer and B. C. Netschert. bibliog f Harvard Bsns R 45:14-16+ N '67
POWER saws. See Saws
POWER supply, Electric. See Electric power
POWER tools. See Electric tools, Portable
POWERED hand tools. See Electric tools, Portable
POWERS, Bertram Anthony
Trade winds; unyielding bargaining table approach. H. R. Mayes. Sat R 50:11-12 My 27 '67
POWERS, Jessica
Only one voice; poem. America 116:853 Je 17 '67
POWERS; story. See Singer, I. B.
POWILLS, Dorothy
Playing cards. See issues of Hobbies
POWLEDGE, Fred
Battle over the Bill of rights. Life 62:22-5+ Mr 31 '67
Girl from V.I.S.T.A. Redbook 129:80-1+ Jl '67
Idea broker in the race crisis. Life 63:72A-72B+ N 3 '67
Is Garrison faking? New Repub 156:13-18 Je 17 '67
PRACTICE (music) See Piano—Instruction and study
PRACTITIONER; story. See Frater, A.
PRADHAN, Panna Lal. See Dart, F. E. jt. auth.
PRADO museum, Madrid
Still another art find: a priceless work by Antonello da Messina. il Life 62:30-30A Ja 27 '67
PRAEGER, Frederick A, incorporated
Praeger acquires Phaidon press. Pub W 191: 35 Mr 27 '67
Praeger discusses CIA book ties. Pub W 191:48 Mr 6 '67
PRAGER, Arthur
With insight and inducement. Sat R 51:79-80 Ja 13 '68
PRAGER, Karsten
Winning back the Montagnards. Reporter 36: 38-40 Mr 23 '67
PRAGUE
Some interesting happenings in Prague. R. Eder. N Y Times Mag p99+ N 12 '67

Description
18th INSEA world congress in Prague, Czechoslovakia. M. F. Andrews. il Sch Arts 66:32-7 Mr '67

Music
Notes from our correspondents. H. Halbreich. Hi Fi 18:20+ Ja '68
Notes from our correspondents. J. Higgins. il Hi Fi 17:16+ Je '67
Prague. P. Eckstein. Opera N 31:33 F 11 '67
Prague; production of Bohuslav Martinu's Greek passion. P. Eckstein. Opera N 31:31 My 13 '67

Theater
Theatre. K. Tynan. New Yorker 43:99-100+ Ap 1 '67
Theatre in Europe; Gate theatre and Dramatic club productions. H. Clurman. Nation 205:60-2 Jl 17 '67

PRAIRIE chickens
Owls, eagles and prairie chicanery. H. Peterson. il Sports Illus 26:46-8+ My 29 '67
PRAIRIE NATIONAL PARK (proposed) See National parks and reserves—United States
PRAIRIES
Abundance of the prairie; Hayden Kalsow Cayler, and Sheeder prairies. K. B. Gale. il Horticulture 45:34-5 Ag '67

PRAISE
    See also
    Encouragement
PRALINE soufflé. See Soufflés
PRAMER, David. See Bartha, R; Higgins, M. L.
    jt. auths.
PRANTERA, Antonio
    Restaurateur; interview. New Yorker 43:43-4
    Mr 18 '67
PRASAD, Kedar N. and Van Woert, M. H.
    Dopamine protects mice against whole-body
    irradiation. bibliog Science 155:470-2 Ja 27
    '67
PRASLIN, Fanny, duchesse de
    Crime of passion, by S. Loomis. Review
    Sat R 50:28-9 My 27 '67. O. Prescott
PRATT, Charles L. and Sackett, G. P.
    Selection of social partners as a function of
    peer contact during rearing. bibliog Sci-
    ence 155:1133-5 Mr 3 '67
PRATT, John Lowell
    J. Lowell Pratt launches new venture. Pub
    W 193:48 Ja 8 '68
PRATT and Whitney aircraft division. See
    United aircraft corporation—Pratt and
    Whitney aircraft division
PRATT ware. See Pottery, English
PRAVDA. See Newspapers—Russia
PRAY for grace, poor little sinner; story. See
    O'Faolain, J.
PRAYER
    Are you there, God? contemporary problem
    of prayer. America 117:340 S 30 '67; Dis-
    cussion. 117:457 O 28 '67
    Communal prayer, back when. A. R. Riel, jr.
    America 116:455 Mr 25 '67
    'Gimme' is dead? M. Novak. Commonweal
    86:174-5 Ap 28 '67; Discussion. 86:379+ Je
    23 '67
    God is not enough? I. J. Gerber. Christian
    Cent 84:684-7 My 24 '67; Discussion. 84:
    676, 997-8, 1524-5 My 24, Ag 2, N 29 '67
    Means to the end. V. P. McCorry. America
    116:325-6 Mr 4 '67
    New prayer. V. P. McCorry. America 116:
    165-4 Ja 28 '67
    Primer of prayer. V. P. McCorry. America
    116:135-6 F 4 '67
PRAYER in the schools. See Public schools
    and religion
PRAYERS
    Mississippi prayer; excerpts. America 116:
    270 F 25 '67
    New grandmother's prayer. S. R. Lyons.
    McCalls 94:70 F '67
    See also
    Lords prayer
PREACHING
    Credibility gap in theology. F. Kirschen-
    mann. Christian Cent 84:498-500 Ap 19 '67;
    Discussion. 84:757 Je 7 '67
    Empty pulpit. il Newsweek 70:89-90 Ag 14 '67;
    Reply. Christian Cent 84:1111 Ag 30 '67
    See also
    Sermons
PREAKNESS race. See Horse racing
PREAMPLIFIERS. See Amplifiers
PRECAMBRIAN period. See Geology, Stratig-
    raphic—Precambrian; Paleontology—Precam-
    brian
PRECAST concrete. See Concrete, Precast
PRECIOUS stones
    Gems and minerals. H. D. Brown. See issues
    of Hobbies
    King of colored gems; H. Stern's jewelry
    business. S. Seegers and K. Seegers. il
    Read Digest 92:203-8 Ja '68
    Legends of gem stones. Good H 165:195 O '67
    See also
    Goldsmithing
PRECIPITATION (meteorology)
    See also
    Rain and rainfall
PRECISION approach radar. See Radar in
    aviation
PRECISION flying. See Aviation—Stunt flying
PRECISION forge. See Forging machinery
PRECISION forge company
    Forge conversion deemed breakthrough; high
    velocity precision machine. J. F. Judge. il
    Aero Tech 21:27-9+ D 4 '67
PRECISION measurement. See Measurement
PREDATOR; story. See Hoyer, L. G.
PREDATOR and rodent control. See United
    States—Fish and wildlife service
PREDATORY animals. See Animals, Predatory
PREDESTINATION. See Free will and de-
    terminism
PREDICTED log competitions. See Navigation
    —Competitions

PREDICTION of scholastic success
    Predicting college success. Time 89:58 Mr 10
    '67
    Written test scores and prediction of success
    in college. H. R. Douglass. il Sch & Soc 95:
    392-4 O 28 '67
PREDICTIONS. See Forecasts
PREDICTIONS, Economic. See Forecasts (eco-
    nomics)
PREFAB fireplaces. See Fireplaces
PREFABRICATED buildings. See Buildings,
    Prefabricated
PREFABRICATED cabins. See Cabins
PREFABRICATED houses. See Houses, Pre-
    fabricated
PREFERRED stocks. See Stocks
PREGNANCY
    Doctor's guide to a healthy pregnancy; ex-
    cerpt from infant world. M. Liley and B.
    Day. il Parents Mag 42:46-7+ Ap '67
    Expectant mother:
        Answers to questions about pregnancy.
        Redbook 129:34+ S '67; 130:24 Ja '68
        Classes to prepare you for childbirth.
        F. W. Goodrich, jr. Redbook 129:26+
        Je '67
        How much weight should you gain during
        pregnancy? R. G. Holly and D. Z.
        Meilach. Redbook 128:31+ F '67
        Is it safe to have surgery during preg-
        nancy? R. H. Barter. Redbook 129:52+
        Jl '67
        Is pregnancy the time to think about
        spacing children? S. G. Kohl. Redbook
        130:29+ N '67
        Postpartum depression. S. H. Gardiner.
        Redbook 129:31+ O '67
        What hormones have to do with preg-
        nancy. R. W. Kistner. Redbook 129:22+
        Ag '67
    Fine art of mothering. N. Shainess. il Parents
    Mag 43:46-7+ Ja '68
    Guarding the unborn. J. Beck. il Todays
    Health 46:38-41+ Ja '68
    Pregnancy: its problems and the importance
    of prenatal care. il Good H 164:141-2 Ja '67
    Problems posed by summer pregnancy. il
    Good H 164:199 Je '67
    Twice a mother in thirty days. E. Keiffer.
    il Good H 164:26+ My '67
    When another baby is on the way. H. A.
    Kaminetzky and D. Z. Meilach. il Parents
    Mag 42:38-9+ Ja '67
    Why healthy mothers need prenatal care; in-
    terview, ed. by E. M. Stern. C. Hunter.
    Redbook 128:57+ Ap '67
        See also
    Abortion
    Childbirth
    Fetus
PREGNANCY, Complications of
    Expectant mother; causes of bleeding. A. L.
    Southam and D. Z. Meilach. Redbook 128:
    40+ Mr '67
    GG vs Rh disease. Newsweek 69:62 Ja 30 '67
    Protecting the unborn baby. A. Kerr. il Mc-
    Calls 94:48+ Jl '67
    What is meant by an ectopic pregnancy.
    Good H 165:175 Ag '67
PREHISTORIC animals. See Animals, Extinct
PREHISTORIC man. See Man, Prehistoric
PREJUDICE
    Opinion: on intellectual arrogance. R. K.
    Price, jr. Mlle 65:88+ My '67
    They told us we must never marry. McCalls
    95:50+ O '67
        See also
    Race prejudice
PRE-KINDERGARTEN schools. See Nursery
    schools
PREMATURE infants. See Infants, Premature
PREMINGER, Otto
    Excerpt from statement before Communica-
    tions subcommittee, October 10, 1967. Cong
    Digest 46:304+ D '67

    about

    Otto the Terrible. T. Meehan. il pors Sat
    Eve Post 240:26-31 Ap 8 '67
PRENATAL care. See Pregnancy
PRENATAL influences
    Better health for all babies; Collaborative
    perinatal project, U.S. Public health service.
    T. C. Wilson and K. Niehans. il Parents
    Mag 42:68-9+ N '67
    Guarding the unborn. J. Beck. il Todays
    Health 46:38-41+ Ja '68
    Prenatal auditory imprinting in chickens. J.
    B. Grier and others. bibliog Science 155:
    1692-3 Mr 31 '67

PRENDERGAST, Joseph
Joseph Prendergast leaves NRPA. L. Gulick. por Parks & Rec 2:30 Jl '67

PRENTICE, Ann E.
Comics scene; ed. by B. Katz. Library J 93:59 Ja 1 '68

PRENTICE-Hall, Incorporated
P-H staff describes production system at AIGA. Pub W 191:102+ My 1 '67

PRENTISS, S. Gilbert
Goals for state library service to state agencies and state institutions. ALA Bul 61:387-92 Ap '67
State library agency and metropolitan library service; adaptation of address. por Library J 92:546-9 F 1 '67

PREPARATORY schools. See Private schools

PREPAREDNESS, Military
See also
United States—Defenses

PRESBYTERIAN church in Canada
Canada's Presbyterians in annual assembly. D. H. Rayner. **Christian Cent** 84:1002-4 Ag 2 '67

PRESBYTERIAN church in New Zealand
Heresy trial; L. G. Geering. M. W. Wilson. Christian Cent 84:1575-6 D 6 '67

PRESBYTERIAN church in the United States
Evangelist from Big Lick; new moderator. Time 89:82 My 26 '67
Presbyterians, U.S, in annual assembly. J. A. Womeldorf. Christian Cent 84:978-80 Jl 26 '67
See also
United Presbyterian church in the United States of America

PRESBYTERIAN church in the United States (South)
Concern v. concerned; Presbyterian group fear church's increasing involvement in social issues. Time 90:50 O 13 '67
Presbyterians, U.S, urged to move 'out'; conference at Montreat. J. A. Womeldorf. Christian Cent 84:1166 S 13 '67

PRESCHOOL children
Choosing for our youngest. A. Rusk. il Library J 92:1294-5 Mr 15 '67
In praise of preschoolers. C. Blunt. il Parents Mag 42:60-1+ O '67
Play materials for many moods; with study-discussion program, by R. Strang. F. R. Horwich. bibliog il PTA Mag 62:16-18, 34-5 D '67
Save them young; New York state's prekindergarten program. M. P. Berson. il Am Ed 3:5-8 Jl '67
School where blind children see; Blind childrens center, Los Angeles. E. M. Dean. il Todays Health 45:50-3 F '67
Somebody at your house ready for nursery school? il Changing T 21:35-6 Jl '67
Tiny tots a go-go; group adjustment program for four & five year olds; Mountain View, Calif. D. Gale. il Parks & Rec 2:26-7+ Ag '67
See also
Child study
Nursery schools
Readiness for school

Education
Early learners; excerpt from Revolution in learning. M. Pines. il McCalls 95:74+ Ja '68
Pound of cure for educational problems. B. J. Paschal. Sch & Soc 95:53-5 Ja 21 '67

Reading
See Childrens reading

PRESCHOOL education. See Education of children; Preschool children

PRESCHOOL literature. See Childrens literature

PRESCOTT, David M. and Goldstein, Lester
Nuclear-cytoplasmic interaction in DNA synthesis. bibliog Science 155:469-70 Ja 27 '67

PRESCOTT, Isabel
Regional report. Home Gard 64:78 My; 56 O '67

PRESCOTT, Orville
Death of a duchess. Sat R 50:28-9 My 27 '67
Disillusionment of a visionary. Sat R 50:31 Ag 26 '67
Eden Down Under. Sat R 50:30-1 S 9 '67
He had a mania for exotica. Sat R 50:27 Jl 8 '67
Mail from the front. Sat R 50:35 Ap 29 '67
Natural world. Sat R 50:42-3 S 2 '67

PRESCRIPTIONS
Handbook of prescription drugs, by R. Burack. Review
Consumer Rep 33:47-8 Ja '68
New Repub 156:7 My 6 '67
Who owns your prescription? Good H 166:168 Ja '68

PRESENT, The
Pleasure to recall. C. Ford. il Read Digest 91:205-6 D '67

PRESERVATION of cells. See Tissues—Culture

PRESERVATION of food. See Canning and preserving

PRESERVATION of landmarks, scenery, etc.
Conservation: keeping watch on the road builders. L. J. Carter. il Science 157:527-9 Ag 4 '67
Gift of land. D. MacDonald. il House B 109:162+ D '67

Japan
Deathwatch in Tokyo; O. Wright's efforts to save husband's Imperial hotel. F. Riley. Sat R 50:40+ D 16 '67

United States
Natural landmark dedicated; Petrified gardens. Nat Parks Mag 41:20 N '67
Preservation: the necessary art. il Fortune 75:159-62 Mr '67
Proposed Lewis and Clark national river; National park service proposes to conserve certain sections of the Missouri. il Parks & Rec 2:22+ Ag '67
Song of San Francisco Bay. M. Reynolds. il Natur Hist 77:6-8+ bibliog(p76) Ja '68
They saved the Big Sur. F. J. Taylor. il Read Digest 91:170-5 N '67

PRESERVES. See Jelly, jam, etc.

PRESERVES, Game. See Game preserves

PRESIDENTIAL advisers. See Public officers

PRESIDENTIAL campaigns
Campaign agonies. R. Moley. Newsweek 69:120 Ap 17 '67
'68 is not like '12 or '32. C. Fritchey. il N Y Times Mag p25-7+ D 17 '67
Speaking out; don't believe what the Liberals tell you. B. Goldwater. Sat Eve Post 240:10+ F 11 '67
Spoiler; Cleveland's Wallace-for-president campaign. il Newsweek 69:34 Ap 3 '67
See also
Campaign funds
National conventions (political)
National conventions, Democratic
National conventions, Republican
Presidential candidates
Television in politics

1964
In a cause that will triumph, by K. Hess. Review
Nat R 19:310+ Mr 21 '67. W. A. Rusher
New Repub 156:28-30 F 11 '67. A. Kopkind
Suite 3505: the story of the draft Goldwater movement, by F. C. White. Review
Nat R il 19:596-7 My 30 '67. M. S. Evans

1968
Big show. il Newsweek 71:17-22 Ja 8 '68
Can the Republicans take over Congress in '68? il U S News 63:26-7 D 25 '67
George Wallace maps his way to the White House. T. L. Knap. New Repub 156:7-9 Ap 29 '67
GOP doings. Nat R 19:453 My 2 '67
Great temptation; war in Vietnam as a political issue for Republicans. K. Crawford. Newsweek 70:35 O 23 '67
How Wallace will run his third-party campaign. R. M. Scammon. il Reporter 37:34-6 O 19 '67
Preview of '68; Johnson's re-election campaign. Time 90:16-18 D 22 '67
Romney, a '68 boom that's in trouble. il U S News 63:56 Jl 17 '67
Romney's week. il Newsweek 69:20-1 My 1 '67
See America first; Gov. Romney to tour nation's cities. Time 90:16 S 8 '67
Stumping from the White House. il Bsns W p 18-20 D 30 '67
They never go back; Kennedy Democrats-in-exile. K. Crawford. Newsweek 70:27 Ag 14 '67
They vote against. K. Crawford. Newsweek 69:30 My 1 '67
Wallace in the West. il Time 90:27 D 8 '67
Why unthinkable? C. P. Case's argument against Vietnam as a political issue. Nation 204:482-3 Ap 17 '67

PRESIDENTIAL candidates

Myth of splendid misery; preparations that candidates make. H. Sidey. il Life 62:32B F 24 '67

1968 nomination? I do not rule it out: Harold Stassen. B. Weinraub. il Esquire 68:97-101 Ag '67

See also
Campaign funds

Anecdotes, facetiae, satire, etc.

Al Capp on the hippie economics; J. K. Galbraith and L. Abolafia. A. Capp. il Nations Bsns 55:64-7 S '67

Caricatures and cartoons

Artists and models. Newsweek 70:98 O 2 '67

1964

Just like old times; Goldwater and Miller recollections over National educational television. Newsweek 70:31 O 2 '67

1968

According to John; Lindsay discusses Republican candidates. Time 90:28 O 13 '67

Anchors aweigh; contenders for GOP nomination. il Time 90:17-21 O 20 '67

Another 1948? four candidates? New Repub 156:4 My 6 '67

Arkansas traveler. Time 89:23 My 5 '67

Around the world, a block away; visit to Latin America. il Time 89:29-30 My 19 '67

Atlantic report; search for a Republican candidate. D. Kiker. Atlan 219:4+ F '67

Big issue: five positions on Vietnam; statements of possible presidential candidates. il Newsweek 70:40-1 Jl 10 '67

Big show. il Newsweek 71:17-22 Ja 8 '68

Bobby's spring offensive. Nat R 19:180-2 F 21 '67

Boxer Reagan of California. New Repub 157:4 Jl 22 '67

Camel crusade; convention nominates Prohibition candidates for 1968. Time 90:16 Jl 7 '67

Careful Kennedy hurry. E. J. Hughes. Newsweek 69:23 Mr 20 '67

Choices, not echoes. Nat R 19:557-8 My 30 '67

Coalition for victory in '68: will LBJ get Republican votes? H. Paolucci. Nat R 19:630-1 Je 13 '67

Dick's lucky palm; headquarters for the Nixon for president committee. Time 89:15 Je 2 '67

Draft-Kennedy conclave. New Repub 157:10-11 O 14 '67

Dump LBJ? il Newsweek 70:24-5 O 9 '67

Election puzzle for '68. il U S News 62:38-41 My 1 '67

Enigma in the South; G. Wallace's appeal to southerners. il Time 89:20-1 My 12 '67

Eugene who? P. Wieck. New Repub 158:14-15 Ja 13 '68

Expert advice: Goldwater suggests proper GOP candidates. il Newsweek 70:29 Jl 3 '67

First things first; new left seeks presidential candidate. Newsweek 70:24 S 11 '67

For '68: rising talk of a Rockefeller-Reagan ticket. il U S News 63:50-1 Jl 3 '67

Gaining strength; Reagan and Rockefeller. il U S News 63:11 Jl 10 '67

Gene McCarthy. New Repub 157:7-8 N 18 '67

General attacks; J. M. Gavin refuses to support Johnson for re-election in 1968. Newsweek 70:22-3 Ag 14 '67

George, Dick, Ronnie. il Newsweek 70:27-8 N 6 '67

George Wallace isn't kidding. J. Witcover. Reporter 36:23-5 F 23 '67

George Wallace: running for God; with excerpts from interview. R. G. Sherrill. il Nation 204:589-96 My 8 '67

Goldwater will have his say. S. Alsop. Sat Eve Post 240:16 Ap 8 '67

GOP for '68. Nat R 19:723-4 Jl 11 '67

GOP hopefuls near starting gate. il Bsns W p38-40 N 18 '67

GOP million-to-one- shot; Rockefeller-Reagan ticket in 1968. E. J. Hughes Newsweek 70:15 S 4 '67

GOP view of '68: why Reagan and Percy may be fighting it out. il Newsweek 69:28-9 My 22 '67

Great Republican rectangle. E. J. Hughes. Newsweek 70:21 N 27 '67

How Republican race shapes up now. il U S News 63:55-6 S 25 '67

How we chose the next president. W. Weaver, jr. pors N Y Times Mag p 12-14 D 31 '67

Hypothesis unbound; Republicans. il Time 89:19 F 3 '67

In business; Republicans. il Time 89:19 F 24 '67

Into the silks. il Time 90:29-30 N 17 '67

Is it really McCarthy? Reporter 37:10 D 14 '67

Is it too late for a man of honesty, high purpose and intelligence to be elected president of the United States in 1968? with editorial comment. S. V. Roberts. il Esquire 68:6+. 89-93+ O '67

Jockeying at the post. R. G. Sherrill; G. Pressman. Nation 205:589-93 D 4 '67

Johnson after Glassboro. W. V. Shannon. Commonweal 86:439-40 Jl 14 '67

Let George do it; Rockefeller supports nomination of Romney. Time 89:29 My 19 '67

Long hot winter; possibilities for New Hampshire primary. il Time 91:13-14 Ja 12 '68

LBJ's chances for a new term. il U S News 64:24-6 Ja 8 '68

McCarthy: critic or challenger? Nation 206:5-6 Ja 1 '68

McCarthy or McCoy? Newsweek 70:30 D 11 '67

Making of a candidate: a look at the Reagan boom. il U S News 63:53-5 Jl 24 '67

Man from PAUSE; proposed society of Republican governors. il Time 89:21 Ap 28 '67

Meditations on the morning line. Nat R 19:1154 O 31 '67

Meet candidate Lyndon Johnson. il Newsweek 70:31-2 N 13 '67

Message for L.B.J from the pros. J. N. Eller. America 116:776 My 27 '67

Middleman Percy. New Repub 157:3-4 Jl 8 '67

Morning line. Nat R 19:941 S 5 '67

Morning line; Republican runners. Newsweek 69:33-4 Ap 3 '67

Move to dump Johnson. il Newsweek 70:25-8 N 27 '67

Mystery guest; G.O.P. victory gala. il Time 89:23-4 Mr 10 '67

NR poll; conservatives' preferences for the 1968 Republican nomination. il Nat R 19:236-7, 340-1, 456, 559, 678, 786, 893-4, 1007, 1251 Mr 7, Ap 4, My 2, 30, Je 27, Jl 25, Ag 22, S 19, N 14 '67

Next, please? Nat R 19:338+ Ap 4 '67

1968 campaign for president. C. B. Luce. McCalls 94:42+ Mr '67

1968 in the crystal ball. W. Lippmann. Newsweek 69:31 Mr 13 '67

1968 presidential preview. il Sr Schol 91:3 O 5 '67

Nixon and Reagan, choice of party pros. il U S News 63:11 D 25 '67

Nixon tells how '68 race stands; interview. R. M. Nixon. il U S News 63:74-80 N 20 '67

Nixon vs. LBJ, '68 choice? survey of party officals. il U S News 62:42-5 Ap 17 '67

Nixon vs. Rockefeller; choice shaping up. il U S News 64:38-40 Ja 1 '68

Non-candidates; Republicans. il Time 90:22-3 S 22 '67

Northern hospitality; Dartmouth college demonstration against G. Wallace. Newsweek 69:36 My 15 '67

Now is the time. New Repub 157:7-8 D 9 '67

Off to an early start; Republican contenders for the presidential nomination. il Bsns W p33-5 My 13 '67

On the road. il Time 90:18 N 3 '67

Operation 1968. W. A. Rusher. il Nat R 19:1115-17+ O 17 '67

Other voices, other booms; rivals for Republican presidential nomination. il Newsweek 70:28 S 25 '67

Peace politics and 1968; third-party candidate for president? A. I. Waskow. Commonweal 86:195-8 My 5 '67

Percy: everybody's second-best man. W. B. Furlong. Harper 235:41-7 S '67

Political talk. Nat R 19:1053-4 O 3 '67

Political weather; views on presidential candidates. K. Crawford. Newsweek 71:30 Ja 22 '68

Politics of war. W. V. Shannon. Commonweal 86:254-5 My 19 '67

Politics: the outlook for '68; war in Vietnam decisive factor in the 1968 presidential campaign. il Newsweek 70:36+ Jl 10 '67

Poll winner: ticket of Rockefeller-Reagan; How South and Southwest rate Johnson in polls. U S News 63:16 O 16 '67

Polls & portents. Time 90:24 Jl 21 '67

Pols here and there; Republican possibilities. Nat R 19:1105-6 O 17 '67

President's every move will be suspect. P. Lisagor. il Nations Bsns 55:23-4 F '67

PRESIDENTIAL candidates—1968—*Continued*
Primary primary; New Hampshire presidential. M. Nolan. Reporter 37:32-4 S 7 '67
Race for the Republican nomination: how it looks now. il U S News 63:37-8 S 11 '67
Reagan on the rise? H. Brandon. Sat R 50:12 Ag 26 '67
Reign of Republican unreason. E. J. Hughes. Newsweek 69:29 Ap 17 '67
Republican cool. K. Crawford. Newsweek 70: 26 D 25 '67
Republican roulette; openings of the Romney and the Nixon for president committees. Reporter 36:16-17 Je 15 '67
Republicans. il Newsweek 69:20-1 My 1 '67
Return to normalcy; Republican governors to confer on presidential nomination. Reporter 37:10-12 N 16 '67
Revving up; Republicans. il Time 90:18 D 22 '67
Richard Nixon's return engagement. G. A. Harrison. New Repub 157:11-12 N 4 '67
Rockefeller in '68? New Repub 156:3-4 Je 10 '67
Rockefeller-Reagan? R. Moley. Newsweek 70: 112 S 18 '67
Rockefeller: Republican dark horse? inside look at '68 strategy. il U S News 62:48-50 My 8 '67
Rocky: he who runs least runs best. J. Cannon. Newsweek 70:34-5 D 18 '67
Rocky's rise. Time 90:26 S 29 '67
Romney and Nixon getting set for the '68 campaign. il U S News 62:14 Ap 3 '67
Romney rubs noses with voters; with report by R. B. Stolley. il Life 62:70-4 Mr 3 '67
Rumblings of 1968. H. Brandon. Sat R 50: 14 F 25 '67
Selecting a president. Nation 205:546 N 27 '67
Senator to the young reporter; Republican convention. Nat R 19:1413-15 D 26 '67
'68 is not like '12 or '32. C. Fritchey. il N Y Times Mag p25-7+ D 17 '67
Slumming it; Romney benefits from intensified competition of two potential rivals. il Newsweek 70:22 S 11 '67
Sons also rise; GOP campaign for 1968 nomination. il Newsweek 70:22-3 O 2 '67
Southern comfort. Newsweek 69:32-3 F 6 '67
Southern Republican strategy for 1968. P. Duke. Reporter 37:21-3 Ag 10 '67
Spoiler; G. Wallace visits North. il Newsweek 69:39-40 My 8 '67
Spring warmth in the great big House; Republican contenders; popularity decrease. H. Sidey. il Life 62:36D My 26 '67
T.R.B. from Washington. New Repub 158:8 Ja 6 '68
Table talk; R. Nixon talks with R. Reagan. il Newsweek 70:34 Ag 7 '67
Tapping the grass roots. J. Burnham. Nat R 19:1063-4 O 3 '67
Temper of the times. il Time 89:27-33 Ap 14 '67
They're off! contest for 1968 Republican presidential nomination. il Newsweek 70:21-2 S 4 '67
Thinking aloud about 1968. F. S. Meyer. Nat R 19:640 Je 13 '67
Top Republicans talk about their choice for '68. il U S News 62:40-1 F 6 '67
Toward a brokered convention. Nat R 19: 285-6 Mr 21 '67
Trade winds; announcements of candidates. J. Beatty, jr. Sat R 50:12+ D 9 '67
Trials of a presidential candidate. M. McGrory. America 116:368 Mr 18 '67
Voice for dissent. Time 90:21-2 D 8 '67
Waiting game; Republican candidates. il Time 90:13-15 Jl 7 '67
Wallace threat. R. Moley. Newsweek 69:100 Ap 3 '67
War, riots, crime, taxes: why Democrats worry about '68. il U S News 63:46-7 Ag 21 '67
Washington desk. G. R. Rosen. Duns R 90:7-8 S '67
Washington desk; Republican possibilities. G. R. Rosen. Duns R 89:7-8 Je '67
What makes Wallace run? J. J. Kilpatrick. il Nat R 19:400-9 Ap 18 '67
What the winning candidate must sense. P. Lisagor. il Nations Bsns 55:19-20 Jl '67
What's happening to the Democrats? il U S News 63:31-3 D 18 '67
Where's George? Republican governors conference. il Newsweek 70:97-8 Jl 10 '67
Who will win the '68 election? countrywide opinion. il Nations Bsns 55:60-2+ N '67
Who's ahead now, Nixon or Romney? U S News 62:19 Ap 24 '67

Why choices narrow for the politicians. P. Lisagor. il Nations Bsns 55:25-6 Mr '67
Why McCarthy challenges LBJ in primaries. U S News 63:24 D 11 '67
Why '68 looks like a close election. il U S News 62:45-6 My 15 '67
Will Bobby's friends trip up LBJ in '68? il U S News 62:53-4 Ap 10 '67
Wing and a prayer; President's Vietnam policy worries Democratic strategists. il Newsweek 69:26 My 22 '67
Word; Gov. Romney to fight for Republican nomination. il Time 90:25 N 24 '67
Would-be candidate for this season: Senator E. McCarthy. W. H. Honan. il N Y Times Mag p27+ D 10 '67
See also names of Presidential candidates E. McCarthy

Anecdotes, facetiae, satire, etc.
Political fiction. B. Laird. New Yorker 43: 42-6 S 16 '67
Politics in the forest. H. Fairlie. New Repub 157:13-15 O 7 '67
Tiddely-pom; concerning New republic article. Newsweek 70:27-8 O 16 '67

Protection
Letter from Washington; selecting a safe place for 1968 conventions. R. H. Rovere. New Yorker 43:98 Ag 19 '67

PRESIDENTIAL communication. See Communication in government
PRESIDENTIAL conventions. See National conventions (political)
PRESIDENTIAL duties. See Presidents—United States—Powers and duties
PRESIDENTIAL elections. See Presidents—United States—Elections
PRESIDENTIAL entertaining. See Government entertaining
PRESIDENTIAL libraries
Presidential libraries gain recognition. F. L. Schick. Hobbies 72:108-9 S '67
Presidential papers library to open next spring. Pub W 192:33-4 O 23 '67
PRESIDENTIAL nominations. See Nominations for office
PRESIDENTIAL polls. See Public opinion polls
PRESIDENTIAL primaries. See Primaries
PRESIDENTIAL scholars. See High school students, Mentally superior
PRESIDENTIAL succession. See Presidents—United States—Succession
PRESIDENTS

France
Black president for France? position of G. Monnerville. il Ebony 23:88-90+ N '67

Indonesia
Tethered scapegoat. il Newsweek 69:52+ Mr 20 '67

United States
If I were president; sixteen famous women give their program for America. il McCalls 95:51-3+ Ja '68
Presidency is back-breaking, but you get to walk to work. T. C. Sorensen. il N Y Times Mag p25+ Mr 19 '67
Talk with an eighty-three-year-old enfant terrible; ed. by H. Brandon. A. R. Longworth. il N Y Times Mag p8-9+ Ag 6 '67
See also
United States—Executive office of the president
Vice-Presidents—United States
White House

Assassination—Anecdotes, facetiae, satire, etc.
Death of a President; a dissent. J. Brennan. Nat R 19:415 Ap 18 '67

Children
Never spill milk on a president; excerpts from Children in the White House. C. Sadler. il McCalls 94:34+ Jl '67

Communication
See Communication in government

Correspondence
Beyond the aid of history; concerning introduction by Allan Nevins to new edition of Richardson's 1905 Messages and papers of the Confederacy. F. E. Vandiver. il Sat R 50:34 My 6 '67

Election
ADA defers; question of L. B. Johnson's renomination. New Repub 157:5-6 O 7 '67; Discussion. 157:11-12 O 14: 34-6 O 28 '67
Dirksen's switch; direct election proposal. New Repub 157:8 O 7 '67

PRESIDENTS—United States—Election—*Cont.*
Hitched to LBJ? case for not renominating L. B. Johnson. New Repub 157:1+ S 30 '67
Next year, a funny thing could happen on the way to the White House. R. L. Strout. il N Y Times Mag p24-5 Jl 23 '67
President dumping; W. H. Taft and L. B. Johnson. Americus. New Repub 157:11-13 O 28 '67; Reply. G. Tyler. 157:44 N 11 '67
This month's feature: moves to change the U.S. electoral system. Cong Digest 46:257-88 N '67
Time to change the presidential system; months between election day and inauguration. D. Lawrence. U S News 62:124 Mr 13 '67
When presidents run for re-election. il U S News 63:49 S 25 '67
Will Westmoreland elect Johnson? S. Alsop. il Sat Eve Post 241:11 Ja 13 '68
    See also
Electoral college
Nominations for office
Presidential campaigns
Presidential candidates

Homes
See United States—Historic houses, etc.

Messages
Beyond the aid of history; concerning introduction by Allan Nevins to new edition of Richardson's 1905 Messages and papers of the Confederacy. F. E. Vandiver. il Sat R 50:34 My 6 '67
Civil rights & consumer messages. Time 89: 18 F 24 '67
Civil rights bill of 1967. America 116:303 Mr 4 '67
LBJ's package for consumers. il Newsweek 69:69 F 27 '67
Marking time; concerning health and education message to Congress. Time 89:22-3 Mr 10 '67
Message of defeat; State of the Union. Nation 204:98-9 Ja 23 '67
President Johnson's special message to Congress: children and youth. L. B. Johnson. il PTA Mag 61:20-2 Mr; 12-14+ Ap '67
Something borrowed; Presidential message on civil rights. Newsweek 69:27-8 F 27 '67
State of the Union. M. Ascoli. Reporter 36:8 Ja 26 '67
State of the Union. il Sci N 91:55+ Ja 21 '67
Time of testing; State of the Union message; with editorial comment. il Bsns W p25-6, 164 Ja 14 '67

Powers and duties
Big issue: Tonkin declaration and the Fulbright resolution. Nation 205:162-3 S 4 '67
Comparative roles of the President and the Congress in foreign affairs; statement, August 17, 1967. N. D. Katzenbach. Dept State Bul 57:333-6 S 11 '67
Congress: its lost sacred powers. T. Coffin. Bul Atomic Sci 23:35-7 D '67
Gulf of Tonkin resolution; text of August 7, 1964. Cur Hist 54:49 Ja '68
Johnson's war powers: just what Congress said; text. U S News 63:8-9 Ag 28 '67
Maker of foreign policy, Congress or the president? D. Lawrence. U S News 63:136+ D 11 '67
Man of the year: L. Johnson. il Time 91:13-14+ Ja 5 '68
Myth of splendid misery. H. Sidey. il Life 62:32B F 24 '67
Philosophy of office and the ache of ambition. H. Sidey. Life 63:30 N 3 '67
Policing the presidency; Senate foreign relations committee. Commonweal 87:324 D 8 '67
Presidency and executive departments: six hats and twelve right arms. il Sr Schol 91: 9-10+ N 30 '67
Protest, power and the future of politics. C. McWilliams. Nation 206:71-7 Ja 15 '68
Rethinking the unthinkable; Fulbright resolution to limit administration's power. Reporter 37:14+ S 21 '67
Why presidents like their job. il U S News 63:56-8 Jl 24 '67

Protection
Four years after the Kennedy assassination: could it happen again? D. Kraslow. il Pop Sci 191:70-3+ N '67
How the President of the U.S. has to travel today, in secret. il U S News 63:52 D 4 '67
Queens retire: new presidential follow-up cars. il Newsweek 70:27 N 6 '67

Public relations
Back to normal. K. Crawford. Newsweek 70: 28 Jl 24 '67
Camera and JFK. J. Neubauer. il Pop Phot 61:88-103+ N '67
Can you top this? Mr Johnson's new image. Newsweek 70:29 D 4 '67
Communication gap; LBJ's monologue with the intellectuals. B. Nelson. il Science 157: 173-6 Jl 14 '67
Consensus of a different kind. il Time 90: 25-6 O 13 '67
Failure of communication. il Time 90:13-14 Ag 25 '67
Intellectuals and the presidency. M. Ways. il Fortune 75:146-9+ Ap '67
It's always the same old question. P. Lisagor. Nations Bsns 55:29-30 O '67
Johnson has the kind of troubles Truman had. C. Phillips. il N Y Times Mag p34-5+ O 22 '67; Discussion. p 16+ N 12; 42 D 10 '67
Johnson treatment. T. Levitt. il Harvard Bsns R 45:114-18+ Ja '67
Letter from Washington; LBJ's credibility gap and public opinion. R. H. Rovere. New Yorker 43:157-60+ S 23 '67
LBJ and the intellectuals. il Newsweek 69: 27-8 Je 5 '67
LBJ at a low ebb. il Newsweek 70:15-16 Ag 21 '67
Music to his ears; favorable public-opinion polls. il Time 90:14 Jl 14 '67
Our naïve President. S. Alsop. il Sat Eve Post 240:14 My 6 '67
Outward bound; Veterans day tour. il Newsweek 70:68 N 20 '67
Political troubles ahead for LBJ. il U S News 63:46-50 S 25 '67
President in trouble. il Newsweek 70:17-21 S 4 '67
Rancors aweigh; Johnson lashes out at critics. il Time 90:31 N 17 '67
Random thoughts on a presidential press conference. Nat R 19:942-3 S 5 '67
Stammering advocate. E. J. Hughes. Newsweek 70:19 O 30 '67
T.R.B. from Washington; hating LBJ. New Repub 156:6 Ap 8 '67; Reply. 156:15-17 Ap 29 '67
There's that gap again. M. McGrory. America 116:240 F 18 '67
Truth about LBJ's credibility. W. Rogers. Look 31:70+ My 2 '67
What's happened to LBJ: a size-up from Congress. U S News 62:54-6 Mr 6 '67
Why the gap between L.B.J. and the Nation; failure to communicate. M. Frankel. il N Y Times Mag p26-7+ Ja 7 '68

Relations with Congress
Action LBJ wants, and the prospects. U S News 63:40 N 13 '67
Anger on the Hill. il Bsns W p33-5 O 14 '67
Atavistic yearning; Johnson's declining prestige. Time 90:26 N 10 '67
Balky Congress faces showdown. il U S News 63:44-5 S 25 '67
Bedtime thoughts; balance between the President and the Congress. Time 90:14 D 1 '67
Best evidence; L. B. Johnson's collision with Wilbur Mills over proposed tax surcharge. Nation 205:388 O 23 '67
Coalition for peace. Nation 204:356 Mr 20 '67
Congressional outlook; what they'll do in '68. il Nations Bsns 55:36-9 D '67
Consensus of a different kind. il Time 90: 25-6 O 13 '67
Drift & dissent; increasing opposition by Congress to Johnson's war policies. il Time 90:9 Ag 11 '67
GOP congressmen get early start on '68; bucking President's programs. il Bsns W p94-8 S 2 '67
If spending is cut 7 billions—. il U S News 63:31-3 O 23 '67
Is it constitutional? Congress's claim to larger share in foreign policymaking. K. Crawford. Newsweek 70:36 S 4 '67
Johnson has the kind of troubles Truman had. C. Phillips. il N Y Times Mag p34-5+ O 22 '67; Discussion. p 16+ N 12; 42 D 10 '67
Looking ahead; what kind of Congress. il U S News 64:27 Ja 8 '68
LBJ at a low ebb. il Newsweek 70:15-16 Ag 21 '67
LBJ vs. Congress: collision course. il U S News 62:23-4 Ap 3 '67
Maker of foreign policy, Congress or the president? D. Lawrence. U S News 63:136+ D 11 '67
Mood indigo. il Time 90:23-5 D 15 '67

PRESIDENTS—United States—Relations with Congress—*Continued*
Moulting of the doves; concerning letter to Ho Chi Minh. America 116:522 Ap 8 '67
No president can destroy it. F. Morley. Nations Bsns 55:31-2 N '67
Political storm over Congress. America 118:6 Ja 6 '68
Pressures mount on LBJ; dissent in the Congress. S. V. Roberts. Commonweal 87:70-1 O 20 '67
Purse-string answer; debate over power of Congress to influence or change the President's conduct of a war. Time 90:12 S 1 '67
Real story of revolt in Congress, as told by members themselves. il U S News 63:36-9 N 13 '67
Report: Washington. E. B. Drew. Atlan 220:4+ N '67
Splendid misery at last understood. M. McGrory. America 117:217 S 2 '67
Surtax scrimmage. W. V. Shannon. Commonweal 87:107-8 O 27 '67
What's happened to LBJ: a size-up from Congress. U S News 62:54-6 Mr 6 '67
What's happening in Congress now. il U S News 63:29-31 O 30 '67

Relations with the press
See Government and the press

Religion
Beyond politics, the reality of faith. H. Sidey. il Life 63:30B Ag 11 '67
John F. Kennedy and American Catholicism, by H. Fuchs. Review
Commentary 4:105-8 N '67. J. O'Gara

Succession
How to succeed; 25th amendment. il Newsweek 69:26-7 Mr 6 '67
If anything happens to a president; 25th amendment. il U S News 62:90 F 27 '67
Succession; Bayh amendment ratified. Newsweek 69:33 F 20 '67
Thirty-eight for twenty-five. Time 89:24 F 17 '67
25th amendment; if a president falters. U S News 62:12 F 10 '67
Twenty-fifth amendment of the United States Constitution; full text. Cur Hist 52:302 My '67
25th amendment ratified. Sr Schol 90:21 F 24 '67

Term
There ought never to be another presidential nominating convention; excerpts from letter, February 5, 1913. W. Wilson. U S News 63:124 O 23 '67
PRESIDENTS, College. See College presidents
PRESIDENT'S commissions, committees, etc;
See name of commission, committee, etc. as subhead under United States; e.g. United States—President's commission on law enforcement and administration of justice; United States—President's committee on selective service; etc.
PRESIDENT'S representatives. See Public officers
PRESLEY, B. J. and others
Manganese and related elements in the interstitial water of marine sediments. bibliog Science 158:906-10 N 17 '67
PRESLEY, J. M.
New horizons for retarded children: an expert's plan. por U S News 62:109-10 My 15 '67
PRESS. See Journalism; News agencies; Newspapers
PRESS, Catholic. See Catholic press
PRESS agencies. See News agencies
PRESS and crime. See Crime and the press
PRESS and government. See Government and the press
PRESS associations. See News agencies
PRESS conferences
Press conference pointers. W. M. Kiplinger, ir Parks & Rec 2:29+ Mr '67
PRESS council. See Newspapers—Great Britain
PRESS forging. See Forging
PRESS photography. See Photography, Journalistic
PRESS releases
See also
Government and the press
PRESSES
Big press argument explodes again at air force meeting. il Tech W 20:25-6 Ja 23 '67
200,000-ton forging press seen needed. M. L. Yaffee. Aviation W 86:78-9+ Ja 30 '67
PRESSES de la cité. See Publishers and publishing—France

PRESSMAN, Gabe
Rockefeller-Lindsay feud. Nation 205.591-3 D 4 '67
PRESSMEN'S home, Tenn.
Last press run for union home; Tennessee retreat to be sold. il Bsns W p66+ S 9 '67
PRESSURE
Buoyancy and pressure; questions and answers. J. Daugherty and M. Daugherty. il Sci Digest 62:91-2 Jl '67
Enthalpy of transformation of a high-pressure polymorph of titanium dioxide to the rutile modification. A. Navrotsky and others. bibliog il Science 158:388-9 O 20 '67
High-pressure dissociation of carbonic and boric acids in seawater. C. Culberson and others. bibliog il Science 157:59-61 Jl 7 '67
Hydraulic compression of mice to 166 atmospheres. J. A. Kylstra and others. bibliog il Science 158:793-4 N 10 '67
Metastable superheated ice in liquid-water inclusions under high negative pressure. E. Roedder. bibliog il Science 155:1413-17 Mr 17 '67
Pi electron systems at high pressure. H. G. Drickamer. bibliog il Science 156:1183-9 Je 2 '67
Quartz: extreme preferred orientation produced by annealing. H. W. Green, 2d. bibliog il Science 157:1444-7 S 22 '67
Sulfide solubilities in alteration-controlled systems. J. J. Hemley and others. bibliog il Science 158:1580-2 D 22 '67

Physiological effects
Animals at very high pressures of helium and neon. K. W. Miller and others. bibliog Science 157:97-8 Jl 7 '67
PRESSURE, Atmospheric. See Atmospheric pressure
PRESSURE cooking
Cooking under pressure; with recipes. il Redbook 128:54+ F '67
Hearty winter soup in a pressure cooker. S. M. Rule. il Good H 166:137 Ja '68
Ragout of beef in 15 minutes. il Ladies Home J 84:130 N '67
PRESSURE groups
Orgies of collective public signature; concerning Hugh R. Trevor-Roper's statement. Life 62:6 F 24 '67
See also
Lobbying
PRESSURE of population. See Population—Overpopulation
PRESSURE suits
See also
Aquanauts—Clothing
PRESSURIZED airplane cabins. See Airplanes—Pressurization
PRESSURIZED containers. See Aerosols
PRESTON, Catherine Lawn
Now that you are married, do not always expect the lover; letter. Am Heritage 19:34-5 D '67
PRETTYMAN, P. E. See Saunders, M. J. jt. auth.
PREVENTICARE. See Insurance, Health—United States
PREVENTION of accidents. See Accidents—Prevention
PREVENTION of crime. See Crime prevention
PREVENTION of cruelty to animals. See Animals—Treatment
PREVENTION of war. See War, Prevention of
PREVIN, André
André Previn succeeds Barbirolli in Houston. por Hi Fi 17:MA2 Ja '67
Bernstein West. por Newsweek 70:61 O 16 '67
In prospect from Previn, a Vaughan Williams cycle. E. Greenfield. il por Hi Fi 17:24+ D '67
PREZIOSO, Sal J.
Fragmentation a luxury. por Parks & Rec 2:15 S '67
Proposed Adirondak Mountains National Park. Parks & Rec 2:14-16+ N '67
about
Trustees name Sal Prezioso NRPA executive vice president and secretary; with editorial comment. il por Parks & Rec 2:13, 15+ Ag '67

PRIBILOF ISLANDS
Emancipation comes to the Pribilofs. M. E. Leary. il Reporter 36:25-9 Mr 9 '67
PRIBRAM, Karl H. and Tubbs, W. E.
Short-term memory, parsing, and the primate frontal cortex. bibliog Science 156:1765-7 Je 30 '67

PRIDEAUX, Tom—*Continued*
No frantic need for making good. Life 62:
93-4 Je 23 '67
Wild Irishman's space journey, with its volcanic splashdown. Life 62:38-9 Ap 28 '67
You're not made a lot of, because so many
others are good too. Life 64:42-3 Ja 5 '68

about
Buff of theater, magic, music and O'Neill.
G. P. Hunt. por Life 63:4 O 13 '67
PRIEST, Pat
Premiere. M. Laurance. il pors U S Camera
30:56-7 O '67
PRIESTS
Clergy manpower for the future. M. W. Car-
dullo. America 117:546-7+ N 11 '67; Reply.
W. J. Mehok. 117:726 D 16 '67
Dear editor: letter. P. Sanford. America 116:
870-3 Je 24 '67; Discussion. 116:inside cover
Je 24; 117:176-82 Ag 19 '67
Friction in Philadelphia; another head rolls.
A. Swidler. Commonweal 87:463-4 Ja 19 '68
How U.S. Catholics view celibacy.il News-
week 69:73 Mr 20 '67
Image of the teaching religious. O. C.
D'Amour. America 116:418 Mr 25 '67
New York priests go back to class. America
116:236-7 F 18 '67
Nigger priest: Father B. Joyce. il Newsweek
69:64 F 20 '67
Part-time priests? recent suggestion of a
German bishop. America 116:410 Mr 25 '67
Pedro house; experiment in St Louis. Amer-
ica 116:716 My 13 '67
Priest as rebel; priests vs. American bishops.
Commonweal 87:6 O 6 '67
Priests' associations go regional. J. J. Hill.
Commonweal 87:69-70 O 20 '67
Speaking out; priests shouldn't marry. E.
C. Kennedy. Sat Eve Post 241:8+ Ja 27 '68
Talking back to Rome. Time 90:66 S 15 '67
Trial by laicization; celibacy and marriage.
P. Declan. Commonweal 87:328-31 D 8 '67
Up-dating the clergy; how far is up? J. F.
Byrnes. America 118:8-10 Ja 6 '68
When priests marry. Christian Cent 84:427
Ap 5 '67
Wounded priest, wounded church; discussion.
America 116:132-3, 296 Ja 28, Mr 4 '67
See also
Association of Chicago priests
Association of Pittsburgh priests
Celibacy
Clergy
Ex-priests, nuns, etc.
National association for pastoral renewal

Salaries
Salaries, not stipends. America 116:365 Mr
18 '67
PRIESTS' dress. See Clergy—Costume
PRIETO, A. and others
Electrical recordings from meningioma cells
during cytolytic action of antibody and
complement. bibliog Science 157:1185-7 S 8
'67
PRIETO, Antonio
Antonio Prieto, 1912-1967. il por Craft Horiz
27:23-5 Jl '67
PRIMARIES
Big show. il Newsweek 71:17-22 Ja 8 '68
Long hot winter; possibilities for New Hamp-
shire primary. il Time 91:13-14 Ja 12 '68
Primary primary; New Hampshire presiden-
tial. M. Nolan. Reporter 37:32-4 S 7 '67
Report: New Hampshire; preview. C. McDow-
ell, jr. Atlan 220:4+ D '67
Whose stalking horse? E. McCarthy's to enter
primary in Massachusetts. Newsweek 70:32
D 18 '67
See also
Nominations for office
PRIMARY education. See Education, Elemen-
tary
PRIMARY elections. See Primaries
PRIMATES
Vitamins D₂ and D₄ in New World primates:
influence on calcium absorption. R. D. Hunt
and others. bibliog il Science 157:943-5 Ag
25 '67
PRIME ministers
See also
Australia—Prime ministers
PRIMERS

Anecdotes, facetiae, satire, etc.
Read it like it is, baby. W. Stanton. il Sat
Eve Post 240:16 Jl 29 '67
PRIMITIVE man. See Man, Primitive

PRIMITIVE musical instruments. See Musical
instruments, Primitive
PRIMITIVE sculpture. See Sculpture, Primitive
PRIMITIVE society. See Society, Primitive
PRIMITIVES, American. See Painting, Amer-
ican
PRIMITIVISM (art) See Art, Primitive
PRIMROSES
It's time to choose primroses. il Sunset
138:227 F '67
Primrose, the flower of spring. W. Wilson.
il Home Gard 54:44-5+ F '67
Primroses. A. Siepman. il Horticulture 45:22-
3 My '67
Untamed primrose. D. E. Rose. Horticulture
45:18 F '67
PRIMULAS. See Primrose
PRINA, Lee Lorick
Parent and child (cont) N Y Times Mag p
112+ Ap 2; 122+ O 8 '67
PRINCE, Alain Wood
Fishing the province of plenty. Outdoor Life
139:56-9+ Je '67
Summer bass discovery. pors Outdoor Life
140:40-1+ Jl '67
PRINCE, George M.
Prefab walk-in coolers and freezers meet
changing demands for food storage. Arch
Rec 141:201-2 Je '67
PRINCE GEORGES COUNTY, Md
See also
Maryland-National capital park and plan-
ning commission
PRINCE GEORGES COUNTY memorial li-
brary, Hyattsville, Md.
Librarians and board fight county takeover.
Library J 92:1399+ Ap 1 '67
Maryland library board backed by Agnew
veto. Library J 92:2108 Je 1 '67
PRINCE Igor; opera. See Borodin, A. P.
PRINCESS and the rose-colored glasses; drama.
See Hark, M. and McQueen, N.
PRINCETON, N.J.
Big dig in Princeton; suburban pool keeper.
L. Bergquist. il Look 31:100+ My 16 '67

Institute for advanced study
Advanced study of social change. Sch & Soc
95:330-1 O 28 '67
Bright new use, and new form, for the moni-
tor skylight; new library. il Arch Rec 141:
151-4 My '67
PRINCETON university
Celibacy, sacred and profane. J. O'Hara.
Holiday 42:28-9 Ag '67
Princeton; breaking the Gothic habit. J. M.
Dixon. il Arch Forum 127:54-61 Jl '67
Princeton faces life. il Newsweek 71:65 Ja 8
'68
Psychedelics at Princeton; booklet issued to
students. Newsweek 70:54 O 2 '67
Scribner archieves presented to Princeton. il
Pub W 191:60-1 Ap 10 '67
Time to serve; adaptation of address, Sep-
tember 18, 1966. R. F. Goheen. Sch & Soc
95:296-8 Sum '67

Art museum
Art museum, Princeton university. H. Black-
lin-Landman. il Antiques 92:670-9 N '67
PRINCIPALS, School. See School superintend-
ents and principals
PRINCIPLES
Rules and decisions. R. O. Johann. America
117:61 Jl 15 '67
PRINTED circuits
Circuit boards for your projects. B. Hartford.
il Pop Mech 127:186 Mr '67
Cutting, punching and drilling of printed
circuit boards. A. Adel. il Pop Electr 28:
57-9 Ja '68
New approach to breadboarding. R. F. Harris.
il Electr World 77:82-3 Ja '67
Space etch. il Electr World 77:85 Ap '67
PRINTERS
See also
International printing pressmen's and assist-
ants' union of North America
International typographical union
Printing industry—Wages and hours
PRINTING
AAUP: short-run production for books and
journals; summary of address, June 12,
1967. R. Gurney. il Pub W 192:66-7+ Jl 3
'67
New points on paper, type; interview. A.
Eisenman. il Pub W 192:62-4+ S 4 '67
1997; enlargement of a future Popular photog-
raphy story. D. B. Eisendrath. il Pop Phot
60:76-7 My '67

PRINTING—*Continued*
Quality control procedures in book manu-
facture; panel discussion. il Pub W 192:
82-4+ Jl 3 '67
Thirty years of typography in America. E. M.
Ettenberg. il Am Artist 31:74-8+ Ap '67
See also
Computers—Printing applications
Lithography
Type and typefounding

Design
AAUP: typographic myths; summary of address, June 12, 1967. C. Zahn. il Pub W
192:74+ Jl 3 '67
Jan Tschichold: proponent of asymmetry and
tradition. P. Standard. il Pub W 191:88-
92+ My 1 '67
Making mechanicals. S. Salter. Pub W 191:
100-1 Je 12 '67
See also
Type and typefounding

History
Master of the playing-cards; Johannes
Gutenberg.D. Powills. il Hobbies 72:124-5+
Mr '67

Legibility
Large print program initiated by Walker;
including mysteries. Library J 92:2345 Je
15 '67
Large print revolution. A. D. Hagle. bibliog
il Library J 92:3008-10 S 15 '67
Large print: trends in a new field. K. Nyren.
il Library J 92:3011-13 S 15 '67
NYPL large print project gets another $21,500
grant. Library J 92:176 Ja 15 '67
See also
Privately printed books

Private presses

Study and teaching
Printing for the child. J. Burgner. il Design
68:10-13 Ja '67

Technique
Printing in three dimensions. G. R. Smith.
il Sch Arts 66:22 F '67
PRINTING (photography) See Photography—
Printing processes
PRINTING, Linoleum block. See Linoleum
block printing
PRINTING, Offset
Color guides for offset printing; report of
convention of the Lithographic platemakers
section, Printing industries of America, inc.
il Pub W 193:62+ Ja 1 '68
Web offset for books: a major NAPL topic.
F. B. Myrick. il Pub W 192:62-3+ O 2 '67
PRINTING industries of America, Incorporated
PIA annual convention: stress is on new
tools for management, labor & plant; sym-
posium. il Pub W 192:58-60+ N 6 '67
PRINTING industry
Bookmaking around the Bay: San Francisco's
second largest industry. R. D. Harlan. il
Library J 92:2369-71 Je 15 '67
Consultant outlines production savings. Pub
W 191:117 Mr 6 '67
See also
International printing pressmen's and assist-
ants' union of North America
Kingsport press, incorporated
Strikes—United States—Printers

Wages and hours
Labor: the revolution begins; report of panel
discussion. il Pub W 192:60+ N 6 '67
PRINTING machinery
DRUPA 67, the gargantuan printing fair. F.
Myrick. il Pub W 192:60-1+ Ag 7 '67
New methods advanced. il Pub W 191:78+
Je 12 '67
New processes and old stupidity. R. L. Tobin.
Sat R 50:93-4 Je 10 '67
See also
Photocomposing machines
PRINTING plates
Offset platemaking in one step by 3M. Pub W
191:118 F 6 '67
PRINTING week. See Special days, weeks and
months
PRINTS
See also
Engravings
Glass prints

Collectors and collecting
Chez Mlle: prints to collect now. D Hampton. il Mlle 65:100-1 My '67

Exhibitions
Crazy-quilt composer; traveling show of prints
by M. Ikeda. Time 90:64+ Jl 14 '67
Some rare American prints in the Midden-
dorf collection; Metropolitan museum of art.
W. J. Shadwell. il Antiques 92:558-62 O '67

Technique
African potato printing. C. McClure. il Sch
Arts 66:32-3 Ap '67
Classroom graphics; use of office duplicating
papers. L. E. Wilson. il Sch Arts 67:22-3
O '67
Clay prints. S. Solomon. il Design 69:14-17
Fall '67
Etching with an eraser. C. L. Ferris. il De-
sign 68:17 Ja '67
Relief printing from cardboard. L. J. Miller.
il Sch Arts 66:21-3 Je '67
See also
Linoleum block printing
PRINZ, Joachim
Germans are worrying the world again. J.
Roddy. il Look 31:18-21 Mr 21 '67
PRISENDORF, Anthony
Benevolent coercion: New York's dope nos-
trum. Nation 204:486-9 Ap 17 '67
Con Edison: the arrogance of power. Nation
204:401-4 Mr 27 '67
Retirement benefits: pension plans on thin
ice. Nation 204:175-8 F 6 '67
PRISON chaplains. See Chaplains, Prison
PRISON education. See Education of prisoners
PRISON escapes. See Escapes
PRISON libraries
Books behind the bars; prisons and jails
served by Multnomah County library, Port-
land, Ore. J. W. Kling. il Library J 92:
1424-5 Ap 1 '67; Reply. M. H. Vedder. 92:
2488 Jl '67
Patient and the inmate; program meetings
of Association of hospital and institution
libraries and American association of state
libraries. P. Goldie. ALA Bul 61:843-4 Jl '67
Prison reading edict raises rights issue. Li-
brary J 93:138 Ja 15 '68
PRISON recreation
Fight on, old Sing Sing U. athletes behind
prison walls. R. H. Boyle. il Sports Illus
26:29-32+ Ja 23 '67
PRISONERS
Prelude to love: three letters; excerpts from
Soul on ice. E. Cleaver. Mlle 65:170+ S '67
See also
Escapes
Political prisoners

Recreation
See Prison recreation

Rehabilitation
Employees who got a second chance. il Na-
tions Bsns 55:90-5 Ap '67
How to rescue America from plumbers, car-
penters, and people like that. J. Fischer;
discussion. Harper 234:6+ Mr '67
Prisons and prison reform. J. P. Conrad.
bibliog f Cur Hist 53:88-93+ Ag '67
Seventh step, by B. Sands. Review
Sat R 50:28 Jl 8 '67. J. Haas
See also
Education of prisoners

Treatment
Down on the farm; Tucker prison farm,
Arkansas. il Newsweek 69:39-40 F 20 '67
Lester's open house; prisoners escape from
Wilkinson County prison work camp to tell
Gov. Maddox about mistreatment. il News-
week 69:24 My 1 '67
Only on Sunday; State penitentiary at Parch-
man allows conjugal visits. il Time 90:49
Ag 18 '67
Rights for prisoners. Time 91:46+ Ja 5 '68

Russia
Fifty years; a literary tribute; selections
from the literature of anti-communism. il
Nat R 19:1176-87 O 31 '67

Anecdotes, facetiae, satire, etc.
Next fifty years: a preview? C. FitzGibbon.
il Nat R 19:1201-4 O 31 '67
PRISONERS, Discharged
He makes decisions after twenty years behind bars. D. Llorens. il Ebony 23:44-6+ Ja
'68

Employment
Deep South boss who hires ex-cons; with report by R. Busch. il Life 63:28-40+ D 15 '67
Fidelity from the frat; employment agency
places ex-cons only. il Time 90:82-3 S 22
'67

PRISONERS, Discharged—*Continued*

Rehabilitation

Helping hand of Jim Redding; activities in the Hough area, Cleveland. V. Pizer. il Read Digest 90:99-103 Je '67

Self-made Lazarus; case of T. Green. il Time 90:58+ O 13 '67

PRISONERS, Education of. See Education of prisoners

PRISONERS, Political. See Political prisoners

PRISONERS as authors

Authors & editors; M. Braly. Pub W 192: 16-17 O 2 '67

PRISONERS of war

Arab stragglers on the Sinai sands. il Life 62:28-9 Je 30 '67

Last-gasp strafing, then into the compound for PW's. il Life 62:68-9 Je 23 '67

See also

Vietnamese war, 1957-   —Prisoners and prisons

PRISONERS of war, Returned

Coming and going; Viet Cong frees American POW. Newsweek 70:24 N 27 '67

Political prisoners; Viet Cong turns over three U.S. prisoners of war. il Time 90:38-9 N 17 '67

Three who came through; released by Viet Cong. Time 90:28 N 24 '67

PRISONERS of war in Vietnam. See Vietnamese war, 1957-   —Prisoners and prisons

PRISONS

See also

Penal colonies

Construction

Medium-control custody and rehabilitation are designed into new prison in Hawaii; Hawaii adult correctional training facility, Pauwela Point, Hawaii. il Arch Rec 141: 144-5 Mr '67

Arkansas

Down on the farm; Tucker prison farm. il Newsweek 69:39-40 F 20 '67

California

Guru of San Quentin. E. Cleaver. Esquire 67:88+ Ap '67

Connecticut

Stone walls do not a prison make; Simsbury dungeon, known as Newgate. W. S. Lee. il Am Heritage 18:40-3+ F '67

Florida

Fatal ruckus; fire at Road prison no. 32. Time 90:16-17 Jl 28 '67

Georgia

Lester's open house; prisoners escape from Wilkinson County prison work camp to tell Gov. Maddox about mistreatment. il Newsweek 69:24 My 1 '67

Greece, Modern

Island in the sun; prison island of Yioúra. il Newsweek 70:36 Ag 28 '67

Hawaii

Medium-control custody and rehabilitation are designed into new prison in Hawaii; Hawaii adult correctional training facility, Pauwela Point, Hawaii. il Arch Rec 141: 144-5 Mr '67

Ireland

Kilmainham gaol: monument to the rising. V. S. Pritchett. il Atlan 219:100-1 F '67

Mississippi

Only on Sunday; State penitentiary at Parchman allows conjugal visits. il Time 90:49 Ag 18 '67

Missouri

Out of purgatory; State penitentiary at Jefferson City. il Time 89:21 Je 23 '67

Oregon

Books behind the bars; prisons and jails served by Multnomah County library, Portland, Ore. J. W. Kling. il Library J 92: 1424-5 Ap 1 '67; Reply. M. H. Vedder. 92: 2488 Jl '67

Russia

Island, by A. Chekhov. Review
New Repub 157:26-8+ O 21 '67. C. Brown
Sat R 50:35-6 O 7 '67. M. Friedberg

Through rose-colored glasses darkly; E. S. Ginzburg's experiences. A. C. Schmidt. Reporter 38:44+ Ja 11 '68

See also

Concentration camps—Russia

South Africa

Commission on human rights strongly condemns the policies of apartheid and repressive measure in South Africa. P. Nedbailo. UN Mo Chron 4:59-68 My '67

Treatment of prisoners in South Africa; meetings of working group of experts. UN Mo Chron 4:87-9 Jl '67

Sweden

Living out. Time 90:83 S 22 '67

United States

Our sick jails can be cured. M. T. Bloom. Read Digest 90:181-2+ F '67

Prisons and prison reform. J. P. Conrad. bibliog f Cur Hist 53:88-93+ Ag '67

PRITCHETT, Victor Sawdon

Books. New Yorker 43:189-90+ Ap 15 '67

Debt of honor; story. New Yorker 43:27-34 D 30 '67

Kilmainham gaol: monument to the rising. Atlan 219:100-1 F '67

PRITTIE, Terence

Palatinate, pick of the lot. Atlan 220:116-18 S '67

Philosopher and his Germany. New Repub 157:30-2 N 11 '67

Report: Turkey. Atlan 220:32+ S '67

PRIVACY

Case of the private I. F. J. Donner. Nation 205:629-33 D 11 '67

Computer; individual privacy; address, March 6, 1967. S. J. Ervin, jr Vital speeches 33:421-6 My 1 '67

Computerized man; cause of privacy; address, May 20, 1967. W. Douglas. Vital Speeches 33:700-4 S 1 '67

Conflict of values: news and privacy; Hill vs. Life. Sr Schol 90:18 F 10 '67

Intruders; Unesco's Director-General looks at ethics in the mass media. R. Maheu. UNESCO Courier 20:23-4 F '67

Is snooping ever justified?. J Brothers. Good H 164:66+ My '67

Mailed junk & privacy bunk; author loses plea to prevent state from selling his name. Time 90:47 Jl 7 '67

National data center and personal privacy. A. R. Miller. Atlan 220:53-7 N '67

Our precious right to be unheard. J. V. Lindsay. Life 63:19 O 6 '67

Personality tests and invasion of privacy. M. L. Gross; J. N. Butcher. NEA J 56:50-2 N '67

Privacy. P. H. Abelson. Science 158:323 O 20 '67

Privacy and behavioral research. Review
New Repub 156:36-8 Je 3 '67. I. R. Wechsler

Privacy and behavioral research; preliminary summary of the report of the panel on privacy and behavioral research. Science 155:535-8 F 3 '67

Privacy and freedom, by A. F. Westin. Review
Nat R 19:1213-14 O 31 '67. F. Mount
New Repub 157:28-9 S 30 '67. R. L. Goldfarb
Sat R 50:42-3 S 16 '67. J. J. Kilpatrick

Privacy: how much need you tell a visting federal investigator? B. Nelson. Science 157:1539-41 S 29 '67

Private lives of several beauties. il Vogue 150:132-5 O 15 '67

Public interest vs. privacy; summary of panel discussion at meeting of Authors guild. il Pub W 191:37-8 Mr 20 '67

Punchcard snoopers. P. Hirsch. il Nation 205: 369-72 O 16 '67; Reply with rejoinder. A. R. Eckler. 205:610+ D 11 '67

Right of privacy, a right in formation. H. F. Pilpel. Pub W 191:40+ Je 26 '67

Right to privacy. Nat R 19:728 Jl 11 '67

Right to privacy. M. Mead. Redbook 128:30+ Ap '67

Right to privacy; act suspended by opposition of prosecutors and policemen. New Repub 157:4 Ag 5 '67

Secrets: why you need them. A. West. Vogue 150:127+ Ag 15 '67

Some words of warning anent privacy. H. F. Pilpel. Pub W 191:45-6 Mr 6 '67

Spy in the corporate structure: and the right to privacy, by E. Engberg. Review
Sat R 50:43-4 S 16 '67. N. Samstag

Students' records: ACE calls for confidentiality. E. Langer. Science 157:525 Ag 4 '67

Supreme court extends press freedoms in overruling Desperate hours verdict. Pub W 191:221 Ja 23 '67

Supreme court overturns Warren Spahn decision. Pub W 191:43 My 29 '67

PRIVACY—*Continued*
Tempest in a snakepit; Massachusetts seeking permanent injunction against showing of Titicut follies. il Newsweek 70:109 D 4 '67
Titicut follies; case against F. Wiseman for exposé on the State hospital for the criminally insane at Bridgewater, Mass. America 117:539 N 11 '67
Truth as private property; Manchester book. A. Gingrich. Esquire 67:6+ Mr '67
Two-way outrage; state charges Titicut follies invaded privacy of inmates. il Time 90:52 D 1 '67
See also
Wire tapping

PRIVATE airplanes. See Airplanes—Private ownership

PRIVATE corporations. See Corporations

PRIVATE detectives. See Detectives

PRIVATE enterprise. See Free enterprise

PRIVATE flying
Cowboy and the Comanche; traveling the rodeo circuit by plane. C. Lofting. il Flying 81:82-6 D '67
Doing the Lindy; private flying across the Atlantic. il Time 90:68 Jl 7 '67
Gone flying, Caribbean by Skyknight; a spendthrift's tour of the islands. J. Gilbert. il Flying 81:70-8 Ag '67
Gone flying to Alaska. R. Blodget. il Flying 80:34-9+ Mr '67
IFR and the single man. M. W. Horowitz. Flying 80:78-9 Ap '67
Is flying for you? C. Conley. il Field & S 72:56-7+ Je '67
Mountain hopping to Aspen in a hot new Debonair. R. B. Weeghman. il Flying 80:34-9 Ap '67
Weekend pilot. F. K. Smith. See issues of Flying
What's a swinger lake you doing on the ground? light aircraft accidents. A. R. Roalman. il Todays Health 45:28-31+ O '67
See also
Airplanes—Private ownership
Airplanes in business

PRIVATE museums. See Museums, Private

PRIVATE police. See Police, Private

PRIVATE schools
Dialogue between public and nonpublic educators; report on convocation. J. Kaminetsky. Sch & Soc 95:425-6 N 11 '67
Getting tough with pot; marijuana smokers discovered at New Jersey's Hun preparatory school. Time 90:110 D 8 '67
How much rubbed off? art teacher at Phillips academy. Andover, Mass. il Time 89:76+ Je 16 '67
In my opinion; fourteen is a good time to leave home; boarding school. J. Wales. Seventeen 26:222-3 Mr '67
New hope for Harlem's bright youth; preparation for prep school class, New York's Wadleigh intermediate school. il Ebony 22:27-30+ My '67
Private schools aren't doomed; Westminster academy, Northbrook, Ill. R. Kirk. Nat R 19:1021 S 19 '67
That old feeling; Phillips academy, Andover, Mass, art show called Feelies. il Newsweek 69:98-9 Ap 3 '67
Traffic jam in the private schools; Dalton schools, New York. R. Schickel. il N Y Times Mag p26-7+ Mr 12 '67; Discussion. p 14+ Ap 2 '67
Two new buildings for a priory school respect tradition but embrace the future; Portsmouth priory complex in rural Rhode Island. il Arch Rec 141:184-6 Mr '67
See also
Education and state
Military schools

Caricatures and cartoons
1967 yearbook. Stevenson. New Yorker 43:34-7 My 27 '67

Desegregation
Negroes in the private schools. C. Merrill. Atlan 220:37-40 Jl '67

PRIVATE secretaries. See Secretaries

PRIVATELY printed books
Fantasano set, printed and bound by hand. il Pub W 192:86-7 S 4 '67

PRIVETT, Katharine
Song of Dorothy Day; poem. Cath World 204:361 Mr '67

PRIZE fighters. See Boxers

PRIZE fighting. See Boxing

PRIZES (rewards) See Rewards, prizes, etc.

PRO DEO. See International university of social studies

PROBABILITIES
How to price industrial products. A. W. Walker. il Harvard Bsns R 45:125-32 S '67
It's more probable than you think. M. Gardner. il Read Digest 91:107-10 N '67
See also
Games, Theory of

PROBATE law and practice
Appeals court upholds ban on How to avoid probate! Pub W 192:29 N 6 '67
Don't let probate take your money away. N. Dacey. il Ladies Home J 84:70+ Ap '67
How to avoid probate! by N. F. Dacey. Review
Consumer Rep 32:390-2 Jl '67
How to avoid probate! decision to be appealed. Pub W 192:47 Jl 17 '67
Issues in the probate verdict. R. H. Smith. Pub W 193:51 Ja 8 '68
Revolt of the nonpersons. il Time 90:46 Jl 21 '67
Taking Dacey off the hook. Time 91:29 Ja 12 '68
See also
Wills

PROBES, Space. See Space probes

PROBLEM children
Boys nobody wanted. S. S. Rosenberg. il Parents Mag 42:35-7+ Ja '67
Scapegoat child. K. D. Fishman. il N Y Times Mag p86+ S 24 '67
Where did we go wrong? H. Tucker. il Ladies Home J 84:110-11+ Mr '67
See also
Child psychiatry
Juvenile delinquency
Runaway boys and girls
Special classes and special schools

PROBLEM drinking. See Alcoholism

PROBLEM solving
Teach your mind to think. R. Hyman and B. Anderson. Read Digest 90:107-10 Mr '67
See also
Thought and thinking

PROBOSCIS monkeys. See Monkeys

PROCEDURE (law)
See also
Criminal procedure

PROCHNOW, Herbert V.
Independence day; address, July 4, 1967. Vital Speeches 33:664-6 Ag 15 '67

PROCTER and Gamble, limited
Lowering the suds; Britain's Board of trade orders company to de-escalate. Time 89:94+ My 12 '67

PROCTER and Gamble company
Clorox case; Supreme court dissolves P&G-Clorox merger. il Consumer Rep 32:360-3 Jl '67
High court dissolves a sudsy conglomerate; P&G-Clorox merger decision. il Bsns W p40-1 Ap 15 '67
New ball game? Supreme court orders Clorox sell off. Newsweek 69:75-6 Ap 24 '67
No guidelines in sight; ten-year-old Procter & Gamble-Clorox chemical merger. Time 89:92+ Ap 21 '67
Now, a tougher barrier to big mergers? U S News 62:12+ Ap 24 '67
Supreme court versus corporate efficiency. R. H. Bork. Fortune 76:92-3+ Ag '67

PROCUREMENT, Military. See United States—Armed forces—Procurement

PRODIGIES, Musical. See Children as musicians

PRODUCT liability. See Liability (law)

PRODUCTION
Pluralism redefined. R. H. Mulford. Sat R 51:33-4 Ja 13 '68
Production outlook. Bsns W p65 Je 17 '67
Production turns down. il Fortune 75:31-2 Mr '67
See also
Gross national product
Inventories
Labor productivity

PRODUCTION, Agricultural
Population, natural resources, and technology. E. A. Ackerman. bibliog f il Ann Am Acad 369:84-97 Ja '67
See also
Food supply

PRODUCTION, Theatrical. See Theatrical production

PRODUCTION control
Third generation, PERT/LOB. P. P. Schoderbek and L. A. Digman. il Harvard Bsns R 45:100-10 S '67
See also
Critical path analysis
Factory management

PRODUCTION costs. See Cost

PRODUCTIVITY, Labor. See Labor productivity

PRODUCTS, Commercial. See Commercial products

PRODUCTS, New
Computer model for new product demand. M. Hamburg and R. J. Atkins. Harvard Bsns R 45:107-10+ Mr '67
CPM for new product introductions. W. Dusenbury. il Harvard Bsns R 45:124-39 Jl '67
Exciting new products. C. Schultz. il Pop Mech 127:150-1 My; 166-7 Je '67
Go-go world of the risk manager. R. Levy. il Duns R 90:38-9+ N '67
Inventions for hire, but not for sale; Sibany mfg. corp. il Bsns W p 136-7+ Mr 25 '67
Mainly for men. See issues of American home
Most dangerous game in marketing. J. Weingarten. il Duns R 89:45+ Je '67
New home products you should know about. il Pop Sci 190:152-5 Ap '67
New products. See issues of Popular electronics
New products: a 1966 sampler. il Fortune 75:188-93 Je 15 '67
New venture management in a large company. R. W. Peterson. il Harvard Bsns R 45:68-76 My '67
Setting a timetable; development of new products. il Bsns W p52-4+ My 27 '67
What's new around the house. E. Kaufman. Redbook 130:69+ Ja '68
What's newest. See issues of Newsweek
See also
American research and development corporation

PRODUCTS, Quality of. See Quality of products

PRODUCTS, Synthetic. See Synthetic products

PROFERA, Peter J.
Permanent tinning of soldering irons. Electr World 78:60 S '67

PROFESSIONAL basketball players. See Basketball players

PROFESSIONAL children. See Children. Professional

PROFESSIONAL education
See also
Library schools and education

PROFESSIONAL ethics
See also
Journalistic ethics
Librarians, Professional ethics for
Scientists, Professional ethics for

PROFESSIONAL football clubs. See Football clubs

PROFESSIONAL football players. See Football players

PROFESSIONAL golfers' association championship. See Golf—Tournaments

PROFESSIONAL golfers' association of America
Par busters. il Time 89:58 Ap 7 '67

PROFESSIONAL sanctions. See Sanctions, Professional

PROFESSIONAL tennis. See Tennis

PROFESSIONAL workers
Jobs for college grads; with list of occupations, salaries and information sources. il Ebony 22:81-2+ Je '67
Power in America, by D. T. Bazelon. Review
Commentary 44:92+ Jl '67. C. V. Woodward
Slaughter on Park avenue; plight of the affluent poor. F. Brennan. Sat R 50:18 Je 24 '67
Supply and demand
Cost of the brain drain. W. F. Mondale. Atlan 220:67-9 D '67

PROFESSIONALISM (sports) See Amateurism (sports)

PROFESSIONS
See also
Occupations
Self employed

PROFESSORS. See College professors and instructors

PROFILE MOUNTAIN
What price concrete? Old Man of the Mountain. C. B. Mitchell. il Am Heritage 18: 112 Ag '67

PROFIT
Pay vs. profit: where the Nation's money really goes; interview, ed. by A. N. Booth. J. Q. Jennings. Read Digest 90:177-80 F '67
Wall Street: the FCC drops a shoe; rules that AT&T's rates should be lowered. C. Morgello. il Newsweek 70:74 Jl 17 '67

Why things cost what they do. il Nations Bsns 55:96-8+ Je '67
See also
Corporations—Finance
Interest
Risk

PROFIT sharing
Big boom in profit sharing: what's back of it; interview. R. W. Galvin; R. L. Wood. U S News 63:64-6 Ag 28 '67
New direction and growth in profit sharing. G. Engen. bibliog f il Mo Labor R 90:1-8 Jl '67
Profit sharing for France. America 117:106 Jl 29 '67
Profit sharing, now it's a de Gaulle must. U S News 63:10 Jl 24 '67
Sharing profits all around. B. L. Masse. America 117:293 S 23 '67
When workers share the pie; united auto workers' demand. il Bsns W p 118+ Jl 22 '67
See also
Bonus system

PROGESTERONE
Progesterone: its possible role in the biosynthesis of cardenolides in digitalis lanata. E. Caspi and D. O. Lewis. bibliog il Science 156:519-20 Ap 28 '67

PROGNOSIS of scholastic success. See Prediction of scholastic success

PROGRAM evaluation and budget committee. See American library association—Program evaluation and budget committee

PROGRAMMED teaching
Innovation in undergraduate teaching. E. M. Williams. bibliog il Science 155:974-9 F 24 '67
Now you can double your learning power. W. Langewiesche. Read Digest 90:112-16 Ap '67
Of students, professors and computers. C. Fincher. il Sch & Soc 95:144-8 Mr 4 '67
Rise of programed instruction; excerpts from History of instructional technology. P. Saettler. bibliog Sch & Soc 95:536-44 D 23 '67
See also
Computers—Educational applications
Teaching machines

PROGRAMMERS, Computer. See Computer workers

PROGRAMMING (computers)
Communicating with computers. J. Kyle. il Electr World 77:50-2+ F '67
Penultimate automatic keyer. P. A. Stark and others. il Electr World 77:36-8+ Je '67
Software gets a hardsell approach. il Bsns W p 171-2+ O 21 '67
Study and teaching
How good are computer schools? il Bsns W p97-8+ O 7 '67

PROGRAMMING languages (computers)
New computer borrows present programs; using Miniflow language. il Tech W 20:40-1 Ja 30 '67

PROGRAMS, School. See School programs

PROGRESS
And children shall lead the way. M. Mead. Redbook 128:46+ F '67
See also
Change
Civilization
Inventions
Science and civilization
Social progress

PROGRESS, Technical. See Technological change

PROGRESSIVE party
Gideon's army, by C. D. MacDougall. Review
Nation 205:186-8 S 4 '67. C. L. Adcock

PROGRESSIVISM (United States politics)
Progressives, ed. by C. Resek. Review
New Repub 156:26+ Je 10 '67. G. W. Johnson

PROHIBITION
India
Repeal for profit; state of Kerala, repeal prohibition. il Time 89:35 My 12 '67
North Carolina
Drinking and winking in North Carolina. B. Shaw. New Repub 156:11-13 Ja 28 '67

PROHIBITION party (United States)
Camel crusade. Time 90:16 Jl 7 '67

PROINSULIN. See Proteins

PROJECT Apollo. See Space flight to the moon

PROJECT Camelot
CIA damage. Sci N 92:32-3 Jl 8 '67

PROJECT English. See English language—Study and teaching

PROJECT Gasbuggy. See Atomic blasting

PROJECT Head Start
Curtain of illusion: the odyssey of the Children's caravan; OEO grant, with list of films and filmstrips. J. Poignand and P. Mann. il Library J 92:860-3 F 15 '67
Follow through. N. Estes. il Am Ed 3:12-14 S '67
For the young: Follow Through program. New Repub 156:7-8 F 25 '67
From Head Start to Follow Through. Sch & Soc 95:404 N 11 '67
Head Start Follow Through. J. Lloyd. il (sup 1) Sr School 90:sup 15 F 24 '67
Head start to what? role of art activities. P. J. Smith. il Sch Arts 66:9-10 Je '67
Help for Head Start. W. D. Boutwell. PTA Mag 61:16 Ap '67
Learning in a lonely place. A. Fischel. Sat R 50:55 Ag 19 '67
President Johnson's special message to Congress; children and youth. il PTA Mag 61:20-2 Mr '67
Project Head Start: the record after two years; interview. E. Zigler. il U S News 62:72-4 Je 19 '67
Slum children must make up for lost time. M. Pines. il N Y Times Mag p66-7+ O 15 '67; Discussion. p 12+ N 5; 42 N 12 '67
Struggle that changed Glen Allan; formation of child development group in Mississippi. D. Nevin. il Life 63:108+ S 29 '67
What's happening in education? W. D. Boutwell. PTA Mag 61:21 F '67
Whites stay away but Negroes put their hopes in Head Start. il Life 63:100-1 S 29 '67

PROJECT Hindsight. See Government research

PROJECT INTREX. See Information storage and retrieval systems

PROJECT method in teaching
Schools and action. Sch & Soc 94:468-70 D 24 '66

PROJECT Mohole. See Mohole project

PROJECT organization. See Business management and organization

PROJECT Plowshare. See Atomic blasting

PROJECT Themis. See Research—Federal aid

PROJECTILES
Army evaluating rocket-assisted artillery projectiles. M. L. Yaffee. il Aviation W 86:82-3+ Je 19 '67

PROJECTION, Light. See Light projection

PROJECTION apparatus. See Projectors

PROJECTION printing. See Photography—Printing processes

PROJECTION screens
At last! superbrite screen! E. Wildi. Mod Phot 31:156 D '67
Make sure the screen is right. G. Gilbert. il U S Camera 30:60-1+ Je '67
Projection screens. Consumer Rep 32:354-5 D '67

PROJECTORS
Auto-focusing for the merry-go-round. J. S. Forney. il Pop Phot 62:82-3 Ja '68
Automatic focusing slide projectors. il U S Camera 30:50-3 Je '67
Beat & offbeat; Rolleiscop projector. N. Rothschild. il Pop Phot 61:48+ O '67
14 oz. of projector. N. Rothschild. il Pop Phot 60:100 Mr '67
One-man band recorder/projector integrates slides, sound, movies; Cinema sound. M. Duitz. il Pop Phot 61:122-3+ D '67
Projection: the new turned-on décor. il House B 109:138-9 S '67
Relaxatrol to automate your slide projector. G. W. Towner. il Pop Electr 25:55-6+ D '66
Rolleiscop projector. M. Laurance. il U S Camera 30:58-9 D '67
Slide projectors: auto focusing is in. L. Drukker. il Pop Phot 61:117 Jl '67
Slide projectors. il Consumer Rep 32:356-60 D '67
See also
Moving picture projectors

PROJECTS (teaching)
Model project for inner-city youth; programs in Philadelphia. America 117:145 Ag 12 '67
Teachers reach the children with affection and new ways; Nashville educational improvement project. il Life 63:102-3+ S 29 '67

PROJECTS to advance creativity in education. See Creative education

PROKOF'EV, Mikhail Alekseevich
Facing the complexities of modern education. UNESCO Courier 20:14-20 N '67

PROKOF'EV, Sergei Sergeevich
David Oistrakh's Red angel conducting debut. J. Diether. Am Rec G 33:474 F '67

Gennady Rozhdestvensky conducts three performances of Prokofiev ballet music, including Cinderella. H. Glass. il Am Rec G 34: 96-9 O '67
Ivan the Terrble, Prokofiev's music towers grandly alone. S. Lowe. il Hi Fi 17:80-1 S '67
Musical souvenir of a famous collaboration. A. Cohn. il por Am Rec G 34:196-7 N '67
Sergei Prokofiev: simultaneously, his last three operas. P. L. Miller. il por Am Rec G 33:468-70+ F '67
Two concerti: Gary Graffman. J. Diether. Am Rec G 33:472-4 F '67
War and peace. Criticism
New Yorker 43:141-2 S 9 '67

PROLINE hydroxylase. See Enzymes

PROLOGUE; ballet. See Ballets—Criticisms

PROMENADE concerts, London. See London—Music

PROMETHEUS bound; drama. See Lowell, R.

PROMISE; drama. See Arbuzov, A. N.

PROMISES to keep; story. See Perrin, U.

PROMOTERS and promoting
Lady is a champ; A. Eaton. M. Kram. il Sports Illus 27:76-8+ N 6 '67

PROMOTION, Sales. See Sales promotion

PROMOTION of employees. See Employees—Promotion

PRONGHORN hunting
Long, long trail. E. Park. il Outdoor Life 140: 46-7+ D '67
One day, one antelope. T. Trueblood. il Field & S 72:16+ S '67
We wanted a western hunt. J. O. Cartier. il Outdoor Life 140:29-31+ S '67
Wyoming antelope B. Milek. il Field & S 72:40-1+ Ag '67

PRONGHORNS
Nature note. il Sci N 91:180 F 25 '67

PRONUNCIATION
See also
English language—Pronunciation

PROPAGANDA
See also
Communication
Moving pictures—Propaganda films
Radio broadcasting—Propaganda
Television broadcasting—Propaganda
Voice of America (radio program)

PROPAGANDA in the schools
On the way to 1984; analysis of film Why Vietnam, and arguments against carrying war propaganda into the classroom. H. S. Commager. il Sat R 50:68-9+ Ap 15 '67; Discussion. 50:72 My 20 '67

PROPAGATION of plants. See Plant propagation

PROPANAL. See Propyl alcohol

PROPELLERS
Performance pointers. il Motor B 119:41-2 Ap '67
Propulsion efficiency starts at the prop. C. Miller. il Motor B 121:87-92 Ja '68 (to be cont)

PROPER, Datus C.
Ultralight fills the gap. Outdoor Life 139: 56-7+ Ap '67

PROPERTY
See also
Capitalism
Eminent domain
Joint tenancy
Real property
Trespass
Wills

PROPERTY insurance. See Insurance, Property

PROPERTY surveying. See Surveying

PROPERTY tax
Property tax scandals: bad laws & crafty assessors. M. Harris. Nation 204:210-12 F 13 '67

PROPERTY values. See Land values

PROPHECIES
Some new prophecies. Life 62:95 Je 16 '67
See also
Astrology
Fortune telling
Prophets

PROPHETS
Gullibility in Washington; J. Dixon's image in the capital. C. Fritchey. Harper 234: 34-8 Je '67
See also
Woodruff. M.

PROPORTION (architecture) See Architecture—Composition, proportion, etc.

PROPULSION, Rocket. See Rocket propulsion

PROPYL alcohol
Propanal may be a precursor of ethylene in metabolism. M. Lieberman and A. T. Kunishi. bibliog il Science 158:938 N 17 '67
PROSEN, Anthony
Mediterranean. Sr Schol 90:sup 18 My 5 '67
PROSPECT park. See Brooklyn—Parks and playgrounds
PROSPERITY
Three reasons for prosperity. E. L. Dale, jr. il N Y Times Mag p33-9+ N 5 '67
See also
Business conditions
United States—Economic conditions
PROST, Stephanie
Bride furnishes her first house, and writes us about it; letter. pors House B 109:105-6 F '67
PROSTAGLANDIN
Prostaglandins: localization in subcellular particles of rat cerebral cortex. K. Kataoka and others. bibliog il Science 157:187-9 S 8 '67
Prostaglandins: members of a new hormonal system. S. Bergström. bibliog il Science 157:382-91 Jl 28 '67
PROSTATE gland
Man's disease every woman should know about; prostatic disease. J. Lentz. Todays Health 45:66-8 Mr '67
PROSTHESIS
Back on their feet; amputees being fitted with artificial limbs. F. Marley. il Sci N 91:120-1 F 4 '67
Instant skin for burned. Sci Digest 63:81 Ja '68
Segmented polyurethane: a new elastomer for biomedical applications. J. W. Boretos and W. S. Pierce. bibliog il Science 158:1481-2 D 15 '67
PROSTITUTION
Courtesans: the demi-monde in 19th century France, by J. Richardson. Review
Newsweek il 70:105-6 O 23 '67. P. D. Zimmerman
Fun city; prostitution increases in New York. Newsweek 70:74 Jl 3 '67
Hooker's market; prostitutes in Manhattan. il Time 90:23 Ag 18 '67
Jelke? Jelke? wasn't he the guy who...? N. Randolph. il Esquire 67:136-9+ Ap '67
See also
Sexual ethics
PROTEAS
From an ancient desert relict to more elegant floral rarities. W. Tijmens. il Natur Hist 76:38-43 Ap '67
PROTEASES
Evolution of structure and function of proteases. H. Neurath and others. bibliog il Science 158:1638-44 D 29 '67
PROTECTION (tariff) See Free trade and protection
PROTECTION against radiation. See Radiation —Safety devices and measures
PROTECTION of animals. See Animals—Protection
PROTECTION of birds. See Birds—Protection
PROTECTION of the president. See Presidents —United States—Protection
PROTECTIVE coatings
How to glass a boat. G. Emory. il Pop Mech 128:129-33+ D '67
Institute reports on... protective coatings for kitchen floors. il Good H 164:6 Mr '67
PROTECTIVE mechanisms (biology) See Defense mechanisms (biology)
PROTECTIVE paint. See Paint, Protective
PROTECTIVE resemblance. See Mimicry (biology)
PROTECTORATES, British. See Great Britain —Protectorates
PROTEIN foods. See Meat substitutes
PROTEIN metabolism
Protein metabolism in the developing brain: influence of birth and gestational age. R. J. Schain and others. bibliog il Science 156: 984-6 My 19 '67
PROTEIN synthesis. See Proteins
PROTEINPOLYSACCHARIDES. See Polysaccharides
PROTEINS
Abductin: a rubber-like protein from the internal triangular hinge ligament of pecten. R. E. Kelly and R. V. Rice. bibliog il Science 155:208-10 Ja 13 '67
Absorption of intact protein molecules across the pulmonary air-tissue barrier. K. G. Bensch and others. bibliog il Science 157: 1204-6 S 8 '67
Autoradiographic plaques for the detection of antibody formation to soluble proteins by single cells. E. Pick and J. D. Feldman. bibliog il Science 156:964-6 My 19 '67

Blastokinin: inducer and regulator of blastocyst development in the rabbit uterus. R. S. Krishnan and J. C. Daniel, jr. bibliog il Science 158:490-2 O 27 '67
Construction of phylogenetic trees. W. M. Fitch and E. Margoliash. bibliog il Science 155:279-84 Ja 20 '67
Crystallization of a sulfate-binding protein (permease) from salmonella typhimurium. A. B. Pardee. bibliog il Science 156:1627-8 Je 23 '67
Decipher protein structure. Sci N 91:119 F 4 '67
Enhanced protein synthesis in a cell-free system from hypertrophied skeletal muscle. M. Hamosh and others. bibliog il Science 157:935-7 Ag 25 '67
Enzymatic solubilization of insoluble proteins at neutral pH. S. Rothberg and R. V. Axilrod. bibliog il Science 156:90-3 Ap 7 '67
Evolution of immunoglobulins: structural homology of Kappa and Lambda Bence Jones proteins. K. Titani and others. bibliog il Science 155:828-30+ F 17 '67
Food proteins: new sources from seeds; address, December 26, 1966. A. M. Altschul. bibliog il Science 158:221-6 O 13 '67
For animal feed first; single cell protein. Sci N 92:417 O 28 '67
Gene structure and protein structure. C. Yanofsky. il Sci Am 216:80-2+ bibliog (p 167) My '67
Heme and globin synthesis control: observations in vivo in beta thalassemia. M. Kreimer-Birnbaum and R. M. Bannerman. bibliog il Science 155:1116-18 Mr 3 '67; Reply with rejoinder. T. G. Gabuzda and others. 157:1079 S 1 '67
Hemoglobin and its reaction with ligands. E. Antonini. bibliog il Science 158:1417-25 D 15 '67
How proteins start. B. F. C. Clark and K. A. Marcker. il Sci Am 218:36-42 bibliog (p 150) Ja '68
Immunoglobulin structure: variation in amino acid sequence and length of human lambda light chains. F. W. Putnam and others. bibliog il Science 157:1050-3 S 1 '67
Insulin biosynthesis: evidence for a precursor. D. F. Steiner and others. bibliog il Science 157:697-700 Ag 11 '67
Iodide transport; inhibition by agents reacting at the membrane. P. R. Larsen and J. Wolff. bibliog il Science 155:335-6 Ja 20 '67
Memory and protein synthesis. B. W. Agranoff. il Sci Am 216:115-22 Je '67
Morphological changes in human scalp hair roots during deprivation of protein. R. B. Bradfield and others. bibliog il Science 157: 438-9 Jl 28 '67
New arms for war on hunger; development of single cell protein. il Bsns W p 160 O 21 '67
Pemoline and magnesium hydroxide: lack of effect on RNA and protein synthesis. H. H. Stein and T. O. Yellin. bibliog il Science 157:96-7 Jl 7 '67
Plasma membranes of rat liver: isolation of lipoprotein macromolecules. M. Barclay and others. bibliog il Science 156:665-7 My 5 '67
Prevention of protein denaturation during exposure to sterilization temperatures. E. W. Chappelle and others. bibliog il Science 155: 1287-8 Mr 10 '67
Protein components in the 40S ribonucleoprotein particles in escherichia coli. E. Otaka and others. bibliog il Science 157:1452-4 S 22 '67
Protein gap. Sci Am 217:41 Jl '67
Protein polices genes. Sci N 91:569 Je 17 '67
Protein structure in days. il Sci N 92:151-2 Ag 12 '67
Protein subunits: a table. bibliog il Science 155:697-8 F 10 '67
Protein-synthesizing activity of the anucleate polar lobe of the mud snail Ilyanassa obsoleta. A. C. Clement and A. Tyler. bibliog il Science 158:1457-8 D 15 '67
Sequenator opens evolutionary doors; machine for analyzing and comparing protein sequences. il Sci N 93:31-2 Ja 13 '68
Structural basis for the inhibition of protein biosynthesis: mode of action of tubulosine. A. P. Grollman. bibliog il Science 157:84-5 Jl 7 '67
Submaxillary gland of mouse: properties of a purified protein affecting muscle tissue in vitro. D. G. Attardi and others. bibliog il Science 156:1253-5 Je 2 '67
Substrate binding properties of mutant and wild-type A proteins of escherichia coli tryptophan synthetase. J. K. Hardman and C. Yanofsky. bibliog il Science 156:1369-71 Je 9 '67

PROTEINS—*Continued*
Temperature effect on protein synthesis in a heat-synchronized protozoan treated with actinomycin D. J. E. Byfield and O. H. Scherbaum. bibliog il Science 156:1504-5 Je 16 '67
Transport of protein by goldfish optic nerve fibers. B. Grafstein. bibliog il Science 157: 196-8 Jl 14 '67
Turnover of rat liver tyrosine transaminase: stabilization after inhibition of protein synthesis. F. T. Kenney. bibliog il Science 156:525-8 Ap 28 '67
Ultrastructure of thrombosthenin, the contractile protein of human blood platelets. D. Zucker-Franklin and others. bibliog il Science 157:945-6 Ag 25 '67

See also
Collagen
Fish flour
Gliadin
Interferon
Plant proteins
Tryptophan

PROTEOLIPIDS. See Lipides

PROTEOLYTIC enzymes. See Proteases

PROTESTANT churches
See also
Catholic church — Relations — Protestant churches
Ecumenical movement
Protestantism

Clergy
See Clergy

Missions
See Missions

Relations
Catholic church
Casualties of Catholic reform; Protestant obligations to ex-priests and nuns. C. Bangs. Christian Cent 84:1554-6 D 6 '67

Theology
See Theology

Colombia
Eye opener on Latin America. M. E. Marty. Christian Cent 84:261-3 Mr 1 '67

Latin America
Ecumenical tangle. J. G. Chamberlin. Christian Cent 85:75-7 Ja 17 '68
See also
Protestant churches—Colombia

United States
War in the Bible belt? concerning S. A. Hill's assessment of the Protestant South. il Newsweek 69:91 Mr 27 '67
See also
Church unity—United States
National council of the churches of Christ in the United States of America

PROTESTANT churches and politics. See Church and politics

PROTESTANT churches and race problems. See Church and race problems

PROTESTANT churches and social problems. See Church and social problems

PROTESTANT colleges. See Denominational colleges

PROTESTANT Episcopal church
Bishop Pike catches attention at Richmond. W. B. Gray. Christian Cent 84:21-2 F 15 '67
Boost for COCU. Christian Cent 84:227-8 F 22 '67; Discussion. 84:470 Ap 12 '67
Coup that impends: Episcopal extremism. L. Kinsolving. il Nation 204:105-9 Ja 23 '67
Death of dialogue; Episcopal committee dismissing heresy, charges against Bishop Pike. W. H. DuBay. Christian Cent 84:1192 S 20 '67; Reply. R. R. Winkelmann. 84: 1530 N 29 '67
End to heresy? report by committee on theological freedom and social responsibilities. Time 90:39 Ag 25 '67
Episcopal report may preclude Pike trial. Christian Cent 84:1147-8 S 13 '67
Episcopal 62nd: a great convention. W. F. Maxwell. Christian Cent 84:1441-2 N 8 '67
Heresy trial postponed. Christian Cent 84: 134 F 1 '67
How to carry out a conviction; Episcopal church poverty programs for urban ghettos. il Time 90:53-4 S 29 '67
In defense of heresy. A. Towne; discussion. Christian Cent 84:211-13, 380-1 F 15, Mr 22 '67
Is heresy dead? report by Episcopal committee. il Newsweek 70:56 Ag 28 '67

Séance in Seattle: ruminations in a ruin. A. Towne. Christian Cent 84:1442-4 N 8 '67
Thorny Episcopal issues; general convention. Newsweek 70:66 O 2 '67

Clergy
Episcopal report card. Newsweek 69:55 My 29 '67
See also
Bishops

PROTESTANT missions. See Missions

PROTESTANT missions in Latin America. See Missions—Latin America

PROTESTANT monasteries. See Monasteries

PROTESTANT reformation. See Reformation

PROTESTANTISM
Are you a Catholic? questioning by a Protestant philosopher. F. Sontag. America 117: 502-5 N 4 '67; Discussion. 118:13-16 Ja 6 '68
Notes on Protestant self-loathing. R. G. Middleton. Christian Cent 84:304-6 Mr 8 '67
Obedient rebel; M. Luther. il Time 89:70-2+ Mr 24 '67
Protestant radicalism; eschatological witness in the world. V. Eller. Christian Cent 84: 1391-5 N 1 '67; Reply. H. Arnold. 84:1633-4 D 20 '67
Radical theology and the death of discourse. L. T. Howe. Christian Cent 84:583-6 My 3 '67
See also
Evangelicalism
Fundamentalism

PROTESTANTS in Africa
African reformation. il Newsweek 71:66-7 Ja 8 '68

PROTESTANTS in Latin America
Ministerial crisis. A. Zambrano and M. Zambrano. Christian Cent 84:818+ Je 21 '67

PROTESTANTS in Mexico
Mexico; annual Juárez march. A. Zambrano and M. Zambrano. Christian Cent 84:820 Je 21 '67

PROTESTS against Vietnamese war. See Vietnamese war, 1957- —Protests, demonstrations, etc, against

PROTHRO, James Thompson, jr
Lock the doors! here comes Tommy! M. Durslag. il por Sports Illus 27:40-4 S 4 '67

PROTHRO, Tommy. See Prothro, J. T. jr

PROTOCOLS of the wise men of Zion
Warrant for genocide, by N. Cohn. Review Commentary 44:80-4 Jl '67. W. Laqueur; Reply. N. Cohn. 44:14+ N '67
Reporter 36:44+ Je 29 '67. W. L. Gundersheimer

PROTON accelerators. See Accelerators (electrons, etc)

PROTONS
Nucleon-meson cascade and shielding. R. G. Alsmiller, jr. bibliog il Science 157:1399-405 S 22 '67
Polarized protons as nuclear probes. L. Rosen. bibliog il Science 157:1127-34 S 8 '67
Radiative-capture studies of the giant dipole resonance. R. E. Segel. bibliog il Science 158:723-30 N 10 '67

PROTOZOA
Genomic exclusion: a rapid means for inducing homozygous diploid lines in tetrahymena pyriformis, syngen 1. S. L. Allen. bibliog il Science 155:575-7 F 3 '67
Temperature effect on protein synthesis in a heat-synchronized protozoan treated with actinomycin D. J. E. Byfield and O. H. Scherbaum. bibliog il Science 156:1504-5 Je 16 '67
See also
Ameba
Euglena
Paramecia
Tetrahymena pyriformis

Culture media
Tetrahymena: effect of freezing and subsequent thawing on breeding performance. E. M. Simon. bibliog il Science 155:694-6 F 10 '67

PROUST, Marcel
Three friends of Proust. P. Kolb. il Vogue 149:86-91 Mr 15 '67

PROVENCE
Going places, finding things in La Côte d'Azur and Provence. K. Bates. il House & Gard 131:56-8+ Ap '67

PROVINCIAL furniture, French. See Furniture, French

PROVING grounds
Five-year goals set for eastern test range. K. Voss. il Tech W 20:24-9+ My 22 '67
MOL launch complex geared to growth: AF satellite test center, Sunnyvale, Calif. W. E. Wilks. il Tech W 20:20-4 Ap 10 '67

PROVING grounds—*Continued*
S-1C test to mark progress in Mississippi. K. Voss. il Tech W 20:28-9 F 6 '67
Shelters downrange; shelters for homestead along Woomera-Talgarno rocket range. il Sci N 91:353 Ap 15 '67
Space-age sights: USA. L. M. Rhodes. il Todays Health 46:24-8+ Ja '68

PROVO, Larry Sherman
Looking younger. por Time 90:82 Jl 14 '67

PROXIES
MGM's own drama: the great proxy war; attempt by Levin group to oust O'Brien management. il Bsns W p 126-8 Mr 4 '67
Newest life of Leo the lion; proxy battles for MGM. Time 90:59 S 1 '67

PROXMIRE, William
Bill Proxmire: a loner to watch. G. R. Rosen. por(p75) Duns R 89:36 Ap '67
Shylock was a piker. por Time 90:23 Jl 21 '67

PROXIMITY alerting systems. See Aeronautic instruments

PRPIC, George J.
New era in Yugoslavia. America 116:528-30 Ap 8 '67

PRUDENTIAL Insurance company of America
Change in standings. Time 89:86 Mr 10 '67
Essential ingredient; public relations programs. L. L. L. Golden. Sat R 50:64-5 Ag 12 '67
Hitting the top. Newsweek 69:77 Mr 13 '67
Pru fights to keep its lead. il Bsns W p 138-40+ Je 24 '67
Rock at the top. Fortune 75:262 Je 15 '67

PRUETT, Harold D.
Designs for log-periodic FM & TV antennas. Electr World 78:46-8+ D '67

PRUITT, Inez
Of course, I'm no psychiatrist. R. Reisig and R. Rapoport. New Repub 156:14-15 Je 24 '67

PRUNE whip. See Desserts

PRUNING
How to prune trees and shrubs. H. Mason. il Bet Hom & Gard 45:68-9+ Mr '67
Pointers on pruning. il Pop Gard 18:70-1 My '67
Pruning, the two basic techniques. il House & Gard 131:198-9 My '67
See also
Fruit trees, Training of

PRUNING apparatus and equipment
Pruning shears. il Consumer Rep 32:320-3 Je '67
Care
Sharpening your pruning shears. il Sunset 139:214+ N '67

PRYCE-JONES, Alan
Theatre. Vogue 149:112 F 1 '67
Traveling with Mile: HemisFair.'68. Mlle 66:113-14 Ja '68

PRYDE, Philip R.
First Soviet national park. bibliog Nat Parks Mag 41:20-3 Ap '67

PRYOR, Lindsey D.
Eucalyptus: tree of the future. por Am For 73:12-15+ F '67

PRYOR, Richard
Beyond laughter. il pors Ebony 22:86-8+ S '67

PRYOR, Tap. See Pryor, T. A.

PRYOR, Taylor Allderdice
Frontiersman of the sea: with interview, ed. by M. Silva. pors Life 63:45-6+ O 27 '67

PRZEWALSKI'S horse. See Horses

PSEUDONYMS
Fool-the-squares. Time 90:58 D 15 '67
What's in a pen name? D. N. Kassman. Writer 80:19-23 My '67

PSILOCYBIN
Psilocybin: reaction with a fraction of rat brain. L. P. Gilmour and R. D. O'Brien. bibliog il Science 155:207-8 Ja 13 '67

PSYCHEDELIC drugs. See Hallucinogenic drugs

PSYCHEDELIC shops. See Stores

PSYCHIATRIC hospitals. See Hospitals, Psychiatric

PSYCHIATRIC social workers. See Social workers

PSYCHIATRISTS
Heal thyself; suicides among psychiatrists. Newsweek 69:112 My 22 '67
Oath of secrecy; concerning college psychiatry. Sci N 91:354 Ap 15 '67
Politics of experience, by R. D. Laing. Review
New Repub 156:24-8+ My 13 '67. R. Coles
Why I am not a psychiatrist. J. Medelman. il Harper 234:46-9 F '67; Discussion. 234:8+ Ap '67

PSYCHIATRY
California's gift to psychotherapy; reality therapy; theories and techniques of W. Glasser. J. Langguth. Harper 234:52-6 Je '67
East-West psychiatry: a happening. Sci N 91:493-4 My 27 '67
Games analysis adds flavor to psychiatry; transactional analysis. P. McBroom. il Sci N 91:308-9 Ap 1 '67
Oriental psychiatry veering West; Japan. S. Griffin. il Sci N 92:254-5 S 9 '67
Personal business; checkup with a psychiatrist. Bsns W p 167-8 My 6 '67
Politics of experience, by R. D. Laing. Review
New Repub 156:24-8+ My 13 '67. R. Coles
Psychiatrist's study reveals inner personality of wrist slashers. il Todays Health 45:79 My '67
Two faces of medicine, by C. Binger. Review
Sat R 50:32+ Ag 12 '67. D. Woods
Unusual facts about psychiatry in new book; The history of psychiatry by F. G. Alexander and S. T. Selesnick. Todays Health 45:68 Je '67
See also
International relations—Psychological aspects
Neuroses
Psychoanalysis

PSYCHIATRY, Forensic. See Forensic psychiatry

PSYCHIATRY, Military
Psychiatry and war; British treatments of neurotics during World war II; excerpts from The unquiet mind. W Sargant. Atlan 219:102-9 My '67

PSYCHIATRY and art. See Art therapy

PSYCHIATRY and religion
Learning from psychiatry. Time 90:87-8 N 17 '67
Ministers: a 200-hour view. H. W. Allison. Christian Cent 84:533-5 Ap 26 '67
See also
American foundation of religion and psychiatry

PSYCHIC energizers. See Antidepressants

PSYCHIC masochism. See Masochism

PSYCHOACTIVE drugs. See Hallucinogenic drugs

PSYCHOANALYSIS
Depth psychology, by D. Wyss. Review
Commentary 43:76-9 Je '67. R. L. Zimmerman; Discussion. 44:24+ O '67
Freud and his own patients. D. M. Kaplan. Harper 235:99-100+ D '67
Freudian analysis founders on Wilson book. P. McBroom. il Sci N 91:88-9 Ja 28 '67
How do you doodle? D. Sara. il Seventeen 26:106-7 Je '67
Performer looks at psychoanalysis. C. Arrau. il Hi Fi 17:50-4 F '67
Psychoanalysis observed, ed. by C. Rycroft. Review
New Repub 156:21-3 My 6 '67. T. S. Szasz
Psychoanalysis: the decline of a golden craft. D. M. Kaplan. il Harper 234:41-6 F '67; Discussion. 234:6+ Ap '67

PSYCHOBIOLOGY
Lithium vs. manic-depression. P. McBroom. il(p561) Sci N 91:575 Je 17 '67
Mind, brain, and humanist values. R. W. Sperry; discussion. Bul Atomic Sci 23:33-4 Ja; 26 F '67

PSYCHOLOGICAL examinations
Model-railroad marriage therapy; Interpersonal behavior game-test. il Life 63:93-4+ O 6 '67
Ten dogs know all about you; reprint. M. Luci. il Seventeen 26:138-9+ Mr '67

PSYCHOLOGICAL literature
Links between the humanities and the literature of the human sciences. I. Bry and L. Afflerbach. Wilson Lib Bul 42:510-25 Ja '68

PSYCHOLOGICAL medicine. See Mental hygiene

PSYCHOLOGICAL research
Psychochemical research strategies in man, symposium, 28-29 December, AAAS annual meeting. A. J. Mandell. Science 158:1496-7 D 15 '67
Rare study tracks half a lifetime. il Sci N 92:275-6 S 16 '67
See also
Child study

PSYCHOLOGICAL stress. See Stress (physiology)

PSYCHOLOGICAL tests. See Psychological examinations

PSYCHOLOGISTS
Freudianism. R. L. Zimmerman. Commentary 43:75-9 Je '67; Discussion. 44:24+ O '67

PSYCHOLOGY
See also
Aggressiveness (psychology)
Attitudes
Behavior (psychology)
Child study
Criminal psychology
Emotions
Experience
Fighting (psychology)
Habit
Human nature
Imagination
Mental hygiene
Motivation (psychology)
Negroes—Psychology
Psychiatry
Psychoanalysis
Psychobiology
Self
Self acceptance
Self evaluation
Sex (psychology)
Social psychology
War—Psychological aspects
Woman—Psychology
also subhead Psychology under various
subjects, e.g. Advertising—Psychology

Bibliography
See also
Psychological literature

Experiments
Case of the wandering IQs. B. Asbell. il Redbook 129:31+ Ag '67
Saga of the barefoot bag on campus; experiment at Oregon state university. J. Riley.
il Life 62:72A-72B Mr 17 '67

Industrial applications
See Psychology, Industrial
PSYCHOLOGY, Animal. See Animal intelli-
gence
PSYCHOLOGY, Comparative
See also
Animals—Habits and behavior
PSYCHOLOGY, Criminal. See Criminal psy-
chology
PSYCHOLOGY, Educational
Kari's handicap, the impediment of creativity.
R. E. Samples. il Sat R 50:56-7+ Jl 15 '67;
Discussion. 50:51+ Ag 19 '67
Talks to teachers on psychology and to stu-
dents on some of life's ideals; excerpts,
with comments by A. I. Gates. W. James.
NEA J 56:34-5 O '67
What turns kids on? Philadelphia cooperative
schools curriculum of concerns program.
T. Borton. il Sat R 50:72-4+ Ap 15 '67
See also
Child study
Intelligence levels
Learning, Psychology of
Thought and thinking
PSYCHOLOGY, Experimental
Cammie; condensation. G. Frank. il Read
Digest 92:209-12+ Ja '68
PSYCHOLOGY, Forensic
See also
Forensic psychiatry
PSYCHOLOGY, Industrial
How to get more work done. J. K. Lagemann.
Read Digest 90:85-7 My '67
See also
Job satisfaction
PSYCHOLOGY, International congress of. See
International congress of psychology
PSYCHOLOGY, National. See National charac-
teristics
PSYCHOLOGY, Pathological
Perverted piety; mortification of the flesh.
Christian Cent 84:428 Ap 5 '67
See also
Mental hygiene
Mind and body
Neuroses
Psychoanalysis
Psychotherapy
PSYCHOLOGY, Physiological
Causality, consciousness, and cerebral organ-
ization. W. R. Hess. bibliog Science 158:
1279-83 D 8 '67
Senses rechanneled. A. Ewing. Sci N 93:74-
5 Ja 20 '68
Stimulus generalization as signal detection
in pigeons. D. S. Blough. bibliog il Science
158:940-1 N 17 '67
See also
Pain
Psychology, Experimental
Sex (psychology)
PSYCHOLOGY, Sex. See Sex (psychology)
PSYCHOLOGY, Social. See Social psychology
PSYCHOLOGY of age. See Age (psychology)

PSYCHOLOGY of learning. See Learning, Psy-
chology of
PSYCHOLOGY of war. See War—Psychological
aspects
PSYCHOMETRICS
Scaling data on inter-nation action. L. E.
Moses and others. bibliog il Science 156:
1054-9 My 26 '67
PSYCHOMOTOR epilepsy. See Epilepsy
PSYCHONEUROSIS. See Neuroses
PSYCHOPHARMACOLOGY
Real STP. Sci N 92:80-1 Jl 22 '67
STP mystery. Sci N 92:56-7 Jl 15 '67
PSYCHOPHYSICS. See Psychology, Physiolog-
ical
PSYCHOSES
See also
Depression, Mental
PSYCHOTHERAPY
Behavioral psychotherapy. A. Bandura. il Sci
Am 216:78-82+ bibliog(p 150) Mr '67
California's gift to psychotherapy; reality
therapy; theories and techniques of W.
Glasser. J. Langguth. Harper 234:52-6 Je
'67
Changing world of living; address. M. Mead.
Sci Digest 62:38-43 S '67
Choosing your psychiatrist. C. Carner. il To-
days Health 45:30-3 Jl '67
Depth psychology, by D. Wyss. Review
Commentary 43:76-9 Je '67. R. L. Zim-
merman; Discussion. 44:24+ O '67
Gross but appropriate; operant conditioning.
Sci N 92:81 Jl 22 '67
Help in a crisis. F. R. Schreiber and M. Her-
man. il Sci Digest 61:18-22 Mr '67
Neurosis is just a bad habit. M. M. Hunt. il
N Y Times Mag p38-9+ Je 4 '67
Oriental psychiatry veering West; Japan. S.
Griffin. il Sci N 92:254-5 S 9 '67
Psychiatry and war; British treatments of
neurotics during World war II; excerpts
from The unquiet mind. W. Sargant. Atlan
219:102-9 My '67
Where religion and psychiatry join hands.
C. W. Hall. Read Digest 90:122-6 Mr '67
See also
Group psychotherapy
Psychiatry and religion
PSYCHOTROPIC drugs. See Psychopharmacol-
ogy
PTARMIGANS
Footprint thieves. G. M. Sutton. il Audubon
69:53-7 N '67
PTERIDINES
Carotenoid biosynthesis in rhodospirillum
rubrum: effect of pteridine inhibitor. N. A.
Nugent and R. C. Fuller. bibliog il Science
158:922-4 N 17 '67
PTOLEMY
Cultural relic of colonial America: J. Logan's
quest for Almagest. E. Wolf, 2d. il Wilson
Lib Bul 41:569-72 F '67
PU-YI, Henry. See Ch'ing Hsüan-t'ung, em-
peror of China
PUBERTY
This is the way a girl grows. A. Lake. il
Seventeen 26:156-7+ Ap '67
What makes boys so different. A. Lake. il
Seventeen 26:108-9+ O '67
See also
Adolescence

Anecdotes, facetiae, satire, etc.
Puberty is . . . W. Allen. il Read Digest
92:99-101 Ja '68
PUBLIC, The
Looking out at John Q. Public. H. Sidey. il
Life 63:46 S 22 '67
PUBLIC address systems. See Loud speaking
apparatus
PUBLIC administration. See Administration,
Public
PUBLIC broadcast laboratory
Air. M. J. Arlen. New Yorker 43:143-4+ N
18; 54+ D 30 '67
Dreary debut. G. B. Porter. Newsweek 70:96
N 20 '67
Ford-fueled controversy. E. Dowling. New
Repub 157:35-7 N 25 '67
Happening on the night of November 5. J.
Fischer. Harper 235:16+ N '67
Meatier than Bonanza. il Bsns W p38 N 4
'67
Opportunities for change. il Time 90:86+ N
10 '67
Public broadcasting corporation; proposed
Public broadcasting act of 1967 to support
noncommercial television and radio. J. Mc-
Laughlin. America 117:9-14 Jl 1 '67
PBL: hypothesis trouble? R. L. Shayon. Sat
R 50:37 D 9 '67
PBL on the brink. il Newsweek 70:102+ N
6 '67

PUBLIC broadcast laboratory—*Continued*
PBL: the great experiment. J. Tebbel. il
Sat R 50:85-7+ N 11 '67
PBL's première. J. McLaughlin. America
117:621-2 N 18 '67
Television. J. Horn. Nation 205:574 N 27 '67
Television; film, Good bye and good luck. E.
Dowling. New Repub 158:44-5 Ja 6 '68
Turn on, tune in, yawn. C. H. Simonds.
Nat R 19:1128-9 O 17 '67
Wait till next week? il Time 90:66+ N 17 '67

PUBLIC buildings
See also
Armories
Embassies (buildings)
Library architecture
also subhead Public buildings under
names of cities, e.g. Glendale, Calif.—Pub-
lic buildings

PUBLIC debt (United States) See Debts, Public—United States

PUBLIC defenders
Is it wrong to handcuff the police? W. J.
Dempsey, jr. Cath World 204:264-9 F '67

PUBLIC domain. See Public lands

PUBLIC education association, New York
Second pair of hands; school volunteer program. N. Gittelson. il N Y Times Mag
p 104+ Mr 19 '67; Discussion. p 100+ Ap 9;
22+ Ap 16 '67

PUBLIC employees. See Government employees

PUBLIC health
Tale of three cities; comparison of common
illnesses and medical services in U.S. Brit-
ain and Yugoslavia. Sci Am 217:59-60 N '67
See also
Air pollution
Food adulteration and inspection
Infant mortality
Meat inspection
Mosquitoes—Extermination
Rats as carriers of infection
Venereal diseases, Campaign against
World health organization

Economic aspects
Work limitations and chronic health prob-
lems. C. Rosenfeld and E. Waldman. il Mo
Labor R 90:38-41 Ja '67

Federal aid
President's new ideas, and a look at the
expense. il U S News 62:104-5 Mr 13 '67

International aspects
Health, population, and economic development.
C. E. Taylor and M.-F. Hall. bibliog Sci-
ence 157:651-7 Ag 11 '67
Health research: a small start for an in-
ternational center. J. Walsh. Science 155:
1088-90 Mr 3 '67
See also
World health organization

Chile
Improving occupational health in Chile; Institute of occupational health and air pollution research. Santiago. il UN Mo Chron
4:79-84 Mr '67

Great Britain
Hidden illness. Sci N 91:522 Je 3 '67
See also
Great Britain—National health service

Korea (Republic)
Birthrate cut; other diseases remain problem.
Sci N 92:130 Ag 5 '67

Latin America
Progress notes; summary of report by the
Pan American health organization. G.
Meek. Américas 19:46 Ja '67
See also
Public health—Chile

United States
Health and well-being. P. R. Lee. bibliog f il
Ann Am Acad 373:193-207 S '67
In pursuit of the nation's health. il Sci N
91:229-30 Mr 11 '67
Patients who make the doctor feverish. M.
Halberstam. il N Y Times Mag p 18-19+
F 5 '67; Discussion. p6+ F 26 '67
Rural health: OEO launches bold Mississippi
project. L. J. Carter. Science 156:1466-8 Je
16 '67
Technological development and their effects
upon health manpower. H. M. Sturm. il Mo
Labor R 90:1-8 Ja '67
See also
Negroes in the United States—Health and
hygiene

PUBLIC health centers. See Health centers

PUBLIC health conferences
See also
World health assembly

PUBLIC health workers. See Health workers

PUBLIC houses (Great Britain) See Bar and
barrooms

PUBLIC houses (Ireland) See Bars and barrooms

PUBLIC housing projects. See Housing projects, Government

PUBLIC institutions. See State institutions

PUBLIC land law review commission. See
United States—Public land law review commission

PUBLIC lands
See also
Submerged lands

United States
Bowhunting on Uncle Sam. G. H. Gillelan.
il Outdoor Life 139:28+ Je '67
Growing crisis on our public land. B. Milek.
il Field & S 72:10-11+ Ja '68
Let's not gamble with our natural resources;
proper management of public lands. J. B.
Craig. Am For 73:9 N '67
Place in the sun. J. B. Craig. il Am For 73:
10-13+ Ag '67
See also
National parks and reserves—United States
United States—Land management. Bureau of
United States—Public land law review com-
mission

PUBLIC libraries. See Libraries

PUBLIC library association. See American library association—Public library association

PUBLIC markets. See Markets, Municipal

PUBLIC meetings
Advice to congressmen; format for a meet-
ing on Vietnam. Nation 205:5-6 Jl 3 '67
See also
Parliamentary practice

PUBLIC officers
Action-intellectuals: chartmakers for our de-
manding future. T. H. White. il Life 62:76-
8+ Je 23 '67
Action-intellectuals; history of academic pen-
etration in American politics. T. H. White.
il Life 62:44-56+ Je 16 '67
Action intellectuals; idea men in American
politics; with biographical sketches. T. H.
White. il Life 62:43-58+ Je 9 '67
Bumper year for political feuds. P. Lisagor.
il Nations Bsns 55:23-4 Ap '67
Elite of the alienated. L. S. Feuer. il N Y
Times Mag p22-3+ Mr 26 '67; Discussion.
p 12+ Ap 9; 12+ Ap 16 '67
In pursuit of a primus; replacement for
Moyers. il Time 89:18-19 Ja 27 '67
Jarring change in Washington; excerpts from
The death of a President. W. Manchester.
il Look 31:50-66 Mr 7 '67
Matters of style. C. Fritchey. Harper 235:38+
D '67
Men of the Pentagon, by C. W. Borklund.
Review
Bul Atomic Sci 23:32-3 D '67. M. A. Kap-
lan
Opening the door; B. Furness inducted as
Special assistant for consumer affairs.
Newsweek 69:26 My 15 '67
Right to privacy. M. Mead. Redbook 128:30+
Ap '67
Scholar who's no. 2 at the White House;
presidential aide W. Rostow. il Bsns W
p 122-3+ Mr 25 '67
Seeking solace amid the shrill dissent; men
around L. B. Johnson. H. Sidey. il Life
63:38B N 17 '67
Those key men advising the President. P.
Lisagor. il Nations Bsns 55:23-4 D '67
To move a nation, by R. Hilsman. Review
Reporter 37:14-19 N 30 '67. M. Greenfield
Troubled flight from Dallas; excerpts from
The death of a President. W. Manchester.
il Look 31:42-8+ F 21 '67
Washington; L. B. Johnson's staff. R. Evans
and R. Novak. Atlan 220:6+ O '67
Who runs this whole U.S. show in the world;
advisers on the President's war council and
the Tuesday lunch procedure. il U S News
62:37-9 Je 5 '67
See also
Cabinet officers
Conflict of interests (public office)
Governors
Municipal officers
Negro public officers
Political ethics
Public service
Rostow, W. W.

PUBLIC officers—*Continued*

Appointment, qualifications, tenure. etc.

How new laws are conceived. P. Lisagor. Nations Bsns 55:19-20 Ag '67

Washington; L. B. Johnson's policies. R. Evans and R. Novak. Atlan 220:13-14+ O '67

Way to get a big federal job? il U S News 63:10 Jl 31 '67

Training

Bureaucrats get their own B-school; Federal executive institute. il Bsns W p69+ Je 10 '67

PUBLIC opinion

Inquiry into a disarmed world. il UNESCO Courier 20:5-9 Ag '67

Public opinion and the OAS. G. de Zéndegui. Américas. 19:inside cover Je '67

Three pragmatists; adverse popular reaction to Erhard. Johnson and Wilson. W. Lippmann. Newsweek 69:29 My 8 '67

See also
Attitudes
Israeli-Arab war, 1967—Public opinion
Public opinion polls
Student opinion
Vietnamese war, 1957- —Public opinion
also subhead Foreign opinion under names of countries, e.g. Great Britain—Foreign opinion

Africa, East

African safari view of the U.N. S. S. Baker. il Sat R 50:41-2 S 9 '67

Australia

See also
Vietnamese war, 1957—Public opinion

Austria

New Austria & the old Nazis. P. Lendvai. Commentary 44:31-8 S '67; Reply with rejoinder. A. Werner. 44:18+ N '67

Belgium

See also
United States—Foreign opinion—Belgian

China (People's Republic)

See also
China (People's Republic)—Foreign opinion

Ethiopia

See also
United States—Foreign opinion—Ethiopian

Europe

See also
United States—Foreign opinion—European

Europe, Eastern

Reality gap in eastern Europe. F. Y. Blumenfeld. Newsweek 70:40-1 O 9 '67

See also
United States—Foreign opinion—European
Vietnamese war, 1957- —Public opinion

Europe, Western

European notebook. H. Brandon. Sat R 50: 16+ Ap 8 '67

Light reaches Europe; condemnation of Thant's role in Middle East crisis. E. Taylor. Reporter 36:12 Je 15 '67

London paper scolds Europe for attacks on U.S; reprint. il U S News 62:98 Ap 24 '67

See also
United States—Foreign opinion—European

France

39,999,999 Frenchmen? anti-Gaullism. Nat R 19:782+ Jl 25 '67

See also
United States—Foreign opinion—French

Germany (Federal Republic)

Germany 1967: impressions gathered by American writers and editors; symposium. Atlan 219:41-56 My '67

See also
Vietnamese war, 1957- —Public opinion

Great Britain

English sickness; state of discontent.   D. W. Brogan. Harper 234:57-62 Je '67

See also
United States—Foreign opinion—British

Greece, Modern

See also
United States—Foreign opinion—Greek

India

Vietnam and the Christian mission: perspective from India. J. A. Bergquist. Christian Cent 84:764-6 Je 7 '67

See also
Great Britain—Foreign opinion—Indian

Israel

How Israelis view their own future. il U S News 62:42 Je 19 '67

Poland

Polish consensus.   R. Terrill. New Repub 156:17-22 My 27 '67

Russia

Paradigm for Russia. J. C. Evans. Christian Cent 84:679-80 My 24 '67

See also
United States—Foreign opinion—Russian

United States

After the riots: a survey, how the flare-ups affected U.S. racial attitudes. il Newsweek 70:18-19 Ag 21 '67

American attitudes on U.S.-Soviet relations. B. G. Lall. il Bul Atomic Sci 23:34-8 Ja '67

American intellectuals and foreign policy. I. Kristol. For Affairs 45:594-609 Jl '67

Congress jittery as public mood shifts. il U S News 63:26-8 Ag 28 '67

Dissent at a dead end. Commonweal 86:597 S 29 '67

Divided we stand: the unpopularity of U.S. wars; Time essay. Time 90:30-1 O 6 '67

Division street: America, by S. Terkel. Review
  Sat R 50:36-7 Ja 28 '67. H. Mitgang

Doves, hawks and morality; attitude of the left to Israel and Vietnam. Nat R 19:723 Jl 11 '67

Good times, but people are unhappy; findings of nationwide survey. U S News 62:50-5 My 22 '67

Great media impact war; concerning Roper and other survey findings. J. Tebbel. il Sat R 50:96-7 Je 10 '67

Hawks, doves through history. il U S News 63:46-7 N 20 '67

How the no. 1 power should use its power. L. Markel. il N Y Times Mag p22-3+ Ja 14 '68

How we feel about our money; Roper research survey findings; with test and editorial comment. M. Gunther. il Sat Eve Post 240: 72-5 D 30 '67

LBJ's popularity: rising sharply, after a rough year. il U S News 63:14 Jl 17 '67

Midsummer soundings; congressmen find out what is on their constituents' minds. il Time 90:13-14 Jl 14 '67

Mood of the country as poll takers find it: findings of Gallup polls. il U S News 63:91-2 D 11 '67

Political weather; views on presidential candidates. K. Crawford. Newsweek 71:30 Ja 22 '68

Poll winner: ticket of Rockefeller-Reagan; How South and Southwest rate Johnson in polls. U S News 63:16 O 16 '67

Press: how clear is its mirror on our world? il Sr Schol 90:6-12 Ap 28 '67

Public attitudes toward crime and law enforcement. J. McIntyre. bibliog f Ann Am Acad 374:34-46 N '67

Real story of revolt in Congress, as told by members themselves. il U S News 63:36-9 N 13 '67

Spirit is dampened. il Bsns W p23-5 Jl 8 '67

Spring warmth in the great big House; L. B. Johnson and Republican presidential contenders. H. Sidey. il Life 62:36D My 26 '67

T.R.B. from Washington; growing disillusionment. New Repub 157:6 S 2 '67

Tapping the grass roots. J. Burnham. Nat R 19:1063-4 O 3 '67

Tense New Year. K. Crawford. Newsweek 71:16 Ja 1 '68

There's not much to laugh about. P. Lisagor. il Nations Bsns 55:23-4 Je '67

To make a difference, by O. Butz. Review
Sat R 50:76-7+ My 20 '67. C. Oglesby

Uneasy America: why? what a nationwide survey shows. il U S News 63:42-6+ S 18 '67

Uneasy lie the states; observations of a British visitor. C. Northcott. Christian Cent 84:1213-14 S 27 '67

View from the heartland; Greenfield, Iowa. H. Sidey. il Life 63:34B Ag 25 '67

Watch the polls, but watch out. H. Sidey. Life 63:21 Jl 21 '67

What the people want. D. Lawrence. U S News 63:100 Ag 21 '67

PUBLIC opinion—United States—*Continued*
Who will win the '68 election? countrywide
opinion. il Nations Bsns 55:60-2+ N '67
Will LBJ get four years more? with charts.
il U S News 63:38-41 N 27 '67
    See also
Israel—Foreign opinion
Israeli-Arab war, 1967—Public opinion
Vietnamese war, 1957- —Public opinion

Vietnam (Democratic Republic)

    See also
Vietnamese war, 1957- —Public opinion

Vietnam (Republic)

    See also
United States—Foreign opinion—Vietnamese
Vietnamese war, 1957—Public opinion
PUBLIC opinion polls
He's up, he's down; presidential polls by
Louis Harris. New Repub 158:10-11 Ja 20 '68
Mood of the country as poll takers find it;
findings of Gallup polls. il U S News 63:91-2
D 11 '67
Watch the polls, but watch out. H. Sidey.
Life 63:21 Jl 21 '67
Yes, no, don't want to know. Sci Am 218:46
Ja '68
    See also
Crossley S-D surveys
PUBLIC ownership. See Government ownership
PUBLIC parking facilities. See Automobile
parking
PUBLIC prayer. See Prayer
PUBLIC records. See Archives
PUBLIC relations
Arts & uses of public relations; Time essay.
Time 90:40-1 Jl 7 '67
Public relations. L. L. L. Golden. See issues
of Saturday review
    See also subhead Public relations under
various subjects, e.g. Supermarkets—Pub-
lic relations
        Bibliography
Books in communications. A. Balk. See issues
of Saturday review
PUBLIC relations, Municipal. See Municipal ad-
vertising
PUBLIC relations consultants
Answer is good performance; (PRSA) licens-
ing proposals. L. L. L. Golden. Sat R 50:
127-8 O 14 '67
    See also
Hill and Knowlton, incorporated
PUBLIC relations society of America
Answer is good performance; licensing pro-
posals. L. L. L. Golden. Sat R 50:127-8 O 14
'67
PUBLIC reports. See Municipal reports
PUBLIC school employees. See School employ-
ees
PUBLIC school teachers. See Teachers
PUBLIC schools
    See also
Courses of study
Negro schools
School management and organization

            Appraisal
    See Evaluation (education)

            Desegregation
Alabama must integrate. Time 89:64 Mr 31 '67
Alone with Lurleen. Christian Cent 84:612 My
10 '67
And the world stopped, waiting; first prize!
Teachers' writing competition. J. Heimo-
witz. NEA J 56:21-3 O '67
Appeal of de facto segregation decision. Sch
& Soc 95:406+ N 11 '67
As nation's capital goes all out for integra-
tion. il U S News 63:54-5 Jl 17 '67
Attacking tokenism; HEW guidelines for
southern states. Sr Schol 89:18-19 Ja 20 '67
Balancing act in Boston. E. Sigel. il Reporter
36:22-4 My 4 '67; Reply with rejoinder. J.
Lee. 36:10-11 Je 15 '67
Big changes in the schools. il U S News 63:
66-9 S 11 '67
Brad. V. H. Ormsby. NEA J 56:20-1 My '67
Brooklyn's bus to equality; white children
taken to P.S. 20 in Negro neighborhood.
B. Bard. il Sat R 50:78-9 F 18 '67
Budding confrontation; no-nonsense order of
Fifth circuit court of appeals. il Time 89:
20-1 Ap 7 '67
Bus in their future? de facto school segre-
gation ruled as unconstitutional. il News-
week 70:48-9 Jl 3 '67
Busing kids to the suburbs; Boston's MET-
CO program. H. Spergel. il Am Ed 3:2-5
Ap '67

Chicago plans desegregation. Sat R 50:73-4
O 21 '67
Classroom struggle; concerning publications
by Peter Schrag and report of the Com-
mission on civil rights. I. Kraft. Nation
205:54-7 Jl 17 '67
Courts take the initiative; Washington court
decision orders reforms in the District of
Columbia public school system. G. Grant.
Sat R 50:65 Jl 15 '67
Danger facing nation's schools? interview.
C. F. Hansen. il U S News 63:40-6+ Jl 24
'67
Decision against de facto; segregation result-
ing from residential patterns. Time 89:58 Je
30 '67
De facto anticlimax; Judge Wright's deci-
sion condemning de facto segregation in
Washington, D.C.'s public schools. M. R.
Berube. Commonweal 86:438-9 Jl 14 '67
Desegregation guidelines. D. S. Seeley. il
Am Ed 3:21-2 F '67
Desegregation success stories: Arkansas and
Texas. Sr Schol 90:sup2 My 12 '67
Does democracy demand degradation? F.
Morley. Nations Bsns 55:29-30 S '67
Does high school integration really work? il
Seventeen 26:160-1 N '67
Extent of elementary school segregation in
seventy-five school systems. Ebony 22:55
Ag '67
Federal guidelines on desegregation of
schools; with comments by C. W. Gibbons
and Z. S. Henderson. D. S. Seeley; R. P.
Gousha and H. E. Row. NEA J 56:41-6
Mr '67
Fight for integrated schools goes on; pro-
grams which help to correct racial imbal-
ance; with discussion group program by
M. R. Sherwin. R. D. Goben. il Parents
Mag 42:10+, 58-9+ Je '67
George vs. the court; Alabama decree. News-
week 69:34 Ap 3 '67
Guidelines for integration upheld in Court
of appeals. Library J 92:830+ F 15 '67
Guidelines on trial. Am Ed 3:18-20 Mr '67
Hobson v. Hansen; ruling for Negro plain-
tiffs in the desegregation case in Wash-
ington, D.C. Reporter 37:20-1 Jl 13 '67
Inside story of the Marshall role in the
school-desegregation decision; excerpts from
address, December 28, 1961. A. H. Kelly.
U S News 62:13 Je 26 '67
Integration: new answer. Sci N 91:185 F 25
'67
Judge Wright faces North; case of Hobson
vs. Hansen and the Board of education
of the District of Columbia. J. Cass. Sat R
50:51-2 Jl 15 '67
Little Rock ten years later. J. Egerton. il Sat
R 50:60-1 D 16 '67
Mrs Governor faces the feds. H. Wolman
Commonweal 86:192-3 My 5 '67
Mixed classes: broadest plan so far; Chicago.
U S News 63:10 S 4 '67
NAACP sues to integrate Alabama schools.
Library J 92:278 Ja 15 '67
New drive to get city Negroes into the
suburbs. il U S News 62:68-9 F 27 '67
New super high school, wave of future for
big cities. il U S News 63:58-9 Jl 10 '67
No more nonsense about ghetto education!
J. Alsop. New Repub 157:18-23 Jl 22 '67;
Same abr. with title Can Negro children
make the grade? Read Digest 91:81-4 N '67;
Discussion. New Repub 157:42-4 S 2; 16-19
S 23; 38-9 O 21; 18-23 N 18 '67
No-progress report. il Newsweek 69:97 Mr
6 '67
Nobody wanted school desegregation: Moore
County, N.C. D. Cooper. il Am Ed 3:2-4
Je '67
Obeying the law? racial balance guidelines.
D. Lawrence. U S News 62:96 F 6 '67
Perils of Lurleen. Newsweek 69:36+ Ap 10 '67
Racial isolation in schools. America 116:301
Mr 4 '67
Racial survey goes North; HEW guidelines.
Sr Schol 91:sup2 N 2 '67
Revolution since Little Rock. il Life 63:92-107
S 29 '67
School integration is still on the agenda. R. L.
Carter. il Sat R 50:70-2+ O 21 '67
Shape of things to come in the public
schools? court ruling against officials of
Washington, D.C. il U S News 63:52 Jl 3
'67
Skelly Wright's sweeping decision; Washing-
ton school system and Carl F. Hansen in-
dicted. A. M. Bickel. New Repub 157:11-12
Jl 8 '67; Reply with rejoinder. M. E. Tigar.
157:41-3 Ag 5 '67
South is told now: integrate all the way.
U S News 62:11 Ap 10 '67

PUBLIC schools—Desegregation—*Continued*
Thirteen years after 1954; Negro pupils in South. A. Poinsett. il Ebony 22:76-7+ Ap '67
Urban school integration: strategy for peace. R. L. Crain and M. Inger. il Sat R 50:76-7+ F 18 '67; Discussion. 50:96-7 My 20 '67
Urges end of racial isolation; recommendation of US commission on civil rights. Sr Schol 90:sup3 Mr 17 '67
Well done, Gardner! Reporter 36:10 Je 1 '67
What about the ghetto? school integration in Chicago. Newsweek 70:49 S 4 '67
What High court rules now on school integration. il U S News 63:49 O 23 '67
What is racial balance in the schools? M. Greenfield. Reporter 36:20-6 Mr 23 '67
What's happening in education; progress in integration. W. D. Boutwell. PTA Mag 61:22 F '67

Employees
See School employees

Finance
See School finance

Health service
School absenteeism rule criticized by PHS physician; school health programs. Todays Health 45:84 O 67

Public relations
See School and the community

Standards
See Education—Standards

Statistics
See Education—Statistics

United States
Children are dying. J. R. Lowe. McCalls 95:4-5 Ja '68
Competition for the public schools; proposals, for providing alternatives to the established system. P. Schrag. Sat R 50:75 Ja 15 '67
Devastating report on U.S. education; concerning Coleman report. il Fortune 76:181-2 Ag '67
Education and the poor; the urban public school. M. R. Berube. Commonweal 86:46-8 Mr 31 '67
Our surprising schools; symposium. il Todays Health 45:43-65+ S '67
Public-school blues; urban-education conference. Newsweek 70:72-4 Jl 24 '67
School crisis: any way out? il Newsweek 70:71-5 S 25 '67
What's going on in schools & colleges. See issues of Changing times
See also
Education—United States
High schools
Rural schools—United States
School districts
School year
Suburban schools
PUBLIC schools (endowed)

England
Assault on privilege. il Time 89:60 Ap 28 '67
Old Boys' dinner; the English institution contrasted with American class reunions. A. Waugh. Nat R 19:750 Jl 11 '67
PUBLIC schools and religion
Christmas in the schools. il NEA J 56:54-7 D '67
Church-state issue in federal aid to education; symposium. bibliog il Wilson Lib Bul 41:682-718 Mr '67; Discussion. 41:884-5, 1014-16; 42:20+, 273+ My-S, N '67
How do you prohibit prayer? il Time 90:53 Ag 25 '67
Shared time in Winona. Sr Schol 91:sup 14 O 12 '67
Should there be prayer in public schools. GH poll; with statements by E. Dirksen and D. Hunter. Good H 164:28+ Mr '67
Teaching of morality has not been tabooed. D. Lawrence. U S News 62:112 F 13 '67

Anecdotes, facetiae, satire, etc.
This is in response: legality of starting each school day with a reading from the first page of the Congressional record. Nat R 19:625-6 Je 13 '67
PUBLIC schools and the community. See School and the community
PUBLIC service
Education and public service. J. W. Eaton. bibliog f Sch & Soc 95:358-60 O 14 '67
Labor management relations in the public service. Mo Labor R 90:III-IV Jl '67

Toward a responsible future; educating children for responsibility. W. D. Carey. il Parents Mag 43:32+ Ja '68
See also
Public officers
PUBLIC service advertising. See Advertising, Public service
PUBLIC service television programs. See Television broadcasting—Public service programs
PUBLIC speaking
Nervous about that speech? excerpt from Business ideas: how to create and present them. S. S. Price. il Nations Bsns 55:84+ Je '67
To make people listen, oral reports. J. Guncheon. il Nations Bsns 55:96+ O '67
Who's who among campus celebrities: guest speakers. il Time 90:61 O 27 '67
See also
Preaching
Speeches, addresses, etc.

Anecdotes, facetiae, satire, etc.
Unaccustomed as I am ... S. Alexander. Life 62:30B My 19 '67
PUBLIC spirit. See Patriotism
PUBLIC television. See Public broadcast laboratory; Television broadcasting, Noncommercial
PUBLIC utilities
Second battle of Antietam; opposition to line towers of Potomac Edison company. Life 62:4 Je 23 '67
See also
Electric utilities
Pacific gas and electric company

Consolidations and mergers
Marriage inside the family; International utilities corp. and Philadelphia's General waterworks corp. il Time 90:100-1 N 10 '67

Public relations
Case of Con Edison. L. L. L. Golden. Sat R 50:96 My 13 '67

Rates
He makes utilities blow fuses; T. Maynard of National utility service, inc. Bsns W p54+ Je 3 '67
Overcharge, by L. Metcalf and V. Reinemer. Review
Pub W 191:41 F 13 '67
PUBLIC welfare

Law
How much is enough in helping the poor? Bsns W p24-6 Jl 29 '67
We've got rights! R. A. Cloward and F. F. Piven. New Repub 157:23-7 Ag 5 '67
What rights for those on welfare? G. M. Sirilla. America 117:349-51 S 30 '67

Maryland
Baltimore clamps down. New Repub 156:6-7 Ap 29 '67
Taking it out on the kids. New Repub 157:9 O 7 '67

Mississippi
Mississippi: starving by the rule book; Commission on civil rights hearings. R. A. Cloward and F. F. Piven. il Nation 204:429-31 Ap 3 '67

New York (state)
Businesslike approach to poverty; Nelson A. Rockefeller's conference on social welfare. R. Stein. Sat R 50:20 D 9 '67

South Carolina
U.S. letter: Columbia. C. Trillin. New Yorker 43:208+ N 25 '67

United States
After thirty years, relief a failure? il U S News 63:44-7 Jl 17 '67
Battle line of welfare: the hungry can't wait. C. I. Schottland. il Nation 204:649-52 My 22 '67
Big stick, small carrot. Time 90:17 Ag 25 '67
Birth of a movement. R. A. Cloward and F. F. Piven. il Nation 204:582-8 My 8 '67
Case for a family allowance; excerpt from testimony before a Senate government operations subcommittee on the federal role in urban problems. D. P. Moynihan. il N Y Times Mag p 13+ F 5 '67; Discussion. p 12+ F 26 '67
Case for the negative income tax. M. Friedman. Nat R 19:239-40 Mr 7 '67
Do we want children's allowances? with table. J. Tobin. New Repub 157:16-18 N 25 '67; Reply with rejoinder. J. C. Vadakin. 157:15-18 D 23 '67

PUBLIC welfare—United States—*Continued*
Down and out; report on public welfare practices in southern states. New Repub 158:10 Ja 6 '68
End of relief as a way of life? il U S News 63:24-6 S 4 '67
End of the handout? what Congress plans. il U S News 63:46 D 25 '67
How it is, getting on welfare; excerpt from Prologue to riots. P. Jacobs. Harper 235:74-5 O '67
Jobs, not checks, new welfare aim. U S News 63:88 Ag 28 '67
Looking for new ways to welfare; Commission on income maintenance programs. Bsns W p26 Ja 6 '68
New poor swell the ranks; 8-million Americans on welfare rolls. il Bsns W p72-4+ N 11 '67
Our obsolete welfare state; address, October 29, 1967. G. Champion. Vital Speeches 34:111-14 D 1 '67
Overdue relief reform. Life 63:4 S 1 '67
People on relief. America 116:672-3 My 6 '67
Plugging welfare gaps. America 116:774 My 27 '67
Poor power; National welfare rights movement. Nation 204:228-9 F 20 '67
Protecting the poor. L. Chazen. Commentary 44:93-6 Ag '67
Public welfare: investment, or giveaway? with press comments. il Sr Schol 90:4-9 Mr 10 '67
Revolt of the nonpersons. il Time 90:46 Jl 21 '67
Unions for people on relief. il U S News 63:36-8 O 30 '67
Welfare labyrinth. Newsweek 70:22+ Ag 28 '67
We've got rights! R. A. Cloward and F. F. Piven. New Repub 157:23-7 Ag 5 '67
What rights for those on welfare? G. M. Sirilla. America 117:349-51 S 30 '67

Washington, D.C.
Consent or starve. New Repub 157:12-13 O 21 '67

PUBLIC works
See also
Municipal engineering

PUBLICITY
Teenagers outside the law: should their names be published? pro and con discussion. Sr Schol 91:14-15+ S 28 '67
See also
Industrial publicity
Public utilities—Public relations
Television in politics

PUBLICITY, Industrial. See Industrial Publicity

PUBLISHERS and libraries. See Libraries and publishers

PUBLISHERS and publishing
Bidding for Che; publishers bid for E. Guevara's diary. Time 90:58+ D 15 '67
Case the court found not very troublesome; concerning suing and prosecuting a publisher. H. F. Pilpel. Pub W 191:86-7 Ja 30 '67
How a publisher can help improve manufacturing. L. Shatzkin. Pub W 192:68+ Ag 7 '67
Most important questions unpublished writers ask. M. Pollack. Writer 80:14-16+ F '67
No captive of the computer. D. Dempsey. Sat R 50:29 N 18 '67
Production planning: a publisher speaks. L. Shatzkin. Pub W 191:84+ My 1 '67
Quality in book production; address, September 20, 1967. H. Williamson. Pub W 192:80+ O 2 '67
Sales supervision: suggestions for managers. Coqui. Pub W 192:42-4 S 18 '67
Techniques in sales of rights; address, March 22, 1967. R. E. Banker. il Pub W 191:30-2 Ap 3 '67
See also
American newspaper publishers association
Authors and publishers
Best sellers
Books—Advertising
Books—Prices
Booksellers and bookselling
Newspaper publishing
Periodicals, Publishing of
Royalties
Subscription books
University presses
also names of publishers, e.g. Harper and Row, publishers, incorporated

Anecdotes, facetiae, satire, etc.
Publishers at play. Nat R 19:892 Ag 22 '67

Art literature
Museum-publisher marriage. D. Dempsey. Sat R 50:45 F 25 '67

Catholic literature
Bold new approach in Catholic education; new catechetical series. il Pub W 191:94 Ap 3 '67
Newsletter for Catholic book trade. Pub W 192:91-2 S 25 '67

Childrens literature
Backing our backlist; Macmillan's children's books. S. Hirschman. il Pub W 192:120-1 Jl 10 '67
Children's books. See issues of Publishers' weekly
Eighteen publishers of children's books charged with price fixing by Justice department; the library market. il Library J 92:1982-5 My 15 '67
Family's always the last to know: a wide open letter to publishers of juvenile books. L. Russ. Pub W 191:26-7 My 8 '67
Joyful challenge. U. Nordstrom. il Sat R 50:39-40 N 11 '67
Libraries make a noise; suits over setting net prices for specially bound library editions. Bsns W p39 My 6 '67
Library binding suit drags on in Chicago. Library J 92:1103 Mr 15 '67
Net pricing and the salesman. D. Melcher. Library J 92:1979-80 My 15 '67
New plaintiffs debate entering library binding suit; State of Michigan joins; Detroit library withdraws. Pub W 191:76 F 27 '67
Publishers consent decrees override legal suits; high prices for children's books in library editions. Library J 82:4563-4 D 15 '67
Random and Golden plan for Doctor Dolittle. Pub W 192:157 Jl 10 '67
U.S. sues eighteen publishers on library bindings, net prices. Pub W 191:32-3 My 1 '67

Computer installations
Machine devised to process paperback returns. il Pub W 191:63-4 Je 19 '67
Order processing systems; summary of discussions on automation at AAUP annual meeting. Pub W 192:31-2 Jl 3 '67

Consolidations and mergers
CBS proposes merger with Holt. Pub W 191:37 Mr 13 '67
Herder & Herder and Burns & Oates in merger. Pub W 191:91 Ja 30 '67
Museum-publisher marriage. D. Dempsey. Sat R 50:45 F 25 '67
Wall Street notes, 1966 book publishing stock prices, mergers and acquisitions. il Pub W 191:55-9 Ja 30 '67

Educational literature
Washington briefing. K. Nyren. Library J 92:3941 N 1 '67

Film books
Literature of film. A. Knight. Sat R 50:51+ N 4 '67

Finance
One book's earnings for author and publisher. P. R. Reynolds. il Pub W 192:42-3 S 11 '67; Reply. L. Hughes. 192:35 O 9 '67

International aspects
International programs; summary of reports of International cooperation committee at AAUP annual meeting. il Pub W 192:27-8 Jl 3 '67
Notes on international co-publishing. Pub W 193:51+ Ja 15 '68
U.S. technology for export. R. H. Smith. Pub W 191:62 Ap 10 '67

Limited editions
Limited editions, unlimited prices. D. Dempsey. Sat R 50:31 My 13 '67

Paperback books
Clarion books: new S&S paperback imprint. il Pub W 191:148 Je 5 '67
Italy: il boom in paperbacks slows down. H. R. Lottman. Pub W 191:31-4 Ap 17 '67
Paperback publishers' report. il Pub W 191:59-61 Ja 30 '67
Paperbacks. See issues of Publishers' weekly
Paperbound bound? book lists. S. Forman and R. L. Collins. il Sr Schol 89:sup28 Ja 20 '67
Plea to publishers from a peripatetic parent; need for paperbacks for teen-agers. C. Heilbrun. il Pub W 192:116-18 Jl 10 '67
Tauchnitz rises again. T. L Christie. Sat R 50:35-6 D 23 '67
Uniform encoding planned for paperback backstraps. il Pub W 191:63 Je 19 '67

PUBLISHERS and publishing—*Continued*

Public relations

Truth as private property; Manchester book. A. Gingrich. Esquire 67:6+ Mr '67

Reference books

Bowker lecture: subscription books; address, May 18, 1967. E. J. McCabe. Pub W 191: 36-40 My 29 '67

Religious literature

Factors in marketing viewed at RPG workshop; symposium. il Pub W 191:26-32 Ap 3 '67

Religious publishing. Commonweal 86:39 Mr 31 '67; Reply. L. H. Wijnhausen. 86:183 Ap 28 '67

Securities

Book publishing stock prices: a monthly report. See first issue of each month of Publishers' weekly

Wall Street notes, 1966 book publishing stock prices, mergers and acquisitions. il Pub W 191:55-9 Ja 30 '67

Statistics

ABPC estimates 1966 sales, reports five-year trends; with tables. Pub W 192:28-31 O 16 '67

1966 in review; sales trends, operations, prices, foreign trade. Pub W 191:46-9 Ja 30 '67

1966: subject analysis of American book title output. il Pub W 191:34-6 Ja 30 '67

Publishers' 1966 output; 1965 and 1966 figures. Pub W 191:36-9 Ja 30 '67

U.K. title production increased 10 per cent in 1966. Pub W 191:91-92 Ja 30 '67

See also
Book industries and trade—Statistics

Taxation

Magazines: tax blow for some? il U S News 62:118-19 Ap 24 '67

Paying taxes on nonprofits. Time 90:64-5 D 22 '67

Taxing the Geographic. Newsweek 69:90 Ap 24 '67

Taxing the tax-exempt. Time 89:86 Ap 21 '67

Technical literature

Evaluation: what should publishers do? summary of ABPC conference. Pub W 191:41 Ap 10 '67

Textbooks

ATPI: past, present and future at 25th anniversary meeting; symposium; with editorial comment. il Pub W 191:26-40, 48 My 29 '67

ATPI president stresses special school market; summary of address. L. C. Deighton. Pub W 191:61 Je 19 '67

Changes in textbook specifications discussed by joint committee. Pub W 192:96 S 4 '67

College publishers to advise USOE; summary of address. P. Muirhead. Pub W 191:78+ F 27 '67

Dialog with publishers; symposium. il Pub W 191:32-4 My 22 '67

Educational publishers study the role of universities; two day conference, sponsored by American textbook publishers institute. il Pub W 192:21-4 D 25 '67

How to get the most out of a modern textbook. R. Rahtz. il Sr Schol 90:sup 12 F 17 '67

1966 in review; education and publishing. Pub W 191:50 Ja 30 '67

Some facts of life for designers; designing textbooks. S. Salter. Pub W 192:86+ Jl 3 '67

Textbook considerations, merchandising. Pub W 191:29-30 My 22 '67

Textbook market, what went wrong? summary of address. R. D. Sackett. Pub W 192:23-4 N 20 '67

What college bookmen are up to in 1967. H. S. Bryant, jr. Pub W 191:42-5 F 13 '67

See also
Textbooks

Africa

Postmark: Pall Mall; debate over agreements made with African nations. G. R. Davies. Pub W 191:23-4 My 15 '67

Canada

Canadian publishing; summary of address. J.-Z. L. Patenaude. Pub W 192:28-9 Jl 24 '67

Coordinated production for Expo 67 guide book. il Pub W 191:99-101 My 1 '67

See also
Toronto university press
University presses

Europe, Western

Impressions of the European scholarly book trade; summary of address. R. G. Underwood. Pub W 192:30-1 Jl 24 '67

France

Editions Arthaud and the Syndicat des editeurs. H. R. Lottman. il Pub W 172:30-2 O 23 '67

Editions Flammarion's new look. H. R. Lottman. il Pub W 191:43-5 F 6 '67

France's great big personal publisher; Presses de la cité. H. R. Lottman. il Pub W 192: 29-32 S 4 '67

French publishers view the U.S. as export market. H. R. Lottman. il Pub W 191:20-3 My 15 '67

Gallimard: synonymous with French literature. H. R. Lottman. il Pub W 193:55-9 Ja 15 '68

Grasset: the firm that won the prizes. H. R. Lottman. Pub W 191:42-4 Mr 6 '67

Laffont: most American publisher in France. H. R. Lottman. Pub W 192:29-31 Ag 7 '67

Literary life in Paris. H. R. Lottman. il Pub W 192:21-3 N 27 '67

Scholarly publishing in France; summary of address. A. Vachon. Pub W 192:29 Jl 24 '67

Germany (Federal Republic)

Oak attracts the lightning; left-wing opposition to Springer publications. il Time 90:53-4 N 24 '67

Tauchnitz rises again. T. L. Christie. Sat R 50:35-6 D 23 '67

Great Britain

U.K. title production increased 10 per cent in 1966. Pub W 191:91-2 Ja 30 '67

See also
Allen, George and Unwin, limited
Collins, William, sons and company, limited

Israel

Israel program for scientific translations. I. Soifer. il Pub W 192:50-1 N 13 '67

Italy

Italy: *il* boom in paperbacks slows down. H. R. Lottman. Pub W 191:31-4 Ap 17 '67

Mexico

Time inc. buys share in Mexican publishing company; Novaro. Pub W 191:91 Ja 30 '67

Norway

Norwegian scholarly publishing; summary of address. T. Andenaes. Pub W 192:29-30 Jl 24 '67

Russia

House of Pravda. W. B. Kerr. il Sat R 50: 60-1 D 9 '67

Spain

Rights and permissions. P. Nathan. Pub W 192:56 O 9; 52 O 16 '67; Correction. 192: 50 D 25 '67

Sweden

Bonniers of Stockholm; a national institution. H. R. Lottman. il Pub W 192:27-9 O 2 '67

Turkey

Note on Turkish publishing; summary of address. M. Carroll. Pub W 192:31 Jl 24 '67

United States

Bennett Cerf's views on trends in publishing. Pub W 192:36 O 16 '67

Conducting a marketing survey for a marketing book. L. Cheskin. il Pub W 193:59-60 Ja 15 '68

End of black book publishing; the Catholic publisher. D. Dempsey. Sat R 50:27 O 14 '67

Hidden hands in publishing; USIA's book development program. D. Wise. New Repub 157:17-18 O 21 '67

Independent publishers: subsidiary rights are their lifeblood. Pub W 191:32-3 Mr 13 '67

Land of opportunity; bids to publish memoir of S. Stalina. il Time 89:54 My 26 '67

1966 in review; legislation that affected publishing. Pub W 191:49 Ja 30 '67

1966 in review; statistics, news and trends in the industry. Pub W 191:46-61 Ja 30 '67

Publishers advise binders to specialize; manufacturer-publisher relations; summary of panel discussion. il Pub W 191:106-7 F 6 '67

Publishers, booksellers exchange views. il Pub W 191:35+ Je 26 '67

Study in intense competition: the review book industry. il Pub W 191:40-2 F 6 '67

Svetlana papers. G. Wills and O. Demaris. il Esquire 68:99-106+ N '67

PUBLISHERS and publishing—United States—
Continued
What college bookmen are up to in 1967. H.
S. Bryant, jr. Pub W 191:42-5 F 13 '67
See also
American book publishers council
Time, incorporated
University presses

PUBLISHERS' book numbers. See Book numbers

PUBLISHERS' publicity association
Program of the week; panel on publicity.
il Pub W 191:33-5 Mr 20 '67
PPA workshop panel gives tips on author
tours. Pub W 192:33-4 N 6 '67

PUBLISHING. See Publishers and publishing

PUBLISHING of periodicals. See Periodicals,
Publishing of

PUBS (Great Britain) See Bars and barrooms

PUBS (Ireland) See Bars and barroms

PUCCINI, Giacomo
La Bohème. Criticism
New Yorker 42:107 Ja 21 '67
New Yorker 42:146+ F 18 '67; Correction.
43:94 F 25 '67
New Yorker 43:124 Ap 1 '67
Opera N 31:18-20 F 4 '67
Opera N 31:24-7 F 4 '67
Butterfly by Barbirolli. R. Jacobson. Sat R
50:56-7+ O 28 '67
Butterfly that satisfies all round. C. L. Os-
borne. Il Hi Fi 17:81-2 S '67
From Butterfly to Wozzeck. H. Kupferberg.
il Atlan 220:124+ N '67
Gianni Schicchi. Criticism
New Yorker 43:147 Mr 4 '67
Sat R 50:114-15 Mr 11 '67
Madame Butterfly. Criticism
Opera N il 31:17-20 Mr 18 '67
New flight for La rondine. I. Kolodin. por Sat
R 50:69+ S 30 '67
Puccini's La rondine, the charm of delicate
felicities. G. Movshon. Hi Fi 17:127-8 O '67
Records:
Madama Butterfly. Opera N 32:30 O
14 '67
La rondine. Opera N 32:30 S 9 '67
Tosca. Opera N 32:30 N 4 '67
La rondine (The swallow) Criticism
Opera N 31:14-15 Mr 11 '67
La rondine: a case that needed presenting.
P. L. Miller. Am Rec G 34:310 D '67
Suor Angelica. Criticism
New Yorker 43:147 Mr 4 '67
Sat R 50:114-15 Mr 11 '67
Swallow returns. G. R. Marek. il Opera N
31:14-15 Mr 18 '67
Il tabarro. Criticism
New Yorker 43:147 Mr 4 '67
Sat R 50:114-15 Mr 11 '67
Tosca. Criticism
New Yorker 43:157-8 O 14 '67
Opera N il 32:17-19 Ja 13 '68

PUCCINIA striiformis. See Rusts (botany)

PUCK's fair. See Festivals—Ireland

PUDDINGS
All it is is rice pudding. il Sunset 139:128
D '67
Good baked puddings. B. L. Henry. il Farm J
91:74 S '67
Molasses cream soufflé. V. V. Voboril. il
Good H 164:110 Ja '67
Pouding, s'il vous plait; bread and butter
pudding. C. Claiborne. il N Y Times Mag
p67-8 F 12 '67

PUEBLO, Colo.
Housing
Scattered sites for public housing win ad-
herents. il Am City 82:97 F '67

PUEBLO Indians
See also
Taos Indians

PUERTO RICAN students in the United States
See also
Spanish speaking students

PUERTO RICANS
Nightmare night in mi barrio. P. Thomas.
il N Y Times Mag p 16-17+ Ag 13 '67

PUERTO RICANS in New York city. See Puerto Ricans in the United States

PUERTO RICANS in the United States
Nightmare night in mi barrio. P. Thomas.
il N Y Times Mag p 16-17+ Ag 13 '67
Puerto Rican pupils and American education;
adaptation of address, August 30, 1966. F.
M Cordasco. bibliog f Sch & Soc 95:116-19
F 18 '67
Summer in the city; projects of R. J. Fox.
M. Cole. il Cath World 205:223-30 Jl '67

La vida: a Puerto Rican family in the culture
of poverty—San Juan and New York, by
O. Lewis. Review
Commentary 43:83-5 F '67. N. Glazer
Nat R 19:426-8 Ap 18 '67. M. Geltman
Natur Hist 76:70+ Ap '67. J. Monserrat
New Yorker 43:154+ Mr 4 '67. N. Hentoff

PUERTO RICO
Puerto Rico: 51st state? America 116:337-8
Mr 11 '67
See also
Booksellers and bookselling—Puerto Rico
Investments, Foreign (in Puerto Rico)
San Juan
Tourist trade—Puerto Rico

Description and travel
¡Que Puerto Rico! L. Blackwood. il Sr Schol
91:sup9 N 2 '67
Travel's picture portfolio. Travel 128:52-7 N
'67

Economic conditions
Boost for Puerto Rico's boom; overwhelming
preference for commonwealth status. il Bsns
W p68-70+ Jl 29 '67

Economic relations
See also
Joint Dominican Republic-Puerto Rican eco-
nomic commission

History
Hostos' Caribbean vision. J. A. Mora. Américas 19:1-2 D '67

Industries
Island boom, with trouble ahead. il U S News
63:104-6 D 4 '67

Moral conditions
La vida: a Puerto Rican family in the culture
of poverty—San Juan and New York, by
O. Lewis. Review
Commentary 43:83-5 F '67. N. Glazer
Nat R 19:426-8 Ap 18 '67. M. Geltman
Natur Hist 76:70+ Ap '67. J. Monserrat
New Yorker 43:154+ Mr 4 '67. N. Hentoff

Politics and government
Commonwealth: si. Sr Schol 91:21 S 21 '67
Fifty-one states? not for a while, anyway.
U S News 63:14 Ag 7 '67
Pocketbook plebiscite; to decide status. Time
90:24-5 Jl 21 '67
Puerto Rican decision. Sr Schol 90:27 My 19 '67
Puerto Rico: commonwealth, state or nation?
G. T. Nunn. Nation 205:4-6 Jl 17 '67
Puerto Rico: yes or no; first status plebiscite
on kind of government to be held. C.
Fritchey. Harper 235:32-4 Jl '67
Something for everyone; plebiscite favors
continuing Puerto Rico's commonwealth
ties. Time 90:20 Ag 4 '67
Status report. il Newsweek 70:35 Ag 7 '67

Social conditions
See also
Puerto Rico—Moral conditions

PUERTO RICO and the United States
Pocketbook plebiscite; to decide status. Time
90:24-5 Jl 21 '67
Puerto Rico: commonwealth, state or nation?
G. T. Nunn. Nation 205:44-6 Jl 17 '67
Puerto Rico: yes or no; first status plebiscite
on kind of government to be held. C.
Fritchey. Harper 235:32-4 Jl '67

PUFF pastry. See Pastry

PUFFBALL fungus. See Fungi

PUGET SOUND
Puget Sound heritage cruise. E. Crimmin. il
Motor B 119:22-7+ My '67

PUGH, Betsy Ann
Twice a mother in thirty days. E. Keiffer. il
pors Good H 164:26+ My '67

PUGH, Richard C.
Predicting job corpsmen's performance on
the tests of general education development.
Sch & Soc 95:268-9 Ap 15 '67

PUGWASH conferences on science and world
affairs
Pugwash fights atrophy. H. J. Barnes. il Sci
N 92:350-1 O 7 '67
Pugwash XVI; with introd. by E. Rabino-
witch. Bul Atomic Sci 23:43-7 Ja '67
Pugwash XVII; official statement. Bul Atomic
Sci 23:46-8 N '67

PUJOL, Jean François, and others
Increased turnover of cerebral norepinephrine
during rebound of paradoxical sleep in the
rat. bibliog Science 159:112-14 Ja 5 '68

PULITZER, Joseph
Man of two worlds. por Time 90:52-3 S 22 '67
Pulitzer, by W. A. Swanberg. Review
Nation 205:502-5 N 13 '67. C. Dreher
New Repub 157:29+ S 30 '67. G. W. Johnson
Sat R 50:128-9 O 14 '67. S. W. Little

PULITZER prizes
Declining honor; H. Salisbury fails to win award. Time 89:41-2 My 12 '67
Fourth for the WSJ: fourth Pulitzer prize since 1961. il Newsweek 69:90 My 15 '67
Light in a dark journey; Anne Sexton winner of the Pulitzer prize for poetry. T. P. McDonnell. America 116:729-31 My 13 '67
1967 Pulitzer prizes awarded; letters prizes go to Malamud, Albee, Goetzmann, Kaplan, Sexton and Davis. il Pub W 191:35-6 My 8 '67
Prize flap; Pulitzer advisory board vetoes Salisbury. il Newsweek 69:89 My 15 '67
Salisbury in '68. Nation 204:613 My 15 '67

PULMONARY emphysema. See Emphysema

PULP mills. See Paper mills

PULSATING stars. See Stars, Variable

PULSE command responder. See Remote control

PULSE generators
Selecting and using pulse generators. J. D. Lenk. il Electr World 77:43-5+ My '67

PULSE time modulation. See Radio pulse time modulation

PUMA hunting
Cougar moves up from vermin to trophy. V. Kraft. il Sports Illus 27:58-62 N 6 '67
Hound man's dream; cougar hunting. D. D. Ellis. il Outdoor Life 140:50-3+ N '67
Man who feeds the trumpeters. J. Turner. il Outdoor Life 139:64-7+ F '67
Silent hunter. J. Lesowski. il Outdoor Life 140:44-7+ Jl '67

PUMAS
Nature note; a lion that purrs. il Sci N 92:100 Jl 29 '67
Our wild lyric soprano. S. P. Young. il Am For 73:26-7+ Ag '67

PUMPING engines. See Fire apparatus, Motor

PUMPING machinery
See also
Sewage pumps

PUMPING stations
Built to be seen; storm-drainage pump station, Foster City, Calif. D. W. Klar. il Am City 82:96-7 My '67
But it doesn't look like a pumping station; Oakland, Calif. il Am City 82:95 Ap '67

PUMPING stations, Sewage. See Sewage pumping

PUMPS
Domestic water supply systems. il Consumer Bul 50:36-40 Je '67

PUMPS, Fuel. See Fuel pumps

PUNCH (beverage)
Anybody for a punch? Am Home 70:113 Jl '67
Sparkling summer punches. P. S. Brown. House & Gard 131:48+ My '67
Successful recipes, punch. il Suc Farm 65:81-2 S '67

PUNCHED card systems
Data processing can save money. G. Lee. il Pub W 191:52-4 Mr 20 '67
High-speed punched-card readers. W. Barden. il Electr World 77:42-5 Ja '67

PUNCHING machinery
Special-shaped punches you can make. W. E. Burton. il Pop Mech 128:172-4 D '67

PUNCTUATION
New punctuation mark; American type founders co. introduces interabang. Time 90:56 Jl 21 '67

PUNISHMENT
Community based correctional treatment: rationale and problems. E. K. Nelson, jr. bibliog f Ann Am Acad 374:82-91 N '67
U.S. crime; punishment and prevention; symposium. bibliog f il Cur Hist 53:65-110+ Ag '67
See also
Capital punishment

PUNTILA and his hired man; drama. See Brecht, B.

PUPIL (eye)
Not-so-private eye: E. H. Hess's Pupillograph measures reactions. il Life 62:80A-80B Ap 21 '67
See also
Eye camera

PUPIL response apparatus. See Eye camera

PUPPETS and puppet plays
Children can make their own. il Sunset 139:91-2+ S '67
Disguising the paper bag for puppetry. S. Rainey. il Sch Arts 67:10-11 N '67
Off Broadway; performance of People is the thing that the world is fullest of, at new Bill Baird theatre, using both marionettes and hand puppets. E. Oliver. New Yorker 43:132 Mr 4 '67
People is the thing the world is fullest of; Bil Baird theatre production at Lincoln Center. T. Lewis. America 116:354 Mr 11 '67
See also
Shadow pantomimes and plays

PUPPIES. See Dogs

PURCELL, Carl
Even on Sunday. il Pop Phot 60:92-3 Ap '67
Micronesia; photographs. Holiday 42:70-5 Jl '67

PURCELL, Dean G. See Dember, W. N. jt. auth.

PURCELL, Henry
Purcell omnibus: Dido & Aeneas, and The Indian Queen. G. L. Mayer. il Am Rec G 33:464-6 F '67
Recital of Purcell songs. G. L. Mayer. Am Rec G 33:466 F '67
Records:
Dido and Aeneas. Opera N 31:34 Mr 11 '67
Music for the theater. Opera N 31:34 Ap 15 '67

PURCELL, William L.
Asian music primer. Am Rec G 33:850-1 My '67

PURCHASING
See also
Consumers
Consumption (economics)
Shopping and shoppers
also subhead Purchasing under various subjects, e.g. Boats—Purchasing

PURCHASING, Cooperative
See also
Purchasing, Municipal

PURCHASING, Government
See also
Contracts, Government
United States—General accounting office

PURCHASING, Household
Fifty ways to stretch food dollars. Redbook 130:67+ Ja '68
Home goods: but what will they think of next? L. A. Mayer. il Fortune 76:114-18+ Ag '67
How to be a super marketer. Bet Hom & Gard 45:92 S '67
See also
Consumer education
Food—Prices

PURCHASING, Military
Arms & the bank; Senate limits arms trade by the U.S. Export-import bank with underdeveloped countries. Time 90:21 Ag 18 '67
Arms and the man who sells them; excerpt from The limits of power. E. J. McCarthy. Atlan 220:82-6 O '67
Arms merchant to the world. S. De Gramont. il N Y Times Mag p38-9+ S 24 '67
Arms sales and foreign policy; excerpts from Arms sales and foreign policy, January 25, 1967. Bul Atomic Sci 23:44-8 S '67
Arms sales racket; Senate foreign relations committee report. Nation 204:229 F 20 '67
Arms trafficker; H. J. Kuss of International logistics negotiations. New Repub 156:4 F 25 '67
Bank-door financing; government arms sales. Newsweek 70:34-5 Ag 7 '67
Big spenders; world defense spending. Nation 204:484-5 Ag 17 '67
Bitter aftertaste; question of Britain's selling arms to South Africa. il Time 90:18 D 29 '67
Crises come, crises go; arms sales by U.S. Nation 205:293 O 2 '67
Dogfight; U.S. and France in aircraft sales race. il Newsweek 70:76 D 18 '67
Gun-peddling; US-USSR, sales policies. New Repub 157:6 Jl 8 '67
How many troops? agreements on German arms purchases in the U.S. il Newsweek 69:44-5 Mr 20 '67
Kill for peace; U.S. underwriting arms races among underdeveloped countries. New Repub 157:7-8 Ag 5 '67
Madness and Armageddon. N. Cousins. Sat R 50:24 N 11 '67
Picking the winners with a new system; life cycle costing vs traditional low-bid practice. il Bsns W p62+ My 13 '67
Push to boost export sales focuses on advanced arms. Aviation W 88:28 Ja 15 '68

PURCHASING, Military—*Continued*
Selling arms abroad; US arms sales. New Repub 156:9-10 F 11 '67
U.S. release selected arms items to Israel and certain Arab states; excerpt from press and radio news briefing, October 24, 1967. R. J. McCloskey. Dept State Bul 57: 652 N 13 '67
U.S.A. arms merchant. P. J. Weber. America 117:157 Ag 12 '67
  See also
United States—Armed forces—Procurement
PURCHASING, Municipal
Don't oversell centralized purchasing. J. T. Walsh. il Am City 82:93+ Ag '67
Petty cash fund handles small-order purchases; Milwaukee. A. L. Lehrbaummer. il Am City 82:95-6 Jl '67
Plugging profit leaks in small-order purchases. T. K. Lindsay. Am City 82:135-7 N '67
Putting EXRY punch in small-order purchases; expedited delivery. R. Price. Am City 82:180 S '67
Setting up a small-city purchasing system; Philadelphia. O. R. Winter. Am City 82: 168+ Je '67
Some dos and don'ts of cooperative purchasing. Am City 82:106+ D '67
State-local cooperative purchasing; Wisconsin. G. W. McGrath. il Am City 82:120+ Mr '67
Streamlined purchasing; San Jose, Calif. J. M. Marzluft and K. South. il Am City 82: 119-20+ My '67
PURDIE, Bernard
Pretty Purdie. New Yorker 43:52-6 N 18 '67
PURDY, Bud. See Purdy, E. W.
PURDY, E. Wilson
Messiah in open town. il por Time 89:24 Ap 28 '67
PURDY, James
Incompleat novelist. W. Coffey. Commentary 44:98+ S '67
James Purdy and the works. R. K. Morris. Nation 205:342-4 O 9 '67
PURDY, Ken W.
Motor racing: more slowdowns. Atlan 220:119-21 D '67
PURIFICATION of water. See Water purification
PURINE metabolism. See Metabolism
PURINES
Enzyme defect associated with a sex-linked human neurological disorder and excessive purine synthesis. J. E. Seegmiller and others. bibliog il Science 155:1682-4 Mr 31 '67
Phosphoribosylamidotransferase: regulation of activity in virus-induced murine leukemia by purine nucleotides. G. H. Reem and C. Friend. bibliog il Science 157:1203-4 S 8 '67
Zeatin and zeatin riboside from a mycorrhizal fungus. C. O. Miller. bibliog Science 157: 1055-7 S 1 '67
PURITANISM
Puritanism, capitalism, democracy, and the new science. L. F. Solt. bibliog f Am Hist R 73:18-29 O '67
Puritanism: the spirit that refuses to play dead; American attitudes. il Bsns W p 194+ Ap 15 '67
  See also
Calvinism
Puritans
PURITANS
Our Puritan roots. L. Baritz. Nation 204:699-700 My 29 '67
PURKINJE cells. See Cells
PURLOINED portrait; drama. See Dias, E. J.
PURNELL, Karl H.
Instructing the peasants. Nation 204:434-5 Ap 3 '67
Marching out the horses. Nation 205:267-9 S 25 '67
Negro in Vietnam. Nation 205:8-10 Jl 3 '67
PUROMYCIN
Puromycin and retention in the goldfish. A. Potts and M. E. Bitterman. bibliog il Science 158:1594-6 D 22 '67
Puromycin effect on memory may be due to occult seizures. H. D. Cohen and S. H. Barondes. bibliog il Science 157:333-4 Jl 21 '67
PURPLE sea urchins. See Sea urchins
PURSES
  Anecdotes, facetiae, satire, etc.
Two for the money and nothing shows. S. Klaw. il Sat Eve Post 240:22 Jl 15 '67
PURSLANE
How to get rid of pigweed. Sunset 138:284 Ap '67

PURVIS, Robert
Robert Purvis & his early challenge to American racism. J. A. Borome. por Negro Hist Bul 30:8-10 My '67
PUT and call transactions
Plunging in puts & calls. il Time 90:104 O 6 '67
Traders take to an arcane art; business in puts and calls. il Bsns W p 153-4+ My 13 '67
PUTMAN, Donald
Art of Donald Putman. F. Whitaker. il por Am Artist 32:50-5+ Ja '68
PUTNAM, Frank W.
Gamma globulins: structure and control of biosynthesis. Science 158:813-14 N 10 '67
—and others
Immunoglobulin structure: variation in amino acid sequence and length of human lambda light chains. bibliog Science 157:1050-3 S 1 '67
PUTNAM, Howard
Suggested intermediate graduate degree. bibliog f Sch & Soc 95:182 Mr 18 '67
PUTNAM, Israel
This hollowed-out ground. C. Carmer. il por Am Heritage 18:58-9+ Je '67
PUTNAM, Judith
(comp) Adult paperbacks. Library J 92:369-403, 2056-82, 3139-73 Ja 15, My 15, S 15 '67
(ed) Books to come (cont) Library J 92:611-90, 1037-62+, 2194-256, 2611-41, 2947-57, 3465-555, 4033-63; 93:100-11 F 1, Mr 1, Je 1, Jl, S 1, O 1, N 1 '67, Ja 1 '68
—and Gersoni, Diane
(comps) Adult paperbacks. Library J 93:324-66 Ja 15 '68
PUTNAM, Leon J.
What hope for hope? Christian Cent 84:1519-21 N 29 '67
PUTNAM'S, G. P, sons
G. P. Putnam's sons will go public in May. Pub W 191:67 Ap 24 '67
PUTTERS (golf) See Golf clubs (sticks)
PUTTING (golf)
Blow for esthetics; croquet style of putting outlawed. P. Ryan. il Sports Illus 26:28-9 Je 5 '67
Chip-putt has some fringe benefits. J. Nicklaus. il Sports Illus 27:64 D 18 '67
One way not to pull is give the ball a push. J. Nicklaus. il Sports Illus 27:72 N 6 '67
Overspin stroke smooths a bumpy route. J. Nicklaus. il Sports Illus 27:56 Jl 17 '67
PUTTING greens
Why not golf right at home? il Sunset 138: 112-14+ My '67
PUZO, Mario
Italians, American style. N Y Times Mag p7+ Ag 6 '67
PYE, Lucian W.
Communism as it wanted to be is through; interview por U S News 62:49-50 Ja 30 '67
Portrait of the Vietcong. Look 32:64-5 Ja 23 '68
PYGMY stars. See Stars, Subdwarf
PYLE, Carter
Hawaiian story. Yachting 122:38-9+ Jl '67
PYLE, Howard
Drive, and stay safe. Parents Mag 42:30 Jl '67
PYNCHON, Thomas
New novel, USA: Thomas Pynchon. R. Sklar. Nation 205:277-80 S 25 '67
PYNE, Joe
TV's new fun game: savagery: television's era of cruelty. B. Williamson. Life 62:25 Ap 7 '67
PYRAMIDS
Atom sleuths seek secret treasures in the pyramids. A. P. Armagnac. il Pop Sci 190: 88-90 Mr '67
PYRANOSE sugars. See Sugars
PYRENEES
  See also
Basque provinces
PYRIMIDINE nucleotides. See Nucleotides
PYRIMIDINES
Growth and sporulation of a pyrimidine spore color mutant of sordaria fimicola. A. S. El-Ani. bibliog il Science 156:88-90 Ap 7 '67
Photoreactivation in vivo of pyrimidine dimers in paramecium DNA. B. M. Sutherland and others. bibliog il Science 158:1699-700 D 29 '67
PYROLYSIS
Burns refuse without a flame. D. A. Hoffman. il Am City 82:102-4 F '67
PYTHAGOREAN theory of music. See Music—Theory

Q

QALQILAH, Jordan
Learning to live with the foe. il Life 63:118-19 S 29 '67
See also
QALQILIYA. See Qalquilah, Jordan

QUACKS and quackery
Facts on quacks: how to lose weight without diet, and other myths. il Todays Health 45:16-18 N '67
Mail-order doctoring, still a menace. R. L. Smith. il Todays Health 45:20-3 Je '67; Same abr. with title Menace of mail-order medicine. Read Digest 91:111-14 O '67
Shocking facts about fake marriage counselors. D. Robinson. Good H 165:74-5+ Jl '67
Use as directed; excerpts from Facts on quacks, what you should know about health quackery. il Todays Health 45:14-15 D '67
See also
Impostors and imposture

QUADE, Quentin L.
Vietnam, is the price too high? America 116:805-9 Je 3 '67

QUAIL shooting
Best quail hunting in the South? G. Gresham. il Field & S 72:34-5+ N '67
Bobtails for bobwhites. D. M. Duffey. il Outdoor Life 140:142-6 O 67
Fun with an old gun. T. Trueblood. il Field & S 72:20+ Ja '68
Hardest bird hunting in Jersey. P. McLain. il Field & S 72:36-9+ D '67
Imp of southern Texas; scaled quail. V. Kraft. Sports Illus 26:41-2+ Ja 30 '67
Kansas quail renaissance. P. Curtis. il Field & S 72:58-9+ O '67

QUAILS
Photoperiodic control of the cloacal gland of the Japanese quail. B. D. Sachs. bibliog il Science 157:201-3 Jl 14 '67
That quail, Robert; excerpt. M. A. Stanger. il Read Digest 90:122-7 Ap '67
See also
Cookery—Game

QUAITI
South Arabia: Nasser and the sultans. J. A. Morris, jr. il Nation 204:358-61 Mr 20 '67
QUAKER relief work. See American Friends service committee
QUAKERS. See Friends, Society of
QUALITY control
Are you selling quality short? W. A. Golomski. il Nations Bsns 55:72-4 D '67
Does zero defects really work? G. Berkwitt; discussion. Duns R 88:18+ D '66
Quality control procedures in book manufacture; panel discussion. il Pub W 192:82-4+ Jl 3 '67
Quality control, testing seen key to future aeronautical advances. J. F. Judge. il Tech W 20:63-4+ Mr 27 '67
QUALITY of products
Buying guide issue (cont) il Consumer Rep 32:1-441 D '67
Dialogue that never happens: marketing and its critics. R. A. Bauer and S. A. Greyser. bibliog f Harvard Bsns R 45:2-4+ N '67
Institute reports on...See issues of Good housekeeping
Long-run economy seen in burn-in tests. il Aviation W 86:84-7 Ja 30 '67
Quality and a pure price index. T. W. Gavett. il Mo Labor R 90:16-20 Mr '67
Speaker for the house. C. Montgomery. See issues of Good housekeeping
Standards and the public interest; address, February 13, 1967. J. H. Hollomon. Vital Speeches 33:364-8 Ap 1 '67
See also
Quality control
Testing
QUANT, Mary
Chez Mlle: Mary Quant at home; excerpts from interview. ed. by E. Blair. pors Mlle 65:82-4+ S '67
about
Mary Quant. limited, kinky success story. M. Cleave. il pors N Y Times Mag p28-9+ Mr 19 '67; Same abr. with title Mary Quant, London's kooky success story. Read Digest 90:109-12 Je '67
QUANTITY cookery. See Cookery, Quantity
QUANTUM mechanics. See Quantum theory
QUANTUM theory
Electrical properties of materials. H. Ehrenreich. il Sci Am 217:194-204 S '67

Kirchhoff-Planck radiation law. J. Agassi. bibliog Science 156:30-7 Ap 7 '67
Optical properties of materials. A. Javan. il Sci Am 217:238-42+ S '67
Selective laser photocatalysis of bromine reactions. W. B. Tiffany and others. bibliog il Science 157:40-3 Jl 7 '67
See also
Time reversal
QUARANTINE, Veterinary
Regulating exotic pets; British problem. F. C. Livingstone. Sci N 92:540 D 2 '67
QUARKS. See Particles (nuclear physics)
QUARRELS
Stop the fighting! bring our girls home! D. Newman and R. Benton. il Mlle 65:48+ S '67
When brothers and sisters fight. B. Bettelheim. il Ladies Home J 84:42+ Ap '67
QUARRY, Jerry
They're still waiting for Jerry. M. Kram. il Sports Illus 27:20-3 N 6 '67
QUARTERBACKS. See Football players
QUARTER-tone music. See Music
QUARTZ
Quartz: extreme preferred orientation produced by annealing. H. W. Green, 2d. bibliog il Science 157:1444-7 S 22 '67
X-ray fabric analysis of hot-worked and annealed quartz. H. R. Wenk and others. il Science 157:1447-9 S 22 '67
QUARTZ crystals
Deformation lamellae parallel to 1013 and 0001 in quartz of the Coeur d'Alene district, Idaho. W. R. Greenwood. bibliog Science 158:1180 D 1 '67
High Q quartz; improved method of quartz crystal growing. il Sci Digest 61:27 Mr '67
QUASARS. See Radio astronomy
QUASHA, George
Lover's request to his beloved; Hieroglyph for a gull; Look there! Mack's at the mike! poems. Poetry 110:382-5 S '67
QUASI-stellar objects. See Radio astronomy
QUASI-stellar radio sources. See Radio astronomy
QUASTEL, J. H.
Membrane structure and function. Science 158:146+ O 6 '67
—See Chan, S. L. jt. auth.
QUATTLEBAUM, Charles A.
Enactments by the 89th Congress relevant to education and training below college grade, 1965-66 Sch & Soc 95:360-3 O 14 '67
QUEBEC (province)
Crisis coming in Canada; with interview with L. Lévesque. il U S News 64:42-6 Ja 15 '68
See also
French Canadians
Gaspé peninsula

Description and travel
Exploring north of nowhere. F. Perry and L. Perry. il Field & S 72:46-9+ Je '67
Steeples and the ferries along the St Lawrence; French Canada. il Sunset 139:22+ O '67
Super '67 vacation: French Canada and a world's fair too. R. Dunlop. il Todays Health 45:24-9+ F '67

Politics and government
De Gaulle's Canadian fiasco. il Newsweek 70:38-9 Ag 7 '67
Free Quebec: how serious a threat? il U S News 63:50 S 11 '67
Nationalism in Quebec, 1967. F. Caloren. Christian Cent 84:913-19, 1102 Jl 12, Ag 30 '67
Quebec's liberty, de Gaulle keeps pushing. U S News 63:16 Ag 14 '67
Spoiler; de Gaulle support of Quebec separatists. il Time 90:22 Ag 4 '67

Religious institutions and affairs
Quebec: secular and free; excerpt from Four o'clock lectures. P. Doucet. Christian Cent 84:910-13 Jl 12 '67
World around us. Christian Cent 84:323-4, 387-9, 1606 Mr 8, 22, D 13 '67
QUEBEC winter carnival. See Carnivals
QUEDENS, Phil
Easy way to make toy building logs. Pop Sci 191:122-3 N '67
QUEEN, Daniel
Electronic guitars and amplifiers. Electr World 77:38-41 F '67
QUEEN, Ellery
House of brass; story. Redbook 130:127-53 Ja '68
QUEEN Elizabeth (ship) See Ocean liners

QUEEN Mary (ship) See Ocean liners
QUEEN of spades; opera. See Tchaikovsky,
  P. I.
QUEENAN, John William
  Accountant of tomorrow; address April 25,
  1966. Vital Speeches 33:200-8 Ja 15 '67
QUEENS, N.Y.

Parks and playgrounds
Park and festival; speeches in honor of
  Flushing Meadows-Corona park. New York-
  er 43:23 Je 17 '67
QUEENS borough public library
  Queens borough trustees refuse union nego-
    tiation. Library J 92:722 F 15 '67
  Queens votes for union in sudden election. Li-
    brary J 92:1783 My 1 '67
QUEENSLAND, Australia
  See also
  Great Barrier Reef
QUEENSLAND ferns. See Ferns
QUENCHING
  Wider use of cryogenic quenching seen. M.
    L. Yaffee. il Aviation W 86:81+ Ap 10 '67
QUENNELL, Peter
  Crusoe's island. Horizon 9:66-83 Spr '67
QUESTER, George H.
  Is the nuclear nonproliferation treaty enough?
    Bul Atomic Sci 23:35-7 N '67
QUESTIONING
  See also
  Police questioning
QUESTIONNAIRES
  Federal paper-work explosion: new form
    bothers universities. B. Nelson. Science 156:
    1468-9 Je 16 '67
  Interdisciplinary communication. R. F. Rush-
    mer. il Science 157:252 Jl 21 '67
QUESTIONS, Childrens. See Childrens ques-
  tions

QUESTIONS and answers

Anecdotes, facetiae, satire, etc.
Answers to questions no one ever asks me,
  alas! L. Rosten. il Look 31:10 Je 27 '67
In place of soft answers. L. Rosten. il Look
  32:14 Ja 23 '68
QUETZALCÓATL
  Way of Quetzalcóatl. T. de Gerez. il Horn
    Bk 43:171-5 bibliog(p 132) Ap '67
QUICK breads. See Bread
QUICKSAND
  Quicksand, the baloney bog. R. Starnes. Field
    & S 72:20+ My '67
QUIE, Albert Harold
  Kicking civil rights upstairs. P. Schrag. Sat
    R 50:49-50 Je 17 '67
  Republican mischief. New Repub 156:4 My 20
    '67
QUIGLEY, Carroll
  Creative writer today. Cath World 206:111-17
    D '67
QUILICO, Louis
  Return of the native; interview, ed. by F.
    Stevenson. pors Opera N 31:16 My 13 '67
QUIMBY, Ian M. G.
  Mark Fisher: an American impressionist. An-
    tiques 91:780-3 Je '67
QUINACRINE. See Atabrine
QUINCY, Mass.
  Quincy builds a new vocational-technical cur-
    riculum. N. Farmer. il Am Ed 3:12-13+
    Jl '67
QUININE
  Quinine cartel on the record. il Sci N 91:302
    Ap 1 '67
  Quinine price comes back to earth; Senate
    exposure of international cartel. il Bsns
    W p 139-40+ Ap 8 '67
QUINN, James Brian
  Technological forecasting. bibliog f Harvard
    Bsns R 45:89-106 Mr '67
QUINN, John Robert
  By candlelight; poem. Christian Cent 84:
    1595 D 13 '67
  Family album; poem. Commonweal 87:120
    O 27 '67
  From porches; poem. Christian Cent 84:896
    Jl 12 '67
QUINTANA, Bernardo
  Incubating industry in Mexico. il pors Bsns
    W p86-8 Je 24 '67
QUINTUPLETS
  How to raise quints without going crazy.
    G. Cameron. il Ladies Home J 84:102-3+
    My '67
  Quints on a picnic; Fischer quintuplets. A.
    Bayer. il Sat Eve Post 240:24-31 S 9 '67
QUISHQUI Puncu. See Indians of South Amer-
  ica—Antiquities—Peru
QUIST, Veronica M.
  Regional report. Home Gard 54:51 Jl '67

QUITO, Ecuador
Description
Summer seminar in Ecuador; travel-study
  program by Ecuador's Ministry of educa-
  tion and U.S. embassy with University of
  Oregon summer session. J. Moorhead. il
  Sr Schol 90:sup 13-14 Mr 3 '67
QUIZZES. See Information tests
QUOIREZ, Françoise. See Sagan, F. pseud.
QUOTAS, import. See Import quotas
QUOTATIONS
  Quotable quotes. See issues of Reader's digest
  Quotemanship, by P. F. Boller, jr. Review
    Sat R 50:56+ Je 10 '67. R. Walters, jr
    See also
  Children—Sayings
  Plagiarism
    also subhead Quotations, maxims, etc.
  under various subjects, e.g. Music—Quota-
  tions, maxims, etc.
QURAISHY, Masood
  Wild game in East Africa. K. Sharma. il U S
    Camera 30:44-7 O '67

R

R-factor genes. See Genes
RCIA. See Retail clerks international associa-
  tion
RDF (radio direction finders) See Radio in
  navigation
REA. See United States—Rural electrification
  administration
REA express. See Railway express agency, in-
  corporated
REM (rapid eye movement) sleep. See Sleep
Rh factors
  Agglutinating specificity for LW factor in
    guinea pig and rabbit anti-Rh serums. P.
    Levine and M. J. Celano. bibliog il Science
    156:1744-6 Je 30 '67
  Controlling Rh mismatch; anti-Rh antibodies
    vaccination. Time 90:60 N 17 '67
  GG vs. Rh disease. Newsweek 69:62 Ja 30 '67
  Unborn baby's fight to live. J. Blank. il
    Redbook 128:74-5+ Mr '67
  Vaccine conquers baby-killer; RhoGAM for
    Rh disease. B. J. Culliton. il Sci N 92:
    520-1 N 25 '67
R. J. Reynolds foods, incorporated. See Rey-
  nolds, R. J., foods, incorporated
RNA. See Ribonucleic acid
ROTC. See United States—Reserve officers
  training corps
RPMI. See Roswell Park memorial institute
RSV (Revised standard version) See Bible—
  Versions
RTCM. See Radio technical commission for
  marine services
RABANNE, Paco
  For the woman who needs added mystery. por
    Life 62:54 My 26 '67
  Now and future Paco Rabanne. il Vogue
    149:204-5+ Mr 1 '67
RABB, Ellis
  APA's big season. M. Gussow. il por News-
    week 71:57 Ja 1 '68
RABBET-miter joints. See Joints (carpentry)
RABBIT hunting
  Best ways to hunt rabbits East to West. J.
    Bashline; C. Carpenter; J. Freeman. il Field
    & S 72:46-7+ Ja '68
  Cottontails are tough critters. D. J. Anderson.
    il Field & S 72:56-7+ S '67
  Hounds to trail ghosts! D. J. Anderson. il
    Field & S 72:48-9+ O '67
  One small gun for all small game. H. Brad-
    shaw. il Field & S 72:54-5+ N '67
  Rabbit hunt, Indian style. J. Downs. il Out-
    door Life 139:54-5+ Je '67
  Runway rabbit hunt. J. S. Flannery. il Out-
    door Life 139:74-6 Mr '67
RABBITS
  Great rabbit war; wild rabbits in Australia.
    H. Earl. il Sci Digest 62:18-20 N '67
    See also
  Cookery—Game
RABI, Isidor Isaac
  Time to leave the house. il por Time 89:46+
    My 26 '67
RABIES
Preventive inoculation
Bite of a shrew, and a life-or-death deci-
  sion. R. B. Stolley. il Life 63:63-4+ Ag 11
  '67

RABIES—Preventive inoculation—*Continued*
Father's decision: case of Michael LeBrun.
il Newsweek 69:67 Mr 20 '67
Life-or-death decision with a happy ending.
S. Frank. il Good H 165:48+ O '67
RABINOWITCH, Eugene
Communications satellites; introduction. Bul
Atomic Sci 23:2-3 Ap '67
New Year's thoughts 1967. Bul Atomic Sci
23:2-3 Ja '67
What is sauce for the goose is sauce for the
gander. Bul Atomic Sci 23:41-3 S '67
RABORG, Frederick A. Jr
Transient nativity; story. Horn Bk 43:772-8
D '67
RACCOON hunting
Great coon hunt. E. A. Bauer. il Outdoor
Life 140:48-9+ N '67
RACCOONS
Nature note. Sci N 92:364 O 14 '67
RACE attitudes. See Attitudes
RACE car drivers. See Automobile drivers
RACE cooperation. See Interracial cooperation
RACE differences. See Racial differences
RACE discrimination
City v. the publisher; abuse of Negroes by
the Lynchburg, Va. press. Time 89:78 My
5 '67
Discrimination against Negroes. O. D. Dun-
can. bibliog f il Ann Am Acad 371:85-103
My '67
International day for the elimination of racial
discrimination; text of message; with text
of resolution adopted October 26, 1966.
Thant. UN Mo Chron 4:1-iii Mr '67
Lynchburg's daily shame; papers' treatment
of Negroes. Newsweek 69:88 My 8 '67
When city bites newspaper, that's news; white
community reacts to racist policies of the
News and Daily advance. Life 62:4 My 12
'67
See also
Discrimination in education
Discrimination in employment
Negroes in the United States—Segregation
Race prejudice
United Nations—Sub-commission on preven-
tion of discrimination and protection of
minorities
RACE horses
Best racehorses in all the world; Argentine
thoroughbred racehorses. W. Tower. il
Sports Illus 26:52-5 My 1 '67
Buckmaker; Buckpasser for stud duty. il
Time 90:65 Jl 7 '67
Building an empire on horses ready to run;
entrepreneur O'Farrell. P. Axthelm. il
Sports Illus 26:45-8 Ja 23 '67
Clarion call: Kentucky Derby won by Proud
Clarion. Time 89:66 My 12 '67
Clarion call: $62.20! third highest payoff in
Derby history. W. Tower. il Sports Illus
26:20-5 My 15 '67
Clarion victory; winner of the Kentucky
Derby. Newsweek 69:68 My 15 '67
Damascus against the world; America's
horse of the year. W. Tower. Sports Illus
27:64 N 6 '67
Derby daze. il Newsweek 69:72 My 8 '67
Derby tip: look for a colt back in the barn.
W. Tower. il Sports Illus 26:22-3 Mr 6 '67
Fastest run in the West; Argentine champion
Forli at Hollywood park. W. Tower. Sports
Illus 26:70 My 29 '67
Fillies may be better than the colts. W.
Tower. Sports Illus 26:54 F 20 '67
Hard ride all the way; ed. by W. Tower.
B. Hartack. il Sports Illus 26:60-4+ Mr
27; 30-2+ Ap 3; 58-62+ Ap 10 '67
Hopeful time for all; photographs by J.
Cooke and others; with account by W.
Tower and D. Jenkins. Sports Illus 27:16-
21 S 4 '67
How to stay in the money; champion thor-
oughbreds for breeding purposes. il Bsns W
p96 Jl 1 '67
In Reality shows that he's for real; Florida
derby winner. W. Tower. il Sports Illus
26:83-5 Ap 10 '67
Invader is there; Ruken, Kentucky Derby
contender. W. Tower. il Sports Illus 26:16-
19 My 1 '67
Painful prognosis for the good Dr Fager;
Kentucky Derby favorites. W. Tower. il
Sports Illus 26:74-8 Ap 24 '67
Passing of the ghost; Native Dancer. il
Time 90:87 N 24 '67
Race track. A. Minor. See issues of New
Yorker
Rushing out of the barn and into the picture;
Damascus, Bay Shore stakes winner. W.
Tower. il Sports Illus 26:54-5 Ap 3 '67

Shades of Silky! Reflected Glory and Ruken,
Flamingo and Santa Anita derby winners.
W. Tower. il Sports Illus 26:18-21 Mr 13
'67
Toe that stopped a show; Santa Anita's big
race won by Howard Keck's Drin. W.
Tower. il Sports Illus 26:52-3 F 6 '67
Why Buckpasser's mission to Paris was
scrubbed. W. Tower. Sports Illus 26:62
Je 26 '67
Winner but not yet king; Damascus winner
of Belmont stakes. W. Tower. il Sports
Illus 26:26-9 Je 12 '67
With an assist from pal Duffy; Damascus at
Pimlico. W. Tower. il Sports Illus 26:26-9
My 29 '67
RACE improvement. See Eugenics
RACE prejudice
Backlash in Boston, and across the U.S. il
Newsweek 70:29-30+ N 6 '67
Bigot, spare that tree; school board kills
federal summer program for white and
Negro underprivileged children in Wake
County, N.C. Nation 205:133 Ag 28 '67
Bigotry's greedy roots; white man's op-
pression of the Negro. Christian Cent 84:
1547-8 D 6 '67
Dark underside. New Repub 157:4 S 30 '67
Death at an early age; excerpt. J. Kozol.
Atlan 220:49-55 S '67
John Bull and Jim Crow; color prejudice in
Britain. Newsweek 69:37 My 1 '67
Portrait of a wretched man: R. Williams of
Monroe, N.C. M. Renek. New Repub 157:11-
13 S 30 '67
Requiem for the urban school; experiences
of H. Kohl and J. Kozol in Boston and
Harlem. E. Z. Friedenberg. il Sat R 50:
77-9+ N 18 '67
Village school downtown, by P. Schrag. Re-
view
New Repub 156:33-5 My 20 '67. J. Kozol
Sat R 50:90 My 20 '67. R. Coles
White pieties and black reality. R. Coles. il
Sat R 50:57-9+ D 16 '67
See also
Anti-Semitism
Jews and Negroes
Negroes in the United States—Segregation
Race problems
Racism

Anecdotes, facetiae, satire, etc.
Love in a small room. M. Finn. il Good H
165:56+ Jl '67
Mission of Melchizedek Truepew. T. W.
Moore. Christian Cent 84:1397-8 N 1 '67
RACE problems
Color of want. W. Gordimer. Nation 204:
313-15 Mr 6 '67
See also
Business and race problems
Church and race problems
Interracial cooperation
Minorities
Race discrimination
Race prejudice
Race relations
also subhead Race problems under names
of continents, countries, etc. e.g. South
Africa—Race problems
RACE problems in literature
From the ashes: voices of Watts, ed. by B.
Schulberg. Review
Sat R 50:78 S 23 '67. P. Thomas
RACE relations
After the riots: a survey, how the flare-ups
affected. U.S. racial attitudes. il Newsweek
70:18-19 Ag 21 '67
And the world stopped, waiting; first prize!
Teachers' writing competition. J. Heimo-
witz. NEA J 56:21-3 O '67
...Because he was black and I was white;
symposium, ed. by E. Sutherland. Mlle 64:
224-5+ Ap '67
Beyond the riots. E. Roper. Sat R 50:24-5 O
7 '67
Black and white, by W. Brink and L. Harris.
Review
Sat R il 50:28 Ag 5 '67. E. R. Lincoln
Black power and the American Christ. V.
Harding; discussion. Christian Cent 84:
214 F 15 '67
Black power: its goals and methods; inter-
view. N. Hare. il U S News 62:64-6+ My 22
'67
Black racism. N. Cousins. Sat R 50:34 S 30 '67
Called to reconciliation; excerpt from In-
strument of thy peace. A. Paton. Christian
Cent 84:1628-9 D 20 '67
Can I practice what I preach? H. J. Burn.
McCalls 94:62+ Ap '67
Comparison of industrial and race conflict. I.
Bernstein. Mo Labor R 90:39-40 Jl '67

RACE relations—*Continued*
From the Oasis. V. Arness. il Ebony 22:112-14+ O '67
How the white problem spawned black power. A. F. Poussaint. il Ebony 22:88-90+ Ag '67
Maybe God will come and clean up this mess. R. Coles. il Atlan 220:103-6 O '67
Memo from the ghetto: the dispirit of '67. E. Dunbar. Look 31:92 S 19 '67
My parents are so narrow-minded! questions and answers. A. Wood. Seventeen 26:210 Mr '67
Negro millionaire's advice to his race; interview. ed. by F. X. Tolbert. H. T. Taylor. U S News 63:68-9 S 4 '67
Negro soldier's memory. W. M. Young, jr. McCalls 95:168 D '67
Nervous Nellies on race relations? school libraries. A. G. Mims. bibliog Library J 92:1291-3+ Mr 15 '67
New Negro mood: urban Negro attitudes; with editorial comment. R. Beardwood. il Fortune 77:127-8, 146-51+ Ja '68
No armistice; arms buying and charges of terrorism. il Newsweek 70:36 O 16 '67
Race wars in the making. G. Lichtheim. Commentary 43:62-6 Ja '67; Discussion. 44:6+ Ag '67
Riots and revolution. F. M. Henley; R. A. Schroth. America 117:150-3 Ag 12 '67
Spirit of Newark, U.S.A. America 117:105 Jl 29 '67
Splitting over Adam: the liberal-Negro breach. F. E. Kearns. Commonweal 85:443 Ja 27 '67
Stranger at the gates, by T. Sugarman. Review
New Repub 156:28+ F 4 '67. E. Sutherland
Surinam: multiracial paradise at the crossroads. E. B. Thompson. il Ebony 22:112-16+ F '67
To our Negro brothers. M. Ascoli. Reporter 37:12 Ag 10 '67
Up from hate. T. Slaughter. il Sat R 50:59 D 16 '67
Way to racial peace in America; interview. R. Wilkins. il U S News 63:80-6 S 25 '67
Which way for the Negro? il Newsweek 69:27-8+ My 15 '67
RACE tracks
Disaster at a thorny barricade; Grand national at Aintree. W. Tower. il Sports Illus 26:32-4+ Ap 17 '67
One tough little guy; S. Silberman, owner of Tropical Park racetrack, Miami. J. Underwood. il Sports Illus 26:54-62 F 6 '67
They never sleep. S. Toperoff. Atlan 220:77-80 O '67
See also
Speedways
RACHAL, Hal
Mitey Mooney. il por Time 90:106+ D 1 '67
RACHLEFF, Owen
Saturday, June 14, 1800. Opera N 32:24-5 Ja 13 '68
RACHLIN, Howard, and Hineline, P. N.
Training and maintenance of keypecking in the pigeon by negative reinforcement. bibliog Science 157:954-5 Ag 25 '67
RACIAL differences
Race & ability; Time essay. Time 90:46-7 S 29 '67
Racial studies: Academy states position on call for new research; statement of National academy of sciences. .Science 158:892-3 N 17 '67
Researching racial inferiority? il Time 89:65 F 3 '67
RACIAL discrimination. See Race discrimination
RACIAL equality. See Equality
RACIAL extinction. See Genocide
RACING. See Airplane racing; Automobile racing; and similar headings
RACING car engines. See Automobile engines
RACING cars. See Automobiles, Racing
RACISM
Black racism. N. Cousins. Sat R 50:34 S 30 '67
Last word (we hope) on George Lincoln Rockwell. F. C. Shapiro. il Esquire 67:101-5+ F '67
Mr Genocide; views of black power militants. S. Alsop. Sat Eve Post 240:14 S 9 '67
See also
Race prejudice
RACKETEERING
Bombs in the bayous; bombing of wells and pipelines in Louisiana. il Newsweek 71:55 Ja 8 '68
New York seeks tighter airport security. R. F. Coburn. Aviation W 88:35 Ja 1 '68

Organized crime in the United States. G. R. Blakey. bibliog f Cur Hist 52:327-33+ Je '67
Scandal in the Bahamas. R. Oulahan and W. Lambert. il Life 62:58-66+ F 3 '67
See also
Mafia
RACKETS, Tennis. See Tennis rackets
RACKHAM, Arthur
Arthur Rackham, 1867-1939. E. Shaffer. il Horn Bk 43:617-21 O '67
Rackham hour; exhibition at Columbia university. New Yorker 43:54-5 D 9 '67
RACKS, Wine. See Wine racks
RADAR
CAL readying radar system to study microwave, plasma. R. Barnhart. il Tech W 20:30+ My 29 '67

Antenna and scanning mechanisms

Radar design offers X- or C-band option. K. J. Stein. il Aviation W 87:106-7+ Ag 14 '67
Technique adds electronic scan to precision monopulse radars. K. J. Stein. il Aviation W 86:77-8+ Je 12 '67

Mapping applications

Bistatic-radar detection of lunar scattering centers with Lunar Orbiter. I. G. L. Tyler and others. il Science 157:193-5 Jl 14 '67

Military applications

Family of radars available for Nike-X use. P. J. Klass. il Aviation W 87:110-11+ O 23 '67
New FPS-85 will not help against FOBS; spacetracking radar complex. F. Burnham. il Aero Tech 21:22-3 D 18 '67
Radar signature analysis; White Sands missile range in New Mexico. E. A. Lacy. il Electr World 77:23-5+ F '67
RCA, Radiation undertaking radar improvements at ETR. il Aero Tech 21:34+ O 23 '67
See also
Radar defense networks
RADAR altimeters. See Altimeters
RADAR defense networks
AWACS moves toward key decisions. Aero Tech 21:8 D 18 '67
AWACS overland radar tests start; new airborne warning and control system. P. J. Klass. il Aviation W 86:87-8+ Ap 10 '67
See also
Guided missiles—Defenses
RADAR detectors. See Detectors
RADAR flares. See Flares
RADAR in astronomy
Radar astronomy. V. R. Eshleman. bibliog il Science 158:585-97 N 3 '67
RADAR in aviation
ARTS in Atlanta; advanced radar traffic system. il Flying 82:32-4 Ja '68
Bullseye GCA radar uses phased array; new precision approach radar to simplify ground control approach. P. J. Klass. il Aviation W 87:56-7+ Jl 3 '67
F-111A flies land profile supersonically. P. J. Klass. il Aviation W 84:84-5+ Ja 23 '67
FAA to seek proposals on terminal radar control. W. Andrews. Aero Tech 21:16-17 N 6 '67
Hughes ADGE consoles shown in Belgium. R. van Osten. il Tech W 21:21 Jl 3 '67
See also
Airports—Traffic control
Transponders
RADAR in navigation
Is radar worthwhile? R. Mitchell. il Motor B 120:38-9+ S '67
New Q-band marine radar. R. Humphrey. il Electr World 77:32-3 Ap '67
Radar for safer boating; excerpts. J. West. il Yachting 121:66-9+ My; 122:47-9+ Jl '67
RADAR in tracking and trailing
Birdwatching seriously. il Sci N 91:245 Mr 11 '67
Radar observations of insects in free flight. K. M. Glover and others; reply R. C. Rainey. bibliog Science 157:98 Jl 7 '67
RADAR interference
USAF boosts North Viet ECM jamming; electronic-countermeasures. C. Brownlow. il Aviation W 86:22-5 F 6 '67
RADAR meteorology
Radar design offers X- or C-band option. K. J. Stein. il Aviation W 87:106-7+ Ag 14 '67
Radar observations of insects in free flight. K. M. Glover and others; reply R. C. Rainey. bibliog Science 157:98 Jl 7 '67
RADAR simulators. See Simulators
RADAR target simulators. See Simulators

RADBURN, N.J. See Fair Lawn, N.J.

RADCLIFFE, George
World striper record tied. Field & S 72:68-9 S '67

RADCLIFFE, Woodward
Doctor and his garden. Pop Gard 18:69-71 D '67
These driveways are prize-winners. Pop Gard 18:66-8 D '67

RADCLIFFE college, Cambridge, Mass.
Courtyard unifies varied elements and spaces; four-level library. il Arch Rec 141:155-8 My '67

RADEMAEKERS, William
Report from east Europe. Fortune 76:77+ O '67

RADER, Dotson
Deadly friendship. New Repub 157:13-15 S 23 '67
Princeton weekend with the SDS. New Repub 157:14-16 D 9 '67

RADFORD, Edward P. Jr. See Little, J. B. jt. auth.

RADIAL saws. See Saws

RADIATION
Background radiation and the birth of the universe. Sci N 92:582 D 16 '67
Charge transfer between raindrops. J. D. Sartor and W. R. Atkinson. bibliog il Science 157:1267-9 S 15 '67
Radiation damage at high temperatures. J. R. Weir, jr. bibliog il Science 156:1689-95 Je 30 '67

See also
Gamma rays
Glass, Effect of radiation on
Heat—Radiation and absorption
Mossbauer effect
X rays

Laws and regulations
Carcinogenic mines; Public contracts act invoked. D. Sanford. New Repub 156:5-6 Je 3 '67

Measurement
Carbon-14 and tritium measurement by means of bremsstrahlung emissions. J. C. Rosen and others. bibliog il Science 157:77-8 Jl 7 '67
Isotropy of cosmic background radiation at 4080 megahertz. R. W. Wilson and A. A. Penzias. bibliog il Science 156:1100-1 My 26 '67
New measurements of the cosmic microwave background. G. E. Mumford. Sky & Tel 35: 10 Ja '68

See also
Remote sensing systems
Television receivers—Color receivers—Radiation hazards

Physiological effects
Dopamine protects mice against whole-body irradiation. K. N. Prasad and M. H. Van Woert. bibliog il Science 155:470-2 Ja 27 '67
Herpes-type virus and chromosome marker in normal leukocytes after growth with irradiated Burkitt cells. W. Henle and others. bibliog il Science 157:1064-5 S 1 '67
Inhibition of lipolytic action of growth hormone and glucocorticoid by ultraviolet and X-radiation. J. N. Fain. bibliog il Science 157:1062-4 S 1 '67
Langerhans cells: uptake of tritiated thymidine. L. Giacometti and W. Montagna. il Science 157:439-40 Jl 28 '67
Oncogenicity by DNA tumor viruses: enhancement after ultraviolet and cobalt-60 radiations. V. Defendi and F. Jensen. bibliog il Science 157:703-5 Ag 11 '67
Radiation and the patterns of nature; excerpts from address, March 24, 1965. G. M. Woodwell. bibliog il Science 156:461-70 Ap 28 '67
Radiation of hemocyanin: inactivation and reactivation of oxygen-carrying capacity. J. Schubert and E. R. White. bibliog il Science 155:1000-3 F 24 '67
Serum alpha globulin fraction: survival-and-recovery effect in irradiated mice. M. G. Hanna, jr. and others. bibliog il Science 157:1458-61 S 22 '67
Ultraviolet irradiation of DNA in vitro and in vivo produces a third thymine-derived product. A. J. Varghese and S. Y. Wang. bibliog il Science 156:955-7 My 19 '67
Warning in Washington; calm in Montreal. Sci N 92:253 S 9 '67

See also
X rays—Physiological effects

Safety devices and measures
Radiation hazards: Senate bill would provide federal regulation. K. Sperry. Science 157: 1292-3 S 15 '67; Discussion. 158:1397-8 D 15 '67
Radiation protection; report on symposium. R. L. Kathren. Science 156:544-6+ Ap 28 '67

RADIATION, Solar. See Solar radiation

RADIATION belts
See also
Van Allen radiation belts

RADIATION in the body. See Radioactive substances in the body

RADIATION shielding. See Shielding (radiation)

RADIATION sickness
Association of illness with prior ingestion of novel foods. S. H. Revusky and E. W. Bedarf. bibliog il Science 155:219-20 Ja 13 '67
Kuboyama and the saga of the Lucky Dragon; reprint, adaptation of The voyage of the Lucky Dragon, by R. E. Lapp. R. Hudson. il UNESCO Courier 20:40-5 Ag '67

RADICAL left (politics) See Right and left (political science)

RADICAL right (politics) See Right and left (political science)

RADICAL right conservatives. See Right and left (political science)

RADICALS (chemistry)
Atom reactions in flow tubes. B. A. Thrush. bibliog il Science 156:470-3 Ap 28 '67
Chlorination of unsaturated compounds in nonpolar media. M. L. Poutsma. bibliog il Science 157:997-1005 S 1 '67
Mechanisms of organic oxidation and reduction by metal complexes. J. K. Kochi. bibliog il Science 155:415-24 Ja 27 '67
Paramagnetic resonance spectra of methyl radicals on porous glass surfaces. M. Fujimoto and others. bibliog il Science 156:1105-6 My 26 '67
Radio reflection by free radicals in earth's atmosphere. J. D. Barry and others. bibliog il Science 156:1730-2 Je 30 '67; Reply with rejoinder. P. L. Bender. 158:1487-8 D 15 '67

RADICALS and radicalism
See also
Right and left (political science)

RADICH, Stephen
Battle over the Bill of rights. F. Powledge. il Life 62:22-5+ Mr 31 '67

RADIN, Alex
Artificial lakes: multi-purpose reservoirs. Parks & Rec 2:16-17+ Ag '67

RADINSKY, Leonard
Relative brain size: a new measure. bibliog Science 155:836-8 F 17 '67

RADIO
See also
Telegraph, Wireless

RADIO, Military. See Radio communication, Military

RADIO, Police. See Police radio

RADIO advertising
Commercial undertaking; Forest Lawn memorial park, commercials on radio. Newsweek 70:92 D 11 '67
FCC ruling on cigarette ads: health groups react warily. L. J. Carter. Science 158:888-92 N 17 '67
Smoking and health: FCC demands an antidote to cigarette ads. L. J. Carter. il Science 157:406-8 Jl 28 '67

RADIO aids to navigation. See Radio in navigation

RADIO amateurs. See Radio operators, Amateur

RADIO amplifiers. See Amplifiers

RADIO and copyright. See Copyright—Broadcasting rights

RADIO and television. See Radio broadcasting and television

RADIO antennas
Antennas for CB and business radio. il Electr World 77:38-9+ Mr '67
Build a stacked-antenna AM radio. A. Trauffer. il Pop Electr 26:40 My '67
Designs for log-periodic FM & TV antennas. H. D. Pruett. il Electr World 78:46-8+ D '67
40-pole; vertical monopole. R. N. Tellefsen. il Pop Electr 27:82 N '67
Hot plasma studied as antenna possibility. G. S. Hunter. il Aviation W 86:77+ F 20 '67
Improve your FM reception. R. Angus. il Hi Fi 17:43-6 Jl '67
Long-boom antennas to map cosmic noise; radio astronomy explorer satellite. W. S. Beller. il Tech W 20:34-5 F 20 '67

RADIO antennas—*Continued*
New antenna aids LaGuardia approaches. K. J. Stein. il Aviation W 86:74+ Je 26 '67
Portable satellite communications link. il Electr World 77:69 F '67
Scrounge, an instant J antenna. A. S. Von Trott. il Pop Electr 25:46+ D '66

RADIO apparatus
Cover story; citizens band and business radio equipment. il Electr World 77:28 Mr '67
Information central; questions and answers. C. J. Schauers. il Pop Electr 26:68-70+ F; 66-8+ Mr; 76-8+ Ap; 81-3 My; 68-70 Je; 27:64-6 Jl '67
See also
Radio instruments

Medical application
See Radio in medicine

RADIO apparatus on aircraft
AF plans study contracts for integrated aircraft unit; communications, navigation and identification system. Aero Tech 21:15 N 6 '67
USAF weighs single transceiver concept. P. J. Klass. il Aviation W 87:75+ D 18 '67
See also
Radio telephone on aircraft

RADIO apparatus on ships, boats, etc.
See also
Radio telephone on ships, boats, etc.

RADIO astronomy
Brightness variations of quasars. G. S. Mumford. Sky & Tel 33:354-5 Je '67
Carbon broadcasts. Sci N 91:593 Je 24 '67
Continent-wide antennas probe space. Sci N 92:370 O 14 '67
Crab nebula in X-rays; radio source mapped. il Sci N 91:330-1 Ap 8 '67
Data, not answers; evidence for big bang comes from study of quasars. Sci N 91:111 F 4 '67
Emission-line variability and distance of quasars. J. Pfleiderer and M. Grewing. bibliog Science 157:544-5 Ag 4 '67
Explosion in astronomy. G. Berry. il Sci Digest 61:43-54 My '67
Farther-out quasar. Time 89:37 Ap 7 '67
Flux density of cassiopeia-A at 3.0 megacycles per second. R. Parthasarathy. bibliog il Science 158:1449-50 D 15 '67
Fourth Texas symposium; relativistic astrophysics. L. C. Green. il Sky & Tel 34:84-8, 153-6 Ag-S '67
Galaxies and quasars at Prague. T. L. Page. il Sky & Tel 34:372-6; 35:16-20 D '67, Ja '68 (to be cont)
Galaxies as gravitational lenses. D. Sadeh. bibliog il Science 158:1176-8 D 1 '67
How near the quasar? Thomas Matthews' new finding. il Time 90:53 D 29 '67
Intensity fluctuations of a relativistically expanding source. A. G. Petschek. bibliog Science 156:239 Ap 14 '67
Is mysterium the message? emission lines produced by the hydroxyl radical. Sci Am 217:50 O '67
Long-boom antennas to map cosmic noise; radio astronomy explorer satellite. W. S. Beller. il Tech W 20:34-5 F 20 '67
Maser here. Hello, there! radiation waves from hydroxyl clouds. Newsweek 70:84 S 11 '67
Measuring quasars. Sci N 91:544-5 Je 10 '67
New ideas on the red shift. T. D. Nicholson. il Natur Hist 76:34-6 F '67
New window to heavens. A. Ewing. il Sci N 91:504-5 My 27 '67
Night at the observatory; studying quasars at Mount Palomar. H. S. F. Cooper, jr. il Horizon 9:108-16 Sum '67
Primeval fireball. P. J. F. Peebles and D. T. Wilkinson. il Sci Am 216:28-37 bibliog (p 155) Je '67
Quasar distance measured. il Sci N 92:607 D 23 '67
Quasar 3C 446. A. J. Wesselink and J. Hunter, jr. il Science 156:103-4 Ap 7 '67
Quasars: rapid light fluctuations. W. H. McCrea. bibliog Science 157:400-2 Jl 28 '67
Quasi-stellar objects: possible local origin. J. Terrell; reply with rejoinder. J. M. Barnothy. bibliog Science 156:264-5 Ap 14 '67
Radio astronomy: NSF scrutinizing proposals for six major instruments. V. K. McElheny. Science 157:732-4 Ag 18 '67
Radio measurements in space; radio astronomy explorer satellite. J. H. Wujek, jr. il Electr World 77:46-7+ My '67
Radio observations of interstellar hydroxyl radicals. A. H. Barrett. bibliog il Science 157:881-9 Ag 25 '67

Radio sources in the vicinity of source M 31. C. M. Varsavsky. bibliog il Science 158:1043-5 N 24 '67
Science in high gear; X-ray astronomy. A. Ewing. il Sci N 92:14-15 Jl 1 '67
Structure of radio sources. Sky & Tel 33:163 Mr '67
Twinkling galaxy; quasar distance observation. Sci Am 217:49-50 D '67
X-ray stars. R. Giacconi. Sci Am 217:36-46 bibliog(p 158) D '67
X rays from a quasar. Time 90:56 Jl 14 '67
X-rays from beyond the Milky way. il Sci N 92:77-8 Jl 22 '67
X-rays from sources 3C 273 and M 87. H. Friedman and E. T. Byram. bibliog il Science 158:257-9 O 13 '67
See also
National radio astronomy observatory, Green Bank, W.Va.
Radio telescope

RADIO astronomy explorer (satellite) *See* Artificial satellites—Astronomical applications

RADIO attenuators
Micro-Precision's attenuator prevents accidental actuation. il Tech W 20:35 Je 26 '67

RADIO beacons
Litton radio relay/beacon tested for jungle air drops. C. D. LaFond. il Tech W 20:34-5 Je 19 '67

RADIO broadcasting

Comedy
See Radio broadcasting—Humor

Conversation programs
Margaret Truman's new life; interview program: Author in the news. G. Shalit. il Look 31:26-8 Ap 18 '67
Truth helps; Boston's WGBH, A chance to grow series. R. L. Shayon. Sat R 50:79 Ap 22 '67

Educational applications
See Radio in education

Foreign language programs
New sound of radio. W. H. Honan. il N Y Times Mag p56-8+ D 3 '67

Frequency allocation
See Radio frequency allocation

History
Radio's heroic age. il Newsweek 70:96-7 N 13 '67
This month's feature: the question of pay television. Cong Digest 46:289-314 D '67

Humor
It's a bird! it's a plane! whoops, it's a bird; Chickenman. Time 89:67+ Je 9 '67
Larry Josephson; interview. L. Josephson. New Yorker 43:25-6 Je 17 '67

Illegal applications
See also
Radio stations, Illegal

International aspects
Protocol to U.S.-Mexico radio agreement enters into force. Dept State Bul 56:224 F 6 '67
U.S. and Mexico resume talks on radio broadcasting agreement. Dept State Bul 56:352-3 F 27 '67
See also
Radio broadcasting—Propaganda

Music
Pop goes Murray; change in record selections over WOR-FM. il Newsweek 70:100+ O 16 '67
Radio: the languishing giant; U.S, Great Britain, Japan. R. Swing. Sat R 50:53 Ag 12 '67
Treasury of Toscanini broadcasts; NBC symphony orchestra album. R. Lawrence. Sat R 50:61-My 27 '67
See also
Disc jockeys
Radio broadcasting—Opera

News
Happening sound; all-news stations. Newsweek 70:84 Ag 28 '67
News, news, news. Time 90:51-2 S 22 '67
Radio: the languishing giant. R. Swing. Sat R 50:51-3 Ag 12 '67
Under military control; American forces network in Europe. Time 91:57 Ja 5 '68

RADIO in aviation
Army evaluates portable beacon system. K. J. Stein. il Aviation W 86:98-9+ Mr 20 '67
New antenna aids LaGuardia approaches. K. J. Stein. il Aviation W 86:74+ Je 26 '67
Tu-114 avionic lack may delay U.S.-Moscow route; concerning installation of VOR/DME. Aviation W 86:40 Ap 3 '67
See also
Decca navigation
Radio apparatus on aircraft
Radio beacons
Tacan

RADIO in education
Truth helps; Boston's WGBH, A chance to grow series. R. L. Shayon. Sat R 50:79 Ap 22 '67
See also
Radio stations, Educational

RADIO in government
See also
Voice of America (radio program)

RADIO in medicine
Ham radio club beams help to distant jungle medics; Project MED-AID of Duke medical center amateur radio club. Todays Health 45:33 Ag '67

RADIO in navigation
Radio navigation aids. J. West. il Yachting 122:51-3+ Ag '67
Sure, you can radio-navigate yourself home. E. L. Hilts. il Pop Sci 191:112-14 S '67

RADIO in politics
See also
Radio broadcasting—Propaganda

RADIO in tracking and trailing
Radio tracking of homing bats. T. C. Williams and J. M. Williams. bibliog il Science 155:1435-6 Mr 17 '67

RADIO instruments
Test equipment for CB and business radio. D. Walker. il Electr World 77:32-3+ Mr '67

RADIO interference
Clatter stopper. I. C. Chapel. il Pop Electr 26:57-8 Je '67

RADIO interferometers. See Interferometers

RADIO interviews. See Interviewing

RADIO laws and regulations
Broadcasting and impartiality. America 118:26-7 Ja 13 '68
Your time is my time; equal-time rule. Newsweek 71:46 Ja 8 '68
See also
United States—Federal communications commission

RADIO Luxembourg. See Radio broadcasting—Luxembourg

RADIO medical service. See Radio in medicine

RADIO modulation. See Modulation (electronics)

RADIO operators, Amateur
Amateur radio. H. S. Brier. See issues of Popular electronics
Short-wave listening, H. Bennett. See issues of Popular electronics

Licenses
New incentive regulations for hams: what happens now? R. M. Brown. il Electr World 78:32-4+ D '67

RADIO plays
Pride and prejudice; dramatization of novel by J. Austen. D. Newman. Plays 26:83-96 Ap '67
Wuthering Heights. L. Olfson. Plays 27:87-96 Ja '68

RADIO program rating. See Radio broadcasting—Program rating

RADIO programs. See Radio broadcasting—Programs

RADIO pulse time modulation
Pulse-counting detector for FM tuners. A. H. Seidman. il Electr World 77:36-8 Ja '67

RADIO receivers
Build a stacked-antenna AM radio. A. Trauffer. il Pop Electr 26:40 My '67
FM/AM clock radios. il Consumer Rep 32:475-7, 298-308 S, D '67
Very small but not very good; Sony ICR 100. il Consumer Rep 32:298-9 Je '67

Frequency modulation receivers
Convert your All-American 5 for 120-meter marine band. J. G. Conner. il Pop Electr 26:71-2+ F '67
Good musical sound from a small radio. il Consumer Rep 32:125-6 Mr '67
Improve your FM reception. R. Angus. il Hi Fi 17:43-6 Jl '67

Integrated circuits used in new hi-fi Am/FM receiver. W. Hannah. il Electr World 77:34-5+ Ja '67
Philco-Ford introduces IC radio. il Electr World 77:72 Ja '67
Put FM in your car. D. J. Sweeney. il Pop Electr 27:83-4 N '67

Installation on automobiles
See Automobiles—Radio equipment

Testing
Aligning FM-stereo receivers without a generator. T. L. Moore. il Electr World 78:33-5+ N '67

Transistor receivers
Build the beginner's FET Regen receiver; field-effect transistors. C. Caringella. il Pop Electr 27:40-6+ S '67
Get more VHF on AM/FM transistor radios. M. W. Tobias. il Pop Electr 26:35-6 Je '67
Introducing the FET set; field effect transistor radio receiver. J. Althouse. il Pop Electr 26:27-30 My '67
New small radios. il Consumer Bul 51:4-8 Ja '68
Pennant race special; four-way earphone adapter. A. F. Burr. il Pop Electr 26:31 My '67
Portable FM. H. Fantel. Opera N 31:27 Je 10 '67
Portable radios that tune in the world. R. M. Benrey. il Pop Sci 190:124-7+ Ja '67
Power output of solid-state receivers. il Electr World 77:74 My '67
Transistor numbers game; transistors in a radio. Consumer Rep 32:463 S '67

Tuning
Knight-kit KG-790 AM-FM stereo tuner. il Electr World 78:16+ S '67
Pulse-counting detector for FM tuners. A. H. Seidman. il Electr World 77:36-8 Ja '67
Staying on the beam with tuning indicators. W. Salm. il Pop Mech 127:194-7 F '67

RADIO receivers, Portable
New dimension in portable radio listening. A. Trauffer. il Pop Electr 26:43 Je '67
Portable radios that tune in the world. R. M. Benrey. il Pop Sci 190:124-7+ Ja '67
Portable VHF receiver from DEI weighs less than 10 lbs. C. D. LaFond. il Tech W 20:32-3 Ap 3 '67
Short wave FM/AM portable radios. il Consumer Rep 32:579-83 N '67
Triple threat radio; Norelco radio-cassette player. C. Conley. il Field & S 72:129 O '67

RADIO receivers, Short wave
EICO model 711 space ranger short-wave receiver. il Pop Electr 27:79 Ag '67
Short wave FM/AM portable radios. il Consumer Rep 32:579-83 N '67
Shortwave, have you listened to it lately? R. Hertzberg. il Pop Mech 128:170-2+ Ag '67

RADIO receivers, Stereophonic
Aligning FM-stereo receivers without a generator. H. L. Moore. il Electr World 78:33-5+ N '67
EW lab tests of new solid-state stereo receivers. J. D. Hirsch. il Electr World 78:25-9+ D '67
Heathkit AR-15; a superb stereo receiver. il Consumer Rep 33:49 Ja '68
Top-notch stereo receiver comes in a kit. R. M. Benrey. il Pop Sci 191:94-5 D '67

RADIO receivers, Superheterodyne
Police special II; public service band receiver. G. J. Whelan. il Pop Electr 27:41-8+ N '67

RADIO reception
See also
Radio receivers—Frequency modulation receivers

RADIO relay systems
Litton radio relay/beacon tested for jungle air drops. C. D. LaFond. il Tech W 20:34-5 Je 19 '67

RADIO service shops
PEMOHT; the Russian radio, TV service-man. L. A. Harlow. il Pop Electr 27:57-8+ Ag '67

RADIO stations
ATS tracking system accurate to 0.5 meter; results obtained by NASA's global ground stations. C. D. LaFond. il Tech W 20:37-9 Ja 30 '67
Beating the system; KRLA pop station in Los Angeles. il Newsweek 70:60 Ag 21 '67
Burning issues; arsonists set fire to trailer station WRKL. il Newsweek 70:51 Ag 7 '67
Chicago's FM war; WFMT and WEFM. A. Balk. Sat R 50:38 Ap 1 '67
Deejays and teen radio; WQAM, teen music station in south Florida. L. M. Savary. America 117:444-5 O 21 '67

RADIOACTIVE dating—*Continued*

Dating and authenticating works of art by measurement of natural alpha emitters. B. Keisch and others. bibliog il Science 155:1238-42 Mr 10 '67

Fossil alpha-particle recoil tracks: a new method of age determination. W. H. Huand and R. M. Walker. bibliog il Science 155: 1103-6 Mr 3 '67

Ionium dating of igneous rocks. K. Kigoshi. bibliog il Science 156:932-4 My 19 '67

Pollen diagrams from sub-Arctic central Canada. H. Nichols. bibliog il Science 155: 1665-8 Mr 31 '67

Potassium: argon dating of iron meteorites. L. Rancitelli and others. bibliog il Science 155:999-1000 F 24 '67

Radioactive dating and low-level counting; report on symposium. V. R. Switsur. Science 157:726 Ag 11 '67

Test of continental drift by comparison of radiometric ages. P. M. Hurley and others. bibliog il Science 157:495-500 Ag 4 '67

Tiny tracks to ancient ages; dating by alpha particle recoil and fission tracks. il Time 90:63 Ag 4 '67

Unraveling the age of earth and man. E. L. Simons. il Natur Hist 76:52-9 F '67

Xenon-iodine dating; sharp isochronism in chondrites. C. M. Hohenberg and others. bibliog il Science **156:233-6 Ap 14 '67**

RADIOACTIVE fallout
See also
Atomic bomb shelters

Measurement

Atmospheric burnup of a plutonium-238 generator. P. W. Krey. bibliog il Science 155:769-71 N 10 '67

Europium-155 in debris from nuclear weapons. A. Aarkrog and J. Lippert. bibliog il Science 157:425-7 Jl 28 '67

Fallout from the Chinese nuclear explosion of 17 June 1967. M. A. Reynolds and others. bibliog il Science 158:1692-3 D 29 '67

Single fallout particles and zirconium-95 from the Chinese nuclear explosion of 9 May 1966. J. O. Baugh and others. bibliog il Science 155:1405-7 Mr 17 '67

Strontium-90 deposition in New York city. H. L. Volchok. bibliog il Science 156:1487-9 Je 16 '67

Physiological effects

Chromosome studies on Marshall islanders exposed to fallout radiation. H. Lisco and R. A. Conard. bibliog Science 157:445-7 Jl 28 '67

Utah

Hazards of iodine-131 fallout in Utah; Norman Bauer memorial symposium. E. W. Pfeiffer. Science 158:397-8 O 20 '67

RADIOACTIVE substances

Atomic black market; risk of fissionable material going astray. Sci N 91:470 My 20 '67
See also
Radioisotopes
Radium
Radon

RADIOACTIVE substances in the body

After ten years: thyroid damage; iodine fallout from nuclear tests. Sci N 93:32 Ja 13 '68

RADIOACTIVE waste disposal

Atom wastes; storage policy rather than disposal. Sci N 91:531 Je 3 '67

RADIOACTIVITY
See also
Nuclear reactions
Radioactive substances
Radium

Aeronautic applications

High-performance gyros seen from radioisotope techniques; utilizing the radioisotope field support principle. R. Pay. il Tech W 20:40-1 My 22 '67

Measurement

Aerial rescue gain seen in debris study; upper atmospheric nuclear debris studies may yield experience in midair retrieval. B. K. Thomas, jr. il Aviation W 87:83+ Ag 21 '67

Radioactivity of lunar rocks. G. S. Mumford. Sky & Tel 33:354 Je '67
See also
Radioactivation analysis
Radiometers

Physiological effects

How harmful is natural radioactivity? current tests in Brazil. T. L. Cullen. America 116:280-2 F 25 '67

Toxic substances and ecological cycles. G. M. Woodwell. il Sci Am 216:24-31 Mr '67; Discussion. 216:6+ Je '67

Underground A-tests may be making us radioactive. N. Wadsworth. il Sci Digest 62: 13-17 S '67

Uranium mining: doubly risky; radioactive dust causing lung cancer. il Sci N 91:469-70 My 20 '67; Reply. A. M. Keefe. 91:589-90 Je 24 '67
See also
Radiation sickness
United Nations—Scientific committee on the effects of atomic radiation

Safety devices and measures
See also
Atomic bomb shelters
Shielding (radiation)

RADIOACTIVITY in time measurement. See Radioactive dating

RADIOCARBON dating

Bering land bridge: evidence of spruce in late-Wisconsin times. P. A. Colinvaux. bibliog il Science 156:380-3 Ap 21 '67

Enclosed bark as a pollen trap. D. P. Adam and others. bibliog il Science 157:1067-8 S 1 '67

Olmec civilization, Veracruz, Mexico: dating of the San Lorenzo phase. M. D. Coe and others. bibliog il Science 155:1399-401 Mr 17 '67

Radiocarbon content of marine shells from the Pacific coasts of Central and South America. R. E. Taylor and R. Berger. bibliog il Science 158:1180-2 D 1 '67

Radiocarbon dating and archeology in North America. F. Johnson. bibliog Science 155: 165-9 Ja 13 '67

Radiocarbon dating of biogenetic opal. L. P. Wilding. bibliog Science 156:66-7 Ap 7 '67; Reply. E. D. Gill. 158:810 N 10 '67

Transitional pre-desert phase in San Diego County, California. J. R. Moriarty. bibliog il Science 155:553-6 F 3 '67

RADIOCHEMISTRY

Stabilization of hydrated electrons in irradiated frozen sugar solutions. W. R. Elliott. bibliog il Science 157:558-9 Ag 4 '67

Tritiated thymidine; effect of decomposition by self-radiolysis on specificity as a tracer for DNA synthesis. M. Wand and others. bibliog il Science 157:436-8 Jl 28 '67
See also
Radioactivation analysis

RADIOGRAPHY
See also
X ray photogrammetry

RADIOISOTOPES

Radioisotope uptake as a measure of synthesis of messenger RNA. D. P. Nierlich. bibliog il Science 158:1186-8 D 1 '67

Sleuths on a widening track; uses in industry, agriculture, medicine, biochemistry and chemistry. Sci N 91:99 Ja 28 '67

Aeronautic applications
See Radioactivity—Aeronautic applications

RADIOLOGY, Medical

Dosimetry: high-energy radiation therapy; report on symposium. L. H. Lanzl and J. S. Laughlin. Science 158:1499-502 D 15 '67

RADIOLYSIS. See Radiochemistry

RADIOMETERS

Ecological dosimetry: radiation levels influenced by plant growth. W. C. Ashby and others. bibliog il Science 155:1430-2 Mr 17 '67

Infrared radiometry. J. R. Collins. il Electr World 78:23-7+ O '67

IR device tested as turbulence detector; infrared scanning radiometer to detect clear air turbulence. R. D. Hibben. il Aviation W 86:61+ F 20 '67

Isotropy of cosmic background radiation at 4080 megahertz. R. W. Wilson and A. A. Penzias. bibliog il Science 156:1100-1 My 26 '67

Primeval fireball. P. J. E. Peebles and D. T. Wilkinson. il Sci Am 216:28-37 bibliog(p 155) Je '67

RADIOTELESCOPE. See Radio telescope

RADIOTHERAPY
See also
Radiology, Medical

RADIUM

Marie Curie; excerpts from Madame Curie, tr. by V. Sheean. E. Curie. il UNESCO Courier 20:14-16+ O '67

Radium-226 and radon-222: concentration in Atlantic and Pacific oceans. W. S. Broecker and others. bibliog il Science 158:1307-10 D 8 '67

RADNOTI, Miklos
Five late poems, tr. by S. Polgar and others.
Nation 205:440 O 30 '67
RADON
Radium-226 and radon-222: concentration in
Atlantic and Pacific oceans. W. S. Broecker
and others. bibliog il Science 158:1307-10
D 8 '67
Radon daughters and the federal govern-
ment. M. Viorst and J. V. Reistrup. Bul
Atomic Sci 23:25-9 O '67
RADOVICH, Jevrosima, and Talmage, D. W.
Antigenic competition: cellular or humoral.
bibliog Science 158:512-14 O 27 '67
RADVÁNYI, János
Crossing the Potomac. il por Time 89:20 My 26
'67
Model defector. por Newsweek 69:22-3 My 29
'67
RADZIWILL, Lee (Bouvier) princess
Princess goes on stage. J. Howard. il pors Life
63:52E-52F+ Jl 14 '67
Public and the private Lee. H. Ehrlich. il pors
Look 32:36-41 Ja 23 '68
Stay tuned for the princess. T. Coleman.
il pors Sat Eve Post 240:28-9 D 16 '67
RAEBURN, Christopher
Ring twice and ask for Mario. Hi Fi 17:
56-7 Ag '67
RAFAEL, Richard V.
San Francisco sampler. por ALA Bul 61:729-38
Je '67
RAFFAELE, Joe, and Baker, E. C.
Way-out West: interviews with four San
Francisco artists. Art N 66:38-41+ Sum '67
RAFFERTY, Max
Other side: hardest of all things to come by;
reply to E. Z. Freidenberg; address, June
27, 1967. por Wilson Lib Bul 42:181-6 O '67
about
Max Rafferty of California. M. Harris. por
Atlan 220:95-101 D '67
RAFTERY, Gerald
Arrivederci, trauma! retiring to a small pub-
lic library. por Library J 92:4475-6 D 15 '67
RAFTS
Adventure as you like it; floating down the
Colorado River in rubber rafts. C. Conley.
il Field & S 72:26-31 Ja '68
RAG dolls. See Dolls
RAGO, Henry
Knowledge of light; Praise of comedy: a dis-
course; Promising; poems. Poetry 110:343-8
Ag '67
Vocation of poetry; address, November 28,
1966. Poetry 110:328-48 Ag '67
RAGOUT. See Stew
RAGTIME; ballet. See Ballets—Criticisms
RAGWEED
Nature note. Sci N 92:340 O 7 '67
RAHAL, James J. jr, and others
Purified staphylococcal alpha toxin: effect
on epithelial ion transport. bibliog Science
155:1118-20 Mr 3 '67
RAHM, Jan
Right tape for the job. Hi Fi 17:52-5 Ag
'67
RAHMAN, Abdul, tunku
Tunku Abdul Rahman's Malaysian miracle.
D. Reed. por Read Digest 90:139-44 F '67
RAHN, Hermann. See Hong, S. K. jt. auth.
RAHNER, Karl
Karl Rahner and heaven. America 117:592-3
N 18 '67
RAHTZ, Robert
How to get the most out of a modern text-
book. Sr Schol 90:sup 12 F 17 '67
RAHV, Philip
Liberal anti-communism revisited. Commen-
tary 44:63-5 S '67
RAIL freight rates. See Railroads—Rates
RAIL mergers. See Railroads—Consolidations
and mergers
RAILROAD buses. See Motor buses on rails
RAILROAD cars. See Railroads—Cars
RAILROAD consolidation. See Railroads—Con-
solidations and mergers
RAILROAD law
Railroad unemployment insurance. M. F.
Riche. bibliog f il Mo Labor R 90:9-18 N
'67
See also
Railroads and state—United States
RAILROAD management. See Railroads—Man-
agement
RAILROAD models
Hills in a hurry for your model-train layout.
H. Clark. il Pop Mech 128:180 D '67
See also
Railroads. Toy

RAILROAD rates. See Railroads—Rates
RAILROAD retirement and unemployment in-
surance acts. See Railroad law
RAILROAD stations. See Railroads—Stations
RAILROAD strikes. See Strikes—United States
—Railroads
RAILROAD supplies industry
Rail car makers bank on tax credit; rein-
statement of the 7 per cent write-off on
capital investment. il Bsns W p 175-6+
Mr 25 '67
RAILROAD trains. See Railroads—Trains
RAILROAD travel
Anyone here remember trains? R. Federico.
il Sat R 50:40-1 D 30 '67
Great train ride; or, romance revived. M.
Gough. il House B 109:110+ Je '67
See also
Railroads—Passenger traffic
RAILROAD unemployment insurance act. See
Railroad law
RAILROAD work rules. See Railroads—Work
rules
RAILROAD workers. See Railroads—Employees
RAILROADS
See also
Locomotives
Rapid transit

Automatic train control
Train ID, a key to better mass transit.
S. B. Fein. il Am City 82:106-7 Ag '67

Cars
Mass and class. W. McQuade. il Arch Forum
126:88 Mr '67
Putting design on the track; Sundberg-Ferar
designs. il Bsns W p94-6+ F 25 '67
See also
Budd company
Railway mail service—Cars

Consolidations and mergers
Coming of the super-railroad. M. J. Barloon.
il Harper 234:63-8 Ap '67; Same abr. with
title Super railroad is overdue. Read Di-
gest 91:163-7 Jl '67
Court clears the track; Atlantic Coast line
and Seaboard air line merger. il Bsns W
p41 Ap 15 '67
Few big railroads for all U.S.? mergers win-
ning official sanction. il U S News 63:116
D 11 '67
Getting closer; Penn Central merger. Time 90:
99-100 O 27 '67
Go-ahead; Chicago and North Western-Chi-
cago Great Western merger. Time 89:90
My 5 '67
Go ahead to merging railroads. il U S News
62:12 Ap 24 '67
High court puts off a wedding; ruling against
Penn-Central merger. Bsns W p24 Ap 1 '67
Northern green light; merger of the Great
Northern railway, the Northern Pacific
railway and the Chicago, Burlington &
Quincy. Newsweek 70:78 D 11 '67
Northerns; creation of the Great Northern
Pacific & Burlington lines, inc. il Time 90:
104 D 8 '67
Penn Central; sidetracked again. il Time 89:
88 Ap 7 '67
Portentous wedding for the South. il Fortune
75:46 Je 1 '67
Rolling & ready; Penn Central partners. il
Time 89:91 F 10 '67
Slow train to nowhere; merger of New York
central and Pennsylvania railroads delayed
again. Newsweek 69:62 Je 26 '67
Still very much alive, big rail mergers. U S
News 62:14 Ap 10 '67

Employees
Rail unions build steam; prepare for 1968
bargaining. Bsns W p72 S 9 '67
Why trucks stopped running and trains might.
il U S News 62:95-6 Ap 24 '67
See also
Railroads—Wages and hours
Strikes—United States—Railroads

Equipment and supplies
See also
Railroad supplies industry

Freight cars
Rail car makers bank on tax credit; reinstatement of the 7 per cent write-off on
capital investment. il Bsns W p 175-6+ Mr
25 '67
See also
Railroads—Freight service

RAILROADS—*Continued*

Freight rates
See Railroads—Rates

Freight service
Blitzing trucks off the highway; shifting long-haul freight traffic from road to rail. il Bsns W p 104-6+ N 11 '67
Coming of the super-railroad. M. J. Barloon. il Harper 234:63-8 Ap '67; Same abr. with title Super railroad is overdue. Read Digest 91:163-7 Jl '67

Government regulation
See Railroads and state—United States

Management
Railroad hypocrisy: nuisance of passengers. W. R. Wright. Nation 204:275-6 F 27 '67

Parlor cars
See Railroads—Cars

Passenger service
High-speed bid for business. il Bsns W p 126-8 F 4 '67
Railroad hypocrisy: nuisance of passengers. W. R. Wright. Nation 204:275-6 F 27 '67

Passenger traffic
Continuous car-belts proposed; car-type passenger conveyor. il Am City 82:114 Ag '67
See also
Commuters

Rates
Carriers get rolling on the rate-hike plea. il Bsns W p70+ Je 3 '67
Freight rates edge higher. Bsns W p34 Ag 5 '67
Just and reasonable, ICC grants railways increase in freight rates. Time 90:68-9 Ag 11 '67
Off on the wrong track; ICC rebuffs Transportation dept.'s effort to influence rates. Bsns W p39 Je 24 '67

Signals
See also
Railroads—Automatic train control

Stations
Train station and the community; conversion to community center, Altamont, N.Y. E. Cowley. il Sch Arts 66:35-8 My '67

Strikes
See Strikes—United States—Railroads

Train speed
Come ride on rails at 100 m.p.h! D. Francis. il Pop 191:106-9 N '67
High-speed bid for business. il Bsns W p126-8 F 4 '67
Supertrain meets VTOL. il Newsweek 70:58 N 6 '67
Third-generation, 300-mph trains urged. J. Rhea. Tech W 20:34 Mr 20 '67
Train ride at 150 miles an hour; Pennsylvania railroad demonstration. il U S News 62:14-15 Je 5 '67
Why high-speed trains run late. il Bsns W p 176 O 7 '67

Trains
Anyone here remember trains? R. Federico. il Sat R 50:40-1 D 30 '67
Last run; Twentieth Century limited. New Yorker 43:20-3 D 23 '67
Third-generation, 300-mph trains urged. J. Rhea. Tech W 20:34 Mr 20 '67
Why high-speed trains run late. il Bsns W p 176 O 7 '67

Wages and hours
Reason for the rails. il Bsns W p 146 Je 10 '67
Sop for skilled rail workers; inequities in pay and 5 per cent increases suggested. Bsns W p76 Mr 18 '67
What the railroad raises will cost. U S News 63:116 S 25 '67
Will railroad terms set a new pattern? il Bsns W p 145 S 23 '67

Work rules
Permissive anarchy; reprint. D. Lawrence. U S News 63:92 Jl 31 '67

Canada
See also
Canadian national railways
Canadian Pacific railway
Great Slave Lake railway

Europe
Europe's TEE trains. R. Tunley. il Travel 128:59-62 Ag '67; Same abr. with title Glamour rides the rails again. Read Digest 91:25-6 Ag '67
Orient express, by M. Barsley. Review Newsweek il 70:75 Jl 3 '67. S. K. Oberbeck

Europe, Western
Luxury on the track; Trans Europe express. il Time 89:65 Je 2 '67

Great Britain
Letter from London ; recent go-slow. M. Panter-Downes. New Yorker 43:52 D 23 '67

Ireland
Of trains, air, and Eire; Atmospheric railway. J. F. Henahan. Sat R 50:4+ N 25 '67

Japan
More zip for the fastest train; Japan's New Tokaido line. il Bsns W p 180+ O 21 '67

United States
Hoot, toot and whistle; railroads of S. M. Pinsly. il Newsweek 69:85-6 Ja 30 '67
Railroads are back in trouble again. il U S News 63:64-5 D 25 '67
See also
Railroads—Consolidations and mergers
Railroads and state—United States
Railway mail service
also names of railroads, e.g. California Western railroad

RAILROADS, Single rail
Travel trend: minibuses, monorails. il Travel 128:12 S '67
Why the latest monorail fell flat on its face; monorail between Tokyo international airport at Haneda and Hamamatsu-Cho station. il Bsns W p 118-19+ F 18 '67

RAILROADS, Toy
New mini-trains: built like a watch! R. Schleicher. il Pop Mech 128:144-5 D '67

RAILROADS and state

Canada
See also
Canadian national railways

United States
Permissive anarchy; reprint. D. Lawrence. U S News 63:92 Jl 31 '67
Report of the special railroad board; issued September 15, 1967. Mo Labor R 90:43-6 N '67

RAILWAY express agency, Incorporated
Unloading the express. Time 90:77 Jl 28 '67

RAILWAY mail service
Changes for the mails; postage up, service down. il U S News 63:76-8 D 11 '67

Cars
Heading for the end of the line; decision to drop railway post office cars. il Bsns W p 110+ N 11 '67

RAILWAY rates. See Railroads—Rates

RAIMONDI, Gianni
Tenor's life; interview, ed. by G. Fitzgerald. por Opera N 31:31 F 4 '67

RAIMONDI, Luigi, abp
Pope's fraternal eyes. por Time 90:62 Jl 14 '67

RAIN and rainfall
Charge transfer between raindrops. J. D. Sartor and W. R. Atkinson. bibliog il Science 157:1267-9 S 15 '67
Hurray! it's raining! E. S. Hill. il Read Digest 90:55-8 Ap '67
See also
Droughts
Runoff

Anecdotes, facetiae, satire, etc.
Rain is hard. H. Böll. il Esquire 67:100 Mr '67

RAIN forests
See also
Olympic National Park

RAIN making
Firing back at hail; suppression by antiaircraft shells. Time 90:89 O 13 '67
New success in fighting fires by making it rain; cloud-seeding. U S News 63:10 Jl 31 '67
Rainmaking projects; India. K. S. Nayar. Sci N 92:229 S 2 '67
Tapping the rivers of the sky. F. E. Dominy. il Am City 82:98-101 Jl '67

RAIN trees
Monkeypod business. B. Sigel. il Am For 73:34-6+ My '67

RAINA, Peter
Intellectual revolt in Poland. T. Szamuely. il
Reporter 36:32-4 Je 1 '67
RAINBOW
Color through a raindrop; the mechanics of
rainbow formation. R. E. Orville and W. C.
Livingston. il Natur Hist 76:44-5 My '67
RAINCOATS
Raincoats. Good H 164:176 Mr '67
RAINDROPS. See Rain and rainfall
RAINE, Kathleen
By the river Eden; poem. New Yorker 43:54
O 21 '67
RAINEY, Gertrude
Mostly modernists. M. Williams. Sat R 50 Jl
29 '67
RAINEY, Robert H.
Natural displacement of pollution from the
Great Lakes. Science 155:1242-3 Mr 10 '67
RAINEY, Sarita R.
Disguising the paper bag for puppetry. Sch
Arts 67:10-11 N '67
Woven structures. Sch Arts 67:6-7 D '67
RAINIER III, prince of Monaco
Our life together; excerpts from A prince's
story. pors Good H 164:100-10 Mr '67
RAINMAKER; story. See Humphrey, W.
RAINMAN, Eva Schindler-. See Schindler-
Rainman, E.
RAINS, Donald W.
Light-enhanced potassium absorption by corn
leaf tissue. bibliog Science 156:1382-3 Je 9
'67
RAINY Sunday; story. See Shyer, M. F.
RAISINS
See also
Cookery—Fruit
RAJAGOPALACHARI, Chakravarti
(tr) See Kamban. Exile of Rama
RAJAN, Sundar
India's opposition scents power. Reporter 36:
35-8 Ap 20 '67
Steady decline of New Delhi's authority. Re-
porter 37:30-3 O 19 '67
RAJCHMAN, Jan A.
Integrated computer memories; with bio-
graphical sketch. Sci Am 217:10, 18-31 bib-
liog(p 134) Jl '67
RAJPUTANA
Is man changing the climate of earth?
adaptation of address. R. A. Bryson. il
Sat R 50:52-5 Ap 1 '67
RAKES, Charles D.
Breakdown reverse voltage transistor and
diode tester. Pop Electr 26:67-71 My '67
RAKE'S progress; opera. See Stravinsky, I. F.
RAKSTIS, Ted J.
How safe are your child's toys? Todays
Health 45:20-3 D '67
RAKU ware. See Pottery, Japanese
RALEIGH, Sir Walter
Raleigh and El Dorado of Guiana. H. T.
Sturcken. il por Américas 19:15-21 Ag '67
RALLIES, Automobile. See Automobile driving
—Competitions
RALSTON, Dennis
Amateur bad boy turns pro perfectionist. K.
Chapin. il por Sports Illus 26:56 Je 19 '67
RALSTON, K. M.
Few ill-chosen words; address, 1964. Horn Bk
43:42-7 F '67
RAM (student newspaper) See College and
school journalism
RAMA RAU, Santha
Invitation to serenity. por Redbook 128:65+
F '67
Letter from abroad: marvelous medicine of
Malabar. McCalls 94:40+ My '67
RAMANUJAN, A. K.
Three poets. P. Legler. Poetry 109:412-14 Mr
'67
RAMAT ha Shofet
I fell in love with kibbutzniks. S. Lo Bello.
il Seventeen 26:136-7+ Mr '67
RAMAT Hashofet. See Ramat ha Shofet
RAMAYANA
Ramayana and the Mahabharata; symposium,
with excerpt from poems and with paint-
ings. bibliog il UNESCO Courier 20:4-45
D '67
RAMBUSCH, Nancy
O blessed deviation. Commonweal 86:363-6
Je 16 '67
RAMJET airplane engines. See Jet airplane
engines
RAMO, Simon
Individual; address, June 9, 1967. Vital
Speeches 33:646-8 Ag 15 '67
Making technology serve society; interview.
pors Nations Bsns 55:66-7+ Jl '67
Science turns to challenge of satisfying hu-
man needs. por Tech W 20:78-9 Ja 23 '67

RAMO-Wooldridge corporation
Making technology serve society; interview.
S. Ramo. il Nations Bsns 55:66-7+ Jl '67
RAMOBOA, Petrus
Huge diamond becomes family's best friend.
il pors Ebony 23:110-15 Ja '68
Petrus and Ernestine find a diamond as big
as an egg. il por Life 63:36-7 N 10 '67
RAMOS, Manuel
Vicente bored in but Ernie merely bored.
B. Ottum. Sports Illus 27:66-8 O 23 '67
RAMOS BUONOMO, Jeannette
El Peyton Place. il por Time 89:23 Mr 31
'67
RAMPAL, Jean Pierre
Pied Piper. H. Saal. por Newsweek 71:62 Ja
1 '68
RAMPART CANYON DAM (proposed) See
Dams—Alaska
RAMPARTS (periodical)
Fall of the archangel. Time 89:77-8 My 5
'67
O'er Ramparts we watch. A. Karlen. il Holi-
day 41:147-9+ Ap '67
Ramparts dropout. Time 90:38 D 1 '67
Ramparts need watching. Nat R 19:393-5
Ap 18 '67
Rebellion at Ramparts. il Newsweek 69:88-9
My 8 '67
Who's to manage the muckraker? il Bsns W
p 171-2+ My 20 '67
RAMS (football club) See Football clubs
RAMSEIER, H.
Leukotactic factor elaborated by mixtures
of genetically dissimilar cells. bibliog Sci-
ence 157:554-6 Ag 4 '67
RAMSEY, Paul
On sexual responsibility; excerpts from Deeds
and rules in Christian ethics. Cath World
205:210-16 Jl '67
Over the slope to total war? Cath World 205:
166-8 Je '67
RANCH life
See also
Cowboys
RANCHES
Big dude drive in the Crazies. A. Chamber-
lin. il Sat Eve Post 240:32-7 Jl 29 '67
King of ranchers: H. Miller. B. Taper. il
Am Heritage 18:20-3+ Ag '67
Peace and peril at Ghost ranch; conference
center at Abiquiu, N.Mex. K. Haselden.
Christian Cent 84:988-90 Ag 2 '67
Where whooping cranes winter; guest ranches
and resorts in the Bandera area. H. Sutton.
il Sat R 50:39-40 Ap 1 '67
RANCITELLI, L. and others
Potassium:argon dating of iron meteorites.
bibliog Science 155:999-1000 F 24 '67
RAND, Ayn
Are America's students flunking capitalism? J.
St John. Nations Bsns 55:90 Jl '67
Cult of angry Ayn Rand. D. J. Hamblin. il
pors Life 62:92-4+ Ap 7 '67
Gospel according to Ayn Rand. M. S. Evans.
Nat R 19:1059-63 O 3 '67
RAND, Christopher
Our far-flung correspondents. New Yorker 43:
152+ S 16 '67
RAND, Lester
Teen-agers and money. NEA J 56:34 My '67
RAND corporation
Action intellectuals; legendary triumphs of the
biggest think-factory. T. H. White. Life 62:
66+ Je 9 '67
Research in California. J. Lear; J. Duscha.
il Sat R 50:64-6+ S 23 '67
Who thinks in a think tank? E. Stern. il
N Y Times Mag p28-9+ Ap 16 '67
RANDALL, Betty
There's more to autumn than the leaves
on the trees. il U S Camera 30:38-41+
O '67
RANDALL, Charles Edgar
America's sweetest tree. Am For 73:16-18+
Ap '67
Black walnut, our vanishing money tree. Am
For 73:14-17+ O '67
Ivy league forest. Am For 73:24-7+ Ap '67
Them were the good old days. Am For 73:26-
9+ My '67
RANDALL, Florence Engel
First chill; story. Redbook 129:76-7 O '67
RANDALL, Harry
Magnificent American iris. Home Gard 54:16-
19 Je '67
RANDALL, J. Parke
Anybody with a camera can be a newsman!
D. P. Blake. il Pop Phot 60:81-3 F '67
RANDALL, James
Build multipurpose FET signal tracer. Pop
Electr 26:43-7+ Ap '67
FET voltmeter. Electr World 77:63-4 F '67
VOM+FET=TVM. Pop Electr 27:57-9 Jl '67

RANDALL, Margaret
Marriage; poem. Poetry 109:325 F '67
about
Six books by seven poets. R. Vas Dias.
Poetry 110:190-2 Je '67
RANDALL, Robert
French way with french fries; summary, ed.
by E. Alston. por Look 31:111-12 O 17 '67
RANDOL, Ward
Explorers club. New Yorker 43:51-2 N 18 '67
RANDOLPH, John
Consensus politics, 1800-1805. L. W. Koenig.
il por Am Heritage 18:4-7+ F '67
RANDOLPH, Norris
Jelke? Jelke? wasn't he the guy who..?
Esquire 67:136-9+ Ap '67
RANDOM house, incorporated
Random and Golden plan for Doctor Dolittle.
Pub W 192:157 Jl 10 '67
Random house opens Maryland warehouse. il
Pub W 192:32-4 Jl 24 '67
U.S. Supreme court refuses to block Howard
Hughes book. Pub W 191:221 Ja 23 '67
RANDOM house dictionary of the English lan-
guage. See English language—Dictionaries
RANGE finders. See View finders
RANGERS (hockey team) See Hockey teams
RANGERS, Texas. See Texas—Police
RANGES, Kitchen. See Electric stoves; Gas
stoves; Stoves
RANKIN, Allen
Super-farmer attacks global poverty. Read
Digest 92:25-6+ Ja '68
RANKING, Student. See Grading and marking
(students)
RANNEY, J. Buckminister. See Moore, M. V.
jt. auth.
RANSOM, Harry Howe
England's secret war. Sat R 50:44 S 16 '67
He wouldn't fly with the hawks. Sat R 50:33-4
O 21 '67
RANSOM
Merchandise returned; return of Kenneth
Young. il Time 89:37 Ap 14 '67
RANSON, Charles Wesley
Drew controversy gets wider airing. T.
Cooper. Christian Cent 84:451-4 Ap 5 '67
Drew's dean summarily dismissed. Christian
Cent 84:102 Ja 25 '67
Student boycott hits Drew university. Chris-
tian Cent 84:526 Ap 26 '67
RANSTEAD, Donald D.
How free is Frei? Commonweal 85:549-50 F
17 '67
RAPA NUI ISLAND. See Easter Island
RAPE
See also
Trials (rape)
RAPE of Lucretia; opera. See Britten, B.
RAPF, Maurice
Life movie review: Battle of Algiers. Life
63:16 O 27 '67
Life movie review; the fair in retrospect.
Life 63:18 N 24 '67
RAPHAEL, Chaim
Battle of the scrolls. Atlan 219:88-92+ My '67
RAPHIOLEPIS indica. See Hawthorns
RAPID transit
Breakthrough in mass transit. il U S News
62:74-6 My 15 '67
Can you use rail rapid transit? P. H. Fried-
lander and others. il Am City 82:120-2 Ap
'67
Continuous car-belts proposed; car-type pas-
senger conveyor. il Am City 82:114 Ag '67
Mass transit. See issues of American city
to April 1967
Mass transit sparks building boom; proposed
southern New Jersey rapid transit line
between Lindenwold Township, N.J., and
Philadelphia. il Am City 82:116-17 F '67
Mass transit, today and tomorrow. il Am
City 82:84-5 D '67 (to be cont)
Mass transit's simple answer. Am City 82:8
Ap '67
Transit expressway proves a success; Pitts-
burgh. il Am City 82:116 D '67
Vehicular revolution; the ruckus it stirs; with
report by C. Welles. il Life 62:34-43 My 12
'67
See also subhead Rapid transit under
names of cities, e.g. Santa Barbara, Calif.
—Rapid transit
RAPIER, James T.
James T. Rapier; congressman from Ala-
bama. N. W. Walton. bibliog f por Negro
Hist Bul 30:6-10 N '67
RAPOLA, J. and Koskimies, O.
Embryonic enzyme patterns; characterization
of the single lactate dehydrogenase isozyme
in preimplanted mouse ova. bibliog Science
157:1311-12 S 15 '67

RAPOPORT, Anatol
Escape from paradox; with biographical
sketch. Sci Am 217:10, 50-6 bibliog(p 134) Jl
'67
RAPOPORT, Roger
In defense of the multiversity. Atlan 219:73-4
Je '67
—See Reisig, R. jt. auth.
RAPPAPORT, Irving, and Zaitlin, Milton
Antigenic study of the protein from a defec-
tive strain of tobacco mosaic virus. bib-
liog Science 157:207-8 Jl 14 '67
RAPPAPORT, Lewis
Using records in U.S. history classes. Sr
Schol 91:sup 10 D 7 '67
RAPPAPORT, R.
Cell division: direct measurement of maxi-
mum tension exerted by furrow of echino-
derm eggs. bibliog Science 156:1241-3 Je 2
'67
RAPPOLD, Marie
Edison recordings of Marie Rappold. R. R.
Wile. pors Hobbies 72:36+ My; 36+ Je '67
RAPUNZEL; drama. See Thane, A.
RARDEN, Imogene Krippner
Friday pathos; poem. Christian Cent 84:367
Mr 22 '67
RARE book division, Library of Congress. See
United States—Library of Congress—Rare
book division
RARE books. See Book rarities
RARE gases. See Gases, Rare
RARE metals. See Metals
RAS, Norberto
Society, technology, and development. bibliog
Américas 18:14-23 D '66; Correction. 19:48
Mr '67
RASCO, José Ignacio
Two Americas. Américas 19:12-17 Jl '67
RASHFORD, Nicholas J.
Parishes in the central city. America 117:
381-3 O 7 '67
RASKIN, A. H.
He leads his teachers up the down staircase.
N Y Times Mag p4-5+ S 3 '67
Labor's middle-class revolt. Reporter 36:24-7
Je 15 '67
More strikes, more inflation: collision course
on the labor front. Sat R 50:32-5+ F 25 '67
Strikes by public employees. Atlan 221:46-51
Ja '68
What's ahead for labor-management relations.
Mo Labor R 90:47 Ap '67
What's wrong with American newspapers?
N Y Times Mag p28-9+ Je 11 '67
RASKIN, Judith
Recordings. M. Mayer. Esquire 67:79+ Ap '67
RASMUSSEN, W. C.
Substations can be good neighbors. Am City
82:142 O '67
RASPBERRY, William
Summer jobs that are going begging; ex-
cerpts from report. U S News 62:8 Je 12 '67
RASPONI, Lanfranco
Burtons in Dahomey. Vogue 149:92-3+ Ap
15 '67
Elusive Romans: easy to like, hard to know;
excerpts from Golden oasis. Vogue 150:
230-1+ N 1 '67
RASPUTIN, Grigorii Efimovich
Nicholas and Alexandra, by R. K. Massie.
Review
Atlan 221:110-12 Ja '68. E. Weeks
Life 63:10 O 6 '67. G. Weales
Sat R 50:34-5 O 7 '67. S. Heitman
Rasputin reconsidered. E. M. Halliday. il por
Horizon 9:80-7 Aut '67
RASPUTIN, Maria
Final accounting. il por Newsweek 70:27-8
O 9 '67
RAT control. See Rats—Extermination
RATCLIFF, John Drury
Are you getting enough sleep? Read Digest
90:109-11 My '67
Day in the life of a bushman. Read Di-
gest 91:29-30+ S '67
Down to the deeps for gold. Read Digest
91:201-2+ Jl '67
I am Joe's heart. Read Digest 90:59-62 Ap
'67
Lifting the curtain of silence. Todays Health
45:66-8+ N '67; Same abr. with title Doc-
tor, I can hear! Read Digest 91:189-90+
N '67
RATES. See Telephone—Rates
RATH packing company
Losing battle of Waterloo. Fortune 75:232 Je
15 '67
RATHS, Louis E. and others
Helping children to clarify values; excerpts
from Values and teaching: working with
values in the classroom. NEA J 56:12-15
O '67

RATICO, Ruth
Needling up on craftsmanship. Sch Arts 66:
38-40 Ap '67
RATING of automobiles. See Automobiles—
Rating
RATING of employees. See Employees—Rating
RATING of radio programs. See Radio broad-
casting—Program rating
RATING of television programs. See Televi-
sion broadcasting—Program rating
RATING services. See Credit—Rating
RATINGS of colleges. See Evaluation (edu-
cation)
RATIONS, Army. See United States—Army—
Commissariat
RATLIFF, Floyd
Nobel prize: three named for medicine,
physiology award. Science 158:469-73 O 27
'67
—and others
Enhancement of flicker by lateral inhibition.
bibliog Science 158:392-3 O 20 '67
RATS
After 50 million years, a respite for rodents.
il Sci N 92:127-8 Ag 5 '67
Most destructive creature on earth. F. War-
shofsky. il Read Digest 91:175-6+ S '67

Extermination

Defeat in Congress for a war on rats. U S
News 63:10 Jl 31 '67
Fate of the Pied Piper; Rat extermination
bill. Nat R 19:841 Ag 8 '67
House now says yes to a war on rats. U S
News 63:14 O 2 '67
Rats: latest national issue. il U S News 63:
35 Ag 14 '67
Rats, riots and politics. Nat R 19:889-90 Ag
22 '67
Rattus trappus: rat-control bill. Sr Schol 91:
40 O 5 '67
Symbol of despair. il Newsweek 70:78+ Ag
14 '67
When a rat riot hit Congress. il U S News
63:10 Ag 21 '67
RATS as carriers of infection
Of rats & men. il Time 90:60+ Ag 11 '67
RATTE, John
Crisis and comparison. America 117:35-7 Jl
8 '67
RATTLESNAKE venom. See Venom
RATTLESNAKES
Rattlesnake jamboree; ed. by B. East. W. L.
Tucker. il Outdoor Life 139:60-3+ Mr '67
RAU, Santha Rama. See Rama Rau, S.
RAUH, Joseph L. Jr
Forever filibuster. New Repub 156:10 F 4 '67
RAUSCH, Howard
Russia's economic reformation. Reporter 37:
33-5 N 16 '67
RAUSCHENBERG, Robert
Books. Vogue 149:111 Mr 1 '67
Interview; ed. by A. Fatt. por Dance Mag
41:57 Ap '67
RAUSCHER virus. See Leukemia viruses
RAUSHENBUSH, Esther
From where I sit. Mlle 66:61+ Ja '68
RAVEN, David
Pudding down the immortals. Horizon 10:120
Wint '68
RAVEN, Peter H. See Ehrlich, P. R. jt. auth.
RAVEN, Susan
First great woman scientist, and much more.
N Y Times Mag p52-3+ D 3 '67
RAVENSBRÜCK concentration camp. See Con-
centration camps—Germany
RAVENSCROFT, George
George Ravenscroft and his contribution to
English glassmaking. J. P. Hudson. bibliog
il Antiques 92:822-31 D '67
RAVIOLO, Victor Gino
Auto news makers. D. MacDonald. por
Motor T 19:30 Ap '67
RAVITCH, Mark M.
Letter to a colleague; story. Esquire 67:106-7
Je '67
RAW food. See Food, Raw
RAWLINS, Winifred
Cry; poem. Christian Cent 85:80 Ja 17 '68
RAWLS, Lou
Soulin' & sweet-talkin'. por Time 89:78 Ja
27 '67
RAWLS, W. E. and others
Effect of amantadine hydrochloride on the
response of human lymphocytes to phyto-
hemagglutinin. bibliog Science 158:506-7
O 27 '67
RAWSON, Robert O. and others
Visceral tissue vascularization: an adaptive
response to high temperature. Science 158:
1203-4 D 1 '67
RAY, David
Steward; poem. Nation 206:22 Ja 1 '68

RAY, Doris D.
Doris D. Ray and Robert Van Houte; inter-
view, ed. by M. S. Fenner. por NEA J 56:
71-2 Mr '67
RAY, H. Cordelia
March; poem. Negro Hist Bul 30:23 F '67
RAY, Henry W.
Freeing pupils from the sit-look-listen syn-
drome. NEA J 56:8-10 Ap '67
RAY, Michèle
Michèle is missing. por Time 89:58 F 3 '67
Michele Ray: now reported a captive of the
Vietcong. il por Life 62:30A F 3 '67
Out of the woods. por Newsweek 69:88+
F 20 '67
RAY, Satyajit
Maestro. New Yorker 43:25-7 Jl 22 '67
RAY, Tarapada
Atlantic report. F. Levine. Atlan 219:30+
Mr '67
RAYBIN, Harry
Help, my child has taken poison! E. M.
Wylie. Good H 164:77+ Je '67; Same abr. il
Read Digest 91:133-7 Ag '67
RAYMER, W. B. See Diener, T. O. jt. auth.
RAYMOND, John
What's become of the leaf rake? Pop Gard
18:76-81 D '67
RAYMOND, Nicholas, and Carty, W. P.
Balaguer's burden: the Trujillo holdings. Re-
porter 37:26-8 N 30 '67
—See Carty, W. P. jt. auth.
RAYMOND, Peter
Wise ways to enjoy Mexico. Todays Health
45:42-7+ O '67
RAYNOR, Vivien
Jackson Pollock in retrospect, he broke the
ice. N Y Times Mag p50-1+ Ap 2 '67
RAYNS, D. G. and others
Transverse tubule apertures in mammalian
myocardial cells: surface array. bibliog Sci-
ence 156:656-7 My 5 '67
RAYTHEON company
Raytheon gets nod on Sam-D development.
W. Andrews. Tech W 20:18-19 My 29 '67
RAZOR blades
See also
Gillette company
RAZOR clams. See Clams
RAZORS
Dry shaver for trips to the wild. il Consumer
Rep 32:512-13 O '67
How Gillette has put on a new face; diver-
sified product line. il Bsns W p58-60+ Ap 1
'67
Men's cordless shavers. il Consumer Bul 50:
19-20 F '67
Men's electric shavers. il Consumer Rep 32:
233-5 Ap; 233-5 D '67
Stahly razor; a spring-driven razor. il Con-
sumer Bul 50:22 Jl '67
REA, D. G. See O'Leary, B. T. jt. auth.
REACTIONS, Chemical. See Chemical re-
actions
REACTORS, Nuclear. See Nuclear reactors
READ, Bill
His beloved words. Sat R 50:39 Jl 22 '67
READ, Sir Herbert
Describing the indescribable. Sat R 50:32-3
Jl 15 '67
Robot as an answer. Sat R 50:30-1 N 18 '67
Whatever happened to the great simplicities?
por Sat R 50:21-3+ F 18 '67

about
Herbert Read as poet. R. J. Mills, jr. Poetry
110:45-7 Ap '67
READABILITY of print. See Printing—Legibil-
ity
READE, Walter, 1916-
Joyce unconfined. il Newsweek 69:104+ Ap 17
'67
READERS (books)
See also
Primers
READERS and libraries. See Libraries and
readers
READER'S digest
Digest that! tactics used to get the Courier
off the ground. New Repub 156:6 Ap 29
'67
Reader's digest goes to college. J. Tebbel. il
Sat R 50:92-3 My 13 '67; Discussion. 50:94-5
Je 10 '67
READERS digest association, Incorporated
Pictures from Pleasantville. il Read Digest
91:158-69 Ag '67
Reader's digest fund. Newsweek 70:84-5 O
9 '67
READERS' guide to periodical literature
Motherly index. B. Katz. Library J 92:555
F 1 '67

READINESS for learning
College? man, you must be kidding! College readiness program, College of San Mateo, Calif. E. Gattmann and others. NEA J 56:8-10 S '67

READINESS for school
Operation Home Start; Hawaiian program teaches parents how to ready their preschool youngsters for formal education. W. G. Cupit. NEA J 56:53-4 S '67
See also
Reading readiness

READING
See also
Books and reading
International reading association

Readiness
See Reading readiness

Remedial teaching
Apple to Mrs Henkell; report on Hennessey, Okla. remedial-accelerated reading program. M. Henkell. Am Ed 3:21-2 Ap '67
Forced reading; Chicago's reading research foundation. il Time 90:57-8 N 3 '67
Gift for all seasons. M. V. Murray. il Am Ed 4:5-7 D '67
Paperbacks for slow readers. H. M. McDonnell. il Sr Schol 89:sup27 Ja 20 '67
Remedial reading roundup, new materials. Library J 92:4212-13 N 15 '67
Sixth graders make terrific tutors; program at Haynes street school; Los Angeles. V. Bartel. il Parents Mag 42:56-7+ S '67
Why many Johnnys still can't read. il U S News 62:72-4 Je 12 '67

Adults
Rights and permissions; children's books for adults. P. Nathan. Pub W 192:36 D 4 '67

Speed improvement
See Reading—Remedial teaching

Study and teaching
Generation of illiterates. R. Kirk. Nat R 19:588 My 30 '67
Helping Johnny read; theories of J. S. Chall. Newsweek 70:66 N 6 '67
How teachers make children hate reading. J. Holt. Redbook 130:50+ N '67
It's quite possible to read. R. Kirk. Nat R 19:146 F 7 '67
Reaching the nonreaders. J. D. McAulay. NEA J 56:15 S '67
Should Johnny read in kindergarten? a report on the Denver experiment; with comment by K. D. Wann. J. E. Brzeinski and others. il NEA J 56:23-6 Mr '67
Sophocles and the sixth graders. D. Broden. NEA J 56:15 N '67
Throw out the textbooks. A. Gordon. il Am Ed 3:5-7 S '67
You're reading, Mr Mitchell! Greenleigh project to test reading systems for adult illiterates. M. W. Clark. NEA J 56:16-19 My '67
See also
Primers
Reading readiness

READING, Choice of. See Books and reading
READING aloud. See Books and reading—Reading aloud
READING and moving pictures. See Moving pictures and reading
READING and television. See Television and reading
READING by children. See Childrens reading
READING in bed. See Books and reading
READING lamps. See Lamps
READING lists
At our corner: Scholastic's expanded summer reading program. Sr Schol 90:sup26 Ap 28 '67
Books for spring reading. R. Girson. il Sat R 50:46-7+ F 25 '67
Paperbound bound? book lists. S. Forman and R. L. Collins. il Sr Schol 89:sup28 Ja 20 '67
Role of the book in combating prejudice; concerning third edition of list: We build together. C. Rollins. il Wilson Lib Bul 42:176-9 O '67
Standard lists, an unstandardized view. J. Shera. Wilson Lib Bul 41:615+ F '67
Summer reading: for children; for adults. L. Nix. PTA Mag 61:22-6 Je '67
See also
Books and reading—Best books
READING machines
High-speed punched-card readers. W. Barden. il Electr World 77:42-5 Ja '67

READING readiness
Read in kindergarten? Changing T 21:21 O '67
Ready for reading? G. L. Wyatt. il Parents Mag 42:46-7+ My '67
Who are the early readers? A. P. Eliasberg. il N Y Times Mag p74+ F 19 '67
READING rooms, Religious. See Libraries, Religious
READING to children. See Books and reading—Reading aloud
READINGS, Dramatic. See Dramatic readings
READY, William
Books: the reader and the writer. Writer 80:21-3+ Jl '67
READY-mixed concrete. See Concrete
READY-to-cook food. See Food—Ready-to-cook food
REAGAN, Gerald M.
Constructive criticism and education. Sch & Soc 95:423-4 N 11 '67
REAGAN, Michael D.
Basic and applied research: a meaningful distinction? bibliog Science 155:1383-6 Mr 17 '67
REAGAN, Nancy (Davis)
Are you ready to be seen? S. Harney. por Ladies Home J 84:34 Ag '67
California's leading lady. S. Gordon. il pors Look 31:36-8 O 31 '67
California's stylish first lady, size 6. il pors Life 62:55-6+ My 19 '67
What is Nancy Reagan really, really like? E. Harris. il por Look 31:40+ O 31 '67
REAGAN, Ronald
Air. M. J. Arlen. New Yorker 43:59-60 D 30 '67
As Berkeley awaits Ronald Reagan. R. Stith. Commonweal 85:443-4 Ja 27 '67
Berkeley story; facts on a big university. il por U S News 62:54-5 F 6 '67
Boxer Reagan of California. New Repub 157:4 Jl 22 '67
California notebook. H. Brandon. Sat R 50:10-11 Je 3 '67
Cal's Kerr ousted. il por Sr Schol 90:13-14 F 17 '67
Chubbmanship. il por Time 90:25 D 15 '67
Credibility in Sacramento. por Time 90:27 N 10 '67
Failure of a peacemaker; California's board of regents dismiss Kerr. il Time 89:60 Ja 27 '67
Fast start. il por Time 90:17 Ag 11 '67
Governor no. Reporter 37:12-13 O 19 '67
Governor Reagan's slightest vestige. A. Rosin and R. H. Simmons. New Repub 156:10 Je 24 '67
Governor talks of sport. A. Wright. il por Sports Illus 26:43-3 Je 26 '67
Happy 50.4th! il por Time 89:24-5 F 17 '67
Has Reagan mastered his role? por Bsns W p 100+ Ag 12 '67
Homecoming day. por Newsweek 70:27 O 9 '67
In the black, with crust. il por Time 89:24-5 Mr 17 '67
Looking stronger for '68: Reagan. por U S News 63:13 Ag 14 '67
Making of a candidate: a look at the Reagan boom. il pors U S News 63:53-5 Jl 24 '67
Matter of principle. J. B. Craig. Am For 73:9 Ag '67
Most happy fellow. il por Newsweek 70:35-6 D 18 '67
Not great, not brilliant, but a good show. J. Duscha. il pors N Y Times Mag p28-9+ D 10 '67
Now Reagan tries a cross-country tour. il por U S News 63:20 O 9 '67
Now that Reagan is governor, how's he doing? R. Evans and R. Novak. il pors Sat Eve Post 240:40-2+ Jl 1 '67
On the run. il por Newsweek 69:28-9 Mr 20 '67
Reagan: a relaxing view. W. F. Buckley, jr. il pors Nat R 19:1319-25+ N 28 '67
Reagan, ex-radical. A. Kopkind. New Repub 157:17-21 Jl 15 '67
Reagan in the State house. W. F. Buckley, jr. Nat R 19:787 Jl 25 '67
Reagan on the rise? H. Brandon. Sat R 50:12 Ag 26 '67
Reagan retreats. Newsweek 69:80-1 F 27 '67
Reagan takes a look ahead: and explains some '67 decisions. por U S News 64:11 Ja 8 '68
Reagan uses his broom. Bsns W p38 Ja 28 '67
Reagan's lesson. Nation 204:166 F 6 '67
Reagan's road show. Time 90:28 O 13 '67
Reagan's week. Nat R 19:1415 D 26 '67
Report from California: the Governor and the university. E. Langer. il por Science 155:1220-4 Mr 10 '67; Discussion. 156:581-2 My 5 '67
Revolt against the poor. P. Kerby. Nation 205:262-7 S 25 '67

REAGAN, Ronald—*Continued*
Right to fulfillment. Time 90:57 N 3 '67
Riots, Reagan and Rockefeller. il Nations Bsns 55:80-2+ N '67
Rockefeller, Romney, Reagan: what kind of governors; a study of the record. il pors U S News 63:54-5+ O 30 '67
Ronald Reagan faces life. A. J. Reichley. il pors Fortune 76:98-103+ Jl '67
Ronald Reagan, governor. A. V. Krebs, jr. Commonweal 85:639-41 Mr 10 '67
Ronald Reagan in the limelight. il por U S News 63:52-3 S 18 '67
Ronald Reagan: Lancelot out of the West. H. Sutton. il por Sat R 50:22-4+ S 23 '67
Ronald Reagan plays surgeon. F. M. Brodie. il Reporter 36:11-16 Ap 6 '67
Ronald Reagan: rising star in the West? il pors Newsweek 69:27-8+ My 22 '67
Ronnie-Bobby show. il por Newsweek 69:26+ My 29 '67
Showmanship at Sacramento. Nation 204:100 Ja 23 '67
Spots on Mr Clean. il pors Newsweek 70:34-5 N 13 '67
Star is born. por Newsweek 69:36+ F 6 '67
Tailored press. Nation 205:676 D 25 '67
Three Rs in California: Reagan, the Regents, and the right. W. Trombley. il por Sat R 50:47-8+ Mr 18 '67
U.S. letter: McFarland. C. Trillin. New Yorker 43:173-4+ N 4 '67
Welcome to the fraternity. il por Time 89:30 My 19 '67
What eighteen smart women think of Ronald Reagan. M. Davidson. il por Good H 166:78-9+ Ja '68
What is Nancy Reagan really, really like? E. Harris. il por Look 31:40+ O 31 '67
What Reagan hath wrought. J. Duscha. New Repub 156:10-12 F 4 '67
Who is Ronald Reagan? por Read Digest 90:102-6 Ap '67
Wounded are many. il por Newsweek 69:87-8 Ja 30 '67

REAL estate. See Real property

REAL estate agents
Is Babbitt dead? survey reveals what real estate people think of their reflected images. L. S. Burns. bibliog f Harvard Bsns R 45:14-16+ S '67
Taking the pain out of moving; homebuying companies helping transferred employees to buy or sell homes. Bsns W p96 Jl 15 '67

REAL estate business
Action in Las Vegas; H. Hughes buys properties around Las Vegas. Time 90:101 S 22 '67
Hughes's buying binge; Las Vegas property. il Newsweek 70:66 Ag 7 '67
Personal business. Bsns W p 163-4 S 30 '67
Speculation in the redwoods. Nat Parks Mag 41:20 F '67
See also
Corporations—Real estate operations
Location in business and industry
Tishman realty and construction company

REAL Presence. See Lords Supper

REAL property
Real estate as a corporate investment. S. L. Hayes, 3d. and L. M. Harlan. Harvard Bsns R 45:144-52+ Jl '67
Who owns America? R. J. Whalen. il Sat Eve Post 240:17-21 D 30 '67
See also
Air rights
Joint tenancy
Land values
Mortgages

Valuation
See also
Assessment

Caribbean Region
Personal business. Bsns W p 155 Je 24 '67

Spain
Search for sun=boom in Spain. il U S News 62:80-1 My 1 '67

REAL property and taxation
Look who's voting to cut your taxes! farmers are gaining new tax relief. J. Carlson. il Farm J 91:30-1+ Ja '67
What does the assessed value of property mean? il Good H 165:160 Jl '67

REALISM in art
European and American realists of the late nineteenth century. A. von Saldern. il Antiques 92:694-705 N '67

REALISM in literature
Realism in children's literature. E. Enright. Horn Bk 43:165-70 Ap '67

REALISM in moving pictures
Is this the world we live in? J. Morgenstern. il Newsweek 70:105-6 O 9 '67

REALITY
See also
Experience

REALS, Lucile Farnsworth
Late nineteenth century brooch. Hobbies 72:98W N '67

REAM, Marsha A.
Sick leave for teachers. NEA J 56:26-7 N '67

REAPPORTIONMENT. See Apportionment (election law)

REAR view mirrors. See Automobiles—Equipment

REARDEN, Jim
Alaska cracks down. Outdoor Life 140:39-41+ O '67

REARDON, John
Keeping the balance; interview. ed. by Q. Eaton. por Opera N 31:27 Ja 7 '67

REASON
Humanness of man. I. Asimov. il NEA J 56:6-8+ D '67

REASONING
Visual and auditory information processing in children and adults. E. C. Carterette and M. H. Jones. bibliog il Science 156:986-8 My 19 '67
See also
Fallacies (logic)
Problem solving

REAVEY, George
(tr) See Evtushenko, E. A. New poems
(tr) See Evtushenko, E. A. Rome: Rhythms of Rome; Heat in Rome
(tr) See Evtushenko, E. A. What pain, my beloved

REBEKAH Harkness foundation dance festival. See Dance festivals

REBELLIONS. See Revolutions

REBHAN, John R.
How to be your own landscape designer. Home Gard 54:52-4 Mr '67

REBUILT automobiles. See Automobiles, Remodeled

RECAPPING of motor bus tires. See Tires, Motor bus—Retreading and recapping

RECESSION, Business. See Business depression

RECIPES. See Cookery

RECIPROCITY
Notes that sank a business. Bsns W p 161-2 Je 24 '67

RECLAMATION of land
How to reclaim blowout areas. A. C. Everson. Suc Farm 65:48 N '67

Pennsylvania
Strip mining in Pennsylvania. G. Ade. il Nat Parks Mag 41:15-17 Mr '67

RECLASSIFICATION. See Classification

RECOGNITION (international law)
China watching. W. F. Buckley, jr. Nat R 19:1161 O 31 '67

RECOIL (gunnery) See Gunnery

RECOMBINATION of genes. See Crossing over (genetics)

RECONNAISSANCE satellites. See Artificial satellites—Military applications

RECONSTRUCTION (Civil war)
Ex parte McCardle: judicial impotency? the Supreme court and Reconstruction reconsidered. S. I. Kutler. bibliog f Am Hist R 72:835-51 Ap '67
James T. Rapier; congressman from Alabama. N. W. Walton. bibliog f Negro Hist Bul 30:6-10 N '67
New reconstruction. il Ebony 23:52-3 Ja '68
Reconstruction of the Nation, by R. W. Patrick. Review
Commentary 44:94+ S '67. D. Donald

RECORD, The (newspaper)
New giant in New Jersey. W. Sullivan. il Sat R 50:100-1+ Je 10 '67

RECORD changers. See Phonograph—Record changers

RECORDERS, Sound. See Sound—Recording and reproducing

RECORDING directors. See Phonograph records—Recording

RECORDING from the manuscripts (record company) See Phonograph record industry—Italy

RECORDING instruments
How it paid to put an idea to the test; market testing of GE letter writer. il Bsns W p 176-8+ O 14 '67
Just like putting a foreman in the cab; installing recording devices on street sweepers in Oakland, Calif. J. E. McCarty and R. Williams. il Am City 82:94-5 Mr '67
See also
Magnetic recorders and recording

RECORDING of sound. See Sound—Recording and reproducing

RECORDS
Paper tiger; copies of government forms. Newsweek 70:83-4 O 9 '67

RECORDS, Family. See Family records

RECORDS, Municipal. See Municipal records

RECORDS, Phonograph. See Phonograph records

RECORDS, Public. See Archives

RECORDS, Sports. See Sports records

RECREATION
Send your park superintendent to school; European recreational facilities. J. A. Smith. Am City 82:44 Ja '67
See also
Childrens amusements
Games
Leisure
Parks
Physical education and training
Play

Activities
Automotive activity in recreation. E. G. West. il Parks & Rec 2:32-3 Ja '67
Give yourself a lift every month. il Farm J 91:76-7 Ja '67
How to get more out of weekends. F. Cross. Read Digest 92:125-8 Ja '68
New trends accent creativity. Parks & Rec 2:17 My '67
Promoting functional play patterns. I. J. Hutchinson, jr. il Parks & Rec 2:29+ S '67
Resourceful director provides special events program; Palm Springs, Calif. H. Haddock. il Parks & Rec 2:34-6 O '67
Riflery included in indoor recreation program; Lancaster recreation program. P. Bomberger. il Parks & Rec 2:40+ Ap '67
Social unrest; park and recreation leaders' response. R. F. Fralick. il Parks & Rec 2:26-8+ N '67
Taxidermy, why not? Vacaville recreation department in California. J. Steinke. il Parks & Rec 2:31+ Ap '67
To meet new urban problems: a new kind of urban park with an endless variety of activities. il Arch Rec 142:110-11 Ag '67
See also
Boats and boating
Dancing
Gardening
Music as recreation
Playground activities
Tennis

Administration
Cowardly lion; a set of demands. J. E. Curtis. Parks & Rec 2:18+ Ag '67
State of New Jersey sets pace; provides board of recreation examiners. D. G. Goodwin. Parks & Rec 2:16+ F '67

Aims and objectives
Businessman looks at the business of pleasure; address, October 31, 1966. S. Coleman. il Am For 73:18-21+ Ja '67
Experimental programs. P. Boehm. Parks & Rec 2:37-8+ D '67
Fallacy of our programs. T. L. Goodale. Parks & Rec 2:39-40+ N '67
Recreation's vital role. H. H. Humphrey. Parks & Rec 2:13 Je '67
Sociologist discusses the meaning of recreative use of leisure. W. L. Stone. bibliog Parks & Rec 2:22+ Ap '67

Economic aspects
Businessman looks at the business of pleasure; address, October 31, 1966. S. Coleman. il Am For 73:18-21+ Ja '67

Exhibitions
Exhibitors to show newest park and recreation products at 1967 congress for recreation and parks. il Parks & Rec 2:48-9 O '67

Federal aid
See Recreation and state

Fees
Golden passport bonus; federal recreation area entrance fee. Outdoor Life 139:44 Ap '67
Golden passport; for federal recreation areas. Nat Parks Mag 41:20 Ag '67
'67 Golden passports; annual permit for entrance to national parks, forests, refuges, and recreational areas. Nat Parks Mag 41:24 Ap '67

Finance
National institute to focus on financing. il Parks & Rec 2:29+ O '67

Revenue facilities and services by lease; Maryland-National capital park and planning commission; address. F. F. Rubini. Parks & Rec 2:45-6 Ja; 36+ Mr '67

Laws and regulations
Legal aspects of recreation. A. M. Farina. Parks & Rec 2:42-3+ Mr '67

Public relations
Establishing local press relations. D. J. Scherer. Parks & Rec 2:36+ O '67
Press conference pointers. W. M. Kiplinger, jr. Parks & Rec 2:29+ Mr '67

Study and teaching
Let's get the elephants out of the Volkswagen. L. E. Taylor. il Parks & Rec 2:18-19+ F '67

Switzerland
Use of high country in Switzerland; North Cascades debate continues using Switzerland as yardstick. A. Netboy; discussion. Am For 73:2 Ja '67

United States
Lifetime sports recreation project to be expanded. il Parks & Rec 2:24 Ja '67
1967, the park and recreation movement in retrospect. il Parks & Rec 2:39-40+ D '67
Over-use of the national parks. W. A. Johnson. il Nat Parks Mag 41:4-7 O '67
See also
Recreation, Rural

History
Trends at a glance; progress of park and recreation services over the past twenty-five years. D. E. Hawkins. il Parks & Rec 2:21+ Jl '67

RECREATION, Industrial. See Industrial recreation

RECREATION, Rural
Rural recreation sites. il Parks & Rec 2:41+ O '67

RECREATION activities. See Recreation—Activities

RECREATION and state
Federal aid institute to be sponsored by NRPA; with editorial comment. Parks & Rec 2:13, 26 F '67
Federal grants for cultural recreation. S. H. Frieswyk. Parks & Rec 2:22+ F '67
First NRPA federal assistance institute. il Parks & Rec 2:32-3 Jl '67

RECREATION areas
Developers help country acquire recreation sites. W. W. Kershow. Parks & Rec 2:4 F '67
Good ground maintenance; address, October 1966. H. S. Conover. Parks & Rec 2:38+ Ap '67
Homage to Basswood Lake; Boundary waters canoe area. H. Clepper. il Am For 73:24-7+ Mr '67
Lake that looked impossible; Cull Canyon regional recreation area. W. P. Mott, jr. il Parks & Rec 2:14-15+ F '67
Recreation land management and the new forestry. L. C. Merriam, jr. bibliog il Nat Parks Mag 41:14-18 Je '67
Recreation needs in urban areas. R. C. Weaver. il Nat Parks Mag 41:10-13 D '67
Red Rock recreation lands. P. M. Tilden. il Nat Parks Mag 41:2 N '67
Seesaw in the Sawtooth. V. Fischer; reply. S. F. Arno. Am For 73:4 Ja '67
Trustees name Sal Prezioso NRPA executive vice president and secretary; with editorial comment. il Parks & Rec 2:13, 15+ Ag '67
What about Mineral King? R. Leadabrand. il Am For 73:18-20+ F '67
Will you have the answer? il Am For 73:19 Je '67
See also
California. University—Berkeley campus—Strawberry Canyon recreation area

RECREATION buildings
Milwaukee County park commission plans recreation complex. il Parks & Rec 2:35+ My '67
Moorestown builds modern neighborhood center. M. B. Berman. il Parks & Rec 2:36-7 My '67
New directions in design for D.C. department. L. C. Lemmon. il Parks & Rec 2:24-5+ My '67
Recreation: a chance for innovative urban design; building types study. New York (city) il Arch Rec 142:109-24 Ag '67

RECREATION centers
Recreation: a change for innovative urban design; building types study. New York (city) il Arch Rec 142:109-24 Ag '67

RECREATION conferences
Coming events. See issues of Parks & recreation
Park and recreation meeting makes waves; third World recreation congress. J. A. Smith. il Am City 82:90-2 Ag '67
See also
National recreation and park association—Meetings
RECREATION for the aged
Senior citizens bowling; Newington, Conn. senior citizens club. C. M. Lemire. il Parks & Rec 2:33+ My '67
Symphony for New York's elder population; Sirovich day center, New York city. G. Bamberger. il Parks & Rec 2:32+ My '67
RECREATION for the handicapped
Community recreation referral project; arthritic patients. P. R. Trommer. il Parks & Rec 2:19+ Ag '67
Nursing home setting; Miller center for nursing care, White Plains, N.Y. D. B. Miller il Parks & Rec 2:38-9+ Ja '67
Weekends at the seashore for physically disabled persons and their families: the Beach Haven excursion. M. D. McMullin and M. Clarke. Parks & Rec 2:24+ Je '67
RECREATION for youth. See Youth—Recreation
RECREATION workers
Cowardly lion; a set of demands. J. E. Curtis. Parks & Rec 2:18+ Ag '67
People in the news. See issues of Parks & recreation
State of New Jersey sets pace; provides board of recreation examiners. D. G. Goodwin. Parks & Rec 2:16+ F '67

Training

Educating recreational professionals. S. S. Frissell, jr. Parks & Rec 2:30+ Ap '67
Education for recreation and park professionals. H. D. Sessoms. il Parks & Rec 2:29-30+ D '67
Executive development program for P&R administrators. Parks & Rec 2:41+ N '67
Recreation education in selected junior or community colleges. W. M. Bartholomew. il Parks & Rec 2:25-6+ Ja '67
Revenue sources management school graduates first class. il Parks & Rec 2:36-7 Ap '67
There is nothing junior about the junior college. P. J. Verhoven. Parks & Rec 2:43-4 O '67
RECRUITING and enlistment. See United States—Armed forces—Recruiting and enlistment
RECRUITING for business and industry. See Employment systems
RECRUITING for librarianship. See Librarians—Recruiting
RECRUITING for school libraries. See School librarians—Recruiting
RECRUITING of athletes. See Athletes—Recruiting
RECRUITING of college football players. See Football players—Recruiting
RECRUITING of engineers. See Engineers—Supply and demand
RECRUITING of scientists. See Scientists—Supply and demand
RECRUITING of teachers. See Teachers—Recruiting
RECRUITMENT; story. See Gaines, C.
RECTIFIERS. See Electric current rectifiers
RECTOR, Milton G.
Drinking & pot parties. PTA Mag 6:4-7 bibliog(p36) Mr '67
RECTORIES. See Parsonages and rectories
RECTUM
Immunoglobulin A: localization in rectal mucosal epithelial cells. E. A. Gelzayd and others. bibliog il Science 157:930-1 Ag 25 '67
RED alder. See Alder
RED algae. See Algae
RED BANK, N.J.
Alert system that blankets a borough. F. E. Brower, jr. il Am City 82:30 My '67
RED dress; story. See Maynard, F. B.
RED filters. See Light filters
RED guard. See Youth movement—China (People's Republic); China (People's Republic)—Politics and government
RED hair. See Hair
RED light. See Light, Colored
RED ROCK LAKES national wildlife refuge. See Bird sanctuaries
RED ROCK recreation area, Nev. See Recreation areas

RED SEA
Confirmation from afar; hot brines and heavy metal deposits. E. T. Degens and D. A. Ross. il Sat R 50:52 S 2 '67
Red Sea: detailed survey of hot-brine areas. J. M. Hunt and others. bibliog il Science 156:514-16 Ap 28 '67
Red Sea's treasure; reprint. W. J. Perkinson. Sci Digest 62:22-4 D '67
See also
Suez Canal
RED shift. See Galactic systems—Spectra
RED Sox (baseball) See Baseball clubs
RED spiders
Here is what spider mites do. il Sunset 139:126 Ag '67
REDBOOK magazine
Redbook enters fifteenth year of homemaking service to readers. R. F. Pomery. Redbook 130:61-2 Ja '68
REDDIN, Thomas J.
Optimist for Los Angeles. por Time 89:50 F 17 '67
REDDING, James
Helping hand of Jim Redding. V. Pizer. il Read Digest 90:99-103 Je '67
REDDY, John
Living legacy of Walt Disney. Read Digest 90:165-70 Je '67
Up from the mud, a second renaissance for Florence. Read Digest 91:205-16+ O '67
Woody Allen's bed of neuroses. Read Digest 91:113-16 Jl '67
REDECORATING. See House decoration
REDEKER, J. A.
ESRO spending crisis hampers programs. Tech W 20:30 Je 19 '67
ESRO II satellite scheduled for WTR launch in April. Tech W 20:24-5 Ap 3 '67
REDEMPTION. See Salvation
REDEVELOPMENT, Urban. See City planning
REDEVELOPMENT programs. See Economic assistance, Domestic
REDFIELD, Alfred C.
Postglacial change in sea level in the western north Atlantic Ocean. bibliog Science 157:687-92 Ag 11 '67
REDFIELD, William
On speaking the speech. por Sat R 50:30-1 Mr 4 '67
REDFORD, Polly
Vanishing tidelands. Atlan 219:75-8+ Je '67; Same abr. Read Digest 91:134-7 S '67
REDGRAVE, Lynn
Beaut of a British bird; ed. by E. Miller. pors Seventeen 26:98-9+ D '67

about

Birds of a father. il pors Time 89:80-2+ Mr 17 '67
REDGRAVE, Michael, family
Beaut of a British bird; ed. by E. Miller. L. Redgrave. il pors Seventeen 26:98-9+ D '67
Redgraves talk about their children. F. M. Eckman. il pors McCalls 94:86-7+ S '67
Those astonishing Redgraves. J. Graham. il pors Good H 166:16+ Ja '68
REDGRAVE, Vanessa
Lively arts; interview, ed. by M. Ronan. por Sr Schol 91:17-18 O 19 '67
Variety of Vanessa; interview, ed. by J. Hamilton. pors Look 31:44-8+ My 2 '67

about

Birds of a father. il pors Time 89:80-2+ Mr 17 '67
Vanessa Redgrave. R. Blackmon. pors Vogue 149:68-77+ F 15 '67
Vanessa Redgrave takes on Isadora. A. West. pors Vogue 150:108-11 N 15 '67
REDL, Fritz
Boys nobody wanted. S. S. Rosenberg. il Parents Mag 42:35-7+ Ja '67
REDLICH, Don
Don Redlich dance concert; Hunter college playhouse. J. Maskey. Dance Mag 42:39+ Ja '68
REDLICH, Fredrick Carl
New dean at Yale. por Time 89:46 Mr 24 '67
REDMOND, James Francis
Chicago; legacy of an ice age; excerpt from Our children's burden. C. Remsberg and B. Remsberg. il por Sat R 50:73-5+ My 20 '67; Discussion. 50:50+ Je 17 '67
REDUCING. See Corpulence
REDUCING diet. See Diet
REDUCING exercises. See Exercise
REDUCING preparations. See Weight reducing preparations

REFUSE and refuse disposal—*Continued*
New solid waste system; using system of
underground ducts. il Sci N 91:150 F 11 '67
On policing a lakeshore; clean-up of the
shores of Jackson Lake, Grand Teton Na-
tional Park. M. W. Payne. il Nat Parks Mag
41:19 Je '67
Outdated thinking; using abandoned coal
strip-mines as repositories for solid wastes
in Maryland. Nat Parks Mag 41:21 Mr '67
Problem of solid waste disposal. il Parks
& Rec 2:27+ S '67
Refuse collection & disposal. See issues of
American city
Two unusual solid-waste solutions; Sioux
City, Ia. F. H. Kerr. il Am City 82:114-15
Ap '67
Visual pollution; sometimes it hides the
scars. il Pop Gard 18:24-5 D '67
Where will we put all that garbage? T.
Alexander. il Fortune 76:148-51+ O '67

See also
Cleaning of cities
Municipal dumps
Radioactive waste disposal
Refuse incinerators
Trade waste
Water pollution
also subhead Sanitary affairs under names
of cities, e.g. Miami, Fla.—Sanitary affairs

Apparatus
Disposers and hoods. J. LemMon. il Suc
Farm 65:102-3 Ja '67
Research
Solid-waste research projects. Am City 82:63
Je '67
REFUSE as fertilizer
Composting works in Houston. E. F. Spitzer.
il Am City 82:97-9 O '67
REFUSE collection. See Refuse and refuse dis-
posal
REFUSE collection trucks
Mammoth trucks and mini scooters; Pasa-
dena, Calif. F. Zapf and H. Giles. il Am
City 82:77-9 Ja '67
Refuse trains, better, faster, safer; Tucson,
Ariz. H. L. Danforth. il Am City 82:102-4
N '67
We're switching to diesel-driven refuse
trucks; Phoenix, Ariz. J. E. Attebery. il
Am City 82:79-80 Ag '67
REFUSE grinders
Food waste disposers. Consumer Rep 27:74-7
D '67
REFUSE incinerators
Cleanest incinerator stack gases; North
Hempstead, L.I, N.Y. L. S. Wegman. il
Am City 82:89-91+ My '67
Don't sell incinerators short. Am City 82:8
Mr '67
Garbage for health and power; burning refuse
to produce power. il Bsns W p82 Jl 1 '67
Incinerators can meet tougher standards;
Hempstead, N.Y. H. Mandelbaum. il Am
City 82:97-8 Ag '67
Refuse is the sweetest fuel; pollution-free
generation of power in municipal incinera-
tors; report on symposium. il Am City 82:
116-18 My '67
Unobstrusive incinerator. il Sunset 139:80
S '67
Worldwide rush to incineration. F. Sebastian.
Am City 82:40 D '67
REFUSE receptacles
How to dress up your garbage can. il Pop
Gard 18:89 My '67
Ninety-four per cent vote aye; disposable
refuse-sack system; Barrington, R.I. il
Am City 82:78-9 Jl '67
Quieting the clang and clatter; paper sacks
replacing garbage cans. il Bsns W p 146+
D 16 '67
Refuse sacks perform indoors; Milwaukee. il
Am City 82:39 N '67
Trash can liners. il Consumer Bul 50:23 Ag
'67
REGAL, Philip J.
Voluntary hypothermia in reptiles. bibliog
Science 155:1551-3 Mr 24 '67
REGAN, Charles L.
King's chapel dead; poem. Commonweal 87:
385 D 22 '67
REGATTAS
Another Marietta mud puddle; third annual
Mid-America regatta on Ohio River. H.
Peterson. il Sports Illus 26:30-1 My 15 '67
Beer can regatta. L. Payne. il Yachting 121:
76-7 Mr '67
Chesapeake, Skipjack regatta. B. Schill and
B. Schill. il Yachting 121:200-2 F '67
Look what Columbus started! Miami regatta.
B. Robinson. il Yachting 122:30 D '67

Month in yachting. See issues of Yachting
Old Jawn was a very bad bear; Harvard un-
defeated. H. Peterson. Sports Illus 26:58-9
My 22 '67
On the circuit. il Yachting 122:32-6+ O '67
Pennsylvania pulls it off; wins intercollegiate
rowing association regatta. H. Peterson. il
Sports Illus 26:60 Je 26 '67
Regatta results. See issues of Yachting
Salt pills and sun hats; pre-Olympic regatta.
B. Robinson. il Yachting 122:26-8+ D '67
Sunfish catch for Spanish point. il Motor B
119:146-7 F '67
REGENCY Hyatt house. See Atlanta—Hotels,
restaurants, etc.
REGENERATION (biology)
L-Asparaginase: inhibition of early mitosis
in regenerating rat liver. F. F. Becker and
J. D. Broome. bibliog il Science 156:1602-3
Je 23 '67
Collagen proline hydroxylase in wound heal-
ing, granuloma formation, scurvy, and
growth. E. Mussini and others. bibliog il
Science 157:927-9 Ag 25 '67
Nerve regeneration: correlation of electrical,
histological, and behavioral events. J. W.
Jacklet and M. J. Cohen. bibliog il Science
156:1640-3 Je 23 '67
Regeneration in crustacean motoneurons:
evidence for axonal fusion. R. R. Hoy and
others. bibliog il Science 156:251-2 Ap 14
'67
Regeneration of rat liver: transfer of humoral
agent by cross circulation. F. L. Moolten
and N. L. R. Bucher. bibliog il Science
158:272-4 O 13 '67
Vertebrate regeneration system: culture in
vitro. S. B. Simpson, jr. and P. G. Cox.
bibliog il Science 157:1330-2 S 15 '67
REGENSBURG, Sophy P.
Women worth watching. por(p30) McCalls
95:103 Ja '68
REGINA award
Medals and magic. R. H. Viguers. Horn Bk
43:24-5 F '67
REGIONAL airlines. See Local service airlines
REGIONAL cooperation. See International co-
operation
REGIONAL education laboratories. See Educa-
tional research
REGIONAL management in business. See Busi-
ness management and organization
REGIONAL planning
Architecture; Zähringer towns, Switzerland.
E. Galantay. Nation 204:283-5 F 27 '67
City pulls itself together; Nashville-Davidson
County merger. J. N. Miller. Read Digest
91:132-6 Jl '67
How to make your land worth more. J.
Carlson. il Farm J 91:34-5+ D '67
Metropolitan government on the way; sum-
mary of address. H. F. Wise. Am City 82:
18+ Je '67
Planned unit development means better com-
munities. M. C. Huntoon, jr. il Am Home
70:124+ Mr '67
Quality environment. A. C. Borg. il Am Home
70:92-7 O '67
Rise of a new political force. il Nations Bsns
55:72-4+ F '67
See also
City planning
Metropolitan areas
Shopping centers

United States
See Regional planning

REGIONALISM
Black-white at home, North-South abroad.
E. Kenworthy. Yale R 57:161-81 D '67
REGISTRATION of airplanes. See Airplanes
—Registration and transfer
REGISTRATION of dogs. See Dogs—Registra-
tion
REGISTRATION of voters. See Voters, Regis-
tration of
REGULATION of lobbying. See Lobbying—
Regulation
REGULATION of prices. See Price regulation
by government
REGULATORY commissions. See Independent
regulatory commissions
REHABILITATION
Boy who wouldn't give up. E. Keiffer. il
Good H 165:56+ S '67
One man's impossible triumph; case of F.
Ellis. B. Merson. il Good H 165:74-5+ Ag
'67
One-track skiers; therapy for amputee
veterans at the Soda Springs ski area,
Donner summit in California. il Life 62:
103+ Ap 14 '67
Patricia Neal: suddenly I wanted to live! S.
Frank. Good H 165:70-1+ Jl '67

REHABILITATION—*Continued*
Rehabilitation, the fight back. G. E. Maxwell. il Todays Health 45:62-7 D '67
Self-sufficiency surfboard. il Time 90:69 S 8 '67
REHABILITATION centers
Community mental health center exploits a sloping site for strong identity; Resthaven community mental health center, Los Angeles. il Arch Rec 141:160-1 F '67
Dynamic master plan keeps retardation center ahead of its time, a model of planned growth; Oregon Fairview home, Salem. il Arch Rec 141:152-3 F '67
How California is licking drug addiction. I. Ross. Read Digest 91:138-42 S '67
One-track skiers; therapy for amputee veterans at the Soda Springs ski area Donner summit in California. il Life 62:103+ Ap 14 '67
REHABILITATION of alcoholics. See Alcoholics—Rehabilitation
REHABILITATION of juvenile delinquents
Charity ends at home; Opportunities inc. search for home in Rhode Island. New Repub 156:9 F 18 '67
I learned my lesson. F. Pickett. il Nations Bsns 55:76+ O '67
Spirit of caring; Bernalillo County, N.Mex, PTA council activities. PTA Mag 62:27 D '67
REHABILITATION of prisoners. See Prisoners—Rehabilitation
REHEARSALS, Operatic. See Operatic production
REHEARSALS, Theatrical. See Theatrical production
REICE, Sylvie
Under twenty-one. McCalls 95:14+ Ja '68
Writing for Ingenue. Writer 80:27 D '67
REICH, Charles A.
Tragedy of justice in Billy Budd. Yale R 56:368-89 Mr '67
REICH, Peter, and Sidel, Victor
Napalm; reprint. Commonweal 87:440-1 Ja 12 '68
—and others
Sleep; effects on incorporation of inorganic phosphate into brain fractions. bibliog Science 157:336-8 Jl 21 '67
REICHARDT, Frederic Carl. See Reichardt, R.
REICHARDT, Rick
Rick (the ripper) Reichardt: California's super Angel. G. Astor. il pors Look 31:64-5+ Jl 25 '67
REICHLEY, A. James
Here come the Republicans. Fortune 76:94-7+ S 1 '67; Same abr. with title Remarkable rebirth of the Republicans. Read Digest 91:80-4 D '67
How Nixon plans to bring it off. Fortune 76:124-7+ D '67
Ronald Reagan faces life. Fortune 76:98-103+ Jl '67
REICHMAN, Ann
Please listen, I have something to say. por Redbook 128:8+ Mr '67
REID, Alastair
Daedalus; poem. New Yorker 43:130 Mr 11 '67
Querida mañana; poem. New Yorker 43:183 Ap 15 '67
REID, Barrett
Books in Australia. por Library J 92:4123-6 N 15 '67
REID, C. P. P. and Woods, F. W.
Atmospheric transfer of carbon-14: a problem in fungus translocation studies. bibliog Science 157:712-13 Ag 11 '67
REID, Charles
Georg Solti's full score. Hi Fi 17:66-70 Ja '67
Ravi Shankar and George Beatles. N Y Times Mag p28-9+ My 7 '67
REID, Ogden Rogers
Terror in a place of doves. Sat R 50:39-40 Ja 28 '67
REIDY, Affonso Eduardo
Two from the first team. il Time 90:90-3 D 8 '67
REIF, Rita
Home (cont) N Y Times Mag p64-5 F 19; 56-7 Ag 13; 134-5 O 8; 106-7 O 22 '67
REIG, Osvaldo A.
Archosaurian reptiles: a new hypothesis on their origins. bibliog Science 157:565-8 Ag 4 '67
REIM, Robert G.
Lend-a-hand plan. por Am City 82:98-9 Mr '67
REIN orchids. See Orchids
REINER, Carl
Something different. Criticism
Nation 205:669-70 D 18 '67
Newsweek 70:96 D 11 '67

REINER, Mary-Lynne
What to do when some are fat and some are thin. Parents Mag 42:94-5 N '67
REINER, S. Theodore
Relax it's only a tax audit. Nations Bsns 55:78-80 My '67
REINERT, Jeanne
Radio control of the brain. Sci Digest 61:32-6 Je '67
Secrets of the people of the jaguar. Sci Digest 62:6-12 S '67
REINFORCED concrete. See Concrete, Reinforced
REINFORCED materials. See Materials
REINHARDT, Adolph
Art world; exhibition of all-black paintings at Jewish museum. H. Rosenberg. New Yorker 43:99-109+ F 25 '67
Master of the minimal; with account by D. Bourdon. il pors Life 62:45-51 F 3 '67
Obituary
Art N 66:23 O '67. T. B. Hess
REINHARDT, Ed
Operation Sunshine. C. W. Wittman. il pors Am Artist 31:27-31 F '67
REINHOLD, Leonora
Induction of coiling in tendrils by auxin and carbon dioxide. bibliog Science 158:791-3 N 10 '67
REINHOLD, Ralph
Obituary
Am Artist 31:4 Mr '67
REINHOLD book corporation
Reinhold book division to be separate subsidiary. il Pub W 192:33-4 D 25 '67
REINOEHL, John H.
Task of the campus is education, not rioting; interview. por U S News 64:36-7 Ja 1 '68
REIS, Donald J. and others
Brain catecholamines: relation to defense reaction evoked by acute brainstem transection in cat. bibliog Science 156:1768-70 Je 30 '67
REISCHAUER, Edwin Oldfather
Time is on our side in Asia. Read Digest 90:55-60 F '67
U.S. policy in Asia: as two ex-envoys see it; excerpts from testimony. por U S News 62:19-20 F 13 '67
What choices do we have in Vietnam? excerpts from Beyond Vietnam: the United States and Asia. Look 31:23-7 S 19 '67
What we should do next in Asia. por Look 31:21-3 Ap 4 '67
about
Clarity of hindsight; US policy in Vietnam. K. Crawford. Newsweek 69:40 F 13 '67
Why stay in Vietnam? New Repub 156:9 F 11 '67
Winter term. il por Newsweek 69:35 F 13 '67
REISIG, Robin, and Rapoport, Roger
Of course, I'm no psychiatrist. New Repub 156:13-15 Je 24 '67
REISS, Albert J. jr, and Black, D. J.
Interrogation and the criminal process. bibliog f Ann Am Acad 374:47-57 N '67
—See Biderman, A. D. jt. auth.
REISS, Howard
Chemical properties of materials; with biographical sketch. Sci Am 217:52, 210-14+ S '67
REISSUES of phonograph records. See Phonograph records—Reissues
REISTRUP, J. V.
Moral sense of the scientists. Science 155:271 Ja 20 '67
—See Viorst, M. jt. auth.
REJECTED manuscripts. See Editors and editing
RELATIVITY (philosophy and logic)
My search for absolutes, by P. Tillich. Review
New Repub 158:36-7 Ja 6 '68. R. Hazelton
RELATIVITY (physics)
Challenging Einstein. Newsweek 69:98+ F 13 '67
Einstein under siege. C. Behrens. il Sci N 91:144 F 11 '67
Flattened star. Sci Am 216:48 Mr '67
Icarus, strange swinger. Sci N 92:490 N 18 '67
New method for the detection of light deflection by solar gravity. L. I. Shapiro. bibliog Science 157:806-8 Ag 18 '67
Nothing with a twist; curved space. I. Asimov. Sci Digest 62:81-2 N '67
See also
Light—Velocity
RELAXATION
Quotations, maxims, etc.
Take it easy; comp. by E. F. Murphy. il N Y Times Mag p6 Ag 27 '67

RELAY running. See Running

RELAYS
    See also
    Electric relays
    Electronic relays
RELAYS, Time limit
    Time-delay relays. J. E. Elpers. il Electr
    World 77:37-40 Ap '67
RELICS and reliquaries
    Old metals; Tibetan chorten. G. Kaler. il
    Hobbies 72:50 O '67
RELIEF. See Unemployment—Relief measures
RELIEF work
    Operation anti-disaster. E. D. Mills. il
    UNESCO Courier 20:16-17+ F '67
    See also
    American Friends service committee
    Food relief
    Medical relief work
    Middle East—Relief work
    Vietnamese war, 1957-—Relief work

    Vietnam (Republic)
    See also
    Medical relief work—Vietnam (Republic)
RELIGION
    Universal religion? excerpts from Peace
    among Christians. W. A. Visser't Hooft.
    Cath World 206:32-5 O '67
    See also
    Atheism
    Christian life
    Christianity
    Faith
    God
    Mysticism
    Public schools and religion
    Religions
    Religious thought
    Revelation
    Secularism
    Television broadcasting—Religious programs
    Theology
    Women and religion
    Youth—Religion
        Bibliography
    Books to come (cont) ed. by J. Putnam. Li-
    brary J 92:2947-57; 93:100-11 S 1 '67, Ja 1
    '68
    Some fall highspots, religious books; Sep-
    tember—December. il Pub W 192:50-69 S
    25 '67
    Some spring highspots, February through
    July religious books. il Pub W 191:44-66
    F 27 '67
        Study and teaching
    Religious education as a humanity. M. H.
    Goldberg. Sch & Soc 95:123-4 F 18 '67
    Religious instruction; faith vs. training. F.
    McQuilkin; G. Moran. Commonweal 86:48-
    50+ Mr 31 '67
    Unit on religion. D. P. Anderson. NEA J 57:35
    Ja '68
RELIGION, Personal. See Christian life
RELIGION, Primitive
    See also
    Paper in religion, folklore, etc.
RELIGION and art. See Art and religion
RELIGION and children. See Children—Religion
RELIGION and communism. See Communism
    and religion
RELIGION and democracy
    Democracy in the church. W. L. Doty; E. C.
    Bianchi. America 117:76-82 Jl 22 '67
RELIGION and education. See Public schools
    and religion
RELIGION and higher education. See Church
    and education
RELIGION and literature
    Literature in the divinity school. Time 90:51
    D 22 '67
    See also
    Religion and poetry
RELIGION and music
    Has jazz a place in the church? H. Dance il
    Sat R 50:46-7 Jl 15 '67
RELIGION and philosophy. See Philosophy and
    religion
RELIGION and poetry
    Poetry, prayer and cosmic reality. Sister M.
    Angelique. Cath World 205:237-44 Jl '67
    Vocation of poetry; address, November 28,
    1966. H. Rago. Poetry 110:328-48 Ag '67
RELIGION and politics. See Church and politics
RELIGION and psychiatry. See Psychiatry and
    religion
RELIGION and science
    Beyond the secular city; theology of H. W.
    Richardson. Newsweek 70:82-3 S 11 '67

Churches and evolution. P. Hefner. Christian
    Cent 84:651-6 My 17 '67
Evolution: implications for religion. T. Dob-
    zhansky. Christian Cent 84:936-41 Jl 19 '67
Is the church powerless in a scientific world?
    M. Mead. Redbook 129:44+ Jl '67
Open windows: southern exposure; scientists
    and theologians discussing science, religion
    and man's future H. L. Smith. Christian
    Cent 84:1311-13 O 18 '67
Science and the goodness of God; excerpt
    from Science and the imagination. W.
    Weaver. il Redbook 130:47+ D '67
Significance of Teilhard. I. G. Barbour.
    Christian Cent 84:1098-102 Ag 30 '67
    See also
    Evolution
    Tennessee evolution controversy
RELIGION and sex. See Sex and religion
RELIGION and social problems. See Church
    and social problems
RELIGION and sociology
    Eastern Europe & the death of God; con-
    ference of Marxist sociologists of religion in
    Prague. N. Birnbaum. Commentary 44:69-73
    Jl '67
    Relevance, community organization and so-
    ciology. S. A. Mueller. Christian Cent 84:
    1282-4 O 11 '67
RELIGION and state. See Church and state
RELIGION and technology
    Electronic culture and the future church;
    reprint. K. Paul. Cath World 205:157-9
    Je '67
RELIGION and war. See War and religion
RELIGION in literature
    See also
    Mysticism in literature
RELIGION in periodicals. See Periodical litera-
    ture
RELIGION in poetry
    See also
    Religion and poetry
RELIGION in the public schools. See Public
    schools and religion
RELIGION of children. See Children—Religion
RELIGIONS
    Impact of world religions on 1967. il Sr
    Schol 91:12-13 O 5 '67
    See also
    Christian Science
    Cults
RELIGIOUS advertising
    Chamber of horrors. Christian Cent 84:1671
    D 27 '67
    Heavenly commercials; Telespots. Newsweek
    70:57-8 O 30 '67
RELIGIOUS architecture. See Church architec-
    ture
RELIGIOUS art. See Christian art and sym-
    bolism
RELIGIOUS conferences
    Canadian Catholics offer milestone confer-
    ence on renewal. E. R. Fairweather. Chris-
    tian Cent 84:1261-6 O 4 '67
    Catholic inter-American cooperation con-
    ference. G. F. Hall. Christian Cent 84:
    252-4 F 22 '67; Reply. L. M. Colonnese. 84:
    472 Ap 12 '67
    Deliberation on the believers church. M.
    Shelly. Christian Cent 84:1077-8+ Ag 23 '67
    Fourth National workshop for Christian unity;
    in California. E. T. Culver. Christian Cent
    84:698-9 My 24 '67
    Laying foundations for a theology of re-
    newal. G. Baum. Commonweal 86:564-5 S
    22 '67
    Methodist women as peace disturbers. B.
    Thompson. Christian Cent 84:1205-6 S 20
    '67
    News and views; excerpts from paper
    adopted at Washington meeting of Chris-
    tians and Jews; ed. by J. Leo. Commonweal
    85:580 F 24 '67
    Of many things; Episcopal seminar held at
    Fordham university. C. J. McNaspy. Amer-
    ica 117:inside cover Jl 22 '67
    Protestant professors hold meeting in Spain.
    T. S. Goslin, 2d. Christian Cent 84:1574 D 6
    '67
    Role of conscience in the modern world;
    conference in Boston under Catholic,
    Jewish and Protestant sponsorship. Amer-
    ica 116:746 My 20 '67
    Theological road show; Catholic congress on
    the theology of church renewal at the Uni-
    versity of Toronto. il Newsweek 70:79 S 4
    '67

RELIGIOUS conferences—*Continued*
Thomas More: conscientious objector; conscience and the civil law, topic at Ecumenical conference on the role of conscience. J. B. Sheerin. Cath World 205:196-8 Jl '67
See also
International congress on religion, architecture and the visual arts
World council of churches
RELIGIOUS controversy. See Controversy
RELIGIOUS cooperation
Catholic inter-American cooperation conference. G. F. Hall. Christian Cent 84: 252-4 F 22 '67; Reply. L. M. Colonnese. 84: 472 Ap 12 '67
Community of Christians; Community of Christ our Brother, an ecumenical experiment in Atlanta. Ga. America 117:144 Ag 12 '67
Dialogue with Mecca; France's Fraternity of Abraham. il Time 89:56-7 Je 2 '67
God is not enough? I. J. Gerber. Christian Cent 84:684-7 My 24 '67; Discussion. 84: 676, 997-8, 1524-5 My 24, Ag 2, N 29 '67
Lutherans and Catholics salute the reformation together. Christian Cent 84:957 Jl 26 '67
Ministry of togetherness; churches of different denominations cooperate to create new ecumenical parishes. il Time 89:72 F 24 '67
New city, new church; ecumenical church planning for Columbia, Md. T. Mathews. Commonweal 86:518-20+ Ag 25 '67
Out of the cold; Missouri synod convention urges its churches to work with other Christians. Time 90:60 Jl 21 '67
Parish without bounds; Community of Christ our Brother. C. Foust. Commonweal 86: 514-15 Ag 25 '67
Renewal and the dynamic of the provisional. G. H. Shriver. Christian Cent 84:1551-3 D 6 '67
Take public relations out of public prayer. Christian Cent 84:196-7 F 15 '67
See also
Ecumenical institute, Chicago
RELIGIOUS dancing. See Dancing in religion, folklore, etc.
RELIGIOUS drama
By the grace of God and Henry Tudor. archbishop. W. H. Auden. il Holiday 42:99-100+ Ag '67
Lord's player; Methodist pastor's dramatic evangelism opposed by conservative churchgoers. il Newsweek 70:58 Ag 21 '67
Seminary drama and the God is dead theme; musical commissioned by Christian theological seminary. R. A. Fangmeier. Christian Cent 84:846-7 Je 28 '67
RELIGIOUS education
Christian education and the Jewish people; address before American academy of religion. L. D. Streiker. Christian Cent 84: 168-71 F 8 '67; Reply. J. E. Krueger. 84:348 Mr 15 '67
Secular ecumenism and the teaching of the faith; excerpt from address. November 22, 1966. A. H. van den Heuvel. Cath World 205: 14-19 Ap '67
Simple child, doubting parent. D. Callahan. Commonweal 86:287-90 My 26 '67
See also
Catholic church—Education
Children—Religion
Denominational colleges
Sunday schools
Theological education
RELIGIOUS experience. See Experience (religion)
RELIGIOUS faith. See Faith
RELIGIOUS freedom. See Religious liberty
RELIGIOUS institutes and workshops
Christian community; five-day institute at Boston college. America 117:49 Jl 15 '67
Lansing renewal program. C. E. Rhodes. America 117:202-3 Ag 26 '67
Report on a workshop; Vatican II's Constitution on the church. America 116:549 Ap 15 '67
RELIGIOUS institutions and affairs
World around us. See issues of Christian century
RELIGIOUS liberty
Elimination of all forms of religious intolerance; discussion by United Nations third committee. UN Mo Chron 4:39-42 N '67
Elimination of all forms of religious intolerance; U.N. third committee consideration. UN Mo Chron 4:83-7 D '67
Freedom at last: Spain. Time 89:37 Mr 3 '67
Matter of one hour; Spain's law on religious freedom. America 117:338 S 30 '67
Religious freedom in Spain. America 117:47 Jl 15 '67
Religious freedom in Spain. E. K. Culhane. America 118:38-40 Ja 13 '68

Religious freedom in Yugoslavia: yes and no. M. Bourdeaux. Christian Cent 84:1228+ S 27 '67
Religious liberty and development of doctrine; interview, ,ed. by E. Gaffney. J. C. Murray. Cath World 204:277-83 F '67
Religious liberty: down the drain in Spain; hostility to pending legislation of religious liberty statute. D. Peerman. Christian Cent 84:742-4 Je 7 '67; Reply. 84:885 Jl 12 '67
World Presbyterian area meeting. D. H. Rayner. Christian Cent 84:250+ F 22 '67
See also
Church and state
RELIGIOUS libraries. See Libraries, Religious
RELIGIOUS life (Christianity) See Christian life
RELIGIOUS literature
College market for religious and related books; summaries of addresses at luncheon of the Religious publishers group. Pub W 191:74-5 F 27 '67
East Germany; theology, East and West. Germanicus. Christian Cent 85:58-9 Ja 10 '68
New kinds of religious books. C. B. Grannis. Pub W 191:82 F 27 '67
See also
Booksellers and bookselling—Religious literature
Catholic literature
Libraries—Religious collections
Publishers and publishing—Religious literature
RELIGIOUS music. See Church music
RELIGIOUS newspapers and periodicals
How to sell to the top religious magazines. E. H. Pitts. Writer 80:31-3 Je '67
See also
Christianity today (periodical)
Risk (periodical)
Venture (periodical)
RELIGIOUS orders
New forms for a new age. America 117:168-9 Ag 19 '67
See also
Franciscans
Jesuits
Paulist fathers
Secular institutes
Sisterhoods
Trappists
RELIGIOUS persecution. See Persecution
RELIGIOUS plays. See Religious drama
RELIGIOUS poverty. See Poverty (virtue)
RELIGIOUS prejudice. See Prejudice
RELIGIOUS publishers group. See American book publishers council—Religious publishers group
RELIGIOUS records. See Phonograph records —Religious records
RELIGIOUS rites and ceremonies. See Rites and ceremonies
RELIGIOUS schools. See Parochial schools; Parochial schools, Catholic
RELIGIOUS services. See Church services
RELIGIOUS thought
Uncharted future of faith. R. Muska. Sat R 50:34-5+ Jl 22 '67
Utopia, by T. Molnar. Review
Cath World 205:312-13 Ag '67. G. L. Vincitorio
See also
Puritanism

Germany (Federal Republic)
Revelation & history; existentialist theologies under attack in Germany. il Time 90:61 Jl 14 '67
RELIGIOUS toleration. See Toleration
RELIGIOUS vocation. See Vocation in religion
RELIQUARIES. See Relics and reliquaries
RELISHES. See Pickles and relishes
RELLI, Corrado Marca-. See Marca-Relli, C.
RELOCATABLE classrooms. See Classrooms
REMARRIAGE
Church and second marriage. J. T. Catoir. Commonweal 86:113-17 Ap 14 '67
Second marriage: their daughters couldn't get along. D. C. Disney. il Ladies Home J 84:18+ Ag '67
REMBRANDT Hermanszoon van Rijn
Portrait of the artist's son Titus. A. Saarinen. il McCalls 95:41-2 Ja '68
REMEDIAL reading. See Reading—Remedial teaching

REMEDIAL teaching
Street academies: new way to reach the ghetto dropout; Harlem's Street academy program. P. Pierce. il Ebony 22:158-60+ Ag '67
See also
Reading—Remedial teaching
Tutors and tutoring
REMICK, Lee
Actress Lee Remick's second talent: decorating! il por Good H 164:100-4+ Ja '67
REMINDERS. See Memorandums
REMINGTON, Frank
Challenge of crime. New Repub 156:38-40 My 20 '67
REMINGTON, Frank L.
Bedtime tales. Todays Health 46:64-7 Ja '68
Medicine's magic needle. Todays Health 45: 58-61 N '67
Stork realities. Todays Health 45:16-17 Mr '67
REMINGTON rifles. See Rifles
REMINISCENCE
Going home again. A. Brien. Holiday 42:12+ N '67
Let the screen door slam. J. Mills. il Read Digest 91:57-9 Jl '67
Pleasure to recall. C. Ford. il Read Digest 91:205-6 D '67
Rothenburg: time remembered. R. Atcheson. il Holiday 42:20+ D '67
Winter is my memory season M. Holmes. il Todays Health 45:24-7+ D '67
REMODELED airplanes; Remodeled automobiles; etc. See Airplanes, Remodeled; Automobiles, Remodeled; etc.
REMODELING (architecture)
Making of a manor house; conversion of a silo and a cattle barn at Southampton, L.I. F. Heard. il House B 109:138-45 D '67
Maltings at Snape; old malthouses converted into a concert hall for Aldeburgh music festival. il Arch Forum 127:66-71 N '67
No structural changes needed for new store front; Chinook bookshop in Colorado Springs. il Pub W 191:66-7 F 6 '67
Old barn with a new bias; Simon's Rock arts center, Great Barrington, Mass. il Arch Forum 126:100-3 Ja '67
Remodeling creates dramatic spaces for this showroom. il Arch Rec 141:180-1 My '67
Renovation scheme adapts old school for future; Joseph H. Wade junior high school, Bronx. il Arch Rec 142:188-9 O '67
Shape-up on the waterfront. il Time 90:36-7 D 29 '67
Where once the alarm sounded; firehouse is home, studio, and office. E. Sverbeyeff. il House B 109:160-3 Mr '67
White elegance in a firehouse. il House & Gard 131:112-17 Je '67
See also
Apartments, Remodeled
Buildings, Remodeled
Houses, Remodeled
REMOTE control
Build the pulse command responder. E. C. Maynard. il Pop Electr 27:33-7 Jl '67
Build the 2+2 remote volume control. L. E. Greenlee. Pop Electr 27:40 O '67
Extending man's grasp. il Time 89:46 F 24 '67
Four tamperproof ways to operate your garage door. R. M. Benrey. il Pop Sci 191: 126-9 N '67
Remote commander. E. C. Maynard. il Pop Electr 27:42-6+ Ag '67
Typing without hands. il Sci Digest 62:75 O '67
REMOTE sensing systems
Remote sensing of natural resources. R. N. Colwell. il Sci Am 218:54-69 Ja '68
REMSBERG, Bonnie, and Remsberg, Charles
Strange struggle of Sy Patt. Good H 166: 88-9+ Ja '68
What four brave women told their children. Good H 164:94-6+ My '67
What went wrong in dreamland? Good H 164:74-5+ F '67
—See Remsberg, C. jt. auth.
REMSBERG, Charles, and Remsberg, Bonnie
Chicago; legacy of an ice age; excerpt from Our children's burden. Sat R 50:73-5+ My 20 '67
What are your chances in a medical emergency? Good H 165:100-1+ N '67
—See Remsberg, B. jt. auth.
REMUS, Gerald J.
Big questions; interview. ed. by R. R. Fleming. pors Am City 82:93-5+ Je '67
RENAL diseases. See Kidneys—Diseases
RENAUX, Robert. See Coffey, J. R. jt. auth.
RENDEZVOUS (space) See Orbital rendezvous (space flight)

RENDULIC, Klaus D. See Müller, E. W. jt. auth.
RENEK, Morris
McNamara establishment. New Repub 156: 32-3 Ap 8 '67
Portrait of a wretched man. New Repub 157: 11-13 S 30 '67
Slum landlords. New Repub 156:4-5 Je 3 '67
Slums and politics. New Repub 156:25-6 Ap 29 '67
Sport section. New Repub 156:25-6 Je 24 '67
Unpolished nigger. New Repub 157:7 S 9 '67
Whistling in a very lively graveyard. New Repub 156:14-15 My 13 '67
RENEWAL (periodical)
Renewal? you're kidding! An evening with God. Christian Cent 84:703 My 24 '67
RENEWAL of copyright. See Copyright—Duration
RENEWAL of the church. See Church renewal
RENFIELD, Richard L.
Policy for Vietnam. Yale R 56:481-505 Je '67
RENO, Marcus Albert
After seventy-eight years: Custer's aide is cleared. il por U S News 62:16 Je 12 '67
Reno's last stand. il por Newsweek 69:35 My 15 '67
Reno's last stand. il por Time 89:22 My 12 '67
RENO, Nev.
Description
Gamesmanship in Nevada. H. Sutton. Sat R 50:54-5 N 4 '67
RENO national championship air races. See Airplane racing
RENOUF, Renee
Visit to India. il Dance Mag 42:48-51 Ja '68
RENT
See also
Landlord and tenant
RENT laws
Whose welfare? New York city rent control law. Nat R 19:622 Je 13 '67
RENTAL services
What can be rented for parties. Good H 165:192 D '67
See also
Automobiles—Renting
Campers and coaches, Truck—Renting
Computers—Renting
RENTING of farm machinery. See Agricultural machinery—Leasing
RENTMEESTER, Co
Action along Highway 13; photographs. Life 62:69-74 Je 2 '67
RENZELMAN, Marilyn
You, the wounded; poem. Mlle 64:97 F '67
REPAIR men. See Repairmen
REPAIR shops
See also
Automobile service stations
REPAIRING
Home repairs a woman can make. il Good H 165:182-3 S '67
Why it's so hard to get things fixed. il U S News 63:46-8 O 16 '67
See also
Calking
Household appliances—Repairing
Houses—Maintenance and repair
Stereophonic sound systems—Repairing
REPAIRMEN
Why it's so hard to get things fixed. il U S News 63:46-8 O 16 '67
REPARATION
Victims of crime deserve a break. I. Ross. Read Digest 91:173-6 Jl '67
REPARATIONS (World war, 1939-1945) See World war, 1939-1945—Reparations
REPARTEE. See Conversation
REPENTANCE
See also
Confession
REPERTORY companies. See Theater—United States
REPERTORY theatre, New Orleans. See New Orleans—Theater
REPLACEMENT; story. See Bankier, W.
REPORT; story. See Barthelme, D.
REPORT cards. See School reports and records
REPORTERS and reporting
Beating dad can be fun: father-son combinations on different papers. il Time 90: 102 O 13 '67
But don't tell anyone I told you; private briefings of Pentagon press corps by top officials. S. M. Hersh. New Repub 157:13-14 D 9 '67
Campaign agonies. R. Moley. Newsweek 69:120 Ap 17 '67
Case in point: Daytona Beach morning journal. B. H. Bagdikian. Esquire 67:125-8+ Mr '67

REPUBLICAN party—*Continued*
Is it too late for a man of honesty, high
purpose and intelligence to be elected presi-
dent of the United States in 1968? with
editorial comment. S. V. Roberts. il Esquire
68:6+, 89-93+ O '67
Is the elephant wising up? Nation 205:675-
6 D 25 '67
Making of a president; contenders for the
presidency of the National federation of
Republican women. il Time 89:21 My 12 '67
Matter of semantics; fund-raising dinner in
Washington. il Newsweek 69:37 Mr 13 '67
Men around Nixon. N. B. Freeman. Nat R
19:1118-19+ O 17 '67
Morning line. Nat R 19:941 S 5 '67
Never in nineteen years. Time 90:23 S 15 '67
New leader for constructive opposition? P.
Lisagor. Nations Bsns 55:25-6 S '67
New revolution? D. Lawrence. U S News 63:
120 N 20 '67
Newsweek delegate count. Newsweek 71:20-1
Ja 8 '68
90th GOP style; Republican State of the
Union message. il Newsweek 69:19-20 Ja 30
'67
Nixon for president in '68? J. Witcover. il
Sat Eve Post 240:93-7 F 25 '67
Nixon tells how '68 race stands; interview.
R. M. Nixon. il U S News 63:74-80 N 20
'67
Nixon vs. Rockefeller: choice shaping up.
il U S News 64:38-40 Ja 1 '68
No consensus: G.O.P. State of the Union
message. il Time 89:18 Ja 27 '67
Off to an early start; Republican contenders
for the presidential nomination. il Bsns W
p33-5 My 13 '67
Omaha handshake; relations between nation-
al G.O.P. organization and Young Republican national federation. il Time 89:19 Je
30 '67
Operation 1968. W. A. Rusher. il Nat R 19:
1115-17+ O 17 '67
Pols here and there. Nat R 19:1105-6 O 17
'67
Portrait of the GOP. R. Moley. Newsweek
70:108 O 30 '67
Premature burial; GOP-southern democratic
axis. Newsweek 69:25 My 29 '67
Race for the Republican nomination: how it
looks now. il U S News 63:37-8 S 11 '67
Raising a war chest; surface unity of Repub-
lican hopefuls. il U S News 62:24 Mr 13 '67
Reign of Republican unreason. E. J. Hughes.
Newsweek 69:29 Ap 17 '67
Report: New Hampshire; preview. C. Mc-
Dowell, jr. Atlan 220:4+ D '67
Republican bug-out. F. S. Meyer Nat R 19:
1208 O 31 '67
Republican cool. K. Crawford. Newsweek 70:
26 D 25 '67
Republican establishment, by S. Hess and
D. S. Broder. Review
Commentary 44:91-2 D '67. A. Hacker
New Repub 157:28+ N 18 '67. R. D. Novak
Republicans stay on the fence for '68; GOP
governors conference. il Bsns W p36-7 D
16 '67
Republicans vs. LBJ, preview of '68 donny-
brook? U S News 63:11 D 25 '67
Return to normalcy; Republican governors to
confer on presidential nomination. Reporter
37:10-12 N 16 '67
Road to Miami Beach. R. Evans and R. Nov-
ak. il Harper 236:21-6 Ja '68
Rockefeller-Reagan? R. Moley. Newsweek 70:
112 S 18 '67
Rockefeller: Republican dark horse? inside
look at '68 strategy. il U S News 62:48-50
My 8 '67
Romney, a '68 boom that's in trouble. il U S
News 63:56 Jl 17 '67
Sons also rise; GOP campaign for 1968 nom-
ination. il Newsweek 70:22-3 O 2 '67
Southern comfort. Newsweek 69:32-3 F 6 '67
Southern Republican strategy for 1968. P.
Duke. Reporter 37:21-3 Ag 10 '67
State of the G.O.P. Commonweal 85:476-7
F 3 '67
State of the Union; a Republican appraisal;
addresses, January 19, 1967. E. M. Dirksen;
G. R. Ford. Vital Speeches 33:258-64 F 15
'67; Excerpts. il U S News 62:72-3 Ja 30
'67
T.R.B. from Washington; myth that TV has
made people hate war. New Repub 156:
inside cover Je 3 '67
Temper of the times. il Time 89:27-33 Ap 14
'67
They're off! contest for 1968 Republican presi-
dential nomination. il Newsweek 70:21-2
S 4 '67
Thinking aloud about 1968. F. S. Meyer.
Nat R 19:640 Je 13 '67

Top Republicans talk about their choice for
'68. il U S News 62:40-1 F 6 '67
Toward a brokered convention. Nat R 19:
285-6 Mr 21 '67
Veepstakes. il Newsweek 70:22-3 Jl 31 '67
Waiting for Rocky. Time 91:12 Ja 19 '68
We want a winner. New Repub 157:7 S 23
'67
What Republican victory means to the Negro
S. Booker. il Ebony 22:88-90+ F '67
Where's George? Republican governors con-
ference. il Newsweek 70:97-8 Jl 10 '67
Wooden army; House Republicans. E. J.
Hughes. Newsweek 70:13 D 25 '67
Wronged far right; reaction to revelations of
CIA subornation of American institutions.
Nation 204:232-4 Mr 13 '67
See also
National conventions, Republican
REQUIEM for a bachelor; story. See Head, A.
RERYCH, Steven
He's a long drink of glop. T. C. Brody. por
Sports Illus 26:56+ Mr 27 '67
RESALE price fixing. See Price maintenance
by industry
RESCUE, incorporated. See Suicide
RESCUE at sea. See Survival after airplane
accidents, shipwrecks, etc.
RESCUE trucks. See Motor trucks, Municipal
RESCUE work
Challenge of winter; assault on Alaska's
Mount McKinley. il Time 89:44 Mr 17 '67
Girl in the well; T. Fregia rescue; Votaw,
Tex. Newsweek 69:39 Mr 27 '67
Lifesaving jobs where you earn as you learn.
T. Berland. il Todays Health 45:36-41+
F '67
Well drillers save trapped girl; Votaw, Tex.
il Am City 82:95 My '67
See also
Airplanes in rescue work
Animals—Protection
Helicopters in rescue work
Survival after airplane accidents, shipwrecks,
etc.
Underwater rescue work
United States—Air force—Air rescue service
United States—Coast guard
RESEARCH
About simultaneous discovery. I. Asimov. Sci
Digest 62:88-9 S '67
Diversity; excerpts from address. J. R. Platt;
discussion. Science 155:402+ Ja 27 '67
LBJ: praise for the value of research. D. S.
Greenberg. Science 156:625 My 5 '67
Research comparisons; some limitations of
international comparisons. C. Freeman.
bibliog il Science 158:463-8 O 27 '67
Research frontier (cont) il Sat R 50:52-5 Ap
1; 51-5 Je 3; 74-5 D 2 '67
Ubiquitous bacterium; worldwide use in sci-
entific experiments. F. Marley. il Sci N 92:
231 S 2 '67
We need scientific diversity. il Sci Digest
61:55-6 My '67
Woman we called *la patronne*; M. Curie.
M. Perey. il UNESCO Courier 20:22-4 O '67
See also
Libraries and research
Research laboratories
also Atmospheric research; and similar
headings

Anecdotes, facetiae, satire, etc.
Swinging with owl one; adaptation of address; reprint. D. S. Greenberg. il Sat R
50:50-1 Ap 1 '67

Cost
Bureau of the budget cost sharing and
effort reports. S. Lang. Science 155:773-4
F 17 '67; Discussion. 155:1489-90+ Mr 24
'67
Revolt against time and effort reports. S.
Lang. Science 158:1268-9 D 8 '67

Economic aspects
Control by accountants. D. Wolfle. Science
156:895 My 19 '67
Research funding growth seen slowing. W. J.
Normyle. Aviation W 87:30-1 Ag 14 '67

Federal aid
Academic research: Foster defends DoD sup-
port in universities; statement. November
2, 1967. J. S. Foster, jr. il Science 158:1032-4
N 24 '67
Academic science and the federal government.
P. Handler. Science 157:1140-6 S 8 '67
Administration of federal aid: a monstrosity
has been created. D. S. Greenberg. Science
157:43-5+ Jl 7 '67

RESEARCH—Federal aid—*Continued*
Basic and applied research: a meaningful distinction? M. D. Reagan. bibliog il Science 155:1383-6 Mr 17 '67; Discussion. 156:313-14 Ap 21 '67
Basic research and financial crisis in the universities; excerpts from address, March 1967. G. Pake. Science 157:517-20 Ag 4 '67; Reply. W. Weaver. 158:1133 D 1 '67
Basic science in mission-oriented endeavor; report on panel discussion. T. L. Campbell. il Science 156:670-2 My 5 '67
Beyond Vietnam: what has science to say to man? J. Lear. Sat R 50:37-9 Jl 1 '67
Bureau of the budget cost sharing and effort reports. S. Lang. Science 155:773-4 F 17 '67; Discussion. 155:1489-90+ Mr 24 '67
Developments in federal policy toward university research; adaptation of address, September 29, 1966. H. Orlans. bibliog Science 155:665-8 F 10 '67
Einstein's angel and the empty temple; excerpt from address. September 29, 1966. H. Orlans. Sat R 50:45-6 Ap 1 '67
Federal economizing: House votes to take it out of R&D. D. S. Greenberg. Science 158:473-4 O 27 '67
Federal funds for science. il Bul Atomic Sci 23:33-8 F '67
Federal paper-work explosion: new form bothers universities. B. Nelson. Science 156:1468-9 Je 16 '67
Federal R&D grants to feel war's pinch. Bsns W p75 D 9 '67
Federal research funds: science gets caught in a budget squeeze. P. M. Boffey. il Science 158:1286-8 D 8 '67
Fine art of grantsmanship. Time 89:59 Mr 17 '67
From the editor's desk; review and forecast, policy. W. Kornberg. Sci N 92:614 D 23 '67
Funds for new graduate students. P. H. Abelson. Science 158:583 N 3 '67
Geographical distribution of NSF grants; letter. J. D. Millett. il Science 156:890 My 19 '67; Reply. H. J. Jerison. 157:991 S 1 '67
Great research boondoggle. W. Schulz. Read Digest 90:91-6 Mr '67
Hindsight: DOD study examines return on investment in research. D. S. Greenberg: Discussion. Science 155:397-8; 157:1512; 159: 34 Ja 27, S 29 '67, Ja 5 '68
Hornig on research policy: public understanding essential to scientific progress; excerpts from address, April 26, 1967. D. F. Hornig. Science 156:628-9 My 5 '67
How much research? address, April 12, 1967. K. S. Pitzer. Science 157:779-81 Ag 18 '67
LBJ's budget: lean fare set forth for research and development. D. S. Greenberg. il Science 155:434-5 Ja 27 '67
Money for research: LBJ's advisers urge scientists to seek public support. D. S. Greenberg. il Science 156:920-2 My 19 '67; Discussion. 157:134+ Jl 14 '67
Money for research: prospects for next year are gloomy. D. S. Greenberg. Science 158: 230-3 O 13 '67
New research grants need action now. Library J 93:133-4 Ja 15 '68
Politics of pure science. D. S. Greenberg. il Sat R 50:62-9 N 4 '67
Process values of university research. J. D. Carroll. bibliog Science 158:1019-24 N 24 '67
Professors and the Pentagon; Montana AAUP attacks DOD's Project Themis grant. il Sat R 50:84 My 20 '67
Project Themis: more research dollars for the have-nots. L. J. Carter. Science 155: 548 F 3 '67
Proposal for an institution for scientific judgment; excerpts from report to U.S. Senate, March 16, 1967. A. Kantrowitz. Science 156:763-4 My 12 '67
R&D looms big in fiscal budgets; McGraw-Hill survey. il Bsns W p68-9+ My 13 '67
Representative Joe Evins: NSF and NASA get a new master of finance. L. J. Carter. il Science 155:806-10 F 17 '67
Research policies hit. Sci N 91:58 Ja 21 '67
Revolt against time and effort reports. S. Lang. Science 158:1268-9 D 8 '67
Science money up only slightly. il Sci N 91: 109-11 F 4 '67
Secret research: tightrope act on Capitol hill. E. Langer. Science 156:1718 Je 30 '67
Summer research subsidies; letter. C. G. Danforth. Science 155:781 F 17 '67
SST, weather watch funding planned. Tech W 20:31 Ja 30 '67
Technology: academy panel sees need for enhancing applied science. D. S. Greenberg. Science 156:1212-14 Je 2 '67

Themis: DOD plan to spread the wealth raises questions in academe. E. Langer. Science 156:48-50, 366 Ap 7, 21 '67; Reply. T. E. Phipps, jr. 156:1307 Je 9 '67
While Themis rolls; Project Themis receives money for basic research funds. Sci N 91:471 My 20 '67
Yankee, go home; opposition to classified research on the campus. il Newsweek 70:66-7 N 13 '67
See also
Government investigations—Government funded research

History
Robert Boyle. M. B. Hall. il Sci Am 217:96-102 Ag '67

International aspects
EEC steps to close the gap; technological gap between western Europe and the United States. J. R. Lambert. Sci N 92:588 D 16 '67
Foreign research: CIA plus Camelot equals troubles for U.S. scholars. E. Langer. Science 156:1583-4 Je 23 '67
Rarest, most precious vital force; preamble of memorandum, June 16, 1926. M. Curie. UNESCO Courier 20:16-17 O '67

Psychological aspects
Creative tensions in the research and development climate. D. C. Pelz. bibliog il Science 157:160-5 Jl 14 '67

Africa, East
East African academy; report on fourth symposium. R. J. Olembo Science 155: 1581-2+ Mr 24 '67

Brazil
How harmful is natural radioactivity? current tests in Brazil. T. L. Cullen. America 116:280-2 F 25 '67

Canada
Is a great tradition eroding? D. Rose and J. Marier. il Sat R 50:53-7 S 2 '67

China (People's Republic)
Research and development in Communist China. L. A. Orleans. bibliog il Science 157: 392-400 Jl 28 '67
See also
Atomic research—China (People's Republic)

Europe, Western
Europe and America: partners in technology; address, November 10, 1966. G. C. McGhee. Dept State Bul 56:148-53 Ja 23 '67

Japan
Collector on Sagami Bay; letter. T. Komai. Science 157:488+ Ag 4 '67

Russia
See also
Atomic research—Russia

Tanzania
Marine lab in East Africa; Kanduchi, Tanzania. C. Weiss. il Sci N 91:552-3 Je 10 '67

United States
Applied science and technological progress; excerpt from report. H. Brooks. bibliog Science 156:1706-12 Je 30 '67; Reply. W. S. Budington. 158:320-1 O 20 '67
Heroes needed; concerning support of applied and basic research. Sci N 91:521 Je 3 '67
Research funding growth seen slowing. W. J. Normyle. Aviation W 87:30-1 Ag 14 '67
Research in America. J. Lear. See issues of Saturday review
Science takes a field trip up the Amazon; Alphea Helix expenditure. il Bsns W p 132-4+ S 16 '67
Think tanks, billions for brainwork. R. Reeves. Read Digest 91:55-60 S '67
See also
Colleges and universities—Research
Government investigations—Government funded research
Government research
Rand corporation
Stanford research institute

RESEARCH, Cooperative
Hope for small nations; regional cooperation. H. J. Barnes. Sci N 92:326-8 S 30 '67

RESEARCH, Freedom of. See Science, Freedom of

RESEARCH and engineering council of the graphic arts industry, incorporated
New methods advanced; annual conference. il Pub W 191:78+ Je 12 '67

RESEARCH and industry. See Industrial research

RESEARCH and technology division. See United States—Air force—Systems command

RESEARCH in colleges. See Colleges and universities—Research

RESEARCH laboratories
Applied science. P. H. Abelson. Science 156: 1555 Je 23 '67
Baedeker for scientists; European laboratories visited by Americans. E. Langer. Science 156:228 Ap 14 '67
Checkerboard square gets new master plan for headquarters and research center; Ralston-Purina: master plan and office building. St. Louis, Mo. il Arch Rec 141:146 Mr '67
Research in California. J. Lear; J. Duscha. il Sat R 50:64-6+ S 23 '67
Think tanks, billions for brainwork. R. Reeves. Read Digest 91:55-60 S '67
    See also
Bell telephone laboratories
Haskins laboratories
United States—National aeronautics and space administration—Electronics research center

RESEARCH librarians. See Libraries—Reference work

RESEARCH libraries
ACLS to study research libraries' needs. Pub W 191:59 Ap 10 '67

RESEARCH organizations. See Associations

RESEARCH ships. See Ships, Research

RESEGREGATION of schools. See Public schools—Desegregation

RESERPINE
Reserpine: effect on structure of heart muscle. D. E. L. Wilcken and others. bibliog il Science 157:1332-4 S 15 '67
Reserpine: inhibition of olfactory blockage of pregnancy in mice. C. J. Dominic; discussion. bibliog Science 155:851-2 F 17 '67

RESERVATIONS, Airline. See Airlines—Reservation systems

RESERVATIONS, Indian. See Indians of North America—Reservations

RESERVE forces (United States) See United States—Armed forces—Reserves

RESERVE officers training corps. See United States—Reserve officers training corps

RESERVES, Bank. See Bank reserves

RESERVOIRS
Artificial lakes: multi-purpose reservoirs. A. Radin. il Parks & Rec 2:16-17+ Ag '67
How to clean a big reservoir; Jerome park reservoir, Bronx. J. L. Marcus. il Am City 82:69-71 N '67
Man-made fishing holes answer pollution threats. il Parks & Rec 2:34-5 Mr '67
Reservoirs don't have to be eyesores; Phoenix, Ariz. R. N. Tayor. il Am City 82:71-2 Jl '67

RESIDENCE (law) See Domicile

RESIDENCE halls. See Dormitories

RESIDUAL oil. See Oil fuel

RESIKA, Paul
Resika's delectable mountains. C. N. White. il por Art N 66:48-9+ Ap '67

RESIN filters. See Cigarette filters

RESINS. See Gums and resins

RESISTANCE, Electric. See Electric resistance

RESISTANCE of bacteria. See Bacteria—Resistance

RESISTANCE to drugs. See Drugs, Resistance to

RESISTANCE to government. See Passive resistance to government

RESISTANCE to insects in plants. See Plants—Disease and pest resistance

RESNAIS, Alain
Strain of genius. H. Alpert. Sat R 50:55 F 4 '67

RESNICK, Joseph Yale
Harvest of scandal. R. G. Sherrill. Nation 205:496-500 N 13 '67

RESNICK, Michael A. and others
Separation of spores from diploid cells of yeast by stable-flow free-boundary electrophoresis. bibliog Science 158:803-4 N 10 '67

RESNICK, Henry
Another sex triangle. Vogue 150:345+ S 1 '67

RESNIK, Henry S.
Brave new words. Sat R 50:28-9 D 9 '67
Passion on a bicycle. Atlan 221:104-5 Ja '68
What culture? what boom? Atlan 217:51-3 F '67

RESOLUTIONS
    See also
New Years resolutions

RESONANCE, Magnetic. See Magnetic resonance

RESONANCE, Nuclear magnetic. See Nuclear magnetic resonance

RESONANCE curves. See Frequency curves

RESORTS. See Seaside resorts; Summer resorts

RESOURCES, Conservation of. See Conservation of resources

RESOURCES, Natural. See Natural resources

RESOURCES and technical services division. See American library association—Resources and technical services division

RESPIRATION
Respiratory exposure to lead: epidemiological and experimental dose-response relationships. J. R. Goldsmith and A. C. Hexter. bibliog il Science 158:132-4 O 6 '67

Measurement
Pulmonary ventilation measured from body surface movements. J. Mead and others. bibliog il Science 156:1383-4 Je 9 '67

RESPIRATION, Artificial
Artificial respiration for a child. C. J. Potthoff. Todays Health 45:66 Jl '67
Mouth-to-mouth resuscitation; reprint. il Yachting 121:66 Je '67

RESPIRATORY apparatus
Artificial gills: they'll let you breathe like a fish. W. Cloud. il Pop Mech 128:69-72+ D '67
Breath of life; Res-Q-Aire, artificial respirator. il Sci Digest 61:75 My '67
Breathe easy in ultrasonic fog. il Life 62:53+ Mr 10 '67
Fog that saves lives. T. Berland. Read Digest 90:33-4+ Mr '67

RESPIRATORY organs

Diseases
I prescribe for coughs and colds. J. D. Wassersug. il Sci Digest 61:67-71 Mr '67
    See also
Asthma
Rhinitis

Insects
Control of spiracles in silk moths by oxygen and carbon dioxide. B. N. Burkett and H. A. Schneiderman. bibliog il Science 156:1604-6 Je 23 '67

RESPONSES to stimuli. See Stimulus and response

RESPONSIBILITY
American rediscovers America. F. C. Painton. il U S News 63:58-62 S 4 '67
Are we spoiling our kids? with group discussion program, by E. J. Le Shan. il Parents Mag 42:46-7+, 84-5 Ja '67
Brotherhood; address, December 11, 1966. J. M. Roche. Vital Speeches 33:285-8 F 15 '67
Fine art of abdicating responsibility; adaptation of address, June 23, 1967. R. H. Dillon. il Library J 92:2885-8 S 1 '67
How children learn the joy of giving. B. Spock. il Redbook 129:41-3+ S '67
Mistaken kindness; when a mother tries to do too much for her children. il Good H 165:24+ O '67
Responsibility of the intellectual; address, April 8, 1964. R. Squirru. il Américas 19:17-22 Je '67
Riddle for tomorrow's world: how to lead a good life; excerpts from address. E. F. Zeigler. Parks & Rec 2:28+ S '67
Samaritans, good and bad. S. Alexander. Life 63:34 O 13 '67

RESPONSIBILITY (law) See Liability (law)

RES-Q-AIRE. See Respiratory apparatus

REST
    See also
Relaxation
Sleep

RESTAURANT guide books. See Guidebooks

RESTAURANTS
Filet and football; film presentations of professional football at restaurants. Newsweek 70:62 N 6 '67

Architecture
Alexander Girard invites you to dine at the Compound. il Arch Forum 126:60-3 Je '67

Automation
My compliments to the chef. C. W. Morton. il Atlan 220:88 Ag '67

Employees
    See also
Waiters and waitresses

RESTAURANTS—*Continued*

Sanitation

How to tell whether a restaurant is clean. il Good H 165:181 S '67

Europe, Western

About feasting en route. M. Gough. il House B 109:252+ N '67
Europe's finest restaurants, 1968. il Holiday 43:103-8+ Ja '68

France

Finest food of France. S. Spitzer. il Holiday 42:70-1+ N '67
Long, sweet day of the sidewalk café. J. Wechsberg. il Holiday 42:50-3+ Ag '67
See also
Paris—Hotels, restaurants, etc.

Hawaii

About feasting en route. M. Gough. il House B 109:252+ N '67

United States

America: stars and gripes; Guide Julliard to American restaurants and hostelries. il Newsweek 69:53-4 My 22 '67
Cooking up profits, southern style; Kentucky fried chicken corp. il Bsns W p 176+ Je 24 '67
Holiday's choice of American restaurants. S. Spitzer and H. Spitzer. il Holiday 42:99-104 Jl '67
Milky way or alimentary canal? pretensions of foreign cooking. J. Wechsberg. Sat R 50:64+ F 25 '67
New England restaurants. Redbook 129:37+ Jl '67
See also
Stouffer's restaurants

RESTHAVEN community mental health center, Los Angeles. See Rehabilitation centers

RESTIF DE LA BRETONNE, Nicolas Edme
Restive spirit. J. Simon. New Repub 158:31-2+ Ja 6 '68

RESTITUTION claims
Epilogue to a sorry drama; Supreme court decision on U.S. debt owed to Japanese-Americans. Life 62:4 Ap 28 '67
Supreme court orders repayment to Japanese Americans. Christian Cent 84:525 Ap 26 '67
Wrong partially righted; settlement of Japanese-Americans' claims for seizure of property during World war II. il Time 89:25 Ap 21 '67

RESTON, James Barrett
Chaos in the Great society. Read Digest 90:49-50 F '67
Cuban diary: bringing up Castro's new man. N Y Times Mag p 11-13+ Ag 13 '67

about

Mr Reston on the press. M. Childs. New Repub 156:23-4 Ap 29 '67
Nuisance value. Newsweek 70:99 O 2 '67
What we do not need. Nation 206:67-8 Ja 15 '68

RESTON, Va.
Are we being en-gulfed? W. Von Eckardt. New Repub 157:21-3 D 9 '67; Reply. F. Flaxman. 157:36 D 23 '67
Can new towns meet a budget? ouster of R. E. Simon. il Bsns W p 103-4 N 18 '67
Dream city (almost) H. Cox; discussion. Commonweal 85:631, 688 Mr 3, 17 '67
End of a dream. il Newsweek 70:30-1 D 4 '67
Lure of living in clustered houses. il House & Gard 131:124-31 My '67
New towns: geological survey has key role in experiment; its new headquarters. L. J. Carter. il Science 158:752-5 N 10 '67
Reston,fiefdom on the Potomac. M. Viorst. il Horizon 9:34-41 Aut '67
Townhouses, Reston, Virginia. il Arch Rec 141:58-61 mid-My '67

RESTORATION of books. See Books—Conservation and restoration
RESTORATION of buildings. See Architecture—Conservation and restoration
RESTORATION of works of art. See Art—Conservation and restoration
RESTORED airplanes. See Airplanes, Restored
RESTRAINT of trade
See also
Boycott
Exclusive agencies
Patents—Licensing
Trusts, Industrial
RESTREPO, Carlos Lleras. See Lleras Restrepo. C.
RESTRICTIONS on travel. See Travel restrictions

RÉSUMÉS of employment. See Applications for positions
RESURRECTION
See also
Jesus Christ—Resurrection and ascension
RESUSCITATION
See also
Cardiac resuscitation
Respiration, Artificial
RETAIL clerks international association
Union in trade: the retail clerks. Mo Labor R 90:III-IV N '67
RETAIL credit. See Credit
RETAIL prices. See Prices
RETAIL trade
Christmas trade: better, but; meaning for business. il U S News 63:15-17 D 25 '67
Long, cold spring for retailers. il Bsns W p34-5 Je 3 '67
People starting to spend more; meaning to business. il U S News 62:34-6 My 15 '67
Ratios of retailing; table. Duns R 90:54-5 S '67
Responsible retailing. W. M. Batten. Duns R 89:83-6 Mr '67
Spring will be a little late this year. il Bsns W p43-4 Mr 25 '67
Uncle Sam wants you to buy something. il Time 89:87-8 Ap 7 '67
Welcome to the consumption community; excerpt from The Americans: the world experience. D. J. Boorstin. il Fortune 76:118-20+ S 1 '67
See also
Canvassing
Chain stores
Charge accounts (retail trade)
Christmas business
Department stores
Distributive education
Drug trade
Grocery trade
Mail order business
Montgomery Ward and company
Penney. J. C. company
Sears, Roebuck and company

Automation
Next revolution in retailing: automated central distribution facility. A. F. Doody and W. R. Davidson. il Harvard Bsns R 45:4-6+ My '67
RETARDED children. See Mentally handicapped children; Slow learning children
RETENTION (psychology)
Motivated forgetting mediated by implicit verbal chaining: a laboratory analog of repression. S Glucksberg and L. J. King. il Science 158:517-19 O 27 '67
Pentylenetetrazol enhances memory function. S. Irwin and A. Benuazizi; reply with rejoinder. J. Pearl and D. B. McKean. il Science 157:220 Jl 14 '67
RETICULAR formation, Brain. See Brain
RÉTIF DE LA BRETONNE, Nicolas Edme. See Restif de la Bretonne, N. E.
RETINA
Acetylcholinesterase: method for demonstration in amacrine cells of rabbit retina. C. W. Nichols and G. B. Koelle. bibliog il Science 155:477-8 Ja 27 '67
Amino acids and the spikes from the retinal ganglion cells. K. Kishida and K. I. Naka. bibliog il Science 156:648-50 My 5 '67
Direction-selective units in rabbit retina: distribution of preferred directions. C. W. Oyster and H. B. Barlow. bibliog il Science 155:841-2 F 17 '67
Early receptor potential: photoreversible charge displacement in rhodopsin. R. A. Cone. bibliog il Science 155:1128-31 Mr 3 '67
Foveal blue-blindness. G. S. Mumford. Sky & Tel 35:10 Ja '68
Goldfish retina: organization for simultaneous color contrast. N. W. Daw. bibliog il Science 158:942-4 N 17 '67
Molecular and thermal origins of fast photoelectric effects in the squid retina. W. A. Hagins and R. E. McGaughy. bibliog il Science 157:813-16 Ag 18 '67
Nobel work. il Newsweek 70:82-3 O 30 '67
Retinal ganglion cells: specification of central connections in larval xenopus laevis. M. Jacobson. bibliog il Science 155:1106-8 Mr 3 '67
Rhodopsin: responses from transient intermediates formed during its bleaching. W. L. Pak and R. J. Boes. bibliog il Science 155:1131-3 Mr 3 '67
Site of visual adaptation. J. E. Dowling. bibliog il Science 155:273-9 Ja 20 '67

RETINA—*Continued*
Vitamin A deficiency: effect on retinal structure of the moth manduca sexta. S. D. Carlson and others. bibliog il Science 158:268-70 O 13 '67
See also
Visual purple
RETIRED librarians. See Librarians, Retired
RETIRED military personnel

Employment
Out of uniform. L. M. Sharpe and A. D. Biderman. il Mo Labor R 90:15-21 Ja; 39-47 F '67
RETIREMENT, Places of
America's retirement islands. N. D. Ford. il Travel 128:56-8+ D '67
Mexico: two views. il Travel 128:24-9 O '67
RETIREMENT from business, etc.
The best is yet to be. L. De Veuve. Christian Cent 84:866-7 Jl 5 '67; Reply. G. Harkness. 84:1318-19 O 18 '67
Closer look at the problems of retired people. il U S News 63:72-3 O 16 '67
How to be happy though retired. il Changing T 21:24-8 N '67
Illness of idleness. il Time 90:44 D 8 '67
Retirement crisis; report on workshop. F. M. Carp. Science 157:102-3 Jl 7 '67
Taking the fear out of retirement. H. G. Earl. il Todays Health 45:64-7 F '67
Tax breaks when you retire. il Changing T 21:27-8 Je '67
When top men retire; six interviews. J. Weingarten. il Duns R 89:32-4+ F '67
See also
Old age pensions
Retirement, Places of
RETIREMENT income
As social security benefits and taxes go up. il U S News 63:109-10 D 18 '67
New tax-free way to invest for your future. Farm J 91:19 F '67
Retirement plan you start now can save tax dollars. F. Bailey, jr. Suc Farm 65:35 S '67
RETIREMENT systems. See Pensions; Pensions, Industrial
RETOUCHING. See Photography—Retouching
RETREADING of motor bus tires. See Tires, Motor bus—Retreading and recapping
RETREATS, Spiritual
Catholic, Protestant laymen share retreat. A. P. Klausler. Christian Cent 84:878 Jl 5 '67

Judaism
Kosher retreat; Institute of Judaism at Wildacres. il Newsweek 70:83 Ag 7 '67
RETRIEVER trials. See Field trials (dogs)
RETROGRADE amnesia. See Amnesia
RETTIE, Dwight F.
Let's save the most important open space, now! Parks & Rec 2:30-1+ My '67
RETURN of Bobby Shafto; drama. See Miller, H. L.
RETURNS policy of booksellers. See Booksellers and bookselling—Returns policy
REUBEN, John P. and others
Crayfish muscle: permeability to sodium induced by calcium depletion. bibliog Science 155:1263-6 Mr 10 '67
REUNIFICATION question, German. See Germany—Union (proposed)
REUNION; story. See Mountzoures, H. L.
REUNIONS, Family. See Family reunions
REUPHOLSTERING. See Upholstery
REUSEABLE launch vehicle. See Space vehicles—Propulsion systems
REUSS, Henry S.
Cuius regio eius religio. Christian Cent 84:1346-8 O 25 '67
Excerpt from testimony before House committee on armed services, June 29, 1966. Cong Digest 46:150+ My '67
Lobby for tax reform; address, August 16, 1967. Vital Speeches 33:722-4 S 15 '67
Our Rube Goldberg tax system. Commonweal 86:280-1 My 26 '67
REUTERS (news agency)
Speed for sale. il Time 90:64 D 22 '67
REUTHER, Walter Philip
Excerpt from address, February 20, 1967. Cong Digest 46:238+ O '67
Reuther: we won't sign until ..; summary of address, March 10, 1967. U S News 62:88 Mr 20 '67

about
After a settlement at Ford. por U S News 63:12 O 30 '67
Auto strike. Nat R 19:1002 S 19 '67

Auto workers' latest demands, will they set the pace for others? por U S News 62:84-5 Mr 27 '67
Bone in Meany's throat. H. Rowen. New Repub 156:9-10 My 6 '67; Correction. 156:42 Je 3 '67
Contract time in Detroit: collision course. il por Newsweek 70:76-8 Jl 17 '67
Fading blue collars. Christian Cent 84:1421 N 8 '67
GM fight delays a family battle. il Bsns W p57-8 D 2 '67
Inside story of the Reuther-Meany fight. por U S News 62:93-5 F 20 '67
Labor's newest split: the price of a Reuther walkout. U S News 62:76-8 F 27 '67
Labor's top council sticks out its chin. por Bsns W p32-3 F 25 '67
Marriage on the rocks. Time 89:20-1 F 10 '67
Mr Reuther's ploy. America 117:462 O 28 '67
Open door. por Time 89:24 Mr 3 '67
Reuther delivers the goods. il Bsns W p51-2+ N 4 '67
Reuther escalates his war on auto companies. por U S News 63:85-6 N 13 '67
Reuther takes a walk. Newsweek 69:80 F 13 '67
Reuther vs. Meany. S. Lens. Commonweal 85:557-9 F 17 '67
Reuther vs. Meany: background to labor's showdown. B. J. Widick. por Nation 204:614-16 My 15 '67
Reuther walks out, but doesn't shut the door. il por Bsns W p66-8 F 11 '67
Split in labor. W. V. Shannon. Commonweal 85:584-5 F 24 '67
Split labor faces a big year. il por Newsweek 69:82-5 F 20 '67
Walter Reuther: he's got to walk that last mile. S. H. Brown. il por Fortune 76:87-9+ Jl '67
Walter Reuther tries to build a fire. S. Lens. Commonweal 86:253-4 My 19 '67
Walter's walkout. Nat R 19:182 F 21 '67
When union members defy their top leaders. il por U S News 62:84-5 Mr 20 '67
Who's angry? il Newsweek 69:63-4 Mr 6 '67
REVELATION
God of revelation. G. Moran. Commonweal 85:499-503 F 10 '67
Post-biblical Christianity. D. Callahan; discussion. Commonweal 85:359+, 606-7 Ja 6, F 24 '67
Revelation & history; existentialist theologies under attack in Germany. il Time 90:61 Jl 14 '67
REVELLE, Roger
International biological program. Science 155:957 F 24 '67
REVELS, Hiram Rhoades
Three Negro senators of the United States. por Negro Hist Bul 30:4-5 Ja '67
REVENUE
See also
Taxation
REVENUE, State. See State finance
REVENUE bonds. See Bonds, Revenue
REVERB adapter. See Electronic apparatus and appliances
REVERBERATION. See Acoustics, Architectural
REVERE, Paul
Paul Revere's shop in miniature. R. Davidson. il Antiques 92:176 Ag '67
REVERSAL of time. See Time reversal
REVIEW board, Civilian. See New York (city)—Police department
REVIEWS of books. See Book reviews
REVISED standard version of the Holy Bible. See Bible—Versions
REVOLUTION, Social. See Social revolution
REVOLUTIONARY action movement. See Terrorism
REVOLUTIONARY war (United States) See United States—History—Revolution
REVOLUTIONISTS
Great human option; concerning books by G. Rudé. E. T. Gargan. Nation 204:216-20 F 13 '67
REVOLUTIONISTS, Latin American
New Latin revolutionaries and the U.S. R. Shaull. Christian Cent 85:69-70 Ja 17 '68
REVOLUTIONS
Biblical basis of the Geneva conference; Conference on church and society. H. Cox. Christian Cent 84:435-7 Ap 5 '67
Christians look at revolution; World conference on church and society. J. C. Bennett. Christian Cent 84:137-8 F 1 '67
Counter-revolution, by J. H. Meisel. Review New Repub 156:24+ Je 10 '67. S. Karnow
Counter-revolutionary reflex. C. C. O'Brien. Commonweal 85:619-21 Mr 3 '67

REVOLUTIONS—*Continued*
Ignoring the storm warnings; causes of counterrevolution in the less developed world. G. Bing. Nation 205:594-6 D 4 '67
Is insurrection brewing in U.S? an expert's appraisal; interview. R. H. Sanger U S News 63:32-7 D 25 '67
Is the revolution dead? J. Burnham. Nat R 19:1162+ O 31 '67
One millionaire and twenty beggars; excerpts from Pax Americana. R. Steel. Harper 234: 81-7 My '67
Revolution, anyone? W. C. Ferkiss. Commonweal 85:480-3 F 3 '67
Riots: schools for revolution? comparative study of the French revolution of 1848 and the current Negro revolutions. L. Kampf. Nation 205:117-18 Ag 14 '67
La violencia. E. von Kuehnelt-Leddihn. Nat R 19:250 Mr 7 '67
See also
France—History—Revolution
Russia—History—Revolution, 1917-1921
REVOLVERS
Colt's Paterson revolvers. C. G. Worman. il Hobbies 72:126-7 Jl '67
Webley-Fosbery automatic revolver. C. G. Worman. il Hobbies 72:122-3 S '67
REVOLVING charge account. See Charge accounts (retail trade)
REVOLVING credit plans. See Credit
REVUE. See Musical comedy, revue, etc.
REVUSKY, S. H. and Bedarf, E. W.
Association of illness with prior ingestion of novel foods. bibliog Science 155:219-20 Ja 13 '67
REWALD, John
Misunderstanding Monet. Art N 66:25+ Ja '68
REWARD (theology)
Prize dopes; Americans going ga-ga over giveaways. R. P. Sessions. Christian Cent 84:306-9 Mr 8 '67
REWARDS, prizes, etc.
And the world stopped, waiting; first prize! Teachers' writing competition. J. Heimowitz. NEA J 56:21-3 O '67
Awards. See issues of Wilson library bulletin
Children's spring book festival winners announced. il Pub W 191:38 My 8 '67
Juvenile book awards: 1966. Library J 92:1303 Mr 15 '67
Letting off steam; Community opinion wins Peabody award for WLIB. il Newsweek 69:114 My 8 '67
Literary prizes and awards, 1966. Pub W 191: 62-5 Ja 30 '67
Prize dopes; Americans going ga-ga over giveaways. R. P. Sessions. Christian Cent 84:306-9 Mr 8 '67
Prize offers and awards. See issues of Writer
Prizes and awards. See issues of Publishers' weekly
Sounding board; Operation Golden Eagle award given to AFA. il Am For 73:40 Ap '67
Soviet educator urges engineer rewards; excerpts from Izvestia. I. F. Obraztsov. Aviation W 87:115+ S 11 '67
T. P. Sevensma prize; announcement. ALA Bul 61:188-90 F '67
Toward the excellent: Health science advancement awards. K. Sperry. Science 157: 662-3 Ag 11 '67
See also names of awards, e.g. Caldecott medal; Newbery medal
also names of organizations, societies, etc. granting awards, e.g. National art education association

Anecdotes, facetiae, satire, etc.

Notables of 1967. E. Moon. Library J 92:4453 D 15 '67
REXALL drug and chemical company
Life in a banana peel factory. il Duns R 89:50-1+ Ap '67
REXINE, John E.
Colgate's high school high ability seminars. Sch & Soc 95:316-18 Sum '67
REXROTH, Kenneth
Among the cypresses at the end of the way of the cross; poem. Atlan 219:110 F '67
Classics revisited. See issues of Saturday review
How poets make a living, if any. Harper 234:90-2+ F '67
Renaissance by the Bay. Sat R 50:35-6 S 23 '67
REY, Jean Max Georges
Pragmatic prophet of a federalist Europe; with editorial comment. il por Bsns W p74-6+,202 S 16 '67
REYNOLDS, Barbara
Hiroshima, Vietnam: sisters in sorrow. Christian Cent 84:636-8 My 10 '67

REYNOLDS, Charles
Amazing weekend with the amazing Ted Serios. por Pop Phot 61:81-4+ O '67
REYNOLDS, Fred
Sweet and swinging. See issues of American record guide
REYNOLDS, James J.
Labor's stake in the Kennedy round; address, July 7, 1967. Dept State Bul 57:137-40 Jl 31 '67
REYNOLDS, Jesse A.
Park maintenance tasks expanding. Parks & Rec 2:39-40+ O '67
REYNOLDS, M. A. and others
Fallout from the Chinese nuclear explosion of 17 June 1967. bibliog Science 158:1692-3 D 29 '67
REYNOLDS, Malvina
Song of San Francisco Bay; with biographical sketch. Natur Hist 77:4, 6-8+ bibliog(p76) Ja '68
REYNOLDS, Margaret
Last exit verdict casts doubt on U.K. obscenity laws. Pub W 192:20-1 D 11 '67
REYNOLDS, Maryan E.
New ALA officer. ALA Bul 61:869-70 Jl '67
REYNOLDS, Maynard C.
Surge in special education. NEA J 56:46-8 N '67
REYNOLDS, Paul R.
One book's earnings for author and publisher. Pub W 192:42-3 S 11 '67
REYNOLDS, Peggy
What your summer weekends hold. Mlle 65: 149-51+ My '67
REYNOLDS, R. J. foods, incorporated
Trying to package entrepreneurs. il Bsns W p 175-6 Ja 28 '67
REYNOLDS, Robert L.
Canyonlands. Am Heritage 18:52-63 O '67
REYNOLDS, Tim
For Sharon & Don: Going home; Catfish goodbye; poems. Poetry 110:370-3 S '67
REYNOLDS, Vaughan
Decorate your tree outdoors. Home Gard 54:47 D '67
REYNOLDS foods. See Reynolds, R. J. foods, incorporated
REYRE, Jean
Paris bank with a flair for empire. il por Bsns W p78-9+ F 18 '67
Tiger in the bank. il por Time 89:68-9 Ja 27 '67
REZEL, Ronald G.
Toggle switches. por Electr World 78:47-9 O '67
RHEA, John
Focal point for education technology seen. Tech W 20:39 My 1 '67
RHEA, Sally Ann
While somewhere; poem. Horn Bk 43:385 Je '67
Das RHEINGOLD; opera. See Wagner, R.
RHEINGOLD breweries, incorporated
Saving the bread for the sandwich; Rheingold's no-carbohydrate beer. il Time 90:74-5 Jl 7 '67
RHENISH stoneware. See Pottery
RHESUS factor. See Rh factors
RHETORIC
See also
English language—Composition
RHEUMATISM
See also
Gout
RHEUMATOID arthritis. See Arthritis
RHINE PROVINCE
See also
Palatinate
RHINE RIVER
Rhine; Europe's river of legend. W. Graves. il Nat Geog Mag 131:449-99 Ap '67
RHINITIES
Why Johnny can't breathe, allergy? J. P. McGovern and S. M. Linde. il Todays Health 45:11-13+ Mr '67
RHINOPLASTY. See Surgery, Plastic
RHOADES, Orille B.
Books reviewed. See issues of Hobbies
RHODE ISLAND
See also
Block Island
Music festivals—Rhode Island

Constitution

Textbook loan law unconstitutional. Christian Cent 84:1309 O 18 '67

Description and travel

Island-hopping off the coast of New England. M. Goodman. il Redbook 129:35-8 Jl '67

Politics and government

Eroded stronghold. Time 89:19 Ap 7 '67

RHODE ISLAND furniture. See Furniture, American

RHODE ISLAND state ballet. See Ballet companies

RHODE ISLAND. University, Kingston
Law of the sea; University of Rhode Island first summer conference. G. Pontecorvo. Bul Atomic Sci 23:46-8 Ap '67

RHODES, Clarence E.
Lansing renewal program. America 117:202-3 Ag 26 '67

RHODES, Lynwood Mark
Fury named Beulah. Todays Health 45:36-41+ D '67
Killer on the rampage; the great flu epidemic. Todays Health 45:24-7+ O '67
Space-age sights: USA. Todays Health 46:24-8+ Ja '68

RHODESIA
Champagne and bigotry. P. Webb. Newsweek 70:78 N 20 '67
Crisis over Rhodesia, by C. B. Marshall. Review
Nat R 19:1339-40 N 28 '67. E. Huxley
Rhodesia: a case history. J. J. Kilpatrick and others. il Nat R 19:512-26 My 16 '67

See also
United Nations—Rhodesia

Commerce
Sanctions busters; nations trading with Rhodesia. Time 90:23-4 S 8 '67
Success story in Africa: how Rhodesia fares under sanctions. il U S News 63:74-5 D 18 '67

Economic conditions
Boycott pinches. Newsweek 69:48 Je 26 '67
Boycotted but unbowed. il Newsweek 69:49 Ap 24 '67
How long can Rhodesia hold out? il Bsns W p46+ Jl 22 '67
Inch or so of pinch. il Time 89:46 Ap 14 '67
While Salisbury bustles. il Time 89:68 Je 30 '67

Foreign relations
Incredible envoy. Newsweek 70:44 Jl 3 '67

History
Rhodesia: sanctions on trial; events leading to rejection of British proposals. J. Hatch. Nation 204:166-9 F 6 '67

Industries
See also
Rhodesia—Economic conditions

Politics and government
Crisis over Rhodesia, by C. B. Marshall. Review
Reporter 37:45 O 19 '67. E. W. Lefever
Deviationist. Newsweek 69:52+ F 6 '67
Leave us alone to solve our own affairs; interview. ed. by A. J. Meyers. I. Smith. il U S News 63:76-8 D 18 '67
No middle way on Rhodesia. A. A. Kee. Christian Cent 84:231-3 F 22 '67
Prospects in Rhodesia. R. Brown. bibliog f Cur Hist 52:162-7+ Mr '67
Rhodesia: sanctions on trial; events leading to rejection of British proposals. J. Hatch. Nation 204:166-9 F 6 '67
Southern Rhodesia and the United Nations: the U.S. position. Dept State Bul 56:366-77 Mr 6 '67
Southern Rhodesia: the issue of majority rule. J. Palmer, 2d. Dept State Bul 56:449-58 Mr 20 '67

Race problems
Prospects in Rhodesia. R. Brown. bibliog f Cur Hist 52:162-7+ Mr '67
Suspense in Rhodesia. Christian Cent 84:773 Je 14 '67
Tranquil no more: Rhodesian African nationalist group. Newsweek 70:45 S 11 '67

RHODODENDRONS
Blazing Oregon trail; native color, azaleas and rhododendrons. R. Friedman. il Home Gard 54:45 Je '67
First to flower; rhododendrons to bloom with daffodils. M. J. Dietz. il Home Gard 54:55-6 Mr '67
Grow azaleas and rhododendrons. il Pop Gard 18:54-5 My '67
Rhododendron color explosion; displays of the Northwest. il Sunset 138:94-7 My '67

RHODOPSIN. See Visual purple

RHODOSPIRILLUM rubrum. See Bacteria, Photosynthetic

RHUBARB
Asparagus & rhubarb. D. Brooks. il Home Gard 54:35-6 Je '67

What you should know about planting rhubarb. Home Gard 54:20 Jl '67
See also
Cookery—Rhubarb

RHYS, Jean
Second time around. G. Kersh. Sat R 50:23 Jl 1 '67

RHYTHMIC phenomena. See Periodicity

RIBA, Vicki
In my opinion. por Seventeen 26:192 Je '67

RIBICOFF, Abraham
Latest ideas on how to save the big cities; interview. por U S News 62:50-2 F 27 '67

about
Trillion dollars to save U.S. cities? por U S News 62:12 F 6 '67

RIBMAN, Ronald
Ceremony of innocence. Criticism
Nation 206:92 Ja 15 '68
New Yorker 43:68+ Ja 6 '68
Newsweek 71:60 Ja 8 '68

RIBONUCLEASE
Decipher protein structure. Sci N 91:119 F 4 '67
Ribonuclease activity in normal and opaque-2 mutant endosperm of maize. C. M. Wilson and D. E. Alexander. bibliog il Science 155:1575-6 Mr 24 '67
Ribonuclease activity in the developing seeds of normal and opaque-2 maize. A. Dalby and I. ab I. Davies. bibliog il Science 155:1573-5 Mr 24 '67
Ribonuclease: recent advances; report on symposium. D. B. Straus. Science 157:1212+ S 8 '67

RIBONUCLEIC acid
Chemical modification of yeast alanine-tRNA with a radioactive carbodiimide. S. W. Brostoff and V. M. Ingram. bibliog il Science 158:666-9 N 3 '67
Competent chick ectoderm; nonspecific response to RNA. N. Hillman and R. Hillman. bibliog il Science 155:1563-5 Mr 24 '67
Cytokinins in the soluble RNA of plant tissues. R. H. Hall and others. bibliog il Science 156:69-71 Ap 7 '67
Cytoplasmic RNA upsets theories. Sci N 92:394 O 21 '67
Delayed hypersensitivity in man; a correlate in vitro and transfer by an RNA extract. D. E. Thor. bibliog il Science 157:1567-9 S 29 '67
Detergent-solubilized RNA polymerase from cells infected with foot-and-mouth disease virus. R. Arlinghaus and J. Polatnick. bibliog il Science 158:1320-2 D 8 '67
Erythrocyte transfer RNA: change during chick development. J. C. Lee and V. M. Ingram. bibliog il Science 158:1330-2 D 8 '67
Fine structure of RNA codewords recognized by bacterial, amphibian, and mammalian transfer RNA. R. E. Marshall and others. bibliog il Science 155:820-6 F 17 '67
Genetic mapping of phenylalanyl-sRNA synthetase in escherichia coli. A. Böck and F. C. Neidhardt. bibliog il Science 157:78-9 Jl 7 '67
Hope to end virus disease. Sci N 92:173-4 Ag 19 '67
How proteins start. B. F. C. Clark and K. A. Marcker. il Sci Am 218:36-42 bibliog(p 150) Ja '68
Magnesium pemoline: failure to affect in vivo synthesis of brain RNA. N. R. Morris and others. bibliog il Science 155:1125-6 Mr 3 '67
Memory pills: new route to brain power. B. H. Frisch. il Sci Digest 62:37-43 Jl '67
Messenger RNA patterns in rat liver nuclei before and after treatment with growth hormone. J. Drews and G. Brawerman. bibliog il Science 156:1385-6 Je 9 '67
Nucleotide sequence of KB cell 5S RNA. B. G. Forget and S. M. Weissman. bibliog il Science 158:1695-9 D 29 '67
Pemoline and magnesium hydroxide: lack of effect on RNA and protein synthesis. H. H. Stein and T. O. Yellin. bibliog il Science 157:96-7 Jl 7 '67
RNA and DNA synthesis in developing eggs of the milkweed bug, oncopeltus fasciatus (Dallas) S. E. Harris and H. S. Forrest. bibliog il Science 156:1613-15 Je 23 '67
Radioisotope uptake as a measure of synthesis of messenger RNA. D. P. Nierlich. bibliog il Science 158:1186-8 D 1 '67
Reformation of functional liver polyribosomes from ribosome monomers in the absence of RNA systhesis. G. A. Stewart and E. Farber. bibliog il Science 157:67-9 Jl 7 '67
Replication of viral RNA: RNA synthetase from escherichia coli infected with phage MS2 or QB. G. Feix and others. bibliog il Science 157:701-3 Ag 11 '67

RIBONUCLEIC acid—*Continued*
Ribonuclease in three dimensions. Sci Am 216:48-50 Mr '67
Ribonucleic acid: control of steroid synthesis in endocrine tissue. D. B. Villee. bibliog il Science 158:652-3 N 3 '67
Ribosomes: effect of interferon on their interaction with rapidly labeled cellular and viral RNA's. W. A. Carter and H. B. Levy. bibliog il Science 155:1254-7 Mr 10 '67
Valyl-transfer RNA: role in repression of the isoleucine-valine enzymes in escherichia coli. M. Freundlich. bibliog il Science 157:823-5 Ag 18 '67
Yeast transfer RNA: a small-angle X-ray study. J. A. Lake and W. W. Beeman. bibliog il Science 156:1371-3 Je 9 '67
RIBONUCLEOPROTEINS. See Nucleoproteins
RIBOSOMES. See Nucleoproteins
RIBOUD, Jean
New gusher for Schlumberger? J. Ross-Skinner. por Duns R 90:91-2 O '67
RIBOUD, Marc
Nomads of Inner Mongolia; photographs. Natur Hist 76:47-50 Je '67

about

Master of timing, master of light. P. Caulfield. il Mod Phot 31:52-9 Mr '67
RIC, pseud.
Confessions of a campus pot dealer. Esquire 68:100-1+ S '67
RICCI, Franco Maria
Ricci's luxury edition aids Florence library. il por Pub W 191:114 F 6 '67
RICCIO, Ottone M.
Ruined dance; poem. Mlle 66:78 D '67
RICE, Berkeley
In Cleveland and Boston, the issue is race. N Y Times Mag p31+ N 5 '67
Most popular dog in America. N Y Times Mag p50-1+ Ja 7 '68
RICE, Betty. See Rice, E. G. jt. auth.
RICE, Charles E.
Human echo perception. bibliog Science 155:656-64 F 10 '67
RICE, E. G. and Rice, Betty
What's on my mind? Sch Arts 66:5-11 Mr '67
RICE, Emmett
Money men. il pors Ebony 22:65-6+ S '67
RICE, Robert
Normal week for crime. N Y Times Mag p8-9+ Je 18 '67
RICE, Robert V. See Kelly, R. E. jt. auth.
RICE, William S.
Pseudo-etchings. Design 68:27 Sum '67
RICE
Breakthrough against hunger: miracle rice for Far East; IR-8. il U S News 63:68-9 D 4 '67
See also
Cookery—Rice
RICE, Wild. See Wild rice
RICE LAKE, Minn.
Reporter at large; wild rice harvest at Lower Rice Lake, in the White Earth Chippewa Indian reservation, Minn. B. Roueché. il New Yorker 43:34-8+ D 23 '67
RICE pudding. See Puddings
RICH, Adrienne
Charleston in the 1860s; poem. Nation 204:526 Ap 24 '67
Night watch; poem. Nation 204:406 Mr 27 '67

about

To solve experience. H. Carruth. Poetry 109:267 Ja '67
RICH, Alan
Imagery in music. House B 109:164+ Je '67
Inertia and enterprise in San Francisco. Sat R 50:42-3 S 23 '67
Siren sounds. House B 109:122-3+ Ja '67
What you can learn from Frère Jacques. House B 109:60+ O '67
RICH, Alexander
Cooperative education in developing countries: two programs; excerpts from address. Bul Atomic Sci 23:43-5 N '67
—See Kim, S. H. jt. auth.
RICH, Buddy
Portrait of Buddy. B. Korall. Sat R 50:64-5 My 27 '67
Profiles. W. Balliett. por New Yorker 42:35-6+ Ja 21 '67
RICH, Leslie
It's fun to yell bravo. Am Ed 3:15-20+ Je '67
RICH, The
Dilemma of being very, very rich. D. Brinkley. Ladies Home J 84:204 N '67

Speaking out: God bless the rich. W. F. Buckley, jr. Sat Eve Post 240:4+ D 30 '67
See also
Millionaires

Anecdotes, facetiae, satire, etc.
Old money, new money. L. H. Lapham. il Sat Eve Post 240:22-3 D 30 '67
RICHARD, Betti
Sculpture of Betti Richard. N. Kent. il pors Am Artist 31:46-51+ N '67
RICHARD III; drama. See Shakespeare, W.
—Plays
RICHARDS, Ben
Make your own six to twelve volt up-verter. Pop Electr 27:67-70 O '67
RICHARDS, Bob
Health, wealth & Wheaties. il por Time 89:85 Je 16 '67
RICHARDS, Donald W.
Radio-telephone answers communication lack. Am City 82:113 Ap '67
RICHARDS, Louise G.
Drug abuse and the value crisis. Sr Schol 91:sup 13-14 N 16 '67
RICHARDS, Pat
How to buy a fishing boat. Pop Mech 127:154+ F '67
RICHARDS, Paul
Things are different in Atlanta. por Sports Illus 26:53-4 Mr 27 '67
RICHARDS, W. P. C. and Cordy, D. R.
Bluetongue virus infection: pathologic responses of nervous systems in sheep and mice. bibliog Science 156:530-1 Ap 28 '67
RICHARDS, Walter
Cruising to Expo 67. Motor B 119:154 F '67
Interlude, enroute to a cup match. Motor B 120:40+ S '67
RICHARDSON, Benjamin
Richardson glass. H. Wakefield. il Antiques 91:632-6 My '67
RICHARDSON, David C.
Bombing: an admiral's report; interview, ed. by E. Martin. por Newsweek 69:49 My 29 '67
RICHARDSON, Dorothy Miller
Dorothy Richardson in limbo. R. Freedman. Nation 205:280-1 S 25 '67
Dorothy Richardson's pilgrimage. M. Ellmann. New Repub 157:23-5 O 28 '67
She was an Edwardian camera. L. Edel. por Sat R 50:29-30 Ag 12 '67
RICHARDSON, Francis
Goldfish; poem. Sat R 50:73 Mr 25 '67
Pactolus; poem. Sat R 50:34 Mr 25 '67
RICHARDSON, Herbert Warren
Beyond the secular city. Newsweek 70:82-3 S 11 '67
RICHARDSON, Jack
English imports on Broadway. Commentary 43:73-5 Je '67
Grace through gambling. Esquire 67:142-4+ Ap '67
Satires. Commentary 43:86-9 Mr '67
Two new plays. Commentary 44:82-4 D '67
RICHARDSON, John Kirk
Brass household candlesticks of the gothic period. Antiques 92:818-21 D '67
RICHARDSON, Larry
Larry Richardson & dance company; 92nd street Y. M. Marks. Dance Mag 42:28+ Ja '68
Larry Richardson, Village theatre. M. Marks. Dance Mag 41:66+ Ag '67
RICHARDSON, Martha
Discipline problems. NEA J 56:61-2 D '67
RICHARDSON, Ralph
Bears look for trouble. por Outdoor Life 140:66-7+ O '67
RICHARDSON, Robert S.
Return of Halley's comet. Sci Digest 62:70-5 N '67
RICHARDSON, William J.
Pay any price? break any mold? America 116:625-9 Ap 29 '67
Reopening the door to China. America 116:850-2 Je 17 '67
RICHFIELD oil corporation
And they lived happily ever after; merger of Atlantic refining and Richfield oil. il Bsns W p 156-8+ Ap 29 '67
RICHLER, Mordecai
Koufax the incomparable. Commentary 42:87-9 N '66; 43:20+ F '67
RICHMAN, Barry M.
Capitalists & managers in Communist China. Harvard Bsns R 45:57-78 Ja '67
RICHMAN, Robin
Happy hippie hunting ground. Life 63:66+ D 1 '67
RICHMOND, Douglas
Baja and back, on a Honda! Pop Mech 128:118-20+ N '67
PM tests BSA's 250-cc Starfire. Pop Mech 128:116-18 D '67

RICHMOND, Douglas—*Continued*
Scrambling cycles. U S Camera 30:46-7+ Ag '67
Spotless darkroom. U S Camera 30:64-5+ My '67
RICHMOND, Theodore J.
Wizard of Paterson. por Newsweek 70:72 N 6 '67
RICHMOND, Va.
How to dovetail construction projects. C. Du-Val. il Am City 82:58 D '67
RICH'S (department store) See Atlanta—Stores
RICHTER, Gerhart
Camera and the brush. K. Young. il U S Camera 30:34 D '67
RICHTERITE. See Amphiboles
RICKENBACKER, Edward Vernon
Captain Eddie. il por Newsweek 70:100+ O 9 '67
One of a kind. W. F. Rickenbacker. Nat R 19:1433-4 D 26 '67
Swashbuckler with a message. E. K. Gann. Sat R 50:28 O 14 '67
RICKENBACKER, William F.
One of a kind. Nat R 19:1433-4 D 26, '67
Records. Nat R 19:866+, 1344-6 Ag 8, N 28 '67
RICKLES, Don
Merchant of venom. por Newsweek 70:118 S 25 '67
Mr Warmth. por Time 90:35 D 29 '67
RICKMAN, Eric
Rooster tales. See issues of Hot rod
RICKOVER, Hyman G.
Admiral Rickover opens up on Pentagon's cost policies; excerpts from testimony, April 18, 1967. por U S News 62:42-3 My 29 '67
Printing week; summary of address, January 16, 1967. por Pub W 191:100+ F 6 '67

about
Implications of the latest Rickover ruling. H. F. Pilpel. Pub W 192:33-4 Jl 31 '67
Rickover tells GE to weigh anchor. por Bsns W p 105+ Je 24 '67
RIDDIFORD, Lynn M.
Antibiotics in the laboratory-rearing of cecropia silkworms. bibliog Science 157:1451-2 S 22 '67
Trans-2-hexenal: mating stimulant for polyphemus moths. bibliog Science 158:139-41 O 6 '67
—and Williams, C. M.
Volatile principle from oak leaves: role in sex life of the polyphemus moth. bibliog Science 155:589-90 F 3 '67
RIDE round the rivers. See Inland navigation
RIDEAU CANAL
Ontario's historic cruiseway; Rideau Canal. J. Lingard. il Yachting 121:73-5+ Je '67
RIDER, Cowl
On learning photography; reprint. U S Camera 31:61 Ja '68
RIDGEWAY, James
Air accidents. New Repub 157:12-14 Ag 5 '67
Antitrust doldrums. New Repub 156:13-15 Mr 18 '67
Behind the scenes at Long Island U. New Repub 156:10-11 Ap 15 '67
Coming up with a slate in California. New Repub 157:9-10 O 14 '67
Crazy kind of carnival. New Repub 157:13-14 S 30 '67
Freak-out in Chicago. New Repub 157:9-12 S 16 '67
On Wisconsin. New Repub 157:8-10 N 4 '67
Patriots on the campus. New Repub 156:12-13 Mr 25 '67
Sedition in Kentucky. New Repub 157:10 S 2 '67
Social problem-solvers. New Repub 156:18-20 Ap 8 '67
Treating mental illness. New Repub 156:13-15 Je 10 '67
Voice of ITT. New Repub 157:17-19 Jl 8 '67
Who needs people. New Repub 156:10-12 My 13 '67
—and Kopkind, Andrew
Playing it straight. New Repub 156:35 Mr 11 '67
—and Sanford, David
Nader affair. New Repub 156:16-18 F 18 '67

about
ITT's press relations. New Repub 157:6-7 S 16 '67; Reply. W. F. Donnelly. 157:36 S 30 '67
RIDGWAY, Sam H. and McCormick, J. G.
Anesthetization of porpoises for major surgery. bibliog Science 158:510-12 O 27 '67
RIDLEY, Charles Price
Investigation into the causes of hyperpedantism. Atlan 221:101-2 Ja '68

RIE, Ellen D. See Rie, H. E. jt. auth.
RIE, Herbert E. and Rie, E. D.
Growing and learning. Cath World 206:13-16 O '67
RIEDEL, W. R.
Radiolarian evidence consistent with spreading of the Pacific floor. bibliog Science 157:540-2 Ag 4 '67
RIEFF, Philip
Lessons from revolution. R. B. Kaiser. America 117:469+ O 28 '67
Psychological man. W. F. Lynch. America 117:635-7 N 25 '67
RIEGEL paper corporation
Sharing the risk in packaging war. il Bsns W p 132-4 Jl 8 '67
RIEGER, Catherine
Survival test; story. Redbook 130:159-85 N '67
RIEGGER, Hal
Clay and fibres: a beginning. Sch Arts 66:19-22 Ap '67
RIEGLE, Donald W. Jr
Best congressmen of the year. Nation 206:34-5 Ja 8 '68
RIEL, Arthur R. Jr
Communal prayer, back when. America 116:455 Mr 25 '67
RIEMENSCHNEIDER, Tilman
Riemenschneider rediscovered. A. Werner. il por Am Artist 31:36-41+ D '67
RIENOW, Leona Train. See Rienow, R. jt. auth.
RIENOW, Robert, and Rienow, L. T.
Crisis in beauty; excerpt from Moment in the sun. pors Liv Wildn 31:50-4 Spr '67
Oil around us. N Y Times Mag p24-5+ Je 4 '67
S. R. O; excerpt from Moment in the sun. N Y Times Mag p62-3+ My 28 '67
RIES, S. K. See Kesner, C. D. jt. auth.
RIESMAN, David
Some questions about the study of American character in the twentieth century. bibliog f Ann Am Acad 370:36-47 Mr '67
RIETH, Marian
No boy. I'm a girl! story. Seventeen 26:132-3 Mr '67
RIETI, Vittorio
Neoclassic delights: the music of Vittorio Rieti. A. Cohn. Am Rec G 33:817-18 My '67
RIFIELD, Phyllis
Fashion-design schools: getting the fantasy out of your system. Mlle 65:120-1+ S '67
If you want to teach. Mlle 64:150-1+ Mr '67
RIFKIN, Murray S.
Variable low-voltage power supply. Electr World 78:79 O '67
RIFLE sheaths. See Sheaths
RIFLE shooting. See Shooting
RIFLE slings. See Rifles
RIFLES
Alaskan arms. W. Page. il Field & S 72:60-4 Ja '68
Amazing new kind of gun, it's not all hot air; the V-L. G. C. Nonte, jr. il Pop Mech 128:120-2+ O '67
ARVN: toward fighting trim; use of new M-16s. il Time 91:31 Ja 5 '68
B. Tyler Henry. C. G. Worman. il Hobbies 71:124-5 F '67
Christian Sharps. C. Worman. il Hobbies 72:126-7 Ap '67
Colonel Greene's rifle. C. G. Worman. il Hobbies 72:122-3 N '67
Hawken rifles. C. Worman. il Hobbies 72:126-7 My '67
How good is our new Vietnam rifle? H. O. Johansen. il Pop Sci 191:70-3+ Ag '67
Kentucky rifle in the Revolutionary war. C. Worman. il Hobbies 72:126-7 Mr '67
Long pants for the 6 mm.'s. W. Page. il Field & S 71:120-4 F '67
M-16, the gun they swear by, and at! D. C. Fales. il Pop Mech 128:128-31+ O '67
Model 1903 Springfield rifle. C. Worman. il Hobbies 72:126-7 Je '67
New Browning rifle. J. O'Connor. il Outdoor Life 140:92+ O '67
New U.S rifle: best yet? or a failure in Vietnam? M-16 controversy; with excerpt from letter from a wounded marine. il U S News 62:8+ Je 5 '67
One small gun for all small game. H. Bradshaw. il Field & S 72:54-5+ N '67
Patrick Ferguson; soldier and gun designer. C. G. Worman. il Hobbies 72:122-3 Ja '68
Peeking out a chuck hole. W. Page. Field & S 71:136-8 Ap '67
Powder pains; M-16 jamming troubles. Time 90:17 S 8 '67
Rifle that's also a shotgun. P. Wahl. il Pop Sci 191:138-9 O '67

RIFLES—*Continued*
Rifle under fire; M-16. il Newsweek 69:26-7 Je 12 '67
Rifle under fire; M-16 report. il Newsweek 70:27-8 O 30 '67
Rimfire news. W. Page. il Field & S 72:142-4+ My '67
Troubles of M-16; was army at fault? U S News 63:16 O 30 '67
The .270 in Africa. J. O'Connor. il Outdoor Life 139:118-22 Mr '67
Under fire; M-16 controversy. il Time 89:31 Je 9 '67
Using a rifle sling. J. O'Connor. il Outdoor Life 140:74+ D '67
See also
Colt industries, incorporated
RIFLES, Air. See Air guns
RIGA, Peter
Catholic and obscenity. por Cath World 205:340-5 S '67
RIGER, Robert
Selection of photographs from Man in sport; exhibition at Baltimore museum of art; excerpts from introduction to catalogue. Am Artist 32:56-9+ Ja '68
RIGG, Robert B.
Military appraisal of the threat to U.S. cities. por U S News 64:68-71 Ja 15 '68
RIGGENBERG, Harold
Scribble cartoons. Design 69:14-15 Wint '67
RIGGING. See Masts and rigging
RIGGS, Austen. See Bonaventura, J. jt. auth.
RIGGS, H. C.
Hydrologic bench marks in the national parks. Nat Parks Mag 41:17-19 Ja '67
RIGHT and left (political science)
Alice in newleftland; national convention on New politics. P. Steinfels. Commonweal 86:608-10 S 29 '67
American Left and Israel. M. Peretz. bibliog f Commentary 44:27-34 N '67
Are Jews still liberals? how they voted on the Civilian review board issue. M. Himmelfarb. Commentary 43:67-72 Ap '67; Discussion. 44:6+ S '67
Better purpose. Nation 204:162-3 F 6 '67
Black power: a third party going nowhere; national conference on New politics. il U S News 63:78 S 18 '67
Black power; new left. il Newsweek 70:40 S 18 '67
Chaos on the left; national conference for New politics. Time 90:23 S 15 '67
Choices, not echoes. Nat R 19:557-8 My 30 '67
Civil disobedience: prelude to revolution? address, October 5, 1967. L. F. Powell, jr. il U S News 63:66-9 O 30 '67
Decline of the anti-Communist left. M. Geltman. il Nat R 19:79-83 Ja 24 '67
Extremists in America: vigilant watchdogs or obstructive dropouts? with press comments. il Sr Schol 90:6-12+ My 5 '67
Fascism and Harvard. Nat R 19:337 Ap 4 '67
First things first; new left seeks presidential candidate. Newsweek 70:24 S 11 '67
Freak-out in Chicago: the national conference of New politics. J. Ridgeway. New Repub 157:9-12 S 16 '67
Good, the true and the beautiful; causes of the right. J. G. Dunne. Sat Eve Post 240:16+ Ag 12 '67
Hippies, political radicals and the church. N. K. Gottwald. Christian Cent 84:1043-5 Ag 16 '67
In defense of dissent. D. Young. Sat R 50:60+ Ap 8 '67
Left in search of itself: the New politics convention. T. Gitlin. Christian Cent 84:1230+ S 27 '67
Left, right and center: essays on liberalism and conservatism in the United States, ed. by R. A. Goldwin. Review
Nat R 20:37+ Ja 16 '68. A. Lejeune
Letter from the Palmer house; national New politics convention, Chicago. R. Adler. New Yorker 43:56-8+ S 23 '67; Discussion. Nation 205:450+, 514+ N 6, 20 '67
Liberal anti-communism revisited; symposium. Commentary 44:31-79 S '67; Discussion. 44:6+ D '67
Limits of the new left. C. Jencks. New Repub 157:19-21 O 21 '67; Correction and Reply. J. Epstein. 157:29 N 4 '67
Little old professors in tennis shoes. J. Hart. Nat R 19:635+ Je 13 '67
Middle of the journey. R. Kirk. Nat R 19:857 Ag 8 '67
New left and American history: some recent trends in United States historiography. I. Unger. bibliog f Am Hist R 72:1237-63 Jl '67
New left & the old right. M. Geltman. il Nat R 19:632-5 Je 13 '67

New left asks faith beyond politics. J. N. Eller. America 116:495 Ap 1 '67
New politics at Chicago. R. Blumenthal. Nation 205:273-6 S 25 '67
New politics comes to the old left. T. J. Wheeler. Nat R 19:1015-17 S 19 '67
New politics; new left meeting in Chicago. K. Crawford. Newsweek 70:45 S 18 '67
New radicals; Time essay. Time 89:26-7 Ap 28 '67
Populism of George Wallace. F. S. Meyer. Nat R 19:527 My 16 '67
Protest, power and the future of politics. C. McWilliams. Nation 206:71-7 Ja 15 '68
Right has nine lives; radical right movement's hold on the body politic. F. J. Cook. Nation 204:330-5 Mr 13 '67
Romantic rebel on the campus. J. Hitchcock. Yale R 57:31-7 O '67
What the new left did to me. P. A. Luce. Read Digest 90:93-7 F '67
When black power runs the new left; national conference for New politics. W. Goodman. il N Y Times Mag p28-9+ S 24 '67
Why Lucky Jim turned right. K. Amis. Nat R 19:1121-2+ O 17 '67
Why young radicals zero in on business. il Nations Bsns 55:31-4 Jl '67
See also
Conservatism
RIGHT- and left-handedness. See Left- and right-handedness
RIGHT and wrong. See Ethics
RIGHT of asylum. See Asylum, Right of
RIGHT of dissent. See Free speech
RIGHT of government employees to strike. See Strikes—United States—Government employees
RIGHT of privacy. See Privacy
RIGHT of search. See Search, Right of
RIGHT to labor
Work and human worth. T. L. Smith. Christian Cent 84:1094-7 Ag 30 '67
RIGHT to speedy trial. See Speedy trial
RIGHT to travel. See Travel regulations
RIGHT to work laws. See Labor laws and legislation—United States
RIGHT wing (politics) See Right and left (political science)
RIGHTS, Bill of (United States) See United States—Constitution—Bill of rights
RIGHTS, Civil. See Civil rights
RIGHTS of the child, Declaration of the. See Child welfare
RIGHTS of way
See also
Eminent domain
RIGHTS of women. See Woman—Equal rights
RIGOLETTO; opera. See Verdi, G.
RIIS plaza. See New York (city)—Parks and playgrounds
RIKER, Audrey Palm. See Burns, J. T. jt. auth.
RIKITAKE, T. See Hagiwara, T. jt. auth.
RIKKI
Rikki cuts out. E. Willis. Sat Eve Post 240:35 Je 3 '67
RIKLIS, Meshulam
Meshulam Riklis: how to build an empire without cash. il por Duns R 90:21 Jl '67
RILEY, Brett
Sidney and the dogs; story. Atlan 220:70-4 D '67
RILEY, Frank
A cross in Heraklion. Sat R 50:47-8+ O 14 '67
Deathwatch in Tokyo. Sat R 50:40+ D 16 '67
RILEY, James Whitcomb
James Whitcomb Riley; notes on the early years; reprint. W. R. Cagle. Hobbies 72:108-9+ Jl '67
RILEY, John
Alcindor. Life 62:106 F 17 '67
Saga of the barefoot bag on campus. Life 62:72A-72B Mr 17 '67
RILEY, Mrs Lowell F.
Dutch life of Riley. il Pop Phot 60:50+ My '67
RILEY, Mike
Baseball's week. Sports Illus 27:73 Ag 14 '67
Rowing. Sports Illus 27:44 Jl 10 '67
RILEY, Nord
Something peculiar at Tulelake. Outdoor Life 140:62-4+ N '67
Stubble-field bird hunt. Field & S 72:64-5+ O '67
RILEY, Pat
Life of Riley, and Dampier. H. L. Masin. il por Sr Schol 90:20 F 10 '67
RILEY, Robert B.
Dreams of tomorrow. Arch Forum 126:66-7+ Ap '67

RILEY, Virginia
Educational secretary in the elementary school. NEA J 56:40 F '67
RIMERS of Eldritch; drama. See Wilson, L.
RIMOIN, David L. See McKusick, V. A. jt. auth.
RIMSKII-KORSAKOV, Nikolai Andreevich
Le coq d'or. Criticism
New Yorker 43:86+ S 30 '67
Opera N 32:6-7 S 23 '67
Opera N il 32:20 N 4 '67
Sat R 50:49 O 7 '67
Legend of the invisible city of Kitezh. Criticism
New Yorker 43:146-8 S 9 '67
Sat R 50:64 S 16 '67
Want to feel like a prince? M. N. Kanny. Am Rec G 34:52 S '67
RINALDI, Giorgio
From Scandinavia to Somalia, a Soviet spy network crumbles. il por U S News 62:44-6 Ap 24 '67
RINFRET, Pierre A.
Political economics; address, November 1, 1966. Vital Speeches 33:278-82 F 15 '67
about
Edie's new mind & manners. Time 89:84 Mr 24 '67
RING counters. See Counting machines and devices
RING of the Nibelung; operas. See Wagner, R.
RINGGENBERG, Harold
Two heads are better than one. Design 68: 14-16 Ja '67
RINGLING brothers, Barnum and Bailey circus. See Circus
RINGO, James
About getting here from there. Am Rec G 33:824+ My '67
From Schirmer, Barber's Antony and Cleopatra. Am Rec G 33:871-2+ My '67
Virgil. Am Rec G 33:460-3 F '67
RINGO, Jim
Iron man. il Newsweek 70:70 D 11 '67
RINGS, Piston. See Piston rings
RINGS of trees. See Tree rings
RINGWORM fungi. See Fungi, Pathogenic
RINK, Larry, family
And there was one. A. Lake. pors Good H 164:90-1+ Mr '67
RIO ARRIBA COUNTY, N.Mex.
Incident in Rio Arriba; attempt by small band of Spanish-Americans to seize land. C. Kentfield. il N Y Times Mag p20-1+ Jl 16 '67
RIO DE JANEIRO
Housing
No time for gaiety; governor's demolition order and construction ban. Newsweek 69:66 Mr 27 '67
RIO DE JANEIRO flood. See Floods—Brazil
RIO GRANDE national life insurance company
Vietnam sparks a family war; heavy losses from military policies. Bsns W p 150 O 21 '67
RIO NEGRO
River of insecticide; contains plant and tree substances similar to insect hormones. il Time 90:76 Ag 25 '67
RIOPELLE, Arthur J.
Snowflake; the world's first white gorilla. Nat Geog Mag 131:442-8 Mr '67
RIOS, Walter B.
After Wieland, business as usual? Hi Fi 17: MA22-3 N '67
RIOT control
Can new non-lethal weapons control riots? E. S. Gardner. il Pop Sci 191:48-52 D '67
Civil-rights bill moves ahead, but—. U S News 63:10 Ag 28 '67
Delicate balance; President says local police have responsibility for keeping the peace. il Newsweek 70:30 S 25 '67
DEW line for riots. Newsweek 70:74 Ag 7 '67
Do we need a federal riot force? pro and con discussion. il Sr Schol 91:22-3 S 21 '67
Getting ready; National guard's training course. New Repub 157:8-9 O 28 '67
GOP steals a march with crime; crime control proposals. Bsns W p 130+ Ag 19 '67
Guns and riots; anti-riot bill passed in House. New Repub 157:4 Ag 5 '67
How much force? parallel strategies for dealing with riots and war. W. V. Kennedy. America 117:278-80 S 16 '67
How rest of world handles riots. il U S News 63:36-8 Ag 14 '67; Same abr. with title How they do it abroad. Read Digest 91:135-6 O '67

Humane policing. E. F. Fennessy, jr. and others. Sat R 50:48 Jl 1 '67
Humane riot control. il Am City 82:165-6 S '67
It's a riot. Reporter 37:16-17 S 21 '67
LBJ raps rioters; summary of address, September 1967. L. B. Johnson. Sr Schol 91:40-1 O 5 '67
Nation seeks ways to cool it. il Bsns W p23-4 Ag 5 '67
National guard, awake or asleep? training program. W. A. McWhirter. il Life 63:85-6+ O 27 '67
Negro militancy; a complicating dimension. Sci N 92:152-3 Ag 12 '67
New kind of war. il Newsweek 70:20-1 Ag 14 '67
New nonlethal weapons. il Life 63:76-7 N 24 '67
No armistice; arms buying and charges of terrorism. il Newsweek 70:36 O 16 '67
Permanent insurrection. il Nat R 19:835-8 Ag 8 '67
Putting out the fires next time; riot-control training. H. B. Meyers. il Fortune 77:174-6+ Ja '68
Quench riots, and look beyond. Life 63:4 Ag 4 '67
Riot control. G. M. Chamberlain. il Am City 82:87-9+ F; 107-9 Mr '67
Riot control: hold the street & seize the high ground. Time 90:16-17 Ag 4 '67
Speaking out; after the riots: force won't settle anything. R. Girardin. Sat Eve Post 240:10+ S 23 '67
Toward next summer, and after. Fortune 76:68 S 1 '67
Watts to Detroit. Nat R 19:885+ Ag 22 '67
What Congress is doing to curb riots. U S News 63:11 Ag 21 '67
See also
Police—Equipment and supplies
RIOT prevention. See Riot control
RIOTS
Why people riot. F. R. Schreiber and M. Herman. il Sci Digest 62:56-60 O '67
See also
Mob violence
Riot control
also subhead Riots under names of countries, cities, etc. e.g. Nashville, Tenn.—Riots
RIPLEY, F. C.
Owner's comments. Yachting 122:60 Jl '67
RIPLEY, S. Dillon
Editor interviews; ed. by M. S. Fenner. pors NEA J 56:91-2 F '67
Elegant lady; address, October 19, 1967. Vital
about
Toys in the attic. il por Newsweek 69:106-7 My 15 '67
RIPPON, John W.
Elastase; production by ringworm fungi. bibliog Science 157:947 Ag 25 '67
RISE up and hear the bells; story. See Rohde, B.
RISK
Better decisions with preference theory. J. S. Hammond, 3d. bibliog f il Harvard Bsns R 45:123-41 N '67
RISK (Insurance) See Insurance—Risks
RISK (periodical)
Updating the theses. Christian Cent 84:1308 O 18 '67
RISOTTO. See Cookery—Rice
RISTOW, Walter W.
Map librarianship. bibliog por Library J 92: 3610-14 O 15 '67
RITES and ceremonies
See also
Confirmation
Coronations
Festivals
Funeral rites and ceremonies
Paper in religion, folklore, etc.
Passover

Germany (Federal Republic)
U.S. business pays tribute to Frankfurt; revival of Piper's court. il Bsns W p 110-12 S 9 '67

India
Living prehistory in India. D. D. Kosambi. il Sci Am 216:104-12+ F '67

Japan
Antlers of Nara. il Natur Hist 76:30-3 F '67
RITTER, Joseph Elmer, cardinal
Cardinal for all seasons. America 116:865 Je 24 '67
Obituary
Commonweal 86:402 Je 30 '67. J. Deedy

RITTER, Norman
Interstate 87. Atlan 220:104-9 S '67
RITTERBUSH, Philip C.
Books. Bul Atomic Sci 23:33-4 N '67
RITUAL. See Rites and ceremonies
RIVER blindness. See Onchocerciasis
RIVER FOREST, Ill.
Million dollar carrels: Oak Park and River
Forest, high school library; with report by
L. Salinger. G. L. Schwilk. il Library J
92:306-10 Ja 15 '67
RIVER herring. See Alewives (fishes)
RIVER navigation. See Inland navigation
RIVER photography. See Photography—Land-
scapes
RIVER trips
How to sell multiple use without half trying;
Clearwater River country, Idaho. V.
Fischer. il Am For 73:34-5+ Ag '67
Hudson River heritage cruise. P. Smyth. il
Motor B 120:21-6+ S '67
On to the Yukon. il Am For 73:40+ Mr '67
Our cruising houseboat. M. Clark. il Yacht-
ing 121:80-1+ Ap '67
River that isn't a river. K. Ferguson. il
Motor B 120:34+ O '67
Short trip up the river. J. Wilson. il Motor B
120:35-7 O '67
Sojourn on the Susquehanna. R. G. Miller.
il Motor B 119:183-4+ Mr '67
Tall trip in short takes. J. Scott and L.
Scott. il Motor B 119:28-31+ Ap '67
Vanishing waterway; a sentimental pilgrim-
age to the Oklawaha River system. E.
White. il Yachting 122:42-3+ N '67
See also
Canoe trips
RIVERA, Luis
On the boards. W. Como. il por Dance Mag
41:22 My '67
RIVERO HAEDO, Elsie Krasting de. See Car-
reño, V. pseud.
RIVERS, Joan
Who are you, Joan? W. H. Manville. il pors
Sat Eve Post 240:67-8 Jl 1 '67
RIVERS, Larry
Blues for Yves Klein. Art N 65:32-3+ F '67
about
Larry Rivers' living room. M. Simons. il
pors Look 31:M20+ Mr 21 '67
RIVERS, Thomas E.
Recreation in the war zone. Parks & Rec
2:26-7 Mr '67
RIVERS, William L.
New winds in the South, new splash in the
North. Sat R 50:75-6+ S 23 '67
RIVERS
Dams and wild rivers: looking beyond the
pork barrel. L. J. Carter. il Science 158:233-
6+ O 13 '67
House committee must choose between four
wild river bills. C. H. Callison. il Audubon
69:70-1 N '67
Meander wavelength of alluvial rivers. S. A.
Schumm. bibliog il Science 157:1549-50 S 29
'67
Mike Frome; activities of the exclusive river-
ways guild. M. Frome. Am For 73:6 N '67
Of time and the rivers; wild rivers bill before
House of representatives. Newsweek 69:86
Je 19 '67
Rivers in the making. H. F. Garner. il Sci
Am 216:84-8+ Ap '67
See also
Estuaries
Water pollution
also names of rivers, e.g. Mississippi
River
Photographs
Cheat River. J. Dominis. Life 63:110-19+ D
22 '67
Regulation
See also
Dams
Flood prevention and control
RIVERSIDE, Calif.
Finance
Smooth tax collections mean soothed tax-
payers. D. R. O'Connor. il Am City 82:94-5
Ag '67
RIVERSIDE buildings. See Building sites
RIVERSIDE church. See New York (city)—
Churches
RIVETS and riveting
Useful riveting tools of unusual type; blind
riveting. il Consumer Bul 50:24-5 Ag '67
RIVIERA
French Riviera, storied playground on the
Azure coast. C. Mitchell. il Nat Geog Mag
131:798-835 Je '67

Going places, finding things in La Côte
d'Azur and Provence. K. Bates. il House &
Gard 131:56-8+ Ap '67
Going places, finding things on the Italian
Riviera. M. Roche. il House & Gard 132:58-
9+ S '67
Marseille to Toulon slowly. il Sunset 138:66+
Ap '67
RIVIERE, Bill
Campfire bakery. Field & S 71:64 F '67
RIZZO, Eugene
(ed) See Bury, J. Moses, Mozart, Pinter
RIZZO, Patrick V.
Convention in Washington. por Sky & Tel 34:
139-42 S '67
ROACH, R. Hopkins
Your teen-ager and smoking. Todays Health
46:68-70+ Ja '68
ROACHES. See Cockroaches
ROAD construction. See Highway engineering
ROAD guards. See Roads—Safety guards
ROAD rallies. See Automobile racing
ROAD runners (birds)
Nature note; roadrunner. Sci N 91:396 Ap 29
'67
ROAD signs
Signs for bicycle routes. il Parks & Rec 2:69
My '67
ROAD traffic
7 billions to cure traffic ills; one state's plan.
il U S News 63:70-2 D 4 '67
See also
Highway engineering
Traffic signs
Sweden
In one instant a left-lane nation swerves
right. il Life 63:38-9 S 15 '67
Now in Sweden it's keep to the right. U S
News 63:14 S 18 '67
Right flank, drive! il Newsweek 70:75 S 11
'67
Sweden tells traffic to keep to the right. il
Bsns W p26-7 S 2 '67
Switch to the right. il Time 90:39-40 S 15
'67
ROADRUNNERS. See Road runners (birds)
ROADS
See also
Driveways
National parks and reserves—Roads
Trails
Finance
Tussle for the highway trust fund; State high-
way officials trying to head off efforts to di-
vert funds. Bsns W p 176+ Je 17 '67
See also
Toll roads
Location
Hardnosed highwaymen ride again; Inter-
state highway program and route planning.
Life 62:4 Ap 14 '67
Maintenance and repair
See also
Roads—Surface treatment
Safety devices and measures
Farewell to wet-weather skids; longitudinal
grooves in California. J. Root. il Pop Mech
127:124-7+ Mr '67
Federal rules for safety on roads; move to
implement Highway safety act of 1966. il
U S News 63:8 Jl 10 '67
Man-made highway hazards that kill. J. A.
Blatnik. il Pop Sci 191:84-8+ N '67
To stay alive on the highways. J. N. Miller.
Read Digest 90:128-31 Ap '67
See also
Reflectors (safety devices)
Safety guards
Highway device that can save your life. il
Sci Digest 61:64-8 Ap '67
Superhighways
See Express highways
Surface treatment
Salt stabilization; how it is done. il Parks &
Rec 2:23+ S '67
Arizona
Aspens turn to gold this month along Ari-
zona's Coronado trail. il Sunset 139:42-4+
O '67
California
After 700 road curves, there's old Mineral
King, your destination or jumping-off place.
il Sunset 138:42-4+ Je '67

ROADS—*Continued*

Canada
Banff to Jasper; snowy and spectacular. il Sunset 138:44 F '67

Central America
See also
Pan American highway

Latin America
Andean awakening. P. Orlandini. il Travel 127:64-6+ My '67
If you want to drive to the Panama Canal; Inter-American highway. il U S News 62:109 Je 5 '67
Peru's path to progress; Marginal forest highway. D. G. Stroetzel. il Read Digest 91:167-70+ S '67
See also
Pan American highway

Nevada
Detour to sleepy Paradise Valley. il Sunset 139:60+ O '67

New York (state)
Interstate 87; routes argument. N. Ritter. il Atlan 220:104-9 S '67
7 billions to cure traffic ills; one state's plan. il U S News 63:70-2 D 4 '67

Northeastern states
Profiles; through the great city. A. Bailey. il New Yorker 43:35-42+ Jl 22 '67

Peru
Regaining a lost habit; effect of Belaúnde's Marginal highway. il Time 90:37 D 8 '67

South America
See Roads—Latin America

Texas
Follow the old road to San Antonio. R. Dunlop. il Todays Health 45:42-9+ Mr '67

United States
Conservation: keeping watch on the road builders. L. J. Carter. il Science 157:527-9 Ag 4 '67
See also
Billboards
Express highways
Pan American highway
Toll roads

ROADS, Brick
See also
Pavements, Brick

ROADS, International
See also
Pan American highway

ROADSIDE improvement
Perils of planned prettiness: highway beautification program. L. S. Hall. Life 62:20 My 12 '67
Youth is action. il Sr Schol 91:6-7 D 14 '67
See also
Billboards

ROALMAN, A. R.
Designed for healthier living: America's new cities. Todays Health 45:46-9+ F '67
How good are auto safety gimmicks? Todays Health 45:38-41 S '67
How to love a parade. Todays Health 45:20-5+ Jl '67
Simplicity is the keynote in Japanese gardening. Pop Gard 18:18-21+ D '67
What's a swinger like you doing on the ground? Todays Health 45:28-31+ O '67

ROAMIN' Jo and Juli; or, How the West was lost; drama. See Boiko, C.

ROASTING. See Cookery—Meat

ROBARDS, Sherman M.
Here come the Japanese. Fortune 75:114-15 Je 1 '67

ROBB, Charles Spittal
How big a White House wedding for Lynda? il por U S News 63:30 S 25 '67
Lynda Bird: no. 1 bride-to-be. W. Hedgepeth. il pors Look 31:53-6+ D 12 '67
Lynda Johnson tells the story of her engagement. L. B. Johnson. por McCalls 95:80-1+ N '67
Man in her life. il por Newsweek 70:29-30 S 25 '67
Real Charlie. il por Time 90:25 S 22 '67
When there's a White House wedding. por U S News 63:16 D 18 '67
White House wedding. il pors Newsweek 70:28-32 D 18 '67

ROBB, Walter L. See Ward, W. J. 3d, jt. auth.

ROBBER flies. See Flies

ROBBERIES and assaults
As good as gold; theft of gold bullion in London. Time 89:29-30 My 12 '67
Bank-robbery boom. il Newsweek 70:41 N 13 '67
Behind the boom in bank robberies. il U S News 63:65-6 O 23 '67
Big business of hijacking. B. Surface. il Read Digest 92:115-19 Ja '68
Brinksmanship; looting of armored car in Boston. il Newsweek 69:33 Je 5 '67
Easier than robbing a bank; truck robberies. B. Surface. il N Y Times Mag p 129+ My 7 '67
Eleventh-hour defendants; first indictments for 1962 mail robbery. il Newsweek 70:24+ Ag 14 '67
Great bullion robbery. Newsweek 69:58 My 15 '67
Spreading a net for hijackers; Operation Alert, radio-warning system. il Bsns W p 171-2 My 6 '67
Whole works; du Pont coin collection stolen. il Newsweek 70:36+ O 16 '67
See also
Burglary and burglars

ROBBERSON, Winifred
Boating business. See issues of Yachting

ROBBINS, Frederic John
How to get out of a steel-lined rut. por Bsns W p86+ Jl 15 '67

ROBBINS, Harold, pseud.
World's best-paid writer. T. Thompson. il pors Life 63:49-50+ D 8 '67

ROBBINS, Jerome
Dancing in semi-silence. W. Terry. Sat R 50:104 O 14 '67

ROBBINS, Jhan
I don't believe in ghosts, but . . . Read Digest 91:105-9 Jl '67
Two little boys from Tayninh. Good H 164:94-5+ Je '67
(ed) See Doxiadis, C. A. House is to live in, a home is to love
—and Robbins, June
I, Sharon, take thee, Jay . . . McCalls 94:108-9+ Mr '67
Little girl is lost. Good H 165:12+ Ag '67
Rest are simply left to die. Redbook 130:80-1+ N '67
We discovered our town. Read Digest 90:88-91 My '67
Woman who hit and ran. McCalls 94:112-13+ F '67

ROBBINS, June
(ed) See Doxiadis, C. A. House is to live in, a home is to love
—See Robbins, Jhan, jt. auth.

ROBBINS, P. W. and others
Direction of chain growth in polysaccharide synthesis. bibliog Science 158:1536-42 D 22 '67

ROBBINS, Richard
Native sons. Cath World 206:81-6 N '67

ROBBINS, W. E. See Svoboda, J. A. jt. auth.

ROBBINS, William H.
Forty-seven places in America to buy land and make money. Esquire 68:141-4+ O '67

ROBE, T. J.
Small-signal high-frequency transistors. por Electr World 78:38-40 Jl '67

ROBENS, Alfred, baron Robens of Woldingham. See Robens of Woldingham, A. R.

ROBENS of Woldingham, Alfred Robens, baron
Lord Coal's role. il por Time 90:84 Ag 18 '67

ROBERSON, Clarence W. Jr
Excerpt from letter, March 10, 1967. Cong Digest 46:159 My '67

ROBERT Joffrey ballet. See City Center Joffrey ballet

ROBERTIS, Eduardo Diego Patricio de
Ultrastructure and cytochemistry of the synaptic region. bibliog Science 156:907-14 My 19 '67
—and others
Cholinergic binding capacity of proteolipids from isolated nerve-ending membranes. bibliog Science 158:928-9 N 17 '67

ROBERTS, Charles
Truth v. death. il por Time 89:26 Mr 17 '67

ROBERTS, David S.
Death in a far place; excerpt from Mountain of my fear. il por Sat Eve Post 241:30-4+ Ja 27 '68

ROBERTS, Don
This is my beat. E. Geller. il por Library J 93:259-64 Ja 15 '68

ROBERTS, G. W.
Reproductive performance and reproductive capacity in less industrialized societies. bibliog f Ann Am Acad 369:37-47 Ja '67

ROBERTS, Gene
Case of Jim Garrison and Lee Oswald. N Y
Times Mag p32-5+ My 21 '67
Kind of black power in Macon County, Ala.
N Y Times Mag p32-3+ F 26 '67
ROBERTS, Henry L.
(comp) Recent books on international rela-
tions. See issues of Foreign affairs
ROBERTS, Jeremy B.   See Palmer, J. K. jt.
auth.
ROBERTS, Leslie
Quiet role of the go-betweens. Sat R 50:40
Ag 12 '67
When Egypt won and UAR lost. Sat R 50:
44-6 N 4 '67
ROBERTS, Llewellyn
He bought a bus. D. Dew. il Sat R 50:58-9+
Je 17 '67
ROBERTS, McLean
My son is on LSD. Ladies Home J 85:38+
Ja '68
ROBERTS, Millard George
Flunking of drop-out U. por Time 89:74+ Ap
14 '67
ROBERTS, Myron
Making of a city. Sat R 50:72-4 S 23 '67
ROBERTS, Paul
Interview with Paul Roberts. por Sr Schol
91:sup9+ O 19 '67
ROBERTS, Percy
Big bark in the Garden. R. H. Boyle. por
Sports Illus 26:48-50 F 13 '67
ROBERTS, Phyllis
Seashore state park. Parks & Rec 2:10-13+
D '67
ROBERTS, Ray
Pictures you can stroke. Design 69:34-5 Wint
'67
ROBERTS, Sidney, and others
Adenosine 3',5'-cyclic phosphate: stimulation
of steroidogenesis in sonically disrupted
adrenal mitochondria. bibliog Science 158:
372-4 O 20 '67
ROBERTS, Steven V.
Dump-Johnson movement. Commonweal 87:
106-7 O 27 '67
Elections: poor guys finish last. Common-
weal 87:291-2 D 1 '67
Is it too late for a man of honesty, high
purpose and intelligence to be elected presi-
dent of the United States in 1968? Esquire
68:89-93+ O '67
Pressures mount on LBJ. Commonweal 87:
70-1 O 20 '67
ROBERTS, Ted
Can we save the falling tower? Sci Digest
61:57-9 My '67
ROBERTS, Wallace I.
New England power. Nation 204:818-21 Je 26 '67
ROBERTS, Walter
Musicians of Bremen town; dramatization
of Grimms' fairy tale. Plays 27:71-4 Ja
'68
ROBERTS, Walter Orr
Walter Orr Roberts, president-elect. W. T.
Golden. por Science 155:853-4 F 17 '67
ROBERTSON, Cliff
Lively arts; interview, ed. by R. Hemming.
por Sr Schol 90:26 Ap 28 '67
ROBERTSON, David H.
Pools in schools. NEA J 56:41 My '67
ROBERTSON, L. S. Jr
How to set up a soil fertility program. Suc
Farm 65:46-7+ S '67
ROBERTSON, O. J.
Animals' Christmas tree; drama. Plays 27:
67-9 D '67
Sleepy little elf; drama. Plays 27:70-2 D '67
ROBERTSON, Ray
Boating. Sports Illus 27:86-8 S 11 '67
ROBERTSOM, Robert
Heliacus, gastropoda: architectonicidae,
symbiotic with zoanthiniaria, coelenterata.
bibliog Science 156:246-8 Ap 14 '67
ROBERTSON, William Owen
Second shock wave; address, January 26,
1967. Vital Speeches 33:408-11 Ap 15 '67
ROBIN, Eugene D. and others
Humoral agent from calf lung producing pul-
monary arterial vasoconstriction. bibliog
Science 156:827-30 My 12 '67
ROBIN, Ralph
Actual assassin; poem. Christian Cent 84:166
F 8 '67
Exaggerators; poem. Christian Cent 84:1550
D 6 '67
Processing data; poem. Christian Cent 85:10
Ja 3 '68
ROBINS
Science proves it, the robin sees the worm.
F. Heppner. il Audubon 69:86-8+ S '67
ROBINSON, Barbara
Big white naked bird; story. McCalls 95:
104-5 N '67
Christmas pageant; story. McCalls 95:112-13
D '67

ROBINSON, Bill
Editor's page. Yachting 122:21 N '67
Powerboating in paradise. il Yachting 122:42-
3+ Jl '67
Texas way. il Yachting 121:76-8+ Ja '67
    about
Yachting's new editor   C. Rimington. por
Yachting 121:37 F '67
ROBINSON, Carrie C.
Negro history week. bibliog Library J 93:
268-9 Ja 15 '68
ROBINSON, Cervin
Modern antiques: 20th century landmarks. il
Arch Forum 126:74-82 Je '67
ROBINSON, Daniel N.
Visual discrimination of temporal order. bib-
liog Science 156:1263-4; 158:1705 Je 2, D 29
'67
ROBINSON, Donald
America's big eye on the sky. Read Digest
90:155-6+ F '67
Shocking facts about fake marriage coun-
selors. Good H 165:74-5+ Jl '67
ROBINSON, Dyann
On the boards. W. Como. por Dance Mag 41:
18 D '67
ROBINSON, Elizabeth C.
Collections make vacation memories. Am
Home 70:118 Jl '67
Common sense and table manners. Am Home
70:126b N '67
Your manners are showing. Am Home 70:60
Mr '67
ROBINSON, Francis
Fortunes of Gallo. Sat R 51:101+ Ja 13 '68
Geraldine Farrar; February 28, 1882-March
11, 1967. Opera N 31:14-15 Ap 15 '67
ROBINSON, Frank
Birds fall down on broken wings.   J. Jares.
il Sports Illus 27:26-8+ Jl 17 '67
ROBINSON, Frank M.
New dimensions in camping for the physic-
ally handicapped. Parks & Rec 2:21+ F '67
ROBINSON, J. H.
Let's update filter-design standards; ex-
cerpts from address, January 1967. bibliog
Am City 82:105-8 Ap '67
ROBINSON, Jack
Jack Robinson photographs Vogue's own
boutique. M. P. R. Thomas. il U S Camera
30:50-1 Ap '67
ROBINSON, Jerome B.
Our summer visitor. Read Digest 90:73-7 F
'67
ROBINSON, Louie
Charles White: portrayer of black dignity.
Ebony 22:25-8+ Jl '67
Death threatens western town. Ebony 22:
60-2+ Je '67
Godfrey Cambridge wins battle of bulges,
loses 117 pounds. Ebony 22:160-2+ O '67
Redd Foxx, prince of clowns. Ebony 22:91-2+
Ap '67
ROBINSON, Thomas E.
Company came to Hollybush. por NEA J 56:
20-1 S '67
ROBINSON, William Albert
Voyage of the Svaap. il por Newsweek 69:16
Je 12 '67
ROBINSON, William G. See Cornish, G. S. jt.
auth.
ROBINSON Crusoe's island. See Juan Fernan-
dez Islands
ROBINSONADES
Crusoe's island. P. Quennell. il Horizon 9:
66-83 Spr '67
ROBISON, Joseph B.
ESEA. Title II: a fictional facade for religious
subsidies. bibliog Wilson Lib Bul 41:708-13
Mr '67
ROBISON, Richard A. See Pantoja-Alor, J. jt.
auth.
ROBISON, Sophia M.
Juvenile delinquency. bibliog f Cur Hist 52:
341-8 Je '67
ROBOTS. See Anatomical models; Automatons
ROBY, Frank Helmuth
Less diversity means more prosperity for
Sola Basic. il por Bsns W p82-4+ Ap 22
'67
ROCHE, Albert
Pilgrim of Downing st. il Look 31:87 My 2 '67
ROCHE, Jack
Mother Goose report. Sat Eve Post 240:22
O 7 '67
ROCHE, James Michael
Brotherhood; address, December 11, 1966. Vital
Speeches 33:285-8 F 15 '67

ROCHE, James Michael—*Continued*
about
GM: test for a new team. por Newsweek 70:83 N 13 '67
Giant GM splits its big problems. il por Bsns W p 134-6+ N 4 '67
Nader affair. J. Ridgeway and D. Sanford. New Repub 156:16-18 F 18 '67
New leaders for a mammoth corporation. por U S News 63:19 N 13 '67
Roche team at G.M. il por Fortune 76:51 D '67

ROCHE, John P.
At the White House, intellectual-in-residence. A. Howard. il pors N Y Times Mag p34-5+ Mr 12 '67
Inconceivable connivance. Time 91:14 Ja 12 '68

ROCHE, Josephine Aspinwall
Battler for miners. por Bsns W p 100-1 Ap 8 '67

ROCHE, Mary, 1907-
Going places, finding things on the Italian Riviera. House & Gard 132:58-9+ S '67

ROCHE, William M.
To be perfectly frank. America 116:376-7 Mr 18 '67

ROCHESTER, N.Y.
Negroes
... And Kodak will ask, how high? troubles with FIGHT. Fortune 75:78 Je 1 '67
FIGHT against Kodak. B. Carter. il Reporter 36:28-31 Ap 20 '67
Fight at Kodak; company racial policies. il Newsweek 69:81+ My 8 '67
FIGHT in color; Negro employment by Kodak. il Time 89:88 My 5 '67
Self-doubt and black pride; Eastman Kodak and the FIGHT organization. R. A. Schroth. America 116:502-5 Ap 1 '67; Reply with rejoinder. P. A. Mallon. 116:664-5 My 6 '67
Shepherds vs. flocks; church involvement in FIGHT assault on Kodak. W. C. Martin. Atlan 220:53-9 D '67

Parks and playgrounds
Mobile playgrounds in Rochester. R. E. Dispenza. il Parks & Rec 2:26+ Je '67

ROCHESTER, N.Y., public library
Open access for children at Rochester proves successful. Library J 93:255 Ja 15 '68
Rochester public library awarded county support. Library J 92:4094 N 15 '67

ROCHESTER, N.Y. University
Bold scale for a restricted site: a science complex for the University of Rochester. il Arch Rec 141:192-5 Ap '67
See also
Eastman school of music, Rochester, N.Y.

ROCK, Irvin, and Harris, C. S.
Vision and touch; with biographical sketches. Sci Am 216:21, 96-104 bibliog(p 167) My '67

ROCK, Maxine A.
We expect to win. Nat Parks Mag 41:12-13 Je '67

ROCK climbing. See Mountaineering
ROCK dams. See Dams
ROCK-eating snails. See Snails
ROCK FALLS, Ill.
Small-city municipal center. il Am City 82:90-1 Ja '67

ROCK garden plants. See Plants, Rock garden
ROCK gardens. See Gardens, Rock
ROCK ISLAND, Ill.
Mini-megalopolis rises along the Mississippi; thriving Quad-cities of Iowa and Illinois. il Bsns W p 168-70 F 25 '67
Our people aren't impressed. J. E. Holzer. il Am City 82:108-9 My '67

ROCK 'n' roll music
Beyond these things; Procol Harum. il Newsweek 70:78 Jl 31 '67
Crawdaddy! first flourishing journal of serious rock criticism. Newsweek 70:114 D 11 '67
Does this Mother know best? F. Zappa, leader of the Mothers of Invention rock group. W. H. Manville. il Sat Eve Post 241:56-7 Ja 13 '68
Face to face with the editor of a rock and roll magazine: Crawdaddy! P. Williams. il Seventeen 26:159 Ap '67
Forget the message; just play; British rock trio called Cream. il Time 90:53 O 27 '67
Four Fifths: hard-luck noise for hire. D. Chapman. il Look 31:M14+ Jl 25 '67
Hi, hi, Hornets; eight-year-old Steve Calvert on drums for his three-brother rock combo. W. Hedgepeth. il Look 31:M21-2 O 17 '67
It's time to start listening. R. Kramer. il N Y Times Mag p80+ S 17 '67

Jefferson airplane loves you; new San Francisco sound: love rock. J. Luce. il Look 31:58-62 My 30 '67
Open up, tune in, turn on; San Francisco sound from the Jefferson Airplane. il Time 89:53 Je 23 '67
Other noises, other notes; Beatles' astonishing inventiveness. il Time 89:63 Mr 3 '67
Paupers arrive. R. Goldstein. Vogue 151:54 Ja 1 '68
Rock: symptom of today's sociological disturbances. G. Lees. il Hi Fi 17:57-61 N '67
Secular music. R. Christgau. il Esquire 67:16+ Je '67
Something heavy; religious rock. il Time 90:50 D 29 '67
Swimming to the moon; The Doors. il Time 90:106 N 24 '67
This way to the egress; The Doors. il Newsweek 70:101 N 6 '67
Tune up, turn disestablishmentarian, drop out. R. Christgau. il Esquire 68:104-5+ S '67
Voice of experience; Jimi Hendrix Experience. il Newsweek 70:90+ O 9 '67

ROCK 'n' roll songs. See Music, Popular (songs, etc)
ROCK paintings. See Cave drawings and paintings
ROCK profiles
See also
Profile Mountain
ROCK salt stabilized roads. See Roads—Surface treatment
ROCK singers. See Singers
ROCKEFELLER, David
Common market for U.S. and Canada? interview. por U S News 63:88-9 Ag 21 '67
about
David Rockefeller, banker's banker. il pors Newsweek 69:72-4+ Ap 3 '67

ROCKEFELLER, John Davison, 1906-
Parents' magazine's 1967 awards. il por Parents Mag 42:52+ D '67

ROCKEFELLER, John Davison, 1938?-
I, Sharon, take thee, Jay. . . . J. Robbins and J. Robbins. por McCalls 94:108-9+ Mr '67
Percy-Rockefeller wedding. il pors Life 62:85-90 Ap 14 '67
Royal wedding. por Newsweek 69:39 Ap 10 '67

ROCKEFELLER, Larry
Around the world. por Flying 81:58-62+ N '67

ROCKEFELLER, Laurance S.
Men who made the world move. H. Bigart. por Sat R 50:54+ Ap 22 '67

ROCKEFELLER, Nelson Aldrich, 1908-
Governor lectures on art; excerpt from address at the New school for social research, New York. por N Y Times Mag p28-31+ Ap 9 '67
Policy and the people. For Affairs 46:231-41 Ja '68
about
Business and Rockefeller. R. Brady. Duns R 90:5 N '67
How T.R.'s giraffes got Rocky thinking about the big job. H. Sidey. il por Life 64:32B Ja 12 '68
Let George do it. Time 89:29 My 19 '67
Nelson Rockefeller: a record to fit the times. D. Norton-Taylor. il pors Fortune 75:96-9+ Je 1 '67
New clue to Rockefeller's political plans. por US News 64:20 Ja 15 '68
Nixon vs. Rockefeller: choice shaping up. il por U S News 64:38-40 Ja 1 '68
Other fellows. il Newsweek 71:21 Ja 22 '68
Revival of Rockefeller. S. Alsop. por Sat Eve Post 240:12 Ag 12 '67
Riots, Reagan and Rockefeller. il Nations Bsns 55:80-2+ N '67
Rockefeller in '68? New Repub 156:3-4 Je 10 '67
Rockefeller-Lindsay feud. G. Pressman. Nation 205:591-3 D 4 '67
Rockefeller: Republican dark horse? il pors U S News 62:48-50 My 8 '67
Rockefeller, Romney, Reagan: what kind of governors; a study of the record. il pors U S News 63:54-7 O 30 '67
Rocky: he who runs least runs best. J. Cannon. por Newsweek 70:34-5 D 18 '67
Rocky (is, is not, may be) running. R. Reeves. il pors N Y Times Mag p30-1+ N 26 '67
Rocky on the rise. por Newsweek 70:20 Ag 28 '67
Rocky's rise. Time 90:26 S 29 '67
Waiting for Rocky. Time 91:12 Ja 19 '68

ROCKEFELLER, Sharon Lee (Percy)
I, Sharon, take thee, Jay. . . J. Robbins and J. Robbins. por McCalls 94:108-9+ Mr '67
Percy-Rockefeller wedding. il pors Life 62: 85-90 Ap 14 '67
Royal wedding. por Newsweek 69:39 Ap 10 '67

ROCKEFELLER, Winthrop
Big Rock of Little Rock. il por Read Digest 90:111-15 Mr '67
On to 1968; tour of Arkansas. il por Time 90:25 Jl 21 '67
Rocky of Little Rock. T. Dearmore. il por Reporter 37:14-18 O 5 '67

ROCKEFELLER Center. See New York (city) —Rockefeller Center

ROCKEFELLER university, New York
See also
Institute for research in animal behavior

ROCKET-assisted projectiles. See Projectiles

ROCKET engines
Gentle rockets. J. Eberhart. il Sci N 91:95+ Ja 28 '67
Marquardt sees $2-billion market for control rockets. W. E. Wilks. il Aero Tech 21:44+ S 11 '67
Missile target powered by hybrid engine; liquid oxidizer and solid fuel. il Aviation W 88:30-1 Ja 15 '68
Nuclear power for spaceships of future? U S News 62:21 Mr 13 '67
Problems spur changes in ascent engine; Apollo lunar module. il Aviation W 88:54-5+ Ja 15 '68
U.S rocket motors; specifications (cont) Aviation W 86:181-6 Mr 6 '67
See also
Ion engines
Solid propellant rockets
Space vehicles—Propulsion systems

Materials
Electroformed nickel motor cases cut cost. il Tech W 20:41 My 8 '67

Testing
Hybrid motor slated for missile target. Aviation W 87:25 S 4 '67
Hybrid rocket passes target missile test. Aviation W 88:24 Ja 8 '68

ROCKET explosions. See Explosions

ROCKET fuel. See Rockets—Fuel

ROCKET models
Getting started in model rocketry. E. Florida. il Pop Mech 128:148-51+ Jl '67

ROCKET motor cases

Materials
See Rocket engines—Materials

ROCKET propulsion
Army studies hybrid rocket MHD power for lasers. R. Lindsey. il Aero Tech 21:48-9 Ag 14 '67
Bell developes two-man pogo for travel on moon, earth. il Tech W 21:26 Jl 3 '67
Gentle rockets. J. Eberhardt. il Sci N 91: 95+ Ja 28 '67
NASA may increase thrust for new X-15; rocket engine power for hypersonic research aircraft. il Aviation W 86:77+ Ap 17 '67
USAF to ground-test toxic propellants. il Aviation W 86:115-18+ Ap 24 '67
See also
Solid propellant rockets

ROCKET sleds
Low-cost sled motor offers versatility; solid-propellant unit is reusable. M. L. Yaffee. il Aviation W 86:50-2 F 20 '67

ROCKETS
Annual world aerospace encyclopedia 1967. il Aero Tech 21:21-32+ Jl 31 '67
Navy eyes small rocket using ABM technique. M. Getler. Tech W 20:24 F 6 '67
See also
Guided missiles
Solid propellant rockets

Control
NASA may ask proposals for Aerobee guidance units. W. S. Beller. il Tech W 20: 32+ Ap 24 '67

Fuel
Pots and pans to missiles; Teflon. Sci Digest 62:23-4 N '67

Materials
Tungsten wire nozzle tested. Aviation W 87: 51 N 27 '67

Testing
UTC claims successful test of largest hybrid rocket. Tech W 20:22 Je 19 '67

USAF to ground-test toxic propellants. il Aviation W 86:115-18+ Ap 24 '67
See also
Space vehicles—Propulsion systems—Testing

Use in research
Barium clouds observed; experiment to study upper-air winds and the diffusion of ionized particles. il Sky & Tel 33:393 Je '67
High-altitude rocket aids debris problem; Astro-Dart meteorological rocket system. R. Barnhart. il Tech W 20:16-17 F 27 '67
Overwater tests planned for air sampler; air-launched air-recoverable rocket. M. L. Yaffee. il Aviation W 86:40-3 F 27 '67
Rocket observations of the eclipse in Brazil. C. A. Accardo. il Sky & Tel 33:77-82 F '67
SESP plans at least three '68 shots; air force's space experiment support program. F. Burnham. il Aero Tech 21:17-18 Ja 1 '68
U.S. research rockets; specifications (cont) Aviation W 86:187 Mr 6 '67

ROCKETS, Atomic powered
How we'll travel beyond the moon; flying nuclear engine, NERVA. W. Von Braun. il Pop Sci 191:84-6+ O '67
NERVA funds to aid manned Mars fly-by. H. Taylor. Tech W 20:18 Mr 6 '67
Upgraded NERVA gets space engine role. il Aero Tech 21:40-3 N 20 '67

Testing
To go to Mars; nuclear rocket program. C. Behrens. il Sci N 91:336-7 Ap 8 '67

ROCKETS, Sounding
Competition to balloons seen from reusable solid rockets. W. E. Wilks. il Tech W 20:25+ Je 19 '67
ESRANGE being expanded for Skylark. K. Lovstuhagen. il Tech W 20:40-1 F 6 '67
Ionospheric sounding rocket use gains. W. J. Normyle. il Aviation W 86:87+ Mr 20 '67
NASA may ask proposals for Aerobee guidance units. W. S. Beller. il Tech W 20: 32+ Ap 24 '67
Rockets bombard the aurora; Aerobee and Javelin. il Sci Digest 61:38-9 My '67

ROCKETTES. See Dancers

ROCKLAND Bog, Me. See Bogs

ROCKS
Farmington meteorite; cristobalite xenoliths and blackening. R. A. Binns. bibliog il Science 156:1222-6 Je 2 '67
Shock effects in certain rock-forming minerals. E. C. T. Chao. bibliog il Science 156:192-202 Ap 14 '67
See also
Batholiths
Metamorphism

Age
Ionium dating of igneous rocks. K. Kigoshi. bibliog il Science 156:932-4 My 19 '67
See also
Geological time

Analysis
Uranium distribution in rocks by fission-track registration in Lexan plastic. J. D. Kleeman and J. F. Lovering. bibliog il Science 156:512-13 Ap 28 '67

ROCKS, Igneous
Andesitic volcanism and seismicity around the Pacific. W. R. Dickinson and T. Hatherton. bibliog il Science 157:801-3 Ag 18 '67
Ionium dating of igneous rocks. K. Kigoshi. bibliog il Science 156:932-4 My 19 '67

ROCKWELL, Ford
Wichita's new living room. Library J 92:4365-6 D 1 '67

ROCKWELL, George Lincoln
Ashes to ashes. il Newsweek 70:23 S 11 '67
Conscience of George Lincoln Rockwell. W. F. Buckley, jr. Nat R 19:1011 S 19 '67
Deadly friendship. D. Rader. New Repub 157: 13-15 S 23 '67
Finis for the Führer. il por Time 90:12 S 1 '67
Last word (we hope) on George Lincoln Rockwell. F. C. Shapiro. pors Esquire 67: 101-5+ F '67
Der tag. il por Newsweek 70:30-1 S 4 '67

ROCKWELL, Norman
Christmas in Stockbridge, Massachusetts, 1967; painting. McCalls 95:101-3 D '67
Education; painting of Russian students. Look 31:48-9 O 3 '67
New kids in the neighborhood; painting. Look 31:52-3 My 16 '67
Willie, the uncommon thrush; picture story. McCalls 94:76-83 Ap '67

ROCKWELL, Orrin Porter
Orrin Porter Rockwell, by H. Schindler. Review
  Sat R 50:36 F 11 '67. M. Brown
ROCKWELL, Willard Frederick, 1888-
Making know-how pay; interview. pors Nations Bsns 55:88-90+ N '67
ROCKWELL, Willard Frederick, 1914-
Eight hats of the chief executive. Duns R 89: 40-1+ Je '67
Rockwells take off for outer space. J. Mecklin. il por Fortune 75:100-4+ Je 1 '67
ROCKWELL-Standard corporation. See North American Rockwell corporation
ROCKY MOUNTAIN goat hunting
Luck beats the odds. E. Park. il Outdoor Life 140:40-1+ S '67
ROCKY MOUNTAINS
Autumn in the Rockies. J. E. Dwyer. il Pop Gard 18:52-5+ D '67
  See also
Hell's Canyon
Teton Range
ROCOCO art. See Art, Rococo
ROD, Divining. See Divining rod
RODBERG, Leonard S.
ABM, some arms control issues. Bul Atomic Sci 23:16-20 Je '67
RODE, Alex
Teacher's dedication to those whose search has failed. il pors Life 62:76-9 Ap 28 '67
RODENTS
  See also
Rats
RODENTS as carriers of infection
Great Bolivian fever mystery; ed. by D. S. Stroetzel. T. Armbrister. il Read Digest 90: 165-6+ F '67
Virus of the California encephalitis complex: isolation from culiseta inornata. O. Morgante and J. A. Shemanchuk. bibliog il Science 157:692-3 Ag 11 '67
RODENTS as laboratory animals. See Laboratory animals
RODEOS
Calf love. H. French. Holiday 41:6 My '67
Cowboy and the Comanche; traveling the rodeo circuit by plane. C. Lofting. il Flying 81:82-6 D '67
Eight seconds on a barrel of dynamite; Negro bullriding cowboy. il Ebony 23:35-6+ D '67
Grey flannel cowboy; L. Mahan. il Time 89:49 Mr 31 '67
He took the bull by the horns; B. Pickett, inventor of bulldogging. J. J. Mundis. il Am Heritage 19:50-5 D '67
Lonely bull rider. il Newsweek 69:89-90 Je 19 '67
Rodeos: a rough ride to glory. O. Bay. il Farm J 91:26-7+ Ag '67
Roughest rides to richest; National finals rodeo. T. C. Brody. il Sports Illus 27:20-2+ D 18 '67
RODEWALD, Diana Kristina
All my life I've loved horses. Seventeen 26: 92-3+ Jl '67
RODGER, Dave A.
Current planetarium activity in Canada. Sky & Tel 34:13-14 Jl '67
RODGER, Robert W.
Borrowing department store techniques to promote library service. por Wilson Lib Bul 42:304-8 N '67
RODGERS, Charles T.
American superiority at the World's great fair; chromolithograph. il Am Heritage 18: 23-5 Ag '67
RODGERS, Dorothy (Feiner)
House in my head; excerpts. House B 109: 124-30+ S; 208-15+ O; 70+, 282-7+ N '67
  about
Chateau the sounds of music built. J. Peter. il pors Look 31:46-7 O 31 '67
RODGERS, Guy
Ballhawk of the Chicago Bulls. il pors Ebony 22:40+ F '67
RODGERS, Johnathan
Basketball's week. Sports Illus 28:56-7 Ja 8 '67
Step to an Olympic boycott. Sports Illus 27: 30-1 D 4 '67
RODGERS, Mary Augusta
Affectionate divorce; story. Redbook 129:70-1 Jl '67
Bless this house; story. Good H 165:69-71 Ag '67
Rhythm of a story. Writer 80:19-21 N '67
RODGERS, Peter
Flat patterns; poem. Harper 234:75 Mr '67
RODGERS, Richard
Chateau the sounds of music built. J. Peter. il por Look 31:44-7 O 31 '67

RODGERS, Rod A.
Is it just for jobs? por Dance Mag 41:26-8 Ap '67
RODIECK, R. W.
Receptive fields in the cat retina: a new type. bibliog Science 157:90-2 Jl 7 '67
RODIN, Auguste
Notes for an essay on Rodin. J. Berger. Nation 205:661-3 D 18 '67
Rodin, homage to a Titan. A. Werner. il por Am Artist 31:45-51+ Ap '67
RODITI, Edouard
Ex-titan of the Tate. Sat R 50:35-6 My 27 '67
RODMAN, Robert L.
It's all in the family. L. J. Kennedy. il Motor B 119:46-7+ My '67
RODMAN, Selden
Balaguer: the first nine months. New Repub 156:19-23 Mr 25 '67
RODRICKS, Joseph V. and others
Solvent contamination from volatile components of a fiberglass glove box. Science 156:1648 Je 23 '67
RODRÍGUEZ-MONEGAL, Emir
Ruben Dario and the resurrection of Hispano-American poetry. UNESCO Courier 20:24-6 O '67
RODRÍGUEZ SAAVEDRA, Carlos
Stone, iron, wood, poverty, truth. Américas 19:20-6 My '67
ROE, Jim
Prize catch for the cruising man. Yachting 121:74-6+ My '67
—and Roe, Jim, Jr
Two Jim Roes test the Glasspar. pors Pop Sci 191:104-6 Jl '67
ROE, Jim, Jr. See Roe, Jim, jt. auth.
ROE, Joann
Plane in every garage. House B 109:34+ S '67
ROE, Robert A.
Skylands of New Jersey. Parks & Rec 2:17+ S '67
ROEDDER, Edwin
Metastable superheated ice in liquid-water inclusions under high negative pressure. bibliog Science 155:1413-17 Mr 17 '67
ROEFER, Martin
'Round the world, family style. por Motor B 120:22-5+ Jl; 27-9+ S '67; 121:107-9 Ja '68
ROELANTS, Gaston
Fleming with a flair. T. Maule. il pors Sports Illus 27:36-43 Jl 17 '67
ROELFS, Robert M.
Liberal-Conservatives; address, August 11, 1967. Vital Speeches 33:746-9 O 1 '67
ROENTGEN, Wilhelm Konrad. See Röntgen, W. K.
ROESSLER, Rudolf
Man called Lucy, by P. Accoce and P. Quet. Review
  Life 62:8 My 12 '67 H. M. Hyde
  Time il por 89:102+ My 5 '67
ROETHKE, Theodore
Completed pattern. M. Benedict. Poetry 109: 262-6 Ja '67
ROGEL, Carole
(comp) Articles and other books received; eastern Europe. Am Hist R 72:1551-2 Jl '67
ROGERS, A. Robert
Wedding cake in Bowling Green. Library J 92:4353-4 D 1 '67
ROGERS, Archibald C.
Toward a national design policy. Arch Rec 141:187-90 Je '67
  about
Building roads without disrupting the city. il Bsns W p 108+ N 18 '67
ROGERS, Barry
New voice from the barrios. R. F. Thompson. il por Sat R 50:53-5+ O 28 '67
ROGERS, Daniel, 1735-1816
Daniel Rogers, silversmiths. M. G. Fales. il Antiques 91:487-91 Ap '67
ROGERS, Daniel, 1753-1792
Daniel Rogers, silversmiths. M. G. Fales. il Antiques 91:487-91 Ap '67
ROGERS, Doug
Doug Rogers theater dance; 92nd street Y. M. Marks. Dance Mag 41:65 F '67
ROGERS, Ginger
Ginger peachy. il pors Time 89:78 F 10 '67
ROGERS, Lawrence H. 1921-
Freedom's last frontier; address, November 17, 1966. Vital Speeches 33:333-9 Mr 15 '67
ROGERS, William P.
Tasks of the ad hoc Committee for South West Africa; statement, January 26, 1967. Dept State Bul 56:302-5 F 20 '67
ROGIN, Gilbert
Boxing. Sports Illus 27:50+ O 9 '67
Uncompleted investigation, furthered and annotated; story. New Yorker 43:37-9 Mr 4 '67

ROGOFF, Gordon
  Fearless Flindt and his dancing Danes. Holiday 41:158+ Ap '67
  Guthrie's Shakespeare. New Repub 156:32-3 Mr 11 '67
ROGUES and vagabonds in literature. See Picaresque literature
ROHDE, Barbara
  Rise up and hear the bells; story. McCalls 94:76-7 Jl '67
ROHLF, John A.
  Your beef business. See issues of Farm journal
ROHR, Bill
  Dream stuff. il pors Newsweek 69:70 Ap 24 '67
ROHR, Frank
  Fearsome 500 for Mona Lou. Motor B 119: 112-14 Je '67
ROHRBACH, Heinrich
  Good small trees for your garden. Horticulture 45:30-1+ O '67
ROHRMAN, F. A. and others
  Industrial emissions of carbon dioxide in the United States: a projection. bibliog Science 156:931-2 My 19 '67
Le ROI se meurt; drama. See Ionesco, E.
ROLAMITE. See Bearings (machinery)
ROLE playing. See Dramatization in education
ROLL your own cigarette machines. See Cigarette-making machines
ROLLAND, Romain
  My debt to Romain Rolland. A. Maurois. por Sat R 50:21+ D 16 '67
ROLLEI cameras. See Cameras
ROLLERS, Hair. See Hair curlers
ROLLERS, Paint. See Paint rollers
ROLLING MEADOWS, Ill.
  Why we began plowing sidewalks. J. McFeggan. il Am City 82:70-1 Ja '67
ROLLING Stones. See Singers
ROLLINS, Alfred B. jr
  Voice as history. Nation 205:518-21 N 20 '67
ROLLINS, Charlemae
  Role of the book in combating prejudice; concerning third edition of list: We build together. por Wilson Lib Bul 42:176-9 O '67
    about
  To Mississippi in the interest of children and books. G. Woods. il Wilson Lib Bul 41:1033 Je '67
ROLLS. See Bread
ROLLS-Royce, limited
  Rolls stressing airbus engine technology. il Aviation W 86:273+ My 29 '67
ROM, Becci
  Face to face with a north woods guide; ed. by T. Merkert. pors Seventeen 26:58 Jl '67
ROMAN, Dick
  Singing in the darkroom. E. Galligan. U S Camera 30:48-9+ Ag '67
ROMAN, Robert C.
  Yankee Doodle Cagney. Dance Mag 41:58-61+ Jl '67
ROMAN Catholic church. See Catholic church
ROMAN curia. See Catholic church—Roman curia
ROMAN law
  Guillaume Budé and the first historical school of law. D. R. Kelly. bibliog f Am Hist R 72:807-34 Ap '67
ROMAN Nose (Cheyenne indian)
  Don't let them ride over us. G. M. Heinzman. il por Am Heritage 18:44-7+ F '67
ROMANCE
  Romance; off-key; memories of being in Vienna when in the twenties. L. Rosten. Look 31:12 My 30 '67
ROMANOV, House of
  Nicholas and Alexandra, by R. K. Massie. Review
    Atlan 221:110-12 Ja '68. E. Weeks
    Life 63:10 O 6 '67. G. Weales
    Sat R 50:34-5 O 7 '67. S. Heitman
ROMANTIC love. See Love
ROMANTIC music. See Music
ROMANTICISM
  European literary scene; international congress, Budapest. R. J. Clements. Sat R 50: 31 N 4 '67
  Our new age of romanticism. P. Gleason. America 117:372-5 O 7 '67
  Romantic rebel on the campus. J. Hitchcock. Yale R 57:31-7 O '67
  Small world of the toy novel. S. Morse. Sat R 50:23+ O 21 '67
  Varieties of criticism. L. L. Martz. Poetry 110:254-5 Jl '67

ROMANTICISM in music. See Music
ROME
  City as an act of will; excerpt from Design of cities. E. N. Bacon. il Arch Rec 141:124-5 Ja '67
    Officials and employees
  Corruption in the Senate; excerpt from Hannibal's legacy. A. J. Toynbee. Atlan 220:56 Jl '67
ROME (city)
  Buying is a Roman art. il Bsns W p 110-14+ Ap 22 '67
  Roman diary. D. Slow. America 116:582-3; 117:18-19 Ap 22, Jl 1 '67
    Art
  Rome. M. Gendel. Art N 66:61 Mr '67
    See also
  Rome (city)—Monuments, statues, etc.
    Churches
  New churches in Rome. America 116:335 Mr 11 '67
    Description
  Literary road to Rome. N. Kotker. il Horizon 9:16-31 Sum '67
  Roman astonishment. S. Alexander. il Life 63:24 S 29 '67
  Rome's Riviera. R. Deardorff. il Travel 128: 61-3 Jl '67
  When in Rome . . . L. Barry. il Pop Phot 61: 46+ D '67
  When in Rome. W. Weaver. il House & Gard 131:60+ Mr '67
    History
    Anecdotes, facetiae, satire, etc.
  Day they built Rome. J. Slate. il Sat Eve Post 240:68-9 Mr 25 '67
    Monuments, statues, etc.
  Roman astonishment. S. Alexander. il Life 63:24 S 29 '67
    Music
  Notes from our correspondents (cont) W. Weaver. Hi Fi 17:22+ Ap; 26+ S; 40+ O '67
  Recordings. M. Mayer. Esquire 67:60+ Je '67
  Rome, Bologna. F. Nuzzo. Opera N 31:33 Mr 11 '67
  Rome; production of Verdi's Alzira. F. Nuzzo. il Opera N 31:31 Ap 1 '67
    Religious institutions and affairs
  American pastor in Rome, by J. F. Cunningham. Review
    Cath World 205:251 Jl '67. J. Kane.
    Sanitary affairs
  Dust to dust. J. Ferris. Sat R 50:4-5 D 23 '67
    Social life and customs
  Elusive Romans: easy to like, hard to know; excerpts from Golden oasis. L. Rasponi. Vogue 150:230-1+ N 1 '67
    Stores
  Boutiques of Paris and Rome. E. Sheppard. il Holiday 42:87-8 N '67
ROME (city) in literature
  Literary road to Rome. N. Kotker. il Horizon 9:16-31 Sum '67
ROME, N.Y.
  Small buses restore transit. F. D. McCutchen. il Am City 82:66 F '67
ROMEO, James
  City; photographs. Fortune 77:136-9 Ja '68
ROMEO and Juliet; ballet. See Ballets—Criticisms
ROMEO and Juliet; opera. See Gounod, C. F.
ROMER, Alfred Sherwood
  Major steps in vertebrate evolution; address, December 28, 1967. bibliog Science 158:1629-37 D 29 '67
ROMER, Joanna, and Roth, Patricia
  Something to talk about on campus. Mlle 65: 320-3 Ag '67
ROMERISCUS. See Reptiles, Fossil
ROMERO, Francisco
  Varona as a philosopher; address, June 4, 1949; biographical sketch by J. C. Torchia-Estrada. por Américas 19:13-18 D '67
ROMERO, Patricia W.
  Justice under law; Hugo L. Black. Negro Hist Bul 30:12-14 F '67
ROMERO, Vicente
  World of dance. W. Terry. Sat R 50:39 Ag 26 '67

ROMMEL, Erwin
Defeat and death of General Rommel. A. McKee. il por N Y Times Mag p44-5+ O 22 '67

ROMNES, Haakon Ingolf
Kappel and Romnes of A.T.&T. por Fortune 75:53 F '67

ROMNEY, George, 1907-
Fourth largest war; address, April 7, 1967. Vital Speeches 33:462-5 My 15 '67; Excerpts. U S News 62:20 Ap 17 '67
Transmission lines. por Parks & Rec 2:17 N '67
U.N. and red China; address, August 18, 1967. Vital Speeches 33:727-30 Ag 14 '67

about

Arkansas traveler. Time 89:23 My 5 '67
As Romney goes to the voters. il por U S News 62:38 Mr 6 '67
As Romney squares away for 1968. por U S News 63:22 N 27 '67
Bell tolls for a galloping ghost. il pors Newsweek 70:27-8 S 25 '67
Brainwashed candidate. il Time 90:22 S 15 '67
Brainwashing furor Romney set off. por U S News 63:22 S 18 '67
. . . But oh you kid! S. Alsop. por Sat Eve Post 240:18 Ap 22 '67
Doubleheader for George; A. Licata's victory. il por Time 89:15 Je 2 '67
George Romney: battered but unbowed. J. Witcover. il pors Sat Eve Post 240:38-42 D 2 '67
George Romney: holy and hopeful. W. V. Shannon. Harper 234:55-62 F '67
George Romney's road-show Hamlet. J. Witcover. Reporter 36:36-7 Mr 23 '67
GOP: it's spring. il por Newsweek 69:31-2 Ap 17 '67
GOP: the man whom. . ? Newsweek 70:30-1 S 18 '67
Having a wonderful time; campaign in New Hampshire. il por Newsweek 70:26 Jl 17 '67
I'm an underdog. il por Newsweek 71:20-1 Ja 22 '68
In business. il por Time 89:19 F 24 '67
In the cold. il Newsweek 71:16-17 Ja 15 '68
In transition. il por Time 90:15-16 Ag 25 '67
Innocent abroad. New Repub 157:6 D 2 '67
Inside Romney. Newsweek 70:18+ D 25 '67
It's official. Newsweek 70:29 N 27 '67
Lenore: Romney's secret weapon. A. Rothenberg. il pors Look 31:34-6+ F 7 '67
Letter from Washington. R. H. Rovere. New Yorker 43:153-60 Ap 22 '67
Listening to another drummer. M. McGrory. America 117:341 S 30 '67
Long, hot century? Time 89:21 Ap 28 '67
Lukewarm at the lake. il por Time 90:16-17 Jl 14 '67
Man enough to pray. il por Time 91:13 Ja 19 '68
Matter of semantics. il por Newsweek 69:37 Mr 13 '67
Mormons and the Negro. il Newsweek 69:80 Mr 6 '67
Morning line. Newsweek 69:33 Ap 3 '67
Notes and comment; concerning his brainwashing statement. New Yorker 43:42 S 23 '67
Poor George. Nation 205:259 S 25 '67
Puzzling front runner. B. Brower. il pors Life 62:84-8+ My 5 '67
Republican choice: now it's Nixon over Romney. il por U S News 62:14 F 20 '67
Rockefeller, Romney, Reagan: what kind of governors; a study of the record. il pors U S News 63:54-5+ O 30 '67
Romantic interlude. il por Newsweek 69:34+ Mr 6 '67
Romney, a '68 boom that's in trouble. il por U S News 63:56 Jl 17 '67
Romney and Nixon: each makes gains in polls. il por U S News 63:12-13 Ag 28 '67
Romney-LBJ feud: who played politics in the rioting? por U S News 63:14 Ag 14 '67
Romney on tour: can he regain lost ground? U S News 63:30 S 25 '67
Romney rubs noses with voters; with report by R. B. Stolley. il pors Life 62:70-4 Mr 3 '67
Romney: salesman on the move. J. J. Kilpatrick. il pors Nat R 19:1372-83+ D 12 '67
Romney sounds an uncertain trumpet. W. Weaver, jr. il pors N Y Times Mag p45-7+ N 19 '67; Reply. J. Whitehall. p39-40 D 10 '67
Romney: still blooper-prone, but very much alive. J. C. Jones. il por Newsweek 70:26 O 9 '67
Romney the incredible. R. Moley. Newsweek 70:116 D 11 '67

Romney the rambler. Nation 204:130-1 Ja 30 '67
Romney: trouble abroad; and at home. il por U S News 64:12 Ja 8 '68
Romney's week. il por Newsweek 69:20-1 My 1 '67
See America first. Time 90:16 S 8 '67
Sleeper. Reporter 37:10-11 O 5 '67
Slumming it. il Newsweek 70:22 S 11 '67
Trials of a presidential candidate. M. McGrory. America 116:368 Mr 18 '67
Two Romneys. il por Time 89:24-5 Mr 3 '67
What makes Romney run: excerpt from Romney's way. T. G. Harris. il por Look 31:92-4+ D 12 '67
What Romney learned on trip abroad. U S News 64:14 Ja 15 '68
Word. il por Time 90:25 N 24 '67
World rambler. il por Newsweek 70:35 D 18 '67

Visit to South Vietnam

Romney goes to the war. il por Time 91:25 Ja 5 '68

ROMNEY, Lenore (LaFount)
Lenore: Romney's secret weapon. A. Rothenberg. il pors Look 31:34-6+ F 7 '67
Mrs Romney's quandary. Christian Cent 84:165 F 8 '67

RONAN, Margaret
Following the films. See issues of Senior scholastic

RONAYNE, Eugene L. See Malvesta, D. jt. auth.

RONBERG, Gary
Baseball. Sports Illus 27:54-6 Ag 14 '67
Bowling. Sports Illus 26:86-8 Ap 10 '67
College football (cont) Sports Illus 27:51-2 S 25; 64-5 N 13 '67
College wrestling. Sports Illus 26:50+ Ap 3 '67
Playing it the Japanese way. Sports Illus 26:30-1 Je 5 '67
Water polo. Sports Illus 27:56+ Ag 21 '67
Wrestling. Sports Illus 26:59-60 F 20 '67

RONDA, Spain
Ronda. il Holiday 42:120-1 D '67

La RONDINE; opera. See Puccini, G.

RÖNTGEN, Wilhelm Konrad
Roentgen's magic rays. T. Berland. il Todays Health 45:58-9+ Mr '67

ROOD, Ronald
Chat mysterieux, uncanny cat. Audubon 69:86-8+ N '67; Same abr. with title Wildcat: wraith with claws. Read Digest 91:25-6+ N '67
Crab that isn't. Audubon 69:38-43 My '67

ROOF gardens
Easy gardening on the skyline. il Pop Gard 18:14-15 My '67
Garden on your roof. P. Truex. il Horticulture 45:30-1+ Ap '67
Weekending in the city. L. Hammel. il N Y Times Mag p24-5 Jl 2 '67

ROOF playgrounds. See Playgrounds, Roof

ROOFING
Gravel protects a felt shed roof. il Sunset 138:129 Ap '67
See also
Shingles

ROOFS
Development house, Morris Township, New Jersey. il Arch Rec 141:98-9 mid-My '67
Interlocking beam system makes possible greater roof spans and clerestories. A. B. Dow. il Arch Rec 142:174-6 S '67
New roofs emphasize shelter and security. il House & Gard 131:142-3 F '67
Replacing their shade tree, a new patio roof. il Sunset 138:184 Je '67
Unusual roof. J. De Long. il House B 109:132-3 S '67
See also
Gutters (roof)
Shells (structural engineering)

ROOKS, Conrad
New film vocabulary. A. Knight. Sat R 50:50 F 11 '67
Self as hero. il por Time 90:106 N 17 '67

ROOM air conditioners. See Air conditioning equipment

ROOM dividers. See Partitions

ROOM furnishings. See Household furnishings

ROOMMATES
Why roommates make the best wives. J. Paulson. Ladies Home J 84:171-3 Mr '67; Same abr. Read Digest 91:203-4 O '67

ROOMS
Garden room. il Flower Grower 54:26-7+ Ja '67
Great ways to use the room you have. il Good H 164:133-41 My '67
Just off the kitchen: a new many-purpose room. R. Martens. il Farm J 91:58-9 S '67
Live-in room. il House & Gard 132:238-41 O '67

ROOMS—*Continued*
Old rooms with new labels. il House & Gard 132:210-17 O '67
One big switch-around room. il House & Gard 132:72-7 Jl '67
Period rooms updated. il McCalls 94:90-5 My '67
Room of his own. il McCalls 94:82-7 Ag '67
Three high spots for a hobby room.   B. Joselyn. il Pop Mech 128:136-41 Jl '67
To get away at home; escape rooms. il House B 109:108-12 Ja '67
Two basic rooms you can add to any house. C. T. Sigman. il Pop Sci 190:162-8 Ap '67
See also
Attics
Bedrooms
Childrens rooms
Dressing rooms
House decoration
Kitchens
Living rooms
Outdoor rooms
Sewing rooms
Studies (rooms)
ROOMS, Remodeled. See Houses, Remodeled
ROONEY, Francis Charles, 1921-
Man in the shoe. R. Levy. il por Duns R 90:78-9+ O '67
ROONEY, Mickey
After Andy Hardy. J. Epstein. Commentary 43:94-7 Mr '67
ROOSA, Robert Vincent
Dollar in trouble; a banker speaks out; interview. por U S News 63:36-7 N 27 '67
about
How paper gold could work. por Fortune 76:81+ Ag '67
Roosa pats dollar's new friend. por Bsns W p 155-6+ S 9 '67
ROOSEN-RUNGE, E. C.
Gastrovascular system of small hydromedusae: mechanisms of circulation. bibliog Science 156:74-6 Ap 7 '67
ROOSEVELT, Eleanor (Roosevelt)
Eleanor Roosevelt: a great lady's last brave days; excerpts from I love a Roosevelt. P. P. Roosevelt. il pors Good H 164:80-3+ Je '67
ROOSEVELT, Franklin Delano, 1882-1945
FF and FDR. por Newsweek 71:73 Ja 15 '68
FDR, by R. G. Tugwell. Review
New Repub 156:25-6 F 25 '67. G. W. Johnson
Greetin's, cousin George. P. L. Cantelon. il pors Am Heritage 19:6-11+ D '67
Mystery of the President's mystery; literary episode in the life of Franklin D. Roosevelt. A. M. Schlesinger, jr. por McCalls 94:55+ Ag '67
ROOSEVELT, Franklin Delano, 1914-
My first trip. McCalls 94:142 My '67
ROOSEVELT, Kermit
What's in it for the United States? Nat R 19:562+ My 30 '67
ROOSEVELT, Patricia Peabody
Eleanor Roosevelt: a great lady's last brave days; excerpts from I love a Roosevelt. por Good H 164:80-3+ Je '67
ROOSEVELT, Theodore
Return of the Rough Rider. I. McManus. il por Am For 73:18-21+ O '67
Teddy Roosevelt and the boy from Syracuse. K. V. Hostick. Hobbies 71:109+ F '67
Theodore Roosevelt, by N. Roosevelt. Review
Sat R il por 50:33 My 6 '67. J. D. Adams
ROOSEVELT memorial. See Washington, D.C. —Monuments, statues, etc.
ROOT, Jonathan
Farewell to wet-weather skids. Pop Mech 127:124-7+ Mr '67
ROOT, Lin, and Ash, Agnes
First 124 years are the hardest. Sat Eve Post 240:79-80+ Je 17 '67
ROOT, William Pitt
Storm: poem. Atlan 219:88-9 Je '67
ROOT cuttings. See Plant propagation
ROOTES motors, Incorporated
More than half American. Time 89:69-70 Ja 27 '67
ROOTS
Greedy tree roots, and why it's sometimes wise to cut them. il Sunset 139:64-5 Jl '67
ROPE
Anchors aweigh. il Motor B 119:40 Ap '67
See also
Knots and splices
ROPER, Elmo
Beyond the riots. Sat R 50:24-5 O 7 '67
Roper remembers Luce; letter. Sat R 50:23+ Ap 29 '67
View of H.H.H. Sat R 50:18-19 Je 17 '67

ROPER, Hugh Redwald Trevor-. See Trevor-Roper. H. R.
ROPER, James
How to save money on food. Redbook 128:66-7+ Mr '67
ROPER, Myra
Guest critic of China. K. A. Wittfogel. Nat R 19:149-52 F 7 '67
ROREM, Ned
Poulenc and Bernac. French song, with pure pleasure the aim. Hi Fi 17:85-6 N '67
about
Fashion of peeping Toms. M. Croyden. Nation 205:568-9 N 27 '67
RORIMER, James Joseph
Profiles: T. P. F. Hoving. J. McPhee. New Yorker 43:55-6+ My 20 '67
RORSCHACH test. See Educational tests and measurements
ROSE, Aaron
Incredible lab of Aaron Rose. A. Francekevich. il por Pop Phot 62:28+ Ja '68
ROSE, Barbara
Art. Vogue 151:60 Ja 1 '68
ROSE, Dixie E.
Untamed primrose. Horticulture 45:18 F '67
ROSE, Dyson, and Marier, John
Is a great tradition eroding? Sat R 50:53-7 S 2 '67
ROSE, Frank Anthony
His and hers. New Repub 156:8-9 My 27 '67
Rose red with anger. por Time 89:49 Ap 21 '67
Visit to Tuscaloosa. N. Cousins. Sat R 50:20+ My 27 '67
ROSE, Herman
Herman Rose: telling and showing. S. Burton. il por Art N 66:36-7+ Sum '67
ROSE, James
American blown glass in the Seigfred collection. Antiques 91:744-7 Je '67
ROSE, Kathleen
In my opinion. por Seventeen 26:170 D '67
ROSE, Richard
Problem of political change in Great Britain. bibliog f Cur Hist 52:264-9+ My '67
ROSE, Stephen C.
Generations and the W.C.C. Christian Cent 84:864-6 Jl 5 '67
Proposals for Uppsala. Christian Cent 84:1123-6 S 6 '67
ROSE, Stuart
Centaur and editor. E. Weeks. Atlan 219:142 Ap '67
ROSE medallion china. See Pottery, Chinese
ROSE potpourri. See Potpourri
ROSE tattoo; drama. See Williams, T.
ROSEBUD reservation, S.D. See Indians of North America—Reservations
ROSELAND ballroom. See Dance halls
ROSELIEP, Raymond
By Lake Monona; poem. Christian Cent 84:1253 O 4 '67
Field cricket; poem. Nation 205:24 Jl 3 '67
From a November journal; poem. Nation 206:59 Ja 8 '68
Marianne Moore; poem. Nation 205:55 Jl 17 '67
Now I lay me; poem. Christian Cent 84:1431 N 8 '67
Our land & our sea & hallelujah. Poetry 111:189-95 D '67
Parents; poem. Cath World 205:230 Jl '67
Shoe repair; poem. Christian Cent 84:1592 D 13 '67
ROSEMAN, Alvin
U.S. economic commitment in southeast Asia. bibliog f Cur Hist 54:7-14+ Ja '68
ROSEMAN, Eugene
In my opinion. por Seventeen 26:268 F '67
ROSEN, Charles A.
Pattern classification by adaptive machines. bibliog Science 156:38-44 Ap 7 '67
ROSEN, Gerald R.
Washington desk. See issues of Dun's review, May 1967-
ROSEN, Jerry C. and others
Carbon-14 and tritium measurement by means of bremsstrahlung emissions. bibliog Science 157:77-8 Jl 7 '67
ROSEN, Louis
Polarized protons as nuclear probes. bibliog Science 157:1127-34 S 8 '67
ROSEN, Martin M.
Successful development effort; address, November 7, 1967. Vital Speeches 34:153-7 D 15 '67
ROSENBAUM, Jean B.
Psychoanalyst's case for celibacy. Cath World 205:107-10 My '67

ROSENBERG, Abraham
Euglena gracilis: a novel lipid energy reserve and arachidonic acid enrichment during fasting. bibliog Science 157:1189-91 S 8 '67
Galactosyl diglycerides: their possible function in euglena chloroplasts. bibliog Science 157:1191-6 S 8 '67

ROSENBERG, Harold
American woman's dilemma: love, self-love, no love. Vogue 149:162-3 My '67
Art world. New Yorker 43:99-100+ F 25; 179-80+ Mr 25; 162+ My 6; 112+ Je 3; 69-73 Jl 1; 76+ Jl 29; 90+ Ag 26; 145-6+ S 23; 189-92+ O 21; 225-8+ N 18; 138+ D 16 '67
Books. New Yorker 43:182+ Ap 22 '67
Homage to Hans Hofmann. Art N 65:49+ Ja '67
Liberal anti-communism revisited. Commentary 44:65-7 S '67
Masculinity: real and put on. Vogue 150:106-7+ N 15 '67
Movement in art. Vogue 149:170-1+ F 1 '67

ROSENBERG, Joseph
Cow's in the meadow, the kid's in the barn. Parents Mag 42:48-9+ My '67

ROSENBERG, Julius and Ethel, case
Rosenberg myth. il Time 89:51 F 24 '67

ROSENBERG, Leon E. and others
Lysine transport in human kidney: evidence for two systems. bibliog Science 155:1426-8 Mr 17 '67

ROSENBERG, Philip, and Mautner, H. G.
Acetylcholine receptor: similarity in axons and junctions. bibliog Science 155:1569-71 Mr 24 '67
—See Hoskin, F. C. G. jt. auth.

ROSENBERG, Roger L.
Reed relays. por Electr World 77:41-3 Ap '67

ROSENBERG, Samuel
Confessions of a trivialist. por Life 62:66-8+ F 24 '67

ROSENBERG, Shirley Sirota
Boys nobody wanted. Parents Mag 42:35-7+ Ja '67
Now's the time to choose next summer's camp. Parents Mag 42:42-3+ Jl '67
(ed) See Goodrich, W. What makes a marriage succeed or fail

ROSENBLAD, Martha
Who's afraid of L. I. Sound? il Yachting 121:61+ F '67

ROSENBLATT, Arthur
Open space design: New York shows how in its park program. Arch Rec 142:110-24 Ag '67

ROSENBLATT, Henry R.
Capsnapper arrests shock hazard and protects electrolytics. Pop Electr 26:23 Ap '67

ROSENBLATT, Herta
At sundown; poem. Cath World 205:216 Jl '67

ROSENBLATT, Jay S.
Nonhormonal basis of maternal behavior in the rat. bibliog Science 156:1512-14 Je 16 '67

ROSENBLATT, Rand, and Schechter, Daniel
Daffodils, unite! New Repub 156:13-14 Ap 15 '67

ROSENBLATT, Richard H. and Losey, G. S. Jr
Alarm reaction of the top smelt, atherinops affinis: reexamination. bibliog Science 158:671-2 N 3 '67

ROSENBLUM, Leonard A. See Kaufman, I. C. jt. auth.

ROSENBLUTH, Marshall N.
Einstein award winner. Sci N 91:279 Mr 25 '67

ROSENCRANTZ and Guildenstern are dead: drama. See Stoppard, T.

ROSENFELD, Albert
Breakthrough by Du Pont: a drug that blocks viruses. Life 62:60A-61 F 10 '67
Drugs that even scare hippies. Life 63:31-2 O 27 '67
Facts, myths and grave hidden dangers. Life 63:20-1 Jl 7 '67
In defense of old folks over twenty-five. Life 63:22 Ag 25 '67
New cigarette filter, a university's dilemma. Life 63:50-1 Jl 28 '67
10,000-to-1 payoff. Life 63:121-2+ S 29 '67

ROSENFELD, Alvin
Economics of triumph. Reporter 37:22-5 Jl 13 '67
Franco's restive workers. Reporter 36:31-3 My 4 '67
West bank waits for an answer. Reporter 37:31-4 O 5 '67

ROSENFELD, David
Color slides on the water. Yachting 122:56+ Jl '67
Rosie remembers. il por Motor B 120:30-3+ Ag '67

ROSENFELD, Morris
Rosie remembers. D. Rosenfeld. il por Motor B 120:30-3+ Ag '67

ROSENFELD, Paul
(comp) Articles and other books received; Low Countries. See issues of American historical review

ROSENHOUSE, Harvey
Come to Haiti and meet Papa Doc's police. New Repub 156:10 Mr 11 '67
Terms of the new treaty for the Panama Canal. New Repub 157:10-11 Jl 22 '67

Der ROSENKAVALIER; opera. See Strauss, R.

ROSENMAN, Samuel I.
Better way to handle strikes. Read Digest 91:106-10 O '67

ROSENSTEIN, Harris
Di Suvero: the pressures of reality. Art N 65:36-9+ F '67
Total and complex. Art N 66:52-4+ My '67

ROSENTHAL, Benjamin Stanley
Excerpt from address, April 28, 1966. Cong Digest 46:80+ Mr '67

ROSENTHAL, Lawrence M.
Accent on youth. por Time 90:97 N 3 '67

ROSENTHAL, M. L.
At full speed. Nation 204:538-9 Ap 24 '67
Journey toward rebirth. Sat R 50:25 S 2 '67
Poems in embryo. Sat R 50:24-5 D 30 '67
Reality, the void abandoned by imagination; Farewell; poems. Poetry 111:161-2 D '67
Voznesensky in translation. Poetry 110:40-2 Ap '67

ROSENZWEIG, Franz
Franz Rosenzweig: a voice for today. H. E. Schaalman. Christian Cent 84:233-6 F 22 '67

ROSES
How that perfect rose happens. il Bet Hom & Gard 45:142-3 F '67
Miniature roses. M. Pinney. il Horticulture 45:20-1 S '67
New roses for 1967. Home Gard 54:57-8 F '67
New roses to treasure. N. G. Breedlove. il Home Gard 54:46+ F '67
Old roses to treasure. M. G. Benzinger. il Home Gard 54:47+ F '67
Rose success in easy stages. A. H. Bello. il Flower Grower 54:52-3+ Ja '67
Roses, planting the new pruning the old. il Home Gard 54:77-9 F '67
Roses; selecting, cutting, preparing for shows. K. P. Jones. il Horticulture 45:26-9+ Je '67
Whatever happened to the old-fashioned rose garden? H. Mason. il Bet Hom & Gard 45:64-9 F '67

All America selections
See Plants—All American selections

History
Mystique of the rose; excerpt from The magic world of roses. M. A. R. Bassity. il Pop Gard 18:58-9+ Mr '67

ROSES, Arrangement of
When arranging your roses. il Pop Gard 18:82-3 Ag '67

ROSETT, Arthur
Negotiated guilty plea. Ann Am Acad 374:70-81 N '67

ROSHWALD, Mordecai
Awakening Olympus. Nation 204:147-8 Ja 30 '67
Cybernetics of blunder. Nation 204:335-6 Mr 13 '67

ROSIN, Alan, and Simmons, R. H.
Governor Reagan's slightest vestige. New Repub 156:10 Je 24 '67

ROSKO. See Pasternak, M.

ROSKO, Milt
Plug for jumbo blues. Outdoor Life 140:56-8+ Ag '67

ROSS, Arnold
Natural world of the post office. Natur Hist 77:28-31 Ja '68

ROSS, Arthur M.
Changing pattern of Negro employment. Ebony 22:38-9 Jl '67
How much cost of living will go up; interview. por U S News 63:70-2+ N 13 '67

ROSS, Bob
Ridgey-didge. Yachting 122:65+ S '67

ROSS, D. A. See Degens, E. T. jt. auth.

ROSS, D. M. and Sutton, L.
Swimming sea anemones of Puget Sound: swimming of actinostola new species in response to stomphia coccinea. bibliog Science 155:1419-21 Mr 17 '67

ROSS, Diane
Poem: My pen is empty. Horn Bk 43:514 Ag '67

ROSS, Elaine
Dinner-for-two cookbook. House & Gard 131:173+ Ap '67
Gourmet diet cook book. House & Gard 131:127+ Je '67

ROSS, Elinor
New York's Alzira; interview, ed. by S. Jenkins, jr. por Opera N 32:16 Ja 20 '68

ROSS, G. T. and others
Luteinizing hormone activity in plasma during the menstrual cycle. bibliog Science 155:1679-80 Mr 31 '67

ROSS, George
Mr Leavitt comes to Harvard. Nation 205:654-8 D 18 '67

ROSS, Herbert
Dancer-choreographer-show doctor now film director Herb Ross talks shop. L. Joel. il pors Dance Mag 41:42-9+ D '67

ROSS, Irwin
Britain's big moat: the Channel. Read Digest 90:21-2+ Je '67
How California is licking drug addiction. Read Digest 91:138-42 S '67
Needed: first aid for ambulance services. Read Digest 90:98-102 F '67
Roy Wilkins, Mr Civil Rights. Read Digest 92:86-91 Ja '68
Victims of crime deserve a break. Read Digest 91:173-6 Jl '67
Who wins a strike? Read Digest 91:101-5 Ag '67

ROSS, Ishbel
American habitat; excerpts from Taste in America. House B 109:200-2 Ap '67

ROSS, James F.
Marriage of Paris and Bologna; address, September 6, 1967. Vital Speeches 33:766-8 O 1 '67

ROSS, James William, Jr
Calcium-selective electrode with liquid ion exchanger. bibliog Science 156:1378-9 Je 9 '67

ROSS, Mignon M. R.
Modified cilia in sensory organs of juvenile stages of a parasitic nematode. bibliog Science 156:1494-5 Je 16 '67

ROSS, Nancy Wilson
Psychedelic trip to revelation. Sat R 50:90-1 Ap 22 '67
Silent witness. Sat R 50:28-9 D 23 '67

ROSS, Roger. See Cross, F. L. jr, jt. auth.

ROSS, Thomas B. See Wise, D. jt. auth.

ROSS, Walter Sanford
Charles and Anne Morrow Lindbergh: America's most remarkable parents; excepts from The last hero; Charles A. Lindbergh. Ladies Home J 85:43-6+ Ja '68
What parents should know about childhood cancer. Read Digest 90:83-7 Mr '67
(ed) See Lepore, M. J. Secret of caring for the patient

ROSS, Warren R.
Bird's-eye view helps win sales and savings. il por W p66-9 Ap 8 '67

ROSS-DUGGAN, John K.
Colonel of the liturgy. America 116:237 F 18 '67

ROSS-SKINNER, Jean
International business. See issues of Dun's review

ROSS Barnett reservoir. See Jackson, Miss.—Water supply

ROSSELLI, Aldo
Descent from the hill; story, tr. by F. Frenaye. Reporter 37:41-4 S 7 '67

ROSSELLI, John
Importance of writing good plays. Reporter 36:44+ My 18 '67

ROSSELLINI, Isabella
New heartbreak in Ingrid Bergman's life. M. S. Davis. il pors Good H 164:54-7+ Ja '67

ROSSELLINI, Renzo
La guerra. Criticism
Opera N 31:21 Je 10 '67
View from the bridge. Criticism
Hi Fi il 18:MA23 Ja '68
Opera N 32:23 N 25 '67
Opera N il 32:20-1 O 14 '67

ROSSI, Jean
Knowledge found in playing cards. il Hobbies 72:122-3 Jl '67

ROSSI, Peter Henry
Adventure capital for research. Sat R 50:68 N 4 '67

ROSSINI, Gioacchino
Ghost of Semiramide. H. Weinstock. Sat R 50:71 Ja 28 '67
On London, the first recording of Rossini's Semiramide. P. L. Miller. il Am Rec G 33:372-5 Ja '67

ROSSVILLE, Ga. fire. See Fires

ROSTEN, Leo
Harold Lasswell: a memoir. Sat R 50:65-7 Ap 15 '67
Murder of a nit-picker. Sat R 50:17 Jl 29 '67
They made our world (cont) Look 31:84-5+ F 7 '67
World of Leo Rosten. See issues of Look
about
Behind the scenes. L. Botto. por Look 31:25 Mr 7 '67

ROSTEN, Norman
Dear Marilyn. McCalls 94:74-5+ Ag '67

ROSTENBERG, Adolph, Jr. See Snyder, J. M. jt. auth.

ROSTOV, Russia
On location in Rostov: filming the new revolution. D. Smith. il Nation 204:268-72 F 27 '67

ROSTOW, Eugene Victor
Another round in the great debate: American security in an unstable world; address, October 17, 1967. Dept State Bul 57:605-11 N 6 '67; Same. Vital Speeches 34:66-70 N 15 '67
Concert and conciliation: the next stage of the Atlantic alliance; address, September 11, 1967. Dept State Bul 57:422-30 O 2 '67; Same. Vital Speeches 34:13-18 O 15 '67
Cooperation for balance-of-payments equilibrium; statement, November 30, 1967. Dept State Bul 57:876-81 D 25 '67
Department opposes elimination of import quotas on extra long staple cotton; statement, July 12, 1967. Dept State Bul 57:236-9 Ag 21 '67
Importance of agricultural development in our strategy for peace; address, May 10, 1967. Dept State Bul 56:856-65 Je 5 '67
Middle East crisis and beyond; address, December 8, 1967. Dept State Bul 58:41-8 Ja 8 '68
Politics of progress; address, February 20, 1967. Dept State Bul 56:398-405 Mr 13 '67
about
Communication task force. America 117:401 O 14 '67
New monitor on communications. por Bsns W p40 Ag 19 '67

ROSTOW, Walt Whitman
Great transition: tasks of the first and second postwar generations; address, February 23, 1967. Dept State Bul 56:491-504 Mr 27 '67
Regionalism and world order; address, June 12, 1967. Dept State Bul 57:66-9 Jl 17 '67
about
Dangerous world of Walt Rostow. J. R. Moskin. il pors Look 31:27-31 D 12 '67
Most happy fella in the White House. T. B. Morgan. il pors Life 63:80-80B+ D 1 '67
Scholar who's no. 2 at the White House. il pors Bsns W p 122-3+ Mr 25 '67
Walt Whitman Rostow. A. Campbell. New Repub 157:15-17 N 4 '67

ROSTROPOVICH, Mstislav
Master cellist. H. Saal. il por Newsweek 69:102+ Mr 13 '67
Music to my ears. I. Kolodin. Sat R 50:114-15 Mr 11 '67
Musical events; concert in Carnegie Hall. W. Sargeant. New Yorker 43:129-30 Mr 18 '67
Rostropovich whirlwind. S. Fleming. Hi Fi 17:MA9+ My '67

ROSWAENGE, Helge
Timeless Tamino; interview, ed. by H. Fantel. por Opera N 31:27 Mr 4 '67

ROSWELL, N.Mex. public library
Police-check on overdues; letter to the editor. G. McShean. Library J 92:2096+ Je 1 '67
Roswell librarian resigns; charges smear campaign. il Library J 92:3943 N 1 '67

ROSWELL Park memorial institute
Major battlefield in war on cancer; RPMI in Buffalo, for diagnosis, therapy, and surgery. il Bsns W p88-9+ Ap 22 '67

ROSZAK, Theodore
A.J. Nation 204:293-4 Mr 6 '67
Life in the instant cities. Nation 204:336-40+ Mr 13 '67

ROTARY engines, Marine. See Marine engines

ROTARY internal combustion engines. See Airplane engines

ROTARY piston engines. See Automobile engines

ROTARY switches. See Electric switches

ROTATING combustion engines. See Automobile engines

ROTE, Kyle, Jr
Second generation. il pors Time 90:73 N 17 '67

ROTENONE
Metabolism of rotenone in vitro by tissue homogenates from mammals and insects. J. Fukami and others. bibliog il Science 155:713-16 F 10 '67

ROTH, Bernhard A.
Cycling out to sea. pors Travel 128:45-9 Ag '67

ROTH, Bernie. See Coates, B. jt. auth.

ROTH, Carolyn C. See Dennison, D. S. jt. auth.

ROTH, Cecil
Caveat emptor Judaeus. Commentary 43:84-6 Mr '67
Jewish art. Commentary 44:88-90 Ag '67
Only kid. Commentary 43:82-5 Ap '67

ROTH, Emery, and sons
Skyline factory. il Newsweek 70:98+ S 18 '67

ROTH, Patricia. See Romer, J. jt. auth.

ROTH, Philip
Jewish patient begins his analysis; story. Esquire 67:104 Ap '67
New man; story. Sat Eve Post 240:50-2 F 11 '67

ROTH, Robert J.
Henry David Thoreau. America 117:761-3 D 23 '67

ROTH, Susan A.
(ed) Books to come. Library J 92:3879-912+ O 15 '67
(comp) Children's paperbacks. Library J 92: 2053-4+, 3137-9 My 15, S 15 '67

ROTH, Ueli
Centre Le Corbusier. Arch Forum 127:82-7 S '67

ROTH, William Matson
Chief trade negotiator tells: where we go from here. pors Nations Bsns 55:54-7 Ag '67
Completing the work of the Kennedy round; address, October 5, 1967. Dept State Bul 57:574-8 O 30 '67
Future work program of GATT; statement, November 23, 1967. Dept State Bul 58:13-15 Ja 1 '68
Issues in future U.S. foreign trade policy; statement, July 11, 1967. Dept State Bul 57: 173-80 Ag 7 '67
Kennedy round enters decisive phase; statement, February 15, 1967. Dept State Bul 56:476-8 Mr 20 '67
Kennedy round holds promise of free-world economic growth; statement, May 23, 1967. Dept State Bul 56:879-80 Je 12 '67
Price of protectionism; statement, October 18, 1967. Dept State Bul 57:648-50 N 13 '67
What happened in the Kennedy round; address, July 7, 1967. Dept State Bul 57:123-7 Jl 31 '67

ROTHBERG, Simon, and Axilrod, G. D.
Enzymatic solubilization of insoluble proteins at neutral pH. bibliog Science 156:90-3 Ap 7 '67

ROTHENBURG, Germany
Rothenburg: time remembered. R. Atcheson. il Holiday 42:20+ D '67

ROTHENSTEIN, Sir John
Ex-titan of the Tate. E. Roditi. Sat R 50:35-6 My 27 '67
Tate in trouble. E. Weeks. Atlan 220:109 Jl '67

ROTHSCHILD, Ernestine
John Martin at school. por Dance Mag 42: 38-40 Ja '68

ROTHSCHILD, Guy, baron de
Rothschild sweeps the cobwebs away. il pors Bsns W p84-6+ D 16 '67

ROTHSCHILD, Miriam
Mimicry; the deceptive way of life; with biographical sketch. Natur Hist 76:5, 44-51 F '67

ROTHSCHILD, Norman
Beat & offbeat. Pop Phot 61:34+ Ag; 32+ S '67
Offbeat. See issues of Popular photography
Photo beat. See issues of Popular photography

ROTHSCHILD, Pauline, baronne de
Moscow: of people, poets, palaces. Vogue 149:82-5+ Ja 15 '67

ROTHSCHILD family
Does R.F. mean *république française* or Rothschild frères? S. de Gramont. il N Y Times Mag p8-9+ Je 25 '67
Rothschild sweeps the cobwebs away. il Bsns W p84-6+ D 16 '67
Rothschild's new image. Newsweek 69:85-6 My 8 '67
Tapping the rivulets. il Time 89:95 My 5 '67

ROTHSTEIN, Arthur
Creative color. See issues of U.S. camera & travel
Sight and insight; excerpts from Look at us; photographs. U S Camera 30:50-1 D '67

ROTHSTEIN, Fred. See Brown, M. E. jt. auth.

ROTHSTEIN, Raphael
Massacre of the innocents. Nation 204:663-4 My 22 '67

ROTHSTEIN, Samuel
In search of ourselves; address, June 1967. Library J 93:156-7 Ja 15 '68

ROTISSERIES. See Electric apparatus and appliances, Domestic

ROTKIN, Charles E.
Photographer pleads his case. pors Pub W 191:90-1+ F 6 '67

ROTORS (helicopters)
Boelkow flight testing prototypes of rigid-rotor Bo-105. il Aviation W 86:80-1+ Je 26 '67
Lockheed tests AH-56A rigid rotor unit. G. S. Hunter. il Aviation W 86:55+ Ap 24 '67

ROTSCHILD, Klára
All strictly from Hungary. il Life 63:72-81 D 8 '67

ROTTERDAM
Harbor
Creative vision of Europort. N. Mostert. il Reporter 37:22-4+ D 28 '67
Working while waiting; Europoort refineries. il Time 90:71 Ag 11 '67

ROUD, Richard
Through an ideology darkly. Sat R 50:13-14+ D 23 '67

ROUDIEZ, Leon S.
Life beneath the lines we wear. Sat R 50:35-6 My 6 '67

ROUECHÉ, Berton
Annals of medicine (cont) New Yorker 43: 110+ My 27 '67
Reporter at large. New Yorker 43:76+ Ag 12; 34-8+ D 23 '67

ROUGH ROCK demonstration school. See Indians of North America—Education

ROUGIER, Michael
Photographer with a sculptor's eye. G. P. Hunt. il por Life 62:3 Ap 28 '67

ROUND houses. See Buildings, Round

ROUNER, Leroy S.
Foreign aid and Christian responsibility. Christian Cent 84:103-5 Ja 25 '67

ROURKE, Elizabeth M.
One cannot tell; poem. Horn Bk 43:737 D '67

ROUS, Francis Peyton
Challenge to man of the neoplastic cell; address, December 13, 1966. bibliog Science 157:24-8 Jl 7 '67

ROUS, Peyton. See Rous, F. P.

ROUS sarcoma. See Sarcoma

ROUSE, Charles C.
Rouse case. New Repub 157:5 Jl 1 '67
Who's fit to be free? J. Ridgeway. New Repub 156:24-6 F 4 '67; Discussion. 156:35-6 F 18 '67

ROUSE, James Wilson
Messianic master builder; interview. pors Life 62:35-6+ F 24 '67

about
Hail Columbia. il por Newsweek 69:65 Je 26 '67
Profiles; through the great city. A. Bailey. New Yorker 43:51-2+ Ag 5 '67

ROUSE, Milford O.
Joys and problems of being a doctor. Todays Health 45:72+ Je '67
Medical education and the AMA. Todays Health 45:88 O '67

about
AMA: some doctors are in revolt, but revolution is not in sight. E. Langer. por Science 157:285-8 Jl 21 '67; Discussion. 157:1261-3 S 15 '67

ROUSE, Roger
Right man in the right place, at last. G. Rogin. il pors Sports Illus 27:32-4+ N 13 '67
Tiger hammers home a sermon. G. Rogin. il pors Sports Illus 27:24-6+ N 27 '67

ROUSSEAS, Stephen
Elections or coup? deadlock in Greece. Nation 204:390-5 Mr 27 '67

ROUSSEAS, Stephen W. and Clements, R. J.
Letter to a tyrant. Nation 205:550-1 N 27 '67

ROUSSEAU, Henri
Toll collector's riddles; with portfolio of reproductions. R. Cowley. Horizon 10:30-43 Wint '68

ROUSSEAU, Jean Jacques
Jean-Jacques Rousseau, by J. Guéhenno. Review
Nation 204:220-1 F 13 '67. J. J. Kaplow
Rousseau and revolution, by W. Durant and A. Durant. Review
Time 90:118+ O 6 '67

ROUSSELLE country school. See Rural schools —United States

ROUTH, Guy
Evolution of an economist. Mo Labor R 90:18-22 F '67
ROUTING machines
How to turn pro with a router. J. Burroughs. il Pop Mech 128:188-91 O '67
Nineteen smart tricks with a router. R. J. De Cristoforo. il Pop Sci 191:140-5 Jl '67
Tilt your router. R. Shoberg. il Pop Mech 128:170-2 S '67
ROUTTENBERG, Aryeh. See Alloway, T. M. jt. auth.
ROUX, Edmonde Charles-. See Charles-Roux, E.
ROVANIEMI, Lapland
Points North. P. L. Adams. Atlan 219:99-100+ Mr '67
ROVERE, Richard H.
Books (cont) New Yorker 43:172-6 Ap 8; 238+ N 11 '67
Germany 1967. Atlan 219:44-6 My '67
Letter from Bonn. New Yorker 43:136+ F 25 '67
Letter from the United Nations. New Yorker 43:67-70+ Jl 8 '67
Letter from Washington. See occasional issues of New Yorker
Liberal anti-communism revisited. Commentary 44:67-8 S '67
Most gifted and successful demagogue this country has ever known. N Y Times Mag p23+ Ap 30 '67
On civil disobedience, 1967. N Y Times Mag p 131 N 26 '67
Reflections. New Yorker 43:60-4+ O 28 '67

about

Civilized eye on the jungle. il por Time 90:65 D 22 '67
ROVNER, Jerome S.
Copulation and sperm induction by normal and palpless male linyphid spiders. bibliog Science 157:835 Ag 18 '67
ROVNYAK, R. M.
Arc, surge, and noise suppression. Electr World 77:46-8 Ap '67
ROW, Howard E. See Gousha, R. P. jt. auth.
ROW houses
Here's a quality house to learn by. V. D. Hahn. il Am Home 70:78-81 O '67
Significance of scale. il Am Home 70:58-9 S '67
ROW spacing of plants. See Plants, Space arrangement of
ROWAN, Carl Thomas
Answer to youth's challenge. por Ebony 22:140-3 Ag '67
How Kennedy's concern for Negroes led to his death. Ebony 22:27-30+ Ap '67
Martin Luther King's tragic decision. Read Digest 91:37-42 S '67
Negro's place in the American dream. Read Digest 90:63-7 Ap '67
(ed) See Ong, Y. L. What is at stake in Vietnam: an Asian view
ROWAN, Helen
Minority nobody knows. Atlan 219:47-52 Je '67
ROWAN, Lawrence C. See Trask, N. J. jt. auth.
ROWBOATS. See Boats and boating
ROWE, Pete
Amateur scientist. Sci Am 216:143-4+ My '67
ROWELL, John A.
Interface. Library J 92:3126, 3823, 4590+ S 15, O 15, D 15 '67
ROWEN, Hobart
Bone in Meany's throat. New Repub 156:9-10 My 6 '67; Correction. 156:42 Je 3 '67
ROWING
Awful upset by the ANZACS; North American rowing championships. M. Riley. il Sports Illus 27:18-19 Ag 21 '67
Crew that grew and grew; Seattle park department rowing program. W. Vance. il Parks & Rec 2:38+ O '67
Parker's pachyderms; Harvard's oarsmen earn right to represent the U.S. at Pan American games. Time 90:50 Jl 14 '67
Streaking Harvards; crew owes success to coach. il Newsweek 69:89 Je 19 '67
Tale of an ancient mariner. P. Gallico. il Sports Illus 27:76-8+ S 25 '67
To Becky with love from all the Harvards; Harvard victory over Vesper boat club of Philadelphia in the U.S. Pan American games. M. Riley. il Sports Illus 27:44 Jl 10 '67
See also
Regattas
ROWLAND, Stanley J. Jr
Views from religion; mental health session. Christian Cent 84:664+ My 17 '67
ROWLEY, Arthur Henderson, baron
Signposts to stature. Sat R 50:34 N 18 '67

ROXBURY riots. See Boston—Riots
ROY publishers, Incorporated
Roy may start company in India. Pub W 191:54 F 13 '67
ROYAL, Darrell
Necessity is the mother of the forward pass. D. Jenkins. il Sports Illus 27:46+ N 6 '67
ROYAL ballet, Great Britain
Ballerina's day; interview. D. Vere. New Yorker 43:34-5 My 20 '67
Letter from London; performance of Paradise lost. M. Panter-Downes. New Yorker 43:163 Ap 15 '67
Music to my ears. I. Kolodin. Sat R 50:26 My 6 '67
Musical events; performance Dream and Song of the earth. W. Sargeant. New Yorker 43:157 My 6 '67
Musical events; performance of Romeo and Juliet. W. Sargeant. New Yorker 43:134 My 27 '67
Musical events; performances of Cinderella and Sleeping beauty. W. Sargeant. New Yorker 43:134 Ap 29 '67
Nureyev and Fonteyn; with report by C. Barnes. il Life 62:126-8+ My 12 '67
Royal pair; U.S. tour. H. Saal. il Newsweek 69:83-4 My 1 '67
Royalty and images. C. Barnes. il Dance Mag 41:48-54 Ap '67
Toe to toe; productions in New York. H. Saal. il Newsweek 69:88-9 Je 5 '67
What's become of Sadler's Wells? two reviews of the Royal ballet season at Metropolitan opera house. J. Maskey; D. Hering. il Dance Mag 41:50-5+ Jl '67
World of dance; review of New York season. W. Terry. il Sat R 50:84-5 Je 10 '67
ROYAL Danish ballet
Fearless Flindt and his dancing Danes. G. Rogoff. il Holiday 41:158+ Ap '67
Royal flash. il Time 89:65+ F 24 '67
ROYAL duck. See Ducks, Wild
ROYAL Dutch-Shell group
Split personalities. Fortune 76:200 S 15 '67
ROYAL family of Great Britain. See Great Britain—Royal family
ROYAL family of Monaco. See Monaco—Royal family
ROYAL palace, Madrid. See Madrid—Historic houses, etc.
ROYAL society for the prevention of cruelty to animals
Kindness and cruelty in Great Britain. G. Carson. il Natur Hist 76:6+ bibliog(p 105) D '67
ROYALTIES
One book's earnings for author and publisher. P. R. Reynolds. il Pub W 192:42-3 S 11 '67; Reply. L. Hughes. 192:35 O 9 '67
Peripatetic reviewer. E. Weeks. Atlan 219:124 Je '67
Rights and permissions; delays in payment. P. Nathan. Pub W 192:48 Jl 31 '67
Susann sues to break contract with publisher. Pub W191:143-4 Je 5 '67
ROYAN, France
Festival for the case-hardened veteran; Royan's international festival of contemporary art. P. Moor. Hi Fi 17:MA26+ Jl '67
ROYAN festival. See Music festivals—France
ROYCE, William F.
Fish and fishing. Bul Atomic Sci 23:26-7 S '67
ROYSTER, Vermont
North by South. il por Time 90:61-2 N 10 '67
Trade winds. H. R. Mayes. Sat R 50:8 D 2 '67
RUARK, Gibbons
Letter to Odysseus; 1965; Blind wish for Randall Jarrell; poems. Poetry 110:391-3 S '67
Yevtushenko and Voznesensky. Poetry 111:121-4 N '67
RUBARTELLI, Franco
Veruschka; photographs. Life 63:45-53 Ag 18 '67
RUBBER, Artificial
Potential aerospace uses seen for nitroso rubber. Aviation W 87:81+ Jl 10 '67
Silicone rubber: a new diffusion property useful for general anesthesia. J. Folkman and others; reply with rejoinder. S. C. Glauser and others. Science 155:1037 F 24 '67
Silicone rubber: oxygen, carbon dioxide, and nitrous oxide measurement in gas mixtures. H. S. Winsey and J. Folkman. bibliog il Science 157:203-4 Jl 14 '67
RUBBER gloves. See Gloves, Rubber

RUBBER industry and trade
  See also
  Government investigations—Rubber industry and trade
  Tire industry and trade
RUBBER industry strikes. See Strikes—United States—Rubber workers
RUBBER rafts. See Rafts
RUBBER tiles
  On rubber floor coverings; sizes of tiles and comparative prices. Consumer Bul 50:30 Ap '67
  Rubber floors and rubber heels help to prevent falls. Consumer Bul 50:29-30 Ap '67
RUBBER workers
  See also
  Strikes—United States—Rubber workers
RUBBERMAID, incorporated
  Rubbermaid takes its turn at wheel; reviving lazy susan devices. il Bsns W p 124+ Ja 28 '67
RUBBINGS
  There's the rub; rubbings of Palenque sarcophagus. il Newsweek 70:87 O 2 '67
RUBBISH disposal. See Refuse and refuse disposal
RUBELLA
  Human fibroblasts infected with Rubella virus produce a growth inhibitor. S. A. Plotkin and A. Vaheri. bibliog il Science 156:659-61 My 5 '67
  Viral inhibition of lymphocyte response to phytohemagglutinin. J. R. Montgomery and others. bibliog il Science 157:1068-70 S 1 '67
RUBEN, Samuel
  Sam Ruben: born to invent. A. Steinberg. il por Read Digest 90:155-7+ My '67
  Wizard of New Rochelle. il por Bsns W p68-70 N 4 '67
RUBENSTEIN, Ben, and Levitt, Morton
  Rebellion and responsibility. Yale R 57:16-30 O '67
RUBENSTEIN, Richard L.
  Did Christians fail Israel? Commonweal 87:297-8 D 1 '67
RUBIDIUM
  Fractionation of potassium/rubidium by amphiboles: implications regarding mantle composition. S. R. Hart and L. T. Aldrich. bibliog il Science 155:325-7 Ja 20 '67
RUBIN, Bonnie B. and Katz, A. M.
  Sodium and potassium effects on skeletal muscle microsomal adenosine triphosphatase and calcium uptake. bibliog Science 158:1189-90 D 1 '67
RUBIN, Harold. See Robbins, H. pseud.
RUBIN, Joan Alleman
  Costumes by Karinska; reprint. Dance Mag 41:49-51+ Je '67
RUBIN, Larry
  Annual checkup; poem. Harper 235:53 Jl '67
  Storm; poem. New Yorker 43:39 Ap 29 '67
  Vitalist; poem. Commonweal 87:443 Ja 12 '68
RUBIN, Louis D.
  Be your own weather prophet. il Read Digest 90:221-4+ Ap '67
RUBIN, Ronald I.
  Promised land grows dim. Sat R 50:35 S 2 '67
  State and the system. Sat R 50:30-1 Je 3 '67
RUBIN, Theodore Isaac
  Psychiatrist's notebook; excerpts from The winner's notebook. por McCalls 95:48+ O '67
  Psychiatrist's notebook; questions and answers. See issues of McCall's to September 1967
RUBIN, William
  Art scholar's loft; the New York apartment of William Rubin. il por Vogue 149:136-43+ Mr 15 '67
RUBINI, F. Frank
  Revenue facilities and services by lease; address. Parks & Rec 2:45-6 Ja; 36+ Mr '67
RUBINSTEIN, Alvin Z.
  Balkan kaleidoscope. Cur Hist 52:220-6+ Ap '67
RUBINSTEIN, Amnon
  Sinai diary; by an Israeli soldier. N Y Times Mag p6+ Jl 2 '67
RUBINSTEIN, Artur
  Lessons of age. il por Time 91:50-1 Ja 12 '68
  Musical events; concert in Carnegie Hall. W. Sargeant. New Yorker 43:63-4 Ja 13 '68
RUBY, Jack
  Jack Ruby (1911-67) Sr Schol 89:18 Ja 20 '67
  Last madness of Jack Ruby; delusions of the new anti-Semitic persecutions. R. Dugger. New Repub 156:19-23 F 11 '67; Discussion. 156:42 F 25 '67
  You all know me! I'm Jack Ruby. G. Wills and O. Demaris. il pors Esquire 67:79-87+ My '67
RUBY-pulsed lasers. See Lasers
RUBY trial. See Trials (murder)
RUCKSACKS. See Packs

RUDD, Hughes
  New York, New York: good-bye, good-bye. Esquire 68:130-1+ O '67
RUDDLE, Nancy H. and Waksman, B. H.
  Cytotoxic effect of lymphocyte-antigen interaction in delayed hypersensitivity. bibliog Science 157:1060-2 S 1 '67
RUDEL, Julius
  Tale of two Juliuses. H. Kupferberg. Atlan 221:106-7 Ja '68
RUDMAN, Herbert C.
  Problems of higher education in the Soviet Union; excerpt from The school and state in the U.S.S.R. bibliog f Sch & Soc 95:153-4+ Mr 4 '67
RUDNICK, Lia
  Face to face with a girl on her toes. por Seventeen 26:157 N '67
RUDOFSKY, Bernard
  Troglodytes; with biographical sketch. por Horizon 9:1-2, 28-39 Spr '67
RUDOLF, Max
  Musical events; two concerts in Carnegie Hall, performed by Cleveland symphony orchestra. W. Sargeant. New Yorker 42:105-6+ Ja 28 '67
RUDOLPH, Lloyd I. and Rudolph, S. H.
  India campaigns: cows, corruption & demonstrations. Nation 204:138-43 Ja 30 '67
RUDOLPH, Paul Marvin
  Curiouser and curiouser. Newsweek 69:95 F 13 '67
  Rudolph style: unpredictable. D. Jacobs. il por N Y Times Mag p46-7+ Mr 26 '67
  Two great architects hit by public taste. E. Goble. Arch Rec 141:9 Mr '67
RUDOLPH, Susanne Hoeber. See Rudolph, L. I. jt. auth.
RUEFF, Jacques
  How sound is the dollar? French view; interview. por U S News 63:56+ D 11 '67
RUETHER, David
  Graphics are crucial! so is emotional impact! J. Scully. il Mod Phot 31:52-61+ My '67
RUETHER, Rosemary
  Divorce: no longer unthinkable. Commonweal 86:117-19+ Ap 14 '67
RUF, K. and Steiner, F. A.
  Steroid-sensitive single neurons in rat hypothalamus and midbrain: identification by microelectrophoresis. bibliog Science 156:667-9 My 5 '67
RUFFLED grouse. See Grouse
RUFFO, Titta
  Collector's releases. A. Favia-Artsay. Hobbies 72:35 Ja '68
  Historical records. A. Favia-Artsay. por Hobbies 72:36+ Mr '67
  Lion of Pisa. M. De Schauensee. por Opera N 31:26-7 Ap 8 '67
RUG making. See Rugs and carpets
RUG pads
  Carpet underlays. il Consumer Bul 50:22-3 Ag '67
RUGBY football
  Day the All-Blacks attained the Zenith: New Zealand vs Wales. G. S. Brown. il Sports Illus 27:26-8+ N 20 '67
  Ferocious Mormons; Church college of Hawaii. Sports Illus 26:12+ My 1 '67
RUGENDAS, Johann Moritz
  Rugendas: historian with pencil and paint. E. Correas. bibliog il por Américas 19:12-19 O '67
RUGGIERI, George D.
  New York aquarium and Osborn laboratories of marine sciences. Science 158:675-6 N 3 '67
RUGGLES, Eugene
  White goddess; Poem at sea on my thirtieth birthday; poems. Poetry 110:241 Jl '67
RUGOWSKI, James A. See Auerbach, R. jt. auth.
RUGS and carpets
  Area rugs. il House & Gard 131:150-5 My '67
  Dental floss and the area rug. A. Heidt. il Design 68:18-19 Sum '67
  New carpets. il Good H 165:128-35 S '67
  Quiet revolution underfoot. P. Hyde. il House B 109:231-5 O '67
  Shopper's guide to carpets & rugs. il Changing T 21:13-15 Je '67
  Shopping for a carpet. il Good H 165:136+ S '67
  Shopping for outdoor carpeting. Bet Hom & Gard 45:144+ My '67
  See also
  Rug pads
RUGS and carpets, Oriental
  Primer on Oriental rugs today. il House & Gard 132:72-3+ S '67
  Primer on oriental rugs today; questions and answers. House & Gard 131:196-7+ My '67

RUGS and carpets, Oriental—*Continued*
Rare rugs; reception at opening of exhibition at Brooklyn museum. New Yorker 43:38-9 My 13 '67
Rugs from the cities of Northwest Persia. House & Gard 132:70+ O '67

RUGS and carpets, Outdoor
Carpets you use out-of-doors. Sunset 139:142-3 O '67
Inside story on the new outdoor carpets. il Good H 156:164 Jl '67

RUINS. See Archeology

RUKEYSER, Muriel
Endless; poem. New Yorker 43:48 O 7 '67

RUKEYSER, William S.
Apollo project: North American's Achilles' heel. Fortune 75:105+ Je 1 '67
$4-billion business Garfield Weston built. Fortune 75:116-21+ Je 1 '67
Getting tough with tenders. Fortune 76:108-10+ Ag '67

RULE, Philip C.
Do vocation ads mislead? America 116:379-80 Mr 18 '67

RULE, Slide. See Calculating devices

RULE of law
American role and world order. L. Gelber. Yale R 56:524-36 Je '67
Legacy of a great American; interview; ed. by R. D. Heffner. G. Clark. il McCalls 94:64+ Ap '67

RULES of order. See Parliamentary practice

RUM
Rum, Spanish speaking, light-bodied. Consumer Rep 32:382-3, 385 Jl '67

RUM-runners. See Bootlegging

RUMANIA
Barbers of the world unite! beards only by special permission. Time 89:33 F 10 '67
See also
Birth rate—Rumania
Moving picture industry—Rumania
Music festivals—Rumania
United States—Commerce—Rumania

Cultural relations
See also
Exchange of persons programs

Economic conditions
Report from east Europe: western ways are catching on. A. Kucherov. il U S News 63:48-50 Jl 10 '67

Economic policy
Two in one; economic reforms. Newsweek 70:61 D 18 '67

Economic relations
Business of Romania is politics. C. Sterling. il Reporter 36:24-7 Ap 20 '67

Foreign relations
...But warm reception for Rumanians in U.S. U S News 63:12 Jl 10 '67
Equilibrists. Newsweek 70:39 Ag 7 '67
Mavericks in Bucharest. il Newsweek 70:36-7 Jl 31 '67

Politics and government
Balkan kaleidoscope. A. Z. Rubinstein. Cur Hist 52:222-4 Ap '67
Business of Romania is politics. C. Sterling. il Reporter 36:24-7 Ap 20 '67
Report from Rumania. T. C. Sorensen. il Sat R 50:14-15 D 30 '67
Winner take all. Time 90:39 D 15 '67

Population
Back to puritanism; low birth rate. Newsweek 69:60 F 6 '67

Social conditions
Report from east Europe: western ways are catching on. A. Kucherov. il U S News 63:48-50 Jl 10 '67

RUMMEL, P. Brooke
To catch a thief. Mlle 65:106-7+ Je '67

RUNAWAY boys and girls
From a hippie's soul: WNEW's A child again broadcast. R. L. Shayon. Sat R 50:46 D 16 '67
Gentle Marcy: a shattering tale; runaway to hippieland. il Newsweek 70:88-9 O 30 '67; Same abr. with title Saga of gentle Marcy. Read Digest 92:62-3 Ja '68
Runaway kids. il Life 63:18-29 N 3 '67
Runaways; Greenwich Village case histories. J. Whitbread. il Look 31:26-32 Jl 25 '67
Runaways; teen-agers who run away to the hippies. il Time 90:46+ S 15 '67

RUNGE, E. C. Roosen-. See Roosen-Runge, E. C.

RUNGE, Evgeniĭ Evgenievich
Big haul in Bonn. il Newsweek 70:31-2 O 30 '67
Covey of spies is flushed in Germany. M. Durham and J. Cook. il Life 63:65-6+ N 3 '67
Flight from the KGB. Sr Schol 91:18-19 N 2 '67
Spies that were left behind. il Time 90:35 O 27 '67
When a red spymaster defected to U.S. U S News 63:11 N 20 '67

RUNKLE, Robert S. See Baldwin, C. L. jt. auth.

RUNNING
And now the one-mile dash. il Time 90:54 Jl 21 '67
Best record yet. P. Axthelm. il Sports Illus 27:16-21 Jl 17 '67
Cheering Kelley home; Boston marathon. il Newsweek 69:94 My 1 '67
Cross country; NCAA championship in Laramie. P. Axthelm. il Sports Illus 27:72-3 D 11 '67
Faster and better and still only no. 2; Villanova's D. Patrick. T. C. Brody. il Sports Illus 26:64-6 Mr 13 '67
First blood of a classic duel; Ryun-Patrick duel at the NCAA indoor half-mile final in Detroit. G. S. Brown. il Sports Illus 26:26-7 Mr 20 '67
Harnessed energy; T. Smith. il Newsweek 69:57-8 Je 12 '67
He is built for chasing beyondness; T. Smith of San Jose state. F. Deford. il Sports Illus 26:34-6+ My 22 '67
Inefficient but fast; J. Hines equals sprinting records. il Time 89:78+ Je 9 '67
It's a long, long, long way to Brighton; London-to-Brighton marathon. G. S. Brown. il Sports Illus 27:70-1 O 16 '67
Jogging for heart and health; it's catching on. il U S News 63:49 D 25 '67
Joyous night for a pixie; G. Lindgren trounced Australia's Ron Clarke. G. S. Brown. il Sports Illus 26:48-50 F 27 '67
Jumping sprinters; dynamics of a runner's step. Sci Am 216:57 Mr '67
Last gasp in Laramie; National collegiate athletic association's cross country championship. il Newsweek 70:68-9 D 11 '67
Learning to care. Newsweek 69:64 Je 26 '67
Over the hills and far ahead; New Zealand's D. McKenzie winner of Boston marathon. T. C. Brody. il Sports Illus 26:62-3+ My 1 '67
Record pace; 1,500 meters record broken by J. Ryun. Newsweek 70:53 Jl 17 '67
Relays and old reliable; Penn-Drake relays. G. S. Brown. il Sports Illus 26:26-7 My 8 '67
Running man; J. Ryun. G. Astor. il Look 31:70-4 Jl 11 '67
Running of the green. R. Delany. il Sports Illus 28:18-23 Ja 15 '68
See you later, Jim Ryun. P. Axthelm. il Sports Illus 27:10-13 Jl 3 '67
Teen-ager on a comeback trail; M. Mulder at Los Angeles times indoor games. G. S. Brown. il Sports Illus 26:22-3 F 20 '67
That last E is for easy, baby! C. Greene of University of Nebraska. T. C. Brody. il Sports Illus 26:51-4 Mr 6 '67
Tommie in a breeze; San Jose state's T. Smith. G. Ronberg. il Sports Illus 26:22-5 My 29 '67
Two guys named Jim had the same idea; Ryun and Hines win at Los Angeles. T. C. Brody. il Sports Illus 26:34-5 Je 12 '67
See also
Hurdle racing

RUNNING aground (boats) See Boats and boating—Accidents

RUNOFF
How to handle feedlot runoff. O. Bay. Farm J 91:44R-44S S '67
Rivers in the making. H. F. Garner. il Sci Am 216:84-8+ Ap '67

RUNWAY lighting. See Airports—Lighting

RUPLEY, D. G.
IC used in new TV kit. Electr World 77:73 Ja '67

RUPPENTHAL, Karl M.
Sonic boom tests. Nation 205:229-30 S 18 '67
Supersonic transport. Nation 204:652-6, 685-9, 786-9 My 22-29, Je 19 '67
about
Getting a lecture from the pilot. il Dors Bsns W p68-9+ Ja 28 '67

RURAL development program. See Rural planning

RURAL electrification administration. See United States—Rural electrification administration

RURAL health. See Public health
RURAL hospitals. See Hospitals, Rural
RURAL life. See Country life
RURAL planning
New kind of poverty war; improving life of poor on farms and in small towns. il Bsns W p44+ D 16 '67
RURAL poverty
United States
See Poor—United States
RURAL recreation. See Recreation, Rural
RURAL schools
Mexico
Sun maiden architect; Dutch girl builds schools for Mexico's Indians. il Life 63:103-4+ O 13 '67
United States
Reunion in Montana; Rousselle country school anniversary. il Time 90:44 S 22 '67
See also
School children—Transportation
RUSDEN, Philip L.
Are your trees in need of food and water? Home Gard 54:42-3 O '67
RUSH, Benjamin
Revolutionary doctor, by C. Binger. Review Sat R 50:52 F 25 '67. M. M. Brown
RUSH, James
Now a way of life. Criticism Commonweal 86:126 Ap 14 '67
RUSH, Myron
Hindsight. Commentary 43:84-6 Je '67
RUSH-Bagot agreement days. See Special days, weeks, and months
RUSHER, William A.
Boys in group II. Nat R 19:310+ Mr 21 '67
Operation 1968. Nat R 19:1115-17+ O 17 '67
RUSHMORE, Robert
Singing voice: ages of man. Opera N 31:26-8 Ap 1 '67
Singing voice: heroes and peach fuzz. Opera N 31:26-8 F 25 '67
Singing voice: indisposed. Opera N 31:28-30 Mr 25 '67
Singing voice: light and soaring. Opera N 31:28-30 F 4 '67
Singing voice: lower and darker. Opera N 31:24-6 F 18 '67
Singing voice: magic. Opera N 31:24-6 Ja 28 '67
Singing voice: national types. Opera N 31:22-5 Mr 18 '67
Singing voice: rarest of all. Opera N 31:28-30 F 11 '67
Singing voice: the lower depths. Opera N 31:28-30 Mr 11 '67
Tenor of James Joyce. Opera N 32:8-12 D 9 '67
RUSK, Alice
Choosing for our youngest. Library J 92:1294-5 Mr 15 '67
RUSK, Dean
American interest in Europe; address, December 2, 1967. Dept State Bul 57:855-9 D 25 '67
American purposes and the pursuit of human dignity; address, August 9, 1967. Dept State Bul 57:343-9 S 18 '67
Building a durable peace; address, January 26, 1967. Dept State Bul 56:269-73 F 20 '67
Central purpose of United States foreign policy; address, August 5, 1967. Dept State Bul 57:251-5 Ag 28 '67
Conversation with Dean Rusk; transcript of interview, ed. by P. Niven. Dept State Bul 56:774-88 My 22 '67
Excerpt from letter, May 11, 1966. Cong Digest 46:172+ Je '67
Firmness and restraint in Viet-Nam; excerpts from address, October 30, 1967. Dept State Bul 57:703-5 N 27 '67
Foreign assistance program for 1968; statement, May 4, 1967. Dept State Bul 56:826-33 My 29 '67
Foreign assistance program; statement, July 14, 1967. Dept State Bul 57:208-15 Ag 14 '67
Humanity's greatest need; address, May 31, 1967. Dept State Bul 56:904-7 Je 19 '67
Keep the faith baby; excerpts from addresses, February 1, 1963 to July 21, 1967. New Repub 157:8-9 Ag 5 '67
1967, a progress report; address, December 6, 1967. Dept State Bul 58:1-5 Ja 1 '68
OAS foreign ministers take steps against Cuban subversion; statements, September 23, 24, 1967. Dept State Bul 57:490-3 O 16 '67
Our foreign policy commitments to assure a peaceful future; address, May 18, 1967. Dept State Bul 56:874-9 Je 12 '67
Our purpose is peace; interview. Dept State Bul 57:821-4 D 18 '67; Same. Read Digest 91:53-9 D '67

Outer space treaty signed by sixty nations at White House ceremony; text of statement, January 27, 1967. Dept State Bul 56:266-7 F 20 '67
Political future of the family of man; address, November 14, 1967. Dept State Bul 57:735-41 D 4 '67
Price of protectionism; statement, October 18, 1967. Dept State Bul 57:634-8 N 13 '67
Road to a lasting peace; address, July 6, 1967. Dept State Bul 57:87-91 Jl 24 '67
Role of the United States in world affairs; address, May 1, 1967. Dept State Bul 56:770-3 My 22 '67
Rusk: our commitment is clear; statement, October 12, 1967. U S News 63:40 O 23 '67
Science and foreign affairs; address, January 24, 1967. Dept State Bul 56:238-42 F 13 '67
Secretary Rusk and Ambassador Bunker discuss Viet-Nam in TV-radio interviews; transcript of interview, September 10, 1967. Dept State Bul 57:411-16 O 2 '67
Secretary Rusk and Ambassador Goldberg urge Senate approval of outer space treaty; statement, March 7, 1967. Dept State Bul 56:600-2 Ap 10 '67
Secretary Rusk and Secretary McNamara discuss developments in Latin America and Viet-Nam; statement, with questions and answers, February 28, 1967. Dept State Bul 56:464+ Mr 20 '67
Secretary Rusk discusses European affairs and Viet-Nam in interview for German television; transcript of interview, February 10, 1967. Dept State Bul 56:358-65 Mr 6 '67
Secretary Rusk discusses prospects for 1967 on Face the nation; transcript of interview, January 1, 1967. Dept State Bul 56:126-32 Ja 23 '67
Secretary Rusk discusses the Punta del Este conference and Viet-Nam on Meet the press; transcript of interview, April 16, 1967. Dept State Bul 56:722-8 My 8 '67
Secretary Rusk discusses Viet-Nam in interview for British television; transcript of interview for Associated television, ltd. January 31, 1967. Dept State Bul 56:274-84 F 20 '67
Secretary Rusk discusses Viet-Nam in interview for foreign television; videotaped, October 16, 1967. Dept State Bul 57:595-602 N 6 '67
Secretary Rusk interviewed on Today program; transcript of interview, January 12, 1967. Dept State Bul 56:168-72 Ja 30 '67
Secretary Rusk on the Middle East; excerpts from address, August 25, 1966. Cur Hist 52:113-14 F '67
Secretary Rusk redefines United States policy on Viet-Nam for student leaders; text of letter, January 4, 1967. Dept State Bul 56:133-6 Ja 23 '67
Secretary Rusk replies to questions on Viet-Nam for Swedish newspaper. Dept State Bul 57:91-4 Jl 24 '67
Secretary Rusk: top defender of U.S. role in Vietnam; excerpts from address, October 24, 1967. por U S News 63:26 N 6 '67
Secretary Rusk urges appropriation of full amount authorized under the Foreign assistance act; statement, November 20, 1967. Dept State Bul 57:801-7 D 11 '67
Secretary Rusk urges congressional support for consular convention with the Soviet Union; statement, January 23, 1967. Dept State Bul 56:247-50 F 13 '67
Secretary Rusk's news conference:
December 21, 1966. Dept State Bul 56:42-8 Ja 9 '67
February 9, 1967. Dept State Bul 56:317-22 F 27 '67
March 28, 1967. Dept State Bul 56:618-24 Ap 17 '67
July 19, 1967. Dept State Bul 57:159-67 Ag '67
September 8, 1967. Dept State Bul 57:383-90 S 25 '67
October 12, 1967. Dept State Bul 57:555-64 O 30 '67
Situation in the Near East; statements, June 5, 6, 1967. Dept State Bul 56:949-51 Je 26 '67
SEATO council reaffirms resolve to repeal aggression; statement, April 18, 1967. Dept State Bul 56:742-4 My 15 '67
Thailand grants U.S. permission to use U Tapao airbase; statement, March 22, 1967. Dept State Bul 56:597-8 Ap 10 '67
Thirteenth anniversary of SEATO; message, September 8, 1967. Dept State Bul 57:391 S 25 '67
U.S. and Mexico complete Chamizal settlement; statement, October 27, 1967. Dept State Bul 57:684-5 N 20 '67

RUSK, Dean—*Continued*
United States commemorates closing of successful AID mission to Iran; remarks, November 29, 1967. Dept State Bul 57:825-6 D 18 '67
U.S.-Japan joint economic committee holds sixth meeting; statement, September 13, with joint communique and news conference, September 15, 1967. Dept State Bul 57:451-9 O 9 '67
U.S. reviews situation in Greece following military takeover; statement, April 28, 1967. Dept State Bul 56:750 My 15 '67
U.S. sets its terms for peace in Vietnam; excerpts from news conference, February 9, 1967. por U S News 62:107-8 F 20 '67
—and Rusk, V. F.
Rusks reminisce. pors PTA Mag 61:24 F '67

about

Dean Rusk at Cornell. Nation 204:516 Ap 24 '67
Demonstration. New Yorker 43:52-3 N 25 '67
Get Rusk movement; is it aimed at LBJ? il pors U S News 63:51-2 N 20 '67
How about it, Mr Rusk? New Repub 157:4 D 23 '67
Indispensables. K. Crawford. Newsweek 70: 42 N 13 '67
Real Dean Rusk. Nation 205:419-20 O 30 '67
Rusk enigma: who runs the State department? S. Simpson. por Nation 204:294-9 Mr 6 '67
Secretary misunderstood. W. Lippmann. Newsweek 70:23 N 6 '67
Tuesday's menu; symbol of what is wrong and sterile in American policy. Nation 204: 708 Je 5 '67
Up from dominoes. Commonweal 87:101-2 O 27 '67

RUSK, Howard A.
Gift of love. Read Digest 90:72 Je '67

about

Napalm story. il por Time 89:63 Mr 24 '67
RUSK, Margaret Elizabeth. See Smith, M. E. R.
RUSK, Virginia Foisle. See Rusk, D. jt. auth.
RUSKAUFF, Bob
Offshore raceboat? Yachting 121:200-1 My '67
Westward ho. See issues of Motor boating
RUSKAY, Joseph A.
Missing taxpayers. New Repub 156:11-14 Ap 29 '67
RUSPOLI, Alessandro
Ruspolis. il por Vogue 150:322-5 S 1 '67
RUSPOLI, Nancy
Ruspolis. il por Vogue 150:322-5 S 1 '67
RUSS, Lavinia
Family's always the last to know: a wide open letter to publishers of juvenile books. Pub W 191:26-7 My 8 '67
RUSSELL, Bertrand Russell, 3d earl
Autobiography: 1914-1918; excerpts from Autobiography of Bertrand Russell 1914-1944. Harper 236:31-9 Ja '68 (to be cont)

about

Bertrand bedazzled by Euclid and free love: The autobiography of Bertrand Russell: 1872-1914. N. Mitford. Life 62:10 Ap 28 '67
Bertrand Russell: prosecutor, judge and jury. B. Levin. il pors N Y Times Mag p24-5+ F 19 '67; Discussion. p 12+ Mr 12; 156 Mr 19; 141+ Ap 16 '67
Birth of a philosopher. G. Lichtheim. Commentary 43:86+ Je '67
Bit of an ass. J. H. Plumb. por Sat R 50: 85-6 Ap 22 '67
Books. G. Steiner. New Yorker 43:101-2+ Ag 19 '67
Books. M. Muggeridge. Esquire 67:64+ Je '67
Dissent ahead. Commonweal 86:251-2 My 19 '67; Reply. J. J. Maher. 86:403+ Je 30 '67
Evil eye. Nat R 19:232-3 Mr 7 '67
Lion at morning. S. Maloff. pors Newsweek 69:106+ Ap 17 '67
Logic and the agony. S. Eimerl. Reporter 36: 47-8+ Je 1 '67
Lord Russell's youth. S. Kauffmann. New Repub 156:18+ Ap 22 '67
Peer's passions. il pors Time 89:114+ Ap 14 '67
Perverse peer. P. P. Witonski. por Nat R 19:592-4 My 30 '67
Reader's choice. O. Handlin. Atlan 219:128-9 My '67
Russell and Wittgenstein. M. Frayn Commentary 43:68-75 My '67
Russell in his prime. R. Sampson. Nation 204:566-8 My 1 '67
Sartre's séance. Time 89:30 My 12 '67

Tragedy of Bertrand Russell. F. Lewis. il pors Look 31:30-2+ Ap 4 '67; Reply with rejoinder. A. J. Toynbee. 31:14 Je 27 '67
Trial begins. il por Newsweek 69:54 My 8 '67
War crimes trial. il Sr Schol 90:28 My 19 '67
RUSSELL, Bill
I am not worried about Ali; ed. by T. Maule. por Sports Illus 26:18-21 Je 19 '67

about

For all the marbles. por Time 89:57-8 F 24 '67
Just too much giant; with report by J. Larner. il pors Life 62:82-4+ Ap 21 '67
RUSSELL, C. J. See Benolken, R. M. jt. auth.
RUSSELL, Findlay E. and others
Venom of the scorpion vejovis spinigerus. bibliog Science 159:90-1 Ja 5 '68
RUSSELL, Francis
Movies (cont) Nat R 19:428-30 Ap 18 '67
Theater Nat R 19:316-17 Mr 21 '67
RUSSELL, George William. See A. E. pseud.
RUSSELL, Jack
Belize. Travel 128:56-60 O '67
RUSSELL, Jane
Where are they now? pors Newsweek 70:22 N 13 '67
RUSSELL, John. See Johnson, G. jt. auth.
RUSSELL, John, 1919-
Calder. Vogue 150:110-15+ Jl '67
Content as combination. Art N 66:52-3+ O '67
London. See issues of Art news
Success that failed. Art N 65:58-61 Ja '67
Why Aubrey Beardsley is back. N Y Times Mag p 14-17+ F 5 '67
RUSSELL, John, viscount Amberley. See Amberley. J. R.
RUSSELL, John L. Jr
Transistors can find treasure. Motor B 119: 138-41 My '67
RUSSELL, John R. and others
Simulation for production. Harvard Bsns R 45:162-4+ S '67
RUSSELL, K. L. and others
Marine dolomite of unusual isotopic composition. bibliog Science 155:189-91 Ja 13 '67
RUSSELL, Mary
American girl's romp in the rich robes of high fashion. il pors Life 63:62-3+ S 1 '67
RUSSELL, Richard Brevard
Et tu, Russell? Nation 204:549 My 1 '67
New view on missiles. por U S News 62:15 Ap 3 '67
RUSSELL cave. See Caves
RUSSELL Stover candies, Incorporated
Sweet success. il Time 89:91 Ap 7 '67
RUSSETT, Bruce M.
Complexities of ballistic missile defense. Yale R 56:354-67 Mr '67
RUSSIA
Edgy anniversary. il Time 90:34 N 17 '67
Keynoting the golden jubilee. il Newsweek 70:46+ N 13 '67
Revolution in retrospect. W. Pfaff. Commonweal 87:71-2 O 20 '67
Russia; symposium. il Nat R 19:1165-206 O 31 '67
Russia: the next fifty years. il Bsns W p81-2+ Ap 29 '67
Russia today; symposium. il Look 31:29-42+ O 3 '67
Russian revolution, fifty years after; symposium. For Affairs 46:1-94 O '67
Russians' jubilee year. il Newsweek 70:40-9+ O 23 '67
Second revolution. il Time 90:32-6 N 10 '67
Soviet achievement; excerpt from The Soviet achievement, 1917-1967. J. P. Nettl. Harper 235:90-4+ O '67
Unfinished revolution, by I. Deutscher. Review
Sat R 50:32-5 D 9 '67. M. Nomad
U.S.S.R. after half a century; symposium. bibliog f il Cur Hist 53:193-235+ O '67
U.S.S.R. today; symposium. il UNESCO Courier 20:4-37 N '67
Where Russia is headed; with interview with G. W. Nutter. il U S News 63:68-77 N 6 '67
With Aurora's roar the birthday begins; Revolution's 50th anniversary celebrations. il Life 63:26-35 N 17 '67
Year of jubilee: the USSR at fifty; with editorial comment. A. Werth. il Nation 205: 418, 424-30 O 30 '67

See also
Aeronautics, Military—Russia
Agricultural administration—Russia
Air travel—Russia
Airlines—Russia
Airplane industry and trade—Russia
Airplanes, Military—Russia

RUSSIA—See also—*Continued*
Architecture—Russia
Art—Russia
Astronomical observatories—Russia
Atomic research—Russia
Automobile industry and trade—Russia
Automobile touring—Russia
Aviation—Russia
Ballet—Russia
Bratsk
Censorship—Russia
Childrens literature—Russia
Cities and towns—Russia
Civil defense—Russia
Clothing industry—Russia
Colleges and universities—Russia
Communism—Russia
Concentration camps—Russia
Daghestan
Economic assistance in Russia
Education—Russia
Electronic apparatus industry and trade—
Russia
Foreign students in Russia
Foreign visitors in Russia
Industrial management and organization—
Russia
Jazz music—Russia
Jews in Russia
Labor and laboring classes—Russia
Merchant marine—Russia
Mines and mineral resources—Russia
Moving picture industry—Russia
Moving pictures—Russia
Music—Russia
National parks and reserves—Russia
Newspapers—Russia
Opera—Russia
Periodicals—Russia
Phonograph record industry—Russia
Postal service—Russia
Prisoners—Russia
Prisons—Russia
Public opinion—Russia
Rostov
Science—Russia
Secret service—Russia
Space research—Russia
Tashkent
Tourist trade—Russia
Trials—Russia
Unemployment—Russia
Uzbekistan
Youth—Russia

Anecdotes, facetiae, satire, etc.
Not so glorious fiftieth. J. Burnham. Nat R
19:1370 D 12 '67

Armed forces
Pride and power in Moscow. il Newsweek 70:
74-5+ N 20 '67
Restraining the red generals. H. Schwartz.
Sat R 50:40 Jl 22 '67
See also
Military service, Compulsory—Russia
Russia—Navy

Appropriations and expenditures
ABM, Mideast war boost Soviet budget.
Aviation W 87:34 O 16 '67

Boundaries
Tension on the Sino-Soviet border. C. P.
Fitzgerald. il For Affairs 45:683-93 Jl '67
War of nerves; Sino-Soviet border. il News-
week 69:44+ Mr 6 '67

Commerce
East-West trade, what it means to business.
il U S News 62:50 Mr 27 '67
See also
Russia—Industries

Commercial treaties and agreements
U.S. and U.S.S.R. conclude talks on fishery
problems. Dept State Bul 56:331-2 F 27 '67

Cultural relations
Motion picture bridge between East and
West. J. Valenti. il Sat R 50:8-9+ D 23 '67

Defenses
Arms and the Soviet Union. V. Zorza; reply.
R. Abrams. New Repub 156:37 F 4 '67
Carrot and stick; U.S. and the U.S.S.R.
might avoid new sprint in arms race.
Newsweek 69:20 Ja 30 '67
China's bomb; US-USSR agreement against
the Chinese. New Repub 157:3-4 Jl 1 '67
Great missile debate. H. W. Baldwin. il Re-
porter 36:23-6 Je 29 '67
If Russia perfects its orbital bomb. U S News
63:6 N 13 '67

McNamara's ABM policy; a failure of com-
munications. N. Moss. il Reporter 36:34-6
F 23 '67
Matter of missiles and megadeaths; issue
that divides Robert S. McNamara and
Joint chiefs of staff. il Newsweek 69:44-8
Mr 27 '67
More questions than answers; Russian anti-
missile missiles. il Bsns W p88 Ja 14 '67
Outward bound; Soviet military power. Nat R
19:1310+ N 28 '67
Parallel reasoning; views of U.S. and Russia
after two decades of arms competition. il
Newsweek 69:35 Mr 13 '67
Shifting equation of nuclear defense. R. J.
Whalen. il Fortune 75:84-7+ Je 1 '67
Soviet ABM cost pegged at $25 billion. Avia-
tion W 87:78 O 23 '67
Soviet ABM philosophy. Aviation W 87:79
O 23 '67
Soviets narrowing ICBM gap. Tech W 20:33
Mr 27 '67
Soviets prepare space weapon for 1968; with
editorial comment. C. Brownlow. il Avia-
tion W 87:21, 30-1 N 13 '67
Strengthened U.S. ICBM forces to offset
Soviet missile defense. P. J. Klass. Avia-
tion W 86:27-8 F 6 '67
U.S. watches the Soviet parade; weaponry
not revolutionary. il Bsns W p46-7 N 11 '67
See also
Aeronautics, Military—Russia
Atomic warfare—Defenses
Russia—Armed forces
Russia—Navy

Description and travel
See also
Automobile touring—Russia

Diplomatic and consular service
Comfortable Communists; new look in Soviet
diplomacy. il Newsweek 70:40+ D 4 '67

Economic conditions
Ahead is change, I don't believe the system
can survive; interview. G. W. Nutter. il
U S News 63:74-7 N 6 '67
China, Russia & the U.S. O. Gass. Commen-
tary 43:43-6 Ap '67
Consumers in the US vs. the USSR. Con-
sumer Bul 51:25-6 Ja '68
East-West trade; address, March 8, 1967. G. P.
Lipscomb. bibliog f Vital Speeches 33:389-94
Ap 15 '67
Economy; snares, hurdles, progress. il News-
week 70:49+ O 23 '67
New look at today's Russia. R. K. Brome. il
U S News 62:70-2+ Je 5 '67
Rose-colored world of Intourist. E. C. Died-
rich. Nat R 19:638-9+ Je 13 '67
Russia loosens its belt. il Bsns W p64-8+
S 30 '67
Solid gold droshky. il Newsweek 69:81 F 13
'67
Stop-go economy goes. Time 90:25-6 Ag 4 '67
Trade with U.S.S.R. and European growth;
address, April 20, 1967. G. W. Ball. Vital
Speeches 33:546-50 Jl 1 '67
What Russia has achieved; at what price. il
U S News 62:55 Mr 13 '67
See also
Agriculture—Russia
Communism—Russia
Labor and laboring classes—Russia
Russia—Industries
Unemployment—Russia

Economic history
Soviet economic growth since the revolution.
M. I. Goldman. bibliog f Cur Hist 53:230-5+
O '67

Economic planning
Creeping capitalism in the Soviet Union?
excerpts from address, 1967. H. Landreth.
bibliog f Harvard Bsns R 45:133-40 S '67

Economic policy
Making the Soviet future work. il Bsns W
p 128-30+ Je 10 '67
Russia's economic reformation. H. Rausch. il
Reporter 37:33-5 N 16 '67
Russia's priorities; butter and guns. il U S
News 63:16 O 23 '67
Soviet aid and trade. M. Kovner. bibliog f
il Cur Hist 53:217-23+ O '67
Soviet economic growth since the revolution.
M. I. Goldman. bibliog f Cur Hist 53:230-5+
O '67
Soviet economic reform. E. G. Liberman. For
Affairs 46:53-63 O '67

RUSSIA—Economic policy—*Continued*
What makes Ivan run? R. A. Freeman.
Nat R 19:246-9 Mr 7 '67; Reply with
rejoinder. E. Lyons. 19:960-2+ S 5 '67
See also
Communism—Russia

Economic relations
Latin America
New Russian offensive. Time 89:30+ Mr 31
'67
Foreign opinion
Cold war, to flare anew or fade? reports from
world capitals. il U S News 63:23-6 Jl 10 '67
Foreign relations
Biggest pie-throwing contest ever? emergency
session of the U.N. General assembly. il
Newsweek 69:18-20 Je 26 '67
Communist dilemma; analysis. F. B. Stevens.
il U S News 62:64-5 Mr 13 '67
Containment has won, but. . . E. Stillman. il
N Y Times Mag p 23+ My 28 '67
Europe versus détente. M. D. Shulman? For
Affairs 45:389-402 Ap '67
Making policy in a divided world. il News-
week 70:62 O 23 '67
Prayers for the Russian people. D. Lawrence.
U S News 62:104 Je 12 '67
Real news on the hot line. Fortune 76:71-2 Jl
'67
Russia's role in Vietnam. C. Emmet. Amer-
ica 117:112-13 Jl 29 '67
Soviet game in the world. il U S News 62:
36-8 Je 26 '67
Thus spake Leonid Brezhnev; excerpts from
address, November 3, 1967. L. Brezhnev.
Reporter 37:19 D 14 '67
Uneven record of Soviet diplomacy. Time
89:15 Je 30 '67
Why Vietnam worries the Russians. W. Att-
wood. Look 31:23-5 Jl 11 '67
See also
Communist strategy
Cuban crisis, 1962
Russia—Boundaries

Arab states
Arms for embracing; growing Soviet penetra-
tion of the Arab world. il Time 91:18-19 Ja
19 '68
Down go the U.S.S.R. and the Arabs again.
il Newsweek 70:28+ Jl 17 '67
Hand of Russia. W. Laqueur. il Reporter 36:
18-20 Je 29 '67
Losers' summit, a peaceless truce. il News-
week 70:29+ Jl 24 '67
Middle East blueprint. New Repub 157:7-8
Jl 15 '67
Soviet blunder that led to Mideast war; the
inside story. il U S News 63:6 Jl 17 '67

China
Russia & China; ancient rivalry for the Asian
land mass. H. Schwartz. il Horizon 10:4-21
Wint '68

China (People's Republic)
Closer to a final split. il Time 89:26 F 17 '67
Communism's great divide. A. Parry. il Re-
porter 36:29-32 Je 1 '67
High invective. il Time 89:25 F 3 '67
High noon in Dairen; Red guards damage
Soviet freighter. Newsweek 70:39 Ag 28 '67
New turn in Vietnam, a deal between Russia
and China. il U S News 62:42-3 Ap 24 '67
Persuading red China to join the U.N. J.
B. Sheerin. Cath World 204:261-3 F '67
Russia vs. red China: what's actually going
on; with analysis by F. B. Stevens. il U S
News 62:36-40 F 20 '67
Russian charge: Peking is hijacking Soviet
jets. il U S News 62:12 Mr 6 '67
Significance of the rift between the Chinese
Communist regime and the Soviet Union;
address, April 1967, with questions and
answers. S. K. Chow. Ann Am Acad 372:
64-71 Jl '67
Tension on the China-Soviet border. A. D.
Barnett. il Look 31:40-2+ O 3 '67

Cuba
Cool days at the Havana summit. il U S
News 63:12 Jl 10 '67
Stopover in Havana; Kosygin visits Castro.
il Time 90:26 Jl 7 '67
Who won the missile confrontation? Nat R
19:838 Ag 8 '67

Egypt
Money and arms for Nasser and a foothold
for Russia. il Life 62:88 Je 16 '67
Why Nasser is no longer a free agent. L.
Muray. New Repub 157:10-11 D 23 '67

Europe
Soviet Russia and the two Europes. S. S.
Anderson. Cur Hist 53:203-7+ O '67

Europe, Western
Changing nature of Soviet and American rela-
tions with western Europe; address, April
1967, with questions and answers. D. S.
McLellan. bibliog f Ann Am Acad 372:16-32
Jl '67
Moscow's new look in western Europe. J.
H. Hedley. Yale R 56:390-6 Mr '67

France
Kosygin in Paris: differences within amity.
A. Werth; reply with rejoinder. P. Baum.
Nation 204:162+ F 6 '67

Great Britain
Chief aim of Kosygin's British trip. il U S
News 62:22 F 20 '67
Communist at Claridge's; Kosygin in Eng-
land. il Newsweek 69:48 F 20 '67
Unsmiling comrade; Kosygin visit. il Time
89:28 F 17 '67

Israel
Playing with fire; change of propaganda target
from Israel to Zionism and world Jewry.
Newsweek 70:30-1 Ag 21 '67

Italy
Ideology & practice; Podgorny in Rome. il
Time 89:31 F 3 '67
Russian in Rome; Podgorny visit. il News-
week 69:52 F 6 '67

Middle East
Did Moscow lose the Mideast war? C. Emmet.
Nat R 19:677 Je 27 '67
Foreign policy: a study in contrasts; US and
USSR. Bsns W p 182 Je 24 '67
Middle East: guidelines for policy. N. Safran
and S. Hoffmann. Nation 204:807-8 Je 26
'67
Region slipping to Russia, and U.S. has a big
stake. J. Law. il U S News 62:32-5 Je 5
'67
Soviet posture in the Middle East. B. Shwad-
ran. Cur Hist 53:331-6+ D '67
Soviet Union in the Middle East. B. Shwa-
dran. Cur Hist 52:72-7+ F '67
Victory without peace? D. Lawrence. U S
News 62:98 Je 26 '67

Sweden
MiGs demonstrated in visit to Sweden. Aviation W 87:18 S 4 '67

Underdeveloped areas
Kremlin and the third world. P. E. Mosely.
For Affairs 46:64-77 O '67

United States
American attitudes on U.S.-Soviet relations.
B. G. Lall. il Bul Atomic Sci 23:34-8 Ja '67
Arctic trip frozen out; coast guard ships
attempting first circumnavigation of the
Arctic Ocean. il Sci N 92:273-4 S 16 '67
Cold war as history, by L. J. Halle. Review
Sat R 50:32-3 O 21 '67. S. K. Padover
Cold war, revisited and re-visioned. C. Lasch.
il N Y Times Mag p26-7+ Ja 14 '68
Cold war, to flare anew or fade? reports from
world capitals. il U S News 63:23-6 Jl 10
'67
Diplomatic counterpoint. il Newsweek 69:
31-4 Je 19 '67
Dual crisis; Vietnam and Middle East situa-
tions stress need for amity. Nation 204:
738-9 Je 12 '67
Fact sheet on U.S.-Soviet relations. J.
Brownell. Sr Schol 91:6-7 O 5 '67
From Stalin to Kosygin; the myths and the
realities. W. A. Harriman. il Look 31:55-
6+ O 3 '67
Hot-line diplomacy; use of link between
Washington and Moscow. il Time 89:15-17
Je 16 '67
Middle East aftermath. H. Brandon. Sat R
50:8 Jl 1 '67
Opportunity for two; prospects for coopera-
tion between Washington and Moscow
dimmed. il Time 89:15-16 Je 23 '67
Postscript to Glassboro. N. Cousins. Sat R
50:18 Jl 29 '67
Russia's strategy in today's world; the view
from Europe. il U S News 63:101-2 N 27 '67
Soviet-American relations: conflict and co-
operation. J. C. Campbell. bibliog f Cur
Hist 53:193-202+ O '67
Storm over Svetlana: Russians ask for delay
in publication of memoir. Newsweek 70:20
Jl 31 '67

RUSSIA — Foreign relations — United States —
Continued
U.N: an arena for peaceful East-West en-
gagement; address, February 24, 1967. J. J.
Sisco. Dept State Bul 56:458-63 Mr 20 '67
U.N, front and center; what is needed to
prevent world war. N. Cousins. Sat R 50:
20 Je 17 '67
United States relations with the Soviet Union;
address, April 21, 1967. N. D. Katzenbach.
Dept State Bul 56:753-6 My 15 '67
United States-Soviet co-operation; incentives
and obstacles; address, April 1967, with
questions and answers. R. C. Tucker. bib-
liog f Ann Am Acad 372:11-15 Jl '67
War of the words. il Bsns W p33-6 Je 24 '67
We should encourage the doves in the Krem-
lin. R. L. Gilpatric. il N Y Times Mag p9+
Jl 30 '67
What's really going on between U.S. and
Russia. il U S News 62:46-50 Mr 27 '67
See also
Glassboro conference, 1967
United States—Treaties—Russia

History

Essential characteristics of the Russian na-
tion in the twentieth century. P. A. Sorokin.
bibliog f Ann Am Acad 370:99-115 Mr '67
Fortress, by R. Payne. Review
Sat R 50:38-9+ My 13 '67. M. Nomad
Lest you forget. . ; quiz, comp. by A. Croce
and C. H. Simonds. Nat R 19:1205-6 O 31 '67
See also
Romanov, House of

Bibliography

Articles and other books received; comp.
by R. V. Allen. See issues of American
historical review

20th century

Fifty years of the Soviet Union. il Newsweek
70:48-9 O 23 '67
On Stalin's triumph, on Stalin's madness. C.
P. Snow. il Esquire 67:114-18+ My '67
Rasputin reconsidered. E. M. Halliday. il
Horizon 9:80-7 Aut '67
Soviet Russia, 1917-1967: fifty years of
thunder. R. Armstrong. il Sat Eve Post
240:25-38+ N 4 '67
Unfinished revolution (1917-1967) by I. Deut-
scher. Review
Time il 90:78+ Jl 21 '67

Revolution, 1917-1921

Coup that changed the world. E. Crankshaw.
il N Y Times Mag p26-7+ F 19 '67
Dissenting view of the day that shook the
world; November 7, 1917. J. Lukacs. il
N Y Times Mag p32-3+ O 22 '67; Dis-
cussion. p12+ N 12 '67; 1112-13 Ja 7 '68
Fall of Nicholas II. il Newsweek 69:46+
Mr 20 '67
Lenin's journey in the sealed train; from
Switzerland into Russia. H. W. Dewey. il
N Y Times Mag p26-7+ Mr 26 '67
Letter from Paris; fiftieth anniversary.
Genêt. New Yorker 43:228 N 25 '67
Lost revolution. il Time 89:32-3 Mr 17 '67
Revolution that shook and upset the world;
with analysis by F. B. Stevens and inter-
view with A. Kerensky. il U S News 62:
54-7+ Mr 13 '67
Russian revolution; its nature and conse-
quences. G. F. Kennan. For Affairs 46:1-21
O '67
Soviet Russia, 1917-1967: fifty years of
thunder. R. Armstrong. il Sat Eve Post
240:25-38+ N 4 '67
Workers' paradise lost; condensation. E.
Lyons. il Read Digest 91:233-7+ N '67
See also
Russia—Politics and government

Revolution, 1917-1921—Bibliography

USSR: the first half-century. R. Barnes. il
Sat R 50:22-3 D 30 '67

Revolution 1917-1921—Study and teaching

Teaching about the Russian revolution. H.
L. Hurwitz. bibliog il Sr Schol 91:sup8-9
N 30 '67

Industries

Businessman sizes up Russia; interview. R. S.
Morse. il U S News 63:50-4 Ag 14 '67
Ivan looks to western ways; economy to adopt
capitalistic techniques. il Bsns W p86+
Ap 29 '67

U.S.S.R. today; metamorphosis of a continent. N. Mikhailov. il UNESCO Courier
20:4-10 N '67
See also
Automobile industry and trade—Russia
Industrial management and organization—Russia

Intellectual life

Around the arts in the Soviet Union. J.
Roddy. il Look 31:109-12 O 3 '67
Arts; somehow, sometimes, brilliant. il News-
week 70:54-6 O 23 '67
Beneath the panoply of power, the intel-
ligentsia hits out at the old order. J. H.
Billington. il Life 63:70-2+ N 10 '67
Other country inside Russia; Soviet writers.
S. Kunitz. il N Y Times Mag p24-5+ Ag
20 '67
Politics. Petition to the presidium. D. Mac-
donald. Esquire 67:16+ F '67
Protesting the fig leaf. il Time 90:35 Jl 21 '67
Reflections on Soviet culture. S. Gerasimov.
il UNESCO Courier 20:21+ N '67
Revolt of the authors. il Newsweek 70:31 Ag
21 '67

Maps

Fast-changing Siberia dominates new Atlas
map. il Nat Geog Mag 131:346-7, sup(folded
map) Mr '67

Military policy

Arms and the Soviet Union. V. Zorza; reply.
R. Abrams. New Repub 156:37 F 4 '67
Soviet Mideast buildup shows tactic shift.
D. C. Winston. Aviation W 87:19-20 N 6 '67
Soviet military policy at the fifty year mark.
T. W. Wolfe. bibliog f Cur Hist 53:208-16+
O '67
See also
Russia—Defenses

Navy

Aim of Russia's growing naval might. il U S
News 63:14 N 6 '67
Collision course; harassment of U.S. naval
vessels conducting exercises on the high
seas. Newsweek 69:62 My 22 '67
Game of chicken; Russians harass U.S.
naval maneuvers. Time 89:35 My 19 '67
Just what are the Russians up to now? Rus-
sian harassment of U.S. warship. il U S
News 62:8 My 22 '67
Looking southward; Soviet buildup in the
Mediterranean. il Time 90:27 D 22 '67
Now Russia builds up power in the Mediter-
ranean; excerpts from address, November
17, 1967. C. D. Griffin. il U S News 63:46+
D 11 '67
Red navy's moves; their meaning. U S News
62:34-5 Je 12 '67
Russia's Sixth fleet; Mediterranean squadron.
il Newsweek 70:39-40 Ag 28 '67
Soviet challenge that is growing; effort by
Soviet warships to harass U.S. naval units
in strategic waters. il U S News 62:15 My
29 '67
Soviet fleet in the Mediterranean. C. Sterling.
il Reporter 37:14-18 D 14 '67
Titan unbound; Russian seapower. R. Moley.
Newsweek 70:80 Jl 24; 84 Ag 7 '67

Politics and government

Fiftieth anniversary; a Soviet watershed? D.
T. Cattell. Cur Hist 53:224-9+ O '67
Freedom on the way for Soviet people? state-
ment, 1917. A. F. Kerensky. U S News 63;
16 N 20 '67
From Stalin to Kosygin; the myths and the
realities. W. A. Harriman. il Look 31:55-
6+ O 3 '67
Other country inside Russia; Soviet writers.
S. Kunitz. il N Y Times Mag p24-5+ Ag 20
'67
Russian revolution; fifty years after; ques-
tions and answers. J. Brownell. il Sr Schol
91:15-18 O 26 '67
Svetlana Allilueyva and the Russian revolu-
tion. D. L. Flaherty. America 117:473-6 O
28 '67
See also
Communism—Russia
Communist party (Russia)
Russia—History—Revolution, 1917-1921

Population

Soviet population theory. D. Wolfle. Science
158:999 N 24 '67

Relations (diplomatic)
Catholic church

See Catholic church—Relations (diplomatic)—Russia

RUSSIA—*Continued*

Religious institutions and affairs

God and Russian women. Newsweek 70:82 S 11 '67

Literature and religion in Russia today; interview, ed. by C. L. Palms. R. Marshall. Cath World 204:362-7 Mr '67

World around us. Christian Cent 84:844+, 1607-8 Je 28, D 13 '67

See also
Baptists in Russia
Christians in Russia
Orthodox Eastern church, Russian
Orthodox Eastern church in Ukraine

Social conditions

Essential characteristics of the Russian nation in the twentieth century. P. A. Sorokin. bibliog f Ann Am Acad 370:99-115 Mr '67

Fifty years: a literary tribute; selections from the literature of anti-communism. il Nat R 19:1176-87 O 31 '67

Kremlin's human dilemma, by M. Hindus. Review Sat R 50:33-4 F 18 '67. H. Schwartz

New look at today's Russia. R. K. Brome. il U S News 62:70-2+ Je 5 '67

Peaceful revolutions ahead. Newsweek 70:41 O 23 '67

Rose-colored world of Intourist. E. C. Diedrich. Nat R 19:638-9+ Je 13 '67

Russian revolution: fifty years after; questions and answers. J. Brownell. il Sr Schol 91:11-13+ N 2 '67

Service please; program to train more people for service jobs. Time 90:37 S 29 '67

See also
Communism—Russia
Jews in Russia
Labor and laboring classes—Russia
Youth—Russia

Social history

Russia before the revolution; excerpts from Workers paradise lost. E. Lyons. il Nat R 19:1166-9 O 31 '67

Social life and customs

On location in Rostov; filming the new revolution. D. Smith. il Nation 204:268-72 F 27 '67

See also
Baltic states—Russian occupation

Travel regulations

See Travel regulations

Treaties
United States
See United States—Treaties—Russia

RUSSIA and China
Angry din of China's joyless New Year. il Life 62:40-1 F 17 '67

RUSSIA and the United States
Another U.S.-Russian contest; exhibits at Expo 67. il U S News 62:96-8 My 22 '67

We don't know much about each other. Look 31:72+ O 3 '67

See also
United States—Foreign opinion—Russian

RUSSIA and the West. See World politics, 1945-

RUSSIA-United States air agreement. See Aviation—International aspects

RUSSIAN air show. See Aviation—Exhibitions

RUSSIAN airways. See Airways

RUSSIAN art. See Art, Russian

RUSSIAN art objects. See Art objects, Russian

RUSSIAN artificial satellites. See Artificial satellites, Russian

RUSSIAN authors. See Authors, Russian

RUSSIAN bonds. See Bonds, Government—Russia

RUSSIAN communist party. See Communist party (Russia)

RUSSIAN cookery. See Cookery, Russian

RUSSIAN culture. See Russia—Intellectual life

RUSSIAN drama
Chekhov's plays. K. Rexroth. Sat R 50:18 Jl 8 '67

RUSSIAN fiction
War and peace. K. Rexroth. Sat R 50:10+ N 11 '67

RUSSIAN Jews. See Jews in Russia

RUSSIAN language
How says itself in Russian? L. A. Harlow. Travel 127:61-2+ Ja '67

Study and teaching

Berlitz taught me Russian in a hurry. J. Roddy. Look 31:M6+ O 3 '67

Teaching Russian in junior high schools; Maplewood, N.Y. an Albany suburb. L. J. Cerri. Sr Schol 90:sup21 My 5 '67

RUSSIAN literature
Literature and religion in Russia today; interview, ed. by C. L. Palms. R. Marshall. Cath World 204:362-7 Mr '67

See also
Authors, Russian
Russian drama
Russian fiction

Bibliography

Continuity of Russian voices. I. Howe. Harper 236:69-70+ Ja '68

Translations into English

Department of amplification; concerning From two to five. by K. I. Chukovskii. tr. and ed. by M. Morton. K. I. Chukovsii New Yorker 42:81-2+ Ja 21 '67; Reply. M. Morton. 43:166+ Ap 8 '67

Grove, Harper both issue Russian novel, Oct. 4. Pub W 192:45-6 S 18 '67

Master and Margarita; the implicit controversy. Pub W 192:33-4 O 2 '67

Rights and wrongs of advertising and translation; concerning The master and Margarita by M. Bulgakov; letter. M. Ginsburg. Pub W 193:45-6 Ja 15 '68

RUSSIAN military assistance. See Military assistance, Russian

RUSSIAN olives. See Oleasters

RUSSIAN Orthodox church. See Orthodox Eastern church, Russian

RUSSIAN painting. See Painting, Russian

RUSSIAN peace corps. See Volunteer service International

RUSSIAN poetry
Poets, red and white. D. Brown. il N Y Times Mag p6+ My 28 '67

Translations into English

Babi Yar; poem; tr. by H. Marshall. Y. Yevtushenko. Am Rec G 34:11 S '67

Call of the lake; From a Transcarpathian diary; poems, tr. by S. Kunitz and V. Dunham. A. Voznesenskii. New Repub 157:28, 31 S 2 '67

In the mountains; tr. by J. Wallace. A. Voznesensky. Mlle 65:104 S '67

New poems; Fears; Tenderness; tr. by G. Reavey. Y. Yevtushenko. Harper 234:65 Mr '67

Reading Hamlet; July 1914; Heart's memory of sun. . . ; tr. by S. Kunitz. A. Akhmatova. Nation 204:528 Ap 24 '67

Restaurant for two; Ballad about nuggets; tr. by J. Updike. Y. Yevtushenko. Life 62:33, 38 F 17 '67

Rome; Rhythms of Rome; Heat in Rome; tr. by G. Reavey. Y. Yevtushenko. il Sat R 50:24-7 Jl 22 '67

Sketch for a poem; tr. by W. J. Smith and V. Dunham. A. Voznesenskii. Harper 235: 52-5 Ag '67

They've taken out our sense of shame; excerpts from poem; translation. A. Voznesenskii. N Y Times Mag p24 Ag 20 '67

To Bela Akhmadulina; Lament for two unborn poems; Self-portrait; Note to E. Yanitskaya, formerly typist to Mayakovsky; Lieutenant Zagorin; tr. by S. Kunitz and V. Dunham. A. Voznesenskii. New Repub 157:31-3 Jl 1 '67

Two poems; Striptease on strike; Winter at the track; tr. by M. Hayward. A. Voznesenskii. Atlan 220:70-2 N '67

What pain, my beloved; tr. by G. Reavey. E. A. Evtushenko. Good H 166:122 Ja '68

RUSSIAN poets. See Poets, Russian

RUSSIAN revolution. See Russia—History—Revolution, 1917-1921

RUSSIAN scientists. See Scientists, Russian

RUSSIAN space probes. See Space probes, Russian

RUSSIAN spies. See Spies

RUSSIAN students
Eager to work for state, and rubles; with report by P. Young. il Life 63:46-53+ N 10 '67

RUSSIAN travel restrictions. See Travel regulations

RUSSIAN youth. See Youth—Russia

RUSSIANS
Essential characteristics of the Russian nation in the twentieth century. P. A. Sorokin. bibliog f Ann Am Acad 370:99-115 Mr '67

Other country inside Russia; Soviet writers. S. Kunitz. il N Y Times Mag p24-5+ Ag 20 '67

RUSSIANS—*Continued*
Paradigm for Russia. J. C. Evans. Christian Cent 84:679-80 My 24 '67
Russia today; symposium. il Look 31:29-42+ O 3 '67
Yalta, the Soviet playground. G. Feifer. il Holiday 42:66-7+ O '67
RUSSIANS in Great Britain
Mistaken identity; dispute over return of V. Tkachenko. il Newsweek 70:40+ O 2 '67
RUSSO, Perry Raymond
D.A. wins a round. il por Time 89:17-18 Mr 24 '67
Thickening the plot. por Newsweek 69:37 Mr 27 '67
RUST. See Corrosion and anticorrosives
RUSTIC furniture. See Furniture, Rustic
RUSTIN, Bayard
Lessons of the long hot summer. Commentary 44:39-45 O '67
On civil disobedience, 1967. N Y Times Mag p 131-2 N 26 '67
Way out of the exploding ghetto. N Y Times Mag p 16-17+ Ag 13 '67
RUSTS (botany)
Atmospheric ions and germination of uredospores of puccinia striiformis. E. L. Sharp. bibliog il Science 156:1359-60 Je 9 '67
RUTELLI, Giovanni
Pseudo-solarizations of Giovanni Rutelli. il Pop Phot 60:92-5 Je '67
RUTGERS university, New Brunswick, N.J.

Graduate school of library service
Rutgers celebrates birthday, creates children's Lit award. Library J 92:284 Ja 15 '67
RUTH, Henry S. Jr
Why organized crime thrives. bibliog f Ann Am Acad 374:113-22 N '67
—See Ohlin, L. E. jt. ed.
RUTH, Jerry
King. W. Youst. il Hot Rod 20:80-2 Mr '67
RUTHENIAN rite. See Catholic church—Byzantine rite (Ruthenian)
RUTHVEN, Grey
Lady poet; poem. Atlan 220:68 O '67
March letters; poem. Atlan 219:91 Je '67
RUTILE. See Titanium dioxide
RUTLEDGE, Carl A. family
Sense of bursting away, utterly free. H. Suydam. il Life 62:74+ F 10 '67
RUTLEDGE, Dana
Sense of bursting away, utterly free. H. Suydam. il pors Life 62:74+ F 10 '67
RUTTENBERG, Derald H.
Obscure tycoon to reckon with. il por Bsns W p 129-30+ My 27 '67
RUTTER, William J. See Lebherz, H. G. jt. auth.
RUTTING season. See Sex behavior
RUYLE, Robert L.
What ground? Pop Electr 27:59-62 Ag '67
RUZICKA, Rudolph
Genius of Rudolph Ruzicka. R. Nash. il por Am Artist 31:44-50+ D '67
RYAN, A. S.
Build an expandable camper. Pop Sci 190:162-6+ My '67
How to add a kitchen to a camper. Pop Sci 190:160-2 Je '67
RYAN, Elizabeth M. See Levy, H. M. jt. auth.
RYAN, James W.
Renin-like enzyme in the adrenal gland. bibliog Science 158:1589-90 D 22 '67
RYAN, M. P. and Colley, R. H.
Preventive maintenance in client-ad agency relations. Harvard Bsns R 45:66-74 S '67
RYAN, Orletta, and Brodsky, Bernard
Class of 1984 (now 5) looks ahead. N Y Times Mag p6-7+ D 31 '67
RYAN, Patricia
Blow for esthetics. Sports Illus 26:28-9 Je 5 '67
RYAN, William
Holy work of Bruno Bettelheim. Commonweal 86:283-6 My 26 '67
RYAN, William L. and Summerlin, Sam
Incredible story of How China got the bomb; excerpts. Look 31:19-25 Jl 25 '67
RYBICKI, Frank, Jr
Home is the soldier ... il por Newsweek 69:25-6 Je 5 '67
RYDER, Norman B.
Character of modern fertility. bibliog f Ann Am Acad 369:26-36 Ja '67
—and Westoff, C. F.
Use of oral contraception in the United States, 1965. Science 153:1199-205; 155:951 S 9 '66, F 24 '67

RYDER, R. M.
Selection of transistors. por Electr World 78:37 Jl '67
RYDER cup matches. See Golf—Tournaments
RYE, N.Y.
Children's library; Rye free reading room. Horn Bk 43:55 F '67
Undebatable joy; the late M. Dalphin, former librarian of Rye free reading room. Horn Bk 43:120+ F '67
RYE
                    Hybrids
    See also
Triticale
RYNNE, Xavier, pseud.
Letter from Vatican City (cont) New Yorker 43:119-20+ S 9 '67
RYUKU ISLANDS
    See also
Okinawa
RYUN, Jim
And now the one-mile dash. por Time 90:54 Jl 21 '67
Best record yet. P. Axthelm. il por Sports Illus 27:16-21 Jl 17 '67
Few high flyers in a hope-filled debut. G. S. Brown. il Sports Illus 26:14-15 Ja 30 '67
First blood of a classic duel. G. S. Brown. il Sports Illus 26:26-7 Mr 20 '67
From no O to no. 1! H. L. Masin. il Sr Schol Schol 90:27 My 5 '67
One, two. Newsweek 69:62 Mr 20 '67
Record pace. Newsweek 70:53 Jl 17 '67
Relays and old reliable G. S. Brown. il Sports Illus 26:26-7 My 8 '67
Running man. G. Astor. il pors Look 31:70-4 Jl 11 '67
Sanctions and sanctimony. Sports Illus 26:11 Mr 6 '67
See you later, Jim Ryun. P. Axthelm. il pors Sports Illus 27:10-13 Jl 3 '67
Two guys named Jim had the same idea. T. C. Brody. il por Sports Illus 26:34-5 Je 12 '67

S

SAILS (simplified aircraft instrument landing system) See Airplanes—Landing
SAR (search and rescue aircraft) See Airplanes, Military—United States
SAS. See Scandinavian airlines system
SBA. See United States—Small business administration
SBIC. See Small business investment companies
SCLC. See Southern Christian leadership conference
SDC. See System development corporation
SDS. See Scientific data systems, incorporated; Students for a democratic society (organization)
SEALs (sea-air-land) units. See United States—Navy—Underwater demolition teams
SEATO. See Southeast Asia treaty organization
SEC. See United States—Securities and exchange commission
SEED (special elementary education for the disadvantaged) See Socially handicapped children—Education
SERT (space electric rocket test) See Artificial satellites
SINS (ship's inertial navigation systems) See Inertial guidance systems
SLR cameras. See Single-lens reflex cameras
SLR lenses. See Lenses, Photographic
SNAP (secondary nuclear auxiliary power) See Space vehicles—Atomic power plants
SNCC. See Student non-violent coordinating committee
SOE (special operations executive) See Secret service—Great Britain
SORC (Southern Ocean racing conference) See Yacht racing
SPD (Social democratic party) See Political parties—Germany (Federal Republic)
SRI. See Stanford research institute
S. S. Pierce company. See Pierce, S. S, company
STOL airplanes. See Airplanes, Short take-off and landing
STP. See Hallucinogenic drugs; Psychopharmacology
STV. See Television broadcasting—Subscription programs

SUNY (State university of New York) See
    New York (state) State university
SURV (standard underwater research vessel)
    See Submarine boats
SAAB. See Airplane industry and trade—Swe-
    den
SAAL, Hubert
    True story of Beverly Sills. N Y Times Mag
    p34-5+ S 17 '67
SAAL, Rollene W.
    Pick of the paperbacks. See issues of Satur-
    day review
SAALBURG, Leslie
    Aftermath. Esquire 67:62+ My '67
SAARINEN, Aline B.
    [Fine art reproductions] McCalls 94:52-4 Je;
    132-5 Jl; 114-15 Ag; 30-1 S; 95:38-9 O; 42-3
    N; 78-9 D '67; 41-2 Ja '68
                   about
Intelluptuously speaking. il por Time 90:86
    N 3 '67
SAAVEDRA, Carlos Rodríguez. See Rodríguez
    Saavedra, C.
SABBATHAIANS
    Sabbatai Zevi and the Jewish imagination.
    R. Alter. Commentary 43:66-71 Je '67
SABBATI Zevi. See Shabthai Tsebi
SABBATIANISM. See Sabbathaians
SABBATIANS. See Sabbathaians
SABBATICAL leave. See College professors and
    instructors—Leaves of absence
SABELLARIA. See Annelids
SABER saws. See Saws
SABIN, Albert B.
    Collaboration for accelerating progress in
    medical research; excerpts from Senate
    committee testimony, March 16, 1967. Sci-
    ence 156:1568-71 Je 23 '67
SABIN, Robert
    J. S. Bach up to date. Am Rec G 34:157 O
    '67
    Last years of Serge Koussevitzky. Am Rec G
    34:22-3 S '67
    Not the music but the man. Am Rec G 33:
    858-60 My '67
SABLE ISLAND
    Sable Island.   F. Bruemmer. il Natur Hist
    76:54-9 Ag '67
SABOL, Edwin
    C. B. DeMille of the pros. T. C. Brody. il
    pors Sports Illus 27:74-6+ N 20 '67
SABSAY, David
    Santa Rosa: a library for today. Library J
    92:4367-8 D 1 '67
SACCHARIDES
    Imine-bonding in membrane transport of
    monosaccharides: invalidity of kinetic
    evidence. P. G. LeFevre. bibliog il Science
    158:274-5 O 13 '67
SACCO-Vanzetti case
    Sacco-Vanzetti: a memoir. A. Felicani. il
    Nation 205:108-12 Ag 14 '67
SACERDOTALIS celibatus. See Encyclicals
SACHAR, Abram Leon
    With status came perplexity. Sat R 50:36+
    O 28 '67
                   about
Brandeis at nineteen. Newsweek 70:94-5 O
    16 '67
Builder in a hurry. il por Time 90:64 S 29 '67
SACHS, Albie
    Reader's choice. O. Handlin. Atlan 219:145
    Ap '67
SACHS, Benjamin D.
    Photoperiodic control of the cloacal gland of
    the Japanese quail. bibliog Science 157:201-3
    Jl 14 '67
SACHS, Nelly
    O the homeless colours; in this amethyst;
    poems, tr. by R. Mead and M. Mead. Mlle
    65:104 S '67
    O the night of the weeping children! poem;
    tr. by M. Hamburger. Harper 235:68 Jl '67
    Ten poems: Agony, metronome of an alien
    star; Chorus of the unborn; When day
    grows empty; Earth, old man of the plan-
    ets; And we who move away; Landscape
    of screams; How many; Sleepwalker; You in
    the night; Vainly. New Yorker 43:30-1 Ag
    5 '67
                   about
From death to rebirth. J. Slater. Sat R 50:36
    N 4 '67
SACK, John
    When Demirgian comes marching home again
    (hurrah? hurrah?) Esquire 69:56-9+ Ja '68
SACKETT, Gene P. See Pratt, C. L. jt. auth.

SACKETT, Ross D.
    Textbook market, what went wrong? sum-
    mary of address. por Pub W 192:23-4 N 20
    '67
SACKETT, Russell
    In a grim city, a secret meeting with the
    snipers. Life 63:27-8 Jl 28 '67
SACKLER, Howard
    Great white hope. Criticism
        Nation 206:93-4 Ja 15 '68
        Newsweek il 70:73 D 25 '67
        Sat R 50:18 D 30 '67
SACKS, William
    Mutarotase in erythrocytes: isolation and
    properties. bibliog Science 158:498-9 O 27
    '67
SACRAMENT of penance. See Confession
SACRAMENTO, Calif.
                  Architecture
Courthouse sets the tone of community beau-
    tification. M. T. Scimens. il Am City 82:
    129 O '67
               Governors mansion
        See Governors mansions
SACRAMENTO COUNTY, Calif.
    We use TV for more than inspection. J. S.
    Haldeman. il Am City 82:112-13+ Mr '67
SACRAMENTS
         See also
    Lords Supper
SACRED books
    Expedition holy book; Maya holy book,
    CEDAM, at Chumpon.   E. Gowen. il
    Américas 19:1-7 S '67
SACRED Heart, Devotion to
    Perennial piety. V. P. McCorry. America 116:
    822, inside back cover Je 3 '67
SACRED music. See Church music
SACRIFICE, Human
    Body in the bog; archaeological detective
    story. G. Bibby. il Horizon 10:44-51 Wint
    '68
SADE, Donatien Alphonse François, comte de
    Hypochondriacal vision. L. Schaffer. New
    Repub 157:26-8 Ag 19 '67
SADEH, Dror
    Galaxies as gravitational lenses. bibliog Sci-
    ence 158:1176-8 D 1 '67
SADHUS
    India's holy men; Tyagis. F. Levine. Atlan
    220:18+ O '67
SADIE, Jan L.
    Labor supply and employment in less devel-
    oped countries. bibliog f Ann Am Acad
    369:121-30 Ja '67
SADIE, Stanley
    Handel operas. Hi Fi 17:69-72 F '67
SADLER, Ann. See Parker, A.
SADLER, Christine
    Never spill milk on a president; excerpts from
    Children in the White House. McCalls 94:
    34+ Jl '67
SADLER, Marion
    American way. Time 91:84-5 Ja 19 '68
SADRUDDIN Aga Khan, prince
    High commissioner for refugees; summary of
    statement, November 20, 1967. UN Mo Chron
    4:87 D '67
SAETTLER, Paul
    Rise of programed instruction; excerpts from
    History of instructional technology. bibliog
    Sch & Soc 95:536-44 D 23 '67
SAFARI. See Hunting—Africa, East
SAFDIE, Moshe
    Concrete ideas from a kibbutz. il por Bsns W
    p 166 Je 24 '67
    Habitat's cluster. R. Boyd. il Arch Forum
    126:36-41 My '67
    Tomorrow's Pueblo: Expo 67's controversial
    Habitat. il por Life 62:74-5+ Mr 31 '67
    Twenty-first century comes to Montreal. R.
    Gustaitis. il Reporter 36:37-8 F 9 '67
SAFELIGHTS.   See   Photography—Apparatus
    and supplies
SAFETY belts
    Buckle-on bill; shoulder harness requirement.
    Sr Schol 91:23 N 16 '67
    Safety harness for '68 cars, after all. il U S
    News 63:8 O 23 '67
    Seat-belt trauma; lap-belt injury. il Newsweek
    69:92 Je 19 '67
SAFETY devices and measures
    Accident-prevention program that works;
    North Miami, Fla. E. J. Connell. il Am
    City 82:147+ O '67
    Bathroom safety. Newsweek 69:65 Je 26 '67
    New help for summer hazards. J. D. Wasser-
    sug. il Sci Digest 62:65-9 Jl '67
    Safe at home. E. Kinard. House B 109:30+
    Ap '67

SAFETY devices and measures—*Continued*
Why you need a safety program; Milwaukee;
excerpts from address. H. G. Hatcher. il
Am City 82:103-5 Ag '67
See also
Accidents
Road signs
Safety belts
also subhead Safety devices and meas-
ures under various subjects, e.g. Automo-
biles—Safety devices and measures
SAFETY education
Safety village; city within a city is teaching
Tampa youngsters accident prevention. il
Travel 127:56-7 Ja '67
See also
Accidents—Prevention
Automobile driving—Study and teaching
SAFETY guards. See Roads—Safety guards
SAFETY movement
See also
Automobiles—Safety devices and measures
SAFETY parade; drama. See Fisher, A.
SAFETY razors. See Razors
SAFFO; opera. See Pacini, G.
SAFRAN, Nadav
Arab-Israeli dispute in perspective. Cur Hist
53:321-30+ D '67
—and Hoffmann, Stanley
Middle East. Nation 204:806-8 Je 26 '67
SAGA administrative corporation
Dishing up 5-million meals every week. il
Bsns W p 188-90 My 6 '67
SAGALL, Solomon
Excerpt from statement before Communica-
tions subcommittee, October 13, 1967. Cong
Digest 46:300-1+ D '67
SAGALYN, Arnold, and Coates, Joseph
Wanted: weapons that do not kill. N Y
Times Mag p6+ S 17 '67
SAGAN, Carl
Mars: a new world to explore. por Nat Geog
Mag 132:820-41 D '67
Unidentified flying objects; reprint from En-
cyclopedia Americana, 1967. Bul Atomic Sci
23:43-4 Je '67
—and Veverka, Joseph
Martian ionosphere: a component due to
solar protons. bibliog Science 158:110-12 O
6 '67
SAGAN, Françoise, pseud.
Help! or something; story. tr. by A. Foulke.
Vogue 150:76-7 Jl '67
SAGE, Tom, pseud.
Gulliver in Greece. Nat R 19:1112-13 O 17 '67
Who'll end up ruling Cyprus? Nat R 19:569-
71 My 30 '67
SAGEBRUSH
Look what they're doing to your land; sage-
brush-killing bad for western wildlife. T.
Trueblood. il Field & S 72:10+ O '67
SAGER, Ruth, and Hamilton, M. G.
Cytoplasmic and chloroplast ribosomes of
chlamydomonas: ultracentrifugal character-
ization. bibliog Science 157:709-11 Ag 11 '67
SAGINAW, Mich.
Modern workshop is more efficient. L. D.
Worth. il Am City 82:112+ D '67
SAHAGÚN, Bernardino de
Feather merchants; excerpt from the 16th
century Aztec manuscript; tr. by C. E.
Dibble and A. J. O. Anderson. Craft Horiz
27:18-23+ Mr '67
Goldworkers and lapidaries; excerpt from the
16th century Aztec manuscript; tr. by C.
E. Dibble and A. J. O. Anderson. Craft
Horiz 27:16-21 S '67
SAHARA DESERT
Dry-land fleet sails the Sahara. J. Du
Boucher. il Nat Geog Mag 132:696-725 N '67
SAHER, José Manuel
Father and son. il por Newsweek 69:59 Ap
10 '67
SAHER, Pablo
Father and son. il por Newsweek 69:59 Ap
10 '67
SAHLOFF, Willard Henry
How Mr Housewares woos his customers. il
pors Bsns W p98-100+ Jl 1 '67
SAIGON
Letter from abroad. E. Steinbeck. il McCalls
94:42+ Je '67
Crime
Crooks in toyland; harbor thieves. Newsweek
69:34 F 27 '67
Economic conditions
Keeping up with the Tran Quan Lacs. L. G.
Martin. il N Y Times Mag p22-3+ Ag 20
'67
Harbor
Pulling the cork from Saigon's bottleneck.
il Bsns W p 114-15 S 23 '67

Newspapers
License vs. liberty. Newsweek 69:41-2 F 13 '67
Social conditions
Cleaning up Saigon. il Time 90:27 D 1 '67
Transportation
Public sector goes to pot in Saigon; or, At
sea in a fuming bus; excerpt. Nguyen-
van-Tao. Nat R 19:1006 S 19 '67
Water supply
Saigon water-works psychology. J. A. Dillen-
er. il Am City 82:92-4 My '67
SAILBOAT building. See Boatbuilding
SAILBOAT racing
At sea without a rudder; interview, ed. by
D. Selby. A. Biehl. il Yachting 121:94+
Ap '67
Explosion of boats; race-rendezvous. il
Yachting 121:108-11 Ja '67
IYRU adopts three new classes. R. N. Bavier.
il Yachting 123:117+ Ja '68
It's a long way to Alviso Slough; race on
lower San Francisco Bay. T. Moore. il
Yachting 123:88-9 Ja '68
Olympic sailing; a rising fever. B. Robinson.
il Yachting 121:88-9+ Ap '67
On the circuit. il Yachting 122:32-6+ O '67
Profiles; F. E. Hood. A. Bailey. New Yorker
43:34-6+ Ag 26 '67
Sailing by Chance. E. S. Gillingham, jr. il
Motor B 119:88-90+ Ap '67
They sail to win. See issues of Yachting
We came for the gold; Olympic sailing his-
tory; excerpt from White sails, black clouds.
J. J. McNamara, jr. il Yachting 122:42-3+
D '67
With the racing classes. E. Horan. See
issues of Yachting
SAILBOATS
Go on, buy the kids a sailboat! il Changing T
21:13-14 Ap '67
How to buy a sailboat. J. Westlake. il Pop
Mech 127:154+ F '67
In defense of the windward plane; Junior
contest article. G. Blair. il Yachting 122:
23+ N '67
IYRU adopts three new classes. R. N. Bavier.
il Yachting 123:117+ Ja '68
Paul Elvström on dinghy techniques. P.
Elvström. il Yachting 122:24-5+ O '67
They sail to win; making an FD fly. B.
Melges. il Yachting 121:56+ Ap '67
See also
Catamarans
Trimarans
Care
Single-handed fit out. J. R. Guthrie. il Mo-
tor B 119:84-5+ Mr '67
Yachting clinic for starboats. Yachting 121:
49+ My '67 (to be cont)
Design
Designs. W. H. deFontaine. See issues of
Yachting
Whaler-sailer? R. W. Carrick. il Yachting 123:
106-8+ Ja '68
Equipment
Yachting's boat show. il Yachting 121:123-
6+ Ja '67; 123:120-2+ Ja '68
Exhibitions
1968 sailboats. il Motor B 121:148-57 Ja '68
Materials
New fiberglass spars. B. Cobb, jr. il Yacht-
ing 122:41+ O '67
Testing
Chrysler's five-boat fleet, fast and fancy! J.
Roe. il Pop Sci 190:104-8+ Je '67
SAILING
Abroad Intrepid; above and below deck. B.
D. Barker, 3d. il Yachting 122:88-90+ S '67
Go on, buy the kids a sailboat! il Changing T
21:13-14 Ap '67
In defense of the windward plane; Junior
contest article. G. Blair. il Yachting 122:
23+ N '67
Paul Elvström on dinghy techniques. P.
Elvström. il Yachting 122:24-5+ N '67
They sail to win. See issues of Yachting
See also
Cruising
Sailboat racing
Yachts and yachting

SAILING—*Continued*

Study and teaching

Girls before the mast; Culver military academy. Summer naval school. B. Kocivar. il Look 31:89-91 Je 13 '67

Malin Burnham and the Pittwater Star fleet. il Yachting 121:48-9 My; 50+ Je '67

Sailing schools in Britain. Sunset 139:39 Jl '67

Sailing schools; with list of schools in U.S. J. H. Winchester. il Travel 127:32-6 My '67

Small craft sailing program in San Diego. J. W. Lucas and M. Miner. il Parks & Rec 2:25+ Ag '67

We learned at school. D. Buchanan. il Yachting 123:83+ Ja '68

SAILING canoes. See Sailboats

SAILING ships. See Sailing vessels

SAILING vessels

Sailing oystermen of Chesapeake Bay. L. Marden. il Nat Geog Mag 132:798-819 D '67

Sailing vessel comes into its own. L. Gottschalk. il UNESCO Courier 20:16-17 My '67

See also
Schooners

SAILING yachts. See Yachts and yachting

SAILMAKER'S bench. See Benches

SAILORS. See Seamen

SAILPLANES. See Gliders (aeronautics)

SAILS

Building draft into a sail. J. Sutphen. il Yachting 121:96-8+ Ja '67

Chris Wilson on spinnakers for small catamarans; excerpt from The international book of catamarans and trimarans. C. Wilson. il Yachting 121:48-9+ Mr '67

Master touch; ed. by K. Krüger. P. Elvström. il Yachting 121:66-8+ Mr '67

Profiles; F. E. Hood. A. Bailey. New Yorker 43:34-6+ Ag 26 '67

Care

Care of sails. K. E. Watts. il Yachting 121:74 Ap '67

SAIN, Johnny

Coach me a little bit. il por Newsweek 69:88-92 Ap 10 '67

SAINSBURY, Jan Arthur

It's a bargain at $1.95. Writer 80:26+ N '67

SAINT, Nicholas

Deep in the heart of Texas; story. Esquire 67:86-9 Mr '67

ST AUGUSTINE, Fla.

New modern base restores the oldest street in America. S. G. Stepp. il Am City 82:93-4 D '67

ST CHARLES, Mo.

Historic houses, etc.

St Charles County historical society museum. J. L. Stoutenburgh. il Hobbies 71:116 F '67

ST CRISPIN bindery, incorporated

Tool-up at St Crispin. D. Dempsey. Sat R 50:27 D 23 '67

ST ELMO'S fire

Nature note. Sci N 91:359 Ap 15 '67

SAINT-JACQUES, Raymond

New bad guy of the movies. C. L. Sanders. il pors Ebony 22:171-2+ Je '67

SAINT Joan; drama. See Shaw, G. B.

ST JOHN, Jeffrey

New generation. See issues of Nation's business

Squall in the Red Sea. Sat R 50:22-3+ Jl 8 '67

ST JOHN, Judith

Second thoughts about Victorian children's fare. por Wilson Lib Bul 41:590-2 F '67

ST JOHN-STEVAS, Norman

Abortion, Catholics, and the law. Cath World 206:149-52 Ja '68

English experience. America 117:707-9 D 9 '67

ST JOHN ISLAND

Leisurely cruise around St John. J. C. Kozlick. il Motor B 120:38-9+ O '67

Virgin Islands National Park. V. B. Moore. il Nat Parks Mag 41:4-8 Ja '67

ST JOHN the Divine, Cathedral of. See New York (city)—St John the Divine, Cathedral of

ST JOHN'S bread. See Carob

ST JOHN'S seminary, Brighton, Mass. See Theological schools

ST JOHN'S university, Jamaica, N.Y.

Academic freedom; lessons from the crisis at St John's. L. J. Carter; discussion. Science 155:778-80 F 17 '67

Better late. . . Commonweal 86:4-5 Mr 24 '67

St John's case. Sch & Soc 95:276+ Sum '67

St John's congress postponed till May; library school boycott by UFCT continues. Library J 92:517+ F 1 '67

ST JOHNSBURY, Vt.

Sixteen years of sweeping at $1.26 per mile. D. T. Clark. il Am City 82:57 F '67

SAINT LAWRENCE ISLAND

Next door to Siberia. M. Miller. il Travel 128:31-7 Ag '67

ST LAWRENCE RIVER

St Lawrence River; key to Canada. H. LaFay. il Nat Geog Mag 131:622-67 My '67

ST LAWRENCE SEAWAY

St Lawrence Seaway tolls to remain at present levels. Dept State Bul 56:554 Ap 3 '67

Seaway stretch. C. H. Winn. il Travel 127:46-9 My '67

ST LOUIS

Banks

See also
Federal reserve bank of St Louis

Bridges

Where everything, almost, went wrong; interstate highway linking St Louis and East St Louis. il Bsns W p62+ Je 10 '67

Economic conditions

St Louis economic blues. W. S. Rukeyser. il Fortune 77:210-12 Ja '68

Education

Miss Leesy's magic; cultural enrichment program. W. D. Cook. il Am Ed 3:8-10 N '67

St Louis study assesses school librarian's role. Library J 92:3100+ S 15 '67

Hotels, restaurants, etc.

Dining in/out with Esquire; Andreino's. Esquire 68:296-8 D '67

Industries

To prevent a chain of super-Watts. bibliog f Harvard Bsns R 45:61-4 S '67

Missouri botanical garden

See Missouri botanical garden

Monuments, statues, etc.

Dream parabola; Jefferson national expansion memorial. il Life 62:45-6 Je 2 '67

Lighting the Gateway arch. il Am City 82:118 D '67

Music

See also
St Louis symphony orchestra

Negroes

St Louis economic blues. W. S. Rukeyser. il Fortune 77:210-12 Ja '68

Newspapers

Classic competitors; Post-dispatch and Globe-democrat. il Time 89:59-60 Je 9 '67

Sour notes in St Louis. Time 90:72 Ag 4 '67

Parks and playgrounds

New paving materials benefit St Louis parks. A. M. Johnson. il Parks & Rec 2:32-3 D '67

ST LOUIS Blues (hockey team) See Hockey teams

ST LOUIS Cardinals (baseball) See Baseball clubs

ST LOUIS Hawks (basketball team) See Basketball teams

ST LOUIS symphony orchestra

Honeymoon is over. T. B. Sherman. Hi Fi 17:MA24-5 My '67

ST MARKS in the Bouwerie. See New York (city)—Churches

ST MARY'S Dominican college, New Orleans

St Mary's Dominican; a sense of quiet energy; John XXIII library. il Library J 92:4355 D 1 '67

ST PATRICK'S cathedral. See New York (city)—St Patrick's cathedral

ST PAUL

Business at work in the Twin Cities. P. Herrera. il Fortune 76:123-4+ Ag '67

ST PAUL civic opera company

Report: St Paul; production of Don Giovanni. A. B. Cutts. Opera N 32:30-1 Ja 20 '68

Report: St Paul; production of Faust. A. B. Cutts. Opera N 32:28-9 D 23 '67

ST PAUL ROCKS

St Peter and St Paul Rocks; a high-temperature, mantle-derived intrusion. W. G. Melson and others. bibliog il Science 155:1532-5 Mr 24 '67

ST PAUL the apostle, Missionary order of. See
Paulist fathers
ST PAUL'S cathedral. See London—St Paul's
cathedral
ST PETER and St Paul Rocks. See St Paul
rocks
ST PETERSBURG, Fla.
Savings in activated-sludge systems. R.
Steytler. il Am City 82:113-15+ My '67

Lighting
Three years, 16,000 new lights. L. H. Andrews. il Am City 82:150 S '67

Newspapers
Men from SHRDLU; Times campaign to
erase mistakes. il Newsweek 69:66 Ap 10
'67
SAINT PIERRE and Miquelon (islands)
White Mist cruises to wreck-haunted St
Pierre and Miquelon. M. B. Grosvenor. il
Nat Geog Mag 132:378-419 S '67
ST ROSE, Sister
Puzzling over Buber; poem. Christian Cent
84:905 Jl 12 '67
ST VINCENT (island)
St Vincent: a troubled isle. E. B. Thompson.
il Ebony 22:84 O '67
St Vincent and Bequia. J. Egan. il Atlan
220:122-3+ D '67
See also
Bequia (island)
SAINTE GENEVIEVE, Mo.

Historic houses, etc.
History in houses, the Bolduc house. G. R.
Brooks. il Antiques 92:96-9 Jl '67
SAINTE-MARIE, Buffy
They talk about freedom; ed. by E. Miller.
por Seventeen 26:150-1+ Ap '67

about
Music to my ears; performance in Philhar-
monic Hall. I. Kolodin. Sat R 50:73 N 11
'67
SAINTS
Good companions; very human saints and
their soulmates. P. McGinley. Mlle 66:122-3+
D '67
Weeding out the saints; Vatican report. il
Newsweek 69:63 Je 5 '67
SAINTS (football club) See Football clubs
SAKAMOTO, Makoto
Flying ring master. por Newsweek 69:88+
Mr 13 '67
SAKELLARAKIS, John
Found: a gold ring. por Horizon 10:102-5 Wint
'68
SAKHALIN
Island, by A. Chekhov. Review
New Repub 157:26-8+ O 21 '67. C. Brown
Sat R 50:35-6 O 7 '67. M. Friedberg
SAKS Fifth Avenue. See New York (city)—
Stores
SALADS
Barbecue salads. il Bet Hom & Gard 45:89-90
Je '67
Best-dressed salads; with recipes. il McCalls
94:92-3+ Ag '67
Bird of paradise salad. il Ladies Home J
84:140 Mr '67
Blender cucumber salad. il Bet Hom & Gard
45:98 My '67
Bride makes chicken salad. il McCalls 94:62
My '67
California salads. il Ladies Home J 84:88-9+
Jl '67
Chicken salads that serve twenty-five. Good H
164:213 My '67
Cool and inviting jellied salads. B. M. Stover.
il Parents Mag 42:62-3+ Ag '67
Cool, cool salads. R. Holmberg. il Bet Hom &
Gard 45:70-1+ Ag '67
Enliven menus with lighthearted salads; with
recipes. G. Maddox. il Todays Health 45:
60-5 Ap '67
Everything's coming up salads. R. Hanna.
il Suc Farm 65:66-7 My '67
Four September salads; with recipes. il Sun-
set 139:66-7 S '67
Green salads. il Bet Hom & Gard 45:103-4
Mr '67
It's a supper salad, and it's Mexican; with
recipe. il Sunset 138:124 Je '67
Potato salad: three choices. Sunset 139:109
Ag '67
Salad classics. il Ebony 22:136+ Ap '67
Salads by the pool. V. T. Habeeb. il Am Home
70:104+ Je '67
Salads: super, hearty, & special; with recipes.
il Redbook 128:94-5+ F '67
Salads; with a foreign flavor; with recipes.
Good H 165:172 S '67

Sole aspic salads. il Sunset 138:156 Ap '67
Soup and salad supper cook book; with menus
and recipes. I. Brooks. il House & Gard 131:
179+ Mr '67
Taste of the Riviera; salade Niçoise. C. Clai-
borne. il N Y Times Mag p23 Jl 2 '67
Three-row garden salad. il Farm J 91:88 O
'67
Unusual make-ahead salads. S. Sarvis. il
Farm J 91:66-7 S '67
Wilted lettuce salad. il Bet Hom & Gard 45:95
Je '67
SALARIES
What's your job worth? M. Mayer. Bet Hom
& Gard 45:42 F '67
See also
Non-wage payments
also subhead Salaries under various sub-
jects. e.g. Government employees—Salaries
SALDERN, Axel von
European and American realists of the late
nineteenth century. Antiques 92:694-705 N
'67
SALDINO, Michael D.
Facts you should know about auto insurance;
interview. ed. by E. D. Fales, jr. Read
Digest 91:65-8 Jl '67
SALDIVAR, Vicente
Vicente bored in but Ernie merely bored. B.
Ottum. Sports Illus 27:66-8 O 23 '67
SALE, J. Kirk, and Apfelbaum, Ben
Report from teeny-boppersville. N Y Times
Mag p24-5+ My 28 '67
SALER, Steve. See Ferber, C. jt. auth.
SALES, Soupy
Sales tacks. H. Hewes. Sat R 50:51 F 11 '67
Transmogrification of Soupy Sales. S. Braun.
pors Esquire 68:104-7+ O '67
SALES, Art. See Art sales
SALES, Book. See Book sales
SALES forecasting. See Business forecasting
SALES management
Art of dividing sales territories. M. A. Brice.
il Duns R 89:47+ My '67
New sales management tool: ROAM; return
on assets managed. J. S. Schiff and M.
Schiff. il Harvard Bsns R 45:59-66 Jl '67
Sales supervision: suggestions for managers;
trade publishing houses. Coqui. Pub W 192:
42-4 S 18 '67
SALES policies
Credit risks & opportunities. R. M. Kaplan.
il Harvard Bsns R 45:83-8 Mr '67
See also
Exclusive agencies
Guaranty of goods
SALES promotion
Christmas spirit pours out early; Schenley
industries' road show. il Bsns W p32-3 N
4 '67
It's a bird! it's a plane! it's industrials! W.
Como. il Dance Mag 41:24-5 Je '67
Teaching the ladies helps pull in traffic; fur-
niture retailers give courses in homemaking.
il Bsns W p 124-7 Ja 13 '68
Treasure from the sea; commercial exploita-
tion of Sir F. Chichester. il Time 89:48 Je
9 '67
See also
Competitions
Coupons
Trading stamps

Anecdotes, facetiae, satire, etc.
Treatment, supermarket style. L. B. Smith.
Atlan 219:125-7 Ap '67
SALESMEN and salesmanship
Company with a heart; Baxter laboratories.
R. Levy. il Duns R 90:49 Ag '67
How to double your sales. P. F. Drucker. il
Nations Bsns 55:80-2+ Mr '67
See also
Advertising
Automobile dealers
Canvassing
Distributive education
Retail clerks international association
Sales management
Sales promotion
SALICYLANILIDE
Salicylanilides: a new group of active un-
couplers of oxidative phosphorylation. R.
L. Williamson and R. L. Metcalf. bibliog
il Science 158:1694-5 D 29 '67
SALII, Lazarus
Trust Territory of the Pacific Islands: state-
ment, June 8, 1967. Dept State Bul 57:376-8
S 18 '67
SALINE irrigation. See Irrigation
SALINE water. See Water, Saline
SALINE water conversion. See Sea water—
Desalting

SALISBURY, Charlotte Y.
Sikkim. Mlle 65:171-4 S '67
SALISBURY, Glenn Wade
Sperm banks debated.   B. J. Culliton. il
Sci N 92:208-9 Ag 26 '67
SALISBURY, Harrison E.
Illuminating the world. Sat R 50:29+ N 11
'67
Is there a way out of the Vietnam war?
excerpt from Behind the lines, Hanoi. por
Sat R 50:29-34+ Ap 8 '67
Kremlin walls won't tremble. Sat R 50:33-4+
O 7 '67
Visit with the enemy; excerpt from Orbit of
China. por Esquire 67:90-1+ My '67
War with China? New Repub 156:25-8 My
20 '67
We talk to; interview by Mademoiselle's guest
editors. por Mlle 65:324 Ag '67

about
Credibility and the Times; abandonment of
balanced reporting. H. K. Smith. Nat R
19:73-4 Ja 24 '67
Declining honor. Time 89:41-2 My 12 '67
Prize flap. il por Newsweek 69:89 My 15 '67
Public and private wars of Harrison E.
Salisbury.   G. Talese. Esquire 67:88-90+
My '67
Watcher along the border. M. Kalb. Sat R
50:51 My 6 '67
SALISBURY, John W. and Hunt, G. R.
Infrared images of tycho on dark moon. bib-
liog Science 155:1098-100 Mr 3 '67
SALISBURY, Ralph J.
Eugene, Oregon, U.S.A: my side yard and
something from an old travel book; poem.
Poetry 110:173 Je '67
SALISBURY, Robert Cecil, 1st earl of
Jacobean diplomatic service. M. Lee, jr. bib-
liog f Am Hist R 72:1264-82 Jl '67
SALISBURY, Conn.
Our far-flung correspondents; waters. C.
Rand. il New Yorker 43:152+ S 16 '67
SALIVARY glands
Submaxillary gland of mouse: properties of a
purified protein affecting muscle tissue in
vitro. D. G. Attardi and others. bibliog il
Science 156:1253-5 Je 2 '67
SALK, Jonas Edward
Probing the molecule for the key to disease.
il pors Bsns W p 122-7 Ag 12 '67
SALK institute for biological studies, San
Diego, Calif.
Probing the molecule for the key to disease.
il Bsns W p 122-7 Ag 12 '67
SALLAL, Abdullah
Desperation of a strongman. Time 90:28+ O
20 '67
SALLES, Elizinha Moreira. See Moreira Salles,
E.
SALM, Walter G.
Staying on the beam with tuning indicators.
Pop Mech 127:194-7 F '67
Stop the music with an automatic tape shut-
off. Pop Mech 128:193-5+ O '67
SALMO salar. See Salmon
SALMON, Robert
Master of the wharves. il Time 90:46-7 Jl
28 '67
SALMON, Stephen R.
Information science and automation. ALA
Bul 61:637-42 Je '67
(ed) Library automation. bibliog por ALA
Bul 61:635-75+ Je '67
—See McCune, L. C. jt. auth.
SALMON
Crisis on the Columbia: huge annual fish loss.
T. Trueblood. il Field & S 72:10-12+ Jl '67
Fish-watching at Taylor Creek; in Eldorado
national forest. il Sunset 139:46+ S '67
Glorious fish; Pacific salmon. il Sunset 139:
44-51 Jl '67
Melancholy fate of salmo salar. A. Netboy.
il Natur Hist 76:52-9 bibliog(p74) Je '67
Return of the salmon; coho returns to rivers
of Washington and Oregon. il Newsweek
70:101-2 S 25 '67
Where East meets West. A. J. McClane. il
Field & S 71:78-80+ Ap '67
Woe is salmon; Alaska's harvest worst since
1899. Time 90:98+ O 13 '67
See also
Cookery—Fish
SALMON, Canned. See Canned food
SALMON fishing
Before you go salmon fishing. Sunset 139:27
Jl '67
Big three of cold-water sport fishing: trout,
char, salmon.   A. J. McClane. il Field & S
72:46+ My '67
Boom and a blunder on Lake Michigan; coho
salmon. H. Babbitt. il Sports Illus 27:67-
8+ O 9 '67

Coho craze in Michigan. J. Chiappetta. il
Field & S 72:42-3+ Ja '68
Fish is caught; Kalum River, N.S; ed. by
J. Cameron. A Reed il Outdoor Life 139:
30-1 Je '67
Glorious fish; Pacific salmon. il Sunset 139:
44-51 Jl '67
I'll take seconds; Atlantic-salmon fishing in
George River. B. Warner. il Outdoor Life
140:60-1+ S '67
Kokanee keep things jumping. W. Curtis.
il Outdoor Life 139:25-6+ Mr '67
Most in fishing ever; interview. G. Anderegg.
il Field & S 71:42-5+ F '67
New fish for the Northeast. A. Davenport.
il Field & S 71:38-9+ Ap '67
Salmon for everyone. W. W. Hunter. il
Field & S 71:58-9+ Mr '67
Skipper called me honey. H. J. Samuels. il
Outdoor Life 139:68-9+ My '67
We float the Yukon and strike it rich. J. S.
Flannery. il Outdoor Life 140:48-52+ Jl '67
SALMONELLA. See Bacteria, Pathogenic
SALMONELLOSIS
What's behind that salmonella scare. R.
Wilmore. Farm J 91:27+ Ja '67
SALOMON, Erich
Erich Salomon: candid historian.   M. R.
Weiss. il Sat R 50:56-7 S 9 '67
Who was Erich Salomon? J. Deschin. por Pop
Phot 61:36+ N '67
SALOMON, L. B.
Stop the dirty-word drain; poem. Atlan 220:
125 O '67
SALOMON brothers and Hutzler (firm)
Homer: bard of the bond market. il Bsns W
p 116-18+ S 23 '67
SALOONS. See Bars and barrooms
SALOYA VALLEY
Saloya. M. B. Pomeroy. il Américas 19:28-33
O '67
SALT
Amateur scientist; on growing crystals of
salt. J. Bailey. il Sci Am 218:131-2 Ja '68
Digital model of evaporite sedimentation. L.
I. Briggs and H. N. Pollack. il Science 155:
453-6 Ja 27 '67
Siliceous urinary calculi in calves: prevention
by addition of sodium chloride to the diet.
C. B. Bailey. bibliog il Science 155:696-7
F 10 '67
Therapeutic uses
Colombian villagers try fluoridated salt. il
Todays Health 45:17 O '67
SALT and pepper shakers
Unique salt and pepper shaker. T. H. Marsh.
il Hobbies 72:84 My '67
SALT LAKE. See Great Salt Lake
SALT LAKE CITY
Education
East high school's drama workshop. J. A.
Christensen. il Sr Schol 90:sup 13 Mr 17 '67
Newspapers
See also
Deseret news
SALT marshes
Vanishing tidelands. P. Redford. Atlan 219:
75-8+ Je '67; Same abr. il Read Digest
91:134-7 S '67
SALT water aquariums. See Aquariums
SALT water fishing
Fishing in the Banana Republics. A. J. Mc-
Clane. il Field & S 72:86-8+ D '67
How to hunt fish by plane; Gulf of Mexico.
G. Gresham. il Field & S 72:42-3+ Je '67
Lure of Libertad. R. B. Whitaker. il Field & S
72:40-1+ Je '67
Revolution in salt water fishing. G. X. Sand.
il Outdoor Life 139:68-71+ F '67
Salt water. G. Heinold. See issues of Outdoor
life
Utopia isle. C. Elliott. il Outdoor Life 140:
44-7+ O '67
With the sport fishermen. N. Benedict. See
issues of Yachting
See also
Barracuda fishing
Bass fishing
Marlin fishing
Swordfish fishing
Tuna fishing

Anecdotes, facetiae, satire, etc.
Voyage of the Sea Serpent. J. Shepherd. il
Field & S 72:58-9+ My '67
SALT water irrigation. See Irrigation
SALTER, George
Obituary
Pub W 192:55 N 13 '67

SALTER, Stefan
Designer's corner. See first issue of each month of Publisher's weekly
SALTMAN, Paul
Science jungle. Harper 234:102-4 F '67
SALTON SEA
Should we save the Salton? B. Behme. il Field & S 72:8-10+ Ag '67
SALTONSTALL, Richard, jr
Life music review. Life 62:15 Je 9 '67
SALTS, Marine. See Sea water
SALTS, Soluble
Digital model of evaporite sedimentation. L. I. Briggs and H. N. Pollack. il Science 155: 453-6 Ja 27 '67
SALVA, Sylvester
Resistor-selection nomogram. Electr World 77:29 Ap '67
SALVAGE
Man's obsession and its rewards. il Life 62: 102 Mr 10 '67
See also
Submarine disasters
SALVAGE (ships)
Magnetometers locate loaded liberty ship. il Sci N 92:319 S 30 '67
Tantalizing treasure of the Andrea Doria. F. Dickenson. il Read Digest 91:150-3 N '67
World's wettest drydock; salvaging of Sweden's great 17th century warship Wasa. R. P. Crossley. il Pop Mech 127:152-5+ My '67
See also
Merritt-Chapman and Scott corporation
SALVAGE (waste)
See also
Refuse, Utilization of
Scrap metal
SALVAGE archeology. See Archeology
SALVATION
City of salvation; excerpt from Free in obedience. W. Stringfellow. Christian Cent 84:331 Mr 15 '67
Faithful one. V. P. McCorry. America 116: 293-4 F 25 '67
First and last truth. V. P. McCorry. America 116:228 F 11 '67
God of the Bible. B. Vawter. Commonweal 85:504-7 F 10 '67
Mystery of salvation. V. P. McCorry. America 116:266 F 18 '67
Redemption of Malcolm X. R. A. Schroth. Cath World 205:346-52 S '67
Salvation in history, by O. Cullmann. Review Christian Cent 84:1323-4 O 18 '67. R. A. Harrisville
Single offering; excerpt from Key words for Lent. G. W. Barrett. Christian Cent 84:299 Mr 8 '67
Theology of hope; theories of German theologians. il Newsweek 70:92+ D 11 '67
SALVATO, Joseph
Single pool plays a dual role. Am City 82:102-3 Ap '67
SALVES. See Ointments
SALVIAS
Some good plants. R. C. Hands. Horticulture 45:56+ F '67
SALZBURG Easter festival. See Music festivals —Austria
SALZBURG festival
Salzburg. D. Stevens. Opera N 32:27-8 O 14 '67
Where Karajan is king. J. Higgins. il Hi Fi 17:MA26-7+ N '67
SALZBURG seminar in American studies
Can we communicate with Europe? P. Kimball. Sat R 50:54-5 Jl 8 '67
SALZGITTER AG. See Steel industry and trade —Germany (Federal Republic)
SALZMAN, Eric
In the cards. Opera N 32:26-7 D 16 '67
Many lives of Lukas Foss. Sat R 50:73-4+ F 25 '67
Prophet in exile. Opera N 32:8-11 Ja 20 '68
(ed) See Silja, A. Grand old lady
(ed) See Tureck, R. And we quote
SALZMANN, Laurence
Discovery; interview, ed. by P. Caulfield. il Mod Phot 31:64-5+ Mr '67
SAM, Nguyen-van-. See Nguyen-van-Sam
SAM Griffith memorial race. See Motor boat racing
SAMAN. See Rain trees
SAMELSON, Harold. See Lempicki, A. jt. auth.
SAMOA, AMERICAN. See American Samoa
SAMOANS
Are the natives friendly? M. Mead. Redbook 128:31+ Mr '67
SAMPERI, Frank
Two poems: On a bridge; Lie down. Poetry 109:380-1 Mr '67

SAMPLERS
Embroider a calendar and use it forever. M. Garrity. il Bet Hom & Gard 45:86 F '67
SAMPLES, Robert E.
Kari's handicap, the impediment of creativity. Sat R 50:56-7+ Jl 15 '67
SAMPLING
See also subhead Analysis under various subjects, e.g. Air—Analysis
SAMPLING (statistical methods)
Machete in the paper jungle; statistical sampling in the Office of education. A. M. Mood. il Am Ed 3:5 O '67
Surveys of population samples for estimating crime incidence. A. D. Biderman. bibliog f il Ann Am Acad 374:16-33 N '67
SAMPSON, Ronald
Russell in his prime. Nation 204:566-8 My 1 '67
SAMPSON, William B. and others
Advances in superconducting magnets; with biographical sketches. Sci Am 216:19, 114-23 bibliog(p 152) Mr '67
SAMSTAG, Nicholas
Classical curses. Sat R 50:30 D 23 '67
Seeing all the evil. Sat R 50:43-4 S 16 '67
Slick-paper pages of the past. Sat R 50:50+ N 25 '67
Woe of wealth. Sat R 50:31-2 Je 24 '67
SAMUEL, Maurice
If the Arabs had won. Look 31:80-2 Jl 25 '67
SAMUELS, Alan
I quit! from solo to chorus. Nation 205:284-5 S 25 '67
SAMUELS, Charles Thomas
Puzzling Miss Stead. New Repub 157:30-1 S 9 '67
Usable critic. Nation 204:764-5 Je 12 '67
SAMUELS, Gertrude
Curbs for the crooked path. Sat R 50:39+ Mr 11 '67
Do women really want the freedom they've won? Redbook 129:54-5+ My '67
Methadone, fighting fire with fire. N Y Times Mag p44-5+ O 15 '67
Statistic named Mary. N Y Times Mag p24-5+ Mr 5 '67
There are 300 Negroes at the University of Alabama. N Y Times Mag p32-3+ My 14 '67
SAMUELS, H. J.
Oriental pig tale. Outdoor Life 139:68-71+ Mr '67
Skipper called me honey. por Outdoor Life 139:68-9+ My '67
Special-extra moose hunt. por Outdoor Life 140:32-5+ N '67
SAMUELS, Leonard
Projectors that bridge the 8-mm gap. Pop Mech 127:154-7 Mr '67
SAMUELSON, Paul Anthony
[Column on economic questions] See issues of Newsweek
Money. Vogue 151:58 Ja 1 '68

about

Evolution of an economist. G. Routh. Mo Labor R 90:18-22 F '67
SAN ANDREAS fault. See Faults (geology)
SAN ANDRÉS Y PROVIDENCIA
San Andrés. il Holiday 42:98-9 N '67
SAN ANTONIO, Tex.
Cleansville; cleanest town in the U.S. Time 89:58 Mr 3 '67
Water utility will offer air conditioning and steam heating. L. F. Campos. il Am City 82:75-7 D '67

Description

Follow the old road to San Antonio. R. Dunlop. il Todays Health 45:42-9+ Mr '67
San Antonio, Texas. il Bet Hom & Gard 45: 14 Ag '67

HemisFair, 1968

Traveling with Mlle; HemisFair-'68. A. Pryce-Jones. il Mlle 66:113-14 Ja '68
World fair in 1968 is planned in Texas. il Arch Rec 141:50-1 Mr '67

Historic houses, etc.

San Antonio's Spanish treasure: Spanish governor's palace. K. Elliott. il Todays Health 45:28-31 S '67

Music

San Antonio. J. Ardoin. Opera N 31:29 My 13 '67
SANASARDO, Paul
Paul Sanasardo and company; 92nd street Y. J. Maskey. Dance Mag 41:34+ F; 79 Ap '67
Paul Sanasardo dance company, 92nd street Y. J. Maskey. Dance Mag 41:80 My '67
Paul Sanasardo dance company, 92nd street Y. M. Marks. Dance Mag 41:78 Mr '67

SAN BERNARDINO, Calif.

Newspapers

Meaning of monopoly. il Newsweek 69:67 Je 12 '67

SAN CARLO opera company
Fortunes of Gallo. F. Robinson. il Sat R 51: 101+ Ja 13 '68

SAN CARLOS, Calif.
Working farm within the city. M. B. Lovell. il Parks & Rec 2:40-1 Ja '67

SANCHEZ-VILELLA, Roberto
El Peyton Place. il por Time 89:23 Mr 31 '67

SANCTIONS (international law)
Do sanctions work? J. Burnham. Nat R 19: 1254 N 14 '67
How long can Rhodesia hold out? il Bsns W p46+ Jl 22 '67
Sanctions busters; nations trading with Rhodesia. Time 90:23-4 S 8 '67
Security council votes mandatory sanctions against Southern Rhodesia; statement, December 12; with text of resolution adopted, December 16, 1966. A. J. Goldberg. Dept State Bul 56:73-8 Ja 9 '67
This month's feature; question of U.S. Rhodesian policy. Cong Digest 46:67-71+ Mr '67

SANCTIONS, Professional
Professional sanctions: what, why, when, where, and how. J. H. Kleinmann. NEA J 57:42-4 Ja '68
Teacher opinion poll; strikes and sanctions. il NEA J 56:38-9 O '67

SANCTUARIES, Bird. See Bird sanctuaries

SANCTUARIES, Wildlife. See Wildlife sanctuaries

SANCTUARY (law) See Asylum, Right of

SAND, George X.
Cook while you drive. Pop Mech 127:122-3 Je '67
Revolution in salt water fishing. Outdoor Life 139:68-71+ F '67

SAND, Ole
DESP: design for educational change in the 70's; excerpts from address, April 1967. Sr Schol 90:sup2 My 5 '67
—See McClure, R. M. jt. auth.

SAND
See also
Bituminous sand
Quicksand

SAND-bottom community. See Ocean bottom

SAND buggies. See Motor vehicles

SAND casting. See Casting (sculpture)

SAND dune hillbillies; drama. See Dias, E. J.

SAND dunes
Nature note. il Sci N 91:420 My 6 '67
This sandy mountain sings; Nevada. il Sunset 138:39 F '67

SAND filtration. See Sewage disposal—Filtration

SAND sailboats. See Sand yachts

SAND sculpture
Art education accessible to all: creative activity on the seashore; project among vacationing youngsters in Egypt. L. Zaky. bibliog il Sch Arts 66:19-23 My '67

SAND trails. See Animal tracks and trails

SAND wedge (golf club) See Golf clubs (sticks)

SAND yachts
Dry-land fleet sails the Sahara. J. Du Boucher. il Nat Geog Mag 132:696-725 N '67

SANDBURG, Carl
Finish; poem. Life 63:52 Ag 4 '67
People, yes; poem; excerpt. PTA Mag 62:8 S '67
about
American troubadour. il por Time 90:17 Jl 28 '67
Carl Sandburg: 1878-1967; with excerpts from poems. H. Mitgang. por Sat R 50:18-19 Ag 12 '67
Poet of the people. por Newsweek 70:49 Jl 31 '67
Years of a poet who sang of America; with excerpts from his writings. il pors Life 63: 44D-51 Ag 4 '67

SANDBURG, Helga
When my father decided not to die after all; poem. Ladies Home J 84:152 O '67
about
Helga Sandburg book banned in Memphis. Library J 92:4210 N 15 '67

SANDERS, Charles L.
Black power at the polls. Ebony 23:23-6+ Ja '68
Comedown for a king. Ebony 22:49-50+ My '67

New bad guy of the movies. Ebony 22:171-2+ Je '67
Odyssey of Charles Wayo. Ebony 22:27-30+ F '67
(ed) See Herrin, M. R. My conflict with East German reds

SANDERS, Doug
Doug tames a pink pussycat. M. Mulvoy. il Sports Illus 26:22-3 Mr 13 '67
King of the Kelloggs. Time 89:44 Mr 17 '67

SANDERS, Flora G. See Austin, E. D. jt. auth.

SANDERS, Harland
Cooking up profits, southern style. il por Bsns W p 176+ Je 24 '67

SANDERS, J. A.
Urbis and orbis: Jerusalem today. Christian Cent 84:967-70 Jl 26 '67

SANDERS, Marion K.
Durable skeptic. Harper 234:115-16 My '67
Uncharted terrain. Harper 235:42 Jl '67

SANDERS, Sol W.
Delta revisited: still "Charlie country". U S News 62:38-40 Ap 17 '67

SANDERS, Stanley
I'll never escape the ghetto. pors Ebony 22: 30-2+ Ag '67

SANDERS, Thomas G.
Brazil's Catholic left. America 117:598-601 N 18 '67

SANDHILL cranes. See Cranes (birds)

SANDIA corporation
Minimum of friction; rolamite bearing. il Bsns W p52 O 21 '67
Rolamite seen as important mechanical design technique. il Aero Tech 21:48-9 O 23 '67

SAN DIEGO, Calif.
Sun and sea build a new San Diego. il Bsns W p 126-7+ My 20 '67

Description
San Diego. P. Deutsch and R. Deutsch. il Redbook 129:64-5+ My '67

Music
San Diego; premiere performance of Henze's Young lord, in English. S. A. Desick. il Opera N 31:31 Mr 25 '67
U.S. premiere: Henze's Young lord. D. Dierks. il Hi Fi 17:MA26-7+ My '67
See also
San Diego opera company

Parks and playgrounds
Need index in park planning. J. D. Parks. il Parks & Rec 2:28+ Mr '67

Sanitary affairs
Burns refuse without a flame. D. A. Hoffman. il Am City 82:102-4 F '67

Theater
La Jolla's hourglass stage. H. Hewes. il Sat R 50:38-9 S 23 '67

SAN DIEGO, Calif. zoological garden
Reporter at large. E. Hahn. New Yorker 43:170+ O 14 '67
San Diego zoo wins notable animal birth awards. il Parks & Rec 2:36+ Ja '67

SAN DIEGO COUNTY, Calif.
How to get the most out of local educational resources. J. M. Huffman. il Sr Schol 90: sup 16 F 3 '67

SAN DIEGO national Shakespeare festival. See Shakespeare festivals

SAN DIEGO opera company
Report: San Diego; production of Salome. S. A. Desick. il Opera N 32:28 D 23 '67

SANDIFER, Dick
You've got to be optimistic in this business. S. Brown. il por Sat Eve Post 240:68-71 D 30 '67

SANDING machines
Look at what you can do with an orbital sander. J. Burroughs. il Pop Mech 128:166-9 D '67

SANDINO, Augusto César
Mr Coolidge's jungle war. R. O'Connor. il por Am Heritage 19:36-9+ D '67
Sandino affair, by N. Macaulay. Review
Bul Atomic Sci 23:56-7 Je '67. W. F. Barber
Newsweek por 69:94-5 Mr 6 '67. P. D. Zimmerman

SANDLER, Carl L. See Inglis, D. R. jt. auth.

SANDS, Bill
Keeping out of debt to society. J. Haas. Sat R 50:28 Jl 8 '67

SANDS, Diana
Passion of Diana Sands. A. Wolff. il pors Look 32:70-3 Ja 9 '68

SANDSON, John
Human synovial fluid: detection of a new component. bibliog Science 155:839-41 F 17 '67

SANDWICH construction
Boeing to cut weight of 747 with use of paper honeycomb. Aviation W 87:43 Jl 10 '67

SANDWICHES
Everyone's delight: the sandwich; with recipes. G. Maddox. il Todays Health 45:52-5 Ag '67
Favorites with the young set. il Ebony 22:152+ Ag '67
Hot sandwiches; with recipes. il Bet Hom & Gard 45:99-100 S '67
Redbook's complete guide to fabulous sandwiches; with recipes. il Redbook 129:92+ Je '67
Summer sandwiches. R. Holmberg. il Bet Hom & Gard 45:72-3+ Ag '67
Three delicious egg sandwiches; recipes. il Sunset 139:115 Jl '67
Time out for lunch. H. G. Tapply. il Field & S 72:72 O '67

SANDY, Stephen
After the Grand Union; poem. Atlan 219:67 F '67
Butterfly and snake; poem. Reporter 36:39 Je 29 '67
Home from the range; Dissolve; poems. Poetry 109:317-20 F '67
Windows; poem. Mlle 66:46 Ja '68

SANE (organization) See National committee for a sane nuclear policy

SANEHOLTZ, Betty J.
Consumer service bureau report. Parents Mag 43:22+ Ja '68

SANFORD, David
Carcinogenic mines. New Repub 156:5-6 Je 3 '67
Countdown on Noyd. New Repub 157:14-15 O 21 '67
Drug on the market. New Repub 157:13-15 Jl 22 '67
Hippie business. New Repub 156:7-8 Je 10 '67
Political party games. New Repub 157:7-8 D 16 '67
Pot bust at Cornell. New Repub 156:17-20 Ap 15 '67
Risks of marijuana. New Repub 156:11-12 Ap 22 '67
Seedier media. New Repub 157:7-8 D 2 '67
Who's against pollution? New Repub 156:8-9 Mr 25 '67
—See Ridgeway, J. jt. auth.

SANFORD, Michael R.
Foolproof control of pigeons and starlings. por Am City 82:116-17 Mr '67

SANFORD, Patrick, pseud.
Dear editor; letter. America 116:870-3; 117:179-82 Je 24, Ag 19 '67

SANFORD, Terry
Are the states obsolete? interview. por U S News 63:82-4+ N 27 '67

SAN FRANCISCO

Architecture
Early consultation works for unity of arts. il Arch Rec 141:180-1 Je '67
Hartford plaza and Old St Mary's rectory. il Arch Rec 141:131-8 My '67
Rockefeller Center West; office-hotel-and-cultural complex. il Time 89:83 F 24 '67
Shape-up on the waterfront. il Time 90:36-7 D 29 '67
Store-office-apartment on a tight urban site: Fox plaza. il Arch Rec 141:175-7 Je '67

Art
Way-out West: interviews with four San Francisco artists. J. Raffaele and E. Baker. il Art N 66:38-41+ Sum '67

Banks
Dean's new desk; Wells Fargo bank. Time 90:99 O 27 '67

Chinatown
Behind the scenes in San Francisco's Chinatown. il Sunset 139:28-9 Jl '67
Chinaman's chance. il Time 90:18 S 8 '67

Churches
Rector, a church and the hippies; All Saints Episcopal church in Haight-Ashbury district. L. Kinsolving. Christian Cent 84:667-8 My 17 '67

City planning
San Francisco redevelopment blues; the downtown section, Yerba Buena. H. Brill. Commonweal 86:383-4 Je 23 '67

Description
Changing north face of San Francisco. il Sunset 139:64-79 N '67
Off-hours in convention city. F. Howard. il Wilson Lib Bul 41:1050-4 Je '67

San Francisco. H. Gilliam. il Wilson Lib Bul 41:1046-9 Je '67
San Francisco and a land of contrast. il Bet Hom & Gard 45:152-3 Ap '67
San Francisco sampler. R. V. Rafael. il ALA Bul 61:729-38 Je '67
Summer days in psychedelphia; touring the Haight-Ashbury district. H. Sutton. il Sat R 50:36+ Ag 19 '67
Travel notes. R. Joseph. Esquire 67:48+ Je '67
Where it's at. M. P. Doss. il Library J 92:2361-4 Je 15 '67

Education
See also
San Francisco state college

Historic houses, etc.
Oldest house in San Francisco adopts the 20th century. F. Heard. il House B 109:142-5 Je '67

Hospitals
Drugs, uses and abuses: young doctor's crusade; Alcohol and drug abuse screening unit at San Francisco general hospital. J. Luce. il Look 31:24-7 Ag 8 '67

Hotels, restaurants, etc.
San Francisco a la carte. R. H. Dillon. il Library J 92:2353-60 Je 15 '67
San Francisco for nobs and no-nobs. R. Joseph. il Esquire 67:116-23 Je '67
San Francisco for visitors. D. Messinesi. Vogue 150:78 Ag 15 '67
San Francisco: gourmet dining on a budget. K. Scannell and others. il ALA Bul 61:740-6 Je '67
Travel notes. R. Joseph. Esquire 67:48+ Je '67

Housing
Housing over highways; proposed plans. il Arch Forum 126:96-9 Ja '67

Industries
Bookmaking around the Bay. R. D. Harlan. il Library J 92:2369-71 Je 15 '67

Intellectual life
Renaissance by the Bay. K. Rexroth. Sat R 50:35-6 S 23 '67

Libraries
New library buildings in the San Francisco Bay area. C. Coolidge and N. Coolidge. ALA Bul 61:733-9 Je '67

Moral conditions
Flowering of the hippies; Haight-Ashbury scene. M. Harris. il Atlan 220:63-72 S '67
Hashbury is the capital of the hippies. H. S. Thompson. il N Y Times Mag p28-9+ My 14 '67
Splendid desire for nothing; concerning hippies in the Haight-Ashbury district. America 116:746-7 My 20 '67

Music
First U.S. Makropulos case. K. D. Wallace. il Hi Fi 17:MA20-MA21 F '67
Inertia and enterprise in San Francisco. A. Rich. il Sat R 50:42-3 S 23 '67
Open up, tune in, turn on; San Francisco sound from the Jefferson Airplane. il Time 89:53 Je 23 '67
San Francisco; Monteverdi commemorative program. W. Aguiar, jr. Opera N 31:27 Ap 15 '67
See also
San Francisco opera company

Negroes
San Francisco story: a dancer rocks the slums; G. Unti founder of Performing arts workshop. G. B. Leonard. il Look 31:94-6 F 7 '67

Newspapers
See also
San Francisco chronicle

Parks and playgrounds
On Golden Gate's redwood trail. il Sunset 138:260+ Ap '67

Police
Our war was with the police department. E. Carruth. il Fortune 77:195-7 Ja '68

Politics and government
Bathos by the Bay; candidates for mayor. il Time 90:20 N 3 '67
Flower of the West? new mayor. il Newsweek 71:24 Ja 22 '68

Rapid transit
BART bogs down. il Newsweek 70:94 N 13 '67

SAN FRANCISCO—*Continued*

Religious institutions and affairs

Bridge to the non-church; Glide foundation. il Time 90:86+ O 20 '67

Social conditions

Love on Haight; drug addicts of the Haight-Ashbury district. il Time 89:27 Mr 17 '67

Social life and customs

San Francisco for nobs and no-nobs. R. Joseph. il Esquire 67:116-23 Je '67

Strange new love land of the hippies. L. Wainwright. Life 62:15-16 Mr 31 '67

Stores

In San Francisco's North Beach, unusual gifts each $10 or less. il Sunset 139:28-30 D '67

Theater

San Francisco Mime. R. Hatch. Nation 205: 637 D 11 '67

San Quentin on stage; Actor's workshop production of R. Cluchey's The cage. D. Zack. New Repub 158:34+ Ja 13 '68

Theatre; mime troupe's productions of Carlo Goldoni's L'Amant militaire and Lope de Rueda's Olive pits. R. F. Sayre. Nation 205: 189-90 S 4 '67

See also

American conservatory theatre

SAN FRANCISCO ballet

Nutcracker has a birthday. il Dance Mag 41: 38-41 D '67

SAN FRANCISCO BAY

Song of San Francisco Bay. M. Reynolds. il Natur Hist 77:6-8+ bibliog(p76) Ja '68

SAN FRANCISCO BAY REGION

Lake that looked impossible; Cull Canyon regional recreation area. W. P. Mott, jr. il Parks & Rec 2:14-15+ F '67

San Francisco Bay area 1966 nurses' negotiations. M. D. Kossoris. Mo Labor R 90:8-12 Je '67

SAN FRANCISCO chronicle

New winds in the South, new splash in the North. W. L. Rivers. il Sat R 50:75-6+ S 23 '67

SAN FRANCISCO 49ers (football club) See Football clubs

SAN FRANCISCO mime troupe. See San Francisco—Theater

SAN FRANCISCO mining exchange. See Exchanges

SAN FRANCISCO mint. See United States—Mint

SAN FRANCISCO opera company

Report: San Francisco; new productions. A. Boucher. il Opera N 32:22-3 N 25 '67

Report: San Francisco; productions at the War memorial. A. Boucher. Opera N 32:29 D 23 '67

Report: San Francisco; productions of Gunther Schuller's The visitation and Gounod's Faust. A. Boucher. il Opera N 32:28 D 16 '67

Revivals reign in the Bay area. A. Frankenstein. il Hi Fi 17:MA22-3+ D '67

San Francisco (cont) A. Boucher. il Opera N 32:19-20 S 9; 23 O 14 '67

San Francisco sound; interview, ed. by F. Merkling. K. H. Adler. il Opera N 32:18-19 S 23 '67

Trojans at War memorial. K. D. Wallace. il Hi Fi 17:MA22-3 Ja '67

Visitation, home produced. A. Frankenstein. il Hi Fi 18:MA18-19 Ja '68

SAN FRANCISCO public library

LSCA and the cities; letter to the editor. W. R. Holman. Library J 92:1391 Ap 1 '67

Public library phoenix. D. E. Belch. il Library J 92:2365-8 Je 15 '67

SAN FRANCISCO state college

Agony at State. il Newsweek 71:59 Ja 22 '68

Chaos on the campus; student suspension. New Repub 158:14-15 Ja 6 '68

Guerrillas on campus; move from protest to resistance. il Newsweek 70:68+ D 18 '67

How to wreck a campus. D. Swanston. il Nation 206:38-41 Ja 8 '68

Preparation for Dow day. J. L. Shover. Nation 205:648-51 D 18 '67

Zen basketball, etc. at San Francisco state. H. Wilner. Esquire 68:98+ S '67

Anecdotes, facetiae, satire, etc.

For sale: one college. E. Solomon. Atlan 219: 111-12 My '67

SAN FRANCISCO Warriors (basketball team) See Basketball teams

SANGER, Marjorie D.

Wonderful world of water play. PTA Mag 61:20-1 Je '67

SANGER, Marjory Bartlett

Ardea's world; excerpts from World of the great white heron: a saga of the Florida Keys. Audubon 69:54-65 Ja '67

SANGER, Richard H.

Is insurrection brewing in U.S? interview. por U S News 63:32-7 D 25 '67

SANGSTER, Donald Burns

His own man. por Time 89:38 Mr 3 '67

One sort of moderation. por Newsweek 69: 50 Mr 6 '67

SANITARY affairs. See subhead Sanitary affairs under names of countries, states, cities, e.g. Stamford, Conn.—Sanitary affairs

SANITATION

See also

Restaurants—Sanitation

SANITATION, Household

See also

Drainage, House

Plumbing

SANITATION equipment. See Municipal equipment

SAN JORGE RIVER

Pre-Columbian ridged fields; agricultural earthworks of South America. J. J. Parsons and W. M. Denevan. il Sci 217:92-100 Jl '67

SAN JOSE, Calif.

Finance

Streamlined purchasing. J. M. Marzluft and K. South. il Am City 82:119-20+ My '67

Water supply

Computerized water system. N. J. Kendall. il Am City 82:99-100 S '67

SAN JOSE state college. See California. State college, San Jose

SAN JUAN, Puerto Rico

Description

San Juan, Puerto Rico. il Bet Hom & Gard 45:13-14 Ag '67

SAN MARINO

Little land of liberty. D. H. Shor. il Nat Geog Mag 132:232-51 Ag '67

SAN MATEO, Calif.

Air rights help to solve a parking problem. P. N. Bay. il Am City 82:84-5 N '67

Flood control brings beauty. R. G. Bezzant. il Am City 82:73 Jl '67

SAN MATEO college, Calif.

College? man, you must be kidding! College readiness program. E. Gattmann and others. NEA J 56:8-10 S '67

SAN MATEO COUNTY, Calif

Man nobody knows; congressional candidates. New Repub 157:11-12 O 21 '67

SANNES, Sanne

Honestly erotic. J. Deschin. por Pop Phot 60:22+ F '67

SAN QUENTIN prison. See Prisons—California

SAN RAFAEL primitive area (proposed) See Wilderness areas—California

SAN RAFAEL wilderness area (proposed) See Wilderness areas—California

SAN SALVADOR ISLAND

October 12, 1492; with editorial comment. H. Martínez-Montero. il Américas 19:inside cover, 1-4 O '67

SANSCHAGRIN, Grover

Man from Moran. C. Peet. il pors Pop Mech 128:136-9+ N '67

SANSKRIT poetry

See also

Ramayana

SANSOM, William

October song; story. McCalls 94:72-3 S '67

SANSON institute of heraldry

Name of the game is names. il Bsns W p 114-15 Je 10 '67

SANTA ANA winds. See Winds

SANTA and the efficiency expert; drama. See Watts, F. B.

SANTA BARBARA, Calif.

Banning the boom. il Time 90:67 O 6 '67

Description

Santa Barbara, California. il Bet Hom & Gard 45:10+ Ag '67

Parks and playgrounds

Santa Barbara's miracle; dump site and hobo village transformed. A. R. Locker. il Parks & Rec 2:42+ N '67

Police

Instant replay aids police work; video-tape recording system. il Am City 82:50 O '67

Rapid transit

City-county transit district. W. W. Wills. il Am City 82:101+ Ap '67

SANTA BARBARA COUNTY, Calif.
City-county transit district. W. W. Wills.
il Am City 82:101+ Ap '67
SANTA BARBARA ISLANDS, Calif.
Following the Santa Monicas as they march
out to sea. il Sunset 138:78-85 Ap '67
SANTA CATALINA ISLAND
Cruising to the Garden of the Hesperides.
R. Kelton. il Motor B 119:28-9+ My '67
SANTA CLAUS
In my opinion: Santa Claus should retire.
K. Rose. Seventeen 26:170 D '67
SANTA CRUZ, Calif.
View from Santa Cruz. J. D. Houston. il
Holiday 41:18+ My '67
SANTAELLA, William. See Benko, G. jt. auth.
SANTA FE, N.Mex.

Hotels, restaurants, etc.
Alexander Girard invites you to dine at the
Compound. il Arch Forum 126:60-3 Je '67
SANTA FE opera association
Phoenix of Santa Fe. Time 90:64 Ag 4 '67
Santa Fe; American premieres of Boulevard
solitude and Cardillac. G. Martin. il
Opera N 32:20-1 S 9 '67
Show goes on: Cardillac & Boulevard soli-
tude. P. J. Smith. il Hi Fi 17:MA20-1 O '67
World of dance; production of Boulevard soli-
tude. W. Terry. il Sat R 50:38 Ag 26 '67
SANTA FE opera house fire. See Opera houses
—Fires and fire protection
SANTA FE railway. See Atchison, Topeka and
Santa Fe railway
**SANTA ROSA-Sonoma County free public li-
brary, Santa Rosa, Calif.**
Santa Rosa: a library for today. D. Sabsay.
il Library J 92:4367-8 D 1 '67
SANTALO, Lois
Year we went back to school. por Redbook
128:10+ F '67
SANTAMARIA, Louis E. S.
Chemway's way. R. Levy. il por Duns R 88:
45+ D '66
SANTANA, Manuel
Reign in Spain of King Manolo. F. Deford.
il pors Sports Illus 27:26-9 Jl 3 '67
SANTAYANA, George
Forty-year visit. S. Kauffmann. New Repub
157:28+ Ag 5 '67
SANTEE, Calif.
Town that launders water. L. A. Stevens.
il Read Digest 90:117-21 Ap '67
SANTO DOMINGO (Republic) See Dominican
Republic
SANTORO, Joel T.
Saddle mount; a deep-water canoe entry.
Parks & Rec 2:25+ Je '67
SANTUCCI, John Joseph
City of Councilman John Santucci is a man
in a wind tunnel. M. Arnold. il pors N Y
Times Mag p56-7+ Ap 16 '67
SANZ DE SANTAMARIA, Carlos
CIAP chairman installed. G. Meek. por
Américas 19:45 My '67
SÃO PAULO biennial. See Art—Exhibitions
SAP
Turgor pressure: direct manometric measure-
ment in single cells of nitella. P. B. Green
and F. W. Stanton. bibliog il Science 155:
1675-6 Mr 31 '67
SAPP, Dorothy W.
Regional report. Home Gard 54:76-7 My '67
SARA, Dorothy
How do you doodle? Seventeen 26:106-7 Je '67
SARAGAT, Giuseppe
President Saragat of Italy visits the United
States; exchange of greetings, September
18, exchange of toasts, and joint statement,
September 19, 1967. Dept State Bul 57:500-3
O 16 '67
SARAH Mellon Scaife foundation
Funds for the younger faculty. Sch & Soc
95:170 Mr 18 '67
SARASOTA, Fla.
What ever happened to Sarasota? P. H. Hiss.
il Arch Forum 126:66-73 Je '67

Theater
Florida findings: Asolo company's audience-
development projects and productions. H.
Hewes. Sat R 50:22 Mr 18 '67
SARATOGA performing arts center
Saratoga performing arts center: highly suc-
cessful solution to an impossible program.
il Arch Rec 141:126-30 F '67
World of dance. W. Terry. Sat R 50:40 Jl
29 '67
SARATOGA SPRINGS, N.Y.
Best in the world; racing and social season.
il Newsweek 70:45 Ag 21 '67
High life at Saratoga, 1837; excerpt from
letter. S. Dawson. il Am Heritage 18:107
Je '67

SARAWAK
Malaysia after confrontation. D. Warner. Re-
porter 36:33-5 Ja 26 '67
SARCOMA
Mutations, chromosomal aberrations, and
tumors in insects treated with oncogenic
virus. W. J. Burdette and J. S. Yoon.
bibliog il Science 155:340-1 Ja 20 '67
SARDINIA
See also
Architecture, Domestic—Sardinia
Nuoro
SARGANT, William Walters
Psychiatry and war; excerpts from The un-
quiet mind. Atlan 219:102-9 My '67
SARGEANT, Winthrop
Books. New Yorker 43:146-8 Je 10; 98+ Ag 12
'67
Doing what comes naturally. Opera N 32:28-9
D 9 '67
Musical events. See issues of New Yorker
Profiles; Z. Mehta. New Yorker 43:53-4+
D 16 '67
SARGENT, John Singer
Sargent in combat. Newsweek 70:88 O 2 '67
SARGENT, Sir Malcolm
Farewell to Sir Malcolm. T. Heinitz. Sat R
50:60 D 2 '67
Proms, hail and farewell to Sir Malcolm.
E. Greenfield. il Hi Fi 17:MA30-1 D '67
SARGENT, T. D.
Cryptic moths: effects on background selec-
tions of painting the circumocular scales.
bibliog Science 159:100-1 Ja 5 '68
SARICH, Vincent M. and Wilson, A. C.
Immunological time scale for hominid evolu-
tion. bibliog Science 158:1200-3 D 1 '67
SARIS, Indian. See Costume—India
SARNOFF, Dorothy
Voice of America. il Mlle 65:70-1 Jl '67
SARNOFF, Robert W.
Communications technology: address, October
10, 1967. Vital Speeches 34:94-6 N 15 '67

about
On his own. il por Time 90:93-4 N 10 '67
SAROYAN, Aram
Nine poems. Poetry 110:374-8 S '67
SAROYAN, Lucy
Lucy Saroyan; photographs. Vogue 149:166-7
My '67
SAROYAN, William
Help, the newsboy hollered; story. McCalls
94:88-9 My '67
Madness in the family; story. Sat Eve Post
240:56-7 Je 17 '67
Sight and insight; excerpts from Look at us.
U S Camera 30:50-1 D '67
Three tales. Sat Eve Post 240:68-70 O 7 '67
SARRAUTE, Nathalie
Life beneath the lines we wear. L. S.
Roudiez. por Sat R 50:35-6 My 6 '67
Le mensonge (Lie) Criticism
New Yorker 42:124 F 11 '67
Le silence. Criticism
New Yorker 42:124 F 11 '67
SARRIS, Andrew
Movers. Sat R 50:10+ D 23 '67
SARSINI, Enrico
Yevtushenko; photographs. Life 62:32-9 F 17
'67

about
Here's the portrait you wanted, Mrs Sarsini.
F. McCulloch. por Life 62:3 Mr 24 '67
SARTON, May
Poet as novelist. M. Van Duyn. Poetry 109:
333 F '67
SARTOR, J. D. and Atkinson, W. R.
Charge transfer between raindrops. bibliog
Science 157:1267-9 S 15 '67
SARTRE, Jean Paul
Jean-Paul Sartre: Christian theist? J. B.
Mow; discussion. Christian Cent 83:1578;
84:146+ D 21 '66, F 1 '67
Letter from Paris. Genêt. New Yorker 43:
170+ My 13 '67
What's wrong with Israel? M. Geltman.
Nat R 19:568-9 My 30 '67
SARVIS, Shirley
Personalized pastry. Farm J 91:106-7 F '67
Roasts to carve before company comes.
Farm J 91:60-2 N '67
Unusual make-ahead salads. Farm J 91:66-7
S '67
SASANO, Takaaki
Weaving colored paper. Design 69:4-5 Wint
'67
SASCHENBRECKER, P. W. See Ecobichon,
D. J. jt. auth.
SASKATCHEWAN

Politics and government
In Canada, socialism loses: a portent for
U.S? il U S News 63:69-70 N 20 '67

SASS, Samuel
Library technicians: instant librarians? excerpts from address, May 28, 1967. bibliog por Library J 92:2123-6 Je 1 '67

SASSOON, Siegfried Lorraine
Obituary
Pub W 192:48 S 18 '67
Some talk of Passchendaele. R. C. Wald. Reporter 37:36-7 N 30 '67

SATAN in literature. See Devil in literature

SATELLITE states. See Europe, Eastern

SATELLITES
Changes in Triton's orbit. G. S. Mumford. Sky & Tel 33:94 F '67
Discovery of Janus, Saturn's tenth satellite. A. Dollfus. il Sky & Tel 34:136-7 S '67
New moons. Sci Am 216:50 Ap '67
Saturn's tenth satellite. G. S. Mumford. il Sky & Tel 33:159 Mr '67
Tenth moon of Saturn; reply with rejoinder. N. Valery. il Sci N 91:348 Ap 15 '67
Tenth satellite of Saturn? il Sky & Tel 33: 71+ F '67

SATINOFF, Evelyn
Disruption of hibernation caused by hypothalamic lesions. bibliog Science 155:1031-3 F 24 '67

SATIRE
Laughing matter? church as subject for comedians. il Newsweek 69:55 My 29 '67
See also
Caricatures and cartoons
also subhead Anecdotes, facetiae, satire, etc, under various subjects, e.g. Peace—Anecdotes, facetiae, satire, etc.

SATISFACTION in work. See Job satisfaction

SATISFACTORY settlement; story. See Gordimer, N.

SATO, Eisaku
Japan's Prime Minister talks to Vietnam and the future of Asia; excerpts from address, November 15, 1967. U S News 63:55-6 N 27 '67
U.S. and Japan reaffirm common objectives and pledge continued cooperation; exchange of greetings and toasts, November 14, with joint communique, November 15, 1967. Dept State Bul 57:742-7 D 4 '67

about
Bouncing back. il por Newsweek 69:49-50 F 13 '67
Complete meeting of the minds. il por Newsweek 70:49-50 N 27 '67
Election victory for Sato. il por Sr Schol 90:13 F 17 '67
Grand tour, Japanese style. il por Newsweek 70:36-8 O 2 '67
Right eye of Daruma. il pors Time 89:24-8 F 10 '67

SATO, Gordon H. See Mohit, B. jt. auth.

SATTA, Sebastiano
Poet in the piazza. il Arch Forum 127:70-5 O '67

SATURDAY evening post
What are we looking for? D. McKinney. Writer 80:14-16+ N '67

SATURDAY review
Adventures in ideas and learning; What I have learned, series to be published. N. Cousin. Sat R 50:22 D 16 '67
American editor's odyssey. B. Moyers. Sat R 50:30-1+ N 11 '67
Conductors at Glyndebourne; libel action in London by Stanley Frederick John Pritchard. Sat R 50:39 D 30 '67
SR's fifteenth annual advertising awards. W. D. Patterson. il Sat R 50:76-83 Ap 8 '67
Ten years of recordings; comp. by G. Jellinek. Sat R 50:50-60 Ag 26 '67
See also
Amy Loveman national award
Anisfield-Wolf awards

SATURDAY review photo contest. See Photography—Competitions

SATURN (planet)
Evaporation of ice in space: Saturn's rings. H. Harrison and R. I. Schoen. bibliog Science 157:1175-6 S 8 '67
More on the 1966-67 apparition of Saturn. L. J. Robinson. il Sky & Tel 33:390-2 Je '67
Observing Saturn's edgewise rings, October, 1966. J. Texereau. il Sky & Tel 33:226-7 Ap '67
Saturn: four rings. Sci N 91:518 Je 3 '67

Satellites
See Satellites

SATURN launch vehicles. See Space vehicles—Propulsion systems

SAUCEPANS. See Kitchen utensils

SAUCERS, Flying. See Flying saucers

SAUCES
Art of saucing vegetables. il Sunset 138:178-9 Ap '67
Cooking with oyster sauce; with recipes. il Sunset 138:147-8 Je '67
Great garlic surprise; aïoli sauce. il Sunset 138:88-9 Ap '67
Memory making; sauces for pastas. il Sunset 138:202+ My '67
Sauces make the difference; with recipes. J. Hunt. il Parents Mag 42:64-5+ Mr '67
Simple sauces; with recipes. il Bet Hom & Gard 45:108 Ap '67
Spaghetti sauces. il Consumer Rep 32:493-5 S '67
What ice cream needs is sauce. il Sunset 138:183 My '67
See also
Tomato sauce

SAUD, king of Saudi Arabia (abdicated 1964)
Misguided monarch. il por Time 89:37 My 5 '67

SAUDI ARABIA
Keeping devils at bay. il Time 91:25 Ja 12 '68
Nasser's drive for south Arabia. L. Mosher. il Reporter 36:24-7 F 9 '67
Nasser's poison gas. Reporter 36:12+ Je 15 '67
See also
Water supply—Saudi Arabia
Women—Saudi Arabia

Politics and government
Tradition and reform in Saudi Arabia. G. Lenczowski. Cur Hist 52:98-104+ F '67

Social conditions
See also
Women—Saudi Arabia

Social life and customs
On being a sheik's wife. A. Shammout. il Sat R 50:71-2+ O 14 '67

SAUER, G. E. and Borst, L. B.
Lambda transition in liquid sulfur. bibliog Science 158:1567-9 D 22 '67

SAUER, Louis W.
Your child's health. See issues of PTA magazine
Your family's health. PTA Mag 62:35-6 S '67

SAUERKRAUT
See also
Cookery—Vegetables

SAULNIER, Raymond J.
Budgetary note. Nat R 19:508 My 16 '67
Tax increase: address, September 19, 1967. Vital Speeches 34:39-41 N 1 '67
Three federal budget concepts; address, March 3, 1967. Vital Speeches 33:400-4 Ap 15 '67

SAUNA
Americanization of the sauna. D. X. Manners. House B 110:115+ Ja '68
Outbuilding is in and the sauna is very in. il Pop Gard 18:52-5 Mr '67
What you should know about saunas. H. Higdon. il Todays Health 45:20-3 Mr '67

SAUNDERS, Arlene
Blonde with brains, interview, ed. by S. Jenkins, jr. por Opera N 32:18 N 25 '67

SAUNDERS, D. S.
Time measurement in insect photoperiodism: reversal of a photoperiodic effect by chilling. bibliog Science 156:1126-7 My 26 '67

SAUNDERS, Diana
On the boards. W. Como. por Dance Mag 42: 20 Ja '68

SAUNDERS, Frederick A.
Physics for the queen. J. Eberhart. il Sci N 91:212-13 Mr 4 '67

SAUNDERS, J. L. and Knoke, J. K.
Diets for rearing the ambrosia beetle xyleborus ferrugineus (fabricius) in vitro bibliog Science 157:460+ Jl 28 '67

SAUNDERS, M. J. and Prettyman, P. E.
Preparation of submicroscopic spider threads for particle studies. bibliog Science 155: 1124-5 Mr 3 '67

SAUSAGE
See also
Cookery—Meat

SAUSALITO, Calif.
Houseboats of Sausalito. A. Garvey. il Arch Forum 126:48-53 Mr '67
No weeds on the front lawn; shipboard living. B. Gilbert. il Sports Illus 26:80-2+ Ap 24 '67

SAUVAJOU caves. See Caves

SAVAGE, John
Girl with fifteen speeds; story. Ladies Home
J 84:94-5 Mr '67
Girls across the water; story. Redbook 128:
86-7 F '67
How to get to page one. Writer 81:9-11+ Ja
'68
SAVAGE sound; story. See Ford, J. H.
SAVAGES. See Man, Primitive
SAVANG, Vong, crown prince of Laos. See Vong
Savang
SAVANNAH, Ga.
Savannah issue; symposium. Antiques 91:
320-73 Mr '67

Architecture

Architectural trends in Savannah. W. C.
Hertridge. il Antiques 91:324-8 Mr '67

Galleries and museums

See also
Telfair academy of arts and sciences

Historic houses, etc.

Andrew Low's house. W. C. Hartridge. il
Antiques 91:350-2 Mr '67
Davenport house. E. N. McKinnon. il An-
tiques 91:339-41 Mr '67
Juliette Gordon Low birthplace. R. K. Mc-
Clendon. il Antiques 91:360-3 Mr '67
Owens-Thomas house. E. V. Jones. il An-
tiques 91:342-6 Mr '67
SAVANNAH (ship) See Ships, Atomic powered
SAVANNAH furniture. See Furniture, Ameri-
can
SAVARY, Louis M.
Deejays and teen radio. America 117:444-5 O
21 '67
SAVE a cat league, incorporated
Cat-savers. New Yorker 43:39-41 Mr 25 '67
SAVILE, George, 1st marquis of Halifax. See
Halifax, G. S.
SAVING and savings
Americans on a saving spree: what it means.
il U S News 63:114-16 S 18 '67
Build a financial legacy for your child. P.
Lindberg. Bet Hom & Gard 45:6+ D '67
Cautious mood in U.S.; saving up: spending
down. il U S News 62:98-9 Mr 27 '67
Consumers hold back. il Bsns W p27 F 11 '67
Making money grow for your children. M.
Feeley. Am Home 70:20-1 Mr '67
New set of priorities; savings spurt. il Time
90:59 S 1 '67
Saving comes back into style. il Bsns W
p28-9 F 11 '67
Savings accounts: which one for you? il
Good H 165:208 N '67
Should your policy also be a savings ac-
count? il Consumer Rep 32:100-7 F '67
Simple savings around your home. M. E.
Dowd. Am Home 70:59+ Ja '67
See also
Bonds
Christmas clubs
Finance, Personal
Investments
Postal savings banks
SAVINGS and loan associations
California's doctor for ailing S&Ls; P. Martin.
Bsns W p77-8+ Ap 1 '67
Countrywide look at the stir in home build-
ing. U S News 62:92-4 Ja 30 '67
Sampling of insured savings and loan associa-
tions that pay 5¼ per cent. Changing T
21:14 Mr '67
See also
Federal savings and loan insurance corpora-
tion
Home savings and loan association of Los
Angeles

Holding companies

Leeching Lytton back to health. Bsns W
p 130+ N 11 '67
SAVINGS banks
Cautious mood in U.S; saving up: spending
down. il U S News 62:98-9 Mr 27 '67
Compound woes of the savings banks. S. H.
Brown. il Fortune 75:124-6+ Mr '67
Wriggling and smarting; reaction to selling
lottery tickets issued by New York state.
New Yorker 43:29-30 Je 10 '67
See also
Postal savings banks
Savings deposits
SAVINGS bonds. See Bonds, Government
SAVINGS deposits

Interest

What compounding adds to your savings. il
Changing T 21:29 O '67

SAVINGS-sharing plan in industry
New slices for Kaiser's melon? Kaiser steel-
United steelworkers long-range sharing
plan. il Bsns W p 149-50 Mr 4 '67
SAVITRI
Marriage of Draupadi; excerpt from Tales
from Indian classics, book 1. UNESCO Cou-
rier 20:8-9 D '67
SAVOY, Gene
Lost city of Pajaten.   S. Tomkievicz. il
Horizon 9:62-7 Aut '67
Pajatén: a lost city found. R. Wood. il por
Américas 19:7-16 Je '67
Wanted: paying guests to trace the lost cities
of Peru. R. Joseph. il Esquire 68:138-9 S '67
SAW horses. See Sawhorses
SAW-mill; opera. See Hawkins, M.
SAW mills. See Sawmills
SAW-whet owls. See Owls
SAWHORSES
Hitch up a team of high-low horses. H. T.
Bodkin. il Pop Mech 128:181 N '67
SAWING
Two saw blades are better than one. R. J.
De Cristoforo. il Pop Sci 191:118-21+ Ag '67
SAWITS, Murray
Model for branch store planning. Harvard
Bsns R 45:140-3 Jl '67
SAWMILLS
Sawmill in Vietnam; excerpt from letter. J.
Cravens. il Am For 73:8+ S '67
SAWS
Bench saw? radial? new kit gives advantages
of both. H. Wicks. il Pop Sci 191:160-2
O '67
Build your own abrasive cutoff machine. R. S.
Walker. il Pop Mech 127:190-2+ F '67   ?
Don't sell your bandsaw short. M. Banis-
ter. il Pop Mech 128:160-2 Jl '67
Don't sell your table saw short. W. C.
Leckey. il Pop Mech 127:166-9 F '67
Electric trim saw puts miter box to shame.
W. C. Leckey. il Pop Mech 127:186-7 F '67
Get double duty from your portable saw. M.
Banister. il Pop Mech 128:184-6 O '67
How Teflon-S improves power-saw blades. R.
J. De Cristoforo. il Pop Sci 191:138-40 D
'67
New chain saw licks vibration. W. C. Leckey.
il Pop Mech 128:208 S '67
New variable-speed saws; saber saws. il Pop
Sci 192:145 Ja '68
Power hacksaw comes in $18.95 kit. P. Mc-
Cafferty. il Pop Sci 192:160-3 Ja '68
Saber saws. il Consumer Rep 32:496-501 S '67
Teflon-coated saw: the slickest yet. il Pop
Sci 190:139 Ap '67
Two saw blades are better than one. R. J.
De Cristoforo. il Pop Sci 191:118-21+ Ag '67
Unimat offers three improved saws. H. Wal-
ton. il Pop Sci 192:146-7+ Ja '68
Use chain saws right. W. J. Fletcher. il Suc
Farm 65:84 Ja '67
Your guide to buying a chain saw. E. F.
Lindsley. il Pop Sci 191:150-4+ O '67
See also
Jigsaws
SAWTOOTH national recreation area, Idaho.
See Recreation areas
SAWTOOTH primitive area. See Wilderness
areas—Idaho
SAWYER, Charles
Launching pad for doves. por Outdoor Life
140:50-1+ S '67
SAWYER, Ruth
To May Massee. Horn Bk 43:229-32 Ap '67
SAXBERG, Borje O. See Knowles, H. P. jt.
auth.
SAXITOXIN. See Toxins and antitoxins
SAXON, Charles David
Cocktail party. J. Peter. il pors Look 31:
82-4+ My 16 '67
SAXOPHONE, Electronic. See Musical instru-
ments, Electronic
SAYERS, Gale
Gale Sayers. Chicago's windy city express.
W. J. McKean. il pors Look 31:58-60+ O 31
'67
Storm over Gale. Sports Illus 27:13 N 6 '67
SAYINGS. See Aphorisms and apothegms;
Quotations
SAYLER, Anne, and Wolfson, Albert
Avian pineal gland: progonadotropic response
in the Japanese quail. bibliog Science 158:
1478-9 D 15 '67
SAYRE, Nora
Desires and disappointments. Reporter 36:48-
50 Ja 26 '67
SAYRE, Robert F.
Theatre. Nation 205:189-90 S 4 '67
SCABBARDS
See also
Sheaths

SCAIFE, Sarah Mellon, foundation. See Sarah Mellon Scaife foundation
SCALE (architecture) See Architecture—Composition, proportion, etc.
SCALES (weighing instruments)
Air force, NASA developing space scales; devices to measure the mass of objects in space. Tech W 20:18 F 20 '67
SCALLOPS
See also
Cookery—Shellfish
SCAMMON, Richard M.
Electoral participation. bibliog f Ann Am Acad 371:59-71 My '67
How Wallace will run his third-party campaign. Reporter 37:34-6 O 19 '67
This is what a baby can look forward to. Life 63:28-9 D 1 '67

about
Shibboleth smasher. por Time 90:24 S 22 '67
SCANDINAVIA
Scandinavia; symposium. il House B 110:70+ Ja '68

Description and travel
Scandinavia observed. A. Heckscher. il House B 110:88-9 Ja '68
SCANDINAVIAN airlines system
SAS expects Bangkok flights to triple. E. H. Kolcum. il Aviation W 87:29+ N 27 '67
SAS gains Moscow-Tokyo route; with editorial comment. Aviation W 86:21, 36-7 Ja 23 '67
SAS plans new Copenhagen cargo center. J. W. Carter. il Aviation W 86:50-1 My 8 '67
SCANDINAVIAN cookery. See Cookery, Scandinavian
SCANDINAVIAN furniture. See Furniture, Scandinavian
SCANDINAVIANS
Scandinavia observed. A. Heckscher. il House B 110:88-9 Ja '68
See also
Icelanders
SCANLAN, John
Meditation in time of war; poem. America 117:616 N 18 '67
SCANLON, John J.
How much should a corporation earn? Harvard Bsns R 45:4-6+ Ja '67
SCANNELL, Karen, and others
San Francisco: gourmet dining on a budget. pors ALA Bul 61:740-6 Je '67
SCANNING beams. See Aeronautic instruments
SCANNING electron microscope. See Electron microscope and microscopy
SCANNING radar. See Radar—Antenna and scanning mechanisms
SCARBROUGH, Marsha
Mlle's guest editors: 1967. por Mlle 65:222-3 Ag '67
SCARLET ibises. See Ibises
SCARLET Pimpernel; drama. See Leech, M. T.
SCARVES
Scarf! various ways of wearing scarves. il Good H 165:83-5 Jl '67
SCATTERGUNS. See Shotguns
SCATTERING (physics)
High-energy scattering. V. D. Barger and D. B. Cline. il Sci Am 217:76-9+ D '67
See also
Radio waves—Scattering
SCENARIO writing. See Moving picture authorship
SCENE designers. See Designers
SCENERY. See Nature
SCENIC areas. See Preservation of landmarks, scenery, etc.—United States
SCENT. See Perfumery
SCENT of ginger; story. See Chidester, A.
SCERRA, Joseph A.
Vietnam reality; address, November 11, 1967. Vital Speeches 34:174-6 Ja 1 '68
SCHAALMAN, Herman E.
Franz Rosenzweig: a voice for today. Christian Cent 84:233-6 F 22 '67
SCHAAP, Dick
Where is Bill Miller? Harper 235:68-72 D '67
SCHACKMUTH, Don
Build this two-in-one chest-crib. Pop Mech 127:172-5 My '67
SCHAEFER, R. J.
Three cheers for the America. por Am For 73:4-7+ S '67
SCHAETZEL, J. Robert
Europe and America, 1967; address, November 10, 1967. Dept State Bul 57:710-15 N 27 '67
SCHAFFER, Leslie
Hypochondriacal vision. New Repub 157:26-8 Ag 19 '67

SCHAFFER, Robert H.
Putting action into planning. Harvard Bsns R 45:158-60+ N '67
SCHAFFNER, Kenneth F.
Antireductionism and molecular biology. bibliog Science 157:644-7; 158:861-2 Ag 11, N 17 '67
SCHAIN, Richard J. and others
Protein metabolism in the developing brain: influence of birth and gestational age. bibliog Science 156:984-6 My 19 '67
SCHALK, Adolph
Samaritans to Hanoi. Commonweal 86:542-4 S 8 '67
SCHALL, James V.
Beginnings of world war III? America 117: 14-17 Jl 1 '67
SCHALL, Roger
Man from Paris. U S Camera 30:50-1 Ag '67
SCHALLER, George B.
Heronry in the house. il Audubon 69:66-7 Jl '67
Life among the gorillas; condensation of The year of the gorilla. Sci Digest 62:6-13 Jl '67
SCHALLER, Lyle E.
Challenge of creative federalism. Christian Cent 84:618-22 My 10 '67
SCHALLY, Andrew V. and others
Enterogastrone inhibits eating by fasted mice. bibliog Science 157:210-11 Jl 14 '67
SCHALOCK, Robert L. and Klopfer, F. D.
Phenylketonuria: enduring behavioral deficits in phenylketonuric rats. bibliog Science 155:1033-5 F 24 '67
SCHANCHE, Donald Arthur
Holiday ins, and outs. Newsweek 69:66-7 Ap 10 '67
SCHANTZ-HANSEN, R. See Alm, A. A. jt. auth.
SCHAPIRO, Shawn, and Norman, R. J.
Thyroxine: effects of neonatal administration on maturation, development, and behavior. bibliog Science 155:1279-81 Mr 10 '67
SCHAUERS, Charles J.
Information central; questions and answers. Pop Electr 26:68-70+ F; 66-8+ Mr; 76-8+ Ap; 81-3 My; 68-70 Je; 27:64-6 Jl '67
SCHECHTER, Daniel. See Rosenblatt, R. jt. auth.
SCHECTER, Jerrold L.
Horatio Alger story, with a Japanese twist. N Y Times Mag p56-7+ S 10 '67
Japan's new bid for leadership. Reporter 36: 31-3 My 18 '67
SCHEDULES, Household. See Home economics
SCHEDULES, School
Flexibility for class time; Stanford school scheduling system. il Time 90:110 D 8 '67
SCHEIBEL, Arnold B. See Globus, A. jt. auth.
SCHEIBER, Harry N.
Report: California textbook fight. Atlan 220: 38+ N '67
SCHEIBER, Walter A.
Council of governments. Am City 82:110-12 My '67
SCHEINGOLD, Stuart A.
Britain wants in. Commonweal 86:84-6 Ap 7 '67
SCHEINMAN, Lawrence
Euratom: nuclear integration in Europe. bibliog f por(back cover) Int Council 563:5-66 My '67
SCHEINSON, Julian
Computer traffic control a hit with baseball fans. Am City 82:152+ O '67
SCHELL, Jonathan
Reporter at large. New Yorker 43:28-40+ Jl 15 '67
SCHELL, Orville
Cage for the innocents. Atlan 221:29-34 Ja '68
Thailand: priviledged sanctuary. New Repub 157:16-19 S 30 '67
SCHELLING, Thomas C. and others
U.S. selective service. Bul Atomic Sci 23:38-40 O '67
SCHENCK, Walter S.
Shoot swirling color from a swinging light. Pop Mech 127:90-1 Je '67
SCHENK, Gretchen Knief
(ed) Extending library service. See issues of Wilson library bulletin to June 1967
SCHENKEN, Howard
Schenken just rolls along. C. Goren. il Sports Illus 26:52-3 F 27 '67
SCHENKER-SPRÜNGLI, O.
Down with decibels! UNESCO Courier 20:4-7 Jl '67
SCHENLEY, James P.
How to pick the right masonry paint. Pop Mech 128:163-70+ O '67
How to refinish hardwood floors. Pop Mech 129:188-90 Ja '68

SCHLOSSBERG, Stephen I.
Excerpt from testimony before Subcommittee on constitutional amendments. August 23, 1967. Cong Digest 46:282+ N '67
SCHLUMBERGER, limited
Dash of Curaçao. Fortune 76:188 S 15 '67
New gusher for Schlumberger? J. Ross-Skinner. Duns R 90:91-2 O '67
SCHMALE, Jack
New unlimiteds. Motor B 119:100+ F '67
Northern Cal roundup. See issues of Motor boating
SCHMID, Rudi. See Diamond, I. jt. auth.
SCHMIDT, Albert C.
Fault is in the stars. Reporter 37:46+ S 7 '67
Pitterman flies; story. Reporter 37:43-6 S 21 '67
Through rose-colored glasses darkly. Reporter 38:44+ Ja 11 '68
SCHMIDT, Warren H. See Lippitt, G. L. jt. auth.
SCHMIDT, William J.
Night singers; poem. Christian Cent 84:1462 N 15 '67
SCHMIDTCHEN, Paul W.
Books. See issues of Hobbies
SCHMIEGE, Don
Backpack sheep hunt; ed. by M. Miller. Field & S 71:44-5+ Mr '67
SCHMITT, Hans A.
Men and politics in East Germany. bibliog f Cur Hist 52:232-7 Ap '67
SCHMITZ, Dennis
There is no sound; poem. Commonweal 86:56 Mr 31 '67
SCHMITZ, Ettore. See Svevo, I. pseud.
SCHMÖLZER, Sepp
Jewelry by Sepp Schmölzer. I. Brynner. il Craft Horiz 27:14-15 S '67
SCHNEIDER, D. R. and others
Gastrin antibodies: induction, demonstration, and specificity. bibliog Science 156:391-2 Ap 21 '67
SCHNEIDER, Daniel J.
Little Black Sambo; poem. Christian Cent 84:863 Jl 5 '67
SCHNEIDER, Howard A.
Ecological ectocrines in experimental epidemiology. bibliog Science 158:597-603 N 3 '67
SCHNEIDER, Jerry A. and others
Increased cystine in leukocytes from individuals homozygous and heterozygous for cystinosis. bibliog Science 157:1321-2 S 15 '67
SCHNEIDER, Sherman
New Garden; interview. New Yorker 42:25-6 F 4 '67
SCHNEIDERMAN, Howard A. See Burkett, B. N. jt. auth.
SCHODDE, Stephen C.
NSA: a national student forum. Sch & Soc 95:86-7 F 4 '67
SCHODERBEK, Peter P. and Digman, L. A.
Third generation, PERT/LOB. Harvard Bsns R 45:100-10 S '67
SCHOEN, Elin
Let's travel. Mlle 65:30+ Jl '67
SCHOEN, R. I. See Harrison, H. jt. auth.
SCHOENBERG, Arnold. See Schönberg, A.
SCHOENBRUN, David
Fall of the French empire in Indochina. Sat R 50:31-3 F 18 '67
Journey to North Vietnam. Sat Eve Post 240:21-5+ D 16 '67
Vietnam legacy. New Repub 156:25-8 F 11 '67
SCHOENDIENST, Albert Fred. See Schoendienst, R.
SCHOENDIENST, Red
Red and his roomie, and the pennant. J. Brosnan. il pors N Y Times Mag p36-7+ S 17 '67
SCHOENDOERFFER, Pierre
Anderson platoon. il pors Ebony 22:69-72+ O '67
Frenchman discovers America in the Vietnam war. il por U S News 63:12 Jl 31 '67
Men at war: a French view. il Time 89:78 F 17 '67
SCHOENER, Allon
Electronic museum. Pop Phot 60:84-7 Ap '67

about

Viewpoint. J. Deschin. por Pop Phot 61:66+ O '67
SCHOENER, Thomas W.
Ecological significance of sexual dimorphism in size in the lizard anolis conspersus. bibliog Science 155:474-7 Ja 27 '67
SCHOENHOFEN, Leo H. 1915-
Three years beyond George Orwell. Duns R 89:43-4+ Mr '67

about

Container seeks a bigger package. il pors Bsns W p 186-8+ O 21 '67
SCHOENMAN, Ralph
Evil eye. Nat R 19:232-3 Mr 7 '67
Tragedy of Bertrand Russell. F. Lewis. il por Look 31:30-2+ Ap 4 '67
SCHOENSTEIN, Ralph
Pet news. Ladies Home J 84:47 F '67
You can't tell the boys from the girls without this scorecard. Ladies Home J 84:24 Jl '67
SCHOFIELD, Mary-Peale
Cleveland arcade; reprint. Arch Forum 127:60-5 S '67
SCHOLANDER, P. F.
Osmotic mechanism and negative pressure. bibliog Science 156:67-9; 158:1210-12 Ap 7, D 1 '67
SCHOLARS
  See also
College professors and instructors
Intellectuals
SCHOLARS, Russian. See Russia—Intellectual life
SCHOLARSHIPS and fellowships
Competition for graduate fellowships. T. O. Brandt. Sch & Soc 95:394 O 28 '67
Congressional critique of scholarship. W. W. Brickman. Sch & Soc 95:69 F 4 '67
Dollars for scholars; funds given by each state PTA. PTA Mag 61:19 Je '67
New hope for Harlem's bright youth; preparation for prep school class, New York's Wadleigh intermediate school. il Ebony 22:27-30+ My '67
What counts most in winning a college scholarship. il Good H 164:198-9 Mr '67
  See also
Citizens scholarship foundation of America, incorporated
Student aid
  also subhead Scholarships and fellowships under various subjects, e.g. Physics—Scholarships and fellowships
SCHOLASTIC ability. See Ability
SCHOLASTIC achievements. See Student achievements
SCHOLASTIC aptitude tests. See Aptitude tests
SCHOLASTIC institute of student opinion. See Scholastic research center
SCHOLASTIC magazines, incorporated
At our corner; Canadian subsidiary, Scholastic-TAB publications, ltd; tenth birthday. il Sr Schol 90:sup22 My 5 '67
At our corner; editorial platform governing selection and treatment of topics for magazines and books. Sr Schol 90:sup21 F 3 '67
At our corner; from press, to post office, to you. Sr Schol 90:sup22 Mr 17 '67
At our corner; 1967 art, photography, and writing awards programs. il Sr Schol 90:sup22 My 12 '67
At our corner; Scholastic conducts paperback book clubs. il Sr Schol 91:sup 16 O 12 '67
At our corner; Scholastic's expanded summer reading program. Sr Schol 90:sup26 Ap 28 '67
At our corner: transparency masters in the teacher editions: Professional relations and curriculum division. Sr Schol 90:sup30 Ap 14 '67
At our corner: VISTA book kits from many publishers. il Sr Schol 90:sup37 Mr 31 '67
Presenting the 1967 Scholastic awards. il Sr Schol 90:17-24+ My 19 '67
Scholastic magazines' new corporate structure. Pub W 192:34 D 25 '67
Search for talented youth; 1967 Scholastic awards program. Sr Schol 90:sup2 My 19 '67
Transparencies; Scholastic's unique service. il Sr Schol 91:sup7 S 21 '67
View of what's new at Scholastic. Sr Schol 91:sup44 S 28; sup30 O 26 '67
[Winners of the 1967 travel story contest] il Sr Schol 90:sup 13-19 My 5 '67
Winners, Scholastic magazine's annual photography contest. il U S Camera 30:66-7 N '67

Library

At our corner. il Sr Schol 90:sup21 Ap 21 '67
SCHOLASTIC research center
What teenagers themselves say: marriage, sex, and families; Institute of student opinion survey. Sr Schol 90:7 My 12 '67
SCHOLASTIC teacher. See Senior scholastic (periodical)
SCHOLASTIC world atlas. See Atlases
SCHOLASTICISM
  See also
Thomism

SCHOLEM, Gershom
Jews and Germans; excerpt from address at World Jewish congress, 1966; tr. by W. J. Dannhauser. Commentary 42:31-8 N '66; 43:18 Mr '67
Reflections on S. Y. Agnon. Commentary 44: 59-66 D '67

about
Sabbatai Zevi and the Jewish imagination. R. Alter. Commentary 43:67-71 Je '67

SCHOLES, W. A.
Kidney grafts successful. Sci N 91:582 Je 17 '67

SCHOLL, Joyce B. See Plank, M. S. jt. auth.

SCHOLLANDER, Don
Old and new pool their talent. K. Chapin. por Sports Illus 27:48+ Ag 21 '67

SCHOMBURG, Arthur A.
Schomburg's ailing collection. il por Ebony 22:55-6+ O '67

SCHOMBURG collection. See New York public library—135th Street branch

SCHOMER, Howard
Vietnam; the war nobody wants? Christian Cent 85:7-8 Ja 3 '68

SCHÖNBERG, Arnold
From one day to the next (Von heute auf morgen) Criticism
New Yorker 43:176-7 My 13 '67
Moses and Aaron. Criticism
Commentary 44:73-5 Jl '67
Hi Fi il 17:MA8+ F '67
Nation 204:124-5 Ja 23 '67
Music; Philharmonic's performance of violin concerto. B. Boretz. Nation 204:124 Ja 23 '67
Musical Hebraism. L. S. Dawidowicz. Commentary 44:75-7 Jl '67
Records; Columbia series. B. Boretz. Nation 205:603-5 D 4 '67

SCHONBERG, Harold C.
Conductor Otto Klemperer; giant on the podium. House B 109:138-9+ Mr '67

SCHÖNFELD, Johann Heinrich
Byron of the baroque. il Time 90:78 S 22 '67

SCHOOL administration. See School management and organization

SCHOOL administrators. See School superintendents and principals

SCHOOL age
Extend the compulsory school age to eighteen? pro and con discussion. Sr Schol 90:4-5 Mr 3 '67

SCHOOL and social and economic problems
Academic sickness in New York; mass resignation of teachers from Bronx junior high school 98 and other problems. il Time 89: 35-6 Mr 24 '67
Academy for hard cases; Philip Schuyler high school, Albany, N.Y. il Time 89:38 Ap 7 '67
Big changes in the schools. il U S News 63: 66-9 S 11 '67
Compensatory education for the disadvantaged. G. W. Jones. bibliog NEA J 56: 21-3 Ap '67
Education and the poor; the urban public school. M. R. Berube. Commonweal 86:46-8 Mr 31 '67
Educational equality. D. Wolfle. Science 156:19 Ap 7 '67; Reply. J. P. Gilbert and F. Mosteller. 156:1435 Je 16 '67
Imperatives remain; President's message. Sat R 50:73 F 18 '67
Poverty programs, civil rights, and the American school. A. S. Carton. Sch & Soc 95:108-9 F 18 '67
Rising expectations and riots. W. D. Boutwell. PTA Mag 62:13-14 O '67
Schools as a social barometer. J. Cass. Sat R 50:75-6 S 16 '67
Teacher opinion poll; teaching in center-city schools. il NEA J 56:63 D '67
See also
Children of migrant laborers—Education
Socially handicapped children—Education

SCHOOL and society (periodical)
Status of School & society, 1966-67. W. W. Brickman. Sch & Soc 95:341 O 14 '67

SCHOOL and the community
From the editor: Project Public Information. Am Ed 3:inside cover S '67
Getting our back-up; Ridgeview PTA, Oklahoma City, forms civil defense auxiliary. il PTA Mag 62:27 S '67
How to get the most out of local educational resources; use of teaching modules in San Diego County, Calif. J. M. Huffman. il Sr Schol 90:sup 16 F 3 '67
Teacher-opinion poll; attitudes toward school. NEA J 56:24 My '67
Teens sound off. J. Guernsey. il Am Ed 3:24-6+ S '67
Urban schools and society. D. Seeley. Cath World 206:19-21 O '67

SCHOOL and the home
Head start on home-school cooperation; low-income communities. il PTA Mag 62:26-8 N '67
Help your child learn more, better, faster. M. Mayer. Bet Hom & Gard 45:18+ S '67
Home and school. A. J. Belanger. Cath World 206:17-18 O '67
How to talk to your child's teacher; parent-teacher conferences. F. Buckvar. il Parents Mag 42:64-5+ S '67
Learning in a lonely place. A. Fischel. Sat R 50:55 Ag 19 '67
Mama goes to nursery school; Malabar street school, East Los Angeles. il Am Ed 3:10-11 S '67
Mothers bring their skills to school. D. Levenson. il Parents Mag 42:48-9+ F '67
Operation Home Start; Hawaiian program teaches parents how to ready their preschool youngsters for formal education. W. G. Cupit. NEA J 56:53-4 S '67
Teacher stretchers; home-visiting aides. il Am Ed 3:27-8 Jl '67
Teachers' gripes about parents; with study-discussion program, by E. Harris and D. Harris. bibliog il PTA Mag 61:8-10+, 31 F '67
What is school for? B. Bettelheim. Ladies Home J 84:54+ O '67
See also
Parents and teachers associations

Caricatures and cartoons
Parents' night. Changing T 21:23 O '67

SCHOOL annuals. See High school annuals

SCHOOL architecture. See School buildings

SCHOOL art. See Art—Study and teaching

SCHOOL athletics
Penny-wise; Cincinnati board of education eliminates interscholastic sports. Sports Illus 26:14-15 Mr 13 '67
Why some boys should stay off the team. F. V. Hein. Todays Health 45:72+ Ag '67
See also
Physical education and training

SCHOOL attendance
U.S. school enrollment, 1966-67. Sch & Soc 95: 4+ Ja 7 '67
See also
Compulsory education

SCHOOL bands. See Bands, School

SCHOOL boards
How much control for neighborhood school boards? Sr Schol 91:sup4 N 30 '67
See also
New York (city)—Education, Board of

SCHOOL bonds. See School finance

SCHOOL books. See Textbooks

SCHOOL budget. See School finance

SCHOOL buildings
Build now pay later. W. Coyne. il Am Ed 3:6-8+ Ap '67
Building types study. il Arch Rec 141:167-86 Mr '67
Curiouser and curiouser; voters in New Canaan, Conn. opposed to high school designed by P. Rudolph. Newsweek 69:95 F 13 '67
New look in schools. H. B. Gores. il Parents Mag 42:48-51+ Ja '67
One-room schoolhouse and how it grew. W. W. Chase. il Am Ed 3:8-12 My '67
Pittsburgh goes back to school. J. Bailey. il Arch Forum 126:40-51 Je '67
School that will vanish; Lincoln elementary school, Columbus. Ind. J. M. Dixon. il Arch Forum 127:48-53 N '67
Schoolhouse in the city. J. J. Morisseau. il Sat R 50:58-9 Mr 18 '67
Schoolhouse in the city; address, July 11, 1967. H. B. Gores. Vital Speeches 33:743-6 O 1 '67
Schools & the summer; vandalism. il Time 90:17 Ag 25 '67
Second boom in school building. G. A. Christie. il Arch Rec 142:83 Jl: 67 Ag '67
Some current answers for urban schools; building types study. il Arch Rec 142:177-92 O '67
Some new directions in systems for education. il Arch Rec 141:167-70 F '67 (to be cont)
Twin schools on three levels; Stuttgart. il Arch Forum 126:80-6 Ap '67

SCHOOL bus accidents. See Traffic accidents

SCHOOL bus transportation. See School children—Transportation

SCHOOL buses

Safety devices and measures
Danger rides the school bus. R. Bugg. il Todays Health 45:20-3+ N '67

SCHOOL children
Special journal feature on the average child; symposium. il NEA J 57:6-16+ Ja '68
See also
Teachers and students

Adjustment
Is your child in the wrong grade? excerpts. L. B. Ames. Ladies Home J 84:119-20+ Je '67
See also
High school students—Adjustment

Grading and promotion
See Grading and marking (students)

Health
See Children—Care and hygiene

Migration
See Children of migrant laborers

Reading
See Childrens reading

Transportation
Busing kids to the suburbs; Boston's METCO program. H. Spergel. il Am Ed 3:2-5 Ap '67
Growing concern about school buses. il Good H 165:201 O '67
He bought a bus; how L. Roberts applied federal funds to the Walden, Vt. system. D. Dew. il Sat R 50:58-9+ Je 17 '67
Wisconsin's fair bus law; transportation for children who attend church-related schools. America 117:47 Jl 15 '67
See also
School buses

SCHOOL construction. See School buildings

SCHOOL discipline
Discipline problems. J. Marcus; M. Richardson; J. Gray. il NEA J 56:60-3 D '67
See also
Corporal punishment
Police services for juveniles

SCHOOL districts
Decentralization dilemma; Bundy proposal. il Time 90:31 D 29 '67
Reorganization really makes a difference. B. W. Kreitlow. il NEA J 56:44-5 My '67

SCHOOL drama. See College and school drama

SCHOOL employees
Other employees in the school; nonteacher bargaining; excerpt from Teachers, administrators, and collective bargaining. E. B. Shils and C. T. Whittier. Mo Labor R 90:42-4 S '67

SCHOOL excursions
How to survive a field trip. G. McMillan and E. Stryker. il NEA J 56:58 O '67

SCHOOL exercises. See School programs

SCHOOL exhibits
Organizing an exhibit. il Design 68:30-1 Ja '67

SCHOOL finance
Bond market (cont of) Education and the bond market. See issues of American education
Build now pay later. W. Coyne. il Am Ed 3:6-8+ Ap '67
Education and the bond market. R. H. Barr and J. Du Von. See issues of American education to March 1967
Rising school expenditures. Sch & Soc 95:132 Mr 4 '67
Schools yes, taxes no; voting against bigger schools budgets. Time 89:44 Je 2 '67
Where school taxes sparked a revolt: Los Angeles. il U S News 62:64 F 27 '67
See also
Colleges and universities—Finance
Federal aid to education

Statistics
How much does your state spend on teachers and pupils? il Parents Mag 42:72 S '67

SCHOOL grading and promotion. See Grading and marking (students)

SCHOOL grounds
School that will vanish; Lincoln elementary school, Columbus, Ind. J. M. Dixon. il Arch Forum 127:48-53 N '67

SCHOOL health service. See Public schools—Health service

SCHOOL houses. See School buildings

SCHOOL laws and legislation

Tennessee
See also
Evolution—Laws and legislation

United States
Education professions development act. H. R. Ellis, 2d. Am Ed 3:20-1 O '67
Fair educational practice act is dead. E. S. Wilson. il Sat R 50:85-6 S 16 '67
See also
Compulsory education
Federal aid to education
Teachers—Contracts

SCHOOL leaving age. See School age

SCHOOL librarians
Continuing education for school librarians; address, January 11, 1967. V. McJenkin. bibliog ALA Bul 61:272-5 Mr '67
Revolution in our schools: individual instruction, new media, electronics. J. Fogarty. il Library J 92:302-3 Ja 15 '67
St Louis study assesses school librarian's role. Library J 92:3100+ S 15 '67
See also
American association of school librarians

Recruiting
We must be doing something wrong; recruiting young blood for school libraries. L. L. Shapiro. il Library J 92:1992-4 My 15 '67

Selection and appointment
Computer to help school librarians find jobs. Library J 92:1685 Ap 15 '67

Supply and demand
School librarian shortage in New Jersey. H. T. Gumaer. ALA Bul 61:555-7 My '67
School library manpower project wins $1.1 million grant; Knapp foundation of North Carolina, inc. Library J 93:249 Ja 15 '68
See also
School librarians—Recruiting

SCHOOL libraries
Comments on school library research. M. L. Woodworth; P. Sullivan. Wilson Lib Bul 41:947-9 My '67
Library of the American school in Japan. L. D. Downs. Horn Bk 43:576-9 O '67
Luaus in the library; or, The curriculum that wasn't; Rock Creek Palisades elementary school, Kensington, Md. M. Murray. il Library J 92:1708-10 Ap 15 '67
Million dollar carrels; Oak Park and River Forest, Ill. high school library; with report by L. Salinger. G. L. Schwilk. il Library J 92:306-10 Ja 15 '67
On libraries and learning; interview, ed. with introd. by E. Geller. H. Howe, 2d. il Library J 92:841-4 F 15 '67
Revolution in our schools: individual instruction, new media, electronics. J. Fogarty. il Library J 92:302-3 Ja 15 '67
School libraries: waiting in the wings; Australia. L. H. McGrath. bibliog Library J 92:4225-7 N 15 '67
School library: an intellectual force? adaptation of address, March 1967. M. V. Gaver. Library J 92:1989-91 My 15 '67
Vote for flexible scheduling; visits by individual students and class groups throughout the school day; discussion. Library J 92:821-2 F 15 '67
See also
Knapp school libraries project
Libraries and schools

Audio-visual materials
See School libraries and audio-visual materials

Automation
School information center. F. L. Goodman. NEA J 56:20-2 F '67

Book selection
See Book selection

Censorship
Censorship in schools rising, says Merritt; summary of statement, 1967. L. C. Merritt. Library J 92:4318+ D 1 '67
Helga Sandburg book banned in Memphis. Library J 92:4210 N 15 '67
Irreverent dissection of libraries; excerpts from address, June 23, 1967, ed. by G. Dusheck. E. Z. Freidenberg. Wilson Lib Bul 42:180 O '67
Other side: hardest of all things to come by; reply to E. Z. Freidenberg; address, June 27, 1967. M. Rafferty. il Wilson Lib Bul 42:181-6 O '67

Film strips
See Libraries—Film strips

SCHOOL libraries—*Continued*

Finance

Swim'st thou in wealth; California's school library puzzle. F. D. Largent and J. W. May. il Am Ed 3:12-13 Je '67

Foreign language collections

Books for Miguel. T. de Gerez. bibliog Library J 92:4587-9+ D 15 '67

Instruction in use

See Libraries—Instruction in use

Paperback books

Aiding unwilling readers; paperbacks do the trick; Ocean township H.S., Oakhurst, N.J. H. M. McDonnell. Sr Schol 90:sup21-2 Mr 31 '67

At our corner; Scholastic conducts paperback book clubs. il Sr Schol 91:sup 16 O 12 '67

Developing a reading public, Ivan Ludington, sr. at work; schools get free paperback books. il Pub W 192:46-7 S 4 '67

Fader plan: Detroit style; Highland Park high school. E. Baur. bibliog il Library J 92:3119-21 S 15 '67

On parade; new paperbacks; symposium. il Sr Schol 89:sup8-9+ Ja 20 '67

Paper tiger. Library J 92:4590 D 15 '67

Paperback boom seen for future school libraries; discussion. Library J 91:5666; 92: 821 N 15 '66, F 15 '67

Pin money for paperbacks; Menlo-Atherton high school, Atherton, Calif. M. Hegland. il Library J 92:2000-1 My 15 '67

School paperback survey destroys some old notions. il Library J 92:3798-9 O 15 '67

Technical processes

Is central processing for you? services in Montgomery County, Md. R. L. Darling; reply. M. Hegland. Library J 92:1267-8 Mr 15 '67

SCHOOL libraries and audio-visual materials

Agents for change: producer or consumer? W. Howell. Library J 92:3812-14 O 15 '67

Cartridge loop: 8mm made easy. L. Forsdale. il Library J 92:2002-4 My 15 '67

Choosing in 8; silent cartridge films. K. E. Vandergrift. Library J 92:2005 My 15 '67

Dimensions of oral history; adaptation of address, September 1966. L. Shores. il Library J 92:979-83 Mr 1 '67

Discovery: a study in audiovisual saturation; school libraries and Encyclopaedia Britannica films. L. Salinger. il Library J 92:849-52 F 15 '67

Equipment. il Library J 92:4599; 93:274 D 15 '67, Ja 15 '68

Highly adaptable package: homemade media kit to provide unit on Japan, in Pennsylvania department of public instruction. M. S. Plank and J. B. Scholl. bibliog il Library J 92:1714-17+ Ap 15 '67

Media librarian and a/v; school library programs. E. Geller. Library J 92:1683 Ap 15 '67

Million dollar carrels: Oak Park and River Forest, Ill. high school library; with report by L. Salinger. G. L. Schwilk. il Library J 92:306-10 Ja 15 '67

Small ways out of chaos; SLJ coverage of the audiovisual field. E. Geller. Library J 92: 4203 N 15 '67

SCHOOL libraries and social and economic problems. See Libraries and social and economic problems

SCHOOL libraries and state

Aid to parochial schools questioned in N.Y. suit; ESEA Title I suit expected to reach Supreme court. Library J 92:277 Ja 15 '67

ALA Washington notes: Brademas and Perkins bills: amendments to Elementary and secondary education act. G. Krettek and E. D. Cooke. Wilson Lib Bul 41:981 My '67

Bugbear of school library education; results of ESEA. J. Rowell; reply. M. Cheeseman. Library J 92:1681 Ap 15 '67

Church-state issue in federal aid to education; symposium. bibliog il Wilson Lib Bul 41:682-718 Mr '67; Discussion. 41:884-5, 1014-16; 42-20+, 273+ My-S, N '67

ESEA extension recommended. G. Krettek and E. D. Cooke. ALA Bul 61:464-6 My '67

ESEA House action pending. G. Krettek and E. D. Cooke. Wilson Lib Bul 41:1077 Je '67

ESEA House vote deferred. G. Krettek and E. D. Cooke. ALA Bul 61:619-20 Je '67

ESEA Title II the first year in review; Elementary and secondary education act of 1965. F. Stevens. Library J 92:311-12+ Ja 15 '67

ESEA to enter third year with increased funding probable. il Library J 92:3097-8 S 15 '67

First year of Title II; summary of address. S. Halperin. il Pub W 192:24-6 N 20 '67

Footnotes to the future. E. Geller. Library J 92:3785-6 O 15 '67

Libraries and Title I; Elementary and secondary education act of 1965. E. Geller. Library J 92:275 Ja 15 '67

Library emphasis continues in state Title II plans; state breakdowns of Title II spending, 1966 and 1967; school library resources. Library J 92:836-7 F 15 '67

New ESEA authorizations. E. Geller. Library J 93:247 Ja 15 '68

1968 education budget still under discussion; future of federal aid explored at D.C. briefing. il Library J 92:3789-92 O 15 '67

1968 OE budget tops 67's by a hair; most library-related programs remain firm; ESEA dominates requests; Title I shows library component. il Library J 92:1275-6+ Mr 15 '67

No student center for New York city either; letter to the editor. H. R. Sattley. Wilson Lib Bul 42:18-20 S '67

President's education proposals sent to Congress; summary, ed. by G. Krettek and E. D. Cooke. L. B. Johnson. Wilson Lib Bul 41:849 Ap '67

Senate ESEA hearings near conclusion; excerpts from testimony, August 15, 1967. ed. by G. Krettek and E. D. Cooke. C. P Bomar. Wilson Lib Bul 42:229 O '67

State aid to parochial schools upheld in New York decision. Library J 92:836 F 15 '67

Titles III: yet once more. J. A. Rowell. Library J 92:3823+ O 15 '67

Two year authorization bill gives ESEA $9.3 billion. Library J 93:249-50+ Ja 15 '68

View from the hill; Education act: second year. E. Geller. il Library J 82:313-17 Ja 15 '67

SCHOOL library Journal

Small ways out of chaos; SLJ coverage of the audiovisual field. E. Geller. Library J 92:4203 N 15 '67

SCHOOL library surveys

Changing attitudes toward the library and the librarian; survey results from two high schools in Knapp school libraries J. L. Walker. il ALA Bul 61:977-81 S '67

St Louis study assesses school librarian's role. Library J 92:3100+ S 15 '67

School paperback survey destroys some old notions. il Library J 92:3798-9 O 15 '67

SCHOOL management and organization

Advancement school; North Carolina kills its dream. D. Cooper. il Nation 206:77-9 Ja 15 '68

Can parents run New York's schools? decentralization experiment. T. R. Brooks. il Reporter 38:20-2 Ja 11 '68

Community control of our schools; Bundy report. J. Featherstone. New Repub 158:16-19 Ja 13 '68

DESP: design for educational change in the 70's; excerpts from address. April 1967. O. Sand. Sr Schol 90:sup2 My 5 '67

Educational tyranny and the ombudsman; protecting pupils and teachers. R. O. Werner.. Sch & Soc 95:391-2 O 28 '67

Give urban schools back to the people? McGeorge Bundy decentralization proposals. J. Cass. Sat R 50:55 D 16 '67

Historical context of educational administration; excerpt from Foundations of educational administration: a behavioral analysis. W. R. Lane and others. bibliog f Sch & Soc 94:482-92+ D 24 '66

Hottest spot in town; excerpt from Issues and problems in contemporary educational administration. K. Goldhammer. il Am Ed 3:2-4 O '67

Problems of school organization and administration. R. Dottrens. Sch & Soc 95:177-80 Mr 18 '67

Siege at the fortress school; decentralization. P. Schrag. Sat R 50:82 N 18 '67

What's wrong with our big-city schools. M. Mayer. il Sat Eve Post 240:21-3+ S 9 '67

See also
Cheating in schoolwork
Classroom management
Colleges and universities—Administration
Corporal punishment
Expulsion from school and college
School boards
School districts
School superintendents and principals
School year

Student participation

Teens sound off. J. Guernsey. il Am Ed 3:24-6+ S '67

SCHOOL management and organization—*Cont.*

Teacher participation

Claimant to power. Time 90:64 O 13 '67

Marvelous potential of professional negotiation. NEA J 56:28-9 N '67

NEA's digest of negotiation research; tables. R. R. Asnard and D. P. Walker. NEA J 56:34-5 S '67

Professional negotiation and grievance procedures. NEA J 56:39 O '67

Resolution on impasse in negotiation situations. NEA J 56:38-9 O '67

Teacher evaluates innovations. G. A. Griffin and J. Devlin. NEA J 56:26-8 D '67

Teacher peer relations and educational change. M. Chesler and R. Fox. NEA J 56:25-6 My '67

Teacher's quest for quality. P. A. Ellis and D. V. Meyer. NEA J 56:24-5 D '67

When the votes are counted. . . R. J. Flynn. NEA J 56:48+ My '67

SCHOOL music

See also

Bands, School

Caricatures and cartoons

School concert. Stevenson. New Yorker 42: 30-1 F 4 '67

SCHOOL of performing arts. See New York (city)—Education

SCHOOL of visual arts. See New York (city) —Education

SCHOOL organization. See School management and organization

SCHOOL partnership program. See School-to-school program

SCHOOL plays. See College and school drama

SCHOOL prayer. See Public schools and religion

SCHOOL principals. See School superintendents and principals

SCHOOL program of Lincoln Center. See Lincoln Center fund for education and artistic advancement

SCHOOL programs

Letter killeth. R. Coles. New Repub 157:19-23 N 4 '67

SCHOOL psychiatrists. See Psychiatrists

SCHOOL public relations. See School and the community

SCHOOL reports and records

Statement on confidentiality of student records; July 7, 1967. Sch & Soc 95:504-6 D 9 '67

What's happening to report cards. il Good H 164:193 My '67

SCHOOL secretaries

Confusions of a school secretary. A. Terrill. Parents Mag 42:88-9 S '67

Educational secretary in the elementary school. V. Riley. NEA J 56:40 F '67

SCHOOL statistics. See Education—Statistics

SCHOOL subjects. See Courses of study

SCHOOL superintendents and principals

Administrator and EDP; deciding on the adoption of a computer system. S. J. Knezevich. il NEA J 56:18-19 F '67

Administrator speaks out; interview. W. Pierce. Am Ed 3:27-9 F '67

Case of the pot-smoking school principal; Mrs G. Brennan of Nicasio, Calif. S. Alexander. Life 63:25 N 17 '67

On the causes of teacher discontent. P. Woodring. Sat R 50:61-2 O 21 '67

Teacher-administrator relationships in the local association; symposium. NEA J 56:49-52 F '67

What is a principal? R. Cline of Villa Heights elementary school, Charlotte, N.C. J. Poppy. il Look 31:34-40 O 17 '67

See also

National association of secondary-school principals

National education association—Department of elementary school principals

SCHOOL surveys. See Educational surveys

SCHOOL swimming pools. See Swimming pools

SCHOOL teachers. See Teachers

SCHOOL teaching. See Teaching

SCHOOL-to-school program

Building a school by long distance; School partnership program. il Sr Schol 91:8-9 N 16 '67

SCHOOL transportation. See School children—Transportation

SCHOOL vacations. See Vacations

SCHOOL volunteer program. See Volunteer workers in education

SCHOOL year

DESP: design for educational change in the 70's; excerpts from address, April 1967. O. Sand. Sr Schol 90:sup2 My 5 '67

Let's try year-round schools; with study discussion program. G. M. Jensen. il Parents Mag 42:33-4, 60-1+ S '67

See also

College year

SCHOOL yearbooks. See High school annuals

SCHOOLEY, Allen H.

Wake collapse in a stratified fluid. Science 157:421-3 Jl 28 '67

SCHOOLHOUSES. See School buildings

SCHOOLS

See also

Courses of study

Military schools

Negro schools

Nursery schools

Parochial schools, Catholic

Private schools

Public schools

School buildings

Trade schools

Statistics

See Education—Statistics

England

See also

Public schools (endowed)—England

United States

How good is your child's school? S. Dorros. il NEA J 56:37-52 S '67

See also

Education—United States

Public schools—United States

Rural schools—United States

SCHOOLS, Elementary. See Education, Elementary

SCHOOLS, Experimental

Advancement school: North Carolina kills its dream. D. Cooper. il Nation 206:77-9 Ja 15 '68

See also

Free universities

Friends world institute, New York

Reed college, Portland, Ore.

SCHOOLS, Medical. See Medical colleges

SCHOOLS, Traveling

Fun on wheels; mobile unit program of the San Pablo, Calif. recreation department. D. L. Howe. il Parents Mag 42:52-3+ Ap '67

SCHOOLS and libraries. See Libraries and schools

SCHOOLS and social and economic problems. See School and social and economic problems

SCHOOLS for American dependents abroad. See American schools abroad

SCHOOLS of nursing. See Nursing schools

SCHOONER racing. See Yacht racing

SCHOONERS

Reborn America. J. Gribbins. il Motor B 120: 36-7 Ag '67

Schooner America sails again. J. Gribbins. il Motor B 119:118-19+ Je '67

Three cheers for the America. R. J. Schaefer. il Am For 73:4-7+ S '67

Design

New America; full-size replica of the famous schooner. B. D. Barker, 3d. il Yachting 121: 70-2+ My '67

SCHOPF, J. William, and Barghoorn, E. S.

Alga-like fossils from the early Precambrian of South Africa. bibliog Science 156:508-12 Ap 28 '67

SCHORER, Mark

Substance of fiction; excerpts from The story: a critical anthology. Writer 80:14-18+ Je '67

SCHORR, Daniel

Shaky legs in Bonn. Sat R 50:28-30 D 16 '67

SCHORR, Friedrich

Historical records. A. Favia-Artsay. por Hobbies 72:33 Ag '67

SCHORRE, Charles

Art directing & everything; address, January 15, 1967. Am Artist 31:26+ Ap '67

SCHORSKE, Carl E.

Transformation of the garden: ideal and society in Austrian literature; address, September 1965. bibliog f Am Hist R 72: 1283-320 Jl '67

SCHOTT, Webster

Civil rights and the homosexual. N Y Times Mag p44-5+ N 12 '67

Life book review (cont) Life 62:17 F 17; 18 Ap 7; 63:8 S 15; 8+ D 8 '67

SCHOTTLAND, Charles I.
Battle line of welfare: the hungry can't wait. Nation 204:649-52 My 22 '67
SCHRAEMLI, Harry
Food of love; tr. by F. Merkling. Opera N 32:6-7 D 30 '67
SCHRAG, Peter
Education in America. Sat R 50:49-50 Je 17 '67
Education's romantic critics. Sat R 50:80-2+ F 18 '67
Golden age, the gathering gloom. Sat R 50: 58-62+ S 23 '67
Homecoming. Reporter 37:44+ N 30 '67
Kids, computers, and corporations. Sat R 50: 78-80+ My 20 '67
Notre Dame: our first great Catholic university. Harper 234:41-9 My '67
Teachers college: John Dewey with a hard nose. Sat R 50:62-4+ D 16 '67
University: power and innocence. Sat R 50: 68-9+ O 21 '67
Voices in the classroom (cont) Sat R 50:92 F 18; 60 Mr 18; 75 Ap 15; 63 Je 17; 66 Jl 15; 61 Ag 19; 87 S 16; 82 N 18 '67
SCHRAGE, Chuck
Is USPS for me? Yachting 123:54 Ja '68
What USPS means. Yachting 121:57 Ja '67
With the power squadrons. See issues of Yachting
SCHRAMM, Harold
Opera and India. Opera N 32:8-12 O 14 '67
SCHREIBER, Flora Rheta
What youngsters' questions tell us. Todays Health 45:34-7 N '67
—and Herman, Melvin
Family is the patient. Sci Digest 61:65-9 Je '67
Help in a crisis. Sci Digest 61:18-22 Mr '67
How to drive your family crazy. Sci Digest 62:65-9 N '67
LSD, one way trip for alcoholics? Sci Digest 62:60-4 Jl '67
Tell your troubles to the group. Sci Digest 61:60-4 My '67
Why people riot. Sci Digest 62:56-60 O '67
SCHREIBER, Jean Jacques Servan-. See Servan-Schreiber, J. J.
SCHREIDER, Frank. See Schreider, H. jt. auth.
SCHREIDER, Helen, and Schreider, Frank
In the footsteps of Alexander the Great. il Nat Geog Mag 133:1-65 Ja '68
SCHREIER, Peter
Dresden tenor; interview, ed. by J. W. Freeman. por Opera N 32:16 Ja 6 '68
SCHREINER, David
Packer snapper. U S Camera 30:60-1+ N '67
SCHREK, Robert, and others
L-Asparaginase: toxicity to normal and leukemic human lymphocytes. bibliog Science 155:329-30 Ja 20 '67
SCHRIEVER, Bernard A.
Military technology and the Great society. por Tech W 20:63-5 Ja 23 '67
Technological forecasts: excerpts from address. Aviation W 87:21 D 4 '67
U.S. space program; address, May 15, 1967. Vital Speeches 34:26-8 O 15 '67
SCHRÖDER, Gerhard
Problem for LBJ: feud between top Germans. U S News 63:16 Ag 21 '67
SCHROEDER, Eva M.
Shrubby clematis for perennial gardens. Home Gard 54:57 Mr '67
Space-saving idea: onions among my tulips. Home Gard 54:69 My '67
SCHROEDER, Fred W. Jr
Reconstructing a Flying Dutchman. Yachting 121:74-5+ Ja '67
SCHROEDER, Lynn. See Ostrander, S. jt. auth.
SCHROEDER, R. J.
Stage. Commonweal 86:208-10 My 5 '67
SCHROTH, Raymond A.
Between the lines. See occasional issues of America
Detroit, 1967. America 117:151-3 Ag 12 '67
Of many things. America 117:inside cover Jl 8 '67
Philadelphia, farewell. America 116:176 F 4 '67
Redemption of Malcolm X. por Cath World 205:346-52 S '67
Self-doubt and black pride. America 116:502-5, 664-5 Ap 1, My 6 '67
SCHUBEL, Max
Op. 1 from Opus one. J. Diether. Am Rec G 33:498 F '67
SCHUBERT, Franz Peter
Records:
Twenty songs. Opera N 31:34 F 25 '67
Winterreise, six songs. Opera N 31:32 Mr 4 '67
Schubert onstage. D. Vaughan. il pors Opera N 32:8-12 Ja 6 '68

Very difficult to resist: Schubert by Wunderlich. H. Glass. Am Rec G 33:634-5 Ap '67
SCHUBERT, Gerald. See Goldreich, P. jt. auth.
SCHUBERT, Jack, and White, E. R.
Radiation of hemocyanin: inactivation and reactivation of oxygen-carrying capacity. bibliog Science 155:1000-3 F 24 '67
SCHUGAR, Leonard
Color at work. il Pop Phot 61:104-5 Jl '67
SCHULBERG, Budd
Biased course in Cohnology. Life 62:11+ Mr 3 '67
It could happen in the schools; interview, ed. by J. Colmenares. NEA J 56:19 D '67

about
Dateline Watts: from the ashes, a solution. A. Nevins. il Sat R 50:79 S 23 '67
SCHULER, Stanley
How to give a child a rare vacation. Am Home 70:54+ Je '67
How to water for greener lawns and gardens. Am Home 70:52+ My '67
New chemicals make the garden behave. House B 109:174+ S '67
Play host to foreign visitors. Am Home 70: 48+ N '67
SCHULLER, Gunther
And we quote; interview, ed. by B. Jacobson. por Hi Fi 17:MA18 S '67
Is opera dead? Opera N 31:8-12 Je 10 '67

about
Thinking big. il por Time 90:84 N 10 '67
Visitation. Criticism
Hi Fi il 18:MA18-19 Ja '68
Life 62:11 Je 30 '67
New Repub 157:32 Jl 15 '67
Sat R 50:39+ Jl 15 '67
SCHULTHESS, Emil
U.S. camera achievement award. por U S Camera 30:40 N '67
SCHULTZ, Barbara
Writing for television. Writer 80:17-18+ My '67
SCHULTZ, Carol
Exciting new products. Pop Mech 127:150-1 My; 166-7 Je '67
SCHULTZ, Gwen
Look to the sun before you plan. Pop Gard 18:40-5+ Mr '67
This fall, don't desert your garden. Pop Gard 18:6-7+ D '67
SCHULTZ, Jerry
Hiphazard Happening. Time 89:89 Ap 21 '67
SCHULTZ, Morton J.
Electronic wonders for better living. Sci Digest 61:37-47 Je '67
Exotic fuels will power tomorrow. Sci Digest 62:45-52 O '67
Giant size prints. U S Camera 30:54-5+ Ap '67
How you can find those hidden causes of engine overheating. Pop Mech 127:140-3+ Je '67
Look what they're doing with glass. Sci Digest 62:44-7+ Jl '67
Plastics: the raw material for nearly everything. Sci Digest 62:45-53 Ag '67
Saturday mechanic. See issues of Popular mechanics
VC firepower, can we match it? Pop Mech 127:97-101+ Je '67
Your steering linkage. Pop Mech 127:164-7+ Mr '67
SCHULTZ, R. E.
Buffet? dining table? here are both in one. Pop Sci 191:165-9 N '67
SCHULTZ, R. Jack
Gynogenesis and triploidy in the Viviparous fish poeciliopsis. bibliog Science 157:1564-7 S 29 '67
SCHULTZ, William J. See Stettner, L. J. jt. auth.
SCHULTZE, Charles Louis
Excerpt from testimony before Joint economic committee of U.S. Congress, February 3, 1967. Cong Digest 46:118+ Ap '67
High officials argue over taxes, spending, inflation; excerpts from hearing before the House ways and means committee, November 30, 1967. por U S News 63:90-2 D 18 '67
President urges action on funds for southeast Asia operations; text of letter to the President; January 24, 1967. Dept State Bul 56: 237 F 13 '67

about
Charlie Schultze's $135 billion book. H. Sidey. il Life 62:32B F 10 '67
Manner of their going. Time 91:14 Ja 19 '68
SCHULTZE, Norbert
When Lilli went to war, for both sides. D. Jewell. il por N Y Times Mag p52-3+ N 19 '67

SCHULZ, Charles M.
New Peanuts happiness book; excerpt. il Mc-
Calls 95:90-1 O '67
Redbook dialogue. por Redbook 130:50-1+ D
'67
That doggone Crosby. il Sports Illus 28:28-33
Ja 8 '68

about

Enough is a warm too much; little books.
W. K. Zinsser. Look 31:11 F 21 '67
Inept heroes, winners at last; with report by
J. Borgzinner. il pors Life 62:74-8+ Mr 17
'67
You're a good man, Charlie Schulz. B. Conrad.
il por N Y Times Mag p32-5+ Ap 16 '67

SCHULZ, William
Great research boondoggle. Read Digest 90:
91-6 Mr '67
Mike Kirwan's big ditch. Read Digest 90:59-
64 Je '67
Our alarming police shortage. Read Digest
92:75-80 Ja '68

SCHÜTZ, Klaus
Problems for a protégé. il por Time 90:34-5
O 27 '67

SCHUMM, S. A.
Meander wavelength of alluvial rivers. bib-
liog Science 157:1549-50 S 29 '67
Rates of surficial rock creep on hillslopes in
western Colorado. bibliog Science 155:560-2
F 3 '67

SCHUSTERMAN, Ronald J.
Attention shift and errorless reversal learning by the California sea lion. bibliog Science 156:833-5 My 12 '67

SCHUTZER, Paul
Found: Paul Schutzer's final twenty-three
frames; photographs. Life 62:30-32A Je 23
'67

about

In memory of Paul Schutzer. G. P. Hunt. por
Life 62:3 Je 16 '67
Photographer's death, his last photographs.
M. Mok. Life 62:34 Je 16 '67

SCHUYLER, George
Blame for the riots as a Negro writer sees
it; reprint. U S News 63:10 Ag 14 '67

SCHUYLER, James
Immediacy is the message. Art N 66:32-3+
Mr '67
Joe Brainard; quotes and notes. por Art N
66:56-7+ Ap '67
Lenore Tawney. Craft Horiz 27:20-5 N '67

SCHUYLER, Keith C.
Selecting a bow for the target archer. Consumer Bul 50:15-18 Je '67

SCHUYLER, Philippa Duke
Americans not everyone knows. C. W. Ferguson. il por PTA Mag 62:12-14 D '67
Philippa Schuyler, RIP. Nat R 19:559 My 30
'67

SCHWALBERG, Bob
Cartier-Bresson today. Pop Phot 60:108-9+
My '67

SCHWALBERG, Carol
Camera collectors and why they grow. U S
Camera 30:48-9+ S '67
Focus on: Wayne Miller. il Pop Phot 60:88-9+
Mr '67
Minute that took fifteen hours. U S Camera
30:66-7+ O '67
R: bel canto. Opera N 32:16 D 30 '67
(ed) See Watson, P. Face to face with a girl
who swims everywhere

SCHWARTZ, Arthur
Something to remember them by. I. Kolodin.
il por Sat R 50:60 F 11 '67

SCHWARTZ, Benjamin I.
Upheaval in China. Commentary 43:55-62 F '67

SCHWARTZ, Daniel
Two-year-old summer; paintings. McCalls
94:72-7 My '67

SCHWARTZ, Fred
Ceramist as educator; excerpts from address,
April 15, 1967. Craft Horiz 27:16-17+ Jl '67
Glen Kaufman. il Craft Horiz 27:14-16 Ja '67

SCHWARTZ, Harry
Look through the bamboo curtain. Sat R
50:51-2 My 6 '67
People and the presidium. Sat R 50:33-4 F
18 '67
Restraining the red generals. Sat R 50:40 Jl
22 '67
Russia & China. Horizon 10:4-21 Wint '68

SCHWARTZ, Herman
Wiretapping and eavesdropping; pros and
cons. bibliog f Cur Hist 53:31-7 Jl '67

SCHWARTZ, Jonathan
Gypsy student; story. Seventeen 26:154-5 Ap
'67

SCHWARTZ, Judith
Two-year-old summer; poem. McCalls 94:72-7
My '67

SCHWARTZ, Lester J. See Peets, C. O. jt. auth.

SCHWARTZ, Marvin D.
More English silver in the Morrison collection. Antiques 91:228-32 F '67

SCHWARTZ, Morton
What Moscow's Washington-watchers see.
N Y Times Mag p50-1+ O 8 '67

SCHWARTZ, Robert, and others
Fake panaceas for ghetto education. New
Repub 157:16-9 S 23 '67
Is desegregation impractical? New Repub 158:
27-9 Ja 6 '68

SCHWARTZ, Tony
Sound for photographers. See issues of Popular photography

SCHWARZKOPF, Elisabeth
Disappearing art. R. Gelatt. Reporter 36:38-
9 My 4 '67

SCHWEBEL, Milton
Theory of educability. bibliog f Sch & Soc
95:306-9 Sum '67

SCHWEICH, Elise
Miss Leesy's magic. W. D. Cook. il por Am
Ed 3:8-10 N '67

SCHWEITZER, Albert
Theodor Binder: Peru's Albert Schweitzer.
A. J. Carley. il Américas 19:1-7 Mr '67

SCHWEITZER, Gertrude
My child is missing; story. Good H 164:62-3
Ja '67
This time tomorrow; story. Good H 165:
79-81 S '67

SCHWEITZER, S. O.
New evidence on problems of reemployment.
bibliog f Mo Labor R 90:12-14 Ag '67

SCHWERIN research corporation
Great TV commercial war; advertising copy-
writer vs advertising-testing corporations. S.
Blum. il N Y Times Mag p32-3+ Ap 9 '67

SCHWETZINGEN festival. See Music festivals
—Germany (Federal Republic)

SCHWEYK in the second World war; drama.
See Brecht, B.

SCHWIEBERT, Ernest
Fishing in the land of fire. pors Field & S
72:48-9+ N '67
Where fishing is a blood sport. Esquire 68:
126-7+ O '67

SCHWILK, Gene L.
Million dollar carrels. Library J 92:306-10 Ja
15 '67

SCHWINN, Arnold and company
When bicycle maker peddles alone; Supreme
court decision concerning Schwinn's marketing systems. Bsns W p39-40 Jl 1 '67

SCIENCE
Beyond Vietnam: what has science to say to
man? symposium. il Sat R 50:39-50 Jl 1; 49-
52 Ag 5; 68 N 4 '67
Books and libraries in the scientific age;
adaptation of address; January 9, 1967. H.
Wooster. bibliog il Library J 92:2511-15 Jl
'67
Isaac Asimov explains (cont of) Please ex-
plain; questions and answers. See issues
of Science digest
New voice of science. H. Downs. Sci Digest
61:83-6 Mr '67
Physical sciences notes. See issues of Science
news
Science and scientists; excerpts from address,
September 1, 1965. C. Hinshelwood. Bul
Atomic Sci 23:31-6 Je '67
Science jungle; frenetic and frustrating. P.
Saltman. Harper 234:102-4 F '67
Science map and guide to the U.S. L.
Thomas. il Pop Sci 190:59-63+ Je '67
Seeing is deceiving; facts disputing tradi-
tional beliefs in folk customs and science.
L. Rosten. Look 31:10 My 2 '67
See also
American association for the advancement of
science
Communication in science
Inventions
Natural history
Research
Technology
also headings beginning Scientific

Authorship

See Technical writing

Awards and prizes

Matthew effect in science; address, August
1967. R. K. Merton. bibliog Science 159:56-63
Ja 5 '68

Bibliography

Book reviews. See issues of Science
Books to come; ed. by J. Putnam. Library J
92:1037-62+, 2611-41, 4033-63 Mr 1, Jl, N 1
'67
Science, technology: highspots. il Pub W 191:
42-58 Ap 10 '67

SCIENCE—Bibliography
Science, technology; November-March highspots. il Pub W 192:31-46 N '67
Scientific and technical books of 1966; one hundred outstanding titles for a general collection; comp. by R. L. Snyder. il Library J 92:969-73 Mr 1 '67

Experiments
See also
Physics—Experiments

Federal aid
See Research—Federal aid

Fiction
See Science fiction

History
Scientific profession in early nineteenth-century America; excerpt from American science in the age of Jackson. G. H. Daniels. bibliog Sch & Soc 95:523-36 D 23 '67
Spread of western science. G. Basalla. bibliog il Science 156:611-22 My 5 '67; Reply. C. S. Smith. 156:1438-9 Je 16 '67

International aspects
Anthropologists' debate: concern over future of foreign research. B. Nelson; discussion. Science 156:1032-5, 157:251-2 My 26, Jl 21 '67
Baedeker for scientists; European laboratories visited by Americans. E. Langer. Science 156:228 Ap 14 '67
Environmental pollution; West Germany, U.S. cooperate. J. Walsh. Science 157:529-31 Ag 4 '67
Fine idea, if... Nation 204:772-3 Je 19 '67
Foreign scientists advise. Sci N 91:58 Ja 21 '67
Hemispheric science. il Sci N 91:401 Ap 29 '67
International biological program. R. Revelle. Science 155:957 F 24 '67
Molecular biology: U.S. and Italy to establish new graduate school. J. Walsh. il Science 156:1582-3 Je 23 '67
Naples station: crisis Italian style at marine biology center. J. Walsh. il Science 156:1066-71 My 26 '67
Natural resources: U.S. and Japan work together. K. Sperry. Science 157:530 Ag 4 '67
Particle physics: new talk of East-West ties. D. S. Greenberg. Science 156:1069 My 26 '67
Radio astronomy; conflict of frequencies; letter. G. W. Swenson, jr. and R. N Bracewell. Science 155:518+ F 3 '67
Research in Japan: U.S. army grants cause controversy. P. M. Boffey. Science 158:748-52 N 10 '67
Science and disarmament. P. Noel-Baker. bibliog f il UNESCO Courier 20:10-21+ Ag '67
Science and foreign affairs; address, January 24, 1967. D. Rusk. Dept State Bul 56:238-42 F 13 '67
Science policy: committee studies international aspects. D. S. Greenberg. Science 155:547 F 3 '67
What's ahead for international science? adaptation of address, September 13, 1966. G. T. Seaborg. il Bul Atomic Sci 23:24-8 Ja '67
See also
Joint United States-Japan committee on scientific cooperation
North Atlantic treaty organization—Science committee
United States—State, Department of—International scientific and technological affairs, Office of

Juvenile literature
See Scientific literature for children

Nomenclature
Vague identities exasperate; letter. C. A. Reed. Science 157:373 Ag 25 '67; Discussion. 158:995-6, 1525 N 24, D 22 '67

Religious aspects
See Religion and science

Social aspects
Man must first choose goals. G. T. Seaborg. il Tech W 20:32-5 Ja 23 '67
Peace on earth: the position of the scientists; statement, May 1967. L. Pauling. Bul Atomic Sci 23:46-8 O '67
Research comparisons; some limitations of international comparisons. C. Freeman. bibliog il Science 158:463-8 O 27 '67
Science turns to challenge of satisfying human needs. S. Ramo. Tech W 20:78-9 Ja 23 '67
Scientists alone can't do the job; excerpts from addresses, September 1967. R. J. Dubos. il Sat R 50:68-71 D 2 '67

Study and teaching
College scene (cont) il Sci Digest 61:25 F '67
Colleges in action. See issues of Science digest
Cross-cultural teaching of science. F. E. Dart and P. L. Pradhan. bibliog il Science 155:649-56 F 10 '67; Reply. G. H. Bartlett, jr. 156:12+ Ap 7 '67
Education comes alive outdoors. R. M. Isenberg. il NEA J 56:34-5 Ap '67
McGraw-Hill offers packaged science program; Science package project to be funded by USOE. il Library J 92:1286-7 Mr 15 '67
Pain & progress in discovery. il Time 90:110+ D 8 '67
See also
Science students
Scientific education
also subhead Study and teaching under names of sciences, e.g. Physics—Study and teaching

Terminology
Fuzziness of fuzz; letter. J. F. A. McManus. Science 157:490-1 Ag 4 '67

Africa
Science and technology in Africa. G. E. A. Lardner. Bul Atomic Sci 23:36-9 Je '67; Reply. M. Dow. 23:42-3 O '67

Africa, East
East Africa: science for development. T. R. Odhiambo. bibliog il Science 158:876-81 N 17 '67

Africa, West
Tale of two nations: Nigeria and Ghana work to recreate basic science organizations. C. Weiss, jr. Sci N 91:460-1 My 13 '67

Canada
See also
Research—Canada

China
Science and civilization in China, by J. Needham. Review; with excerpts
Horizon il 10:52-63 Wint '68. D. J. de S. Price

China (People's Republic)
Mainland China: an emerging power. P. H. Abelson. Science 157:373 Jl 28 '67

Cuba
Biologist visits Cuba. G. C. Gorman. Science 156:889 My 19 '67

Europe, Eastern
See also
Council for economic mutual assistance

France
Some new targets defined for French science policy. J. Walsh. Science 156:626-30 My 5 '67

Great Britain
British science policy: the case for growth. J. Walsh. Science 158:1030-1 N 24 '67
Molecular biology: British groups push enzyme-structure studies. N. Calder. Science 156:367-9 Ap 21 '67
Their decision-making process bothers some of the British. J. Walsh. Science 155:1654-6 Mr 31 '67

Italy
Naples station: crisis Italian style at marine biology center. J. Walsh. il Science 156:1066-71 My 26 '67

Latin America
Doctor Killian notes progress in Latin American science program. Dept State Bul 57:717 N 27 '67
Scientific explorers in Latin America. E. Uzcátegui. il Américas 19:3-11 Jl '67

Russia
Science: first-rate, also second best. il Newsweek 70:47 O 23 '67
700,000 scientists in the U.S.S.R. in 1967. M. A. Lavrent'ev. il UNESCO Courier 20:31-2+ N '67
Siberia's oasis for scientists; Academic town: Akademgorodok. il Bsns W p74-6+ Jl 22 '67
Soviet genetics: first Russian visit since 1930's offers a glimpse. E. Langer. il Science 157:1153 S 8 '67; Reply. T. Dobzhansky. 158:577 N 3 '67

South Africa
Science in South Africa: the effects of apartheid. E. Langer. Science 155:1387-9 Mr 17 '67

SCIENCE—*Continued*

Switzerland
Training for engineering and technology in Switzerland; excerpt from Science in Switzerland. J. M. Luck. bibliog f il Sch & Soc 94:499-502 D 24 '66

Underdeveloped areas
Ever widening gap; address, December 27, 1966. P. M. S. Blackett. bibliog Science 155: 959-64 F 24 '67; Discussion. 156:314+, 1312-13 Ap 21, Je 9 '67

SCIENCE (periodical)
Instructions for contributors. Science 158: 1709-10 D 29 '67
Readers' judgment. D. Wolfle. Science 156: 1181 Je 2 '67
Upward spiral of costs and dues; letter with reply. E. B. Hook; D. Wolfle. Science 158:854-5 N 17 '67

SCIENCE, Ethics of. See Scientists, Professional ethics for

SCIENCE, Freedom of
AEC proposals, a threat to scientific freedom. H. P. Green. Bul Atomic Sci 23:15-17 O '67
Classified research in the university; statement and recommended guidelines, July 29, 1967. Bul Atomic Sci 23:45-6 O '67

SCIENCE adviser, Office of. See United States—State, Department of—International scientific and technological affairs, Office of

SCIENCE advisory committee. See United States—President's science advisory committee

SCIENCE and art. See Art and science

SCIENCE and civilization
American scientist: man or superman? M. Gunther. il Sat Eve Post 240:30-6+ D 16 '67
American transition. Z. Brzezinski. New Republic 157:18-21 D 23 '67
Applied science. P. H. Abelson. Science 156:1555 Je 23 '67
Cross-cultural teaching of science. F. E. Dart and P. L. Pradhan. bibliog il Science 155: 649-56 F 10 '67; Reply. G. H. Bartlett, jr. 156:12+ Ap 7 '67
Epitaph for an age; reprint. J. W. Krutch. il N Y Times Mag p 10-11+ Jl 30 '67; Discussion. p4+ Ag 13; 10+ Ag 20 '67
Ever widening gap; address, December 27, 1966. P. M. S. Blackett. bibliog Science 155: 959-64 F 24 '67; Discussion. 156:314+, 1312-13 Ap 21, Je 9 '67
History of mankind; excerpts. il UNESCO Courier 20:4-31 Ny '67
LBJ: praise for the value of research. D. S. Greenberg. Science 156:625 My 5 '67
Moral sense of the scientists. J. V. Reistrup. Science 155:271 Ja 20 '67
On Max Born's reflections. L. Williams. Bul Atomic Sci 23:27-8 F '67
Organization of inquiry, by G. Tullock. Review Nat R 19:645+ Je 13 '67. W. J. Holman, 3d
Pure-science ideal and democratic culture. G. H. Daniels. bibliog Science 156:1699-705 Je 30 '67
Revolution is here. H. Pryor. il Sci Digest 61:13-17 Mr '67
Science education today, public policy tomorrow. A. B. Grobman. il NEA J 56:8-10 Mr '67
Science, technology, and change. J. McHale. bibliog f il Ann Am Acad 373:120-40 S '67
Shall we play God? L. Augenstein. Christian Cent 84:1314-18 O 18 '67; Reply. C. W. Kirkpatrick. 84:1571 D 6 '67
Weather modification: implications of the new horizons in research; excerpts from address, December 28, 1966. T. F. Malone. bibliog Science 156:897-901 My 19 '67
What man can make of man: genetic programing; competence of biologists to determine the optimal genotype. K. H. Hertz. Christian Cent 84:807-10 Je 21 '67

SCIENCE and industry. See Industrial research

SCIENCE and religion. See Religion and science

SCIENCE and society. See Science and civilization

SCIENCE and state
Air force: study relates troubled relationship with research. D. S. Greenberg. Science 156:1463-6 Je 16 '67; Reply. L. Edson. 157:877 Ag 25 '67
Battery additives: AID's chagrin. D. S. Greenberg. Science 156:627 My 5 '67
Congress faces space policies. E. Q. Daddario. Bul Atomic Sci 23:11-16 My '67
Cross-cultural research and government policy. R. L. Beals. Bul Atomic Sci 23:18-24 O '67

Epitaph for an age; reprint. J. W. Krutch. il N Y Times Mag p 10-11+ Jl 30 '67; Discussion. p4+ Ag 13; 10+ Ag 20 '67
Federal paper-work explosion; new form bothers universities. B. Nelson. Science 156:1468-9 Je 16 '67
Federal science policy; excerpts from address, December 30, 1966. P. Handler. Science 155:1063-6 Mr 3 '67
Hindsight: DOD study examines return on investment in research. D. S. Greenberg; discussion. Science 155:397-8; 157:1512; 159:34 Ja 27, S 29 '67, Ja 5 '68
Hornig on research policy: public understanding essential to scientific progress; excerpts from address, April 26, 1967. D. F. Hornig. Science 156:628-9 My 5 '67
In science policy, who holds the power? Sci N 91:326 Ap 8 '67
It's time for science to act its political age; excerpts from address, December 1966. D. S. Greenberg. Bul Atomic Sci 23:36-7 O '67
Naples station: crisis Italian style at marine biology center. J. Walsh. il Science 156:1066-71 My 26 '67
Office of science and technology. P. H. Abelson. Science 156:173 Ap 14 '67
Politics of pure science. D. S. Greenberg. il Sat R 50:62-9 N 4 '67
Proposal for an institution for scientific judgment; excerpts from report to U.S. Senate, March 16, 1967. A. Kantrowitz. Science 156:763-4 My 12 '67
Pure-science ideal and democratic culture. G. H. Daniels. bibliog Science 156:1699-705 Je 30 '67
Research and development in Communist China. L. A. Orleans. bibliog il Science 157:392-400 Jl 28 '67
Science, foreign affairs, and the State department; address, May 17, 1967. H. Pollack. Dept State Bul 56:910-17 Je 19 '67
Science, technology, and American foreign policy, by E. B. Skolnikoff. Review Sat R 50:62 Je 10 '67. K. W. Thompson
Senate declines change. Sci N 91:86 Ja 28 '67
Some new targets defined for French science policy. J. Walsh. Science 156:626-30 My 5 '67
Their decision-making process bothers some of the British. J. Walsh. Science 155:1654-6 Mr 31 '67
200 bev: harmony prevails as physicists close ranks. D. S. Greenberg. Science 155:983-5 F 24 '67
University basic research. L. A. DuBridge. Science 157:648-50 Ag 11 '67
Weather modification: implications of the new horizons in research; excerpts from address, December 28, 1966. T. F. Malone. bibliog Science 156:897-901 My 19 '67
See also
Research—Federal aid

SCIENCE and the humanities
Links between the humanities and the literature of the human sciences. I. Bry and L. Afflerbach. Wilson Lib Bul 42:510-25 Ja '68
Technological know-how plus know-what; bridging the gulf. Life 62:4 Ap 7 '67
Unity in a university: the two cultures; address, April 25, 1967. C. M. Allen. Vital Speeches 33:730-4 S 15 '67

SCIENCE and war. See War and science

SCIENCE as a profession
Rarest, most precious vital force; preamble of memorandum, June 16, 1926. M. Curie. UNESCO Courier 20:16-17 O '67
Scientific profession in early nineteenth-century America; excerpt from American science in the age of Jackson. G. H. Daniels. bibliog Sch & Soc 95:523-36 D 23 '67

SCIENCE books for children. See Scientific literature for children

SCIENCE citation index
Citation indexing and evaluation of scientific papers. J. Margolis. bibliog il Science 155:1213-19 Mr 10 '67; Discussion. 156:890+ My 19 '67

SCIENCE city. See Akademgorodok, Siberia

SCIENCE clubs of America
See also
Science talent search

SCIENCE drama
Book that saved the earth. C. Boiko. Plays 27:37-42 Ja '68

SCIENCE fairs
International fair opens in San Francisco. P. McBroom. il Sci N 91:452 My 13 '67

SCIENCE fiction
Dreams of tomorrow. R. B. Riley. il Arch Forum 126:66-7+ Ap '67
Evolution and ideation; twenty-fifth annual World science fiction convention. New Yorker 43:38 S 16 '67

SCIENTISTS—*Continued*

Ethics
See Scientists, Professional ethics for

Political activities
Partisan attack on research. P. H. Abelson. Science 156:1315 Je 9 '67; Discussion. 157:368 Jl 28 '67
Scientists and engineers for L.B.J: a war and three years later. E. Langer. Science 157: 1533-6 S 29 '67
Scientists and engineers for McCarthy. P. M. Boffey. Science 158:1554 D 22 '67
Scientists and government decisions; Unesco symposium. Sch & Soc 95:378-9 O 28 '67
Scientists in foreign affairs: where do we go now? adaptation of address, April 1966. F. A. Long. il Bul Atomic Sci 23:14-18 Mr '67
Smale case: tracing the path that led to NSF's decision. D. S. Greenberg. Science 157:1536-9 S 29 '67

Public relations
Money for research: LBJ's advisers urge scientists to seek public support. D. S. Greenberg. il Science 156:920-2 My 19 '67; Discussion. 157:134+ Jl 14 '67

Supply and demand
Brain drain. D. Wolfle; discussion. Science 155:513-14+, 1361; 156:1030+ F 3, Mr 17, My 26 '67
Brain drain: foreign aid for U.S. il U S News 62:78-81 My 22 '67
Brain drain: how poor nations give to the rich. W. F. Mondale. Sat R 50:24-6 Mr 11 '67
Brain drain refrain. Sci N 91:281 Mr 25 '67
Brain drain; the sound and the fury. il Sci N 91:255-6 Mr 18 '67
Brains across the sea. R. Schiller. Read Digest 90:72-6 Mr '67
British brain drain doubled in six years, survey finds. H. J. Coleman. Aviation W 87: 62-3+ O 30 '67
Fewer brains hear U.S.A.'s siren song. il Bsns W p 100+ My 27 '67
Help wanted: engineers and scientists. R. Schiller. Read Digest 90:193-4+ F '67
India's brain drain. Sch & Soc 95:57-8+ Ja 21 '67
Military research: a decline in the interest of scientists? B. Nelson. Science 156:364-6 Ap 21 '67
Mr Brain drain; New York firm's London recruiting drives. il Life 62:101-2 Mr 17 '67
Route to the top: government to campus. D. S. Greenberg. Science 156:1352 Je 9 '67
Wealth attracts talent: taking creative talent from growing societies. R. Jorrin. Nation 204:425-7 Ap 3 '67
White paper on brain drain; Japanese science and technology. M. Cohen. Sci N 93:76 Ja 20 '68
Why U.S. is lure for Britain's brains. U S News 63:12+ O 23 '67

SCIENTISTS, African
Today's schools prepare tomorrow's African scientists. N. C. Otieno. il UNESCO Courier 20:33-6 Je '67

SCIENTISTS, American
American scientist: man or superman? M. Gunther. il Sat Eve Post 240:30-6+ D 16 '67
See also
Federation of American scientists

SCIENTISTS, British
See also
Davy, H.

SCIENTISTS, Canadian
Is a great tradition eroding? D. Rose and J. Marier. il Sat R 50:53-7 S 2 '67

SCIENTISTS, Chinese
See also
Tsien, H. S.

SCIENTISTS, Exchange of. See Exchange of persons programs

SCIENTISTS, Japanese
Brain drain touches lightly; conditions in Japan. S. Griffin. Sci N 91:480-1 My 20 '67

SCIENTISTS, Professional ethics for
Anthropologists overwhelmingly approve research ethics statement. B. Nelson. Science 156:365 Ap 21 '67
P-M bomb. L. Cranberg. Bul Atomic Sci 23: 37-40 D '67
Privacy and behavioral research; preliminary summary of the report of the panel on privacy and behavioral research. Science 155:535-8 F 3 '67

SCIENTISTS, Russian
700,000 scientists in the U.S.S.R. in 1967. M. A. Lavrent'ev. il UNESCO Courier 20:31-2+ N '67
See also
Kurchatov, I. V.

SCIENTISTS as astronauts. See Astronauts

SCILLY ISLANDS
England's Scillies, the flowering isles. A. Villiers. il Nat Geog Mag 132:126-45 Jl '67

SCIMENS, Mike T.
Courthouse sets the tone of community beautification. Am City 82:129 O '67

SCINDIA, Vijaya Raje, maharani
End of the maharajas. F. Levine. Atlan 219: 112-14 Ap '67

SCLERAL lenses. See Contact lenses

SCLEROSIS, Multiple
Day I stopped worrying about tomorrow. Redbook 129:8+ My '67
MS clue. Sci N 91:472 My 20 '67

SCOFIELD, Nanette E.
So your mother is going to work. Seventeen 26:362+ Ag '67

SCOFIELD reference Bible. See Bible—Versions

SCOGGIN, Margaret C.
(comp) Outlook tower. See issues of Horn book magazine

SCOLIOSIS. See Spine—Abnormities and deformities

SCONCES. See Candlesticks

SCONES
Scones to bake on a "girdle"; with recipes. il Sunset 139:90 Jl '67

SCOOTERS. See Ice boats and ice boating; Motor scooters

SCOOTERS, Childrens
Build a sail-powered winter skater: summer scooter. il Pop Mech 128:152-3 N '67

SCOPES, John Thomas
Editor's bookshelf. P. Woodring. por Sat R 50:64 Mr 18 '67
John T. Scopes redividus. Christian Cent 84:429 Ap 5 '67
Monkey trial. J. W. Krutch. Commentary 43:83-4 My '67

SCOPES. See Oscillographs

SCOPES trial. See Tennessee evolution controversy

SCORE project. See United States—Small business administration

SCORGIE, Helen C.
Enjoy the many forms of daffodils. Horticulture 45:20-1 Ag '67

SCORPIONS
Venom of the scorpion vejovis spinigerus. F. E. Russell and others. bibliog il Science 159:90-1 Ja 5 '68

SCOTCH literature. See Scottish literature

SCOTCH PLAINS, N.J.
Take special care of your equipment. A. Milton. il Am City 82:108-9 S '67

SCOTFORD, John R.
Aftermath of the church building boom. Christian Cent 84:1650-3 D 27 '67

SCOTLAND
North rises again. il Time 90:42+ N 10 '67
See also
Architecture—Scotland
Booksellers and bookselling—Scotland
Education—Scotland
Hunting—Scotland

Home rule
Scotland the brave. Newsweek 70:51-2 N 27 '67

Politics and government
See also
Scotland—Home rule

Religious institutions and affairs
World around us (cont) Christian Cent 84: 448, 842-4, 1174; 85:90-1 Ap 5, Je 28, S 13 '67 Ja 17 '68

SCOTT, Bobby
Jays turned into eagles. G. Ronberg. il Sports Illus 26:28-9 My 22 '67

SCOTT, Clifford
Chicagoan makes horse sense pay off. il pors Ebony 23:130-2+ D '67

SCOTT, David
Closing in on the Loch Ness monster. Read Digest 90:86-90 F '67

SCOTT, David H.
Scott's corner. See issues of Flying

SCOTT, Douglas W.
Story of Seven Ponds. Audubon 69:82 S '67

SCOTT, E. Colvin
Should boys play football? Parents Mag 42: 84-6+ N '67

SCOTT, Eugene L.
Great Scott! Gene won another one. Sports Illus 27:46-8+ O 2 '67

SCOTT, H. Fred
Behind the scenes at Britain's best shipper. Pub W 192:27-9 O 23 '67

SCOTT, Herbert
At the bus stop; poem. Ladies Home J 84:133 F '67

SCOTT, Hugh
Man from T'ang. il por Time 89:14 Je 2 '67

SCOTT, J. B.
How to be a failure at hunting. Field & S 72:62-3+ My '67

SCOTT, John Finley
Where to get bad advice about college. Ladies Home J 84:76+ N '67

SCOTT, John W. and Pfaffmann, Carl
Olfactory input to the hypothalamus: electrophysiological evidence. bibliog Science 158:1592-4 D 22 '67

SCOTT, Joseph, and Scott, Lenore
Tall trip in short takes. pors Motor B 119:28-31+ Ap '67

SCOTT, Ken
Something for the boys. il por Newsweek 69:58 Ap 24 '67

SCOTT, Lenore. See Scott, J. jt. auth.

SCOTT, Paul
Build yourself this carbon arc welder for $5. Pop Mech 128:174-6 S '67
How to make your own lawn spiker. Pop Sci 191:131 Jl '67

SCOTT, Robert
Keys to selling your house. Am Home 70:130+ Mr '67

SCOTT, Robert Falcon
Ends of the earth. R. L. Tobin. il Sat R 50:25-6 Jl 1 '67
Scott of the Antarctic, by R. Pound. Review
Newsweek por 69:100 My 22 '67. S. Maloff
Sci Digest il 62:85-6 Jl '67

SCOTT, Robert Lee, 1908–
General proposes insurrection. Christian Cent 84:1092 Ag 30 '67

SCOTT, Ronald F.
Feel of the moon; with biographical sketch. Sci Am 217:20, 34-43 bibliog(p 154) N '67
—See O'Keefe, J. A. jt. auth.

SCOTT, Vernon
Mia Farrow's swinging life with Frank Sinatra. Ladies Home J 84:84+ My '67

SCOTT, Winfield
How to make it to the White House without really trying; Z. Taylor in Mexican war. D. Lavender. il por Am Heritage 18:26-7+ Je '67

SCOTT, Winfield Townley
Uses of poetry; North Easter; Bring; poems. Poetry 111:36-8 O '67

SCOTT paper company
Enriching life by broad experience; interview. T. B. McCabe. Nations Bsns 55:52-3+ Je '67
Scott's towels bring reader howls. Consumer Rep 32:461 S '67

SCOTTI, Thomas M. See Bergs, V. V. jt. auth.

SCOTTISH ballads. See Ballads, Scottish

SCOTTISH literature
Scottish history tales. S. N. Leodhas. Horn Bk 43:323-7 Je '67

SCOTTISH poetry
See also
Ballads, Scottish

SCOTTO, Anthony
New front man on the mob-run piers. S. Smith. il por Life 63:102+ S 8 '67

SCOTTO, Renata
Butterfly by Barbirolli. R. Jacobson. Sat R 50:56-7+ O 28 '67
Music to my ears. I. Kolodin. Sat R 50:105 Ap 22 '67

SCOTTSBLUFF, Neb.
Where businessmen gave their community a future. il Nations Bsns 55:92-4+ F '67

SCOTTSDALE, Ariz.
Scottsdale, Arizona. il Bet Hom & Gard 45:16+ Ag '67

SCOUR in swine. See Swine—Diseases and pests

SCOUT dogs. See Dogs, War use of

SCOUTING, Basketball. See Basketball scouting

SCOUTING, Football. See Football scouting

SCOUTS and scouting
What parents should know about scouting. il Good H 164:152-3 F '67
See also
Boy scouts
Girl scouts

SCOVEL, Carl
Year Thanksgiving came early. McCalls 95:72+ N '67

SCOVEL, Myra
Mountain Sunday; poem. Am For 73:45 Ag '67

SCOVOTTI, Jeanette
And we quote; interview. ed. by G. Movshon. por Hi Fi 17:MA18 Je '67

SCRAMBLERS. See Motorcycles

SCRAP metal
Industry looks up to copper mine in the sky; old copper wire and cable lines reclaimed. il Bsns W p 177-8+ S 16 '67

SCRAPERS
What spade bits can do for you. R. J. DeCristoforo. il Pop Sci 190:126-9 Je '67

SCRAPIE disease. See Sheep—Diseases and pests

SCRATCHES
First aid. C. J. Potthoff. Todays Health 45:84 My '67

SCREEN houses. See Garden houses, shelters, etc.

SCREEN printing. See Silk screen printing

SCREEN writing. See Moving picture authorship

SCREENS (engineering)
See also
Sewage disposal—Screening

SCREENS (projection) See Projection screens

SCREENS (sun)
For privacy, ventilation, light. il Sunset 138:112 F '67
Panels that tame wind and sun. il Pop Gard 18:34-7 My '67
These simple screens give daytime privacy. il Sunset 139:114 O '67
To intercept the fierce afternoon sun. il Sunset 139:66 Ag '67
To keep out the morning sun. il Sunset 139:71 Ag '67

SCREENS (wind)
Panels that tame wind and sun. il Pop Gard 18:34-7 My '67

SCREW threads
Thread restoration. J. Thawley. il Hot Rod 20:46-7 D '67

SCREW worms. See Screwworms

SCREWS
How Phillips fastens onto its profits; Posidriv, the new screw design. il Bsns W p 154+ N 11 '67

SCREWWORMS
Screwworms sneak back; sterilization campaign in Texas. F. Sartwell. il Sci N 91:238-9 Mr 11 '67

SCRIABIN, Alexander Nicholaevich. See Skriabin, A. N.

SCRIBBLE drawing. See Drawing

SCRIBNER, Barbara Colvin
Planning to remodel or add a bathroom? Am Home 70:140+ My '67

SCRIBNER, Charles, Jr
Future of the bookstore; summary of address. por Pub W 192:22 D 4 '67

SCRIBNER, Charles, sons
Scribner archives presented to Princeton. il Pub W 191:60-1 Ap 10 '67

SCRIPT writing. See Television authorship

SCRIPTS, Moving picture. See Moving picture authorship

SCRIVEN, Michael
Let's be sexumenical. R. Kirk. Nat R 19:1430 D 26 '67

SCRIVER, C. R. and Wilson, O. H.
Amino acid transport: evidence for genetic control of two types in human kidney. bibliog Science 155:1428-30 Mr 17 '67

SCROLLS from the Dead Sea. See Dead Sea scrolls

SCRUTON, Judson
While proctoring a selective service college qualification exam; poem. Christian Cent 84:202 F 15 '67

SCUBA. See Diving apparatus

SCUBA diving. See Diving, Submarine

SCUBA duba; drama. See Friedman, B. J.

SCULLY, Ed
Ed Scully on basics. See issues of Modern photography

SCULLY, James
Grandson; poem. New Yorker 43:42 My 20 '67

SCULPTORS
See also
Sculpture

SCULPTORS materials. See Artists materials

SCULPTURAL space. See Space

SCULPTURAL weaving. See Weaving

SCULPTURE
Art world; environmental art. H. Rosenberg. New Yorker 43:189-92+ O 21 '67
Evaporating environments; dry ice sculpture. il Time 91:30 Ja 12 '68
Gallery '68; high art and low art. P. Leider. il Look 32:14-21 Ja 9 '68

SCULPTURE—*Continued*
Instant sculpture. T. Conway. il Design 69: 31-3 Wint '67
Issue of innovation; contemporary sculpture. E. F. Fry. il Art N 66:40-3+ O '67
Moments for tomorrow; out in public places. il Newsweek 69:97-8 F 27 '67
Number is 581-4570, but don't call it, let it call you; environmental telephone booth. il Time 90:58 Jl 7 '67
Picasso: the ninth decade; interview. ed. by S. Gauthier. P. Picasso; J. Picasso. il Look 31:86-8 N 28 '67
Sculpture public again. B. Rose. Vogue 151: 60 Ja 1 '68
Shape of art for some time to come; primary structures. il Life 63:38-43+ Jl 28 '67
Spoon sculpture. R. Knight. il Design 68: 20-2 Sum '67
Twittering galaxy of electronic sculptures. il Life 62:112-14+ Ap 7 '67
UCLA's outstanding displays of modern sculpture. il Sunset 138:96-7 F '67
    See also
Art—Expertising
Bronzes
Casting (sculpture)
Decoration and ornament, Architectural
Garden ornaments
Metal sculpture
Monuments
Paper sculpture
Portrait sculpture
Sand sculpture
Wire sculpture
Wood carving
    also subhead Monuments, statues, etc. under names of cities, e.g. Chicago—Monuments, statues, etc.

Exhibitions
Beauty & bongos; UCLA campus outdoor sculpture court. il Time 89:70 Je 16 '67
Jacob Epstein: Edward Schimman collection on view at Fairleigh Dickinson university. Rutherford, N.J. K. Kuh. il Sat R 50:48-9 Mr 25 '67
Land of funk; show at Berkeley's art museum, University of California. il Newsweek 69:106 Ap 24 '67
Master of the monumentalists. il Time 90:80-6 O 13 '67
Pittsburgh's mini-international. K. Kuh. il Sat R 50:45-7 D 2 '67
Responding to the moment; Guggenheim's fifth International exhibition. il Time 90:64+ O 27 '67
Up with funk; show of funk art at the Berkeley museum. il Time 89:60E My 5 '67
White wings in the sunlight; exhibition of American sculpture of the sixties at the Los Angeles County museum. il Time 89: 80-3 My 12 '67
Year-end notes from a critic's diary. K. Kuh. il Sat R 50:34-5 D 30 '67
    See also
Museum of modern art, New York

Philosophy
See Art—Philosophy

Private collections
See Art—Private collections

Study and teaching
New dimensions in sculpture; papier-mâché. J. Belik. il Sch Arts 66:9-12 Ja '67
Sculpture for a school atrium. M. F. Tressler. il Sch Arts 66:15-18 Ja '67

Materials
Doodle-naks; assemblages of junk-pile heritage. M. L. Skelton. il Sch Arts 67:38-9 D '67
Woven structures. S. R. Rainey. il Sch Arts 67:6-7 D '67

Technique
Form determinants. D. Irving. il Sch Arts 66: 12-17 Je '67
Sculpture of Spero Anargyros. F. Whitaker. il Am Artist 31:32-7+ F '67
SCULPTURE, American
American sculpture in wood and stone. R. Davidson. il Antiques 92:480+ O '67
Art; T. Smith exhibition in Philadelphia. M. Kozloff. il Nation 204:125-6 Ja 23 '67
Master of the monumentalists. il Time 90: 80-6 O 13 '67
Third dimension; exhibition at Los Angeles County museum of art's special exhibits building. il Newsweek 69:92-4 My 8 '67

Why scale? Los Angeles County museum's survey of U.S. sculpture. J. Wechsler. il Art N 66:32-5+ Sum '67
    See also
Anargyros, S.
Breer, R.
Calder, A.
Di Suvero, M.
Gabo, N
Gallo, F
Greenough, H.
Grosvenor, R.
Liberman, A.
Nakian, R.
Nevelson, L.
Newman, B.
Nivola, C.
Richard, B.
Smith, T
Westermann, H. C.
SCULPTURE, Architectural. See Decoration and ornament, Architectural
SCULPTURE, British
English sculpture in California. il Antiques 92:736+ N '67
    See also
Adam, R.
Epstein, J.
SCULPTURE, Buddhist
Buddhas and Bodhisattvas. G. Kaler. il Hobbies 72:50 Jl '67
Maitreya Buddha of the future. G. Kaler. il Hobbies 72:50 Ag '67
SCULPTURE, Cambodian
Moving tragedies in stone. il UNESCO Courier 20:32-3 D '67
SCULPTURE, Childrens. See Childrens art
SCULPTURE, Dutch
Hoge Veluwe National Park. D. B. Huyck. il Am For 73:22-5+ F '67
SCULPTURE, English. See Sculpture, British
SCULPTURE, Eskimo. See Eskimos—Art
SCULPTURE, Finnish
    See also
Hiltunen, E. W.
SCULPTURE, French
    See also
Duchamp-Villon, R.
Laurens, H.
Rodin, A.
SCULPTURE, German
    See also
Haese, G.
SCULPTURE, Greek
    See also
Philolaos
SCULPTURE, Italian
    See also
Canova, A.
Michelangelo Buonarroti
SCULPTURE, Metal. See Metal sculpture
SCULPTURE, Mexican
    See also
Zuniga, R.
SCULPTURE, Photography of. See Photography of works of art
SCULPTURE, Polynesian
Polynesia: the indwelling power. A. Wardwell. il Art N 66:38-9+ N '67
SCULPTURE, Pre-Columbian
Newest ancient art; exhibition of objects from J. C. Leff collection of Ancient art of Latin America at the Brooklyn museum. J H Kay il Américas 19:9-16 Ap '67
SCULPTURE, Primitive
Isle of eyeless watchers; statues of Easter Island. L. S. De Camp. il Sci Digest 62:6-12 O '67
    See also
Sculpture, Pre-Columbian
SCULPTURE, Spanish
    See also
Picasso, P
SCULPTURE, Venezuelan
    See also
Marisol
SCULTHORP, Elsie Louise
Border plants with blue foliage. House B 109: 64+ O '67
Plant a crooked tree. House B 109:38+ My '67
SCUTT, Der
Modern updated. B. Plumb. il N Y Times Mag p20-1 D 31 '67
SEA. See Ocean
SEA anemones
Heliacus, gastropoda: architectonicidae, symbiotic with zoanthiniaria, coelenterata. R. Robertson. bibliog il Science 156:246-8 Ap 14 '67
Permanent resident. C. Barsi. il Atlan 220:100-1 Jl '67
Swimming sea anemones of Puget Sound: swimming of actinostola new species in response to stomphia coccinea. D. M. Ross and L. Sutton. bibliog il Science 155:1419-21 Mr 17 '67

SEA birds
Accidents and hazards
See Birds—Accidents and hazards

SEA BRIGHT, N.J.
Profiles: through the great city. A. Bailey. New Yorker 43:65-9 Jl 29 '67

SEA change; story. See Grau, S. A.

SEA coasts. See Coasts

SEA cows. See Manatees

SEA elephants. See Elephant seals

SEA food
See also
Cookery—Fish
Cookery—Shellfish
Lobsters
Oysters

SEA ice. See Ice

SEA ISLANDS
See also
Johns Island

SEA law. See Maritime law

SEA level changes
Holocene changes in sea level: evidence in Micronesia. F. P. Shepard and others. bibliog il Science 157:542-4 Ag 4 '67
Postglacial change in sea level in the western north Atlantic Ocean. A. C. Redfield. bibliog il Science 157:687-92 Ag 11 '67
Sea levels 7,000 to 20,000 years ago. K. O. Emery and L. E. Garrison. bibliog il Science 157:684-7 Ag 11 '67
Vertebrate evidence of a low sea level in the middle pliocene. S. D. Webb and N. Tessman. bibliog il Science 156:379 Ap 21 '67

SEA lions. See Seals (animals)

SEA otters
Brand-new horror for harried husbands. D. Connelly. il Sports Illus 27:64+ N 27 '67

SEA planes. See Seaplanes

SEA power
Merchant marine; address, February 13, 1967. T. N. Downing. Vital Speeches 33:478-80 My 15 '67
Titan unbound; Russian seapower. R. Moley. Newsweek 70:80 Jl 24; 84 Ag 7 '67
U.S. seapower; address, September 28, 1967. T. H. Moorer. Vital Speeches 34:83-5 N 15 '67

SEA products. See Marine resources

SEA Robin (buoy) See Buoys

SEA salt. See Salt

SEA shells. See Shells (conchology)

SEA slugs. See Nudibranchs

SEA sounds. See Ocean sounds

SEA sparrow missile system. See Guided missiles—Launching from ships

SEA urchins
Adenosine triphosphate usage by flagella. C. J. Brokaw. bibliog il Science 156:76-8 Ap 7 '67
Negative growth and longevity in the purple sea urchin strongylocentrotus purpuratus (Stimpson) T. A. Ebert. bibliog il Science 157:557-8 Ag 4 '67
See also
Embryology—Echinoderms

SEA wasp. See Jellyfish

SEA water
Gaseous hydrocarbons in sea water: determination. J. W. Swinnerton and V. J. Linnenbom. bibliog il Science 156:1119-20 My 26 '67
High-pressure dissociation of carbonic and boric acids in seawater. C. Culberson and others. bibliog il Science 157:59-61 Jl 7 '67
Ion pairing of magnesium sulfate in seawater: determined by ultrasonic absorption. F. H. Fisher. bibliog Science 157:823 Ag 18 '67
Manganese and related elements in the interstitial water of marine sediments. B. J. Presley and others. bibliog il Science 158:906-10 N 17 '67
Ocean as a chemical system. L. G. Sillén. bibliog il Science 156:1189-97 Je 2 '67
Oxygen-18 variations in sulfate ions in sea water and saline lakes. A. Longinelli and H. Craig. bibliog il Science 156:56-9 Ap 7 '67
Radium-226 and radon-222: concentration in Atlantic and Pacific oceans. W. S. Broecker and others. bibliog il Science 158:1307-10 D 8 '67
Red Sea: detailed survey of hot-brine areas. J. M. Hunt and others. bibliog il Science 156:514-16 Ap 28 '67
Silica in sea water: control by silica minerals. F. T. MacKenzie and others. bibliog il Science 155:1404-5 Mr 17 '67

Analysis
Radio-controlled model boat samples air and plankton. H. E. Schlichting, jr. and J. E. Hudson, jr. il Science 156:238-9 Ap 14 '67

Bacteriology
Life in a dead sea, Great Salt Lake. P. A. Zahl. il Nat Geog Mag 132:252-63 Ag '67

Desalting
Diesels in the desert. il Time 90:32 S 8 '67
Drinkable sea water; new plant at Key West. Time 90:17 Jl 28 '67
Dwight Eisenhower's proposal for our time; atomic desalting plants for the Near East. L. L. Strauss. il Nat R 19:1008-10 S 19 '67
Like no other water works; Key West, Fla. builds the nation's largest desalting plant. W. S. Foster. il Am City 82:91-3 O '67
Progress in water desalination; report. UN Mo Chron 4:50 My '67
Proposal for the Middle East: atomic desalting plants. Nation 205:322 O 9 '67
Reverse osmosis techniques star at water conference. J. F. Judge. il Tech W 20:21-2 My 29 '67
Scale control cuts desalting costs; Eilat, Israel, plant. R. A. Tidball. il Am City 82:68-9+ Ja '67
7.75 MGD water plant; Tijuana. E. Zubryn. Sci N 92:230 S 2 '67
United States joins dedication of Jidda desalting plant site; remarks, February 5, 1967. S. L. Udall. Dept State Bul 56:561-3 Ap 3 '67
Water pollution, conversion pose great R&D challenges. J. F. Judge. il Tech W 20:46-7+ Je 5 '67
Water, water everywhere, and now to drink. il Newsweek 70:69-70 Jl 31 '67

Pollution
Desert in the sea; putrid sediment giving off gas in the Cape Lookout Bight. Sci N 91:115 F 4 '67
Oil around us. R. Rienow and L. T. Rienow. il N Y Times Mag p24-5+ Je 4 '67
Thermal addition to the marine environment; report on meeting. J. B. Pearce. Science 157:1080 S 1 '67
Valley of death in the sea; San Pedro basin, Calif. J. Ludwigson. il Sci N 91:218 Mr 4 '67
See also
Oil pollution of rivers, harbors, etc.

Temperature
Oxygen solubility in sea water: thermodynamic influence of sea salt. E. J. Green and D. E. Carritt. bibliog il Science 157:191-3 Jl 14 '67

SEA water irrigation. See Irrigation

SEA waves, Seismic. See Seismic sea waves

SEABOARD air line railway-Atlantic Coast line merger. See Railroads—Consolidations and mergers

SEABOARD air line railway company
Seaboard safari. W. E. Towell. il Am For 73:34-5+ S '67

SEABOARD world airlines
Seaboard to equip DC-8s with Omnitrac. K. J. Stein. il Aviation W 86:45 Ap 10 '67
Transpacific route case: three all-cargo carriers aim at major market in Pacific case. H. D. Watkins. il Aviation W 86:48-50+ Je 12 '67

SEABORG, Glenn T.
Atomic energy; address, August 31, 1967. Vital Speeches 33:752-6 O 1 '67; Excerpts. Science 158:226-30 O 13 '67
Cybernetic age: an optimist's view. Sat R 50:21-3 Jl 15 '67
Man must first choose goals. por Tech W 20:32-5 Ja 23 '67
What's ahead for international science? adaptation of address, September 13, 1966. Bul Atomic Sci 23:24-8 Ja '67
Worldwide nuclear power: progress and problems. Dept State Bul 56:90-7 Ja 16 '67

SEABROOK, John Martin
Marriage inside the family. por Time 90:100-1 N 10 '67

SEADROMES. See Airports, Floating

SEAFARING life
See also
Voyages

SEAGER, Allan
Class of '67: the gentle desperadoes. Nation 204:778 Je 19 '67

SEAGOING laboratories. See Ships, Research

SEAGREN, Bob
He sizzles at the end of a sizzle stick. J. Underwood. il pors Sports Illus 26:32-4+ F 20 '67
Wayward pole. il Time 89:57 F 24 '67

SEAL BEACH Leisure World, Calif. See Aged—Housing

SEAL hunting
Whitecoat in peril. D. H. Pimlott. il Audubon 69:76-81 S '67

SEALAB projects. See Underwater laboratories

SEALE, Bobby
Call of the Black Panthers. S. Stern. il por N Y Times Mag p 10-11+ Ag 6 '67

SEALING compositions
Designing building exteriors with sealants in mind. R. Farrell. il Arch Rec 144:169-74 Ja '67
New calks seal your house permanently. M. E. Dowd. Am Home 70:82+ S '67

SEALS (animals)
Alpha-glycerophosphate dehydrogenase and glucose-6-phosphate dehydrogenase in tissues of the Weddell seal. G. H. Fried and others. bibliog il Science 155:1560-1 Mr 24 '67
Attention shift and errorless reversal learning by the California sea lion. R. J. Schusterman. bibliog il Science 156:833-5 My 12 '67
Our summer visitor. J. B. Robinson. il Read Digest 90:73-7 F '67
Pressure regulation in the middle ear cavity of sea lions; a possible mechanism. S. Odend'hal and T. C. Poulter; discussion. bibliog il Science 155:489; 157:99 Ja 27, Jl 7 '67
Whitecoat in peril. D. H. Pimlott. il Audubon 69:76-81 S '67
See also
Elephant seals

SEALs (sea-air-land) units. See United States Navy—Underwater demolition teams

SEAMAN, Barbara
Dangers of birth-control operations. Ladies Home J 84:50 Jl '67

SEAMANS, Robert C. Jr
Text of preliminary report on Apollo 204 fire cause. Tech W 20:20+ F 13 '67; Same. Aviation W 86:34-5 F 13 '67

SEAMEN
Aboard Intrepid; above and below deck. B. D. Barker, 3d. il Yachting 122:88-90+ S '67
Brains and muscles. il Yachting 122:81-7 S '67
Tom Corkett on crew selection. T. Corkett. Yachting 121:124 Je '67
See also
National maritime union of America

SEANCES. See Spiritualism

SEAPLANES
Swan song for the seaplane. il Sr Schol 91:20 N 16 '67

Floats
New products. il Flying 81:98+ D '67

SEARCH, Right of
Interrupted cruise; encounter with Red guards of the Chinese coast. C. Hancke and B. Hancke. il Yachting 122:44-5+ Ag '67

SEARCH warrants. See Warrants (law)

SEARCHLIGHTS
Compact searchlights designed by Xerox for Viet battle needs. Aviation W 86:23 Je 26 '67
EOS readying new, compact searchlights for Vietnam use. il Aero Tech 21:54 O 23 '67

SEARLE, Ronald
Modern Rake's progress; drawings. Holiday 43:72-83 Ja '68
Searle's cats. il Look 31:58-9 S 19 '67

SEARS, Paul Bigelow
Patterns of life; excerpts from Patterns of life; the unseen world of plants. Audubon 69:58-63 Mr '67

SEARS, Roebuck and company
Luck of Clarence Jackson. il Time 90:64 S 1 '67
Plenitude of Sears. Fortune 75:292+ Je 15 '67
Rivals join Sunbeam's lawn party. il Bsns W p 184-5 My 6 '67
Spain's shoppers say *bienvenido* to Sears. il Bsns W p92-4+ Ap 15 '67

SEASCAPES. See Marine painting

SEASHORE
See also
Beaches
Coasts

SEASHORE houses. See Beach architecture

SEASHORE state park, Virginia. See Virginia —Parks and reserves

SEASIDE gardens. See Gardens, Seaside

SEASIDE regional center, Conn. See State institutions

SEASIDE resorts

Great Britain
Britain's great, ghastly ooze; fight against oil from the Torrey Canyon shipwreck off the Cornish coast. il Newsweek 69:48-51 Ap 10 '67

Spain
Siren song of Sotogrande; photographs by E. Haas; with account by L. Smith. Sports Illus 26:34-41 Mr 6 '67

SEASON of endings; story. See McInerny, R.

SEASON of renewal; story. See Fritz, J.

SEASONAL cycles. See Periodicity

SEASONAL industries
Seasonality and construction. R. J. Myers and S. Swerdloff. il Mo Labor R 90:1-8 S '67

SEASONING
See also
Garlic

SEASONS
See also
Spring

SEAT belts. See Safety belts

SEATON, Esta
Paradox; poem. Christian Cent 84:775 Je 14 '67

SEATTLE
Plywood sandwich raises arena profits. il Am City 82:88-9 Ja '67

Metropolitan district
City's answer to water pollution. il U S News 63:112-13 O 2 '67
How Seattle is beating water pollution; Metro's project. E. Clark. il Harper 234: 91-5 Je '67

Music
See also
Seattle opera association

Politics and government
Politics on the split-level frontier; Jocelyn Marchisio. J. Poppy. il Look 31:94+ My 16 '67

Recreation
Crew that grew and grew; Seattle park department rowing program. W. Vance. il Parks & Rec 2:38+ O '67

Sanitary affairs
City's answer to water pollution. il U S News 63:112-13 O 2 '67

SEATTLE boat show. See Boats—Exhibitions

SEATTLE childrens zoo. See Zoological gardens

SEATTLE opera association
Arts at fever pitch. W. Johnson. Hi Fi 17: MA22-3+ Mr '67
Music under Mount Rainier. Newsweek 69: 105 Ap 24 '67
Seattle; performance of Delibes's Lakmé. F. J. Warnke. il Opera N 31:23 Je 10 '67
Seattle; production of Turandot. F. J. Warnke. Opera N 31:31 Mr 11 '67
Seattle's Soldat; production by association's fledgling company. il Time 89:74 Mr 10 '67

SEATTLE opera company
Seattle (cont) F. J. Warnke. il Opera N 32:22 N 4 '67

SEATTLE public library
Scale and character for a residential area; Magnolia branch library. il Arch Rec 142: 182-3 S '67

SEATTLE SuperSonics (basketball team) See Basketball teams

SEAVER, Tom
Mets find a young phenom. J. Jares. por Sports Illus 26:64-6 Je 26 '67

SEAWRIGHT, James
Twittering galaxy of electronic sculptures. il pors Life 62:112-14+ Ap 7 '67

SEBASTIAN, Frank
Worldwide rush to incineration. Am City 82:40 D '67

SECAUCUS, N.J.
On the track. Sports Illus 27:13 N 20 '67

SECESSION
Faces from the past: J. C. Calhoun. R. M. Ketchum. il Am Heritage 18:18-19 O '67

SECOND committee of the General assembly. See United Nations—Economic and financial committee

SECOND honeymoon; story. See Knowlton, R. A.

SECONDARY boycott. See Boycott

SECONDARY education. See Education, Secondary

SECONDARY recovery of oil. See Oil field flooding

SECONDARY schools. See High schools

SECONDHAND jets. See Airplanes, Used

SECONDHAND yachts. See Yachts, Used

SECONDS. See Time measurements

SECRET agents. See Spies

SECRET cupboards. See Cupboards

SECRET police, Russian. See Secret service— Russia

SECRET service
Other cloaks, other daggers. Sr Schol 90:10-11 Mr 31 '67
Secrets of the secret services. L. Farago. Sat R 50:31-2 N 18 '67
  See also
Spies

Confederate States of America
  See United States—History—Civil war—Secret service—Confederate States

Great Britain
Espionage establishment; excerpt. D. Wise and T. B. Ross. il Sat Eve Post 240:50-3+ N 4 '67
Establishment man; case of H. Philby. Newsweek 70:45-6 O 16 '67
Not-so-secret service; chief of M.I.6. il Newsweek 70:31 O 30 '67
Scandal rocks MI-6. Sr Schol 91:21 O 26 '67
Set Europe ablaze. E. H. Cookridge. Review Sat R 50:44 S 16 '67. H. H. Ransom
Stranger than spy fiction: the story of double agent Philby. U S News 63:19-20 O 16 '67

Israel
New ghosts; Shin Bet's secret deal with Moslem Morocco. il Newsweek 69:49 Mr 6 '67

Russia
CIA: other side of the story, what reds are doing; methods of the KGB. il U S News 62:96-8 Mr 13 '67
Covey of spies is flushed in Germany. M. Durham and J. Cook. il Life 63:65-6+ N 3 '67
Espionage establishment; excerpt. D. Wise and T. B. Ross. il Sat Eve Post 240:76-80+ N 18 '67
Flight from the KGB. Sr Schol 91:18-19 N 2 '67
KGB. W. Rogers. Look 31:105 O 3 '67

United States
Broken seal, by L. Farago. Review Sat R 50:31+ Je 3 '67. J. M. Allison
CIA: only a part of big U.S. intelligence network. il U S News 62:29 Mr 6 '67
Organizational intelligence, by H. L. Wilensky. Review Reporter 37:54-6 N 2 '67. G. A. Craig
U.S. intelligence community. il Sr Schol 90: 16 Mr 21 '67
  See also
Presidents—United States—Protection
United States—Central intelligence agency

Civil war
  See United States—History—Civil war—Secret service

Vietnam (Democratic Republic)
Ho's underground in South Vietnam. D. Warner. il Reporter 37:20-2 N 30 '67
SECRET societies
  See also
Ku Klux klan

Africa
  See also
Mau Mau
SECRETARIAT for non-believers. See Vatican—Secretariat for non-believers
SECRETARIAT of the United Nations. See United Nations—Secretariat
SECRETARIES
New-style secretaries. R. Hoffmann. Mlle 65: 162-3+ O '67
Secretaries: 1967 style. J. Weingarten. il Duns R 89:45-6+ Mr '67
  See also
School secretaries
SECRETARIES of defense (United States)
Heirs apparent. il Time 90:26 D 8 '67
SECRETARY General of the United Nations. See United Nations—Secretary General
SECRETS
Secrets: why you need them. A. West. Vogue 150:127+ Ag 15 '67
SECRETS, Trade. See Trade secrets
SECRETS of a clock watcher; story. See McGinnis, L. S.
SECTIONALISM
  See also
Regionalism
SECTS
  See also
Cults
Mennonites
Shakers
Unitarians

SECULAR institutes
Role of secular institutes. L. Avery. America 116:187-8 F 4 '67
  See also
Opus Dei
SECULARISM
Cold feet in the promised land; excerpt from Sex is dead and other postmortems. E. H. Brill. Christian Cent 84:432-5 Ap 5 '67; Discussion. 84:688 My 24 '67
Secular and the sacred. R. F. Capon. il America 116:307-12 Mr 4 '67; Discussion. 116:515 Ap 8 '67
SECULARIZATION
Colloquium on secularity; ecumenical encounter at the University of Notre Dame. W. J. Sullivan. America 117:743 D 16 '67
SECURITIES
  See also
Bonds
Dividends
Investment banking
Investments, Foreign
Manipulation (securities)
Stock exchange
Stocks
  also subhead Securities under various subjects, e.g. Petroleum industry and trade —Securities

Marketing
Wall Street: the market looks to its defenses. C. Morgello. il Newsweek 70:81 O 23 '67
Wall Street's own watchdogs; compliance men to prevent stock frauds. il Bsns W p90-2+ Jl 29 '67

Regulation
Contract sales, a crackdown. U S News 63: 104 O 2 '67

Valuations
Investing in a dividend boost. G. E. MacDougal. il Harvard Bsns R 45:87-92 Jl '67
SECURITIES and exchange commission. See United States—Securities and exchange commission
SECURITIES as gifts
  See also
Gifts for children
SECURITY. See International security
SECURITY, Internal. See Internal security
SECURITY analysts. See Investments—Advisers
SECURITY and insecurity (psychology)
Babes in the wood; ed. by D. C. Disney. Ladies Home J 84:18+ F '67
Frustration quotient. P. D. Weidig. il NEA J 57:38-9 Ja '68
SECURITY classification (government documents)
AEC proposals, a threat to scientific freedom. H. P. Green. Bul Atomic Sci 23:15-17 O '67
Classified research in the university; statement and recommended guidelines, July 29, 1967. Bul Atomic Sci 23:45-6 O '67
SECURITY council of the United Nations. See United Nations—Security council
SECURITY measures in industry. See Industry—Security measures
SECURITY service. See Secret service
SEDER. See Passover
SEDIMENTATION and deposition
Aluminum-26 in Pacific sediment: implications. J. T. Wasson and others. bibliog il Science 155:446-8 Ja 27 '67
Digital model of evaporite sedimentation. L. I. Briggs and H. N. Pollack. il Science 155:453-6 Ja 27 '67
Foraminiferal ooze: solution at depths. W. H. Berger. bibliog il Science 156:383-5 Ap 21 '67
Iodide abundance in oilfield brines in Oklahoma. A. G. Collins and G. C. Egleson. bibliog il Science 156:934-5 My 19 '67
Isoprenoid acids in recent sediments. M. Blumer and W. J. Cooper. bibliog il Science 158:1463-4 D 15 '67
Meander wavelength of alluvial rivers. S. A. Schumm. bibliog il Science 157:1549-50 S 29 '67
Sedimentary phosphate method for estimating paleosalinities. B. W. Nelson. bibliog il Science 158:917-20 N 17 '67
  See also
Deep sea deposits
SEDITIOUS libel
  See also
Trials (seditious libel)
SEDRO-WOOLLEY, Wash.
Happening at Hoogdal: an unidentified beeping object. T. Beauchamp. Look 31:42-3 N 14 '67
SEE mother run! story. See Mills, J.
SEED catalogs. See Catalogs, Seed and plant
SEEDING
Seeding a lawn. il Bet Hom & Gard 45:10+ S '67

SEEDING machinery
Faster planting in narrow rows. il Farm J 91:34-5+ Ap '67
Once-over planters cut costs, stop weeds. il Farm J 91:42-3+ Mr '67
Plant faster, spray weeds too. il Farm J 91:30-1+ My '67
Same wagon loads seed and fertilizer. il Farm J 91:50Q O '67

SEEDS
Apple fruit-set: evidence for a specific role of seeds. F. G. Dennis, jr. bibliog il Science 156:71-3 Ap 7 '67
Food proteins: new sources from seeds; address, December 26, 1966. A. M. Altschul. bibliog il Science 158:221-6 O 13 '67
Mitotic reactivation of the terminal bud and cambium of white ash. H. B. Tepper and C. A. Hollis. bibliog il Science 156:1635-6 Je 23 '67
Seed dormancy: breaking by uncouplers and inhibitors of oxidative phosphorylation. L. A. T. Ballard and A. E. G. Lipp. bibliog il Science 156:398-9 Ap 21 '67
Seeds. B. Black. Horticulture 45:28-9+ F '67
See also
Germination
Grasses—Seed

Germination
See Germination

SEEDS, Age of. See Age (plants)

SEEGER, Pete
So long, Woody, it's been good to know ya. Life 63:8 N 10 '67
about
Big and muddy. il por Newsweek 70:118 S 25 '67

SEEGERS, Kathleen, and Seegers, Scott
Brazil's magic mountain. Américas 19:20-7 Mr '67
—See Seegers, S. jt. auth.

SEEGERS, Scott
Death and the friendly river. Read Digest 92:42-7 Ja '68
—and Seegers, Kathleen
King of colored gems. Read Digest 92:203-8 Ja '68
—See Seegers, K. jt. auth.

SEEGMILLER, J. Edwin, and others
Enzyme defect associated with a sex-linked human neurological disorder and excessive purine synthesis. bibliog Science 155:1682-4 Mr 31 '67

SEEING eye dogs. See Dogs as guides

SEELEY, David S.
Desegregation guidelines. Am Ed 3:21-2 F '67
Tool or Trojan horse? NEA J 56:41-3 Mr '67
Urban schools and society. Cath World 206:19-21 O '67

SEFTON, William
Open-frame rotary switches. por Electr World 78:57-60 O '67

SEGAL, David I.
Nerve of Edmund Wilson. Commonweal 87:117-18+ O 27 '67

SEGAL, Julius. See Luce, G. G. jt. auth.

SEGAL, George, 1924-
Conversation with George Segal; interview, ed. by D. Cyr. Sch Arts 67:30-1 N '67

SEGAL, Ronald
Dying minds. por UNESCO Courier 20:24-6 Mr '67

SEGAL, Sheldon. See Corfman, P. A. jt. auth.

SEGAL, Stanton. See Cuatrecasas, P. jt. auth.

SEGEL, Ralph E.
Radiative-capture studies of the giant dipole resonance. bibliog Science 158:723-30 N 10 '67

SEGHERS, Hercules Pietersz
Labors of Hercules Seghers; exhibition in Amsterdam. J. G. van Gelder. il Art N 66:26-9+ S '67

SEGINSKI, John
3½ square. U S Camera 30:54-5+ Mr '67

SEGREGATION, Social
Trouble is the ghetto? or let's take another look. E. Goble. Arch Rec 142:9 S '67
See also
Discrimination in housing
Negroes in the United States—Segregation

SEGREGATION in education
Again, integration; NAACP campaign to end de facto segregation in metropolitan areas. Sat R 50:69 D 16 '67
Controversial report on education; what it really means. J. S. Coleman. U S News 63:44-5 D 25 '67
Extent of elementary school segregation in seventy-five school systems. Ebony 22:55 Ag '67

Is desegregation impractical? R. Schwartz and others. New Repub 158:27-9 Ja 6 '68
Northern bias to be probed; HEW investigation of de facto segregation in northern city schools. Sat R 50:69 D 16 '67
Racial isolation in public education. W. W. Brickman. Sch & Soc 95:209 Ap 1 '67
Slow pace in Dixie; all-Negro schools. il Newsweek 70:43 Ag 21 '67
See also
Negroes in the United States—Education
Negroes in the United States—Segregation
SEGREGATION of Negroes. See Negroes in the United States—Segregation

SEIBERLING, Dorothy
How dare they do it? Life 63:123-4 O 13 '67
True path lies buried under stone and myth. Life 62:60+ Mr '67

SEIBERT, Deni
Delaware delights. Travel 127:46-7 Ap '67

SEIBOLD, Edward Albert
Cathey, where's Cathey? il por Newsweek 70:42+ S 18 '67

SEIDLIN, Joseph
From logs to logistics; excerpts from address, December 9, 1965. Sch & Soc 95:420-3 N 11 '67

SEIDMAN, Arthur H.
Pulse-counting detector for FM tuners. Electr World 77:36-8 Ja '67

SEIGAL, Walter
Eleven ideas from the CBS dream darkroom. M. D. Grennan. il Pop Phot 61:124-7+ D '67

SEILACHER, Adolf
Fossil behavior. Sci Am 217:72-6+ Ag '67

SEINGALT, Giacomo Girolamo Casanova de. See Casanova de Seingalt, G. G.

SEISMIC sea waves
What causes those giant killer waves. W. Kreh. il Pop Mech 129:98-101+ Ja '68

SEISMOLOGICAL stations
Seismic station; plans for station in southern Norway. H. J. Barnes. Sci N 92:137 Ag 5 '67

SEISMOLOGY
Building to a quake? B. Tufty. il Sci N 91:550-1 Je 10 '67
Excitation of surface waves by events in southern Algeria. R. C. Liebermann and P. W. Pomeroy. bibliog il Science 156:1098-100 My 26 '67
Phase changes in the upper mantle. D. L. Anderson. bibliog il Science 157:1165-6+ S 8 '67
Sea-floor spreading near the Galapagos. E. M. Herron and J. R. Heirtzler. bibliog il Science 158:775-80 N 10 '67
Seismic delay times: correlation with other data. M. N. Toksöz and J. Arkani-Hamed. bibliog il Science 158:783-5 N 10 '67
See also
Earth movements

SEITZ, Nick
What I'd like my son to be. Parents Mag 42:50-3 Je '67

SEKI, Tsutomu
Another for the amateurs. il por Time 91:37 Ja 12 '68

SELBY, Don
(ed) See Biehl. A. At sea without a rudder
—See Inch, B. jt. auth.

SELBY, Earl
Youthful shoplifting: a national epidemic. Read Digest 90:95-9 Ap '67

SELBY, Richard
Uncommon eye of Richard Selby. P. Caulfield. il Mod Phot 31:76-81 Ap '67

SELDEN, David. See Cogen, C. jt. auth.

SELDEN, Marguerite C.
Tulip poplars and protozoa on the Chopawamsic. P. Thomson. il NEA J 56:32-3 O '67

SELECTION, Natural. See Natural selection

SELECTION of librarians. See Librarians—Selection and appointment

SELECTION of students. See Student selection

SELECTION of teachers. See Teachers—Selection and appointment

SELECTIVE service, Military. See Military service, Compulsory

SELENOLOGY. See Moon

SELEY, Jason
Constructions in chrome. il por Time 89:66 Mr 10 '67

SELF
Emerging self. A. Moore. Cath World 206:180-2 Ja '68

SELF acceptance
Perfect wife and mother. McCalls 94:24+ Ag '67

SELF appraisal. See Self evaluation

SELF defense
Personal business. Bsns W p 113-14 Ag 5 '67
See also
Judo
SELF defense for women
How can a girl defend herself? arrest for
using tear-gas gun. il Time 89:71 F 10 '67
SELF determination. National
America today; address, June 27, 1967. L. B.
Johnson. Vital Speeches 33:605-8 Jl 15 '67;
Excerpts. Dept State Bul 57:59-60 Jl 17 '67
Understanding people's wars. G. W.
Shepherd, jr. Christian Cent 84:1185-8 S 20
'67
SELF-developing cameras. See Cameras
SELF employed
Going into business for yourself. J. D. Bier-
man. Parents Mag 42:12+ N '67
Machines that make money for you. H.
Shuldiner. il Pop Sci 191:62-4 Jl '67
One way to feather the nest; Keogh retire-
ment plan. il Bsns W p 145 N 11 '67
Owning your own business: how tough? how
wise? il Sr Schol 90:14-16+ My 12 '67
Soon, it will be easier to build your own
pension. il U S News 63:82-3 S 4 '67
SELF estimate. See Self evaluation
SELF evaluation
Are you making the most of yourself? B.
Haldane. il Pop Sci 190:76-8 Je '67
Crises in a developing organization. G. L.
Lippitt and W. H. Schmidt. il Harvard
Bsns R 45:102-12 N '67
Is Babbitt dead? survey reveals what real
estate people think of their reflected
images. L. S. Burns. bibliog f Harvard
Bsns R 45:14-16+ S '67
Management of disappointment. A. Zaleznik.
bibliog f Harvard Bsns R 45:59-70 N '67
Secret of self-renewal. A. Gordon. Read Di-
gest 90:103-6 F '67
What injures a child's self-esteem? with
study-discussion program, by E. Harris
and D. Harris. V. S. Sherman. bibliog il
PTA Mag 61:23-5, 35 Mr '67
SELF expression. See Personality
SELF government in education
Bearded sockless radical of Moo U: D. Smith,
president of the Government of the student
body. W. C. Murray. il N Y Times Mag
p25+ Ap 9 '67; Discussion. p 12+ Ap 23 '67
Honorable code? Air force academy. Sr Schol
90:20 Mr 17 '67
Marriage of Paris and Bologna: the evolving
undergraduate school; address, September
6, 1967. J. F. Ross. Vital Speeches 33:766-8
O 1 '67
Minors no more; Statement on rights and free-
doms of students. Newsweek 70:47 Jl 31 '67
Now it's student power. B. Paisner. il Life
63:91-2 O 20 '67
Student participation. Sch & Soc 95:214 Ap
1 '67
Student power. il Newsweek 70:94-5 O 23 '67
Student power, for what? R. Kirk. Nat R
19:1386 D 12 '67
Student unrest. D. Wolfle. Science 158:443 O
27 '67
SELF importance. See Self love
SELF incrimination
Massiah v. United States; text of majority
opinion and excerpts from minority dissent.
Cur Hist 53:43-5 Jl '67
Miranda v. Arizona discussed. Am City 82:52
Je '67
Miranda v. Arizona; Supreme court decision;
excerpts. Cur Hist 52:359-62+ Je '67
SELF knowledge. See Self evaluation
SELF love
Homecoming; finding myself. J. K. Martine.
McCalls 95:68+ N '67
See also
Autism
SELF murder. See Suicide
SELF mutilation
Girls who cut themselves; slashers in mental
hospitals. Sci N 92:496 N 18 '67
SELF pity. See Self love
SELF ratings. See Self evaluation
SELF realization
Happiness: new light on an old subject; inter-
view. J. K. Lagemann. Read Digest 91:117-
20 O '67
SELFISH story; story. See Gold, H.
SELFISHNESS
Gospel according to Ayn Rand. M. S. Evans.
Nat R 19:1059-63 O 3 '67
SELIGMAN, Ben B.
High cost of eating. Commentary 44:48-52
Jl; 14+ O '67
SELKIRK, Alexander
Crusoe's island. P. Quennell. il Horizon 9:66-
83 Spr '67

SELL, Stephen
Report on a marathon. Am Rec G 33:802+
My '67
SELLARS, Dorothy Rainer
Dance teacher in the community. por Dance
Mag 41:68-9 N; 74-6 D '67; 42:84-5 Ja '68
SELLERS, Rose Z.
Overloaded bandwagon. Wilson Lib Bul 41:
915-19 My '67
SELLING
See also
Marketing
SELWAY-BITTERROOT wilderness area. See
Wilderness areas—Idaho
SELYE, Hans
Ischemic necrosis: prevention by stress. bib-
liog Science 156:1262-3 Je 2 '67
SEMANTICS
Componential analysis; kinship studies in cul-
tural anthropology. W. H. Goodenough. bib-
liog il Science 156:1203-9 Je 2 '67
How much do they really understand? AP
survey findings of understanding of words
common in World war II. R. L. Tobin.
Sat R 50:81-2 My 13 '67
SEMEN
Adenosine triphosphate usage by flagella. C.
J. Brokaw. bibliog il Science 156:76-8 Ap
7 '67
Sperm banks debated. B. J. Culliton. il
Sci N 92:208-9 Ag 26 '67
Spermatophore formation and sperm transfer
in ornithodoros ticks. B. Feldman-Muhsam.
bibliog il Science 156:1252-3 Je 2 '67
SEMENENKO, Serge
Improbable Bostonian. Time 90:68 Jl 21 '67
$1,000,000 misunderstanding. Time 90:75 Ag 18
'67
Semenenko steps out. por Newsweek 70:60 Jl
24 '67
SEMICONDUCTOR diodes. See Diodes
SEMICONDUCTOR lasers. See Lasers
SEMICONDUCTORS
High-voltage, high-power semiconductors. J.
H. Wujek, jr. il Electr World 79:48-50 Ja
'68
Light-emitting semiconductors. F. F. More-
head, jr. il Sci Am 216:108-13+ bib-
liog (p 168) My '67
Low-cost semiconductors for the consumer
market. J. S. MacDougall. il Electr World
78:37-9 S '67
New frontiers in semiconductors. il Electr
World 77:78-9 Mr '67
Semiconductor switching of low-power cir-
cuits. A. Harris. il Electr World 77:33-5 Je
'67
See also
Electric current rectifiers

Testing
Semiconductor test set. M. Gross. il Electr
World 78:74-6 N '67
SEMINAR in American studies. See Salzburg
seminar in American studies
SEMINARIANS. See Theological students
SEMINARIES. See Theological schools
SEMINARS
International seminar on apartheid, racial dis-
crimination and colonialism in southern
Africa; United Nations. UN Mo Chron 4:40-
7 Ag '67
Regional seminar in Warsaw on economic and
social rights. UN Mo Chron 4:69 Ag '67
Seminar on civic and political rights of
women; United Nations. UN Mo Chron 4:
69-70 Ag '67
There's no business like seminar business.
J. Weingarten. il Duns R 90:36-7+ S '67
See also
Freedom studies center
Salzburg seminar in American studies
SEMINARY libraries. See Theological libraries
SEMINOLE Indians
Indian givers; Federal claims court upholds
1964 verdict. Newsweek 69:43-4 Je 26 '67
Very small happening at Forty Mile Bend;
Fla. A. Hurwitz. il NEA J 56:71-2 S '67
SEMONIN, Paul F.
Politics of copper: proxy fight in the Congo.
Nation 204:303-6 Mr 6 '67
SEMPLE, Robert B. jr
Slum planners. New Repub 157:8-10 Jl 22 '67
SENATE (United States) See United States—
Congress—Senate
SENATE ethics committee. See United States
—Congress—Senate—Standards and con-
duct, Committee on
SENATE foreign relations committee. See
United States—Congress—Senate—Foreign
relations committee

SENATE investigations. See Government investigations

SENATORIAL candidates. See Candidates, Political

SENATORS
Chuck Percy: political Twiggy. G. Wills. il Nat R 19:458-64 My 2 '67
Doves in trouble? their problem in '68. il U S News 62:78-9 Je 5 '67
Elephant gets glamor; freshmen lawmakers giving the Grand old party new image. W. Martin. il Nations Bsns 55:38-9+ My '67
Lords proprietors of Congress; chairmen of Senate's sixteen standing committees. A. Krock. pors N Y Times Mag p28-9+ Ja 22 '67
New quintet but no harmony. M. McGrory. America 116:141 Ja 28 '67
Occupation: farmer; avocation: Senator: Aiken of Vt. J. Herbers. il N Y Times Mag p24-5+ Ja 29 '67
Public business that's clothed in privacy. A. H. Sypher. il Nations Bsns 55:35-6 N '67
Seven sitting doves; Democrats who speak out. P. F. Healy. New Repub 156:8-10 Je 3 '67
Who belongs to the Senate's inner club? C. Fritchey. Harper 234:104+ My '67
  See also
United States—Congress—Senate

SENDAK, Maurice
Fine book for children by a secret child: hidden world of Maurice Sendak. R. Phelps. il Life 63:8 D 15 '67

SENEGAL
  See also
Festivals—Senegal

SENG, Sister M. Angelica
Poverty, paternalism and protest. Cath World 204:352-5 Mr '67

SENIOR citizens. See Aged

SENIOR scholastic (periodical)
Games for the classroom; Scholastic teacher's panelists' evaluations. il Sr Schol 91:sup 12-13 N 9 '67

SENIORITY, Employee
Job tenure of workers, January 1966. H. R. Hamel. il Mo Labor R 90:31-7 Ja '67

SENSATION. See Senses and sensation

SENSE of humor. See Humor

SENSE of mission; story. See Hazzard, S.

SENSES and sensation
Hand them a *frobish*; learning through the five senses. R. M. Bilenker. il NEA J 56: 30-1+ O '67
Mind: an essay on human feeling, by S. K. Langer. Review
  New Yorker 43:98+ Ag 12 '67. W. Sargeant
Senses rechanneled. A. Ewing. Sci N 93:74-5 Ja 20 '68
Sensory coding; report on conference. G. G. Somjen. Science 158:399-400+ O 20 '67
  See also
Brain
Pain
Psychology, Physiological

SENSING systems, Remote. See Remote sensing systems

SENSORS, Remote. See Remote sensing systems

SENSORY cortex. See Cerebral cortex

SEPARATION of Dinah Delbanco; story. See Hazzard, S.

SEPER, Franjo, cardinal
Shake-up in the curia. il por Newsweek 71: 78-9 Ja 22 '68

SEPHTON, Nancy E.
I was free! Redbook 129:10+ O '67

SEPULCHRAL monuments
Death's head, cherub, urn and willow. J. Deetz and E. S. Dethlefsen. il Natur Hist 76:28-37 Mr '67
Knight's tombstone at Jamestown, Virginia. J. P. Hudson. il Antiques 91:760-1 Je '67

SEQUATCHIE; story. See Meyers, W.

SEQUENATOR. See Biological apparatus and supplies

SEQUOIA national forest. See National forests

SEQUOIA NATIONAL PARK
After 700 road curves, there's old Mineral King, your destination or jumping-off place. il Sunset 138:42-4+ Je '67
Mineral King; construction of highway through Sequoia-Kings Canyon National Park. A. W. Smith. Nat Parks Mag 41:2 Jl '67
Preliminary wilderness plan for Sequoia-Kings Canyon National Parks and the surrounding region. il Nat Parks Mag 41:9-13 Ja '67
What about Mineral King? R. Leadabrand. il Am For 73:18-20+ F '67

SERBIA
  History
  European war
  See European war, 1914-1918—Serbia

SERBIAN language. See Serbo-Croatian language

SERBIN, Max
For all string players, indispensable. Am Rec G 33:852 My '67

SERBO-Croatian language
War of words. il Time 89:31-2 Ap 7 '67

SERGEANT major. See United States—Army—Non-commissioned officers

SERIAL art. See Modernism (art)

SERIAL publications
Price indexes for 1967: serial services. N. B. Brown and W. H. Huff. il Library J 92: 2527-8 Jl '67

SERIES, Book
Series of series. Z. Sutherland. Sat R 50:35 Je 17 '67

SERIOS, Ted
Amazing weekend with the amazing Ted Serios. C. Reynolds; D. B. Eisendrath, jr. il pors Pop Phot 61:81-7+ O '67; Reply. J. Eisenbud. 61:31-2+ N '67
Man who thinks pictures; with report by P. Welch. il pors Life 63:112+ S 22 '67

SERKIN, Peter
Boy who hates circuses. por Time 89:65 F 24 '67
Peter Serkin: it is what the music does for him. R. Sabin. il por Am Rec G 34:54 S '67
Young excitement in music. A. Rich. por House B 109:102-3+ Jl '67

SERMONS
I'm sorry you came! visiting preachers' sermon on Vietnam. J. M. Hopkins. Christian Cent 85:14-15 Ja 3 '68
Politics in the pulpit; concerning sermon delivered in church at Chevy Chase Circle, Washington, D.C. America 117:104 Jl 29 '67
Secular sermons. il Time 89:93-4 Mr 10 '67
  See also
Preaching

SEROTONIN
Aminoacidemias: effects on maze performance and cerebral serotonin. C. M. McKean and others. bibliog il Science 157:213-15 Jl 14 '67
5-Hydroxytryptamine in the carotid body of the cat. S. R. Chiocchio and others. bibliog il Science 158:790-1 N 10 '67
Serotonin release from brain slices by electrical stimulation: regional differences and effect of LSD. T. N. Chase and others. bibliog il Science 157:1461-3 S 22 '67
Serotonin: release in the forebrain by stimulation of midbrain raphé. G. K. Aghajanian and others. bibliog il Science 156:402-3 Ap 21 '67

SERPENTINE
Geochemical evidence of present-day serpentinization. I. Barnes and others. bibliog il Science 156:830-2 My 12 '67

SERRANO, Frank
Mama goes to nursery school. il por Am Ed 3:10-11 S '67

SERRIN, William, and Goltz, Gene
Detroit's press profiteers. Reporter 38:32-3 Ja 11 '68

SERUM
Agglutinating specificity for LW factor in guinea pig and rabbit anti-Rh serums. P. Levine and M. J. Celano. bibliog il Science 156:1744-6 Je 30 '67
Serum from two horses offers another chance for life; antilymphocyte globulin. il Life 63:30-1 D 15 '67
Serum osmolality in the coelacanth, latimeria chalumnae: urea retention and ion regulation. G. E. Pickford and F. B. Grant. bibliog il Science 155:568-70 F 3 '67
  See also
Serotonin

SERUM globulins
Carboxy-terminal amino acids of γA and γM heavy chains. C. A. Abel and H. M. Grey. bibliog il Science 156:1609-10 Je 23 '67
Colostral immunoglobulin-A; synthesis in vitro of T-chain by rabbit mammary gland. R. Asofsky and P. A. Small, jr. bibliog il Science 158:932-3 N 17 '67
Concanavalin A reaction with human normal immunoglobulin G and myeloma immunoglobulin G. M. A. Leon. bibliog il Science 158:1325-6 D 8 '67
Evolution of immunoglobulins: structural homology of Kappa and Lambda Bence Jones proteins. K. Titani and others. bibliog il Science 155:828-30+ F 17 '67
Immunoglobulin A: localization in rectal mucosal epithelial cells. E. A. Gelzayd and others bibliog il Science 157:930-1 Ag 25 '67

SERUM globulins—*Continued*
Immunoglobulin structure: variation in amino acid sequence and length of human lambda light chains. F. W. Putnam and others. bibliog il Science 157:1050-3 S 1 '67

Light chains of rabbit immunoglobulin: assignment to the kappa class. R. F. Doolittle and K. H. Astrin. bibliog il Science 156:1755-7 Je 30 '67

Mouse immunoglobulin allotypes: detection with rabbit antiserums. J. E. Coe. bibliog il Science 155:562+ F 3 '67

Red cells coated with immunoglobulin G: binding and sphering by mononuclear cells in man. A. F. LoBuglio and others. bibliog il Science 158:1582-5 D 22 '67

Serum alpha globulin fraction: survival-and-recovery effect in irradiated mice. M. G. Hanna, jr. and others. bibliog il Science 157:1458-61 S 22 '67

Two types of lambda polypeptide chains in human immunoglobulins. D. Ein and J. L. Fahey. bibliog il Science 156:947-8 My 19 '67

Ultrastructure of gamma M immunoglobulin and alpha macroglobulin: electro-microscopic study. S. E. Svehag and others. bibliog il Science 158:933-6 N 17 '67

See also
Haptoglobins

SERVAN-SCHREIBER, Jean Jacques
U.S. business taking over Europe? excerpts from American challenge. por U S News 63:103-4 N 20 '67

about
Invasion stirs a cry for action. por Bsns W p42 D 30 '67

SERVANT of two masters; drama. See Goldoni, C.

SERVANT of two masters; opera. See Giannini, V.

SERVICE, Compulsory non-military
National service proposal. J. M. Swomley, jr; discussion. Christian Cent 84:282,441-2 Mr 1, Ap 5 '67

SERVICE, Length of. See Seniority, Employee

SERVICE, Public. See Public service

SERVICE community. See Community service

SERVICE corps of retired executives. See United States—Small business administration

SERVICE industries
Address book. E. Kinard. See issues of House beautiful
America's huge catered affair. il Newsweek 70:60-2 S 4 '67
Rise of the service conglomerates. G. J. Berkwitt. il Duns R 90:67-8+ D '67
Service, please; Russian program to train more people for service jobs. Time 90:37 S 29 '67
See also
Moving and storage companies
Repairing

Securities
Payoff in services. il Duns R 90:111-12 S '67

SERVICE men
Before you sign an instalment contract; regulations that protect servicemen. il Changing T 21:19-21 Ag '67
Social inequities; Project Transition; address, November 7, 1967. R. S. McNamara. Vital Speeches 34:102 D 1 '67
Two who stayed home. Time 90:28 N 24 '67
See also
Furloughs
Soldiers

Laws and legislation
Law that helps servicemen with debts; Soldiers' and sailors' civil relief act. il Changing T 21:39-41 F '67

SERVICE men, Discharged
Re-entry problem of the Vietvets. W. B. Furlong. il N Y Times Mag p23+ My 7 '67

Benefits
What Congress is asked to do for veterans. U S News 62:14 F 13 '67

Education
How new GI bill may help you. F. Bailey, jr. Suc Farm 65:16 Ja '67

Employment
Oh, you're back? il Time 91:15 Ja 12 '68

SERVICE mens families
At home with the prisoners' families. M. Byers. il Life 63:34-34B O 20 '67
Do I have a daddy? J. Headley. il Redbook 130:10+ D '67
Going for broke; plight of the married enlisted man. il Newsweek 70:100+ D 4 '67
Special report on the families of the men in Vietnam. J. Whitbread. il Parents Mag 42:53-5+ O '67

SERVICE mens housing. See Housing—United States

SERVICE mens letters. See Letters from servicemen

SERVICE ribbons. See Decorations of honor

SERVICEBERRIES
Small tree for small gardens. C. M. Fitch. il Home Gard 54:61-2 F '67

SERVING carts
Barbecue cart you can build. G. Florida. il Pop Sci 190:158-9 My '67

SESSIONS, Robert Paul
Prize dopes. Christian Cent 84:306-9 Mr 8 '67

SESSOMS, H. Douglas
Education for recreation and park professionals. Parks & Rec 2:29-30+ D '67

SET theory. See Algebra, Boolean

SETON, Anya
Writer's requisites. Writer 80:19+ Ag '67

SETON, Cynthia Propper
Traveling with children. Atlan 220:126-9 O '67

SETON, Ernest Thompson
By a thousand fires, by J. M. Seton. Review
Newsweek por 70:108+ D 18 '67. S. K. Oberbeck

SETON, Julia (Clements) lady. See Clements, J.

SETON, Mary
Swing to small families. Parents Mag 42:56-7+ O '67

SETTERS
Happy is a dog with friends; English setter. il Look 31:M10+ Jl 11 '67
Two weeks' leave. C. Ford. il Field & S 72:6+ O '67

SETTING-in of winter; story. See Coates, R. M.

SEUSS, Dr, pseud. See Geisel, T. S.

SEUSS, Juergen
Where there's smoke. . . il U S Camera 30:80-1 O '67

SEVAREID, Eric
Dissent or destruction? Look 31:21-3 S 5 '67

SEVEN Ponds nature center. See Nature centers

SEVEN RIVERS library system, Iowa
Farmer Jones's information network. N. Neafie. il Library J 92:1586-7 Ap 15 '67

SEVERIN, Timothy
Passion of Hernando de Soto; excerpt from Explorers of the Mississippi. Am Heritage 18:26-31+ Ap '67
Preposterous pathfinder; excerpt from Explorers of the Mississippi. Am Heritage 19:56-63 D '67

SEVERINO, Tony
He always leaves them laughing. por Flying 80:94-5 Ap '67

SEVILLE, Jack
How to buy a cruiser. Pop Mech 127:155-6+ F '67
How to buy a runabout. Pop Mech 127:153+ F '67

SEVILLE, Spain
Murder and jasmine; Santa Cruz quarter. E. Cox. Sat R 50:63-4+ N 18 '67

SEWAGE disposal
First results with oxidation ditches on the farm. A. Phelps. il Farm J 91:48L+ Ja '67
Sewerage and sewage purification. See issues of American city
Sewers 300 feet down; Mexico city. E. Zubryn. Sci N 92:204 Ag 26 '67
Tests chemical treatment of storm overflow; pollution control project. il Am City 82:36 N '67
See also
Sewage incinerators
Sewage lagoons
Sewage pumping
Water pollution

Activated sludge method
Rapid-bloc system accelerates treatment; Milpitas, Calif. R. E. Boone. il Am City 82:80-3 Ja '67
Savings in activated-sludge systems; St Petersburg, Fla. R. Steytler. il Am City 82:113-15+ My '67

Chlorination
How Chicago saved $2.5 million; chlorination facilities. V. W. Bacon. il Am City 82:16 O '67

SEWAGE disposal—*Continued*

Filtration

Drinking water from sewage? Nassau County, N.Y. A. Gruenwald. il Am City 82:92-3 Mr '67

Membranes will cut treatment costs; Stamford, Conn. R. W. Okey. il Am City 82:124 Je '67

Phosphate removal

Battle of Lake Erie: eutrophication and political fragmentation. K. Sperry. il Science 158:351-5 O 20 '67

Better phosphate removal. Am City 82:28 Ja '67

What third-stage sewage treatment means. A. Machis. il Am City 82:110+ S '67

Screening

Fine screens for combined sewage; Portland, Ore. Am City 82:42 D '67

SEWAGE disposal plants

Better than the pilot model; Cedar Rapids, Ia, water pollution control plant. J. W. Gerlich. il Am City 82:94-6 O '67

Big but compact; New York city's thirteenth water-pollution-control plant. J. Cunetta. il Am City 82:137-9 O '67

City's answer to water pollution. il U S News 63:112-13 O 2 '67

Contact stabilization saves a million dollars; Winfield, Kan. R. L. Brown. il Am City 82:89-91 Mr '67

How Seattle is beating water pollution; Metro's project. E. Clark. il Harper 234:91-5 Je '67

LAS detergents relieve stream-foam problems; biodegradability and removal from sewage treatment plants. il Am City 82:107+ N '67

Sewage treatment plant designed to enhance a riverfront. il Arch Rec 142:108-9 D '67

Sewerage and sewage purification. See issues of American city

Sewerage program wins by 10-1 vote; Monroe, N.C. J. E. Hinkle and R. A. McCoy, jr. il Am City 82:74-5 Jl '67

What third-stage sewage treatment means. A. Machis. il Am City 82:110+ S '67

Automatic control

Instrumentation for today and tomorrow; sewage-treatment plant, Brockton, Mass. il Am City 82:113-15 F '67

Maintenance and repair

Concentrate on preventive maintenance. E. F. Spitzer. il Am City 82:72-4 N; 78-80 D '67

SEWAGE incinerators

Incinerator's role in sludge disposal; excerpt from paper presented before American society of sanitary engineering. P. J. Cardinal, jr. il Am City 82:108-10 D '67

SEWAGE lagoons

Town that launders water. L. A. Stevens. il Read Digest 90:117-21 Ap '67

SEWAGE pumping

Eighty tons go into a wet hole; sewage pumping station, Oakland Park, Fla. il Am City 82:42 D '67

SEWAGE pumps

Pumping polyelectrolytes is tricky. C. P. Baugher. Am City 82:28 Jl '67

SEWAGE treatment in space. See Life support systems (space environment)

SEWAGE treatment plants. See Sewage disposal plants

SEWARD, William Henry

GOP mainstream. R. Moley. Newsweek 70:126 N 13 '67

Warm celebration for Seward's icebox. il por Sr Schol 90:6-7 Mr 31 '67

SEWELL, David O.

Critique of cost-benefit analyses of training; excerpt from Training the poor. bibliog f Mo Labor R 90:45-51 S '67

SEWELL, W. R. Derrick

Pipedream or practical possibility? Bul Atomic Sci 23:9-13 S '67

SEWER cleaning

In an emergency, call a contractor to solve a critical sewer-cleaning problem at high speed; New York. M. M. Cohn. il Am City 82:84-5 Ag '67

SEWER inspection

We use TV for more than inspection; Sacramento County, Calif. J. S. Haldeman. il Am City 82:112-13+ Mr '67

SEWER pipes

Heavy pipe on the half shell; New Orleans. il Am City 82:28 Ag '67

SEWERAGE

Separate those sewers; Tacoma, Wash. J. A. Bronow. il Am City 82:94-6 F '67

Two storm-water solutions. Am City 84:42 F '67

Maintenance and repair

Horn foretells sewer overflows; McPherson, Kan. C. E. Stacy. il Am City 82:58 My '67

SEWERS. See Sewerage

SEWING

Everybody's sewing like mad! il Changing T 21:41-3 My '67

Home sewing with permanent press fabrics. il Consumer Bul 50:4-6 Je '67

How to organize your sewing. Bet Hom & Gard 45:121 Je '67

Making a shirt for dad. C. Houck. il Parents Mag 42:130 S '67

Teaching a child to sew. C. Houck. il Parents Mag 42:27 Ag '67

See also

Hats

Needlework

SEWING equipment

See also

Thimbles

SEWING machines

Get the most out of your sewing machine. Bet Hom & Gard 45:120 F '67

Zigzag sewing machines. il Consumer Bul 50:19-25 D '67

SEWING patterns. See Patterns (dress)

SEWING rooms

Kitchen satellite: family room/hideaway sewing center. S. Kaiser. il Farm J 91:60-1 S '67

To inspire your creative talents, H&G designs a sewing studio. il House & Gard 131:168-71 Ap '67

SEX

Future of sex. M. McLuhan and G. B. Leonard. Look 31:56-60+ Jl 25 '67

Is marriage dying, too? excerpt from Sex is dead and other postmortems. E. H. Brill. Christian Cent 84:268-70 Mr 1 '67

Opinion: on the sex hang-up. M. Farange. Mlle 65:38+ Jl '67

Sex and money: the modern equation. A. Brien. il Holiday 42:12+ O '67

Anecdotes, facetiae, satire, etc.

Who killed the stork? McCall's Who's who in American sex circles. il McCalls 95:38-9 Ja '68

SEX (biology)

See also

Gynandromorphism

SEX (psychology)

Love's body, by N. O. Brown. Review

Commentary 43:71-5 F '67. H. Marcuse; Reply. N. O. Brown. 43:83-4 Mr '67

Nation 204:405-7 Mr 27 '67. K. Burke

Parental nudity. B. Bettelheim. il Ladies Home J 84:56 Ag '67

Sexual roles being reversed, says psychiatrist; theories of Ralph R. Greenson. Todays Health 45:85 Ap '67

SEX, Change of. See Change of sex

SEX and religion

Catholic and obscenity. P. Riga. Cath World 205:340-5 S '67; Reply. M. A. Hill. 206:105-8 D '67

New morality: some questions. T. A. Wassmer. America 117:132 Ag 5 '67

On sexual responsibility; excerpts from Deeds and rules in Christian ethics. P. Ramsey. Cath World 205:210-16 Jl '67

Sex and the Christian; the erotic and the scriptures. J. Blenkinsopp. Commonweal 87:435-9 Ja 12 '68

Trial by marriage. Time 89:110+ Ap 14 '67

See also

Skoptsi

SEX behavior

Alienated youth. J. Down. il Sch & Soc 95:252-4 Ap 15 '67

Duel in the Rockies; bighorn rutting activity. J. S. Crawford. il Outdoor Life 140:54-7+ O '67

Girls, or boys, who needs them? F. Nelson. il Nat R 19:1067-9 O 3 '67

Hormone-mediated nutritional control of sexual behavior in male dung flies. W. Foster. bibliog Science 158:1596-7 D 22 '67

Maternal behavior in the domestic cock under the influence of alcohol. J. K. Kovach. bibliog il Science 156:835-7 My 12 '67

Mating behavior: facilitation in the female rat after cortical application of potassium chloride. L. G. Clemens and others. bibliog il Science 157:1208-9 S 8 '67

On being a woman; you don't have to say more than no. J. Brothers. Good H 164:22+ Ja '67

Role differentiation in copulating cicada killer wasps. N. Lin. bibliog il Science 157:1334-5 S 15 '67

SEX behavior—*Continued*
Sex and the Christian: the erotic and the scriptures. J. Blenkinsopp. Commonweal 87:435-9 Ja 12 '68
Sex and the single standard. C. R. Pangborn. Christian Cent 84:648-50 My 17 '67; Discussion. 84:872-3 Jl 5 '67
Sex on campus; a new ethic but not sex for kicks. J. L. Walsh. Commonweal 85:590-1+ F 24 '67
Teen-agers and sex: a student report. A. Lake. il Seventeen 26:88-9+ Jl '67
Testosterone regulation of sexual reflexes in spinal male rats. B. L. Hart. bibliog il Science 155:1283-4 Mr 10 '67
Twin meiosis and other ambivalences in the life cycle of schizosaccharomyces pombe. H. Gutz. bibliog il Science 158:796-8 N 10 '67
Your secret life. D. Newman and R. Benton. Mlle 64:38 F; 90+ Mr '67
See also
Courtship of insects
SEX chromosomes. See Chromosomes
SEX crimes
See also
Indecent assault
SEX differences
How different are they? excerpt from Development of sex differences, ed. by E. E. Maccoby. S. F. Yolles. il N Y Times Mag p64-5+ F 5 '67
Is feminine psychology justified? H. Gavin and K. O'Hara. Cath World 205:282-5 Ag '67
Rare study tracks half a lifetime. il Sci N 92:275-6 S 16 '67
Sex differences in taste preference for glucose and saccharin solutions. E. S. Valenstein and others. bibliog il Science 156:942-3 My 19 '67
What makes boys masculine. B. Bettelheim. Ladies Home J 84:41-2 S '67
Who goes there? Polish athlete fails sex test. Newsweek 70:97 S 25 '67
SEX education. See Sex instruction
SEX hormones. See Hormones, Sex
SEX in literature
Literature vs. trash: where can we draw the line? M. Lerner. Redbook 129:60-1+ Ag '67
SEX in moving pictures. See Moving pictures—Moral aspects
SEX in television programs. See Television broadcasting—Moral aspects
SEX instruction
Experiment in sex education. J. Gorsuch. Read Digest 91:138-42 N '67
Father speaks out on sex. R. F. Hettlinger. il Parents Mag 42:44-5+ Je '67
Films and filmstrips for sex education. V. M. Falconer. Sr Schol 90:sup25 Ap 28 '67
It's a long way from the birds and bees. W. B. Furlong. il N Y Times Mag p24-5+ Je 11 '67
New sex education. W. Goodman. il Redbook 129:62-3+ S '67
On teaching children about sex; Time essay. Time 89:36-7 Je 9 '67
Pedagogy of sex. W. Simon and J. H. Gagnon. il Sat R 50:74-6+ N 18 '67
Pill and the pupil. il Newsweek 70:72 Jl 24 '67
Sex and sexuality: the crucial difference. W. H. Masters and V. E. Johnson. il Read Digest 90:123-6 F '67
Sex education in modern schools; forum in Chicago. il PTA Mag 61:17-18 Je '67
Sex education: what do children actually learn? M. F. Iseman. McCalls 95:36-7+ Ja '68
Shameful neglect of sex education; with study-discussion program by C. Smallenburg and H. Smallenburg. P. Friggens. bibliog il PTA Mag 61:4-7, 36-7 My '67; Same abr. with title Case for enlightened sex education. Read Digest 90:73-7 My '67
What's happening in sex education? symposium. Sr Schol 90:sup 13-14+ Ap 21 '67
Where did babies come from? famous women recall how they learned the facts of life. S. Birmingham. il McCalls 94:65+ S '67

Anecdotes, facetiae, satire, etc.
Karen and the facts of life. F. Maynard. il Good H 164:37-9 F '67
SEX organs. See Generative organs
SEX perversion
See also
Homosexuality
SEX ratio
Extraordinary sex ratios. W. D. Hamilton. bibliog il Science 156:477-88 Ap 28 '67

SEX relations
Copulation and sperm induction by normal and palpless male linyphiid spiders. J. S. Rovner. bibliog Science 157:835 Ag 18 '67
Most delicate problem in marriage. S. Frank. il Good H 164:87+ Mr '67
No moral revolution discovered, yet. Sci N 93:60-1 Ja 20 '68
Opinion: on men at war. J. Kazickas. Mlle 64:124+ Mr '67
Sex and class; L. Rainwater survey findings. Newsweek 69:100+ Ap 17 '67
Stop the fighting! bring our girls home! D. Newman and R. Benton. il Mlle 65:48+ S '67

Anecdotes, facetiae, satire, etc.
Love song of David H. Myers. D. H. Myers. Esquire 68:80+ N '67
SEX-role inversion. See Change of sex
SEX surgery. See Generative organs—Surgery
SEXTON, Alan W. and Gersten, J. W.
Isometric tension differences in fibers of red and white muscles. bibliog Science 157:199 Jl 14 '67
SEXTON, Anne
Nude swim; poem. Harper 235:107 D '67
about
Light in a dark journey; winner of the Pulitzer prize for poetry. T. P. McDonnell. por America 116:729-31 My 13 '67
O yellow eye. P. Legler. Poetry 110:125-7 My '67
SEXUAL behavior. See Sex behavior
SEXUAL diseases. See Venereal diseases
SEXUAL ethics
Anything goes: taboos in twilight. il Newsweek 70:74-8 N 13 '67
Father speaks out on sex. R. F. Hettlinger. il Parents Mag 42:44-5+ Je '67
Husband stealer, American style. S. Knickerbocker. il Vogue 149:192-3+ My '67
Innocent game that disrupts marriage. N. M. Lobsenz. il Redbook 128:64-5+ Ap '67; Same abr. with title Innocent game that can disrupt marriage. Read Digest 91:122-4 Jl '67
Is marriage still sacred? what does love mean? A. Whitman. Redbook 128:68-9+ F '67
New case for chastity. E. Gordon. Read Digest 92:81-5 Ja '68
New morality. U. Bronfenbrenner. Sat R 50:47 Jl 1 '67
Not a case history, not a statistic: our daughter. J. March. il McCalls 94:76-7+ Ag '67
Of many things; U.S. college students. J. McLaughlin. America 117:527 N 11 '67
On sexual responsibility; excerpts from Deeds and rules in Christian ethics. P. Ramsey. Cath World 205:210-16 Jl '67
Redbook dialogue; I. Marvin; J. Carson. il Redbook 130:74-5+ N '67
Sex and sexuality: the crucial difference. W. H. Masters and V. E. Johnson. il Read Digest 90:123-6 F '67
Sex and the single standard. C. R. Pangborn. Christian Cent 84:648-50 My 17 '67; Discussion. 84:872-3 Jl 5 '67
Sex, morality, and the turned-on generation; with press comments. il Sr Schol 90:6-11+ My 12 '67
Sex on campus; a new ethic but not sex for kicks. J. L. Walsh. Commonweal 85:590-1+ F 24 '67
Sex: our changing times; address, March 27, 1967. W. I. Nichols. Vital Speeches 33:445-8 My 1 '67
Taking sex seriously. Christian Cent 84:644-5 My 17 '67; Discussion. 84:873 Jl 5 '67
Too much sex too soon? dating in adolescence. B. Spock. Redbook 130:26+ Ja '68
Why I believe in sex before marriage. S. Milas. Redbook 130:10+ N '67
You shall not commit adultery. H. A. Bosley. Read Digest 91:139-42 O '67
See also
Marriage
Sex and religion
Sex instruction
Sex relations
SEXUAL maturity. See Puberty
SEXUAL sterilization. See Sterilization, Sexual
SEYBOLD, John W.
Break-even point in computer composition; summary of report. Pub W 191:73 Ap 3 '67
SEYMOUR, Dan
New boss for the biggest. il pors Time 89:87 Je 23 '67
SEYMOUR, Peter
Hydra adio, Hydra hello. Sat R 50:56+ O 14 '67

SFAKIA. See Sphakia, Crete
Uno SGUARDO dal ponte; opera. See Rossellini, R.
SHABECOFF, Philip
Fox and the bear are cautious partners. N Y Times Mag p20-1+ F 5 '67
SHABTHAI Tsebi
Sabbatai Zevi and the Jewish imagination. R. Alter. Commentary 43:66-71 Je '67
SHACKELFORD, Lyne T.
Lyne T. Shackelford; advocates strong design; with biographical sketch. il por Am Artist 31:36-7+ Mr '67
SHACKLETON, Robert
Shackleton committee reports academic libraries plight. Library J 92:957 Mr 1 '67
SHAD fishing
Oh shad, poor shad. L. Green. il Field & S 72:52-5+ My '67
SHADBLOWS. See Serviceberries
SHADBOLT, Maurice
Paradise in search of a future. Nat Geog Mag 132:202-31 Ag '67
SHADE, Christine Sinrud
As frail as a sparrow. McCalls 94:74+ Mr '67
SHADE plants. See Plants, Shade
SHADE trees. See Trees; Trees in cities
SHADES, Electric light. See Electric lamps— Shades
SHADOW bride; story. See Eden, D.
SHADOW pantomimes and plays
Shadows and light on the Ramayana; Cambodia's shadow theater. il UNESCO Courier 20:34-5+ D '67
SHADOWGRAMS
Photograms. P. Holtra. il Sch Arts 66:13-17 F '67
Pictures without a lens; photograms. il Pop Phot 61:55-8 S '67
SHADOWPLAY; ballet. See Ballets—Criticisms
SHADWELL, Wendy J.
Some rare American prints in the Middendorf collection. Antiques 92:558-62 O '67
SHAEFFER, Joseph R. and others
Rabbit hemoglobin biosynthesis: use of human hemoglobin chains to study molecule completion. bibliog Science 158:488-90 O 27 '67
SHAFER, Raymond Philip
Debut of a wallflower. por Time 89:21 My 26 '67
SHAFFER, Ellen
Arthur Rackham, 1867-1939. Horn Bk 43:617-21 O '67
Potter, pirates, and punctuation. por Wilson Lib Bul 41:598-602 F '67
SHAFFER, Kenneth R.
Inept library consultants attacked by Shaffer; excerpts from address, October 5, 1967. Library J 92:3946 N 1 '67
SHAFFER, Peter
Black comedy. Criticism
Commentary 43:74-5 Je '67
Life il 62:70A-70B+ Mr 10 '67
Nation 204:285-6 F 27 '67
New Yorker 43:91 F 25 '67
Newsweek 69:102-3 F 20 '67
Reporter 36:50+ Mr 9 '67
Sat R 50:59 F 25 '67
Time il 89:70 F 17 '67
Vogue 149:54 Mr 15 '67
White lies. Criticism
Nation 204:286 F 27 '67
New Yorker 43:91 F 25 '67
Reporter 36:50+ Mr 9 '67
Sat R 50:59 F 25 '67
SHAFFER, Robert H.
Peace corps: antidote for provincialism. Sch & Soc 95:261-3 Ap 15 '67
SHAFTEL, Fannie R. and Shaftel, George
Role-playing as a learning method for disadvantaged children; excerpt from Role-playing for social values: decision-making in the social studies. bibliog f Sch & Soc 94:494-8 D 24 '66
SHAFTEL, George. See Shaftel, F. R. jt. auth.
SHAFTING
See also
Automobiles—Transmission
SHAHN, Ben
Mellowed militant. il por Time 90:72-3+ S 15 '67
SHAINESS, Natalie
Fine art of mothering. Parents Mag 43:46-7+ Ja '68
SHAKERS
Serene twilight of a once-sturdy sect: the Shakers; with report by D. Martin. il Life 62:58-68+ Mr 17 '67
SHAKESPEARE, William
Man who knew Shakespeare. P. H. Johnson. il Holiday 42:34+ N '67

Anniversaries, etc.
Anniversary; wreath-laying ceremony conducted by Shakespeare club of New York city. New Yorker 43:35-6 My 6 '67

Authorship
Devil Will shake. R. P. Lister. Atlan 219: 122+ Ap '67

Characters
Theater; Men and women of Shakespeare. H. Hewes. Sat R 50:51 F 11 '67

Plays
Theatre; Bristol Old Vic company's productions at the City Center: Measure for measure and Hamlet. J. McCarten. New Yorker 43:91 F 25 '67

Anecdotes, facetiae, satire, etc.
MacBird; an historical review. D. C. Buell. New Repub 156:27-8 F 18 '67

Antony and Cleopatra
Egyptian dish and a swinger: Antony and Cleopatra in Stratford, Ontario. T. Prideaux. Life 63:10 S 8 '67
Rare spirits; Michael Langham's production at Stratford, Ontario. H. Hewes. il Sat R 50:22 Ag 19 '67

As you like it
Men without women; all-male version staged by London's national theater company. il Time 90:72 O 13 '67

Hamlet
Anti-Hamlet of Joseph Papp. R. Brustein. New Repub 158:23+ Ja 20 '68
Bristol Old Vic; performance in New York. A. West. Vogue 149:93 Ap 1 '67
Hamlet; J. Papp's version. il Time 91:55 Ja 5 '68
Mocking bard; Bristol Old Vic's Broadway debut. Time 89:60 F 24 '67
Off Broadway; J. Papp's production. E. Oliver. New Yorker 43:68+ Ja 6 '68
Other Old Vic; Bristol Old Vic production in New York. M. Gussow. il Newsweek 69: 99-100 F 27 '67
Slings, arrows and confetti; J. Papp's production. R. A. Sokolov. Newsweek 71:60 Ja 8 '68
Theatre; Bristol Old Vic production in New York. H. Clurman. Nation 204:317-18 Mr 6 '67
Theater of shattered focus; J. Papp's production. H. Hewes. Sat R 51:95 Ja 13 '68
Theatre; J. Papp's production. H. Clurman. Nation 206:92-3 Ja 15 '68

Measure for measure
Guthrie's Shakespeare; production of the Bristol Old Vic at N.Y. city center. G. Rogoff. New Repub 156:32-3 Mr 11 '67
Mocking bard; Bristol Old Vic's Broadway debut. Time 89:60 F 24 '67
Other Old Vic; Bristol Old Vic production in New York. M. Gussow. Newsweek 69: 100 F 27 '67
Theatre; Bristol Old Vic production in New York. H. Clurman. Nation 204:317-18 Mr 6 '67

Merchant of Venice
Theater; production by the American Shakespeare festival theatre. H. Hewes. Sat R 50:34 Jl 29 '67

Midsummer night's dream
Theatre; production at Loretto-Hilton center for the performing arts. Webster college. T. Lewis. America 116:604-5 Ap 22 '67

Richard III
Breakaway bit for the bard: Shakespeare and Gogol in Stratford, Ontario. T. Prideaux. Life 63:12 Ag 4 '67

Staging and acting of plays
Letters from an actor, by W. Redfield. Review
Sat R 50:30-1 Mr 4 '67. B. Atkinson
SHAKESPEARE club of New York. See New York (city)—Clubs
SHAKESPEARE festival, Stratford, Ontario
Breakaway bit for the bard: Shakespeare and Gogol in Stratford, Ontario. T. Prideaux. Life 63:12 Ag 4 '67
Egyptian dish and a swinger: Antony and Cleopatra in Stratford, Ontario. T. Prideaux. Life 63:10 S 8 '67
Outpost of habitual culture. il Time 89:53 Je 30 '67

SHAKESPEARE festival, Stratford, Ontario
—Continued
Rare spirits; Michael Langham's production of Antony and Cleopatra. H. Hewes. il Sat R 50:22 Ag 19 '67
Theatre; current season. J. Novick. Nation 205:220-2 S 11; 285-6 S 25 '67
SHAKESPEARE festivals
Bard at Balboa; San Diego festival. H. Hewes. Sat R 50:24 Ag 26 '67
Shakespeare comes to Utah's Cedar City. il Sunset 139:36 Jl '67
Shakespeare trail; Ashland, Ore. festival. H. Hewes. Sat R 50:38 S 2 '67
See also
Shakespeare festival, Stratford, Ontario
SHAKING hands. See Hand shaking
SHALE
Chromium and nickel in the fig tree shale from South Africa. R. V. Danchin. bibliog il Science 158:261-2 O 13 '67
Isoprenoid and dicarboxylic acids isolated from Colorado Green River shale (Eocene) P. Haug and others. bibliog il Science 158:772-3 N 10 '67
Perhydro-β-carotene in the Green River shale. M. T. J. Murphy and others. bibliog il Science 157:1040-2 S 1 '67
SHALES, Oil. See Oil shales
SHALIT, Gene
What's happening. See issues of Ladies' home journal
SHALLCROSS, Doris J.
Creative problem-solving course. NEA J 56:57 F '67
SHALLIT, Joseph
We're up to Deuteronomy. Read Digest 91:19-20+ Jl '67
SHAM. See Fraud
SHAMMOUT, Anne
On being a sheik's wife. Sat R 50:71-2+ O 14 '67
SHAMPOOS
Consumer service bureau report; something special in shampoos. M. B. Keiser. il Parents Mag 42:8+ Ag '67
Taming the raging mane. il Mlle 65:140-1 S '67
SHANAHAN, Edward K.
Drumming up votes for the poverty program. New Repub 156:7-8 Je 17 '67
SHANE, Ted
Roamer's ramblings. See issues of Travel to August 1967
SHANKAR, Ravi
Raga is all the rage! ed. by E. Miller. por Seventeen 26:346+ Ag '67
about
His sitar sound rocks the U.S. J. Borgzinner. il pors Life 63:35-6+ Ag 18 '67
Ravi Shankar and George Beatles. C. Reid. il pors N Y Times Mag p28-9+ My 7 '67
Shankar and his magic sitar. I. Kolodin. Sat R 50:55-6 S 30 '67
SHANKER, Albert
Cost of militancy. Time 90:40 D 22 '67
He leads his teachers up the down staircase. A. H. Raskin. il por N Y Times Mag p4-5+ S 3 '67
Shrewd union leader takes his teachers out. il Life 63:32-5 S 22 '67
SHANKS, Ann Zane
Woman on the run. E. Bennett. il U S Camera 30:44-5+ S '67
SHANNON, Dell, pseud. See Linington, E.
SHANNON, James A.
Medicine moves toward systems techniques. por Tech W 20:72-3+ Ja 23 '67
about
Basic science in mission-oriented endeavor. T. L. Campbell. por Science 156:670-2 My 5 '67
Medical research: NIH wants divorce from PHS. L. J. Carter. il por Science 156:45-8 Ap 7 '67
NIH: as the time approaches for Shannon's retirement. D. S. Greenberg. il por Science 158:1165-7 D 1 '67
NIH wants independence. B. J. Culliton. il por Sci N 91:478-9 My 20 '67
Succession at NIH. P. H. Abelson. Science 156:459 Ap 28 '67
SHANNON, John P. See Harlow, F. H. jt. auth.
SHANNON, Peter M.
Changing law in a changing church. America 116:248-50 F 18 '67
Reform of canon law; reprint. Cath World 206:53-6 N '67
SHANNON, Walter S.
Forest practices and watershed management in California; address. Am For 73:6-7+ My '67

SHANNON, William V.
Case for the war. Commonweal 87:326-7 D 8 '67
George Romney: holy and hopeful. Harper 234:55-62 F '67
National affairs. See issues of Commonweal
SHANNON airport. See Airports—Ireland
SHANOR, Donald R.
Report: Poland. Atlan 220:36+ D '67
SHANTYTOWNS. See Squatters
SHAPE of the earth. See Earth—Figure
SHAPE perception. See Perception
SHAPIRO, David
Poem; We have come to be saved. From a pest. Nation 204:190 F 6 '67
SHAPIRO, Fred C.
Last word (we hope) on George Lincoln Rockwell. Esquire 67:101-5+ F '67
Life and death of a great newspaper. Am Heritage 18:97-112 O '67
Successor to Floyd McKissick may not be so reasonable. N Y Times Mag p32-3+ O 1 '67
SHAPIRO, Gilbert
Many lives of Georges Lefebvre. bibliog f Am Hist R 72:502-14 Ja '67
SHAPIRO, Harry L.
Books in review. Natur Hist 76:68+ Je '67
SHAPIRO, Harvey
An end; poem. Harper 235:102 O '67
As I come home; poem. Nation 206:61 Ja 8 '68
Events; poem. Nation 205:150 Ag 28 '67
For WCW; For Delmore Schwartz; Days and nights; Blue Max; Sister; poems. Poetry 110:159-63 Je '67
Hello there! poem. Nation 205:222 S 11 '67
Tractors; poem. Nation 204:665 My 22 '67
Years; poem. Nation 204:157 Ja 30 '67
about
Art in transition. L. Lieberman. Poetry 109:398-9 Mr '67
Past reordered. D. Ignatow. Nation 204:531-2 Ap 24 '67
SHAPIRO, Irwin I.
New method for the detection of light deflection by solar gravity. bibliog Science 157:806-8 Ag 18 '67
Resonance rotation of Venus. bibliog Science 157:423-5 Jl 28 '67
SHAPIRO, Joseph
Induced rapid release and uptake of phosphate by microorganisms. bibliog Science 155:1269-71 Mr 10 '67
SHAPIRO, Karl
Class of '67: the gentle desperadoes. Nation 204:776-7 Je 19 '67
Five poems. New Yorker 43:38 Ag 12 '67
From white-haired lover; fourteen poems. Poetry 111:1-14 O '67
SHAPIRO, Kenneth
Underground channels. H. Junker. New Repub 157:33-4 S 9 '67
SHAPIRO, Lillian L.
We must be doing something wrong: recruiting young blood for school libraries. por Library J 92:1992-4 My 15 '67
SHAPLEIGH family
Shapleigh coat-of-arms. H. K. Eilers. il Hobbies 72:116-17+ Ag '67
SHAPLEN, June H. See Durdin, P. jt. auth.
SHAPLEN, Robert
Letter from Bangkok. New Yorker 43:142+ Mr 18 '67
Letter from Cambodia (cont) New Yorker 43:66+ Ja 13 '68
Letter from Saigon (cont) New Yorker 42:150+ F 18; 43:149-54+ O 7 '67
Letter from South Vietnam (cont) New Yorker 43:37-8+ Je 17 '67
Viet Nam: crisis of indecision. For Affairs 46:95-110 O '67
SHARED time for religious instruction. See Public schools and religion
SHAREHOLDERS. See Stockholders
SHAREHOLDERS meetings. See Stockholders meetings
SHARKS
Hydrocarbons in digestive tract and liver of a basking shark. M. Blumer. il Science 156:390-1 Ap 21 '67
Shark! P. Benchley. Holiday 42:68-9+ N '67
Shark! overrated demon or genuine scourge? W. Hartley and E. Hartley. il Sci Digest 61:6-13 Je '67
SHARMA, Uma
Uma Sharma; MacMillan theatre. J. Maskey. Dance Mag 42:22 Ja '68
SHARON, William
Althea and the judges. B. W. Maccracken. il por Am Heritage 18:60-3+ Je '67

SHARP, Bob
Bob Sharp on navigation. Yachting 121:81+
Je '67
SHARP, E. L.
Atmospheric ions and germination of uredo-
spores of puccinia striiformis. bibliog Sci-
ence 156:1359-60 Je 9 '67
SHARP, Margery
In pious memory; story; excerpt from novel.
Ladies Home J 84:101-8 Ap '67
SHARP, Ulysses Simpson Grant, 1906-
Stand firm in Vietnam! interview. ed. by D.
Reed. por Read Digest 92:102-6 Ja '68

about

How to win the war; Admiral Sharp's pre-
scription. por U S News 63:22 O 2 '67
SHARPE, Eileen
Young start in art. Todays Health 45:58-61
S '67
SHARPENERS
Homemade sharpener for home-improvement
tools. W. G. Waggoner. il Pop Sci 191:
144-6+ S '67
SHARPS, Christian
Christian Sharps. C. Worman. il Hobbies
72:126-7 Ap '67
SHARPS rifles. See Rifles
SHARR, F. A.
Like an ambitious young man. por Library J
92:4110-12 N 15 '67
SHASTA daisies
Fresh as a daisy. il Home Gard 54:48 Jl '67
SHATTUCK, Dennis
Ford's new clean machine. Motor T 19:74-6
D '67
SHATTUCK, George E.
Shysters, moochers, and gyp artists are ex-
ploiting our students! NEA J 56:66-7 D '67
SHATZKIN, Leonard
How a publisher can help improve manufac-
turing. Pub W 192:68+ Ag 7 '67
Production planning; a publisher speaks. Pub
W 191:84+ My 1 '67
That solid backlist title; how many to print?
Pub W 191:31-2 Je 12 '67
SHAUL, W. Dennis
We were right. por Mlle 65:233+ Ag '67
SHAULL, Richard
New Latin revolutionaries and the U.S. Chris-
tian Cent 85:69-70 Ja 17 '68
SHAVING lotions. See Cosmetics for men
SHAW, Arthur
U.S. letter: Connecticut. C. Trillin. New York-
er 43:76+ Ja 6 '68
SHAW, Bernard. See Shaw, G. B.
SHAW, Bynum
Drinking and winking in North Carolina.
New Repub 156:11-13 Ja 28 '67
SHAW, Clay L.
Charge of conspiracy. por Newsweek 69:36-7
Ap 3 '67
D.A. wins a round. Time 89:17-18 Mr 24 '67
JFK death: a new investigation, but—.
U S News 62:16 Mr 13 '67
New Orleans: act I. J. Cohen and N. C.
Chriss. il Reporter 36:17-20 Ap 6 '67
New Orleans plot? Sr Schol 90:18-19 Ap 14
'67
Odd company. il por Time 89:24 Mr 10 '67
Thickening the plot. Newsweek 69:37 Mr 27
'67
SHAW, Dale
Accidents happen to other people. Redbook
128:76-7+ Ap '67
SHAW, George Bernard
Arms and the man. Criticism
America 117:63 Jl 15 '67
Devil's disciple. Criticism
America 116:880 Je 24 '67
Saint Joan. Criticism
New Yorker 43:57 Ja 13 '68
Newsweek il 71:78-9 Ja 15 '68
Time il 91:40 Ja 12 '68
Shaw at the stake; TV adaptation of Saint
Joan. R. L. Shayon. Sat R 50:37 D 30 '67
SHAW, H. B.
Mother, I do not hate to die. J. C. Phifer.
il Am Heritage 18:32-3+ F '67
SHAW, Irwin
Choice of wars. Criticism
Sat R 50:51 Ap 15 '67
SHAW, Ralph R.
Quo vadis? librarian's role in a democratic
culture; adaptation of address, February
6, 1967. por Library J 92:2881-4 S 1 '67
SHAW, Robert, 1916-
Downbeat for a new era. il por Time 90:53
O 27 '67
SHAW, Robert, 1927-
Highest paid, oldest unknown actor in the
world. T. Thompson. il pors Life 63:35-6+
N 3 '67

Like a knife. S. Kauffmann. New Repub
156:27 F 4 '67
Man in the glass booth. Criticism
Time il 90:44+ Ag 11 '67
Vogue 150:70 O 15 '67
SHAW, Russell. See Koob, C. A. jt. auth.
SHAWN, Ted
O, brother sun and sister moon. W. Terry. il
por Sat R 50:39-40 Jl 29 '67
SHAW'S garden, St Louis. See Missouri bo-
tanical garden
SHAYON, Robert Lewis
TV and radio. See issues of Saturday re-
view
SHEARER, Lloyd
Inside stuff. il por Newsweek 69:76 Je 26 '67
SHEATHS
Rifles on horseback. W. Page. il Field &
S 71:146-50 Mr '67
SHEBOYGAN, Wis.
Designed for six major functions; municipal
service building. R. E. Fleischer. il Am
City 82:104-7 S '67
SHECTER, Leonard
Baseball. Sports Illus 27:61-2+ Jl 17; 58+ D
18 '67
Humiliation of a hero. Sports Illus 26:66-71
Je 12 '67
Toughest man in pro football. Esquire 69:68-
71+ Ja '68
SHEDD, Margaret Cochran
Literary life south of the Rio Grande. J. K.
Hutchens. il Sat R 50:42-4 F 25 '67
SHEDD, Mark
Revolution in Philadelphia. Newsweek 70:70
D 18 '67
SHEDESKY, Pat
Regional report. Home Gard 54:58-9 Ag '67
SHEDS
Storage unit can be good looking. H. Mason
and others. il Bet Hom & Gard 45:54-5
Ap '67
SHEEAN, Vincent
Mary Garden, February 20, 1874-January 3,
1967. Opera N 31:6-7 F 4 '67
(tr) See Curie, E. Marie Curie
SHEED, Wilfrid
Films. See issues of Esquire
Jones boy forever. Atlan 219:68-72 Je '67
Life theater review. Life 62:8 F 24 '67
Speaking out. por Sat Eve Post 240:10+
Mr 25 '67
Theatre. Vogue 149:42 Ja 15 '67
SHEEHAN, Edward R. F.
In the forest of fear. Sat Eve Post 240:30-2+
Ag 12 '67
Making of a president, Uganda style. N Y
Times Mag p36-7+ Ja 22 '67
SHEEHAN, Ethna
Bountiful harvest of children's books. Amer-
ica 117:514+ N 4 '67
SHEEHAN, Marjorie W.
Papier-mâché project. Sch Arts 67:16-17 D '67
SHEEHAN, Neil
You don't know where Johnson ends and
McNamara begins. N Y Times Mag p29-31+
O 22 '67
SHEEHAN, Robert
Portrait of the artist as a businessman.
Fortune 75:144-8+ Mr '67
Proprietors in the world of big business. For-
tune 75:178-83+ Je 15 '67
Those retired management missionaries.
Fortune 76:106-9+ S 1 '67
SHEEHAN, Susan
Vietnamese woman; excerpt from Ten Viet-
namese. McCalls 94:48+ Mr '67
SHEEN, Fulton John, bp
Awaiting confirmation. por Newsweek 69:64
F 27 '67
Catholic bishop wants troops withdrawn from
Vietnam. Christian Cent 84:1036 Ag 16 '67
Conversion. por Newsweek 70:90 Ag 14 '67
Day of reconciliation. W. F. Buckley, jr.
Nat R 19:948 S 5 '67
New career for Sheen. il por Time 89:47-8
F 10 '67
SHEEP
News. Farm J 91:44J S '67
What's new. See issues of Successful farming

Diseases and pests

Disease theory skips DNA; study of kuru
and scrapie. F. Marley. il Sci N 91:169-
70 F 18 '67
See also
Foot-and-mouth disease
SHEEP, Wild. See Mountain sheep
SHEEP breeding
Lambs on slats: how are they doing? J.
Bickers and O. Bay. Farm J 91:42L D '67
SHEEP killer; story. See Gillespie, A.

SHEERIN, John B.
Editorial. See issues of Catholic world
SHEETS
Bed sheets; permanent press. il Consumer Bul 50:6-9 F '67
Institute reports on. . . new no-iron sheets and pillowcases. il Good H 164:6 F '67
Lively sheets. il House & Gard 131:166-9+ Mr '67
SHEFFTZ, Melvin
Maverick historian. New Repub 156:19-21 Ap 29 '67
SHEIL, Bernard James, abp
Where are they now? por Newsweek 69:16 Mr 20 '67
SHELBURNE, Mary Willis
Morning and evening; poem. Cath World 205: 345 S '67
SHELBURNE FALLS, Mass.

Gardens
To beautify America: a bridge becomes a bower. J. P. Fairhurst. il Home Gard 54: 10+ Ag '67
SHELBURNE museum, Shelburne, Vt.
Electra's hobby. il Time 90:58-63 Jl 7 '67
SHELDON, Paul B.
Experiences with sea anchors. Yachting 123: 92-3+ Ja '68
First aid afloat. Yachting 121:61-5 Je '67
SHELL decoration. See Decoration and ornament
SHELL game; story. See Cusack, I. L.
SHELL oil company
From inside out. L. L. L. Golden. Sat R 50: 65 D 9 '67
High-octane world of Shell. J. Poindexter. il Duns R 90:40-2+ O '67
Soft sell on the links. il Bsns W p62-7 Ja 6 '68
SHELL oil's Wonderful world of golf. See Golf—Tournaments
SHELLFISH
See also
Cookery—Shellfish
Lobsters
Oysters
SHELLFISH fisheries
Sailing oystermen of Chesapeake Bay. L. Marden. il Nat Geog Mag 132:798-819 D '67
SHELLS (conchology)
Cosmetic shell. A. G. Melvin. il Hobbies 72: 118 D '67
Glory of the sea. A. G. Melvin. il Hobbies 71:130 F '67
More on glory of the sea. A. G. Melvin. il Hobbies 72:124 Je '67
Patterns in shells. A. G. Melvin. il Hobbies 72:130 Mr '67
Precious wentletrap. A. G. Melvin. il Hobbies 72:119 N '67
Radiocarbon content of marine shells from the Pacific coasts of Central and South America. R. E. Taylor and R. Berger. bibliog il Science 158:1180-2 D 1 '67
What is a shell dealer? A. G. Melvin. il Hobbies 72:130 Ap '67
See also
Abalones
SHELLS (projectiles) See Cartridges; Projectiles
SHELLS (structural engineering)
Bini shell; Columbia university; interview. D. Bini. New Yorker 43:28-9 Je 3 '67
Interval in a street; Civic center synagogue. New York. il Arch Forum 127:64-9 O '67
New thin-shell forming technique uses a balloon to both lift and mold concrete. il Arch Rec 141:191-2 Je '67
Prestressed foundation resists roof thrusts. R. M. Gensert. il Arch Rec 142:173-6 N '67
SHELLY, Maynard
World's Mennonites meet in Amsterdam. Christian Cent 84:1109-10 Ag 30 '67
SHELNUTT, Eve
Affectionately, Harold; story. Mlle 65:278-9 Ag '67
SHELTERS, Atomic bomb. See Atomic bomb shelters
SHELTERS, Garden. See Garden houses, shelters, etc.
SHELTON, William
Contacts for sale. Sat R 50:84-5+ My 13 '67
Neck and neck in the space race. Fortune 76:166-8+ O '67
SHELUS, Peter J.
Spectrogram of Gamma Cassiopeiae. Sky & Tel 33:220 Ap '67
SHELVES
Balcony shelves for apartment dwellers. L. O. Rexrode. il Pop Sci 191:175 O '67
Box shelves are in style. J. B. Johnstone. il Pop Sci 190:167 My '67

Handsome and distinctive. W. C. Lammey; C. L. Widdicombe; J. E. Reppert. il Pop Mech 129:162-7 Ja '68
How to shelve a window. il Pop Gard 18:8 My '67
Standard-and-bracket shelf systems. il Consumer Rep 32:334-7 Je '67
SHELVING, Library. See Library furniture and equipment
SHEMANCHUK, Joseph A. See Morgante, O. jt. auth.
SHEMER, Naomi
Song that took a city. L. Gottlieb. Read Digest 91:112-15 D '67
SHENANDOAH NATIONAL PARK
Facets of wilderness. D. Lambert. il Liv Wildn 31:10-18 Spr '67
Wilderness plan for Shenandoah National Park and the surrounding region. il Nat Parks Mag 41:18-19 S '67
SHENKER, Israel
King & the coup. Time 89:31 My 12 '67
SHENKER, Morris
Deeper debt of gratitude to the mob. W. Lambert. il pors Life 63:38-38B N 10 '67
SHEPARD, Francis P. and others
Holocene changes in sea level: evidence in Micronesia. bibliog Science 157:542-4 Ag 4 '67
SHEPARD, George H. and James, Jesse
Police; do they belong in the schools? Am Ed 3:2-4 S '67
SHEPARD, Marietta Daniels
Literacy programs in Colombia; adaptation of report. Wilson Lib Bul 41:829-33 Ap '67
SHEPARD, Thomas Z.
Some reflections on recording the Boulez Wozzeck. pors Am Rec G 33:1067-72 Ag '67
SHEPHERD, George W. Jr
Understanding people's wars. Christian Cent 84:1185-8 S 20 '67
SHEPHERD, Jack
Drugs, a personal LSD experience. Look 31:23 Ag 8 '67
SHEPHERD, Jean
200-shot Daisy and the ultimate plink. Field & S 72:66-7+ S '67
Voyage of the Sea Serpent. Field & S 72:58-9+ My '67
SHEPLEY, James Robinson
Letter from the publisher. B. M. Auer. il por Time 89:11 F 3 '67
SHEPP, Archie
Junebug graduates tonight! Criticism Nation 204:411-12 Mr 27 '67
SHEPPARD, Eugene
Boutiques of Paris and Rome. Holiday 42: 78-81+ N '67
SHEPPARD, Roger. See Kramer, M. jt. auth.
SHEPRO, David, and Fulton, G. P.
Microcirculation and shock. Science 157:1211-12 S 8 '67
SHERA, Jesse H.
Librarians against machines. bibliog Science 156:746-50 My 12 '67; Same. Wilson Lib Bul 42:65-73 S '67
Without reserve. See issues of Wilson library bulletin
SHERATON corporation of America
ITT Sheraton. Newsweek 70:72 N 6 '67
Room at the inns: ITT buys Sheraton corp. Time 90:94 N 3 '67
SHERBET. See Ice cream, ices, etc.
SHEREFF, Ruth
Liberals in wonderland. Commonweal 86:198-9+ My 5 '67
SHERIDAN, Jennie
How to dry herbs. Horticulture 45:18 S '67
SHERIDAN, Michael P.
Campus corner (cont) America 116:279, 722, 877; 117:318 F 25, My 13, Je 24, S 23 '67
Student freedom. America 116:856 Je 17 '67
Students in social action. America 117:565 N 11 '67
Theology and academic freedom. America 116:681-2 My 6 '67
SHERIDAN, Thomas
Thomas Sheridan of Smock-Alley, by E. K. Sheldon. Review
Sat R 50:29 Je 17 '67. P. Burton
SHERIDAN, Walter
NBC's supersleuth. il por Newsweek 70:116 O 23 '67
SHERIFF; story. See Midwood, B.
SHERIFFS
Kind of black power in Macon County, Ala; L. D. Amerson, first Negro sheriff in Alabama. G. Roberts. il N Y Times Mag p32-3+ F 26 '67
New look in southern sheriffs. il Ebony 22:120-2+ My '67
SHERMAN, Bennett
Techniques tomorrow. See issues of Modern photography

SHERMAN, Edward F.
Dissenters and deserters. New Repub 158:23-6
Ja 6 '68
SHERMAN, Jerome Kalman
Sperm banks debated. B. J. Culliton. il Sci N
92:208-9 Ag 26 '67
SHERMAN, John K.
Mischievous opera at the Tyrone Guthrie.
Hi Fi 17:MA21+ Ap '67
SHERMAN, Louis
What's ahead for labor-management rela-
tions. Mo Labor R 90:44-5 Ap '67
SHERMAN, Margaret E.
Where and how of student travel. Sat R 50:
38+ F 18 '67
SHERMAN, Robert
Recordings reports: stage and screen. Sat R
50:52 Jl 29; 56 D 2 '67
SHERMAN, Roy V.
Residence requirements drop for city jobs.
Am City 82:108+ Je '67
SHERMAN, Thomas B.
Honeymoon is over. Hi Fi 17:MA24-5 My '67
SHERMAN, Vivian S.
What injures a child's self-esteem? PTA
Mag 61:23-5 bibliog(p35) Mr '67
SHERMAN antitrust law. See Trusts, Indus-
trial—Law

SHERRELL, Elliot
Made in Italy export house manager. il pors
Ebony 22:75-6+ F '67
SHERRIFFS, Alex C.
Convenient myths; address, May 19, 1967.
Vital Speeches 33:669-72 Ag 15 '67
SHERRILL, Robert G.
A.B.C. & ITT: marriage in haste. Nation
204:361-4 Mr 20 '67
Architect, spare our Capitol. N Y Times
Mag p30-1+ Ap 16 '67
Bastille day on the Potomac. Nation 205:454-5
N 6 '67
Faith of Eugene McCarthy. Nation 205:589-
91 D 4 '67
George Wallace: running for God; with ex-
cerpts from interview. Nation 204:589-96 My
8 '67
Harvest of scandal. Nation 205:496-500 N 13
'67
Hatfield: the Oregon enigma. Nation 205:38-
44 Jl 17 '67
How to succeed on the Potomac: be an in-
vestigator. N Y Times Mag p44-5+ O 8 '67
It isn't true that nobody starves in America.
N Y Times Mag p22-3+ Je 4; 59 Jl 30 '67
Jet noise is getting awful. N Y Times Mag
p24-5+ Ja 14 '68
Lobby on target. N Y Times Mag p27+ O 15;
85 N 5; 42 N 19 '67
90th Congress: slapping at symbols. Nation
205:142-5 Ag 28 '67
Political happening named Claude Kirk. N Y
Times Mag p34-5+ N 26 '67
Professor & the CIA. Nation 204:258-60 F
27 '67
Strange decorum of Lester Maddox. Nation
204:553-6 My 1 '67
Surfmanship and salesmanship. N Y Times
Mag p 12-14+ Jl 16 '67
U.S. civil service: rebels on the Potomac.
Nation 204:265-8 F 27 '67
U.S. civil service: Washington's bland bond-
age. Nation 204:239-42, 436 F 20, Ap 3 '67
SHERRILL, William W.
For the Fed, a man with no label. por Bsns
W p40 My 6 '67
Neither tight nor easy—for now; appoint-
ment to the Federal reserve board. por
Time 89:87 My 5 '67
SHERROD, Robert Lee
Notes on a monstrous war. pors Life 62:
20-9 Ja 27 '67
about
Return of Robert Sherrod. G. P. Hunt. por
Life 62:3 Ja 27 '67
SHERRY, Paul H.
Church or college: either, but not both. Chris-
tian Cent 84:1247-50 O 4 '67
SHERRY. See Wine
SHERRY; musical comedy. See Musical com-
edies, revues, etc.—Criticisms, plots, etc.
SHERWIN, Chalmers William
Quick-access pool for world data. Bsns W
p78+ Je 17 '67
Shift at Commerce. Sci N 91:545-6 Je 10 '67
—and Isenson, R. S.
Project Hindsight. bibliog Science 156:1571-7
Je 23 '67
SHERWIN, Michael
Stereo Christmas goodies under $30. Hi Fi
17:64-6 D '67
SHERWIN-Williams company
New gloss at Sherwin-Williams; modern
management and marketing techniques. il
Bsns W p 154-6+ Jl 15 '67

SHERWOOD, Lyn
Shooting the bull. U S Camera 30:64-5+ Je
'67
SHERWOOD, Terry
Up, virago! poem. Nat. R 19:180 F 21 '67
SHESTOV, Lev
Tyrant necessity. W. Herberg. Sat R 50:50-1
F 4 '67
SHEVRIN, Aliza
(tr) See Singer, I. B. Letter writer
(tr) See Singer, I. B. My adventures as an
idealist
SHIBLEY, George P. and others
Leukemogenic activity of ether-extracted
Rauscher leukemia virus. bibliog Science
156:1610-13 Je 23 '67
SHIDELER, Mary McDermott
Coup de grâce. Christian Cent 83:1499-502;
84:272-3 D 7 '66, Mr 1 '67
SHIELD, William
Records:
Rosina. Opera N 31:34 Ap 15 '67
SHIELDING (electricity)
Conductive-foil tape seals interference. P. J.
Klass. il Aviation W 87:87-9 Jl 24 '67
SHIELDING (heat)
Ablation thermal protection systems. E. W.
Ungar. bibliog il Science 158:740-4 N 10 '67
New high-temperature materials studied. Avi-
ation W 88:41 Ja 1 '68
Tantalum elevon built for 3,000F test. M. L.
Yaffee. il Aviation W 88:36-9+ Ja 1 '68
See also
Guided missiles—Shielding (heat)
Space vehicles—Shielding (heat)
SHIELDING (radiation)
Nucleon-meson cascade and shielding. R. G.
Alsmiller, jr. bibliog il Science 157:1399-405
S 22 '67
Radiation-resistant transistor studied. il Avia-
tion W 87:112 O 16 '67
See also
Space vehicles—Shielding (radiation)
SHIELDS, A. Randolph
Strangers in high places. Liv Wildn 30:29-30
Aut '66
SHIELDS, Ellen
Armadillo's prayer. Horn Bk 43:632 O '67
SHIGEMORI, Mirei
Simplicity is the keynote in Japanese garden-
ing. A. R. Roalman. il por Pop Gard 18:18-
21+ D '67
SHIH, Hsio-yen
Mad Ming monks and eccentric exiles. Art N
66:36-9+ Ap '67
SHIH, Pen-shan
I fought in red China's sports war; ed. by
L. Velie. por Read Digest 90:73-8 Je '67
SHILLELAGH (guided missile) See Guided
missiles
SHILS, Edward
Intellectuals and the future. Bul Atomic Sci
23:7-14 O '67
SHILS, Edward B. and Whittier, C. T.
Other employees in the school: nonteacher
bargaining; excerpt from Teachers, ad-
ministrators, and collective bargaining. Mo
Labor R 90:42-4 S '67
SHIMAZU, Takashi
Glycogen synthetase activity in liver: regu-
lation by the autonomic nerves. bibliog
Science 156:1256-7 Je 2 '67
SHIMKIN, Michael
Educational publishing reorganized at S&S.
por Pub W 191:48 F 6 '67
SHIMOKAWA, Keishi, and Kasal, Zenzaburo
Ethylene formation from ethyl moiety of
ethionine. bibliog Science 156:1362-3 Je 9
'67
SHINDELL, Sidney
Week we met the Swiss. Sat R 50:44 Jl 22 '67
SHINER, Don
Antlered dinnerware. Design 69:18-19 Fall '67
Build a pretty little privy for your weekend
retreat. Pop Mech 127:156-9+ Ap '67
Need space? you can live in a carport. Pop
Sci 191:138-43 S '67
Woodpile art bonanza. Design 68:20-2 Mr '67
SHINGLES
How to reroof your house; asphalt shingles.
il Pop Mech 127:152-5 Je '67
How to reroof your house with wood shakes
and shingles. W. C. Leckey. il Pop Mech
128:154-8 Jl '67
SHINN, Sydniciel
Show-me state recruits. ALA Bul 61:205-7
F '67
SHIP and boat models
Monitor. Oriental style. il Sci Digest 62:28-9
Ag '67
Tank testing America; model test. P. DeSaix.
il Yachting 122:69+ S '67
SHIP building. See Shipbuilding
SHIP subsidies
Unshipshape industry. il Newsweek 69:76-8
Je 12 '67

SHIPBOARD games. See Games

SHIPBUILDING
About to become the biggest; Japan's Ishi-
kawajima-Harima heavy industries co. il
Time 91:85 Ja 19 '68
Europe's shipbuilders up anchor; building
supertankers. il Bsns W p88-90 O 14 '67
Lakes boat operators sight a brighter day. il
Bsns W p 118-20 N 25 '67
New shipbuilding techniques; Japan leading
the world. S. Griffin. il Sci N 91:580-1 Je 17
'67
Polish bottoms up. il Newsweek 71:56 Ja 8
'68
Tankers on Tyne; British firms merge. il Time
90:97-8 N 3 '67
Three cheers for the America. R. J. Schaefer.
il Am For 73:4-7+ S '67
Unshipshape industry. il Newsweek 69:76-8
Je 12 '67
Virtue triumphant. J. Burnham. Nat R 19:
398 Ap 18 '67
See also
American shipbuilding company
Avondale shipyards, incorporated
Hulls (naval architecture)
Newport News shipbuilding and dry dock
company
Shipyards
Warships
Yacht building

SHIPMAN, John R.
International patent planning. Harvard
Bsns R 45:56-72 Mr '67

SHIPMENT of goods
See also
Distribution of goods
Railroads—Freight service

SHIPPING
See also
Merchant marine
Panama Canal
Shipbuilding

International aspects
Long way around; effects of Suez Canal
closing. il Bsns W p26+ Jl 22 '67

Denmark
Follow the star; A. P. Møller co. Time 90:
104-5 N 24 '67

United States
Lakes boat operators sight a brighter day. il
Bsns W p 118-20 N 25 '67
Maritime industry's expensive new box;
trailer-size cargo containers. H. B. Meyers.
il Fortune 76:150-4+ N '67
See also
Merchant marine—United States
Ship subsidies

SHIPPING companies
See also
Container system (freight handling)

SHIPPING containers. See Containers for shipping

SHIPPING fever. See Cattle—Diseases and
pests

SHIPPING subsidies. See Ship subsidies

SHIPS
Ahoy? loss of ship carrying obsolete am-
munition. il Time 90:25 S 15 '67
Kilotons of TNT, 3,500 feet down. il Sci N
92:296 S 23 '67
Magnetometers locate loaded liberty ship. il
Sci N 92:319 S 30 '67
See also
Hospital ships
Ice breaking vessels
Merchant marine
Ocean liners
Sailing vessels
Salvage
Schooners
Shipwrecks
Tank ships
Tugboats
Viking ships
Warships
Yachts and yachting

Fires and fire protection
Fire at sea! D. Harlander. il Yachting 121:
197-9 My '67
IMCO subcommittee recommends new passen-
ger-ship standards. Dept State Bul 56:102
Ja 16 '67
See also
Aircraft carriers—Fires and fire protection

Food service
Groaning board. C. W. Morton. Atlan 219:
110-11 Je '67

History
Pride of the seas; merchant navy; with port-
folio of paintings. C. B. Mitchell. bibliog il
Am Heritage 19:64-88 D '67

Launching
See also
Aircraft carriers—Launching

Loading and unloading
See Loading and unloading

Manufacture
See Shipbuilding

Safety devices and measures
New international rules for passenger-ship
safety. W. K. Miller. Dept State Bul 56:
173-8 Ja 30 '67
President urges ratification of new ship
safety rules; White House announcement,
February 15, 1967. Dept State Bul 56:429
Mr 13 '67

SHIPS, Atomic powered
Nuclear ship faces mothballs; world's only
nuclear-powered merchant ship, NS Savan-
nah. il Bsns W p36-7 Mr 4 '67
Outlook now for atomic-powered ships; moth-
balling of Savannah. il U S News 62:11
F 6 '67
Sink the Savannah? il Newsweek 69:80 F 6 '67
So long to the Savannah? W. Kelley. il Sci
Digest 62:49-52 D '67
Technology and politics meet; nuclear ship
Savannah to remain afloat. il Sci N 91:591
Je 24 '67
Troubled seas; Senate hearings on fate of
Savannah. Time 89:20 Je 16 '67
See also
Warships, Atomic powered

SHIPS, Hospital. See Hospital ships

SHIPS, Research
Aboard the navy's newest seagoing laboratory; Silas Bent. J. F. Pearson. il Pop
Mech 127:124-7+ Ap '67
Biology afloat; Alpha Helix, research ship
operated by the Scripps institution of
oceanography. Sci Am 216:50+ Mr '67
From the log of the Te Vega. R. L. Bolin.
il Natur Hist 76:24-31 Ag '67
Gulf oil gets research ship. Tech W 20:46-7
My 22 '67
Navy intensifies surveys near USSR; anti-
submarine warfare-undersea warfare sur-
vey project. R. W. Niblock. il Tech W 21:
29-30 Jl 3 '67
Soviet Union bars completion of U.S. scientific
voyage; statement, August 31, 1967. Dept
State Bul 57:362 S 18 '67
U.S. navy studying Swedish hydrographic
ship, techniques. R. W. Niblock. il Aero
Tech 21:48-9 D 4 '67
U.S. offers Indian government oceanographic
research vessel. Dept State Bul 57:23 Jl 3
'67
World's newest hydrographic ship; USNS
Kane. F. J. Sweeney. il Motor B 120:25-6+
D '67

SHIPS, Training. See Training ships

SHIPS flags. See Flags

SHIPS papers
See also
Yachts—Registration

SHIPWORKERS
Taft-Hartley reopens the shipyards. Bsns
W p86 Mr 18 '67

SHIPWRECKS
Britain's great, ghastly ooze; fight against
oil from the Torrey Canyon shipwreck off
the Cornish coast. il Newsweek 69:48-51
Ap 10 '67
In the oily wake of a tragedy at sea. il U S
News 62:18 Ap 10 '67
Letter from London; battle to finish off the
Torrey Canyon. M. Panter-Downes. New
Yorker 43:158 Ap 15 '67
Letter from Paris; two Brittany departments:
Côtes du Nord and Finistère devastated
areas, because of wreck of Torrey Canyon.
Genêt. New Yorker 43:166+ Ap 29 '67
Locate Turkish warship. Pop Mech 127:229
F '67
Oil globs coat Cornwall; wreck of tanker
Torrey Canyon. il Sr Schol 90:17 Ap 14 '67
Oil, oil everywhere; water pollution problem
posed by breakup of oil tanker Torrey
Canyon. il Sci N 91:328 Ap 8 '67
Oily flotsam that fouled fair England; with
report by J. Hicks. il Life 62:26-35 Ap 14 '67
Operation Canute; fighting the oil from
tanker Torrey Canyon, aground off Cornish
coast. il Time 89:28 Ap 7 '67

SHIPWRECKS—*Continued*
Ship of foolishness; grounded Amaryllis. il Life 62:87-8 My 26 '67
Tanker's messy wake; wreck of the Torrey Canyon. Bsns W p 128 Ap 1 '67
Tantalizing treasure of the Andrea Doria. F. Dickenson. il Read Digest 91:150-3 N '67
Two kinds of tankers, clean and dirty; Torrey Canyon wreck. C. Kentfield. il N Y Times Mag p24-5+ My 14 '67
See also
Collisions at sea
Salvage (ships)
SHIPYARD employees. See Shipworkers
SHIPYARDS
New ways for the shipyards. T. Alexander. il Fortune 76:114-21 Jl '67
See also
Shipbuilding
SHIRAZ-Persepolis festival. See Music festivals —Iran
SHIRLEY, George
And we quote; interview, ed. by G. Movshon. por Hi Fi 18:MA21 Ja '68
SHIRLEY, James R.
War protest in wartime. New Repub 156:15-16 My 6 '67
SHIRLEY, Wayne
Ives's holidays: a glorious fourth, and no anticlimax. Hi Fi 17:79-80 S '67
SHIRLEY poppies. See Poppies
SHIRTS
Durable press shirts. il Consumer Bul 50:22-7 S '67
Making a shirt for dad. C. Houck. il Parents Mag 42:130 S '67
Making the turtles move; can turtlenecks replace the button-down shirts? il Bsns W p 152 N 11 '67
Turtlenecks. il Newsweek 70:86 N 27 '67
SHISH kebab cookery. See Cookery—Meat
SHIVER, Ray A.
Instrumentation tape recorder. Electr World 78:44-7 N; 44-5+ D '67
SHIVERS, Allan
Boom times ahead; address, October 31, 1967. Vital Speeches 34:146-8 D 15 '67
Serving the people's interest; interview. pors Nations Bsns 55:40-1+ My '67
Social security; address, September 25, 1967. Vital Speeches 34:92-4 N 15 '67
SHIVERS, J. S.
Special recreation needs of teenagers. Parks & Rec 2:20+ Ag '67
SHNEIDERMAN, Samuel Loeb
Polands anti-Semitic Maoist underground. Reporter 36:21-3 Ja 26 '67
SHOBERG, Ray
Here's an easy way to make an abrasive cutoff machine. Pop Mech 128:184-5 N '67
Tilt your router. Pop Mech 128:170-2 S '67
SHOCK
Microcirculation and shock; report on international interdisciplinary conference. D. Shepro and G. P. Fulton. Science 157:1211-12 S 8 '67
See also
Electric shock
SHOCK, Anaphylactic. See Anaphylaxis
SHOCK absorbers
Just a smoothie; new drive line damper. E. Rickman. il Hot Rod 20:76 F '67
See also
Automobiles—Shock absorbers
SHOCK waves
Atmosphere effect on sonic boom probed. W. C. Wetmore. il Aviation W 87:72-3+ N 27 '67
Supersonic transport: heat, cold, radiation & the boom. K. M. Ruppenthal. il Nation 204:685-9 My 29 '67
See also
Sonic boom
SHOCKLEY, William Bradford
Researching racial inferiority? il por Time 89:65 F 3 '67
SHOE industry. See Shoes—Trade and manufacture
SHOE laces. See Shoelaces
SHOELACES
Knotty problem of shoelaces. il Changing T 21:37-8 O '67
SHOEMAKERS' holiday; musical comedy. See Musical comedies, revues, etc.—Criticisms, plots, etc.
SHOES
Five myths about your feet. H. L. DuVries. il Todays Health 45:49-51 Ag '67
If you take hiking seriously, the first thing you know you get serious about boots. il Sunset 139:58-60+ Ag '67
Important steps in choosing children's shoes. il Good H 164:210+ Ap '67
Up with legs; high-rise boots for women. il Time 90:65 O 20 '67
What mothers must know about children's shoes. il Redbook 128:80-5 Mr '67
Your children's foot comfort depends on quality shoes and good fit; Parents' magazine certified children's shoe fitter. M. B. Keiser. il Parents Mag 42:28-9 Jl '67

Trade and manufacture
Man in the shoe; Melville shoe corp. R. Levy. il Duns R 90:78-9+ O '67
SHOES, Rubber, plastic, etc.
Footrace in synthetics; man-made shoe materials called poromerics. il Bsns W p40 F 25 '67
Nonskid boots; inexpensive way to fix your waders. C. L. Howard. il Field & S 72:88 My '67
SHOES for astronauts. See Astronauts—Clothing
SHOLOKHOV, Mikhail Aleksandrovich
Revolution in the Cossack world. I. Weil. por Sat R 50:33 Je 17 '67
SHOMON, Joseph J.
Wake up foresters, you're needed. il Am For 73:12-15+ My '67
Will a park die in Brooklyn? Audubon 69:80-1 Mr '67
SHOOTING
Birds and bows. B. Dalrymple. il Field & S 72:42-5+ Jl '67
Flinching and flinchers. J. O'Connor. il Outdoor Life 140:72+ Ag '67
Haw's magic never-miss. R. Starnes. Field & S 71:28+ Mr '67
Help for lousy shots. W. Page. il Field & S 72:90-2+ O '67
Shooting. J. O'Connor. See issues of Outdoor life
Shooting; ed. by W. Page. See issues of Field & stream
Standing position. J. O'Connor. il Outdoor Life 140:68+ Jl '67
Triggers and trigger control. J. O'Connor. il Outdoor Life 139:108-12 F '67
Wager on a woodchuck. C. Vinson. il Outdoor Life 139:64-5+ Ap '67
Wingshooting in Saskatchewan. M. Ellis. il Field & S 72:56-7+ Ag '67
See also
National rifle association
also Pheasant shooting; Pigeon shooting; and similar headings

Anecdotes, facetiae, satire, etc.
Something peculiar at Tulelake. N. Riley. il Outdoor Life 140:62-4+ N '67
200-shot Daisy and the ultimate plink. J. Shepherd. il Field & S 72:66-7+ S '67

Study and teaching
First pheasant; instruction in gun handling. R. Barlow. il Field & S 72:50-1 N '67
Quick kill; instinct-shooting techniques. il Time 90:16 Jl 14 '67
Riflery included in indoor recreation program; Lancaster recreation program. P. Bomberger. il Parks & Rec 2:40+ Ap '67
SHOOTING ranges
Cooperation builds a target range; police pistol range, Baltimore County, Md. W. E. Fornoff. il Am City 82:64 Ap '67
Under-cover archery. G. H. Gillelan. il Outdoor Life 140:94+ D '67
SHOOTING stars. See Meteors
SHOP indicators. See Measuring instruments
SHOPLIFTING
Housewives' crime, and what makes them do it? F. Maynard. il Good H 165:98-9+ O '67
One out of sixty is a shoplifter; with report by C. Welles. il Life 63:66B-72B D 15 '67
Thief in the store. Pub W 191:38 My 22 '67
'Tis the season to be shoplifting. il Bsns W p20+ D 23 '67
'Tis the season to be wary. il Time 90:49 D 15 '67
What crime costs you; losses to business. il Nations Bsns 55:44-6+ Je '67
Youthful shoplifting: a national epidemic. E. Selby. Read Digest 90:95-9 Ap '67
SHOPPING and shoppers
Around-the-world bargain hunt. il NEA J 57:48-9 Ja '68
Mirror mannequin; new method of buying clothes. il Time 90:67-8 O 6 '67
Smart moves in the shopping game. il Seventeen 26:152-3 O '67

SHOPPING and shoppers—*Continued*
Spending less & saving more. Time 89:88 Mr 3 '67
What it takes to be a smart shopper. il Changing T 21:39-44 S '67
See also
Christmas shopping

Europe, Western
Shopping in Europe. E. Benson. Craft Horiz 27:23+ My '67

Great Britain
Devaluation at work; European shoppers in London. il Time 91:83 Ja 19 '68

Italy
Flood of U.S. buyers hits Florence as usual. il Bsns W p 126-8+ Mr 18 '67
SHOPPING arcades. See Arcades
SHOPPING centers
Harvard square, where all Boston makes the scene. il Bsns W p 144-6 O 28 '67
Homes on the range; Irvine ranch's Fashion island near Los Angeles. il Time 90:94+ S 22 '67
Pedestrian mall or plaza? Washington, D.C. W. S. Foster. il Am City 82:101 My '67
Store designers help ring the cash registers; suburban branches in the U.S. il Bsns W p42-6+ Jl 1 '67
SHOPSMITHS. See Workshops—Equipment
SHOR, Donna Hamilton
Little land of liberty. Nat Geog Mag 132: 232-51 Ag '67
SHOR, George G. Jr
Seismic refraction profile in Coral Sea basin. bibliog Science 158:911-13 N 17 '67
SHORE batteries. See Fortification
SHORE birds
Reporter at large. P. Matthiessen. New Yorker 43:40-4+ My 27; 42-4+ Je 3 '67
SHORES, Louis
Dimensions of oral history; adaptation of address, September 1966. por Library J 92:979-83 Mr 1 '67
SHORRIS, Earl
Love is dead. N Y Times Mag p26-7+ O 29 '67
SHORT, James M. and Goldstein, J. I.
Rapid methods of determining cooling rates of iron and stony iron meteorites. bibliog Science 156:59-61 Ap 7 '67
SHORT, Willis
Willis Short on boat preparation. Yachting 121:123-4 Je '67
SHORT cake. See Shortcake
SHORT haul airlines. See Local service airlines
SHORT measures. See Weights and measures
SHORT men. See Stature
SHORT selling. See Stocks—Short selling
SHORT stories
How to get to page one. J. Savage. Writer 81:9-11+ Ja '68
Selling touch. C. Boyd. Writer 81:16-17+ Ja '68
Short-short story. R. W. Alexander. Writer 80:17-18 Ag '67
Sound of the story. J. Buechler. Writer 80: 19-21 Je '67
Your technique is showing. M. Wilson. Writer 80:19-21 Ja '67
See also
Christmas stories
Fiction—Technique
Fiction in periodicals and newspapers
SHORT subject films. See Moving pictures— Short subject films
SHORT take-off and landing airplanes. See Airplanes, Short take-off and landing
SHORTCAKE
Look what's happened to shortcake! with recipes. il McCalls 94:90-1+ Je '67
Spring shortcakes. il Bet Hom & Gard 45:91-2 My '67
SHORTIA galacifolia. See Oconee bells
SHORTT, S. L.
Key man in cosmetics. J. Ross-Skinner. il Duns R 90:65 D '67
SHOSTAK, Stanley
Bud movement in hydra. bibliog Science 155: 1567-8 Mr 24 '67
SHOSTAKOVICH, Dmitrii Dmitrievich
As before, but even better: Katerina Ismailova. G. L. Mayer. Am Rec G 45:14 S '67
Babi Yar. J. Diether. il Am Rec G 34:4-6+ S '67
Execution of Stepan Razin; score composed to a Yevtushenko text. Am Rec G 34:12-14 S '67

Records:
Katerina Ismailova. Opera N 32:34 N 25 '67
Russians have arrived, thanks to Melodiya/ Angel. B. Jocobson. il por Hi Fi 17:67-8 Mr '67
SHOT
More with fours. W. Page. il Field & S 72: 72-4+ N '67
SHOT putting
Now two wizards of oomph: R. Matson and N. Steinhauer. T. C. Brody. il Sports Illus 26:58-9 F 13 '67
One man's meet; world record holder. il Time 89:58 Ap 21 '67
Whale of an artist; N. Steinhauer. il Time 89:42 F 10 '67
SHOTGUNS
European shotgun. J. O'Connor. il Outdoor Life 139:94+ My '67
Ever patterned your shotgun? H. G. Tapply. il Field & S 72:52 Ja '68
Fun with an old gun. T. Trueblood. il Field & S 72:20+ Ja '68
Gifts that last a lifetime. T. Trueblood. il Field & S 72:12+ D '67
How does the 28-gauge? W. Page. il Field & S 72:116-20 Je '67
Shotguns. J. B. Miller. il Consumer Bul 50: 31-7 O '67
Shotguns; buying the right boom. il Pop Mech 128:118-21 S '67
Shotguns, parts and accessories. J. B. Miller. il Consumer Bul 50:21-4 N '67
Two more shotguns tested: Winchester 1200 and Winchester 1400. il Consumer Bul 51: 24 Ja '68
Upland guns and loads. J. O'Connor. il Outdoor Life 140:68+ S '67
SHOUP, David Monroe
Plain talk. Nation 204:483-4 Ap 17 '67
SHOVER, John L.
Preparation for Dow day. Nation 205:648-51 D 18 '67
SHOW cases. See Exhibition cases
SHOW-off; drama. See Kelly, G. E.
SHOW windows
Unusual window display stirs controversy, pickets; Taylor's paperback books. New York city; display of propaganda books by Mao and books dealing with John Birch society. il Pub W 191:50 F 6 '67
SHOWER baths
Shower power. il Mlle 66:80-1 Ja '68
SHOWMOBILE. See Theater, Traveling
SHOWROOMS
New York showroom uses brick and natural wood for display of exotic leathers. il Arch Rec 141:178-9 My '67
Remodeling creates dramatic spaces for this showroom. il Arch Rec 141:180-1 My '67
SHRAGO, Earl, and others
Carbohydrate supply as a regulator of rat liver phosphoenolpyruvate carboxykinase activity. bibliog Science 158:1572-3 D 22 '67
SHRAKE, Edwin
Buffalo hunt; excerpt from Blessed McGill. Sports Illus 27:60-70 D 25 '67
Pro football (cont) Sports Illus 27:69-72+ S 25; 74-5 N 13 '67
SHRIMPS
Poisoning with DDT; effect on reproductive performance of artemia. D. S. Grosch. il Science 155:592-3 F 3 '67
See also
Cookery—Shellfish
SHRIMPTON, Jean Rosemary
Cover girl; very private thoughts of a very public figure. J. Graham. il pors Good H 165:26+ Ag '67
SHRINES
See also
Holy places
Pilgrims and pilgrimages
Relics and reliquaries
SHRINES, War. See War memorials
SHRIVER, George Hite
Renewal and the dynamic of the provisional. Christian Cent 84:1551-3 D 6 '67
SHRIVER, Robert Sargent, 1915-
Nickel revolution. I. Mothner. Look 31:34+ Je 13 '67
Observations of an optimist. America 117: 594-5 N 18 '67
SHRUBS
Best trees and shrubs for the colorful fruits of fall. D. Wyman. il Home Gard 54:22-3 O '67
Forsythia & flowering almond & mahonia & lilac. M. J. Dietz. il Home Gard 54:62-3 Ap '67
Grow them for greens. il Sunset 138:272 Ap '67

SHRUBS—*Continued*
Plants for dry places. G. W. Kelly. il Horticulture 45:32-3 Jl '67
Shrubs for summer flowers. il Am Home 70:30 Jl '67
See also
Evergreens

Pruning
See Pruning

SHUB, Elizabeth
(tr) See Singer, I. B. Letter writer
(tr) See Singer, I. B. My adventures as an idealist

SHUFFLEBOARD
Hustle of Texas Billy. G. Rogin. il Sports Illus 27:58-64+ S 4 '67

SHUGG, Roger W.
Publishing in two worlds; summary of address. Pub W 193:39-43 Ja 8 '68

SHUKAIRY, Ahmad
Palestine refugees: perennial source of trouble. J. H. Huizinga. il Reporter 36:33-5 My 18 '67

SHULDINER, Herbert
Du Pont's slick new Teflon-S. Pop Sci 191:136-8+ D '67
Great UFO probe. Pop Sci 191:120-3 O '67
Lively '68 snowmobiles heat up the winter scene. Pop Sci 191:80-3+ N '67
Machines that make money for you. Pop Sci 191:62-4 Jl '67

SHULMAN, Marshall D.
Europe versus détente? For Affairs 45:389-402 Ap '67

SHULMAN, Milton
Kill three; story. Sat Eve Post 240:50-3 O 21; 62-6 N 4 '67

SHULMAN, Morton
How to hit it big. Newsweek 70:92+ S 25 '67

SHUMAN, Helen Glossner
Early start for seeds, under fluorescent lights. Home Gard 54:88-9 Ap '67

SHUMLIN, Herman
Spofford; dramatization of Reuben, Reuben, by P. De Vries. Criticism
Nation 206:27 Ja 1 '68
New Yorker 43:43 D 23 '67
Newsweek 70:73 D 25 '67
Sat R 50:18 D 30 '67

SHUMSKY, Jeff
Dig we must! pors Seventeen 26:146-7+ S '67

SHUNAMAN, Fred
Can dry cells be recharged? Pop Electr 27:41-5 Jl '67

SHURE, Leonard
Music to my ears; recital in Carnegie Hall. I. Kolodin. Sat R 50:47 F 18 '67

SHURTLEFF, Malcolm C.
New pesticides are safer, more effective, easier to use. Pop Gard 18:80-1+ Mr '67

SHUSTER, Alvin
Let's take the kids to Washington; excerpts from Washington: the New York times guide to the Nation's capital. Parents Mag 42:50-1+ Mr '67

SHUSTER, George Nauman
Reason can prevail. Sat R 50:34 Je 24 '67

SHUTTERS
Using shutters for light control and for privacy. il Sunset 138:126+ My '67

SHUTTERS, Camera. See Camera shutters

SHUTTLE service, Airline. See Airlines—Shuttle service

SHWADRAN, Benjamin
Soviet posture in the Middle East. Cur Hist 53:331-6+ D '67
Soviet Union in the Middle East. Cur Hist 52:72-7+ F '67

SHYER, Marlene Fanta
Feud; story. Good H 165:100-1 O '67
Just a simple bride; story. Good H 164:90-1 My '67
Rainy Sunday; story. Redbook 129:82-3 Je '67
Stuff of a plot. Writer 80:15-16 My '67
Trouble with anchovies; story. McCalls 94:128-9 F '67

SIALIC acids
Gangliosides in isolated neurons and glial cells. D. M. Derry and L. S. Wolfe. bibliog il Science 158:1450-2 D 15 '67
Sialic acid in HeLa cells: effect of hydrocortisone. R. Carubelli and M. J. Griffin. bibliog il Science 157:693-4 Ag 11 '67

SIBANY manufacturing corporation
Inventions for hire, but not for sale. il Bsns W p 136-7+ Mr 25 '67

SIBELIUS, Jean Julius Christian
Finland's memorial to Jean Sibelius. C. Willard. il Look 31:M16+ O 17 '67
Lorin Maazel's beautiful Sibelius: vibrancy, tension, plasticity. J. Diether. Am Rec G 33:591-2 Mr '67

SIBERIA
See also
Akademgorodok

Description and travel
Siberia: Russia's frozen frontier. D. Conger. il Nat Geog Mag 131:297-345 Mr '67

Maps
Fast-changing Siberia dominates new Atlas map. il Nat Geog Mag 131:346-7. sup (folded map) Mr '67

SIBERIAN irises. See Irises

SIBLINGS
Best of friends: worst of enemies. F. Buckvar. il Parents Mag 42:42-3+ D '67
How to outwit a toddler. A. Arnold. il Parents Mag 42:41-3+ Mr '67
My charming, freeloading brother. il Good H 164:32+ Ja '67
My step-family and me. il Seventeen 26:304-5+ Ag '67
When brothers and sisters fight. B. Bettelheim. il Ladies Home J 84:42+ Ap '67
See also
Children, First-born

SICILY
See also
Gardens—Sicily
Licodia Eubea

Social conditions
Tools for a new world. D. Dolci. Sat R 50:13-16 Jl 29 '67

SICK, The
Fear of death: patients with fatal diseases. il Newsweek 69:56 F 27 '67
Hospital of the future? remodeling plans for Georgetown hospital, Washington, D.C. W. R. Young. il Read Digest 90:161-3+ My '67
Logistics of dying. D. Sudnow. il Esquire 68:102-3+ Ag '67
No bed rest for kids. Sci Digest 62:73-4 O '67
When giving flowers. J. B. Carson. Horticulture 45:46 N '67
See also
Chronically ill

SICK leave
Sick leave for teachers. M. A. Ream. il NEA J 56:26-7 N '67

SICKELS, Elizabeth Galbraith
Thimblemakers in America. Antiques 92:372-3 S '67

SICKERT, Walter Richard
Sickert's unsentimental journey. M. Kozloff. il Art N 66:50-3+ Ap '67

SICKLE cells. See Cells

SICKLE cell anemia. See Anemia

SICKLES, Daniel Edgar
Verdicts of history: husband's revenge. T. J. Fleming. il por Am Heritage 18:65-75 Ap '67

SICKLES, Theresa (Bagioli)
Verdicts of history: husband's revenge; Daniel E. Sickles case. T. J. Fleming. il por Am Heritage 18:66-75 Ap '67

SICKNESS
See also
Medical service, Cost of
Sick, The

SICKNESS absence. See Absenteeism

SICKNESS insurance. See Insurance, Health

SICRE, José Gómez-. See Gómez-Sicre, J.

SIDDIQUI, Wasim A. and others
Stearic acid as plasma replacement for intracellular in vitro culture of plasmodium knowlesi. bibliog Science 156:1623-5 Je 23 '67

SIDE-blotched lizard. See Lizards

SIDEBAND filters. See Radio filters

SIDEL, Victor. See Reich, P. jt. auth.

SIDEMAN, Janet
Death of a dropout. New Repub 156:11-14 Je 3 '67

SIDERS, Harvey
Cantata with lyrics by Hitler. Life 63:14 S 29 '67

SIDEWALK cafes. See Restaurants

SIDEWALKS
How to promote sidewalk construction; excerpts from report; Lincoln, Neb. R. Holsinger. il Am City 82:80-2 Jl '67

SIDEY, Hugh
Around the world with Lyndon B. Magellan. Life 64:24B-24D Ja 5 '68
Presidency. See issues of Life
Time of imperative privacy as crises pile up. Life 63:22-9 Ag 18 '67
You can have anything you want, said L.B.J. I owe it to you. Life 63:38-9 D 8 '67

SIDING (building)
Barn fever; use of weathered barn siding. il Time 91:27 Ja 12 '68
What covers the side of your house? House B 109:40+ O '67
Which kind of siding for your house? il Changing T 21:21-3 S '67
SIDNEY and the dogs; story. See Riley, B.
SIE, Cheoukang
Spirit of bamboo; interview. New Yorker 43: 36-7 My 6 '67
SIEBER, Roy
Art of primitive arts. Art N 66:28-43+ Ja '68
SIEFER, Kristine
Curl up and read. Seventeen 26:22 O '67
SIEGEL, B. Z. and Galston, A. W.
Indoleacetic acid oxidase activity of apoperoxidase. bibliog Science 157:1557-9 S 29 '67
SIEGEL, Marcia B.
Building an organization. Dance Mag 41:51+ Ag '67
SIEGEL, Robert H.
Ash Wednesday in Chicago; poem. Christian Cent 84:174 F 8 '67
Hanscom air field; poem. Atlan 219:90 Je '67
SIEGEL, S. M. and others
Living relative of the microfossil kakabekia. bibliog Science 156:1231-4 Je 2 '67
SIEGLER corporation. See Lear Siegler, incorporated
SIEMEL, Sasha
Cat man returns. pors Outdoor Life 139:46-9+ My '67
SIEMILLER, Paul LeRoy
Bullheaded leader of aerospace labor. B. Brower. il pors Life 64:60-2+ Ja 19 '68
SIENA, Italy
Medieval commune and internal violence; police power and public safety in Siena, 1287-1355. W. M. Bowsky. bibliog f Am Hist R 73:1-17 O '67
SIEPMAN, Anne
Primroses. Horticulture 45:22-3 My '67
SIEPMANN, Charles A.
Television. J. Horn. Nation 205:702 D 25 '67
SIERRA BLANCA, N.Mex.
Skiing the silver country. F. R. Smith. il Sports Illus 26:40-7 F 20 '67
SIERRA club
Conservation comes of age; California movement. S. Thurber. il Nation 204:272-5 F 27 '67
Eliot Porter: medication to conservation. J. Deschin. il Pop Phot 61:70+ D '67
Fighting Sierrans. Newsweek 70:50-1 D 25 '67
Sierra club caper. R. Starnes. Field & S 72: 10+ S '67
SIERRA LEONE
End of the exception. Time 89:29 Mr 31 '67
No. 10; military coup. il Newsweek 69:52+ Ap 10 '67
Seatmates on flight 321. Time 89:32 Ap 7 '67
See also
Education—Sierra Leone
SIERRA national forest. See National forests
SIERRA NEVADA, Calif.
Sierra Nevada batholith. P. C. Bateman and J. P. Eaton. bibliog il Science 158:1407-17 D 15 '67
See also
Kings Canyon National Park
SIERRA NEVADA earthquake. See Earthquakes—United States
SIEVERS, Harry J.
Dream is of peace. America 117:705 D 9 '67
Of many things. America 116:inside cover Je 3 '67
(ed) See McCarthy, E. J. Interview with McCarthy
SIGEL, Barbara
Monkeypod business. Am For 73:34-6+ My '67
SIGEL, Efrem
Balancing act in Boston. Reporter 36:22-4 My 4; 11 Je 15 '67
SIGHT
Early receptor potential: photoreversible charge displacement in rhodopsin. R. A. Cone. bibliog il Science 155:1128-31 Mr 3 '67
Is your night driving in focus? W. J. Toth. Am Home 70:31+ S '67
Minimum condition for stereopsis and anomalous contour. R. B. Lawson and D. C. Mount. bibliog il Science 158:804-6 N 10 '67
Safety check; red-light blindness. W. L. DeGinder. il Flying 81:96-7 Ag '67
Simple home test detects lazy eye; amblyopia ex anopsia. Todays Health 46:11 Ja '68
Site of visual adaptation. J. E. Dowling. bibliog il Science 155:273-9 Ja 20 '67; Reply with rejoinder. P. Gouras. 157:583-5 Ag 4 '67

Stereopsis based on vernier acuity cues alone. B. Julesz and G. J. Spivack. bibliog il Science 157:563-5 Ag 4 '67
Vision and the hunter. R. V. McCormick. il Field & S 72:54-5+ S '67
Vision and touch. I. Rock and C. S. Harris. il Sci Am 216:96-104 bibliog(p 167) My '67
Visual adaptation to gradual change of intensity. S. M. Anstis. il Science 155:710-11 F 10 '67
Visual and auditory information processing in children and adults. E. C. Carterette and M. H. Jones. bibliog il Science 156:986-8 My 19 '67
See also
Night vision
SIGHT (animals)
Direction-selective units in rabbit retina: distribution of preferred directions. C. W. Oyster and H. B. Barlow. bibliog il Science 155:841-2 F 17 '67
Dissociation of the visual placing response into elicited and guided components. A. Hein and R. Held. bibliog il Science 158: 390-2 O 20 '67
Eyes have it. D. M. Duffey. il Outdoor Life 140:112-16 Ag '67
Molecular isomers in vision. R. Hubbard and A. Kropf. il Sci Am 216:64-70+ bibliog(p 155) Je '67
Receptive fields in the cat retina: a new type. R. W. Rodieck. bibliog il Science 157: 90-2 Jl 7 '67
Single fibers of cat optic nerve: thresholds to light. W. D. Heiss and D. C. Milne. bibliog il Science 155:1571-2 Mr 24 '67
Total luminous flux: a possible response determinant for the normal monkey. P. Schilder and others. bibliog il Science 158:806-9 N 10 '67
Visual form discrimination after removal of the visual cortex in cats. S. S. Winans. bibliog il Science 158:944-6 N 17 '67
Visually guided reaching in infant monkeys after restricted rearing. R. Held and J. A. Bauer, jr. bibliog il Science 155:718-20 F 10 '67
SIGHT (birds)
Science proves it, the robin sees the worm. F. Heppner. il Audubon 69:86-8+ S '67
SIGHTS for bows. See Bow sights
SIGHTS for firearms. See Firearms—Sights
SIGMA delta chi
Sigma delta chi's new look. J. Tebbel. il Sat R 50:84+ Ap 8 '67
SIGMAN, Carl T.
In your home: let there be natural light. Pop Sci 190:142-6 Mr '67
Two basic rooms you can add to any house. Pop Sci 190:162-8 Ap '67
SIGMUND, Paul E.
Chile: open season on President Frei. Reporter 37:33-5 S 21 '67
Chile's Christian democrats. America 117:602-4 N 18 '67
SIGN language
See also
Deaf—Means of communication
SIGNAL generators
Build an IC Testone: utility square-wave generator. D. Lancaster. il Pop Electr 28: 27-9 Ja '68
Build the amligner. D. Lancaster. il Pop Electr 26:60-1+ F '67
Knight-kit model KG-687 sweep/marker generator. il Electr World 79:82-3 Ja '68
Multi-waveform generator; hi-fi testing. M. Chan. il Pop Electr 27:52-4+ S '67
Scope sweep generator; calibrating the horizontal sweep of an oscilloscope. R. G. Teeter. il Electr World 77:80-1 F '67
Signal-powered signal squarer. L. Solomon. il Pop Electr 27:48 O '67
Tone-selective signaling; the new look. L. Solomon. il Electr World 78:88-90 S '67
SIGNAL lights, Automobile. See Automobiles—Signal lights
SIGNAL oil and gas company
Alphabet soup; Signal and Allis-Chalmers merge. Newsweek 70:85-6 D 11 '67
Mack strikes oil in Signal deal. Bsns W p60 My 13 '67
Signal accomplishment; acquires Allis-Chalmers. il Time 90:104+ D 8 '67
SIGNAL tracers. See Testing instruments
SIGNAL tracing. See Radio receivers—Testing
SIGNALS, Interplanetary. See Interplanetary communication
SIGNATURES (writing)
Autopen; excerpts from The collector. M. A. Benjamin. il Hobbies 72:108-9+ O '67
Record prices mark Charles Hamilton's 1966-67 auctions. K. V. Hostick. Hobbies 72:108-9 D '67

SIGNERS of the Constitution. See United States—Constitution—Signers

SIGNORET, Simone
You can see that I'm not twenty years old. B. Weinraub. il pors Sat Eve Post 240:38-41 F 25 '67

SIGNS and signboards
Inn sign revived. T. Haynes. il Am Artist 31:61-5 N '67
Signs of the times. Newsweek 70:88-9 O 23 '67
Unique park entrances. J. Bellinger. il Parks & Rec 2:85-6 My '67
See also
Billboards
Road signs
Street signs
Traffic signs

Anecdotes, facetiae, satire, etc.
Notes and comment; signs on buses and subway trains. New Yorker 43:51 N 25 '67

SIHANOUK, Norodom. See Norodom Sihanouk

SIKES, Robert L. F.
Excerpt from remarks, May 25, 1967. Cong Digest 46:217+ Ag '67

SIKKIM
Guns of Natu La; Sino-Indian fighting. il Newsweek 70:50 S 25 '67
India vs. China: new war for U.S. too? il U S News 63:16 S 25 '67
Sikkim: in the high Himalayas. C. Y. Salisbury. il Mlle 65:171-4 S '67
Vivid variety of India. L. Van Der Post. il Holiday 42:82-3+ N '67

SILAGE
Corn silage, the only roughage cows need. N. Reeder. il Farm J 91:32-3+ N '67
Feed your grain wet? C. E. Ball. il Farm J 92:B6-8 Ja '68
How to feed silage. D. Malena. il Suc Farm 65:38-9 Ag '67
How to make corn silage. C. E. Sommers. il Suc Farm 65:34-5+ Ag '67
See also
Silos

SILAGE handling
Vacuum-sealed silage: how it fed out. il Farm J 91:46L+ My '67

SILAS Bent (ship) See Ships, Research

SILBERMAN, Arlene
Portion of thyself. Read Digest 90:157-60 Mr '67
Tell it like it is. Read Digest 91:15-16+ N '67
Things that live. Good H 164:51+ Ja '67

SILBERMAN, Charles E.
Little bird that casts a big shadow. Fortune 75:108-11+ F '67

SILBERMAN, Saul
One tough little guy. I. Underwood. il pors Sports Illus 26:54-62 F 6 '67

SILBERSTEIN, Gerard E.
Serbian campaign of 1915; its diplomatic background. bibliog f Am Hist R 73:51-69 O '67

Le SILENCE; drama. See Sarraute, N.

SILENT night; drama. See Hollingsworth, L.

SILICA
Silica in alkaline brines. B. F. Jones and others. bibliog il Science 153:1310-14 D 8 '67
Silica in sea water; control by silica minerals. F. T. MacKenzie and others. bibliog il Science 155:1404-5 Mr 17 '67
Structure of silica glass. J. F. G. Hicks. bibliog il Science 155:459-61 Ja 27 '67
See also
Tridymite

SILICATES
See also
Amphiboles
Fresnoite
Sodium silicates

SILICON-carbide diodes. See Diodes

SILICON compounds
Chemistry of silicon difluoride; address, June 28, 1965. J. C. Thompson and J. L. Margrave. bibliog il Science 155:669-71 F 10 '67

SILICON controlled rectifiers. See Electric current rectifiers

SILICON difluoride. See Silicon compounds

SILICONE gaskets. See Gaskets

SILICONE rubber. See Rubber, Artificial

SILICONES
Guide to silicone masonry water repellents. C. A. Bergeson. Arch Rec 141:181-2 Ja '67
Silicones could have saved sea life; Torrey Canyon disaster. Sci N 92:343-4 O 7 '67

SILJA, Anja
Grand old lady; interview, ed. by E. Salzman. pors Opera N 32:18-19 O 14 '67

SILK, George
U.S. coast guard; photographs. Life 63:28-43 Jl 7; 36-50+ Jl 14 '67

SILK
Silk road. J. Morris. il Horizon 9:4-23 Aut '67

SILK moths. See Moths

SILK routes. See Trade routes

SILK screen printing
Made in the shade; decorated window shades. J. A. Hasek. il Sch Arts 67:10-11 D '67

SILKWORMS
Antibiotics in the laboratory-rearing of cecropia silkworms. L. M. Riddiford. bibliog Science 157:1451-2 S 22 '67

SILL, William B.
How to add a typewriter table to a desk. Pop Sci 192:155 Ja '68
Triple-duty armrest for your car. Pop Sci 191:121 N '67

SILLEN, Lars Gunnar
Ocean as a chemical system. bibliog Science 156:1189-97 Je 2 '67

SILLITOE, Alan
Canals; story. Reporter 36:36-43 Je 1 '67

SILLS, Beverly
And we quote; ed. by C. L. Osborne. por Hi Fi 17:MA23 My '67
Three in one; interview, ed. by R. D. Daniels. por Opera N 31:27 F 11 '67

about
True story of Beverly Sills. H. Saal. il pors N Y Times Mag p34-5+ S 17 '67; Discussion. p97 O 1 '67
Two for the C-note. il por Newsweek 70:86 O 2 '67

SILONE, Ignazio, pseud.
Ignazio Silone: study in integrity. I. Origo. por Atlan 219:86-93 Mr '67

SILOS
Boom in sealed silos. R. Wilmore. il Farm J 91:28-9+ S '67
How to store silage. P. B. Jones. il Suc Farm 65:36-7 Ag '67
Need more room for corn? il Farm J 91:24-5+ Ag '67

SILVA, Artur da Costa e. See Costa e Silva, A. da

SILVER, Adele Zeldman
Keeping behind the times in Cleveland. Reporter 36:40+ Je 29 '67

SILVER, Isidore
Corporate ombudsman. bibliog f Harvard Bsns R 45:77-87 My '67
Crime, American style: the President's commission. Commonweal 86:141-2 Ap 21 '67

SILVER, Martin A.
Odyssey. Am Rec G 33:636-8 Ap '67
Three flutists. Am Rec G 34:104-5 O '67

SILVER, Nathan
Art of human use. Nation 204:629-31 My 15 '67

SILVER, Robert Harold
Lower Manhattan expressway. Arch Forum 127:66-9 S '67

SILVER, Sidney L.
Avalanche transistor circuits. Electr World 78:30-2 S '67

SILVER, W. S.
Biological nitrogen fixation. Science 157:100-2 Jl 7 '67

SILVER
Hi-ho silver, prices away! Mod Phot 32:98+ Ja '68
See also
Silverware

Prices
Playing for coin; silver certificates and rush on silver. il Newsweek 70:68-70 Ag 28 '67
Shining silver. il Time 90:76 Jl 28 '67
Silver goes free, with strings. il Bsns W p 136 My 27 '67
Silver price calms down. Bsns W p 138 Je 17 '67
Silver rush is on. Bsns W p24 Jl 22 '67
Silver; who gets the bonanza? U S News 63:90-1 Ag 7 '67
Suddenly, a crisis in silver, how it happened, what it means. il U S News 62:102 Je 5 '67
With the lid blown off silver prices. il U S News 63:86-8 Jl 31 '67

SILVER as money
Blowing the whistle. Newsweek 69:74 My 29 '67
Case of the vanishing silver; new crisis for U.S. coin system. U S News 62:99 Mr 27 '67
Silver goes free, with strings. il Bsns W p 136 My 27 '67
Silver looks brighter; Treasury reserves low. il Time 89:61 Je 2 '67
Silver situation. C. French. Hobbies 72:102 N '67

SILVER as money—*Continued*
Suddenly, a crisis in silver, how it happened, what it means. il U S News 62:102 Je 5 '67
Trading in cartwheels. il Fortune 75:221-2+ My '67
SILVER certificates. See Paper money—United States
SILVER in house decoration. See Color in house decoration
SILVER jewelry. See Jewelry
SILVER mines and mining

United States
There may be joy in Leadville, if silver pans out; Colorado. il Bsns W p 128-30 D 2 '67
SILVER-zinc batteries. See Storage batteries
SILVERBERG, Robert
John Hunter, brash genius of pathology; excerpt from The great doctors. Todays Health 45:44-5+ F '67
Visits to vanished cultures. Sat R 50:58 N 25 '67
SILVERMAN, S. M. and Lloyd, J. W. F.
Optical environment in Gemini space flights. bibliog Science 157:917-19 Ag 25 '67
SILVERMAN, Sanford L. See Gettleman, M. E. jt. comp.
SILVERS, Willys K. and Billingham, R. E.
Genetic background and expressivity of histocompatibility genes. bibliog Science 158:118-19 O 6 '67
—and others
Mixed leukocyte reactions and histocompatibility in rats. bibliog Science 155:703-4 F 10 '67
—See Mintz, B. jt. auth.
SILVERSMITHS
Daniel Rogers, silversmiths. M. G. Fales. il Antiques 91:487-91 Ap '67
Savannah silver and silversmiths. J. A. Williams. il Antiques 91:347-9 Mr '67
SILVERSTEIN, Murray. See Van Der Ryn, S. jt. auth.
SILVERSTEIN, Robert M. and others
Sex attractant of the black carpet beetle. bibliog Science 157:85-7 Jl 7 '67
SILVERSWORDS
Silversword of Haleakala National Park. il Nat Parks Mag 41:8-9 O '67
SILVERWARE
American and English silver. R. Davidson. il Antiques 91:386+ Mr '67
Daniel Rogers, silversmiths. M. G. Fales. il Antiques 91:487-91 Ap '67
English silver; toilet set of 1679. R. Davidson. il Antiques 92:814+ D '67
Form and ornament in early Canadian silver. J. E. Langdon. il Antiques 92:78-83 Jl '67
How to buy sterling silver flatware. Am Home 70:24 Ja '67
More English silver in the Morrison collection. M. D. Schwartz. il Antiques 91:228-32 F '67
Opulence in silver. M. B. Davidson. il Antiques 92:342-3 S '67
Savannah silver and silversmiths. J. A. Williams. il Antiques 91:347-9 Mr '67
Silver box is not square. il Vogue 149:158-9+ Je '67
Silver leads a double life. il Seventeen 26:120-1 D '67
Stars predict your silver. il Seventeen 26:152-3 Ap '67
What's it for? seventeen handsome pieces of silver. il House & Gard 131:16-17 Je '67
See also
Cups
Epergnes

Exhibitions
Great silver from three centuries; English, Dutch, and American; Sterling and Francine Clark art institute, Williamstown, Mass. il Antiques 92:332-5 S '67
SIMCOX, Carroll Eugene
Episcopal editor denounces Saul Alinsky. Christian Cent 84:1452 N 15 '67
SIMMONS, Geoffrey Roy
Simmonds' search for excellence. R. Levy. por Duns R 89:50-1+ My '67
SIMMONS, W. Austin
Barbados: twenty-third member state of the OAS. Américas 19:3-12 D '67
SIMMONS aerocessories, Incorporated. See Simmonds precision products incorporated
SIMMONS precision products, Incorporated
Simmonds' search for excellence. R. Levy. Duns R 89:50-1+ My '67
SIMMONS, Charles B.
Toys for Christmas. Antiques 92:848-9 D '67
SIMMONS, Charles Wesley
Odyssey of Charles Wayo. C. L. Sanders. il por Ebony 22:27-30+ F '67

SIMMONS, E. Romayne, and Holland, D. J.
Salome and the king. Dance Mag 41:52-3 N '67
SIMMONS, Ernest J.
Out of the drawer, into the light. Sat R 50:35-6+ N 11 '67
SIMMONS, J. L. and Winograd, Barry
Hang-loose ethic; excerpts from It's happening. NEA J 56:18-20+ O '67
SIMMONS, Joseph Edgar
Two poems; Keats' trodden weed; The sea harp's spray. Yale R 57:100-2 O '67
SIMMONS, Robert H. See Rosin, A. jt. auth.
SIMON
Simon says (cont) por Mod Phot 31:28 Jl; 74+ N; 30+ D '67; 32:107 Ja '68
SIMON, Abbey
And we quote; interview. ed. by S. Fleming. por Hi Fi 17:MA19 Je '67
SIMON, Anne W.
Vintage mind; excerpts from The new years. McCalls 95:75+ Ja '68
SIMON, Ellen M.
Tetrahymena: effect of freezing and subsequent thawing on breeding performance. bibliog Science 155:694-6 F 10 '67
SIMON, Hilda
Lithography and the artist. S. Salter. Pub W 191:106-7 Mr 6 '67
SIMON, Joan
Wry and healthy humanist. Life 63:23 O 13 '67
SIMON, John
Restive spirit. New Repub 158:31-2+ Ja 6 '68
Stage. See issues of Commonweal
(tr) See Kästner, E. Reiteration of a feeling
SIMON, John K.
Solitary metaphysicians. Sat R 50:29-30 D 2 '67
SIMON, Kate
London for sale. Holiday 42:91-6 Ag '67
SIMON, Mayo
Happiness. Criticism
Nation 205:573 N 27 '67
Walking to Waldheim. Criticism
Nation 205:573 N 27 '67
SIMON, Neil
Star-spangled girl. Criticism
America 116:264 F 18 '67
Vogue 149:60 F 15 '67
Take a letter. G. Ace. Sat R 50:12 Ja 28 '67
SIMON, Norton
Antidisestablishmentarianism at Wheeling steel. D. Cordtz. il por Fortune 76:104-9+ Jl '67
Bath in steel. il por Time 89:97 Ap 28 '67
Simon keeps the experts guessing. por Bsns W p 140+ Ap 29 '67
Simon's new recipe. il por Bsns W p 180 N 18 '67
SIMON, Paul
Quiet campaign: one state's story. Sat R 50:20 Jl 15 '67
SIMON, Paul, 1942?-
Simon & Garfunkel; interview. New Yorker 43:24-7 S 2 '67
We talk to; interview by Mademoiselle's guest editors. por Mlle 65:326 Ag '67

about
People are talking about... por Vogue 149:110-11 Je '67
Simon & Garfunkel in action. M. Ames. il pors Hi Fi 17:62-6 N '67
Syncopated times. por Newsweek 69:98+ F 6 '67
Two fine rockers roll their own. S. Kanfer. Life 62:18 Ap 21 '67
SIMON, Robert Edward, 1914-
Can new towns meet a budget? il pors Bsns W p 103-4 N 18 '67
End of a dream. il por Newsweek 70:30-1 D 4 '67
Reston. M. Viorst. il por Horizon 9:34-41 Aut '67
SIMON, William, and Gagnon, J. H.
Pedagogy of sex. Sat R 50:74-6+ N 18 '67
SIMON and Schuster, Incorporated
Calories author guilty; faces jail and fine. Pub W 191:40 My 22 '67
Clarion books: new S&S paperback imprint. il Pub W 191:148 Je 5 '67
Educational publishing reorganized at S&S. Pub W 191:48 F 6 '67
Three S&S vice-presidents to join Knopf in March. il Pub W 193:61 Ja 15 '68
SIMONDS, C. H.
Cars, cars, cars. Nat R 19:757-8 Jl 11 '67
Children's books. Nat R 19:1342-3 N 28 '67
Television. Nat R 19:210-12, 534-6, 1128-9 F 21, My 16, O 17 '67

SIMONDS, C. H.—*Continued*
(comp) NR's annual guide to unsatisfactory people. Nat R 19:1428-9 D 26 '67
(ed) Very special edition of The New York times. Nat R 19:580-5 My 30 '67
—See Croce, A. jt. comp.

SIMONS, Elwyn L.
Earliest apes; with biographical sketch. Sci Am 217:14; 28-35 D '67
Unraveling the age of earth and man; with biographical sketch. por Natur Hist 76:5, 52-9 F '67

SIMONSON, Solomon
Future of television: misunderstanding the medium. Cath World 206:126-31 D '67

SIMONT, Marc
Downhill to Enchilada; reproductions of paintings. Sports Illus 26:40-4 My 1 '67

SIMONTON, Wesley
Clearinghouse for library science. por Wilson Lib Bul 42:383-5 D '67

SIMPLE Simon's reward; drama. See Miller, H. L.

SIMPLICIA, Sister M. See M. Simplicia, Sister

SIMPLICIUS simplicissimus. See Periodicals— Germany (Federal Republic)

SIMPSON, Dwight James
Israel after victory. Cur Hist 53:341-5+ D '67
Israel: the unrelenting battle. Cur Hist 52: 78-83+ F '67

SIMPSON, Harvey
Pair of talented preservers. por Fortune 75:162 Mr '67

SIMPSON, Louis
Dead horses and live issues. Nation 204:520-2 Ap 24 '67
New books of poems. Harper 235:89-91 Ag '67
Poems from memory; Jamaicas; Night in Odessa. Harper 235:73 D '67
Son of the Romanovs; poem. Harper 235:104 N '67

SIMPSON, Myrtle
First woman across Greenland's ice. pors Nat Geog Mag 132:264-79 Ag '67

SIMPSON, O. J.
All the way with O.J. D. Jenkins. il Sports Illus 27:16-21 N 27 '67
Great one confronts O.J. D. Jenkins. il pors Sports Illus 27:32-4+ N 20 '67
O.J. J. Bonfante. il pors Life 63:74A-74B+ O 27 '67
Sportsman of the year, and two to remember. il por Sports Illus 27:24-5 D 25 '67
Three for the trophy. il Newsweek 70:94 N 27 '67

SIMPSON, S. A.
Sailing through the Tuamotus. Travel 128: 30-5 D '67

SIMPSON, S. B. Jr, and Cox, P. G.
Vertebrate regeneration system: culture in vitro. bibliog Science 157:1330-2 S 15 '67

SIMPSON, Smith
Rusk enigma: who runs the State department? Nation 204:294-9 Mr 6 '67

SIMSBURY, Conn.
Stone walls do not a prison make: dungeon, known as Newgate. W. Lee. il Am Heritage 18:40-3+ F '67

SIMULATION, System. See System simulation

SIMULATORS
How to walk on the moon; gravity simulator. J. Berry. il Pop Mech 128:228+ O '67; Same. Sci Digest 62:6-8 N '67
Manned lunar simulator test completed. R. G. O'Lone. il Aviation W 37:64-5+ S 11 '67
Radar simulator uses digital computer. B. M. Elson. il Aviation W 87:97+ O 16 '67
SDC marketing first hardware in years; digital radar simulator. W. E. Wilks. il Tech W 20:37+ My 8 '67
See also
Tank ship simulators

SIN
Adam's fall: the task of reinterpretation. M. Flick. Cath World 205:42-6 Ap '67
Sin and forgiveness. V. P. McCorry. America 117:inside back cover S 16 '67
See also
Confession
Good and evil

Anecdotes, facetiae, satire, etc.
Sin-drome: America, nation of sin bores. R. Baker. McCalls 95:5 Ja '68

SINANTHROPUS. See Man, Prehistoric

SINATRA, Frank
Action in Las Vegas. Time 90:101 S 22 '67
Dean Martin talks about: his drinking, the Mafia, Frank Sinatra, women, Bobby Kennedy; interview, ed. by O. Fallaci. D. Martin. il Look 31:78-85+ D 26 '67
Mia Farrow's swinging life with Frank Sinatra. V. Scott. Ladies Home J 84:84+ My '67

Performance and the pain. G. Lees. il por Hi Fi 17:95 My '67
Render unto Caesars. il por Newsweek 70: 32 S 25 '67
Working Sinatras. J. Hamilton. il pors Look 31:86-90+ O 31 '67

SINATRA, Frank, family
TV Christmas with the Martins and the Sinatras. il pors Look 31:76-7 D 26 '67

SINATRA, Nancy
Mini Mata Hari. por Time 89:62+ My 5 '67

SINCLAIR, Dorothy
Implications of cooperation. Wilson Lib Bul 41:939-42 My '67

SINCLAIR, John H. and others
Mitochondrial-satellite and circular DNA filaments in yeast. bibliog Science 156:1234-7 Je 2 '67

SINCLAIR, Upton
Remembering Uppie. E. Ainsworth. por Sat R 50:32-3 S 30 '67

SING-out America movement. See Moral rearmament

SINGAPORE
Lee Kuan Yew's fight for survival. D. Warner. Reporter 37:36-8 N 2 '67
Rugged society. il Time 89:38+ Ap 21 '67

Description and travel
Persistence of Singapore. R. McKie. il Holiday 42:32-41+ Ag '67

Economic conditions
Rugged society; Communist-inspired demonstrations. il Newsweek 69:46-7 Je 26 '67

Economic policy
Economic development board at work. il UN Mo Chron 4:95-100 Je '67

Foreign relations
Prime Minister of Singapore visits the United States; exchange of greetings and toast, October 17, with joint statement, October 18, 1967. L. B. Johnson; K. Y. Lee. Dept State Bul 57:612-15 N 6 '67

Industries
Economic development board at work. il UN Mo Chron 4:95-100 Je '67

Politics and government
Rugged society; Communist-inspired demonstrations. il Newsweek 69:46-7 Je 26 '67

SINGER, Isaac Bashevis
Extreme Jews. Harper 234:55-62 Ap '67
Letter writer; story, tr. by A. Shevrin and E. Shub. New Yorker 43:26-36 Ja 13 '68
Match for a princess; story. Redbook 129: 68-9 Ag '67
My adventures as an idealist; story; tr. by A. Shevrin and E. Shub. Sat Eve Post 240: 68-73 N 18 '67
Pigeons; story. Esquire 68:76-9 Ag '67
Powers; story. Harper 235:76-8 O '67
Slaughterer; story, tr. by M. Ginsburg. New Yorker 43:60-5 N 25 '67

about
Authors & editors. por Pub W 192:17-18 O 16 '67
Old Jew in new times. J. Chametzky. Nation 205:436-8 O 30 '67
Two worlds of Isaac Singer. C. R. Hughes. America 117:611-13 N 18 '67

SINGER, Maxine F.
In vitro synthesis of DNA: a perspective on research. Science 158:1550-1 D 22 '67

SINGER, Norman
And we quote; interview. ed. by S. Fleming. por Hi Fi 17:MA16 O '67

SINGER, Siegfried Fred
Planetary engineering. por Sat R 50:41-2 Jl 1 '67
Zodical dust and deep-sea sediments. bibliog Science 156:1080-3 My 26 '67
about
New twist for an old theory. il Time 89:64 F 3 '67

SINGER building. See New York (city)— Architecture

SINGERS
Ancient Russian rarities. A. Favia-Artsay. il Hobbies 72:35+ D '67
At the piano; excerpts. I. Newton. il Opera N 31:6-7 Je 10 '67
Baddies: Rolling Stones. il Time 89:54 Ap 28 '67
Beatles vs. Stones; Rolling Stones as rivals. J. Kroll. il Newsweek 71:62-3 Ja 1 '68
Debuts & reappearances; New York concerts. il Hi Fi 17:MA16-21+ My '67

SINGERS—*Continued*
English supreme fifteen; those who recorded in years before electrical methods of capturing sound. J. Walsh. il Hobbies 71:37-8 F; 72:37-8 Mr '67
Evolution; the Monkees. Time 89:70 F 17 '67
Greatest quartet basso. J. Walsh. il Hobbies 72:38-9+ N '67
Just call us super group; the Mamas and the Papas. W. Kloman. il Sat Eve Post 240:36-41 Mr 25 '67
Long gone Macushla; The Dubliners. il Time 90:66 O 13 '67
Luvs story; girls' band. M. English. il Look 31:M14-16+ My 2 '67
Mama, papa & the kids; the Cowsills. il Time 90:81 O 20 '67
Monkee talk; symposium, ed. by E. Miller. il Seventeen 26:302-3+ Ag '67
Musical whirl; photographs. See issues of High fidelity incorporating Musical America
Nashville the sounds and the symbols; country and western scene. G. Lees. il Hi Fi 17:57-61 Ap '67
Pop music: the most? or just a mess? A. G. Aronowitz. il Sat Eve Post 240:70-5 Jl 15 '67
Queen bees; female singers in rock groups. il Newsweek 71:77-8 Ja 15 '68
Singing voice: lower and darker. R. Rushmore. il Opera N 31:24-6 F 18 '67
Singing voice: national types. R. Rushmore. il Opera N 31:22-5 Mr 18 '67
Too young to cry; sixteen year old little J. Ian. H. Saal. il Newsweek 69:114 Je 19 '67
Tune up, turn disestablishmentarian, drop out. R. Christgau. il Esquire 68:104-5+ S '67

See also
Beatles
Negro singers
Opera singers
also names of singers, e.g. D. Warwick

Anecdotes, facetiae, satire, etc.
Man and his matrix. G. Cotler. New Yorker 43:164-7 S 9 '67

SINGH, Brajesh
Her journey of no return; S. Stalin. M. H. Zim. il Life 62:66-7 Mr 24 '67

SINGH, Roderick P. and Meyer, D. B.
Primordial germ cells in blood smears from chick embryos. bibliog Science 156:1503-4 Je 16 '67

SINGING
Great singers, by H. Pleasants. Review
Am Rec G 33:864+ My '67. G. L Mayer
Sat R 50:69 Mr 25 '67. H. Weinstock
Lively arts; interview, ed. by R. Hemming. L. Kazan. Sr Schol 91:30 N 16 '67
Mystery of performing; ed. by P. M. Katona, tr. by A. M. Lingg. G. Souzay. il Opera N 32:8-11 N 25 '67
R: bel canto. C. Schwalberg. Opera N 32:16 D 30 '67
They talk about freedom; ed. by E. Miller. B. Sainte-Marie. il Seventeen 26:150-1+ Ap '67

See also
Embellishment (vocal music)
Singers
Vaudeville
Voice

Competitions
Chances to be heard; Metropolitan opera regional auditions. R. Eyer. Opera N 32:14-15 Ja 6 '68
Council surprises; finals of the Metropolitan opera national council's regional auditions. A. M. Lingg. il Opera N 32:13 D 9 '67
Young opera singers, their care and training; International competition for young opera singers. P. Hart. Hi Fi 17:MA24-5 O '67

SINGLE cell protein. See Proteins

SINGLE convention on narcotic drugs, 1961
President urges accession to 1961 single convention on narcotics; texts of letter and report. L. B. Johnson; N. D. Katzenbach. Dept State Bul 56:671-3 Ap 24 '67
While you weren't looking; Senate ratifies a new international treaty. New Repub 157:7 Jl 8 '67

SINGLE-lens reflex cameras
Beat & offbeat; German SLR's. N. Rothschild. Pop Phot 61:32+ S '67
Fast lenses for 35mm cameras. Consumer Rep 32:393 Jl '67
Good buys in used SLR's. il Mod Phot 31:72-3+ S '67
Keppler looks over the SLR's & lenses. H. Keppler. Mod Phot 31:77+ Je '67

Keppler on the SLR. H. Keppler. See issues of Modern photography
Reflections on the reflex. W. Clark. U S Camera 31:31 Ja '68
Reply to the SLR know-it-alls. N. Rothschild. il Pop Phot 60:71-3+ Ap '67
Simon says. Simon. il Mod Phot 31:74+ N '67
SLR viewing: what a mess! B. Sherman. il Mod Phot 31:92-5+ N '67
SLR's may look alike, but. . . D. L. Miller. il Mod Phot 31:84-91 Ag '67
Singular reflexes are done with mirrors. W. Lane. Travel 128:65 Ag '67
Six single-lens-reflex cameras. il Consumer Bul 50:11-14 Ap '67
35; a flood of lens-metering SLRs! C. W. Kennedy. il Pop Phot 60:102-3 Je '67
35mm SLR cameras. il Consumer Rep 32:73-7 F '67
2¼ SLR systems compared. D. L. Miller. il Mod Phot 31:60-1 Mr '67
What's what in SLR? D. L. Miller. il Mod Phot 31:62-7 My '67
Will pros take to the new Contarex? W. Clark. il U S Camera 30:44-5 F '67

SINGLE men
Boys & girls together; apartments for singlesonly: South Bay clubs, Los Angeles. C. Mangel. il Look 31:M8+ Ag 22 '67
Income taxes are unfair to us single people. il Changing T 21:13-16 Ag '67; Discussion. 21:31-3 N '67
Last resort; singles weekend scene at Catskills hotels. il Newsweek 71:52-3 Ja 15 '68
New crop of bachelors. il Ebony 22:48-50+ Je '67
New rules for the singles game; helping singles meet each other. il Life 63:60-6 Ag 18 '67
Pleasures & pain of the single life; Time essay. Time 90:26-7 S 15 '67

SINGLE rail railroads. See Railroads, Single rail

SINGLE women
Boys & girls together; apartments for singlesonly: South Bay clubs, Los Angeles. C. Mangel. il Look 31:M8+ Ag 22 '67
Defense of women who refuse to marry. S. Blum. il Redbook 130:50-1+ Ja '68
Half a hundred eligible girls. il Ebony 22:44-6+ F '67
Income taxes are unfair to us single people. il Changing T 21:13-16 Ag '67; Discussion. 21:31-3 N '67
Last resort; singles weekend scene at Catskills hotels. il Newsweek 71:52-3 Ja 15 '68
Man talk; les *misérables*. D. Newman and R. Benton. Mlle 65:12 Jl '67
New girl in town, what she seeks & what she finds. J. Paulson. il Ladies Home J 85:62-3+ Ja '68
New rules for the singles game; helping singles meet each other. il Life 63:60-6 Ag 18 '67
Opinion: on late bloomers. S. Temple. Mlle 66:52-3+ D '67
Pill and the girl next door. D. Hubert. il Mlle 64:162-3+ Mr '67
Pleasures & pain of the single life; Time essay. Time 90:26-7 S 15 '67
Should doctors prescribe contraceptives for unmarried girls? F. R. Talbot. il Ladies Home J 85:37+ Ja '68
Spinsters are smarter. Sci Digest 63:20-1 Ja '68

SINGLETON, Carlton M. and Brown, S. M.
To the hills and hollows. Am Ed 3:22-5 Jl '67

SINGLETON, Henry E.
Making big waves with small fish. il por Bsns W p36-9 D 30 '67
Teledyne's takeoff. il por Time 90:102 O 6 '67

SINK holes. See Sinkholes

SINKHOLES
Drought or sinkholes. il Sci N 91:520 Je 3 '67
Sinkhole formation by groundwater withdrawal: Far West Rand, South Africa. R. M. Foose. bibliog il Science 157:1045-8 S 1 '67

SINKIANG province, China
War of nerves; Sino-Soviet border. il Newsweek 69:44+ Mr 6 '67

SINO-INDIAN border dispute, 1957-
Guns of Natu La; Sino-Indian fighting. il Newsweek 70:50 S 25 '67
India vs. China: new war for U.S. too? il U S News 63:16 S 25 '67

SINOLOGY. See Chinese studies (Sinology)

SINSHEIMER, Robert
End of the beginning. Bul Atomic Sci 23:8-12 F '67

SIOTIS, Jean
ECE in the emerging European system. bibliog f por Int Concil 561:5-70 Ja '67

SIOUX CITY, la.
To all the world, welcome! D. J. Hamblin. il Life 63:46-53 S 1 '67

Sanitary affairs
Two unusual solid-waste solutions. F. H. Kerr. il Am City 82:114-15 Ap '67
SIOUX Indians. See Dakota Indians
SIQUEIROS, David Alfaro
Art for the active. il Time 89:72 F 17 '67
SIRIKIT Kitiyakara, consort of Bhumibol Adulyadej, king of Thailand
Visit with the king & queen of Thailand. G. Zimmermann. il pors Look 31:86-91 Je 27 '67
SIRILLA, George M.
What rights for those on welfare? America 117:349-51 S 30 '67
SIROCCO. See Winds
SIROVICH symphony orchestra
Symphony for New York's elder population. G. Bamberger. il Parks & Rec 2:32+ My '67
SISAL hemp
Henequen diseased; situation in Yucatan. E. Zubryn. Sci N 92:403 O 21 '67
SISCO, Joseph J.
Institutions for order; address, December 7, 1966. Dept State Bul 56:64-9 Ja 9 '67
Recent international developments concerning the ocean and ocean floor; statement, November 29, 1967. Dept State Bul 58:17-19 Ja 1 '68
U.N: an arena for peaceful East-West engagement; address, February 24, 1967. Dept State Bul 56:458-63 Mr 20 '67
United States reviews problems of control of peaceful uses of atomic energy; statement, December 5, 1967. Dept State Bul 58:63-5 Ja 8 '68
SISSMAN, L. E.
Dying; an introduction; poem. New Yorker 43:34-5 Je 3 '67
Going home, 1945; poem. New Yorker 43:31-3 Je 24 '67
Life in Alabaster street; poem. New Yorker 43:52 S 16 '67
Love-making; April; middle age; poem. Atlan 221:58 Ja '68
New England: dead of winter; poem. New Yorker 42:42 F 18 '67
Sunday morning, Watkins Glen; poem. New Yorker 43:100 O 28 '67
Two encounters; poem. New Yorker 43:56 Ap 15 '67
SISTER cities. See Intercommunity cooperation
SISTER schools. See School-to-school program
SISTERHOODS
Crisis in Catholic education. D. Callahan. il N Y Times Mag p34-5+ Ap 23 '67
Experiment in sisterhood; idea of Austin, Tex, diocese. America 117:72 Jl 22 '67
Grennan affair; American Catholic college is being secularized. V. P. McCorry. America 116:149-50 Ja 28 '67; Discussion. 116:138, 298 Ja 28, Mr 4 '67
Image of the teaching religious. O. C. D'Amour. America 116:418 Mr 25 '67
In praise of nuns; letter. T. F. Reilly. America 117:288-9 S 23 '67
Jacqueline Grennan: ex-nun. R. B. Kaiser. il Look 31:106-10 My 30 '67
Medium is absurd. D. M. Burton. Commonweal 86:340-2 Je 9 '67
Nun: a joyous revolution. il Newsweek 70:45-8 D 25 '67
Nuns that quit. R. B. Kaiser. il Ladies Home J 84:82-3+ Ap '67
Pope addresses mother superiors; concerning adaptation of rules. America 116:491 Ap 1 '67
Raise your voice: renewal of religious life; address, May 27, 1967. B. Meyers. Vital Speeches 33:661-4 Ag 15 '67
Reform as experiment: Sisters of the immaculate heart of Mary in California. Commonweal 87:160 N 10 '67
Senate of sisters in Cleveland; initial meeting of the Senate for religious women. America 116:492 Ap 1 '67
Sisters administer parishes; Brazil. America 116:490 Ap 1 '67
Sister's on the other line; listing of nuns as phone subscribers. N. Perrin. New Yorker 43:150+ N 18 '67
Woman's angle; four nuns named to curia. il Newsweek 70:72 O 16 '67
See also
Vocation (in religion)

Anecdotes, facetiae, satire, etc.
Get thee to a nunnery, Ophelia de Sade! P. J. Laux. il America 116:420-2 Mr 25 '67; Discussion. 116:609-10, 617 Ap 29 '67

Sisters to form baseball team. P. J. Laux. il America 117:552 N 11 '67
SISTERS of Loretto. See Sisterhoods
SITAR
Ravi Shankar and George Beatles. C. Reid. il N Y Times Mag p28-9+ My 7 '67
SITE planning. See Housing projects—Site Planning
SITE values. See Land values
SITES, Building. See Building sites
SITHI-AMNUAI, Paul
Strange fellows, those American executives. por Nations Bsns 55:60-2+ Jl '67
SITOSTEROLS
Conversion of beta sitosterol to cholesterol blocked in an insect by hypocholesterolemic agents. J. A. Svoboda and W. E. Robbins. bibliog il Science 156:1637-8 Je 23 '67
SITWELL, Dame Edith
Dame Edith Sitwell, by E. Salter. Review
  New Repub 157:21-2 D 2 '67. S. Spender
Two ladies of legend. D. Hoffman. Reporter 37:41-3 D 28 '67
SIVAK, Andrew, and Van Duuren, B. L.
Phenotypic expression of transformation: induction in cell culture by a phorbol ester. bibliog Science 157:1443-4 S 22 '67
SIVERD, Clifford David
Siverd of American cyanamid. por Fortune 76:59 N '67
SIX nations. See Iroquois Indians
SIX year term for president. See Presidents—United States—Term
SIXTEEN magazine
Meet Gloria Stavers. W. Kloman. il Sat Eve Post 240:80+ N 4 '67
SIXTH committee of the United Nations. See United Nations—Legal committee
SIZE of man. See Body size
SJODIN, R. A. and Beaugé, L. A.
Strophanthidin-sensitive transport of cesium and sodium in muscle cells. bibliog Science 156:1248-50 Je 2 '67
SKAKEL, Patricia
And then, the mother. por Newsweek 69:31 My 29 '67
SKATING
Crystal and steel on the ice; World skating championships. B. Ottum. il Sports Illus 26:24-7 Mr 13 '67
Elegance on ice; P. Fleming wins Women's international figure skating championships. il Newsweek 69:88 Mr 13 '67
First time on ice skates. il Sunset 138:33-4 F '67
Growing up & staying there; women's world figure-skating champion. il Time 89:76+ Mr 10 '67
SKATING rinks
Ice skating, Whitemarsh style. D. R. Koontz. il Parks & Rec 2:27 Ja '67
We switched from cows to roller skates. E. M. Pearson. Farm J 91:60D Mr '67
SKEELS, Harold Manville
Case of the wandering IQs. B. Asbell. Redbook 129:31+ Ag '67
SKEET (game)
Skeet shooting scores a bull's-eye; Highland Park, Ill. D. Fritz. il Am City 82:94 Jl '67
SKELETON
Echinoderm calcite: single crystal or polycrystalline aggregate. K. M. Towe. bibliog il Science 157:1048-50 S 1 '67
SKELTON, Mary L.
Doodle-naks. Sch Arts 67:38-9 D '67
SKELTON, Red
I'm nuts and I know it. B. Davidson. il pors Sat Eve Post 240:66-72+ Je 17 '67
SKELTON, Robin
Voices; poem. Poetry 110:33-7 Ap '67
SKETCHING. See Drawing
SKEWER cookery. See Barbecue cookery
SKI bobs and bobbing
Ski bob bobbing along. il Time 89:52+ Mr 17 '67
SKI cabins. See Cabins
SKI clothing. See Clothing and dress—Sports clothes
SKI lodges. See Lodges (architecture)
SKI resorts. See Winter resorts
SKIDDING of airplanes. See Airplanes—Skidding
SKIERS
See also
  Killy, J. C.
SKIING. See Skis and skiing

SKILLED labor
Brain drain: a U.S. dilemma. H. G. Grubel; discussion. Science 155:1495-7 Mr 24 '67
Canada's brain drain ceases; skilled craftsman emigration to the U.S. Bsns W p 110 Ap 29 '67
Variability by skill in cyclical unemployment. M. S. Cohen and W. H. Gruber. bibliog f il Mo Labor R 90:8-11 Ag '67
Worker skills in current defense employment. M. A. Rutzick. il Mo Labor R 90:17-20 S '67

SKILLETS
Pick a perfect frying pan. il Changing T 21:24 Jl '67

SKILLIN, Edward Simeon
Change of editors. J. O'Gara. Commonweal 86:255-6 My 19 '67

SKIMMER investigation platform. See Ground effect machines

SKIN
Skin. R. F. Rushmer and others; reply. C. A. Larson Science 155:488 Ja 27 '67
When your skin turns dry. T. Berland. il Todays Health 46:12-15 Ja '68
  See also
Moles (dermatology)
Sunburn

Care and hygiene
Beauty life: feeding your face. il Mlle 65:126-7 Je '67
Beauty treatment from a $20 gadget? facial sauna. il Consumer Rep 32:245-7 My '67
Can great skin be created? Vogue 150:112-13+ Ag 15 '67
Capsule guide to skin care. McCalls 94:178 Mr '67
Do you have oily skin? il Redbook 129:84-5+ Je '67
Facial saunas. il Seventeen 26:218 N '67
Facing it: your skin care. A. F. Cronin. il Parents Mag 43:24+ Ja '68
Facing up to college. Mlle 65:250-1 Ag '67
How to cleanse your skin. Am Home 71:22 Ja '68
How-what-when for your type of skin. il Seventeen 26:122-5 S '67
Skin-care strategy for the six most common problems. il Good H 164:96-7 Mr '67
Steam: the new beauty essential. S. Harney. il Ladies Home J 84:92 F '67
When your skin turns dry. T. Berland. il Todays Health 46:12-15 Ja '68

Diseases
Better protection against diaper rash. Todays Health 46:77 Ja '68
Danger signals on the skin. il Todays Health 45:8+ F '67
How your skin reflects your health. T. Sternberg. il Sci Digest 62:21-5 Ag '67
Skin-care strategy for the six most common problems. il Good H 164:96-7 Mr '67
Sun ban; diseases caused by sun's rays. il Time 89:65 My 12 '67
  See also
Allergy
Eczema

SKIN, Artificial. See Prosthesis

SKIN, Color of. See Color of man

SKIN diving
Practical skin-diving. S. Anderson. il Yachting 122:58-9+ N '67
Skin diving: why it appealed to Mr Holt. il U S News 64:9 Ja 1 '68
Sport of scuba. F. M. Paulson. il Field & S 72:84-7 Jl '67

SKIN grafting. See Transplantation of organs, tissues, etc.

SKIN pigment. See Color of man

SKINNER, Constance Lindsay, award. See Constance Lindsay Skinner award

SKINNER, Cornelia Otis
Madame Sarah; condensation. Read Digest 90:227-30+ Ap '67

SKINNER, Harry
Self-contained drill speeds sign-post installation. Am City 82:133 Ap '67

SKINNER, Jean Ross-. See Ross-Skinner, J.

SKIS and skiing
Cup for Canada. il Time 89:60 Ap 7 '67
Encore Napoleon; North American ski championships. il Time 89:43-4 Mr 24 '67
Fastest man on any mountain; J. C. Killy. D. Jenkins. il Sports Illus 26:18-21 Mr 27 '67
Lafayette, they are back; French ski champions at Franconia, N.H; photographs by M. E. Newman; with account by D. Jenkins. Sports Illus 26:20-5 Mr 20 '67
Little tiger takes the cup; Canada's N. Greene at the wild west classic at Jackson Hole, Wyo. B. Ottum. il Sports Illus 26:22-3 Ap 3 '67

One-track skiers; therapy for amputee veterans at the Soda Springs ski area Donner summit in California. il Life 62:103+ Ap 14 '67
Outdoor woman. il McCalls 95:16 Ja '68
Ski fun for everyone; review. P. Idleman. il Consumer Bul 50:18 N '67
Sudden streak for Nancy; Canada's N. Greene, a sensation on the European ski circuit. D. Jenkins. il Sports Illus 26:10-13 Ja 30 '67
  See also
Ski bobs and bobbing

Accidents and injuries
Après-ski legality. il Time 89:45 Ja 27 '67
How to avoid the twelve most common skiing accidents. K. N. Anderson. il Sci Digest 62:7-12 D '67

Equipment
France puts its stamp on the snow; ski fashion and equipment business. il Bsns W p 192-4 Mr 18 '67
Short-ee skis, your short cut to winter fun. W. I. Fischman. il Pop Sci 191:108-10+ D '67
Simple holder flattens ski boots. il Pop Sci 191:151 D '67

Safety devices and measures
Skiing safety tips from the AMA. Sci Digest 62:12 D '67

Study and teaching
Short-ee skis, your short cut to winter fun. W. I. Fischman. il Pop Sci 191:108-10+ D '67

California
Skiing the Sierras. E. Gay. il Todays Health 45:28-33+ N '67

Chile
Skiing in Chile; photographs by R. Rowan. Holiday 41:70-7 F '67

France
France, a go-go place for the games; photographs by E. Haas; with account by F. R. Smith. il Sports Illus 27:46-62 N 13 '67
Let's travel: ski scoops 1967-68. J. Silver. Mlle 66:106+ N '67
Trouble with being no. 1; J. C. Killy. Time 91:33 Ja 19 '68

Idaho
Changing Sun Valley. il Sunset 138:74-81 F '67
It's the only life for me! P. Street. il Seventeen 26:92-3 D '67

New England
Skiing bare-to-good, with some pain. J. Skow. il Sat Eve Post 240:24-9 Mr 11 '67

New Mexico
Skiing the silver country; Sierra Blanca ski area. F. R. Smith. il Sports Illus 26:40-7 F 20 '67

Northwestern states
Ski drama with a big third act: skiing in the Tetons. F. Kappler. Life 62:21 Mr 17 '67

Sweden
Sweden's strenuous ski scramble. J. H. Winchester. il Read Digest 90:107-10 F '67

United States
America's ski book. Review Consumer Bul il 50:43 D '67. P. Idleman
Best ski news. D. Messinesi. Vogue 151:46 Ja 1 '68
Let's travel: ski scoops 1967-68. J. Silver. Mlle 66:106+ N '67
Making the snow scene, on or off skis. J. Egan. il Mlle 66:171-2+ N '67
New exhilaration: skiing at sixty! C. W. Casewit. il Travel 127:37-9 F '67
Skiing with a twist; the hosteling way. S. Y. Herman. il Sr Schol 91:sup 12-13 N 2 '67

Vermont
Lookout at Sugarbush. J. H. Ingersoll. il House B 109:150-3 D '67

Western states
Western powder. E. Bowen. il Mlle 66:189-90+ N '67

SKLAR, Robert
Hot and cold societies. Reporter 36:52 Ap 6 '67
Maimed generation. Reporter 36:51-2 F 23 '67
New novel, USA: Thomas Pynchon. Nation 205:277-80 S 25 '67

SKLAR, Robert—*Continued*
  To strive, to seek, to find. Reporter 37:48+
    Ag 10 '67
  Tolkien & Hesse: top of the pops. Nation 204:
    598-601 My 8 '67
  Word people on film people. Reporter 37:52+
    D 14 '67
SKODA. See Automobile industry and trade—
  Czechoslovakia
SKODAK, Marie
  Case of the wandering IQs. B. Asbell. Red-
    book 129:31+ Ag '67
SKOL international corporation
  Beer without a country. J. Ross-Skinner.
    il Duns R 90:71-2+ N '67
  World quaffers call for Skol. il Bsns W p74+
    S 30 '67
SKOLIMOWSKI, Jerzy
  Movers. A. Sarris. por Sat R 50:39 D 23 '67
SKOLNIKOFF, Eugene B.
  Birth and death of an idea: research in AID.
    Bul Atomic Sci 23:38-40 S '67
SKOOGFORS, Judy
  American jewelry today. Craft Horiz 27:26-
    7 N '67
SKOPTSI
  Some place to hide; a home in the Danube
    delta. F. V. Grunfeld. il Reporter 37:32-4
    N 30 '67
SKOPTZI. See Skoptsi
SKOW, John
  Dueling with slingshots at 180 mph. Sat Eve
    Post 240:70-5 Je 3 '67
  Farewell to Hells Canyon. Sat Eve Post 240:
    76-83 Jl 1 '67
  I must go down to the beach again, must I?
    Sat Eve Post 240:18 Ap 8 '67
  I want to smoke pot; story. Sat Eve Post
    241:42-5 Ja 27 '68
  Island that borrows its children. Sat Eve Post
    240:87-91 Mr 25 '67; Same abr. Read Digest
    90:79-83 Je '67
  Question in the ghetto: can Cleveland escape
    burning? Sat Eve Post 240:38-42+ Jl 29 '67
  Skiing bare-to-good, with some pain. Sat Eve
    Post 240:24-9 Mr 11 '67
SKRIABIN, Aleksandr Nikolaevich
  Scriabin's opera. F. Bowers. por Opera N
    31:6-7 Mr 4 '67
SKROWACZEWSKI, Stanislaw
  Lively arts; interview, ed. by R. Hemming.
    por Sr Schol 90:21 Mr 17 '67

                about
  Big five plus one? por Time 90:84-5 N 10 '67
SKUJINS, J. J. and McLaren, A. D.
  Enzyme reaction rates at limited water ac-
    tivities. bibliog Science 158:1569-70 D 22 '67
SKUNKS

        Anecdotes, facetiae, satire, etc.
  Wayward skunk. C. Ford. il Field & S 72:6+
    S '67
SKURNIK, W. A. E.
  Nigeria in crisis. Cur Hist 52:142-8+ Mr '67
SKVORECKY, Josef
  Letter from Prague. Nation 205:470-3 N 6
    '67
SKY, Color of
        See also
  Sunset phenomena
SKY diving. See Parachuting
SKY-Hook. See Artificial satellites
SKYLANDS of New Jersey. See New Jersey—
  Parks and reserves
SKYLIGHTS
  Almost the whole ceiling is a translucent sky-
    light. il Sunset 138:130 Ap '67
  Easy-to-build skylight. D. Huff. il Pop Sci
    190-174 My '67
  Fact sheet: short course in skylights. il Am
    Home 70:110+ S '67
SKYSCRAPERS
  Chicago's multi-use giant; John Hancock
    center. il Arch Rec 144:137-44 Ja '67
  Hartford plaza; office building in San Fran-
    cisco. il Arch Rec 141:132-6 My '67
  Pittsburgh skyscraper achieves breakthrough
    in steel fireproofing; United States steel
    corporation. il Arch Rec 141:165-72 Ap '67
  They'll commute by elevator in 100-story
    tower; John Hancock center, Chicago. A. P.
    Armagnac. il Pop Sci 190:100-1 My '67
  Total energy in high-rise, two applications.
    il Arch Rec 142:153-4 D '67
SKYTTE, Bengt
  Bengt Skytte's project of a universal uni-
    versity in 1667. W. W. Brickman. por
    Sch & Soc 95:483 D 9 '67
SLACKMAN, Charles B.
  In the finest tradition of our armed forces.
    Esquire 67:140-1 Ap '67

SLADE, David H.
  Modeling air pollution in the Washington,
    D.C, to Boston megalopolis. bibliog Science
    157:1304-7 S 15 '67
SLANDER. See Libel and slander
SLANG
  English, hip and ofay; English exercise book.
    Play it cool for the ghetto child. il News-
    week 69:70 Ap 10 '67
  Glossary of campus slang. L. B. Johnson. il
    McCalls 94:56 Ap '67
  Introduction to boont: if you call a man a
    haireem, smile. il Sunset 138:34 Mr '67
  Ridgey-didge; or, How to communicate with
    an Australian, we think. B. Ross. il Yacht-
    ing 122:65+ S '67
        See also
  Jargon
SLAPPEY, Sterling G.
  Trends: tomorrow's businessmen. Nations
    Bsns 55:87 D '67
SLATE, John
  Day they built Rome. Sat Eve Post 240:68-9
    Mr 25 '67
SLATER, Joseph
  From death to rebirth. Sat R 50:36 N 4 '67
SLATTED barn floors. See Barns and stables
  —Floors
SLATTED floors (swine houses) See Swine
  houses—Floors
SLAUGHTER, L. W.
  On time. See issues of Hobbies

                about
  Obituary
    Hobbies 71:46 F '67
SLAUGHTER, Robert E.
  Educator and the industrialist. NEA J 56:27-9
    F '67
SLAUGHTER, Thedford
  Up from hate. Sat R 50:59 D 16 '67
SLAUGHTERER; story. See Singer, I. B.
SLAUGHTERING and slaughterhouses
        See also
  Meat inspection
SLAVE trade
  Captain Canot, American slave-trader visits
    the African town of Timbo. T. Canot. il
    Negro Hist Bul 30:10 O '67
  Slavery still plagues the earth; lack of action
    by UN. R. L. Tobin. Sat R 50:24+ My 6 '67
  Slavery: the crime the world ignores; function
    of the Anti-slavery society in London. N.
    Mostert. il Reporter 38:29-31 Ja 11 '68
SLAVERY
  Slavery: the crime the world ignores; function
    of the Anti-slavery society in London. N.
    Mostert. il Reporter 38:29-31 Ja 11 '68
        See also
  Slave trade
                Africa
  Africa remembered, ed. by P. D. Curtin. Re-
    view
      Sat R 50:39-41 Je 10 '67. C. Miller

                Middle East
  Slavery still plagues the earth; lack of action
    by UN. R. L. Tobin. Sat R 50:24+ My 6 '67

                United States
  John Brown, fanatic or precursor of free-
    dom? Negro Hist Bul 30:4-5 My '67
  Robert Purvis & his early challenge to
    American racisms. J. A. Borome. Negro
    Hist Bul 30:8-10 My '67
        See also
  Abolitionists
  Secession
            Insurrections, etc.
        See also
  Southampton insurrection, 1831
SLAVIC languages
                Alphabet
  Clement of Ohrid, Slavic educator. il Sch &
    Soc 95:175-6 Mr 18 '67
SLAVITT, David R.
  Lute; poem. Yale R 56:552-3 Je '67
SLAYMAKER family
  To see America: houseful of our history; with
    report by D. J. Hamblin. il Life 63:44-56
    Ag 25 '67
SLED dog racing. See Dog racing
SLED dogs
  Sled-dog fact and fiction. D. M. Duffey. il
    Outdoor Life 140:118+ N '67
SLEDS
  Dragster sled. il Pop Mech 127:170-1 F '67
SLEDS, Rocket. See Rocket sleds

SLEEP
Are you getting enough sleep? Philip M. Tiller, jr. survey. J. D. Ratcliff. Read Digest 90:109-11 My '67
Autonomic basis for the rise in brain temperature during paradoxical sleep. M. A. Baker and J. N. Hayward. bibliog il Science 157:1586-8 S 29 '67
Brain stem structures responsible for the electroencephalographic patterns of desynchronized sleep. O. Candia and others. bibliog il Science 155:720-2 F 10 '67
Eye-opening discoveries about sleep. H. Fantel. il Pop Mech 128:104-7+ N '67
Increased turnover of cerebral norepinephrine during rebound of paradoxical sleep in the rat. J. F. Pujol and others. bibliog il Science 159:112-14 Ja 5 '68
Long day's journey into the insomniac's night. E. Diamond. il N Y Times Mag p30-1+ O 1 '67; Same abr. with title Inside insomnia. Read Digest 92:131-4 Ja '68; Same with title Insomniac's nightmare, sleep. Sci Digest 63:62-7 Ja '68
Magic of sleep. D. V. Whipple. il Parents Mag 42:50-1+ My '67
Nature's sleeping potion? humoral factor. Sci Am 217:56+ O '67
Neurons in paradoxical sleep and motivated behavior. W. D. Mink and others. bibliog il Science 158:1335-7 D 8 '67
Rapid eye movement sleep deprivation: a central-neural change during wakefulness. J. H. Dewson, 3d, and others. bibliog il Science 156:403-6 Ap 21 '67
Reassuring report for women who have trouble sleeping. G. G. Luce and J. Segal. il McCalls 94:102-3+ F '67
Sleep: effects on incorporation of inorganic phosphate into brain fractions. P. Reich and others. bibliog il Science 157:336-8 Jl 21 '67
Sleep: the effect of electroconvulsive shock in cats deprived of REM sleep. H. B. Cohen and others. bibliog il Science 156:1646-8 Je 23 '67
Solving the mystery of sleep. M. Fishbein. Sci Digest 62:43-4 Ag '67
State as a determinant of infants' heart rate response to stimulation. M. Lewis and others. bibliog il Science 155:486-8 Ja 27 '67
States of sleep. M. Jouvet. il Sci Am 216: 62-8+ bibliog(p 146) F '67
When bedtime brings problems... J. J. Cox. il Todays Health 45:39-41 My '67
Why do you dream? rapid eye movement sleep. M. Gunther. il Sat Eve Post 240:84-7 D 2 '67
You and your sleep. B. Gaines. See issues of Ladies' home journal
See also
Dreams

SLEEPING, Outdoor
Get a good sleep. C. B. Colby. il Outdoor Life 140:104-8 N '67

SLEEPING bags
Great gift: a good bag. il Sunset 139:33+ D '67

SLEEPING beauty; ballet. See Ballets—Criticisms

SLEEPING Chinese beauty; drama. See Locke, K.

SLEEPING medicines. See Barbiturates

SLEEPLESSNESS. See Insomnia

SLEEPY little elf; drama. See Robertson, O. J.

SLENCAK, Robert J.
It's just a simple cold. Flying 81:74 N '67

SLEPECKY, R. A. See Northrop, J. jt. auth.

SLEPIAN, Ed
Fuel cell. Motor B 119:38-40+ My '67

SLEVIN, Joseph R.
Washington desk. See issues of Dun's review

SLIDE projectors. See Projectors

SLIDE rule
Common slide rule for reactance calculations. G. B. Houck, jr. Electr World 78:93 S '67

SLIDE viewers. See Transparencies—Viewers

SLIDING. See Coasting

SLIMMER, Pete
They left Pan Am for riches in Fiji. il por Bsns W p82-3+ S 16 '67

SLINGS for rifles. See Rifles

SLIP covers
Cover it colorful. il Good H 164:144-50 Ap '67
Slipcovers are not only for summer. Am Home 70:136-7 O '67

SLIPPED disc. See Spine—Abnormities and deformities

SLIPS (clothing) See Underwear

SLIVKA, Marie
Friendly town. PTA Mag 61:8-10 Je '67

SLOAN, John
Artist-teacher in America. D. G. Byrd. bibliog il Sch Arts 66:25-30 F '67

SLOAN-Kettering Institute for cancer research
Science vs. democracy; NIH blanket. J. Lear. Sat R 50:57-61 N 4 '67

SLOANE, Louise
Let yourself grow. Am Home 70:74 O '67

SLOANE, William
Inscrutable; poem. Sat R 50:20 S 30 '67

SLOAT, James G.
Super-simple transistor tester. Pop Sci 191: 96-8 D '67

SLOAT, Warren
Exploration of color. Sat R 50:33 Ag 5 '67

SLOATSBURG, N.Y.
We don't read water meters any more; automatic system. J. Babcook. il Am City 82: 86-7 Jl '67

SLOGANS
Manner of speaking; of poetry and sloganeering. J. Ciardi. Sat R 51:14 Ja 6 '68

SLOOP racing. See Yacht racing

SLOSKY, Bill
Do flash & filters improve underwater pictures? il Mod Phot 31:88-9+ Je '67

SLOVAK literature
See also
Czech literature

SLOW, David, pseud.
End of a beginning. America 117:564-5 N 11 '67
First week of the synod. America 117:442-3 O 21 '67
Lay congress ends. America 117:512-13 N 4 '67
Roman diary. America 116:582-3; 117:18-19 Ap 22, Jl 1 '67
Synod and lay congress, Roman diary. America 117:477-8 O 28 '67
Synod of bishops, Roman diary. America 117: 410-11 O 14 '67

about
Reactions to a Jonathan Swift; letters to the editor. America 117:671 D 2 '67

SLOW learning children
Case of the wandering IQs; study findings of H. M. Skeels and M. Skodak. B. Asbell. il Redbook 129:31+ Ag '67
Gymnastics for the retarded. T. J. Denman. il Parks & Rec 2:44+ Mr '67
Hereditary learning disabilities; minimal brain dysfunction. Sci N 91:411 Ap 29 '67
Shadow children. by C. Ellingson. Review Sat R 50:72 D 16 '67. E. W. Colvin

Education
From a young American, with love; Dian Hamilton working in school for retarded children south of Manila. J. R. Moskin. il Look 31:50-2+ My 30 '67
Giving the retarded a chance; Human development program, West Springfield, Mass. D. R. Snyder. il NEA J 56:24-5 S '67
New horizons for retarded children: an expert's plan. J. M. Presley. il U S News 62: 109-10 My 15 '67

SLOWDOWN strikes. See Strikes—United States

SLUGS
Angiostongylus cantonensis; proof of direct transmission with its epidemiological implications. D. Heyneman and B. L. Lim. bibliog il Science 158:1057-8 N 24 '67

SLUGS, Sea. See Nudibranchs

SLUM children. See Socially handicapped children

SLUM clearance. See Slums; Urban renewal

SLUMS
Bringing new jobs into the ghettos; companies putting up plants in slum areas. il Bsns W p84-6 D 2 '67
Crisis in the cities: does business hold the key? with comments by business leaders. il Duns R 90:31-5 N '67
Failure in the slums. W. F. Buckley, jr. Nat R 19:341 Ap 4 '67
Finding a profit in slum streets; Pittsburgh group called Action-housing. il Bsns W p52-4+ F 4 '67
Oakland presents its case for salvaging a ghetto. J. Bailey. il Arch Forum 126:42-5 Ap '67
$1-billion plunge to rebuild slums; insurance industry pledge for mortgage loans. Bsns W p46 S 16 '67
Poverty in the ghetto, the view from Watts. P. Bullock. Mo Labor R 90:26 F '67
Slums: cancer in the heart of our cities. il Sr Schol 90:8-12 F 3 '67
Sprouting slums; the *campesinos* leave their past. J. Bishop. Commonweal 86:172-3 Ap 28 '67

SLUMS—*Continued*

To prevent a chain of super-Watts. A. J. Cervantes. bibliog f Harvard Bsns R 45: 55-65 S '67; Excerpts. il U S News 63:108-11 O 9 '67

Which plan for slum renewal? plans sponsored by Senators Percy and Kennedy, or the new Administration plan. Bsns W p77-8 Ag 26 '67

Writing a policy for the ghetto. il Bsns W p 118+ S 9 '67

You can't run away. il Newsweek 70:17-18 Jl 31 '67

Zeroing in on slums. Sr Schol 91:19-20 D 7 '67

SLURRY seal. See Pavements—Surface treatment

SLUTZ, Merton H.
Magnetic game. Pop Mech 127:175 F '67

SMALE, Stephen
Handler statement on Smale case. P. Handler. Science 157:1411 S 22 '67

No NSF cote for the Vietnam dove. Sci N 92:319 S 30 '67

Political science. New Repub 157:9 S 30 '67; Reply. S. Lang. 157:27-8 O 14 '67

Smale and NSF: a new dispute erupts. D. S. Greenberg. Science 157:1285 S 15 '67

Smale case. Nation 205:291-2 O 2 '67

Smale case: tracing the path that led to NSF's decision. D. S. Greenberg. Science 157:1536-9 S 29 '67

Smale: NSF shifts position. D. S. Greenberg. Science 158:98 O 6 '67

Smale: NSF's records do not support the charges. D. S. Greenberg. Science 158:618-19 N 3 '67

SMALL, Parker A. jr. See Asofsky, R. jt. auth.

SMALL arms. See Firearms

SMALL business
Foreign scout for the small man; E. M. Lang of Resources & facilities corp. il Bsns W p 131-2+ O 21 '67

Going into business for yourself. J. D. Bierman. Parents Mag 42:12+ N '67

How can you turn your hobby into a business? P. Lindberg. Bet Hom & Gard 45:6+ N '67

Meeting the competition of giants. A. Gross. Harvard Bsns R 45:172-4+ My '67

Owning your own business: how tough? how wise? il Sr Schol 90:14-16+ My 12 '67

Problems of small merchant examined in SBA booklet. Pub W 191:50 Ap 17 '67

Technological innovation: panel stresses role of small firms; with editorial comment. B. Nelson. Science 155:1201, 1229-31 Mr 10 '67

See also
Self employed
Student business

Finance

Putting the poor out of business; unhappy career of the Economic opportunity loan program. M. Levy. il Nation 204:750-3 Je 12 '67

SMALL business administration. See United States—Small business administration

SMALL business investment companies
SBICs get the pruning treatment. il Bsns W p84+ Je 10 '67

SMALL claims courts
How a small-claims court works. il Good H 165:198 O '67

SMALL states. See States, Small

SMALLEY, Katherine N. See Smalley, R. L. jt. auth.

SMALLEY, R. L. and Smalley, K. N.
Brown and white fats: development in the hamster. bibliog Science 157:1449-51 S 22 '67

SMALLPEICE, Sir Basil
Great Cunard gamble. R. Nuttall. il Duns R 90:51+ N '67

SMALLPOX
Barrier down; U.S. and Mexico recognize the end of a scourge. E. Zubryn. Sci N 92:67 Jl 15 '67

Deadline for smallpox; global eradication forecast. D. A. Ehrlich. il Sci N 92:568-9 D 9 '67

Smallpox campaign; launched by the World health organization. Sci N 92:261 S 9 '67

WHO takes on smallpox. Sci N 91:574 Je 17 '67

See also
Vaccination

SMART, Margaret
Reference books of 1966. Library J 92:1573-7 Ap 15 '67

SMART set (periodical)
And middle-class daydreams. K. S. Lynn. Nation 204:279-81 F 27 '67

SMATHERS, Eugene
Evangelist from Big Lick. Time 89:82 My 26 '67

SMEARS, Political. See Presidential campaigns

SMELL
Olfactory input to the hypothalamus: electrophysiological evidence. J. W. Scott and C. Pfaffmann. bibliog il Science 158:1592-4 D 22 '67

SMELT fishing
Down by the old smelt stream. T. Janes. il Outdoor Life 140:48-9+ D '67

SMELTER workers. See International union of mine, mill and smelter workers

SMIRNOW, Louis
Yellow peonies for the future. Home Gard 54:71 Mr '67

SMITH, A. Paul
Rust: the uninvited guest. Yachting 121:68+ Ap '67

Troubleshooting tactics. Motor B 119:30-2 Je '67

SMITH, Adam, pseud.
This is a kids' market. They're all under 30. Life 63:47-8 Jl 28 '67

SMITH, Al
Yet another first step; interview. New Yorker 43:35 Ap 8 '67

SMITH, Anthony Peter
Master of the monumentalists. il por Time 90:80-6 O 13 '67

SMITH, Anthony Wayne
Last call for park wilderness! address, April 1967. Nat Parks Mag 41:2+ My '67

SMITH, Beverly Bush
Lunches kids like. See issues of Parents' magazine and better homemaking

What to do with the children until company comes. por Redbook 129:6+ Ag '67

SMITH, Bradford, jr
Case of the isolated executive. Duns R 89: 34-5+ Ja '67

SMITH, Bradford A.
Rotation of Venus: continuing contradictions. bibliog Science 158:114-16 O 6 '67

SMITH, Brenton H.
Provocative history. Nat R 19:644-5 Je 13 '67

Triumph of the Will (and Ariel) Nat R 20:40-1 Ja 16 '68

SMITH, Charles L.
Taming your TV tuner. Pop Electr 26:51-4 Mr '67

SMITH, Charles L.
High octane. Christian Cent 84:999 Ag 2 '67

SMITH, Charlie
First 124 years are the hardest. L. Root and A. Ash. il pors Sat Eve Post 240:79-80+ Je 17 '67

SMITH, Chloethiel Woodard
Profiles: through the great city. A. Bailey. New Yorker 43:59-63 Ag 5 '67

She makes the city a place for living. il por Bsns W p76-8+ Je 3 '67

SMITH, Cossie L.
Portable turntable for competitive swimming. por Parks & Rec 2:27+ My '67

SMITH, Cyril Stanley
Materials; with biographical sketch. Sci Am 217:48, 68-79 S '67

SMITH, David
Africa-to-Europe: a treacherous stretch outswum by a swinger. il por Life 63:30-1 Jl 21 '67

SMITH, David Elvin
Drugs, uses and abuses: young doctor's crusade. J. Luce. il pors Look 31:24-8 Ag 8 '67

SMITH, David H.
R factors mediate resistance to mercury, nickel, and cobalt. bibliog Science 156:1114-16 My 26 '67

SMITH, David Loeffler
New Bedford artists of the nineteenth century. Antiques 92:689-93 N '67

SMITH, Desmond
On location in Rostov: filming the new revolution. Nation 204:268-72 F 27 '67

Vietnam by helicopter. Nation 204:745-50 Je 12 '67

SMITH, Dido
Bertil Vallien. Craft Horiz 27:8-13+ S '67

Louise Nevelson. Craft Horiz 27:44-9+ My '67

Report on the first International congress of religion, architecture, and the visual arts. Craft Horiz 27:34-7+ N '67

SMITH, Donald R.
Bearded, sockless radical of Moo U. W. C. Murray. il por N Y Times Mag p25+ Ap 9 '67; Discussion. p 12+ Ap 23 '67

Shaking up Moo U. Newsweek 69:97 Mr 6 '67

SMITH, Dorothy J.
College reference librarian and the faculty. por Library J 92:1588-9 Ap 15 '67

SMITH, Edith
Spunky widow runs modern pilot school. il pors Ebony 22:38-40+ O '67
SMITH, Edmund Ware
Dark deeds on Dobsis Lake. Field & S 72: 32-3+ Jl '67
Now you're cooking on wood. Field & S 71: 56-7+ Mr '67
SMITH, Edward H.
Biography of Rev Harden Smith, Baptist minister, 1829-1929. Negro Hist Bul 30:19+ Ap '67
SMITH, Elinor Goulding
Hairpiece. Atlan 219:119-20 Mr '67
Old folks at, home? Atlan 220:118-19 D '67
SMITH, Elwyn A.
What ought seminaries to be? Cath World 205:160-4 Je '67
SMITH, Ethel Sabin
Ceylon sidetrip. Travel 128:30-5+ S '67
SMITH, Frank Kingston
Weekend pilot. See issues of Flying
SMITH, Fred R.
Keys to a reefbound realm. Sports Illus 28: 37-9 Ja 15 '68
SMITH, G. Roland
Printing in three dimensions. Sch Arts 66:22 F '67
SMITH, Gordon S.
Making fast. Motor B 119:122 My '67
Short splice. Motor B 120:38 D '67
There's a hitch to it. Motor B 119:52 Je '67
SMITH, Guy Gibson
Challenge for the Guy Smiths. S. Booker. il pors Ebony 23:146-8+ D '67
Interracial marriage for Rusk's daughter. por U S News 63:16 O 2 '67
Marriage of enlightenment. il pors Time 90: 28-31 S 29 '67
Mr & Mrs Smith. il por Newsweek 70:23-4 O 2 '67
Wedding pictures from the Rusk album. il pors Life 63:32-3 O 6 '67
SMITH, H. Allen
August. Sat R 50:6 Je 24 '67
Case of the reluctant jar lid. Read Digest 90:127-8 Mr '67
Deluxe hardship tours. Travel 127:43-5 Ap '67
English: how she is talked. Read Digest 91: 109-11 D '67
Green bottles down the Rio Grande. Field & S 71:46-7+ F '67
How strong the toes? Sat R 50:4+ N 18 '67
Most nerve-shattering word in the language. Read Digest 90:100-1 Ap '67
Nobody knows more about chili than I do. Holiday 42:68-9+ Ag '67

about
Great chili championship fix. G. Cartwright. il por Sports Illus 27:80-2+ D 11 '67
SMITH, Hannis S.
Seamless web: the systems approach to library service; address, November 1966. por ALA Bul 61:180-5 F '67
SMITH, Harden
Biography of Rev Harden Smith, Baptist minister, 1829-1929. E. H. Smith. Negro Hist Bul 30:19+ Ap '67
SMITH, Harmon L.
Open windows; southern exposure. Christian Cent 84:1311-13 O 18 '67
SMITH, Hartland B.
Build a Hart-65 transmitter. Pop Electr 27: 41-7+ O '67
Build the camper's cuzzin. Pop Electr 26: 55-8 Mr '67
SMITH, Hedrick
Aden is a little Vietnam for Britain. N Y Times Mag p 12-14+ Jl 23 '67
SMITH, Herbert F.
Ascent to God after the council. America 116:283-5 F 25 '67
SMITH, Howard, and Newfield, Jack
How not to flop at pop. McCalls 95:78-9+ N '67
SMITH, Howard K.
Credibility and the Times. Nat R 19:73-4 Ja 24 '67
SMITH, Howard W.
Congressional outlook; less liberal laws ahead; interview. pors National Bsns 55:42-4 D '67
SMITH, Ian Douglas
Leave us alone to solve our own affairs; interview. ed. by A. J. Meyers. pors U S News 63:76-8 D 18 '67

about
Deviationist. Newsweek 69:52+ F 6 '67
SMITH, Irving H.
Research papers and the small college library. por Library J 92:544-5 F 1 '67

SMITH, J. Austin
Park and recreation meeting makes waves. Am City 82:90-2 Ag '67
Send your park superintendent to school. Am City 82:44 Ja '67
SMITH, J. Crispin. See Craig, F. A. jt. auth.
SMITH, J. Frederick
Never ending joy of shooting women; photographs. U S Camera 30:50-3 F '67
SMITH, Jean
I learned to feel black. por Redbook 129:64-5+ Ag '67
SMITH, Jean Edward
Red Prussianism of the German Democratic Republic. bibliog Bul Atomic Sci 23:24-30 My '67
SMITH, Joe A.
Two who stayed home. por Time 90:28 N 24 '67
SMITH, John E.
Instant college libraries; interview. ed. by J. Cushman. por Library J 92:540-3 F 1 '67
SMITH, Joseph E. and Osburn, B. I.
Glutathione deficiency in sheep erythrocytes. bibliog Science 158:374-5 O 20 '67
SMITH, Kendric C. and O'Leary, M. E.
Photoinduced DNA-protein cross-links and bacterial killing: a correlation at low temperatures. bibliog Science 155:1024-6 F 24 '67
SMITH, Kirk
Cookouts for the young set. Pop Gard 18: 56-9 Ag '67
For winter health and energy plan bigger better brunches. Pop Gard 18:72-5+ Mr '67
Garden parties for weight watchers. Pop Gard 18:48-51+ My '67
SMITH, L. S. See Woolfolk, E. O. jt. auth.
SMITH, Lacey Baldwin
England's second family. Horizon 9:68-79 Aut '67
SMITH, Lendon Howard
Bringing up baby for a million mothers; interview. ed. by S. O'Quin. pors Life 64:38-9+ Ja 19 '68
Pediatrician's almanac. por McCalls 95:34 Ja '68

about
TV doctor. il por Time 89:62 Je 16 '67
SMITH, Lorris B.
Treatment, supermarket style. Atlan 219:125-7 Ap '67
SMITH, Lyle J.
Football knee. Outdoor Life 140:42-3+ O '67
SMITH, McGregor, Jr
Enjoying nature; on a nature hike across Florida. Audubon 69:69-72 Ja '67
How to keep 'em rolling when the going gets tough. Pop Mech 128:106-9+ Jl '67
SMITH, Margaret (Chase)
Sick movies, a menace to children. Read Digest 91:139-42 D '67
SMITH, Margaret Elizabeth (Rusk)
Challenge for the Guy Smiths. S. Booker. il pors Ebony 23:146-8+ D '67
Interracial marriage for Rusk's daughter. por U S News 63:16 O 2 '67
Marriage of enlightenment. il pors Time 90: 28-31 S 29 '67
Mr & Mrs Smith. il por Newsweek 70:23-4 O 2 '67
Wedding pictures from the Rusk album. il pors Life 63:32-3 O 6 '67
SMITH, Margoret
Left for me; poem. New Yorker 43:42 My 27 '67
SMITH, Marie
Glittering state dinner, excerpts from Entertaining in the White House. Good H 165: 226 D '67
SMITH, Marshall
One more Somoza. Life 62:82 Ap 28 '67
SMITH, Michael
Let's travel: student style. Mlle 65:156+ Ag '67
SMITH, Mike
No wilderness wasted. Parks & Rec 2:20+ Je '67
SMITH, Neal Griffith
Visual isolation in gulls; with biographical sketch. Sci Am 217:19, 94-102 O '67
SMITH, Ned
How to field dress a deer. Field & S 72: 52-3+ O '67
SMITH, Oliver
Interview; ed. by A. Fatt. il por Dance Mag 41:51 Mr '67
SMITH, Patricia Marie
Pat Smith's special war in Vietnam. F. Chinnock. il por Read Digest 90:195-6+ Je '67
SMITH, Patrick J.
Book reviews Hi Fi 17:MA28-30 Ja '67
High emotions, radiant melos, in a first Beatrice di Tenda. Hi Fi 17:76+ D '67
Met's Flute: apotheosis of Chagall? Hi Fi 17:MA10-11 My '67

SMITH, Patrick J.—*Continued*
Show goes on: Cardillac & Boulevard solitude. Hi Fi 17:MA20-1 O '67
View from the bridge. Hi Fi 18:MA23 Ja '68
(ed) See Caldwell, S. And we quote

SMITH, Paula
Caseworker and the client. T. R. Brooks. il pors N Y Times Mag p26-7+ Ja 29 '67

SMITH, Peter J.
Head start to what? Sch Arts 66:9-10 Je '67

SMITH, Phillip
Dead heart of Australia; Australian outback; poems. Am For 73:51 Je '67
More poems from Down Under. Am For 73: 38-9 My '67
Poems from Down Under: Australian redgums; Northern pine. Am For 73:48 F '67

SMITH, Philip M.
Some problems and opportunities at Mammoth Cave National Park. Nat Parks Mag 41:14-19 F '67

SMITH, R. W. and Fuller, M.
Alpha-hematite: stable remanence and memory. bibliog Science 156:1130-3 My 26 '67

SMITH, Ralph Lee
Mail-order doctoring, still a menace. Todays Health 45:20-3 Je '67; Same abr. with title Menace of mail-order medicine. Read Digest 91:111-14 O '67

SMITH, Ralph V.
Behind the riots; excerpt of address. Am Ed 3:2-4+ N '67

SMITH, Sir Reginald Verdon-. See Verdon-Smith, R.

SMITH, Richard G.
Kenai national moose range. il Liv Wildn 30: 24-32 Wint '66

SMITH, Robert Benjamin
Suddenly, without warning or reason, it happens. P. Hamill. Good H 164:98-9+ Ap '67
Two states of mind. il por Time 90:50 N 3 '67

SMITH, Robert C.
John Hall, a busy man in Baltimore. Antiques 92:360-6 S '67

SMITH, Robert Lloyd
Robert Lloyd Smith and the Farmers' improvement society, a self-help movement in Texas. P. M. Carter. bibliog Negro Hist Bul 29:175-6 Fall '66

SMITH, Roysce
Bookman abroad. Pub W 192:44-8 N 20 '67
Books a la mode in Paris. Pub W 192:35-6 N 27 '67

SMITH, Ruth
(comp) Calendar of coming events. See issues of Motor boating

SMITH, Sandy
Fix. Life 63:22-3+ S 1 '67
From a governor and a D.A. an offer of resignation. Life 63:34-6 S 29 '67
Mobsters in the marketplace: money, muscle, murder. Life 63:98-102+ S 8 '67
—and Lambert, William
Mob finds a patsy in a mayor's inner circle. Life 64:46-51 Ja 5 '68
—See Wheeler, K. jt. auth.

about
Reunion on the gangland beat. G. P. Hunt. por Life 62:3 Ap 21 '67

SMITH, Scottie Fitzgerald
Christmas radiance at the White House. House & Gard 132:134-5+ D '67

SMITH, Shine
Shine Smith: Navajo friend. B. Goldwater. McCalls 95:168-9 D '67

SMITH, Stanford
Freedom is everybody's business; address, February 27, 1967. Vital Speeches 33:361-4 Ap 1 '67

SMITH, Susan A.
Village woman; poem. Mlle 65:306 Ag '67

SMITH, T. E.
Control of mortality. bibliog f Ann Am Acad 369:16-25 Ja '67

SMITH, T. Lynn
Hunger and antiquated farming in Latin America. Cath World 205:268-75 Ag '67

SMITH, Terence
New new frontier of Ted Sorensen. N Y Times Mag p24-5+ Mr 26 '67

SMITH, Tex
Brakes and how to use them. Flying 81:71-2 D '67

SMITH, Timothy L.
Work and human worth. Christian Cent 84: 1094-7 Ag 30 '67

SMITH, Tommie
Harnessed energy. il por Newsweek 69:57-8 Je 12 '67
He is built for chasing beyondness. F. Deford. il por Sports Illus 26:34-6+ My 22 '67

Jetting into gear. il por Time 89:76 Mr 10 '67
Tommie in a breeze. G. Ronberg. il pors Sports Illus 26:22-5 My 29 '67

SMITH, Tony
Art; exhibition in Philadelphia. M. Kozloff. Nation 204:125-6 Ja 23 '67
Art world; eight monumental presences in Bryant park. H. Rosenberg. New Yorker 43:108-9 F 25 '67
Presences in the park. il por Time 89:74 F 10 '67

SMITH, Van Dyke
Modern argonauts. Ebony 22:99-102+ Mr '67

SMITH, Victoria Young
Judo black belt queen. il pors Ebony 22: 107-8+ Ap '67

SMITH, Walker
Lighted switching devices. por Electr World 78:40-3 O '67

SMITH, Warren
Family man. M. Orovan. il U S Camera 30: 60-1 Mr '67

SMITH, William James
Stage. Commonweal 85:567-8, 657-8; 86:393-4 F 17, Mr 10, Je 23 '67

SMITH, William Jay
Desert scene; poem. New Repub 157:24 O 28 '67
Winter morning; poem. New Yorker 43:46 D 16 '67
(tr) See Voznesenskiĭ, A. Sketch for a poem

SMITH, Willie
Still roaring. il por Time 90:38+ Jl 28 '67

SMITH, Kline and French laboratories
When sniffles can be beautiful; Contac, cold remedy. il Bsns W p69-70+ Ja 14 '67

SMITH families
Smiths coats-of-arms. H. K. Eilers. il Hobbies 72:116-17 Ja '68

SMITH of Wootton Major; story. See Tolkien, J. R. R.

SMITHIES, Oliver
Antibody variability; excerpts from address, June 3, 1967. bibliog Science 157:267-73 Jl 21 '67
—See Claflin, A. J. jt. auth.

SMITHIES, Ronald H.
You and your diet. See issues of Good housekeeping, June 1967-

SMITHSONIAN Institution
Editor interviews; ed. by M. S. Fenner. S. D. Ripley. NEA J 56:91-2 F '67
Is this museum necessary? question of a national armed forces museum. Nation 204: 100 Ja 23 '67
More beautiful than Taj Mahal; National armed forces museum. Christian Cent 84: 491-2 Ap 19 '67
National war park. A. V. Krebs, jr. Commonweal 87:161 N 10 '67
Slumming at the Smithsonian; proposal that a railroad flat be added to the Institution. Life 62:4 F 3 '67
Smithsonian: biographer to the world. S. O'Faolain. il Holiday 42:44-9+ Ag '67
Smithsonian outpost; Cooper union museum. New Yorker 43:49-50 O 21 '67
Toys in the attic; new life under S. D. Ripley's direction. il Newsweek 69:106-7 My 15 '67

Astrophysical observatory
SAO standard earth. R. N. Watts, jr. Sky & Tel 34:89-90 Ag '67

Museum of history and technology
Infinity in eight minutes; sculpture piece in front of new museum. il Time 89:66 Ap 7 '67

SMITS, Anna
Students weave and pattern future. D. L. Thompson. il Sch Arts 67:32-3 D '67

SMOG
Billion-dollar smog hoax! J. M. Callahan. il Motor T 19:68-70 Mr '67
Cars are poison. Sci N 91:162 F 18 '67
Ingredients of poisoned air. Sr Schol 90:11 Mr 17 '67
Menace in the skies. il Time 89:48-52 Ja 27 '67
Publisher's memo. R. Brock. Hot Rod 20:6 Mr '67
What to do about the discomfort of smog. il Good H 165:200 O '67

SMOG control devices. See Automobile engines —Exhaust

SMOKE
New test measures deadly smoke density. il Am City 82:10 Ja '67
See also
Cigarette smoke
Smog

SMOKE cookery. See Barbecue cookery
SMOKESTACKS. See Chimneys

SMOKING
Crusading against cigarettes; World conference on smoking & health; with editorial comment. il Bsns W p39-40, 202 S 16 '67
How I didn't give up smoking; experience at antismoking clinic. S. Maloff. il Newsweek 70:64-5 N 6 '67
How to stop smoking; World conference on smoking and health. il Newsweek 70:97-8 S 25 '67
Personal business; so you want to quit smoking. Bsns W p 171-2 S 16 '67
Project spotlights smoking dangers. Sr Schol 90:sup9 Ap 14 '67
Right to breathe pure air: letter. G. Turbeville. Science 158:315 O 20 '67
Smoking and health education: a national overview; National conference on smoking and health; excerpt from address, September 22, 1967. R. L. Davis. PTA Mag 62:27-8 D '67
What teachers can do about smoking. A. Paroni. il Sr Schol 91:sup 18 N 16 '67
Youth lights up the smoking problem; students' views. PTA Mag 62:28 S '67
See also
Cigarettes
SMOKING, Cigarette. See Cigarettes
SMOKING of cigarettes. See Cigarettes
SMØRREBRØD. See Cookery, Danish
SMOTHERS brothers
Brothers irreverent. pors Newsweek 70:90 D 4 '67
Brothers Smothers, Tom and Dick. G. Fox. il pors Sat Eve Post 240:32-5 S 23 '67
Mothers' brothers. il Time 89:41 Je 30 '67
Smothers brothers: the naughtiest boys on TV. B. Rollin. il pors Look 31:68-9+ Je 13 '67
SMUGGLING
Bootlegging is back: now it's cigarettes. il U S News 63:22 N 6 '67
Hot butter; smuggling across border between Ireland and Northern Ireland. il Newsweek 70:63-4 Jl 31 '67
Strange case of James Mellaart; or, The tale of the missing Dorak treasure; with editorial comment by J. J. Thorndike. K. Pearson and F. Connor. il Horizon 9:2-3, 4-15 Sum '67
SMYRNA, Tenn.
Sam Davis museum and shrine. J. L. Stoutenburgh. il Hobbies 71:115 F '67
SMYTH, Pete
Chartering, Caribbean style. il Motor B 120: 26-8+ O '67
Hudson River heritage cruise. il Motor B 120: 21-6+ S '67
TLC. Motor B 120:46 D '67; 121:322 Ja '68
SNACK bars
Municipally operated refreshment stands. il Parks & Rec 2:41+ My '67
Quickie snack counters. il Bet Hom & Gard 45:98 O '67
SNACKS
California drive-in snacks. P. Cannon. il Ladies Home J 84:86-7+ Jl '67
Desserts and snacks for the keep-slim crowd; with recipes. il Good H 164:120-33 Mr '67
Great snacking; recipes. il Bet Hom & Gard 46:56-9 Ja '68
Mini-meals for the now generation. il Parents Mag 42:64-5 Ag '67
We trim a snack tree; with recipes. il Farm J 91:78-9 Ja '67
SNAIL fever. See Schistosomiasis
SNAIL-killing flies. See Flies
SNAILS
Calcareous septa formed in snail shells by larvae of snail-killing flies. L. V. Knutson and others. bibliog il Science 156:522-3 Ap 28 '67
Lithophagic snail from southern British Honduras. A. K. Craig. bibliog il Science 158: 795-6 N 10 '67
Natural history. Hobbies 72:119 S '67
SNAILS; story. See Highsmith, P.
SNAITH, William Theodore
Renaissance skipper. il por Time 90:101-2 S 22 '67
SNAKE bite. See Venom
SNAKE RIVER
High court questions need of dam on Snake River. Am For 73:38 Jl '67
Snake River submarines. H. D. Bishop. il Am For 73:24-5+ Je '67
SNAKE RIVER dams. See Dams
SNAKE venom. See Venom

SNAKES
Oxygenation properties of snake hemoglobin. B. Sullivan. bibliog il Science 157:1308-10 S 15 '67
See also
Venom
SNAKES, Color of. See Color of animals
SNAP. See Space vehicles—Atomic power plants
SNAPE Maltings concert hall, England. See Concert halls
SNEAD, Edwin
Amateur scientist. Sci Am 216:142 Je '67
SNELBECKER, Glenn E. and Arffa, M. S.
Summer school integration in a suburb. Sch & Soc 95:303-5 Sum '67
SNELL, David
How it feels to die. por Life 62:38-40+ My 26 '67; Same abr. Read Digest 91:106-10 Ag '67
SNETSINGER, K. G. See Keil, K. jt. auth.
SNIDER, Arthur J.
Medicine (cont of) Progress of medicine. See issues of Science digest
SNIPE shooting
Snipe safari. E. Zern. il Field & S 72:120-3 N '67
SNOBS and snobbishness
Speaking out; what's wrong with being a snob? V. S. Naipaul. Sat Eve Post 240:12+ Je 3 '67
SNOOKER shark; story. See Harrison, W.
SNOW, Charles Percy, baron Snow of Leicester. See Snow of Leicester, C. P. S.
SNOW, Mitzi
Things with string. Sch Arts 66:13-14 Ja '67
SNOW of Leicester, Charles Percy Snow, baron
G. H. Hardy: the pure mathematician; excerpts from Variety of men. Atlan 219: 106-10+ Mr '67
Lloyd George: Britain's great radical; excerpt from Variety of men. Atlan 219:68-70+ F '67
On Albert Einstein; excerpt from Variety of men. Commentary 43:45-55 Mr '67
On Stalin's triumph, on Stalin's madness. Esquire 67:114-18+ My '67
Unwitting rival; excerpt from Variety of men. Sat R 50:48-9 Ap 1 '67
about
Gaze behind the lens. C. Bedient. Nation 205: 59-60 Jl 17 '67
SNOW
Nature note; cup crystals. il Sci N 91:108 F 4 '67
SNOW and ice removal
Clean the snow off the parking lots first; St Cloud, Minn. S. Knapp. il Am City 82: 86-7 Ag '67
How to enhance your wintermobility. il Am City 82:34 N '67
Our plows had to stop plowing; Portland, Me. T. Griffin. il Am City 82:75-7 N '67
Sand, salt and calcium chloride; West Hartford, Conn. T. Nosek. il Am City 82:82-3 D '67
Snow removal. See issues of American city
Tips for conscientious snowfighters; excerpts from The snowfighter's handbook. H. R. Malott. il Am City 82:24 S '67
Why we began plowing sidewalks; Rolling Meadows, Ill. J. McFeggan. il Am City 82: 70-1 Ja '67
SNOW blowers, throwers, etc.
How to buy the right snow thrower. E. F. Lindsley. il Pop Sci 191:133-5+ D '67
Right way to run a snowblower. il Pop Mech 128:124-8 D '67
Throw away your snow shovel. il Pop Gard 18:68-71+ Mr '67
SNOW in Petrograd; story. See Brodeur, P.
SNOW melters. See Snow removal equipment; Snow removal equipment, Municipal
SNOW plows
Squeegee blades move every snowflake. il Am City 82:100-1 O '67
SNOW queen; drama. See Leech, M. T.
SNOW removal equipment
Stationary melter licks snow-disposal problem; Narragansett electric company, Providence, R. I. F. J. Casey. il Am City 82:118+ F '67
SNOW removal equipment, Municipal
Chemical corrosion argument rekindled at snow conference. Am City 82:35 Je '67
Melter makes the snow disappear; Berwyn, Ill. il Am City 82:45 D '67
No more equipment rental; Southhampton Township, Pa. il Am City 82:45 D '67
Take special care of your equipment; Scotch Plains, N.J. A. Milton. il Am City 82:108-9 S '67
SNOW slides. See Avalanches

SNOW storms. See Snowstorms

SNOW throwers. See Snow blowers, throwers, etc.

SNOW tire studs. See Tires, Automobile

SNOW White; story. See Barthelme, D.

SNOW White and friends; drama. See Cheatham, V.

SNOWDON, Antony Charles Robert Armstrong-Jones, 1st earl of
Arabian horses, a new surge in America; photographs. Vogue 150:198-201 D '67
Calder; photographs. Vogue 150:110-15 Jl '67

about

Life-styles: royalty in our time. A. Haden-Guest. il por Esquire 69:88-91+ Ja '68

SNOWFLAKE flowers. See Water snowflake

SNOWMAN, Abominable. See Animals, Mythical

SNOWMAN who overstayed; drama. See Boiko, C.

SNOWMASS, Colo. See Winter resorts

SNOWMASS-AT-ASPEN, Colo. See Winter resorts

SNOWMOBILES
Hot sport on snow; snowmobile marathon in Rhinelander, Wis. il Bsns W p 136-7 Ja 28 '67
Ice fishing a la cart. H. Bradshaw. il Pop Mech 129:132-4+ Ja '68
Lively '68 snowmobiles heat up the winter scene. H. Shuldiner. il Pop Sci 191:80-3+ N '67
'68: the big year for snowmobiles. D. C. Fales. il Pop Mech 128:138-41+ O '67
Skiing with gas. il Time 89:47-8 F 17 '67
Snowmobiles for winter fun. il Am City 82:21 S '67
Snowmobiles start a new camping craze. H. Shuldiner. il Pop Sci 191:148-50+ D '67
Snowmobility; new cold-weather diversion. il Newsweek 71:58 Ja 8 '68
Through Yellowstone on a snowmobile. D. C. Fales. il Pop Mech 128:104-9+ D '67

SNOWSHOE hare hunting. See Rabbit hunting

SNOWSLIDES. See Avalanches

SNOWSTORMS
Blizzard of '67; Northeast. J. Gilbert. il Flying 80:90 Ap '67
Chicago digs itself out. il Bsns W p36 F 4 '67
Cry for help from the proud Navajo; photographs. R. Crane. Life 64:14-23 Ja 5 '68
Deadly windfall; storm hits Navajo reservation in Arizona. il Time 91:23 Ja 5 '68
Notes and comment; blizzard report; New York. New Yorker 42:32-4 F 18 '67
24-million-ton snow job; Chicago. il Time 89:21 F 3 '67
Worst snow in Chicago's history. il Life 62:62-70 F 10 '67
See also
Aviation—Storm hazards

SNOWY night on west Forty-ninth street; story. See Brennan, M.

SNYDER, Donald R.
Giving the retarded a chance. NEA J 56:24-5 S '67

SNYDER, James D.
Great power robbery. Nations Bsns 55:96-7+ Mr '67

SNYDER, Jean Maclean, and Rostenberg, Adolph, jr
Common sense about moles. Todays Health 46:74-5 Ja '68

SNYDER, Louis L.
Beyond human judgment. Sat R 50:43-4 F 4 '67
More than cement and barbed wire. Sat R 50:44 Je 10 '67
Wehrmacht meets it match. Sat R 50:28-9 Mr 18 '67

SNYDER, Margaret
Behavioral sciences and family planning. Science 158:677-80+ N 3 '67

SNYDER, Monroe B.
Examination of methods used in a study of decision-making. por ALA Bul 61:1319-23 D '67

SNYDER, Richard L.
(comp) Scientific and technical books of 1966. por Library J 92:969-73 Mr 1 '67

SNYDER, Solomon H. and others
2,5-Dimethoxy-4-methyl-amphetamine, STP: a new hallucinogenic drug. bibliog Science 158:669-70 N 3 '67

SO dark a night; story. See Glenday, A.

SOAP
Glossary of soap terms. il Good H 164:196 Je '67

SOAP bubbles and films
Efflux time of soap bubbles and liquid spheres. A. V. Grosse. bibliog il Science 156:1220-2 Je 2 '67

SOAP industry and trade
Lowering the suds; Britain's Board of trade orders Lever brothers & associates ltd. and Procter & Gamble ltd. to de-escalate. Time 89:94+ My 12 '67
Sudsy experiment in Britain; Unilever and P&G in promoting their brands. Bsns W p50 Ap 29 '67

SOAP operas. See Television broadcasting—Drama

SOARING (aeronautics) See Gliding and soaring

SOBELL, Morton
Rosenberg myth. il por Time 89:51 F 24 '67

SOBILOFF, Hy
Elegy for twelve. Poetry 110:155-6 Je '67

SOCCER
Alive and kicking? National professional soccer league and United soccer association talking of merger. Sports Illus 27:9-10 Jl 24 '67
Baseball gets a brawny rival; U.S. debut in April. il Bsns W p26-8 Ap 1 '67
Dangerous game. Sports Illus 27:11 O 2 '67
Fierce holy war in a violent city; Celtic-Rangers fans in Glasgow. H. McIlvanney. il Sports Illus 28:40-3 Ja 15 '68
Hello, Emment! hello, Horst! professional soccer for US. il Time 89:65 Ap 14 '67
How to watch TV's newest sport; soccer. W. J. McKean. il Look 31:89-93 My 2 '67
I want my bloody game back; U.S. televised version of soccer. D. Morgan. il Sports Illus 27:52-4 Ag 28 '67
Kickoff for a Babel of booters; televised soccer. T. Maule. Sports Illus 26:68+ Ap 24 '67
Knees-up for the hot Spurs. H. McIlvanney. il Sports Illus 26:32-4+ Je 5 '67
Name of the game is soccer. G. Astor. il Look 31:94 My 2 '67
Pro soccer's U.S. kickoff. il Life 62:91-2+ My 12 '67
Soccer is simple? il Newsweek 69:70-1 Ap 24 '67
Spiking the side-kick issue; U.S. kickers against the best English soccer kickers. E. Shrake and J. Lovesey. il Sports Illus 26:38-42 Ap 10 '67
Think soccer; North America's big-league soccer. il Newsweek 70:56 S 11 '67
True football gets its big chance. M. Kane. il Sports Illus 26:22-3 Mr 27 '67
See also
United soccer association

Economic aspects

Soccer business kicks off. W. Berry. il Duns R 90:49-50+ N '67

SOCCER fans. See Sports fans

SOCCER players
His majesty: Edson Arantes do Nascimento. Time 91:43 Ja 5 '68

SOCHUREK, Howard
Gifts from out there; photographs. Esquire 67:92-101 My '67

SOCIAL action
Stewardship and social action. W. H. Jennings. Christian Cent 84:1593-5 D 13 '67

SOCIAL adjustment. See Adjustment, Social

SOCIAL agencies
Organization woman; HEW integrates welfare agencies into social and rehabilitation service. Time 90:14 S 1 '67

SOCIAL and economic council of the United Nations. See United Nations—Economic and social council

SOCIAL and economic security
Challenge of human aspirations. J. T. Hill, jr. Duns R 89:23-4+ Ja '67
Coming crisis in welfare; objections to Milton Friedman's negative income tax. H. Hazlitt. Nat R 19:416-18 Ap 18 '67
Lavish welfare schemes ahead. il Nations Bsns 55:34-5 Ag '67
Rebuilding the welfare system. Bsns W p200 N 18 '67
Social security in trouble. America 116:412 Mr 25 '67
See also
Pensions, Industrial

Europe, Western

If you think welfare costs are high in U.S. U S News 62:45 Ja 30 '67

Great Britain

Britain: going broke on welfare. il U S News 62:31 F 6 '67

SOCIAL and economic security—Great Britain
—*Continued*
Britain rethinks the welfare state. America
117:675 D 2 '67
Justifying the means. Newsweek 70:47-8 S
4 '67

New Zealand
Wool & Welfare. Time 90:79 Jl 28 '67

Sweden
Sad experience with social security. A.
Zanker. il U S News 62:90-1 Ap 24 '67;
same abr. with title Behind the façade of
Sweden's great society. Read Digest 91:
157-9 Jl '67

Uruguay
Where the welfare state runs wild. S. G.
Slappey. il Nations Bsns 55:38-9+ Ap '67
SOCIAL aspects of art. See Art and society
SOCIAL attitudes. See Attitudes; Moral at-
titudes
SOCIAL behavior. See Manners and customs
SOCIAL behavior of animals. See Animals—
Habits and behavior
SOCIAL change
Case for a national social science foundation;
address, May 6, 1967. F. R. Harris. Science
157:507-9 Ag 4 '67
Change, in concert with society. J. S. Gow,
jr. and M. Thompson. NEA J 56:22-3 D '67
Changing world of living; address. M. Mead.
Sci Digest 62:38-43 S '67
Company president is a Berkeley student. H.
J. Leavitt. Harvard Bsns R 45:152-4+ N '67
Cultural evolution today. J. H. Steward.
Christian Cent 84:203-7 F 15 '67
Cursing of the fig tree; fruitless human insti-
tutions. R. Hull, jr. Christian Cent 84:1429-
31 N 8 '67
Hippies, political radicals and the church.
N. K. Gottwald. Christian Cent 84:1043-5
Ag 16 '67
Intellectuals and the future. E. Shils. Bul
Atomic Sci 23:7-14 O '67
Nobody knows the quandaries I've seen; ex-
cerpt from I've only got two hands, and
I'm busy wringing them. J. Goodsell. il
Read Digest 91:211-12 Jl '67
Revolution of 1976. M. Novak. Commonweal
86:441-3 Jl 14 '67; Discussion. 86:550-3 S
8 '67
Scholar in a nowhere world. A. Heckscher.
Yale R 57:47-55 O '67
Science, technology, and change. J. McHale.
bibliog f il Ann Am Acad 373:120-40 S '67
Science to fix everything; do we need sophis-
tication? excerpts from address, ed. by E.
Goble. R. C. Wood. Arch Rec 142:9 Jl '67
Social change means new social studies;
seminar at Arden house, Columbia uni-
versity's Harriman campus. H. P. Boss. Sr
Schol 90:sup2 Ap 21 '67
Sociological and institutional changes in
American life: their implications for the
library. R. W. Conant. ALA Bul 61:528-36
My '67
Toward a communal society. D. Bell. il Life
62:112-14+ My 12 '67
Why people riot. F. R. Schreiber and M.
Herman. il Sci Digest 62:56-60 O '67
See also
Social progress
Social revolution
SOCIAL classes
Making it; excerpt. N. Podhoretz. Harper
235:59-62+ D '67
Many lives of Georges Lefebvre. G. Shapiro.
bibliog f Am Hist R 72:502-14 Ja '67
On Who intervened in 1788? J. Kaplow. bibliog
f Am Hist R 72:497-502 Ja '67
Speaking out: what's wrong with being a
snob? V. S. Naipaul. Sat Eve Post 240:12+
Je 3 '67
See also
Upper classes

Latin America
Latin American middle sectors; address, April
11, 1967. J. J. Johnson. Vital Speeches 33:
638-40 Ag 1 '67
SOCIAL conditions
Appeals to reason; Pope's agenda for a new
humanism. New Repub 156:7-8 Ap 8 '67
Populorum progressio; fifth encyclical of Pope
Paul. il Time 89:70 Ap 7 '67
We must make haste; Pontiff's Populorum
progressio message. il Newsweek 69:84 Ap
10 '67
See also
Civilization
Poverty
Social problems
also subhead Social conditions under
names of countries, states, cities, etc. e.g.
Chicago—Social conditions

SOCIAL conflict
Black, green and red rebellions; how a con-
gress of psychologists and others under-
stood them. N. H. Cassem. America 118:33-
5 Ja 13 '68
SOCIAL dancing. See Dancing
SOCIAL democrats (Germany) See Political
parties—Germany (Federal Republic)
SOCIAL development. See Social progress
SOCIAL diseases. See Venereal diseases
SOCIAL drinking. See Drinking customs
SOCIAL education
Shortchanged children of suburbia, by A.
Miel. Review
Sat R 50:89 My 20 '67. J. H. Martin
Shortchanged in suburbia; excerpts from
Shortchanged children of suburbia. A. Miel.
Sr Schol 90:sup4 My 12 '67
See also
Civil rights—Study and teaching
Sex instruction
Social sciences—Study and teaching
SOCIAL equality. See Equality
SOCIAL ethics
Elements for a social ethic, by G. Winter.
Review
Christian Cent 84:208-10 F 15 '67. J. D.
Bettis
See also
Christian ethics
Sexual ethics
SOCIAL evolution. See Social change
SOCIAL games. See Games
SOCIAL history
See also
Great Britain—Social history
Urbanization
SOCIAL, humanitarian and cultural committee
of the United Nations. See United Nations
—Social, humanitarian and cultural com-
mittee
SOCIAL hygiene. See Venereal diseases
SOCIAL institutions
Recent developments in research on social
institutions. R. M. Williams, jr. bibliog f
Ann Am Acad 374:171-84 N '67
SOCIAL interaction
Selection of social partners as a function of
peer contact during rearing. C. L. Pratt
and G. P. Sackett. bibliog il Science 155:
1133-5 Mr 3 '67
See also
Sociometry
SOCIAL isolation
Experiential deprivation and later behavior.
J. L. Fuller. bibliog il Science 158:1645-52
D 29 '67
These are three of the alienated. S. Kelman.
il N Y Times Mag p38-9+ O 22 '67; Dis-
cussion. p40+ N 12 '67
See also
Loneliness
SOCIAL justice. See Justice
SOCIAL legislation
See also
Public welfare—Law

United States
Congress and the crisis in our cities. J.
Bailey. Arch Forum 127:54-7 S '67
Dealing out the poor; proposed reforms to
the aid to dependent children program.
Nation 205:164 S 4 '67
End of relief as a way of life? il U S News
63:24-6 S 4 '67
New welfare; women and children last;
amendments to new social security bill.
R. A. Cloward and F. F. Piven. Common-
weal 86:541-2 S 8 '67
See also
Family allowances
Old age pensions—United States
SOCIAL measurements. See Sociometry
SOCIAL norm
Politics of experience, by R. D. Laing. Re-
view
New Repub 156:24-8+ My 13 '67. R. Coles
SOCIAL planning

United States
See United States—Social policy
SOCIAL policy
See also
United States—Social policy
SOCIAL problems
On church and state. M. Ascoli. Reporter
36:18 Ap 20 '67
Redbook dialogue. R. Kennedy; O. Lewis. il
Redbook 129:74-5+ S '67
Social breakdown. N. Goldman. bibliog f il
Ann Am Acad 373:156-79 S '67

SOCIAL problems—*Continued*
Social reform goes ecumenical. B. L. Masse. America 116:339 Mr 11 '67
See also
Church and social problems
Crime and criminals
Homosexuality
Illegitimacy
Juvenile delinquency
Libraries and social and economic problems
Marriage
Migrant labor
Narcotic habit
Poor
Prostitution
Public welfare
Race discrimination
Race problems
School and social and economic problems
Slums
Social action
Suicide
Technology and civilization
Unemployables
War
Woman—Social and moral questions
SOCIAL problems and art. See Art and society
SOCIAL problems in literature
Christmas carol; excerpt from introduction to A Christmas carol in two Christmas classics. E. Johnson. Sat R 50:13+ D 30 '67
SOCIAL progress
Ten commitments. J. W. Gardner. Sat R 50:39-40 Jl 1 '67
Third committee adopts social development proposal. UN Mo Chron 4:88-9 D '67
See also
Social change

Statistics

New goals for social information. B. M. Gross and M. Springer. bibliog f il Ann Am Acad 373:208-18 S '67
SOCIAL psychology
Hooked on law enforcement. E. Z. Friedenberg. il Nation 205:360-5 O 16 '67
Recent trends: deviant behavior and social control. D. J. Bordua. bibliog f Ann Am Acad 369:149-63 Ja '67
What nature reveals about peacemaking; theories of W. Trotter. J. F. Wharton. Sat R 50:14-16 My 27 '67
Why people riot. F. R. Schreiber and M. Herman. il Sci Digest 62:56-60 O '67
See also
Adjustment, Social
Attitudes
Criminal psychology
Leadership
Morale, National
Public, The
Public opinion
Social conflict
War—Psychological aspects
SOCIAL reform. See Social problems; Social revolution
SOCIAL research. See Social science research
SOCIAL responsibility. See Responsibility
SOCIAL revolution
Counterrevolutionary America; adaptation of address. R. L. Heilbroner. Commentary 43:31-8 Ap '67; Discussion. 44:6+ Jl '67
Counter-revolutionary reflex. C. C. O'Brien. Commonweal 85:619-21 Mr 3 '67
Lessons from revolution; report of symposium at the University of San Francisco. R. B. Kaiser. America 117:469+ O 28 '67
Message to a world in ferment. America 117:461 O 28 '67
Real nature of the world revolution; the drive for human rights; what this portends for U.S. policy. A. Larson. Sat R 50:15-18 Je 3 '67
Report on the geosocial revolution. B. Fuller. Sat R 50:31-3+ S 16 '67
Revolution, anyone? V. C. Ferkiss. Commonweal 85:480-3 F 3 '67
Riots and revolution. F. M. Henley; R. A. Schroth. America 117:150-3 Ag 12 '67
SOCIAL science research
Adventure capital for research. P. H. Rossi. Sat R 50:68 N 4 '67
Cross-cultural research and government policy. R. L. Beals. Bul Atomic Sci 23:18-24 O '67
Do we need social observatories? H. D. Lasswell. Sat R 50:49-52 Ag 5 '67
Foreign area research guidelines adopted; announcement, December 19, 1967. Dept State Bul 58:55-9 Ja 8 '68
Foundation, yes and no. Sci N 91:160 F 18 '67
Little learning; criticisms by Reuss subcommittee. Reporter 36:10-11 My 18 '67

Methodological problems in the study of organized crime as a social problem. D. R. Cressey. bibliog f Ann Am Acad 374:101-12 N '67
Place of values in the study of society. C. E. Beck and J. Barak. bibliog f Sch & Soc 95:122-3 F 18 '67
Recent developments in research on social institutions. R. M. Williams, jr. bibliog f Ann Am Acad 374:171-84 N '67
R; social research. H. G. Hohorst; D. C. Burnham. il Sat R 51:56+ Ja 13 '68
Risks of research; legal complications for sociologists. il Time 90:40 D 22 '67
Social science study. Sci N 91:422 My 6 '67
Social sciences: expanded role urged for Defense department. D. S. Greenberg. Science 158:886-8 N 17 '67; Reply with rejoinder. H. David and G. M. Lyons. 158:1624-5 D 29 '67
Social sciences: progress slow on House and Senate bills. D. S. Greenberg. Science 157:660-2 Ag 11 '67
See also
Sociometry

Federal aid

Social science: federal agencies agree to end covert support. D. S. Greenberg. Science 159:64-6 Ja 5 '68
SOCIAL sciences
Impact of the social sciences, by K. E. Boulding. Review
Commentary 43:101-4 Ap '67. W. J. Dannhauser
Social sciences notes (title varies) See issues of Science news
See also
Behavior (psychology)
Behavioral sciences
Political science

Bibliography

New paperbacks for teaching social studies. il Sr Schol 89:sup8-9+ Ja 20 '67
What's new in social studies; summaries of articles and reports, ed. by H. L. Hurwitz (cont) Sr Schol 90:sup 19 Mr 10 '67

Research

See Social science research

Study and teaching

Federal support for the social studies; excerpts from New frontiers in the social studies: action and analysis. J. S. Gibson. Sr Schol 90:sup9+ F 24 '67
For social studies teachers. F. R. McElwain. il Sr Schol 91:sup27 S 28 '67
New paperbacks for teaching social studies. il Sr Schol 89:sup8-9+ Ja 20 '67
New social studies. D. M. Fraser. NEA J 56:24-6 N '67
Social change means new social studies; seminar at Arden house, Columbia university's Harriman campus. H. P. Boss. Sr Schol 90:sup2 Ap 21 '67
Social myth vs. social science. R. G. Hanvey. Sat R 50:80-1+ N 18 '67
Social studies look to the future; excerpts from New frontiers in the social studies. S. H. Engle. Sr Schol 91:sup29+ S 28 '67
Teachers know the score in Nassau County; new Social studies planning and service center. W. A. Zeralsky and E. Schester. il Sr Schol 91:sup 17-20 O 26 '67
See also
Citizenship. Education for
History—Study and teaching
National council for the social studies
Social education
SOCIAL scientists
Action intellectuals. T. H. White. il Life 62:78+ Je 23 '67
SOCIAL security. See Insurance, Social; Social and economic security
SOCIAL security act, 1935
Social security. P. A. Samuelson. Newsweek 69:88 F 13 '67
SOCIAL security act amendments
Here's the rub; social-security bill restricts aid to families with dependent children. il Newsweek 71:16 Ja 15 '68
It looks like money in the bank; new social security bill. Bsns W p 134 D 16 '67
Nectar & pickle juice. Time 91:12 Ja 12 '68
Social security drifting off course. D. Cordtz. il Fortune 76:104-7+ D '67
Social security in conference; bills approved. America 117:703 D 9 '67
Sweetening the pot of social security. il Bsns W p 115-16 N 25 '67

SOCIAL security act amendments—*Continued*
Who foots what bill for social security? Congress to pay pensions of the lower-income workers. il Bsns W p 110-11 Ja 13 '68
SOCIAL security benefits. See Insurance, Social
—United States; Old age pensions—United States
SOCIAL segregation. See Segregation, Social
SOCIAL statistics
See also
Cities and towns—Statistics
SOCIAL status
How important is the color of a man's collar? il Good H 165:20+ N '67
See also
Middle classes
Social classes
SOCIAL stratification. See Social classes
SOCIAL studies. See Social sciences
SOCIAL welfare
Challenge of creative federalism. L. E. Schaller. Christian Cent 84:618-22 My 10 '67
See also
Public welfare
United Nations—Commission on social development
SOCIAL work
See also
Legal aid
Social workers
SOCIAL workers
Caseworker and the client. T. R. Brooks. il N Y Times Mag p26-7+ Ja 29 '67
Professionals who help humanity; psychiatric and medical social workers. T. Berland. il Todays Health 45:52-5+ Ap '67
You'd better count me out; concerning social action programs. R. B. Miller. America 116: 590-3 Ap 22 '67
SOCIALISM
Capitalism, socialism, and the future of the industrial state; excerpts from The new industrial state. J. K. Galbraith. Atlan 219: 61-7 Je '67
Three big ism's and how they grew. il Sr Schol 91:16-21+ S 28 '67
See also
Communism

Africa
Africa's need: African socialism. J. O'Connor. Cath World 205:358-64 S '67

Algeria
Algerian socialism's slow leak. J. Harriss. New Repub 156:19 My 6 '67

Canada
In Canada, socialism loses: a portent for U.S? defeat of Cooperative commonwealth federation (CCF) in Saskatchewan. il U S News 63:69-70 N 20 '67

Great Britain
High price of socialism. A. Lejeune. Nat R 19:1384 D 12 '67
In Britain the walls keep closing in. B. Wenham. New Repub 157:9 S 2 '67
See also
Labor party (Great Britain)

Tanzania
Paving Tanzania's way with good intentions: the Arusha declaration. A. Delius. Reporter 37:41-3 Jl 13 '67
Report. Atlan 219:32-4+ Je '67
SOCIALISM, Christian
Christian socialism's day. T. Molnar. Nat R 19:348-9 Ap 4 '67
SOCIALIZED medicine. See Medical service, State
SOCIALLY handicapped children
Friendly town; Cleveland's vacation and medical examination programs for disadvantaged children. M. Slivka. il PTA Mag 61: 8-10 Je '67
How there's a White House plan for the Nation's children. il U S News 62:30-1 F 20 '67
Poverty and mental retardation. Sci Am 217: 50 D '67
See also
Negro children

Education
Are we driving teachers out of ghetto schools? concerning John S. Roberts junior high school. S. Levey. il Am Ed 3:2-4 My '67
Awareness of dignity; new uses and meanings of dance education. il Dance Mag 41:38-41 N '67
Big debate: teaching by pressure or by discovery. il Life 62:44-7 Mr 31 '67
Boys nobody wanted. S. S. Rosenberg. il Parents Mag 42:35-7+ Ja '67
Break for lonely losers; Upward bound. il Time 89:40 My 26 '67

Coleman report: another look. D. L. Burleson. Sr Schol 91:sup6 N 30 '67
Coleman report: Equality of educational opportunity; excerpts. J. Alsop; A. M. Mood. il NEA J 56:26-8+ S '67
College? man, you must be kidding! College readiness program, College of San Mateo, Calif. E. Gattmann and others. NEA J 56: 8-10 S '67
Computer tutors for ghetto pupils. A. Poinsett. il Ebony 23:91-4+ D '67
Education of the underprivileged. bibliog f Sch & Soc 95:108-10+ F 18 '67
Federal aid vs. poverty. Sch & Soc 95:250 Ap 15 '67
Games work with underachievers; North Carolina advancement school. D. C. Farran. il Sr Schol 91:sup 10-11 N 9 '67
Googol! abstract math keeps slum kids interested in school. J. Benet. il Am Ed 3:9-10 O '67
Help and no help for ghetto children; bussing to white schools. Sci N 92:486 N 18 '67
Help for neglected children. Sch & Soc 95: 485 D 9 '67
Lights are on; and the whole family goes to school at night; Operation Reach. M. A. Marlar. il Am Ed 3:21-4 My '67
Miss Leesy's magic; cultural enrichment program in St Louis schools. W. D. Cook. il Am Ed 3:8-10 N '67
Model project for inner-city youth; programs in Philadelphia. America 117:145 Ag 12 '67
Ned O'Gorman: worker at Harlem library and day care center; interview. New Yorker 43: 54-5 D 2 '67
New hope for city schools; More effective schools. B. B. Gotthold. il Parents Mag 42: 68-70+ S '67
Paying for American education. H. Howe, 2d. il PTA Mag 62:5-8 S '67
Role-playing as a learning method for disadvantaged children; excerpt from Role-playing for social values; decision-making in the social studies. F. R. Shaftel and G. Shaftel. bibliog f Sch & Soc 94:494-8 D 24 '66
School crisis; any way out? il Newsweek 70: 71-5 S 25 '67
Special assignment; creative arts in the disadvantaged elementary school. H. Topper. il Sch Arts 66:5-8 F '67
Special Journal feature on the impoverished child; symposium. bibliog il NEA J 56:21-33 Ap '67
Talent training for culturally deprived adolescents. Sch & Soc 95:514+ D 23 '67
Taste of college; Upward bound programs. P. Dranov. il Am Ed 3:25-7 Ap '67
Teacher corps. C. Conner. il Am Ed 3:13-19 Ap '67
Teacher education for the deprived: a new pattern; Operation fair chance, project in experimental teacher education at California state college centers at Hayward. E. G. Olsen. Sch & Soc 95:232-4 Ap 1 '67
This way out; slum youngsters choose college; three students at the University of California. A. Allen. il Am Ed 3:2-4+ Jl '67
To America's PTA leaders a message from the Vice-President of the United States. H. H. Humphrey. PTA Mag 61:19 Je '67
To the hills and hollows; story of the Appalachia Educational laboratory. C. M. Singleton and S. M. Brown. il Am Ed 3:22-5 Jl '67
Vice-President; appearance on J. Carson's tonight show and meeting with participants of Double discovery. New Yorker 43:23-5 Ag 12 '67
Why the schools flunk out; concerning the Coleman report. C. S. Benson. il Nation 204:463-6 Ap 10 '67
See also
Children of migrant laborers—Education
Project Head Start
United States—National advisory council on the education of disadvantaged children

SOCIETY. See subhead Social life and customs under names of countries, states, cities, e.g. Washington, D.C.—Social life and customs
SOCIETY, High. See Upper classes
SOCIETY, Primitive
Changing world of living; address. M. Mead. Sci Digest 62:38-43 S '67
Conserving behavior. H. Welch. Sat R 50: 49-50 Jl 1 '67
Cross-cultural teaching of science. F. E. Dart and P. L. Pradhan. bibliog il Science 155:649-56 F 10 '67; Reply. G. H. Bartlett, jr. 156:12+ Ap 7 '67
See also
Indians of North America—Culture
Man, Primitive
SOCIETY and art. See Art and society
SOCIETY and law. See Jurisprudence

SOCIETY and literature. See Literature and society
SOCIETY and the individual. See Individual and society
SOCIETY and war. See War and society
SOCIETY ISLANDS
See also
Bora-Bora (island)
SOCIETY of automotive engineers
Europeans firm on aerospace transporter. W. E. Wilks. Tech W 20:36-7 Mr 13 '67
SOCIETY of Friends. See Friends, Society of
SOCIETY of illustrators
Art directing & everything; address, January 15, 1967. C. Schorre. Am Artist 31:26+ Ap '67
Illustrators 67; ninth annual SI exhibit. il Pub W 191:80+ Ap 3 '67
SOCIETY of Jesus. See Jesuits
SOCIOLOGY
Sociology of national character. D. Martindale. bibliog f il Ann Am Acad 370:30-5 Mr '67
See also
Age groups
Culture
Evolution
Individualism
Man—Influence of environment
Race problems
Regionalism
Religion and sociology
Social problems

Methodology
See also
Sociometry
SOCIOLOGY, Christian
See also
Christianity and economics
Church and social problems
SOCIOLOGY, Industrial
Sinews of industrial society. C. F. Ware and others. il UNESCO Courier 20:24-6 My '67
SOCIOLOGY, Religious. See Religion and sociology
SOCIOLOGY, Rural
See also
Farm ownership
SOCIOLOGY, Urban
E. T. Hall and the human space bubble. W. Kloman. il Horizon 9:42-7 Aut '67
Light in the frightening corners. il Time 90: 10-15 Jl 28 '67
Plight of our cities. il Sr Schol 89:4-8+ Ja 20 '67
See also
Cities and towns
Urban renewal
Urbanization
SOCIOLOGY and economics. See Economics—Social and ethical aspects
SOCIOMETRY
Social goals and indicators for American society; symposium, ed. by B. M. Gross. bibliog f il Ann Am Acad 371:1-177 My; 373: 1-218 S '67
SOCKS. See Hosiery
SOCRATES
Socrates and Aristophanes, by L. Strauss. Review
Nat R 19:423-4 Ap 18 '67. S. Parry
SOD
Instant lawn from sod. Am Home 71:110 Ja '68
SODA, Takemune
New deal for women: longer life expectancy in Japan. D. A. Ehrlich. Sci N 91:599 Je 24 '67
SODIUM chloride. See Salt
SODIUM cyclamate. See Sugar substitutes
SODIUM discharge lamps. Electric lamps
SODIUM humate. See Humic acids
SODIUM in the body
Activation analysis of soluble and fixed sodium in mammalian hair. G. S. Kennington. bibliog il Science 155:588-9 F 3 '67; Reply with rejoinder. J. P. W. Houtman. 156:1397 Je 9 '67
Cochlear function and sodium and potassium activated adenosine triphosphatase. W. Kuijpers and others. bibliog il Science 157: 949-50 Ag 25 '67
Crayfish muscle; permeability to sodium induced by calcium depletion. J. P. Reuben and others. bibliog il Science 155:1263-6 Mr 10 '67
Regulation of intracellular sodium concentrations in rat diaphragm muscle. H. A. Fozzard and D. M. Kipnis. bibliog il Science 156:1257-60 Je 2 '67

Sodium-potassium adenosine triphosphatase: acyl phosphate intermediate shown to be L-glutamyl-γ-phosphate. A. Kahlenberg and others. bibliog il Science 157:434-6 Jl 28 '67
Sodium transport: inhibitory factor in sweat of patients with cystic fibrosis. J. A. Mangos and N. R. McSherry. bibliog il Science 158:135-6 O 6 '67
Strophanthidin-sensitive transport of cesium and sodium in muscle cells. R. A. Sjodin and L. A. Beaugé. bibliog il Science 156: 1248-50 Je 2 '67
SODIUM silicates
Hydrous sodium silicates from Lake Magadi, Kenya: precursors of bedded chert. H. P. Eugster. bibliog il Science 157: 1177-80 S 8 '67
SODIUM vapor lamps. See Electric lamps, Sodium vapor
SOFIAN, Naid
(comp) SR's check list of the week's new books. See issues of Saturday review
SOFOKIDIS, Jeanette H.
Instant campus. Am Ed 3:15-19 S '67
SOFT drink industry
See also
Canada dry corporation
Coco-Cola company
Moxie company
Pepsi-Cola company
SOFT drinks. See Beverages
SOFTBALL
In Stratford, nobody beats the Raybestos Brakettes; Women's national softball tournament. C. Kirkpatrick. il Sports Illus 27:92-3 S 11 '67
SOGLO, Christophe
Seasonal coup. por Time 90:24 D 29 '67
SOHN, David A.
New media. Sr Schol 90:sup 16-17 My 19 '67
SOHYO. See Trade unions—Japan
SOIFER, Israel
Doctor Maurice Spitzer: pioneer of the Judaic book art. Pub W 192:83-4+ S 4 '67
Israel program for scientific translations. Pub W 192:50-1 N 13 '67
SOIKE, Kenneth. See Allen, M. jt. auth.
SOIL analysis. See Soils—Analysis
SOIL bacteriology
See also
Soil microbiology
SOIL conditioners
Ten soil conditioners. il Sunset 138:266-7 My '67
SOIL conservation
Soil conservation in perspective, by R. B. Held and M. Clawson. Review
Am For 73:31+ Mr '67. M. Bush
SOIL erosion. See Erosion
SOIL fertility
How to set up a soil fertility program. L. S. Robertson, jr. il Suc Farm 65:46-7+ S '67
See also
Fertilizers and manures
SOIL maps. See Soil surveys
SOIL microbiology
Dieldrin: degradation by soil microorganisms. F. Matsumura and G. M. Boush. bibliog il Science 156:959-61 My 19 '67
Living relative of the microfossil kakabekia. S. M. Siegel and others. bibliog il Science 156:1231-4 Je 2 '67
Martian wolf trap in action; soil samples to be examined for evidence of living organisms. il Sci Digest 61:72-3 Je '67
Pesticide transformation to aniline and azo compounds in soil. R. Bartha and D. Pramer. bibliog il Science 156:1617-18 Je 23 '67
Stereoscan electron microscopy of soil microorganisms. T. R. G. Gray. bibliog il Science 155:1668-70 Mr 31 '67
SOIL moisture
Low subsoil moisture? what to do. R. J. Fee. il Suc Farm 65:47 Mr '67
Surfactants help make water wetter. J. M. Boodley. il Horticulture 45:28-9 Jl '67
SOIL preparation in gardens. See Gardening—Soil preparation
SOIL surveys
Are you paying too much for sewer contractors' guesswork; soil-engineering survey, Hillsdale, N.J. R. R. Fleming. il Am City 82:112-14 O '67; Reply. O. Freeman. 82:21+ D '67
Is that lot safe to build on? soil survey can tell you before it's too late. il Changing T 21:22-4 Ag '67
SOIL testing. See Soils—Analysis

SOILS
What's new. See issues of Successful farming
See also
Erosion
Humic acids

Analysis
How to set up a soil fertility program. L. S. Robertson, jr. il Suc Farm 65:46-7+ S '67
What does soil analysis mean? F. E. Bear. Horticulture 45:26-7 Mr '67
Your soil, is it alkaline or is it acid? E. Forester. il Home Gard 54:30 Mr '67

Mineral content
Micronutrients, what's the score? C. E. Sommers and L. Chesnin. il Suc Farm 65:26-7+ D '67

Sulfate content
Sulfate reduction in soil: effects of redox potential and pH. W. E. Connell and W. H. Patrick, jr. bibliog il Science 159:86-7 Ja 5 '68

Testing
See Soils—Analysis

Water content
See Soil moisture

SOILS, Minerals in. See Soils—Mineral content

SOKA Gakkai (sect)
Soka Gakkai stirs the ashes of nationalism; Japan's quasi-religious Komeito party. il Bsns W p 114+ F 11 '67

SOKOLOFF, A. and others
Tribolium castaneum: morphology of aureate revealed by the scanning electron microscope. bibliog Science 157:443-5 Jl 28 '67

SOKOLOFF, Alice Hunt
Dry stalks of autumn. Sat R 50:48-9+ O 28 '67

SOKOLOW, Anna
Anna Sokolow dance company, Hunter college playhouse. J. Maskey. Dance Mag 41:36 My '67

SOLA Basic Industries
Less diversity means more prosperity for Sola Basic. il Bsns W p82-4+ Ap 22 '67

SOLANO, Armando Ochoa-. See Ochoa-Solano, A.

SOLAR atmosphere. See Sun—Atmosphere

SOLAR batteries
Cell studies spur solar power advances. G. S. Hunter. il Aviation W 87:94-5+ Ag 28 '67
Requirements for solar arrays spurring new techniques. G. S. Hunter. il Aviation W 87:72-7+ Ag 14 '67

SOLAR corona. See Sun—Corona

SOLAR energy
Solar stills for sheep; solar-powered desalination equipment. W. A. Scholes. Sci N 92:204+ Ag 26 '67

SOLAR flares
Pioneer 7 doubling as sun weatherman. R. Pay. il Tech W 20:20+ F 27 '67
Position of planets linked to solar flare prediction. R. Pay. il Tech W 20:35-8 My 15 '67
Rare flare. il Sci N 91:592-3 Je 24 '67

SOLAR gravity. See Gravitation

SOLAR magnetic fields. See Magnetic field (cosmic physics)

SOLAR models. See Astronomical models

SOLAR probes. See Space probes

SOLAR prominences. See Sun—Prominences

SOLAR radiation
Circulation of the sun's atmosphere. V. P. Starr and P. A. Gilman. il Sci Am 218:100-2+ bibliog(p 152) Ja '68
Diamagnetic solar-wind cavity discovered behind moon. D. S. Colburn and others. bibliog il Science 158:1040-2 N 24 '67
Radiant solar energy and the function of black homeotherm pigmentation: an hypothesis. W. J. Hamilton, 3d. and F. Heppner. bibliog il Science 155:196-7 Ja 13 '67; Reply with rejoinder. R. B. Cowles. 158:1340-1 D 8 '67
Skin-pigment regulation of vitamin-D biosynthesis in man. W. F. Loomis. bibliog il Science 157:501-6 Ag 4 '67; Reply with rejoinder. F. R. Freemon. 158:579-80 N 3 '67
Solar X-rays and flares. il Sky & Tel 34:144 S '67
Spectrometer will evaluate solar plasma. G. S. Hunter. il Aviation W 86:55 F 27 '67
See also
Solar flares
Sunspots
Van Allen radiation belts

SOLAR research. See Sun

SOLAR rotation. See Sun—Rotation

SOLAR spectrum. See Spectrum, Solar

SOLAR telescope. See Telescope

SOLAR wind spectrometers. See Spectrometers

SOLARIZATION
Controlled solarization. J. Cornell. il U S Camera 30:46-7+ S '67

SOLDER and soldering
Electronic soldering. J. McNarney. il Pop Electr 27:53-6 Jl '67

SOLDERING apparatus
Permanent tinning of soldering irons. P. J. Profera. Electr World 78:60 S '67
Soldering tools now acceptable. il Consumer Rep 32:298 Je '67
Wen's single-post soldering gun. C. P. Gilmore. il Pop Sci 191:126-8+ Ag '67

SOLDIERS
When Beatniks land in the army. il U S News 62:52-4 Je 5 '67

Protection
See Arms and armor

SOLDIERS; drama. See Hochhuth, R.

SOLDIERS, Negro. See United States—Army—Negroes

SOLDIERS families. See Service mens families

SOLDIERS letters. See Letters from servicemen

SOLDIERS publications
See also
Overseas weekly

SOLDIERS singing
See also
European war, 1914-1918—Songs and music

SOLDIER'S tale; opera. See Stravinsky, I. F.

SOLHEIM, Wilhelm G. 2d
Southeast Asia and the West. bibliog Science 157:896-902 Ag 25 '67

SOLID electrolytes. See Electrolytes

SOLID helium. See Helium, Solid

SOLID propellant rockets
Air-augmented, solid-propellant system analyzed by Lockheed. Aviation W 86:79 F 13 '67
Army evaluating rocket-assisted artillery projectiles. M. L. Yaffee. il Aviation W 86:82-3+ Je 19 '67
Increased solid propellant life reported. J. F. Judge. il Tech W 20:24 Ap 24 '67
NASA funds voted to continue solid rockets. Tech W 20:21 My 1 '67
Rocket to propel lunar seismic grenades; ultra-small solid rocket motors. W. E. Wilke. il Aero Tech 21:23-4 Ja 1 '68
Schedule is still uncertain in big solid rocket future. W. Hansen. Aviation W 86:20 Je 26 '67

Materials
Nickel casing is electroformed on Lockheed monolithic rocket. il Aviation W 86:75 My 15 '67

Sterilization
Sterilizable propellant developed by UTC. R. Lindsey. il Tech W 20:30 Mr 13 '67

Testing
Aiming to save solid boosters; Aerojet test fires its third solid rocket motor. Bsns W p 115 Je 24 '67
Exit cone destruction mars third 260-in. rocket firing. J. F. Judge. il Tech W 20:20-2 Je 26 '67
Low-cost sled motor offers versatility; solid-propellant unit is reusable. M. L. Yaffee. il Aviation W 86:50-2 F 20 '67

SOLID state amplifiers. See Amplifiers

SOLID-state flashers. See Electric lamps, Flashing

SOLID wastes. See Refuse and refuse disposal

SOLIDS
Chemical properties of materials. H. Reiss. il Sci Am 217:210-14+ S '67
Solid state. N. Mott. il Sci Am 217:80-9 S '67
See also
Zone refining

SOLIS-COHEN, Lita H.
Living with antiques (cont) Antiques 92:336-40 S '67

SOLITRON devices, incorporated
When a suitor knocks; courtship of Amphenol by Solitron. il Bsns W p 121-2 N 11 '67

SOLITUDE
See also
Loneliness

SOLMAN, Joseph
Stormy revelations. Nation 204:345-6 Mr 13 '67

SOLOMON, Alan R.
New New York art scene: who makes it? excerpts from New York: the new art scene. Vogue 150:102-7+ Ag 1 '67

SOLOMON, Anthony M.
Cotton in the world trade arena; address, March 10, 1967. Dept State Bul 56:555-60 Ap 3 '67
Economic integration of Latin America; address, September 29, 1967. Dept State Bul 57:534-40 O 23 '67
Revival of trade between the Communist bloc and the West. bibliog f Ann Am Acad 372:105-12 Jl '67
United States foreign trade policy and the developing countries; statement, July 12, 1967. Dept States Bul 57:180-90 Ag 7 '67
Why the United States should expand peaceful trade with eastern Europe; address, March 2, 1967. Dept State Bul 56:518-23 Mr 27 '67

SOLOMON, Eric
For sale: one college. Atlan 219:111-2 My '67

SOLOMON, Jane
Cafeteria now bookstore at University of Florida. Pub W 192:68-9 N 13 '67

SOLOMON, Leslie
Automobile diagnostic center. Electr World 77:48-52+ My '67
Tone-selective signaling; the new look. Electr World 78:88-90 S '67

SOLOMON, Richard H.
China return. Yale R 57:148-60 O '67

SOLOMON, Syd
Clay prints. Design 69:14-17 Fall '67

SOLOMON R. Guggenheim museum, New York
Fire. New Yorker 43:39-40 Ap 15 '67

SOLOMONSON, Vicky
Some children are special. R. Kramer. il por N Y Times Mag p87+ N 5 '67

SOLOTAROFF, Theodore
Authentic voice. Commentary 43:91-2 My '67
Desert within. New Repub 157:29-31 S 2 '67
Kind of survival. New Repub 156:21-2+ My 13 '67
Life book review. Life 62:10 Je 23 '67
Primer for survival. New Repub 157:22-5 O 14 '67

about

Authors & editors. por Pub W 192:183-5 Ag 28 '67

SOLT, Leo F.
Puritanism, capitalism, democracy, and the new science. bibliog f Am Hist R 73:18-29 O '67

SOLTI, Georg
Georg Solti's full score. C. Reid. il pors Hi Fi 17:66-70 Ja '67

SOLUBLE coffee. See Coffee

SOLUBLE salts. See Salts, Soluble

SOLUTION (chemistry)
Solvated electron. J. L. Dye. il Sci Am 216:76-83 F '67

SOLVANG, Calif.
Traveler's choice. M. Johnson. Travel 128:9 O '67

SOLVENTS
Chlorination of unsaturated compounds in nonpolar media. M. L. Poutsma. bibliog il Science 157:997-1005 S 1 '67
Solvent contamination from volatile components of a fiberglass glove box. J. V. Rodricks and others. Science 156:1648 Je 23 '67

SOLZHENITSYN, Aleksandr Isaevich
Man of courage. por Newsweek 69:44 Je 12 '67
Soviet censors on the defensive. Life 63:4 Jl 28 '67

SOMALILAND, FRENCH
Mini-Vietnam; referendum; riots. il Newsweek 69:48 Ap 3 '67
Troops quell riots. il Sr Schol 90:19 Ap 7 '67
Victory for trouble. il Time 89:30 Mr 31 '67

SOMAN, Florence Jane
Girl with love in her eyes; story. Good H 165:76-7 Jl '67
One unhappy bachelor; story. Good H 165:90-1 N '67

SOMATIC cells. See Cells

SOMAYAJULU, B. L. K.
Beryllium-10 in a manganese nodule. bibliog Science 156:1219-20 Je 2 '67

SOMEBODY'S valentine; drama. See Newman, D.

SOMEONE missing at the manger; story. See Hill, E. S.

SOMERO, George N. and DeVries, A. L.
Temperature tolerance of some Antarctic fishes. bibliog Science 156:257-8 Ap 14 '67

SOMERS, Florence
New movies. See Issues of Redbook

SOMETHING about heaven; story. See Austin, A.

SOMETHING different; drama. See Reiner, C.

SOMETHING else; story. See Amft, M. J.

SOMEWHERE music; story. See Boles, P. D.

SOMMER, Sally R. and others
Food and water intake after intrahypothalamic injections of carbachol in the rabbit. bibliog Science 156:983-4 My 19 '67

SOMMER, Theo
Bonn changes course. For Affairs 45:477-91 Ap '67

SOMOZA DEBAYLE, Anastasio
Friendship's toll. il por Newsweek 69:56 F 13 '67
One more Somoza. M. Smith. il por Life 62:82 Ap 28 '67
Where a dynasty was extended, but—. por U S News 62:22 F 20 '67

SONAR
Piezoelectric property of otoliths. R. W. Morris and L. R. Kittleman. bibliog il Science 153:363-70 O 20 '67
See also
Echolocation (physiology)

SONATAS
See also
Phonograph records—Sonatas

SONG of the earth; ballet. See Ballets—Criticism

SONG of the Lusitanian bogey; drama. See Weiss, P.

SONG writers. See Composers

SONGS
See also
Phonograph records—Songs

SONGS, American
Trade winds; Arthur Schwartz's list of ten best songs written this century. H. R. Mayes. Sat R 50:8+ Mr 4 '67
See also
Folk songs, American

SONGS, Popular. See Music, Popular (songs, etc)

SONIC boom
Atmosphere effect on sonic boom probed. W. C. Wetmore. il Aviation W 87:72-3+ N 27 '67
Ban the boom? F. Mount. il Nat R 19:850-4 Ag 8 '67
Banning the boom. il Time 90:67 O 6 '67
Carpet of sound. il Fortune 75:117 F '67
Ground effects may slow SST. Sci N 92:102 Jl 29 '67
Incredible SST. W. V. Shannon. Commonweal 86:462-3 Jl 28 '67
Supersonic boom carpet. il UNESCO Courier 20:18-19 Jl '67

Psychological aspects
Boom or bust? Ministry of technology measures British tolerance of sonic noise. Newsweek 70:61 Jl 17 '67
Boom that's brewing a storm; Boeing's SST. il Bsns W p64-5+ O 28 '67
Lowering the boom. Newsweek 70:80 Ag 14 '67
Sonic boom tests. K. M. Ruppenthal. Nation 205:229-30 S 18 '67

SONNET, Philip E.
Fire and venom: synthesis of a reported component of solenamine. bibliog Science 156:1759-60 Je 30 '67

SONOMA state hospital, Calif. See State institutions

SONORAN DESERT NATIONAL PARK (proposed) See National parks and reserves—United States

SONORAY machines. See Testing instruments

SONS
See also
Fathers

SONS and fathers. See Parent-child relationship

SONS of Martha; story. See McKenna, R.

SONTAG, Frederick
Are you a Catholic? America 117:502-5 N 4 '67

SONY corporation. See Japan—Industries

SONY corporation of America
What nudists look at; advertisement for Sony portable television set. il Newsweek 70:66 Jl 24 '67

SOPRANOS. See Singers

SORCERY. See Witchcraft

SORDARIA fimicola. See Ascomycetes

SORELL, Walter
Dance. Horizon 9:96-105 Sum '67

SORENSEN, Theodore Chaikin
Dialogue with Bonn. Sat R 50:28-9 My 20 '67
Do we need peace candidates? Sat R 50:32-3 F 4 '67
May 29, 1967 would have been John Kennedy's 50th birthday. McCalls 94:58-9 Je '67

SORENSEN, Theodore Chaikin—*Continued*
Presidency is back-breaking, but you get to walk to work. N Y Times Mag p25+ Mr 19 '67
Quiet campaign to rewrite the Constitution. Sat R 50:17-20 Jl 15 '67
Report from Rumania. Sat R 50:14-15 D 30 '67
War in Vietnam: how we can end it. Sat R 50:19-22 O 21 '67

about
New new frontier of Ted Sorensen. T. Smith. il pors N Y Times Mag p24-5+ Mr 26 '67
SORGHUM
Hybrids
Let's take another look at the high-yielding grass forages. C. E. Sommers. il Suc Farm 65:34-5+ Je '67
SORGMAN, Dara
On destruction. Nat Parks Mag 41:15 O '67
SORIA, Dorle J.
Artist life. See issues of High fidelity incorporating Musical America
SOROKIN, Constantine
New high-temperature chlorella. bibliog Science 158:1204-5 D 1 '67
SOROKIN, Pitirim A.
Essential characteristics of the Russian nation in the twentieth century. bibliog f Ann Am Acad 370:99-115 Mr '67
SORRELL tree. See Sourwood
SORRELLS, Helen
But if we should; poem. Reporter 37:43 Ag 10 '67
Prodigal's mother; poem. Commonweal 87: 467 Ja 19 '68
Searcher; poem. Reporter 36:46 Je 1 '67
SORRENTINO, Gilbert
Football poem I; Land of cotton; Long gone blues; Some bright paintings; poems. Poetry 110:174-7 Je '67
SORRENTINO, Joe
Dropout who made good. il por Time 89:59 Je 30 '67
SORROW
Cup of sorrow in every woman's life; interview, ed. by J. Graham. P. L. Travers. Ladies Home J 84:68+ F '67
See also
Bereavement
SOTH, Lauren
Closing the world food gap. Bul Atomic Sci 23:49-2 N '67
SOTHEBY and company
Autographs; fascinating sales at Sotheby's. K. V. Hostick. Hobbies 72:108-9 Ja '68
SOTO, Hernando de
Passion of Hernando de Soto; excerpt from Explorers of the Mississippi. T. Severin. il Am Heritage 18:26-31+ Ap '67
SOTOGRANDE colony. See Seaside resorts— Spain
SOUFFLÉS
Praline soufflé. il Sunset 139:168 N '67
Soufflé spiked with spinach; with menu and recipes by E. Graves. il Life 62:110-11+ F 17 '67
SOUL
Searching for the soul; will of James Kidd. il Time 89:63 Je 23 '67
SOUL music. See Jazz music
SOULAGES, Pierre
Letter from Paris; one-man show at the musée National d'art moderne. Genêt. New Yorker 43:178+ Ap 15 '67
SOULE, Claire Whitaker
Three spectators; poem. Christian Cent 84: 371 Mr 22 '67
SOULE, George
Pied Piper from down East. D. Barnes. il por Sports Illus 28:34-7 Ja 8 '68
SOUND
See also
Acoustics. Architectural
Music—Acoustics and physics
Noise
Voice
Apparatus
Introduction to audio components. il Consumer Rep 32:267-322 D '67
Sound for photographers. T. Schwartz. See issues of Popular photography
What's new in sight and sound. R. Freas. Am Home 70:50+ O '67
See also
Audio dealers
Audio-visual equipment
Detectors
Earphones

Magnetic recorders and recording
Moving pictures—Sound effects
Stethoscope, Electric

Physiological effects
Audiogenic seizure susceptibility induced in C57B1/6J mice by prior auditory exposure. K. R. Henry. bibliog il Science 158:938-40 N 17 '67

Recording and reproducing
Records, circa 1987. G. R. Marek. il Sat R 50:64-5+ Ag 26 '67
Sonic policy. H. Fantel. Opera N 31:34 Mr 4 '67
Sound. J. Wesson. See issues of U.S. camera & travel
Sound advice. See issues of Modern photography
Sound for photographers. T. Schwartz. See issues of Popular photography
Sound of sound-on-sound. I. Berger. Sat R 50:57 D 2 '67
What's new in sight and sound. R. Freas. Am Home 70:50+ O '67
See also
Audio fairs
High fidelity sound systems
Phonograph records—Recording

Stereophonic recording and reproducing
Audio. H. Fantel. See issues of Opera news
See also
Stereophonic sound systems
SOUND and light; story. See Carter, M.
SOUND equipment. See Sound—Apparatus
SOUND measurement
Noisy chorus of the sea. W. N. Tavolga. il Natur Hist 76:20-7 Ap '67
SOUND of music; musical comedy. See Musical comedies, revues, etc.—Criticisms, plots, etc.
SOUND production by animals
Mike Frome; voices of wolves in Algonquin Provincial Park, Ontario. M. Frome. Am For 73:5+ Ja '67
SOUND production by insects. See Insect sounds
SOUND suppressors
Doctor Dolby's dilly. I. Berger. Sat R 50:74-5 Mr 25 '67
SOUND waves
Danger of sounds we cannot hear. il UNESCO Courier 20:28-9 Jl '67
Noisy sun. il Sci N 92:251 S 9 '67
See also
Doppler effect
Damping
Damping factor debate; amplifier damping factors. G. L. Augspurger. il Electr World 77:46-7 Ja '67
SOUNDERS. See Depth indicators
SOUNDING and soundings
See also
Depth indicators
SOUNDING rockets. See Rockets. Sounding
SOUNDPRINTING
See also
Voiceprints
SOUNDPROOFING
Simple ways to sound-condition your home. M. C. Huntoon, jr. Am Home 70:110 My '67
Sound advice; or, How to lower the noise level in your home. il Good H 164:188+ F '67
SOUNDS of the sea. See Ocean sounds
SOUPS
American classic; Philadelphia pepper pot. C. Claiborne. il N Y Times Mag p 108+ My 14 '67
Borden company vs. chicken little; USDA vs Wyler's chicken noodle soup mix. Consumer Rep 32:349 Jl '67
Cold soups with a foreign flavor. il Good H 165:146 Ag '67
Good soup. S. Spitzer. il Holiday 42:74-7+ O '67
H&G's gourmet's guide; Mary's chicken soup; with recipe. House & Gard 131:184 Ap '67
Leeks and potatoes join in a soup. il Sunset 139:123 D '67
Quick-change soups. il Redbook 129:92-3+ Jl '67
Sea fare at the dock. V. T. Habeeb. il Am Home 70:102+ Je '67
Soup and salad supper cook book; with menus and recipes. I. Brooks. il House & Gard 131: 179+ Mr '67
Soups to suit the summer. C. Claiborne. il N Y Times Mag p58 Je 18 '67
Spectacular soups, hot or cold; with recipes. il Ladies Home J 84:86+ Ag '67

SOUPS—*Continued*
Splendid soupe for September; with recipe. il Sunset 139:116 S '67
Sunday-night soups; with recipes. H. McCully. il House B 109:152+ F '67
Tureen parties; meal-in-a-dish soups. il Ebony 23:98+ Ja '68

SOURDOUGH. See Dough

SOURIRE, Sister. See Luc Dominique

SOURITZ, Elizabeth
Report from Russia. Dance Mag 41:28-9+ S '67

SOURWOOD
Sourwood, an outstanding small tree. E. S. Henderson. il Horticulture 45:33 N '67

SOUTAR, Andrew. See Berger, W. H. jt. auth.

SOUTH, Kent. See Marzluft, J. M. jt. auth.

SOUTH
See also
American literature—Southern states
Colleges and universities—Southern states
Confederate States of America
Education—Southern states
Fishing—Southern states
Justice, Administration of—Southern states
Negroes in the United States—South

Description and travel
Atlanta and the Old South. il Bet Hom & Gard 45:154-5 Ap '67

History
See also
Negroes in the United States—History
Reconstruction (Civil war)
Secession

Politics
Impact of Negro votes on southern politics. R. Cleghorn and P. Watters. il Reporter 36:24-5+ Ja 26 '67
See also
Southern governors conference

Race problems
See Negroes in the United States—South

Religious institutions and affairs
War in the Bible belt concerning S. A. Hill's assessment of the Protestant South. il Newsweek 69:91 Mr 27 '67

Social conditions
See also
Southern conference for human welfare

SOUTH AFRICA
South Africa, D. L. Niddrie. bibliog il Focus 17:1-6 Je '67
See also
Automobile industry and trade—South Africa
Dassen Island
Geology—South Africa
Gold mines and mining—South Africa
Great Karoo
Hunting—South Africa
Immigration and emigration—South Africa
Investments, Foreign (in South Africa)
Justice, Administration of—South Africa
Labor supply—South Africa
Paleontology—South Africa
Prisons—South Africa
Science—South Africa
Trade unions—South Africa
Trials—South Africa
United Nations—South Africa

Defenses
U.K. rejects South Africa defense order. H. J. Coleman. Aviation W 87:20 D 25 '67

Foreign relations
Vorster's practical approach. N. Mostert. il Reporter 36:15-19 My 4 '67

Intellectual life
Effects of apartheid on culture; symposium. bibliog il UNESCO Courier 20:14-17+ Mr '67

Native races
See also
South Africa—Race problems

Politics and government
Goldwater in South Africa. S. Uys. New Repub 158:15-17 Ja 6 '68
Touch of sweet reasonableness. il Time 89:28-9 Mr 31 '67

Race problems
Apartheid: symposium. il UNESCO Courier 20:4-34 Mr '67

Apartheid with a smile; Vorster adds cunning to brute force in perpetuating apartheid. Christian Cent 84:526 Ap 26 '67
Challenge of fear. A. Paton. Sat R 50:19-21+ S 9 '67
Commission on human rights strongly condemns the policies of apartheid and repressive measures in South Africa. P. Nedbailo. UN Mo Chron 4:59-68 My '67
Effects of apartheid on education, science, culture and information in South Africa; summary of report. UN Mo Chron 4:43-63 Mr '67
House of apartheid. M. De Villiers. il Nation 204:741-4 Je 12 '67
House of bondage, by E. Cole and T. Flaherty. Review
Nation 205:569-70 N 27 '67. L. Levitt
New Repub 157:22+ O 28 '67. S. Kauffmann
Science in South Africa: the effects of apartheid. E. Langer. Science 155:1387-9 Mr 17 '67
Shade of difference; R. Van der Walt reclassified as colored. il Newsweek 69:40+ F 27 '67
Silence about apartheid; seventh anniversary of the Sharpeville massacre at Johannesburg. America 116:516 Ap 8 '67
South Africa, an imperial dilemma, by B. Sacks. Review
Sat R 50:41 Je 10 '67. G. Godsell
Southern Baptists withdraw from South Africa crusade. Christian Cent 84:581-2 My 3 '67
Trade union rights in South Africa; UN working group. UN Mo Chron 4:47 Ag '67
'Twas a famous victory. Nat R 19:177-8 F 21 '67
See also
United Nations—South Africa
United Nations—Special committee on the policies of apartheid of the government of the Republic of South Africa

Religious institutions and affairs
Apartheid and the church; excerpt from Unesco report on apartheid. UNESCO Courier 20:33-4 Mr '67
World around us (cont) Christian Cent 84:356-8, 702, 949-50, 1001-2, 1472+ Mr 15, My 24, Jl 19, Ag 2, N 15 '67
See also
Reformed church in South Africa

SOUTH AFRICAN culture. See South Africa—Intellectual life

SOUTH AFRICAN frogs. See Frogs

SOUTH AFRICAN political prisoners. See Political prisoners

SOUTH AMERICA
Inside South America, by J. Gunther. Review
Newsweek 69:101 F 6 '67. S. Schmidt
See also
Gardens—South America
Tierra del Fuego

Commerce
See Latin America—Commerce

Defenses
See Latin America—Defenses

Description and travel
Gardener goes to South America. R. Bailey. il House & Gard 132:168-9+ D '67

Education
See Education—Latin America

Politics
See Latin America—Politics

SOUTH AMERICAN literature. See Latin American literature

SOUTH ARABIA (Federation)
Note:
For material after November 1967, see South Yemen (People's Republic)
As the British pull out: another big vacuum. J. Law. il U S News 63:64-5 N 27 '67
Countdown. Newsweek 70:73-4 N 20 '67
Gone with the wind. il Time 90:37-8 S 15 '67
Itching toward independence. Time 90:47 N 10 '67
Muddling through. il Newsweek 70:53-4 S 18 '67
Sheiks under siege. Time 90:20 S 8 '67
Snatching power. Newsweek 70:40 S 11 '67
South Arabia: Nasser and the sultans. J. A. Morris, jr. il Nation 204:358-61 Mr 20 '67
Yoke of independence. Time 90:40 N 24 '67

SOUTH CAROLINA
See also
Architecture—South Carolina
Fishing—South Carolina
Johns Island
Libraries—South Carolina
Public welfare—South Carolina

Race problems
Religion and race in South Carolina, M. P. Harrington. Christian Cent 84:320-3 Mr 8 '67

Religious institutions and affairs
World around us. Christian Cent 84:320-3 Mr 8 '67
SOUTH CAROLINA state college, Orangeburg
Fight for quality on two Negro campuses. P. Clancy. il Reporter 37:37-9 Jl 13 '67
SOUTH DAKOTA
See also
Hunting—South Dakota

History
See also
Wounded Knee Creek, Battle of, 1890
SOUTH Pacific; musical comedy. See Musical comedies, revues, etc.—Criticisms, plots. etc.
SOUTH PACIFIC championship drag races. See Automobile racing
SOUTH PACIFIC dragfest. See Automobile racing
SOUTH SEA ISLANDS
Keys to a reefbound realm. F. R. Smith. il Sports Illus 28:37-9 Ja 15 '67
See also
Bora-Bora (island)
Cook Islands
Easter Island
Fiji
Guam
Line Islands
Micronesia
Nauru (island)
New Caledonia
New Hebrides
Tahiti
Tuamotu Islands
SOUTH SEA ISLANDS in literature
Literary adventures in paradise: the beachcomber books. A. G. Day. il Holiday 42:6+ Jl '67
SOUTH TYROL. See Tyrol
SOUTH VIETNAM. See Vietnam (Republic)
SOUTH YEMEN (People's Republic)
Double trouble. Newsweek 70:49-50 D 11 '67
Leap in the dark. Newsweek 70:46+ D 4 '67
See also
United Nations—South Yemen (People's Republic)
SOUTHAM, Anna L. and Mellach, D. Z.
Expectant mother. Redbook 128:40+ Mr '67
SOUTHAMPTON insurrection, 1831
Books; The fire last time. G. Steiner. New Yorker 43:236+ N 25 '67
Into the mind of Nat Turner. R. A. Sokolov. il Newsweek 70:65-9 O 16 '67
Note on the history; inaccuracies of W. Styron's novel. H. Aptheker. Nation 205:375-6 O 16 '67
SOUTHARD, Helen F.
Time of tension. PTA Mag 62:12 S '67
SOUTHARD, J. B.
Momentum transport in turbulent flow between concentric rotating cylinders. bibliog Science 156:1725-7 Je 30 '67
SOUTHARD, Samuel C.
Increased pressure good for children. por Todays Health 45:63-4 S '67
SOUTHEAST ASIA. See Asia, Southeastern
SOUTHEAST ASIA treaty organization
Present viability of NATO, SEATO, and CENTO; address, April 1967, with questions and answers. A. E. P. Duffy. Ann Am Acad 372:33-9 Jl '67
SEATO council reaffirms resolve to repeal aggression; statement, April 18, with text of final communique, April 20, 1967. D. Rusk. Dept State Bul 56:742-7 My 15 '67
SEATO: false alibi; American involvement in Vietnam. J. A. Joyce. il Christian Cent 84:1424-9 N 8 '67; Reply. W. R. Espy. 84:1600 D 13 '67
Thirteenth anniversary of SEATO; message, September 8, 1967. D. Rusk. Dept State Bul 57:391 S 25 '67
SOUTHEAST Asian studies
Scholar shortage; lack of Vietnam scholars. Newsweek 70:56 Ag 28 '67
Void on Viet Nam. Time 90:58-9 Ag 25 '67
SOUTHEASTERN Baptist theological seminary, Wake Forest, N.C. See Theological schools

SOUTHEASTERN regional ballet festival. See Dance festivals
SOUTHERN AFRICA. See Africa, Southern
SOUTHERN Baptist convention. See Baptists in the United States
SOUTHERN Baptists. See Baptists in the United States
SOUTHERN CALIFORNIA university, Los Angeles
A/V index revamped in major media project; by USC: National information center for educational media (NICEM) Library J 92:1280+ Mr 15 '67
Computer-controlled manikin developed by Aerojet, USC. il Tech W 20:20 Ap 3 '67
McGraw-Hill grant backs USC media project; National information center for educational media. Pub W 191:53 F 13 '67
SOUTHERN Christian leadership conference
Negroes go national with demands for jobs; SCLC's Operation Breadbasket. Bsns W p37-8 Ag 19 '67
SOUTHERN conference educational fund
Kentucky's coal beds of sedition. P. Good. il Nation 205:166-9 S 4 '67
Sedition in Kentucky. J. Ridgeway. New Repub 157:10 S 2 '67
SOUTHERN conference for human welfare
And promises to keep, by T. A. Krueger. Review
Sat R 50:66-7 Je 10 '67. E. Yoder, jr
SOUTHERN furniture exposition. See Furniture—Exhibitions
SOUTHERN furniture manufacturers association
Furniture market gets new polish. il Bsns W p38-40 Ap 22 '67
SOUTHERN governors conference
Gone fishing; Gov. Maddox tries to incite anti-federalist posturing. il Newsweek 70:34+ S 25 '67
On racial front; a quiet South and a troubled North; why. il U S News 63:76-7 S 25 '67
Whistlin' Dixie; the southern governors in caucus. J. H. Ford; discussion. 219:32-3 F '67
SOUTHERN ILLINOIS university
In from the Three I league. J. Jares. il Sports Illus 26:18-19 Ja 30 '67
Out of nowhere. il Newsweek 69:102-3 Je 12 '67
SOUTHERN nations. See Nations
SOUTHERN ocean racing conference. See Yacht racing
SOUTHERN Pacific company
Switch at Southern Pacific. N. Willatt. il Duns R 90:47-8+ O '67
SOUTHERN Presbyterian church. See Presbyterian church in the United States (South)
SOUTHERN regional education board
Southern regional education board: continuity and change. J. L. Miller, jr. Sch & Soc 95:184-5 Mr 18 '67
SOUTHERN writers. See Authors, American
SOUTHWEST
Navajo country; excerpts from Navajo wildlands. S. C. Jett. il Audubon 69:22-7 Ja '67
See also
Botany—Southwestern states
Education—Southwestern states
Hunting—Southwestern states
Water supply—Southwestern states

Description and travel
Big sky country. Redbook 130:37-44 N '67

Social conditions
Mexican-Americans make themselves heard. M. Alisky. Reporter 36:45-6+ F 9 '67
SOUTHWEST AFRICA
South West Africa cases. H. Highet. bibliog f il Cur Hist 52:154-61 Mr '67
See also
Namib Desert
United Nations—Southwest Africa

Native races
Ghosts of Windhoek. N. Mostert. Reporter 37:39-42 S 21 '67
SOUTHWEST airmotive company, Dallas
Big operator in big D. A. Trammell. il Flying 81:72-4 O '67
Service firm building two new hangars. Aviation W 87:123+ Ag 14 '67
SOUTHWEST ALABAMA farmers cooperative association
Shriver makes it; OEO grant. New Repub 156:9 My 27 '67
SOUTHWEST Indians. See Indians of North America
SOUTHWESTERN regional ballet festival. See Dance festivals

SOUVANNA Phouma, prince of Laos
As an Asian neutralist sees U.S. stake in Vietnam; interview. por U S News 63:106-7 N 6 '67
Prince Souvanna Phouma of Laos meets with President Johnson; exchange of toasts and statement, October 20, 1967. Dept State Bul 57:653-4 N 13 '67

about

Two Asian leaders who support U.S. role in Vietnam. por U S News 63:22 O 30 '67
SOUVENIR spoons. See Spoons
SOUVENIRS
Souvenir detectors; Civil war memento collectors in the South. il Time 89:53 Mr 24 '67
SOUZAY, Gérard
Mystery of performing; ed. by P. M. Katona, tr. by A. M. Lingg. Opera N 32:8-11 N 25 '67
SOVIET air show. See Aviation—Exhibitions
SOVIET CENTRAL ASIA. See Asia, Central
SOVIET education. See Education—Russia
SOVIET encyclopedias. See Encyclopedias
SOVIET government. See Russia—Politics and government
SOVIET Russian poetry. See Russian poetry
SOVIET Union. See Russia
SOVIET writers. See Authors, Russian
SOVIET youth. See Youth—Russia
SOW bugs. See Wood lice
SOWS. See Swine
SOYBEANS
Beans vs. corn, which will net you most in 1967? A. G. Mueller and H. Guither. il Suc Farm 65:104 Mr '67
Chemical weed control in soybeans. il Suc Farm 65:83+ Mr '67
Growth regulators, how they work for you. C. E. Sommers. il Suc Farm 65:44 Je '67
How to get top soybean prices every year. J. Bickers. il Farm J 91:39+ Mr '67
How to put more beans in your bin. C. E. Sommers. il Suc Farm 65:40+ Jl '67
Midwest soybean yields impress southern farmers. Farm J 91:42B D '67
Narrow rows and proper seeding rate essential for top yields. C. E. Sommers. il Suc Farm 65:50-1+ Mr '67
Nature note; China cow. Sci N 91:172 F 18 '67
Seed selection, first step to top yields. W. D. Pardee and C. E. Sommers. il Suc Farm 65:36-7 Ja '67
Should you fertilize soybeans? C. E. Sommers. il Suc Farm 65:46-7+ F '67
Solid-seed soybeans: OK if you stop weeds. D. Hagen. il Farm J 91:56J-56K Ja '67
South's big soybean boom. D. Seim. il Farm J 91:27-9+ N '67
Those big soybean yields. D. Seim. il Farm J 91:39+ F '67
Ways to boost soybean profits. C. E. Sommers. il Suc Farm 65:40-1+ Ag '67
You can grow fifty-bu. soybeans. D. Seim. il Farm J 92:C6+ Ja '68

Diseases and pests

How to control soybean diseases. J. J. Feight and C. E. Sommers. il Suc Farm 65:40-1+ Ap '67
How to control soybean insects. Suc Farm 65:46+ My '67
SOYER, Raphael
East side story. D. L. Shirey. il por Newsweek 70:112+ N 13 '67
SOYINKA, Akinwande Oluwole. See Soyinka, W.
SOYINKA, Wole
Strong breed. Criticism
Nation 205:606 D 4 '67
New Yorker 43:133-4 N 18 '67
Time il 90:50+ N 17 '67
Trials of Brother Jero. Criticism
Nation 205:606 D 4 '67
New Yorker 43:133-4 N 18 '67
Time 90:50+ N 17 '67
SPAAK, Paul Henri
European statesman backs U.S. role in Asia; interview. por U S News 62:64-6 Mr 6 '67
SPACE
Space search. L. J. Anderson and others. il Sch Arts 67:21-4 S '67
SPACE (architecture)
Five small-scale communities; projects in design by Hok; with introd. by G. Obata. il Arch Rec 141:141-50 Mr '67
Space and gadgets. G. Nelson. il Am Home 70:16 S '67
Subject is space. il Am Home 70:51-71 S '67

SPACE, Outer

Exploration

Biologist in the solar system. C. S. Pittendrigh. il Bul Atomic Sci 23:4-10 Mr '67
Moon exploration: advent of the new engineering. I. Asimov. Tech W 20:46-8 Ja 23 '67
Planetary investigations; excerpt from Space research; directions for the future. il Bul Atomic Sci 23:10 My '67
Post-Apollo era, decisions facing NASA. A. H. Brown. Bul Atomic Sci 23:11-16 Ap '67
Visual aspects of trans-stellar space flight. S. Moskowitz. il Sky & Tel 33:290-4 My '67
See also
Space probes

International control

Administration urges Senate approval of UN space treaty. Tech W 20:17 Mr 13 '67
Assembly adopts three resolutions; with text of treaty. UN Mo Chron 4:35-46 Ja '67
Committee recommends postponement of conference. UN Mo Chron 4:16-17 Mr '67
International control in space: 1967; text of the treaty. Bul Atomic Sci 23:46-8 Mr '67
Loophole seen in space treaty. Sci N 91:565-6 Je 17 '67
More Soviet space cooperation not expected. Aviation W 87:27 O 16 '67
Outer limits? Time 89:21 My 5 '67
Outer space, strategy, and arms control. W. C. Clemens, jr. Bul Atomic Sci 23:24-8 N '67
Outer space treaty. S. Gorove. Bul Atomic Sci 23:44-5 D '67
Outer space treaty signed by sixty nations at White House ceremony; texts of statements made when signing, January 27, 1967. Dept State Bul 56:266-9 F 20 '67
President calls for Senate ratification on treaty on outer space; message to the Senate, February 7, 1967. L. B. Johnson. Dept State Bul 56:386-8 Mr 6 '67
Secretary Rusk and Ambassador Goldberg urge Senate approval of outer space treaty; statements, March 7, 1967. D. Rusk; A. J. Goldberg. Dept State Bul 56:600-12 Ap 10 '67
Space treaty expected to pass Senate. Tech W 20:11 Ap 24 '67
Space treaty: what it will and will not do. U S News 62:13 My 8 '67
Treaty on the exploration of space; text. Cur Hist 52:175-7 Mr '67
Treaty opened for signature; peaceful uses of outer space. UN Mo Chron 4:9-10 F '67
U.N. General assembly endorses outer space treaty; statements, December 17, 19; with text of resolution adopted December 19, 1966. A. J. Goldberg. Dept State Bul 56:78-84 Ja 9 '67
White House ceremony marks entry into force of outer space treaty; statements, October 10, 1967. Dept State Bul 57:565-8 O 30 '67
SPACE and time
How much space does a man need? J. K. Lagemann. Read Digest 91:72-6 Ag '67
See also
Relativity (physics)
Time reversal
SPACE biology
Biologist in the solar system. C. S. Pittendrigh. il Bul Atomic Sci 23:4-10 Mr '67
New life detection methods studied by Martin's RIAS. Tech W 20:44 My 15 '67
SPACE blankets. See Blankets
SPACE bomb. See Artificial satellites—Military applications
SPACE cabin atmospheres. See Space vehicles —Cabin atmospheres
SPACE centers
Space-age sights: USA. L. W. Rhodes. il Todays Health 46:24-8+ Ja '68
See also
United States—National aeronautics and space administration
SPACE environment chamber. See Testing laboratories
SPACE flight
Abandoning the planets to Russia. Time 91:64 Ja 5 '68
Chronology of fiscal 1967. Aero Tech 21:121-5 Jl 31 '67
NASA moves to add AAP flights in fiscal 1969. H. Taylor. Aero Tech 21:14 O 9 '67
Neck and neck in the space race; U.S. and Russia. W. Shelton. il Fortune 76:166-8+ O '67
Next five years in space. W. Ley. il Pop Mech 127:93-7+ F '67
Recent American successes in space. Sky & Tel 35:13 Ja '68

SPACE flight—*Continued*
Roster of space activity. R. N. Watts, jr. il Sky & Tel 35:13-15 Ja '68
Second decade. M. Getler. Aero Tech 21:136+ N 20 '67
Soviet and U.S. activity; recent flurry of space activity. Sci N 92:466 N 11 '67
Sputnik plus ten. il Newsweek 70:88-9 O 9 '67
See also
Ground support systems (space flight)
International astronautical federation
Orbital rendezvous (space flight)
United States—National aeronautics and space administration

Accidents
Shared sorrow. R. Hotz. Aviation W 86:11 My 1 '67
See also
Space flight—Manned flights—Komarov flight, 1967

Astronomical observations
Optical environment about the OGO-III satellite. C. Wolff. bibliog il Science 158:1045-6 N 24 '67
Optical environment in Gemini space flights. E. P. Ney and W. F. Huch; discussion. Science 155:354, 1136 Ja 20, Mr 3 '67
Optical environment in Gemini space flights. S. M. Silverman and J. W. F. Lloyd. bibliog il Science 157:917-19 Ag 25 '67
Ultraviolet stellar spectroscopy on Gemini 11. K. G. Henize and others. bibliog il Science 155:1407-8 Mr 17 '67

Communication problems
10-100 GHz band windows seen increasing data rates; experiment for applications technology satellite. W. S. Beller. il Tech W 20:38-9 F 27 '67

Economic aspects
Space: what's in it for industry; address, October 16, 1967. J. R. Moore. Vital Speeches 34:76-9 N 15 '67

Food problems
U.S. Russian scientists view algae as principal space food. H. J. Coleman. Aviation W 87:88-9 Ag 14 '67

International aspects
Astronauts and cosmonauts, unite! E. Diamond. Newsweek 69:68-9 My 8 '67
Blessing and evils of space travel. M. Born; discussion. Bul Atomic Sci 23:24-5 F; 40-2 O '67
Conversation about Venus; Soviet-U.S. dialogue via Britain. J. Lear. Sat R 50:60-1 N 4 '67
In orbit; conference: Astronautics international. New Yorker 43:52-4 D 9 '67
Pennant on Venus. R. S. Lewis. il Bul Atomic Sci 23:19-24 N '67
Space diplomacy; excerpts from address. R. F. Packard. Aviation W 86:17 Mr 20 '67
Strong U.K. national space effort urged. Aviation W 87:33 Ag 14 '67
World unity urged on space programs; 18th congress of the International astronautical federation. D. E. Fink. Aviation W 87:21-2 O 2 '67
See also
United Nations—Committee on the peaceful uses of outer space

Manned flights
Apollo 4 success may perk up schedule. il Aero Tech 21:20 N 20 '67
Chances slim for '67 manned Apollo flight. il Tech W 20:22 Mr 6 '67
Chastening of NASA. C. Dreher. Nation 205:269-73 S 25 '67
Colossus; manned flights to the planets; interview. A. C. Clarke. New Yorker 43:25 My 27 '67
Declaration of confidence; recovery of the Apollo program. W. J. Coughlin. Tech W 20:58 My 22 '67
Exploration race: moon or sea? J. Lear. il Sat R 50:51-5 Mr 4 '67
Goal and no goal: a new policy in space. R. S. Lewis. Bul Atomic Sci 23:17-20 My '67
Industry participation slated for AAP follow-on work: Apollo applications program. il Tech W 20:23 F 6 '67
Manned Apollo flight delayed until 1968. Aviation W 86:320 Mr 6 '67
Manned Mars flights studied for 1970s. W. J. Normyle. il Aviation W 86:62-3+ Mr 27 '67
Manned planetary vehicle study proposed. I. Stone. Aviation W 87:87+ O 2 '67
NASA details sweeping Apollo revisions. W. J. Normyle. Aviation W 86:24-6 My 15 '67

NASA revises manned flight plan. W. J. Normyle. Aviation W 86:26-9 Ap 24 '67
NASA: the image misfires. W. Hines. Nation 204:517-19 Ap 24 '67
NASA weighs impact of Apollo accident. Aviation W 86:29 F 6 '67
Never on Mars. A. Glasser. il Sci Digest 61:81-3 F '67
New Soviet manned flights anticipated. M. Getler. Tech W 20:16 Mr 13 '67
New vigor by Soviets expected in manned space flight. D. Winston. il Aviation W 86:140-3+ Mr 6 '67
Next manned Apollo shot off for at least three-six months. Tech W 20:13 F 6 '67
Sixteen experiments contend for 1st AAP flight. A. Hill. Tech W 20:37 My 29 '67
Space committee voice hope Apollo will resume schedule. H. M. David. Tech W 20:18 Ap 24 '67
Visual aspects of trans-stellar space flight. S. Moskowitz. il Sky & Tel 33:290-4 My '67
Voyager, manned fly-by may be combined. A. Hill. Tech W 20:20 Mr 13 '67
White House pushing manned flight development for 1970s; Apollo applications program. W. J. Normyle. Aviation W 86:30-1 Ja 30 '67
See also
Space, Outer—Exploration

Accidents
See Space flight—Accidents

Anecdotes, facetiae, satire, etc.
In the finest tradition of our armed forces. C. B. Slackman. il Esquire 67:140-1 Ap '67

Extravehicular activity
EVA study aids future mission planning. W. J. Normyle. Aviation W 86:44-6 F 27 '67
New ideas solve the weird problems of space walking. W. Von Braun. il Pop Sci 190:110-11+ F '67

Komarov flight, 1967
Correcting the fatal flaws; slowdown in Soviet manned launchings after fatal flight of Soyuz I. il Newsweek 69:64-5+ My 8 '67
Death of a cosmonaut. Time 89:45-6 My 5 '67
Fatal space trip. Sr Schol 90:18-19 My 5 '67
Gagarin helps fight false Soyuz rumors. Aviation W 86:66+ Je 19 '67
Grim turn in space. il Sci Digest 62:23 Jl '67
New Soyuz flight forecast in try to meet schedule. W. J. Normyle. Aviation W 86:22 My 1 '67
Premonition of fire; Komarov's fatal flight. Time 89:44 My 12 '67
Russians may now share U.S. moon landing delays; with editorial comment. H. Taylor. il Tech W 20:17-18, 50 My 1 '67
Secrecy, tragedy mark Soviet flight. il Sci N 91:421-2 My 6 '67
Shadow on Soviet moon race; Cosmonaut Komarov killed. Bsns W p42-3 Ap 29 '67
Shared sorrow. R. Hotz. Aviation W 86:11 My 1 '67
Soyuz-1 disaster. R. N. Watts, jr. Sky & Tel 33:363 Je '67

Meteorological aspects
See Meteorology, Aeronautic

Physiological aspects
Biological hazards in space cited. W. J. Normyle. Aviation W 87:17 Ag 21 '67
Can we keep our astronauts alive in space? K. V. Brown. il Pop Mech 128:82-5+ Ag '67
Endurance limits in space. W. Hartley and E. Hartley. il Sci Digest 61:40-7 Ap '67
First in-flight studies of metabolism. Sci N 91:159 F 18 '67
Hazards of 1,000-day space flight cited; report on conference. W. J. Normyle. Aviation W 87:75+ S 11 '67
I spent ninety minutes in hell. R. Gannon. il Pop Sci 191:66-9 Jl '67
See also
Life support systems (space environment)
Space vehicles—Cabin atmospheres
Weightlessness

Psychological aspects
I spent ninety minutes in hell. R. Gannon. il Pop Sci 191:66-9 Jl '67

Safety devices and measures
Views on space flight emergencies marked by diversity. R. D. Hibben. il Aviation W 86:72-3+ My 8 '67

SPACE flight—*Continued*

Social aspects

Selling the space program; excerpts from address. E. C. Welsh. Aviation W 87:11 Jl 24 '67

Terminology

Space jargon. J. Daugherty and M. Daugherty. il Sci Digest 63:88-90 Ja '68

Space sterilization shorthand proposed. R. van Osten and J. A. Redeker. Aero Tech 21:46-7 Ag 14 '67

SPACE flight accidents. See Space flight—Accidents

SPACE flight centers. See Space centers

SPACE flight simulators

I spent ninety minutes in hell. R. Gannon. il Pop Sci 191:66-9 Jl '67

Simulator fire review focuses on filter. Tech W 20:34 F 27 '67

USAF investigation report; electric arcing blamed in simulator fire. Aviation W 86:115-17 Ap 17 '67

SPACE flight to Mars

Industry to get systems work on Mariner/Mars '71 mission. Tech W 20:16 Mr 20 '67

Looking beyond Project Apollo; NASA pressing for funds for mission to Mars. Bsns W p90 Ja 21 '67

Manned Mars flights studied for 1970s. W. J. Normyle. il Aviation W 86:62-3+ Mr 27 '67

Mars; a new world to explore. C. Sagan. il Nat Geog Mag 132:820-41 D '67

Mars data refined. Sci N 91:198 F 25 '67

NASA pushing Mars fly-by for Post-Apollo. H. Taylor. Tech W 20:14-15 F 27 '67

NERVA funds to aid manned Mars fly-by. H. Taylor. Tech W 20:18 Mr 6 '67

Planetary program decision due next month. H. Taylor. Aero Tech 21:14-15 N 6 '67

To go to Mars; nuclear rocket program. C. Behrens. il Sci N 91:336-7 Ap 8 '67

See also

Space probes

SPACE flight to the moon

After Apollo, a colony on the moon. I. Asimov. il N Y Times Mag p30-2+ My 28 '67; Same. Sci Digest 62:44-8+ S '67

Alsep array cut for first moon missions. R. D. Hibben. il Aviation W 86:63+ Ap 3 '67

AAP forecast for fiscal 1969; $450 million. il Aero Tech 21:29-32 N 20 '67

Apollo; calm to come. Sci N 91:401 Ap 29 '67

Apollo; can do? technology and management improvements. il Newsweek 69:94 My 22 '67

Apollo 4 closes gaps to lunar mission. W. J. Normyle. il Aviation W 87:26-8 N 20 '67

Apollo 4 launch to test moon vehicle in nine-hr. flight. Aero Tech 21:17 N 6 '67

Apollo; great flaws in Apollo program as reported in 1965. New Repub 156:6 My 13 '67

Apollo landing site choices. Sci N 91:85 Ja 28 '67

Apollo team finds big reason to smile; successful launching of Apollo/Saturn V system. il Bsns W p62-4 N 18 '67

Apollo 204 fire; new Apollo schedule awaits end of probe. H. Taylor and H. David. il Tech W 20:16-20 Ap 17 '67

Astronauts turn aquanauts as NASA shakes up the lagging moon program. il Life 62:34-5 My 19 '67

Back to the job; aim for a lunar landing by 1970. il Time 89:27-8 My 19 '67

Bidding for moon in 1968; NASA's new timetable to the moon. il Bsns W p80+ F 25 '67

Block 1 manned Apollo missions scrapped in scheduling revision. W. J. Normyle. Aviation W 86:33 F 13 '67

Exit robots, enter man; Surveyor 7 and preparation for launching of the first lunar module. il Newsweek 71:80 Ja 22 '68

Exploration race; moon or sea? J. Lear. il Sat R 50:51-5 Mr 4 '67

First lunar module launch due in January. Aviation W 87:20 N 6 '67

High hopes for the moon shot; chance for lunar landing before 1970. il Bsns W p60-2+ Ap 15 '67

Is moon program in real trouble? il U S News 62:29-32 F 13 '67

Is the race to the moon worth what it costs? J. E. Webb says yes; G. E. Moore says no; Good housekeeping poll. il Good H 164:12+ Je '67

Lunar module set for first space ride. il Bsns W p42 Ja 13 '68

Lunar-power-generator. il Sci Digest 62:35 O '67

Man on the moon; how soon? interview. W. Von Braun. Read Digest 90:136-9 Mr '67

Manned Apollo flight slips to mid-1968. Aviation W 87:18-19 O 2 '67

NASA again revises schedule for Apollo. Aviation W 87:33 N 13 '67

NASA paring landing sites for Apollo. A. Hill. Aero Tech 21:19 D 18 '67

NASA sets safer trim for Apollo; admit fire could have been averted. Bsns W p 160+ Mr 4 '67

NASA to set up Apollo lunar exploration office. H. Taylor. Aero Tech 21:18-19 Ja 1 '68

New Soviet ships aid lunar capabilities. H. Taylor. Aero Tech 21:14 S 11 '67

New space station, long lunar stay-times off until late '70s. A. Hill. il Aero Tech 21:33-4+ N 20 '67

On rocky road to the moon; practical meaning of Apollo disaster. il U S News 62:64 Ap 24 '67

Post-Apollo; NASA's plans get boost from LBJ and PSAC. L. J. Carter. il Science 155:1084-7 Mr 3 '67

Race to the moon; playing with human lives. W. Lippmann. Newsweek 69:31 F 13 '67

Sixteen experiments contend for 1st AAP flight. A. Hill. Tech W 20:37 My 29 '67

Surveyor to sample lunar soil composition. il Tech W 20:17 Ap 3 '67

Third Lunar Orbiter assigned to affirm Apollo landing sites. W. J. Normyle. Aviation W 86:32 Ja 23 '67

Tribute to Apollo I. il Sci Digest 61:9-12 Mr '67

Voyage; Columbus voyage and Apollo mission. W. J. Coughlin. Tech W 20:50 My 29 '67

Why should man go to the moon? Time essay. Time 89:22-3 F 10 '67

See also

Moon—Exploration

Orbital rendezvous (space flight)

Anecdotes, facetiae, satire, etc.

Money up the drain. G. Ace. Sat R 50:8 O 28 '67

Cost

NASA raises tab on moon-landing. il Bsns W p52-3 Ja 14 '67

International aspects

Moon race; after two tragedies. U S News 62:57 My 8 '67

Luna flights

Luna 13 stabs the moon. R. N. Watts, jr. Sky & Tel 33:97 F '67

Manned flights

Manned Soviet circumlunar flight predicted next year. H. Taylor. Aero Tech 21:19 D 4 '67

Orbiter flights

Lunar Orbiter 5. R. N. Watts, jr. Sky & Tel 34:157 S '67

Lunar Orbiter 5 takes unusual pictures. R. N. Watts, jr. il Sky & Tel 34:216-17 O '67

Lunar Orbiter photo quality attributed to tape recorders. R. Pay. il Tech W 20:29-30 Ap 24 '67

Lunar Orbiter team lauded for effort as program is ended. Aero Tech 21:18 S 11 '67

NASA solving camera system problems on Orbiter 4. il Aviation W 86:20-1 My 22 '67

Orbiter 4 to follow Surveyor 3 success. il Tech W 20:20 My 1 '67

Orbiter struggles on; Orbiter 4 in elliptical orbit around the moon. il Sci N 91:496-7 My 27 '67

Orbiters studied for planetary missions. W. J. Normyle. il Aviation W 87:30-2 O 23 '67

Sharp eye of Orbiter V. il Bsns W p55+ Ag 19 '67

Snapping the moon's face; Orbiter 5 pictures. il Time 90:36 Ag 18 '67

Orbiter 1 and Orbiter 2 flights

More on Orbiter 2. R. N. Watts, jr. il Sky & Tel 33:96-7 F '67

Orbiter 3 flight

Apollo site P-1 scanned by Orbiter 3; with photographs. Aviation W 86:20-2 F 27 '67

Cameras on Orbiter 3 scan Apollo, Surveyor landing sites. Aviation W 86:25 F 20 '67

Orbiter 3 achieves initial lunar orbit. Aviation W 86:40 F 13 '67

Surveyor flight, 1967

Moon sampler; soft-landing Surveyor 3. il Sci N 91:352 Ap 15 '67

Surveyor flights

Apollo role seen for next four Surveyors. il Tech W 20:19 Ap 24 '67

Astronauts may find moon a bit like home; findings of Surveyor V. il Bsns W p80-2 O 7 '67

SPACE flight to the moon—Surveyor flights
—*Continued*
Dead on arrival; Surveyor 4. Time 90:69 Jl
28 '67
Dig at the moon. il Time 89:51 Ap 28 '67
Earthlike moon. Time 90:90-1 O 6 '67
Feel of the moon. R. F. Scott. il Sci Am
217:34-43 bibliog(p 154) N '67
Happy landings; Surveyor 5 and Biosatellite
2. Newsweek 70:98 S 25 '67
How Surveyor 5 was saved. R. N. Watts, jr.
il Sky & Tel 34:305-7 N '67
In the lunar highlands. J. Lear. il Sat R 51:
95-8 Ja 6 '68
Last Surveyor to study lunar highlands. G.
S. Hunter. il Aviation W 87:40-1 D 25 '67
Little spacecraft that could. il Time 90:61 N
24 '67
Lunar Orbiter 5 takes unusual pictures; Sur-
veyor 5 to test moon's surface composition.
R. N. Watts, jr. il Sky & Tel 34:217-18
O '67
Moon scoop and Soyuz I; Surveyor 3. il News-
week 69:63 My 1 '67
Moon's soil tested. Sr Schol 91:13-14 O 19 '67
Moonsnaps: a fabulous new approach to the
science of photography. J. Lear. il Sat R
50:45-8 Ag 5 '67
Of gnats and moonbeams; Surveyor 5 and
Biosatellite 2. il Newsweek 70:67 S 18 '67
One for the scientists; Surveyor 7. il Time 91:
75 Ja 19 '68
Space chemistry set tests moon's makeup;
Surveyor V will help clear way for manned
Apollo landing. il Bsns W p48 S 16 '67
Surveyor 5 is alive and on the moon. il Time
90:54 S 22 '67
Surveyor 5 lunar chemistry data studied. I.
Stone. il Aviation W 87:28-9 S 18 '67
Surveyor V; reports. bibliog il Science 158:
631-52 N 3 '67
Surveyor 4 mission ends in signal loss. Avia-
tion W 87:29 Jl 24 '67
Surveyor mission to the moon. J. H. Wujek,
jr. il Electr World 78:41-3 N '67
Surveyor reports. il Sci N 91:425 My 6 '67
Surveyor resumes operation on moon. Avia-
tion W 87:33 O 23 '67
Surveyor 7 investigates lunar highlands. il
Aviation W 88:32-3 Ja 15 '68
Surveyor 3 enters lunar night. il Aviation W
86:27 My 8 '67
Surveyor 3 indicates firm lunar surface. G. S.
Hunter. il Aviation W 86:19-21 My 1 '67
Surveyor 3 on the moon. R. N. Watts, jr. il
Sky & Tel 33:361-3 Je '67
Surveyor 3 sends lunar surface photos. il
Aviation W 86:30-1 Ap 24 '67
Surveyor's moon. il Sci N 91:517-18 Je 3 '67
Virtuosity on the moon. il Time 89:45 My 5
'67
What U.S. learned from new robot on the
moon. U S News 62:14 My 1 '67
SPACE flight to Venus
Manned Mars flights studied for 1970s; Venus
missions also contemplated. W. J. Normyle.
il Aviation W 86:62-3+ Mr 27 '67
Venus 4 underscores U.S. delay. Aviation W
87:26 O 23 '67
See also
Space probes
SPACE heaters. See Electric heaters; Heaters
SPACE medicine
Astronaut monitoring devices groomed for
civilian markets. Tech W 20:22 Ap 17 '67
Four firms deliver spacesuits for MOL. H.
M. David. Tech W 20:38-9 F 13 '67
See also
Space flight—Physiological aspects
SPACE navigation. See Navigation (space
flight)
SPACE people. See Life on other planets
SPACE perception
Behavioral compensation with monocular vis-
ion. R. H. Day and others. bibliog il Science
156:1129-30 My 26 '67
Traffic signals and depth perception. B. R.
Bugelski. bibliog Science 157:1464-5 S 22 '67
SPACE photography
Camera's eye too slow; cloud satellites. il
Sci N 92:153-4 Ag 12 '67
Crazy mixed-up planets; pictures taken by
U.S. navy's DODGE satellite. il Newsweek
70:58-9+ N 6 '67
Eyes of Lunar Orbiter. il U S Camera 30:
18+ F '67
First color portrait of an angry earth. il Life
63:107 N 10 '67
Gifts from out there; with photographs by
H. Sochurek. Esquire 67:92-101 My '67
Historic color portrait of earth from space;
DODGE satellite. K. F. Weaver. il Nat
Geog Mag 132:726-31 N '67
How Lunar Orbiters took dramatic moon
pictures. A. P. Armagnac. il Pop Sci 191:85
D '67

Moonsnaps: a fabulous new approach to the
science of photography. J. Lear. il Sat R
50:45-8 Ag 5 '67
Photography of the earth's cloud satellites
from an aircraft. C. Wolff and others.
bibliog il Science 157:427-9 Jl 28 '67
Sharper eye on the sky; new photographic
emulsion. il Sci Digest 61:61-2 Ap '67
Techniques tomorrow. B. Sherman. Mod Phot
31:42+ O '67
See also
Moon—Photographs, maps, etc.

Apparatus and supplies
Microdot making portable lamp for astro-
nauts in space work. il Aviation W 87:117+
Ag 21 '67
SPACE power systems. See Space vehicles—
Power supply
SPACE probes
Date with Venus; Mariner 5 and Venus 4.
Time 89:33 Je 30 '67
Dec. 13 Pioneer launch set; Ames studies
new missions. Aero Tech 21:52-3 N 6 '67
Double probe sketches planet's portrait; Rus-
sia's Venus 4 and U.S. Mariner 5. il Sci N
92:439-40 N 4 '67
Five sunblazers scheduled; first launch due
in 1968. il Tech W 20:19 F 27 '67
Greenhouse planet. il Newsweek 70:52+ O 30
'67
JPL seeking prime role on Mariner/Mars '71
probe. H. Taylor. Tech W 20:15 My 22 '67
Lockheed study shows probe to Halley's
comet is feasible. il Aero Tech 21:56 Ag 28
'67
Mariner V flight, reports. bibliog il Science
158:1665-90 D 29 '67
Mariner 5 midcourse maneuver succeeds;
Venus flyby. Aviation W 86:21 Je 26 '67
New circumlunar probe; Explorer 35. R. N.
Watts, jr. il Sky & Tel 34:156-7 S '67
Planetary probes are long-term goals. Avia-
tion W 86:138-9 Mr 6 '67
Pole-sitting spacecraft is Venus-bound; Mar-
iner 5. il Sci N 91:207 Mr 4 '67
Preliminary results from the Venus probes.
R. N. Watts, jr. Sky & Tel 34:365 D '67
Racing to Venus. il Newsweek 70:48 Jl 3 '67
Secrets of Venus that Russia unlocked. il
U S News 63:14 O 30 '67
Soviet, U.S. contradictions? Venus 4, Mariner
5 space probes. il Sr Schol 91:16 N 2 '67
Soviets, U.S. launch probes toward Venus
two days apart; Venus 4 and Mariner 5.
Aviation W 86:24 Je 19 '67
Space: 1971 Mariner mission knifed by budget-
cutters. L. J. Carter. Science 157:658-60 Ag
11 '67
Two touches of Venus. il Time 90:74 O 27 '67
U.S. tries to renew Mariner 4 contact. Avia-
tion W 86:40 Je 12 '67
Venus revealed; findings of Russia's Venus 4
and the U.S.'s Mariner 5. Time 90:45 N 3 '67
Voyager, manned fly-by may be combined.
A. Hill. Tech W 20:20 Mr 13 '67
Warm touch of Venus; Soviet's Venera-4 re-
ports. il Bsns W p49 O 21 '67
SPACE probes, Russian
Conversation about Venus; Soviet-U.S. dia-
logue via Britain. J. Lear. Sat R 50:60-1
N 4 '67
Double probe sketches planet's portrait; Ve-
nus 4. il Sci N 92:439-40 N 4 '67
Early cutoff of transmissions from Venus 4
unexplained. H. Rausch. il Aviation W 87:
17-18 N 6 '67
Fouled antenna impairs Venus 4 mission. il
Aviation W 87:24-5 O 30 '67
Soviets, U.S. launch probes toward Venus
two days apart; Venus 4 and Mariner 5.
Aviation W 86:24 Je 19 '67
SPACE propulsion. See Space vehicles—Pro-
pulsion systems
SPACE rescue work
Industry offers wide range of space rescue
system plans. H. M. David. Tech W 20:30-1
Mr 20 '67
Lifeboats for astronauts. il Time 90:62 Ag
4 '67
Orbiting rescue vehicle proposed by GPI;
Orpheus rescue system. K. Voss. il Tech
W 20:32-3 Ap 10 '67
Rescue service for astronauts. il Time 89:55
Mr 10 '67
Space rescue methods urged by Congress.
Tech W 20:35 Mr 6 '67
Views on space flight emergencies marked by
diversity. R. D. Hibben. il Aviation W 86:
72-3+ My 8 '67
SPACE research
Chronology of fiscal 1967. Aero Tech 21:121-5
Jl 31 '67

SPACE research—*Continued*
Impact of space research on science and technology. H. E. Newell and L. Jaffe. il Science 157:29-39 Jl 7 '67
Next five years in space. W. Ley. il Pop Mech 127:93-7+ F '67
Space at the crossroads. R. Hotz. Aviation W 87:21 O 9 '67
Space notes. Sci N 91:166, 191, 247, 283, 298 F 18-25, Mr 11, 25-Ap 1 '67
Upward bound; accomplishments and objectives. il Newsweek 70:89 O 9 '67
　See also
Artificial satellites—Use in research
International council of scientific unions—Committee on space research
United Nations—Committee on the peaceful uses of outer space

Economic aspects
Concern mounts over long-term support. il Aero Tech 21:66-70 N 20 '67
Modest goals, benefits seen key to future. J. Rhea. il Aero Tech 21:21-2+ S 11 '67
Space program: a citizen's return on investment; address, September 13, 1967. J. L. Helms. Vital Speeches 34:176-81 Ja 1 '68

International aspects
Astronauts and cosmonauts, unite! E. Diamond. Newsweek 69:68-9 My 8 '67
Conversation about Venus; Soviet-U.S. dialogue via Britain. J. Lear. Sat R 50:60-1 N 4 '67
NASA international; agreements between NASA and nineteen countries. J. Eberhart. il Sci N 91:576-7 Je 17 '67
NASA official raps Soviets at AAS meeting. Aero Tech 21:47 D 4 '67
Space diplomacy; excerpts from address. R. F. Packard. Aviation W 86:17 Mr 20 '67
Tyranny of realism. D. E. Kash. Bul Atomic Sci 23:16-20 F '67
　See also
United Nations—Committee on the peaceful uses of outer space

Military applications
Military's drive to move into space; a decade of delays. il U S News 63:38 N 20 '67

Europe, Western
Booster recovery continues as Europe space challenge. R. G. O'Lone. Aviation W 86:369+ My 29 '67
Europe irons out issues in initial space programs. W. C. Wetmore. il Aviation W 86:146-7+ Mr 6 '67
That technology gap. W. J. Coughlin. Tech W 20:50 Ap 10 '67
　See also
European space research organization

France
French space budget totaling $141 million. D. E. Fink. Aviation W 87:24-5 N 6 '67
French space program begins new phase; scientific mission of Diademe series. W. C. Wetmore. il Aviation W 86:50-1+ Mr 27 '67
Increase forecast in French space budget. il Aviation W 86:360-1+ My 29 '67

Great Britain
Strong U.K. national space effort urged. Aviation W 87:33 Ag 14 '67

Italy
Italy's African space triumph; launch from sea-borne pad; with report by M. Durham. il Life 62:101-2+ My 26 '67

Japan
Dispute clouds Japan aerospace efforts. R. F. Coburn. il Aviation W 88:47+ Ja 8 '68
Japan bids for a place in space; third attempt to loft small satellite into earth orbit. il Bsns W p 158-9 Mr 4 '67
Japan may share rocket range. W. A. Scholes. Sci N 93:10+ Ja 6 '68

Russia
Cosmos flights seen ICBM aids. P. J. Klass. Aviation W 87:26-7 O 16 '67
House unit reports Soviet payload gains. D. C. Winston. il Aviation W 87:96-8 D 4 '67
New Soviet manned flights anticipated. M. Getler. Tech W 20:16 Mr 13 '67
New Soviet ships aid lunar capabilities. H. Taylor. Aero Tech 21:14 S 11 '67
New Soyuz flight forecast in try to meet schedule. W. J. Normyle. Aviation W 86:22 My 1 '67
New vigor by Soviets expected in manned space flight. D. Winston. il Aviation W 86:140-3+ Mr 6 '67

Pennant on Venus. R. S. Lewis. il Bul Atomic Sci 23:19-24 N '67
Robot on the moon. il Sci Digest 61:33-4 Mr '67
Second decade. M. Getler. Aero Tech 21:136+ N 20 '67
Soviet space efforts detailed. Sci N 92:534-5 D 2 '67
Soviet space spectacular? D. L. Flaherty. America 116:370-2 Mr 18 '67
Who is ahead in the space race now? il U S News 63:78-9 O 9 '67

United States
After Apollo, what? Sci Am 216:50 Ap '67
America's lag in space race. il U S News 63:43-5 N 6 '67
Are we to abandon the planets to the Soviet Union? J. A. Van Allen. Science 158:1405 D 15 '67
Blessings and evils of space travel. H. C. Urey. Bul Atomic Sci 23:24-5 F '67
Exploitation of space technology boosted; special report: AAS annual meeting; with editorial comment. W. J. Coughlin and others. il Tech W 20:18-20, 50 My 8 '67
First AAP flight slips to 1969 due to NASA budget cuts. H. Taylor. il Aero Tech 21:18 Ag 14 '67
Fund cuts redirect space plans. Aviation W 87:32 Ag 14 '67
Future space program. P. H. Abelson. Science 155:1367 Mr 17 '67
Industry told of responsibility to continue space program. W. S. Beller and C. D. LaFond. il Tech W 20:46-7 My 15 '67
Interest in space found lagging. Aviation W 87:72 D 18 '67
Karth: practical benefits needed to buoy space science; ed. by W. S. Beller. J. E. Karth. il Tech W 20:18-19 Ap 3 '67
Mars fly-by project dies as two MSC contracts are cancelled. A. Hill. Aero Tech 21:16-17 O 23 '67
Martin wins Apollo applications integration contract. Aero Tech 21:10 Jl 31 '67
NASA identifies twenty-one promising new missions. Tech W 20:20 Je 12 '67
[NASA issue] ed. by H. Taylor. il Aero Tech 21:24-34+ N 20 '67
NASA pushes planetary program. W. J. Normyle. Aviation W 87:16-17 N 27 '67
NASA realigns '67 money in four areas. H. M. David. Tech W 20:17 F 20 '67
NASA seeking alternatives for Voyager. H. Taylor. il Aero Tech 21:16-17 Ag 28 '67
NASA: walking orders; post-Apollo space program. il Sci N 92:57-8 Jl 15 '67
NASA's full calendar. il Bsns W p88+ Ja 21 '67
NASA's post-moon pitch: research. J. Eberhart. il Sci N 91:60-1 Ja 21 '67
New capabilities broaden scientific goals. W. J. Normyle. il Aviation W 86:54-5+ Ja 23 '67
New markets for aerospace technology; symposium; with editorial comment. il Tech W 20:20-4+, 66 Je 5 '67
Pennant on Venus. R. S. Lewis. il Bul Atomic Sci 23:19-24 N '67
Planetary exploration: how to get by the budget-cutters? L. J. Carter. Science 158:1025-8 N 24 '67
Planetary program support seen lacking. W. J. Normyle. Aviation W 87:32-3 D 11 '67
Post-Apollo: NASA's plans get boost from LBJ and PSAC. L. J. Carter. il Science 155:1084-7 Mr 3 '67
Priority shift blocks space plans. W. J. Normyle. Aviation W 87:26-7 S 11 '67
Science advisers urge balanced program. Aviation W 86:133+ Mr 6 '67
Science and space policy. Bul Atomic Sci 23:2-24 Mr: 9-10 Ap: 2-20 My '67
Science and space policy; symposium. il Bul Atomic Sci 23:2-24 Mr '67
Second decade. M. Getler. Aero Tech 21:136+ N 20 '67
$7 billion NASA budget seen following Mars goal. il Tech W 20:16 F 20 '67
Single new space goal rejection urged; integrated NASA-Defense dept. plan for lunar exploration, planetary and applications missions. W. J. Normyle. Aviation W 86:19 F 20 '67
Smog control; gloom about space program. M. Getler. Aero Tech 21:62 N 6 '67
Space pace; U.S. space program threatened. M. Getler. Aero Tech 21:62 O 23 '67
Space program: a citizen's return on investment; address, September 13, 1967. J. L. Helms. Vital Speeches 34:176-81 Ja 1 '68
Space race hits economy hurdle. il Bsns W p41-2+ Ja 13 '68
Space: two safe trips. Sci N 92:299 S 23 '67

SPACE research—United States—*Continued*
That technology gap. W. J. Coughlin. Tech W 20:50 Ap 10 '67
U.S. space funding to grow moderately. il Aviation W 86:123-6 Mr 6 '67
U.S. space program: a long view; address, May 15, 1967. B. A Schriever. Vital Speeches 34:26-8 O 15 '67
Who is ahead in the space race now? il U S News 63:78-9 O 9 '67
See also
Space flight
United States—National aeronautics and space administration

SPACE scales. See Scales (weighing instruments)

SPACE science and applications, Office of. See United States—National aeronautics and space administration—Space science and applications, Office of

SPACE science board. See National academy of sciences—Space science board

SPACE shoes. See Astronauts—Clothing

SPACE-simulation chambers. See Testing laboratories

SPACE stations
Air force is climbing to a wild new yonder; manned orbit laboratory (MOL) program. il Bsns W p26-8 Jl 8 '67
Four firms deliver spacesuits for MOL. H. M. David. Tech W 20:38-9 F 13 '67
Fund cuts force two-year stretch in MOL. Aviation W 87:22 N 27 '67
MOL computer weds two technologies. R. Pay. il Tech W 20:26-7 Ap 3 '67
MOL cost up $700 million to $2.2 billion. M. Getler. Tech W 20:14 My 8 '67
MOL increases opportunities in military space activities. il Aviation W 86:117-19 Mr 6 '67
MOL launch complex geared to growth. W. E. Wilks. il Tech W 20:20-4 Ap 10 '67
MSC awards space station study pacts. Tech W 20:22+ Mr 27 '67
NASA plans ahead; Apollo applications. il Sci N 91:137 F 11 '67
NASA pushes orbital workshop program; orbital applications center. G. S. Hunter. il Aviation W 86:70-1+ Mr 20 '67
New space station, long lunar stay-times off until late '70s. A. Hill. il Aero Tech 21:33-4+ N 20 '67
Orbiting factory seen for 1990's. Sci N 91:466 My 20 '67
RCA planning AAP studies of solar effects; proposed manned orbiting meteorological observatory. R. Barnhart. il Tech W 20:35 F 6 '67
S-IVB support as interim space station. il Aero Tech 21:29-30+ Jl 17 '67
S-IVB workshop undergoes design, schedule changes. A. Hill. il Aero Tech 21:26-8+ O 9 '67

Economic aspects
Space station commercial potential cited. E. H. Kolcum. Aviation W 87:22-3 O 2 '67

Equipment
Space cherrypickers. il Sci Digest 62:21 N '67
SPACE suits. See Astronauts—Clothing
SPACE systems division. See United States—Air force—Systems command
SPACE technology
Commercial development of space urged. il Aviation W 86:67+ My 15 '67
Exploitation of space technology boosted; special report: AAS annual meeting; with editorial comment. W. J. Coughlin. and others. il Tech W 20:18-20, 50 My 8 '67
House unit reports Soviet payload gains. D. C. Winston. il Aviation W 87:96-8 D 4 '67
Manned planetary vehicle study proposed. 1. Stone. Aviation W 87:87+ O 2 '67
NASA pushes orbital workshop program. G. S. Hunter. il Aviation W 86:70-1+ Mr 20 '67
NASA studies ATS-3 switch to new position over Pacific. B. K. Thomas, jr. Aviation W 87:20 N 27 '67
New capabilities broaden scientific goals. W. J. Normyle. il Aviation W 86:54-5+ Ja 23 '67
Post-Apollo program potential emerging. W. J. Normyle. il Aviation W 86:126-7+ Mr 6 '67
Risk of knowing space. Life 62:4 My 5 '67
Space suit and life support projects escape trimming. il Aero Tech 21:100-5 N 20 '67
Space technology and progress. W. Von Braun. Tech W 20:36-8 Ja 23 '67
World technology grows in sophistication. H. J. Coleman. il Aviation W 87:79+ S 4 '67

SPACE technology conference
Europeans firm on aerospace transporter. W. E. Wilks. Tech W 20:36-7 Mr 13 '67
No joint agreement in sight on reusable space hardware. il Tech W 20:38-9 My 22 '67

SPACE telemetry
Nimbus-D telemetry eyed for new uses. il Aero Tech 21:31+ N 6 '67
PCM telemetry for C-5A evolved from space effort. C. D. LaFond. il Tech W 20:32-3 Ap 17 '67
VHF voice relayed via ATS-3 to 707. Aviation W 87:28 N 27 '67

SPACE vehicle models
LTV designs service vehicles for space. E. J. Bulban. il Aviation W 86:79-80 My 8 '67
Paris air show; Soviet displays again dominate exposition. H. Taylor. il Tech W 20: 12-15 Je 5 '67
Pint-sized Surveyor. il Sci Digest 62:30-1 Ag '67

SPACE vehicles
Annual world aerospace encyclopedia 1967. il Aero Tech 21:21-32+ Jl 31 '67
Astrolog; current status of U.S. missile and space programs. il Aero Tech 21:38-9 Ja 1 '68
Orbiting rescue vehicle proposed by GPI; Orpheus rescue system. K. Voss. il Tech W 20:32-3 Ap 10 '67
Saturn 5 success quickens Apollo pace. Aviation W 87:32-3 N 13 '67
U.S. & international spacecraft; specifications (cont) Aviation W 86:177-8 Mr 6 '67
Voyager teams to be picked within year. H. Taylor. il Tech W 20:18-19 Mr 20 '67

Atmospheric entry
Extended Athena program improved by man in the loop; successful flight-test of the first FATE vehicle. W. Wilks. il Tech W 20:17 Ap 24 '67
NASA still trying to solve problem of re-entry blackout. il Aero Tech 21:50 O 23 '67
Recoverable vehicle patents eyed for future space use. W. E. Wilks. il Tech W 20:36-7 Ap 3 '67
Spacecraft ground landings under study; testing of glide parachutes. G. Alexander. il Aviation W 86:48-9+ Je 5 '67
USAF nears manned lifting body tests. B. K. Thomas, jr. il Aviation W 87:99-101 Jl 10 '67

Atomic power plants
Fuel capsules of Snap-29 are being tested. Aviation W 88:33 Ja 15 '68
GE reports successful tests of radioisojet microthruster; propulsion system using nuclear power source. il Tech W 20:34-5 My 8 '67
SNAP-27 readied for tests with ALSEP; Apollo lunar surface experiments package. W. S. Beller. il Tech W 20:23-5 My 1 '67
Support continues for Snap development. il Aviation W 86:161+ Mr 6 '67
Turbo-alternator power units pass tests for AEC at TRW. W. S. Beller. il Tech W 20:36-7 My 29 '67

Cabin atmospheres
Accident reviving ECS gas controversy. Aviation W 86:34-6 F 6 '67
Apollo 204; oxygen environment a peril in space? K. Voss and others. il Tech W 20: 12-17 F 6 '67
Apollo's final seconds. il Newsweek 69:96+ F 13 '67
Atmosphere inside a spacecraft. R. N. Watts, jr. il Sky & Tel 33:139-40 Mr '67
Beating the spacecraft fire peril. A. P. Armagnac. il Pop Sci 190:96-8+ Je '67
Biological hazards in space cited. W. J. Normyle. Aviation W 87:17 Ag 21 '67
Carbon dioxide removal unit developed by Ham Standard. Tech W 20:29 Ap 10 '67
Hatch redesign, safety features considered for Apollo modules. Aviation W 86:23-4 F 20 '67
Oxygen question. Time 89:18 F 10 '67
Respiration in space: a warning. Sci N 91: 306 Ap 1 '67
Soviets expected to change future spacecraft atmospheres. Tech W 20:31 My 8 '67
Study shows helium increases fire hazards. H. M. David. il Tech W 20:22-3 Mr 13 '67
Tragedy breeds change; proposed two-gas system. Sci N 91:161 F 18 '67
Troubles with Apollo. Sci N 91:136 F 11 '67

Control systems
GE electric microthruster using Teflon wax as fuel; testing its applicability to spacecraft attitude stabilization. J. Rhea. il Tech W 21:22 Jl 3 '67

SPACE vehicles—Control systems—*Continued*

Microelectronic unit readied for Saturn 1U; advanced control signal processor. il Aero Tech 21:40 O 23 '67

New missions seen dictating tracking system changes. A. Hill. Tech W 20:16 Ap 3 '67

New Soyuz flight forecast in try to meet schedule. W. J. Normyle. Aviation W 86:22 My 1 '67

100-ft.-lb.-sec. momentum produced by 65-lb. CMG. il Aero Tech 21:40-1 Ag 28 '67

Design

Apollo changes slip first manned flight to mid-1968. A. Hill. Aero Tech 21:21 S 25 '67

Chances slim for '67 manned Apollo flight. il Tech W 20:22 Mr 6 '67

Contract awards, proposal bids advance Voyager design work. Aviation W 86:68 My 29 '67

Design changes shown in block 2 Apollo boilerplate; with photographs. Aviation W 86:22-3 My 22 '67

Enlarged Gemini proposed as space ferry. G. Alexander. il Aviation W 86:20-1 Je 19 '67

Manned planetary vehicle study proposed. I. Stone. Aviation W 87:87+ O 2 '67

NAA facing heavy loss of AAP funding. H. Taylor and H. M. David. il Tech W 20:19-22 My 15 '67

NASA details sweeping Apollo revisions. W. J. Normyle. Aviation W 86:24-6 My 15 '67

Rescue study urges major design changes. H. Taylor. il Tech W 20:16 Ap 24 '67

Tests of modified Apollo systems set this fall. Aviation W 86:40 Je 12 '67

Electric equipment

Inquiry focuses on electrical systems. il Aviation W 86:30-4 F 6 '67

Electronic equipment

Electrostatic accelerometer scores firsts in Agena flight. il Aero Tech 21:41-2 Ag 28 '67

Planar electroluminescent cell developed. B. M. Elson. il Aviation W 87:101+ D 11 '67

Pointing system tested in space. Aviation W 87:27 D 11 '67

Equipment

EG&G lights help monitor Saturn tanks. Aero Tech 21:41 N 6 '67

Extra gear in Apollo ship. Aero Tech 21:10 N 6 '67

Flexi-firm tether. il Time 89:86-7 Ap 14 '67

Handyman tools for space. il Sci Digest 62:32 S '67

One step nearer a lunar landing; Surveyor III spacecraft equipped with mechanical shovel. il Bsns W p74-6 Ap 29 '67

Orbiter 4 to follow Surveyor 3 success. il Tech W 20:20 My 1 '67

Orbiter sends back pictures of moon's equatorial gap. G. S. Hunter. il Aviation W 87:28-30 Ag 14 '67

RCA developing laser beam camera unit. K. J. Stein. il Aviation W 87:83+ O 16 '67

Soil probes for space: penetrometers. S. V. Jones. il Sci Digest 62:82-3 D '67

Surveyor 3 sends lunar surface photos. il Aviation W 86:30-1 Ap 24 '67

Surveyor to sample lunar soil composition; Surveyor C. il Tech W 20:17 Ap 3 '67

Three new cameras headed for space use. W. S. Beller. il Tech W 20:42+ My 22 '67

See also

Artificial satellites—Equipment

Life support systems (space environment)

Escape devices

Escape cocoon. S. V. Jones. il Sci Digest 62: 81 O '67

Hatch redesign, safety features considered for Apollo modules Aviation W 86:23-4 F 20 '67

MSC begins design work on space escape system. A. Hill. il Aero Tech 21:21-2 Ag 14 '67

NASA designs new Apollo hatch. W. J. Normyle. il Aviation W 86:22-3 Mr 20 '67

NASA plans to order study of astronaut escape devices. Aviation W 87:46 N 27 '67

New hatch slashes Apollo egress time. il Aviation W 86:26-7 My 15 '67

Space escape capsule ideas under study for air force. W. E. Wilks. il Tech W 20:24-5 My 15 '67

Fires and fire protection

Apollo contractor criticisms, fixes summarized for House committee; text of summary. Aviation W 86:28-9 Ap 24 '67

Apollo fire believed hottest near ECU. G. Alexander. Aviation W 86:22-3 F 20 '67

Apollo; great flaws in Apollo program as reported in 1965. New Repub 156:6 My 13 '67

Apollo story: we never thought... il Sci N 91:373-4 Ap 22 '67

Apollo 204. J. G. Dunne. Sat Eve Post 240: 20+ Je 17 '67

Apollo 204 fire forcing design changes. il Tech W 20:18-19 F 13 '67

Apollo 204 fire; new Apollo schedule awaits end of probe. H. Taylor and H. David. il Tech W 20:16-20 Ap 17 '67

Apollo 204; oxygen environment, a peril in space? K. Voss and others. il Tech W 20: 12-17 F 6 '67

Apollo 204 review. W. J. Coughlin. Tech W 20:50 Ap 17 '67

Apollo water-glycol line breaks studied. G. Alexander. Aviation W 86:25-6 F 27 '67

Apollo's final seconds. il Newsweek 69:96+ F 13 '67

Blind spot; concerning report on the Apollo disaster. il Time 89:22-3 Ap 21 '67

Board presses Apollo 204 investigation. G. Alexander. Aviation W 86:34-6 F 13 '67

Board reports on Apollo fire investigation; text of inquiry report. il Aviation W 86: 100-1+ Ap 17 '67

Death by miscalculation; Apollo changes. il Newsweek 69:94 Mr 13 '67

Fire in the spacecraft! il Newsweek 69:25-9 F 6 '67

Fire kills three astronauts. il Sr Schol 90: 16 F 10 '67

Fire test critical for Apollo module. Aviation W 87:19-20 O 2 '67

Fire tests lift Apollo vehicle confidence. il Aviation W 87:43 D 25 '67

Fireproofing Apollo. il Time 90:38 S 1 '67

How soon the moon? three months investigation of the Apollo 204 fire. il Time 89:86 Ap 14 '67

Inquest on Apollo. il Time 89:18-19 F 10 '67

Inquiry focuses on electrical systems. il Aviation W 86:30-4 F 6 '67

Is moon program in real trouble? il U S News 62:29-32 F 13 '67

NASA implements board findings; with text of summary findings and editorial comment. W. J. Normyle. il Aviation W 86:21, 26-33 Ap 17 '67

NASA sets safer trim for Apollo; admit fire could have been averted. Bsns W p 160+ Mr 4 '67

NASA to detail Apollo fire impact. D. C. Winston. Aviation W 86:16-17 My 8 '67

On tragedy; deaths of the Apollo astronauts. W. J. Coughlin. Tech W 20:50 F 6 '67

Ricky road to the moon; Apollo tragedy and another fire during air force test. il Bsns W p25-7 F 4 '67

Search begins in the scorched capsule. il Life 62:30-1 F 10 '67

Simulator fire review focuses on filter. Tech W 20:34 F 27 '67

Study shows helium increases fire hazards. H. M. David. il Tech W 20:22-3 Mr 13 '67

Ten desperate minutes; Apollo fire; eyewitness reports; interviews; ed. by M. Smith and others. il Life 62:113-14 Ap 21 '67

Text of NASA summary of Phillips report; with editorial comment. S. Phillips. Tech W 20:39-40, 50 Ap 24 '67

Text of preliminary report on Apollo 204 fire cause. R. C. Seamans, jr. il Tech W 20: 20+ F 13 '67; Same. Aviation W 86:34-5 F 13 '67

To strive, to seek, to find, and not to yield: death of three astronauts. il Time 89:13-16 F 3 '67

Tragedy at Cape Kennedy. Nation 204:195-6 F 13 '67

Tragedy at the Cape. R. Hotz. Aviation W 86: 17 F 6 '67

USAF investigation report: electric arcing blamed in simulator fire. Aviation W 86: 115-17 Ap 17 '67

Verdict on Apollo. il Newsweek 69:89-90 Ap 24 '67

We knew that someday... Sci N 91:112 F 4 '67

Fuel

See Rockets—Fuel

Fuel tanks

Radiation shielding developed for cryogenic fuel storage. J. F. Judge. il Tech W 20:30 Ap 3 '67

Landing systems

How we'll bring spacemen down on land. W. Von Braun. il Pop Sci 190:86-7+ Mr '67

SPACE vehicles—Landing systems—*Continued*

Moon

Exhaust effects on LM surfaces predicted. D. A. Anderton. il Tech W 20:34-5 Ap 17 '67

How we'll land on the moon. W. Von Braun. il Pop Sci 191:45-7+ Ag '67

Lunar descent, ascent engines to simulate roles in earth orbit. W. J. Normyle. Aviation W 87:19 D 25 '67

MSC defining AAP land recovery ideas. A. Hill. Tech W 20:22 My 1 '67

NASA considers lunar module changes. Aviation W 86:18 Mr 13 '67

NASA mounts effort to control lunar module weight problems. W. J. Normyle. Aviation W 87:32 O 16 '67

New lunar module versions taking shape. M. Getler. il Tech W 20:28-9+ Je 29 '67

Soil test indicates clear vision for astronauts in lunar landing. il Aviation W 87:23 N 27 '67

Some landing systems omitted from lunar module test flight. Aviation W 88:29 Ja 15 '68

Surveyor 5 lunar chemistry data studied. I. Stone. il Aviation W 87:28-9 S 18 '67

Launching

AS-501 move set to launch Complex. Aviation W 87:32-3 Ag 28 '67

Mariner-5 launch sequence. R. N. Watts, jr. il Sky & Tel 34:89 Ag '67

Russians sketch Vostok launch; sequence parallels U.S. method. il Aviation W 86:117 Je 12 '67

Saturn V automatic checkout uses multiple-media displays. il Aero Tech 21:41-2 D 4 '67

Saturn 5 mission will simulate key lunar landing flight events. W. J. Normyle. Aviation W 87:21 S 25 '67

SESP plans at least three '68 shots; air force's space experiment support program. F. Burnham. il Aero Tech 21:17-18 Ja 1 '68

That puzzling problem for space launches: weather. W. Von Braun. il Pop Sci 191:102-4 S '67

See also
Artificial satellites—Launching

Launching pads

Monitoring system to provide data on Saturn V vibrations. il Tech W 20:30 Ap 24 '67

Launching sites

Alligator on the pad! L. B. Taylor, jr. il Sci Digest 62:53-7 D '67

Maintenance and repair

LTV designs service vehicles for space. E. J. Bulban. il Aviation W 86:79-80 My 8 '67

Materials

See also
Shielding (heat)

Orbits

Orbiters studied for planetary missions. W. J. Normyle. il Aviation W 87:30-2 O 23 '67

Power supply

Cell studies spur solar power advances. G. S. Hunter. il Aviation W 87:94-5+ Ag 28 '67

Eight areas to get 80 per cent-90 per cent of funds. il Aero Tech 21:58+ N 20 '67

Radiation shielding developed for cryogenic fuel storage. J. F. Judge. il Tech W 20:30 Ap 3 '67

Requirements for solar arrays spurring new techniques. G. S. Hunter. il Aviation W 87:72-7+ Ag 14 '67

Views mixed on high-power generation for spacecraft; report on Intersociety energy conversion engineering conference. P. J. Klass. il Aviation W 87:96-7+ S 11 '67

Waste makes haste: rocket fuel made of human waste. J. Eberhart. il Sci N 92:236-7 S 2 '67

See also
Space vehicles—Atomic power plants

Propulsion systems

Air force buys Titans for 1969-71 missions. Aviation W 87:23 Jl 31 '67

Apollo 4 closes gaps to lunar mission. W. J. Normyle. il Aviation W 87:26-8 N 20 '67

Apollo team finds big reason to smile; successful launching of Apollo/Saturn V system. il Bsns W p62-4 N 18 '67

Biggest blastoff yet; Saturn V. il Bsns W p34 S 2 '67

Biggest; success of Saturn 5. il Newsweek 70:68-9+ N 20 '67

Blast to the moon; Saturn V. il Sr Schol 91:24 N 30 '67

Doctor Von Braun's all-purpose space machine; Saturn V. G. Bylinsky. il Fortune 75:142-9+ My '67

First stage solid considerations. Aero Tech 21:15 D 4 '67

French reveal three new launch vehicles. L. Doty. il Aviation W 86:24-5 Je 5 '67

High energy engines get OART go-ahead. J. F. Judge. il Aero Tech 21:77-8+ N 20 '67

Improved Agena to increase launch vehicle payload 25 per cent. R. Lindsey. Tech W 20:29-30 My 29 '67

Improvements under way on Titan vehicles. W. E. Wilks. il Tech W 20:24-5+ My 29 '67

LM ascent engine snags may delay first manned shot. Aero Tech 21:17 Ag 14 '67

Marquardt sees $2-billion market for control rockets. W. E. Wilks. il Aero Tech 21:44+ S 11 '67

Mission problems beset electric propulsion. J. F. Judge. il Aero Tech 21:27-9 S 11 '67

Moon rocket's debut: colossal; success of Saturn V. il U S News 63:41 N 20 '67

Moonward bound; Saturn 5. il Time 90:84-5 N 17 '67

NASA may swap two Apollo boosters. Aviation W 86:23 Mr 20 '67

NASA postpones decision on new booster for mid-1970's. Tech W 20:26 Mr 27 '67

Need seen for intermediate class of launch vehicles. Tech W 20:31 Je 19 '67

New launch vehicle for mid-'70s seen. Aero Tech 21:17 O 9 '67

No joint agreement in sight on reusable space hardware. il Tech W 20:38-9 My 22 '67

NERVA funds to aid manned Mars fly-by. H. Taylor. Tech W 20:18 Mr 6 '67

Russians sketch Vostok launch; sequence parallels U.S. method. il Aviation W 86:117 Je 12 '67

Saturn 5 success quickens Apollo pace. Aviation W 87:32-3 N 13 '67

Saturn 5 trajectory near predicted data. Aviation W 87:28 N 20 '67

Saturn flight data meet NASA objectives. W. J. Normyle. il Aviation W 87:28-30 D 4 '67

Space MAC urged for launch economy. R. G. O'Lone. il Aviation W 86:49+ My 22 '67

Studies show feasibility of Minuteman as launch vehicle. il Aero Tech 21:25 Ag 14 '67

Stupendous Saturn V: the free world's largest space vehicle. il Pop Mech 128:96-9+ Jl '67

Supersonic aircraft studied as launchers. W. J. Normyle. Aviation W 86:54+ Je 26 '67

Titan, modified Saturn in NASA future. R. W. Niblock. il Aero Tech 21:106-8 N 20 '67

To go to Mars; nuclear rocket program. C. Behrens. il Sci N 91:336-7 Ap 8 '67

U.S. launch vehicles; International launch vehicles; specifications (cont) Aviation W 86:179-80 Mr 6 '67

Upgraded NERVA gets space engine role. il Aero Tech 21:40-3 N 20 '67

See also
Ion engines
Rocket engines
Solid propellant rockets
Space vehicles—Atomic power plants

Design

Saturn 5 only a beginning. J. Eberhart. il Sci N 92:472-3 N 11 '67

Safety devices and measures

Measuring missile explosions. E. A. Lacy and C. N. Golub. il Electr World 78:23-6 S '67

Testing

Excellence aloft; exuberance in the bunker; Apollo's Saturn 5 rocket. il Sci N 92:513-14 N 25 '67

French trying to learn cause of Coralie misfire. Aviation W 87:35 Ag 14 '67

GE seeking flight test microthruster; solid-propellant electrical thruster system. W. C. Wetmore. il Aviation W 86:62-3+ Ja 30 '67

Impact of the supershot; Saturn V. il Life 63:28-30 N 24 '67

Lower stage retrorocket firing found harmless to S-4B stage. il Aviation W 86:61+ Je 5 '67

Lunar descent, ascent engines to simulate roles in earth orbit. W. J. Normyle. Aviation W 87:19 D 25 '67

MOL launch complex geared to growth. W. E. Wilks. il Tech W 20:20-4 Ap 10 '67

S-1C test to mark progress in Mississippi. K. Voss. il Tech W 20:28-9 F 6 '67

Saturn V shot set for Sept. Tech W 20:19 Je 26 '67

Snag for Saturn; maiden flight of Saturn 5 rocket postponed. il Newsweek 70:72 Ag 28 '67

SPACE vehicles—*Continued*

Recovery

Apollo module survives flight. il Aviation W 87:29 N 20 '67

Booster recovery continues as Europe space challenge. R. G. O'Lone. Aviation W 86:369+ My 29 '67

Higher L/D lifting bodies may face strong challenge. il Aero Tech 21:30-1 Ag 14 '67

Lift from the lifting body; air force SV-5D. il Time 89:73-4 Mr 17 '67

NASA sets plan to quarantine returning lunar mission crew. A. Hill. il Aero Tech 21:52-3 Ag 28 '67

Recoverable vehicle patents eyed for future space use. W. E. Wilks. il Tech W 20:36-7 Ap 3 '67

Second prime lifting body lost after successful test flight. Aviation W 86:23 Mr 13 '67

Spacecraft ground landings under study; testing of glide parachutes. G. Alexander. il Aviation W 86:48-9+ Je 5 '67

Safety devices and measures

Apollo 204 fire; new Apollo schedule awaits end of probe. H. Taylor and H. David. il Tech W 20:16-20 Ap 17 '67

Inside story of the new Apollo. P. Ditzel. il Pop Sci 191:96-100 N '67

Rocketing out of emergencies. W. Von Braun. il Pop Sci 190:112-14 Ap '67

Science and space policy; editorial introduction. R. S. Lewis. Bul Atomic Sci 23:9-10 Ap '67

See also

Space vehicles—Escape devices

Space vehicles—Fires and fire protection

Shielding (heat)

Self-regulating cooling method developed by Martin/Orlando. Tech W 20:37-8 Mr 13 '67

Shielding (radiation)

Radiation shielding developed for cryogenic fuel storage. J. F. Judge. il Tech W 20:30 Ap 3 '67

Stability and stabilizers

GE electric microthruster using Teflon wax as fuel; testing its applicability to spacecraft attitude stabilization. J. Rhea. il Tech W 21:22 Jl 3 '67

See also

Gyroscopes

Sterilization

Contamination safeguards grow in cost, complexity. Aviation W 87:68+ Ag 7 '67

JPL scientists challenge sterilization goals. H. M. David. Tech W 20:32-3 My 1 '67

NASA sets plan to quarantine returning lunar mission crew. A. Hill. il Aero Tech 21:52-3 Ag 28 '67

Planetary contamination I: the problem and the agreements. N. H. Horowitz and others. bibliog Science 155:1501-5 Mr 24 '67; Discussion. 156:1436; 157-582-3 Je 16, Ag 4 '67

Planetary contamination II: Soviet and U.S. practices and policies. B. C. Murray and others. bibliog il Science 155:1505-11 Mr 24 '67

Putting heat on Voyager. Time 89:51 Ap 28 '67

Space sterilization shorthand proposed. R. van Osten and J. A. Redeker. Aero Tech 21: 46-7 Ag 14 '67

Testing

Extended Athena program improved by man in the loop; successful flight-test of the first FATE vehicle. W. Wilks. il Tech W 20:17 Ap 24 '67

Lift from the lifting body; air force SV-5D. il Time 89:73-4 Mr 17 '67

NASA: the image misfires. W. Hines. Nation 204:517-19 Ap 24 '67

New Apollo hatch passes crucial test. il Aero Tech 21:20 D 4 '67

Saturn-Apollo test flight. il Sky & Tel 35: 12-13 Ja '68

Saturn 5 mission will simulate key lunar landing flight events. W. J. Normyle. Aviation W 87:21 S 25 '67

Some landing systems omitted from lunar module test flight. Aviation W 88:29 Ja 15 '68

Tests of modified Apollo systems set this fall. Aviation W 86:40 Je 12 '67

Tracking

America's big eye on the sky. D. Robinson. il Read Digest 90:155-6+ F '67

New missions seen dictating tracking system changes. A. Hill. Tech W 20:16 Ap 3 '67

Orbiter 5 to continue work on selenodesy. Aviation W 87:32 O 23 '67

S-Band signals pierce re-entry blackout. W. E. Wilks. il Aero Tech 21:44-5 D 4 '67

Sea-and-air armada to aid flight to moon. W. Von Braun. il Pop Sci 190:112-13+ Ja '67

Surveyor I: location and identification. L. H. Spradley and others. il Science 157:681-4 Ag 11 '67

Tracking ships to use lasers for accuracy; flexure monitor system. Aero Tech 21:54 N 6 '67

U.S. space tracking capability to double. B. M. Elson. il Aviation W 88:64-7 Ja 1 '68

Voluntary sky-watch aids re-entry study. Aviation W 87:38-9 D 11 '67

See also

Ground support systems (space flight)

Transportation

Mini Guppy begins certification testing. G. S. Hunter. il Aviation W 87:72-3+ Jl 3 '67

SPACE vehicles, French

French reveal three new launch vehicles. L. Doty. il Aviation W 86:24-5 Je 5 '67

SPACE vehicles, Russian

Russian mystery shots. Time 90:37 S 8 '67

Soviets expected to change future spacecraft atmospheres. Tech W 20:31 My 8 '67

Stealing the show in Paris; Russians display space vehicles. il Time 89:87 Je 9 '67

Variety of Russian spacecraft displayed; Paris air show; photographs. Aviation W 86:84-5+ Je 12 '67

SPACESUITS. See Astronauts—Clothing

SPACEWALK. See Space flight—Manned flights—Extravehicular activity

SPACKS, Barry

Long song, a wife song, a cat song, a rain song. New Yorker 43:32 S 2 '67

Outrageously blessed; poem. New Yorker 43: 40 S 30 '67

Robert's song. Poetry 109:367-8 Mr '67

SPADE bits. See Scrapers

SPAGHETTI. See Macaroni

SPAGHETTI sauce. See Sauces

SPAHN, Warren Edward

Supreme court overturns Warren Spahn decision. Pub W 191:43 My 29 '67

SPAIN

See also

Asturias

Basque provinces

Censorship—Spain

Childrens literature—Spain

Church and state in Spain

Colleges and universities—Spain

Costume—Spain

Elections—Spain

Granada

Lanjarón

Marbella

Moving picture industry—Spain

Palma de Mallorca

Publishers and publishing—Spain

Real property—Spain

Ronda

Seaside resorts—Spain

Seville

Trade unions—Spain

Antiquities

Problematical pleistocene artifact assemblage from northwestern Spain. E. De Aguirre and K. W. Butzer. bibliog il Science 157:430 Jl 28 '67

Army

Politics and the military in Spain, by S. G. Payne. Review

Sat R il 50:42-3 Je 10 '67. B. Welles

Colonies

Hernandarias; upper Peru to the Plate River. V. Carreño. il Américas 19:27-35 My '67

See also

Canary Islands

Latin America—History

Commercial treaties and agreements

United States and Spain sign cotton textile agreement. il Dept State Bul 57:726-8 N 27 '67

Constitution

Franco's restive workers. A. Rosenfeld. il Reporter 36:31-3 My 4 '67

Description and travel

Hemingway's Spain. M. Hemingway. il Sat R 50:48-9+ Mr 11 '67

SPAIN—*Continued*

Foreign relations

Great Britain

End of the road for the Rock? il U S News 62:56 My 22 '67

History

Rediscovery of America; Institute of Hispanic culture. G. de Zéndegui. il Américas 19:1-8 Ja '67

Bibliography

Articles and other books received; comp. by C. J. Bishko. See issues of American historical review

Spanish American war

See United States—History—Spanish American war, 1898

Civil war, 1936-1939

Spain: the vital years, by L. Bolin. Review Nat R 19:1081 O 3 '67. A. Lunn Sat R 50:42 O 7 '67

Intellectual life

Rediscovery of America; Institute of Hispanic culture. G. de Zéndegui. il Américas 19: 1-8 Ja '67

Spanish scene. C. Brossard. il Look 31:98-100+ N 14 '67

Politics and government

Franco will have no choice: why liberalization in Spain is inevitable. P. Ben. New Repub 156:13-14 F 18 '67

Franco's reforms; fact and façade? Christian Cent 84:195-6 F 15 '67

Politics and the military in Spain, by S. G. Payne. Review Sat R il 50:42-3 Je 10 '67. B. Welles

Spanish scene. C. Brossard. il Look 31:98-100+ N 14 '67

Struggle for freedom; freedom-of-religion bill. Time 89:30+ F 24 '67

See also
Elections—Spain
Spain—Constitution

Religious institutions and affairs

Freedom at last. Time 89:37 Mr 3 '67

1968: year of human rights. America 118:2 Ja 6 '68

Religious freedom in Spain. E. K. Culhane. America 118:38-40 Ja 13 '68

Religious liberty: down the drain in Spain; hostility to pending legislation of religious liberty statute. D. Peerman. Christian Cent 84:742-4 Je 7 '67; Reply. 84:885 Jl 12 '67

Spain's religious liberty statute in jeopardy. Christian Cent 84:261 Mr 1 '67

See also
Catholic church in Spain

Riots

Out! out! il Newsweek 69:54 F 13 '67

Unaccustomed tumult. Time 89:34 F 10 '67

Social conditions

Unrest in Spain. Nat R 19:236 Mr 7 '67

SPANGLER, Hayward G.

Ant stridulations and their synchronization with abdominal movement. bibliog Science 155:1687-9 Mr 31 '67

SPANIARDS

Spaniard and the seven deadly sins, by F. Diaz-Plaja. Review Sat R 50:36+ O 7 '67. B. Welles

Spanish scene. C. Brossard. il Look 31:98-9+ N 14 '67

See also
Basques

SPANIARDS in the United States

See also
Tampa, Fla.—Ybor City

SPANIELS

Bobtails for bobwhites. D. M. Duffey. il Outdoor Life 140:142-6 O '67

SPANIER, Francis Joseph

Muggsy. R. Gehman. il por Sat R 50:117+ Mr 11 '67

SPANIER, Muggsy. See Spanier, F. J.

SPANISH. See Spaniards

SPANISH AMERICAN architecture in the United States. See Architecture, Spanish American (United States)

SPANISH AMERICAN history. See Latin America—History

SPANISH AMERICAN literature. See Latin American literature

SPANISH AMERICAN war. See United States —History—Spanish American war, 1898

SPANISH AMERICANS in the United States. See Latin Americans in the United States

SPANISH colonial architecture. See Architecture, Spanish American (United States)

SPANISH colonies in America. See Spain— Colonies

SPANISH cookery. See Cookery, Spanish

SPANISH dancing. See Dancing, Spanish

SPANISH furniture. See Furniture, Spanish

SPANISH governor's palace. See San Antonio, Tex.—Historic houses, etc.

SPANISH HARLEM riot, 1967. See New York (city)—Riots

SPANISH language in Mexico

Anecdotes, facetiae, satire, etc.

Late late lovers. E. H. Lopez. Atlan 220:95+ Jl '67

SPANISH SAHARA

Bonanza in the desert; Spanish government and IMC mine phosphate deposits. il Time 89:64-5 Je 2 '67

SPANISH speaking students

Bilingual education; legislative proposals. New Repub 157:9 O 21 '67; Discussion. 157:44-5 N 18 '67

Knocking down the language walls; proposed amendment to ESEA to establish bi-lingual education programs. F. M. Cordasco. Commonweal 87:6-8 O 6 '67

SPARANO, Vin T.

(ed) Where to go fishing, vacationing, hunting. See issues of Outdoor life

SPARGUR, Ronn

Recognition of death; poem. Christian Cent 84:398 Mr 29 '67

SPARK, Muriel

Alice Long's dachshunds; story. New Yorker 43:36-40 Ap 1 '67

Edinburgh villanelle; poem. New Yorker 43: 24 Ag 26 '67

Exotic departures. New Yorker 42:31-2 Ja 28 '67

Fruitless fable; poem. Reporter 37:44 S 7 '67

Messengers; poem. New Yorker 43:44 S 16 '67

She wolf; poem. New Yorker 42:40 F 4 '67

SPARK plugs

How to clean and adjust your spark plugs. H. Carrier. il Pop Sci 190:103-7 My '67

How to time your sparks. H. Carrier. il Pop Sci 191:115-19 Jl '67

SPARKMAN, John

Senator Sparkman looks at the economy; interview. ed. by G. R. Rosen. por Duns R 90:49-50+ O '67

about

Senators, the funds, and the law. il por Fortune 75:152-3 My '67

SPARKPLUGS. See Spark plugs

SPARROW, John Hanbury Angus

Mystery makers. il Time 90:21 D 22 '67

SPARTA, N.J.

Regional refuse-disposal solution. P. Braun. il Am City 82:96-7 D '67

SPAS. See Health resorts, watering places, etc.

SPATER, George A.

American way. por Time 91:84-5 Ja 19 '68

American's new pilot. Newsweek 71:75 Ja 22 '68

SPAULDING, Asa Timothy

World of the wealthy Negro. B. Surface. il por N Y Times Mag p 10-11+ Jl 23 '67

SPAULDING-Moss, incorporated

New bindery triples Spaulding-Moss capacity. il Pub W 191:116 F 6 '67

SPAWNING

Coronary disease in spawning steelhead trout salmo gairdnerii. R. L. Van Citters and N. W. Watson. bibliog il Science 159:105-7 Ja 5 '68

Starfish gonad: action and chemical identification of spawning inhibitor. S. Ikegami and others. bibliog il Science 158:1052-3 N 24 '67

SPEAKERS (House of representatives) See United States—Congress—House of representatives—Speakers

SPEAKERS, Guest. See Public speaking

SPEAKING. See Public speaking; Voice

SPEARS, C. J.

Rapid copy stand. U S Camera 31:50-1+ Ja '68

SPECIAL classes and special schools

Hexagonal cottages create human scale in state-supported school for mentally retarded; Woodbridge state school, Woodbridge, N.J. il Arch Rec 141:150-1 F '67

If you want to teach: roundup of teaching jobs off the beaten track. P. Rifield. il Mlle 64:150-1+ Mr '67

SPECIAL classes and special schools—*Continued*
Rapport, basic ingredient for teaching; excerpts from Summer education for children of poverty. O. M. Wilson. il NEA J 56:31-3 Ap '67
Reaching the nonreaders. J. D. McAulay. NEA J 56:15 S '67
Surge in special education. M. C. Reynolds. il NEA J 56:46-8 N '67
Where unwed mothers stay in school. J. H. Pollack. il Todays Health 45:24-7 S '67
World without 1; University of Chicago's Orthogenic school for autistic children. il Newsweek 69:70-1 Mr 27 '67
See also
Slow learning children—Education
SPECIAL committee of twenty-four on colonialism. See United Nations—Special committee on the situation with regard to implementation of declaration on granting of independence to colonial countries and peoples
SPECIAL days, weeks, and months
Are we communicating? summary of statement prepared for World communications day by United States bishops' committee for social communications. America 116:673 My 6 '67
Auspicious crane: model of castle on exhibit for New York city's Japan week celebration; interview, tr. by J. Kawai. K. Komoda. New Yorker 43:43-4 Mr 11 '67
Cows in the meadow: Central park sheep meadow to celebrate Greater New York dairy month. New Yorker 43:19-20 Je 24 '67
Let's clear the air! cleaner air week; ed. by P. D. Eimon. il Am City 82:132+ Ag '67
Printing week: summaries of addresses. H. G. Rickover; D. Lacy. il Pub W 191:100+ F 6 '67
Rush-Bagot agreement days; proclamation. L. B. Johnson. Dept State Bul 56:800 My 22 '67
To the praise of his glory; Week of prayer for Christian unity. Christian Cent 85:36 Ja 10 '68
World law day, 1967; proclamation. L. B. Johnson. Dept State Bul 57:171-2 Ag 7 '67
See also names of special days, weeks, and months, e.g. Pan American day and week
SPECIAL drawing rights. See International monetary fund; Money—International aspects
SPECIAL forces of the United States army. See United States—Army—Special forces
SPECIAL libraries association
On the rocks? annual convention, New York, 1967. E. Moon. il Library J 92:2491, 2529-37 Jl '67; Reply. E. Ferguson. 92:2855 S 1 '67
SLA annual awards presented in N.Y. Library J 92:2507 Jl '67
SPECIAL operations executive. See Secret service—Great Britain
SPECIALISTS
Aunt Effie and the brass; what is the expert really expert at. W. F. Whyte. Nation 205:134-5 Ag 28 '67

Supply and demand
Brain drain: foreign aid for U.S; why scientists, engineers, technicians and doctors come here. il U S News 62:78-81 My 22 '67
Brain drain: how poor nations give to the rich. W. F. Mondale. Sat R 50:24-6 Mr 11 '67
Brains across the sea. R. Schiller. Read Digest 90:72-6 Mr '67
SPECIALIZATION
See also
Specialists
SPECIE
See also
Natural selection
Phylogeny
SPECIFICATIONS
See also subhead Specifications under various subjects, e.g. Automobiles—Specifications
SPECK, Richard
All deliberate, little speed. Time 89:60 Mr 24 '67
Born to raise hell, by J. Altman and M. Ziporyn. Review
Newsweek il por 70:108+ S 25 '67. S. K. Oberbeck
Mind of a murderer; excerpt from Born to raise hell. J. Altman and M. Ziporyn. il pors Sat Eve Post 240:27-31+ Jl 1; 38-40+ Jl 15 '67
Suddenly, without warning or reason, it happens. P. Hamill. Good H 164:98-9+ Ap '67
SPECK, Richard, trial. See Trials (murder)

SPECTACLES. See Eyeglasses
SPECTER, Arlen
Republican Specter. il por Time 89:26-7 Mr 17 '67
Search for an heir. Time 90:33 O 27 '67
SPECTOR, Robert Donald
Lyre in the larger pattern. Sat R 50:45 Je 10 '67
New poetry of protest. Sat R 50:38-40 F 11 '67
SPECTROHELIOGRAPH
OSO 4 ultraviolet solar observations. il Sky & Tel 34:362-5 D '67
OSO reveals the sun in ultraviolet. il Sci N 92:559 D 9 '67
SPECTROMETERS
Exploring the universe in infrared; use of multiplex interferometric Fourier spectrometer. A. Ewing. il Sci N 91:384-5 Ap 22 '67
Isotopic analysis of rare gases with a laser microprobe. G. H. Megrue. bibliog il Science 157:1555-6 S 29 '67
Spectrometer will evaluate solar plasma; solar wind spectrometer for Apollo lunar surface experiments package. G. S. Hunter. il Aviation W 86:55 F 27 '67
Thousand-inch 'scope for infrared scan; multiplex interferometric Fourier spectrometer. il Sci N 91:350 Ap 15 '67
SPECTROPHOTOMETRIC cell sorter. See Physiological apparatus
SPECTROPHOTOMETRY
Pollution detection; using Beckman ultraviolet spectrophotometer. Sci N 91:115 F 4 '67
SPECTRUM

Absorption spectra
See Absorption spectra
SPECTRUM, Solar
Ratio of blue to red light: a brief increase following sunset. T. B. Johnson and others. bibliog il Science 155:1663-5 Mr 31 '67
SPECTRUM analysis
Chemical bonding information from photoelectron spectroscopy. C. S. Fadley and others. bibliog il Science 157:1571-3 S 29 '67
High-resolution nuclear magnetic resonance spectroscopy. R. C. Ferguson and W. D. Phillips. bibliog il Science 157:257-67 Jl 21 '67
Laser's grandfather; a Kastler's optical pumping technique. G. M. Spruch. il Sat R 50:56-9 Mr 4 '67
Paramagnetic resonance spectra of methyl radicals on porous glass surfaces. M. Fujimoto and others. bibliog il Science 156:1105-6 My 26 '67
See also
Absorption spectra
SPECULATION
Big casino. il Time 90:94 N 17 '67
Commodities churn in a crisis; how futures reacted to the Mideast crisis. il Bsns W p 146-8 Je 17 '67
Gamblers' market; warning of speculative activity. il Time 90:68 Jl 21 '67
How the smart money is playing it smart; ducking the blue chips. il Bsns W p 154-6 S 23 '67
Merits of speculation; Time essay. Time 90:26-7 S 22 '67
Old fever returns to the street; speculative fever. il Bsns W p 149-50 Mr 11 '67
Speculation in stocks: a growing worry. il U S News 63:103-4 O 2 '67
Speculative spree alarms Amex. il Bsns W p36 Jl 15 '67
Stock speculation: a new warning. U S News 63:80 Jl 24 '67
Upside-down market. il Newsweek 70:90-2 N 13 '67
Wall Street: plungers and swingers. C. Morgello. il Newsweek 70:61 Jl 24 '67
Wall Street: speculators' choice. C. Morgello. Newsweek 70:91 N 13 '67
See also
Arbitrage
Brokers
Investments
Stock exchange
Stocks
SPEECH
See also
Conversation
English language—Study and teaching
Public speaking
Stammering
Voice
Study and teaching
See Speech education
SPEECH, Freedom of. See Free speech
SPEECH, Liberty of. See Free speech

SPIDERS, Red. See Red spiders

SPIEGEL, Marshall
News on wheels. Sr Schol 91:38-9 S 28; 26
N 2; 19 D 14 '67

SPIEGEL, Der. See Periodicals—Germany (Federal Republic)

SPIES
Aeroflot: Soviet spy line? il U S News 62:64 My 29 '67
Covey of spies is flushed in Germany. M. Durham and J. Cook. il Life 63:65-6+ N 3 '67
Espionage establishment; excerpt. D. Wise and T. B. Ross. il Sat Eve Post 240:29-31+ O 21; 50-3+ N 4; 76-80+ N 18 '67
Lesson of Philby. Nat R 19:1155 O 31 '67
When a red spymaster defected to U.S. U S News 63:11 N 20 '67
See also
Espionage
Loginov, IU.
Philby, H. A. R.
Roessler, R.
Secret service
Trials (espionage)
Wynne, G.

SPIES, industrial
Big corporations can have their own CIA. New Repub 156:18 F 18 '67
Bitten by a bug; chairman of Amphenol corp. makes charge of corporate espionage. Newsweek 70:85-6 N 20 '67
How to steal $4 billion. il Newsweek 69:76-8 My 1 '67

SPIES and dolls; drama. See Murray, J.

SPIES in literature
Bond and I; techniques of Ian Fleming; Len Deighton; John Le Carré. S. Eimerl. Reporter 37:55-8 Jl 13 '67
Lucky Jim Bond. il Newsweek 69:61 My 8 '67
Many lives of James Bond. il Esquire 67:73-85 Mr '67

SPILHAUS, Athelstan F.
Geotechnology objectives demand imaginative planning. por Tech W 20:68-71 Ja 23 '67
about
Cities under glass. il por Newsweek 71:44-5 Ja 8 '68
Should U.S. cities be torn down? U S News 64:10 Ja 8 '68

SPILLER, Burton L.
Crouse oddities. Field & S 72:46-7+ N '67

SPINAL column. See Spine

SPINAL cord
Surgery
Claim of mended spine questioned. Bsns W p96 D 2 '67
Miracle surgery case; dispute over operation by G. Murray. il Newsweek 70:56+ D 11 '67
Rejoining the spinal cord. il Time 90:70 N 24 '67
Repairing the paraplegic. il Newsweek 70:66 N 27 '67
Spinal cord spliced, paralyzed patient starts recovery. Sci N 92:534 D 2 '67

SPINAL curvature. See Spine—Abnormities and deformities

SPINDLETOP. See Oil wells

SPINE
Biped's burden. il Newsweek 70:59 O 16 '67
Abnormities and deformities
New heartbreak in Ingrid Bergman's life; daughter's illness. M. S. Davis. il Good H 164:54-7+ Ja '67
Slipped disk. Todays Health 46:77-8 Ja '68

SPINELLO, Matt P.
On the citizens band. See issues of Popular electronics

SPINNAKERS. See Sails

SPINNER, Thomas J. Jr
From defeat to disaster. Nation 204:588-9 My 8 '67

SPINNING reels. See Fishing tackle

SPINOZA, Benedictus de
Varieties of Jewish experience. M. Himmelfarb. Commentary 44:54-61 Jl '67

SPINRAD, Bernard I.
New role for the national laboratories; text of declaration. Bul Atomic Sci 23:30-1 Ja '67

SPINRAD, R. J.
Automation in the laboratory. Science 158:55-60 O 6 '67

SPINS, Airplane. See Airplanes—Spinning

SPINSTERS. See Single women

SPIRACLES (insects) See Respiratory organs —Insects

SPIRATONE adapters. See Lenses, Photographic

SPIREAS
Choice creeping shrub. M. Haislip. Home Gard 54:14 F '67

SPIRIT. See Soul

SPIRIT, Holy. See Holy Spirit

SPIRITS. See Ghosts

SPIRITS, Photography of. See Photography of apparitions

SPIRITUAL life
See also
Christian life

SPIRITUAL-mindedness. See Spirituality

SPIRITUAL retreats. See Retreats, Spiritual

SPIRITUALISM
Medium's message; televised séance with Bishop Pike. il Newsweek 70:57 O 9 '67
Messages through the medium; beliefs of Bishop Pike. il Time 90:55 O 6 '67

SPIRITUALITY
Fifield concept of spirituality. A. B. Haines. Christian Cent 84:1332-4 O 18 '67

SPIRO, Al
Burning issues. il por Newsweek 70:51 Ag 7 '67

SPIROGRAPH. See Drawing instruments

SPITBALL pitching. See Pitching (baseball)

SPITTLE insects. See Froghoppers

SPITZ, Mark
All out to be number 1; with report by B. Bruns. il pors Life 63:47-8+ S 15 '67
Old and new pool their talent. K. Chapin. por Sports Illus 27:48+ Ag 21 '67
Times came for two teens. K. Chapin. il por Sports Illus 26:97-9 Ap 17 '67

SPITZER, David L.
Hoffa taint. New Repub 156:5 Je 10 '67

SPITZER, Elroy F.
Cities play a major role in eutrophication. Am City 82:99+ Ag '67
Continuous ion-exchange softening. Am City 82:118-20 Je '67
Which trees and what street surfacing. Am City 82:97+ Jl '67

SPITZER, Helen. See Spitzer, S. jt. auth.

SPITZER, Maurice
Doctor Maurice Spitzer: pioneer of the Judaic book art. I. Soifer. il Pub W 192:83-4+ S 4 '67

SPITZER, Richard C.
Today's Catholic schools. Cath World 206:167-70 Ja '68

SPITZER, Silas
Dining in Chicago. Holiday 41:84-6+ Mr '67
Finest food of France. Holiday 42:70-1+ N '67
Good soup. Holiday 42:74-7+ O '67
—and Spitzer, Helen
Holiday's choice of American restaurants. Holiday 42:99-104 Jl '67

SPIVACK, G. J. See Julesz, B. jt. auth.

SPIVACK, Kathleen
Fat-lipped, you formless; poem. Atlan 220:91 Jl '67

SPIVAK, Lawrence E.
Making news with a news show. il por Sr Schol 91:5 N 2 '67

SPLEEN cells. See Cells

SPLICERS, Television. See Couplings, Electric

SPLICES. See Knots and splices

SPLICING amateur moving pictures. See Moving pictures, Amateur—Editing

SPLICING of moving pictures. See Moving pictures—Editing

SPLIT-level houses. See Architecture, Domestic

SPOCK, Benjamin
Children must be protected from the harm of race. Negro Hist Bul 30:14 Ap '67
First hours. Redbook 130:65-71+ N '67
How children learn the joy of giving. por Redbook 129:41-3+ S '67
[Monthly column] See issues of Redbook
—and Hathaway, M. L.
Montessori and traditional American nursery schools, how they are different, how they are alike. por Redbook 128.20+ Mr '67
about
Doctor's dilemma. il por Time 91:14-15 Ja 12 '68
Law and Dr. Spock. Newsweek 71:18+ Ja 15 '68
Peace, man, says baby doctor Spock. R. Reeves. il pors N Y Times Mag p8-9+ Jl 16 '67
SANE warning. Christian Cent 84:1419-20 N 8 '67; Reply. R. J. Neuhaus. 84:1600 D 13 '67

SPOFFORD; drama. See Shumlin, H.

SPOKEN English. See English language—Pronunciation

SPOKEN phonograph records. See Phonograph records—Spoken records

SPOLETO festival. See Festivals—Italy

SPONGA, Edward J.
Jesuits face the future. America 116:208-11+ F 11 '67

SPONGES
Carbon replicas of siliceous sponge spicules. R. W. Drum. il Science 157:581-2 Ag 4 '67

SPONGES, Artificial
Collagen-coated cellulose sponge: three-dimensional matrix for tissue culture of Walker tumor 256. J. Leighton and others. bibliog il Science 155:1259-61 Mr 10 '67

SPONSORED television programs. See Television advertising

SPONSORS, Advertising. See Television advertising

SPOOLCRAFT. See Spools

SPOOLS
Who'll spool? you'll! Christmas presents. il Seventeen 26:162-3+ N '67

SPOON sculpture. See Sculpture

SPOON thermometer. See Thermometers, Cooking

SPOONS
American souvenir spoons. D. Anderson. il(cover) Hobbies 72:84-5 Je '67
Charming tradition: the Christmas spoon. il House & Gard 132:46-7 D '67

SPORANGIOPHORES
Phycomyces sporangiophores: fungal stretch receptors. D. S. Dennison and C. C. Roth. il Science 156:1386-8 Je 9 '67

SPORES (botany)
Atmospheric ions and germination of uredospores of puccinia striiformis. E. L. Sharp. bibliog il Science 156:1359-60 Je 9 '67
Growth and sporulation of a pyrimidine spore color mutant of sordaria fimicola. A. S. El-Ani. bibliog il Science 156:88-90 Ap 7 '67
Life cycle and variation of prototheca wickerhamii. A. S. El-Ani. bibliog il Science 156:1501-3 Je 16 '67
Separation of spores from diploid cells of yeast by stable-flow free-boundary electrophoresis. M. A. Resnick and others. bibliog il Science 158:803-4 N 10 '67
Sporulation mutations induced by heat in bacillus subtilis. J. Northrop and R. A. Slepecky. bibliog il Science 155:838-9 F 17 '67
Twin meiosis and other ambivalences in the life cycle of schizosaccharomyces pombe. H. Gutz. bibliog il Science 158:796-8 N 10 '67
See also
Sporophytes

SPOROPHYTES
Gametophytes of four tropical fern genera reproducing independently of their sporophytes in the southern Appalachians. D. R. Farrar. bibliog Science 155:1266-7 Mr 10 '67

SPORT equipment. See Sporting goods

SPORT fisheries and wildlife, Bureau of. See United States—Interior, Department of—Sport fisheries and wildlife, Bureau of

SPORT fishing boats. See Fishing boats

SPORT trophies. See Trophies, Sport

SPORTING goods
For the outdoor man. il House & Gard 132:26 N '67
1967 buyers guide for the park, recreation, zoo, and golf markets. Parks & Rec 2:69-72+ Ja '67
What's new. See issues of Outdoor life

SPORTING goods catalogs. See Catalogs, Mail order

SPORTS
Who won? Time 89:51 Mr 31 '67
World travel calendar, 1968. T. L. Christie. Sat R 51:74+ Ja 6 '68
Yes, darling, but who was on third? sport, as camp as anything. G. O'Connor. il Sports Illus 26:42-4+ Ap 24 '67
See also
Amateurism (sports)
Athletes
Jews—Sports
Mountaineering
Pan-American games
Photography of sports
Rowing
School athletics
Television broadcasting—Sports
Umpires (sports)
also names of Sports, e.g. Horse racing

Accidents and injuries
Bad trip; parachutists drown in Lake Erie. il Time 90:38+ S 8 '67

Last jump; parachutists drown in Lake Erie. il Newsweek 70:25 S 11 '67
What to do in the event of injury during a sporting event. E. Maxwell. Todays Health 45:78 D '67
See also
Baseball—Accidents and injuries
Football—Accidents and injuries

Photographs
Selection of photographs from Man in sport: exhibition at Baltimore museum of art. Am Artist 32:56-9+ Ja '68

Records
See Sports records

Africa
Diplomatic strides; United States information agency youth officer coaches African athletes. il Newsweek 70:105-6 O 30 '67

Australia
Australia; country of champs; with report by G. Johnston. il Vogue 150:158-66+ S 15 '67

China (People's Republic)
I fought in red China's sports war; ed. by L. Velie. P. S. Shih. Read Digest 90:73-8 Je '67

England
See also
Soccer

Ireland
See also
Hurling (game)

Italy
See also
Basketball

Scotland
See also
Soccer

United States
For the record. See issues of Sports illustrated
Golden age of sport; Time essay. Time 89: 18-19 Je 2 '67
Sporting life. R. Lardner. il Holiday 41:28+ Mr '67
Sports. See issues of Newsweek
Sports. H. L. Masin. See issues of Senior scholastic
Tahoe's Incline leans on total sport; Incline Village launched on impetus of sport. P. Knight. il Sports Illus 27:42-6 S 25 '67
See also
Soccer

SPORTS arenas. See Stadiums

SPORTS car club of America. See Automobile clubs

SPORTS car drivers. See Automobile drivers

SPORTS car racing. See Automobile racing

SPORTS cars
New skin for a familiar tiger of the road; Chevrolet Corvette. K. Chapin. il Sports Illus 27:62-3 S 25 '67
Piranha. il Motor T 19:26-7 Jl '67
Symbol; XKE 2+2. J. G. Schmidt. il Motor T 19:96-7 O '67
See also
Automobiles, Racing

Testing
Gordon Johncock tests AMC's Javelin. G. Johncock. il Pop Mech 128:128-30+ N '67
Hottest 'Vette yet. E. Dahlquist. il Hot Rod 20:32-4+ My '67
Shelby GT 500 & 427 Sting Ray. S. Kelly. il Motor T 19:24-9 Ap '67
Sting Ray & Shelby GT. S. Kelly. il Motor T 19:43-5 My '67

SPORTS cars, Foreign. See Automobiles, Foreign

SPORTS clothes. See Clothing and dress—Sports clothes

SPORTS clubs
Club for secret swingers; Burning tree golf club. C. Price. il Esquire 67:154+ Ap '67
Gentleman's game; National singles championships at West Side tennis club, Forest Hills, N.Y. R. Lynes. il Harper 235:26+ D '67

SPORTS fans
Cup course. J. Gribbins. il Motor B 120:28+ Ag '67
Don't gripe about a splinter; how to be happy, and keep a boy happy, at a football game. B. Palmer. il Seventeen 26:128-9+ O '67
Fierce holy war in a violent city; Celtic-Rangers fans in Glasgow. H. McIlvanney. il Sports Illus 28:40-3 Ja 15 '68

SPORTS fans—*Continued*
Instant football; a survival guide for women only. B. Lang. il McCalls 95:44+ O '67
Life styles: the boxing fan. R. Christgau. il Esquire 67:120-3 My '67
National pastime; violence of soccer fans in Great Britain. il Newsweek 70:32 Ag 21 '67
See also
Basketball fans

SPORTS films. See Moving pictures—Sports films

SPORTS for women
New outdoor woman. il McCalls 94:10+ Jl '67
Outdoor woman. il McCalls 95:16 Ja '68
Sporting life of summer; medal winners. il Seventeen 26:96-105 Jl '67
See also
Physical education and training of women
Softball
Women as athletes

SPORTS in literature
John R. Tunis: a commitment to values. W. J. Jacobs. Horn Bk 43:48-54 F '67

SPORTS journalism
Lady-killer; L. Merchant of New York post vs old ladies of the press. Sports Illus 26:9 Ap 3 '67
My feuds with officials and the press; ed. by W. Tower. B. Hartack. il Sports Illus 26:30-2+ Ap 3 '67
Play by play; Boston newspapers' coverage of Red Sox games. il Newsweek 70:88 S 18 '67
Sporting life; sports pages services for gambling. il Newsweek 70:60 O 9 '67

SPORTS museums. See Museums

SPORTS officiating
Mona Lisa's mustache; H. Kessler as referee of Clay-Terrell fight. Sports Illus 26:11 F 20 '67

SPORTS promoting. See Promoters and promoting

SPORTS records
Mighty minnows; records set in Women's A.A.U. swimming championships. il Time 90:52 S 1 '67
New Dean on the list of great nonhitters; D. Chance of Minnesota Twins. C. Kirkpatrick. il Sports Illus 27:42-3 Jl 24 '67

SPORTS unions. See Trade unions

SPORTSMANSHIP
Speaking out: I like to risk my life. A. Alvarez. Sat Eve Post 240:10+ S 9 '67

Anecdotes, facetiae, satire, etc.
Everybody's welcome. C. Ford. Field & S 72:6+ Je '67

SPORTSMEN
See also
Hunters

Health and hygiene
See Men—Health and hygiene

SPORTSWOMEN. See Women as athletes

SPOT meters. See Exposure meters

SPOT removers. See Cleaning compositions

SPOTS, Removal of. See Cleaning

SPOTTING (photography) See Photography—Printing processes

SPRADLEY, L. Harold, and others
Surveyor 1: location and indentification. Science 157:681-4 Ag 11 '67

SPRAGUE, G. F.
Agricultural production in the developing countries. Science 157:774-8 Ag 18 '67

SPRAGUE, Marshall
Love in the park; excerpt from A gallery of dudes. Am Heritage 18:8-13+ F '67

SPRAINS
First aid. C. J. Potthoff. Todays Health 45:74 Mr '67
Strains and sprains. A. F. Benjamin. Am Home 70:34 N '67

SPRAY guns. See Spraying apparatus

SPRAY-on starch. See Starch (for clothes)

SPRAY process. See Steel metallurgy

SPRAYING and dusting
For top quality fruit follow a regular spray program. il Pop Gard 18:78-9+ My '67
How to reduce spray drift. Suc Farm 65:87 Mr '67
In the early calm, you can dust in a business suit. il Sunset 138:296 My '67
Legal aspects of crop spraying. Suc Farm 65:98 Mr '67
New okays boost no-mix sprays; undiluted chemicals. J. Bickers. il Farm J 91:24-5+ Jl '67

Spruce budworm mortality as a function of aerial spray droplet size. C. M. Himel and A. D. Moore. bibliog il Science 156:1250-1 Je 2 '67
See also
Pesticides

SPRAYING apparatus
How to make a good sprayer better. E. E. Florida. il Pop Mech 127:157 Je '67
Plant faster, spray weeds too. il Farm J 91:30-1+ My '67
Quick, Henry, the fogger! A. M. Watkins. il Pop Sci 191:138-40+ Ag '67
Rotary spray paint gun. il Consumer Bul 51:40 Ja '68
This month's cover story; insecticide fogger. D. Malena. il Suc Farm 65:65 Ag '67
See also
Aerosols

SPRING, Anselm M.
Anselm M. Spring: he has pictures to burn. il Pop Phot 60:94-5 Ap '67

SPRING
March madness. R. Baker. il Read Digest 90:15-16 Mr '67
Notes and comment. New Yorker 43:39 Ap 22 '67

Drama
Waking the daffodil. R. Bennett. Plays 26:73-4 Ap '67

SPRING cleaning. See House cleaning

SPRING VALLEY, N.Y.
Private school's campus fulfills community needs; Lakeside school. il Audubon 69:80-1 My '67

SPRING wheat. See Wheat

SPRINGER, Axel
Oak attracts the lightning. il por Time 90:53-4 N 24 '67

SPRINGER, Lois E.
One bell collector's luck. Hobbies 72:123 S '67

SPRINGER, Michael. See Gross, B. M. jt. auth.

SPRINGER spaniels. See Spaniels

SPRINGFIELD, Mass.

Industries
How a city took care of itself; reaction to closure of armory. il Nations Bsns 55:48-51 S '67

SPRINGNATIONALS. See Automobile racing

SPRINGS
Rivers of fresh water. D. J. Belcher. Sat R 50:46 Jl 1 '67

SPRINKLERS
Do-it-yourself underground sprinkler. il Pop Gard 18:66-7 My '67
Lawn sprinklers. il Consumer Rep 32:448-51 Ag '67
Lawn sprinklers. Consumer Rep 32:185-9 D '67
Sprinkler in a brick walkway. il Sunset 139:159 O '67

SPRINTING. See Running

SPROTT, Richard L.
Barometric pressure fluctuations: effects on the activity of laboratory mice. bibliog Science 157:1206-7 S 8 '67

SPROUL, Allan
LBJ or the Fed: who's right? Duns R 89:35+ F '67

SPROUTING. See Germination

SPRUCE
Great Smokies Park botanical discovery; disjunct stand of spruce on Miry Ridge. Nat Parks Mag 41:22 Ja '67

Diseases and pests
See also
Spruce budworms

SPRUCE budworms
Spruce budworm mortality as a function of aerial spray droplet size. C. M. Himel and A. D. Moore. bibliog il Science 156:1250-1 Je 2 '67

SPRUCH, Grace Marmor
Laser's grandfather. Sat R 50:56-9 Mr 4 '67

SPRÜNGLI, O. Schenker-. See Schenker-Sprüngli, O.

SPUMONI. See Ice cream, ices, etc.

SPURGEON, Emily
Season's greetings from days gone by. Hobbies 72:98N-98P D '67

SPUTNIK (periodical) See Periodicals—Russia

SPY stories. See Spies in literature

SPY who returned to the fold; story. See Campbell, J. F.

SPYING. See Spies

SPYRI, Johanna
Heidi; dramatization. See Thane, A.

SQUAB. See Cookery—Poultry

SQUALUS (submarine boat) See Submarine disasters

SQUARE knotting. See Macramé

SQUARE-wave generators. See Signal generators

SQUASHES
See also
Cookery—Vegetables

SQUATTER settlements. See Squatters

SQUATTERS
Squatter settlements; Peru's shantytowns. W. Mangin. il Sci Am 217:21-9 bibliog(p 156) O '67

SQUIDS
Effects of tetrodotoxin on excitability of squid giant axons in sodium-free media. A. Watanabe and others; reply with rejoinder. J. W. Moore and others. bibliog Science 157:220-1 Jl 14 '67
Homology of retractile filaments of vampire squid. R. E. Young. bibliog il Science 156:1633-4 Je 23 '67
Molecular and thermal origins of fast photoelectric effects in the squid retina. W. A. Hagins and R. E. McGaughy. bibliog il Science 157:813-16 Ag 18 '67
Penetration of an organophosphorous compound into squid axon and its effects on metabolism and function. F. C. G. Hoskin and P. Rosenberg. bibliog il Science 156:966-7 My 19 '67
Squids; jet-powered torpedoes of the deep. G. L. Voss. il Nat Geog Mag 131:386-411 Mr '67
See also
Cookery—Shellfish

SQUIRREL hunting
Errant Eric. M. Ellis. il Field & S 72:38-9+ N '67
It's a waiting game for squirrels. J. Houston. il Field & S 72:68-9+ O '67
Ways for fox squirrels. J. Olt. il Outdoor Life 140:62-4+ S '67

SQUIRREL monkeys. See Monkeys

SQUIRRELS
White tails and yellow pines. J. G. Hall. il Nat Parks Mag 41:9-11 Ap '67

SQUIRRU, Rafael
Belated homage; poem. Américas 19:39 N '67

SRERE, Paul A.
Enzyme concentrations in tissues. bibliog Science 158:936-7 N 17 '67

STAAR, Richard F.
Hard line in Poland. bibliog f Cur Hist 52:208-13+ Ap '67

STABILE, Toni
Poisons & cosmetics. Nation 206:16-19 Ja 1 '68

STABILITY, Family. See Family

STABILIZATION of prices. See Price regulation by government—United States

STABLES. See Barns and stables

STACK, Nancy
Americans not everybody knows. PTA Mag 61:26-7 F '67

STACKPOLE, Peter
35mm techniques. See issues of U.S. Camera & travel

STADIUM blankets. See Blankets

STADIUMS
Better break for the fans: mammoth sports palaces. il Time 91:68 Ja 5 '68
Plywood sandwich raises arena profits: Seattle, Wash. il Am City 82:88-9 Ja '67
Pop! goes the ball game; Houston's Astrodome. G. Astor. il Look 31:52-3+ Ag 8 '67
Slow death by committee in Boston: Fenway park only stadium. M. Mulvoy. Sports Illus 26:79-81 Je 12 '67
Space frame in a Swedish forest: Landskrona tennis hall, Landskrona, Sweden. il Arch Forum 126:104-7 Ja '67
Stadiums of the '60s; with photographs by N. Leifer. Sports Illus 27:30-7 Jl 10 '67
Underground activity supports above-ground action; turf at Busch memorial stadium, St. Louis. il Am City 82:129+ S '67
See also
New York (city)—Madison Square Garden

STAERZL, Richard E.
Build $6 electronic tachometer. Pop Electr 26:61-2 Ap '67

STAFFORD, Jean
Books. Vogue 150:74 Ag 15; 69 O 15 '67

STAFFORD, William
Earth dweller; poem. Sat R 50:20 D 2 '67
Five-book shelf. Poetry 111:184-8 D '67
Good horse; poem. Sat R 50:16 Jl 29 '67
Portrait of a refugee musician; Priest lake; In fur; Brother; In fog; That weather; Monuments for a friendly girl at a tenth grade party; in Sublette's barn; poems. Poetry 109:250-9 Ja '67
Publius Vergilius Maro; poem. Nation 205:573 N 27 '67
Sidesaddle on the ocean. Poetry 109:270-1 Ja '67
Sound from the earth; poem. Nation 205:634 D 11 '67
You, Walter Cronkite; poem. Sat R 50:71 F 25 '67
about
Place and movement. H. Adams. Poetry 110:42-4 Ap '67

STAFFORD HARBOR, Va.
New town that conserves the landscape. il Arch Rec 141:151-8 Ap '67

STAGE. See Acting; Theater; Theater buildings

STAGE coaches. See Coaches and coaching

STAGE costume. See Costume, Theatrical

STAGE music
Stage band. R. Kerr. il Opera N 31:24-5 F 25 '67
See also
Phonograph records—Stage music

STAGE photography. See Photography, Theatrical

STAGE scenery. See Opera—Stage scenery

STAGECOACHES. See Coaches and coaching

STAGG, Anne
Colonial Williamsburg. House & Gard 131:52+ My '67
Discoveries at Expo. House & Gard 132:192-7 S '67
House in the life of a playwright. House & Gard 132:160-3+ D '67
How to delight your guests. House & Gard 132:65-71 Jl '67
Museum village: Mystic seaport. House & Gard 132:22+ S '67
Old Salem. House & Gard 131:20+ Je '67

STAGGERS, Harley O.
Reason for the rails. il por Bsns W p 146 Je 10 '67

STAHL, Jere
Jere total tuned. J. McFarland. il pors Hot Rod 20:72-4 O '67

STAIN repellents
Spray starch, yes; soil repellent, hardly; Colgate's Pruf! il Consumer Rep 33:6-7 Ja '68

STAINED glass. See Glass painting and staining

STAINS, Removal of. See Cleaning

STAINS and staining
There's good news about exterior finishes. Pop Gard 18:18-19 My '67
See also
Wood finishing

STAIRCASE; drama. See Dyer, C.

STAIRS, G. R.
Insect pests: microbial control. Science 157:464+ Jl 28 '67

STAIRWAYS
These stairs just fold flat. il Sunset 138:134+ Ap '67

STALIN, Iosif
No help from Svetlana; Russian-language copies of memoirs in London. il Time 90:26+ Ag 11 '67
On Stalin's triumph, on Stalin's madness. C. P. Snow. il pors Esquire 67:114-18+ My '67
Svetlana's Letters: another view of Stalin. il por Newsweek 70:42-3 Ag 14 '67
To a ghost about ghosts. G. Wills. Nat R 19:1077+ O 3 '67
What Stalin really did. pors U S News 63:38-43 Ag 28 '67

STALIN, Iosif, family
Historian's assessment of a Soviet family chronicle; appraisal of Twenty letters to a friend, by S. Stalina. J. H. Billington. il Life 63:106A+ S 22 '67
Intimate recollections of Stalin's daughter; excerpt from Twenty letters to a friend. S. Stalina. il pors Life 63:103-116B S 15; 91-105 S 22 '67
Svetlana. M. Gordey. New Repub 157:17-21 Jl 1 '67
Twenty letters to a friend, by S. Alliluyeva. Review
Esquire 69:40+ Ja '67. M. Muggeridge
New Repub 157:25-6 O 14 '67
Newsweek il pors 70:92+ O 2 '67
Sat R 50:33-4+ O 7 '67. H. E. Salisbury
Time il por 90:108 S 29 '67

STALINA, Svetlana Iosifovna
Horror of communism, as Stalin's daughter tells it. por U S News 62:22 My 8 '67

STALINA, Svetlana Iosifovna—*Continued*
Intimate recollections of Stalin's daughter; excerpt from Twenty letters to a friend. pors Life 63:103-116B S 15; 91-105 S 22 '67
To Boris Leonidovich Pasternak; tr. by M. Hayward. Atlan 219:133-40 Je '67

about

Authors & editors; Mme Alliluyeva as a writer and a Soviet intellectual. il por Pub W 191:24-5 My 8 '67
Battle of the books. por Newsweek 70:41-2 Ag 14 '67
Blow to the reds: Stalin's daughter defects. il por U S News 62:19 Mr 20 '67
BOMC pays record price for Alliluyeva memoirs. Pub W 191:40-1 My 22 '67
Books. E. Wilson. New Yorker 43:232+ D 9 '67
Chase. Time 89:30 Mr 24 '67
European notebook. H. Brandon. Sat R 50: 11+ S 23 '67
First, love... il por Newsweek 69:40+ My 8 '67
First words from Svetlana; article in the Atlantic magazine. Time 89:33 Je 2 '67
General and the refugee. E. J. Hughes. Newsweek 69:23 My 15 '67
Hare and the hounds. Newsweek 69:53 Ap 3 '67
Hello there, everybody; with statement. il por Time 89:37-8 Ap 28 '67
Historian's assessment of a Soviet family chronicle. J. H. Billington. il Life 63: 106A+ S 22 '67
International intrigue over Alliluyeva memoirs. Pub W 192:30 Ag 14 '67
Land of opportunity; bids to publish memoir. por Time 89:54 My 26 '67
Letter from Paris. Genêt. New Yorker 43: 129-30 My 27 '67
Life with father. Newsweek 70:42 S 18 '67
Life with father. A. Campbell. New Repub 157:25-6 O 14 '67
Message loud and clear; what Stalin's daughter means to the Kremlin. F. B. Stevens. U S News 62:22 My 8 '67
New beginning. Sr Schol 90:19 My 5 '67
No help from Svetlana; Russian-language copies of memoirs in London. il por Time 90: 26+ Ag 11 '67
Oh dad, poor dad! daughter's found religion, and thinks communism's bad! il por Time 89:25 My 5 '67
Out of the shadows. Newsweek 70:35-6 O 16 '67
Real Svetlana Stalin story. J. Kobler and P. Wyden. il pors Ladies Home J 84:59-63+ Ag '67
Search for Svetlana. il Newsweek 69:62 Mr 27 '67
Stalin's daughter. il pors Newsweek 69:51-2 Mr 20 '67
Stalin's daughter and the Russian church. M. Bourdeaux. Christian Cent 84:1330-2 O 18 '67
Stalin's daughter crosses over. M. McGrory. America 116:717 My 13 '67
Storm over Svetlana. Newsweek 70:20 Jl 31 '67
Surprise from the past. il por Time 89:32 Mr 17 '67
Svetlana. M. Gordey. New Repub 157:17-21 Jl 1 '67
Svetlana: a love story. T. Morris. por McCalls 94:74-5+ Jl '67
Svetlana Alliluyeva and the Russian revolution. D. L. Flaherty. America 117:473-6 O 28 '67
Svetlana, as I know her. E. d'Astier de la Vigerie. Ladies Home J 84:61+ Ag '67
Svetlana era; Soviet intellectuals swear never again. J. Laber. Commonweal 86:390-2 Je 23 '67
Svetlana goes west. il por Sr Schol 90:14-15 Mr 31 '67
Svetlana here to find self-expression. pors Life 62:72A-72B My 5 '67
Svetlana Stalin; with report by M. H. Zim. il pors Life 62:64A-67 Mr 24 '67
Svetlana papers. G. Wills and O. Demaris. il pors Esquire 68:99-106+ N '67
Svetlana: who needs her? A. Werth. Nation 205:469-70 N 6 '67
Svetlana's book due Oct. 16 from Harper. Pub W 191:31 My 1 '67
Svetlana's future; excerpt from Svetlana: the story of Stalin's daughter. M. Ebon. por Good H 165:79-80+ O '67
Svetlana's trip to freedom; with report by R. Korengold. il pors Newsweek 69:21-4 My 1 '67
To a ghost about ghosts. G. Wills. Nat R 19:1077+ O 3 '67
To speak the truth; essay in the Atlantic. Newsweek 69:34-5 Je 5 '67

Twenty letters to a father. A. Schlesinger, jr. Atlan 220:90-5 N '67
Twenty unread letters. il por Newsweek 70: 80A D 4 '67
What Stalin really did. por U S News 63: 38-43 Ag 28 '67
STALLING of automobiles. See Automobiles— Stopping
STALLS. See Barns and stables—Equipment
STALLS, Loafing. See Barns and stables— Equipment
STALSON, Helena. See Kauffman, K. M. jt. auth.
STAMATOYANNOPOULOS, George, and others
Athens variant of glucose-6-phosphate dehydrogenase. bibliog Science 157:831-3 Ag 18 '67
STAMFORD, Conn.

Sanitary affairs
Membranes will cut treatment costs. R. W. Okey. il Am City 82:124 Je '67

Water supply
Magnetic float switch ends sticky problem. E. A. Bell. il Am City 82:52 Mr '67
STAMLER, Jeremiah
Un-American activities: court rule aids Stamler in contempt case. K. Sperry. Science 158:1294-5 D 8 '67
STAMMERING
Please listen, I have something to say. A. Reichman. il Redbook 128:8+ Mr '67
STAMP, Terence
Hollywood scene; ed. by E. Miller. pors Seventeen 26:56-7 N '67
STAMPEDE! story. See Flynn, R.
STAMPS, Food. See Food relief
STAMPS, Postage. See Postage stamps
STANBURY, Louis
Pictures you can stroke. R. Roberts. il por Design 69:34-5 Wint '67
STANCHIONS. See Barns and stables—Equipment
STANDARD, Paul
Jan Tschichold: proponent of asymmetry and tradition. Pub W 191:88-92+ My 1 '67
Kredel: renaissance man among illustrators. Pub W 192:68-9+ S 4 '67
Who designed and cut the Arrighi types? Pub W 192:82-3 N '67
STANDARD brands paint company, Los Angeles
Paint your wagon. N. Willatt. il Duns R 89:59+ Mr '67
STANDARD of living
Diverse $10,000-and-over masses. L. A. Mayer. il Fortune 76:114-17+ D '67
Pass the paper napkins, please; excerpt from Half the battle. B. Vaughan. Read Digest 91:81-3 O '67
Rates of population growth and standards of living; excerpt from address, June 1967. J. E. Meade. Mo Labor R 90:55-8 S '67
Shadowy statistics; moderate living standard. Fortune 76:98 D '67
See also
Income
Luxury
Poverty
STANDARD oil company (New Jersey)
Clean-sea code. il Parks & Rec 2:37-8 N '67
Long-term view from the 29th floor. il Time 90:56-9+ D 29 '67
New keeper for Esso's tiger? Bsns W p48 Ap 22 '67
STANDARD-shift transmission. See Automobiles—Transmission
STANDARD underwater research vessel. See Submarine boats
STANDARDS (ethics) See Ethics
STANDARDS, Labor. See Labor standards
STANDARDS, Library. See Libraries—Standards
STANDARDS, Light. See Street lighting fixtures
STANDARDS, National bureau of. See United States—Standards, National bureau of
STANDARDS in education. See Education—Standards
STANDER, Lionel
Who is the world's foremost actor? H. Lawrenson. il por Esquire 68:180-3+ D '67
STANDIFER, Leon C. See Gosselink, J. G. jt. auth.
STANDING congressional committees. See United States—Congress—Committees
STANDPIPES
This standpipe will store water, just beautifully; Peoria Heights, Ill. il Am City 82:159 Mr '67

STARR, Victor P. and Gilman, P. A.
Circulation of the sun's atmosphere; with biographical sketch. Sci Am 218:19, 100-2+ bibliog(p 152) Ja '68

STARRS, James E.
Forbidding fruits of capital punishment. Cath World 205:286-92 Ag '67

STARRY, Allan R. See Leidy, T. R. jt. auth.

STARS
Astronomy. J. Stokley. See issues of Science news
Deep-sky wonders. W. S. Houston. See issues of Sky and telescope
How stars are born; theory of E. Parker. Newsweek 71:45 Ja 8 '68
See also
Constellations
Milky way
Occultations

Atlases
Photographic star atlases. H. C. Ingrao and E. Kasparian. bibliog il Sky & Tel 34:284-7 N '67

Brightness
See Stars—Magnitudes

Catalogs
Messier album. J. H. Mallas and E. Kreimer. See issues of Sky and telescope
Some new notes on Messier's catalogue. K. G. Jones. il Sky & Tel 33:156-8 Mr '67

Clusters
Over-reddened stars in clusters. G. S. Mumford. Sky & Tel 34:289 N '67
See also
Nebulae

Magnitudes
Laboratory exercises in astronomy, variable stars in M15. O. Gingerich. il Sky & Tel 34:239-42 O '67

Measurements
See Astronomical measurements

Observations
Stellar evolution: comparison of theory with observation. I. Iben, jr. bibliog il Science 155:785-96 F 17 '67

Radiation
Optical identification of an X-ray source in Cygnus. G. S. Mumford. Sky & Tel 34:82 Ag '67
X-ray stars. R. Giacconi. il Sci Am 217:36-46 bibliog(p 158) D '67

Spectra
Hazards of playing with matches; likely explanation for potassium flare stars. G. S. Mumford. il Sky & Tel 34:380 D '67
Hazards of smoking; likely explanation for potassium flare stars. Sci Am 217:60-1 N '67
Late-type stars. M. Hack. il Sky & Tel 33:74-6, 153-5 F-Mr '67
Lithium in old stars. G. S. Mumford. Sky & Tel 33:94 F '67
Spectrogram of Gamma Cassiopeiae. P. J. Shelus. il Sky & Tel 33:220 Ap '67
Ultraviolet spectra in Orion. il Sky & Tel 33:162 Mr '67
Ultraviolet spectra of stars. A. B. Underhill and D. C. Morton. bibliog il Science 158:1273-9 D 8 '67
Ultraviolet stellar spectroscopy on Gemini 11. K. G. Henize and others. bibliog il Science 155:1407-8 Mr 17 '67

Temperature
Infrared stars; interaction between stars and interstellar clouds. H. L. Johnson. bibliog il Science 157:635-8 Ag 11 '67
Late-type stars. M. Hack. il Sky & Tel 33:74-6, 153-5 F-Mr '67

STARS, Double
Backyard astronomer; the sun and double stars. J. S. Pickering. il Natur Hist 76:60+ Ag '67
Measuring the position angle of a double star. G. Gleason. il Sky & Tel 33:117-18 F '67
Origin of binary stars. S. Huang. bibliog il Sky & Tel 34:368-70 D '67

STARS, Magnetic. See Magnetism, Stellar

STARS, New
Alcock's nova in Delphinus. il Sky & Tel 34:150-1 S '67
Identification of Cassiopeia A? supernova explosion. G. S. Mumford. Sky & Tel 34:221 O '67
More about Nova Delphini 1967. il Sky & Tel 34:300-1 N '67

Naked-eye nova. Sci N 92:81 Jl 22 '67
New supernova theory. Sci N 91:258 Mr 18 '67
Nova T Pyxidis brightens again. il Sky & Tel 33:143 Mr '67
Photograph exploding stars. il Sci Digest 62:32 O '67
Supernova remnants. G. S. Mumford. Sky & Tel 33:211 Ap '67
Visibility of Nova Delphini near conjunction. L. J. Robinson. il Sky & Tel 35:61 Ja '68
What causes a supernova outburst? G. S. Mumford. Sky & Tel 34:221 O '67

STARS, Photography of. See Astronomical photography

STARS, Subdwarf
Debate rages in a professionally low key; pygmy stars. Sci N 92:104 Jl 29 '67

STARS, Variable
Cepheid pulsations. A. N. Cox and J. P. Cox. il Sky & Tel 33:278-82 My '67
Laboratory exercises in astronomy, variable stars in M15. O. Gingerich. il Sky & Tel 34:239-42 O '67
NGC 2313: a variable nebula; 18-minute variable star. G. S. Mumford. Sky & Tel 33:211 Ap '67
Nature of AG Pegasi. il Sky & Tel 34:381-2 D '67
Variable star notes from Prague. il Sky & Tel 34:366-8 D '67
Youngest stars; T Tauri variables. G. H. Herbig. il Sci Am 217:30-6 Ag '67
See also
Cepheids

STARS and stripes (newspaper)
News by the numbers. il Newsweek 69:66 F 6 '67

STARVATION
See also
Famines

STASIOR, Richard A.
Small-signal low-frequency transistors. por Electr World 78:53-6 Jl '67

STASSEN, Harold Edward
1968 nomination? B. Weinraub. pors Esquire 68:97-101 Ag '67

STATE, The
See also
Church and state
Individual and state

STATE aid to education. See Education and state

STATE aid to libraries. See Libraries and state

STATE and agriculture. See Agricultural administration

STATE and art; State and church; etc. See Art and state; Church and state; etc.

STATE and local relations
Expanding functions of state and local governments, 1965-70. J. C. Wakefield. il Mo Labor R 90:9-14 Jl '67

STATE and municipal relations
New force focuses on urban ills. il Bsns W p75-6+ Je 24 '67

STATE archives. See Archives—United States

STATE ballet of Rhode Island. See Ballet companies

STATE bonds
New route out of traffic jams? New York's $2.5-billion transportation bond issue. il Bsns W p 160+ N 4 '67
Rhodes at the crossroads: voters defeat Ohio bond commission. M. I. Urofsky. New Repub 156:7-8 My 20 '67
Where bond issues won, lost. U S News 63:116-17 N 20 '67

STATE budget. See Budget, State

STATE candidates. See Candidates, Political

STATE colleges. See Colleges and universities, State

STATE control of education. See Education and state

STATE courts. See Courts, State

STATE department (United States) See United States—State, Department of

STATE education associations. See Educational associations

STATE elections. See Elections—United States

STATE employees
Employment effect of state and local government spending. J. C. Wakefield. il Mo Labor R 90:15-17 Ag '67
State and local government manpower in 1975. H. V. Stambler. il Mo Labor R 90:13-17 Ap '67

Salaries
Twenty-four states to test wage-hour law. U S News 62:86 Mr 20 '67

STATE encouragement of science, literature and art
See also
Art and state

STATE expenditures. See State finance

STATE farms. See Collective farms

STATE finance

Ronald Reagan faces life. A. J. Reichley. il Fortune 76:98-103+ Jl '67

Should Uncle share the wealth? il Nations Bsns 55:35-7+ Ap '67

Where state & local governments get money. il Changing T 21:20 F '67

Where the money comes from. il Time 89:17-18 F 10 '67

See also

Taxation, State

Federal aid

Governors get role in federal largesse; Washington promises funds. il Bsns W p46-7 Mr 25 '67

If U.S. shares taxes with states: where money will go; with chart. U S News 62:118+ Mr 20 '67

Money for the states; revenue sharing plan. J. A. Pechman. New Repub 156:15-17 Ap 8 '67; Discussion. 156:28-9 Ap 22 '67

Sharing revenue with the states; argument against the Heller plan. L. H. Keyserling. il New Repub 156:14-18 Mr 25 '67

States-man; F. Bryant's mission to solve federal aid problems. Newsweek 69:35-6 Mr 20 '67

Subsidy or windfall; federal revenue sharing. R. Moley. Newsweek 70:100 O 2 '67

Tax sharing with states: plan that's in trouble. U S News 62:104-6 F 27 '67

Tax sharing without strings: the answer to states' needs? with pro and con discussion. il Sr Schol 90:13-15 My 5 '67

Walter Heller's federalist papers. M. Nolan. il Reporter 36:13-17 Je 1 '67

STATE forests. See Forests, State

STATE governments

Are the states obsolete? interview. T. Sanford. il U S News 63:32-4+ N 27 '67

From defiance to détente. il Time 89:22 Ja 27 '67

In bad shape. Time 90:19-20 Ag 4 '67

More of the obvious; defects in governmental systems. D. Lawrence. U S News 63:100 Jl 24 '67

Program for curing inertia in states. U S News 63:10 Jl 24 '67

States: middlemen in the federal structure. il Sr Schol 91:11-13 N 30 '67

See also

Governors

STATE hospitals, Psychiatric. See Hospitals, Psychiatric

STATE institution libraries. See Libraries, Institution

STATE institutions

Dynamic master plan keeps retardation center ahead of its time, a model of planned growth; Oregon Fairview home, Salem. il Arch Rec 141:152-3 F '67

Question of priorities; views of Niels Erik Bank-Mikkelsen on Sonoma state hospital, Calif. Nation 205:516 N 20 '67

Tragedy and hope of retarded children; experiment at Seaside regional center, Conn. B. Blatt and C. Mangel. il Look 31:96-9+ O 31 '67

See also

Special classes and special schools

STATE legislation. See Legislation—United States

STATE legislatures

On to Philadelphia! concerning Article V. Nat R 19:338 Ap 4 '67

There's ferment in the statehouse. il Nations Bsns 55:78-80+ Je '67

STATE liability. See Government liability

STATE libraries. See Libraries, State

STATE library associations. See Library associations

STATE lotteries. See Lotteries

STATE medicine. See Medical service, State

STATE of the Union messages. See Presidents —United States—Messages

STATE ownership. See Government ownership

STATE parks and reserves

See also

National conference on state parks

also subhead Parks and reserves under names of states, e.g. New Jersey—Parks and reserves

STATE police. See Police, State

STATE regulation of industry. See Industry and state

STATE senators. See Senators

STATE taxation. See Taxation, State

STATE technical services, Office of. See United States—Commerce, Department of—State technical services, Office of

STATE trade missions. See Trade missions

STATE universities. See Colleges and universities. State

STATE university of New York. See New York (state). State university

STATE visits. See Visits of state

STATEN ISLAND

Cottage: A. Austen house and esplanade. New Yorker 43:35-6 S 30 '67

STATEN ISLAND nature center. See Nature centers

STATES (Africa)

Birth of a new Africa. G. d'Arboussier. il UNESCO Courier 20:4-8+ Je '67

STATES (United States)

Chart of the fifty states (cont) Sr Schol 91:32-3 O 5 '67

See also

State governments

STATES, New

Happy calypso of new semi-states; former British crown colonies in the Caribbean. il Life 62:36-9 Mr 17 '67

New mini-states of the Caribbean. W. P. Carty and N. Raymond. Reporter 36:40-2 Mr 9 '67

Vatican and the third world; ally in their struggle against underdevelopment. T. P. Melady. America 117:641-3 N 25 '67

See also

Underdeveloped areas

STATES, Small

Influence of small states in a changing world; address, April 1967, with questions and answers. W. A. Wilcox. Ann Am Acad 372:80-92 Jl '67

STATES' rights party. See Political parties— United States

STATESMEN

Echoes across the centuries. J. H. Plumb. Sat R 50:34-5 Ja 28 '67

Key world figures as Khrushchev rates them; excerpts from NBC documentary, Khrushchev in exile. N. S. Khrushcev. il U S News 63:12-13 Jl 24 '67

STATIC electricity. See Electricity, Static

STATION wagons

Brief look at the station wagons. il Consumer Rep 32:211-12 Ap '67

1968 station wagons. Changing T 21:32 D '67

Station wagons (cont) Consumer Bul 50:25 My '67

Three-seat wagon as a family car. il Changing T 22:33-6 Ja '68

Testing

Chevrolet Sportvan and Dodge Sportsman. J. P. Norbye. il Pop Sci 190:136-9 My '67

Road testing four station wagons: Ford Country Squire, Plymouth Fury III, Chevrolet Caprice, Ford Falcon Futura. il Consumer Rep 32:139-45 Mr '67

Sportswagons offer surprising comfort and amazing visibility. J. Dunne. il Pop Sci 190:138-9 My '67

STATIONERY

Paper fancies. il Seventeen 26:54-5 N '67

Where is my pen? R. Warfield. House & Gard 132:240-1 N '67

STATIONS, Railroad. See Railroads—Stations

STATIONS of the cross

Picture stations; concerning J. Dieuzaide's photographs. D. Gelatt. Pop Phot 61:120-1+ D '67

STATISTICAL methods

Radioactive dating and low-level counting; report on symposium. V. R. Switsur. Science 157:726 Ag 11 '67

The (±) reference: accuracy of estimated mean components in average response studies. H. Schimmel. bibliog il Science 157:92-4 Jl 7 '67

See also

Sampling (statistical methods)

STATISTICS

Science & snares of statistics; Time essay. Time 90:29 S 8 '67

See also

Inter-American statistical institute

also subhead Statistics under various subjects, e.g. Unemployment—Statistics

STATISTICS of sampling. See Sampling (statistical methods)

STATUES

See also

Portrait sculpture

also subhead Monuments, statues, etc. under names of cities, e.g. Chicago—Monuments, statues, etc.

STATURE
Big Lew measures his lonely world; with account by J. Riley. il Life 62:105-6+ F 17 '67
Giants grow up; New York Giants football players. M. Mulvoy. il Sports Illus 27:26-9 D 4 '67
Growth: the short and tall of it; report prepared in cooperation with the American academy of pediatrics. A. Kerr. il McCalls 94:50+ Ap '67
Long and short of it; why I married a man who is shorter than I am. A. H. Freeman. il McCalls 95:68+ O '67

STATUS, Social. See Social status

STATUS of women, Commission on the. See United Nations—Commission on the status of women

STAUB, Daniel. See Staub, R.

STAUB, Rusty
Basement bargain. il por Newsweek 70:53-4 Ag 28 '67
Houston's boy is now a man. G. Ronberg. il por Sports Illus 27:54-6 Ag 14 '67

STAUBER, Leslie A. See Ott, K. J. jt. auth.

STAUROLITE
Staurolite: sectoral compositional variations L. S. Hollister and A. E. Bence. bibliog il Science 158:1053-6 N 24 '67

STAVERS, Gloria Frances
Meet Gloria Stavers. W. Kloman. il por Sat Eve Post 240:80+ N 4 '67

STAVROPOULOS, Constantin A.
United Nations commission on international trade law. UN Mo Chron 4:89-94 Ap '67

STEAD, Christina
Puzzling Miss Stead. C. T. Samuels. New Repub 157:30-1 S 9 '67

STEADY dating. See Dating

STEAHLY, Vivian Emrick
Stimulating the student writer. NEA J 56: 64-6 N '67

STEAK. See Cookery—Meat

STEAK tartare. See Food, Raw

STEAKS. See Beef

STEALING
New device perfected for detecting thieves. Pub W 191:67 F 13 '67
Sneak thieves in the office & ways to stop them; pilfering in offices. il Changing T 21:37 Ap '67
Success story; case of E. Knowles. il Newsweek 69:33-4 Je 12 '67
Tighter security on cargo sought. R. F. Coburn. Aviation W 87:26-9 S 4 '67
What crime costs you; losses to business. il Nations Bsns 55:44-6+ Je '67
See also
Art thefts
Automobiles, Theft of
Burglary and burglars
Shoplifting

STEAM, Natural
Tapping the heat engine; concerning geothermal energy rights. il Sci N 92:8-9 Jl 1 '67

STEAM automobiles. See Automobiles, Steam

STEAM cleaning
U.S.-made steam unit cleans flood-begrimed Florence. il Am City 82:94 D '67

STEAM engines, Toy. See Engines, Toy

STEAM irons, Electric. See Electric irons

STEAM locomotives. See Locomotives

STEAM pipe lines
Rebellion: water-main break and steam explosion at Seventh avenue and Sixteenth street. New Yorker 43:22-3 Ja 13 '68

STEAM power plants
Geothermal steam plant; Cierro Prieto, Baja Calif. E. Zubryn. Sci N 92:423 O 28 '67
Tapping the heat engine; concerning geothermal energy rights. il Sci N 92:8-9 Jl 1 '67

STEAMSHIP lines
Keeping French glory afloat; French line under E. Lanier. il Bsns W p90-2+ Ja 14 '67
Once over lightly; French line's live theater. H. Hewes. Sat R 50:48 Je 24 '67
See also
Cunard steamship company
Merchant marine

Consolidations and mergers
Chip at the barnacles; merger of three West coast companies. il Time 91:57-8 Ja 12 '68
Toward a new flag; proposed merger of American president, Pacific Far East and American mail line. il Newsweek 71:56-7 Ja 8 '68

STEAMSHIPS and steamboats
See also
Ocean liners

STEARIC acid
Stearic acid as plasma replacement for intracelular in vitro culture of plasmodium knowlesi. W. A. Siddiqui and others. bibliog il Science 156:1623-5 Je 23 '67

STEARNS, Chuck
Fastest man on water skis, 119 mph. il pors Life 62:82-5 Ja 27 '67

STEARNS, Richard G.
We were wrong. por Mlle 65:232+ Ag '67

STECKLER, Larry
Hot antennas for cool color. Pop Mech 127: 93-6+ Je '67

STEDMAN, Jane W.
If the tights fit. Opera N 31:6-7 Ja 7 '67
Rough and ready. Opera N 31:14-15 Mr 4 '67
Singing in the plains. Opera N 31:29-31 F 25 '67

STEEGMULLER, Francis
Letter from Florence. New Yorker 42:50+ Ja 28 '67

STEEL, Ronald
American empire; excerpts from Pax Americana. Commonweal 86:335-9 Je 9 '67
Greener grass on the other side. New Repub 156:27-9 Ap 8 '67
One millionaire and twenty beggars; excerpts from Pax Americana. Harper 234:81-7 My '67
What can the UN do? Commentary 43:84+ My '67
Yellow peril revisited; excerpts from Pax Americana. Commentary 43:58-65 Je '67

STEEL
Cold working
High-pressure process wins Detroit's heart; cold extrusion technique for steel. il Bsns W p 112-13 My 6 '67

Prices
Bloodless boost. Newsweek 70:68 S 11 '67
Going up. Time 90:97 D 15 '67
Steel begs Congress for an import shield. il Bsns W p 169-70 Je 10 '67
Steel industry takes a big bite; latest price increases. Bsns W p47 D 9 '67
Steel prices edge up. Bsns W p27 Ag 26 '67
Steel prices stir capital jitters; Administration to prevent further boosts. Bsns W p37 S 9 '67
Steel steps up the war on imports. il Bsns W p36+ F 11 '67

STEEL, Galvanized
Paints that won't peel on galvanized steel. Farm J 91:48 Ap '67

STEEL alloys
Ductile, strong steel. Sci N 92:177 Ag 19 '67

STEEL castings
See also
Continuous casting

STEEL construction
Nine stories hang from steel straps for two high-rise dormitories. il Arch Rec 142:151-2 D '67
Pittsburgh skyscraper achieves breakthrough in steel fireproofing; United States steel corporation. il Arch Rec 141:165-72 Ap '67

STEEL extrusion. See Extrusion process

STEEL industry and trade
Consolidations and mergers
Where two's company in steel; pact between Wheeling steel and Pittsburgh steel. il Bsns W p38-9 My 6 '67

Government ownership
British steel is given the date; nationalization effective July 28. Bsns W p68 My 6 '67

International aspects
See also
International iron and steel institute

Securities
Simon keeps the experts guessing; sale of Wheeling stock to Pittsburgh steel. Bsns W p 140+ Ap 29 '67

Wages and hours
See also
Collective bargaining—Steel industry

Australia
See also
Broken Hill proprietary company

Germany (Federal Republic)
Göring's legacy; Salzgitter AG. il Time 90:101-2 D 15 '67
Melding steel; two major companies announce merger plans. Time 90:104 S 22 '67

STEEL industry and trade—*Continued*

Great Britain

British steel braces for nationalization. il Bsns W p80+ F 4 '67

British steel is given the date; nationalization effective July 28. Bsns W p68 My 6 '67

British steel process stirs industry debate; spray process may help streamline industry. il Bsns W p66-8 Mr 4 '67

Costly shibboleth; nationalization of steel industry. Time 89:31 F 3 '67

Steelmaking in midair; spraying process promises cheaper production. F. C. Livingstone. il Sci N 91:454-5 My 13 '67
See also
British steel corporation

United States

Cargo of grief for U.S. steelmakers; foreign competitors. il Fortune 76:140-1 O '67

Great rush; stockpiling. Newsweek 71:73 Ja 22 '68

Hard case of steel; competition from abroad. J. Davenport. il Fortune 76:116+ O '67; Reply. J. P. Roche. 76:106 N '67

Inflation: who is really to blame? summary of address. R. M. Blough. U S News 63:16 D 18 '67

New spur for steel's also-ran: CF&I steel corp. il Bsns W p 188-90+ My 13 '67

Revolution in steel: new products, new uses. il U S News 63:72-3 O 23 '67

Steel begs Congress for an import shield. il Bsns W p 169-70 Je 10 '67

Steel gets ready for the roller coaster; boom and bust in 1968. il Bsns W p 150+ D 2 '67

Steel goes afield. il Bsns W p42+ S 30 '67

Steel tries to break an old bind: asks USW to end crisis bargaining. Bsns W p 166 N 18 '67

Steelmakers are iffy. il Bsns W p30 My 27 '67

What's in a name? limitation on imports urged by steel industry. M. Friedman. Newsweek 70:91 N 20 '67

Where one of nation's biggest industries is having trouble. il U S News 62:87-8 F 20 '67
See also
Collective bargaining—Steel industry
Strikes—United States—Steel industry and trade
United steelworkers of America
also names of steel companies, e.g. Granite City steel company

STEEL metallurgy

British steel process stirs industry debate; spray process may help streamline industry. il Bsns W p66-8 Mr 4 '67

Self-healing steel; transformation-induced plasticity steel. Time 90:37 Ag 18 '67

Steelmaking in midair; spraying process promises cheaper production. F. C. Livingstone. il Sci N 91:454-5 My 13 '67

STEEL sculpture. See Metal sculpture

STEEL strikes. See Strikes—United States—Steel industry and trade

STEEL workers
See also
United steelworkers of America

STEELE, Robert
Movies. Christian Cent 84:506 Ap 19 '67

STEELE, Tommy
Tommy Steele; interview. ed. by E. Miller. pors Seventeen 26:78-9+ Jl '67

STEELHEAD trout fishing. See Trout fishing

STEELHEADS (fish) See Trout

STEELWORKERS union. See United steelworkers of America

STEEN, Leslie
Lansing. Michigan's 8mm film workshop. Sr Schol 91:sup8-9 O 26 '67

STEERE, William Campbell
New York botanical garden. research and education. Science 158:539-41 O 27 '67

STEERING gear, Automobile. See Automobiles—Steering gear

STEERS, Chris
Turn the yearbook back to the students. NEA J 56:74 F '67

STEERS, Nina A.
Ariabella; story, excerpts. Américas 19:31-6 D '67

STEGNER, Wallace
California: the experimental society. Sat R 50:28 S 23 '67

Class of '67: the gentle desperadoes. Nation 204:780-1 Je 19 '67

Hard experience talking. Sat R 50:25 Ag 19 '67

Last chance for the Everglades. Sat R 50:22-3+ My 6 '67

STEICHEN, Edward
If this should be my last trip to Europe ..; ed. by R. Joseph. por Esquire 67:82-5+ F '67
about
Focus on: Wayne Miller. C. Schwalberg. il por Pop Phot 60:88-9+ Mr '67

STEIG, Jeremy
Jazz. W. Balliett. New Yorker 43:130-2 Mr 18 '67

Jazz concerts; quintet: Jeremy and the Satyrs, in garden of Museum of modern art. W. Balliett. New Yorker 43:80 Ag 5 '67

Piper of Pan. P. D. Zimmerman. il por Newsweek 70:74 Ag 7 '67

STEIG, William
Bestiary. il New Yorker 43:52-3 Mr 11 '67

STEIN, Bennett H.
(ed) See Garcia, A. Graves and grizzlies

STEIN, David
Dealing from Park avenue. Time 89:75 My 26 '67

STEIN, Donald G. See Brink. J. J. jt. auth.

STEIN, Gertrude
Letter from Paris. Genêt. New Yorker 43: 174+ Mr 25 '67

Miss Stein and the ladies. C. M. De Morinni. New Repub 157:17-19 N 11 '67

Together again. por Time 89:34+ Mr 17 '67

STEIN, Herbert
Case for the tax surcharge. Reporter 37:26-9 O 19 '67

STEIN, Herman H. and Yellin, T. O.
Pemoline and magnesium hydroxide: lack of effect on RNA and protein synthesis. bibliog Science 157:96-7 Jl 7 '67

STEIN, Leonard
How goes the new music? Sat R 50:43-5 S 23 '67

STEIN, M. L.
So you want to teach journalism. Sat R 51:112-13+ Ja 13 '68

STEIN, Ralph
Ralph Stein on vintage cars. See issues of Motor trend

STEIN, Robert
Businesslike approach to poverty. Sat R 50:20 D 9 '67

Changing needs of magazines. Writer 81:14-15 Ja '68

STEIN and Day, incorporated
Court denies injunction against Chicago tribune; alleged improper listing of The arrangement. Pub W 192:157-8 Jl 10 '67

Publisher retaliates for book banning; offer free copies of Kazan book to Mount Pleasant, Iowa. Library J 92:2103 Je 1 '67

Stein & Day happening cannot happen in park. Pub W 192:36 S 4 '67

Stein and Day sues Chicago tribune; alleged improper listing of The arrangement. Pub W 191:44 My 29 '67

STEINBACK, M. S.
Relay coil considerations. por Electr World 77:44-5 Ap '67

STEINBAUM, Martin Jay
Young artists in orbit. por Sch Arts 67:32-3 O '67

STEINBECK, Elaine Scott
Letter from abroad. McCalls 94:42+ Je '67

STEINBECK, John
Camping is for the birds. por Pop Sci 190: 160+ My '67
about
Steinbeck up front. por Newsweek 69:71 Ja 30 '67

STEINBERG, Alfred
GAO: the taxpayer's best friend. Read Digest 91:133-7 N '67

Sam Ruben: born to invent. Read Digest 90:155-7+ My '67

STEINBERG, Benjamin
Lesson of experience. il Newsweek 69:102 F 20 '67

STEINBERG, Daniel, and others
Refsum's disease; nature of the enzyme defect. bibliog Science 156:1740-2 Je 30 '67

STEINBERG, Jane
College crime, and punishment. Mlle 65:316+ Ag '67

Mother government's helpers. Mlle 66:138-9+ D '67

Return of the native. Mlle 64:216-17+ Ap '67

STEINBERG, Leo
Deliberate speed. Art N 66:42-7+ Ap '67

STEINBERG, Michael
At the opera: mod Stravinsky, brilliant Bartók. Hi Fi 17:MA20-1 Jl '67

Musician as writer. Commentary 43:96-7+ My '67

STEINBERG, Saul
　Our false-front culture. il Look 32:46-9 Ja 9 '68
STEINBERG, Stephen. See Stark, R. jt. auth.
STEINBRENNER, George
　Takeover on the lakes. il por Bsns W p29-30 Ag 26 '67
STEINEM, Gloria
　Party. Vogue 149:50-7+ Ja 15 '67
　Women for all seasons. McCalls 94:86-7+ My '67
　(ed) See Capote, T. Go right ahead and ask me anything
STEINEMANN, Maurine
　Distaff architect aids Chicago renewal. il por Am City 82:92 Ag '67
STEINER, Dinah Eva Kweiki
　Ghana's control tower girl. il pors Ebony 22: 115-16+ S '67
STEINER, Donald F. and others
　Insulin biosynthesis: evidence for a precursor. bibliog Science 157:697-700 Ag 11 '67
STEINER, F. A. See Ruf, K. jt. auth.
STEINER, George
　Books (cont) New Yorker 42:111-14+ Ja 21; 43:142-4+ Ap 1; 137-8+ Je 3; 101-2+ Ag 19; 236+ N 25 '67

about

　Doom-haunted prodigy. D. Littlejohn. Commonweal 87:113+ O 27 '67
STEINER, George
　Books (cont) New Yorker 42:111-14+ Ja 21; 43:142-4+ Ap 1; 137-8+ Je 3 '67
STEINER, Gerolf
　Snouters, by Harald Stümpke. Natur Hist 76:8-13 Ap '67
STEINER, James F.
　Excerpt from testimony, March 10, 1966. Cong Digest 46:57+ F '67
STEINER, Jean Francois
　Revolt at Treblinka; tr. by H. Weaver. Sat Eve Post 240:34-6+ My 20; 38-40+ Je 3 '67

about

　Author. M. Sterling. por Sat R 50:32-3 My 13 '67
　Authors & editors. por Pub W 191:22-3 Ap 17 '67
　Nazi war victims on trial. A. Donat. Sat R 50:32-4 My 13 '67
　Survival of the Jews. B. Bettelheim. New Repub 157:23-30 Jl 1 '67
　Treblinka: heroism or fantastic apology? J. Greenfeld. Life 62:8+ My 19 '67
STEINER, Nyle A.
　How to sputter thin films of metal onto glass and experiment with them; ed. by C. L. Stong. Sci Am 217:134+ O '67
STEINER, Sattva
　Quo vadis, economist Johnson? Christian Cent 84:1285 O 11 '67
STEINFELS, Peter
　Case for withdrawal. Commonweal 86:585-7 S 22 '67
　Letter from an editor. Commonweal 87:352-5 D 15 '67
STEINHARD, Walter
　Program planning. Motor B 119:96+ F '67
STEINHART aquarium, San Francisco, Calif.
　See Aquariums
STEINHAUER, Neal
　Now two wizards of oomph. T. C. Brody. il por Sports Illus 26:58-9 F 13 '67
　Whale of an artist. il por Time 89:42 F 10 '67
STEINKE, Jerry
　Taxidermy, why not? Parks & Rec 2:31+ Ap '67
STEINMAN, Robert M. and others
　Voluntary control of microsaccades during maintained monocular fixation. bibliog Science 155:1577-9 Mr 24 '67
STEINMANN, Marion
　Handful of Jews vs. 10,000 Romans. Life 63: 124+ D 8 '67
　Leif's brief career as a missionary. Life 63:60+ S 15 '67
STEINMEIER, Dorothy E.
　Overlooked Indiana. Travel 127:28-33 Je '67
STEINMETZ, Lawrence L.
　Do him a favor, fire him! Nations Bsns 55: 96-8 N '67
STEINMULLER, David
　Immunization with skin isografts taken from tolerant mice. bibliog Science 158:127-9 O 6 '67
STELLA, Frank
　Art; exhibition at the Castelli gallery. M. Kozloff. Nation 205:667-8 D 18 '67
　Minimal cartwheels. Time 90:64-5 N 24 '67

　New cut in art; with report by D. Bourdon. il pors Life 64:44-9+ Ja 19 '68
　What's that, the '68 Stella? wow. F. Castle. il Art N 66:46-7+ Ja '68
STELLA, Sal
　Build the electronic stethoscope. Pop Electr 26:33-5 My '67
STELLAR interferometers. See Interferometers
STELLAR magnetism. See Magnetism, Stellar
STELLAR magnitudes. See Stars—Magnitudes
STELLAR models. See Astronomical models
STELLAR molecules. See Molecules
STELLAR radiation. See Stars
STELLER, Georg Wilhelm
　Journey among barbarians; condensation of Where the sea breaks its back. C. Ford. il Audubon 69:24-31 Mr '67
STELLING, A. Carl, and Mitchell, N. D.
　County parks and open space planning. Parks & Rec 2:28-9+ Ap '67
STELZER, Irwin M. and Netschert, B. C.
　Hot war in the energy industry. bibliog f Harvard Bsns R 45:14-16+ N '67
STENEK, Stanley
　Ossining answers teen entertainment turmoil. Parks & Rec 2:21+ Ag '67
STENGEL, Casey
　Baseball's grand old man. E. Howard. por Read Digest 91:185-8+ O '67
　Casey at the bat. J. K. Hutchens. por Sat R 50:29+ Ap 15 '67
STENGEL, Charles Dillon. See Stengel, C.
STENNIS, John Cornelius
　Case of Senator Dodd: the charges and a reply; excerpts. U S News 62:44-5 Je 26 '67
　Shortages and sanctuaries; key senators report on Vietnam; excerpts. U S News 62: 38-9 Ap 10 '67
STEPHANI, D.
　Amplitude modulation tester. Electr World 79: 51 Ja '68
STEPHEN D; drama. See Leonard, H.
STEPHENS, Jim
　I skippered a Swift. por Pop Mech 128:92-5+ Jl '67
STEPHENS, Johnny
　Those great pictures in Grand prix, how they were made. R. Dempewolff. il pors Pop Mech 127:77-81+ Mr '67
STEPHENS, Olin J.
　Designer's comments; Palawan. Yachting 121: 115-16 My '67

about

　Two Intrepid men. F. Rohr, jr. il por Motor B 120:26-7+ Ag '67
　World's greatest designer who wants no geraniums. B. Bruns. il por Life 63:65 Jl 28 '67
　Yachting interviews. B. Robinson. il por Yachting 122:74+ S '67
STEPHENS, Robert
　People are talking about... por Vogue 149: 180-1 Mr 1 '67
STEPHENS, W. R.
　Infrared heat extends recreation season. Parks & Rec 2:31+ Ja '67
STEPHENS, William M.
　Exploring a coral atoll. il Yachting 121:62-4+ F '67
STEPLADDERS. See Ladders
STEPP, Scott G.
　New modern base restores the oldest street in America. Am City 82:93-4 D '67
STEPPARENTS
　How I'm raising my second family. C. Marshall. il Good H 166:76-7+ Ja '68
　My step-family and me. il Seventeen 26:304-5+ Ag '67
　Second marriage: their daughters couldn't get along. D. C. Disney. il Ladies Home J 84: 18+ Ag '67
STEPS, Garden. See Garden steps
STERENBORG, Robert H.
　How to get a doctor in a farm community. Suc Farm 65:51+ Jl '67
STEREO cabinets. See Loud speaking apparatus—Cabinets
STEREO cartridges. See Phonograph—Stereophonic pickup
STEREO fluoricon. See Fluoroscopy
STEREO vision. See Sight
STEREOLOGY
　Stereology; report of International congress for stereology. H. Elias. Science 156:1137+ My 26 '67
STEREOPHONIC phonograph records. See Phonograph records—Stereophonic records

STEVENS, Sylvester Kirby—*Continued*
Stevens' book vindicated by Pennsylvania court; judge terms book true and excellent history; with editorial comment. Pub W 191:144+, 152 Je 5 '67
U.S. Court of appeals denies Stevens' motion for injunction restraining Helen Frick. Pub W 191:52 F 13 '67
STEVENS, Wallace
Wallace Stevens: the ironic eye. F. Lentricchia, jr. Yale R 56:336-53 Mr '67

about

Tireless conscience. R. Howard. Poetry 111:39-40 O '67
STEVENS, Walter W.
Conquest; poem. Christian Cent 85:42 Ja 10 '68
Limited conflict; poem. Christian Cent 84:741 Je 7 '67
STEVENSON, Adlai Ewing, 1931?-
Let's muffle the sound of guns; interview, ed. by W. B. Furlong. por Good H 164:64-5+ Ja '67
STEVENSON, Adlai, institute of international affairs. See Adlai Stevenson institute of international affairs
STEVENSON, Charles
Great society's wondrous war budget. Read Digest 90:49-54 Ap '67
How secure is your social security? Read Digest 91:75-80 O '67
STEVENSON, Florence
800th anniversary festival. Hi Fi 17:MA30 Ag '67
Oscar the first. Opera N 31:8-13 Mr 18 '67
(ed) See Ludgin, C. All American
STEVENSON, Grace T.
Training for growth; the future for librarians; address, January 11, 1967. bibliog por ALA Bul 61:278-81+ Mr '67
STEVENSON, James
Reporter at large. New Yorker 43:141-2+ S 16 '67
STEVENSON, Janet
Family divided. Am Heritage 18:4-25+ Ap '67
STEVENSON, Robert P.
Shop talk. See issues of Popular science monthly
STEVENSON Institute of international affairs. See Adlai Stevenson institute of international affairs
STEW
Bride makes Irish stew. il McCalls 94:78 Mr '67
Busy-day oven stews. B. L. Henry and D. Groves. il Farm J 91:72-3 My '67
Greek stews with low calorie sauces. Sunset 139:186 N '67
Hearty stews. il Bet Hom & Gard 45:115-16 O '67
Ragout of beef in 15 minutes; pressure cooker. il Ladies Home J 84:130 N '67
Surprises that sharpen a stew; beef stew; with menu and recipes by E. Graves. il Life 63:94-5+ O 20 '67
These three family stews all have famous cousins. Sunset 138:245 My '67
STEWARD, Julian H.
Cultural evolution today. Christian Cent 84:203-7 F 15 '67
STEWARD observatory. See Astronomical observatories
STEWARDESSES, Air. See Airlines—Hostesses
STEWARDSHIP, Christian
Stewardship and social action. W. H. Jennings. Christian Cent 84:1593-5 D 13 '67
STEWART, Douglas J.
Apollo, the destroyer. New Repub 156:15 F 18 '67
Hobbit war. Nation 205:332-4 O 9 '67
STEWART, Elisabeth
Stewart covers up. P. L. Levin. Sat Eve Post 240:35 Je 3 '67
STEWART, Ellen
Their hearts belong to La Mama. J. Greenfeld. il por N Y Times Mag p 10-11+ Jl 9 '67
STEWART, F. K.
Happy hundred! Sr Schol 90:sup 13 F 10 '67
What's new and different about Canadian education? Sr Schol 90:sup2 F 10 '67
STEWART, George Rippey
Affair of passion. Nation 204:795-6 Je 19 '67
STEWART, Gloria A. and Farber, Emmanuel
Reformation of functional liver polyribosomes from ribosome monomers in the absence of RNA synthesis. bibliog Science 157:67-9 Jl 7 '67
STEWART, J. George
Architect, spare our Capitol. R. Sherrill. il por N Y Times Mag p30-1+ Ap 16 '67

STEWART, Jackie
Jackie Stewart tests ... por Pop Mech 127:98-100+ F '67
STEWART, James R.
Instant ID cards for tighter security. Am City 82:151 O '67
STEWART, John J.
Try climbing your family tree. Read Digest 91:103-7 S '67
STEWART, John M. See Ansoff, H. I. jt. auth.
STEWART, Mathew W. See DiMateo, L. P. jt. auth.
STEWART, Natacha
By a lake in the Bois; story. New Yorker 43:52-5 O 14 '67
Portraits in a village; story. New Yorker 42:32-8 F 4 '67
STEWART, O. E.
Ripe blueberries. Horticulture 45:29 Ag '67
STEWART, Potter
Is the war legal? two justices pose questions; summary of testimony. por U S News 63:16 N 20 '67
STEWART, Robert
Carving of trees; poem. America 116:853 Je 17 '67
Project Head Start; summer, 1967; poem. America 117:225 S 2 '67
Ragpickers; poem. America 116:378 Mr 18 '67
STEWART, Robert Haslam
America's most beautiful valley. S. Storm. il Am For 73:38-40+ Ja '67
STEWART, Thomas
And we quote; interview, ed. by C. L. Osborne. por Hi Fi 17:MA11 N '67

about

Lively arts; interview, ed. by R. Hemming. il por Sr Schol 91:27-8 O 26 '67
STEWART, W. D. P.
Nitrogen-fixing plants. bibliog Science 158:1426-32 D 15 '67
STEWART, William Huffman
NIH wants independence. B. J. Culliton. il por Sci N 91:478-9 My 20 '67
STEWS. See Stew
STEYTLER, Robert
Savings in activated-sludge systems. Am City 82:113-15+ My '67
STICKNEY, John
Non-toxic psychedelia for squares. Life 63:12 Ag 11 '67
STIEVE, Helen
Dear me, it's deer hunting season again! Farm J 91:45+ N '67
STILEMAN family
Stileman coat-of-arms. H. K. Eilers. il Hobbies 72:114-15+ S '67
STILL, James
Man on troublesome. D. Cadle. Yale R 57:236-55 D '67
STILL, Joseph W.
Love your enemies. Bul Atomic Sci 23:30 Mr '67
STILL life painting
Masterpiece recipes. il Redbook 129:78-83+ My '67
STILL life photography. See Photography—Still life
STILLINGER, Elizabeth
Adam revolution in furniture. Antiques 91:218-22 F '67
Living with antiques. Antiques 91:503-7 Ap; 92:214-17 Ag '67
STILLMAN, Edmund O.
Containment has won, but ... N Y Times Mag p23+ My 28 '67
Holy terrors of Munster. Horizon 9:90-5 Sum '67
Konrad Lorenz. Horizon 9:60-5 Spr '67
Short war and the long war. N Y Times Mag p7+ Je 18 '67
STIMMEL, Thomas S.
Prayerful Oregonian. New Repub 156:17-18 My 6 '67
STIMSON, Thomas E.
Campers; twelve ways to add comfort and convenience. Pop Mech 127:124-7+ My '67
Cheese it, the copters! Pop Mech 127:74-7+ Je '67
How fast is too fast? Pop Mech 128:71-4+ S '67
How young is too young? Pop Mech 128:132-5+ O '67
Tuffy, the navy's deep sea lifeguard. Pop Mech 128:66-9+ Jl '67
STIMULANTS
Chill of death; cocktail glass chillers. Newsweek 70:60 O 16 '67
Mellow yellow; banana skins, newest ticket to a psychedelic trip. il Newsweek 69:93 Ap 10 '67
Perils of periwinkle; smoking dried leaves. Newsweek 69:68 Je 26 '67

STIMULANTS—*Continued*

Tripping on banana peels; mellow yellow craze. il Time 89:52 Ap 7 '67

Trips that kill; fumes from cocktail-glass chiller. il Time 90:77 O 13 '67

Psychological effects

Seeds of wit. R. G. G. Price. Atlan 220:93-5 Jl '67

STIMULUS and response

Activity and responsivity in rats after magnesium pemoline injections. G. Beach and D. P. Kimble. bibliog il Science 155:698-701 F 10 '67

Behavioral acts elicited by stimulation of single, identifiable brain cells. A. O. D. Willows. bibliog il Science 157:570-4 Ag 4 '67

Brain signals and learning. Sci Am 217:42 Jl '67

Dissociation of the visual placing response into elicited and guided components. A. Hein and R. Held. bibliog il Science 158: 390-2 O 20 '67

Early receptor potential: photoreversible charge displacement in rhodopsin. R. A. Cone. bibliog il Science 155:1128-31 Mr 3 '67

Evoked cortical potentials: relation to visual field and handedness. R. G. Eason and others. bibliog il Science 156:1643-6 Je 23 '67

Fast light-evoked potential from leaves. T. G. Ebrey. bibliog il Science 155:1556-7 Mr 24 '67

Information delivery and the sensory evoked potential. S. Sutton and others. bibliog il Science 155:1436-9 Mr 17 '67

Intracellular olfactory response of hippocampal neurons in awake, sitting squirrel monkeys. T. Yokota and others. bibliog il Science 157:1072-4 S 1 '67

Lateral hypothalamus: hoarding behavior elicited by electrical stimulation. L. J. Herberg and J. E. Blundell. bibliog il Science 155:349-50 Ja 20 '67

Neural basis of the sense of flutter-vibration. V. B. Mountcastle and others. bibliog il Science 155:597-600 F 3 '67

Not-so-private eye; E. H. Hess's Pupillograph measures reactions. il Life 62:80A-80B Ap 21 '67

Oxygen tension changes evoked in the brain by visual stimulation. K. J. Gijsbers and R. Melzack. bibliog il Science 156:1392-3 Je 9 '67

Perceived number and evoked cortical potentials. M. R. Harter and C. T. White. bibliog il Science 156:406-8 Ap 21 '67

Phycomyces sporangiophores: fungal stretch receptors. D. S. Dennison and C. C. Roth. il Science 156:1386-8 Je 9 '67

Radio control of the brain. J. Reinert. il Sci Digest 61:32-6 Je '67

Resistance shifts accompanying the evoked cortical response in the cat. K. A. Klivington and R. Galambos. bibliog il Science 157: 211-13 Jl 14 '67

Serotonin release from brain slices by electrical stimulation: regional differences and effect of LSD. T. N. Chase and others. bibliog il Science 157:1461-3 S 22 '67

Serotonin: release in the forebrain by stimulation of midbrain raphé. G. K. Aghajanian and others. bibliog il Science 156:402-3 Ap 21 '67

Single fibers of cat optic nerve: thresholds to light. W. D. Heiss and D. C. Milne. bibliog il Science 155:1571-2 Mr 24 '67

Somatosensory thalamic neurons: effects of cortical depression. H. J. Waller and S. M. Feldman. bibliog il Science 157:1074-7 S 1 '67

State as a determinant of infants' heart rate response to stimulation. M. Lewis and others. bibliog il Science 155:486-8 Ja 27 '67

Stimulus generalization as signal detection in pigeons. D. S. Blough. bibliog il Science 158:940-1 N 17 '67

Thalamic reticular system and central grey: self-stimulation. R. M. Cooper and L. H. Taylor. bibliog il Science 156:102-3 Ap 7 '67

Transfer following operant conditioning in the curarized dog. A. H. Black. bibliog il Science 155:201-3 Ja 13 '67

Visual discrimination of temporal order. D. N. Robinson. bibliog Science 156:1263-4 Je 2 '67; Reply with rejoinder. D. H. Thor. 158: 1704-5 D 29 '67

Visual reaction times on a circle about the fovea. W. H. Payne. il Science 155:481-2 Ja 27 '67

Visually guided reaching in infant monkeys after restricted rearing. R. Held and J. A. Bauer, jr. bibliog il Science 155:718-20 F 10 '67

STINE, G. Harry

Prowling mind of Henri Coanda. Flying 80: 64-8 Mr '67

STINGS, Insect. See Insect bites and stings

STINNETT, Caskie

Samoa. Holiday 42:54-5+ Jl '67

Speaking of travel. See issues of Holiday

STINNETT, Loni

My love is like a red, red rose; story. McCalls 95:108-9 O '67

STIRLING, Monica

Summer of a dormouse; story. McCalls 94: 70-3 Je '67

STITCHERY. See Embroidery

STITH, Richard

As Berkeley awaits Ronald Reagan. Commonweal 85:443-4 Ja 27 '67

STITT, Virginia S.

Stay young & beautiful. Parents Mag 42:40 O; 54 N; 18 D '67

STIVENS, Dal

Red dog dingo. Holiday 42:105-6+ S '67

STOCK, Brian

Report; Canada. Atlan 220:10+ Jl; 48+ O '67

STOCK, Dennis

Tokaido; photographs. Holiday 41:34-45 Je '67

STOCK, Robert

Sitting on the lid in Cleveland. Commonweal 86:358-9 Je 16 '67

STOCK averages. See Stocks—Price indexes and averages

STOCK-car racing. See Automobile racing

STOCK control. See Inventories

STOCK control (bookstores) See Booksellers and bookselling—Stock

STOCK dividends. See Dividends

STOCK exchange

Bob Cratchit hours; Stock exchange shortens daily trading sessions to help paperwork delays. il Time 90:75 Ag 18 '67

Danger ahead in the stock market. il U S News 63:63-4 N 20 '67

How experts see stock market now. il U S News 63:42-4 Ag 7 '67

Regionals: will the SEC spoil success? Fortune 76:242+ N '67

Sixteen stock exchanges? why so many? il Changing T 21:45-7 F '67

Stock market: behind its ups and downs. Sr Schol 90:4-8 Ap 21 '67

Stock market gets off Mideast roller coaster. il Bsns W p42 Je 10 '67

Stock market outlook. W. Maynard. Duns R 89:17+ F '67

Stock market's effort to dig out. U S News 63:96 Ag 21 '67

Stocks of the 200; performances on world exchanges. J. Main. il Fortune 76:151-2+ S 15 '67

When security analysts look ahead; with excerpts from address by W. M. Martin, jr. il U S News 62:56-8 My 29 '67

See also

Arbitrage

Brokers

Government investigations—Stock exchange

Manipulation (securities)

Put and call transactions

Speculation

United States—Securities and exchange commission

Crisis, October 1929

Big crash and the rocky road to reform. Sr Schol 90:6-7 Ap 21 '67

Regulation

Are give-ups on the way out? SEC rules against commission splitting with regional exchanges. il Bsns W p 125-6+ Ja 14 '67

How traders beat the 70 per cent margin; unregulated loan companies reappearing. il Bsns W p51-2 Ap 8 '67

Terminology

Glossary. Sr Schol 90:5 Ap 14 '67

Europe, Western

Europe tries to spur its capital markets; hampered by conservative stand of governments and investors. il Bsns W p 160-2 Ja 28 '67

In foul weather, a wild blue yonder; stock prices soar in London and Paris. Time 90: 104 S 22 '67

London

Stock tenders, British style. J. Ross-Skinner. il Duns R 90:32-5+ S '67

Luxembourg

Luxembourg versus de Gaulle. J. Ross-Skinner. il Duns R 90:41-2 Jl '67

STOCK exchange—*Continued*

New York (city)

Big board lists a chief; R. W. Haack to succeed. G. Keith Funston. Bsns W p 134 Ap 29 '67

Big board's choice. Newsweek 69:70 My 1 '67

Changing the guard. Newsweek 70:94+ S 25 '67

Close-up of today's stock market; interview. G. K. Funston. U S News 63:62-5 Jl 3 '67

Good wife; bull market. il Time 90:67 Ag 11 '67

Haack of the big board. il Fortune 75:39 Je 1 '67

Happy birthday, big board. il Time 89:88 My 26 '67

Hot market's blizzard of paper. il Newsweek 70:51 Ag 21 '67

Johnson's plan yields some quick dividends. il Bsns W p82-4 Ja 6 '68

Market warms up; State of the Union message dispels uncertainty. il Bsns W p25-6 Ja 21 '67

Market's frenzy is short-lived; following restoration of the 7 per cent tax credit. Bsns W p36 Mr 18 '67

New president; interview. R. W. Haack. New Yorker 43:49 N 4 '67

New stock indexes get there first; New York stock exchange indicators. il Bsns W p 124+ F 25 '67

Old fever returns to the street; speculative fever. il Bsns W p 149-50 Mr 11 '67

Over-the-counter stocks. il Changing T 21:25-8 Ag '67

Problems of plenty pinch the big board; growth pains pose challenges. il Bsns W p 102-4+ Ag 26 '67

Speculative fervor. il Time 89:91 Mr 17 '67

Taxing the tape; trading almost frantic. Time 89:88 F 17 '67

Wall Street. See issues of Newsweek

Wall Street rides with the punch; after devaluation. il Bsns W p 124-6 N 25 '67

Wall St. talks. See issues of Business week

Wall Street under fire. R. A. Phalon. il Duns R 89:39-40+ Ap '67

Wall Street's view is foggy; stock market for 1968. il Bsns W p 16-17 D 30 '67

Why big board hopes to tame a paper tiger; using extra time to catch up with back office work. il Bsns W p96 Ag 12 '67

See also

National stock exchange

Statistics

Volume & vigor. Time 89:87 Ap 7 '67

Toronto

Queen Bee gets stung; MacMillan accused of wash trading. Time 89:98 Mr 17 '67

STOCK exchange, American. See American stock exchange

STOCK gambling. See Speculation

STOCK margin requirements. See Stock exchange—Regulation

STOCK market. See Stock exchange

STOCK market charts. See Stocks—Price indexes and averages

STOCK option contracts. See Put and call transactions

STOCK purchase options

Finding the right silver for the executive palm; stock-option plan still the favorite. il Bsns W p90+ Jl 22 '67

Wall Street: caution, men at work. C. Morgello. il Newsweek 70:65 Jl 3 '67

STOCK purchase warrants

Wall Street: caution, men at work. C. Morgello. il Newsweek 70:65 Jl 3 '67

What warrants are worth. il Fortune 75:208+ Mr '67

STOCK speculation. See Speculation

STOCK tenders. See Stocks—Tender offers

STOCKBRIDGE, Mass.

Home for Christmas; with painting by N. Rockwell. McCalls 95:100-3 D '67

STOCKBROKERS. See Brokers

STOCKER, Joseph

Help for Spanish-speaking youngsters. Am Ed 3:17-18+ My '67

STOCKHAUSEN, Karlheinz

Contents of Kontarsky. O. Daniel. por Sat R 50:47+ D 30 '67

Conversation with Stockhausen; with excerpts from interview. J. Marks. il por Sat R 50:63-5 S 30 '67

Flashes of a mad logic. il Time 89:73 F 10 '67

Via Nonesuch, a trip to another brave new world. A. Cohn. por Am Rec G 34:190-1 N '67

STOCKHOLDERS

Buying and selling stocks. il Sr Schol 90:8 Ap 21 '67

Wall Street: the rally from afar; vacationing investors. C. Morgello. Newsweek 70:64 Jl 31 '67

See also

Executives as stockholders

Proxies

Anecdotes, facetiae, satire, etc.

Stockholder bit. M. Berry. il Look 31:72 Je 27 '67

STOCKHOLDERS meetings

Fight that swirls around Eastman Kodak; battle over more jobs for Negroes. il Bsns W p38-41 Ap 29 '67

New threat for employers? what a Negro group seeks from Kodak; FIGHT dispute over hiring agreement. il U S News 62: 74-5 My 8 '67

Spring: the voice of the treasurer. il Newsweek 69·69 My 1 '67

STOCKHOLM

City planning

Piet Hein and his 7000 grooks. J. Hicks. il Read Digest 90:193-4+ Mr '67

Music

Report: Stockholm; Royal opera productions. K. Atterberg. Opera N 32:33 D 16 '67

Stockholm: production of Tristan und Isolde. K. Atterberg. il Opera N 31:32 F 11 '67

STOCKLIN, William A.

For the record. See issus of Electronics world

STOCKS

As company officials step up sales of their own stocks; with charts. U S News 63: 100-1 S 11 '67

Best bets for 1967. il Duns R 89:95-6+ Ja '67

Bonds vs. stocks: growing dilemma. il U S News 63:87-9 D 18 '67

Buying stock: is the price right? il Changing T 21:21-3 N '67

Changing signals for investors; what investment advisers see ahead. il U S News 62: 48-50 My 15 '67

Computer-leasing stocks. A. M. Louis. il Fortune 76:167-8+ Jl '67

Go-go market in the little stocks; with report by A. Smith. il Life 63:44B-45+ Jl 28 '67

Guide for smog-bound investors; companies making pollution control devices. il Bsns W p 110+ Jl 22 '67

Ins & outs of convertible securities. il Changing T 21:43-5 Mr '67

Investment manager looks at stocks; interview. L. Levy. il Duns R 90:44-5+ S '67

Outlook for investors: as the analysts see it. il U S News 64:40-2 Ja 8 '68

Six stocks for growth. il Duns R 89:81-2 F '67

Stocks: before investing, read this. Good H 164:207 Ap '67

Veteran fund manager views the market; interview. T. R. Price. il Duns R 90:47-9 D '67

Wall Street:

Butter over guns. C. Morgello. Newsweek 70:70 Jl 10 '67

Is the glamour turning to tinsel? C. Morgello. il Newsweek 71:74 Ja 22 '68

Lure of two+two=five; conglomerate stocks. il Newsweek 69:82-3 My 8 '67

New-listing game; on the Big board. C. Morgello. il Newsweek 69:80 Mr 13 '67

Oil and the Mideast crisis. C. Morgello. il Newsweek 69:75 Je 12 '67

Performance stocks C. Morgello. Newsweek 70:72 O 30 '67

Restrained optimism for '68. C. Morgello. il Newsweek 70:83 D 11 '67

Small investor switches. C. Morgello. il Newsweek 70:76 D 4 '67

Sweetest stocks of '67. C. Morgello. il Newsweek 70:59 D 25 '67

Take me to your leaders: office equipment and airlines. C. Morgello. il Newsweek 69:58 Je 26 '67

Wang! new hot issues. Newsweek 70:81+ S 18 '67

What investors need to know now; interviews. M. Freeman; D. Kennedy; R. Naess. il U S News 63:38-43 D 4 '67

What makes a glamour stock? C. Mathews. il Duns R 90:36-7+ O '67

When stock issues miss the boat. il Bsns W p 162+ Ap 15 '67

Why stocks feel better; first-quarter earnings. il Bsns W p42 Ap 22 '67

See also

Bonds

Computers—Investment applications

STOCKS—See also—*Continued*
Corporations
Corporations—Finance
Investment banking
Speculation
Stock exchange
Television apparatus industry and trade—
  Securities

Insider trading

Corporate disclosure; insider trading. A. Fleischer, jr. bibliog f Harvard Bsns R 45: 129-35 Ja '67

Marketing

Buying and selling stocks. il Sr Schol 90:8 Ap 21 '67
How funds are dominating the stock market now. il U S News 62:109-10 Ap 17 '67
Over-the-counter stocks. il Changing T 21:25-8 Ag '67
Question about volume. il Fortune 75:221 My '67
Rumors & rigging; indictments in case of stock price of Chicago's Pentron electronics corp. Time 89:102+ Je 9 '67
Wall Street: don't sell on strike news. C. Morgello. il Newsweek 70:75 S 18 '67
What is reviving the OTC; over-the-counter securities market. il Bsns W p93-4+ F 4 '67
Where to buy the future, and the hereafter; over-the-counter trading. il Newsweek 69:82-4 Ap 24 '67
  See also
National association of securities dealers

Odd lots

Is the odd-lotter always wrong? il Bsns W p 147-8 My 6 '67

Price indexes and averages

As Wall Street watches hemlines; corresponding highs and lows in Dow-Jones average. il U S News 62:94 My 29 '67
Back to the 900s? il Time 89:65 Ja 27 '67
Brave bulls. Newsweek 70:70 Ag 14 '67
Bright spots in a fuzzy market. il Duns R 88:75-6+ D '66
Bulls look ahead. il Bsns W p38 My 20 '67
Close-up of today's stock market; interview. G. K. Funston. U S News 63:62-5 Jl 3 '67
Discounting the dip. Time 89:87 My 5 '67
Fear of credit crunch harries Wall Street. il Bsns W p 120+ O 28 '67
How long will stocks keep it up? il Bsns W p93-4 Ag 12 '67
How market acted when pound fell. il U S News 63:37 D 4 '67
Hypothesis about the stock market. il Fortune 76:239 N '67
If you pitch darts to pick stocks. il U S News 63:9 Ag 28 '67
Investing in the 500; market performance of largest industrial corporations. A. M. Louis. il Fortune 75:305-6+ Je 15 '67
Is the odd-lotter always wrong? il Bsns W p 147-8 My 6 '67
Jitters on the stock market; what the price slide showed. il U S News 62:122 Mr 13 '67
Johnson's plan yields some quick dividends. il Bsns W p82-4 Ja 6 '68
Leg of the bear; how far will stocks fall? il Bsns W p43-4 N 11 '67
Market spurts ahead. il Bsns W p34 Ag 5 '67
Market warms up; State of the Union message dispels uncertainty. il Bsns W p25-6 Ja 21 '67
Markets run scared as tax bill falters. il Bsns W p30-1 N 4 '67
New stock indexes get there first; New York stock exchange indicators. il Bsns W p 124+ F 25 '67
Plotting a course to buy, buy, buy; chartists predicting the Dow will reach or top 900. il Bsns W p 115-16 Ap 8 '67
Profits gain a bit more. il Bsns W p44 O 14 '67
Rallying round the blue chips. il Time 90: 75 Jl 28 '67
Rush is on for low-priced stocks. il U S News 63:90-1 Jl 17 '67
Sagging Du Pont casts shadow over the Dow. il Bsns W p 113+ Ap 8 '67
Selectivity: key to investment success. il Changing T 21:31-6 Je '67
Speculation in stocks: a growing worry. il U S News 63:103-4 O 2 '67
Story the stock market is telling about the future. il U S News 62:88-90 My 8 '67
Wall Street:
  Analyzing the analysts. C. Morgello. il Newsweek 69:85 Ap 17 '67
  Autumn leaves aswirl. C. Morgello. il Newsweek 70:70 S 11 '67
  Blue chips vs. performers. C. Morgello. il Newsweek 70:59 Ag 7 '67

Dow also rises. C. Morgello. il Newsweek 70:87 S 25 '67
End of the blue-chip blues? C. Morgello. il Newsweek 69:83 My 22 '67
Faith, hope, and clarity? C. Morgello. il Newsweek 69:75 Je 19 '67
Gauging the conglomerates. C. Morgello. il Newsweek 70:82 O 9 '67
Gold bugs. C. Morgello. Newsweek 69:80 Ap 24 '67
Impact of devaluation. C. Morgello. il Newsweek 70:80-1 N 27 '67
Life on the pogo stick. C. Morgello. il Newsweek 69:75 Je 5 '67
Next target for the Dow. C. Morgello. il Newsweek 69:81 Mr 27 '67
Prices outpace profits. C. Morgello. il Newsweek 69:73 My 1 '67
Schizophrenic market. C. Morgello. il Newsweek 69:67 Mr 6 '67
Stronger than the Dow. C. Morgello. il Newsweek 69:80 Ja 30 '67
Temporary roadblock? C. Morgello. Newsweek 69:80 F 20 '67
That old siren song. C. Morgello. Newsweek 69:82 F 13 '67
Three averages. C. Morgello. Newsweek 69:79 My 15 '67
Why the Dow is lagging. C. Morgello. il Newsweek 69:73 F 27 '67
Word right now is caution. C. Morgello. il Newsweek 71:63 Ja 15 '68
Wall Street gets more edgy; considerable disagreement about the outlook from here. il Bsns W p42 S 23 '67
Wall Street rides with the punch; after devaluation. il Bsns W p 124-6 N 25 '67
Wall Street's view is foggy; stock market for 1968. il Bsns W p 16-17 D 30 '67
What happened to the Dow. il Fortune 75: 223 Ap '67
Which way for stocks in '68? C. Mathews. il Duns R 90:36-7+ N '67

Short selling

Wall Street: the tax-selling season. C. Morgello. Newsweek 70:86 N 20 '67

Tender offers

Getting tough with tenders. W. S. Rukeyser. il Fortune 76:108-10+ Ag '67
Stock tenders, British style. J. Ross-Skinner. il Duns R 90:32-5+ S '67
Tactics of cash takeover bids. S. L. Hayes, 3d. and R. A. Taussig. il Harvard Bsns R 45:135-48 Mr '67
Tender offers find rougher going. il Bsns W p 134+ My 6 '67
Tender war. il Time 89:101-2 Je 9 '67

Terminology

What's your investor I.Q? quiz. Nations Bsns 55:42-3+ Je '67
STOCKTON, Calif.

Galleries and Museums

Stopover in Stockton, to explore the delightful Haggin museum. il Sunset 139:44 N '67
STODELLE, Ernestine
College or career for dancers? Adelphi's answer. Dance Mag 41:60-3 Mr '67
Connecticut commission on the arts ventures a seminar. Dance Mag 41:30-1+ O '67
STOESSINGER, John G.
Recent books on international relations. For Affairs 46:205-23 O '67
STOFA, John
Break, a wrench and a march of new quarterbacks. E. Shrake. il por Sports Illus 27:69-72+ S 25 '67
STOFFEL, Lester L.
Public library development in Illinois. por Library J 92:210-13 Ja 15 '67
STOJANOVIC, Milka
Music to my ears. I. Kolodin. Sat R 50:89 N 25 '67
STOKES, Carl Burton
Black breakthrough. il por Newsweek 70:30+ O 16 '67
Black power at the polls. C. L. Sanders. il pors Ebony 23:23-6+ Ja '68
Focus on Cleveland. S. Friedman. Nat R 19: 1335-6 N 28 '67
Historic Election day for America. D. Jackson. il pors Life 63:36-7 N 17 '67
In Cleveland and Boston, the issue is race. J. M. Naughton. il N Y Times Mag p30+ N 5 '67
Into the mud. Time 90:19 N 3 '67
Negro marches toward city hall. il por Bsns W p36-7 O 7 '67
Real black power. il pors Time 90:23-7 N 17 '67
Rematch in Cleveland. por Time 90:24 S 15 '67

STOKES, Carl Burton—*Continued*
Score one for Stokes, and Negroes up for mayor. il pors Life 63:36-7 O 13 '67
Second chance for Cleveland. J. Barden. Commonweal 87:103-4 O 27 '67
Stokes in Cleveland. New Repub 157:11 O 28 '67
Stokes on trial in Cleveland. il por Bsns W p41 N 18 '67
U.S. letter: Cleveland. C. Trillin. New Yorker 43:210-14+ O 14 '67
Vindicative victory. il por Time 90:29 O 13 '67

STOKES, George
Balloonacy! por Travel 127:60-2 Ap '67

STOKES, Roy
To America, with daughters: in search of Robert McCloskey. Horn Bk 43:419-23 Ag '67
Trading stamp mentality; adaptation of address, 1966. por Library J 92:3595-600 O 15 '67

STOKES, Sewell. See Morley, R. jt. auth.

STOKESBURY, Leon
Lamar tech football team has won its game; poem. New Yorker 43:60 O 21 '67

STOKLEY, James
Astronomy. See issues of Science news

STOKOWSKI, Leopold Anton Stanislaw
Letter from Paris; rehearsal sessions with orchestra at the conservatorie. Genet. New Yorker 43:114-15 F 25 '67
Musical events; concert performed by Philadelphia orchestra in Philharmonic Hall. W. Sargeant. New Yorker 43:220-1 N 18 '67
Stokowski leads Stravinsky as Vanguard tries the Dolby system. P. G. Davis. il pors Hi Fi 17:16+ F '67

STOLEN automobiles. See Automobiles, Theft of

STOLLE, John F.
How to manage physical distribution. Harvard Bsns R 45:93-100 Jl '67

STOLLE, Red
Trimarans. il Yachting 122:48-9+ D '67 30 '67

STOLLEY, Richard B.
Bite of a shrew, and a life-or-death decision. por Life 63:63-4+ Ag 11 '67
Crisis worse than anyone imagined: report. Life 62:24-5 F 24 '67
Gustav Hertz's unfinished bike ride. Life 63:25-9 Jl 21 '67
Shrewd blend of pop-rock-schmaltz. Life 62:84A+ Je 9 '67
World of energy, some ad-lib bumbles. Life 62:74 Mr 3 '67

STOLZ, Mary
How much of a story is real? Writer 80:9-10+ Mr '67

STONE, Chuck
Report: Gary, Ind. Atlan 220:28-30+ O '67

STONE, Doug
Hotshot Charlie rides again. Esquire 68:111-15 O '67

STONE, I. F.
Izzy. il por Newsweek 71:52 Ja 22 '68
One man in time. S. W. Little. Sat R 51:117 Ja 13 '68
Stone's throw. A. Campbell. New Repub 158:37+ Ja 6 '68

STONE, Jeremy J.
Beginning of the next round? Bul Atomic Sci 23:20-5 D '67

STONE, Martin
On the run. por Time 90:101 O 13 '67

STONE, Millard E.
Conservation; address, June 13, 1967. Vital Speeches 33:625-8 Ag 1 '67

STONE, Polly Mariner
History in houses: West. Antiques 91:768-71 Je '67

STONE, Robert
Hard experience talking. W. Stegner. Sat R 50:25 Ag 19 '67

STONE, Ron, and Napier, Jeff
Pollution pickle revisited. Motor B 121:318-19 Ja '68

STONE, Ruth
Wild asters; poem. New Yorker 53:187 N 11 '67

STONE, Stanley
Rhode Island furniture at Chipstone. Antiques 91:207-13, 508-13 F: Ap '67

STONE, Walter L.
Sociologist discusses the new meaning of recreative use of leisure. bibliog Parks & Rec 2:22+ Ap '67

STONE, William Clement
Stone is new president of Hawthorn books. Pub W 191:67 Ap 24 '67

STONE, William T.
Washington report. See issues of Yachting

STONE age
Ex occidente lux; excavation at Lepenski Vir. il Newsweek 71:48 Ja 15 '68

STONE construction
Stillman house, Litchfield, Connecticut. il Arch Rec 141:54-7 mid-My '67

STONE dams. See Dams

STONE implements and weapons
Problematical pleistocene artifact assemblage from northwestern Spain. E. De Aguirre and K. W. Butzer. bibliog il Science 157:430 Jl 28 '67

STONE rubbings. See Rubbings

STONEBRIDGE priory. See Retreats, Spiritual

STONEHENGE, England
Beauty and mystery of Stonehenge. H. Fast. il Sat R 50:52-4 F 4 '67
Building bridges between disciplines; Stonehenge as an astronomical observatory. Sci N 92:440-1 N 4 '67
Stones of Wiltshire. D. Cohen. il Sci Digest 62:16-21 D '67

STONEWARE. See Pottery

STONEWORK. See Stone construction

STONEWORK, Decorative. See Decoration and ornament, Architectural

STONG, C. L.
(ed) Amateur scientist. See issues of Scientific American

STOOP, Norma McLain
My mother was good-bye; poem. Ladies Home J 84:137 Ap '67

STOP baths (photography) See Photography—Fixing

STOPPARD, Tom
Playwright Tom Stoppard: go home British boy genius! W. Hedgepeth. il pors Look 31:92-6 D 26 '67
Rosencrantz and Guildenstern are dead. Criticism
Commentary 44:82-4 D '67
Commonweal 87:171-2 N 10 '67
Look il 31:92-6 D 26 '67
Nat R 19:1393-5 D 12 '67
Nation 205:476 N 6 '67
New Repub 157:25-6 N 4 '67
New Yorker 43:179-80 My 6 '67
New Yorker 43:105 O 28 '67
New Yorker 43:52 N 4 '67
Newsweek il 70:90+ O 30 '67
Reporter 37:39-40 N 16 '67
Sat R 50:28 N 4 '67
Time 90:84 O 27 '67
Travel 128:22 D '67
Vogue 150:72 N 15 '67
Tom Stoppard. K. Halton. il por Vogue 150:112-13 O 15 '67
What's all this about? por Newsweek 70:72 Ag 7 '67

STOPPING of automobiles. See Automobiles—Stopping

STORAGE
See also
Moving and storage companies
also subhead Storage under various subjects, e.g. Corn—Storage

STORAGE batteries
Battery bulletin. C. W. Kennedy. il Pop Phot 61:74-7+ S '67
Battery care for fast starts. il Suc Farm 65:72 Ja '67
Leesona Moos battery draws oxygen for cathode from air. J. A. Strasser. il Aero Tech 21:38-9 N 6 '67
New know-how: choosing and using batteries. Good H 165:192 N '67
Reduced size, greater power claimed for new battery. il Aero Tech 21:43-4 Ag 14 '67
Saving mony in buying an automobile storage battery. il Consumer Bul 50:25-8 F '67
When I pushed the starter nothing happened. E. B. Forsyth. il Motor B 119:34-5+ My '67

Additives
Battery additives: AID's chagrin. D. S. Greenberg. Science 156:627 My 5 '67

History
That mysterious little black box. L. Heiner. il Yachting 123:96-7+ Ja '68

Testing
Build a combination battery charger and tester. H. H. Stover. il Pop Electr 27:33-7 Ag '67

STORAGE battery chargers
Build a combination battery charger and tester. H. H. Stover. il Pop Electr 27:33-7 Ag '67
Superspeed recharger for nickel-cadmium cells. R. M. Benrey. il Pop Sci 191:144-6 O '67

STORAGE elements (computers) See Magnetic memory (computers)

STORAGE in the home
Bold, beautiful, and buildable. D. Jordan. il
  Bet Hom & Gard 45:70-5 F '67
Bright ideas to stretch space. il Am Home
  70:76+ S '67
Build a storage bench for lounging. il Pop
  Gard 18:76-7 My '67
Clever answers to storage problems. il Bet
  Hom & Gard 45:120 S '67
Find a kitchen; places to put appliances and
  equipment in your kitchen. M. Davidson. il
  Ladies Home J 84:112-13 Mr '67
It's tough all over, n'est-ce-pas? B. Plumb.
  il N Y Times Mag p 104-5 Mr 12 '67
More storage anyone? Am Home 70:121 Mr
  '67
Storage ideas, room by room. N. Seney. il
  Bet Hom & Gard 45:6+ O '67
Three high spots for a hobby room. B. Josel-
  yn. il Pop Mech 128:136-41 Jl '67
Three unique ways to beat the storage short-
  age. il Pop Mech 128:136-41 S '67
Try these storage ideas in your farm home.
  J. LemMon. il Suc Farm 65:62-5 My '67
Weekend projects for your weekend home.
  il Pop Mech 127:152-5 Ap '67
    See also
  Kitchen cabinets
  Storage walls
STORAGE of bulbs. See Bulbs—Storage
STORAGE of grain. See Grain—Storage
STORAGE tanks. See Water tanks
STORAGE walls
Bold, beautiful, and buildable. D. Jordan.
  il Bet Hom & Gard 45:70-5 F '67
Hidden in the wall, firewood, hi-fi, chairs,
  TV. il Sunset 139:122-3 N '67
Instead of a sideboard, a storage wall. il Sun-
  set 139:76 Jl '67
New built-in for the kitchen wall. il Pop Sci
  191:163 O '67
Storage wall for a family room. F. L. Green-
  wald. il Pop Sci 190:145-8 F '67
Walls that entertain! il Bet Hom & Gard
  45:53-4 Mr '67
Walls that work. il Bet Hom & Gard 45:114
  Ap '67
STORE hours
    See also
  Business hours
STORES
Building types study. il Arch Rec 141:171 My
  '67
Psychedelicatessen; shops for psychedelic ac-
  cessories. il Time 89:78+ F 24 '67
Suburbia: where the action is in stores.
  G. A. Christie. il Arch Rec 141:83 Ja '67
    See also
  Retail trade
    also subhead Stores under names of
  cities, e.g. Atlanta—Stores

    Safety measures
NRMA issues guidelines for civil disorder
  areas. Pub W 192:42 Ag 14 '67
STORES, Remodeled. See Remodeling (archi-
  tecture)
STORIES. See Anecdotes; Fairy tales; Short
  stories; Story telling
STORK is a wonderful bird; story. See Ger-
  ber, M. J.
STORM, Sydney
America's most beautiful valley. Am For 73:
  38-40+ Ja '67
STORM KING (mountain)
This hollowed-out ground; battle of Fort
  Montgomery and retreat to Butter Hill.
  C. Carmer. il Am Heritage 18:58-9+ Je '67
STORM water. See Sewerage
STORMS
Beware the big ones! E. R. Greeff. il Yacht-
  ing 121:70-1+ Mr '67
Gales for Christmas. D. J. Tinius. il Motor
  B 120:39+ D '67
Ordeal of the Petrel. E. D. Fales, jr. il Pop
  Mech 127:68-72+ Je '67
    See also
  Hail
  Hurricanes
  Snowstorms
  Thunderstorms
  Tornadoes
  Winds
STORY (periodical)
Story magazine acquired by Four winds
  press. Pub W 191:89 Ja 30 '67
STORY of Gilbert and Sullivan; drama. See
  Leech, M. T.
STORY of Miss Sadie Graine; story. See Haz-
  zard, S.
STORY telling
How to develop students' storytelling skills.
  S. Cochell. Sr Schol 90:sup24 Mr 31 '67

World of storytelling; preconference institute
  of Children's services division. D. Ander-
  son. ALA Bul 61:828-9 Jl '67
STORY telling records. See Phonograph records
  —Childrens records
STORYTELLING. See Story telling
STOTT, E. B.
Down we go. Flying 80:78 My '67
STOUFFER, Charles William
Pictograph cave in Kings Canyon National
  Park. il Nat Parks Mag 41:16-17 My '67
STOUFFER foods corporation
Out at the ballpark; Stouffer foods corp.
  approves Litton industries' buy-out offer.
  il Time 89:94 Ap 21 '67
STOUFFER-Litton merger. See Business con-
  solidations and mergers
STOUFFER'S restaurants
Puritan restaurant swings à la mod: pitching
  its image at the young crowd. il Bsns W
  p62-3 F 4 '67
STOUGHTON, Cecil
Full record. il por Time 89:19 F 24 '67
STOUTENBURGH, John L. jr
Museum world. See issues of Hobbies
STOVER, Harley H.
Build a combination battery charger and
  tester. Pop Electr 27:33-7 Ag '67
STOVES
How to shop for a range. Bet Hom & Gard
  45:130-1 Je '67
New ranges. il Redbook 128:92-5 Mr '67
What to look for in a range. V. T. Habeeb.
  il Am Home 70:86 S '67
    See also
  Electric stoves
  Electronic stoves
  Gas stoves

    Care
On the spot with oven cleaners. Am Home 70:
  132 O '67
STOVES, Franklin
Wonderful Franklin stove. J. Gould. il Field
  & S 71:52-3+ Mr '67
STOVES, Outdoor. See Camp stoves
STOWAWAYS
Memo from the Mary's last stowaway. T.
  Barry. il Look 31:122 N 14 '67
STOWE house, Buckinghamshire. See England
  —Historic houses, etc.
STRAGE, Mark
Art of re-creativity. Esquire 69:92-7 Ja '68
STRAIN, Paula M.
Adirondacks, forever wild. Liv Wildn 30:32-3
  Aut '66
Trails for tomorrow; review. Liv Wildn 31:
  55-9 Spr '67
STRAINS. See Muscles—Wounds and injuries
STRAINS and stresses
Prestressed foundation resists roof thrusts.
  R. N Gensert. il Arch Rec 142:173-6 N '67
STRAMENTOV, Konstantin
Architects of silence. UNESCO Courier 20:8-
  12 Jl '67
STRAND, Harold P.
Man-sized dryer blows hot or cold. Pop Mech
  127:192-3 Ap '67
STRAND, Mark
Babies; poem. New Yorker 43:48 S 30 '67
Dream; poem. New Yorker 43:34 Ag 19 '67
Last bus; poem. New Yorker 43:62 O 14 '67
Man in the mirror; poem. New Yorker 43:50
  Mr 11 '67
Man in the tree; poem. New Yorker 43:30 D
What to think of; poem. New Yorker 43:172
  Ap 22 '67
STRAND, Paul
Paul Strand at seventy-six; interview. ed.
  by J. Deschin. por Pop Phot 60:14+ Mr '67
STRANG, Ruth
War talk and war games. PTA Mag 62:
  20-3 bibliog(p33) Ja '68
STRANGE fare; story. See Hudson, H.
STRANGER, Joyce
Breed of giants; story. Sat Eve Post 240:44-7
  Je 3 '67
STRANGER come home; story. See Buck, P. S.
STRANGWAY, David W. and others
Stable magnetic remanence in antiferromag-
  netic goethite. bibliog Science 158:785-7 N
  10 '67
  —See McMahon, B. E. jt. auth.
STRASBERG, Lee
Clap hands, here comes Strasberg. il por Time
  90:78 O 6 '67
STRASBOURG festival. See Music festivals—
  France
STRASSMANN, W. Paul
Books. Bul Atomic Sci 23:52-3 Je '67
STRATEGY
AFA convention demands new strategy, cites
  technology. W. E. Wilks. Tech W 20:17 Mr
  20 '67

STRATEGY—*Continued*
Graduated response fallacy. D. Graham. Yale
R 57:90-8 O '67
Reconsideration of the criteria for deterrence.
J. Barton. Bul Atomic Sci 23:41-4 D '67
We need a new strategy in Vietnam. Bsns W
p 132 Ag 12 '67
See also
Military art and science
United States—History—Revolution—Strategy
Vietnamese war, 1957- —Strategy
STRATEGY, Communist. See Communist strat-
egy
STRATES, James E.
Lot of quarters. W. K. Zinsser. il Look 31:
18 S 5 '67
STRATFORD, Ontario. Shakespeare festival.
See Shakespeare festival, Stratford. Ontario
STRATFORD-ON-AVON
Stratford-on-Avon. N. Marsh. il Atlan 219:
116+ F '67
Traveler's choice. K. B. Peavy. Travel 128:
11 S '67
STRATIGRAPHIC geology. See Geology, Strati-
graphic
STRATTON, Charles Sherwood
General Tom Thumb and other midgets. V.
A. McKusick and D. L. Rimoin. il por Sci
Am 217:102-6+ bibliog(p 136) Jl '67
STRAUS, David B.
Ribonuclease: recent advances. Science 157:
1212+ S 8 '67
STRAUSS, Claude Lévi-. See Lévi-Strauss, C.
STRAUSS, Johann, 1825-1899
Blue Danube waltzes on. H. Fantel. il Read
Digest 90:174-7+ My '67
Die fledermaus. Criticism
Opera N il 31:17-20 Ja 7 '67
Opera N il por(cover) 31:24-5 Ja 7 '67
Vintage Strauss. R. Freed. Sat R 50:88 F 25
'67
STRAUSS, Josef
Farewell to Feuerfest; concerning translation
of title. R .Freed. Sat R 50:74 S 30 '67
Vintage Strauss. R. Freed. Sat R 50:88 F
25 '67
STRAUSS, Leo
Jerusalem and Athens. Commentary 43:45-57
Je '67
STRAUSS, Lewis Lichtenstein
Dwight Eisenhower's proposal for our time.
Nat R 19:1008-10 S 19 '67
about
More war or real progress in Mideast. il por
U S News 63:58-60 Ag 7 '67
STRAUSS, Richard
Friedenstag. Criticism
Opera N 31:24 Je 10 '67
Records:
Der Rosenkavalier. Opera N 32:34 Ja 6 '68
Richard Strauss, the life of a non-hero, by
G. Marek. Review
Am Rec G 33:858-60 My '67. R. Sabin
New Yorker 43:175 Ap 22 '67. W. Sargeant
Sat R il por 50:56+ My 27 '67. R. Breuer
Der Rosenkavalier. Criticism
Hi Fi 17:MA12-13 My '67
New Yorker 43:93 F 25 '67
New Yorker 43:127 Ap 1 '67
New Yorker 43:137-8 S 23 '67
Sat R 50:115 Mr 11 '67
Strauss as musician and man. G. R. Marek.
il pors Opera N 31:8-12 Ap 8 '67
Triumph! London's new Elektra. G. L. Mayer.
il Am Rec G 34:274-7 D '67
Woman without a shadow (Die frau ohne
schatten) Criticism
Opera N 32:25 S 23 '67
STRAUSZ-HUPÉ, Robert
Sagacity of Dr Strausz-Hupé. R. Kirk. Nat
R 19:1276 N 14 '67
STRAVINSKY, Igor Fedorovich
Dolly system of recording. L'histoire du
soldat conduced by Leopold Stokowski. J.
Diether. il por Am Rec G 33:624-6 Ap '67
Histoire du soldat (Soldier's tale) Criticism
Time il 89:74 Mr 10 '67
In celebration, Stravinsky's 85th. C. J. Luten.
Am Rec G 33:1008 Jl '67
Musical events. W. Sargeant. New Yorker
43:190-2 N 4 '67
Rake's progress. Criticism
New Yorker 43:83 Je 24 '67
Records:
Mavra and Les noces: Pulcinella: Oedipus
Rex; Persephone; Symphony of psalms.
por Opera N 32:34 D 30 '67
Rite of spring like none other. il por H. Glass.
Am Rec G 34:59 S '67
Stravinsky. R. Craft. il pors Look 31:50-4+
D 26 '67
Stravinsky at eighty-five. R. Evett. New Re-
pub 157:27-8 D 16 '67

Stravinsky and the microphone. D. Hamilton.
il pors Hi Fi 17:56-60 Je '67
Stravinsky: the composer and his works, by
E. W. White. Review
Am Rec G 33:862-4 My '67. C. J. Luten
Hi Fi por 17:MA28 Ap '67. D. Hamilton
Three new discs continue Columbia's Stra-
vinsky canon. D. Hamilton. por Hi Fi 17:
69-70 Ag '67
World's greatest pictures: Stravinksy by
Newman. J. Scully. il pors Mod Phot 31:
70-1+ My '67
STRAWBERRIES
Strawberries. G. M. Darrow. il Horticulture
45:16-17+ Jl '67
Strawberries and flowers; border with a
bonus. I. M. Walters. il Home Gard 54:85-7
Ap '67
See also
Cookery—Fruit
STRAWBERRY CANYON recreation area. See
California. University—Berkeley campus—
Strawberry Canyon recreation area
STRAYHORN, Billy
Strayhorn and the Duke. B. Korall. Sat R
50:71-2 S 16 '67
STREAMER chamber. See Counters (electrons,
ions, etc)
STREAMERS (fishing flies) See Fishing lures,
flies, etc.
STREET, Donald M. Jr
Gunkholing the lesser Antilles. Yachting 122:
52-3+ N '67
STREET, Penny
It's the only life for me! pors Seventeen 26:
92-3 D '67
STREET cleaning
Soviet streets are the cleanest. A. Bjoerkman.
il Am City 82:102-3 Je '67
Street cleaning. See issues of American city
STREET cleaning apparatus
Eliminated: one expensive rehandling opera-
tion; four-wheel sweepers clean the streets
and haul the debris; Baltimore. E. Moore.
il Am City 82:76-7 Jl '67
See also
Leaf gatherers
Refuse collection trucks
STREET lighting
Another all-mercury city; Chesterfield, Ind.
il Am City 82:128 N '67
Bright lights, brighter future; Buchanan,
Mich. D. D. Tammer. il Am City 82:158 O
'67
Congressmen push for better street lighting.
Am City 82:136 F '67
Lighting puts a final touch on a downtown
renewal; Hollidaysburg, Pa. J. M. Mitchell.
il Am City 82:110 Ag '67
Minimum lighting not good enough; Maple-
wood, Mo. Am City 82:122 D '67
More light to grow by; Kansas City, Mo.
C. F. Sharpe. il Am City 82:120 D '67
Outdoor lighting. See issues of American city
Police cite need for more residential light-
ing. Am City 82:188 S '67
Maintenance
Maps tell us where the lights are; Hagers-
town. Md. R. E. Roulette. il Am City 82:116
Jl '67
STREET lighting fixtures
Breakaway poles promise fewer deaths. il Am
City 82:126 N '67
STREET markers. See Street signs
STREET name signs. See Street signs
STREET names
On the street, lane, circle or drive where
you live. J. L. O'Neill. Am Home 71:40
Ja '68
STREET paving. See Pavements
STREET records. See Municipal records
STREET repairing.   See Streets—Maintenance
and repair
STREET signs
Good signs reflect a city's image; Galveston.
J. Impey. il Am City 82:156-7 S '67
Good street-sign program; High Point, N.C.
R. V. Moss. il Am City 82:156 O '67
Make street signs big enough to read; Phoe-
nix, Ariz. C. E. Haley. il Am City 82:133-4
F '67
Street signs hit home; indoor and outdoor
decor. J. Peter. il Look 31:M30+ N 28 '67
STREET sweepers. See Street cleaning appara-
tus
STREET trades
Great food markets of the world. il Life 62:
64-81 My 12 '67
STREET traffic
Drive in U.S. to break traffic jams. il U S
News 63:50-2 O 23 '67

STREET traffic—*Continued*
How other countries fight the rush hours;
western Europe, Japan, India. il U S News
63:52-3 O 23 '67
See also
Road traffic
Traffic police
also subhead Street traffic under names
of cities, e.g. Turin, Italy—Street traffic
STREET trees. See Trees in cities
STREETS
See also
Arcades
Block parties
Sidewalks
also subhead Streets under names of
cities, e.g. Toronto—Streets

Lighting
See Street lighting

Maintenance and repair
New modern base restores the oldest street
in America; St Augustine, Fla. S. G. Stepp.
il Am City 82:93-4 D '67
No more paving secrets or underground mysteries; Denver. F. A. Wikgren. il Am City
82:28 Mr '67

Nomenclature
See Street names
STREICHER, Lee
Filter backwash gets special treatment. Am
City 82:94-5 N '67
STREIKER, Lowell D.
Christian education and the Jewish people;
address. Christian Cent 84:168-71 F 8 '67
Communication between faiths. Sat R 50:37
N 11 '67
Drama. Christian Cent 84:870-1, 1071-2, 1106,
1527-8, 1604 Jl 5. Ag 23-30. N 29. D 13 '67
Philadelphian frolics. Christian Cent 84:815-16
Je 21 '67
STREISAND, Barbra
Funny girl goes West; with report by J.
Hallowell. il pors Life 63:139-42 S 29 '67
Funny girl makes a movie. il pors N Y Times
Mag p34-5 S 24 '67
Her name is Barbra. M. W. Lear. por Red-
book 130:54-5+ Ja '68
Mama Barbra. I. Mothner. il pors Look 31:
74-8 Jl 25 '67
What makes a Barbra special. il pors Bsns W
p64-8+ My 20 '67
STRENGTH, Muscular. See Muscular power
STRENGTH of materials
See also
Fracture of solids
Metals—Strength
STREPTOMYCIN
Phenotypic masking and sterptomycin de-
pendence. L. Gorini and others. bibliog il
Science 157:1314-17 S 15 '67
STREPTONIGRIN. See Antibiotics
STRESHINSKY, Shirley G.
How to choose the right name for your baby.
Parents Mag 42:62-3+ O '67
STRESS (physiology)
Children under pressure: four doctors' views;
symposium. il Todays Health 45:62-5 S '67
Creative tensions in the research and devel-
opment climate. D. C. Pelz. bibliog il Sci-
ence 157:160-5 Jl 14 '67
Does emotional tension make you ill? P.
Deutsch and R. Deutsch. Read Digest 91:
122-5 D '67
Don't let tension push you around. C.
Mitchell. il Pop Sci 191:79-82+ O '67
Fighting and death from stress in a cock-
roach. L. S. Ewing. bibliog il Science 155:
1035-6 F 24 '67
Frustration quotient. P. D. Weidig. il NEA
J 57:38-9 Ja '68
Inner-harmony secrets of people under pres-
sure. D. V. Cleary. il Todays Health 45:
62-5 N '67
Ischemic necrosis: prevention by stress. H.
Selye. bibliog il Science 156:1262-3 Je 2 '67
Isometric tension differences in fibers of red
and white muscles. A. W. Sexton and J. W.
Gersten. bibliog il Science 157:199 Jl 14 '67
Social breakdown. N. Goldman. bibliog f il
Ann Am Acad 373:156-79 S '67
Stress in fight & flight. il Time 89:57 Ap 14
'67
Tension, anxiety, and nervous distress: how
to cope with everyday pressures. Bet Hom
& Gard 45:26+ Ap '67
STRESSES. See Strains and stresses

STRETCH, Bonnie Barrett
Bundy report. Sat R 50:70-1 D 16 '67
Fate of Negro colleges. Sat R 50:77 Ap 15
'67
Overhauling Negro colleges. Sat R 50:86 N
18 '67
STRETTON, Hesba
Second thoughts about Victorian children's
fare. J. St John. il Wilson Lib Bul 41:590-2
F '67
STRICK, Joseph
Things I am here to read, seaspawn and sea-
wrack. il Life 62:58 Mr 31 '67
STRICKLAND, Hiram D.
I died a soldier. Read Digest 90:103 My '67
STRICKLAND, Mrs J. P.
I am a tired housewife. U S News 62:112 Mr
27 '67
STRICKLAND, Virgil E.
Current priorities in education. Sch & Soc 95:
51-3 Ja 21 '67
STRICKMAN, Robert Louis
Columbia filter raises a cloud of questions.
por Bsns W p20-1 Jl 22 '67
New cigarette filter, a university's dilemma.
A. Rosenfeld. il por Life 63:50-1 Jl 28 '67
New dark horse entry; low-tar filter. il Sci
N 92:104-5 Jl 29 '67
New safe cigarette filter. L. David. Good H
165:92-3+ N '67
Strickman filter. il por Time 90:43 Jl 21 '67
STRIDULATIONS. See Insect sounds
STRIKE insurance. See Insurance, Strike
STRIKES
See also
Lockouts

Economic aspects
Labor woes cloud outlook for economy. il
Bsns W p38-9 O 14 '67
What the subway strike cost in lost time. Am
City 82:26 D '67
Who wins a strike? I. Ross. Read Digest 91:
101-5 Ag '67

Law
See Labor laws and legislation—United
States

Canada
If you think U.S. has labor troubles—. il U S
News 62:77-9 F 13 '67

France
Letter from Paris; workers political strike
for purely political reasons. Genêt. New
Yorker 43:126-7 My 27 '67
Looking backward; nationwide strikes. il
Newsweek 69:47 Ap 3 '67

Great Britain
British dock strike ends, but-. U S News
63:98 D 11 '67
In Britain: strikes, labor violence, and calls
for regulation of unions. U S News 63:82
O 30 '67
Letter from London; recent go-slow on the
railways. M. Panter-Downes. New Yorker
43:52 D 23 '67
U.K. acts to avert BOAC strike. Aviation W
87:40 D 11 '67
Why Britain risked a rail strike. il Bsns W
p 118 O 28 '67

Japan
Shuntō: Japanese labor's spring wage offensive. R. Evans, jr. bibliog f il Mo Labor R
90:23-8 O '67

Spain
Out! out! il Newsweek 69:54 F 13 '67
Unaccustomed tumult. Time 89:34 F 10 '67

United States
As strike crises pile up for LBJ: new push
for new law. U S News 62:97 Ap 17 '67
Avco strike heats up pressure for a law. il
Bsns W p 114 Jl 1 '67
Bargaining hurdles that are still ahead; truck-
ing settlement boosts demands in other
industries. il Bsns W p 160+ Ap 22 '67
Bargaining's bite hits small business: unions
pressing hard at all levels. Bsns W p 154+
My 6 '67
City troubled by strike threats; New York.
U S News 62:65-6 Ap 3 '67
Divide and conquer isn't so easy. Bsns W
p59-60 Je 10 '67
Era of growing strife in U.S. il U S News
63:41-3 S 25 '67
For unions in '68: strikes, big raises, election
losses. U S News 64:74-5 Ja 8 '68
Guns of April. il Time 89:35 Ap 14 '67
How to avoid strikes that hurt the Nation.
Bsns W p200 Ap 22 '67
Huelga: new goals for labor. E. Nelson, jr.
il Nation 204:724-5 Je 5 '67

STRIKES—United States—*Continued*
It's definite now: no permanent law to stop
big strikes; recent, current and threatened
strikes. U S News 63:66-8 Jl 31 '67
Labor; threatened slowdowns or strikes involving fire department, radio and television networks, and, once again, newspapers, New York city. New Yorker 43:31-3
Ap 8 '67
Major strikes, but small gains. U S News 63:
73 Jl 10 '67
New militancy. il Time 90:21 S 22 '67
Playing the patsy; strikes and threats of
strikes. il Time 89:22 Ap 21 '67
Rethinking the right to strike. Fortune 76:
113-14 O '67; Reply. F. Spreng. 76:106 N
'67
Review of work stoppages during 1966. H.
N. Fullerton. il Mo Labor R 90:39-42 Ag
'67
Strikes force the issue in Congress; tough,
wide-ranging legislation against strikes. il
Bsns W p44+ Ap 29 '67
These are the issues that are bringing strike
threats. il U S News 62:95-6+ Ap 10 '67
What will strife cost? Bsns W p27-9 Ap 8
'67
When strikers must be rehired. U S News
64:68 Ja 1 '68
Why strikes are getting harder to settle. il
U S News 63:74-5 O 16 '67
Why trucks stopped running and trains might.
il U S News 62:95-6 Ap 24 '67
Work stoppages; tables. See issues of Month-
ly labor review
Worst year. il Time 90:93-4 O 13 '67

Agricultural workers
See Strikes—United States—Farm labor

Airlines
Escaping a holiday air strike. Bsns W p98 Mr
25 '67

Apartment house employees
Apartment mess. il Newsweek 69:72 Je 12 '67
Canapés on the sidewalk, angina at eight. il
Time 89:35 Je 9 '67

Automobile industry and trade
At the showdown stage in the auto dispute;
offer to United auto workers union by
General motors, Ford and Chrysler. U S
News 63:70-2 S 11 '67
Auto bargaining complications. America 117:
263 S 16 '67
Auto strike. Nat R 19:1002 S 19 '67
Auto strike talks go into gear. il Newsweek
70:77-8 O 23 '67
Auto strike to upset business? il U S News
63:35-7 S 18 '67
Auto workers' war chest: loaded for a long
strike; UAW investments. il U S News
62:80+ Je 5 '67
Costly from any point of view. il Time 90:
91 S 15 '67
Detroit tries brinkmanship; forcing UAW
officials to name specific priorities. Bsns W
p 115-16 Ag 26 '67
Everyone was lined up, ready for a Ford
shutdown. il Life 63:36-9 S 22 '67
Everything is on ice. Newsweek 70:82 S 25
'67
Ford dealers battle the storm; lack of new
cars to sell. il Bsns W p44-5 O 21 '67
Ford strike. New Repub 157:7-8 S 23 '67
Ford takes the blow; Reuther pulls UAW
out. il Bsns W p35-6 S 9 '67
High cost of strikes: what auto union is
learning. il U S News 63:81-2 O 23 '67
Mood is adamant; neither Ford nor UAW is
ready to bargain. il Bsns W p37-8 S 16 '67
Now auto dispute heads for showdown. U S
News 63:70-1 Jl 17 '67
Now the showdown at General motors; what
a strike would do. U S News 63:95-6 N 20
'67
Pressures on Reuther, and Ford. il News-
week 70:71-4+ S 18 '67
Starting to talk, & sell. il Time 90:94 O 20
'67
Strike woes multiply. il Bsns W p35-6 O 7
'67
Toward a settlement. Time 90:89-90 O 27 '67
What the auto strike is costing the workers.
il U S News 63:104 O 9 '67

Farm labor
Delano: the story of the California grape
strike. by J. G. Dunne. Review
New Repub 157:23-6 D 2 '67. M. Duber-
man; Reply. W. L. Kircher. 158:46 Ja
6 '68
Strike! California's grape pickers. J. G.
Dunne. il Sat Eve Post 240:32-6+ My 6 '67

Trouble in the melon patch; Texas Rangers
break up picket lines in pickers' strike. il
Newsweek 69:38+ Je 19 '67

Farmers
Crackdown; NFO injunction. il Newsweek 69:
76 Ap 10 '67
Curds & woe. il Time 89:22 Mr 31 '67
Dairy farmers protest. America 116:523 Ap
8 '67
Dairymen rebel. il Sr Schol 90:18 Ap 14 '67
NFO milk dumping, what did it do? N.
Reeder. il Farm J 91:28-9+ My '67
Spilled milk. il Newsweek 69:68 Ap 3 '67
When dairy farmers went on strike. il U S
News 62:53 Ap 3 '67

Government employees
Can new state law end public worker strikes?
Condon-Wadlin act replaced with heavy
fines on organizations. il Bsns W p98 Ap
8 '67
Ineffective injunctions; public employees'
strikes. il Time 90:77 S 29 '67
More costly strikes ahead; rising strength of
public employee unions. il Nations Bsns
55:38-42 N '67
Strikes against government. B. L. Masse.
America 117:609-10 N 18 '67
Strikes by public employees. A. H. Raskin.
Atlan 221:46-51 Ja '68

Government intervention
As strike crisis grows: new talk of controlling unions; proposals for a permanent
ban on crippling work stoppages. il U S
News 62:72-3 My 8 '67
Riding the rails again. il Bsns W p 17-19 Jl
22 '67
When government takes a hand in wage
fights: more for unions? U S News 63:92
O 2 '67
When the president steps in; history of presidential intervention. il Bsns W p 122-4 Je
17 '67
Whiff of chaos; bill creates panel to mediate
the dispute. il Time 90:15 Jl 28 '67

Maritime workers
Back of the latest maritime strike. U S News
62:78 Je 26 '67

Miners
Copper's holy war. il Newsweek 71:75-6 Ja
22 '68
Crucial copper talks move to Washington;
to end eight-week old copper strike. Bsns
W p38 S 9 '67
Little union-busting? copper workers strike.
Nation 206:70 Ja 15 '68
One strike that drags on and on; copper
industry. U S News 64:76 Ja 8 '68
River of poison; pollutants released in Clark
Fork River by strike at copper mine. il
Newsweek 70:70 Ag 28 '67
Strain of a five-month strike. il Bsns W p
160-2+ N 18 '67
Strike that adds to the dollar's troubles;
copper workers. il U S News 64:78-9 Ja 15
'68
Toll of five-month strike: who is hurt and
how much. il U S News 63:94-6 D 11 '67
Tug of war; copper workers strike. il Time
90:69 D 22 '67
Why the copper strike goes on. U S News
63:78-9 D 4 '67

Newspapers
Detroit papers: shutdown again. U S News
63:79 D 4 '67
Detroit's press profiteers. W. Serrin and G.
Goltz. il Reporter 38:32-3 Ja 11 '68
Putting on the pressure; strike of newspaper
workers. il Newsweek 71:47-8 Ja 8 '68
Too impatient to talk; Detroit's two strike-
prone newspapers closed down. il Time 90:
84+ D 8 '67

Police
When policemen strike in a big city; Detroit.
il U S News 63:73-4 Jl 3 '67

Printers
Anti-union vote at Kingsport certified by
NLRB and U.S. Court of appeals; four-year
strike near end. Pub W 192:47 Jl 17 '67
Kingsport press four years later, an assess-
ment. il Pub W 191:62-3+ My 1 '67
Quasi-boycott of Kingsport press in Detroit.
Pub W 191:89 Ja 30 '67
Two unions decertified in Kingsport election.
Pub W 191:226+ Ja 23 '67

Radio industry
Management takes to the microphones. il
Bsns W p28 Ap 8 '67
Portrait of the artists. il Time 89:46 Ap 7 '67

STRIKES—United States—*Continued*

Railroads

Can Congress settle the rails? impasse between carriers and the shopcraft unions. Bsns W p92+ My 13 '67

Can the unions block LBJ's plan to prevent a railroad strike? U S News 62:114 My 15 '67

Frustrating bargaining laws; strike threat. Life 62:4 My 19 '67

Rail crisis: all hands stand pat; six shopcraft unions threatening to strike. Bsns W p 104 Jl 15 '67

Railroad peace plan. Sr Schol 90:26-7 My 19 '67

Riding the rails again. il Bsns W p 17-19 Jl 22 '67

Strike law may go broad gauge; impasse on anti-strike legislation. Bsns W p 148+ Je 24 '67

When government takes a hand in wage fights; more for unions? U S News 63:92 O 2 '67

When the president steps in. il Bsns W p 122-4 Je 17 '67

Whiff of chaos; bill creates panel to mediate the dispute. il Time 90:15 Jl 28 '67

Why the House rejected LBJ's plan to head off rail strike. U S News 62:77 Je 26 '67

Rubber workers

Rubber workers try the boycott weapon. il Bsns W p 121-2 Je 3 '67

Strike that's a mystery; what's behind rubber dispute. il U S News 62:81-3 My 29 '67

Tire makers roll again; industry lamenting higher costs. il Bsns W p30 Jl 29 '67

U.S. lends a hand to end rubber strike. Bsns W p 150 Je 24 '67

Why tire workers walked out. U S News 62:96 My 1 '67

Steel industry and trade

Can steel strike be avoided? U S News 63:84 O 23 '67

Teachers

Autumn of their discontent: teachers walk out on schools. Library J 92:3792+ O 15 '67

Back of the rash of teachers' strikes; with charts. U S News 63:54 S 18 '67

Back to school, bitterly. Time 90:64 S 29 '67

Back to school? teachers from New York to Oakland threatening to strike. il Newsweek 70:80-1 S 11 '67

Catholic school strikes. America 117:370 O 7 '67

Catholic school teachers picket. America 116:711 My 13 '67

Displays of blackboard power. America 117:294-5 S 23 '67; Reply. B. L. Johnson. 117:398 O 14 '67

Driving a hard bargain. Newsweek 70:54 O 2 '67

If 100,000 teachers go on strike. il U S News 63:74-5 Ag 14 '67

Just the beginning? Sr Schol 91:34+ S 28 '67

Meanwhile, back in Philadelphia; strike of lay teachers in the diocesan high school system. A. Swidler. Commonweal 86:191-2 My 5 '67

More militant mood. il Time 89:66 Mr 3 '67

More teachers favor strikes. Sr Schol 91:sup 29 O 26 '67

Pursuit of power. il Time 90:43 S 22 '67

Shock of public strikes; with editorial comment. il Life 63:8, 30D-35 S 22 '67

Should teachers be allowed to strike? pro and con discussion. il Sr Schol 91:14-15 O 12 '67

Strikes against states: two tests; New York city and Detroit. U S News 63:93 O 2 '67

Teacher opinion poll; strikes and sanctions. il NEA J 56:38-9 O '67

Teacher power. il Newsweek 70:65 S 18 '67

Teacher shortages and strikes plague nation's school openings; report of NEA survey. Sr Schol 91:sup2 O 5 '67

Teacher strikes. W. D. Boutwell. PTA Mag 62:14-15 O '67

Teacher strikes: who won? P. Janssen. Sat R 50:66 O 21 '67

Teachers defy antistrike laws; New York and Detroit. U S News 63:116 S 25 '67

Teachers' revolt. Nation 205:260 S 25 '67

Teachers strike hard; push for better pay and working conditions. il Bsns W p43-4 S 16 '67

Teachers' strikes: a threat to opening of schools. il U S News 63:70-2 S 4 '67

Test of strength. il Time 90:50 S 15 '67

Trouble in the classroom: teacher walkouts in parochial schools. il Time 89:56 Je 2 '67

Work stoppages and teachers: history and prospect. R. W. Glass. il Mo Labor R 90:43-6 Ag '67

Teamsters

Guns of April. il Time 89:35 Ap 14 '67

Teamsters start to slip bridle; steel naulers' strike. il Bsns W p 113-14 O 28 '67

Tough test for labor; congressional pressure for laws to curb transportation tie-ups. il Bsns W p33-5 Ap 15 '67

Why trucks stopped running and trains might. il U S News 62:95-6 Ap 24 '67

Television industry

AFTRA the fact. New Repub 156:7 Ap 29 '67

Due to circumstances; AFTRA strike. il Newsweek 69:86 Ap 10 '67

Hour of amateurs. il Time 89:88 Ap 14 '67

Management takes to the microphones. il Bsns W p28 Ap 8 '67

Portrait of the artists. il Time 89:46 Ap 7 '67

Show-stopper; AFTRA strike ends. Sr Schol 90:22-3 Ap 28 '67

Still out. Newsweek 69:119 Ap 17 '67

What the strike in TV won. U S News 62:97 Ap 24 '67

When $100,000-a-year men go on strike. il U S News 62:98-9 Ap 17 '67

Transportation workers

What the subway strike cost in lost time. Am City 82:26 D '67

Truck drivers

Terror on the highway; independent steel haulers. il Newsweek 70:83-4 O 16 '67

STRINDBERG, August

Dance of death. Criticism
New Yorker 43:158+ Ap 15 '67
Sat R il 50:36 Jl 1 '67

STRINDBERG, Johan August. See Strindberg, A.

STRINER, Herbert E.

Technological displacement as a micro phenomenon. Mo Labor R 90:30-1 Mr '67

STRING quartets

Now we are 20; the Juilliard quartet. H. Saal. il Newsweek 69:107 Ap 10 '67

See also

Phonograph records—String quartet music

STRINGED instruments

Family of twang. F. V. Grunfeld. Reporter 36:39-40+ Ap 20 '67

Orchestra in opera: kingdom of strings. R. Lawrence. il Opera N 32:26-9 D 30 '67

See also

Guitar

Sitar

STRINGFELLOW, William

Great society as a myth; adaptation of address; reprint. por Cath World 205:83-9 My '67

STRIP coal mining. See Coal mines and mining—Stripping operations

STRIP mine dumps, Reclamation of. See Reclamation of land

STRIP mining. See Coal mines and mining—Stripping operations

STRIP rust. See Rusts (botany)

STRIPED bass fishing. See Bass fishing

STRIPER fishing. See Bass fishing

STROETZEL, Donald S.

(ed) See Armbrister, T. Great Bolivian fever mystery

STROETZEL, Dorothy Gow

Peru's path to progress. Read Digest 91:167-70+ S '67

STROHL, William A. and others

Adenovirus tumorigenesis: role of the viral genome in determining tumor morphology. bibliog Science 156:1631-3 Je 23 '67

STROKES, Apoplectic. See Cerebral hemorrhage

STROM, Susan

Schools and the pregnant teen-ager. Sat R 50:80-1+ S 16 '67

STROMATOLITES. See Algae, Fossil

STROMINGER, Jack L. and Ghuysen, J. M.

Mechanisms of enzymatic bacteriolysis. bibliog Science 156:213-21 Ap 14 '67

STRONG breed; drama. See Soyinka, W.

STRONGYLOCENTROTUS purpuratus. See Sea urchins

STROPHANTHIDIN

Strophanthidin-sensitive transport of cesium and sodium in muscle cells. R. A. Sjodin and L. A. Beaugé. bibliog il Science 156:1248-50 Je 2 '67

STROUT, Richard L.

India's gigantic effort at modernization. New Repub 157:12 D 23 '67

Next year, a funny thing could happen on the way to the White House. N Y Times Mag p24-5 Jl 23 '67

STROVNIK, Robert

Long Island lens. il U S Camera 30:72-3 N '67

STRUCTURAL engineering
Architectural engineering. il Arch Rec 142: 125-35 Ag; 205-16 S; 149-50 D '67
Engineers achieve surprising savings by post-tensioning apartment flat plate slabs. il Arch Rec 141:193-6 Je '67
Field day for engineers: Expo 67. H. Comstock. il Pop Mech 127:88-92 My '67
Miniature megastructure; Yamanashi communications center. V. C. Mahler. il Arch Forum 127:35-43 S '67
New town; Grand Isle, prefabricated mining town in the Gulf of Mexico. J. Johansen. il Arch Forum 127:44-53 S '67
See also
Shells (structural engineering)
STRUCTURAL geology. See Geology, Structural
STRUHSAKER, Thomas T.
Behavior of vervet monkeys and other cercopithecines. bibliog Science 156:1197-203 Je 2 '67
STRUNK, Norman
This can be a good time to buy a house. Am Home 70:30+ Mr '67
STRYCHNINE
Strychnine caper. S. P. Young il Am For 73: 20-3+ Je '67
Strychnine onslaught. S. P. Young. il Am For 73:32-3+ Jl '67
STRYKER, Evelyn. See McMillan, G. jt. auth.
STUART, Alastair M.
Alarm, defense, and construction behavior relationships in termites isoptera. bibliog Science 156:1123-5 My 26 '67
STUART, Dabney
Tourist; poem. New Yorker 43:205 O 28 '67
about
Seven poets. R. Tillinghast. Poetry 110:260-1 Jl '67
STUART, E. S. and Moscona, A. A.
Embryonic morphogenesis: role of fibrous lattice in the development of feathers and feather patterns. bibliog Science 157:947-8 Ag 25 '67
STUART, Gilbert
Philosopher of the face; retrospective at the National gallery. B. N. O'Doherty. il Art N 66:42-5+ Sum '67
Presidential painter. il por Newsweek 70:56-8 Jl 17 '67
STUART, James
Letter from London. See issues of Antiques
STUART, Jesse
Eye of the April sun; poem. Am For 73:19 Ap '67
Mick, the dreamer; a story of the soil. Am For 73:34-7+ F '67
This is my land; poem. Am For 73:51 Jl '67
STUART, Jessica Jane
God sends October; poem. Am For 73:55 O '67
STUART-STUBBS, Basil
Trial by computer; excerpts from address, April 1967. Library J 92:4471-4 D 15 '67
STUBBORN old lady; story. See Hayes. P. T.
STUBBS, Basil Stuart-. See Stuart-Stubbs, B.
STUBBS, Harry C.
Views on science books. Horn Bk 43:767-8 D
STUCKER, Gilbert F.
Mullica: river of iron. il Nat Parks Mag 41: 10-15 S '67
STUD farms. See Horse breeding
STUDEBAKER, John Ward
Doctor Studebaker retires. por Sr Schol 91: sup3 D 7 '67
STUDENT achievements
Academic casualties. Sch & Soc 95:248 Ap 15 '67
Coleman report: Equality of educational opportunity; excerpts. J. Alsop; A. M. Mood. il NEA J 56:26-8+ S '67
Dropout who made good; valedictorian of Harvard law school. il Time 89:59 Je 30 '67
Eighth grade rebel; a student speaks. L. Hedgecock. NEA J 56:19 S '67
Excessive educational pressures. P. H. Abelson. Science 156:741 My 12 '67; Discussion. 156:1685; 157:1117 Je 30, S 8 '67
Games work with underachievers; North Carolina advancement school. D. C. Farran. il Sr Schol 91:sup 10-11 N 9 '67
Instant measurement; comprehensive random achievement monitor. Sch & Soc 95:208-9 Ap 1 '67
International study of achievement in mathematics, ed. by T. Husén. Review
Sat R il 50:68-9 Jl 15 '67. M. Beberman
Needed: a university for the C+ student. H. A. Fitzgerald. il Look 32:52 Ja 23 '68
Our happy underachiever. J. Lewis. il Parents Mag 42:48-9+ Ap '67

Our special hell: student failures; need for funds to help them. J. Nugent. Sr Schol 90:sup 13 My 19 '67
Problems of high school students in relation to grade achievement. J. C. Marshall. bibliog f il Sch & Soc 95:237-8 Ap 1 '67
Underachievers need help. Sr Schol 91:sup3 O 19 '67
Which personality succeeds in college? D. Klein. il Seventeen 26:148-9+ My '67
Wide, wide world of Walter Winshall; student's simultaneous studies in Harvard law school and M.I.T.'s Sloan school of management. Time 89:76 Je 23 '67
STUDENT activities
Clark Kerr calls it the exaggerated generation. C. Kerr. il N Y Times Mag p28-9+ Je 4 '67
Equality for your fellow man; Student homophile league. Time 89:52 My 12 '67
Mood at Berkeley. C. J. McNaspy. America 116:817-18 Je 3 '67
Painting the ocean red, etc. at Columbia university; Warmth movement. D. Carlinsky and B. Lefkowitz. Esquire 68:99+ S '67
Relaxing from coast to coast; spring-vacation invasion. il Newsweek 69:30-3 Ap 3 '67
Something to talk about on campus. J. Romer and P. Roth. il Mlle 65:320-3 Ag '67
Spies, J.G; campus-spy game. il Newsweek 69:112 Mr 27 '67
See also
College students—Political activities
National intercollegiate flying association
Parents and teachers associations—Student participation
Student unions
STUDENT aid
Answer to youth's challenge; proposal that middle class Negroes contribute education funds to needy students. C. Rowan. il Ebony 22:140-3 Ag '67
College: what it costs, how to pay for it. il Changing T 21:7-13 S '67
How to get money for college. L. T. Trimble. il Am Ed 3:9-11 Jl '67
Loans to college students; borrowing against future earnings. Sch & Soc 95:373 O 28 '67
Looking ahead to college costs. M. Feeley. il Am Home 70:38+ D '67
See also
Student loans
Theological students—Aid
STUDENT attitudes. See Attitudes
STUDENT business
Campus entrepreneurs. il Newsweek 70:88-90 S 25 '67
STUDENT Christian movements
European S.C.M.s and political action. K. Chamberlain. Christian Cent 84:418-19 Mr 29 '67
STUDENT clubs. See Student activities
STUDENT conferences
See also
United States national student association
STUDENT counselors
See also
Personnel service in education
STUDENT demonstrations
And leave the marching to us; Proxy Pickets. il Time 89:23 My 5 '67
Case of *kulturkrankheit*; West Germany's students. Time 89:28 Je 30 '67
Chaos on the campus; San Francisco state college suspensions. New Repub 158:14-15 Ja 6 '68
Crackdown on protesters. il Time 90:54 N 10 '67
Crackdown starts on student riots; with interview with J. H. Reinoehl. il U S News 64:34-7 Ja 1 '68
Daffodils, unite! issues of the sit-in at the London school of economics. R. Rosenblatt and D. Schechter. New Repub 156:13-14 Ap 15 '67
Dow at Harvard: the right to recruit on college campuses. M. Ford. New Repub 157: 11-13 N 11 '67
Enmity in the North; Dartmouth college demonstrations against G. Wallace. il Time 89:20 My 12 '67
Face of justice; Cincinnati protest, December 1967 by Antioch students. A. L. Denman. New Repub 158:12 Ja 20 '68
Feeding the fire; riots at University of Madrid. Newsweek 69:36+ My 29 '67
Festival in Berlin. J. Maguire. Sat R 50:75+ N 11 '67
Guerrillas on campus; move from protest to resistance at S.F. state. il Newsweek 70: 68+ D 18 '67
How to prevent riots; student-faculty committee report at Berkeley. il Time 91:34 Ja 19 '68

STUDENT demonstrations—*Continued*

How to wreck a campus; violence at San Francisco state college. D. Swanston. il Nation 206:38-41 Ja 8 '68

Ire against fire; demonstrations against firm making napalm. il Time 90:57 N 3 '67

London school of economics & Berkeley. A. Lejeune. Nat R 19:473-4 My 2 '67

Marcher; current state of American protest; interview. C. Charvez. New Yorker 43:28 My 27 '67

Mr Leavitt comes to Harvard. G. Ross. Nation 205:654-8 D 18 '67

New campus cry; student power, but a crackdown starts. il U S News 63:6+ N 13 '67

Oakland; how to lose in winning; Berkeley student sit-in at induction center. J. S. Hadsell. Christian Cent 84:1476-8 N 15 '67

On Wisconsin; faculty and police vs students during anti-Dow chemical demonstrations. J. Ridgeway. New Repub 157:8-10 N 4 '67

Princeton weekend with the SDS. D. Rader. New Repub 157:14-16 D 9 '67

Racial violence in the high schools. U S News 63:12 N 6 '67

Rebellion and responsibility. B. Rubenstein and M. Levitt. Yale R 57:16-30 O '67

Rebellion in Europe. il Time 90:39 D 22 '67

Summer of discontent; Vietnam Summer. il Newsweek 69:103 Je 12 '67

Tough line on protests. il Sat R 50:69 D 16 '67

Ugly new mood. Newsweek 70:68 N 27 '67

U.S. letter: Connecticut; A. Shaw, Dow chemical company recruiter. C. Trillin. New Yorker 43:76+ Ja 6 '68

Unrest on the campus; reasons why. il U S News 62:12 My 1 '67

War on campus; what happened when Dow recruited at Harvard. R. J. Samuelson. il Science 158:1289-94 D 8 '67

What teeth does the draft law have? il U S News 63:22-3 D 25 '67

STUDENT drinking. See Liquor problem—United States

STUDENT employment

Employment of school age youth, October 1966. V. C. Perrella. il Mo Labor R 90:20-6 Ag '67

Going to Europe, the hard way; summer job. D. Klein. il Seventeen 26:152-3 D '67

Job for the summer. D. Klein. il Seventeen 26:140+ Je '67

McCall's guide to summer jobs. McCalls 94:114-17 F '67

Mother's not-so-little helper. D. Klein. il Seventeen 26:214-16 Mr '67

Open letter to employers; plea for summer jobs. H. H. Humphrey. U S News 62:79 Je 12 '67

Summer in space for ghetto youths; education experiment, working at Goddard space flight center. il Bsns W p44 S 9 '67

Summer jobs that are going begging; excerpts from report. W. Raspberry. U S News 62:8 Je 12 '67

There's still time to earn money; symposium. il Seventeen 26:66-7+ Jl '67

Wanted: kids for summer jobs. il Changing T 21:38 Mr '67

STUDENT exchange programs. See Students, Interchange of

STUDENT fees. See Colleges and universities—Finance

STUDENT forums. See Forums (discussion and debate)

STUDENT government. See Self government in education

STUDENT health. See College students—Health and hygiene

STUDENT homophile league. See Student activities

STUDENT life

Campus turmoil: a religious dimension. T. A. Langford. Christian Cent 84:172-4 F 8 '67

Girls, or boys, who needs them? F. Nelson. il Nat R 19:1067-9 O 3 '67

Necker checkers; rules that regulate student life. il Newsweek 69:96 My 8 '67

Relaxing from coast to coast; spring-vacation invasion. il Newsweek 69:30-3 Ap 3 '67

Room-mates. il Esquire 68:94-7 S '67

Stanford's open dorm policy. Sch & Soc 95:293 Sum '67

See also

College students

Student activities

STUDENT loans

Ed op bank. Sat R 50:73 O 21 '67

Educational loans. R. C. Jancauskas. America 116:440-1+ Mr 25 '67

How to get money for college. L. T. Trimble. il Am Ed 3:9-11 Jl '67

Loans to Cuban refugee students. Sch & Soc 94:476 D 24 '66

Paying for college; loan plan receives chilly reception. D. S. Greenberg. Science 157:1412+ S 22 '67

To foot the bill; proposed Educational opportunity bank. Sci N 92:296-7 S 23 '67

STUDENT newspapers. See College and School journalism

STUDENT nonviolent coordinating committee

As rioting spreads, the search for answers. il U S News 63:26-8 Ag 14 '67

Black racists attack Jews. Christian Cent 84:1211 S 27 '67

Frantic search for notoriety. Life 63:4 S 1 '67

Man from SNCC. Newsweek 69:45 My 22 '67

Odyssey of a man, and a movement. P. Good. il N Y Times Mag p5+ Je 25 '67

Politics. D. Macdonald. Esquire 68:44+ N '67

Radical speaks in defense of S.N.C.C. S. Lynd. il N Y Times Mag p50-1+ S 10 '67; Discussion. p4+ O 1; 36+ O 8 '67

Squirm, baby, squirm! Nat R 19:943-4 S 5 '67

SNCC and the Jews. il Newsweek 70:22 Ag 28 '67

STUDENT opinion

Concern on the campus; excerpts from To make a difference, ed. by O. Butz. il Time 89:90 Je 9 '67

Cool generation and the church; symposium. Commonweal 87:11-23 O 6 '67; Discussion. 87:5, 152-5 O 6, N 3 '67

Five college students speak out; questions and answers, ed. by L. F. McKernan; discussion. Cath World 205:134-8 Je '67

How do you double-date on a camel? visiting high-school students from fifty-eight countries. L. B. Johnson. il McCalls 94:48+ S '67

Letter to LBJ; college students protest our involvement in Vietnam. Sat R 50:64 Ag 19 '67

Minds of high school seniors; impressions gathered from reactions to essay on the open mind. F. B. Maynard. New Repub 156:11-12 My 20 '67

Secondary sources; high-school students' judgments about the Vietnamese war. il Newsweek 70:88+ Jl 10 '67

Student involvement in the liturgy; survey findings of attitudes of Catholic college freshmen toward the mass. W. J. Farrell. il Cath World 205:199-204 Jl '67

To make a difference, by O. Butz. Review Sat R 50:76-7+ My 20 '67. C. Oglesby

Urug and the Grungey; day of the campus hero is over. il Newsweek 70:54 D 4 '67

Who are the activists? E. Van Loon. il Am Ed 4:2-4+ D '67

STUDENT participation in school government. See Self government in education

STUDENT peace movement. See Pacifism

STUDENT personnel work. See Personnel service in education

STUDENT press association. See United States student press association

STUDENT program of Lincoln Center. See Lincoln Center fund for education and artistic advancement

STUDENT records. See School reports and records

STUDENT rights. See Intellectual liberty; Students—Civil rights

STUDENT selection

Art of the application. Newsweek 71:37 Ja 1 '68

Data on college vacancies; program conducted by educational service bureau in Illinois. Sch & Soc 95:7 Ja 7 '67

STUDENT self government. See Self government in education

STUDENT self-support. See College students—Employment

STUDENT teachers

Student teacher named Gail; Gail Holliday at Garfield high school, Los Angeles. D. Barclay. il Sch Arts 66:3-4 Ja '67

Why not a draft to get new teachers? H. Taylor. Look 31:80+ Je 27 '67

STUDENT tours. See Student travel

STUDENT travel

All students aboard! (a compendium of opportunities) A. L. Zeigler. Sat R 50:57-8+ F 18 '67

Discover America; this is the year! L. Jonckheere. il Sr School 90:sup 18-19 Ap 7 '67

Let's travel: student style. M. Smith. il Mlle 65:156+ Ag '67

Let's travel: student travel news. J. Silver. Mlle 66:34+ Ja '68

Personal business; student tours and study programs abroad. Bsns W p 135 Ap 8 '67

Six girls and one man; tours of the Netherlands office for foreign student relations. J. Silver. il Mlle 65:193-4+ O '67

STUDENT travel—*Continued*
Where and how of student travel. M. E. Sherman. Sat R 50:38+ F 18 '67
See also
Travel study courses
STUDENT tutors. See Tutors and tutoring
STUDENT unions
Duquesne, dramatic change in campus scale. W. R. Cooper. il Arch Forum 127:78-85 Jl '67
Relations with the student union; symposium. il Pub W 191:36-7 My 22 '67
STUDENT withdrawals. See Dropouts
STUDENTS
See also
Art students
College students
Federal aid to education
Foreign students in the United States
Graduate students
High school students
Medical students
Negro students
Theological students

Civil rights
Academic freedom: judges support student rights. L. J. Carter. Science 158:477-9 O 27 '67
National rally for student power. J. Brann. Nation 205:658-60 D 18 '67

Employment
See Student employment

Grading and promotion
See Grading and marking (students)

Rating
See also
High school students—Rating
STUDENTS, Interchange of
Teenage ambassadors abroad; exchange programs for high-school students. C. Lauren and F. G. Conn. il Parents Mag 42:54-7+ My '67
See also
Experiment in international living (organization)
STUDENTS, Married
See also
High school students, Married
STUDENTS, Mentally superior. See College students, Mentally superior; High school students, Mentally superior
STUDENTS and teachers. See Teachers and students
STUDENTS contests. See Competitions
STUDENTS for a democratic society (organization)
Princeton weekend with the SDS. D. Rader. New Repub 157:14-16 D 9 '67
SDS: protest is not enough. R. Blumenthal. il Nation 204:656-60 My 22 '67
STUDENTS of theology. See Theological students
STUDENTS vocabularies. See Vocabulary
STUDIES (rooms)
Homework havens all through the house. il Good H 165:112-18 Ag '67
STUDIOS
In his former studio an artist creates an art-filled second home. il House B 109:132-5 Je '67
Light, silence, and space. A. Michelson. il Vogue 149:142-3+ Mr 15 '67
Studio by the sea. il House & Gard 131:86-9 Je '67
To get away at home: escape rooms. il House B 109:108-12 Ja '67
See also
Artists studios
STUDIOS, Dance. See Dance studios
STUDIOS, Moving picture. See Moving picture studios
STUDS, Automobile. See Automobile engines
STUDS, Tire. See Tires, Automobile
STUDY
High school homework vs. college preparation. D. Klein. il Seventeen 26:52+ S '67
See also
Courses of study
STUDY carrels. See School libraries
STUDY guides
Study in intense competition: the review book industry. il Pub W 191:40-2 F 6 '67
STUDY tours. See Travel study courses
STUFFED toys. See Toys
STUFFING. See Cookery—Poultry
STUHLER, James
Vietnam. E. Galligan. il U S Camera 31:48-9+ Ja '68

STUMPS. See Trees
STURCKEN, H. Tracy
Raleigh and El Dorado of Guiana. Américas 19:15-21 Ag '67
STURGEON, Everett
Contemporary machine embroidery. Sch Arts 66:23-7 Ap '67
STURGEON (submarine boat) See Submarine boats, Atomic powered
STURGEON fishing
Snake River submarines. H. D. Bishop. il Am For 73:24-5+ Je '67
STURGEONS
See also
Caviar
STURMER, Barbara
Our borrowed year. por McCalls 94:20+ My '67
STURROCK, Jock
Tough skipper to run a fast Dame. R. Robertson. il Sports Illus 27:86-8 S 11 '67
STURTZ Shirley
Block to block. Sch Arts 67:18-21 O '67
STÜSSY, Jan
Man in a box. il por Time 90:86 O 6 '67
STUTTERING. See Stammering
STUTTGART, Germany

Architecture
Twin schools on three levels; Stuttgart. il Arch Forum 126:80-6 Ap '67

Music
Stuttgart; heir to Wieland Wagner's battle against tradition. E. D. Echols. Opera N 31:30 Mr 4 '67
Stuttgart; production of Les Troyens. H. Koegler. Opera N 31:32 Ap 8 '67
Stuttgart; Walter Felsenstein production of Weber's Freischütz. H. Koegler. Opera N 32:32 Ja 13 '68
STYCOS, J. Mayone
Prospects for population control. Christian Cent 84:1458-62 N 15 '67
STYLE, Literary
Challenge of words. S. Babb. Writer 81:12-13 Ja '68
House of the seven ushers and how they grew: a look at Jamesian Gothicism. M. Banta. Yale R 57:56-65 O '67
Longing for spring again; interview. G. Fielding. Cath World 204:296-300 F '67
Prejudice and hope; reprint. V. Peterson. Writer 80:21-4 F '67
Substance of fiction; excerpts from The story: a critical anthology. M. Schorer. Writer 80:14-18+ Je '67
Words and style. E. Weeks. Writer 80:22-3+ Ap '67
World elsewhere, by R. Poirier. Review Nation 205:58-9 Jl 17 '67. A. Trachtenberg
See also
Literary criticism
Literature
Words

Anecdotes, facetiae, satire, etc.
Portrait of a babe. T. Meehan. il Sat Eve Post 240:22 Mr 25 '67
STYLE, Musical. See Composition (music)
STYLE In dress. See Fashion
STYLE shows. See Fashion shows
STYLING, Automobile. See Automobiles—Design
STYRON, William
Author. P. Meras. por Sat R 50:30 O 7 '67
Confessions of Nat Turner; excerpts from novel. Harper 235:51-102 S '67; Same. por Life 63:54 O 13 '67

about
Books. G. Steiner. New Yorker 43:236+ N 25 '67
Into the mind of Nat Turner. R. A. Sokolov. il pors Newsweek 70:65-9 O 16 '67
Nat Turner's sword. R. A. Schroth. America 117:416 O 14 '67
Note on the history. H. Aptheker. Nation 205:375-6 O 16 '67
Novelist as a rebel slave. il pors Life 63:51-2 O 13 '67
Styron unlocked. J. Phillips. il por Vogue 150:216-17+ D '67
STYLITES, Simeon, pseud. See Luccock, H. E.
SUBCONSCIOUSNESS
Responses of human somatosensory cortex to stimuli below threshold for conscious sensation. B. Libet and others. bibliog il Science 158:1597-600 D 22 '67
Short reactions stay unconscious; neurological basis in sensory cortex for unconscious processes. Sci N 92:631-2 D 30 '67

SUBCONTRACTING
Two-way contracting. W. M. Lowry. il Harvard Bsns R 45:131-7 My '67
See also
Contracts, Government—Subcontracting
SUBJECT cataloging. See Cataloging
SUBJECT headings
Many changes, no alteration; analysis of Library of Congress subject headings, seventh edition. J. E. Daily. bibliog il Library J 92:3961-3 N 1 '67; Reply. A. L. Phinazee. 93:15 Ja 1 '68
SUBJECTS, School. See Courses of study
SUBMARINE archeology. See Archeology, Submarine
SUBMARINE boats
Business takes the deep plunge; U.S. companies to launch subs to explore the sea's possibilities. il Bsns W p74-6 Je 17 '67
Deep sea exploration. E. Wenk, jr. il Sat R 50:43-4 Jl 1 '67
DSRV cost said to almost triple the initial estimate. R. Lindsey. Aero Tech 21:29 D 18 '67
Down in the sea in a bubble. J. Ludwigson. il Sci N 91:240-1 Mr 11 '67
First plastic underwater hull big enough for men readied. Tech W 20:39-40 My 8 '67
Glass reinforced plastic hull set for delivery soon to DSRV; deep submergence rescue vehicle. il Aero Tech 21:39+ N 6 '67
I became an aquanaut, third class. D. C. Fales. il Pop Mech 127:110-11+ My '67
Litton proposing off-the-shelf sub design; dry diver transport vehicle. C. D. LaFond. il Tech W 20:30-1+ Mr 6 '67
Manned submersibles for research. H. A. Arnold. bibliog il Science 158:84-90+ O 6 '67
NAA ready to begin building submersible; Beaver Mark IV model. W. E. Wilks. il Tech W 20:36-7 My 1 '67
Our first ferry to the bottom of the sea; Deep Diver. E. A. Link. il Pop Sci 191:47-9+ Jl '67
Rescue from the deep! W. B. Hendrickson, jr. il Pop Mech 129:124-6+ Ja '68
Sights sub, wants same; Russians want to buy Star III. il Newsweek 69:73 Mr 6 '67
600-ft. dives planned by OSI; Deep Diver, new submersible. Tech W 20:41 My 15 '67
Star III sub leased by NOO for ocean-floor mapping. R. W. Niblock. Tech W 20:40 F 27 '67
Submarine in a fish pond; display at University of Pennsylvania. il Sci Digest 63:77 Ja '68
Submarine shuttle bus; Deep Diver. il Life 62:51-2+ Ap 21 '67
SURV to tackle the North Sea. il Sci N 93:45-6 Ja 13 '68
Taxi for the deep frontier; project Man-in-sea goes mobile. K. MacLeish. il Nat Geog Mag 133:138-50 Ja '68
United States and foreign; undersea research vehicles. il Aero Tech 21:111+ Jl 31 '67
Work beneath the waves. il Time 91:68-75 Ja 19 '68
See also
Submarine vehicles

Accidents
See Submarine disasters

Airplane combination
Fantastic flying sub. S. M. Gallager. il Pop Mech 128:114-17 S '67

Electronic equipment
MIT readying DSRV system based on Polaris, Apollo data. Aero Tech 21:18 S 25 '67
Rickover tells GE to weigh anchor; manufacturers of propulsion equipment decline to bid. Bsns W p 105+ Je 24 '67
Undersea electronic needs focus on repackaging methods. J. Rhea. Aero Tech 21:42 S 25 '67

Materials
Funding restraints threaten DSSP materials R&D base. J. F. Judge. il Aero Tech 21: 33-5 S 25 '67

Power supply
DSSP prepares for new fuel cell effort. Aero Tech 21:37 S 25 '67

Regulation
AIAA meeting hears call for steps to regulate submersibles. R. W. Niblock. Aero Tech 21:50 N 6 '67
SUBMARINE boats, Atomic powered
Deterrents at sea; U.S.'s Will Rogers and France's Redoubtable commissioned. il Newsweek 69:110 Ap 10 '67

New type of nuclear submarine in offing. M. Getler. Tech W 20:16 My 1 '67
Second Sturgeon enters service; nuclear-powered submarine. il Bsns W p74 My 6 '67
SUBMARINE cables. See Cables, Submarine
SUBMARINE disasters
Rescuer; diving bell inventor saves crew of Squalus. P. Maas. il Sat Eve Post 240: 36-40+ S 23 '67
SUBMARINE diving. See Diving, Submarine
SUBMARINE geology
Blake outer ridge; development by gravity tectonics. J. E. Andrews. bibliog il Science 156:642-5 My 5 '67
Drilling on Midway atoll, Hawaii. H. S. Ladd and others. bibliog il Science 156: 1088-94 My 26 '67
SUBMARINE moving picture photography. See Moving picture photography, Submarine
SUBMARINE oil well drilling. See Oil well drilling, Submarine
SUBMARINE painting. See Painting, Submarine
SUBMARINE photography. See Photography, Submarine
SUBMARINE rescue work. See Underwater rescue work
SUBMARINE research. See Oceanographic research
SUBMARINE vehicles
Underwater hot rod; Pegasus. J. Fix. il Pop Mech 128:100-2 D '67
SUBMARINE warfare
A-New system readied for tests on P-3C. C. M. Plattner. il Aviation W 86:72-3+ Mr 27 '67
Aircraft, the one indispensable arm of the entire anti-submarine warfare team. S. Thurmond. Aero Tech 21:23-4 D 4 '67
On the record; interview. C. B. Martell. Aero Tech 21:42-3 N 6 '67
See also
Guided missiles—Launching from submarine boats
SUBMERGED lands
Law comes to the sea floor. J. Ludwigson. il Sci N 91:474 My 20 '67
U.S. claims to undersea territory urged by Rogers. Tech W 20:15 Ap 10 '67
Vanishing tidelands. P. Redford. Atlan 219: 75-8+ Je '67; Same abr. il Read Digest 91:134-7 S '67
SUBMERSIBLE boats. See Submarine boats
SUBMERSION
See also
Underwater physiology
SUBOTNICK, Morton
Electronic music with nary a blurp or a whine or a krontch. A. Frankenstein. il por Hi Fi 17:75-6 D '67
SUB-PLANES. See Submarine boats—Airplane combination
SUBSCRIPTION books
Bowker lecture; subscription books; address, May 18, 1967. E. J. McCabe. Pub W 191: 36-40 My 29 '67
SUBSCRIPTION television programs. See Television broadcasting—Subscription programs
SUBSCRIPTION tickets. See Tickets
SUBSIDENCES (earth movements)
Geological subsidence. S. S. Marsden, jr. and S. N. Davis. il Sci Am 216:93-100 Je '67
SUBSIDIES
See also
Agricultural administration—United States
Economic assistance, Domestic
Family allowances
Ship subsidies
also subhead Federal aid under various subjects, e.g. Housing—Federal aid
SUBSONIC aerodynamics. See Aerodynamics
SUBSONIC airplane engines. See Jet airplane engines
SUBSTATIONS, Electric. See Electric substations
SUBSTITUTE products
See also
Milk substitutes
SUBSTRATA communications. See Radio communication, Underground
SUBURBAN churches
Low-rise in suburbia; other possibilities in the apartment house ministry. G. J. Micheals. Christian Cent 84:871-2 Jl 5 '67
SUBURBAN life
Report on suburbia; symposium. ed. by J. Peter and M. Simons. il Look 31:25-36+ My 16 '67
View from the picture window; are the suburbs really perfect? M. Mead. Redbook 129:28+ O '67
SUBURBAN newspapers. See Newspapers—United States

SUBURBAN offices. See Location in business and industry

SUBURBAN schools
Busing kids to the suburbs; Boston's METCO program. H. Spergel. il Am Ed 3:2-5 Ap '67
New drive to get city Negroes into the suburbs. il U S News 62:68-9 F 27 '67

SUBURBS
Decentralization of jobs. D. K. Newman. bibliog f il Mo Labor R 90:7-13 My '67
Report on suburbia: symposium. ed. by J. Peter and M. Simons. il Look 31:25-36+ My 16 '67
Rise of suburban power. Christian Cent 84: 1275-6 O 11 '67
White exodus to suburbia steps up. H. J. Gans. il N Y Times Mag p24-5+ Ja 7 '68
Wooing white collars to suburbia; office parks. il Bsns W p96-8 Jl 8 '67
See also
Regional planning

SUBVERSIVE activities
Violence of politics; Mau Maus of Harlem and C.I.C.'s of St Louis. il Esquire 68:46-7 Jl '67
See also
Communism—United States
Political crimes and offenses

Vietnam (Republic)
Ho's underground in South Vietnam. D. Warner. il Reporter 37:20-2 N 30 '67
Vietcong cadre of terror; operations of F-100 unit. D. Moser. il Life 64:19-29 Ja 12 '68

SUBWAY stations
Remodeled subway station is prototype for improvement of Boston's transit system. il Arch Rec 142:36 N '67

SUBWAYS
Subways can be beautiful. il Time 90:65-6 O 20 '67
Subways don't have to be miserable. il Fortune 75:177+ Ap '67
See also subhead Subways under names of cities, e.g. Montreal—Subways

SUCARYL. See Sugar substitutes

SUCCESS
How to succeed in business? work in Washington. il Fortune 75:127-33 Mr '67
If this be heresy; address, April 26, 1967. M. Upton. Vital Speeches 34:37-9 N 1 '67; Excerpts with title It's time to stand up for the upperdog. il U S News 63:62-3 Jl 10 '67
Making know-how pay; interview. W. F. Rockwell. Nations Bsns 55:88-90+ N '67
Self-made man as father. A. A. Messer. N Y Times Mag p 123+ Mr 19 '67
Want to be a success? reprint. D. C. McClelland. il Sci Digest 61:69-74 Ap '67

SUCCESS story; story. See Glaze, E.

SUCCESSION, Presidential. See Presidents— United States—Succession

SUCCULENT plants
Gardener's synopsis of useful succulents. D. Barrows. il Home Gard 54:26-34 Jl '67
How to grow succulents in the home. il Good H 164:198-9 Mr '67
See also
Cactus
Flowering stones

SUCH a quiet thing; story. See Tucker, H.

SUCKER fishing
Old fishing hole. D. J. Anderson. il Field & S 72:46-7+ Jl '67

SUCKING, Thumb. See Thumb sucking

SUDAN
Sudan's donkey-back midwives; with photos by Paul Almasy. Todays Health 46:16-18 Ja '68
See also
Elections—Sudan

Economic conditions
Economic development in the Sudan; photographs. UN Mo Chron 4:95-102 Ap '67

History
Mystic hero met a tragic end in the deathtrap of Khartoum. E. Kern. il Life 63: 66-7 O 6 '67

Politics and government
See also
Elections—Sudan

Race problems
Africa's hidden race war. il U S News 63:56 O 23 '67

SUDAN grass

Hybrids
Let's take another look at the high-yielding grass forages. C. E. Sommers. il Suc Farm 65:34-5+ Je '67

SUDNOW, David
Logistics of dying. Esquire 68:102-3+ Ag '67

SUEKER, K. H.
One-tube low-frequency converter. Electr World 78:28-9 Jl '67

SUENENS, Léon Joseph, cardinal
Of many things. America 116:197+ F 11 '67

SUERO, Orlando. See Orlando, 1925-

SUEZ CANAL
Long way around. il Bsns W p26+ Jl 22 '67
Roots of bitterness; with report by E. Kern. il Life 63:52-70+ O 6 '67
Suez follies. J. Burnham. Nat R 19:1422 D 26 '67

SUEZ crisis. See Egypt—History—Invasion, 1956

SUFFOLK COUNTY, N.Y.
Reporter at large; race between O. G. Pike and J. M. Catterson, jr. for seat in House of representatives from First congressional district. R. Harris. New Yorker 43:48-50+ Ap 8 '67

SUFFRAGE
See also
Voters, Registration of
Voting

United States
In my opinion; eighteen-year-olds aren't ready to vote. B. Glasgow. Seventeen 26:266 S '67
See also
Negroes in the United States—Politics and suffrage

SUGA, Nobuo, and Campbell, H. W.
Frequency sensitivity of single auditory neurons in the gecko coleonyx variegatus. bibliog Science 157:88-90 Jl 7 '67

SUGAR
See also
Glucose

Manufacture and refining
See also
Holly sugar corporation

Physiological effects
Nitrate ions: potentiation of increased permeability to sugar associated with muscle contraction. J. O. Holloszy and H. T. Narahara. bibliog il Science 155:573-5 F 3 '67

SUGAR in the body
Aldolase reaction with sugar diphosphates. A. H. Mehler and M. E. Cusic, jr. bibliog il Science 155:1101-3 Mr 3 '67

SUGAR industry and trade
How life has changed in a Cuban sugar mill town. J. Yglesias. il N Y Times Mag p8-9+ Jl 23 '67
Report; Northeast Brazil. J. A. Page. Atlan 221:20-3 Ja '68

SUGAR maple. See Maple

SUGAR substitutes
Bitter battle over sweets. il Sci N 92:199-200 Ag 26 '67

SUGARMAN, Daniel A. and Hochstein, Rollie
How to cool your anger. Seventeen 26:144-5+ Ap '67
How to handle a crisis. Seventeen 26:150-1+ S '67
One and only you? excerpt from The Seventeen guide to knowing yourself. Seventeen 26:300-1+ Ag '67
Question of conscience. Seventeen 26:140-1+ F '67
Your dreams both day and night. Seventeen 26:84-5+ Jl '67

SUGARMAN, George
Wood: George Sugarman. W. Castle. il pors Craft Horiz 27:30-3 Mr '67

SUGARS
Anomeric bond-character in the pyranose sugars. H. M. Berman and others. bibliog il Science 157:1576-7 S 29 '67
Stabilization of hydrated electrons in irradiated frozen sugar solutions. W. R. Elliott. bibliog il Science 157:558-9 Ag 4 '67
See also
Lactose
Saccharides
Trehalose

SUGGESTION systems
Employee suggestions win cash; Dade County, Fla. il Am City 82:80 Ag '67

SUGIYAMA, Taketoshi, and others
Chromosome abnormality in rat leukemia induced by 7,12-dimethylbenz[a]anthracene. bibliog Science 158:1058-9 N 24 '67

SUHARTO, 1925-
Blossoming of Pak Harto. il por Time 90:39 N 17 '67
End of the line for Sukarno? por Sr Schol 90:16 Mr 10 '67
Indonesia wobbles toward recovery. G. R. Packard, 3d. il por N Y Times Mag p34-5+ O 1 '67

SUHARTO—*Continued*
Strong-man Suharto's job: to rebuild the nation that Sukarno wrecked. il por U S News 62:14+ Mr 6 '67
SUICIDE
Autocide: question of road fatalities. il Time 89:23 Mr 10 '67
Heal thyself; suicides among psychiatrists. Newsweek 69:112 My 22 '67
How to cure depression. F. R. Schreiber and M. Herman. Sci Digest 61:12-15 F '67
Lifeline for would-be suicides; with list of suicide-prevention centers. J. N. Bell. il Todays Health 45:30-3+ Je '67
Suicides rising. D. A. Ehrlich. Sci N 92:229 S 2 '67
Too young to die: help for teenagers by Rescue, incorporated; interview, ed. by R. W. O'Donnell. K. B. Murphy. il Sr Schol 91: sup7-8 N 16 '67
Ultimately sorrowful. Christian Cent 84:1415 N 1 '67
Why children commit suicide. M. Gunther. il Sat Eve Post 240:86-9 Je 17 '67
SUITS, Mens. See Clothing and dress—Men
SUITS at law. See Actions and defenses
SUJI-craft. See Wire sculpture
SUKARNO, 1901-
As the trap closes on Indonesia's Sukarno. por U S News 62:20 F 27 '67
Building pressure. Time 89:26 F 24 '67
Bung Karno at bay. D. Warner. il Reporter 36:41-4 F 9 '67
End in view. il por Newsweek 69:48-9 Mr 6 '67
End of the line for Sukarno? por Sr Schol 90:16 Mr 10 '67
Fall of Sukarno ,by T. Vittachi. Review Nation 205:217-19 S 11 '67. A. Josey
Indonesia's night of terror. H. Sutton. il por Sat R 50:25-8+ F 4 '67
Now he's going, now he isn't. Time 89:31-2 Mr 3 '67
Strong-man Suharto's job: to rebuild the nation that Sukarno wrecked. il por U S News 62:14+ Mr 6 '67
Tethered scapegoat. il Newsweek 69:52+ Mr 20 '67
Thousand cuts. il Newsweek 69:65 Mr 27 '67
SULFA ointment. See Ointments
SULFAMYLON
Medicine's dramatic strides against burns. J. H. Winchester. Read Digest 90:177-80+ Ap '67
SULFATE in soils. See Soils—Sulfate content
SULFATES
Crystallization of a sulfate-binding protein (permease) from salmonella typhimurium. A. B. Pardee. bibliog il Science 156:1627-8 Je 23 '67
Oxygen-18 composition of oceanic sulfate. R. M. Lloyd. bibliog il Science 156:1228-31 Je 2 '67
Oxygen-18 variations in sulfate ions in sea water and saline lakes. A. Longinelli and H. Craig. bibliog il Science 156:56-9 Ap 7 '67
SULFHYDRYL group. See Mercapto group
SULFIDES
Niningerite: a new meteoritic sulfide. K. Keil and K. G. Snetsinger. bibliog il Science 155:451-3 Ja 27 '67
Sulfide solubilities in alteration-controlled systems. J. J. Hemley and others. bibliog il Science 158:1580-2 D 22 '67
SULFITE oxidase. See Oxidases
SULFOXIDES
See also
Methyl sulfoxide
SULFUR
Booming brimstone. Time 90:88+ S 29 '67
Diminishing the role of sulfur oxides in air pollution. P. H. Abelson. Science 157:1265 S 15 '67
Lambda transition in liquid sulfur. G. E. Sauer and L. B. Borst. bibliog il Science 158:1567-9 D 22 '67

Prices
Squeeze on sulfur. Bsns W p54 Mr 25 '67
SULFUR butterflies. See Butterflies
SULFUR dioxide
Cutting down the reek of pollution; residual oil with high sulfur content major contributor to big-city smog. il Bsns W p79-80+ Ja 28 '67
Sulphur dioxide threatens forests; pollution in Sweden. H. J Barnes. Sci N 92:519 N 25 '67
SULFUR mines and mining
Mexico
Unlocking a rich store of sulfur; Isthmus of Tehuantepec. il Bsns W p60 Ap 22 '67

United States
New town; Grand Isle, prefabricated mining town in the Gulf of Mexico. J. Johansen. il Arch Forum 127:44-53 S '67
See also
Freeport sulphur company
SULFUR mustard. See Mustard gas
SULFUR oxides
Disulfur monoxide: production by desulfovibrio. W. P. Iverson. bibliog il Science 156:1112-14 My 26 '67
SULIOTIS, Elena
Adventure on the high C. por Time 90:65 N 17 '67
Music to my ears; role of Norma in American opera society production. I. Kolodin. Sat R 50:75+ N 25 '67
SULKIN, Sidney
Ride in; poem. Harper 235:98 D '67
SULLIVAN, Sir Arthur Seymour. See Gilbert, W. S. jt. auth.
SULLIVAN, Boling
Oxygenation properties of snake hemoglobin. bibliog Science 157:1308-10 S 15 '67
SULLIVAN, Darrell T. See Widmoyer, F. B. jt. auth.
SULLIVAN, Ed
Ed Sullivan's biggest show: the story of his life. por Ladies Home J 84:68-71+ Je '67

about
After nineteen TV years, only Ed Sullivan survives. J. Barthel. il pors N Y Times Mag p24-5+ Ap 30 '67
Plenty of nothing. il pors Time 90:47-8 O 13 '67
Twenty years: Ed Sullivan; with report by W. Warga. il por Life 63:80-4 O 20 '67
SULLIVAN, Eugene
Golden needle; story. Redbook 130:56-7 D '67
SULLIVAN, Frank
Greetings, friends! poem. New Yorker 43:27 D 23 '67
SULLIVAN, Fred R.
Where are tomorrow's markets? Duns R 90: 40-1+ N '67
SULLIVAN, John
Profiles; Ootacamund, India. M. Panter-Downes. New Yorker 43:70+ Mr 4 '67
SULLIVAN, John L.
Arrested by detectives Valesares and Sullivan, charge: murder. B. J. Friedman. il pors Sat Eve Post 240:38-42+ Ap 22 '67
SULLIVAN, Kevin
Labor of love and learning. Nation 205:149-50 Ag 28 '67
Simplicity behind the disguises. Nation 204: 341-3 Mr 13 '67
Yeats and all that crowd. Nation 205:501-2 N 13 '67
SULLIVAN, Leon H.
Curing explosive disillusionment; address, October 27, 1967. Vital Speeches 34:117-19 D 1 '67
He helps the poor help themselves; interview. pors Nations Bsns 55:42-4+ Jl '67

about
Solving the Q.N. problem. il por Time 89: 25-6 Mr 3 '67
Teaching people to hold jobs: the Philadelphia plan. il por U S News 64:58-9 Ja 1 '68
SULLIVAN, Mark
Face of the future at General motors. Fortune 76:84-6 Jl '67
SULLIVAN, Martin Gloster
Preacher for the empire's parish. por Time 89:63-4 Je 23 '67
SULLIVAN, Maureen
Poet, Spanish Harlem; poem. Christian Cent 84:806 Je 21 '67
SULLIVAN, Pamela Wylie
Coming-out party; story. Seventeen 26:150-1 My '67
Miriam; story. Seventeen 26:150-1 N '67
SULLIVAN, Peggy
Feedback from the field. Wilson Lib Bul 41:948-9 My '67
SULLIVAN, Walter
Was Einstein wrong? reprint. Sci Digest 61: 75-8 Ap '67
SULLIVAN, Warren
Publisher's impression of the store. Pub W 191:27-9 My 22 '67
SULLIVAN, William J.
Colloquium on secularity. America 117:743 D 16 '67
SULLIVAN, Wilson
Biggest job shop in the world. Sat R 50:124-5+ O 14 '67
Corporate publication. Sat R 50:62-3 Ag 12 '67
New giant in New Jersey. Sat R 50:100-1+ Je 10 '67

SULLIVAN award. See Amateur athletic union of the United States

SULLY, Francois
Thirty-five miles from Saigon. New Repub 157:11-12 Ag 5 '67
Vietnam: the eye of the storm. New Repub 157:13-16 Jl 15 '67

SULPHUR. See Sulfur

SULZBERGER, Cyrus Leo
Water vs. hatred. Read Digest 91:144+ O '67

SUMMER
Exciting summer furniture, food, projects, equipment. D. Popplestone. il Bet Hom & Gard 45:46-65+ Je '67
100 days of summer. L. Lerman. il Mlle 65:125-7 My '67
Season gone but not forgotten; 1967. il Newsweek 70:19-20 S 11 '67

Anecdotes, facetiae, satire, etc.
Let the screen door slam. J. Mills. il Read Digest 91:57-9 Jl '67

SUMMER cabins. See Cabins
SUMMER camping. See Camping
SUMMER camps. See Camps
SUMMER cookery. See Cookery
SUMMER days; story. See Creal, M.
SUMMER drinks. See Beverages
SUMMER furniture. See Furniture, Summer
SUMMER hang-up; story. See Hoag, M. D.

SUMMER homes
Roadside bargain; misleading roadside advertising. J. Heath. il Consumer Bul 50:18-19 Jl '67
Summering simply. B. Plumb. il N Y Times Mag p54-5 Ag 6 '67

SUMMER jobs for students. See Student employment
SUMMER lady; story. See Mann, P.
SUMMER meals. See Meals
SUMMER music camps. See Music camps
SUMMER of a dormouse; story. See Stirling, M.
SUMMER photography. See Photography
SUMMER reading. See Books and reading

SUMMER resorts
Good life in the Ponderosa; Incline Village developments, Nevada. H. Sutton. il Sat R 50:51-2+ O 21 '67
Princely resorts: Mediterranean resorts. il Holiday 43:38-55 Ja '68
See also
Newport, R.I.

SUMMER safety devices and measures. See Safety devices and measures

SUMMER schools
Let's travel: to a British school. W. Petschek. Mlle 65:96+ S '67
Summer in study; textile arts teachers. D. Van Dommelen il Sch Arts 66:9-16 My '67
Summer school integration in a suburb. G. E. Snelbecker and M. S. Arffa. il Sch & Soc 95:303-5 Sum '67
Summer shorts. P. Schrag. Sat R 50:66 Jl 15 '67
Sunshine students. il Newsweek 70:46 Jl 31 '67
Talent in the ghetto; New York city's Brownsville section. E. M. Zaslow. il Am Ed 3:24-7 Mr '67
To America's PTA leaders a message from the Vice-President of the United States. H. H. Humphrey. PTA Mag 61:19 Je '67
What? study on my vacation? summer courses or summer reading. D. Klein. il Seventeen 26:252-3 Ap '67
World guide to summer study. L. Jonckheere. Sr Schol 90:sup 15-19 Mr 3 '67

SUMMER serenade; story. See Cave, H.
SUMMER vacations. See Vacations
SUMMER workshops. See Educational workshops

SUMMERLIN, Sam. See Ryan, W. L. jt. auth.

SUMMERLIN, W. Newson
Paroles for sale; corruption on Georgia parole board. il por Newsweek 71:15-16 Ja 1 '68

SUMMERS, Hollis
Delivery; poem. Sat R 50:41 N 18 '67
State of statues; poem. Christian Cent 84:813 Je 21 '67

SUMMERS, Nevin M. Jr
Winning biologist. Sci N 91:259 Mr 18 '67

SUMMERSKILL, John
Chaos on the campus. New Repub 158:14-15 Ja 6 '68

SUMMERSON, Sir John
Morals and mime: essential Hogarth. Art N 65:22-5+ F '67

SUMMIT conferences. See International conferences

SUMNER, William Graham
Pest of glory. E. J. Hughes. Newsweek 70:13 Ag 21 '67

SUN
Flattened star. Sci Am 216:48 Mr '67
Noisy sun. il Sci N 92:251 S 9 '67
Oblateness of the sun. G. S. Mumford. Sky & Tel 33:283 My '67
Pioneer 7 doubling as sun weatherman. R. Pay. il Tech W 20:20+ F 27 '67
Scopes for solar study; taking the first radio moving pictures of the sun; experiments at Culgoora, Australia. il Sci N 91:222 Mr 4 '67
Sun and space solar measurements. J. H. Wujek, jr. il Electr World 78:32-3 O '67
Sun, moon, and planets this month. See issues of Sky and telescope
U.S, USSR push continuing solar studies. H. J. Coleman. Aviation W 87:67 Ag 7 '67
What is the true shape of the sun? J. Ashbrook. bibliog il Sky & Tel 34:229-30 O '67; Discussion. 34:371 D '67
See also
International years of the quiet sun
Solar radiation
Sunspots

Atmosphere
Circulation of the sun's atmosphere. V. P. Starr and P. A. Gilman. il Sci Am 218:100-2+ bibliog(p 152) Ja '68

Corona
Coronal polar plumes. Sky & Tel 34:214 O '67
Coronal studies at the eclipse in Bolivia. J. M. Malville. il Sky & Tel 33:136-9 Mr '67
Ground observers report on November's eclipse; symposium. il Sky & Tel 33:144-8 Mr '67

Observations
Backyard astronomer; the sun and double stars. J. S. Pickering. il Natur Hist 76:60+ Ag '67

Prominences
Giant prominence photographed in March. il Sky & Tel 33:276-7 My '67

Rising and setting
See also
Twilight

Rotation
Rapid rotation of the solar interior. A. J. Deutsch. bibliog Science 156:236-7 Ap 14 '67
Rotation of the sun. P. Goldreich and G. Schubert. bibliog il Science 156:1101-2 My 26 '67; Reply. R. H. Dicke. 157:960 Ag 25 '67
Solar oblateness and fluid spin-down. B. E. McDonald and R. H. Dicke. bibliog il Science 158:1562-4 D 22 '67
Was Einstein wrong? reprint. W. Sullivan. il Sci Digest 61:75-8 Ap '67

Spectrum
See Spectrum, Solar

SUN, Distance to. See Astronomical distances
SUN, Photography of. See Astronomical photography
SUN burn. See Sunburn
SUN compass. See Compass
SUN dials. See Sundials

SUN glasses
Beauty life: on being a shady lady. il Mlle 64:160-1 Mr '67
Hot shades for the bright sun. G. Plaut. il Look 31:78-9 My 30 '67
Looking for laughs. il Life 62:41-2 Je 16 '67
What sun glare can do to your driving. J. Berry. il Pop Mech 128:78-80+ Jl '67
What you should know about sunglasses. P. W. Kearney. Read Digest 90:68-71 Je '67

SUN light. See Sunlight

SUN oil company
From an icy quagmire, half the world's oil; Fort McMurray plant. il Newsweek 70:78-80 O 2 '67

SUN rooms
My sunporch plants, and how I care for them. E. D. Ballard. il Horticulture 45:22-5 N '67

SUN screens. See Screens (sun)
SUN spots. See Sunspots
SUN tan. See Tan
SUN tan preparations. See Cosmetics

SUN VALLEY, Idaho
Changing Sun Valley. il Sunset 138:74-81 F '67
Sun Valley set. S. Birmingham. il Holiday 42:62-7+ N '67

SUN VALLEY, Idaho—*Continued*
Sun Valley's rosier glow. il Bsns W p 122-6 S 30 '67
Tower of stone in Sun Valley. H. Morrison. il House B 109:154-7 D '67

SUNAY, Cevdet
Turkey and the United States reaffirm bonds of friendship and cooperation; exchange of greetings and exchange of toasts, April 3, 1967, with joint communique. Dept State Bul 56:652-7 Ap 24 '67

SUNBEAM corporation
Rivals join Sunbeam's lawn party. il Bsns W p 184-5 My 6 '67

SUNBURN
Don't let the sun make you sick! A. F. Benjamin. Am Home 70:39 Jl '67
Drugs and sun: when they don't mix. il Good H 165:159 Jl '67
Effects of too much sun; skin cancer, also prematurely aged skin. Consumer Rep 32:364 Jl '67
Play safe with sunburn. P. Kalman. il Field & S 71:72-4+ F '67

SUNDAES. See Ice cream, ices, etc.

SUNDAY after Christmas; story. See Gallant, M.

SUNDAY like the others; story. See Cullinan, E.

SUNDAY schools
Bye-bye, Sunday school. E. C. Parker. Christian Cent 84:1038-9 Ag 16 '67; Reply. E. D. Schlenker. 84:1290 O 11 '67

SUNDBERG, Carl
Putting design on the track. il pors Bsns W p94-6+ F 25 '67

SUNDEW
Life on the sticky sundew. E. Eisner. il Natur Hist 76:32-5 Je '67

SUNDGAARD, Arnold
Of love rembered. Criticism
New Yorker 43:92 F 25 '67

SUNDIALS
Timely sculpture for the garden, and the ancient art of dialing. A. S. Gochman. il Home Gard 54:26-7 Ag '67
Unusual kind of sundial; ed. by C. L. Stong. il Sci Am 217:137-9 N '67

SUNFISH fishing
Ice-out bluegills. C. Patterson. il Outdoor Life 139:52-3+ Mr '67

SUNFISHES
See also
Cookery—Fish

SUNFLOWER, Miss.
Sunflower in the spring; rerun election. New Repub 156:10 Ap 8 '67

SUNGLASSES. See Sun glasses

SUNKEN gardens. See Gardens, Sunken

SUNKEN treasure. See Treasure trove

SUNLIGHT
Of sunlight and shadow. A. Whitman. Read Digest 90:27-8+ F '67
See also
Plants, Effect of light on

SUNPORCHES. See Sun rooms

SUNROOMS. See Sun rooms

SUNSET (periodical)
A.I.A.-Sunset Western home awards. il Sunset 139:74-89 O '67
Laurence William Lane. por Sunset 138:31 Ap '67

SUNSET phenomena
Volcanic sunset-glow stratum: origin. A. B. Meinel and M. P. Meinel. bibliog Science 155:189 Ja 13 '67

SUNSET STRIP. See Los Angeles—Streets

SUNSHADES. See Umbrellas

SUNSHINE, Irving
Be wary! be wise! keep children alive! PTA Mag 61:17 Mr '67

SUNSHINE. See Sunlight

SUNSHINE circuit (horse show) See Horse shows

SUNSPOTS
Circulation of the sun's atmosphere. V. P. Starr and P. A. Gilman. il Sci Am 218:100-2+ bibliog(p 152) Ja '68
February's large sunspot group. il Sky & Tel 33:326-7 My '67
Variation in atmospheric carbon-14 activity relative to a sunspot-auroral solar index. J. R. Bray. bibliog il Science 156:640-2 My 5 '67
White-light solar flare and the May 25th aurora. il Sky & Tel 34:57-9 Ji '67
See also
Solar flares

SUNSTROKE
Don't let the sun make you sick! A. F. Benjamin. Am Home 70:39 Jl '67

SUOR Angelica; opera. See Puccini, G.

SUPEK, Ivan
New directions in education. Bul Atomic Sci 23:31-3 My '67

SUPENSKY, Thomas G.
Working with clay. il Sch Arts 67:16-28 N '67

SUPER 8 cameras. See Moving picture cameras

SUPER markets. See Supermarkets

SUPER Skunk railroad. See California Western railroad

SUPER stock nationals. See Automobile racing

SUPERCHARGERS
See also
Airplane engines—Superchargers
Automobile engines—Superchargers

SUPERCONDUCTIVE magnets. See Magnets

SUPERCONDUCTIVITY
Frigid perpetual motion machines of tomorrow. W. S. Bacon. il Pop Sci 190:92-5+ Mr '67
Superconductivity and the d-shell. J. J. Engelhardt and others. bibliog il Science 155:191-3 Ja 13 '67
Superconductivity at 20 degrees Kelvin. B. T. Matthias and others. bibliog il Science 156:645-6 My 5 '67
Superconductivity of metallic aluminum antimonide. J. Wittig. bibliog il Science 155:685-6 F 10 '67

SUPERCONDUCTORS
Hotter superconductors. Sci Am 217:42 Jl '67

SUPERHETERODYNE receivers. See Radio receivers, Superheterodyne

SUPERHIGHWAYS. See Express highways

SUPERINTENDENTS, School. See School superintendents and principals

SUPERIOR, LAKE
See also
Isle Royale National Park

SUPERIOR men. See Great men

SUPERMARKETS
Smart moves in the shopping game. il Seventeen 26:152-3 O '67

Public relations
Supermarket gives the women an inning; ladies fairs, sponsored by Wetterau foods, inc, in Ark. and Mo. il Bsns W p66-8 Ap 29 '67

SUPERNATURAL
God and the supernatural. L. Dewart. Commonweal 85:523-8 F 10 '67

SUPERNOVAE. See Stars, New

SUPERPOWERS. See Great powers

SUPERSONIC air travel. See Air travel

SUPERSONIC airplane engines. See Jet airplane engines

SUPERSONIC airplanes. See Airplanes, Supersonic

SUPERSONIC boom. See Sonic boom

SUPERSONIC business planes. See Airplanes, Business

SUPERSONICS (basketball team) See Basketball teams

SUPERSTITION
Superstitions of the sea. J. W. Giles. Motor B 119:116-20 F '67
See also
Astrology

SUPERTANKERS. See Tank ships

SUPPÉ, Franz von
Records:
Boccaccio. Opera N 31:34 Ja 7 '67

SUPPERS
Company's coming to a late supper; with menu. Am Home 70:92 D '67
Graduation galas; commencement supper; with menu and recipes. il McCalls 94:92-3+ Je '67
Happy New Year buffet; with recipes. il Ladies Home J 85:74-5+ Ja '68
Late little super; with menus. il Good H 164:134-5 Mr '67
Late supper entertaining; with recipes. il Bet Hom & Gard 46:60-1+ Ja '68
Popular dishes for potluck suppers. B. L. Henry. il Farm J 91:64-5 O '67
Soup and salad supper cook book; with menus and recipes. I. Brooks. il House & Gard 131:179+ Mr '67
Super supper cakes; one-dish meals. il Redbook 129:90-6+ O '67

SUPPES, Patrick
Teacher and computer-assisted instruction. NEA J 56:15-17 F '67

SUPPLEMENTAL airlines. See Local service airlines

SUPPLEMENTARY employment
Moonlighting. M. Friedman. Newsweek 70: 85 S 18 '67
Moonlighting, an economic phenomenon. H. R. Hamel. il Mo Labor R 90:17-22 O '67
SUPPLY and demand
Why does more money mean higher interest. il Bsns W p 134-6 O 14 '67
See also
Consumption (economics)
SUPPLY and demand of teachers. See Teachers —Supply and demand
SUPREME court of the United States—See United States—Supreme court
SUPREME courts, State. See Courts, State
SUPREME headquarters, Allied powers, Europe. See North Atlantic treaty organization —Headquarters
SURDAM, Ronald C. See Goodwin, J. H. jt. auth.
SURF fishing. See Salt water fishing
SURF riding
Dory boat surfing offers newest water sports fun. A. Wechter. il Motor B 120:107+ S '67
Fresh-water surfing. il Todays Health 45:56-7 Je '67
Hanging five. W. Murray. il Holiday 42:62-7 S '67
Runouts, kickouts, and popouts at Gilgo beach. New Yorker 43:24 Je 17 '67
Surfmanship and salesmanship. R. Sherrill. il N Y Times Mag p 12-14+ Jl 16 '67; Reply. B. E. Simon. p31 Ag 6 '67
Surf's up: the wet-set revolution. il Newsweek 70:52-6 Ag 14 '67
Take a surfer out of the surf and what have you got? G. Greene. il Ladies Home J 84:172-4+ O '67
You should have been here an hour ago; excerpt. P. Edwards. il Sat Eve Post 240: 32-9 Jl 1 '67

Safety devices and measures
Surf safety school. M. C. Cronin. il Parks & Rec 2:16-17+ Jl '67
SURFACE, Bill
Big business of hijacking. Read Digest 92:115-19 Ja '68
Buffalo is back! Read Digest 90:189-92+ My '67
Easier than robbing a bank. N Y Times Mag p 129+ My 7 '67
Rangers don't have no inferiority complex no more. N Y Times Mag p46-7+ Mr 12 '67
Should reporters buy news? Sat R 50:85-6 My 13 '67
World of the wealthy Negro. N Y Times Mag p 10-11+ Jl 23 '67
SURFACE active substances
Surfactants help make water wetter. J. W. Boodley. il Horticulture 45:28-9 Jl '67
SURFACE chemistry
Carbon dioxide, oxygen separation: facilitated transport of carbon dioxide across a liquid film. W. J. Ward, 3d and W. L. Robb. bibliog il Science 156:1481-4 Je 16 '67
Catalysis of ester hydrolysis by mixed micelles containing N-α-myristoyl-L-histidine. A. Ochoa-Solano and others. bibliog il Science 156:1243-4 Je 2 '67
Chromatographic silica gel: surface area determined by adsorption. R. L. Hoffmann and others. bibliog il Science 157:550-1 Ag 4 '67
Efflux time of soap bubbles and liquid spheres. A. V. Grosse. bibliog il Science 156:1220-2 Je 2 '67
Forces between lecithin bimolecular leaflets are due to a disordered surface layer. V. A. Parsegian. bibliog il Science 156:939-42 My 19 '67
Paramagnetic resonance spectra of methyl radicals on porous glass surfaces. M. Fujimoto and others. bibliog il Science 156:1105-6 My 26 '67
Surface tension and surface structure of water. W. F. Claussen. bibliog il Science 156:1226-7 Je 2 '67
Transition-state models and hydrogen-isotope effects. R. E. Weston, jr. bibliog il Science 158:332-42 O 20 '67
SURFACE phenomena. See Surface chemistry
SURFACE to air missiles. See Guided missiles
SURFACE to surface missiles. See Guided missiles
SURFACE treatment of highways. See Roads— Surface treatment
SURFACTANTS. See Surface active substances
SURFBOARDS
Self-propelled surfboard needs no surf. il Pop Mech 128:26 Ag '67
SURFING. See Surf riding

SURGERY
Expectant mother: is it safe to have surgery during pregnancy? R. H. Barter. Redbook 129:52+ Jl '67
When someone in your family faces surgery. G. M. Knox. Bet Hom & Gard 45:16+ N '67
See also
American college of surgeons
Cesarean section
Cryogenic surgery
Transplantation of organs, tissues, etc.
also subhead Surgery under names of organs and regions of the body, e.g. Ear— Surgery
SURGERY, Cosmetic. See Surgery, Plastic
SURGERY, Experimental
Doctors' dilemma; ethics of surgical experimentation. Sci N 93:57 Ja 20 '68
SURGERY, Facial
Mirror, mirror on the wall; woman who had her face lifted. E. Byrd. McCalls 94:76+ F '67
SURGERY, Neonatal. See Infants, Newborn— Surgery
SURGERY, Plastic
Noses out of joint; detecting psychologically unfit patients for plastic surgery. il Newsweek 69:112 My 22 '67
Plastic surgery brings brighter lives to thousands of youngsters; services provided by the Children's hospital medical center, Boston. Todays Health 45:41 Mr '67
What plastic surgery can do for you. A. Hamilton. il Sci Digest 61:60-4 Je '67
What's new in medicine: guide to cosmetic surgery. A. Kerr. il McCalls 94:46+ My '67
SURGICAL instruments and apparatus
Instant appendectomy? portable emergency surgery room. il Sci Digest 62:28 D '67
SURGICAL operations. See Surgery
SURGICAL research
See also
American college of surgeons
SURINAM
Surinam: multiracial paradise at the crossroads. E. B. Thompson. il Ebony 22:112-16+ F '67
Time is short and the water rises; condensation. J. Walsh and R. Gannon. il Read Digest 91:213-22+ Jl '67
See also
Costume—Surinam
SURPLUS food supply. See Food supply
SURPLUS products, Agricultural
Who will hold grain stocks? D. Hanson. Suc Farm 65:6 Ja '67
SURROGATE law. See Probate law and practice
SURTAX. See Income tax—United States
SURTSEY (island) See Volcanoes
SURVEYING
Surveyor: an old career has a new look; Cross & Ghent, certified land surveyors, Alexandria, Va. il Changing T 21:42-4 Je '67
See also
Electronics in surveying
Hydrographic surveying
SURVEYS. See Educational surveys; Television surveys; and similar headings
SURVEYS, Soil. See Soil surveys
SURVIVABILITY (airplanes) See Airplanes. Military—Safety devices and measures
SURVIVAL (after airplane accidents, shipwrecks, etc)
Adrift and alone. J. Hahn. il Yachting 122:44-6+ D '67; 123:94-5+ Ja '68
Aerial rescue gain seen in debris study; upper atmospheric nuclear debris studies may yield experience in midair retrieval. B. K. Thomas, jr. il Aviation W 87:83+ Ag 21 '67
But we're alive! D. Agee. il Read Digest 90: 104-8 Je '67
Courage of Karla Little. J. G. Hubbell. il Read Digest 91:149-54 Jl '67
Cry in the night. C. E. Akridge. il Outdoor Life 139:54-5+ F '67
Death and the friendly river. S. Seegers. il Read Digest 92:42-7 Ja '68
I'm the second-luckiest pilot alive. D. K. Tooker. il Read Digest 91:64-9 O '67
Long voyage home. H. Bourdens; J. Bourdens. il Newsweek 69:64-5 Ap 17 '67
Man who refused to die; R. Gauchie. L. Elliott. il Read Digest 91:73-80 N '67
Please hurry, someone; ordeal of A. Oien family after crash in mountains of northern California. H. H. Martin. il Sat Eve Post 241:30-2+ Ja 13 '68
Survival in the North. R. Blodget. il Flying 80:40-1 Mr '67
They dropped me in the middle of the ocean and left me there. R. Gannon. il Pop Sci 191:90-3+ O '67

SURVIVAL after death. See Immortality

SURVIVAL test; story. See Rieger, C.

SUSANN, Jacqueline
Why women are so much smarter than men. por Ladies Home J 84:97+ N '67

about

Susann sues to break contract with publisher. Pub W 191:143-4 Je 5 '67

SUSPENSE stories. See Fiction

SUSPENSION from school and college. See Expulsion from school and college

SUSQUEHANNA RIVER
Sojourn on the Susquehanna. R. G. Miller. il Motor B 119:183-4+ Mr '67

SUSSEX university. See Colleges and universities—England

SUSSKIND, David
Me, David Susskind and the greatest man in the world. R. L. Foreman. Esquire 68: 69+ S '67

SUSSMAN, Cornelia, and Sussman, Irving
Case of Camilo Torres: the problem of obedience. Cath World 204:356-61 Mr '67

SUSSMAN, Irving. See Sussman, C. jt. auth.

SUSSMAN, M. V. and Huang, C. C.
Continuous gas chromatography. bibliog Science 156:974-6 My 19 '67

SUTCLIFFE, James H.
Happy Handel festival. Hi Fi 17:MA28-9+ S '67

SUTHERLAND, B. M. and others
Photoreactivation in vivo of pyrimidine dimers in paramecium DNA. bibliog Science 158:1699-700 D 29 '67

SUTHERLAND, Dorothy B.
Chicago clinic panel examines different kinds of edition. Pub W 191:51-2 F 6 '67
Trade winds. Sat R 50:10+ Je 10 '67

SUTHERLAND, Elizabeth
(ed) . . . Because he was black and I was white. Mlle 64:224-5+ Ap '67
Stranger in Mississippi. New Repub 156:28+ F 4 '67

SUTHERLAND, Joan
Donizetti's Daughter, raised by the Bonynges. E. Greenfield. il por Hi Fi 17:24+ O '67
Ghost of Semiramide. H. Weinstock. Sat R 50:71 Ja 28 '67
Music under Mount Rainier. Newsweek 69:105 Ap 24 '67
Sutherland's Beatrice. H. Weinstock. por Sat R 50:57 O 28 '67

SUTHERLAND, Zena
Books for young people. See issues of Saturday review
Stocking full of wealth. Sat R 50:34-6 D 16 '67

SUTPHEN, Jack
Building draft into a sail. Yachting 121:96-8+ Ja '67

SUTTON, George Miksch
Footprint thieves. il Audubon 69:53-7 N '67

SUTTON, Horace
Booked for travel. See issues of Saturday review
From motion to mobilism. Sat R 50:27-9+ Ap 22 '67
Indonesia's night of terror. Sat R 50:25-8+ F 4 '67
Montreal lights up. Sat R 50:51-3 Ap 29 '67
New Caledonia. Holiday 42:20+ Jl '67
Politics in the Palmlands. Sat R 50:22-7+ S 23 '67
Powers that make California go. Vogue 150: 148-53 Ag 15 '67

SUTTON, Johanna G.
Disadvantaged and the public library. Wilson Lib Bul 41:946-7 My '67

SUTTON, L. See Ross, D. M. jt. auth.

SUTTON, Samuel, and others
Information delivery and the sensory evoked potential. bibliog Science 155:1436-9 Mr 17 '67

SUYDAM, Henry West, 1926-1966
Sense of bursting away, utterly free. Life 62:74+ F 10 '67

SUZANNE; story. See Trott, S.

SUZUKI, Shinichi
Every child a prodigy. D. Chapman. il por Look 31:M24+ N 28 '67
Invasion from the Orient. il Time 90:46 N 3 '67

SVEHAG, S. E. and others
Ultrastructure of gamma M immunoglobulin and alpha macroglobulin: electro-microscopic study. bibliog Science 158:933-6 N 17 '67

SVERBEYEFF, Elizabeth
Architect's choice: townhouse transformed. House B 109:132-5 F '67

SVEVO, Italo, pseud.
Italo Svevo, the man and the writer, by P. N. Furbank. Review
New Yorker 43:137-8+ Je 3 '67. G. Steiner

SVOBODA, J. A. and Robbins, W. E.
Conversion of beta sitosterol to cholesterol blocked in an insect by hypocholesterolemic agents. bibliog Science 156:1637-8 Je 23 '67

SWADOS, Harvey
Bridge on the River Jordan. N Y Times Mag p32-3+ N 26 '67
Fred Friendly and Friendlyvision. N Y Times Mag p30-1+ Ap 23 '67
Germany 1967. Atlan 219:49-50 My '67

SWALLOW, William
Get more use from your stepladder. Am Home 70:126 N '67

The SWALLOW; opera. See Puccini, G.

SWAMPS. See Marshes

SWAN, Jon
Fall; poem. New Yorker 43:156 N 25 '67
Netherlands' birdscape; poem. New Yorker 43: 52 Jl 1 '67
One, two, three; poem. Atlan 221:45 Ja '68

SWAN, Joyce Ferris
Let me count the ways. . . Farm J 91:97 F '67

SWAN lake; ballet. See Ballets—Criticisms

SWANN, Donald
Hat: tenth anniversary of collaboration; interview. New Yorker 43:46-8 Mr 11 '67

about

Flann and Swanders. il por Newsweek 69: 100 Ja 30 '67
Mixed bag from Britain. D. Morgan. Reporter 36:52 Mr 9 '67

SWANS
Trumpeter returns from oblivion; at Red Rock Lakes national wildlife refuge. R. C. Murphy. il Read Digest 90:190-2+ Je '67

SWANSON, Steve
Resurrection; poem. Christian Cent 84:309 Mr 8 '67

SWANSTON, David
How to wreck a campus. Nation 206:38-41 Ja 8 '68

SWAP funds. See Investment trusts

SWAPPING. See Barter

SWARD, Robert
Landscape and language. Poetry 109:407-11 Mr '67

SWAZILAND
Africa: new nations and new alignments. N. Mostert. il Reporter 36:27-31 Je 29 '67
Swazis prepare for the inde-pen-dance. L. Norman. Sat R 50:48+ S 30 '67

SWEARING
Anatomy of swearing, by A. Montagu. Review
Sat R 50:30 D 23 '67. N. Samstag
Dialogue with mothers: when children use bad language. B. Bettelheim. Ladies Home J 84:48 Mr '67

SWEATING. See Perspiration

SWEDEN
See also
Aerospace industries—Sweden
Air mail service—Sweden
Airplane industry and trade—Sweden
Airplanes, Military—Sweden
Architecture, Domestic—Sweden
Automobile industry and trade—Sweden
Banks and banking—Sweden
Göteborg
Hospitals—Sweden
Labor and laboring classes—Sweden
Money—Sweden
Munitions industries—Sweden
Prisons—Sweden
Publishers and publishing—Sweden
Road traffic—Sweden
Skis and skiing—Sweden
Social and economic security—Sweden
Uppsala
Warships—Sweden
Water pollution—Sweden

Economic conditions
See also
Labor and laboring classes—Sweden

History
Queen Christina. J. H. Elliott. il Horizon 9: 66-79 Sum '67

Industries
Wallenberg boys, and how they grew; Sweden's premier industrial dynasty. il Bsns W p 114-18+ F 25 '67

Labor policy
How Sweden keeps them working. il Bsns W p 100-2 Jl 15 '67

SWEDEN—*Continued*

Moral conditions

Sex and society in Sweden, by B. Linnér. Review
  Sat R 50:26 Jl 29 '67. G. Krupp
Sex education: the Swedish system. E. Adams. il Sr Schol 90:sup 16-17 Ap 21 '67

Social conditions

Sex and society in Sweden, by B. Linnér. Review
  Sat R 50:26 Jl 29 '67. G. Krupp
  See also
Social and economic security—Sweden

SWEDES
Swedish character in the twentieth century. G. Carlsson. bibliog f Ann Am Acad 370:93-8 Mr '67

SWEDISH opera. See Opera, Swedish

SWEDISH pottery. See Pottery, Swedish

SWEDROE, Paul
Hybrid ixoras. Horticulture 45:44 Ap '67

SWEENEY, David J.
Put FM in your car. Pop Electr 27:83-4 N '67

SWEENEY, Frank
Shakedown cruise family style. Yachting 121:91-3+ Ja '67

SWEENEY, Frank James
World's newest hydrographic ship. il Motor B 120:25-6+ D '67

SWEENEY, Joseph
Lawyer's view. Newsweek 69:51-2 Ap 10 '67

SWEENEY, Pat
Winter pears; poem. America 117:415 O 14 '67

SWEEP generators. See Signal generators

SWEEPERS, Lawn. See Lawn sweepers

SWEEPERS, Street. See Street cleaning apparatus

SWEET, Herman R.
Remarkable miltonias. Horticulture 45:38-9+ Je '67

SWEET corn. See Corn, Sweet

SWEET potatoes
Instant fu-fu for West Africa; mixing yam and instant mashed potato. Sci N 91:430-1 My 6 '67

SWEETENING agents. See Sugar substitutes

SWENBERG, Mei-lie L. and others
Muscarine: isolation from cultures of clitocybe rivulosa. bibliog Science 155:1259 Mr 10 '67

SWENSON, G. W. Jr, and Bracewell, R. N.
Radio astronomy: conflict of frequencies; letter. Science 155:518+ F 3 '67

SWENSON, Karen
Visit; poem. Nation 205:598 D 4 '67

SWENSON, Marlette E. See Hasler, A. D. jt. auth.

SWENSON, May
His suicide; poem. Poetry 109:330-1 F '67
Naked in Borneo; poem. New Yorker 42:32 Ja 21 '67
  about
Five-book shelf. W. Stafford. Poetry 111:184-5 D '67

SWEZEY, Ken
Physics for fun: Bernoulli's paradox. Pop Sci 191:88-9+ O '67

SWIDLER, Arlene
Friction in Philadelphia. Commonweal 87:463-4 Ja 19 '68
Meanwhile, back in Philadelphia. Commonweal 86:191-2 My 5 '67

SWIDLER, Leonard
Theology in the American university. Cath World 205:205-9 Jl '67

SWIFT, Donald J. P. See Stanley, D. J. jt. auth.

SWIFT, Joan
Snow; poem. Reporter 37:46 N 16 '67

SWIFT, Jonathan
Swift conviviality: tercentenary symposium. Dublin. V. Mercier. Nation 205:151-3 Ag 28 '67

SWIFT, Lloyd W.
Wildlife management in Turkey. Am For 73:34-5+ Je '67

SWIFT, Mary Grace
Ballet in Communist China. Dance Mag 41:60-5 N '67

SWIFT and company
Hog butcher for the world. R. Levy. il Duns R 89:36-8 F '67

SWIGGUM, Pearl
Sisters under the skin. Farm J 91:55 Ag '67

SWIMMING
Africa-to-Europe: a treacherous stretch outswum by a swinger; Morocco-Gibraltar swim. il Life 63:30-1 Jl 21 '67

Face to face with a girl who swims everywhere; ed. by C. Schwalberg. P. Watson. Seventeen 26:309 Ag '67
He's a long drink of glop; S. Rerych, junior at North Carolina state. T. C. Brody. Sports Illus 26:56+ Mr 27 '67
Naiad's triumph; brilliant performances of U.S. swimmers at Pan-American games. il Time 90:40 Ag 4 '67
Old and new pool their talent; D. Schollander and M. Spitz. K. Chapin. Sports Illus 27:48+ Ag 21 '67
Stanford's big new splash; G. Buckingham star of American swimming. K. Chapin. Sports Illus 26:24-5 Ap 3 '67
Swimming makes a splash at Morehouse. il Ebony 22:56-8+ My '67
Times came for two teens; M. Spitz and F. Haywood. K. Chapin. il Sports Illus 26:97-9 Ap 17 '67

Anecdotes, facetiae, satire, etc.

Swimming lesson. L. Conversi. Atlan 219:112-13 Je '67

SWIMMING pools
All summer is a holiday, at home! il Good H 165:98-9 Jl '67
Big dig in Princeton; suburban pool keeper. L. Bergquist. il Look 31:100+ My 16 '67
Do-it-yourself steel pool for $1250. il Pop Mech 127:170-1 My '67
Have a summer vacation in your own backyard. il Parents Mag 42:91+ Mr '67
How to keep kids out of the swimming pool. Changing T 21:11 Ag '67
Instant swimming pool for everyone, for less than the price of a compact car. il Pop Gard 18:42-3+ Ag '67
Keep your cool in a pool. il Am Home 70:51-3 Jl '67
New shapes of the pool. il House B 109:120-4 Je '67
Pool at the desert's edge among boulders. il Sunset 138:102 Je '67
Pool is to use the year around. il Pop Gard 18:46-9 Mr '67
Pools in schools. D. H. Robertson. il NEA J 56:41 My '67
Pools in the schools; program sponsored by the National swimming pool foundation of Washington, D.C. M. Dowd. il Parks & Rec 2:24+ Ag '67
Portable swimming pools. il Parks & Rec 2:22 My '67
Single pool plays a dual role; Tempe, Ariz. J. Salvato. il Am City 82:102-3 Ap '67
Their new pool is in the tree-tops. il Sunset 138:108-9 My '67

Care

Getting your pool sparkling again. Sunset 138:150-1 My '67
Readying your pool for winter. Sunset 139:131 N '67

Equipment

Poolside living. il Sunset 139:48-51 Ag '67
Portable turntable for competitive swimming. C. L. Smith. il Parks & Rec 2:27+ My '67

Heating

Wipe windows with warmth; system for an indoor-outdoor swimming pool. il Am City 82:104-5 Je '67

Lighting

Lighting gets more people in the swim; system used in Aurora, Colo. T. R. Knapp. il Am City 82:130+ Je '67

Safety devices and measures

Accent on safety. il Pop Gard 18:40-1+ Ag '67

SWIMMING pools, Municipal
Inflatable roof puts outdoor pool indoors; town of Mamaroneck, N.Y. il Am City 82:12 N '67

SWIMMING suits. See Bathing suits

SWINDALE, L. D. and Fan, P.-F.
Transformation of gibbsite to chlorite in ocean bottom sediments. bibliog Science 157:799-800 Ag 18 '67

SWINDLERS and swindling. See Fraud

SWINE
Hog extra; symposium. See issues of Farm journal
In praise of pigs. R. C. Davids. il Read Digest 91:223-4+ D '67
News. See issues of Farm journal
Pigs aren't so dumb. Sci Digest 62:26-7 D '67
What's new. See issues of Successful farming
Your complete guide for selecting today's modern meat-hog! J. Harvey. il Suc Farm 65:40-5 S '67

SWITZERLAND
See also
Airplanes, Military—Switzerland
Architecture—Switzerland
Banks and banking—Switzerland
Cities and towns—Switzerland
Education—Switzerland
Forests and forestry—Switzerland
Fribourg
Opera—Switzerland
Science—Switzerland
Tourist trade—Switzerland

Description and travel
Travel's picture portfolio. il Travel 127:54-9
F '67

History
Bibliography
Articles and other books received; comp. by
A. H. Price. See issues of American
historical review

Social life and customs
Midsummer dream. P. Devlin. il Vogue 149:
152-7+ Je '67
Week we met the Swiss. S. Shindell. Sat R
50:44 Jl 22 '67
SWOBODA'S tragedy; story. See Hazzard, S.
SWOMLEY, John M. Jr
Conscience and the draft. Christian Cent 84:
833-5 Je 28 '67
Twenty-five years of conscription. Christian
Cent 84:465-8 Ap 12 '67
SWORD cactus; story. See Moore, J.
SWORDFISH fishing
Gladius the gladiator. il Time 90:40 S 8 '67
SYBURG, Jane
Romeo and renewal. Cath World 206:21-3 O
'67

SYDNEY, Australia
Description
Sydney: lively, glistening. D. Messinesi.
Vogue 150:70+ S 15 '67
SYDNEY national opera house. See Opera
houses
SYKES, Gerald
Local guru. J. Hart. il Nat R 19:912 Ag 22
'67
SYLVANIA electric products, incorporated
U.S. camera achievement award. U S Cam-
era 30:44 N '67
SYLVESTER, Arthur
Speaking out. por Sat Eve Post 240:10+ N
18 '67
SYMBIOSIS
Symbiosis: effects of a mutualistic fungus
upon the growth and reproduction of xyleb-
orus ferrugineus. D. M. Norris and J. K.
Baker. bibliog Science 156:1120-2 My 26 '67
See also
Indian pipes (plants)
SYMBIOTIC algae. See Algae
SYMBOLISM
Chinese symbolism; crane. G. Kaler. il
Hobbies 71:50 F '67
Giving peace the bird. il Sr Schol 91:26 S 28
'67
See also
Christian art and symbolism
SYMBOLISM in literature
Advise and learn. R. L. Fish. Writer 80:22-4
Je '67
SYMBOLS
Magic of symbols. E. M. Bower. il NEA J
57:28-31+ Ja '68
See also
Cryptography
SYMINGTON, James Wadsworth
Genial Jim. il pors Newsweek 71:81-2 Ja 22
'68
SYMINGTON, Stuart
Shortages and sanctuaries; key senators re-
port on Vietnam; excerpts. U S News 62:
38-9 Ap 10 '67
Vietnam revisited; as Symington sees it
now; excerpts from report. por U S News
62:13 Ap 3 '67
SYMMETREL. See Amantadine hydrochloride
SYMONDS, Gardiner
Tenneco lands Kern County. il por Bsns W
p96-8+ Jl 22 '67
SYMPATHY
I'll never live among strangers again. V. Han-
cock. McCalls 94:20+ S '67
Things that live; expressions of sympathy.
A. Silberman. il Good H 164:51+ Ja '67
SYMPHONIES
Musical events. W. Sargeant. New Yorker
43:142+ My 20 '67
See also
Phonograph records—Symphonies

SYMPHONY of the New World
Lesson of experience. il Newsweek 69:102 F
20 '67
SYMPHONY orchestras. See Orchestras
SYNAGOGUES
Contemporary synagogue art, by A. Kampf.
Review
Commentary 44:88-90 Ag '67. C. Roth
Interval in a street; Civic center synagogue,
New York. il Arch Forum 127:64-9 O '67
SYNAPSES
Crayfish muscle fiber: ionic requirements for
depolarizing synaptic electrogenesis. M.
Ozeki and H. Grundfest. bibliog il Science
155:478-81 Ja 27 '67
Direct synaptic connection mediating both ex-
citation and inhibition. H. Wachtel and
E. R. Kandel. bibliog il Science 158:1206-8 D
1 '67
Opposite synaptic actions mediated by dif-
ferent branches of an identifiable inter-
neuron in aplysia. E. R. Kandel and oth-
ers. bibliog il Science 155:346-9 Ja 20 '67
Origin of synaptic noise. J. I. Hubbard and
others. bibliog il Science 157:330-1 Jl 21 '67
Synaptic connections between a transplanted
insect ganglion and muscles of the host.
J. W. Jacklet and M. J. Cohen. bibliog il
Science 156:1638-40 Je 23 '67
Synaptic loci on parietal cortical neurons:
terminations of corpus callosum fibers. A.
Globus and A. B. Scheibel. bibliog il Sci-
ence 156:1127-9 My 26 '67
Synaptic noise as a source of variability
in the interval between action potentials.
W. H. Calvin and C. F. Stevens. bibliog il
Science 155:842-4 F 17 '67
Synaptic vesicles of inhibitory and excitatory
terminals in the cerebellum. L. M. H. Lar-
ramendi and others. bibliog il Science 156:
967-9 My 19 '67
Tetraethylammonium ions: effect of pre-
synaptic injection on synaptic transmission.
K. Kusano and others. bibliog il Science
155:1257-9 Mr 10 '67
Ultrastructure and cytochemistry of the syn-
aptic region. E. D. P. de Robertis. bibliog
il Science 156:907-14 My 19 '67
SYNCHRONIZING
Master time technique eases obstacles: syn-
chronizing aircraft time standards. P. J.
Klass. Aviation W 87:85-8+ Jl 10 '67
SYNDICAT des editeurs. See Publishers and
publishing—France
SYNDICATE materials, Newspaper. See News-
papers—Syndicate service
SYNDICATES (finance)
Going shopping with lady luck; Brazil's un-
usual installment buying plans, consortium.
il Bsns W p 152+ D 16 '67
Message for industry; excerpts from ad-
dress. R. H. Charles. Aviation W 86:11
Mr 13 '67
SYNDROMES
Chromosomal breakage induced by extracts
of human allogeneic lymphocytes. P. J. Fial-
kow. bibliog il Science 155:1676-7 Mr 31 '67
SYNGE-HUTCHINSON, Patrick
Some English and German porcelain in an
English collection. Antiques 91:614-19 My '67
SYNOD of bishops, 1967
Bishops' synod. G. MacEoin. Commonweal
86:546-8 S 8 '67
Bishops' synod. J. M. Johnson. Christian Cent
84:1608+ D 13 '67
Bishops' synod, a decisive perhaps. J. O'Gara.
Commonweal 87:162-3 N 10 '67
Catholic updating: how far and how fast?
synods of bishops. il U S News 63:16 O 9
'67
Clear voice in Rome. il Newsweek 70:57 O 30
'67
Dossier on the synod. America 117:193 Ag 26
'67
End of a beginning. D. Slow. il America 117:
564-5 N 11 '67
First week of the synod. D. Slow. America
117:442-3 O 21 '67
Historic synod in Rome. il Newsweek 70:57-8
O 9 '67
How much updating for the Catholics? il
U S News 63:10 N 13 '67
In the cellar of broken heads; synod of the
Catholic bishops. il Time 90:55-6 O 6 '67
Of many things; Edward Schillebeeckx com-
ments on the synod of bishops. T. N.
Davis. America 117:237 S 9 '67
Of many things; questions facing the synod
of bishops in Rome. T. N. Davis. America
117:inside cover Ag 26 '67
Peace, justice and freedom; Synod of bishops.
America 117:399 O 14 '67
Pope Paul's alarm. Christian Cent 84:1307-8
O 18 '67

TABLE decoration
Alfresco go-togethers. il House B 109:114-15 Jl '67
Candlelight cookbook of glamorous recipes and glowing tables for your holiday entertaining. il Good H 165:88-107 D '67
Fringed frilly pants. il Am Home 70:91 D '67
Put tulips on your table. il Bet Hom & Gard 45:111 My '67
Stitch-and-paste table settings. il Bet Hom & Gard 45:125 N '67
Switch-about centerpiece; surtout de table. il House & Gard 133:92-3 Ja '68
Winning winter arrangements. il Bet Hom & Gard 45:106 F '67
See also
Garnishes
TABLE for two; story. See Frazier, W.

TABLE linen
Alfresco go-togethers. il House B 109:114-15 Jl '67
Care and safekeeping of table linens; how to keep them spot-free and crisply laundered. House & Gard 131:216+ Ap '67
Double damask with new dash. il House & Gard 131:176-7 Mr '67
Smart-as-paint table covers. il Bet Hom & Gard 45:122 Je '67

TABLE manners. See Etiquette
TABLE saws. See Saws
TABLE setting
Breakfast, lunch, and dinner at Tiffany's. M. White. il Ladies Home J 84:114-15 My '67
Christmas dinner in your own tradition. il Ladies Home J 84:84-7 D '67
First, feast the eyes. E. Sverbeyeff. il House B 109:258-61 N '67
If food looks good, family will cheer; with recipes. il Redbook 130:76-7+ Ja '68
Picnic; a bite-size vacation. il House B 109:116-17+ Jl '67
Tables set for compliments. il McCalls 95:108-11 N '67
Turn the table on china. il Am Home 70:60-1 N '67
Two for the money; double life accessories. il Redbook 130:94-5 N '67

TABLE shuffleboard. See Shuffleboard
TABLE-side cookery. See Cookery
TABLE silver. See Silverware
TABLE tennis
Coach Mao calls off the game; Japanese win the world championship. D. Miles. Sports Illus 26:59 My 1 '67
More pong than ping. P. Keese. il N Y Times Mag p 149-51+ O 22 '67

TABLECLOTHS. See Table linen
TABLES
Basic best buys in party tables. il House & Gard 132:90-1 Jl '67
Buffet? dining table here are both in one. R. E. Schultz. il Pop Sci 191:165-9 N '67
Build this butterfly-trestle table. W. C. Lammey. il Pop Mech 127:172-4 F '67
Coffee table that solves a problem; storage for books. C. G. Bucher. il Pop Sci 191:124-7 D '67
Entertaining tables. il House B 109:296-7 N '67
How to add a typewriter table to a desk. W. B. Sill. il Pop Sci 192:155 Ja '68
How to build H&G's cutting table. il House & Gard 131:211 Ap '67
How to reproduce a Pembroke table. H. Wicks. il Pop Sci 192:168-71 Ja '68
How you can build a Scandinavian flip-top table. D. Huff. il Pop Sci 190:144-7+ Je '67
Magazine-go-round end table. E. Waltner and W. Waltner. il Pop Mech 127:170-1 Ap '67
Two coffee tables out of the past. J. Payne; H. Wicks. il Pop Sci 191:120-3 Jl '67
Wood sunburst; symphony in wood; gift table for F. E. Hornaday. il Am For 73:36-8 Ap '67

TABLES turned; drama. See Brown, J.
TABLEWARE
Antique oyster plates. il(p 1) Hobbies 72:80 My '67
Art of the picnic; with recipes. il Sunset 139:38-45 Ag '67
Dessert plates. il House & Gard 131:34+ Mr '67

TABLEWARE, Horn
Antlered dinnerware. D. Shiner. il Design 69:18-19 Fall '67

TABORI, George
Niggerlovers. Criticism
New Yorker 43:152-3 O 14 '67
Newsweek 70:109 O 16 '67

TACAN
Compact micro-Tacan slated for delivery. P. J. Klass. il Aviation W 86:55-7+ Je 19 '67

TACHOMETERS
Build $6 electronic tachometer. R. E. Staerzl. il Pop Electr 26:61-2 Ap '67
IC engine tachometer and red line indicator; application of integrated circuits to automotive electronics. R. A Hirschfeld. il Electr World 77:37-9 My '67
New approach to engine tachometers. R. L. Carroll. il Electr World 78:71 S '67
TACKLE boxes. See Fishing—Implements and appliances
TACOMA, Wash.
Never never land; lifesized fiberglassed storybook characters in Point Defiance park. il Parks & Rec 2:18-19 Je '67
Power lines go off the street. il Am City 82:112 My '67

Sanitary affairs
Separate those sewers. J. A. Bronow. il Am City 82:94-6 F '67
TACONIS, Kryn
This proud land, this Canada; photographs. Look 31:20-30 Ag 22 '67
TACONITE
Billion-dollar comeback; iron-range country of northeastern Minnesota. il Nations Bsns 55:38-41 Ag '67
TACTAIR autopilot. See Automatic pilot (airplanes)
TACTICAL air command. See United States—Air force—Tactical air command
TACTICAL air navigation. See Tacan
TACTICAL articulated swimmable carrier. See Motor vehicles, Amphibious
TACTICAL fighter, Experimental. See Airplanes, Military—United States
TACTICAL landing approach radio. See Airplanes—Landing
TADPOLES
Histones in the wild-type and the anucleolate mutant of xenopus laevis. L. Berlowitz and M. L. Birnstiel. bibliog il Science 156:78-80 Ap 7 '67
TAEUBER, Conrad
Population and food supply; excerpts from papers submitted to the United Nations world population conference. bibliog f Ann Am Acad 369:73-83 Ja '67
TAEUBER, Irene (Barnes)
Demographic transitions and population problems in the United States; excerpts from The Changing population of the United States: 1900 to 1960. bibliog f Ann Am Acad 369:131-40 Ja '67
TAFFEL, Tom
From touchdown to take-off. A. Blinderman. il pors U S Camera 30:70-1+ D '67
TAFT, Seth Chase
In Cleveland and Boston, the issue is race. J. M. Naughton. il N Y Times Mag p30+ N 5 '67
Into the mud. Time 90:19 N 3 '67
TAFT, William Howard, 1857-1930
President dumping. Americus. New Repub 157:11-13 O 28 '67; Reply. G. Tyler. 157:44 N 11 '67
TAFT-Hartley law. See Labor laws and legislation—United States—Taft-Hartley law
TAGGART, Ross E.
Burnap collection today. Antiques 92:850-3 D '67
TAGLIABUE, John
Noticed; poem. Atlan 219:113 My '67
Part of a Hindu festival; poem. Poetry 110:83-7 My '67

about
Five poets. D. W. Baker. Poetry 111:201-2 D '67
TAGS, identification. See Identification tags, bracelets, etc.
TAHITI
Possibility of paradise. C. Lucas. il Atlan 220:120+ N '67
Tahiti. G. J. W. Goodman. il Holiday 41:46-63+ F '67
TAHOE, LAKE
Tahoe's Incline leans on total sport; Incline Village launched on impetus of sport. P. Knight. il Sports Illus 27:42-6 S 25 '67
TAI, Chiaki, and Halasz, N. A.
Histocompatibility antigen transfer in utero: tolerance in progeny and sensitization in mother. bibliog Science 158:125-6 O 6 '67
TAIT, L. Gordon
Seminary and preseminary education: analyses of two A.A.T.S. reports. Christian Cent 84:536+ Ap 26 '67
TAIWAN
U.S. scientific team visits Republic of China. Dept State Bul 57:585 O 30 '67
See also
Dancing—Taiwan
Natural resources—Taiwan

TAIWAN—*Continued*

Commercial treaties and agreements

U.S. and China exchange notes on Cotton textile agreements. il Dept State Bul 57: 694-7 N 20 '67

Economic conditions

Boom in the other China. il U S News 62: 88-90 Mr 27 '67

Model; Taiwan a model for Asian economic development. il Time 89:92+ My 12 '67

Foreign relations

Vice President of the Republic of China visits the United States; exchange of greetings and exchange of toasts, May 9; with joint statement, May 10, 1967. L. B. Johnson; C. Yen. Dept State Bul 56:846-50 Je 5 '67

Industries

Taiwan. il Focus 17:1-6 D '66

Politics and government

Ready & waiting. Time 89:28+ Ja 27 '67

TAJ MAHAL
Taj Mahal; with report by W. A. McWhirter. il Life 63:44-60+ N 3 '67

TAKEMITSU, Toru
In an icy forest. il Time 90:65 N 17 '67

TAKROUNA. See Tunisia—Antiquities

TALAR landing system. See Airplanes—Landing

TALBERT, William F.
Tennis. Sports Illus 26:60+ Mr 13 '67

TALBOT, Frederic R. pseud.
Should doctors prescribe contraceptives for unmarried girls? Ladies Home J 85:37+ Ja '68

TALBOT, William
Stage. Commonweal 86:126 Ap 14 '67

TALBOT, William, family
How to delight your guests; visiting the Talbots of Washington, Conn. A. Stagg. il pors House & Gard 132:65-71 Jl '67

TALBOT, William S.
Jasper F. Cropsey, child of the Hudson River school. Antiques 92:713-17 N '67

TALENT agents. See Theatrical agencies

Il TALENTO mysterioso; story. See Meehan, T.

TALER. See Money—Germany

TALES of Hoffmann; opera. See Offenbach, J.

TALESE, Gay
Corry papers. Esquire 67:92-4+ Je '67
Getting even; story. Mlle 65:158-9 My '67
Party's over. Esquire 68:168-72 D '67
Public and private wars of Harrison E. Salisbury. Esquire 67:88-90+ My '67

TALK. See Conversation

TALKING books
LC talking books go to handicapped. Library J 92:2104 Je 1 '67
Library service to the handicapped; change of name for Division for the blind. E. Hamer and A. McCormick. ALA Bul 61: 250-1 Mr '67
New hope for the handicapped; Division for the blind and physically handicapped at the Library of Congress. C. Gallozzi. bibliog il Library J 92:1417-20 Ap 1 '67

TALL and fascinating stranger; story. See Blyth, M.

TALL men. See Stature

TALLER, Herman
Calories author guilty; faces jail and fine. Pub W 191:40 My 22 '67

TALLMAN. Frank
Great antiques: Nieuport 28. Flying 81:64-7 Jl '67
Reno '66. Flying 80:40-3 F '67

about

Publisher's memo. E. D. Muhlfeld. il Flying 81:6 Jl '67
Spirit of St Louis' takes new turn over Paris. il pors Bsns W p 196-8 My 13 '67

TALLON, James
Camera hunting a coyote; photographs. Field & S 72:40-1 D '67

TALMAGE, David W.   See Radovich, J. jt. auth.

TALMEY, Allene
Cholesterol. Vogue 150:148-9 S 15 '67
Fatigue: what to do about it. Vogue 149: 98-9 F 15 '67
Pill; latest experiments in birth control. Vogue 149:114-15 Ap 15 '67
What to do about fat; plus the commonsense diet. Vogue 149:126-7 Mr 15 '67

TALOUMIS, George
Gardening by the sea. Pop Gard 18:24-9+ Ag '67
To water or not to. Home Gard 54:84 F '67

TAMIRIS, Helen
Testament to Tamiris; 92nd street Y. M. Marks. Dance Mag 41:88 Je '67

TAMMANY Hall
Boss Jones of Tammany Hall. A. Hiss. il N Y Times Mag p32-3+ F 19 '67
Tammany picked an honest man; excerpts. L. Thomas. il Am Heritage 18:34-9+ F '67; Discussion. 18:50 O '67

TAMPA, Fla.
New equipment is less costly than old; findings of sanitation department. il Am City 82:114-15+ S '67
Safety village; city within a city is teaching Tampa youngsters accident prevention. il Travel 127:56-7 Ja '67

Ybor City

Ebullient Ybor. K. Johnson. il Travel 127:52-3 F '67

TAMPONE, Dominic
Inventive inventory. il por Newsweek 70:62-3 D 25 '67

TAN
Effects of too much sun; skin cancer, also prematurely aged skin. Consumer Rep 32: 364 Jl '67
Sun ban; diseases caused by sun's rays. il Time 89:65 My 12 '67
Tyrosinase inhibition; its role in suntanning and in albinism. L. T. Y. Chian and G. F. Wilgram. bibliog il Science 155:198-200 Ja 13 '67

TANDON, S. N. and Wasson, J. T.
Indium variations in a petrologic suite of L-group chondrites. bibliog Science 158: 259-61 O 13 '67

TANGE, Kenzō
Miniature megastructure. V. C. Mahler. il Arch Forum 127:35-43 S '67

TANGERINES

Diseases and pests

See also
Mal secco disease of citrus

TANGLEWOOD music festival. See Berkshire symphonic festival

TANGO; drama. See Mrozek, S.

TANK ship simulators
Maneuvering in miniature. L. Aigner. il Pop Mech 129:136-7 Ja '68

TANK ships
Anarchy at sea; need for size and routes control. Nation 204:549+ My 1 '67
Big-tanker rush. il Newsweek 70:77 N 6 '67
Europe's shipbuilders up anchor; building supertankers. il Bsns W p88-90+ O 14 '67
Oil around us. R. Rienow and L. T. Rienow. il N Y Times Mag p24-5+ Je 4 '67
Sunken time bombs full of oil! D. C. Fales. il Pop Mech 128:97-101+ N '67
Tankers move the oil that moves the world. G. H. Wierzynski. il Fortune 76:80-5+ S 1 '67
Two kinds of tankers, clean and dirty. C. Kentfield. il N Y Times Mag p24-5+ My 14 '67

Chartering

Tankers strike it rich; chartering combats Suez Canal closure. il Newsweek 70:70+ Jl 17 '67

TANKERS. See Tank ships

TANKS, Airplane. See Airplanes—Fuel tanks

TANKS, Military
Germans eye MBT 70 alternative. Tech W 21: 17 Jl 3 '67
Tank goes anywhere, and fast; MBT-70. il Pop Sci 192:132 Ja '68
Tank of the future for U.S. army: MBT-70. il U S News 63:10 O 23 '67
Weapons for present & future; MBT-70. il Time 90:21 O 20 '67

TANNENBAUM, Libby
Degas: illustrious and unknown; with excerpt from La Cigale by H. Meilhac and L. Halévy. Art N 65:50-5+ Ja '67

TANNER, Elaine
Winning ways of Winnipeg. J. Underwood. il pors Sports Illus 27:20-5 Ag 7 '67

TANNER, Henry
Congo is still an active volcano. N Y Times Mag p52-3+ S 10 '67; Same abr. Read Digest 91:135-8 D '67
France's Communists make a formidable comeback. N Y Times Mag p54-5+ N 19 '67

TANNER, Henry Ossawa
Henry Ossawa Tanner. J. Perreault. il Art N 66:47+ D '67

TANNER, J. M.
Earlier maturation in man; with biographical sketch. Sci Am 218:19, 21-7 Ja '68
TANNER, Paul Francis, bp
Die-hards. S. J. Adamo. **America** 117:255-inside back cover S 9 '67
TANNER, Wilson P. Jr
Senses rechanneled. A. Ewing. Sci N 93:74-5 Ja 20 '68
TANTRUMS. See Temper
TANZANIA
Tanzania's brand of socialism pleases. E. A. Hawley. Christian Cent 84:512 Ap 19 '67
See also
Christians in Tanzania
Costume—Tanzania
National parks and reserves—Tanzania
Research—Tanzania
Socialism—Tanzania

Economic policy
Dog days; program of African socialism. il Newsweek 69:46 Mr 6 '67
Nyerere: Operation bootstrap, or backstep? interview, ed. by P. Webb. J. Nyerere. Newsweek 69:47 Mr 6 '67

Politics and government
Follow that car! il Newsweek 70:45 Ag 7 '67
Socialism, tribal style. il Newsweek 69:55-6 F 20 '67
TAO, Nguyen-van-. See Nguyen-van-Tao
TAOS, N.Mex.
D. H. Lawrence in Taos. P. S. Beagle. Holiday 42:44-5+ S '67
TAOS Indians
National council champions Taos Pueblo Indians; restoration of land to Indians. Christian Cent 84:932 Jl 19 '67
TAP dancing

Study and teaching
Tap for young children (title varies) (cont) A. Gilbert. Dance Mag 41:74-5 F; 84-5 Ap '67 (to be cont)
TAPE, Magnetic. See Magnetic tape
TAPE cartridge. See Magnetic tape
TAPE-recorder music. See Music, Concrete
TAPE recorders and recording. See Magnetic recorders and recording
TAPE recordings
Independence Hall reconstruction sound system; Knott's berry farm, Calif. J. P. Nelson. il Electr World 78:32-3 Jl '67
New records and tapes. il Sr School 90:sup 16+ Mr 10 '67
Tape deck. R. D. Darrell. See issues of High fidelity incorporating Musical America
Voice as history. A. B. Rollins, jr. Nation 205:518-21 N 20 '67
Xerox U; listening courses prepared by the Xerox corp. il Time 91:73 Ja 5 '68
See also
Automobiles—Tape equipment
Oral history
Editing
Sound advice; tape editing. M. A. Matzkin. il Mod Phot 31:24+ Ag '67

Stereophonic recordings
Stereotape reviews. J. W. Barker and others. See issues of American record guide to May 1967
TAPER, Bernard
King of ranchers. Am Heritage 18:20-3+ Ag '67
Profiles; C. Abrams. New Yorker 42:38-42+ F 4; 45-8+ F 11 '67
TAPESTRY
Medieval flowers for today's gardens; plants taken from Unicorn tapestries at New York's Cloisters; ed. by E. McDonald. T. P. Miller. il House B 109:158-61 D '67

Exhibitions
Third international tapestry biennial. E. Billeter. il Craft Horiz 27:8-15 Jl '67
TAPPLY, H. G.
Sportsman's notebook. See issues of Field & stream
TAR sand. See Bituminous sand
TARANTO, Italy
Art. M. Grosser. Nation 206:60-2 Ja 8 '68
TARAXEIN
Lead on schizophrenia. Sci N 91:141 F 11 '67
TARCHER, Martin
Leadership; address, March 7, 1967. Vital Speeches 33:404-8 Ap 15 '67

TARGAN, Barry
And their fathers who begat them; story. Esquire 74:108 Ja '68
TARIFF
Bargain at Le Bocage. il Time 89:90+ My 26 '67
Completing the work of the Kennedy round; address, October 5, 1967. W. M. Roth. Dept State Bul 57:574-8 O 30 '67
Economic necessities and Atlantic communities. A. C. Neal. il For Affairs 45:694-705 Jl '67
End of the Round. New Repub 156:7 My 27 '67
Farmers and the Kennedy round. il Farm J 91:74 Je '67
Improving export earnings of developing countries; statement, January 18, 1967. W. M. Blumenthal. Dept State Bul 56:430-6 Mr 13 '67
It is high noon in Geneva; closing minutes of the Kennedy round. Life 62:4 Ap 14 '67
Kennedy round. M. Friedman. Newsweek 70:80 Jl 17 '67
Kennedy round: a hard task well done. Life 62:4 My 26 '67
Kennedy round agreements signed at Geneva. Dept State Bul 57:95-101 Jl 24 '67
Kennedy round enters decisive phase; statement, February 15, 1967. W. M. Roth. Dept State Bul 56:476-8 Mr 20 '67
Kennedy round holds promise of free-world economic growth; statements, May 16, 23, 1967. L. B. Johnson; W. M. Roth. Dept State Bul 56:879-80 Je 12 '67
Kennedy round: proud chapter in the history of international commerce; symposium. Dept State Bul 57:123-40 Jl 31 '67
Kennedy round staging to replace staging under interim agreements; a proclamation. L. B. Johnson. Dept State Bul 57:800 D 11 '67
Kennedy round: success. il Newsweek 69:80-2 My 29 '67
Kennedy round: the iceberg moves. il Newsweek 69:77 My 22 '67
Kennedy round turns into a cliff-hanger; trade talks in Geneva. il Bsns W p 162+ Mr 18 '67
Last round in Kennedy round. Sr Schol 90:27-8 My 19 '67
More or less trade. New Repub 156:2 Je 10 '67
Offering trade to the poor; system of tariff preferences to developing countries. Bsns W p 109 D 9 '67
Progress achieved in reducing nontariff barriers to trade. Dept State Bul 57:860-1 D 25 '67
Round's end; agreement to sweeping tariff reductions. Time 90:76+ Jl 7 '67
Tariff walls tumble; steps that led to freer trade; with editorial comment. il Bsns W p33-6, 192 My 20 '67
Toward agreement; Kennedy round. il Time 89:121 My 19 '67
United States achieves removal of foreign import restrictions. Dept State Bul 56:245-6 F 13 '67
What you got and lost in the tariff slashes; Kennedy round agreements affecting farm commodities. C. W. Gifford. Farm J 91:21+ Ag '67
Who gets what from the Kennedy round? E. L. Dale, jr. New Repub 156:15-16 F 11 '67
Who's helped, who's hurt by new deal on tariffs. il U S News 62:34-5 My 29 '67
See also
Commercial treaties and agreements
Free trade and protection
General agreement on tariffs and trade

United States
Again the candlemakers. Nat R 19:1157-8 O 31 '67
Backward march; quota legislation. il **Time** 90:89 O 27 '67
Business' stake in the Kennedy round; address, July 7, 1967. A. B. Trowbridge. Dept State Bul 57:127-32 Jl 31 '67
Chemical makers come to a boil; tariff deals in Kennedy round. Bsns W p36+ My 27 '67
Chief trade negotiator tells: where we go from here. W. Roth. il Nations Bsns 55:54-7 Ag '67
End in sight; Kennedy-round deadline. Newsweek 69:92 Mr 20 '67
Fair labor standards for world trade. R. B. Schwenger. Mo Labor R 90:27-31 N '67
Fighting to keep trade walls; reaction against the Kennedy round of tariff-cutting. il Bsns W p36-7 O 14 '67
Financial prohibition; proposal for tax on imports as well as on tourism. H. C. Wallich. Newsweek 71:76 Ja 22 '68
Freeman answers cheap food charges. O. L. Freeman. Farm J 91:35-6 Ag '67

TARIFF—United States—*Continued*
Issues in future U.S. foreign trade policy; statement, July 11, 1967. W. M. Roth. Dept State Bul 57:173-80 Ag 7 '67
Kennedy round: a hard task well done. Life 62:4 My 26 '67
More or less trade. New Repub 156:2 Je 10 '67
More trade, less aid; OAS call to cut tariffs. America 117:496 N 4 '67
President Johnson reaffirms support for free flow of trade; statement, October 12, 1967. L. B. Johnson. Dept State Bul 57:573 O 30 '67
President modifies escape-clause duty rates on sheet glass; Escape-clause duty rates on watch movements terminated. Dept State Bul 56:216-17 F 6 '67
Protectionism, a policy of retreat; address, October 30 ,1967. N. D. Katzenbach. Dept State Bul 57:686-9 N 20 '67; Same. Vital Speeches 34:119-21 D 1 '67
Steel begs Congress for an import shield. il Bsns W p 169-70 Je 10 '67
Tariff walls tumble; steps that led to freer trade; with editorial comment. il Bsns W p33-6, 192 My 20 '67
Trade warriors; Trade expansion act and import quota bills. New Repub 157:5-7 N 11 '67
U.S. tariff & trade policies: failure to consult industry; address, July 11, 1967. R. G. Wingerter. Vital Speeches 34:28-32 O 15 '67
Where tariffs go down; sampling of Kennedy round tariff cuts. il Bsns W p 18 Jl 1 '67
Wrong war at the wrong time; backlash to global tariff cuts. Fortune 76:98 D '67
See also
Duty free importation
Free trade and protection
United States—Commercial treaties and agreements
United States—Tariff commission
TARIFF, Exemption from. See Duty free importation
TARIFF commission. See United States—Tariff commission
TARIFF on antiques
Antiques and United States tariff legislation, 1816-1966. W. D. Garrett. il Antiques 92: 546-51 O '67
TARIFF on watches
Escape-clause duty rates on watch movements terminated. Dept State Bul 56:217 F 6 '67
TARKENTON, Francis
Right between the ears. il por Time 89:44+ Mr 17 '67
Two for the football show: the swinger and the square. J. Lake. il por N Y Times Mag p40-1+ N 5 '67
—and Olsen, Jack
Always leave those monsters laughing. por Sports Illus 27:38-45 Ag 7 '67
Better to scramble than lose. pors Sports Illus 27:74-80+ Jl 17 '67 (to be cont)
Dear Norm: I cannot return. Sports Illus 27: 36-42 Jl 31 '67
Pro rookie's ups and downs. pors Sports Illus 27:22-7 Jl 24 '67
TARPON fishing
Going fishing with the Kid. J. Underwood. il Sports Illus 27:60-70 Ag 21 '67
New world record tarpon on a fly. S. Apte. il Outdoor Life 140:30-3+ Ag '67
Troublesome tarpon. T. McNally. il Outdoor Life 139:72-3+ Mr '67
TARRANT, John
It's a long, long, long way to Brighton. G. S. Brown. il por Sports Illus 27:70-1 O 16 '67
TARTAS, Joseph
New tetrode transisitor. Electr World 77:34-5 F '67
TARTS
New plan for flan. J. Hewitt. il N Y Times Mag p66 Ag 27 '67
Tasty berry tarts. il Sunset 138:110-11 My '67
Upside-down apple pie. il Sunset 139:184 N '67
TARTUFFE; drama. See Moliére, J. B. P.
TARZAN (literary character) See Characters in literature
TASHKENT, Russia
Uzbek. M. Harari. il Vogue 149:146+ Ap 1 '67
TASK force on communication policy. See United States—President's task force on communication policy
TASMANIA
Ash Wednesday; most disastrous fire in Australian history. il Time 89:29-30 F 17 '67
Nature's blitz. Newsweek 69:57 F 20 '67
TASSELL, Leslie E.
Pack hunt with camels. Outdoor Life 139: 46-9+ Je '67

TASSONE, G. L.
Don't clean the refrigerator. Writer 80:29-30 O '67
TASTE
Chemicals that tickle your taste buds; flavor potentiators; reprint. il Sci Digest 62:52-5 N '67
Orientation by taste in fish of the genus ictalurus. J. E. Bardach and others. bibliog il Science 155:1276-8 Mr 10 '67
Polydipsia elicited by the synergistic action of a saccharin and glucose solution. E. S. Valenstein and others. bibliog il Science 157:552-4 Ag 4 '67
Sex differences in taste preference for glucose and saccharin solutions. E. S. Valenstein and others. bibliog il Science 156:942-3 My 19 '67
TASTE (aesthetics) See Aesthetics
TASTE of metal; story. See Updike, J.
TATE, James
Coda; poem. New Yorker 43:85 Ag 19 '67
Trust; poem. Nation 204:700 My 29 '67
Whole world's sadly talking to itself; W. B. Yeats; Pity ascending with the fog; poems. Poetry 110:239-40 Jl '67
about
At full speed. M. L. Rosenthal. Nation 204: 538-9 Ap 24 '67
TATE, James Hugh Joseph
Search for an heir. Time 90:33 O 27 '67
TATE, Sharon
Dames in the Valley of the dolls. B. Rollin. il pors Look 31:53-6+ S 5 '67
Sexy little me. J. Bowers. il pors Sat Eve Post 240:26-31 My 6 '67
TATE gallery, London
Brave day hideous night, by J. Rothenstein. Review
Atlan 220:109 Jl '67. E. Weeks
Sat R 50:35-6 My 27 '67
Mo(o)re for the Tate. Time 89:66 Mr 10 '67
TATTOOING
How to tattoo like a lady. il Redbook 130:64-5 Ja '68
Laserasing tattoos. il Time 90:68 O 20 '67
TAUBINGER, Laszlo M.
Letter from Vienna. Nat R 19:909 Ag 22 '67
Peking's defectors abroad. Nat R 19:414 Ap 18 '67
TAUBMAN, Howard
Measure of greatness. Opera N 31:8-13 Ap 1 '67
TAUC, Jan
Electronic properties of amorphous materials. bibliog Science 158:1543-8 D 22 '67
TAUCHNITZ, Bernhard, freiherr von
Tauchnitz rises again. T. L. Christie. Sat R 50:35-6 D 23 '67
TAUCHNITZ, Christian Bernhard, freiherr von. See Tauchnitz. B. von
TAUFA'AHAU Tupou IV, king of Tonga
Hail to the new king of Tonga. J. Bonfante. il pors Life 63:58-65 Jl 21 '67
On a tropical isle, big week for a big king. il por U S News 63:16 Jl 17 '67
What a king should be. il por Time 90:32 Jl 14 '67
TAUSSIG, Robert A. See Hayes, S. L. 3d, jt. auth.
TAVARES, Paulo, bp
Macao's Communists challenge Catholics. R. W. Fox. Christian Cent 85:54 Ja 10 '68
TAVEL, Ronald
Non-communications. P. Michelson. New Repub 156:35-8 Mr 4 '67
TAVERNER, Sonia
Brief biography. S. Goodman. pors Dance Mag 41:58-9 O '67
TAVOLGA, William N.
Noisy chorus of the sea; with biographical sketch. Natur Hist 76:7, 20-7 Ap '67
TAWNEY, Lenore
Lenore Tawney: her new work. J. Schuyler. il pors Craft Horiz 27:20-5 N '67
TAX, Sol
War and the draft. Natur Hist 76:54-8 bibliog (p70) D '67
TAX auditing
Big brother reads the tax returns. G. Astor. il Look 31:82+ Ap 18 '67
Relax it's only a tax audit. S. T. Reiner. il Nations Bsns 55:78-80 My '67
Unhappy returns from the IRS' computers; income tax returns checked by central data processing machines. il Bsns W p73-4+ F 25 '67
TAX avoidance. See Tax planning
TAX collection
Smooth tax collections mean soothed taxpayers; Riverside, Calif. D. R. O'Connor. il Am City 82:94-5 Ag '67

TAX collection—*Continued*
Tax speedups & corporate liquidity. J. E. Miles. il Harvard Bsns R 45:2-4+ Jl '67
See also
United States—Internal revenue service

TAX consultants
Storefront tax service earns a good return; H & R Block, inc, Kansas City, Mo. il Bsns W p 196-8+ Mr 25 '67

TAX credits. See Investment tax credit

TAX deductions. See Income tax—Deductions

TAX evasion
Protest group to hold back tax. U S News 63:105 O 2 '67
Spurious sacrifice; campaign for tax refusal. Reporter 37:12-13 O 5 '67
See also
Tax planning

TAX exemption. See Taxation, Exemption from

TAX forms
    Anecdotes, facetiae, satire, etc.
Sweetly flows the dun. F. P. Tullius. New Yorker 43:44-5 Ap 15 '67

TAX planning
End-of-year tax planning; shifting income. Bet Hom & Gard 45:35 D '67
Keep your tax records month by month. M. Feeley. Am Home 70:49 My '67
Personal business: tax hints for executives on the move. Bsns W p 137-8 Jl 15 '67
Power not to tax: sound long range planning; address, October 30, 1967. C. R. Kirk, jr. Vital Speeches 34:141-4 D 15 '67
Wall Street: the tax-selling season. C. Morgello. Newsweek 70:86 N 20 '67

TAX returns
Easier tax paying coming; interview. S. S. Cohen. Nations Bsns 55:42-3+ Mr '67
Smooth tax collections mean soothed taxpayers: Riverside, Calif. D. R. O'Connor. il Am City 82:94-5 Ag '67
When and how to file an amended tax return. Suc Farm 65:103 Mr '67
When should you file an amended tax return. P. Lindberg. Bet Hom & Gard 45:6+ Ap '67

    Auditing
See Tax auditing

TAX selling. See Tax planning

TAX write-off program. See Amortization deductions

TAXATION
    See also
Assessment
Income tax
    also subhead Taxation under various subjects, e.g. Church property—Taxation

    Brazil
Tragic end of Travancas the Terrible. Time 90:24 D 29 '67

    California
How California taxes may rise. U S News 62:121-2 Mr 20 '67
Value of positive pain. Time 89:23 Ap 28 '67

    Canada
Starting over on taxes: here is Canada's plan. il U S News 62:120-1 Mr 13 '67
Tax plan for Canada switches the burden; report of Carter royal commission. Bsns W p40 Mr 4 '67
Tax reform: Canada shows the way. D. G. M. Coxe. il Nat R 19:688-90 Je 27 '67
See also
Taxation—Ontario

    Europe, Western
Taxes in major nations: how the burden in U.S. compares. il U S News 62:63 F 27 '67

    Germany (Federal Republic)
Common market gets common tax; switch to French-style tax on value added. il Bsns W p65-6+ D 9 '67

    Ohio
Another sign of taxpayer revolt. U S News 62:106 My 22 '67

    Ontario
Rendering unto Caesar. Christian Cent 84: 1244 O 4 '67; Discussion. 84:1570 D 6 '67

    Switzerland
Forest that pays the taxes: Juriens, village in foothills of Jura Mountains. P. C. Fraley. Am For 73:25+ Ja '67

    United States
Arguing the tax hike; testimony before Ways & means, NAM for a rise, Chamber of commerce against. Bsns W p30 Ag 26 '67

Argument for a tax increase. America 117: 168 Ag 19 '67
Best evidence; L. B. Johnsons collision with Wilbur Mills over proposed tax surcharge. Nation 205:388 O 23 '67
Big tax spree in the U.S. il U S News 63: 25-7 Ag 21 '67
Case for taxes. America 117:52 Jl 15 '67
Case for the tax surcharge. H. Stein. il Reporter 37:26-9 O 19 '67
Cautious eye on the tax package. Bsns W p 124-5 F 4 '67
Chairman Mills, he wouldn't budge when LBJ pushed. il U S News 63:19 D 4 '67
Closing tax loopholes: who's to be squeezed? il U S News 63:63-4 S 18 '67
Congress still ducking an increase in taxes. Bsns W p43 O 21 '67
Cooling things by spending less, or taxing more? il Newsweek 70:57-8 S 4 '67
Cost of bad timing on taxes. Bsns W p 158 Ag 19 '67
Deadlock on taxes; no cut in spending, on 10 per cent surcharge. Bsns W p39 S 30 '67
First of the month; Writers and editors war tax protest. C. Amory. Sat R 50:6 O 7 '67; Discussion. 50:12+ O 21; 60 N 11; 8+ N 18 '67
Getting the budget under control; stalemate over spending and taxation. Bsns W p 190 O 14 '67
Going up; the deficit, wages, taxes. il Newsweek 70:60-1 Jl 31 '67
Gold taxes, inflation & co. Nat R 19:1052-3 O 3 '67
Higher taxes? no. M. Friedman. Newsweek 69:86 Ja 30 '67
How much, and when? surcharge sought by Johnson. il Bsns W p25-7 Ag 12 '67
How much tax? Time 90:15 Ag 25 '67
How secure is your social security? C. Stevenson. Read Digest 91:75-80 O '67; Reply. America 117:591 N 18 '67
If taxes are raised: effects on business and you. il U S News 63:49-50 Jl 31 '67
If taxes aren't raised: one view; excerpts from testimony, September 14, 1967. W. M. Martin, jr. U S News 63:125 S 25 '67
If U.S. shares taxes with states: where money will go; with chart. U S News 62: 118+ Mr 20 '67
In case taxes aren't raised—. il U S News 63:33-5 N 13 '67
Johnson swings the ax on spending; cut federal budget to win tax increase. il Bsns W p30-1 Jl 15 '67
Latest on the taxing and spending squabble. U S News 63:96-7 O 30 '67
Lobby for tax reform; address, August 16, 1967, H. S. Reuss. Vital Speeches 33:722-4 S 15 '67
Looking for the whites of the enemy's eyes; arguments for tax increase. il Time 90:73-4 Jl 7 '67
Lower spending, higher taxes; urges Fed chairman Martin. Bsns W p40 N 18 '67
LBJ's answer. Newsweek 70:79+ N 27 '67
LBJ's economics meets the critics. Bsns W p32-3 F 11 '67
LBJ's tax hike gains big-name support. il Bsns W p41-2 S 16 '67
Mills takes his time on tax rise. il Bsns W p31 Ag 19 '67
Moribund surtax; need for higher taxes to curb inflation. il Time 90:21-2 S 22 '67
National economic policy for '67; excerpts from addresses before the Joint economic committee of Congress, February 16. J. Tobin; A. H. Hansen. New Repub 156:17-19 Mr 4 '67
New tax surcharge. P. A. Samuelson. Newsweek 70:75 Ag 14 '67
Non-tax increase. H. C. Wallich. Newsweek 69:94 Mr 20 '67
Open letter to Wilbur Mills. P. A. Samuelson. Newsweek 70:81 N 6 '67
Our Rube Goldberg tax system; exorcising the deficit demon. H. S. Reuss. Commonweal 86:280-1 My 26 '67
Pigeonhole power; battle over tax-surcharge bill and budget cuts. il Newsweek 70:25-6 O 16 '67
Plain talk to LBJ on a tax rise: excerpts from address, November 20, 1967. W. D. Mills. U S News 63:102 D 4 '67
Power not to tax: sound long range planning; address, October 30, 1967. C. R. Kirk. jr. Vital Speeches 34:141-4 D 15 '67
Price hikes, yes; tax hike, hmm. . . il Newsweek 70:71 O 2 '67
Price of tax delay; more inflation and higher interest rates. il Bsns W p41-3 N 11 '67
Prudent tax policy. P. A. Samuelson. Newsweek 69:86 Mr 27 '67
Quo vadis, economist Johnson? S. Steiner. Christian Cent 84:1285 O 11 '67

TAXATION—United States—*Continued*
Raise taxes or cut spending. America 116:803 Je 3 '67
Rising consensus for a tax hike. Newsweek 70:59 Jl 24 '67
Sharing revenue with the states; argument against the Heller plan. L. H. Keyserling. il New Repub 156:14-18 Mr 25 '67
Shifts in the effect of taxes on the CPI; tables. J. A. Royse. il Mo Labor R 90:47-50 Jl '67
Should the President set tax rates? G. W. McKinney, jr. il Duns R 90:33-4 Jl '67
Slaughter on Park avenue; plight of the affluent poor. F. Brennan. Sat R 50:18 Je 24 '67
Soul-searching on taxes. J. A. Pechman. New Repub 157:11-12 S 23 '67; Reply. M. Carnoy and D. Mueller. 157:10-11 O 7 '67
Spending and taxes. Bsns W p 148 Jl 8 '67
Support, and opposition: for the President's tax-surcharge plan. U S News 63:84 S 4 '67
Surtax scrimmage. W. V. Shannon. Commonweal 87:107-8 O 27 '67
Tax boost? here's the way congressmen feel now. il U S News 63:89-90 Ag 7 '67
Tax hike chances still look slim. Bsns W p40 D 2 '67
Tax hike is almost certain to come. il Bsns W p31-2 Je 3 '67
Tax hike? Mills grinds slowly. il Newsweek 70:77 D 11 '67
Tax hike still has a chance. il Bsns W p35-6 O 14 '67
Tax increase: back to life again. il U S News 63:98+ D 4 '67
Tax increase; the federal budget; address, September 19, 1967. R. J. Saulnier. Vital Speeches 34:39-41 N 1 '67
Tax: painful but necessary; proposed increase. Life 63:4 Ag 18 '67
Tax revolt. W. Lippmann. Newsweek 70:25 O 23 '67
Tax revolt brewing? signs across U.S. il U S News 63:29-31 O 16 '67
Tax rise blocked again, how and why it happened. U S News 63:8 D 11 '67
Tax rise? Wilbur Mills is the key man; excerpts from statements. W. Mills. U S News 63:29 S 25 '67
Tax sharing with states: plan that's in trouble. U S News 62:104-6 F 27 '67
Tax sharing without strings: the answer to states' needs? with pro and con discussion. il Sr Schol 90:13-15 My 5 '67
Tax troubles: letter. L. H. Keyserling. New Repub 157:39-40 O 21 '67
Tax with a question mark. Fortune 75:101-2 F; 76:65-6 Ag '67
Taxes and expenditures; address, November 20, 1967. W. D. Mills. Vital Speeches 34:130-2 D 15 '67
Taxing situation. il Ebony 23:64-5 D '67
10 per cent more; surcharge on all corporate and individual income taxes. il Time 90:10 Ag 11 '67
Tithing for war; case against the Johnson surtax. H. Kasper. Commonweal 87:50-2 O 13 '67
To tax or not to tax. America 116:174 F 4 '67
Tough talk on U.S. tax policies. U S News 62:111 My 1 '67
U.S. taxpayer: fit to be tithed. il Newsweek 70:65-6+ Ag 14 '67
War and taxes; stand against the tax increase. Nation 206:36-7 Ja 8 '68
Way out of the tax thicket? L. E. Kust. Nations Bsns 55:82-4 F '67
What proposed hikes in taxes would mean to you. il U S News 63:48-9 Ag 14 '67
What taxes and spending do to the economy. il Nations Bsns 55:50-2+ N '67
What's happened to a simple tax plan. U S News 62:109 My 1 '67
What's wrong with the way we raise revenues. F. Morley. il Nations Bsns 55:27-8 Je '67
Where the tax bill bogged down. Bsns W p35 Ap 22 '67
Why budget problems may raise your taxes. U S News 64:85-6 Ja 8 '68
Why you can look for a tax rise. il U S News 62:42-4 Je 5 '67
Will Congress raise taxes? interview. W. D. Mills. U S News 63:52-5 O 9 '67
Your taxes: out of hand? with views of top economists. il U S News 62:60-3 F 27 '67
  See also
Corporations—Taxation
Income tax—United States
Inheritance tax
Property tax
Real property and taxation

Tax evasion
Taxation, Exemption from
Taxation, State
United States—Internal revenue service

  Anecdotes, facetiae, satire, etc.
$10,000-a-year man. G. Ace. Sat R 50:8 S 9 '67

TAXATION, Double
Income tax conventions enter into force; Canada, Trinidad and Tobago. Dept State Bul 58:66-7 Ja 8 '68
Income tax convention signed with Trinidad and Tobago; Department statement, December 23, 1966. Dept State Bul 56:84-5 Ja 9 '67
Supplementary estate-tax protocol with Greece enters into force. Dept State Bul 57:809 D 11 '67
United States and France sign income tax convention. Dept State Bul 57:268-9 Ag 28 '67

TAXATION, Exemption from
Bargains in tax-free bonds? il U S News 63:94-5 Ag 21 '67
Bond doggie. P. Stern. New Repub 156:8-9 My 6 '67
Boost for Puerto Rico's boom. il Bsns W p68-70+ Jl 29 '67
Crackdown on tax-free groups: who's under fire and how. U S News 63:78-80 Jl 24 '67
Financial record-keeping simplified; method for dancers. R. L. Gorewitz. Dance Mag 42:88-90 Ja '68
Foundations as easy as ABC; Americans building constitutionally. Time 91:46 Ja 5 '67
Giveaways of property; a growing boom. il U S News 64:96-8 Ja 15 '68
In lieu of taxes; Twentieth century fund contribution. America 118:27 Ja 13 '68
Magazines: tax blow for some? il U S News 62:118-19 Ap 24 '67
Missing taxpayers; loopholes favoring special groups. J. A. Ruskay. New Repub 156:11-14 Ap 29 '67
Power to untax; tax exempt organizations. Nat R 19:1156 O 31 '67
Some pay, some don't; inquiry on unrelated business activity of tax-exempt organizations. New Repub 157:5-6 Jl 22 '67
Stick-in-the-HUDs; tax inducements to private enterprise to provide jobs in the ghettos. Nat R 19:1056 O 3 '67
Tax exemption. D. Wolfle. Science 157:493 Ag 4 '67
Tax incentive that's coming under fire; industrial-aid bonds. il U S News 62:94-6 Je 12 '67
Taxing the geographic. Newsweek 69:90 Ap 24 '67
Taxing the tax-exempt. Time 89:86 Ap 21 '67
  See also
Church property—Taxation

TAXATION, Municipal. See Local taxation

TAXATION, State
Coming: an epidemic of state tax increases. U S News 62:113-15 F 20 '67
Monster; Iowa service tax. Newsweek 70:78+ O 16 '67
Now that your federal tax is paid—. il U S News 62:78 My 1 '67
State and local taxes: up almost 10 per cent, but cities ask more. U S News 62:110 My 1 '67
State taxes: upward trend. U S News 62:86 F 13 '67
What's wrong with the way we raise revenues. F. Morley. il Nations Bsns 55:27-8 Je '67
Where state & local taxes go. il Changing T 21:24-5 O '67

TAXATION for education. See School finance

TAXATION of bonds, securities, etc.
Foreign stocks yield a fast buck; buying foreign stocks abroad and selling them in the U.S. il Bsns W p 117-18 Jl 15 '67
  See also
Taxation, Exemption from

TAXATION of corporations. See Corporations—Taxation

TAXATION of securities. See Taxation of bonds, securities, etc.

TAXCO, Mexico
Wayward wanderer. M. Gough. il House B 109:122+ Mr '67

TAXES. See Taxation

TAXICAB drivers
Overheard in suburbia: cabdriver. W. Hedgeneth. Look 31:M26 My 16 '67
Trade winds; some rules applicable to New York city. J. Beatty, jr. il Sat R 50:14 My 6 '67

TAXICAB drivers—*Continued*
Where are the taxis? occupational hazard; violent crime. New York city. il Time 89: 48 F 3 '67
TAXICABS
Cringe: odd corporation names for fleet-owned taxicabs. New Yorker 43:39 S 16 '67
Taxis clock up woes for the urban planner. il Bsns W p50-1 D 23 '67
Where are the taxis? New York city. il Time 89:48 F 3 '67
TAXIDERMY
Taxidermy, why not? Vacaville recreation department in California. J. Steinke. il Parks & Rec 2:31+ Ap '67
See also
Fishes—Collection and preservation
TAYLOR, Alan John Percivale
Maverick historian. M. Shefftz. New Repub 156:19-21 Ap 29 '67
TAYLOR, Alice. See Crist, R. E. jt. auth.
TAYLOR, Andrew, family
Negro millionaire's advice to his race; interview. ed. by F. X. Tolbert. H. T. Taylor. U S News 63:68-9 S 4 '67
TAYLOR, Ann (Bonfoey)
American westerns, 1967. il pors Vogue 149: 238-41 My '67
TAYLOR, Calvin W. and Ellison, R. L.
Biographical predicators of scientific performance. bibliog Science 155:1075-80 Mr 3 '67
TAYLOR, Carl E. and Hall, M.-F.
Health, population, and economic development. bibliog Science 157:651-7 Ag 11 '67
TAYLOR, Cecil
Four lives in the bebop business, by A. B. Spellman. Review
Nation 204:378-9 Mr 20 '67. B. Kremen
Trials of Cecil Taylor. M. Williams. por Sat R 50:120 Mr 11 '67
TAYLOR, Duncan Norton-. See Norton-Taylor, D.
TAYLOR, Edmond
De Gaulle surveys the damage. Reporter 36: 29-30 Ap 6 '67
De Gaulle's economic reforms. Reporter 37: 24-6 N 2 '67
Europe's obsession with U.S. economic power. Reporter 37:25-7 D 28 '67
French elections. Reporter 36:16 Mr 23 '67
Light reaches Europe. Reporter 36:12 Je 15 '67
Political war intensifies. Reporter 36:20-2 Je 29 '67
Temporary victory for de Gaulle. Reporter 36: 27-8+ Je 15 '67
TAYLOR, Edward Plunket
When a tycoon flunks retirement. il pors Bsns W p 142-4+ D 2 '67
TAYLOR, Eleanor Ross
After twenty years; Bulletin; Pause, in flight; poems. Poetry 109:241-4 Ja '67
Sylvia Plath's last poems. Poetry 109:260-2 Ja '67
TAYLOR, Elizabeth, 1932-
Burtons in Dahomey. L. Rasponi. il por Vogue 149:92-3+ Ap 15 '67
Happy anniversary, Elizabeth and Richard; tributes from their friends. por McCalls 94:68-9+ Je '67
His Liz: a scheming charmer. R. Burton. il pors Life 62:78-9+ F 24 '67
Liz Taylor festival. A. Knight. Sat R 50:26 O 28 '67
On location with Richard and Liz: why they're never dull. C. Brossard. il pors Look 31:64-7 Je 27 '67
Peter Glenville talks about the Burtons. P. Glenville. il pors Vogue 150:282-5+ S 1 '67
Rise and fall and rise of Elizabeth Taylor. L. Israel. il pors Esquire 67:96-9+ Mr '67
Voyage with the Burtons. C. G. Pepper. il pors McCalls 95:56-60+ Ja '68
TAYLOR, Elsie
My art is my feelings made visible. por Farm J 91:106-7+ Mr '67
TAYLOR, Emily
Keeping house with Emily Taylor. See issues of Good housekeeping
TAYLOR, Frank J.
They saved the Big Sur. Read Digest 91:170-5 N '67
TAYLOR, Fred G.
Visit to Bielefeld. Hobbies 72:122-3 Ag '67
TAYLOR, George V.
Noncapitalist wealth and the origins of the French revolution; excerpts from address, December 30, 1965. bibliog f Am Hist R 72:469-96 Ja '67
TAYLOR, Harold
Why not a draft to get new teachers? Look 31:80+ Je 27 '67

TAYLOR, Hobart, 1920-
Money men. il pors Ebony 22:65-6+ S '67
TAYLOR, Hobart T.
Negro millionaire's advice to his race; interview. ed. by F. X. Tolbert. por U S News 63:68-9 S 4 '67
TAYLOR, Kathryn S.
Growing wild flowers from seed. Horticulture 45:30-3 My '67
TAYLOR, L. B. jr
Alligator on the pad! Sci Digest 62:53-7 D '67
TAYLOR, L. H. See Cooper, R. M. jt. auth.
TAYLOR, Lee, jr
Rewarding race in Detroit. K. Chapin. il por Sports Illus 27:22-3 Jl 10 '67
TAYLOR, Loren E.
Let's get the elephants out of the Volkswagen. Parks & Rec 2:18-19+ F '67
TAYLOR, Mark M.
Clematis. Horticulture 45:54+ D '67
TAYLOR, Maxwell Davenport
Cause in Vietnam is being won. por N Y Times Mag p36-7+ O 15 '67
General Taylor discusses recent developments in Viet-Nam; statement at press conference, January 30, 1967. Dept State Bul 56: 285-7 F 20 '67
Mr Clifford and General Taylor report on talks on Viet-Nam with allied leaders; transcript of a press conference, August 5, 1967. Dept State Bul 57:256-60 Ag 28 '67

about
Debate and disquiet. il por Newsweek 69:35-6 F 6 '67
Fulbright versus Taylor. A. Campbell. New Repub 156:26-7 F 25 '67
TAYLOR, Paul
World of dance. W. Terry. il por Sat R 51:96 Ja 13 '68
TAYLOR, Peter
Mrs Billingsby's wine; story. New Yorker 43:56-60 O 14 '67
TAYLOR, Philip B. jr
Progress in Venezuela. Cur Hist 53:270-4+ N '67
TAYLOR, R. E. and Berger, Rainer
Radiocarbon content of marine shells from the Pacific coasts of Central and South America. bibliog il Science 158:1180-2 D 1 '67
TAYLOR, Raymond L.
Report of the eighth Washington meeting. por Science 155:860-9 F 17 '67
TAYLOR, Richard K.
Property rights and human rights. Christian Cent 84:1120-2 S 6 '67
TAYLOR, Theodore
Girl who took risks; story. Sat Eve Post 240: 50-5 Jl 15 '67
TAYLOR, Zachary
How to make it to the White House without really trying. D. Lavender. il por Am Heritage 18:26-7+ Je '67
TAYLOR, Zack
How to outwit a hurricane! Motor B 120:46-7+ Ag '67
Look at the latest in houseboats! Read Digest 91:145-8 Jl '67
New look at life jackets. Motor B 119:45-6+ F '67
TAYOR, Richard N.
Reservoirs don't have to be eyesores. Am City 82:71-2 Jl '67
TAZIEFF, Haroun
Menace of extinct volcanoes; reprint. UNESCO Courier 20:4-6+ O '67
TCHAIKOVSKY, Peter Ilyitch
Efrem Kurtz's balletic Tchaikovsky, a subtle instinct for musical drama. G. L. Mayer. Am Rec G 34:240 N '67
Four Tchaikovsky suites. C. J. Luten. il Am Rec G 33:555 Mr '67
Markevitch's magnificent Manfred. J. Diether. Am Rec G 33:594 Mr '67
On crossroads, a superb Tchaikovsky serenade. M. N. Kanny. Am Rec G 34:60 S '67
Queen of spades (Pique dame) Criticism
New Yorker 42:157 F 11 '67
New Yorker 43:142-4 S 9 '67
Sat R 50:46-7 F 18 '67
Records:
Eugene Onegin, Queen of spades (excerpts) Opera N 31:34 F 25 '67
Queen of spades. Opera N 32:38 D 9 '67
Tchaikovsky's Pique dame: a spine-chiller from today's Bolshoi. C. L. Osborne. il Hi Fi 17:87-8 N '67
Thief. M. K. Argus. Sat R 50:4 Ja 28 '67
TCHELITCHEW, Paul
Romantic in an unromantic age. G. Davenport. Nat R 19:1389+ D 12 '67

TEA

Tea therapy; with recipes. E. Alston. il Look 31:80-1 Ap 18 '67

To make a good cup of tea. il Ladies Home J 85:26 Ja '68

TEA ceremony. See Japan—Social life and customs

TEACH corps. See National education association—Teach corps

TEACHER corps. See United States—National teacher corps

TEACHER education, Experimental. See Teachers—Education

TEACHER grievances. See Teachers grievances

TEACHER librarians. See School librarians

TEACHER participation in school administration. See School management and organization—Teacher participation

TEACHER pupil relations. See Teachers and students

TEACHER shortage. See Teachers—Supply and demand

TEACHER strikes. See Strikes—United States —Teachers

TEACHERS

Do teachers talk too much? with study-discussion program, by E. Harris and D. Harris. J. Holt. bibliog il PTA Mag 62: 2-4, 34 O '67

Editor interviews; ed. by M. S. Fenner. S. J. Wright. NEA J 56:63-4 My '67

First-grade teacher is a V.I.P. L. L. Prina. il N Y Times Mag p 122+ O 8 '67

If we are to be leaders. R. M. McClure and O. Sand. NEA J 56:28-31 D '67

Roger Tenney: teacher of the year. C. Mangel. il Look 31:64-9 My 2 '67

Talk about teaching. A. Grant. il Mlle 64: 148-9+ Mr '67

Teacher-administrator relationships in the local association; symposium. NEA J 56: 49-52 F '67

Teacher and the instructional materials center. H. C. Hartsell. il Sr Schol 90:sup 13 F 3 '67

Teachers then and now. M. Bonn. il Am Ed 3:13-19 O '67

Why the schools flunk out; concerning the Coleman report. C. S. Benson. il Nation 204:463-6 Ap 10 '67

See also

Collective bargaining—Teachers
College professors and instructors
Courses of study
Dance teachers
National education association
Negro teachers
Sanctions, Professional
School and the home
School management and organization— Teacher participation
School superintendents and principals
Teachers unions
Teaching

Adjustment

Are we driving teachers out of ghetto schools? S. Levey. il Am Ed 3:2-4 My '67

Beginning teacher. A. L. Townes. NEA J 56: 69-70 O '67

Beginning teacher. NEA J 56:69-70 O; 72-3 80 D '67; 57:67 Ja '68

Teacher peer relations and educational change. M. Chesler and R. Fox. NEA J 56:25-6 My '67

Anecdotes, facetiae, satire, etc.

Green teacher and the gossip queen. NEA J 56:21-2 Mr '67

No greater reward P. H. Kendall. il Atlan 219:113 F '67

Certification

Teacher gap, and how to close it. F. B. Maynard. Read Digest 91:50-4 Ag '67

Contracts

Striking teachers return to classrooms; New York and Detroit. Sr Schol 91:sup2 O 19 '67

Teacher-Board of ed. contract talks; National institute on collective negotiations in public education conferences. Sr Schol 91:sup4 O 12 '67

Dismissal

Monkeys and miniskirts. America 116:620-1 Ap 29 '67

Education

Career teacher cadre. Sch & Soc 94:470+ D 24 '66

Education professions development act. H. R. Ellis. 2d. Am Ed 3:20-1 O '67

Federal funds; teacher training. Am Ed 3:30-1 S '67

Problems and developments in teacher education in the U.S.S.R. N. Grant. bibliog f il Sch & Soc 95:451-5 N 25 '67

Summer seminar in Ecuador. J. Moorhead. il Sr Schol 90:sup 13-14 Mr 3 '67

Summer study tour of New York and New England. D. Minor. il Sr Schol 90:sup21 Mr 3 '67

Teacher education for the deprived: a new pattern; Operation fair chance, project in experimental teacher education at California state college centers at Hayward. E. G. Olsen. Sch & Soc 95:232-4 Ap 1 '67

See also

Art teachers—Education
National commission on teacher education and professional standards
Student teaching
Summer schools
Teachers institutes

Hours of teaching

See Teaching load

Insurance

Accidental death and dismemberment insurance. NEA J 56:18 S '67

Leaves of absence

See also

College professors and instructors—Leaves of absence

Oaths of allegiance, etc.

See Loyalty. Oaths of

Pensions

See also

Carnegie foundation for the advancement of teaching

Placement

See Teachers—Selection and appointment

Political activities

Mugwump or full participant? J. A. Cooper. NEA J 56:18 Mr '67

Political activity; questions and answers. J. H. Starie. NEA J 56:40 O '67

Political life of American teachers, by H. Zeigler. Review
  New Repub 157:31+ S 30 '67. J. Kozol

Teacher unrest spreads. Sr Schol 91:sup2 N 9 '67

Qualifications

Good pupils, poor teachers. M. T. Bloom. il Redbook 128:72-3+ F '67

See also

Teachers—Certification

Rating

See also

College professors and instructors—Rating

Recruiting

Why not a draft to get new teachers? H. Taylor. Look 31:80+ Je 27 '67

See also

Association for school, college and university staffing

Salaries

47-hour work week, $6,253 annual salary. il Sr Schol 90:sup4 F 17 '67

How much does your state spend on teachers and pupils? il Parents Mag 42:72 S '67

More militant mood. il Time 89:66 Mr 3 '67

Salaries; recent research report of the NEA. Sch & Soc 95:373-4 O 28 '67

Teachers' salaries, 1966-67. G. N. Steiber. il NEA J 56:36-7 O '67

Terre Haute library pay scale ties salaries to school rates; New York state: librarians surging ahead of local teaching pay scales. Library J 92:958 Mr 1 '67

See also

Sick leave
Strikes—United States—Teachers

Selection and appointment

American education placement service. G. E. Arnstein. bibliog f Sch & Soc 95:298-301 Sum '67

Computer to help school librarians find jobs. Library J 92:1685 Ap 15 '67

NEA search locates teachers and jobs; interview, ed. by J. Lloyd. G. Arnstein. Sr Schol 91:sup4+ O 26 '67

NEA's computer system; matching job applicants and teacher vacancies. Sch & Soc 95:284+ Sum '67

Statistics

Profile of the American public school teacher, 1966. H. Davis. NEA J 56:12-15 My '67

Supply and demand

American federation of teachers' position paper; statement; July 18-20, 1966. C. Cogen and D. Selden. Sch & Soc 95:87-91 F 4 '67

TEACHERS—Supply and demand—*Continued*
Shortage worsens. Sch & Soc 95:43 Ja 21 '67
Statement on the teacher shortage; September 9, 1966. Sch & Soc 95:91-2 F 4 '67
Teacher gap, and how to close it. F. B. Maynard. Read Digest 91:50-4 Ag '67
Teacher shortages and strikes plague nation's school openings; report of NEA survey. Sr Schol 91:sup2 O 5 '67
Teachers: enough or good enough? il Am Ed 3:back cover Jl '67
See also
Teachers—Recruiting

Teaching load
See Teaching load

Tenure
See also
Teachers—Dismissal

TEACHERS, interchange of
Washington report; Teacher-exchange program. J. Lloyd. Sr Schol 91:sup4 N 2 '67

TEACHERS aides
Have traveled, will teach; Peace corpsmen come home with ideas. M. Bonn. il Am Ed 3:1-3 F '67
How teacher aides feel about their jobs. A. C. Harding. il NEA J 56:17-19 N '67
Introduction to success; teenage trainees working with preschool youngsters. H. C. Lyon, jr. il Am Ed 3:5-6+ My '67
Mothers bring their skills to school. D. Levenson. il Parents Mag 42:48-9+ F '67
Paraprofessionals. J. H. Starie and M. Stevenson. NEA J 56:74 S '67
Teacher aides. Sch & Soc 95:38-9 Ja 21 '67
Teacher aides have wide-range responsibilities. S. Holzman. Sr Schol 91:sup2+ N 30 '67
Teacher opinion poll; how the profession feels about teacher aides. il NEA J 56:16-17 N '67
Teacher stretchers; home-visiting aides. il Am Ed 3:27-8 Jl '67

TEACHERS and libraries. See Libraries and schools

TEACHERS and students
Brad. V. H. Ormsby. NEA J 56:20-1 My '67
Campus turmoil: a religious dimension. T. A. Langford. Christian Cent 84:172-4 F 8 '67
Classroom incident. See issues of NEA journal
Closing the gap. H. Howe. 2d. Parents Mag 42:50+ S '67
Crippled and health-impaired children. F. P. Connor. il NEA J 56:37-9 N '67
Crucible case; teacher exonerated of molesting charge. Newsweek 70:33 S 25 '67
Death at an early age; excerpt. J. Kozol. Atlan 220:49-55 S '67
Drama at Baldwin high; investigation of teacher charged with molesting girl. il Newsweek 70:65-6 S 18 '67
Editor's notebook. M. S. Fenner. NEA J 56:88 D '67
Eighth grade rebel; a student speaks. L. Hedgecock. NEA J 56:19 S '67
Giving faces to the faceless. J. E. Mizer. il NEA J 57:6-8 Ja '68
Happenings in education; marks of a good teacher. W. D. Boutwell. il PTA Mag 62:27-8 Ja '68
Helping children to clarify values; excerpts from Values and teaching; working with values in the classroom. L. E. Raths and others. il NEA J 56:12-15 O '67
Libraries of the future for the liberal arts college; faculty vs. librarians. R. T. Jordan. il Library J 92:537-9 F 1 '67; Correction, 92:1096 Mr 15 '67; Reply. L. Hubbard. 92:1392 Ap 1 '67
Matching teachers and pupils; excerpts from Classroom grouping for teachability. H. A. Thelen. il NEA J 56:18-20 Ap '67
Question of conduct; accusations of molestation against teacher. il Time 90:52 S 15 '67
Self-fulfilling prophecies. Sci Am 217:54+ N '67
Teacher-opinion poll; attitudes toward school. NEA J 56:24 My '67
Teacher's quest for quality. P. A. Ellis and D. V. Meyer. NEA J 56:24-5 D '67
These techniques work for me. K. W. Muster. il NEA J 56:16-18 S '67
Turmoil in higher education; interview, ed. by G. B. Leonard and T. G. Harris. C. Kerr. il Look 31:17-21 Ap 18 '67

TEACHERS associations. See Educational associations

TEACHERS attitudes. See Attitudes

TEACHERS certificates. See Teachers—Certification

TEACHERS college, Columbia university
Teachers college: John Dewey with a hard nose. P. Schrag. il Sat R 50:62-4+ D 16 '67

TEACHERS conferences. See Educational conferences

TEACHERS contracts. See Teachers—Contracts

TEACHERS ethics
Prohibited speech. NEA J 56:54-5 Ap '67

TEACHERS grievances
Grievance procedures. J. H. Starie and D. L. Conrad. NEA J 56:63 N '67
It burns me up (cont) NEA J 56:85 S; 63 O; 77 N '67
On the causes of teacher discontent. P. Woodring. Sat R 50:61-2 O 21 '67
Teachers' gripes about parents; with study-discussion program, by E. Harris and D. Harris. bibliog il PTA Mag 61:8-10+, 31 F '67

TEACHERS institutes
Hawaii: innovation seminars. L. E. Hunt. Sr Schol 91:sup4 S 28 '67

TEACHERS loyalty oaths. See Loyalty, Oaths of

TEACHERS salaries. See Teachers—Salaries

TEACHERS tours. See National education association—Division of educational travel

TEACHERS unions
Down the up staircase; striking teachers. il Sat Eve Post 240:96 O 21 '67
Parochial school teachers organize. Sr Schol 91:sup6 S 28 '67
Pursuit of power. il Time 90:43 S 22 '67
Teachers strike hard; push for better pay and working conditions. il Bsns W p43-4 S 16 '67
See also
American federation of teachers
United federation of teachers

TEACHERS writing competition. See Literature—Competitions

TEACHING
Agony and the ecstasy of teaching. M. C. Hunter. NEA J 56:36-8 F '67
Big debate: teaching by pressure or by discovery. il Life 62:44-7 Mr 31 '67
How team teaching works in Tulsa; East central high school. J. L. Armstrong. il Sr Schol 90:sup 17 Ap 14 '67
If you want to teach: roundup of teaching jobs off the beaten track. P. Rifield. il Mlle 64:150-1+ Mr '67
Reaching and teaching the gifted. E. M. Drews. il NEA J 56:8-11+ N '67
Reducing the behavior gap. M. D. Fantini and G. Weinstein. NEA J 57:22-5 Ja '68
School as a center of inquiry, by R. J. Schaefer. Review
Sat R 50:66-7 Mr 18 '67. F. G. Jennings
Some very special teachers' pets; three experimental federally financed education projects in Connecticut. E. Pinto. il Sr Schol 90:sup 16 Ap 7 '67
Talk about teaching. A. Grant. il Mlle 64:148-9+ Mr '67
Team teaching. W. Georgiades; J. R. Fraenkel; R. E. Gross. bibliog NEA J 56:14-17 Ap '67
These techniques work for me. K. W. Muster. il NEA J 56:16-18 S '67
Things are happening in Cleveland Heights; Roxboro junior high school. il Sr Schol 91:sup3-9 S 21 '67
Thirty-six children, by H. Kohl. Review
New Repub 157:23-6+ D 23 '67. J. Featherstone
Video tape in the classroom, helping teachers study themselves and their teaching techniques. G. Perry. il Sr Schol 90:sup21 My 12 '67
Walls come tumbling down; team teaching center established by the Weber County school district in Ogden, Utah, under Title III grant. W. T. Greenleaf. Am Ed 3:22 Mr '67
What's happening in education? methods. W. Abraham. il Todays Health 45:47-51 S '67
See also
Audio-visual instruction
Classroom management
Colleges and universities—Teaching
Courses of study
Discussion method (education)
Education
Education, Experimental
Individual instruction
Montessori method of education
Motivation (education)
Programmed teaching
Psychology, Educational
Remedial teaching
Teachers

Aids and devices
Communications: the undiscovered country; adaptation of address, 1966. D. M. Grieco. bibliog il Library J 92:845-8 F 15 '67

TEACHING—Aids and devices—*Continued*
Education comes alive outdoors. R. M. Isenberg. il NEA J 56:34-5 Ap '67
Educational consultant and commercially produced instructional media. J. L. Peyser. bibliog f Sch & Soc 95:301-3 Sum '67
Evaluating educational materials. R. H. Smith. Pub W 191:38 Ap 3 '67
Freeing pupils from the sit-look-listen syndrome. H. W. Ray. il NEA J 56:8-10 Ap '67
Games for the slums; pinball machine to teach mathematics. Sci N 91:402 Ap 29 '67
Games in the classroom. E. Carlson. il Sat R 50:62-4+ Ap 15 '67
Games in the classroom; symposium, ed. by J. S. Coleman. il Sr Schol 91:sup3+ N 9 '67
How mechanized should the classroom be? G. M. Torkelson and E. A. Torkelson. NEA J 56:28-30 Mr '67
How to get the most out of local educational resources; use of teaching modules in San Diego County, Calif. J. M. Huffman. il Sr Schol 90:sup 16 F 3 '67
Instructional materials in the mathematics classroom. D. A. Johnson. NEA J 56:39-40 My '67
Instructional resources in the teaching of art history. R. M. Diamond. il Sch Arts 66:24-8 Je '67
Man-made world, a new course for high schools; Engineering concepts curriculum project. E. E. David, jr. and J. G. Truxal. il Science 156:914-20 My 19 '67
Materials for teaching about Canada. Sr Schol 90:sup6 F 10 '67
New educational materials (cont) Sr Schol 90:sup 18-20 F 3; sup30+ F 17; sup 16+ Mr 10; sup23-4+ Ap 14; sup 19 Ap 21; sup 17-19 My 12; sup21 My 19; 91:sup33-5 S 28; sup20 O 5; sup 15 O 19; sup 10-12 O 26; sup 17 N 16 '67
Non-book materials; new design problems. il Pub W 192:98-100 N 6 '67
Realities of the learning market; address, August 9, 1966. H. Howe, 2d. il Library J 92:297-301 Ja 15 '67
Remedial reading roundup, new materials. Library J 92:4212-13 N 15 '67
Roundup of new teaching tools. il Sr Schol 91:sup24-5 O 26 '67
Schoolman's guide to Marshall McLuhan. J. M. Culkin. il Sat R 50:51-3+ Mr 18 '67
Sex education; new teaching materials. D. Burleson. il Sr Schol 90:sup 14 Ap 21 '67
Small school, big curriculum; use of self-study education kits at Anatone high school, state of Washington. J. Guernsey. il Am Ed 3:11+ O '67
Some new directions in systems for education. il Arch Rec 141:167-70 F '67 (to be cont)
Technology in higher education: the winds of change blow stronger; report of conference sponsored by the American educational publishers institute. il Pub W 193:35-8 Ja 8 '68
Treasures without tariffs; concerning Beirut and Florence agreements. D. H. Fenn, jr. il Am Ed 3:23-4+ Ap '67
Using tape to teach note-taking. C. G. Woodhouse. NEA J 56:53 D '67
Washington developments in education; summaries of addresses. L. Hausman; M. Johnson; W. M. Robinson. il Pub W 191:30-4 My 29 '67
What's happening in education? materials. W. Abraham. il Todays Health 45:51-5 S '67
Will we recognize tomorrow's elementary school. W. D. Hedges. il NEA J 56:9-12 D '67
See also
Audio-visual aids
Computers—Educational applications
Film strips
Instructional materials centers
Moving pictures in education
Phonograph in education
Teaching machines
Telephone in education
Workbooks (education)

TEACHING as a profession
Career teacher cadre. Sch & Soc 94:470+ D 24 '66
Commitment to action. B. Alonso. NEA J 56:29 S '67
Teacher-opinion poll; improvement in teaching as a profession. il NEA J 56:62 Ap '67
Teaching as beneficiary of service. Sch & Soc 95:68-9 F 4 '67

TEACHING assistants. See College professors and instructors

TEACHING load
47-hour work week. $6,253 annual salary. il Sr Schol 90:sup4 F 17 '67
Forty-seven hour week; teaching load of public school teachers. Sch & Soc 95:276 Sum '67

TEACHING machines
Automation's value for education. Sch & Soc 95:140-1 Mr 4 '67
Teaching machines: what's ahead? excerpts. Todays Health 45:56-7 S '67
See also
Computers—Educational applications
Programmed teaching

TEACHING priests. See Priests

TEACHING sisters. See Sisterhoods

TEAK boats. See Boats—Materials

TEAM flying. See Aeronautics, Military

TEAM management (business) See Executives

TEAM teaching. See Teaching

TEAMS, Baseball. See Baseball clubs

TEAMSTERS
See also
Strikes—United States—Teamsters

TEAMSTERS union. See International brotherhood of teamsters, chauffeurs, warehousemen, and helpers of America

TEATRO Juarez, Guanajuato, Mexico. See Opera houses

TEBBEL, John
Britain's chronic press crisis. Sat R 50:49-50 Jl 8 '67
Britain's troubled air. Sat R 50:60-1 Ag 12 '67
Century of The world almanac. Sat R 50:62-3 D 9 '67
Children's TV, European style. Sat R 50:70-1+ F 11 '67
Great media impact war. Sat R 50:96-7 Je 10 '67
Making the British press responsible. Sat R 50:118+ O 14 '67
People and jobs. Sat R 50:8-12+ D 30 '67
PBL: the great experiment. Sat R 50:85-7+ N 11 '67
Readers's digest goes to college. Sat R 50:92-3 My 13 '67
Sigma delta chi's new look. Sat R 50:84+ Ap 8 '67
Wall Street publishing giant. Sat R 51:110-11+ Ja 13 '68
What happens to J-school graduates. Sat R 50:126-7+ Mr 11 '67

TEBBETTS, Birdie
Big-leaguer big in the boondocks. D. Wolf. il pors Life 63:28-31 S 1 '67

TEBBETTS, George Robert. See Tebbetts, B.

TECHCRETE. See Concrete, Precast

TECHNICAL assistance
See also
Community development
Industrialization
Underdeveloped areas

TECHNICAL assistance, American
Interdepartmental committee on water for peace surveys world water problems; text of memorandum, and excerpt from report Dept State Bul 56:758-65 My 15 '67

TECHNICAL assistance in Italy
Educational aid to flood-ravaged Florence. W. W. Brickman. Sch & Soc 95:289 Sum '67

TECHNICAL assistance in Latin America
Technical assistance; activities of the OAS. G. Meek. Américas 19:46 Je '67

TECHNICAL assistance in Russia
American aid to Russia. il U S News 62:60-1 Mr 13 '67

TECHNICAL assistance in the Dominican Republic
Inter-American volunteers for development. Américas 19:inside cover Ap '67

TECHNICAL assistance in Vietnam
After victory, what? A. Gerber. Bul Atomic Sci 23:27 Mr '67
Agents of the other war: U.S. county agents in Viet Nam. Time 89:23 Ja 27 '67

TECHNICAL cooperation, International. See International cooperation

TECHNICAL education
Getting off the road to technology gap: McNamara's view. D. S. Greenberg. Science 155:1089 Mr 3 '67; Discussion. 156:451-2 Ap 28 '67
Quincy builds a new vocational-technical curriculum. N. Farmer. il Am Ed 3:12-13+ Jl '67
School that breeds France's business elite; Ecole Polytechnique, Paris. il Bsns W p 184-6+ My 20 '67
Teacher-opinion poll; technology and education. il NEA J 56:70 Mr '67

TECHNICAL education—*Continued*
Training for engineering and technology in Switzerland; excerpt from Science in Switzerland. J. M. Luck. bibliog f il Sch & Soc 94:499-502 D 24 '66
  See also
Engineering education
Massachusetts institute of technology, Cambridge
Trade schools
Vocational education
TECHNICAL information
Data transfer: explosion and remedies; ABPC conference at Arden house. il Pub W 191: 35-41 Ap 10 '67
Government-wide technology transfer sought. Aero Tech 21:31 O 9 '67
TECHNICAL literature
Literature program of engineering societies; report on conference. S. Klein. Science 155: 1698-9 Mr 31 '67
TECHNICAL measurement corporation
Suit underscores proprietary data issue. K. J. Stein. Aviation W 86:56-7+ F 27 '67
TECHNICAL processes in libraries. See Libraries—Technical processes
TECHNICAL schools. See Technical education
TECHNICAL universities. See Technical education
TECHNICAL workers. See Technicians in industry
TECHNICAL writing
Sounder thinking through clearer writing. F. P. Woodford. Science 156:743-5 My 12 '67; Discussion. 157:6, 876 Jl 7, Ag 25 '67
TECHNICIANS, Electronic. See Electronic workers
TECHNICIANS, Laboratory. See Laboratory technicians
TECHNICIANS, Medical. See Medical workers
TECHNICIANS in industry
Foreign talent heads where the action is. il Bsns W p 196+ S 9 '67
Put people on your balance sheet. J. S. Hekimian and C. H. Jones. bibliog f il Harvard Bsns R 45:105-13 Ja '67
  See also
Electronic workers
Engineers
TECHNIQUE (music) See Piano—Instruction and study; Violin playing
TECHNOLOGICAL aids in education. See Teaching—Aids and devices
TECHNOLOGICAL change
Adjusting manpower requirements to constant change. Mo Labor R 90:36-41 O '67
American transition. Z. Brzezinski. New Repub 157:18-21 D 23 '67
Big gap in economic theory. H. M. Boettinger. bibliog f Harvard Bsns R 45:51-8 Jl '67
Bringing the future into focus. Nations Bsns 55:82-3+ D '67
Civilian technology: NASA study finds little spin-off. D. S. Greenberg. Science 157:1016-18 S 1 '67; Discussion. 158:438 O 27 '67
Continuing education; address. December 16, 1966. H. A. Moreen. Vital Speeches 33:244-7 F 1 '67
Giant corporations resist change. Sci N 92: 346 O 7 '67
How to close the technology gap; exchanges of technological knowledge between the U.S. and Europe. Bsns W p 156 Ap 8 '67
Invention and economic growth, by J. Schmookler. Review
  Fortune 76:191-2 S 1 '67. I. Kristol
Military technology and the Great society. B. A. Schriever. il Tech W 20:63-5 Ja 23 '67
New jobs with a big future. il Changing T 21:6-10 N '67
New technological era: a view from the law. H. P. Green. Bul Atomic Sci 23:12-18 N '67
Old worlds to conquer; technology gap. H. Martyn. Nation 204:427-9 Ap 3 '67
Privacy. P. H. Abelson. Science 158:323 O 20 '67
Remedial technology must be supported by information. C. S. Draper. il Tech W 20: 56-8+ Ja 23 '67
Report on the geosocial revolution. B. Fuller. Sat R 50:31-3+ S 16 '67
Technological forecasting. J. B. Quinn. bibliog f il Harvard Bsns R 45:89-106 Mr '67
Technological forecasts; excerpts from address. B. A. Schriever. Aviation W 87:21 D 4 '67
Technological innovation: panel stresses role of small firms; with editorial comment. B. Nelson. Science 155:1201, 1229-31 Mr 10 '67
Technology and change, by D. A. Schon. Review
  New Repub 157:32-4 Jl 22 '67. R. Nader
Technology assessment. D. Wolfie. Science 158:209 O 13 '67

Twenty-first century: the world you'll live in. W. Cronkite. il Pop Sci 190:98-101 Ap '67
U.S. economic giant keeps growing. E. L. Dale, jr. il N Y Times Mag p30-1+ Mr 19 '67
TECHNOLOGICAL research. See Industrial research
TECHNOLOGICAL unemployment. See Unemployment, Technological
TECHNOLOGY
Beyond Vietnam: what has science to say to man? symposium. il Sat R 50:39-50 Jl 1; 49-52 Ag 5; 68 N 4 '67
Competition of materials. W. O. Alexander. il Sci Am 217:254-6+ S '67
NAS charts goals for applied technology. J. F. Judge. Tech W 20:36-7 Je 19 '67
Science and scientists; excerpts from address, September 1, 1965. C. Hinshelwood. Bul Atomic Sci 23:31-6 Je '67
Strategies for a technology-based business. H. I. Ansoff and J. M. Stewart. il Harvard Bsns R 45:71-83 N '67
Technology notes. See issues of Science news
  See also
Inventions

Bibliography

Books to come; ed. by J. Putnam. Library J 92:1037-62+, 2611-41, 4033-63 Mr 1, Jl, N 1 '67
Science, technology: highspots. Pub W 191: 42-58 Ap 10 '67
Science, technology: November-March highspots. il Pub W 192:31-46 N 13 '67
Scientific and technical books of 1966; one hundred outstanding titles for a general collection; comp. by R. L. Snyder. il Library J 92:969-73 Mr 1 '67

International aspects

Address to OECD council, Paris, April 7, 1967. H. H. Humphrey. Dept State Bul 56:683-5 My 1 '67
Atlantic industrial community looks to the future; address, June 2, 1967. A. B. Trowbridge. Dept State Bul 57:70-6 Jl 17 '67; Same with title Atlantic industrial community. Vital Speeches 33:688-92 S 1 '67
Common market lure. D. Fishlock. Sci N 91:555+ Je 10 '67
European discontent with the technology gap. P. H. Abelson. Science 155:783 F 17 '67
Goals for technology; symposium; with editorial comment. il Tech W 20:31-42+, 102 Ja 23 '67
Great American purchase; massive and continuing penetration of Europe. A. de Borchgrave. il Newsweek 69:36-8 F 27 '67
NATO: a North Atlantic technology organization? J. Walsh. Science 155:985-6+ F 24 '67
North Atlantic council meets at Luxembourg; text of communique, June 14, 1967. Dept State Bul 57:14-16 Jl 3 '67
Old worlds to conquer; technology gap. H. Martyn. Nation 204:427-9 Ap 3 '67
Tale of two cities; British and French investment in advanced technology. M. Getler. Aero Tech 21:58 D 4 '67
Technological revolution and the world of the 1970's; address, December 6, 1966. H. H. Humphrey. Dept State Bul 56:164-8 Ja 30 '67
Three gaps: economic, technological & educational; address, February 24, 1967. R. S. McNamara. Vital Speeches 33:357-61 Ap 1 '67

TECHNOLOGY and civilization
Air. M. J. Arlen. New Yorker 43:135-8 Ap 1 '67
Applied science and technological progress; excerpt from report. H. Brooks. bibliog Science 156:1706-12 Je 30 '67; Reply. W. S. Budington. 158:320-1 O 20 '67
Congress searches for foresight. il Sci N 91: 301-2 Ap 1 '67
Consultation on technology and human values. G. M. Schurr. Christian Cent 84:874-6 Jl 5 '67
Cool millennium, by G. Sykes. Review
  Sat R 50:31-2 Je 24 '67. N. Samstag
Corporation: sociological and technological developments; address, April 20, 1967. T. J. Gordon. Vital Speeches 33:500-5 Je 1 '67
Cybernetic age: an optimist's view. G. T. Seaborg. Sat R 50:21-3 Jl 15 '67
Engineering, civilization, and society; excerpts from address, November 8, 1966. A. B. Kinzel. Science 156:1343-5 Je 9 '67
Eutechnics, motif for new technology. J. Lederberg. il Tech W 20:49-50+ Ja 23 '67
First decade of the noösphere. N. P. Hurley. America 117:171-3 Ag 19 '67

TECHNOLOGY and civilization—*Continued*
Historical roots of our ecologic crisis; address, December 26, 1966. L. T. White, jr. Science 155:1203-7 Mr 10 '67; Same with title What hath man wrought? il Américas 19:11-19 My '67; Same with title Saint Francis and the ecologic backlash. il Horizon 9:42-7 Sum '67
History of mankind; excerpts. il UNESCO Courier 20:4-31 My '67
Impact of space research on science and technology. H. E. Newell and L. Jaffe. il Science 157:29-39 Jl 7 '67
Individual and the good technological society; address, June 9, 1967. S. Ramo. Vital Speeches 33:646-8 Ag 15 '67
McLuhan montage. il Library J 92:1701-3 Ap 15 '67
Making technology serve society; interview. S. Ramo. il Nations Bsns 55:66-7+ Jl '67
Marshall McLuhan: communications explorer. N. P. Hurley. America 116:241-3 F 18 '67
Message of Marshall McLuhan. il Newsweek 69:53-7 Mr 6 '67
Moves planned to shape technical growth. Aero Tech 21:22 Ag 14 '67
Myth of the machine: technics and human development, by L. Mumford. Review
  Harper 235:106+ O '67. A. Temko
New industrial state, by J. K. Galbraith. Review
  Bul Atomic Sci 23:30-2 N '67. R. Eisner
New study-discussion program on human values. Sch & Soc 94:478-9 D 24 '66
New technological era: a view from the law. H. P. Green. Bul Atomic Sci 23:12-18 N '67
Policy and the people. N. A. Rockefeller. For Affairs 46:231-41 Ja '68
Printing week; summary of address, January 16, 1967. H. G. Rickover. il Pub W 191:100+ F 6 '67
Research and development in Communist China. L. A. Orleans. bibliog il Science 157:392-400 Jl 28 '67
Science and technology in Africa. G. E. A. Lardner. Bul Atomic Sci 23:36-9 Je '67
Science, technology, and change. J. McHale. bibliog f il Ann Am Acad 373:120-40 S '67
Society, technology, and development. N. Ras. bibliog il Américas 18:14-23 D '66; Correction. 19:48 Mr '67
Technology: academy panel sees need for enhancing applied science. D. S. Greenberg. Science 156:1212-14 Je 2 '67
Technology and the environment: a new concern on Capitol hill. L. J. Carter. Science 157:784-6 Ag 18 '67
To talk of many things; address, April 5, 1967. H. F. Heller. Vital Speeches 33:697-700 S 1 '67
Understanding McLuhan (in part) R. Kostelanetz. il N Y Times Mag p 18-19+ Ja 29 '67; Discussion. p 12+ F 12 '67
Understanding Marshall McLuhan; or, Will TV put a zombie in your future? Sr Schol 90:13-16 Ap 28 '67
Vision 67: communications' role in man's survival and growth; report of conference. Pub W 192:58-9 D 4 '67
Who's in charge here? M. Getler. Aero Tech 21:62 Ag 14 '67
  See also
Technological change

Study and teaching
Man-made world, a new course for high schools; Engineering concepts curriculum project. E. E. David, jr. and J. G. Truxal. il Science 156:914-20 My 19 '67

TECHNOLOGY and law
New technological era: a view from the law. H. P. Green. Bul Atomic Sci 23:12-18 N '67

TECHNOLOGY and religion. See Religion and technology

TECHNOLOGY and society
But then came man; address, May 4, 1967. S. L. Udall. Vital Speeches 33:569-73 Jl 1 '67

TECHNOLOGY utilization program. See Minnesota. University, Minneapolis

TECHNOLOGY week (periodical)
Letter to our readers; change of name from Technology week to Aerospace technology. W. W. Parrish. Tech W 21:8 Jl 3 '67
Memo from the publisher (cont) A. C. Boughton. il Tech W 20:11 Mr 6 '67
Memo from the publisher; National space club's tribute to William J. Coughlin. il Tech W 20:9 Mr 27 '67

TEDDER, Arthur William Tedder, 1st baron
Cord to Anglo-American accord. B. Pitt. Sat R 50:30 O 14 '67
Peripatetic reviewer. E. Weeks. il Atlan 220:124-5 S '67
Pitfalls of command. G. F. Eliot. Nat R 19:1024-5+ S 19 '67

TEELE, Roy E.
From the East. Poetry. 109:272-5 Ja '67
TEEN-age audiences. See Audiences
TEEN-age buying. See Youth market
TEEN-age clothes. See Clothing and dress
TEEN-age codes. See Youth—Management and training
TEEN-age drinking. See Liquor problem—United States
TEEN-age employment. See Youth—Employment
TEEN-age entertaining. See Entertaining
TEEN-age fads. See Fads
TEEN-age marriage. See High school students, Married
TEEN-age parties. See Entertaining
TEEN-age periodicals. See Periodicals
TEEN-age reading. See Books and reading; Reading lists; Youth—Reading
TEEN-age singers. See Singers
TEEN-age slang. See Slang
TEEN-age smoking. See Smoking
TEEN-age spending. See Budget, Personal
TEEN-age tours. See Travel—Economic aspects
TEEN-agers. See Youth
TEETER, Robert G.
Scope sweep generator. Electr World 77:80-1 F '67
TEETH
Wrinkling of molar crowns: new evidence. B. S. Kraus and S. W. Oka. bibliog il Science 157:328-9 Jl 21 '67
  See also
Dental research
Dentifrices

Care and hygiene
Dentists advise: have missing teeth replaced. il Todays Health 45:79 Ap '67
Family dental care: what are the facts? il Bet Hom & Gard 45:36+ Je '67
Now, keep your teeth forever. S. Englebardt. il Sci Digest 61:55-61 Mr '67
Oral hygiene appliances; water pressure devices. il Consumer Bul 50:4-8 Ap '67
Pearly gates. il Mlle 66:82-3 Ja '68
Perfect teeth; how can you have them? questions, with answers by division heads of U.C.L.A. school of dentistry; ed. by C. Phillips. Vogue 150:130-1+ O 15 '67
Taking care of your teeth. E. Chappell. Am Home 71:103 Ja '68
When a child's teeth need straightening. D. Bressler. il Parents Mag 42:82-3+ N '67
Your teeth can last a lifetime. L. Galton. il Pop Sci 191:76-8+ N '67
  See also
Dentists

Diseases
Now, keep your teeth forever. S. Englebardt. il Sci Digest 61:55-61 Mr '67
TEETH (animals)
Lepidocrocite, an apatite mineral, and magnetite in teeth of chitons, polyplacophora. H. A. Lowenstam. bibliog il Science 156:1373-5 Je 9 '67
Tell age of cattle by their teeth. J. Herrick. il Suc Farm 65:50H Ap '67
TEETH, Artificial
Dentists advise: have missing teeth replaced. il Todays Health 45:79 Ap '67
TEETH, Fossil
American Jurassic symmetrodonts and Rhaetic pantotheres. A. W. Crompton and F. A. Jenkins, jr. bibliog il Science 155:1006-9 F 24 '67
Elephant teeth from the Atlantic continental shelf. F. C. Whitmore, jr. and others. bibliog il Science 156:1477-81 Je 16 '67
TEFLON
GE electric microthruster using Teflon wax as fuel. J. Rhea. il Tech W 21:22 Jl 3 '67
Repairs for scratched Teflon. Consumer Bul 50:16 F '67
TEFLON-coated cookware. See Kitchen utensils
TEFLON-coated irons. See Electric irons
TEFLON coated tools. See Tools
TEHUANTEPEC, ISTHMUS OF
Unlocking a rich store of sulfur. il Bsns W p60+ Ap 22 '67
TEILHARD DE CHARDIN, Pierre
Jacques Maritain on aggiornamento. R. A. Graham. America 116:348-9 Mr 11 '67
Religion of Teilhard de Chardin, by H. de Lubac. Review
  Commonweal 87:109-11 O 27 '67. T. Merton

TEILHARD DE CHARDIN, Pierre—*Continued*
Significance of Teilhard. I. G. Barbour. Christian Cent 84:1098-102 Ag 30 '67
Teilhard de Chardin album, by J. Mortier and M.-L. Auboux. Review
    Christian Cent 84:440 Ap 5 '67. M. E. Marty

TEJA, Devika
Curry: hot or not; with recipes. E. Alston. il por Look 31:78-80 S 5 '67

TEKTITES
Aftermath of a cataclysm; reversal of the earth's magnetic field. il Time 89:44 My 12 '67
Cosmic reversal? Sci Am 216:52 Je '67
Oxygen isotopes: experimental vapor fractionation and variations in tektites. L. S. Walter and R. N. Clayton. bibliog il Science 156:1357-8 Je 9 '67
Some notes on tektites. D. Futrell. il Sky & Tel 33:272-5 My '67
Tektites and geomagnetic reversals. B. P. Glass and B. C. Heezen. il Sci Am 217:32-8 Jl '67
Tektites are terrestrial. H. Faul; reply. C. M. Botley and A. Dauvillier. bibliog Science 156:337 My 12 '67
Tektites that were partially plastic after completion of surface sculpturing. H. H. Nininger and G. I. Huss. bibliog il Science 157:61-2 Jl 7 '67
Were comets the midwives at the birth of man? theories of R. J. Uffen. J. Lear. il Sat R 50:57-62 My 6 '67; Discussion. 50:52-6 Ag 5 '67

TELECOMMUNICATION
Behind the communications mess; outdated laws and conflicting regulatory policies. il Bsns W p66-8+ N 18 '67
Tuning in the telepaper; printed messages by television. Newsweek 69:77 Je 26 '67
    See also
Communications satellites
Facsimile transmission
Telegraph, Wireless

TELECOMMUNICATION union, international.
See International telecommunication union

TELEDYNE, incorporated
Litton's "children": Kidde and Teledyne. Fortune 75:321-2 Je 15 '67
Making big waves with small fish. il Bsns W p36-9 D 30 '67
Teledyne's takeoff. il Time 90:102 O 6 '67

TELEFACTORS. See Automatons

TELEFAX. See Facsimile transmission

TELEGRAPH, Wireless
Coherer; early history of radio communications. H. B. Davis. il Pop Electr 26:47-9 My '67

TELELECTURES. See Telephone in education

TELEMANN, Georg Philipp
From Telefunken, a commemorative first recording of G. P. Telemann's The day of judgment; with reviews of other new Telemann releases. J. W. Barker; P. L. Miller. il Am Rec G 33:906-10 Je '67
Records:
    St Matthew passion. Opera N 31:34 Mr 25 '67
Telemania. R. Gelatt. Reporter 36:46+ Ja 26 '67

TELEMETER
    See also
Remote sensing systems
Space telemetry

TELEMETER (physiological apparatus)
Radio pill: symbol of a new science; R. S. Mackay's radio telemetry. Todays Health 45:16+ Ap '67

TELEMETRY, Biological. See Biotelemetry

TELEMETRY, Space. See Space telemetry

TELEMETRY, Wildlife. See Biotelemetry

TELEMETRY tracking. See Space vehicles—Tracking

TELEPATHY
Amazing weekend with the amazing Ted Serios. C. Reynolds; D. B. Eiseidrath, jr. il Pop Phot 61:81-7+ O '67; Reply. J. Eisenbud. 61:31-2+ N '67
Man who thinks pictures; with report by P. Welch. il Life 63:112+ S 22 '67
Telepsyche: the meeting of minds. R. C. O'Brien. il Holiday 41:8+ F '67
    See also
Extrasensory perception

TELEPHONE
Phone of the future; custom-fitted phone service. Changing T 21:6 Jl '67
    See also
Radio telephone
Radio telephone on ships, boats, etc.

Anecdotes, facetiae, satire, etc.
Dial A for attention. M. L. Harvey. il Read Digest 91:24B O '67
How to work the London telephone, think of Allah. T. S. Matthews. Mlle 64:208-10 Mr '67

Answering service
Ringing success. Newsweek 69:89-89A Je 12 '67

Apparatus and supplies
Family communications. today and tomorrow. M. B. Keiser. il Parents Mag 42:15-16 My '67

Computer combination
Computer's little helpers multiply. il Bsns W p 116-20 Ag 5 '67

Data transmission systems
Why Ma Bell chops up the signals; digital communication systems. il Bsns W p82-4 Ja 13 '68

Laws and regulations
New jolt for Ma Bell and friends. Bsns W p91 Ag 19 '67

Radio telephone connection
New jolt for Ma Bell and friends. Bsns W p91 Ag 19 '67

Rates
Ceiling on earnings for AT&T: the effects. il U S News 63:42 Jl 17 '67
Decoding FCC's signal; commission's decision on AT&T's rate structure. il Bsns W p 120+ Jl 15 '67
FCC says talk must be cheaper; AT&T ordered to cut rates. Bsns W p38 Jl 8 '67
    See also
Government investigations—American telephone and telegraph company

Religious applications
Select your life line with care; Life line international. Christian Cent 84:1484 N 22 '67

Wire tapping
    See Wire tapping

TELEPHONE; story. See Glaze, E.

TELEPHONE, Dial
Yet another first step: new dial tone part of Touch-tone story. A. Smith. New Yorker 43:35 Ap 8 '67

TELEPHONE calls
What you can do about those obscene telephone calls. W. B. Furlong. il Good H 165:82-3+ S '67

TELEPHONE companies
    See also
American telephone and telegraph company
Bell telephone system
General telephone and electronics company

Employees
How to be happy though retired. il Changing T 21:24-8 N '67
    See also
Telephone companies—Wages and hours

Securities
Why Ma Bell looks good again; AT&T's stock perking up. il Bsns W p 152+ Mr 11 '67

Wages and hours
Employment and wage trends in Bell system companies. L. E. Lewis and J. C. Bush. il Mo Labor R 90:38-41 Mr '67

TELEPHONE employees. See Telephone companies—Employees

TELEPHONE in education
In a class by themselves: Tele-class program, Los Angeles; reprint. C. E. Cassidy. il Sr Schol 90:sup 10-11 Ap 14 '67

TELEPHONE lines

Underground
Plot to bury the Bell system. il Parks & Rec 2:17-18 D '67

TELEPHONE lines, Underground. See Telephone lines—Underground

TELEPHOTO lenses. See Lenses, Photographic

TELEPHOTOGRAPHY
How pros hold teles. M. A. Matzkin. il Mod Phot 31:74-5 Ag '67
Oh, what a telescopic morning! P. Stackpole. U S Camera 30:26+ Ap '67
Telephotos: How we use them; symposium. il Mod Phot 31:76-83 Ag '67

TELEPSYCHE (machine) See Telepathy

TELESCOPE

All-reflection Schmidt telescope for space research. L. C. Epstein. il Sky & Tel 33: 204-7 Ap '67

Astronomy's crucial requirements; letter. L. H. Aller. Science 155:953-4 F 24 '67

Can a small telescope be too powerful? Consumer Bul 50:29 O '67

Cooke triplet astrographic lens for the amateur. R. J. Donnel. il Sky & Tel 33: 312-19 My '67

Giant telescope to eye the sun. A. P. Armagnac. il Pop Sci 190:102-3 Ap '67

Gleanings for ATM's; ed. by R. E. Cox. See issues of Sky and telescope

Harem of telescopes. J. Ashbrook. il Sky & Tel 33:346+ Je '67

Inexpensive finder and guide telescope. R. C. Hartman. il Sky & Tel 34:187 S '67

Join the in-group and look to the stars. G. Heberton. il Pop Gard 18:50-3+ Ag '67

Night at the observatory; studying quasars at Mount Palomar. H. S. F. Cooper, jr. il Horizon 9:108-16 Sum '67

Ninety-eight-inch Isaac Newton telescope; Royal Greenwich observatory in Sussex. P. L. Brown. il Sky & Tel 34:356-61 D '67

Optical astronomy in perspective. H. W. Babcock. bibliog il Science 156:1317-22 Je 9 '67

Science versus spectaculars; concerning statements of B. Lovell and Fred Hoyle. Nation 204:612 My 15 '67

Southern hemisphere telescope to be built in Chilean Andes. Dept State Bul 56:728 My 8 '67

Supereyes for astronomers. il Sci Digest 63: 21 Ja '68

Telescopes. il Consumer Rep 32:607-14 N '67

Telescopes and automation. S. P. Maran. bibliog il Science 158:867-71 N 17 '67

Thousand-inch 'scope for infrared scan. il Sci N 91:350 Ap 15 '67

Two 150-inch telescopes for southern hemisphere. Sky & Tel 34:71 Ag '67

World's biggest camera; Kitt Peak national observatory solar telescope. C. M. Cardon. il Arch Forum 127:44-9 O '67

See also

Mirrors for telescope

History

What is an English mounting? O. Gingerich. il Sky & Tel 34:293-5 N '67

TELESCOPE mirrors. See Mirrors for telescopes

TELESCOPE mountings

Amateur scientist. E. Snead. il Sci Am 216: 142 Je '67

Twin-telescope observatory on wheels. N. G. Oberle. il Sky & Tel 34:108-12 Ag '67

TELESCOPIC photography. See Telephotography

TELESCOPIC sights. See Firearms—Sights

TELETYPE

Teletypewriters for bookstores: improving communications. il Pub W 192:41-2 Ag 21 '67

See also

Hot line (Washington and Moscow)

TELETYPEWRITERS. See Teletype

TELEVISION

Radio & television news. F. H. Belt. Electr World 79:23-4 Ja '68

Color

See Television, Color

History

Look back into the tube. D. Karp. il N Y Times Mag p50-1+ N 19 '67

Industrial application

See Television in industry

Photographic aspects

Only politicians get pro treatment now on TV. P. Stackpole. U S Camera 30:18 My '67

Pop photo white paper; NBC newsfilm. H. V. Fondiller. il Pop Phot 60:112-16+ Mr '67

Police applications

See Television in criminal investigation

Scientific applications

All-digital displays studied for NASA mission center. il Tech W 20:22 F 20 '67

Social aspects

See Television broadcasting—Social aspects

Wire line connection

Wiring your home for TV. G. Zappa. il Pop Electr 26:44 Je '67

TELEVISION, Airborne. See Television stations, Educational

TELEVISION, Closed circuit

Media; Channel one theatre television. P. Velde. Commonweal 87:147-8 N 3 '67

Underground channels. H. Junker. New Repub 157:33-4 S 9 '67

See also

Television in industry

TELEVISION, Color

Around the world with color TV; new European color-television systems. R. M. Benrey. il Pop Sci 190:102-5+ Mr '67

Color-TV in the marketplace. il Electr World 79:31-3 Ja '68

Color TV makes the scene again. il Bsns W p 153-4 S 16 '67

Letter from Paris. Genêt. New Yorker 43: 228+ N 25 '67

Whirlpool of color; color TV in Europe. Newsweek 70:62-3 S 4 '67

TELEVISION, Community antenna. See Television antennas

TELEVISION, Stereoscopic

What's new? TV in 3D. P. R. Farber. il U S Camera 30:35+ Ap '67

TELEVISION academy of arts and sciences. See Academy of television arts and sciences

TELEVISION actors and actresses. See Television broadcasting—Performers

TELEVISION advertising

Art of bamboozlement; concerning theories of John Kenneth Galbraith. R. L. Shayon. Sat R 50:37 Jl 29 '67

Color line and commercials; LDF-Plotkin survey of Negroes in commercials. R. L. Shayon. il Sat R 50:52 N 4 '67

Color the ad dollar a paler green. Bsns W p93-4 Ag 26 '67

Commercially yours; stars and the ads. J. Crist. Ladies Home J 84:70 Mr '67

FCC ruling on cigarette ads: health groups react warily. L. J. Carter. Science 158: 888-92 N 17 '67

Football in five-quarter time; eighteen minutes per game for commercials. Consumer Rep 32:297 Je '67

German sponsors fight for TV time. il Bsns W p92-4+ Ja 21 '67

Great TV commercial war; advertising copywriter vs advertising-testing corporations. S. Blum. il N Y Times Mag p32-3+ Ap 9 '67

Homelies. il Time 89:104+ Ap 28 '67

Honor without profit. Time 90:81-2 D 8 '67

Letter from Paris. Genêt. New Yorker 43: 231-2 N 25 '67

Master of the mini-ha-ha. il Time 90:77 N 24 '67

Moment musical; scores for commercials. il Newsweek 70:106 N 27 '67

Not all of the time; time for commercials in televising soccer games. Sports Illus 26:10 Ap 17 '67

Notes and comment: art of the television commercial. New Yorker 42:31 F 18 '67

Notes and comment; proposed bills to limit cigarette advertising. New Yorker 43:41 S 23 '67

Now, back to our commercial; sales-within-sales messages. R. L. Shayon. Sat R 50:49 Je 24 '67

Other voices; use of actors to provide off-screen dialogue in commercials. il Newsweek 69:60 Je 19 '67

Plan for a TV network without commercials. U S News 61:8 F 6 '67

Platformate illusion by courtesy of Shell's advertising men. il Consumer Bul 51:26 Ja '68

Real masters of television. R. Eck. Harper 234:45-52 Mr '67; Same abr. with title Why TV is the way it is. Read Digest 90:78-82 My '67

Saving radiance; quality programs, absence of commercials on public TV. W. K. Zinsser. Look 31:15 Mr 21 '67

TV advertisers load up on buckshot: one-minute, scatter-plan commercials. il Bsns W p74-6+ Ap 8 '67

This war is being brought you by; War in the skies and the B. F. Goodrich company. C. W. Morton. il Atlan 220:92 Jl '67

Time for the truth; FCC ruling on fair time for ads and programs on smoking dangers. New Repub 156:7 Je 17 '67

Watch the commercial go by; longest advertisement in TV history preceding the Easter showing of The robe. il Bsns W p82+ Mr 25 '67

What makes a Barbra special. il Bsns W p64-8+ My 20 '67

TELEVISION advertising—*Continued*
Why they are doing all that; Hertz's commercials. il Time 91:71-2 Ja 5 '68
You might say they invented Saturday morning; networks to extol the virtues of ready-to-eat cereals. il Fortune 76:130-1 D '67

Anecdotes, facetiae, satire, etc.
FCC, FTC, KO, TV. G. Ace. Sat R 50:4 Ag 12 '67
Notes and comment; new attractions of this season. New Yorker 43:41 O 7 '67

TELEVISION advertising, Religious. See Religious advertising

TELEVISION amplifiers. See Amplifiers

TELEVISION and children. See Television broadcasting and children

TELEVISION and moving pictures. See Moving pictures and television

TELEVISION and radio broadcasting. See Radio broadcasting and television

TELEVISION and reading
Baby dolls are gone; effect of TV. N. Larrick. bibliog il Library J 92:3815-17 O 15 '67

TELEVISION antennas
Appeals court upholds CATV's copyright liability. Pub W 191:143 Je 5 '67
Cable: parasite or panacea? R. Angus. il Hi Fi 17:50-5 D '67
Class struggle on TV; Manhattan cable television and Teleprompter services in New York city. Nation 206:70 Ja 15 '68
CATV comes down from the hills; community antenna television in New York selling pure reception. il Bsns W p64-6+ S 16 '67
CATV: past, present & future. J. E. Hastings. il Electr World 78:23-6+ Ag '67
CATV: promise and peril. N. Johnson. Sat R 50:87-8+ N 11 '67
Designs for log-periodic FM & TV antennas. H. D. Pruett. il Electr World 78:46-8+ D '67
For whom does the system toll? E. A. Lacy. il Pop Electr 26:64-7 Je '67
Hot antennas for cool color. L. Steckler. il Pop Mech 127:93-6+ Je '67
Selecting antennas. Pop Electr 26:45+ Je '67
TV antenna sampler. il Pop Electr 26:46-7 Je '67
Untenable reception from a TV antenna; Skyprobe. il Consumer Rep 32:512 O '67
Unusual TV antenna; described in Soviet electronics hobbyist journal. J. Zelle. Pop Electr 26:68 Ap '67
Wiring your home for TV. G. Zappa. il Pop Electr 26:44 Je '67

TELEVISION apparatus
CBS video cartridge plays through TV sets; electronic video recording. N. Eisenberg. Hi Fi 17:24 N '67
Click, click, it's Casals; Electronic video recording. Newsweek 70:59 S 11 '67
Lone inventor with a genie complex; electronic video recording. L. Edson. il N Y Times Mag p28-9+ D 17 '67
TV's wider horizons; electronic video recording. il Bsns W p30 S 2 '67
What you should know about TV color bar generators. R. Cornell. il Pop Electr 26:48-52+ Ap '67
Your own ETV station; electronic video recording. Time 90:53 S 8 '67
See also
Video tape recorders and recording

Manufacture
Color-TV in the marketplace. il Electr World 79:31-3 Ja '68

TELEVISION apparatus industry and trade
Adventures of Nick Carter. T. J. Murray. il Duns R 89:50-2+ Ap '67
Color TV: blue. Time 90:69 Ag 11 '67

Securities
Color TV makes the scene again. il Bsns W p 153-4 S 16 '67

TELEVISION apparatus on automobiles
Is car TV practical? M. Lamm. il Motor T 19:34+ Ap '67

TELEVISION audiences
Problem of sanitation; questioning the little reaction to ghastly scenes of Vietnamese dead. Nation 206:5 Ja 1 '68
Viewing from the top; nation's leaders and tastemakers il Time 90:77-8 N 24 '67
When everybody loses; controversy over quality-audience defections. R L. Shayon. Sat R 50:60 F 25 '67

TELEVISION authorship
If I could only write; TV scripts. G. Ace. Sat R 50:8 O 14 '67
Writing for television. B. Schultz. Writer 80:17-18+ My '67

TELEVISION awards. See Academy of television arts and sciences

TELEVISION broadcasting
Johnny Carson: the battle for TV's midnight millions. H. Van Horne. il Look 31:78-9+ Jl 11 '67
See also
Video tape recorders and recording

Advertising
See Television advertising

Anecdotes, facetiae, satire, etc.
Capsule case history of TV. H. Humphrey. Holiday 42:54-5 O '67
How to get rich in show business. L. Wyse. il Ladies Home J 84:64+ My '67

Animal programs
See Animals on television programs

Animated cartoons
Pterodactyl for breakfast. E. Dowling. New Repub 157:39+ N 18 '67

Billiards
See Television broadcasting—Sports

Book programs
Rights and permissions; new series over the entire National educational television network scheduled to begin in November. P. Nathan. Pub W 192:60 Jl 17 '67

Censorship
Challenge in the South; U.S. Court of appeals forces FCC to schedule public hearing on WLBT's current application for license renewal. Newsweek 69:63 My 29 '67

Children, Effect on
See Television broadcasting and children

Childrens programs
Batman and the comic profanation of the sacred. M. C. Hyers. Christian Cent 84:1322-3 O 18 '67
Children's TV, European style. J. Tebbel. Sat R 50:70-1+ F 11 '67
Gene and Jack and the beanstalk. V. H. Swisher. il Dance Mag 41:52-3 F '67
Irrigation for the wasteland; Carnegie report. C. B. Grannis. Pub W 191:127 F 20 '67
Pterodactyl for breakfast. E. Dowling. New Repub 157:39+ N 18 '67
Report on TV for children. F. Orme. il Parents Mag 42:40-1+ F '67
Time out for television. See issues of PTA magazine

Christmas programs
Nights before Christmas. il Time 90:34 D 29 '67
Show business puts its holiday foot forward. J. Barthel. il Good H 165:56+ D '67

Comedy
See Television broadcasting—Humor

Conversation programs
Author on TV. R. Armour. il Pub W 192:48-9 D 25 '67
Baron von sneer; Alan Burke show. Newsweek 70:96 N 13 '67
Finite variety; Carson/Griffin shows. S. Eimerl. il Reporter 36:42-5 F 23 '67
Hate hour; late-night Los Angeles television. J. G. Dunne. Sat Eve Post 240:24+ D 2 '67
How now, Brown wren? Outrageous opinions. il Time 90:74 O 20 '67
Inka dinka doo; Sam Yorty show. N. White. New Repub 158:11-12 Ja 20 '68
Intercontinental palaver or pith? CBS's Town meeting of the world. R. L. Shayon. Sat R 50:79 Je 10 '67
Joey vs. Johnny; Joey Bishop show. Newsweek 69:52 My 1 '67
Letter from London; B.B.C. presentation of L. Woolf in random recollections to M. Muggeridge. M. Panter-Downes. New Yorker 43:164+ Ap 15 '67
Midnight idol; J. Carson's Tonight. il Time 89:104-6+ My 19 '67; Same abr. with title Johnny Carson: TV's midnight idol. Read Digest 91:153-7 Ag '67
Mommy's boy; Mike Douglas show. il Time 90:78+ O 6 '67
So you want to be a TV star; two minutes miniprogram in Minneapolis and Duluth. il Time 90:81 D 15 '67
TV's new fun game: savagery: television's era of cruelty: Joe Pyne and Alan Burke shows. B. Williamson. Life 62:25 Ap 7 '67

TELEVISION broadcasting—Conversation programs—*Continued*
Vice-President; appearance on J. Carson's Tonight show and meeting with participants of Double discovery. New Yorker 43: 23-5 Ag 12 '67

Criticism
See Television criticism

Dancing
Gene and Jack and the beanstalk. V. H. Swisher. il Dance Mag 41:52-3 F '67
Looking at television. A. Barzel. See issues of Dance magazine
Special for the special Fred Astaire and partner Barrie Chase. V. H. Swisher. il Dance Mag 42:24-6 Ja '68

Documentary programs
Africa: interrupted journey. R. L. Shayon. Sat R 50:48 O 7 '67
African odyssey; ABC's Africa. il Newsweek 70:59 S 11 '67
Air; CBS documentary Vietnam, perspective: air war in the North. M. J. Arlen. New Yorker 43:148+ Mr 4 '67
Air; C.B.S. reports: what about Ronald Reagan? M. J. Arlen. New Yorker 43:59-60 D 30 '67
Anderson platoon; Frenchman films Viet war. il Ebony 22:69-72+ O '67
China epic in fine fragments; Xerox's China spectacular. China: the roots of madness. C. Elliott. Life 62:10 Ja 27 '67
China watching; China: the roots of madness. Newsweek 69:63 F 20 '67
CBS on the Warren report. A. M. Bickel. New Repub 157:29-30 Jl 15 '67; Reply with rejoinder. W. Lister. 157:30-2+ Ag 19 '67
Frenchman discovers America in the Vietnam war; Anderson platoon. il U S News 63:12 Jl 31 '67
Fruits of hatred; China: the roots of madness. il Time 89:57 Ja 27 '67
Germans: analysis of a defamation. G. Krodel. Christian Cent 84:1653-6 D 27 '67
Harmless deception? circumstances behind NBC's Khrushchev in exile. R. L. Shayon. Sat R 50:42 Ag 5 '67
How to cover wars; CBS and NBC programs on Israeli victory. R. L. Shayon. Sat R 50: 22 Ag 12 '67
Intelluptuously speaking; coverage of the arts. il Time 90:86 N 3 '67
Men at war: a French view; documentary on Viet Nam. il Time 89:78 F 17 '67
Morley Safer's sojourn; Red China diary. R. L. Shayon. Sat R 50:61 S 16 '67
N.E.T.'s A time for burning; involvement of the Augustana Lutheran church, Omaha, with civil rights. J. M. Ferrer, 3d. Life 62:12 F 10 '67
Nikita in exile; documentary by NBC. il Newsweek 70:100 Jl 17 '67
Not-so-cool medium; M. McLuhan and The medium is the massage. R. L. Shayon. Sat R 50:46 Ap 15 '67
Of bears & bygones. il Time 90:86 N 10 '67
Peripatetic reviewer. E. Weeks. Atlan 219: 124-6 My '67
Poignant war report on men, not heroes: The Anderson platoon; French documentary on Vietnam war. S. Heckscher. Life 62:12 Je 30 '67
Same mud same blood; documentary on the Negro GI in Vietnam. Newsweek 70:90 D 4 '67
Saving face; series called Your dollar's worth for NET. il Time 90:86 N 3 '67
Schooner's screen test; schooner yacht America's Sail to glory. J. Gribbins. il Motor B 120:38+ Ag '67
Senior citizen Khrushchev; NBC program, Khrushchev in exile—his opinions and revelations. il Time 90:71 Jl 7 '67
Sexual revolution in living color. H. Van Horne. McCalls 95:46+ O '67
Something of a shambles; The J.F.K. conspiracy. Time 89:42 Je 30 '67
Son of 20th century; 21st century. Time 89: 66 F 17 '67
TV and radio; biography of H. G. Wells produced by the British broadcasting company. R. L. Shayon. Sat R 50:50 Ja 28 '67
Television; Same mud, same blood; Good bye and good luck. E. Dowling. New Repub 158:43-5 Ja 6 '68
This war is being brought you by; War in the skies and B. F. Goodrich company. C. W. Morton. il Atlan 220:92 Jl '67
Through the looking glass; CBS documentary shot in red China. il Newsweek 70:77 Ag 14 '67

Two for the seesaw; programs on Garrison investigation and Warren commission report. il Newsweek 70:82 Jl 3 '67
See also
Public broadcast laboratory

Drama
Air; drama: The final war of Olly Winter. M. J. Arlen. New Yorker 42:136+ F 18 '67
Drama of aging; Loring Mandel's Do not go gentle into that good night. R. L. Shayon. Sat R 50:62 N 18 '67
From anxiety to identity; Arthur Miller's The crucible. R. L. Shayon. Sat R 50:48 My 27 '67
Harry Dolan's first; Losers weepers. R. L. Shayon. Sat R 50:39 Mr 18 '67
Lesson of Auschwitz; The investigation. R. L. Shayon. Sat R 50:46 My 6 '67
Secret storm; soap opera. A. Waugh. il Nat R 19:1438 D 26 '67
Shaw at the stake. R. L. Shayon. Sat R 50:37 D 30 '67
This is the network that is; outstanding productions of the British broadcasting corporation. il Time 89:50 Mr 10 '67

Educational applications
See Television in education

Football
See Television broadcasting—Sports

Golf
See Television broadcasting—Sports

Government programs
See also
Television broadcasting—Municipal programs

History
This month's feature; the question of pay television. Cong Digest 46:289-314 D '67

Horror programs
Ghoul show; Dark shadows becomes popular afternoon program. il Newsweek 70:60 Ag 21 '67

Humor
Air. M. J. Arlen. New Yorker 42:75-6 Ja 21 '67
Big hand for shot-down western; NBC's pilot Sheriff who?? J. M. Ferrer, 3d. Life 63:16 S 15 '67
Jackie Gleason: anything I can't lick appeals to me. B. Davidson. il Sat Eve Post 240: 30-7 F 11 '67
Marlo Thomas: That girl is some girl. B. Rollin. il Look 31:124+ O 17 '67
Mothers' brothers. il Time 89:41 Je 30 '67
Smothers brothers; the naughtiest boys on TV. B. Rollin. il Look 31:68-9+ Je 13 '67
Success is a warm puppy; Gomer Pyle, U.S.M.C. il Time 90:88 N 10 '67

Interference
See Television interference

International aspects
TV programme girdling the world; Our world. P. de Latil. UNESCO Courier 20:38 N '67

Laws and regulations
See Television laws and regulations

Medical programs
TV doctor; The children's doctor. il Time 89:62 Je 16 '67

Moral aspects
Lesson of Auschwitz; watching The investigation on television. R. L. Shayon. Sat R 50:46 My 6 '67
Non-news explosion. J. Brennan. Nat R 19: 849 Ag 8 '67
Sex and violence in TV films. America 117: 576 D 2 '67
Sexual revolution in living color. H. Van Horne. McCalls 95:46+ O '67

Moving pictures
Appeals court upholds CATV's copyright liability. Pub W 191:43 Je 5 '67
Coming soon on TV; every night at the movies. B. Davidson. il Sat Eve Post 240: 30-3 O 7 '67
Fab? chaos; the Beatles TV film. Magical mystery tour. il Time 91:60-1 Ja 5 '68
Fight over M-G-M; money grabs movies. il Newsweek 69:68-70 Mr 6 '67
Flick boom. il Newsweek 70:104 N 6 '67
Lively arts; Hollywood musicals of 1930's and 1940's. P. Hudson and R. Hemming. il Sr Schol 91:42-3 S 28 '67

TELEVISION broadcasting—Moving pictures
—*Continued*
Onward and upward with the arts. P. Kael.
New Yorker 43:120+ Je 3 '67
Over the rainbow; NBC wins rights to Wizard
of Oz. Time 90:60 Ag 25 '67
Play it again, Sam, and again; Late show.
W. Markfield. il Sat Eve Post 240:72-6+
Ap 22 '67
Watch the commercial go by; longest advertisement in TV history preceding the
Easter showing of The robe. il Bsns W
p82+ Mr 25 '67
See also
Moving pictures and television
Television broadcasting—Sports films

Municipal programs
Fellow citizens; mayors' television program.
Newsweek 70:75 D 25 '67

Music
Direct dial to a fine music hour: new Bell
telephone hour. J. M. Ferrer, 3d. Life 62:12
Mr 10 '67
Rare fusion; Bell telephone's El Prado program. R. L. Shayon. Sat R 50:67 My 13 '67
Whom the bell extols; Bell telephone hour.
il Newsweek 71:54 Ja 1 '68

Musical comedies, revues, etc.
Weapon was humor; Harry Belafonte's A
time for laughter. R. L. Shayon. Sat R
50:44 Ap 29 '67

Nature programs
New trails; Trail of Stanley and Livingstone
and Sharks. il Time 91:44 Ja 19 '68

News
Can you believe your eyes? H. Fairlie. il
Horizon 9:24-7 Spr '67; Same abr. with title
Unreal world of television news. Read
Digest 91:127-30 Ag '67
Casting the NET wider. il Newsweek 69:60
Ja 30 '67
Due to circumstances beyond our control, by
F. W. Friendly. Review
America 116:564 Ap 15 '67. J. McLaughlin
Filling the front page. il Time 90:80 O 27 '67
Great sellout to soap opera; excerpt from
Due to circumstances beyond our control.
F. W. Friendly. il Life 62:84+ Mr 17 '67
Into the heartland; C. Kuralt's essays. il
Newsweek 71:54 Ja 1 '68
Maintaining the public welfare; exposés by
L. Gordon. Time 90:51 S 22 '67
Mission: impossible; CBS and NBC conflict
over heart transplant operations. il Time
91:52 Ja 12 '68
Newman-at-large; news commentator. il
Newsweek 69:79 Je 26 '67
Non-news explosion. J. Brennan. Nat R 19:
849 Ag 8 '67
Pop photo white paper; NBC newsfilm. H. V.
Fondiller. il Pop Phot 60:112-16+ Mr '67
Race and the news media, ed. by P. L.
Fisher and R. L. Lowenstein. Review
Sat R 50:68 D 9 '67. S. W. Little
Racial stress and the mass media; address,
September 21, 1967. E. W. Lower. Vital
Speeches 34:53-9 N 1 '67
Rather not; President forbids use of taped
interview. Time 89:38 Je 23 '67
Retrieving a lost rocket; excerpt from Due
to circumstances beyond our control. .
F. W. Friendly. il Life 62:70-2+ Mr 24 '67
Riot beat. il Newsweek 70:78 Ag 14 '67
Riot coverage, plus & minus. il Time 90:62
Ag 25 '67
Six-man dialogue; Huntley-Brinkley report
revamped. Newsweek 70:109 S 18 '67
TV news explosion. J. Harden. il Sat R 50:
72-3 F 11 '67
Television: race and news media. J. Horn.
Nation 205:638 D 11 '67
Television; revamped format of the Huntley-
Brinkley report. J. Horn. Nation 205:477-8
N 6 '67
TV's editorial voice. il Newsweek 69:93-93A+
My 15 '67
Travels with Charley; C. Kuralt's reports
from small towns. il Time 91:44+ Ja 19 '68
See also
Television broadcasting—War news

Anecdotes, facetiae, satire, etc.
News to sleep by. G. Ace. Sat R 50:10 My
27 '67

Performers
Activism. Hollywood style. il Newsweek 70:74
Ag 28 '67
Color line and commercials; LDF-Plotkin survey of Negroes in commercials. R. L. Shay-
on. il Sat R 50:52 N 4 '67

Color on TV. R. D. Colle. il Reporter 37:23-5
N 30 '67
Finite variety; Carson/Griffin shows. S.
Eimerl. il Reporter 36:42-5 F 23 '67
Look back into the tube. D. Karp. il N Y
Times Mag p50-1+ N 19 '67
Negro stereotype. B. Porter. il Newsweek
69:59-60 Ap 3 '67
Sense of style. G. Frazier. Esquire 67:31-2+
Ap '67

Political programs
See Television in politics

Program production
Doctor Jonathan Miller operates on Alice;
dramatization of Alice in Wonderland for
BBC television. W. H. Honan. il N Y
Times Mag p24-7 Ja 22 '67
Jackie Gleason: anything I can't lick appeals
to me. B. Davidson. il Sat Eve Post 240:
30-7 F 11 '67
Lights, camera, blam! producing American
sportsman show. il Newsweek 71:46 Ja 8 '68
Me, David Susskind and the greatest man in
the world. R. L. Foreman. Esquire 68:69+
S '67
See also
Television—Photographic aspects

Program rating
At the halfway mark. Time 91:52 Ja 12 '68
CBS widens its lead; A. C. Nielsen co. ratings.
il Bsns W p48+ O 28 '67
For your listening pleasure; a PTA guide to
evaluating and improving TV and radio
programs. PTA Mag 61:31-3 Mr '67
Honor without profit. Time 90:81-2 D 8 '67
Nielsen rating for a box of spaghetti. D. D.
Trainer. il N Y Times Mag p 12-13+ Jl 30
'67
Plethora of angles. C. H. Simonds. il Nat R
19:210-12 F 21 '67
See also
Schwerin research corporation

Programming
Fairness doctrine: Fred J. Cook and John F.
Banzhaf, 3d. actions; rulings by FCC. R. L.
Shayon. Sat R 50:53 Jl 15 '67
Real masters of television R. Eck. Harper
234:45-52 Mr '67; Same abr. with title Why
TV is the way it is. Read Digest 90:78-82
My '67

Programs
Ad hoc hookup; United network produces the
Las Vegas show. Time 89:50 My 12 '67
After nineteen TV years, only Ed Sullivan
survives. J. Barthel. il N Y Times Mag
p24-5+ Ap 30 '67
Air (cont) M. J. Arlen. New Yorker 43:187-
8 Mr 18 '67
Another TV season coming up. Changing T
21:6 Ag '67
Comic-strip formula. il Newsweek 70:61 O 2
'67
Dino's breezy way to easy money; Dean
Martin show. B. Williamson. Life 62:18 My
26 '67
Ed Sullivan's biggest show: the story of
his life. E. Sullivan. il Ladies Home J
84:68-71+ Je '67
End of the road; The fugitive. il Newsweek
70:84 Ag 28 '67
Farewell to TV; new season. N. Compton.
Commentary 43:7-9 Ja '67
Funny-side up; Dean Martin show. il Newsweek 69:97+ Mr 20 '67
Gallic-American spectacular; TV revue. il
Ebony 22:36+ Ap '67
Games pretty people play; Dating game and
others. il Newsweek 70:56 Jl 31 '67
Generals or musicians? television during the
Arab-Israeli war. R. L. Shayon. Sat R
50:33 Jl 1 '67
How to succeed casually; Mike Douglas show.
il Newsweek 69:60+ Je 19 '67
Idiot's lantern; current television season.
America 117:404 O 14 '67
Intercontinental palaver or pith? CBS's Town
meeting of the world. R. L. Shayon. Sat R
50:79 Je 10 '67
Life TV review. See occasional issues of Life
Look and listen. P. Hudson. See issues of
Senior scholastic
Look back into the tube. D. Karp. il N Y
Times Mag p50-1+ N 19 '67
Looking & listening. P. Hudson. See issues
of Senior scholastic
Making news with a new show; Meet the
press, news interview program. il Sr Schol
91:5 N 2 '67
Mike Douglas lights up screen of daytime
TV. il Bsns W p86-8 Jl 22 '67

TELEVISION broadcasting—Programs—*Cont.*
Networks take cue from Stage 67; ABC's success with cultural TV series. il Bsns W p60-2+ F 25 '67
Peripatetic reviewer. E. Weeks. Atlan 219: 124 My '67
Plethora of angles. C. H. Simonds. il Nat R 19:210-12 F 21 '67
Problem, solution industry. C. H. Simonds. Nat R 19:534-6 My 16 '67
Program for public-TV. L. Markel. il N Y Times Mag p25+ Mr 12 '67; Discussion. p22+ Ap 2 '67
Same old new season; autumn schedule. il Newsweek 70:77-8 S 4 '67
Sam's show; mayor of Los Angeles as TV host. il Time 89:22 Mr 31 '67
Sex and security; The pursuit of pleasure. Newsweek 69:90 My 15 '67
Sight and sound. L. Hershey. See issues of McCall's
Smile! canceled Candid camera. Time 89:63 Mr 3 '67
Smile, you're off; victims of CBS's new schedule. il Newsweek 69:86 Mr 6 '67
Specials or nothing. il Time 90:69 S 15 '67
Spotlight! E. Miller. See issues of Seventeen
Super-veep; need for a show with a political hero. D. Compton. Atlan 219:118+ Ap '67
Television. See issues of Time
Television; entertainment invasion of the socio-political domain. J. Horn. Nation 204: 667-8 My 22 '67
TV-radio. See issues of Newsweek
TV's autumn of reappraisal. R. C. Albrook. il Fortune 76:134-9+ O '67
TV's Sally Field: The flying nun. B. Rollin. il Look 31:M18-20+ N 14 '67
Time listings. See issues of Time
Time out for television. See issues of PTA magazine
Twenty years: Ed Sullivan; with report by W. Warga. il Life 63:80-4 O 20 '67
Two of another kind; Treasure Isle and Baby game. il Newsweek 71:51 Ja 15 '68
What makes a Barbra special. il Bsns W p64-8+ My 20 '67
Who decides what gets on TV, and why. S. Blum. il N Y Times Mag p8-9+ S 3 '67; Reply. Mrs B. Schulz. p41 O 8 '67
See also
Academy of television arts and sciences
Public broadcast laboratory
Television broadcasting—Drama
Television criticism

Anecdotes, facetiae, satire, etc.
Air; ten most shows of 1967. M. J. Arlen. New Yorker 43:185-8 N 4 '67
Real girls ask for mint frappés. W. Stanton. il Sat Eve Post 240:20 F 25 '67
Three networks in search of a dollar. R. Lasson. Esquire 69:46 Ja '68

Propaganda
Little white dacha halfway up the next block; Russian film Ivan Ivanovich. Nat R 19: 340 Ap 4 '67

Psychological aspects
Getting the message. il Time 90:47 O 13 '67

Public service programs
Anti-cigarette advertising. America 117:433 O 21 '67
Cigarette issue; health agencies failure to support FCC rule. R. L. Shayon. Sat R 50:58 O 21 '67
Free press & fancy packages. A. Q. Mowbray. Nation 205:621-3 D 11 '67
Job show; Chicago television program offers help to unemployed. Newsweek 70:57 Jl 31 '67
TV and radio; programs sponsored by Philadelphia gas works. R. L. Shayon. Sat R 51:39 Ja 6 '68

Quiz programs
Sign off, please; What's my line? ends. il Newsweek 70:109 S 18 '67

Religious programs
Catholic hour loses its magic. America 117: 700 D 9 '67; Discussion. 117:753-4, 771-2 D 23 '67
Religious television. J. McLaughlin. America 117:326-7+ S 23 '67; Reply. C. E. Reilly, jr. 117:528 N 11 '67
Wizard of Hatch End; center for training sessions in radio and television techniques. J. McLaughlin. America 117:140-inside back cover Ag 5 '67

Anecdotes, facetiae, satire, etc.
In living color; Mount of Olives church's Easter service televised. C. Elrod. Christian Cent 84:375-6 Mr 22 '67
New TV series announced. P. J. Laux. il America 117:553+ N 11 '67

Science fiction
Interplanetary Spock; Star Trek. R. L. Shayon. Sat R 50:46 Je 17 '67
TV's Star Trek; how they mix science fact with fiction. J. W. Wright. il Pop Sci 191:72-4 D '67

Soccer
See Television broadcasting—Sports

Social aspects
Batman and the comic profanation of the sacred. M. C. Hyers. Christian Cent 84: 1322-3 O 18 '67
Electronic culture and the future church; reprint. K. Paul. Cath World 205:157-9 Je '67
Letter from London; documentary film on B.B.C.; Cathy come home. M. Panter-Downes. New Yorker 42:145-6+ F 11 '67
Problem, solution industry. C. H. Simonds. Nat R 19:534-6 My 16 '67
Soap opera, Denver style; KRMA-TV programs for the poor. Nation 205:581 D 4 '67
See also
Television broadcasting—Psychological aspects

Sports
Air. M. J. Arlen. New Yorker 43:158+ Ap 29 '67
Breaks in the game; television influencing professional sports. il Newsweek 69:66 Je 5 '67
Companies tee off to win more friends; tournaments under corporate sponsorship. il Bsns W p28 S 2 '67
Eye on the Masters; CBS at the 1966 Masters, Augusta, Ga. D. Jenkins. il Sports Illus 26:90-2+ Ap 10 '67
Golden age of sport; Time essay. Time 89: 18-19 Je 2 '67
How to watch football on TV. W. B. Furlong. il Pop Mech 128:87-9+ O '67
Hustler; first in series of pool games over Chicago's WFLD-TV. Newsweek 70:100 Jl 17 '67
I want my bloody game back; U.S. televised version of soccer. D. Morgan. il Sports Illus 27:52-4 Ag 28 '67
Kickoff for a Babel of booters; televised soccer. T. Mule. Sports Illus 26:68+ Ap 24 '67
Locker in the living room. il Time 90:73 O 20 '67
Mustangs and Tigers on Madison avenue; sportscasting and coverage. R. L. Tobin. Sat R 50:83-4 N 11 '67; Discussion. 50: 58-9+ D 9 '67; 51:108 Ja 13 '68
Schooner's screen test; schooner yacht America's Sail to glory. J. Gribbins. il Motor B 120:38+ Ag '67
Super stakes; Super bowl. Newsweek 69:60 Ja 30 '67
Time-outs and other nonsense in TV sports. R. L. Tobin. Sat R 50:57-8 D 9 '67
Would you let this man interview you? sportscaster. H. Cosell. M. Cope. il Sports Illus 26:70-2+ Mr 13 '67

Sports films
C. B. DeMille of the pros; filming football games. T. C. Brody. il Sports Illus 27:74-6+ N 20 '67

Subscription programs
Boost for pay-TV. Newsweek 70:56-7 Jl 31 '67
Pay TV; better entertainment, or trouble for the industry? il U S News 62:96-7 My 8 '67
Subscription TV; address, October 11, 1967. J. S. Wright. Vital Speeches 34:79-83 N 15 '67
This month's feature: the question of pay television. Cong Digest 46:289-314 D '67

Travel films
New trails; Trail of Stanley and Livingstone and Sharks. il Time 91:44 Ja 19 '68

War news
Air. M. J. Arlen. New Yorker 43:139-42+ My 27 '67
Air; CBS documentary, Vietnam perspective; air war in the North. M. J. Arlen. New Yorker 43:148+ Mr 4 '67
Air; C.B.S. news show about Con Thien, by correspondent J. Laurence. M. J. Arlen. New Yorker 43:161-4+ S 30 '67

TELEVISION broadcasting—War news—*Cont.*
Air; Morley Safer's Vietnam. M. J. Arlen.
 New Yorker 43:184+ Ap 15 '67
Air; political candidates and Vietnamese war.
 M. J. Arlen. New Yorker 43:215-18 D 2 '67
Air; television and the press in Vietnam.
 M. J. Arlen. New Yorker 43:173-80+ O 21
 '67
Anderson's platoon; French documentary on
 Viet Nam war. il Newsweek 69:79-80 Je
 26 '67
For all to see; television's image of the Mid-
 dle East struggle. R. L. Shayon. Sat R 50:
 38 Jl 8 '67
Glimpse of the Viet Cong; French docu-
 mentary Time 90:81-2 D 15 '67
Honest persuader views an imprecise instru-
 ment; interview, ed. by A. Henehan. J. W.
 Chancellor. Sr Schol 90:20 Ap 28 '67
How bloody can it be? il Newsweek 70:75 D
 25 '67
How to cover wars; CBS and NBC programs
 on Israeli victory. R. L. Shayon. Sat R 50:
 22 Ag 12 '67
Mortars at martini time. il Time 90:86+
 D 1 '67
Poignant war report on men, not heroes: The
 Anderson platoon; French documentary on
 Vietnam war. S. Heckscher. Life 62:12 Je
 30 '67
Press: room for improvement. il Newsweek
 70:76+ Jl 10 '67
Problem of sanitation; questioning the little
 reaction to ghastly scenes of Vietnamese
 dead. Nation 206:5 Ja 1 '68
Sermon, extempore; excerpts from CBS interview with two U.S. soldiers. Nation
 204:739-40 Je 12 '67
T.R.B. from Washington; myth that TV has
 made people hate war. New Repub 156:
 inside cover Je 3 '67

Weather forecasts
Weather broadcast information. Yachting
 121:204-5 Je '67

Westerns
Hot as a pistol: Gunsmoke. il Newsweek 70:
 96 N 20 '67
Television; V. DeCosta suit. J. Horn. Nation
 206:59 Ja 8 '68

Yacht racing
See Television broadcasting—Sports

Youth programs
Listening to youth; Dorothy Gordon youth
 forums. D. Gordon. il Wilson Lib Bul 42:
 194-8 O '67

Belgium
Who paints the image? French TV band's
 anti-American feature: Contrastes. J.
 Burnham. Nat R 19:76 Ja 24 '67

Brazil
Television is the message down in Rio. il
 Bsns W p86-8 Je 17 '67

Canada
See also
Canadian broadcasting corporation

Europe, Eastern
Red tube. il Time 91:53 Ja 12 '68

Europe, Western
Race is to the daft; Games without bounda-
 ries on Eurovision. il Time 90:69-70 S 15 '67
Whirlpool of color; color TV in Europe.
 Newsweek 70:62-3 S 4 '67

France
But first, a message; television commercials
 to weaken power of press. Newsweek 70:50
 N 27 '67
Letter from Paris. Genêt. New Yorker 43:
 228+ N 25 '67
Men at war: a French view; documentary
 on Viet Nam. il Time 89:78 F 17 '67

Germany (Federal Republic
German sponsors fight for TV time. il Bsns
 W p92-4+ Ja 21 '67
Real-life manhunt; crime search program.
 il Newsweek 70:90+ D 4 '67

Great Britain
Air. M. J. Arlen. New Yorker 43:182-8 My 13
 '67
Bird of prey; Series of Birds most controversial new show. il Time 90:68 N 17 '67
Britain's troubled air. J. Tebbel. Sat R 50:
 60-1 Ag 12 '67

Doctor Jonathan Miller operates on Alice;
 dramatization of Alice in Wonderland for
 BBC television. W. H. Honan. il N Y Times
 Mag p24-7+ Ja 22 '67
Healthy convulsion in British television. R.
 Beardwood. il Fortune 76:47-8+ Ag '67
Letter from London; B.B.C. presentation of
 L. Woolf in random recollections to M.
 Muggeridge. M. Panter-Downes. New
 Yorker 43:164+ Ap 15 '67
Letter from London; documentary film on
 B.B.C.: Cathy come home. M. Panter-
 Downes. New Yorker 42:145-6+ F 11 '67
Public TV and the networks; BBC and ITV.
 B. Wenham. New Repub 156:19-20 My 13 '67;
 Reply. M. Wynne. 156:41-2 Je 3 '67
Television abroad; viewers have a choice.
 U S News 62:62 Je 12 '67
This is the network that is. il Time 89:50 Mr
 10 '67

Japan
Ah, so; program of inventions on Tokyo's
 Channel 12. Newsweek 71:94 Ja 22 '68
Television abroad; viewers have a choice.
 U S News 62:62 Je 12 '67

United States
Due to circumstances beyond our control, by
 F. W. Friendly. Review
 Sat R 50:30-1 Ap 1 '67. R. J. Landry
Fred Friendly and Friendlyvision. H. Swados.
 il N Y Times Mag p30-1+ Ap 23 '67
Friendly persuasion; concerning book Due to
 circumstances beyond our control. R. L.
 Shayon. Sat R 50:71 Ap 8 '67
Great sellout to soap opera; excerpt from Due
 to circumstances beyond our control. F.
 W. Friendly. il Life 62:84+ Mr 17 '67
Need for public television; summary of ad-
 dress at National book committee luncheon,
 March 7, 1967. F. W. Friendly. Pub W 191:
 35 Mr 20 '67
Retrieving a lost rocket; excerpt from Due
 to circumstances beyond our control ... F.
 W. Friendly. il Life 62:70-2+ Mr 24 '67
Television. J. Horn. Nation 204:476-7, 570-1,
 667-8; 205:414, 574, 638, 702 Ap 10, My 1, 22,
 O 23, N 27, D 11, D 25 '67
Television fiasco; interview. F. W. Friendly.
 il U S News 62:58-62 Je 12 '67
Top of my head. G. Ace. See issues of Satur-
 day review
When everybody loses; controversy over qual-
 ity-audience defections. R. L. Shayon. Sat
 R 50:60 F 25 '67
 See also
Alfred I. duPont awards
Columbia broadcasting system
United network company
United States—Federal communications com-
 mission

 Anecdotes, facetiae, satire, etc.
Air. W. W. Mudlark. New Yorker 42:122+
 F 4 '67

TELEVISION broadcasting, Noncommercial
Coming: a new era in public TV. Changing
 T 21:6 D '67
Future of television: misunderstanding the
 medium. S. Simonson. Cath World 206:126-
 31 D '67
Public television now, public newspapers
 later? D. Lawrence. U S News 63:116 N
 27 '67
Television. J. Horn. Nation 205:702 D 25
 '67
TELEVISION broadcasting and children
King-size problem. G. Ace. Sat R 50:7 D 2 '67
 See also
Television broadcasting—Childrens programs
TELEVISION broadcasting and reading. See
 Television and reading
TELEVISION broadcasting for children. See
 Television broadcasting—Childrens programs
TELEVISION broadcasting stations. See Tele-
 vision stations
TELEVISION cabinets
How to hide the television set. il House B
 109:38 Ap '67
TELEVISION camera tubes
Camera tube uses solid-state target electrode.
 il Electr World 77:54 My '67
TELEVISION cameras
Japanese shrink TV camera. Sci N 91:353 Ap
 15 '67
TELEVISION censorship. See Television broad-
 casting—Censorship
TELEVISION channels. See Television stations
TELEVISION circuits
Inside the 1968 color sets. F. H. Belt. il
 Electr World 79:41-5+Ja '68
IC used in new TV kit. D. G. Rupley. il Electr
 World 77:73 Ja '67
Troubleshooting new color chassis. L. Allen.
 il Electr World 79:38-40+ Ja '68

TELEVISION commercials. See Television advertising

TELEVISION couplings. See Couplings, Electric

TELEVISION criticism
Tuned in, turned off. Newsweek 70:93 O 16 '67

TELEVISION drama. See Television broadcasting—Drama

TELEVISION editorials. See Editorials

TELEVISION in criminal investigation
Real-life manhunt; crime search program in Germany. il Newsweek 70:90+ D 4 '67

TELEVISION in education
Airborne TV studied by emerging nations. W. C. Wetmore. il Aviation W 88:37+ Ja 8 '68
Antidote to boredom: Carnegie report. New Repub 156:7-8 F 11 '67
Blueprint for public TV; report by Carnegie commission. il Newsweek 69:89 F 6 '67
Carnegie report urges national ETV setup. Sr Schol 90:sup4 F 10 '67
Dial a lesson; TV dial-select system at Hall high school, West Hartford, Conn. C. L. Towne. il Sr Schol 90:sup 14 F 3 '67
Ford proposes satellites to serve educational TV. Library J 92:279 Ja 15 '67
Irrigation for the wasteland; Carnegie report. C. B. Grannis. Pub W 191:127 F 20 '67
Microwave ETV system planning & installation. L. G. Lawrence. il Electr World 77:34-6 My '67
Saving radiance; quality programs, absence of commercials on public TV. W. K. Zinsser. Look 31:15 Mr 21 '67
TV and learning. J. McLaughlin. America 116:841-3 Je 10 '67
Television's role in education. H. R. Cassirer. Sch & Soc 95:354-8 O 14 '67
Viability of video; televised lectures and demonstrations. il Time 90:50 O 20 '67
What's happening in education? new proposals regarding TV. W. D. Boutwell. PTA Mag 61:11 Mr '67
Who runs educational TV? D. Walker. New Repub 156:35-7 F 11 '67
    See also
Television stations, Educational

TELEVISION in industry
Infrared television. F. C. Livingstone. Sci N 92:519 N 25 '67

TELEVISION in medicine
Internal TV; color TV cystoscope. Time 89:65 My 12 '67

TELEVISION in politics
Air; political candidates and Vietnamese war. M. J. Arlen. New Yorker 43:215-18 D 2 '67
Camera and JFK. J. Neubauer. il Pop Phot 61:88-103+ N '67
Candidates on television. P. Barnes. New Repub 157:7-8 Jl 22 '67
Ronnie-Bobby show; R. Kennedy and R. Reagan on Town meeting of the world. il Newsweek 69:26+ My 29 '67
Shorter conventions and campaigns. R. L. Tobin. Sat R 50:24 Ap 15 '67

    Anecdotes, facetiae, satire, etc.
Super-veep; need for a show with a political hero. D. Compton. Atlan 219:118+ Ap '67

TELEVISION in sewer inspection. See Sewer inspection

TELEVISION industry
    See also
Strikes—United States—Television industry
Television apparatus industry and trade

    Brazil
Television is the message down in Rio. il Bsns W p86-8 Je 17 '67

    United States
CBS wins some bullish reviews. il Bsns W p 121-3 Ja 21 '67
Due to circumstances beyond our control, by F. Friendly. Review Time 89:46+ Ap 7 '67
Program for public-TV. L. Markel. il N Y Times Mag p25+ Mr 12 '67; Discussion. p22+ Ap 2 '67
Public TV and the networks. B. Wenham. New Repub 156:19-20 My 13 '67; Reply. M. Wynne. 156:41-2 Je 3 '67
Real masters of television. R. Eck. Harper 234:45-52 Mr '67; Same abr. with title Why TV is the way it is. Read Digest 90:78-82 My '67

TELEVISION information office
Evaluations of television. America 117:260-1 S 16 '67

TELEVISION interference
Ghost town; question of Manhattan's proposed World trade center buildings interfering with television transmission. Newsweek 70:51 Ag 7 '67
NBFM routs 6-meter TVI. R. L. Winklepleck. il Pop Electr 26:73-6 F '67
Notes and comment; effects from watching channels not in regular operation in N.Y. New Yorker 43:19 Je 24 '67

TELEVISION interviews. See Interviewing

TELEVISION laws and regulations
Broadcasting and impartiality. America 118:26-7 Ja 13 '68
FCC ruling on cigarette ads: health groups react warily. L. J. Carter. Science 158:888-92 N 17 '67
Noncommercial TV and radio. America 116:715-16 My 13 '67
Public broadcasting corporation; proposed Public broadcasting act of 1967 to support noncommercial television and radio. J. McLaughlin. America 117:9-14 Jl 1 '67
    See also
United States—Federal communications commission

TELEVISION performers. See Television broadcasting—Performers

TELEVISION photography. See Television—Photographic aspects

TELEVISION production. See Television broadcasting—Program production

TELEVISION program rating. See Television broadcasting—Program rating

TELEVISION programs. See Television broadcasting—Programs

TELEVISION receivers
Gadgets to improve TV; are they any good? R. M. Benrey. il Pop Sci 190:118-21 F '67
Monochrome TV sets; 18-inch black-and-white. il Consumer Rep 32:135-8 Mr '67
Television receivers; color and black-and-white. il Consumer Bul 50:9-15 D '67
Two new TV kits from Heath. B. Hartford. il Pop Mech 127:168-70+ Je '67

    Color receivers
Color for $200? B. Hartford. il Pop Mech 128:122-7+ N '67
Color TV makes the scene again. il Bsns W p 153-4 S 16 '67
Color TV sets. Consumer Rep 32:312-19 D '67
Color TV; what's new for '68. R. M. Benrey. il Pop Sci 191:92-4 S '67
¿Cómo está, RCA? J. Ross-Skinner. il Duns R 89:63 Ap '67
Earth's magnetic field & color TV. Electr World 77:71 Ja '67
Inside the 1968 color sets. F. H. Belt. il Electr World 79:41-5+ Ja '68
Large-screen color TV. il Consumer Rep 33:16-20 Ja '68
180 square inches of color TV. il Pop Electr 27:62-3 Jl '67
Small-screen color television set: 14-inch-diagonal RCA Victor not satisfactory. Consumer Rep 32:350 Jl '67
Television receivers; color and black-and-white. il Consumer Bul 50:9-15 D '67
What to look for in color TV sets. R. Freas. il Am Home 70:38+ Mr '67

    Manufacture
    See Television apparatus—Manufacture

    Radiation hazards
Owners of GE color TV sets take note; sets may emit excessive X-radiation. Consumer Rep 32:349 Jl '67
Perils of TV; excessive amounts of X-rays. Newsweek 70:53 Ag 7 '67
TV radiation assessed; X-ray emission from color TV sets. Sci N 92:11 Jl 1 '67
TV that can bite; color sets emit mild X-ray beam. Bsns W p61 My 27 '67
Too much radiation from two sets. il Consumer Rep 33:18 Ja '68
X-ray hazard in TV sets; GE color-TV. Consumer Bul 50:4+ O '67
X-rays in the living room; X-ray-producing potential of TV sets. Time 90:62 Ag 4 '67

    Repairing
TV servicing, the modular approach. W. A. Stocklin. Electr World 79:6 Ja '68
Troubleshooting new color chassis. L. Allen. il Electr World 79:38-40+ Ja '68

    Tuning
New color-TV tuning indicator. W. H. Buchsbaum. il Electr World 78:68-9 D '67

    Installation
Installing the system. il Pop Electr 26:52-3+ Je '67
Wiring your home for TV. G. Zappa. il Pop Electr 26:44 Je '67

TELEVISION receivers—*Continued*

Interference
See Television interference

Repairing
Computerized servicing. W. A. Stocklin. Electr World 77:6 Ap '67
Quality of TV repair services. il Consumer Rep 32:108-12 F '67
Servicing the system. il Pop Electr 26:54+ Je '67

Solid-state receivers
See Television receivers—Transistor receivers

Transistor receivers
Coat pocket TV. L. Solomon. il Pop Electr 27:31-5 O '67
Inside the 1968 color sets. F. H. Belt. il Electr World 79:41-5+ Ja '68
Tiny TV set with a large fault; transistorized Symphonic Minni TV. il Consumer Rep 32: 184 Ap '67
What to look for in a miniscreen TV. L. Buckwalter. il Pop Mech 128:90-3+ D '67

Repairing
TV servicing, the modular approach. W. A. Stocklin. Electr World 79:6 Ja '68

Tuning
Taming your TV tuner. C. L. Smith. il Pop Electr 26:51-4 Mr '67

TELEVISION receivers, Portable
Coat pocket TV. L. Solomon. il Pop Electr 27:31-5 O '67
$70 TV set, and not bad, either: Admiral PN 904's. il Consumer Rep 32:66 F '67
What to look for in a miniscreen TV. L. Buckwalter. il Pop Mech 128:90-3+ D '67

TELEVISION receivers industry. See Television apparatus industry and trade

TELEVISION reception
Cable: parasite or panacea? R. Angus. il Hi Fi 17:50-5 D '67
CATV comes down from the hills; community antenna television in New York selling pure reception. il Bsns W p64-6+ S 16 '67
Earth's magnetic field & color TV. Electr World 77:71 Ja '67

TELEVISION relay systems
See also
Communications satellites

TELEVISION repairing. See Television receivers apparatus—Repairing

TELEVISION script writing. See Television authorship

TELEVISION scripts. See Television authorship

TELEVISION service shops
Computerized servicing. W. A. Stocklin. Electr World 77:6 Ap '67
PEMOHT; the Russian radio, TV serviceman. L. A. Harlow. il Pop Electr 27:57-8+ Ag '67

TELEVISION stations
Air; new developments. M. J. Arlen. New Yorker 42:138-40 F 18 '67
Challenge in the South; U.S. Court of appeals forces FCC to schedule public hearing on WLBT's current application for license renewal. Newsweek 69:63 My 29 '67
Notes and comment; effects from watching channels not in regular operation in N.Y. New Yorker 43:19 Je 24 '67
WLBT vs. United church of Christ. America 117:493 N 4 '67
See also
Columbia broadcasting system
United network company

TELEVISION stations, Educational
Airborne TV studied by emerging nations. W. C. Wetmore. il Aviation W 88:37+ Ja 8 '68
Board has a TV station; WNYE-TV. Sat R 50:76 Ap 15 '67
Boost for poor brother; Carnegie solution. Time 89:55 F 3 '67
Candid camera on TV; Carnegie commission's report. Nation 204:324 Mr 13 '67
Closing the TV quality gap; Public television; Carnegie commission's proposals. R. L. Tobin. Sat R 50:73-4+ Ap 8 '67
Coming up in TV; Ford and federal funds. New Repub 157:4 N 4 '67
Educational television. New Repub 156:8-9 Mr 11 '67
ETV goes way out and brings the world to Samoa. M. L. Fiedler. il Am Ed 3:14-17 Mr '67

ETV's historic opportunity; Ford foundation's proposal for a new structure to finance noncommercial television vs. the Carnegie plan. R. L. Shayon. Sat R 50:71 F 18 '67
Growth of educational television. Sch & Soc 95:39 Ja 21 '67
House divided; Public broadcasting act of 1967. R. L. Shayon. Sat R 50:18 S 2 '67
Implementing the Carnegie plan. R. L. Shayon. Sat R 50:63 My 20 '67
Most dangerous game; geopolitical crisis game over Boston's educational station, WGBX. Newsweek 71:51 Ja 15 '68
Prodigious satellites; Comsat, ma Bell and ETV. E. B. Lambeth. il Nation 204:109-12 Ja 23 '67
Public television. J. McLaughlin. America 116:567 Ap 15 '67
Public TV: a power struggle. J. Morgenstern. il Newsweek 69:90-2+ Je 5 '67
Public TV: a wasteland oasis. Life 62:4 F 17 '67
Public TV and the networks. B. Wenham. New Repub 156:19-20 My 13 '67; Reply. M. Wynne. 156:41-2 Je 3 '67
Public TV around the corner? concerning report of Carnegie commission on educational TV. il U S News 62:91 Mr 13 '67
Public television; concerning report of the Carnegie commission on educational television. Nation 204:197 F 13 '67
Swing: Q.E.D; station KQED. Time 90:81 D 8 '67
Television; financing ETV. Nation 205:414 O 23 '67
Television; financing public television. J. Horn. Nation 204:570-1 My 1 '67

TELEVISION surveys
Color line and commercials; LDF-Plotkin survey of Negroes in commercials. R. L. Shayon. il Sat R 50:52 N 4 '67
Great media impact war; concerning Roper and other survey findings. J. Tebbel. il Sat R 50:96-7 Je 10 '67
Popping the question; viewers' opinions registered by telephone. Time 90:73-4 O 20 '67

TELEVISION transmission
Selecting transmission lines. il Pop Electr 26:50-1 Je '67
See also
Television, Color

Interference
See Television interference

TELEVISION vocabulary. See Vocabulary

TELEVISION wiring. See Electric wire and wiring

TELEVISION writing. See Television authorship

TELFAIR academy of arts and sciences, Savannah, Ga.
Telfair and its paintings. L. T. Cheney. il Antiques 91:353-9 Mr '67

TELL me how long the train's been gone; story. See Baldwin, J.

TELLE, Paul. See Graham, E. R. jt. auth.

TELLEFSEN, Robert N.
Build the emitter dipper. Pop Electr 25:47-9 D '66
40-pole. Pop Electr 27:82 N '67

TELLER, Edward
Dollars vs. lives: a U.S. choice; interview. pors U S News 62:44-8 My 29 '67
Dormant nuclear revolution. por Tech W 20: 39-42 Ja 23 '67
about
Teller attacks breeder safety. il Sci N 92: 200+ Ag 26 '67

TELLICO DAM (proposed) See Dams

TEMIANKA, Henri
Creators in a creative society. Sat R 50:30+ S 23 '67

TEMKO, Allan
Lewis Mumford at seventy-two. Harper 235: 106+ O '67
about
Civic consciences. por Time 89:66+ Mr 31 '67

TEMPE, Ariz.
Single pool plays a dual role. J. Salvato. il Am City 82:102-3 Ap '67

TEMPER
Emotional first aid? L. L. Prina. il N Y Times Mag p 112+ Ap 2 '67
How to handle children's tantrums. il Good H 164:152-3 F '67
See also
Anger

TEMPERATURE

Isotopic paleotemperatures. C. Emiliani; discussion. Science 156:410; bibliog 157:722-5 Ap 21, Ag 11 '67
See also
Metals. Effect of temperature on
Stars—Temperature

Measurement

Temperature measurements from oxygen isotope ratios of fish otoliths. I. Devereux. il Science 155:1684-5 Mr 31 '67
Temperature measurements in noctilucent clouds. J. S. Theon and others. il Science 157:419-21 Jl 28 '67
Warm-hearted city; mapping the heat island of Corvallis, Ore. Sci Am 216:52 Ap '67
See also
Thermometers and thermometry

Physiological effects

Multiple temperature-sensitive spots innervated by single nerve fibers. D. R. Kenshalo and E. S. Gallegos. bibliog il Science 158:1064-5 N 24 '67
Temperature compensation in short-duration time-measurement by an intertidal amphipod. J. T. Enright. bibliog il Science 156:1510-12 Je 16 '67
Temperature effect on protein synthesis in a heat-synchronized protozoan treated with actinomycin D. J. E. Byfield and O. H. Scherbaum. bibliog il Science 156:1504-5 Je 16 '67
Temperature tolerance of some Antarctic fishes. G. N. Somero and A. L. DeVries. bibliog il Science 156:257-8 Ap 14 '67
Tiliqua scincoides: temperature-sensitive units in lizard brain. M. Cabanac and others. bibliog il Science 158:1050-1 N 24 '67
Visceral tissue vascularization: an adaptive response to high temperature. R. O. Rawson and others. il Science 158:1203-4 D 1 '67

TEMPERATURE, Animal and human

Autonomic basis for the rise in brain temperature during paradoxical sleep. M. A. Baker and J. N. Hayward. bibliog il Science 157:1586-8 S 29 '67
Radiant solar energy and the function of black homeotherm pigmentation: an hypothesis. W. J. Hamilton, 3d. and F. Heppner. bibliog il Science 155:196-7 Ja 13 '67; Reply with rejoinder. R. B. Cowles. 158:1340-1 D 8 '67
Regulation of body temperature in the blue-tongued lizard. H. T. Hammel and others. bibliog il Science 156:1260-2 Je 2 '67
Thermoregulation in the desert iguana dipsosaurus dorsalis. S. M. McGinnis and L. L. Dickson. bibliog il Science 156:1757-9 Je 30 '67; Reply with rejoiner. C. B. DeWitt. 158:809-10 N 10 '67
Voluntary hypothermia in reptiles. P. J. Regal. bibliog il Science 155:1551-3 Mr 24 '67

TEMPERATURE, Atmospheric. See Atmospheric temperature

TEMPLE, Robert W.

ABCs of brakes. Pop Mech 127:138-42+ My '67
ABCs of smog-control devices. il Pop Mech 123:154-9+ N '67

TEMPLE, Sarah pseud.

Opinion: on late bloomers. Mlle 66:52-3+ D '67

TEMPLE, Shirley

Baby take a bow. il pors Newsweek 70:21-2 S 11 '67
Black out. New Repub 157:7 N 25 '67
Entertainment culture. A. Berger. Nation 205:228-9 S 18 '67
Holy lollipop! S. Temple to run for Congress in '68? por Newsweek 69:64 Je 19 '67
How do you fight Shirley Temple? J. Duscha. il por Reporter 37:21-3 N 2 '67
Little Miss candidate. L. Williams. il pors Look 31:86+ N 14 '67
Little Shirley Temple lives. S. Alexander. Life 63:17 N 3 '67
Miscasting of Shirley. Nation 205:580-1 D 4 '67
Mrs Black & the neighbors. il por Time 90:27-8 N 10 '67
Mrs Black for Congress. il por Time 90:16 S 8 '67
Moms and pops, arise! il por Newsweek 70:35 N 6 '67
Now it's Shirley Temple for Congress. por U S News 63:20 S 11 '67
Politics American style. J. N. Eller. America 117:265 S 16 '67
Politics of entertainment. A. Berger. Nation 205:422-4 O 30 '67
Shirley runs but not on the Temple ticket. il pors Life 63:27 S 8 '67

TEMPLE, Truman R.

Program for overcoming the handicap of dialect. New Repub 156:11-12 Mr 25 '67

TEMPLE, Willard

That old college try; story. Good H 164:52-3 Ja '67

TEMPLES

Should the Temple be rebuilt? il Time 89:56 Je 30 '67

Egypt

See also
Abu Simbel, Temples of

Hawaii

God Lono has many faces; City of refuge national historical park. il Sunset 139:29+ O '67

TEMPURA. See Cookery, Japanese

TEN-penny tragedy; drama. See Elfenbein, J. A.

TEN THOUSAND ISLANDS

Not a park to go barefoot in. J. Olsen il Sports Illus 26:58-60+ Ap 3 '67

TENA, Lucero

In search of new talent. W. Terry. il Sat R 50:48-9 N 4 '67
Lucero Tena and ensemble; Henry Miller's theatre. D. Hering. por Dance Mag 41:30 D '67

TENANCY. See Farm tenancy

TENANT unions. See Landlord and tenant

TENANTS. See Landlord and tenant

TENDER offers. See Stocks—Tender offers

TENDONS

Snap! crack! pop! ruptured Achilles' tendon. il Newsweek 70:111 S 18 '67

TENNECO, Incorporated

Tenneco lands Kern County. il Bsns W p96-8+ Jl 22 '67

TENNESSEE

See also
Fishing—Tennessee
Hunting—Tennessee
Reelfoot Lake

Legislature

Some lessons of reapportionment. B. Kovach. Reporter 37:26+ S 21 '67

TENNESSEE cypress. See Bald cypress

TENNESSEE evolution controversy

Center of the storm, by J. T. Scopes and J. Presley. Review
Newsweek 69:94+ F 20 '67. S. K. Oberbeck
Time 89:102+ F 17 '67
John T. Scopes redivivus. Christian Cent 84:429 Ap 5 '67
Monkey trial. J. W. Krutch. Commentary 43:83-4 My '67
Monkeys, titans, and soda pop; Scopes trial. Sr Schol 90:5 My 5 '67

TENNESSEE VALLEY authority

TVA: the halo slips; Land between the lakes dispute. J. Egerton. il Nation 205:11-15 Jl 3 '67

TENNEY, Roger

Key to teaching music; interview. por NEA J 56:69-70 D '67

about
Roger Tenney: teacher of the year. C. Mangel. il pors Look 31:64-9 My 2 '67

TENNIS

Amateur bad boy turns pro perfectionist. K. Chapin. il Sports Illus 26:56 Je 19 '67
And the last shall be first; ambition of promoter Wally Dill. K. Chapin. il Sports Illus 27:44-5 Jl 24 '67
Anyone for sense? need for competition between pros and amateurs. il Time 90:57 S 15 '67
Anyone? U.S. Davis cup team loses to Ecuador. Time 89:55 Je 30 '67
Best losers in the world; U.S. Davis cup team. B. Collins. il Sports Illus 27:44-6 Jl 3 '67
Bomb at Wimbledon; defending champion beaten in first round. il Time 90:65 Jl 7 '67
Gentleman's game; National singles championships at West Side tennis club, Forest Hills, N.Y. R. Lynes. il Harper 235:26+ D '67
Great Scott! Gene won another one. E. L. Scott. il Sports Illus 27:46-8+ O 2 '67
He's old hat to Australians; J. Newcombe winner at Wimbledon. F. Deford. il Sports Illus 27:30-3 S 4 '67
King-size tennis; winner of All-England championships at Wimbledon. Newsweek 70:53 Jl 17 '67

TENNIS—*Continued*
Mental muscle on court; C. Pasarall. il Time 89:69-70 Mr 3 '67
Murderous pleasures of tennis. N. Hentoff. Atlan 219:98-100 Ap '67
No alibi; U.S. toppled by Ecuador. Newsweek 70:70 Jl 3 '67
Pay's the thing; pro tennis has gone big time. Time 89:69 Je 23 '67
Plays tennis like a man, speaks out like, Billie Jean King. H. Higdon. il N Y Times Mag p28-9+ Ag 27 '67; Reply. J. C. Smith. p97 O 1 '67
Reign in Spain of King Manolo. F. Deford. il Sports Illus 27:26-9 Jl 3 '67
Seeing red; Rod Laver wins U.S. championship. il Newsweek 70:50 Jl 31 '67
Some beer for Newk, a waltz for Billie. F. Deford. il Sports Illus 27:22-5 Jl 17 '67
Sporting scene; 1967 United States lawn tennis championships. H. W. Wind. New Yorker 43:94+ S 30 '67
Tennis, everyone? British lawn tennis association erases distinction between amateur and professional. il Newsweek 70:49 D 25 '67
Tonic for a game with tired blood; professional tennis. F. Deford. Sports Illus 27:68+ D 11 '67
Two little words; British lawn tennis association deletes amateur and professional division. Time 90:45 D 22 '67
Two times one equals zero; timing error of amateur and pro tournaments in New York. W. F. Talbert. il Sports Illus 26:60+ Mr 13 '67
Two who didn't stay away; B. J. King and J. Newcombe at Forest Hills. K. Chapin. il Sports Illus 27:97-8+ S 18 '67
What the deuce is going on? G. Plimpton. il Sports Illus 27:34-6+ S 18 '67
Wimbledon à la King. il Time 90:53 Jl 21 '67
See also
Paddle tennis
United States lawn tennis association

Accidents and injuries
Getting the elbow is a pain. J. Lipscomb. il Sports Illus 26:38-40+ Je 5 '67

Study and teaching
Lead-up games and activities in tennis instruction. P. J. Xanthos. il Parks & Rec 2:32+ S '67

TENNIS courts
Courtship; synthetic turf called Centercourt. Newsweek 69:70 My 8 '67
Space frame in a Swedish forest; Landskrona tennis hall, Landskrona, Sweden. il Arch Forum 126:104-7 Ja '67
See also
Paddle tennis courts

Lighting
New tennis-court lighting results in net sayings; Miami, Fla. il Am City 82:124 My '67
Tennis after dark, anyone? Dallas, Tex. il Am City 82:132 Je '67

TENNIS players
And the last shall be first; ambition of promoter Wally Dill. K. Chapin. il Sports Illus 27:44-5 Jl 24 '67
Best losers in the world; U.S. Davis cup team. B. Collins. il Sports Illus 27:44-6 Jl 3 '67
Sporting scene; 1967 United States lawn tennis championships. H. W. Wind. New Yorker 43:94+ S 30 '67
U.S. men are losers; views of B. J. King. B. Bruns. il Life 63:109+ S 22 '67
What the deuce is going on? G. Plimpton. il Sports Illus 27:34-6+ S 18 '67
See also
Santana, M.

TENNIS rackets
Big steel; Wilson sporting goods co.'s new steel-framed racket. Newsweek 71:56 Ja 8 '68
Some steel; T2000 steel rackets. il Time 90:70+ S 22 '67
Swinging the steelies. il Newsweek 70:77 S 25 '67

TENNYSON, Alfred Tennyson, 1st baron
Tennyson's Isle of Wight. N. Braybrooke. il Sat R 50:60-1+ Mr 11 '67

TENORS, Operatic. See Opera singers

TENRECS
Most unappetizing beast imaginable. il Sci Digest 62:13-15 D '67

TENSION (psychology) See Fatigue; Stress (physiology)

TENTH man; drama. See Chayefsky, P.

TEOTIHUACÁN, Mexico
Teotihuacán. R. Millon. il Sci Am 216:38-48 bibliog(p 155) Je '67
TEPPER, Herbert B. and Hollis, C. A.
Mitotic reactivation of the terminal bud and cambium of white ash. bibliog Science 156:1635-6 Je 23 '67
TEPPER, Scott
Conflict or compromise. Sat R 50:41-2 S 30 '67
TEQUILA
Exports put extra kick in tequila; Mexico's national drink. il Bsns W p90 Ja 13 '68
Tequila without hands. il Esquire 67:90-1 Mr '67
TER-ARUTUNIAN, Rouben
Interview; ed. by A. Fatt. il por Dance Mag 41:53 Mr '67
TERATOLOGY. See Abnormalities (animals); Deformities
TERHUNE, Albert Payson
Kind and canny canines. R. H. Boyle. il Sports Illus 28:50-6 Ja 15 '68
TERIYAKI. See Cookery, Japanese
TERKEL, Studs
Division street; America. R. A. Schroth. America 116:381 Mr 18 '67
Talk of the town. por Newsweek 69:63 F 20 '67
TERMINAL buildings, Airport. See Airport buildings
TERMINAL radar control. See Radar in aviation
TERMINALLY-guided missiles. See Guided missiles
TERMINE, John D. and Posner, A. S.
Infrared analysis of rat bone; age dependency of amorphous and crystalline mineral fractions. bibliog Science 153:1523-5; 155:607-8 S 23 '66, F 3 '67
TERMINOLOGY. See subhead Terminology under various subjects, e.g. Politics—Terminology
TERMITES
Alarm, defense, and construction behavior relationships in termites isoptera. A. M. Stuart. bibliog il Science 156:1123-5 My 26 '67
New Asiatic invader; Formosan termite, with recommendations by USDA Forest research advisory committee. K. B. Pomeroy. il Am For 73:22-4+ Ja '67
Termites, and how to keep them at bay. il House & Gard 131:48+ Ap '67; Same abr. Read Digest 91:176-80 O '67
TERMS and phrases, English. See English language—Terms and phrases
TERPENES
Perhydro-β-carotene in the Green River shale. M. T. J. Murphy and others. bibliog il Science 157:1040-2 S 1 '67
TERRACE, H. S.
Discrimination learning and inhibition. bibliog Science 154:1677-80; 156:988-9 D 30 '66, My 19 '67
TERRACE gardens. See Roof gardens
TERRAIL, Claude
Gourmets' delight is lean on profits. il por Bsns W p62-4 D 30 '67
TERRAZZO
How to maintain terrazzo floors. J. C. Ferguson. il Am City 82:92-3 Ja '67
TERRAZZO; story. See Logan, M. Z.
TERRE HAUTE, Ind.
Water supply
Continuous ion-exchange softening. E. F. Spitzer. il Am City 82:118-20 Je '67
TERRELL, Dave
How to make a horse say cheese. U S Camera 30:64 Ap '67
TERRELL, Ernie
Cruel Ali with all the skills. T. Maule. il Sports Illus 26:18-21 F 13 '67
Left that was. T. Maule. il pors Sports Illus 26:14-17 F 6 '67
Vicente bored in but Ernie merely bored. B. Ottum. Sports Illus 27:66-8 O 23 '67
TERRELL, James
Quasi-stellar objects; possible local origin. bibliog Science 154:1281-8; 156:265 D 9 '66, Ap 14 '67
TERRES, John K.
Eagles over Hawk Mountain; excerpt from Flashing wings. Audubon 69:28-33 Jl '67
TERRESTRIAL magnetism. See Magnetism, Terrestrial
TERRILL, Audrey
Confusions of a school secretary. Parents Mag 42:88-9 S '67
TERRILL, Ross
China and Vietnam. New Repub 155:16-20 O 29 '66; Correction. 156:37 Ja 28 '67

TEXAS—*Continued*

Politics and government

Invitation to a brawl; candidates for governorship. il Time 90:17 D 1 '67
LBJ will make it despite a GOP trend. G. Olds. New Repub 158:13-14 Ja 20 '68
Who gets the crown? candidates for governorship. il Newsweek 71:22 Ja 22 '68

Religious institutions and affairs

Punt on the five-yard line; four Paulist priests fired from diocese by Bishop Gorman. il Time 89:56 Je 16 '67

TEXAS floods. See Floods—United States

TEXAS instruments, incorporated
Texas instruments: all systems go. J. B. Weiner. il Duns R 89:28-31+ Ja '67

TEXAS Rangers. See Texas—Police

TEXAS southern university, Houston, Tex.
Love and hate and a very fast hundred. P. Axthelm. il Sports Illus 26:66+ Je 5 '67
Stokely generation; riots at Texas southern university. il Newsweek 69:24-5 My 29 '67

TEXAS. University, Austin
University of Texas philosophical colloquia. il Sch & Soc 94:476+ D 24 '66

TEXEREAU, Jean
Observing Saturn's edgewise rings, October, 1966. il Sky & Tel 33:226-7 Ap '67

TEXTBOOK publishers institute, American. See American textbook publishers institute

TEXTBOOKS
Evaluating educational materials. R. H. Smith. Pub W 191:38 Ap 3 '67
NEA sets new guidelines for textbook purchases. Pub W 192:29-30 N 6 '67
Negro in textbooks: reading, 'riting and racism. L. Bennett, jr. il Ebony 22:130-2+ Mr '67
School books; reprint. M. Van Doren. Pub W 191:35 My 29 '67
Treatment of minorities in textbooks. Sch & Soc 95:323-4 Sum '67
Treatment of minorities in textbooks; resolutions by NEA. il Negro Hist Bul 30:8-10 Mr '67
What our children read; excerpt from The American schoolbooks. H. Black. il Sat Eve Post 240:27-9+ O 7 '67
Where ghetto schools fail; excerpt from Death at an early age. J. Kozol. il Atlan 220:107-10 O '67
See also
Publishers and publishing—Textbooks
United States—History—Textbooks

Bibliography

What's new in textbooks. Sr Schol 90:sup 14 F 17 '67

Prices

Trials and tribulations of textbook price indexing. B. M. Conant. il ALA Bul 61:197-9 F '67

United States

See Textbooks

TEXTILE design
Africa abstracted; Julian Tomchin's designs. il Look 31:36-40 Jl 25 '67
Glen Kaufman. F. Schwartz. il Craft Horiz 27:14-16 Ja '67
Jack Lenor Larsen; his retrospective exhibition at Amsterdam's Stedelijk museum. J. L. Larsen. il Craft Horiz 27:22-5 S '67
Thoughts on designing for textiles. N. Belfer. il Sch Arts 66:34-7 Ap '67
Thousand and one patterns: a new decorative delight worthy of Scheherazade. il House & Gard 132:104-9 Ag '67
Thinking in colour. . . il Vogue 150:98-9 Ag 15 '67

TEXTILE fabrics
Complete recovery. il House B 109:52+ My '67
From the Victorian era; new fabric inspirations. G. Monypenn. il House B 109:192-3 Ap '67
Great unlooked-fors; refreshing new roles for an old familiar friend-fabric. il House & Gard 132:250-5 N '67
How to paint walls and furniture with fabric. il House & Gard 132:288-9+ N '67
How to wake up an old-fashioned house without spending a fortune: color and pattern. il House & Gard 131:116-19 F '67
Neutrals coming in. il House B 109:156-7 S '67
Pictures you can stroke. R. Roberts. il Design 69:34-5 Wint '67
Textile arts; symposium; ed. by D. B. Van Dommelen. il Sch Arts 66:4-30 Ap '67

Throw away as you go away. il Travel 128:14-15 S '67
World's gone dotty. il Am Home 70:90-1 My '67
See also
Textile finishing

Color

Making up to flamboyant fashions. il McCalls 94:104-5+ Ap '67

Creasing

See Creasing of textiles

Finishing

See Textile finishing

Fireproofing

See Fireproofing of textiles

TEXTILE fabrics, Bonded web
Textile engineering seen as spur to composite market; astrocarb, laminated fabric for aerospace use. il Tech W 20:29 Je 12 '67

TEXTILE fabrics, Fire resisting
What you should know about flammable fabrics; synthetic flameproof fabrics. H. Manchester. Read Digest 90:42 My '67

TEXTILE fabrics, Flammable
Some burning questions. J. Daugherty and M. Daugherty. il Sci Digest 61:90-2 Je '67
What you need to know about flammable fabrics. il Consumer Bul 50:16-17 Mr '67
What you should know about flammable fabrics. H. Manchester. Read Digest 90:37-8+ My '67

TEXTILE fabrics, Fur-like. See Fur, Artificial

TEXTILE fabrics, Laminated. See Textile fabrics, Bonded web

TEXTILE fabrics, Wrinkle resistant
Building an easy-care wardrobe? it's as easy as durable press. il Good H 164:236+ Ap '67
Candid look at permanent press. B. G. Wadsworth. il Ladies Home J 84:34 Ap '67
Durable press shirts. il Consumer Bul 50:22-7 S '67
Home sewing with permanent press fabrics. il Consumer Bul 50:4-6 Je '67
How to care for durable press. il McCalls 94:50 S '67
Institute answers your questions on children's clothes that need no ironing. G. Wham. il Good H 165:182+ Ag '67
Permanent-press fabric, the farm wife's newest helper. il Suc Farm 65:56-7 Ag '67

TEXTILE fiber products identification act. See Labels

TEXTILE fibers, Synthetic
Shopping for outdoor carpeting. Bet Hom & Gard 45:144+ My '67

TEXTILE finishing
Candid look at permanent press. B. G. Wadsworth. il Ladies Home J 84:34 Ap '67
Durable-press sheets & pillowcases. il Consumer Rep 32:264-6 My '67
Home sewing with permanent press fabrics. il Consumer Bul 50:4-6 Je '67
Permanent-press fabric, the farm wife's newest helper. J. LemMon. il Suc Farm 65:56-7 Ag '67
See also
Creasing of textiles
Woolen and worsted finishing

TEXTILE industry

Great Britain

Textile tycoonery. J. Ross-Skinner. Duns R 89:54-5 Ja '67

United States

Tariff commission to report on textile and apparel industries; statement, October 4, 1967. L. B. Johnson. Dept State Bul 57:529 O 23 '67
See also
Munsingwear, incorporated
Stevens, J. P, and company

TEXTILE labels. See Labels

TEXTILE machinery industry

Great Britain

Tea without sympathy; Roberts-Arundal plant to close. Newsweek 71:46 Ja 1 '68

TEXTILE workers
See also
Woolen and worsted mills—Wages and hours

TEXTILE workers union of America
Can AFL-CIO win its textile siege? il Bsns W p94+ Mr 25 '67

TEXTRON, incorporated
When half a loaf is the answer; Textron bond issue. il Bsns W p 118+ Jl 8 '67

TEXTURED walls. See Wall coverings

THAI, Vu-van-. See Vu-van-Thai
THAI airways international. See Airlines—
Thailand
THAILAND
Hopes and fears in booming Thailand. P. T.
White. il Nat Geog Mag 132:76-125 Jl '67
How the guerrillas came to Koh Noi. P.
Braestrup. il N Y Times Mag p30-1+ D
10 '67
    See also
Air travel—Thailand
Airlines—Thailand
Americans in Thailand
Communism—Thailand
Guerrillas—Thailand
United States—Foreign relations—Thailand

Defenses
In the pattern; new agreement with the U.S.
Commonweal 87:323-4 D 8 '67

Foreign relations
Is Thailand getting fed up with America?
U S News 64:6 Ja 8 '68
Letter from Bangkok. R. Shaplen. New
Yorker 43:135-6+ Mr 18 '67
Thailand: a fighting ally for U.S. in Asia.
il U S News 62:46-8 F 27 '67
United States and Thailand; address, May 3,
1967. G. Martin. Dept State Bul 56:851-5
Je 5 '67
United States and Thailand pledge to continue
close cooperation to promote peace; ex-
change of greetings and exchange of toasts,
June 27, with joint statement, June 29, 1967.
L. B. Johnson; King Bhumibol Adulyadej.
Dept State Bul 57:61-4 Jl 17 '67
Visit with the king & queen of Thailand.
G. Zimmermann. il Look 31:86-91 Je 27 '67

Politics and government
Northeast Thailand: tomorrow's Viet Nam?
J. L. S. Girling. For Affairs 46:388-97 Ja '68
Thailand: a fighting ally for U.S. in Asia.
il U S News 62:46-8 F 27 '67
Thailand: privileged sanctuary; government's
leaders. O. Schell. New Repub 157:17-18
S 30 '67
Visit with the king & queen of Thailand.
G. Zimmermann. il Look 31:86-91 Je 27 '67
    See also
Communism—Thailand
THALASSEMIA. See Anemia
THALER, Mike
Another roundup. il Opera N 31:14-16 Ap 8 '67
Roundup. il Opera N 31:14-16 Ja 7 '67
THALER, Richard
Pot bust at Cornell. D. Sanford. New Repub
156:19-20 Ap 15 '67
THALER. See Money—Germany
THALIDOMIDE
Clue to the mechanism. Sci N 92:10-11 Jl 1 '67
THAMES RIVER, England
Cruising up or down the Thames. Sunset 138:
60 F '67
Ground water to bolster river flow and pre-
vent the use of valuable land for reservoirs.
C. E. Tiffen. il Am City 82:139+ S '67
THANE, Adele
Brave little tailor; dramatization of Grimms'
fairy tale. Plays 26:49-58 F '67
Cinderella; drama. Plays 27:57-68 O '67
Gift for Hans Brinker; dramatization of Hans
Brinker, or The silver skates, by M. M.
Dodge. Plays 27:61-6. 86 Ja '68
Heidi; dramatization of story by J. Spyri.
Plays 26:85-96 Mr '67
King Thrushbeard; dramatization of Grimms'
fairy tale. Plays 27:45-54 N '67
Merry Tyll and the three rogues; drama-
tization of a German folk tale. Plays 27:
33-41, 65 D '67
Rapunzel; dramatization of Grimms' fairy
tale. Plays 26:79-88. 96 F '67
Swineherd; dramatization of story by H. C.
Andersen. Plays 26:75-81 Mr '67
THANG, Nguyen-duc-. See Nguyen-duc-Thang
THANH, Nguyen-chi-. See Nguyen-chi-Thanh
THANKS to butter-fingers; drama. See Miller,
H L.
THANKSGIVING day
Exporting Thanksgiving; International Thanks-
giving fellowship program. A. Balk. Sat R
50:26 N 4 '67

Drama
First Thanksgiving. D. Newman. Plays 27:
75-8 N '67
Thanks to butter-fingers. H. L. Miller. Plays
27:35-44 N '67

Fiction
Prize pumpkin. R. P. T. Coffin. il PTA Mag
62:31-2 N '67

THANKSGIVING dinners
Change in the traditional Thanksgiving din-
ner; with recipes. il Sunset 139:86-7 N '67
Deluxe menu for holiday meals. il Good H
165:130-44+ N '67
Preparing a turkey dinner. Redbook 130:110 N
'67
Thanksgiving buffet. il Ebony 23:158+ N '67
Try turkey with a modern twist. G. Maddox.
il Todays Health 45:46-51 N '67
Turkey dinner, never easier than this. il Bet
Hom & Gard 45:92-3+ N '67
THANKSGIVING proclamations
Was God listening when we gave thanks?
President's Thanksgiving proclamation.
Christian Cent 84:1516 N 29 '67; Discussion.
85:29 Ja 3 '68
THANKSGIVING visitor; story. See Capote, T.
THANT, 1909-
Address of Secretary-General to convocation
of Pacem in terris II; text of address. UN
Mo Chron 4:83-6 Je '67
Address to OAU; summary. UN Mo Chron
4:26-7 O '67
Crisis; interview, with excerpts from reports.
New Yorker 43:19-21 Jl 29 '67
Denuclearization of Latin America; text of
message, January 31, 1967. UN Mo Chron
4:13-14 F '67
Exchange of messages; with officers and
men of UNEF, May 19, 1967. UN Mo Chron
4:59-61 Je '67
Human rights day 10 December 1967; message.
UN Mo Chron 4:iii-iv D '67
International day for the elimination of racial
discrimination; text of message. UN Mo
Chron 4:i-iii Mr '67
Introduction to the annual report of the
Secretary-General on the work of the or-
ganization. UN Mo Chron 4:93-137 O '67
Middle East crisis; address, June 27, 1967.
Vital Speeches 33:591-602 Jl 15 '67; Same
with title Withdrawal of UNEF. UN Mo
Chron 4:135-60 Jl '67
New Year message, 1967. UN Mo Chron 4:i-ii
Ja '67
Press conference at headquarters; September
16, 1967. UN Mo Chron 4:23-6 O '67
Press conference at headquarters; summary,
January 10, 1967 UN Mo Chron 4:11-13 F '67
Secretary-General's press conference; March
28, 1967. UN Mo Chron 4:67-77 Ap '67
Situation in Viet-Nam. UN Mo Chron 4:30
Mr' 67
Southern Rhodesia; report of Secretary-Gen-
eral. UN Mo Chron 4:13-14 Mr '67
Statement on population growth. UN Mo
Chron 4:105-6 Ja '67
Statement regarding Viet-Nam; May 11, 1967.
UN Mo Chron 4:56-9 Je '67
United Nations day 1967; message. UN Mo
Chron 4:iii-iv O '67
United Nations: the human factor; address,
July 30, 1967. Vital Speeches 33:724-7 S 15
'67; Same. UN Mo Chron 4:75-83 Ag '67;
Excerpts with title Is U Thant unfair to
U.S? por U S News 63:16 Ag 14 '67
United States accepts U.N. Secretary-Gen-
eral's proposal for ending the Viet-Nam
conflict; text of aide memoire, March 14,
1967. Dept State Bul 56:624-5 Ap 17 '67
U.S. reaffirms desire for peace in Viet-Nam;
exchange of letters with A. J. Goldberg,
December 30, 1966. Dept State Bul 56:138-9
Ja 23 '67

    about
Appeal to reason. Commonweal 86:275-6 My 26
'67
Appeals to reason. New Repub 156:8 Ap 8 '67
Did U Thant bungle the Middle-East crisis?
por U S News 62:19 Je 5 '67
Hanoi strengthens LBJ's hand. il por News-
week 69:31-2 Ap 10 '67
Inscrutable East side. Nat R 19:1054 O 3 '67
Light reaches Europe; condemnation of role
in Middle East crisis. E. Taylor. Reporter
36:12 Je 15 '67
Spokesman for the university. America 116:
621 Ap 29 '67
Stage manager for U.N.'s twilight hour? por
U S News 62:14 Je 12 '67
Story of forty-eight hours. M. Greenfield.
il Reporter 36:19-23 Je 15 '67
UNEF: U Thant's report. Reporter 37:18+ Jl
13 '67
Up with U Thant! Christian Cent 84:228-9
F 22 '67
Visit to Europe and Asia. UN Mo Chron 4:
29-32 My '67
THAT old college try; story. See Temple, W.
THAT summer, that fall; drama. See Gilroy,
F. D.
THAT'S why I loved Chauncey Meadors; story.
See Munson, G.

THAYER, Charles W.
American era ends in Germany. Look 31:
25-9 My 2 '67
Yugoslavia: the bellwether keeps turning
right. Read Digest 91:63-8 S '67

THAYER, Ernest Lawrence
Casey at the bat; excerpts from The an-
notated Casey at the bat. M. Gardner. il
Am Heritage 18:64-8 O '67

THAYER, Mary Van Rensselaer
Jacqueline Kennedy's years in the White
House; excerpts. McCalls 95:12-15+ D '67;
8-9+ Ja '68 (to be cont)

THEATER
Avant-garde images of America. A. Croce;
P. P. Witonski. Nat R 19:261-6 Mr 7 '67
Engineers had all the fun; nine evenings:
theatre and engineering. 69th Regiment
armory. D. Hering; reply. S. Lieberman.
Dance Mag 41:27 F '67
Teaching contemporary drama: existentialism
and the theatre of the absurd. R. M.
Weatherford. Sr Schol 90:sup7 Mr 17 '67
See also
Acting
Actors and actresses
Ballet
College theater
Comedy
Drama
Happenings (theater)
Mime
Shadow pantomimes and plays
Vaudeville

Bibliography
Bibliography of contemporary drama. Sr Scol
90:sup 14 Mr 17 '67
New books for teaching drama. J. L. Mersand.
Sr Schol 90:sup 18-19 Mr 17 '67

Costume
See Costume, Theatrical

Finance
What makes an angel successful; with editorial comment. il Bsns W p56-8+, 163 O 7
'67

History
See also
Theater—United States—History

Moral and religious aspects
Theatre goes to war; anti-war plays at off-
Broadway theater. C. Hughes. America 116:
759-61 My 20 '67
Theater of commitment; excerpt from address. E. Bentley; discussion. Commentary
43:6+ Mr '67

Political aspects
Actos: Teatro campesino, a theatrical part
of the United farmworkers organizing committee. New Yorker 43:23-5 Ag 19 '67
New grapes; el Teatro campesino (the Farm
workers' theater) performs for migrant
workers. il Newsweek 70:79 Jl 31 '67

Stage music
See Stage music

Stage scenery
Masked & bared; drawings from Duke of
Devonshire's collection of display at Wash-
ington's National gallery. il Time 89:82 Ap
14 '67
See also
Opera—Stage scenery

Afghanistan
Theatrical nights with the Afghans. G.
Wright. Sat R 51:91-2 Ja 13 '68

Cambodia
Shadows and light on the Ramayana. il
UNESCO Courier 20:34-5 D '67

Czechoslovakia
See also
Prague—Theater

England
See also
English drama

Europe
Anarchists of the anti-word; Living theater,
emigrants from off-Broadway. il Time 90:
93 D 1 '67
Becks in Paris; Living theatre, Paris production of Mysteries and smaller pieces. R.
Pasolli. Nation 205:540-1 N 20 '67

France
See also
Paris—Theater

Germany (Democratic Republic)
See also
Berlin (East Berlin)—Theater

Great Britain
Best of breed; Britain's national theater on
Canadian tour. il Time 90:64 N 3 '67
British theater: a sense of destiny. R. Gil-
man. il Newsweek 69:85-7 Ap 3 '67
Olivier triumphant; National theatre's pro-
duction of Strindberg's The dance of death.
H. Hewes. il Sat R 50:36 Jl 1 '67
See also
London—Theater

India
See also
Moving pictures—India

Italy
Before and after the deluge. R. Feist. America 116:151-3 Ja 28 '67
Theatre abroad. K. Tynan. New Yorker 43:
86+ O 21 '67

United States
APA'S big season. M. Gussow. il Newsweek
71:57 Ja 1 '68
Brewing with yeast; Repertory around the
country. H. Hewes. Sat R 50:47 Mr 25 '67
Rep comes high, but it's worth it. T. Prideaux.
Life 62:17 Je 2 '67
Repertory headaches. T. Lewis. America
117:284-5 S 16 '67
Theatre. T. Lewis. See issues of America
Trade winds; 1927 season. H. R. Mayes.
Sat R 50:14 S 9 '67
See also
American conservatory theatre
American drama
American theatre wing
Federal theater project
Theater, Negro
Yale university—Drama school
also subhead Theater under names of cit-
ies, e.g. Nashville, Tenn.—Theater

History
Plainsman and ballerina. L. Moore. il Dance
Mag 41:46-9 O '67

THEATER, Amateur. See Amateur theatricals

THEATER, Negro
Breaking new ground; Ford foundation grant
to establish Negro ensemble company. Newsweek 69:90 My 29 '67
Repertory; Negro ensemble company. il Time
91:40 Ja 12 '68

THEATER, Traveling
This stage goes where the action is: show-
mobile, Hoyt Lakes, Minn. A. Lohmann.
Am City 82:33 Mr '67
See also
American conservatory theatre

THEATER and state
Three giant steps; Dance magazine reports
on three government funded conferences;
symposium. Dance Mag 41:46-51+ Ag '67

THEATER architecture. See Theater buildings

THEATER Atlanta. See Atlanta—Theater

THEATER buildings
La Jolla's hourglass stage. H. Hewes. il Sat
R 50:38-9 S 23 '67
New theater: a center for Baltimore; Charles
center theater. J. M. Dixon. il Arch Forum
126:72-9 My '67
Uncolloquial colloquium; Canadian theatre
centre's international exchange of ideas on
design. H. Hewes. Sat R 50:45 Jl 15 '67
See also
Concert halls
Opera houses

THEATER conferences
Uncolloquial colloquium; Canadian theatre
centre's international exchange of ideas on
design of theaters. H. Hewes. Sat R 50:45
Jl 15 '67

THEATER festivals. See Drama festivals

THEATRE of the absurd. See Theater

THEATER programs
See also
Playbill (periodical)

THEATER tickets
Play's the costly thing. G. Ace. Sat R 50:8
Je 3 '67

THEATERS. See Theater buildings

THEATRICAL agencies
Power behind the 90 percent. il Newsweek
69:84-6 F 13 '67
Ten percenters of Hollywood. B. Wolfe. il
N Y Times Mag p26-8+ Je 18 '67

THEATRICAL costume. See Costume, Theatrical

THEATRICAL make-up. See Make-up, Theatrical

THEATRICAL photography. See Photography, Theatrical

THEATRICAL production
Follies of Broadway. J. O'Hara. Holiday 41: 23+ F '67
Hoofer; a musical in two acts; auditions for musical Henry sweet Henry. New Yorker 43:30-3 Je 10 '67
Looking for crummies; m.c. in musical Cabaret; interview. J. Grey. New Yorker 43: 34-6 Mr 4 '67
Memo to: the Dollys, from: David Merrick. il Time 90:44 Ag 11 '67
Playwright Tom Stoppard: go home British boy genius! debut of Rosencrantz and Guildenstern are dead. W. Hedgepeth. il Look 31:92-6 D 26 '67
R. and G, G, and R; interview. B. Murray; J. Wood. New Yorker 43:52 N 4 '67
Reflections on a Broadway flop; Mata Hari. R. Estrada. il Dance Mag 42:58-61 Ja '68
Run-through; rehearsal of Hellzapoppin '67 for Expo 67. New Yorker 43:21-2 Jl 8 '67
What makes an angel successful; with editorial comment. il Bsns W p56-8+, 163 O 7 '67
Where the pre-Nazis play; Cabaret. J. M. Flagler. il Look 31:72-4+ Mr 7 '67
See also
College and school drama
Dance production
Greek drama—Production, Modern
Operatic production
Shakespeare, William—Staging and acting of plays
Women as theatrical managers, etc.

THEATRICALS, Amateur. See Amateur theatricals

THEFT. See Shoplifting; Stealing

THEISEN, Earl
How to make portraits with warmth, meaning and interest. A. Rothstein. U S Camera 30:14+ F '67

THEISM
God and contemporary philosophy. J. Collins. Commonweal 85:528-34 F 10 '67

THELEN, Herbert A.
Matching teachers and pupils; excerpts from Classroom grouping for teachability. NEA J 56:18-20 Ap '67
What's new in grouping. PTA Mag 62:22-5 bibliog(p33) S '67

THELIN, Murray
One man's fight against hemophilia. P. Deutsch and R. Deutsch. il por Todays Health 45:40-3 Ag '67; Same abr. with title Doctor Thelin's fight against hemophilia. Read Digest 91:90-4 Ag '67

THEME writing. See English language—Composition

THEOBALD, Robert
Excerpt from address, December 9, 1966. Cong Digest 46:244+ O '67
Goal of full unemployment; excerpt from The guaranteed income. New Repub 156: 15-18 Mr 11 '67

THEODORAKIS, Mikis
Absent defendant. por Newsweek 70:52+ N 27 '67

THEODORE Roosevelt memorial island. See Washington, D.C.—Monuments, statues, etc.

THEODORE ROOSEVELT NATIONAL MEMORIAL PARK
Badlands and Teddy's park. G. M. Johnson. il Liv Wildn 31:20-7 Spr '67
Roosevelt memorial dedicated. il Parks & Rec 2:26-8 D '67

THEOLOGIANS
Credibility gap in theology. F. Kirschenmann. Christian Cent 84:498-500 Ap 19 '67; Discussion. 84:757 Je 7 '67
New theologian. by V. Mehta. Review
    Nation 204:188-9 F 6 '67. G. Vahanian
Open windows; southern exposure; scientists and theologians discussing science, religion and man's future. H. L. Smith. Christian Cent 84:1311-13 O 18 '67
Putting optimism to pasture. Christian Cent 84:885 Jl 12 '67

THEOLOGICAL education
Crisis in Canadian theological education. N. K. Clifford. Christian Cent 84:897-9 Jl 12 '67
Key term in theological education for the Negro; compensatory. H. H. Mitchell. Christian Cent 84:530-3 Ap 26 '67
Needs of theological education. Sch & Soc 95:174-5 Mr 18 '67
Seminary and preseminary education; analyses of two A.A.T.S. reports. T. C. Oden; L. G. Tait. Christian Cent 84:536+ Ap 26 '67

Theology in the American university; proposals for ecumenical theological courses. L. Swidler. Cath World 205:205-9 Jl '67
See also
Clergy—Education
Religious education
Theological schools

THEOLOGICAL libraries
Seminary library sets a high architectural standard for the archdiocese of Boston; St John's seminary. il Arch Rec 142:101-2 Ag '67

THEOLOGICAL school professors. See College professors and instructors

THEOLOGICAL schools
Alma moves to Berkeley. America 117:536 N 11 '67
Better training for a better clergy; American association of theological schools study. il Time 89:50 F 3 '67
Center for theological studies established in Rochester. Christian Cent 84:1342 O 25 '67
Ecumenical move at Berkeley; Graduate theological union. America 117:730 D 16 '67
Is there a new establishment of religion? R. E. Wentz. Christian Cent 84:463-5 Ap 12 '67
News: roundup; seminaries. Christian Cent 84:572-4 Ap 26 '67
Seminary community; a critique. L. B. Mead. Christian Cent 84:563+ Ap 26 '67
Seminary education: separate and unequal. R. J. McNamara. America 116:533-6 Ap 8 '67
Seminary library sets a high architectural standard for the archdiocese of Boston; St John's seminary. il Arch Rec 142:101-4 Ag '67
Southern Baptist seminaries challenged. G. H. Shriver, jr. Christian Cent 84:601-2 My 3 '67
Squeeze play; resignation of R. J. Arnott. Newsweek 69:61 Ja 30 '67
Toward fewer and better seminaries. Christian Cent 84:1147 S 13 '67; Discussion. 84:1403 N 1 '67
Upgrading the seminaries; Episcopal ministerial education program. Time 90:82 S 8 '67
What ought seminaries to be? E. A. Smith. Cath World 205:160-4 Je '67
Where the action is; need for Jesuit seminaries to move to urban academic centers. Newsweek 70:72 Jl 31 '67
See also names of theological schools, e.g. Christian theological seminary, Indianapolis

Curriculum
Literature in the divinity school. Time 90: 51 D 22 '67

Directories
Directory of seminary offerings. il Christian Cent 84:537-63 Ap 26 '67

THEOLOGICAL students
It'll be different; students from Holy Name seminary enroll at Edgewood, a Catholic women's college. America 117:366 O 7 '67
News and views; plan to involve seminarians in Peace corps opposed. Commonweal 86: 562 S 22 '67
Seminarians and Vietnam. Christian Cent 84: 1605 D 13 '67
Seminary education: separate and unequal. R. J. McNamara. America 116:533-6 Ap 8 '67
Theological students today. N. Pittenger. Christian Cent 84:527-9 Ap 26 '67
What ought seminaries to be? E. A. Smith. Cath World 205:160-4 Je '67

Aid
Financial aid for the theological student. W. A. Imler. Christian Cent 84:568+ Ap 26 '67

THEOLOGY
Adam's fall: the task of reinterpretation. M. Flick. Cath World 205:42-6 Ap '67
Canadian Catholics offer milestone conference on renewal. E. R. Fairweather. Christian Cent 84:1261-6 O 4 '67
Catholic looks at Bonhoeffer. W. Kuhns. Christian Cent 84:830-2 Je 28 '67
Comfortable idolatries; Protestant and Catholic fundamentalism. J. Opie, jr. Cath World 205:151-6 Je '67
Dangerous ambiguity; letter to the editor. R. Lawler. America 117:259 S 16 '67; Discussion. 117:397 O 14 '67
Empirical faith; ideas of J. A. Pike. Time 90:66 S 15 '67
Fabric of Paul Tillich's theology, by D. H. Kelsey. Review
    Christian Cent 84:473 Ap 12 '67. K. Hamilton

THEOLOGY—*Continued*
Faith and dogmatic pluralism. A. Dulles. America 116:728 My 13 '67; Reply. R. Philbin. 116:844 Je 17 '67
Frontline theology, ed. by D. Peerman. Review Christian Cent 84:310-12 Mr 8 '67. W. Ashby
God is evolving, not dead; with excerpt from If this be heresy, by J. A. Pike. K. S. Latourette. Sat R 50:45-6 S 16 '67
History and theology. R. H. Bryant. Christian Cent 84:944-5 Jl 19 '67
Hope in a posthuman era. S. Keen. Christian Cent 84:106-9 Ja 25 '67
Lutheran dogmatics. W. H. Lazareth. Christian Cent 84:1376-8 O 25 '67
Maritain asks some questions. J. Collins. America 118:29-32 Ja 13 '68
Peasant of the Garonne, by J. Maritain. Review
Cath World 204:368-71 Mr '67. T. Molnar
Nat R 19:696-7+ Je 27 '67. P. Burnham
Politics and the sacred; man's ambivalent concept of the sacred. T. Eagleton. Commonweal 87:402-6 D 29 '67; Reply. T. Merton. 87:479 Ja 19 '68
Refresher course in theology. C. Wessels. il America 116:648-9 Ap 29 '67
Requiem aeternam homini. R. E. Wentz. Christian Cent 84:113-14 Ja 25 '67
Secular and the sacred. R. F. Capon. il America 116:307-12 Mr 4 '67; Discussion. 116:515 Ap 8 '67
Secular ecumenism in action; excerpt from address, November 20, 1966. G. A. Lindbeck. Cath World 205:7-13 Ap '67
Systematic theology, by P. Tillich. Review New Repub 157:36-8 Ag 5 '67. R. Hazelton
Theological basis of the Geneva conference; World conference on church and society. P. Lønning. Christian Cent 84:270-1 Mr 1 '67
Theology: made in U.S.A. T. F. O'Meara. Cath World 205:231-6 Jl '67
See also
Angels
Christianity
Death of God theology
Eschatology
Free will and determinism
God
Good and evil
Heresy
Love (theology)
Mary, Virgin—Theology
Modernism
Protestantism
Religion and science
Revelation
Salvation
Secularism
Soul
Theism

Bibliography
Uncharted future of faith. R. Muska. Sat R 50:34-5+ Jl 22 '67

Study and teaching
At the feet of greatness; pastor-theologian K. Barth, at the University of Basel, Switzerland. J. C. Evans. Christian Cent 84:335 Mr 15 '67
Sell-out in college theology. D. O. Dugan. America 117:605+ N 18 '67
Theological ferment in Canada? J. A. Davidson. Christian Cent 84:900-2 Jl 12 '67
See also
Theological education
Theological schools
THEOLOGY, Doctrinal
See also
Mary, Virgin—Theology
THEOLOGY, Liberal. See Modernism
THEON, J. S. and others
Temperature measurement in noctilucent clouds. Science 157:419-21 Jl 28 '67
THEORETICAL astronomy. See Astronomy
THEORY of games. See Games, Theory of
THEORY of sets. See Algebra, Boolean
THERA (island)
Is this Atlantis? D. Cohen. il Sci Digest 62:66-9 O '67
Promise of Thera. E. Vermeule. Atlan 220:83-4+ D '67
Volcano that shaped the western world; Santorini eruption; theories of A. Galanopoulos. J. Lear; discussion. Sat R 49:93-4 D 3 '66; 50:74 F 4; 55-6 Ap 1 '67
THERAPEUTICS
See also
Drugs
Psychotherapy
Ultrasonic waves—Medical applications
also subhead Therapy under names of diseases, e.g. Cancer—Therapy

THERAPISTS, Physical. See Physical therapists
THEREMIN
Music à la theremin; all-electronic musical instrument. L. E. Garner, jr. il Pop Electr 27:29-33+ N '67
THERE'S a girl in my soup; drama. See Frisby, T.
THÉRÈSE, Sister Mary. See Mary Thérèse, Sister
THERMAL conductivity. See Heat conductivity
THERMAL-knit underwear. See Underwear
THERMAL pollution. See Sea water—Pollution; Water pollution
THERMIONIC converters
Energy converters readied for space, cars. Tech W 20:39 Ap 17 '67
THERMOCOUPLES
Inventor of the month, electricity for years; generator uses thermoelectric alloy. S. V. Jones. il Sci Digest 61:17 F '67
THERMODYNAMICS
Maxwell's demon. W. Ehrenberg. il Sci Am 217:103-10 bibliog(p 156) N '67
Perpetual motion machines. S. W. Angrist. il Sci Am 218:114-22 Ja '68
Surface tension and surface structure of water. W. F. Claussen. bibliog il Science 156:1226-7 Je 2 '67
Thermodynamics in Einstein's thought. M. J. Klein. bibliog Science 157:509-16 Ag 4 '67
THERMOELECTRIC generators. See Electric generators
THERMOELECTRICITY
See also
Thermocouples
THERMOGRAPHY, Infrared. See Photography, Infrared
THERMOLUMINESCENCE. See Luminescence
THERMOMAGNETISM
Tesla's thermomagnetic motor; demonstration device to show the effects of temperature on magnetism. A. S. Cookfair. il Pop Electr 25:70-1+ D '66
THERMOMETERS, Cooking
Mixing spoon-thermometer all in one. il Consumer Bul 50:40 Jl '67
THERMOMETERS and thermometry
Amateur scientist; sensitive electronic thermometer used for making a study in micrometerology. D. A. Kohl. il Sci Am 216:135-6+ Je '67
Choosing an outdoor thermometer. Good H 165:201 N '67
Temperature-depth measurements in the ocean. J. Althouse. il Electr World 78:33-6+ S '67
Temperature monitor; general utility temperature indicator. S. Horwitz. il Electr World 78:58 N '67
THERMONUCLEAR bombs. See Hydrogen bombs
THERMONUCLEAR reactions. See Nuclear fusion
THERMONUCLEAR war. See Atomic warfare
THERMOS containers
Vacuum bottles and insulated food jars. il Consumer Bul 50:34-8 My '67
THEROUX, Paul
On cowardice. Commentary 43:41-4 Je '67
THESES. See Dissertations, Academic
THEUS, Mrs Charlton M.
Furniture in Savannah. Antiques 91:364-9 Mr '67
Living with antiques. Antiques 92:194-7 Ag '67
THIAMINE. See Vitamins—Vitamin B1
THIBODEAU, Ralph
Church music revisited. Commonweal 86:204-6 My 5 '67
THICH Nhat Hanh. See Nhat Hanh
THICH Tri Quang. See Tri Quang
THIELKE, Rosemary
Our integrated Milwaukee neighborhood. America 117:566-7 N 11 '67
THIEME, Lars Werner
Portuguese people and places. U S Camera 31:74-5 Ja '68
THIEU, Nguyen-van-. See Nguyen-van-Thieu
THIEVES
Crooks in toyland; harbor thieves, Saigon. Newsweek 69:34 F 27 '67
See also
Burglary and burglars
Shoplifting
THIMBLES
Thimblemakers in America. E. G. Sickels. il Antiques 92:372-5 S '67
THIMMESCH, Nick
Metaphysics of automotive design. Esquire 68:188-9+ D '67
Young mayor seeks an answer in the ashes. Life 63:56+ Ag 11 '67

THINKING. See Thought and thinking
THIOPENTAL. See Pentothal sodium
THIRD committee of the General assembly.
See United Nations—Social, humanitarian
and cultural committee
THIRD girl; story. See Christie, A.
THIRD party movement. See Political parties
—United States; Progressive party
THIRRING, Hans
Can a scientist be a optimist? por Sat R
50:17-20+ O 28 '67
THIRRING, Josef Hans. See Thirring, H.
THIRST
Anticholinergic blockade of centrally induced
thirst. R. A. Levitt and A. E. Fisher;
reply with rejoinder. A. Routtenberg. bib-
liog il Science 157:838-41 Ag 18 '67
Neural correlates of food and water intake in
the rat. J. N. Coury. bibliog il Science 156:
1763-5 Je 30 '67
Polydipsia elicited by the synergistic action
of a saccharin and glucose solution. E. S.
Valenstein and others. bibliog il Science
157:552-4 Ag 4 '67
35mm films. See Photography—Films
THIS cursed fog; story. See Montaña, A.
THIS time tomorrow; story. See Schweitzer, G.
THOENES, Piet
Rebels from affluence: Provos of Holland. Na-
tion 204:494-7 Ap 17 '67
THOM, Robert
Montgomery Clift: a small place in the sun.
Esquire 67:104-5+ Mr '67
THOMAS Aquinas, Saint
See also
Thomism
THOMAS More, Saint. See More, T.
THOMAS, Alexander, and others
Persistent child; excerpt adapted from Tem-
perament and behavior disorders in chil-
dren. Parents Mag 42:35-7+ D '67
THOMAS, Ambroise
Hamlet. Criticism
New Yorker 43:164 My 13 '67
THOMAS, B. K. Jr
C-5A design refined to hit drag targets. Avia-
tion W 87:187+ N 20 '67
THOMAS, Bob
Is there a real Dean Martin? Good H 165:96-
7+ N '67
Racing's elusive pot of gold. Motor T 19:46-
8+ F '67
THOMAS, Charles Walker
First Negro president of the D.C. Board of
education: Wesley S. Williams. Negro Hist
Bul 29:177-8+ Fall '66
THOMAS, D. des S. and Mullins, J. T.
Role of enzymatic wall-softening in plant
morphogenesis: hormonal induction in
achlya. bibliog Science 156:84 Ap 7 '67
THOMAS, Danny
Marlo Thomas: That girl is some girl. B.
Rollin. il por Look 31:124+ O 17 '67
THOMAS, Delia
From Aardvark to Zymurgy. bibliog Li-
brary J 92:4582-6 D 15 '67
Matriarch of the nursery. bibliog Library J
92:1300-2 Mr 15 '67
THOMAS, Donald W. See Mayer, J. jt. auth.
THOMAS, Dorothy
Holy stove; story. Redbook 130:48-9 Ja '68
Violets are brief; story. Redbook 128:78-9 Ap
'67
THOMAS, Dylan
Books. H. Moss. New Yorker 43:185-9 O 7
'67
Fallen angel. S. Moss. New Repub 156:19-20
Je 10 '67
His beloved words. B. Read. Sat R 50:39 Jl
22 '67
Poems in embryo. M. L. Rosenthal. Sat R
50:24-5 D 30 '67
Prodigal. por Time 89:74+ Je 30 '67
THOMAS, Evan Welling, 1920-
Art of amiable persistence. il por Time 89:77
My 5 '67
Litmus with a voice. por Newsweek 69:98+
My 15 '67
THOMAS, John Charles
Affectionately recalled: John Charles Thomas.
P. L. Miller. Am Rec G 33:635 Ap '67
THOMAS, Kelly E.
Open door. Flying 82:93 Ja '68
THOMAS, Lately, pseud.
Tammany picked an honest man; excerpts.
Am Heritage 18:34-9+ F '67
THOMAS, Lowell Jackson, 1892-
Science map and guide to the U.S. por Pop
Sci 190:59-63+ Je '67
THOMAS, Marlo
Marlo Thomas: That girl is some girl. B.
Rollin. il pors Look 31:124+ O 17 '67

THOMAS, Mary P. R.
Never ending joy of shooting women. U S
Camera 30:52 F '67
THOMAS, Norman
Norman Thomas: a combative life. R. N.
Baldwin. New Repub 158:11-12 Ja 13 '68
Politics. D. MacDonald. Esquire 67:34-5 Mr '67
THOMAS, Paul
Hanuman, leader of the monkeys, beloved
by millions; excerpts from Epics, myths
and legends of India. UNESCO Courier 20:
16-17 D '67
THOMAS, Piri
From arson to a thousand candles. Sat R
50:78 S 23 '67
Nightmare night in *mi barrio*. N Y Times
Mag p 16-17+ Ag 13 '67
about
Exploration of color. W. Sloat. Sat R 50:33
Ag 5 '67
Knuckle-hard code of the barrio. M. Mad-
docks. Life 62:8 Ja 9 '67
Machismo. E. Bendiner. Nation 205:283-4 S
25 '67
THOMAS, Rachele
Challenge of fatherhood. Parents Mag 42:41-
3+ Je '67
New approach to discipline. Parents Mag 42:
58-9+ bibliog(p30) My '67
THOMAS, Richard L.
How to dismount from an elephant. Harper
234:102-3 My '67
THOMAS, Samuel W.
History in houses. Antiques 91:223-7 F '67
THOMAS, Stanley W.
Solid-state circuit breaker operates within
microseconds. Electr World 78:31 Jl '67
THOMAS, Will
Metalworking tricks on a jigsaw. Pop Sci
190:154-6 Je '67
THOMAS Cranmer of Canterbury; drama. See
Williams, C.
THOMISM
Belief and Mr Dewart. M. Novak. Common-
weal 85:485-8 F 3 '67; Discussion. 85:634+;
86:103 Mr 10, Ap 7 '67
Philosophy in the Catholic university. J.
Donceel; discussion. America 115:470-1; 116:
99+, 580-2, 767-8 O 22 '66, Ja 21, Ap 22,
My 27 '67
Truth of belief. E. MacKinnon. America 116:
554-6 Ap 15 '67
THOMPSON, Alice
Beauty at home. Am Home 70:22 Ja; 26 Mr '67
THOMPSON, Arthur Leonard Bell. See Clifford,
F. pseud.
THOMPSON, Benjamin
World around us: toward an architecture of
joy and human sensibility. Arch Rec 142:
153-8 S '67
THOMPSON, Betty
Leslie E. Cooke, ecumenical servant. Christian
Cent 84:334-5 Mr 15 '67
Philippe Maury, 1916-1967. Christian Cent 84:
806 Je 21 '67
THOMPSON, Diana Lee
Students weave and pattern future. Sch Arts
67:32-3 D '67
THOMPSON, Era Bell
Black leaders of the West Indies. Ebony 22:
76-82+ O '67
Japan's rejected. Ebony 22:42-4+ S '67
Profile of a prime minister. Ebony 22:124-8+
Ap '67
Surinam: multiracial paradise at the cross-
roads. Ebony 22:112-16+ F '67
THOMPSON, Hunter S.
Hashbury is the capital of the hippies. N Y
Times Mag p23-9+ My 14 '67
THOMPSON, J. C. and Margrave, J. L.
Chemistry of silicon difluoride; address, June
28, 1966. bibliog Science 155:669-71 F 10 '67
THOMPSON, J. Walter, company
New boss for the biggest. il Time 89:87 Je
23 '67
THOMPSON, James H. W.
Air of intrigue. Time 89:32+ My 5 '67
American abroad. il por Newsweek 69:54 Ap
10 '67
Walk in the jungle. il por Time 89:27 Ap 7 '67
THOMPSON, John
Observations. Commentary 44:81-5 N; 77-80
D '67
THOMPSON, Josiah
Cross fire that killed President Kennedy; ex-
cerpt from Six seconds in Dallas. Sat Eve
Post 240:27-31+ D 2 '67
about
Back to Dallas. por Time 90:54-5 N 24 '67
Life sues to enjoin book on assassination
of Kennedy. Pub W 192:32 D 25 '67
New assassination theory. il por Newsweek
70:29-30+ N 27 '67

THOMPSON, Kenneth W.
Bridge between two cultures. Sat R 50:62 Je
10 '67
THOMPSON, Lawrance
First love. Read Digest 91:55-8 Ag '67
THOMPSON, Lee (Eitingon)
Letter from the publisher. G. Valk. por
Sports Illus 26:4 F 27 '67
THOMPSON, Margaret W.
Genetic counseling. PTA Mag 61:12-15 F '67
THOMPSON, Margery. See Gow, J. S. jr, jt.
auth.
THOMPSON, Robert Farris
Esthetics in traditional Africa. Art N 66:44-5+
Ja '68
New voice from the barrios. Sat R 50:53-5+
O 28 '67
THOMPSON, Sir Robert Grainger Ker
Ten-to-twenty-year war in South Vietnam?
interview. ed. by J. Fromm. por U S News
62:92-4 F 13 '67
THOMPSON, Scott
Nigeria. Atlan 219:16+ Ap '67
THOMPSON, Sylvia Vaughn
Quenching crystals: granite. Vogue 151:151-
3+ Ja 1 '68
THOMPSON, Thomas
Cairo diary of U.S. humiliation. Life 62:70+
Je 23 '67
Highest paid, oldest unknown actor in the
world. Life 63:35-6+ N 3 '67
Mia. Life 62:75-81 My 5 '67
Never a champ like Nino. Life 62:78+ Je 2
'67
New far-out Beatles. Life 62:100-2+ Je 16 '67
What he did is nothing short of miraculous.
Life 63:51-2+ N 17 '67
Whatever happened to Elaine May? Life 63:
54-54B+ Jl 28 '67
World's best-paid writer. Life 63:49-50+ D
8 '67
THOMPSON, Tracy
Some kinship with the pigeons; poem. Chris-
tian Cent 84:719 My 31 '67
THOMPSON, William C.
Man who washed his hands Criticism
America 116:264 F 18 '67
THOMPSON Ramo Wooldridge, incorporated.
See TRW, incorporated
THOMPSONVILLE, Conn. See Enfield, Conn.
THOMS, Wayne
Second-hand super cars. Motor T 19:44-5 Je
'67
THOMSON, Helen
Take it easy with teen-agers. Todays Health
45:33-5 F '67
THOMSON, James Claude, 1931-
Dragon under glass: time for a new China
policy. Atlan 220:55-61 O '67
JFK's foreign policy. New Repub 157:23-6 Jl
15 '67
Minutes of a White House meeting, summer
1967. Atlan 219:67-8 My '67
THOMSON, Jean C.
(ed) Books to come. Library J 92:1341-79 Mr
15 '67
(comp) Children's paperbacks (cont) Li-
brary J 92:367-9 Ja 15 '67
THOMSON, Peggy
Tulip poplars and protozoa on the Chopa-
wamsic. NEA J 56:32-3 O '67
THOMSON, Roy Herbert, 1st baron Thomson
of Fleet. See Thomson of Fleet, R. H. T.
THOMSON, Virgil
Musician as writer. M. Steinberg. Commen-
tary 43:96-7+ My '67
Virgil. J. Ringo. por Am Rec G 33:460-3 F '67
THOMSON of Fleet, Roy Herbert Thomson,
1st baron
Into Britain's parlor with his hat on. D. Nor-
ton-Taylor. il por Fortune 75:136-9+ F '67
Strength in the afternoon. il por Time 90:45
S 8 '67
THOMSON organization, limited
Into Britain's parlor with his hat on: Lord
Thomson of Fleet. D. Norton-Taylor. il
Fortune 75:136-9+ F '67
THOR, Daniel E.
Delayed hypersensitivity in man: a correlate
in vitro and transfer by an RNA extract.
bibliog Science 157:1567-9 S 29 '67
THORAZINE. See Chlorpromazine
THÓRDARSON, Thórbergur
Sweet suffering in Iceland. P. M. Mitchell.
Sat R 50:58 N 11 '67
THOREAU, Henry David
From the Thoreauvian well. P. H. Oehser.
por Liv Wildn 30:27-9 Aut '66
Gift from Walden woods; with excerpts from
writings. W. Harding. il por Home Gard
54:29-36 D '67
Henry David Thoreau. R. J. Roth. America
117:761-3 D 23 '67
Thoreau lyceum founded. Liv Wildn 30:43
Aut '66

Trees, the original inhabitants. O. A. Ste-
vens. Am For 73:8+ F '67
Was Thoreau a hippie? P. Woodring. Sat R
50:68 D 16 '67
Who was Henry Thoreau? J. W. Krutch. il
Sat R 50:18-19+ Ag 19 '67
THORIUM
Primary oxidation variation and distribution
of uranium and thorium in a lava flow.
N. D. Watkins and others. bibliog il Sci-
ence 155:579-81 F 3 '67
THORNE, Joan
Each one had a home; poem. New Yorker 43:
28 Ja 6 '68
THORNE, Kip S.
Gravitational collapse; with biographical
sketch. Sci Am 217:20, 88-92+ bibliog(p
154+) N '67
THORNS, U. See Lindemann, B. jt. auth.
THORP, Nathan D.
On hearing the Epistle; poem. Christian Cent
84:1281 O 11 '67
THORPE, James
Understanding Anglo-American civilization.
por Wilson Lib Bul 41:580-5 F '67
THORPE, Jeremy
Yeasty man called Jeremy; interview. ed.
by J. Hicks. pors Life 62:37-8+ Je 2 '67
THORPE, Thomas
Good enough for Galileo. P. Boulay. Am Ed
4:15-18 D '67
THORSON, Thomas B. and others
Potamotrygon spp: elasmobranchs with low
urea content. bibliog Science 158:375-7 O 20
'67
THOSE wonderful shots of Killarney; story.
See Espy, H. C.
THOUGHT and language
Language and reality. R. W. Funk. Chris-
tian Cent 84:1378-9 O 25 '67
THOUGHT and thinking
Class of 1984 (now 5) looks ahead. O. Ryan
and B. Brodsky. il N Y Times Mag p6-7+
D 31 '67
Creative problem-solving course. D. J. Shall-
cross. NEA J 56:57 F '67
Discourse on thinking, by M. Heidegger. Re-
view
Commentary 44:106+ D '67. L. Abel
Man's new dialogue with man; Time essay.
Time 89:34-5 Je 30 '67
See also
Attention
Intellect
Problem solving
Reason
THOUGHT transference. See Telepathy
THREAD
Soluble basting thread. S. V. Jones. il Sci
Digest 62:80-1 Jl '67
THREADS, Screw. See Screw threads
THREATT, Frank
Deep South boss who hires ex-cons; with
report by R. Busch. il pors Life 63:38-40+
D 15 '67
THREE dimensional photography. See Stereo-
photography
THREE-dimensional television. See Television,
Stereoscopic
THREE wise men. See Magi
THREITOL
Heat inactivation of the relaxing site of
actomyosin: prevention and reversal with
dithiothreitol. H. M. Levy and E. M. Ryan.
bibliog il Science 156:73-4 Ap 7 '67
THRIFT
See also
Domestic finance
Saving and savings
THROAT
See also
Larynx
Diseases
See also
Goiter
THROMBOSIS
Clot that kills; how thrombi form. il Life 64:
30-1 Ja 19 '68
THROMBOSTHENIN. See Proteins
THROUGH-lens meters. See Exposure meters
THROWERS, Snow. See Snow blowers, throw-
ers, etc.
THRUSH, B. A.
Atom reactions in flow tubes. bibliog Sci-
ence 156:470-3 Ap 28 '67
THULINE, H. C. and others
Autosomal phosphogluconic dehydrogenase
polymorphism in the cat, felis catus L. bib-
liog Science 157:431-2 Jl 28 '67
THUMB, Tom. See Stratton, C. S.

THUMB sucking
Nail-biting and thumb-sucking: habit or need? B. Bettelheim. Ladies Home J 84:32 F '67

THUNA, Lee
Natural look. Criticism
New Yorker 43:121 Mr 18 '67

THUNDERSTORMS
Charge transfer between raindrops. J. D. Sartor and W. R. Atkinson. bibliog il Science 157:1267-9 S 15 '67

THURBER, F. B.
So Kit sank. Yachting 123:90+ Ja '68

THURBER, James
James Thurber, I love you. E. C. Acosta. il Sat Eve Post 240:88-9 My 20 '67

THURBER, Scott
Conservation comes of age. Nation 204:272-5 F 27 '67

THURMOND, Strom
Aircraft, the one indispensable arm of the entire anti-submarine warfare team. por Aero Tech 21:23-4 D 4 '67
Panama Canal; address, September 2, 1967. Vital Speeches 34:103-6 D 1 '67
Through the looking glass; address, February 15, 1967. Vital Speeches 33:343-8 Mr 15 '67

THYMES
Some good plants. R. C. Hands. Horticulture 45:61 F '67

THYMIDINE
Langerhans cells: uptake of tritiated thymidine. L. Giacometti and W. Montagna. il Science 157:439-40 Jl 28 '67
Tritiated thymidine: effect of decomposition by self-radiolysis on specificity as a tracer for DNA synthesis. M. Wand and others. bibliog il Science 157:436-8 Jl 28 '67

THYMINE
Ultraviolet irradiation of DNA in vitro and in vivo produces a third thymine-derived product. A. J. Varghese and S. Y. Wang. bibliog il Science 156:955-7 My 19 '67

THYMUS gland
Loss of thymus-distinctive serological characteristics in mice under certain conditions. M. Schlesinger and V. K. Golakai. bibliog il Science 155:1114-16 Mr 3 '67
Neoplastic transformation of rat thymic cells induced in vitro by Gross leukemia virus. H L. Ioachim. bibliog il Science 155:585-7 F 3 '67

THYNNE, Henry Frederick, 6th marquis of Bath. See Bath. H. F. T.

THYROCALCITONIN. See Thyroid extracts

THYROID extracts
Iodine determined in purified thyrocalcitonin. P. Blanquet and others. bibliog il Science 158:381-3 O 20 '67
Thyrocalcitonin: evidence for release in a spontaneous hypocalcemic disorder. C. C. Capen and D. M. Young. bibliog il Science 157:205-6 Jl 14 '67

THYROID gland
Creatine phosphokinase in thyroid: isoenzyme composition compared with other tissues. F. A. Graig and J. C. Smith. bibliog il Science 156:254-5 Ap 14 '67
Thyroid: your energy gland. Todays Health 45:14-15 Ap '67
See also
Goiter

THYROXINE
Thyroxine: effects of neonatal administration on maturation, development, and behavior. S. Schapiro and R. J. Norman. bibliog il Science 155:1279-81 Mr 10 '67
Thyroxine interaction with actinomycin D and possible biological implications. K. H. Kim and others. bibliog il Science 156:245-6 Ap 14 '67

THYSSEN, Fiona, baroness
Fiona's Paris favorites. il pors Life 62:91-7 Mr 3 '67

TIBBER, Robert
Food for love; story. Ladies Home J 84:80-1 Je '67

TIBET
Civilization
Vivid variety of India. L. Van Der Post. il Holiday 42:105-6+ N '67

TIBETAN art. See Art, Tibetan

TIBETAN bronzes. See Bronzes

TIC-TAC-TOE (game) See Games

TICK bites. See Insect bites and stings

TICKETS
Recordings; subscription series. M. Mayer. Esquire 69:36+ Ja '68
See also
Airlines—Tickets
Opera tickets
Theater tickets

TICKS
Spermatophore formation and sperm transfer in ornithodoros ticks. B. Feldman-Muhsam. bibliog il Science 156:1252-3 Je 2 '67

TICKTACKTOE. See Games

TIDAL marshes. See Salt marshes

TIDAL rhythms. See Periodicity

TIDAL waves. See Seismic sea waves

TIDBALL, Robert A.
Scale control cuts desalting costs. Am City 82:68-9+ Ja '67

TIDELANDS. See Submerged lands

TIDEROCK corporation. See Business consultants

TIDES
Deep-sea tides: a program. W. H. Munk and B. D. Zetler. Science 158:884-6 N 17 '67

TIEGEL, Eliot
Notes from our correspondents. Hi Fi 17:18+ Ag '67

TIEMANN, Norbert
New way to spell Nebraska. il por Time 89: 23 Ap 28 '67

TIEMPO, Edith L.
Our land & our sea & hallelujah. R. Roseliep. Poetry 111:189-90 D '67

TIEN, Nguyen-van-. See Nguyen-van-Tien

TIERRA DEL FUEGO
Frosty days in the land of fire. A. Hornos. Sat R 50:67-70 N 11 '67

TIFFANY, W. B. and others
Selective laser photocatalysis of bromine reactions. bibliog Science 157:40-3 Jl 7 '67

TIFFEN, C. E.
Ground water to bolster river flow. Am City 82:139+ S '67

TIGAR, Michael E.
In defense of Skelly Wright; letter. New Repub 157:41-3 Ag 5 '67

TIGER, Dick
Tiger hammers home a sermon. G. Rogin. il pors Sports Illus 27:24-6+ N 27 '67

TIGER or disciple; drama. See Giraudoux, J.

TIGERS (baseball) See Baseball clubs

TIJERINA, Reies Lopez
Incident in Rio Arriba. C. Kentfield. il por N Y Times Mag p20-1+ Jl 16 '67
Peace and peril at Ghost ranch. K. Haselden. Christian Cent 84:989-90 Ag 2 '67
Tijerina brass. il Newsweek 69:37-8 Je 19 '67
Tijerina; with interview. G. W. Grayson, jr. Commonweal 86:464-6 Jl 28 '67
Tijerina's Republic of San Joaquin del Rio de Chama. G. W. Grayson, jr. New Repub 157: 10-11 Jl 1 '67
Wild days again on the American frontier. il U S News 62:14 Je 19 '67

TIJMENS, Willem Jan
From an ancient desert relict to more elegant floral rarities; with biographical sketch. Natur Hist 76:7, 36-43 Ap '67

TILE floors. See Floors, Tile

TILE setting
Now you can lay a Spanish tile floor. A. Lees. il Pop Mech 127:106-9+ Je '67

TILES
Research shows how to construct successful tile-metal lath partitions. il Arch Rec 142: 181-2 N '67
See also
Rubber tiles

TILGHMAN, William Matthew
Last frontier marshal; condensation. F. Miller. il por Read Digest 90:201-4+ Je '67

TILLACK, Robert H.
Enclosed rotary switches. Electr World 78:39 O '67

TILLAGE
New tillage ideas stop soil blowing. D. Hagen. il Farm J 91:30+ N '67

TILLETT, Gladys A.
U.N. commission on the status of women holds 20th session. Dept State Bul 57:218-21 Ag 14 '67

TILLICH, Paul
Fabric of Paul Tillich's theology, by D. H. Kelsey. Review
Christian Cent 84:473 Ap 12 '67. K. Hamilton
Religion of Paul Tillich. M. Novak. bibliog f Commentary 43:53-65 Ap '67

TILLINGHAST, Richard
Pilot into poet. New Repub 157:28-9 S 9 '67
Seven poets. Poetry 110:258-66 Jl '67
Winter insomnia; Passage; poems. Poetry 110:394-6 S '67

TIME
See also
Present, The

Systems and standards
Selecting frequency and time standards. I. Math. il Electr World 77:40-1+ My '67

TIME (periodical)
He ran the course. il Time 89:28-33 Mr 10 '67
Letter from the publisher; man of the year.
J. R. Shepley. Time 91:11 Ja 5 '68
Quenchless me and omphalocentric you;
Time's man of the year, January 6, 1967. W.
K. Zinsser. il Horizon 9:120 Sum '67
TIME, Daylight saving. See Daylight saving
TIME, incorporated
He ran the course. il Time 89:28-33 Mr 10 '67
Henry Luce: founder publishing empire. U S
News 62:24 Mr 13 '67
Henry R. Luce: his Time and Life. il News-
week 69:68-70+ Mr 13 '67
Orderly succession: Henry R. Luce's will.
Newsweek 69:76 Mr 20 '67
Supreme court extends press freedoms in
overruling Desperate hours verdict.
Pub W 191:221 Ja 23 '67
Taking up where Luce left off. Bsns W p38
Mr 4 '67
Time inc. buys share in Mexican publishing
company. Pub W 191:91 Ja 30 '67
Time-Life's Story of great music. D. Hamil-
ton. il Hi Fi 17:59-62 D '67
    See also
General learning corporation
TIME and space. See Space and time
TIME compressor. See Magnetic recorders and
recording
TIME-delay switches. See Electric switches
TIME for the gentle people; drama. See Coble,
T.
TIME-Life international
Time-Life caper: Brazil's Yankee network;
infiltration of communications media. E.
Blum. il Nation 204:678-81 My 29 '67
TIME-Life records. See Time, incorporated
TIME limit relays. See Relays, Time limit
TIME measurements
How to build the magic box that goes click
. . . click . . . click. R. M. Benrey. il Pop
Sci 190:166-7 Mr '67
Third second; new definition. Sci Am 218:46
Ja '68
    See also
Sundials
TIME payment sales. See Instalment plan
TIME reversal
Time reversal search. Sci N 91:448 My 13 '67
TIME sharing computers. See Computers—Co-
operative use
TIMERS. See Timing devices
TIMES, London
Better than a backslap; by-lines. Newsweek
69:66 F 6 '67
Great haunch forward. Time 91:56 Ja 5 '68
Swinging lady. il Time 90:34-5 Ag 11 '67
TIMES, Los Angeles. See Los Angeles times
TIMES, New York. See New York times
TIMES-Mirror company
Meaning of monolopy. il Newsweek 69:67 Je 12
'67
Times-Mirror expands again. Time 89:47 Mr
10 '67
TIMING devices
Build a firing-range timer. C. F. Hadlock. il
Pop Electr 26:37-9 Je '67
Call timer for your telephone. R. F. Graf. il
Pop Sci 192:112-13 Ja '68
Elapsed time indicator. il Pop Electr 25:84
D '66
Suicide timer used on ERS; electrochemical
satellite destruct timers to silence trans-
mitters. Aero Tech 21:42 D 4 '67
Wide-range electronic timer. G. L. Jackson.
il Electr World 78:56-7 N '67
TIMMS, Edward H.
Man who knew Shakespeare. P. H. Johnson.
por Holiday 42:34+ N '67
TIN can sculpture. See Metal sculpture
TIN cans
    See also
American can company
Beer containers
Continental can company
TIN ware. See Tinware
TINIUS, Dan J.
Gales for Christmas. il por Motor B 120:39+
D '67
TINKER, Frank A.
Drive-aways. Travel 128:61-2+ O '67
TINNAPPEL, Harold
Hybrid peonies. il Horticulture 45:20-1+ My
'67
TINNEY, E. Roy
Engineering aspects. Bul Atomic Sci 23:21-5
S '67
TINSLEY, Russell
Texas brag lake. por Outdoor Life 140:42-3+
S '67

TINTYPES
Ferrotypes: gems on coated iron. il Pop Phot
60:99+ My '67
TINWARE
Tin collecting. M. H. Hommel. il Hobbies
72:98DD-98EE N '67
TIPPETT, Sir Michael
Music to my ears; production of King Priam
at Covent Garden. I. Kolodin. Sat R 50:24
Je 17 '67
Semblance of a resemblance. O. Daniel.
Sat R 50:113 O 14 '67
TIPPING
Dutch finger in the dike against tipping.
Life 63:4 D 15 '67
Intelligent woman traveler. F. Koltun. Mlle
64:203-4 Mr '67
TIPTON, Stuart Guy
Problems of prosperity; excerpts from ad-
dress. Aviation W 87:21 D 11 '67
    about
Airlines challenge general aviation fees. H.
D. Watkins. Aviation W 87:36-7 O 23 '67
Federal airport corporation urged. L. Doty.
Aviation W 87:16-17 S 4 '67
TIRE chains. See Chains
TIRE industry and trade
Akron turns onto a wider road. il Bsns W
p 184-5+ N 18 '67
    See also
Goodyear tire and rubber company
    Wages and hours
Tire makers roll again; industry lamenting
higher costs. il Bsns W p30 Jl 29 '67
TIRE valves
Must new tires have new valves? Consumer
Bul 50:30 D '67
TIREDNESS. See Fatigue
TIRES, Automobile
Akron turns onto a wider road. il Bsns W
p 184-5+ N 18 '67
And what are radials? D. Chu. il Sr Schol
90:32 My 12 '67
Are you neglecting the tires on your car?
il Good H 164:166 My '67
Better bone up on these new kinds of tires.
il Changing T 21:33-6 My '67
Can studs unchain winter drivers? R. Schill-
ing. il Motor T 19:80-1 F '67
Charlotte world 600. R. Brock. il Hot Rod
20:50-2 Ag '67
Fighting the fifth wheel; spare tires. il Time
89:73 F 3 '67
How the tire industry polices safety. Con-
sumer Rep 32:410-11 Ag '67
Radial-plies: a dramatic advance in tires.
P. W. Kearney. il Read Digest 90:129-32
Mr '67
Should unsafe tires be recalled? Consumer
Rep 33:5 Ja '68
Soon, federal rules for safer tires. U S News
63:11 Jl 31 '67
Stud tires for sportsmen. J. Chiappetta. il
Field & S 72:58-9+ S '67
Tires have changed, do you really know how
to make the right choice this year? D. L.
Gregg. il Bet Hom & Gard 45:54-5 Ag '67
What you should know about buying tires.
D. MacDonald. il Motor T 20:47-51 Ja '68
What's with those new tires? G. Booth. il
Pop Mech 128:96-9+ S '67
Where do you begin to shop for tires? il Good
H 156:128 Jl '67
World 600; the rub was in the rubber. B.
Myers. il Motor T 19:56-7 Ag '67
    Prices
Can you assure greater safety by buying the
most expensive tires? Consumer Bul 50:14
Ag '67
    Repairing
Which tire repair method to specify. D. L.
Gregg. Bet Hom & Gard 45:162-3 N '67
    Retreading and recapping
    See also
Tires, Motor bus—Retreading and recapping
    Testing
Instant check on tire pressure? Consumer Rep
32:186-7 Ap '67
130 mph on these tires? K. Vining. il Pop
Mech 128:120-2+ D '67
TIRES, Motor bus
    Retreading and recapping
How safe are regrooved tires? il Bsns W
p 184+ S 16 '67
    Testing
How safe are regrooved tires? il Bsns W
p 184+ S 16 '67

TIRES, Rubber
Radial-plies: a dramatic advance in tires. P. W. Kearney. il Read Digest 90129-32 Mr '67

TIRES, Tractor
Bigger tires for tractors? Suc Farm 65:72B Ja '67

TIROS (satellite) See Artificial satellites— Meterological applications

'TIS pity she's a whore; drama. See Ford, J.

TISHMAN realty and construction company
Stretching the skyline. il Time 91:58 Ja 12 '68

TISSUES
Calcified tissues; report on Gordon research conference. G. Nichols, jr. Science 157:961-2 Ag 25 '67
Collagen proline hydroxylase in wound healing, granuloma formation, scurvy, and growth. E. Mussini and others. bibliog il Science 157:927-9 Ag 25 '67
Distribution of circulation rates within a single tissue type. B. A. Hills. bibliog il Science 157:942-3 Ag 25 '67
Enzyme concentrations in tissues. P. A. Srere. bibliog il Science 158:936-7 N 17 '67
Toxohormone from normal tissues. J. Olivares and others. bibliog il Science 157:327-8 Jl 21 '67
See also
Embryonic tissues
Membranes (biology)

Culture
Adaptation of an insect cell line, Grace's antheraea cells, to medium free of insect hemolymph. C. E. Yunker and others. il Science 155:1565-6 Mr 24 '67
Cell aggregation: its enhancement by a supernatant from cultures of homologous cells. J. E. Liljen and A. A. Moscona. bibliog il Science 157:70-2 Jl 7 '67
Cell cultures; report on third annual meeting of Committee on cell cultures of the permanent section on microbiological standardization of the international association of microbiological societies. F. T. Perkins and L. Hayflick. Science 155:723-4 F 10 '67
Cell, tissue, and organ culture; report on second decennial review conference. M. F. Dolan. Science 156:672-3 My 5 '67
Collagen-coated cellulose sponge: three-dimensional matrix for tissue culture of Walker tumor 256. J. Leighton and others. bibliog il Science 155:1259-61 Mr 10 '67
Deuterium oxide: direct action on sympathetic ganglia isolated in culture. M. R. Murray and H. H. Benitez. bibliog il Science 155:1021-4 F 24 '67
Electrical recordings from meningioma cells during cytolytic action of antibody and complement. A. Prieto and others. bibliog il Science 157:1185-7 S 8 '67
Eosinophilic response in glioblastoma tissue culture after addition of autologous lymphocytes. J. Ciembroniewicz and O. Kolar. bibliog il Science 157:1054-5 S 1 '67
Human collagenase: identification and characterization of an enzyme from rheumatoid synovium in culture. J. M. Evanson and others. bibliog il Science 158:499-502 O 27 '67
Improved in vitro survival of normal, functional spleen cells. B. Mohit and G. H. Sato. bibliog il Science 157:449-51 Jl 28 '67
Lactic dehydrogenase and metabolism of human leukocytes in vitro. A. D. Bloom and others. bibliog il Science 156:979-81 My 19 '67
Metachromatic leukodystrophy. sulfatide lipidoses. cultured in vitro. H. Cravioto and others. bibliog il Science 156:243-5 Ap 14 '67
Phenotypic expression of transformation: induction in cell culture by a phorbol ester. A. Sivak and B. L. Van Duuren. bibliog il Science 157:1443-4 S 22 '67
Radiation chimeras and genetics of somatic cells. A Lengerová. bibliog il Science 155: 529-35 F 3 '67
Seizure discharges evoked in vitro in thin section from guinea pig hippocampus. C. Yamomoto and N. Kawai. bibliog il Science 155:341-2 Ja 20 '67
Stearic acid as plasma replacement for intracellular in vitro culture of plasmodium knowlesi. W. A. Siddiqui and others. bibliog il Science 156:1623-5 Je 23 '67
Transforming activity of green monkey SA7, C8 adenovirus in tissue culture. A. D. Alstein and others. bibliog il Science 158: 1455-7 D 15 '67
Vertebrate regeneration system: culture in vitro. S. B. Simpson, jr. and P. G. Cox. bibliog il Science 157:1330-2 S 15 '67

TISTOU of the green fingers; story. See Druon, M.

TITAN (boosters) See Space vehicles— Propulsion systems

TITANI, Koiti, and others
Evolution of immunoglobulins: structural homology of Kappa and Lambda Bence Jones proteins. bibliog Science 155:828-30+ F 17 '67

TITANIUM
Diffusion bonding techniques changing aerospace industry. J. F. Judge. il Tech W 20:28-31 My 1 '67
Fresnoite: unusual titanium coordination. P. B. Moore and J. Louisnathan. bibliog il Science 156:1361-2 Je 9 '67
New bonding process may cut titanium engine blade weight. Aviation W 86:37 Ap 3 '67
Russian titanium exports growing. Aviation W 87:20 Ag 21 '67

TITANIUM dioxide
Enthalpy of transformation of a high-pressure polymorph of titanium dioxide to the rutile modification. A. Navrotsky and others. bibliog il Science 158:388-9 O 20 '67
Shock-wave compression and X-ray studies of titanium dioxide. R. G. McQueen and others. bibliog il Science 155:1401-4 Mr 17 '67

TITLE; story. See Barth, J.

TITLES, Music. See Music titles

TITO
Now Tito cracks down on old-line Communists. il por U S News 64:93-4 Ja 15 '68
Tito the liberal, Tito the Stalinist. M. M. Mestrovic. Commonweal 85:477-8 F 3 '67
Titoism's failure. G. Bailey. il Reporter 36: 16-20 Ja 26 '67

TITUS, Harold
(ed) Conservation. See issues of Field & stream to December 1967

TIVOLI park. See Copenhagen—Parks and playgrounds

TKACHENKO, Vladimir
Confused case of the abducted Russian. il pors Life 63:30 S 29 '67
Mistaken identity. il por Newsweek 70:40+ O 2 '67

TO be an athlete; story. See Corfman, E. L.

TO clothe the naked; drama. See Pirandello, L.

TO find my heart again; story. See Kaufman, L.

TO keep your cool; story. See Amft, M. J.

TOAD venom. See Venom

TOADS
Mystery of Mima mounds. R. C. Davids. il Farm J 91:17 Ag '67
Plague of toads; bufus marinus. L. Gebhart. il Sci N 92:38-9 Jl 8 '67
See also
Frogs
Tadpoles

TOAST
Toast with the most; with recipes. il Ladies Home J 84:72 Mr '67

TOASTERS, Electric. See Electric toasters

TOBACCO
See also
Nicotiana
Smoking

Physiological effects
Antismoke signals. L. W. Sauer. PTA Mag 61:27-8 Ap '67
Drugs and tobacco; films. V. Falconer. Sr Schol 91:sup 16 N 16 '67
New warning for cigarette smokers. il U S News 63:40 S 4 '67
Search for a safer cigarette. G. Bylinsky. il Fortune 76:146-9+ N '67
Smoke signs: the signal remains red; excerpts from address. D. Horn. PTA Mag 62:25 S '67
Smoking & safety: Senate commerce subcommittee hearings to investigate progress of research. il Time 90:16-17 S 1 '67
See also
Smoking

TOBACCO Industry and trade
Where there's smoke; British government to abolish cigarette coupons. il Time 90:94 N 3 '67
While Salisbury bustles. il Time 89:68 Je 30 '67
See also
Cigarettes
Lorillard, P, company

Advertising
See also
Cigarettes—Advertising

TOBACCO mosaic virus
Antigenic study of the protein from a defective strain of tobacco mosaic virus. I. Rappaport and M. Zaitlin. bibliog il Science 157:207-8 Jl 14 '67

TOBACCO mosaic virus—*Continued*
Aucuba strain of tobacco mosaic virus: an unusual aggregate. H. E. Warmke. bibliog Science 156:262-3 Ap 14 '67
TOBACK, James
Norman Mailer today. Commentary 44:68-76 O '67
TOBAGO
See also
Trinidad and Tobago
TOBIAS, Marc Weber
Get more VHF on AM/FM transistor radios. Pop Electr 26:35-6 Je '67
TOBIN, James
Do we want children's allowances? New Republic 157:16-18 N 25; 17 D 23 '67
Excerpt from address, December 9, 1966. Cong Digest 46:250+ O '67
It can be done! New Repub 156:14-18 Je 3 '67
We can do better than this; excerpt from address, February 16, 1967. New Repub 156:17-18 Mr 4 '67
TOBIN, Richard L.
(ed) Communications. See issues of Saturday review
Ends of the earth. Sat R 50:25-6 Jl 1 '67
Hunger is the big story. por Cath World 205:26-30 Ap '67
Like your cigarette should; reprint. Writer 80:34 Ja '67
Ring of the Piper's tune. Sat R 50:72-3 Mr 25 '67
They lost the war in one battle. Sat R 50:23-4 S 2 '67
When dynamite rains from the sky. Sat R 50:18-19 Ag 5 '67
TOBOGGANS and tobogganing
Tobogganing in your shirtsleeves; chutes in Cleveland's Rocky River reservation. O. D. Graham. il Parks & Rec 2:23+ My '67
TOCH, Hans
Last word on the hippies. Nation 205:582-8 D 4 '67
TODAK, Joseph. See Zirlin, S. jt. auth.
TODAS (tribe) See India—Native races
TODD, Carl David
Stable, low-cost reference power supplies. Electr World 78:39-41+ D '67
TODD, John H. and others
Chemical communication in social behavior of a fish, the yellow bullhead (ictalurus natalis) bibliog Science 158:672-3 N 3 '67
TODD, Richard
Eastern view of Stanford: from ivy to eucalyptus. Harper 235:83-8 Ag '67
TODDIE, Jean
Lady with the lute; story. Seventeen 26:160-1 S '67
TOES
Anecdotes, facetiae, satire, etc.
How strong the toes? H. A. Smith. il Sat R 50:4+ N 18 '67
TOFFEE. See Candy
TOFFLER, Alvin
Art of measuring the arts. Ann Am Acad 373:141-55 S '67
TOGGLE switches. See Electric switches
TOGO

Commercial treaties and agreements
Ratifications exchanged with Togo on commercial treaty. Dept State Bul 56:181 Ja 30 '67
TOILET
See also
Beauty, Personal
Perfumery
TOILET articles
Beauty aids for the Sybarite in you. il House & Gard 132:57-8 N '67
TOILET preparations
Checking out the men. Vogue 149:64+ Je '67
Give beauty for Christmas. Am Home 70:28+ D '67
How Gillette has put on a new face; diversified product line. il Bns W p58-60+ Ap 1 '67
See also
Cosmetics
Deodorants
Shampoos
TOILET water. See Perfumery
TOILETS
How to repair your toilet tank. G. Daniels and L. Weaver. il Pop Sci 190:169-74 Ap; 169-73 My '67
TOJO, Hideki
Lonely goose. S. K. Oberbeck. por Newsweek 70:93 Jl 17 '67
TOKAIDO. See Japan
TOKAIDO line. See Railroads—Japan

TOKLAS, Alice B.
Alice B. Toklas. G. A. Harrison. New Repub 156:24+ Mr 18 '67
Grave of Alice B. Toklas. O. Friedrich. il Esquire 69:98-103+ Ja '68
Letter from Paris. Genêt. New Yorker 43:174+ Mr 25 '67
Obituary
Pub W 191:42 Mr 20 '67
Together again. por Time 89:34+ Mr 17 '67
TOKSÖZ, M. Nafi, and Arkani-Hamed, J.
Seismic delay times: correlation with other data. bibliog Science 158:783-5 N 10 '67
TOKYO

Architecture
Skyline changes; Japan's first skyscraper able to resist earthquakes. S. Griffin. il Sci N 92:85 Jl 22 '67

Crime
How world's biggest city keeps crime rate low. il U S News 63:75-6 O 9 '67

Elections
Tangled Tokyo; gubernatorial campaign. il Newsweek 69:50-2 Ap 24 '67

Hotels, restaurants, etc.
Deathwatch in Tokyo; O. Wright's efforts to save husband's Imperial hotel. F. Riley. Sat R 50:40+ D 16 '67
Down comes the landmark; Imperial hotel. il Time 90:90 D 8 '67
Remember the Hilton; Tokyo Hilton hotel take-over. Newsweek 69:84-5 My 8 '67

Music
Tokyo. E. C. Wilkes. il Opera N 31:32-3 Mr 11 '67
Tokyo; Italian opera sponsored by NHK, the government-owned Japanese radio-TV network. E. C. Wilkes. Opera N 32:28 N 25 '67

Parks and playgrounds
Reporter at large; Ueno zoological garden and Tama zoological park. E. Kahn. New Yorker 43:110+ S 23 '67

Rapid transit
Why the latest monorail fell flat on its face. il Bsns W p118-19+ F 18 '67

Social conditions
Tangled Tokyo. il Newsweek 69:51-2 Ap 24 '67

Transportation
See also
Tokyo—Rapid transit
TOKYO Shibaura electric company. See Electric apparatus industry
TOLANSKY, S. and Komatsu, H.
Abundance of type II diamonds. Science 157:1173-5 S 8 '67
TOLBERT, Frank X.
(ed) See Taylor, H. T. Negro millionaire's advice to his race
TOLEDO, Ohio

Newspapers
Sigh of relief in Toledo; strike settled. Time 89:64 Mr 24 '67
TOLERATION
Religious intolerance; aborted International convention on the elimination of religious intolerance. America 117:672 D 2 '67
Tolerance draft collapses; United Nations statement on religious tolerance. Christian Cent 84:1517 N 29 '67
TOLKIEN, John Ronald Reuel
Smith of Wootton Major; story. Redbook 130:58-61 D '67

about
Can America kick the hobbit? C. Elliott. Life 62:10 F 24 '67
Lord of the rings. R. A. Schroth. America 116:254 F 18 '67
Tolkien & Hesse: top of the pops. R. Sklar. Nation 204:598-601 My 8 '67
Why Frodo lives. J. Crist. Ladies Home J 84:58 F '67
TOLKMITH, Henry, and others
Imidazole: fungitoxic derivatives. bibliog Science 158:1462-3 D 15 '67
TOLL roads
Toll roads: are too many being built? U S News 63:14 S 11 '67
TOLL television. See Television broadcasting—Subscription programs
TOLMAN family
Bog; Rockland Bog, Me. L. Dietz. il Field & S 72:56-7+ My '67
TOLNAY, Thomas
Matter of time; poem. Christian Cent 85:77 Ja 17 '68

TOLSTOI, Lev Nikolaevich, graf
How much land does a man need? dramatization. See Leech, M. T.
War and peace; dramatization. See Neumann, A. and others
about
Tolstoy, by H. Troyat. Review
Atlan 220:142+ D '67. O. Handlin
Harper 235:108+ D '67. J. Kaplan
Life 63:8+ D 8 '67. W. Schott
Newsweek por 70:103+ D 18 '67. S. Maloff
Time il 90:79 D 22 '67
War and peace. K. Rexroth. Sat R 50:10+ N 11 '67

TOLSTOY, Leo. See Tolstoi, L. N.

TOM Jones (literary, character) See Characters in literature

TOM Thumb. See Stratton, C. S.

TOM Tinker Ellis; story. See Moray, A.

TOMAJAN, William H.
Color inventions. Sch Arts 66:29-30 Ja '67

TOMALIN, Nicholas
Theater. Nat R 19:702-3 Je 27 '67

TOMASZ, Alexander
Choline in the cell wall of a bacterium: novel type of polymer-linked choline in pneumococcus. bibliog Science 157:694-7 Ag 11 '67

TOMATO sauce
Tomato sauce primer. M. Hudson. Am Home 70:108 N '67

TOMATOES
See also
Cookery—Vegetables

TOMBOY and the dragon; drama. See Miller, H. L.

TOMBS
De mortuis. J. H. Plumb. il Horizon 9:40-1 Spr '67
See also
Taj Mahal

TOMBSTONES. See Sepulchral monuments

TOMCIK, Dan
Varitone electronic saxophone. Electr World 77:30+ F '67

TOMKIEVICZ, Shirley
Lost city of Pajaten. Horizon 9:62-7 Aut '67

TOMKINS, Calvin
Human comedy: the love wave. Sat Eve Post 240:16 S 9 '67
Man and whose world? New Yorker 43:24 Ag 26 '67
Profiles; J. Levine. New Yorker 43:55-6+ S 16 '67
Profiles; S. B. Gould. New Yorker 43:67-8+ N 18 '67

TOMLINSON, Charles
Way of a world; Clouds; Words for the madrigalist; Logic; On the principle of blowclocks; End; Rumour; Beautiful aeroplane; poems. Poetry 111:67-75 N '67
—and Gifford, Henry
Versions of César Vallejo; poem. Poetry 109:229-34 Ja '67

TOMPKINS, John S. See Finney, P. B. jt. auth.

TOMPKINS square
Mathematical games; beauties of the square. M. Gardner. il Sci Am 218:124-6 Ja '68

TONE dialing. See Telephone, Dial

TONET furniture. See Furniture, Bentwood

TONGA (islands)
Hail to the new king of Tonga. J. Bonfante. il Life 63:58-65 Jl 21 '67
Tongans respond to Alan Walker mission; youth convention plus mission. H. R. Henderson. Christian Cent 84:416+ Mr 29 '67
What a king should be; coronation of Tupou IV. il Time 90:32 Jl 14 '67

TONGASS national forest, Alaska. See National forests

TONINI, Dino
Anatomy of the flood. UNESCO Courier 20:35-8 Ja '67

TONKIN GULF, Battle of. See Vietnamese crisis, 1964

TONSOR, Stephen J.
Conservatism and history. Nat R 19:700-1 Je 27 '67
Passional I. Nat R 19:208-10 F 21 '67
Prophet of modernity. Nat R 20:41-3 Ja 16 '68

TONY awards. See American theatre wing

TONY party (Great Britain) See Conservative party (Great Britain)

TOO bad, so sad; story. See Kjelgaard, B.

TOOF, Mary E.
Traveler's choice. Travel 127:9 My '67

TOOKER, D. K.
I'm the second-luckiest pilot alive. Read Digest 91:64-9 O '67

TOOKER, Frank H.
Build the R-matcher. Pop Electr 27:84 N '67
Low-cost high-quality electronic voltmeter. Pop Electr 27:57-61+ N '67
Throw together a Quintupler. Pop Elecr 28:64 Ja '68

TOOKER, George
Contemporary Florentine; exhibition at Manhattan's Durlacher bros. gallery. il por Time 89:72 Ap 21 '67

TOOL boxes, racks, etc.
Rattle-free case for car tools. P. McCafferty. il Pop Sci 191:130-1 N '67

TOOL cases. See Tool boxes, racks, etc.

TOOL holders. See Holding devices (machine work)

TOOLS
Cutting, punching and drilling of printed circuit boards. A. Adel. il Pop Electr 28:57-9 Ja '68
Du Pont's slick new Teflon-S; coated tools. H. Shuldiner. il Pop Sci 191:136-8+ D '67
New tools for home upkeep. il Pop Sci 191:164-5 O '67
Roundup of new tools for home and workshop. il Pop Sci 190:152-3 Ja '67
Shop talk. R. P. Stevenson. See issues of Popular science monthly
Shopping for tools. See occasional issues of Popular mechanics
Special tools you may not have heard of. il Pop Sci 191:134-5 Ag '67
Tools from wire. W. E. Burton. il Pop Mech 128:168-9 Jl '67
See also
Electric tools, Portable
Garden tools, equipment and supplies

Care
How to take care of your home-care tools. J. Burroughs. il Pop Sci 190:202+ Ap '67

TOOMEY, Bill
All dressed up and fit to kill. J. Underwood. il por Sports Illus 26:24-6+ Je 19 '67

TOOP, Nicole S.
Light-hearted entertaining on a gold-plated shoestring. Parents Mag 42:78-9+ O '67

TOOTH powders and pastes. See Dentifrices

TOOZE, Ruth (Tibbits)
Can the forces of virtue defeat John Barleycorn? W. Kloman. il por Sat Eve Post 240:85-9 Mr 11 '67

TOPAZ; story. See Uris, L.

TOPEKA, Kan.
Twenty-two minutes over Topeka . . . E. D. Fales, jr. il Pop Mech 127:82-7+ Mr '67

Education
Fitness time in Topeka. J. Corcoran. il Am Ed 3:21-3+ S '67

TOPEKA, Kan. zoological park. See Zoological gardens

TOPEROFF, Sam
Errata for fall; poem. Atlan 220:120 D '67
Orpheus devises a plan; poem. Atlan 220:94 Ag '67
They never sleep. Atlan 220:77-80 O '67

TOPIARY work
Portable topiary. il House & Gard 133:124-5+ Ja '68
Topiary & espalier. il Home Gard 54:27-34 O '67

TOPOGRAPHICAL surveying
See also
Military topography

TOPOGRAPHY, Military. See Military topography

TOPPER, Harvey
Special assignment: creative arts in the disadvantaged elementary school. Sch Arts 66:5-8 F '67

TOPPER, Yale J. See Voytovich, A. E. jt. auth.

TORK, Peter
Monkee talk; interview, ed. by E. Miller. por Seventeen 26:303+ Ag '67

TORKELSON, Emily A. See Torkelson, G. M. jt. auth.

TORKELSON, Gerald M. and Torkelson, E. A.
How mechanized should the classroom be? NEA J 56:28-30 Mr '67

TORNABENE, Lyn
I passed as a teenager; excerpts. por Ladies Home J 84:113-18 Je '67
about
Adult spy goes to high school. il pors Life 62:97-8 My 5 '67

TORNADOES
Electric currents accompanying tornado activity. M. Brook. bibliog il Science 157:1434-6 S 22 '67

TORNADOES—*Continued*
Ill wind in Indiana. J. P. Blank. il Read Digest 90:66-71 Mr '67
Time of the twisters; Midwest aftermath. il Newsweek 69:28 My 1 '67
Tornadoes, a mystery. il Sci N 91:422-3 My 6 '67
Tornadoes: mechanism and control. S. A. Colgate. bibliog il Science 157:1431-4 S 22 '67
Tornadoes: puzzling phenomena and photographs. L. B. Loeb. Science 155:1037 F 24 '67
Twenty-two minutes over Topeka . . . E. D. Fales, jr. il Pop Mech 127:82-7+ Mr '67
University in a windstorm; Washburn university, Topeka, Kan. A. F. Engelbert. il Sch & Soc 95:119-21 F 18 '67
TORNEK, Terry Eliot
DRIVE: teamsters in politics. Nation 203: 663-5; 204:194 D 19 '66, F 13 '67
TORONTO
Description
Going places, finding things in Montreal and Toronto. J. Wilson. il House & Gard 132:28+ Ag '67
Hospitals
Quo vadis: R for the nursing shortage. D. MacDonald. il Read Digest 91:15-16+ S '67
Music
See also
Toronto symphony orchestra
Politics and government
Metro: Toronto's answer to urban sprawl. J. N. Miller. Read Digest 91:85-9 Ag '67
Streets
Quick-set slurry replaces sand seal. A. W. Pellegrino. il Am City 82:109-12 Ap '67
TORONTO Maple Leafs (hockey team) See Hockey teams
TORONTO public library
Second thoughts about Victorian children's fare. J. St John. il Wilson Lib Bul 41:590-2 F '67
TORONTO symphony orchestra
Musical events; concert in Carnegie Hall; conducted by S. Ozawa. W. Sargeant. New Yorker 43:169 Ap 15 '67
TORONTO, University
Preview of Toronto. J. K. Hutchens. Sat R 50:28-9+ Je 10 '67
TORONTO university press
AAUP: short-run production for books and journals; summary of address, June 12, 1967. R. Gurney. il Pub W 192:66-7+ Jl 3 '67
Preview of Toronto. J. K. Hutchens. Sat R 50:28-9+ Je 10 '67
University of Toronto relocates its press. il Pub W 191:80-2+ F 6 '67
TORPEDOES
Civil war torpedo. il Hobbies 72:127 Ag '67
TORRANCE, J. W.
I joined about flyin' from dat; reprint. Flying 80:6 Mr '67
TORRANCE, Calif.
Anyone for singles? South Bay club. il Newsweek 69:70 My 8 '67
TORREALBA JUAREZ, Carlos T.
Pajatén: a lost city found. R. Wood. il pors Américas 19:7-16 Je '67
TORRES, Camilo
Case of Camilo Torres: the problem of obedience. C. Sussman and I. Sussman. Cath World 204:356-61 Mr '67
Latin America: rise of a new non-Communist left. G. A. Geyer. por Sat R 50:22 Jl 22 '67
Synod of bishops and dissent. J. B. Sheerin. Cath World 206:98-9 D '67
TORREY Canyon (tanker) See Shipwrecks
TORREY pine. See Pine
TORS, Ivan
King of the beasties. il por Time 89:67-8 Je 16 '67
Lovingest animal lover. il pors Life 63:41-2+ S 29 '67
TORTILLA press. See Kitchen utensils
TORTILLAS
See also
Cookery, Mexican
TORTUGAS, Fla. See Dry Tortugas
TOSCA; opera. See Puccini, G.
TOSCA (operatic character) See Characters in opera
TOSCANINI, Arturo
Appointment in Milan. G. R. Marek. il Hi Fi 17:42-7 Mr '67
Convegno Toscanini. I. Kolodin. il Sat R 50: 34+ Jl 1 '67
Divine autocrat. M. Davenport. il pors Opera N 31:6-13 Mr 25 '67

First hundred years of Toscanini; symposium. il pors Sat R 50:53-63 Mr 25 '67
Forum for Toscanini. J. W. Freeman. il Opera N 32:6-7 S 9 '67
Imperfect and nonpareil. R. Gelatt. Reporter 37:39-40 D 28 '67
In life a Democrat, in the arts a dictator. il por Sr Schol 90:3+ Mr 10 '67
Maestro at 100. C. J. Luten. il Am Rec G 33:720-1 My '67
Maestro's century. por Newsweek 69:109 Mr 27 '67
Salute from the ranks. il por Time 89:80+ My 5 '67
Toscanini celebration, Italian style. G. R. Marek. il por Hi Fi 17:MA26-7 Je '67
Toscanini legacy. Hi Fi 17:41 Mr '67
Toscanini reissues. C. J. Luten. por Am Rec G 33:998-1000 Jl '67
Toscanini reissues, a tribute at last honorably paid. B. H. Haggin. por Hi Fi 17:71-2 Ag '67
Toscanini treasury of historic broadcasts. B. H. Haggin. por Hi Fi 17:73-5 Je '67
World-wide calendar of Toscanini observances. Sat R 50:65 Mr 25 '67
Bibliography
Toscanini bibliography; comp. by R. Jacobson. Sat R 50:64-5 Mr 25 '67
TOSI, Henry L.
Administrators' development program. por Wilson Lib Bul 42:406-10 D '67
TOSTADAS. See Cookery, Mexican
TOTA, LAKE
Save some time for Lake Tota; Colombia. il Sunset 139:32+ N '67
TOTALITARIANISM and literature
Reactionaries, by J. Harrison. Review
Commentary 44:82+ Ag '67. D. Donoghue; Reply with rejoinder. C. M. Silverman. 44:8+ N '67
Nat R il 19:809+ Jl 25 '67
New Repub 157:19-20+ S 16 '67. I. Howe
TOTEM poles
Alaska's vanishing art (cont) K. Kuh. Sat R 50:23+ Mr 25 '67
TOTH, Stephen M.
Discovery. J. Scully. il Mod Phot 31:68-9+ My '67
TOTH, William J.
Most from your automobile. See issues of American home
TOUCH
Ears and eyes in your skin. A. J. Snider. il Sci Digest 61:75-6 Je '67
Vision and touch. I. Rock and C. S. Harris. il Sci Am 216:96-104 bibliog (p 167) My '67
TOUCH football
It was only a game of touch. G. V. Packard. il Sports Illus 27:108-10+ S 18 '67
TOUCH of magic; story. See Jensen, E.
TOUPES. See Wigs
TOUR d'argent (restaurant) See Paris—Hotels, restaurants, etc.
TOUR de France (bicycle race) See Bicycle racing
TOURAINE festival. See Music festivals—France
TOUREL, Jennie
And we quote; ed. by S. Fleming. por Hi Fi 17:MA19 D '67
TOURING ballet companies. See Ballet companies
TOURIST blight. See Landscape protection
TOURIST trade
Call of the world. il Time 89:86-7 Ap 28 '67
Capital place for tourists. il Bsns W p 122-4 Ag 5 '67
Coming battle of the gaps; conflicting pressures of the travel, technological gaps and gold gaps. W. D. Patterson. Sat R 51:24+ Ja 6 '68
Far-off places are calling again. il Bsns W p 176+ My 20 '67
Going abroad this winter? do's, don't's and prices for travelers. il U S News 63:104-6 N 13 '67
Mike Frome. M. Frome. Am For 73:3+ Je '67
Minority report. F. P. Keyes. Travel 127: 58-9+ Mr '67
Peaceful traveler in a fractious world; symposium. il Sat R 50:37-48+ O 14 '67
Trip abroad? what to expect. il U S News 62:70-4+ Ap 24 '67
Twenty years of travel; symposium. il Sat R 50:27-33+ Ap 22 '67
See also
Travel—Economic aspects
Travel agencies
Africa
Natural world; East Africa. O. Prescott. il Sat R 50:42-3 S 2 '67

TOURIST trade—*Continued*

Africa, East
Well traveled camera. H. Keppler. il Mod Phot 31:142+ D '67

Alaska
One way to plan an Alaska trip is to put air, sea, and land legs together. il Sunset 138:28 Mr '67

Bahama Islands
Travel notes. R. Joseph. Esquire 67:60+ Mr '67
Traveler, consider my Bahamas. ; interview, ed. by R. Joseph. B. Ives. il Esquire 67:120-1+ Mr '67

Black Sea Region
Red Miami on the Black Sea. il U S News 63:84-5 Ag 28 '67

Caribbean Region
Boom in the Caribbean. A. Waugh. Nat R 19:86+ Ja 24 '67
100 ways of summer traveling in the West Indies and Mexico. T. Van Doren. Mlle 65:190-4 My '67

Cuba
Biologist visits Cuba. G. C. Gorman. Science 156:889 My 19 '67

Egypt
Plight of tourist guide no. 25. A. Carthew. il Sat R 50:42-3 O 14 '67

Europe
Times are changing in Europe, too. il Changing T 21:45-6 S '67
Unbelievable explosion; adaptation of address. L. Harris. il Sat R 51:43-4+ Ja 6 '68

Europe, Western
Traveling with Mlle: Europe on the cheap. L. Gottlieb. il Mlle 64:165-72+ F '67

Far East
Gold rush over Pacific; for tourist traffic. il U S News 62:88-9 Mr 6 '67
Latest boom in travel. il U S News 63:90-2 O 9 '67

Fiji
They left Pan Am for riches in Fiji. il Bsns W p82-3+ S 16 '67

France
Caveat tourist; new rules for tourist discount. Time 90:107-8 D 8 '67
Gaullism empties bistros; slump in tourism. il Bsns W p92-3 S 2 '67

Greece, Modern
Mail from Athens. R. Goodman. Sat R 50:46 O 14 '67
Troika and the tourists. T. L. Christie. il Sat R 50:44-6 O 14 '67

Hawaii
Gold rush over Pacific; for tourist traffic. il U S News 62:88-9 Mr 6 '67
Travel notes. R. Joseph. il Esquire 67:10+ My '67

Hong Kong
Letter from Hong Kong. J. Y. Dickinson. Holiday 42:24+ S '67

Ireland
Irish firm in ban on U.S. rights to Dublin. W. J. Normyle. il Aviation W 87:39+ Jl 31 '67
Let's travel: to Shannonside. J. Silver. il Mlle 65:90+ S '67

Israel
Israel for the tourist. J. Comay. il Holiday 42:137-40+ D '67
No truce on the tourists' front; Israel promoting hard. il Bsns W p40 Jl 15 '67
Packing in the pilgrims. il Newsweek 70:79 Jl 24 '67
Travel notes. R. Joseph. Esquire 68:31-2+ S '67

Italy
Let's travel: student style. M. Smith. il Mlle 65:156+ Ag '67

Jordan
What's left after the tornado? T. L. Christie. Sat R 50:41 O 14 '67

Kenya
East African holiday. il Newsweek 70:117+ N 13 '67

Mexico
100 ways of summer traveling in the West Indies and Mexico. T. Van Doren. Mlle 65:190-4 My '67

Middle East
Holy Land; symposium. il Sat R 50:38-41+ O 14 '67

Pacific countries
Strong promotion urged to lure U.S. tourists to Pacific Region. Aviation W 87:43 O 16 '67

Peru
Wanted: paying guests to trace the lost cities of Peru. R. Joseph. il Esquire 68:138-9 S '67

Portugal
Suggested tours in Portugal. Travel 127:55 Je '67
Touring Portugal by car, a 1,500 mile loop. il Sunset 138:38+ Mr '67

Puerto Rico
Shangri-la or hamburger heaven? T. Moscoso. il Sat R 51:53-4+ Ja 6 '68

Russia
Capitalists are welcome. il Newsweek 70:66 S 4 '67
Tips about trips to the U.S.S.R. il Time 90:54-63 Jl 28 '67

Switzerland
Middle-income elegance in Switzerland. N. S. Hazelton. Nat R 19:910 Ag 22 '67

United States
Coming battle of the gaps; conflicting pressures of the travel, technological gaps and gold gaps. W. D. Patterson. Sat R 51:24+ Ja 6 '68
Discovering America. il Time 90:97 O 20 '67
Fifty-one vacation stop-offs that will add real excitement to your trip; attractions in the United States. R. Dunlop. il Pop Mech 127:100-3+ Ap '67
Speaking out; tourist, stay home! W. M. Whitehill. il Sat Eve Post 240:8+ Ag 12 '67
Swinging Americans. A. Chamberlin. Mlle 64:222-3+ Ap '67
Through darkest America with camera and checkbook. A. Carthew. il N Y Times Mag p30-1+ Ag 27 '67; Discussion. p22+ S 24 '67
See also
United States—Travel service

Vietnam (Republic)
Positive approach. Newsweek 69:37 Je 12 '67

Virgin Islands
Let's travel. Mlle 65:34 Jl '67

TOURISTS. See Travelers
TOURISTS and customs administration. See Customs service and tourists
TOURISTS bureaus. See Information services
TOURNAMENT players. See Bridge players
TOURNAMENTS. See Basketball tournaments
TOURNAMENTS, Bridge. See Bridge tournaments
TOURNEDOS Rossini. See Cookery—Meat
TOURS, Garden. See Garden tours
TOURS, Industrial. See Industrial tours
TOURS, Package. See Travel
TOUSTER, Saul
Spun on a thread. J. Logan. Nation 205:601-2 D 4 '67
TOWBOATS. See Tugboats
TOWE, Kenneth M.
Echinoderm calcite: single crystal or polycrystalline aggregate. bibliog Science 157:1048-50 S 1 '67
TOWELL, William Earnest
Do residents control resident game? Am For 73:20-1+ Jl '67
Parks are for people. Am For 73:5+ O '67
Seaboard safari. por Am For 73:34-5+ S '67
Sustained yield and balanced use. Am For 73:11 S '67
This I believe. Am For 73:11 F '67
TOWELS
Terry towels; how to buy them, how to keep them beautiful. J. Van Leeuwen. il Good H 166:152 Ja '68
What we've learned about terry towels. il Good H 166:6 Ja '68
See also
Paper towels

TOWER, John Goodwin
Excerpt from debate, August 18, 1966. Cong Digest 46:45+ F '67
Reds' road; like Jersey turnpike. por U S News 62:34 F 27 '67

TOWER, Whitney
Horse racing. See issues of Sports illustrated

TOWER of London
Tower of London. F. Leary. il Horizon 10: 73-81 Wint '68

TOWER of Pisa. See Pisa—Campanile (leaning tower)

TOWER-Soudan state park. See Minnesota— Parks and reserves

TOWER suite. See New York (city)—Hotels, restaurants, etc.

TOWERS
Useless towers of Mexico; Satellite city. il Fortune 75:166 F '67

TOWING
Beware the highway's bad samaritans. J. Joseph. Motor T 19:83-4+ Jl '67

TOWING equipment. See Automobiles—Equipment

TOWN planning. See City planning

TOWNE, Anthony
Consume all these kingdoms; poem. Christian Cent 84:888 Jl 12 '67

TOWNE, Charles L.
Dial a lesson. Sr Schol 90:sup 14 F 3 '67

TOWNER, Gary W.
Relaxatrol to automate your slide projector. Pop Electr 25:55-6+ D '66

TOWNS. See Cities and towns

TOWNS, Models of. See Models of cities, towns, etc.

TOWNS, New. See New towns

TOWNSEND, Benjamin
Albright-Knox-Buffalo: work in progress. Art N 65:30-8+ Ja '67; Correction. 66:6 Mr '67

TOWNSEND, James Roger
Mao's revolution. Nation 204:781-6 Je 19 '67

TOWNSEND, John Rowe
Didacticism in modern dress. Horn Bk 43: 159-64 Ap '67

TOXICOLOGY. See Poisons

TOXINS and antitoxins
Anaphylatoxin in its relation to the complement system. J. Jensen. bibliog il Science 155:1122-3 Mr 3 '67
Ciguatoxin: isolation and chemical nature. P. J. Scheuer. bibliog Science 155:1267-8 Mr 10 '67
Effects of tetrodotoxin on excitability of squid giant axons in sodium-free media. A. Watanabe and others; reply with rejoinder. J. W. Moore and others. bibliog Science 157:220-1 Jl 14 '67
Potency difference between the zwitterion form and the cation forms of tetrodotoxin. G. Camougis and others. bibliog il Science 156:1625-7 Je 23 '67
Purified staphylococcal alpha toxin: effect on epithelial ion transport. J. J. Rahal, jr. and others. bibliog il Science 155:1118-20 Mr 3 '67
Saxitoxin and tetrodotoxin: comparison of nerve blocking mechanism. T. Narahashi and others. bibliog il Science 157:1441-2 S 22 '67
Tetrodotoxin blocks a graded sensory response in the eye of limulus. R. M. Benolken and C. J. Russell. bibliog il Science 155:1576-7 Mr 24 '67; Reply with rejoinder. H. Grundfest. 156:1771 Je 30 '67
Tetrodotoxin derivatives: chemical structure and blockage of nerve membrane conductance. T. Narahashi and others. bibliog il Science 156:976-9 My 19 '67
Tetrodotoxin: effects on brain metabolism in vitro. S. L. Chan and J. H. Quastel. bibliog il Science 156:1752-4 Je 30 '67
Tetrodotoxin; possible model for new local anesthetics. F. A. Fuhrman. il Sci Am 217:60-2+ Ag '67

TOXOHORMONE
Toxohormone from normal tissues. J. Olivares and others. bibliog il Science 157:327-8 Jl 21 '67

TOXOPLASMOSIS
Parasites tagged. Sci N 91:594 Je 24 '67

TOY building logs. See Toys

TOY engines. See Engines, Toy

TOY houses. See Doll houses

TOY industry
Toys from Jutland; Lego toymaking business. il Time 90:72 D 22 '67

TOY railroads. See Railroads, Toy

TOY typewriters. See Typewriters

TOYNBEE, Arnold Joseph
Corruption in the Senate; excerpt from Hannibal's legacy. Atlan 220:56 Jl '67
Peace, empire, and world government; introduction to Major peace treaties of modern history, 1648-1966, ed. by F. L. Israel. Sat R 50:17-21 Ap 29 '67
Sir Lewis Namier and history; excerpt from Acquantances. Harper 234:55-61 My '67
Toynbee on America; interview, ed. by J. Hicks. por Life 63:108-108B+ D 8 '67

about

Gaze behind the lens. C. Bedient. Nation 205:59-60 Jl 17 '67
Last of the old school. F. Mount. Nat R 19: 859-61 Ag 8 '67
Toynbee the biographer. A. Campbell. New Repub 156:26-7 Je 24 '67

TOYON
It bears red berries in time for Christmas; California holly or Christmas berry. il Sunset 139:150 D '67

TOYOTA (automobile) See Automobiles, Foreign

TOYS
All the world's a toy. C. Johnson. Nation 204:506-7 Ap 17 '67
Cardboard pets and woolly pillows; make a merry menagerie. il Bet Hom & Gard 45: 48-50 D '67
Christmas sleight of hand; toys from mittens and gloves. il Ladies Home J 84:182 N '67
Classic toys test your physics know-how; interview, ed. by W. S. Griswold. J. S. Miller. il Pop Sci 190:116-21+ Ap '67
Consumer service bureau report; toys to stimulate creativity; Lego building toys. M. B. Keiser. il Parents Mag 42:17-18 O '67
Delightful trifles for the young set. il House & Gard 132:60 N '67
Easy way to make toy building logs. P. Quedens. il Pop Sci 191:122-3 N '67
G.I. Joe talks; Hassenfeld bros. products. Newsweek 69:99 Mr 13 '67
Head start in architecture; blocks. il Sunset 138:122 F '67
How safe are your child's toys? T. J. Rakstis. il Todays Health 45:20-3 D '67
Never-never land of construction toys. il House & Gard 132:54 N '67
Noisy, yes; deafening, no; Daisy sonic mystery gun. il Consumer Rep 32:124 Mr '67
On and off the avenue (cont) New Yorker 43:105-6+ D 9 '67
Right toys for your preschooler. A. Wennblom. il Farm J 91:48-9 N '67
Science toys for Christmas. il Changing T 21: 41-3 N '67
Science toys urged for poorer nations. Sci N 91:111 F 4 '67
Scrap blocks for toy making. il Sunset 139:76 D '67
Still another dangerous toy; Wonder plastic balloons. Consumer Rep 32:350 Jl '67
They are box blocks. il Sunset 139:54-7 D '67
Three toys that make geometric patterns; Magic Designer, Spirograph, Super-Circle Designer. il Consumer Rep 32:564 N '67
Toys and games. il Consumer Bul 50:33-6 D '67
Toys that prove incontestably that there is a Santa Claus. il House & Gard 132:238-9 N '67
War talk and war games; with study-discussion program. R. Strang. bibliog il PTA Mag 62:20-3, 33 Ja '68
What's new for children. N. Pierce. il Parents Mag 43:16 Ja '68
Whirligigs revisited. il McCalls 95:92-5 D '67
Wonder year of Xmas toys. il Ebony 23: 122-4+ N '67
See also
Christmas gifts for children
Creative playthings, incorporated
Doll houses
Toy industry

Collectors and collecting
Toys for Christmas. C. B. Simmons. il Antiques 92:848-9 D '67

TOZZI, Giorgio
Tozzi's Sachs. I. Kolodin. Sat R 50:56 Ja 28 '67

TRACHTENBERG, Alan
High cost of professionalism. Nation 204:565-6 My 1 '67
Mind-expanding verbs. Nation 205:58-9 Jl 17 '67

TRACING
Instant sketches from photo prints. B. Corley. il Pop Mech 128:156-7 D '67

TRACK athletes. See Athletes

TRACK athletics
All dressed up and fit to kill; national decath-
lon championship, Los Angeles. J. Under-
wood. il Sports Illus 26:24-6+ Je 19 '67
Best-kept secrets; decathlon men. J. Under-
wood. il Sports Illus 26:82-6+ Je 12 '67
Few high flyers in a hope-filled debut; Los
Angeles invitational indoor track meet. G.
S. Brown. il Sports Illus 26:14-15 Ja 30 '67
Higher & faster; A.A.U. track and field
championship. Time 89:54 Je 30 '67
Jetting into gear; best sprinter in the world.
il Time 89:76 Mr 10 '67
One, two; NCAA indoor championships. il
Newsweek 69:62 Mr 20 '67
Pop fare for a popular fair; Americas vs.
Europe track-and-field meet. J. Underwood.
il Sports Illus 27:22-4+ Ag 21 '67
Smashing start to the season; best dash men
met in San Francisco. P. Axthelm. il Sports
Illus 28:46-7 Ja 15 '68
Smoking performance at a no-smoke affair;
University of southern California track team
at NCAA championships. P. Axthelm. il
Sports Illus 26:56+ Je 26 '67
Thank heaven for. . ; Fairfield girls' track
team. B. Gilbert. il Sports Illus 27:72-4+ N
27 '67
Two for the record; National AAU champion-
ships. il Newsweek 70:70 Jl 3 '67
See also
Running
Shot putting
TRACKING radar. See Radar in tracking and
trailing
TRACTION (automobiles) See Automobiles—
Traction
TRACTOR engines
Tractor tune-up in your farm shop. il Suc
Farm 65:91 F '67
TRACTOR industry and trade
See also
Caterpillar tractor company
TRACTOR tires. See Tires, Tractor
TRACTORS
Farm women describe my dream tractor. G.
W. Wormley. il Farm J 91:84-5+ Ap '67
Gravely's 50th anniversary tractor. E. F.
Lindslev. il Pop Sci 192:138-42+ Ja '68
Home tractor; jack-of-all jobs. J. Hand. il
Pop Sci 190:148-51 Ap '67
How to get full value from a home tractor.
C. L. Brek. il Pop Sci 191:166+ Jl '67
How to use tractor weights. Suc Farm 65:76
Ja '67
Midget yard-dozer you can build. C. E. Rhine.
il Pop Sci 190:83-7 My '67
Riding mower or tractor, which for you? J.
Hand. il Pop Sci 190:144-7 Ap '67
Suburban or baby tractors. il Consumer Bul
50:10-15 Mr '67
You can't call them toys anymore. J. M. Lis-
ton. il Pop Mech 127:98-101+ My '67

Fuel
Get best possible tractor fuel economy. Suc
Farm 67:88 Ja '67

Testing
Back to the old drawing board; testing Allis-
Chalmers equipment. il Am City 82:58 Ap
'67

Transmission
Now: a farm tractor you never shift; new
hydrostatic transmission. G. W. Wormley.
il Farm J 91:32 Jl '67
TRACTORS, Municipal
Machine for all seasons; tractor-dozer on
wheels. il Am City 82:10 D '67
TRACY, Honor
British remnant. New Repub 157:28-30 D 23
'67
Greed for collective guilt. New Repub 156:
25-6 Mr 25 '67
TRACY, Spencer
Last visit with two undimmed stars; inter-
view, ed. by J. Hamilton. pors Look 31:
26-30+ Jl 11 '67

about
He could wither you with a glance. S.
Kramer. il pors Life 62:69-70+ Je 30 '67
Old Bucko. il pors Newsweek 69:43-4 Je 19
'67
TRADE. See Commerce
TRADE agreements
Heat builds for higher wages. Bsns W p31
My 6 '67
Major collective bargaining agreements ex-
piring in [month] tables (title varies) See
issues of Monthly labor review
Pace quickens for wages. Bsns W p29-30 Ag 5
'67

Wage changes under 1966 major agreements.
J. E. Talbot, jr. il Mo Labor R 90:13-20
Je '67
Will railroad terms set a new pattern? il
Bsns W p 145 S 23 '67
See also
Collective bargaining
TRADE balance. See Balance of payments
TRADE cycles. See Business cycles
TRADE expansion act. See Tariff—United
States
TRADE fairs. See Exhibitions
TRADE journals
Sky writing; airlines publishing their own
magazines. il Newsweek 70:86 Jl 17 '67
TRADE marks
Chrysler corp. assembles a new identity;
Pentastar as symbol. il Bsns W p59+ Ap 29
'67
Sacred cow at Borden; Elsie the cow. il
Duns R 89:44 My '67
Story behind:
Birds eye. Changing T 21:26 Jl '67
Fruit of the loom. il Changing T 22:24
Ja '68
National lead's Dutch boy. il Changing
21:40 My '67
Reddy Kilowatt. il Changing T 21:40 N
'67
Trademark of the Hartford insurance
group. Changing T 21:32 S '67
Trademarks on glass. A. G. Peterson. il Hob-
bies 72:90-1 D '67
What's in a name? R. Ross-Skinner. Duns R
89:47-8 F '67
TRADE missions
States take a stab at salesmanship; sending
trade missions abroad to drum up sales.
il Bsns W p71-2+ F 18 '67
TRADE names
Fencing in Esso's brand. Bsns W p98 Ja 21
'67
Generic drugs favored. B. J. Culliton. Sci N
91:206-7 Mr 4 '67
Pill consumers' report; higher prices for
brand-name drugs. il Time 89:62+ My 26 '67
Story behind:
Birds eye. Changing T 21:26 Jl '67
Fruit of the loom. il Changing T 22:24
Ja '68
National lead's Dutch boy. il Changing
21:40 My '67
Reddy Kilowatt. il Changing T 21:40 N
'67
War of the suds; Lite vs. Lite. il Newsweek
70:80-1 O 2 '67
TRADE regulation
See also
Foreign trade regulation
TRADE relations
Developments in industrial relations. See
issues of Monthly labor review
TRADE routes
Silk road. J. Morris. il Horizon 9:4-23 Aut
'67
TRADE schools
How South hopes to keep Negroes; technical
training schools. il U S News 63:42-4 O 2 '67
TRADE secrets
Cost disclosure showdown nears. D. C. Win-
ston. Aviation W 87:16-17 O 2 '67
How to steal $4 billion. il Newsweek 69:76-8
My 1 '67
Suit underscores proprietary data issue. K.
J. Stein. Aviation W 86:56-7+ F 27 '67
TRADE union leaders. See Trade unions—Of-
ficials
TRADE union mergers. See Trade unions—Con-
solidations and mergers
TRADE unions
Foreign labor briefs. See issues of Monthly
labor review
Trade union approaches to income and price
policy; excerpt from Non-wage incomes and
prices policy. Mo Labor R 90:52-7 Ja '67
See also
Boycott
Collective bargaining
Industrial relations
Strikes

Consolidations and mergers
Steps toward union mergers. Mo Labor R 90:
III-IV Mr '67

Dues, fees, etc.
Where unions are getting help from the
courts. il U S News 62:76-7 Je 26 '67

Ethical aspects
See Labor ethics

History
Labor melts a link with its fiery past; Smelter workers merger into the USW ends an
era. il Bsns W p 109-10+ Ja 28 '67

TRADE unions—*Continued*

International aspects

Fair labor standards for world trade. R. B. Schwenger. Mo Labor R 90:27-31 N '67
See also
International labor organization

Investments

Auto workers' war chest: loaded for a long strike; UAW investments. il U S News 62: 80+ Je 5 '67

Jurisdictional disputes

Where everything, almost, went wrong; interstate highway bridge linking St Louis and East St Louis. il Bsns W p62+ Je 10 '67

Law

See Labor laws and legislation; Labor laws and legislation—United States

Membership

Fresh breezes in the labor movement. G. Tyler. New Repub 156:13-15 My 20 '67
How to negotiate with municipal labor unions. Am City 82:50-1 Mr '67
How unions are gaining and losing members; chart. U S News 63:105 D 18 '67
Profile of union members: who they are, what they think. U S News 63:75 Jl 24 '67
When a worker refuses to strike. U S News 62:37 Mr 27 '67
Where unions have most growth potential; unionism among public employees. il Bsns W p76-8 O 21 '67
Why unions think they can get more now. il Nations Bsns 55:35-7+ F '67

Negro membership

And organized labor gets involved, too. Sr Schol 91:10 N 2 '67
Case against the unions. T. O'Hanlon. il Fortune 77:170-3+ Ja '68
Craft unions are hurting; plans to end all-white unions. New Repub 157:9 Jl 15 '67
Crafts ease their stand on bias. Bsns W p 133-4 D 9 '67
Cram course for Negro apprentices; joint apprenticeship program of the Workers defense league and the A. Philip Randolph education fund. il Bsns W p88-90+ N 25 '67
Negro and apprenticeship, by F. R. Marshall and V. M. Briggs, jr. Review
Reporter 37:56+ N 2 '67. K. Goodall
Will labor feel a backlash? labor's liberal wing campaigns for Negro rights. il Bsns W p69-70 Ag 5 '67

Officials

Bullheaded leader of aerospace labor; R. Siemiller of I.A.M. B. Brower. il Life 64:60-2+ Ja 19 '68
Business image tops labor, government; college students. J. St John. Nations Bsns 55:114 O '67
Labor maps a try harder strategy. Bsns W p 152+ Mr 4 '67

Political activities

AFL-CIO gets wooed for 1968. il Bsns W p76+ D 16 '67
DRIVE: teamsters in politics: Democrat Republican independent voter education. T. E. Tornek; reply with rejoinder. B. Weissman. Nation 204:194 F 13 '67
Holding back on foreign trade. Bsns W p83-4 S 2 '67
Labor's stand on Vietnam. America 117:403 O 14 '67
Vietnam: labor's love lost. D. Ireland. Commonweal 87:292-3 D 1 '67
Where labor throws its weight around. il Nations Bsns 55:44-9 Ag '67
Where unions are getting help from the courts. il U S News 62:76-7 Je 26 '67
Why unions think they can get more now. il Nations Bsns 55:35-7+ F '67

Recreation activities

UAW structure emphasizes recreation, leisure-time activities and conservation. O. M. Madar. Parks & Rec 2:31+ N '67

Argentina

End of a truce; crackdown of General labor confederation. il Time 89:40 Mr 17 '67
How one country in Latin America is cracking down on labor unions. U S News 62:86 Mr 27 '67
Toothless lion; falling out among Peronist union. Newsweek 69:48 Je 12 '67

Canada

Canadian unions press for U.S.-size wages. Bsns W p90+ Ja 6 '68

France

De Gaulle gets blame for decline in jobs. il Bsns W p 134 Ja 21 '67

Great Britain

Common paradox: white-collar organization in Britain; excerpt from Trade union growth and recognition. G. S. Bain. bibliog f il Mo Labor R 90:42-7 O '67
Mixture as before. Newsweek 70:53 D 18 '67
See also
Trades union congress

Japan

Shuntō: Japanese labor's spring wage offensive. R. Evans, jr. bibliog f il Mo Labor R 90:23-8 O '67

Latin America

Why a Christian democratic labor organization? Latin American confederation of Christian syndicalists. J. Goldsack. America 116:154-6 Ja 28 '67

Mexico

Coco loco; battle over labor union leadership. Newsweek 70:46 S 4 '67

South Africa

Trade union rights in South Africa; UN working group. UN Mo Chron 4:47 Ag '67

Spain

Franco's restive workers. A. Rosenfeld. il Reporter 36:31-3 My 4 '67

United States

Bargaining's bite hits small business; unions pressing hard at all levels. Bsns W p 154+ My 6 '67
Battler for democracy in unions. B. L. Masse. America 117:53 Jl 15 '67
Big worry for unions: conservative gains in '68. il U S News 63:66-7 D 25 '67
Boom times ahead; address, October 31, 1967. A. Shivers. Vital Speeches 34:146-8 D 15 '67
Development of labor law in 1966. G. C. Smith. Mo Labor R 90:12-17 F '67
Developments in industrial relations. See issues of Monthly labor review
For unions in '68: strikes, big raises, election losses. U S News 64:74-5 Ja 8 '68
Fresh breezes in the labor movement. G. Tyler. New Repub 156:13-15 My 20 '67
From the top union leaders: latest on '67 wage demands. il U S News 62:74-5 Mr 6 '67
It's hard to satisfy local unions; concerns of young unionists. B. L. Masse. America 117:149 Ag 12 '67
Labor at Bal Harbour. B. J. Widick. Nation 206:6-8 Ja 1 '68
Labor jottings. Nat R 19:784-5 Jl 25 '67
Labor month in review. See issues of Monthly labor review
Labor revolution, by G. Tyler. Review
Commentary 43:91-3 Je '67. L. A. Coser
New Repub 156:26-8 Mr 25 '67. M. R. Berube
Now your taxes train pickets; unions infiltrating poverty programs. il Nations Bsns 55:37-9+ Mr '67
On labor horizon for '68: big demands, turmoil, strikes. U S News 63:105-7 D 18 '67
Primer for a theory of white-collar unionization. V. Lombardi and A. J. Grimes. bibliog f Mo Labor R 90:46-9 My '67
Rethinking the right to strike. Fortune 76:113-14 O '67; Reply. F. Spreng. 76:106 N '67
Roots of union power. W. Wingo. il Nations Bsns 55:44-9 Ag; 70-2+ S; 104+ O '67
Split labor faces a big year. il Newsweek 69:82-5 F 20 '67
Trade-off becomes the word. B. L. Masse. America 116:520 Ap 8 '67
Trade winds; unyielding bargaining table approach of a Bertram Powers. H. R. Mayes. Sat R 50:11-12 My 27 '67
Unionization of engineers and technicians. A. Kleingartner. bibliog f il Mo Labor R 90: 29-35 O '67
Unions call the signals; NFL and AFL players plan to register with the National labor relations board as a bona fide union. il Bsns W p26 Ja 13 '68
What will strife cost? il Bsns W p27-9 Ap 8 '67

TRADE unions—United States—*Continued*
White House at bay; maritime unions attack on administration policy. Bsns W p 124+ Je 3 '67
  See also
American federation of labor and Congress of industrial organizations
Arbitration, Industrial—United States
Building trades unions
Featherbedding (industrial relations)
Strikes—United States
  also names of unions, e.g. International brotherhood of teamsters, chauffeurs, warehousemen and helpers of America

TRADE waste
Watery grave for Lake Michigan? result of industrial waste. il Bsns W p 103-4+ O 21 '67
  See also
Water pollution

TRADEMARKS. See Trade marks

TRADERS, Indian. See Indian traders

TRADES union congress
Jeers from the ranks; TUC condemns Wilson's economic policies. Newsweek 70:51-2 S 18 '67
Labor turns on Wilson. America 117:290 S 23 '67
National wage policies in Europe and the U.S. E. M. Kassalow. Mo Labor R 90:36-7 Mr '67

TRADING. See Barter

TRADING cards. See Advertising cards

TRADING posts. See Indians of North America—Trading posts

TRADING stamps
To the manor bought; King Korn offers English lord of the manor title. il Newsweek 69:74 My 29 '67
Trading stamps start to look more like money; Stampak's package gimmick. il Bsns W p68 Ap 1 '67

TRADITIONAL furniture. See Furniture

TRAFFIC. See Road traffic

TRAFFIC accidents
Accidents happen to other people. D. Shaw. il Redbook 128:76-7+ Ap '67
Auto safety devices cut head-on injuries. Todays Health 45:12 D '67
Bad design blamed for highway accidents. Am City 82:154 S '67
Big pile-up of 1966; New York thruway. E. D. Fales, jr. il Pop Mech 127:122-7+ F '67
Danger rides the school bus. R. Bugg. il Todays Health 45:20-3+ N '67
Death rides on two wheels; motorcycle accidents. F. Warshofsky. il Read Digest 91:151-2+ O '67
Drugs & driving, a deadly mix! J. Pickering. il Motor T 19:58-60 My '67
Growing concern about school buses. il Good H 165:201 O '67
Highway device that can save your life. il Sci Digest 61:64-8 Ap '67
How fast is too fast? T. Stimson. il Pop Mech 128:71-4+ S '67
I hunted twenty years to find my father's killer. W. Lee and B. Lindeman. il Sat Eve Post 240:74-9 Ag 26 '67
Young killers; high accident rate and death toll of young male drivers. il Time 90:46 Ag 25 '67
Your youngster and the motorcycle. H. E. Dark. il Todays Health 45:20-4 My '67
  See also
Automobile driving
Automobiles—Safety devices and measures
Drinking and traffic accidents
Insurance, Automobile
Safety belts

Prevention
See Traffic safety

Statistics
Another holiday that death didn't take; July 4 week-end. U S News 63:10 Jl 17 '67

TRAFFIC accidents and alcoholism. See Drinking and traffic accidents

TRAFFIC congestion. See Street traffic

TRAFFIC control, Airport. See Airports—Traffic control

TRAFFIC control, Airway. See Air traffic control

TRAFFIC control towers, Airport. See Airports—Control towers

TRAFFIC courts
Traffic jam. il Time 89:36 Je 30 '67

TRAFFIC engineering
Mathematical theory of automobile traffic. D. C. Gazis. bibliog il Science 157:273-81 Jl 21 '67
  See also subhead Street traffic under names of cities, e.g. New York (city)—Street traffic

TRAFFIC fines. See Fines (penalties)

TRAFFIC markings
Disposable stencils cut marking costs; Kalamazoo, Mich. R. B. Carroll. il Am City 82:98 Ja '67
Instant-dry traffic lines; bridges, tunnels and air terminals. L. Bender. il Am City 82:112 Ag '67

TRAFFIC police
Selective enforcement; R to prevent auto accidents. J. N. Miller. il Read Digest 91:147-51 D '67
Your best friend on the road, the police officer. W. J. Toth. Am Home 70:58-9 Mr '67

TRAFFIC regulations
Sweden tells traffic to keep to the right. il Bsns W p26-7 S 2 '67
Traffic control. See issues of American city
  See also
Automobile parking
Helicopters in traffic regulation
Photography in traffic regulation
Traffic police

TRAFFIC safety
Automotive safety; community action; address, June 5, 1967. B. J. Nichols. Vital Speeches 33:628-31 Ag 1 '67
How young is too young? T. Stimson. il Pop Mech 128:132-5+ O '67
Night inspection weed out traffic hazards; Costa Mesa, Calif. il Am City 82:122 N '67
Selective enforcement; R to prevent auto accidents. J. N. Miller. il Read Digest 91:147-51 D '67
U.S. and the automobile; driving research laboratory in Providence, R.I. Sci Am 216:58+ My '67
  See also
Roads—Safety devices and measures

TRAFFIC safety agency. See United States—National traffic safety agency

TRAFFIC signals
9, 8, 7... stop; Abilene, Tex. R. G. Taylor. il Am City 82:129 My '67

Control
Optics operate signals in emergencies; Buena Park, Calif. J. W. Verbeck. il Am City 82:125+ Mr '67
Solid-state flashers for light displays. A. A. Adem. il Electr World 78:83-4 Ag '67

TRAFFIC signs
Mercuries outshine fluorescents for sign lighting. il Am City 82:122 D '67
Signs of color. il Time 90:84 N 24 '67
Watch those road signs. W. J. Toth. il Am Home 70:42-3 N '67

TRAGEDY
Tragedy and comedy, by W. Kerr. Review Life 62:18 My 19 '67. T. Prideaux

TRAHAN, Marian, and Minudri, Regina
(eds) Adult books for young adults. por Library J 92:3209-15, 3870-2+, 4272-8, 4636-40; 93:313-16 S 15, O 15, N 15, D 15 '67, Ja 15 '68

TRAIL riders of the wilderness
On to the Yukon. il Am For 73:40+ Mr '67

TRAIL scooter. See Motor scooters

TRAILER hitches
  See also
Automobiles—Equipment

TRAILER-size containers. See Container system (freight handling)

TRAILERS
  See also
Automobile trailers

TRAILING plants. See Climbing plants

TRAILS
Enjoying nature; on a nature hike across Florida. M. Smith, jr. il Audubon 69:69-72 Ja '67
Footpath in the wilderness; Long Trail, Green Mountains, Vt. J. T. Starr. il Am For 73:24-6+ Jl '67
Let's saddle up! il Am For 73:26-7 F '67
New lure for tourists; trail Lyndon trod. il U S News 63:54-5 N 20 '67
Signs for bicycle routes. il Parks & Rec 2:69 My '67
Trails for tomorrow; review. il Liv Wildn 31:55-9 Spr '67
Wayfaring along the Ozark trail. R. Dunlop. il Todays Health 45:44-9 Ap '67

TRAILS—*Continued*
What trails for America? F. Graham, jr. il Audubon 69:46-52 N '67
Wisconsin's whistle-stop nature trail; Elroy-Sparta trail. il Audubon 69:78-9 My '67
   See also
National parks and reserves—Trails
TRAIN speed. See Railroads—Train speed
TRAIN travel. See Railroad travel
TRAINED nurses. See Nurses and nursing
TRAINER, Dixie Dean
Nielsen rating for a box of spaghetti. N Y Times Mag p 12-13+ Jl 30 '67
TRAINING airplanes. See Airplanes, Training
TRAINING camps. See Military training camps
TRAINING of animals. See Animals—Training; Bears—Training
TRAINING of birds. See Birds—Training
TRAINING of children. See Children—Management and training
TRAINING of dogs. See Dogs—Training
TRAINING schools for delinquents. See Reformatories
TRAINING ships
Tiny tankers train pilots. il Pop Sci 191:80-1 D '67
TRAINS. See Railroads—Trains
TRAINS, Toy. See Railroads, Toy
TRAITORS
   See also
Treason
Trials (treason)
TRAITS of character. See Character analysis
TRAMWAYS, Aerial. See Cableways
TRANQUILIZING drugs
More on drug abuse; question whether Librium and Valium should be restricted. Sci N 91:232 Mr 11 '67
Tranquilizers, and other psychoactive drugs: how well do they work? Consumer Rep 32:544-50 O '67
   See also
Drugs—Physiological effects
Reserpine
TRANQUILLI, Secondo. See Silone, I. pseud.
TRANSAMERICA corporation
Unveiling Transamerica. Newsweek 70:80B D 4 '67
TRANSATLANTIC cables. See Cables, Submarine
TRANSATLANTIC flights. See Aviation—Transatlantic flights
TRANSATLANTIC race. See Yacht racing
TRANSATLANTIC voyages. See Voyages
TRANSCEIVERS. See Radio telephone
TRANSCENDENCE of God
God: language and transcendence. D. B. Burrell. Commonweal 85:511-16 F 10 '67
TRANSCO. See Transcontinental gas pipe line corporation
TRANSCONTINENTAL flights. See Aviation—Transcontinental flights
TRANSCONTINENTAL gas pipe line corporation
Getting a gas line submerged; more heat for Long Islanders. il Bsns W p 160-2 N 11 '67
TRANSFER of employees. See Employees, Transfer of
TRANSFER students. See College students
TRANSFERRIN
Transferrin D₁: identity in Australian aborigines and American Negroes. A. C. Wang and others. bibliog il Science 156:936-7 My 19 '67
TRANSFERRIN polymorphism. See Polymorphism (biology)
TRANSFORMERS. See Electric transformers
TRANSFUSION of blood. See Blood—Transfusion
TRANSHEXENAL. See Insect sex attractants
TRANSIENT nativity; story. See Raborg, F. A. jr
TRANS INTERNATIONAL airlines, incorporated
Supplemental sees rising tour business. Aviation W 86:41 Ja 23 '67
TRANSISTOR circuits
Avalanche transistor circuits. S. L. Silver. il Electr World 78:30-2 S '67
Bias compensation for transistor output stages. P. Halliday. il Electr World 78:76-8 Ag '67
Field-effect transistor circuits. J. H. Wujek, jr. and M. E. McGee. il Electr World 77:32-3+ My '67
Solderless breadboard. A. A. Mangieri. il Pop Electr 25:54 D '66

TRANSISTOR curve tracer. See Testing instruments
TRANSISTOR radios. See Radio receivers—Transistor receivers
TRANSISTOR testers. See Testing instruments
TRANSISTORS
FET voltmeter; transistorized version uses field-effect transistor. J. Randall. il Electr World 77:63-4 F '67
Hi-fi. I. B. Berger Esquire 67:36+ Mr '67
Introducing the FET set; field effect transistor radio receiver. J. Althouse. il Pop Electr 26:27-30 My '67
Meet Mr FET, the transistor that thinks it's a tube. L. E. Garner, jr. il Pop Electr 26: 47-53+ F '67
New frontiers. H. Fantel. Opera N 32:29 S 23 '67
New tetrode transistor. J. Tartas. il Electr World 77:34-5 F '67
Radiation-resistant transistor studied. il Aviation W 87:112 O 16 '67
Salute to the transistor. P. J. Klass. Aviation W 88:21 Ja 15 '68
Solid state. L. Garner. See issues of Popular electronics
Transistors can find treasure. J. L. Russell, jr. il Motor B 119:138-41 My '67
Transistors on trial. il Hi Fi 17:48-52 Mr '67
Transistors; symposium. il Electr World 78: 37-60 Jl '67
War is over, the transistor has won! J. Wesson. U S Camera 30:34+ Jl '67
Years of stereo and solid state. I. Berger. Sat R 50:70-1 Ag 26 '67
   See also
Television receivers—Transistor receivers
Transistor circuits

Control uses

Solid-state flashers for light displays. A. A. Adem. il Electr World 78:83-4 Ag '67
Solid-state ring counters and chasers for light displays. A. A. Adem. il Electr World 78:84-5 S '67
Switching transistors. S. Fierro. il Electr World 78:57-60 Jl '67

Testing

Breakdown reverse voltage transistor and diode tester. C. D. Rakes. il Pop Electr 26:67-71 My '67
Super-simple transistor tester. J. G. Sloat. il Pop Sci 191:96-8 D '67
Transistor curve tracer. M. Chan. il Electr World 79:55-8+ Ja '68
Versatile transistor tester. M. J. Moss. il Electr World 78:56-8 Ag '67
TRANSIT (satellite) See Artificial satellites—Navigational applications
TRANSIT expressway. See Rapid transit
TRANSIT systems. See Rapid transit
TRANSITION elements. See Transition metals
TRANSITION metals
Superconductivity and the d-shell; isotope effects on transition temperatures. J. J. Engelhardt and others. bibliog il Science 155:191-3 Ja 13 '67
TRANSLATING machines
Machine translation. Sci N 91:265 Mr 18 '67
TRANSLATIONS and translating
Israel program for scientific translations. I. Soifer. il Pub W 192:50-1 N 13 '67
New National book award established for translations. Pub W 191:52-3 F 13 '67
   See also
American literature—Translations into Russian
Childrens literature—Translating
Russian literature—Translations into English
TRANSLOCATION in plants. See Plants—Translocation
TRANSLUCENS; ballet. See Ballets—Criticisms
TRANSMISSION, Automobile. See Automobiles—Transmission
TRANSMISSION lines. See Electric lines
TRANSPACIFIC routes. See Airways
TRANS-PACIFIC yacht race. See Yacht racing
TRANSPARENCIES
Making and using transparencies. K. B. Culver. il Sr Schol 91:sup 10-11 S 28 '67
Of teachers and transparencies. J. H. Joy. Sr Schol 90:sup 17 F 3 '67
Transparencies: Scholastic's unique service. il Sr Schol 91:sup7 S 21 '67

Anecdotes, facetiae, satire, etc.

Next slide, please. C. Ford. Field & S 72: 6+ Jl '67

Copying

Creative copying. W. D. Griffin. il U S Camera 30:40-1+ S '67

TRANSPORTATION—*Continued*

Canada

Canada frees the reins on its railroaders. il Bsns W p96-8+ Je 24 '67

Europe

See also
Railroads—Europe

Germany (Federal Republic)

Blitzing trucks off the highway; shifting long-haul freight traffic from road to rail. il Bsns W p 104-6+ N 11 '67

Radical surgery; plan to clear highways of trucks and revive railroads. Newsweek 70: 86 O 16 '67

Great Britain

Blitzing trucks off the highway; shifting long-haul freight traffic from road to rail. il Bsns W p 104-6+ N 11 '67
See also
Railroads—Great Britain

Japan

See also
Railroads—Japan

Latin America

See also
Waterways—Latin America

New York (state)

7 billions to cure traffic ills; one state's plan. il U S News 63:70-2 D 4 '67

Philippines

Barging ahead; Luzon stevedoring co. biggest commercial cargo handler in southeast Asia. Time 90:72 Ag 25 '67

Underdeveloped areas

Transport development; report by the Secretary-General. UN Mo Chron 4:49-50 My '67

United States

Transportation forecast for the year 2000. M. L. Feldman. il Sat R 51:42 Ja 13 '68

Trucks, trains, planes, boats, all in one company? il U S News 63:118-20 S 25 '67

Vehicular revolution; the ruckus it stirs; with report by C. Welles. il Life 62:34-43 My 12 '67

Water-rail coordination; address, September 6, 1967. W. J. Barta. Vital Speeches 34:4-7 O 15 '67
See also
Aeronautics, Commercial—United States
United States—Transportation, Department of

Vietnam (Republic)

Leave the driving to us; nationwide bus service. il Newsweek 69:46 F 6 '67

TRANSPORTATION, Automotive
See also
Trucking

TRANSPORTATION, High speed
Computer express roars past Fuji; French aerotrain; U.S. pneumatic project. il Life 62:40-3 My 12 '67

DOT to build air cushion research vehicle. H. Taylor. Aero Tech 21:17-18 O 23 '67

Megalopolis unbound, by C. Pell. Review Reporter 36:56-8 Mr 23 '67. C. W. Griffin, jr

Profiles; through the great city. A. Bailey. il New Yorker 43:40-2 Jl 22 '67

Third-generation, 300-mph trains urged. J. Rhea. Tech W 20:34 Mr 20 '67
See also
Railroads—Train speed

TRANSPORTATION, Military
Aircraft variety marks airlift to Vietnam. C. Brownlow. il Aviation W 86:76-9 My 15 '67
See also
Airplanes, Military transport
United States—Military airlift command
Vietnamese war, 1957- —Transportation

TRANSPORTATION, Municipal. See Rapid transit

TRANSPORTATION of school children. See School children—Transportation

TRANSPORTATION of works of art
Flight of the bird; portrait of Ginevra del Benci. il Time 89:72 Mr 3 '67

TRANSPORTATION to airports. See Airports —Transportation problems

TRANSSEXUALISM. See Change of sex

TRANS WORLD airlines
Eastern TWA to cooperate on Concorde, 747 support. Aviation W 87:38 D 4 '67

Hilton's fortunes ride on the jets; TWA's new partner, Hilton international. il Bsns W p50-4+ Jl 1 '67

Mr Z; bomb threats to TWA. Newsweek 69:33 Je 12 '67

Places to put them; preliminary merger agreement between Hilton international and TWA. Time 89:67 Ja 27 '67

Transpacific route case; TWA stresses forging round-the-world service link. H. D. Watkins. il Aviation W 86:32-4+ F 20 '67

TWA completes major financing program. Aviation W 87:31 D 25 '67

TWA Hilton. Newsweek 69:78 Ja 30 '67

TWA plans to buy ten more 747s in $455-million Boeing purchase. Aviation W 87:37 O 23 '67

TWA untangles its finances. Bsns W p22 D 23 '67

TRAN-van-Dinh
Exercise in deception. Commonweal 86:582-4 S 22 '67

Ky v Buddhists, round two. New Repub 156: 15-19 My 13 '67

South Vietnam leaders. New Repub 158:29 Ja 6 '68

South Vietnam's captive vote. New Repub 157:15-16 S 2 '67

TRAP shooting
First shootoff of the franchises; nation-wide skeet and trap contest. W. Page. il Field & S 71:12+ Mr '67

TRAPPING
See also
Fur trade

TRAPPISTS
Getting the word; rule of silence relaxed. Time 90:41 Ag 11 '67

TRAPS
Trapping mammals about the home. E. M. Mills. il Consumer Bul 50:24-6 Jl '67
See also
Mousetraps

TRASH. See Refuse and refuse disposal

TRASH cans. See Refuse receptacles

TRASK, Margaret
Children's library scene. bibliog Library J 92:4222-4 N 15 '67

TRASK, Newell J. and Rowan, L. C.
Lunar Orbiter photographs: some fundamental observations. bibliog Science 158:1529-35 D 22 '67

TRAUFFER, Art
Build a stacked-antenna AM radio. Pop Electr 26:40 My 67

New dimension in portable radio listening. Pop Electr 26:43 Je '67

TRAVANCAS, Orlando
Tragic end of Travancas the Terrible. Time 90:24 D 29 '67

TRAVEL
Around the world on a camera. A. N. Podell. il U S Camera 30:62-3+ Jl '67

Booked for travel. H. Sutton. See issues of Saturday review

Escape mechanisms. M. Gough. il House B 109:76+ Ja '67

Family travel. See issues of Better homes and gardens

Five people who go places: their travel notes. il Vogue 149:142-7+ Ap 1 '67

How to cope with holiday travel. Bet Hom & Gard 45:28+ D '67

How to leave home and like it. M. Gough. See issues of House beautiful

Intelligent woman traveler; excerpts from Complete guide for the intelligent woman traveler. F. Koltun. Mlle 64:203-8 Mr '67

Let's travel: fall-winter news. Mlle 65:104+ O '67

Let's travel: winter budget brainstorms. J. Silver. il Mlle 66:62+ D '67

[Month] travel in and beyond the West. See issues of Sunset

My first trip; six famous travelers confess why, how and when they first left home. McCalls 94:36+ My '67

Roamer's ramblings. T. Shane. See issues of Travel to August 1967

Roaming the globe with travel. See issues of Travel

Speaking of travel. C. Stinnett. See issues of Holiday

Surprise, surprise. S. Hazzard. Mlle 65:98+ Je '67

Take a fashion lesson; how to choose double-time travel clothes. Seventeen 26:232 My '67

Tourist tips. C. J. McNaspy. America 117:23-4 Jl 1 '67

Travel. L. Barry. See issues of Popular photography

Travel (cont) il Life 62:50-61+ Je 23; 63:78-87+ S 8 '67

TRAVEL—*Continued*
Travel & camera. See issues of U.S. camera & travel
Travel notes. H. French. Holiday 41:4+ Ap; 6+ My; 4+ Je '67
Travel notes. See issues of Flower grower, the home garden (cont as) Home garden & flower grower
Travel notes. R. Joseph. See issues of Esquire
Travel schemes to guard against. il Good H 164:194 Mr '67
Travel that comes in a package. il Changing T 21:25-9 My '67
Traveletters; questions and answers. Sr Schol 90:sup20 Mr 3 '67
Twenty years of travel; symposium. il Sat R 50:27-33+ Ap 22 '67
Well traveled camera. See issues of Modern photography
Well worth the trip. M. Gough. House B 109:96+ F '67
    See also
Air travel
Automobile touring
Cruising
Garden tours
Guidebooks
Luggage
Motor bus travel
Packing of luggage
Railroad travel
Tourist trade
Travels
Vacations
Youth hostels

Anecdotes, facetiae, satire, etc.

Around the world with Flo. R. Gehman. Holiday 42:30+ S '67
Deluxe hardship tours. H. A. Smith. il Travel 127:43-5 Ap '67
East of New York, south of Madrid, down to Kenya. F. R. Buckley. Vogue 149:82-5 Ap 1 '67
Go away madly. J. L. O'Neill. Am Home 70:44 Ja '67
Shoprite tours. R. Lasson and D. Eynon. il Atlan 220:102+ Jl '67

Bibliography

Bookshelf for tripping. L. Barry. il Pop Phot 62:60+ Ja '68
Bound to travel. S. Robinson. il McCalls 95:76+ D '67

Economic aspects

Expenditures for foreign travel by U.S. residents; U.S. receipts from foreign visitors for travel in the United States and payments to U.S. transocean carriers. il Aviation W 88:20 Ja 8 '67
Miniprice tours for budget-minded teachers; NEA tours in capsule. il NEA J 57:50-1 Ja '68
President Johnson appoints special task force on travel. Dept State Bul 57:828 D 18 '67
Problems of prosperity; excerpts from address. S. G. Tipton. Aviation W 87:21 D 11 '67
Teen travel talk. il Seventeen 26:219 My '67
Travel curbs? possible effects. il U S News 64:35 Ja 15 '68
    See also
Tourist trade

Health aspects

Bon voyage, bonne santé; how to stay healthy on foreign soil. P. N. Mathless. il NEA J 57:46-9 Ja '68
How to stay healthy and happy while traveling. J. D. Wassersug. il Sci Digest 62:73-7 Ag '67
Intelligent woman traveler. F. Koltun. Mlle 64:205-6 Mr '67
On your vacation, eat with care! Consumer Bul 50:27-8 Jl '67
Personal business; latest on travel health. Bsns W p 141-2 Je 3 '67
Travel well. E. N. Dye. See issues of Travel
Travelers' comforts. N. S. Hazelton. Nat R 19:475+ My 2 '67
Traveling in good health. P. Wright. il Holiday 41:135-9 Ap '67
Weight watching for wanderers. J. H. Winchester. il Travel 128:49-51 N '67

Photographs

Scrapbook 1947-1967: a traveler's retrospective. Sat R 50:32-3 Ap 22 '67

Taxation

Tourist gets hit. il Bsns W p 18-19 Ja 6 '68
Travel-tax proposal. Christian Cent 85:67 Ja 17 '68

TRAVEL (periodical)
    See also
Mr Travel award
TRAVEL, Space. See Space flight
TRAVEL agencies
Cost study planned in agent fee dispute. il Aviation W 86:42 Mr 20 '67
On tour with the overprivileged. H. Sutton. il Sat R 50:46-7 Je 24 '67
Russian tourism is rough-and-ready, but it has to get better; Intourist. C. S. Wren. il Look 31:121 O 3 '67
TRAVEL agents
Booked for travel, by computer. il Bsns W p 181-2 S 9 '67
How to choose a travel agent. Bet Hom & Gard 45:33 S '67
How to use an agent. L. Barry. Pop Phot 61:26+ N '67
TRAVEL and education. See Student travel
TRAVEL books. See Travel literature
TRAVEL bureaus. See Information services
TRAVEL films. See Moving pictures—Travel films
TRAVEL folders. See Travel literature
TRAVEL guides. See Guidebooks
TRAVEL literature
From Bogotá to B.A: two nineteenth-century travel books. J. N. Goodsell. Sat R 50:37 Jl 15 '67
World as a gift; comp. by B. Moore. Sat R 50:36 D 2 '67
Your society offers four new books. M. B. Grosvenor. il Nat Geog Mag 131:868-75 Je '67
    See also
Guidebooks

Anecdotes, facetiae, satire, etc.

Traveling with Mlle: how to read a travel folder. K. D. Fishman. il Mlle 66:141-2+ D '67
TRAVEL manners. See Etiquette
TRAVEL regulations
America to Moscow nonstop: what it's like to fly Russian; Aeroflot. R. K. Brome. il U S News 62:62-4 My 29 '67
Department issues public notices on travel to restricted areas. Dept State Bul 56:564-5 Ap 3 '67
Department seeks criminal penalties on travel to restricted areas; letter, December 11, 1967, with proposed bill. N. deB. Katzenbach. Dept State Bul 58:53-5 Ja 8 '68
Economic curbs imperil industry; with editorial comment. C. Brownlow. Aviation W 88.11, 16-19 Ja 8 '68
Present travel restrictions extended through March 15. Dept State Bul 56:102-3 Ja 16 '67
Russian tourism is rough-and-ready, but it has to get better. C. S. Wren. il Look 31:121 O 3 '67
There are no aliens; International tourist year and the U.S. N. Cousins. Sat R 50:28+ Mr 11 '67
Tourist gets hit. il Bsns W p 18-19 Ja 6 '68
Travel cuts could blunt airline growth. L. Doty. Aviation W 88:19-21 Ja 8 '68
U.S. amends travel restrictions resulting from Near East conflict. Dept State Bul 57:41 Jl 10 '67
U.S. passports valid for travel to Iraq, Jordan, and Yemen. Dept State Bul 57:459 O 9 '67
U.S. passports valid for travel to United Arab Republic. Dept State Bul 57:799 D 11 '67
TRAVEL study courses
Personal business: student tours and study programs abroad. Bsns W p 135 Ap 8 '67
Summer seminar in Ecuador; travel-study program by Ecuador's Ministry of education and U.S. embassy with University of Oregon summer session. J. Moorhead. il Sr Schol 90:sup 13-14 Mr 3 '67
Summer study tour of New York and New England. D. Minor. il Sr Schol 90:sup21 Mr 3 '67
Year of the students; eastern and western grantees of the East-West center, University of Hawaii. H. Sutton. Sat R 50:50+ F 18 '67
    See also
Experiment in international living (organization)
Foreign study
TRAVEL tax. See Travel—Taxation
TRAVEL trailers. See Automobile trailers
TRAVEL with children
How to make travel with children easier. il Good H 165:156-7 Jl '67

TRAVEL with children—*Continued*
Let's take the kids to Washington; excerpts from Washington; the New York times guide to the Nation's capital. A. Shuster. il Parents Mag 42:50-1+ Mr '67
'Round the world, family style. M. Roefer. il Motor B 120:22-5+ Jl; 27-9+ S '67; 121: 107-9 Ja '68
Should you take your children to Europe? Bet Hom & Gard 45:31 Jl '67
Traveling with children. C. P. Seton. il Atlan 220:126-9 O '67

TRAVELERS
Covered with Old Glory; advice to American tourists; excerpt from Maiden voyages. R. Girson. Sat R 50:48-50 My 6 '67
How grand it was! excerpts from Europe: the grand tour. L. Martin and S. Martin. Sat R 50:41-3 My 27 '67
Intelligent woman traveler; excerpts from Complete guide for the intelligent woman traveler. F. Koltun. Mlle 64:203-8 Mr '67
Letters of introduction. A. Waugh. Nat R 19:420 Ap 18 '67
Minority report. F. P. Keyes. Travel 127:58-9+ Mr '67
No truce on the tourists' front; Israel promoting hard. il Bsns W p40 Jl 15 '67
Those were the years that were: vets, jets, mods, and minis. G. Bocca. il Sat R 50:47+ Ap 22 '67
Tips for the travelling photographer. A. Rothstein. U S Camera 30:13-14 My '67
What an American consul can do for you; helping American travelers in foreign countries. Good H 165:197 O '67
See also
Voyages
Women as travelers

Anecdotes, facetiae, satire, etc.
You, too, can be anti-American. R. Baker. il N Y Times Mag p36-7+ Ap 23 '67
TRAVELERS insurance. See Insurance, Travelers
TRAVELING bags. See Luggage
TRAVELING hospitals. See Hospitals, Traveling
TRAVELING schools. See Schools, Traveling
TRAVELING theater. See Theater, Traveling
TRAVELS
Just a minute, Mrs Gulliver, by M. Considine. Review
Sat R 50:41-2 Jl 8 '67. H. Sutton
Maiden voyages, by R. Girson. Review
Sat R il 50:34 Ap 29 '67. E. Kimbrough
See also
Travel
Travelers
Vacations
Voyages
Voyages around the world
TRAVEN, B. pseud
Great Traven mystery. A. West. New Yorker 43:82+ Jl 22 '67
TRAVERS, Depaul
Evolution of the high school student. por Cath World 205:139-44 Je '67
TRAVERS, Pamela Lyndon
Cup of sorrow in every woman's life; interview, ed. by J. Graham. Ladies Home J 84:68+ F '67
TRAVERSE CITY, Mich.
Traverse City, Michigan. il Bet Hom & Gard 45:20+ Ag '67
TRAVIA, Anthony John
Other half of the state government. R. Reeves. il pors N Y Times Mag p24-5+ Ap 2 '67
La TRAVIATA; opera. See Verdi, G.
TRAVIS, Clifford K.
Update your old shopsmith with this two-way stand. Pop Mech 128:148-51 Ag '67
TRAVIS, William D. T.
Army of the Cumberland; paintings, with text by B. Catton. il por Am Heritage 19:40-9 D '67
TRAWLS and trawling
Trolling doubles. H. G. Tapply. il Field & S 72:54 Jl '67
TRAYS
Trays can simplify your life. B. Banks. il House B 109:41-3 S '67
TREADWELL, Porter Atkins
New year at Crab hill. Life 64:20B Ja 19 '68
TREASON
Benedict Arnold: how the traitor was unmasked; excerpt from George Washington in the American revolution. J. T. Flexner. il Am Heritage 18:6-15 O '67
Benedict Arnold: the aftermath of treason. M. Lomask. bibliog il Am Heritage 18:16-17+ O '67
See also
Trials (treason)

TREASURE; story. See Williams, L.
TREASURE dream; story. See Ayer, E.
TREASURE finders. See Metal detectors
TREASURE trove
Diving for treasure in the pirate city; Port Royal, Jamaica. H. H. Martin. il Sat Eve Post 240:63-7 Ag 12 '67
Ill-starred treasure comes into its own; auction of items of K. Wagner's Spanish treasure trove at New York's Parke-Bernet galleries. il Life 62:100-2 Mr 10 '67
Modern argonauts. V. D. Smith. il Ebony 22:99-102+ Mr '67
They dive for wrecks. J. R. Berry. il Pop Mech 127:92-4+ Mr '67
Transistors can find treasure. J. L. Russell, jr. il Motor B 119:138-41 My '67
Trove come true; salvage of an armada wrecked in 18th century off Florida at Manhattan's Parke-Bernet galleries. il Time 89: 74-5+ F 10 '67
TREASURY department (United States) See United States—Treasury department
TREAT, Ida
Flash flood underground. Holiday 42:48-9+ O '67
TREATIES
Conventions and agreements; ratified by UN. UN Mo Chron 4:73-4 Ag '67
International law commission and the law of treaties. H. Waldock. UN Mo Chron 4:69-76 My '67
Peace with justice; United Nations treaties; address, July 10, 1967. E. Warren. Vital Speeches 33:644-6 Ag 15 '67
U.S. discusses draft articles on the law of treaties; statement, October 20, 1967. R. D. Kearney. Dept State Bul 57:719-22 N 27 '67
See also
Antarctic treaty, 1959
North Atlantic treaty organization
also subhead Treaties under names of countries, e.g. United States—Treaties
TREATMENT of prisoners. See Prisoners—Treatment
TREATY of Moscow. See Nuclear test ban treaty, 1963
TREBLINKA concentration camp. See Concentration camps—Poland
TREE, Penelope
After the twig, the tree? pors Time 90:74 O 13 '67
Penelope Tree. P. Devlin. il pors Vogue 150: 162-5 O 1 '67
TREE breeding
Tubelings for tomorrow. A. A. Alm and R. Schantz-Hansen. il Am For 73:16-18 S '67
TREE drawing and painting. See Trees in art
TREE grafting. See Grafting
TREE houses
Building permits for tree houses! Life 63:4 Jl 14 '67
Front-yard tree house has to be presentable. il Sunset 139:70 Jl '67
Safety in the trees; building inspector requires parents to obtain tree-house building permits. il Time 90:68+ Jl 7 '67
TREE planting
Ground rules for tree planting. il Am Home 70:114-15 N '67
Here's how to plant a tree. il Bet Hom & Gard 45:122+ Ap '67
How to plant a good tree. il House & Gard 132:272-3 O '67
It pays to give a tree a proper start. D. Barrows. il Home Gard 54:40 N '67
Spring planting! il Bet Hom & Gard 45:134+ My '67
Tubelings for tomorrow. A. A. Alm and R. Schantz-Hansen. il Am For 73:16-18 S '67
When I plant a tree. H. R. Hodgson. il Am For 73:26-7+ Ja '67
TREE rings
Climate and tree rings in Mesa Verde. D. O'Bryan. il Nat Parks Mag 41:17-19 Ap '67
Tree ring indices: a circumpolar comparison. R. K. Haugen. bibliog il Science 158:773-5 N 10 '67
TREE roots. See Roots
TREE stumps. See Trees
TREES
All about trees; questions and answers. J. Daugherty and M. Daugherty. il Sci Digest 61:90-2 My '67
Best trees and shrubs for the colorful fruits of fall. D. Wyman. il Home Gard 54:22-3 O '67
Fantastic trees, by E. A. Menninger. Review
Am For il 73:28-30 Mr '67. C. B. Craig
Growing investment in shade and beauty. H. Mason and others. il Bet Hom & Gard 45:66-7 Ap '67

TREES—*Continued*
Silhouettes of distinctive trees. T. E. Avery. il Am For 73:24-6 S '67
Terraces and trees. il Home Gard 54:53-6+ Ap '67
Three tricks with trees. il Pop Gard 18:10 My '67
Trees across the plains. J. P. Jackson. il Am For 73:34-5+ N '67
Trees of Hawaii. S. M. Jepsen. il Am For 73:18-21+ D '67
Trees, the original inhabitants. O. A. Stevens. Am For 73:8+ F '67
Trees to grow by the sea. il Pop Gard 18:14-15 Ag '67
Twenty best trees to plant. C. Calkins. il House B 109:128-31+ F '67
Want to save a stump? polyethylene glycol treatment. il Pop Sci 190:175 My '67
What a good tree can do for you. il House & Gard 132:232-3+ O '67
  See also
Flowering trees
Forest conservation
Fruit trees
Grafting
Topiary work
Tree planting
Tree rings
  also names of trees, e.g. Walnut trees

Planting
  See Tree planting

Pruning
  See Pruning

TREES, Age of
Oldest living thing in the world; bristlecone pines. A. Hamilton. il Sci Digest 62:37-8 O '67
TREES, Care of
Are your trees in need of food and water? R. L. Rusden. il Home Gard 54:42-3 O '67
TREES, Dwarf
Alpine conifers as bonsai. il Sunset 139:234+ O '67
Lilliputian world of the bonsai. N. F. Busch. il Read Digest 91:182-6+ S '67
Up with the bonsai. il Sunset 139:100-1 O '67
TREES, Effect of radiation on. See Plants, Effect of radiation on
TREES, Fossil
Tridymite pseudomorphs after wood in Virginian lower cretaceous sediments. R. S. Mitchell. bibliog il Science 158:905-6 N 17 '67
  See also
Petrified Forest National Park
TREES, Historic
Oak in paradise. A. R. Chapman. il Am For 73:27+ S '67
Social register: eighty-five new champs. K. B. Pomeroy and L. C. Littlecott. il Am For 73:28-33 S '67
TREES, Photography of. See Photography of flowers, plants, trees, etc.
TREES, Training of
Topiary & espalier. il Home Gard 54:27-34 O '67
  See also
Fruit trees, Training of
TREES, Watering of. See Trees, Care of
TREES in art
Let's progress beyond the lollipop tree. C. J. Alkema. il Design 68:4-8 Sum '67
TREES in cities
Don't say it's not worthwhile to plant a tree. il Home Gard 54:38-9 N '67
Mall idea. il Sunset 139:70-5 S '67
Trees for St James. il Time 90:84 N 24 '67
Which trees and what street surfacing; regional APWA meeting. E. F. Spitzer. il Am City 82:97+ Jl '67
Why city folks need trees. G. E. Hafstad. il Am For 73:18-21 Ag '67
Woodsman; trees in Central park; interview. C. O'Shea. New Yorker 43:41-3 Mr 18 '67
TREFETHEN, Florence
Poet's workshop. Writer 80:21-4 S; 22-5 N '67; 81:27-30 Ja '68
TREGEAR, Geoffrey W. See Catt, K. J. jt. auth.
TREGO, Charlotte
Drop city. Arch Forum 127:74-5 S '67
TREHALOSE
Trehalose regulation of glucose-6-phosphate hydrolysis in blowfly extracts. S. Friedman. bibliog il Science 159:110-11 Ja 5 '68
TREIDLER, Adolph
Cover; linoleum cut. il Am Artist 31:4 Mr '67
TREIGLE, Norman
And we quote; interview. ed. by C. L. Osborne. por Hi Fi 17:MA19 S '67
Treigle approach; interview. ed. by F. Stevenson. por Opera N 31:13 F 25 '67

about
Two for the C-note. il por Newsweek 70:86 O 2 '67
TRELLISES
Build a garden trellis. il Pop Gard 18:56-7 My '67
Shade, screening, savory fare: all for 50 cents. L. H. Graffam. Home Gard 54:30 My '67
Two good-looking trellises. il Sunset 138:116 Ap '67
TRENCH, Sir David
Can Hong Kong be defended? interview. por U S News 62:36-7 My 29 '67
TRESPASS
Laying down the law to number-one lawman; trespassory eavesdrops. I. Younger. New Repub 156:11-13 Mr 4 '67
TRESSLER, Marcile F.
Sculpture for a school atrium. Sch Arts 66:15-18 Ja '67
TRESTLE tables. See Tables
TREVOR, William
Daftness falls from the air. L. Graver. New Repub 156:35-7 F 4 '67
TREVOR-ROPER, Hugh Redwald
Understanding Mao; or, look back to Stalin. N Y Times Mag p28-9+ F 12 '67
TRI Quang
Buddhists are back. il por Newsweek 70:49 O 9 '67
Conversation with a monk. J. Mirsky. por Nation 205:678-81 D 25 '67
Monk without a cause. il por Time 90:35-6 O 6 '67
TRIAL by jury. See Jury
TRIAL of Mother Goose; drama. See Miller, H. L.
TRIALS
And the moral of the Baker case is . . . R. Harwood. New Repub 156:17-19 F 4 '67
Bailey & the Boston strangler. il Time 89:40 Ja 27 '67
Baker case: a glimpse of inside politics. il U S News 62:42-3 F 6 '67
Baker found guilty. Sr Schol 90:22 F 24 '67
Bobby Baker trial: a rare look at politics behind the scenes. il U S News 62:8+ Ja 30 '67
Dead men tell no tales; Bobby Baker trial. il Time 89:22-3 Ja 27 '67
Friend in need; trial of Bobby Baker. Newsweek 69:29 Ja 30 '67
Guilty; Baker case. il Newsweek 69:33-4 F 6 '67
Inside the Baker case: the jurors' story. il U S News 62:39 F 13 '67
Secret of box G-302; Baker trial. Time 89:20-1 F 3 '67
T.R.B. from Washington; Baker case. New Repub 156:6 Ja 28 '67
Talk tactics; case of H. (Kayo) Konigsberg. il Time 89:76+ Ap 21 '67
Unaccustomed defeat; DeSalvo guilty. Newsweek 69:30 Ja 30 '67
Verdicts of history; with editorial comment (cont) T. J. Fleming. bibliog il Am Heritage 18:65-75 Ap; 28-33+ Ag; 19:22-7+ D '67
Winning loser; E. B. Williams loses case of Bobby Baker. il Time 89:66+ F 10 '67
  See also
Evidence (law)
Jury
Newspaper court reporting
Nuremberg trials

Bolivia
Judgment on Régis Debray. Newsweek 70:60 N 27 '67
Who, me? trial of R. Debray. Newsweek 70:42 O 9 '67

Brazil
Cracking down on Castro; trial of J. R. Debray. Nation 205:324-5 O 9 '67

France
L'affaire est finie; Ben Barka trial ends. Time 89:39 Je 16 '67

Germany (Federal Republic)
How secret the confessional? case of murders by J. Bartsch in Germany. il Time 90:51 D 22 '67

Great Britain
Last exit verdict casts doubt on U.K. obscenity laws. M. Reynolds. Pub W 192:20-1 D 11 '67
Test by jury; H. Selby, jr's Last exit to Brooklyn found obscene. Time 90:53 D 1 '67

TRIALS—*Continued*

Greece, Modern
Absent defendant. Newsweek 70:52+ N 27 '67

Korea (Republic)
Judgment on thirty-one; South Korean intellectuals charged with spying for North Korea in a net-work controlled from East Germany. Time 90:33 D 22 '67

Massachusetts
Banned in Massachusetts; Titicut follies. Time 91:65 Ja 19 '68
Two-way outrage; state charges Titicut follies invaded privacy of inmates. il Time 90:52 D 1 '67

Mississippi
Changing times. il Newsweek 70:28-9 O 30 '67
I never hit nobody; acquittal for eight white men on trial for violence to Negro school-children. il Time 89:48 Je 16 '67
Jury convicts seven; KKK case. Sr Schol 91:18 N 2 '67
Justice turns a corner in Mississippi; verdict on 1964 killings of civil rights workers. America 117:495 N 4 '67
Philadelphia murders; lynching of three civil rights workers. il Newsweek 70:32-3 O 23 '67
Reckoning in Meridian; seven men guilty of conspiracy. il Time 90:32-3 O 27 '67
Time of trial; charges of conspiracy to deprive slain civil rights workers of constitutional rights. il Time 90:22 O 20 '67

Russia
Chain reaction. il Newsweek 71:29-31 Ja 8 '68
Moscow trial; the perils of literature. il Newsweek 71:35 Ja 22 '68
Off with the mask; trial of intellectuals accused of anti-Soviet agitation. il Time 91:21-2 Ja 19 '68

South Africa
Jungle law; South-West African nationalists tried for terrorism. Reporter 37:14 D 28 '67

Yugoslavia
Matter of definiiton; M. Mihajlov faces new trial. il Newsweek 69:38 My 1 '67

TRIALS (espionage)
Judgment on thirty-one; South Korean intellectuals charged with spying for North Korea in a net-work controlled from East Germany. Time 90:33 D 22 '67

TRIALS (libel)
Authors & editors; Dr. S. K. Stevens sued by H. C. Frick. Pub W 191:176-7 Ja 23 '67
Blacklisted! story of J. H. Faulk; condensation of The jury returns. L. Nizer. il Read Digest 90:201-4+ Mr '67
Church libel suit; libel action against A. D. Pont by two liberal theologians of the Dutch Reformed in South Africa. America 117:47 Jl 15 '67
Conductors at Glyndebourne; libel action in London by Stanley Frederick John Pritchard, against Saturday review. Sat R 50:39 D 30 '67
Final arguments heard in Frick-Stevens libel case. il Pub W 191:222-6 Ja 23 '67
Frick-Stevens battle enters new phase. Pub W 192:44 Ag 21 '67
History and privacy; dismissal of Frick lawsuit. America 116:848 Je 17 '67
Interim report on South Africa libel trial. Christian Cent 84:677 My 24 '67
Justice wins a case in South Africa. Christian Cent 84:828-9 Je 28 '67
Stevens' book vindicated by Pennsylvania court; judge terms book true and excellent history; with editorial comment. Pub W 191:144+, 152 Je 5 '67
See also
Trials (seditious libel)

TRIALS (murder)
Bailey for the defense. il Newsweek 69:35-6+ Ap 17 '67
Case for the defense; famous attorneys talk of famous cases. il Esquire 68:51-4 Jl '67
Coppolino verdict. il Newsweek 69:42 My 8 '67
Disposal of Jack Ruby. G. Wills and O. Demaris. Esquire 67:131-5+ Je '67
High ground; LSD was basis of murder acquittal of S. Kessler. Newsweek 70:37 N 6 '67
House of death; R. Speck trial. il Newsweek 69:43-4 Ap 17 '67
How secret the confessional? case of murders by J. Bartsch in Germany. il Time 90:51 D 22 '67

Insulin shocker; W. Archerd accused of using insulin as a murder weapon. il Newsweek 70:25-6 D 25 '67
Judgment on Speck. Newsweek 69:29 Ap 24 '67
Justice vs. journalism; Speck trial. il Newsweek 69:37 Mr 6 '67
Mary Coppolino's own story; ed. by E. Linn. M. Coppolino. Good H 165:72-3+ Ag '67
Masakin in Peoria; first week of the Speck trial. il Time 89:36 Ap 14 '67
Mississippi mud. Nat R 19:1158 O 31 '67
Press & Richard Speck. Time 89:49 Mr 3 '67
Reliving a murder; Thomas Kidwell verdict. il Time 90:38 D 29 '67
That's it, Jack; J. Kirschke. Newsweek 71:29 Ja 22 '68
Tiny red mark; Coppolino's second murder trial. il Newsweek 69:28 Ap 24 '67
Tracing the untraceable; trial of Dr Carl Coppolino. il Time 89:24-5 My 5 '67
Two states of mind; insanity pleas. il Time 90:50 N 3 '67
Verdicts of history; husband's revenge; Daniel E. Sickles case. T. J. Fleming. il Am Heritage 18:65-75 Ap '67

TRIALS (obscenity)
Landmark decision in the war on pornography; Polly King case in Cincinnati. O. K. Armstrong. Read Digest 91:93-7 S '67
Last exit verdict casts doubt on U.K. obscenity laws. M. Reynolds. Pub W 192:20-1 D 11 '67
Love in California: The love book trial. A. V. Krebs, jr. Commonweal 86:359-61 Je 16 '67
Test by jury; H. Selby, jr's Last exit to Brooklyn found obscene in Great Britain. Time 90:53 D 1 '67

TRIALS (perjury)
Shutting up big-mouth; D. Andrews found guilty of having committed perjury three times during J. Garrison's investigation. il Time 90:48+ Ag 25 '67

TRIALS (poisoning)
Milk-shake Mary; Mary Koshiol found guilty of attempted murder of husband. Newsweek 70:25 Jl 31 '67

TRIALS (rape)
Lucky death sentence; retrial of Giles brothers. il Time 90:81 N 10 '67

TRIALS (seditious libel)
Verdicts of history; a scandalous, malicious and seditious libel. T. J. Fleming. il Am Heritage 19:22-7+ D '67

TRIALS (slander) See Trials (libel)

TRIALS (treason)
Verdicts of history; trial of John Brown. T. J. Fleming. bibliog il Am Heritage 18:28-33+ Ag '67

TRIALS, Military. See Courts martial

TRIALS, War crime. See Nuremberg trials; World war, 1939-1945—War criminals

TRIALS of Brother Jero; drama. See Soyinka, W.

TRIANGLE conduit and cable company
Three-sided figure. R. Levy. Duns R 90:48-9+ S '67

TRIBES and tribal systems
Kenya report: market in brides. L. Fellows. il N Y Times Mag p 12+ F 19 '67
Living prehistory in India. D. D. Kosambi. il Sci Am 216:104-12+ F '67
See also
Society, Primitive

TRIBOLIUM. See Flour beetles

TRIBUNE (Chicago) See Chicago tribune

TRICHINA and trichinosis
Trichinosis knocks pork exports. Farm J 91:72H F '67

TRICHLOROPHENOXYACETIC acid
Drafting a weed killer; 2,4,5-T to defoliate Vietnam jungles. il Bsns W p37 Ap 22 '67
2,4,5-Trichlorophenoxyacetic acid: effect on ethylene production by fruits and leaves of fig tree. E. C. Maxie and J. C. Crane. bibliog il Science 155:1548-50 Mr 24 '67

TRI-CITIES opera
Binghamton; performance of Rossini's Barbiere di Siviglia. J. Browning. Opera N 31:30 Ap 8 '67

TRICK photography. See Photography, Trick

TRICKS
See also
Conjuring

TRICONTINENTAL conference, Havana, 1966
OAS council: report recommends anti-Communist measures; study of the first Tricontinental conference, Havana, January 1966. G. Meek. il Américas 19:42-3 Ja '67

TRIDYMITE
Tridymite pseudomorphs after wood in Virginian lower cretaceous sediments. R. S. Mitchell. bibliog il Science 158:905-6 N 17 '67

TRILLIN, Calvin
Barnett Frummer learns to distinguish packaged paprika from the real article; story. New Yorker 43:36-8 Ap 8 '67
Lester Drentluss, a Jewish boy from Baltimore, attempts to make it through the summer of 1967. Atlan 221:43-5 Ja '68
Reporter at large. New Yorker 43:56-8+ Ap 22; 41-6+ Je 10 '67
U.S. letter. New Yorker 43:210-14+ O 14; 173-4+ N 4; 208+ N 25; 128+ D 16 '67; 76+ Ja 6 '68

TRILLING, Diana
Germany 1967. Atlan 219:46-7 My '67
Liberal anti-communism revisited. Commentary 44:73-6 S '67

TRILLING, Lionel
Liberal anti-communism revisited. Commentary 44:76 S '67

TRIMARANS
Fun³, a big time in the Bahamas. E. Horan. il Yachting 122:50-1+ N '67
Getting there is more than half the fun. N. Brower. il Motor B 120:29-31+ O '67
Trimarans, an owner's frank appraisal. R. Stolle. il Yachting 122:48-9+ D '67

TRIMBLE, La Valle T.
How to get money for college. Am Ed 3:9-11 Jl '67

TRIMBLE, Lester
And we quote; interview, ed. by S. Fleming. por Hi Fi 17:MA10 N '67

TRIMESTER system. See College year

TRIMMERS, Lawn. See Lawn mowers

TRINIDAD (island)
See also
Birds—Trinidad (island)

TRINIDAD and Tobago
Forward-looking nation. A. J. Lowe. il Américas 19:23-30 Je '67
Trinidad and Tobago. A. J. Lowe. il Américas 19:1-10 My '67
Trinidad and Tobago country review. G. Meek. Américas 19:45 N '67

TRINITY
In defense of heresy. A. Towne; discussion. Christian Cent 84:211-13 F 15 '67

TRINITY ALPS. See Klamath Mountains

TRINITY college, Dublin. See Colleges and universities—Ireland

TRIP out on Red Lizzie; story. See Kersh, G.

TRIPODS, Camera. See Camera tripods

TRIPOLI, Nancy
Twinkle twinkle little UFO. Flying 81:85 S '67

TRIPPE, Juan Terry
Men who made the world move. H. Bigart. por Sat R 50:60-1 Ap 22 '67

TRISTAN and Isolde; opera. See Wagner, R.

TRITERPENES. See Terpenes

TRITICALE
Birth of a super-food; combining wheat and rye into a new and larger form. J. Bird. il Sat Eve Post 240:62+ Jl 1 '67
New grain you may be growing; wheat-rye cross. N. Grove. il Farm J 91:44P+ S '67

TRITIUM
Radioactive wastes from fusion reactors. F. L. Parker. bibliog il Science 159:83-4 Ja 5 '68

TRITON (satellite) See Satellites

TRIUMPH for two; drama. See Corson, H. W.

TRIVIA collecting. See Collectors and collecting

TRIVIA contest. See Competitions

TROCCHI, Alexander
Other culture. B. Farrell. il por Life 62:96-7 F 17 '67

TROGDON, Gertrude
Exporting Thanksgiving. A. Balk. Sat R 50: 26 N 4 '67

TROGLODYTES. See Cave dwellers

TROJAN men; opera. See Berlioz, H.

TROJAN war
Lost: the Trojan war. M. I. Finley. il Horizon 9:50-5 Spr '67

TROJAN women; opera. See Garwood, M.

TROLL motors. See Electric motors

TROLLING. See Trawls and trawling

TROLLOPE, Anthony
Case of contemptible efficiency. L. Conger. Writer 80:9-10 S '67

TROMBLEY, William
Three Rs in California; Reagan, the Regents, and the right. Sat R 50:47-8+ Mr 18 '67

TROMMER, Philip R.
Community recreation referral project. por Parks & Rec 2:19+ Ag '67

TROPHIES, Sport
Three for the trophy; Heisman trophy. il Newsweek 70:94 N 27 '67

TROPICAL ferns. See Ferns

TROPICAL Park racetrack, Miami. See Race tracks

TROPICAL plants
See also
Bromeliads

TROPICS
See also
Caribbean Region

Diseases and hygiene
See also
Malaria

TROPOSPHERIC radio wave propagation
Air force to test portable tropo radio; tropospheric scatter telecommunications. C. D. LaFond. il Tech W 20:23-5 Mr 20 '67
Bell tropo unit to begin tests at Eglin. C. D. LaFond. il Tech W 20:30+ Je 12 '67

TROPOSPHERIC scatter communications. See Tropospheric radio wave propagation

TROTT, Susan
Suzanne; story. Mlle 65:34 My '67

TROTTER, Wilfred
What nature reveals about peacemaking. J. F. Wharton. Sat R 50:14-16 My 27 '67

TROTTING races. See Harness racing

TROUBLE with anchovies; story. See Shyer, M. F.

TROUBLE with marriage; story. See Madocs, R.

TROUHANOVA, Natalia Vladimirovna
La Péri: 1912. L. Joffe. il pors Dance Mag 41:40-2 Ap '67

TROUT, Lawana
We ain't unteachable, just unteached. NEA J 56:24-6 Ap '67

TROUT
Coronary disease in spawning steelhead trout salmo gairdnerii. R. L. Van Citters and N. W. Watson. bibliog il Science 159:105-7 Ja 5 '68

TROUT fishing
Art of worm fishing. W. Davis. il Outdoor Life 139:78+ Mr '67
Big fly: big trout. V. C. Marinaro. il Outdoor Life 139:56-9+ Mr '67
Big three of cold-water sport fishing: trout, char, salmon. A. J. McClane. il Field & S 72:44+ My '67
Big trout are my meat. K. Asper and J. Hayes. il Outdoor Life 139:66-9+ Ap '67
Big tumbling creek K. Mink. il Outdoor Life 139:62-5 Je '67
Boom in steelheads. R. Gerlach. il Outdoor Life 139:40-3+ Je '67
Bull trout testimonial. L. C. Newlun. il Field & S 71:56-7+ Ap '67
Cutthroats of southeast arm. G. A. Barrus. il Field & S 72:34-5+ Jl '67
Deschutes steelhead. J. Gartner. il Field & S 72:40-1+ Jl '67
Dig 'em out of the bushes; New York's Ausable River. W. Davis. il Outdoor Life 140:54+ Jl '67
Don't fish while I'm talking. R. Manning. il Atlan 220:123 O '67
Easy way to catch trout. H. G. Tapply. Field & S 72:72 Je '67
Fall steelheads are back. J. O. Cartier. il Outdoor Life 140:58-9+ O '67
Fish the headwaters for trout. C. Elliott. il Outdoor Life 139:58-61+ My '67
Fishing a floating island. J. Martin. il Outdoor Life 140:42-3+ Jl '67
Fishing in the land of fire. E. Schwiebert. il Field & S 72:48-9+ N '67
Fishing the big ones. T. Trueblood. il Field & S 72:22+ Ag '67
Fishing the Klamath Loop. M. Hayden. il Outdoor Life 140:36-9+ S '67
Float trip for rainbows. W. Davis. il Outdoor Life 139:28+ My '67
Great hatch. E. W. McCray. il Outdoor Life 140:24-7+ Jl '67
High water and flies only. B. Warner. il Field & S 71:44-5+ Ap '67
How to fish high lakes. H. Wixom. il Outdoor Life 140:42-3+ Ag '67
How to read a trout stream. A. J. McClane. il Field & S 72:78-81 Ja '68
Lakers on top; Great Bear Lake in Northwest Territories. W. Davis. il Outdoor Life 139: 94+ F '67
Little T for big trout. C. Elliott. il Outdoor Life 140:44-7+ N '67
Mackinaw on a fly. E. Park. il Field & S 71: 42-3+ Ap '67
Midsummer night rainbows. J. Hayes. il Field & S 72:94-7+ Ja '68
Natural baits for trout. T. Trueblood. il Field & S 71:26+ Ap '67
New angle for anglers; trout preserves. Newsweek 70:30 Jl 31 '67

TRUST TERRITORY OF THE PACIFIC IS-LANDS—*Continued*
Sprawling trust. il Time 90:32+ N 3 '67
Trust Territory of the Pacific Islands; statements, June 8, 1967. E. Anderson; W. R. Norwood; L. Salii. Dept State Bul 57:365-78 S 18 '67

TRUSTEES. See Trusts and trustees

TRUSTEES, Library. See Libraries—Trustees, boards, committees, etc.

TRUSTEES of colleges. See College trustees

TRUSTEESHIP council. See United Nations—Trusteeship council

TRUSTS, Charitable. See Charitable uses and trusts

TRUSTS, Industrial
Case for conglomerates. Fortune 75:163-4 Je 15 '67
Too big for antitrust to handle? il Bsns W p70-2 Jl 8 '67
    See also
Business consolidations and mergers
Corporations
Monopolies

International trusts
Quinine caper; activities of German-Dutch dominated international cartel. New Repub 156:9 Ap 8 '67

Law
Antitrust hears a kind word; highlights of study released by FTC economist, W. F. Mueller. il Bsns W p78+ Jl 29 '67
Antitrust slowdown? A. M. Bickel. New Repub 156:15-18 My 20 '67; Reply with rejoinder. R. L. Wright. 156:32-3 Je 10 '67
Banking and the antitrust laws. W. T. Lifland. bibliog f Harvard Bsns R 45:138-44 My '67
Big business and the law. Sr Schol 90:11 Ap 7 '67
Crybaby act? Senate antitrust and monopoly subcommittee investigates newspapers. Newsweek 70:70 Jl 24 '67
Finding homes for merger orphans; problems of divestiture. il Bsns W p 154+ D 9 '67
Give us a merger policy. J. Weingarten. il Duns R 90:43-4+ D '67
Library shelving firms pay antitrust damages; Oregon and California. Library J 92:1403 Ap 1 '67
Meaning of monopoly; Justice department case against Times Mirror co, purchase of San Bernardino newspapers. il Newsweek 69:67 Je 12 '67
New ball game? Supreme court ruling on Procter-Clorox and conglomerate mergers. Newsweek 69:75-6 Ap 24 '67
No guidelines in sight; ten-year-old Procter & Gamble-Clorox chemical merger. Time 89:92+ Ap 21 '67
Now, a tougher barrier to big mergers? U S News 62:12+ Ap 24 '67
Short pause for new rules; Justice department's antitrust division protests ITT-ABC merger. Time 89:82+ Mr 24 '67
Supreme court versus corporate efficiency. R. H. Bork. Fortune 76:92-3+ Ag '67
Taking the crusade out of antitrust. il Bsns W p59-62 My 20 '67
Waiting for fresh legal guidelines; business decisions the Supreme court must make. Bsns W p38-9 S 23 '67

United States
    See also
United States—Justice, Department of—Antitrust division

TRUSTS, Investment. See Investment trusts

TRUSTS and trustees
Use a trust to avoid probate? Suc Farm 65:30B N '67
Who will look out for the kids if something happens to you? il Changing T 21:37-8 My '67

TRUTH, Sojourner
Sojourner Truth, the first sit-in. M. Harlowe. por Negro Hist Bul 29:173-4 Fall '66

TRUTH
Of many things; church's attitude toward truth and truthfulness. T. N. Davis; discussion. America 116:267, 496-501 F 25, Ap 1 '67

TRUTH drugs. See Narcoanalysis

TRUTHFULNESS
Of many things; church's attitude toward truth and truthfulness. T. N. Davis; discussion. America 116:267, 496-501 F 25, Ap 1 '67
Reflections; truth and politics. H. Arendt. New Yorker 43:49-52+ F 25 '67
Tell it like it is. A. Silberman. Read Digest 91:15-16+ N '67

TRUXAL, J. G. See David, E. E. jt. auth.

TRYON, Alice F. and Vida, Gabor
Platyzoma: a new look at an old link in ferns. bibliog Science 156:1109-10 My 26 '67

TRYPAN blue
Lysosomal enzyme inhibition by trypan blue; a theory of teratogenesis. F. Beck and others. bibliog il Science 157:1180-2 S 8 '67

TRYPTOPHAN
Substrate binding properties of mutant and wild-type A proteins of escherichia coli tryptophan synthetase. J. K. Hardman and C. Yanofsky. bibliog il Science 156:1369-71 Je 9 '67
Tryptophan hydroxylation: measurement in pineal gland, brainstem, and carcinoid tumor. W. Lovenberg and others. bibliog il Science 155:217-19 Ja 13 '67

TSAI, Gerald, jr
Tsai touch no longer seems so golden. il por Bsns W p80+ Mr 4 '67

TSCHICHOLD, Jan
Jan Tschichold: proponent of asymmetry and tradition. P. Standard. il por Pub W 191:88-92+ My 1 '67

TSHOMBE, Moise
Abduction in the air. il por Time 90:19-20 Jl 14 '67
Certain apprehension. il por Time 90:26 Ag 4 '67
Clemency. Commonweal 86:484 Ag 11 '67
End of Moise Tshombe. Nat R 19:840-1 Ag 8 '67
India-rubber man. il por Newsweek 70:34+ Jl 17 '67
Let Tshombe go. Nat R 19:1250 N 14 '67
Matter of justice. America 117:125 Ag 5 '67
Moise Tshombe on the way to his kidnaping. il pors Life 63:28D-30 Jl 14 '67
One-way trip; Algeria's supreme court orders extradition. il por Newsweek 70:38 Jl 31 '67
Plot and counter-plot. K. Kyle. New Repub 157:13-16 S 16 '67
Too hot to handle? Nat R 19:890 Ag 22 '67
Tshombe scowls in Algerian detention as Congo writhes. il por Life 63:32B Jl 21 '67

TSIEN, Hsue-shen
Bitter tea of Dr Tsien. M. Viorst. por Esquire 68:125-9+ S '67
Incredible story of How China got the bomb; excerpts. W. L. Ryan and S. Summerlin. il por Look 31:19-25 Jl 25 '67

TSUKADA, Matsuo
Chenopod and amaranth pollen: electron-microscopic identification. bibliog Science 157:80-2 Jl 7 '67

TSUNAMIS. See Seismic sea waves

TUAMOTU ISLANDS
Sailing through the Tuamotus. S. A. Simpson. il Travel 128:30-5 D '67

TUBBS, W. E. See Pribram, K. H. jt. auth.

TUBERCULIN
Passive transfer of tuberculin reactivity in vitro. P. Fireman and others. bibliog il Science 155:337-8 Ja 20 '67

TUBEROUS begonias. See Begonias

TUBMAN, William Vacanarat Shadrach
Resilient uncle. por Time 91:35 Ja 5 '68

TUBULOSINE
Structural basis for the inhibition of protein biosynthesis: mode of action of tubulosine. A. P. Grollman. bibliog il Science 157:84-5 Jl 7 '67

TUCHMAN, Barbara (Wertheim)
Can history use Freud? the case of Woodrow Wilson. Atlan 219:39-44 F '67
Historian's opportunity. Sat R 50:27-31+ F 25 '67
How we entered World war I. N Y Times Mag p40-1+ Mr 5 '67
In the wake of war; time and reality in the Middle East. Atlan 220:62-9 N '67
Israel's swift sword. Atlan 220:56-62 S '67
Missing element; excerpts from address. McCalls 94:28+ Je '67; Excerpts. PTA Mag 61:20-2 My '67

TUCK, Jim
Primitives: Catholicism's submerged third. Cath World 204:284-8 F '67

TUCKER, Harold W.
Greater role in education seen for public libraries; summary of statement, May 15, 1967. Library J 92:2322+ Je 15 '67

TUCKER, Helen
Such a quiet thing; story. Ladies Home J 84:98-9 N '67
Where did we go wrong? Ladies Home J 84:110-11+ Mr '67

TUCKER, Marcia
Natkin: overtones at outskirts. Art N 66:48-9+ Mr '67

TUCKER, Richard
Recordings. M. Mayer. Esquire 68:16+ O '67

TUCKER, Robert C.
United States-Soviet co-operation: incentives and obstacles; address. April 1967, with questions and answers. bibliog f Ann Am Acad 372:1-15 Jl '67

TUCKER, Walter L.
Rattlesnake jamboree; ed. by B. East. Outdoor Life 139:60-3+ Mr '67

TUCKERMAN, Anne Weill-. See Weill-Tuckerman, A.

TUCKWELL, Barry
Music to my ears; Carnegie Hall concert. I. Kolodin. Sat R 50:44 Mr 25 '67

TUCSON, Ariz.

Description
Booked for travel. H. Sutton. Sat R 50:43 Mr 18 '67

Education
Tucson's tale of two cultures. NEA J 56:56:62+ F '67

Police
Radio-telephone answers communication lack. D. W. Richards. il Am City 82:113 Ap '67

Sanitary affairs
Refuse trains, better, faster, safer. H. L. Danforth. il Am City 82:102-4 N '67

TUDOR, Antony
Tudor and the Royal ballet. S. J. Cohen. il Sat R 50:74-5 My 13 '67
Tudor in form, company in stride. I. Kolodin. Sat R 50:62 My 20 '67

TUFTS university, Medford, Mass.

Lincoln Filene center for citizenship and public affairs
Subject: human rights. J. H. Sofokidis. il Am Ed 4:12-14 D '67

TUFTY, Barbara
Man and his science. Sci N 91:188-9 F 25 '67

TUGBOATS
Man from Moran. C. Peet. il Pop Mech 128:136-9+ N '67

TUGGLE, Robert A.
People and their feelings. Opera N 31:8-13 Mr 4 '67

TUITION fees. See Colleges and universities— Finance

TULIP trees
Nature note. il Sci N 91:492 My 27 '67

TULIPS
Choice tulips for planting this fall. R. Mark. il Horticulture 45:24-5 O '67
Lust for tulips. A. West. il Vogue 150:192-7+ D '67
Rainbow of tulip color. il Home Gard 54:20-1 S '67
There's variety in tulips. P. F. Frese. il Pop Gard 18:48-51 D '67
What price tulips? J. Bryan, 3d. il Holiday 41:62-3 Ap '67

TULLIUS, F. P.
Billy Brown shoes in west Hollywood. New Yorker 43:31-3 My 27 '67
Frog week at the 7-11, near West Hollywood. New Yorker 43:40-2 S 9 '67
Oldies but goodies. New Yorker 43:56 D 9 '67
Sweetly flows the dun. New Yorker 43:44-5 Ap 15 '67

TULLOCK, Gordon
Where scientists fear to tread. Nat R 19:531-2 My 16 '67

TULSA, Okla.
Ministers: a 200-hour view. H. W. Allison. Christian Cent 84:533-5 Ap 26 '67

Education
How team teaching works in Tulsa: East central high school. J. L. Armstrong. il Sr Schol 90:sup 17 Ap 14 '67

TULSA, Okla. city-county library system
Fine arts festival in Tulsa. B. Hagist and F. Neighbors. il Wilson Lib Bul 42:309-11 N '67

TUMIN, Melvin
Teaching in America. Sat R 50:77-9+ O 21 '67

TUMOR viruses
Oncogenicity by DNA tumor viruses; enhancement after ultraviolet and cobalt-60 radiations. V. Defendi and F. Jensen. bibliog il Science 157:703-5 Ag 11 '67
See also
Adenoviruses

TUMORS
Cell-bound immunity to autologous and syngeneic mouse tumors induced by methylcholanthrene and plastic discs. I. Hellström and K. E. Hellström. bibliog il Science 156:981-3 My 19 '67

Challenge to man of the neoplastic cell; address, December 13, 1966. P. Rous. bibliog Science 157:24-8 Jl 7 '67
Eosinophilic response in glioblastoma tissue culture after addition of autologous lymphocytes. J. Ciembroniewicz and O. Kolar. bibliog il Science 157:1054-5 S 1 '67
Hepatomas; report on symposium. S. Weinhouse. Science 158:542-3 O 27 '67
Herpes-type virus and chromosome marker in normal leukocytes after growth with irradiated Burkitt cells. W. Henle and others. bibliog il Science 157:1064-5 S 1 '67
Insulin biosynthesis: evidence for a precursor. D. F. Steiner and others. bibliog il Science 157:697-700 Ag 11 '67
Leukemia and tumors. L. W. Sauer. PTA Mag 61:33-4+ My '67
Loss of thymus-distinctive serological characteristics in mice under certain conditions. M. Schlesinger and V. K. Golakai. bibliog il Science 155:1114-16 Mr 3 '67
Murine lymphoma: augmented growth in mice with pertussis vaccine-induced lymphocytosis. M. Hirano and others. bibliog il Science 158:1061-4 N 24 '67
Zeroing in on mono; relationship between mononucleosis and Burkitt's lymphoma. Newsweek 71:61 Ja 22 '68
See also
Melanoma

TUMORS, Blood. See Leukemia

TUMORS, Malignant. See Cancer

TUNA fish
Oxygen consumption of red and white muscles from tuna fishes. M. S. Gordon. bibliog il Science 159:87-90 Ja 5 '68
See also
Cookery—Fish

TUNA fishing
Tuna slaughter; American study of Japanese tuna fishing in tropical Atlantic. L. Gebhart. il(p585) Sci N 91:597 Je 24 '67

TUNG-Sol electric incorporated-Wagner electric corporation merger. See Business consolidations and mergers

TUNING, Radio. See Radio receivers—Tuning

TUNIS, John R.
John R. Tunis: a commitment to values. W. J. Jacobs. Horn Bk 43:48-54 F '67

TUNIS

Galleries and museums
Art. M. Grosser. Nation 204:634-6 My 15 '67

TUNISIA
Art of plain talk; improvements under Bourguiba régime. il Time 90:40 S 29 '67
See also
Architecture, Domestic—Tunisia

Antiquities
Art. M. Grosser. Nation 204:634-6 My 15 '67
Takrouna. M. H. Goldfinger. il Arch Forum 127:98-106 Jl '67

Art
See also
Tunis—Galleries and museums

Foreign relations
Tunisia and Egypt. il Atlan 219:28+ Ap '67

TUNISIA, National museum. See Tunis—Galleries and museums

TUNISIAN architecture. See Architecture, Tunisian

TUNLEY, Roul
America's ten best hospitals. Ladies Home J 84:34+ F '67
Europe's TEE trains. Travel 128:59-62 Ag '67; Same abr. with title Glamour rides the rails again. Read Digest 91:25-6 Ag '67
Why not compulsory hospital insurance? Sat R 50:12-14 Jl 8 '67
Why we need more nurses, now. Redbook 129:68-9+ Jl '67

TUNNELS and tunneling
Corkscrew tunnel gives driving new twist; near Drammen, Norway. D. Scott. il Pop Sci 191:62-3 Ag '67
Dig we must, and faster. il Bsns W p 135-6 F 11 '67
Rapid excavation. T. E. Howard. il Sci Am 217:74-6+ bibliog(p 154) N '67

TUNNEY, Gene
My most unforgettable character. Read Digest 90:75-80 Ap '67

TUPOLEV, Andreï Nikolaevich
Heroes who man Soviet drawing-boards. por Bsns W p66 Mr 18 '67

TUPPER, Harmon
SCORE spells help for the small businessman. Read Digest 90:19+ Mr '67

TURANDOT; opera. See Busoni, F.

TURBINE generators. See Electric generators

TURBINES
See also
Gas turbines, Aircraft

TURBINES, Mercury. See Mercury turbines

TURBOFAN engines. See Gas turbines, Aircraft

TURBOJETS. See Gas turbines, Aircraft

TURBOPROP airplane engines. See Gas turbines, Aircraft

TURBOSUPERCHARGERS. See Airplane engines—Superchargers

TURBULENCE detector. See Aeronautic instruments

TURCO, Lewis
Arras tapestry; poem. Poetry 111:166 D '67
Of laureates and lovers. Sat R 50:31-3+ O 14 '67

TURECK, Rosalyn
And we quote; ed. by E. Salzman. por Hi Fi 17:MA17 Ap '67
about
Music to my ears; Carnegie Hall recital. I. Kolodin. Sat R 51:97 Ja 13 '68
Tureck talks Bach. S. Fleming. il por Hi Fi 17:MA9+ O '67

TURF, Artificial
How to put down an instant lawn. R. Capotosto. il Pop Sci 191:178-81 O '67
Mod sod. il Time 89:57 My 12 '67

TURGENEV, Ivan Sergeevich
Turgenev's Traviata; story, excerpt from On the eve, tr. by G. Gardiner. por Opera N 32:24-5 D 30 '67

TURIN, Italy
Street traffic
Turin tries computer traffic control. il Am City 82:136 Ap '67

TURKEY
See also
Americans in Turkey
Cappadocia
Earthquakes—Turkey
European war, 1914-1918—Turkey
Miletus
Opera—Turkey
Publishers and publishing—Turkey
Antiquities
Ancient Ararat; discovery of Urartian treasures at Altintepe. T. Özgüç. il Sci Am 216:38-46 bibliog(p 150) Mr '67
Strange case of James Mellaart; or, The tale of the missing Dorak treasure; with editorial comment by J. J. Thorndike. K. Pearson and P. Connor. il Horizon 9:2-3, 4-15 Sum '67
See also
Aphrodisias
Foreign relations
New regime in Turkey. R. C. Lawson. Cur Hist 52:105-10+ F '67
Out of the past: Cyprus on the brink. il Newsweek 70:37-8 D 4 '67
Shadows of war; threat of invasion of Cyprus. il Time 90:22-3 D 1 '67
Still ticking; situation in Cyprus; Paradise lost. il Newsweek 70:48-9 D 11 '67
Turkey: a U.S. ally that is warming up to Russia. il U S News 63:52-3 D 11 '67
Turkey and the United States reaffirm bonds of friendship and cooperation; exchange of greetings and exchange of toasts, April 3, 1967, with joint communique. C. Sunay; L. B. Johnson. Dept State Bul 56:652-7 Ap 24 '67
See also
Cyprus
History
Dead hand of the Ottomans. E. Kern. il Life 63:70+ O 6 '67
Old order on the road to oblivion; Ottoman Empire. E. Kern. il Life 63:48-57 O 20 '67

European war, 1914-1918
See European war, 1914-1918—Turkey

Politics and government
Turkey: a U.S. ally that is warming up to Russia. il U S News 63:52-3 D 11 '67
Turkey; emerging democracy. A. Yalcin. For Affairs 45:706-14 Jl '67
See also
Political parties—Turkey

Social life and customs
In Turkey, everything comes up roses; experiences in small Turkish seacoast village. A. Friendly. il Harper 234:85-9 F '67

TURKEY, Frozen. See Poultry, Frozen

TURKEY as food. See Cookery—Poultry

TURKEY carving. See Carving (meat, etc)

TURKEY hunting
I have the last gobble. G. Gresham. il Outdoor Life 139:58-9+ Ap '67
Thanksgiving comes twice a year out West. V. Kraft. il Sports Illus 26:60+ Je 5 '67

TURKEY point. See Wilderness areas—Florida

TURKEYS
Turkeys: the new look, and how they got that way. il Good H 165:199 N '67

TURKEYS, Wild
Gobblers get their wings; restocking programs. G. Heinzman. il Outdoor Life 139:56-9+ F '67
See also
Turkey hunting

TURKISH cookery. See Cookery, Turkish

TURMAN, James A.
Decisions from the field. Am Ed 3:20-1 Jl '67

TURNBULL, Andrew
Fitzgerald as teacher. Harper 234:106 F '67
Thomas Wolfe arrives; excerpt from Thomas Wolfe. Atlan 220:60-6 D '67

TURNBULL, Colin M.
Nature of reality. Natur Hist 76:58+ My '67

TURNCOATS
See also
Defectors, Political

TURNER, Arthur Campbell
Britain in the western alliance. bibliog f Cur Hist 52:257-63+ My '67

TURNER, C.
Beginning of tomorrow; story. Good H 164:100-1 Je '67
One of the family; story. Good H 165:94-5 S '67

TURNER, Donald Frank
Antitrust slowdown? A. M. Bickel. New Repub 156:15-18 My 20 '67; Reply with rejoinder. R. L. Wright. 156:32-3 Je 10 '67
New watchdog for the admen? il por Bsns W p94-6 F 18 '67
Taking the crusade out of antitrust. il por Bsns W p59-62 My 20 '67

TURNER, Evan H.
Living with antiques. Antiques 92:91-5 Jl '67

TURNER, Jack
Man who feeds the trumpeters. pors Outdoor Life 139:64-7+ F '67
World's biggest grizzly? pors Outdoor life 139:41-3+ Mr '67

TURNER, Joseph Mallord William
Elemental Turner; with a gravure portfolio. J. Canaday. Horizon 9:88-105 Spr '67
J. M. W. Turner, by J. Lindsay. Review Nation 204:345-6 Mr 13 '67. J. Solman

TURNER, Morris
Elementary guide to civil rights bird watching. il Ebony 22:68-9+ Mr '67

TURNER, Myron
Two poems: At the place of transformation; The lioness triumphs over the radio. Yale R 56:429-30 Mr '67

TURNER, Nat
Books. G. Steiner. New Yorker 43:236+ N 25 '67
Confessions of a rebel: 1831. C. V. Woodward. New Repub 157:25-8 O 7 '67
Nat Turner's sword. R. A. Schroth. America 117:416 O 14 '67
Novelist as a rebel slave. il Life 63:51 O 13 '67
Peripatetic reviewer. E. Weeks. Atlan 220:130+ N '67
Rise and slay! J. Thompson. Commentary 44:81-5 N '67
Styron's Nat Turner. S. O'Connell. Nation 205:373-4 O 16 '67

TURNER, Nicholas
(ed) See Le-xuan-Chuyen. Why I defected from the Vietcong

TURNER, Paul
How high are you? Flying 81:82-3 N '67

TURNER, Pete
Turner; excerpts from address. il Pop Phot 60:90-9+ Mr '67

TURNER'S Negro insurrection, 1831. See Southampton insurrection, 1831

TURNING
Flat turnings from round stock. W. E. Burton. il Pop Mech 127:186-7 My '67
How to get started in metal turning (cont) W. C. Lammey. il Pop Mech 127:176-9+ F; 170-3 Mr '67 (to be cont)

TURNIP yellow mosaic virus. See Viruses, Plant

TURNTABLES
See also
Phonograph—Turntables

TURQUOISE trail; story. See Nunn, J. A.

TURTLE fishing
Reporter at large; voyage of Caymanians to the Miskito Bank, Nicaragua. P. Matthiessen. il New Yorker 43:120+ O 28 '67
TURTLENECK shirts. See Shirts
TURTLES, Green
Caribbean green turtle. imperiled gift of the sea. A. Carr. il Nat Geog Mag 131:876-90 Je '67
Comeback for the sea turtle, breeding and raising. W. Hartley and E. Hartley. il Sci Digest 62:33-7 S '67
100 turtle eggs; excerpt from So excellent a fishe. A. Carr. il Natur Hist 76:46-51 Ag; 40-3+ O '67
Reporter at large; voyage of Caymanians to the Miskito Bank, Nicaragua. P. Matthiessen. il New Yorker 43:120+ O 28 '67
Visual accommodation in the green turtle. D. W. Ehrenfeld and A. L. Koch. bibliog il Science 155:327-8 F 17 '67
TUSIANI, Joseph
Easter rite; poem. Cath World 205:41 Ap '67
Old and new trends in contemporary Italian literature. Cath World 205:112-15 My '67
TUTEN, Frederic
Books. Vogue 150:227 S 1; 69 S 15 '67
TUTENKHAMUN, king of Egypt
Letter from Paris; exhibition at the Petit palais. Genêt. New Yorker 43:141 Je 10 '67
Return of Tut; treasures on exhibition in Paris. il Newsweek 69:118 Mr 13 '67
Tutankhamnia. il Time 89:76 Mr 17 '67
TUTIMABA wilderness (proposed) See Wilderness areas—Idaho
TUTORIAL method in education. See Tutors and tutoring
TUTORS, Volunteer. See Volunteer workers in education
TUTORS and tutoring
Pint-size tutors learn by teaching; excerpt from Staffing for better schools. il Am Ed 3:20+ Ap '67
Sixth graders make terrific tutors. V. Bartel. il Parents Mag 42:56-7+ S '67
Teaching ethics and moral values in the schools. W. Fallaw. Christian Cent 84:1153-7 S 13 '67; Reply. L. R. Ward. 84:1498 N 22 '67
Tutor style; significance of tutoring programs in upgrading education of disadvantaged children. P. Schrag. Sat R 50:92 F 18 '67
TVETEN, Lowell H.
Ionospherically propagated sea scatter. bibliog Science 157:1302-4 S 15 '67
TWAIN, Mark, pseud. See Clemens, S. L.
TWEEDY-HOLMES, Karen
Thy name is woman. il Pop Phot 61:69-72 O '67
TWELFTH amendment. See United States—Constitution—Amendments
TWELFTH night. See Epiphany
TWENTIETH Century limited (train) See Railroads—Trains
TWENTY-first century
Mapping management to the 21st century. il Bsns W p 112-14 S 2 '67
TWENTY-five cent job; story. See Cavanaugh, A.
TWIGGY (model)
Twiggy talks about the Twiggy look. por Ladies Home J 84:62 Je '67

about

Arrival of Twiggy. il pors Life 62:33-4+ F 3 '67
Is it a girl? is it a boy? no, it's Twiggy. il pors Look 31:84-6+ Ap 4 '67
Justin looks at Twiggy. N. Davies. il pors Mlle 65:76 Jl '67
My girl Twiggy, by her mum. Mrs N. Hornby. il pors Mlle 65:122-3+ Jl '67
My name is Twiggy. O. Fallaci. por Sat Eve Post 240:60-1 Ag 12 '67
Reporter at large. T. Whiteside. New Yorker 43:64-6+ N 4 '67
Twig. il pors Newsweek 69:62 Ap 3 '67
Twiggy. il pors Seventeen 26:116-19 Mr '67
Twiggy. il U S Camera 30:34 Ag '67
Twiggy; click! click! il pors Newsweek 69:62-6 Ap 10 '67
Twiggy haute couture. P. Devlin. il pors Vogue 149:64-5+ Mr 15 '67
Twiggy makes U.S. styles swing too. il pors Life 62:99 Ap 14 '67
Twiggy who? J. Kerr. pors McCalls 94:62-3+ Jl '67
What Twiggy's got. J. Crist. il Ladies Home J 84:60 Je '67
TWILIGHT
Dusk, the magic hour. E. S. Hill. il Read Digest 91:128-30 N '67

TWIN circle (periodical) See Catholic press
TWIN-lens cameras
Six-format TLR. J. S. Forney. il Pop Phot 62:81 Ja '68
TWINING, Nathan F.
America's clear and present danger; interview. Read Digest 90:49-55 Mr '67
TWINING plants See Climbing plants
TWINS
Twice a mother in thirty days. E. Keiffer. il Good H 164:26+ My '67
TWITTY, Victor, and others
Amphibian orientation: an unexpected observation. bibliog Science 155:352-3 Ja 20 '67
TWO character play; drama. See Williams, T.
2,4,5-T. See Trichlorophenoxyacetic acid
TWO hearts, vulnerable; story. See McInerny, R.
200 MPH club meet. See Automobile racing
TWO Leggings (Crow Indian)
Horse thief and the historian. M. Brown. Sat R 50:36-7 S 9 '67
Other side camp. B. Catton. Am Heritage 18:80-2 O '67
TWO thousand (year)
Excerpts from The year 2000. A. J. Wiener and H. Kahn. il Natur Hist 76:10-12+ N '67
Herman Kahn's thinkable future. il Bsns W p 114-16+ Mr 11 '67
Life in the year 2000. C. A. Doxiadis. il NEA J 56:12-14 N '67
1984 plus sixteen. Time 90:58-9 Jl 21 '67
Will the future work? il Newsweek 70:54 O 16 '67
Year 2000, by H. Kahn and A. J. Wiener. Review
  Time 90:106 N 10 '67
TWO-way radio. See Radio telephone, Portable
TWO-wheeled automobiles. See Automobiles
TWO wishes for Christmas; story. See Knowlton, R. A.
TWO-year colleges. See Junior colleges
TYAGIS. See Sadhus
TYBEL, Irv
Color & content! il Pop Phot 61:106-13+ Jl '67
TYDINGS, Joseph D.
Speaking out; they want to tamper with the Constitution. por Sat Eve Post 240:10+ Je 17 '67
TYLER, Albert. See Clement, A. C. jt. auth.
TYLER, Anne
Feather behind the rock; story. New Yorker 43:26-30 Ag 12 '67
Flaw in the crust of the earth; story. Reporter 37:43-6 N 2 '67
TYLER, G. L. and others
Bistatic-radar detection of lunar scattering centers with Lnunar Orbiter I. Science 157:193-5 Jl 14 '67
TYLER, Gus
Criminal and the community. Cur Hist 53:102-6+ Ag '67
Fresh breezes in the labor movement. New Repub 156:13-15 My 20 '67
TYMS, James D.
Sensitive to youth. Christian Cent 84:594-5 My 3 '67
TYNAN, Kenneth
Theatre abroad. New Yorker 43:99-100+ Ap 1; 86+ O 21 '67
TYNER, Paul
How you play the game; story. New Yorker 42:34-42 Ja 28 '67
TYPE and typefounding
New punctuation mark; American type founders co. introduces interabang. Time 90:56 Jl 21 '67
Who designed and cut the Arrighi types? P. Standard. Pub W 192:82-3 N 6 '67
TYPESETTING
  See also
Phototypesetting
TYPESETTING machines
Technology: demise of hot metal? report of forum. Pub W 192:66+ N 6 '67
  See also
Computers—Printing applications
TYPEWRITER desks. See Desks
TYPEWRITER tables. See Tables
TYPEWRITERS
Portable typewriters (cont) il Consumer Rep 32:259-64 D '67
Toy typewriters. il Consumer Bul 50:32-4 F '67
TYPEWRITERS, Electronic
Typing without hands. il Sci Digest 62:75 O '67
TYPEWRITERS, Telephone. See Teletype
TYPHA. See Cattails

TYPOGRAPHICAL union, International. See In-
international typographical union
TYPOGRAPHY. See Printing
TYRMAND, Leopold
Reporter at large. New Yorker 43:67-8+
N 11 '67
Upper class in eastern Europe. Reporter 38:
14-19 Ja 11 '68
TYROL
Terror in the Tyrol; German-speaking peoples
want self-rule. America 117:125 Ag 5 '67
Traveler's choice; Austrian Tyrol. J. A.
Teusch. Travel 127:19 Ja '67
TYRONE Guthrie theatre. See Minneapolis—
Theater
TYROSINASE
Tyrosinase inhibition: its role in suntanning
and in albinism. L. T. Y. Chian and G. F.
Wilgram. bibliog il Science 155:198-200 Ja
13 '67
TYROSINE
Biosynthesis of the morphine alkaloids. G. W.
Kirby. bibliog il Science 155:170-3 Ja 13 '67
Daily rhythm in tyrosine concentration in
human plasma: persistence on low-protein
diets. R. J. Wurtman and others. bibliog il
Science 158:660-2 N 3 '67
Failure of cycloheximide to induce tyrosine
transaminase in the anesthetized rat. C.
Mavrides and E. A. Lane. bibliog il Science
156:1376-8 Je 9 '67; Reply with rejoinder.
S. Fiala and E. S. Fiala. 157:1591 S 29 '67
Suppression by actidione of development of
rat liver L-tyrosine: 2-oxoglutarate amino-
transferase activity. P. F. Benson and
P. M. Young. bibliog il Science 159:97 Ja
5 '68
Turnover of rat liver tyrosine transaminase:
stabilization after inhibition of protein syn-
thesis. F. T. Kenney. bibliog il Science
156:525-8 Ap 28 '67
TYRRELL, C. Gordon
Winterthur, the gardens of Mr and Mrs Hen-
ry Francis du Pont. Horticulture 45:36-7+
My '67
TZ'U hsi, empress dowager of China
Last great empress of China, by C. Haldane.
Review
Newsweek il por 69:100+ F 6 '67. S
Schmidt

U

UAW. See United automobile, aerospace and
agricultural implement workers of Amer-
ica
UCLA. See California. University—Los Angeles
campus
UFCT. See American federation of teachers
UFO (unidentified flying object)   See Flying
saucers
UFT. See United federation of teachers
UFWOC. See American federation of labor
and Congress of industrial organizations—
United farm workers organizing committee
UHF television stations. See Television stations
UJA. See United Jewish appeal
UL. See Underwriters' laboratories, incorpor-
ated
UN. See United Nations
UNAMACE (united automatic map compila-
tion equipment) See Mapping, Aerial—
Equipment
UNC. See United network company
UNCTAD. See United Nations conference on
trade and development
UNCURK. See United Nations commission for
the unification and rehabilitation of Korea
UNEF (United Nations emergency force) See
United Nations—Armed forces
UNESCO. See United Nations educational, sci-
entific and cultural organization
UNHCR. See United Nations—High commission-
er for refugees
UNICEF. See United Nations children's fund
UNIDO. See United Nations industrial devel-
opment organization
UNRWA. See United Nations relief and works
agency for Palestine refugees in the Near
East
UPI. See United press international
URW. See United rubber, cork, linoleum and
plastic workers of America
U.S. camera & travel (periodical)
Aerospace companies honored for photography
achievements: U.S. camera achievement
awards. il U S Camera 30:48 Mr '67

USBE. See United States book exchange
USDA. See United States—Agriculture, De-
partment of
USES. See United States—Employment service
USI. See United States industries, incorporated
USIA. See United States—Information agency
USLTA. See United States lawn tennis associa-
tion
USNSA.   See United States national student
association
USOE. See United States—Education, Office of
USPS. See United States power squadrons,
incorporated
USS Liberty. See Warships—United States
USSPA. See United States student press asso-
ciation
USSR (Union of Soviet Socialist Republics)
See Russia
USWA. See United steelworkers of America
UTC. See United aircraft corporation—United
technology center
UWF. See United world federalists
UCHIDA, Genko
Technology in China; with biographical
sketch. Sci Am 215:28, 37-45 N '66; 216:9 F
'67
UCHIYAMA, Ayako
Ayako & dance company; 92nd street Y. M.
Marks. Dance Mag 41:32 Jl '67
Ayako Uchiyama co; Alice Condodina and
co, Clark center for the performing arts.
J. Maskey. Dance Mag 41:31-2 Ag '67
UDALL, Ermalee Webb
Four corners, three cultures. Redbook 130:40-1
N '67
My first trip. McCalls 94:36 My '67
UDALL, Lee. See Udall, E. W.
UDALL, Morris King
Udall's gamble; excerpts from address. New
Repub 157:10 N 18 '67
UDALL, Stewart Lee
But then came man; address, May 4, 1967.
Vital Speeches 33:569-73 Jl 1 '67
Our perilous population implosion. Sat R 50:
10-13 S 2 '67
Price of protectionism; statement, October
18, 1967. Dept State Bul 57:638-42 N 13 '67
United States joins dedication of Jidda de-
salting plant site; remarks, February 5,
1967. Dept State Bul 56:561-3 Ap 3 '67
about
Mike Frome. M. Frome. Am For 73:3+ O '67
UDENFRIEND, Sidney
Molecular biology: drug firm to establish
new research center. D. S. Greenberg. por
Science 157:408-9 Jl 28 '67
UDIN, Anne
Take a bow. G. Goulder. por Pub W 191:54-5
My 8 '67
UENISHI, Nobuko
Getting to know the Noh. Mlle 66:144-5+
N '67
UFFEN, Robert J.
Were comets the midwives at the birth of
man? J. Lear. il por Sat R 50:57-62 My 6
'67; Discussion. 50:52-6 Ag 5 '67
UGANDA
See also
Buganda

Politics and government
King's story: President Obote decrees total
abolition of Buganda. Newsweek 70:45 Jl
3 '67
Making of a president, Uganda style. E. R.
F. Sheehan. il N Y Times Mag p36-7+ Ja
22 '67
Tough shepherd; new constitution. Time 90:
38+ O 13 '67
UGGAMS, Leslie
Why I married an Australian; ed. by H.
Curnow. pors Ebony 22:140-2+ My '67
about
Leslie, a cool bombshell; with report by T.
Prideaux. il pors Life 62:88-90+ Je 23 '67
Leslie Uggams, star in a new galaxy. il pors
Newsweek 70:63-7 Jl 17 '67
People are talking about. . . por Vogue 150:
78-9 Jl '67
UGLINESS. See Aesthetics
UINTA MOUNTAINS
High Uintas. M. F. Foster. il Liv Wildn 30:
11-13 Wint '66
UINTAS wilderness area (proposed) See Wil-
derness areas—Utah
UKAI, Nobushige
Foreign study, perils and possibilities. Sat R
50:88+ F 18 '67

UKRAINE
See also
Orthodox Eastern church in Ukraine
ULBRICHT, Walter
Berlin again? Newsweek 71:31 Ja 8 '68
With friends like these. Newsweek 69:49-50
F 20 '67
ULCERATIVE colitis. See Colitis
ULCERS
See also
Peptic ulcers
ULCERS, Swine. See Swine—Diseases and pests
ULFFERS, Dirk
Exposure. U S Camera 30:61+ D '67
ULFUNG, Ragnar
Viking guest; interview, ed. by Q. Eaton. por
Opera N 32:27 Ja 13 '68
ULIN, Richard O.
Are English teachers teachable? Sch & Soc
95:363-6 O 14 '67
ULLMAN, Henry L.
Frog comes to Hawaii; with biographical
sketch. Natur Hist 76:5, 36-7 My '67
ULLMAN, Victor
In darkest America. Nation 205:177-80 S 4 '67
ULLMANN, Bill
Memo on menswear: news, views and advice.
Good H 166:156-7 Ja '68
ULRYCH, T. J.
Oceanic basalt leads: a new interpretation
and an independent age for the earth. bib-
liog Science 158:252-6 O 13 '67
ULTIMOBRANCHIAL glands. See Glands
ULTRALIGHT spinning reels. See Fishing
tackle
ULTRAMICROMETERS. See Micrometers
ULTRASONIC scanning. See Ultrasonic waves
—Medical applications
ULTRASONIC test instruments. See Testing
instruments
ULTRASONIC waves
Sound assesses fish; determining whether
meat or fish have been frozen. T. Weiss-
mann. il Sci N 92:405 O 21 '67

Medical applications
Brain scans by ultrasound; Makow scanner.
il Sci N 91:62 Ja 21 '67
ULTRAVIOLET lenses.   See Lenses, Photo-
graphic
ULTRAVIOLET rays

Physiological effects
Induction of mutants with altered DNA com-
position: effect of ultraviolet on bacterium
paracoli 5099. G. F. Gause and others. bib-
liog il Science 157:1196-7 S 8 '67
Photoinduced DNA-protein cross-links and
bacterial killing: a correlation at low tem-
peratures. K. C. Smith and M. E. O'Leary.
bibliog il Science 155:1024-6 F 24 '67
UMBILICAL connectors. See Connectors
UMBRELLAS
Sunshades, parasols, and umbrellas. A. W.
Murray. il Antiques 91:492-5 Ap '67
UMBRIAN festival. See Music festivals—Italy
UMEZAWA, Hamao, and others
Phosphorylative inactivation of aminoglyco-
sidic antibiotics by escherichia coli carry-
ing R factor. Science 157:1559-61 S 29 '67
UMPIRES (sports)
Highlight; incident at Houston's Astrodome.
il Sports Illus 26:89 My 29 '67
Jocko; excerpts. J. Conlan and R. Creamer.
il Sports Illus 26:70-2+ Je 26; 27:36-9 Jl
3 '67
Nobody loves an umpire; excerpts from Jocko.
J. Conlan and R. Creamer. il Sports Illus
26:70-2+ Je 26 '67
UN-AMERICAN activities committee.   See
United States—Congress—House of rep-
resentatives—Un-American activities com-
mittee
UNCOMPLETED investigation, furthered and
annotated; story. See Rogin. G.
UNCONSCIOUSNESS. See Coma; Subconscious-
ness
UNDER another's sky; story. See Doran, J.
UNDER sentence of death; story. See White,
D.
UNDERACHIEVERS
Advancement school: North Carolina kills
its dream. D. Cooper. il Nation 206:77-9
Ja 15 '68
UNDERDEVELOPED areas
And children shall lead the way. M. Mead.
Redbook 128:46+ F '67
Human hunger as a policy determinant; ad-
dress, November 3, 1967. H. J. Waters. Dept
State Bul 57:764-8 D 4 '67

Ignoring the storm warnings; causes of
counterrevolution. G. Bing. Nation 205:594-6
D 4 '67
Improving export earnings of developing
countries; statement, January 18, 1967.
W. M. Blumenthal. Dept State Bul 56:
430-6 Mr 13 '67
Of, by and for the rich. Nation 205:549-50
N 27 '67
Offering trade to the poor; system of tariff
preferences to developing countries. Bsns
W p 109 D 9 '67
Political-economic web: crisis in development:
text of address. H. Brown. il Bul Atomic
Sci 23:2-7 D '67
Problems of independence: a look at the third
world; interview. B. Ben Yahmed. U S News
63:80-1 S 4 '67
Scandal of the century: rich and poor. A. de
Borchgrave. il Newsweek 70:38-40 O 30 '67
Slide toward violence in the hungering world.
H. I. Schiller. Bul Atomic Sci 23:4-6 Ja
'67; Reply with rejoinder. H. W. Salzberg.
23:63-4 Je '67
UN and the have-nots: alternatives to ex-
plosion. J. Boyd. Nation 204:562-4 My 1 '67
United States foreign trade policy and the
developing countries; statement, July 12,
1967. A. M. Solomon. Dept State Bul 57:
180:90 Ag 7 '67
See also
Agriculture—Underdeveloped areas
Birth control—Underdeveloped areas
Birth rate—Underdeveloped areas
Communism—Underdeveloped areas
Economic assistance in underdeveloped areas
Education—Underdeveloped areas
Food supply—Underdeveloped areas
Housing—Underdeveloped areas
Immigration and emigration—Underdeveloped
areas
International basic economy corporation
Investments, Foreign (in underdeveloped
areas)
Labor supply—Underdeveloped areas
Land tenure—Underdeveloped areas
Medical service—Underdeveloped areas
Science—Underdeveloped areas
States, New
Unemployment—Underdeveloped areas
United States—Economic relations—Underde-
veloped areas
United States—Foreign relations—Under-
developed areas
UNDEREMPLOYMENT. See Part time em-
ployment
UNDERGRADUATES. See College students
UNDERGROUND; story. See West, J.
UNDERGROUND atomic testing.   See Atomic
bombs—Testing, Underground
UNDERGROUND factories
Cavemen in Kansas City. il Newsweek 69:
78-80 My 1 '67
UNDERGROUND movies. See Moving pictures
UNDERGROUND press.   See Newspapers—
United States
UNDERGROUND radio. See Radio communi-
cation, Underground
UNDERGROUND structures
Troglodytes; putting architecture under-
ground. B. Rudofsky. il Horizon 9:28-39
Spr '67
UNDERGROUND telephone lines. See Tele-
phone lines—Underground
UNDERGROUND water. See Water, Under-
ground
UNDERHILL, Anne B. and Morton, D. C.
Ultraviolet spectra of stars. bibliog Science
158:1273-9 D 8 '67
UNDERPRIVILEGED children. See Socially
handicapped children
UNDERSEA Gardens, Santa Barbara.   See
Aquariums
UNDERSEA light. See Light—Transmission
thru sea water
UNDERSEA research vehicles. See Submarine
boats
UNDERSTANDING. See Knowledge, Theory of
UNDERTAKERS and undertaking
See also
National funeral directors association
UNDERWATER archeology. See Archeology,
Submarine
UNDERWATER breathing apparatus. See Div-
ing apparatus
UNDERWATER cables. See Cables, Submarine
UNDERWATER demolition teams. See United
States—Navy—Underwater demolition teams
UNDERWATER drilling
Britain's bonanza at the bottom of the sea.
J. H. Winchester. il Read Digest 91:138-43
Ag '67

UNDERWATER explosions
U.S. protests Soviet failure to give notice of scientific tests; text of note, December 8, 1967. Dept State Bul 58:16 Ja 1 '68

UNDERWATER laboratories
Air from the sea for oceanauts. il Sci N 92:66 Jl 15 '67
Ecological studies during Project Sealab II. T. A. Clarke and others. bibliog il Science 157:1381-9 S 22 '67
Now, the ocean; Sealab III. J. Ludwigson. il Sci N 92:40-1 Jl 8 '67
Submarine shuttle bus; Deep Diver. il Life 62:51-2+ Ap 21 '67
Undersea hardware still untrustworthy; Sealab 2 experiment. il Sci N 91:408-9 Ap 29 '67

UNDERWATER moving picture photography. See Moving picture photography, Submarine

UNDERWATER oil well drilling. See Oil well drilling, Submarine

UNDERWATER photography. See Moving picture photography, Submarine; Photography, Submarine

UNDERWATER physiology
Air from the sea for oceanauts. il Sci N 92:66 Jl 15 '67
Diving women of Korea and Japan. S. K. Hong and H. Rahn. il Sci Am 216:34-43 My '67

UNDERWATER rescue work
Rescue from the deep! W. B. Hendrickson, jr. il Pop Mech 129:124-6+ Ja '68
Rescuer; diving bell inventor saves crew of Squalus. P. Maas. il Sat Eve Post 240:36-40+ S 23 '67
Tuffy, the navy's deep sea lifeguard. T. Stimson. il Pop Mech 128:66-9+ Jl '67

UNDERWATER research. See Oceanographic research

UNDERWATER sounds. See Ocean sounds

UNDERWATER structures
Cities under the ocean floor. B. H. Frisch. il Sci Digest 62:36-42 Ag '67

UNDERWATER suits. See Aquanauts—Clothing

UNDERWATER thermometers. See Thermometers and thermometry

UNDERWATER vehicles. See Submarine vehicles

UNDERWEAR
Thermal underwear. il Consumer Rep 32:553-5 O '67
What you should know before buying a slip. il Good H 164:198 My '67
Winter warmers: underwear and innerwear to keep the sportsman warm. il Consumer Bul 51:21-3 Ja '68
  See also
Brassieres

UNDERWOOD, George C.
Trade-offs in relay selection. por Electr World 77:58-60 Ap '67

UNDERWOOD, John
College football (cont) Sports Illus 27:65-7 D 11 '67
One tough little guy. Sports Illus 26:54-62 F 6 '67

UNDERWOOD, Paul Atkins
Djami jewel. J. Beckwith. il Art N 66:40-1+ D '67

UNDERWOOD, Richard G.
Impressions of the European scholarly book trade; summary of address. Pub W 192:30-1 Jl 24 '67

UNDERWRITERS' laboratories, incorporated
Head start on safety by Underwriters' laboratories. Consumer Bul 50:17-18 D '67

UNEMPLOYABLES
Business takes new role: training unemployables. il U S News 63:97-8 N 13 '67
Unemployable; survey findings. Newsweek 69:30 My 1 '67
Unemployables; new federal study. Time 89:22 Ap 28 '67

UNEMPLOYMENT
Foreign labor briefs. See issues of Monthly labor review
  See also
Labor supply
Right to labor
Unemployables

Relief measures
After thirty years, relief a failure? il U S News 63:44-7 Jl 17 '67
Development of jobs; address, September 2, 1967. F. H. Cassell. bibliog f Vital Speeches 34:59-64 N 1 '67
Employer of last resort; L. B. Johnson's proposals. Time 90:10 D 29 '67
Luring business into the ghettos. il Newsweek 70:77 O 16 '67
New business for business: reclaiming human resources. G. Burck. il Fortune 77:158-61+ Ja '68

Quiet progress in the cities; programs to alleviate poverty. Life 63:4 O 6 '67
Screening people in; three broad new approaches. Time 90:17 N 3 '67
  See also
Anti-poverty program, 1964-
Federal art project
Federal writers project
Urban coalition (organization)

Statistics
Comparative unemployment rates, 1964-66. A. F. Neef and R. A. Holland. il Mo Labor R 90:18-20 Ap '67
How many unemployed? New Repub 157:10 S 30 '67; Discussion. 157:7-8, 27 O 14; 36-7 O 28 '67
Jobs go begging, but not all over. Bsns W p 105-6 F 18 '67
Unemployment among youth: the explosive statistic! il Ebony 22:127-9 Ag '67
Where are the jobless? New Repub 158:8 Ja 20 '68

Europe, Western
Another boom tiring; Europe's layoffs rise. il U S News 62:82-3 Ja 30 '67

France
De Gaulle gets blame for decline in jobs. il Bsns W p 134 Ja 21 '67

Michigan
Effect of economic change on the Michigan labor force. P. S. Barth. Mo Labor R 90:29 Mr '67

Russia
Russia's crisis: lack of jobs. il U S News 63:98-9 D 18 '67

Underdeveloped areas
Labor supply and employment in less developed countries. J. L. Sadie. bibliog f il Ann Am Acad 369:121-30 Ja '67

United States
Aftermath of summer. Newsweek 70:78 O 23 '67
Decentralization of jobs. D. K. Newman. bibliog f il Mo Labor R 90:7-13 My '67
Full employment and workers' education. E. Hardin. il Mo Labor R 90:21-5 My '67
How many unemployed? New Repub 157:10 S 30 '67; Discussion. 157:7-8, 27 O 14; 36-7 O 28 '67
Job seekers face thinner pickings. il Bsns W p44 Je 10 '67
Jobs that were lost when minimum wage went up. il U S News 63:71-3 Jl 10 '67
New evidence on problems of reemployment. S. O. Schweitzer. bibliog f il Mo Labor R 90:12-14 Ag '67
Rise in unemployment. Fortune 76:20 Ag '67
Throwing inflation a tricky curve; Phillips curve to gauge what must be given up in price stability for a cut in unemployment. il Bsns W p62+ Ag 19 '67
Unemployment among youth: the explosive statistic! il Ebony 22:127-9 Ag '67
Variability by skill in cyclical unemployment. M. S. Cohen and W. H. Gruber. bibliog f il Mo Labor R 90:8-11 Ag '67
Why job figures jump. il Bsns W p37 N 18 '67
Why the unemployed look for work. K. D. Hoyle. il Mo Labor R 90:32-8 F '67
  See also
Labor supply—United States
Unemployment—Relief measures
Unemployment surveys

UNEMPLOYMENT, Technological
Automation, computers, and the decline and fall of work. il Sr Schol 91:6-9+ O 26 '67
Technological displacement as a micro phenomenon. H. E. Striner. Mo Labor R 90:30-1 Mr '67
Technology and the Negro. Sci Am 217:102 S '67

UNEMPLOYMENT surveys
Means of adjustment to technological displacement. J. A. Pichler. Mo Labor R 90:32-3 Mr '67

UNGAR, E. W.
Ablation thermal protection systems. bibliog Science 158:740-4 N 10 '67

UNGAR, Sanford J.
Moving the mikveh. Commentary 44:89-91 S; 12 D '67

UNGER, Donald L.
Sneezin' season is here. Todays Health 45:3 Jl '67

UNGER, Irwin
New left and American history: some recent trends in United States historiography. bibliog f Am Hist R 72:1237-63 Jl '67

UNICON.   See Information storage and retrieval systems
UNICORN tapestries. See Tapestry
UNICYCLES
Only one wheel to a customer! R. Gannon. il Pop Sci 190:86-9+ Je '67
UNIDENTIFIED flying objects.   See Flying saucers
UNIFIED field theories
Can you please give an explanation of the Unified field theory? I. Asimov. Sci Digest 61:86 F '67
UNIFORMS, Police
Scotland yard skirts maxi to mini. il Life 63:32-3 S 29 '67
UNILEVER, limited. See Lever brothers and Unilever, limited
UNIMATION, incorporated
Robots: makers of Unimate industrial robot; interview. T. H. Lindbom. New Yorker 43:20-2 Je 24 '67
Unimation head sees 5,000 full-time robots in five years.   R. Barnhart. il Tech W 20: 38-9 F 20 '67
UNION carbide chemicals company. See Union carbide corporation
UNION carbide corporation
Exhibits: involving the viewer. il Wilson Lib Bul 41:727-9 Mr '67
UNION catalog of Library of Congress.   See United States—Library of Congress—Union catalog
UNION minière. See Mining industry and finance—Congo (capital Kinshasa)
UNION of American Hebrew congregations
Temple Emanu-El protests. Time 89:56 Je 2 '67
UNION of Soviet Socialist Republics. See Russia
UNION oil company of California
Fred Hartley and his well-oiled multiplying machine. T. O'Hanlon. il Fortune 75:156-61+ Ap '67
UNION shops. See Open and closed shop
UNION wide collective bargaining. See Collective bargaining, Industry wide
UNIONS, Teachers. See Teachers unions
UNIT construction
Dropping in, speeding up; rehabilitating slum structure in forty-eight hours. il Time 89: 60 Ap 21 '67
Instant rehab does it in hours. il Arch Rec 141:187-8 My '67
Instant rehab not so instant; New York's drop-in kitchen-bathroom core concept. il Arch Rec 141:175-6 Ja '67
Instant renewal; HUD's instant rehabilitation project. il Newsweek 69:84-6 Ap 24 '67
Out of slums into instant homes in forty-eight hours. il Life 62:57-8+ My 12 '67
See also
Modular coordination (architecture)
UNITARIAN Universalist association
Growing avant-garde. Time 89:106+ Ap 14 '67
Look at Unitarian Universalist goals. R. B. Tapp. Christian Cent 84:515-18 Ap 19 '67
UNITARIANS
Spry downgrader of divinity; interview, ed. by C. Altman. D. M. Greeley. il Life 63:31-2+ Jl 28 '67
What Unitarians believe. Newsweek 69:94 Ap 17 '67
UNITAS, Johnny
It's Johnny U. again. T. Maule. il por Sports Illus 27:14-17 O 2 '67
UNITED air lines
Conflict over 737 crew size intensifies. Aviation W 87:37-8 S 11 '67
$690-million order will give United all-jet fleet in 1969. J. W. Carter. Aviation W 87:28 Jl 31 '67
Transpacific route case: United takes dual position in application. H. D. Watkins. il Aviation W 86:36-7+ Mr 13 '67
United buys seventy-nine new jets. Bsns W p29 Jl 29 '67
United high-speed bag system installation at O'Hare delayed. R. F. Coburn. Aviation W 86:50 Ap 17 '67
United opens new LA air-freight facility. il Aviation W 86:57 Ja 30 '67
UNITED aircraft corporation

Hamilton standard division
Facility to put UAC in boron filament field. il Aero Tech 21:48 Ja 1 '68

Pratt and Whitney aircraft division
P&W keys airbus engine work to JT9D. I. Stone. Aviation W 87:45 Jl 10 '67

United technology center
Sterilizable propellant developed by UTC. R. Lindsey. il Tech W 20:30 Mr 13 '67
UTC claims successful test of largest hybrid rocket. Tech W 20:22 Je 19 '67
UNITED automobile, aerospace and agricultural implement workers of America
After a settlement at Ford. U S News 63:12 O 30 '67
And now for G.M. il Time 90:96 N 17 '67
Any way in sight to head off an auto strike? il U S News 62:93-5 My 1 '67
At the showdown stage in the auto dispute; offer to United auto workers union by General motors, Ford and Chrysler. U S News 63:70-2 S 11 '67
Auto bargaining complications. America 117: 263 S 16 '67
Auto firm's call for help from union. U S News 63:85 Ag 21 '67
Auto strike talks go into gear. il Newsweek 70:77-8 O 23 '67
Auto strike to upset business? il U S News 63:35-7 S 18 '67
Auto workers' latest demands, will they set the pace for others? U S News 62:84-5 Mr 27 '67
Auto workers shrug at the big issues; will strike if they have to. il Bsns W p 152-3+ Ag 19 '67
Auto workers' war chest: loaded for a long strike. il U S News 62:80+ Je 5 '67
Best contract we've ever had. il Newsweek 70:85 N 20 '67
Biggest pay demand in history? Reuther states his terms. il U S News 63:72-4 Jl 24 '67
Bone in Meany's throat: AFL-CIO pullout? H. Rowen. New Repub 156:9-10 My 6 '67; Correction. 156:42 Je 3 '67
Contract time in Detroit: collision course. il Newsweek 70:76-8 Jl 17 '67
Costly from any point of view. il Time 90:91 S 15 '67
Detroit tries brinkmanship; forcing UAW officials to name specific priorities. Bsns W p 115-16 Ag 26 '67
Detroit's labor talks race down to the wire; threshing out compromises. il Bsns W p21-2 S 2 '67
Down to the wire in Detroit; Ford-UAW. il Newsweek 70:67-8 S 11 '67
Ford accord. Sr Schol 91:14 N 9 '67
Ford sets costly pattern; GM and Chrysler next on UAW's bargaining calendar; with editorial comment. il Bsns W p37-9, 164 O 28 '67
Ford takes the blow. il Bsns W p35-6 S 9 '67
Gut issues start to pain Detroit; auto contract talks approach. il Bsns W p 138+ My 27 '67
High cost of strikes: what auto union is learning. il U S News 63:81-2 O 23 '67
How UAW has propped up income; protections for pay, health, and old age. il Bsns W p83-4+ N 11 '67
Inside story of the Reuther-Meany fight. il U S News 62:93-5 F 20 '67
Labor peace in '68? il Bsns W p 17-18 D 23 '67
Labor's newest split: the price of a Reuther walkout. U S News 62:76-8 F 27 '67
Latest on auto-contract talks: General motors makes demands. U S News 63: 75-6 Ag 14 '67
Long, large & difficult; U.A.W. labor demands. il Time 90:67 Jl 21 '67
Men with the skills get restive over pay; craftsmen in the auto industry. il Bsns W p83-4 Mr 11 '67
Mr. Reuther's ploy. America 117:462 O 28 '67
Mood is adamant; neither Ford nor UAW is ready to bargain. il Bsns W p37-8 S 16 '67
Now the showdown at General motors: what a strike would do. U S News 63:95-6 N 20 '67
Reuther delivers the goods; contracts by UAW with Ford motor co. and Caterpillar tractor co. il Bsns W p51-2+ N 4 '67
Reuther escalates his war on auto companies. il U S News 63:85-6 N 13 '67
Reuther nears showdown; UAW votes to replenish strike fund. Bsns W p 150 O 14 '67
Reuther vs. Meany, a labor rift widens. U S News 62:10 F 13 '67
Reuther vs. Meany: background to labor's showdown. B. J. Widick. Nation 204:614-16 My 15 '67
Reuther walks out, but doesn't shut the door; UAW resignations from AFL-CIO posts. il Bsns W p66-8 F 11 '67

UNITED NATIONS—*Continued*

Advisory committee on the application of science and technology to development

Application of science and technology to development; seventh session. UN Mo Chron 4:72-3 Je '67
Science and technology. UN Mo Chron 4:96-7 D '67

Armed forces

Exchange of messages; between U Thant and officers and men of UNEF, May 19, 1967. Thant. UN Mo Chron 4:59-61 Je '67
Soldiering for peace, by C. von Horn. Review
Nat R il 19:861+ Ag 8 '67. J. B. Burnham

Forces in Cyprus

Appeal for contributions. UN Mo Chron 4:48 Je '67
Diary of a U.N. peacekeeper.   J. Waern. Sat R 50:19-21+ N 18 '67
Financial postion of UNFICYP. UN Mo Chron 4:11 F '67
Security council adopts resolution; with text. UN Mo Chron 4:22-7 Ja '67
Special council extends UNFICYP; with text of resolution. UN Mo Chron 4:81-7 Jl '67
United Nations force in Cyprus extended through June 1967; statement, December 15, 1966. A. J. Goldberg. Dept State Bul 56:179-81 Ja 30 '67
U.N. peace force in Cyprus again extended for six months; statement, June 19, 1967. R. F. Pedersen. Dept State Bul 57:52-3 Jl 10 '67

Forces in the Middle East

Diary of a U.N. peacekeeper.   J. Waern. Sat R 50:19-21+ N 18 '67
Many attempts to police the peace. il Life 62:84 Je 16 '67
Middle East crisis; address, June 27, 1967. Thant. Vital Speeches 33:591-602 Jl 15 '67; Same with title Withdrawal of UNEF. UN Mo Chron 4:135-60 Jl '67
Situation in the Middle East; Security council statements. UN Mo Chron 4:3-26 Je '67
Story of forty-eight hours; U Thant's part in UNEF withdrawal. M. Greenfield. il Reporter 36:19-23 Je 15 '67
United Nations as the keeper of world peace; with excerpts from exchange of letters between H. F. Byrd, jr. and A. J. Goldberg. il U S News 62:31 Je 5 '67
UNEF: U Thant's report. Reporter 37:18+ Jl 13 '67
Withdrawal of United Nations emergency force: some questions answered. UN Mo Chron 4:87-94 Je '67

Assembly

See United Nations—General assembly

Bibliography

What can the UN do? new books. R. Steel. Commentary 43:84+ My '67

Budget

See United Nations—Finance

Capital development fund

First pledging conference for Capital development fund. UN Mo Chron 4:43-4 N '67

Charter

United Nations: the human factor; address, July 30, 1967. Thant. Vital Speeches 33:724-7 S 15 '67; Same. UN Mo Chron 4:75-83 Ag '67

Commission for the unification and rehabilitation of Korea

Assembly adopts resolution; with text. UN Mo Chron 4:64-8 Ja '67
U.N. objectives for unification of Korea reaffirmed; statement, November 16, 1967. with text of resolution. W. S. Broomfield. Dept State Bul 57:844-5 D 18 '67

Commission on human rights

Ad hoc study group; proposal for establishing regional commissions. UN Mo Chron 4:33-4 O '67
Commission on human rights strongly condemns the policies of apartheid and repressive measures in South Africa. P. Nedballo. UN Mo Chron 4:59-68 My '67
Periodic reports on human rights; ad hoc committee. UN Mo Chron 4:41 Mr '67
Treatment of prisoners in South Africa; meetings of working group of experts. UN Mo Chron 4:87-9 Jl '67

Twenty-third session concluded. UN Mo Chron 4:43-50 Ap '67
Twenty-third session opens in Geneva. UN Mo Chron 4:31 Mr '67
See also
United Nations—Sub-commission on prevention of discrimination and protection of minorities

Commission on international trade law

Assembly elects members. UN Mo Chron 4:54 N '67
Progressive development of the law of international trade. UN Mo Chron 4:136-8 Ja '67
United Nations commission on international trade law. C. A. Stavropoulos. UN Mo Chron 4:89-94 Ap '67

Commission on social development

Eighteenth session; questions of social policy. UN Mo Chron 4:53-61 Ap '67

Commission on the status of women

Commission concludes twentieth session. UN Mo Chron 4:61-4 Ap '67
Commission opens twentieth session. UN Mo Chron 4:34-7 Mr '67
U.N. commission on the status of women holds 20th session. G. A. Tillett. Dept State Bul 57:218-21 Ag 14 '67

Committee for programme and coordination

Enlarged committee for programme and coordination; first session. UN Mo Chron 4:48 N '67
Enlarged committee for programme and coordination; plan to review the operational and research activities of the United Nations. UN Mo Chron 4:32 O '67

Committee of twenty-four

See United Nations—Special committee on the situation with regard to implementation of declaration on granting of independence to colonial countries and peoples

Committee on development planning

Committee on development planning; second session. UN Mo Chron 4:43-5 My '67

Committee on housing, building and planning

See United Nations—Economic and social council

Committee on information from non-self-governing territories

United Nations and the decolonization of non-self-governing territories. J. W. S. Malecela. UN Mo Chron 4:84-96 Ag '67

Committee on invisibles and financing relating to trade

See United Nations conference on trade and development

Committee on the peaceful uses of outer space

Assembly adopts three resolutions; with text of treaty. UN Mo Chron 4:35-46 Ja '67
Committee adopts report to Assembly. UN Mo Chron 4:14-15 O '67
Committee recommends postponement of conference. UN Mo Chron 4:16-17 Mr '67
General assembly adopts resolutions; with texts. UN Mo Chron 4:55-7 D '67
Ninth session of committee. UN Mo Chron 4:18-19 My '67
Outer space conference: Assembly sets new date. UN Mo Chron 4:46-8 Je '67
Peaceful uses of outer space; recommendations of committee; draft resolutions adopted by First committee. UN Mo Chron 4:27 N '67
President calls for Senate ratification on treaty on outer space; message to the Senate, February 7, 1967. L. B. Johnson. Dept State Bul 56:386-8 Mr 6 '67
Recent advances in international cooperation in space; statement, August 29, 1967. A. W. Frutkin. Dept State Bul 57:401-3 S 25 '67
Secretary Rusk and Ambassador Goldberg urge Senate approval of outer space treaty; statements, March 7, 1967. D. Rusk; A. J. Goldberg. Dept State Bul 56:600-12 Ap 10 '67
U.N. General assembly endorses outer space treaty; statements, December 17, 19; with text of resolution adopted, December 19, 1966. A. J. Goldberg. Dept State Bul 56:78-84 Ja 9 '67

UNITED NATIONS—*Continued*

Committee on the question of defining aggression
Question of defining aggression: Committee considers draft resolution. UN Mo Chron 4:79-81 Je '67
Question of defining aggression; fourth session of committee. UN Mo Chron 4:51-8 My '67
U.N. on aggression; excerpts from proceedings. Reporter 36:11 Je 1 '67

Committee on trust and non-self-governing territories
See United Nations—Trusteeship committee

Credentials committee
Committee's report approved. UN Mo Chron 4:80 Ja '67
Credentials; Assembly approves report. UN Mo Chron 4:27 Je '67

Delegates
Our heroes at the U.N. C. Fritchey. Harper 234:30+ F '67

Department of economic and social affairs
Promotion of private foreign investment; report. UN Mo Chron 4:51-2 Ap '67

Department of social affairs
See United Nations—Department of economic and social affairs

Development program
Andean Indian programme in Colombia; photographs. UN Mo Chron 4:77-84 My '67
Assistance programme in Congo. UN Mo Chron 4:73-4 Je '67
Economic development board at work; Singapore. il UN Mo Chron 4:95-100 Je '67
Fourth session of UNDP governing council. UN Mo Chron 4:115-18 Jl '67
Mekong discussions. UN Mo Chron 4:97-8 D '67
New pre-investment projects approved; third session of UNDP governing council. UN Mo Chron 4:14-25 F '67
1967 UNDP pledging conference. UN Mo Chron 4:42-4 N '67
Progress report on a global partnership; international assistance. P. G. Hoffman. UN Mo Chron 4:64-73 Mr '67
UN and the have nots: alternatives to explosion. J. Boyd. Nation 204:562-4 My 1 '67
U.S. to contribute to UNDP/FAO fisheries project in Viet-Nam. Dept State Bul 56:964 Je 26 '67

Documents
See United Nations—Publications

Economic and financial committee
Assembly asks study of training of personnel; recommendation from the Second committee. UN Mo Chron 4:78-82 D '67
Assembly decisions on economic matters. UN Mo Chron 4:106-15 Ja '67
World economic problems; Second committee adopts five recommendations. UN Mo Chron 4:33-7 N '67

Economic and social council
Arrangements for 1968 conference of social welfare ministers. UN Mo Chron 4:32 O '67
Assembly fills vacancies. UN Mo Chron 4:63-4 D '67
Committee on non-governmental organizations; report adopted. UN Mo Chron 4:50-1 My '67
Forty-first session concluded. UN Mo Chron 4:122-4 Ja '67
Housing, building and planning; fifth session. UN Mo Chron 4:49 N '67
Natural resources; world-wide survey proposed. UN Mo Chron 4:49 My '67
Non-governmental organizations. UN Mo Chron 4:53 Ap '67
Progress in water desalination; report. UN Mo Chron 4:50 My '67
Resumes forty-third session. UN Mo Chron 4:89-91 D '67
Transport development; report by the Secretary-General. UN Mo Chron 4:49-50 My '67
See also
United Nations—Commission on social development

Meetings, 1967
Economic and social council concludes forty-second session. UN Mo Chron 4:112-15 Jl '67
Forty-second session; meetings in May. UN Mo Chron 4:61-5 Je '67
Forty-third session concluded. UN Mo Chron 4:60-5 Ag '67

Economic commission for Africa
ECA conference in industry and finance. UN Mo Chron 4:27 F '67
Eight session held at Lagos. UN Mo Chron 4:32-4 Mr '67

Economic commission for Asia and the Far East
Annual session held in Tokyo. UN Mo Chron 4:39-43 My '67
Economic commission for Asia and the Far East; twenty years of progress. il UN Mo Chron 4:78-88 Ap '67

Economic commission for Europe
ECE in the emerging European system. J. Siotis. bibliog f il Int Concil 561:5-70 Ja '67
Twenty-second session held in Geneva. UN Mo Chron 4:45-7 My '67

Economic commission for Latin America
Twelfth session. UN Mo Chron 4:65-8 Je '67

Emergency force
See United Nations—Armed forces

Employees
See also
United Nations—Secretariat

Finance
As we said before. Reporter 36:8-10 Je 29 '67
Assembly decisions on economic matters. UN Mo Chron 4:106-15 Ja '67
Budget estimates for 1968. UN Mo Chron 4:50-4 N '67
Estimates, 1967. UN Mo Chron 4:127-34 Ja '67
Expenditures and appropriations. UN Mo Chron 4:101-6 D '67
Population trust fund. UN Mo Chron 4:67-8 Ag '67

First committee
See United Nations—Political and security committee

Fourth committee
See United Nations—Trusteeship committee

General assembly
Emergency sessions
Adjournment of session; fifth special session. UN Mo Chron 4:26 Je '67
Admission of failure. Newsweek 70:37 Jl 31 '67
Argument indeed: Soviet attack, Israeli retort; with excerpts from addresses. A. Kosygin; A. Eban. il Life 62:24-5 Je 30 '67
Biggest pie-throwing contest ever? emergency session of the U.N. General assembly. il Newsweek 69:18-20 Je 26 '67
Conclusion of emergency special session. UN Mo Chron 4:3-6 O '67
Down go the U.S.S.R. and the Arabs again. il Newsweek 70:28+ Jl 17 '67
Fifth emergency special session of U.N. General assembly adjourns; statement, with text of resolution, July 21, 1967. A. J. Goldberg. Dept State Bul 57:216-18 Ag 14 '67
Israel's surprise weapon; envoy Eban. il U S News 63:20 Jl 3 '67
Letter from the United Nations. R. H. Rovere. New Yorker 43:67-70+ Jl 8 '67
Mission from Moscow; special session on peace in the Middle East. Time 89:22 Je 23 '67
No practical help; General assembly debates Middle East crisis. Time 90:24 Jl 7 '67
Opening of fifth special session. UN Mo Chron 4:3-10 My '67
Psychedelic debate; General assembly Mideast debate. il Time 89:22 Je 30 '67
Report from the U.N. General assembly; Middle East debate. C. M. Eichelberger. Sat R 50:16-17 Ag 12 '67
Russia vs. U.S. who really won? voting details. il U S News 63:6-7 Jl 17 '67
Situation in the Middle East. UN Mo Chron 4:7-32 Ag '67
Situation in the Middle East; fifth emergency special session of the General assembly; with text of resolutions and record of roll-call votes. UN Mo Chron 4:32-80 Jl '67
U.N. debate unfolds. il Newsweek 70:18-21 Jl 3 '67
U.N. General assembly holds fifth emergency session; United States offers proposals for peace in the Middle East; statements, June 17, 19 and 20, 1967. A. J. Goldberg. Dept State Bul 57:47-52 Jl 10 '67
U.N. summit; emergency session. C. M. Eichelberger. Sat R 50:14 Jl 1 '67

UNITED NATIONS—General assembly—Emergency sessions—*Continued*
U.S. does not concur in request for U.N. General assembly session; text of letter, June 15, 1967. A. J. Goldberg. Dept State Bul 57:12-13 Jl 3 '67
Waiting for a compromise. P. Ben. New Repub 157:9-10 Jl 1 '67
Wall of words; U.S, USSR proposals on Palestine question. A. Weill-Tuckerman. Nation 205:2-4 Jl 3 '67
War of the words; debate over Mideast crisis. il Bsns W p33-6 Je 24 '67

Sessions (21st)

Conclusion of twenty-first session. UN Mo Chron 4:3-6 Ja '67
ENDC at the General assembly. H. A. Jack. il Bul Atomic Sci 23:30-3 F '67
[Elimination of all forms of racial discrimination; text of resolution adopted October 26, 1966] UN Mo Chron 4:ii-iii Mr '67
U.N. adopts international covenants on human rights; statement, December 12, 1966; with texts of the human rights covenants. P. R. Harris. Dept State Bul 56:104-21 Ja 16 '67
Work of the 21st session of the U.N. General assembly; statement, December 21, 1966. A. J. Goldberg. Dept State Bul 56:98-102 Ja 16 '67

Sessions (22d)

Agenda of the 22d regular session of the U.N. General assembly. Dept State Bul 57:545-8 O 23 '67
Assembly concludes debate. UN Mo Chron 4:9-11 N '67
Chill winds on the East River. il Time 90:21 S 29 '67
Effects of atomic radiation; Assembly adopts report; with text of resolution. UN Mo Chron 4:11-12 N '67
For whom is time working? A. Tuckerman. Nation 205:386-7 O 23 '67
General assembly debate; Middle East. P. Ben. New Repub 157:15-16 S 30 '67
General assembly 22nd session; photographs. UN Mo Chron 4:37-40 O '67
General debate; summaries of representatives' statements. UN Mo Chron 4:41-92 O; 57-121 N '67
Glassboro spirit? Sr Schol 91:38-9 O 5 '67
Issues before 22nd General assembly. bibliog f il Int Concil 564:5-206 S '67
Now: a Communist in a key U.N. spot. il U S News 63:22 O 2 '67
Opening of twenty-second session. UN Mo Chron 4:6-10 O '67
Provisional agenda, twenty-second session of U.N. General assembly. Dept State Bul 57:239-42 Ag 21 '67
Record of the month. See issues of UN monthly chronicle
Small hello. Newsweek 70:38 O 2 '67

High commissioner for human rights (proposed)

Global ombudsman. W. Korey. Sat R 50:20 Ag 12 '67
High commissioner for human rights. UN Mo Chron 4:40 Mr '67

High commissioner for refugees

High commissioner for refugees; summary of statement, November 20, 1967. Sadruddin Aga Kahn. UN Mo Chron 4:87 D '67
Pledges for refugee programmes. UN Mo Chron 4:124-5 Ja '67
UNHCR executive committee opens spring session. UN Mo Chron 4:74-5 Je '67

Industrial development organization

Industrial development; Assembly takes note of symposium arrangements. UN Mo Chron 4:33 N '67

International law commission

Assembly adopts resolutions. UN Mo Chron 4:134-5 Ja '67
International law commission and the law of treaties. H. Waldock. UN Mo Chron 4:69-76 My '67
International law commission; nineteenth session. UN Mo Chron 4:71-2 Ag '67
Nineteenth session opens. UN Mo Chron 4:81-2 Je '67

International narcotics control board

Buying off the farmers. D. A. Ehrlich. Sci N 93:15 Ja 6 '68
International control of narcotic drugs; administrative arrangements. UN Mo Chron 4:71-2 Je '67

Legal affairs, Office of

Conventions and agreements; list. UN Mo Chron 4:31-2 F '67

Legal committee

Assembly adopts resolutions; reports of the International law commission. UN Mo Chron 4:134-5 Ja '67
General assembly adopts resolutions; principles of international law concerning friendly relations and co-operation among states. UN Mo Chron 4:135 Ja '67
Programme of assistance in international law. UN Mo Chron 4:138-9 Ja '67
Right of asylum; resolution adopted by General assembly. UN Mo Chron 4:139 Ja '67
Sixth committee recommendations. UN Mo Chron 4:109-12 D '67
Sixth committee recommendations; report of the International law commission. UN Mo Chron 4:55-6 N '67

Membership

Southern Yemen admitted to United Nations; statement, December 12, 1967. A. J. Goldberg. Dept State Bul 58:65 Ja 8 '68
U.N. General assembly again rejects move to change Chinese representation; statement. November 21, 1967; with text of resolutions. L. H. Fountain. Dept State Bul 57:829-33 D 18 '67

Political and security committee

Assembly adopts three resolutions; with text of treaty. UN Mo Chron 4:35-46 Ja '67
Convention on prohibition of nuclear weapons; consideration by First committee. UN Mo Chron 4:69-72 D '67
Denuclearization of Latin America; consideration in First committee. UN Mo Chron 4:18-22 N '67
Denuclearization of Latin America; First committee's recommendation to Assembly. UN Mo Chron 4:72-3 D '67
General assembly adopts resolutions; with texts. UN Mo Chron 4:27-35 Ja '67
Peaceful uses of outer space; recommendations of committee; draft resolutions adopted by First committee. UN Mo Chron 4:27 N '67

Population commission

Concludes fourteenth session. UN Mo Chron 4:92-5 D '67

Public information, Office of

New publishing unit formed at UN; External publishing relations. Pub W 192:24 D 11 '67

Publications

United Nations statistical yearbook. UN Mo Chron 4:71 Ag '67
World economic survey. UN Mo Chron 4:70 Ag '67
See also
United Nations—Public information, Office of
United Nations educational, scientific and cultural organization—Publications

Bibliography

Current U.N. documents: a selected bibliography. See issues of Department of state bulletin
Recent publications; descriptive list. See issues of UN monthly chronicle

Scientific committee on the effects of atomic radiation

Assembly adopts resolution; with text. UN Mo Chron 4:62-4 Ja '67
Effects of atomic radiation; Assembly adopts report; with text of resolution. UN Mo Chron 4:11-12 N '67

Second committee

See United Nations—Economic and financial committee

Secretariat

Personnel questions; nationality composition of the United Nations secretariat. UN Mo Chron 4:107-9 D '67

Secretary General

Spokesman for mankind; proposal for an annual report on the state of mankind. F. K. Kelly. Sat R 50:22 N 18 '67

Security council

Assembly fills vacancies. UN Mo Chron 4:63 D '67
Situation in the Middle East; Security council adopts resolution; with text. UN Mo Chron 4:3-9 N '67

UNITED NATIONS—Security council—*Cont.*

Meetings, 1966

Record of the month:
Cyprus. UN Mo Chron 4:22-7 Ja '67
Southern Rhodesia. UN Mo Chron 4:6-22 Ja '67

Meetings, 1967

Congo: Security council adopts resolutions; with text of resolution. UN Mo Chron 4:32-9 Ag '67
Record of the month:
Cyprus. UN Mo Chron 4:3-8 D '67
Democratic Republic of Congo. UN Mo Chron 4:20-8 D '67
Situation in the Middle East. UN Mo Chron 4:3-26 Je; 3-7 Ag; 8-20 D '67
Security council extends UNFICYP; with text of resolution. UN Mo Chron 4:81-7 Jl '67
Situation in the Middle East; action of Security council, with text of resolutions. UN Mo Chron 4:4-32 Jl '67
U.N. condemns violations of Middle East cease-fire; statements, October 24, 25, 1967. A. J. Goldberg. Dept State Bul 57:690-2 N 20 '67
U.N. Security council continues consideration of the crisis in the Near East; statements, May 29-31, 1967. A. J. Goldberg. Dept State Bul 56:920-9 Je 19 '67
U.N. Security council continues debate on Near East; Soviet proposal condemning Israel rejected; statements, June 10, 13 and 14, with text of letter, June 9, texts of resolutions June 12 and 14, and texts of draft resolutions June 13, 14, 1967. A. J. Goldberg. Dept State Bul 57:3-12 Jl 3 '67
U.N. Security council demands a cease-fire in the Near East; statements, June 6, 8 and 9, with texts of Security council resolutions, June 6, 7 and 9 and U.S. draft resolutions May 31 and June 8, 1967. A. J. Goldberg. Dept State Bul 56:934-49 Je 26 '67

Sixth committee

See United Nations—Legal committee

Social, humanitarian and cultural committee

Human rights questions; discussion in Third committee. UN Mo Chron 4:37-42 N '67
Resolutions adopted by the General assembly; social and humanitarian questions. UN Mo Chron 4:115-22 Ja '67
Social and humanitarian questions; discussions in U.N. third committee. UN Mo Chron 4:82-9 D '67

Social commission

See United Nations—Commission on social development

Special committee of twenty-four on colonialism

See United Nations—Special committee on the situation with regard to implementation of declaration on granting of independence to colonial countries and peoples

Special committee on peace-keeping operations

Assembly defers report to special session. UN Mo Chron 4:68-79 Ja '67
Assembly renews appeal for contributions; text of resolution. UN Mo Chron 4:37-46 Je '67
Meeting of Special committee. UN Mo Chron 4:10-13 Mr '67
Meetings of Working group A. UN Mo Chron 4:3-11 Ap '67
Meetings of working groups. UN Mo Chron 4:10-18 My '67
Peace-keeping operations; with text of draft resolutions. UN Mo Chron 4:73-4 D '67
Special committee's report. UN Mo Chron 4:13 O '67

Special committee on principles of international law concerning friendly relations and co-operation among states

Principles of international law concerning friendly relations and co-operation among states; second session. UN Mo Chron 4:72-3 Ag '67

Special committee on the policies of apartheid of the government of the Republic of South Africa

Committee begins consideration of programme of work. UN Mo Chron 4:7-9 F '67
Committee discusses form of report to General assembly. UN Mo Chron 4:15-17 O '67

Meetings of Special committee. UN Mo Chron 4:3-6 Mr; 16-18 Ap; 49-50 Je '67
Sub-committee to visit Europe and Africa. UN Mo Chron 4:19 My '67

Special committee on the situation with regard to implementation of declaration on granting of independence to colonial countries and peoples

Adopts resolutions and report; with texts. UN Mo Chron 4:19-42 Ap '67
Assembly adopts resolution; with text. UN Mo Chron 4:3-6 Mr; 16-18 Ap; 49-50 Je '67
Conclusion of meetings in Africa; with text of resolutions. UN Mo Chron 4:89-111 Jl '67
Reports of sub-committees. UN Mo Chron 4:30-2 N '67
Special committee of twenty-four; action during September. UN Mo Chron 4:17-22 O '67
Special committee of twenty-four; adopts resolution on Gibraltar; with text of resolution. UN Mo Chron 4:48-59 Ag '67
Special committee of twenty-four; meetings in Africa. UN Mo Chron 4:51-6 Je '67
Special committee of twenty-four; meetings in April. UN Mo Chron 4:20-9 My '67
United Nations and the decolonization of non-self-governing territories. J. W. S. Malecela. UN Mo Chron 4:84-96 Ag '67

Special political committee

Apartheid in South Africa; committee adopts resolution. UN Mo Chron 4:64-9 D '67
Apartheid in South Africa; committee discusses report. UN Mo Chron 4:23-6 N '67
Assembly defers report to special session. UN Mo Chron 4:68-79 Ja '67
Peace-keeping operations; with text of draft resolutions. UN Mo Chron 4:73-4 D '67
Special political commitee adjourns debate; peaceful settlement of disputes. UN Mo Chron 4:104-5 Ja '67

Sub-commission on prevention of discrimination and protection of minorities

Sub-commission concludes Geneva session. UN Mo Chron 4:45-7 N '67
Sub-commission meets. UN Mo Chron 4:28-30 F '67

Task force on nuclear arms escalation

Nuclear time bomb: excerpts from report on the effects of possible use of nuclear weapons, and security and economic implications of wider acquisition and further development. il Sat R 50:16-19+ D 9 '67

Technical assistance program

See also
United Nations—Development program

Third committee

See United Nations—Social, humanitarian and cultural committee

Treaties

See Treaties

Trusteeship committee

Foreign interests in colonial territories; consideration by Fourth committee. UN Mo Chron 4:74-8 D '67
Fourth committee's recommendations approved. UN Mo Chron 4:98-103 Ja '67
Southern Rhodesia; recommendations of Fourth committee. UN Mo Chron 4:12-18 N '67

Trusteeship council

Assembly fills vacancies. UN Mo Chron 4:63-4 D '67
Thirty-fourth session. UN Mo Chron 4:75-9 Je; 120-34 Jl '67
Trust territory of Nauru; with text of resolution. UN Mo Chron 4:99-101 D '67
Trust Territory of the Pacific Islands; statements, June 8, 1967. E. Anderson; W. R. Norwood; L. Salii. Dept State Bul 57:365-78 S 18 '67

Voting

Installation of mechanical means of voting; Sixth committee recommendations. UN Mo Chron 4:111-12 D '67

Aden

Appointment of mission. UN Mo Chron 4:17-18 Mr '67
Assembly takes note of report of special mission. UN Mo Chron 4:46-9 D '67
General assembly adopts resolution; with text. UN Mo Chron 4:87-94 Ja '67

Africa

Address to OAU; summary. Thant. UN Mo Chron 4:26-7 O '67
UN: the grip loosens. Nat R 19:507 My 16 '67

UNITED NATIONS—*Continued*

Asia, Southeastern
Co-ordination of investigations of lower Mekong Basin; thirty-first session of the committee. UN Mo Chron 4:37-9 Mr '67

Barbados
Assembly admits Barbados to membership. UN Mo Chron 4:51-2 Ja '67

China (People's Republic)
Assembly decision. UN Mo Chron 4:28-35 D '67

China, the United Nations, and the United States; address, March 28, 1967. D. H. Popper. Dept State Bul 56:689-95 My 1 '67

Persuading red China to join the U.N. J. B. Sheerin. Cath World 204:261-3 F '67

U.N. and red China; address, August 18, 1967. G. Romney. Vital Speeches 33:727-30 S 15 '67

U.N. General assembly again rejects move to change Chinese representation; statement, November 21, 1967, with text of resolutions. L. H. Fountain. Dept State Bul 57:829-33 D 18 '67

Congo (capital Kinshasa)
Assistance programme in Congo. UN Mo Chron 4:73-4 Je '67

Congo: Security council adopts resolution; with text of resolution. UN Mo Chron 4: 32-9 Ag '67

Council condemns interference in internal affairs of Congo; with text of resolution. UN Mo Chron 4:20-8 D '67

Cyprus
Council calls for moderation and restraint. UN Mo Chron 4:3-8 D '67

See also
United Nations—Armed forces—Forces in Cyprus

Gibraltar
Special committee of twenty-four: adopts resolution on Gibraltar; with text of resolution. UN Mo Chron 4:48-59 Ag '67

Great Britain
Lion is not dead. A. Tuckerman. Nation 205: 612 D 11 '67

See also
United Nations—Cyprus
United Nations—Gibraltar

Greece, Modern
See also
United Nations—Cyprus

Israel
Emergency meeting of ISMAC. UN Mo Chron 4:10 F '67

U.N. censure of Israel; text of resolution. Cur Hist 52:113 F '67

Korea
Assembly adopts resolution; with text. UN Mo Chron 4:64-8 Ja; 49-55 D '67

Korean question; committee adopts resolution. UN Mo Chron 4:22-3 N '67

Report on North Korean violations of DMZ transmitted to U.N; letter, with text of report. A. J. Goldberg. il Dept State Bul 57:692-4 N 20 '67

See also
United Nations commission for the unification and rehabilitation of Korea

Latin America
Denuclearization of Latin America; consideration in First committee. UN Mo Chron 4:18-22 N '67

Denuclearization of Latin America; First committee's recommendation to Assembly. UN Mo Chron 4:72-3 D '67

Middle East
Admission of failure. Newsweek 70:37 Jl 31 '67

Argument indeed: Soviet attack, Israeli retort; with excerpts from addresses. A. Kosygin; A. Eban. il Life 62:24-5 Je 30 '67

Biggest pie-throwing contest ever? emergency session of the U.N. General assembly. il Newsweek 69:18-20 Je 26 '67

Conclusion of emergency special session. UN Mo Chron 4:3-6 O '67

Crisis; interviews. Thant; F. Y. Chai; R. Bunche. New Yorker 43:19-23 Jl 29 '67

Did U Thant bungle the Middle-East crisis? U S News 62:19 Je 5 '67

Diplomatic counterpoint. il Newsweek 69:31-4 Je 19 '67

Edging ahead; Soviet Union joins in unanimous Security council vote for British resolution. Newsweek 70:33+ D 4 '67

Egypt and Israel; Security council resolution condemns cease-fire violation. New Repub 157:6-7 N 4 '67

Fifth emergency special session of U.N. General assembly adjourns; statement, with text of resolution, July 21, 1967. A. J. Goldberg. Dept State Bul 57:216-18 Ag 14 '67

General assembly debate. P. Ben. New Repub 157:15-16 S 30 '67

Great de-mythification; cease-fire resolution. A. Weill-Tuckerman. Nation 204:770-1 Je 19 '67

Is peace possible? address, March 12, 1967. F. B. Morse. Vital Speeches 33:452-5 My 15 '67

King pleads the Arab case. il Life 63:24-5 Jl 7 '67

Kosygin's aim at U.N: victory in a propaganda carnival. il U S News 62:6 Je 26 '67

Letter from Washington. R. H. Rovere. New Yorker 43:90+ Je 24 '67

Light reaches Europe; condemnation of Thant's role in Middle East crisis. E. Taylor. Reporter 36:12 Je 15 '67

Madness and Armageddon. N. Cousins. Sat R 50:24 N 11 '67

Middle East blueprint. New Repub 157:7-8 Jl 15 '67

Middle East crisis; address, June 20, 1967. A. J. Goldberg. Vital Speeches 33:603-5 Ji 15 '67

Mission from Moscow; special session on peace in the Middle East. Time 89:22 Je 23 '67

Mission impossible; reactions to Gunnar V. Jarring's arrival. Newsweek 71:33-4 Ja 1 '68

Next battlefield: the U.N. il Bsns W p29-30 Je 17 '67

No practical help; General assembly debates Middle East crisis. Time 90:24 Jl 7 '67

Object lesson in the Middle East. America 116: 867 Je 24 '67

Propaganda in the UN; Price of peace; Hammarskjold vs. U Thant. America 117:3 Jl 1 '67

Psychedelic debate; General assembly Mideast debate. il Time 89:22 Je 30 '67

Russia vs. U.S. who really won? voting details. il U S News 63:6-7 Jl 17 '67

Security council adopts resolution; with text. UN Mo Chron 4:8-20 D '67

Security council affirms principles for peace in the Middle East; requests Secretary-General to send special representative; statements with text of resolution. A. J. Goldberg. Dept State Bul 57:834-44 D 18 '67

Situation in the Middle East; action by the United Nations. UN Mo Chron 4:3-80 Jl '67

Situation in the Middle East; action of Security council and fifts emergency special session of the General assembly, with text of resolutions. UN Mo Chron 4:3-32 Ag '67

Situation in the Middle East; report on Jerusalem; General assembly and Security council. UN Mo Chron 4:11-13 O '67

Situation in the Middle East; Security council adopts resolution; with text. UN Mo Chron 4:3-9 N '67

Situation in the Near East; White House releases, June 5-8, 1967. Dept State Bul 56:549-52 Je 26 '67

Spiral of defiance; Security council action. A. Tuckerman. Nation 205:482-3 N 13 '67

Staving off a second front. il Time 89:11-12 Je 2 '67

Story of forty-eight hours; U Thant's part in UNEF withdrawal. M. Greenfield. il Reporter 36:19-23 Je 15 '67

Third front; U Thant's mission. A. Weill-Tuckerman. Nation 204:706-7 Je 5 '67

U.N. adopts resolutions on aid to refugees and status of Jerusalem; rejects other resolutions dealing with the Middle East crisis; statements, July 3, 4, 1967, with text of resolutions. A. J. Goldberg. Dept State Bul 57:108-13 Jl 24 '67

U.N. condemns violations of Middle East cease-fire; statements, October 24, 25, 1967. A. J. Goldberg. Dept State Bul 57:690-2 N 20 '67

U.N. debate unfolds. il Newsweek 70:18-21 Jl 3 '67

U.N. General assembly holds fifth emergency session; United States offers proposals for peace in the Middle East; statements, June 17, 19 and 20, 1967. A. J. Goldberg. Dept State Bul 57:47-52 Jl 10 '67

U.N. Security council continues consideration of the crisis in the Near East; statements, May 29-31, 1967. A. J. Goldberg. Dept State Bul 56:920-9 Je 19 '67

UNITED NATIONS—Middle East—*Continued*

U.N. Security council continues debate on Near East; Soviet proposal condemning Israel rejected; statements, June 10, 13 and 14, with text of letter, June 9, texts of resolutions June 12 and 14, and texts of draft resolutions June 13, 14, 1967. A. J. Goldberg. Dept State Bul 57:3-12 Jl 3 '67

U.N. Security council demands a cease-fire in the Near East; statements, June 6, 8 and 9, with texts of Security council resolutions, June 6, 7 and 9 and U.S. draft resolutions May 31 and June 8, 1967. A. J. Goldberg. Dept State Bul 56:934-49 Je 26 '67

U.N. summit. C. M. Eichelberger. Sat R 50:14 Jl 1 '67

United Nations; the human factor; address, July 30, 1967. Thant. Vital Speeches 33:724-7 S 15 '67; Same. UN Mo Chron 4:75-83 Ag '67

U.S. abstains on U.N. resolution on Jerusalem; urges steps toward durable peace in Near East; statement, July 14, 1967, with text or resolution. A. J. Goldberg. Dept State Bul 57:148-51 Jl 31 '67

United States calls for restraint in the Near East; statements, May 23, 24, 1967. L. B. Johnson; A. J. Goldberg. Dept State Bul 56:870-3 Je 12 '67

Unsettlement is the Middle East prospect. P. Ben. New Repub 157:10-11 N 25 '67

Victory without peace? D. Lawrence. U S News 62:98 Je 26 '67

Waiting for a compromise. P. Ben. New Repub 157:9-10 Jl 1 '67

Wall of words; U.S, USSR proposals on Palestine question. A. Weill-Tuckerman. Nation 205:2-4 Jl 3 '67

War of the words. il Bsns W p33-6 Je 24 '67
See also
United Nations—Armed forces—Forces in the Middle East

Nauru (Island)

Council's recommendation; with text of resolution. UN Mo Chron 4:99-101 D '67

Portugal

Assembly adopts resolution; with text. UN Mo Chron 4:35-44 D '67

General assembly adopts resolution; Portuguese territories; with text. UN Mo Chron 4:94-8 Ja '67

Rhodesia

Assembly adopts resolution; with text. UN Mo Chron 4:44-6 D '67

Report of the Secretary-General. UN Mo Chron 4:18 Ap '67

Rhodesia; U.N. policy dictatorial; address, January 12, 1967. P. J. Fannin. Vital Speeches 33:264-7 F 15 '67

Security council adopts resolution; with text. UN Mo Chron 4:6-22 Ja '67

Security council votes mandatory sanctions against Southern Rhodesia; statement, December 12; with text of resolution adopted, December 16, 1966. A. J. Goldberg. Dept State Bul 56:73-8 Ja 9 '67

Southern Rhodesia and the United Nations: the U.S. position. Dept State Bul 56:366-77 Mr 6 '67

Southern Rhodesia; recommendations of Fourth committee. UN Mo Chron 4:12-18 N '67

Southern Rhodesia; report of Secretary-General. Thant. UN Mo Chron 4:13-14 Mr '67

This month's feature; question of U.S. Rhodesian policy. Cong Digest 46:67-71+ Mr '67

U.S, U.N. and U.K; participation in U.N.'s economic sanctions against Rhodesia. R. Moley. Newsweek 69:104 Je 12 '67

South Africa

Apartheid in South Africa; committee adopts resolution. UN Mo Chron 4:64-9 D '67

Apartheid in South Africa; committee discusses report. UN Mo Chron 4:23-6 N '67

Assembly adopts resolutions; with texts. UN Mo Chron 4:52-62 Ja '67

Council approves letter to South Africa; concerning status of South West Africa. UN Mo Chron 4:39-40 Ag '67

Treatment of prisoners in South Africa; meetings of working group of experts. UN Mo Chron 4:87-9 Jl '67

South Yemen (People's Republic)

Southern Yemen admitted to United Nations; statement, December 12, 1967. A. J. Goldberg. Dept State Bul 58:65 Ja 8 '68

Southwest Africa

Ad hoc committee organizes work. UN Mo Chron 4:3-7 F '67

Assembly action; elects 11-member council. UN Mo Chron 4:87 Jl '67

Assembly adopts resolution. UN Mo Chron 4:27-37 Je '67

Assembly considers report and proposals; fifth special session. UN Mo Chron 4:4-10 My '67

Committee approves report. UN Mo Chron 4:11-16 Ap '67

Committee considers suggestions for administration of territory. UN Mo Chron 4:6-10 Mr '67

Council approves letter to South Africa. UN Mo Chron 4:39-40 Ag '67

Drawn-out fight for South-West Africa. Reporter 36:20-1 My 4 '67

South West Africa; Council discusses report to Assembly. UN Mo Chron 4:28-30 N '67

Tasks of the ad hoc Committee for South West Africa; statement, January 26, 1967. W. P. Rogers. Dept State Bul 56:302-5 F 20 '67

United States urges dialog regarding South West Africa; statements, April 26 and May 19, 1967; with text of resolution. A. J. Goldberg. Dept State Bul 56:888-94 Je 12 '67

Spain

See also
United Nations—Gibraltar

Syria

Emergency meeting of ISMAC. UN Mo Chron 4:10 F '67

Turkey

See also
United Nations—Cyprus

United States

Human rights conventions; statement, February 23, 1967. A. J. Goldberg. Dept State Bul 56:524-9 Mr 27 '67

Human rights treaties: why is the U.S. stalling? W. Korey. For Affairs 45:414-24 Ap '67

Our heroes at the U.N. C. Fritchey. Harper 234:30+ F '67

Public diplomacy at the United Nations; address, July 27, 1967. A. J. Goldberg. Dept State Bul 57:262-5 Ag 28 '67

U.N. General assembly holds fifth emergency session; United States offers proposals for peace in the Middle East; statements, June 17, 19 and 20, 1967. A. J. Goldberg. Dept State Bul 57:47-52 Jl 10 '67

U.S does not concur in request for U.N. General assembly session; text of letter, June 15, 1967. A. J. Goldberg. Dept State Bul 57:12-13 Jl 3 '67

U.S. participation in the U.N. during 1965; text of message, March 9, 1967. L. B. Johnson. Dept State Bul 56:566-8 Ap 3 '67

U.S. participation in the U.N. during 1966; text of letter, November 15, 1967. L. B. Johnson. Dept State Bul 58:59-60 Ja 8 '68

Why Goldberg opts out. il Bsns W p40-1 D 16 '67

Vietnam

Call it up! M. Mansfield urges revival of U.S. draft resolution. Nation 205:5 Jl 3 '67

End the war talks at the U.N, but—. U S News 63:8 O 2 '67

How vital Vietnam? il Sr Schol 90:19 F 10 '67

Press conference at headquarters; summary. January 10, 1967. Thant. UN Mo Chron 4:11-13 F '67

Prod from the Senate; Mansfield-Morse resolutions. Nation 205:484-5 N 13 '67

Responsibility of the United Nations in the search for peace in Viet-Nam; statement, November 2, 1967. A. J. Goldberg. Dept State Bul 57:667-72 N 20 '67

Stirrings in the elephant grass; an invitation from the Security council to the National liberation front. A. Tuckerman. Nation 206:3-4 Ja 1 '68

United Nations as the keeper of world peace; with excerpts from exchange of letters between H. F. Byrd, jr. and A. J. Goldberg. il U S News 62:31 Je 5 '67

U.N. truce plan falters. Sr Schol 90:19 Ap 14 '67

U.S. reaffirms desire for peace in Viet-Nam; exchange of letters, December 30, 31, 1966. A. J. Goldberg; Thant. Dept State Bul 56:137-9 Ja 23 '67

U.S. renews bid; Viet debate. Sr Schol 91:7 O 12 '67

Uses of the U.N; NLF program circulated. Newsweek 70:38 D 25 '67

UNITED NATIONS childrens' fund

Center on children's cultures; agency within framework of United States committee for UNICEF. A. Pellowski. bibliog il Wilson Lib Bul 42:209-13 O '67

UNITED NATIONS childrens' fund—*Continued*
Executive board 1967 session. UN Mo Chron 4:119-20 Jl '67
What UNICEF means to children. B. Spock. il Redbook 129:20+ O '67
UNITED NATIONS conference on trade and development
Conference on olive oil to prolong agreement. UN Mo Chron 4:64-5 Ap '67
Invisibles and financing related to trade; second session. UN Mo Chron 4:37-9 My '67
New perspectives on trade and development. I. Frank. For Affairs 45:520-40 Ap '67
Preparatory work on shipping problems. UN Mo Chron 4:52 Ap '67
Scandal of the century; rich and poor; need for global redistribution of wealth. A. de Borchgrave. il Newsweek 70:38-40 O 30 '67
Special session held on rubber problems. UN Mo Chron 4:92 D '67
Trade and development board; concludes fifth session. UN Mo Chron 4:28-31 O '67
Trade and development board; fifth session. UN Mo Chron 4:65-6 Ag '67
UNCTAD calendar for 1967. UN Mo Chron 4:126 Ja '67
UNCTAD committee on shipping; second session. UN Mo Chron 4:32 Mr '67
UNITED NATIONS day
United Nations day 1967; messages. C. Manescu; Thant. UN Mo Chron 4:i-iv O '67
United Nations day, 1967; proclamation. L. B. Johnson. Dept State Bul 57:295 S 4 '67
UNITED NATIONS educational, scientific, and cultural organization
For Florence and Venice; appeal. R. Maheu. il UNESCO Courier 20:4-5 Ja '67
Magna carta for teachers adopted at Unesco. Sch & Soc 94:479-80 D 24 '66
Partners for peace, students of UNESCO; study project sponsored by the National PTA and the Department of classroom teachers. PTA Mag 61:25 F '67
Unesco in the service of peace. V. De Lipski. il UNESCO Courier 20:28-30 F '67
Unesco seminar on education for international understanding. Sch & Soc 95:62 Ja 21 '67
See also
International conference on public education
International music council

Publications
Country divided; excerpts from the Unesco report on apartheid. il UNESCO Courier 20:7-13+ Mr '67
Figures for a developing world; third edition of Unesco statistical yearbook. UNESCO Courier 20:36 Ap '67
UNESCO and the search for peace. il UNESCO Courier 20:64-6 Ag '67
UNITED NATIONS emergency force. See United Nations—Armed forces
UNITED NATIONS general assembly. See United Nations—General assembly
UNITED NATIONS human rights day. See Human rights day and week
UNITED NATIONS industrial development organization
Industrial development board; first session. UN Mo Chron 4:32-7 My '67
Industrial development board; first session concluded. UN Mo Chron 4:68-71 Je '67
Industrial promotion service; International symposium on industrial development. UN Mo Chron 4:66-7 Ag '67
Special industrial services; first year completed. UN Mo Chron 4:50 il Ap '67
UNITED NATIONS institute for training and research
United Nations institute for training and research; programmes and activities. UN Mo Chron 4:74-8 Mr '67
UNITED NATIONS international atomic energy agency. See International atomic energy agency
UNITED NATIONS international children's emergency fund. See United Nations children's fund
UNITED NATIONS organization for industrial development. See United Nations industrial development organization
UNITED NATIONS relief and works agency for Palestine refugees in the Near East
Pledges for refugee programmes. UN Mo Chron 4:124-5 Ja '67
Refugees; slender resources over-taxed. UN Mo Chron 4:80-1 Jl '67
Strange world of UNRWA. G. Bailey. il Reporter 37:20-3 N 16 '67
UNRWA report. UN Mo Chron 4:47-8 N '67
UNITED NATIONS seminars. See Seminars

UNITED NATIONS university (proposed)
Idea of a world university, by M. Zweig. Review
  Bul Atomic Sci 23:34-5 O '67. E. U. Condon
UNITED network company
Ad hoc hookup; United network produces the Las Vegas show. Time 89:50 My 12 '67
Network fade-out. Newsweek 69:84 Je 12 '67
Pop goes the network. il Newsweek 69:90+ My 15 '67
United we fall. Time 89:70 Je 9 '67
UNITED Presbyterian church in the United States of America
At last, the new creed. Time 89:56 Je 2 '67
Confession of 1967; Presbyterian church's proposed new creedal statement. Christian Cent 84:364-5 Mr 22 '67
Peace and peril at Ghost ranch; conference center at Abiquiu, N. Mex. K. Haselden. Christian Cent 84:988-90 Ag 2 '67
Radical confession; fresh statement of doctrine. Newsweek 69:63 Je 5 '67
United Presbyterian general assembly. R. A. Balcomb. Christian Cent 84:788+ Je 14 '67
UNITED Presbyterian general assembly. See United Presbyterian church in the United States of America
UNITED press international
Live wires. il Newsweek 71:46-7 Ja 15 '68
UNITED professional planning, Incorporated
R for M.D.'s. Newsweek 69:83 Mr 27 '67
UNITED rubber, cork, linoleum and plastic workers of America
Push for blue-collar salaries; negotiations for status and security through guaranteed annual wage. il Bsns W p 135-6+ F 25 '67
Strike that's a mystery; what's behind rubber dispute. il U S News 62:81-3 My 29 '67
Unions mass for copper showdown; rubber walkout is stalemated. Bsns W p 156+ My 20 '67
UNITED soccer association
Soccer is simple? il Newsweek 69:70-1 Ap 24 '67
UNITED STATES
America today; address, June 27, 1967. L. B. Johnson. Vital Speeches 33:605-8 Jl 15 '67
America's destiny; address, May 14, 1967. J. A. Farley. Vital Speeches 33:636-8 S 1 '67
Doctor Edgar Friedenberg; our most devastating critic; statement, ed. by C. Brossard. E. Z. Friedenberg. Look 31:73-5 My 30 '67
Not all this country is tense, troubled. il U S News 63:34-7 Ag 7 '67
Second centennial. Nation 206:66-7 Ja 15 '68
This is my land. P. Kunhardt. Life 62:20D Je 2 '67
Toynbee on America; interview, ed. by J. Hicks. A. Toynbee. il Life 63:108-108B+ D 8 '67
Trends; the state of the Nation. F. Morley. See issues of Nation's business
Wondrous world of 1990; outlook for young people. il U S News 62:62-6 Ja 30 '67
See also
Americanism
Americans
States (United States)
also names of sections, states, e.g. West; *also* subhead United States under various subjects, e.g. Hospitals—United States

Advanced research projects agency
See United States—Defense, Department of—Advanced research projects agency

Advisory board on national parks, historic sites, buildings and monuments
Advisory board meets; proposed additions to existing national parks. Nat Parks Mag 41:20 Jl '67

Agency for international development
AID report on Viet-Nam commodity programs submitted to President Johnson; letter of transmittal, January 9, 1967; with text of report. W. S. Gaud. Dept State Bul 56:200-16 F 6 '67
Battery additives; AID's chagrin. D. S. Greenberg. Science 156:627 My 5 '67
Birth and death of an idea; research in AID. E. B. Skolnikoff. Bul Atomic Sci 23:38-40 S '67
Blunder in Laos; how USAID disrupted one of the most successful programs for cooperation between Asian nations. M. A. Bernad. America 117:766-9 D 23 '67
Budget message of the President; excerpts; with excerpts from The budget of the United States government for the fiscal year ending June 30, 1968. L. B. Johnson. il Dept State Bul 56:233-5 F 13 '67

UNITED STATES—Agency for international development—*Continued*
Charting new seas for U.S. capital; new AID program of entended risk guarantees. Bsns W p 130 Ap 8 '67
Commercial matter; Senate subcommittee investigates payments of South Vietnamese importers by U.S. drug companies. Newsweek 70:30 Ag 14 '67
Fantasy in Vietnam. J. Osborne. New Repub 156:13-15 My 27 '67
Food for the future. M. Jones. il Américas 19:30-3 Jl '67
Importance of agricultural development in our strategy for peace; address, May 10, 1967. E. V. Rostow. Dept State Bul 56:856-65 Je 5 '67
Management of the war: a tale of two capitals. W. Guzzardi, jr. il Fortune 75:134-9+ Ap '67
Secretary Rusk urges appropriation of full amount authorized under the Foreign assistance act; statement, November 20, 1967. D. Rusk. Dept State Bul 57:801-7 D 11 '67
Selling Congress on foreign aid. America 116:550-1 Ap 15 '67
United States commemorates closing of successful AID mission to Iran; remarks, November 29, 1967 and message from the President. D. Rusk; L. B. Johnson. Dept State Bul 57:825-7 D 18 '67
Vietnam, a doctor's journal; U.S. military public health assistance program at Camau hospital. J. J. Weiss. Commentary 43:55-8 My '67

Agricultural research center, Beltsville, Md.

U.S.D.A. agricultural research center, Beltsville, Md. V. R. Boswell. il Horticulture 45:36-7 F '67

Agriculture, Department of

Farmers get closer to the market. il Bsns W p 110-12+ S 16 '67
Foot-and-mouth alert! test of defenses against the world's costliest animal disease. J. A. Rohlf. il Farm J 91:25-7+ My '67
New Asiatic invader; Formosan termite, with recommendations by USDA Forest research advisory committee. K. B. Pomeroy. il Am For 73:22-4+ Ja '67
Remote sensing techniques considered most promising; promotion of agricultural satellites. il Tech W 20:58 Je 5 '67
We're still in the jungle; meat products promotion and conflict of interest. R. Nader New Repub 157:11-12 Jl 15 '67
See also
United States—Agricultural research center, Beltsville, Md

Air force

Air force is climbing to a wild new yonder; manned orbit laboratory (MOL) program. il Bsns W p28-9 Jl 8 '67
Big press argument exploded again at air force meeting. il Tech W 20:25-6 Ja 23 '67
Flying saucers; sightings and study of UFO's. W. Rogers. il Look 31:76-80 Mr 21 '67
Shopping for new aircraft. il Bsns W p62+ Ag 26 '67
200,000-ton forging press seen needed. M. L. Yaffee. Aviation W 86:78-9+ Ja 30 '67
U.S. plans long-term tactical buildup. B. K. Thomas, jr. il Aviation W 86:75-81 Mr 6 '67
See also
Air bases
Airplanes, Military—United States

Air rescue service

AF, navy move toward new SAR craft; search and rescue aircraft. Tech W 20:16 My 15 '67
HH-53B readied for southeast Asia role as interim CARA; combat aircrew rescue aircraft. C. Brownlow. il Aviation W 87:64-5+ Jl 3 '67
U.S. to increase air rescue capability in southeast Asia. C. Brownlow. il Aviation W 86:40-1+ My 1 '67

Appropriations and expenditures

Aerospace budget. R. Hotz. Aviation W 86:17 Ja 30; 21 F 13 '67

Ballistic systems division

AF divisions near merger; possible recombination of Systems command's space systems div. and Ballistic systems div. Tech W 20:37 Ap 3 '67

Extended Athena program improved by man in the loop. W. Wilks. il Tech W 20:17 Ap 24 '67

Cambridge research laboratories

AF Cambridge labs spending 10 per cent of R&D on limited war. R. Barnhart. il Tech W 20:22-3 Ap 24 '67

Communication systems

Air force to test portable tropo radio; tropospheric scatter telecommunications. C. D. LaFond. il Tech W 20:23-5 Mr 20 '67
U.S. air force; command & control; address, May 24, 1967. R. P. Klocko. Vital Speeches 33:648-51 Ag 15 '67

Education

See also
United States air force academy, Colorado Springs

Forces in France

U.S. troops leave France. M. Buckley. America 116:563-4 Ap 15 '67

Forces in Libya

Backlash of Mideast war: Libya turns on the U.S; Wheelus field at stake. il U S News 63:48 Ag 21 '67
Is U.S. to lose its last air base in Africa? Wheelus air base. il U S News 62:6 Je 26 '67

Forces in Thailand

Thai ally; missions over North Vietnam. F. Sully. il Newsweek 69:51 Mr 27 '67
Thailand grants U.S. permission to use U Tapao airbase; statement, March 22, 1967. D. Rusk. Dept State Bul 56:597-8 Ap 10 '67

Forces in Vietnam

Old man & the MIGs; America's top MIG killer. il Time 89:16 Je 2 '67
Rolling the thunder; W. W. Momyer; the man who is running the air war. il Time 90:23 D 29 '67
USAF F-4C carries varied ordnance loads; photographs. Aviation W 86:75-8 Ap 24 '67

History

Billy Mitchell affair, by B. Davis. Review Newsweek il 69:98+ Je 19 '67. S. K. Oberbeck

Procurement

Air force to centralize software services under new command. D. C. Winston. Aviation W 87:30 D 11 '67
C-5A pioneers in subcontract relations. il Aviation W 87:243-5+ N 20 '67
GAO scrutinizes one-step procurement. D. C. Winston. Aviation W 86:63+ Je 19 '67
USAF hits industry attitude on tighter contract control. K. Johnsen. Aviation W 87:113-14 O 9 '67
USAF request stresses tactical aircraft. D. C. Winston. il Aviation W 86:26-7 Ja 30 '67

Research

Air force: study relates troubled relationship with research. D. S. Greenberg. Science 156:1463-6 Je 16 '67; Reply. L. Edson. 157:877 Ag 25 '67

Systems command

AF divisions near merger; possible recombination of Systems command's space systems div. and Ballistic systems div. Tech W 20:37 Ap 3 '67
Air force seeks new equipment to meet research and development needs; upgrading of research and development laboratories of research and technology division. R. W. Niblock and others. il Tech W 20:107+ Mr 27 '67
Computers cut topographic survey costs; Electromagnetic compatibiliy analysis center employing site analysis model. C. D. LaFond. il Tech W 20:20-1 F 20 '67
USAF, industry studying ABM concepts. Aviation W 86:84-5+ My 15 '67
USAF investigation report: electric arcing blamed in simulator fire. Aviation W 86:115-17 Ap 17 '67

Tactical air command

TAC profiting from Nellis' expanded role. C. M. Plattner. il Aviation W 86:98-9+ My 8 '67

Air force, Army

Army asks large aircraft gain. il Aviation W 86:29 Ja 30 '67

Air force, Navy

A-New system readied for tests on P-3C. C. M. Plattner. il Aviation W 86:72-3+ Mr 27 '67

UNITED STATES—*Continued*

Anti-Communist measures
See Communism—United States—Anti-Communist measures; United States—Foreign relations—Anti-Communist measures

Anti-poverty program
See Anti-poverty program, 1964-

Antiquities
See also
Indians of North America—Antiquities

Appalachian regional commission
Opportunity and action in Appalachia. Mo Labor R 90:III-IV Ja '67

Appropriations and expenditures
Agencies reach for scalpels. Bsns W p44 D 9 '67

Arithmetic fluff haunts LBJ on Hill; disparity in spending cuts. Bsns W p59 D 9 '67

Billions for war and world aid, but as for the Great society—. il U S News 63:28-9 Jl 31 '67

Blunt broadax; ineffective budget cuts for scientific research. Sci N 92:415 O 28 '67

Budget cuts. H. C. Wallich Newsweek 70:86 O 23 '67

Can you spare a dime? regular appropriation bills. Newsweek 70:36 N 6 '67

Change of heart? Senate committees vote funds for slum aid. Newsweek 70:21 S 11 '67

Congress sours on new spending ideas. il U S News 63:31 Ag 21 '67

Congressional record. New Repub 157:7-8 D 23 '67

Defending the dollar. il Time 90:13-14 D 1 '67

Discretionary funds. D. Wolfle. Science 157:879 Ag 25 '67

End of the caper; funding policy for U.S. organizations abroad. Newsweek 69:33 Ap 10 '67

Fiscal responsibility. M. Friedman. Newsweek 70:68 Ag 7 '67

Forestry in the federal budget; fiscal year ending June 30, 1968. il Am For 73:10 Mr '67

George Mahon wields a powerful ax. il Bsns W p 110-12+ F 18 '67

GOP digs in its heels. Bsns W p42+ Je 24 '67

Great society faces future; changes Congress is making; cuts in spending. il U S News 63:32-3 Jl 10 '67

Grudging progress. Time 90:30-1 N 17 '67

Guns, butter: must we choose? address, August 4, 1967. W. Morse. Vital Speeches 32:714-17 S 15 '67

House that lost its head; budget-cutters. S. Maloff. Commonweal 87:135-6 N 3 '67

How your tax money is wasted. il Nations Bsns 55:94-5+ My '67

It's time to define our priorities. Fortune 76:119-20 N '67

Job corps comes up to a test. il Bsns W p 145-6+ O 14 '67

Locked horns. New Repub 157:7 N 4 '67

Mike Frome; false economy by federal government. M. Frome. Am For 73:3+ D '67

Mike Kirwan's big ditch; Lake Erie-Ohio River Canal; pork barrel project. W. Schulz. Read Digest 90:59-64 Je '67

New policy outlined on funds for U.S. voluntary organizations; statement, March 29, 1967, and text of report. L. B. Johnson. Dept State Bul 56:665-8 Ap 24 '67

Pigeonhole power; battle over tax-surcharge bill and budget cuts. il Newsweek 70:25-6 O 16 '67

Pinchpenny fever. Newsweek 70:26-7 O 30 '67

President requests $400 million for Latin American loans. Dept State Bul 56:887 Je 12 '67

Putting off the tax bill till '68. Time 90:30-1 O 27 '67

Revolt on the hill. Time 90:27 O 6 '67

Signs read slow for R&D; funds short of last year's appropriations. il Bsns W p70-2 F 4 '67

So proudly we hail. New Repub 157:8 Jl 15 '67

Spending and taxes. Bsns W p 148 Jl 8 '67

State of the Union. il Sci N 91:55+ Ja 21 '67

They sure know how to spread it around. A. H. Sypher. il Nations Bsns 55:31-2 Ap '67

Unfinished business. Time 90:25 N 10 '67

What LBJ wants on taxes and money; State of the Union message. Bsns W p26-7 Ja 14 '67

Where charity begins; largest public-works bill since 1963. Time 90:19 Ag 4 '67
See also
Budget—United States
Government spending policy
United States—Economic policy
  also subhead Appropriations and expenditures under names of government departments, e.g. United States—Defense, Department of—Appropriations and expenditures

Armed forces
Growing drain on U.S. combat strength. U S News 62:14 Ap 17 '67

How U.S. could meet a new military test. il Bsns W p38-40 Je 10 '67
See also
Service men
United States—Air force
United States—Army
United States—Coast guard
United States—Defense, Department of
United States—Joint chiefs of staff
United States—Marine corps
United States—Navy

Appropriations and expenditures

Admiral Rickover opens up on Pentagon's cost policies; excerpts from testimony, April 18, 1967. H. Rickover. il U S News 62:42-3 My 29 '67

Big squeeze. R. Hotz. Aviation W 87:21 Ag 14 '67

Biggest arms bill yet; where money goes. il U S News 63:9 S 4 '67

Dollars vs. lives; a U.S. choice; interview. E. Teller. il U S News 62:44-8 My 29 '67

Fiscal year 1968 budget; with editorial comment. il Tech W 20:14-20+, 50 Ja 30 '67

Freedom, and the mighty military machine. il Sr Schol 90:9-13 Ap 21 '67

House votes more AMSA, FDLS funds. Tech W 20:21 My 1 '67

Major cuts believed unlikely in $6 billion DOT request; with editorial comment. H. Taylor. Aero Tech 21:18-19, 70 Jl 17 '67

Man under the gun in military research; Pentagon research chief. il Bsns W p60-2+ D 16 '67

Senate approves F-111B production fund. D. C. Winston. Aviation W 86:22-3 Mr 27 '67

Senate gets $70.1 billion defense appropriation bill. Aero Tech 21:19 Ag 14 '67

Services face deep program cuts. C. Brownlow. Aviation W 87:22-3 Ag 7 '67

Special budget report; Viet requirements boost budget. Aviation W 86:22-38 Ja 30 '67

U.K. F-111 order seen periled by Buy American amendment. Aero Tech 21:17 S 25 '67
See also
United States—Defense, Department of—Appropriations and expenditures

Desertions

Dissenters and deserters. E. F. Sherman. New Repub 158:23-6 Ja 6 '68

Education

Retraining the rejects, an army success story. il U S News 63:82-3 N 6 '67

Social inequities; Defense department programs; address, November 7, 1967. R. S. McNamara. Vital Speeches 34:98-103 D 1 '67
See also
United States—Army—Education

Equipment and supplies

Superiority and innovation in U.S. defense forces. B. G. Lall. il Bul Atomic Sci 23:11-13 Mr '67

Forces in Asia

USA in Asia. J. R. Moskin. il Look 31:29-35 My 30 '67

Forces in Ethiopia

Ethiopia; the over-present Americans. N. G. Kotler. il Nation 204:236-9 F 20 '67

Forces in Europe

As U.S. starts a pullback of troops from Europe. U S News 62:10 My 15 '67

Can America reduce its troops in Europe? opponents: M. Mansfield, H. M. Jackson. il U S News 62:12 Mr 20 '67

Conversation with Dean Rusk; transcript of interview, ed. by P. Niven. D. Rusk. Dept State Bul 56:782-83 My 22 '67

How many troops? agreement between Washington and Bonn. il Newsweek 69:44-5 Mr 20 '67

How West German leader sees U.S. role in Europe; interview, ed. by R. A. Haeger. K. G. Kiesinger. U S News 63:52-4 Jl 10 '67

UNITED STATES—*Continued*

Army

Barracks and quarters

Shipping out; Oakland's overseas processing center. J. G. Dunne. Sat Eve Post 240:18-19 S 9 '67

Cavalry

Black Jack of the 10th; J. J. Pershing. R. O'Connor. il Am Heritage 18:14-17+ F '67

Commissariat

Gourmet C-rations; long range patrol subsistence. Newsweek 70:95 N 13 '67

Communications

See Radio communication, Military

Corps of engineers

Dams and wild rivers; looking beyond the pork barrel. L. J. Carter. il Science 158:233-6+ O 13 '67

Don't pull the plug on the Everglades. J. Browder. il Am For 73:12-15+ S '67

Desertion

Aggressive campaign. il Time 91:21 Ja 19 '68

Conscientious AWOLS; European organizations aiding deserters. T. Land. Nation 205: 488-91 N 13 '67

Deserters go underground; AWOL's in Amsterdam. S. De Gramont. Sat Eve Post 241: 27 Ja 27 '68

Education

Drop-ins; remedial reading and writing classes. Newsweek 70:50-1 O 30 '67

See also

United States military academy, West Point

Equipment and supplies

Pentagon escalates war on payments gap; overseas sales of military equipment. il Bsns W p22-3 Ja 13 '68

See also

Rifles

Tanks, Military

Forces in Europe

Good-by to all that; departure from France. il Newsweek 69:59-60 Mr 27 '67

U.S. troops leave France. M. Buckley. America 116:563-4 Ap 15 '67

Forces in Vietnam

Action along Highway 13; 11th Armored cavalry regiment. il Life 62:69-74 Je 2 '67

Anderson platoon; Frenchman films Viet war. il Ebony 22:69-72+ O '67

Day's work; First infantry division in Cambodian border area. E. Martin. il Newsweek 70:47 D 18 '67

Digging out the V.C.; U.S. 1st Cavalry airmobile. il Time 90:38 S 29 '67

Draftee is sent to fight; Pfc. Steven C. Stone. C. S. Wren. il Look 31:28-33 N 28 '67

GI's in Vietnam; praise from a Dutch general; excerpts from report. M. W. J. M. Broekmeijer. U S News 63:14 O 16 '67

Men of third squad, second platoon, C company, third battalion. T. Buckley. il N Y Times Mag p34-5+ N 5 '67; Discussion. p40+ N 26 '67

New ceiling for GI's in Vietnam; will it stick this time? il U S News 63:8 Ag 14 '67

Sociologist appraises the G.I. C. C. Moskos, jr. il N Y Times Mag p32-3+ S 24 '67

U.S. paratroopers in a stepped-up war; battle jump. D. Moser. il Life 62:72-7 Mr 10 '67

U.S. weapons in Vietnam; are they good enough? interview. H. W. O. Kinnard. il U S News 62:68-71 F 6 '67

Vietnam by helicopter; operations of First air cavalry division. D. Smith. il Nation 204: 745-50 Je 12 '67

West Point goes to war. il Newsweek 70:46-56 Jl 10 '67

Yanks and the gooks. M. Wallace; T. Koppel. Nation 204:811-13 Je 26 '67

Hospitals

See Hospitals, Military

Libraries

Black marble moat for Fort Campbell. G. Piersall. il Library J 92:4381-3 D 1 '67

Medical Corps

W.I.A; activities in Vietnam. R. Nessen. il Todays Health 45:20-7 Ap '67

Negroes

Black Jack of the 10th; J. J. Pershing. R. O'Connor. il Am Heritage 18:14-17+ F '67

Courage beyond the call of duty. W. L. Katz. il Sat R 50:30-1 Je 17 '67

Non-commissioned officers

Army's topmost sarge; W. O. Wooldridge, first sergeant major. il Life 63:51-2+ S 22 '67

Officers

Patton's peer; General Abrams. il Time 89: 34 Ap 14 '67

See also

Generals

Parachute troops

U.S. paratroopers in a stepped-up war; battle jump; men of the 173rd Airborne brigade in Vietnam. D. Moser. il Life 62:72-7 Mr 10 '67

Post exchanges

See United States—Armed forces—Post exchanges

Procurement

Army to request bids on new LOH orders. D. C. Winston. Aviation W 87:18-19 Jl 31 '67

Army's ADSAF seen worth $100 million-plus to industry. C. D. LaFond. Tech W 20:36-7 Ap 10 '67

How the army zeroed in on the M-16; negotiations with Colt to purchase the production rights. Bsns W p68 Je 24 '67

Public relations

Research in Japan; U.S. army grants cause controversy. P. M. Boffey. Science 158:748-52 N 10 '67

Recruiting and enlistment

Why not abolish the draft? B. K. Chapman. Nat R 19:303-5 Mr 21 '67

Reserves

Trimming the totem; army reserve and national guard reorganization plan. Time 89:32 Je 9 '67

Special forces

B-52s & Green Berets. il Time 89:27-8 Mr 31 '67

John Wayne's Green Beret. Nation 205:614 D 11 '67

Whom the gods love. J. F. Mason. il Reporter 37:21-5 S 21 '67

Army library service

See United States—Army—Libraries

Army research office

Our magicians of limited war. J. G. Hubbell. Read Digest 90:181-2+ My '67

Art

See Art—United States; Art, American

Atomic energy commission

AEC centrifuge ban puts industry in spin. il Bsns W p99-100 Je 10 '67

AEC digs deep for big blast; new test series. il Bsns W p 140+ S 16 '67

AEC proposals, a threat to scientific freedom. H. P. Green. Bul Atomic Sci 23:15-17 O '67

AEC revamps warheads to penetrate ABM defenses. Tech W 20:20 F 6 '67

AEC to start new warhead production. K. Johnsen. il Aviation W 86:37-8 Ja 30 '67

AEC weapons expert blasts DOD technology. Tech W 20:15-16 Mr 27 '67

Bottling up the atom; AEC determination to control production of enriched uranium-235 in gas centrifuges. il Newsweek 69:86 Je 19 '67

Building a hotter fire under irradiated foods; preserving food by using radioisotopes or electronics under AEC contract. il Bsns W p91-2 Ap 8 '67

Large new projects demand systems management skills. W. S. Beller. il Tech W 20:28+ Je 5 '67

New boom in uranium as peace needs grow; report of survey. il U S News 63:64-5 O 16 '67

New force in vaccines; developed at AEC center. Bsns W p 127 Ag 12 '67

New role for the national laboratories; text of declaration. B. I. Spinrad. Bul Atomic Sci 23:30-1 Ja '67

Thermal pollution; Senator Muskie tells AEC to cool it. B. Nelson. Science 158:755-6 N 10 '67

Thinning the reactor jungle. C. Behrens. il Sci N 91:360-1 Ap 15 '67

Useless secrecy and the world bomb balance. Sci N 92:31 Jl 8 '67

See also

Ernest Orlando Lawrence memorial awards

UNITED STATES—Atomic energy commission
—*Continued*

Appropriations and expenditures

AEC boosts weapon, breeding funding.
Tech W 20:27 Ja 30 '67
New missile warheads get $715 million. il
Aero Tech 21:18 O 9 '67

Attorney General

See United States—Justice, Department
of

Boundaries

Ceremonies at U.S.-Mexican border; remarks,
October 28, 1967; with Declaration of the
Presidents. L. B. Johnson. Dept State Bul
57:683-4 N 20 '67
Chamizal to Mexico. il Sr Schol 91:15 N 9 '67
**Out of the thicket; U.S.-Mexican border dis-
pute settled.** Time 90:19 N 3 '67
U.S. and Mexico complete Chamizal settle-
ment; statement, October 27, 1967, with
White House announcement. D. Rusk. Dept
State Bul 57:684-5 N 20 '67

Budget, Bureau of the

Budget bureau: reviewing science in a new
context. L. J. Carter. il Science 157:1413 S
22 '67
McNamara-style budget bureau. Bsns W
p 129+ S 23 '67
Roles of the Bureau of the budget: excerpts
from address, September 30, 1966. W. D.
Carey. Science 156:206-8+ Ap 14 '67

Business economics, Office of

Building a base for forecasters. il Bsns W
p 117-19 Je 10 '67

Cabinet

Exodus of JFK men from the Cabinet? il U S
News 63:24 D 11 '67
Presidency and executive departments: six
hats and twelve right arms. il Sr Schol
91:9-10+ N 30 '67
They're not jobs for little men. A. H.
Sypher. Nations Bsns 55:33-4 S '67
Time to change the presidential system. D.
Lawrence. U S News 62:124 Mr 13 '67
See also
Secretary of defense (United States)

**Cabinet committee on Mexican
Americans**

Cabinet meeting in El Paso. P. D. Ortego.
Nation 205:624-7 D 11 '67

Capitol

Architect, spare our Capitol. R. Sherrill. il
N Y Times Mag p30-1+ Ap 16 '67
Capitol hill's ugliness club. H. Lewis. il
Atlan 219:60-6 F '67
Our national Capitol. B. Finnegan. il Hobbies
72:115-17 Je '67
Renovation proposal: capital plan, or Capitol
punishment? il Sr Schol 90:14 F 24 '67
See also
Washington, D.C.

Census

Census-eye view of sales in '70s; buying population will keep on growing. il Bsns W
p 120-2+ Je 10 '67
Short count: uncounted persons in 1960.
Newsweek 70:29 Jl 3 '67
Where we go after 200-million. il Bsns W
p96-7+ N 4 '67

Census, Bureau of the

Punchcard snoopers. P. Hirsch. il Nation 205:
369-72 O 16 '67; Reply with rejoinder. A. R.
Eckler. 205:610+ D 11 '67

Central intelligence agency

Anthropologists overwhelmingly approve re-
search ethics statement. B. Nelson. Sci-
ence 156:365 Ap 21 '67
Books; C.I.A.: cultural penetration. M. Mug-
geridge. Esquire 68:12+ S '67
CIA and the American conscience. America
116:305 Mr 4 '67
CIA and the kiddies. il Newsweek 69:25-7
F 27 '67
C.I.A. and the students; with editorial com-
ment. W. C. McWilliams. Commonweal 85:
611-14 Mr 3 '67
CIA campus caper. Sat Eve Post 240:92 Mr
25 '67
C.I.A. caper. Christian Cent 84:300-1 Mr 8
'67
CIA chickens home to roost. Nat R 19:230-2
Mr 7 '67
CIA controversy: secret aid bared; with press
comments. Sr Schol 90:16-17 Mr 3 '67
CIA damage. Sci N 92:32-3 Jl 8 '67

CIA: how does it fit in an open society?
il Sr Schol 90:8-16+ Mr 31 '67; Correc-
tion. 90:9 My 19 '67
CIA orphans. Nat R 19:288 Mr 21 '67
CIA: other side of the story, what reds are
doing. il U S News 62:96-8 Mr 13 '67
CIA stooges; secret subsidies to National
student association. New Repub 156:5-6 F
25 '67
CIA subsidized college bookstore co-op. Pub
W 191:48 Mr 6 '67
Closing CIA's cashbox. Time 89:18 Ap 7 '67
Come the revelations; concerning T. Braden's
Saturday evening post article and state-
ments. New Repub 156:7-8 My 27 '67
Corruption. Nation 204:290-1 Mr 6 '67
Cultural cold war; excerpt from Towards a
new past. C. Lasch. Nation 205:208-12 S 11
'67; Discussion. 205:309, 340-1 O 2-9 '67
End of the caper. Newsweek 69:33 Ap 10 '67
Espionage establishment; excerpt. D. Wise
and T. B. Ross. Sat Eve Post 240:53+ N 4
'67
Evasion by definition. Nation 204:452 Ap 10
'67
Former ambassador says: a few kind words
for the CIA. W. Attwood. Look 31:70-1
Ap 18 '67
Funny money; CIA-conduit Texas-based foun-
dations. Nation 205:581 D 4 '67
Guevara, Debray and the CIA. R. Gott. il
Nation 205:521-30 N 20 '67
House of glass; funneling money through
maze of philanthropic funds. il Newsweek
69:28+ Mr 6 '67
House of spooks. Nation 205:260 S 25 '67
How to care for the CIA orphans; Time
essay. Time 89:42-3 My 19 '67
Insufficiency of frankness; subsidizing cul-
tural publications. Nation 204:678 My 29 '67;
Reply. S. Spender. 204:802+ Je 26 '67
Is Garrison faking? F. Powledge. New Repub
156:13-18 Je 17 '67
Issue is integrity; statement, February 20,
1967; ed. by C. B. Grannis. H. S. Commager. Pub W 191:42 Mr 13 '67
Keeping it in the family; Presidents committee on CIA reform. New Repub 156:8 Ap
8: 5 Ap 22 '67
Lessons of the CIA mess. Life 62:4 Mr 3
'67
Liberal anti-communism revisited; symposium.
Commentary 44:31-79 S '67; Discussion. 44:
6+ D '67
Literary Bay of Pigs; subsidies to cultural
freedom publications. A. Werth. Nation
204:710-11 Je 5 '67; Reply. S. Spender. 204:
802+ Je 26 '67
Matter of intelligence. Reporter 36:12 Mr
9 '67
Modern dilemma: two views of the NSA-CIA
crisis by present and former NSA officers.
R. G. Stearns; W. D. Shaul. il Mlle 65:232-
3+ Ag '67
New policy outlined on funds for U.S. volun-
tary organizations; statement, March 29,
1967, and text of report. L. B. Johnson.
Dept State Bul 56:665-8 Ap 24 '67
No laughing matter; CIA and its involvement
with private citizens. Christian Cent 84:332
Mr 15 '67
Notes on the CIA shambles. J. Burnham.
Nat R 19:294 Mr 21 '67
Of many things; CIA and NSA. T. N. Davis.
America 116:inside cover F 25 '67
Orders from top? il Sr Schol 90:17-18 Mr
10 '67
Pandora's cashbox. il Time 89:23 Mr 3 '67
Playing it straight; financing of organizations
to fight communism. New Repub 156:5-9
Mr 4 '67; Correction. 156:9 Mr 11 '67; Dis-
cussion. 156:35 Mr 11; 26+ Ap 1 '67
Political science; CIA, ethics stir otherwise
placid convention. R. J. Samuelson. Science
157:1414-17 S 22 '67
Politics. D. Macdonald. Esquire 67:72+ Je
'67
Praeger discusses CIA book ties. Pub W
191:48 Mr 6 '67
Preserving democracy, C.I.A. style. H. K.
Flad and M. F. Flad. Commonweal 85:614-15
Mr 3 '67
Professor & the CIA; Operations and policy
research, inc. funds. R. G. Sherrill. Nation
204:258-60 F 27 '67; Reply. R. B. Luce.
204:386 Mr 27 '67
Ramparts need watching. Nat R 19:393-5
Ap 18 '67
Ramparts we watch; subsidized student or-
ganizations. K. Crawford. Newsweek 69:38
Mr 6 '67
Secret spending by CIA; LBJ sets some limits.
U S News 62:16 Ap 10 '67
Silent service. il Time 89:13-17 F 24 '67

UNITED STATES—Central intelligence agency
—*Continued*
Speaking out, I'm glad the CIA is immoral.
T. W. Braden. Sat Eve Post 240:10+ My 20
'67
Spies for C.I.A. or deserving students? P. G.
Altbach. Christian Cent 84:352-4 Mr 15 '67
Subversion by government. N. Cousins. Sat
R 50:22-3 Mr 4 '67
That CIAche; four possible plans of Rusk
committee. New Repub 158:12-13 Ja 6 '68
To tell or not to tell; CIA story. W. V.
Shannon. Commonweal 86:308-9 Je 2 '67
Union furor over CIA money. U S News
62:86 My 22 '67
Unknowable CIA; analysis of Walter Lipp-
mann's articles in the Washington post. C.
Felix. il Reporter 36:20-4 Ap 6 '67
Watching the CIA at work around the world.
il U S News 62:28-30 Mr 6 '67
We must not fight fire with fire. J. W. Ful-
bright. il N Y Times Mag p27+ Ap 23 '67
What was so wrong? Thomas Braden pub-
lishes case for the defense. Newsweek 69:
37+ My 22 '67
Why the CIA gave money to U.S. college
students. U S News 62:10 F 27 '67

Caricatures and cartoons
Viewpoints; as cartoonists view the CIA-NSA
controversy. Sr Schol 90:13 Mr 31 '67

Church history
Impact of Christian Science on the American
churches, 1880-1910. R. J. Cunningham. bibliog f Am Hist R 72:885-905 Ap '67

Civil aeronautics board
Airlines eye Pacific as next plum. il Bsns W
p50-2+ F 11 '67
Board bureau urges intensified competition in
transpacific case. Aviation W 87:35-6 Ag
7 '67
Board denies air taxi jet weight limit exemp-
tion. Aviation W 86:29 F 27 '67
Board proposes substantial hike in airline
overbooking penalties. H. D. Watkins. Avia-
tion W 86:39 Ja 23 '67
Board shifts policy on subsidies. il Avia-
tion W 86:36-7 Ap 10 '67
Board's blackout investigation hinges on fu-
ture United position. Aviation W 88:45 Ja
15 '68
Cargo, charter proposals hit by airlines. H. D.
Watkins. Aviation W 87:37 D 4 '67
CAB conditionally approves IATA fares.
Aviation W 86:31 Mr 13 '67
CAB cuts domestic airmail rates. L. Doty.
Aviation W 87:34 S 11 '67
CAB defers major Northwest awards. Avia-
tion W 86:39 Ap 17 '67
CAB eases backhaul limitations for overseas
military charters. H. D. Watkins. Aviation
W 87:28 N 6 '67
CAB, FAA propose to charge industry, in-
dividuals for services. Aviation W 86:32
Mr 13 '67
CAB faces problem in Pan Am route bid. R.
G. O'Lone. Aviation W 86:39 My 1 '67
CAB hurls legal rebuff at Alitalia. L. Doty.
Aviation W 87:35 O 23 '67
CAB mood spurs route filings from three all-
cargo carriers. H. D. Watkins. Aviation W
86:27-8 My 1 '67
CAB plans more innovation in policies. H. D.
Watkins. il Aviation W 86:223-31+ Mr 6 '67
CAB proposes local service subsidy cuts.
Aviation W 86:75 My 29 '67
CAB reverses examiner awards in U.S.-Ca-
nadian air service. Aviation W 86:41 Ap
10 '67
CAB service scrutiny concerns carriers. H. D.
Watkins. Aviation W 86:41+ Ap 3 '67
CAB will tighten route case procedures. J.
W. Carter. Aviation W 87:38-9 O 23 '67
CAB withdraws subsidy from Northeast.
J. W. Carter. Aviation W 88:29 Ja 8 '68
Complaint surge concerns board. H. D. Wat-
kins. il Aviation W 86:37-8 Mr 20 '67
Fare structure study ready; preliminary
CAB findings due. Aviation W 86:37-8 Ap
10 '67
Filings snarl excursion fare plans. R. F.
Coburn. Aviation W 86:38 Ap 3 '67
Little impact on paperwork seen in CAB's
user charge imposition. Aviation W 88:44
Ja 15 '68
Long-term inclusive tour plans clouded. H. D.
Watkins. Aviation W 87:29 Jl 31 '67
Major shift seen in blocked-space policy; com-
bination airlines to sell blocked freight
space. J. W. Carter. Aviation W 87:41 O 9
'67
Mixed earnings cloud fare issue. H. D. Wat-
kins. Aviation W 87:25-6 N 27 '67

Murphy urges continued airlines, CAB independence. H. D. Watkins. Aviation W 88:
28 Ja 8 '68
New procedure set to strengthen locals. Aviation W 87:40-1 O 16 '67
Plan for southern route case disputed. H.
D. Watkins. Aviation W 86:45 Ap 17 '67
Policy shift seen in Hawaii awards. Aviation W 87:41 S 18 '67
State dept. to press for new talks on U.S.
rights to Dublin. J. W. Carter. Aviation W
86:38-9 Ja 23 '67

Civil air patrol
Big red and the new CAP. A. Trammell. il
Flying 80:80-1 Mr '67

Civil defense, Office of
Fallout shelter survey: Civil defense says
there is no place like home. K. Sperry.
Science 158:894-5 N 17 '67

Civil rights commission
See United States—Commission on civil
rights

Civil service
U.S. civil service: Washington's bland
bondage. R. G. Sherrill. Nation 204:239-42 F
20 '67; Reply with rejoinder. J. W. Macy,
jr. 204:418+ Ap 3 '67

Civil service commission
Bureaucrats get their own B-school; Federal
executive institute. il Bsns W p69+ Je
10 '67
Contractor support service called illegal. Avia-
tion W 87:19-20 O 30 '67
Rights in conflict. Reporter 37:10+ O 19 '67
U.S. civil service: rebels on the Potomac.
R. G. Sherrill. Nation 204:265-8 F 27 '67
U.S. civil service: Washington's bland bond-
age. R. G. Sherrill. Nation 204:239-42 F 20 '67
See also
Loyalty investigations

Civilization
America fouls its dream. D. F. Dowd. il
Nation 204:198-203 F 13 '67
American way of life, by A. Montagu. Review
Sat R 50:63+ Ap 8 '67. C. M. Curtis
Challenges of our times. D. Lawrence. U S
News 62:108 My 8 '67
Dialogue between the generations; sympo-
sium. il Harper 235:45-60+ O '67
Gloom, gloom, gloom, and scarce one ray of
light; excerpts from The anti-imperialists:
twelve against empire, 1898-1900. R. L.
Beisner. il Am Heritage 18:65-71 Ag '67
Like a conquered province, by P. Goodman.
Review
Sat R 50:27-8 S 2 '67. C. M. Curtis
Nation at odds. il Newsweek 70:16-20 Jl 10
'67
Toward a communal society. D. Bell. il Life
62:112-14+ My 12 '67
See also
Americanism
United States—Popular culture
United States—Social conditions

Climate
Alaska's mighty rivers of ice; new clues to
our climate. M. M. Miller. il Nat Geog
Mag 131:194-217 F '67

Coast and geodetic survey
For 160 years, nautical chartmakers for the
Nation. H. D. Nygren. il Motor B 120:21-4+
D '67
Washington clipboard; standardizing govern-
ment-produced aeronautical charts. R.
Burkhardt. Flying 80:20 My '67

Coast guard
Safeguard your passage; Coast guard's in-
formation form for yachtsmen. J. Hart. il
Yachting 122:47 D '67
Saved by a whisker. H. Waters. il Motor B
119:74+ Mr '67
U.S. coast guard; with photographs by G.
Silk. il Life 63:36-50+ Jl 14 '67
U.S. coast guard; with report and interview
with T. McAdams, ed. by G. Silk. il Life
63:28-45+ Jl 7 '67
See also
United States coast guard academy, New
London, Conn.

Boats
Arctic trip frozen out; coast guard ships at-
tempting first circumnavigation of the
Arctic Ocean. il Sci N 92:273-4 S 16 '67

UNITED STATES—*Continued*

Coast guard auxiliary

Free boating education. il **Motor B** 120:106 Ag '67

Under the blue ensign. B. Woodward. See issues of Motor boating

U.S. Coast guard auxiliary. R. Birnn. See issues of Yachting

Commerce

Business' stake in the Kennedy round; address, July 7, 1967. A. B. Trowbridge. Dept State Bul 57:127-32 Jl 31 '67

Foreign scout for the small man; E. M. Lang of Resources & facilities corp. il **Bsns W** p 131-2+ O 21 '67

Issues in future U.S. foreign trade policy; statement, July 11, 1967. W. M. Roth. Dept State Bul 57:173-80 Ag 7 '67

Marketing abroad. E. W. Spencer. **Duns R** 89:24 My '67

President Johnson sets goal of substantial export increase; remarks, May 23, 1967. L. B. Johnson. Dept State Bul 56:886-7 Je 12 '67

President transmits Kennedy round trade agreement to the Congress; message, November 27, 1967. L. B. Johnson. Dept State Bul 57:883-5 D 25 '67

Push to boost export sales focuses on advanced arms. Aviation W 88:28 Ja 15 '68

Steel steps up the war on imports. il **Bsns W** p36+ F 11 '67

U.S. in world trade; address, March 22, 1967. B. K. Wickstrum. Vital Speeches 33:535-8 Je 15 '67

See also
Import quotas
Merchant marine—United States
Tariff—United States
World trade week

Canada

Common market for U.S. and Canada? interview. D. Rockefeller. **U S News** 63:88-9 Ag 21 '67

Communist countries

Aid to our enemies; address, August 27, 1967. K. E. Mundt. Vital Speeches 34:44-8 N 1 '67

Constructive initiatives in East-West relations; address, February 17, 1967. F. D. Kohler. Dept State Bul 56:406-13 Mr 13 '67

East-West relations; address, December 11, 1966. F. D. Kohler. Vital Speeches 33:196-200 Ja 15 '67

East-West trade; address, March 8, 1967. G. P. Lipscomb. bibliog f Vital Speeches 33:389-94 Ap 15 '67

President hails U.S. council's support of East-West trade; exchange of letters with text of U.S. council statement. L. B. Johnson; C. H. Phillips. Dept State Bul 56:696-9 My 1 '67

This month's feature: moves to expand U.S.-Soviet-bloc trade. Cong Digest 46:162-92 Je '67

See also
United States—Commerce—Europe, Eastern

Europe, Eastern

Address to North Atlantic council. Paris, April 7, 1967. H. H. Humphrey. Dept State Bul 56:681-3 My 1 '67

East-West trade: an avenue toward world peace; address, May 4, 1967. A. B. Trowbridge. Dept State Bul 56:881-5 Je 12 '67

Revival of trade between the Communist bloc and the West. A. M. Solomon. bibliog f Ann Am Acad 372:105-12 Jl '67

Road to trade; East-West trade relations act. H. J. Berman and J. R. Garson. Nation 204:626-8 My 15 '67

Short-sighted view of trade; East-West trade bill. Life 62:4 Ap 7 '67

United States and eastern Europe in perspective; address, April 29, 1967. W. A. Harriman. Dept State Bul 56:315-21 My 29 '67

Great Britain

Under debate: plan for closer **U.S.-British** ties. U S News 62:13 Mr 6 '67

What cheaper pound means to Americans. U S News 63:36 D 4 '67

Japan

See also
Joint United States-Japan committee on trade and economic affairs

Korea (Republic)

U.S. investment and trade mission visits Korea. Dept State Bul 56:554 Ap 3 '67

Latin America

More trade, less aid; OAS call to cut tariffs. America 117:496 N 4 '67

Mexico

Mexican-U.S. trade committee holds second meeting; joint communique, December 21, 1966. Dept State Bul 56:70-1 Ja 9 '67

Mexican-U.S. trade committee holds third meeting; joint communique, December 9, 1967. Dept State Bul 58:10 Ja 1 '68

Middle East

Mideast war's effect on U.S. business. il **U S News** 62:48-9 Je 19 '67

Rumania

Report from Rumania. T. C. Sorensen. il **Sat R** 50:14-15 D 30 '67

Russia

Businessman sizes up Russia; interview. R. S. Morse. il **U S News** 63:50-4 Ag 14 '67

East-West trade; address, March 8, 1967. G. P. Lipscomb. bibliog f Vital Speeches 33:389-94 Ap 15 '67

East-West trade; an avenue toward world peace; address, May 4, 1967. A. B. Trowbridge. Dept State Bul 56:881-5 Je 12 '67

More or less trade. New Repub 156:2 Je 10 '67

Trade with U.S.S.R. and European growth; address, April 20, 1967. G. W. Ball. Vital Speeches 33:546-50 Jl 1 '67

What's really going on between U.S. and Russia. il **U S News** 62:46-50 Mr 27 '67

Underdeveloped areas

United States foreign trade policy and the developing countries; statement, July 12, 1967. A. M. Solomon. Dept State Bul 57:180-90 Ag 7 '67

Commerce, Department of

Can Alexander Trowbridge change Commerce? G. R. Rosen. il **Duns R** 90:33-4+ Ag '67

Foreign direct investment curbs summarized. Aviation W 88:17 Ja 8 '68

New double yoke for Labor and Commerce; President Johnson's plan to put the two departments together. il **Bsns W** p 140 Ja 14 '67

New voice on economic policy; proposed merger of Commerce and Labor depts. il **Bsns W** p 157-8+ F 18 '67

Shift at Commerce; new assistant secretary for science and technology. Sci N 91:545-6 Je 10 '67

Togetherness; proposed business-labor merger. New Repub 156:9 Ja 28 '67

Trowbridge steps up at Commerce. **Bsns W** p31 My 27 '67

$25 million available for industry R&D. C. D. LaFond. il **Tech W** 20:51-2+ Je 5 '67

Up from oblivion; new Commerce secretary. Time 89:13 Je 2 '67

State technical services, Office of

Agricultural extension for industry begins; federal-state program to disseminate information on technology. **Tech W** 20:40-1 F 13 '67

Commercial treaties and agreements

Ratifications exchanged with Togo on commercial treaty. Dept State Bul 56:181 Ja 30 '67

Road test for auto trade accord il **Bsns W** p55-6 Je 17 '67

U.S. and China exchange notes on cotton textile agreements. il Dept State Bul 57:694-7 N 20 '67

United States and India sign new cotton textile agreement; announcement, with text of U.S. note, August 31, 1967. il Dept State Bul 57:398-400 S 25 '67

U.S. and Israel conclude new cotton textile agreement; Department announcement; with text of U.S. note, January 27, 1967. il Dept State Bul 56:389-92 Mr 6 '67

United States and Israel sign new cotton textile agreement; Department announcement, with text of U.S. note. Dept State Bul 57:243-5 Ag 21 '67

United States and Jamaica sign new cotton textile agreement. il Dept State Bul 57:622-4 N 6 '67

United States and Malta conclude cotton textile agreement. Dept State Bul 57:23-4 Jl 3 '67

United States and Mexico sign cotton textile agreement. Dept State Bul 56:964-5 Je 26 '67

UNITED STATES—Commercial treaties and agreements—*Continued*

U.S. and Pakistan conclude new cotton textile agreement; Department announcement and text of U.S. note. il Dept State Bul 57:114-16 Jl 24 '67

United States and Poland sign cotton textile agreement. Dept State Bul 56:612 Ap 10 '67

United States and Portugal amend cotton textile agreement. W. T. Bennett, jr. il Dept State Bul 57:548-9 O 23 '67

U.S. and Portugal sign new cotton textile agreement. Dept State Bul 56:699 My 1 '67

United States and Spain sign cotton textile agreement. il Dept State Bul 57:726-8 N 27 '67

U.S. and U.S.S.R. conclude talks on fishery problems. Dept State Bul 56:331-2 F 27 '67

U.S. and Yugoslavia exchange notes on cotton textile arrangements. il Dept State Bul 57:586-9 O 30 '67

U.S. Philippines exchange notes on cotton textile arrangements. il Dept State Bul 57:511-14 O 16 '67

Commission of fine arts

Commissars for instant beauty. J. N. Eller. America 116:306 Mr 4 '67

Commission on civil rights

Civil rights commission. E. B. Drew. Atlan 220:16-19 Ag '67

Mississippi: starving by the rule book; hearings on public welfare administration. R. A. Cloward and F. F. Piven. il Nation 204:429-31 Ap 3 '67

Urges end of racial isolation. Sr Schol 90: sup3 Mr 17 '67

What is racial balance in the schools? special report on race and education. M. Greenfield. il Reporter 36:20-6 Mr 23 '67

Commission on marine science, engineering and resources

Lawrence to head marine commission. S. Montgomery. Tech W 20:40 My 15 '67

See also

National council on marine resources and engineering development

Commission on noxious and obscene matters and materials

Obscenity legislation waits Senate action. Library J 92:3579-80 O 15 '67

Senate votes commission on obscene materials. Library J 92:2321 Je 15 '67

Committee for economic development

See Committee for economic development

Communicable disease center

U.S. wages world war on epidemics; Atlanta's communicable disease center. il Bsns W p 104-6+ Mr 11 '67

Community relations service

Keeping it cool; attempts to temper the tone of riot coverage. Time 90:44 Jl 14 '67

Congress

Close look inside today's Congress; effect of the Powell and Dodd cases. il U S News 62:44-8 Ap 10 '67

Congress at work, 1967; ed. by D. Reische. il Sr Schol 90:3-20 F 24 '67

Congress: representing the people. il Sr Schol 91:6-8+ N 30 '67

Congressional outlook; less liberal laws ahead; interview. H. W. Smith. il Nations Bsns 55:42-4 D '67

Congressional seat for the District of Columbia? pro and con discussion. il Sr Schol 91:14-15 N 2 '67

Dangerous delay on the Hill. R. L. Tobin. Sat R 50:18 Mr 18 '67

Report; mood on both sides. D. Kiker. Atlan 219:6+ My '67

Senate declines change. Sci N 91:86 Ja 28 '67

What about ethics in Congress? the story insiders tell. il U S News 62:47-50 Je 5 '67

What we think of Congress. J. N. Eller. America 117:75 Jl 22 '67

Why is Congress so boring? S. Alsop. il Sat Eve Post 240:16 N 4 '67

See also

Congressional record

Congressmen

Legislation—United States

Lobbying

Presidents—United States—Relations with Congress

Committees

Congressional committees: a system of specialization. il Sr Schol 90:10-11+ F 24 '67

Ferment on Capitol hill; challenge to authority of committee chairmen and to seniority system. il Bsns W p31-2 F 25 '67

Keeping Congress honest; move to create a standing ethics committee. D. Bonafede. il Newsweek 69:29-30 Ap 3 '67

Powerhouse behind the atom; Joint committee's latest goal: development of U.S. anti-ballistic missile system. il Bsns W p 160-2 S 16 '67

Who's really running the new Congress. il Nations Bsns 55:40-3+ F '67

Joint economic committee

Magic numbers; proposals for money supply increase rate. H. C. Wallich. Newsweek 69:82 Ap 10 '67

What it takes to reach $1-trillion; with tables. Bsns W p84-6+ F 11 '67

Powers and duties

Comparative roles of the President and the Congress in foreign affairs; statement, August 17, 1967. N. D. Katzenbach. Dept State Bul 57:333-6 S 11 '67

Congress: its lost sacred powers. T. Coffin. Bul Atomic Sci 23:35-7 D '67

Congressional outlook; will they get control of spending? il Nations Bsns 55:40-1 D '67

Is it constitutional? Congress's claim to larger share in foreign policymaking. K. Crawford. Newsweek 70:36 S 4 '67

Money for NSF: the odyssey of a research agency's budget. D. S. Greenberg. il Science 158:357-61 O 20 '67

New leader for constructive opposition? P. Lisagor. Nations Bsns 55:25-6 S '67

Rethinking the unthinkable; Fulbright resolution to limit administration's power. Reporter 37:14+ S 21 '67

Technology assessment. D. Wolfle. Science 158:209 O 13 '67

Privileges and immunities

Public business that's clothed in privacy. A. H. Sypher. il Nations Bsns 55:35-6 N '67

Resolutions

Sabotage in the Senate; Punta del Este resolution and J. W. Fulbright. Reporter 36:9+ Ap 20 '67

Rules and practice

Speaking out; Congress needs reform. C. L. Weltner. Sat Eve Post 240:12+ O 7 '67

Viewpoints: congressional reform; symposium. Sr Schol 90:18-19 F 24 '67

Voting

Package of mischief; 1966 Civil rights act; Senate rejection. New Repub 157:4 S 23 '67

89th Congress

Enactments by the 89th Congress relevant to education and training below college grade, 1965-1966. C. A. Quattlebaum. Sch & Soc 95:360-3 O 14 '67

90th Congress

Congress puts off the tough decisions. Bsns W p38-40 D 16 '67

Disappointing ninetieth. America 117:128 Ag 5 '67

Divided government. New Repub 157:4 N 4 '67

Drift & dissent; increasing opposition by Congress to Johnson's war policies. il Time 90:9 Ag 11 '67

Ferment on Capitol hill; challenge to authority of committee chairmen and to seniority system. il Bsns W p31-2 F 25 '67

GOP shows its hand; Republican leaders in Congress. Bsns W p32-3 Ja 21 '67

Hope for reform on Capitol hill? H. J. Sievers. America 118:28 Ja 13 '68

Laundry list; legislative proposals. Newsweek 69:32+ Mr 27 '67

New Congress starts to rock LBJ's boat. il Bsns W p28-9 Ja 14 '67

90th Congress; slapping at symbols. R. G. Sherrill. Nation 205:142-5 Ag 28 '67

90th GOP style; Republican State of the Union. il Newsweek 69:19-20 Ja 30 '67

President's program. Newsweek 69:32 Mr 27 '67

T.R.B. from Washington; period of lost control. New Repub 157:4 O 28 '67

Washington: a city divided. M. McGrory. America 117:126 Ag 5 '67

90th Congress—1st session

Absent consensus; issues on agenda. New Repub 157:5-6 S 23 '67

Action LBJ wants, and the prospects. U S News 63:40 N 13 '67

UNITED STATES—Congress—Senate—Foreign relations committee—*Continued*
Doves, hawks and flutterers in the Foreign relations committee. M. Kalb. il N Y Times Mag p56-8+ N 19 '67; Discussion. p42 D 3: 16+ D 17 '67
How about it, Mr Rusk? invitation to discuss southeast Asia policy refused. New Repub 157:4 D 23 '67
Maker of foreign policy, Congress or the President? D. Lawrence. U S News 63:136+ D 11 '67
Policing the presidency. Commonweal 87:324 D 8 '67
Purse-string answer; debate over power of Congress to influence or change the President's conduct of a war. Time 90:12 S 1 '67
Sabotage in the Senate; Punta del Este resolution and J. W. Fulbright. Reporter 36:9+ Ap 20 '67
Senate role in foreign policy. America 117: 264 S 16 '67
Uncovering the enemy. D. Lawrence. U S News 63:100 O 16 '67

Senate—Rules and practice

Forever filibuster. J. L. Rauh, jr. New Repub 156:10 F 4 '67
Political habit; filibuster. K. Crawford. Newsweek 69:31 Ja 30 '67
Rule 22. Reporter 36:16+ F 9 '67
Scenario; filibuster intact. Newsweek 69:20 Ja 30 '67

Senate—Standards and conduct, Committee on

Anti-Dodd report. W. F. Buckley, jr. Nat R 19:560 My 30 '67
At Dodd hearings: the accusations, the senator's defense. il U S News 62:8 Mr 27 '67
Beginning of the end. Newsweek 69:36 My 8 '67
Case of Senator Dodd: the charges and a reply; excerpts. T. J. Dodd; J. C. Stennis. il U S News 62:44-5 Je 26 '67
Censure for Dodd? recommendation of ethics committee. Sr Schol 90:19 My 12 '67
Crime and punishment in the club. R. Yoakum. New Repub 156:8-9 My 13 '67
Deeper debt of gratitude to the mob; E. V. Long vindicated. W. Lambert. il Life 63:38-38B N 10 '67
Different kind of censure debate. M. McGrory. America 117:31 Jl 8 '67
Dodd and Powell; ethics of the Dodd issue. Nation 204:387-8 Mr 27 '67
Dodd dilemma. Commonweal 86:404 Je 30 '67
Dodd report revisited. Nat R 19:624-5 Je 13 '67
Dodd that failed; Ethics committee hearings. R. Yoakum. New Repub 156:10-13 Ap 1 '67
Dogging Dodd; fresh allegations; committee not reopening investigation. Newsweek 69: 26-7 Ap 24 '67
Findings in the Dodd case; with text of resolution of censure. il U S News 62:70-1 My 8 '67
For Dodd and Yale; arguments put forward for defense. R. Yoakum. New Repub 156:6-8 Je 3 '67
Testifying for Dodd. R. Yoakum. New Repub 156:12-13 Mr 18 '67
To tell or not to tell; Dodd case. W. V. Shannon. Commonweal 86:308-9 Je 2 '67
Undoing of Dodd. il Time 89:21-2 My 5 '67
What Dodd did. il Newsweek 69:30-1 Mr 27 '67

Voting

Ghost vote; teller vote falsified on NASA budget bill. Nation 205:37 Jl 17 '67

Constitution

Action intellectuals; our Constitution, a mudbank left by receding tides of history. T. H. White. il Life 62:84+ Je 23 '67
Are judges remaking America? il U S News 63:36-8 D 18 '67
Assembly of rare minds for a Constitution. T. H. White. il Life 62:46-56 Je 16 '67
Constitutional convention, the facts; with interview with E. Dirksen. il U S News 62: 62-6 Je 5 '67
On to Philadelphia! concerning Article V. Nat R 19:338 Ap 4 '67
Quiet campaign to rewrite the Constitution. T. C. Sorensen. Sat R 50:17-20 Jl 15 '67
Speaking out; they want to tamper with the Constitution; states calling for a national constitutional convention. J. D. Tydings. Sat Eve Post 240:10+ Je 17 '67

Amendments

Convention to amend the Constitution? U S News 62:10 Ap 3 '67

If Congress names next president. il U S News 63:34-5 D 18 '67
If Powell comes in, will 14th amendment go out? D. Lawrence. U S News 62:124 Mr 20 '67
Rectifying an error of 100 years ago; failure of sixteen states to ratify Fourteenth amendment, reprint. D. Lawrence. U S News 63:100+ O 30 '67
Succession; Bayh amendment ratified. Newsweek 69:33 F 20 '67
This month's feature: moves to change the U.S. electoral system. Cong Digest 46:257-88 N '67
See also
Presidents—United States—Succession
Presidents—United States—Term

Bill of rights

Essay: filial piety and the First amendment; Frick v. Stevens. O. Jensen. il Am Heritage 18:2-4 O '67
Extending the Fifth; confessions obtained under threat of removal from office. Time 89: 40+ Ja 27 '67
Is it wrong to handcuff the police? W. J. Dempsey, jr. Cath World 204:264-9 F '67
Responsible for the abuse of that liberty; First amendment. R. L. Tobin. Sat R 51: 107-8 Ja 13 '68
Teaching the Bill of rights; with study-discussion program, by C. Smallenburg and H. Smallenburg. J. U. Newman. bibliog il PTA Mag 62:2-5, 36 N '67

Signers

Assembly of rare minds for a Constitution. T. H. White. il Life 62:46-56 Je 16 '67

Constitutional convention, 1787

Assembly of rare minds for a Constitution. T. H. White. il Life 62:46-56 Je 16 '67

Constitutional convention (proposed)

Constitutional convention, the facts; with interview with E. Dirksen. il U S News 62: 62-6 Je 5 '67
Dirksen caper. New Repub 156:2 Ap 29 '67
One man, one vote. E. S. Cahn and J. C. Cahn. New Repub 156:11-12 Ap 8 '67
Quiet campaign: one state's story. P. Simon. Sat R 50:20 Jl 15 '67
Quiet campaign to rewrite the Constitution. T. C. Sorensen. Sat R 50:17-20 Jl 15 '67
Speaking out; they want to tamper with the Constitution. J. D. Tydings. Sat Eve Post 240:10+ Je 17 '67
Unconventional convention. Reporter 36:6-8 Ap 6 '67
We, the people; drive to invoke second convention. il Newsweek 69:28-9 Ap 3 '67

Constitutional law

See also
United States—Supreme court

Consumer advisory council

Betty Furness's new Consumer council Consumer Rep 32:514-15 O '67
Blitzing the consumer. Nation 204:133 Ja 30 '67

Council of economic advisers

Building a base for forecasters. il Bsns W p 117-19 Je 10 '67
Good-bye to guideposts; LBJ unleases unions, report. il U S News 62:87-8 F 6 '67
Good-by to LBJ's Mr Chips. il Newsweek 71:57-8 Ja 15 '68
Government economists: in today, out tomorrow. il Sr Schol 90:10-13 Mr 10 '67
Hitting the guideposts; CEA policies. Bsns W p 114+ F 4 '67
Is U.S. really filled with poverty? J. B. Parrish. il U S News 63:50-3 S 4 '67
Ivied council. Time 91:11 Ja 12 '68
New switch in the troika; C. J. Zwick to replace C. L. Schultze. Bsns W p32 Ja 13 '68
Policy for '67; flexible. il Newsweek 69:73-4 F 6 '67
Report of Council of economic advisers. il Dept State Bul 56:336-50 F 27 '67
Road for '67; bumpy but upward; reports by Johnson and CEA, with charts. Bsns W p 156-8 Ja 28 '67
Shift at top for LBJ's economic team: new policy to come? il U S News 64:19 Ja 15 '68
Steady beat at the CEA; A. Okun, CEA chairman. Bsns W p19 Ja 6 '68

UNITED STATES—*Continued*

Council of social advisers
(proposed)
Council of social advisers: new approach to welfare priorities? R. J. Samuelson. Science 157:49-50 Jl 7 '67

Court of military appeals
Miranda in uniform; case of Michael Tempia. Time 89:50 My 5 '67

Courts
See Courts—United States

Crime commission
See United States—President's commission on law enforcement and administration of justice

Cultural relations
Cultural exchanges between Communist countries and the United States. F. C. Barghoorn. bibliog f Ann Am Acad 372:113-23 Jl '67
International programs: Frankel resigns from State. D. S. Greenberg. Science 158:1436 D 15 '67
Motion picture bridge between East and West. J. Valenti. il Sat R 50:8-9+ D 23 '67
Sports ambassadors; service athletes and coaches participate in competitions, clinics and demonstrations in foreign countries. R. F. Mendenhall. il Parks & Rec 2:20+ F '67
United States and Morocco sign cultural agreement. Dept State Bul 56:351-2 F 27 '67
See also
Exchange of persons programs
United States—Information agency
United States—State, Department of—Educational and cultural affairs, Bureau of

Culture, Popular
See United States—Popular culture

Customs, Bureau of
See Customs service—United States

Defense, Department of
Academic research: Foster defends DoD support in universities; statement, November 2, 1967. J. S. Foster, jr. il Science 158:1032-4 N 24 '67
Alternate command center set for DOD manned flights. Tech W 20:34 Je 26 '67
Battle for brainpower; difficulty to recruit first-rate scientists and engineers. Bsns W p78 F 25 '67
Exit McNamara. Sr Schol 91:15 D 14 '67
Greater DOD ocean role hinted by Foster; statement revealed at the fourth military symposium on oceanography. R. W. Niblock. Tech W 20:22 My 22 '67
Hindsight: DOD study examines return on investment in research. D. S. Greenberg; discussion. Science 155:397-8; 157:1512; 159:34 Ja 27, S 29 '67, Ja 5 '68
Housing: Defense department starts new research program. D. S. Greenberg. Science 158:1432-4 D 15 '67
How the Pentagon works. A. Yarmolinsky. il Atlan 219:56-71 Mr '67
Irreversible revolution. Time 90:23 D 8 '67
Letter from Washington; R. McNamara's replacement. R. H. Rovere. New Yorker 43:150-4 D 9 '67
Men of the Pentagon, by C. W. Borklund. Review
Bul Atomic Sci 23:32-3 D '67. M. A. Kaplan
New no. 2: Deputy Defense Secretary. il Newsweek 69:37 Je 19 '67
New no. 2: Deputy Defense Secretary. Time 89:17 Je 23 '67
Pentagon builds a monster; search for management system. il Bsns W p 198-9 F 18 '67
Pentagon, by C. R. Mollenhoff. Review
New Repub 156:32-3 Ap 8 '67. M. Renek
Reporter 36:51-2 Mr 23 '67. W. Beecher
Pentagon crackdown on a critic? U S News 62:8 F 6 '67
Pentagon portfolio; assets of $183.6 billion. Time 89:21 Ja 27 '67
Social inequities; Defense department programs; address, November 7, 1967. R. S. McNamara. Vital Speeches 34:98-103 D 1 '67
Tension in the tank; control over the Pentagon. il Time 89:26-7 My 19 '67
Themis: DOD plan to spread the wealth raises questions in academe. E. Langer. Science 156:48-50, 366 Ap 7, 21 '67; Reply. T. E. Phipps, jr. 156:1307 Je 9 '67

Top candidate for defense chief. il U S News 63:18 D 18 '67
Untangling the alliances; universities and the Pentagon. G. Kolko. il Nation 205:645-8 D 18 '67
What went wrong in the Pentagon; a 73-billion dollar operation. il U S News 63:41-3 D 11 '67
What will happen now to the Pentagon's whiz kids? il U S News 64:26-8 Ja 1 '68
Whiz kid steps aside. Bsns W p31-3 D 2 '67
See also
Pentagon building, Arlington, Va.
Secretaries of defense (United States)

Advanced research projects agency
ARPA stresses advanced ABM research. il Aviation W 87:83+ O 23 '67
RFP's due soon from DOD on missile interceptor stage. Tech W 20:15 Ap 24 '67
Seismic station; plans for station in southern Norway. H. J. Barnes. Sci N 92:137 Ag 5 '67

Appropriations and expenditures
Astronomy of war; defense appropriations bill. Time 89:18 Je 23 '67
DOD seeks funds for expanded inventories of aircraft, missiles. il Aviation W 86:23-6 Ja 30 '67
Education of Robert McNamara. D. Kiker. Atlan 219:49-55 Mr '67
Employment effect of defense expenditures. R. P. Oliver. il Mo Labor R 90:9-16 S '67
Extra $8-billion Viet need seen. D. C. Winston. Aviation W 86:16-17 My 1 '67
Feast at the Pentagon. S. Watzman. Nation 205:686-9 D 25 '67
$40 billion and you. New Repub 156:4 Mr 4 '67
House slashes defense funds $1.3 billion. il Aviation W 86:25-6 Je 19 '67
Plateau of power; military budget. il Time 89:18 F 3 '67
President urges action on funds for southeast Asia operations; text of letter to Speaker of the House; and text of letter to President; January 24, 1967. L. B. Johnson; C. L. Schultze. Dept State Bul 56:236-7 F 13 '67
Project Themis: more research dollars for the have-nots. L. J. Carter. Science 155:548 F 3 '67
Senate unit slashes F-111B funds. K. Johnsen. Aviation W 87:26 Ag 14 '67
Slighted ship, sank same; navy's fast deployment logistics ship. W. J. Coughlin. Tech W 20:50 Ap 3 '67
War is [deleted]; censored excerpts from joint meeting of two committees considering supplemental appropriation for Vietnam war. New Repub 156:5-6 Ap 22 '67

Defense intelligence agency
What will happen now to the Pentagon's whiz kids? il U S News 64:26-8 Ja 1 '68

Procurement
Congress approves $21 billion for Defense dept. procurement. il Aviation W 86:69+ My 29 '67
DOD, industry clash on support awards. D. C. Winston. Aviation W 86:32-3 Ap 24 '67
DOD procurement slash to spur debate. Aviation W 87:30-1 Jl 10 '67
DOD to demand contractor record audit. D. C. Winston. Aviation W 87:28 O 9 '67
DOD to start post-award audits. Aviation W 87:26-7 D 4 '67
Dispute flares on DOD payments. Aviation W 87:16-17 D 25 '67
EA-6A aircraft buy in $70.3 billion DOD appropriations bill. Tech W 20:12 Je 19 '67
Go-ahead is imminent for improved A-7. W. Andrews. il Tech W 20:16-17 Je 19 '67
McDonnell Douglas led DOD '67 awards. il Aero Tech 21:14-16 D 18 '67
Pentagon data bank to monitor sixty-five firms. Aviation W 87:57+ O 30 '67
Price of admission into the defense business. M. Meyerson. il Harvard Bsns R 45:111-23 Jl '67

Research
Social sciences: expanded role urged for Defense department. D. S. Greenberg. Science 158:886-8 N 17 '67; Reply with rejoinder. H. David and G. M. Lyons. 158:1624-5 D 29 '67

Defenses
About the draft. il Nat R 19:556 My 30 '67
Anti-ballistic missile debate. J. I. Coffey. For Affairs 45:403-13 Ap '67
Billions for Vietnam, but back in U.S.— il U S News 62:41 Ap 17 '67

UNITED STATES—Defenses—*Continued*
Billions to stop a missile attack. il U S News 63:33-5 O 2 '67
Carrot and stick; U.S. and the U.S.S.R. might avoid new sprint in arms race. Newsweek 69:20 Ja 30 '67
China's bomb; US-USSR agreement against the Chinese. New Repub 157:3-4 Jl 1 '67
Congress debates the ABM. B. G. Lall. Bul Atomic Sci 23:28-33 S '67
Congressional interest in ABM heightens. D. C. Winston. Aviation W 87:68-9 O 23 '67
Defense fantasy now come true; U.S. ABM system; interview, ed. by R. B. Stolley. R. S. McNamara. il Life 63:28-28C S 29 '67
$40 billion and you. New Repub 156:4 Mr 4 '67
Gaps in the ABM debate. B. G. Lall. Bul Atomic Sci 23:45-6 Ap '67
Great missile debate. H. W. Baldwin. il Reporter 36:23-6 Je 29 '67
Green light for ABM. Time 90:20 S 22 '67
Green light; to install ABM system. Newsweek 70:31 S 25 '67
How U.S. could meet a new military test. il Bsns W p38-40 Je 10 '67
McNamara explains limited missile defense for U.S; text of address, September 18, 1967. R. S. McNamara. U S News 63:106-11 O 2 '67
McNamara policy; road to disaster. F. S. Meyer. Nat R 19:856+ Ag 8 '67
McNamara's ABM policy: a failure of communications. N. Moss. il Reporter 36:34-6 F 23 '67
McNamara's plan for defending the U.S. in a nuclear age; statement, January 26, 1967. R. S. McNamara. U S News 62:38-9 F 6 '67
Matter of missiles and megadeaths; issue that divides Robert S. McNamara and Joint chiefs of staff. il Newsweek 69:44-8 Mr 27 '67
Missile-defense debate intensifies. C. Brownlow. il Aviation W 87:55-6+ O 23 '67
Missing card; opposition to ABM system. il Time 90:22-3 S 29 '67
National security; address, October 11, 1967. H. M. Jackson. Vital Speeches 34:34-7 N 1 '67
New defense line in Pacific; Marianas. il U S News 63:52-4 Ag 7 '67
New shape of Armageddon. il Bsns W p56-8+ F 11 '67
On walking softly. W. J. Coughlin. Tech W 20:58 My 15 '67
Overstated case. J. Burnham. Nat R 19:185 F 21 '67
Parallel reasoning; views of U.S. and Russia after two decades of arms competition. il Newsweek 69:35 Mr 13 '67
Pentagon gazette. M. Getler. Aero Tech 21:136 Jl 31 '67
Pentagon's urgent worry: can U.S. missiles survive Russia's X-ray defenses. il U S News 62:36-7 F 6 '67
Second place in the arms race. W. D. Jacobs. il Nat R 19:186-9 F 21 '67
Secretary McNamara comments on risks of anti-ballistic-missile system; interview, ed. by J. Mossman, February 15, 1967. R. S. McNamara. Dept State Bul 56:442-7 Mr 20 '67
Secretary of defense. W. J. Coughlin. Tech W 20:50 Mr 6 '67
Shifting equation of nuclear defense. R. J. Whalen. il Fortune 75:84-7+ Je 1 '67
Sino-Soviet threat; testimony. R. S. McNamara. Aviation W 86:11 F 27 '67
Status of major U.S, European defense, aerospace programs. Aviation W 86:62-6 Mr 6 '67
Superiority and innovation in U.S. defense forces. B. G. Lall. il Bul Atomic Sci 23:11-13 Mr '67
Technology-gap debate; excerpts from address. J. S. Foster. Aviation W 86:11 My 22 '67
Thin or thick ABMs for U.S? Sr Schol 91:38 O 5 '67
$30-billion Nike-X debate, special report. il Bsns W p76-80+ Ja 14 '67
Tipping the balance of terror? U.S. to deploy anti-ballistic-missile defenses. il Newsweek 70:19-21 O 2 '67
U.S. Secretary of defense testifies; excerpts from address, January 23, 1967. R. S. McNamara. il Bul Atomic Sci 23:21-4 Je '67
U.S. stressing new re-entry technology. E. H. Kolcum. Aviation W 86:26-7 F 6 '67
See also
Aeronautics, Military—United States
Air bases
Airplanes, Military—United States
Atomic warfare—Defenses
Guided missiles—Defenses

Radar defense networks
United States—Air force
United States—Armed forces
United States—Army
United States—Coast guard
United States—Defense, Department of
United States—Navy

Description and travel
Discover America; this is the year! L. Jonckheere. il Sr Schol 90:sup 18-19 Ap 7 '67
Let's travel in the U.S.A. Mlle 64:226-9 Ap '67
Redbook's guide to Canada's fair. M. Cohen. il Redbook 128:21-6 Ap '67
Science map and guide to the U.S. L. Thomas. il Pop Sci 190:59-63+ Je '67
See these sights that others miss. il Changing T 21:19-22 Je '67
Wayfaring along the Ozark trail. R. Dunlop. il Todays Health 45:44-9 Ap '67

Diplomatic and consular service
American ambassador: Joseph C. Grew and the development of the United States diplomatic tradition, by W. H. Heinrichs. Review
Sat R 50:47-8 F 4 '67. J. M. Allison
Ecuador asks recall of U.S. ambassador; texts of notes. Dept State Bul 57:621-2 N 6 '67
New team for the U.S. in Vietnam. il U S News 62:20 Mr 27 '67
U.S. mission chiefs in Europe meet at Bonn. Dept State Bul 56:599 Ap 10 '67
What an American consul can do for you; helping American travelers in foreign countries. Good H 165:197 O '67
See also
Ambassadors
United States—State, Department of

Economic conditions
And fifty years of capitalism; Time essay. Time 90:33 N 17 '67
Antaeus and Hercules; beneficial effects of Vietnamese war. Nation 205:390+ O 23 '67
Barometer falling. il Fortune 75:35-6 F '67
Better year coming for business: a preview of the gains and losses. il U S News 64:29-31 Ja 8 '68
Can we stay prosperous? S. Chase. Sat R 50:20-2 F 11 '67
Cheery cherry blossoms. Time 89:97 Ap 21 '67
Cities in U.S. where business is best; with charts. U S News 62:34-7 Ap 3 '67
Consumers in the US vs. the USSR. Consumer Bul 51:25-6 Ja '68
Detours on the road. il Fortune 76:35-6 D '67
Economic crisis, please go away! D. Lawrence. U S News 63:124 N 6 '67
Economics in action. See issues of Senior scholastic
Economy. R. Lekachman. Duns R 90:11 N; 11 D '67
Economy: a minority view. J. C. Cooper. il Duns R 89:40-1+ My '67
Economy: seesaw; influence of war in Vietnam. il Newsweek 70:62+ Jl 10 '67
Economy set to warm up; Wharton model. il Bsns W p26-7 My 27 '67
Economy takes a spurt, but ... il Newsweek 71:45 Ja 1 '68
Eight questions for 1968. A. Hacker. Sat R 51:102-3 Ja 6 '68
Entering the new economy. D. S. Ammer. Harvard Bsns R 45:2-4+ S '67
Flattened curve, but a happy line. il Newsweek 69:75 Ap 24 '67
Going up: the deficit, wages, taxes. il Newsweek 70:60-1 Jl 31 '67
How's business? Nat R 19:1247-8 N 14 '67
Is U.S. really filled with poverty? J. B. Parrish. il U S News 63:50-3 S 4 '67; Reply. New Repub 157:4 O 7 '67
It's a go-go economy; Wharton school prediction. il Bsns W p21-3 Ag 26 '67
Labor month in review. See issues of Monthly labor review
Lesson on controlling expansion; highlights of Productivity, prices and incomes, by Congress' Joint economic committee. il Bsns W p62+ Jl 15 '67
London helps to clear economic fog in U.S; American economists forecasting rapid growth in U.S. Bsns W p33-4 N 25 '67
Looking for the whites of the enemy's eyes; arguments for tax increase. il Time 90:73-4 Jl 7 '67
Milestones to the future. il Time 90:23-4 N 10 '67
New industrial state, by J. K. Galbraith. Review
Fortune 76:90-1+ Jl '67. I. Kristol

UNITED STATES—Economic conditions—*Cont.*
Off to a speedy start. il Bsns W p 11-13 D 30 '67
Passing the inflated buck. Newsweek 70:75 D 18 '67
Pause that refreshed. il Bsns W p35 Ap 15 '67
Senator Sparkman looks at the economy; interview, ed. by G. R. Rosen. J. Sparkman. il Duns R 90:49-50+ O '67
Soaring stocks and easing money. il Newsweek 69:77 Ja 30 '67
Sobering up the statistics. Fortune 75:35-6 My '67
Spend and spend and spend; why Congress balks. il U S News 64:15-17 Ja 1 '68
Spirit is dampened. il Bsns W p23-5 Jl 8 '67
Sterling's lesson for the dollar. Life 63:4 D 1 '67
Taxes: the high cost of waiting. Bsns W p 162 D 9 '67
U.S. economy enters a new era. W. Bowen. il Fortune 75:110-15+ Mr '67
Upturn. il Time 89:95 Ap 28 '67
What happens when Fed changes its tune? potent effect on economy. il Bsns W p 188+ Ap 15 '67
When business really will boom in U.S. il U S News 62:42-6 F 20 '67
When will the bubble burst? S. Alsop. Sat Eve Post 240:11 D 30 '67
Why America carries the world's burden. il U S News 62:34-7 Mr 6 '67
See also
Business conditions
Consumption (economics)
Cost of living—United States
Debts, Public—United States
Finance—United States
Free trade and protection
Negroes in the United States—Economic conditions
Prices—United States
Prosperity
Strikes—United States
Taxation—United States
Unemployment—United States
United States—Industries
Wages—United States

Economic cooperation administration

Secretary Rusk urges appropriation of full amount authorized under the Foreign assistance act; statement, November 20, 1967. D. Rusk. Dept State Bul 57:801-7 D 11 '67

Economic history

Growth has its pains; NABE survey, with editorial comment. il Bsns W p31-3, 188 O 7 '67

Economic opportunity, Office of

Birth of a movement. R. A. Cloward and F. F. Piven. il Nation 204:582-8 My 8 '67
Curtain of illusion: the odyssey of the Children's caravan; OEO grant, with list of films and filmstrips. J. Poignand and P. Mann. il Library J 92:860-3 F 15 '67
Enter the Urban coalition; antipoverty maneuvering on the Senate floor. New Repub 157:10-11 O 21 '67
Helping the poor find justice; Legal services program. W. Greene. il Reporter 36:16-18 My 18 '67
Is war on poverty stirring up rioters? U S News 63:8 Jl 31 '67
Nickel revolution. I. Mothner. Look 31:34+ Je 13 '67
Poverty bill's progress. Time 90:28 O 13 '67
Putting the poor out of business; unhappy career of the Economic opportunity loan program. M. Levy. il Nation 204:750-3 Je 12 '67
Rural health: OEO launches bold Mississippi project. L. J. Carter. Science 156:1466-8 Je 16 '67
Sputtering war on poverty. B. L. Masse. America 116:346-8 Mr 11 '67
See also
Anti-poverty program, 1964-

Economic policy

After Vietnam, what? symposium; ed. by G. R. Rosen. il Duns R 89:33-5+ Je '67
Better than gold; Lyndon Johnson's proposals to cut deficit. New Repub 158:5-6 Ja 13 '68
Bigger benefits, bigger taxes: latest idea for Great society; with chart. U S News 62: 28-30 F 6 '67
Billions for aid, clamor for more. il U S News 63:60 S 18 '67

Blow-up in the cities; cause of riots and the need for the Administration to get priorities in perspective. New Repub 157:5-7 Ag 5 '67
Buck stops here. il Newsweek 71:64-6 Ja 15 '68
Cheating the people; continuous inflation. D. Lawrence. U S News 62:112 Ap 17 '67
Defending the dollar. P. A. Samuelson. Newsweek 71:69 Ja 15 '68
Deficit comes home to roost; new economics; with editorial comment. G. Burck. il Fortune 76:67, 90-3+ S 1 '67
Economics and politics: do they mix? Sr Schol 91:12-14 O 26 '67
Economy. R. Lekachman. Duns R 90:11 N; 11 D '67
Employment and the new economics. L. H. Keyserling. il Ann Am Acad 373:102-19 S '67
Finetuning; fiscal and monetary motions destabilize the economy. H. C. Wallich. Newsweek 69:85 My 29 '67
Fiscal responsibility. M. Friedman. Newsweek 70:68 Ag 7 '67
Gold rush: defending the dollar. il Newsweek 70:68-70+ D 4 '67
High officials argue over taxes, spending, inflation; excerpts from hearing before the House ways and means committee, November 30, 1967. il U S News 63:90-2 D 18 '67
How Washington makes its forecast; economic troika. il Bsns W p80-2+ D 30 '67
International trade and investment; address, March 7, 1967. P. Chambers. Vital Speeches 33:371-5 Ap 1 '67
Is Congress neglecting the poor? excerpts from address, July 31, 1967. G. H. Mahon. U S News 63:46 Ag 14 '67
LBJ or the Fed: who's right? A. Sproul. il Duns R 89:35+ F '67
LBJ's economics meets the critics. Bsns W p32-3 F 11 '67
More realistic policy for 1967. Bsns W p 192 Ja 28 '67
National economic policy for '67; excerpts from addresses before the Joint economic committee of Congress, February 16. J. Tobin; A. H. Hansen. New Repub 156:17-19 Mr 4 '67
New deal and the states. J. T. Patterson. bibliog f Am Hist R 73:70-84 O '67
New economics: can it beat the business cycle? il Sr Schol 91:20+ O 12 '67
New economics gets its lumps. il Bsns W p96-8 My 13 '67
1967 State of the Union message; excerpts. L. B. Johnson. Cur Hist 52:238-40+ Ap '67
Oracle views the economy; W. M. Martin's testimony. il Newsweek 69:77 F 20 '67
Other shoe; lessons from the British experience. H. C. Wallich. Newsweek 70:82 D 4 '67
Policy for '67: flexible. il Newsweek 69:73-4 F 6 '67
Political economics; address, November 1, 1966. P. A. Rinfret. Vital Speeches 33:278-82 F 15 '67
Problems of success; excerpts from address. M. Bundy. Time 90:25 D 8 '67
Qualified optimism. Time 89:17 F 3 '67
Radical economics of Milton Friedman. J. Davenport. Fortune 75:130-2+ Je 1 '67
Return of the prodigal dollar? Nat R 20:13-14+ Ja 16 '68
Safeguarding tomorrow's growth; address, November 16, 1966. R. G. Dunlop. Vital Speeches 33:252-6 F 1 '67
State of the Union; a Republican appraisal; address, January 19, 1967. G. R. Ford. Vital Speeches 33:260-4 F 15 '67; Excerpts. U S News 62:73 Ja 30 '67
State of the Union; address, January 10, 1967. L. B. Johnson. Vital Speeches 33:226-34 F 1 '67; Excerpts. Dept State Bul 56:158-63 Ja 30 '67
Tax increase; the federal budget; address, September 19, 1967. R. J. Saulnier. Vital Speeches 34:39-41 N 1 '67
Test of intelligence and will; painful policy decisions on U.S. fiscal affairs. Bsns W p 160 D 2 '67
Testing year for the economy. America 116: 205 F 11 '67
Tithing of war. H. Kasper. Commonweal 87: 50-2 O 13 '67
What it takes to reach $1-trillion; with tables. Bsns W p84-6+ F 11 '67
Where it stands: Congress and LBJ's Great society program. Sr Schol 90:17 F 24 '67
Where new economics went wrong: advisers to four presidents explain; symposium. il U S News 64:36-9 Ja 15 '68
Why fiscal policy must be flexible. Bsns W p200 My 13 '67

UNITED STATES—Economic policy—*Continued*
With statistics that are steadier than the arguments; witnesses before Senate-House joint economic committee. il Time 89:35 F 17 '67
See also
Budget—United States
Committee for economic development
Economic assistance, Domestic
Finance—United States
Government spending policy
Import quotas
Income tax—United States
Price regulation by government—United States
Tariff—United States
Taxation—United States
United States—Appropriations and expenditures
United States—Council of economic advisers

Economic relations

Busy bully. Commonweal 85:476 F 3 '67
Doors ajar, one stuck. New Repub 156:3-4 Ap 22 '67
Economic necessities and Atlantic communities. A. C. Neal. il For Affairs 45:694-705 Jl '67
International economic policies; excerpts from Economic report of the President and annual report of the Council of economic advisers. il Dept State Bul 56:333-50 F 27 '67
Our evolving international strategy; address, April 6, 1967. R. A. Peterson. Vital Speeches 33:429-34 My 1 '67
See also
Economic assistance, American
United States—Commerce
United States—Commercial treaties and agreements

Argentina

U.S.-Argentine trade committee holds second meeting; text of joint communique, July 5, 1967. Dept State Bul 57:146-7 Jl 31 '67

Canada

See also
Joint United States-Canadian committee on trade and economic affairs

Europe, Eastern

Why the United States should expand peaceful trade with eastern Europe; address, March 2, 1967. A. M. Solomon. Dept State Bul 56:518-23 Mr 27 '67

Japan

See also
Joint United States-Japan committee on trade and economic affairs

Latin America

Alliance for urgency; Punta del Este conference of hemisphere chiefs. il Time 89: 28-9 Ap 21 '67
Is there a Latin America? R. Hilton. il Nation 204:457-63 Ap 10 '67
Optimism and obstacles; Punta del Este summit. il Newsweek 69:42-3 Ap 24 '67
Reflections on the Inter-American conference of Chiefs of state; excerpts from address, April 21, 1967. S. M. Linowitz. Dept State Bul 56:729-31 My '67

Rhodesia

U.S. implements U.N. sanctions against Southern Rhodesia; White House announcement; with executive order. Dept State Bul 56:145-7 Ja 23 '67

Underdeveloped areas

Does the U.S. exploit the developing nations? D. S. French. Commonweal 86:257-9 My 19 '67

Education, Office of

At 100, still a radical? Sr Schol 90:3 Mr 3 '67
Blow at federal control of schools. U S News 62:10 Je 5 '67
Cabinet status for USOE? R. H. Smith. Pub W 192:36 D 25 '67
Century of cooperation. J. W. Gardner; W. G. Carr; H. Howe. 2d. il NEA J 56:61-2 S '67
College publishers to advise USOE; summary of address. P. Muirhead Pub W 191:78+ F 27 '67
Court endorses USOE guidelines. Sr Schol 89:sup4 Ja 20 '67
Decisions from the field, what OE's decentralization means to schools and colleges. J. A. Turman. il Am Ed 3:20-1 Jl '67
Focal point for education technology seen. J. Rhea. Tech W 20:39 My 1 '67

Future of federal aid explored at D.C. briefing; conference. il Library J 92:3790-2 O 15 '67
Guidelines on trial. Am Ed 3:18-20 Mr '67
Library materials grants to colleges tripled. Library J 92:2863+ S 1 '67
Library research due for $3.5 million boost. Library J 92:2691-2+ Ag '67
Library training expansion charted by OE for 1967-68. Library J 92:951 Mr 1 '67
Machete in the paper jungle; statistical sampling in the Office of education. A. M. Mood. il Am Ed 3:5 O '67
1968 OE budget tops 67's by a hair; most library-related programs remain firm; ESEA dominates requests; Title I shows library component. il Library J 92:1275-6+ Mr 15 '67
Organizational changes in the USOE Bureau of research. ALA Bul 61:622 Je '67
Science package project to be funded by USOE; Media fellowships offered under Higher ed. act. Library J 92:1286-7 Mr 15 '67
300 years at a glance; with editorial comment. il Am Ed 3:inside cover, 7-13 Mr '67
Tough, blunt master of U.S. schools: H. Howe, 2d. il Life 62:37-8+ F 10 '67
U.S. office of education announces plans to decentralize. Library J 92:277 Ja 15 '67
U.S. Office of education's century of service to international education. W. W. Brickman. Sch & Soc 95:136-7 Mr 4 '67
USOE regional offices. ALA Bul 61:1087 O '67
USOE's $4 billion budget. R. H. Smith and W. Buchanan. Pub W 191:53 F 6 '67
View from the hill; Education act: second year. E. Geller. il Library J 92:313-17 Ja 15 '67
Washington report: happy 100th to USOE, ESEA accomplishments; summary of address, March 2, 1967, ed. by J. Lloyd. H. Howe, 2d. Sr Schol 90:sup6 Ap 14 '67

Educational research and development, Bureau of

Aerospace techniques may meet needs. J. Rhea. il Tech W 20:28-9 F 27 '67
Clearinghouse for library science. W. Simonton. il Wilson Lib Bul 42:383-5 D '67
ERIC and the need to know. L. G. Burchinal. NEA J 56:65-72 F '67
Feasibility study on clearinghouse for copyrights and computers; with editorial comment. Pub W 192:33, 38 S 4 '67
Prototype project for copyrights and computers; feasibility study of mechanism to handle requests for copyright clearances. Pub W 192:35 Jl 31 '67

Library services and educational facilities, Division of

New team at the top; with editorial comment. R. M. Fry. il Library J 93:19, 43-8 Ja 1 '68

Library services branch

Librarians skeptical of OE decentralization. Library J 92:515-16 F 1 '67
Library services branch launches talent hunt. Library J 92:951-2 Mr 1 '67
LSB reorganization due; Fry appointed director. Library J 92:175 Ja 15 '67
Washington report: from the Library services branch. P. P. Price and H A. Carl. See issues of ALA bulletin to March 1967
Washington report: from the Library services branch. R. M. Fry and H. A. Carl. ALA Bul 61:803-4 Jl '67

Research, Bureau of

New research grants need action now. Library J 93:133-4 Ja 15 '68

Emergency planning, Office of

Security of incompetence. Nation 205:388-9 O 23 '67

Employment service

American education placement service. G. E. Arnstein. bibliog f Sch & Soc 95:298-301 Sum '67

Engineer corps

See United States—Army—Corps of engineers

Environmental science services administration

ESSA ocean institute set for Miami area. il Tech W 20:15 My 1 '67
Filling a weather gap; launching of ESSA-4. Sci N 91:135 F 11 '67

UNITED STATES—Environmental science services administration—*Continued*
Storm stalkers get jump on hurricanes; U.S. weather team at Miami. il Bsns W p 106-8 Jl 15 '67
$25 million available for industry R&D. C. D. LaFond. il Tech W 20:51-2+ Je 5 '67

Executive departments

Chaos in the Great society. J. Reston. Read Digest 90:49-50 F '67
Foreign area research guidelines adopted; announcement, December 19, 1967. Dept State Bul 58:55-9 Ja 8 '68
How to care for the CIA orphans; Time essay. Time 89:42-3 My 19 '67
New policy outlined on funds for U.S. voluntary organizations; statement, March 29, 1967, and text of report. L. B. Johnson. Dept State Bul 56:665-8 Ap 24 '67
Regulating federal regulators; agencies face increasingly complex decisions. il Bsns W p24-5 Ja 13 '68
Robert Kennedy on: government injustice to business. R. F. Kennedy. Nations Bsns 55: 70-2+ Je '67
See also
Presidents—United States

Executive office of the president

Overlooking the obvious; need for reorganization. D. Lawrence. U S News 63:96 Jl 11 '67

Exiles
See Exiles

Expenditures
See United States—Appropriations and expenditures

Farm credit administration
Who's in charge here? Farm J 91:114 Ap '67

Federal airport corporation
See Federal airport corporation (proposed)

Federal aviation administration

Air accidents; House commerce committee hearing. J. Ridgeway. New Repub 157:12-14 Ag 5 '67
Air taxis, commuters face new rules. Aviation W 86:43 Ap 17 '67
ATA urges major control improvements. Aviation W 87:36 Ag 28 '67
Atlanta tests support automation plans. P. J. Klass. il Aviation W 87:51+ S 4 '67
Basic reaction. R. Burkhardt. Flying 81:32 S '67
Category 2 rules set for general aviation. Aviation W 86:35 My 15 '67
Charge and counter charge. R. B. Parke. Flying 81:36 Jl '67
CAB, FAA propose to charge industry, individuals for services. Aviation W 86:32 Mr 13 '67
DC-6, -7 inspections easing restrictions. Aviation W 86:322 Mr 6 '67
Economic gains forecast for SST. il Aviation W 86:26-7 My 22 '67
FAA maps a route to more air safety. Bsns W p40 S 23 '67
FAA plans new communications systems. H. Taylor. il Tech W 20:18-19 Je 19 '67
FAA proposes sweeping use fees. D. A. Brown. Aviation W 86:26 My 1 '67
FAA urges training at remote airports. Aviation W 86:45+ Ap 24 '67
FAA will aid 386 U.S. airports; Alaska, Texas top beneficiaries. Aviation W 87:17-18 S 4 '67
$15 billion SST market predicted by FAA official. il Tech W 20:17 My 22 '67
Fiscal 1969 fund talks crucial for ATC. P. J. Klass. il Aviation W 87:76-7+ Ag 28 '67
How the SST will be financed. Time 89:88-9 My 26 '67
Human problems in traffic control. D. A. Brown. il Aviation W 87:44-5+ O 2; 100-1+ O 9; 102-3+ O 16 '67
New FAA standards set guidelines. Sci N 92:344 O 7 '67
Threat to air safety seen in funding cut. Aviation W 87:37 Ag 7 '67

Appropriations and expenditures

Congress votes $25.6 million more than FAA budget request. Aviation W 87:33 O 23 '67
Criticism of ATC operation broadens. Aviation W 87:100-1+ O 9 '67
FAA limits hiring, travel pending money bill passage. D. A. Brown. Aviation W 87:39 Ag 14 '67
McKee warns fund reductions could threaten aviation safety. Aviation W 87:25 Ag 21 '67
Short-changing FAA. Nation 205:292-3 O 2 '67

Federal bureau of investigation

Cultural shock; employee fired for unbecoming conduct sues to be reinstated. Newsweek 70:30 O 2 '67
Federal law enforcement. F. M. Vinson, jr. bibliog f Cur Hist 53:15-22+ Jl '67
Patriots on the campus; FBI's activities at Duke university. J. Ridgeway. New Repub 156:12-13 Mr 25 '67
Trade winds; N. Ollestad's view of the FBI. J. Beatty, jr. Sat R 50:6 Jl 8 '67
Washington. D. Kiker. il Atlan 219:6+ Ap '67
See also
Loyalty investigations

National crime information center
Now; instant crime control in your town. J. E. Hoover. il Pop Sci 190:67-9+ Ja '67

Federal communications commission

A.B.C. & ITT: marriage in haste; Justice department requests FCC reopen case. R. G. Sherrill. il Nation 204:361-4 Mr 20 '67
Behind the communications mess; outdated laws and conflicting regulatory policies. il Bsns W p66-8+ N 18 '67
Busy signal; telephone from your airplane. R. B. Parke. il Flying 81:34 S '67
Challenge in the South; U.S. Court of appeals forces FCC to schedule public hearing on WLBT's current application for license renewal. Newsweek 69:63 My 29 '67
Cliffhanger for ABC; proposed merger with ITT back in FCC's lap after second round of hearings. Bsns W p36-7 Je 3 '67
Decoding FCC's signal; commission's decision on AT&T's rate structure. il Bsns W p 120+ Jl 15 '67
Fairness doctrine; Fred J. Cook and John F. Banzhaf, 3d. actions; rulings. R. L. Shayon. Sat R 50:50 Jl 15 '67
FCC bears down on CB. W. A. Stocklin. Electr World 77:6 My '67
FCC proposes CB type acceptance; manufacturers blamed for CB malpractices; with editorial comment. il Pop Electr 26:78-9 My '67
FCC ruling on cigarette ads; health groups react warily. L. J. Carter. Science 158:888-92 N 17 '67
FCC says talk must be cheaper; AT&T ordered to cut rates. Bsns W p38 Jl 8 '67
FCC smoke ruling; radio and television stations must represent antismoking groups. Newsweek 69:84 Je 12 '67
ITT and ABC merger. New Repub 156:8-9 F 25 '67
Is the FCC dead? E. B. Drew. Atlan 220:29-36 Jl '67
Jam that the FCC can't spread; citizen's band and small-business airwaves jammed. il Bsns W p 176-8 F 25 '67
Quiet merger; approval of American broadcasting companies-International telephone and telegraph corporation merger. R. L. Shayon. Sat R 50:56 F 4 '67
Smoking and health; FCC demands an antidote to cigarette ads. L. J. Carter. il Science 157:406-8 Jl 28 '67
Sovereign state of Bell. N. L. Parks. Nation 205:430-5 O 30 '67
Tension in the air; mobile radio users. Bsns W p46 D 9 '67
This month's feature: the question of pay television. Cong Digest 46:289-314 D '67
Time for the truth; FCC ruling on fair time for ads and programs on smoking dangers. New Repub 156:7 Je 17 '67
Wall Street: the FCC drops a shoe; rules that AT&T's rates should be lowered. C. Morgello. il Newsweek 70:74 Jl 17 '67
Weston, Jackson, the F.C.C. and Pastore. N. Sharp. Christian Cent 84:1268 O 4 '67
Who will Bell the colossus? N. L. Parks. Nation 205:391-3 O 23 '67

Federal convention, 1787
See United States—Constitutional convention, 1787

Federal council for science and technology
Governmental information systems; summary of addresses at ABPC conference. A. A. Aines; M. S. Day. Pub W 191:38-9 Ap 10 '67
President enlarges Council for science and technology. Dept State Bul 57:798-9 D 11 '67

Federal council on the arts and the humanities
See United States—National foundation on the arts and the humanities

UNITED STATES—*Continued*

Federal deposit insurance corporation
See Federal deposit insurance corporation

Federal housing administration
Belated effort to save our cities. M. Nolan. il Reporter 37:16-21 D 28 '67
Can FHA switch for slum housing problem? il Bsns W p 146+ D 9 '67
Facts about FHA: low income housing; address, August 23, 1967. R. C. Weaver. Vital Speeches 33:734-6 S 15 '67
FHA speeds up processing, revises some standards. Arch Rec 141:81 Je '67
Low income programs; address, August 7, 1967. E. W. Brooke. Vital Speeches 33:719-22 S 15 '67
Unfair housing authority. J. Eisen. Commonweal 87:8-9 O 6 '67

Federal mediation and conciliation service
Can you force labor peace? views of experts in labor, management, and government. il Bsns W p 128+ Ja 21 '67
Rank and file flexes its muscle; reject negotiated settlements for heftier contracts. Bsns W p61-2 S 9 '67

Federal power commission
Another jolt for the utilities; Middle Atlantic power failure. il Bsns W p 148-9 Je 10 '67
Guarding against more blackouts. Bsns W p54 D 30 '67
It's open season on utilities; public pressure for more federal controls. il Bsns W p41-2+ Jl 22 '67
Power blackouts and the FPC. Nation 204: 773 Je 19 '67
Transmission lines; the placement of power lines and the preservation of aesthetic value. L. C. White. Parks & Rec 2:19+ D '67
Why the power failures and why more may come. il U S News 62:76-7 Je 19 '67

Federal reserve board
Another signal; order for increase in the reserves of its member banks. Time 91:70 Ja 5 '68
Back at the bank. il Time 89:87 Ap 7 '67
Billion-dollar decision. il Time 89:81 Mr 24 '67
Blocking the threat to the dollar. Bsns W p 160 N 25 '67
Current monetary policy. M. Friedman. il Newsweek 70:80 O 30 '67
Dilemma for Johnson: who is to manage dollar. il U S News 62:72 Mr 13 '67
Fear of credit crunch harries Wall Street. il Bsns W p 120+ O 28 '67
Fed gets set to pull harder on reins. Bsns W p45-6 D 9 '67
Fed holds to its easy money course. Bsns W p 108 Ag 26 '67
Fed may lighten its touch. Bsns W p29-30 4 '67
Fed sticks to its course. il Bsns W p36-7 Ap 15 '67
Fed takes a fresh step toward ease; reducing reserve requirements of banks. il Bsns W p34-5 Mr 4 '67
Fed tries a tricky act on the tightrope; economy in danger of overheating. il Bsns W p 145-6 O 21 '67
Fed tunes up a drifting economy. il Newsweek 69:77 Mr 13 '67
Fed uses new tools to sharpen policy. Bsns W p 168 F 18 '67
Fed will play it tight, but not overdo it. il Bsns W p86-7 D 30 '67
Fed's unenviable task. Bsns W p 174 N 11 '67
For the Fed, a man with no label; W. W. Sherrill. Bsns W p40 My 6 '67
Inflation's arch-enemy at the Fed; W. M. Martin. il Bsns W p72-3+ Ap 22 '67
Keeping the Fed on middle ground; passing up chance to pack board with liberals. il Bsns W p 36-7 F 25 '67
Latest move toward easier money. U S News 62:111 Ap 17 '67
LBJ's $1 billion Fed appointment. il Newsweek 69:75 Ap 10 '67
Martin stays on as top U.S. money man; Fed chairman. Bsns W p21 Ap 1 '67
Now there's plenty of money; Federal reserve board reduces discount rate. Time 89:95 Ap 14 '67
Selective stimulus. Time 89:86-7 Mr 10 '67
What happens when Fed changes its tune? potent effect on economy. il Bsns W p 188+ Ap 15 '67
What the Fed watchers watch. il Bsns W p 158+ Mr 25 '67

Who's afraid of the big blank check? attempt to stamp out uncoded checks. Time 90:95 S 15 '67
Why the President renamed Martin as head of the Fed. U S News 62:23 Ap 10 '67
Worst is over in housing; Fed and White House push recovery. il Bsns W p27 Ja 21 '67

Federal trade commission
Antitrust slowdown? A. M. Bickel. New Republic 156:15-18 My 20 '67; Reply with rejoinder. R. L. Wright. 156:32-3 Je 10 '67
Can FTC stunt growth of smokers? Bsns W p34 Jl 8 '67
Federal trade commission charged with censorship. Library J 92:2866 S 1 '67
FTC hits false advertising of health books. S. Wagner. Pub W 192:35-6 Jl 24 '67
FTC lifts merger fog for some; sets formal guidelines. Bsns W p33-4 Ja 21 '67
Fighting aspirin ads three ways; proposed FTC rules. il Bsns W p38 Jl 15 '67
Little old lady with a tough new look. il Newsweek 70:82-3 O 23 '67
Mergers make FTC feathers fly. il Bsns W p 124+ My 6 '67
Rodale seeks court review of free speech issue in book advertising. S. Wagner. Pub W 192:36-7 O 9 '67
Tough questions for recruiters; is an employment counselor an employment agency? Bsns W p42 D 23 '67

Federal water pollution control administration
Murky waters; attempts to ensure states submit adequate proposals. Newsweek 70:61 Ag 21 '67
States struggle with water standards. il Sci N 92:34 Jl 8 '67
Watery grave for Lake Michigan? result of industrial waste. il Bsns W p 104+ O 21 '67
What third-stage sewage treatment means. A. Machis. il Am City 82:110+ S '67

Fish and wildlife service
Predators, prejudice, & politics. M. Frome. il Field & S 72:24-6+ D '67

Food and drug administration
Amendment needs amendment; Federal food, drug and cosmetic act. Consumer Rep 32: 247 My '67
Bitter pills for vitamins. Bsns W p28+ Ja 13 '68
Do streptomycin and sirloin mix? Bsns W p 104-5 Jl 1 '67
Drug makers make a difference. B. J. Culliton. il Sci N 91:382-3 Ap 22 '67
FDA: how it guards drug safety. Good H 166:167 Ja '68
FDA prescribes a bitter pill; crack down on pharmaceutical advertising. il Bsns W p58-60 F 4 '67
FDA seizes anticancer drug. Sci N 91:142-3 F 11 '67
FPC gets OK at last; FDA's regulations on fish protein concentrate. Sci N 91:138 F 11 '67
Goddard: revolution comes hard. B. J. Culliton. Sci N 91:91 Ja 28 '67
Limits on children's aspirin. il Time 89:67 Mr 17 '67
Lions and the lambs. Sci N 92:250 S 9 '67
MS-222: vanished and banished? letter with reply. W. A. van Bergeijk; F. J. Kingma. Science 158:438 O 27 '67
Money wasted on unneeded vitamins; proposed regulations of dietary supplements and vitamin-enriched foods. B. J. Culliton. il Sci N 91:146 F 11 '67
Science predicts a growing danger; Legator-Verrett report on pesticide effects on humans. il Bsns W p42+ My 13 '67
Something fishy; FDA surveys of fish processing plants. R. Nader. New Repub 158: 19-21 Ja 6 '68

Foreign opinion
American promise. W. Lippmann. Newsweek 70:21 O 9 '67
As others see us. See issues of Saturday review
As outside world sees riots in America. il U S News 63:12 Ag 7 '67
Battlefield report; foreign reaction to Detroit riots. Newsweek 70:70 Ag 7 '67
Cold war, to flare anew or fade? reports from world capitals. il U S News 63:23-6 Jl 10 '67
Domestic public affairs: international impacts; address, April 20, 1967. C. H. Malik. Vital Speeches 33:538-41 Je 15 '67

UNITED STATES—Foreign opinion—*Continued*
Foreign research: CIA plus Camelot equals troubles for U.S. scholars. E. Langer. Science 156:1583-4 Je 23 '67
Hands across the sea? roundup of foreign executives' attitudes. il Duns R 90:28-9 Ag '67
How do you double-date on a camel? visiting high-school students from fifty-eight countries. L. B. Johnson. il McCalls 94:48+ S '67
Humphrey's complaint: U.S. image is bad. U S News 62:16 Ap 24 '67
I love America. J. Morris. Read Digest 90: 147-8+ Ap '67
London paper scolds Europe for attacks on U.S; reprint. il U S News 62:98 Ap 24 '67
Tarnished image abroad. il Newsweek 70:60-1 Jl 10 '67
U.S. from abroad. H. C. Wallich. Newsweek 70:82 O 2 '67
When the world looks at U.S, a study in power. il U S News 63:24-6 Jl 24 '67

Anecdotes facetiae satire etc.
...But do as we say; observations on elective process. M. Greenfield. Reporter 37:14-16 S 7 '67

Belgian
Who paints the image? French TV band's anti-American feature; Contrastes. J. Burnham. Nat R 19:76 Ja 24 '67

Brazilian
Something wild; revival of anti-Americanism. Newsweek 71:43 Ja 15 '68

British
Anti-Americanism is now non-U. P. Worsthorne. il N Y Times Mag p34-5+ Ap 9 '67; Discussion. p 12 Ap 30 '67
New backing in Britain for U.S. Vietnam policy. U S News 62:10 F 6 '67

Ethiopian
Ethiopia: the over-present Americans. N. G. Kotler. il Nation 204:236-9 F 20 '67

European
Americans, why aren't you liked? Y. Chabas. Christian Cent 84:1127-8 S 6 '67
America's troubles: the European view; race problem and the war in Vietnam. E. M. von Kuehnelt-Leddihn. Nat R 19:78 Ja 24 '67
Can we communicate with Europe? P. Kimball. Sat R 50:54-5 Jl 8 '67
Europe minus America. New Repub 157:7-8 O 21 '67
European statesman backs U.S. role in Asia; interview. P. H. Spaak. il U S News 62:64-6 Mr 6 '67
How the no. 1 power should use its power. L. Markel. il N Y Times Mag p22-3+ Ja 14 '68
Humphrey's mission. W. Lippmann. Newsweek 69:23 Ap 24 '67
Making the rounds with HHH. il Newsweek 69:56-7 Ap 17 '67
They're all afraid of America: how the European sees the war. P. Ben. New Repub 156:7-8 My 13 '67
Youth movement comes to Europe. J. Fromm. il U S News 63:56-8 O 16 '67

French
De Gaulle on America. Nat R 19:1106+ O 17 '67
French opinion on an American war. M. Buckley. America 116:810-11 Je 3 '67
Guide to the U.S.A. for Frenchmen only. P. Daninos. il Read Digest 91:25-6+ O '67
Let's understand the French. F. Morley. il Nations Bsns 55:27-8 My '67

Greek
Bugging the press; reprint of dispatch in New York times, March 2, 1967. C. Poulos. Nation 204:421 Ap 3 '67

Irish
Opinion: on writing about America. F. O'Connor. Mlle 64:148+ Ap '67

Latin American
Anti-U.S. ferment in Latin America. E. M. Smith. Christian Cent 84:1445-6 N 8 '67

Russian
What Moscow's Washington-watchers see. M. Schwartz. il N Y Times Mag p50-1+ O 8 '67

Vietnamese
As the Vietnamese see us. F. Sully. il Newsweek 70:61-2 Jl 10 '67

Ky v Buddhists, round two. Tran-van-Dinh. New Repub 156:15-19 My 13 '67
Playing with fire; new anti-Americanism. Newsweek 70:36 O 23 '67

Foreign population
See also
Immigrants in the United States
also Italians in the United States, and Immigration and emigration—United States

Foreign relations
American crisis: Vietnam, Cuba & the Dominican Republic; transmutation from the political to the military. T. Draper. bibliog f Commentary 43:27-43 Ja '67; Discussion. 43:6+ My '67
American intellectuals and foreign policy. I. Kristol. For Affairs 45:594-609 Jl '67
American role and world order. L. Gelber. Yale R 56:524-36 Je '67
Another round in the great debate: American security in an unstable world; address, October 17, 1967. E. V. Rostow. Dept State Bul 57:605-11 N 6 '67; Same. Vital Speeches 34:66-70 N 15 '67
Anti-Communist empire; concerning books by Theodore Draper and Ronald Steel. T. J. Farer. Nation 205:213-15 S 11 '67
Arms sales and foreign policy; excerpts from Arms sales and foreign policy, January 25, 1967. Bul Atomic Sci 23:44-8 S '67
Arrogance of power, by J. W. Fulbright. Review
  Bul Atomic Sci 23:30-2 O '67. W. Goldstein
  Sat R 50:33 F 11 '67. F. Altschul
Brassy trumpet; concerning Maxwell D. Taylor's book Responsibility and response. Nation 204:357 Mr 20 '67
Building a durable peace; address, January 26, 1967. D. Rusk. Dept State Bul 56:269-73 F 20 '67
Central purpose of United States foreign policy; address, August 5, 1967. D. Rusk. Dept State Bul 57:251-5 Ag 28 '67
Comparative roles of the President and the Congress in foreign affairs; statement, August 17, 1967. N. D. Katzenbach. Dept State Bul 57:333-6 S 11 '67
Diplomacy of a new age, by D. Perkins. Review
  Sat R 50:64 Je 10 '67. F. Altschul
Domestic public affairs: international impacts; address, April 20, 1967. C. H. Malik. Vital Speeches 33:538-41 Je 15 '67
Doors ajar, one stuck. New Repub 156:3-4 Ap 22 '67
Exhilarating crucible of crisis. H. Sidey. il Life 62:32B Je 23 '67
Fact sheet on U.S. alliances. Sr Schol 91:11-12 O 5 '67
First team; foreign-policy advisers. il Newsweek 70:23 Jl 17 '67
Foreign policy for the future; address, May 1967. C. Frankel. il PTA Mag 62:2-4 S; 10-12 O '67
Fulbright versus Taylor. A. Campbell. New Repub 156:26-7 F 25 '67
Fulbright's guerrilla war; national commitment hearings. W. V. Shannon. Commonweal 86:544-5 S 8 '67; Reply. R. V. Ellinger. 86:618-19 S 29 '67
Future of NATO: meaning to U.S; with excerpt from address by H. Cleveland. il U S News 63:60-4 S 11 '67
Hardening up? Nat R 19:454 My 2 '67
Helped or hindered in the world? extent Vietnamese war affects U.S. role abroad. il Newsweek 70:57-8 Jl 10 '67
Hostage; views of Edward Weintal and Charles Bartlett in Facing the brink. Newsweek 69:44 Mr 13 '67
How not to be a world power. H. S. Commager. il N Y Times Mag p28-9+ Mr 12 '67
How the no. 1 power should use its power. L. Markel. il N Y Times Mag p22-3+ Ja 14 '68
I am tired of your gimmicks. G. E. Brown, jr. Nation 205:614-17 D 11 '67
Illusions of distance. A. Wohlstetter. bibliog f For Affairs 46:242-55 Ja '68
Implications of change for United States foreign policy; remarks, May 22, 1967. Z. Brzezinski. Dept State Bul 57:19-23 Jl 3 '67
Importance of agricultural development in our strategy for peace; address, May 10, 1967. E. V. Rostow. Dept State Bul 56:856-65 Je 5 '67
In memoriam; argument between isolationists and interventionists. K. Crawford. Newsweek 69:35 Je 5 '67
Intellectual and American foreign policy; address, August 8, 1967. J. A. Gronouski. Dept State Bul 57:432-5 O 2 '67

UNITED STATES—Foreign relations—Anti-Communist measures—*Continued*
Seventeen years in east Asia; address. May 3, 1967. W. P. Bundy. Dept State Bul 56: 790-5 My 22 '67
Tightrope in Thailand. E. Klein. il Newsweek 69:52-3 Je 19 '67
20th anniversary of the Truman doctrine; text of letter and messages. L. B. Johnson. Dept State Bul 56:546-7 Ap 3 '67
Uncovering the enemy; scope and basic functions of the Senate foreign relations committee. D. Lawrence. U S News 63:100 O 16 '67
Up from dominoes; concerning D. Rusk's yellow peril speech. Commonweal 87:101-2 O 27 '67
What the Communists are after, in Vietnam and elsewhere. M. Padev; J. G. Campaigne. Read Digest 91:142-4 Jl '67
Where America is winning in the world. il Nations Bsns 55:35-7+ Je '67
Will the American people stay awake? D. Lawrence. U S News 63:130 S 18 '67

Bibliography
Congressional documents relating to foreign policy. See issues of Department of state bulletin

History
America's long dream in Asia. W. LaFeber. Nation 205:456-9 N 6 '67
America's role in world affairs: reflections on a year of anniversaries; address, November 27, 1967. N. deB. Katzenbach. Dept State Bul 57:815-20 D 18 '67
GOP mainstream; American interests in the Pacific. R. Moley. Newsweek 70:126 N 13 '67
Greetin's, cousin George; 1939 visit to the United States by King George VI and his queen. P. L. Cantelon. il Am Heritage 19:6-11+ D '67
To move a nation, by R. Hilsman. Review Reporter 37:14-19 N 30 '67. M. Greenfield

Afghanistan
Prime Minister of Afghanistan visits the United States; exchange of greetings, exchange of toasts, and joint statement, March 28, 1967. M. H. Maiwandwal; L. B. Johnson. Dept State Bul 56:627-32 Ap 17 '67

Africa
Africa and America; address, March 31, 1967. J. Palmer, 2d. Dept State Bul 56:646-51 Ap 24 '67
View from outside. J. Burnham. Nat R 19: 128 F 7 '67

Africa, Southern
Lost heritage: African good will. R. E. Dodge. Christian Cent 84:1395-6 N 1 '67
United States, the United Nations, and southern Africa; address, January 27, 1967. A. J. Goldberg. Dept State Bul 56:289-94 F 20 '67

Asia
America in Asia. W. Lippmann. Newsweek 70:31 N 20 '67
American purposes and the pursuit of human dignity; address, August 9, 1967. D. Rusk. Dept State Bul 57:343-9 S 18 '67
America's long dream in Asia. W. LaFeber. Nation 205:456-9 N 6 '67
Asia after Vietnam. R. M. Nixon. For Affairs 46:111-25 O '67; Same. il U S News 63: 86-91 O 23 '67
Asian perspectives; address, July 11, 1967. H. Kaplan. Dept State Bul 57:230-5 Ag 21 '67
Beyond Vietnam, by E. O. Reischauer. Review
  New Repub 157:23-6 N 25 '67. S. S. Harrison
  Reporter 37:48+ D 14 '67. J. Mecklin
  Time 90:112+ N 17 '67
East Asia today; address, January 20, 1967. W. P. Bundy. Dept State Bul 56:323-7 F 27 '67
Our new western frontier. J. H. Moskin. il Look 31:36-40+ My 30 '67
Papier-maché tiger? J. O'Gara. Commonweal 85:675 Mr 17 '67
Secretary misunderstood; concerning D. Rusk's press conference, October 12, 1967. W. Lippmann. Newsweek 70:23 N 6 '67
Time is on our side in Asia. E. O. Reischauer. Read Digest 90:55-60 F '67
U.S. mission chiefs in Asian and Pacific area meet at Baguio; text of communique, March 7, 1967. Dept State Bul 56:517 Mr 27 '67
U.S. policy in Asia: as two ex-envoys see it; excerpts from testimony. E. O. Reischauer; G. F. Kennan. U S News 62:19-20 F 13 '67

What is our picture of Asia? A. Axelbank. New Repub 158:17-19 Ja 6 '68
What we should do next in Asia. E. O. Reischauer. il Look 31:21-3 Ap 4 '67

Asia, Southeastern
Assent from academe; statement from scholars after debate in Tuxedo, N.Y. il Time 90:10-11 D 29 '67
Dawks and the hoves. K. Lamott. Nation 205:564-5 N 27 '67
How about it, Mr Rusk? New Repub 157:4 D 23 '67
Perspective on Vietnam. J. K. Fairbank. New Repub 158:15-17 Ja 20 '68
Seventeen years in east Asia; address. May 3, 1967. W. P. Bundy. Dept State Bul 56: 790-5 My 22 '67
Thailand and the southeast Asia; address, January 18, 1967. G. Martin. Dept State Bul 56:193-9 F 6 '67
To move a nation, by R. Hilsman. Review New Repub 157:23-6 Jl 15 '67. J. C. Thomson, jr
U.S. commitment in southeast Asia; symposium. biblog f Cur Hist 54:1-47+ Ja '68
Yellow peril. K. Crawford. Newsweek 70:29 O 30 '67
See also
Humphrey, H. H.—Visit to Southeast Asia, 1967

Brazil
President-elect of Brazil visits the United States; exchange of toasts, January 26, 1967. A da Costa e Silva; L. B. Johnson. Dept State Bul 56:242-4 F 13 '67

Cambodia
About, face! N. Sihanouk changes his tune. Newsweek 71:41 Ja 8 '68
Borderline success; violations to be investigated by ICC. il Newsweek 71:32 Ja 22 '68
In hot pursuit; reactions to U.S. pursuit of North Vietnamese inside borders. A. Campbell. New Repub 158:19-21 Ja 13 '68
New balance. il Newsweek 71:14-15 Ja 15 '68

Cameroon Republic
President of Cameroon visits the United States; exchange of toasts, October 24, 1967. L. B. Johnson; A. Ahidjo. Dept State Bul 57:654-6 N 13 '67

Canada
Canada and the United States, a centennial retrospective. B. Hutchison. il Am Heritage 18:6-12+ Je '67
Is Canada for sale? Canadian attitudes toward U.S. control of Canadian industry. Christian Cent 84:134-5 F 1 '67

Chile
See also
Project Camelot

China (People's Republic)
China and the hydrogen bomb. N. Cousins. Sat R 50:16 Jl 8 '67
China and Vietnam. R. Terrill. New Repub 155:16-20 O 29 '66; Correction. 156:37 Ja 28 '67
China: the people's middle kingdom and the U.S.A. by J. K. Fairbank. Review Sat R 50:45 S 30 '67. C. T. Hu
China, the United Nations, and the United States; address, March 28, 1967. D. H. Popper. Dept State Bul 56:689-95 My 1 '67
Communist China; address, February 13, 1967. U. A. Johnson. Dept State Bul 56: 420-4 Mr 13 '67
Diagnosing the dragon; U.S.-China watchers. il Time 89:21-2 Ja 27 '67
Dragon under glass: time for a new China policy. J. C. Thomson, jr. Atlan 220:55-61 O '67
Going up? Rusk-Humphrey revelations on purpose of U.S. Vietnam commitment. New Repub 157:5-7 O 28 '67
Papier-maché tiger? J. O'Gara. Commonweal 85:675 Mr 17 '67
Pentagon euphoria; Chinese border violations. Nation 205:163 S 4 '67
RFK's new moves to stand apart from LBJ; excerpts from address, February 8, 1967. R. F. Kennedy. il U S News 62:21 F 20 '67
Taunting the dragon. Christian Cent 84: 1117-18 S 6 '67
War with China? H. E. Salisbury. New Repub 156:25-8 My 20 '67
Yellow peril. K. Crawford. Newsweek 70:29 O 30 '67
Yellow peril revisited; excerpts from Pax Americana. R. Steel. Commentary 43:58-65 Je '67

UNITED STATES—Foreign relations—*Cont.*

Communist countries

Concert and conciliation: the next stage of the Atlantic alliance; address, September 11, 1967. E. V. Rostow. Dept State Bul 57: 422–30 O 2 '67; Same. Vital Speeches 34:13–18 O 15 '67

East-West relations; address, December 11, 1966. F. D. Kohler. Vital Speeches 33:196–200 Ja 15 '67

Through the looking glass; address, February 15, 1967. S. Thurmond. Vital Speeches 33: 343–8 Mr 15 '67

See also
United States—Commerce—Communist countries

Congo (capital Kinshasa)

Congo and the Senate. New Repub 157:6–7 Jl 22 '67

Cuba

Does a deal bar U.S. from action against Cuba? il U S News 63:54–5 Ag 28 '67

Waves from Cuba; policy re-examination needed. Nation 205:132–3 Ag 28 '67

Ethiopia

Emperor of Ethiopia visits the United States; exchange of greetings, February 13, 1967; exchange of toasts, February 14, 1967. Haile Selassie I; L. B. Johnson. Dept State Bul 56:425–8 Mr 13 '67

Europe

Dynamic new policy toward the new Europe. W. Goldstein. Bul Atomic Sci 23:17–22 Ap '67

Secretary Rusk discusses European affairs and Viet-Nam in interview for German television; transcript of interview, February 10, 1967. D. Rusk. Dept State Bul 56:358–65 Mr 6 '67

Seeking alternatives to de Gaulle. Life 62:4 F 10 '67

Europe, Eastern

United States and eastern Europe in perspective; address, April 29, 1967. W. A. Harriman. Dept State Bul 56:815–21 My 29 '67

United States policy in east Europe. M. Petrovich. bibliog f Cur Hist 52:193–9+ Ap '67

Europe, Western

Changing nature of Soviet and American relations with western Europe; address, April 1967, with questions and answers. D. S. McLellan. bibliog f Ann Am Acad 372: 16–32 Jl '67

Europe versus détente? M. D. Shulman? For Affairs 45:389–402 Ap '67

Gathering at the grave; meetings at funeral of K. Adenauer. il Time 89:28–9 My 5 '67

How not to lead an alliance. B. Brodie. il Reporter 36:18–24 Mr 9 '67

KGK, meet LBJ; discussion of U.S. commitment to the security of Europe. il Newsweek 70:19 Ag 28 '67

LBJ's mission in Europe; decision to attend funeral of Konrad Adenauer. il U S News 62:33–4 My 1 '67

On three fronts; search for a stable new relationship. il Newsweek 69:49–50 My 15 '67

Time for the delicate touch. H. Brandon Sat R 50:6–7 Mr 18 '67

U.S.-European relations: appraisal and future policy. B. G. Lall. Bul Atomic Sci 23:45–7 Je '67

See also
Atlantic community
Humphrey, H. H.—Visit to Europe, 1967

Far East

Our new western frontier. J. R. Moskin. il Look 31:36–40+ My 30 '67

France

Good-by to all that; U.S. army departure ceremony. il Newsweek 69:59–60 Mr 27 '67

See also
France and the United States

Germany

Swastika and the eagle, by J. V. Compton. Review
Atlan 220:100 Ag '67. O. Handlin

Germany (Federal Republic)

American era ends in Germany. C. W. Thayer. il Look 31:25–9 My 2 '67

Building a bridge to Bonn; discussions concerning nuclear nonproliferation, the Kennedy round, and monetary reform. il Bsns W p35–6 Ap 29 '67

Burying Der Alte, and an era. il Newsweek 69:50–1+ My 8 '67

Dialogue with Bonn; some suggestions for what might, but won't be said at the Kiesinger-Johnson meeting in Washington. T. C. Sorensen. Sat R 50:28–9 My 20 '67

How West German leader sees U.S. role in Europe; interview, ed. by R. A. Haeger. K. G. Kiesinger. U S News 63:52–4 Jl 10 '67

LBJ in Europe: a little summit; Johnson-Kiesinger talks. il U S News 62:35 My 8 '67

Maiden comes of age. il Time 89:18 F 17 '67

President Johnson attends funeral of Konrad Adenauer; exchange of remarks, April 26, statement, and message, April 19, 1967. K. G. Kiesinger; L. B. Johnson. Dept State Bul 56:751–2 My 15 '67

President Johnson meets with German chancellor; exchange of greetings, statements and exchange of toasts, August 15; with joint statement, August 16, 1967. K. G. Kiesinger; L. B. Johnson. Dept State Bul 57:325–30 S 11 '67

Repairing the alliance. il Time 90:16–17 Ag 25 '67

Ghana

General Ankrah of Ghana visits the United States; exchange of toasts, October 10, 1967. L. B. Johnson; J. A. Ankrah. Dept State Bul 57:571–3 O 30 '67

Great Britain

LBJ-Wilson talks: end of grand alliance? il U S News 62:20 Je 5 '67

Our only real ally; with editorial comment. S. Alsop. il Sat Eve Post 240:16, 84 Jl 1 '67; Same abr. without editorial comment. Read Digest 91:43–5 S '67

President Johnson confers with British Prime Minister; remarks, June 2, 1967. L. B. Johnson; H. Wilson. Dept State Bul 56: 963–4 Je 26 '67

Suez crisis; a footnote to history. W. W. Aldrich For Affairs 45:541–52 Ap '67

U.S., U.N. and U.K; participation in the U.N.'s economic sanctions against Rhodesia. R. Moley. Newsweek 69:104 Je 12 '67

Greece, Modern

Case of Greece; arms shipments. Nation 205: 195–6 S 11 '67

Elections or coup? deadlock in Greece; American role in politics. S. Rousseas. Nation 204:390–5 Mr 27 '67

Greek coup. Nation 204:581 My 8 '67

Less U.S. muscle, more leverage. Life 62:4 Je 2 '67

No aid for Greece. Nation 205:452 N 6 '67

Our tragedy in Greece. Nation 204:643–4 My 22 '67

Saving Greece from the Greeks; background to military coup. B. D. Nossiter. New Repub 156:9–10 My 20 '67

What happened in Greece; 1947 to 1967. M. Goldbloom. Commentary 44:68–74 D '67

Indonesia

Vice President Humphrey visits Viet-Nam, Malaysia, and Indonesia; remarks, toast, and joint communique, October 30–November 6, 1967. H. H. Humhprey. Dept State Bul 57:790–2 D 11 '67

Iran

Case of Iran. Nation 205:196 S 11 '67

President Johnson and the Shah of Iran hold talks at Washington; exchange of remarks and exchange of toasts, August 22, with joint statement, August 23, 1967. L. B. Johnson; Mohammed Reza Pahlevi. Dept State Bul 57:358–62 S 18 '67

United States commemorates closing of successful AID mission to Iran; remarks, November 29, 1967 and message from the President. D. Rusk; L. B. Johnson. Dept State Bul 57:825–7 D 18 '67

Israel

Mutual aid. il Newsweek 71:38 Ja 22 '68

Urbis and orbis: Jerusalem today. J. A. Sanders. Christian Cent 84:967–70 Jl 26 '67

Italy

President Saragat of Italy visits the United States; exchange of greetings, September 18, exchange of toasts, and joint statement, September 19, 1967. L. B. Johnson; G. Saragat. Dept State Bul 57:500–3 O 16 '67

Ivory Coast

President Johnson holds meeting with president of Ivory Coast; exchange of toasts, August 17, 1967. F. Houphouet-Boigny; L. B. Johnson. Dept State Bul 57:330–2 S 11 '67

UNITED STATES—Foreign relations—*Cont.*

Japan

Changing flags; U.S. yields Bonins. il Sr Schol 91:18 D 7 '67

Research in Japan: U.S. army grants cause controversy. P. M. Boffey. Science 158: 748-52 N 10 '67

U.S. and Japan reaffirm common objectives and pledge continued cooperation; exchange of greetings and toasts, November 14, with joint communique, November 15, 1967. L. B. Johnson; E. Sato. Dept State Bul 57:742-7 D 4 '67

See also

Japan—Foreign relations—United States

Panay (gunboat) incident

United States—Treaties—Japan

Korea (Republic)

U.S. and Korea pledge continued friendship and cooperation; exchange of greetings, exchange of toasts, with joint statement, March 14, 1967. I. K. Chung; L. B. Johnson. Dept State Bul 56:548-53 Ap 3 '67

See also

Korean war, 1950-1953—American participation

Laos

In hot pursuit; reactions to U.S. pursuit of North Vietnamese inside borders. A. Campbell. New Repub 158:19-21 Ja 13 '68

President Johnson welcomes Crown Prince of Laos; toast, November 9, 1967. L. B. Johnson. Dept State Bul 57:752 D 4 '67

Prince Souvanna Phouma of Laos meets with President Johnson; exchange of toasts and statement, October 20, 1967. L. B. Johnson; Souvanna Phouma. Dept State Bul 57:653-4 N 13 '67

Latin America

Can Castro start a new Vietnam? P. D. Bethel. Nat R 19:130-4 F 7 '67

Legacy of Che Guevara; civil and military presence. N. Gall. bibliog f Commentary 44: 39-44 D '67

New Latin revolutionaries and the U.S. R. Shaull. Christian Cent 85:69-70 Ja 17 '68

Our stake in a big awakening. R. N. Goodwin. il Life 62:66-8+ Ap 14 '67

United States and the Latin American left wings. J. J. Johnson. Yale R 56:321-35 Mr '67

See also

Alliance for progress

Inter-American conferences

Mexico

Amigos reunited, Diaz Ordaz and LBJ. il U S News 63:28 N 6 '67

United States and Mexico reaffirm friendship and good will; exchange of toasts, statements, October 26-28, 1967, with joint communique, Presidents' action program, and ceremonies at U.S.-Mexican border. L. B. Johnson; G. Diaz Ordaz. Dept State Bul 57:673-84 N 20 '67

Middle East

ABC's of Israeli-Arab conflict; the U.S. role. il U S News 62:44-6 Je 19 '67

As America sees Mideast: time is on U.S. side. il U S News 62:34-5 Je 26 '67

But what do we do about the Arabs? D. Cordtz. il Fortune 76:74-9+ S 1 '67

Changing of the guard in the Middle East. H. L. Hoskins. Cur Hist 52:65-6+ F '67

Exhilarating crucible of crisis. H. Sidey. il Life 62:32B Je 23 '67

Foreign policy: a study in contrasts; US and USSR. Bsns W p 182 Je 24 '67

Fortunate failure; triumph of Israel, also a victory for the U.S. K. Crawford. Newsweek 69:45 Je 19 '67

Is peace possible? address, March 12, 1967. F. B. Morse. Vital Speeches 33:452-5 My 15 '67

Letter from Washington. R. H. Rovere. New Yorker 43:90+ Je 24 '67

Middle East crisis and beyond; address, December 8, 1967. E. V. Rostow. Dept State Bul 58:41-3 Ja 8 '68

Middle East: guidelines for policy. N. Safran and S. Hoffmann. Nation 204:806-8 Je 26 '67

Military appraisal: U.S. stake in the Mideast. M. S. Johnson. U S News 62:37 Je 19 '67

Moral stakes in the Mid-East. W. V. Shannon. Commonweal 86:361-2 Je 16 '67

Muddled tale of two wars. E. J. Hughes. Newsweek 69:17 Je 26 '67

New deal for the Midde East; responsibility of USSR and US. Nation 204:802-3 Je 26 '67

Open-ended wars. M. Ascoli. Reporter 37:18 Jl 13 '67

Opportunity for two; prospects for cooperation between Washington and Moscow dimmed. il Time 89:15-16 Je 23 '67

Plunging into the Mideast crisis. il Bsns W p30-2 Je 17 '67

Secretary Rusk on the Middle East; excerpts from address, August 25, 1966. D. Rusk. Cur Hist 52:113-14 F '67

Situation in the Near East; White House releases, June 5-8, 1967. Dept State Bul 56: 549-52 Je 26 '67

Staving off a second front. il Time 89:11-12 Je 2 '67

Test of patience & resolve. il Time 89:29-30 Je 9 '67

Trouble shooter Bundy; the job: peace in Mideast. U S News 62:21 Je 19 '67

Unfinished war. M. Ascoli. Reporter 36:12 Je 29 '67

U.N. Security council continues debate on Near East; Soviet proposal condemning Israel rejected; statements, June 10, 13 and 14, with text of letter, June 9, texts of resolutions June 12 and 14, and texts of draft resolutions June 13, 14, 1967. A. J. Goldberg. Dept State Bul 57:3-12 Jl 3 '67

U.N. Security council demands a cease-fire in the Near East; statements, June 6, 8 and 9, with texts of Security council resolutions, June 6, 7 and 9 and U.S. draft resolutions May 31 and June 8, 1967. A. J. Goldberg. Dept State Bul 56:934-49 Je 26 '67

U.S. absence. M. Ascoli. Reporter 36:18 Je 15 '67

U.S. abstains on U.N. resolution on Jerusalem; urges steps toward durable peace in Near East; statement, July 14, 1967, with text of resolution. A. J. Goldberg. Dept State Bul 57:148-51 Jl 31 '67

United States calls for restraint in the Near East; statements, May 23, 24, 1967. L. B. Johnson; A. J. Goldberg. Dept State Bul 56:870-3 Je 12 '67

U.S. in the 1967 Middle East crisis. H. N. Howard. Cur Hist 53:337-40+ D '67

Washington handled the crisis well. Life 62:4 Je 16 '67

What's in it for the United States? K. Roosevelt. Nat R 19:562+ My 30 '67

Morocco

King Hassan II of Morocco visits the United States; exchange of greetings and exchange of toasts, February 9, 1967. Hassan II; L. B. Johnson. Dept State Bul 56:328-31 F 27 '67

Nepal

King Mahendra of Nepal visits the United States; exchange of greetings and toasts, with joint communique, November 1, 1967. L. B. Johnson; Mahendra. Dept State Bul 57:706-9 N 27 '67

Nicaragua

Sandino affair, by N. Macaulay. Review Bul Atomic Sci 23:56-7 Je '67. W. F. Barber

Niger

President Johnson meets with President of Niger; exchange of greetings and exchange of toasts, September 26, 1967. D. Hamani; L. B. Johnson. Dept State Bul 57:541-3 O 23 '67

Panama

Is U.S. facing another crisis over the Panama Canal? il U S News 62:104-5 Mr 27 '67

See also

United States—Treaties—Panama

Philippines

Depth and durability of U.S.-Philippine relations; address, June 29, 1967. W. M. Blair, jr. Dept State Bul 57:203-7 Ag 14 '67

U.S.-Philippine relations: where we stand today; address, March 9, 1967. E. M. Braderman. Dept State Bul 56:660-4 Ap 24 '67

Rhodesia

Back in the corner. Nat R 19:340 Ap 4 '67

Rhodesia; U.N. policy dictatorial; address, January 12, 1967. P. J. Fannin. Vital Speeches 33:264-7 F 15 '67

Security council votes mandatory sanctions against Southern Rhodesia; statement, December 12, 1966. A. J. Goldberg. Dept State Bul 56:73-7 Ja 9 '67

Southern Rhodesia and the United Nations; the U.S. position. Dept State Bul 56:366-77 Mr 6 '67

Southern Rhodesia: the issue of majority rule. J. Palmer, 2d. Dept State Bul 56:449-58 Mr 20 '67

UNITED STATES—Foreign relations—Rhodesia
—*Continued*
This month's feature; question of U.S. Rhodesian policy. Cong Digest 46:67-71+ Mr '67
U.S., U.N. and U.K; participation in the U.N.'s economic sanctions against Rhodesia. R. Moley. Newsweek 69:104 Je 12 '67

Rumania
. . . But warm reception for Rumanians in U.S. U S News 63:12 Jl 10 '67

Russia
American attitudes on U.S.-Soviet relations. B. G. Lall. il Bul Atomic Sci 23:34-8 Ja '67
Cold war as history, by L. J. Halle. Review
   Sat R 50:32-3 O 21 '67. S. K. Padover
Cold war, revisited and re-visioned. C. Lasch. il N Y Times Mag p26-7+ Ja 14 '68
Cold war, to flare anew or fade? reports from world capitals. il U S News 63:23-6 Jl 10 '67
Containment has won, but. . . E. Stillman. il N Y Times Mag p23+ My 28 '67
Continuing cold war. K. Crawford. Newsweek 69:34 Je 12 '67
Diplomatic counterpoint. il Newsweek 69:31-4 Je 19 '67
Dual crisis; Vietnam and Middle East situations stress need for amity. Nation 204:738-9 Je 12 '67
Europe versus détente? M. D. Shulman. For Affairs 45:389-402 Ap '67
Fact sheet on U.S.-Soviet relations. J. Brownell. Sr Schol 91:6-7 O 5 '67
Fortunate failure; triumph of Israel, also a victory for the U.S. K. Crawford. Newsweek 69:45 Je 19 '67
From Stalin to Kosygin; the myths and the realities. W. A. Harriman. il Look 31:55-6+ O 3 '67
From the iron curtain to the open door; address, March 5, 1967. H. H. Humphrey. Dept State Bul 56:486-90 Mr 27 '67; Same with title New engagement. Vital Speeches 33:386-9 Ap 15 '67; Excerpts. U S News 62:22 Mr 13 '67
Hot-line diplomacy; use of link between Washington and Moscow. il Time 89:15-17 Je 16 '67
Middle East aftermath. H. Brandon. Sat R 50:8 Jl 1 '67
Middle East crisis: a trial balance. L. Binder. il Bul Atomic Sci 23:2-7+ S '67
Opportunity for two; prospects for cooperation between Washington and Moscow dimmed. il Time 89:15-16 Je 23 '67
Our foreign policy commitments to assure a peaceful future; address, May 18, 1967. D. Rusk. Dept State Bul 56:874-9 Je 12 '67
Parting of the ways. J. O'Gara. Commonweal 85:618 Mr 3 '67
Postscript to Glassboro. N. Cousins. Sat R 50:18 Jl 29 '67
Russia's role in Vietnam. C. Emmet. America 117:112-13 Jl 29 '67
Russia's strategy in today's world; the view from Europe. il U S News 63:101-2 N 27 '67
Soviet-American relations: conflict and cooperation. J. C. Campbell. bibliog f Cur Hist 53:193-202+ O '67
Time for the delicate touch. H. Brandon. Sat R 50:6-7 Mr 18 '67
U.N: an arena for peaceful East-West engagement; adress, February 24, 1967. J. J. Sisco. Dept State Bul 56:458-63 Mr 20 '67
U.N. front and center; what is needed to prevent world war. N. Cousins. Sat R 50:20 Je 17 '67
U.S. protests Soviet failure to give notice of scientific tests; text of note, December 8, 1967. Dept State Bul 58:16 Ja 1 '68
United States relations with the Soviet Union; address, April 21, 1967. N. D. Katzenbach. Dept State Bul 56:753-6 My 15 '67
United States-Soviet co-operation: incentives and obstacles; address, April 1967, with questions and answers. R. C. Tucker. bibliog f Ann Am Acad 372:11-15 Jl '67
War of the words. il Bsns W p33-6 Je 24 '67
We and they. M. Ascoli. Reporter 37:12-13 N 30; 12-13 D 14 '67
We should encourage the doves in the Kremlin. R. L. Gilpatric. il N Y Times Mag p9+ Jl 30 '67
What's really going on between U.S. and Russia. il U S News 62:46-50 Mr 27 '67
See also
Cuban crisis. 1962
Glassboro conference. 1967
United States—Treaties—Russia

Singapore
Prime Minister of Singapore visits the United States; exchange of greetings and toast, October 17, with joint statement, October 18, 1967. L. B. Johnson; K. Y. Lee. Dept State Bul 57:612-15 N 6 '67

South Africa
How the United States protects South Africa. J. Lelyveld. Atlan 219:77-9 Ap '67
'Twas a famous victory. Nat R 19:177-8 F 21 '67

Taiwan
Vice President of the Republic of China visits the United States; exchange of greetings and exchange of toasts, May 9; with joint statement, May 10, 1967. L. B. Johnson; C. Yen. Dept State Bul 56:846-50 Je 5 '67

Thailand
Is Thailand getting fed up with America? U S News 64:6 Ja 8 '68
Letter from Bangkok. R. Shaplen. New Yorker 43:135-6+ Mr 18 '67
Senate approves U.S.-Thai treaty of amity and economic relations. Dept State Bul 57:477 O 9 '67
Thailand: a fighting ally for U.S. in Asia. il U S News 62:46-8 F 27 '67
Thailand and southeast Asia; address, January 18, 1967. G. Martin. Dept State Bul 56:193-9 F 6 '67
Thailand: where we came in; summary of foreign policy roundtable conference at Washington university. R. Buckhout. Nation 205:305-8 O 2 '67
Tightrope in Thailand. E. Klein. il Newsweek 69:52-3 Je 19 '67
United States and Thailand; address, May 3, 1967. G. Martin. Dept State Bul 56:851-5 Je 5 '67
United States and Thailand pledge to continue close cooperation to promote peace; exchange of greetings and exchange of toasts, June 27, with joint statement, June 29, 1967. L. B. Johnson; King Bhumibol Adulyadej. Dept State Bul 57:61-4 Jl 17 '67
See also
United States—Treaties—Thailand

Turkey
Turkey and the United States reaffirm bonds of friendship and cooperation; exchange of greetings and exchange of toasts, April 3, 1967, with joint communique. C. Sunay; L. B. Johnson. Dept State Bul 56:652-7 Ap 24 '67

Underdeveloped areas
Counterrevolutionary America; adaptation of address. R. L. Heilbroner. Commentary 43:31-8 Ap '67; Discussion. 44:6+ Jl '67
Revolution, anyone? Americans are conditioned to overrate its importance. V. C. Ferkiss. Commonweal 85:480-3 F 3 '67

Vietnam
Vietnam: the neglected debate; reconstruction of our foreign policy. J. Nuveen. Christian Cent 84:399-403 Mr 29 '67

Vietnam (Democratic Republic)
Closed channel; communication between the U.S. and the Viet Cong. Newsweek 70:40 D 11 '67
Negotiations now? reflections on a meeting with the enemy; DRV and NLF-U.S. talks in Czechoslovakia. C. Jencks. New Repub 157:19-23 O 7 '67
United States reaffirms policy toward National liberation front; Department statement, December 8, 1967. Dept State Bul 57:854 D 25 '67

Vietnam (Republic)
Ambassador Bunker dedicates new U.S. embassy at Saigon; remarks, September 29, 1967. E. Bunker. Dept State Bul 57:584-5 O 30 '67
American crisis. T. Draper. bibliog f Commentary 43:27-48 Ja '67; Discussion. 43:6+ My '67
American group to observe elections in Viet-Nam; background, with press interview, August 28, 1967. H. C. Lodge. Dept State Bul 57:349-51 S 18 '67
Bell of decision rings out in Vietnam. T. H. White. il Life 63:54-6+ S 1 '67
Bitter heritage, by A. M. Schlesinger, jr. Review
   New Repub 156:25-8 F 11 '67. Schoenbrun
   Time il 89:77 F 3 '67
Burgeoning boss picks an old hand; E. Bunker for Vietnam. H. Sidey. il Life 62:32B Mr 24 '67
Changing the guard; ambassadorial change? il Newsweek 69:26 Mr 20 '67
Clarity of hindsight; views of G. Kennan and E. Reischauer. Newsweek 69:40 F 13 '67

UNITED STATES—Foreign relations—Vietnam
(Republic)—*Continued*
Debate and disquiet; concerning three books
about the wisdom of U.S. policy in Viet-
nam. il Newsweek 69:35-6 F 6 '67
Guam gambit; personnel replacements in
Saigon. Nat R 19:334 Ap 4 '67
Human tragedy of Vietnam. V. S. Kearney.
America 117:376-7+ O 7 '67; Discussion. 117:
529-32 N 11 '67
Mr Bundy discusses Viet-Nam on Meet the
press; transcript of interview, August 27,
1967. W. P. Bundy. Dept State Bul 57:352-7
S 18 '67
Our new team in Saigon. D. Warner. il Re-
porter 37:25-6+ S 7 '67
Path to Viet-Nam: a lesson in involvement;
address, August 15, 1967. W. P. Bundy.
Dept State Bul 57:275-87 S 4 '67; Same.
Vital Speeches 33:706-13 S 15 '67
President Johnson's press conference of
November 17; excerpts. L. B. Johnson. Dept
State Bul 57:775-80 D 11 '67
Quiet American goes to Vietnam; E. Bunker
to replace H. C. Lodge. R. Eder. il N Y
Times Mag p28-9+ Mr 26 '67
Secretary Rusk discusses Viet-Nam in inter-
view for British television; transcript of
interview for Associated television, ltd. January 31, 1967. D. Rusk. Dept State Bul
56:274-84 F 20 '67
Secretary Rusk interviewed on Today pro-
gram; transcript of interview, January 12,
1967. D. Rusk. Dept State Bul 56:168-72
Ja 30 '67
Secretary Rusk redefines United States policy on Viet-Nam for student leaders; text
of letter to 100 student leaders, January 4,
1967; with text of students' letter to President Johnson, December 29, 1966. D. Rusk.
Dept State Bul 56:133-7 Ja 23 '67; Correc-
tion. 56:192 F 6 '67
Something in the wind. New Repub 157:4
O 14 '67
Thanks, but no thanks; concerning editorial
in the London Economist. New Repub 158:
6 Ja 20 '68
To move a nation, by R. Hilsman. Review
Nation 204:726-8 Je 5 '67. M. W. Browne
To seek a newer world, by R. F. Kennedy.
Review
New Repub 157:30+ D 2 '67. G. A. Harri-
son
Two USAs; concerning R. F. Kennedy's
March 2, 1967 speech. M. Ascoli. Reporter
36:18-19 Mr 23 '67
What next? Nation 205:227-8 S 18 '67
Why stay in Vietnam? views of Kennan and
Reischauer. New Repub 156:9 F 11 '67
Why U.S. is in Vietnam: an official explana-
tion. W. P. Bundy. U S News 63:48-9
D 18 '67
See also
Vietnamese crisis, 1964
Vietnamese war, 1957- —American participa-
tion

Foreign service
Labyrinth in foggy bottom; excerpts from
The reds and the blacks. W. Attwood. Atlan
219:45-50 F '67; Same abr. Read Digest 90:
121-4 Je '67
Let the poor old Foreign service alone. S.
Alsop. il Sat Eve Post 240:14 Mr 11 '67
Reds and the blacks, by W. Attwood. Review
Sat R 50:64 Ap 8 '67. T. P. Melady

Foreign service institute
Foreign service institute: patterns of profes-
sional development. J. N. Cortada and A.
G. Hope. Dept State Bul 56:218-23 F 6 '67

Forest products laboratory
Penetrating stain for rough and weathered
wood. il Consumer Bul 50:25 Ag '67

Forest service
History
Them were the good old days. C. E. Randall.
il Am For 73:26-9+ My '67

General accounting office
Closer eye on contractors; non-competitive
fixed-price contracts. Bsns W p 158 O 21 '67
Feast at the Pentagon. S. Watzman. Nation
205:686-9 D 25 '67
GAO cries for help. Nation 204:389 Mr 27 '67
GAO scrutinizes one-step procurement. D. C.
Winston. Aviation W 86:63+ Je 19 '67
GAO: the taxpayer's best friend. A. Stein-
berg. Read Digest 91:133-7 N '67
World's biggest client needs professional brief-
ing. Arch Rec 141:81-2 Ap '67

Geological survey
New towns: geological survey has key role
in experiment; its new headquarters. L. J.
Carter. il Science 158:752-5 N 10 '67

Government
See United States—Politics and government

Government printing office
Biggest job shop in the world. W. Sullivan.
il Sat R 50:124-5+ O 14 '67

Government procurement, Commission
on (proposed)
Procurement study bill deferred to 1968. K.
Johnsen. Aviation W 87:77+ N 27 '67

Government publications
See Government publications

Health, education and welfare,
Department of
Attacking tokenism; HEW guidelines for
southern states. Sr Schol 89:18-19 Ja 20
'67
Bad case of inflation; HEW report to Pres-
ident Johnson. Bsns W p35 Mr 4 '67
Birth control: U.S. programs off to slow start.
E. Langer. Science 156:765-7 My 12 '67
Clean air: carrot and stick; amendments to
the Air quality act of 1967. il Sci N 91:374
Ap 22 '67
Congress starts clearing the air; air-pollu-
tion-control bill. il Bsns W p 109 Jl 22 '67
Guidelines on trial. Am Ed 3:18-20 Mr '67
Organization woman; HEW integrates welfare
agencies into social and rehabilitation serv-
ice. Time 90:14 S 1 '67
Putting a dollar sign on life; guide to where
its money should go. Bsns W p86-8 Ja 21
'67
Racial survey goes North; HEW guidelines.
Sr Schol 91:sup2 N 2 '67
War budget holds huge R&D expansion in
check. H. M. David. il Tech W 20:33+ Je
5 '67
Well done, Gardner! Reporter 36:10 Je 1 '67

Appropriations and expenditures
HEW budget passed; further delays pre-
dicted. Pub W 192:30-1 N 20 '67
Integrating America, the problems; inter-
view. J. W. Gardner. il U S News 62:64-9
My 8 '67

Historic houses, etc.
Great celebrations in historic American
houses. P. Hyde and J. L. Hendrix. il House
B 109:263-73 N '67
Ike's Gettysburg farm: a gift to the Nation.
il U S News 63:17 D 11 '67
On the banks of the Pedernales; President
Johnson's boyhood home. H. Sutton. Sat R
50:45-6 Ap 8 '67
Treasure house on the prairie; D. D. Eisen-
hower's boyhood home. B. Hibbs. il Read
Digest 90:146-52 My '67
See also
Mount Vernon (historic house)
also subhead Historic houses, etc. under
names of states, cities, etc. e.g. Vermont-
Historic houses, etc.

History
Divided we stand: the unpopularity of U.S.
wars; Time essay. Time 90:30-1 O 6 '67
See also
Education—United States—History
Frontier and pioneer life—United States
Michigan. University, Ann Arbor—Clements
library of American history
United States—Church history
United States—Foreign relations—History
United States—Social history
also subhead History under names of
regions, states, etc. e.g. Maryland—History

Bibliography
Articles and other books received; comp. by
W. Gray. See issues of American historical
review
New books on American history (cont) H.
L. Hurwitz. Sr Schol 90:sup 10 F 17 '67
New books on U.S. history. W. K. Richards.
Sr Schol 91:sup8 O 5 '67

Discovery and exploration
See also
America—Discovery and exploration

Historiography
New left and American history: some recent
trends in United States historiography. I.
Unger. bibliog f Am Hist R 72:1237-63 Jl '67

UNITED STATES—History—*Continued*

Sources

Reference books for U.S. history. M. L. Allison. Sr Schol 90:sup 11 F 17 '67

Study and teaching

Past and present: the twain shall meet; Enfield high school, Thompsonville, Conn. F. S. Gross. Sr Schol 91:sup 13 O 5 '67
Using records in U.S. history classes; discography. L. Rappaport. il Sr Schol 91:sup 10 D 7 '67

Textbooks

California s law on Negro history. Negro Hist Bul 30:21-2 F '67
Report: California textbook fight. H. N. Scheiber. Atlan 220:38+ N '67

Colonial period

See also
Maryland—History
New England—History—Colonial period
Puritans

Revolution

Benedict Arnold: how the traitor was unmasked; excerpt from George Washington in the American revolution. J. T. Flexner. il Am Heritage 18:6-15 O '67
Firebrand of the revolution. A. Winston. il Am Heritage 18:60-4+ Ap '67
Well-off, middle-aged rebels. S. K. Padover. Sat R 50:30-1 Ag 19 '67
See also
Boston massacre, 1770

Revolution—Campaigns and battles

Providence rides a storm: plan to take Boston's Dorchester Heights; excerpts from George Washington in the American revolution. J. T. Flexner. il Am Heritage 19: 12-17+ D '67
This hollowed-out ground; battle of Fort Montgomery and retreat to Butter Hill, now Storm King Mountain. C. Carmer. il Am Heritage 18:58-9+ Je '67

Revolution—Strategy

History lesson: Britain drops a domino. D. Felix. New Repub 157:10-11 N 11 '67

Constitutional period, 1789-1809

Consensus politics, 1800-1805. L. W. Koenig. il Am Heritage 18:4-7+ F '67

1815-1861

Strange stillbirth of the Whig party. L. L. Marshall. bibliog f Am Hist R 72:445-68 Ja '67

War with Mexico, 1845-1848

How to make it to the White House without really trying; Z. Taylor. D. Lavender. il Am Heritage 18:26-7+ Je '67
Mexican war dove; A. Lincoln. H. Mitgang. New Repub 156:23-4 F 11 '67

Civil war

See also
Confederate States of America
Grand army of the Republic
See also
Secession

Civil war—Bibliography

Lincolniana in 1966. B. E. Wheeler. il Hobbies 71:35+ F; 72:114-15+ Mr '67

Civil war—Journalists

Generals and the news spy; concerning T. W. Knox. T. L. Christie. Sat R 50:60-1+ Jl 8 '67

Civil war—Naval operations

Civil war torpedo. il Hobbies 72:127 Ag '67

Civil war—Negro troops

Selection of officers and non-commissioned officers of Negro troops in the Union army, 1863-1865. J. W. Blassingame. bibliog f Negro Hist Bul 30:8-11 Ja '67

Civil war—Pictorial works

Army of the Cumberland: a panorama show by W. D. T. Travis. B. Catton. il Am Heritage 19:40-9 D '67

Civil war—Press reports and censorship

Generals and the news spy; concerning T. W. Knox. T. L. Christie. Sat R 50:60-1+ Jl 8 '67

Civil war—Regimental histories

Army of the Cumberland: a panorama show by W. D. T. Travis. B. Catton. il Am Heritage 19:40-9 D '67

Civil war—Secret service—Confederate States

Mother, I do not hate to die. J. C. Phifer. il Am Heritage 18:32-3+ F '67

1865-

Gloom, gloom, gloom, and scarce one ray of light; excerpts from The anti-imperialist: twelve against empire, 1898-1900. R. L. Beisner. il Am Heritage 18:65-71 Ag '67

1865-1898

See also
Little Big Horn, Battle of the, 1876
Reconstruction (Civil war)
Wounded Knee Creek, Battle of, 1890

Spanish American war, 1898

Presidential leadership in foreign affairs: William McKinley and the Turpie-Foraker amendment. P. S. Holbo. bibliog f Am Hist R 72:1321-35 Jl '67

Philippine insurrection, 1899-1901

See Philippines—History—Insurrection, 1899-1901

1933-1945

First New deal, by R. Moley. Review
Nat R 19:424+ Ap 18 '67. M. S. Evans
New deal and the states. J. T. Patterson. bibliog f Am Hist R 73:70-84 O '67

World war, 1939-1945

See World war, 1939-1945—United States

Korean war, 1950-1953

See Korean war, 1950-1953—American participation

House of representatives

See United States—Congress—House of representatives

Housing and urban development, Department of

Belated effort to save our cities. M. Nolan. il Reporter 37:16-21 D 28 '67
Ex-city manager named HUD deputy for housing assistance. Am City 82:47 D '67
Hit the deck; running! concerning HUD's Model neighborhoods under the Demonstration cities act, and Program guide. K. Nyren. Library J 92:715 F 15 '67; Discussion. 92:1549-50, 2312+ Ap 15, Je 15 '67
How HUD helps mass transportation to mold our cities C. M. Haas. il Am City 82:113-14 N '67
Our homes: are they livable? report. Sr Schol 90:19 Mr 10 '67
Start in urban problem solving. Sr Schol 89:3 Ja 20 '67
This month's feature: the demonstration cities controversy. Cong Digest 46:36-64 F '67
$20 million urban research budget called just first step. Tech W 20:38 Je 5 '67

Indian affairs, Bureau of

New era for the American Indian. R. L. Bennett. il Natur Hist 76:6-8+ F '67
See also
Indians of North America—Government relations
Institute of American Indian art, Santa Fe

Industries

Labor's stake in the Kennedy round; address, July 7, 1967. J. J. Reynolds. Dept State Bul 57:137-40 Jl 31 '67
New industrial state, by J. K. Galbraith. Review
Commentary 44:77-83 O '67. M. Harrington
New Yorker 43:85-6+ Ja 6 '68. N. Bliven
U.S. economic giant keeps growing. E. L. Dale, jr. il N Y Times Mag p30-1+ Mr 19 '67
See also
Food industry and trade
Industrial mobilization
Shipbuilding
United States—Economic conditions
also subhead Industries under names of sections, states, cities, e.g. New York (city)—Industries
also subhead United States under names of industries. e.g. Automobile industry and trade—United States

UNITED STATES—*Continued*

Information agency

Atlanta bookseller is star in USIA film for overseas. il Pub W 192:42 N 6 '67

Deliberations on IMG start in Senate committee. Pub W 191:33-4 Ap 3 '67

Diplomatic strides; United States information agency youth officer coaches African athletes. il Newsweek 70:105-6 O 30 '67

Hidden hands in publishing. D. Wise. New Repub 157:17-18 O 21 '67

How the U.S. tells its story to the world; interview. L. H. Marks; J. Chancellor. il U S News 62:76-9 F 20 '67

Professor & the CIA; Operations and policy research. inc. funds. R. G. Sherrill. Nation 204:258-60 F 27 '67; Reply. R. B. Luce. 204: 386 Mr 27 '67

Voice of America: memorandum to John Daly. R. J. Walton. il Nation 205:135-8 Ag 28 '67; Reply with rejoinder. J. Chancellor. 205:258+ S 25 '67

Intellectual life

Art on trial. A. Kazin. Harper 235:51-5 O '67

Cultural cold war; excerpt from Towards a new past. C. Lasch. Nation 205:198-212 S 11 '67; Discussion. 205:309, 340-1 O 2-9 '67

Sociological and institutional changes in American life: their implications for the library. R. W. Conant. ALA Bul 61:528-36 My '67

Thirties: when culture came to Main Street; excerpt from Just around the corner. R. Bendiner. Sat R 50:19-21 Ap 1 '67

To Mr Kazin; art will not disappear. B. Dunlap. Harper 235:55 O '67

See also
American literature
Books and reading
Education—United States
United States—Popular culture

Interior, Department of

Alaska's art in peril. K. Kuh. Sat R 50:23+ Mr 25 '67

Mr Freeman's response to reorganization; bill to redesignate the Department of the interior as the Department of natural resources. J. B. Craig. Am For 73:11+ D '67

Water pollution, conversion pose great R&D challenges. J. F. Judge. il Tech W 20:46-7+ Je 5 '67

See also
United States—Federal water pollution control administration

Sport fisheries and wildlife,
Bureau of

New federal policy for animal damage control. Audubon 69:4 S '67

Internal revenue service

Easier tax paying coming; interview. S. S. Cohen. Nations Bsns 55:42-3+ Mr '67

Inside internal revenue. by W. Surface. Review
Sat R 50:38 Mr 4 '67

129 billion dollars in taxes: the miracle of April 15; excerpts from address. March 17, 1967. S. S. Cohen. il U S News 62:100-1 Ap 17 '67

Sierra club caper. R. Starnes. Field & S 72:10+ S '67

Tax exemption. D. Wolfle. Science 157:493 Ag 4 '67

Tax threat to nonprofits; Internal revenue proposes to tax publications of nonprofit organizations. Bsns W p 131 My 6 '67

To tax and to please; address, December 15, 1966. S. S. Cohen. Vital Speeches 33:268-72 F 15 '67

Tyranny in the Internal revenue service. J. Barron. Read Digest 91:42-9 Ag '67

Tyranny in the Internal revenue service, true or false? reaction from the IRS. Read Digest 91:101 N '67

Interoceanic canal commission

Interoceanic canal study commission submits third annual progress report; announcement and letter of transmittal, August 8, 1967. L. B. Johnson. Dept State Bul 57:302-3 S 4 '67

Interstate commerce commission

Freight rates edge higher. Bsns W p34 Ag 5 '67

Just and reasonable, ICC grants railways increase in freight rates. Time 90:68-9 Ag 11 '67

Job corps

Corps in the Cradle; Cradle of forestry. K. B. Pomeroy. il Am For 73:20-3 S '67

Disadvantaged youth employed by Washington state parks. J. M. Willits. Parks & Rec 2:34+ Ap '67

How much is a boy worth? Job corps camps. J. B. Craig. Am For 73:18-19 Jl '67

Job corps comes up to a test. il Bsns W p 145-6+ O 14 '67

Life in job corps: what a camp is like; Camp Schenck, N.C. il U S News 63:58-9 Ag 14 '67

Operational problems of the Job corps. S. A. Levitan. il Mo Labor R 90:27 F '67

Pioneering with the Job corps; camp near Curlew, Wash; North central regional library, Wenatchee, Wash. J. H. Pardee. il Library J 92:748-9 F 15 '67

Predicting job corpsmen's performance on the tests of general education development. R. C. Pugh. Sch & Soc 95:268-9 Ap 15 '67

Scandal in the Job corps. G. Caesar. Read Digest 90:118-22 F '67

Joint chiefs of staff

How to prevent a nuclear war; warning to Americans; with statement by E. G. Wheeler. il U S News 62:31-3 My 15 '67

What went wrong in the Pentagon: a 73-billion-dollar operation. il U S News 63:41-3 D 11 '67

Justice, Department of

All in the family; R. Clark and T. C. Clark. il Time 89:22 Mr 10 '67

Coplon case dismissed. D. Kraslow. New Repub 156:10-11 F 18 '67

Federal law enforcement. F. M. Vinson, jr. bibliog f Cur Hist 53:15-22+ Jl '67

How will Clark tip the scales? new attorney General at Justice department. Bsns W p 160+ Mr 11 '67

Juridical chairs; R. Clark appointment; T. Clark retirement. il Newsweek 69:36-7 Mr 13 '67

Laying down the law to number-one lawman; trespassory eavesdrops. I. Younger. New Repub 156:11-13 Mr 4 '67

Low-key and liberal; Attorney General Clark. F. P. Graham. il N Y Times Mag p30-1+ Ap 2 '67

Mr Clark: what kind of attorney general? U S News 62:22 Mr 13 '67

Antitrust division

Again, talk of breaking up GM. il U S News 63:69 N 13 '67

Antitrust slowdown? A. M. Bickel. New Repub 156:15-18 My 20 '67; Reply with rejoinder. R. L. Wright. 156:32-3 Je 10 '67

Cliffhanger for ABC; proposed merger with ITT back in FCC's lap after second round of hearings. Bsns W p36-7 Je 3 '67

Drug companies go on trial. Bsns W p80 N 4 '67

Eye on IBM. il Newsweek 69:81 F 13 '67

IBM comes under antitrusters' gaze; complaints from competitors. il Bsns W p34 Ja 14 '67

ITT-ABC hearings. New Repub 156:4-5 Ap 22 '67

Poke at the power of patent holders; Justice dept. investigating corporate patent holders. Bsns W p36-7 F 18 '67

Salve for drug buyers; damage suit confronts five major distributors of tetracycline drugs. Bsns W p22 Ja 6 '68

Time of decision on bank mergers; Justice dept. claims that 1966 law did not relax rules on mergers. il Bsns W p 100+ Ja 28 '67

Trust-busters of '67: heroes or villains? il Newsweek 69:77-8+ My 8 '67

Why ITT-ABC wedding faces delay; pressure from Justice dept. il Bsns W p38-9 Mr 18 '67

Civil rights division

Bearing down on job bias. Bsns W p 18-19 D 23 '67

Criminal division

Creme de la crime: attack on organized crime. New Repub 157:7 D 2 '67

Labor, Department of

Education and the labor market; with study-discussion program, by C. Smallenburg and H. Smallenburg. bibliog il PTA Mag 61:24-6, 36-7 Ap '67

New double yoke for Labor and Commerce; President Johnson's plan to put the two departments together. il Bsns W p 140 Ja 14 '67

New voice on economic policy; proposed merger of Commerce and Labor depts. il Bsns W p 157-8+ F 18 '67

Togetherness: proposed business-labor-merger. New Repub 156:9 Ja 28 '67

UNITED STATES—Labor, Department of —*Continued*

Federal contract compliance, Office of

Slough of equality. Nation 204:196-7 F 13 '67

Labor policy

Labor's middle-class revolt. A. H. Raskin. il Reporter 36:24-7 Je 15 '67

See also
Labor laws and legislation—United States
United States—National labor relations board

Labor statistics, Bureau of

See also
Index numbers

Land management, Bureau of

One-sided candor; oil companies file suit. Nation 205:293-4 O 2 '67
Place in the sun. J. B. Craig. il Am For 73: 10-13+ Ag '67
Wilderness and public lands. T. L. Kimball. il Liv Wildn 30:14-17 Wint '66

Library of Congress

Librarian of Congress reports year of growth; summary of report. L. Q. Mumford. Library J 92:2496 Jl '67
Library for all the Nation. I. Wolfert. il Read Digest 91:235-41 D '67
Madison library designs scored as inadequate. Library J 92:2496 Jl '67
Madison library model unveiled at LC. il Library J 92:2983+ S 15 '67
Third building for Library of Congress: James Madison memorial. il Wilson Lib Bul 32:132 O '67
Washington report: from the Library of Congress. E. Hamer and A. McCormick. See issues of ALA bulletin

Automation

Library of Congress automation program: a progress report to the stockholders. B. E. Markuson. bibliog il ALA Bul 61:647-55 Je '67
LC duplicating two machine-readable cataloging files. E. Hamer and A. McCormick. ALA Bul 61:1295 D '67
Marc II cataloging format recommended as standard. Library J 93:136 Ja 15 '68

Division for the blind and physically handicapped

LC talking books go to handicapped. Library J 92:2104 Je 1 '67
Library service to the handicapped; change of name for Division for the blind. E. Hamer and A. McCormick. ALA Bul 61: 250-1 Mr '67
New hope for the handicapped. C. Gallozzi. bibliog il Library J 92:1417-20 Ap 1 '67

Legislative reference service

Effective advisers to Congress; Science policy division of Library of Congress. F. Sartwell. Sci N 91:335 Ap 8 '67

Manuscript division

National union catalog of MSS adds fourth volume. Library J 92:182 Ja 15 '67
Quarterly notes: recent acquisitions (cont) K. V. Hostick. Hobbies 72:108+ Je; 108+ Ag; 108 N '67

Moving picture collections

National film collection planned for LC. Library J 93:134 Ja 15 '68

Rare book division

Bibliographical soufflé, so to speak. F. R. Goff. il Wilson Lib Bul 41:576-9 F '67

Union catalog

British firm gets NUC publishing contract. Library J 92:959 Mr 1 '67
Publisher selected for National union catalog. Pub W 191:55-6 F 13 '67

Literary landmarks
See Literary landmarks

Literature
See American literature

Maps

See also
Maps, Pictorial

Marine corps

For next marine boss: three candidates. il U S News 63:16 S 18 '67
Marines get a new leader. il U S News 63:18 D 18 '67

Forces in Vietnam

Bearing the brunt at Con Thien. D. Warner. il Reporter 37:18-21 O 19 '67; Correction. 37:10 N 2 '67
Bitterest battlefield; marine camps near Demilitarized zone. il Time 90:28 S 22 '67
Brutal battle at Con Thien; why U.S. marines are hanging on. il U S News 63:40-1 O 9 '67
Building a nation beyond the killing; new emphasis on land control, population security and nation building. il Time 89:32-3 F 3 '67
Changing the guard; General Walt appointed marine corps director of personnel. il Newsweek 69:47 My 29 '67
How the marines fight the other war; pacification program of the combined-action company. S. Dickerman. il Reporter 36:31-3 Ap 6 '67
Inside the cone of fire, Con Thien. D. D. Duncan. il Life 63:28D-42C O 27 '67
It's more than a shooting war for American GI's. H. Handleman. il U S News 63:36-8 O 23 '67
Key victory for marines, but was the battle necessary? three hills overlooking U.S. base at Khe Sanh. il U S News 62:8+ My 15 '67
Leader for all reasons; L. Walt returns to U.S. il Time 89:32 Je 9 '67
Quick and the dead; case of First Sergeant Churchill. il Newsweek 70:35 N 13 '67
Siege at Con Thien. il Newsweek 70:49-50 O 9 '67
Their mission: defend, befriend; pacification program of Echo two, Combined action platoon. D. Moser. il Life 63:24-9+ Ag 25 '67
Two wars of General Lew Walt. C. Leinster. il Life 62:77-80+ My 26 '67
Up Hill 881 with the marines. il Life 62:40-44A My 19 '67
Viet Nam buildup? battle of the hills: near Khe Sanh. il Sr Schol 90:26-7 My 19 '67
Vietnam: the eye of the storm; situation in provinces known as Eye Corps. F. Sully. New Repub 157:13-16 Jl 15 '67
Vietnam: the issue and the response; address, April 24, 1967. W. M. Greene, jr. Vital Speeches 33:509-12 Je 1 '67
Why U.S. marines took war to North Vietnam's doorstep. il U S News 62:40 My 29 '67

History

Mr Coolidge's jungle war. R. O'Connor. il Am Heritage 19:36-9+ D '67

Officers

Cerebral commandant. il Time 90:25 D 15 '67
Management marine; new commandant. Newsweek 70:33 D 18 '67

Marine science commission
See United States—Commission on marine science, engineering and resources

Maritime administration

$25 million available for industry R&D. C. D. LaFond. il Tech W 20:51-2+ Je 5 '67

Merchant marine
See Merchant marine—United States

Military airlift command

Biggest airlift to Vietnam crosses Pacific. il Aviation W 88:68-9 Ja 1 '68
Buying better airlift; excerpt from address, March 31, 1967. R. H. Charles. Aviation W 86:21 Ap 3 '67
C-5A to revolutionize U.S. military airlift. J. D. Hendricks. il Aviation W 87:167-9+ N 20 '67
Carriers push effort to improve MAC terms after CAB rebuff. Aviation W 88:31 Ja 8 '68
Demand for cargo charter seen continuing downward trend. Aviation W 87:29 O 30 '67
Flying Tiger defends back-haul charters. H. D. Watkins. Aviation W 86:38-9 Ap 24 '67
MAC charter demands take dip. H. D. Watkins. Aviation W 87:22-3 S 25 '67
Sagging MAC cargo hits charters; Transpacific piston operations suspended. H. D. Watkins. Aviation W 86:27-8 Je 19 '67
U.S. airlift capacity slated to climb 400 per cent in six years. Aviation W 86:81 Mr 6 '67

Military missions
See Military missions

Military policy

America's clear and present danger; interview. N. F. Twining. Read Digest 90:49-55 Mr '67

UNITED STATES—Military policy—*Continued*
Commander-in-chief who leaves his generals alone. H. Sidey. il Life 63:38 D 1 '67
Crises come, crises go; arms sales. Nation 205:293 O 2 '67
Et tu, Russell? fast deployment logistics proposal. Nation 204:549 My 1 '67
Fish to the cats. Nation 205:290-1 O 2 '67
Nike-X go-ahead followed fierce struggle. il Aviation W 87:70+ O 23 '67
Overestimating the power of power. L. J. Halle. New Repub 156:15-17 Je 10 '67
Protest, power and the future of politics. C. McWilliams. Nation 206:71-7 Ja 15 '68
Who runs this whole U.S. show in the world? advisers on the President's war council and the Tuesday lunch procedure. il U S News 62:37-9 Je 5 '67
    See also
United States—Defenses

Militia

    See also
United States—National guard

Mint

Case of the walking coins; thefts by San Francisco mint employees. il Newsweek 69: 83 Mr 27 '67

Missions

See Missions—United States

Monetary policy

See Monetary policy

Moral conditions

Another three Rs: the development of the individual; address, September 13, 1967. J. A. Howard. Vital Speeches 34:18-22 O 15 '67
Anything goes: taboos in twilight. il Newsweek 70:74-8 N 13 '67
Can we still be shocked? W. K. Zinsser. il Look 31:11 D 12 '67
Discount on gorgeous; a society without trust. P. A. Hart. Nation 205:400-1 O 23 '67
Generation gap. J. Poppy. il Look **31:26-32** F 21 '67
Great society as a myth; adaptation of address; reprint. W. Stringfellow. Cath World 205:83-9 My '67
I am a tired housewife. Mrs J. P. Strickland. U S News 62:112 Mr 27 '67
If this be heresy; address, April 26, 1967. M. Upton. Vital Speeches 34:37-9 N 1 '67; Excerpts with title It's time to stand up for the upperdog. il U S News 63:62-3 Jl 10 '67
Indecent society. New Repub 156:5-6 My 13 '67
Is there a sick society in the U.S? il U S News 63:49-51 Ag 28 '67
Like a conquered province. by P. Goodman. Review
    Sat R 50:27-8 S 2 '67. C. M. Curtis
Missing elements: moral courage; excerpts from address. B. W. Tuchman. McCalls 94: 28+ Je '67; Excerpts. PTA Mag 61:20-2 My '67
Moral double bookkeeping. Nation 204:546 My 1 '67
Only half-civilized. Christian Cent 84:523-4 Ap 26 '67
Pop goes America. P. Michelson. New Repub 157:25-8 S 2 '67
Revolution. D. Lawrence. U S News 62:116 My 22 '67
Sex, morality, and the turned-on generation; with press comments. il Sr Schol 90:6-11+ My 12 '67
    See also
Crime and criminals—United States

Narcotics, Bureau of

U.S. bureau of narcotics. M. L. Harney. bibliog f Cur Hist 53:23-30+ Jl '67

National advisory commission on civil disorders

After Detroit. il Time 90:18-19 Ag 4 '67
Report: Washington. E. B. Drew. Atlan 220: 13-14 N '67

National advisory commission on health manpower

Health crisis: LBJ panel calls for reshaping American medicine. P. M. Boffey. Science 158:1160-2 D 1 '67
National campaign to prevent catastrophes; glaring inadequacies in health care. Sci N 92:535-6 D 2 '67

National advisory commission on libraries

Balancing the Commission. E. Moon. Library J 92:35 Ja 1 '67; Correction. 92:713 F 15 '67
Calling the commission; symposium. il Library J 92:1802-7, 1901-5 My 1-15 '67
It's a date; don't be late; opportunity to communicate our convictions about American librarianship. E. Moon. Library J 92:949 Mr 1 '67
National commission hears ARL group. Library J 92:2493-4 Jl '67
National commission meets in Chicago. Library J 92:1882 My 15 '67
National commission meets in New York. Library J 92:1101 Mr 15 '67
National commission's task described by Dan Lacy; summary of address, May 25, 1967. D. Lacy. Library J 92:2494 Jl '67
National library commission meets in Pikeville, Ky. il Library J 92:4089 N 15 '67
Report from Pikeville, Kentucky; with testimony by R. Caudill. K. Molz. il Wilson Lib Bul 42:397-402+ D '67
Six members added to National commission. Library J 92:721 F 15 '67
Six more named to library advisory group. Pub W 191:123 F 20 '67
Spirit of Pikeville. K. Nyren. il Library J 92:4465-70 D 15 '67

National advisory committee on aeronautics

NACA si, NASA no. W. J. Coughlin. Tech W 20:132 Mr 27 '67

National advisory council on the education of disadvantaged children

Washington report; Title I of ESEA. J. Lloyd. Sr Schol 90:sup8 F 3 '67

National advisory health council

Policing the consequences of science. J. Lear. Sat R 50:65-7 D 2 '67; Discussion. 51:104-5 Ja 6 '68

National aeronautics and space administration

America's lag in space race. il U S News 63: 43-5 N 6 '67
Apollo contractor criticisms, fixes summarized for House Committee; text of summary. Aviation W 86:28-9 Ap 24 '67
Apollo story: we never thought... il Sci N 91:373-4 Ap 22 '67
Apollo 204 fire forcing design changes. il Tech W 20:18-19 F 13 '67
Apollo 204; review board pushes investigation at Cape. K. Voss and others. Tech W 20:17 F 6 '67
Back to the job; aim for a lunar landing by 1970. il Time 89:27-8 My 19 '67
Board presses Apollo 204 investigation. G. Alexander. Aviation W 86:34-6 F 13 '67
Board reports on Apollo fire investigation; text of inquiry report. il Aviation W 86: 100-1+ Ap 17 '67
Contractor support service called illegal. Aviation W 87:19-20 O 30 '67
Full Phillips report demanded by Rep. Ryan. Tech W 20:19 My 1 '67
Governmental information systems; summary of addresses at ABPC conference. A. A. Aines; M. S. Day. Pub W 191:38-9 Ap 10 '67
High hopes for the moon shot; chance for lunar landing before 1970. il Bsns W p60-2+ Ap 15 '67
How soon the moon? three months investigation of the Apollo 204 fire. il Time 89:86 Ap 14 '67
Jim Webb's earthy management of space. J. Mecklin. il Fortune 76:82-7+ Ag '67
Lunar programs shift weighed. Aviation W 87:21 D 18 '67
Lunar programs united in single office. W. J. Normyle. Aviation W 88:22 Ja 8 '68
NACA si, NASA no. W. J. Coughlin. Tech W 20:132 Mr 27 '67
NASA and the media. Nation 204:677 My 29 '67
NASA centers feel fund cuts. Aviation W 83: 31 D 4 '67
NASA considers lunar module changes. Aviation W 86:18 Mr 13 '67
NASA details sweeping Apollo revisions. W. J. Normyle. Aviation W 86:24-6 My 15 '67
NASA evaluates bids to study lift-engine exhaust ingestion. G. S. Hunter. Aviation W 86:87+ Je 19 '67
NASA implements board findings; with text of summary findings and editorial comment. W. J. Normyle. il Aviation W 86:21, 26-33 Ap 17 '67
NASA international. J. Eberhart. il Sci N 91:576-7 Je 17 '67
[NASA issue] ed. by H. Taylor. il Aero Tech 21:24-34+ N 20 '67

UNITED STATES—National aeronautics and space administration—*Continued*

Manned spacecraft center

All-digital displays studied for NASA mission center. il Tech W 20:22 F 20 '67
Impatient Gulliver above our roofs. R. Bradbury. il Life 63:31-7 N 24 '67
Lunar lock-up; lunar receiving laboratory. il Sci N 91:165 F 18 '67
Lunar receiving laboratory. J. C. McLane, jr. and others. bibliog il Science 155:525-9 F 3 '67
MSC awards space station study pacts. Tech W 20:22+ Mr 27 '67
New missions seen dictating tracking system changes. A. Hill. Tech W 20:16 Ap 3 '67
Quarantine for moon travelers; Lunar receiving laboratory. il Time 90:52 D 29 '67

Marshall space flight center

LTV designs service vehicles for space. E. J. Bulban. il Aviation W 86:79-80 My 8 '67

Procurement

ERC awarding more guidance contracts. R. Barnhart. Tech W 20:34 Ap 3 '67
Industry participation slated for AAP follow-on work; Apollo applications program. il Tech W 20:23 F 6 '67
NAA facing heavy loss of AAP funding. H. Taylor and H. M. David. il Tech W 20:19-22 My 15 '67
NASA lists top 100 contractors. Aviation W 87:69-70+ O 2 '67
NASA soon to award AAP integration, payload contracts. H. Taylor. Tech W 20:17-18 Ap 10 '67
Top 50 NASA contractors, first half of FY '67. Tech W 20:13 My 15 '67

Space science and applications, Office of

NASA identifies twenty-one promising new missions. Tech W 20:20 Je 12 '67
NASA's post-moon pitch: research. J. Eberhart. il Sci N 91:60-1 Jl 21 '67
OSSA emphasizes small-scale studies. Aviation W 86:17 Je 26 '67

National bureau of standards
See United States—Standards, National bureau of

National commission on food marketing

To market we go; with editorial comment. E. Dowling. New Repub 156:9, 22-4 Ja 28 '67

National council on marine resources and engineering development

Comsat-type oceanology organization urged. il Tech W 20:34 Mr 27 '67
Exploration race: moon or sea? concerning transition report. J. Lear. Sat R 50:54-5 Mr 4 '67
Marine council evaluating special projects. R. W. Niblock. il Tech W 20:37-9 Je 12 '67
Marine sciences council reports priorities of executive branch. B. Nelson. il Science 155:1389+ Mr 17 '67
National effort takes shape. il Sci N 91:277-8 Mr 25 '67
Ocean budget doubled by new formula. il Tech W 20:28+ Ja 30 '67
Presidential ocean program stresses nine special areas. R. Niblock. il Tech W 20:33 Mr 13 '67
Year of transition. W. J. Coughlin. Tech W 20:50 Mr 20 '67

National crime commission
See United States—President's commission on law enforcement and administration of justice

National data center (proposed)

Data center safeguards promised. Sci N 91:278 Mr 25 '67
National data center and personal privacy. A. R. Miller. Atlan 220:53-7 N '67
Spy in the corporate structure: and the right to privacy, by E. Engberg. Review Sat R 50:43-4 S 16 '67. N. Samstag

Anecdotes, facetiae, satire, etc.

Day the computers got Waldon Ashenfelter. B. Elliott and R. Goulding. Atlan 220:58-61 N '67

National foundation for the social sciences (proposed)

Case for a national social science foundation; address, May 6, 1967. F. R. Harris. Science 157:507-9 Ag 4 '67
CIA damage. Sci N 92:32-3 Jl 8 '67

National foundation on the arts and the humanities

All's well that ends well; first awards to painters and sculptors. T. B. Hess. Art N 65:21 F '67
America sings: Sarah Caldwell's National opera; grant. H. Kupferberg. il Atlan 220:120-2 S '67
Building an organization; National endowment's initial grants to Association of American dance companies. M. B. Siegel. Dance Mag 41:51+ Ag '67
Delights in a mixed bag of grants. R. H. Smith. Pub W 191:59 F 13 '67
Endowing the arts; National council on the arts program of assistance to writers. D. Dempsey. Sat R 50:25 Ag 12 '67
Funnies on Capitol hill. D. S. Greenberg. Science 155:1222 Mr 10 '67
National endowment awards go to five authors. Pub W 192:49 Jl 17 '67
Pot shots at culture; dispute over comic study grant. New Repub 156:17 Ap 22 '67
Refurbishing American authors; grant to MLA. D. Dempsey. Sat R 50:30+ Je 10 '67

National guard

Changing the guard; annual conference of the National guard association. il Time 90:24-5 S 29 '67
Getting ready; riot training course. New Repub 157:8-9 O 28 '67
Guard under fire; House armed services subcommittee investigation of handling of riots. il Newsweek 70:22 S 4 '67
It's time to change the guard; Time essay. Time 90:24-5 O 20 '67; Same abr. with title National guard, time for a change. Read Digest 92:135-9 Ja '68
Look at new weapons to cope with riots. il U S News 64:6-7 Ja 1 '68
Military appraisal of the threat to U.S. cities. R. B. Rigg. U S News 64:68-71 Ja 15 '68
National guard and Negroes. America 117:213 S 2 '67
National guard, awake or asleep? training program. W. A. McWhirter. il Life 63:85-6+ O 27 '67
National guard shape-up is overdue. Life 63:4 O 27 '67
National guardsmen; Michigan national guard in Detroit riots. New Repub 157:5-6 S 9 '67
New furor over the national guard. il U S News 62:6 Je 12 '67
New kind of war. il Newsweek 70:20-1 Ag 14 '67
Nightmare journey; violence against Negroes during riots in Detroit. B. Clark. il Ebony 22:121-4+ O '67
Putting out the fires next time; riot-control training. H. B. Meyers. il Fortune 77:174-6+ Ja '68
Trimming the totem; army reserve and national guard reorganization plan. Time 89:32 Je 9 '67

National institute of child health and human development

New morality. U. Bronfenbrenner. Sat R 50:47 Jl 1 '67

National institute of general medical sciences

Comparative medicine; report on workshop conference. W. I. Gay. Science 158:1220+ D 1 '67

National institute of mental health

Psychoses and the womb. Newsweek 69:84 F 6 '67

National institutes of health

Advancement of the Nation's health. P. H. Abelson. Science 158:53 O 6 '67
After all, we're at war; NIH feels the pinch. Sci N 92:78-9 Jl 22 '67
Collaboration for accelerating progress in medical research; excerpts from Senate committee testimony, March 16, 1967. A. B. Sabin. Science 156:1568-71 Je 23 '67
Information exchange groups to be discontinued; letter. E. A. Confrey; reply. W. V. LBJ at NIH; President offers kind words for basic research. E. Langer. il Science 157:403-5 Jl 28 '67
Medical research: NIH wants divorce from PHS. L. J. Carter. il Science 156:45-8 Ap 7 '67

UNITED STATES—National institutes of health
—*Continued*
NIH: as the time approaches for Shannon's retirement. D. S. Greenberg. il Science 158: 1165-7 D 1 '67
NIH budget: House committee sticks to administration figure. D. S. Greenberg. Science 156:1071-3 My 26 '67
NIH: Fountain committee issues bitter attack on programs. D. S. Greenberg. Science 158: 611-14 N 3 '67
NIH: Lister Hill criticizes LBJ budget. E. Langer. Science 156:1471 Je 16 '67
NIH wants independence. B. J. Culliton. il Sci N 91:478-9 My 20 '67
Policing the consequences of science. J. Lear. Sat R 50:65-7 D 2 '67; Discussion. 51:104-5 Ja 6 '68
Progress in medicine; latest findings. U S News 62:12 My 22 '67
Science vs. democracy; NIH blanket grant to Sloan-Kettering institute and HSAA award. J. Lear. Sat R 50:57-61 N 4 '67
Succession at NIH. P. H. Abelson. Science 156:459 Ap 28 '67
Toward the excellent: Health science advancement awards. K. Sperry. Science 157: 662-3 Ag 11 '67

National labor relations board
Does NLRB's bias swing union elections? study by economist. J. Krislov. il Bsns W p60 D 2 '67
Employer protest: pre-union bias. U S News 62:87 Mr 20 '67
How government fattens unions. W. Wingo. il Nations Bsns 55:70-2+ S '67
Justice too long deferred. B. L. Masse. America 117:238 S 9 '67
Lockout, the other dimension. W. A. Lewis. bibliog f Mo Labor R 90:1-7 Ag '67
Significant decisions in labor cases. See Issues of Monthly labor review

National library of medicine
Information environment studied by NLM project. Library J 92:725 F 15 '67
NLM names committees to advise on grants. Library J 92:1397 Ap 1 '67
NLM's medicine collection; letter to the editor. J. B. Blake. Library J 92:507-8 F 1 '67

National military establishment
See United States—Defense, Department of

National park service
Building for the National park service: designed to respect an historic site; Interpretive facilities building, Harpers Ferry, W.Va. il Arch Rec 142:136-9 O '67
Earthquake lake; inclusion in National registry of natural landmarks. C. H. Giles. il Nat Parks Mag 41:7 N '67
Fiftieth anniversary of the National park service 1916-1966. S. A. Cain. Liv Wildn 30:16-18 Aut '66
Interpretive facilities center; Harpers Ferry center. R. C. Byrd. il Parks & Rec 2:23-4+ D '67
National park experience. D. Lambert. il Nat Parks Mag 41:4-8 My '67
Parks are for people; balancing park use and preservation of resources. W. E. Towell. Am For 73:5+ O '67

National parks and reserves
See National parks and reserves—United States

National planning
See National planning

National science board
National science board: its place in national policy. E. A. Walker. Science 156:474-7 Ap 28 '67; Reply. I. H. Abbott. 156:1549-50 Je 23 '67

National science foundation
Federal R&D grants to feel war's pinch. Bsns W p75 D 9 '67
Federal science policy; excerpts from address, December 30, 1966. P. Handler. Science 155:1063-6 Mr 3 '67
$500 million budget breakthrough possible. Sci N 92:345 O 7 '67
Geographical distribution of NSF grants; letter. J. D. Millett il Science 156:890 My 19 '67; Reply. H. J. Jerison. 157:991 S 1 '67
Kennedy backs NSF. Sci N 92:489-90 N 18 '67
Handler statement on Smale case. P. Handler. Science 157:1411 S 22 '67

Money for NSF: the odyssey of a research agency's budget. D. S. Greenberg. il Science 158:357-61 O 20 '67
NSF issues administrative study; concerning Systems for measuring and reporting the resources and activities of colleges and universities. D. S. Greenberg. Science 158: 890 N 17 '67
NSF issues new education survey. D. S. Greenberg. Science 158:96 O 6 '67
NSF, metric bills advance. Sci N 91:208 Mr 4 '67
NSF: same ceiling. Sci N 91:519-20 Je 3 '67
No NSF cote for the Vietnam dove. Sci N 92:319 S 30 '67
Political science. New Repub 157:9 S 30 '67
Reply. S. Lang. 157:27-8 O 14 '67
Smale and NSF: a new dispute erupts. D. S. Greenberg. Science 157:1285 S 15 '67
Smale case. Nation 205:291-2 O 2 '67
Smale case: tracing the path that led to NSF's decision. D. S. Greenberg. Science 157:1536-9 S 29 '67
Smale: NSF shifts position. D. S. Greenberg. Science 158:98 O 6 '67
Smale: NSF's records do not support the charges. D. S. Greenberg. Science 158:618-19 N 3 '67

National security agency
CIA's big sister. Time 90:22 N 3 '67

National security council
Charting the enemy's strength; with charts of North Vietnamese combat power. Bsns W p82-4 Ag 12 '67
Who runs this whole U.S. show in the world? il U S News 62:38 Je 5 '67

National student association
See United States national student association

National teacher corps
Boon from the beadle; House subcommittee votes funds. il Time 90:16 Jl 7 '67
Educational bargain worth keeping. Life 62:4 Mr 17 '67
Ford road school votes aye for the Teacher corps. R. Van Doren. il NEA J 56:28-30 Ap '67
National teacher corps. il PTA Mag 61:12-15 My '67
Promotion time. il Newsweek 69:111-12 Mr 27 '67
Slum kids' hope. C. Ferber and S. Saler. New Repub 156:8-10 Ap 15 '67
Teacher corps. C. Conner. il Am Ed 3:13-19 Ap '67
Washington report. J. Lloyd. Sr Schol 91:sup7 O 5 '67

National traffic safety agency
Horsetrading? car safety deadline. il Sr Schol 89:16-17 Ja 20 '67
LBJ's safety boss: babe in bureaucracy's jungle. A. Rothenberg. il Look 31:101-3 My 30 '67
New auto rules: safe or sorry? il Newsweek 69:79 F 13 '67
Truce and progress; concerning safety requirements. il Time 89:87 F 10 '67

National water commission
Need for a new water policy. A. W. Smith. Nat Parks Mag 41:2+ S '67
Water resources: Congress favors taking a new look. L. J. Carter il Science 157:906 Ag 25 '67

Naval air systems command
Naval space group doubling staff to handle bigger load. il Aviation W 87:121+ S 11 '67

Naval material command
See United States—Navy department—Naval material command

Naval ship research and development center
Navy will add labs to ship R&D center. R. W. Niblock. il Aero Tech 21:54-5 Ag 28 '67

Navy
Deep ocean technology may spur funding. R. W. Niblock and S. Montgomery. il Tech W 20:40-2+ Je 5 '67
Navy intensifies surveys near USSR; antisubmarine warfare-undersea warfare survey project. R. W. Niblock. il Tech W 21:29-30 Jl 3 '67

UNITED STATES—Navy—*Continued*
Navy's plan for handling other Vietnams. il U S News 63:59-60 O 23 '67

Our limited war in the South China Sea. D. Reed. Read Digest 90:88-92 Ap '67

U.S. seapower; address, September 28, 1967. T. H. Moorer. Vital Speeches 34:83-5 N 15 '67

See also
Logistics
Naval maneuvers
Naval research
United States—Coast guard
United States—Navy department
Warships—United States

Appropriations and expenditures

Funding restraints threatens DSSP materials R&D base. J. F. Judge. il Aero Tech 21:33-5 S 25 '67

House may restore Senate cuts in FDLS. Tech W 20:10+ Mr 27 '67

New ship defense missile gets funding; unguided conventional air-launched weapons. Tech W 20:25 F 6 '67

Services' tactical missile budget requests detailed. Tech W 20:18 F 6 '67

War budget slows national momentum; setbacks to oceanology program. R. W. Niblock and S. Montgomery. il Aero Tech 21:30-2 S 25 '67

Boats

Aerospace techniques eyed for naval use. J. F. Judge. Tech W 20:42-4 My 15 '67

Honeywell gun for Vietnam patrol boats. C. D. LaFond. il Tech W 20:30 F 6 '67

New inshore warfare projects move ahead. Aero Tech 21:26 Ag 28 '67
See also
Armored vessels
Warships—United States

Crimes and misdemeanors

Arnheiter incident. il Time 90:18-19 D 1 '67
Raising Caine; case of M. A. Arnheiter. Newsweek 70:31A D 4 '67

Desertions

Aggressive campaign. il Time 91:21 Ja 19 '68
Caviar & encomiums; four desert from aircraft carrier Intrepid as protest against Viet Nam war. il Time 90:15-16 D 1 '67
Just average: four deserters from the navy in Russia. il Newsweek 70:43 D 4 '67

History

Rehearsal for World war II; Japanese bombing of U.S.S. Panay. D. Perry. il Am Heritage 18:40-5+ Ap '67; Reply. 18:51 O '67

Procurement

A-7A maintenance test may set trend. E. J. Bulban. il Aviation W 87:79+ S 18 '67
Down to the sea. M. Getler. Tech W 21:50 Jl 3 '67
Navy set to brief industry on huge new VAST program. Aero Tech 21:52+ S 11 '67
Navy to fund initial F-111B procurement. il Aviation W 86:28 Ja 30 '67

Underwater demolition teams

Supercommandos of the wetlands; Sea-airland unit's exploits in Vietnam. J. G. Hubbell. il Read Digest 90:49-54 Je '67
Unconventional commandos. Time 91:18-19 Ja 12 '68

Navy department

Comer arrives; new chief of naval operations. il Time 89:33 Je 9 '67

Naval material command

Rickover tells GE to weigh anchor; manufacturers of propulsion equipment decline to bid. Bsns W p 105+ Je 24 '67

Navy space systems activity
See United States—Naval air systems command

Office of education
See United States—Education, Office of

Officials and employees
See Government employees; Public offices

Patent office

Lines are drawn for patent law fight; a presidential Commission's report. il Bsns W p56-8+ Ja 28 '67

Patent system proposals: how practical? Presidential commission urges many changes. G. E. Frost. bibliog f Harvard Bsns R 45:111-22 S '67
See also
Patents

Peace corps

Disheartened volunteers. Reporter 37:11 D 14 '67
From a young American, with love; Dian Hamilton working in school for retarded children south of Manila. J. R. Moskin. il Look 31:50-2+ My 30 '67
Have traveled, will teach; Peace corpsmen come home with ideas. M. Bonn. il Am Ed 3:1-3 F '67
Idealistic Americans; Peace corps volunteers. L. B. Johnson. McCalls 95:64+ N '67
Middle-class revolutionaries are home; Returned peace corps volunteers. J. Harkison. il Mile 66:104-5+ Ja '68
More for more. Time 90:32 O 27 '67
Peace corps: antidote for provincialism. R. H. Shaffer. Sch & Soc 95:261-3 Ap 15 '67
Peace corps: now we are seven. J. H. Vaughn. il Sat R 51:21-3+ Ja 6 '68
Peace corps returnees. F. Pollock. Nations 205:15-17 Jl 3 '67
President transmits fifth annual report of Peace corps to Congress. L. B. Johnson. Dept State Bul 56:529 Mr 27 '67
Teaching as benficiary of service. Sch & Soc 95:68-9 F 4 '67
Well, can she? recruiting drive produces fewer volunteers. Newsweek 71:23 Ja 15 '68
See also
School-to-school program

Politics and government

Affairs of state. S. Alsop. See issues of Saturday evening post
Better job for McNamara; concerning article in Columbia university forum, by T. J. Farer. Nation 204:674-5 My 29 '67
Cronkite's alarm. Nation 204:260-1 F 27 '67
Elite of the alienated. L. S. Feuer. il N Y Times Mag p22-3+ Mr 26 '67; Discussion. p 12+ Ap 9; 12+ Ap 16 '67
Empty society; excerpts from Massey lectures. P. Goodman; discussion. Commentary 43:26+ Mr '67
Eugene McCarthy's mission. W. Lippman. Newsweek 70:25 D 18 '67
Focus on Washington. Cato. See issues of National review
Freedom and order: a commentary on the American political scene, by H. S. Commager. Review
Sat R 50:37-8 Ja 28 '67. D. Young
Great disfranchisement; central political drama of 1968. E. J. Hughes. Newsweek 71:15 Ja 8 '68
Great society is a sick society. J. W. Fulbright. il N Y Times Mag p30-1+ Ag 20 '67; Discussion. p2 S 3; 42+ S 10 '67
How the President feels about his troubles. il U S News 63:50-1 S 18 '67
In the Nation, by A. Krock. Review
Nat R il 19:97-8 Ja 24 '67. M. S. Evans
Johnson talks about peace, politics, and problems at home; excerpts from interview, December 19, 1967. L. B. Johnson. il U S News 64:44-5 Ja 1 '68; Dept State Bul 58:33-8 Ja 8 '68
Laugh, Casca, laugh! G. W. Johnson. Sat R 50:16+ D 2 '67
Letter from Washington. R. H. Rovere. See occasional issues of New Yorker
LBJ, near great. W. V. Shannon; reply with rejoinder. H. Cox. Commonweal 85:563-5 F 17 '67
LBJ weighs his mistakes. U S News 64:40-1 Ja 15 '68
National affairs. See issues of Newsweek
New orientation in American government. B. M. Gross and M. Springer. bibliog f Ann Am Acad 371:1-19 My '67
New revolution? military-industrial-government complex. Commonweal 87:397 D 29 '67
Next for LBJ: agonizing reappraisal. il U S News 63:32-4 Ag 14 '67
Notes & asides. W. F. Buckley,, jr. Nat R 19:1314 N 28 '67
Notes by the way. J. Burnham. Nat R 19:1063-4, 1111+ O 3-17 '67
Our government(s) at work, 1967-'68 edition. il Sr Schol 91:4-20+ N 30 '67
Paul Douglas: man ahead of his time. C. Mangel. Look 31:103-4+ Je 13 '67
Peace politics: calculus for '68. E. Kenworthy. Nation 206:46-50 Ja 8 '68
Political horrors: the war, central to the politics of 1967. K. Crawford. Newsweek 69:40 My 15 '67

UNITED STATES—Politics and government
—*Continued*
Political troubles ahead for LBJ. il U S News 63:46-50 S 25 '67
Politics as usual? K. Crawford. Newsweek 70:42 N 27 '67
Politics, by A. Ribicoff and J. O. Newman. Review
  New Repub 156:28-9 Mr 11 '67. G. W. Johnson
Politics 1968: address, December 12, 1967. L. B. Johnson. Vital Speeches 34:162-5 Ja 1 '68; Excerpt. Dept State Bul 58:39-40 Ja 8 '68
Politics of sham. E. J. Hughes. Newsweek 70:25 S 18 '67
Power in America, by D. T. Bazelon. Review
  New Repub 156:31-2 Mr 25 '67. G. W. Johnson
Presidency. H. Sidey. See issues of Life
President's every move will be suspect. P. Lisagor. il Nations Bsns 55:23-4 F '67
Protest, power and the future of politics. C. McWilliams. Nation 206:71-7 Ja 15 '68
Reformation and American political life. R. de V. Williamson. Christian Cent 84:1343-5 O 25 '67; Reply. R. G. Cheffey. 84:1633 D 20 '67
Report: Washington (cont of) Atlantic report: Washington. D. Kiker. See issues of Atlantic
Sense of crisis. Nation 205:485-6+ N 13 '67
Shape of American politics. Commentary 43: 25-40 Je '67; Reply. Nat R 19:728-9 Jl 11 '67
Storm warnings. Nation 205:515-16 N 20 '67
T.R.B. from Washington. See issues of New republic
They're not jobs for little men. A. H. Sypher. Nations Bsns 55:33-4 S '67
To seek a newer world, by R. F. Kennedy. Review
  New Repub 157:29-30+ D 2 '67. G. A. Harrison
Trends: Washington mood. P. Lisagor. See issues of Nation's business
Two USAs; concerning R. F. Kennedy's March 2, 1967 speech. M. Ascoli. Reporter 36:18-19 Mr 23 '67
U.S. commitment to peace: a shield for threatened nations; address, December 4, 1967. L. B. Johnson. Dept State Bul 57:851-4 D 25 '67
Washington front. See issues of America
Washington outlook. See issues of Business week
What ails America? withering away of the public's trust in government. H. J. Morgenthau. New Repub 157:17-21 O 28 '67
What we do not need; J. Reston's national union proposal. Nation 206:67-8 Ja 15 '68
What's new in Washington. See issues of Successful farming
Will we make it? New Repub 158:9-10 Ja 6 '68
  See also
Candidates, Political
Congressmen
Conservatism
Democratic party
Elections—United States
Farmers—Political activities
Federal and state relations
Legislation—United States
Lobbying
Local government—United States
Political parties—United States
Presidential campaigns
Presidential candidates
Presidents—United States—Election
Presidents—United States—Powers and duties
Presidents—United States—Relations with Congress
Pressure groups
Progressive party
Progressivism (United States politics)
Republican party
State governments
Suffrage—United States
Trade unions—Political activities
United States—Congress
United States—Constitution
United States—Executive departments
Vice-Presidents—United States
  also subheads Politics, Politics and government under sections, states, cities, e.g. South—Politics; Florida—Politics and government

Anecdotes, facetia, satire, etc.
America: a nation in utter confusion. T. Meehan. il Sat Eve Post 240:16 My 6 '67
Hoax or horror? a book that shook White House; concerning Report from Iron Mountain on the possibility and desirability of peace. il U S News 63:48 N 20 '67
Iron Mountain lies beyond credibility gap. I. Kristol. Fortune 77:185-6 Ja '68

On the possibility and desirability of peace; excerpts from Report from Iron Mountain. bibliog f Esquire 68:129-37+ D '67
Peace games; concerning Report from Iron Mountain. Time 90:44 N 17 '67
Peace games, war games; Report from Iron Mountain on the possibility and desirability of peace. Christian Cent 84:1588 D 13 '67
Report from Iron Mountain on the possibility and desirability of peace. Review
  Newsweek il 70:103-103B D 4 '67. H. Junker
Way back in '68. G. Ace. il Sat Eve Post 240:22 O 21 '67

Bibliography
Book marks. H. M. Christman. Nation 204: 507-9 Ap 17 '67

Caricatures and cartoons
Bobby doll. Nat R 19:242-5 Mr 7 '67

Popular culture
Art on trial. A. Kazin. Harper 235:51-5 O '67
Cultivating the arts of poverty. F. A. J. Ianni. il Sat R 50:60-2+ Je 17 '67
Culture: the new joy; United States pavilion at Expo 67. W. K. Zinsser. Look 32:8 Ja 9 '68
Is American history a happening? M. Fishwick. Sat R 50:19-21 My 13 '67
Now let the festivities proceed; popular dissemination of violence. D. Newman and R. Benton. il Esquire 68:55-8 Jl '67
Onward and upward with the arts; the put-on. J. Brackman. New Yorker 43:34-6+ Je 24 '67
Our false-front culture. S. Steinberg. il Look 32:46-9 Ja 9 '68
To Mr Kazin; art will not disappear. B. Dunlap. Harper 235:55 O '67
Underground, incorporated. R. Cravens and G. Cravens. Mlle 64:164-5+ Ap '67
What culture? what boom? H. S. Resnik. Atlan 219:51-3 F '67
What does it mean? W. K. Zinsser. il Look 31:14 My 16 '67
What options do youth have? symposium; with study-discussion program, by C. Smallenburg and H. Smallenburg. bibliog il PTA Mag 62:2-5, 34 Ja '68

Anecdotes, facetiae, satire, etc.
Genius scene. D. Goodrich. Look 31:M24 My 2 '67

Population
Demographic transitions and population problems in the United States; excerpts from The changing population of the United States: 1900 to 1960. I. B. Taeuber. bibliog f Ann Am Acad 369:131-40 Ja '67
How your state's population will grow. il U S News 62:45 F 20 '67
Makeup of America: a look at the future. il U S News 64:54-5 Ja 8 '68
No more population explosion for the U.S? il U S News 62:48-50 Ap 17 '67
Now 200 million Americans. il U S News 63: 46-9 N 6 '67
Our perilous population implosion. S. L. Udall. Sat R 50:10-13 S 2 '67
People: the more the merrier? il Sr Schol 91: 21 N 16 '67
Population. P. A. Samuelson. Newsweek 69:82 Je 12 '67
Population shifts: business effect; how age groups are changing. il U S News 62:52-3 Je 26 '67
Rush to the cities eases off; National planning assn. study. il Bsns W p90+ Je 24 '67
200 million: not far from a madding crowd. il Newsweek 70:89-90 N 27 '67
200 million: profile of U.S. il U S News 63: 80-1 N 27 '67
United States reaches 200 million population. Christian Cent 84:1485 N 22 '67
Win, place, show in the population sweeps; 200 millionth American; with report by R. Scammon. il Life 63:26-31 D 1 '67
  See also
Birth rate—United States
Migration, Internal
United States—Census

Post office department
Apolitical postmaster; O'Brien's plea for the removal of the post office from cabinet rank. Reporter 36:6+ Ap 20 '67
Changes for the mails: postage up, service down. il U S News 63:76-8 D 11 '67
Handle with care: proposed changes. Newsweek 69:34 Ap 17 '67
How to head off mail crisis: interview. L. F. O'Brien. U S News 62:59-62 Ap 24 '67

UNITED STATES—Post office department
—*Continued*
Idea: a corporation to run the Post office;
excerpts from address, April 3, 1967. L. F.
O'Brien. U S News 62:54 Ap 17 '67
It's now or never for the post office. D.
Cordtz. il Fortune 75:134-9+ Mr '67
Mr O'Brien's leviathan. R. Moley. Newsweek
69:96 My 1 '67
New design for the postal service; address,
April 3, 1967. L. F. O'Brien. Vital Speeches
33:418-21 My 1 '67
People gap seen retarding postal R&D. J.
Rhea. il Tech W 20:59-60 Je 5 '67
Post office protects consumers against fraud.
Consumer Bul 50:19-20 N '67
Post office seeks proposals on $23 million
package. Tech W 20:35 Mr 20 '67
Progress above politics; L. O'Brien's re-
organization scheme. il Time 89:33 Ap 14
'67
U.S. mail wail. Sr Schol 90:21-2 Ap 28 '67
With higher postal rates, will the mails im-
prove? il U S News 62:8 Ap 17 '67
See also
Postal censorship
Postal service—United States

President's advisory committee on foreign assistance programs

General advisory committee on foreign assistance programs. Dept State Bul 57:294 S 4
'67

President's commission on civil disorders

See United States—National advisory
commission on civil disorders

President's commission on law enforcement and administration of justice

Calling Dick Tracy; report recommends sci-
entific research. Newsweek 69:34 Je 12 '67
Challenge of crime in a free society. Report
by the President's commission on law
enforcement and administration of justice.
Review
New Repub 156:38-40 My 20 '67. F. Rem-
ington
Combating crime; symposium, ed. by L. E.
Ohlin and H. S. Ruth, jr. bibliog f il Ann
Am Acad 374:1-184 N '67
Compromise report on crime. J. P. Mac-
Kenzie. New Repub 156:15-16 F 4 '67
Cost of crime: 20 billions; what to do: a new
approach. il U S News 62:74-5 F 27 '67
Crime, American style: the President's
commission. I. Silver. Commonweal 86:141-
2 Ap 21 '67
Crime and politics; findings of the Presi-
dent's commission. G. Geis. Nation 205:115-
16 Ag 14 '67
Crime & the Great society; findings of com-
mission; Time essay. Time 89:20-1 Mr 24
'67
Crime commission report. Nat R 19:122-4 F 7
'67
Crime in our communities. J. Moorhead.
PTA Mag 61:2-3 Ap '67
Crime; interview, ed. by W. Rogers. N. D.
Katzenbach. Look 31:101-4+ Mr 7 '67
Crisis worse than anyone imagined: report.
R. B. Stolley. il Life 62:24-5 F 24 '67
Expected rise in crime; concerning commis-
sion's report. America 117:48 Jl 15 '67
High crime, poor justice. P. McBroom. il Sci
N 91:186-7 F 25 '67
Neglect of children as a cause of crime; re-
port. D. Lawrence. U S News 62:96 Mr 6
'67
Official cover-up: a flagrant case in point;
Blakey findings reduced to footnotes. Life
63:103 S 8 '67
Permanent punishment; task force's recom-
mendations for reform. Time 89:54 Je 2 '67
Response to crime. Sci N 91:172 F 18 '67
This month's feature: Congress & the na-
tional crime problem. Cong Digest 46:193-
224 Ag '67
U.S. crime: a renaissance? il Newsweek 69:
31-3 F 27 '67
War on crime. Sr Schol 90:23 F 24 '67

President's commission on the assassination of President Kennedy

Acquittal for Oswald; concerning the movie
Rush to judgment. J. J. Graham. Com-
monweal 86:149-51 Ap 21 '67
CBS on the Warren report. A. M. Bickel.
New Repub 157:29-30 Jl 15 '67; Reply with
rejoinder. W. Lister. 157:30-2+ Ag 19 '67
Failure of the Warren report. A. M. Bickel;
discussion. Commentary 43:7-8+ Ap '67

More on the Kennedy assassination charges;
concerning J. Garrison's TV broadcast. il U S
News 62:55-6 Je 12 '67
Persistent devils; CBS news inquiry: the War-
ren report. R. L. Shayon. Sat R 50:46 Jl 22
'67
Reporter at large; the buffs. C. Trillin. New
Yorker 43:41-6+ Je 10 '67

Anecdotes, facetiae, satire, etc.

Realism at the grassy knoll; Warren report
and national schizophrenia. A. C. Watson.
Christian Cent 84:1596-7 D 13 '67

President's committee on employment of the handicapped

President's committee on the handicapped.
America 117:215 S 2 '67

President's committee on selective service

Selective objection and the public interest:
present law is unconstitutional. W. Arnold.
Christian Cent 84:1218-21 S 27 '67

President's council on youth opportunity

Recreation's vital role. H. H. Humphrey.
Parks & Rec 2:13 Je '67

President's equal employment opportunity commission

Bigger stick to fight job bias. il Bsns W
p84+ Mr 18 '67
Broader effort on job bias. Bsns W p56+ Jl
15 '67
Equal employment opportunity: probing and
problems. Mo Labor R 90:III-IV O '67
Opening the record on jobs for Negroes; industry-by-industry survey of minority hiring. il Bsns W p 128+ Ag 12 '67
Processing employment discrimination cases.
A. W. Blumrosen. Mo Labor R 90:25-6 Mr
'67
Slough of equality. Nation 204:196-7 F 13 '67

President's science advisory committee

Federal science policy; excerpts from address, December 30, 1966. P. Handler. Science 155:1063-6 Mr 3 '67
Science advisers report. Sci N 91:159 F 18 '67
Science advisers urge balanced program.
Aviation W 86:133+ Mr 6 '67
World food supply faces twenty-year deadline. il Sci N 92:8 Jl 1 '67
World food supply: PSAC panel warns of impending famine. L. J. Carter. Science 156:
1578-9 Je 23 '67

President's task force on communication policy

Communication task force. America 117:401
O 14 '67

Public health service

Air pollution: the Feds move to abate Idaho
pulp mill stench. B. Nelson. il Science 157:
1018-21 S 1 '67
Better health for all babies; Collaborative
perinatal project. T. C. Wilson and K.
Niehans. Parents Mag 42:68-9+ N '67
Negro graduates: PHS study reports opinions
and problems. B. Nelson. Science 158:99-100
O 6 '67
See also
United States—National institutes of health

Driving research laboratory

I drove through a town that isn't. W. S.
Bacon. il Pop Sci 191:76-9+ Jl '67

Public land law review commission

Growing crisis on our public land. B. Milek.
il Field & S 72:10-11+ Ja '68
New look at the public lands. M. A. Pearl.
il Nat Parks Mag 41:8-12 F '67
Uncle Sam, landowner. il Sr Schol 90:2-5
F 3 '67

Public roads, Bureau of

Bureau of public roads, devastator. R. Kirk.
Nat R 19:202 F 21 '67

Race problems

America's troubles: the European view. E.
M. von Kuehnelt-Leddihn. Nat R 19:78 Ja
24 '67
Gentile beast. Christian Cent 84:299-300 Mr 8
'67
See also
Church and race problems
Congress of racial equality
National Catholic conference for interracial
justice
Negroes in the United States
also subhead Race problems under names
of states, e.g. Mississippi—Race problems

UNITED STATES—*Continued*

Relations (diplomatic)

Catholic church
See Catholic church—Relations (diplomatic)—United States

Religious Institutions and affairs

Apostle to the affluent; suburban minister. W. Hedgepeth. Look 31:41 My 16 '67
Japanese view of religion in the U.S. H. Shimmi. Christian Cent 85:61-2 Ja 10 '68
See also
Catholic church—Relations (diplomatic)—United States
Catholic church in the United States
Christian Science
Church and state
Churches—United States
Lutheran church in the United States
Mennonites
Methodist church in the United States
Missions—United States
Mormons and Mormonism
Negroes in the United States—Religion
Presbyterian church in the United States
Presbyterian church in the United States (South)
Protestant churches—United States
Protestant Episcopal church
Puritans
United Church of Christ
United States—Church history
    also subhead Religious institutions and affairs under names of states, cities, e.g. Chicago—Religious institutions and affairs

Reserve forces

See United States—Armed forces—Reserves

Reserve officers training corps

Brush with the R.O.T.C. W. C. Findley. Christian Cent 84:1222-3 S 27 '67

Revenue

See also
Taxation—United States

Riots

After the long, hot summer, where do we go? E. W. Brooke. il Look 31:24-7 S 5 '67
American tragedy, 1967. A. Balk. Sat R 50:34 S 16 '67
Anarchy growing threat to big cities? il U S News 63:28-30 Ag 7 '67
Antiriot bill. Nat R 19:785 Jl 25 '67
Archie's ABCs. A. Moore. Sports Illus 27:9 Ag 21 '67
As outside world sees riots in America. il U S News 63:12 Ag 7 '67
As rioting spread, the search for answers. il U S News 63:26-8 Ag 14 '67
Billy Graham's plea to President Johnson; reprint from Washington star and Congressional record, July 21, 1966. D. Lawrence. U S News 63:92 Ag 7 '67
Blame for the riots as a Negro writer sees it; reprint. G. Schuyler. U S News 63:10 Ag 14 '67
Blow-up in the cities; cause of riots. New Repub 157:5-7 Ag 5 '67
Burning the fire trucks. Christian Cent 84:1059-60 Ag 23 '67
Cage and the curfew. il Newsweek 70:18-20 Ag 14 '67
Can a disorderly society survive? excerpts from The effects of planned, mass disobedience of our laws, September 1966. C. E. Whittaker. U S News 63:27 Jl 31 '67
Collective organizer. J. Burnham. Nat R 19:895 Ag 22 '67
Conspicuous irrationality. Christian Cent 84:987 Ag 2 '67
Crisis coverage; conference on the mass media and race relations at Columbia university. Newsweek 70:60+ O 30 '67
Cry of the ghetto. il Sat Eve Post 240:80 Ag 26 '67
Era of growing strife in U.S. il U S News 63:41-3 S 25 '67
Explosion in the cities; with editorial comment. il Bsns W p21-3, 124 Jl 29 '67
Fever chart. il Newsweek 70:18-19 Jl 31 '67
From anarchy to tyranny. Christian Cent 84:1035-6 Ag 16 '67
Great disgrace. E. J. Hughes. Newsweek 70:17 Ag 7 '67
Great society is a sick society. J. W. Fulbright. il N Y Times Mag p30-1+ Ag 20 '67; Discussion. p2 S 3; 42+ S 10 '67
Hot summers and short tempers; bill under way. Nation 205:36-7 Jl 17 '67
How long, oh Lord, how long? il Ebony 22:106-7 S '67

How to cool it; measures to avert racial violence in slums. il Time 89:21 Je 30 '67
How to start a riot. E. J. Younger. U S News 63:56-8 Ag 21 '67
How to start a riot; address, August 2, 1967. E. J. Younger. Vital Speeches 33:759-63 O 1 '67
If you have any doubts about Rap Brown inciting riots; excerpts from news conference, July 27, 1967. H. R. Brown. il U S News 63:8 Ag 7 '67
In cities, July was month of violence. U S News 63:26-7 Ag 7 '67
Insurers tot up riot tab. il Bsns W p26-7 Jl 29 '67
Is Castro behind guerrilla war in U.S. cities? il U S News 63:23-5 Ag 14 '67
Is war on poverty stirring up rioters? U S News 63:8 Jl 31 '67
Keeping it cool; attempts to temper the tone of riot coverage. Time 90:44 Jl 14 '67
LBJ's ideas on how to stop riots in the Nation's cities; address, July 27, 1967. L. B. Johnson. il U S News 63:56-7 Ag 7 '67; Same with title Rioting in the cities. Vital Speeches 33:642-4 Ag 15 '67
Maybe God will come and clean up this mess. R. Coles. il Atlan 220:103-6 O '67
Military appraisal of the threat to U.S. cities. R. B. Rigg. U S News 64:68-71 Ja 15 '68
Mind over mayhem. il Time 89:19 Je 23 '67
Negro militancy; a complicating dimension. Sci N 92:152-3 Ag 12 '67
Now: move in Congress to curb agitators. U S News 63:8 Jl 31 '67
Plague of riots. Newsweek 70:28+ Ag 7 '67
Politics as usual; Republican coordinating committee statement. Nation 205:99-100 Ag 14 '67
Poverty: phony excuse for riots? yes, says a key senator; excerpt from address, July 17, 1967. R. Byrd. U S News 63:14 Jl 31 '67
Psychiatrists seek secrets of the riots. J. H. Pollack. il Todays Health 45:24-7+ N '67
Quench riots, and look beyond. Life 63:4 Ag 4 '67
Race and the news media, ed. by P. L. Fisher and R. L. Lowenstein. Review
    Sat R 50:68 D 9 '67. S. W. Little
Race troubles: record of 109 cities. il U S News 63:28-30 Ag 14 '67
Racial stress and the mass media; address, September 21, 1967. E. W. Lower. Vital Speeches 34:53-9 N 1 '67
Racial violence inevitable or preventable? il Sr Schol 91:8-13 O 13 '67
Real story of the riots and who's behind them; excerpts from testimonies. il U S News 63:64-7 Ag 21 '67
Reason why; findings of U.S. civil rights commission special report. Newsweek 70:30 D 4 '67
Revolution or slave despair? W. V. Shannon. Commonweal 86:603-4 S 29 '67
Riot control. G. M. Chamberlain. il Am City 82:87-9+ F: 107-9 Mr '67
Riot forecast: more violence in new year. il U S News 64:62 Ja 8 '68
Riot season: how hot will it get? il U S News 62:23-4 Je 26 '67
Riots and our national response. J. M. Gessell. Christian Cent 84:1063-5 Ag 23 '67
Riots and politics: meaning for '68. il U S News 63:62 Ag 7 '67
Riots and revolution. F. M. Henley; R. A. Schroth. America 117:150-3 Ag 12 '67
Riots and root causes. Commonweal 86:483-4 Ag 11 '67
Riots: schools for revolution? comparative study of the French revolution of 1848 and the current Negro revolutions. L. Kampf. Nation 205:117-18 Ag 14 '67
Riots: the more there are, the less we understand. R. J. Samuelson. Science 157:663-5 Ag 11 '67; Reply. J. Boeke. 158:577 N 3 '67
Rising tide of racial violence. il U S News 63:7 Jl 10 '67
Seeds of hope; riots bringing end to apathy. America 117:169 Ag 19 '67
Shooting bloody; Community relations service recommendations for riot reporting. il Newsweek 70:69 Jl 24 '67
Speech that touched a tender nerve in Congress; excerpts from address, July 25, 1967. T. G. Abernethy. U S News 63:33 Ag 7 '67
Spreading fire. il Time 90:9-10 Jl 28 '67
Summer calculus. il Newsweek 69:31+ Je 26 '67
Summer riots. New Repub 156:8 Je 24 '67
This year's riot. New Repub 156:6 Ap 8 '67
Time of violence & tragedy. il Time 90:12-13 Ag 4 '67
U.S. race-riot outlook for '67; what Negro leaders predict. il U S News 62:42-5+ My 1 '67

UNITED STATES—Riots—*Continued*

Unrest and revolt, Humphrey's views; excerpts from address, July 31, 1967. H. H. Humphrey. U S News 63:10 Ag 14 '67

Urban riots: hottest summer yet. il Sr Schol 91:17-18 S 21 '67

Violence in the cities: a better place to live; address, July 31, 1967. J. V. Lindsay. Vital Speeches 33:674-7 S 1 '67

Violence; symposium. il Nation 205:101-7+ Ag 14 '67

Washington desk. G. R. Rosen. Duns R 90: 7-8 S '67

Watts to Detroit. Nat R 19:885+ Ag 22 '67

Way out of the exploding ghetto. B. Rustin. il N Y Times Mag p 16-17+ Ag 13 '67; Discussion. p67+ S 10 '67

We should be ashamed. D. D. Eisenhower. Read Digest 91:67-71 Ag '67

What can be done? il Newsweek 70:31-2 Ag 7 '67

What happens when rioters get into court. il U S News 63:52 Ag 28 '67

What has happened to America? R. M. Nixon. Read Digest 91:49-54 O '67

Whitey hasn't learned. New Repub 157:4 S 9 '67

Who riots and why. R. N. McMurry. il Nations Bsns 55:72-5 O '67

See also

Riot control

also subhead Riots under names of cities, e.g. Detroit—Riots

Rural electrification administration

Electric power: new uses, new sources. more demand; interview. W. J. Clapp. il U S News 62:74-8 Mr 27 '67

Rural recreation sites. il Parks & Rec 2:41+ O '67

Science and technology, Office of

Office of science and technology. P. H. Abelson. Science 156:173 Ap 14 '67

White House science office: report urges expanded role. B. Nelson. Science 156:50-1 Ap 7 '67

Securities and exchange commission

Are give-ups on the way out? SEC rules against commission splitting with regional exchanges. il Bsns W p 125-6+ Ja 14 '67

Big crash and the rocky road to reform. Sr Schol 90:6-7 Ap 21 '67

Funds talk it over with SEC; tough recommendations on the fund business. Bsns W p 118 Ap 1 '67

Mutual funds under fire: their side of the dispute; interview. F. S. Williams. U S News 63:80-2 S 18 '67

Mutual funds warm for a fight. Bsns W p 149 Je 17 '67

Profit reporting by divisions? T. J. Murray. il Duns R 89:29-31+ My '67

Reforming the funds. P. A. Samuelson. Newsweek 69:74 Mr 6 '67

Stiffer rules for mutuals? lower costs to investors; SEC's proposals. il U S News 62:118+ My 15 '67

Why the government is worried about the stock market; interview H. F. Owens. U S News 63:65-7 N 20 '67

Senate

See United States—Congress—Senate

Small business administration

Merchants count up the losses; riot damages. Bsns W p28 Ag 5 '67

Putting the poor out of business; unhappy career of the Economic opportunity loan program. M. Levy. il Nation 204:750-3 Je 12 '67

SBIC's get the pruning treatment. il Bsns W p84+ Je 10 '67

SCORE spells help for the small businessman. H. Tupper. Read Digest 90:19+ Mr '67

Social conditions

Addictive society; habitual users of narcotics. Christian Cent 84:331-2 Mr 15 '67

American wound. Commonweal 86:307 Je 2 '67

Challenge for free men in a mass society; with report by B. Hooper. il Life 62:60-74+ Ap 21 '67

Eight questions for 1968. A. Hacker. Sat R 51:102-3 Ja 6 '68

Empty society; excerpts from Massey lectures. P. Goodman; discussion. Commentary 43:26+ Mr '67

Hot summer hallucinogenics. Life 62:4 Je 2 '67

Poverty, inequality, and conflict. S. M. Miller and others. bibliog f il Ann Am Acad 373: 16-52 S '67

Sex: our changing times; address, March 27, 1967. W. I. Nichols. Vital Speeches 33:445-8 My 1 '67

Temper of our time, by E. Hoffer. Review Nat R 19:203-4 F 21 '67. A. W. Green Sat R 50:41-2 Ap 8 '67. M. R. Konvitz

Toward a communal society. D. Bell. il Life 62:112-14+ My 12 '67

U.S. domestic crisis? excerpts from address, December 27, 1967. J. W. Gardner. U S News 64:12 Ja 8 '68

See also

Child welfare—United States

Cities and towns—United States

Cost of living—United States

Crime and criminals—United States

Divorce—United States

Negroes in the United States

Poor—United States

United States—Population

Women—United States

Youth—United States

also subhead Social conditions under names of cities, states, e.g. New York (city)—Social conditions

Bibliography

Home scene (cont) W. L. Lucey. America 116:690+ My 6 '67

History

See United States—Social history

Social history

Babbitts & bohemians, by E. Stevenson. Review Atlan il 220:110-13 N '67. L. Kronenberger

Cultural roots of American law enforcement. W. G. Carleton. bibliog f Cur Hist 53:1-7+ Jl '67

History in a self-governing culture; address, December 29, 1966. R. F. Nichols. Am Hist R 72:411-24 Ja '67

Just around the corner: a highly selective history of the thirties, by R. Bendiner. Review Newsweek 69:106+ My 8 '67. S. Maloff Reporter 37:51-2 Ag 10 '67

See also

Education—United States—History

Negroes in the United States—History

Social life and customs

American way of life, by A. Montagu. Review Sat R 50:63+ Ap 8 '67. C. M. Curtis

Challenge for free men in a mass society; with report by B. Hooper. il Life 62:60-74+ Ap 21 '67

Protestant establishment, by E. D. Baltbell. Review Nation 204:439-41 Ap 3 '67. V. K. Dibble

Social life of married couples: its pleasures and problems; survey findings. M. M. Hunt. il McCalls 94:67-9+ My '67

Some questions about the study of American character in the twentieth century. D. Riesman. bibliog f Ann Am Acad 370:36-47 Mr '67

Swinging Americans. A. Chamberlin. Mlle 64: 222-3+ Ap '67

See also

Christmas—United States

Drinking customs

Suburban life

also subhead Social life and customs under names of cities, e.g. New York (city)—Social life and customs

Social policy

Autopsy for a Great society. P. Schrag. Sat R 50:63 Je 17 '67

Bigger benefits, bigger taxes: latest idea for Great society; with chart. U S News 62:28-30 F 6 '67

Death of a slogan: the Great society 1967. R. Lekachman. Commentary 43:56-61 Ja '67; Discussion. 43:16+ My '67

Freedom's last frontier: business; address. November 17, 1966. L. H. Rogers, 2d. Vital Speeches 33:333-9 Mr 15 '67

Fulbright on riots. K. Crawford. Newsweek 70:28 Ag 21 '67

Future-planners. A. Kopland. New Repub 156:19-23 F 25 '67; Discussion. 156:36-7 Mr 11; 34 Mr 25 '67

Grapes of wrath. K. Crawford. Newsweek 70: 36 Ag 7 '67

Great society as a myth; adaptation of address; reprint. W. Stringfellow. Cath World 205:83-9 My '67

UNITED STATES—Social policy—*Continued*
Great society faces future; changes Congress is making; cuts in spending. il U S News 63:32-3 Jl 10 '67
How much is enough in helping the poor? Bsns W p24-6 Jl 29 '67
Integrating America, the problems; interview. J. W. Gardner. il U S News 62:64-9 My 8 '67
Is Congress neglecting the poor? excerpts from address, July 31, 1967. G. H. Mahon. U S News 63:46 Ag 14 '67
Is the Great society now a sick society? excerpts from address, August 8, 1967. J. W. Fulbright. U S News 63:16 Ag 21 '67
Letter from Washington; suggested rehabilitation of American cities. R. H. Rovere. New Yorker 43:88+ Ag 19 '67
Mrs LBJ: saleslady for Great society. il U S News 62:22 Mr 27 '67
1967 State of the Union message; excerpts. L. B. Johnson. Cur Hist 52:238-40+ Ap '67
Price of empire; address, August 8, 1967. J. W. Fulbright. bibliog Vital Speeches 33: 678-82 S 1 '67; Excerpts. U S News 63:16 Ag 21 '67
Price of hope offered and then denied; curtailing or eliminating educational and social programs. R. H. Smith. Pub W 192:38 Jl 31 '67
Priority of worries. K. Crawford. Newsweek 70:27 Ag 28 '67
Rebuilding the welfare system. Bsns W p200 N 18 '67
Social goals and indicators for American society; symposium, ed. by B. M. Gross. bibliog f il Ann Am Acad 371:1-177 My; 373:1-218 S '67
State of the Union. il Sci N 91:55+ Ja 21 '67
State of the Union; a Republican appraisal; address, January 19, 1967. G. R. Ford. Vital Speeches 33:260-4 F 15 '67; Excerpts. U S News 62:73 Ja 30 '67
State of the Union; address, January 10, 1967. L. B. Johnson. Vital Speeches 33: 226-34 F 1 '67; Excerpts. Dept State Bul 56:158-63 Ja 30 '67
Taking the Great society seriously. M. Harrington; discussion. Harper 234:4, 81-4 F '67
Ten commitments. J. W. Gardner. Sat R 50: 39-40 Jl 1 '67
Two issues in planning; excerpts from address. P. Goodman. Commentary 44:75-7 Ag '67
What next? need for new programs to ease the ghettos' anguish. il Time 90:11-12 Ag 11 '67
Where it stands: Congress and LBJ's Great society program. Sr Schol 90:17 F 24 '67

Standards, National bureau of
Concept of a national measurement system. R. D. Huntoon. bibliog il Science 158:67-71 O 6 '67
Electron beams: National bureau of standards and the new technology. H. W. Koch. bibliog il Science 156:321-8 Ap 21 '67
Joint institute for laboratory astrophysics; National bureau of standards and University of Colorado. R. H. Garstang. il Sky & Tel 33:150-2 Mr '67
National standard reference data system. E. L. Brady and M. B. Wallenstein. bibliog il Science 156:754-62 My 12 '67

State, Department of
Anatomy of the State department, by S. Simpson. Review
Sat R 50:30-1 Je 3 '67. R. I. Rubin
Department issues 1967 edition of Treaties in force. Dept State Bul 56:288 F 20 '67
Department names advisory panel on international law. Dept State Bul 57:661 N 13 '67
Exit McNamara. Nation 205:610-11 D 11 '67
First team: foreign-policy advisers. il Newsweek 70:23 Jl 17 '67
Labyrinth in foggy bottom; excerpts from The reds and the blacks. W. Attwood. Atlan 219:45-50 F '67; Same abr. Read Digest 90: 121-4 Je '67
National policy statement on international book and library activities; text. Library J 92:515 F 1 '67; Same. ALA Bul 61:186 F '67
Nazi murder plot; excerpts from While six million died. A. D. Morse. il Look 31:49-52+ N 14 '67
No. 2 man at State is a cooler-downer. V. S. Navasky. il N Y Times Mag p3+ D 24 '67
Publications. See issues of Department of state bulletin
Relativity in foreign policy. T. L. Hughes. For Affairs 45:670-82 Jl '67

Rusk enigma: who runs the State department? S. Simpson. Nation 204:294-9 Mr 6 '67
State department in trouble? what's going on inside. il U S News 63:45-7 Jl 3 '67
State examines itself. Nation 204:291-2 **Mr 6** '67
Tragic gap; concerning editorial of September. 9, 1967. N. Cousins. Sat R 50:24+ O 21 '67
See also
United States—Foreign service

African affairs, Bureau of
Advisory panel named for African affairs bureau. Dept State Bul 56:651 Ap 24 '67

Educational and cultural affairs, Bureau of
State department's poetic powerhouse; K. Louchheim. H. Ehrlich. il Look 31:118+ O 17 '67

International scientific and technological affairs, Office of
Pollack to head State science office. D. S. Greenberg. Science 157:292 Jl 21 '67
Science, foreign affairs, and the State department; address, May 17, 1967. H. Pollack. Dept State Bul 56:910-17 Je 19 '67
State department science: how good? F. Sartwell. Sci N 91:123 F 4 '67

Near Eastern and South Asian affairs, Bureau of
Advisers named for Near Eastern and South Asian bureau. Dept State Bul 56:72 Ja 9 '67

Overseas schools, Office of
Road to Taipei: University-to-school project. R. Forbes and H. R. Wire. il Am Ed 3:5-7 N '67

Science adviser, Office of
See United States—State, Department of —International scientific and technological affairs, Office of

Statistics
And fifty years of capitalism; Time essay. Time 90:33 N 17 '67
So proudly we hail. New Repub 157:8 Jl 15 '67
What the 1970's will bring. il Changing T 22: 6-16 Ja '68
See also
United States—Census

Subversive activities control board
Safe target. Time 90:19 N 3 '67

Supreme court
Are judges remaking America? il U S News 63:36-8 D 18 '67
Chief; influence of E. Warren. il Time 90:108+ N 17 '67
Chosing a justice. Time 89:75 Ap 21 '67
Discrimination in reverse? D. Lawrence. U S News 63:88 S 4 '67
Guessing about obscenity. Time 90:50 N 3 '67
Ignore Earl Warren? Newsweek 70:30 O 16 '67
Is the Supreme court really supreme? E. H. Methvin. il Read Digest 91:80-5 Jl '67
Justice under law: Hugo L. Black. P. W. Romero. Negro Hist Bul 30:12-14 F '67
Kite flying & other games. Time 90:16 Jl 28 '67
LBJ's turn to change the Court. il U S News 62:70 Mr 13 '67
Negro justice; first Negro associate justice. il Time 89:18 Je 23 '67
On the obscene scene. Reporter 36:10 Je 29 '67
Shift in the Supreme court; what one new justice can mean. il U S News 62:67-8 Ap 24 '67
Supreme court asks a question: is it fair? S. Alsop. il Sat Eve Post 240:42-4+ O 21 '67
U.S. Supreme court. il Sr Schol 91:36-7 O 5 '67
What the session holds. Time 90:49 O 20 '67
With another liberal on High court. U S News 63:21 S 11 '67
With Mr Marshall on the Supreme court. il U S News 62:12-13 Je 26 '67

Decisions
Angelic vision of the Warren court: New York laws designed to keep subversives off the staffs and faculties of public schools and state colleges declared unconstitutional. Nat R 19:122 F 7 '67
Approving dual citizenship. Time 89:76 Je 9 '67
Blow to bank mergers; Supreme court backs Justice's antitrusters, takes a dim view of Bank merger act of 1966. Bsns W p23 Ap 1 '67

UNITED STATES—Supreme court—Decisions
—*Continued*
Clorox case; Supreme court dissolves P&G-Clorox merger. il Consumer Rep 32:360-3 Jl '67
Combing out the bugs; new standards for snooping. Newsweek 71:14 Ja 1 '68
Cops, crooks and bugs. Nat R 19:676 Je 27 '67
Cop's right(?) to stop and frisk; decisions the Supreme court must make. F. P. Graham. il N Y Times Mag p44-5+ D 10 '67
Court raps price cuts; regional price differences illegal. Bsns W p50 Ap 29 '67
Court v. King; upholds 1963 conviction. Time 89:20 Je 23 '67
Crime, confessions and the Supreme court; Miranda decision. G. L. Chamberlain. America 117:32-4 Jl 8 '67
Criminal and the law; excerpts from Lawyers and laws. M. Mayer. il Sat Eve Post 240: 25-7+ F 11 '67
Feinberg law, 6-3, 4-5; loyalty oaths declared unconstitutional. America 116:200-1 F 11 '67
Get a warrant; Supreme court rules on warrantless searches of private property. Time 89:48 Je 16 '67
Good Court gets better. Christian Cent 84: 827-8 Je 28 '67
Helping prosecutors; Supreme court decision on mere-evidence rule. Time 89:75 Je 9 '67
High court denies Stevens' plea. Pub W 191: 43 My 29 '67
High court dissolves a sudsy conglomerate; P&G-Clorox merger decision. il Bsns W p40-1 Ap 15 '67
High court hints a softer tone. Bsns W p40 Je 17 '67
High court puts off a wedding; ruling against Penn-Central merger. Bsns W p24 Ap 1 '67
High court questions need of dam on Snake River. Am For 73:38 Jl '67
High court snaps into action; major decisions in business area. Bsns W p50+ D 9 '67
In the matter of Gault; excerpts from United States Supreme court decision and from the dissent, May 15, 1967. Cur Hist 53:112-13+ Ag '67
Inside story of the Marshall role in the school-desegregation decision; excerpts from address, December 28, 1961. A. H. Kelly. U S News 62:13 Je 26 '67
Is it wrong to handcuff the police? W. J. Dempsey, jr. Cath World 204:264-9 F '67
Is the Supreme court really supreme? E. H. Methvin. il Read Digest 91:80-5 Jl '67
Limits of libel. il Newsweek 69:76-7 Je 26 '67
Loyalty laws; Supreme court upholds academic freedom. L. J. Carter. Science 155: 987 F 24 '67
Massiah v. United States; text of majority opinion and excerpts from minority dissent. Cur Hist 53:43-5 Jl '67
Mergers make FTC feathers fly. il Bsns W p 124+ My 6 '67
Miranda v. Arizona discussed. Am City 82:52 Je '67
Miranda v. Arizona; excerpts. Cur Hist 52: 359-62+ Je '67
Mr Jones goes to Washington; Supreme court will hear arguments in major open-housing case. J. Galloway. Commonweal 87:374-5 D 22 '67
Move to moderation. il Time 89:45-6+ Je 23 '67
Obscenity cases; May 8 decision triggers R. Ginzberg appeal. A. M. Bickel. New Repub 156:15-17 My 27 '67
Open issue; Supreme court reverses California's 1964 initiative vote on open housing. Newsweek 69:30+ Je 12 '67
Passional I; discussion of pornography. S. J. Tonsor. Nat R 19:208-10 F 21 '67
Police, judges tell Congress; criminals get the breaks; excerpts from hearings by Senate judiciary committee's subcommittee on criminal laws and procedures. il U S News 62:44-5 Mr 27 '67
Right to associate; Right to be left alone. America 118:2-3 Ja 6 '68
Saying no to Proposition 14; California supreme court decision upheld by U.S. Supreme court. il Time 89:75 Je 9 '67
Self-reversal; Feinberg law. Time 89:47 F 3 '67
Significant decisions in labor cases. See issues of Monthly labor review
Supreme court decisions that changed U.S. U S News 63:37 D 18 '67
Supreme court extends press freedoms in overruling Desperate hours verdict. Pub W 191: 221 Ja 23 '67
Supreme court; internal security cases. A. M. Bickel. New Repub 158:21-2 Ja 6 '68
Supreme court overturns Warren Spahn decision. Pub W 191:43 My 29 '67

Supreme court review, 1966; ed. by P. B. Kurland. Review
  Commentary 44:103-7 S '67. A. S. Goldstein
Supreme court rules; treat juvenile offenders like adults. U S News 62:12 My 29 '67
Supreme court versus corporate efficiency. R. H. Bork. Fortune 76:92-3+ Ag '67
Supreme court; what can business expect? F. P. Graham. il Duns R 90:29-31+ S '67
Term's end; major decisions of 1966; with case histories. J. J. Kilpatrick. il Nat R 19:789-93+ Jl 25 '67
Toward free and responsible speech. Nat R 19:673-4 Je 27 '67
Unconstitutional bugging; Fourth amendment is applicable. New Repub 158:11 Ja 6 '68
Unplugging bugging. Time 90:43 D 29 '67
Vital informers; question of the secret informer. Time 89:73 Mr 31 '67
Waiting for fresh legal guidelines; business decisions the Supreme court must make. Bsns W p38-9 S 23 '67
Warren revolution, by L. B. Bozell. Review
  Nat R 19:642-4 Je 13 '67. M. Diamond
What did the Supreme court say? journals of the Court opinions. G. Cranberg. il Sat R 50:90-2 Ap 8 '67; Discussion 50:82 My 13 '67
What High court rules now on school integration; decisions on other cases. il U S News 63:49 O 23 '67
When bicycle maker peddles alone; Supreme court decision concerning Schwinn's marketing system. Bsns W p39-40 Jl 1 '67
Will boycott rule put brake on technology? labor's right to resist automation. il Bsns W p 104+ Ap 29 '67

History
Ex parte McCardle; judicial impotency? the Supreme court and Reconstruction reconsidered. S. I. Kutler. bibliog f Am Hist R 72:835-51 Ap '67

Tariff commission
Tariff commission to report on textile and apparel industries; statement, October 4, 1967. L. B. Johnson. Dept State Bul 57: 529 O 23 '67

Technical assistance program
See Technical assistance, American

Territories and possessions
See also
Trust Territory of the Pacific Islands
Virgin Islands

Trade policy
See United States—Commerce

Transportation, Department of
DOT budget request imminent, new House committee set up; special subcommittee. H. Taylor. Tech W 20:15 Ap 3 '67
Hot seat; concerning first secretary of the department of transportation. R. B. Parke. il Flying 80:30 My '67
Off on the wrong track; ICC rebuffs effort to influence rates. Bsns W p39 Je 24 '67
$600 million for R&D seen in fiscal '69. H. Taylor. il Tech W 20:22-4+ Je 5 '67
Third-generation, 300-mph trains urged; study by Office of high speed ground transportation. J. Rhea. Tech W 20:34 Mr 20 '67
Transportation outlook. Bsns W p63 Jl 1 '67
Welcome to chaos. W. J. Coughlin. Tech W 20:50 Je 19 '67

Travel regulations
See Travel regulations

Travel service
Different kind of shortage; foreign visitors. il U S News 62:98-9 F 27 '67

Treasury department
Low-blow for the working girl; amused press reaction to dismissal of clerks in 1869. E. M. Halliday. il Am Heritage 18:98-9 Ap '67
Prudent tax policy. P. A. Samuelson. Newsweek 69:86 Mr 27 '67
Some pay, some don't; inquiry on unrelated business activity of tax-exempt organizations. New Repub 157:5-6 Jl 22 '67
See also
United States—Internal revenue service

Treaties
American empire; excerpts from Pax Americana. R. Steel. Commonweal 86:335-9 Je 9 '67
Department issues 1967 edition of Treaties in force. Dept State Bul 56:288 F 20 '67

UNITED STATES—Treaties—*Continued*
Forty-three places U.S. can get into war. il
U S News 62:36 Je 5 '67
Fulbright's guerrilla war; national commit-
ment hearings. W. V. Shannon. Common-
weal 86:544-5 S 8 '67; Reply. R. V. Ellinger.
86:618-19 S 29 '67
Treaty information. See issues of Department
of state bulletin
United States collective defense arrangements;
map. Dept State Bul 57:460-1 O 9 '67
While you weren't looking; Senate ratifies a
new international treaty. New Repub 157:7
Jl 8 '67
See also
United   States—Commercial   treaties   and
agreements

Japan
Okinawa's future and Far-East security;
hope of reversion of 1951 peace treaties.
M. E. Weinstein. Reporter 37:39-40 N 2 '67

Panama
As treaty dispute heats up, terms of U.S.-
Panama pacts; reprint. il U S News 63:71
Ag 28 '67
Deal on Panama Canal: rough transit ahead;
new treaties. il U S News 63:41 Jl 10 '67
Panama Canal; proposed treaties; address,
September 2, 1967. S. Thurmond. Vital
Speeches 34:103-6 D 1 '67
Speaking softly; U.S. agrees to surrender
sovereignty over the Canal Zone. il News-
week 70:25-6 Jl 17 '67
Terms of the new treaty for the Panama
Canal. H. Rosenhouse. New Repub 157:10-11
Jl 22 '67
U.S. and Panama reach agreement on texts
of new canal treaties. Dept State Bul 57:65
Jl 17 '67

Russia
Anti-missive missive: question of legisla-
tive fate of the U.S.-Soviet consular treaty.
il Newsweek 69:32 F 6 '67
Bipartisan span; consular treaty ratified.
Newsweek 69:38 Mr 27 '67
Bridges or spies; consular controversy. Sr
Schol 90:15 F 17 '67
Casting out devils; congressional struggle
over the consular treaty. Commonweal 85:
583-4 F 24 '67
Clearing it with Hoover; consular treaty.
New Repub 156:9 F 4 '67
Constructive initiatives in East-West rela-
tions; address, February 17, 1967. Dept
State Bul 56:411-12 Mr 13 '67
Consular treaty, a bridge to Russia? U S
News 62:16 Mr 27 '67
Horatius at the bridge; proposed consular
treaty. Newsweek 69:35 F 13 '67
Matter of mutual advantage; consular treaty.
Time 89:19-20 F 3 '67
No two sides: proposed Soviet-American con-
sular treaty. Nation 204:227-8 F 20 '67
Not right now, please; proposed consular ac-
cord with the Soviet Union. Nat R 19:178+
F 21 '67
President urges ratification of Consular pact
with U.S.S.R.; statement, February 2, 1967.
L. B. Johnson. Dept State Bul 56:287-8 F
20 '67
Righteous wreckers; Senate debate over a
consular convention between Moscow and
Washington. E. J. Hughes. Newsweek 69:21
F 20 '67
Secretary Rusk urges congressional support
for consular convention with the Soviet
Union; statement, January 23, 1967. D.
Rusk. Dept State Bul 56:247-50 F 13 '67
Senate okays pact, 66-28; consular treaty.
Sr Schol 90:17 Mr 31 '67
Symbolic span; U.S.-Soviet consular treaty
ratified by Senate. Time 89:15 Mr 24 '67
Whys of a treaty with the Russians. il U S
News 62:51-2 Mr 13 '67

Thailand
In the pattern; new agreement. Commonweal
87:323-4 D 8 '67

Vital statistics
See also
Birth rate—United States
Mortality

Weather bureau
Pilots' weather outlook. R. Blodget. il Flying
81:38-43 Ag; 53-5 S '67
See also
United States—Environmental science serv-
ices administration

Wildlife services, Division of
See United States—Interior, Department
of—Sport fisheries and wildlife, Bureau of

Womens air force
Our flying Nightingales in Vietnam. K.
Drake. il Read Digest 91:73-9 D '67

Work projects administration
See also
Federal art project
Federal writers project
UNITED   STATES   agricultural   stabilization
and conservation service
Crop allotments: power behind the cotton.
P. Marcuse. il Nation 206:43-6 Ja 8 '68
UNITED STATES air force academy, Colorado
Springs
Crack in the façade; latest cheating scandal.
il Newsweek 69:117 Mr 13 '67
Honorable code? Sr Schol 90:20 Mr 17 '67
Scandal in Colorado Springs. Time 89:66 Mr 3
'67
Why the cadets cheat. J. A. Heise. il Nation
204:622-6 My 15 '67; Discussion. 205:2+ Jl
3 '67
UNITED STATES amateur golf championship.
See Golf—Tournaments
UNITED STATES and Canada; United States
and Mexico; etc. See Canada and the United
States; Mexico and the United States; etc.
UNITED STATES and the European war. See
European war, 1914-1918—United States
UNITED STATES book exchange
U.S. book exchange seeks expansion. Library
J 92:2498 Jl '67
UNITED STATES camera (periodical)
U.S. camera achievement awards. il U S
Camera 30:39-45 N '67
U.S. camera achievement awards presenta-
tions. il U S Camera 31:62-3 Ja '68
UNITED STATES-Canadian committee on trade
and economic affairs. See Joint United
States-Canadian committee on trade and
economic affairs
UNITED STATES Catholic relief services. See
National Catholic welfare conference
UNITED STATES cavalry. See United States
—Army—Cavalry
UNITED STATES coast guard academy, New
London, Conn.
New hands to staff proud ranks. G. Silk. il
Life 63:30-43 Jl 7 '67
UNITED STATES conference on church and
society. See National council of the church-
es of Christ in the United States of America
UNITED   STATES   flag.   See   Flags—United
States
UNITED STATES foreign service. See United
States—Foreign service
UNITED STATES Grand prix. See Automobile
racing
UNITED STATES gypsum company
Trials of man from big business. Life 62:
60 My 12 '67
UNITED STATES in art
See also
West in art
UNITED STATES industries, incorporated
Taking USI out of the limelight. Bsns W
p51-2+ Ja 21 '67
UNITED   STATES   information   agency.   See
United States—Information agency
UNITED STATES-Japan committee on scien-
tific cooperation. See Joint United States-
Japan committee on scientific cooperation
UNITED   STATES-Japan   cooperative   science
program. See Science—International aspects
UNITED STATES lawn tennis association
Sporting scene. H. W. Wind. New Yorker
43:94+ S 30 '67
Vote for the 19th century; USLTA against
open tennis. B. Collins. Sports Illus 26:76-
7 Je 12 '67
UNITED STATES marshals
Last frontier marshal; condensation. F. Miller.
il Read Digest 90:201-4+ Je '67
UNITED STATES military academy, West
Point
High life at Saratoga, 1837; excerpt from
letter. S. Dawson. il Am Heritage 18:107
Je '67
Tom Cahill: Army's accidental coach. T.
Cohane. il Look 31:116-19+ N 28 '67
Well, ma, I'm still here; goat of the gradu-
ating class. H. H. Martin. il Sat Eve Post
240:67a N 18 '67
West Point goes to war. il Newsweek 70:46-56
Jl 10 '67
UNITED STATES military public health as-
sistance program. See United States—
Agency for international development

UNITED STATES national student association
Black power: five shades of gray. F. Mills-paugh. Mlle 66:94+ Ja '68
CIA and the kiddies. il Newsweek 69:25-7 F 27 '67
C.I.A. and the students; with editorial comment. W. C. McWilliams. Commonweal 85:611-14 Mr 3 '67
CIA controversy: secret aid bared; with press comments. Sr Schol 90:16-17 Mr 3 '67
CIA: how does it fit in an open society? il Sr Schol 90:8-16+ Mr 31 '67; Correction. 90:9 My 19 '67
CIA stooges. New Repub 156:5-6 F 25 '67
Modern dilemma: two views of the NSA-CIA crisis by present and former NSA officers. R. G. Stearns; W. D. Shaul. il Mlle 65:232-3+ Ag '67
National rally for student power. J. Brann. Nation 205:658-60 D 18 '67
NSA: a national student forum. S. C. Schodde. Sch & Soc 95:86-7 F 4 '67
National student association congress; with editorial comment. P. J. Weber. America 117:236-7, 251-2 S 9 '67
NSA's 20th; annual congress. Nat R 19:945-6 S 5 '67
New NSA; twentieth congress. N. White. New Repub 157:11 S 2 '67
Now it's student power; annual congress. B. Paisner. il Life 63:91-2 O 20 '67
Of many things; CIA and NSA. T. N. Davis. America 116:inside cover F 25 '67
Preserving democracy, C.I.A. style. H. K. Flad and M. F. Flad. Commonweal 85:614-15 Mr 3 '67
Repairing an image. Newsweek 70:55 Ag 28 '67
Silent service. il Time 89:13-17 F 24 '67
Spies for C.I.A. or deserving students? P. G. Altbach. Christian Cent 84:352-4 Mr 15 '67
Student power! Newsweek 70:49 S 4 '67
Student power at College Park; 20th congress. R. Blumenthal. Nation 205:165 S 4 '67
When the cover was blown. il U S News 62:97 Mr 13 '67
Why the CIA gave money to U.S. college students. US News 62:10 F 27 '67

Caricatures and cartoons
Viewpoints; as cartoonists view the CIA-NSA controversy. Sr Schol 90:13 Mr 31 '67
UNITED STATES naval oceanographic office, Suitland, Md.
Star III sub leased by NOO for ocean-floor mapping. R. W. Niblock. Tech W 20:40 F 27 '67
UNITED STATES naval postgraduate school, Monterey, Calif.
In Monterey the navy asks you in. il Sunset 139:40+ Jl '67
UNITED STATES Open golf championship. See Golf—Tournaments
UNITED STATES plywood corporation-Champion papers incorporated merger. See Business consolidations and mergers
UNITED STATES power squadrons, incorporated
Free boating education. il Motor B 120:106 Ag '67
Is USPS for me? C. Schrage. Yachting 123:54 Ja '68
Underway with the USPS. See issues of Motor boating
What USPS means. C. Schrage. Yachting 121:57 Ja '67
With the power squadrons. C. Schrage. See issues of Yachting
UNITED STATES-Russia air agreement. See 'Aviation—International aspects
UNITED STATES savings bonds. See Bonds, Government
UNITED STATES steel corporation
Bigger job at big steel; new president. Bsns W p37 Je 3 '67
It's Gott to be good; new president. Time 89:102 Je 9 '67
New boss at the Corporation; E. H. Gott. il Bsns W p 140-2+ Jl 8 '67
Recasting a basic industry; interview. R. Blough. il Nations Bsns 55:54-5+ S '67
UNITED STATES student press association
Exploring the gap; meeting. il Newsweek 69:88 F 20 '66
UNITED STATES tax court building. See Courthouses
UNITED STATES travel service. See United States—Travel service
UNITED STATES women's Open golf championship. See Golf—Tournaments
UNITED steelworkers of America
Bargaining brightens in can talks; wages on productivity basis. Bsns W p 101-2 Ja 13 '68

Merger toughens metal unions; MMSW merger into USW. Bsns W p 104 Ja 28 '67
New slices for Kaiser's melon? Kaiser steel-United steelworkers long-range sharing plan. il Bsns W p 149-50 Mr 4 '67
Steel tries to break an old bind; asks USW to end crisis bargaining. Bsns W p 166 N 18 '67
Tough stands stymie a copper settlement; workers set to strike eight companies. il Bsns W p 111-12 Jl 8 '67
USW signs holdout; Mesta machine co. Bsns W p66 Je 10 '67
Walkouts hurt the USW. Bsns W p56 N 4 '67
UNITED steelworkers of America-International union of mine, mill and smelter workers merger. See Trade unions—Consolidations and mergers
UNITED technology center. See United aircraft corporation—United technology center
UNITED world federalists
United world federalists assembly. H. Y. Williams. Christian Cent 84:1077 Ag 23 '67
UNIVAC computers. See Computers—Digital computers
UNIVERSAL and international exhibition of 1967. See Montreal—Worlds fair, 1967
UNIVERSAL automatic map compilation equipment. See Mapping, Aerial—Equipment
UNIVERSAL city. See Moving picture studios
UNIVERSAL declaration of human rights
Human rights day 10 December 1967; texts of messages. C. Manescu; Thant. UN Mo Chron 4:i-iv D '67
Human rights treaties: why is the U.S. stalling? W. Korey. For Affairs 54:414-24 Ap '67
UNIVERSE
Antimatter and creation. A. Ewing. il Sci N 91:64+ Ja 21 '67
Cosmological element production. R. V. Wagoner. biblig il Science 155:1369-76 Mr 17 '67
Data, not answers; evidence for big bang comes from study of quasars. Sci N 91:111 F 4 '67
Primeval fireball. P. J. E. Peebles and D. T. Wilkinson. il Sci Am 216:28-37 bibliog(p 155) Je '67
See also
Cosmogony
Cosmology
Earth
Galactic systems
Harmony of the spheres
Man
Milky way
UNIVERSITIES. See Colleges and universities
UNIVERSITY bookstores. See College bookstores
UNIVERSITY extension
Community service; tuition-free Ithaca neighborhood college. Time 90:82 N 17 '67
UNIVERSITY government. See Colleges and universities—Administration
UNIVERSITY governors. See College officials
UNIVERSITY libraries. See College libraries
UNIVERSITY of Southern California. See Southern California university, Los Angeles
UNIVERSITY of Sussex. See Colleges and universities—England
UNIVERSITY of Texas. See Texas. University, Austin
UNIVERSITY of the United Nations. See United Nations university (proposed)
UNIVERSITY of Toronto. See Toronto. University
UNIVERSITY presidents. See College presidents
UNIVERSITY presses
AAUP views publishing scene in Canada and abroad; symposium. il Pub W 192:27-31 Jl 24 '67
Challenging future of scholarly publishing. M. Muntyan; M. Jeanneret. il Sat R 50:14-17 Je 10 '67
Literature of film. A. Knight. Sat R 50:51+ N 4 '67
Professional seminars mark annual meeting of AAUP; symposium; with editorial comment. il Pub W 192:22-33, 38 Jl 3 '67
Publishing in two worlds; summary of address. R. W. Shugg. Pub W 193:39-43 Ja 8 '68
Quarter-century of milestones. Sat R 50:31-2+ Je 10 '67
Scholarly madness. il Time 90:39 Jl 7 '67
Trade winds; news from various presses. D. B. Sutherland. Sat R 50:10+ Je 10 '67
University approach; reprint. D. P. Geddes. Sat R 50:24+ Je 10 '67
See also
Association of American university presses
Toronto university press

UNIVERSITY professors. See College professors and instructors

UNIVERSITY regents. See College officials

UNIVERSITY research. See Colleges and universities—Research

UNIVERSITY students. See College students

UNIVERSITY-to-school project. See United States—State, Department of—Overseas schools, Office of

UNIVERSITY trustees. See College trustees

UNKNOWN soldier and his wife; drama. See Ustinov, P.

UNMARRIED mothers. See Mothers, Unmarried

UNMARRIED women. See Single women

UNRUH, Jesse Marvin
Jesse Unruh: the scholar as ringmaster. H. Sutton. por Sat R 50:25 S 23 '67

UNSINKABLE lifeboats. See Lifeboats, Unsinkable

UNTERECKER, John
Fish, 1936-1940: Buffalo, New York; 1965; Collioure, France; poems. Yale R 56:432-3 Mr '67

UNTERMEYER, Louis
Conrad Aiken: our best known unread poet. Sat R 50:28-9+ N 25 '67
Meters of wisdom and innocence. Sat R 50: 31 D 2 '67
Poet or poetaster? Sat R 50:27 Jl 1 '67
Way of seeing and saying. Sat R 50:31+ My 6 '67

UNTI, Gloria
San Francisco story: a dancer rocks the slums. G. B. Leonard. il pors Look 31: 94-6 F 7 '67

UPDIKE, John
Antigua; poem. New Yorker 42:46 F 11 '67
Books (cont) New Yorker 43:223-4+ D 2 '67
Memories of Anguilla, 1960; poem. New Repub 157:21 N 11 '67
Museums and women; story. New Yorker 43: 57-61 N 18 '67
Subway love; poem. New Repub 156:26 My 20 '67
Taste of metal; story. New Yorker 43:49-51 Mr 11 '67
(tr) See Evtushenko, E. A. Restaurant for two; Ballad about nuggets

about

John Updike: chronicler of the time of the death of God. K. Hamilton. Christian Cent 84:745-8 Je 7 '67

UPDIKE, S. J. and Hicks, G. P.
Reagentless substrate analysis with immobilized enzymes. bibliog Science 158:270-2 O 13 '67

UPHAUS, Robert A. and Katz, J. J.
Deuterium isotope effect on carbon isotope fractionation in photosynthesis. bibliog Science 155:324-5 Ja 20 '67

UPHOLSTERY
Big bold stitches. il House & Gard 131:148-9 My '67
Complete recovery. il House B 109:52+ My '67
Here's how to make removable upholstery. il Am Home 70:58 O '67
Ins and outs of buying unholstered furniture. il Good H 165:188+ O '67
See also
Automobiles—Upholstery

Terminology

Upholstered furniture terms. il Am Home 70: 46 Je '67

UPPER classes
Beautiful people, by M. Bender. Review
Reporter 37:39-40+ N 30 '67. G. Culligan
Protestant establishment, by E. D. Baltzell. Review
Nation 204:439-41 Ap 3 '67. V. K. Dibble
Saratoga story. il Time 90:56+ Ag 18 '67
Upper class in eastern Europe. L. Tyrmand. il Reporter 38:14-19 Ja 11 '68

UPPER hand; story. See Benson, A.

UPPSALA, Sweden
Uppsala 1968. Christian Cent 84:707-8 My 31 '67

UPSIDE-down cake. See Cake

UPTON, Miller
If this be heresy; address, April 26, 1967. Vital Speeches 34:37-9 N 1 '67; Excerpts with title It's time to stand up for the upperdog. por U S News 63:62-3 Jl 10 '67

UPWARD bound (program) See Socially handicapped children—Education

URANIUM
Controlled technology; gas-centrifuge process for production of uranium 235. Sci Am 216: 50 Je '67
Policy on uranium; Australia. W. A. Scholes. il Sci N 92:278 S 16 '67
Primary oxidation variation and distribution of uranium and thorium in a lava flow. N. D. Watkins and others. bibliog il Science 155:579-81 F 3 '67
Tight lid on U-235 production method; using gas centrifuge for uranium separation. il Sci N 91:327-8 Ap 8 '67
Uranium distribution in rocks by fission-track registration in Lexan plastic. J. D. Kleeman and J. F. Lovering. bibliog il Science 156:512-13 Ap 28 '67

URANIUM bullets. See Bullets

URANIUM mines and mining
New boom in uranium as peace needs grow; report of survey by AEC. il U S News 63: 64-5 O 16 '67

Safety devices and measures

Carcinogenic mines; Public contracts act invoked. D. Sanford. New Repub 156:5-6 Je 3 '67
Is uranium mining a hazard to health? battle between government and mine operators. il Bsns W p 107-8+ Je 3 '67
Radon daughters and the federal government. M. Viorst and J. V. Reistrup. Bul Atomic Sci 23:25-9 O '67

United States

Uranium industry gets new punch. il Bsns W p72-4 N 25 '67
Uranium mining: doubly risky; radioactive dust causing lung cancer. il Sci N 91:469-70 My 20 '67; Reply. A. M. Keefe. 91:589-90 Je 24 '67

URARTU
Ancient Ararat; discovery of Urartian treasures at Altintepe. T. Özgüç. il Sci Am 216:38-46 bibliog(p 150) Mr '67

URBAN America, Incorporated
What's needed for new cities. il Am City 82: 104+ Ap '67

URBAN coalition (organization)
Advice to the Urban coalition. E. Ginzberg. il Reporter 37:18-20 S 7 '67
American tragedy, 1967; urban crisis and aims of Urban coalition. A. Balk. Sat R 50:34 S 16 '67
Anti-rioters at work; urban coalition consisting of city and state officials, civil rights organizations, and groups of businessmen. il Bsns W p34+ Ag 12 '67
Enter the Urban coalition; antipoverty maneuvering on the Senate floor. New Repub 157:10-11 O 21 '67
Jobs are a must for Negroes; aims of Urban coalition. Life 63:4 S 15 '67
Politics of consortium; Urban coalition. M. Miles. New Repub 157:11-13 S 9 '67
Problem behind the problem; Urban coalition. Nation 205:197 S 11 '67
Report: Washington. E. B. Drew. Atlan 220: 8+ N '67
Search for solutions; newly formed Urban coalition; with excerpts from program. il Time 90:9-11 S 1 '67
Urban coalition. il Ebony 23:130-2+ N '67

URBAN freeways. See Express highways

URBAN growth. See Cities and towns—Growth

URBAN journalism center. See Northwestern university, Evanston, Ill.—Medill school of journalism

URBAN league, National. See National urban league

URBAN redevelopment. See City planning; Urban renewal

URBAN renewal
Bankrolling the slum clearance job; insurance companies. il Bsns W p58+ O 14 '67
Beginnings of wisdom; Ribicoff committee hearings. W. Klein. Nation 205:112-15 Ag 14 '67
Big first step; life insurance industry to invest $1 billion in the slums. Time 90:23-4 S 22 '67
Big-sky man hemmed in by the city; L.B.J.'s urban efforts. H. Sidey. il Life 63: 28B Jl 28 '67
Bill that must be paid. America 117:194 Ag 26 '67
Billion dollar bubble; insurance companies to invest in slum areas. Commonweal 86:598 S 29 '67
Business rebuilds the slums. il Nations Bsns 55:40-1+ Je '67

URBAN renewal—*Continued*

Cities in a race with time, by J. R. Lowe. Review
Reporter 37:43-4 D 28 '67. W. Klein
Sat R 50:26-7 Ag 5 '67. L. C. Fitch

City meets the space age; summer study on science and urban development. Woods Hole, Mass J. Bailey. Arch Forum 126:60-3+ Ja '67

Comprehensive district planning privately sponsored guides rehabilitation of six blocks in Brooklyn. il Arch Rec 142:142-9 Jl '67

Corporate imperialism for the poor. R. A. Cloward and F. F. Piven. il Nation 205:365-7 O 16 '67

Crisis in the cities: does business hold the key? with comments by business leaders. il Duns R 90:31-5 N '67

Design-in; at New York's Central park mall. il Newsweek 69:72 My 22 '67

Detroit: up from the ashes; New Detroit committee program. il Newsweek 71:48-50 Ja 1 '68

Distaff architect aids Chicago renewal. il Am City 82:92 Ag '67

Further probe into housing rehabilitation; Lancaster, Pa. Am City 82:44+ N '67

Ghetto is people; involving the community in planning. J. Aumente. Nation 205:555-7 N 27 '67

Giving the past a future; Burns—Jackson, Dayton, Ohio. H. Meeker. il Arch Forum 126:56-61 My '67

How business is helping to rebuild cities. il U S News 62:90-2 Mr 20 '67

How Detroit gropes toward racial peace. il Bsns W p83-4 N 25 '67

How to clean up the Nation's slums? il Newsweek 70:64-5+ Ag 28 '67

How to stop riots. L. Bennett, jr. il Ebony 22:29-32+ O '67

Insurance in the slums. New Repub 157:7-8 S 30 '67

It helps to be in trouble; Camden, N.J. il Am City 82:67-8 N '67

Latest ideas on how to save the big cities; with interview with A. A. Ribicoff. il U S News 62:50-2 F 27 '67

Mayors' dilemma.; projects to aid Negro ghetto areas of Mount Vernon and New York rebuffed. il Newsweek 70:21-2 Ag 14 '67

Megastructure for renewal. il Arch Forum 126:58-9 Je '67

Model aid starts flowing to cities; sixty-three cities chosen. il Bsns W p86 N 25 '67

Mortgages for the slums. W. McQuade. Fortune 77:162-3 Ja '68

New force focuses on urban ills. il Bsns W p75-6+ Je 24 '67

New kind of team: three trade associations, a non-profit citizens' group and HUD, combine to rehab slum; planning in Cleveland. il Arch Rec 142:150-2 Jl '67

Numbers game: sums for slums. Time 90:19 Ag 18 '67

$1-billion plunge to rebuild slums; insurance industry pledge for mortgage loans. Bsns W p46 S 16 '67

People: the new voice in renewal; Shaw area of Washington, D.C. E. P. Berkeley. il Arch Forum 127:72-7 N '67

Philadelphia renews renewal. J. Bailey. il Arch Forum 126:64-7 Mr '67

Potholes in the road to renewal. il Bsns W p 183 F 18 '67

Promise denied; Cleveland's urban renewal program. Time 89:34 Je 9 '67

Recreation needs in urban areas. R. C. Weaver. il Nat Parks Mag 41:10-13 D '67

Redesigning the cities is what's happening; design-in at New York's Central park. il Bsns W p40-1 My 20 '67

She makes the city a place for living; townhouse projects of C. W. Smith. il Bsns W p76-8+ Je 3 '67

Slum housing: a billion-dollar baby; life-insurance companies to invest in slum redevelopment. il Newsweek 70:81 S 25 '67

Slums: cancer in the heart of our cities. il Sr Schol 90:8-12 F 3 '67

This month's feature: the demonstration cities controversy. Cong Digest 46:36-64 F '67

To save a slum; Bedford-Stuyvesant restoration corp. il Newsweek 70:48 N 20 '67

Trillion dollars to save U.S. cities? U S News 62:12 F 6 '67

Urban redoubt. W. H. Dougherty, jr; J. A. Norton. il Sat R 51:34+ Ja 13 '68

Urban unrest: whose problem is it? address, August 25, 1967. L. W. Moore. Vital Speeches 33:749-52 O 1 '67

Urgent future, by A. Mayer. Review
Arch Rec 142:131-4 D '67. L. Mumford

Violence in the cities: a better place to live; address, July 31, 1967. J. V. Lindsay. Vital Speeches 33:674-7 S 1 '67

Which plan for slum renewal? plans sponsored by Senators Percy and Kennedy, or the new Administration plan. Bsns W p77-8 Ag 26 '67

Zeroing in on slums. Sr Schol 91:19-20 D 7 '67
See also
City planning
Urban America, incorporated
Urban coalition (organization)

URBAN sociology. See Sociology, Urban

URBANA, Ill.

Architecture
Architecture strongly manipulated in space and scale; Christian science organization building. il Arch Rec 141:137-42 F '67

URBANISM. See Cities and towns

URBANIZATION
Deeper shame of the cities. M. Ways. Fortune 77:132-5+ Ja '68

Life in the year 2000. C. A. Doxiadis. il NEA J 56:12-14 N '67

Profiles: through the great city. A. Bailey. il New Yorker 43:35-42+ Jl 22; 35-8+ Jl 29; 32-6+ Ag 5 '67

Through the great city, by A. Bailey. Review
Reporter 37:49-50 O 5 '67. C. W. Griffin, jr; Reply with rejoinder. A. Bailey. 37:10-11 N 2 '67
See also
Urban America, incorporated

URBANIZED areas. See Metropolitan areas

URBMOBILES. See Automobiles, Electric

URDU poetry

Translations into English
Wind and the trees; Why does it happen so? tr. by A. Ali. D. Ahmed. Horn Bk 43:237-8 Ap '67

UREA
Enzyme reaction rates at limited water activities. J. J. Skujins and A. D. McLaren. bibliog il Science 158:1569-70 D 22 '67

Ornithine-urea cycle activity in xenopus laevis: adaptation in Saline. R. L. McBean and L. Goldstein. bibliog il Science 157:931-2 Ag 25 '67

Potamotrygon spp: elasmobranchs with low urea content. T. B. Thorson and others. bibliog il Science 158:375-7 O 20 '67

Supplement that's all urea. D. Braun. il Farm J 91:36+ O '67

Urea and its formation in coelacanth liver. G. W. Brown, jr. and S. G. Brown. bibliog il Science 155:570-3 F 3 '67

Urea works best with long-feds. D. Seim. Farm J 91:38D Je '67

UREASE
Enzyme reaction rates at limited water activities. J. J. Skujins and A. D. McLaren. bibliog il Science 158:1569-70 D 22 '67

UREDOSPORES. See Spores (botany)

URETHANS
Depression of circulating interferon response in Balb/c mice after urethan treatment. J. De Maeyer-Guignard and E. De Maeyer. bibliog il Science 155:482-4 Ja 27 '67

Segmented polyurethane; a new elastomer for biomedical applications. J. W. Boretos and W. S. Pierce. bibliog il Science 158:1481-2 D 15 '67

URINALYSIS. See Urine—Analysis

URINE
See also
Hematuria

Analysis
Collagen-like fragments: excretion in urine of patients with Paget's disease of bone. S. M. Krane and others. bibliog il Science 157:713-16 Ag 11 '67

Honing a diagnostic weapon; urinalysis. F. Marley. il Sci N 92:595 D 16 '67

Incontinence
How to help the child who wets his bed. J. Mendels. il Parents Mag 42:38-9+ Jl '67

URIS, Auren
Get rid of that run-down feeling. Nations Bsns 55:82-4 Jl '67

Make the most of your weaknesses. Nations Bsns 55:74-6 Ap '67

URIS, Leon
Girls who fought for Israel. por Ladies Home J 84:83-6 S '67

Topaz; story; excerpt from novel. Look 31:37-42 S 5; 37-40 S 19 '67

URLANIS, Boris
John Graunt's offspring. UNESCO Courier 20: 4-9 F '67
UROFSKY, Melvin I.
High noon at Catholic U. Nation 205:303-5 O 2 '67
Rhodes at the crossroads. New Repub 156: 7-8 My 20 '67
URUGUAY

Economic conditions
Too much of a good thing. il Time 90:41 N 17 '67
Where the welfare state runs wild. S. G. Slappey. il Nations Bsns 55:38-9+ Ap '67

Social conditions
See also
Social and economic security—Uruguay
US; drama. See Dramas—Criticism, plots, etc.—Single works
USED automobiles; Used planes; etc. See Airplanes, Used; Automobiles Used; etc.
USED car industry. See Automobile industry and trade—Used cars
USSERY, Bobby
Clarion call: $62.20! W. Tower. il por Sports Illus 26:20-5 My 15 '67
USTINOV, Peter
Luxury. Vogue 150:147 N 1 '67

about
Halfway up the tree. Criticism
America 117:724 D 9 '67
Nation 205:572-3 N 27 '67
New Yorker 43:131 N 18 '67
Sat R 50:70 N 25 '67
Time 90:50 N 17 '67
Unknown soldier and his wife. Criticism
America 117:139 Ag 5 '67
Christian Cent 84:1131 S 6 '67
Commonweal 86:472-3 Jl 28 '67
Life 63:12 Ag 25 '67
New Yorker 43:94 Jl 15 '67
Newsweek 70:67 Jl 17 '67
Sat R 50:48 Jl 22 '67
Time 90:75 Jl 14 '67
Vogue 150:225 S 1 '67
Ustinov. New Yorker 43:23-5 Jl 15 '67
USURY laws
Why this year's usury may be next year's interest. il U S News 64:70-1 Ja 1 '68
UTA stansburiana. See Lizards
UTAH
See also
Birds—Utah
Fishing—Utah
Geology—Utah
Glen Canyon
Great Salt Lake
Hunting—Utah
Mormons and Mormonism
Natural Bridges National Monument
Radioactive fallout—Utah
Uinta Mountains
Wilderness areas—Utah
Zion National Park

Description and travel
Travel report. L. Barry. il Pop Phot 60: 90-1+ F '67

Parks and reserves
See also
Canyonlands National Park
UTAH civic ballet. See Ballet companies
UTAH Shakespearean festival. See Shakespeare festivals
UTAH. University, Salt Lake City
Old bones store sells out; dinosaur store. il Sci Digest 62:65-6 Ag '67
U TAPAO airbase. See Air bases
UTERUS
Blastokinin: inducer and regulator of blastocyst development in the rabbit uterus. R. S. Krishnan and J. C. Daniel, jr. bibliog il Science 158:490-2 O 27 '67
Intrauterine devices: effects on ultrastructure of human endometrium. R. M. Wynn. bibliog il Science 156:1508-10 Je 16 '67; Reply with rejoinder. W. A. Krotoski. 157:1465 S 22 '67
See also
Placenta

Surgery
Operation every woman should understand; hysterectomy. G. Naismith. Todays Health 45:50-1+ Ap '67

UTILITY billing. See Billing
UTILITY rates. See Public utilities—Rates
UTILITY rooms. See Rooms
UTILIZATION of land. See Land utilization
UTLEY, Beatrice S.
History in houses. Antiques 92:210-13 Ag '67
UTLEY, Freda
Open question. Nat R 19:848+ Ag 8 '67
UTOPIAS
Utopia, by T. Molnar. Review
Cath World 205:312-13 Ag '67. G. L. Vincitorio
Nat R 19:916-17 Ag 22 '67. F. D. Wilhelmsen
UYS, Stanley
Goldwater in South Africa. New Repub 158: 15-17 Ja 6 '68
UZBEKISTAN
Uzbek. M. Harari. il Vogue 149:146+ Ap 1 '67
UZCÁTEGUI, Emilio
Bolivia. Ecuador. Paraguay: historians. Américas 19:19-28 F '67
Scientific explorers in Latin America. Américas 19:3-11 Jl '67
UZZLE, Burk
To see America: spring's old sweet challenge; photographs. Life 62:62-71 My 19 '67
Something of Carolyn in all his pictures. G. P. Hunt. por Life 62:3 My 19 '67
UZZLE, Carolyn
We all shared every chore. Life 62:72+ My 19 '67
about
Something of Carolyn in all his pictures. G. P. Hunt. por Life 62:3 My 19 '67

V

VASCAR (visual average speed computer and recorder) See Speed indicators
VAST (versatile avionics shop test) See Airplanes, Military—Electronic equipment—Testing
VD. See Venereal diseases
VDIG (vertical display indicator group system) See Aeronautic instruments—Display systems
VIP (versatile information processor) See Space telemetry
VISTA. See Volunteers in service to America
V-L rifle. See Air guns
VOA. See Voice of America (radio program)
VOM. See Voltohmmeters
VOR/DME (very high frequency omnidirectional range/distance measuring equipment) See Radio in aviation
V/STOL (vertical or short take-off and landing) See Airplanes—Vertical take-off and landing
VTOL. See Airplanes, Vertical take-off and landing
VTVM (vacuum tube voltmeters) See Voltmeters
VACATION clothing. See Clothing and dress
VACATION houses
Cabins and vacation houses. il Consumer Bul 50:17 Jl '67
Cedar outpost; a weekend hideaway. J. H. Ingersoll. il House B 110:20 Ja '68
Eight vacation houses. il Arch Rec 141:157-64 Je '67
Escape to the snows of Vermont; the ivory tower. E. Sverbeyeff. il House B 109:82-7 Ja '67
Escape to the Texas prairie; open-and-shut shelter. J. DeLong. il House B 109:80-1+ Ja '67
Four mountain houses. il Sunset 138:86-93 F '67
High on a Long Island bluff, shingle shelter. il House B 109:74-7+ Jl '67
Homes for all seasons. il Holiday 42:62-5 O '67
Imaginative vacation houses. il House & Gard 131:86-103 Je '67
In an abandoned mill a city couple fashions a roomy weekend retreat. E. Sverbeyeff. il House B 109:136-41 Je '67
Instant vacation house for under $6000. il Am Home 70:112 Je '67
Living in a work of art; G. Bunshaft's weekend home, on Long Island. J. Peter. il Look 32:64-6 Ja 9 '68

VACATION houses—*Continued*
Load of leisure living; prefabricated vacation house erected on Block Island; with report by S. Mahoney. il Life 63:108-11+ S 8 '67
Quality vacation house on a limited budget. M. C. Huntoon, jr. Am Home 70:46+ Jl '67
Riviera house on a hilltop. il Arch Rec 141:148-50 Je '67
Scandinavian way; year-round vacation retreat in Adirondacks. B. Plumb. il N Y Times Mag p 116-17 O 15 '67
Snowflake house for snow-filled weekends. il House & Gard 132:170-1 D '67
This vacation house is pre-planned for expansion. N. Seney. il Bet Hom & Gard 45:72-5 Je '67
Updating a vacation house. il Am Home 70:84 Jl '67
Vacation fortress on Sardinia. il Arch Forum 126:64-5 Je '67
Vacation from care. il Am Home 70:76-7 Je '67
Vacation home for all seasons. R. Charles. il Parents Mag 42:120-4+ N '67
Vacation homes. il Pop Mech 127:142-59 Ap '67
Vacation house in the woods; year-round hideaway in Finland. il House B 110:102-3 Ja '68
Vacation house that arrives like a nice big Christmas package; mobile home. N. Seney. il Bet Hom & Gard 45:106-7 D '67
Weekend place. il Sunset 139:56-7 Ag '67
Well-built, well-kept house. J. H. Ingersoll. il House B 109:36+ O '67
See also
Summer homes

Anecdotes, facetiae, satire, etc.
How does the land lie? B. Coates and B. Roth. il Outdoor Life 140:30-1+ Jl '67
Please don't move the piano. J. L. O'Neill. Am Home 70:44 Jl '67

VACATION photography. See Photography
VACATION projects
Friendly town; Cleveland's vacation and medical examination programs for disadvantaged children. M. Slivka. il PTA Mag 61:8-9 Je '67
VACATION reading. See Books and reading
VACATION safety devices and measures. See Safety devices and measures
VACATION schools. See Summer schools
VACATION villages
California: planned pleasure; new condominium communities. D. Messinesi. Vogue 150:76-8 Ag 15 '67
Charlie Fraser's island paradise; Hilton Head, S.C. A. J. Reichley. il Fortune 76:171+ O '67
Club Méditerranée. A. Mayor. il Holiday 42:62-7+ Ag '67
Club on Corfu; a Club Méditerranée village. R. H. Buck. il Sr Schol 91:sup 11 N 2 '67
How to have a second home on the club plan. House B 109:90+ Ja '67
Shoestring vacations with a Midas touch; Club Méditerranée. il Bsns W p42-3 S 9 '67
VACATIONS
Adventure trips to the far outposts; to the Amazon Basin and Antarctica; with report by M. Leatherbee. il Life 63:78-87+ S 8 '67
Cow's in the meadow, the kid's in the barn; farm vacations. J. Rosenberg. il Parents Mag 42:48-9+ My '67
Dream vacation. F. Maynard. il Good H 165:48+ Ag '67
Eight ways to have an extra vacation without leaving town. P. Beshiri. il Parents Mag 42:36-7+ Jl '67
Escaping in midwinter. A. Waugh. Nat R 19:302+ Mr 21 '67
Flight of the snowbirds. A. J. McClane. il Field & S 71:86-92 F '67
How to get more out of weekends. F. Cross. Read Digest 92:125-8 Ja '68
Long summer commute; businessmen's weekend visits to family in summer homes. il Time 90:58 Jl 21 '67
Ten special vacation tours. Bet Hom & Gard 45:16 Mr; 50 Ap '67
There's no place like home, somebody else's; home-swapping vacations. J. A. M. Graham and W. Cross. Read Digest 91:49-50+ Jl '67
Try a farm vacation. J. H. Winchester. il Read Digest 90:19-20+ My '67
Up to the minute vacation tips. W. J. Toth. Am Home 70:52-3 Je '67

Weekends at the seashore for physically disabled persons and their families; the Beach Haven excursion. M. D. McMullin and M. Clarke. Parks & Rec 2:24+ Je '67
What your summer weekends hold. P. Reynolds. il Mlle 65:149-51+ My '67
Where to go fishing, vacationing, hunting; ed. by V. T. Sparano. See issues of Outdoor life
See also
Camping
Fresh air charity
VACCARIELLO, Barbara
L.A. police: as seen from Olympus. Nat R 19:77 Ja 24 '67
VACCINATION
Deadline for smallpox; global eradication forecast. D. A. Ehrlich. il Sci N 92:568-9 D 9 '67
Eczema & vaccination. Time 89:65 My 12 '67
Get vaccinated against flu this year? Consumer Rep 32:551 O '67
See also
Measles—Vaccination
Smallpox
VACCINES
New force in vaccines; developed at AEC center. Bsns W p 127 Ag 12 '67
New vaccines that will prevent disease. il Good H 164:189-91 Je '67
Vaccine conquers baby-killer; RhoGAM for Rh disease. B. J. Culliton. il Sci N 92:520-1 N 25 '67
See also
Influenza—Vaccines
Mumps—Vaccines
VACHON, Andre
Scholarly publishing in France; summary of address. Pub W 192:29 Jl 24 '67
VACUUM apparatus
Yard vacuums: new year-round tool. C. E. Rhine. il Pop Sci 190:142-3 F '67
VACUUM bottles. See Thermos containers
VACUUM cleaner bags. See Paper bags
VACUUM cleaners
Built-in vacuum cleaner systems. il House & Gard 131:164-5 F '67
How to install a built-in vacuum system. W. Leckey. il Pop Mech 128:158-63+ S '67
New sawdust collector for radial arms. R. J. De Cristoforo. il Pop Sci 191:152-3 Jl '67
Vacuum cleaners. Consumer Rep 32:100-7 D '67
Vacuum cleaners. il Consumer Rep 32:128-34 Mr '67
See also
Hoover company
VACUUM cleaning
Built-in vacuum cleaning systems. il Consumer Bul 50:11-14 My '67
VACUUM tube voltmeters. See Voltmeters
VACUUM tubes
New tetrode transistor. J. Tartas. il Electr World 77:34-5 F '67
See also
Cathode ray tubes
Diodes
VADAKIN, James C.
Helping the children. New Repub 157:15-18 D 23 '67
VAGANOV, Igor
If they've found another assassin, let them name names and produce their evidence. J. Berendt. il por Esquire 68:80-2+ Ag '67
VAGNOZZI, Egidio, abp
Delegate leaves. Commonweal 86:358 Je 16 '67
Pope's fraternal eyes. Time 90:62 Jl 14 '67
VAGRANCY
Voiding vagrancy. Time 90:81 N 10 '67
VAGUS nerves. See Nerves
VAHANIAN, Gabriel
Gourmet theologian. Nation 204:188-9 F 6 '67
VAHERI, Antti. See Plotkin, S. A. jt. auth.
VAHLE, Ronald W.
Power transistors. por Electr World 78:45-8 Jl '67
VAIL, Thomas Van Husen
Cordial welcome for Newhouse. il Time 89:47 Mr 10 '67
VAIL, Colo. See Winter resorts
VAIMAN, Mikhail
Music to my ears; Carnegie Hall debut. I. Kolodin. Sat R 50:47 F 18 '67
VALDOVINOS, Carlos
Francisco de Miranda; a vindication. bibliog Américas 19:28-35 Mr '67
VALENCIA, Calif.
Life in the instant cities. T. Roszak. il Nation 204:336-40+ Mr 13 '67

VALENSTEIN, Elliot S. and others
Polydipsia elicited by the synergistic action of a saccharin and glucose solution. bibliog Science 157:552-4 Ag 4 '67
Sex differences in taste preference for glucose and saccharin solutions. bibliog Science 156:942-3 My 19 '67

VALENTI, Jack
Marquess of Halifax: eloquent paradox. Sat R 50:22-3+ N 4 '67
Motion picture bridge between East and West. Sat R 50:8-9+ D 23 '67
Voltaire's timeless eminence. Sat R 50:27+ Mr 11 '67

about
Czar of the movie business. V. Canby. il pors N Y Times Mag p38-9+ Ap 23 '67

VALENTINE, Helen
Young wife's world. See issues of Good housekeeping

VALENTINE, Jean
Orpheus and Eurydice; December; poems. Poetry 110:3-5 Ap '67
Two poems: The couples; For S., at the boat pond. Yale R 56:430-1 Mr '67

VALENTINES
Young hearts and valentines; comp. by B. Adler. il Good H 164:84-5 F '67

VALENTINES day
Dagmar's panel for Valentine's day. il Sunset 138:110 F '67
Lost your heart? better find it before February 13! il Seventeen 26:244 F '67

Drama
Somebody's valentine. D. Newman. Plays 26:75-8 F '67

VALENTINO
New Valentino. il por Time 89:70 Mr 10 '67
V for Valentino. il por Life 63:91-4+ D 1 '67

VALESARES, Pete
Arrested by detectives Valesares and Sullivan, charge: murder. B. J. Friedman. il pors Sat Eve Post 240:38-42+ Ap 22 '67

VALIUM. See Tranquilizing drugs

VALL, Seymour
How to be a Jewish mother; dramatization of book by D. Greenburg. Criticism Newsweek il 71:60 Ja 8 '68

VALLEJO, César
Intensity & height; poem. Nation 204:540 Ap 24 '67

about
Translating César Vallejo. C. Eshleman. Nation 204:540 Ap 24 '67

VALLEY mould and iron corporation
Ingot mold maker casts new horoscope. il Bsns W p74-6+ Ag 5 '67

VALLEYS
See also
Rivers

VALLIEN, Bertil
Bertil Vallien. D. Smith. il por Craft Horiz 27:8-13+ S '67

VALONIA ventricosa. See Algae

VALUABLE papers. See Family records

VALUATION
When an appraiser is needed. il Good H 165:201 N '67
See also
Assessment

VALUATION (psychology) See Value (psychology)

VALUE (philosophy) See Worth

VALUE (psychology)
Hang-loose ethic; excerpts from It's happening. J. L. Simmons and B. Winograd. NEA J 56:18-20+ O '67
Helping children to clarify values; excerpts from Values and teaching: working with values in the classroom. L. E. Raths and others. il NEA J 56:12-15 O '67
Individual and group values. R. M. Williams, jr. bibliog f il Ann Am Acad 371:20-37 My '67
These are three of the alienated. S. Kelman. il N Y Times Mag p38-9+ O 22 '67; Discussion. p40+ N 12 '67

VALUE analysis
Value engineering for the electronics industry. F. H. Posser. il Electr World 78:41-4 Ag '67

VALUE engineering. See Value analysis

VALUE Line investment survey (firm)
Value Line vs. all comers. Fortune 76:240+ N '67

VALUE of college education. See College education, Value of

VALVES
See also
Automobile engines—Valves
Tire valves

VAMPIRE squids. See Squids

VAN ALLEN, James A.
Are we to abandon the planets to the Soviet Union? Science 158:1405 D 15 '67

about
Abandoning the planets to Russia; concerning editorial in Science. por Time 91:64 Ja 5 '68

VAN ALLEN radiation belts
Earth is viewed as dc. generator. Aviation W 87:19 N 27 '67
High voltage in the sky. il Time 90:54 D 1 '67

VAN ARSDALE, Harry
Gap in labor-management relations; interview, ed. by T. J. Murray. por Duns R 90:29-30+ Jl '67

VANCE, Cyrus Roberts
U.S. joins in efforts to avert war in eastern Mediterranean; statement, December 5, 1967. Dept State Bul 57:860 D 25 '67

about
Heirs apparent. il por Time 90:26 D 8 '67
Top candidate for defense chief. il por U S News 63:18 D 18 '67

VANCE, Sarah R.
Disillusioned first-timer comments on the ABA convention. Pub W 192:172-3 Jl 10 '67

VANCE, William
Crew that grew and grew. Parks & Rec 2:38+ O '67

VANCIL, Richard F.
So you're going to have a planning department! Harvard Bsns R 45:88-96 My '67

VAN CITTERS, Robert L. and Watson, N. W.
Coronary disease in spawning steelhead trout salmo gairdnerii. bibliog Science 159:105-7 Ja 5 '68

VAN CLIBURN international quadrennial piano competitions. See Music—Competitions

VANCOUVER opera association
Vancouver; performance of Lucia di Lammermoor. R. Sunter. Opera N 31:31 My 13 '67

VANDALISM
On destruction. D. Sorgman. Nat Parks Mag 41:15 O '67
Schools & the summer. il Time 90:17 Ag 25 '67
Wreckreation: what can teenagers do about vandalism? il Sr Schol 90:21-3 My 12 '67

VAN DE GRAAFF accelerators. See Accelerators (electrons, etc)

VAN DEN HAAG, Ernest
Case for pornography is the case for censorship and vice versa. Esquire 67:134-5 My '67
Psychoanalysis and fantasy. Nat R 19:295-8+ Mr 21 '67

VANDERBILT, Amy
[Monthly column] See issues of Ladies' home journal

VANDERBILT, Sanderson
Obituary
New Yorker 42:132 F 4 '67

VANDERGRIFT, Kay E.
Choosing in 8. Library J 92:2005 My 15 '67

VAN DER KROEF, Justus M.
Letter from Colombo. Nat R 20:34-5 Ja 16 '68

VAN DER POST, Laurens
Ageless mosaic of India. Holiday 42:38-47+ O '67
Vivid variety of India. Holiday 42:82-3+ N '67

VAN DER RYN, Sim. and Silverstein, Murray
Berkeley, how do students really live? Arch Forum 127:90-7 Jl '67

VANDERSLICE, Thomas A.
Four problems, four opportunities. Sat R 51:48+ Ja 13 '68

VAN DER WALT, Ronnie
Shade of difference. por Newsweek 69:40+ F 27 '67

VAN DEUSEN, Hobart M.
Books in review. Natur Hist 76:64-9 Mr '67

VAN DINE, Alan C.
Eagles in disguise. Sat R 51:8+ Ja 13 '68
What is littature? Sat R 50:4+ Ap 22 '67
Who's afraid of the new math? Parents Mag 42:62-3+ S '67

VANDIVER, Frank E.
Beyond the aid of history. Sat R 50:34 My 6 '67

VAN DOMMELEN, David B.
Primitive weaving as a contemporary idiom. Sch Arts 66:6-10 Ap '67
(ed) Textile arts. por Sch Arts 66:4-30 Ap '67
VAN DOREN, Mark
School books; reprint. por Pub W 191:35 My 29 '67
So fair a world it was; poem. Nation 204:565 My 1 '67
VAN DOREN, Ron
Ford road school votes aye for the Teacher corps. NEA J 56:28-30 Ap '67
VAN DOREN, Tandy
100 ways of summer traveling in the West Indies and Mexico. Mlle 65:190-4 My '67
VAN DUSSELDORP, Ralph A.
Systems approach. NEA J 56:24-6 F '67
VAN DUUREN, Benjamin L. See Sivak, A. jt. auth.
VAN DUYN, Mona
Poet as novelist. Poetry 109:332-9 F '67
VAN DYKE, Dick
Triumph of a square. S. Gordon. il pors Look 31:88-92 Ap 18 '67
VANELLA, Betty
And now for golf. il por Time 89:76 F 24 '67
VAN HOBOKEN, Jon
Yachting interviews: Jon Van Hoboken. B. Robinson. il por Yachting 122:41+ Ag '67
VAN HORNE, H. H.
Lead feed, but keep costs in line. Suc Farm 65:66 S '67
VAN HORNE, Harriet
Johnny Carson. Look 31:78-9+ Jl 11 '67
Sexual revolution in living color. McCalls 95: 46+ O '67
VAN HOUTE, Robert
Doris D. Ray and Robert Van Houte; interview, ed. by M. S. Fenner. por NEA J 56:71-2 Mr '67
VANISHING Easter egg; drama. See Miller, H. L.
VAN ITALLIE, Jean-Claude
America hurrah. Criticism
Christian Cent 84:596-7 My 3 '67
Commentary 43:87-8 Mr '67
New Yorker 42:69-70 Ja 21 '67
Reporter 36:49-50 Mr 9 '67
VANITY on the gridiron; story. See Kerouac, J.
VAN LOON, Eric
Who are the activists? Am Ed 4:2-4+ D '67
VAN NORDEN, Langdon
New man at the helm. F. Merkling. por Opera N 31:16-17 Je 10 '67
VAN OVERBEEK, J. and others
Dormin (abscisin II) inhibitor of plant DNA synthesis? bibliog Science 156:1497-9 Je 16 '67
VAN PATTEN, James
Case for individual man in the educational environment. Sch & Soc 95:231-2 Ap 1 '67
VAN RIJN, Ignatius, pseud.
Dutch pastoral council. America 116:373-5 Mr 18 '67
VAN RIPER, Paul P.
Dimensions of manpower: problems and policies. bibliog Wilson Lib Bul 41:800-9 Ap '67
VAN Savang, crown prince of Laos. See Vong Savang
VAN SCHMUS, W. R. and Koffman, D. M.
Equilibrium temperatures of iron and magnesium in chondritic meteorites. bibliog Science 155:1009-11 F 24 '67
VANSTON, A. Rorke
New deal in design for the mentally retarded. Arch Rec 141:148-9 F '67
VAN WAGENER, Isabella. See Truth, S.
VAN WOERT, Melvin H. See Prasad, K. N. jt. auth.
VAN ZELE, Helen
African violets. Horticulture 45:24 D '67
VANZETTI, Bartolomeo
See also
Sacco-Vanzetti case
VAPOR baths. See Baths, Vapor
VAPORIZERS
Electric vaporizers. il Consumer Rep 33:39-44 Ja '68
VARGHESE, A. J. and Wang, S. Y.
Ultraviolet irradiation of DNA in vitro and in vivo produces a third thymine-derived product. bibliog Science 156:955-7 My 19 '67
VARIABLE annuities. See Annuities
VARIABLE frequency oscillators. See Oscillators
VARIABLE stars. See Stars, Variable
VARIATION (biology) See Mutation (biology)
VARICOSE veins
Looking after your legs. A. Kerr. McCalls 94: 48+ Ag '67

VARIETY stage. See Vaudeville
VARNER, Joseph E. See Kok, B. jt. auth.
VARNISH and varnishing
There's good news about exterior finishes. Pop Gard 18:18-19 My '67
VARONA, Enrique José
Varona as a philosopher. F. Romero. por Américas 19:13-18 D '67
VARSAVSKY, Carlos M.
Radio sources in the vicinity of source M 31. bibliog Science 158:1043-5 N 24 '67
VASA (ship) See Warships—Sweden
VASCULAR system
Corridors of the heart; with photographs by L. Nilsson. Life 64:22-31 Ja 19 '68
Gastrovascular system of small hydromedusae: mechanisms of circulation. E. C. Roosen-Runge. bibliog il Science 156:74-6 Ap 7 '67
VAS DIAS, Robert
Six books by seven poets. Poetry 110:186-95 Je '67
VASSAR college, Poughkeepsie, N.Y.
Banns published: Yale and Vassar. il Am Heritage 18:112 Je '67
Can Vassar find happiness in New Haven? with report by D. Seiberling. il Life 63: 118-20+ O 13 '67
Group and I. S. Lanahan. McCalls 94: 59+ Jl '67
Her own mistress; Yale's affiliation proposal declined. Time 90:85 D 1 '67
No match; no merger with Yale. Newsweek 70:54 D 4 '67
Vassar-Yale match? Sch & Soc 95:280+ Sum '67
VATICAN
See also
Catholic church
Catholic church—Relations (diplomatic)
Papacy

Finance
Anecdotes, facetiae, satire, etc.
Secret of Vatican finances revealed. P. J. Laux. il America 117:553 N 11 '67

Library
Propose ecumenical center in Rome. Christian Cent 84:333-4 Mr 15 '67

Secretariat for non-believers
Difficult dialogue with non-believers. R. Butler. Cath World 205:95-100 My '67
VATICAN council, 2d
Change strikes Catholic university. J. B. Sheerin. Cath World 205:132-3 Je '67
Peasant of the Garonne, by J. Maritain. Review
Nat R 19:696-7+ Je 27 '67. P. Burnham
Reformation Roman-style; excerpt from Methodist observer at Vatican II. A. C. Outler. Cath World 204:341-5 Mr '67
Religious liberty and development of doctrine; interview, ed. by E. Gaffney. J. C. Murray. Cath World 204:277-83 F '67
Roman diary. D. Slow. America 116:582-3; 117:18-19 Ap 22, Jl 1 '67
Vatican II, contraception and Christian marriage. T. Mackin. America 117:54-7 Jl 15 '67; Discussion. 117:314-17 S 23 '67
VATICAN library. See Vatican—Library
VAUDEVILLE
Bubbles: survivor of Buck & Bubbles, the great song-and-dance team; interview. J. Bubbles. New Yorker 43:21-3 Ag 26 '67
VAUGHAN, Bill
Pass the paper napkins, please; excerpt from Half the battle. Read Digest 91:81-3 O '67
Worth of a wife. Read Digest 91:206 N '67
VAUGHAN, Denis
Schubert onstage. Opera N 32:8-12 Ja 6 '68
VAUGHAN, Roger
Gulf between parents. Life 63:104A-104B+ N 17 '67
Real Great society. Life 63:76+ S 15 '67
VAUGHAN, Sarah
Words for Sarah Vaughan. M. Williams. por Sat R 50:81 Ag 26 '67
VAUGHAN WILLIAMS, Ralph
Records:
Hodie. Opera N 32:34 D 23 '67
Vaughan Williams: four works, one, a first on records. J. Diether. il Am Rec G 33:552-4 Mr '67
VAUGHN, Jack Hood
Peace corps: now we are seven. Sat R 51:21-3+ Ja 6 '68
VAUGHN, Robert
First of the month; excerpt from anti-Vietnam war speech with interview, ed. by C. Amory. Sat R 50:4+ Je 3 '67

VAULTING (sport)
He sizzles at the end of a swizzle stick; Southern Cal's B. Seagren. J. Underwood. il Sports Illus 26:32-4+ F 20 '67
Wayward pole; pole passing underneath bar. Time 89:57 F 24 '67

VAWTER, Bruce
God of the Bible. Commonweal 85:504-7 F 10 '67

VAYDA, Andrew P.
Hypotheses about functions of war. Natur Hist 76:48-50 bibliog(p69) D '67

VEAL
Raising and selling veal. R. Vilstrup and J. Crowley. il Suc Farm 65:46L Mr '67
See also
Cookery—Meat

VECTOR analysis
Toward nuclear truth; Vector-axial vector theory of weak interactions. il Sci N 91: 287 Mr 25 '67

VEEDER, Nicholas Phipps
Top brass takes to the road to sell steel. il por Bsns W p90-1 Ja 28 '67

VEGA, Juan Bautista
Expedition holy book. E. Gowen. il pors Américas 19:1-7 S '67

VEGETABLE breeding. See Plant breeding

VEGETABLE gardening
Botanist in the vegetable garden. J. W. Wilson. il Horticulture 45:18-19+ Jl '67
Is vegetable gardening profitable? L. J. Hering. il Horticulture 45:38-9+ Mr '67
Summer in the vegetable garden. G. Morrison. il Horticulture 45:26+ Ag '67
Sure you can grow vegetables! il Changing T 21:36-7 Mr '67
Vegetables for every garden. il Home Gard 54:36-40 Mr '67
See also
Herbs

VEGETABLES
Choice food garden for the gourmet chef. K. Rigg. il Pop Gard 18:76-7+ Ag '67
New plants for 1967. il Flower Grower 54:38-42+ Ja '67
See also
Cookery—Vegetables
Vegetable gardening
also names of vegetables, e.g. Asparagus

VEGETABLES, Frozen

Anecdotes, facetiae, satire, etc.
Tell me pretty billboard; conversation with package of garden-fresh frozen peas. N. Perrin. New Yorker 43:166+ Ap 22 '67

VEGETATION detectors. See Detectors

VEHICLE rapid fire weapon system. See Weapons systems

VEINS
Venous system. J. E. Wood. Sci Am 218: 86-8+ Ja '68
See also
Varicose veins

VELA project. See Atomic bombs—Testing, Detection of

VELÁSQUEZ, Jorge
Transistors from Panama. il por Time 90:50-1 Ag 11 '67

VELDE, Paul
Media. Commonweal 87:147-8, 334-5, 471-2 N 3, D 8 '67, Ja 19 '68
Stage. Commonweal 85:681-2; 86:175-7 Mr 17, Ap 28 '67
Woman in a field; poem. Commonweal 87:88 O 20 '67

VELIE, Lester
Behind the lines. Read Digest 90:26 My '67
Japan's quiet war against Mao. Read Digest 91:116-20 Ag '67
Let's take our ships out of the bottle. Read Digest 90:132-6 F '67
(ed) See Shih, P. S. I fought in red China's sports war
(ed) See Wang, C. T. I was a Red guard

VELIS, Andrea
Also in the cast. . . por Opera N 32:8-12 D 16 '67

VELOCITY of light. See Light—Velocity

VENDING machines

Anecdotes, facetiae, satire, etc.
Tell me pretty billboard; conversation with coffee vending machine. N. Perrin. New Yorker 43:169-70+ Ap 22 '67

VENEREAL diseases
Shocking facts about VD. P. Deutsch and R. Deutsch. Parents Mag 42:44-5 Ja '67
VD: a major health problem. S. D. Furst, jr. Parents Mag 42:104 N '67

Venereal disease: the unmentionable menace. il Sr Schol 90:10-11 My 12 '67
What you should know about VD—and why. by B. Webster. Review Sr Schol 91:sup27 N 30 '67
See also
Syphilis

VENEREAL diseases, Campaign against
VD detectives; doctors and nurses in Boston. Time 90:32 S 1 '67

VENEZUELA
See also
Caroni River
Guerrillas—Venezuela
Margarita Island
Petroleum industry and trade—Venezuela
Yachts and yachting—Venezuela

Economic conditions
Progress in Venezuela. P. B. Taylor, jr. Cur Hist 53:270-4+ N '67

Politics and government
Progress in Venezuela. P. B. Taylor, jr. Cur Hist 53:270-4+ N '67

VENEZUELA and the United States
See also
International basic economy corporation

VENICE
Venice under water. R. Lynes. Harper 234: 33+ Mr '67

Architecture
Is Venice sinking? excerpt from Antiquities in peril. T. L. Christie. il Sat R 50:40+ Mr 25 '67

Art
Evening of splendor for the love of Venice; fund raising ball for artisan flood victims. il Life 63:40-5 S 22 '67
Years to repair the damage. B. Molajoli. il UNESCO Courier 20:6-11 Ja '67

Description
Venice, the forever city. M. Gough. il House B 109:120+ S '67

VENICE biennale. See Music festivals—Italy

VENICE in art
Venice preserved; Venetian views exhibition at the Doges palace. M. Gendel. il Art N 66:54-7+ S '67

VENISON
See also
Cookery—Game

VENN, Grant
Federal library legislation, programs, and services; introduction. ALA Bul 61:1049 O '67

VENOM
Beware the brown recluse; most venomous spider. il Time 90:53 Ag 18 '67
Danger in the woods! T. McMorrow and H. M. Farkas. il Travel 128:56-8 Ag '67
Fire ant venom; synthesis of a reported component of solenamine. P. E. Sonnet. bibliog il Science 156:1759-60 Je 30 '67
How it feels to die. J. Grindell. il Outdoor Life 140:29-31+ N '67
Most snake-bitten man in the world. W. Hartley and E. Hartley. il Sci Digest 62: 13-17 O '67
Plague of toads; bufus marinus. L. Gebhart. il Sci N 92:38-9 Jl 8 '67
Snakebite: the forgotten menace. B. East. il Read Digest 90:132-6 Je '67
Venom of the scorpion vejovis spinigerus. F. E. Russell and others. bibliog il Science 159:90-1 Ja 5 '68
See also
Rattlesnakes

VENORA, Lee
And we quote; ed. by C. L. Osborne. por Hi Fi 17:MA16 Ja '67

La VENTANA; ballet See Ballets—Criticisms

VENTILATION
Ventilation for a sun-baked attic. il Sunset 138:134+ My '67

VENTURE (periodical)
Poetic venture; Armed forces chaplains board drops name from list of recommended reading. il Newsweek 69:64 F 27 '67

VENUS (planet)
Earth's secretive sister. J. Eberhart. il Sci N 92:86-7 Jl 22 '67
Life in the clouds; conditions on Venus. Sci N 92:320 S 30 '67
Venus' inferior conjunction. il Sky & Tel 34: 116-17 Ag '67
See also
Space flight to Venus

VENUS (planet)—*Continued*

Atmosphere

Crazy mixed-up planets; findings of Mariner 5 and Venus 4. il Newsweek 70:58-9+ N 6 '67

Dried up Venus? Newsweek 69:65 Je 12 '67

Early cutoff of transmissions from Venus 4 unexplained. H. Rausch. il Aviation W 87: 17-18 N 6 '67

Mariner V data indicate ionosphere, corona on Venus. Aero Tech 21:49 N 6 '67

Rendezvous with Venus; U.S. and Russian probes. Sci Am 217:50 D '67

Soviet, U.S. contradictions? Venus 4, Mariner 5 space probes. il Sr Schol 91:16 N 2 '67

Venus, a hellhole. il Sci Digest 63:16-18 Ja '68

Venus atmosphere found refractive. G. S. Hunter. Aviation W 87:22-3 O 30 '67

Venus: atmospheric evolution. M. O. Dayhoff and others. bibliog il Science 155:556-8 F 3 '67

Venus is dead, & too hot. Time 89:87-8 Je 9 '67

Venus revealed; findings of Russia's Venus 4 and the U.S.'s Mariner 5. Time 90:45 N 3 '67

Venus: volcanic eruptions may cause atmospheric obscuration. G. T. Davidson and A. D. Anderson. bibliog Science 156:1729-30 Je 30 '67; Reply with rejoinder. J. Weertman. 158:395-6 O 20 '67

Contamination

Planetary contamination II; Soviet and U.S. practices and policies. B. C. Murray and others. bibliog il Science 155:1505-11 Mr 24 '67; Discussion. 157:487 Ag 4 '67

Rotation

Resonance rotation of Venus. I. I. Shapiro. bibliog il Science 157:423-5 Jl 28 '67

Rotation of Venus; continuing contradictions. B. A. Smith. bibliog il Science 158:114-16 O 6 '67

VENUS probes. See Space probes

VERBA, Sidney
Democratic participation. bibliog f Ann Am Acad 373:53-78 S '67

VERBAL learning. See Learning, Psychology of

VERBECK, J. W.
Optics operate signals in emergencies. Am City 82:125+ Mr '67

VERDERY, John D.
Innocent rebels. Parents Mag 42:46-7+ Ag '67

VERDI, Giuseppe
Afternoon at Sant'Agata. S. Hughes. il por Opera N 32:8-13 D 30 '67

Aida. Criticism
Opera N 32:17-19 Ja 20 '68
Opera N il 31:17-20 F 25 '67
Sat R 50:89 F 25 '67
Sat R 51:97 Ja 13 '68

Un ballo in maschera. H. Glass. il Am Rec G 33:904-5 Je '67

Ernani. Criticism
Opera N 32:30 Ja 13 '68

Falstaff. Criticism
New Yorker 43:154 O 14 '67
Opera N il 32:17-19 D 16 '67
Opera N il 32:24-5 D 16 '67
Sat R 50:54 O 21 '67

Family resemblance. C. D. Alper. il Opera N 31:21-3 F 18 '67

La forza del destino (Force of destiny) Criticism
New Yorker 43:178-9 O 7 '67
Sat R 50:106 O 14 '67
Sat R 50:73 N 11 '67

Masked ball (Un ballo in maschera) Criticism
New Yorker 43:80 Je 24 '67

Montserrat Caballé in La Traviata. P. L. Miller. il Am Rec G 34:194-5 N '67

Music to my ears. I. Kolodin. Sat R 50:50+ Ap 8 '67

Otello. Criticism
New Yorker 43:155-6 Mr 11 '67
Opera N 31:24-5 Mr 11 '67
Opera N 32:27 N 25 '67
Opera N 32:32 Ja 20 '68
Opera N il 31:17-20 Mr 11 '67
Sat R 50:41 Mr 18 '67

Records:
Un ballo in maschera. il Opera N 31:34 Ap 15 '67
Falstaff. il Opera N 31:34 F 11 '67
Five arias from Verdi operas. Opera N 31:34 F 25 '67
La forza del destino. Opera N 31:32 Mr 18 '67

La Traviata. il Opera N 32:34 N 25 '67

Rigoletto. Criticism
Opera N il 31:17-20 Ap 8 '67

La Traviata. Criticism
Dance Mag il 41:29-30+ Mr '67
Hi Fi il 17:MA6 D '67
New Yorker 43:93-4 F 25 '67
New Yorker 43:138-9 S 23 '67
New Yorker 43:84 S 30 '67
Opera N 31:24-6 Mr 25 '67
Opera N il 31:17-20 Mr 25 '67
Opera N il 32:17-19 D 30 '67
Sat R 50:105 Ap 22 '67

Il Trovatore. Criticism
New Yorker 42:121 F 4 '67
Opera N il 31:17-20 F 18 '67
Sat R 50:62+ F 25 '67

Verdian Requiem by La Scala. I. Kolodin. Sat R 50:49-50 N 4 '67

Verdi's fathers. S. Hughes. Opera N 31:24-5 Ap 8 '67

VERDON, René
He cooked for the Kennedys. il por Newsweek 70:17 D 18 '67

VERDON-SMITH, Sir Reginald
Verdon-Smith of Lloyds bank. por Fortune 75:51 Ap '67

VERDY, Violette
World of dance. W. Terry. por(p43) Sat R 50:64 S 9 '67

VERE, Diana
Ballerina's day; interview. New Yorker 43:34-5 My 20 '67

VERHOVEN, Peter J.
There is nothing junior about the junior college. Parks & Rec 2:43-4 O '67

VERITY, William E.
I crossed the Atlantic in a 12-foot sloop. por Pop Sci 190:104-8+ Ja; 94-9+ F '67

VERMEULE, Emily
Promise of Thera. Atlan 220:83-4+ D '67

VERMICULITE
Chemical exfoliation of vermiculite and the production of colloidal dispersions. G. F. Walker and W. G. Garrett. bibliog il Science 156:385-7 Ap 21 '67

VERMONT
From sword to scythe in Champlain country. E. A. Starbird. il Nat Geog Mag 132:153-201 Ag '67
See also
Architecture, Domestic—Vermont
Booksellers and bookselling—Vermont
Education—Vermont
Skis and skiing—Vermont

Historic houses, etc.
Rockefeller home designated historic landmark; address. C. A. T. Johnson. il Parks & Rec 2:23+ Ag '67

VERNON, Jeremy
Maybe tomorrow, maybe the next day. W. C. Heinz. il pors Sat Eve Post 241:65-9 Ja 27 '68

VERNON, Raymond
Multinational enterprise & national sovereignty. Harvard Bsns R 45:156-8+ Mr '67

VERONA, Italy

Music
Verona (cont) E. Davidson. Opera N 32:28 O 14 '67

VERREAUX eagles. See Eagles

VERRIER, Anthony
Report from Arabia. Fortune 76:77+ N '67

VERSAILLES, Palaces of
Fresh wind through Versailles. V. Lawford. il Vogue 150:120-7+ Ag 1 '67

VERSATILE avionics shop test. See Airplanes, Military—Electronic equipment—Testing

VERSIFICATION
Turning on the light; art and craft of light verse. R. Armour. Writer 80:33-5+ Ap '67
See also
Poetics

VERSTEEGH, Byron
How to keep 'em rolling when the going gets tough. M. Smith, jr. il por Pop Mech 128:106-9+ Jl '67

VERTEBRATES
Major steps in vertebrate evolution; address, December 28, 1967. A. S. Romer. bibliog il Science 158:1629-37 D 29 '67
Natural free-running period in vertebrate animal populations. C. H. Lowe and others. bibliog il Science 156:531-4 Ap 28 '67

VERTICAL density currents. See Hydrodynamics

VERTICAL display indicator group system. See Aeronautic instruments—Display systems

VERTICAL-scale engine instruments. See Aeronautic instruments

VERTICAL take-off and landing airplanes. See Airplanes, Vertical take-off and landing

VERUSCHKA
Veruschka; with report by R. Chelminski. il pors Life 63:45-55 Ag 18 '67

VERVET monkeys. See Monkeys

VERY high frequency omnidirectional range. See Radio in aviation

VERY Narcissus; story. See Huber, K.

VESELL, Elliot S.
Induction of drug-metabolizing enzymes in liver microsomes of mice and rats by softwood bedding. bibliog Science 157:1057-8 S 1 '67

VESTA (asteroid) See Asteroids

VESTAL, David
Cartier-Bresson today. Pop Phot 60:139 My '67
David in Adamsland. il Pop Phot 61:90-101+ D '67
Home cooking. Pop Phot 61:102-3+ Ag '67
(comp) Thirty years of books that shaped photography. Pop Phot 60:104-7+ My '67

VETERANS. See Service men, Discharged

VETERINARY instruments and apparatus
Dairy health first aid kit. J. W. Bailey. Suc Farm 65:135-6 Mr '67

VETERINARY medicine
Are drugs safe on the farm? FDA orders study of medicated feed additives. Bsns W p54 Ja 14 '67
Contracts save your money and your vet. L. A. Baker. Farm J 91:D10 Je '67
Do streptomycin and sirloin mix? Bsns W p 104-5 Jl 1 '67
Vet contract makes money. R. C. Black. il Farm J 91:66T+ Mr '67
Veterinary helps. J. W. Bailey. See issues of Successful farming
What to do about four common diseases. J. G. Clark. il Farm J 91:B12 Mr '67

VETERINARY quarantine. See Quarantine, Veterinary

VEVERKA, Joseph. See Sagan, C. jt. auth.

VIA, Bernard S.
High rise; poem. Christian Cent 84:617 My 10 '67

VIABILITY of seed. See Germination

VIAL, Pedro
Pedro Vial and the roads to Santa Fe, by N. M. Loomis and A. P. Nasatir. Review Sat R 50:52 Je 10 '67. B. Garfield

VIBRAPHONE
Jazz and the vibraphone. M. Williams. il Sat R 50:78-9 N 11 '67
Vibe tribe; vibraharp players. il Newsweek 69:105 My 15 '67

VIBRATION
Vibration analysis finds a tool. il Sci N 93:19-20 Ja 6 '68

Measurement
Monitoring system to provide data on Saturn V vibrations. il Tech W 20:30 Ap 24 '67

VIBURNUMS
Add a viburnum to your garden. D. Wyman. il Horticulture 45:38-9+ O '67
Double file viburnum. il Flower Grower 54:43 Ja '67

VICE
Wicked cities of the world. G. Feifer. il Holiday 43:72-83 Ja '68
See also
Prostitution

VICE-PRESIDENTIAL candidates
Where is Bill Miller? D. Schaap. Harper 235: 68-72 D '67

VICE-PRESIDENTS

United States
Humphrey-Nixon law. Nation 204:514 Ap 24 '67
No longer a hot subject. il Time 90:16 Jl 28 '67
Veepstakes. il Newsweek 70:22-3 Jl 31 '67

Powers and duties
Hubert Humphrey's scientific role: from ocean depths to outer space. B. Nelson. il por Science 155:981-3 F 24 '67

VICE-PRESIDENTS (in business) See Executives

VICENZO, Roberto de
Champ from the Pampas. il por Time 90:70 Jl 28 '67
They all love a Latin. G. S. Brown. il pors Sports Illus 27:12-15 Jl 24 '67

VICKERS, Jon
Postscript on Vickers; an interview, ed. by S. Jenkins, jr. pors Am Rec G 33:736-7+ My '67

VICKERS, Jonathan
Living with antiques in England. Antiques 92:208-9 Ag '67

VICTOR, Florence
Rigoletto; poem. Nation 205:346 O 9 '67; Correction. 205:418 O 30 '67

VICTOR talking machine company. See Radio corporation of America—RCA Victor division

VICTORIAN furniture. See Furniture, English

VIDA, Gabor. See Tryon, A. F. jt. auth.

VIDAL, Gore
Holy family. bibliog f Esquire 67:99-103+ Ap '67

VIDEO tape recorders and recording
Ampex makes a play for the home market. il Bsns W p 164-6+ Je 17 '67
Directory of most popular, low-priced video tape recorders. il Electr World 78:40-1 S '67
Getting it on tape; video-taped evidence. il Time 90:49 D 22 '67
Instant replay aids policy work; videotape recording system in Santa Barbara, Calif. il Am City 82:50 O '67
Long base line interferometry: a new technique. N. W. Broten and others. il Science 156:1592-3 Je 23 '67
RCA aiming at aircraft market for recorders; airborne continuous video recorders. il Aero Tech 21:36 O 9 '67
Reliving a murder; video taped evidence used in murder trial. il Time 90:38 D 29 '67
Underground channels. H. Junker. New Repub 157:33-4 S 9 '67
Video tape in the classroom, helping teachers study themselves and their teaching techniques. G. Perry. il Sr Schol 90:sup21 My 12 '67
Video tape: mass medium for individualized instruction. G. Pensinger. il Sr Schol 91: sup22-3 O 26 '67
Video tape recorders. il House & Gard 131: 18+ F '67
VTR topics. N. Eisenberg. See issues of High fidelity incorporating Musical America
Video tape recorders used in tests by Miami police. il Tech W 20:29 Je 19 '67

VIDEO tape recorders on airplanes. See Video tape recorders and recording

VIDEO tape recordings
Video tape vaudeville; Audio fidelity records. L. Klein. il Pop Phot 60:75+ F '67

VIDEOCOMP. See Phototypesetting

VIENNA
Thousand violins. A. Gingrich. il Esquire 67: 110-11+ My '67

Art
Reunion in Vienna; Kunsthistorisches museum shows collection for first time since 1938. il Time 90:34 Ag 4 '67

Description
Franz Werfel's Vienna. J. Wechsberg. il Sat R 50:62+ Mr 11 '67

History
Last waltz in Vienna. S. C. Burchell. il Horizon 10:82-101 Wint '68

Music
Notes from our correspondents. K. Blaukopf. Hi Fi 17:22+ Mr; 22+ Ag '67
Report: Vienna; productions at the State opera. J. Wechsberg. Opera N 32:32 D 30 '67
Vienna. J. Wechsberg. il Opera N 32:23-4 S 9 '67
Vienna; production of Wagner's Fliegende Holländer. J. Wechsberg. Opera N 31:32 Ap 1 '67
Vienna; State opera's new production of Le nozze di Figaro. J. Wechsberg. Opera N 31:27 Je 10 '67

VIENNA philharmonic orchestra
How it should be played. Time 90:66 O 13 '67

VIENNA state opera. See Opera—Austria

VIENNESE cookery. See Cookery, Austrian

VIENNESE pastry. See Pastry

VIERECK, Peter
Killed by a car at twenty-one; poem. Christian Cent 84:656 My 17 '67
Modern litany; poem. New Repub 156:22 Je 10 '67

VIERNO, Louis C.
Make your own Tiffany shade. Pop Mech 128:166-9 Ag '67

VIET rock; drama. See Terry, M.

VIETNAM
See also
Hunting—Vietnam
Political parties—Vietnam

Bibliography
Nationalism and communism. O. Handlin. Atlan 219:140-3 Mr '67
Vietnam: charted on a distorted map. M. O. Hatfield. il Sat R 50:20-2+ Jl 1 '67

History
Fact sheet on Viet Nam. il Sr Schol 91:4 O 5 '67
Two thousand years of war in Viet-Nam. B. F. Fall. il Horizon 9:4-23 Spr '67
Vietnam: the neglected debate; reconstruction of our foreign policy. J. Nuveen. Christian Cent 84:399-403 Mr 29 '67

Nationalism
Struggle and the war. F. FitzGerald. il Atlan 220:72-82+ Ag '67

Native races
See also
Montagnards

Politics and government
Viet Nam: crisis of indecision. R. Shaplen. For Affairs 46:95-110 O '67

VIETNAM (Democratic Republic)
Enemy land at war; North Vietnam. J. R. Moskin. il Look 31:45-51 Jl 25 '67
North Vietnam under siege; with report by L. Lockwood. il Life 62:33-44D Ap 7 '67
Visit to the North Vietnamese. J. P. Brown. Christian Cent 85:18-21 Ja 3 '68
Visit with the enemy; excerpt from Orbit of China. H. E. Salisbury. Esquire 67:90-1+ My '67
Voices of the Vietcong. D. Halberstam. Harper 236:45-52 Ja '68
See also
Foreign vistors in Vietnam (Democratic Republic)
Hanoi
Hospitals—Vietnam (Democratic Republic)
Medical relief work—Vietnam (Democratic Republic)
Political parties—Vietnam
Secret service—Vietnam (Democratic Republic)

Air force
Air war: end of a MIG sanctuary. il U S News 63:12 N 6 '67

Army
Awkward facts; Communists use Cambodia as base area and sanctuary. il Newsweek 70:46 D 4 '67
Buildup on the border; North Vietnamese infiltrators in Cambodia. il Time 90:27-8 D 1 '67
Cambodia: growing base for Vietnam reds. il U S News 63:62-3 D 11 '67
Charlie, come home! propaganda to urge Viet Cong to defect. il Time 89:32-3 F 10 '67
Is this overkill? Viet Cong 9th division. New Repub 158:8 Ja 13 '68
More and more Soviet arms keep war going. il U S News 62:31 Ap 3 '67
Proof of who is running Hanoi's war. U S News 62:10 Mr 27 '67
Puzzle at the Pentagon; decline in infiltration. il Newsweek 69:56 Ja 30 '67
Saigon vs. Washington; infiltration figures. Newsweek 69:44 F 6 '67
Special war; operations against Ho Chi Minh trail. il Time 89:34 My 19 '67
Versatile enemy. il Time 90:28+ Jl 21 '67
Wanted: a new commissar; General Nguyen Chi Thanh dies. Time 90:21 Jl 14 '67

Defenses
Charting the enemy's strength; with charts of North Vietnamese combat power. Bsns W p82-4 Ag 12 '67
North Viets quickly return Phuc Yan to full operation. il Aviation W 87:22-3 N 6 '67
Scarred countryside on the alert for máy-bay-my. il Life 62:36-9 Ap 7 '67

Economic conditions
Story of red triumph, Saigon failure? il U S News 63:9 D 25 '67

Foreign opinion
American
Other side, by S. Lynd and T. Hayden. Review New Repub 156:27-9 Ap 8 '67. R. Steel

Foreign relations
China and North Vietnam: the limits of the alliance. I. C. Ojha. bibliog f Cur Hist 54:42-7 Ja '68
How Hanoi controls the Vietcong. J. H. Weiss. il Reporter 38:27-8 Ja 11 '68
Negotiations now? reflections on a meeting with the enemy; DRV and NLF-U.S. talks in Czechoslovakia. C. Jencks. New Repub 157:19-23 O 7 '67

Politics and government
How Hanoi sees the war. D. Warner. il Reporter 37:17-20 Ag 10 '67
Trials of Ho; likely successors as president. il Time 90:37 N 24 '67

Relief work
See also
Medical relief work—Vietnam (Democratic Republic)

VIETNAM (Democratic Republic) and the United States
Visit to the North Vietnamese. J. P. Brown. Christian Cent 85:18-21 Ja 3 '68

VIETNAM (Republic)
Bell of decision rings out in Vietnam. T. H. White. il Life 63:54-6+ S 1 '67
Filipino in Vietnam. America 117:446 O 21 '67
Other Vietnam; behind battlefronts and headlines. J. Bingham. Mlle 65:179+ O '67
Secretary McNamara discusses the situation in Viet-Nam; statement, July 12, 1967. R. S. McNamara. Dept State Bul 57:167-70 Ag 7 '67
Seven Asian and Pacific nations consult on efforts in Viet-Nam; text of communique, April 21, 1967. Dept State Bul 56:747-9 My 15 '67
South Viet Nam: big little country. E. Sparn. Sr Schol 91:5 O 5 '67
Who holds what in Vietnam now. il U S News 62:35 My 22 '67
See also
Agriculture—Vietnam (Republic)
Americans in Vietnam
Catholics in Vietnam
Child welfare—Vietnam (Republic)
Church and state in Vietnam (Republic)
Economic assistance in Vietnam (Republic)
Education—Vietnam (Republic)
Elections—Vietnam (Republic)
Hospitals—Vietnam (Republic)
Labor and laboring classes—Vietnam (Republic)
Land tenure—Vietnam (Republic)
Libraries—Vietnam (Republic)
Medical relief work—Vietnam (Republic)
Morale. National—Vietnam (Republic)
Newspapers—Vietnam (Republic)
Peasantry—Vietnam (Republic)
Phuoc Vinh
Police—Vietnam (Republic)
Political campaigns—Vietnam (Republic)
Political parties—Vietnam
Technical assistance in Vietnam
Tourist trade—Vietnam (Republic)
Transportation—Vietnam (Republic)
United Nations—Vietnam (Republic)
United States—Armed forces—Forces in Vietnam
United States—Foreign relations—Vietnam (Republic)
Vietnamese crisis, 1964
Vietnamese war, 1957- —Public opinion
Women—Vietnam (Republic)

Armed forces
Hatchet man; drive to eliminate corruption and inefficiency. Newsweek 70:49 Ag 28 '67
In Vietnam: whose war is it now? il U S News 63:21-2 Jl 24 '67

Army
A.R.V.N. can fight! M. Novak. Christian Cent 84:1310 O 18 '67
ARVN: toward fighting trim. il Time 91:31 Ja 5 '68
Buddying up; on-the-job training for ARVN units. il Newsweek 70:28+ Ag 14 '67
Building up the ARVN. il Time 90:24-5 Ag 4 '67
Kennedy on TV; concerning remarks on American intervention and South Vietnamese army. K. Crawford. Newsweek 70:39 D 11 '67
Return to Vietnam; why this bewildering war will not be won. D. Halberstam. il Harper 235:47-58 D '67
Struggle to rescue the people. J. Mecklin. il Fortune 75:126-33+ Ap '67
Their lions, our rabbits. M. D. Perry. il Newsweek 70:44+ O 9 '67

VIETNAM (Republic)—Army—_Continued_
Their mission: defend, befriend; pacification program of Echo two, Combined action platoon. D. Moser. il Life 63:24-9+ Ag 25 '67
Thieu on top. il Time 90:23-4 Jl 7 '67
Troubled army. Nation 205:324 O 9 '67
Vietnamese army starts to fight; with interview with C. W. Abrams. jr. il U S News 63:62-5 D 4 '67
Yanks and the gooks. M. Wallace; T. Koppel. Nation 204:811-13 Je 26 '67

Constitution 1

Document as valuable as divisions. Life 62: 4 Mr 31 '67
Ky figure; new constitution. Newsweek 69: 38 Ap 3 '67
Step by step. il Newsweek 69:43A+ Ap 10 '67
Vote of confidence in a civilian future. il Time 89:22-3 Mr 24 '67

Defenses

Alarm belt; barrier below the Demilitarized zone. il Time 90:20-1 S 15 '67
Barring the way; McNamara's line. il Newsweek 70:29 S 18 '67
Can a wall slow down the war in Vietnam; Demilitarized zone. il Bsns W p44-6 S 16 '67
Electronic wall, yet. Commonweal 86:563-4 S 22 '67
McNamara's fence against the reds; will it really work? il U S News 63:8 S 18 '67
McNamara's gimmick; barrier project. Nation 205:258 S 25 '67
McNamara's line. New Repub 157:8 S 23 '67
Vietnam, fencing in the North; U.S. plan for a barrier of electronic devices. A. Hamilton. New Repub 157:19-21 Jl 8 '67

Description and travel

Behind the headlines in Viet Nam. P. T. White. il Nat Geog Mag 131:149-89 F '67
Portfolio of drawings of Vietnam. J. Nielsen. il Am Artist 31:58-63 Ap '67

Economic conditions

Economic situation in Viet-Nam. L. B. Johnson; D. E. Lilienthal; R. W. Komer. Dept State Bul 56:467-71 Mr 20 '67
Fat cats of _lam phat_; consequences of inflation. Newsweek 69:44 My 1 '67
Mr Lilienthal to head U.S. team studying Vietnamese development. Dept State Bul 56:69 Ja 9 '67
Other war for U.S. bankers; in Vietnam, Chase Manhattan and Bank of America fight inflation. il Bsns W p92+ O 14 '67
They pay the bill for war. il Bsns W p34-6 Ap 8 '67
Vietnam's other war; battered economy. il Bsns W p99-102+ S 23 '67
See also
Saigon—Economic conditions

Economic policy

Mr Lilienthal discusses Viet-Nam's economic development program; news briefing, December 6. 1967. D. E. Lilienthal. Dept State Bul 57:864-7 D 25 '67

History

ABC's of the war in Vietnam; questions and answers. il U S News 62:37-9 Mr 20 '67

Politics and government

After the elections. New Repub 157:7-8 S 2 '67
Ambassador Goldberg reports on his trip to Asia; transcripts of news conferences, March 6. 8. 1967. A. J. Goldberg. Dept State Bul 56:505-14 Mr 27 '67
Buddhists are back; ganging up on Thieu. il Newsweek 70:49 O 9 '67
Caging the white dove; case of Truong Dinh Dzu. M. Novak. Commonweal 87:72-3 O 20 '67
Cause in Vietnam is being won. M. D. Taylor. il N Y Times Mag p36-7+ O 15 '67
Cleanup time; concerning Nguyen-huu-Co. Newsweek 69:44 F 6 '67
Fighting on two fronts; military and diplomatic. il Bsns W p45 Mr 25 '67
Ky v Buddhists, round two; dealing with United Buddhist church's call for cease-fire and peace. Tran-van-Dinh. New Repub 156: 15-19 My 13 '67
Letter from Washington (cont) R. H. Rovere. New Yorker 42:94+ Ja 21 '67
Low Ky; dismissal of General Co. il Time 89:32 F 3 '67

Monk without a cause. il Time 90:35-6 O 6 '67
Naïveté versus reality in Vietnam; excerpts from Worlds in conflict. D. W. Brogan. Atlan 220:48-55 Jl '67
NLF's terms for peace. G. M. Kahin. New Repub 157:13-17 O 14 '67
New look at Vietnam mess: the way it all began; excerpts from statement by Senate Republican policy committee, May 1, 1967. il U S News 62:68-71 My 15 '67
Policy for Vietnam. R. L. Renfield. Yale R 56:481-505 Je '67
Politics in South Vietnam. C. A. Joiner. bibliog f Cur Hist 54:35-41+ Ja '68
Report. Atlan 221:12+ Ja '68
Secretary Rusk and Ambassador Bunker discuss Viet-Nam in TV-radio interviews; transcripts of interviews, September 10, 1967. D. Rusk; E. Bunker. Dept State Bul 57:411-21 O 2 '67
Secretary Rusk's news conference of September 8, 1967. D. Rusk. Dept State Bul 57: 383-90 S 25 '67
South Vietnam leaders; Prime minister's action program. Tran-van-Dinh. New Repub 158:29 Ja 6 '68
South Vietnam's no. 1 dove. S. Weinraub. il N Y Times Mag p43+ O 8 '67
Stake worth fighting for; inauguration of president and vice president. il Time 90:25 N 3 '67
Struggle and the war. F. FitzGerald. il Atlan 220:72-82+ Ag '67
Ten-to-twenty-year war in South Vietnam? interview, ed. by J. Fromm. R. Thompson. il U S News 62:92-4 F 13 '67
Thieu and Ky squeak through. il Newsweek 70:41-2 O 16 '67
Thieu sworn in. il Sr Schol 91:22 N 16 '67
Toughest year. il Newsweek 70:40 N 6 '67
Viet Cong. by D. Pike. Review
New Yorker 42:112+ Ja 28 '67. J. Alsop
Vietnam makes ready for another beginning; inauguration of President Nguyen Van Thieu; with editorial comment. il Bsns W p42-3, 164 O 28 '67
Vietnam: the need for a loyal opposition. D. Warner. Reporter 37:23-5 D 14 '67
Voice for the countryside. Time 90:35-6 O 13 '67
Vote for the future. il Time 90:28-32 S 15 '67
We put him in; J. W. Fulbright's opinion of Ky. K. Crawford. Newsweek 69:42 F 6 '67
Welcoming a government. il Time 90:39+ N 10 '67
What else can we do? W. Pfaff. Commonweal 85:641-2 Mr 10 '67
What role for the NLF? H. Brandon. Sat R 50:5 D 30 '67
What we can do to end the agony of Vietnam; excerpts from To seek a newer world, with editorial comment. R. F. Kennedy. Look **31:34-6+ N 28 '67**
See also
Elections—Vietnam (Republic)
Vietnam (Republic)—Constitution

Relief work

See also
Medical relief work—Vietnam (Republic)
Vietnamese war. 1957- —Relief work

Religious institutions and affairs

Conversation with a monk. J. Mirsky. Nation 205:678-81 D 25 '67
See also
Church and state in Vietnam (Republic)

Social conditions

Human cost. J. Finn. Commonweal 86:573-4 S 22 '67
Progress in Vietnam; concerning Richard Critchfield's report in the Washington star. New Repub 156:7-8 Mr 18 '67; Discussion. 156:28-9 Ap 1; 27-8 Ap 22 '67
Reporter at large; village of Ben Suc. J. Schell. il New Yorker 43:28-40+ Jl 15 '67
Village of Ben Suc. by J. Schell. Review
Nation 206:55-6 Ja 8 '68. J. Mirsky

Social life and customs

They're off! Phu tho hippodrome. Saigon's race track. il Newsweek 69:44 Ap 10 '67

Social policy

Heart of the matter; pacification program. il Newsweek 69:48+ My 22 '67
U.S. support of pacification effort in Viet-Nam reorganized; statement, May 11, 1967. E. Bunker. Dept State Bul 56:844-5 Je 5 '67

VIETNAM (Republic)—*Continued*

Statistics

Vietnam: those computer reports; U.S. army information on pacification. W. J. Lederer. New Repub 157:13-14 D 23 '67

VIETNAM (Republic) and the United States
How Saigon sees US. New Repub 158:8 Ja 6 '68
Yanks and the gooks. M. Wallace; T. Koppel. Nation 204:811-13 Je 26 '67
See also
United States—Foreign opinion—Vietnamese

VIETNAM Summer. See Vietnamese war, 1957- —Protests, demonstrations, etc, against

VIETNAMESE
Enemy land at war; North Vietnam. J. R. Moskin. il Look 31:45-51 Jl 25 '67
For whose interests? R. R. Banville. Christian Cent 84:118+ Ja 25 '67
Human tragedy of Vietnam. V. S. Kearney. America 117:376-7+ O 7 '67; Discussion. 117: 529-32 N 11 '67
Journey to North Vietnam. D. Schoenbrun. il Sat Eve Post 240:21-5+ D 16 '67
Keeping up with the Tran Quan Lacs. L. G. Martin. il N Y Times Mag p22-3+ Ag 20 '67
Ten Vietnamese, by S. Sheehan. Review Newsweek 69:93-4 F 27 '67. S. K. Oberbeck
Time il 89:104+ Mr 3 '67
Thirty-seven year war of the village of Tananhoi. L. G. Martin. il N Y Times Mag p30-1+ O 29 '67
Viet Nam, the people. F. FitzGerald. il Vogue 149:174-5+ My '67
Vietnam: those computer reports; U.S. army information on pacification. W. J. Lederer. New Repub 157:13-14 D 23 '67
Vietnamese labor force in transition. M. B. Zuzik. Mo Labor R 90:32-5 N '67
Visit to the North Vietnamese. J. P. Brown. Christian Cent 85:18-21 Ja 3 '68
See also
Montagnards
Peasantry—Vietnam (Republic)

VIETNAMESE businesswomen. See Business and professional women

VIETNAMESE crisis, 1964
Fulbright's dilemma; dispute about the Tonkin Gulf resolution. il Newsweek 70:18-19 Ag 28 '67
Gulf of Tonkin resolution; text of August 7, 1964. Cur Hist 54:49 Ja '68

VIETNAMESE in the United States
Face to face with a Vietnamese girl in New York. J. Lee. Seventeen 26:161 My '67

VIETNAMESE refugees. See Refugees, Vietnamese; Vietnamese war, 1957- —Refugees

VIETNAMESE soldiers. See Vietnam (Republic)—Army

VIETNAMESE studies. See Southeast Asian studies

VIETNAMESE villages. See Villages

VIETNAMESE war, 1957-
Acheson on negotiation; excerpts from televised interview. D. Acheson. Reporter 37:28-9 D 28 '67
Ambassador Lodge discusses Viet-Nam in New York times interview. H. C. Lodge. Dept State Bul 56:795-800 My 22 '67
Ambassador Lodge discusses Viet-Nam in interview on Meet the press; transcript of radio and television program, September 17, 1967. H. C. Lodge. Dept State Bul 57:464-9 O 9 '67
As war heats up. U S News 64:20-1 Ja 8 '68
Battles in the monsoon, by S. L. A. Marshall. Review
Nat R 19:752-3 Jl 11 '67. G. F. Eliot
Beginning of the end? report from Gen. W. C. Westmoreland. il Newsweek 70:28 D 4 '67
Brighter side of the Vietnam war; Communists badly shaken. il U S News 62:40-1 Ap 10 '67
Building a nation beyond the killing; new emphasis on land control, population security and nation building. il Time 89:32-3 F 3 '67
C-123s defoliate jungle stronghold of Viet Cong; photographs. Aviation W 86:82-5 My 8 '67
Cambodia: growing base for Vietnam reds. il U S News 63:62-3 D 11 '67
Cards on the table; General Westmoreland's visit to the U.S. il Time 89:17-21 My 5 '67
China, Russia & the U.S. O. Gass. bibliog f Commentary 43:39-42 Ap '67; Reply. D. Clifford. 44:24+ S '67

Commanding General reports on the Vietnam war; excerpt from address, April 24, 1967. W. C. Westmoreland. U S News 62:42-4 My 8 '67
Conversation with Dean Rusk; transcript of interview, ed. by P. Niven. D. Rusk. Dept State Bul 56:774-81 My 22 '67
Conversation with Dulles; footnote on Suez and Vietnam. L. Jefferson. Nat R 19:681-2 Je 27 '67
Dark portents; war nearing point of no return. E. J. Hughes. Newsweek 69:19 My 29 '67
Decisive battles near in Vietnam war? G. C. Troelstrup. il U S News 62:52-3 My 1 '67
Devils of *Tet*; violations of cease-fire. il Time 89:27-8 F 17 '67
Election, a barrier and talk of peace. il Newsweek 70:27-8+ S 18 '67
End of Vietnam war in sight? interview. H. K. Johnson. il U S News 63:44-8 S 11 '67
End the war talks? what General Wheeler thinks. E. G. Wheeler. U S News 64:10 Ja 1 '68
Enemy's weapons. il Time 89:24 Mr 24 '67
Escalation from Hanoi; Communists continue to increase pressure in the South. il Time 89:32-3 My 19 '67
Farewell assessment of Vietnam. F. McCulloch. il Life 63:34-34A D 15 '67
For whose interests? R. R. Banville. Christian Cent 84:118+ Ja 25 '67
Fourth largest war; address, April 7, 1967. G. Romney. Vital Speeches 33:462-5 My 15 '67; Excerpts. U S News 62:20 Ap 17 '67
Fresh look at the Vietnam war. J. N. Wallace. il U S News 63:62-6 S 25 '67
From Algeria to Vietnam. J. Kaplow. Commonweal 86:260-2 My 19 '67
General Taylor discusses recent developments in Viet-Nam; statement at press conference, January 30, 1967. M. D. Taylor. Dept State Bul 56:285-7 F 20 '67
Halt Vietnam bombing? U S News 62:15 Ap 3 '67
Home-front war; visit to U.S. by Gen. William C. Westmoreland. il Newsweek 69:31-6 My 8 '67
How goes the war? il Newsweek 71:17-20+ Ja 1 '68
How long will it last? M. Frankel. il N Y Times Mag p28-9+ Ap 30 '67
How reds cashed in on bombing pause. il U S News 62:33-9 Mr 27 '67
How the marines fight the other war; pacification program of the combined-action company. S. Dickerman. il Reporter 36: 31-3 Ap 6 '67
If war now spreads in Asia: bigger burden for U.S. il U S News 64:29-31 Ja 15 '68
Journey to North Vietnam. D. Schoenbrun. il Sat Eve Post 240:21-5+ D 16 '67
Leaning on Vietnamese; U.S. leaders ask more effort. il U S News 63:20+ O 30 '67
McNamara's reports on nine Vietnam visits, the record. R. S. McNamara. il U S News 63:23 Jl 24 '67
Missile defense, nuclear spread and Vietnam. D. R. Inglis. Bul Atomic Sci 23:49-52 My '67
Mr Clifford and General Taylor report on talks on Viet-Nam with allied leaders; transcript of press conference, August 5, 1967. M. D. Taylor; C. M. Clifford. Dept State Bul 57: 256-60 Ag 22 '67
NLF's new program. D. Warner. Reporter 37: 23-4+ O 5 '67
Negotiations now? reflections on a meeting with the enemy; DRV and NLF-U.S. talks in Czechoslovakia. C. Jencks. New Repub 157:19-23 O 7 '67
New turn in Vietnam, a deal between Russia and China. U S News 62:42-3 Ap 24 '67
Non-debate; ADA and M. L. King's stands. K. Crawford. Newsweek 69:46 Ap 17 '67
Notes on a monstrous war. R. Sherrod. il Life 62:20-9 Ja 27 '67
Now the ninth coming; R. S. McNamara's latest visit to Vietnam. il Newsweek 70:21-2 Jl 17 '67
Offense is the worst defense. E. Rabinowitch; discussion. Bul Atomic Sci 23:32-3 Ja; 26 F '67
On not knowing when to stop; danger that red China might enter the war. Nation 204:548 My 1 '67
Operation Dragnet; combined military and police campaign to discover Viet Cong members. M. Perry. il Newsweek 70:43-4 Jl 24 '67
Political horrors; the war, central to the politics of 1967. K. Crawford. Newsweek 69:40 My 15 '67
Politics. D. MacDonald. Esquire 67:30+ Mr '67

VIETNAMESE war, 1957- —*Continued*
President Johnson holds talks with Australian Prime Minister; remarks, June 1, 1967. L. B. Johnson; H. E. Holt. Dept State Bul 56: 960-3 Je 26 '67
Press conference at headquarters; September 16, 1967. Thant. UN Mo Chron 4:23-6 O '67
Problem is not with this government. .; excerpts from press conference. L. B. Johnson. Time 89:22 Mr 17 '67
Profiles in opportunism; C. H. Percy resolution for greater Asian military support. Nation 205:387-8 O 23 '67
Progress. Time 90:22-3 N 24 '67
Prologue. Nation 204:675-6 My 29 '67
Real stalemate; debate at home. Time 90:24 N 10 '67
Report. il Atlan 220:14+ S '67
Report of success in the war; situation in central provinces. il U S News 63:24-5 D 25 '67
Report on Viet-Nam; address, November 17, 1967. E. Bunker. Dept State Bul 57:781-4 D 11 '67
Reporter at large; village of Ben Suc. J. Schell. il New Yorker 43:28-40+ Jl 15 '67
Return to Vietnam; why this bewildering war will not be won. D. Halberstam. il Harper 235:47-58 D '67
Rivals for the Vietcong? W. Pfaff. Commonweal 85:615-17 Mr 3 '67
Saigon vs. Washington; new note of optimism in evaluations of the military progress. Newsweek 69:44 F 6 '67
Secretary McNamara discusses the situation in Viet-Nam; statement, July 12, 1967. R. S. McNamara. Dept State Bul 57:167-70 Ag 7 '67
Secretary Rusk and Secretary McNamara discuss developments in Latin America and Viet-Nam; statements, with questions and answers, February 28, 1967. D. Rusk; R. S. McNamara. Dept State Bul 56:464-6 Mr 20 '67
Secretary Rusk discusses European affairs and Viet-Nam in interview for German television; transcript of interview, February 10, 1967. D. Rusk. Dept State Bul 56:358-65 Mr 6 '67
Secretary Rusk discusses the Punta del Este conference and Viet-Nam on Meet the press; transcript of interview, April 16, 1967. D. Rusk. Dept State Bul 56:722-8 My 8 '67
Secretary Rusk discusses Viet-Nam in interview for foreign television; videotaped, October 16, 1967. D. Rusk. Dept State Bul 57:595-602 N 6 '67
Secretary Rusk replies to questions on Viet-Nam for Swedish newspaper. D. Rusk. Dept State Bul 57:91-4 Jl 24 '67
Seven Asian and Pacific nations consult on efforts in Viet-Nam; text of communique, April 21, 1967. Dept State Bul 56:747-9 My 15 '67
Shortages and sanctuaries; key senators report on Vietnam; excerpts. J. Stennis; S. Symington. il U S News 62:38-9 Ap 10 '67
Situation in Viet-Nam. Thant. UN Mo Chron 4:30 Mr '67
Stakes in Vietnam. K. T. Young. Cur Hist 54:22-8+ Ja '68
Stalled war: now what? il U S News 63:25-6 Jl 17 '67
Statement regarding Viet-Nam; May 11, 1967. Thant. UN Mo Chron 4:56-9 Je '67
Struggle and the war. F. FitzGerald. il Atlan 220:72-82+ Ag '67
T.R.B. from Washington; inevitable consequences of U.S. escalation. New Repub 156:4 My 6 '67; Reply. V. H. Edmonds. 156:43 Je 3 '67
Taking stock; Defense secretary's ninth visit to Viet Nam. il Time 90:20-1 Jl 14 '67
That man and that boy; L. B. Johnson-R. Kennedy feud. il Newsweek 69:25-6 Mr 20 '67
Time of the jabberwock; views of statesmen. E. J. Hughes. Newsweek 7023 D 11 '67
Toughened mood; concerning Senate speech on ending war. Time 89:21 Mr 10 '67
Trouble in I corps; marines guard five northern provinces. il Newsweek 69:38 Je 5 '67
Truth about war in Vietnam: facts vs. propaganda. il U S News 63:40-3 Jl 31 '67; Same abr. with title Sobering truth about the war. Read Digest 91:85-8 O '67
Two thousand years of war in Viet-Nam. B. F. Fall. il Horizon 9:4-23 Spr '67
Viet-Nam and the international law of self-defense; address, December 13, 1966. L. C. Meeker. Dept State Bul 56:54-63 Ja 9 '67

Vietnam balance sheet. H. W. Baldwin. il Reporter 37:14-18 O 19 '67
Vietnam: comparisons and convictions; address, November 7, 1967. H. K. Johnson. Vital Speeches 34:168-71 Ja 1 '68
Vietnam: last chance? E. G. Martin. il Newsweek 70:64-5 S 25 '67
Vietnam revisited; as Symington sees it now; excerpts from report. S. Symington. U S News 62:13 Ap 3 '67
Vietnam revisited: change in the war as seen by a veteran observer. S. W. Sanders. il U S News 62:31-2 Mr 6 '67
Vietnam: slow, tough but coming along. H. Donovan. il Life 62:68+ Je 2 '67
Vietnam the incubator. Commonweal 86:459-60 Jl 28 '67
Vietnam; the situation today; address, April 28, 1967. W. C. Westmoreland. Vital Speeches 33:450-2 My 15 '67; Same with title Report to the Congress by the commander of U.S. military forces in Viet-Nam. Dept State Bul 56:738-41 My 15 '67; Excerpts. U S News 62:44-5 My 8 '67
Vietnam war and American life; symposium. il Newsweek 70:16-26+ Jl 10 '67
Vietnam: war tide turning to U.S? with report by H. Handleman. il U S News 63: 50-3 N 27 '67
View from Hanoi. Nation 205:66-7 Jl 31 '67
Village of Ben Suc, by J. Schell. Review Nation 206:55-6 Ja 8 '68. J. Mirsky
War for southeast Asia. R. Hotz. Aviation W 86:21 Ap 24 '67
War on the third front; impact of Westmoreland's U.S. mission. Nation 204:610-11 My 15 '67
War; symposium. il Commonweal 86:569-87 S 22 '67
Westmoreland's Progress report. A. Hamilton. il New Repub 157:15-18 D 16 '67
What General Westmoreland told Congress; excerpts from address, April 28, 1967. W. C. Westmoreland. U S News 62:44-5 My 8 '67
White House report: we are more optimistic than we dare say. U S News 63:23 Ag 28 '67
Why Vietnam worries the Russians. W. Attwood. Look 31:23-5 Jl 11 '67
Will China intervene? the stakes in Vietnam. W. C. McWilliams. Commonweal 85:553-5 F 17 '67
See also
Conscientious objectors
Guam conference, 1967
Mines. Military
Vietnam (Democratic Republic)—Army

Aerial operations

AC-47 broadens Viet attack envelope. C. Brownlow. il Aviation W 86:54-5+ Ap 17 '67
Air force North Vietnam effort dependent on Thai bases. C. Brownlow. il Aviation W 86:26-9 Ap 3 '67
Air losses spark Phuc Yen strike. C. Brownlow. il Aviation W 87:16-17 O 30 '67
Air war advances detailed for Congress. Aviation W 87:24-5 O 2 '67
Air war, by F. Harvey. Review New Repub 158:23-6 Ja 13 '68. H. R. Coursen, jr
Air war: end of a MIG sanctuary. il U S News 63:12 N 6 '67
Airpower over North Vietnam. R. Hotz. Aviation W 87:21 S 11 '67
Airpower over North Vietnam; excerpts from statement. J. P. McConnell. Aviation W 87:21 Ag 28 '67
Airpower over North Vietnam; excerpts from statements. R. S. McNamara. Aviation W 87:11 S 4 '67
Antiseptic war; bombing by navy attack planes. E. Martin. il Newsweek 69:48-9 My 29 '67
Aunt Effie and the brass; congressional hearings and expert judgment. W. F. Whyte. Nation 205:134-5 Ag 28 '67
B-52's move to Thai bases; from Guam to Thailand. il Sr Schol 90:17-18 Ap 7 '67
Bagel strategy; attempt to isolate Haiphong. il Newsweek 70:58+ S 25 '67
Bomb restriction criticism has little effect on supplemental. D. C. Winston. Aviation W 86:17-18 F 20 '67
Bombing: an admiral's report; interview. ed. by E. Martin. D. C. Richardson. il Newsweek 69:49 My 29 '67
Bombing controversy; bombing of North Viet Nam. il Time 89:21-2 Mr 3 '67

VIETNAMESE war, 1957- —Aerial operations
—Continued
Bombing criticism expands in Congress; public
exchange between Sen. Symington and Mc-
Namara on the bombing of MiG bases in
North Vietnam; with editorial comment.
D. C. Winston. il Aviation W 86:21, 28-9
Ap 10 '67
Bombing of civilians; the Red cross stand.
A. Joyce. Christian Cent 84:480 Ap 12 '67
Bombing of the innocents; U.S. air raids in
North Vietnam. W. F. Buckley, jr. Nat R
19:293 Mr 21 '67
Bombing question in Viet Nam; viewpoints.
Sr Schol 90:20 Ap 14 '67
Bombing; Senate preparedness investigating
subcommittee hearings. New Repub 157:6
S 9 '67
Bombing story; U.S. bombing policy as re-
ported in London's Economist. Time 89:63
Mr 24 '67
Busiest bombing month. il Time 90:19-20
S 8 '67
Carrier pilots show little stress in North Viet-
nam raids. C. M. Plattner. il Aviation W
86:80-1+ Ap 24 '67
Carriers launch strikes against Vietnam.
photographs. Aviation W 86:50-3 F 27 '67
Case for bombing pause number seven. Life
63:4 O 20 '67
Change   of   weather;   Operation   Rolling
Thunder. Time 90:23 D 29 '67
Cost goes up again; bombing of Thai Nguyen
iron and steel complex. il Time 89:30 Mr
17 '67
Dangerous air war becomes deadly. il U S
News 63:41 S 18 '67
Deaf ear to the military; Stennis committee
inquiry into conduct of U.S. air offensive
against North Viet Nam. Time 90:14 S 8
'67
Diminishing heartland; bombing along the
Red River. il Time 89:23 Je 2 '67
Diminishing returns; increased pitch of air
war. il Newsweek 70:38 S 4 '67
Efficient thunder; bombing of Hanoi's out-
skirts. il Time 89:25 My 12 '67
Full story of Lyndon Johnson's world war III
remark; U.S. attack of oil-storage facilities
at Haiphong. il U S News 62:21 My 29 '67
General LeMay's god. Christian Cent 84:229 F
22 '67
Generals vs. Vietnam strategy; excerpts from
testimonies   before   Senate   preparedness
investigation subcommittee. G. L. Meyers;
H. K. Johnson; W. M. Greene, jr. U S
News 63:114 N 6 '67
Hanoi: cool to peace; Washington: new heat
in war debate. il U S News 63:8+ O 16 '67
High-level dispute; how much does bombing
help? il U S News 62:10 Mr 6 '67
If U.S. hadn't pulled its punch; excerpts
from testimony, August 1967. J. P. McCon-
nell. U S News 63:10 O 16 '67
Improved North Viet air capability cited. E.
H. Kolcum. Aviation W 87:32 D 4 '67
Into exile; air strike against two MIG bases.
il Time 90:24 N 3 '67
Into the barrel; missions from Thai bases.
il Time 90:34-5 O 13 '67
Into the buffer zone; bombing within twelve
miles of China. il Time 90:14-15 Ag 25 '67
Is the national honor being bombed? N.
Cousins. Sat R 50:22 S 9; 24+ O 21 '67
Laurels for 1967. R. Hotz. Aviation W 87:
11 D 25 '67
Let's fight to win in Vietnam; proposal to
bomb military targets in North Vietnam.
F. V. Drake. Read Digest 90:67-72 My '67
LBJ and RFK: now a sharper rift on war.
U S News 62:14 Mr 13 '67
McNamara backs bomb policy in defending
present limitations. D. C. Winston. Avia-
tion W 86:19 F 27 '67
McNamara on bombing the North; excerpts
from report. R. S. McNamara. Time 90:19
S 1 '67
McNamara's non-war. J. Burnham. Nat R
19:1012-14 S 19 '67
Major U.S. bastion springs up in Thailand.
il Bsns W p38-9 My 13 '67
Marine North Viet air effort spurred by DMZ
violation. C. Brownlow. il Aviation W 86:
72-3+ Ap 10 '67
Meyers deplores Viet air war gradualism;
testimony before the Senate Armed services
preparedness   investigating   subcommittee.
G. L. Meyers. Aviation W 87:55+ N 6 '67
Military voice; schism between the Joint
chiefs and the Department of defense. Na-
tion 205:228 S 18 '67
Mini-barrier; actions over North Vietnam. il
Newsweek 69:44 My 1 '67

Mr Bundy discusses Viet-Nam on Meet the
press; transcript of interview. August 27,
1967. W. P. Bundy. Dept State Bul 57:352-7
S 18 '67
More escalation, why? bombing MIG airfields.
Nation 204:579-80 My 8 '67
More of the same; air force chief McConnell
supports bombing. il Time 90:27 O 13 '67
Navy develops package air strike tactic. C.
Brownlow. il Aviation W 86:16-19 F 27
'67
Needs outpace strong Viet recon gains. C.
Brownlow. il Aviation W 86:19-22 Mr 13 '67
New bombing strategy; reduced number of
untouched targets. il Time 90:29 S 22 '67
New fury in the bombing war; but will Hanoi
quit? il U S News 63:6 S 4 '67
New light on wrangle over civilian casual-
ties; concerning report in New York times
by R. W Apple, jr. U S News 62:11 Mr 6
'67
New phase in air war against North Vietnam?
U S News 63:22 S 25 '67
New targets. il Time 89:31 My 5 '67
New turn in the air war over North Vietnam.
il U S News 63:6 O 23 '67
New Viet strikes approach China border. il
Aviation W 87:19-20 Ag 21 '67
North Viet air loss rate slashed. C. Brown-
low. Aviation W 87:26-7 Ag 28 '67
North Viets quickly return Phuc Yen to full
operation. il Aviation W 7:22-3 N 6 '67
Notes and comment; concerning McNamara's
testimony before the Senate preparedness
subcommittee   on   the   bombing   of   North
Vietnam. New Yorker 43:37 S 16 '67
One bridge, one buffalo; bombing of Long
Bein bridge near Hanoi. Time 90:27 Ag 18
'67
Over the slope to total war? P. Ramsey.
Cath World 205:166-8 Je '67
Pentagon euphoria; Chinese border viola-
tions. Nation 205:163 S 4 '67
President reviews U.S. position on bombing
of North Viet-Nam; text of letter, March
1, 1967. L. B. Johnson. Dept State Bul 56:
514-16 Mr 27 '67
Quick strikes follow truce in Viet. C. Brown-
low. Aviation W 88:16 Ja 1 '68
Racing the monsoon; increased bombing near
China's border. il Time 90:18 S 1 '67
Report from North Vietnam. J. Gerassi. New
Repub 156:13-15 Mr 4 '67
Rift over North Viet restrictions widens. D.
C. Winston. Aviation W 87:22-3 S 4 '67
RFK vs. LBJ. il Sr Schol 90:18 Mr 17 '67
Rolling the thunder; W. W. Momyer, the
man who is running the air war. il Time
90:23 D 29 '67
Secretary Rusk and Ambassador Bunker dis-
cuss Viet-Nam in TV-radio interviews;
transcripts of interviews, September 10,
1967. D. Rusk; E. Bunker. Dept State Bul
57:411-21 O 2 '67
Secretary Rusk's news conference of October
12, 1967. D. Rusk. Dept State Bul 57:555-64
O 30 '67
Senate's bombing inquiry finds McNamara at
fault; excerpts from report by Senate pre-
paredness investigating subcommittee. U S
News 63:102-3 S 11 '67
Seven more; MIG-17s downed. il Time 89:32
My 19 '67
Sitting ducks who call the shots. K. V.
Brown. il Pop Mech 129:89-92+ Ja '68
Skirmishing for peace; resumption of bomb-
ing as lunar New Year's truce ends. il
Bsns W p33-4 F 18 '67
Stemming the flow? stopping men and ma-
terials from reaching Communist-led forces
in South Vietnam. Sr Schol 89:19 Ja 20 '67
Stennis committee reports; excerpts. Nat R
19:1000-1 S 19 '67
Stop the bombing? J. Fischer. Harper 235:16+
O '67
Tactical air power curtailment seen causing
excessive losses; with editorial comment.
D. C. Winston. Aviation W 87:11, 17-18 O
30 '67
Tempo of North Viet air war increases. D. C.
Winston. Aviation W 87:28-9 O 16 '67
To bomb or not to bomb: how LBJ decides;
report. J. P. Sutherland. il U S News
63:8 Ag 28 '67
To bomb or not to bomb MIG airfields. il
U S News 62:12 Ap 17 '67
Two nights of war; a B-52 returns, a boy
is wounded. J. R. Moskin. il Look 31:54
My 30 '67
USAF boosts North Viet ECM jamming. C.
Brownlow. il Aviation W 86:22-5 F 6 '67

VIETNAMESE war, 1957- —Aerial operations
—Continued
USAF chief defends Viet effectiveness. R. G. O'Lone. Aviation W 86:89-90 Mr 27 '67
USAF effectiveness, loss rate improving. C. Brownlow. il Aviation W 86:28-32 F 13 '67
USAF, Navy bombard MIG installations at Hoa Lac, Kep bases in North Vietnam; with photographs. Aviation W 86:18-23 My 8 '67
U.S. bombs Haiphong, MIGs. il Sr Schol 90: 16 My 5 '67
U.S. dilemma: if bomb it must; bombing strategy debated. il Newsweek 69:21-2 My 29 '67
U.S. ends investigation of incident involving Soviet ship at Haiphong; text of a U.S. note, July 13, 1967. Dept State Bul 57:170-1 Ag 7 '67
U.S. informs U.S.S.R. of new facts on air actions at Cam Pha. Dept State Bul 57:44 Jl 10 '67
U.S. rejects Soviet charges of attacks on ship at Cam Pha; text of note, June 3, 1967. Dept State Bul 56:953 Je 26 '67
U.S. to increase air rescue capability in southeast Asia. C. Brownlow. il Aviation W 86:40-1+ My 1 '67
Viet MiG-base strikes shun key targets. il Aviation W 86:17-18 My 1 '67
Viet operations spur new A-6 interest. C. Brownlow. il Aviation W 86:67+ Ap 24 '67
Viet target envelope may expand; USAF tactical commanders press to hit MiG bases, factories, other military support facilities. C. Brownlow. il Aviation W 86: 16-21 Mr 27 '67
Vietnam: a first step; bombing of North Vietnam. il Sat Eve Post 240:86 F 11 '67
Vietnam: same game, new rules; bombings near China. il Newsweek 70:17-18 Ag 28 '67
Visit with the enemy; excerpt from Orbit of China. H. E. Salisbury. Esquire 67:90-1+ My '67
Warmed-over Bertrand Russell; facts worth more. America 116:546 Ap 15 '67
What 2½ years of bombing has done to North Vietnam. il U S News 63:34-5 S 11 '67
Who's credible now? President's letter, Ho's reply, R. Kennedy's reaction. K. Crawford. Newsweek 69:36 Ap 3 '67
Why new furor over bombing in Vietnam. il U S News 63:24 Ag 28 '67
See also
Helicopters—Military applications

Statistics
DOD admits higher air losses. Aviation W 86:16 F 20 '67
New totals on plane losses in Vietnam. il U S News 62:16 F 20 '67

Aims
See Vietnamese war, 1957- —War aims

American participation
ABC's of the war in Vietnam; questions and answers. il U S News 62:37-9 Mr 20 '67
Advice & dissent. Sr Schol 91:20 S 21 '67
Ambassador Bunker assesses current situation in Viet-Nam; news conference, November 13, 1967. E. Bunker. Dept State Bul 57:748-51 D 4 '67
American policy: the Vietnam war; address, September 29, 1967. L. B. Johnson. Vital Speeches 34:2-4 O 15 '67; Same with title Why we are in Vietnam. il U S News 63:80-2 O 16 '67; Same with title Answering aggression in Viet-Nam. Dept State Bul 57; 519-22 O 23 '67
American purposes and the pursuit of human dignity; address, August 9, 1967. D. Rusk. Dept State Bul 57:343-9 S 18 '67
Arrogance of power, by J. W. Fulbright. Review
 Sat R 50:33 F 11 '67. F. Altschul
As a top general sees the war now; excerpts from statements, January 1967. E. G. Wheeler. U S News 62:14 Ja 30 '67
As an Asian neutralist sees U.S. stake in Vietnam; interview. Souvanna Phouma. il U S News 63:106-7 N 6 '67
As the military sees it: failure of a strategy. M. S. Johnson. U S News 62:33-4 My 8 '67
Ask not what. . . excerpts from address. K. Boulding. New Repub 157:7 O 7 '67
Assent from academe; statement from scholars after debate in Tuxedo, N.Y. il Time 90:10-11 D 29 '67
Back to normal. K. Crawford. Newsweek 70: 28 Jl 24 '67

Bitter heritage, by A. M. Schlesinger, jr. Review
 Atlan 219:138+ Mr '67. O. Handlin.
 Sat R il 50:39-41 F 4 '67. B. B. Fall
Bitterest fighting still ahead. Sr Schol 90:17 My 12 '67
Brass alibi; concerning statements of E. G. Wheeler. Nation 206:35-6 Ja 8 '68
Bugging the press; reprint of dispatch in New York times, March 2, 1967. C. Poulos. Nation 204:421 Ap 3 '67
Case for the war. W. V. Shannon. Commonweal 87:326-7 D 8 '67; Discussion. 87:395+ D 29 '67
China's cautious American policy. I. C. Ojha. bibliog f Cur Hist 53:135-40+ S '67
Complex and difficult problems in Viet-Nam; excerpt from address, October 17, 1967. N. D. Katzenback Dept State Bul 57:602-4 N 6 '67
Congress tries to recapture its birthright; questioning the President's expanding authority. Christian Cent 84:1277-8 O 11 '67
Conscience, Congress and the Court. W. More. America 117:634 N 25 '67
Courage to change. New Repub 156:3-4 Ap 1 '67
Course holds steady; despite caustic criticism on homefront. il Bsns W p35-6 N 18 '67
Cruel pendulum. H. Brandon. Sat R 50:10+ My 20 '67
Curse of confusion; M. L. King's attack on U.S. policy. E. J. Hughes. Newsweek 69:17 My 1 '67
Cybernetics of blunder. M. Roshwald. Nation 204:335-6 Mr 13 '67
Dissenting from the dissenters; administration spokesmen. il Newsweek 70:25-6 N 6 '67
Doctor King's boycott. il Sr Schol 90:15-16 Ap 21 '67
Doves, hawks and flutterers in the Foreign relations committee. M. Kalb. il N Y Times Mag p56-8+ N 19 '67; Discussion. p42 D 3; 16+ D 17 '67
Drift & dissent; increasing opposition by Congress to Johnson's war policies. il Time 90:9 Ag 11 '67
Emperor's new face. Nat R 19:1104 O 17 '67
Escalation and East Asia; excerpt from The United States in Vietnam. G. M. Kahin and J. W. Lewis. il Bul Atomic Sci 23:20-4 Ja '67
European's view of the Vietnam war. J. H. Huizinga. il Reporter 36:30+ Mr 9 '67
Evidence at Stockholm; Bertrand Russell's International war crimes tribunal. G. Julin; C. Oglesby. il Nation 204:712-21 Je 5 '67
A father speaks to the President in behalf of a son killed in Vietnam; exchange of letters by L. B. Johnson; W. J. D. Hunter; P. G. Goulding. il U S News 62:46-7 My 8 '67
Fighting on two fronts: military and diplomatic. il Bsns W p45 Mr 25 '67
Firmness and restraint in Viet-Nam; excerpts from address, October 30, 1967. D. Rusk. Dept State Bul 57:703-5 N 27 '67
From Con Thien to Capitol hill. il Sr Schol 91:11-12 O 19 '67
From Saigon to Detroit. W. Pfaff. Commonweal 86:567-8 S 22 '67
From Vietnam to isolationism? J. B. Sheerin. Cath World 206:50-1 N '67
Fulbright versus Taylor. A. Campbell. New Repub 156:26-7 F 25 '67
Fulbright's dilemma; dispute about the Tonkin Gulf resolution. il Newsweek 70: 18-19 Ag 28 '67
Galbraith plan to end the war; with reply by W. P. Bundy. J. K. Galbraith. il N Y Times Mag p29-31+ N 12 '67
General Taylor discusses recent developments in Viet-Nam; statement at press conference, January 30, 1967. M. D. Taylor. Dept State Bul 56:285-7 F 20 '67
Generals sing an old song. P. Devillers. Nation 205:233-8 S 18 '67
Going up? Rusk-Humphrey revelations on purpose of U.S. Vietnam commitment. New Repub 157:5-7 O 28 '67
Good hatchet job; concerning Senate staff report. New Repub 156:2 My 27 '67
GOP: it's spring; G. Romney speaks out. il Newsweek 69:31-2 Ap 17 '67
GOP white paper; dissent on Vietnam rejected by Senator Dirksen and others. Nation 204:642-3 My 22 '67
Great society is a sick society. J. W. Fulbright. il N Y Times Mag p30-1+ Ag 20 '67 Discussion. p2 S 3; 42+ S 10 '67
Great what-is-it; Republican Senate staff paper opposes Johnson war effort. Newsweek 69:25-6 My 15 '67

VIETNAMESE war, 1957- —American participa-
tion—*Continued*
Talks with GI's on their way to combat in
Vietnam. J. N. Wallace. il U S News
64:56-7 Ja 15 '68
Their security and ours. Nat R 19:1153-4
O 31 '67
Time of decision for LBJ: what comes next
in the war. il U S News 62:31-3 My 8 '67
To Hanoi with candor; concerning statement
by senators addressed to Hanoi. il Time
89:13-14 My 26 '67
To move a nation, by R. Hilsman. Review
New Repub 157:23-6 Jl 15 '67. J. C. Thom-
son, jr
Tougher U.S. stance: grind the enemy down;
escalating manpower and money commit-
ments to Vietnam. il Bsns W p36-7 Ap 29
'67
Toward national unity over Vietnam. N.
Cousins. Sat R 50:20-1 D 2 '67
Treadmill to disaster. J. O'Gara. Commonweal
86:569-72 S 22 '67
Two Asian leaders who support U.S. role in
Vietnam. il U S News 63:22 O 30 '67
Two rallies; gatherings in Los Angeles. Na-
tion 204:804-5 Je 26 '67
United Nations: the human factor; address,
July 30, 1967. Thant. Vital Speeches 33:
724-7 S 15 '67; Same. UN Mo Chron 4:75-83
Ag '67; Excerpts with title Is U Thant un-
fair to the U.S? U S News 63:16 Ag 14 '67
U.S. achievements in Viet-Nam; address,
January 17, 1967. E. G Wheeler. Dept State
Bul 56:186-92 F 6 '67
U.S. misadventure in Vietnam. H. J. Morgen-
thau. Cur Hist 54:29-34 Ja '68
Up from dominoes; concerning D. Rusk's
yellow peril speech. Commonweal 87:101-2
O 27 '67
Up with U Thant! Christian Cent 84:228-9 F
22 '67
Viet Cong, by D. Pike. Review
New Yorker 42:112+ Ja 28 '67. J. Alsop
Vietnam and the birds; letter. G. McGovern.
New Repub 157:28 S 23 '67
Vietnam: believe me, he can kill you. R.
Armstrong. il Sat Eve Post 240:29-35+ Mr
25 '67
Vietnam: charted on a distorted map. M. O.
Hatfield. il Sat R 50:20-2+ Jl 1 '67
Vietnam is no mistake. J. McDermott. Nation
204:203-6 F 13 '67
Vietnam, is the price too high? Q. L. Quade.
America 116:805-9 Je 3 '67
Vietnam isolationists. E. J. Hughes. News-
week 70:59 Jl 10 '67
Vietnam: its effect on the Nation; address,
August 11, 1967. M. S. Eccles. Vital Speeches
33:717-19 S 15 '67
Vietnam: joining the issues. E. W. Lefever.
Cath World 205:72-7 My '67; Reply. W. V.
O'Brien. 205:169-70 Je '67
Vietnam: let's not be children; administration
spokesmen defend policy. il Newsweek 70:
29-30 O 23 '67
Vietnam, 1968; moral issues confronted, sym-
posium. Christian Cent 85:3-8+ Ja 3 '68
Vietnam: no exit. Sat Eve Post 240:90 O 7
'67
Vietnam our position today, address, March
15, 1967. L. B. Johnson. Vital Speeches 33:
354-7 Ap 1 '67; Same with title Defense of
Viet-Nam: key to the future of free Asia.
Dept State Bul 56:534-9 Ap 3 '67; Excerpts.
U S News 62:10 Mr 27 '67
Vietnam reality; the dissenters; address,
November 11, 1967. J. A. Scerra. Vital
Speeches 34:174-6 Ja 1 '68
Vietnam: study in ironies. R. Niebuhr. New
Repub 156:11-12 Je 24 '67; Reply. M. Gor-
don. 157:36-7 Jl 22 '67
Vietnam: the charges and the facts. E. Lyons.
Read Digest 91:57-63 O '67
Vietnam: the issue and the response; ad-
dress, April 24, 1967. W. M. Greene, jr. Vital
Speeches 33:509-12 Je 1 '67
Vietnam: the logic of withdrawal; excerpt.
H. Zinn. Nation 204:170-5 F 6 '67
Vietnam: the President's next big decision.
S. Alsop. il Sat Eve Post 240:25-8 Mr 25 '67
Vietnam: world war III, Communist style;
address, October 23, 1967. W. F. Bennett.
U S News 63:108-13 N 6 '67
View from Vietnam. H. Brandon. Sat R 50:
16+ N 25 '67
Voice for the voiceless: results of U.S. press
polls. Nation 205:421+ O 30 '67
Voice of a soldier in Vietnam; letter. D. E.
Capurro. U S News 62:112 Je 5 '67
Voices of doubt. Nation 205:548 N 27 '67
War in Vietnam: how we can end it. T.
C. Sorensen. Sat R 50:19-22 O 21 '67; Dis-
cussion. 50:25 N 11; 23 N 18 '67

Warning to Hanoi from U.S. war critics. U S
News 62:14-15 My 29 '67
Was God listening when we gave thanks?
President's Thanksgiving proclamation.
Christian Cent 84:1516 N 29 '67; Discussion.
85:29 Ja 3 '68
Way out for U.S. in Vietnam war? report
from the scene. W. S. Merick. il U S News
63:28-32 Jl 17 '67
We and they. M. Ascoli. Reporter 27:12-13
N 30; 12-13 D 14 '67
We cannot accept a Communist seizure of
Vietnam. R. A. Scalapino; discussion. New
Repub 155:5-7 D 24 '66; N Y Times Mag p
12+ Ja 22 '67
What choices do we have in Vietnam? ex-
cerpts from Beyond Vietnam: the United
States and Asia. E. O. Reischauer. il Look
31:23-7 S 19 '67
What is at stake in Vietnam: an Asian view;
interview, ed. by C. T. Rowan. Y. L. Ong.
Read Digest 91:118-21 N '67
What we should do next in Asia. E. O. Rei-
schauer. il Look 31:21-3 Ap 4 '67
When is a war really a war? questions and
answers. il U S News 62:43 Mr 13 '67
Who runs the war in Viet Nam? Time essay.
Time 90:20 Ag 25 '67
Why are we in Vietnam? R. Christopher. il
Newsweek 70:36+ N 27 '67
Why don't you speak out, senator? G. Mc-
Govern. New Repub 156:10-11 Mr 18 '67
Why no war declaration? with statement by
R. S. McNamara. il U S News 62:31-3 My 22
'67
Why President Johnson sticks to his Viet-
nam guns. U S News 63:12 S 4 '67
Why the U.S. can't quit Vietnam. il U S
News 63:44-6 N 13 '67
Why U.S. is in Vietnam: an official explana-
tion. W. P. Bundy. U S News 63:48-9 D 18
'67
Why unthinkable? L. B. Johnson and es-
calation. Nation 204:482-3 Ap 17 '67
Why we are in Vietnam; address, September
29, 1967. L. B. Johnson. il U S News 63:
80-2 O 16 '67
Wobble on the war on Capitol hill; congres-
sional mind-changing on Vietnam. D. Oberdorfer. il N Y Times Mag p30-1+ D 17 '67
See also
Conscientious objectors
United States—Armed forces—Forces in Vietnam

Anecdotes, facetiae, satire, etc.
Death of seven zipperheads. W. Eastlake. il
Nation 205:530-1 N 20 '67

Art
Portfolio of drawings of Vietnam. J. Nielsen.
il Am Artist 31:58-63 Ap '67

Atrocities
Belfries & red berets. il Time 89:22-3 Je 2
'67
Debugging the VC; Associated press and New
York times reports. Nat R 19:1002+ S 19 '67
Guilty minority; first U.S. war crimes trial
to come out of Vietnam. il Time 91:31-2
Ja 5 '68
Massacre at Dak Son; Viet Cong attack. il
Time 90:32-3 D 15 '67
Off with their hands. il Newsweek 69:44 My
15 '67
Singled out for terror. Time 89:25 My 26 '67
Teaching by example; civilian massacre at
Dak Son. Newsweek 70:47 D 18 '67
Terrorism, weapon of warfare. W. F. Buck-
ley, jr. Nat R 19:237 Mr 7 '67
Two sides of atrocity; Americans commit-
ting atrocities receive sentences. il Time
90:38 Jl 14 '67
Vietcong cadre of terror; operations of F-100
unit. D. Moser. il Life 64:19-29 Ja 12 '68
Who speaks for the civilian dead in South
Vietnam? Read Digest 90:119-21 Mr '67
Why the step-up in atrocity stories? Chris-
tian Cent 85:5 Ja 3 '68

Australian participation
For undaunted criticism. R. Mathias. Christian Cent 84:1502+ N 22 '67

Bibliography
Bookmarks: Vietnam guide; comp. by M. E.
Gettleman and S. L. Silverman. Nation 205:
215-17 S 11 '67
Nationalism and communism. O. Handlin.
Atlan 219:140-3 Mr '67
Vietnam: an end in itself? A. C. Brackman.
Sat R 50:32-4 O 28 '67

VIETNAMESE war, 1957- —Casualties—*Cont.*
Napalm story; findings of H. Rusk. il Time 89:63 Mr 24 '67
New light on wrangle over civilian casualties; concerning report in New York times, by R. W. Apple, jr. U S News 62:11 Mr 6 '67
Price of war: a missing limb, an aching heart. il Newsweek 70:24-5 Jl 10 '67
Real story of war casualties. il U S News 63: 35 O 30 '67
Sacrifices in Viet-Nam marked in Memorial day messages; exchange of messages, May 30, 1967. L. B. Johnson; Nguyen van Thieu. Dept State Bul 56:917 Je 19 '67
Scarifying debate; Howard Rusk's dismissal of napalm toll challenged by Committee of responsibility. il Newsweek 69:118 Ap 17 '67
Secret weapons: Viet Cong booby trap. il Newsweek 69:36 Je 12 '67
Sorry 'bout that; paucity of official news on civilian casualties; reply with rejoinder. M. D. Reynolds. New Repub 156:34 F 18 '67
Those civilian war casualties. America 116: 710 My 13 '67
Two nights of war: a B-52 returns, a boy is wounded. J. R. Moskin. il Look 31:54 My 30 '67
Unanswered questions. Time 90:23 S 15 '67
U.S. deaths in Vietnam: a definition of escalation. C. Istock. Bul Atomic Sci 23: 62-3 Je '67
U.S. war casualties: 50,000 in '67? il U S News 62:16 F 13 '67
Vietnam: bigger battles, mounting tolls. il U S News 62:6 Ap 3 '67
Victims; investigation of civilian casualties. Nation 205:404 O 23 '67
Vietnam's daily toll: twenty-six U.S. dead. il U S News 64:12 Ja 15 '68
W.I.A; medical personnel activities and facilities. R. Nessen. il Todays Health 45:20-7 Ap '67
War's deadly toll: a new weekly peak. U S News 62:10 Je 5 '67
Why more GI's are dying in battle. il U S News 62:11 Ap 10 '67
See also
Committee of responsibility to save war-burned and war injured Vietnamese children

Causes

Why U.S. troops are in Vietnam. D. Lawrence. U S News 62:124+ My 15 '67

Censorship

War is [deleted]; censored excerpts from joint meeting of two committees considering supplemental appropriation for Vietnam war. New Repub 156:5-6 Ap 22 '67

Children

Louie, the boy on the cover. D. Moser. il Life 63:3 Ag 25 '67
Scarifying debate; Howard Rusk's dismissal of napalm toll challenged by Committee of responsibility. il Newsweek 69:118 Ap 17 '67
Two little boys from Tayninh. J. Robbins. il Good H 164:94-5+ Je '67
Vietnam's war-ravaged children; refugee center at Quang Ngai by American Friends service committee. C. Brossard. il Look 31: 22-5 Ap 18 '67

Children and the war

See War and children

Construction

See Vietnamese war, 1957- —Engineering and construction

Cost

Speaking out: Vietnam costs more than you think. V. Hartke. il Sat Eve Post 240:10+ Ap 22 '67
Vietnam prognosis: more men and money. il Bsns W p29 Ag 12 '67
War and taxes; stand against the tax increase. Nation 206:36-7 Ja 8 '68

Damage to property

See Vietnamese war, 1957- —Destruction and pillage

Destruction and pillage

North Vietnam under siege; with report by L. Lockwood. il Life 62:33-44D Ap 7 '67
Report from North Vietnam. J. Gerassi. New Repub 156:13-15 Mr 4 '67
Too blind stupid to see; obliteration of Ben Suc. J. Mirsky. il Nation 205:397-400 O 23 '67

Unrepentant, unyielding; interview with Viet Cong prisoners, after destruction of Ben-Suc in Iron triangle. B. B. Fall. New Repub 156:19-24 F 4 '67
Uprooting the Vietnamese; Iron triangle: hardcore Communist areas. New Repub 156: 9-10 Ja 28 '67

Economic aspects

After Vietnam, what? symposium; ed. by G. R. Rosen. il Duns R 89:33-5+ Je '67
Antaeus and Hercules; effects on U.S. Nation 205:390+ O 23 '67
Beating the Great society into swords. Christain Cent 84:581 My 3 '67
Biggest arms bill yet: where money goes. il U S News 63:9 S 4 '67
Converting lives into money. Christian Cent 84:333 Mr 15 '67
Defense orders start to peak out. il Bsns W p44-6 O 28 '67
Employment effect of defense expenditures. R. P. Oliver. il Mo Labor R 90:9 -16 S '67
Extra $8-billion Viet need seen. D. C. Winston. Aviation W 86:16-17 My 1 '67
House cuts Viet fund bill $61.6 million. D. C. Winston. Aviation W 86:24 Mr 20 '67
Phrase rediscovered; the military-industrial complex; profiting from defense contracts. Nation 205:420-1 O 30 '67
There to stay; effect of Vietnamese war on business. il Newsweek 70:68 Jl 10 '67
Vietnam and the poor. Sat Eve Post 240:98 F 25 '67
Vietnam: its effect on the Nation; address, August 11, 1967. M. S. Eccles. Vital Speeches 33:717-19 S 15 '67
Vietnam keeps heat on. il Bsns W p33-4 Ja 28 '67
Vietnam war in perspective; with charts. U S News 63:42-4 N 20 '67
See also
Industrial mobilization
War finance—United States

Education and the war

On campus: fear and anger; effect of war. il Newsweek 70:87-8+ Jl 10 '67
Sad young men: effects on U.S. graduate programs. New Repub 157:10 D 9 '67
Scholars and soldiers, a crisis of values. M. Windmiller. Nation 205:651-4 D 18 '67
Secondary sources; high-school students' judgments about the Vietnamese war. il Newsweek 70:88+ Jl 10 '67

Engineering and construction

Will civilian builders go to war again? military construction program in Vietnam. il Bsns W p 153-4+ Ap 15 '67

Equipment and supplies

Aid to our enemies; address, August 27, 1967. K. E. Mundt. Vital Speeches 34:44-8 N 1 '67
Biggest boom; U.S. command, communications and supply network. il Time 89:26-9 My 12 '67
From factory to foxhole: a 10,000-mile pipeline to war; excerpts from address, May 12, 1967. F. S. Besson, jr. il U S News 62: 98-9 Je 19 '67
Latest on weapons for the U.S. arsenal. il U S News 62:10-11 Je 12 '67
On the volcano's edge; dangers in loading of ammunition for Vietnam. T. Plate. il Newsweek 70:26 Jl 10 '67
Photos and letters upstage the Guam show; resupply activities by North Vietnam during Tet truce. il Life 62:26-7 Mr 31 '67
Russia: the enemy in Vietnam il U S News 62:27-9 Ja 30 '67
Sniffing out the enemy; E-63 manpack personnel detector. il Time 89:88 Je 9 '67
Sustained Viet buildup urged to 1972. C. Brownlow. il Aviation W 86:26-9 Ja 23 '67
U.S. weapons in Vietnam; are they good enough? interview. H. W. O. Kinnard. il U S News 62:68-71 F 6 '67
Viet-generated advances reach theater; testing sensors and electronic-counter-measures hardware. C. Brownlow. il Aviation W 86: 68-9+ My 22 '67
Viet requirements boost budget. E. H. Kolcum. il Aviation W 86:22-3 Ja 30 '67
War and weapons in Vietnam. Bul Atomic Sci 23:59-60 My '67
War at crisis; mobilization ahead? il U S News 62:29-31 Je 12 '67
See also
Rifles
Weapons

VIETNAMESE war, 1957- —Moral and religious aspects—*Continued*

Vietnam, 1968; moral issues confronted, symposium. Christian Cent 85:3-8+ Ja 3 '68

Vietnam: reappraisal from Down Under. A. Walker. Christian Cent 84:835-6 Je 28 '67

Vietnam: some basic considerations. G. A. Elston. Cath World 205:78-82 My '67. Reply. W. V. O'Brien. 205:160-70 Je '67

Vietnam statements by scientists abroad. Bul Atomic Sci 23:47-8 Ja '67

You can be righteous but not right. A. H. Sypher. il Nations Bsns 55:33-4 Mr '67

Naval operations

Battleship returns; New Jersey to be reactivated. R. Moley. Newsweek 69:104 My 29 '67

Footnote to history; J. White's account of Gulf of Tonkin incident. Nation 205:676-7 D 25 '67

I skippered a Swift. J. Stephens. il Pop Mech 128:92-5+ Jl '67

In Vietnam, a comeback for ironclads; Monitors. il U S News 63:14 Jl 3 '67

Ironclads rise again! river battleships for Vietnam duty. R. Zimmerman. il Pop Mech 128:96-9 D '67

Life on the river; Detachment Alpha, mine squadron eleven. il Newsweek 69:42 F 13 '67

Operation Sea Dragon. R. Steele. il Newsweek 70:38-9 S 4 '67

Our limited war in the South China Sea. D. Reed. Read Digest 90:88-92 Ap '67

Picket line; Operation Market Time. Newsweek 70:26 Jl 31 '67

Role for a relic; preliminary demothballing of New Jersey. Time 89:32 Je 9 '67

Tiger sharks strike in the Vietnam swamps. W. Cloud. il Pop Mech 128:131-4+ N '67

Yankee station; inviting retaliation; in the Gulf of Tonkin. T. W. Pew. jr. Nation 205:141-2 Ag 28 '67

Negroes

Air; propaganda. M. J. Arlen. New Yorker 43:100+ D 16 '67

Democracy in the foxhole. il Time 89:15-19 My 26 '67; Same abr. with title Negro's bright badge of courage. Read Digest 91:59-64 Ag '67

Dixie town fetes war hero; Medal of honor winner Lawrence Joel is hailed by Winston-Salem. R. Lantz. il Ebony 22:27-8+ Je '67

Greeting from Victor Charlie; propaganda aimed at the Negro fighting man. il Time 91:20-1 Ja 19 '68

King-talk. Nat R 19:395-6 Ap 18 '67

Negro and Vietnam. Nation 205:37-8 Jl 17 '67

Negro in Vietnam. K. H. Purnell. il Nation 205:8-10 Jl 3 '67

Negro view: a special anguish. M. Kupfer. il Newsweek 70:34+ Jl 10 '67

Negroes in the Vietnam war. America 116:827-8 Je 10 '67

Viet Nam: every youth must face the fact of involvement; with report on Ulysses C. Kendall. il Ebony 22:23-6+ Ag '67

When the Negroes in Vietnam come home; with excerpts from interviews. W. M. Young, jr. Harper 234:63-9 Je '67

Parachute troops

See United States—Army—Parachute troops

Peace and mediation

All, all honorable men; diplomacy of the Johnson administration. M. Novak. il Commonweal 86:580-2 S 22 '67

Ambassador Goldberg reports on his trip to Asia; transcripts of news conferences, March 6, 8, 1967. A. J. Goldberg. Dept State Bul 56:505-14 Mr 27 '67

Ambassador on the war. A. Goldberg. Newsweek 70:56 Jl 10 '67

Appeals to reason; U Thant's peace proposal. New Repub 156:8 Ap 8 '67

Are peace hints real? Hanoi may be ready to discuss peace; with editorial comment. Bsns W p28, 132 Ja 13 '68

Back to the fighting; peace efforts during truce. il Time 89:24 F 24 '67

Bid for peace, and a rebuff; letter to President Ho chi Minh, February 2, with reply February 15, 1967. L. B. Johnson; Ho-chi-Minh. il U S News 62:26-7 Ap 3 '67

Case for withdrawal. P. Steinfels. il Commonweal 86:585-7 S 22 '67

Chances for peace. Commonweal 87:427-8 Ja 12 '68

Chances for peace. il Newsweek 69:25-31 F 20 '67

China, Russia & the U.S. O. Gass. bibliog f Commentary 43:39-42 Ap '67; Reply. D. Clifford. 44:24+ S '67

Chorus of one; concerning R. F. Kennedy's To seek a newer world. Time 90:26 N 24 '67

Coalition government? NLF proposals. M. Ascoli. Reporter 38:8 Ja 11 '68

Day of reconciliation; National day of prayer for peace and reconciliation. W. F. Buckley, jr. Nat R 19:948 S 5 '67

Deal on peace talks? Thieu offers bombing pause. U S News 63:22 O 23 '67

Department gives facts regarding Ashmore-Baggs contacts with Hanoi. Dept State Bul 57:462-3 O 9 '67

Debate and disquiet; concerning three books about the wisdom of U.S. policy in Vietnam. il Newsweek 69:35-6 F 6 '67

Different kind of conclusion; U.S. policymakers weigh evidence from Viet Cong. il Time 90:23 D 15 '67

Do truce talks mean peace? interview. M. W. Clark. U S News 62:42-4 Mr 20 '67

Embarrassing Mr Kennedy. America 116:366-7 Mr 18 '67; Discussion. 116:544-5 Ap 15 '67

Ending the war. New Repub 157:5-7 Jl 15 '67

Fence walking North Carolina Baptists; North Carolina Baptist state convention. Christian Cent 84:1620 D 20 '67

Fine Irish hand? Nat R 19:1309-10 N 28 '67

Fourteen points for peace in southeast Asia. Dept State Bul 56:284-5 F 20 '67

Fulbright's proposals for peace; excerpt from Arrogance of power. Christian Cent 84:132 F 1 '67

Future indicative; change of mood in statement from Hanoi. il Time 91:9-10 Ja 12 '68

Galbraith plan to end the war; with reply by W. P. Bundy. J. K. Galbraith. il N Y Times Mag p29-31+ N 12 '67

General in arms; interview, ed. by E. J. Hughes. J. M. Gavin. Newsweek 70:28-9 O 16 '67

Generals sing an old song. P. Devillers. Nation 205:233-8 S 18 '67

Getting out; discussion. Commonweal 85:441+ Ja 27 '67

Hanoi: cool to peace; Washington: new heat in war debate. il U S News 63:8+ O 16 '67

Hanoi strengthens LBJ's hand; rebuff of U Thant's appeal. il Newsweek 69:31-2 Ap 10 '67

Hatfield on LBJ; President's demands demonstrate insensitivity or indifference. M. O. Hatfield. New Repub 156:18 My 6 '67

Help from the hyperhawks; Hanoi's wrath over U Thant's plan. Time 89:16 Ap 7 '67

Ho keeps saying no; two years, forty-five peace feelers. U S News 63:42 Ap 10 '67

How long will it last? M. Frankel. il N Y Times Mag p28-9+ Ap 30 '67

In pursuit of the elusive peace feelers. H. Sidey. Life 62:42B F 17 '67

Inscrutable East side. Nat R 19:1054 O 3 '67

Is peace coming tomorrow? J. B. Sheerin. Cath World 205:4-6 Ap '67

Is there a way out of the Vietnam war? excerpt from Behind the lines. Hanoi. H. Salisbury. il Sat R 50:29-34+ Ap 8 '67

Is there real hope in the peace rumors? il Bsns W p30-1 F 11 '67

It's time for some guidance for Hanoi. Fortune 75:102 F '67

It's time to negotiate. W. S. Ellis. Christian Cent 84:590-1 My 3 '67

Just war; judging the Vietnam war. Commonweal 87:371-2 D 22 '67

Kosygin in Britain; the peace almost within our grasp. Life 62:32-32A F 24 '67

Laying out the facts for Hanoi. Bsns W p 166 My 27 '67

Let there be peace; acting as his own ambassador; R. F. Kennedy. K. Crawford. Newsweek 69:46 F 20 '67

Letter from Saigon. R. Shaplen. New Yorker 42:150+ F 18 '67

Letter from Washington. R. H. Rovere. New Yorker 43:176-8+ Mr 18 '67

Listening to bubbles from Hanoi. il Time 89:15-16 F 10 '67

Look at what peace would mean. Bsns W p 140 F 11 '67

Men at war; RFK vs. LBJ. il Newsweek 69:33-4 Mr 13 '67

Message from Pope Paul VI; text of message, September 22, 1967. Paul VI. UN Mo Chron 4:26 O '67

Mr Johnson's two-step; coalition for peace. Nation 204:355-6 Mr 20 '67

Moulting of the doves; concerning letter to Ho-chi-Minh. America 116:522 Ap 8 '67

VIETNAMESE war, 1957- —Peace and mediation—*Continued*
NLF's terms for peace. G. M. Kahin. New Repub 157:13-17 O 14 '67
Negotiate what? Nat R 19:178 F 21 '67
Negotiate with the reds? Dean Acheson's advice; interview. D. Acheson. U S News 63:50-1 D 18 '67
Negotiation now! Christian Cent 84:1148 S 13 '67
New bid for Viet peace talks? Sr Schol 91:24 N 16 '67
New president of South Vietnam speaks out; interview, ed. by W. S. Merick. Nguyen-van-Thieu. U S News 63:32-4 O 30 '67
Notes and comment. New Yorker 43:47 O 14 '67
Numbers game in Vietnam; calculation of number of villagers of South Vietnam now under government control. M. Novak. il Commonweal 87:373-4 D 22 '67
On the subject of pain; D. Acheson's views on negotiations. N. Cousins. Sat R 50:22 D 23 '67
One single, simple act of trust; activities during truce. Newsweek 69:23-4 F 27 '67
Opinion: on fighting the problem. G. W. Ball. Mlle 65:200+ Ag '67
Other war; R. F. Kennedy, middleman in peace relay; with report by E. Weintal. Newsweek 69:31-2 F 20 '67
Pacific mission; L. B. Johnson's proposals. il Time 90:9-10 D 29 '67
Peace? hints, signs, hopes; with report of Paris message by E. Weintal. il Newsweek 69:33-4 F 13 '67
Peace moves next in Vietnam? W. S. Merick. il U S News 63:38-40 S 18 '67
Peace on earth: the position of the scientists; statement, May 1967. L. Pauling. Bul Atomic Sci 23:47-8 O '67
Peace ploy: what's Hanoi up to now? U S News 64:10 Ja 15 '68
Peace politics: calculus for '68. E. Kenworthy. Nation 206:46-50 Ja 8 '68
Perils of probing; visit of H. Ashmore to North Viet Nam. Time 90:22 S 29 '67
Persevering for peace; address, May 12, 1967. A. J. Goldberg. Dept State Bul 56:838-44 Je 5 '67
Politics 1968; address, December 12, 1967. L. B. Johnson. Vital Speeches 34:162-5 Ja 1 '68; Excerpt. Dept State Bul 58:39-40 Ja 8 '68
Politics of peacemaking. E. J. Hughes. Newsweek 71:17 Ja 22 '68
President Johnson invites Hanoi to shipboard peace talks; remarks, November 11, 1967. L. B. Johnson. Dept State Bul 57:747-8 D 4 '67
President Johnson's proposal for negotiation on Viet-Nam rejected by Ho chi Minh; exchange of letters; February 8, 15, 1967, with Department statement. L. B. Johnson; Ho-chi-Minh. Dept State Bul 56:595-7 Ap 10 '67
Problems of peace. K. Crawford. Newsweek 69:33 F 27 '67
Prod from the Senate; Mansfield-Morse resolutions. Nation 205:484-5 N 13 '67
Public opinion and Vietnam; disturbing signs that basic U.S. policy calling for negotiations may be shifting. N. Cousins. Sat R 50:22 Ap 29 '67
Rancors aweigh; Johnson lashes out at critics. il Time 90:31 N 17 '67
Real achievement in Vietnam. Bsns W p 180 F 25 '67
Reds' plan: fight while talking. il U S News 62:54 My 15 '67
Regional solution for Viet Nam. Vu-van-Thai. For Affairs 46:347-61 Ja '68
RSVP. Nat R 19:554 My 30 '67
Responsibility of the United Nations in the search for peace in Viet-Nam; statement, November 1, 1967. A. J. Goldberg. Dept State Bul 57:667-72 N 20 '67
Rhetorical escalation. W. Pfaff. Commonweal 85:673-4 Mr 17 '67
RFK wants out. Commonweal 85:668 Mr 17 '67
Rome haul; meeting between the President and the Pope at the Vatican. il Newsweek 71:40 Ja 8 '68
Rover boys retaliate. Nat R 19:1054+ O 3 '67
Rusk: our commitment is clear; statement, October 12, 1967. D. Rusk. U S News 63:40 O 23 '67
Secretary-General's press conference; March 28, 1967. Thant. UN Mo Chron 4:67-77 Ap '67
Secretary Rusk and Ambassador Bunker discuss Viet-Nam in TV-radio interviews; transcripts of interviews, September 10, 1967. D. Rusk; E. Bunker. Dept State Bul 57:411-21 O 2 '67

Secretary Rusk discusses prospects for 1967 on Face the nation; transcript of interview, January 1, 1967. D. Rusk. Dept State Bul 56:126-32 Ja 23 '67
Secretary Rusk discusses Viet-Nam in interview for British television; transcript of interview for Associated television, ltd, January 31, 1967. D. Rusk. Dept State Bul 56:274-84 F 20 '67
Secretary Rusk's news conference of February 9, 1967. D. Rusk. Dept State Bul 56:317-22 F 27 '67
Secretary Rusk's news conference of March 28, 1967. D. Rusk. Dept State Bul 56:618-24 Ap 17 '67
Secretary Rusk's news conference of September 8, 1967. D. Rusk. Dept State Bul 57:383-90 S 25 '67
Secretary Rusk's news conference of October 12, 1967. D. Rusk. Dept State Bul 57:555-64 O 30 '67
Skirmishing for peace; resumption of bombing as lunar New Year's truce ends. il Bsns W p33-4 F 18 '67
Slow grind; U.S.'s cautious refusal to jump into negotiations. il Newsweek 71:32-4 Ja 22 '68
Some olive branch! New Repub 157:5-6 D 23 '67
Something in the wind? change in Hanoi's bargaining position. il Newsweek 71:13-14 Ja 15 '68
Still wishing, still nothing. il Time 89:17-18 F 17 '67
Stirrings in the elephant grass; an invitation from the Security council to the National liberation front. A. Tuckerman. Nation 206:3-4 Ja 1 '68
Stockholm conference reveals hard truths; World conference on Vietnam. H. A. Jack. Christian Cent 84:1168+ S 13 '67
Swinging Senator; R. Kennedy and French peace formula. Nation 204:226-7 F 20 '67
Talk of a Greek solution for Vietnam. A. Hamilton. New Repub 157:10-11 S 23 '67
Talk with Ho Chi Minh; interview, ed. by W. C. Baggs. Ho-chi-Minh. il Sat Eve Post 240:26-7 D 16 '67
Talking of peace. New Repub 156:7-8 F 18 '67
Temptation of Lyndon Johnson. W. Lippmann. Newsweek 69:21 F 27 '67
Time to end the war. V. Cadden. McCalls 95:4 Ja '68
Time to negotiate. Nation 204:260 F 27 '67
Trip to Guam, and a no from Ho. il Newsweek 69:25-8 Ap 3 '67
Tuning in on all channels. Time 91:11-12 Ja 19 '68
United States accepts U.N. Secretary-General's proposal for ending the Viet-Nam conflict; text of aide memoire, March 14, with texts of U.S. replies, March 15, 18, 1967. Thant. Dept State Bul 56:624-6 Ap 17 '67
U.S. asks U.N. Secretary-General for help in seeking peace; text of letter, December 19, 1966. A. J. Goldberg. Dept State Bul 56:63-4 Ja 9 '67
United States peace aims in Viet-Nam; address, February 10, 1967. A. J. Goldberg. Dept State Bul 56:310-16 F 27 '67
United States reaffirms policy toward National liberation front; Department statement, December 8, 1967. Dept State Bul 57:854 D 25 '67
U.S. sets its terms for peace in Vietnam; excerpts from news conference, February 9, 1967. D. Rusk il U S News 62:107-8 F 20 '67
U.S. viewpoint on four current world problems; statement, September 21, 1967. A. J. Goldberg. Dept State Bul 57:483-6 O 16 '67
Vietnam and the fourth group. H. Cousins. Sat R 50:22 Ap 1 '67
Vietnam as a matter of conscience. America 118:5-6 Ja 6 '68
Viet Nam; crisis of indecision. R. Shaplen. For Affairs 46:95-110 O '67
Vietnam settlement. Commonweal 85:581-2 F 24 '67
Vietnamese mandate to talk. Life 63:4 S 15 '67
Visit to Washington; summary of talks with government officials concerning article, Vietnam and the fourth group. N. Cousins. Sat R 50:22+ Ap 22 '67
Voice from the think tank; editor accuses administration of vetoing peace moves. Newsweek 70:21-2 O 2 '67
War and peace; President Johnson's press conference. Nation 204:322-3 Mr 13 '67

VIETNAMESE war, 1957- —Peace and mediation—*Continued*

War in Vietnam: how we can end it. T. C. Sorensen. Sat R 50:19-22 O 21 '67; Discussion. 50:25 N 11; 23 N 18 '67

Way out for U.S. in Vietnam war? report from the scene. W. S. Merick. il U S News 63:28-32 Jl 17 '67

What are we waiting for? Commonweal 87: 459-60 Ja 19 '68

What negotiations in Viet Nam might mean; Time essay. Time 90:22-3 D 22 '67

What we can do to end the agony of Vietnam; excerpts from To seek a newer world, with editorial comment. R. F. Kennedy. Look 31:34-6+ N 28 '67

What's in a word? meetings between spokesmen of the United States and the Viet Cong. Newsweek 70:48 D 18 '67

What's your plan? Nation 205:643-4 D 18 '67

When an ex-editor made a bid for peace. U S News 63:12 O 2 '67

Where the real obstacles to peace are. Bsns W p 146 Ap 1 '67

Who's credible now? President's letter, Ho's reply, R. Kennedy's reaction. K. Crawford. Newsweek 69:36 Ap 3 '67

Will there be a real truce? il U S News 62: 33-5 F 20 '67

Year of ram stumbles in. Sr Schol 90:15 Mr 3 '67

See also
United Nations—Vietnam (Republic)

Anecdotes, facetiae, satire, etc.

Birthday way out of Vietnam. H. Mitgang. Atlan 220:116+ D '67

Personal narratives

Battles in the monsoon. S. L. A. Marshall. Review
 Nation 205:85-6 Jl 31 '67. J. N. Morris

Combat general tells what Vietnam war is like; interview, ed. by W. S. Merick. L. W. Walt. il U S News 62:36-9 My 22 '67

Farm boy's thoughts in Vietnam; letter. J. W. Lanning. Farm J 91:50N+ O '67

I care; excerpts from letters. J. Jacobs. Time 89:18-19 Mr 31 '67

I skippered a Swift. J. Stephens. il Pop Mech 128:92-5+ Jl '67

I smell Charlies all around; Operation Junction City; with report by F. Sully. il Newsweek 69:23-5 Mr 6 '67

Letter from abroad. E. Steinbeck. il McCalls 94:42+ Je '67

Mail from the front. O. Prescott. Sat R 50: 35 Ap 29 '67

My visit to Vietnam; ed. by W. Rogers. O. N. Bradley and K. Bradley. il Look 31:29-35 N 14 '67

Notes on a monstrous war. R. Sherrod. il Life 62:20-9 Ja 27 '67

Sermon, extempore; excerpts from CBS interview with two U.S. soldiers. Nation 204: 739-40 Je 12 '67

They also serve; interviews with servicemen; ed. by M. Liebman. il Nat R 19:1327-31 N 28 '67

Tourist at the Vietnam war. B. Hooper. Life 63:14 Jl 7 '67

Up front in Vietnam: condensation. D. Reed. il Read Digest 91:189-94+ S '67

Vietnam, a doctor's journal; report on An Xuyen province. J. J. Weiss. Commentary 43:52-9 My '67

Vietnam by helicopter; operations of First air cavalry division. D. Smith. il Nation 204:745-50 Je 12 '67

Vietnam: slow, tough but coming along. H. Donovan. il Life 62:68+ Je 2 '67

Vietnam: the eye of the storm; situation in provinces known as Eye Corps. F. Sully. New Repub 157:13-16 Jl 15 '67

Viet Nam, the people. F. FitzGerald. il Vogue 149:174-5+ My '67

Voices of the Vietcong. D. Halberstam. Harper 236:45-52 Ja '68

When Demirgian comes marching home again (hurrah? hurrah?) J. Sack. Esquire 69:56-9+ Ja '68

Photography

Action along Highway 13; with photographs by C. Rentmeester. Life 62:69-74 Je 2 '67

Artist and the camera-John Groth. il U S Camera 30:62-5 N '67

Cameras and combat. M. Krawetz. il U S Camera 30:68+ Jl '67

Capa; his traditions remain. il Pop Phot 60: 87+ Je '67

Enemy land at war; North Vietnam. J. R. Moskin. il Look 31:45-51 Jl 25 '67

Gnat of Hill 881; C. Leroy freelance photographer in Vietnam. il Time 89:42 My 12 '67

Inside the cone of fire, Con Thien. D. D. Duncan. il Life 63:28D-42C O 27 '67

North Vietnam under siege; with report by L. Lockwood. il Life 62:33-44D Ap 7 '67

Photography in the front line; Pictures of the year award winners. M. R. Weiss. il Sat R 50:134-5 Mr 11 '67

Up Hill 881 with the marines; with photographs by C. Leroy. Life 62:40-44A My 19 '67

Vietnam; with photographs by J. Stuhler and D. Lyman. E. Galligan. U S Camera 31:48-9+ Ja '68

Poetry

Poetic Venture; concerning poem by twelve-year-old. il Newsweek 69:64 F 27 '67

Response to a war. W. Berry. Nation 204:527-8 Ap 24 '67

Press reports and censorship

Air; television and the press. M. J. Arlen. New Yorker 43:173-80+ O 21 '67

Another battleground reporting the war in Viet Nam. il Sr Schol 90:17-19 Ap 28 '67

Are we being told the truth about Vietnam? C. Fritchey. Harper 234:121-2+ Mr '67

But don't tell anyone I told you; private briefings of Pentagon press corps by top officials. S. M. Hersh. New Repub 157:13-14 D 9 '67

Con Thien story. il Newsweek 70:92 O 16 '67

Credibility gap: who's to blame, the government or the public? discussion. Sr Schol 91:8-10 O 19 '67

Debunking the VC; Associated press and New York times reports. Nat R 19:1002+ S 19 '67

Gap prone: need for government information on bombing policy. K. Crawford. Newsweek 70:39 S 25 '67

Pianissimo persuasion. Nation 205:579-80 D 4 '67

Press: room for improvement. il Newsweek 70:76+ Jl 10 '67

Whose benefit? whose doubt? growing split between U.S. administration and press in Vietnam. il Newsweek 70:68+ N 13 '67

Prisoners and prisons

Cage for the innocents; detainees in Chulai camp. O. Schell. Atlan 221:29-34 Ja '68

Fight to make the Vietcong let him go: case of G. C. Hertz; with report by R. B. Stolley. il Life 63:22-9 Jl 21 '67

Hanoi's Pavlovians; apparent attempts to brainwash U.S. prisoners held in the North. il Time 89:33-4 Ap 14 '67

Inside the Hanoi Hilton; concerning pictures in Life magazine and on NBC. il Newsweek 70:60 O 30 '67

Mildred Harrison's Viet Nam ordeal. P. Avery. il Ebony 22:88-90+ My '67

Our Lord in Vietnam. W. Eastlake. Nation 205:491-2 N 13 '67

P.O.W; North Vietnam: are U.S. prisoners mistreated? W. Rogers. Look 31:53-5 Jl 25 '67

Sequel to Gus Hertz's story. he's alive. G. P. Hunt. Life 63:3 Ag 11 '67

U.S. expresses concern at plight of prisoners in North Viet-Nam; statement. July 17, 1967. Dept State Bul 57:170 Ag 7 '67

U.S. prisoners and an eerie puppet show; with statement by Averell Harriman. L. Lockwood. il Life 62:44-44A Ap 7 '67

U.S. prisoners in North Vietnam; with report by M. Byers. il Life 63:21-34B O 20 '67

U.S. protests Hanoi's violation of Geneva convention on POW's; Department statement. Dept State Bul 56:825 My 29 '67

Why they confess. il Newsweek 69:70 Ap 17 '67

See also
Prisoners of war, Returned

Propaganda

Air; Negro soldier in Vietnam. M. J. Arlen. New Yorker 43:100+ D 16 '67

Charlie, come home! propaganda to urge Viet Cong to defect. il Time 89:32-3 F 10 '67

Evil eye. Nat R 19:232-3 Mr 7 '67

Greetings from Victor Charlie; propaganda aimed at the Negro fighting man. il Time 91:20-1 Ja 19 '68

Westmoreland caper. Commonweal 86:221-2 My 12 '67

While chatting with a poet; letter to Mayor Lindsay on the Support our boys in Vietnam parade. Nat R 19:558-9 My 30 '67

VIETNAMESE war, 1957- —*Continued*

Protests, demonstrations, etc,
against

After protesters burned a U.S. flag. il U S
News 62:12+ My 1 '67
Amherst community referendum. D. J. Flie-
gel. Nation 204:757 Je 12 '67
. . .And a round of war protests, too. il U S
News 62:10+ Ap 24 '67
And further . . . Nat R 19:452 My 2 '67
And murmur: Vietnam; self immolation of
Vietnamese student and Buddhist nun. Thich
Nu Nhat Chi Mai. Christian Cent 84:829
Je 28 '67; Reply. A. F. Ledebuhr. 84:1072-3
Ag 23 '67
Anti-anti-Vietniks at work. Nat R 19:1105 O
17 '67
Anti-war demonstrations; are they moral?
address, May 22, 1967. M. Arnold. Vital
Speeches 33:565-6 Jl 1 '67
Antiwar protests: a weapon for Communists.
U S News 63:12 N 13 '67
Arts: protest on all sides. il Newsweek 70:
83-6 Jl 10 '67
As Lincoln watched; march on the Pentagon.
R. A. Schroth. America 117:644 N 25 '67
Banners of dissent; demonstration at the
Pentagon. il Time 90:23-9 O 27 '67
Bastille day on the Potomac; march on
Washington. R. G. Sherrill. Nation 205:
454-5 N 6 '67
Battle of the Pentagon; Washington march
of October 1967. B. Jackson. il Atlan 221:
35-42 Ja '68
Because of Vietnam, in conscience, I must
break the law; civil disobedience. R. M.
Brown. il Look 31:48+ O 31 '67
Bertrand Russell: prosecutor, judge and jury.
B. Levin. il N Y Times Mag p24-5+ F 19
'67; Discussion. p 12+ Mr 12; 156 Mr 19;
141+ Ap 16 '67
Burning issue. il Time 89:20-1 Ap 28 '67
Burning words, yes; burning cards, no; case
of D. J. Miller. Time 89:51-2 F 24 '67
Catholics picket Cardinal Spellman. Christian
Cent 84:133 F 1 '67
Concerned and committed. K. Haselden.
Christian Cent 84:197-8 F 15 '67; Discussion.
84:410 Mr 29 '67
Conversion: Bishop Sheen's call for unilateral
withdrawal. Newsweek 70:90 Ag 14 '67
Counter-punch. Nat R 19:508 My 16 '67
Crazy kind of carnival; Seth Freeman's Expo
'67 Vietnam in San Francisco. J. Ridgeway.
New Repub 157:13-14 S 30 '67
Damned fool; case of R. Lockman. Nation
205:357 O 16 '67
Dance protest for Viet Nam I and 2, Hunter
playhouse. M. Marks. Dance Mag 41:79 Mr
'67
Dead end to disaster; Martin Luther King
and Benjamin Spock in Chicago. Christian
Cent 84:427-8 Ap 5 '67
Dean Rusk at Cornell. Nation 204:516 Ap 24 '67
Demonstration: people against D. Rusk at the
New York Hilton. New Yorker 43:52-3 N 25
'67
Demonstrations during mass; incident at St
Patrick's cathedral, New York. America
116:172 F 4 '67
Did Communists spark the Pentagon march?
U S News 63:16 D 4 '67
Dilemma of dissent; peace march in New
York. il Time 89:20-2 Ap 21 '67
Disobedience now! the Stanford statement. J.
Neugeboren. Commonweal 86:367-9 Je 16 '67;
Discussion. 86:443-5 Jl 14 '67
Dissent ahead; meeting of International war
crimes tribunal. Commonweal 86:251-2 My
19 '67; Reply. J. J. Maher. 86:403+ Je 30 '67
Dissent among the dissenters; Stop the draft
and end the war week. il Time 90:26-7 D 15
'67
Dissent: An act of respect for the Vietnamese
people. program in Washington Square
Methodist church. New Yorker 42:29-31 F
11 '67
Dissent in Canada. Christian Cent 84:772-3
Je 14 '67
Dissenters and deserters. E. F. Sherman. New
Repub 158:23-6 Ja 6 '68
Doctor King's crusade: how he hopes to end
the war. U S News 62:14 My 8 '67
Doctor's dilemma. il Time 91:14-15 Ja 12 '68
Doing their thing: Stop the draft week. il
Newsweek 70:41 D 18 '67
Draft crackdown? il Sr Schol 91:18-19 D 7 '67
Draft may not be used to silence dissent. il
Time 89:66 F 10 '67
Escalation of dissent; RESIST organization;
statement of the Catholic intellectuals. Com-
monweal 87:102-3 O 27 '67; Reply. P.
Garver. 87:193+ N 17 '67

Evidence at Stockholm; Bertrand Russell's
International war crimes tribunal. G. Julin;
C. Oglesby. il Nation 204:712-21 Je 5 '67
Fearsome five; conspiracy charge against
Benjamin Spock and others. New Repub
158:7-8 Ja 20 '68
Fighting travesty with travesty; picketing
high mass at St Patrick's cathedral, New
York city. Christian Cent 84:164 F 8 '67
First of the month; Writers and editors war
tax protest. C. Amory. Sat R 50:6 O 7 '67;
Discussion. 50:12+ O 21; 60 N 11; 8+ N 18
'67
Foes of war march on Pentagon. il Bsns W
p43 O 28 '67
Games men play; Bertrand Russell's war
crimes tribunal. Newsweek 69:42+ My 15
'67
Goals of dissent; evaluation of the protest
movement. L. Grauman, jr. Nation 205:617-
21 D 11 '67
Guerrilla war on the campus; reprisals against
activators. New Repub 156:6-7 My 20 '67
Hangover from a demonstration; weekend
peace demonstrations in Washington, D.C.
America 117:495-6 N 4 '67
Honest dissent vs. ugly disorder. Life 63:4
N 10 '67
Honest protest and the big lie; peace march
and rally in New York. L. Wainwright. Life
62:30B Ap 28 '67
In the White House; question of the march
on the Pentagon being planned in Hanoi.
New Repub 157:9 D 9 '67
Interns' dissent; congressional interns sign
anti-Vietnam letter. S. S. Goldschlager.
New Repub 157:16 Ag 19 '67
King speaks for peace; at Coliseum in Chi-
cago and at Riverside church in New York
city. Christian Cent 84:492-3 Ap 19 '67
Let the Negro do it; antiwar whites exploit
Negro dilemma. K. Crawford. Newsweek
69:46 My 8 '67
Letter from Stanford; Humphrey and the
now generation. J. Neugeboen. New Repub
156:32-5 Mr 18 '67
Life with father; draft boards could not
punish protesters. Newsweek 69:40 F 13
'67
Limits of decorum; demonstration against
Dean Rusk at the Foreign policy associa-
tion dinner. Nation 205:548 N 27 '67
Long-winded lady; high-school students'
demonstration on Washington place. New
Yorker 43:35-7 Ap 29 '67
Love. . .peace. . . il Newsweek 70:26-7 N 6
'67
March for peace, a summing up; Washington
march. U S News 63:20 N 6 '67
March on the Pentagon. il Newsweek 70:20-1
O 30 '67
Militant clergy; critics fire back. il U S News
63:66-8 N 27 '67
More in sorrow than anger; Student confer-
ence at Cornell. Nation 204:324-5 Mr 13 '67
More protests, growing lawlessness: how far
will it go? il U S News 63:6+ D 18 '67
Morning after; antiwar marchers at the Pen-
tagon. Time 90:17 N 3 '67
Morton the realist. Nation 205:354-5 O 16 '67
Musings from Baltimore city jail. P. Ber-
rigan. Commonweal 87:195-6 N 17 '67
New kind of war profiteering. A. H. Sypher.
il Nations Bsns 55:33-4 D '67
No hope? U.S. peace groups. Nation 205:261
S 25 '67
Nuremberg revisited; case of Capt. H. Levy.
il Newsweek 69:23-4 My 29 '67
Nürnberg & Viet Nam; case of Captain
Howard Levy. il Time 89:20 My 26 '67
On a pleasant Sunday; self immolations in
California. Nation 205:517 N 20 '67
On civil disobedience, 1967; symposium. N Y
Times Mag p27-9+ N 26 '67
On the march again: New York; San Fran-
cisco. P. Good; M. Wax. Nation 204:550-3
My 1 '67
On White House sidewalk, violence in a rally;
Women strike for peace members. il U S
News 63:8 O 2 '67
Orgies of collective public signature; concern-
ing Hugh R. Trevor-Roper's statement.
Life 62:6 F 24 '67
Our national priorities are upside down;
publishers to issue open letter to President.
C. B. Grannis. Pub W 192:35 N 6 '67
Pacifism or politics? Nat R 19:450-2 My 2 '67
Patriotism and Vietnam; concerning W. C.
Westmoreland's speech against critics of
U.S. policy. N. Cousins. Sat R 50:26+ My
13 '67

VIETNAMESE war, 1957- —Public opinion
—*Continued*
Heat on the Hill; Republicans' rising criticism of the war. il Time 90:26-7 O 13 '67
How Hanoi sees the war. D. Warner. il Reporter 37:17-20 Ag 10 '67
How South Vietnamese feel about the war; survey. il U S News 62:12 Ap 3 '67
How the U.S. public now feels about Vietnam. L. Harris. Newsweek 69:24-5 F 27 '67
Ike to war critics: be moderate in dissent; excerpts from news conference, October 13, 1967. D. W. Eisenhower. il U S News 63:22 O 23 '67
In Vietnam debate: mounting criticism of LBJ and his answer. il U S News 63:6 O 9 '67
Into the dovecote; Republicans. il Newsweek 70:26-7 O 16 '67
Letter from Washington. R. H. Rovere. New Yorker 43:88+ Ag 19 '67
Letter to LBJ; college students protest our involvement in Vietnam. Sat R 50:64 Ag 19 '67
List grows; opposition to our entanglement in Vietnam. Nation 205:450-1 N 6 '67
LBJ and the war: a lag in public support? il U S News 62:11 Mr 20 '67
LBJ meets professors on Vietnam. B. Nelson. Science 158:231 O 13 '67
LBJ's supporters: varying plumage. il Newsweek 70:22-4 Jl 10 '67
Medium as she is massaged; excerpts from Authors take sides on Vietnam. Nat R 20:18-19 Ja 16 '68
New sophistication; poll of representative American adults. il Newsweek 70:20-2 Jl 10 '67
Notes and comment. New Yorker 43:25-6 Je 3 '67
Notes and comment; concerning article in the Times by A. Miller. New Yorker 43:19 Ja 13 '68
Other wound. R. A. Schroth. America 116:816 Je 3 '67
Petition syndrome; collective public signature by professors. Time 89:43 F 24 '67
Pianissimo persuasion. Nation 205:579-80 D 4 '67
Politics '68: beyond the water's edge; critiques of administration's war policy. il Newsweek 70:23-4 O 9 '67
Question of priorities. il Time 90:13-14 S 8 '67
Report; Japanese attitude. J. M. Truitt. Atlan 219:15-16 Je '67
Reporter at large; war in Kansas. C. Trillin. New Yorker 43:56-8+ Ap 22 '67
Revolution of 1976. M. Novak. Commonweal 86:441-3 Jl 14 '67; Discussion. 86:550-3 S 8 '67
Self-corrective process; freedom of dissent. il Time 89:17-18 My 12 '67
Seminarians and Vietnam. Christian Cent 84:1605 D 13 '67
Senator Brooke and Dr King. Nation 204:452-3 Ap 10 '67
Should we get out of Vietnam? GH readers are split 42 to 46 percent. il Good H 166:10+ Ja '68
Showdown in U.S. over Vietnam war. il U S News 63:21-3 Ag 28 '67
Smell of crisis. E. J. Hughes. Newsweek 70:29 N 13 '67
Tale of three towns; attitudes to Vietnamese war. il Newsweek 70:25-6 Jl 10 '67
They're all afraid of America; how the Europeans see the war. P. Ben. New Repub 156:7-8 My 13 '67
Thunder from a distant hill. il Time 90:21-6 O 6 '67
Torment for everyone. America 116:868 Je 24 '67
Toward national unity over Vietnam. N. Cousins. Sat R 50:20-1 D 2 '67
Vietnam and the fourth group. N. Cousins. Sat R 50:22 Ap 1 '67
Views on Vietnam; statements by clergy. Christian Cent 85:24 Ja 3 '68
Voice for the voiceless; results of U.S. press polls. Nation 205:421+ O 30 '67
Vote for peace; South Vietnam elections. New Repub 157:5-6 S 16 '67
Who guards the Guardian? Nat R 19:558 My 30 '67
Will U.S. emulate France; lose the Vietnam war at home? U S News 63:46 N 13 '67
World around us; views of Australian church leaders. Christian Cent 84:820-2 Je 21 '67
Zinn position; poll results of Sunday gazette-mail of Charleston, W.Va. Nation 205:131 Ag 28 '67

Refugees
See Refugees, Vietnamese

Relief work
Building a nation beyond the killing; new emphasis on land control, population security and nation building. il Time 89:32-3 F 3 '67
Call to suffering; religious samaritans. il Time 90:84-5 S 22 '67
Chauvinistic Catholic charity; American Catholic relief services. Commonweal 87:159-60 N 10 '67
End this war; IVS workers withdraw. Nation 205:322-3 O 9 '67
How the marines fight the other war; pacification program of the combined-action company. S. Dickerman. il Reporter 36:31-3 Ap 6 '67
Letter from South Vietnam. R. Shaplen. New Yorker 43:37-8+ Je 17 '67
NLF's terms for peace; U.S. pacification effort. G. M. Kahin. New Repub 157:13-17 O 14 '67
Relief and Vietnam. Christian Cent 84:1292 O 11 '67
Struggle to rescue the people. J. Mecklin. il Fortune 75:126-33+ Ap '67
Their mission: defend, befriend; pacification program of Echo two, Combined action platoon. D. Moser. il Life 63:24-9+ Ag 25 '67
Toughest question; International voluntary services resignations. il Newsweek 70:32 O 2 '67
Unrequited love; resignation of four top I.V.S. officials. Time 90:39 S 29 '67
Viet aides quit; International voluntary services. il Sr Schol 91:39-40 O 5 '67
Viet-Nam civilian service awards presented by President Johnson; remarks, August 16, 1967. L. B. Johnson. Dept State Bul 57:288-90 S 4 '67
Vietnam's war-ravaged children; refugee center at Quang Ngai by American Friends service committee. C. Brossard. il Look 31:22-5 Ap 18 '67

Russian participation
Now Russia escalates the war. il U S News 63:39-41 O 9 '67

Science
In science: a selective squeeze. il Newsweek 70:72-5 Jl 10 '67
Vietnam: call for scientific help; letter. E. C. Pollard. Science 157:755-6 Ag 18 '67; Discussion. 158:438+ O 27 '67

Social aspects
Fulbright on riots. K. Crawford. Newsweek 70:28 Ag 21 '67

Songs and music
Vietnam blues; protest songs. T. Phillips. il N Y Times Mag p 12+ O 8 '67

Statistics
Charting the enemy's strength; with charts of North Vietnamese combat power. Bsns W p82-4 Ag 12 '67
Credibility Giap; enemy fabrications. Newsweek 69:50 Mr 13 '67
How the generals view the war now. L. Norman. il Newsweek 69:28-9 Mr 27 '67
Numbers game in Vietnam; calculation of number of villagers of South Vietnam now under government control. M. Novak. il Commonweal 87:373-4 D 22 '67
Statistics of death. Time 89:31 My 19 '67
Vietnam: those computer reports; U.S. army information on pacification. W. J. Lederer. New Repub 157:13-14 D 23 '67

Strategy
Air war advances detailed for Congress. Aviation W 87:24-5 O 2 '67
Another turn of the screw; L. B. Johnson policy. Nation 204:386 Mr 27 '67
Army to bolster air strength in Vietnam. C. Brownlow. il Aviation W 86:28-30+ Mr 20 '67
As the North sees it. Time 90:27-8 O 20 '67
Barefoot at the wake; Provisional reconnaissance units. Time 90:24-5 N 3 '67
Beyond Vietnam, by E. O. Reischauer. Review
  Sat R 50:34 O 28 '67. A. C. Brackman
Bigger war ahead in Vietnam. il U S News 62:37-40 Mr 27 '67
Bitterest battlefield; marine camps near Demilitarized zone. il Time 90:28 S 22 '67

VIETNAMESE war, 1957- —Strategy—*Cont.*

Bombing criticism expands in Congress; public exchange between Sen. Symington and McNamara on the bombing of MiG bases in North Vietnam; with editorial comment. D. C. Winston. il Aviation W 86:21, 28-9 Ap 10 '67

Can a wall slow down the war in Vietnam; Demilitarized zone. il Bsns W p44-6 S 16 '67

Chill winds on the East River; U.S. Ambassador A. Goldberg's speech before the General assembly. il Time 90:21 S 29 '67

Close-up of McNamara's fence: how it works, why it's disputed. il U S News 64:24-5 Ja 1 '68

Combat general tells what Vietnam war is like; interview, ed. by W. S. Merick. L. W. Walt. il U S News 62:36-9 My 22 '67

Communist step-up. il Time 91:20 Ja 19 '68

Courage to change. New Repub 156:3-4 Ap 1 '67

Cruel pendulum. H. Brandon. Sat R 50:10+ My 20 '67

Demonstration cities; hit-and-run attacks against South Vietnam's cities. Newsweek 69:36 Je 12 '67

Elusive General Gavin. R. J. Whalen. Harper 235:110+ N '67

Escalation again, by both sides. il Newsweek 69:19-20 My 1 '67

Escalation and East Asia; excerpt from The United States in Vietnam. G. M. Kahin and J. W. Lewis. il Bul Atomic Sci 23:20-4 Ja '67

Free fire zone in Vietnam; will it keep out invading reds? il U S News 62:31 Je 12 '67

Frontier offensive; border battles. il Time 90: 15-16 D 22 '67

General in arms; interview, ed. by E. J. Hughes. J. M. Gavin. Newsweek 70:28-9 O 16 '67

Generals vs. Vietnam strategy; excerpts from testimonies before Senate preparedness investigating subcommittee. G. L. Meyers; H. K. Johnson; W. M. Greene, jr. U S News 63:114 N 6 '67

Graduated response fallacy. D. Graham. Yale R 57:90-8 O '67

Hanging on with Giap; North Vietnamese strategy. il Newsweek 70:36 O 23 '67

Hanoi's summer offensive: a bigger war in prospect. D. Warner. il Reporter 36:31-4 Je 29 '67

Herbicides in Vietnam. A. W. Galston. New Repub 157:19-21 N 25 '67

How and when the war may end. W. S. Merick. il U S News 64:21-3 Ja 8 '68

How much force? parallel strategies for dealing with riots and war. W. V. Kennedy. America 117:278-80 S 16 '67

How the battle got turned around. C. J. V. Murphy. il Fortune 75:140-5+ Ap '67

How the generals view the war now. L. Norman. il Newsweek 69:28-9 Mr 27 '67

How to end the bombing and de-escalate. A. de Borchgrave. il Newsweek 69:43 My 15 '67

How to fight the war in Vietnam; interview. E. G. Wheeler. il U S News 62:38-45 F 27 '67

How to win the war; Admiral Sharp's prescription. U S News 63:22 O 2 '67

Ike's tactics: hot pursuit in Vietnam; television interview. D. D. Eisenhower; O. N. Bradley. il U S News 63:22-D 11 '67

Illegitimi non carborundum; US escalation and reactions of dissenting senators. New Repub 156:5 My 6 '67

Illustrious support; Robert F. Kennedy accuses Lyndon Johnson of reversing his brother's politics. Time 90:22 D 8 '67

In hot pursuit; North Vietnamese attack from sanctuaries inside Cambodia and Laos. A. Campbell. New Repub 158:19-21 Ja 13 '68

Ineffectual strategy. R. Hotz. Aviation W 86:17 My 15 '67

Is this a limited war? D. G. Porter. Commonweal 86:9-11 Mr 24 '67

Johnson is still playing to win. il Bsns W p 14-17 D 23 '67

Just a baby step; plan to authorize U.S. troops to enter Cambodia. il Newsweek 70: 38 D 25 '67

Korean general tells how to beat the Viet Cong; interview, ed. by C. G. Troelstrup. M. S. Chae. il U S News 62:56-7 My 15 '67

Let's fight to win in Vietnam; proposal to bomb military targets in North Vietnam. F. V. Drake. Read Digest 90:67-72 My '67

Letter from South Vietnam. R. Shaplen. New Yorker 43:37-8+ Je 17 '67

Letter from Washington (cont) R. H. Rovere. New Yorker 42:94+ Ja 21 '67

Lure of the lonely patrol: forcing the enemy to fight; expert execution of the newest allied infantry tactic. il Time 89:39-40 Ap 14 '67

Marine North Viet air effort spurred by DMZ violation. C. Brownlow. il Aviation W 86: 72-3+ Ap 10 '67

Meyers deplores Viet air war gradualism; testimony before the Senate Armed services preparedness investigating subcommittee. G. L. Myers. Aviation W 87:55+ N 6 '67

Mini-barrier; U.S. engineers attempt to shut off Vietnamese infiltration route. il Newsweek 69:44 My 1 '67

Mini-truce in Vietnam. New Repub 156:7 F 25 '67

Mr Johnson's two- step: coalition for peace. Nation 204:355-6 Mr 20 '67

More men or new thinking? Nat R 19:779 Jl 25 '67

More non-escalation. Commonweal 85:637-8 Mr 10 '67

Navy develops package air strike tactic. C. Brownlow. il Aviation W 86:16-19 F 27 '67

No letup in Vietnam: strategy after Guam. il U S News 62:25-8 Ap 3 '67

Notes and comments. New Yorker 43:37-8 My 13 '67

Now a new kind of war in Vietnam: failure of a strategy? il U S News 62:39-42 Mr 13 '67

One-way traffic on a two-way street. il Time 89:19-20 Ap 28 '67

Outlook in Vietnam war: more of the same. il U S News 63:43-4 Ag 21 '67

Paucity of choice. il Time 90:19-20 S 15 '67

Politics '68: beyond the water's edge; critiques of administration's war policy. il Newsweek 70:23-4 O 9 '67

Pressures mount. il Time 90:17-18 Ag 18 '67

Progress report on the war in Viet-Nam; address, November 21, 1967. W. C. Westmoreland. Dept State Bul 57:785-8 D 11 '67; Excerpts. il U S News 63:20 D 4 '67

Reds' plan: fight while talking. il U S News 62:54 My 15 '67

Re-examining the conduct of the war. Life 64:4-5 Ja 5; 4 Ja 12 '68

Reformation of war, by J. F. C. Fuller. Review

New Repub il 156:39-41 Ap 8 '67. A. Brynes

Relentless pressure. il Time 90:34 O 13 '67

Retreat to reason. Nation 204:707-8 Je 5 '67

Rift over North Viet restrictions widens. D. C. Winston. Aviation W 87:22-3 S 4 '67

Robert McNamara and the process of military decision. G. F. Eliot. Nat R 19:189+ F 21 '67

Secret battle over Vietnam; excerpts from To move a nation. R. Hilsman. il U S News 62:71 Je 19 '67

Stop the bombing? J. Fischer. Harper 235:16+ O '67

Sustained Viet buildup urged to 1972. C. Brownlow. il Aviation W 86:26-9 Ja 23 '67

Sweep and countersweep. il Newsweek 69: 50 Mr 13 '67

Tactical turnabout; Viet Cong mortar raids. il Newsweek 69:51-2 Mr 27 '67

Ten-to-twenty-year war in South Vietnam? interview, ed. by J. Fromm. R. Thompson. il U S News 62:92-4 F 13 '67

13¢ killers; snipers of the U.S. army and marine corps. il Time 90:36+ O 27 '67

Three more notches; campaign to interrupt North Viet Nam's flow of arms and men to the Communist troops in the South. il Time 89:34-5 Mr 10 '67

Thunder from a distant hill. il Time 90:21-6 O 6 '67

Time of decision for LBJ: what comes next in the war. il U S News 62:31-3 My 8 '67

Timetable for peace; excerpts from address. W. C. Westmoreland. Aviation W 87:11 N 27 '67

Today the Pentagon, tomorrow the World bank. Nat R 19:1362+ D 12 '67

Treadmill to disaster. J. O'Gara. Commonweal 86:569-72 S 22 '67

Turning the tables; long-range reconnaissance patrols probe deep into VC terrain. il Newsweek 70:40-1 Ag 21 '67

U.S. proposes 10-mile buffer area north and south of Viet-Nam DMZ; Department statement, April 19, 1967. Dept State Bul 56:750 My 15 '67

Viet target envelope may expand; USAF tactical commanders press to hit MiG bases, factories, other military support facilities. C. Brownlow. il Aviation W 86: 16-21 Mr 27 '67

VILLAGE theater ballet. See Ballet companies

VILLAGES
Thirty-seven year war of the village of Ta-nanhoi. L. G. Martin. il N Y Times Mag p30-1+ O 29 '67

VILLAGES, Historical. See Historical museums

VILLAS, Italian. See Architecture, Domestic—Italy

VILLAVICIOSA, Spain
Incident at Villaviciosa. R. Lynes. Harper 235:26+ O '67

VILLEE, Dorothy B.
Ribonucleic acid: control of steroid synthesis in endocrine tissue. bibliog Science 158:652-3 N 3 '67

VILLELLA, Edward
Delicate balance. H. Saal. il por Newsweek 69:97 Ja 30 '67
Villella: a dancing Harlequin reborn. W. Terry. il pors Sat R 50:42-4 Ag 12 '67

VILLIARD, Paul
Collectors. il Audubon 69:85-7 My '67
Nature and the camera. Natur Hist 76:50+ Mr: 68+ Ag '67

VILLIERS, Alan
England's Scillies, the flowering isles. Nat Geog Mag 132:126-45 Jl '67

VILLON, Jacques, pseud.
Father of modern print-making. L. Campbell. il Art N 66:38-9+ D '67

VILLON, Raymond Duchamp-. See Duchamp-Villon, R.

VINACKE, Harold M.
Continuing Chinese revolution. Cur Hist 53: 161-6+ S '67

VINCENT, Donald E.
New England state university libraries' regional processing center. ALA Bul 61:672-3 Je '67

VINCENT, Harvey
Ambitious six-week repertory. Hi Fi 17: MA15+ N '67

VINCENT, Jean Louis
Life in Peking: report from a long nose. N Y Times Mag p25-7+ F 26 '67

VINCITORIO, Gaetano L.
New books. Cath World 205:312-13 Ag '67

VINEGAR
Vinegar: its kinds and uses. Good H 164:195 Je '67

VINES. See Climbing plants

VINEYARDS. See Grapes

VINING, Keith
130 mph on these tires? Pop Mech 128:120-2+ D '67

VINSON, Carlos
Wager on a woodchuck. Outdoor Life 139: 64-5+ Ap '67
Yankee walleyes see red. Outdoor Life 139: 44-5+ Je '67

VINSON, Fred M. Jr
Federal law enforcement. bibliog f Cur Hist 53:15-22+ Jl '67

VINTON, John
Nation's capital: out on a limb? Hi Fi 17: MA24+ Mr '67

VINYL floor coverings. See Floor coverings

VINYL wall coverings. See Wall coverings

VIOLENCE
Esquire: a special section on violence; symposium. il Esquire 68:39-66+ Jl '67
Principles & heresies. F. S. Meyer. Nat R 20: 36 Ja 16 '68
Speaking out; children should learn about violence. B. Bettelheim. Sat Eve Post 240: 10+ Mr 11 '67
Teaching violence as a means towards social justice. F. A. J. Ianni. il Cath World 206: 160-4 Ja '68
Violence in America; Time essay. Time 90: 18-19 Jl 28 '67
Violence in American society. G. Geis. Cur Hist 52:354-8+ Je '67
Violence studies frustrating. C. Behrens. Sci N 92:381 O 14 '67
Violence; symposium. il Nation 205:101-7+ Ag 14 '67
La violencia. E. von Kuehnelt-Leddihn. Nat R 19:250 Mr 7 '67

VIOLENCE in television programs. See Television broadcasting—Moral aspects

VIOLENT deaths
Trade winds; American writers who came to a violent end; ed. by H. R. Mayes. W. Brockway. Sat R 50:16 N 4 '67

VIOLETS are brief; story. See Thomas, D.

VIOLIN

Construction

Physics for the queen. J. Eberhart. il Sci N 91:212-13 Mr 4 '67

Instruction and study

Every child a prodigy; Japanese violinists. D. Chapman. il Look 31:M24+ N 28 '67
See also
Violin playing

VIOLIN cellists. See Cellists

VIOLIN making. See Violin—Construction

VIOLIN music
See also
Violin playing

VIOLIN playing
History of violin playing from its origins to 1761, by D. D. Boyden. Review
Am Rec G il 33:852 My '67. M. Serbin
See also
Violin—Instruction and study

VIOLINISTS
See also
Buswell, J. O.
Perlman, I.

VIOLINS of St Jacques; opera. See Williamson, M.

VIORST, Milton
Bitter tea of Dr Tsien. Esquire 68:125-9+ S '67
Bobby Baker has it made. Esquire 68:90-2+ Jl '67
Reston. Horizon 9:34-41 Aut '67
—and Reistrup, J. V.
Radon daughters and the federal government. Bul Atomic Sci 23:25-9 O '67

VIRAL endocarditis. See Endocarditis

VIRGIN Mary. See Mary, Virgin

VIRGIN ISLANDS
Bargains in the sun; 50th anniversary of Transfer day. il Time 89:21 Ap 7 '67
See also
St John Island
Tourist trade—Virgin Islands

Description and travel

Our Virgin Islands, fifty years under the flag. C. Mitchell. il Nat Geog Mag 133: 66-103 Ja '68
Travel's picture portfolio. Travel 128:50-5 D '67
Virgin Islands. J. Faber. il U S Camera 31:52-3+ Ja '68
Virgin Islands U.S.A. il Sr Schol 90:3+ Mr 17 '67

Politics and government

Virgin Islands U.S.A. il Sr Schol 90:3+ Mr 17 '67

VIRGIN ISLANDS, BRITISH. See British Virgin Islands

VIRGIN ISLANDS NATIONAL PARK
Virgin Islands National Park. V. B. Moore. il Nat Parks Mag 41:4-8 Ja '67

VIRGINIA
See also
Architecture, Domestic—Virginia
Fishing—Virginia
Gardens—Virginia
Shenandoah National Park

Description and travel

Exploring history's heartland. G. C. Bennett. il Travel 128:56-60 Jl '67

Historic houses, etc.

Exploring history's heartland. G. C. Bennett. il Travel 128:56-60 Jl '67
George Mason country. H. D. Crawford. il Am For 73:18-21+ N '67
Poplar forest; Thomas Jefferson's retreat from busy Monticello. il House B 109:72+ Ja '67
See also
Mount Vernon (historic house)

Parks and reserves

Seashore state park; approved master plan for Virginia park preserves unspoiled natural areas. P. Roberts. il Parks & Rec 2:10-13+ D '67

VIRGINIA 500 race. See Automobile racing

VIRGINIA. University, Charlottesville
Contemporary solution, sympathetic to tradition: proposals for a university center at the University of Virginia. il Arch Rec 141:190-1 Ap '67
Designed in deference to Mr Jefferson: a fine arts center for the University of Virginia. il Arch Rec 141:186-9 Ap '67

VIRTANEN, Reino
French national character in the twentieth century. bibliog f Ann Am Acad 370:82-92 Mr '67

VIRUS diseases
Hope to end virus disease. Sci N 92:173-4
Ag 19 '67
What you can do about the virus. E. Crim-
min. il Sci Digest 61:77-80 F '67

Vaccines
Live virus vaccines, benefactors with a
catch. R. DeLong. bibliog il Sci Digest 63:
33-8 Ja '68

VIRUS research
Arbovirus infections of laboratory workers.
R. P. Hanson and others. bibliog il Science
158:1283-6 D 8 '67
Building a bacterial virus. W. B. Wood and
R. S. Edgar. il Sci Am 217:60-6+ Jl '67
Helping the body to fight viruses; sub-
stances spur formation of interferon. Bsns
W p80+ S 23 '67

VIRUSES
Assembly of a virus. Sci Am 216:56+ My '67
Bluetongue virus infection: pathologic re-
sponses of nervous systems in sheep and
mice. W. P. C. Richards and D. R. Cordy.
bibliog il Science 156:530-1 Ap 28 '67
Concurrent isolation from patient of two ar-
boviruses. chikungunya and dengue type 2.
R. M. Myers and D. E. Carey. bibliog il
Science 157:1307-8 S 15 '67
Genetics manipulates life. B. Frisch. il Sci
Digest 61:49-51 Mr '67
Herpes-type virus and chromosome marker in
normal leukocytes after growth with irradi-
ated Burkitt cells. W. Henle and others.
bibliog il Science 157:1064-5 S 1 '67
Induction of cancer by viruses. R. Dulbecco.
il Sci Am 216:28-37 bibliog(p 146) Ap '67
Lymphocytic choriomeningitis: production of
antibody by tolerant infected mice. M. B. A.
Oldstone and F. J. Dixon. bibliog il Science
158:1193-5 D 1 '67
Myxovirus-like structures in a case of human
chronic polymyositis. S. M. Chou. bibliog il
Science 158:1453-5 D 15 '67
Replication of viral RNA: RNA synthetase
from escherichia coli infected with phage
MS2 or Qβ. G. Feix and others. bibliog il
Science 157:701-3 Ag 11 '67
Ribosomes: effect of interferon on their in-
teraction with rapidly labeled cellular and
viral RNA's. W. A. Carter and H. B. Levy.
bibliog il Science 155:1254-7 Mr 10 '67
Viral hemorrhagic encephalopathy of rats.
A. H. ElDadah and others. bibliog il Sci-
ence 156:392-4 Ap 21 '67
Virus-induced erythropoiesis in hypertrans-
fused-polycythemic mice. E. A. Mirand. bib-
liog il Science 156:832-3 My 12 '67
Virus-induced peliosis hepatis in rats. V.
V. Bergs and T. M. Scotti. bibliog il Sci-
ence 158:377-8 O 20 '67
Virus-like particles in normal and tumorous
tissues of drosophila. H. Akai and others.
bibliog il Science 157:810-13 Ag 18 '67
See also
Adenoviruses
Bacteriophage
Fetus, Effects of viruses on the
Virus diseases
Virus research
also names of viruses, e.g. Herpes sim-
plex virus

Culture media
Virus-like particles in established murine
cell lines: electron-microscopic observations. D. A. Kindig and W. H. Kirsten.
bibliog il Science 155:1543-5 Mr 24 '67
Virus particles and murine leukemia virus
complement-fixing antigen in neoplastic
and nonneoplastic cell lines. W. T. Hall
and others. bibliog il Science 156:85-8 Ap
7 '67

Culture mediums
Detergent-solubilized RNA polymerase from
cells infected with foot-and-mouth disease
virus. R. B. Arlinghaus and J. Polatnick.
bibliog il Science 158:1320-2 D 8 '67

Resistance
Helping the body to fight viruses; substances
spur formation of interferon. Bsns W
p80+ S 23 '67
Interferon binding: the first step in establishment of antiviral activity. R. M. Friedman. bibliog il Science 156:1760-1 Je 30
'67

VIRUSES, Plant
Potato spindle tuber virus: a plant virus with
properties of a free nucleic acid. T. O.
Diener and W. B. Raymer. bibliog il Sci-
ence 158:378-81 O 20 '67
Tubular structures associated with turnip
yellow mosaic virus in vivo. J. H. Hitch-
born and G. J. Hills. bibliog il Science 157:
705-6 Ag 11 '67
VISAS. See Passports
VISCERAL muscle. See Muscle
VISCOUNT, Bill Martin-. See Martin-Vis-
count, B.
VISIBLE speech. See Deaf—Means of commu-
nication
VISION. See Sight
VISION (animals) See Sight (animals)
VISIONARY gleam; story. See Warner, S. T.
VISIT and search, Right of. See Search, Right
of
VISITATION; opera. See Schuller, G.
VISITOR services. See Information services
VISITS of state
An evening at the de Gaulles'; gala recep-
tion during the official visit to France of
the King of Nepal. P. Feldkamp. Atlan
219:114-18 My '67
VISSER'T HOOFT, Willem Adolf
Universal religion? excerpts from Peace among
Christians. Cath World 206:32-5 O '67
VISTA. See Volunteers in service to America
VISTA system. See Communications satellites
VISUAL aids. See Audio-visual aids
VISUAL instruction. See Audio-visual instruc-
tion
VISUAL memory. See Memory
VISUAL perception. See Perception
VISUAL pigment. See Retina
VISUAL purple
Molecular isomers in vision; chemistry of rho-
dopsin. R. Hubbard and A. Kropf. il Sci Am
216:64-70+ bibliog(p 155) Je '67
Rhodopsin: responses from transient inter-
mediates formed during its bleaching.
W. L. Pak and R. J. Boes. bibliog il Sci-
ence 155:1131-3 Mr 3 '67
VISUAL stimulus. See Stimulus and response
VITAL statistics
Don't tell it to the computer; V. Packard;
discussion. N Y Times Mag p 12+ Ja 29
'67
See also
Demography
Infant mortality
Population
VITAMIN P. See Bioflavonoids
VITAMINS
How vitamins work. I. Asimov. Sci Digest 62:
88-9 Jl '67
Money wasted on unneeded vitamins. B. J.
Culliton. il Sci N 91:146 F 11 '67
Vitamins in your diet. A. F. Benjamin. Am
Home 70:40 Ja '67
See also
Bioflavonoids

Vitamin A
Vitamin A deficiency: effect on retinal structure of the moth manduca sexta. S. D.
Carlson and others. bibliog il Science 158:
268-70 O 13 '67

Vitamin B₁
Conditioning with delayed vitamin injections.
J. Garcia and others. bibliog il Science 155:
716-18 F 10 '67

Vitamin D
Skin pigment regulation of vitamin-D bio-
synthesis in man. W. F. Loomis. bibliog il
Science 157:501-6 Ag 4 '67; Reply with rejoinder. F. R. Freemon. 158:579-80 N 3 '67
Vitamin D & the races of man. il Time 90:
52-3 Ag 18 '67
Vitamin D, key to color? Sci N 92:177 Ag 19
'67
Vitamins D₂ and D₃ in New World primates:
influence on calcium absorption. R. D. Hunt
and others. bibliog il Science 157:943-5 Ag
25 '67
VITÉ, J. P.
Sex attractants in frass from bark beetles.
bibliog Science 156:105 Ap 7 '67
VITICULTURE
Home with the winos; vineyards in California. H. Sutton. il Sat R 50:44-5 Ag 12 '67

VITICULTURE—*Continued*

History

Search for good wine. M. A. Amerine; reply. R. D. Gerard. Science 155:951 F 24 '67

VIVIAN Beaumont theater. *See* Lincoln Center for the performing arts, New York—Vivian Beaumont theater

VIVISECTION

Pain is cruel, but disease is cruel, too. L. Galton il N Y Times Mag p30-1+ F 26 '67; Discussion. p21+ Mr 19 '67
See also
Animal experimentation
Surgery, Experimental

VLACHOS, Helen
Barbs of defiance. il Time 90:36+ O 6 '67
Helen of Athens. por Newsweek 70:42 O 9 '67

VO-nguyen-Giap
As the North sees it. por Time 90:27-8 O 20 '67
Hanging on with Giap. il Newsweek 70:36 O 23 '67

VOBORIL, Virginia V.
Dessert of the month. *See* issues of Good housekeeping

VOCABULARY
Man of many words: V. Nabokov. G. Hicks. Sat R 50:31-2 Ja 28 '67; Discussion. 50:30 F 18 '67
No strings attached. P. W. Schmidtchen. il Hobbies 72:104-6+ O; 104+ N '67
Student vocabulary; from Wales. F. C. Livingston. Sci N 92:379 O 14 '67
Who says it's proper English? television vocabulary; its influence on standard English. J. W. Krutch. Sat R 50:19-21+ O 14 '67; Reply. J. Stein. 50:31 N 25 '67
See also
Words

VOCABULARY tests
It pays to increase your word power. P. Funk. *See* issues of Reader's digest

VOCAL cords. *See* Larynx

VOCATION (in religion)
Do vocation ads mislead? P. C. Rule. America 116:379-80 Mr 18 '67
Fishers of men. V. P. McCorry. America 116: inside back cover Je 10 '67
No shortage of vocations? il America 116:800 Je 3 '67
Of many things. T. N. Davis. America 116: 707 My 13 '67
Too many vacant places; observing world day of prayer for vocations. America 116: 519 Ap 8 '67

VOCATIONAL education
Just try to find a job without it. M. L. Barlow. il Am Ed 4:8-9 D '67
Quincy builds a new vocational-technical curriculum. N. Farmer. il Am Ed 3:12-13+ Jl '67
Tomorrow is now; educating for 21st century manpower needs. H. A. Matthews. il Am Ed 3:21-2 Je '67
See also
Agricultural education
Distributive education
Trade schools

Federal aid
See Federal aid to education

United States
See Vocational education

VOCATIONAL guidance
Can you predict your child's future? G. Davenel. il Parents Mag 42:33-5+ Ag '67
Career counseling. Sr Schol 91:sup6 O 5 '67
College and career; questions and answers. H. Zuckerman. Sr Schol 90:26 My 5 '67
See also
Occupations
Personnel service in education

VOCATIONAL rehabilitation
See also
United States—President's committee on employment of the handicapped

VODKA
Vodka, the Russian little water. Consumer Rep 32:381, 383-4 Jl '67

VOGELSANG, Guenter
New men of iron at Krupp. il por Bsns W p 106-8 Ag 12 '67

VOGT, Evon Z. *See* Hyman, R. jt. auth.

VOGUE (periodical)
Jack Robinson photographs Vogue's own boutique. M. P. R. Thomas. il U S Camera 30:50-1 Ap '67

VOICE
Put your best voice forward; reprint. S. S. Price. il Read Digest 90:133-5 Mr '67
Singing voice: ages of man. R. Rushmore. il Opera N 31:26-8 Ap 1 '67
Singing voice: heroes and peach fuzz; operatic tenors. R. Rushmore. il Opera N 31: 26-8 F 25 '67
Singing voice: indisposed. R. Rushmore. il Opera N 31:28-30 Mr 25 '67
Singing voice: magic. R. Rushmore. il Opera N 31:24-6 Ja 28 '67
Singing voice: national types. R. Rushmore. il Opera N 31:22-5 Mr 18 '67
Singing voice: rarest of all. R. Rushmore. il Opera N 31:28-30 F 11 '67
Singing voice: the lower depths. R. Rushmore. il Opera N 31:28-30 Mr 11 '67
Your voice; the most personal thing about you. M. V. Moore and J. B. Ranney. il Todays Health 45:60-1+ D '67
See also
Automatic speech recognition

VOICE of America (radio program)
Change of voice; J. Chancellor leaves Voice of America. Time 89:41 Je 2 '67
How the U.S. tells its story to the world; interview. L. H. Marks; J. Chancellor. il U S News 62:76-9 F 20 '67
International broadcasting and the changing world audience; address, April 1967, with questions and answers. J. W. Chancellor. Ann Am Acad 372:72-9 Jl '67
Leaving the Voice. Newsweek 69:63 My 29 '67
Memo for John Daly; Vietnamese war reports. Nation 205:517 N 20 '67
Sound of music; Music—U.S.A. most popular radio program in eastern Europe. il Newsweek 69:50+ Je 5 '67
Voice of America: memorandum to John Daly. R. J. Walton. il Nation 205:135-8 Ag 28 '67; Reply with rejoinder. J. Chancellor. 205:258+ S 25 '67
VOA technique; concerning account of antiwar demonstrations of April 15. Nation 204:709 Je 5 '67

VOICE prints. *See* Voiceprints

VOICEPRINTS
Sound judgement. il Time 89:66 Je 23 '67
Valuable clues from sounds made visible. il Life 63:56A-56B Jl 21 '67
Verdi and the pirates; pirated recordings. G. Fitzgerald. il Opera N 31:14-15 F 25 '67

VOIGT, Melvin J.
Information access. por Library J 92:1802 My 1 '67

VOLANAKIS, Minos
(tr) *See* Euripides. Iphigenia in Aulis

VOLCANIC rocks. *See* Rocks, Igneous

VOLCANO ISLANDS
What U.S. is giving back to Japan. il U S News 63:54 N 27 '67

VOLCANOES
Andesitic volcanism and seismicity around the Pacific. W. R. Dickinson T. Hatherton. bibliog il Science 157:801-3 Ag 18 '67
Creation of an island; Metis Shoal of the Tonga Islands. Sci N 93:8 Ja 6 '68
Explosion that changed the world; Santorini explosion. R. Schiller. il Read Digest 91: 122-7 N '67
Menace of extinct volcanoes; reprint. H. Tazieff. il UNESCO Courier 20:4-6+ O '67
Surtsey; an island emerges. J. Kane. il Natur Hist 76:22-7 Mr '67
Volcanic sunset-glow stratum: origin. A. B. Meinel and M. P. Meinel. bibliog Science 155:189 Ja 13 '67
Volcano that shaped the western world; Santorini eruption; theories of A. Galanopoulos. J. Lear; discussion. Sat R 49:93-4 D 3 '66; 50:74 F 4; 55-6 Ap 1 '67
Volcano warnings. il Newsweek 70:61 Ag 21 '67
See also
Craters
Kilauea (crater)
Lava

VOLCHOK, H. L.
Strontium-90 deposition in New York city. bibliog Science 156:1487-9 Je 16 '67

VOLK, John
Know this about food stamps? Farm J 91: 17 Ap '67

VOLKSWAGEN. *See* Automobiles, Foreign

VOLLEYBALL
Playing it the Japanese way. G. Ronberg. il Sports Illus 26:30-1 Je 5 '67

VOLMIER, Roberta
Two women. M. Orovan. il pors U S Camera 30:46-7 Mr '67

VOLO di notee; opera. See Dallapiccola, L.

VOLT ohmmeter. See Voltohmmeters

VOLTAIRE, François Marie Arouet de
Voltaire's timeless eminence. J. Valenti. il por Sat R 50:27+ Mr 11 '67

VOLTMETERS
Case for the transistorized multimeter; new type of test equipment. L. Solomon. il Pop Electr 28:30-5+ Ja '68
Digital voltmeters. J. D. Lenk. il Electr World 78:37-40 N '67
Electronic kinks. R. O. Pedersen. il Pop Mech 129:144 Ja '68
FET voltmeter; transistorized version uses field-effect transistor. J. Randall il Electr World 77:63-4 F '67
Low-cost high-quality electronic voltmeter. F. H. Tooker. il Pop Electr 27:57-61+ N '67
New breed of digital voltmeter. A. H. Seidman. il Electr World 78:23-7 N '67
Pocket CB meter. H. L. Davidson. il Pop Mech 127:182-3+ Mr '67
R. F. sniffer; field strength meter. J. Ashe. il Pop Electr 26:55-6 Je '67
VOM+FET=TVM. J. Randall. il Pop Electr 27:57-9 Jl '67
See also
Voltohmmeters

VOLTOHMMETERS
Measure A.C. amps & watts with your VOM; ammeter adapter. N. Johnson. il Pop Electr 28:61-3+ Ja '68
New VOM kit! il Pop Electr 26:54 F '67
VOM+FET=TVM. J. Randall. il Pop Electr 27:57-9 Jl '67

VOLUNTARY arbitration. See Arbitration, Industrial

VOLUNTARY health agencies. See Health agencies, Voluntary

VOLUNTEER firemen. See Firemen

VOLUNTEER service
Community-based volunteers; in Illinois mental health therapy. P. Douglass and others. Parks & Rec 2:26+ Ap '67
Doctors' wives help the housebound. il Todays Health 45:56-7 D '67
Girl scouts pitch in. E. W. Brice. il Am Ed 3:32 Jl '67
Great persuader. V. Lawford. il Vogue 149:194-7+ My '67
Involving the layman; park and recreation field. Parks & Rec 2:15 Jl '67
Pedro house; experiment in St Louis. America 116:716 My 13 '67
Retired? well, get busy! il Changing T 21:17-19 Mr '67
Search for purpose. il Life 62:66-75 Ap 28 '67
Volunteers to America program gets underway. Dept State Bul 56:244 F 13 '67
Way back for troubled youngsters; mental health volunteers in Los Angeles County help former psychiatric patients. S. Gordon. il Parents Mag 42:66-7+ N '67
Yes, you can go home again; a community program serving the elderly and chronically ill of Rochester and Monroe County, N.Y. M. A. Brice. Todays Health 45:54-6 D '67
See also
Community service
Teachers aides
Volunteer workers in education

VOLUNTEER service, International
Japan's Peace corps. America 117:290 S 23 '67
Red peace corps; International youth service of solidarity and friendship. Time 90:30 D 1 '67
Reverse peace corps; Volunteers to America from Asia, Africa and Latin America. il Time 89:20 Je 16 '67
Symbolic atonement in Israel. D. Wigoder. Mlle 64:130-1+ F '67
Volunteers to America begin training programs. Dept State Bul 57:235 Ag 21 '67
Wanted: volunteers to work overseas. il Changing T 21:44 N '67
See also
International voluntary services (organization)
United States—Peace corps

VOLUNTEER system, Military. See Military service, Voluntary

VOLUNTEER workers in education
Let me help you learn; school volunteer program. T. J. Fleming. Redbook 129:46+ O '67
Second pair of hands; school volunteer program. N. Gittelson. il N Y Times Mag p 104+ Mr 19 '67; Discussion. p 100+ Ap 9; 22+ Ap 16 '67

VOLUNTEERS In service to America
At our corner; VISTA book kits from many publishers including Scholastic. il Sr Schol 90:sup37 Mr 31 '67
Girl from V.I.S.T.A; experiences of J. Honrath as a worker in the mountains of eastern Kentucky. F. Powledge. il Redbook 129:80-1+ Jl '67
Kentucky's coal beds of sedition. P. Good. il Nation 205:166-9 S 4 '67
Sedition in Kentucky. J. Ridgeway. New Repub 157:10-11 S 2 '67
VISTA. E. O'Hara. il Am Ed 3:27-9 S '67

VOLUNTEERS to America. See Volunteer service, International

VOLZ, E. C.
Unusual annuals. Horticulture 45:22-3 Ap '67

VON ABELE, Rudolph
On a child burned to death in Vietnam; poem. New Repub 156:28 Ja 28 '67

VON BRAUN, Wernher
[Articles on space technology and space flight] See issues of Popular science monthly
Man on the moon: how soon? interview. Read Digest 90:136-9 Mr '67
Space man's look at Antarctica. por Pop Sci 190:114-16+ My '67
Space technology and progress. por Tech W 20:36-8 Ja 23 '67

about
Doctor Von Braun's all-purpose space machine. G. Bylinsky. il Fortune 75:142-9+ My '67

VON DREELE, W. H.
Bobby in '72? poem. Nat R 19:1014 S 19 '67
But does he project? Toward tomorrow; poems. Nat R 19:286, 305 Mr 21 '67
Changing the guard; RIP; poems. Nat R 19:1364, 1369 D 12 '67
Christmas in New York; poem. Nat R 19:1414 D 26 '67
Courtesy call; poem. Nat R 19:834 Ag 8 '67
Harold Wilson blows his bloody top; poem. Nat R 19:1310 N 28 '67
I, a honky; poem. Nat R 19:903 Ag 22 '67
In your heart you know he's right; They're just kids; poems. Nat R 19:230, 261 Mr 7 '67
Listen to the dove; Recessional; poems. Nat R 19:392, 409 Ap 18 '67
Margaret Sanger, where are you? poem. Nat R 19:456 My 2 '67
My candidate; poem. Nat R 19:946 S 5 '67
My most recent position; poem. Nat R 19:1007 S 19 '67
Napalm for Cairo? And now, Biafra; Let us escalate together, prudently; poems. Nat R 19:621, 625, 639 Je 13 '67
New economics; Consider the lobster; poems. Nat R 19:1248, 1274 N 14 '67
O ye of little faith; poem. Nat R 19:507 My 16 '67
On declarations; poem. Nat R 19:673 Je 27 '67
Onward, Christian soldiers; poem. Nat R 19:1160 O 31 '67
Priest that made Milwaukee famous; poem. Nat R 19:1054 O 3 '67
Rockefeller awakes. . . again; poem. Nat R 19:124 F 7 '67
Sonnet to a liberal mama. Nat R 19:724 Jl 11 '67
Storm warning; poem. Nat R 19:336 Ap 4 '67
Thoughts on the Wallace candidacy after having read Frank Meyer's analysis; poem. Nat R 19:557 My 30 '67
Trading with the State department; poem. Nat R 20:20 Ja 16 '68
Yemen is in Arabia; poem. Nat R 19:571 My 30 '67

VON ECKARDT, Wolf
Are we being en-gulfed? New Repub 157:21-3 D 9 '67
Redesigning American airports. Harper 234:66-8+ Mr '67
Toward a better community. Am Home 70:40+ Je; 12+ S; 45-7 N '67

about
Civic consciences. por Time 89:66+ Mr 31 '67

VON heute auf morgen; opera. See Schönberg, A.

VON HOFF, Byron
Big pitch by a baseball baby. W. J. McKean. il pors Look 31:53-8 Je 27 '67

VON HOFFMAN, Nicholas
Conviction of Captain Levy. New Repub 156:9-11 Je 17 '67

VONG Savang, crown prince of Laos
President Johnson welcomes Crown Prince of Laos; toast, November 9, 1967. Dept State Bul 57:752 D 4 '67

VONK, Johannes Franciscus Marie
Conductors; interview. New Yorker **42:28-30**
Ja 28 '67

VON KÁRMÁN, Theodore
Budapest brain in aerodynamics. R. L. Bisplinghoff. por Sat R 50:29-30 O 14 '67

VON KARMAN center. See Aerojet-General
corporation

VON MEIER, Kurt
Love, mysticism, and the hippies. Vogue 150:
84-6+ N 15 '67

VON MOLTKE, Henry
Teaching in a church-related college. bibliog f Sch & Soc 95:230-1 Ap 1 '67

VONNEGUT, Bernard
When will we change the weather? with biographical sketch. por Natur Hist 76:4, 82-9
bibliog(p 105) D '67

VONNEGUT, Kurt, 1922-
Manner of speaking. J. Ciardi. Sat R 50:16+
S 30 '67

VON RECKLINGHAUSEN, Daniel R.
Integrated-circuit i.f. amplifier used in new
FM receiver. Electr World 77:34-6+ Ap '67

VON TROTT, Albert S.
Scrounge, an instant J antenna. Pop Electr
25:46+ D '66

VORARLBERG
Pleasures of the Vorarlberg. N. S. Hazelton.
Nat R 19:1020+ S 19 '67

VORSTER, Balthazar Johannes
Apartheid with a smile. Christian Cent 84:
526 Ap 26 '67
Touch of sweet reasonableness. por Time
89:28-9 Mr 31 '67

VOSBURGH, Frederick G. See Truslow, F. K.
jt. auth.

VOSS, Gilbert L.
Squids; jet-powered torpedoes of the deep.
Nat Geog Mag 131:386-411 Mr '67

VOSS, Virginia
With a telling tongue. Mlle 64:152-3+ Mr '67

VOTAW, Tex.
Well drillers save trapped girl. il Am City
82:95 My '67

VOTE, Labor. See Trade unions—Political activities

VOTERS, Registration of
Gone North; Department of justice invokes
the Fifteenth amendment in Gary, Ind.
New Repub 157:10 N 18 '67
Sunflower in the spring; rerun elections in
Sunflower and Moorhead, Miss, caused by
discrimination against prospective Negro
registrants. New Repub 156:10 Ap 8 '67

VOTH, Alden
Portugal in Africa; Angola and Mozambique.
Sat R 50:52+ S 16 '67

VOTING
Electoral participation. R. M. Scammon. bib-
liog f Ann Am Acad 371:59-71 My '67
Press and twenty-four-hour voting; Frank
Stanton's proposal for national elections. R.
L. Tobin. Sat R 50:49-50 Ag 12 '67
They vote against. K. Crawford. Newsweek
69:30 My 1 '67
Twenty-four hour election day. J. McLaughlin.
America 117:488 O 28 '67
See also
Referendum
United Nations—Voting
United States—Congress—Voting
Voters, Registration of

VOTING age. See Suffrage—United States

VOTING machines
Signs $6.4 million contract for new voting
system; Los Angeles County. Am City 82:50
N '67
What good are voting machines? il Changing
T 21:39-41 Je '67

VOTING records, Congressmen. See Congressmen

VOTIPKA, Thelma
Thelma Votipka featured on LP. A. Favia-
Artsay. il por Hobbies 71:36+ F '67

VOURAS, Paul P.
Jordan. bibliog Focus 17:1-6 F '67

VOW of poverty. See Poverty, Vow of

VOYAGE to Cythera; story. See Drabble, M.

VOYAGER (space vehicle) See Space vehicles

VOYAGES
Bahamas to Maine. E. Hiscock. il Yachting
122:50-1+ Jl '67
Caviar and mutiny; Queen Mary's last voyage.
il Newsweek 70:42 D 18 '67
Extreme magic; cruising up the Yugoslav-
ian coast. T. Capote. il Vogue 149:84-9+
Ap 15 '67

Great northeast cruise; East by West's 2650-
mile voyage. J. West and C. West. il Motor
B 121:77-82 Ja '68 (to be cont)
I crossed the Atlantic in a 12-foot sloop.
W. E. Verity. il Pop Sci 190:94-9+ F '67
I crossed the Atlantic in a 12-foot sloop; the
preparations. W. E. Verity. il Pop Sci 190:
104-8+ Ja '67
Kayak odyssey from the Inland Sea to Tokyo.
D. Dimancescu. il Nat Geog Mag 132:295-337
S '67
Loneliness of the long-distance sailor. H.
Gordon. il N Y Times Mag p30-2+ Ja 22
'67
Nine seas and an ocean. R. Evinrude. il Yacht-
ing 122:38-40+ O '67
'Round the world, family style. M. Roefer.
il Motor B 120:22-5+ Jl '67
Stornoway progress report. M. Petersen. See
issues of Motor boating
To the South Seas in Loon. G. B. Pinchot. il
Yachting 122:44-6+ Jl; 42-3+ Ag '67
We just sailed the Atlantic, said my husband
casually. J. Mustoe and E. Yourke. il
Redbook 129:62-3+ Ag '67
See also
Cruising
Explorations
Ocean travel

Anecdotes, facetiae, satire, etc.
Incredible Caribbean adventures of one Art
Buchwald and family. A. Buchwald. il La-
dies Home J 84:106-7+ N '67
Victory no. 743 at sea; L. Dork first man to
make solo crossing of the Atlantic, east to
west, on inflated rubber horse. G. Cotler.
New Yorker 43:128+ Ap 1 '67; Same.
Yachting 122:58+ Jl '67

VOYAGES, Imaginary
See also
Robinsonades

VOYAGES around the world
Derring-do off Cape Horn; F. Chichester's
voyage. il Time 89:71 Mr 31 '67
14,000 miles singlehanded; reprint. G. Chichester. il Yachting 121:62-5+ My '67
Home is the sailor. L. Wainwright. Life 62:
26A Je 9 '67
Old man and the sea. il Newsweek 69:61-5 Je
12 '67
'Round the world, family style. M. Roefer.
il Motor B 120:22-5+ Jl; 27-9+ S '67; 121:
107-9 Ja '68
Tale of two heroes, Gipsy Moth IV and
her one-man crew. F. Chichester. il Life
62:28-37+ Je 9 '67; Same abr. with title
Around the world with Gipsy Moth IV.
Read Digest 91:46-52 S '67
Voyage completed. G. Chichester. il Yachting 122:38-40+ Ag '67
Voyage of the Svaap. il Newsweek 69:16 Je
12 '67

VOYTOVICH, Anthony E. and Topper, Y. J.
Hormone-dependent differentiation of immature mouse mammary gland in vitro.
bibliog Science 158:1326-7 D 8 '67

VOZNESENSKII, Andrei
Call of the lake; From a Transcarpathian
diary; poems. tr. by S. Kunitz and V.
Dunham. New Repub 157:28, 31 S 2 '67
In the mountains; poem, tr. by J. Wallace.
Mlle 65:104 S '67
Sketch for a poem; poem, tr. by W. J. Smith
and V. Dunham. Harper 235:52-5 Ag '67
They've taken out our sense of shame; ex-
cerpts from poem; translation. por N Y
Times Mag p24 Ag 20 '67
To Bela Akhmadulina; Lament for two un-
born poems; Self-portrait; Note to E Yanit-
skaya, formerly typist to Mayakovsky;
Lieutenant Zagorin; poems, tr. by S. Kunitz
and V. Dunham. New Repub 157:31-3 Jl 1
'67
Two poems: Striptease on strike; Winter at
the track; tr. by M. Hayward. Atlan 220:
70-2 N '67

about
Notes and comment. New Yorker 43:19 Ag 26
'67
Revolt of the authors. por Newsweek 70:31
Ag 21 '67
Spit in time. por Time 90:29 Ag 18 '67
Voznesensky in translation. M. L. Rosenthal.
Poetry 110:40-2 Ap '67
Yevtushenko and Voznesensky. G. Ruark.
Poetry 111:121-4 N '67

VROMAN, Clyde
Accepted or rejected? interview, ed. by D.
Klein. por Seventeen 26:134-5+ Mr '67

VROOM, Barbara
Weekend confrontation with the soc. rels.; story. New Yorker 43:199-200+ D 2 '67
VU-van-Thai
Regional solution for Viet Nam. For Affairs 46:347-61 Ja '68

W

WBA. See World boxing association
WBAI (radio station) See Radio stations
WCTU. See Woman's Christian temperance union
WESCON. See Western electronics show and convention
WHO. See World health organization
WLBT, Jackson, Miss. See Television stations
WMO. See World meteorological organization
WNBA. See Women's national book association
W. R. Grace and company. See Grace, W. R, and company
WSCF. See World student Christian federation
WXUR (radio station) See Radio stations
WACHTEL, Howard, and Kandel, E. R.
Direct synaptic connection mediating both excitation and inhibition. bibliog Science 158:1206-8 D 1 '67
WACKENHUT, George R.
Governor Kirk's not-so-secret police. F. Murray. por Reporter 36:27-30 Mr 23 '67
Governor Kirk's private eyes. F. J. Cook. il Nation 204:616-22 My 15 '67
Great Wackenhut. Nation 204:292-3 Mr 6 '67
When a state opens its own war on crime. il por U S News 62:61-2 My 22 '67
WADDINGHAM, John
Art with a deadline. il por Am Artist 31:54-62 My '67
WADDINGTON, C. J.
Paleomagnetic field reversals and cosmic radiation. bibliog Science 158:913-15 N 17 '67
WADE, James
In Japan: new Bayreuth productions. Hi Fi 17:MA24-5+ Jl '67
WADERS (boots) See Shoes, Rubber, plastic, etc.
WADLEIGH Intermediate school. See New York (city)—Education
WADSWORTH, Nelson
Underground A-tests may be making us radioactive. Sci Digest 62:13-17 S '67
WAERN, Jonas
Diary of a U.N. peacekeeper. Sat R 50:19-21+ N 18 '67
WAFFLES
Chicken-pecan waffles. il Bet Hom & Gard 45:88 My '67
WAGE agreements. See Trade agreements
WAGE bargaining. See Collective bargaining
WAGE differentials
Hourly earnings differentials by region and size of city. V. R. Fuchs. il Mo Labor R 90:22-6 Ja '67
Where the top dollar is going; National bureau of economic research studies hourly wages il Bsns W p 175-6 Mr 11 '67
WAGE payment plans
Push for blue-collar salaries; negotiations for status and security through guaranteed annual wage. il Bsns W p 135-6+ F 25 '67
See also
Wages—Annual wage
WAGE-price policy. See Price regulation by government—United States
WAGE stabilization. See Wages—Regulation
WAGES
Foreign labor briefs. See issues of Monthly labor review
See also
Income
Labor cost
Non-wage payments
Overtime
Profit sharing
Salaries
Tipping
Trade unions

Annual wage
Shape of the salary plan; UAW guaranteed annual salary scheme. il Bsns W p 102-3 Jl 29 '67

Trading blue collars for white; guaranteed annual wage and salaries, UAW goals in 1967 bargaining. il Bsns W p43-4+ Ap 1 '67
See also
Automobile industry and trade—Wages and hours

Cost of living adjustments
Living costs get critical again. il Bsns W p62+ F 11 '67

Dismissal wage
Guaranteed wage catches on: the way it will work. U S News 63:84+ N 6 '67

Economic aspects
Beyond the guidelines: wage-price policy for 1967; excerpt from Maintaining price stability and reducing unemployment. Mo Labor R 90:47-9 Mr '67
Does inflation pay? what workers find. il U S News 64:18-19 Ja 1 '68
Hitting the guideposts; CEA policies. Bsns W p 114+ F 4 '67
Living costs, wages, and wage policy. H. M. Douty. bibliog f il Mo Labor R 90:1-7 Je '67
Next: new threat of inflation? impact of auto-wage hike. U S News 63:39-41 N 6 '67
Where the top dollar is going; National bureau of economic research studies hourly wages. il Bsns W p 175-6 Mr 11 '67

Regulation
National wage policies in Europe and the U.S. E. M. Kassalow. Mo Labor R 90:36-7 Mr '67
New slant for the guideposts; tougher rules for management on prices and profits. Bsns W p29-30 Ja 28 '67

Statistics
Earnings in motion picture theater industry, April 1966. C. M. O'Connor. bibliog f Mo Labor R 90:48-51 Ap '67
Wages and supplementary benefits in metropolitan areas. K. J. Hoffmann. il Mo Labor R 90:48-54 Je '67
See also
Wage differentials

Canada
Canadian unions press for U.S.-size wages. Bsns W p90+ Ja 6 '68
If you think U.S. has labor troubles—. il U S News 62:77-9 F 13 '67
Now it's a wage explosion for workers in Canada. il U S News 63:76-8 Ag 28 '67

Europe
See also
Wages—Regulation

France
Profit sharing, now it's a de Gaulle must. U S News 63:10 Jl 24 '67

Great Britain
Britain's plan to curb raises. U S News 62:113-14 My 15 '67
Britain's wage freeze: a success, but what comes later? il U S News 63:72 Jl 17 '67
Why Britain froze wages; with editorial comment. R. Harrod. il Duns R 88:32-3+ D '66

Japan
Composition of wages and supplements: U.S.-Japan comparisons. J. L. Norwood. il Mo Labor R 90:30-4 My '67
Shuntō: Japanese labor's spring wage offensive. R. Evans, jr. bibliog f il Mo Labor R 90:23-8 O '67
Wages in Japan and the United States; similarities and contrasts in wage systems. J. L. Norwood. il Mo Labor R 90:25-8 Ap '67

United States
Already, a wage pattern for '68: bigger raises than in '67. il U S News 64:67 Ja 1 '68
As profits go down, wages keep going up. U S News 62:112 My 15 '67
Bigger and bigger raises; no end in sight. il U S News 63:80-1 Ag 7 '67
Composition of wages and supplements: U.S.-Japan comparisons. J. L. Norwood. il Mo Labor R 90:30-4 My '67
Earnings and hours; tables. See issues of Monthly labor review

WAGES—United States—*Continued*
From the top union leaders: latest on '67 wage demands. il U S News 62:74-5 Mr 6 '67
Good-bye to guideposts: LBJ unleashes unions, report of Council of economic advisers. il U S News 62:87-8 F 6 67
Hourly earnings differentials by region and size of city. V. R. Fuchs. il Mo Labor R 90:22-6 Ja '67
How much is a raise really worth? U S News 64:79 Ja 15 '68
How workers are faring in 1967: biggest raises in many years. il U S News 63:97-8 N 20 '67
Succession of pay raises, and now; gains since 1952. il U S News 63:40-1 N 6 '67
Wage changes under 1966 major agreements. J. E. Talbot, jr. il Mo Labor R 90:13-20 Je '67
Wage developments in manufacturing, 1966. G. Ruben. il Mo Labor R 90:31-8 Ag '67
Wages in Japan and the United States; similarities and contrasts in wage systems. J. L. Norwood. il Mo Labor R 90:25-8 Ap '67
   See also
Government employees—Salaries
Minimum wage—United States
Wages—Regulation
   also subhead Wages and hours under names of industries, e.g. Cleaning and dyeing industry—Wages and hours

WAGES, Annual. See Wages—Annual wage

WAGGONER, Paul E.
Mulches. Horticulture 45:10+ Ag '67

WAGGONER, William G.
Homemade sharpener for home-improvement tools. Pop Sci 191:144-6+ S '67
Your drill can power a paint shaker. Pop Sci 190:166-7 Ja '67

WAGGONNER, Joe David, 1918-
Excerpt from address, April 5, 1966. Cong Digest 46:93+ Mr '67

WAGNER, Bartlett A. and Conley, James
Experiment with brainstorming: creative playground activities. Parks & Rec 2:21+ S '67

WAGNER, Frank
One exercise that does everything. E. L. Gross. il Vogue 151:118-21 Ja 1 '68

WAGNER, Kip
Man's obsession and its rewards. il por Life 62:102 Mr 10 '67

WAGNER, Nancy M.
160-acre kindergarten. NEA J 56:41-2 F '67

WAGNER, Philip
War with the birds. Harper 234:80-4 Ap '67

WAGNER, Richard, 1813-1883
Armchair opera. R. Gelatt. Reporter 36:44+ Ap 6 '67
Deutsche grammophon's Die Walküre. H. Glass. Am Rec G 33:734-6 My '67
Karajan's Walkuere and a brave new Ring begins. C. L. Osborne. Hi Fi 17:67-9 My '67
Lohengrin. Criticism
   Hi Fi 17:MA7+ F '67
Die Meistersinger von Nürnberg. Criticism
   Sat R 50:46-7 Mr 4 '67
Records:
   Götterdämmerung excerpts. Opera N 31:34 F 18 '67
   Die Walküre. Opera N 31:34 Ap 1 '67
Das Rheingold. Criticism
   Opera N 32:15-17 N 25 '67
Ring East and West. S. Jenkins, jr. il Opera N 32:15-17 N 25 '67
Ring resounding, by J. Culshaw. Review
   Hi Fi il 17:18+ D '67. G. Movshon
Salzburg; Herbert von Karajan staging of Wagner's Ring. J. H. Sutcliffe. il Opera N 31:30 My 13 '67
Tristan and Isolde. Criticism
   Opera N 32:22 N 25 '67
Von Karajan's Easter festival. P. Moor. il Hi Fi 17:MA21+ Je '67
Wagner operas on records; a discography (cont) C. L. Osborne. Hi Fi 17:44+ Ja '67
Die Walküre. Criticism
   New Yorker 43:192-3 D 2 '67
   New Yorker 43:225 D 9 '67
   Newsweek il 70:112 D 4 '67
   Opera N 32:15-17 N 25 '67
   Sat R 50:48-9+ D 9 '67
   Time il 90:116 D 1 '67
World of Wieland Wagner. G. London. il Sat R 50:59-60+ Ja 28 '67
   See also
Bayreuth festival

WAGNER, Susan
FTC hits false advertising of health books. Pub W 192:35-6 Jl 24 '67
Rodale seeks court review of free speech issue in book advertising. Pub W 192:36-7 O 9 '67

WAGNER, Walter F. Jr
Emerson Goble won't like this a bit, but... Arch Rec 142:9 D '67

WAGNER, Wieland
Wieland Wagner, elaborate mourning, future uncertainties. P. Moor. por Hi Fi 17:MA3 Ja '67
World of Wieland Wagner. G. London. il pors Sat R 50:59-60+ Ja 28 '67

WAGNER, Wolfgang
After Wieland, business as usual? W. B. Rios. il Hi Fi 17:MA22-3 N '67

WAGNER, Wolfgang, family
Squabble in the Wagner family: widow vs. brother. Hi Fi 17:MA2 Mr '67

WAGNER electric corporation-Tung-Sol electric incorporated merger. See Business consolidations and mergers

WAGONER, David
Blues to be sung in a dark voice; poem. Nation 205:218 S 11 '67
Magic night at the reformatory; poem. Nation 205:182 S 4 '67
March of Coxey's army; Getting above ourselves on Sunday; Getting out of jail on Monday; Archeological notes; poems. Poetry 110:211-21 Jl '67
Stretching; poem. Sat R 50:112 S 23 '67

   about
Opposite methods. H. Carruth. Poetry 109:400-1 Mr '67
Poet as novelist. M. Van Duyn. Poetry 109:336-7 F '67

WAGONER, Robert V.
Cosmological element production. bibliog Science 155:1369-76 Mr 17 '67

WAHL, Paul
Coming: home sound movies for everyone. Pop Mech 128:74-5 Jl '67
How to shoot flashy color without a flash. Pop Mech 129:160-1+ Ja '68
Personal-use report: Instamatic 804. Pop Sci 190:126-7 F '67
Real scoop on scopes. Pop Mech 128:112-15+ D '67
Rifle that's also a shotgun. Pop Sci 191:138-9 O '67
Stop that action with a stutter strobe. Pop Mech 128:174-5+ N '67
Try a new air rifle. Pop Sci 192:92-5 Ja '68
World's fastest color film. Pop Mech 128:96-8 Ag '67

WAHL, Werner H. and Kramer, H. H.
Neutron-activation analysis; with biographical sketches. Sci Am 216:14, 68-72+ bibliog(p 146) Ap '67

WAIKIKI. See Honolulu

WAILING wall. See Jerusalem

WAIN, John
E pluribus unum. New Repub 156:25-6+ My 27 '67
Greats man. New Repub 157:25-8 N 18 '67
Mr Day Lewis' pale fire. New Repub 156:21-4 Je 24 '67
Mr MacLeish's new play. New Repub 157:25-6+ Jl 22 '67

WAINWRIGHT, Loudon
View from here. See issues of Life

WAITERS and waitresses

   Anecdotes, facetiae, satire, etc.
Genus: waiter; species: New York. L. Rosten. il Look 31:8 N 28 '67

WAKE COUNTY, N.C.
Bigot, spare that tree; school board kills federal summer program for white and Negro underprivileged children. Nation 205:133 Ag 28 '67

WAKEFIELD, Dan
Return to paradise. Atlan 219:102-4+ F '67

WAKEFIELD, Hugh
Richardson glass. Antiques 91:632-6 My '67

WAKEFIELD seafoods, Incorporated
King crab. il Time 89:92 Ap 7 '67

WAKIN, Edward
America's ecumenical encounter. Sat R 50:32 My 6 '67

WAKING the daffodil; drama. See Bennett, R.

WAKOSKI, Diane
Canoer; poem. New Yorker 43:94 Jl 15 '67

WAKSMAN, Byron H. See Lubaroff, D. M; Ruddle, N. H. jt. auths.

WALCOTT, Charles. See Michener, M. C. jt. auth.

WALD, George
Good beginning. il por Time 90:56 O 27 '67
Nobel prize: three named for medicine, physiology award. J. E. Dowling. por Science 158:468-9 O 27 '67
Nobel prize winners. por Sci N 92:437-8 N 4 '67
Nobel work. il por Newsweek 70:82-3 O 30 '67
Wald urges Cambridge Vietnam referendum. R. J. Samuelson. il por Science 158:617 N 3 '67

WALD, Richard C.
Some talk of Passchendaele. Reporter 37:36-7 N 30 '67

WALD, S.
Build a battery-less dwell meter. Pop Electr 27:40 N '67

WALDEGRAVE, William
Dizzy, man and myth. Nat R 19:257+ Mr 7 '67

WALDEN, Vt.
He bought a bus; how L. Roberts applied federal funds. D. Dew. Sat R 50:58-9+ Je 17 '67

WALDMAN, Diane
Remarkable commonplace. Art N 66:28-31+ O '67

WALDMAN, Eric
Book review (cont) America 116:190 F 4 '67

WALDMEIR, Pete
Baseball. Sports Illus 27:64 S 25 '67

WALDO, Bruce
Irving Center for the arts. Parks & Rec 2:17+ Je '67

WALDOCK, Sir Humphrey
International law commission and the law of treaties. UN Mo Chron 4:69-76 My '67

WALDRON, Robert
Around the world with swash and buckle. Am Heritage 18:56-9+ Ag '67

WALES, Jane
In my opinion. por Seventeen 26:222-3 Mr '67

WALES, Nym
Old China hands. New Repub 156:13-15 Ap 1 '67

WALES
See also
Aberfan
Coal mines and mining—Wales

Social life and customs
Road to Llanystumdwy. J. Morris. Harper 234:94-7 Ap '67

WALFORD, Roy L.
Matter of life and death. Atlan 220:65-70 Ag '67

WALGREEN company
From Myrtle & malteds. il Time 90:78 Jl 28 '67

WALINSKY, Louis J.
Victorious Israel's look and mood. New Repub 157:9-10 Jl 8 '67

WALKER, Alan
Vietnam: reappraisal from Down Under. Christian Cent 84:835-6 Je 28 '67
Where Pentecostalism is mushrooming. Christian Cent 85:81-2 Ja 17 '68

about
Tongans respond to Alan Walker mission. H. R. Henderson. Christian Cent 84:416+ Mr 29 '67

WALKER, Arleigh W.
How to price industrial products. Harvard Bsns R 45:125-32 S '67

WALKER, Chip
Art festival brightens busy city square. Parks & Rec 2:24-5+ S '67
Innsbruck's unique zoo. Parks & Rec 2:20-1+ Ap '67
Photography can work for you. Parks & Rec 2:24-5+ Jl '67

WALKER, David
Test equipment for CB and business radio. Electr World 77:32-3+ Mr '67
Who runs educational TV? New Repub 156:35-7 F 11 '67

WALKER, Eric A.
National science board: its place in national policy. Science 156:474-7 Ap 28 '67

WALKER, G. F. and Garrett, W. G.
Chemical exfoliation of vermiculite and the production of colloidal dispersions. bibliog Science 156:385-7 Ap 21 '67

WALKER, Gerald
First of the month; Writers and editors war tax protest. C. Amory. Sat R 50:6 O 7 '67; Discussion. 50:12+ O 21; 60 N 11; 8+ N 18 '67

WALKER, Harry
Harry the hat. J. R. McDermott. il pors Life 62:105-8+ Ap 7 '67
Pirates: Pittsburgh's confidence guys. I. R. McVay. il pors Look 31:64-9 My 30 '67

WALKER, Howell
New South Wales. Nat Geog Mag 132:591-635 N '67

WALKER, Jerry L.
Changing attitudes toward the library and the librarian. por ALA Bul 61:977-81 S '67

WALKER, Jimmy
Act of Providence. H. L. Masin. il por Sr Schol 90:24 Mr 17 '67
That Providence cannonball. F. Deford. il pors Sports Illus 26:18-19 Ja 23 '67

WALKER, John
National gallery after a quarter century. Nat Geog Mag 131:348-71 Mr '67

WALKER, Joseph A.
Mid-air! mid-air! mid-air! K. Wheeler. il Read Digest 90:127-31 F '67

WALKER, Laurence C.
Trees, for business or pleasure? Am For 73:16-17+ My '67

WALKER, Margaret
For my people; poem. Negro Hist Bul 30:20 Ja '67

WALKER, Michael J. and Lowen, Janice
Vanishing American. Am For 73:6-9+ O '67

WALKER, Norman
Norman Walker and dance company, Brooklyn academy of music. J. Maskey. Dance Mag 41:77 Ap '67

WALKER, R. M. See Huand, W. H. jt. auth.

WALKER, Ron
Ron Walker: for connoisseurs or cowboys. V. H. Swisher. il por Dance Mag 41:22-3+ Ap '67

WALKER, Ronald S.
Build your own abrasive cutoff machine. Pop Mech 127:190-2+ F '67

WALKER, Ted
Bow; story. New Yorker 43:34-7 S 2 '67
Haircut; story. New Yorker 43:50-4 S 23 '67
Journey back; poem. New Yorker 43:64 N 25 '67
Pythons; poem. New Yorker 43:99 D 9 '67

about
Three poets. P. Legler. Poetry 109:411-12 Mr '67

WALKER, William Aiken
Pack of rebels. il Am Heritage 18:28-9 Je '67

WALKER, William S.
Composer uses printing presses for inspiration. il por Pub W 191:116-17 Mr 6 '67

WALKER and company
Large print program initiated by Walker; including mysteries. Library J 92:2345 Je 15 '67

WALKER cup. See Golf—Tournaments

WALKIE-talkies. See Radio telephone, Portable

WALKING
Antiquity of human walking. J. Napier. il Sci Am 216:56-66 Ap '67
Gait study measures problems of balance. il Sci N 91:293 Mr 25 '67
Odyssey of Charles Wayo; Ghanaian boy walks Sahara and Europe in fantastic quest of American education. C. L. Sanders. il Ebony 22:27-30+ F '67
Personal business; walking your way to better health. Bsns W p 173-4 Ap 22 '67
Step to catastrophe; walking is one controlled fall after another. A. J. Snider. Sci Digest 62:56-7 N '67
See also
Trails

WALKING happy; musical comedy. See Musical comedies, revues, etc.—Criticisms, plots, etc.

WALKING shoes. See Shoes

WALKING to Waldheim; drama. See Simon, M.

Die **WALKÜRE;** opera. See Wagner, R.

WALL, James M.
Movies (cont) Christian Cent 84:1432+ N 8 '67

WALL coverings
Exciting new wall coverings. il Good H 164:156 My '67
How to paint walls and furniture with fabric. il House & Gard 132:288-9+ N '67
New coverings for your walls. il Pop Sci 191:150-2 S '67
Twenty-three beautiful, practical wall treatments. P. Rumely and N. Cordts. il Bet Hom & Gard 45:68-81 N '67
Vinyl/fabric wall coverings. il Consumer Rep 32:282-5 My '67

WALL hangings
How to wake up an old-fashioned house without spending a fortune: color and pattern. il House & Gard 131:116-19 F '67

WALL shelves. See Shelves

WALL Street Journal
Fourth for the WSJ; fourth Pulitzer prize since 1961. il Newsweek 69:90 My 15 '67
Scavengers of the press. Nation 205:580 D 4 '67
Wall Street publishing giant. J. Tebbel. Sat R 51:110-11+ Ja 13 '68

WALL-to-wall carpeting. See Rugs and carpets

WALLACE, Anthony F. C.
Psychological preparations for war. Natur Hist 76:50-4 bibliog(p70) D '67

WALLACE, DeMille L.
Mystique of aggression. Christian Cent 84:503-5 Ap 19 '67

WALLACE, George Corley
How Wallace sees the issues; interview. por U S News 62:57-8+ Mr 20 '67
Wallace on Reagan an' NR; interview, ed. by T. Anderson. Nat R 19:1004 S 19 '67

about
As the Wallace drive takes shape. il por U S News 64:20 Ja 15 '68
California countdown. il Newsweek 71:13-14 Ja 1 '68
Enigma in the South. il por Time 89:20-1 My 12 '67
Enmity in the North. il Time 89:20 My 12 '67
George Wallace: a gross and simple heart. T. Wicker. il por Harper 234:41-9 Ap '67
George Wallace for President? S. Alsop. por Sat Eve Post 240:18 Mr 25 '67
George Wallace isn't kidding. J. Witcover. Reporter 36:23-5 F 23 '67
George Wallace maps his way to the White House. T. L. Knap. New Repub 156:7-9 Ap 29 '67
George Wallace: running for God; with excerpts from interview. R. G. Sherrill. il por Nation 204:589-96 My 8 '67
Goat vote. Time 89:23 My 5 '67
Godzilla's back in town. Nat R 19:508 My 16 '67
Governor and Mister Wallace. M. Frady. il por Atlan 220:35-40 Ag '67
He who throws stones. Newsweek 70:28 N 6 '67
How Wallace fared on his trip North. por U S News 62:12 My 8 '67
How Wallace will run his third-party campaign. R. M. Scammon. il Reporter 37:34-6 O 19 '67
Northern hospitality. Newsweek 69:36 My 15 '67
On the campaign trail with Wallace. il U S News 62:20 My 15 '67
Out West with candidate Wallace. L. Leamer. New Repub 157:11-13 D 16 '67
Populism of George Wallace. F. S. Meyer. Nat R 19:527 My 16 '67
Preview of Wallace's appeal to the North. J. Witcover. New Repub 156:9-10 My 27 '67
Queen of Alabama and the prince consort. R. Jenkins. il pors N Y Times Mag p26-7+ My 21 '67
Spoiler. il Newsweek 69:34 Ap 3; 39-40 My 8 '67
Stand up for George. il por Newsweek 70:31-2 D 4 '67
Third party in '68? the George Wallace story. il pors U S News 62:54-7 Mr 20 '67
Wallace in the West. il Time 90:27 D 8 '67
Wallace race in '68; as governors see it. por U S News 63:77 S 25 '67
Wallace threat. R. Moley. Newsweek 69:100 Ap 3 '67
Wallaces: more clues to '68 plans. por U S News 62:14 Ja 30 '67
Wallace's new math. il por Newsweek 71:18 Ja 15 '68
What George is doing. K. Crawford. Newsweek 69:45 My 22 '67
What makes Wallace run? J. J. Kilpatrick. il por Nat R 19:400-9 Ap 18 '67

WALLACE, Henry Agard
Henry A. Kennedy? K. Crawford. Newsweek 69:36 Mr 20 '67

WALLACE, Joe
(tr) See Voznesenskiĭ, A. In the mountains

WALLACE, Kenneth Dean
First U.S. Makropulos case. Hi Fi 17:MA20-MA21 F '67

Thirtieth Bach festival: ready, willing, and Abel. Hi Fi 17:MA22-3+ O '67
Trojans at War memorial. Hi Fi 17:MA22-3 Ja '67
(ed) See Krips, J. And we quote

WALLACE, Lurleen (Burns)
From defiance to détente. il por Time 89:22 Ja 27 '67
Governor and Mister Wallace. M. Frady. il por Atlan 220:35-40 Ag '67
Ma 'n' pa. il por Newsweek 69:24 Ja 30 '67
Mrs Governor faces the feds. H. Wolman. Commonweal 86:192-3 My 5 '67
Political complications. il por Newsweek 70:26-7 Jl 17 '67
Queen of Alabama and the prince consort. R. Jenkins. il pors N Y Times Mag p26-7+ My 21 '67
Wallaces: more clues to '68 plans. por U S News 62:14 Ja 30 '67

WALLACE, Mary
Just across a bridge. Sat R 50:37+ Je 17 '67
Man on the corner; story. Redbook 130:78-9 N '67
That summer at Folly cove. Sat R 50:44-5+ Ag 26 '67

WALLACE, Mike
Deserters. Nation 204:811-12 Je 26 '67

WALLACE, Robert
Ballad of the mouse. New Yorker 43:62 N 11 '67
Dictionary armadillo; poem. Harper 234:97 Ap '67
For Lawson and Ann; from Strew of tacks; poems. Poetry 110:249-50 Jl '67
Giacometti's dog; poem. Sat R 50:14 Mr 18 '67
Turtle; poem. Reporter 36:54 Ja 26 '67

WALLACE, Sarah L.
Many shall run to and fro, and knowledge will be increased. Wilson Lib Bul 41:908-9 My '67
Who is listening? address, April, 1967. por Wilson Lib Bul 42:295-300 N '67

WALLENBERG family
Wallenberg boys, and how they grew; Sweden's premier industrial dynasty. il pors Bsns W p 114-18+ F 25 '67

WALLENSTEIN, Merrill B. See Brady, E. L. jt. auth.

WALLER, Cinda
Black power, a teenager's concept; poem. Negro Hist Bul 30:12 Ja '67

WALLER, Hardress J. and Feldman, S. M.
Somatosensory thalamic neurons: effects of cortical depression. bibliog Science 157:1074-7 S 1 '67

WALLETS. See Purses

WALLEYE fishing. See Perch fishing

WALLICH, Henry C.
[Column on economic questions] See issues of Newsweek

WALLIS, C. Lamar
Memphis: a seven branch salvo. Library J 92:4373-6 D 1 '67

WALLPAPER
Use wallpaper imaginatively! J. LemMon. il Suc Farm 65:104-5 F '67
See also
Paper-hanging

WALLPAPERING. See Paper-hanging

WALLS
Continuing study of the window wall by Eliot Noyes. il Arch Rec 141:173-80 Ap '67
Decorative ways with walls. il Good H 165:116-21 O '67
Glistening news: silver walls. il House & Gard 131:136-9 F '67
How to mold character into drab walls. W. C. Leckey. il Pop Mech 127:144-5 F '67
Wind, sun, rain and the exterior wall. il Arch Rec 142:205-16 S '67
See also
Storage walls

Maintenance and repair
Repairing drywalls: R for popped nails, cracks and holes. S. J. Howard. il Pop Mech 128:154-7 O '67

WALLS, Glass
New geometry in stone and glass. il House B 109:178-82 Ap '67

WALNUT trees
Black walnut, our vanishing money tree. C. E. Randall. il Am For 73:14-17+ O '67

WALPOLE, Robert, 1st earl of Orford. See Orford. R. W.

WALRAVEN, Jan. See De Valois, R. L. jt. auth.

WALSH, Chad
Heart's heat; poem. Commonweal 87:300 D
1 '67
Meditation on abstract nouns; poem. Sat R
50:20 Je 17 '67
Mid-August; poem. Christian Cent 84:1042 Ag
16 '67
Prayer to the hanged man; poem. Christian
Cent 84:680 My 24 '67
Sequence of saviors; poem. Christian Cent
84:899 Jl 12 '67

WALSH, Jim
Favorite pioneer recording artists. See issues
of Hobbies

WALSH, John, and Gannon, Robert
Time is short and the water rises; condensation. pors Read Digest 91:213-22+ Jl '67

WALSH, John J.
Patch it right the first time. Am City 82:118-
19 Mr '67

WALSH, John S.
Biggest fair ever: Canada's Expo 67. Good
H 164:172+ Ap '67

WALSH, John T.
Don't oversell centralized purchasing. Am
City 82:93+ Ag '67

WALSH, Joseph L.
Sex on campus. Commonweal 85:590-1+ F
24 '67

WALSH, Moira
Films. See issues of America

WALSH, Richard J.
Catholic hour; letter. America 117:753 D 23
'67

WALSH, Thomas F.
Electric cars: coming back? Todays Health
45:56-9+ My '67

WALT, Lewis W.
Combat general tells what Vietnam war is
like; interview, ed. by W. S. Merick. por
U S News 62:36-9 My 22 '67

about

Changing the guard. il por Newsweek 69:47
My 29 '67
Leader for all reasons. il por Time 89:32 Je
9 '67
Two wars of General Lew Walt. C. Leinster
il pors Life 62:77-80+ My 26 '67
Vietnam: the eye of the storm. F. Sully.
New Repub 157:15-16 Jl 15 '67

WALT Disney productions. See Disney, Walt,
productions

WALTER, Claire
Expo 67. U S Camera 30:24-5+ F '67

WALTER, James Willis
One-man show in empire building. il pors
Bsns W p 122-3+ S 16 '67

WALTER, Louis S. and Clayton, R. N.
Oxygen isotopes: experimental vapor fractionation and variations in tektites. bibliog Science 156:1357-8 Je 9 '67

WALTER Kidde and company. See Kidde, Walter, and company

WALTERS, Barbara
California woman. Ladies Home J 84:77+ Jl
'67
Wish you were here. por Ladies Home J 84:
56 F; 62 Ap '67
(ed) See Carson, J. Trouble with $1,500,000 a
year

WALTERS, Ida M.
Strawberries and flowers; border with a
bonus. Home Gard 54:85-7 Ap '67

WALTERS, Raymond, Jr
Other men's punch lines. Sat R 50:56+ Je 10
'67

WALTERS, William H.
Diamond alchemy. R. Levy. por Duns R 89:50-
1+ Je '67

WALTERS art gallery, Baltimore
Baltimore bounty. H. A. La Farge. il Art N
66:44-7+ Mr '67
Sparkle in the storerooms. il Time 90:84-5
D 15 '67

WALTNER, Elma, and Waltner, Willard
Magazine-go-round end table. Pop Mech 127:
170-1 Ap '67
Make this tile-top chess and checkerboard.
Pop Mech 128:146-7+ D '67
—See Waltner, W. jt. auth.

WALTNER, Willard, and Waltner, Elma
Bird cafeteria. Pop Mech 127:86 F '67
—See Waltner, E. jt. auth.

WALTON, Harry
Dremel's powerful new Moto-tool. Pop Sci
191:168-70 O '67
How to machine your own D bits. Pop Sci
191:172-4 O '67
Unimat offers three improved saws. Pop Sci
192:146-7+ Ja '68

WALTON, Henry
H. Walton here and abroad. E. Gaines. Il
Antiques 92:218-19 Ag '67

WALTON, Izaak
Compleat angler. K. Rexroth. Sat R 50:28
S 16 '67

WALTON, Norman W.
James T. Rapier; congressman from Alabama.
bibliog f Negro Hist Bul 30:6-10 N '67

WALTON, Richard J.
Voice of America; memorandum to John
Daly. Nation 205:135-8, 258+ Ag 28, S 25 '67

WALTZES
Blue Danube waltzes on. H. Fantel. il Read
Digest 90:174-7+ My '67

WAND, Martin, and others
Tritiated thymidine; effect of decomposition
by self-radiolysis on specificity as a tracer
for DNA synthesis. bibliog Science 157:436-8
Jl 28 '67

WANDERER (periodical)
Most happy anniversary. America 117:49 Jl 15
'67

WANDERONE, Rudolph Walter, Jr
Hustler. Newsweek 70:100 Jl 17 '67

WANER, John L.
Making book on Mr Daley. E. S. Gilbreth.
Nation 204:396-8 Mr 27 '67

WANG, An-chuan, and others
Transferrin D1: identity in Australian aborigines and American Negroes. bibliog Science 156:936-7 My 19 '67

WANG, Chao-tien
I was a Red guard; ed. by L. Velie. por
Read Digest 90:55-60 My '67
Nobody dared stop us: defector from Red
guards; interview. ed. by K. M. Chrysler.
por U S News 62:57 Ja 30 '67

WANG, Shih Yi. See Varghese, A. J. jt. auth.

WANG laboratories, incorporated
Wang! new hot issues. Newsweek 70:81+
S 18 '67

WANGENSTEEN, Owen H.
Fertile seedbed of transplant surgery. por
Bsns W p98-100 Ja 6 '67

WANKEL engines. See Automobile engines

WANN, Kenneth D.
Comment on the Denver experiment. NEA J
56:25-6 Mr '67

WANT ads. See Advertising, Classified

WAPITI. See Elk

WAPITI hunting. See Elk hunting

WAR
Arms and influence, by T. C. Schelling. Re-
view
Bul Atomic Sci 23:25-6 Mr '67. H. Bull
Human idiosyncrasy, anthropologists con-
clude. Sci N 92:583-4 D 16 '67
Is this a limited war? D. G. Porter. Com-
monweal 86:9-11 Mr 24 '67
Peace and war, by R. Aron. Review
New Repub 156:26-8+ Mr 4 '67. S. Hoff-
mann
Prologue; neglected premonitory rumblings.
Nation 204:675-6 My 29 '67
Reformation of war, by J. F. C. Fuller. Re-
view
New Repub il 156:39-41 Ap 8 '67. A.
Brynes
Small wars: the peril escalates. S. Melman.
Nation 204:774-5 Je 19 '67
Understanding people's wars. G. W. Shep-
herd, jr. Christian Cent 84:1185-8 S 20 '67
War or peace? symposium. bibliog il UNESCO
Courier 20:4-66 Ag '67
See also
Aggression (international law)
Atomic warfare
Chemical warfare
Conscientious objectors
European war, 1914-1918
Gases in warfare
Pacifism
Peace
Strategy
Vietnamese war, 1957-
War and society

Anecdotes, facetiae, satire, etc.

Digging at Iron Mountain. Sci N 92:557-8
D 9 '67
Hoax or horror? a book that shook White
House; concerning Report from Iron Moun-
tain on the possibility and desirability of
peace. il U S News 63:48 N 20 '67
Iron Mountain lies beyond credibility gap. I.
Kristol. Fortune 77:185-6 Ja '68
Mount of Megiddo. Christian Cent 84:855 Je 28
'67

WAR—Anecdotes, facetiae, satire, etc.—*Cont.*
On the possibility and desirability of peace;
excerpts from Report from Iron Mountain.
bibliog f Esquire 68:129-37+ D '67
Peace games; concerning Report from Iron
Mountain. Time 90:44 N 17 '67
Peace games, war games; Report from Iron
Mountain. Christian Cent 84:1588 D 13 '67
Report from Iron Mountain on the possibility
and desirability of peace. Review
Nat R 19:1388-9 D 12 '67. J. Burnham
Newsweek il 70:103-103B D 4 '67. H.
Junker

Economic aspects

Complex-complex; distrust of military-in-
dustrial complex. M. Getler. Aero Tech 21:
58 Ja 1 '68
Wall Street: if peace breaks out. C. Morgello.
il Newsweek 69:78 F 6 '67
See also
Industrial mobilization
Vietnamese war, 1957- —Economic aspects

Moral aspects
See War and morals

Political aspects
See Politics and war

Psychological aspects

Anatomy of courage, by Lord Moran. Review
Sat R il 50:37 My 13 '67. F. J. Braceland
Does man really want peace? N. F. S. Ferre.
Sat R 50:10-12 Jl 1 '67
Psychological preparations for war. A. F. C.
Wallace. Natur Hist 76:50-4 bibliog(p70)
D '67

Social aspects
See War and society

WAR, Causes of
Soviet blunder that led to Mideast war: the
inside story. il U S News 63:6 Jl 17 '67
WAR, Declaration of
Is a declaration of a state of war needed? D.
Lawrence. U S News 62:104+ My 29 '67
Is the war legal? two justices pose questions;
summary of testimony. P. Stewart; W. O.
Douglas. il U S News 63:16 N 20 '67
To declare or not to declare? Nat R 19:1247
N 14 '67
When is a war really a war? questions and
answers. il U S News 62:43 Mr 13 '67
Why no war declaration? with statement by
R. S. McNamara. il U S News 62:31-3 My
22 '67
WAR, Ethics of. See War and morals
WAR, Laws of
See also
War, Declaration of
WAR, Prevention of
Back from the brink; with editorial comment.
il Bsns W p35-6, 192 Je 10 '67
Beginnings of world war III? J. V. Schall.
America 117:14-17 Jl 1 '67
Can a scientist be an optimist? J. H. Thirring.
Sat R 50:17-20+ O 28 '67
Exploring the hopeful possibilities. Bsns W
p 130 F 4 '67
Legacy of a great American; interview; ed.
by R. D. Heffner. G. Clark. il McCalls 94:
64+ Ap '67
Small wars: the peril escalates. S. Melman.
Nation 204:774-5 Je 19 '67
U.N. front and center; what is needed to pre-
vent world war. N. Cousins. Sat R 50:20 Je
17 '67
WAR, Psychology of. See War—Psychological
aspects
WAR aims
See also
Vietnamese war, 1957—War aims
WAR and art
Arts: protest on all sides. il Newsweek 70:83-
6 Jl 10 '67
WAR and children
War talk and war games; with study-discus-
sion program. R. Strang. bibliog il PTA
Mag 62:20-3, 33 Ja '68
See also
Committee of responsibility to save war-
burned and war injured Vietnamese children
Refugee children
Vietnamese war, 1957- —Children
WAR and civilization
War: the anthropology of armed conflict and
aggression; symposium. bibliog il Natur
Hist 76:39-70 D '67

Why men fight; concerning symposium ex-
ploring causes and consequences of armed
conflict. il Newsweek 70:62 D 11 '67
WAR and culture. See War and civilization
WAR and disease
War and disease: an anthropological perspec-
tive. A. Alland, jr. Natur Hist 76:58-61 bib-
liog(p70) D '67
WAR and education
See also
Vietnamese war, 1957- —Education and the
war
WAR and industry. See War—Economic aspects
WAR and literature
Bookskrieg; instant books about the instant
war. il Newsweek 70:52 Jl 3 '67
How Mideast-crisis books sell. Pub W 192:47
Jl 24 '67
WAR and morals
En route to a massacre? J. F. Wharton. Sat
R 50:19-21 N 4 '67
Guernica to Vietnam: the capacity for horror.
H. Cox. Commonweal 86:164-5 Ap 28 '67
Hawks, doves through history. il U S News
63:46-7 N 20 '67
Opinion: on men at war. J. Kazickas. Mlle
64:124+ Mr '67
Peace and modern war in the judgment of
the church, by K. Hörmann. Review
Cath World 204:186-7 D '66. M. V. Gan-
non; Reply. R. A. Buglione. 204:322-3
Mr '67
Research and re-sensitization. N. Cousins.
Sat R 50:20+ Ag 5 '67
War and the individual conscience. J. Mc-
Laughlin. America 117:649-50 N 25 '67
War protest in wartime. J. R. Shirley. New
Repub 156:15-16 My 6 '67
See also
Vietnamese war, 1957- —Moral and religious
aspects
WAR and peace; drama. See Neumann, A. and
others
WAR and peace; opera. See Prokof'ev, S. S.
WAR and petroleum. See Petroleum—Interna-
tional aspects
WAR and politics. See Politics and war
WAR and religion
Blade of a righteous sword; reprint. F. B.
Harris. U S News 62:120 Ap 24 '67
See also
Israeli-Arab war, 1967—Moral and religious
aspects
Vietnamese war, 1957- —Moral and religious
aspects
WAR and science
Science, ecology and war; chemical and bio-
logical weapons. il Sci N 92:511-12 N 25 '67
See also
Vietnamese war, 1957- —Science
WAR and society
Effects of warfare on the biology of the hu-
man species. F. B. Livingstone. Natur Hist
76:61-5 bibliog(p70) D '67
See also
Atomic warfare—Social aspects
Vietnamese war, 1957- —Social aspects
WAR correspondents
Cost of war; three correspondents lose lives on
Israeli front. il Time 89:73-4 Je 16 '67
Covering the crisis; correspondents in Israel.
il Newsweek 69:82+ Je 19 '67
He was too brave; reporters killed in Israeli-
Arab war. il Newsweek 69:84 Je 19 '67
See also
Korean war, 1950-1953—War correspondents
United States—History—Civil war—Journalists
Vietnamese war, 1957. —War correspondents
WAR crime trials. See Nuremberg trials;
World war, 1939-1945—War criminals
WAR criminals. See World war, 1939-1945—
War criminals
WAR dogs. See Dogs, War use of
WAR drama. See War in literature
WAR films. See Moving pictures—War films
WAR finance
See also
Taxation—United States
Vietnamese war, 1957- —Cost
WAR games
Most dangerous game; geopolitical crisis
game over Boston's educational station,
WGBX. Newsweek 71:51 Ja 15 '68
See also
Naval maneuvers
WAR heroes. See Heroes; Vietnamese war, 1957-
—Heroes

WAR in art
Art: drawings from hell; M. Lasansky's Nazi drawings. C. Willard. Look 31:78+ F 21 '67
Guernica as art history. J. Masheck. il Art N 66:32-5+ D '67
See also
Vietnamese war, 1957- —Art
WAR in literature
Theatre goes to war; anti-war plays at off-Broadway theater. C. Hughes. America 116:759-61 My 20 '67
WAR industries. See Munitions industries
WAR inventions. See Inventions
WAR materials
See also
Vietnamese war, 1957- —Equipment and supplies
WAR memorials
Arizona: the ship that became a shrine. J. G. Hubbell. il Read Digest 91:64-8 D '67
WAR neuroses. See Neuroses
WAR news
See also
Korean war, 1950-1953—War correspondents
Television broadcasting—War news
Vietnamese war, 1957- —War correspondents
WAR objectors. See Conscientious objectors
WAR of 1870. See Franco-German war, 1870-1871
WAR on poverty (program) See Anti-poverty program, 1964-
WAR orphans
No ordinary man; Arthur N. McMellon memorial orphanage in Vietnam. H. A. Mulligan il Read Digest 91:127-31 Jl '67
WAR pictures
See also
United States—History—Civil war—Pictorial works
World war, 1939-1945—Photography
WAR poetry
See also
Vietnamese war, 1957- —Poetry
WAR powers. See Presidents—United States—Powers and duties
WAR propaganda
See also
Israeli-Arab war, 1967—Propaganda
Moving pictures—Propaganda films
WAR psychology. See War—Psychological aspects
WAR relief
See also
Fund raising
WAR ships. See Warships
WAR songs
See also
European war, 1914-1918—Songs and music
Israeli-Arab war, 1967—Songs and music
World war, 1939-1945—Songs and music
WAR tax (United States) See Taxation—United States
WAR toys. See Toys
WAR use of dogs. See Dogs, War use of
WAR veterans. See Service men, Discharged
WARBLERS
Colima warbler census in Big Bend's Chisos Mountains. R. H. Wauer. il Nat Parks Mag 41:8-10 N '67
WARD, Aileen
Last century's literary puzzle. Sat R 50:41 N 4 '67
WARD, Barbara (Lady Jackson)
Interview with Barbara Ward; ed. by R. D. Heffner. por McCalls 94:48+ Je '67
Stevenson institute of international affairs. Christian Cent 84:862-3 Jl 5 '67
WARD, Fred
Fred Ward's $25,000 tripod; interview, ed. by J. Neubauer. Pop Phot 60:69 Je '67
WARD, Gene
One man's way. il U S Camera 30:66-7 D '67
WARD, Harry Frederick
Tribute to a social prophet: H. F. Ward. L. H. Ball. Christian Cent 84:152-3 F 1 '67
WARD, Henry
Nothing grand. Time 90:20 N 3 '67
WARD, Hiley H.
Pre-fab housing and the church in Detroit. Commonweal 86:602-3 S 29 '67
WARD, John Harris
Pathfinder for nuclear power. il por Bsns W p76-8 Mr 11 '67
WARD, Pat
Jelke? Jelke? wasn't he the guy who. . ? N. Randolph. il por Esquire 67:136-9+ Ap '67

WARD, Rodger
Can we beat the British at the brickyard? por Pop Mech 127:116-18+ My '67
Rodger Ward tests the Charger R/T. por Pop Mech 128:73-5 D '67
Two champagne cars: $15,000 vs. $4000. pors Pop Mech 127:114-17 Mr '67
WARD, William
Twiggy. il por U S Camera 30:34 Ag '67
WARD, William F. See Hahn, E. W. jt. auth.
WARD, William J. 3d, and Robb, W. L.
Carbon dioxide oxygen separation: facilitated transport of carbon dioxide across a liquid film. bibliog Science 156:1481-4 Je 16 '67
WARDENS, Game. See Game wardens
WARDER, John Aston
John Aston Warder, first president of the American forestry association. L. S. V. Banks. il por Am For 73:10-13+ N '67
WARDS. See Guardian and ward
WARDWELL, Allen
Continental decorative arts at the Art institute of Chicago. Antiques 92:508-23 O '67
Polynesia: the indwelling power. Art N 66:38-9+ N '67
WARE, Caroline F.
Women as citizens. por Américas 19:26-30 D '67
—and others
Era of synthetic materials. UNESCO Courier 20:26-8 My '67
Sinews of industrial society. UNESCO Courier 20:24-6 My '67
WARE, George Washington
Tennessee rebels. L. Jackson. New Repub 157:9-10 S 9 '67
WARE, Leon
Doing what comes naturally. Writer 80:21-2 Mr '67
WAREHOUSES
Random house opens Maryland warehouse. il Pub W 192:32-4 Jl 24 '67
WARFARE, Submarine. See Submarine warfare
WARFIELD, Rebecca
Does your eye lack the nerve for a change? House & Gard 132:218-19 O '67
How to be inhospitable without really trying. House & Gard 132:88-9 Jl '67
Where is my pen? House & Gard 132:240-1 N '67
WARGA, Wayne
He really comes to life off camera. Life 63:82-4 O 20 '67
He sits alone, trying to get mad. Life 62:107-8 My 19 '67
WARHAWK aviation service, Incorporated
Spunky widow runs modern pilot school. il Ebony 22:38-40+ O '67
WARHOL, Andy
Current cinema: avant-garde *****. B. Gill. New Yorker 43:74 Ja 6 '68
Raggedy Andy Warhol. R. Corliss. Commonweal 86:469-70 Jl 28 '67
We talk to: interview by Mademoiselle's guest editors. por Mlle 65:325 Ag '67
WARI-WILLKA. See Huari, Peru
WARING, Eugene V.
Get the tax bills out on time. Am City 82:110-11 Je '67
WARING, James
Works by Joseph Cino, Deborah Lee, Charles Stanley & James Waring, Judson memorial church. J. Anderson. Dance Mag 41:37+ Mr '67
WARING, M. W.
Witnesses; story, excerpt from novel. Ladies Home J 84:155-66 O '67
WARING, Richard H. and Cleary, B. D.
Plant moisture stress: evaluation by pressure bomb. bibliog Science 155:1248+ Mr 10 '67
WARKENTIN, Adena. See Banks, B. jt. auth.
WARM air heating. See Heating
WARM and golden war; story. See Luard, N.
WARM blooded animals. See Temperature, Animal and human
WARM SPRINGS reservation, Oregon. See Indians of North America—Reservations
WARMKE, H. E.
Aucuba strain of tobacco mosaic virus: an unusual aggregate. bibliog Science 156:262-3 Ap 14 '67
WARNCKE, Ruth
Cooperation between ALA and state library associations; address, September 1966. ALA Bul 61:191-6 F '67
Library services to children in the mosaic of administration; address, July 1967. ALA Bul 61:1324-7 D '67

WARNECKE, John Carl
On the Square. il por Newsweek 70:88 O 2 '67
WARNER, Bob
High water and flies only. Field & S 71:44-5+
Ap '67
I'll take seconds. por Outdoor Life 140:60-1+
S '67
WARNER, Denis
Bearing the brunt at Con Thien. Reporter
37:18-21 O 19 '67; Correction. 37:10 N 2 '67
Bung Karno at bay. Reporter 36:41-4 F 9
'67
First steps toward an Asian Common market.
Reporter 36:24+ My 18 '67
Hanoi's summer offensive: a bigger war in
prospect. Reporter 36:31-4 Je 29 '67
Ho's underground in South Vietnam. Re-
porter 37:20-2 N 30 '67
How Hanoi sees the war. Reporter 37:17-20
Ag 10 '67
Indonesia after Sukarno. Reporter 36:34-7 Je
15 '67
Lee Kuan Yew's fight for survival. Reporter
37:36-8 N 2 '67
Malaysia after confrontation. Reporter 36:33-
5 Ja 26 '67
NLF's new program. Reporter 37:23-4+ O 5
'67
Our new team in Saigon. Reporter 37:25-6+
S 7 '67
South Vietnam exists. Reporter 37:18-20 S 21
'67
Vietnam: the need for a loyal opposition. Re-
porter 37:23-5 D 14 '67
Who is Wilfred Burchett? Reporter 36:18-21
Je 1 '67
WARNER, Leslie Harry
New growth circuit at GT&E. J. Poindexter.
il por Duns R 90:42-4+ N '67
WARNER, Sylvia Townsend
Brief ownership. New Yorker 43:140+ O 7 '67
Visionary gleam; story. New Yorker 43:36-41
Je 3 '67
WARNING labels. See Labels
**WARNING lights. See Automobiles—Safety de-
vices and measures**
WARRANTS (law)
Consent or starve; hearings on search war-
rants. New Repub 157:12-13 O 21 '67
Get a warrant; Supreme court rules on war-
rantless searches of private property. Time
89:48 Je 16 '67
**WARRANTS, Stock purchase. See Stock pur-
chase warrants**
WARRANTY
Holes in the warranty umbrella; with editorial
comment. R. B. Weeghman. Flying 81:32,
65-7 Ag '67
How to beef about new car bugs. V. L.
Oertle. Motor T 19:64-5 D '67
Lengthening reach of liability; damage suits
against the manufacturers. il Bsns W
p 100+ S 16 '67
My compliments to the chef. C. W. Morton.
il Atlan 220:88 Ag '67
Saving money in buying an automobile stor-
age battery. il Consumer Bul 50:25-8 F '67
Taking the mystery out of appliance guaran-
tees. Redbook 130:62+ Ja '68
Warranties: the promise and the reality.
Consumer Rep 32:194-7 Ap '67
See also
Guaranty of goods
WARREN, Betty
Paintings of Betty Warren. N. Kent. il por
Am Artist 31:36-41+ My '67
WARREN, David
How to build a Shaker candlestand, and
candlestick, too. Pop Sci 191:144-5 N '67
WARREN, Earl
How Chief Justice Warren changed his mind;
excerpt from address, October 20, 1948. por
U S News 62:66 Je 5 '67
Peace with justice; address, July 10, 1967.
Vital Speeches 33:644-6 Ag 15 '67
about
Chief. il pors Time 90:108+ N 17 '67
Earl Warren, by L. Katcher. Review
New Repub 157:34-5 Ag 5 '67. G. W. John-
son
Earl Warren: defender of human rights. M.
N. Eldridge. por Negro Hist Bul 30:11-13
My '67
Evolution of the justice. D. Young. Sat R
50:48+ N 18 '67
Impeach Earl Warren. C. W. Morton. Atlan
219:118 Ap '67
Warren making a try at fence-mending?
por U S News 62:24 Ap 24 '67
Warren: the man, the court, the era, by J. D.
Weaver. Review
New Repub 157:36-7 O 7 '67. A. M. Bickel

Warrens on tour: this time in Europe. U S
News 63:8 Jl 17 '67
Warrens on tour; why U.S. paid expenses. por
U S News 62:14 Je 12 '67
WARREN, Nina P. (Meyers)
Warrens on tour; why U.S. paid expenses. por
U S News 62:14 Je 12 '67
WARREN, Robert Penn
Fairy story; poem. New Yorker 43:123 Mr 18
'67
Myth on Mediterranean beach; poem. Sat R
50:38 F 25 '67
Where the slow fig; poem. New Yorker 43:145
Je 10 '67
Whiteness of fog on wintry mountains; poem.
Reporter 37:49 S 21 '67
about
Line of light. E. Coleman. Poetry 110:416-19
S '67
**WARREN commission. See United States—
President's commission on the assassina-
tion of President Kennedy**
**WARREN report. See United States—Presi-
dent's commission on the assassination of
President Kennedy**
WARSAW
Education
Maria Sklodowska: the dreamer in Warsaw.
L. Infeld. il UNESCO Courier 20:20-2 O '67
Music
Notes from our correspondents. K. Blau-
kopf. Hi Fi 17:26+ F '67
WARSAW convention
Supreme court agrees to review Warsaw con-
vention limitations. Aviation W 87:39 N 13
'67
WARSAW pact, 1955
Bucharest declaration; Political consultative
committee of the Warsaw pact nations,
Bucharest, July 4-6, 1966; excerpts. Cur
Hist 53:236-7 O '67
**WARSAW university. See Colleges and univer-
sities—Poland**
WARSH, Lewis
Always there; In the ocean air; Crystals; Con-
tinuum; poems. Poetry 110:169-72 Je '67
WARSHIPS
See also
Aircraft carriers
Armored vessels
Armaments
Monitor, Oriental style. il Sci Digest 62:28-9
Ag '67
New helicopter ship landing aid built. K. J.
Stein. il Aviation W 87:93-4+ S 25 '67
New ship defense missile gets funding; un-
guided conventional air-launched weapons.
Tech W 20:25 F 6 '67
Great Britain
Nelson's flagship. C. W. Morton. il Atlan 220:
114+ N '67
Sweden
World's wettest drydock; salvaging of great
17th century warship Wasa. R. P. Crossley.
il Pop Mech 127:152-5+ My '67
United States
Arizona: the ship that became a shrine.
J. G. Hubbell. il Read Digest 91:64-8 D '67
Battleship returns; New Jersey to be reac-
tivated. R. Moley. Newsweek 69:104 My 29
'67
Battleship vs. bombs: a new chapter; reacti-
vation of U.S.S. New Jersey. U S News 63:
12 Ag 14 '67
Down to the sea. M. Getler. Tech W 21:50
Jl 3 '67
Et tu, Russell? fast deployment logistics pro-
posal. Nation 204:549 My 1 '67
FDLS scuttled by Congress; one-year delay
anticipated; navy's fast deployment logis-
tics ship. Tech W 20:19 My 29 '67
FDL ship drawing congressional fire; fast
deployment logistic ship project. D. C.
Winston. Aviation W 86:96-7 F 13 '67
Fiddle-diddle; Senate passes bill to prevent
building fast deployment logistics ships.
New Repub 156:5-6 Ap 1 '67
Finis; Navy court of inquiry reviews Israeli
assault against Liberty. il Newsweek 70:24
Jl 3 '67
House may restore Senate cuts in FDLS.
Tech W 20:10+ Mr 27 '67
Inquest for Liberty. il Time 90:15 Jl 7 '67
June 8, at 1400 hours; story of USS Liberty.
J. J. Kilpatrick. il Nat R 19:952-8 S 5 '67

WARSHIPS—United States—*Continued*
Liberty signals: misrouted, misread. U S News 63:7 Jl 10 '67
Logland jam. il Time 89:20 Mr 31 '67
Mystery of attack on U.S.S. Liberty. il U S News 62:33 Je 26 '67
Navy planning RFP's in fall for new class of destroyers. M. Getler. Tech W 20:17-18 My 15 '67
Navy setting DXGN development timetable: nuclear-powered missile frigates, non-nuclear DX destroyers. W. Andrews. Aero Tech 21:14-15 Ja 1 '68
Navy's LFSS looms as heir to battleship; landing force support ship. M. Getler. Tech W 20:14-15 My 22 '67
New destroyer, missile ships may be industry-designed. Tech W 20:24 F 6 '67
New Jersey gets set to sail for Vietnam. il Bsns W p30-1 Ag 12 '67
Our biggest naval guns to boom again, in Vietnam; battleship New Jersey. A. P. Armagnac. il Pop Sci 191:68-71+ D '67
Role for a relic; preliminary demothballing of New Jersey. Time 89:32 Je 9 '67
Slighted ship, sank same; navy's fast deployment logistics ship. W. J. Coughlin. Tech W 20:50 Ap 3 '67
Unexplained casualty: U.S.S. Liberty. il Life 62:28-9 Je 23 '67
Virtue triumphant; Fast deployment logistics ships. J. Burnham. Nat R 19:398 Ap 18 '67
See also
Armored vessels

WARSHIPS, Atomic powered
Defense money; conversion of the navy to nuclear power recommended. il Sci N 91:471 My 20 '67
Navy setting DXGN development timetable; nuclear-powered missile frigates, non-nuclear DX destroyers. W. Andrews. Aero Tech 21:14-15 Ja 1 '68

WARSHOFSKY, Fred
Death rides on two wheels. Read Digest 91:151-2+ O '67
Most destructive creature on earth. Read Digest 91:175-6+ S '67

WARTS
Are warts dangerous? Sci Digest 61:84-5 Ap '67

WARWICK, Dionne
Spreading the faith. il por Time 90:75 Jl 14 '67

WARWICK, James F.
Art and a high school humanities program. Sch Arts 66:5-8 Je '67
Display units. Sch Arts 67:30-1 S '67
Scrap block printing. Sch Arts 67:14-15 O '67

WAS her face red! drama. See Paradis, M. B.
WASA (ship) See Warships—Sweden
WASHBURN, O. A.
We fish the box at last. por Outdoor Life 140:54-5+ D '67

WASHBURN university, Topeka, Kan.
Taking care of the student boom; relocatable classrooms. il Bsns W p64+ Ja 21 '67
University in a windstorm. A. F. Engelbert. il Sch & Soc 95:119-21 F 18 '67

WASHBURNE, Elihu Benjamin
American in Paris. S. Hess. il por Am Heritage 18:18-27+ F '67

WASHING machines
Automatic clothes washers. il Consumer Rep 27:77-85 D '67
Automatic washing machines. il Consumer Bul 50:10-16 S '67
Automatic washing machines. il Consumer Rep 32:248-55 My '67
Inventing backward; hand operated washing machine; interview. W. Young; R. R. Walton. New Yorker 43:38-40 D 16 '67
What to look for in washers and dryers. V. T. Habeeb. il Am Home 70:138 O '67

WASHING of clothes. See Laundry
WASHINGTON, Bennetta B.
Women worth watching. por(p30) McCalls 95:104 Ja '68

WASHINGTON, George
Benedict Arnold: how the traitor was unmasked; excerpt from George Washington in the American revolution. J. T. Flexner. il por Am Heritage 18:6-15 O '67
First in their hearts; condensation. T. J. Fleming. il por Read Digest 90:209-12+ F '67
Mr Washington's day. il por Sr Schol 90:2 F 17 '67

Providence rides a storm; excerpts from George Washington in the American revolution. J. T. Flexner. il por Am Heritage 19:12-17+ D '67
Samuel Frances, revolutionary patriot and citizen-extraordinary; excerpt from address, August 16, 1966. J. W. Davis. Negro Hist Bul 30:11 N '67

Drama

Date with Washington. M. Hark and N. McQueen. Plays 26:33-42, 58 F '67
Martha Washington's spy. E. J. Dias. Plays 26:59-67 F '67

WASHINGTON, George, family
Paul's Washington family in oil on canvas. G. D. Guadagni. il Antiques 91:519+ Ap '67

WASHINGTON, Walter E.
D.C. gets a new mayor. America 117:291-2 S 23 '67
First mayor of the Nation's capital. il por Negro Hist Bul 30:4-5 N '67
For nation's capital: Negro mayor with a tough assignment. il por U S News 63:21 S 18 '67
Negro mayor for nation's capital? por U S News 63:12 S 4 '67
This is the year. il por Sr Schol 91:4-5 O 12 '67
Two firsts for Washington. por Time 90:23-4 S 15 '67
Washington's Washington. il por Newsweek 70:31 S 18 '67

WASHINGTON, D.C.
Melt the snow on underground parking ramps. il Am City 82:52 Ag '67
Siege of Georgetown. il Newsweek 70:34-5 O 23 '67
See also
Architecture, Domestic—Washington, D.C.
Maryland-National capital park and planning commission
Public welfare—Washington, D.C.
White House

Airports

Airport in the sky near the White House? il U S News 62:14 F 27 '67

Anti-poverty program

Pride, inc; D.C.'s cool answer to hot summers. il Ebony 23:82-4+ D '67
$300,000 payroll for Catfish; program called Pride inc. S. McBee. il Life 63:34 Ag 25 '67

Architecture

Architect, spare our Capitol. R. Sherrill. il N Y Times Mag p30-1+ Ap 16 '67
Capitol hill's ugliness club. H. Lewis. il Atlan 219:60-6 F '67
New home for a new organization; new Mills building. il Parks & Rec 2:22-3 Ja '67
On the Square; new federal courthouse in Lafayette square. il Newsweek 70:88 O 2 '67

Buildings

See Washington, D.C.—Architecture

City planning

Completing the Federal Triangle: a problem of style. il Arch Rec 142:124-7 D '67
New faces for l'Enfant. il Time 90:52+ Ag 11 '67
New grandeur for flowering Washington. J. Judge. il Nat Geog Mag 131:500-39 Ap '67
Pedestrian mall or plaza? W. S. Foster. il Am City 82:101 My '67
Profiles; through the great city. A. Bailey. New Yorker 43:58-63 Ag 5 '67

Clubs

Club for secret swingers; Burning tree golf club. C. Price. il Esquire 67:154+ Ap '67

Crime

Are tougher laws coming to curb crime? U S News 64:8 Ja 8 '68
Crime in Washington; advice from the police. U S News 62:13 Ja 30 '67
Crisis in crime: what Congress did; anticrime bill for the District of Columbia. il U S News 63:8 D 25 '67
Even under Capitol dome, more crime. U S News 62:15 F 13 '67
Life in the Nation's capital, where crime and despair rule; reprint from the Washington star, week of January 16, 1967. H. Johnson. il U S News 62:76-8 Ja 30 '67
New yardstick on the rise in crime. U S News 62:12 F 27 '67
Solution for the plague of crime? U S News 62:18 Mr 13 '67

WASHINGTON, D.C.—Crime—*Continued*
Story of hoodlums in the Nation's capital;
Senate subcommittee hearings. il U S News
62:14 My 8 '67
Tourists in peril from capital's criminals?
il U S News 63:13 Jl 3 '67
Youth and crime. Sr Schol 90:9 F 17 '67

Description

Capital place for tourists. il Bsns W p 122-4
Ag 5 '67
Let's take the kids to Washington; excerpts
from Washington: the New York times
guide to the Nation's capital. A. Shuster. il
Parents Mag 42:50-1+ Mr '67
Step by step through Washington. R. Deardorff. il Travel 128:30-5+ Jl '67
Vacation guide to Washington, D.C; excerpts
from Washington, the New York times'
guide to the Nation's capital. B. Dubivsky.
il Seventeen 26:130-1+ Ap '67
Washington: a reporter's memoir; introduction to Washington: The New York times
guide to the Nation's capital. T. Wicker.
il Sat R 50:49-50+ S 9 '67

Education

Appeal of de facto segregation decision. Sch
& Soc 95:406+ N 11 '67
As nation's capital goes all out for integra-
tion. il U S News 63:54-5 Jl 17 '67
Bus in their future? de facto school segre-
gation ruled as unconstitutional. il Newsweek
70:48-9 Jl 3 '67
Courts take the initiative; Washington court
decision orders reforms in the District of
Columbia public school system. G. Grant.
Sat R 50:65 Jl 15 '67
Danger facing nation's schools? interview.
C. F. Hansen. il U S News 63:40-6+ Jl
24 '67
De facto anticlimax; Judge Wright's decision
condemning de facto segregation in Wash-
ington, D.C.'s public schools. M. R. Berube.
Commonweal 86:438-9 Jl 14 '67
D.C. may drop track system. Sr Schol 90:
sup2+ Ap 14 '67
End of the line; superintendent of schools
resigns. Newsweek 70:54 Jl 17 '67
Going to school in D.C: what one family
found. U S News 63:55 Jl 17 '67
Hobson v. Hansen; ruling for Negro plaintiffs
in the desegregation case. Reporter 37:20-1
Jl 13 '67
Judge Wright faces North; case of Hobson
vs. Hansen and the Board of education of
the District of Columbia. J. Cass. Sat R
50:51-2 Jl 15 '67
Mrs McNamara's crusade: Reading-is-fun-
damental project. H. Brandon. Sat R 50:9-
10 Je 17 '67
National monument to failure; public school
system. S. L. Jacoby. il Sat R 50:71-3+
N 18 '67
No more nonsense about ghetto education!
J. Alsop. New Repub 157:18-20 Jl 22 '67;
Same abr. with title Can Negro children
make the grade? Read Digest 91:81-4 N '67;
Discussion. New Repub 157:42-4 S 2; 16-19
S 23; 38-9 O 21; 18-23 N 18 '67
Reading is fun in Washington; Reading is
fun-damental committee (RIF) K. Lumley.
il Sr Schol 90:sup 1-2 Mr 31 '67
Shape of things to come in the public schools?
il U S News 63:52 Jl 3 '67
She won't be back; Webster girls school,
public school for pregnant girls. E. Good-
man and E. Ferber. il Am Ed 3:6-8 O '67
Skelly Wright's sweeping decision. A. M.
Bickel. New Repub 157:11-12 Jl 8 '67; Reply
with rejoinder. M. E. Tigar. 157:41-3 Ag 5
'67
Tracked or railroaded? civil-rights groups
challenge system. il Newsweek 69:59 Ap 24
'67
Tulip poplars and protozoa on the Chopawamsic; educational camping at Prince
William Forest park. P. Thomson. il NEA
J 56:32-3 O '67

Education, Board of

First Negro president of the D.C. Board of
education: Wesley S. Williams. il Negro
Hist Bul 29:177-8+ Fall '66
Judge Wright faces North; case of Hobson
vs. Hansen and the Board of education.
J. Cass. Sat R 50:51-2 Jl 15 '67
Whose home rule? opposition to new super-
intendent. il Newsweek 70:66 N 6 '67

Galleries and museums

Washington's petrified forest on the Mall;
Joseph Herman Hirshhorn museum and
sculpture garden. C. Foley. il Am For 73:22-
3+ D '67
See also
Dumbarton Oaks research library and collec-
tion
Smithsonian institution

Gardens

Garden of American history: at the White
House; photographs. Horst; with account
by V. Lawford Vogue 149:160-7+ F 1 '67

Highway department

Washington fights creeping concrete. H.
Leavitt. il Reporter 36:39-41 Ja 26 '67

Historic houses, etc.

Rejuvenation at Blair House. il House & Gard
133:106-7+ Ja '68

Hospitals

Emergency! what Alexandria (Virginia)
hospital is doing. T. Irwin. il Todays Health
45:34-9 Ap '67
Hospital of the future? remodeling plans.
W. R. Young. il Read Digest 90:161-3+
My '67
Rouse case. New Repub 157:5 Jl 1 '67
Who's fit to be free? confinement of C. C.
Rouse in John Howard pavilion of St
Elizabeth's hospital. J. Ridgeway. New
Repub 156:24-6 F 4 '67; Discussion. 156:
35-6 F 18 '67

Hotels, restaurants, etc.

Revelry in Washington. V. Curtis. il Travel
127:50-1 F '67

Housing

People: the new voice in renewal. E. P.
Berkeley. il Arch Forum 127:72-7 N '67
She makes the city a place for living; town-
house projects of C. W. Smith. il Bsns W
p76-8+ Je 3 '67
Veep lives his convictions; resident of integrated neighborhood. R. Lantz. il Ebony
22:75-8+ My '67

Libraries

See also
United States—Library of Congress

Monuments, statues, etc.

Back at the drawing board; Breuer efforts
rejected. Time 89:44 F 3 '67
Happy birthday, T.R; Roosevelt memorial. il
Time 90:22 N 3 '67
Return of the Rough Rider; Theodore Roos-
evelt memorial island. I. McManus. il Am
For 73:18-21+ O '67

Music

See also
National symphony orchestra
Opera society of Washington

National zoological park

See National zoological park, Washington, D.C.

Negroes

Capital's bourgeoisie. C. Fritchey. Harper
235:37-40 O '67
Life in the Nation's capital, where crime
and despair rule; reprint from the Wash-
ington star, week of January 16, 1967. H.
Johnson. il U S News 62:76-8 Ja 30 '67
People: the new voice in renewal. E. P.
Berkeley. il Arch Forum 127:72-7 N '67
Research scientist lends a hand to capital's
poor. il Ebony 22:124-6+ Mr '67
Will Negroes rule the Nation's capital? il
U S News 63:8 Ag 21 '67

Newspapers

Bastille day on the Potomac; Press and
Post; peace march coverage. R. G. Sherrill.
Nation 205:445 N 6 '67

Parks and playgrounds

See also
Glen Echo amusement park

Police

Are police reaching a breaking point? ex-
cerpts from report in The Washington post,
February 8, 1967. U S News 62:17 F 20 '67
Bastille day on the Potomac; savagery com-
mitted by marshals during peace march.
R. G. Sherrill. Nation 205:454-5 N 6 '67

WASHINGTON, D.C.—Police—*Continued*
Crime in Washington: advice from the police.
U S News 62:13 Ja 30 '67
New powers for police; District of Columbia
anticrime bill. Time 91:24 Ja 5 '68

Politics and government

Congressional seat for the District of Columbia? pro and con discussion. il Sr Schol
91:14-15 N 2 '67
Council of governments. W. A. Scheiber. il
Am City 82:110-12 My '67
D.C. gets a new mayor. America 117:291-2
23 '67
For nation's capital: Negro mayor with a
tough assignment. il U S News 63:21 S 18
'67
Mayor for Washington. Newsweek 70:27-8 Ag
21 '67
Running the capital. New Repub 156:9 Mr 11
'67
Semi-self-government. Time 90:20 Ag 18 '67
This is the year. il Sr Schol 91:4-5 O 12 '67
Toward home rule. C. Fritchey. Harper 235:
38-40 O '67
Two firsts for Washington. Time 90:23-4
S 15 '67
Washington's Washington; commissioner-
designate. il Newsweek 70:31 S 18 '67
Will Negroes rule the Nation's capital? il
U S News 63:8 Ag 21 '67

Public buildings

Air rights structure for the Department of
labor; over the freeway tunnel. il Arch Rec
142:116-19 D '67
Completing the Federal Triangle: a problem
of style. il Arch Rec 142:124-7 D '67
Federal office building designed to span a
freeway. il Arch Rec 142:120-3 D '67
Justice on a pedestal; U.S. tax court building. il Arch Forum 127:76-9 S '67
New faces for l'Enfant. il Time 90:52+ Ag 11
'67
See also
Embassies (buildings)
United States—Capitol

Rapid transit

Getting Washington to work on time. il Bsns
W p60+ S 30 '67

Recreation

New directions in design for D.C. department.
L. C. Lemmon. il Parks & Rec 2:24-5+ My
'67

Religious institutions and affairs

Commitment on the Potomac; nondenominational Church of the Saviour. il Time 89:
94+ Je 9 '67

Riots

When a rat riot hit Congress. il U S News
63:10 Ag 21 '67

Social life and customs

Glittering state dinner, excerpts from Entertaining in the White House. M. Smith.
Good H 165:226 D '67
Good night, ladies; Dancing class balls to
end. Newsweek 70:31-2 D 11 '67
Living it up in Washington. M. Cheshire. il
Nations Bsns 55:58-9 Jl '67
Nancy Dickerson: Washington's most serious butterfly. B Rollin. il Look 31:28-30
S 5 '67
Talk with an eighty-three-year-old enfant
terrible; ed. by H. Brandon. A. R. Longworth. il N Y Times Mag p8-9+ Ag 6 '67
Wayward Washington; excerpt from Washington: the New York times guide to the
Nation's capital. R. Baker. il Holiday 41:64-
9+ F '67

Street traffic

Unscrambling Washington traffic. il Bsns W
p 198 S 16 '67
Washington fights creeping concrete. H.
Leavitt. il Reporter 36:39-41 Ja 26 '67; Reply with rejoinder. J. De Lorenzi. 36:8+
F 23 '67

Theater

Different Lincoln memorial; Ford's theatre
to re-open. PTA Mag 62:33 D '67
Ford's theatre; interview. S. Syrjala. New
Yorker 42:19-20 Ja 21 '67
Theater: production of Great white hope by
the Arena stage. H. Hewes. Sat R 50:18
D 30 '67

Theatre; Washington theater club's production of The waters of Babylon. R. Pasolli.
Nation 204:573-4 My 1 '67
Tragic cakewalk; Arena stage production of
H. Sackler's Great white hope. J. Novick.
Nation 206:93-4 Ja 15 '68

Transportation

Washington fights creeping concrete. H.
Leavitt. il Reporter 36:39-41 Ja 26 '67;
Reply with rejoinder. J. De Lorenzi. 36:8+
F 23 '67
See also
Washington, D.C.—Rapid transit

WASHINGTON (state)
How the state of Washington conserves its
razor clam population. J. Copland. il Parks
& Rec 2:41+ Mr '67
See also
Architecture, Domestic—Washington (state)
Cascade Range
Columbia River
Forests and forestry—Washington (state)
Gardens—Washington (state)
Mercer Island
Olympic National Park
Olympic Peninsula
Wenatchee Valley
Wilderness areas—Washington (state)

Parks and reserves

Disadvantaged youth employed by Washington state parks. J. M. Willits. Parks &
Rec 2:34+ Ap '67
State parks of Washington. C. M. Ouellette. il Travel 128:45-9 Jl '67

WASHINGTON college, Chestertown, Md.
Game on the eastern shore; photographs by
R. Meek; with account by R. M. Mechem.
il Sports Illus 26:30-5 Mr 27 '67

WASHINGTON correspondents. See Reporters
and reporting

WASHINGTON march, 1968 (proposed) See
Civil rights demonstrations

WASHINGTON opera society
Washington; production of Massenet's
Werther. F. C. Smith. il Opera N 31:28
Mr 4 '67

WASHINGTON post and Times herald
Book world supplement for Washington,
Chicago. Pub W 192:34 Jl 3 '67
For attribution; challenges "background only"
government information. Time 89:56 My 19
'67
Journalism's two faces. New Repub 157:5-6 Jl
1 '67
Power behind the Post; publisher and socialite K. Graham. il Bsns W p 158-60+
My 27 '67

WASHINGTON Redskins (football club) See
Football clubs

WASHINGTON suburban sanitary commission
What third-stage sewage treatment means.
A. Machis. il Am City 82:110+ S '67

WASHINGTON university, St Louis
Taste on the campus; Steinberg hall gallery.
il Time 90:50-1 Jl 21 '67

WASHKANSKY, Louis
End & beginning. il por Time 90:32 D 29 '67
First human hearts transplanted. il Sci N
92:581 D 16 '67
Gift of a heart. il por Life 63:24-7 D 15 '67
Heart: miracle in Cape Town. il por Newsweek 70:86-90 D 18 '67
History-making operation. il por U S News
63:63 D 18 '67
Progress, then a setback. por Time 90:36
D 22 '67
Ultimate operation. il por Time 90:64-6+
D 15 '67
Watching and learning; heart transplant
patient catches pneumonia. il pors Newsweek 70:41 D 25 '67
We climbed Everest. Newsweek 71:52 Ja 1 '68

WASIK, John
Best way. Newsweek 70:33 O 9 '67
Case of paracide. Time 90:28-9 O 6 '67

WASKOW, Arthur I.
Do we need peace candidates? Sat R 50:33
F 4 '67
Education of peacemakers. Sat R 50:12-15+
Ag 12 '67
Infallibility of Eustace Tilley. Nation 205:
450+ N 6 '67
Peace politics and 1968. Commonweal 86:195-8
My 5 '67

WASN'T he nice, Pete? wasn't he nice? story.
See Dillon, J.

WASON, Betty
I designed my own kitchen. Parents Mag
42:85-9 O '67

WASPS
Foundress associations in polistine wasps: dominance hierarchies and the evolution of social behavior. M. J. West. bibliog Science 157:1584-5 S 29 '67
Nature note; weevil killer; bathyplectes curculionis. il Sci N 91:564 Je 17 '67
Role differentiation in copulating cicada killer wasps. N. Lin. bibliog il Science 157:1334-5 S 15 '67

WASSERBERGER, George
Mark Cross puts well-tanned look on West coast. il por Bsns W p66-8 D 2 '67

WASSERMAN, John L.
Bob Dylan through a lens darkly. Life 63:10 Ag 11 '67

WASSERMAN, Paul, and Bundy, M. L.
Manpower blueprint; reprint. pors Library J 92:197-200 Ja 15 '67

WASSERSUG, Joseph D.
How to stay healthy and happy while traveling. Sci Digest 62:73-7 Ag '67
I prescribe. . . See issues of Science digest
New help for summer hazards. Sci Digest 62:65-9 Jl '67

WASSMER, Thomas
Crucial question about abortion. Cath World 206:57-61 N '67
New morality: some questions. America 117: 132 Ag 5 '67
Questions about questions. Commonweal 86: 416-18 Je 30 '67

WASSON, Donald
(comp) Source material. See issues of Foreign affairs

WASSON, E. Hornsby
Business trends; address, July 21, 1967. Vital Speeches 33:694-7 S 1 '67

WASSON, John T. and others
Aluminum-26 in Pacific sediment: implications. bibliog Science 155:446-8 Ja 27 '67
—See Tandon, S. N. jt. auth.

WASTE, Disposal of. See Refuse and refuse disposal; Water products

WASTE, Utilization of
See also
Refuse, Utilization of

WASTE disposal plants. See Sewage disposal plants

WASTE in government spending. See United States—Appropriations and expenditures

WASTE products
Laws to control farm wastes; are they coming? D. Malena. Suc Farm 65:31 Ag '67
See also
Scrap metal

WASTE recycling. See Refuse and refuse disposal

WASTE water purification. See Water purification

WATANABE, Akira, and others
Effects of tetrodotoxin on excitability of squid giant axons in sodium-free media. bibliog Science 155:95-7; 157:221 Ja 6, Jl 14 '67

WATANABE, Takeshi
Asian development bank. UN Mo Chron 4: 33-7 F '67

WATANABE, Tsutomu
Infectious drug resistance; with biographical sketch. Sci Am 217:14, 19-27 D '67

WATCHES
Watch out for this watch; Germinal-Voltaire watches. Consumer Rep 32:64 F '67
Watches to watch. il Life 62:105 Ap 21 '67
What's new in watch stylings. Good H 164: 200 Mr '67

Collectors and collecting
English watches. L. W. Slaughter. il Hobbies 72:46-7 My; 46-7 Je; 46-7 Jl '67 (to be cont)

WATCHES, Electric
Swiss find a rival for Accutron. il Bsns W p82+ Ap 1 '67

WATER
How pure is well water? Good H 164:155 F '67
Manner of speaking; changing constancy of water that lures man. J. Ciardi. Sat R 50:15 Mr 18 '67
Surface tension and surface structure of water. W. F. Claussen. bibliog il Science 156:1226-7 Je 2 '67
Taste of water. Sci Am 216:60 F '67
See also
Hydrologic research
Ice
Runoff
Springs

Analysis
Amazon River: environmental factors that control its dissolved and suspended load. R. J. Gibbs. bibliog il Science 156:1734-7 Je 30 '67
Deuterium and oxygen-18 in natural waters: analyses compared. E. Halevy and B. R. Payne. il Science 156:669 My 5 '67

Heavy water
See Deuterium oxide

Pollution
See Water pollution

Purification
See Water purification

WATER, Freezing of. See Freezing

WATER, Saline
Confirmation from afar; hot brines and heavy metal deposits in deeps of the Red Sea. E. T. Degens and D. A. Ross. il Sat R 50:52 S 2 '67
Silica in alkaline brines. B. F. Jones and others. bibliog il Science 158:1310-14 D 8 '67
See also
Salt water

WATER, Underground
Ground water to bolster river flow and prevent the use of valuable land for reservoirs; Britain's Thames conservancy. C. E. Tiffen. il Am City 82:139+ S '67
Iodide abundance in oilfield brines in Oklahoma. A. G. Collins and G. C. Egleson. bibliog il Science 156:934-5 My 19 '67
See also
Springs
Wells

WATER absorption by plants. See Plants—Absorption of water

WATER birds
See also
Shore birds
also names of water birds, e.g. Swans

Accidents and hazards
See Birds—Accidents and hazards

WATER buffaloes
Water buffalo. W. R. Cockrill. il Sci Am 217:118-25 D '67

WATER chestnuts
See also
Cookery—Water chestnuts

WATER closets. See Toilets

WATER color painting
Nolde: art without audience. J. Gollin. il Art N 65:48-9+ F '67
On composition in landscape; excerpts from Starting with watercolor. R. Hilder. il Am Artist 31:42-7 My '67
Ray Harm; the other side of the window. il House B 109:164-5+ Mr '67
Water color page. See issues of American artist
Whites in watercolor. E. A. Whitney. il Am Artist 31:34-7 Ap '67

WATER conservation
Water-conservation rules for the home. Good H 164:189 My '67

WATER desalting. See Sea water—Desalting

WATER distribution
Big questions; interview, ed. by R. R. Fleming. G. J. Remus. il Am City 82:93-5+ Je '67
See also
Water pipes
Water tanks

WATER districts
Mr and Mrs Willing Water; female water-district manager. il Am City 82:30 N '67

WATER divining. See Divining rod

WATER for peace conference. See International conference on water for peace

WATER fronts
Bay: Savannah's water front. A. C. Hunter. il Antiques 91:332-3 Mr '67
Six ways to fight waterfront blight. il Am City 82:72-3 Ja '67

WATER gardens
Low-upkeep back yard complete with stream. il Pop Gard 18:32-3 My '67
Water gardens of Italy's Villa d'Este. M. J. Dietz. il Home Gard 54:58-9 Ap '67
See also
Garden pools

WATER heaters
How to choose a water heater. il Bet Hom & Gard 45:114-15 F '67

WATER in the body
Australian desert mice: independence of exogenous water. R. E. MacMillen and A. K. Lee. bibliog il Science 158:383-5 O 20 '67
Water balance in desert arthropods. E. B. Edney. bibliog il Science 156:1059-66 My 26 '67
See also
Perspiration

WATER injection in oil fields. See Oil field flooding

WATER lilies
Day and night bloomers, and dazzlers all. il Sunset 138:98-101 Mr '67

WATER mains. See Water pipes

WATER meters
We don't read water meters any more; automatic system; Sloatsburg, N.Y. J. Babcook. il Am City 82:86-7 Jl '67

WATER molds. See Molds (botany)

WATER paint. See Paint

WATER pipes
Rebellion: water-main break and steam explosion at Seventh avenue and Sixteenth street. New Yorker 43:22-3 Ja 13 '68
Tight sheathing tops tunneling; Cincinnati. C. M. Bolton. il Am City 82:159-60 Je '67

WATER plants. See Aquatic plants

WATER play, Childrens. See Play

WATER pollution
America's healthiest cities. N. Faber. Ladies Home J 84:178+ O '67
Calm heads and clean waters. F. Rohr. il Motor B 121:86+ Ja '68
Cities play a major role in eutrophication; report on symposium. E. F. Spitzer. il Am City 82:99+ Ag '67
Clean up the Hudson. J. A. Clay. il Am For 73:12-15 Je '67
Do farms cause water pollution. L. Palmer and R. Wilmore. Farm J 91:64G+ F '67
Dying Lake Michigan. Newsweek 70:110A+ N 13 '67
Effluent society: cleaning up the mess. il Newsweek 69:84-6 My 22 '67
Energy needs versus environmental pollution: a reconciliation? L. Green, jr. bibliog Science 156:1448-50 Je 16 '67; Reply. R. G. Minet. 157:1373 S 22 '67
Eutrophication; report on first international symposium. A. D. Hasler and M. E. Swenson. Science 158:278+ O 13 '67
Fouled nest. W. J. Coughlin. Tech W 20:50 F 27 '67
Its name is mud. R. Starnes. Field & S 71:18+ Ap '67
Laws to control farm wastes, are they coming? D. Malena. Suc Farm 65:31 Ag '67
Natural displacement of pollution from the Great Lakes. R. H. Rainey. il Science 155:1242-3 Mr 10 '67; Reply. H. C. Curl, jr. 156:1179 Je 2 '67
Pesticide pollution control. H. P. Nicholson. bibliog il Science 158:871-6 N 17 '67
Pollution from run-off; dirt and trash washed into streams and lakes. Am City 82:54-5 Ag '67
Pollution in the East: once upon a river. E. S. Grant. il Am For 73:4-7+ Jl '67
Pollution in the West: industry struggles with pollution problems. A. Netboy. il Am For 73:8-11+ Jl '67
Pollution pickle revisited. R. Stone and J. Napier. il Motor B 121:318-19 Ja '68
Pollution predicament: marine sanitary systems. R. W. Carrick. Yachting 121:112+ Ja '67
Recycled water: here's your chance to be involved. il Pop Gard 18:28-9 D '67
River of poison; pollutants released in Clark Fork River by strike at copper mine. il Newsweek 70:70 Ag 28 '67
Salvaging the Lakes; Great Lakes pollution. Time 89:60 Ap 21 '67
$300 billion for clean air and water. il U S News 62:42-5 Ap 3 '67
Time to fish or cut bait. J. B. Craig. Am For 73:12-13 Ja '67
Water pollution, conversion pose great R&D challenges. J. F. Judge. il Tech W 20:46-7+ Je 5 '67
Watery grave for Lake Michigan? result of industrial waste. il Bsns W p 103-4+ O 21 '67

Whatever happened to water pollution? peanuts for water-pollution abatement. Am City 82:6 O '67; Reply. F. C. DiLuzio. 82:21+ D '67
See also
Oil pollution of rivers, harbors, etc.
Sea water—Pollution
United States—Federal water pollution control administration

Thermal pollution
Thermal pollution: Senator Muskie tells AEC to cool it. B. Nelson. Science 158:755-6 N 10 '67

Sweden
Polluted fish sale banned; methyl mercury found in fish. H. J. Barnes. Sci N 92:564 D 9 '67

WATER pollution control administration. See United States—Federal water pollution control administration

WATER pollution control federation
Products at the Water pollution control federation meeting. il Am City 82:193+ O '67

WATER polo
Team so good it makes two; Pan-American tryouts. G. Ronberg. il Sports Illus 27:56+ Ag 21 '67

WATER purification
Aerojet moving into water purification. J. F. Judge. il Tech W 20:26-8 Mr 6 '67
Clearing up the water; way to isolate viruses. Newsweek 69:98 Mr 6 '67
Disinfection by electrohydraulic treatment. M. Allen and K. Soike. il Science 156:524-5 Ap 28 '67
Drinking water from sewage? Nassau County, N.Y. A. Gruenwald. il Am City 82:92-3 Mr '67
Filter backwash gets special treatment; Los Angeles. L. Streicher. il Am City 82:94-5 N '67
How to clean wastewater for reuse. G. Culp and S. Hansen. bibliog il Am City 82:96-9 Je '67
Our people aren't impressed; arguments that algae makes Mississippi River water hard to treat; Rock Island, Ill. J. E. Holzer. il Am City 82:108-9 My '67
What third-stage sewage treatment means. A. Machis. il Am City 82:110+ S '67
You can have safe water. Suc Farm 65:58-9 S '67

Desalting
Desalting dominates international water conference. il Am City 82:82-3 Ag '67
Solar stills for sheep; solar-powered desalination equipment. W. A. Scholes. Sci N 92:204+ Ag 26 '67
See also
Sea water—Desalting

WATER repellents
Guide to silicone masonry water repellents. C. A. Bergeson. Arch Rec 141:181-2 Ja '67

WATER reservoirs. See Reservoirs

WATER resources development
Interdepartmental committee on water for peace surveys world water problems; text of memorandum, and excerpt from report. Dept State Bul 56:758-65 My 15 '67
NARWRS stands for: North Atlantic regional water resources study. Motor B 120:90-2 Jl '67
See also
North American water and power alliance
United States—National water commission

WATER skis and skiing
Fastest man on water skis, 119 mph. il Life 62:82-5 Ja 27 '67
Water skiing and the law. M. M. Dolan. il Motor B 120:34-5 Jl '67

Study and teaching
Learn to water-ski the instant way. W. Heyman. il Motor B 120:32-3+ Jl '67

WATER snowflake
They have snowflake flowers. il Sunset 139:136 Jl '67

WATER softening
Continuous ion-exchange softening; Terre Haute, Ind. water works corporation. E. F. Spitzer. il Am City 82:118-20 Je '67

WATER springs. See Springs

WATER sprinklers. See Sprinklers

WATER storage
See also
Standpipes
Water tanks

WATER supply
Some pertinent comments on water problems; summary of address, May 2, 1967. R. L. Nace. Nat Parks Mag 41:21 Ag '67
Water supply and treatment. See issues of American city
See also
Dams
Droughts
International conference on water for peace
Plumbing
Pumping stations
Reservoirs
Water pipes
Water purification
Waterworks
Wells

Fluoridation
Fluoridation story: putting the smile on young faces. V. L. Diefenbach. il Todays Health 45:60-1 F '67
Fluorides benefit adults, too. Am City 82:12 Ja '67

International aspects
Water international. J. Ludwigson. il Sci N 91:502-3 My 27 '67

Arizona
See also
Central Arizona project (proposed)

Australia
Creating an inland sea in the central desert. W. A. Scholes. Sci N 92:540 D 2 '67

California
Death threatens western town: arsenic-laden water in Allensworth. L. Robinson. il Ebony 22:60-2+ Je '67

Canada
See also
North American water and power alliance

Cyprus
Water resources development in Cyprus; photographs. UN Mo Chron 4:73-80 F '67

Egypt
See also
Irrigation—Egypt

Florida
County water system proved best; Manatee County, Fla. P. A. Cessna. il Am City 82:105-7+ F '67
Defense of the Everglades. A. W. Smith. Nat Parks Mag 41:2 Ag '67
Inadequate water supply threatens Everglades National Park. R. W. Allin. il Parks & Rec 2:37+ O '67
Last chance for the Everglades. W. Stegner. il Sat R 50:22-3+ My 6 '67
Water for Everglades National Park. Nat Parks Mag 41:2 D '67

Israel
Scale control cuts desalting costs; Eilat ,Israel, plant. R. A. Tidball. il Am City 82:68-9+ Ja '67
To resume river diversion. M. Dean. il Sci N 92:203 Ag 26 '67

Jamaica
Water plant sparks tourist development; Jamaica, West Indies. il Am City 82:94+ Ja '67

Michigan
Water, ground, surface, treated or raw; Alma, Mich. J. D. McNaughton. il Am City 82:104-6 Mr '67

Middle East
Dwight Eisenhower's proposal for our time; atomic desalting plants. L. L. Strauss. il Nat R 19:1008-10 S 19 '67
More war or real progress in Mideast. il U S News 63:58-60 Ag 7 '67
Proposal for the Middle East: atomic desalting plants. Nation 205:322 O 9 '67
Water to cool the Middle East; Strauss-Eisenhower proposal. Life 63:4 Ag 18 '67
Water vs. hatred; Lewis Strauss scheme. C. L. Sulzberger. Read Digest 91:144+ O '67

Northwestern states
From sagebrush to crops: as water rescues arid land. il U S News 63:123-4+ D 11 '67

Saudi Arabia
United States joins dedication of Jidda desalting plant site; remarks, February 5, 1967. S. L. Udall. Dept State Bul 56:561-3 Ap 3 '67

Southwestern states
Colorado River fight nears climax; compromise solution. il Bsns W p 162+ Ap 29 '67
From sagebrush to crops: as water rescues arid land. il U S News 63:123-4+ D 11 '67
Grand Canyon: dam it or not? pro and con discussion. il Sr Schol 90:6-7 F 3 '67
Trouble for boom in desert. il U S News 62:92-4+ My 15 '67
Water and the Southwest. V. Fischer. il Am For 73:14-17+ N '67
Wheat belt prays for rain. il Bsns W p44 Ap 15 '67

Texas
Unusual pipe-bedding technique; Texas Panhandle. F. E. Dominy. il Am City 82:90-3 F '67 (to be cont)

United States
Big questions; interview, ed. by R. R. Fleming. G. J. Remus. il Am City 82:93-5+ Je '67
Engineers of prophecy; NAWAPA proposals. D. B. Luten and G. Gould, jr. il Nation 205:70-4 Jl 31 '67
Water pollution, conversion pose great R&D challenge. J. F. Judge. il Tech W 20:46-7+ Je 5 '67
See also
North American water and power alliance
also subhead Water supply under names of cities, e.g. Oakland, Calif.—Water supply

Bibliography
Nation of waterhogs? I. McManus. Am For 73:43-4 Mr '67

WATER supply engineering
Condensation of atmospheric moisture from tropical maritime air masses as a freshwater resource. R. D. Gerard and J. L. Worzel. bibliog il Science 157:1300-1 S 15 '67; Reply. R. G. W. Willcocks. 158:1525 D 22 '67
See also
Dams
Hydraulic engineering
Waterworks

WATER tanks
Esthetic water tanks. il Parks & Rec 2:21-2 My '67
It's coniped, in a photo finish; Clara, Miss. il Am City 82:34 O '67
New tank goes in an old one; reservoir, Arendtsville, Pa. R. M. Best. il Am City 82:125-6 O '67
See also
Standpipes

WATER vapor
Enzyme reaction rates at limited water activities. J. J. Skujins and A. D. McLaren. bibliog il Science 158:1569-70 D 22 '67

WATER wells. See Wells

WATER witching. See Divining rod

WATER works. See Waterworks

WATERFRONTS. See Water fronts

WATERING of gardens, lawns, etc.
Completely automated watering systems; Edina, Minn. D. G. Brauer. il Am City 82:96-7 Mr '67
How to water for greener lawns and gardens. S. Schuler. Am Home 70:52+ My '67
Right way to water lawns and gardens. Good H 165:173 Ag '67
Turfgrass irrigation. A. W. Marsh. il Parks & Rec 2:43-4+ Ja '67
Underground activity supports above-ground action; turf at Busch memorial stadium, St Louis. il Am City 82:129+ S '67
See also
Garden hose

WATERING of plants
To water or not to. G. Taloumis. Home Gard 54:84 F '67

WATERING places. See Health resorts, watering places, etc.

WATERLOO, Ia.
Darkness meets its Waterloo. K. Fox. il Am City 82:132 Mr '67

WATERMAN, Alan T.
Obituary
Science por 158:1293 D 8 '67. G. M. Parrillo

WATERMAN, Charles F.
Hunting the ridge runners. Field & S 72:
44-5+ O '67
WATERMAN-Bic pen corporation
Mightier than the pencil. il por Time 89:
92+ Mr 17 '67
WATERMELONS
See also
Cookery—Fruit
WATERPROOF gloves. See Gloves, Rubber
WATERPROOFING
GE's new Traffic topping waterproofs a sun
deck. B. W. Powell. il Pop Sci 190:138-41+
Je '67
Waterproofing a parking garage; Mount Ver-
non, N.Y. P. Brienza. il Am City 82:142-3
S '67
WATERS, Harold
Five flashes east. Yachting 123:76-7+ Ja '68
Saved by a whisker. Motor B 119:74+ Mr
'67
WATERS, Harry F.
Dolls at war. N Y Times Mag p71+ Je 4 '67
WATERS, Herbert J.
Human hunger as a policy determinant; ad-
dress, November 3, 1967. Dept State Bul
57:764-8 D 4 '67
WATERS, John M. Jr.
How to avoid getting in trouble with your
boat; condensation from Rescue at sea. por
Pop Mech 127:161-3+ F '67
WATERS, Richard D.
Lord's player. il por Newsweek 70:58 Ag 21
'67
WATERS of Babylon; drama. See Arden, J.
WATERSHEDS
Forest practices and watershed management
in California; address. W. S. Shannon. il
Am For 73:6-7+ My '67
High watersheds. A. W. Smith. Nat Parks
Mag 41:2 Je '67
WATERWAYS
See also
Rivers

Brazil
See also
Amazon River

Canada
IJC issues report on improvement of Cham-
plain waterway. Dept State Bul 57:107 Jl
24 '67
See also
St Lawrence Seaway

Latin America
Wild plan for South America's wilds. T.
Alexander. il Fortune 76:148-50+ D '67

United States
Changing West coast; Florida story. R.
Marston. il Yachting 122:40-1+ N '67
Gold Coast to Gulf coast by boat. F. M.
Paulson. il Field & S 72:34-7 Ja '68
IJC issues report on improvement of Cham-
plain waterway. Dept State Bul 57:107 Jl 24
'67
Michigan's inland waterway B. Glowacki. il
Travel 128:48-51+ S '67
New Gulf coast ICW link. W. H. Kendall. il
Motor B 119:49 F '67
See also
Florida Ship Canal project
Mississippi River
Potomac River
St Lawrence Seaway
WATERWORKS
Saigon water-works psychology. J. A.
Dillener. il Am City 82:92-4 My '67
Taste and odor control; potassium perman-
ganate in water supply, Marion, Ohio. C. G.
Whysall. il Am City 82:9-100 D '67
Water supply and treatment. See issues of
American city
Water utility will offer air conditioning and
steam heating; San Antonio, Tex. L. F.
Campos. il Am City 82:75-7 D '67
See also
American water works association
Filter plants
Pumping stations

Automation
Computerized water system. N. J. Kendall.
il Am City 82:99-100 S '67
Our honeymoon with automation; experience
of Gary-Hobart water corp. H. D. Harman.
il Am City 82:112-13 Je '67
WATKINS, A. M.
Quick, Henry, the fogger! Pop Sci 191:138-
40+ Ag '67

WATKINS, Dallas
One photographer's ESP. E. Hannigan. il
U S Camera 30:16+ My '67
WATKINS, John V.
People and plants of Madeira. Horticulture
45:42-3 Je '67
Portugal, land of gardeners. Horticulture 45:
36-7+ O '67
WATKINS, Lucian B.
Prayer of the race that God made black;
poem. Negro Hist Bul 30:21 Ap '67
WATKINS, Mel
Parent and child. N Y times Mag p 127+
D 3 '67
WATKINS, N. D. and Goodell, H. G.
Geomagnetic polarity change and faunal ex-
tinction in the southern ocean. bibliog
Science 156:1083-7 My 26 '67
—and others
Primary oxidation variation and distribution
of uranium and thorium in a lava flow.
bibliog Science 155:579-81 F 3 '67
WATKINS, Ted
Mighty, mighty Watts. por Time 90:11 S 1
'67
WATKINS, Vernon
Against controversy; poem. New Yorker 43:
146 O 7 '67
Crinoid; poem. New Yorker 43:171 Ap 8 '67
Four poems; Fingernail sunrise; Dry prophet;
Many-peopled night; Fisherman. New York-
er 43:58-9 D 9 '67
WATLINGS ISLAND. See San Salvador Island
WATNEY Mann, limited
Tapping profits. Time 89:108 Je 9 '67
WATSON, Albert W.
Excerpt from remarks, March 15, 1967. Cong
Digest 46:191 Je '67
WATSON, Allan C.
Realism at the grassy knoll. Christian Cent
84:1596-7 D 13 '67
WATSON, Arthel
Champion country picker. por Time 90:40+
Ag 25 '67
Doc Watson: musicmaker from Appalachia.
C. S. Wren. il pors Look 32:M6-8 Ja 23 '68
WATSON, Charles S. Jr
Bald cypress swamp in Indiana. Nat Parks
Mag 41:13 Ag '67
WATSON, Donald
(tr) See Ionesco, E. Exit the king
WATSON, Dorothy
NEA teach corps. Sr Schol 90:sup6-7 Mr 3 '67
WATSON, Emmett
Menace in our northern parks. Sports Illus
27:62-4+ O 30 '67
WATSON, James D.
Double helix; the discovery of the structure
of DNA; excerpts. por Atlan 221:76-94+ Ja
'68 (to be cont)
WATSON, Lillian. See Watson, P.
WATSON, Nolan W. See Van Citters, R. L. jt.
auth.
WATSON, Pokey
Face to face with a girl who swims every-
where; ed. by C. Schwalberg. por Seventeen
26:309 Ag '67
WATSON, Robert
Art in transition. L. Lieberman. Poetry 109:
395-6 Mr '67
WATSON, Thomas J. 1914-
Co-owner's comments; Palawan. Yachting
121:86-7+ My '67
This changing world; address, October 5, 1967.
Vital Speeches 34:48-50 N 1 '67; Excerpts.
por U S News 63:60-1 N 13 '67
WATSON-WATT, Sir Robert
Where are they now? il por Newsweek 69:
18 Mr 27 '67
WATT, Douglas
Concert records (cont) New Yorker 43:161-
2+ Mr 11 '67
WATT, Sir Robert Watson-. See Watson-Watt.
R.
WATTERS, Pat. See Cleghorn, R. jt. auth.
WATTS, Andre
Young excitement in music. A. Rich. por
House B 109:102-3+ Jl '67
WATTS, Daniel H.
Speaking out. por Sat Eve Post 241:6+ Ja
13 '68
about
Black anti-Semitism. Time 89:51 Mr 17 '67
WATTS, Frances B.
Merry mix-up; drama. Plays 26:73-7 My '67
Santa and the efficiency expert; drama. Plays
27:59-65 D '67

WATTS, Kenneth E.
Care of sails. Yachting 121:74 Ap '67
WATTS, Raymond N. Jr
Aerospace convention in Boston. Sky & Tel 33:96-7 F '67
Atmosphere inside a spacecraft. Sky & Tel 33:139-40 Mr '67
First applications technology satellite. Sky & Tel 33:288-9 My '67
How Surveyor 5 was saved. Sky & Tel 34: 305-7 N '67
International satellite geodesy. Sky & Tel 33: 214-15 Ap '67
Lunar Orbiter 5 takes unusual pictures. Sky & Tel 34:216-18 O '67
Photographs by Lunar Orbiter 4. Sky & Tel 34:27-31 Jl '67
Roster of space activity. Sky & Tel 35:13-15 Ja '68
Surveyor 3 on the moon. Sky & Tel 33:361-4 Je '67
WATTS, Calif. See Los Angeles
WATTS manufacturing company. See Aerojet-General corporation
WATTS writers workshop. See Educational workshops
WATZMAN, Sanford
Feast at the Pentagon. Nation 205:686-9 D 25 '67
WAUER, Roland H.
Colima warbler census in Big Bend's Chisos Mountains. il Nat Parks Mag 41:8-10 N '67
WAUGH, Alec
Delectations. See issues of National review
My brother Evelyn; excerpts from My brother Evelyn and other literary portraits. Atlan 219:53-60 Je '67
PEN in Africa. Nat R 19:1018-19 S 19 '67
Wine and wit. Nat R 19:974+ S 5 '67
WAUGH, Evelyn
My brother Evelyn; excerpts from My brother Evelyn and other literary portraits. A. Waugh. Atlan 219:53-60 Je '67
WAVES
See also
Seismic sea waves
WAX, Mel
Knowledge bonanza. Nation 204:178-81 F 6 '67
On the march again: San Francisco. Nation 204:552-3 My 1 '67
WAX plants
Hoyas. R. F. Manda. il Horticulture 45:24-5+ Je '67
WAXES
There have been changes made in floor waxes. il Consumer Bul 50:16-21 Ag '67
Three easy recipes for finishing furniture with wax. il Pop Mech 128:174-5 O '67
WAY of the cross. See Stations of the cross
WAY, way off Broadway; drama. See Huff, B. T.
WAYMAN, Stan
Dawn people; photographs. Life 63:40-46D D 22 '67
Lonely, relentless pursuit of the ghosts of the North. Life 62:59-60 Je 2 '67

about
Focus on Stan Wayman: 35-mm for tigers or tankers. J. Neubauer. il pors Pop Phot 61: 106-7+ Ag '67
From raccoons to white wolves. G. P. Hunt. por Life 62:3 Je 2 '67
WAYNE, John
Duke at sixty. il pors Time 89:67 Je 9 '67
John Wayne, superhawk. J. Barthel. il pors N Y Times Mag p4-5+ D 24 '67; Reply with rejoinder. p4+ Ja 14 '68
John Wayne's Green Beret. Nation 205:614 D 11 '67
WAYNE, N.J.
Jews and Christians in suburbia. R. Stark and S. Steinberg. Harper 235:73-8 Ag '67; Discussion. 235:4+ O '67
Trouble in Wayne; concerning defeat of Jews in school board election. il Newsweek 69:80 F 27 '67
WAYNE state university, Detroit
Risks of marijuana. D. Sanford. New Repub 156:12 Ap 22 '67
WAYNESBURG college, Waynesburg, Pa.
Waynesburg: a study in religion on the campus; dismissal of D. C. Benson. J. P. Park. Christian Cent 84:1084-6 Ag 23 '67
WAYO, Charles W.
Odyssey of Charles Wayo. C. L. Sanders. il pors Ebony 22:27-30+ F '67

WAYS, Max
Europe's new nationalism. Read Digest 91: 60-4 Jl '67
Henry R. Luce and American business. Fortune 75:115-16+ Ap '67
Intellectuals and the presidency. Fortune 75: 146-9+ Ap '67
WAYS and means committee. See United States—Congress—House of representatives —Ways and means committee
WAZNYS, Peter
Precision rotary commutating switches. Electr World 78:43 O '67
WE bombed in New Haven; drama. See Heller, J.
WE don't let nobody run in our halls! story. See Welsh, T.
WEALES, Gerald
Cabaret uptown and down. Reporter 36:49-50 Mr 9 '67
Don't drink the water. Reporter 36:43-4 Ap 20 '67
Less stately mansions. Reporter 37:34-5 N 30 '67
New Haven bound. Reporter 36:44-6 Je 15 '67
One man's 1930's. Reporter 37:51-2 Ag 10 '67
Park in the playhouse. Reporter 36:47-8 Ap 6 '67
Stargazing at Lincoln Center. Reporter 36:50-2 My 18 '67
To be and not to be. Reporter 37:39-40 N 16 '67
Working wives. Reporter 37:38-9 D 28 '67
WEALTH
See also
Income
Millionaires
Prosperity
WEALTH, Distribution of
Challenge to the opulent nations; summary of address. G. Díaz Ordaz. America 117:538 N 11 '67
Noncapitalist wealth and the origins of the French revolution; excerpts from address, December 30, 1965. G. V. Taylor. bibliog f il Am Hist R 72:469-96 Ja '67
Rich and the poor. Nation 204:388 Mr 27 '67
Scandal of the century: rich and poor; need for global redistribution of wealth. A. de Borchgrave. il Newsweek 70:38-40 O 30 '67
Task Americans are called to; concerning Franz Koenig's statement. America 117: 236 S 9 '67
WEAPON systems. See Weapons systems
WEAPONS
Enemy's weapons. il Time 89:24 Mr 24 '67
VC firepower, can we match it? M. Schultz. il Pop Mech 127:97-101+ Je '67
See also
Firearms
Pistols
Rockets
WEAPONS control. See Disarmament
WEAPONS systems
Army considering multiple rocket systems; MARS program. W. Andrews. Aero Tech 21:18 D 4 '67
Captured bases stripped of Russian gear. Aviation W 87:69-70 Jl 24 '67
Chemical and biological warfare: the weapons and the policies. E. Langer. il Science 155:299-303 Ja 20 '67
Fubini cites second thoughts on tactical weaponry needs. Aviation W 87:19 S 4 '67
New gun program has large potential; vehicle rapid fire weapon system. Aero Tech 21:18 O 23 '67
New shape of armageddon. il Bsns W p56-8+ F 11 '67
North Viet air loss rate slashed. C. Brownlow. Aviation W 87:26-7 Ag 28 '67
Penetration aids programs. Aviation W 87:99 O 23 '67

Testing
Crucial testing phase nears for Phoenix. B. Miller. il Aviation W 87:59-60+ S 11 '67
JTF-2 begins new tests of low level penetration capabilities. W. E. Wilks. il Aero Tech 21:28-9 Ag 14 '67
WEARINESS. See Fatigue
WEATHER
Have you ever seen such crazy weather? il U S News 63:10 S 4 '67
June in January; and a winter blizzard. il Newsweek 69:36 F 6 '67
May went that-a-way. il Time 89:33-4 Je 9 '67

WEATHER—*Continued*
Rain in Maine, etc. il Newsweek 70:29 S 4 '67
Something is wrong with the weather. il U S News 63:38-40 Jl 10 '67
Weather on rampage all across the U.S. il U S News 62:8 Je 26 '67
Wet blanket; one of dankest summers on record. il Newsweek 70:59 Ag 21 '67
Wild weather, what it's doing. il U S News 62:12 Je 5 '67
See also
Climate
Cold weather
Droughts

WEATHER bureau (United States) See United States—Weather bureau

WEATHER control
Can we change the weather? R. Fee. il Suc Farm 65:22 S '67
Change the weather, change the world. D. Peters. Harper 234:98-101 My '67
Climate modification by atmospheric aerosols. R. A. McCormick and J. H. Ludwig. bibliog Science 156:1358-9 Je 9 '67
Planetary engineering. S. F. Singer. Sat R 50:41-2 Jl 1 '67
Russian hail-suppression experiments. W. O. Roberts. Science 156:1580 Je 23 '67
Tailored weather. J. Ludwigson. il Sci N 91: 432-3 My 6 '67
Warm fog suppression in large-scale laboratory experiments. R. J. Pilié and others. il Science 157:1319-20 S 15 '67
Weather control due. Sci N 91:521 Je 3 '67
Weather modification. J. E. Fletcher. il Science 158:276-7 O 13 '67
Weather modification: implications of the new horizons in research; excerpts from address, December 28, 1966. T. F. Malone. bibliog Science 156:897-901 My 19 '67
When will we change the weather? B. Vonnegut. il Natur Hist 76:82-9 bibliog(p 105) D '67
See also
Rain making

WEATHER forecasts
Be your own weather prophet. L. D. Rubin. il Read Digest 90:221-4+ Ap '67
Good summer rains for the Midwest. I. P. Krick. Farm J 91:22 Ap '67
How accurate are weather forecasts? Good H 164:193 Mr '67
How to improve the weather report. Changing T 21:6 O '67
Pilots' weather outlook. R. Blodget. il Flying 81:38-43 Ag; 53-5 S '67
Stretching the limit on weather forecasts; World meteorologists meet in Geneva. il Bsns W p90-3 Ap 1 '67
Weather preview for sportsmen. il Field & S 72:66-7 O; 22+ N; 58-9+ D '67; 50-1+ Ja '68
What's new. See issues of Successful farming
World weather watch: meteorologists of the world unite; fifth congress of the World meteorological organization. J. Walsh. Science 156:1470-2 Je 16 '67
Your weather. See issues of Farm journal
See also
Artificial satellites—Meteorological applications
Computers—Meteorological applications
Radio broadcasting—Weather forecasts
Television broadcasting—Weather forecasts

Anecdotes, facetiae, satire, etc.
Rain followed by global interpretations. R. Lasson. Look 31:113 Je 13 '67

WEATHER instruments. See Meteorological instruments

WEATHER models
Modeling air pollution in the Washington, D.C. to Boston megalopolis. D. H. Slade. bibliog il Science 157:1304-7 S 15 '67

WEATHER modification. See Weather control

WEATHER predictions. See Weather forecasts

WEATHER research
Global weather; new developments presented at meeting of AAAS. P. H. Abelson. Science 155:153 Ja 13 '67
Position of planets linked to solar flare prediction. R. Pay. il Tech W 20:35-8 My 15 '67
Weather surveillance by satellite; Tiros, Nimbus, and successor ESSA satellites are providing global weather information. J. H. Wujek, jr. il Electr World 77:23-5 Mr '67
See also
National center for atmospheric research

WEATHERFORD, R. M.
Teaching contemporary drama. Sr Schol 90: sup7 Mr 17 '67

WEATHERS, Felicia
Winner; interview, ed. by Q. Eaton. por Opera N 31:13 Je 10 '67

WEATHERWAX, J. R. See Duggan, R. E. jt. auth.

WEAVER, C. J.
Vacation harvest. Travel 127:38-40 Mr '67

WEAVER, Charles E. and others
Mössbauer analysis of iron in clay minerals. bibliog Science 156:504-8 Ap 28 '67

WEAVER, Helen
(tr) See Steiner, J. F. Revolt at Treblinka

WEAVER, Kenneth F.
Historic color portrait of earth from space. Nat Geog Mag 132:726-31 N '67
Magnetic clues help date the past. Nat Geog Mag 131:696-701 My '67

WEAVER, Loyd, and Daniels, George
Half-bath is a do-it-yourself job. Pop Sci 191:153-8 S; 155-8 O '67
Home-plumbing know-how. Pop Sci 192:151-4 Ja '68
—See Daniels, G. jt. auth.

WEAVER, Robert Clifton
Excerpt from statement, February 28, 1966. Cong Digest 46:44+ F '67
Facts about FHA: address, August 23, 1967. Vital Speeches 33:734-6 S 15 '67
Recreation needs in urban areas. Nat Parks Mag 41:10-13 D '67

about
Start in urban problem solving. por Sr Schol 89:3 Ja 20 '67

WEAVER, Warren, 1894-
Science and the goodness of God; excerpt from Science and the imagination. Redbook 130:47+ D '67

WEAVER, Warren, 1923-
Romney sounds an uncertain trumpet. N Y Times Mag p45-7+ N 19 '67

WEAVER, William
After the flood, the operas open. Hi Fi 17: MA30 Mr '67
Donizetti's Pia de' Tolomei. Hi Fi 17:MA31 N '67
Don't fence Dvorak in. Hi Fi 17:51-4 My '67
Notes from our correspondents (cont) Hi Fi 17:22+ Ap; 26+ S; 40+ O '67
Old and new at the Umbrian festival. Hi Fi 17:MA27+ D '67
Revivals: Donizetti and Paisiello. Hi Fi 17: MA27 Ja '67
Tenth Festival of two worlds. Hi Fi 17: MA27+ O '67
Thirtieth Maggio musicale. Hi Fi 17:MA27+ S '67
Verdi and Giordano revived. Hi Fi 17:MA36-7 My '67
When in Rome. House & Gard 131:60+ Mr '67
(ed) See Dallapiccola, L. Solo flight

WEAVING
Expanding aerospace usage looms for woven components. W. E. Wilks. il Tech W 20: 24-5+ Je 12 '67
Needling up on craftsmanship. R. Ratico. il Sch Arts 66:38-40 Ap '67
Olga Amaral. N. Znamierowski. il Craft Horiz 27:28-31+ My '67
Sculptural weaving. O. Johnson. il Sch Arts 67:18-28 D '67
Students weave and pattern future; learning to teach at University of Minnesota. D. L. Thompson. il Sch Arts 67:32-3 D '67
Textile arts; symposium; ed. by D. B. Van Dommelen. il Sch Arts 66:4-30 Ap '67
3D woven forms. L. Campbell. il Sch Arts 66:17-18 My '67
Weaving colored paper. T. Sasano. il Design 69:4-5 Wint '67
Weaving with a straw loom; plastic drinking straws. S. M. David. il Sch Arts 67:4-5 D '67
Woven structures. S. R. Rainey. il Sch Arts 67:6-7 D '67

Study and teaching
Summer in study; textile arts teachers. D. Van Dommelen. il Sch Arts 66:9-16 My '67

WEB-building spiders. See Spiders

WEB offset printing. See Printing, Offset

WEBB, Chick
King of the Savoy. B. Korall. il por Sat R 50:51+ D 30 '67

WEBB, James Edwin
Goal is worth the billions. Good H 164:14
Je '67
High hopes for the moon shot. il por Bsns W
p60-2+ Ap 15 '67
[Space age] Aero Tech 21:24-5 N 20 '67

about

Jim Webb's earthy management of space. J.
Mecklin. il por Fortune 76:82-7+ Ag '67
NASA and the media. Nation 204:677 My 29
'67
Pitchman for NASA's trip to the moon. il
pors Bsns W p70-2+ My 27 '67

WEBB, Paul
Weight loss in men in space. bibliog Science
155:558-60 F 3 '67

WEBB, Robert B. and Malina, M. M.
Mutagenesis in escherichia coli by visible
light. bibliog Science 156:1104-5 My 26 '67

WEBB, Ryland E. and Horsfall, Frank, Jr
Endrin resistance in the pine mouse. bibliog
Science 156:1762 Je 30 '67

WEBB, S. David, and Tessman, Norman
Vertebrate evidence of a low sea level in
the middle pliocene. bibliog Science 156:379
Ap 21 '67

WEBER, David C.
Stanford: precision instrument for undergraduates. Library J 92:4351-2 D 1 '67

WEBER, Eugen Joseph
Moral in an amoral world. Sat R 50:34-5 Ag 5
'67

WEBER, George
Enzyme regulation. Science 155:1137-8+ Mr
3 '67

WEBER, Jean
The line. Opera N 32:6-7 N 25 '67

**WEBER, Karl Maria Friedrich Ernst, freiherr
von**
Records:
Der freischütz. Opera N 32:34 D 23 '67

WEBER, Paul J.
Groppi's war on Milwaukee. America 117:342-
3 S 30 '67
National student association congress. America 117:251-2 S 9 '67
Of many things. America 117:inside cover Jl
1; inside cover Jl 15 '67
On wearing the Roman collar. America 116:
560-2 Ap 15 '67
U.S.A. arms merchant. America 117:157 Ag 12
'67

WEBER, Stormy
Use and misuse of marine radio-telephones.
Motor B 120:30-1+ Jl '67
Walkie-talkie may solve your short-range
communications problems. Motor B 119:104+
Ap '67

WEBERN, Anton von
Third International Webern festival. J. Noble.
Hi Fi 17:MA19 Ja '67

WEBERN festival. See Music festivals—
New York (state)

WEBLEY-Fosbery revolver. See Revolvers

WEBSTER, John
Duchess of Malfi. Criticism
Sat R 50:21 Mr 4 '67

WEBSTER college, Webster Groves, Mo.
Crisis in Catholic education. D. Callahan.
il N Y Times Mag p34-5+ Ap 23 '67
Grennan affair; American Catholic college is
being secularized. V. P. McCorry. America
116:149-50 Ja 28 '67; Discussion. 116:138, 298
Ja 28, Mr 4 '67
Jacqueline Grennan: ex-nun. R. B. Kaiser. il
Look 31:106-10 My 30 '67
Loretto Hilton center for the performing
arts: a new approach to multi-purpose de-
sign. il Arch Rec 141:122-5 F '67
Real world of Jacqueline Grennan. P. J. Doyle.
il Sat R 50:58-9+ Jl 15 '67
Theatre; production of Oh, what a lovely
war at Loretto-Hilton center. T. Lewis.
America 116:604-5 Ap 22 '67
Uncloistered theater; Loretto-Hilton center of
the performing arts. H. Hewes. Sat R 50:
45 F 18 '67
Webster college. Commonweal 85:442 Ja 27
'67

WEBSTER girls school. See Washington, D.C.
—Education

WECHSBERG, Joseph
Education of the American palate: of mousse
and menu. Sat R 50:37-8+ Ap 22 '67
Franz Werfel's Vienna. Sat R 50:62+ Mr 11
'67
Grand tour: as it was. Sat R 51:59-61+ Ja 6
'68

Letter from Berlin (cont) New Yorker 43:165-
6+ N 18 '67
Long, sweet day of the sidewalk café. Holiday
42:50-3+ Ag '67
Milky way or alimentary canal? Sat R 50:64+
F 25 '67
124 rooms, twenty baths, elevators, central
heating, fit for a prince. Esquire 68:217-21+
D '67
Who can understand genius? Holiday 42:60-
1+ S '67
(ed) See Janowitz, G. Karajan's choice

WECHSLER, Irving R.
Claims of privacy. New Repub 156:36-8 Je
3 '67

WECHSLER, Judith
Why scale? Art N 66:32-5+ Sum '67

WECHTER, Arnold
Dory boat surfing offers newest water sports
fun. Motor B 120:107+ S '67

WED enterprises, incorporated
Living legacy of Walt Disney: Mineral King
and Disney world projects. J. Reddy. il
Read Digest 90:165-70 Je '67

WEDDING anniversaries
Cause of optimism for mankind. F. Morley.
il Nations Bsns 55:29-30 D '67
Surprise, Sonny & Cher; with recipes. il
Ladies Home J 84:136-8+ O '67

WEDDING anniversary parties. See Entertaining

WEDDING gifts
What to give the bride. J. Gillies. il Farm J
91:63 Je '67

WEDDING music
Music to marry by. Newsweek 70:97 Jl 17 '67

WEDDINGS
Able Bess's spectacular: Lynda Bird John-
son's White House wedding. il Time 90:
26-7 D 8 '67
Captain courageous; wedding of L. B. John-
son and marine Captain Charles Spittal
Robb. il Time 90:29 D 15 '67
Entertaining people; party ideas from every-
where. il McCalls 94:10 Je '67
For time & eternity; Mormon marriage of
Governor Romney's son. il Time 90:46 S
1 '67
Percy-Rockefeller wedding. il Life 62:85-90
Ap 14 '67
Royal wedding; J. D. Rockefeller-S. L.
Percy. il Newsweek 69:39 Ap 10 '67
Wedding etiquette. A. Vanderbilt. Ladies
Home J 84:56 My '67
White House wed-in. il Newsweek 70:30-1
D 11 '67
White House wedding. il Newsweek 70:28-32
D 18 '67
Who pays which costs? il Good H 164:195
Je '67

Quotations, maxims, etc.
June and weddings; comp. by E. F. Murphy.
il N Y Times Mag p98 Je 4 '67

WEDEL, Waldo R.
Salvage archeology in the Missouri River
basin. bibliog Science 156:589-97 My 5 '67

WEDEMEYER-WELLER, Maria von
Bonhoeffer's love letters. por Time 90:100 D
1 '67
Martyr's love. por Newsweek 70:84 D 4 '67

WEDGE, Bryant
Psychiatry and international affairs; excerpts
from address, October 12, 1966. bibliog Science 157:281-5 Jl 21 '67

WEDGWOOD, Josiah and sons, limited
Improving with age. il Time 89:93 My 26 '67

WEED, Florence Collins
Teaching high school students about C_2H_5OH.
Sr Schol 91:sup20 N 16 '67

WEEDS
See also
Candelillas

Chemical control
Apply atrazine early, plant corn faster. Farm
J 91:67 Ja '67
Chemical weed control in soybeans. il Suc
Farm 65:83+ Mr '67
Latest way to kill soybean weeds. J. Bickers.
il Farm J 91:33+ Ap '67
Postemergence weed control for corn. Suc
Farm 65:70 Ap '67
Solid-stand soybeans: OK if you stop weeds.
D. Hagen. il Farm J 91:56J-56K Ja '67

WEEDS—*Continued*
Successful farming's guide to poisonous plants. C. E. Sommers. il Suc Farm 65:77-82 Mr '67

Treating soil to kill weeds; pre-emergence weed killer. Sunset 139:198+ N '67
See also
Calcium cyanamid
Dicamba
Herbicides
                         Control
How to get rid of pigweed. Sunset 138:284 Ap '67

WEEGEE, pseud. See Fellig, A.

WEEGHMAN, Richard B. See Halford, R. G.; Paquette, M. jt. auths.

WEEKEND confrontation with the soc. rels.; story. See Vroom, B.

WEEKEND vacations. See Vacations

WEEKS, Edward Augustus
Peripatetic reviewer. See issues of Atlantic
Words and style. Writer 80:22-3+ Ap '67

WEEKS, I. D.
What is right in higher education? Sch & Soc 95:353-4 O 14 '67

WEEKS, Jack
Big bloody cockbird; story. Sat Eve Post 240:70-3 Mr 11 '67

WEEKS, Ramona
Thoughts while going over the North Pole in a balloon with Major Andre; poem. Yale R 56:426-7 Mr '67

WEEKS, Special. See Special days, weeks and months

WEEMS, David B.
Build the mixed twelve speaker system. Pop Electr 26:74-7+ Mr '67
Instant non-fat speaker enclosure. Pop Electr 27:53-4 N '67
Princess Cinderella. Pop Electr 27:38-40 Jl '67
Three-corner space saver. Pop Electr 27:57-61 O '67

WEESNER, Theodore
Andrew his son; story. New Yorker 43:54-63 N 4 '67

WEEVILS
See also
Alfalfa weevils

WEFER, Marion
(ed) See Keckley, E. Another assassination, another widow, another embattled book

WEGMAN, Leonard S.
Cleanest incinerator stack gases. Am City 82:89-91+ My '67

WEHNER, Herbert
Grinder ground. por Newsweek 69:54 Je 19 '67

WEIDIG, Phyllis D.
Frustration quotient. NEA J 57:38-9 Ja '68

WEIDMAN, Charles
Charles Weidman & co. Expression of Two arts theatre. J. Anderson. Dance Mag 41:82 Mr '67
Charles Weidman and Theatre dance company; Village theatre. M. Marks. Dance Mag 41:32 Ag '67

WEIDMAN, Jerome
Good man, bad man; story. Sat Eve Post 240:48-53 Jl 1 '67

WEIGAND, Hermann John
Hermann J. Weigand and a letter from Thomas Mann: the critical dialogue. T. Ziolkowski; T. Mann. Yale R 56:537-49 Je '67

WEIGHING machines
See also
Scales (weighing instruments)

WEIGHT (physiology)
Battle of the bulge: height-weight tables unrealistic. Newsweek 69:103 My 29 '67
See also
Corpulence
Diet
Exercise
Weight watchers, incorporated

WEIGHT of airplanes. See Airplanes—Weight

WEIGHT reducing preparations
Facts on quacks: how to lose weight without diet, and other myths. il Todays Health 45:16-18 N '67
In dubious battle; gimmicks to help lose weight. Newsweek 69:62 F 20 '67
See also
Drugs—Physiological effects

WEIGHT throwing
See also
Shot putting

WEIGHT watchers, incorporated
Beauty checkout; add up ounces, subtract pounds. Vogue 151:34 Ja 1 '68
Changing lost pounds into dollars. il Bsns W p 106+ Mr 4 '67
See you lighter. il Time 89:52+ Ap 7 '67

WEIGHTLESSNESS
Weight loss in men in space. P. Webb. bibliog il Science 155:558-60 F 3 '67

WEIGHTS and measures
How long is a yard? short measure of Twinz self-adhering plastic sheeting. il Consumer Bul 50:40 N '67
See also
Cookery—Measurements
Measurement
Metric system

WEIL, Irwin
Revolution in the Cossack world. Sat R 50:33 Je 17 '67

WEIL, James L.
To her hand; Mr Weil; Your father; poems. Poetry 109:376-7 Mr '67

WEIL, Rolf A.
Freedom for education; address, April 16, 1967. Vital Speeches 33:541-4 Je 15 '67

WEILER, Helen
Teen-age artists. Sch Arts 67:38-9 O '67

WEILL-TUCKERMAN, Anne
For whom is time working? Nation 205:386-7 O 23 '67
Great de-mythification. Nation 204:770-1 Je 19 '67
Lion is not dead. Nation 205:612 D 11 '67
Spiral of defiance. Nation 205:482-3 N 13 '67
Third front. Nation 204:706-7 Je 5 '67
Wall of words. Nation 205:2-4 Jl 3 '67

WEINBAUM, George. See Fischman, D. A. jt. auth.

WEINBERG, Alvin M.
Basic science in mission-oriented endeavor. T. L. Campbell. por Science 156:670-2 My 5 '67

WEINBERG, Harold
Courtroom crack-up. il por Time 90:108 N 17 '67

WEINBERG, Susan S.
Navions unite. Flying 80:70-1 Ap '67

WEINER, Harold N.
Art of fund-raising. por Wilson Lib Bul 42:289-92 N '67

WEINER, Herbert
Ebbing of euphoria. Reporter 37:16-19 N 16 '67

WEINGARTEN, Violet
Fertility rite; story. Sat Eve Post 240:54-7 Ag 12 '67

WEINRAUB, Bernard
Alan Arkin talks about what it's like to be a star. N Y Times Mag p30-1+ Mr 12 '67
1968 nomination? Esquire 68:97-101 Ag '67
South Vietnam's no. 1 dove. N Y Times Mag p43+ O 8 '67
You can see that I'm not twenty years old. Sat Eve Post 240:38-41 F 25 '67

WEINRIB, David
See-through sculpture. S. Burton. il Art N 66:36-7+ Mr '67

WEINS, Leo M.
Wilson company changes. Wilson Lib Bul 41:661-2 Mr '67

WEINSHEIMER, Doris Wilson
Make a miniature water garden. Home Gard 54:22+ F '67

WEINSTEIN, Gerald. See Fantini, M. D. jt. auth.

WEINSTEIN, Martin E.
Okinawa's future and Far-East security. Reporter 37:39-40 N 2 '67

WEINSTEIN, Stephen Zachary
Ye friendly tobacconist. il por Time 90:28 N 10 '67

WEINSTOCK, Arnold
Weinstock wins. il por Time 90:103 N 24 '67

WEINSTOCK, Herbert
Authentic Prince Igor. Sat R 50:84 N 25 '67
Ghost of Semiramide. Sat R 50:71 Ja 28 '67
Janáček on Dostoevsky. Sat R 50:63 My 27 '67
Messiah by Mackerras. Sat R 50:70 Ap 29 '67

WEINSTOCK, Herbert—*Continued*
Music to my ears. Sat R 50:64+ S 16 '67
New Handel Hercules. Sat R 50:67 S 30 '67
Orfeo out of Orphée. Sat R 50:81 F 25 '67
Singers Pleasants and unpleasant. Sat R 50:
69 Mr 25 '67
Sutherland's Beatrice. Sat R 50:57 O 28 '67
WEINTRAUB, Stanley
Even Guérnica was myth. Sat R 50:42 O 7 '67
Molded by painful reality. Sat R 50:37-8+ Je
10 '67
WEIR, J. R. Jr
Radiation damage at high temperatures. bib-
liog Science 156:1689-95 Je 30 '67
WEIR, William C.
Enigma of infertility. PTA Mag 62:6-8 O '67
WEISBERGER, Bernard A.
Here come the Wobblies! Am Heritage 18:
30-5+ Je '67
WEISKOPF, Herman
Baseball's week. See issues of Sports illus-
trated published during baseball season
WEISMEHL, Leonard Alain
Some new directions in French architecture.
Arch Rec 142:161-8 O '67
WEISS, Benjamin, and Costa, Erminio
Adenyl cyclase activity in rat pineal gland;
effects of chronic denervation and norepine-
phrine. bibliog Science 156:1750-2 Je 30 '67
WEISS, Charles, Jr
Marine lab in East Africa. il Sci N 91:552-3
Je 10 '67
Rear-guard ecology. Sci N 91:595 Je 24 '67
Tale of two nations. Sci N 91:460-1 My 13 '67
WEISS, Joseph H.
How Hanoi controls the Vietcong. Reporter
38:27-8 Ja 11 '68
WEISS, Joseph Jacob
Vietnam, a doctor's journal. Commentary 43:
52-9 My '67
WEISS, Margaret R.
California exposed. Sat R 50:50-3 S 23 '67
Erich Salomon: candid historian. Sat R
50:56-7 S 9 '67
Karsh's one-man show at Expo 67: centen-
nial salute. Sat R 50:54-7 Ap 29 '67
Labyrinth: film in a framework. Sat R 50:
51-3+ Jl 8 '67
Learning through the lens. Sat R 50:55+ Je
17 '67
Lens on the locks. Sat R 50:57-9 Ag 12 '67
Masada revisited. Sat R 50:24-5 N 4 '67
Mutual concern. Sat R 50:66-7 D 9 '67
PFA-V: the museum is the message. Sat R
50:37-44 My 6 '67
Photography in the front line. Sat R 50:134-5
Mr 11 '67
SR's photo contest. Sat R 51:64 Ja 6 '68
Toni Frissell, in her fashion. Sat R 50:48-9
O 21 '67
WEISS, Miriam
Days of hope and glamour; story. Redbook
128:68-9 Mr '67
WEISS, Peter
Song of the Lusitanian bogey, tr. by L. Bax-
andall. Criticism
New Yorker 43:57-8 Ja 13 '68
Newsweek 71:79 Ja 15 '68
Time il 91:40 Ja 12 '68
WEISS, Piero
Son of nature. Opera N 31:26-7 Mr 11 '67
WEISS, Theodore
Life of. . ; poem. New Yorker 43:28 Ag 26
'67
WEISSENBERG, Alexis
Music to my ears; recital in Philharmonic
Hall. I. Kolodin. Sat R 50:58 N 18 '67
WEISSKOPF, Victor F.
Nobel prizes; physics. Science 158:745-6 N 10
'67
WEISSMAN, Sherman M. See Forget, B. G. jt.
auth.
WEISSMANN, Tom E.
Microwave dryer. Sci N 91:582 Je 17 '67
WEITZ, John
High cost of making the scene. J. Krantz. il
pors Ladies Home J 84:106-7+ S '67
WEITZNER, Dorothea M.
Baggage bike. S. V. Jones. il Sci Digest 62:78
Ag '67
WELCH, Charles
Simple test for shutter speed. Pop Mech 128:
163-9 S '67
WELCH, Curby
Face to face. il Seventeen 26:88 F '67
WELCH, Edna E.
Hot crayon fantasies. Design 68:30-2 Mr '67
WELCH, Helen M.
Price indexes for 1967: U.S. periodicals. Li-
brary J 92:2526-7 Jl '67

WELCH, Herbert, bp
Unfinished piece of business; excerpts from
As I recall my past century. Read Digest 91:
150-2 Ag '67
WELCH, Holmes
Conserving behavior. Sat R 50:49-50 Jl 1 '67
WELCH, Mary Scott
Complete dictionary of home entertaining.
Redbook 129:111-18 O '67
Redbook guide for brides. Redbook 129:98-106
My '67
WELCH, Paul
Haunted man still trying to find believers.
Life 63:114 S 22 '67
WELCH, Raquel
Raquel. J. Hamilton. il pors Look 31:M8-10 Ag
8 '67
Sudden stardom of Raquel Welch. R. W.
Lewis. il pors Sat Eve Post 240:32-5 N 18
'67
WELCH, Robert Henry Winborne
Mutiny in the Birch society. J. Phelan. il
pors Sat Eve Post 240:21-5 Ap 8 '67
WELCH, W. Bruce. See Parsons, C. jt. auth.
WELCH, Walter
Dwarf iris. Horticulture 45:26-7+ S '67
WELCH, Wayne Lee
It was that damned book. B. Davidson. il por
Sat Eve Post 240:81-9 Ap 8 '67
WELD, Theodore Dwight
Family divided; Grimké family. J. Steven-
son. il por Am Heritage 18:4-25+ Ap '67
WELDERS
Build yourself this carbon arc welder for $5.
P. Scott. il Pop Mech 128:174-6 S '67
WELFARE, Public. See Public welfare
WELFARE agencies. See Social agencies
WELFARE state. See Social and economic
security
WELFARE work. See Public welfare
WELFARE work in industry
New NAM; project aimed at enlisting young
executives to help train the jobless and
participate in other poverty programs.
Newsweek 69:76+ My 15 '67
See also
Chaplains, Industrial
WELFARE workers. See Social workers
WELL rescues. See Rescue work
WELL water. See Water
WELLEMEYER, Marilyn
How Columbus started building two land-
marks per year. Life 63:86+ N 17 '67
WELLER, Maria von Wedemeyer-. See Wede-
meyer-Weller, M. von
WELLES, Benjamin
No stereotypes in Spain. Sat R 50:36+ O 7
'67
Reign in Spain. Sat R 50:42-3 Je 10 '67
WELLES, Chris
Bitterest fight: new mass transit vs. more
highways. Life 62:39 My 12 '67
Grueling interview for executives after bigger
jobs. Life 63:69-70+ Je 18 '67
Multimillion reach of Wall Street's mad Aus-
trian. Life 62:43-4+ Mr 10 '67
Most of the snitches are respectable house-
wives. il Life 63:72-72B D 15 '67
Why did it happen and what will it do to the
U.S? Life 63:36-7 D 1 '67
WELLES, Orson
Falstaff as Orson Welles. J. Morgenstern and
R. Sokolov. il pors Newsweek 69:96+ Mr
27 '67
Orson Welles: there ain't no way. P. Kael.
New Repub 156:27-32 Je 24 '67
WELLES, Patricia
Babyhip; story, excerpt. Ladies Home J 84:
135-46 S '67
WELLING, Richard
Drawings of Richard Welling. N. Kent. il
por Am Artist 31:52-9 F '67
WELLINGTON, Cary L.
Whiz of Wellington park. R. Levy. il por
Duns R 89:36-7+ F '67
WELLINGTON electronics, incorporated
Whiz of Wellington park. R. Levy. il Duns R
89:36-7+ F '67
WELLIVER, Neil
Welliver's travels. R. Downes. il por Art N
66:34-6+ N '67
WELLS, George S.
Reservations please! Travel 127:32-7 Mr '67
WELLS, H. G.
H. G. Wells: he was a seer but a disappointed
scientist. J. Walsh. Science 155:181-2 Ja 13
'67
Unwitting rival; excerpt from Variety of
men. C. P. Snow. il Sat R 50:48-9 Ap 1 '67
Which H. G. Wells was right? R. L. Shayon.
Sat R 50:50 Ja 28 '67
WELLS, John. See Ingrams, R. jt. auth.

WELLS, Mary
Girl who painted the planes. Bsns W p 106
Ja 21 '67
Sledge-hammer sell; with report by N. Belli-
veau. il pors Life 63:101-2+ O 27 '67
WELLS, Philip V. and Berger, Rainer
Late pleistocene history of coniferous wood-
land in the Mohave Desert. bibliog Science
155:1640-7 Mr 31 '67
WELLS, Rich, Greene, Incorporated
Sledge-hammer sell; AMC campaign; with re-
port by N. Belliveau. il Life 63:101-2+ O 27
'67
Taking off with talk; Manhattan's new ad-
vertising agency. il Time 89:61-2 Je 2 '67
WELLS, Wesley R.
Maple syrup: what consumers ought to know
about it. Am For 73:28-9+ Ja '67
WELLS
He knows where to drill for water. G. L.
Morris. il Pop Mech 128:124-6+ O '67
Impact of homo sapiens upon an alligator
wishing well; Steinhart aquarium, San
Francisco, Calif. E. S. Herald and others.
il Parks & Rec 2:30+ S '67
See also
Fountains
WELLS, Oil. See Oil wells
WELLS FARGO bank, San Francisco. See San
Francisco—Banks
WELLS FARGO express company
Occurrence; rescue of dog from East River
by drivers. New Yorker 42:20-3 Ja 21 '67
WELSH, Edward C.
Selling the space program; excerpts from
address. Aviation W 87:11 Jl 24 '67
WELSH, Terry
We don't let nobody run in our halls! story.
NEA J 57:40-1 Ja '68
WELSH castles. See Castles
WELSHANS, Merle T.
Using credit for profit making. Harvard
Bsns R 45:141-7+ Ja '67
WELTNER, Charles L.
Speaking out. por Sat Eve Post 240:12+ O 7
'67
WELTNER, William, Jr
Stellar and other high-temperature mole-
cules. bibliog Science 155:155-64 Ja 13 '67
WELWITSCHIA
From an ancient desert relict. W. Tijmens.
il Natur Hist 76:36-7 Ap '67
WENATCHEE VALLEY, Wash.
Vacation harvest. C. J. Weaver. il Travel
127:38-40 Mr '67
WENDEL, Clara E.
Monolithic concrete in Orlando. Library J
92:4363-4 D 1 '67
WENDEL, William Hall
Is there a perfect merger? Duns R 89:37-8+
Ap '67
WENGER, H. Leslie
Should mercy killing be permitted? yes. por
Good H 164:82+ Ap '67
WENHAM, Brian
All-time high. New Repub 157:13 Ag 19 '67
Can Harold Wilson make it work? New Repub
157:11-12 D 9 '67
Coming to grips with the color bar in Britain.
New Repub 156:14-15 Ja 28 '67
Curbing the drug traffic in Britain. New
Repub 156:9-10 Mr 18 '67
In Britain the walls keep closing in. New
Repub 157:9 S 2 '67
Patient is getting restless. New Repub 156:
7-9 Ap 22 '67
Public TV and the networks. New Repub
156:19-20 My 13 '67
Troubled times of George Brown. New Re-
pub 157:11-13 N 18 '67
WENK, Edward, Jr
Deep sea exploration. por Sat R 50:43-4 Jl
1 '67
WENK, H. R. and others
X-ray fabric analysis of hot-worked and an-
nealed flint. Science 157:1447-9 S 22 '67
WENKHAM, Robert
Kauai National Park. il Nat Parks Mag 41:
4-8 Mr '67
WENNBLOM, Audrey
Right toys for your preschooler. Farm J 91:
48-9 N '67
WENNER, Adrian M.
Honey bees: do they use the distance infor-
mation contained in their dance maneuver?
bibliog Science 155:847-9 F 17 '67
—and Johnson, D. L.
Honeybees: do they use direction and distance
information provided by their dancers? bib-
liog Science 158:1076-7 N 24 '67

WENTWORTH, Vivian
Storm; poem. Farm J 91:113 Mr '67
WENTZ, Richard E.
Is there a new establishment of religion?
Christian Cent 84:463-5 Ap 12 '67
Requiem aeternam homini. Christian Cent 84:
113-14 Ja 25 '67
WENZLICK, Roy
Why land boom has slowed; interview. por
U S News 63:95-6 Jl 24 '67
WERBOFF, Jack. See Cairns, R. B. jt. auth.
WERFEL, Franz V.
Franz Werfel's Vienna. J. Wechsberg. il por
Sat R 50:62+ Mr 11 '67
WERNER, Alfred
Ballerinas and bathers. Reporter 36:44+ Ap
20 '67
Draughtsmanship of Edgar Degas. Am Artist
31:47-53+ O '67
Generalić, a Croatian peasant painter. Am
Artist 31:40-5+ F '67
Invisible made visible. Reporter 36:46+ Mr
23 '67
Riemenschneider rediscovered. por Am Artist
31:36-41+ D '67
Rodin, homage to a Titan. Am Artist 31:
45-51+ Ap '67
WERNER, Ray O.
Educational tyranny and the ombudsman.
Sch & Soc 95:391-2 O 28 '67
WERNICK, Robert
Battle of the redwoods. Sat Eve Post 240:
90-5 Ap 22 '67
Small and solid on a savage site. Life 62:
105-6 My 5 '67
WERSHAW, R. L. and others
Sodium humate solution studied with small
angle X-ray scattering. bibliog Science 157:
1429-31 S 22 '67
WERT, Robert Joseph
Search for distinction. il por Time 90:61 O 27
'67
WERTH, Alexander
Do svidanyia, Ilya. Nation 205:344-6 O 9 '67
French vote: why be surprised? Nation 204:
422-4 Ap 3 '67
Kosygin in Paris: differences within amity.
Nation 203:693-6; 204:181 D 26 '66, F 6 '67
Literary Bay of Pigs. Nation 204:710-11 Je
5 '67
Middle East ulcer. Nation 205:311-14 O 2 '67
Nonpersonality cult. Nation 204:790-2 Je 19 '67
Svetlana: who needs her? Nation 205:469-70
N 6 '67
Year of jubilee: the USSR at fifty. Nation
205:424-30 O 30 '67
WERTHEIM, Debra
Curl up and read. Seventeen 26:70 Ag '67
WESLEY, Wallace Ann
Let's improve health education. Todays
Health 45:88 S '67
WESLEYAN university, Middletown, Conn.
Affluent miniversity. il Time 89:45 My 26 '67
WESLEYAN university press
Dance magazine's annual awards 1966. il
Dance Mag 41:39+ Mr '67
WESSEL, Morris A.
What do children ask the doctor? Parents
Mag 42:61-3+ N '67
WESSELINK, A. J. and Hunter, J. Jr
Quasar 3C 446. Science 156:103-4 Ap 7 '67
WESSELS, Cletus
Refresher course in theology. America 116:
648-9 Ap 29 '67
WESSON, Jerry
Sound. See issues of U.S. camera & travel
WEST, Allan M.
King-size job for local associations. NEA J
56:19-20 Mr '67
about
Assistant executive secretary for field opera-
tions and urban services Allan M. West.
por NEA J 56:75 D '67
WEST, Anthony
Great Traven mystery. New Yorker 43:82+
Jl 22 '67
Lust for tulips. Vogue 150:192-7+ D '67
Miss Millard; story. New Yorker 43:132 N 11
'67
Mr Keogh; story. New Yorker 43:29-38 Jl 8 '67
Secrets: why you need them. Vogue 150:127+
Ag 15 '67
Theatre. See issues of Vogue
World that the American woman has invented
for herself. Vogue 149:234-6 My '67
WEST, Carolyn. See West, J. jt. auth.
WEST, E. Gordon
Automotive activity in recreation. por Parks
& Rec 2:32-3 Ja '67

WEST, Jack
Electronic navigation. See issues of Yachting
Radar for safer boating; excerpts. Yachting
121:66-9+ My '67
—and West, Carolyn
Great northeast cruise. pors Motor B 121:77-82 Ja '68 (to be cont)

WEST, Jessamyn
California woman: her unmistakable style.
Ladies Home J 84:76+ Jl '67
Underground; story. por Good H 166:73-5
Ja '68

WEST, Mae
Mirror, mirror, on the ceiling: how'm I doin'?
H. Lawrenson. il pors Esquire 68:72-4+ Jl
'67

WEST, Mary Jane
Foundress associations in polistine wasps:
dominance hierarchies and the evolution
of social behavior. bibliog Science 157:1584-5 S 29 '67

WEST, Morris L.
Testimony of a 20th century Catholic. America 117:678-81+ D 2 '67

WEST, Paul
Education of wombats. Commonweal 87:143-6
N 3 '67
Perpetuating the obsolete. Commonweal 87:203-5 N 17 '67

WEST Dame Rebecca
Was it really like this in Dallas? Reporter
36:37-9 My 18 '67

WEST, Richard
Elephants to the rescue. N Y Times Mag
p85-7 Je 11 '67

WEST, Ruth, and Hotchner, Geraldine
In praise of older men; ed. by H. Ehrlich.
Look 31:80-5 N 28 '67

WEST
Autumn in the Rockies. J. E. Dwyer. il Pop
Gard 18:52-5+ D '67
Points West. J. Didion and J. G. Dunne. Sat
Eve Post 240:8-9+ Je 3; 20+ Je 17; 24-5
Jl 1; 20+ Jl 29; 20+ Ag 26; 22-3 S 23; 26+
O 21; 24+ N 18; 24+ D 2; 18 D 16; 14 D 30
'67; 241-14 Ja 13 '68
Points West. J. G. Dunne and J. Didion. Sat
Eve Post 240:20-1 Jl 15; 16+ Ag 12; 18-19 S
9; 24-5 O 7; 22-3 N 4 '67; 241:16 Ja 27 '68
See also
Fishing—Western states
Frontier and pioneer life—United States
Hunting—Western states
Pacific coast
Skis and skiing—Western states
Southwest

Climate
For gardeners in the West, a new bookful
of answers; Sunset western garden book.
il Sunset 138:74-81 Mr '67

Description and travel
Grandeur of the Great Divide. N. Morgan.
il Holiday 41:42-59+ My '67
Las Vegas and the high desert. il Bet Hom &
Gard 45:78-9 Mr '67
[Month] travel in and beyond the West. See
issues of Sunset
San Francisco and a land of contrast. il Bet
Hom & Gard 45:152-3 Ap '67
West coast wanderings. P. Noyes. See issues
of Travel
See also
Automobile touring—Western states
Southwest—Description and travel

Economic conditions
See also
Ranches

Industries
See also
California—Industries
Ranches

WEST ALLIS, Wis.
Low-cost leaf collection without special
equipment. R. E. Hahn. il Am City 82:54
Ap '67

WEST BERLIN. See Berlin (West Berlin)

WEST Coast airlines
Mini-liner; air service between Seattle and
Port Angeles. il Travel 128:23 Ag '67
West Coast replaces DC-3s with Navajos. il
Aviation W 87:85 Jl 3 '67

WEST END opera association
Report: Ontario, Cal. production of Tosca.
W. Aguiar, jr. Opera N 32:29 D 23 '67

WEST EUROPEAN aerospace industry association. See Eurospace

WEST HARTFORD, Conn.
Sand, salt and calcium chloride. T. Nosek.
il Am City 82:82-3 D '67

Education
Dial a lesson; TV dial-select system at Hall
high school. C. L. Towne. il Sr Schol 90:
sup 14 F 3 '67

WEST in art
Death on the range; with paintings by H.
Jackson. D. G. Lowe. il Am Heritage 18:
48-9+ O '67
Painter of the old West; Joe Grandee. W.
Gard. il Am Artist 31:56-7+ Je '67
Recollections of an Old West illustrator. L. F.
Bjorklund. il Pub W 192:76-8+ N 6 '67

WEST INDIES
Black leaders of the West Indies. E. B.
Thompson. il Ebony 22:76-82+ O '67
See also
Anguilla (island)
Barbados
Caribbean Region
Haiti
Jamaica
Virgin Islands

Description and travel
Gunkholing the lesser Antilles. D. M. Street.
jr. il Yachting 122:52-3+ N '67
Upbeat for the off-beat. Travel 127:69 Mr '67
See also
Barbados—Description and travel

WEST INDIES, BRITISH
Almost independent. il Time 89:39-40 Mr 10
'67
See also
Bequia (island)
Grenadines (islands)
Jamaica

WEST INDIES, FRENCH
See also
Guadeloupe, (islands)

WEST POINT military academy. See United
States military academy. West Point

WEST REDDING, Conn.
Tune in the kids with records and films;
John Reed middle school. S. Jacoby and
R. Lavigne. il Sr School 91:sup9 D 7 '67

WEST Side tennis clubs, Forest Hills. See
Sports clubs

WEST SPRINGFIELD, Mass.
Giving the retarded a chance; Human development program. D. R. Snyder. il NEA J
56:24-5 S '67

WEST VIRGINIA

Economic conditions
Luring the poor out of the hills. il Bsns W
p74-6+ Jl 1 '67
Why pump-prime a gushing economy? il Nations Bsns 55:50-2+ Ap '67

Social conditions
Rougher road of Russell Hicks; Mingo County.
I. Mothner. il Look 31:29-33 Je 13 '67

WEST VIRGINIA pulp and paper company
New gospel at Westvaco. R. Levy. Duns R
89:48-50+ Mr '67
Seminars on book publishing topics; report
on panel discussion (cont) il Pub W 191:86-8 F 6; 65-6+ Ap 3 '67

WESTCHESTER aircraft maintenance association
Cooperative group improves maintenance. R.
F. Coburn. Aviation W 86:75-6 F 27 '67

WESTCHESTER classic golf tournament. See
Golf—Tournaments

WESTCHESTER COUNTY, N.Y.
Crime in the suburbs. il Newsweek 70:24 Jl
31 '67

WESTCHESTER golf classic. See Golf—Tournaments

WESTCOTT, Cynthia
H&G's 1967 guide to plant protection. House
& Gard 131:34+ Ap '67

WESTERDICK, Connie
Meet Miss Connie. J. Doussard. il pors Am
For 73:31+ D '67

WESTERFIELD, Nancy G.
Ship's mass; poem. Reporter 36:50 Mr 23 '67

WESTERFIELD, Putney
Forces of change. por Pub W 191:22-3 My 1
'67

WESTERMANN, H. C.
Carpenter Gothic. M. Friedman. il por Art N
66:30-1+ Mr '67

WESTERN air lines, incorporated
Transpacific route case: Western ties route
bid to fare-cut plan. R. G. O'Lone. il Aviation W 86:54-5+ F 13 '67

WESTERN alliance. See International relations

WESTERN and Atlantic railroad
Great chase. il Newsweek 69:84 Mr 13 '67
WESTERN books exhibition. See Book exhibits
WESTERN civilization. See Civilization
WESTERN conference of teamsters
Workers on the farms; agreement with
United farm workers organizing committee.
N. C. Mills. New Repub 157:9 S 23 '67
WESTERN electric company
Bell, Western electric play key Nike role. il
Aviation W 87:118-23 O 23 '67
WESTERN electronics show and convention
Integrated circuits spotlighted at WESCON.
J. Rhea. Aero Tech 21:18 Ag 28 '67
WESTERN films. See Moving pictures—Westerns
WESTERN GERMANY. See Germany (Federal Republic)
WESTERN hemisphere

Defenses
See also
Organization of American states—Inter-American defense board
WESTERN home awards
A.I.A.-Sunset Western home awards. il Sunset 139:74-89 O '67
Announcing the 1967-1968 Western home awards. il Sunset 138:40-1 F '67
WESTERN Pacific railroad
National asset; California Zephyr. il Time 89:84 F 24 '67
WESTERN policy. See International relations
WESTERN publishing company
Pegasus starts publishing; division of Western. Pub W 191:147 Je 5 '67
WESTERN RESERVE university, Cleveland, Ohio

Health sciences center
Western Reserve university: three schools on one base. il Arch Rec 142:202-3 S '67
WESTERN states. See West
WESTERN stories
See also
Television broadcasting—Westerns
WESTERN testing, incorporated
Vanishing breed; cattle clubs assets missing. Bsns W p40 Jl 15 '67
WESTERN union telegraph company

Anecdotes, facetiae, satire, etc.
Case of the missing! A. Kelley. Atlan 219:112-13 My '67
WESTHEIMER, David
How to write a novel. Writer 80:14-15+ D '67

about
My sweet Charlie. Criticism
Vogue 149:42 Ja 15 '67
WESTIN, Alan F.
Benchmarks. Commonweal 87:429 Ja 12 '68
Newsbook on privacy. por Time 90:102 S 29 '67
WESTIN, Av
Meatier than Bonanza. il Bsns W p38 N 4 '67
WESTINGHOUSE broadcasting company
Marketers meet the minds; London meeting. R. L. Shayon. Sat R 50:50 D 2 '67
WESTINGHOUSE electric corporation
Here's one for the road; Westinghouse Markette. il Bsns W p33 Ap 8 '67
Westinghouse invents a new Westinghouse. J. McDonald. il Fortune 76:142-7+ O '67
Westinghouse lights up. Fortune 75:240 Je 15 '67
Westinghouse plugs in. il Bsns W p94-6+ Je 17 '67
See also
Westinghouse learning corporation
WESTINGHOUSE learning corporation
New educational corporation at Westinghouse. il Sch & Soc 95:292 Sum '67
Westinghouse grows as teacher. Bsns W p40 Ja 21 '67
WESTLAKE, John
How to buy a sailboat. Pop Mech 127:154+ F '67
WESTMINSTER academy, Northbrook, Ill. See Private schools
WESTMINSTER kennel club show. See Dog shows
WESTMORELAND, William Childs
Commanding General reports on the Vietnam war; excerpt from address, April 24, 1967. por U S News 62:42-4 My 8 '67

Progress report on the war in Viet-Nam; address, November 21, 1967. Dept State Bul 57:785-8 D 11 '67; Excerpts. Aviation W 87:11 N 27 '67 por U S News 63:20 D 4 '67
Vietnam; address, April 28, 1967. Vital Speeches 33:450-2 My 15 '67; Same with title Report to the Congress by the commander of U.S. military forces in Viet-Nam. Dept State Bul 56:738-41 My 15 '67; Excerpts. U S News 62:44-5 My 8 '67

about
Bitterest fighting still ahead. por Sr Schol 90:17 My 12 '67
Cards on the table. il pors Time 89:17-21 My 5 '67
General and the refugee. E. J. Hughes. Newsweek 69:23 My 15 '67
Home-front war; visit to U.S. il pors Newsweek 69:31-6 My 8 '67
Patriotism and Vietnam. N. Cousins. Sat R 50:26+ My 13 '67
Right to answer dissent. Life 62:4 My 12 '67
T.R.B. from Washington. New Repub 156:4 My 13 '67
Tougher U.S. stance: grind the enemy down. il por Bsns W p36-7 Ap 29 '67
War on the third front. Nation 204:610-11 My 15 '67
Westmoreland caper. Commonweal 86:221-2 My 12 '67
Westmoreland's mission: explaining the war. il pors U S News 62:20 My 8 '67
Westmoreland's Progress report. A. Hamilton. il New Repub 157:15-18 D 16 '67
Will Westmoreland elect Johnson? S. Alsop. il por Sat Eve Post 241:11 Ja 13 '68
WESTOFF, Charles F. See Ryder, N. B. jt. auth.
WESTON, George, limited
$4-billion business Garfield Weston built. W. S. Rukeyser. il Fortune 75:116-21+ Je 1 '67
WESTON, Ralph E. Jr
Transition-state models and hydrogen-isotope effects. bibliog Science 158:332-42 O 20 '67
WESTON, Robert J.
New service commitment. Sat R 51:32-3 Ja 13 '68
WESTON, Willard Garfield
$4-billion business Garfield Weston built. W. S. Rukeyser. il Fortune 75:116-21+ Je 1 '67
WESTON, Ill.
Accidental village; Senate authorizes location of AEC atom smasher. Newsweek 70:27-8 Jl 24 '67
Civil rights at Weston and beyond. Sci N 92:56 Jl 15 '67
Making a mockery of Title VI; question of a site for government's proposed atomic accelerator plant. Christian Cent 84:886 Jl 12 '67
200-bev accelerator: moving into a WASP's nest? B. Nelson. il Science 156:1713-16 Je 30 '67
WESTRICK, C. W.
Make your own metal castings. Pop Mech 128:162-5 Ag '67
WESTVACO. See West Virginia pulp and paper company
WETHERILL, G. W.
Stone meteorites: time of fall and origin. bibliog Science 159:79-82 Ja 5 '68
WETMORE, Alexander
Re-creating Madagascar's giant extinct bird. por Nat Geog Mag 132:488-93 O '67
WETTACH, Thomas S.
Wisconsin's river road. Travel 127:58-61 My '67
WETTING agents
See also
Surface active substances
WEXFORD festival. See Music festivals—Ireland
WEXLER, Sol
Destruction of molecules by nuclear transformations. bibliog Science 156:901-7 My 19 '67
WEYBRIGHT, Victor
Revolutionary in books. E. Weeks. Atlan 220:136-8 O '67
WEYER, Susan
Hang-up; story. McCalls 95:54-5 Ja '68
WEYERMAN, Andrew M.
Bound to the world. Christian Cent 84:1161 S 13 '67
WHALEN, Charles W. Jr
Excerpt from address at Ohio state university, April 5, 1967. Cong Digest 46:232+ O '67

WHALEN, John P.
Authors & editors; summary of address. por Pub W 191:45 Ap 24 '67

WHALEN, Richard J.
Elusive General Gavin. Harper 235:107-8+ N '67

Shifting equation of nuclear defense. Fortune 75:84-7+ Je 1 '67

Who owns America? Sat Eve Post 240:17-21 D 30 '67

WHALES
Coral corral? proposal to raise plankton-eating whales. Sci Am 216:52+ Mr '67

Whale. J. M. Lindbergh. il Life 63:48-50+ D 22 '67
See also
International whaling commission

WHARTON, Don
Five common frauds, and how to avoid them. Read Digest 91:69-72 D '67

Incredible career of Grandma Moses. Read Digest 91:145-50+ S '67

Seven tips on insuring your home. Read Digest 91:77-80 Ag '67

WHARTON, John F.
En route to a massacre? Sat R 50:19-21 N 4 '67

What nature reveals about peacemaking. Sat R 50:14-16 My 27 '67

WHARTON model. See Economics—Mathematical models

WHAT a way to go! story. See Cusack, I. L.

WHAT did we do wrong? drama. See Denker, H.

WHAT I need don't come in suitcases; story. See Maloney, R.

WHAT mistletoe? story. See Stanton, W.

WHATLEY, Joseph L.
Battle for breath. Todays Health 45:42-3+ F '67

What parents can do to take the scare out of surgery. Todays Health 45:40-4 Jl '67

WHEAT
Fall-seeded spring wheat yields 14 per cent more. D. Hagen. il Farm J 91:71 N '67

Tetraploid wheats: seed protein electrophoretic patterns of the emmer and timopheevi groups. B. L. Johnson. bibliog il Science 158:131-2 O 6 '67

History
Birth of wheat and maize farming. J. Hawkes. il UNESCO Courier 20:6-7 My '67

Hybrids
See also
Triticale

Prices
Will wheat prices come back? O. Bay. Farm J 91:60B Mr '67

World's big wheat crops: a worry for Canada. il U S News 63:64 O 23 '67

WHEAT protein. See Gliadin

WHEAT-rye hybrids. See Triticale

WHEAT strip rust. See Rusts (botany)

WHEAT trade
See also
International grains arrangement

WHEATON college, Wheaton, Ill.
Fundies, infidels, and free inquiry; a profile of Wheaton in Illinois. C. Hilberry. il Mlle 65:160-1+ My '67

WHEDON, G. Donald
Battling the bone-thinner. Todays Health 45: 66-8 S '67

WHEEL adapters. See Automobiles—Wheels

WHEEL barrows. See Wheelbarrows

WHEEL of love; story. See Oates, J. C.

WHEELBARROWS
Wheels in the garden. il Sunset 138:78-9 Je '67

WHEELER, Bruce E.
Lincolniana in 1966. Hobbies 71:35+ F; 72: 114-15+ Mr '67

WHEELER, C. Herbert, Jr
Today's new tools for tomorrow's practice; excerpts from address. Arch Rec 142:93-4 D '67

WHEELER, Earle Gilmore
As a top general sees the war now; excerpts from statements, January 1967. por U S News 62:14 Ja 30 '67

End the war talks? what General Wheeler thinks. por U S News 64:10 Ja 1 '68

How to fight the war in Vietnam; interview. por U S News 62:38-45 F 27 '67

U.S. achievements in Viet-Nam; address, January 17, 1967. Dept State Bul 56:186-92 F 6 '67

Warning to Americans, in the words of the U.S. military chiefs; statement, March 6, 1967. por U S News 62:32-3 My 15 '67

about
Brass alibi. Nation 206:35-6 Ja 8 '68
Tension in the tank. il por Time 89:26-7 My 19 '67

WHEELER, Harvey
World is the problem. Nation 205:358-60 O 16 '67

WHEELER, Helen
Films for the community college library. Wilson Lib Bul 42:411-14 D '67

WHEELER, Keith
Mid-air! mid-air! mid-air! Read Digest 90: 127-31 F '67
—and Smith, Sandy
Murf the Surf and his jewel-studded jinx. Life 62:92-4+ Ap 21 '67

WHEELER, Timothy J.
New politics comes to the old left. Nat R 19:1015-17 S 19 '67

WHEELING steel corporation
Antidisestablishmentarianism at Wheeling steel. D. Cordtz. il Fortune 76:104-9+ Jl '67

Bath in steel. il Time 89:97 Ap 28 '67

Simon keeps the experts guessing; sale of Wheeling stock to Pittsburgh steel. Bsns W p 140+ Ap 29 '67

Where two's company in steel; pact with Pittsburgh steel. il Bsns W p38-9 My 6 '67

WHEELOCK, John Hall
Graceful reticence. Poetry 110:123-5 My '67

WHEELS
See also
Automobiles—Wheels

WHELAN, George J.
Police special II. Pop Electr 27:41-8+ N '67

WHELAN, Thomas J.
Mayor tells how firmness stopped riots; interview. por U S News 63:40-2 Ag 14 '67; Same abr. with title How to stop riots. Read Digest 91:132-5 O '67

WHEN a girl is twenty-five; story. See McInerny, R.

WHEN do we eat? drama. See Hark, M. and McQueen, N.

WHEN it really counts; story. See Alexander, R. W.

WHEN Michael calls; story. See Farris, J.

WHERE did the summer go? story. See Gordon, E. E.

WHERE the ivy fails to grow; story. See Zeigerman, G.

WHIG party (United States)
Strange stillbirth of the Whig party. L. L. Marshall. bibliog f Am Hist R 72:445-68 Ja '67

WHIPPLE, A. B. C.
One old salt deserves another. Life 63:20 N 10 '67

WHIPPLE, Dorothy Vermilya
Magic of sleep. Parents Mag 42:50-1+ My '67

WHIRLIGIGS. See Toys

WHISKEY
Canadian imports and domestic blend whiskies. Consumer Rep 32:94-6 F '67

Urban bourbon. il Esquire 67:108-9 My '67

WHISKEYTOWN LAKE
Traveler's choice. E. D. Clason. Travel 128:11 Jl '67

WHISTLER, James Abbott McNeill
Tough dandy. il Newsweek 71:93 Ja 22 '68

WHITAKER, Frederic
Sculpture of Spero Anargyros. Am Artist 31: 32-7+ F '67

WHITAKER, Robert B.
Latest bass bonanza. Outdoor Life 140:23-5+ Ag '67

Lure of Libertad. Field & S 72:40-1+ Je '67

WHITAM, Frederick L.
God is square. Nat R 19:182-3 F 21 '67

WHITBREAD, Jane
Babies make good teachers. Parents Mag 42: 33-5+ Jl '67

Medicine: for a healthier future. Parents Mag 43:42-3+ Ja '68

Runaways. Look 31:26-32 Jl 25 '67

Special report on the families of the men in Vietnam. Parents Mag 42:53-5+ O '67

WHITBREAD, Thomas
Best place to read Carlyle; poem. Harper 235:
32 Ag '67

WHITE, Al
Mid-air! mid-air! mid-air! K. Wheeler. il
Read Digest 90:127-31 F '67

WHITE, C. T. See Harter, M. R. jt. auth.

WHITE, Charles
Charles White: portrayer of black dignity. L.
Robinson. il pors Ebony 22:25-8+ Jl '67

WHITE, Charles J.
Ten minutes to live. W. R. Young. il por Read
Digest 90:198-200+ My '67

WHITE, Charles W.
East of the border: New Brunswick and
Fundy National Park. Redbook 129:40-1 Jl
'67

WHITE, Claire Nicolas
Resika's delectable mountains. Art N 66:
48-9+ Ap '67

WHITE, Sir Dick Goldsmith
Not-so-secret service. il Newsweek 70:31 O 30
'67

WHITE, Dori
Under sentence of death; story. Redbook
129:82-3 S '67

WHITE, E. B.
Survival through adaptation; poem. New
Yorker 43:50 Ap 15 '67

WHITE, E. R. See Schubert, J. jt. auth.

WHITE, Edward Higgins, 2d
Fire in the spacecraft! il pors Newsweek
69:25-9 F 6 '67
Honored son returns to West Point. il Life
62:22-3 F 10 '67
To strive, to seek, to find, and not to yield.
il por Time 89:13-16 F 3 '67
We knew that someday . . . Sci N 91:112 F 4
'67
White. il pors Life 62:22-3 F 3 '67

WHITE, Elgin
Cruising in northern Florida. Motor B 119:
42-5+ Mr '67
Vanishing waterway. Yachting 122:42-3+ N
'67

WHITE, Eugene W. and White, W. B.
Electron microprobe and optical absorption
study of colored kyanites. bibliog Science
158:915-17 N 17 '67

WHITE, George Abbott
Grandmother; poem. Christian Cent 84:1348 O
25 '67

WHITE, Jim
Build the QRP midget. Pop Electr 27:51-2 Jl
'67

WHITE, Joe
Lead up to a lifetime sport; junior bowling.
Parks & Rec 2:30-1+ Ag '67

WHITE, John
Footnote to history. Nation 205:676-7 D 25 '67

WHITE, John, 1925?-
Adventure in affinities. il Time 91:48 Ja 5 '68

WHITE, Katharine S.
Onward and upward in the garden (cont)
bibliog New Yorker 43:193-6+ N 4; 200+
N 11; 113-14+ D 16 '67

WHITE, Kevin Hagan
In Cleveland and Boston, the issue is race.
B. Rice. il pors N Y Times Mag p31+ N
5 '67

WHITE, Lee C.
Transmission lines. Parks & Rec 2:19+ D
'67

WHITE, Lynn Townsend, 1907-
Historical roots of our ecologic crisis; address, December 26, 1966. Science 155:1203-
7 Mr 10 '67; Same with title What hath
man wrought? Américas 19:11-19 My '67;
Same with title Saint Francis and the ecologic backlash. Horizon 9:42-7 Sum '67
Jacopo Aconcio as an engineer. bibliog f Am
Hist R 72:425-44 Ja '67

WHITE, Mary Alice, and Boehm, A. E.
Child's world of marks. NEA J 57:12-13 Ja
'68

WHITE, Neal
Inka dinka doo. New Repub 158:11-12 Ja 20
'68
New NSA. New Repub 157:11 S 2 '67
Post office box. New Repub 157:21 Ag 19 '67

WHITE, Onna
View from the road; dances of Illya darling.
R. Hicklin. il por Dance Mag 41:24-7+
Mr '67

WHITE, Paul Dudley
My own prescription for life. por Sat R 50:
17-20 D 16 '67

WHITE, Peter T.
Behind the headlines in Viet Nam. Nat Geog
Mag 131:149-89 F '67
Hopes and fears in booming Thailand. Nat
Geog Mag 132:76-125 Jl '67

WHITE, Philip L.
(ed) Let's talk about food. See issues of Today's health

WHITE, Raymond E.
Rights of students in the classroom. Sch &
Soc 95:263-4 Ap 15 '67

WHITE, Richard Grant
Magnificent Truffl. R. Ellsworth. Opera N
32:6 Ja 20 '68

WHITE, Robert Joseph
Dead body & the living brain; with questions and answers. O. Fallaci. il por Look
31:99-101+ N 28 '67

WHITE, Ruth
Compose concrete music for your compositions. por Dance Mag 41:58-61 S '67

WHITE, Theodore H.
Action intellectuals. Life 62:43-58+ Je 9; 44-
56+ Je 16; 76-8+ Je 23 '67
Armor churns up the Syrian hills. Life 62:20-
24C Je 23 '67
Bell of decision rings out in Vietnam. Life
63:54-6+ S 1 '67

WHITE, Tyner
I get there firstmost with the bestmost; poem.
Atlan 220:46 Ag '67

WHITE, Vera Randal
You can't buy people; story. Sat Eve Post
240:78-80 My 6 '67

WHITE, Wallace
Against a backdrop; story. Atlan 219:75-80
Mr '67

WHITE, William B. See White, E. W. jt. auth.

WHITE ants. See Termites

WHITE Chimneys. See Pennsylvania—Historic
houses, etc.

WHITE collar workers. See Office workers

WHITE EARTH Chippewa Indian reservation,
Minn. See Indians of North America—
Reservations

WHITE fat. See Fat

WHITE flies
Counterattack on whiteflies. Sunset 138:210 Je
'67

WHITE footed mice. See Mice, White footed

WHITE geese. See Geese, Wild

WHITE herons. See Herons

WHITE House
Christmas radiance at the White House. S. F.
Smith. il House & Gard 132:134-5+ D '67
Cool Swiss at the stove of state. H. Haller.
il Life 63:35-6+ Jl 21 '67
Garden of American history: at the White
House; photographs. Horst; with account by
V. Lawford. Vogue 149:160-7+ F 1 '67
Jacqueline Kennedy's years in the White
House; excerpts. M. V. Thayer. il McCalls
95:12-15+ D '67; 8-9+ Ja '68 (to be cont)
Mrs Johnson's private White House world.
H. Sidey. il Life 63:42 S 15 '67
Vignettes of change around the mansion. H.
Sidey. Life 63:26B S 1 '67
See also
Presidents—United States

WHITE House conferences

Anecdotes, facetiae, satire, etc.
Minutes of a White House meeting, summer
1967. J. C. Thomson, jr. Atlan 219:67-8 My
'67

WHITE House happening; drama. See Kirstein,
L.

WHITE House press photographers association photo contest. See Photography—
Competitions

WHITE House receptions. See Government entertaining

WHITE House staff. See Public officers

WHITE House youth conference on natural
beauty and conservation
Look to youth. J. W. Corson. il Parks & Rec
2:20-2+ D '67
Youth to the rescue. il Pop Gard 18:82-4
Mr '67

WHITE lies; drama. See Shaffer, P.

WHITE motor company
Hard drive of White motor. J. Berry. il D₁₁ns
R 88:37-8+ D '66

WHITE MOUNTAINS
New Hampshire's White Mountain huts. A. E.
Kessler. il Travel 127:37-40 Je '67

WHITE PINE, Mich.
How White Pine got to pay dirt. il Bsns W p 120-2 Jl 29 '67
WHITE Sox (baseball) See Baseball clubs
WHITE tailed deer hunting. See Deer hunting
WHITE wolves. See Wolves
WHITEFISH fishing
Bonefish of the North. J. Parry. il Field & S 72:60-1+ D '67
WHITEFORD, Andrew Hunter
Impasse in Latin America. Christian Cent 85:71-4 Ja 17 '68
WHITEHEAD, Edward
Dissertation on beards, and other hairy recollections. Bsns W p9 D 2 '67

about

Some bristly thoughts on victory through hair power: barbers, beards and bangs. W. Zinsser. Life 64:10 Ja 19 '68
WHITEHEAD, Eric
Hockey. Sports Illus 26:80-2 Ap 10 '67
WHITEHEAD, Ralph
Anatomy of a riot. Commonweal 86:492-4 Ag 11 '67
WHITEHILL, Joseph
Bobby; story. Atlan 219:57-62 My '67
WHITEHILL, Walter Muir
Speaking out. por Sat Eve Post 240:8+ Ag 12 '67
WHITEHORN, Ethel. See McMahan, I. jt. auth.
WHITELEY, Brett
Plaster apocalypse. il por Time 90:78 N 10 '67
WHITEMAN, Paul
Jazz king. il por Newsweek 71:26 Ja 8 '68
WHITEMARSH, Pa.
Ice skating, Whitemarsh style. D. R. Koontz. il Parks & Rec 2:27 Ja '67
WHITES of their eyes; drama. See Willment, F.
WHITESIDE, Thomas
Reporter at large. New Yorker 43:64-6+ N 4 '67
WHITFIELD, Mal
Diplomatic strides. il por Newsweek 70:105-6 O 30 '67
WHITING, John
Devils; dramatization of Devils of Loudun, by A. Huxley. Criticism Sat R 50:50 Ap 15 '67
WHITING, Leonard
New Romeo and Juliet. M. Simons. il pors Look 31:52-5+ O 17 '67
People are talking about... por Vogue 150:88-9 Ag 1 '67
WHITMAN, Alden
I'm no ghoul. por Newsweek 70:71 Ag 7 '67
WHITMAN, Ardis
Is marriage still sacred? what does love mean? Redbook 128:68-9+ F '67
Of sunlight and shadow. Read Digest 90:27-8+ F '67
WHITMAN, Charles Joseph
Suddenly, without warning or reason, it happens. P. Hamill. Good H 164:98-9+ Ap '67
WHITMAN, Robert
Drawing in the dark. il por Time 90:64 O 27 '67
WHITMORE, Frank C. Jr, and others
Elephant teeth from the Atlantic continental shelf. bibliog Science 156:1477-81 Je 16 '67
WHITNEY, Josiah Dwight
Sheepherder versus the geologist. il por Audubon 69:47-9 Ja '67
WHITNEY, Marie Louise Schroeder Hosford
Saratoga story. il pors Time 90:56+ Ag 18 '67
Woman who lost $780,000 in jewels but still has everything. G. Greene. il pors Ladies Home J 84:108-9+ N '67
WHITNEY, Norman J.
Number one pacifist. Christian Cent 84:622-4 My 10 '67
WHITNEY, Phyllis A.
Writing the Gothic novel. Writer 80:9-13+ F '67
WHITNEY, Thomas P.
Russian storyteller: Alexander Green. Horn Bk 43:551-60 O '67
WHITNEY museum of American art, New York
Neck & neck; survey of painting at the Whitney. il Time 90:46-7 D 22 '67
New impresario for the showcase. il Time 90:64 N 24 '67

WHITSON, G. L. and others
Cell synchrony. Science 157:1219-20+ S 8 '67
WHITTAKER, Charles E.
Can a disorderly society survive? excerpts from The effects of planned, mass disobedience of our laws, September 1966. por U S News 63:27 Jl 31 '67
Planned, mass violations of our laws; address, February 14, 1967. Vital Speeches 33:322-8 Mr 15 '67; Excerpts. por U S News 62:15 F 27 '67
WHITTAKER corporation
Ready when you are, B.D. N. Willatt. Duns R 90:56-8 D '67
Thread that ties diversity together. il Bsns W p74-6+ D 2 '67
WHITTEMORE, Reed
Brothers in loss. Sat R 50:26 S 2 '67
WHITTIER, Anthony
Do you need a lawn edger? Pop Sci 191:124-6+ Jl '67
WHITTIER, C. Taylor. See Shils, E. B. jt. auth.
WHITWORTH, Kathy
Miss Avis against Miss Hertz. M. Mulvoy. il por Sports Illus 27:62-3 N 27 '67
WHITWORTH, William
Profiles; P. Molé. New Yorker 43:63-4+ O 21 '67
WHO is Harry Kellerman and why is he saying those terrible things about me? story. See Gardner, H.
WHOLE city's down below; drama. See Nolan, P. T.
WHOLE wheat bread. See Bread
WHOLESALE prices. See Prices
WHOLESALE trade
Ratios of the wholesalers; table. Duns R 90:88-9 O '67
WHOLESALERS, Book. See Book jobbers
WHOOPING cranes. See Cranes
WHO'S happy now? drama. See Hailey, O.
WHO'S who in library service
Whose who's who? letter to the editor. W. R. Eshelman. Library J 92:1876 My 15 '67; Reply. L. Ash. 92:2487 Jl '67
WHO'S who in the USSR
Aging elite. Sch & Soc 95:39 Ja 21 '67
WHYSALL, Charles G.
Taste and odor control. Am City 82:99-100 D '67
WHYTE, Jean
Man's world. bibliog pors Library J 92:4120-2 N 15 '67
WHYTE, William Foote
Aunt Effie and the brass. Nation 205:134-5 Ag 28 '67
WIBBERLEY, Leonard
Conversing with the people of history. Writer 80:13-14+ My '67
WICHITA, Kan, public library
Wichita's new living room. F. Rockwell. il Library J 92:4365-6 D 1 '67
WICHITA FALLS, Tex.
Computer puts more go on city streets. R. L. Wilshire. il Am City 82:116+ N '67
WICK, Robert H.
Responsibility of colleges and universities; address, October 29, 1966. Vital Speeches 33:240-4 F 1 '67
WICKED cooks; drama. See Grass, G.
WICKER, Tom
George Wallace: a gross and simple heart. Harper 234:41-9 Ap '67
Washington: a reporter's memoir. por Sat R 50:49-50+ S 9 '67
WICKERSHAM, James C.
It's the old Moxie. il Bsns W p42 My 20 '67
WICKS, Harry
How to make the sailmaker's bench. Pop Sci 191:122-3 Jl '67
Nine good gluing tricks. Pop Sci 191:146-7 N '67
WICKSTRUM, B. K.
U.S. in world trade; address, March 22, 1967. Vital Speeches 33:535-8 Je 15 '67
WIDDOP, Walter
Collectors' releases. A. Favia-Artsay. Hobbies 72:36 Ap '67
WIDICK, B. J.
Labor at Bal Harbour. Nation 206:6-8 Ja 1 '68
Labor meets for peace. Nation 205:561-3 N 27 '67
Motown blues. Nation 205:102-4 Ag 14 '67
Reuther vs. Meany: background to labor's showdown. Nation 204:614-16 My 15 '67
What worries Detroit. Nation 205:68 Jl 31 '67

WIDMER, Thomas F.
Cost of flying. Flying 80:94-7 F '67
WIDMOYER, Fred B. and Sullivan, D. T.
Grapes for the Southwest. Horticulture 45:
22-5 S '67
Native plants of the Southwest. Horticulture 45:46-9 Ap '67
WIDNALL, William Beck
Excerpt from debate. October 13, 1966. Cong
Digest 46:47+ F '67
WIDOM, B.
Intermolecular forces and the nature of the
liquid state; address, April 1966. bibliog Science 157:375-82 Jl 28 '67
WIDOWS
Facts every wife should learn about widowhood. Good H 165:154 Jl '67
If only we had spoken. M. Parton. il McCalls 95:66+ O '67
WIECK, Paul R.
Caged liberals. New Repub 157:11-12 Ag 19
'67
Eugene who? New Repub 158:14-15 Ja 13 '68
How the Young were kept in line. New Repub
157:9-10 D 2 '67
Keeping milk off the market. New Repub
156:9-10 Ap 22 '67
McCarthy in Chicago. New Repub 157:9-11
D 16 '67
When will RFK surface? New Repub 157:23-6
O 21 '67
Young democrats and old pros. New Repub
157:13-15 N 25 '67
WIENER, Anthony J. and Kahn, Herman
Excerpts from The year 2000. Natur Hist
76:10-12+ N '67
WIERZYNSKI, Gregory H.
G.E.'s $200-million ticket to France. Fortune
75:92-5+ Je 1 '67
Tankers move the oil that moves the world.
Fortune 76:80-5+ S 1 '67
WIESBADEN, Germany

Music

Wiesbaden; performance of Der Rosenkavalier. F. Stevenson. il Opera N 31:25 Je 10 '67
WIESEL, Elie
Will Soviet Jewry survive? Commentary 43:
47-52 F '67

about

Jews of silence. D. Stern. Commonweal 86:
232-4 My 12 '67
WIESENFELD, Stephen L.
Sickle-cell trait in human biological and cultural evolution; excerpt from address,
January 1967. bibliog Science 157:1134-40
S 8 '67
WIESENTHAL, Simon
Hunters become the hunted. A. Donat. Sat
R 50:32-3 Ap 15 '67
Intercontinental op; searching out of Nazi
war criminals. il por Time 89:98+ Mr 31
'67
Murderers among us. pors Sat Eve Post 240:
42-4+ F 25; 38-9+ Mr 11 '67
Penny a head. por Time 89:40 Mr 10 '67
WIESER, S.
Calgary's planetarium and museum. Sky &
Tel 34:14-15 Jl '67
WIESNER, Gwen
Centralized duplicating. Am City 82:98-9 F
'67
WIESNER, Jerome B.
Case against an antiballistic missile system.
por Look 31:25-7 N 28 '67
Cold war is dead, but the arms race rumbles
on. Bul Atomic Sci 23:6-9 Je '67
Strategy for arms control. Sat R 50:17-20
Mr 4 '67

about

Action intellectuals. T. H. White. il Life 62:
74A-74B Je 16 '67
WIEZELL DE ESPÍNOLA, Elsa
Seven Paraguayan poets. Américas 19:31-6
Je '67
WIGGAM, Lionel
North of Scarsdale; poem. Atlan 219:127
Ap '67
WIGHT, ISLE OF
Tennyson's Isle of Wight. N. Braybrooke. il
Sat R 50:60-1+ Mr 11 '67
WIGNER, Eugene P.
Twenty-five years with the bomb; interview,
ed. by A. Wolff. Look 31:58+ D 26 '67

WIGODER, Devorah
Symbolic atonement in Israel. Mlle 64:130-1+
F '67
WIGREN, Harold E.
New copyright law for the new Congress.
Sch & Soc 95:50-1 Ja 21 '67
WIGS
Big switch to braids. il Seventeen 26:140-1
My '67
Contessa Consuelo Crespi, the marvellous
coiffure she does herself with three hairpieces. il Vogue 149:122-5 Je '67
Gold in the hills; sacrificial hair used for
wig-making in India. il Newsweek 69:62 Je
26 '67
Hairy experience; more men wearing hairpieces. il Newsweek 70:78 Jl 24 '67
How to have a wardrobe of hotshot hairpieces sans selling your graduation watch.
il Mlle 64:138-9 F '67
100 ways of summer: switched-on hair. il
Mlle 65:146-7 My '67
Project: you. il Ladies Home J 84:67 Ap '67
Short classic curls. G. Plaut. il Look 31:
M12-14 Ap 18 '67
You can live without a wig. il Redbook 129:
80-3+ O '67
WIINBLAD, Björn
Artist's garden home. M. Duckett. il House
B 110:98-9+ Ja '68
WIKGREN, J. Arthur
Quit guessing about maintenance costs. Am
City 82:84-5 Ja '67
WILBUR, Richard
Walking to sleep; poem. New Yorker 43:32-3
D 23 '67
Wood; poem. New Yorker 43:42 My 6 '67
WILCKEN, D. E. L. and others
Reserpine: effect on structure of heart muscle. bibliog Science 157:1332-4 S 15 '67
WILCOX, Wayne A.
Influence of small states in a changing world;
address, April 1967, with questions and answers. Ann Am Acad 372:80-92 Jl '67
WILD animal pets. See Pets
WILD boar hunting
Oriental pig tale. H. J. Samuels. il Outdoor
Life 139:68-71+ Mr '67
WILD boars
Down an unknown jungle river. Z. Grey. il
Field & S 72:42-3+ N '67
WILD dogs
See also
Dingoes
WILD duck; drama. See Ibsen, H.
WILD flowers
Growing wild flowers from seed. K. S. Taylor.
il Horticulture 45:30-3 My '67
Wild flowers for natural beauty, when the
builder leaves trees. il Home Gard 54:52-3
F '67
Wild flowers of the United States; comp. by
H. W. Rickett. Review
New Yorker 42:149-50+ D 10 '66. K. S.
White; Reply. D. Malcolm. 42:101-3 Ja
28 '67
See also
Cylburn wildflower preserve and garden
center, Baltimore, Md.
WILD food. See Food
WILD horses. See Horses
WILD life. See Wildlife
WILD nights; story. See Kaufman, L.
WILD rice
Reporter at large; harvest at Lower Rice
Lake, in the White Earth Chippewa Indian
reservation, Minn. B. Roueché. il New
Yorker 43:34-8+ D 23 '67
WILD rivers. See Rivers
WILD sheep. See Mountain sheep
WILD West shows. See Rodeos
WILDCAT hunting. See Bobcat hunting
WILDCATS. See Bobcats
WILDE, Oscar
Happy prince; story. Ladies Home J 84:62-3
D '67

about

Importance of writing good plays. J. Rosselli.
il Reporter 36:44+ My 18 '67
Second visit: younger son's repeat trip to
United States; interview. V. Holland. New
Yorker 43:41-2 Ap 15 '67
WILDER, Amos N.
Journey of the Magi; poem. Christian Cent
84:1649 D 27 '67

WILDER, Laura (Ingalls)
Books, children, and women. R. H. Viguers. Horn Bk 43:152-3 Ap '67
WILDER, R. L.
Role of intuition. bibliog Science 156:605-10 My 5 '67
WILDER, Thornton Niven
Meaning in a disordered university. J. B. Martin. Harper 234:107-8 Ap '67
Old age inaugural. R. H. Goldstone. por Sat R 50:27-8 Ap 1 '67
Thornton Wilder. S. Kauffmann. New Repub 156:26+ Ap 8 '67
WILDERNESS areas
Cumberland Gap park wilderness hearing announced. Nat Parks Mag 41:21 My '67
Dams and wild rivers; looking beyond the pork barrel. L. J. Carter. il Science 158:233-6+ O 13 '67
Do we ask enough? il Liv Wildn 30:2+ Aut '66
Facets of wilderness. D. Lambert. il Liv Wildn 31:10-18 Spr '67
Homage to Basswood Lake; Boundary waters canoe area. H. Clepper. il Am For 73:24-7+ Mr '67
Last call for park wilderness! address, April 1967. A. W. Smith. Nat Parks Mag 41:2+ My '67
Mike Frome; management and use of wilderness and national parks. M. Frome. Am For 73:3+ O '67
Miners ridge threatened; Glacier Peak wilderness area. Liv Wildn 31:60 Spr '67
More wilderness hearings. Nat Parks Mag 41:20 F '67
Park wilderness planning; editorial. A. W. Smith. Nat Parks Mag 41:2 F '67
TVA: the halo slips; Land between the lakes dispute. J. Egerton. il Nation 205:11-15 Jl 3 '67
Various wilderness hearings. Nat Parks Mag 41:22 Mr '67
Wilderness in the Nation's capital; Anacostia River. J. W. Higgs. il Am For 73:34-7 Ja '67
See also
Forests, State
Wildlife sanctuaries

Roads
Primitive area road opposed; Gore Range-Eagle Nest primitive area. Liv Wildn 30:44 Aut '66

Alaska
Denali interlude. W. Peterson. il Audubon 69:44-55 My '67

California
California wilderness area; San Rafael wilderness area. Nat Parks Mag 41:20 Mr '67
San Rafael and the condor; concerning the proposed San Rafael primitive area. Audubon 69:57 My '67
San Rafael wilderness. Liv Wildn 30:2 Wint '66

Colorado
Primitive area road opposed; Gore Range-Eagle Nest primitive area. Liv Wildn 30:44 Aut '66
Wilderness vs. I-70; Gore Range-Eagles Nest primitive area. Nat Parks Mag 41:20-1 N '67

Florida
No wilderness wasted; Turkey point developed by Florida power & light co. M. Smith. Parks & Rec 2:20+ Je '67

Idaho
Backpacking with Joe; trip to Selway-Bitterroot wilderness area. L. R. Jones. il Liv Wildn 30:24-6 Aut '66
Family in the wilderness; camping in the Selway-Bitterroot wilderness area. N. Boyd. il Liv Wildn 30:36-41 Wint '66
How to sell multiple use without half trying; Clearwater River country. V. Fischer. il Am For 73:34-5+ Ag '67
New chance for the Upper Selway. Liv Wildn 30:34-41 Aut '66
On the Snake River lavas. G. A. Jayne. il Natur Hist 76:44-7 O '67
Proposed Tutimaba wilderness. R. J. Contor. il Liv Wildn 30:3-10 Wint '66
Seesaw in the Sawtooth. V. Fischer; reply. S. F. Arno. Am For 73:4 Ja '67

Maine
Mike Frome; questioning the future of woods in a rapidly changing land. M. Frome. Am For 73:5+ My '67

Montana
Proposed Lewis and Clark national river; National park service proposes to conserve certain sections of the Missouri. il Parks & Rec 2:22+ Ag '67

New Hampshire
Great Gulf wilderness. R. F. Moseley, jr. il Liv Wildn 31:3-9 Sp '67

Northwestern states
Use of high country in Switzerland; North Cascades debate continues using Switzerland as yardstick. A. Netboy; discussion. Am For 73:2 Ja '67
See also
Wilderness areas—Washington (state)

Texas
Farewell to Texas, by W. O. Douglas. Review
Liv Wildn 31:48-9 Spr '67. P. A. Gunter

Utah
High Uintas. M. F. Foster. il Liv Wildn 30:11-13 Wint '66
Southern Utah park and monument hearings. Nat Parks Mag 41:18 D '67

Washington (state)
Amen, Mr Justice; proposal to incorporate the Pickett Range into a wilderness area. W. O. Douglas. Am For 73:30-1+ N '67
Copper company vs. the North Cascades. P. Brooks. il Harper 235:48-50 S '67
North Cascades. il Nat Parks Mag 41:20-1 Je '67
North Cascades National Park: copper mining vs. conservation. K. Sperry. il Science 157:1021-4 S 1 '67; Discussion. 158:205; 159: 31-2+ O 13 '67, Ja 5 '68

Wyoming
Sesame trout and sourdough; Bridger wilderness; photographs by Bruce Davidson; with account by P. Knight. il Sports Illus 27:30-3+ Jl 31 '67

WILDERNESS society
New chance for the Upper Selway. il Liv Wildn 30:34-41 Aut '66
Wilderness council in Yellowstone. il Liv Wildn 30:42-3 Aut '66

WILDHABER, Ernest
Big wheel in gears. S. V. Jones. por Sci Digest 61:23 Mr '67

WILDING, L. P.
Radiocarbon dating of biogenetic opal. bibliog Science 156:66-7 Ap 7 '67

WILDLIFE
Close look at wildlife in America; with editorial note. B. Gilbert. il Sat Eve Post 240:32-6, 74 S 9 '67
Outdoors. T. Williams. il Esquire 68:190+ O '67
Wild world; symposium. il Life 63:4+ D 22 '67

WILDLIFE conservation
Aldabra; biology may lose a unique island ecosystem. J. Walsh. il Science 157:788-90 Ag 18 '67
Animals from the Amazon basin; letter. P. G. Heltne. Science 157:134 Jl 14 '67; Reply. A. M. Fletcher. 157:991-2 S 1 '67
Big lift for bighorns; water to Santa Catalina Mountains. T. Foust. il Outdoor Life 139: 70-3+ Ap '67
Can Africa's wildlife be saved? il Newsweek 70:70-1 S 4 '67
Endangered species program seen in perspective. il Audubon 69:4-5 My '67
Look what they're doing to your land; sagebrush-killing bad for western wildlife. T. Trueblood. il Field & S 72:10+ O '67
New federal policy for animal damage control. Audubon 69:4 S '67
Of tortoises and men. J. Ludwigson. il Sci N 92:156-7 Ag 12 '67
Predators, prejudice, & politics. M. Frome. il Field & S 72:24-6+ D '67
Reporter at large; conference at the San Diego zoo. E. Hahn. New Yorker 43:170+ O 14 '67

WILDLIFE conservation—*Continued*
Speaking out; hunting is a dirty business. B. Gilbert. Sat Eve Post 240:10+ O 21 '67
Time is short and the water rises, by J. Walsh and R. Gannon. Review
Newsweek il 70:68 Ag 21 '67. S. K. Oberbeck
Way of the dinosaur. Time 89:53 Mr 24 '67
Who should pay for conservation? Audubon 69:4 Jl '67
Wildlife management in Turkey. L. W. Swift. il Am For 73:34-5+ Je '67
Yellowstone wildlife in winter. W. A. Allard. il Nat Geog Mag 132:636-61 N '67
   See also
Animals—Protection
Bird sanctuaries
Birds—Protection

WILDLIFE Jewelry. See Jewelry
WILDLIFE photographs. See Animals—Photographs
WILDLIFE photography. See Photography of animals
WILDLIFE populations. See Animal populations
WILDLIFE sanctuaries
Great swamp is good for nothing,. but life, knowledge, peace and hope; Morris County, N.J. B. Atkinson. il N Y Times Mag p32-6+ F 12 '67; Discussion. p 14+ Mr 5 '67
It's elk-watching season; Hardware ranch elk refuge. il Sunset 139:47 D '67
Kenai national moose range. R. G. Smith. il Liv Wildn 30:24-32 Wint '66
Last great strand; Corkscrew swamp sanctuary. P. Matthiessen. il Audubon 69:64-71 Mr '67
Profiles: Great Swamp national wildlife refuge. A. Bailey. New Yorker 43:57-8+ Jl 29 '67
Refuge wilderness hearings. Nat Parks Mag 41:24 Ap '67
Udjung Kulon; Indonesia. il Life 63:80-91+ D 22 '67
We expect to win; Mason Neck, Va. M. A. Rock. il Nat Parks Mag 41:12-13 Je; 21 S '67
Wilderness ignored: the Aleutian Islands. M. Frome. il Audubon 69:28-40 Ja '67
Wilderness plan for the Moosehorn refuge; Washington County, Me. Nat Parks Mag 41:20-1 My '67
   See also
Bird sanctuaries
Game preserves
Nairobi National Park

   Roads
Roads in wildlife refuges. Liv Wildn 30:46 Aut '66
WILDLIFE services, Division of. See United States—Interior, Department of—Sport fisheries and wildlife, Department of
WILDLIFE telemetry. See Biotelemetry
WILDMAN, John Hazard
Like a dying tree; poem. Commonweal 86:423 Je 30 '67
WILDMAN, S. G. See Chen, J. L. jt. auth.
WILE, Raymond R.
Edison recordings of Marie Rappold. Hobbies 72:36+ My; 36+ Je '67
WILENSKY, Harold L.
Impact of change on work and leisure; excerpt from address. Mo Labor R 90:21-2 S '67
WILENTZ, Joan
Canadian booksellers: a coming of age. Pub W 191:55-7 Je 19 '67
WILEY, George Alvin
Poor power. Nation 204:228-9 F 20 '67
WILEY, Marcia
Cabin talk. See issues of Yachting
Waterfront news. See issues of Yachting
WILGRAM, George F. See Chian, L. T. Y. jt. auth.
WILHELM, Eugene J. Jr
Park for Patagonia. Am For 73:32-3+ D '68
Return of the elk to Appalachia. Nat Parks Mag 41:16 Ja '67
WILHELMS, Fred T.
Which way to a curriculum for adolescents? NEA J 56:12-15 D '67
WILHELMSEN, Frederick D.
Perpetual itch. Nat R 19:916-17 Ag 22 '67
Speaking out. por Sat Eve Post 240:10+ Jl 15 '67

WILHITE, Lynn
Consummation; poem. Commonweal 87:55 O 13 '67
WILKEN, D. F. and Guither, Harold
Oats compete with corn? Suc Farm 65:98 F '67
WILKERSON, Rick
Rick Wilkerson: top goblin. E. Horan. il por Yachting 121:61 Ja '67
WILKES-BARRE, Pa.
Moving the mikveh. S. J. Ungar. Commentary 44:89-91 S '67
WILKINS, Maurice
Double helix; the discovery of the structure of DNA; excerpts, with editorial comment. J. D. Watson. il por Atlan 221:76-94+ Ja '68 (to be cont)
WILKINS, Roy
Way to racial peace in America; interview. pors U S News 63:80-6 S 25 '67
   about
Roy Wilkins. Mr Civil Rights. I. Ross. por Read Digest 92:86-91 Ja '68
WILKINSON, Charles B. and Atwater, J. D.
Diet you can live with; and exercises you might even enjoy; excerpts from Guide to modern physical fitness. por Look 31:99-100+ O 17 '67
WILKINSON, David T. See Peebles, P. J. E. jt. auth.
WILKINSON, Eugene P.
Where are they now? pors Newsweek 69:10 Ja 30 '67
WILKINSON, Stephan
Learning to fly. Holiday 41:101-6 Je '67
WILKS, Sally
Little by little we created a privacy. por Home Gard 54:68-70 Mr '67
WILL, Frederic
Three for the age; Bomarc; It depends; Ubi terrarum? poems. Commonweal 86:203 My 5 '67
   about
Four poets. H. Carruth. Poetry 111:43-5 O '67
WILL, Hubert L.
Crime and coverage. New Repub 157:34-7+ S 2 '67
WILLAMETTE RIVER
Pollution in the West: industry struggles with pollution problems. A. Netboy. il Am For 73:8-11+ Jl '67
WILLARD, Charlotte
Art: drawings from hell. Look 31:78+ F 21 '67
Art in motion. Look 31:48-50 Ap 18 '67
WILLATT, Norris
Last gold rush. Duns R 90:41-3+ S '67
Paint your wagon. Duns R 89:59+ Mr '67
Power push at PG&E. Duns R 90:39-40+ Ag '67
School where cars are born. Duns R 89:45-6+ Ap '67
Switch at Southern Pacific. Duns R 90:47-8+ O '67
Tall man in the saddle. Duns R 90:35-6 Jl '67
WILLCOX, Donald J.
Guide to writers' conferences. Writer 80:46-8 Ap '67
Robert Bourdon, blacksmith in wrought iron. Am Artist 32:32-7 Ja '68
WILLCOX, William
Growing pains of the multiversity. Atlan 220:45-7 Jl '67
WILLEM Alexander, prince of the Netherlands
After 116 years, a plump little Dutch prince. S. Mahoney. il pors Life 62:46-46A My 12 '67
WILLEMOËS, Peter
Recordist Peter Willemoës and other royal Danes. R. Naur. il por Hi Fi 17:14+ Ap '67
WILLEY, Harold, Jr
Luck of the Willeys. por Outdoor Life 140:56-7+ D '67
WILLIAM Addison Dwiggins award
New England book show, books tour the region; award to Burton Jones. Pub W 191:90+ Mr 6 '67
WILLIAMS, Andre
Marine's longest night. J. R. Moskin. il pors Look 31:30-5 My 2 '67
WILLIAMS, Andy
Boy in the mansion next door. L. Williams. il pors Look 31:84-91 S 19 '67
WILLIAMS, Ashbel C.
Let's close our tragic cancer gap. Todays Health 45:88+ Ap '67

WILLIAMS, Billy
Baseball's gentle iron man. D. Llorens. il
pors Ebony 22:50-2+ Jl '67
WILLIAMS, Carroll M.
Third-generation pesticides; with biographical
sketch. Sci Am 217:10, 13-17 Jl '67
—See Riddiford, L. M. jt. auth.
WILLIAMS, Charles
Thomas Cranmer of Canterbury. Criticism
Holiday 42:99-100+ Ag '67
WILLIAMS, Charles R.
Regional management overseas. Harvard Bsns
R 45:87-91 Ja '67
WILLIAMS, Dave
Dauntless Dave. J. Underwood. il pors Sports
Illus 26:64-9+ Je 19 '67
WILLIAMS, Dick
Slight revival of hope in Boston. J. Jares. il
pors Sports Illus 26:66-8+ My 15 '67
Virtue is rewarded. M. Mulvoy. il Sports
Illus 27:12-17 Ag 21 '67
WILLIAMS, Dudley
Brief biography. S. Goodman. pors Dance
Mag 41:58-9 Mr '67
WILLIAMS, Edward Bennett
Winning loser. il por Time 89:66+ F 10 '67
WILLIAMS, Everard M.
Innovation in undergraduate teaching. bibliog
Science 155:974-9 F 24 '67
WILLIAMS, Francis S.
Mutual funds under fire: their side of the
dispute; interview. por U S News 63:80-2
S 18 '67
WILLIAMS, George Huntston
To be perfectly frank. America 116:452-3
Mr 25 '67
WILLIAMS, George L.
School censorship in Fascist Italy and the
U.S. bibliog f Sch & Soc 95:185-8 Mr 18
'67
WILLIAMS, George Washington
Notes on George W. Williams. W. A. Page.
por Negro Hist Bul 30:12 O '67
WILLIAMS, Gerhard Mennen
Excerpt from address, January 28, 1966. Cong
Digest 46:90+ Mr '67
WILLIAMS, Gray, Jr
Making of In memory of my feelings. Pub W
193:60+ Ja 1 '68
WILLIAMS, Hosea L.
Homesick in freedomland. il por Newsweek
69:37-8 F 13 '67
WILLIAMS, J. Harvie
Excerpt from testimony before Subcommittee
on constitutional amendments, May 16, 1967.
Cong Digest 46:279+ N '67
WILLIAMS, James A.
Savannah silver and silversmiths. Antiques
91:347-9 Mr '67
WILLIAMS, Janet M. See Williams. T. C. jt.
auth.
WILLIAMS, Joan
Pariah; story. McCalls 94:80-1 Ag '67
You-are-thereness in fiction. Writer 80:20-1+
Ap '67
WILLIAMS, John A.
Negro; three families. Holiday 41:58-61+ Mr
'67
This is my country too: a pessimistic post-
script. Holiday 41:8+ Je '67
WILLIAMS, John M.
Man overboard! Yachting 121:82+ My '67
WILLIAMS, L. Pearce
Michael Faraday and the physics of 100 years
ago; excerpts from Michael Faraday, a
biography. bibliog Science 156:1335-42 Je 9
'67
WILLIAMS, Lawrence
Girl with the hometown look; story. Good H
165:90-1 S '67
Matter of living; story. Redbook 129:64-5
Jl '67
Pride of my heart; story. Good H 164:92-3
My '67
Treasure; story. Good H 164:92-3 Mr '67
WILLIAMS, Lloyd
On Max Born's reflections. Bul Atomic Sci
23:27-8 F '67
WILLIAMS, Lucille Pickett
Why Meredith quit the race with Powell.
U S News 62:16 Mr 27 '67
WILLIAMS, M. Woodbridge
Dive at Buck Island. Nat Parks Mag 41:4-7
Ag '67
WILLIAMS, Martin
Jazz and the vibraphone. Sat R 50:78-9 N
11 '67

Mostly modernists (cont) Sat R 50:120 Mr 11;
75 Ap 29; 77 My 13; 91 Je 10; 49 Jl 15;
45 Jl 29; 81 Ag 26; 71 S 30; 59 D 2 '67
WILLIAMS, Melvin G.
Martin Luther: portraits in prose. Christian
Cent 84:1366+ O 25 '67
WILLIAMS, Miller
Done to his mistress; poem. Sat R 50:31 Mr
25 '67
Widow; poem. Sat R 50:35 Ap 1 '67
WILLIAMS, Mona Strader (Bush) See Bis-
marck, M. S. B. W.
WILLIAMS, Norman, Jr
(ed) Zoning and planning decisions. See Is-
sues of American city
WILLIAMS, Paul
Face to face with the editor of a rock and
roll magazine. pors Seventeen 26:159 Ap '67

about

Crawdaddy! por Newsweek 70:114 D 11 '67
WILLIAMS, Ralph. See McCarty, J. E. jt.
auth.
WILLIAMS, Ralph Vaughan. See Vaughan
Williams, R.
WILLIAMS, Raymond
Britain's press crisis. Nation 204:466-7 Ap 10
'67
Letter from London. Nation 205:51-2 Jl 17 '67
WILLIAMS, Robert Franklin
How red China stirs U.S. racial strife. il
por U S News 63:11 S 4 '67
Portrait of a wretched man. M. Renek. New
Repub 157:11-13 S 30 '67
WILLIAMS, Robin M. Jr
Individual and group values. bibliog f Ann
Am Acad 371:20-37 My '67
Recent developments in research on social in-
stitutions. bibliog f Ann Am Acad 374:171-
84 N '67
WILLIAMS, Suzanne
Face to face with a girl who has gone to
jail for what she believes. por Seventeen
26:153+ S '67
WILLIAMS, Ted
Going fishing with the Kid. J. Underwood.
il pors Sports Illus 27:60-70 Ag 21 '67
WILLIAMS, Tennessee
Kingdom of earth; text. Esquire 67:98-100+
F '67

about

Glass menagerie. Criticism
Sat R 50:71 N 25 '67
Rose tattoo. Criticism
Nat R 19:99 Ja 24 '67
Two character play. Criticism
Time il 90:63 D 22 '67
WILLIAMS, Thomas
Outdoors. Esquire 68:190+ O '67
WILLIAMS, Timothy C. and Williams, J. M.
Radio tracking of homing bats. bibliog Sci-
ence 155:1435-6 Mr 17 '67
WILLIAMS, Toni
Touring the big top. il pors Ebony 23:53-4+
D '67
WILLIAMS, W. H. A.
Wexford. Opera N 32:14-17 O 14 '67
WILLIAMS, Wesley Samuel
First Negro president of the D.C. Board of
education: Wesley S. Williams. il por Negro
Hist Bul 29:177-8+ Fall '66
WILLIAMS, William Appleman
Cold-war revisionists. Nation 205:492-5 N 13
'67
WILLIAMS, William Carlos
Art as redemption. S. P. Zitner. Poetry 111:
41-2 O '67
WILLIAMS brothers company
Profits from a pigmy. Fortune 75:326 Je 15
'67
WILLIAMS engine company, incorporated
Will steamers make it back on auto market?
il Bsns W p85-6 D 9 '67
WILLIAMSBURG, Va.
Agreement relating to the painting of the
St George Tucker house; contract of 1798.
il House B 109:42 My '67
Colonial Williamsburg. A. Stagg. il House &
Gard 131:52+ My '67
Color discovery in Williamsburg. M. Gough.
il House B 109:167-71 My '67
Well worth the trip. M. Gough. House B
109:161 F '67

Churches

Daffy datelines for a critical sermon; incident
at Bruton parish church. H. Sidey. il Life
63:38B N 24 '67

WILLIAMSBURG, Va.—*Continued*

Historic houses, etc.
Twelfth night in Williamsburg, circa 1780. P. Hyde and J. L. Hendrix. il House B 109: 270-3 N '67

Music
Music for the celebration of Twelfth night in the manner of colonial Williamsburg. House B 109:108-9 N '67

WILLIAMSBURG student burgesses. See Forums (discussion and debates)

WILLIAMSON, Bruce
Life movie review. Life 62:8 F 24; 17 Ap 28; 18 My 26 '67
Life TV review. Life 62:25 Ap 7 '67

WILLIAMSON, Claire
What happens when you drink. Redbook 129: 62-3+ Jl '67

WILLIAMSON, Dereck
Block that thrip! Sat R 50:8-9 Ap 1 '67
Current happenings. Sat R 50:8+ D 9 '67
Nab blonde, 8, as a porridge thief. Sat Eve Post 240:18 My 20 '67

WILLIAMSON, Donald G.
So you think you're indispensable. il por Nations Bsns 55:56-8+ D '67

WILLIAMSON, Hugh
Quality in book production; address, September 20, 1967. Pub W 192:80+ O 2 '67

WILLIAMSON, John D.
Women, and boats. Motor B 120:82 S '67

WILLIAMSON, Malcolm
Australian parenthesis. Time 90:78+ S 8 '67
Britain's avant-garde. P. L. Miller. Am Rec G 33:623 Ap '67
Records:
    Happy prince. Opera N 31:34 F 11 '67
Sophisticated children's opera. P. L. Miller. Am Rec G 33:518 F '67
Violins of St Jacques. Criticism
    Hi Fi il 17:MA26-MA27 F '67

WILLIAMSON, René de Visme
Reformation and American political life. Christian Cent 84:1343-5 O 25 '67

WILLIAMSON, Robert L. and Metcalf, R. L.
Salicylanilides: a new group of active uncouplers of oxidative phosphorylation. bibliog Science 158:1694-5 D 29 '67

WILLIAMSON, Ruth Lundgren
Companionway. See issues of Motor boating

WILLIAMSTOWN, Mass.
    See also
Sterling and Francine Clark art institute

WILLINGHAM, John R.
Class of '67: the gentle desperadoes. Nation 204:779 Je 19 '67

WILLIS, Benjamin Coppage
Chicago: legacy of an ice age; excerpt from Our children's burden. C. Remsberg and B. Remsberg. il por Sat R 50:73-5+ My 20 '67; Discussion. 50:50+ Je 17 '67

WILLIS, Charles Fountain, 1918-
Flying with Dan McGrew. il por Newsweek 70:78 D 11 '67

WILLIS, Ellen
Rikki cuts out. Sat Eve Post 240:35 Je 3 '67
Sound of Bob Dylan. Commentary 44:71-8 N '67

WILLIS, James E.
We send out bills in envelopes automatically. Am City 82:149+ O '67

WILLIS bill. See Communism—United States—Anti-Communist measures

WILLITS, John M.
Disadvantaged youth employed by Washington state parks. por Parks & Rec 2:34+ Ap '67

WILLMENT, Frank
Whites of their eyes; drama. Plays 26:89-95 F '67

WILLOW Brook (historic house) See Baltimore —Historic houses, etc.

WILLOW ptarmigans. See Ptarmigans

WILLOWS, A. O. D.
Behavioral acts elicited by stimulation of single, identifiable brain cells. bibliog Science 157:570-4 Ag 4 '67

WILLRICH, Mason
International control of civil nuclear power. Bul Atomic Sci 23:31-8 Mr '67

WILLS, Garry
Buckley, Buckley, bow wow wow. Esquire 69:72-6+ Ja '68
Ghostly wisdom. Nat R 19:369-71 Ap 4 '67
Lachrymose Mr Manchester. Nat R 19:591-2 My 30 '67
To a ghost about ghosts. Nat R 19:1077+ O 3 '67

—and Demaris, Ovid
Disposal of Jack Ruby. Esquire 67:131-5+ Je '67
Svetlana papers. Esquire 68:99-106+ N '67
You all know me! I'm Jack Ruby! Esquire 67:79-87+ My '67

WILLS, Maury
They may have been a headache but they never were a bore. B. Bavasi and J. Olsen. il pors Sports Illus 26:30-4+ My 29 '67

WILLS, Sidney Hayward
General acceptance, looking around for trouble. il por Fortune 75:152-4+ F '67

WILLS, W. W.
City-county transit district. Am City 82:101+ Ap '67

WILLS
Do you need a will? J. D. Bierman. Parents Mag 42:42+ S '67
Inheritance of headaches; dispute over will of Alice Byron Atwood. il Time 90:81-2 N 10 '67
Nine questions to ask before you make a will; with answers. N. G. P. Krausz. Farm J 91:92-3 Mr '67
Searching for the soul; will of James Kidd. il Time 89:63 Je 23 '67
Soul searchers all; will of James Kidd. il Newsweek 69:43 Je 26 '67
Strange quest of James Kidd. D. J. Hamblin. il Life 62:76-8+ Mr 3 '67
What you need to know about handling your estate. il U S News 62:64-70 F 13 '67
    See also
Inheritance

WILMERDING, John
George Caleb Bingham: a new find. Antiques 92:556-7 O '67

WILMORE, Rex
What's behind that salmonella scare. Farm J 91:27+ Ja '67

WILNER, Herbert
Long live the king. Sat Eve Post 240:85-9 N 18 '67
Zen basketball, etc. at San Francisco state. Esquire 68:98+ S '67

WILPERT, Czarina
Look in the mirror and over the wall. Commonweal 86:224-5 My 12 '67
Shadow of the concordat. Commonweal 86:333-4 Je 9 '67

WILSHIRE, Roy
Computer puts more go on city streets. Am City 82:116+ N '67

WILSON, Allan C. and others
Enzymatic identification of fish products. bibliog Science 157:82-3 Jl 7 '67
—See Sarich, V. M. jt. auth.

WILSON, C. M. and Alexander, D. E.
Ribonuclease activity in normal and opaque-2 mutant endorsperm of maize. bibliog Science 155:1575-6 Mr 24 '67

WILSON, Charles McMoran, 1st baron Moran. See Moran, C. M. W.

WILSON, Dick
China's economic situation. Bul Atomic Sci 23:3-8 N '67

WILSON, Edmund
Books. New Yorker 43:231-2+ D 9 '67
Dr McGrath; text. Commentary 43:60-7 My '67
Profiles; memoirs. New Yorker 43:50-2+ Ap 29; 52-4+ My 6; 54-6+ My 13 '67
Reporter at large. New Yorker 43:38-40+ Ag 19 '67

    about
Critic with a sacred calling. T. Solotaroff. Life 62:10 Je 23 '67
Edmund Wilson: his life and books. A. Kazin. por Atlan 220:80-3 Jl '67
Interpreter of modern consciousness. G. Hicks. Sat R 50:17-18 Jl 1 '67

WILSON, Edward O. and others
First mesozoic ants. bibliog Science 157: 1038-40 S 1 '67

WILSON, Ernest Henry
Ernest H. "Chinese" Wilson, the man and his plants. D. S. Manks. il pors Horticulture 45:28-30 N '67

WILSON, Eugene S.
Fair educational practice act is dead. Sat R 50:85-6 S 16 '67

WILSON, George
Fiji's flying financier and PR man. por Bsns W p88 S 16 '67

WILSON, George C.
But don't tell anyone I told you. S. M. Hersh. New Repub 157:13-14 D 9 '67

WILSON, Gertrude
 I'm not a flag-waver, but I've learned a
  lot! McCalls 94:34+ Ag '67
WILSON, H. W, company
 Educational research and the hidden author.
  J. W. Keating. Sch & Soc 95:350-1 O 14 '67
 Wilson company changes. Wilson Lib Bul
  41:661-2 Mr '67
  See also
 Readers guide to periodical literature
WILSON, Harold
 Common market; address, May 8, 1967. Vital
  Speeches 33:482-94 Je 1 '67
 Remarks by Prime Minister Wilson. Dept
  State Bul 56:963-4 Je 26 '67

  about

 After the fall. Time 90:23-4 D 1 '67
 Atlantic report. Atlan 219:22+ F '67
 Bitter aftertaste. il por Time 90:18 D 29 '67
 Can Cabinet shake-up cure Britain's ills?
  por U S News 63:36 S 11 '67
 Clobbering of Harold Wilson. P. Crane. Amer-
  ica 116:683 My 6 '67
 Craving for substance. Newsweek 69:46-7 Ap
  3 '67
 D for indefensible? Newsweek 70:83-4 Jl 17
  '67
 De Gaulle, non! Britain's application to join
  the Common market. A. Lejeune. Nat R
  19:637+ Je 13 '67
 Facing facts. Newsweek 70:40+ S 11 '67
 Fast shuffle at 10 Downing. C. Brogan. il
  Nat R 19:1065-6 O 3 '67
 Four U.S. teenagers meet Britain's Prime
  Minister. R. Hemming. il por Sr Schol 91:
  17 D 14 '67
 Jeers from the ranks. Newsweek 70:51-2 S
  18 '67
 Labor turns on Wilson. America 117:290 S
  23 '67
 Letter from London (cont) M. Panter-
  Downes. New Yorker 43:80+ Ag 19; 226-8+
  N 11; 150-3 D 2; 49-50+ D 23 '67
 Libel and the P.M. Newsweek 71:47 Ja 15 '68
 Moment of daring. il por Time 90:23 S 8
  '67
 Outbluffing the outraged. Time 90:36-7 O 13
  '67
 Prime Minister sues. Time 91:28 Ja 12 '68
 Question of character; accuses Colonel Lohan.
  Time 90:31-2 Jl 7 '67
 Sea of troubles. Newsweek 69:56 Mr 13 '67
 Signs of a break in U.S.-British ties. il por
  U S News 62:14 F 6 '67
 Three pragmatists. W. Lippmann. Newsweek
  69:29 My 8 '67
 Wilson barks back. Time 89:36 Mr 10 '67
WILSON, Helen Van Pelt
 Beauty of a long-range plan. Home Gard
  54:56-8 My '67
 Day-lilies are her delight. Home Gard 54:37
  Jl '67
 Here is a garden that began with a plan.
  Home Gard 54:32-4 Mr '67
 Regional report. Home Gard 54:82 My '67
 To grace a wall or window. Home Gard 54:
  48-9 Ag '67
WILSON, Henry Hall, 1921-
 How to succeed. il por Newsweek 69:27 Mr
  20 '67
 New job, old territory. il por Time 89:91-2
  Mr 17 '67
WILSON, Hugh
 British Virgin Islands. Travel 127:42-5 My
  '67
WILSON, J. Tuzo
 Advice for the Establishment; excerpt from
  address. Sat R 50:50-1 S 2 '67

  about

 Canada's unappreciated roles as scientific
  innovator; with excerpts from address. J.
  Lear. il por Sat R 50:45-50 S 2 '67
WILSON, Jack
 Classic action at a vintage auction. Motor T
  19:74-7 Ap '67
WILSON, James Q.
 Guide to Reagan country: the political cul-
  ture of southern California. Commentary
  43:37-45 My; 44:22+ S '67
WILSON, James W.
 Botanist in the vegetable garden. Horticulture
  45:18-19+ Jl '67
WILSON, Jane
 Cop art. Esquire 68:87-9 Jl '67
WILSON, Jesse R.
 One of a kind. Christian Cent 84:687-8 My 24
  '67

WILSON, John
 Hamp; dramatization of novel by J. L. Hod-
  son. Criticism
   America 116:508+ Ap 1 '67
   New Yorker 43:123 Mr 18 '67
   Time il 89:62 Mr 17 '67
WILSON, John S.
 Folk music. Hi Fi 17:136 Ja '67
 Jazz. See issues of High fidelity incorporating
  Musical America
WILSON, Johnny
 Short trip up the river. Motor B 120:35-7 O '67
 Southward ho. See issues of Motor boating
WILSON, José
 Going places, finding things in Montreal and
  Toronto. House & Gard 132:20+ Ag '67
WILSON, Joseph Chamberlain
 Profiles; Xerox corporation, formerly Haloid
  company. J. Brooks. il New Yorker 43:46-
  50+ Ap 1 '67
WILSON, Joseph Ruggles
 Thomas Woodrow Wilson, by S. Freud and
  W. C. Bullitt. Review
   New Repub 156:27-30 Ja 28 '67. R. Coles
   New Yorker 42:111-14+ Ja 21 '67. G.
   Steiner
WILSON, Keith
 From Graves registry; Note to a sister;
  Classes; poems. Poetry 109:302-9 F '67

  about

 Landscape and language. R. Sward. Poetry
  109:407-8 Mr '67
WILSON, Kemmons
 Homely hints on how to make $90 million.
  il por Newsweek 69:60-1 Je 26 '67
WILSON, Kenneth M.
 Documenting some Mt. Washington art glass.
  Antiques 92:367-71 S '67
WILSON, Lanford
 Rimers of Eldritch. Criticism
   America 116:354-5 Mr 11 '67
   New Yorker 43:132+ Mr 4 '67
   Sat R 50:30 Mr 11 '67
   Time il 89:52 Mr 3 '67
WILSON, Lois E.
 Classroom graphics. Sch Arts 67:22-3 O '67
WILSON, Merna
 Your technique is showing. Writer 80:19-21
  Ja '67
WILSON, O. H. See Scriver, C. R. jt. auth.
WILSON, O. Meredith
 Rapport, basic ingredient for teaching; ex-
  cerpts from Summer education for children
  of poverty. NEA J 56:31-3 Ap '67
WILSON, Orlando Winfield
 Criminology lesson. por Newsweek 69:32-3 My
  29 '67
 Professional policeman. B. Davidson. pors
  Holiday 41:13-17+ Mr '67
WILSON, P. M.
 Build this handy arc-welding gun. Pop Sci
  190:149-51 F '67
WILSON, Peter M.
 High rise on the low lands. Motor B 121:110-
  12 Ja '68
WILSON, R. B. and Cooney, A. M.
 Western Australia's Mundrabilla meteorite
  Sky & Tel 33:72-3 F '67
WILSON, R. W. and Penzias, A. A.
 Isotropy of cosmic background radiation at
  4080 megahertz. bibliog Science 156:1100-1
  My 26 '67
WILSON, Robert Wesley
 Nouveau Frisco. Time 89:66-7+ Ap 7 '67
WILSON, Robley, Jr
 Maine: the lobster; Maine: from the Mid-
  west; The bachelor; poems. Reporter 37:
  50+ O 5 '67
 Rocking chair; poem. Atlan 220:109 N '67
 Weekends at the cove; poem. Reporter 37:62
  Jl 13 '67
WILSON, Samuel Vaughan
 On target. il por Newsweek 69:40-1 Mr 20
  '67
WILSON, Scott
 Two unknowns seek movie fame as killers;
  In cold blood. S. Gordon. il pors Look 31:
  114+ Je 13 '67
WILSON, T. A.
 Expanding jet age; address, October 9, 1967.
  Vital Speeches 34:88-92 N 15 '67
WILSON, Thelma C. and Niehans, Ken
 Better health for all babies. Parents Mag 42:
  68-9+ N '67
WILSON, William
 Explosion that never went boom. Sat R 50:
  54-6 S 23 '67
 House of a thousand treasures. House B 109:
  124-7+ F '67

WILSON, William Edward
Maryland, their Maryland. Am Heritage 18: 8-19+ Ag '67
WILSON, William Henry
Wilson of Addessograph Multigraph. por Fortune 76:59 O '67
WILSON, Woodrow
There ought never to be another presidential nominating convention; excerpts from letter, February 5, 1913. U S News 63:124 O 23 '67

about

Can history use Freud? the case of Woodrow Wilson. B. W. Tuchman. Atlan 219:39-44 F '67
Case for Woodrow Wilson. A. S. Link. Harper 234:85-8+ Ap '67
Freudian analysis founders on Wilson book. P. McBroom. il por Sci N 91:88-9 Ja 28 '67
Thomas Woodrow Wilson, by S. Freud and W. C. Bullitt. Review
Nat R 19:307-8+ Mr 21 '67. T. S. Szasz
New Repub 156:27-30 Ja 28 '67. R. Coles
Newsweek il por 69:92-3 Ja 30 '67. S. Maloff
Time il por 89:82-3 Ja 27 '67
Wilson, Bullitt, Freud. R. Moley. Newsweek 69:104 F 20 '67
Woodrow Wilson, by H. W. Bragdon. Review New Repub 157:32-3 D 23 '67. C. N. Degler
WILSON library bulletin
See also
John Cotton Dana publicity awards
WILTED lettuce salad. See Salads
WILTON, Conn.
We discovered our town. J. Robbins and J. Robbins. il Read Digest 90:88-91 My '67
WINANS, Sarah S.
Visual form discrimination after removal of the visual cortex in cats. bibliog Science 158:944-6 N 17 '67
WIMBLEDON tennis tournaments. See Tennis
WINCHESTER, Alice
Canadian chronology in brief, 1605-1867. Antiques 92:62-5 Jl 17 '67
WINCHESTER, James H.
Britain's bonanza at the bottom of the sea. Read Digest 91:138-43 Ag '67
How drugs can control blood pressure. Read Digest 91:143-6 D '67
Medical miracles in South Vietnam. Pop Sci 191:70-3+ Jl '67
Medicine's dramatic strides against burns. Read Digest 90:177-80+ Ap '67
Rescuing newborns with minisurgery. Todays Health 46:52-6 Ja '68
Sailing schools. Travel 127:32-6 My '67
Sweden's strenuous ski scramble. Read Digest 90:107-10 F '67
Tough angel of the battlefield. Todays Health 45:30-3+ My '67
Try a farm vacation. Read Digest 90:19-20+ My '67
Weight watching for wanderers. Travel 128: 49-51 N '67
WIND, Herbert Warren
Sporting scene (cont) New Yorker 42:102+ F 4; 43:138+ Ap 29; 56-8+ Jl 8; 94+ S 30 '67
WIND instruments
Orchestra in opera: play of the winds. R. Lawrence. il Opera N 32:13-16 D 16 '67
Orchestra in opera: ring of the brasses. R. Lawrence. il Opera N 32:10-13 D 23 '67
WIND mills. See Windmills
WIND RIVER wilderness area. See Wilderness areas—Wyoming
WIND tunnels
Moving probe used at AEDC wind tunnel. il Aero Tech 21:35 N 6 '67
WINDASS, Stanley
Christians and violence. Commonweal 86:11-13 Mr 24 '67
WINDHAUSEN, John D.
Religion in Russia: the status of Christians. Nat R 19:1174-5 O 31 '67
WINDMILLER, Marshall
Scholars and soldiers, a crisis of values. Nation 205:651-4 D 18 '67
WINDMILLS
Windmill Island; Windmill Island city park, Holland, Mich. H. H. Holt. il Am For 73: 24-6+ D '67
Windmills. B. Finnegan. il Hobbies 71:118-19 F '67
WINDOW curtains and draperies. See Curtains and draperies

WINDOW gardening
Garden room. il Flower Grower 54:26-7+ Ja '67
To grace a wall or window. H. V. Wilson. il Home Gard 54:48-9 Ag '67
WINDOW glass. See Glass
WINDOW shades
Care of window shades. E. Taylor. il Good H 165:227 S '67
Window wizardry. il House & Gard 131:128-39+ Mr '67
WINDOWS
Bay windows add space, increase light. il House & Gard 131:144-5 F '67
Continuing study of the window wall by Eliot Noyes. il Arch Rec 141:173-80 Ap '67
Do something spectacular with ordinary windows! P. Rumely and C. Garner. il Bet Hom & Gard 45:64-9 O '67
Dress up your windows. il Am Home 70:136 Mr '67
New windows and doors slide on air. W. E. Burton. il Pop Sci 190:158-9 Ap '67
Window wizardry. il House & Gard 131:128-39+ Mr '67
See also
Curtains and draperies
Glass painting and staining
Skylights
WINDS
Nature note; foehn. Sci N 91:483 My 20 '67
Nature note; sirocco. Sci N 91:516 Je 3 '67
Opal phytoliths in a North Atlantic dust fall. D. W. Folger and others. bibliog il Science 155:1243-4 Mr 10 '67
Out of a clear blue sky; gales at Sand Pit, Lloyds Neck, Long Island. F. Nostrand. il Yachting 122:42-3+ O '67
Santa Ana; hot wind in Los Angeles. J. Didion. Sat Eve Post 240:20+ Ag 26 '67
See also
Hurricanes
Tornadoes
WINDS, Solar. See Solar radiation
WINDSHIELDS (airplane) See Airplanes—Windshields
WINDSOR, Edward, duke of. See Edward VIII, king of Great Britain
WINDSOR, Wallis (Warfield) duchess of
Return of Britain's prodigal prince. il por U S News 62:23 Je 19 '67
WINDWARD ISLANDS. See West Indies
WINE
Bread & wine. il McCalls 94:102-7 Mr '67
Choosing the wine for the bird. J. A. Beard. House & Gard 131:126+ Je '67
Corkscrew: offbeat wines for dinner for two. H. Johnson. House & Gard 131:172+ Ap '67
Drink and be merry, by V. Holland. Review Nat R 19:974+ S 5 '67. A. Waugh
Five prima donnas of the wine world. C. Churchill. il House B 109:150-1+ Mr '67
Golden grape; California wines. Newsweek 70:113-14 D 18 '67
New and views; Christian Brothers wine. J. Deedy. Commonweal 87:458 Ja 19 '68
No debate: the wines of California. H. Johnson. Vogue 150:32+ Ag 15 '67
Palatinate, pick of the lot. T. Prittie. il Atlan 220:116-18 S '67
Sherry. H. Johnson. House & Gard 131:148+ F '67
Smart way to buy wine; excerpts from Wine. H. Johnson. House & Gard 132:202+ S '67
Traveler's guide to the native drinks and wines of Italy. R. Neville. House & Gard 131:178+ Mr '67
Who will have a sherry? use of the word sherry. il Time 89:93 Mr 3 '67
Wine primer; excerpts from The world of wines. C. Churchill. House B 109:58+ Jl '67
Wines of America. A. Waugh. Nat R 19:528+ My 16 '67
Wines of the Rhine and the Moselle. H. Johnson. House & Gard 133:126+ Ja '68
Wines to drink young. A. Bespaloff. House & Gard 132:260+ N '67
See also
Cookery—Wine
Grapes

Advertising

Issue at the bar; court decision on use of name "Sherry." il Newsweek 70:74 Ag 14 '67

Anecdotes, facetiae, satire, etc.

My life with the grape (nut) G. Greene. il Sat Eve Post 240:16 Mr 11 '67

History

Search for a good wine. M. A. Amerine; reply. R. D. Gerard. Science 155:951 F 24 '67

WINE as gifts
Gift of cheer. W. Clifford. il House B 109: 163+ D '67
WINE auctions. See Auctions
WINE cellars
Good living begins in the wine cellar. G. Burck. il Fortune 75:122-9 Je 1 '67
WINE racks
Wine racks in new shapes and sizes. il House & Gard 131:46-7 Ap '67
WINE trade
Gospel of the grape; France's foremost wine exporter. il Newsweek 69:98+ My 29 '67
New York's vintners take a bigger sip. il Bsns W p52-4 D 23 '67
Subtle shift; New York producers. il Time 89:67 Ja 27 '67
WINFIELD, Kan.
Contact stabilization saves a million dollars, R. L. Brown. il Am City 82:89-91 Mr '67
WING, Jill
Climb far, climb high. pors Seventeen 26: 90-1+ Jl '67
WING shooting. See Shooting
WINGERTER, Robert G.
U.S. tariff & trade policies; address, July 11, 1967. Vital Speeches 34-28-32 O 15 '67
WINGO, Hal
In five minutes everyone on this ship became a man. Life 63:22 Ag 11 '67
WINICK, Charles
Drug addiction and crime. bibliog f Cur Hist 52:349-53+ Je '67
WINKLEPLECK, R. L.
Build the incredible VFO. Pop Electr 26:69-71 Ap '67
NBFM routs 6-meter TVI. Pop Electr 26:73-6 F '67
Stamp out auto theft. Pop Electr 26:59-61 Mr '67
WINN, Chester H.
Seaway stretch. Travel 127:46-9 My '67
WINNICK, Pauline
It's the latest, it's the greatest, it's the li-ber-ee. Am Ed 3:5-7 Je '67
—and Horn, W. A.
Liaison librarian. Am Ed 4:26-7 D '67
—and Lyman, H. H.
Library services to the disadvantaged and handicapped. bibliog f ALA Bul 61:1065-74 O '67
WINNIPEG, Manitoba
And the melody lingered on. B. Ottum. il Sports Illus 27:18-21 Ag 14 '67
Winning ways of Winnipeg. J. Underwood. il Sports Illus 27:20-5 Ag 7 '67
WINOGRAD, Barry. See Simmons, J. L. jt. auth.
WINSEY, H. Stuart, and Folkman, Judah
Silicone rubber: oxygen, carbon dioxide, and nitrous oxide measurement in gas mixtures. bibliog Science 157:203-4 Jl 14 '67
WINSHALL, Walter
Wide, wide world of Walter Winshall. por Time 89:76 Je 23 '67
WINSOR, Harry B.
Becoming your own landlord. PTA Mag 62: 24-6 Ja '68
WINSTEAD, Warren J.
Novel ideas at Nova U. il por Time 89:58 Je 30 '67
WINSTON, Alexander
Firebrand of the revolution. Am Heritage 18:60-4+ Ap '67
WINSTON, Harry
Huge diamonds becomes family's best friend. il por Ebony 23:112-15 Ja '68
WINSTON-SALEM, N.C.
Old Salem. A. Stagg. il House & Gard 131:20+ Je '67
WINSTONE, Howard
Vicente bored in but Ernie merely bored. B. Ottum. Sports Illus 27:66-8 O 23 '67
WINTER, Edward
Firing glass enamels on aluminum. por Design 68:12-16 Mr '67
Making a copper enamel bowl. Design 69:23-8 Fall '67
WINTER, Gibson
Parishfield community. Christian Cent 84: 776-8 Je 14 '67
WINTER, Otto R.
Setting up a small-city purchasing system. Am City 82:168+ Je '67
WINTER, Ruth
Somebody had to be first. Todays Health 45: 66-9 Ap '67
WINTER
See also
December
Snowstorms

WINTER bouquets. See Flowers, Dried
WINTER camping. See Camping
WINTER carnivals. See Carnivals
WINTER fishing. See Fishing, Winter
WINTER gardening
If you want a winter-blooming garden. il Good H 165:186 S '67
See also
Window gardening
WINTER Olympics, 1968. See Olympic games, 1968
WINTER proofing. See Houses—Maintenance and repair
WINTER resorts
For the big snows, go West; Snowmass-at-Aspen. il Time 90:57 D 22 '67
Good life in the Ponderosa; Incline Village developments, Nevada. H. Sutton. il Sat R 50:51-2+ O 21 '67
In search of winter golf. C. Price. il Holi-day 42:119-24 N '67
Letter from Vail, Colorado. C. Lindsay. Holi-day 43:26+ Ja '68
Skiing in Chile; photographs by R. Rowan. Holiday 41:72-7 F '67
Skis, bikes, polo and $$$; Snowmass, Colo. il Sports Illus 28:24-7 Ja 8 '68
Snowmass. il Newsweek 70:65 D 25 '67
See also
Aspen, Colo.
Sun Valley, Idaho
WINTER sports
Winter is my memory season. M. Holmes. il Todays Health 45:24-7+ D '67
See also
Coasting
Ice boats and ice boating
Skis and skiing
Toboggans and tobogganing
WINTER sports, Photography of. See Photog-raphy of sports
WINTER travel. See Travel
WINTER vacation cabins. See Cabins
WINTER vacations. See Vacations
WINTERICH, John Tracy
Book collecting, anyone? Sat R 50:129-30+ Mr 11 '67
Criminal record. See last issue of each month of Saturday review
—and Glixon, D .M.
(ed) Your literary I.Q. See issues of Saturday review
WINTERKILL; story. See Ford, J. H.
WINTERNATIONALS. See Automobile rac-ing
WINTERNITZ, Adolfo
Stone, iron, wood, poverty, truth. C. Rod-riguez Saavedra. il Américas 19:22-6 My '67
WINTERS, Jonathan
Silly putty. por Newsweek 71:50-1 Ja 15 '68
WINTERS, Robert
Canada and the United States; address, October 31, 1966. Vital Speeches 33:214-17 Ja 15 '67
WINTERTHUR gardens. See Gardens—Dela-ware
WINTERTHUR museum. See Henry Francis Du Pont Winterthur museum
WINTON, Kay Grogan
Hamburger, thrifty, versatile, sure to please. Parents Mag 42:70-1+ Ja '67
WIRE, Howard R. See Forbes, R. jt. auth.
WIRE jewelry. See Jewelry
WIRE sculpture
Creative fun with wire sculpture; Suji kit. il Design 68:9-11 Sum '67
Wrap it up. G. F. Brommer. il Sch Arts 67: 12-15 N '67
WIRE tapping
I wonder who's bugging us now. Christian Cent 84:956-7 Jl 26 '67
Intruders, by E. V. Long. Review Reporter 36:50-1 Ap 20 '67. A. Clymer
Taking out the bugs. Reporter 36:12+ Ja 26 '67
Taps, bugs & spies; anything to get Hoffa; new evidence and Chattanooga trial. F. J. Cook. il Nation 204:230-6 F 20 '67
Why not Hoffa? Nation 204:132 Ja 30 '67
Wiretapping and eavesdropping; pros and cons. H. Schwartz. bibliog f Cur Hist 53: 31-7 Jl '67
WIRE tools. See Tools
WIRELESS telegraph. See Telegraph, Wireless
WIREMAN, Billy O.
Man behind the word; address, May 6, 1967. Vital Speeches 33:692-4 S 1 '67

WIRETAPPING. See Wire tapping

WIRING, Electric. See Electric wire and wiring

WIRTZ, William Willard
Excerpt from statement, July 13, 1966. Cong Digest 46:10+ Ja '67

WISCASSET, Me.
Holiday discovery of the month. il Holiday 42:90-1 O '67

WISCONSIN
See also
Crime and criminals—Wisconsin
Finance—Wisconsin
Fishing—Wisconsin
Hunting—Wisconsin

Historic houses, etc.
History in houses: West, the Old Indian agency house. P. M. Stone. il Antiques 91:768-71 Je '67

WISCONSIN. University, Madison
Building to walk through. il Arch Forum 127: 60-3 O '67

On Wisconsin; faculty and police vs students during anti-Dow chemical demonstrations. J. Ridgeway. New Repub 157:8-10 N 4 '67

WISDOM
Reward and promise; Louis Bouyer's explanation of the significance of the Mary-Wisdom theme and the Assumption of Mary. V. P. McCorry. America 117:inside back cover Ag 12 '67

WISE, Bill
Nothing like creatures for creature comfort. Life 62:76-9 F 3 '67

Out hunting or fishing 100 days a year. Life 63:104 D 8 '67

Sabbath in the Sinai for Israeli tourists. Life 63:30-30A Ag 11 '67

WISE, David
Hidden hands in publishing. New Repub 157: 17-18 O 21 '67

—and Ross, T. B.
Espionage establishment; excerpt. Sat Eve Post 240:29-31+ O 21; 50-3+ N 4; 76-80+ N 18 '67

WISE, Dorothy
Grandma shot out the lights. T. O'Leary. il por Sports Illus 27:52-4 Jl 10 '67

WISE, Harold
Doctors meet the people. M. K. Sanders. Harper 236:56-62 Ja '68

WISE, T. A.
Bristol-Meyers' hard sell. Fortune 75:118-21+ F '67

Hill & Knowlton's world of images. Fortune 76:98-101+ S 1 '67

How McDonnell won Douglas. Fortune 75: 155-6+ Mr '67

WISE men of the East. See Magi

WISEMAN, Frederick
Stripped bare at the follies. R. Coles. New Repub 158:18+ Ja 20 '68

Tempest in a snakepit. il por Newsweek 70: 109 D 4 '67

Titicut follies. America 117:539 N 11 '67

WISH for an afternoon; story. See Bonham, M.

WISHING tree; story. See Faulkner, W.

WISHING wells. See Wells

WISTER, Gertrude S.
Uncommon bulbs next fall. Horticulture 45: 18-21+ Ap '67

WIT and humor. See Humor

WITCHCRAFT
Black arts, by R. Cavendish. Review
Newsweek il 70:66+ Ag 21 '67. S. K. Oberbeck

WITCOVER, Jules
Fulbright's prospects. New Repub 156:4-5 Je 10 '67

George Romney: battered but unbowed. Sat Eve Post 240:38-42 D 2 '67

George Romney's road-show Hamlet. Reporter 36:36-7 Mr 23 '67

George Wallace isn't kidding. Reporter 36: 23-5 F 23 '67

Nixon for president in '68? Sat Eve Post 240: 93-7 F 25 '67

Nixon: the reentry problem. New Repub 156: 11-12 Je 17 '67

Preview of Wallace's appeal to the North. New Repub 156:9-10 My 27 '67

WITHHOLDING tax
Personal business; how to save more pay for your pocket. Bsns W p 141-2 Ja 21 '67

WITKIN, Richard
Why the flak around the F-111. N Y Times Mag p32-5+ Ap 2 '67

WITMER, Jack R.
Midwesterner cruises east. il Yachting 122: 52-4+ D '67

WITNESSES
Credible psychopath. Time 89:40 Ja 27 '67
Noninvolvement, British style; apathy toward crime. il Time 90:49 Ag 18 '67
Should paid witnesses say so? witnesses at congressional hearings paid by tobacco industry. il Bsns W p 168+ S 9 '67
When defendants testify. Time 90:51 N 3 '67
See also
Evidence (law)
Perjury

WITNESSES; story. See Waring, M. W.

WITONSKI, Peter P.
Literary historian awash. Nat R 19:1214-16 O 31 '67
London. Nat R 19:265-6 Mr 7 '67
Perverse peer. Nat R 19:592-4 My 30 '67
Report on the quarterlies. Nat R 19:431-4 Ap 18 '67

WITT, Harold
Dinosaurs; poem. New Repub 157:21 D 16 '67

WITTFOGEL, Karl A.
Guest critic of China. Nat R 19:149-52 F 7 '67

WITTGENSTEIN, Ludwig
Russell and Wittgenstein. M. Frayn. Commentary 43:68-75 My '67

WITTIG, Jörg
Superconductivity of metallic aluminum antimonide. bibliog Science 155:685-6 F 10 '67

WITTMAN, Charles W.
Operation Sunshine. Am Artist 31:27-31 F '67

WITTNER, Dale
Killing of Billy Furr, caught in the act of looting meat. Life 63:21-2 Jl 28 '67

WITTY, Helen S.
From seeds to stately gardens. Sat R 50:48-9 N 25 '67
Fun and fancy of growing herbs. Home Gard 54:40-8 My '67
Season's fare. See issues of Flower grower, the home garden (cont as) Home garden & flower grower

WIVES
High cost of success; reprint. J. Barnett. il Sci Digest 62:26-9 O '67

How to be a good wife; with discussion group program, by E. G. Neisser. D. R. Mace. il Parents Mag 42:24+, 44-5+ F '67

Perfect wife. C. Carney. il Redbook 129:12+ S '67

When father's a traveling man. C. Levine. il Parents Mag 42:54-5+ Je '67

When wives confide in friends, are marriages helped, or harmed? S. Blum. il Redbook 128:70-1+ Mr '67

Worth of a wife. B. Vaughan. Read Digest 91:206 N '67

Young wife's world. H. Valentine. See issues of Good housekeeping
See also
Ambassadors wives
Governors wives
Husbands
Marriage

WIVES, Common law. See Marriage, Common law

WIXOM, Hartt
How to fish high lakes. Outdoor Life 140:42-3+ Ag '67

WOBBLIES. See Industrial workers of the world

WODEHOUSE, P. G.
Very fond of dogs. Holiday 42:24+ Ag '67

WOESTENDIEK, William J.
Freedom to travel. il por Newsweek 69:54 F 27 '67

WOETZEL, Robert K.
Genesis of crime. Cur Hist 52:321-6 Je '67

WOHLERS, H. C. See Jackson, W. E. jt. auth.

WOHLFORTH, Robert
Depression made lively. Nation 205:474-6 N 6 '67

WOHLSTETTER, Albert
Illusions of distance. bibliog f For Affairs 46: 242-55 Ja '68

WOIWODE, L.
History lesson; story. New Yorker 43:47-50 S 30 '67
On this day; story. New Yorker 43:44-9 S 9 '67
Pheasants; story. New Yorker 43:62-6 N 18 '67

WOJTUSIK, Henry J.
You have to want industry. Am City 82:86-7
D '67
WOLF, David
Big-leaguer big in the boondocks. Life 63:
28-31 S 1 '67
about
Baseball expertise put to good use. G. P.
Hunt. il por Life 63:3 S 8 '67
WOLF, Edwin, 2d
Cultural relic of colonial America. por Wilson
Lib Bul 41:569-72 F '67
WOLF, John B.
Arab refugee problem. bibliog f Cur Hist 53:
352-8+ D '67
WOLF, M. J. and others
Subcellular structure of endosperm protein
in high-lysine and normal corn. bibliog
Science 157:556-7 Ag 4 '67
WOLF, Peter
First modern urbanist. Arch Forum 127:50-5
O '67
WOLF, Peter, associates
Set to go. J. Ardoin. il Opera N 31:6-7 Mr 18
'67
WOLF, Robert E.
Politics of conservation. Am For 73:45 Ja '67
WOLF hunting
Diving for wolves in ice water. B. Gilbert.
il Sports Illus 26:62-6+ F 20 '67
Family of white wolves; with report by S.
Wayman. il Life 62:50-7+ Je 2 '67
WOLFE, Bernard
Ten percenters of Hollywood. N Y Times Mag
p26-8+ Je 18 '67
WOLFE, Henry C.
Saga of a deadly dynasty. Sat R 50:27 Ag 19
'67
WOLFE, L. S. See Derry, D. M. jt. auth.
WOLFE, Thomas
Thomas Wolfe arrives; excerpts from Thomas
Wolfe, A. Turnbull. Atlan 220:60-6 D '67
Thomas Wolfe's Berlin. C. H. Holman. il
por Sat R 50:66+ Mr 11 '67
WOLFE, Thomas K.
How you can be as well-informed as Tom
Wolfe. Esquire 68:138+ N '67
Pause, now, and consider some tentative
conclusions about porno-violence. Esquire
68:59+ Jl '67
WOLFE, Thomas W.
Soviet military policy at the fifty year mark.
bibliog f Cur Hist 53:208-16+ O '67
WOLFE, Tom. See Wolfe, T. K.
WOLFENSBERGER, Wolf
Ethical issues in research with human sub-
jects. bibliog Science 155:47-51, 1618 Ja 6,
Mr 31 '67
WOLFERT, Ira
Chickens: cheaper by the million. Read Digest
91:97-100 Ag '67
Global jet-away. Travel 128:65-6+ N '67;
Same abr. with title What it's like to fly
around the world. Read Digest 91:219-20+
N '67
Library for all the Nation. Read Digest 91:
235-41 D '67
WOLFF, Bernard P.
Bridges. il U S Camera 30:68-9 Je '67
WOLFF, Charles
Optical environment about the OGO-III satel-
lite. bibliog Science 158:1045-6 N 24 '67
—and others
Photography of the earth's cloud satellites
from an aircraft. bibliog Science 157:427-9
Jl 28 '67
WOLFF, J. See Larsen, P. R. jt. auth.
WOLFF, Kurt
Designer's corner. S. Salter. Pub W 191:110
F 6 '67
WOLFF, Max
Educational park concept. por Wilson Lib
Bul 42:173-5+ O '67
WOLFF, Philippe
Dawn of the geographic spirit. UNESCO
Courier 20:14-15 My '67
Numerals open new mathematical horizons.
UNESCO Courier 20:11 My '67
WOLFLE, Dael
Policing the consequences of science. J. Lear.
Sat R 50:65-7 D 2 '67; Discussion. 51:104-5
Ja 6 '68
WOLFMAN, Augustus
Wolfman on printing. See issues of Modern
photography
WOLFSON, Albert. See Sayler, A. jt. auth.
WOLFSON, Louis Elwood
Downed eagle. Time 90:104 D 8 '67
Verdict on Wolfson. Newsweek 70:81+ O 9 '67

WOLMAN, Harold
Mrs Governor faces the feds. Commonweal
86:192-3 My 5 '67
WOLMAN, Jerry
Dark skies for Philadelphia's no. 1 Eagle. il
por Bsns W p 100 D 9 '67
In deep water. por Time 90:103 N 24 '67
Woman's woes. por Newsweek 70:82-3 N 27
'67
WOLPERT, Stanley
Today in Tel Aviv. Nation 205:7-8 Jl 3 '67
WOLSELEY, Garnet Joseph Wolseley, viscount
Model of a modern major general delivered
the decisive blow. E. Kern. il por Life 63:
64-5 O 6 '67
WOLTERS, Larry
Cradle of 10,000 babies. Todays Health 45:47-8
Ag '67
WOLVES
Family of white wolves; with report by S.
Wayman. il Life 62:50-7+ Je 2 '67
Mike Frome; voices of wolves in Algonquin
Provincial Park, Ontario. M. Frome. Am
For 73:5+ Ja '67
Old regularity. S. P. Young. il Am For 73:
34+ Ap '67
Strychnine caper. S. P. Young. il Am For
73:20-3+ Je '67
Strychnine onslaught. S. P. Young. il Am
For 73:32-3+ Jl '67
Wolves were the worst. O. A. Fredrickson. il
Outdoor Life 139:60-1+ Je '67
Photographs
See Animals—Photographs
WOLVES, Photography of. See Photography of
animals
WOMAN
New femininity. Vogue 149:88-9+ Ja 15 '67
On being a woman. J. Brothers. See issues
of Good housekeeping
See also
Beauty, Personal
Marriage
Mothers
Sex differences
Single women
also headings beginning Women
Anecdotes, facetiae, satire, etc.
Feminine mistaque. A. Bouchwald. il Read
Digest 91:55-6 O '67
My career as a girl-watcher. R. Armour. il
Read Digest 91:21-2+ Ag '67
Crime
Jail birds; photographs by Melvin Sokolsky.
Esquire 68:64-6 Jl '67
Diseases
Disease: symptoms and treatment of the
most common female disorders. il Good H
164:138-40 Ja '67
Dress
See Clothing and dress
Education
See Colleges for women
Employment
After graduation, a job in New York? A.
Grant. il Mlle 65:144-5+ Je '67
Calling it quits. M. A. Brice. Mlle 64:192-3+
Ap '67
Low blow for the working girl; amused press
reaction to dismissal of clerks in 1869 from
Treasury department. E. M. Halliday. il
Am Heritage 18:98-9 Ap '67
Sex and equal employment rights. Mo La-
bor R 90:III-IV Ag '67
Women college graduates seven years later.
J. A. Wells. il Mo Labor R 90:28-32 Jl '67
See also
Married women—Employment
Woman—Equal rights
Woman—Occupations
Equal rights
Draft declaration on the elimination of dis-
crimination against women; discussion in
United Nations third committee. UN Mo
Chron 4:37-9 N '67
General assembly adopts Declaration on the
elimination of discrimination against
women; recommended by Third committee,
with text. UN Mo Chron 4:82, 113 D '67
How much of a man's world is it? D. Klein.
il Seventeen 26:210+ N '67

WOMAN—Equal rights—*Continued*
Is it now or never for women? C. B. Luce. McCalls 94:48+ Ap '67
No revolution for the woman of Algiers. F. Lewis. il N Y Times Mag p28-9+ O 29 '67
111 cheers for womankind. J. F. Fixx. McCalls 95:5 Ja '68
Seminar on civic and political rights of women; United Nations. UN Mo Chron 4: 69-70 Ag '67

Health and hygiene
Latest medical facts about your most intimate health concerns. il Good H 164:135-48 Ja '67
Redbook guide to the health problems of young women. A. Lake. Redbook 129:21-8 S '67
See also
Beauty, Personal
Menopause

Legal status laws, etc.
See also
Woman—Equal rights

Occupations
How much of a man's world is it? D. Klein. il Seventeen 26:210+ N '67
Styles in educated females. T. McCormack. Nation 204:117-18 Ja 23 '67
See also
Business and professional women
Models (persons)
Negro women—Occupations
Nurses and nursing
Secretaries
Woman—Employment

Professions
See Woman—Occupations

Psychology
American woman's dilemma: love, self-love, no love. H. Rosenberg. Vogue 149:162-3 My '67
Are women basically unco-operative? M. Mead. Redbook 130:32+ Ja '68
Birth control and your emotions. J. Brothers. il Good H 165:50+ Jl '67
Blue Mondays and what to do about them. J. Brothers. il Good H 165:46+ N '67
Hidden habits of women; facts about home accidents. C. B. Hicks. il Todays Health 45:28-31+ D '67
Is feminine psychology justified? H. Gavin and K. O'Hara. Cath World 205:282-5 Ag '67
Man talk; *les misérables.* D. Newman and R. Benton. Mlle 65:12 Jl '67
On being a woman. J. Brothers. See issues of Good housekeeping
Sexual roles being reversed, says psychiatrist; theories of Ralph R. Greenson. Todays Health 45:85 Ap '67
World that the American woman has invented for herself. A. West. Vogue 149: 234-6 My '67

Quotations, maxims, etc.
Collections by Chanel; women and their world; tr. by J. Barry. G. Chanel. McCalls 94: 12 Je; 44 Jl; 40 Ag; 54 S; 95:24 O; 72 D '67

Rights of women
See Woman—Equal rights

Social and moral questions
California woman: her amazing sexual freedom. G. R. Bach. Ladies Home J 84:63+ Jl '67
Women in a contraceptive culture. P. Koval. Commonweal 87:381-2 D 22 '67
See also
Divorce
WOMAN as president. See Women as public officers
WOMAN who gave of herself; story. See Bayer, A.
WOMAN without a shadow; opera. See Strauss, R.
WOMAN'S Christian temperance union
Can the forces of virtue defeat John Barleycorn? W. Kloman. il Sat Eve Post 240:85-9 Mr 11 '67
WOMEN
Sisters under the skin. P. Swiggum. Farm J 91:55 Ag '67

Photographs
Guide to some special birds; photographs from J. d Green's book Birds of paradise. Life 63:79-81+ N 24 '67

Africa
Way to Rehema's house, by H. Spencer. Review
Sat R 50:28-9 D 23 '67. N. W. Ross

Algeria
No revolution for the woman of Algiers. F. Lewis. il N Y Times Mag p28-9+ O 29 '67

France
Courtesans: the demi-monde in 19th century France, by J. Richardson. Review
Newsweek il 70:105-6 P. D. Zimmerman

Germany (Federal Republic)
He, she, it; frau status for unmarried women over age of thirty. J. Gould. Atlan 220:91 Ag '67

Great Britain
Guide to some special birds; photographs from J. d Green's book Birds of paradise. Life 63:79-81+ N 24 '67

Hungary
Girls of Budapest. S. Kirkland. il Life 63:82+ D 8 '67

India
On the role of women. G. D. Berreman; reply with rejoinder. S. A. Durrani. Bul Atomic Sci 23:28-9 Mr '67
What it's like to be a girl in India today. J. Baer. il Seventeen 26:136-9+ F '67

Israel
When my mother, Rachel, went down to Jericho. R. Dayan. McCalls 94:24+ S '67

Kenya
Kenya report: market in brides. L. Fellows. il N Y Times Mag p 12+ F 19 '67

Latin America
Latin America's Methodist women. M. Barber. Christian Cent 84:247-8 F 22 '67
Women as citizens; conference with advice from Overseas education fund of the League of women voters of the United States. C. F. Ware. il Américas 19:26-30 D '67

Saudi Arabia
On being a sheik's wife. A Shammout. il Sat R 50:71-2+ O 14 '67

United States
American woman 1967. il Vogue 149:159-67+ My '67
Battle of the sexes is over, who won? we did. il Ladies Home J 84:66+ F '67
California woman; symposium. il Ladies Home J 84:61-81+ Jl '67
Freckled superwoman; concerning Ladies' home journal report on California women. Time 90:67 Jl 28 '67
How to be a California girl; Robynne Hoover's regimen. R. J. Kaiser. il Look 31:M20-2+ D 26 '67
I was free! trapped housewife. N. E. Sephton. il Redbook 129:10+ O '67
New American woman; the L.A. woman. il Esquire 67:57-62+ F '67
O blessed deviation. N. Rambusch. Commonweal 86:363-6 Je 16 '67
On the role of women. G. D. Berreman; reply with rejoinder. S. A. Durrani. Bul Atomic Sci 23:28-9 Mr '67
Young mothers answer back: you don't have to feel trapped! letters; with editorial comment. Redbook 129:61, 116-18+ Jl '67
See also
Divorce—United States
Married women—Employment
Negro women

Vietnam (Republic)
Power set. F. Fitzgerald. Vogue 149:154-5+ F 1 '67
Vietnamese woman; excerpt from Ten Vietnamese. S. Sheehan. McCalls 94:48+ Mr '67
WOMEN, Famous
Face of the hour: the strong face. il Vogue 150:154-9 O 1 '67

WOMEN, Famous—*Continued*
Where did babies come from? famous women recall how they learned the facts of life. S. Birmingham. il McCalls 94:65+ S '67
See also
Celebrities
WOMEN, Negro. See Negro women
WOMEN, Tall. See Stature
WOMEN and men
Battle of the sexes. F. R. Schreiber and M. Herman. il Sci Digest 61:22-4 Ap '67
Battle of the sexes is over, who won? we did. il Ladies Home J 84:66+ F '67
Battle of the sexes; reversal of male-female roles. il Newsweek 70:52 Ag 7 '67
Charming a man; ten men discuss what turns them on. Mlle 65:50-1+ Jl; 253+ Ag '67
F. Lee Bailey; a new breed of hero; interview, ed. by M. McLaughlin. F. L. Bailey. Mlle 65:64-5+ Jl '67
Girls, or boys, who needs them? F. Nelson. il Nat R 19:1067-9 O 3 '67
Husband hunting? the chances. U S News 63:68 O 2 '67
Man talk; ways women test men. D. Newman and R. Benton. Mlle 64:88 Ap '67
What a man really wants in a woman. J. Brothers. Good H 164:58+ F '67
What makes boys so different. A. Lake. il Seventeen 26:108-9+ O '67
Why so many husbands feel inadequate. R. J. Levin. il Redbook 129:61+ S '67
Why women are so much smarter than men. J. Susann. Ladies Home J 84:97+ N '67
WOMEN and politics
Politics on the split-level frontier; Jocelyn Marchisio from Seattle. J. Poppy. il Look 31:94+ My 16 '67
State department's poetic powerhouse; K. Louchheim. H. Ehrlich. il Look 31:118+ O 17 '67
Women as citizens; conferences with advice from Overseas education fund of the League of women voters of the United States. C. F. Ware. il Américas 19:26-30 D '67
Women who make state laws; Negro women holding state legislative posts. il Ebony 22:27-30+ S '67
See also
Women as public officers
WOMEN and religion
Women in the world of religion, by E. T. Culver. Review
Christian Cent 84:345 Mr 15 '67. M. Frakes
WOMEN and the church
O blessed deviation. N. Rambusch. Commonweal 86:363-6 Je 16 '67
Woman intellectual and the church; symposium. Commonweal 85:446-56+ Ja 27 '67; Discussion. 85:611+ Mr 3 '67
See also
Church women united (organization)
WOMEN and war
See also
Israeli-Arab war, 1967—Women and war
Vietnamese war, 1957- —Women and the war
WOMEN as air pilots
I completed Amelia Earhart's flight. A. H. Pellegreno. il McCalls 95:48+ N '67
Skirts flying. S. Buegeleisen. See issues of Flying
WOMEN as architects
Sun maiden architect; Dutch girl builds schools for Mexico's Indians. il Life 63:103-4+ O 13 '67
WOMEN as astronomers
Faces from the past: M. Mitchell. R. M. Ketchum. il Am Heritage 18:26-7 Ag '67
WOMEN as athletes
In Stratford, nobody beats the Raybestos Brakettes; Women's national softball tournament. C. Kirkpatrick. il Sports Illus 27:92-3 S 11 '67
Ladies first! il Sr Schol 90:20 Mr 3 '67
Mosaic in X & Y; Polish athlete barred on medical grounds. il Time 90:70 S 29 '67
Teen-ager on a comeback trail; M. Mulder at Los Angeles times indoor games. G. S. Brown. il Sports Illus 26:22-3 F 20 '67
Thank heaven for..; Fairfield girls' track team. B. Gilbert. il Sports Illus 27:72-4+ N 27 '67
Who goes there? Polish athlete fails sex test. Newsweek 70:97 S 25 '67
See also
Sports for women

WOMEN as authors
Face to face with a teen-age novelist. S. Hinton. Seventeen 26:133 O '67; Correction. 26:20 N '67
Lachrymose ladies; address, September 15, 1966. J. Manthorne. bibliog Horn Bk 43:375-84, 501-13. 622-30 Je-Ag, O '67
Not by bread alone... P. P. Leimbach. Farm J 91:101+ Mr '67
See also
Women as journalists
WOMEN as brokers
Poolside broker; F. Farkas. il Newsweek 70:70-1 Ag 14 '67
WOMEN as college professors and instructors
With a telling tongue. V. Voss. il Mlle 64:152-3+ Mr '67
WOMEN as engineers
Women engineers. Sci Digest 61:26 F '67
WOMEN as executives
How good are women bosses? il Changing T 21:15-17 Ap '67
WOMEN as foresters
Why I want to be a forester. D. J. Starr. Am For 73:6 Ag '67
WOMEN as guides. See Guides
WOMEN as journalists
Overheard in suburbia; editor. W. Hedgepeth. Look 31:88 My 16 '67
WOMEN as millionaires. See Millionaires
WOMEN as ministers
See also
American association of women ministers
WOMEN as novelists. See Women as authors
WOMEN as photographers
Thy name is woman. K. Tweedy-Holmes. il Pop Phot 61:69-72 O '67
WOMEN as physicians
Americans not everybody knows; E. Blackwell. N. Stack. il PTA Mag 61:26-7 F '67
Drop those prejudices against women doctors. A. Lake. Good H 164:88-9+ My '67
WOMEN as public officers
If I were president; sixteen famous women give their program for America. il McCalls 95:51-3+ Ja '68
WOMEN as reporters
I'll do anything. il Newsweek 69:58 F 13 '67
WOMEN as theatrical managers, etc.
Spotlight off-stage. A. Grant. Mlle 66:157+ N '67
WOMEN as travelers
First woman across Greenland's ice. M. Simpson. il Nat Geog Mag 132:264-79 Ag '67
WOMEN college graduates. See College graduates, Women
WOMEN golf players. See Golfers
WOMEN in airplane racing. See Airplane racing
WOMEN in automobile racing
Female and the fueler. J. McFarland. il Hot Rod 20:30-1 Mr '67
WOMEN in boating
Cabin talk. M. Wiley. See issues of Yachting
Companionway. R. L. Williamson. See issues of Motor boating
Girl watcher's gallery. P. Smyth. il Motor B 121:116-17 Ja '68
Girls before the mast: Culver military academy; Summer naval school. B. Kocivar. il Look 31:89-91 Je 13 '67
She sails while he drives; interview, ed. by S. Lowell. M. D. G. Muncey. il Motor B 120:44-5+ S '67
Women, and boats. J. D. Williamson. Motor B 120:82 S '67

Anecdotes, facetiae, satire, etc.
Interlude, enroute to a cup match. W. Richards. il Motor B 120:40+ S '67
WOMEN in fishing. See Fishing
WOMEN in politics. See Women and politics
WOMEN in sports. See Sports for women
WOMEN shoppers. See Shopping and shoppers
WOMEN'S clothes. See Clothing and dress
WOMENS clothing industry. See Clothing industry
WOMENS colleges. See Colleges for women
WOMEN'S national book association
WNBA holds cocktail party for its 50th anniversary. il Pub W 192:27 N 27 '67
WNBA's contribution to the community of books. C. B. Grannis. Pub W 192:29 N 27 '67
See also
Amy Loveman national award
Constance Lindsay Skinner award

WOMENS pages in newspapers. See News-papers—Womens pages

WOMENS periodicals. See Periodicals for women

WOMENS shoes. See Shoes

WOMEN'S wear daily
Shaking up Women's wear. il Time 90:46+ S 8 '67
Sly fox in fashion's chicken house; interview; ed. by D. Lurie. J. Fairchild. il Life 62:43-4+ Mr 17 '67

WONDERFUL town; musical comedy. See Musical comedies, revues, etc.—Criticisms, plots, etc.

WOOD, Abigail
Young living; questions and answers. See issues of Seventeen

WOOD, Frederic C. jr
Should birth control be available to un-married women? Good H 164:12 F '67

WOOD, Gar
Gar Wood: an old sea dog is up to new tricks. J. Fix. il pors Pop Mech 128:82-5+ Jl '67

WOOD, J. Edwin
Venous system; with biographical sketch. Sci Am 218:19, 86-8+ Ja '68

WOOD, James B.
Solid-state microphone transformer. Electr World 77:68 Mr '67

WOOD, James Playsted
Honest audience. Horn Bk 43:612-16 O '67

WOOD, John
R. and G. G. and R; interview. New Yorker 43:52 N 4 '67

WOOD, John R. jr
He oils the wheels at Clark equipment. por Bsns W p70-1+ Ap 15 '67

WOOD, Rawson L.
Big boom in profit sharing: what's back of it; interview. por U S News 63:64-6 Ag 28 '67

WOOD, Robert
Pajatén: a lost city found. Américas 19:7-16 Je '67

WOOD, Robert C.
Science to fix everything; do we need sophistication? excerpts from address, ed. by E. Goble. Arch Rec 142:9 Jl '67

WOOD, Thomas H.
Genetic recombination in escherichia coli: clone heterogeneity and the kinetics of segregation. bibliog Scence 157:319-21 Jl 21 '67

WOOD, William B. and Edgar, R. S.
Building a bacterial virus; with biographical sketches. Sci Am 217:10, 60-6+ Jl '67

WOOD
Wood on wood; in Norway, a great tradition. il House B 110:90-1 Ja '68
See also
Walnut trees

Diseases and pests
See also
Termites

WOOD, Fossil. See Trees, Fossil

WOOD as fuel
Now you're cooking on wood. E. W. Smith. il Field & S 71:56-7+ Mr '67

WOOD block prints. See Wood engravings

WOOD boxes. See Woodbins

WOOD carving
Artistry in wood. il House B 109:14+ D '67
Carpenter Gothic; work of H. C. Wester-mann. M. Friedman. il Art N 66:30-1+ Mr '67
Colorful candlestick birds. il Design 69:26-7 Wint '67
Louise Nevelson. D. Smith. il Craft Horiz 27:44-9+ My '67
Monkeypod business. B. Sigel. il Am For 73:34-6+ My '67
Riemenschneider rediscovered. A. Werner. il Am Artist 31:36-41+ D '67
Wood: George Sugarman. W. Castle. il Craft Horiz 27:30-3 Mr '67

WOOD chip mulch. See Mulching

WOOD construction
Wonderful world of wood. il Pop Gard 18:72-5 D '67

WOOD cuts. See Wood engravings

WOOD engravings
Genius of Rudolph Ruzicka. R. Nash. il Am Artist 31:44-50+ D '67
My woodcut technique. S. Hurwitz. il Am Artist 31:30-5+ My '67
Traveling collection of historic woodcuts. N. Kent. il Am Artist 31:26-31 D '67

WOOD finishing
Classic piano finish: most [ ] J. Hand. il Pop Sci 190:148-[ ]
Confetti coating for countertops [ ] LaBarge. il Pop Mech 129:168-7[ ]
How to refinish hardwood floors [ ] Schenley. il Pop Mech 129:188-90 J[ ]
Penetrating stain for rough and wea[ ] wood. il Consumer Bul 50:25 Ag '6[ ]
Smart tricks for finishing fir plywood. [ ] Hand. il Pop Sci 190:164-7+ F '67
Wonderful world of wood. il Pop Gard 18:74-5 D '67
Wood floor finishes. il Consumer Bul 50:31-3 N '67

WOOD floors. See Floors, Wood

WOOD-infesting beetles. See Beetles

WOOD lice
Amateur scientist; how to study learning in the sow bug. J. Frost. il Sci Am 216:142-3 My '67

WOOD paneling. See Paneling

WOOD pavements. See Pavements, Wood

WOOD pulp and paper mill waste. See Trade waste

WOOD pulp industry
Pollution in the West: industry struggles with pollution problems. A. Netboy. il Am For 73:8-11+ Jl '67

WOODBINS
Here is where the wood goes. il Sunset 138:124 F '67

WOODBLOCK printing. See Block printing

WOODCHUCK hunting
Peeking out a chuck hole. W. Page. Field & S 71:136-8 Ap '67
Wager on a woodchuck. C. Vinson. il Outdoor Life 139:64-5+ Ap '67

WOODCHUCKS
See also
Cookery—Game

WOODCOCK, George
Before chaos, one last chance. Commonweal 86:109-11 Ap 14 '67
Lessons through the barrel of a gun. Commonweal 86:81-4 Ap 7 '67
Moral man. Commentary 44:104-6+ O '67

WOODCOCKS
Waiting for the woodcock. H. Borland. il Audubon 69:56-7 Mr '67

WOODEN toys. See Toys

WOODFORD, F. Peter
Sounder thinking through clearer writing. Science 156:743-5 My 12 '67

WOODHOUSE, C. G.
Using tape to teach note-taking. NEA J 56:53 D '67

WOODHOUSE, Martin
Authors & editors. por Pub W 191:33 Ja 30 '67

WOODHULL, Victoria (Claflin) See Martin, V. C. W.

WOODLEY, Inez
My son, the shepherd; story. Redbook 130:52-3 D '67

WOODPECKERS
Ivory-bill flies still. J. V. Dennis. il Audubon 69:38-45 N '67
Ivory-billed woodpecker. Nat Parks Mag 41:20 O '67

WOODRING, Carl
Common axis of private lives. Sat R 50:42 N 4 '67

WOODRING, Paul
Editor's bookshelf. See issues of Saturday review
There'll be fewer little noses. Sat R 50:54-5 Mr 18 '67
View from the campus. Sat R 50:68 D 16 '67
—and Cass, James
(eds) Education in America. See issues of Saturday review

WOODRUFF, Maurice
Seer through a third eye. J. Howard. il pors Life 62:91-2+ Je 16 '67

WOODS, Arline
On the boards. W. Como. por Dance Mag 41:18 D '67

WOODS, David
View from the couch. Sat R 50:32+ Ag 12 '67

WOODS, Frank W. See Reid, C. P. P. jt. auth.

WOODS, George
To Mississippi in the interest of children and books. Wilson Lib Bul 41:1028-33 Je '67

February 1968

luxurious of all.
and floors, L.
Ja. '68 J P.
'68
thered

'67
: What the
r; Now the
e known for
-73 Mr '67

. Poetry 109:

ogical labora-

marine biol-
7:1288-92 S 15
'67

aphic institu-

nd MIT pool
r. il Science

hell. S. C. jt.

WOODSMEN
Last of the axmen. B. Geagan. il Field & S 71:60-1+ Mr '67
See also
Lumberjacks

WOODSON, Carter G.
Historian and scholar; poem. Negro Hist Bul 30:7 Mr '67

WOODSTOCK, N.Y.
Merry muses of Woodstock. il Holiday 42:56-9 N '67

WOODVILLE, Richard Caton, 1825-1855
Down from the attic. il Time 90:40-1+ S 1 '67
Gentlemanly genre; retrospective exhibition of work at the Corcoran gallery, Washington, D.C. F. Grubar. il por Art N 66:32-5 My '67

WOODWARD, Bliss
Under the blue ensign. See issues of Motor boating

WOODWARD, C. Vann
Confessions of a rebel: 1831. New Repub 157:25-8 O 7 '67
New politics. Commentary 44:92+ Jl '67
White man, white mind. New Repub 157:28-30 D 9 '67

WOODWARD stakes. See Horse racing

WOODWELL, George M.
Radiation and the patterns of nature; excerpts from address, March 24, 1965. bibliog Science 156:461-70 Ap 28 '67
Toxic substances and ecological cycles; with biographical sketch. Sci Am 216:19, 24-31 Mr; 8 Je '67
—and others
DDT residues in an East coast estuary: a case of biological concentration of a persistent insecticide. bibliog Science 156:821-4 My 12 '67

WOODWIND instruments. See Wind instruments

WOODWORKING
Wood sunburst: symphony in wood; gift table for F. E. Hornaday. il Am For 73:36-8 Ap '67
See also
Joints (carpentry)

Projects

Build a bar just for the fun of it. W. C. Leckey. il Pop Mech 128:136-42 Ag '67
Build this butterfly-trestle table. W. C. Lammey. il Pop Mech 127:172-4 F '67
Build this sleekly styled split-level typing desk. M. Banister. il Pop Mech 129:156-9+ Ja '68
Christmas gifts from your workshop. il Pop Mech 128:176-80 N '67
Five new woodworking projects. il Pop Sci 190:160-4 Mr '67
Five winter workshop projects. il Pop Sci 190:142-7 Ja '67
Handsome and distinctive. W. C. Lammey; C. L. Widdicombe; J. E. Reppert. il Pop Mech 129:162-7 Ja '68
How to build a coffee-table music center. H. V. Huston. il Pop Sci 191:129-33+ Ag '67
New coverings for your floors. il Pop Sci 191:166-7 S '67
Quickie copying stand from plywood scrap. P. Wahl. il Pop Mech 128:128-9 Ag '67
Two coffee tables out of the past. J. Payne; H. Wicks. il Pop Sci 191:120-3 Jl '67

Two one-evening quickies; artist's-palette sandwich board, and stay-in-view card file. il Pop Sci 192:144 Ja '68
Walk the ball. M. H Slutz. il Pop Mech 128:142-3 D '67
Weekend projects for your home. il Pop Mech 127:146-50 Je '67
Weekend projects for your home. A. Lambrecht and others. il Pop Mech 128:132-5 Ag '67
Weekend projects from textured hardboard. il Pop Mech 128:150-3+ O '67
What you can make with counter-top cut-outs. H. Wicks. il Pop Sci 191:114-17 N '67
Wordless workshop. R. Doty. See issues of Popular science monthly
Workshop wonders; colorful storage racks, toy cabinet, mice-people and doll's house. il Bet Hom & Gard 45:56-8 D '67
See also names of projects, e.g. Candlesticks

WOODWORKING machinery
See also
Routing machines

WOODWORTH, Mary L.
Searching for the library's participation in education. Wilson Lib Bul 41:947-8 My '67

WOODYARD, David O.
Campus concerns. Christian Cent 84:110-12 Ja 25 '67

WOOL, Ira G. See Low, R. B. jt. auth.

WOOL dyeing. See Dyes and dyeing

WOOLCOCK, Penny
Curl up and read. Seventeen 26:96 F '67

WOOLDRIDGE, William O.
Army's topmost sarge. il pors Life 63:51-2+ S 22 '67

WOOLEN and worsted fabrics
How to care for washable woolens. Am Home 70:109 Ja '67

WOOLEN and worsted finishing
No-wrinkle for wools; permanent press woolens. Bsns W p 132 Ja 28 '67

WOOLEN and worsted mills

Wages and hours

Earnings in wool yarn and broadwoven fabric mills, 1966. E. J. Caramela. il Mo Labor R 90:59-62 Je '67

WOOLF, Leonard Sidney
Books. W. Maxwell. New Yorker 43:63-4+ D 23 '67
Letter from London; B.B.C. presentation in random recollections to M. Muggeridge. M. Panter-Downes. New Yorker 43:164+ Ap 15 '67
Thorn for triflers and dictators. L. Edel. Sat R 50:55-6 N 25 '67
To the Woolf house. S. Poss. Nation 204:187-8 F 6 '67
Twilight in Bloomsbury. J. M. Edelstein. New Repub 157:26+ N 25 '67

WOOLF, Virginia (Stephen)
Downhill all the way, by L. Woolf. Review New Yorker 43:63-4+ D 23 '67. W. Maxwell

WOOLFOLK, E. O. and Smith, L. S.
Chemical education in Negro colleges. Negro Hist Bul 30:7-11 F '67

WOOLLEN, Evans
Recent work of Evans Woollen. il Arch Rec 141:140-50 My '67

WOOLSON, Edwin A. See Nash, R. G. jt. auth.

WOOLY thymes. See Thymes

WOOMERA missile range. See Proving grounds

WOOSTER, Harold
Books and libraries in the scientific age; adaptation of address, January 9, 1967. bibliog por Library J 92:2511-15 Jl '67

WOOTTON, Barbara Frances (Adam) baroness of Abinger. See Wootton of Abinger, B. F. A.

WOOTTON of Abinger, Barbara Frances (Adam) baroness
Champion of the impossible dream. B. D. Diamonstein. Sat R 50:50+ Je 10 '67

WORCESTER, Donald E.
(comp) Articles and other books received; Latin America. See issues of American historical review

WORD blindness
Shadow children, by C. Ellingson. Review Sat R 50:72 D 16 '67. E. W. Colvin
When film is film. il Newsweek 70:48 Jl 31 '67

WORD tests. See Vocabulary tests

WORLD council of churches—*Continued*
To speak or not to speak; meeting in The Hague. America 116:671 My 6 '67
Unity at Uppsala; assembly to consider universal implications of unity. Christian Cent 84:739-40 Je 7 '67
Uppsala 1968. Christian Cent 84:707-8 **My 31** '67
Uppsala-bound. G. Murray. Christian Cent 85:59 Ja 10 '68
What happened at Geneva; World conference on church and society. Christian Cent 84: 494 Ap 19 '67
World council and world; annual meeting of churches' Central committee. H. E. Fey. Christian Cent 84:1151-2 S 13 '67
WCC: preparation for 1968. America 117:730 D 16 '67
World council; radical reorganization in information interpretation and publishing services. G. Murray. Christian Cent 84:1410 N 1 '67
WORLD cup matches. See Golf—Tournaments
WORLD economic unity. See International economic integration
WORLD economics. See Economic conditions
WORLD festival of Negro arts. See Festivals—Senegal
WORLD flights. See Aviation—World flights
WORLD food program. See Food supply
WORLD food supply. See Food supply
WORLD fund. See International monetary fund
WORLD government. See International organization
WORLD health assembly
World drug law sought. D. A. Ehrlich. Sci N 91:566 Je 17 '67
WORLD health organization
Babel at WHO. Sci N 91:545 Je 10 '67
City sickness. Sci N 91:522 Je 3 '67
Health research: a small start for an international center. J. Walsh. Science 155:1088-90 Mr 3 '67
River blindness afflicts 200,000,000; biological-medical-social attack on black flies. D. A. Ehrlich. il Sci N 92:16-17 Jl 1 '67
U.S. to aid WHO in developing drug reaction reporting system. Dept State Bul 56:918-19 Je 19 '67
World health: bad. D. A. Ehrlich. Sci N 91:481+ My 20 '67
WHO aims at worms. D. A. Ehrlich. Sci N 92:115 Jl 29 '67
WHO begins research; division of epidemiology and communications science. D. A. Ehrlich. Sci N 92:130 Ag 5 '67
WHO takes on smallpox. Sci N 91:574 Je 17 '67
See also
World health assembly
WORLD health service (proposed)
World health service proposed by Ciba head. Sci N 91:431 My 6 '67
WORLD jet aircraft, incorporated
World jet agreement to sell PD-808 in U.S. is cancelled. Aviation W 86:21 F 20 '67
WORLD journal tribune, New York
Death in the afternoon; New York's WJT folds. il Bsns W p40-1 My 13 '67
Death of the widget. F. J. Cook. Nation 204: 645-6 My 22 '67
Gone and forgotten. S. Kauffmann. New Repub 156:24+ My 27 '67
Life and death of a great newspaper. F. C. Shapiro. il Am Heritage 18:97-112 O '67
Look, Manchester sue N.Y. World journal tribune. Pub W 191:53 F 13 '67
New processes and old stupidity. R. L. Tobin. Sat R 50:94 Je 10 '67
New showcase for daily WJT's book coverage. Pub W 191:36 Ap 17 '67
Suicide in Manhattan. il Newsweek 69:88-9 My 15 '67
Void in Manhattan; reasons for shut down. il Time 89:41 My 12 '67
Why another big paper had to close down. il U S News 62:16 My 15 '67
Why our paper died. G. Merlis. il Nat R 19: 572-3+ My 30 '67
Why the WJT folded. New Repub 156:5 My 20 '67
World journal tribune ceases publication. Pub W 191:25 My 15 '67
WORLD law. See International law

WORLD law day. See Special days, weeks and months
WORLD maps
Economic map of the world. (cont) Sr Schol 91:24-5 O 5 '67
World: polar projection. Sr Schol 91:28 O 5 '67
WORLD meteorological congress
Federov at WMC. il Sci N 91:423 My 6 '67
WORLD meteorological organization
Stretching the limit on weather forecasts; World meteorologists meet in Geneva. il Bsns W p90-3 Ap 1 '67
World weather watch: meteorologists of the world unite. J. Walsh. Science 156:1470-2 Je 16 '67
WORLD opinion. See Public opinion
WORLD organization. See International organization
WORLD Pentecostal conference. See Pentecostal churches
WORLD petroleum congress
Oil technicians get the global slant; International congress of the petroleum industry in Mexico city. il Bsns W p 130-2 Ap 15 '67
WORLD politics
See also
Balance of power
Great powers
International politics

Study and teaching
Editor interviews Paul A. Miller on International education act; ed. by M. S. Fenner. P. A. Miller. NEA J 56:63-4 Ap '67
WORLD politics, 1945-
American promise. W. Lippmann. Newsweek 70:21 O 9 '67
Around the world: prospects for '68. il U S News 64:50-2 Ja 8 '68
Beginnings of world war III? J. V. Schall. America 117:14-17 Jl 1 '67
Can we end the cold war? M. Frankel. il N Y Times Mag p20-1+ Ja 29 '67; Reply with rejoinder. L. T. Kiss. p37 F 26 '67
Clouds over the Golden Horn. J. Burnham. Nat R 19:342 Ap 4 '67
Cold war as history. by L. J. Halle. Review New Repub 157:32 S 9 '67. A. Campbell
Constructive initiatives in East-West relations; address, February 17, 1967. F. D. Kohler. Dept State Bul 56:406-13 Mr 13 '67
Containment has won, but. . . E. Stillman. il N Y Times Mag p23+ My 28 '67
Current documents. See issues of Current history
Great transition: tasks of the first and second postwar generations; address, February 23, 1967. W. W. Rostow. Dept State Bul 56: 491-504 Mr 27 '67
Illusions of distance. A. Wohlstetter. bibliog f For Affairs 46:242-55 Ja '68
Implications of change for United States foreign policy; remarks, May 22, 1967. Z. Brzezinski. Dept State Bul 57:19-23 Jl 3 '67
News, mostly good, beyond Viet Nam; Time essay. Time 89:16-17 Ap 7 '67
Origins of the cold war. A. Schlesinger, jr. For Affairs 46:22-52 O '67; Reply. W. A. Williams. Nation 205:492-5 N 13 '67
Peace, empire, and world government; introduction to Major peace treaties of modern history, 1648-1966, ed. by F. L. Israel. A. Toynbee. Sat R 50:20-1 Ap 29 '67
Persuading red China to join the U.N. J. B. Sheerin. Cath World 204:261-3 F '67
Politics of progress; address, February 20, 1967. E. V. Rostow. Dept State Bul 56:398-405 Mr 13 '67
Sunset; power vacuum of the Indian Ocean. J. Burnham. Nat R 19:843 Ag 8 '67
Travail of Britain. W. Lippmann. Newsweek 70:23 D 4 '67
Twenty years of cold war. Commonweal 86: 3-4 Mr 24 '67
U.S. and world affairs annual; 1967-68 edition ,symposium, ed. by E. Sparn and others. il Sr Schol 91:2-41 O 5 '67
War we are in. by J. Burnham. Review Nat R 19:1279 N 14 '67. C. B. Marshall
We and they. M. Ascoli. Reporter 27:12-13 N 30; 12-13 D 14 '67
Week's wars. Nat R 19:779-80+ Jl 25 '67
What is sauce for the goose is sauce for the gander. E. Rabinowitch. Bul Atomic Sci 23:41-3 S '67

WORLD politics, 1945- —*Continued*
When did the cold war begin? D. F. Fleming.
Nation 206:53-5 Ja 8 '68
Worldgram; from the capitals of the world.
See issues of U.S. news & World report
Worlds in conflict, by D. W. Brogan. Review
Sat R 50:24+ S 2 '67. R. Barnes
See also
Communist strategy

WORLD population. See Population

WORLD Presbyterian alliance. See Alliance of
Reformed churches throughout the world
holding the Presbyterian system

WORLD recreation congress. See Recreation
conferences

WORLD revolution. See Social revolution

WORLD series (baseball)
Aftermath of a bittersweet World series. W.
Leggett. il Sports Illus 27:61-3 O 23 '67
El Birdos fly high; St Louis Cardinals vs
Boston Red Sox. W. Leggett. il Sports Il-
lus 27:22-9 O 16 '67
Day the old pros won. il Time 90:42 O 20 '67
Heroic tale. il Time 90:55-6 O 13 '67
Spotting scene (cont) R. Angell. New Yorker
43:176+ O 28 '67
Yaz vs. Lou. il Newsweek 70:90 O 16 '67

WORLD series tickets. See Baseball—Tickets

WORLD student Christian federation
European S.C.M.s and political action. K.
Chamberlain. Christian Cent 84:418-19 Mr
29 '67

WORLD tariffs. See Tariff

WORLD trade. See Commerce

WORLD trade week
World trade week, 1967; a proclamation. L.
B. Johnson. Dept State Bul 56:756-7 My 15
'67

WORLD unity. See International organization

WORLD university. See United Nations university (proposed)

WORLD war, 1914-1918. See European War
1914-1918

WORLD war, 1939-1945
Fall of Japan, by W. Craig. Review
Atlan 220:129-30 S '67. O. Handlin

Aerial operations

See also
London—Air raids
Midway, Battle of, 1942

Atrocities

Art: drawings from hell; M. Lasansky's Nazi
drawings. C. Willard. Look 31:78+ F 21 '67
Death in Rome, by R. Katz. Review
America 116:190 F 4 '67. E. Waldman
Nation 204:663-4 My 22 '67. R. Rothstein
Death in Rome focuses new controversy on
Vatican; 335 Romans killed as reprisal.
Pub W 191:47-8 F 6 '67
Dina Mironovna Pronichev remembers Babi
Yar; excerpt from novel, Babi Yar. A.
Kuznetsov; reply. E. Litvin. il N Y Times
Mag p 121+ Ap 30 '67
Going to the baths; Auschwitz atrocities;
letter. A. Maltz. New Repub 157:34+ S 30
'67
Intercontinental op; searching out of Nazi
war criminals. il Time 89:98+ Mr 31 '67
Murderers among us. S. Wiesenthal. il Sat
Eve Post 240:42-4+ F 25; 38-9+ Mr 11 '67
Nazi murder plot; excerpts from While six
million died. A. D. Morse. il Look 31:49-52+
N 14 '67
Ravine of the dead: Babi Yar. il Time 89:
96 Ap 7 '67
See also
Concentration camps
World war, 1939-1945—War criminals

Bibliography

Curl up and read. E. Campbell. Seventeen
26:234 S '67

Campaigns and battles

Rare photos recall the agony of Bataan;
Death march and surrender. il Life 62:26-33
Ap 21 '67

Africa

Defeat and death of General Rommel. A.
McKee. il N Y Times Mag p44-5+ O 22 '67

Pacific

Back to Bataan; U.S. veterans join in anni-
versary ceremonies. Newsweek 69:50 Ap
24 '67
See also
Midway, Battle of, 1942
Philippine Sea, Battles of the, 1944

Catholic church

Death in Rome, by R. Katz. Review
Nation 204:663-4 My 22 '67. R. Rothstein
Three popes and the Jews, by P. E. Lapide.
Review
Commentary 44:100-5 N '67. G. Lewy
Sat R 50:27-8 S 9 '67. B. E. Olson

Diplomatic history

Broken seal, by L. Farago. Review
Life 62:12 Mr 17 '67. C. Elliott

Jews

Heroism of Staszek Jackowski. R. Gruber. il
Sat R 50:19-21+ Ap 15 '67
Murderers among us. S. Wiesenthal. il Sat
Eve Post 240:42-4+ F 25; 38-9+ Mr 11 '67
Murderers among us: the Simon Wiesenthal
memoirs, ed. by J. Wechsberg. Review
Sat R 50:32-3 Ap 15 '67. A. Doant
Nazi murder plot; excerpts from While six
million died. A. D. Morse. il Look 31:49-52+
N 14 '67
Nazi war victims on trial; concerning Tre-
blinka, by J. F. Steiner. A. Donat. Sat R
50:32-4 My 13 '67
Reader's choice: concerning Treblinka by
Jean-François Steiner. O. Handlin. Atlan
219:128 Je '67
Revolt at Treblinka; excerpts from Treblinka,
tr. by H. Weaver. J. F. Steiner. il Sat
Eve Post 240:34-6+ My 20; 38-40+ Je 3 '67
Survival of the Jews; concerning J. Steiner's
Treblinka. B. Bettelheim. New Repub 157:
23-30 Jl 1 '67; Discussion. 157:32+ Jl 15;
34+ S 30 '67
Test of democracy, by L. Yahil. Review
Commentary 44:97-8+ O '67. E. Livneh
Three popes and the Jews, by P. E. Lapide.
Review
Commentary 44:100-5 N '67. G. Lewy
Treblinka, by J. F. Steiner. Review
Harper 235:92+ Jl '67. D. Caute
Treblinka: heroism or fantastic apology? J.
Greenfeld. Life 62:8+ My 19 '67

Medical and sanitary affairs

See also
Neuroses

Memorials and monuments

See War memorials

Moral and religious aspects

See also
World war, 1939-1945—Catholic church

Naval operations

See also
Midway, Battle of, 1942
Philippine Sea, Battles of the, 1944

Personal narratives

Blast of war 1939-1945, by H. MacMillan.
Review
Atlan 221:114 Ja '68. O. Handlin
Catch-22 revisited. J. Heller. il Holiday 41:44-
61+ Ap '67
Diaries and letters of Harold Nicolson: the
war years, 1939-1945, ed. by N. Nicolson.
Review
Life 62:6 Je 30 '67. A. Cooke
New Yorker 43:170+ S 9 '67. N. Bliven
Sat R 50:27-8 Je 17 '67. J. Lukacs
When dynamite rains from the sky. R. L.
Tobin. Sat R 50:18-19 Ag 5 '67
With prejudice, by Lord Tedder. Review
Nat R 19:1024-5+ S 19 '67. G. F. Eliot
Sat R 50:30 O 14 '67. B. Pitt.

Photography

Rare photos recall the agony of Bataan;
Death march and surrender. il Life 62:26-33
Ap 21 '67
There was a time: Salween River campaign.
E. Galligan. il U S Camera 30:48-9 Jl '67

Prisoners and prisons

Rare photos recall the agony of Bataan;
Death march and surrender. il Life 62:26-33
Ap 21 '67
Year Thanksgiving came early. C. Scovel. Mc-
Calls 95:72+ N '67
See also
Concentration camps

Refugees

See also
Refugee children

WORLD war, 1939-1945—*Continued*

Reparations

Tough cheese; investigating compensation fund for British victims. Newsweek 71:32 Ja 8 '68

Restitution claims
See Restitution claims

Songs and music

When Lilli went to war, for both sides. D. Jewell. il N Y Times Mag p52-3+ N 19 '67

Underground movements
Poland

Heroism of Staszek Jackowski. R. Gruber. il Sat R 50:19-21+ Ap 15 '67

War criminals

I knew, I did nothing; former SS officials Slottke, Zoepf and Harster. il Newsweek 69:58 F 6 '67

Judging the judges; first Nazi judge ever tried in a German court, convicted of war crimes. Time 90:30+ Jl 14 '67

Justice denied; shielding Nazi murderers of postal employees in Danzig; letter. G. C. Fuz. Nation 205:386 O 23 '67

Murderers among us: the Simon Wiesenthal memoirs, ed. by J. Wechsberg. Review Sat R 50:32-3 Ap 15 '67. A. Donat

Penny a head; arrest of F. Stangl in Brazil. Time 89:40 Mr 10 '67

Sunday kind of hate; village of Marzabotto votes to keep German war criminal in prison. Newsweek 70:43 Jl 31 '67

Symbolic punishment; three sentenced for sending Dutch Jews to concentration camps. Newsweek 69:50 Mr 6 '67

Trapping no. 3; arrest of Franz Paul Stangl. Newsweek 69:63 Mr 13 '67

White-gloved killers; attempt to avenge Dutch Jewry. il Newsweek 69:48 Ja 30 '67
See also
Nuremberg trials

Africa
See also
World war, 1939-1945—Campaigns and battles—Africa

Germany

Defeat and death of General Rommel. A. McKee. il N Y Times Mag p44-5+ O 22 '67

Great Britain

Breaking wave, by T. Taylor. Review Sat R il 50:28-9 Mr 18 '67. L. L. Snyder

Set Europe ablaze, by E. H. Cookridge. Review Sat R 50:44 S 16 '67. H. H. Ransom
See also
London—Air raids

Italy

Death in Rome, by R. Katz. Review America 116:190 F 4 '67. E. Waldman Sat R 50:42-3 F 4 '67. W. Guzzardi, jr

Japan

Fall of Japan, by W. Craig. Review Sat R 50:44 S 30 '67. J. M. Allison

Fall of Japan; excerpt. W. Craig. il Sat Eve Post 240:36-8+ Ag 26 '67
See also
Midway, Battle of, 1942
Philippine Sea, Battles of the, 1944

Philippines
See also
Philippine Sea Battles of the 1944

United States

America's concentration camps, by A. R. Bosworth. Review Christian Cent 84:409-10 Mr 29 '67. M. Polner Sat R 50:29 Mr 18 '67. H. Mitgang Time il 89:100+ F 17 '67

Authors and editors; forthcoming book on America's concentration camps. Pub W 191:39 F 6 '67

Issei and Nisei, by D. Kitagawa. Review Sat R 51:89 Ja 13 '68. L. Katcher

Swastika and the eagle, by J. V. Compton. Review Atlan 220:100 Ag '67. O. Handlin
See also
Midway, Battle of, 1942

WORLDS Columbian exposition, 1893. See Chicago—Worlds Columbian exposition, 1893

WORLDS fair, Montreal. See Montreal—Worlds fair, 1967

WORLDS fair, San Antonio, Tex. See San Antonio, Tex.—HemisFair, 1968

WORLDS fairs. See Exhibitions

WORMAN, Charles G.
Kentucky rifle in the Revolutionary war. Hobbies 72:126-7 Mr '67

WORMS, Fossil
Fossilization of an ancient, Devonian, soft-bodied worm. B. Cameron. bibliog il Science 155:1246-8 Mr 10 '67

WORMS, Hog. See Swine—Diseases and pests

WORMS, Intestinal and parasitic
See also
Hookworms

WORMS, Sea. See Annelids

WORMSLOE (historic house) See Georgia—Historic houses, etc.

WORRELL, Elizabeth
Oral interpretation. NEA J 56:37-9 Mr '67

WORRY
See also
Anxiety

WORSHIP
Bound to the world; theology of worship. A. M. Weyerman. Christian Cent 84:1161 S 13 '67
Let my people go. J. N. Eller. America 117:405 O 14 '67
See also
Church attendance

WORSTHORNE, Peregrine
Anti-Americanism is now non—U. N Y Times Mag p34-5+ Ap 9 '67

WORTH, Edith
On a roof in Hong Kong. il Dance Mag 41:30-2 Je '67

WORTH, Frank
Assembly line for oil paintings. Design 69:20-2 Fall '67

WORTH, Irene
Theater. H. Hewes. Sat R 50:51 F 11 '67

WORTH, Larry D.
Modern workshop is more efficient. Am City 82:112+ D '67

WORTH
New art selection process. I. Fleminger. Art N 65:56-7+ Ja '67
Requiem aeternam homini. R. E. Wentz. Christian Cent 84:113-14 Ja 25 '67

WORTHAM, Anne
(comp) Why, all other things being equal, it's better to live in Peking than in Reykjavik. Esquire 67:110-11 Mr '67

WORTHINGTON, Minn.

Negroes

Minnesota town integrates, and survives. il Ebony 22:74-6+ Mr '67

WORTHY, William
American Negro is dead. Esquire 68:126-30+ N '67
(comp) Black power establishment. Esquire 68:131-3 N '67

WORTMAN, Doris Nash
Doris Nash Wortman, 1890-1967. J. R. Cominsky. por Sat R 50:19 Je 24 '67

WORZEL, J. Lamar
Lamont geological observatory. Science 158:948-9 N 17 '67
—See Gerard, R. D. jt. auth.

WOUNDED, Vietnamese war. See Vietnamese war, 1957- —Casualties

WOUNDED KNEE CREEK, Battle of, 1890
Tragic prescience of George Catlin; ed. by R. S. Gallagher. G. Catlin. Am Heritage 18:72 O '67

WOUNDS
Collagen proline hydroxylase in wound healing, granuloma formation, scurvy, and growth. E. Mussini and others. bibliog il Science 157:927-9 Ag 25 '67

WOVEN jewelry. See Jewelry

WOVEN sculpture. See Sculpture—Study and teaching—Materials

WRAPP, H. Edward
Good managers don't make policy decisions; excerpts from address, April 27, 1967. Harvard Bsns R 45:91-9 S '67

WRAPPING of packages
Christmas yarn with a new twist. M. White. il Ladies Home J 84:78-9+ D '67
Gift bags easy to make and colorful. il Sunset 139:75 D '67

WRAPPING of packages—*Continued*
Gifts on the go; send-away Christmas packages. il Ladies Home J 84:98-103 D '67
Home-grown gift wraps. il Bet Hom & Gard 45:60-2 D '67
Labeled for Christmas. il McCalls 95:124-5 D '67
Pretty packages without ribbon. il Am Home 70:30 D '67
Surprise packages; shoe box Christmas wrapping. il Redbook 130:72-3+ D '67
Why not a package as much fun as what's inside? il Sunset 139:58-9 D '67
Wrapping is the magic; famous designers create Christmas packages. il House & Gard 132:144-7 D '67

WREATHS, Christmas. See Christmas wreaths

WRECKING
Tallest: Singer building to come down. New Yorker 43:37-8 S 9 '67

WRECKS. See Shipwrecks

WRENCHES
How to squeeze more from your plier wrench. W. E. Burton. il Pop Mech 127:186-9 Ap '67

WRESAT. See Artificial satellites, Australian

WRESTLING
Delicious dessert for a hungry Spartan crew; Michigan state the 1967 tournament winner. G. Ronberg. il Sports Illus 26:50+ Ap 3 '67
Mighty mouse leads the way; M. Caruso of Lehigh university. G. Ronberg. il Sports Illus 26:59-60 F 20 '67
See also
Judo

WRIGHT, Alfred
Golf (cont) Sports Illus 27:46-7 Jl 10; 94-5 S 11; 56+ O 30; 76-8 N 13 '67

WRIGHT, Arthur F. and Hall, J. W.
Chinese and Japanese historiography: some trends, 1961-1966. bibliog f Ann Am Acad 371:178-93 My '67

WRIGHT, Ben
Golf. Sports Illus 26:59-60+ My 29 '67

WRIGHT, Charles
Daughters of Blum; poem. New Yorker 42: 103 Ja 28 '67

WRIGHT, Frank Lloyd
Frank Lloyd Wright. by N. K. Smith. Review
Nation 204:121-2 Ja 23 '67. S. Paul

WRIGHT, G. Scott, Jr
Films, fad or fine art? Sch Arts 66:31-5 Ja '67
Teaching about the screen arts. Sch Arts 66:41-3 My '67
Teaching art through film making. Sch Arts 66:36-9 Je '67

WRIGHT, Glen
Theatrical nights with the Afghans. Sat R 51:91-2 Ja 13 '68

WRIGHT, James Claud
Clean money for Congress. Harper 234:98-102+ Ap '67

WRIGHT, James Skelly
De facto anticlimax. M. R. Berube. Commonweal 86:438-9 Jl 14 '67
Does democracy demand degradation? F. Morley. Nations Bsns 55:29-30 S '67
Skelly Wright's sweeping decision. A. M Bickel. New Repub 157:11-12 Jl 8 '67; Reply with rejoinder. M. E. Tigar. 157:41-3 Ag 5 '67

WRIGHT, Jay
Historical days; poem. Nation 205:374 O 16 '67
Idiotic and politic; poem. Yale R 56:427-9 Mr '67

WRIGHT, Joseph Sutherland
Excerpt from statement before Communications subcommittee. October 10, 1967. Cong Digest 46:296+ D '67
Subscription TV; address, October 11, 1967. Vital Speeches 34:79-83 N 15 '67

WRIGHT, Lee
Put flood-plain management first. Am City 82: 98-9 N '67

WRIGHT, Marcus A.
Experiment in a rural system. por Wilson Lib Bul 42:301-3 N '67

WRIGHT, Mary Kathryn
Miss Avis against Miss Hertz. M. Mulvoy. il Sports Illus 27:62-3 N 27 '67

WRIGHT, Mickey. See Wright, M. K.

WRIGHT, Myron Arnold
Guaranteed income; address, March 2, 1967. Vital Speeches 33:368-71 Ap 1 '67

WRIGHT, Nathan, Jr
Psychology behind black power; interview; reprint. por Sci Digest 63:58-61 Ja '68
Wright concept of black power; excerpts from Black power and urban unrest. Sat R 50:26-7 Ag 12 '67

WRIGHT, Olgivanna Lloyd
Deathwatch in Tokyo. F. Riley. Sat R 50: 40+ D 16 '67

WRIGHT, Phyllis
Medicine, today; ed. by V. Cohn. See issues of Ladies' home journal
Traveling in good health. Holiday 41:135-9 Ap '67

WRIGHT, Quincy
Books. Bul Atomic Sci 23:32-4 O '67

WRIGHT, Skip
Take a surfer out of the surf and what have you got? G. Greene. il pors Ladies Home J 84:172-4+ O '67

WRIGHT, Stephen Junius
Editor interviews; ed. by M. S. Fenner. pors NEA J 56:63-4 My '67

about

Peace and the racial revolution. por Sch & Soc 95:138 Mr 4 '67

WRIGHT, Sylvia
Pad cluttered with the fallout of all his careers. Life 62:42+ Je 30 '67

WRIGHT, W. Warren
Operate and release times of relays. Electr World 77:54-5 Ap '67

WRIGHT, William R.
Railroad hypocrisy; nuisance of passengers. Nation 204:275-6 F 27 '67

WRIGHT DRY VALLEY. See Antarctic Regions

WRIGHTSTONE, J. Wayne
Ability grouping and the average child. NEA J 57:9-11+ Ja '68

WRIST slashing. See Self-mutilation

WRISTON, Walter Bigelow
You can't get there from here; address, October 25, 1967. Vital Speeches 34:85-8 N 15 '67

about

Moore and Wriston of First national city. por Fortune 76:27 Jl '67
Plum at First national city. il por Time 89: 86-7 Je 16 '67

WRITERS. See Authors

WRITERS, World congress of. See PEN club

WRITERS conferences. See Authors conferences

WRITERS cramp
It's not in the mind. Sci Digest 62:61 N '67

WRITERS project, Federal. See Federal writers project

WRITERS vocabulary. See Vocabulary

WRITERS workshops. See Educational workshops

WRITING
See also
Communication
Penmanship
Signatures (writing)

WRITING (authorship) See Authorship

WRITING (composition) See English language —Composition

WRITING, Chinese. See Chinese language— Writing

WRITING paper. See Stationery

WRONG, Dennis H.
Liberal anti-communism revisited. Commentary 44:77-9 S '67

WRONG way home; story. See Knowlton, R.

WROUGHT iron work. See Ironwork

WU, Han
What the villain did. il Newsweek 69:43 My 1 '67

WUJEK, Joseph H. Jr
Electronic challenges in the SST program. Electr World 78:26-7+ Jl '67
EROS, an airborne collision avoidance system. Electr World 78:35-8+ D '67
High-voltage, high-power semiconductors. Electr World 79:48-50 Ja '68
Medical instrumentation systems. Electr World 79:46-7+ Ja '68
Radio measurements in space. Electr World 77:46-7+ My '67
Sun and space solar measurements. Electr World 78:32-3 O '67

WUJEK, Joseph H. jr—*Continued*
Surveyor mission to the moon. Electr World 78:41-3 N '67
Weather surveillance by satellite. Electr World 77:23-5 Mr '67
—and McGee, M. E.
Field-effect transistor circuits. Electr World 77:32-3+ My '67
WULIGER, Robert
(ed) See Niemöller, M. Niemoeller reports on Vietnam
WUNDERLICH, Fritz
Wunderlich's Lieder, an artistry almost fully in flower. P. G. Davis. por Hi Fi 17:83-4 Ja '67
WUNDERLIN, Linda
Lightning; poem. Horn Bk 43:386 Je '67
WURLITZER, Rudolph
Fastest gun in the West. Sat Eve Post 240: 80-2 Mr 11 '67
WURTMAN, Richard J.
Ambiguities in the use of the term circadian. bibliog Science 156:104 Ap 7 '67
—and others
Daily rhythm in tyrosine concentration in human plasma: persistence on low-protein diets. bibliog Science 158:660-2 N 3 '67
WUTHERING Heights; drama. See Olfson, L.
WYANT, Rowena
Business failures. See issues of Dun's review
WYANT, William K. Jr
That lost bomb. New Repub 156:36-7 My 20 '67
WYATT, Gertrud L.
Ready for reading? Parents Mag 42:46-7+ My '67
WYCHE, Bubba
Wyche has moved to more elegant quarters. J. Underwood. il por Sports Illus 27:14-17 O 30 '67
WYCHE, Paul
Real, live superman. Ebony 22:97-8+ S '67
WYCKOFF, Donald L.
Meet Donald L. Wyckoff. por Craft Horiz 27:5 N '67
WYDEN, Barbara
Parent and child. N Y Times Mag p63+ Ag 20 '67
—See Wyden, P. jt. auth.
WYDEN, Peter, and Wyden, Barbara
Doctors' own diet. Ladies Home J 84:61+ F '67
—See Kobler, J. jt. auth.
WYETH, Andrew
Andrew Wyeth turns his attention from landscapes to portraits. il Horizon 9:86-7 Spr '67
Appalled & amazed. por Time 89:68 F 24 '67
Mass sport of Wyeth-watching; exhibition at the Whitney museum. L. Wainwright. Life 62:27 Mr 10 '67
Wyeth at the Whitney. F. Getlein. New Repub 156:33-4 Mr 11 '67
Wyeth's world. il por Newsweek 69:76-9 Mr 6 '67
WYLIE, Evan McLeod
Help, my child has taken poison! Good H 164:77+ Je '67; Same abr. Read Digest 91:133-7 Ag '67
Pills drivers shouldn't take. Read Digest 90:83-5 F '67
WYLIE, Philip
McNamara's missile defense. Pop Sci 192:59-62+ Ja '68
UFOs: the sense and the nonsense. por Pop Sci 190:76-9 Mr '67
WYMAN, Donald
Add a viburnum to your garden. Horticulture 45:38-9+ O '67
Best trees and shrubs for the colorful fruits of fall. Home Gard 54:22-3 O '67
Evergreen groundcovers. Horticulture 45:14-17 N '67
WYMAN-Gordon company
Raising the pressure fourfold. il Bsns W p126-8 F 18 '67
WYNN, Jimmie
Wynn of the losers. il por Time 90:64 Jl 7 '67
WYNN, Ralph M.
Intrauterine devices: effects on ultrastructure of human endometrium. bibliog Science 156:1508-10; 157:1465 Je 16, S 22 '67
WYNN, Wilton
Report from Milan. Fortune 76:39+ Jl '67
WYNNE, Greville
Contact on Gorki street; condensation. por Read Digest 91:185-90+ Ag '67
about
Battle of the books. por Newsweek 70:56+ S 25 '67

WYNNE, Jim
Wynne becomes world offshore champion. M. Crook. il Yachting 121:54+ Ja '67
WYOMING
See also
Fishing—Wyoming
Grand Teton National Park
Hunting—Wyoming
Paleontology—Wyoming
WYOMING, Ohio
Mrs Potts and her dancing tots. B. Rollin. il Look 31:105-7 My 16 '67
WYPER, W. W.
Aqua glider: a great new sportscraft you can build. Pop Sci 191:50-3 Ag '67
WYSE, Lois
How to get rich in show business. Ladies Home J 84:64+ My '67
Love poems for the very married: Nothing; Sunday; I just talked to you on the telephone; Zipped; Half-squeezed; Cozy heart. Ladies Home J 84:64 Ap '67
WYSZYŃSKI, Stefan, cardinal
Polish Catholic left. J. J. Kulczyski. America 116:556-9 Ap 15 '67
Polish church and Communist state. H. H. Ward. Christian Cent 84:288+ Mr 1 '67
WYZANSKI, Charles Edward, 1906-
It's up to the young to solve the problem. New Repub 157:15-16 O 21 '67

X

X-15 (airplane) See Airplanes, Experimental
X RAY apparatus and equipment
X-ray exposures; Senate commerce committee to start hearings on ionizing radiation hazards of electronic products. R. Nader. New Repub 157:11-12 S 2 '67; Discussion. 157:37-8 S 30 '67
X-RAY astronomy. See Radio astronomy
X-RAY defense. See Guided missiles—Defenses
X RAY photogrammetry
Gifts from out there; with photographs by H. Sochurek. Esquire 67:92-101 My '67
X-RAY stars. See Stars—Radiation
X RAYS
How to zap an ICBM. il Time 89:46 My 26 '67
Optical identification of an X-ray source in Cygnus. G. S. Mumford. Sky & Tel 34:82 Ag '67
Roentgen's magic rays. T. Berland. il Todays Health 45:58-9+ Mr '67
Science in high gear; X-ray astronomy. A. Ewing. il Sci N 92:14-15 Jl 1 '67
X rays from a quasar. Time 90:56 Jl 14 '67
X-rays from beyond the Milky way. il Sci N 92:77-8 Jl 22 '67
See also
Television receivers—Radiation hazards

Archeological applications
Atom sleuths seek secret treasures in the pyramids. A. P. Armagnac. il Pop Sci 190:88-90 Mr '67

Physiological effects
Increased litter size in the rat X-irradiated during the estrous cycle before mating. E. W. Hahn and W. F. Ward. bibliog il Science 157:956-7 Ag 25 '67
Protection through parabiosis against the lethal effects of exposure to large doses of X-rays. H. W. Carroll and D. J. Kimeldorf. bibliog Science 156:954-5 My 19 '67; Reply with rejoinder. S. Warren. 157:582 Ag 4 '67
Ray of danger. il Newsweek 70:63 S 11 '67
Sulfur mustard and X-rays: differences in expression of lethal damage. F. Mauro and M. M. Elkind. bibliog il Science 155:1561-3 Mr 24 '67
TV radiation assessed; X-ray emission from color TV sets. Sci N 92:11 Jl 1 '67
X-ray excess. il Time 90:69 S 8 '67
X-ray exposures; Senate commerce committee to start hearings on ionizing radiation hazards of electronic products. R. Nader. New Repub 157:11-12 S 2 '67; Discussion. 157:37-8 S 30 '67
X-ray hazard in TV sets; GE color-TV. Consumer Bul 50:4+ O '67

XANTHOS, Paul J.
Lead-up games and activities in tennis instruction. Parks & Rec 2:32+ S '67

XENAKIS, Yannis
Iannis Xenakis: formula for new music. J. Maguire. il pors Sat R 50:51-3 Je 24 '67

XENON-Iodine dating. See Radioactive dating

XENOPHORA. See Mollusks

XENOPUS laevis. See Frogs

XEROX corporation
Bowker stockholders approve sale to Xerox corporation. Pub W 193:24 Ja 1 '68
EOS eyes new markets as Xerox unit. J. F. Judge. Tech W 20:36 My 8 '67
New reference service created by Xerox; Education division's DATRIX (direct access to reference information) Library J 92:2107 Je 1 '67
Profiles; formerly Haloid company. J. Brooks. il New Yorker 43:46-50+ Ap 1 '67
Tightening the ship; work force cutback. Newsweek 70:52 Ag 21 '67
Xerox annual report: a guided tour. M. Buhagiar. il Fortune 75:184-7+ Je 15 '67
Xerox U; listening courses. il **Time 91:73** Ja 5 '68

XYLEBORUS ferrugineus. See Beetles

Y

YAF. See Young Americans for freedom (organization)

YWCA. See Young women's Christian association

YABLONSKY, Lewis
Ah, wilderness. New Repub 156:23-4 Ap 1 '67

about
Risks of research. il por Time 90:40 D 22 '67

YACHT building
Boat is born; Intrepid. il Sports Illus 26:32-7 Je 26 '67

YACHT clubs
Small boat paradise; Mission Bay YC, San Diego, Calif. B. Crabtree. il Yachting 121:73+ My '67
Yachting two miles up; Grand Lake YC. I. T. Kingsley. il Yachting 122:50-1+ D '67

Anecdotes, facetiae, satire, etc.
Constitutional crisis; annals of the West Bay yacht club. J. Dugald. il Motor B 119:50-1 Mr '67
No new business; annals of the West Bay yacht club. J. Dugald. il **Motor B 119:47-8** F '67
Stacked deck; annals of the West Bay yacht club. J. Dugald. il Motor B 120:40-1 D '67
Woman's touch; annals of the West Bay yacht club. J. Dugald. il Motor B 119:33+ Je '67

YACHT decoration
Mutiny, decorous and decorative, on the Bountiful. M. Corbman. il Motor B 120:44-7 O '67

YACHT flags. See Flags

YACHT management
Put your boat in business. R. P. Murdock. il Motor B 120:40+ O '67

YACHT ownership. See Yachts—Purchasing

YACHT racing
America cup report: the pace increases. T. Anable, jr. il Motor B 119:126+ My '67
America's cup course, 1967. il Yachting 122:91 S '67
America's cup eliminations. E. B. Morris. Yachting 121:300 Ja '67
America's cup news; ed. by B. D. Barker, 3d. See issues of Yachting
America's cup report. il Motor B 119:126+ My; 118-19+ Je '67
America's cup report: the thirty-day gun. J. Gribbins. il Motor B 120:37 S '67
America's cup, special section; symposium. il Motor B 120:21-39+ Ag '67
Australians set sail for the cup; America's cup race. il Bsns W p34-5 Ag 19 '67
Boat to beat; Intrepid selection favorite for America's cup. il Newsweek 69:90 Je 19 '67
Bus & his bag; America's cup observation trials. il Time 90:53 Jl 21 '67
Cupmanship; Intrepid to defend America's cup. Newsweek 70:69 S 4 '67

Dark sky over Tara; excerpt from White sails, black clouds. J. J. McNamara, jr. il Sports Illus 27:54-62 Ag 7 '67
Deep water racing. B. D. Barker, 3d. See issues of Yachting
Editor's page; challenges for the America's cup. B. Robinson. Yachting 122:21 N '67
Fresh hand for Montego Bay; SORC. N. Hoyt. il Sports Illus 26:100+ Ap 17 '67
If at first; shakedown for America's cup yacht racing off Sydney, Australia. il Time 89:58+ Ap 7 '67
In twenty fatal minutes Australia's try was doomed; Dame Pattie in America's cup race. C. Mitchell. il Sports Illus 27:26-8+ S 25 '67
Into the finals; America's cup elimination trials. il Time 90:57 Ag 25 '67
Intrepid a likely winner. W. S. Cox. il Sports Illus 26:38-9 Je 26 '67
Intrepid all the way; final series of trials to select American defender for America's cup. il Newsweek 70:53 Ag 28 '67
Intrepid approach; launching of Intrepid yacht for America's cup. il Time 89:40 My 5 '67
Intrepid for the defense. Time 90:52 S 1 '67
Intrepid gentleman; contender for America's cup. il Time 90:64-8 Ag 18 '67
Intrepid indeed; America's cup race. il Time 90:70 S 22 '67
Intrepid is the word; contenders for America's cup. il Time 89:80 Je 16 '67
It's Transpac time; symposium. il Yachting 121:78-81+ Je '67
Month in yachting. See issues of Yachting
New twelve and three also-rans; selecting America's cup defender. C. Mitchell. il Sports Illus 27:26-8+ Ag '67
Nine intrepid men; crew of Intrepid for America's cup. J. Gould. il Esquire 67:108-10+ Ap '67
Offshore proving ground; Bermuda to Denmark race. B. D. Barker, 3d. il Yachting 121:80-2+ My '67
On the racing circuit. See issues of Motor boating
Pity Pattie; America's cup race. il Newsweek 70:76 S 25 '67
Quest for the cup. il Yachting 122:76-80 S '67
Racing east to Halifax. B. D. Barker, 3d. il Yachting 121:70-2 Je '67
Regatta results. See issues of Yachting
Sailors' date with Diamond Head. L. J. Kennedy. il Motor B 119:28-9+ Je '67
Same old story; America's cup. B. Robinson. il Yachting 122:34-5+ N '67
SORC crown for Guinevere. F. Rohr. il Motor B 119:132-7+ My '67
Special art of match racing; excerpts from A view from the cockpit. R. N. Bavier. il Yachting 122:62-4+ S '67
Spending and spatting; America's cup. il Newsweek 69:74 Ap 17 '67
Sturock and Wright of the Dame Pattie. il Life 63:119-20+ S 15 '67
There was more than one race; excerpts from America, the story of the world's most famous yacht. C. Boswell. il Yachting 122:70-1+ S '67
There's life in the old girl yet Columbia, America's cup heroine of 1958. C. Phinizy. il Sports Illus 27:26-9 Jl 10 '67
There's nothing like Hood's Dame; Australian yacht for America's cup. C. Phinizy. il Sports Illus 26:76-82+ Je 5 '67
Those Aussies again; their America's cup preparations. B. Robinson. il Yachting 121:54-7+ My '67
To no one's surprise: Intrepid, to defend the America's cup. C. Mitchell. il Sports Illus 27:28-9 S 4 '67
Tough skipper to run a fast Dame; J. Sturock. R. Robertson. il Sports Illus 27:86-8 S 11 '67
Two taut ships eye the grandest prize; Intrepid and Dame Pattie in America's cup race. il Newsweek 70:62-5 S 18 '67
Well geared for the America's cup. R. Lieder. il Sports Illus 27:45 Jl 31 '67
With the racing classes. E. Horan. See issues of Yachting
Yacht races: why there's so much interest; America's cup race. il U S News 63:14 S 25 '67
Yachting interviews: Columbia's Gerry Driscoll; interview, ed. by B. Crabtree. **G.** Driscoll. il Yachting 121:48-9+ F '67
See also
International yacht racing union
Sailboat racing

YACHT racing—*Continued*

Caricatures and cartoons

Cup runneth and runneth; America's cup race. Sports Illus 27:26-8+ O 30 '67

History

America's cup chronicle. J. Gribbins. Motor B 120:39 Ag '67
Around the rock; Fastnet race. A. F. Loomis. il Yachting 123:78-9+ Ja '68
Cup chronology, a digest of the competition since 1851. A. F. Loomis. il Yachting 122:66-8+ S '67

YACHT racing fans. See Sports fans

YACHTING (periodical)
Yachting's new editor. C. Rimington. Yachting 121:37 F '67

YACHTS

Care

Ordeal of the Petrel. E. D. Fales, jr. il Pop Mech 127:68-72+ Je '67
Willis Short on boat preparation. W. Short. Yachting 121:123-4 Je '67

Chartering

Chartering, Caribbean style. P. Smyth. il Motor B 120:26-8+ O '67
Fun³, a big time in the Bahamas. E. Horan. il Yachting 122:50-1+ N '67
Lady's not for racing. J. Clegg. il Motor B 120:42-3+ S '67
Put your boat in business. R. P. Murdock. il Motor B 120:40+ O '67
Special time in Maine. E. Horan. bibliog il Yachting 122:54-6+ Ag '67

Crews
See Seamen

Design

Boats we meet: Bonita II. J. Emmett. il Yachting 121:56-7 F '67
Buddy Friedrich on Dragon slaying. G. S. Friedrichs, jr. il Yachting 122:30-1+ Ag; 54+ S '67
Designs. W. H. deFontaine. See issues of Yachting
Dream into Treasure. J. Guzzwell. il Yachting 121:78-80+ Mr '67
From dream to reality (cont) E. L. Parks. il Motor B 119:50-2+ F '67
Intrepid: a shapely radical; with report by B. Burns. il Life 63:60-3+ Jl 28 '67
Kakki M; a yacht with many unusual features. R. Krantz. il Yachting 123:116+ Ja '68
Nothing like a dame? Dame Pattie. il Time 89:38-9 Ja 27 '67
Other man's boat; Anna Maria. J. Atkin; J. J. Osborn. il Yachting 122:64-5+ D '67
Other man's boat; Circe. T Chamberlin; L. F. Herreshoff. il Yachting 122:52-3+ O '67
Other man's boat; Palawan. T. J. Watson, jr; O. J. Stephens. il Yachting 121:86-7+ My '67
Other man's boat; Radian. T. E. Colvin; R. Kauffman. il Yachting 121:92-3+ Je '67
Other man's boat; Rainbow's End. C. Hamlin; S. R. Thayer. il Yachting 121:74-5+ Mr '67
Other man's boat; Wee Beastie. F. C. Ripley, jr; N. S. Potter. il Yachting 122:60-1 Jl '67
Reborn America. J. Gribbins. il Motor B 120:36-7 Ag '67
Story of Ona. G. F. McClish. il Motor B 121:93-6+ Ja '68
There's nothing like Hood's Dame; Australian yacht for America's cup. C. Phinizy. il Sports Illus 26:76-82+ Je 5 '67
What is a twelve meter? il Yachting 122:72-3 S '67
Why Intrepid won. B. Bavier. il Yachting 122:36+ N '67
Yachting interviews. B. Robinson. il Yachting 122:74-5+ S '67

Documentation
See Yachts—Registration

Equipment

Aboard Intrepid; above and below deck. B. D. Barker, 3d. il Yachting 122:88-90+ S '67
Clearing the decks; Intrepid's winches below deck. Newsweek 70:68-9 Jl 24 '67
Come aboard John Wayne's fabulous yacht. J. W. Wright. il Pop Sci 191:64-7+ Ag '67

Mutiny, decorous and decorative, on the Bountiful. M. Corbman. il Motor B 120:44-7 O '67
Yachting's boat show. il Yachting 121:123-6+ Ja '67; 123:120-2+ Ja '68

Exhibitions

Boat show calendar. Yachting 123:119+ Ja '68
Boat show 1968. il Motor B 121:125-96+ Ja '68

Interior decoration
See Yacht decoration

Launching

Licensed launchman. D. B. Truslow. Yachting 121:128-9 Je '67

Licensing
See Yachts—Registration

Materials

Titian; the largest aluminum yacht. il Yachting 121:113+ Ja '67

Purchasing

Personal business. Bsns W p 137-8 Ag 19 '67

Registration

How to measure a yacht, for documentation. W. T. Stone. Yachting 121:260+ Ap '67

Repairing

Bob Alexander on damage control. B. Alexander. Yachting 121:125 Je '67

Testing

Tank testing America; model test. P. DeSaix. il Yachting 122:69+ S '67

YACHTS, Model. See Ship and boat models

YACHTS, Remodeled
Come aboard John Wayne's fabulous yacht. J. W. Wright. il Pop Sci 191:64-7+ Ag '67
Lady's not for racing. J. Clegg. il Motor B 120:42-3+ S '67

YACHTS, Used
Personal business. Bsns W p 137-8 Ag 19 '67

YACHTS and yachting
America's cup news; ed. by B. D. Barker, 3d. See issues of Yachting
America's cup report: the gang's all here. T. Anable, jr. il Motor B 119:100+ Ap '67
Bahamas bearings. G. F. McClish. See issues of Motor boating
Boat for St Croix. B. Robinson. il Yachting 122:46+ N '67
Calendar of coming events. comp. by R. Smith. See issues of Motor boating
Chesapeake log. W. B. Matthews, jr. See issues of Motor boating
Committee is charged, America's cup committee. F. Rohr, jr. il Motor B 120:29 Ag '67
Guardians of the cup. F. Rohr, jr. il Motor B 120:24-5+ Ag '67
Jamaica by jib. M. Z. Lenci. il Travel 128:44-9 O '67
Man and his boat, Wild Goose. A. R. Mansfield, jr. il Yachting 121:78-9+ Ap '67
Midwest watch. Motor B 119:157-9 Ap '67
News from yachting centers. See issues of Yachting
1967 logbook. il Motor B 121:61-76 Ja '68
Northern Cal roundup. J. Schmale. See issues of Motor boating
Northwest gales. E. Crimmin. See issues of Motor boating
Off my chest. See issues of Yachting
Pacific yachting; symposium. il Yachting 122:37-46+ Jl '67
Proof of the pudding; custom cruiser. J. Hart. il Yachting 121:91+ Ap '67
Quest for the cup. il Yachting 122:76-80 S '67
Reception committee for the Dame; candidates for the defense. R. W. Carrick. il Motor B 120:34-5+ Ag '67
'Round the world, family style. M. Roefer. il Motor B 120:22-5+ Jl; 27-9+ S '67; 121:107-9 Ja '68
Sailing yacht research; report on symposium. B. Chance and others. Science 156:411-12 Ap 21 '67
Seasoned skipper. See issues of Motor boating
Southern yachting; down the islands from Florida; symposium. il Yachting 122:37-53+ N '67

YARROWS
Say yes to yarrows. il Home Gard 54:40-1 Jl '67
Yarrows bloom and bloom. il Sunset 138:260-1 Mr '67
YASHIMA, Taro, pseud.
Golden village. G. L. Johnson. il por Horn Bk 43:183-91 Ap '67
YASTRZEMSKI, Carl
Hero of baseball's hottest pennant race. il pors Newsweek 70:62-6 O 2 '67
Heroic tale. il por Time 90:55 O 13 '67
Sportsman of the year. il por Sports Illus 27:22-3 D 25 '67
Yaz. il pors Life 63:56A-56B Ag 18 '67
YATES, Elizabeth
Why did you end your story that way? Horn Bk 43:709-14 D '67
YATES, Frederick Langdon
He was too brave. il por Newsweek 69:84 Je 19 '67
YAZOO CITY, Miss.
Poverty: the hungry world of Teresa Pilgrim. W. Hedgepeth. il Look 31:40·4 D 26 '67
Yazoo years; excerpt from North toward home. W. Morris. il Sat Eve Post 240:38-42+ O 7 '67
YBOR CITY. See Tampa, Fla.
YCAZA, Carlos Manuel de
Vacation for Manny; disqualification and suspension. il Time 89:80-1 Je 16 '67
Wrong American. W. Tower. il por Sports Illus 27:18-21 N 20 '67
YCAZA, Manuel. See Ycaza, C. M. de
YEAR round schools. See School year
YEARBOOKS, High school. See High school annuals
YEARDLEY, Sir George
Knight's tombstone at Jamestown, Virginia. P. J. Hudson. il Antiques 91:760-1 Je '67
YEAST bread. See Bread
YEASTS
Chemical modification of yeast alanine-RNA with a radioactive carbodiimide. S. W. Brostoff and V. M. Ingram. bibliog il Science 158:666-9 N 3 '67
Mitochondrial-satellite and circular DNA filaments in yeast. J. H. Sinclair and others. bibliog il Science 156:1234-7 Je 2 '67
Separation of spores from diploid cells of yeast by stable-flow free-boundary electrophoresis. M. A. Resnick and others. bibliog il Science 158:803-4 N 10 '67
Twin meiosis and other ambivalences in the life cycle of schizosaccharomyces pombe. H. Gutz. bibliog il Science 158:796-8 N 10 '67
Yeast transfer RNA: a small-angle X-ray study. J. A. Lake and W. W. Beeman. bibliog il Science 156:1371-3 Je 9 '67
YEATS, William Butler
Bring in the whisky now. Mary. F. O'Connor. New Yorker 43:36-40+ Ag 12 '67
Eminent domain, by R. Ellmann. Review Nation 205:501-2 N 13 '67. K. Sullivan
Mann, Yeats, and the truth of art. L. Conversi. Yale R 56:506-23 Je '67
Old Ez and Uncle William. D. Hoffman. Reporter 37:59-62 N 2 '67
YEH, Jen. See Fisher, H. W. jt. auth.
YELLIN, Tobias O. See Stein, H. H. jt. auth
YELLOWSTONE LAKE. See Yellowstone National Park
YELLOWSTONE NATIONAL PARK
Adventuring westward. E. A. Bauer. il Outdoor Life 139:50-3+ My '67
Perceptions and reflections on Yellowstone. R. Dolgner. il Liv Wildn 30:19-23 Aut '66
Studying the black bear in Yellowstone National Park. O. E. Bray. il Nat Parks Mag 41:10-12 Ag '67
Wilderness council in Yellowstone. il Liv Wildn 30:42-3 Aut '66
Yellowstone elk herd. Nat Parks Mag 41:20 Ag '67
Yellowstone wildlife in winter. W. A. Allard. il Nat Geog Mag 132:636-61 N '67
YEMELYANOV, Vassily Semyonovich. See Emel'ianov, V. S.
YEMEN
Anyone for cribbage? two U.S. foregin-aid officials arrested. Newsweek 69:52 My 15 '67
Countdown. Newsweek 70:73-4 N 20 '67

Deferred payment; civil war renewed. Newsweek 70:61 D 18 '67
Desperation of a strongman; Nasser calling soldiers home. Time 90:28+ O 20 '67
Eyewitness story: journey into a forgotten war. J. Law. il U S News 62:58-60 Ap 3 '67
Guess again; Republicans still in control of Sanaa. il Newsweek 70:32+ D 25 '67
How Nasser used poison gas; statements and medical report. R. Janin; W. Brutschin; D. E. Lauppi. U S News 63:60 Jl 3 '67
In new detail, Nasser's gas war. il U S News 63:9 Jl 10 '67
Mid-East blow-up? il Sr Schol 90:25 My 19 '67
Nasser's drive for south Arabia. L. Mosher. il Reporter 36:24-7 F 9 '67
Nasser's poison gas. Reporter 36:12+ Je 15 '67
Revolt within a war. il Time 89:36+ F 17 '67
Revolutionary gains. Newsweek 69:48+ Ap 3 '67
Siege of San'a. il Time 90:39 D 15 '67
When friends fall out. Time 90:37-8 N 17 '67
See also
Egypt—Foreign relations—Yemen
YEN, Chia-kan
Vice President of the Republic of China visits the United States; exchange of greetings and exchange of toasts, May 9; with joint statement, May 10, 1967. Dept State Bul 56:846-50 Je 5 '67
YEOMANS, G. Allan
Why major in speech? address, December 9, 1966. Vital Speeches 33:303-6 Mr 1 '67
YEVTUSHENKO, Yevgeny Aleksandrovich. See Evtushenko, E. A.
YGLESIAS, Helen
Films. Nation 205:349-50 O 9 '67
1967 non-definitive list. Nation 205:663-5 D 18 '67
YGLESIAS, José
Che Guevara: the best way to die. Nation 205:463-5 N 6 '67
Goodbye land. New Yorker 43:51-60+ Mr 18; 48-56+ Mr 25 '67
How life has changed in a Cuban sugar mill town. N Y Times Mag p8-9+ Jl 23 '67
Reporting on Cuba. New Repub 157:23-6 Jl 8 '67
YIDDISH folk songs. See Folk songs, Jewish
YLVISAKER, Paul N.
New force focuses on urban ills. il por Bsns W p75-6+ Je 24 '67
YOAKUM, Robert
Crime and punishment in the club. New Repub 156:8-9 My 13 '67
Dodd that failed. New Repub 156:10-13 Ap 1 '67
For Dodd and Yale. New Repub 156:6-8 Je 3 '67
Testifying for Dodd. New Repub 156:12-13 Mr 18 '67
What hath Dodd wrought? New Repub 157:13-16 Jl 8 '67
YOCUM, Harrison, G.
Cactus. Horticulture 45:34-5 Je '67
YODER, Edwin M. Jr
Harmony of confederacy. Sat R 50:66-7 Je 10 '67
Victorian party man. Sat R 50:29-30 Mr 4 '67
Voices from burning slums. Sat R 50:28-9 Ag 26 '67
YOGA
It's a sort of mini-yoga; exercises for French skiers. B. Ottum. il Sports Illus 26:20-1 Mr 27 '67
YOGURT
Big yogurt binge; Société Danone leads French yogurt market. Time 90:80 Ag 4 '67
Dannon fattens up on nothing but yogurt. il Bsns W p82+ S 9 '67
YOKOTA, Toshikatsu, and others
Intracellular olfactory response of hippocampal neurons in awake, sitting squirrel monkeys. bibliog Science 157:1072-4 S 1 '67
YOLEN, Will
Build your own reentry kite. Pop Sci 191:112-14 Jl '67
YOLLES, Stanley F.
Parent and child (cont) N Y Times Mag p64-5+ F 5 '67
Unraveling the mystery of schizophrenia. Todays Health 45:42-3+ Ap '67
YOO, T. J. and others
Specific binding activity of isolated light chains of antibodies. bibliog Science 157:707-9 Ag 11 '67
YOON, Jong Sik. See Burdette, W. J. jt. auth.
YOORS, Jan
Margaret Mead reviews The gypsies. M. Mead. Redbook 129:52+ S '67

YOURLO, Elizabeth. See Yourlo, Y. jt. auth.

YOURLO, Youry, and Yourlo, Elizabeth
Question and answer (cont) Dance Mag 41:18 F; 30-1 Ap '67

YOUSKEVITCH, Igor
Igor Youskevitch ballet romantique; Village theatre. J. Maskey. Dance Mag 41:33+ Ag '67
Prelude to a dancing dynasty. W. Terry. il por Sat R 50:37-8 Jl 8 '67

YOUSKEVITCH, Maria
Prelude to a dancing dynasty. W. Terry. il por Sat R 50:37-8 Jl 8 '67

YOUST, Will
King. il Hot Rod 20:80-2 Mr '67

YOUTH
Dropouts with a mission; the hippies; with report by H. Hertzberg. il Newsweek 69:92-5 F 6 '67
Journal miss. M. Kadison. See issues of Ladies' home journal
Junior journal; a monthly report from, by, and for the younger journal set (title varies) (cont) M. Kadison. il Ladies Home J 84:68 Mr '67
Love hippies. W. K. Zinsser. il Look 31:4 Ap 18 '67
Question from youth. America 117:7 Jl 1 '67
Under twenty-five. D. J. Leary. Cath World 206:121-4 D '67
When teen-agers talk of marriage. B. Spock. Redbook 129:26+ Ag '67
See also
Adolescence
Boys
Church work with youth
College students
Discipline
Girls
High school students
Libraries—Work with young people
Negro youth
Puberty
Young men
Young women

Adjustment
See Adjustment, Social

Attitudes
See Attitudes

Caricatures and cartoons
Misery loves company; excerpts. S. Heller. Good H 164:98-9 Je '67

Employment
Disadvantaged youth employed by Washington state parks. J. M. Willits. Parks & Rec 2:34+ Ap '67
Education and the labor market; with study-discussion program, by C. Smallenburg and H. Smallenburg. bibliog il PTA Mag 61:24-6, 36-7 Ap '67
Employment of high school graduates and dropouts in 1966. E. Waldman. il Mo Labor R 90:15-21 Jl '67
Employment of school age youth, October 1966. V. C. Perrella. il Mo Labor R 90:20-6 Ag '67
Keeping cities cool. il Bsns W p46+ Je 10 '67
Needed, two million jobs; letter. H. H. Humphrey. Am For 73:8 Je '67
Social unrest; park and recreation leaders response. R. F. Fralick. il Parks & Rec 2:26-8+ N '67
See also
Baby sitters
Labor camps
Student employment
United States—Job corps

Health and hygiene
How you can beat fatigue. A. Lake. il Seventeen 26:112-13+ Je '67
More power to you. il Sr Schol 91:40-1 S 28 '67
What happens behind the doctor's door. A. Lake. il Seventeen 26:102-3+ D '67
Why you need a doctor of your own. A. Lake. il Seventeen 26:146-7+ F '67

Management and training
Sex, morality, and the turned-on generation; with press comments. il Sr Schol 90:6-11+ My 12 '67
Teenagers speak out about codes of conduct. T. Irwin. il Parents Mag 42:43-5+ Ap '67
What kind of mates will our teen-agers be? T. Irwin. il Todays Health 45:20-3 S '67

Your teen-ager and smoking. R. H. Roach. il Todays Health 46:68-70+ Ja '68
See also
Adolescence
Discipline

Nutrition
See also
Children—Nutrition

Political activities
Face to face with a boy who loves politics; ed. by A. Eiseman. J. Katzenberg. Seventeen 26:111 Je '67
Turned-on teenagers; local government. P. D. Eimon. il Am City 82:164+ O '67
Who leads today's youth? round table discussion from 1967 student burgesses at Williamsburg. il Sr Schol 90:4-9+ Ap 14 '67
Why young radicals zero in on business. il Nations Bsns 55:31-4 Jl '67

Reading
Books for the new breed; adaptation of address, 1966. J. Igo. il Library J 92:1704-5 Ap 15 '67; Reply. R. Wyndham. 92:3781-2 O 15 '67
For whom do they write? Z. Sutherland. Sat R 50:34 Ag 19 '67
Plea to publishers from a peripatetic parent; need for paperbacks for teen-agers. C. Heilbrun. il Pub W 192:116-18 Jl 10 '67
Publishers hear YA panel talk about reading tastes. Library J 92:284+ Ja 15 '67
Tolkien & Hesse; top of the pops. R. Sklar. Nation 204:598-601 My 8 '67
See also
Reading lists

Recreation
Ossining answers teen entertainment turmoil; Cellar discotheque. S. Stenek. il Parks & Rec 2:21+ Ag '67
Special recreation needs of teenagers. J. S. Shivers. il Parks & Rec 2:20+ Ag '67

Religion
Adolescent religion, by C. W. Stewart. Review
Christian Cent 84:594-5 My 3 '67. J. D. Tyms
Gap between the generations; ed. by L. F. McKernan. Cath World 205:134-8 Je '67
Teens talk about religion; panel discussion, ed. by L. E. Miller, jr. il Seventeen 26:146-7+ Ap '67

Social life and customs
American adolescent, a bewildering analgam. T. R. Leidy and A. R. Starry. il NEA J 56:8-12 O '67

Czechoslovakia
Some interesting happenings in Prague. R. Eder. il N Y Times Mag p32-3+ N 12 '67

England
See Youth—Great Britain

Europe, Western
Youth movement comes to Europe. J. Fromm. il U S News 63:56-8 O 16 '67

France
Britain and France build a common market of youth. S. De Gramont. il N Y Times Mag p7+ Jl 16 '67

Germany (Democratic Republic)
Voices and yearnings of youth. il Life 62:66-7 My 26 '67

Germany (Federal Republic)
Symbolic atonement in Israel. D. Wigoder. Mlle 64:130-1+ F '67
See also
German students

Great Britain
Biba: London's mini mecca. H. Ehrlich. il Look 31:92-5+ N 14 '67
Exotic departures. M. Spark. New Yorker 42:31-2 Ja 28 '67
Letter from London; drugs and the young. M. Panter-Downes. New Yorker 43:83-4 Ag 19 '67
Maybe young people aren't so bad, after all; government commission recommends lowering legal age. il U S News 63:11 Jl 31 '67
Teen travel talk; an informal look at London, where youth keeps calling the tune. il Seventeen 26:206 Ap '67

YOUTH—*Continued*

India

What it's like to be a girl in India today. J. Baer. il Seventeen 26:136-9+ F '67

Italy

See also
Youth market

Netherlands

Rebels from affluence: Provos of Holland. P. Thoenes. il Nation 204:494-7 Ap 17 '67

Russia

Facing the complexities of modern education. M. A. Prokof'ev. il UNESCO Courier 20:14-20 N '67

Russian revolution: fifty years after; questions and answers. J. Brownell. il Sr Schol 91:11-13+ N 2 '67

Soviet youth and the antireligion drive. M. Bourdeaux. Christian Cent 84:844+ Je 28 '67

We want to live our own lives; with report by P. Young. il Life 63:42-54+ N 10 '67

United States

Ah, wilderness; the hippie culture. L. Yablonsky. New Repub 156:23-4 Ap 1 '67

Bleachies, beachies and blasters on a summer-in at Waikiki; chicks and good guys from the mainland. D. Jenkins. il Sports Illus 27:48-54 Jl 24 '67

Case for young rebels. J. Brothers. Good H 164:61-2 Je '67

Contemporary youth culture; symposium. il NEA J 56:8-20+ O '67

Cousin Brucie; balm for adolescence. D. R. Maxey. il Look 31:M10-12+ Mr 7 '67

Don't trust anyone over thirty. M. M. Hunt. Redbook 129:59-61+ Je '67

Farm girls have a speak-in; Farm journal teen board speaks for the good teen. Polly. il Farm J 91:76-7 O '67

Frantic romantics. A. Cooke. Mlle 66:82-3+ D '67

In defense of old folks over twenty-five. A. Rosenfeld. Life 63:22 Ag 25 '67

In defense of our young people. D. Hanson. Suc Farm 65:6 S '67

In my opinion; teen-agers take themselves too seriously. K. Callanan. Seventeen 26:262 My '67

In my opinion: teenyboppers should find their own place and stay in it. A. Helm. Seventeen 26:254 N '67

Lively arts; interview, ed. by R. Hemming. H. Mancini. Sr Schol 90:17 F 3 '67

Love is dead. E. Shorris. il N Y Times Mag p26-7+ O 29 '67

Meet the restless generation; with editorial comment. il Changing T 21:inside cover, 6-11 Je '67

New generation. J. St John. See issues of Nation's business

Our mysterious children. il Sat Eve Post 240:102 S 23 '67

Report from teeny-boppersville. J. K. Sale and B. Apfelbaum. il N Y Times Mag p24-5+ My 28 '67

Reporter at large: Sunset Strip. R. Adler. New Yorker 43:116+ F 25 '67

Search for purpose. il Life 62:66-79 Ap 28 '67

Spotlight on hippies. il U S News 62:61-3 My 8 '67

Teen-agers and sex: a student report. A. Lake. il Seventeen 26:88-9+ Jl '67

Teen scene. See issues of Seventeen

Teenagers who take but don't give. M. Gross. il Good H 164:66+ Mr '67

That girl in Albuquerque; Carol Chinberg: brilliant in school, housemother for her motherless family. il Look 31:M18+ Ap 4 '67

These are three of the alienated. S. Kelman. il N Y Times Mag p38-9+ O 22 '67; Discussion. p40+ N 12 '67

To redeem the worst, to better the best; concerning Presidential message to Congress. Time 89:19 F 17 '67

Under twenty-one. S. Reice. il McCalls 95:14+ Ja '67

What can the young believe? R. F. Kennedy. New Repub 156:11-12 Mr 11 '67; Reply. H. Fairlie. 156:12-14 Ap 8 '67

What options do youth have? symposium; with study-discussion program, by C. Smallenburg and H. Smallenburg. bibliog il PTA Mag 62:2-5+, 34 Ja '68

What our young people are really saying; excerpt from To seek a newer world. R. F. Kennedy. Ladies Home J 85:35+ Ja '68

What should an American citizen be; address, January 3, 1967. J. E. Davis. Vital Speeches 33:238-40 F 1 '67

What's the matter with the younger generation? S. Brown. Read Digest 90:57-60 Mr '67

Why the generation gap begins at thirty. C. D. B. Bryan. il N Y Times Mag p 10-11+ Jl 2 '67

Youth is action. il Sr Schol 91:6-7 D 14 '67

Youthquake: a report. America 116:828 Je 10 '67

See also
College students
Dating
Negro youth
United States—Job corps
Youth market

YOUTH-adult relationship

Alienated vs. society; symposium. bibliog f il Sch & Soc 95:252-68 Ap 15 '67

Are parents to blame for student behavior? excerpts from address, May 11, 1967. S. L. Halleck. il U S News 62:74-5 My 29 '67

Closing the gap. H. Howe, 2d. Parents Mag 42:50+ S '67

Dialogue between the generations; symposium. il Harper 235:45-60+ O '67

Don't trust anyone over thirty. M. M. Hunt. Redbook 129:59-61+ Je '67

From where I sit; college students and the generational gap. E. Raushenbush. Mlle 66:61+ Ja '68

Gap between the generations; ed. by L. F. McKernan. Cath World 205:134-8 Je '67

Generation gap. J. Poppy. il Look 31:26-32 F 21 '67

Generation gap. K. Crawford. Newsweek 69:48 Mr 13 '67

Generation gap; Washington gathering of campus newspaper editors and people in the establishment. G. Grant. Sat R 50:61 Mr 18 '67

Generations and the W.C.C. S. C. Rose. Christian Cent 84:864-6 Jl 5 '67

How bridge the gap between generations? Quaker-provided forum at Pendle Hill. A. A. Hunter. Christian Cent 84:324-6 Mr 8 '67

How is youth to be served? H. Fairlie. New Repub 156:12-14 Ap 8 '67

Of many things; problem of communicating with the younger generation. P. K. Cuneo. America 116:328 Mr 11 '67

Our troubled youth; address, August 18, 1967. R. W. Menninger. Vital Speeches 34:121-5 D 1 '67

They act as if we'd invented sin; report of interviews with women students at Stanford university and mothers of college students. L. B. Johnson. McCalls 94:32+ Je '67

Under twenty-five. D. J. Leary. Cath World 206:121-4 D '67

We can close the generation gap. G. R. Bach. il Ladies Home J 85:36+ Ja '68

What our young people are really saying; excerpt from To seek a newer world. R. F. Kennedy. Ladies Home J 85:35+ Ja '68

Young and the old. V. P. McCorry. America 117:452-inside back cover O 21 '67

YOUTH associations

Real Great society; New York slum kids team up to fight poverty. R. Vaughan. il Life 63:76+ S 15 '67
See also
Young Americans for freedom (organization)

YOUTH conferences

See also
White House youth conference on natural beauty and conservation

YOUTH forums. See Forums (discussion and debate)

YOUTH group achievement awards

P/M's thirteenth annual youth awards. Parents Mag 42:43-4+ O '67

YOUTH hostels

Skiing with a twist; the hosteling way. S. Y. Herman. il Sr Schol 91:sup 12-13 N 2 '67

YOUTH market

Lot more than a sheepskin; graduation industry. il Bsns W p 124-6 Je 24 '67

YOUTH market—*Continued*
Retailers smile uneasily. il Bsns W p29-30 Ag 19 '67
Second shock wave; address, January 26, 1967. W. O. Robertson. Vital Speeches 33: 408-11 Ap 15 '67
Shysters, moochers, and gyp artists are exploiting our students! G. E. Shattuck. NEA J 56:66-7 D '67
Where is new Bohemia going? J. Gruen. Vogue 150:101+ Ag 1 '67
Young Italy spends big. Bsns W p 184 My 13 '67

YOUTH movement

China (People's Republic)
Backward, march! il Newsweek 69:43 Mr 6 '67
Children's crusade. Newsweek 70:39-40 Ag 21 '67
China puzzle: old man in a hurry. C. P. Fitzgerald. il Nation 204:326-9 Mr 13 '67
Convulsion in Communist China, and what it means to the U.S. D. Chu. Sr Schol 90:6-11+ Mr 3 '67
Cruelty and insanity made me a fugitive. S. T. Ma. il Life 62:24-9+ Je 2 '67
I was a Red guard; ed. by L. Velie. C. T. Wang. Read Digest 90:55-60 My '67
Mao and the struggle for China. il Newsweek 69:32-9+ Ja 30 '67
Mao's cultural revolution. C. P. Fitzgerald. Nation 205:325-8 O 9 '67
Mao's worst crisis; Red guards. M. Omori. New Repub 156:17-19 Ja 28 '67
Muzzling the dragons; Red guards, driven out of the city and presumably back to school or work on the farms. il Time 89:34 Mr 10 '67
Nobody dared stop us: defector from Red guards; interview, ed. by K. M. Chrysler. C. T. Wang. U S News 62:57 Ja 30 '67
Red guard invasion. L. Muray. New Repub 156:15 F 25 '67
Ridicule and bullets widen the great rift; Red guards scourge Soviet Union. il Life 62:30-1 F 24 '67
Third man; rebuke from Chou. il Time 89:34 Mr 3 '67
Upheaval in China. B. I. Schwartz. Commentary 43:55-62 F '67
See also
China (People's Republic)—Politics and government

YOUTH periodicals. See Periodicals
YOUTH programs, Radio. See Radio broadcasting—Youth programs
YOUTH programs, Television. See Television broadcasting—Youth programs
YUCATAN
See also
Mayas
YUDKIN, Vivian
Abortion: one girl's story. Read Digest 91: 69-72 Jl '67
YUGOSLAV folk art. See Folk art
YUGOSLAV language. See Serbo-Croatian language
YUGOSLAV reporters. See Reporters and reporting
YUGOSLAVIA
Balkan way; bombing of embassies and consulates. il Newsweek 69:39 F 13 '67
See also
Censorship—Yugoslavia
Church and state in Yugoslavia
Communism—Yugoslavia
Communist party (Yugoslavia)
Music festivals—Yugoslavia
Trials—Yugoslavia

Antiquities
Ex occidente lux; excavation at Lepenski Vir. il Newsweek 71:48 Ja 15 '68

Commercial treaties and agreements
U.S. and Yugoslavia exchange notes on cotton textile arrangements. il Dept State Bul 57: 586-9 O 30 '67

Economic policy
Adam Smitović on the Sava. G. Burck. il Fortune 75:128-33+ My '67
Capital proposition; precedent-breaking foreign-investment code. Time 89:94 Ap 7 '67
Economic reform in Yugoslavia. S. S. Anderson. bibliog f Cur Hist 52:214-19+ Ap '67

Politics and government
Yugoslavia: the bellwether keeps turning right. C. W. Thayer. il Read Digest 91:63-8 S '67
See also
Communism—Yugoslavia
Communist party (Yugoslavia)

Religious institutions and affairs
Religious freedom in Yugoslavia: yes and no. M. Bourdeaux. Christian Cent 84:1228+ S 27 '67
See also
Catholic church in Yugoslavia

Social policy
Communist country giving up on communism. il U S News 62:104-5 My 8 '67
YUKIC, Thomas S.
Impact of a distinctive university recreation area. Parks & Rec 2:35-6 N '67
YUKON
Canada's Far North; a land on the move. I. Baird. il UNESCO Courier 20:14-17+ Ap '67
Passage to the Yukon. K. Lamott. il Holiday 41:68-9+ My '67
See also
Dawson

Description and travel
North to adventure. T. H. Inkster. il Travel 127:41-5 Je '67
YULETIDE. See Christmas
YUN, Isang
Dream of Liu-Tung. Criticism Opera N 32:31 Ja 13 '68
YUNCKER, Barbara
Keep up with medicine. See issues of Good housekeeping
YUNICK, Henry. See Yunick, S.
YUNICK, Smokey
How we broke 266 speed records with Camaros. Pop Sci 192:102-5+ Ja '68
Say, Smokey; questions and answers. See issues of Popular science monthly

about
Is it is or is it isn't, legal? J. McFarland. il Hot Rod 20:42-4 D '67
When stock cars don't finish. Pop Sci 191: 65-9+ N '67
Where there's fire, there's Smokey. J. McFarland. il pors Hot Rod 21:48-50 Ja '68
YUNIS, Jorge, J. See Hill, R. N. jt. auth.
YUNKER, Conrad E. and others
Adaptation of an insect cell line, Grace's antheraea cells, to medium free of insect hemolymph. Science 155:1565-6 Mr 24 '67
YURCHENCO, Henrietta
Folk music. See issues of American record guide
Nearing completion: the child ballads. Am Rec G 33:845-7 My '67
YURCHISON, George
All-electric high-rise demonstrates economies. il Arch Rec 141:215-18 Ap '67
YURIKO
Yuriko and dance company. 92nd street Y. J. Maskey. Dance Mag 41:76+ Mr '67
YUSUPOV, Feliks Feliksovich, kníaz'. See fUsupov, F. F.

Z

ZD (zero defects) See Quality control
ZACHARIAS, Jerrold Reinach
Zach's way. por Newsweek 70:97-97A O 16 '67
ZACK, David
Theater. New Repub 158:34+ Ja 13 '68
ZADIG, Ernest A.
Toy that became a steering machine. Pop Sci 192:82-5+ Ja '68
ZAGOREN, Ruby
Fragile ones; poem. Horn Bk 43:182 Ap '67
Reassurance; poem. Ladies Home J 84:153 Ap '67
ZAGORIA, Donald S.
There is very real danger of a civil war: interview. por U S News 62:56 Ja 30 '67
ZAGREB, Yugoslavia

Music
Notes from our correspondents. E. Helm. Hi Fi 17:25-6 Ag '67
Notes from our correspondents. K. Blaukopf. Hi Fi 17:26+ Ja '67

ZILLIACUS, Konni
Deutscher and Zilliacus. Nation 205:165-6 S 4 '67

ZIM, Marvin Hugo
Her journey of no return. Life 62:66-7 Mr 24 '67

ZIMAN, John
Thermal properties of materials; with biographical sketch. Sci Am 217:52, 180-8 S '67

ZIMMERMAN, John G.
Splash of strange hues in baseball's most frantic week. il Sports Illus 27:26-31 O 9 '67

ZIMMERMAN, Robert
Ironclads rise again! Pop Mech 128:96-9 D '67

ZIMMERMAN, Robert L.
Freudianism. Commentary 43:75-9 Je; 44:30 O '67

ZINC-air batteries. See Storage batteries

ZINC in the body
Zinc retention in rabbits; effect of previous diet. E. R. Graham and P. Telle. bibliog il Science 155:691-2 F 10 '67

ZINDER, Norton D. and Lyons, L. B.
Cell lysis: another function of the coat protein of the bacteriophage f2. bibliog Science 159:84-6 Ja 5 '68
—See Horiuchi, K. jt. auth.

ZINGONE, Renzo
Planning cities for profit. Time 89:95 F 10 '67

ZINGONIA, Italy
Planning cities for profit. Time 89:95 F 10 '67

ZINKIN, Sheila, and Miller, A. J.
Recovery of memory after amnesia induced by electroconvulsive shock. bibliog Science 155:102-4; 156:1397 Ja 6, Je 9 '67

ZINN, Howard
Vietnam: the logic of withdrawal; excerpt. Nation 204:170-5 F 6 '67

ZINNES, Harriet
Five poets. D. W. Baker. Poetry 109:402 Mr '67

ZINNIAS
Eight zinnia types, scene stealers all. il Sunset 138:256-7 Ap '67

ZINSSER, William Knowlton
Apple a day keeps the flexowriter away. Horizon 9:120 Aut '67
Fringe benefits. Horizon 9:120 Spr '67
I can't give you anything but. Sat Eve Post 240:20 F 11 '67
Looking around with Zinsser. See alternate issues of Look
Pitfalls of pop's pompous pop-off. Life 64:6 Ja 5 '68
Quenchless me and omphalocentric you. Horizon 9:120 Sum '67
Some bristly thoughts on victory through hair power: barbers, beards and bangs. Life 64:10 Ja 19 '68

ZIOLKOWSKI, Theodore
Hermann J. Weigand and a letter from Thomas Mann: the critical dialogue. Yale R 56:537-44 Je '67

ZION NATIONAL PARK
Virgin River country. O. S. Pettingill, jr. il Audubon 69:6-10+ Jl '67

ZIONISM
Aryanization of the Jewish state, by M. Selzer. Review
    Commentary 44:92-4+ D '67. S. Avineri
Israel, by R. Sanders. Review
    Commentary 43:88-9 F '67. E. Grossman
See also
Israel
Jewish-Arab relations
Jews

ZIPORYN, Marvin. See Altman, J. jt. auth.

ZIPSER, David
Orientation of nonsense codons on the genetic map of the lac operon. bibliog Science 157:1176-7 S 8 '67

ZIRCONIUM
Single fallout particles and zirconium-95 from the Chinese nuclear explosion of 9 May 1966. J. O. Baugh and others. bibliog il Science 155:1405-7 Mr 17 '67

ZIRLIN, Sandra, and Todak, Joseph
Motivation to the abstract. Sch Arts 66:29-31 Je '67

ZIRNER, Ludwig
Singing in the plains. J. W. Stedman. il por Opera N 31:29-31 F 25 '67

ZITNER, S. P.
Art as redemption. Poetry 111:41-2 O '67
Urgency and deference. Poetry 110:423-4 S '67

ZIZANIA aquatica. See Wild rice

ZNAMIEROWSKI, Nell
Olga Amaral. Craft Horiz 27:28-31+ My '67

ZOANTHUS. See Sea anemones

ZODIAC parties. See Entertaining

ZODIACAL dust. See Matter, Interstellar

ZODIACAL light
Zodiacal band. G. S. Mumford. Sky & Tel 33:94 F '67

ZOHARY, Daniel. See Ladizinsky, G. jt. auth.

ZOLA, Emile
Letter from Paris. Genêt. New Yorker 43:139-41 Je 10 '67

ZOLA, Joan
Portrait of a bureaucrat. Nat R 19:410-12 Ap 18 '67
What manner of book is this? Nat R 19:864-6 Ag 8 '67

ZOLL, Stephen
And the vanishing East. Nation 205:694-6 D 25 '67
Birmingham and Rubenstein on the destiny of our crowd. Commonweal 87:208-9 N 17 '67

ZOLLNER, Fred
Big Z and his misfiring Pistons. M. Cope. il pors Sports Illus 27:26-8+ D 18 '67

ZOLOTOW, Charlotte
Writing for children. Writer 80:36-8 Ap '67

ZOMOSA, Maximiliano
Brief biography. S. Goodman. pors Dance Mag 41:60-1 D '67

ZONE refining
Zone refining. W. G. Pfann. il Sci Am 217:62-70+ bibliog(p 158) D '67

ZONING
Check home zoning before you buy. R. B. Erickson. Am Home 70:128 N '67
How to make your land worth more. J. Carlson. il Farm J 91:34-5+ D '67
Zoning and planning decisions; ed. by N. Williams. See issues of American city

ZOO conferences
Primer congreso mundial de zoological. M. A. Dankworth. il Parks & Rec 2:26+ Jl '67
Reporter at large; conference at the San Diego zoo. E. Hahn. New Yorker 43:170+ O 14 '67

ZOOLOGICAL gardens
Conventional wisdom: how wise? animal breeding in captivity. il Sci N 91:217 Mr 4 '67
Innsbruck's unique zoo. C. Walker. il Parks & Rec 2:20-1+ Ap '67
Loving touch; new children's zoo at Seattle's Woodland park. il Time 89:75-6 Je 23 '67
New giraffe house for Denver. J. Frazier. il Parks & Rec 2:32+ Mr '67
Noble zoo of the mad marquess; Longleat, England. il Life 62:63-4+ Je 30 '67
Operation Noah's ark, how Topeka, Kansas became more zoo conscious. G. H. Clarke. il Parks & Rec 2:27+ Je '67
Repoorter at large. E. Hahn. New Yorker 43:38-40+ S 2; 96+ S 23; 117-18+ S 30; 170+ O 14 '67
Small mammal exhibits feature moats and grottoes; Miami's Crandon park zoo. J. H. Amon. il Parks & Rec 2:45 O '67
Zoos on the go. il Parks & Rec 2:38-9+ My '67
See also
San Diego, Calif. zoological garden
Zoo conferences

Employees
Zoo's who. A. Grant. il Mlle 65:167+ My '67

ZOOLOGICAL specimens

Collection and preservation
See also
Insects—Collection and preservation
Taxidermy

ZOOLOGY
See also
Desert fauna

Ecology
See also
Insects—Ecology

Africa
Beast-watching: African treasure hunt. J. Huxley. il Holiday 42:36-43+ S '67
Destruction of Eden. L. Brown. il Audubon 69:36-53 Jl '67

ZOOLOGY—Africa—*Continued*
Other Africa; excerpts from Nature's paradise. J. Bartlett and D. Bartlett. il Audubon 69:68-75 S '67
Safari, anyone? photographic safaris. E. A. Bauer. il Audubon 69:22-7 Jl '67

Africa, East
Easy adventure: East Africa. S. M. Howland. il Travel 128:30-5 N '67
See how they run. R. Graves. il Life 63:51-2+ Jl 21 '67

Alaska
Journey among barbarians; condensation of Where the sea breaks its back. C. Ford. il Audubon 69:21-31 Mr '67

Arctic Regions
See also
Musk oxen

Australia
Great rabbit war; wild rabbits. H. Earl. il Sci Digest 62:18-20 N '67
Two for extinction; numbat and marsupial mole. il Sci Digest 61:22-4 F '67
See also
Koalas

Bering Island
Journey among barbarians; condensation of Where the sea breaks its back. S. Ford. il Audubon 69:24-31 Mr '67

Galápagos Islands
Galapagos eerie cradle of new species. R. T. Peterson. il Nat Geog Mag 131:540-85 Ap '67

Hawaii
Frog comes to Hawaii; importing dendrobates auratus from Panama. H. L. Ullman. il Natur Hist 76:36-7 My '67

Indonesia
Udjung Kulon. il Life 63:80-91+ D 22 '67

Panama
Fantastic creatures of northern Panama jungles. Hobbies 72:125 Jl '67
ZOOLOGY, Economic
Interior backs bill on imports, 'gators. C. H. Callison. il Audubon 69:70-1 N '67
Will Congress stop commerce in endangered wildlife? C. H. Callison. il Audubon 69:20-1 Jl '67
ZOOLOGY, Marine. See Marine fauna
ZOOM lenses
Keppler on the SLR. H. Keppler. il Mod Phot 31:30+ N '67
Matzkin on movies. M. A. Matzkin. Mod Phot 31:22+ O '67; 32:28 Ja '68
1,000mm to 4,000mm. P. Farber. il U S Camera 30:52-3 N '67
Tele converter that zooms. H. Keppler. il Mod Phot 31:82-3 F '67
Zoom lens that's also a Macro. N. Rothschild. il Pop Phot 61:80-3 Ag '67
Zoom 1000-4000mm. $135. H. Keppler. il Mod Phot 31:66-7 Mr '67
ZOOPLANKTON. See Plankton
ZOOS. See Zoological gardens
ZORINA, Vera
Practical streak; interview, ed. by G. Martin. pors Opera N 32:14 S 23 '67

about
Zorina. il por Newsweek 70:90 O 9 '67

ZORTHIAN, Barry
Mark of Zorthian; with report by M. Parker. il pors Life 62:51-2+ My 12 '67
ZUBEK, Theodoric
Church in Czechoslovakia today. America 117: 115-17 Jl 29 '67
ZUBROD, C. Gordon
Closing in on leukemia. il por Bsns W p87-8 O 7 '67
ZUBRYN, Emil
Ancient apartments. Sci N 92:106 Jl 29 '67
Barrier down. Sci N 92:67 Jl 15 '67
Heat exacts a toll. Sci N 91:558 Je 10 '67
ZUCKER, Joel
In search of knowledge. il U S Camera 30: 86-7 O '67
ZUCKER-FRANKLIN, Dorothea, and others
Ultrastructure of thrombosthenin, the contractile protein of human blood platelets. bibliog Science 157:945-6 Ag 25 '67
ZUCKERMAN, Harold
College and career; questions and answers. Sr Schol 90:26 My 5 '67
ZUCKERMAN, Harriet
Sociology of the Nobel prizes; with biographical sketch. Sci Am 217:20, 25-33 bibliog(p 154) N '67
ZUCKERMAN, Pinchas
Cookie & Pinky come through. por Time 89:78 My 26 '67
ZUKOFSKY, Louis
A-18; poem. Poetry 110:281-303 Ag '67
A-19; poem. Poetry 111:82-111 N '67

about
Louis Zukofsky. H. Carruth. Poetry 110:420-2 S '67
Of notes and horses. H. Kenner. Poetry 111: 112-21 N '67
ZUNIGA, Raul
Spoon sculpture. R. Knight. il pors Design 68:20-2 Sum '67
ZWEIG, Paul
French chronicle. Poetry 111:124-9 N '67
Looking out at night over rooftops; poem. Nation 204:766 Je 12 '67
Marriage; Anger; There are women; poems. Poetry 110:386-9 S '67
Messages in a bottle. Nation 204:281-3 F 27 '67
Murderous solvent. Nation 204:536-8 Ap 24 '67
Three poems against violent death. Nation 205:94 Jl 31 '67
Woman in a window; poem. Nation 205:506 N 13 '67
ZWEIG, Stefan
Los Angeles. A. Goldberg. Opera N 31:24 Je 10 '67
ZWEMER, Samuel Marinus
One of a kind. J. R. Wilson. Christian Cent 84:687-8 My 24 '67
ZWERLING, Israel
Treating mental illness. J. Ridgeway. New Repub 156:13-15 Je 10 '67
ZWETTLER, Lea
Competition: stimulus to successful Seattle shop. il Pub W 191:53 My 8 '67
ZWICK, Charles J.
New switch in the troika. por Bsns W p32 Ja 13 '68
ZWOLLO, Tonny
Sun maiden architect. il pors Life 63:103-4+ O 13 '67